KT-379-514

Concise Oxford Russian Dictionary

Concise Oxford Russian Dictionary

Revised Edition

Based on the *Oxford Russian Dictionary*

Russian-English
Edited by Marcus Wheeler and Boris Unbegaun

English-Russian
Edited by Paul Falla

Thematic Wordfinder
Prepared by David Taylor

Guide to Exploring the Internet
Prepared by Geoffrey Rolfe

OXFORD UNIVERSITY PRESS

1998

OXFORD
UNIVERSITY PRESS

Great Clarendon Street, Oxford OX2 6DP

Oxford University Press is a department of the University of Oxford.
It furthers the University's objective of excellence in research, scholarship,
and education by publishing worldwide in

Oxford New York

Auckland Bangkok Buenos Aires Cape Town Chennai
Dar es Salaam Delhi Hong Kong Istanbul Karachi Kolkata
Kuala Lumpur Madrid Melbourne Mexico City Mumbai Nairobi
São Paulo Shanghai Taipei Tokyo Toronto

Oxford is a registered trade mark of Oxford University Press
in the UK and in certain other countries

Published in the United States
by Oxford University Press Inc., New York

Single volume first published 1993
Concise edition first published 1996
This revised edition published 1998

British Library Cataloguing in Publication Data

Data available

Library of Congress Cataloging in Publication Data

Data available

ISBN 0-19-860152-2

10 9 8 7 6

Printed in Great Britain by
Clays Ltd
Bungay, Suffolk

Contents

Preface

The *Concise Oxford Russian Dictionary* is an abridgement of The *Oxford Russian Dictionary*, published in 1993.

The Dictionary, which is intended primarily, though by no means exclusively, for English-speaking users at college or university level, contains approximately 120,000 words and phrases. Since it is a general-purpose rather than specialist work, technical, archaic, old-fashioned, and slang terms are included sparingly, but attention has been paid to ensuring generous coverage of idioms and phrases, as well as to the provision of syntactical information. For the convenience of users whose native language is not English all headwords in the English-Russian section are transcribed into the International Phonetic Alphabet. Such transcription has not been supplied in the Russian-English section since Russian pronunciation is generally phonetic.

Native Russian assistance in the task of abridgement was rendered by Tanya Kolker and Vladimir Raivitch. The principles of arrangement, provision of grammatical information etc., are given in the Guide to the Use of the Dictionary which follows.

Guide to the Use of the Dictionary

Russian-English Section

Presentation

1. A separate headword is given for each entry. Where appropriate, a substantial quantity of idiomatic and illustrative phraseology is included.

2. The following devices are used to save space:

(i) The first letter of the headword, followed by a full point, represents the whole headword. Thus:

това́рный ... т. соста́в (= **това́рный соста́в**)

(ii) The swung dash, in conjunction with a vertical stroke, represents that part of the headword which is to the left of the vertical stroke. Thus:

роди́м|ый ... ~ое пятно́ (= **роди́мое пятно́**)

exceptions: the swung dash is not used in indicating the genitive singular of nouns or the 1st and 2nd persons singular of the present tense of verbs with unchanged stress (for examples, see below: *Grammatical Information*: *Nouns* and *Verbs*); and, in cross-references from the imperfective to the perfective verbal aspect, it may, when preceded by a prefix, represent the entire headword. Thus:

ста́|рить, ю, ишь *impf.* (*of* **со~**) ... (= *of* **соста́рить**)

Pronunciation

3. With the general exception of monosyllables, stress is indicated for every Russian word. A stress mark above the swung dash, where this sign represents two or more syllables, indicates shift of stress to the syllable immediately preceding the vertical stroke dividing the headword. Thus:

запи|са́ть, шу́, ~́шешь ... (= **запишу́, запи́шешь**)

4. Conversely, a stress mark above a syllable to the right of the swung dash indicates shift of stress away from the syllable(s) represented by the swung dash. Thus:

до́ктор, а, *pl.* **~а́ ...** (= **доктора́**)

5. Where a variant stress is permissable, both variants are shown. Thus:

скобл|и́ть, ю́, ~́ишь (= **ско́блишь** *or* **скобли́шь**)

Phraseology

6. Idiomatic phrases are frequently duplicated in entries for the component words. Phrases consisting of adjective and noun, however, are normally entered under the adjective component.

Meaning

7. Separate meanings of a word are indicated by means of Arabic numerals. Thus:

риско́ванный ... 1. risky. **2.** risqué.

8. Shades of meaning, represented by translations not considered strictly synonymous, are indicated by means of a semicolon: translations considered synonymous — by a comma. Thus:

выно́сливый ... hardy; robust, sturdy.

9. Homonyms are indicated by repetition of the headword as a separate entry, followed by a superscript Arabic numeral. Thus:

газ¹, а *m.* gas.
газ², а *m.* gauze.

It should be noted that there is no accepted all-embracing criterion for differentiating homonymy from polysemy (plurality of meanings of a single word) or 'meaning' from 'shade of meaning'.

Explanation

10. Where necessary for the avoidance of ambiguity explanatory glosses are given in brackets in italic type. Thus:

интерпрета́тор, а *m.* interpreter (*expounder*). [i.e. *not* translator]

11. This device is used in particular in the case of words denoting specifically Russian or Soviet concepts (e.g. **ка́ша, микрорайо́н, толка́ч**) and makes it possible to use one-word transliterations rather than clumsy paraphrases as a substitute for a translation.

12. Indications of style or usage are given, where appropriate, in brackets. Thus: (*coll.*), (*dial.*); (*fig.*), (*joc.*); (*agric.*), (*pol.*), etc.

Grammatical Information

13. The following grammatical information is given:

Nouns

The genitive singular ending and gender of all nouns are shown. Thus:

мо́лот, а *m.* hammer.
мо́лни|я, и *f.* lightning.
молок|о́, а́ *nt.* milk.
пья́ниц|а, ы *c.g.* drunkard.

Other case endings are shown where declensions or stress is, in relation to generally accepted systems of classification, irregular. Thus:

англича́н|ин, ина, *pl.* **~е, ~** *m.* Englishman.
бор|ода́, оды́, *a.* **∠оду,** *pl.* **∠оды, ~о́д,** *d.* **~ода́м** *f.* beard.

(But the inserted vowel in the genitive plural ending of numerous feminine nouns with nominative singular ending **-ка** is not regarded as irregular, e.g. **анлича́нка,** *g. pl.* **англича́нок.**)

Variant genitive case endings of certain *pluralia tantum* are indicated by a hyphen. Thus:

порт|ки́, о́к-ко́в *no sg.* ... (= **порто́к** *or* **портко́в**)

Nouns ending **-ость** derived from adjectives have not been included where an appropriate English rendering can be obtained by adding *-ness* to the corresponding adjective (e.g., **зо́ркий ...** sharpsighted ... **зо́ркость ...** sharpsightedness ...).

Where an abbreviation is marked (*indecl.*) this indicates that, although not usually declined, it may be declined in order to avoid ambiguity. Thus:

переда́ча информа́ции ТАССом (*opp.* **ТАССа** *or* **ТАССу**)

Adjectives

Only the masculine nominative singular of the full form of the adjective is shown. Endings of the short forms, where these are found, are shown in brackets. Thus:

глу́п|ый (~, ~а́, ~о) ...

The neuter short form ending is omitted where stress is as for the feminine. Thus:

нау́ч|ный (~ен, ~на)

Verbs

Endings are shown of the 1st and 2nd persons singular of the present tense (or of the 1st person only of verbs with infinitive ending **-ать, -ова́ть, -ять, -еть** which retain stem and stress unchanged throughout the present tense). Thus:

говор|и́ть, ю́, и́шь ...
чита́|ть, ю ...

Other endings of the present tense and endings of the past tense are shown where formation or stress are irregular. Thus:

ид|ти́, у́, ёшь, *past* **шёл, шла, шло ...**
стере́|чь, гу́, жёшь, гу́т, *past* **~̈г, ~гла́ ...**

Participles and gerunds, and forms of the passive voice, are not shown unless having special semantic or syntactical features. Verbal aspects: the imperfective aspect is normally treated as the basic form of the simple verb, a cross-reference to the relevant perfective form being shown in brackets. Thus:

чита́|ть, ю *impf.* (*of* **про~**) ...

The corresponding entry is:

прочита́|ть, ю *pf. of* **чита́ть**

In the case, however, of compound verbs formed by means of a prefix, the perfective aspect is treated as the basic form. Thus:

зачит|а́ть, а́ю *pf.* (*of* **~́ывать**) ...

Since, in a number of cases, a correspondence cannot, for semantic or other reasons, be firmly established (e.g. **иска́ть-сыска́ть**), the absence of a corresponding aspect is not necessarily noted.

Meanings and phraseology are shown under the basic form in each case unless peculiar to the other aspect.

Prefixes and Combining Forms

A number of prefixes and combining forms are shown as separate entries.Thus:

до...[1] *vbl. pref.*
гидро... *comb. form* hydro-
сов... *comb. form, abbr. of* **~е́тский**

Numerous compounded words, the meaning of which is judged sufficiently clear from a knowledge of the meaning of the prefix and the root-word, have, to save space, been excluded from the dictionary.

English-Russian Section

Orthography

1. The English spelling follows British usage; less usual American variations are noted, but not, e.g., such spellings as **honor**, or (as a rule) variants in which **e** replaces **ae** or **oe.** (See also paragraph 10 below.)

2. Russian cardinal numbers, given without 'tags' denoting inflection, are to be read in the nominative form. (This does not apply to year-dates).

3. Secondary stress is not indicated in Russian words unless they are hyphenated (or unless the syllable in question contains the letter ё). If stress is optional, as between two vowels, an accent is placed on both. When prepositions attract the accent from a noun, or не from a verb, the fact is shown by a stress mark; otherwise monosyllables are not generally shown as stressed. A form such as инди́|ец (*fem.* -а́нка) means that the feminine noun is stressed on the penultimate syllable only (cf. paragraph 36(iii)).

Pronunciation

4. For the convenience of users whose native language is not English all headwords are transcribed into the International Phonetic Alphabet. An exception is made for those abbreviations, such as BBC, whose component letters are pronounced individually. Transcriptions are supplied, however, where an abbreviation is pronounced in the same way as its expansion, e.g. **c.** meaning 'century'. In compound words where the second element is listed elsewhere only the first element is generally transcribed.

A key to the phonetic symbols used is supplied below, immediately before the list of abbreviations used in the Dictionary.

Arrangement and presentation of entries: principal rules

5. These matters are explained in detail in paragraphs 10–39 below. Attention is drawn to the nesting principle (paragraph 21) and to the fact that compounds, whether hyphenated or written as one word, are listed under the first element and not the second: e.g. **pen-knife** under **pen**, not **knife.** As regards the placing of idioms see paragraph 22; and for the placing of labels such as (*coll.*) and (*sl.*), see paragraph 25. Paragraphs 35–39 deal with the presentation of Russian grammatical information, including verb aspects.

6. Attention is also drawn to paragraphs 24–25 on the subject of usage labels and their position; and to the fact that the oblique stroke / signifies an alternative affecting *one* word on either side of it (paragraphs 30–32).

7. For the use of the vertical stroke and swung dash (~) see paragraphs 16–17; for the approximate sign (≃), paragraph 25.

8. The gender of nouns in ь is only marked when they are *masculine* (paragraph 35(*a*)).

9. Many Russian nouns have an adjectival form (e.g. го́род — городско́й) corresponding to the attributive use of their English equivalent. Such adjectives are frequently given under the English noun-entry, preceded by the abbreviation '*attr.*'

Presentation: detailed rules

10. Headwords are printed in bold roman type except for non-naturalized foreign words and expressions, for which bold italic is used. Alternative spellings (including some of the less classifiable American variants) are presented alongside the preferred spelling in full or abbreviated form, or shown in brackets: these variants appear again in alphabetical sequence (unless adjacent to the main entry), as cross-references. Thus:

cosy (*US* **cozy**) **cozy** = **cosy**
hicc|up, -ough
curts(e)y

11. Similar treatment is applied to words in which an alternative termination can be used without affecting the sense. Thus:

spars|eness, -ity

Here as elsewhere (paragraphs 16–17), a vertical stroke (divider) is placed after those letters which are common to both forms and which, in the alternative form as shown, are replaced by a hyphen.

12. Also presented as headwords are a few two-word expressions of which the first element does not qualify for an individual entry, e.g. **Boxing Day; Parkinson's disease.**

13. Separate headword entries with superscript numerals are made for words which, though identical in spelling, differ in basic meaning and origin (**fine** as noun and verb; **fine** as adjective and adverb), or in pronunciation and/or stress (**house** and **supplement** as nouns and as verbs), or both (**tear** meaning 'teardrop' and **tear** meaning 'rip').

14. Separate entries for adverbs in '-ly' are made only when they have meanings or usage (idiom, compounds, etc.) which cannot conveniently be treated under the corresponding adjective. Examples are **hardly, really,** and **surely.** When there is no separate entry, and no instance of the adverb in the adjectival entry, it can be assumed that the corresponding Russian adverb is also formed regularly from the adjective. Thus **clumsy** неуклю́жий, нело́вкий implies that the Russian for 'clumsily' is неуклю́же or нело́вко; **critical** крити́ческий implies that 'critically' can be translated крити́чески, and so on.

15. Gerundive and participial forms of English verbs, used as nouns or adjectives, are often accommodated within the verb entry (transitive or intransitive as appropriate). Thus:

revolving doors is found under **revolve** *v.i.*
a retarded child is found under **retard** *v.t.*

but in certain cases, for the sake of clarity, such forms have been treated as independent headwords, e.g.

packing *n.*; **flying** *n.* and *adj.*; **barbed** *adj.*

16. Some headwords are divided by a vertical stroke in order that the unchanging letters preceding the stroke may subsequently be replaced, in inflected forms, by a swung dash. Where there is no divider, the swung dash represents the headword *in toto*, e.g.

house ... **keep ~** ... **~hold** ... **~-painter**

17. The vertical divider is also used in both English and Russian to separate the main part of a word from its termination when it is necessary to show modifications or alternative forms of the latter: e.g. paragraphs 10, 35(*c*), and 36.

18. Within the headword entry each grammatical function has its own paragraph, introduced by a part-of-speech indicator (in this order): *n.*, *pron.*, *adj.*, *adv.*, *v.t.*, *v.i.*, *prep.*, *conj.*, *int.* A combined heading, e.g. **adagio** *n.*, *adj.*, *& adv.*, may sometimes be used for convenience; the most common instance is *v.t. & i.* when the two moods are not clearly distinguishable, or when the Russian intransitive is expressed by means of the suffix -ся.

19. Verb-adverb combinations forming 'phrasal verbs' normally appear in a separate paragraph headed '*with advs.*', immediately following simple verb usage; they are given in alphabetical order of the adverb, transitive and intransitive usage within each phrasal verb being separated. Only when the possible combinations are very few and uncomplicated are they contained within the *v.t.* or *v.i.* paragraph.

20. There are also a few verbs (e.g. **go**) where idiomatic usage with prepositions is extensive and complex enough to call for a separate paragraph headed '*with preps.*'.

21. Hyphenated or single-word compounds in which the headword forms the first element are brought together or 'nested' under the headword in a final paragraph headed '*cpds.*'. Here the headword is represented by a swung dash, and the second element, in bold type, determines the alphabetical sequence. An exception is made to the 'nesting' principle in some cases where compounds are particularly numerous, e.g. those beginning with such elements as **'back', 'by', 'out', 'over'** etc. Forms like **'bull's eye'** and **'Englishman'** (despite the reduced 'a') are treated as compounds. Phrases such as **'labour exchange'** will generally be found in the main paragraph of the entry for the first noun, in some cases preceded by '*attr.*' (for 'attributive').

22. Adjective-noun expressions generally appear under the adjective unless this has relatively little weight, as in **'good riddance'**; but some may also be repeated under the noun, e.g. **'French bean'** and **'French horn'.** Idioms of a more complex nature, and proverbs, are generally entered under the first noun, but here too the rule is not inflexible and some duplication may be found.

23. Within an entry differences of meaning or application are defined by synonym, context, or other means. Major differences may be distinguished by numerals in bold type. Thus:

> **gag** *n.* **1.** (*to prevent speech etc.*) … (*surgery*) … (*parl.*) … (*fig.*) …
> **2.** (*joke*) …

24. A second type of label indicates status or level of usage: e.g. *arch*(aic), *liter*(ary), *coll*(oquial), *sl*(ang), *vulg*(ar). It may apply to the headword as a whole, to one of its functions or meanings, or to a single phrase or sentence, and is placed accordingly. Thus:

> **pep** (*coll.*) *n.* … *v.t.* (*usu.* ~ **up**)
> **tart** *n.* **1.** (*flat pie*) … **2.** (*sl., prostitute*) … *v.t.* ~ **up** (*coll., embellish*) …
> **bell** *n.* … **that rings a** ~ (*fig., coll.*)

25. In cases where Russian has an expression corresponding closely in level of usage to a given colloquialism, vulgarism, or slang term in English, the status label (*coll.*), (*sl.*) etc. is placed *after* the Russian, and should be understood to apply equally to the preceding English equivalent. In other cases a 'literary' (non-colloquial) Russian translation is given, and the status label is placed immediately after the English. When both literary and colloquial Russian translations are given for the same English expression, the label appears *before* the second, colloquial one. Russian expressions, especially idioms or proverbs, which parallel rather than translate English ones are preceded by the symbol ≃.

26. The use of the comma or the semicolon to separate Russian words offered as translations of the same English word reflects a greater or lesser degree of equivalence; in the latter case an auxiliary English gloss is often used to express the nuance of difference. Thus:

> **inexhaustible** *adj.* (*unfailing*) неистощи́мый, неисчерпа́емый; …
> (*untiring*) неутоми́мый.

27. When shades of meaning of an adjective or verb have been defined in this way, and similar distinctions exist between derivative abstract nouns, the glosses are not usually repeated. Thus:

> **bookish** *adj.* (*literary, studious*) кни́жный; (*pedantic*) педанти́чный
> **bookishness** *n.* кни́жность; педанти́чность

28. To avoid ambiguity the semicolon is always used when the alternatives are complete phrases or sentences, and also in most cases between synonymous verbs. Thus:

> **what is he getting at?** что он хо́чет сказа́ть?; куда́ он гнёт?
> **allow** *v.t.* позв|оля́ть, -о́лить; разреш|а́ть, -и́ть

Idiom and illustration

29. The examples of characteristic and idiomatic usage in both languages, which illustrate and supplement the standard Russian equivalents, may consist of phrases or finite sentences. In the former case, where a verb is concerned, both aspects are generally given in Russian; in the latter, one or other aspect is chosen according to the context. For the method of giving aspectual information see paragraphs 36–39 below.

30. In both English and Russian there are many instances when one word in a phrase or sentence may be replaced by a synonymous alternative. This is shown by means of a comma in English, and an oblique stroke in Russian. Thus:

> **have, get one's hair cut** стри́чься, по-
> **my better half** моя́ дража́йшая/лу́чшая полови́на
> **lose one's hair** (*lit.*) лысе́ть, об-/по- (either prefix may be used to form the perfective)

31. Non-synonymous alternatives are linked by the oblique stroke in *both* languages. Thus:

> **high/low tension** высо́кое/ни́зкое напряже́ние

32. In all cases the oblique stroke expresses an alternative of only *one* word on either side of it. Other alternatives are shown in the form '(*or* ...)'. Thus:

> **the estate came (*or* was brought) under the hammer**
> **I could do with a drink** я охо́тно (*or* с удово́льствием) вы́пил бы

33. Optional extensions of words, phrases or sentences, which may be included at discretion, e.g. for greater clarity, are shown within brackets, and in ordinary roman or Cyrillic type.

34. Italics within brackets are used for such matters as labels of meaning and usage (paragraphs 24–25) and in connection with Russian grammatical information (paragraph 35). Russian italics (without stress marks) are used for brief definitions or explanations of English terms which have no counterpart in Russian: see e.g. at **commuter**; also to specify noun-objects of certain verbs in order to limit their application to that implicit in the English, e.g.

> **wall up** *v.t.* заде́л|ывать, -ать (*дверь/окно*)

Grammatical Information

35. The following grammatical information is given in respect of words offered as translations of headwords:

(*a*) the gender of *masculine* nouns ending in -ь, except when this is made clear by an accompanying adjective (e.g. **polar bear** бе́лый медве́дь) or by the existence of a corresponding 'female' form (see (*e*) below).

(*b*) the gender of nouns (e.g. neuters in -мя, masculines in -а and -я, foreign borrowings in -и and -у) whose final letter does not serve as an indicator of gender. Nouns of common gender are designated (*c.g.*). Indeclinable nouns are designated (*indecl.*), preceded by a gender indicator if required. The many adjectives used as nouns (e.g. портно́й) are not specially marked.

(*c*) the gender (or, for *pluralia tantum*, the genitive plural termination) and number (*pl.*) of all plural nouns which translate a headword or compound. Thus:

> **timpani** *n.* лита́вры (*f. pl.*).
> **pliers** *n.* щипц|ы́ (*pl.*, *g.* -о́в); кле́щ|и (*pl.*, *g.* -е́й).

This information, however is not given if the singular form has already appeared in the same entry, nor in the case of neuter plurals with an accompanying adjective, where the number and gender are self-evident from the terminations. Plurals of adjectives used substantivally are shown as (*pl.*).

(*d*) the nominative plural termination (-á or -я́) of certain masculine nouns when this form denotes a meaning different from that of the plural in -ы or -и, e.g.

icon ... óбраз (*nom. pl.* -á).

(*e*) the forms of nouns used where Russian differs from English in making a verbal distinction between male and female. Thus:

teacher учи́тель (*fem.* -ница)

(*f*) aspectual information: see paragraphs 36–39 below.

(*g*) case usage with prepositions, e.g. **before** до+*g.*

(*h*) the case, with or without preposition, required to provide an equivalent to an English transitive verb. Thus:

attack *v.t.* нап|ада́ть, -а́сть на+*a.*

If no case is thus indicated, it is to be taken that the Russian verb is transitive.

(*i*) When English and Russian terms are equivalent as they stand, bút both may be regularly extended e.g. by a prepositional phrase, the Russian idiom may be made explicit as in (*h*), but in brackets. Thus:

condole *v.i.* соболе́зновать (*impf.*) (+*d.*)

(*j*) Use is also made of oblique cases of the Russian pronouns кто and что (in brackets and italics) to indicate case/preposition usage after a verb. Thus:

suit (*adapt*) *v.t.* приспос|а́бливать, -о́бить (*что к чему*); соглас́ов|ывать, -а́ть (*что с чем*)

Aspects

36. Aspectual information is given on all verbs (except быть, *impf.*) offered as renderings in infinitive form (except when they are subordinate to the finite verb in a sentence). If the verb is mono-aspectual, or used in a phrase to which only one aspect applies, it is designated either imperfective (*impf.*) or perfective (*pf.*) as the case may be. With verbs of motion a distinction is made between determinate (*det.*) and indeterminate (*indet.*) forms, the imperfective aspect being assumed unless otherwise stated. Bi-aspectual infinitives are shown as (*impf.*, *pf.*). In all other cases both aspects are indicated (the imperfective always preceding the perfective) as in the following examples:

(i) получ|а́ть, -и́ть; возра|жа́ть, -зи́ть; сн|оси́ть, -ести́.
(ii) позв|оля́ть, -о́лить; встр|еча́ть, -е́тить.
(iii) пока́з|ывать, -а́ть (i.e. *pf.* показа́ть); очаро́в|ывать, -а́ть.
(iv) гоня́ть, гнать; брать, взять; вынужда́ть, вы́нудить.
(v) смотре́ть, по-; греть, по- (i.e. *pf.* погре́ть); мости́ть, вы́- (i.e. *pf.* вы́мостить); лысе́ть, об-/по-.
(vi) и|мпровизи́ровать, сы-.

37. It will be seen from the above that

(i) when the first two or more letters of both aspects are identical, a vertical divider in the imperfective separates these letters from those which undergo change in the perfective. The perfective is then represented by the changed letters, preceded by a hyphen.

(ii) a 'change' includes change of stress only if the stress shifts *back* in the perfective to the previous vowel: the divider then precedes this vowel in the im•erfective.

(iii) if it shifts forward, only the stressed syllable of the perfective is shown.

(iv) when the two aspects have only their first letter in common, or are in fact different verbs, or both begin with вы- (which is always accented in the perfective), both are given in full.

(v) perfectives of the type 'prefix+imperfective' are shown by giving the prefix only, followed by a hyphen. Prefixes are unstressed except for вы́-. Alternative prefixes are separated by an oblique stroke.

38. Where a verb has two possible imperfective or perfective forms, the alternative form is shown in brackets. Thus:

разв|ора́чивать (*or* -ёртывать), -ерну́ть.
возвра|ща́ться, -ти́ться (*or* верну́ться).
пали́ть (*or* опа́ливать), о-.

39. When two or three verbs separated by an oblique stroke are followed by the indication (*pf.*) or (*impf.*) this applies to both or all of them.

PHONETIC SYMBOLS USED IN THE DICTIONARY

Consonants

b	*b*ut	j	*y*es	p	*p*en	w	*w*e	ð	*th*is
d	*d*og	k	*c*at	r	*r*ed	z	*z*oo	ŋ	ri*ng*
f	*f*ew	l	*l*eg	s	*s*it	ʃ	*sh*e	x	lo*ch*
g	*g*et	m	*m*an	t	*t*op	ʒ	deci*s*ion	tʃ	*ch*ip
h	*h*e	n	*n*o	v	*v*oice	θ	*th*in	dʒ	*j*ar

Vowels

æ	c*a*t	iː	s*ee*	uː	t*oo*	əʊ	n*o*	aɪə	f*ire*
ɑː	*ar*m	ɒ	h*o*t	ə	*a*go	eə	h*air*	aʊə	s*our*
e	b*e*d	ɔː	s*aw*	aɪ	m*y*	ɪə	n*ear*		
ɜː	h*er*	ʌ	r*u*n	aʊ	h*ow*	ɔɪ	b*oy*		
ɪ	s*i*t	ʊ	p*u*t	eɪ	d*ay*	ʊə	p*oor*		

(ə) signifies the indeterminate sound as in gard*e*n, carn*a*l, and rhyth*m*.

(r) at the end of a word indicates an r that is sounded when a word beginning with a vowel follows, as in *clutter up* and *an acre of land*.

The mark ˜ indicates a nasalized sound, as in the following sounds that are not natural in English: æ̃ (t*im*bre) ɑ̃ (él*an*) ɔ̃ (garç*on*)

The main or primary stress of a word is shown by ˈ preceding the relevant syllable; any secondary stress in words of three or more syllables is shown by ˌ preceding the relevant syllable.

Abbreviations used in the Dictionary

a.	accusative
abbr.	abbreviat|ion, -ed (to)
abs.	absolute
abstr.	abstract
acad.	academic
acc.	according
act.	active
adj., adjs.	adjectiv|e, -al; -es
admin.	administration
adv., advs.	adverb, -ial; -s
aeron.	aeronautics
agric.	agriculture
alg.	algebra
anat.	anatomy
anc.	ancient
anthrop.	anthropology
approx.	approximate(ly)
arch.	archaic
archaeol.	archaeology
archit.	architecture
astrol.	astrology
astron.	astronomy
attr.	attributive
Austral.	Austral(as)ian
aux.	auxiliary
bibl.	biblical
biol.	biology
bot.	botany
Br.	British; British usage
c.g.	common gender
chem.	chemistry
cin.	cinema(tography)
coll.	colloquial
collect.	collective
comb.	combin|ation, -ing
comm.	commerc|e, -ial
comp.	comparative
comput.	computing
concr.	concrete
conj., conjs.	conjunction; -s
cpd., cpds.	compound; -s
cul.	culinary
d.	dative
decl.	decl|ined, -ension
def. art.	definite article
det.	determinate
dial.	dialect(al)
dim.	diminutive
dipl.	diploma|cy, -tic
disp.	disputed
eccl.	ecclesiastical
econ.	economics
educ.	education, -al
elec.	electric|al, -ity
ellipt.	elliptical
emph.	empha|size(s), -sizing, -tic
eng.	engineering
Eng.	English
entom.	entomology
esp.	especially
ethnol.	ethnology
euph.	euphemis|m, -tic
exc.	except
excl.	exclamation
expr.	express|ed, -es, -ing, -ion
f.	feminine
fem.	female
fig.	figurative
fin.	financ|e, -ial
Fr.	French
freq.	frequentative
fut.	future (tense)
g.	genitive
geod.	geodesy
geog.	geography
geol.	geology
geom.	geometry
ger.	gerund
Ger.	German
Gk.	Greek
g.pl.	genitive plural
gram.	grammar
g.sg.	genitive singular
her.	heraldry
hist.	histor|y, -ical
hort.	horticulture
i.	instrumental; intransitive in '*v.i.*'
imper.	imperative
impers.	impersonal
impf.	imperfective
ind.	indirect
indecl.	indeclinable
indef.	indefinite
indet.	indeterminate
inf.	infinitive
inst.	instantaneous
int.	interjection
interrog.	interrogative
intrans.	intransitive
iron.	ironical
Ital.	Italian
joc.	jocular
journ.	journalism
Lat.	Latin
leg.	legal
ling.	linguistics
lit.	literal
liter.	literary
log.	logic
m.	masculine

math. mathematics
mech. mechanics
med. medicin|e, -al
metall. metallurgy
meteor. meteorology
mil. military
min. mineralogy
mod. modern
mus. music(al)
myth. mythology

n. noun
naut. nautical
nav. naval
neg. negative
nn. nouns
nom. nominative
nom.-a. nominative-accusative
nt. neuter
num., nums. numer|al, -ical; -als

obj. object
obs. obsolete
oft. often
onomat. onomatopeia
opp. opposite (to); as opposed to
opt. optics
o.s. oneself

p. prepositional (case)
See also p.p. *and* p.p.p.
palaeog. palaeography
parl. parliamentary
part. participle
pass. passive
path. pathology
pej. pejorative
pers. person(s); personal
pert. pertaining
pf. perfective
pharm. pharmaceutical
phil. philosophy
philol. philology
phon. phonetic(s)
phot. photography
phr., phrr. phrase; -s
phys. physic|s, -al
physiol. physiology
pl. plural
poet. poet|ical, -ry
pol. political
poss. possessive
p.p. past participle
p.p.p. past participle passive
pr. pronounce(d); pronunciation
pred. predicate; predicative
pref. prefix
prep., preps. preposition; -s
pres. present (tense)

pret. preterite
pron., prons. pronoun; -s
propr. proprietary term
pros. prosody
prov., provs. proverb; -s
psych. psychology

radiol. radiology
rail. railway
refl. reflexive
rel. relative
relig. religion
rhet. rhetorical
Rom. Roman
Ru. Russian

Sc. Scottish
sc. scilicet
sg. singular
sl. slang
s.o. someone
soc. social
stat. statistics
sth. something
subj. subject
suff. suffix
superl. superlative
surv. surveying

t. transitive in 'v.t.'
tech. technical
teleg. telegraphy
teleph. telephony
text. textiles
theatr. theatr|e, -ical
theol. theology
thg. thing
trans. transitive
trig. trigonometry
TV television
typ. typography

univ. university
US United States;
United States usage
usu. usually

v. verb
var. various
v.aux. auxiliary verb
vbl. verbal
vet. veterinary
v.i. intransitive verb
voc. vocative
v.t. transitive verb
vulg. vulgar(ism)
vv. verbs

zool. zoology

The Russian -н. in illustrative phrases within entries stands for the enclitic -нибудь (in the words кто-нибудь, что-нибудь, etc.).

This dictionary includes some words which are, or are asserted to be, proprietary names or trade marks. These words are labelled (*propr.*). The presence or absence of this label should not be regarded as affecting the legal status of any proprietary name or trade mark.

A (*abbr. of* **ампе́р**) amp, ampere.

а[1] *conj.* **1.** and; while, whereas; **вот ма́рки, а вот три рубля́ сда́чи** here are the stamps and here is three roubles change; **она́ лю́бит о́перу, а я предпочита́ю кино́** she likes opera, whereas I prefer the cinema; **а и́менно** namely; to be exact. **2.** but; yet (*or not translated*); **пора́ идти́ — а мы то́лько что пришли́!** 'It's time to go.' 'But we've only just come!'; **я иду́ не в кино́, а в теа́тр** I am going to the theatre, not to the cinema. **3.: а то** or (else), otherwise.

а[2] *interrog. particle* (*coll.*) eh?; what('s that)?; huh?

а[3] *int.* (*expr. surprise, annoyance, pain, etc.*; *coll.*) ah, oh; **а ну его́!** oh, to hell with him!

абажу́р, а *m.* lampshade.

абба́т, а *m.* abbot.

аббати́с|а, ы *f.* abbess.

абба́тств|о, а *nt.* abbey.

аббревиату́р|а, ы *f.* abbreviation; acronym.

аберра́ци|я, и *f.* aberration.

абза́ц, а *m.* paragraph; **нача́ть с но́вого ~а** to begin a new line, new paragraph.

абитурие́нт, а *m.* (*college, university*) entrant.

абонеме́нт, а *m.* subscription; season ticket.

абонеме́нтн|ый *adj.*: **~ая ка́рточка** reader's *or* borrower's card; **~ая пла́та** (*TV, radio*) licence fee.

абоне́нт, а *m.* subscriber; (*library*) borrower, reader; (*theatre, etc.*) season-ticket holder.

аборда́ж, а *m.* (*naut.*) boarding; **взять на а.** to board.

абориге́н, а *m.* aboriginal.

абориге́нный *adj.* aboriginal; native.

або́рт, а *m.* abortion; miscarriage; **сде́лать а.** to have an abortion.

абракада́бр|а, ы *f.* gibberish, gobbledygook.

абрико́с, а *m.* **1.** apricot. **2.** apricot-tree.

абрико́с|овый *adj. of* ~

а́брис, а *m.* contour(s); outline.

абсе́нт, а *m.* absinthe.

абсолю́т, а *m.* (*phil.*) the absolute.

абсолюти́зм, а *m.* (*pol.*) absolutism.

абсолюти́ст, а *m.* (*pol.*) absolutist.

абсолю́т|ный (~ен, ~на) *adj.* absolute; **а. слух** (*mus.*) perfect pitch.

абсорби́р|овать, ую *impf. and pf.* to absorb.

абсо́рбци|я, и *f.* absorption.

абстине́нци|я, и *f.* (*med.*) withdrawal symptoms; **наркоти́ческая а.** drug withdrawal symptoms.

абстраги́р|овать, ую *impf. and pf.* to abstract.

абстра́кт|ный (~ен, ~на) *adj.* abstract.

абстракциони́зм, а *m.* abstractionism.

абстракциони́ст, а *m.* abstractionist.

абстра́кци|я, и *f.* abstraction.

абсу́рд, а *m.* absurdity; **довести́ до ~а** to carry to the point of absurdity.

абсу́рдност|ь, и *f.* absurdity.

абсу́рд|ный (~ен, ~на) *adj.* absurd.

абсце́сс, а *m.* abscess.

аванга́рд, а *m.* **1.** advance-guard, van; vanguard (*also fig.*). **2.** (*fig.*) avant-garde.

авангарди́зм, а *m.* avant-gardism.

авангарди́ст, а *m.* avant-gardist.

авангард|и́стский *adj. of* ~ **2.**

аванга́рд|ный *adj. of* ~ **1.**

аванза́л, а *m.* ante-room.

аванпо́ст, а *m.* (*mil.*) outpost; forward position (*also fig.*).

ава́нс, а *m.* **1.** advance (*of money*); **получи́ть а.** to receive an advance. **2.** (*pl. only*; *fig.*) advances, overtures.

аванси́р|овать, ую *impf. and pf.* to advance (*money*).

ава́нсом *adv.* in advance, on account.

авансце́н|а, ы *f.* (*theatr.*) proscenium.

авантю́р|а, ы *f.* **1.** (*pej.*) adventure; escapade. **2.** (risky) venture.

авантюри́зм, а *m.* adventurism.

авантюри́ст, а *m.* adventurist.

авантюр|исти́ческий *adj. of* **~изм**

авантюри́стк|а, и *f.* adventuress.

авантю́р|ный (~ен, ~на) *adj.* adventurous; **а. рома́н** (*liter.*) adventure story.

авари́йно-спаса́тельн|ый *adj.* (emergency-)rescue.

авари́йност|ь, и *f.* accident rate.

авари́йн|ый *adj.* **1.** *adj. of* **ава́рия; а. компле́кт** survival kit; **~ая маши́на** breakdown van; (*aeron.*): **~ая поса́дка** crash landing; **а. сигна́л** distress signal. **2.** emergency, spare.

ава́ри|я, и *f.* **1.** crash, accident; wreck; **потерпе́ть ~ю** to crash, have an accident. **2.** breakdown.

авгу́р, а *m.* augur.

а́вгуст, а *m.* August.

а́вгуст|овский *adj. of* ~

а́виа (*abbr. of* **авиапо́чтой**) '(by) airmail'.

авиа... *comb. form* (*abbr. of* **авиацио́нный**)

авиабиле́т, а *m.* airline ticket.

авиадеса́нт, а *m.* **1.** airborne assault landing. **2.** airborne assault force.

авиадеса́нтник, а *m.* paratrooper.

авиадеса́нтн|ый *adj.* airborne assault; **~ые войска́** airborne assault troops.

авиадиспе́тчер, а *m.* air-traffic controller.

авиадиспе́тчерск|ий *adj.*: **~ая слу́жба** (air) flight control.

авиакатастро́ф|а, ы *f.* air crash.

авиакомпа́ни|я, и *f.* airline, air carrier.

авиакосми́ческий = авиацио́нно-косми́ческий

авиали́ни|я, и *f.* airway, air route.

авиано́с|ец, ца *m.* aircraft carrier.

авиапереброс́к|а, и *f.* airlift.

авиаписьм|о́, а́, *pl.* **~а, авиапи́сем, ~ам** *nt.* air(mail) letter; aerogram(me).

авиапо́чт|а, ы *f.* air mail.

авиараке́т|а, ы *f.* air-launched missile.

авиаспо́рт, а *m.* aerial sports.

авиасъёмк|а, и *f.* aerial surveying.
авиа́тор, а *m.* aviator.
авиатра́нспортн|ый *adj.*: **~ая компа́ния** airline, air carrier.
авиатра́сс|а, ы *f.* air route, air lane.
авиацио́нно-косми́ческ|ий *adj.* aerospace.
авиацио́нн|ый *adj. of* **авиа́ция; ~ая шко́ла** flying school.
авиа́ци|я, и *f.* **1.** aviation. **2.** (*collect.*) aircraft. **3.** aeronautics.
авиача́ст|ь, и *f.* air force unit.
авиашко́л|а, ы *f.* flying school.
ави́зо *nt. indecl.* (*comm.*) advice (note).
авока́до *nt. indecl.* avocado (*tree*); **плод а.** avocado (*fruit*).
аво́сь *particle* (*coll.*) perhaps; **на а.** on the off-chance.
аво́ськ|а, и *f.* (*coll.*) string (shopping) bag.
авра́л, а *m.* **1.** (*naut.*) all-hands evolution; (*as int.*) all hands on deck! **2.** (*coll.*) rush job.
авра́л|ьный *adj.*: **~ьная рабо́та = авра́л**
авро́ра, ы *f.* (*poet.*) aurora, dawn.
австрали́|ец, йца *m.* Australian.
австрали́|йка, йки *f. of* **~ец**
австрали́йский *adj.* Australian.
Австра́ли|я, и *f.* Australia.
австри́|ец, йца *m.* Austrian.
австри́|йка, йки *f. of* **~ец**
австри́йский *adj.* Austrian.
А́встри|я, и *f.* Austria.
авто... *comb. form* **1.** self-, auto-. **2.** *abbr. of* (*i*) **автомати́ческий** *and* (*ii*) **автомоби́льный**
автоава́ри|я, и *f.* road accident.
автоба́з|а, ы *f.* motor-transport depot.
автобиографи́ческий *adj.* autobiographical.
автобиогра́фи|я, и *f.* autobiography.
авто́бус, а *m.* bus; (*inter-city vehicle*) coach.
автовладе́л|ец, ьца *m.* car owner.
автовокза́л, а *m.* bus terminal; coach station.
автово́р, а *m.* (*coll.*) car thief.
автого́нк|а, и *f.* car-race.
автого́нщик, а *m.* racing-driver.
авто́граф, а *m.* autograph.
автода́ч|а, и *f.* mobile home, caravan.
автодоро́г|а, и *f.* road; highway.
автодоро́жник, а *m.* highway engineer.
автодоро́жн|ый *adj.* road-transport; highway.
автодро́м, а *m.* **1.** vehicle testing point. **2.** motor-racing circuit.
автожи́р, а *m.* autogyro.
автозаво́д, а *m.* motor-car factory.
автозапра́вочн|ый *adj.*: **~ая ста́нция** petrol station.
автозапра́вщик, а *m.* petrol tanker.
автоинспе́ктор, а *m.* traffic inspector.
автоинспе́кци|я, и *f.* traffic inspectorate.
автоинформа́тор, а *m.* **1.** recorded (telephone) message. **2.** answerphone.
автока́р, а *m.* motor trolley.
автокаранда́ш, а́ *m.* propelling pencil.
автокатастро́ф|а, ы *f.* road accident.
автоколо́нк|а, и *f.* petrol pump.
автоколо́нн|а, ы *f.* motorcade; convoy.
автокра́т, а *m.* autocrat.
автократи́ческий *adj.* autocratic.
автокра́ти|я, и *f.* autocracy.
автокро́сс, а *m.* autocross.
авто́л, а *m.* motor oil.
автола́вк|а, и *f.* mobile shop.
автолиха́ч, а́ *m.* reckless driver, road-hog.
автомагистра́л|ь, и *f.* motorway.
автомастерск|а́я, о́й *f.* car repair garage.
автома́т, а *m.* **1.** automatic machine, slot-machine; **де́нежный а.** cash dispenser; **стира́льный а.** washing machine; **суши́льный а.** drier; **телефо́н-а.** pay phone; **торго́вый а.** vending machine; (*fig.*) automaton, robot. **2.** (*mil.*) (*coll.*) sub-machine-gun.
автоматиза́ци|я, и *f.* automation.
автоматизи́рованн|ый *adj.* computer-aided; **~ое проекти́рование** CAD, computer-aided design.
автоматизи́р|овать, ую *impf. and pf.* to automate.
автома́тик|а, и *f.* **1.** automation. **2.** automatic equipment.
автомати́ческ|ий *adj.* **1.** (*tech.*) automatic, self-acting; **~ая винто́вка** automatic (rifle); **~ая ру́чка** fountain-pen. **2.** (*fig.*) automatic, involuntary.
автомати́ч|ный (~ен, ~на) = ~еский 2.
автома́т|ный *adj. of* **~ 2.**
автома́тчик, а *m.* (*mil.*) sub-machine-gunner.
автомаши́н|а, ы *f.* motor vehicle.
автомобилево́з, а *m.* (*vehicle*) transporter.
автомоби́л|ь, я *m.* motor vehicle; (motor)car; **легково́й а.** (passenger) car; **грузово́й а.** lorry.
автомоби́ль|ный *adj. of* **~**
автомо́йк|а, и *f.* car wash.
автомотодро́м, а *m.* race-track.
автоно́ми|я, и *f.* autonomy.
автоно́м|ный (~ен, ~на) *adj.* autonomous.
автоотве́тчик = автоинформа́тор
автопо́езд, а, *pl.* **~а́** *m.* articulated lorry; juggernaut.
автопортре́т, а *m.* self-portrait.
автоприце́п, а *m.* trailer, caravan; **жило́й а.** camper, mobile home.
автопроисше́стви|е, я *nt.* road accident.
а́втор, а *m.* author; composer; (*fig.*) architect; **а. резолю́ции** mover of resolution.
автора́лли *nt. indecl.* (car) rally.
автoралли́ст, а *m.* rallyist, rally driver.
автореферáт, а *m.* (author's) abstract.
авториза́ци|я, и *f.* authorization.
авториз|о́ванный *p.p.p. of* **~ова́ть** *and adj.* authorized.
авториз|ова́ть, у́ю *impf. and pf.* to authorize.
авторитари́зм, а *m.* authoritarianism.
авторитари́ст, а *m.* (*pol.*) authoritarian, hard-liner.
авторита́р|ный (~ен, ~на) *adj.* authoritarian.
авторите́т, а *m.* authority.
авторите́тност|ь, и *f.* authoritativeness; trustworthiness.
авторите́т|ный (~ен, ~на) *adj.* authoritative; trustworthy; **а. исто́чник** an authoritative source.
а́втор|ский *adj. of* **~; ~ское пра́во** copyright; *as n.* **~ские, ~ских** royalties.
а́вторско-правово́й *adj.* copyright.
а́вторств|о, а *nt.* authorship.
автору́чк|а, и *f.* fountain-pen.
автоса́н|и, е́й *no sg.* sledge car, motor sleigh.
автосекрета́р|ь, я́ *m.* answerphone, (telephone) answering machine.
автоспо́рт, а *m.* motor sports.
автоста́нци|я, и *f.* bus station; coach station.
автосто́п, а *m.* hitch-hiking.
автостоя́нк|а, и *f.* car park.
автостра́д|а, ы *f.* **= автомагистра́ль**
автосуфлёр, а *m.* Autocue (*propr.*), teleprompter.
автотелефо́н, а *m.* car phone.
автотра́нспорт, а *m.* motor transport.
автотра́сс|а, ы *f.* highway.
автотрюка́ч, а́ *m.* stunt driver.
автотури́зм, а *m.* motor touring.
автотури́ст, а *m.* motor tourer.
автофурго́н, а *m.* van.
автоцисте́рн|а, ы *f.* tanker.
автошко́л|а, ы *f.* driving school; **преподава́тель** (*m.*) **~ы** driving instructor.
ага́ *int.* (*expr.* (*i*) *comprehension*, (*ii*) *malicious pleasure*) ah!; aha!
ага́т, а *m.* (*min.*) agate.

ага́т|овый *adj. of* ~
аге́нт, а *m.* (*in var. senses*) agent.
аге́нтств|о, а *nt.* agency; **а. печа́ти** news agency; **а. (для) по́мощи** aid agency; **бракопосре́дническое а.** marriage bureau.
агенту́р|а, ы *f.* **1.** secret service. **2.** (*collect.*) agents.
агиогра́фи|я, и *f.* hagiography.
агит... *comb. form, abbr. of* **агитацио́нный**
агита́тор, а *m.* (*pol.*) agitator; canvasser; campaigner; electioneer.
агитацио́н|ный (~ен, ~на) *adj.* (*pol.*) agitation; **~ная речь** campaign speech.
агита́ци|я, и *f.* (*pol.*) agitation; drive; **вести́ ~ю** to campaign; **предвы́борная а.** electioneering.
агити́р|овать, ую *impf.* **1.** (*impf. only*) (*pol.*) to agitate, campaign. **2.** (*pf.* **с~**) (*coll.*) to canvass.
аги́тк|а, и *f.* (*pol.*) propaganda piece (*plays, posters, etc.*).
агитпу́нкт, а *m.* agitation centre.
а́гн|ец, ца *m.*: **прики́нуться ~цем** to play the innocent.
агно́стик, а *m.* agnostic.
агностици́зм, а *m.* agnosticism.
агности́ческий *adj.* agnostic.
агонизи́р|овать, ую *impf. and pf.* to be in one's death agony.
аго́ни|я, и *f.* (*med. and fig.*) death-throes.
агра́рный *adj.* agrarian.
агрега́т, а *m.* **1.** (*tech.*) unit, assembly. **2.** aggregate.
агрега́тный *adj.* modular.
агресси́в|ный (~ен, ~на) *adj.* aggressive.
агре́сси|я, и *f.* (*pol.*) aggression.
агре́ссор, а *m.* aggressor.
агро... *comb. form* agro-, agricultural, farm.
агроно́м, а *m.* agronomist.
агроно́ми|я, и *f.* agronomics; agricultural science.
агроте́хник, а *m.* agricultural technician.
агроте́хник|а, и *f.* agricultural technology.
агрохими́ческий *adj.* agrochemical.
ад, а *m.* hell; (*fig.*) bedlam; **душе́вный а.** mental torment, anguish.
ада́мов *adj.*: **~о я́блоко** Adam's apple.
ада́жио (*mus.*) **1.** *adv.* **2.** *n.*; *nt. indecl.* adagio.
адапта́ци|я, и *f.* (*in var. senses*) adaptation.
ада́птер, а *m.* **1.** (*tech.*) adapter. **2.** (*mus.*) pick-up.
адвенти́ст, а *m.* (*relig.*) (Seventh-day) Adventist.
адвока́т, а *m.* barrister; (*fig.*) advocate.
адвокату́р|а, ы *f.* **1.** the profession of barrister. **2.** (*collect.*) the Bar, the legal profession.
адеква́т|ный (~ен, ~на) *adj.* identical, coincident; adequate.
адено́ид, а *m.* (*med.*) adenoid.
аде́пт, а *m.* adherent, disciple.
администрати́вн|ый *adj.* administrative.
администра́тор, а *m.* administrator; manager (*of hotel, theatre, etc.*).
администра́торск|ая, ой *f.* (*hotel*) reception.
администра́ци|я, и *f.* administration; management.
администри́р|овать, ую *impf.* to administer; manage.
адмира́л, а *m.* admiral.
адмиралте́й|ский *adj. of* **~ство**
адмиралте́йств|о, а *nt.* the Admiralty.
адмира́л|ьский *adj. of* ~; **а. кора́бль** flagship.
а́дрес, а, *pl.* **~а́, ~о́в** *m.* (*in var. senses*) address; **в а.** (*+g.*) (*fig.*) aimed at, directed at; **не по ~у** (*fig.*) to the wrong quarter.
адреса́т, а *m.* addressee.
а́дрес|ный *adj. of* ~; **~ная кни́га** directory; **а. стол** address bureau.
адрес|ова́ть, у́ю *impf. and pf.* to address, direct.
адрес|ова́ться, у́юсь *impf. and pf.* (**к**+*d.*) to address o.s. (to).
Адриати́ческ|ое мо́р|е, ~ого ~я *nt.* the Adriatic (Sea).
а́дски *adv.* (*coll.*) infernally, terribly.
а́дск|ий *adj.* infernal, diabolical; (*fig.*) hellish, intolerable; **~ая ску́ка** infernal bore.
адсо́рбци|я, и *f.* (*chem.*) adsorption.
адъюта́нт, а *m.* (*mil.*) aide-de-camp; **ста́рший а.** adjutant.
аж *adv. and conj.* (*coll.*) **1.** (*adv.*) **аж до** right up to; **аж на** (*+a.*) right on to. **2.** (*conj.*) so that, until; **она́ так закрича́ла, аж се́рдце похолоде́ло** she cried enough to break one's heart.
ажиота́ж, а *m.* **1.** (*comm.*) stockjobbing. **2.** (*fig.*) stir, hullabaloo.
ажу́р, а *m.* (*comm.*): **учёт в ~е** the accounts are up to date; **всё в (по́лном) ~е** (*fig., coll.*) everything's fine.
ажу́рн|ый *adj.* open-work; (*fig.*) delicate, fine.
аз, а́ *m.* **1.** az (*Slavonic name of the letter A*). **2.** (*usu. pl.*; *coll.*) basics, rudiments; **начина́ть с ~о́в** to begin at the beginning; **ни ~а́ не знать** (**о**+*p.*) not to know the first thing (about).
аза́ли|я, и *f.* (*bot.*) azalea.
аза́рт, а *m.* heat; excitement; fervour; **войти́ в а.** to grow heated, excited.
аза́рт|ный (~ен, ~на) *adj.* heated; venturesome; **~ная игра́** game of chance.
а́збук|а, и *f.* alphabet; the ABC (*also fig.*); **а. Мо́рзе** Morse code; **дакти́льная а.** sign language.
а́збучн|ый *adj.* alphabetical; **~ая и́стина** truism.
Азербайджа́н, а *m.* Azerbaijan.
азербайджа́н|ец, ца *m.* Azerbaijani.
азербайджа́н|ка, ки *f. of* **~ец**
азербайджа́нский *adj.* Azerbaijani.
азиа́т, а *m.* Asian; Asiatic.
азиа́т|ка, ки *f. of* ~
азиа́т|ский *adj. of* ~
а́зимут, а *m.* (*astron.*) azimuth.
А́зи|я, и *f.* Asia.
азо́т, а *m.* (*chem.*) nitrogen; **о́кись ~а** nitric oxide.
азотистоки́слый *adj.* (*chem.*) nitrite.
азо́тистый *adj.* (*chem.*) nitrous.
азотноки́слый *adj.* (*chem.*) nitrate.
азо́тн|ый *adj.* (*chem.*) nitric; **~ая кислота́** nitric acid.
а́ир, а *m.* (*bot.*) sweet flag.
а́ист, а *m.* (*zool.*) stork.
ай *int.* (*expr.* (*i*) *fear,* (*ii*) *surprise and/or pleasure*) oh!; ow, ouch; **ай, бо́льно!** ow, that hurts!; **ай да** (*expr. approval*) what a ...!; **ай да молоде́ц!** well done!
айв|а́, ы́ *f.* **1.** quince. **2.** quince-tree.
айво́вый *adj.* quince.
айда́ *int.* (*coll.*) come along!; let's go!
айкидо́ *nt. indecl.* aikido.
а́йсберг, а *m.* iceberg.
академи́зм, а *m.* academic manner.
акаде́мик, а *m.* academician.
академи́ческий *adj.* academic(al); **а. мир** academia, academe; **а. о́тпуск** sabbatical (leave).
академи́ч|ный (~ен, ~на) *adj.* academic, theoretical.
акаде́ми|я, и *f.* academy.
а́кань|е, я *nt.* 'akanie' (*pronunciation of unstressed Russian 'o' as 'a'*).
а́ка|ть, ю *impf.* to pronounce unstressed Russian 'o' as 'a'.
ака́ци|я, и *f.* (*bot.*) acacia.
аквала́нг, а *m.* aqualung.
акваланги́ст, а *m.* skin diver.
акваланги́ст|ка, ки *f. of* ~
аквамари́н, а *m.* (*min.*) aquamarine.
аквапла́н, а *m.* aquaplane; **ката́ться на ~е** to aquaplane.

акварели́ст, а *m.* water-colourist.
акваре́л|ь, и *f.* water-colours; **писа́ть ~ ью** to paint in water-colours.
акваре́льный *adj.* water-colour.
аква́риум, а *m.* aquarium.
аквато́ри|я, и *f.* (*defined*) waters, water area.
акведу́к, а *m.* aqueduct.
акклиматиза́ци|я, и *f.* acclimatization.
акклиматизи́р|овать, ую *impf. and pf.* to acclimatize.
акклиматизи́р|оваться, уюсь *impf. and pf.* to become acclimatized.
аккомпанеме́нт, а *m.* (*mus.*) accompaniment (*also fig.*); **под а.** (*+g.*) to the accompaniment of.
аккомпаниа́тор, а *m.* (*mus.*) accompanist.
аккомпани́р|овать, ую *impf.* (*+d.*, **на**+*p.*; *mus.*) to accompany.
акко́рд, а *m.* (*mus.*) chord; **заключи́тельный а.** (*fig.*) finale; **взять а.** to strike a chord.
аккордео́н, а *m.* accordion.
аккордеони́ст, а *m.* accordionist.
акко́рдн|ый *adj.*: **~ая пла́та** payment by the job; **~ая рабо́та** piecework.
аккредити́в, а *m.* (*fin.*) letter of credit.
аккредит|ова́ть, у́ю *impf. and pf.* to accredit.
аккумули́р|овать, ую *impf. and pf.* to accumulate.
аккумуля́тор, а *m.* (*tech.*) accumulator; battery.
аккумуля́ци|я, и *f.* accumulation.
аккура́тност|ь, и *f.* **1.** exactness, thoroughness. **2.** tidiness, neatness.
аккура́т|ный (~ен, ~на) *adj.* **1.** exact, thorough. **2.** tidy, neat.
акмеи́зм, а *m.* (*liter.*) acmeism.
акмеи́ст, а *m.* (*liter.*) acmeist.
акри́л, а *m.* acrylic.
акри́л|овый *adj. of* **~**
акроба́т, а *m.* acrobat.
акроба́тик|а, и *f.* acrobatics.
акро́ним, а *m.* acronym.
акрости́х, а *m.* acrostic.
акселера́т, а *m.* (*med.*) early developer, maturer.
акселера́тор, а *m.* accelerator.
акселера́ци|я, и *f.* (*med.*) early development, maturation; **а. ро́ста** accelerated growth.
аксельба́нт, а *m.* aiguillette.
аксессуа́р, а *m.* **1.** accessory. **2.** *pl.* (*theatr.*) props.
аксио́м|а, ы *f.* axiom.
акт, а *m.* **1.** act; **полово́й а.** sexual intercourse. **2.** (*theatr.*) act. **3.** (*leg.*) deed, document; instrument; **обвини́тельный а.** indictment.
актёр, а *m.* actor.
актёр|ский *adj. of* **~**
актёрств|о, а *nt.* acting; (*fig.*) affectation, posing.
акти́в[1]**, а** *m.* (*fin.*) assets; (*fig.*) asset.
акти́в[2]**, а** *m.* (*pol.*) most active members; **парти́йный а.** party activists.
активиза́ци|я, и *f.* intensification.
активизи́р|овать, ую *impf. and pf.* to intensify; to stimulate, promote.
активи́ст, а *m.* (*pol.*) activist (*active member of political or social organization*).
акти́в|ный (~ен, ~на) *adj.* active, energetic.
акти́ни|я, и *f.* sea anemone.
а́ктов|ый *adj.*: **а. зал** assembly hall.
актри́с|а, ы *f.* actress.
актуа́льност|ь, и *f.* topicality.
актуа́л|ьный (~ен, ~ьна) *adj.* topical, current.
аку́л|а, ы *f.* (*zool.*) shark (*also fig.*).
акупункту́р|а, ы *f.* acupuncture
аку́стик, а *m.* sound-man, sound technician.
аку́стик|а, и *f.* acoustics.
акусти́ческий *adj.* acoustic.
акуше́р, а *m.* obstetrician.
акуше́рк|а, и *f.* midwife.
акуше́рский *adj.* obstetric(al).
акуше́рств|о, а *nt.* obstetrics; midwifery.
акце́нт, а *m.* accent.
акценти́р|овать, ую *impf. and pf.* to accent, accentuate.
акце́пт, а *m.* (*comm.*) acceptance.
акцепт|ова́ть, у́ю *impf. and pf.* (*comm.*) to accept.
акци́з, а *m.* (excise-)duty; **обложи́ть ~ом** to excise.
акционе́р, а *m.* shareholder, stockholder.
акционе́р|ный *adj. of* **~**; **~ное о́бщество** joint-stock company.
а́кци|я[1]**, и** *f.* (*fin.*) share; **обыкнове́нная а.** ordinary share; **привилегиро́ванная а.** preference share.
а́кци|я[2]**, и** *f.* action.
алба́н|ец, ца *m.* Albanian.
Алба́ни|я, и *f.* Albania.
алба́н|ка, ки *f. of* **~ец**
алба́нский *adj.* Albanian.
а́лгебр|а, ы *f.* algebra.
алгебраи́ческий *adj.* algebraic(al).
алгори́тм, а *m.* algorithm.
алеба́рд|а, ы *f.* (*hist.*) halberd.
алеба́стр, а *m.* alabaster.
александри́т, а *m.* (*min.*) alexandrite.
але́|ть, ю *impf.* (*of* **за~**) **1.** to redden, flush. **2.** to show red.
Алжи́р, а *m.* **1.** Algeria. **2.** Algiers.
алжи́р|ец, ца *m.* Algerian.
алжи́р|ка, ки *f. of* **~ец**
алжи́рский *adj.* Algerian.
а́либи *nt. indecl.* (*leg.*) alibi; **установи́ть а.** to establish an alibi.
алиме́нт|ы, ов *no sg.* (*leg.*) alimony, maintenance.
ал|ка́ть, ~чу, ~чешь *impf.* (*+g.*; *poet.*) to hunger (for), crave (for).
алка́ш, а́ *m.* (*coll.*, *pej.*) boozer, dipso.
алкоголи́зм, а *m.* alcoholism.
алкого́лик, а *m.* alcoholic; (*coll.*) drunkard.
алкоголи́ческий *adj.* alcoholic.
алкого́л|ь, я *m.* alcohol; **прове́рить на а.** to breathalyze.
алкого́льный *adj.* alcoholic.
алкоме́тр, а *m.* breathalyzer.
Алла́х, а *m.* Allah; **А. его́ ве́дает** God knows; **одному́ ~у изве́стно** God alone knows.
аллегори́ч|еский *adj.* allegorical.
аллегори́ч|ный (~ен, ~на) = **~еский**
аллего́ри|я, и *f.* allegory.
алле́гро (*mus.*) **1.** *adv.* **2.** *n.*; *nt. indecl.* allegro.
аллерге́н, а *m.* allergen.
алле́ргик, а *m.* allergy sufferer.
аллерги́|я, и *f.* allergy.
алле́|я, и *f.* **1.** path, walk, ride. **2.** avenue.
аллига́тор, а *m.* alligator.
аллилу́йя *nt. indecl. and as int.* hallelujah.
аллитера́ци|я, и *f.* alliteration.
алло́ *int.* hello!
аллопа́т, а *m.* (*med.*) allopath(ist).
аллопа́ти|я, и *f.* (*med.*) allopathy.
аллопати́ческий *adj.* (*med.*) allopathic.
аллювиа́льный *adj.* (*geol.*) alluvial.
аллю́ви|й, я *m.* (*geol.*) alluvium.
аллю́р, а *m.* gait (*of horses*).
алма́з, а *m.* (uncut) diamond.
ало́э *nt. indecl.* (*bot.*) aloe; (*med.*) aloes.
алта́р|ь, я́ *m.* **1.** (*eccl.*) altar; **возложи́ть, принести́ на а.** (*+g.*) to sacrifice (to). **2.** (*eccl.*) chancel; sanctuary.
алфави́т, а *m.* alphabet.
алфави́тно-цифрово́й *adj.* alphanumeric.
алфави́тный *adj.* alphabetical; **а. указа́тель** index.

алхи́мик, а *m.* alchemist.
алхи́ми|я , и *f.* alchemy.
а́лчност|ь, и *f.* greed, avidity, cupidity.
а́лч|ный (~ен, ~на) *adj.* greedy, grasping.
а́лчущ|ий *pres. part. of* **алка́ть**
а́л|ый (~, ~а) *adj.* scarlet.
алыч|а́, и́ *f.* cherry-plum.
альбатро́с, а *m.* albatross.
альбино́с, а *m.* (*med.*) albino.
альбо́м, а *m.* album.
алько́в, а *m.* alcove.
а́льма-ма́тер *f. indecl.* Alma Mater.
альмана́х, а *m.* literary miscellany.
альпака́ *c.g. indecl. and nt. indecl.* **1.** *c.g.* alpaca (*animal*). **2.** *nt.* alpaca (*fabric*).
альпи́йский *adj.* alpine.
альпина́ри|й, я *m.* rock garden.
альпини́зм, а *m.* mountaineering.
альпини́ст, а *m.* mountain-climber.
А́льп|ы, ~ *no sg.* the Alps.
альт, а́, *pl.* **~ы́** *m.* (*mus.*) **1.** alto (*voice or singer*). **2.** viola.
альтернати́в|а, ы *f.* alternative.
альтернати́в|ный (~ен, ~на) *adj.* alternative.
альти́ст, а *m.* viola-player.
альтруи́зм, а *m.* altruism.
альтруи́ст, а *m.* altruist.
альтруисти́ческий *adj.* altruistic.
а́льф|а, ы *f.* alpha; **от ~ы до оме́ги** from A to Z.
альфо́нс, а *m.* (*pej.*) gigolo.
алья́нс, а *m.* alliance.
алюми́ниевый *adj.* aluminium.
алюми́ни|й, я *m.* aluminium.
а-ля́ *prep.* à la.
аляпова́т|ый (~, ~а) *adj.* garish, cheap-looking; crude(ly fashioned).
а-ля фурше́т, а *m.* buffet; fork lunch *or* supper.
Амазо́нк|а, и *f.* the Amazon (*river*).
амазо́нк|а, и *f.* **1.** (*myth.*) Amazon. **2.** horsewoman.
амальга́м|а, ы *f.* (*chem. and fig.*) amalgam.
амальгами́р|овать, ую *impf. and pf.* to amalgamate.
амба́р, а *m.* barn, granary; warehouse, storehouse.
амба́р|ный *adj. of* **~**
амбицио́з|ный (~ен, ~на) *adj.* arrogant, conceited.
амби́ци|я, и *f.* **1.** (*obs.*) pride; arrogance; **вломи́ться в ~ю** to take umbrage. **2.** *pl.* claims (to) (**на**+*a.*).
а́мбр|а, ы *f.* amber; **се́рая а.** ambergris.
амбразу́р|а, ы *f.* (*mil., archit.*) embrasure.
амбро́зи|я, и *f.* ambrosia.
амбулато́ри|я, и *f.* (*med.*) out-patients department (*of hospital*); (*general practioner's*) surgery.
амбулато́р|ный *adj. of* **~ия; а. больно́й** out-patient.
амбушю́р, а *m.* (*mus.*) mouthpiece.
амво́н, а *m.* (*eccl.*) ambo, pulpit.
амёб|а, ы *f.* (*zool.*) amoeba.
Аме́рик|а, и *f.* America.
америка́н|ец, ца *m.* American.
американи́зм, а *m.* (*ling.*) Americanism.
американи́стик|а, и *f.* American studies.
америка́н|ка, ки *f. of* **~ец**
америка́нск|ий *adj.* American; **~ие го́ры** Big Dipper; **а. замо́к** Yale (*propr.*) lock; **а. оре́х** Brazil nut.
амети́ст, а *m.* (*min.*) amethyst.
амети́ст|овый *adj. of* **~**
аминокислот|а́, ы́ *f.* (*chem.*) aminoacid.
ами́нь *particle* (*eccl.*) amen.
аммиа́к, а *m.* (*chem.*) ammonia.
аммиа́чный *adj.* (*chem.*) ammoniac.
аммо́ни|й, я *m.* (*chem.*) ammonium.
амнисти́р|овать, ую *impf. and pf.* to amnesty.
амни́сти|я, и *f.* amnesty.
аморали́зм, а *m.* (*phil.*) amoralism.
амора́льност|ь, и *f.* amorality; immorality.
амора́л|ьный (~ен, ~ьна) *adj.* amoral; immoral.
амортиза́тор, а *m.* (*tech.*) shock-absorber.
амортиза́ци|я, и *f.* **1.** (*econ.*) amortization. **2.** (*tech.*) shock-absorption.
амортизи́р|овать, ую *impf. and pf.* to amortize.
амо́рф|ный (~ен, ~на) *adj.* amorphous.
ампе́р, а, *g. pl.* **а.** *m.* (*phys.*) ampere.
амплиту́д|а, ы *f.* amplitude.
амплуа́ *nt. indecl.* (*theatr.*) type; (*fig.*) role.
а́мпул|а, ы *f.* ampoule.
ампута́ци|я, и *f.* (*med.*) amputation.
ампути́р|овать, ую *impf. and pf.* (*med.*) to amputate.
Амстерда́м, а *m.* Amsterdam.
амуле́т, а *m.* amulet.
амуни́ци|я, и *f.* (*collect.*) (*mil., hist.*) accoutrements.
Аму́р, а *m.* **1.** (*myth.*) Cupid. **2.: аму́ры** (*pl. only*) (*coll.*) intrigues, love affairs.
аму́р|иться, юсь *impf.* (**с**+*i.*; *coll.*) to flirt (with), have an affair (with).
аму́рн|ый *adj.* (*coll.*) love; amorous; **~ые дела́** love affairs; **~ые пи́сьма** love letters.
амфетами́н, а *m.* (*pharm.*) amphetamine.
амфи́би|я, и *f.* (*zool., bot.*) amphibian.
амфитеа́тр, а *m.* (*hist.*) amphitheatre; (*theatr.*) circle.
АН *f. indecl.* (*abbr. of* **Акаде́мия нау́к**) Academy of Sciences.
анаболи́ческий *adj.*: **а. стеро́ид** anabolic steroid.
анагра́мм|а, ы *f.* anagram.
ана́лиз, а *m.* analysis; **а. кро́ви** blood test; **(радио)углеро́дный а.** carbon-dating.
анализи́р|овать, ую *impf.* to analyse.
анали́тик, а *m.* analyst.
аналити́ческий *adj.* analytic(al).
ана́лог, а *m.* analogue.
аналоги́ческ|ий *adj.* analogical; **~ое рассужде́ние** reasoning by analogy.
аналоги́ч|ный (~ен, ~на) *adj.* analogous; **~ные слу́чаи** analogous cases.
анало́ги|я, и *f.* analogy; **по ~и** (**с**+*i.*) by analogy (with); **проводи́ть ~ю** to draw an analogy.
анало́|й, я *m.* (*eccl.*) lectern.
ана́льный *adj.* anal.
анана́с, а *m.* pineapple.
анана́с|ный *adj. of* **~**
анана́с|овый *adj. of* **~; а. сок** pineapple juice.
ана́пест, а *m.* (*liter.*) anapaest.
анархи́зм, а *m.* (*pol.*) anarchism.
анархи́ст, а *m.* (*pol.*) anarchist.
анархи́ческий *adj.* anarchic(al).
ана́рхи|я, и *f.* anarchy.
ана́том, а *m.* anatomist.
анатоми́р|овать, ую *impf. and pf.* (*med.*) to dissect.
анатоми́ческий *adj.* anatomic(al).
анато́ми|я, и *f.* anatomy.
ана́фем|а, ы *f.* (*eccl.*) anathema; excommunication; (*fig.*): **преда́ть ~е** to anathematize.
анафема́тств|овать, ую *impf.* (*eccl.*) to excommunicate.
анахоре́т, а *m.* hermit, anchorite; (*fig.*) recluse.
анахрони́зм, а *m.* anachronism.
анахрони́ческий *adj.* anachronistic.
анаш|а́, и́ *f.* (*sl.*) pot, hash; **закру́тка ~и́** joint (= *marijuana cigarette*).
анаши́ст, а *m.* (*sl.*) pot smoker; hash-head.
анга́р, а *m.* (*aeron.*) hangar.
а́нгел, а *m.* angel; **а. во плоти́** (*coll.*) (an absolute) angel; **день ~а** name-day.
а́нгельск|ий *adj.* angelic (*also fig.*).
анги́н|а, ы *f.* (*med.*) quinsy; tonsillitis.
англизи́ровать, ую *impf. and pf.* to anglicize.

англи́йск|ий *adj.* **1.** English; **~ая боле́знь** rickets; **~ая була́вка** safety-pin; **~ая соль** Epsom salts. **2.** British.
англика́н|ец, ца *m.* Anglican.
англика́н|ка, ки *f. of* **~ец**
англика́нский *adj.* (*eccl.*) Anglican.
англи́стик|а, и *f.* Anglistics.
англици́зм, а *m.* Anglicism.
англича́н|ин, ина, *pl.* **~е, ~** *m.* Englishman.
англича́нк|а, и *f.* Englishwoman.
А́нгли|я, и *f.* **1.** England. **2.** Britain.
а́нгло-бу́рск|ий *adj.*: **~ая война́** Boer War.
англоговоря́щий = англоязы́чный 1.
англома́н, а *m.* anglomane.
англоса́кс, а *m.* Anglo-Saxon.
англосаксо́нский *adj.* Anglo-Saxon.
англофи́л, а *m.* anglophile.
англофо́б, а *m.* anglophobe.
англоязы́чный *adj.* **1.** English-speaking, anglophone. **2.** English-language.
анго́рск|ий *adj.* Angora; **~ая шерсть** Angora (wool).
анда́нте *adv.* (*mus.*) andante.
А́нд|ы, ~ *no sg.* the Andes.
анекдо́т, а *m.* **1.** anecdote, story. **2.** joke.
анекдоти́ческий *adj.* anecdotal.
анекдоти́ч|ный (~ен, ~на) *adj.* humorous.
анекдо́тчик, а *m.* raconteur.
анеми́ческий *adj.* anaemic.
анеми́ч|ный (~ен, ~на) *adj.* anaemic, pale.
анеми́|я, и *f.* anaemia.
анемо́н = анемо́на
анемо́н|а, ы *f.* (*bot.*) anemone.
анеро́ид, а *m.* aneroid (barometer).
анестези́р|овать, ую *impf. and pf.* (*med.*) to anaesthetize; **~ующее сре́дство** anaesthetic.
анестези́|я, и *f.* (*med.*) anaesthesia.
аними́зм, а *m.* animism.
аними́ст, а *m.* animist.
ани́с, а *m.* (*bot.*) **1.** anise. **2.** anise apples.
ани́совк|а, и *f.* (*coll.*) anisette.
ани́с|овый *adj. of* **~**; **~овое се́мя** aniseed; **~овая во́дка** anisette.
анке́т|а, ы *f.* questionnaire; poll, survey; **ви́зовая а.** visa application-form.
анкла́в, а *m.* enclave.
анна́л|ы, ов *no sg.* annals.
аннекси́р|овать, ую *impf. and pf.* (*pol.*) to annex.
анне́кси|я, и *f.* (*pol.*) annexation.
аннота́ци|я *f.* annotation; blurb.
аннoти́р|овать, ую *impf. and pf.* to annotate.
аннули́р|овать, ую *impf. and pf.* to annul, nullify; to cancel; to abrogate.
аннуля́ци|я, и *f.* annulment; cancellation; abrogation.
ано́д, а *m.* (*phys.*) anode.
анома́ли|я, и *f.* anomaly.
анома́л|ьный (~ен, ~ьна) *adj.* anomalous.
анони́м, а *m.* anonymous author.
анони́мк|а, и *f.* (*coll.*) **1.** poison-pen letter. **2.** anonymous telephone call.
анони́м|ный (~ен, ~на) *adj.* anonymous.
анони́мщик, а *m.* (*coll.*) **1.** poison-pen writer. **2.** anonymous telephone caller.
ано́нс, а *m.* announcement, notice; (*cin.*) trailer.
анонси́р|овать, ую *impf. and pf.* (*+a. or* **о***+p.*) to announce.
анора́к, а *m.* anorak.
аноре́кси|я, и *f.* anorexia; **больно́й (***fem.* **больна́я) ~ей** anorexic (*pers.*).
анорма́л|ьный (~ен, ~ьна) *adj.* abnormal.
анса́мбл|ь, я *m.* **1.** harmony. **2.** (*mus.*, *theatr.*) ensemble, company.
антагони́зм, а *m.* antagonism.
антагони́ст, а *m.* antagonist.
Антаркти́д|а, ы *f.* Antarctica.
Анта́рктик|а, и *f.* the Antarctic.
антаркти́ческий *adj.* Antarctic.
анте́нн|а, ы *f.* **1.** (*zool.*) antenna. **2.** (*tech.*) aerial, antenna; **ко́мнатная а.** indoor aerial.
анте́нн|ый *adj. of* **~а**
анти... *pref.* anti-.
антиалкого́льн|ый *adj.*: **~ое движе́ние** temperance movement.
антиа́томный *adj.*: **а. марш** antinuclear march.
антибио́тик, а *m.* (*med.*) antibiotic.
антивеществ|о́, а *nt.* antimatter.
антигеро́|й, я *m.* anti-hero.
антидепресса́нт, а *m.* (*med.*) antidepressant.
антидо́пинговый *adj.*: **а. контро́ль** dope testing.
антизапотева́тел|ь, я *m.* demister.
антиква́р, а *m.* antiquary.
антиквариа́т, а *m.* (*collect.*) antiques.
антиква́рный *adj.* antiquarian; vintage.
антило́п|а, ы *f.* (*zool.*) antelope.
антино́ми|я, и *f.* antinomy.
антипати́ч|ный (~ен, ~на) *adj.* antipathetic.
антипа́ти|я, и *f.* antipathy.
антипо́д, а *m.* antipode.
антиприга́рный *adj.* non-stick.
антираке́т|а, ы *f.* anti-missile missile, antimissile.
антираке́тчик, а *m.* ban-the-bomb campaigner.
антисанитари́|я, и *f.* insanitary conditions.
антисанита́р|ный *adj.* insanitary.
антисеми́т, а *m.* anti-Semite.
антисемити́зм, а *m.* anti-Semitism.
антисеми́тский *adj.* anti-Semitic.
антисе́птик, а *m.* antiseptic.
антисе́птик|а, и *f.* **1.** antisepsis. **2.** (*collect.*) antiseptics.
антисепти́ческий *adj.* antiseptic.
антисоveти́зм, а *m.* anti-Sovietism.
антисове́тский *adj.* anti-Soviet.
антисове́тчик, а *m.* anti-Soviet propagandist.
антисове́тчин|а, ы *f.* anti-Soviet propaganda.
антите́з|а, ы *f.* antithesis.
антите́зис, а *m.* (*phil.*) antithesis.
антите́л|о, а *nt.* antibody.
антитети́ческий *adj.* antithetical.
антифри́з, а *m.* antifreeze.
антицикло́н, а *m.* (*meteor.*) anti-cyclone.
античелове́ческий *adj.* inhuman.
анти́чност|ь, и *f.* antiquity.
анти́чный *adj.* ancient; classical; **а. мир** the ancient world.
антоло́ги|я, и *f.* (*liter.*) anthology.
анто́новк|а, и *f.* Antonovka (*variety of apple*).
анто́новск|ий *adj.*: **~ие я́блоки = анто́новка**
антра́кт, а *m.* **1.** (*theatr.*) interval. **2.** (*mus.*) entr'acte.
антраци́т, а *m.* (*min.*) anthracite.
антреко́т, а *m.* entrecôte.
антрепренёр, а *m.* impresario.
антресо́л|ь, и *f.* (*usu. pl.*) **1.** mezzanine. **2.** shelf.
антропо́ид, а *m.* anthropoid.
антропо́лог, а *m.* anthropologist.
антропологи́ческий *adj.* anthropological.
антрополо́ги|я, и *f.* anthropology.
антропоме́три|я, и *f.* anthropometry.
антропоморфи́зм, а *m.* anthropomorphism.
антропоморфи́ческий *adj.* anthropomorphic.
антропомо́рфный *adj.* anthropoid.
антропофа́г, а *m.* cannibal.
антропофа́ги|я, и *f.* cannibalism.
анфа́с *adv.* full face.
анфила́д|а, ы *f.* suite (of rooms).
анча́р, а *m.* (*bot.*) upas(-tree).
анчо́ус, а *m.* anchovy.

аншла́г, а *m.* notice; (*theatr.*) full house; **спекта́кль идёт с ~ом** the show is sold out, the house is full.
а́ншлюс(с), а *m.* anschluss.
аню́тины: а. гла́зки (*bot.*) pansy.
ао́рт|а, ы *f.* (*anat.*) aorta.
апарта́мен|ты, ов *pl.* (*sg.* **~, ~а** *m.*) apartment.
апартеид, а *m.* apartheid.
апати́ч|ный (~ен, ~ на) *adj.* apathetic.
апа́ти|я, и *f.* apathy.
апа́ч, а *m.* Apache.
апелли́р|овать, ую *impf. and pf.* to appeal.
апелля́нт, а *m.* (*leg.*) appellant.
апелл|яцио́нный *adj. of* **~я́ция; а. суд** Court of Appeal.
апелля́ци|я, и *f.* (*leg.*) appeal.
апельси́н, а *m.* **1.** orange. **2.** orange-tree.
апельси́н|ный *adj. of* **~**
апельси́нов|ый *adj.* orange; **~ое варе́нье** orange marmalade.
аперити́в, а *m.* apéritif.
аплоди́р|овать, ую *impf.* (+*d.*) to applaud.
аплодисме́нт|ы, ов *pl.* (*sg.* **а., ~а** *m.*) applause; **бу́рные а.** tumultuous applause.
апло́мб, а *m.* aplomb, assurance.
апоге́|й, я *m.* (*astron.*) apogee; (*fig.*) climax.
Апока́липсис, а *m.* (*bibl.*) (the Book of) Revelation, the Apocalypse.
апокалипти́ческий *adj.* apocalyptic.
апокриф|и́ческий *adj. of* **апо́криф**
апокрифи́ч|ный (~ен, ~на) *adj.* (*coll.*) apocryphal.
апо́криф|ы, ов *pl.* Apocrypha.
аполити́чност|ь, и *f.* political indifference.
аполити́ч|ный (~ен, ~на) *adj.* apolitical; politically indifferent.
апологе́т, а *m.* apologist.
апологе́тик|а, и *f.* apologetics.
аполо́ги|я, и *f.* apologia.
апоплекси́ческий *adj.* (*med.*) apoplectic.
апопле́кси|я, и *f.* (*med.*) apoplexy.
апо́рт *int.* fetch! (*command to dog*)
апостерио́ри *adv.* (*phil.*) a posteriori.
апостерио́рный *adj.* (*phil.*) a posteriori.
апо́стол, а *m.* **1.** apostle (*also fig.*). **2.** (*eccl.*, *liter.*) Books of the Apostles (*the Acts of the Apostles and the Epistles*).
апо́стольник, а *m.* wimple.
апо́стольский *adj.* apostolic.
апостро́ф, а *m.* apostrophe.
апофео́з, а *m.* apotheosis.
аппара́т, а *m.* **1.** apparatus; appliance; **копирова́льный а.** photocopier; **косми́ческий лета́тельный аппара́т** spacecraft; **ку́хонный а.** food processor; **слухово́й а.** hearing aid; **факсими́льный а.** fax (machine); **фотографи́ческий а.** camera. **2.** (*physiol.*): **пищевари́тельный а.** digestive system. **3.** (*admin.*): **госуда́рственный а.** machinery of State; **суде́бный а.** judicial system. **4.** staff, personnel.
аппара́тно-програ́ммн|ый *adj.* (*comput.*) firmware; **~ые сре́дства** firmware.
аппара́тн|ый *adj.* (*comput.*) hardware; **~ые сре́дства** hardware.
аппарату́р|а, ы *f.* (*tech.*, *collect.*) apparatus, equipment; (*comput.*) hardware.
аппара́тчик, а *m.* **1.** (machine) operative. **2.** (*pol.*) apparatchik.
аппе́ндикс, а *m.* (*anat.*) appendix.
аппендици́т, а *m.* (*med.*) appendicitis.
апперко́т, а *m.* uppercut.
аппети́т, а *m.* appetite; **прия́тного ~а!** bon appétit!
аппети́т|ный (~ен, ~на) *adj.* **1.** appetizing, mouth-watering. **2.** fetching, dishy (*of female*).
аппликату́р|а, ы *f.* (*mus.*) fingering.
апплика́ци|я, и *f.* (*tech.*) appliqué work.
апплике́ *adj. indecl.* plated.
апре́л|ь, я *m.* April; **пе́рвое ~я** April Fool's Day; **с пе́рвым ~я!** April Fool!
апре́ль|ский *adj. of* **~**
априо́ри *adv.* (*phil.*) a priori.
априо́р|ный (~ен, ~на) *adj.* (*phil.*) a priori.
апроба́ци|я, и *f.* approbation.
апроби́р|овать, ую *impf. and pf.* to approve.
апси́д|а, ы *f.* (*archit.*) apse.
апте́к|а, и *f.* chemist's (shop); **как в ~е** (*coll.*, *joc.*) just so, exactly right.
апте́карский *adj.* chemist's; pharmaceutical.
апте́кар|ша, ши *f. of* **~ь**
апте́кар|ь, я *m.* chemist; pharmacist.
апте́чк|а, и *f.* first-aid set; medicine chest; **а. для ремо́нта шин** tyre repair kit.
апчхи́ *int.* atishoo.
ар, а *m.* are (*unit of land measurement*).
а́ра *m. indecl.* macaw.
ара́б, а *m.* Arab, Arabian.
арабе́ск, а *m.* arabesque.
арабе́ск|а, и *f.* = **~**
араби́ст, а *m.* Arabist, Arabic scholar.
ара́б|ка, ки *f. of* **~**
ара́бск|ий *adj.* Arab; Arabian; Arabic; **~ие ци́фры** arabic numerals; **а. язы́к** Arabic.
араме́йский *adj.* Aramaic.
аранжи́р|овать, ую *impf. and pf.* (*mus.*) to arrange.
аранжиро́вк|а, и *f.* (*mus.*) arrangement.
ара́п, а *m.* (*sl.*) cheat, swindler; **на ~а** by bluffing.
ара́пник, а *m.* riding crop.
араука́ри|я, и *f.* araucaria, monkey-puzzle tree.
ара́хис, а *m.* peanut, groundnut; **а. в са́харе** peanut brittle.
ара́хисов|ый *adj.*: **~ая па́ста** peanut butter; **~ое ма́сло** groundnut oil.
арб|а́, ы́, *pl.* **~ы** *f.* bullock-cart.
арбале́т, а *m.* arbalest, crossbow.
арби́тр, а *m.* arbiter, arbitrator; umpire, referee.
арбитра́ж, а *m.* arbitration.
арбу́з, а *m.* water-melon.
Аргенти́н|а, ы *f.* Argentina.
аргенти́н|ец, ца *m.* Argentinian.
аргенти́н|ка, ки *f. of* **~ец**
аргенти́нский *adj.* Argentine.
арго́ *nt. indecl.* argot, slang.
арго́н, а *m.* (*chem.*) argon.
арготи́зм, а *m.* slang expression.
арготи́ческий *adj. of* **арго́**
аргуме́нт, а *m.* argument.
аргумента́ци|я, и *f.* reasoning, argumentation.
аргументи́р|овать, ую *impf. and pf.* to argue; (*pf. only*) to prove.
ареа́л, а *m.* (*bot. and zool.*) natural habitat; (*fig.*) region.
аре́н|а, ы *f.* arena, ring.
аре́нд|а, ы *f.* lease; **сдать в ~у** to rent, lease (*of owner, landlord*); **взять в ~у** to rent, lease (*of tenant*).
аренда́тор, а *m.* tenant, lessee.
аре́нд|ный *adj. of* **~а; ~ная пла́та** rent; **а. подря́д** contract for lease (*of land*).
аренд|ова́ть, у́ю *impf. and pf.* to rent, lease (*of tenant*).
аре́ст, а *m.* arrest; **сиде́ть, находи́ться под ~ом** to be under arrest; **каза́рменный а.** confinement to barracks; **а. иму́щества** seizure, sequestration.
арест|ова́ть, у́ю *pf.* (*of* **~о́вывать**) to arrest; to sequestrate.
аресто́выва|ть, ю *impf. of* **арестова́ть**
ари́дный *adj.* arid.
ари́|ец, йца *m.* Aryan.

арийский *adj.* Aryan.
аристократ, а *m.* aristocrat.
аристократ|ический *adj.* aristocratic.
аристократи|я, и *f.* aristocracy.
арифметик|а, и *f.* arithmetic.
арифметический *adj.* arithmetical.
арифмометр, а *m.* calculating machine.
ари|я, и *f.* (*mus.*) aria.
арк|а, и *f.* arch.
аркад|а, ы *f.* (*archit.*) arcade.
аркадский *adj.* Arcadian.
аркан, а *m.* lasso.
аркан|ить, ю, ишь *impf.* (*pf.* **за~**) to lasso.
Арктик|а, и *f.* the Arctic.
арктический *adj.* arctic.
арлекин, а *m.* harlequin.
арлекинад|а, ы *f.* harlequinade.
армадил, а *m.* armadillo.
арматур|а, ы *f.* (*collect.*) fittings; steel *or* ferro-concrete reinforcement.
арматур|ный *adj. of* **~а**
арматурщик, а *m.* (*tech.*) fitter.
арме|ец, йца *m.* soldier.
армейский *adj. of* **армия**
Армени|я, и *f.* Armenia.
арми|я, и *f.* army; **А. Спасения** Salvation Army.
армян|ин, ина, *pl.* **~е, ~** *m.* Armenian.
армян|ка, ки *f. of* **~ин**
армянский *adj.* Armenian.
арник|а, и *f.* (*bot., med.*) arnica.
аромат, а *m.* scent, odour, aroma, fragrance; (*of wine*) bouquet.
ароматизатор, а *m.* (*cul.*) flavouring.
ароматический = ароматный
ароматич|ный (~ен, ~на) = ароматный
аромат|ный (~ен, ~на) *adj.* aromatic, fragrant.
арочный *adj.* arched, vaulted.
арпедж|ио (*mus.*) **1.** *adv.* **2.** *n.*; *sg. nt. indecl.*, *pl.* **~ии, ~ий** arpeggio.
арсенал. а *m.* arsenal.
арт. *abbr. of* **артиллерия**
арт... *comb. form, abbr. of* **артиллерийский**
артач|иться, усь, ишься *impf.* (*coll.*) to jib, be restive.
артезианский *adj.*: **а. колодец** artesian well.
артел|ь, и *f.* artel (*workers' or peasants' co-operative*).
артель|ный *adj. of* **~**; (*coll.*) common, collective; **на ~ных началах** on collective principles.
артельщик, а *m.* member of an artel.
артериальный *adj.* (*anat.*) arterial.
артериосклероз, а *m.* (*med.*) arteriosclerosis.
артери|я, и, *f.* artery.
артикл|ь, я *m.* (*gram.*) article.
артикулир|овать, ую *impf.* (*ling.*) to articulate.
артикуляци|я, и *f.* (*ling.*) articulation.
артиллерийск|ий *adj.* (*mil.*) artillery; **а. обоз** artillery-train; **а. склад** ordnance depot.
артиллери|я, и *f.* artillery.
артист, а *m.* **1.** artist(e); **оперный а.** opera singer; **а. балета** ballet dancer. **2.** (*fig.*) artist, expert; **он — а. своего дела** he is a real artist (at his job).
артистизм, а *m.* artistry, virtuosity.
артистическ|ий *adj.* artistic; *as n.* **~ая, ~ой** *f.* green-room, dressing-room.
артистичност|ь, и *f.* = **артистизм**
артист|ка, ки *f. of* **~**
артишок, а *m.* (*bot.*) artichoke.
артрит, а *m.* (*med.*) arthritis; **больной ~ом** arthritic (*pers.*).
арф|а, ы *f.* harp.
арфист, а *m.* harpist.
арфистк|а, и *f. of* **~**
архаизм, а *m.* archaism.
архаический *adj.* archaic.
архаич|ный (~ен, ~на) *adj.* archaic.
архангел, а *m.* archangel.
архангельский *adj.* archangelic.
археолог, а *m.* archaeologist.
археологический *adj.* archaeological.
археологи|я, и *f.* archaeology.
архи... *comb. form* arch-.
архив, а *m.* archives; **сдать в а.** (*coll.*) to shelve, throw out, leave out of account.
архивариус, а *m.* archivist.
архив|ный *adj. of* **~**
архидьякон, а *m.* archdeacon.
архиепископ, а *m.* archbishop.
архиере|й, я *m.* member of higher orders of clergy (*bishop, archbishop or metropolitan*).
архимандрит, а *m.* (*eccl.*) archimandrite.
архимиллионер, а *m.* multi-millionaire.
архипелаг, а *m.* archipelago.
архитектор, а *m.* architect.
архитектур|а, ы *f.* architecture.
архитектурный *adj.* architectural.
архитрав, а *m.* (*archit.*) architrave.
аршин, а *m.* **1.** arshin (*old Russ. measure, equivalent to 71 cm*). **2.** rule one arshin in length; **мерить на свой а.** to measure by one's own yardstick; **как будто а. проглотил** (*coll.*) as stiff as a poker.
аршинн|ый *adj.* (*coll.*) huge, whopping great; **~ая борода** great long beard; **~ые заголовки** banner headlines.
арьергард, а *m.* (*mil.*) rearguard.
арьергардный *adj.* (*mil.*) rearguard.
ас, а *m.* (*air*) ace.
асбест, а *m.* asbestos.
асбестовый *adj.* asbestos.
асептик|а, и *f.* (*med.*) asepsis.
асептический *adj.* (*med.*) aseptic.
асимметрический *adj.* asymmetrical.
асимметрич|ный (~ен, ~на) *adj.* asymmetrical.
асимметри|я, и *f.* asymmetry.
аскет, а *m.* ascetic.
аскетизм, а *m.* asceticism.
аскетический *adj.* ascetic.
асоциальный *adj.* anti-social.
аспект, а *m.* aspect, perspective.
аспид, а *m.* (*zool.*) asp; (*fig.*) viper.
аспидный *adj.*: **а. сланец** slate.
аспирант, а *m.* post-graduate student.
аспирантур|а, ы *f.* **1.** post-graduate study. **2.** (*collect.*) post-graduate students.
аспирин, а *m.* (*med.*) aspirin.
ассамбле|я, и *f.* **1.** assembly. **2.** (*hist.*) ball.
ассенизационный *adj.*: **а. обоз** (*collect.*) sewage-disposal men.
ассенизаци|я, и *f.* sewage disposal.
ассигновани|е, я *nt.* (*fin.*) assignation, appropriation, allocation.
ассигн|овать, ую *impf. and pf.* (*fin.*) to assign, appropriate, allocate.
ассигновк|а, и *f.* (*fin.*) assignment; grant (*of funds*).
ассимилир|овать, ую *impf. and pf.* to assimilate.
ассимиляци|я, и *f.* assimilation.
ассистент, а *m.* **1.** assistant. **2.** (*in university, etc.*) junior member of teaching or research staff.
ассистир|овать, ую *impf.* (+*d.*) to assist.
ассонанс, а *m.* assonance.
ассорти *nt. indecl.*: **шоколадное а.** chocolate assortment.
ассортимент, а *m.* assortment; range (*of goods*).
ассоциаци|я, и *f.* association.
ассоциир|овать, ую *impf. and pf.* (**с**+*i.*; *phil.*) to associate (with).
астероид, а *m.* (*astron.*) asteroid.

астигмати́зм, а *m.* (*med.*) astigmatism.
а́стм|а, ы *f.* (*med.*) asthma.
астма́тик, а *m.* (*med.*) asthmatic.
астмати́ческий *adj.* (*med.*) asthmatic.
а́стр|а, ы *f.* (*bot.*) aster.
астра́льный *adj.* astral.
астро́лог, а *m.* astrologer.
астрологи́ческий *adj.* astrological.
астроло́ги|я, и *f.* astrology.
астроля́би|я, и *f.* astrolabe.
астроно́м, а *m.* astronomer.
астрономи́ческий *adj.* astronomic(al).
астроно́ми|я, и *f.* astronomy.
астрофи́зик|а, и *f.* astrophysics.
асфа́льт, а *m.* asphalt.
асфальти́р|овать, ую *impf. and pf.* (*pf. also* **за~**) (*tech.*) to asphalt.
асфа́льтовый *adj.* asphalt.
асфи́кси|я, и *f.* (*med.*) asphyxia.
атави́зм, а *m.* atavism.
атависти́ческий *adj.* atavistic.
ата́к|а, и *f.* attack.
атак|ова́ть, у́ю *impf. and pf.* to attack, charge, assault.
атама́н, а *m.* **1.** (*hist.*) ataman (*Cossack chieftain*). **2.** (*coll.*) (gang-)leader, (robber) chief.
ата́с (*sl.*): **стоя́ть на ~е** to keep lookout; *int.* watch out!; beware!
атеи́зм, а *m.* atheism.
атеи́ст, а *m.* atheist.
атеисти́ческий *adj.* atheistic.
ателье́ *nt. indecl.* studio; **портно́вское а.** tailor's shop; **а. мод** fashion house.
атланти́зм, а *m.* (*pol.*) Atlanticism.
Атланти́ческ|ий океа́н, ~ого ~а *m.* the Atlantic Ocean; the Atlantic.
а́тлас, а *m.* atlas.
атла́с, а *m.* satin.
атла́сный *adj.* satin.
атле́т, а *m.* athlete; (*circus*) strongman.
атлети́зм, а *m.* **1.** athleticism. **2.** body-building.
атле́тик|а, и *f.* athletics; **лёгкая а.** (track-and-field) athletics; **тяжёлая а.** weightlifting.
атлети́ческий *adj.* athletic.
атмосфе́р|а, ы *f.* atmosphere.
атмосфери́ческий *adj.* atmospheric.
атмосфе́рн|ый *adj.* atmospheric.
ато́лл, а *m.* atoll.
а́том, а *m.* atom.
а́томн|ый *adj.* atomic; **~ая бо́мба** atomic bomb; **а. вес** (*chem.*) atomic weight.
атомохо́д, а *m.* nuclear-powered vessel.
атрибу́т, а *m.* attribute.
атропи́н, а *m.* (*med.*) atropine.
атрофи́р|оваться, уюсь *impf. and pf.* to atrophy.
атрофи́|я, и *f.* atrophy.
атташе́ *m. indecl.* (*dipl.*) attaché.
аттеста́т, а *m.* testimonial; certificate; pedigree; **а. зре́лости** school-leaving certificate.
аттестацио́нн|ый *adj.*: **~ая комми́сия** examination board.
аттеста́ци|я, и *f.* **1.** attestation. **2.** testimonial.
аттест|ова́ть, у́ю *impf. and pf.* to attest, recommend.
аттракцио́н, а *m.* (*theatr.*) attraction; (*fairground*) sideshow; **парк ~ов** amusement park.
ату́ *int.* (*hunting*) tally-ho!; halloo!
ать-два *int.* (*mil.*) hep, two!
ау́ *int.* halloo!
аудие́нци|я, и *f.* audience.
аудиовизуа́льный *adj.* audiovisual.
аудиоречево́й *adj.* audiolingual.
аудито́ри|я, и *f.* **1.** auditorium; lecture-hall. **2.** (*collect.*) audience; **зри́тельская а.** viewers; **слу́шательская а.** listeners.
ау́ка|ть, ю *impf.* to halloo.
ау́к|аться, аюсь *impf.* (*of* **~нуться**) to halloo to one another.
ау́к|нуть, ну, нешь *pf. of* **~ать**
ау́к|нуться, нусь *pf. of* **~аться; как ~нется, так и откли́кнется** serves you, *etc.*, right; do as you would be done by.
аукцио́н, а *m.* auction; **продава́ть с ~а** to auction.
аукционе́р, а *m.* = **аукциони́ст**
аукциони́ст, а *m.* auctioneer.
аукцио́н|ный *adj. of* **~; а. зал** auction room.
ау́л, а *m.* aul (*mountain village in Caucasus or Central Asia*).
ауспи́ци|и, й *no sg.* auspices.
а́ут, а *m.* (*sport*) out (*also as int.*).
аутенти́ч|ный (~ен, ~на) *adj.* authentic.
ауто́пси|я, и *f.* autopsy, post-mortem.
аутса́йдер, а *m.* (*pol.*) outsider.
афа́зи|я, и *f.* (*med.*) aphasia.
афга́н|ец, ца *m.* Afghan; Afghan war vet(eran).
Афганиста́н, а *m.* Afghanistan.
афга́н|ка, ки *f. of* **~ец**
афга́нский *adj.* Afghan.
афе́р|а, ы *f.* (*coll.*) speculation; trickery.
афери́ст, а *m.* speculator; trickster.
афи́ш|а, и *f.* poster, placard; **театра́льная а.** playbill; **раскле́йщик ~** billsticker
афиши́р|овать, ую *impf.* to parade, advertise.
афори́зм, а *m.* aphorism.
афористи́ческий *adj.* aphoristic.
афористи́ч|ный (~ен, ~на) *adj.* aphoristic.
А́фрик|а, и *f.* Africa.
африка́анс, а *m.* Afrikaans.
африка́нер, а *m.* Afrikaner.
африка́н|ец, ца *m.* African.
африка́н|ка, ки *f. of* **~ец**
африка́нск|ий *adj.* African.
аффе́кт, а *m.* fit of passion.
аффекта́ци|я, и *f.* affectation.
аффекти́рованный *adj.* affected.
ах *int.* ah! oh!
а́ха|ть, ю *impf.* (*coll.*) to gasp; to sigh.
ахилле́сов *adj.*: **~а пята́** Achilles heel; **~о сухожи́лие** (*anat.*) Achilles tendon.
ахине́|я *f.* (*coll.*) nonsense; **нести́ ~ю** to talk nonsense.
а́х|нуть, ну, нешь *pf.* **1.** *pf. of* **~ать; он и а. не успе́л** before he knew where he was. **2.** (*coll.*) to bang.
а́ховый *adj.* (*coll.*) **1.** breath-taking; **он па́рень а.** he is a great bloke. **2.** rotten.
ахромати́зм, а *m.* achromatism.
ахромати́ческий *adj.* achromatic.
ахтерште́в|ень, ня *m.* (*naut.*) stern-post.
ахти́ *int.* (*coll.*) alas!; **а. мне!** woe is me!; **не а. как, не а. како́й** not particularly, not particularly good; **он был студе́нтом не а. каки́м** he was not the brightest of students.
ацетиле́н, а *m.* (*chem.*) acetylene.
ацето́н, а *m.* (*chem.*) acetone.
ацте́к, а *m.* Aztec.
ашу́г, а *m.* ashug (*folk poet/singer in the Caucasus*).
аэра́ри|й, я *m.* sun terrace.
аэро... *comb. form* aero-; air-, aerial.
аэро́бик|а, и *f.* aerobics.
аэроби́ст, а *m.* aerobicist.
аэроби́ст|ка, ки *f. of* **~**
аэроби́ческий = аэро́бный
аэро́бн|ый *adj.* aerobic; **~ая гимна́стика** aerobics, aerobic exercises.
аэро́бус, а *m.* air bus.
аэровокза́л, а *m.* air terminal.

аэрогра́мм|а, ы *f.* aerogramme; air letter
аэро́граф, а *m.* air brush.
аэродина́мик|а, и *f.* aerodynamics.
аэродинами́ческ|ий *adj.* aerodynamic; **~ая труба́** wind tunnel.
аэродро́м, а *m.* aerodrome.
аэрозо́л|ь, я *m.* aerosol, spray; **а. для воло́с** hair spray.
аэро́н, а *m.* travel sickness pill.
аэрона́вт, а *m.* aeronaut; balloonist.
аэрона́втик|а, и *f.* aeronautics.
аэропо́рт, а *m.* airport.
аэроса́н|и, е́й *no sg.* aero-sleigh.
аэросе́в, а *m.* aerial sowing.
аэросни́м|ок, ка *m.* aerial photograph.
аэроста́т, а *m.* balloon.
аэроста́тик|а, и *f.* aerostatics.
аэросъёмк|а, и *f.* aerial survey.
аэрохо́д, а *m.* hovercraft, air cushion vehicle (*abbr.* ACV).
АЭС *f. indecl.* (*abbr. of* **а́томная электроста́нция**) atomic power station.
аятолл|а́, ы́ *m.* ayatollah.

Б

б *particle* = **бы** (*after words ending in vowel*).
б. (*abbr. of* **бы́вший**) former, ex-, one-time; **Санкт-Петербу́рг (б. Ленингра́д)** St Petersburg (formerly Leningrad).
ба *int.* (*coll.*) hullo!; well! (*expr. surprise*) **~! кого́ я ви́жу!** well I never, if it isn't …
ба́б|а[1], **ы** *f.* **1.** married peasant woman. **2.** (*coll.*) woman; **сне́жная б.** snowman. **3.** (*coll.*) 'old woman', sissy (*said of a man*).
ба́ба[2], **ы** *f.* baba (*cylindrical cake*); **ро́мовая б.** rum-baba.
ба́ба-яга́, ба́бы-яги́ *f.* Baba-Yaga (*witch in Russ. folk-tales*).
бабёнк|а и *f.* (*coll.*) bimbo, bit of skirt.
ба́б|ий *adj.* (*coll.*) women's; womanish; **~ье ле́то** Indian summer; **~ьи ска́зки** old wives' tales.
ба́бк|а[1], **и** *f.* = **ба́бушка**
ба́бк|а[2], **и** *f.* **1.** (*anat.*) pastern. **2.** knuckle-bone; **~и** (*pl.*) babki (*Russ. children's game*).
ба́бник, а *m.* (*coll.*) womanizer.
ба́бочк|а, и *f.* butterfly; **ночна́я б.** moth.
бабуи́н, а *m.* (*zool.*) baboon.
ба́бушк|а, и *f.* grandmother; (*coll.*) old woman; gran(nie) (*as mode of address*).
ба́бушкин *adj.* grandmother's; **~ы ска́зки** old wives' tales.
бага́ж, а́ *m.* luggage; **сдать свои́ ве́щи в б.** to register one's luggage.
бага́жник, а *m.* luggage compartment; roof rack; boot (*of motor-car*).
бага́жнич|ек, ка *m.* glove compartment.
бага́ж|ный *adj. of* **~**; **б. ваго́н** luggage van; **~ная квита́нция** luggage receipt.
баг|о́р, ра́ *m.* boat-hook.
багре́ц, а́ *m.* crimson.
багрове́|ть, ю *impf.* (*of* **по~**) to turn crimson.
багро́в|ый (~, ~а) *adj.* crimson.
багря́н|ец, ца *m.* crimson.
багря́н|ый (~, ~а) *adj.* (*poet.*) crimson.
бадминто́н, а *m.* badminton.
бадминтони́ст, а *m.* badminton-player.
бад|ья́, ьи́, *g. pl.* **~е́й** *f.* tub.
ба́з|а, ы *f.* **1.** (*in var. senses*) base; depot; centre; **б. да́нных** database; **плаву́чая б.** factory ship. **2.** basis; **на ~е** (+*g.*) on the basis (of); **подвести́ ~у (под**+*a.*) to give good grounds (for) .
база́льт, а *m.* basalt.
база́льтовый *adj.* basaltic.
база́р, а *m.* market; bazaar; **пти́чий б.** bird-colony on sea-shore; (*fig., coll.*) din, racket.
база́р|ить, ю, ишь (*impf.*) to wrangle, squabble.
база́р|ный *adj. of* **~**; (*coll.*) of the market-place, rough, crude; **~ная ба́ба** noisy woman, fishwife.
базили́к, а *m.* (*bot.*) basil; **б. души́стый** sweet basil.
бази́ли́к|а, и *f.* (*archit.*) basilica.
бази́ровани|е, я *nt.*: **раке́та назе́много/морско́го ~я** ground-based/sea-launched missile.
бази́р|овать, ую *impf.* (**на**+*p.*) to base (on).
бази́р|оваться, уюсь *impf.* (**на**+*p.*) to be based (on), to rest (on).
ба́зис, а *m.* base; basis.
ба́зов|ый *adj.* **1.** basic. **2.: б. ла́герь** base camp.
базу́к|а, и *f.* bazooka.
ба́иньки = **бай-ба́й**
бай-ба́й *int.* bye-byes; **пора́ б.!** time for bye-byes!
байба́к, а́ *m.* (*zool.*) steppe marmot; (*fig.*) lie-abed.
байда́рк|а, и *f.* **1.** (Aleutian) canoe. **2.** (*sport*) kayak.
байда́рочник, а *m.* canoeist.
байда́р|очный *adj. of* **~ка**
ба́йк|а[1], **и** *f.* flannelette.
ба́йк|а[2], **и** *f.* (*coll.*) fairy story, cock-and-bull story.
ба́йковый *adj.* flannelette.
ба́йт, а *m.* (*comput.*) byte.
бак[1], **и** *m.* cistern; tank.
бак[2], **и** *m.* (*naut.*) forecastle.
бакала́вр, а *m.* bachelor (*holder of bachelor's degree*).
бакале́йн|ый *adj.* grocery; **~ая ла́вка** grocer's shop.
бакале́йщик, а *m.* grocer.
бакале́|я, и *f.* (*collect.*) groceries.
ба́кен, а *m.* (*naut.*) buoy.
бакенба́рд|ы, ~ *pl.* (*sg.* **~а, ~ы** *f.*) side-whiskers.
ба́кенщик, а *m.* buoy-keeper.
ба́к|и, ~ *no sg.* = **бакенба́рды**
баккара́ *nt. indecl.* baccarat (card-game).
бакла́г|а, и *f.* flask, water-bottle.
баклажа́н, а *m.* (*bot.*) aubergine, egg-plant.
бакла́н, а *m.* (*zool.*) cormorant.
бактериа́льный *adj.* bacterial.
бактерио́лог, а *m.* bacteriologist.
бактериологи́ческ|ий *adj.* bacteriological; **~ая война́** bacteriological, germ warfare.
бактериоло́ги|я, и *f.* bacteriology.
бактерици́дный *adj.* germicidal.
бакте́ри|я, и *f.* bacterium.
бал, а, о ~е, на ~у́, *pl.* **~ы́** *m.* ball, dance; **ко́нчен б.!** it's all over; that's that.
балабо́л|ить, ю, ишь *impf.* (*coll.*) to chatter idly, gas.
балабо́лк|а, и *c.g.* (*coll.*) chatterbox, gasbag.
балага́н, а *m.* **1.** booth (*at fairs*). **2.** low farce; (*fig.*) farce.
балага́н|ить, ю, ишь *impf.* (*coll.*) to play the fool.
балага́н|ный *adj. of* **~**; farcical.
балага́нщик, а *m.* (*coll.*) **1.** showman. **2.** clown, joker.
балагу́р, а *m.* joker, clown.
балагу́р|ить, ю, ишь *impf.* to jest, joke.
балагу́рств|о, а *nt.* foolery, buffoonery.
балала́ечник, а *m.* balalaika-player.
балала́|ечный *adj. of* **~йка**
балала́йк|а, и *f.* balalaika.

баламу́т, а *m.* (*coll.*) trouble-maker.
баламу́|тить, чу, тишь *impf.* (*of* **вз~**) (*coll.*) to stir up, trouble (*water*); (*fig.*) to upset.
бала́нс, а *m.* balance; **торго́вый б.** balance of trade.
балансёр, а *m.* tightrope-walker.
баланси́р, а *m.* (*tech.*) **1.** balance-wheel (*in clock*). **2.** (balance) beam.
баланси́р|овать, ую *impf.* **1.** (*impf. only*) to keep one's balance, balance. **2.** (*pf.* **с~**) (*bookkeeping*) to balance.
балахо́н, а *m.* (*coll.*) loose-fitting garment.
балбе́с, а *m.* (*coll.*) booby, nitwit.
балд|а́, ы́ *c.g.* (*fig., coll.*) blockhead.
балдахи́н, а *m.* canopy.
балери́н|а, ы *f.* ballerina.
бале́т, а *m.* ballet; **б. на льду́** ice review.
балетме́йстер, а *m.* ballet-master.
бале́т|ный *adj. of* **~**
балетома́н, а *m.* balletomane.
балетома́ни|я, и *f.* balletomania.
ба́лк|а[1], **и** *f.* beam; girder.
ба́лк|а[2], **и** *f.* gully.
балка́нский *adj.* Balkan.
Балка́н|ы, ~ *no sg.* the Balkans.
балко́н, а *m.* balcony; (*theatr.*) upper circle.
балл, а *m.* **1.** mark (*in school*); **вы́сший б.** an 'A'; **проходно́й б.** pass mark. **2.** (*sport*) point. **3.** (*meteor.*): **ве́тер в пять ~́ов** wind force 5.
балла́д|а, ы *f.* **1.** ballad. **2.** (*mus.*) ballade.
балла́ст, а *m.* ballast (*also fig.*).
балли́стик, а *m.* ballistics expert.
балли́стик|а, и *f.* ballistics.
баллисти́ческий *adj.* ballistic.
балло́н, а *m.* **1.** balloon (*vessel*); container (*of glass, metal, or rubber*); carboy; **аэрозо́льный б.** spray can; **б. с кислоро́дом** oxygen cylinder. **2.** (*motor-car, etc.*) balloon tyre.
баллоти́р|овать, ую *impf.* to ballot (for), vote (for).
баллоти́р|оваться, уюсь *impf.* **1.** (**в**+*a.*, **на**+*a.*) to stand (for), be a candidate (for); **б. на до́лжность секретаря́ па́ртии** to stand for secretary of the party. **2.** (*pass. of* **~овать**) to be put to the vote.
баллотиро́вк|а, и *f.* **1.** vote, ballot, poll. **2.** voting, balloting, polling.
баллотиро́в|очный *adj. of* **~ка; б. бюллете́нь** ballot paper.
бало́в|анный *p.p.p. of* **~а́ть** *and adj.* (*coll.*) spoiled.
бал|ова́ть, у́ю *impf.* (*of* **из~**) to spoil; to pamper.
бал|ова́ться, у́юсь *impf.* **1.** to get up to mischief. **2.** (**с**+*i. coll.*) to play, fool about (with). **3.** (+*i.*; *coll.*) to dabble (in).
ба́лов|ень, ня *m.* **1.** spoilt child; pet, favourite; **б. судьбы́** favourite of fortune. **2.** naughty child.
баловни́к, а́ *m.* (*coll.*) **1.** naughty child; mischief-maker. **2.** pet; favourite.
баловств|о́, а́ *nt.* (*coll.*) **1.** spoiling, over-indulgence; petting, pampering. **2.** mischief.
балти́|ец, йца *m.* sailor of the (Russian) Baltic Fleet.
балти́йский *adj.* Baltic.
балы́к, а́ *m.* balyk (*cured fillet of sturgeon, etc.*).
ба́льза, ы *f.* balsa(wood).
бальза́м, а *m.* balsam; (*fig.*) balm.
бальзами́р|овать, ую *impf.* (*of* **на~**) to embalm.
бальзамиро́вк|а, и *f.* embalming.
бальзамиро́вщик, а *m.* embalmer.
ба́л|ьный *adj. of* **~; ~ьное пла́тье** ball-dress; **~ьные та́нцы** ballroom dancing.
балюстра́д|а, ы *f.* (*archit.*) balustrade.
баля́син|а, ы *f.* baluster.
бамбу́к, а *m.* bamboo.
бамбу́к|овый *adj. of* **~**
бана́льност|ь, и *f.* **1.** banality. **2.** banal remark; platitude.
бана́л|ьный (~ен, ~ьна) *adj.* banal, trite.
бана́н, а *m.* banana.
бананово́з, а *m.* banana boat.
бана́н|овый *adj. of* **~**
ба́нд|а, ы *f.* band, gang.
банда́ж, а́ *m.* **1.** bandage; **грыжево́й б.** truss. **2.** **спорти́вный б.** athletic supporter; jockstrap. **3.** (*tech.*) tyre, band (*of metal*).
бандеро́л|ь, и *f.* **1.** wrapper (*for dispatching printed matter by post*). **2.** 'printed matter'; **отправля́ть ~ью** to send as printed matter.
банди́т, а *m.* bandit; thug; **вооружённый б.** armed robber.
бандити́зм, а *m.* banditry; thuggery; **возду́шный б.** air piracy; **вооружённый б.** armed robbery.
банди́т|ский *adj. of* **~**
банди́тств|овать, ую *impf.* to rampage.
банду́р|а, ы *f.* (*mus.*) bandura (*Ukrainian string instrument similar to large mandoline*).
бандури́ст, а *m.* (*mus.*) bandura-player.
банк, а *m.* **1.** (*fin.*) bank (*also in card-games*); **Всеми́рный б.** World Bank. **2.** faro (*card-game*).
ба́нк|а[1], **и** *f.* (*glass*) jar; tin, can.
ба́нк|а[2], **и** *f.* bank, shoal.
банке́т[1], **а** *m.* banquet.
банки́р, а *m.* banker.
банки́р|ский *adj. of* **~; б. дом** banking-house.
банкно́т, а *m.* (*fin.*) bank-note.
ба́нк|овский *adj. of* **~; б. биле́т** bank-note; **б. слу́жащий** bank clerk; **~овская кни́жка** bank-book.
банкомёт, а *m.* banker (*at cards*); croupier.
банкро́т, а *m.* bankrupt; **объявля́ть ~ом** to declare bankrupt.
банкро́|титься, чусь, тишься *impf.* (*of* **о~**) to become bankrupt (*also fig.*).
банкро́тств|о, а *nt.* bankruptcy.
ба́н|ный *adj. of* **~я**
бант, а *m.* bow; **завяза́ть ~́ом** to tie in a bow.
ба́нщик, а *m.* bath-house attendant.
ба́н|я, и *f.* (Russian) baths; bath-house; **крова́вая б.** blood-bath; **фи́нская б.** sauna; **зада́ть ~ю** (+*d.*; *coll.*) to give (s.o.) what for.
бапти́ст, а *m.* Baptist.
баптисте́ри|й, я *m.* baptist(e)ry.
бапти́стский *adj.* Baptist.
бар[1], **а** *m.* bar; **пивно́й б.** pub.
бар[2], **а** *m.* (*naut.*) (sand-)bar.
бар[3], **а** *m.* (*phys.*) bar (*unit of atmospheric pressure*).
бараба́н, а *m.* drum (*also tech.*).
бараба́н|ить, ю, ишь *impf.* to drum; to patter.
бараба́н|ный *adj. of* **~; ~ная дробь** drum-roll; **~ная перепо́нка** (*anat.*) ear-drum, tympanum.
бараба́нщик, а *m.* drummer.
бара́к, а *m.* hut.
бара́н, а *m.* ram; (wild) sheep.
бара́н|ий *adj.* **1.** sheep's; **согну́ть в б. рог** (*coll.*) to make (s.o.) knuckle under. **2.** sheepskin. **3.** mutton.
бара́нин|а, ы *f.* mutton; lamb.
бара́нк|а, и *f.* **1.** baranka (*ring-shaped roll*). **2.** (*coll.*) (steering-)wheel.
барахл|о́, а́ *nt.* (*collect.*; *coll.*) **1.** old clothes; jumble; odds and ends. **2.** trash, junk.
бара́хо́лк|а, и *f.* (*coll.*) flea market.
барах|о́льный *adj. of* **~ло́**
барах|о́льщик, а *m.* (*coll.*) dealer in second-hand goods.
бара́хта|ться, юсь *impf.* (*coll.*) to flounder; to wallow.
бара́|чный *adj. of* **~к**
бара́ш|ек, ка *m.* **1.** young ram; lamb. **2.** lambskin. **3.** (*tech.*) wing nut, thumbscrew. **4.** (*bot.*) catkin.
бара́шковый *adj.* lambskin.
барбитура́т, а *m.* barbiturate.

барбóс, а *m.* (*coll.*) watch-dog.
бард, а *m.* bard.
бардáк, á *m.* (*coll.*) chaos.
барельéф, а *m.* bas-relief.
бáрж|а, и *f.* barge.
барж|á, ú, *g. pl.* **~éй = бáржа**
бáри|й, я *m.* (*chem.*) barium.
бáр|ин, а, *pl.* **~е** *and* **~ы, ~** *m.* barin (*member of landowning gentry*); landowner; gentleman; **жить ~ином** to live like a lord.
барúт, а *m.* (*min.*) barytes.
баритóн, а *m.* baritone.
бáрич, а *m.* barin's son; (*coll., pej.*) = **бáрин**
бáрк|а, и *f.* wooden barge.
баркарóл|а, ы *f.* (*mus.*) barcarole.
баркáс, а *m.* launch; long boat.
бáрмен, а *m.* barman, bartender.
барóграф, а *m.* barograph.
барóкко *nt. indecl.* baroque.
барóметр, а *m.* barometer.
барометрúческий *adj.* barometric.
барóн, а *m.* baron.
баронéсс|а, ы *f.* baroness.
барóнский *adj.* baronial.
барóнств|о, а *nt.* barony.
бáрочник, а *m.* bargee.
бáр|очный *adj. of* **~ка**
барóчный *adj.* baroque.
баррикáд|а, ы *f.* barricade.
баррикадúр|овать, ую *impf.* (*of* **за~**) to barricade.
баррикáдник, а *m.* barricader.
баррикáд|ный *adj. of* **~а**
барс, а *m.* (*zool.*) ounce, snow leopard.
бáрск|ий *adj. of* **бáрин; б. дом** manor-house; **жить на ~ую нóгу** to live like a lord.
бáрственный *adj.* lordly, grand.
бáрств|о, а *nt.* **1.** lordliness. **2.** (*collect.*) gentry.
бáрств|овать, ую *impf.* to live in idleness and plenty.
барсýк, á *m.* badger.
барсýчий *adj.* **1.** *adj. of* **барсýк. 2.** badger-skin.
бáртер, а *m.* (*econ.*) barter.
бáртер|ный *adj. of* **~; ~ная эконóмика** barter economy.
бархáн, а *m.* (sand-)dune.
бáрхат, а *m.* velvet.
бархатúст|ый (~, ~а) *adj.* velvety.
бáрхатк|а, и *f.* piece of velvet; velvet ribbon.
бáрхатный *adj.* **1.** velvet; **б. сезóн** autumn season, autumn months. **2.** (*fig.*) velvety.
бáрщин|а, ы *f.* (*hist.*) corvée.
бáрын|я, и *f.* barin's wife; lady; mistress; (*as term of address employed by peasants, servants, etc.*) madam.
барыш, á *m.* profit.
барышник, а *m.* **1.** profiteer; speculator; spiv. **2.** horse-dealer.
барышнича|ть, ю *impf.* to profiteer; (*+i.*) to speculate (in).
барышничеств|о, а *nt.* profiteering; speculation.
бáрыш|ня, ни, *g. pl.* **~ень** *f.* **1.** girl of gentry family; (*as term of address employed by peasants, servants, etc.*) miss. **2.** (*coll.*) girl, young lady. **3.** (*coll., obs.*) female assistant; **телефóнная б.** (*female*) telephone operator.
барьéр, а *m.* barrier (*also fig.*); **звуковóй б.** sound barrier; (*sport*) hurdle; **взять б.** to clear a hurdle; **постáвить когó-н. к ~у** to make s.o. fight a duel.
барьерúст, а *m.* hurdler.
бас, а, *pl.* **~ы** *m.* (*mus.*) bass.
бáс|енный *adj. of* **~ня**
басúст|ый (~, ~а) *adj.* (*coll.*) bass.
ба|сúть, шý, сúшь *impf.* (*coll.*) to speak (*or* sing) in a deep voice.
баскетбóл, а *m.* basketball (*sport*).
баскетболúст, а *m.* basket-ball player.
баснопúс|ец, ца *m.* (*liter.*) fabulist.
баснослóв|ный (~ен, ~на) *adj.* **1.** mythical, legendary. **2.** (*fig., coll.*) fabulous.
бáс|ня, ни, *g. pl.* **~ен** *f.* **1.** fable. **2.** (*fig., coll.*) fable, fabrication.
бас|óвый *adj. of* **~; б. ключ** (*mus.*) bass clef.
бас|óк, кá *m.* (*mus.*) **1.** low bass (voice). **2.** bass-string.
бассéйн, а *m.* **1.** (*man-made*) pool; reservoir; **б. для плáвания** swimming-pool. **2.** (*geog.*) basin; **каменноýгольный б.** coalfield.
бáста *int.* (*coll.*) that's enough!; that'll do!
бастиóн, а *m.* (*mil. and fig.*) bastion.
баст|овáть, ýю *impf.* to (go on) strike; to be on strike.
баст|ýющий *pres. part. of* **~овáть** *and adj.* striking; *as n.* **б., ~ ýющего** *m.* striker.
баталúст, а *m.* painter of battle-pieces.
батáли|я, и *f.* (*coll.*) fight; row, squabble.
батальóн, а *m.* (*mil.*) battalion.
батальóн|ный *adj. of* **~; б. командúр** battalion commander; *as n.* **б., ~ного** *m.* = **б. командúр**
батарé|ец, йца *m.* (*mil.; coll.*) gunner.
батарéйк|а, и *f.* (*electric*) battery.
батарé|йный *adj. of* **~я**
батарé|я, и *f.* (*mil. and tech.*) battery; **аккумулятóрная б.** storage battery; **б. отоплéния** radiator;
батúст, а *m.* cambric, lawn.
батúст|овый *adj. of* **~**
батисфéр|а, ы *f.* bathysphere.
батóн, а *m.* **1.** (*long*) loaf of bread. **2.** stick (*of confectionery*).
батрáк, á *m.* farm-labourer.
батрá|цкий *adj. of* **~к**
батрáчеств|о, а *nt.* **1.** farm work. **2.** (*collect.*) farm-labourers.
батрáч|ить, у, ишь *impf.* to work as a farm-labourer.
баттерфляúст, а *m.* butterfly swimmer.
баттерфлá|й, я *m.* butterfly (*swimming stroke*).
батýт, а *m.* (*sport*) trampoline.
батутúст, а *m.* trampolinist.
батутúст|ка, ки *f. of* **~**
батýт|ный *adj. of* **~; б. спорт** trampolining.
бáтюшк|а, и *m.* **1.** (*obs.*) father; **как вас по ~е?** what is your patronymic? **2.** (*as mode of address to priest*) father. **3.** (*coll.*) old chap!; my dear fellow!
бáтюшки *int.*: **б. (мой)!** good gracious!
баýл, а *m.* trunk.
бах *int.* bang!
бахвáл, а *m.* (*coll.*) braggart, boaster.
бахвáл|иться, юсь, ишься *impf.* (*coll.; +i.*) to brag (of).
бахвáльств|о, а *nt.* (*coll.*) bragging.
бахром|á, ы́ *f.* fringe.
бахрóмчатый *adj.* fringed.
бахч|á, и *f.* (water-)melon plantation; pumpkin (gourd) field.
бахчéвник, а *m.* melon-grower.
бахчевóдств|о, а *nt.* melon-growing.
бахч|евóй *adj. of* **~á; ~евы́е культýры** melons and gourds.
бац *int.* = **бах**
бацúлл|а, ы *f.* bacillus.
бациллоносúтел|ь, я *m.* (bacillus-)carrier.
бáшенк|а, и *f.* turret.
бáш|енный *adj. of* **~ня; ~енные часы́** tower clock.
башк|á, ú *no g. pl., f.* (*coll.*) head; pate; **глýпая б.** blockhead.
башкúр, а *m.* Bashkir.
башкúрский *adj.* Bashkir.
башковúт|ый (~, ~а) *adj.* (*coll.*) brainy.
башмáк, á *m.* shoe (*also tech.*); **быть под ~óм у когó-н.** to be under s.o.'s thumb.
башмá|чный *adj. of* **~к**

башма|чо́к, чка́ *m. dim. of* **~к; вя́заный б.** bootee.
ба́ш|ня, ни, *g. pl.* **~ен** *f.* tower; turret.
ба|шу́, си́шь *see* **~си́ть**
баю́ка|ть, ю *impf.* to sing lullabies (to).
ба́юшки-баю́ *int.* lullaby.
бая́н, а *m.* (*mus.*) bayan (*kind of accordion*).
баяни́ст, а *m.* (*mus.*) bayan-player.
бде́ни|е, я *nt.* vigil.
бди́тельност|ь, и *f.* vigilance, watchfulness.
бди́тел|ьный (~ен, ~ьна) *adj.* vigilant, watchful.
бег, а, о ~е, на ~у́, *pl.* **~а́, ~о́в** *m.* **1.** run, running; **~о́м, на ~у́** at the double; **на всём ~у́** at full speed; **оздорови́тельный б.** jogging. **2.** (*sport*) race; **б. на вре́мя** time trial. **3.** (*pl.*) the races (*for horses harnessed, not ridden*); trotting races; **быть на ~а́х** to be at the races. **4.: быть в ~а́х** to be on the run.
бе́га|ть, ю *impf.* (*indet. of* **бежа́ть**) **1.** to run (about); (**за**+*i.*; *coll.*) to run (after), chase (after). **2.** (*of s.o.'s eyes*) to rove, roam.
бегемо́т, а *m.* hippopotamus.
бегле́ц, а *m.* fugitive.
бе́глост|ь, и *f.* fluency; dexterity.
бе́гл|ый *adj.* **1.** runaway, fugitive. **2.** fluent, quick. **3.** superficial; cursory; **б. взгляд** fleeting glance.
бег|ово́й *adj. of* **~; ~ова́я доро́жка** running-track; **~ова́я ло́шадь** racehorse.
бего́м *adv.* running; at the double.
бего́ни|я, и *f.* (*bot.*) begonia.
беготн|я́, и́ *f.* (*coll.*) running about; bustle.
бе́гств|о, а *nt.* flight; escape; **обрати́ть в б.** to put to flight; **обрати́ться в б.** to take to flight.
бе|гу́, ~жи́шь *see* **~жа́ть**
бегу́н, а́ *m.* runner.
бед|а́, ы́, *pl.* **~ы** *f.* **1.** misfortune; trouble; **на ~у́** unfortunately; **на свою́ ~у́** to one's cost; **пришла́ б. — отворя́й воро́та** (*prov.*) it never rains but it pours. **2.** (the) trouble, the matter; *as pred.* it is awful!; **б. в том, что** the trouble is (that); **про́сто б.!** it's simply awful!; **б. мне с ним** (*coll.*) he's nothing but trouble; **не б.!** it doesn't matter. **3.** (*coll.*) an awful lot.
бедла́м, а *m.* bedlam.
бedне́|ть, ю *impf.* (*of* **о~**) (+*i.*) to grow poor (in).
бе́дност|ь, и *f.* poverty (*also fig.*); indigence.
беднот|а́, ы́ *f.* **1.** (*collect.*) the poor. **2.** (*coll.*) poverty.
бе́д|ный (~ен, ~на) *adj.* poor; meagre; (*fig.*) barren.
бедня́г|а, и *m.* (*coll.*) poor devil.
бедня́жк|а, и *c.g.and f.* (*coll.*) **1.** *c.g. dim. of* **бедня́га. 2.** *f. of* **бедня́га.**
бедня́к, а́ *m.* pauper.
бедня́|цкий *adj. of* **~к**
бедо́в|ый (~, ~а) *adj.* (*coll.*) mischievous; daring.
бедоку́р, а *m.* (*coll.*) mischief-maker.
бедоку́р|ить, ю, ишь *impf.* (*of* **на~**) (*coll.*) to make mischief.
бедола́г|а, и *c.g.* poor devil.
бе́дренный *adj.* (*anat.*) femoral.
бед|ро́, ра́, *pl.* **~ра, ~ер, ~рам** *nt.* **1.** thigh; hip. **2.** (*joint of meat*) leg.
бе́дствен|ный (~, ~на) *adj.* disastrous, calamitous.
бе́дстви|е, я *nt.* calamity, disaster; **сигна́л ~я** distress signal.
бе́дств|овать, ую *impf.* to live in poverty.
бедуи́н, а *m.* bedouin.
бедуи́н|ский *adj. of* **~**
беж *adj. indecl.* beige.
бе|жа́ть, гу́, жи́шь, гу́т *impf.* (*det. of* **бе́гать**) **1.** to run; (*fig.*) to fly. **2.** (*impf. and pf.*) to escape.
бе́жевый *adj.* beige.
бе́жен|ец, ца *m.* refugee.
бе́жен|ка, ки *f. of* **~ец**
без *prep.+g.* without; in the absence of; minus, less; **б. вас** in your absence; **б. че́тверти час** a quarter to one; **б. ма́лого** (*coll.*) almost, all but; **быть б. ума́ (от)** to be crazy (about).
без... *pref.* in-, un-, -less.
безавари́йный *adj.* accident-free.
безала́бер|ный (~ен, ~на) *adj.* disorderly; slovenly.
безалкого́льный *adj.* non-alcoholic; **б. напи́ток** soft drink.
безапелляцио́н|ный (~ен, ~на) *adj.* peremptory, categorical.
безбе́д|ный (~ен, ~на) *adj.* well-to-do, comfortable.
безбиле́тник, а *m.* fare dodger.
безбиле́тный *adj.* ticketless; **б. пассажи́р** fare dodger; (*on ship*) stowaway.
безбо́жи|е, я *nt.* atheism.
безбо́жник, а *m.* atheist.
безбо́жно *adv.* (*coll.*) shamelessly, outrageously.
безбо́жн|ый *adj.* **1.** irreligious, anti-religious. **2.** (*coll.*) outrageous.
безбол́езнен|ный (~, ~на) *adj.* painless.
безборо́дый *adj.* beardless (*also fig.*).
безбоя́знен|ный (~, ~на) *adj.* fearless.
безбра́чи|е, я *nt.* celibacy.
безбра́чный *adj.* celibate.
безбре́ж|ный (~ен, ~на) *adj.* boundless.
безбу́р|ный (~ен, ~на) *adj.* calm, peaceful.
безве́ст|ный (~ен, ~на) *adj.* unknown; obscure.
безве́тренный *adj.* calm.
безве́три|е, я *nt.* calm.
безви́н|ный (~ен, ~на) *adj.* guiltless.
безвку́сиц|а, ы *f.* lack of taste; **что за б.!** what bad taste!
безвку́с|ный (~ен, ~на) *adj.* tasteless (*also fig.*).
безвла́сти|е, я *nt.* anarchy.
безво́д|ный (~ен, ~на) *adj.* arid; waterless.
безво́дь|е, я *nt.* aridity.
безвозвра́т|ный (~ен, ~на) *adj.* irrevocable; **~ная ссу́да** permanent loan.
безвозду́шный *adj.* airless.
безвозме́здный *adj.* free (of charge); **б. труд** unpaid work.
безво́ли|е, я *nt.* lack of will; weak will.
безволо́сый *adj.* hairless, bald.
безво́л|ьный (~ен, ~ьна) *adj.* weak-willed.
безвре́д|ный (~ен, ~на) *adj.* harmless.
безвре́менн|ый *adj.* untimely, premature; **~ая кончи́на** untimely decease.
безвы́ездно *adv.* uninterruptedly, without a break.
безвы́ездн|ый *adj.* uninterrupted; **~ое пребыва́ние** continuous residence.
безвы́ход|ный (~ен, ~на) *adj.* hopeless, desperate.
безгла́с|ный (~ен, ~на) *adj.* (*fig.*) silent, dumb.
безголо́в|ый (~, ~а) *adj.* **1.** headless; (*iron.*) brainless. **2.** (*fig., coll.*) scatter-brained.
безголо́с|ый *adj.* weak (*of voice*); voiceless.
безгра́мотност|ь, и *f.* illiteracy.
безгра́мот|ный (~ен, ~на) *adj.* illiterate (*also fig.*); ignorant.
безграни́ч|ный (~ен, ~на) *adj.* infinite, limitless, boundless.
безгре́шност|ь, и *f.* innocence.
безгре́ш|ный (~ен, ~на) *adj.* innocent, sinless.
безда́рност|ь, и *f.* **1.** lack of talent. **2.** (*coll.*) mediocrity.
безда́р|ный (~ен, на) *adj.* talentless, undistinguished; third-rate; **б. актёр** ham; **б. певе́ц** third-rate singer.
бе́здар|ь, и *f.* (*coll.*) mediocrity.
безде́йствен|ный (~, ~на) *adj.* inactive.
безде́йстви|е, я *nt.* inaction, idleness.
безде́йств|овать, ую *impf.* to be inactive; to lie idle; not to work (*of a machine, etc.*).
безде́лиц|а, ы *f.* trifle, bagatelle.

безделу́шк|а, и *f.* knick-knack.
безде́ль|е, я *nt.* idleness.
безде́льник, а *m.* idler, loafer.
безде́льни|ца, цы *f. of* **~к**
безде́льнича|ть, ю *impf.* to idle, loaf.
безде́л|ьный (~ен, ~ьна) *adj.* (*coll.*) idle.
безде́нежный *adj.* **1.** penniless. **2.** (*econ.*) non-monetary.
безде́нежь|е, я *nt.* impecuniousness.
безде́т|ный (~ен, ~на) *adj.* childless.
безде́ятельност|ь, и *f.* inactivity, inertia.
безде́ятел|ьный (~ен, ~ьна) *adj.* inactive; sluggish.
бе́здн|а, ы *f.* **1.** abyss, chasm. **2.** (*coll.*) heaps, stacks of; **б. хлопо́т** a (whole) stack of troubles.
бездо́жд|е, я *nt.* dry weather, drought.
бездоказа́тел|ьный (~ен, ~ьна) *adj.* unsubstantiated.
бездо́м|ный (~ен, ~на) *adj.* homeless; **~ная ко́шка** stray cat.
бездо́нный *adj.* bottomless.
бездоро́жь|е, я *nt.* **1.** absence of roads. **2.** bad condition of roads; season when roads are impassable.
безду́м|ный (~ен, ~на) *adj.* unthinking; feckless.
безду́ши|е, я *nt.* heartlessness, callousness.
безду́ш|ный (~ен, ~на) *adj.* **1.** heartless, callous. **2.** (*fig.*) soulless.
безе́ *nt. indecl.* meringue.
безжа́лост|ный (~ен, ~на) *adj.* ruthless, pitiless.
безжи́знен|ный (~, ~на) *adj.* lifeless, inanimate; (*fig.*) spiritless.
беззабо́т|ный (~ен, ~на) *adj.* carefree, light-hearted; careless.
беззаве́т|ный (~ен, ~на) *adj.* selfless, whole-hearted; **~ная хра́брость** selfless courage.
беззако́ни|е, я *nt.* **1.** lawlessness. **2.** unlawful act.
беззако́н|ный (~ен, ~на) *adj.* **1.** illegal, unlawful. **2.** (*poet.*) lawless, wayward.
беззасте́нчив|ый (~, ~а) *adj.* shameless; **б. лгун** brazen liar; **~ая ложь** barefaced lie.
беззащи́т|ный (~ен, ~на) *adj.* defenceless, unprotected.
беззвёзд|ный (~ен, ~на) *adj.* starless.
беззву́ч|ный (~ен, ~на) *adj.* soundless, noiseless.
безземе́ль|е, я *nt.* lack of land.
безземе́льный *adj.* landless.
беззло́би|е, я *nt.* good nature.
беззло́б|ный (~ен, ~на) *adj.* good-natured.
беззу́б|ый *adj.* toothless; (*fig.*) impotent.
безле́с|ный (~ен, ~на) *adj.* woodless; treeless.
безле́сь|е, я *nt.* **1.** woodless tract. **2.** absence of forest.
безли́кий *adj.* featureless; faceless, impersonal.
безли́ч|ный (~ен, ~на) *adj.* **1.** characterless, impersonal. **2.** (*gram.*) impersonal.
безлю́д|ный (~ен, ~на) *adj.* uninhabited; sparsely populated; solitary, unfrequented.
безлю́дь|е, я *nt.* absence of human life; **на б. и Фома́ дворяни́н** (*prov.*) in the land of the blind the one-eyed is king.
безме́н, а *m.* steelyard.
безме́р|ный (~ен, ~на) *adj.* immense, boundless.
безмо́зглый *adj.* (*coll.*) brainless.
безмо́лви|е, я *nt.* silence; **цари́т б.** silence reigns.
безмо́лв|ный (~ен, ~на) *adj.* silent, mute, speechless; **~ное согла́сие** tacit consent.
безмо́лвств|овать, ую *impf.* to keep silent.
безмоло́чный *adj.* dairy-free.
безмяте́жност|ь и *f.* serenity, placidity.
безмяте́ж|ный (~ен, ~на) *adj.* serene, placid.
безнадёж|ный (~ен, ~на) *adj.* hopeless; despairing.
безнадзо́рный *adj.* neglected.
безнака́занно *adv.* with impunity; **э́то ему́ не пройдёт б.** he won't get away with this.
безнака́занност|ь, и *f.* impunity.
безнака́зан|ный (~, ~на) *adj.* unpunished.
безнали́чный *adj.* non-cash; **б. расчёт** (*fin.*) clearing.
безнало́говый *adj.* tax-free.
безнача́ли|е, я *nt.* anarchy.
безно́гий *adj.* legless; one-legged.
безнра́вственност|ь, и *f.* immorality.
безнра́вствен|ный (~, ~на) *adj.* immoral.
безо *prep.* (*before g. of* **весь** *and* **вся́кий**) = **без**
безоби́д|ный (~ен, ~на) *adj.* inoffensive.
безо́блачност|ь и *f.* cloudlessness; (*fig.*) serenity.
безо́блач|ный (~ен, ~на) *adj.* cloudless; (*fig.*) serene, unclouded.
безобра́зи|е, я *nt.* **1.** ugliness. **2.** outrage. **3.** (*as pred; coll.*) it's a disgrace!
безобра́|зить, жу, зишь *impf.* (*of* **о~**) to disfigure, mutilate.
безобра́зник, а *m.* (*coll.*) **1.** hooligan. **2.** naughty child.
безобра́знича|ть, ю *impf.* (*coll.*) to behave disgracefully; to make a nuisance of o.s.
безобра́з|ный (~ен, ~на) *adj.* **1.** ugly. **2.** disgraceful, outrageous.
безогля́дный *adj.* reckless, impetuous.
безоговоро́чн|ый (~а, ~о) *adj.* unconditional, unreserved.
безопа́сност|ь, и *f.* safety, security; **реме́нь ~и** seat belt.
безопа́с|ный (~ен, ~на) *adj.* safe, secure; **~ная бри́тва** safety razor.
безору́ж|ный (~ен, ~на) *adj.* unarmed.
безоско́лочн|ый *adj.*: **~ое стекло́** safety glass.
безоснова́тел|ьный (~ен, ~ьна) *adj.* groundless.
безостано́вочный *adj.* unceasing; non-stop.
безотве́т|ный (~ен, ~на) *adj.* **1.** unrequited. **2.** meek.
безотве́тственност|ь, и *f.* irresponsibility.
безотве́тствен|ный (~, ~на) *adj.* irresponsible.
безотка́зный *adj.* **1.** dependable, trusty. **2.** trouble-free.
безотлага́тельный *adj.* urgent.
безотлу́чно *adv.* continually; **она́ нахо́дится б. до́ма** she never gets out.
безотлу́ч|ный (~ен, на) *adj.* ever-present; continuous.
безотноси́тельно *adv.* **(к)** irrespective (of).
безотра́д|ный (~ен, ~на) *adj.* cheerless.
безотчёт|ный (~ен, ~на) *adj.* **1.** not subject to control. **2.** unconscious, instinctive.
безоши́боч|ный (~ен, ~на) *adj.* correct; faultless, infallible.
безрабо́тиц|а, ы *f.* unemployment.
безрабо́тн|ый *adj.* unemployed; *as n.* **~ые, ~ых** *pl.* the unemployed.
безра́дост|ный (~ен, ~на) *adj.* joyless; dismal.
безразде́л|ьный (~ен, ~ьна) *adj.* undivided; **~ьная власть** complete sway; **~ьное иму́щество** indivisible property.
безразли́чи|е, я *nt.* indifference.
безразли́чно (*adv.*) indifferently; **относи́ться б. (к)** to be indifferent (to); **б. кто, где** no matter who, where.
безразли́ч|ный (~ен, ~на) *adj.* indifferent; **мне ~но** it's all the same to me.
безразме́р|ный (~ен, ~на) *adj.*: **~ныеноски́** stretch socks.
безрассу́д|ный (~ен, ~на) *adj.* reckless; foolhardy.
безрассу́дств|о, а *nt.* recklessness, foolhardiness.
безрасчёт|ный (~ен, ~на) *adj.* uneconomical.
безрезульта́т|ный (~ен, ~на) *adj.* futile; unsuccessful.
безро́г|ий *adj.* hornless; **~ое живо́тное** pollard.

безро́д|ный (~ен, ~на) *adj.* without kith or kin.
безро́пот|ный (~ен, ~на) *adj.* uncomplaining, resigned; submissive.
безрука́вк|а, и *f.* sleeveless jacket *or* blouse.
безру́кий *adj.* **1.** armless. **2.** one-armed. **3.** (*fig.*) clumsy.
безры́бь|е, я *nt.*: **на б. и рак ры́ба** (*prov.*) in the land of the blind the one-eyed is king.
безубы́точ|ный (~ен, ~на) *adj.* (*comm.*) break-even.
безуда́р|ный (~ен, ~на) *adj.* (*ling.*) unaccented, unstressed.
безу́держ|ный (~ен, ~на) *adj.* unrestrained; impetuous.
безукори́знен|ный (~, ~на) *adj.* irreproachable; impeccable.
безу́м|ец, ца *m.* madman.
безу́ми|е, я *nt.* **1.** madness, insanity. **2.** (*fig.*) madness; folly; **довести́ до ~я** to drive mad; **люби́ть до ~я** to love to distraction.
безу́мно *adv.* madly; terribly, dreadfully.
безу́м|ный (~ен, ~на) *adj.* **1.** (*fig.*) mad, crazy. **2.** (*coll.*) terrible, awful; **~ные це́ны** absurd prices.
безумо́лч|ный (~ен, ~на) *adj.* incessant (*of noise*).
безу́мств|о, а *nt.* madness; foolhardiness.
безу́мств|овать, ую *impf.* to behave like a madman; to rave.
безупре́ч|ный (~ен, ~на) *adj.* irreproachable.
безуса́дочный *adj.* pre-shrunk, shrinkproof.
безусло́вно *adv.* **1.** unconditionally, absolutely. **2.** (*coll.*) of course, undoubtedly.
безусло́вност|ь, и *f.* certainty.
безусло́в|ный (~ен, ~на) *adj.* **1.** unconditional, absolute. **2.** indisputable.
безуспе́ш|ный (~ен, ~на) *adj.* unsuccessful.
безуста́нный *adj.* tireless, indefatigable.
безу́сый *adj.* having no moustache; (*fig.*) callow.
безуте́ш|ный (~ен, ~на) *adj.* inconsolable.
безуча́стност|ь, и *f.* apathy, indifference.
безуча́ст|ный (~ен, ~на) *adj.* apathetic, indifferent.
безъя́дерный *adj.* nuclear-free.
безыде́йност|ь, и *f.* lack of principle(s); lack of ideological content.
безыде́|йный (~ен, ~йна) *adj.* unprincipled; lacking ideals; lacking ideological content.
безызве́стност|ь, и *f.* **1.** uncertainty. **2.** obscurity.
безызве́ст|ный (~ен, ~на) *adj.* unknown, obscure.
безымя́нн|ый *adj.* nameless; anonymous; **б. па́лец** ring-finger.
безынициати́в|ный (~ен, ~на) *adj.* lacking initiative, unenterprising.
безыску́сствен|ный (~ен, ~на) *adj.* artless, ingenuous.
безысхо́д|ный (~ен, ~на) *adj.* irreparable; interminable; perpetual.
бе́й(те) *imper. of* **бить**
бейсбо́л, а *m.* baseball.
бейсболи́ст, а *m.* baseball player.
бека́р, а *m.* (*also as indecl. adj.*) (*mus.*) natural.
бека́с, а *m.* (*zool.*) snipe.
беко́н, а *m.* bacon.
Белару́с|ь, и *f.* Belarus.
белен|а́, ы́ *f.* (*bot.*) henbane.
беле́ни|е, я *nt.* bleaching.
белёный *adj.* bleached.
белёсый *adj.* whitish.
беле́|ть, ю *impf.* (*of* **по~**) **1.** to grow white. **2.** (*no pf.*) to show up white.
беле́|ться, юсь *impf.* to show up white.
белиберд|а́, ы́ *f.* (*coll.*) nonsense, rubbish.
белизн|а́, ы́ *f.* whiteness.
бели́л|а, ~ *no sg.* **1.** whitewash. **2.** ceruse.
бели́льный *adj.* bleaching.
бел|и́ть, ю́, ~́ишь *impf.* **1.** (*pf.* **по~**) to whitewash. **2.** (*pf.* **на~**) to white(n) (*one's face, etc.*). **3.** (*pf.* **вы́~**) to bleach.
бе́л|ичий *adj. of* **~ка**[1]; **б. мех** squirrel (fur).
бе́лк|а[1], **и** *f.* squirrel; **верте́ться как б. в колесе́** to run round in circles.
бе́лк|а[2], **и** *f.* (*coll.*) bleaching.
белладо́нн|а, ы *f.* (*bot.*) belladonna.
беллетриза́ци|я, и *f.* fictionalization.
беллетризи́р|овать, ую *impf. and pf.* to fictionalize.
беллетри́ст, а *m.* fiction writer.
беллетри́стик|а, и *f.* (*liter.*) fiction.
беллетристи́ческий *adj.* (*liter.*) fictional.
бело... *comb. form* white-.
белобры́с|ый (~, ~а) *adj.* (*coll.*) tow-haired.
белова́т|ый (~, а) *adj.* whitish.
белови́к, а́ *m.* fair copy.
белово́й *adj.* clean, fair; **б. экземпля́р** fair copy.
белогварде́|ец, йца *m.* (*pol.*) White Guard.
белогварде́|йский *adj. of* **~ец**
белоголо́вый *adj.* **1.** white-haired. **2.** fair(-haired).
белодере́в|ец, ца *m.* joiner.
бел|о́к[1], **ка́** *m.* (*biol., chem.*) albumen; protein.
бел|о́к[2], **ка́** *m.* white (of egg); glair.
бел|о́к[3], **ка́** *m.* white (of the eye).
белокро́ви|е, я *nt.* (*med.*) leucaemia.
белоку́р|ый (~, ~а) *adj.* blond(e), fair(-haired).
белоли́ц|ый (~, ~а) *adj.* pale, white-faced.
белору́с, а *m.* Belorussian.
белору́с|ка, ки *f. of* **~**
белору́сский *adj.* Belorussian.
белору́чк|а, и *c.g.* (*coll., pej.*) shirker.
Белосне́жк|а, и *f.* Snow-White.
белосне́ж|ный (~ен, ~на) *adj.* snow-white.
белошве́йк|а, и *f.* seamstress.
белошве́йн|ый *adj.* linen; **~ая мастерска́я** seamstress's workshop.
белу́г|а, и *f.* beluga, white sturgeon; **реве́ть ~ой** to bellow.
белу́|жий *adj. of* **~га**
белу́х|а, и *f.* white whale.
бе́л|ый (~, ~а́, ~о) *adj.* **1.** white; **~ая берёза** silver birch; **б. медве́дь** polar bear. **2.** (*opp. dark and in var. fig. senses*) white; fair; **~ое зо́лото** 'white gold' (= *cotton*); **б. у́голь** 'white coal' (= *water power*); **средь ~а дня** in broad daylight; *as n.* **~ые, ~ых** *pl.* white-skinned people, white men. **3.** clean; blank; **б. лист** clean sheet (*of paper*); **~ая страни́ца** blank page (*in book*); **~ые стихи́** blank verse. **4.** (*pol.*) White (*also as n.*).
бельги́|ец, йца *m.* Belgian.
бельги́|йка, йки *f. of* **~ец**
бельги́йский *adj.* Belgian.
Бе́льги|я, и *f.* Belgium.
бель|ё, я́ *nt.* (*collect.*) linen; **да́мское б.** lingerie; **ни́жнее б.** underclothes.
бель|ево́й *adj. of* **~ё**; **б. шкаф** linen cupboard.
бельме́с, а *m.*: **ни ~а** (*coll.*) nothing; **он ни ~а не понима́ет** he hasn't a clue.
бельм|о́, а́, *pl.* **~́а** *nt.* **1.** (*med.*) wall-eye; **как б. на глазу́** (*fig.*) a thorn in the flesh.
бельэта́ж, а *m.* **1.** first floor. **2.** (*theatr.*) dress circle.
беля́к, а́ *m.* white hare.
бемо́л|ь, я *m.* (*also as indecl. adj.*) (*mus.*) flat.
бенедикти́н|ец, ца *m.* (*eccl.*) Benedictine.
бенедикти́нский *adj.* (*eccl.*) Benedictine.
бенефи́с, а *m.* (*theatr.*) benefit performance.
бенефи́с|ный *adj. of* **~**; **б. спекта́кль** benefit performance.
бенефициа́ри|й, я *m.* (*leg.*) beneficiary.
бенефициа́нт, а *m.* (*theatr.*) artist for whom benefit performance is given.
бензи́н, а *m.* benzine; petrol; **неэтили́рованный б.** unleaded petrol.

бензи́н|овый *adj. of* ~
бензино́ме́р, а *m.* petrol gauge.
бензо... *comb. form, abbr. of* **бензи́новый**
бензоба́к, а *m.* petrol tank.
бензово́з, а *m.* petrol tanker.
бензоколо́нк|а, и *f.* petrol pump.
бензо́л, а *m.* (*chem.*) benzol, benzene.
бензохрани́лищ|е, а *nt.* petrol tank.
бенуа́р, а *m.* (*theatr.*) boxes (*on level of the stalls*).
бе́рег, а, о ~е, на ~у́, *pl.* **~а́** *m.* bank; shore; land (*opp.* sea); **на ~у́ мо́ря** at the seaside; **вы́броситься на́ берег** to run aground; **вы́йти из ~о́в** to burst its banks; **сойти́ на б.** to go ashore.
бер|ёг, ~егла́ *see* **бере́чь**
берегов|о́й *adj.* coastal; waterside; **б. ве́тер** offshore wind; **~о́е пра́во** (*leg.*) right of salvage.
бере|гу́, ~жёшь, ~гу́т *see* **бере́чь**
бере|ди́ть, жу́, ди́шь *impf.* (*of* **раз~**) (*coll.*) to irritate; **б. ста́рые ра́ны** (*fig.*) to re-open old wounds.
бережли́вост|ь, и *f.* thrift, economy.
бережли́в|ый (~, ~а) *adj.* thrifty, economical.
бе́режност|ь, и *f.* care; caution; solicitude.
бе́реж|ный (~ен, ~на) *adj.* careful; cautious; solicitous.
берёз|а, ы *f.* birch.
Берёзк|а, и *f.* Beryozka (*hard-currency shop*)
березня́к, а́ *no pl., m.* **1.** birch grove. **2.** birch-wood.
берёз|овый *adj. of* **~а; ~овая ка́ша** (*coll.*) the birch; a flogging.
бере́йтор, а *m.* riding-master.
бере́мене|ть, ю, ешь *impf.* (*of* **за~**) (*coll.*) to become pregnant.
бере́ме|нная (~нна) *adj.* (*+i.*) pregnant (with).
бере́менност|ь, и *f.* pregnancy; gestation.
берёст|а, ы *no pl., f.* birch-bark.
берёст|овый *adj. of* **~а**
берестяно́й = берёстовый
бере́т, а *m.* beret.
бер|е́чь, егу́, ежёшь, егу́т, *past* **~ёг, ~егла́** *impf.* **1.** to take care (of), look after; to keep, guard; **б. ка́ждую копе́йку** to count every penny; **б. та́йну** to keep a secret. **2.** to spare; to spare the feelings (of).
бер|е́чься, егу́сь, ежёшься, егу́тся, *past* **~ёгся, ~егла́сь** *impf.* **1.** to be careful, take care. **2.** (*+g. or +inf.*) to beware (of); **~еги́тесь переда́ть!** mind you don't eat too much! **3.** *pass. of* **~е́чь**
бе́ркут, а *m.* golden eagle.
Берли́н, а *m.* Berlin.
берли́нск|ий *adj.* Berlin; **~ая лазу́рь** Prussian blue.
берло́г|а, и *f.* den, lair.
берму́д|ы, ов *no sg.* Bermuda shorts.
бер|у́, ёшь *see* **брать**
берцо́в|ый *adj.* (*anat.*): **больша́я ~ая кость** shinbone, tibia; **ма́лая ~ая кость** fibula.
бес, а *m.* demon, evil spirit; **рассыпа́ться ме́лким ~ом** (**пе́ред**+*i.*; *coll.*) to ingratiate o.s. (with).
бесе́д|а, ы *f.* **1.** talk, conversation; **б. по душа́м** heart-to-heart. **2.** discussion; **провести́ ~у** to give a talk.
бесе́дк|а, и *f.* summer-house.
бесе́д|овать, ую *impf.* (**с**+*i.*) to talk, converse (with).
бесён|ок, ка, *pl.* **~я́та, ~я́т** *m.* imp, little devil (*also fig.*).
бе|си́ть, шу́, ~сишь *impf.* (*of* **вз~**) (*coll.*) to enrage, madden, infuriate.
бе|си́ться, шу́сь, ~сишься *impf.* (*of* **вз~**) **1.** to go mad (*of animals*). **2.** (*fig.*) to rage, be furious.
беска́мерн|ый *adj.*: **~ая ши́на** tubeless tyre.
бескла́ссовый *adj.* classless.
бескозы́рк|а, и *f.* (peakless) cap.
бескомпроми́с|сный (~ен, на) *adj.* uncompromising.
бесконе́чно *adv.* infinitely, endlessly; (*coll.*) extremely.
бесконе́чност|ь, и *f.* endlessness; infinity; **до ~и** endlessly.
бесконе́ч|ный (~ен, на) *adj.* endless; infinite; interminable; **~ная дробь** (*math.*) recurring decimal.
бесконтро́л|ьный (~ен, ~ьна) *adj.* uncontrolled; unchecked.
бескоры́сти|е, я *nt.* disinterestedness.
бескоры́ст|ный (~ен, ~на) *adj.* disinterested; unselfish.
беско́стный *adj.* boneless.
бескофеиновый *adj.* decaffeinated.
бескра́йний *adj.* boundless.
бескро́в|ный (~ен, ~на) *adj.* **1.** anaemic, pale. **2.** bloodless; **~ная револю́ция** bloodless revolution.
бескры́лый *adj.* wingless; (*fig.*) uninspired, pedestrian.
бескульту́рь|е, я *nt.* lack of culture.
бесनова́тый *adj.* possessed.
бесн|ова́ться, у́юсь *impf.* to be possessed; to rage, rave.
бесо́вский *adj.* devilish, diabolical.
беспа́лый *adj.* lacking one *or* more fingers *or* toes.
беспа́мят|ный (~ен, ~на) *adj.* (*coll.*) forgetful.
беспа́мятств|о, а *nt.* **1.** unconsciousness; **впасть в б.** to lose consciousness. **2.** frenzy, delirium; **быть в ~е** to be beside o.s.; to be delirious.
беспардо́нный *adj.* shameless, brazen.
беспарти́йн|ый *adj.* non-party; *as n.* **б., ~ого** *m., and* **~ая, ~ой** *f.* non-party man, woman.
беспате́нтный *adj.* unlicensed.
бесперебо́йный *adj.* uninterrupted; regular.
беспереса́дочный *adj.* direct; **б. по́езд** through train.
бесперспекти́в|ный (~ен, ~на) *adj.* having no prospects; hopeless.
беспеча́л|ьный (~ен, ~ьна) *adj.* carefree.
беспе́чност|ь, и *f.* carelessness, unconcern.
беспе́ч|ный (~ен, ~на) *adj.* careless, unconcerned; carefree.
беспило́тный *adj.* unmanned.
беспи́сьменный *adj.* having no written language.
беспла́новост|ь, и *f.* absence of plan.
беспла́новый *adj.* planless.
беспла́тно *adv.* free of charge, gratis.
беспла́т|ный (~ен, ~на) *adj.* free, gratuitous; **б. биле́т** free ticket, complimentary ticket.
бесплацка́ртный *adj.* without reserved seat(s); **б. по́езд** train with unreserved seats only; **б. пассажи́р** passenger travelling without reserving a seat.
беспло́ди|е, я *nt.* sterility, barrenness; infertility.
беспло́дност|ь, и *f.* fruitlessness, futility.
беспло́д|ный (~ен, ~на) *adj.* **1.** sterile, barren; infertile. **2.** (*fig.*) fruitless, futile.
беспло́тный *adj.* (*relig.*; *poet.*) incorporeal.
бесповоро́тн|ый (~а, ~о) *adj.* irrevocable, final.
бесподо́б|ный (~ен, ~на) *adj.* matchless; incomparable; superlative; **~но!** *int.* superb!; splendid!
беспозвоно́чн|ый *adj.* (*zool.*) invertebrate; *as n.* **~ое, ~ого** *nt.* invertebrate.
беспоко́|ить, ю, ишь *impf.* **1.** (*pf.* **о~**) to disturb, bother. **2.** (*pf.* **по~**) to disturb, worry.
беспоко́|иться, юсь, ишься *impf.* **1.** (*pf.* **о~**) (**о**+*p.*) to worry, be worried *or* anxious (about). **2.** (*pf.* **по~**) (*coll.*) to worry, put o.s. out; **не ~йтесь!** don't trouble!; don't worry!
беспоко́|йный (~ен, ~йна) *adj.* **1.** agitated; anxious; uneasy; **~йное состря́ние** a state of agitation. **2.** disturbing; restless, fidgety.
беспоко́йств|о, а *nt.* **1.** agitation; anxiety; unrest; **с ~ом** anxiously. **2.** disturbance.
бесполе́з|ный (~ен, ~на) *adj.* useless.
беспо́л|ый *adj.* sexless; asexual.
беспо́мощ|ный (~ен, ~на) *adj.* helpless, powerless; (*fig.*) feeble; **б. ум** feeble intellect.
беспоро́ч|ный (~ен, ~на) *adj.* blameless, irre-

proachable, immaculate; **~ное зача́тие** (*relig.*) the Immaculate Conception.
беспоря́д|ок, ка *m.* disorder, confusion; (*pl. only*; *pol.*) disturbances; riots.
беспоря́доч|ный (~ен, ~на) *adj.* disorderly; untidy.
беспоса́дочный *adj.*: **б. перелёт** non-stop flight.
беспо́чвен|ный (~, ~на) *adj.* groundless; unsound.
беспо́шлинн|ый *adj.* (*econ.*) duty-free; **~ая торго́вля** free trade.
беспоща́д|ный (~ен, ~на) *adj.* merciless, relentless.
беспра́ви|е, я *nt.* **1.** lawlessness; arbitrariness. **2.** lack of rights.
беспра́вност|ь, и *f.* = **беспра́вие 2.**
беспра́в|ный (~ен, ~на) *adj.* without rights; deprived of rights.
беспреде́л, а *m.* (*coll.*) anarchy, chaos; **ценово́й б.** outrageous prices.
беспреде́л|ьный (~ен, ~ьна) *adj.* boundless, infinite.
беспрекосло́в|ный (~ен, ~на) *adj.* unquestioning, absolute.
беспрепя́тствен|ный (~, ~на) *adj.* free, clear, unimpeded.
беспреры́вно *adv.* continuously; uninterruptedly; non-stop.
беспреры́в|ный (~ен, ~на) *adj.* continuous; uninterrupted.
беспреста́нно *adv.* continually, incessantly.
беспреста́н|ный (~ен, ~на) *adj.* continual; incessant.
беспрецеде́нт|ный (~ен,~на) *adj.* unprecedented.
беспри́был|ьный (~ен, ~ьна) *adj.* non-profit-making.
беспризо́рник, а *m.* waif, street urchin.
беспризо́рн|ый *adj.* **1.** neglected. **2.** stray, homeless; *as n.* **б., ~ого** *m.* waif, street urchin.
бесприме́р|ный (~ен, ~на) *adj.* unexampled, unparalleled.
беспри́месный *adj.* unalloyed.
беспринци́п|ный (~ен, ~на) *adj.* unscrupulous, unprincipled.
беспристра́сти|е, я *nt.* impartiality.
беспристра́стност|ь, и *f.* impartiality.
беспристра́ст|ный (~ен, ~на) *adj.* impartial, unbias(s)ed.
беспричи́нн|ый *adj.* causeless; pointless.
бесприю́т|ный (~ен, ~на) *adj.* homeless.
беспробу́д|ный (~ен, ~на) *adj.* **1.** deep (*of sleep*). **2.** unrestrained (*of drunkenness*).
беспроводно́й *adj.*: **б. телефо́н** cordless telephone.
беспро́волочный *adj.* wireless; **б. телегра́ф** wireless.
беспро́игрышн|ый *adj.* safe; risk-free.
беспросве́т|ный (~ен, ~на) *adj.* **1.** pitch-dark; **~ная тьма** pitch darkness. **2.** (*fig.*) hopeless; unrelieved.
беспроце́нтный *adj.* (*fin.*) interest-free.
беспу́тник, а *m.* (*coll.*) debauchee.
беспу́тнича|ть, ю *impf.* (*coll.*) to lead a dissipated life.
беспу́т|ный (~ен, ~на) *adj.* dissipated, dissolute.
беспу́тств|о, а *nt.* dissipation, debauchery.
бессвя́зност|ь, и *f.* incoherence.
бессвя́з|ный (~ен, ~на) *adj.* incoherent.
бессеме́йный *adj.* having no family.
бессемя́нный *adj.* seedless.
бессерде́ч|ие, ия *nt.* = **~ность**
бессерде́чност|ь, и *f.* heartlessness; callousness.
бессерде́ч|ный (~ен, ~на) *adj.* heartless; callous.
бесси́ли|е, я *nt.* impotence; debility; (*fig.*) feebleness.
бесси́л|ьный (~ен, ~ьна) *adj.* impotent, powerless.
бессисте́м|ный (~ен, ~на) *adj.* unsystematic.
бесcла́ви|е, я *nt.* infamy.
бесcла́в|ить, лю, ишь *impf.* (*of* **о~**) to defame.
бесcла́в|ный (~ен, ~на) *adj.* infamous; inglorious.
бессле́дно *adv.* without leaving a trace; completely, utterly.
бессле́дн|ый *adj.* without leaving a trace; complete.
бессслове́с|ный (~ен, ~на) *adj.* dumb, speechless; (*fig.*) silent; **~ные живо́тные** dumb animals; (*theatr.*) **~ная роль** non-speaking part.
бессме́н|ный (~ен, ~на) *adj.* permanent; continuous.
бессме́рти|е, я *nt.* immortality.
бессме́рт|ный (~ен, ~на) *adj.* immortal; undying.
бессмы́слен|ный (~, ~на) *adj.* senseless; foolish; meaningless, nonsensical.
бессмы́слиц|а, ы *f.* nonsense.
бессо́вест|ный (~ен, ~на) *adj.* **1.** unscrupulous, dishonest. **2.** shameless, brazen.
бессодержа́тел|ьный (~ен, ~ьна) *adj.* empty; tame; dull.
бессозна́тел|ьный (~ен, ~ьна) *adj.* **1.** unconscious. **2.** involuntary.
бессо́нниц|а, ы *f.* insomnia, sleeplessness.
бессо́нный *adj.* sleepless.
бесспо́рно *adv.* indisputably; undoubtedly.
бесспо́р|ный (~ен, ~на) *adj.* indisputable, incontrovertible.
бессро́чн|ый *adj.* without time-limit; **б. о́тпуск** indefinite leave.
бесстра́сти|е, я *nt.* **1.** impassiveness, impassivity. **2.** impartiality.
бесстра́ст|ный (~ен, ~на) *adj.* **1.** impassive. **2.** impartial.
бесстра́ши|е, я *nt.* fearlessness, intrepidity.
бесстра́ш|ный (~ен, ~на) *adj.* fearless, intrepid.
бессты́дник, а *m.* shameless person.
бессты́дниц|а, ы *f.* shameless woman, hussy.
бессты́д|ный (~ен, ~на) *adj.* shameless.
бессты́дств|о, а *nt.* shamelessness.
бессчётный *adj.* innumerable.
беста́ктност|ь, и *f.* **1.** tactlessness. **2.** tactless action.
беста́кт|ный (~ен, ~на) *adj.* tactless.
бестала́н|ный (~ен, ~на) *adj.* untalented.
бестеле́с|ный (~ен, ~на) *adj.* incorporeal.
бе́сти|я, и *f.* (*coll.*) rogue; **то́нкая б.** sly rogue.
бестолко́вщин|а, ы *f.* (*coll.*) disorder, confusion.
бестолко́в|ый (~, ~а) *adj.* **1.** slow-witted, muddle-headed. **2.** disconnected, incoherent.
бе́столоч|ь, и *f.* (*coll.*) muddle-headed person (*also collect.*).
бестсе́ллер, а *m.* best-seller (*book*).
бесфо́рмен|ный (~, ~на) *adj.* shapeless, formless.
бесхара́ктер|ный (~ен, ~на) *adj.* lacking in character; weak-willed.
бесхи́трост|ный (~ен, ~на) *adj.* artless; unsophisticated; ingenuous.
бесхо́зн|ый *adj.* ownerless; **~ое иму́щество** property in abeyance.
бесхозя́йственност|ь, и *f.* thriftlessness; bad management.
бесхозя́йствен|ный (~, ~на) *adj.* thriftless; improvident.
бесхребе́т|ный (~ен, ~на) *adj.* (*fig.*) spineless.
бесцве́т|ный (~ен, ~на) *adj.* colourless; (*fig.*) colourless, insipid.
бесце́л|ьный (~ен, ~ьна) *adj.* aimless; idle.
бесце́н|ный (~ен, ~на) *adj.* priceless, invaluable.
бесце́н|ок, ка *m.* (*coll.*): **купи́ть за б.** to buy for a song.
бесцеремо́н|ный (~ен, ~на) *adj.* unceremonious; familiar; cavalier.
бесчелове́чност|ь, и *f.* inhumanity.
бесчелове́ч|ный (~ен, ~на) *adj.* inhuman.
бесче́|стить, щу, стишь *impf.* (*of* **о~**) to dishonour, disgrace.
бесче́ст|ный (~ен, ~на) *adj.* dishonourable; disgraceful.
бесче́сть|е, я *nt.* dishonour; disgrace.
бесчи́нств|о, а *nt.* excess; enormity.

бесчи́нств|овать, ую *impf.* to commit excesses.
бесчи́слен|ный (~, ~на) *adj.* innumerable.
бесчу́вственност|ь, и *f.* **1.** insensibility. **2.** insensitivity.
бесчу́вствен|ный (~, ~на) *adj.* **1.** insensible. **2.** insensitive, unfeeling.
бесчу́встви|е, я *nt.* **1.** loss of consciousness; **пья́ный до ~я** dead drunk; **бить до ~я** to knock senseless. **2.** insensitivity.
бесшаба́ш|ный (~ен, ~на) *adj.* (*coll.*) reckless.
бесшо́вный *adj.* (*tech.*) seamless; jointless.
бесшоссе́йный *adj.* unsurfaced.
бесшу́м|ный (~ен, ~на) *adj.* noiseless.
бе́тел|ь, я *m.* betel.
бето́н, а *m.* (*tech.*) concrete.
бетони́р|овать, ую *impf.* (*tech.*) to concrete.
бето́нный *adj.* (*tech.*) concrete.
бетоново́з, а *m.* concrete-delivery truck.
бетономеша́лк|а, и *f.* (*tech.*) concrete mixer.
бефстро́ганов *m. indecl.* (*cul.*) beef Stroganoff.
бечев|а́, ы́ *no pl., f.* tow-rope.
бечёвк|а, и *f.* string, twine.
бечевни́к, а́ *m.* tow-path.
бечев|о́й *adj. of* **~а́**; **~а́я тя́га** towing; *as n.* **~а́я, ~о́й** *f.* tow-path.
бе́шенств|о, а *nt.* **1.** (*med.*) hydrophobia; rabies. **2.** fury, rage; **довести́ до ~а** to enrage.
бе́шен|ый *adj.* **1.** rabid, mad; **~ая соба́ка** mad dog. **2.** furious; violent; **~ая ско́рость** furious pace; **~ые це́ны** (*coll.*) exorbitant prices.
бзик, а *m.* (*coll.*) quirk, oddity; **он с ~ом** he's loopy.
биатло́н, а *m.* biathlon.
биатлони́ст, а *m.* biathlete.
библеи́зм, а *m.* Biblical expression.
библе́йский *adj.* biblical.
библио́граф, а *m.* bibliographer.
библиографи́ческий *adj.* bibliographical.
библиогра́фи|я, и *f.* bibliography.
библиоте́к|а, и *f.* library.
библиоте́кар|ша, ши *f. of* **~ь**
библиоте́кар|ь, я *m.* librarian.
библиотекове́дени|е, я *nt.* library science.
библиоте́|чный *adj. of* **~ка**
библиофи́л, а *m.* bibliophile.
би́бли|я, и *f.* bible; the Bible.
би́бльдрук, а *m.* India paper.
бива́к, а *m.* (*mil.*) bivouac, camp; **стоя́ть ~ом, на ~ах** to bivouac, camp.
би́в|ень, ня, *pl.* **~ни, ней** *m.* tusk.
бигуд|и́, е́й *no sg.* (*also indecl.*) (hair) curlers.
бидо́н, а *m.* can, churn; **б. для молока́** milk-can.
бие́ни|е, я *nt.* beating; throb; **б. се́рдца** heartbeat; **б. пу́льса** pulse.
бижуте́ри|я, и *f.* costume jewellery.
биза́н|ь, и *f.* (*naut.*) mizzen; **б.-ма́чта** mizzen-mast.
би́знес, а *m.* business; **рекла́мный б.** advertising.
бизнесме́н, а *m.* businessman.
бизнесме́нк|а, и *f.* (*coll.*) businesswoman.
бизо́н, а *m.* (*zool.*) bison.
бики́ни *nt. indecl.* bikini.
биле́т, а *m.* ticket; card; **входно́й б.** entrance ticket, permit; **креди́тный б.** banknote; **обра́тный б.** return ticket; **экзаменацио́нный б.** examination question(-paper) (*at oral examination*).
билетёр, а *m.* ticket-collector.
билетёр|ша, ши *f. of* **~**; (*in cinema, etc.*) usherette.
билл|ь, я *m.* (*pol.*) bill.
би́л|о, а *nt.* **1.** (*tech.*) beater. **2.** gong.
билья́рд, а *m.* **1.** billiard-table. **2.** billiards; **игра́ть в б.** to play billiards.
бильярди́ст, а *m.* billiards player.
билья́рд|ный *adj. of* **~**; **б. шар** billiard ball; *as n.* **~ная, ~ной** *f.* billiard-room.
бимс, а *m.* (*naut.*) beam, transom.
бино́кл|ь, я *m.* binoculars; **театра́льный б.** opera glasses.
бинокуля́рный *adj.* binocular.
бино́м, а *m.* (*math.*) binomial.
бинт, а́ *m.* bandage.
бинт|ова́ть, у́ю *impf.* to bandage.
био... *comb. form* bio-.
био́граф, а *m.* biographer.
биографи́ческий *adj.* biographical.
биогра́фи|я, и *f.* biography.
био́лог, а *m.* biologist.
биологи́ческий *adj.* biological.
биоло́ги|я, и *f.* biology.
биомедици́нский *adj.* biomedical.
биоресу́рс|ы, ов *no sg.* bioresources.
биори́тм|ы, ов *no sg.* biorhythms.
биоста́нци|я, и *f.* biological research station.
биотехноло́ги|я, и *f.* biotechnology.
биосфе́р|а, ы *f.* biosphere.
биохими́ческий *adj.* biochemical.
биохи́ми|я, и *f.* biochemistry.
бипла́н, а *m.* biplane.
би́рж|а, и *f.* **1.** exchange; **фо́ндовая б.** stock-exchange; **б. труда́** labour exchange.
биржеви́к, а́ *m.* stockbroker.
бирж|ево́й *adj. of* **~а**; **б. ма́клер** stockbroker.
би́рк|а, и *f.* label; tag.
Би́рм|а, ы *f.* Burma.
бирма́н|ец, ца *m.* Burmese, Burman.
бирма́н|ка, ки *f. of* **~ец**
бирма́нский *adj.* Burmese.
бирюз|а́, ы́ *no pl., f.* turquoise.
бирюзо́вый *adj.* turquoise.
бирю́к, а́ *m.*(*fig.*) lone wolf, unsociable person; **смотре́ть ~о́м** (*coll.*) to look gloomy, morose.
бирю́льк|а, и *f.* spillikin; **игра́ть в ~и** to play at spillikins; (*fig.*) to occupy o.s. with trifles.
бис *int.* encore; **сыгра́ть, спеть на б.** to play, sing an encore.
бисексуа́льный *adj.* bisexual.
би́сер, а *no pl., m.* beads; **мета́ть б. пе́ред сви́ньями** (*fig.*) to cast pearls before swine.
би́серин|а, ы *f.* bead.
би́сер|ный *adj. of* **~**; (*fig.*) tiny, minute.
биси́р|овать, ую *impf. and pf.* to repeat, give an encore.
бискви́т, а *m.* sponge-cake.
бискви́т|ный *adj. of* **~**; **б. руле́т** Swiss roll.
бит, а *m.* (*comput.*) bit.
бит|а́, ы́ *f.* (*sport*) bat.
би́тв|а, ы *f.* battle.
битко́м *adv. only in phr.* **б. наби́ть** (*coll.*) to pack, crowd; **авто́бус был б. наби́т** the bus was packed.
би́тник, а *m.* beatnik.
би́товый *adj.* (*comput.*) bit-mapped.
бит|о́к, ка́ *m.* (*round*) rissole.
биту́м, а *m.* (*min.*) bitumen.
битумино́зный *adj.* (*min.*) bituminous.
би́т|ый (~, ~а) *p.p.p. of* **~ь** *and adj.*: **б. час** (*coll.*) a full hour, a good hour; **~ое стекло́** broken glass.
бить, бью, бьёшь *impf.* **1.** (*pf.* **по~**) to beat (*a person, an animal, etc.*). **2.** (*pf.* **по~**) to beat, defeat (*in war, sports or games*). **3.** (**уда́рить** *used in place of pf.*) to strike, hit; **б. кнуто́м** to whip, flog. **4.** (*impf. only*) to strike, hit; to beat, thump, bang; **б. в бараба́н** to beat a drum; **б. в ладо́ши** to clap one's hands; **б. по столу́** to bang on the table; **б. за́дом** to kick (*of a horse*). **5.** (*impf. only*) to kill, slaughter (*animals*); **б. гарпуно́м** to harpoon. **6.** (*impf. only*) to break, smash (*crockery, etc.*). **7.** (**уда́рить** *used in place of pf.*) to combat, fight (against), wage war (on); to damage, injure; **б. по хулига́нству** to com-

bat hooliganism; **б. по карма́ну** to cost one a pretty penny. **8.** (*pf.* **про~**) to strike, sound; **б. (в) наба́т** to sound the alarm; **б. отбо́й** to beat a retreat (*also fig.*); (*impers.*): **бьёт пять** it is striking five. **9.** (*impf. only*) to spurt, gush; **б. ключо́м** to gush out, well up; (*fig.*) to be in full swing. **10.** (*impf. only*) to shoot, fire; (*with fire-arms; also fig.*) to hit; to have a range (of); **б. из духово́го ружья́** to fire an air-gun; **б. в цель** to hit the target (*also fig.*); **б. на́ два киломе́тра** to have a range of two kilometres. **11.** (*impf. only*; **на**+*a.*) to strive (for, after); **б. на эффе́кт** to strive after effect.

бит|ьё, ья́ *nt.* (*coll.*) beating, flogging; smashing.

би́ться, бьюсь, бьёшься *impf.* **1.** (**с**+*i.*) to fight (with, against); **б. на поеди́нке** to fight a duel. **2.** (*of the heart*) to beat; **се́рдце его́ переста́ло б.** his heart stopped beating. **3.** (**о**+*a.*) to knock (against), hit (against), strike; **б. голово́й о́б стену** to bang one's head against a brick wall. **4.** to writhe, struggle; **б. в исте́рике** to writhe in hysterics. **5.** (**над**+*i.*; *fig.*) to struggle (with), exercise o.s. (over); **б. над зада́чей** to rack one's brains over a problem. **6.** (*of crockery, etc.*) to break, smash. **7.**: **б. об закла́д** to bet, wager.

бифште́кс, а *m.* beefsteak.

бифште́ксн|ая, ой *f.* steakhouse.

би́цепс, а *m.* (*anat.*) biceps.

бич, а́ *m.* whip, lash; (*fig.*) scourge.

бич|ева́ть, у́ю *impf.* to flog; (*fig.*) to lash, castigate.

бичу́ющ|ий *adj.*: **~ая сати́ра** scathing satire.

бишь *particle* (*expr. effort to recall name, etc.*; *coll.*) now (*or not translated*); **как б. его́ зову́т?** what was the name now?; **то б.** that is to say.

бла́г|о[1], **а** *nt.* good, the good; blessing; **о́бщее б.** the common weal; **жела́ю вам всех благ!** I wish you every happiness; **всех благ!** (*coll.*) all the best! **ни за каки́е ~а** not for the world.

бла́го[2] *conj.* (*coll.*) since; seeing that; **скажи́те ему́ сейча́с, б. он здесь** tell him now since he is here.

благове́рн|ый *now used only facetiously as n.*; **б., ~ого** *m.* husband; **~ая, ~ой** *f.* wife.

бла́говест, а *m.* ringing of church bell(s).

бла́гове|стить, щу, стишь *impf.* (*pf.* **от~**) to ring for church.

Благове́щени|е, я *nt.* (*eccl.*) the Annunciation.

благове́щен|ский *adj. of* **~ие**

благови́д|ный (~ен, ~на) *adj.* specious, plausible.

благоволе́ни|е, я *nt.* goodwill, kindness; favour; **по́льзоваться чьим-н. ~ем** to be in favour with s.o.

благовол|и́ть, ю́, и́шь *impf.* (**к**+*d.*) to be favourably disposed (toward), favour; **~и́те** (+*inf.*) have the kindness (to); **~и́те отве́тить на э́то письмо́** kindly answer this letter.

благовоспи́танност|ь, и *f.* good manners; good breeding.

благовоспи́тан|ный (~, ~на) *adj.* well-mannered; well brought up.

благогове́|йный (~ен, ~йна) *adj.* reverential.

благогове́ни|е, я *nt.* reverence; veneration.

благогове́|ть, ю *impf.* (**пе́ред**+*i.*) to revere, venerate.

благодар|и́ть, ю́, и́шь *impf.* (*of* **по~**) to thank; **~ю́ вас (за**+*a.*) thank you (for).

благода́рност|ь, и *f.* **1.** gratitude; **не сто́ит ~и** don't mention it. **2.** (*usu. pl.*) thanks, acknowledgement of thanks. **3.** (*mil.*) citation, commendation.

благода́р|ный (~ен, ~на) *adj.* **1.** grateful. **2.** rewarding; worthwhile.

благодаря́ *prep.*+*d.* thanks to, owing to; **б. тому́, что** owing to the fact that.

благода́т|ный (~ен, ~на) *adj.* beneficial; abundant; **б. край** land of plenty.

благода́т|ь, и *f.* **1.** plenty, abundance. **2.** (*relig.*) grace.

благоде́нств|овать, ую *impf.* to prosper, flourish.

благоде́тел|ь, я *m.* benefactor.

благоде́тельниц|а, ы *f.* benefactress.

благоде́тел|ьный (~ен, ~ьна) *adj.* beneficial.

благодея́ни|е, я *nt.* good deed; blessing, boon.

благоду́шеств|овать, ую *impf.* (*coll.*) to take life easily.

благоду́ши|е, я *nt.* placidity, equability; good humour.

благоду́ш|ный (~ен, ~на) *adj.* placid, equable; good-humoured.

благожела́тел|ь, я *m.* well-wisher.

благожела́тел|ьный (~ен, ~ьна) *adj.* well-disposed; benevolent; **~ьная реце́нзия** favourable review.

благожела́тельност|ь, и *f.* goodwill; benevolence.

благозву́чи|е, я *nt.* euphony.

благозву́чност|ь *f.* euphony.

благозву́ч|ный (~ен, ~на) *adj.* euphonious; melodious.

благ|о́й[1] *adj.* good; **~а́я мысль** a happy thought; **~и́е наме́рения** good intentions.

благ|о́й[2] *adj.*: **~и́м ма́том** (*coll.*) at the top of one's voice.

благонадёжност|ь, и *f.* reliability, trustworthiness; loyalty.

благонадёж|ный (~ен, ~на) *adj.* reliable, trustworthy; loyal.

благообра́з|ный (~ен, ~на) *adj.* good-looking; fine, fine-looking.

благополу́чи|е, я *nt.* well-being; welfare.

благополу́чно *adv.* well, all right; happily; safely.

благополу́ч|ный (~ен, ~на) *adj.* successful; safe; **б. коне́ц** happy ending.

благоприя́т|ный (~ен, ~на) *adj.* favourable; propitious; **~ные ве́сти** good news.

благоприя́тств|овать, ую *impf.* (+*d.*) to favour.

благоразу́ми|е, я *nt.* prudence; sense.

благоразу́м|ный (~ен, ~на) *adj.* prudent; sensible.

благоро́д|ный (~ен, ~на) *adj.* noble; **б. мета́лл** precious metal.

благоро́дств|о, а *nt.* nobleness; nobility.

благоскло́нност|ь, и *f.* favour; **по́льзоваться чьей-н. ~ью** to be in s.o.'s good graces.

благоскло́н|ный (~ен, ~на) *adj.* favourable, gracious.

благослове́ни|е, я *nt.* (*eccl. and fig.*) blessing; **с ~я** (+*g.*) with the blessing (of).

благослове́н|ный (~, ~на) *adj.* (*eccl., poet.*) blessed.

благослов|и́ть, лю́, и́шь *pf.* (*of* **~ля́ть**) **1.** to bless; to give one's blessing (to). **2.** to be grateful to; **б. свою́ судьбу́** to thank one's stars.

благослов|и́ться, лю́сь, и́шься *pf.* (*of* **~ля́ться**) (*coll.*) **1.** (**у**+*g.*) to receive the blessing (of). **2.** to cross o.s.

благослов|ля́ть(ся), ля́ю(сь) *impf. of* **~и́ть(ся)**

благосостоя́ни|е, я *nt.* well-being, welfare.

благотвори́тел|ь, я *m.* philanthropist.

благотвори́тельност|ь, и *f.* charity, philanthropy.

благотвори́тельный *adj.* charitable, philanthropic; **б. база́р** charity fête.

благотво́р|ный (~ен, ~на) *adj.* beneficial; wholesome, salutary.

благоустра́ива|ть, ю *impf. of* **благоустро́ить**

благоустро́ен|ный (~, ~на) *p.p.p. of* **благоустро́ить** *and adj.* well-equipped; comfortable; **б. дом** house with all modern conveniences.

благоустро́|ить, ю, ишь *pf.* (*of* **благоустра́ивать**) to equip with services and utilities, to improve.

благоустро́йств|о, а *nt.* equipping with services and utilities.

благоуха́ни|е, я *nt.* fragrance.

благоуха́нный *adj.* fragrant, sweet-smelling.

благоуха́|ть, ю *impf.* to be fragrant, to smell sweet.

благочести́в|ый (~, ~а) *adj.* pious, devout.

благоче́сти|е, я *nt.* piety.

блаже́н|ный (~, ~на) *adj.* blessed, blissful; (*eccl.*)

the Blessed; **~ной па́мяти** of blessed memory.
блаже́нств|о, а *nt.* bliss.
блаже́нств|овать, ую *impf.* to be in a state of bliss.
блажь, и *f.* (*coll.*) whim, caprice.
бланк, а *m.* form; **анке́тный б.** questionnaire; **запо́лнить б.** to fill in a form.
блат, а *m.* **1.** pull; string-pulling; **получи́ть по ~́у** to obtain through connections. **2.** thieves' cant.
блатн|о́й *adj.*: **~а́я му́зыка** thieves' cant.
бл|ева́ть, ю́ю, юёшь *impf.* (*vulg.*) to puke.
блево́тин|а, ы *f.* (*vulg.*) **1.** vomit. **2.** (*fig.*) filth.
бледне́|ть, ю, ешь *impf.* (*of* **по~**) to grow pale; to pale.
бледноли́ц|ый *adj.* pale; *as n.* **б., ~ого** *m.* paleface.
бле́дност|ь, и *f.* paleness, pallor.
бле́д|ный (~ен, ~на́, ~но) *adj.* pale, pallid; **б. как полотно́** white as a sheet; (*fig.*) colourless, insipid.
бле́йзер, а *m.* blazer.
блёклый *adj.* faded; wan.
блёк|нуть, ну, нушь, *past* **~, ~ла** *impf.* (*of* **по~**) to fade; to wither.
блеск, а *m.* brilliance; shine; splendour, magnificence; (*as int., sl.*) **б.!** great!; super!; **во всём ~́е** in all (one's) glory; **прида́ть б.** to add lustre (to); **игра́ть с ~́ом на роя́ле** to play the piano brilliantly.
блесн|а́, ы́, *pl.* **~̈ы** *f.* spoon-bait.
блесн|у́ть, у́, ёшь *pf.* to flash; to shine; **у меня́ ~у́ла мысль** a thought flashed across my mind.
бле|сте́ть, щу́, сти́шь *and* **~́щешь** *impf.* to shine (*also fig.*); to glitter; to sparkle; **её глаза́ ~сте́ли ра́достью** her eyes shone with joy; **он не ~́щет умо́м** he's no genius.
блёстк|а, и *f.* **1.** sparkle; **~и остроу́мия** flashes of wit. **2.** spangle, sequin; **усе́янный ~ами** spangled.
блестя́щ|ий (~, ~а, ~е) *pres. part. of* **блесте́ть** *and adj.* shining, bright; (*fig.*) brilliant.
блеф, а *m.* bluff.
блеф|ова́ть, у́ю *impf.* (*coll.*) to bluff.
бле|щу́, ~́щешь *see* **~сте́ть**
бле́яни|е, я *nt.* bleat(ing).
бле́|ять, ю, ешь *impf.* to bleat.
ближа́йш|ий *superl. of* **бли́зкий**; nearest; next; immediate; **в ~ем бу́дущем** in the near future; **б. нача́льник** immediate superior; **б. ро́дственник** next of kin; **при ~ем рассмотре́нии** on closer examination.
бли́|же *comp. of* **~зкий, ~зко** nearer; (*fig.*) closer.
ближневосто́чный *adj.* Middle East; Middle Eastern.
бли́жн|ий *adj.* **1.** near; neighbouring. **2.** (*mil.*) close; **б. ого́нь** close (range) fire. **3.** near, close (*of kinship*); *as n.* **б., ~его** *m.* (*fig.*) one's neighbour; **люби́ть ~его** to love one's neighbour.
близ *prep.+g.* near, close to, by.
бли́|зиться, жусь, зишься *impf.* to approach, draw near.
бли́з|кий (~ок, ~ка́, ~ко) *adj.* **1.** near, close; **на ~ком расстоя́нии** a short way off; at close range. **2.** (*of time*) near; imminent; **~кое бу́дущее** the near future. **3.** intimate, close; **б. друг** close friend; **быть ~ким с кем-н.** to be on intimate terms with s.o; *as n.* **~кие, ~ких** one's nearest and dearest. **4. (к)** like; similar (to); close (to); **б. нам по ду́ху челове́к** kindred spirit.
бли́зко *adv.* **1. (от)** near, close (to); close by. **2.** *as pred.* it is not far; **ему́ б. ходи́ть** he has not far to go.
близлежа́щий *adj.* neighbouring, near-by.
близне́ц, а́ *m.* twin; **Б~ы́** (*astron.*) Gemini.
близору́к|ий (~, ~а) *adj.* short-sighted (*also fig.*).
близору́кост|ь, и *f.* short-sightedness; (*med.*) myopia (*also fig.*).
бли́зост|ь, и *f.* nearness, proximity; intimacy.
блик, а *m.* speck, patch of light.
блин, а́ *m.* pancake; **пе́рвый б. ко́мом** (*prov.*) practice makes perfect.
блинда́ж, а́ *m.* (*mil.*) dug-out.
бли́нн|ая, ой *f.* pancake parlour
бли́нчик, а *m.* pancake; fritter.
блиста́тел|ьный (~ен, ~ьна) *adj.* brilliant, splendid.
блиста́|ть, ю *impf.* to shine; **б. отсу́тствием** (*iron.*) to be conspicuous by one's absence.
блиц, а *m.* flash (attachment).
блиц(-) *comb. form* lightning ...; whirlwind ...; **~визи́т** flying visit.
бли́цкриг, а *m.* blitzkrieg.
блок[1], а *m.* (*tech.*) block, pulley, sheave.
блок[2], а *m.* (*pol.*) bloc.
блок[3], а *m.* module; carton.
блока́д|а, ы *f.* blockade.
блокга́уз, а *m.* (*mil.*) blockhouse.
блоки́р|овать, ую *impf. and pf.* **1.** to blockade. **2.** (*rail.*) to block.
блоки́р|оваться, уюсь *impf. and pf.* **1.** *pass. of* **~ова́ть. 2. (с**+*i.*; *pol.*) to form a bloc with.
блокно́т, а *m.* notebook, notepad.
блонди́н, а *m.* fair-haired man.
блонди́нк|а, и *f.* blonde (*woman*).
блох|а́, и́, *pl.* **~́и, ~а́м** *f.* flea.
бло́чный *adj.* modular.
бло|ши́ный *adj. of* **~ха́; б. уку́с** flea-bite.
бло́ш|ки, ек *f.* tiddly-winks.
блу|ди́ть, жу́, ~́дишь *impf.* (*coll.*) to wander, roam.
блу́д|ный *adj. of* **~; б. сын** prodigal son.
блужда́ни|е, я *nt.* wandering, roaming.
блужда́|ть, ю *impf.* to roam, wander; to rove; **б. по у́лицам** to roam the streets.
блужда́|ющий *pres. part. of* **~ть; б. огонёк** will-o'-the-wisp.
блу́з|а, ы *f.* (working) blouse; smock.
блу́зк|а, и *f.* blouse.
блю́деч|ко, ка, *pl.* **~ки, ~ек, ~кам** *nt.* saucer; small dish.
блю́д|о, а *nt.* dish (*concr. and abstr.*); **обе́д из трёх ~** three-course dinner; **вку́сное б.** a tasty dish.
блюдоли́з, а *m.* (*coll.*) lickspittle.
блю|ду́, дёшь *see* **~сти́**
блю́д|це, ца, *g. pl.* **~ец** *nt.* saucer.
блю|сти́, ду́, дёшь, *past* **~л, ~ла́** *impf.* to guard, watch over; **б. зако́ны** to abide by the law; **б. поря́док** to keep order.
блюсти́тел|ь, я *m.* keeper, guardian; **б. поря́дка** (*coll., iron.*) arm of the law.
блю|ю́, ёшь *see* **блева́ть**
бля́д|ский *adj.* (*vulg.*) *of* **~ь**; fucking.
бляд|ь, и *f.* (*vulg.*) tart, whore (*esp. as term of abuse*); *as int.* fuck!
бля́х|а, и *f.* name plate; number plate.
боа́ *m. indecl. and nt. indecl.* **1.** *m.* (*zool.*) boa, boa-constrictor. **2.** *nt.* boa; **мехово́е б.** fur boa.
боб, а́ *m.* bean; **оста́ться на ~а́х** (*coll.*) to get nothing for one's pains.
боб|ёр, ра́ *m.* beaver (fur).
боб|о́вый 1. *adj. of* **~; б. стручо́к** bean-pod. **2.** *as n.* **~о́вые, ~о́вых** leguminous plants.
бобр, а́ *m.* beaver.
бо́брик, а *m.* (*text.*) beaver, castor; **во́лосы ~ом** (*coll.*) French crop; crew cut.
бобр|о́вый *adj. of* **~**; beaver; beaver-fur.
бобслейст, а *m.* bobsleigher.
бо́бсле|й, я *m.* bobsleigh; bobsleighing.
бобы́л|ь, я́ *m.* solitary, lonely man; **жить ~ём** to lead a solitary, lonely existence.
Бог, а, *voc. sg.* **Бо́же** *m.* God; god; **Бо́же мой!** good God!, my God!; **Б. зна́ет!, Б. весть!** God knows!; **Б. его́ зна́ет!** who knows!; **не дай Б.!** God forbid!; **ра́ди ~́а!** for God's sake!; **Б. с ним!** blow it; **сла́ва ~́у** thank God!
богаде́л|ьня, ьни, *g. pl.* **~ен** *f.* almshouse, workhouse.
богате́|ть, ю, ешь *impf.* (*of* **раз~**) to grow rich.

богáтств|о, а *nt.* **1.** riches, wealth; **прирóдные ~а** natural resources. **2.** (*fig.*) richness, wealth.
богáт|ый (~, ~а) *adj.* (+*i.*) rich (in), wealthy; **~ая растúтельность** luxuriant vegetation; **б. переплёт** a luxurious binding; **б. óпыт** wide experience; *as n.* **б., ~ого** *m.* rich man.
богатыр|ский *adj. of* **~ь;** heroic; (*fig.*) powerful, mighty; **~ское сложéние** powerful physique.
богатыр|ь, я́ *m.* **1.** bogatyr (*hero in Russ. folklore*). **2.** (*fig.*) Hercules; hero.
богáч, á *m.* rich man; **~и́** (*collect.*) the rich.
богéм|а, ы *f.* bohemians; bohemianism; **представúтель** (*m.*) **~ы** bohemian.
богéмный *adj.* bohemian.
богúн|я, и *f.* goddess (*also fig.*).
богобоя́знен|ный (~, ~на) *adj.* god-fearing.
богоúзбранный *adj.* (*rel.*): **б. нарóд** the Chosen people.
Богомáтер|ь, и *f.* Mother of God; **Собóр парúжской ~и** (the cathedral of) Notre Dame.
богомóл, а *m.* (*zool.*) praying mantis.
богомóл|ец, ьца *m.* **1.** devout person. **2.** pilgrim.
богомóл|ка, ки *f.* **1.** (*zool.*) = **~. 2.** *f. of* **~ец**
богомóль|е, я *nt.* pilgrimage.
богомóл|ьный (~ен, ~ьна) *adj.* religious, devout.
богоотстýпник, а *m.* apostate.
богоотстýпничеств|о, а *nt.* apostasy.
Богорóдиц|а, ы *f.* the Virgin Mary.
богослóв, а *m.* theologian.
богослóви|е, я *nt.* theology.
богослóвский *adj.* theological.
богослужé|бный *adj. of* **~ние;** liturgical; **~бная кнúга** prayer-book.
богослужéни|е, я *nt.* divine service, worship; liturgy.
боготвор|úть, ю́, úшь *impf.* to worship, idolize.
богохýльник, а *m.* blasphemer.
богохýльный *adj.* blasphemous.
богохýльств|о, а *nt.* blasphemy.
богохýльств|овать, ую *impf.* to blaspheme.
Богоявлéни|е, я *nt.* (*eccl.*) Epiphany.
бод, а *m.* (*comput.*) baud.
бодá|ть, ю *impf.* (*of* **за~**) to butt.
бодá|ться, юсь *impf.* to butt (*intrans.*).
бодлúв|ый (~, ~а) *adj.* given to butting.
бодн|ýть, ý, ёшь *pf.* to butt, give a butt.
бодр|úть, ю́, úшь *impf.* to stimulate, invigorate.
бодр|úться, ю́сь, úшься *impf.* to try to keep one's spirits up.
бóдрост|ь, и *f.* cheerfulness; courage; good spirits.
бóдрств|овать, ую *impf.* to stay awake; to keep vigil.
бóдр|ый (~, ~á, ~о) *adj.* cheerful, bright; hale and hearty.
бодр|я́щий *pres. part. of* **~úть** *and adj.* invigorating, bracing.
боевúк, á *m.* **1.** fighter; militant. **2.** (*coll.*) hit.
боевúтост|ь, и *f.* fighting spirit.
боев|óй *adj.* **1.** fighting, battle; **~ы́е дéйствия** combat operations; **б. дух** fighting spirit; **~óе крещéние** baptism of fire; **б. патрóн** live cartridge. **2.** urgent. **3.** (*coll.*) militant; energetic.
боеголóвк|а, и *f.* (*mil.*) warhead.
боеготóвност|ь, и *f.* combat readiness.
боеприпáс|ы, ов *no sg.* ammunition.
боеспосóбност|ь, и *f.* (*mil.*) fighting efficiency.
боеспосóб|ный (~ен, ~на) *adj.* (*mil.*) battle-worthy.
бо|éц, йцá *m.* **1.** fighter; private soldier; **петýх-б.** fighting-cock. **2.** slaughterman.
божб|á, ы *f.* swearing.
Бóже *see* **Бог**
бóжеск|ий *adj.* (*coll.*) fair; **~ая ценá** a fair price.
божéственност|ь, и *f.* divinity; divine nature.
божéствен|ный (~, ~на) *adj.* divine (*also fig.*).
божеств|ó, á *nt.* deity, divine being.
бóж|ий, ья, ье *adj.* God's; **я́сно, как б. день** it is as clear as could be; **~ья корóвка** (*zool.*) ladybird.
бож|úться, ýсь, ~úшься *impf.* (*of* **по~**) to swear.
бож|óк, кá *m.* idol (*also fig.*).
бо|й, я, *pl.* **~ú, ~ёв** *m.* **1.** battle, action, combat; **в ~ю́** in action; **без ~я** without striking a blow. **2.** fight; **б. быкóв** bullfight. **3.** *pl.* fighting. **4.** striking, strike (*of a clock*); **часы́ с ~ем** striking clock; **барабáнный б.** drum-beat. **5.** killing, slaughter(ing); **б. китóв** whaling.
бó|йкий (~ек, ~йкá, ~йко) *adj.* **1.** smart; **б. ум** ready wit; **б. язы́к** glib tongue. **2.** lively; brisk; busy.
бойкóт, а *m.* boycott.
бойкотúр|овать, ую *impf.* to boycott.
бойнúц|а, ы *f.* embrasure.
бóйн|я, и, *g. pl.* **бóен** *f.* slaughter-house, abattoir; (*fig.*) slaughter, butchery, carnage.
бойцóвый *adj.* fighting; **б. петýх** fighting-cock.
бóйче *comp. of* **бóйк|ий, ~о**
бок, а, о ~е, на ~ý, *pl.* **~á** *m.* side; flank; **на ~ý** on one side; **б. ó б.** side by side; **пóд ~ом** nearby, close by; **с ~ нá б.** from side to side.
бокáл, а *m.* (wine)glass, goblet.
боков|óй *adj.* side; lateral; **~áя ýлица** side-street; **отпрáвиться на ~ýю** (*coll.*) to turn in, go to bed.
бóком *adv.* **1.** sideways. **2.: вы́йти б.** (*coll.*) to turn out badly.
бокс[1]**, а** *m.* (*sport*) boxing.
бокс[2]**, а** *m.* short back and sides (*hair-style*).
боксёр, а *m.* (*sport*) boxer.
боксúр|овать, ую *impf.* (*sport*) to box.
боксúт, а *m.* (*min.*) bauxite.
болвáн, а *m.* (*coll.*) **1.** blockhead, twit. **2.** block (*esp. for shaping headgear*). **3.** (*in card-games*) dummy.
болвáнк|а, и *f.* **1.** (*tech.*) pig (*of iron, etc.*); **желéзо в ~ах** pig-iron. **2.** block (*for shaping headgear*).
Болгáри|я, и *f.* Bulgaria.
болгáр|ин, ина, *pl.* **~ы, ~** *m.* Bulgarian.
болгáр|ка, ки *f. of* **~ин**
болгáрский *adj.* Bulgarian.
болев|óй *adj. of* **боль**
бóлее *adv.* more; **б. тóлстый** thicker; **б. и б.** more and more; **б. или мéнее** more or less; **б. всегó** most of all; **тем б., что** especially as.
болéзненност|ь, и *f.* **1.** sickliness; abnormality, morbidity. **2.** painfulness.
болéзнен|ный (~, ~на) *adj.* **1.** sickly; unhealthy; (*fig.*) abnormal, morbid; **~ное любопы́тство** morbid curiosity. **2.** painful.
болéзн|ь, и *f.* illness; disease; sickness; (*fig.*) abnormality; **б. Дáуна** Down's syndrome; **морскáя б.** seasickness.
болéльщик, а *m.* (*coll.*) fan, supporter.
болерó *nt. indecl.* bolero.
болé|ть[1]**, ю, ешь** *impf.* **1.** (+*i.*) to be ill (with); **б. душóй (за**+*a.*) to be worried (about). **2.** (**за**+*a.*; *coll.*) to be a fan (of), support.
бол|éть[2] *1st and 2nd pers. not used,* **~úт** *impf.* to ache, hurt; **у меня́ зýбы ~я́т** I have toothache; **у меня́ душá ~úт (о**+*p.*) my heart bleeds (for, over).
болеутоля́ющ|ий *adj.* analgesic; **~ее срéдство** (*med.*) analgesic.
боливú|ец, йца *m.* Bolivian.
боливú|йка, йки *f. of* **~ец**
боливúйский *adj.* Bolivian.
Болúви|я, и *f.* Bolivia.
болиголóв, а *m.* (*bot.*) hemlock.
болúд, а *m.* (*astron.*) fireball.
болóнк|а, и *f.* lap-dog.
болóтист|ый (~, ~а) *adj.* marshy, boggy, swampy.
болóтн|ый *adj.* marsh; **б. газ** marsh gas.
болóт|о, а *nt.* marsh, bog; **торфянóе б.** peatbog.

болт, á *m.* (*tech.*) bolt.
болтáнк|а, и *f.* (*aeron.*; *coll.*) bumpiness, rough air.
болтá|ть[1], ю *impf.* **1.** to stir; to shake. **2.** (+*i.*) to dangle.
болтá|ть[2], ю *impf.* (*coll.*) to chatter, jabber (away); **б. по-францýзски** *etc.* to jabber away in French.
болтá|ться, юсь *impf.* (*coll.*) **1.** to dangle, swing; to hang loosely. **2.** to hang about, loaf.
болтлúвост|ь, и *f.* garrulity, talkativeness.
болтлúв|ый (~, ~а) *adj.* garrulous, talkative; loose-tongued.
болтовн|я́, ú *f.* (*coll.*) chatter; gossip.
болтýн, á *m.* (*coll.*) **1.** chatterbox; gas-bag. **2.** gossip.
бол|ь, и *f.* pain; ache; **зубнáя б.** toothache.
больнúц|а, ы *f.* hospital; **лечь в ~у** to go (in)to hospital; **лежáть в ~е** to be in hospital.
больнú|чный *adj. of* **~ца; б. лист** medical certificate.
бóльно *adv.* **1.** badly. **2.** *as pred.* it is painful (*also fig.*); **мне б. дышáть** it hurts me to breathe .
бол|ьнóй (~ен, ~ьнá) *adj.* ill, sick; diseased; sore (*also fig.*), painful; **б. вопрóс** sore subject; **~ьнóе мéсто** sore spot; *as n.* **б., ~ьнóго** *m.*, **~ьнáя, ~ьнóй** *f.* patient; invalid; **амбулатóрный б.** out-patient; **б. гемофúлией** haemophiliac (*pers.*).
бóльше 1. (*comp. of* **большóй** *and* **велúкий**) bigger, larger; greater. **2.** (*comp. of* **мнóго**) more; **чем б... тем б.** the more ... the more; **б. тогó** and what is more; **б. не** no more, no longer; **он б. не живёт на той ýлице** he does not live in that street anymore.
большевúзм, а *m.* Bolshevism.
большевúк, á *m.* Bolshevik.
большевúстский *adj.* Bolshevik.
бóльш|ий *comp. of* **~óй** *and* **велúкий;** greater, larger; **~ей чáстью, по ~ей чáсти** for the most part; **сáмое ~ее** at most.
большинств|ó, á *nt.* majority; most (of); **в ~é слýчаев** in most cases; **б. голосóв** a majority vote.
больш|óй *adj.* big, large; great; large-scale; (*coll.*) grown-up; **~áя бýква** capital (letter); **б. пáлец** thumb; **б. пáлец ногú** big toe; **когдá я бýду б.** when I grow up.
большýщий *adj.* (*coll.*) huge.
болячк|а, и *f.* sore; scab; (*fig.*) defect.
бол|я́щий *pres. part. of* **~éть[2]**; *as n.* **б., ~я́щего** *m.* (*usu. joc.*) the patient.
бóмб|а, ы *f.* bomb; **зажигáтельная б.** petrol bomb.
бомбардúр, а *m.* **1.** (*mil.*, *hist.*) bombardier. **2.** (*aeron.*) bomb-aimer. **3.** (*sport*) striker.
бомбардир|овáть, ýю *impf.* to bombard; to bomb.
бомбардирóвк|а, и *f.* bombardment; bombing.
бомбардирóвочный *adj.* bombing.
бомбардирóвщик, а *m.* **1.** bomber; **пикúрующий б.** dive-bomber. **2.** (*coll.*) bomber pilot.
бомбёжк|а, и *f.* (*coll.*) bombing.
бомб|úть, лю, úшь *impf.* to bomb.
бóмб|овый *adj. of* **~а**
бомбодержáтел|ь, я *m.* bomb-rack.
бомбометáни|е, я *nt.* bomb-release.
бомбоубéжищ|е, а *nt.* air-raid shelter, bomb shelter.
бомж, а *m.* (*abbr. of* ***без определённого мéста жúтельства***) homeless person, vagrant.
бóндар|ь, я/я́ *m.* cooper.
бóнз|а, ы, *g. pl.* **~** *m.* (*fig.*) superior, distant person; bigwig; **партúйный б.** Party boss.
бóн|ы, ~ *pl.* (*sg.* **~а, ~ы** *f.*) **1.** cheques; vouchers, tokens. **2.** emergency paper money.
бор[1], а, о ~е, на ~ý, *pl.* **~ы́, ~óв** *m.* coniferous forest.
бор[2], а *m.* (*chem.*) boron.
бордéл|ь, я *m.* (*coll.*) brothel.
бордó 1. *nt. indecl.* claret. **2.** *as adj.* claret-coloured.
бордóвый *adj.* claret-coloured.
бордю́р, а *m.* border (*of fabric*, *wallpaper*, *etc.*).
бор|éц, цá *m.* **1.** (**за**+*a.*) fighter (for); campaigner; activist; **б. за мир** peace campaigner; **б. за правá жéнщин** women's liberationist. **2.** (*sport*) wrestler.
боржóм, а *m.* (*and* **~и,** *nt. indecl.*) Borzhomi (*variety of mineral water*).
борз|áя, óй *f.*: **английская б.** greyhound; **рýсская б.** borzoi, Russian wolfhound.
борз|óй *adj. of* **~áя**
борзопúс|ец, ца *m.* (*iron.*) hack writer.
бормашúн|а, ы *f.* (dentist's) drill.
бормотáни|е, я *nt.* muttering.
бормо|тáть, чý, ~чешь *impf.* to mutter.
бормотýн, á *m.* (*coll.*) mutterer.
борм|очý, óчешь *see* **~отáть**
бóрн|ый *adj.* (*chem.*) boric, boracic, **~ая кислотá** boric, boracic acid.
бóров[1], а *m.* hog; (*fig.*) obese man.
бóров[2], а, *pl.* **~á** *m.* (*tech.*) horizontal flue.
бор|овóй *adj. of* **~[1]**
бор|одá, оды́, *a.* **~оду,** *pl.* **~оды, ~óд, ~одáм** *f.* **1.** beard. **2.** wattle (*of bird*).
бородáвк|а, и *f.* wart.
бородáвчатый *adj.* warty.
бородáт|ый (~, ~а) *adj.* bearded.
бородáч, á *m.* **1.** (*coll.*) bearded man. **2.** (*zool.*) bearded vulture, lammergeyer.
борóдк|а, и *f.* small beard, tuft.
бор|оздá, озды́, *a.* **~озду** *and* **~оздý,** *pl.* **~озды, ~óзд, ~оздáм** *f.* furrow.
бороз|дúть, жý, дúшь *impf.* (*pf.* **из~**) to furrow; **морщúны ~дúли егó лоб** (*fig.*) wrinkles furrowed his brow; **б. океáны** (*poet.*) to plough the seas.
борóздчатый *adj.* furrowed; grooved.
бор|онá, оны́, *a.* **~ону,** *pl.* **~оны, ~óн, ~онáм** *f.* (*agric.*) harrow.
борон|úть, ю́, úшь *impf.* (*of* **вз~**) (*agric.*) to harrow.
борон|овáть, ýю *impf.* (*of* **вз~**) = **~úть**
бороньб|á, ы́ *f.* (*agric.*) harrowing.
бор|óться, ю́сь, ~ешься *impf.* to wrestle; (*fig.*) to struggle, fight; **б. со своéй сóвестью** to wrestle with one's conscience.
борт, а, о ~е, на ~ý, *pl.* **~á, ~óв** *m.* **1.** side (*of a ship*); **на ~ý** on board (*ship* or *aircraft*); **вы́бросить зá б.** to throw overboard (*also fig.*); **человéк за ~ом!** man overboard! **2.** coat-breast. **3.** cushion (*billiards*).
бортмехáник, а *m.* (*aeron.*) flight engineer.
борт|овóй *adj. of* **~; б. журнáл** (ship's) log(-book).
бортпроводнúк, á *m.* air steward.
бортпроводнúц|а, ы *f.* stewardess; air hostess.
борщ, á *m.* (*cul.*) bor(t)sch.
борьб|á, ы́ *f.* **1.** (*sport*) wrestling; **америкáнская б.** all-in wrestling. **2.** (*fig.*) struggle, fight; **кампáния по ~é с престýпностью** crime-prevention campaign.
босикóм *adv.* barefoot; **ходúть б.** to go barefoot.
Бóсни|я и Герцеговúн|а, ~и и ~ы *f.* Bosnia and Herzegovina.
бос|óй (~, ~á, ~о) *adj.* bare; barefoot(ed); **на ~ý нóгу** barefoot.
босонóгий *adj.* barefoot(ed).
босонóжк|а, и *f.* **1.** barefoot girl or woman. **2.** (*pl.*) sandals; mules.
бося́к, á *m.* tramp; down-and-out.
бося́|цкий *adj. of* **~к**
бот, а *m.* boat.
ботанизúрк|а, и *f.* (*coll.*) plant-collecting box.
ботанизúр|овать, ую *impf.* to collect plants (*for study*).
ботáник, а *m.* botanist.
ботáник|а, и *f.* botany.
ботанúческий *adj.* botanical; **б. сад** botanical gardens.
ботв|á, ы *f.* leafy tops of root vegetables (*esp. beet leaves*).

ботви́нь|я, и *f.* botvinia (*cold soup of fish, pot-herbs, and kvass*).
бо́тик|и, ов *pl.* (*sg.* ~, ~**а** *m.*) (high) over-shoes.
боти́н|ок, ка, *g. pl.* **б.** *m.* (*ankle-high*) boot.
бо́цман, а *m.* (*naut.*) boatswain.
боча́р, а́, *pl.* ~**ы́** *m.* cooper.
бо́чк|а, и *f.* barrel, cask; (*fig.*) **де́ньги на ~у** cash on the nail.
бочко́м *adv.* sideways.
бочо́н|ок, ка *m.* small barrel, keg.
боязли́вост|ь, и *f.* timidity, timorousness.
боязли́в|ый (~, ~а) *adj.* timid, timorous.
бо́язно *adv. as pred.* (+*d.*; *coll.*) to be afraid, frightened, **ей б. остава́ться одно́й по вечера́м** she is frightened of being left alone in the evening.
боя́зн|ь, и *f.* (+*g. or* **пе́ред**+*i.*) fear (of), dread of; **из ~и** for fear of, lest; **он переменил фами́лию из ~и, что бу́дут смея́ться над ним** he changed his name for fear of being laughed at.
боя́р|ин, ина, *pl.* ~**е,** ~ *m.* (*hist.*) boyar.
боя́р|ский *adj. of* ~
боя́рств|о, а *nt.* (*collect.*; *hist.*) the boyars.
боя́рышник, а *m.* (*bot.*) hawthorn.
бо|я́ться, ю́сь, и́шься *impf.* (+*g.*) to fear, be afraid (of); **~ю́сь, что он (не) прие́дет** I am afraid that he will (not) come; **~ю́сь сказа́ть** I would not like to say.
бра *nt. indecl.* sconce; lamp-bracket.
брава́д|а, ы *f.* bravado.
брави́р|овать, ую *impf.* (+*i.*) to brave, defy.
бра́во *int.* bravo!
браву́р|ный (~ен, ~на) *adj.* (*mus.*) bravura.
бра́вый *adj.* gallant; manly.
бра́г|а, и *f.* home-brewed beer.
бразд|ы́, ~ *now only in phr.* **б. правле́ния** the reins of government.
брази́л|ец, ьца *m.* Brazilian.
Брази́ли|я, и *f.* Brazil.
брази́льский *adj.* Brazilian.
бразил|ья́нка, ья́нки *f. of* ≁**ец**
бра́йлевский *adj.*: **б. шрифт** Braille.
Брайл|ь, я *m.*: **шрифт ~я** Braille.
брак[1], а *m.* marriage; matrimony; **свиде́тельство о** ≁**е** marriage certificate; **рождённый вне** ≁**а** born out of wedlock.
брак[2], а *m.* waste; defective products, rejects.
брако́ван|ный (~, ~а) *p.p.p. of* **бракова́ть** *and adj.*defective.
брак|ова́ть, у́ю *impf.* (*of* **за~**) to reject (*manufactured articles*; *also fig.*).
брако́вщик, а *m.* sorter (*of manufactured articles*).
брако́вщиц|а, ы *f. of* **брако́вщик**
бракоде́л, а *m.* (*coll.*) bad workman.
браконье́р, а *m.* poacher.
браконье́рств|о, а *nt.* poaching.
бракоразво́дный *adj.* divorce.
бракосочета́ни|е, я *nt.* wedding, nuptials.
бра́мсел|ь, я *m.* (*naut.*) topsail.
брандспо́йт, а *m.* **1.** fire-pump. **2.** nozzle.
бран|и́ть, ю́, и́шь *impf.* (*of* **вы́~**) to reprove; to scold; to abuse, curse (*coll.*).
бран|и́ться, ю́сь, и́шься *impf.* **1.** (*of* **по~**) (**с**+*i.*) to quarrel (with). **2.** to swear, curse (*intrans.*).
бра́нн|ый *adj.* abusive; **~ое сло́во** swearword.
бран|ь, и *f.* swearing; abuse; bad language.
брасле́т, а *m.* bracelet; watchband.
брасс, а *m.* (*sport*) breast stroke.
брат, а, *pl.* ≁**ья,** ≁**ьев** *m.* **1.** brother; **сво́дный б.** stepbrother; **двою́родный б.** cousin. **2.** (*fig.*) brother; comrade; ≁**ья-писа́тели** fellow-writers.
брата́ни|е, я *nt.* fraternization.
брата́|ться, юсь *impf.* (*of* **по~**) (**с**+*i.*) to fraternize (with).
бра́т|ец, ца *m. affectionate or patronizing dim. of* ~; (*as term of address*) mate, pal.
брати́ш|ка, ки, *g. pl.* ~**ек** *m.* (*coll.*) **1.** little brother. **2.** = **брат 2.**
бра́ти|я, и, *g. pl.* ~**й** *f.* (*collect.*) brotherhood, fraternity (*also fig.*).
братоуби́йственный *adj.* fratricidal (*also fig.*).
братоуби́йств|о, а *nt.* fratricide (*act*).
братоуби́йц|а, ы *m.* fratricide (*agent*).
бра́тск|ий *adj.* brotherly, fraternal; **б. приве́т** fraternal greetings; **~ая моги́ла** communal grave.
бра́тств|о, а *nt.* (*abstr. and concr.*) brotherhood, fraternity.
бра|ть, беру́, берёшь, *past* ~**л,** ~**ла́, ло** *impf.* (*of* **взять**). **1.** (*in var. senses*) to take; **б. курс (на**+*a.*) to make (for), head (for); **б. нача́ло (в**+*p.*) to originate (in); **б. приме́р (с**+*g.*) to follow the example (of); **б. сло́во** to take the floor; **б. в плен** to take prisoner; **б. на себя́** to take upon o.s.; **б. под аре́ст** to place under arrest; **б. кого́-н. по́д руку** to take s.o.'s arm. **2.** to take; to get, obtain; to book; to hire; **б. верх** to get the upper hand; **б. такси́** to take a taxi; **б. своё** to get one's way; to make itself felt; **б. взаймы́** to borrow; **б. напрока́т** to hire. **3.** to seize; to grip; **б. власть** to seize power; **б. за се́рдце** to move deeply. **4.** to exact; to take (= *to demand*, *require*); **б. штраф** to exact a fine; **б. сло́во с кого́-н.** to get s.o.'s word; **б. вре́мя** to take time. **5.** to take; to surmount; **б. барье́р** to clear a hurdle. **6.** (*usu.*+*neg.*; *coll.*) to work, operate; to be effective; **э́ти но́жницы не беру́т** these scissors don't cut.
бра́|ться, беру́сь, берёшься, *past* ~**лся,** ~**ла́сь,** ~**ло́сь** *impf.* (*of* **взя́ться**). **1.** *pass. of* ~**ть. 2.** (**за**+*a.*) to touch, lay hands (upon); **не бери́сь за то́рмоз!** don't touch the brake! **3.** (**за**+*a.*) to take up; to get down (to); **б. за де́ло** to get down to business; **б. за перо́** to take up the pen. **4.** (**за**+*a. or* +*inf.*) to undertake; to take upon o.s.; **б. за поруче́ние** to undertake a commission; **не беру́сь суди́ть** I do not presume to judge. **5.** (*3rd pers. only*) (*coll.*) to appear, arise; **не зна́ю, отку́да у них де́ньги беру́тся** I don't know where they get their money from. **6.: б. за ум** (*coll.*) to come to one's senses.
бра́т|ья[1] *see* ~
бра́ть|я[2], и *f.* = **бра́тия**
брахма́н, а *m.* Brahmin.
бра́чн|ый *adj.* marriage; conjugal; **б. во́зраст** marriageable age; **~ая жизнь** married life; **~ое свиде́тельство** marriage certificate; **~ое опере́ние** (*zool.*) breeding plumage.
бра́шпиль, я *m.* (*naut.*) windlass, capstan.
бреве́нчатый *adj.* log, made of logs.
брев|но́, на́, *pl.* ≁**на,** ≁**ен,** ≁**нам** *nt.* log, beam.
бред, а, о ≁**е, в ~у́** *m.* delirium; ravings; (*fig.*) gibberish; **быть в ~у́** to be delirious.
бре́д|ень, ня *m.* drag-net.
бре́|дить, жу, дишь *impf.* to be delirious, rave; (+*i.*; *fig.*) to be mad about.
бре́дн|и, ей *no sg.* ravings; fantasies.
бредово́й *adj.* **1.** delirious. **2.** (*fig.*) fantastic, nonsensical.
бредо́вый *adj.* crackpot, crazy.
бре|ду́, дёшь *see* ~**сти́**
бре́|жу, дишь *see* ~**дить**
бре́зг|ать, аю, аешь *impf.* (*of* **по~**) (+*i.*) to be squeamish (about).
брезгли́вост|ь, и *f.* squeamishness, fastidiousness; disgust.
брезгли́в|ый (~, ~а) *adj.* squeamish, fastidious.
брезе́нт, а *m.* tarpaulin.
брезе́нтовый *adj.* tarpaulin.
бре́зж|ить(ся), ~ит(ся) *impf.* to dawn; to glimmer; **~ила заря́** dawn was breaking.

брёл, á *see* **брести́**
брело́к, а *m.* (*bracelet*) charm.
бре́м|я, ~ени, ~енем, ~ени *nt.* burden; load.
бре́нди *m. and nt. indecl.* brandy.
бре́нн|ый (~а, ~о) *adj.*: **~ые оста́нки** mortal remains.
бренч|а́ть, у́, и́шь *impf.* **1.** (*+i.*) to jingle. **2.** (*coll.*) to strum; **б. на роя́ле** to strum on the piano.
бр|ести́, еду́, едёшь, *past* **~ёл, ~ела́** *impf.* to trudge (along); to shuffle..
брете́льк|а, и *f.* shoulder-strap.
бре|ха́ть, шу́, ~шешь *impf.* (*coll.*) **1.** to yelp, bark. **2.** (*fig.*) to tell lies.
брехн|я́, и́ *no pl., f.* (*coll.*) lies; nonsense.
бреху́н, á *m.* (*coll.*) liar.
бреш|у́, ~ешь *see* **бреха́ть**
бреш|ь, и *f.* breach; (*fig.*) gap, deficit.
бре́|ю, ешь *see* **бри́ть**
бре́ющий *pres. part. of* **брить; б. полёт** hedge-hopping flight.
бриг, а *m.* brig.
брига́д|а, ы *f.* **1.** (*mil.*) brigade. **2.** brigade, (work-)team; **поездна́я б.** train crew.
бригади́р, а *m.* brigade-leader; team-leader; foreman.
брига́дник, а *m.* member of a brigade, team.
брига́д|ный *adj. of* **~а**
бри́дер, а *m.* breeder reactor.
бридж, а *m.* bridge (*card-game*).
бри́дж|и, ей *no sg.* breeches.
бриджи́ст, а *m.* bridge player.
бриз, а *m.* breeze.
брике́т, а *m.* briquette.
брил|лиа́нт, а *and* **~ья́нт, а** *m.* (cut) diamond, brilliant.
бриллиа́нт|овый *adj. of* **~**
брил|ья́нт = ~лиа́нт
брил|ья́нтовый = ~лиа́нтовый
брита́н|ец, ца *m.* Britisher, Briton.
брита́н|ка, ки *f. of* **~ец**
брита́нский *adj.* British.
Брита́ни|я, и *f.* Britain.
Брита́нск|ие остров|а́, ~их ~о́в *no sg.* the British Isles.
бри́тв|а, ы *f.* razor; **безопа́сная б.** safety razor.
бри́твенн|ый *adj.* shaving; **~ые принадле́жности** shaving equipment.
бри́т|ый (~, ~а) *p.p.p. of* **~ь** *and adj.* clean-shaven.
бр|ить, е́ю, е́ешь *impf.* (*pf.* **по~**) to shave.
бритьё, я́ *nt.* shave; shaving.
бр|и́ться, е́юсь, е́ешься *impf.* to shave, have a shave.
бри́финг, а *m.* (press) briefing.
бри́чк|а, и *f.* (*obs.*) britzka (*light carriage*).
бров|ь, и, *pl.* **~и, ~е́й** *f.* eyebrow; brow; **хму́рить ~и** to knit one's brows, frown; **он и ~ью не повёл** he did not turn a hair; **попа́сть не в б., а (пря́мо) в глаз** (*prov.*) to hit the nail on the head.
брод, а *m.* ford; **не зна́я ~у, не су́йся в во́ду** (*prov.*) look before you leap.
броди́льный *adj.* (*tech.*) fermentative.
бро|ди́ть[1], жу́, ~дишь *impf.* to wander, roam; to amble, stroll; **б. по магази́ну** to browse round a shop; **б. в потёмках** (*fig.*) to be in the dark.
бро|ди́ть[2], ~дит *impf.* to ferment.
бродя́г|а, и *m.* tramp, vagrant; down-and-out.
бродя́жнича|ть, ю *impf.* to be a tramp, be on the road.
бродя́жничеств|о, а *nt.* vagrancy.
бродя́ч|ий *adj.* vagrant; nomadic; wandering, roving; (*fig.*) restless; **~ая соба́ка** stray dog.
броже́ни|е, я *nt.* fermentation; **б. умо́в** (*fig.*) intellectual ferment.
бро|жу́, ~дишь *see* **~ди́ть**
бро́кер, а *m.* broker.
бро́кколи *f. indecl.* broccoli.
бром, а *m.* (*chem.*) bromine; (*med.*) bromide.
бро́мистый *adj.* (*chem.*) bromide; **б. на́трий** sodium bromide.
бро́м|овый *adj. of* **~**
броне... *comb. form* (*mil.*) armoured-.
бронеавтомоби́л|ь, я *m.* armoured car.
бронебо́йный *adj.* armour-piercing.
броневи́к, á *m.* = **бронеавтомоби́ль**
бронев|о́й *adj.* armoured; **~ы́е пли́ты** (*mil.*) armour plating.
бронежиле́т, а *m.* bulletproof vest.
бронемаши́н|а, ы *f.* = **бронеавтомоби́ль**
броненос|ец[1], ца *m.* (*naut.*) battleship.
броненос|ец[2], ца *m.* (*zool.*) armadillo.
броненосный *adj.* armoured.
бронепо́езд, а *m.* armoured train.
бронета́нков|ый *adj.* (*mil.*) armoured; **~ые ча́сти** armoured units.
бронетранспортёр, а *m.* armoured personnel carrier, APC.
бро́нз|а, ы *f.* bronze.
бронзир|ова́ть, у́ю *impf. and pf.* to bronze.
бро́нзов|ый *adj.* bronze; bronzed, tanned; **б. век** (*archeol.*) the Bronze Age; **б. зага́р** sunburn, sun-tan.
брониро́в|анный *p.p.p. of* **~а́ть** *and adj.* armoured.
брони́р|овать, ую *impf.* (*of* **за~**) to reserve, book.
бронир|ова́ть, у́ю *impf. and pf.* to armour.
бронх, а *m.* (*anat.*) bronchial tube.
бронхиа́льный *adj.* (*anat.*) bronchial.
бронхи́т, а *m.* (*med.*) bronchitis.
бро́н|я *f.* reservation.
брон|я́, и́ *f.* armour; armour-plating.
броса́|ть, ю *impf.* (*of* **бро́сить**). **1.** to throw, toss, fling; cast; **б. обвине́ния** to hurl accusations; **б. тень** to cast a shadow; (**на**+*a.*; *fig.*) to cast aspersions (on); **б. я́корь** to drop anchor; **б. на ве́тер** to throw away, waste. **2.** to leave, abandon, desert; **б. му́жа** to desert one's husband; **б. ору́жие** to lay down one's arms; **б. рабо́ту** to throw up one's work. **3.** (*+inf.*) to give up; **он ~л кури́ть** he gave up smoking.
брос|а́ться, а́юсь *impf.* **1.** (*impf. only*) (*+i.*) to throw at one another, pelt one another (with). **2.** (*impf. only*) (*+i.*) to throw away; **б. деньга́ми** to throw away, squander one's money. **3.** (*pf.* **~иться**) (**на, в**+*a.*) to throw o.s. (on, upon), rush (to); **б. на коле́ни** to fall on one's knees; **б. в объя́тия** (*+d.*) to fall into the arms (of). **4.** (*pf.* **~иться**): **б. в глаза́** to be striking, arrest attention. **5.** (*pf.* **~иться**) (*+inf.*) to begin, start.
бро́|сить, шу, сишь *pf. of* **~са́ть; ~сь(те)!** stop it!
бро́|ситься, шусь, сишься *pf. of* **~са́ться**
бро́с|кий (~ок, ~ка́, ~ко) *adj.* (*coll.*) bright, loud, garish; **б. га́лстук** loud tie.
бро́совый *adj.* **1.** worthless; low-grade. **2.: б. э́кспорт** (*econ.*) dumping.
брос|о́к, ка́ *m.* **1.** throw; **штрафно́й б.** (*sport*) free throw. **2.** bound; spurt.
бро́шк|а, и *f.* brooch.
бро́|шу, сишь *see* **~сить**
брош|ь, и *f.* brooch.
брошю́р|а, ы *f.* pamphlet, brochure.
брудерша́фт, а *m. only in phr.* **вы́пить (на) б.** to drink 'Bruderschaft'.
брус, а, *pl.* **~ья, ~ьев** *m.* squared beam; **паралле́льные ~ья** (*sport*) parallel bars.
брусни́к|а, и *f.* cowberry.
брусни́|чный *adj. of* **~ка**
брус|о́к, ка́ *m.* bar; ingot; **точи́льный б.** whetstone.
бру́ствер, а *m.* (*mil.*) breastwork, parapet.
бру́тто *adj. indecl.* gross; **вес б.** gross weight.
брыж|и, ей *no sg.* ruff, frill.
бры́з|гать, жу, жешь *impf.* (*of* **~нуть**) (*+i.*) **1.** to splash, spatter; to gush, spurt; **б. гря́зью (на**+*a.*)

to splash mud (on to). **2.** (*pres.* **~жу** *or* **~гаю**) to sprinkle.
брызга|ться, юсь *impf.* (*coll.*) to splash; to splash o.s., one another.
брызг|и, ~ *no sg.* **1.** spray, splashes (*of liquids*). **2.** fragments (*of stone, glass, etc.*).
брыз|жу, жешь *see* **~гать**
брыз|нуть, ну, нешь *pf. of* **~гать**
брык|ать, аю *impf.* (*of* **~нуть**) to kick.
брыка|ться, юсь *impf.* to kick; (*fig.*) to kick, rebel.
брык|нуть, ну, нёшь *pf. of* **~ать**
брынз|а, ы *f.* brynza (*sheep's milk cheese*).
брысь *int.* shoo! (*to a cat*).
брюзг|а, и *c.g.* grumbler.
брюзглив|ый (~, ~а) *adj.* grumbling, peevish.
брюзж|ать, у, ишь *impf.* to grumble.
брюкв|а, ы *f.* (*bot.*) swede.
брюкв|енный *adj. of* **~а**
брюк|и, ~ *no sg.* trousers; **б.-юбка** culottes.
брюнет, а *m.* dark-haired man.
брюнетк|а, и *f.* brunette.
Брюссел|ь, я *m.* Brussels.
брюссельск|ий *adj.* Brussels; **~ая капуста** Brussels sprouts.
брюх|о, а, *pl.* **~и** *nt.* (*coll.*) belly; paunch.
брюшин|а, ы *f.* (*anat.*) peritoneum; **воспаление ~ы** (*med.*) peritonitis.
брюшк|о, а, *pl.* **~и, ~ов** *nt.* abdomen; (*coll.*) paunch.
брюшной *adj.* abdominal; **б. тиф** typhoid (fever).
бряк *int.* bang!; crash!
брякань|е, я *nt.* (*coll.*) clatter.
бряк|ать, аю *impf.* (*of* **~нуть**) (*coll.*) **1.** (*+i.*) to clatter. **2.** to let fall with a bang; (*fig.*) to drop a clanger. **3.** to blurt out.
бряк|аться, аюсь *impf.* (*of* **~нуться**) (*coll.*) to crash, fall heavily.
бряк|нуть(ся), ну(сь), нешь(ся) *pf. of* **~ать(ся)**
бряцани|е, я *nt.* **1.** rattling. **2.** rattle; clang; clank, clanking; **б. оружием** sabre-rattling.
бряца|ть, ю *impf.* (*+i. or* **на***+p.*) to rattle; to clang; to clank; **б. оружием** (*fig.*) to indulge in sabre-rattling.
БТР *m. indecl.* (*abbr. of* **бронетранспортёр**) APC (*armoured personnel carrier*).
буб|ен, на, *g. pl.* **~ен** *m.* tambourine.
бубен|ец, ца *m.* little bell.
бубенчик, а *m.* **1.** *dim. of* **бубенец. 2.** (*bot.*) harebell, campanula.
бублик, а *m.* boublik (*thick, ring-shaped bread roll*).
буб|на, ны, *g. pl.* **~ён** *f.* (*cards*) (*pl.*) diamonds.
бубн|ить, ю, ишь *impf.* (*of* **про~**) (*coll.*) to grumble; to mutter; to drone on (*of a speaker*).
бубновый *adj.* (*cards*) diamond; **б. туз** ace of diamonds.
бубон, а *m.* (*med.*) bubo.
бубон|ный *adj. of* **~; ~ная чума** bubonic plague.
буг|ор, ра *m.* mound, knoll; bump, lump.
бугор|ок, ка *m.* **1.** *dim. of* **~**; knob, protuberance. **2.** (*med.*) tubercle.
бугорчатый *adj.* **1.** covered with lumps. **2.** (*bot.*) tuberous.
бугрист|ый (~, ~а) *adj.* hilly; bumpy.
Будапешт, а *m.* Budapest.
буддизм, а *m.* Buddhism.
буддийский *adj.* Buddhist.
буддист, а *m.* Buddhist.
будет 1. *3rd pers. sg. fut. of* **быть. 2.** *as pred.* (*coll.*) that's enough; that'll do; **б. вам писать** it's time you stopped writing.
будильник, а *m.* alarm clock.
бу|дить, жу, ~дишь *impf.* **1.** (*pf.* **раз~**) to wake, awaken, call. **2.** (*pf.* **про~**) (*fig.*) to rouse, arouse; to stir up; **б. мысль** to set (one) thinking.
будк|а, и *f.* box, booth; stall; **караульная б.** sentry-box; **собачья б.** dog kennel; **телефонная б.** telephone booth.
буд|ни, ней, *sg.* (*obs. or coll.*) **~ень, ~ня** *m.* **1.** weekdays; **по ~ням** on weekdays. **2.** humdrum life; colourless existence.
будний *adj.*: **б. день** weekday.
будничн|ый *adj.* **1.: б. день** weekday; **~ое расписание** weekday timetable. **2.** dull, humdrum.
буднишний *adj.* = **будничный**
будораж|ить, у, ишь *impf.* (*of* **вз~**) (*coll.*) to disturb; to excite.
будто 1. *conj.* as if, as though. **2.** *conj.* that (*implying doubt as to the truth of a statement*); **он утверждает, б. свободно говорит на десяти языках** he maintains that he speaks ten languages fluently. **3.** (*also* **б. бы, как б.**) *particle* (*coll.*) apparently; **она б. должна ухаживать за отцом** apparently she has to look after her father.
буд|у, ешь *fut. of* **быть**
будуар, а *m.* boudoir.
будуар|ный *adj. of* **~**
будучи *pres. ger. of* **быть** being.
будущ|ий *adj.* future; next; **~ее время** (*gram.*) future tense; **в ~ем году** next year; **~ая мать** expectant mother; **в б. раз** next time; *as n.* **~ее, ~его** *nt.* (*i*) the future; **в ближайшем ~ем** in the near future, (*ii*) (*gram.*) future tense.
будущност|ь, и *f.* future; **ему предстоит блестящая б.** a brilliant future lies before him.
будь(те) *imper. of* **быть** (*sg. also used in place of* **если***+main v. to form protasis of conditional sentences*) **будьте добры, б. любезны** (*+inf. or imper.*) please; would you be good enough (to); **будь, что будет** come what may; **не будь вас, всё бы пропало** but for you all would have been lost.
бу|ёк, йка *m.* (*naut.*) anchor-buoy, lifebuoy.
буер, а *pl.* **а** *m.* ice-yacht.
буерист, а ice-yachtsman.
буерный *adj.*: **~ спорт** ice-yachting.
буженин|а, ы *f.* boiled salted pork.
бу|жу, ~дишь *see* **~дить**
буз|а, ы *f.* (*coll.*) row; **поднять ~у** to kick up a row.
бузин|а, ы *f.* (*bot.*) elder.
бузотёр, а *m.* (*coll.*) troublemaker, hell-raiser.
бу|й, я, *pl.* **~и, ~ёв** *m.* buoy.
буйвол, а *m.* (*zool.*) buffalo.
буйвол|овый *adj. of* **~**
бу|йный (~ен, ~йна, ~йно) *adj.* **1.** wild; violent, turbulent; tempestuous; ungovernable; **б. сумасшедший** violent lunatic. **2.** luxuriant, lush.
буйств|о, а *nt.* unruly conduct.
буйств|овать, ую *impf.* (*coll.*) to create uproar; to run riot.
бук, а *m.* beech.
бук|а, и *c.g.* (*coll.*) **1.** bogy(man), bugbear. **2.** (*fig.*) unsociable, surly person; **смотреть ~ой** to look surly.
букашк|а, и *f.* small insect.
букв|а, ы, *g. pl.* **~** *f.* letter (*of the alphabet*); **б. в ~у** literally; **б. закона** (*fig.*) the letter of the law.
буквально *adv.* literally; word for word.
буквальн|ый *adj.* literal; **б. перевод** word-for-word translation.
буквар|ь, я *m.* ABC; primer.
буквенно-цифровой *adj.* alphanumeric.
буквенный *adj.* in letters.
буквоед, а *m.* pedant.
буквоедств|о, а *nt.* pedantry.
букет, а *m.* **1.** bouquet; posy. **2.** bouquet; aroma.
букинист, а *m.* second-hand bookseller.
букинистический *adj.*: **б. магазин** second-hand bookshop.
буклет, а *m.* (fold-out) leaflet.
букмекер, а *m.* bookmaker; bookie.

бу́ковый *adj.* beech(en); **б. жёлудь** beechnut.
букси́р, а *m.* **1.** tug, tugboat. **2.** tow-rope; **взять на б.** to take in tow (*also fig.*); **тяну́ть на ~е** to have in tow.
букси́р|ный *adj. of* **~; б. парохо́д** steam tug.
букси́р|овать, ую *impf.* to tow.
буксиро́вк|а, и *f.* towing.
буксова́ни|е, я *nt.* skidding, wheel-spin.
букс|ова́ть, у́ю *impf.* to skid.
булав|а́, ы́ *f.* mace.
була́вк|а, и *f.* pin; **англи́йская б.** safety-pin.
була́в|очный *adj. of* **~ка**
булими́|я, и *f.* bulimia.
бу́лк|а, и *f.* (white) loaf; roll; **сдо́бная б.** bun.
бу́лл|а, ы *f.* (*Papal*) bull.
бу́лочн|ая, ой *f.* bakery; baker's shop.
бу́лочник, а *m.* baker.
бульты́х *int.* plop!; splosh!
бултых|а́ться, а́юсь *impf.* (*coll.*) **1.** (*pf.* **~ну́ться**) to (fall) plop. **2.** (*impf. only*) to splash *or* thrash (about).
булты́х|нуться, нусь-ну́сь, нешься-нёшься *pf. of* **~а́ться**
булы́жник, а *m.* cobble-stone (*also collect.*).
бульва́р, а *m.* avenue; boulevard.
бульва́р|ный *adj. of* **~; ~ная пре́сса** the tabloids; gutter press; **б. рома́н** cheap novel.
бульва́рщин|а, ы *f.* (*pej.*) pulp literature.
бульдо́г, а *m.* bulldog.
бульдо́зер, а *m.* bulldozer.
бульдозери́ст, а *m.* bulldozer driver.
бу́лькань|е, я *nt.* gurgling.
бу́лька|ть, ю *impf.* to gurgle.
бульо́н, а *m.* broth; stock.
бультерье́р, а *m.* bull terrier.
бум[1]**, а** *m.* (*coll.*) **1.** (*econ.*) boom. **2.** newspaper sensation.
бум[2]**, а** *m.* (*sport*) beam.
бум[3] *int.* boom!
бума́г|а, и *f.* **1.** paper; **газе́тная б.** newsprint; **почто́вая б.** notepaper; **2.** document; (*pl.*) (official) papers; **це́нные ~и** (*fin.*) securities.
бумагомара́тел|ь, я *m.* (*coll.*) scribbler; ink-slinger.
бумагопряде́ни|е, я *nt.* cotton-spinning.
бумагопряди́льн|ый *adj.* cotton-spinning; **~ая фа́брика** cotton mill.
бумагопряди́л|ьня, ьни, *g. pl.* **~ен** *f.* cotton mill.
бума́жк|а, и *f.* **1.** *dim. of* **бума́га**; scrap of paper. **2.** note; (paper) money.
бума́жник, а *m.* wallet.
бума́|жный *adj. of* **~га**; **1.** (*fig.*) (existing only on) paper; **б. змей** kite; **~жная фа́брика** paper-mill. **2.** cotton; **~жная пря́жа** cotton yarn.
бумажо́нк|а, и *f.* (*coll.*) scrap of paper.
бумера́нг, а *m.* boomerang.
бу́нгало *nt. indecl.* bungalow.
бу́нкер, а *m.* (*tech.*) bunker.
бунт[1]**, а,** *pl.* **~ы́** *m.* revolt; riot; mutiny.
бунт[2]**, а́** *m.* bale; packet; bundle.
бунта́рский *adj.* **1.** seditious; mutinous. **2.** (*fig.*) rebellious; turbulent; **б. дух** rebellious spirit.
бунта́рств|о, а *nt.* rebelliousness.
бунта́р|ь, я́ *m.* **1.** rebel (*also fig.*); insurgent; mutineer; rioter. **2.** inciter to mutiny, rebellion.
бунт|ова́ть, у́ю *impf.* **1.** (*pf.* **взбунтова́ться**) to revolt, rebel; to mutiny; to riot. **2.** (*pf.* **вз~**) to incite to revolt, mutiny.
бунт|ова́ться, у́юсь *impf.* = **~ова́ть 1.**
бунт|ово́й *adj. of* **~**[2]
бунтовско́й *adj.* rebellious, mutinous.
бунтовщи́к, а́ *m.* rebel, insurgent; mutineer; rioter.
бур[1]**, а** *m.* (*tech.*) auger.
бур[2]**, а** *m.* Boer.
бур|а́, ы́ *f.* (*chem.*) borax.
бура́в, а́, *pl.* **~а́** *m.* (*tech.*) auger; gimlet.
бура́в|ить лю, ишь *impf.* to bore, drill.
бура́вчик, а *m.* gimlet.
бура́н, а *m.* snow-storm (*in steppes*).
бургоми́стр, а *m.* burgomaster.
бургу́ндск|ий *adj.* Burgundian; *as n.* **~ое, ~ого** *nt.* burgundy (*wine*).
бурд|а́, ы́ *f.* slops.
бурдю́к, а́ *m.* (*wine, water-, etc.*) skin.
буреве́стник, а *m.* stormy petrel.
бур|ево́й *adj. of* **~я**; stormy.
бурело́м, а *m.* wind-fallen trees.
буре́ни|е, я *nt.* (*tech.*) boring, drilling.
буре́|ть, ю, еш *impf.* (*of* **по~**) to grow brown.
буржуа́ *m. indecl.* bourgeois.
буржуази́|я, и *f.* bourgeoisie; **ме́лкая б.** petty bourgeoisie.
буржуа́з|ный (~ен, ~на) *adj.* bourgeois.
буржу́|й, я *m.* (*coll.*) bourgeois.
буржу́й|ка, ки *f.* **1.** *f. of* **~. 2.** (*coll.*) small stove.
буржу́йский *adj.* (*coll.*) bourgeois.
бури́льный *adj.* (*tech.*) boring.
бури́льщик, а *m.* borer; driller, drill-operator.
бур|и́ть, ю́, и́шь *impf.* (*tech.*) to bore; to drill.
бу́рк|а, и *f.* felt cloak (*worn in Caucasus*).
бу́рк|ать, аю *impf.* (*of* **~нуть**) (*coll.*) to mutter; growl.
бу́рк|нуть, ну, нешь *pf. of* **~ать**
бурла́к, а́ *m.* barge hauler.
бурла́|цкий *adj. of* **~к**
бурли́в|ый (~, ~а) *adj.* turbulent; seething.
бурл|и́ть, ю́, и́шь *impf.* to seethe, boil up (*also fig.*).
бу́р|ный (~ен, ~на́) *adj.* **1.** stormy, rough; impetuous; **~ные аплодисме́нты** thunderous applause. **2.** rapid; energetic; **б. рост** rapid growth.
буров|о́й *adj.* boring; **~а́я вы́шка** derrick.
бу́рский *adj.* Boer.
буру́н, а́ *m.* breaker; bow-wave.
бурунду́к, а́ *m.* (*zool.*) chipmunk.
бурч|а́ть, у́, и́шь *impf.* (*of* **про~**) (*coll.*) **1.** to mumble, mutter; to grumble. **2.** (*impf. only*) to rumble; to bubble; (*impers.*): **у меня́ ~и́т в животе́** my stomach is rumbling.
бу́р|ый (~, ~а́, ~о) *adj.* brown.
бурья́н, а *m.* tall weeds.
бу́р|я, и *f.* storm (*also fig.*); **б. в стака́не воды́** storm in a teacup.
буря́т, а, *g. pl.* **б.** *m.* Buryat.
буря́т|ка, ки *f. of* **~**
буря́тский *adj.* Buryat.
бу́син|а, ы *f.* bead.
буссо́л|ь, и *f.* surveying compass.
бу́с|ы, ~ *no sg.* beads.
бутафо́р, а *m.* (*theatr.*) property-man.
бутафо́ри|я, и *f.* (*theatr.*) properties; dummies (*in shop window*); (*fig.*) window-dressing, sham.
бутафо́р|ский *adj. of* **~ия**
бутербро́д, а *m.* sandwich.
бутербро́дн|ая, ой *f.* sandwich bar.
бути́л, а *m.* (*chem.*) butyl.
бутиле́н, а *m.* (*chem.*) butylene.
буто́н, а *m.* **1.** bud. **2.** (*coll.*) pimple.
бутонье́рк|а, и *f.* buttonhole, posy.
бу́тс|ы, ~ *pl.* (*sg.* **~а, ~ы** *f.*) football boots.
буту́з, а *m.* (*coll.*) chubby lad.
буты́лк|а, и *f.* bottle.
буты́лочк|а, и *f.* small bottle; vial, phial.
буты́лочник, а *m.* glass-blower.
буты́л|очный *adj. of* **~ка; ~очного цве́та** bottle-green.
буты́л|ь, и *f.* large bottle; carboy, drum.
бу́фер, а, *pl.* **~а́** *m.* **1.** buffer. **2.** bumper. **3.** (*pl., sl.*) boobs, knockers.

бу́фер|ный *adj. of* ~; **~ное госуда́рство** (*pol.*) buffer state.
буфе́т, а *m.* **1.** sideboard. **2.** buffet, refreshment room; (refreshment) bar, counter.
буфе́т|ный *adj. of* ~
буфе́тчик, а *m.* barman, bartender.
буфе́тчиц|а, ы *f.* barmaid; counter assistant.
буффо́н, а *m.* buffoon.
бух *int.* bang!; plonk!; plop!; *as pred.* **он б. на зе́млю** he fell to the ground with a thud.
буха́нк|а, и *f.* loaf (of bread).
Бухаре́ст, а *m.* Bucharest.
бу́х|ать, аю *impf.* (*of* **~нуть**) **1.** to thump, bang; **б. кулако́м в дверь** to bang on the door with one's fist. **2.** to let fall with a thud. **3.** to thud, thunder. **4.** (*fig., coll.*) to blurt out.
бу́х|аться, аюсь *impf.* (*of* **~нуться**) (*coll.*) to fall heavily; to plonk o.s. down.
бухга́лтер, а, *pl.* **~ы** *m.* book-keeper; accountant.
бухгалте́ри|я, и *f.* **1.** book-keeping. **2.** counting-house.
бухга́лтерский *adj.* book-keeping; account; **~ая кни́га** account book.
бу́х|нуть[1]**, ну, нешь,** *past* **~нул** *pf. of* **~ать**
бу́х|нуть[2]**, ну, нешь,** *past* **~, ~ла** *impf.* to swell, expand.
бу́х|нуться, нусь, нешься *pf. of* **~аться**
бу́хт|а, ы *f.* (*geog.*) bay.
бу́хточк|а, и *f.* creek, cove, inlet.
бу́хты-бара́хты *only in phr.* (*coll.*) **с б.-б.** offhand; off the cuff; suddenly.
бу́ч|а, и *f.* (*coll.*) row.
буш|ева́ть, у́ю *impf.* to rage; (*fig.*) to rage, storm.
бу́шел|ь, я *m.* bushel.
бушла́т, а *m.* (*naut.*) pea-jacket.
бу́шпри́т, а *m.* (*naut.*) bowsprit.
буя́н, а *m.* (*coll.*) rowdy, brawler.
буя́н|ить, ю, ишь, *impf.* (*coll.*) to make a row; to brawl.
бы (*abbr.* **б**) *particle* **1.** *indicates hypothetical sentence* (*see also* **е́сли**): **я мог бы об э́том догада́ться** I might have guessed it; **бы́ло бы о́чень прия́тно вас ви́деть** it would be very nice to see you. **2.** **(+ни)** *forms indef. prons.*: **кто бы ни** whoever; **что бы ни** whatever; **как бы ни** however; **кто бы ни пришёл** whoever comes; **что бы ни случи́лось** whatever happens; **как бы то ни́ было** be that as it may. **3.** *expr. wish*: **я бы вы́пил пи́ва** I should like a drink of beer. **4.** *expr. polite suggestion or exhortation*: **вы бы отдохну́ли** you should take a rest.
быва́|ло 1. *see* **~ть. 2.** *particle indicating repetition of an action in past time*: **моя́ мать б. ча́сто пе́ла э́ту пе́сню** my mother would often sing this song.
быва́л|ый *adj.* **1.** experienced; worldly-wise. **2.** (*coll.*) habitual, familiar; **э́то де́ло ~ое** this is nothing new.
быва́|ть, ю *impf.* **1.** to happen; to take place; to be held. **2.** to be (*regularly or as a rule*); to frequent; **он ~ет ка́ждый день в кабине́те с девяти́ часо́в утра́** he is in his office every day from nine a.m.; **они́ ре́дко ~ют в теа́тре** they seldom go to the theatre. **3.** to be inclined to be, tend to be; **он ~ет раздражи́телен** he is inclined to be irritable. **4.: как ни в чём не ~ло** (*coll.*) as if nothing had happened.
бы́вш|ий *p.p. of* **быть** *and adj.* former, ex-; onetime; **го́род Санкт-Петербу́рг, б. Ленингра́д** St. Petersburg, formerly Leningrad.
бык[1]**, а́** *m.* **1.** bull; ox; **рабо́чий б.** draught ox; **бой ~о́в** bullfight; **взять ~а́ за рога́** (*fig.*) to take the bull by the horns; **здоро́в, как б.** as strong as an ox. **2.** male (*of certain horned animals*); **оле́ний б.** stag.
бык[2]**, а́** *m.* pier (*of a bridge*).
был|ево́й *adj. of* **~ина**
были́н|а, ы *f.* (*liter.*) bylina (*Russ. traditional heroic poem*).
были́нк|а, и *f.* blade of grass.
были́н|ный *adj. of* **~а**; epic.
было *particle* (just) about to, on the point of; **он пое́хал б. с ни́ми, но заболе́л** he was all set to go with them, but he fell ill; **чуть б.** very nearly; **я чуть б. не забы́л** I very nearly forgot; **они́ чуть б. не уби́ли его́** they all but killed him.
был|о́й *adj.* past, bygone; **в ~ы́е времена́** in days of old; *as n.* **~о́е, ~о́го** *nt.* (*poet.*) the past.
был|ь, и *f.* true story.
быль|ё, я́ *nt.*: **~ём поросло́** long forgotten.
быстрин|а́, ы́, *pl.* **~ы** *f.* (*geog.*) rapid(s).
быстроде́йствующий *adj.* high-speed; quick-acting.
быстрозаморо́женный *adj.* (quick-)frozen.
быстроно́гий *adj.* (*poet.*) fleet-footed.
быстросбо́рный *adj.* quick-assembly.
быстросо́хнущий *adj.* quick-dry(ing).
быстрот|а́, ы́ *f.* rapidity, quickness; speed.
быстрохо́д|ный (~ен, ~на) *adj.* fast, high-speed.
бы́стр|ый (~, ~а́, ~о) *adj.* rapid, fast, quick.
быт, а, о ~е, в ~у́ *no pl., m.* way of life; life; daily life; **дома́шний б.** family life; **слу́жба ~а** consumer services.
быти|е́, я́ *nt.* (*phil.*) being, existence; **кни́га Б~я́** (*bibl.*) Genesis.
бы́тност|ь, и *f. only in phr.* **в б.** during a given period; **в б. мою́ студе́нтом** in my student days; **в б. его́ в Ри́ме** during his time in Rome.
быт|ова́ть, у́ет *impf.* to occur, be current.
быт|ово́й *adj. of* ~; everyday; **~овые прибо́ры** domestic appliances; **~ова́я ЭВМ** home computer; **~ово́е явле́ние** everyday occurrence.
быть *pres. not used exc. 3rd pers. sg.* **есть** *and* (*obs.*) *3rd pers. pl.* **суть,** *fut.* **бу́ду, бу́дешь,** *past* **был, была́, бы́ло (не́ был, не была́, не́ было)** *imper.* **бу́дь(те)** (*see also* **бу́дет, бу́дь(те), бы́ло, есть**).
I. 1. to be (= *to exist*); **есть таки́е лю́ди** there are such people, such people do exist. **2.: б. у** (*see also* **есть**) to be in the possession (of); **у них была́ прекра́сная да́ча** they had a lovely dacha. **3.** to be (= *to be situated, be located*); **(к)** to come (to), be present (at); **здесь был тракти́р** there used to be an inn here; **где вы бы́ли вчера́?** where were you yesterday?; **он тут был не при чём** he had nothing to do with it; **на ней была́ ро́зовая ко́фточка** she had on a pink blouse. **4.** to be, happen, take place; **э́того не мо́жет б.!** it cannot be!; **что с ним бы́ло?** what happened to him?; **как б.?** what is to be done?; **так и б.** so be it.
II. *as aux. v.* to be.
быча́ч|ий *adj. of* **бык**[1]; **~ья ко́жа** oxhide.
бы́чий *adj.* = **быча́чий**
быч|о́к[1]**, ка́** *m.* steer.
быч|о́к[2]**, ка́** *m.* goby.
быч|о́к[3]**, ка́** *m.* (*coll.*) cigarette butt.
бью, бьёшь *see* **бить**
бюва́р, а *m.* writing-case.
бюдже́т, а *m.* budget.
бюдже́тный *adj.* budgetary; **б. год** fiscal year.
бюллете́н|ь, я *m.* **1.** bulletin; **информацио́нный б.** newsletter. **2. (избира́тельный) б.** voting-paper. **3. (больни́чный) б.** medical certificate; **быть на ~е** (*coll.*) to be on sick-leave.
бю́ргер, а *m.* burgher.
бюро́ *nt. indecl.* **1.** bureau, office; **б. нахо́док** lost-property office; **туристи́ческое б.** travel agency. **2.** bureau, writing-desk.
бюрокра́т, а *m.* bureaucrat.
бюрократи́зм, а *m.* bureaucracy; red tape.
бюрократи́ческий *adj.* bureaucratic.
бюрокра́ти|я, и *f.* bureaucracy (*also collect.*).
бюст, а *m.* bust; bosom.
бюстга́льтер, а *m.* bra(ssière).

бя́з|евый *adj. of* **~ь**
бяз|ь, и *f.* coarse calico.

В

В (*abbr. of* **восто́к**) E, East.
в *prep.*
I. *+a. and p.* **1.** (*+a.*) into, to; (*+p.*) in, at; **пое́хать в Москву́** to go to Moscow; **роди́ться в Москве́** to be born in Moscow; **сесть в ваго́н** to get into the carriage; **сиде́ть в ваго́не** to be in the carriage; **разби́ть на куски́** to smash to pieces; **привести́ в восто́рг** to delight; **быть в восто́рге** to be delighted. **2.** *in reference to external attributes*: **руба́шка в кле́тку** check(ed) shirt; **лицо́ в весну́шках** freckled face. **3.** (*+nom.-a. pl. and p. pl.*) *in reference to occupation*: **пойти́ в стенографи́стки** to become a shorthand-typist. **4.** *in reference to calendar units and periods of time*: **в понеде́льник** on Monday; **в январе́** in January; **в четы́ре часа́** at four o'clock; **в четвёртом часу́** between three and four; **в на́ши дни** in our day; **в тече́ние** (*+g.*) during, in the course (of).
II. *+a.* **1.** *in reference to objects through which vision is directed*: **смотре́ть в окно́** to look out of the window; **смотре́ть в бино́кль** to look through binoculars. **2.** *in attribution of resemblance*: **быть в кого́-н.** to take after s.o.; **она́ вся в тётю** she is the image of her aunt. **3.** *indicating aim or purpose*: for, as; **сказа́ть в шу́тку** to say for a joke. **4.** *in specification of quantitative attributes*: **моро́з в де́сять гра́дусов** ten degrees of frost; **высото́й в три ме́тра** three metres high. **5.** (*+***раз** *and comp. adv.*) *indicates comparison in numerical terms*: **в два ра́за бо́льше** twice as big, twice the size. **6.** *of time*: in, within; **наде́юсь ко́нчить чернови́к за ме́сяц** I hope to finish the rough draft in a month. **7.** *indicates game or sport played*: **игра́ть в ка́рты, футбо́л** to play cards, football.
III. *+p.* **1.** at a distance of; **в трёх киломе́трах от го́рода** three kilometres from the town. **2.** in; of (= *consisting of*, *amounting to*); **пье́са в трёх де́йствиях** play in three acts; **ра́зница в двух копе́йках** a difference of two kopecks.
в. (*abbr. of* **век**) C, century.
ва-ба́нк *adv.* (*cards*) **игра́ть, идти́ ва-б.** to stake everything; (*fig.*) to stake one's all.
вавило́нск|ий *adj.* Babylonian; **~ое столпотворе́ние** babel; **~ая ба́шня** the tower of Babel.
ваго́н, а *m.* **1.** carriage, coach; **мя́гкий, жёсткий в.** soft-seated, hard-seated carriage; **бага́жный в.** luggage van; **в.-рестора́н** dining-car; **спа́льный в.** sleeping-car. **2.** wagon-load; (*fig., coll.*) loads, lots; **вре́мени у нас в.** we have masses of time.
вагоне́тк|а, и *f.* truck; trolley.
ваго́н|ный *adj. of* **~**; **в. парк** rolling-stock.
вагоновожа́т|ый, ого *m.* tram-driver.
важне́цк|ий *adj.* (*coll.*) good, good-quality.
ва́жничани|е, я *nt.* airs and graces.
ва́жнича|ть, ю *impf.* (*coll.*) to give o.s. airs; (*+i.*) to plume o.s. (on).
ва́жност|ь, и *f.* **1.** importance; significance; **не велика́ в.** (*coll.*) it's of no consequence. **2.** pomposity, pretentiousness.
ва́ж|ный (~ен, ~на́, ~но) *adj.* **1.** important; weighty; **~ная ши́шка** (*coll.*) bigwig. **2.** pompous, pretentious.
ва́з|а, ы *f.* vase, bowl.
вазели́н, а *m.* Vaseline (*propr.*).
вазо́н, а *m.* (flower-)pot.
вака́нси|я, и *f.* vacancy.
вака́нт|ный (~ен, ~на) *adj.* vacant, unfilled.
ва́кс|а, ы *f.* (shoe) polish; blacking.
ва́к|сить, шу, сишь *impf.* (*of* **на~**) to black, polish.
ва́куум, а *m.* vacuum.
вакхана́ли|я, и *f.* (*usu. pl.*) bacchanalia.
вакци́н|а, ы *f.* vaccine.
вакцина́ци|я, и *f.* vaccination.
вакцини́р|овать, ую *impf. and pf.* to vaccinate.
ва́к|шу, сишь *see* **~сить**
вал[1]**, а,** *pl.* **~ы́** *m.* billow, roller.
вал[2]**, а,** *pl.* **~ы́** *m.* bank, earthen wall.
вал[3]**, а,** *pl.* **~ы́** *m.* (*tech.*) shaft.
вал[4]**, а** *m.* (*econ.*) gross output.
вале́жник, а *no pl., m.* (*collect.*) windfallen trees, branches.
вал|ёк, ька́ *m.* (*tech.*) **1.** roller. **2.** swingle-tree.
ва́лен|ки, ок *pl.* (*sg.* **~ок, ~ка** *m.*) valenki (*felt boots*).
вале́нтност|ь, и *f.* (*chem.*) valency.
валерья́н|а, ы *f.* (*bot.*) valerian.
валерья́нк|а, и *f.* (*coll.*) tincture of valerian.
валерья́нов|ый *adj.* (*med.*): **~ые ка́пли** tincture of valerian.
вале́т, а *m.* (*cards*) knave, jack.
ва́лик, а *m.* **1.** (*tech.*) roller, cylinder; spindle, shaft; platen. **2.** bolster.
вал|и́ть[1]**, ю́, ~́ишь** *impf.* **1.** (*pf.* **по~** *and* **с~**) to throw down, bring down; to overthrow; **в. кого́-н. с ног** to knock s.o. off his feet; **в. дере́вья** to fell trees. **2.** (*pf.* **с~**) to heap up, pile up; **в. вину́** (**на***+a.*) to lump the blame (on).
вал|и́ть[2]**, и́т** *impf.* (*coll.*) to flock, throng, pour; **вало́м в.** to throng; **лю́ди ~и́ли на стадио́н** people were flocking to the stadium; **снег ~и́т кру́пными хло́пьями** the snow is coming down in large flakes; **дым ~и́л из трубы́** smoke was belching from the chimney.
вал|и́ться, ю́сь, ~́ишься *impf.* (*of* **по~** *and* **с~**) to fall, collapse; to topple over; **в. от уста́лости** to drop from tiredness.
ва́лк|а, и *f.* felling.
ва́л|кий (~ок, ~ка́, ~ко) *adj.* unsteady, shaky; **ни ша́тко, ни ~ко** middling; neither good nor bad.
валли́|ец, йца *m.* Welshman.
валли́йк|а, и *f.* Welshwoman.
валли́йский *adj.* Welsh.
валово́й *adj.* (*econ.*) gross; **в. дохо́д** gross income.
вало́м *see* **вали́ть**[2]
валто́рн|а, ы *f.* (*mus.*) French horn.
валу́н, а́ *m.* boulder.
ва́льдшнеп, а *m.* (*zool.*) woodcock.
вальс, а *m.* waltz.
вальси́р|овать, ую *impf.* to waltz.
вальц|ева́ть, у́ю *impf.* (*tech.*) to roll.
вальцо́вк|а, и *f.* (*tech.*) **1.** rolling. **2.** rolling press.
вальцо́в|ый *adj.* (*tech.*); **~ая ме́льница** rolling-mill.
вальц|ы́, о́в *no sg.* (*tech.*) rolling press.
валю́т|а, ы *f.* (*fin., econ.*) **1.** currency; **курс ~ы** rate of exchange. **2.** (*collect.*) foreign exchange, hard currency.
валю́тно-фина́нсов|ый *adj.*: **~ая би́ржа** foreign exchange market.
валю́т|ный *adj. of* **~а**; currency.
валю́тчик, а *m.* (*coll.*) currency speculator.
валя́льщик, а *m.* fuller.
ва́ляный *adj.* felt.
валя́|ть, ю *impf.* **1.** (*impf. only*) to drag; **в. по́ полу**

to drag along the floor. **2.** (*pf.* **вы~**) to roll, drag; **в. в грязи́** to drag in the mire. **3.** (*pf.* **с~**) to knead. **4.** (*pf.* **с~**) to full; to felt. **5.: в. дурака́** (*coll.*) to play the fool.
валя́|ться, юсь *impf.* **1.** to roll (about). **2.** (*coll.*) to lie about; loll; **её оде́жда ~лась везде́ по ко́мнате** her clothes lay scattered all over the room.
вам *d. of* **вы**
ва́ми *i. of* **вы**
вампи́р, а *m.* **1.** vampire. **2.** (*zool.*) vampire-bat.
вана́ди|й, я *m.* (*chem.*) vanadium.
вanда́л, а *m.* (*hist. and fig.*) Vandal; vandal.
вандали́зм, а *m.* vandalism.
вани́л|ь, и *f.* vanilla.
вани́ль|ный *adj. of* **~**
ва́нн|а, ы *f.* bath; **сидя́чая в.** hip-bath; **взять ~у, приня́ть ~у** to take a bath.
ва́нночк|а, и *f. dim. of* **ва́нна**; (*phot.*) developing tray; **глазна́я в.** eye-bath.
ва́нн|ый *adj. of* **~а**; *as n.* **~ая, ~ой** *f.* bathroom.
ва́нька-вста́нька, ва́ньки-вста́ньки *m.* tumbler (*toy*).
вар, а *m.* pitch; cobbler's wax.
вара́н, а *m.* (*zool.*) monitor lizard.
ва́рвар, а *m.* barbarian.
варвари́зм, а *m.* (*ling., liter.*) barbarism.
ва́рварский *adj.* barbarian; (*fig.*) barbaric.
ва́рварств|о, а *nt.* barbarity.
ва́рев|о, а *nt.* (*coll., pej.*) broth; slop.
ва́режк|а, и *f.* mitten.
варен|е́ц, ца́ *m.* fermented boiled milk.
варе́ние = ва́рка
варе́ник, а *m.* varenik (*curd or fruit dumpling*).
варёный *adj.* **1.** boiled. **2.** (*coll.*) limp.
варе́нь|е, я *nt.* preserve(s), jam.
вариа́нт, а *m.* reading, variant; version; option; scenario; model; **нулево́й в.** (*pol.*) zero option.
вариа́ци|я, и *f.* variation.
варико́зный *adj.* (*anat.*) varicose.
вар|и́ть, ю́, ~́ишь *impf.* (*of* **с~**) **1.** to boil; to cook; **в. глинтве́йн** to mull wine; **в. пи́во** to brew beer. **2.** to found (*steel*).
вар|и́ться, ю́сь, ~́ишься *impf.* (*of* **с~**) **1.** to boil (*intrans.*); to cook (*intrans.*). **2.** *pass. of* **~и́ть**
ва́рк|а, и *f.* boiling; cooking; **в. варе́нья** preserve-making; **в. желе́за** iron-founding; **в. пи́ва** brewing.
Варша́в|а, ы *f.* Warsaw.
варша́вский *adj.* (of) Warsaw.
варьете́ *nt. indecl.* variety (show).
варьи́р|овать, ую *impf.* to vary, modify.
варя́г, а *m.* (*hist.*) Varangian.
варя́жский *adj.* (*hist.*) Varangian.
вас *g., a., and p. of* **вы**
васил|ёк, ька́ *m.* (*bot.*) cornflower.
васил|ько́вый *adj. of* **~ёк**; cornflower blue.
васса́л, а *m.* vassal.
васса́льн|ый *adj.* vassal; **~ая зави́симость** vassalage.
ва́т|а, ы *f.* cotton wool; wadding; **са́харная в.** candy-floss.
вата́г|а, и *f.* band, gang.
ватерклозе́т, а *m.* water-closet.
ватерли́ни|я, и *f.* (*naut.*) water-line.
ватерпа́с, а *m.* (*tech.*) water-level, spirit-level.
ватерполи́ст, а *m.* water polo player.
ватерпо́ло *nt. indecl.* (*sport*) water polo.
Ватика́н, а *m.* the Vatican.
ватика́н|ский *adj. of* **В~**
вати́н, а *m.* batting, sheet wadding.
ва́тник, а *m.* quilted jacket.
ва́тн|ый *adj.* wadded, quilted; **~ое одея́ло** quilt.
ватру́шк|а, и *f.* curd tart; cheese-cake.
ватт, а, *g. pl.* **в.** *m.* (*elec.*) watt.
ва́учер, а *m.* voucher.
ва́учеризаци|я, и *f.* (*pol.*) voucherization.
ва́фельниц|а, ы *f.* waffle-iron.
ва́ф|ля, ли, *g. pl.* **~ель** *f.* waffle; wafer.
вахла́к, а́ *m.* (*coll.*) lout; sloven.
ва́хт|а, ы *f.* (*naut.*) watch; **стоя́ть на ~е** to keep watch.
ва́хт|енный *adj. of* **~а** (*naut.*); **в. журна́л** log(-book); **в. команди́р** officer of the watch; *as n.* **в., ~енного** *m.* watch.
вахтёр, а *m.* janitor, porter.
ваш, ~́его; *f.* **~́а, ~́ей;** *nt.* **~́е, ~́его;** *pl.* **~́и, ~́их** *possessive pron.* your(s); **э́то в. каранда́ш** this is your pencil; **э́тот каранда́ш в.** this pencil is yours; **не ~́е де́ло** it is none of your business; *as n.* **~́и, ~́их** your people, your folk.
Вашингто́н, а *m.* Washington.
ваяни́|е, я *nt.* (*obs.*) sculpture.
вая́тел|ь, я *m.* (*obs.*) sculptor.
вая́|ть, ю *impf.* (*of* **из~**) to sculpt; to carve, chisel.
вбега́|ть, ю *impf.* (**в**+*a.*) to run (into).
вбе|жа́ть, гу́, жи́шь, гу́т *pf. of* **~га́ть**
вбер|у́, ёшь *see* **вобра́ть**
вбива́|ть, ю *impf. of* **вбить**
вбира́|ть, ы *impf. of* **вобра́ть**
вбить, вобью́, вобьёшь *pf.* (*of* **вбива́ть**) to drive in, hammer in; (*sport*) **в. мяч в воро́та** to score a goal; (*coll.*) **в. в го́лову** (+*d.*; *fig.*) to knock into s.o.'s head; **в. себе́ в го́лову** to get into one's head.
вблизи́ *adv.* **(от)** close by; not far (from); **они́ живу́т где́-то в.** they live somewhere nearby; **рассма́тривать в.** to examine closely.
вбок *adv.* sideways, to one side.
вбра́сыва|ть, ю *impf. of* **вбро́сить**
вброд *adv.*: **переходи́ть в.** to wade; to ford.
вв. (*abbr. of* **века́**) C, centuries.
вва́лива|ть, ю *impf. of* **ввали́ть**
вва́лива|ться, юсь *impf. of* **ввали́ться**
ввал|и́ть, ю́, ~́ишь *pf.* to hurl, heave into.
ввал|и́ться, ю́сь, ~́ишься *pf.* **1.** (*coll.*) to tumble into, sink into. **2.** (*fig., coll.*) to burst into. **3.** to become hollow, sunken; **с ~и́вшимися щека́ми** hollow-cheeked.
введе́ни|е, я *nt.* **1.** leading in(to). **2.** introduction; preamble.
вве|ду́, дёшь *see* **~сти́**
ввез|ти́, у́, ёшь, *past* **~̈, ~ла́** *pf.* (*of* **ввози́ть**) to import.
ввек *adv.* (*now only used before neg.*) ever; **я э́того в. не забу́ду** I shall not forget it as long as I live.
вверг|а́ть, а́ю *impf. of* **~́нуть**
вве́рг|нуть, ну, нешь, *past* **~, ~ла** *pf.* (*of* **~а́ть**) (**в**+*a.*) to cause to fall (into); to reduce (to); **в. в темни́цу** to cast into a dungeon; **в. в отча́яние** to drive to despair.
вве́р|ить, ю, ишь *pf.* (*of* **~я́ть**) to entrust; confide.
вве́р|иться, юсь, ишься *pf.* (*of* **~я́ться**) (+*d.*) to trust (in), put o.s. in the hands of.
вверн|у́ть, у́, ёшь *pf.* (*of* **ввёртывать**) **1.** to screw in, insert. **2.** (*fig., coll.*) to insert, put in; **ему́ не удало́сь в. ни слове́чка** he could not get a word in.
ввёртыва|ть, ю *impf. of* **ввернуть**
вверх *adv.* up, upward(s); **идти́ в. по ле́стнице** to go upstairs; **в. по тече́нию** upstream; **в. дном** upside down; topsy-turvy; **в. нога́ми** head over heels.
вверху́ *adv. and prep.*+*g.* above, overhead; **в. страни́цы** at the top of the page.
вверя́|ть(ся), ю(сь) *impf. of* **вве́рить(ся)**
вве|сти́, ду́, дёшь, *past* **~̈л, ~ла́** *pf.* (*of* **вводи́ть**) to introduce, bring in; **в. мо́ду** to introduce a fashion; **в. в заблужде́ние** to mislead; **в. в искуше́ние** to lead into temptation; **в. в курс чего́-н.** to acquaint with the facts of sth.
ввива́|ть, ю *impf. of* **ввить**

ввиду́ *prep.+g.* in view (of); **в. того́, что** as; **в. того́, что вы прие́хали** as you have come.

ввин|ти́ть, чу́, ти́шь *pf.* (*of* **~́чивать**) (**в**+*a.*) to screw (in); **в. што́пор в про́бку** to insert a corkscrew into a cork.

вви́нчива|ть, ю *impf. of* **ввинти́ть**

ввить, вовью́, вовьёшь *pf.* (*of* **ввива́ть**) to weave in.

ввод, а *m.* **1.** bringing in; **в. в бой** (*mil.*) throwing into battle; engagement. **2.** (*elec.*) lead-in. **3.** (*comput.*) input; **в. да́нных** data input.

вво|ди́ть, жу́, ~́дишь *impf. of* **ввести́**

вво́дн|ый *adj.* introductory; (*gram.*) **~ое сло́во** parenthetic word.

вво|жу́[1], **~́дишь** *see* **вводи́ть**

вво|жу́[2], **~́зишь** *see* **ввози́ть**

ввоз, а *no pl., m.* **1.** importation. **2.** import; (*collect.*) imports.

вво|зи́ть, жу́, ~́зишь *impf. of* **ввезти́**

ввозн|о́й *adj.* imported; import; **~а́я по́шлина** import duty.

вво́лю *adv.* (*coll.*) = **вдо́воль**

ВВС *no sg., indecl.* (*abbr. of* **вое́нно-возду́шные си́лы**) Air Force.

ввысь *adv.* up, upward(s).

ввя|за́ть, жу́, ~́жешь *pf.* (*of* **~́зывать**) to knit in; (*fig.*) to involve.

ввя|за́ться, жу́сь, ~́жешься *pf.* (**в**+*a.*; *coll.*) to meddle (in); to get mixed up (in); **в. в неприя́тную исто́рию** to get mixed up in a nasty business.

ввя́зыва|ть(ся), ю(сь) *impf. of* **ввяза́ть(ся)**

вгиба́|ть, ю *impf. of* **вогну́ть**

вглубь *adv. and prep.+g.* deep down; deep into, far into; **в. лесо́в** into the heart of the forest.

вгля|де́ться, жу́сь, ди́шься *pf.* (*of* **~́дываться**) (**в**+*a.*) to peer (at).

вгля́дыва|ться, юсь *impf. of* **вгляде́ться**

вгоня́|ть, ю *impf. of* **вогна́ть**

вгры́з|ться, у́сь, ёшься *pf.* (*coll.*) to get one's teeth into (*of animals*).

вда|ва́ться, ю́сь, ёшься *impf. of* **~́ться**

вдав|и́ть, лю́, ~́ишь *pf.* (*of* **~́ливать**) to press in.

вда́влива|ть, ю *impf. of* **вдави́ть**

вда́лблива|ть, ю *impf. of* **вдолби́ть**

вдалеке́ *adv.* in the distance; **в. от** a long way from.

вдали́ *adv.* in the distance, far off; **в. от го́рода** far away from the city; **держа́ться в.** to keep aloof, keep one's distance; **исчеза́ть в.** to vanish into thin air.

вдаль *adv.* afar, at a distance; **гляде́ть в.** to look into the distance.

вд|а́ться, а́мся, а́шься, а́стся, ади́мся, ади́тесь, аду́тся *pf.* (*of* **вдава́ться**) (**в**+*a.*) to jut out (into); **в. в подро́бности** to go into detail.

вдвига́|ть(ся), ю(сь) *impf. of* **вдви́нуть(ся)**

вдви́|нуть, ну, нешь *pf.* (*of* **~га́ть**) to push in(to).

вдви́|нуться, нусь, нешься *pf.* (*of* **~га́ться**) to push in, squeeze in.

вдво́е *adv.* twice; double; **в. бо́льше** twice as much, twice as big; **сложи́ть в.** to fold double.

вдвоём *adv.* the two together; **они́ в. написа́ли статью́** the two of them together wrote the article.

вдвойне́ *adv.* twice, double; doubly (*also fig.*); **плати́ть в.** to pay double.

вдева́|ть, ю *impf. of* **вдеть**

вде́л|ать, аю *pf.* (*of* **~ывать**) (**в**+*a.*) to fit (into), set (into).

вде́лыва|ть, ю *impf. of* **вде́лать**

вде́н|у, ешь *see* **вдеть**

вдёргива|ть, ю *impf. of* **вдёрнуть**

вдёрн|уть, у, ешь *pf.* (*of* **вдёргивать**) to pull through; to thread; **в. ни́тку в иглу́** to thread a needle.

вде́сятеро *adv.* ten times; **в. бо́льше** ten times as much.

вдесятеро́м *adv.* ten together; **мы в.** ten of us.

вде|ть, ~́ну, ~́нешь *pf.* (*of* **~ва́ть**) (**в**+*a.*) to put in(to); **в. ни́тку в иглу́** to thread a needle.

вдоба́вок *adv.* in addition; moreover; into the bargain.

вдов|а́, ы́, *pl.* **~́ы** *f.* widow; **соло́менная в.** (*coll.*) grass widow.

вдове́|ть, ю *impf.* (*of* **о~**) to be a widow(er); to be widowed.

вдов|е́ц, ца́ *m.* widower.

вдо́воль *adv.* (*coll.*) **1.** in abundance; **у нас вся́кого ро́да фру́ктов в.** we have abundance of every kind of fruit. **2.** enough; **он нае́лся в.** he ate his fill.

вдовств|о́, а́ *nt.* widowhood; widowerhood.

вдо́вств|овать, ую *impf.* (*obs.*) to be a widow, a widower; **~ующая императри́ца** the Dowager Empress.

вдо́в|ый (~) *adj.* widowed.

вдого́нку *adv.* after, in pursuit of; **бро́ситься вдого́нку** (**за**+*i.*) to rush (after).

вдолб|и́ть, лю́, и́шь *pf.* (*of* **вда́лбливать**) (*coll.*) **в. кому́-н. в го́лову** to drum, din into s.o.'s head.

вдоль 1. *prep.* (+*g. or* **по**+*d.*) along; **в. бе́рега** along the bank; **я поплы́л в. по реке́** I sailed down the river. **2.** *adv.* lengthwise, longways; **разре́зать мате́рию в.** to cut material lengthwise; **в. и поперёк** in all directions, far and wide; **он зна́ет Шекспи́ра в. и поперёк** he knows Shakespeare inside out.

вдо́сталь *adv.* (*coll.*) = **вдо́воль**

вдох, а *m.* (*coll.*) breath; **сде́лать глубо́кий в.** to take a deep breath.

вдохнове́ни|е, я *nt.* inspiration.

вдохнове́нный *adj.* inspired.

вдохнови́тел|ь, я *m.* inspirer; inspiration (*of persons*); **он — наш в.** he is an inspiration to us.

вдохнов|и́ть, лю́, и́шь *pf.* (*of* **~ля́ть**) (+*a. or* **на**+*a.*) to inspire (to).

вдохновля́|ть, ю *impf. of* **вдохнови́ть**

вдохн|у́ть, у́, ёшь *pf.* (*of* **вдыха́ть**) (**в**+*a.*) **1.** to breathe in, inhale. **2.** to inspire (with), instil (into); **в. му́жество в кого́-н.** to instil courage into s.o.

вдре́безги *adv.* to pieces, to smithereens; **разби́ть в.** to smash to smithereens; **в. пьян** (*coll.*) dead drunk.

вдруг *adv.* **1.** suddenly, all of a sudden; **все в.** all together. **2.** *as interrog. particle* (*coll.*) what if, suppose; **а в. они́ узна́ют?** what if they find out?

вдува́|ть, ю *impf. of* **вдуть**

вду́м|аться, аюсь *pf.* (*of* **~ываться**) (**в**+*a.*) to think over, ponder, meditate (on).

вду́мчив|ый (~, ~а) *adj.* pensive; thoughtful.

вду́мыва|ться, юсь *impf. of* **вду́маться**

вду́н|уть, у, ешь *pf.* = **вдуть**

вду|ть, ~́ю, ~́ешь *pf.* (*of* **~ва́ть**) to blow into; **в. во́здух в ши́ну** to inflate, blow up a tyre.

вдыха́ни|е, я *nt.* inhalation.

вдыха́тельный *adj.* (*med.*) respiratory.

вдыха́|ть, ю *impf. of* **вдохну́ть**

вегетариа́н|ец, ца *m.* vegetarian.

вегетариа́нский *adj.* vegetarian.

вегетариа́нств|о, а *nt.* vegetarianism.

вегета́ци|я, и *f.* vegetation.

ве́да|ть, ю *impf.* (+*i.*) to manage, be in charge of.

ве́дени|е, я *nt.* authority; jurisdiction.

веде́ни|е, я *nt.* conduct; **в. де́ла** conduct of an affair.

ве́дома *only in phrr.*: **без в., с в.; без моего́ в.** unknown to me; **с моего́ в.** with my knowledge.

ве́домост|ь, и, *pl.* **~и, ~е́й** *f.* **1.** list, register; **платёжная в.** pay-roll; **в. расхо́дов** expense-sheet. **2.** (*pl. only*) Gazette; **Моско́вские ~и** Moscow Gazette.

ве́домственный *adj.* departmental.

ве́домств|о, а *nt.* department.

вед|ро́, ра́, *pl.* **~̈ра, ~ер** *nt.* bucket, pail.

вед|у́, ёшь *see* **вести́**
веду́щ|ий *pres. part. act. of* **вести́** *and adj.* leading; (*tech.*) **~ее колесо́** driving-wheel; *as n.* **в., ~его** *m.* presenter; compère; anchorman.
ведь *conj.* **1.** you see, you know; **она́ всё покупа́ет но́вые пла́тья — в. она́ о́чень бога́та** she is always buying new dresses — she is very rich, after all. **2.** is it not?; is it?; **в. э́то пра́вда?** it's the truth, isn't it?
ве́дьм|а, ы *f.* **1.** witch. **2.** (*coll.*) hag, harridan.
ве́дьм|овский *adj. of* **~а**
ведьмовско́й = ве́дьмовский
ве́ер, а, *pl.* **~а́** *m.* fan (*also fig.*); **обма́хиваться ~ом** to fan o.s.
веерообра́зный *adj.* fan-shaped.
ве́жливост|ь, и *f.* politeness, courtesy.
ве́жлив|ый (~, ~а) *adj.* polite, courteous.
везде́ *adv.* everywhere; **в. и всю́ду** here, there and everywhere.
вездесу́щ|ий (~, ~а) *adj.* ubiquitous; omnipresent.
вездехо́д, а *m.* (*mil.*) all-terrain vehicle (*abbr.* ATV).
везе́ни|е, я *nt.* luck.
вез|ти́, у́, ёшь, *past* **~, ~ла́** *impf.* (*of* **по~**) (*det. of* **вози́ть**) **1.** to cart, convey, carry (*of beasts of burden or vehicle*). **2.** (*coll.*) (*impers.+d.*) to have luck; **ему́ не ~ёт в ка́рты** he is unlucky at cards.
везу́чий *adj.* (*coll.*) lucky.
вей[1] *imper. of* **вить**
вей[2] *imper. of* **ве́ять**
век, а, о ~е, на ~у́, *pl.* **~а́** (*obs.* **~и**) *m.* **1.** century. **2.** age; **ка́менный в.** Stone Age; **сре́дние ~а́** the Middle Ages; **испоко́н ~о́в** from time immemorial; **отжи́ть свой в.** to have had one's day; **в кои-то ~и** once in a blue moon; **во ~и ~о́в** for all time; **в. живи́ — в. учи́сь!** (*prov.*) live and learn! **3.** life, lifetime; **на моём ~у́** in my lifetime. **4.** *as adv.* for ages; **мы с ва́ми в. не вида́лись** we haven't seen each other for ages.
ве́к|о, а, *pl.* **~и, ~** *nt.* eyelid.
веково́й *adj.* ancient, age-old.
векселеда́тел|ь, я *m.* (*comm.*) drawer (*of a bill*).
ве́ксел|ь, я, *pl.* **~я́** *m.* promissory note; bill of exchange.
вёл, ~а́ *see* **вести́**
веле́невый *adj.* vellum.
веле́ни|е, я *nt.* command, behest; dictates.
вел|е́ть, ю́, и́шь *impf. and pf.* (*+d. and inf. or* **что́бы**) **1.** to order; **я ~е́л ему́ сде́лать э́то** *or* **что́бы он сде́лал э́то** I ordered him to do this. **2.: не в.** to forbid.
велика́н, а *m.* giant.
вели́к|ий (~, ~а, ~о́) *adj.* **1.** (*short form* **~а, ~о**) great; **~ие держа́вы** the Great Powers; **Екатери́на Вели́кая** Catherine the Great. **2.** (*short form* **~а́, ~о́,** *pl.* **~и́**) big, large; **но́ги у неё о́чень ~и́** she has very big feet; **от ма́ла до ~а** (*coll.*) young and old. **3.** (*short form only*; **~а́, ~о́,** *pl.* **~и́**) (*+d. or* **для**) too big; **э́ти брю́ки мне ~и́** these trousers are too big for me.
Великобрита́ни|я, и *f.* Great Britain.
великоду́ши|е, я *nt.* magnanimity.
великоду́ш|ный (~ен, ~на) *adj.* magnanimous.
великоле́пи|е, я *nt.* splendour, magnificence.
великоле́п|ный (~ен, ~на) *adj.* **1.** splendid, magnificent. **2.** excellent, marvellous; **~ная иде́я** an excellent idea.
великопо́стный *adj.* (*eccl.*) Lenten.
велича́вост|ь, и *f.* stateliness, majesty.
велича́в|ый (~, ~а) *adj.* stately, majestic.
велича́йш|ий *adj.* (*superl. of* **вели́кий**) greatest, extreme; **де́ло ~ей ва́жности** a matter of supreme importance; **с ~им удово́льствием** with the greatest of pleasure.
велича́|ть, ю *impf.* (*folk poet.*) to sing the praises of.
вели́чественност|ь, и *f.* majesty, grandeur.
вели́чествен|ный (~, ~на) *adj.* majestic, grand.
вели́честв|о, а *nt.* majesty; **ва́ше в.** Your Majesty.
вели́чи|е, я *nt.* greatness; grandeur; **ма́ния ~я** megalomania.
величин|а́, ы́, *pl.* **~ы, ~а́м** *f.* **1.** size. **2.** (*math.*) quantity, magnitude; value; **постоя́нная в.** constant. **3.** great figure; **литерату́рная в.** an eminent literary figure.
вело... *comb. form* bicycle-, cycle-.
велодро́м, а *m.* cycle track; velodrome.
велокро́сс, а *m.* cyclo-cross.
велосипе́д, а *m.* bicycle; cycle; **па́рный в.** tandem.
велосипеди́ст, а *m.* bicyclist; cyclist.
велосипе́д|ный *adj. of* **~**
велотренажёр, а *m.* exercycle, exercise bicycle.
велофигури́ст, а *m.* trick cyclist.
вельве́т, а *m.* velveteen; **в. в ру́бчик** corduroy.
вельве́товый *adj.* velveteen; corduroy.
вельмо́ж|а, и *m.* (*iron.*) grandee.
вельмо́ж|ный *adj. of* **~а**
веля́рный *adj.* (*ling.*) velar.
Ве́н|а, ы *f.* Vienna.
ве́н|а, ы *f.* (*anat.*) vein; **расшире́ние ~** varicose veins.
венге́р|ка, ки *f.* **1.** *f. of* **венгр. 2.** Hungarian dance. **3.** dolman (*jacket*).
венге́рск|ий *adj.* Hungarian.
венгр, а *m.* Hungarian.
Ве́нгри|я, и *f.* Hungary.
венери́ческий *adj.* (*med.*) venereal.
ве́н|ец, ца *m.* Viennese.
вен|е́ц, ца́ *m.* **1.** crown; (*fig.*) completion, consummation. **2.** (*fig.*) wedding; **вести́ под в.** to marry, lead to the altar. **3.** (*poet.*) wreath, garland. **4.** (*astron.*) corona.
венециа́н|ец, ца *m.* Venetian.
венециа́н|ка, ки *f. of* **~ец**
венециа́нск|ий *adj.* Venetian.
Вене́ци|я, и *f.* Venice.
вене́чный *adj.* **1.** (*anat.*) coronary. **2.** *adj. of* **вене́ц**
ве́нзел|ь, я, *pl.* **~я́, ~е́й** *m.* monogram; **~я́ писа́ть** (*coll.*) to walk unsteadily (*of a drunken person*).
ве́ник, а *m.* besom.
ве́н|ка, ки *f. of* **~ец**
вен|о́зный *adj. of* **~а**; venous.
вен|о́к, ка́ *m.* wreath, garland.
ве́нск|ий *adj.* Viennese.
вентили́р|овать, ую *impf.* (*of* **про~**) to ventilate (*also fig.*).
ве́нтил|ь, я *m.* (*tech.*) valve; (*mus.*) mute.
вентиля́тор, а *m.* ventilator; extractor (fan).
вентиля́ци|я, и *f.* ventilation.
венцено́с|ец, ца *m.* (*epithet of monarch*; *rhet.*) wearer of crown, crowned head.
венча́|льный *adj. of* **~ние; ~льное кольцо́** wedding ring; **в. наря́д** wedding dress.
венча́ни|е, я *nt.* **1.: в. на ца́рство** coronation. **2.** wedding ceremony.
венча́|ть, ю *impf.* **1.** (*pf.* **в.** *and* **у~**) to crown. **2.** (*pf.* **у~**) (*fig.*) to crown; **коне́ц ~ет де́ло** all's well that ends well. **3.** (*pf.* **об~** *and* **по~**) to marry.
венча́|ться, юсь *impf.* **1.** (*pf.* **об~** *and* **по~**) to be married, marry. **2.** *pass. of* **~ть**
ве́нчик, а *m.* **1.** *dim. of* **вене́ц. 2.** (*bot.*) corolla.
ве́нчурный *adj.* venture; **в. капита́л** venture capital.
вепр|ь, я *m.* wild boar.
ве́р|а, ы *f.* (**в**+*a.*) faith, belief (in); **приня́ть на ~у** to take on trust; **дать ~у** (*+d.*) to give credence (to).
вера́нд|а, ы *f.* veranda.
ве́рб|а, ы *f.* willow; willow-branch.
verbе́н|а, ы *f.* (*bot.*) verbena.
верблю́д, а *m.* camel; **одного́рбый в.** dromedary;

двугóрбый в. Bactrian camel.
верблюжа́тник, а *m.* camel driver.
верблю|жий *adj. of* **~д; ~жья шерсть** camel's hair.
верблюж|óнок, óнка, *pl.* **~áта, ~áт** *m.* camel foal.
вéрб|ный *adj. of* **~а; ~ное воскресéнье** (*eccl.*) Palm Sunday.
верб|овáть, ýю *impf.* (*of* **за~** *and* **на~**) to recruit, enlist; (*fig.*) to win over.
вербóвк|а, и *f.* recruiting.
вербóвщик, а *m.* recruiter.
вéрбов|ый *adj.* willow; osier; **~ая корзи́на** wicker basket.
верди́кт, а *m.* verdict.
верёвк|а, и *f.* cord, rope; string; (*fig.*) noose; **в. для белья́** clothes-line.
верёв|очный *adj. of* **~ка**
верени́ц|а, ы *f.* row, file, line; **в. лошадéй** a string of horses; **в. идéй** a series of ideas.
вéреск, а *m.* (*bot.*) heather.
веретен|ó, á, *pl.* **веретёна, веретён** *nt.* spindle.
верещ|áть, ý, и́шь *impf.* (*coll.*) to squeal; to chirp (*of a cricket, etc.*).
верзи́л|а, ы *c.g.* (*coll.*) lanky person.
вери́г|и, ~ *pl.* (*sg.* **~а, ~и** *f.*) chains, fetters (*worn by ascetics*; *also fig.*).
вери́тельн|ый *adj.*: **~ая грáмота** (*dipl.*) credentials.
вéр|ить, ю, ишь *impf.* (*of* **по~**) (*+d. or* **в***+a.*) to believe, have faith (in); to trust (in); **в. в Бóга** to believe in God; **в. в привидéния** to believe in ghosts; **э́тому человéку никтó не ~ит** no one believes that man; **он не ~ит своéй женé** he does not trust his wife; **в. нá слово** to take on trust; **я не ~ил свои́м глазáм** I could not believe my eyes.
вéр|иться, ится *impf.* (*impers.+d.*): **мне ~ится с трудóм** I find it hard to believe.
вермишéл|ь, и *f.* vermicelli.
вéрмут, а *m.* vermouth.
верн|ée *adv.* (*comp. of* **~о**) rather; **писáтель и́ли, в., писáка** a writer or, rather, a hack.
вернисáж, а *m.* **1.** private viewing. **2.** opening-day (*of an exhibition*).
вéрн|о *adv. of* **~ый**; *as particle* (*coll.*) probably, I suppose; **вы, в., ужé слыхáли нóвости** you have probably already heard the news.
вéрност|ь, и *f.* **1.** faithfulness, loyalty. **2.** truth, correctness.
верн|ýть, ý, ёшь *pf.* (*of* **возвращáть**) **1.** to give back, return. **2.** to get back, recover, retrieve; **в. здорóвье** to recover one's health.
верн|ýться, ýсь, ёшься *pf.* (*of* **возвращáться**) to return, revert (*also fig.*); **в. домóй** to return home.
вéр|ный (~ен, ~нá, ~но) *adj.* **1.** faithful, loyal, true; **в. свои́м убеждéниям** true to one's convictions. **2.** true, correct; **в. слух** a good ear; **~ны ли вáши часы́?** is your watch right? **3.** sure, reliable; **~ная кóпия** faithful copy; **в. при́знак** sure sign. **4.** certain, sure; **~ная смерть** certain death.
вéровани|е, я *nt.* belief, creed.
вéр|овать, ую *impf.* (**в***+a.*) to believe (in).
вероисповéдани|е, я *nt.* creed, denomination; **свобóда ~я** freedom of religion.
верол óм|ный (~ен, ~на) *adj.* treacherous, perfidious.
веролóмств|о, а *nt.* treachery, perfidy.
вероотстýпник, а *m.* apostate.
вероотстýпничеств|о, а *nt.* apostasy.
вероучéни|е, я *nt.* (*relig.*) dogma.
вероя́ти|е, я *nt.*: **по всемý ~ю** in all probability.
вероя́тно *adv.* probably.
вероя́тност|ь, и *f.* probability; **по всей ~и** in all probability.
вероя́т|ный (~ен, ~на) *adj.* probable, likely; **э́то вполнé ~но** it is highly probable; **в. наслéдник** heir presumptive.
вéрси|я, и *f.* version.
верст|á, ы́, *a.* **~ý** *and* **~у,** *pl.* **~ы, ~** *f.* verst (*old Russ. measurement, equivalent to approx. 1 kilometre*); verst-post; **зá ~у** (*coll.*) far off; **колóменская в.** (*coll.*) beanpole, lanky person.
верстáк, á *m.* (*tech.*) joiner's *or* locksmith's bench.
верстá|ть, ю *impf.* (*of* **с~**) (*typ.*) to impose, make up into pages.
вёрстк|а, и *f.* (*typ.*) **1.** imposing, imposition. **2.** made-up matter.
верст|овóй *adj. of* **~á; в. столб** milestone.
вéртел, а *m.* spit; skewer.
вертéп, а *m.* cave, den (*of thieves, etc.*).
вер|тéть, чý, ~тишь *impf.* (*+a. or i.*) to twirl, turn round and round; **в. трóстью** to twirl a cane; **онá ~тит им, как хóчет** she can twist him round her little finger.
вер|тéться, чýсь, ~тишься *impf.* **1.** to rotate, turn (round), revolve (*also fig.*); **егó фами́лия ~тéлась у меня́ на кóнчике языкá** his name was on the tip of my tongue; **в. под ногáми** (*coll.*) to be under one's feet. **2.** (*coll.*) to move (among), mix (with); **он бóльшей чáстью ~тится среди́ инострáнцев** he mixes mostly with foreigners. **3.** (*coll.*) to fidget. **4.** (*coll.*) to prevaricate.
вертикáл|ь, и *f.* vertical line; file (*on chessboard*).
вертикáльный *adj.* (*math.*) vertical.
вертихвóстк|а, и *f.* (*coll.*) flirt, coquette.
вёрт|кий (~ок, ~кá, ~ко) *adj.* (*coll.*) nimble, agile.
вертлю́г, á *m.* **1.** (*anat.*) head of the femur. **2.** (*tech.*) swivel.
вертлю́|жный *adj. of* **~г**
вертля́в|ый (~, ~а) *adj.* (*coll.*) **1.** restless, fidgety. **2.** flighty, frivolous.
вертодрóм, а *m.* heliport.
вертолёт, а *m.* helicopter; **боевóй в.** helicopter gunship, combat helicopter.
вертýшк|а, и *f.* (*coll.*) **1.** revolving object (*e.g. door, bookcase*). **2.** whirligig, teetotum (*toy*). **3.** flirt, coquette. **4.** turntable.
вéр|ующий *pres. part. act. of* **~овать**; *as n.* **в., ~ующего** *m.* believer.
верф|ь, и *f.* dockyard; shipyard.
верх, а, *pl.* **~и́** *m.* **1.** top, summit (*also fig.*); **совещáние в ~áх** (*pol.*) summit conference; **в. глýпости** the height of folly. **2.** upper part, upper side; bonnet, hood (*of vehicle*); **«верх!»** (*sign*) 'this side up'; (*fig.*) **~и́** (*pl. only*) upper crust (*of society*); (*mus.*) high notes; **взять, одержáть в. (над)** to gain the upper hand (over). **3.** outside, top; right side (*of material*); **хватáть ~и́, нахватáться ~óв** (*fig., coll.*) to get a smattering (of), acquire a superficial knowledge (of).
вéрхн|ий *adj.* upper; **~яя одéжда** outer clothing; **~яя палáта** (*pol.*) upper chamber; **в. я́щик** top drawer.
верхóвн|ый *adj.* supreme; **~ое комáндование** high command; **В. Совéт** Supreme Soviet.
верховóд, а *m.* (*coll.*) boss, leader.
верховó|дить, жу, дишь *impf.* (*+i.*; *coll.*) to lord it over, boss around.
верх|овóй[1] *adj. of* **~óм; ~овáя ездá** (horseback) riding; **~овáя лóшадь** saddle-horse; *as n.* **в., ~овóго** *m.* rider.
верховóй[2] *adj.* up-river.
верхóвь|е, я, *g. pl.* **~ев** *nt.* upper reaches.
верхогля́д, а *m.* (*coll.*) superficial person.
верхогля́дств|о, а *nt.* (*coll.*) superficiality.
верхолáз, а *m.* steeplejack.
вéрхом *adv.* **1.** on high ground. **2.** quite full, brimfull; **нали́ть стакáн в.** to pour out a full glass.
верхóм *adv.* astride; on horseback; **éздить в.** to ride.
верхýшк|а, и *f.* **1.** top, summit; apex. **2.** (*fig., coll.*)

bosses; **профсою́зная в.** trade-union bosses.
вер|чу́, ∽тишь *see* **∽тéть**
вéрш|а, и *f.* fish-trap.
верши́н|а, ы *f.* **1.** top, summit; peak; (*fig.*) peak, acme. **2.** (*math.*) vertex; apex.
верш|и́ть у́, и́шь *impf.* **1.** (+*i.*) to manage, control; **в. всéми делáми** to run the whole show. **2.** (+*a.*) to decide.
верш|óк, кá *m.* vershok (*old Russ. measure of length, equivalent to 4.4 cm*).
вес, а, *pl.* **∽á** *m.* **1.** weight; **ли́шний в.** excess baggage; (*fig.*) weight, authority; **∽ом в сто фу́нтов** weighing a hundred pounds; **держáться на ∽у́** to be balanced; **прибáвить, убáвить в ∽е** to put on, lose weight. **2.** system of weights; **аптéкарский в.** apothecaries' weight. **3.: удéльный в.** specific gravity.
веселé|ть, ю *impf.* (*of* **по∽**) to become gay, become bright.
весел|и́ть, ю́, и́шь *impf.* (*of* **по∽**) to cheer, gladden; to amuse.
весел|и́ться, ю́сь, и́шься *impf.* (*of* **по∽**) to enjoy o.s.; to amuse o.s.
вéсело *adv.* gaily, merrily; *as pred.* (+*d.*) to enjoy o.s.; **мне в. бы́ло смотрéть на вас** I enjoyed seeing you.
весёлост|ь, и *f.* gaiety; cheerfulness.
весёл|ый (вéсел, ∽á, вéсело) *adj.* gay, merry; cheerful; **у негó ∽ое настроéние сегóдня** he is in good spirits today.
весéл|ье, ья, *g. pl.* **∽ий** *nt.* gaiety, merriment.
вес|éльный *adj. of* **∽лó; ∽éльная лóдка** rowing-boat.
вёсельный = весéльный
весельчáк, á *m.* (*coll.*) convivial fellow.
вес|éнний *adj. of* **∽нá**; vernal.
вé|сить, шу, сишь *impf.* to weigh (*intrans.*); **∽сит три тóнны** it weighs three tons.
вéс|кий (∽ок, ∽ка) *adj.* weighty.
вес|лó, лá, *pl.* **∽̈ла, ∽̈ел, ∽̈лам** *nt.* oar; scull; paddle; **подня́ть ∽̈ла** to rest on one's oars.
вес|нá, ны́, *pl.* **∽̈ны, ∽̈ен, ∽̈нам** *f.* spring (*season*).
весну́ш|ки, ек *pl.* (*sg.* **∽ка, ∽ки** *f.*) freckles.
весну́шчатый *adj.* freckled.
весóм|ый (∽, ∽а) *adj.* (*phys.*) ponderable; (*fig.*) weighty; heavy.
вест, а *m.* (*naut.*) **1.** west. **2.** west wind.
вéстерн, а *m.* western (*film*).
ве|сти́, ду́, дёшь, *past* **∽̈л, ∽лá** *impf.* (*det. of* **води́ть**) **1.** (*pf.* **по∽**) to lead; to conduct; to take. **2.** (*pf.* **про∽**) (+*i.* **по**+*d.*) to run (over), pass (over, across); **в. смычкóм по стру́нам** to run one's bow over the strings. **3.** (*pf.* **про∽**) to conduct; to carry on; **в. войну́** to wage war; **в. огóнь** (**по**+*d.*) to fire (on); **в. переговóры** to carry on negotiations; **в. перепи́ску** (**с**+*i.*) to correspond (with); **в. прáвильный óбраз жи́зни** to lead a regular life. **4.** (*impf. only*) to drive; **в. корáбль** to navigate a ship; **в. самолёт** to pilot an aircraft. **5.** (*impf. only*) to conduct, direct, run; **в. дéло** to run a business; **в. хозя́йство** to keep house. **6.** (*impf. only*) to keep, conduct; **в. кни́ги** to keep books, keep accounts; **в. протокóл** to keep minutes. **7.** (*impf. only*): **в. себя́** to behave, conduct o.s. **8.** (*impf. only*) (**к**) to lead (to) (*also fig.*); **кудá ∽дёт э́та дорóга?** where does this road lead (to)? **9.** (*impf. only*): **в. своё начáло (от)** to originate (in).
вестибю́л|ь, я *m.* hall, lobby.
вест-и́ндский *adj.* West Indian.
ве|сти́сь, ду́сь, дёшься, *past* **вёлся, ∽лáсь** *impf.* (*of* **по∽**) **1.** *pass. of* **∽сти́. 2.** (*usu. impers.*; *coll.*) to be observed (*of customs, etc.*); **так ∽дётся ужé три́ста лет** this has been the custom for three hundred years.
вéстник, а *m.* **1.** messenger, herald. **2.** (*in title of publications*) Bulletin.
вéстни|ца, ицы *f. of* **∽к 1.**
вéсточк|а, и *f.* (*coll.*) news; **дáйте о себé ∽у, как тóлько приéдете** drop me a line as soon as you arrive.
вест|ь[1], и, *pl.* **∽и, ∽éй** *f.* (piece of) news; **пропáсть бéз ∽и** (*mil.*) to be missing (in action).
весть[2] *only in phrr.*: **Бог в.** God knows; **не в. что** goodness knows, heaven knows what; **не (Бог) в. какóй** trifling, insignificant.
вес|ы́, óв *no sg.* **1.** scales, balance; **пружи́нные в.** spring balance. **2. В.** the Scales, Libra (*sign of the Zodiac*).
весь, вся, всё, *g.* **всегó, всей, всегó,** *pl.* **все, всех** *pron.* all; **весь день** all day; **вся Фрáнция** the whole of France; **он весь в отцá** he is the image of his father; **вы́йти весь** to be used up; **бумáга вся вы́шла** the paper is all used up; **во в. гóлос** at the top of one's voice; **во всю мочь** with all one's might; **от всегó сéрдца** from the bottom of one's heart, with all one's heart; **при всём том** for all that, moreover; **вот и всё** that's all; **всегó (хорóшего)!** good-bye!, all the best!; *as n.* **всё, всегó** *nt.* everything; **все, всех** *no sg.* all, everyone; **всем, всем, всем!** attention, everyone!
весьмá *adv.* very, highly.
ветви́ст|ый (∽, ∽а) *adj*: branchy, spreading.
ветврáч, á *m.* vet.
ветв|ь, и, *pl.* **∽и, ∽éй** *f.* branch, bough; (*fig.*) branch.
вéт|ер, ра *m.* **1.** wind; (*fig.*) **бросáть словá на в.** to talk idly; **у негó в. в головé** he is a thoughtless fellow; **подби́тый ∽ром** (*coll.*) (*i*) empty-headed, (*ii*) light, flimsy.
ветерáн, а *m.* veteran.
ветеринáр, а *m.* veterinary surgeon.
ветѐринáри|я, и *f.* veterinary science; veterinary medicine.
ветеринáрный *adj.* veterinary.
ветер|óк, кá *m.* breeze.
вéтк|а, и *f.* branch; twig; **железнодорóжная в.** branch-line.
вет|лá, лы́, *pl.* **∽̈лы, ∽̈ел** *f.* (*bot.*) white willow.
вéто *nt. indecl.* veto; **наложи́ть в.** (**на**+*a.*) to veto.
вéточк|а, и *f.* twig, sprig, shoot.
вéтош|ь, и *f.* old clothes, rags.
вéтреник, а *m.* (*coll.*) empty-headed, frivolous person.
вéтрени|ца[1], цы *f. of* **∽к**
вéтрениц|а[2], ы *f.* (*bot.*) anemone.
вéтрен|ый (∽, ∽а) *adj.* **1.** windy; **зáвтра бу́дет ∽о** it will be windy tomorrow. **2.** (*fig.*) empty-headed, frivolous.
ветровóй *adj. of* **вéтер**
ветромéр, а *m.* (*phys.*) anemometer.
ветря́нк|а, и *f.* (*coll.*) chicken-pox.
ветрян|óй *adj.* wind(-powered); **∽áя мéльница** windmill.
вéтрян|ый *adj.*: **∽ая óспа** chicken-pox.
вéтх|ий (∽, ∽á, ∽о) *adj.* old, ancient; dilapidated, tumbledown; **В. завéт** the Old Testament.
ветхозавéтный *adj.* Old Testament; (*fig.*) antiquated.
вéтхост|ь, и *f.* decrepitude; dilapidation.
ветчин|á, ы́ *no pl.*, *f.* ham.
ветчи́н|ный *adj. of* **∽á**
ветшá|ть, ю *impf.* (*of* **об∽**) to decay; to become dilapidated; to become decrepit.
вéх|а, и *f.* landmark (*also fig.*); milestone.
вéч|е, а *nt.* (*hist.*) veche (*popular assembly in medieval Russ. towns*).
вéчер, а, *pl.* **∽á** *m.* **1.** evening; **по ∽áм** in the evenings. **2.** party; evening, soirée.
вечерé|ть, ет *impf.* (*impers.*) to grow dark; **∽ет** night is falling.
вечери́нк|а, и *f.* (evening-)party.
вечéрн|ий *adj. of* **вéчер; ∽яя заря́** twilight, dusk;

~ие кýрсы evening classes; **~яя шкóла** night-school.
вечéр|ня, ни, *g. pl.* **~ен** *f.* (*eccl.*) vespers.
вéчером *adv.* in the evening.
вéчер|я, и *f.*: **Тáйная в.** (*bibl.*) the Last Supper.
вéчно *adv.* for ever, eternally; always; **онú в. ссóрятся** they are always quarrelling.
вечнозелёный *adj.* (*bot.*) evergreen.
вéчност|ь, и *f.* eternity; **кáнуть в в.** to sink into oblivion; **цéлую в.** (*coll.*) for ages.
вéч|ный (~ен, ~на) *adj.* **1.** eternal, everlasting; **~ная мерзлотá** permafrost; **заснýть ~ным сном** to take one's last sleep. **2.** endless; perpetual.
вéшалк|а, и *f.* **1.** peg, rack, stand. **2.** tab (*on clothes for hanging on pegs*). **3.** cloak-room.
вéша|ть[1], ю *impf.* (*of* **повéсить**) to hang; **в. бельё на верёвку** to hang washing on a line.
вéша|ть[2], ю *impf.* (*of* **взвéсить**) to weigh, weigh out; **в. фунт кóфе** to weigh out a pound of coffee.
вéша|ться[1], юсь *impf.* (*of* **повéситься**) **1.** *pass. of* **~ть[1]**; to be hung; to be hanged. **2.** to hang o.s. **3.**: **в. на шéю комý-н.** (*coll.*) to run after; **онá всё ~ется молоды́м офицéрам на шéю** she is always running after young officers.
вéша|ться[2], юсь *impf.* (*of* **с~**) to weigh o.s.
вé|шу, сишь *see* **~сить**
веш|ý, úшь *see* **~úть**
вещáни|е, я *nt.* **1.** prophesying. **2.** (*radio*) broadcasting.
вещá|ть, ю *impf.* **1.** (*coll.*) to pontificate, lay down the law. **2.** (*radio*) to broadcast.
вещ|евóй *adj. of* **~ь; в. мешóк** hold-all; kit-bag; **в. склад** storage warehouse, store; (*mil.*) stores.
вещéственн|ый *adj.* material; **~ые доказáтельства** material evidence.
веществ|ó, á *nt.* substance; matter; **взры́вчатое в.** explosive; **питáтельное в.** nutrient.
вещúзм, а *m.* materialism.
вéщий *adj.* (*poet.*) prophetic.
вещ|úца, úцы *f. dim. of* **~ь**; little thing; bagatelle.
вещ|ь, и, *pl.* **~и, ~éй** *f.* **1.** (*in var. senses*) thing; **э́то в.!** (*expr. approval*; *coll.*) that's quite sth.! **2.** (*pl.*) things (= (*i*) *belongings*; *baggage*; (*ii*) *clothes*); **со всéми ~áми** bag and baggage. **3.** (*of artistic productions*) work; piece.
вéялк|а, и *f.* (*agric.*) winnowing-fan; winnowing-machine.
вéяни|е, я *nt.* **1.** (*agric.*) winnowing. **2.** blowing (*of wind*). **3.** (*fig.*) current (*of opinion*), tendency, trend.
вé|ять, ю, ешь *impf.* **1.** (*agric.*) to winnow. **2.** (*intrans.*) to blow (*of wind*); **~ял прохлáдный ветерóк** a cool breeze was blowing; (*impers.*,+*i.*): **~ет веснóй** spring is in the air; **~ет нóвыми идéями** new ideas are in the air. **3.** to wave, flutter.
вживá|ться, юсь *impf. of* **вжúться**
вжú|ться, вýсь, вёшься *pf.* (**в**+*a.*; *coll.*) to get used (to); **он с трудóм ~вётся в воéнную жизнь** he will find it hard to get used to army life.
взад *adv.* (*coll.*) back; **в. и вперёд** backwards and forwards, to and fro.
взаúмност|ь, и *f.* reciprocity; return (*of affection*); **отвечáть комý-н. ~ью** to reciprocate s.o.'s feelings; **любóвь без ~и** unrequited love.
взаúм|ный (~ен, ~на) *adj.* mutual, reciprocal.
взаимодéйстви|е, я *nt.* interaction; (*mil.*) co-operation, co-ordination.
взаимодéйств|овать, ую *impf.* to interact; (*mil.*) to co-operate.
взаимоотношéни|е, я *nt.* interrelation.
взаимопóмощ|ь, и *f.* mutual aid; mutual assistance.
взаимосвя́з|ь, и *f.* interrelationship.
взаймы́ *adv.*: **взять в.** to borrow; **дать в.** to lend, loan.
взамéн *prep.*+*g.* instead (of); in return (for), in exchange (for).
взапертú *adv.* **1.** under lock and key. **2.** in seclusion.
взáпуски *adv.*: **бéгать в.** to chase one another.
взбáдрива|ть, ю *impf. of* **взбодрúть**
взбаламý|тить, чу, тишь *pf. of* **баламýтить**
взбáлмошный *adj.* (*coll.*) unbalanced, eccentric.
взбáлтыва|ть, ю *impf. of* **взболтáть**
взбегá|ть, ю *impf.* (*of* **взбежáть**) to run up; **в. по лéстнице** to run upstairs.
взбе|жáть, гý, жúшь, гýт *pf. of* **~гáть**
взбелен|úться, ю́сь úшься *pf.* (**на**+*a.*; *coll.*) to become enraged (with).
взбе|сúть(ся), шý(сь), ~сишь(ся) *pf. of* **бесúть(ся)**
взбивá|ть, ю *impf. of* **взбить**
взбирá|ться, юсь *impf. of* **взобрáться**
взбúт|ый (~, ~а) *p.p.p. of* **~ь; ~ые сли́вки** whipped cream.
вз|бить, обью́, обьёшь *pf.* (*of* **~бивáть**) **1.** to beat up; **в. сли́вки** to whip cream. **2.** to fluff (up).
взбодр|úть, ю *pf.* (*of* **взбáдривать**) to cheer up; to encourage.
взболтá|ть, ю *pf.* (*of* **взбáлтывать**) to shake (up) (*liquids*).
взбороз|дúть, жý, дúшь *pf. of* **бороздúть**
взборон|úть, ю́, úшь *pf. of* **боронúть**
взбредá|ть, ю *impf. of* **взбрестú**
взбре|стú, дý, дёшь, *past* **взбрёл, ~лá** *pf.* (*of* **~дáть**) (**на**+*a.*; *coll.*) to mount with difficulty; **в. в гóлову, на ум** to come into one's head; **емý ~лó на ум, что все егó ненавúдят** he got it into his head that everyone hated him.
взбудорáж|ить, у, ишь *pf. of* **будорáжить**
взбунт|овáть(ся), ýю(сь) *pf. of* **бунтовáть(ся)**
взбух|áть, áю *impf. of* **~нуть**
взбýх|нуть, ну, нешь, *past* **~, ~ла** *pf.* (*of* **~áть**) to swell out.
взбýчк|а, и *f.* (*coll.*) **1.** thrashing, beating. **2.** reprimand; **получúть ~у** to be hauled over the coals.
взвáлива|ть, ю *impf. of* **взвалúть**
взвал|úть, ю́ ~ишь *pf.* (*of* **~ивать**) to load, lift (onto); **всю рабóту ~úли на нóвого учúтеля** (*coll.*) the new teacher was loaded with all the work; **всю винý ~úли на негó** he was made to shoulder all the blame.
взвé|сить, шу, сишь *pf.* (*of* **~шивать** *and* **вéшать**) to weigh; (*fig.*) to weigh, consider.
взве|стú, дý, дёшь, *past* **~л, ~лá** *pf.* (*of* **взводúть**) **1.** to lead up, take up; **в. курóк (ружья́)** to cock (a gun). **2.** (**на**+*a.*) to impute (to); **на генерáла ~лú обвинéние в поражéнии** blame for the defeat was laid at the general's door.
взвéшен|ный (~, ~а, ~о) *adj.* carefully thought out.
взвéшива|ть, ю *impf. of* **взвéсить**
взвивá|ть(ся), ю(сь) *impf. of* **взвúть(ся)**
взвизг, а *m.* (*coll.*) scream; yelp (*of a dog*).
взвúзгива|ть, ю *impf. and freq. of* **взвúзгнуть**
взвúзгн|уть, у, ешь *pf.* to scream, cry out; to yelp (*of a dog*).
взвин|тúть, чý, тúшь *pf.* (*of* **взвúнчивать**) (*coll.*) to excite, work up; **в. цéны** to inflate prices.
взвúнчен|ный (~, ~а) *p.p.p. of* **взвинтúть** *and adj.* excited, worked up; highly-strung, nervy; **нéрвы у негó всегдá ~ы** he is always on edge; **~ные цéны** inflated prices.
взвúнчива|ть, ю *impf. of* **взвинтúть**
взвить, взовью́, взовьёшь *pf.* (*of* **взвивáть**) to raise.
взвúться, взовью́сь, взовьёшься *pf.* (*of* **взвивáться**) to rise; to fly up, soar (*of birds*); to be raised, go up (*of flags, etc.*); **зáнавес взвúлся рóвно в вóсемь часóв** the curtain went up at eight o'clock exactly.
взвод[1], а *m.* (*mil.*) platoon.

взвод[2], **а** *m.* (cocking) notch (*of guns*); **на боево́м ~е** cocked; **на пе́рвом ~е** at half-cock; **быть на ~е** (*coll.*) to be in one's cups.
взво|ди́ть, жу́, ~дишь *impf. of* **взвести́**
взво́д|ный *adj. of* ~[1]; *as n.* **в., ~ного** *m.* platoon commander.
взволно́ван|ный (~, ~а) *p.p.p. of* **взволнова́ть** *and adj.* agitated, disturbed; anxious, worried.
взволн|ова́ть, у́ю *pf. of* **волнова́ть**
взволн|ова́ться, у́юсь *pf. of* **волнова́ться**
взво́|ю, ешь *see* **взвыть**
взвыва́|ть, ю *impf. of* **взвыть**
взв|ыть, о́ю, о́ешь *pf.* (*of* **~ыва́ть**) to howl.
взгляд, а *m.* **1.** look; glance; gaze, stare; **бро́сить в.** (**на**+*a.*) to glance (at); **на в.** to judge from appearances; **на пе́рвый в., с пе́рвого ~а** at first sight. **2.** view; opinion; **на мой в.** in my opinion.
взгля́дыва|ть, ю *impf. of* **взгляну́ть**
взглян|у́ть, у́, ~ешь *pf.* (**на**+*a.*) to look (at); to cast a glance (at).
взгромозжда́|ть, ю *impf. of* **взгромозди́ть**
взгромозжда́|ться, юсь *impf. of* **взгромозди́ться**
взгромоз|ди́ть, жу́, ди́шь *pf.* (*coll.*) to pile up.
взгромоз|ди́ться, жу́сь, ди́шься *pf.* (*coll.*) to clamber up.
взгрустн|у́ть, у́, ёшь *pf.* (*coll.*) to feel sad, depressed.
взгрустн|у́ться, ётся *pf.* (*impers.*, +*d.*; *coll.*) to feel sad, depressed; **ему́ ~у́лось** he feels depressed.
вздёргива|ть, ю *impf. of* **вздёрнуть**
вздёрнут|ый (~, ~а) *p.p.p. of* **~ь; в. нос** snub nose.
вздёрн|уть, у, ешь *pf.* (*coll.*) **1.** to hitch up; to jerk up. **2.** to hang.
вздор, а *no pl.*, *m.* (*coll.*) nonsense; **городи́ть, моло́ть в.** to talk nonsense.
вздо́р|ить, ю, ишь *impf.* (*of* **по~**) (*coll.*) to squabble.
вздо́р|ный (~ен, ~на) *adj.* (*coll.*) **1.** foolish, stupid. **2.** cantankerous, quarrelsome.
вздорожа́|ть, ю *pf. of* **дорожа́ть**
вздох, а *m.* sigh; deep breath; **испусти́ть после́дний в.** to breathe one's last.
вздохн|у́ть, у́, ёшь *pf.* (*of* **вздыха́ть**) **1.** to sigh. **2.** (*coll.*) to take breath; **дава́йте ~ём!** let's pause for breath!
вздра́гива|ть, ю *impf.* (*of* **вздро́гнуть**) to shudder, quiver.
вздремн|у́ть, у́, ёшь *pf.* (*coll.*) to have a nap, doze.
вздро́гн|уть, у, ешь *pf.* (*of* **вздра́гивать**) to start; to wince, flinch.
вздува́|ть, ю *impf. of* **вздуть**[1]
взду́ма|ть, ю *pf.* (+*inf.*; *coll.*) to take it into one's head; **не ~й(те)** mind you don't; **не ~йте ныря́ть здесь!** don't try to dive in here!
взду́ма|ться, ется *pf.* (*impers.*, +*d.*; *coll.*) to take it into one's head; **ему́ ~лось пое́хать в Аме́рику** he took it into his head to go to America.
взду́ти|е, я *nt.* (*med.*) swelling.
взду́т|ый (~, ~а) *p.p.p. of* **~ь** *and adj.* swollen.
взду́|ть, ю, ешь *pf.* (*of* **вздува́ть**) to blow up, inflate.
взду́|ться, юсь, ешься *pf.* to swell (*intrans.*).
вздыма́|ть, ю *impf.* to raise.
вздыма́|ться, юсь *impf.* to rise; **~лась мгла над о́зером** mist was rising over the lake.
вздыха́|ть, ю *impf.* (*of* **вздохну́ть**) **1.** to breathe; to sigh. **2.** (**о, по**+*p.*) to pine (for); to long, sigh (for).
взима́|ть, ю *impf.* to levy, collect, raise (*taxes*).
взла́мыва|ть, ю *impf. of* **взлома́ть**
взлеза́|ть, ю *impf. of* **взлезть**
взлез|ть, у, ешь, *past* **~, ~ла** *pf.* (*of* **~а́ть**) to climb up.
взлеле́|ять, ю, ешь *pf. of* **леле́ять**
взлёт, а *m.* (upward) flight (*also fig.*); (*aeron.*) take-off; **в. фанта́зии** flight of fancy.
взлета́|ть, ю *impf. of* **взлете́ть**
взле|те́ть, чу́, ти́шь *pf.* (*of* **~га́ть**) to fly up; to take off; **в. на во́здух** to explode, blow up (*also fig.*).
взлёт|ный *adj. of* ~; (*aeron.*): **~ная доро́жка** runway; **~но-поса́дочная полоса́** landing strip.
взлом, а *m.* breaking open, breaking in; **кра́жа со ~ом** house-breaking.
взлома́|ть, ю *pf.* (*of* **взла́мывать**) to break open, force; to smash; **в. замо́к** to force a lock.
взло́мщик, а *m.* burglar, house-breaker.
взлохма́|тить, чу, тишь *pf. of* **лохма́тить** *and* **~чивать**
взлохма́|ченный (~чен, ~чена) *p.p.p. of* **~тить** *and adj.* tousled; dishevelled.
взлохма́чива|ть, ю *impf.* to tousle.
взлюб|и́ть, лю́, ~ишь *pf.*, *only with neg.*; **не в. с пе́рвого взгля́да** to take an instant dislike (to).
взман|и́ть, ю́, и́шь *pf. of* **мани́ть 2.**
взмах, а *m.* wave (*of hand*); flap, flapping (*of wings*); stroke (*of oars, etc.*); **одни́м ~ом** at one stroke.
взма́хива|ть, ю *impf. of* **взмахну́ть**
взмахн|у́ть, у́, ёшь *pf.* (+*i.*) to wave, flap.
взметн|у́ть, у́, ёшь *pf.* (*of* **взмётывать**) (+*i.*) to throw up, fling up; **в. рука́ми** to fling up one's hands.
взметн|у́ться, у́сь ёшься *pf.* to leap up, fly up; **и́скры ~у́лись из-под копы́т коня́** sparks flew up from the horse's hoofs.
взмётыва|ть, ю *impf. of* **взметну́ть**
взмётыва|ться, юсь *impf. of* **взметну́ться**
взмол|и́ться, ю́сь, ~ишься *pf.* (**о**+*p.*) to beg (for); to beseech.
взмо́рь|е, я *nt.* sea-shore; seaside.
взму|ти́ть, чу́, ти́шь *pf. of* **мути́ть**
взмыва́|ть, ю *impf. of* **взмыть**
взмы́лива|ть(ся), ю(сь) *impf. of* **взмы́лить(ся)**
взм|ыть, о́ю, о́ешь *pf.* (*of* **~ыва́ть**) to soar (up).
взнос, а *m.* payment; fee, dues; subscription; **профсою́зный в.** trade-union dues.
взнузда́|ть, ю *pf.* to bridle.
взну́здыва|ть, ю *impf. of* **взнузда́ть**
взобра́|ться, взберу́сь, взберёшься, *past* **~лся, ~ла́сь** *pf.* (*of* **взбира́ться**) (**на**+*a.*) to climb (up), clamber (up).
взобь|ю́, ёшь *see* **взбить**
взовь|ю́, ёшь *see* **взвить**
взо|йти́, йду́, йдёшь, *past* **~шёл, ~шла́,** *p.p.* **~ше́дший** *pf.* (*of* **всходи́ть** *and* **восходи́ть**) (**на**+*a.*) to mount, ascend; to rise; **в. на трибу́ну** to mount the platform; **со́лнце ~шло́ в пять часо́в сего́дня** the sun rose at five o'clock today.
взор, а *m.* look; glance; **обрати́ть на себя́ ~ы пу́блики** to come into the public eye.
взорв|а́ть, у́, ёшь *pf.* (*of* **взрыва́ть**) **1.** to blow up; to detonate. **2.** (*fig.*) to exasperate, madden; (*impers.*): **его́ ~а́ло, когда́ они́ сообщи́ли о свое́й помо́лвке** he exploded when they announced their engagement.
взорв|а́ться, у́сь, ёшься *pf.* (*of* **взрыва́ться**) to blow up, burst, explode (*also fig.*).
взо|шёл, шла́ *see* **~йти́**
взра|сти́ть, щу́, сти́шь *pf.* to grow, cultivate; to bring up, nurture.
взра́щива|ть, ю *impf. of* **взрасти́ть**
взра|щу́, сти́шь *see* **~сти́ть**
взрев|е́ть, у́, ёшь *pf.* to let out a roar.
взре́ж|у, ешь *see* **взре́зать**
взре́|зать, жу, жешь *pf.* to cut open.
взреза́|ть, ю *impf. of* **взре́зать**
взре́зыва|ть, ю *impf.* = **взреза́ть**
взро́сл|ый *adj.* grown-up, adult; *as n.* **в., ~ого** *m.*; **~ая, ~ой** *f.*

взрыв, а *m.* explosion; (*fig.*) burst, outburst; **в. аплодисме́нтов** burst of applause.
взрыва́|ть[1], **ю** *impf. of* **взорва́ть**
взрыва́|ть[2] *impf. of* **взрыть**
взрыва́|ться, юсь *impf. of* **взорва́ться**
взрывн|о́й *adj.* explosive; **~а́я волна́** blast.
взрывоопа́сн|ый *adj.*: **~ая ситуа́ция** explosive situation.
взрывча́тк|а, и *f.* (*coll.*) explosive.
взры́вчат|ый *adj.* explosive; **~ое вещество́** explosive.
взр|ыть, о́ю, о́ешь *pf.* (*of* **~ыва́ть**[2]) to plough up, turn up.
взрыхл|и́ть, ю́, и́шь *pf.* to loosen, break up.
взрыхля́|ть, ю *impf. of* **взрыхли́ть**
взъеда́|ться, юсь *impf. of* **взъе́сться**
взъезжа́|ть, ю *impf. of* **взъе́хать**
взъерепе́н|иться, юсь ишься *pf. of* **ерепе́ниться**
взъеро́шен|ный (~, ~а) *p.p.p. of* **взъеро́шить** *and adj.* tousled, dishevelled.
взъеро́ш|ить, у, ишь *pf.* (*of* **~ивать**) (*coll.*) to tousle, rumple.
взъ|е́сться, е́мся, е́шься, е́стся, еди́мся, еди́тесь, едя́тся, *past* **~е́лся** *pf.* (*of* **~еда́ться**) (**на**+*a.*; *coll.*) to pitch into, go for (*fig.*).
взъе́|хать, ду, дешь *pf.* (*of* **~зжа́ть**) to mount, ascend (*in a vehicle or on an animal*).
взыва́|ть, ю *impf. of* **воззва́ть**
взыгра́|ть, ю *pf.* **1.** to leap (for joy); **се́рдце во мне ~ло** my heart leapt. **2.** to become disturbed; **мо́ре ~ло** the sea grew rough.
взыска́ни|е, я *nt.* penalty; punishment; **подве́ргнуться ~ю** to incur a penalty.
взыска́тел|ьный (~ен, ~ьна) *adj.* exacting; demanding; severe.
взы|ска́ть, щу́, ~́щешь *pf.* (*of* **~́скивать**) **1.** to exact; to recover; **в. долг (с**+*g.*) to recover a debt (from). **2.** to call to account, make answer (for); **не ~щи́(те)!** (*coll.*) please forgive (me)!; don't be hard on (me)!
взы́скива|ть, ю *impf. of* **взыска́ть**
взы|щу́, ~́щешь *see* **~ска́ть**
взя́ти|е, я *nt.* taking; capture.
взя́тк|а, и *f.* **1.** bribe; backhander. **2.** (*cards*) trick.
взя́точник, а *m.* bribe-taker.
взя́точничеств|о, а *nt.* bribery, bribe-taking.
взя|ть, возьму́, возьмёшь, *past* **~л, ~ла́, ~́ло** *pf.* (*of* **брать**) **1.** *see* **брать. 2.** (*coll.*) to conclude, suppose; **с чего́ вы ~́ли, что он не́мец?** what gave you the idea that he is a German? **3.: в. да, в. и, в. да и...** (*coll.*) to do sth. suddenly; **он ~л да убежа́л** he up and ran; **он возьми́ да скажи́** he up and spoke.
взя́|ться, возьму́сь, возьмёшься, *past* **~лся, ~ла́сь, ~ло́сь** *pf.* (*of* **бра́ться**); **отку́да ни возьми́сь** (*coll.*) from nowhere, out of the blue.
виаду́к, а *m.* viaduct.
вибра́тор, а *m.* (*elec.*) vibrator; (*radio*) oscillator.
вибра́ци|я, и *f.* vibration.
вибри́р|овать, ую *impf.* to vibrate; to oscillate.
вива́ри|й, я *m.* vivarium.
виве́рр|а, ы *f.* (*zool.*) civet.
вивисе́кци|я, и *f.* vivisection.
вигва́м, а *m.* wigwam.
виго́н|ь, и *f.* vicuña; vicuña wool.
вид[1], **а** *m.* **1.** air, look; appearance; aspect; **у вас хоро́ший в.** you look well; **име́ть мра́чный в.** to look gloomy; **сде́лать в. бу́дто** to make it appear that, pretend that; **для ~́у** for the sake of appearances; **на в., с ~́у** in appearance; **знать по ~́у** to know by sight; **под ~́ом** (+*g.*) under the guise (of); **ни под каки́м ~́ом** on no account. **2.** shape, form; condition; **в хоро́шем ~́е** in good condition, in good shape. **3.** view; **ко́мната с ~́ом на го́ры** room with a view of the mountains; **в. сбо́ку** side-view; **откры́тка с ~́ом** picture postcard. **4.** (*pl.*) prospect; **~́ы на бу́дущее** prospects for the future. **5.** sight; **потеря́ть и́з ~у** to lose sight (of); **упусти́ть и́з ~у** (*fig.*) to lose sight (of); **быть на ~у́** to be in the public eye; **при ~́е** (+*g.*) at the sight (of); **в ~у́** (+*g.*) in sight (of); **име́ть в ~у́** (*i*) to plan, intend, (*ii*) to mean; **что вы име́ли в ~у́, говоря́ э́то?** what did you mean when you said that?, (*iii*) to bear in mind; **име́й(те) в ~у́** bear in mind; don't forget.
вид[2], **а** *m.* **1.** (*biol.*) species; **исчеза́ющий в.** endangered species. **2.** kind, sort. **3.** (*gram.*) aspect; **соверше́нный, несоверше́нный в.** perfective, imperfective aspect.
ви́дан|ный (~, ~а) *p.p.p. of* **вида́ть; ~ное ли э́то де́ло?** have you ever heard of such a thing?
вида́|ть, ю *impf.* (*of* **у~**) (*coll.*) to see; **ничего́ подо́бного я не ~л** I have never seen such a thing.
вида́|ться, юсь *impf.* (*of* **по~**) (**с**+*i.*; *coll.*) to meet; to see one another.
ви́дени|е, я *nt.* sight, vision.
виде́ни|е, я *nt.* vision, apparition.
видео... *comb. form* video-.
видеоза́пис|ь, и *f.* video recording.
видеока́мер|а, ы *f.* video camera.
видеокассе́т|а, ы *f.* video cassette.
видеоконфере́нци|я, и *f.* video-conferencing.
видеомагнитофо́н, а *m.* video recorder.
видеотелефо́н, а *m.* videophone.
ви́|деть, жу, дишь *impf.* (*of* **у~**) to see; **в. кого́-н. насквозь** to see through s.o.; **в. во сне** to dream (of); **его́ то́лько и ~дели** (*coll.*) he was gone in a flash; **~дишь (ли)?; ~дите (ли)?** (*coll.*) (do) you see?
ви́|деться, жусь, дишься *impf.* **1.** to see one another; (**с**+*i.*) to see. **2.** (*pf.* **при~**) to appear; **ему́ ~делся стра́шный сон** he had a terrifying dream.
ви́димо *adv.* evidently; **он, в., чу́вствовал себя́ оскорблённым** evidently he was offended.
ви́димо-неви́димо *adv.* (*coll.*) in immense quantity; **наро́ду бы́ло в.-н** there was an immense crowd.
ви́димост|ь, и *f.* **1.** visibility. **2.** outward appearance. **3.: по (всей) ~и** to all appearances.
ви́дим|ый (~, ~а) *p.p.p. of* **ви́деть** *and adj.* **1.** visible. **2.** apparent, evident; **без ~ой причи́ны** with no apparent cause. **3.** apparent, seeming.
видне́|ться, юсь, ешься *impf.* to be visible; **на горизо́нте ~лись огни́ корабля́** a ship's lights could be seen on the horizon.
ви́дно 1. *adv.* obviously, evidently; *as pred.* it is obvious; **всем бы́ло в., что он лжёт** it was obvious to everyone that he was lying; **как в. из ска́занного** as is clear from the statement. **2.** *adv. as pred.* visible; in sight; **конца́ ещё не в.** the end is not yet in sight; **бы́ло хорошо́ в.** visibility was good.
ви́д|ный *adj.* **1. (~ен, ~на́, ~но)** visible; conspicuous. **2.** distinguished, prominent.
видово́й[1] *adj. of* **вид**[1]; **в. фильм** travel film, travelogue.
видово́й[2] *adj.* (*of* **вид**[2]) **1.** (*biol.*) species. **2.** (*gram.*) aspectual.
видоизмене́ни|е, я *nt.* **1.** modification, alteration. **2.** type, variety.
видоизмен|и́ть, ю́, и́шь *pf.* (*of* **~я́ть**) to modify, alter.
видоизмен|и́ться, ю́сь, и́шься *pf.* (*of* **~я́ться**) **1.** to alter (*intrans.*). **2.** *pass. of* **~я́ть**
видоизмен|я́ть(ся), я́ю(сь) *impf. of* **~и́ть(ся)**
ви́з|а, ы *f.* visa.
визави́ 1. *adv.* opposite; **они́ сиде́ли в.** they sat opposite one another. **2.** *n.*; *c.g. indecl.* the person opposite, facing; **мы с мои́м в. завяза́ли разгово́р** I

struck up a conversation with the person opposite me.
византи́йский *adj.* Byzantine.
визг, а *m.* scream, squeal, yelp.
визгли́в|ый (~, ~а) *adj.* **1.** shrill. **2.** given to screaming, squealing, yelping.
визж|а́ть, у́, и́шь *impf.* to scream; to squeal; to yelp.
визи́р, а *m.* **1.** (*mil.*) sight. **2.** (*phot.*) view-finder.
визи́р|овать¹, ую *impf. and pf.* (*pf. also* **за~**) to visa, visé (*passport*).
визи́р|овать², ую *impf. and pf.* to sight; to take a sight (on).
визи́р|ь *m.* vizier.
визи́т, а *m.* (*official*) visit; call; **прийти́ с ~ом к кому́-н.** to pay s.o. a visit.
визи́тк|а, и *f.* **1.** morning coat. **2.** business card.
визи́т|ный *adj. of* **~**; **~ная ка́рточка** visiting card; (business) card.
ви́к|а, и *no pl., f.* vetch.
вика́ри|й, я *m.* (*eccl.*) vicar.
ви́кинг, а *m.* Viking.
вико́нт, а *m.* viscount.
викториа́нский *adj.* Victorian.
виктори́н|а, ы *f.* quiz.
ви́лк|а, и *f.* **1.** fork. **2.** (*elec.*) plug.
ви́лл|а, ы *f.* villa.
ви́ллис, а *m.* (*mil.*) jeep.
вилообра́з|ный (~ен, ~на) *adj.* forked.
ви́л|ы, ~ *no sg.* pitchfork; **э́то ещё ~ами на воде́ пи́сано** (*fig.*) it is still in the air.
вильн|у́ть, у́, ёшь *pf.* **1.** *pf. of* **виля́ть. 2.** to glide away; to turn off sharply, sidetrack.
виля́ни|е, я *nt.* **1.** wagging. **2.** (*fig.*) prevarication; evasions.
виля́|ть, ю *impf.* (*of* **вильну́ть**) **1.** to wag; **в. хвосто́м** to wag one's tail; **хвост у соба́ки всё вре́мя ~л** the dog's tail was wagging the whole time. **2.** (*fig.*) to prevaricate; to be evasive.
вин|а́, ы́, *pl.* **~́ы** *f.* fault, guilt; blame; **свали́ть ~у́ (на+***a.***)** to lay the blame (on).
винегре́т, а *m.* Russian salad; (*fig.*) medley, farrago.
вини́тельный *adj.* (*gram.*) **в. паде́ж** accusative case.
вин|и́ть, ю́ и́шь *impf.* **(в+***p.***)** to accuse (of).
виннока́менн|ый *adj.* (*chem.*) tartaric.
ви́нн|ый *adj.* wine; **в. ка́мень** (*chem.*) tartar; **~ая кислота́** tartaric acid; **в. спирт** alcohol.
вин|о́, а́, *pl.* **~́а** *nt.* wine.
винова́т|ый (~, ~а) *adj.* guilty; to blame; **мы все ~ы в э́том** we are all to blame for this; **~!** sorry!
вино́вник, а *m.* author, initiator; culprit; **в. преступле́ния** perpetrator of a crime; **в. побе́ды** architect of victory.
вино́вность, и *f.* guilt.
вино́в|ный (~ен, ~на) *adj.* **(в+***p.***)** guilty (of); **призна́ть себя́ ~ным** to plead guilty.
виногра́д, а (у) *m.* **1.** vine. **2.** (*collect*) grapes.
виногра́дарств|о, а *nt.* viticulture; wine-growing.
виногра́дар|ь, я *m.* wine-grower.
виногра́дин|а, ы *f.* (*coll.*) grape.
виногра́дник, а *m.* vineyard.
винногра́д|ный *adj. of* **~**; **~ная лоза́** vine; **в. сезо́н** vintage; **~ное су́сло** must.
виноде́л, а *m.* wine-grower.
виноде́ли|е, я *nt.* wine-making.
виноку́р, а *m.* distiller.
винокуре́ни|е, я *nt.* distillation.
виноку́р|енный *adj. of* **~е́ние; в. заво́д** distillery.
виноторго́в|ец, ца *m.* wine-merchant.
винт, а́ *m.* **1.** screw. **2.** propeller.
ви́нт|ик, а *m. dim. of* **~**; **у него́ ~а не хвата́ет** (*coll.*) he has a screw loose; he's not all there.
винто́вк|а, и *f.* rifle.
винт|ово́й *adj. of* **~**; spiral; **~ова́я ле́стница** spiral staircase.
винтообра́з|ный (~ен, на) *adj.* spiral.
винье́тк|а, и *f.* vignette.
вио́л|а, ы *f.* viol; viola.
виолончели́ст, а *m.* cellist.
виолонче́л|ь, и *f.* cello.
вира́ж¹, а *m.* (*phot.*) intensifier; **в.-викса́ж** tone-fixing bath.
вира́ж², а́ *m.* **1.** turn. **2.** bend, curve.
виртуо́з, а *m.* virtuoso.
виртуо́зност|ь, и *f.* virtuosity.
виртуо́з|ный (~ен, на) *adj.* masterly.
вируле́нт|ный (~ен, ~на) *adj.* (*med.*) virulent.
ви́рус, а *m.* (*med.*) virus; bug.
ви́русный *adj.* viral.
ви́рш|и, ей *no sg.* **1.** (*liter.*) (syllabic) verses (*based on Polish form*). **2.** (*coll.*) doggerel.
ви́селиц|а, ы *f.* gallows, gibbet.
ви|се́ть, шу́, си́шь *impf.* to hang; to be hanging, be suspended; **в. в во́здухе** to be up in the air.
ви́ски *nt. indecl.* whisky; **шотла́ндское в.** Scotch (whisky).
виско́з|а, ы *f.* **1.** (*tech.*) viscose. **2.** (*coll.*) rayon.
виско́з|ный *adj. of* **~а**
вислоу́х|ий (~, ~а), *adj.* lop-eared.
ви́смут, а, *m.* (*chem.*) bismuth.
ви́сн|уть, у, ешь *impf.* **(на+***p.***)** to hang (*on*); to droop.
вис|о́к, ка́ *m.* (*anat.*) temple.
високо́сный *adj.*: **в. год** leap-year.
вист, а *m.* whist (*card-game*).
висю́льк|а, и *f.* (*coll.*) pendant.
вися́чий *adj.* hanging; **в. замо́к** padlock; **в. мост** suspension bridge.
витами́н, а *m.* vitamin.
витами́н|ный *adj.* **1.** *adj. of* **~**; **~ная недоста́точность** vitamin deficiency. **2.** vitamin-packed.
витамин|о́зный = ~́ный
вита́|ть, ю *impf.* (*liter.*) to be; to wander (*of thoughts*); to hover; **он ~ет в ми́ре фанта́зий** he inhabits a world of fantasy; **в. в облака́х** to be up in the clouds; **смерть ~ла над ней** death was hovering over her.
витиева́т|ый (~, ~а) *adj.* flowery, ornate.
вит|о́й *adj.* twisted; spiral; **~а́я ле́стница** spiral staircase.
вит|о́к, ка́ *m.* **1.** (*tech.*) spire. **2.** circuit (*of planet by space vehicle*); lap (*sport*). **3.** (*fig.*) round; **но́вый в. го́нки вооруже́ний** a new spiral in the arms race.
витра́ж, а *m.* stained-glass window.
витри́н|а, ы *f.* **1.** (shop-)window; **оформле́ние ~ы** window dressing. **2.** show-case.
ви|ть, вью, вьёшь, *past* **~л, ~ла́, ~́ло** *impf.* (*of* **с~**) to twist, wind; **в. венки́** weave garlands; **в. гнездо́** to build a nest; **в. верёвки из кого́-н.** (*coll.*) to twist round one's little finger.
ви́|ться, вьюсь, вьёшься, *past* **~лся, ~ла́сь, ~ло́сь** *impf.* (*of* **с~**) **1.** to wind, twine. **2.** to curl, wave (*of hair*). **3.** to hover, circle (*of birds*). **4.** to writhe, twist (*of reptiles*).
ви́тяз|ь, я *m.* (*poet., arch.*) knight; hero.
вихля́|ть, ю *impf.* (*coll.*) to reel.
вихля́|ться, юсь *impf.* (*coll.*) to wobble.
вих|о́р, ра́ *m.* forelock.
вихра́ст|ый (~, ~а) *adj.* (*coll.*) shaggy.
вихр|ь, я *m.* **1.** whirlwind; **сне́жный в.** blizzard **2.** (*fig.*) vortex.
ви́це-... *comb. form* vice-.
вице-коро́л|ь я́ *m.* viceroy.
ВИЧ *m. indecl.* (*abbr. of* **ви́рус иммунодефици́та челове́ка**) (*med.*) HIV (*human immunodeficiency virus*); **инфици́рованный В.** HIV-positive.
вишнё|вк|а, и *f.* cherry brandy.
вишнёвый *adj.* **1.** cherry; **в. сад** cherry orchard. **2.** cherry-coloured.

ви́ш|ня, ни, *g. pl.* **~ен** *f.* **1.** cherry-tree. **2.** cherry; (*collect.*) cherries.

вка́лыва|ть, ю *impf.* **1.** *impf. of* **вколо́ть. 2.** *impf. only* (*sl.*) to slog away.

вка́пыва|ть, ю *impf. of* **вкопа́ть**

вка|ти́ть, чу́, ⁓тишь *pf.* (*of* **⁓тывать**) **1.** to roll into, onto; to wheel in, into. **2.** (*fig., coll.*) to give, administer; **в. пощёчину** (*+d.*) to slap in the face.

вка|ти́ться, чу́сь, ⁓тишься *pf.* (*of* **⁓тываться**) to roll in (*intrans.*); (*coll.*) to run in.

вка́тыва|ть(ся), ю(сь) *impf. of* **вкати́ть(ся)**

вклад, а *m.* **1.** (*fin.*) deposit; investment. **2.** endowment; (*fig.*) contribution.

вкла́дк|а, и *f.* supplementary sheet.

вклад|но́й 1. *adj. of* **~. 2.** supplementary, inserted; **в. лист** loose leaf.

вкла́дчик, а *m.* depositor; investor.

вкла́дыва|ть, ю *impf. of* **вложи́ть**

вкла́д|ыш, а *m.* = **~ка**

вкле́ива|ть, ю *impf. of* **вкле́ить**

вкле́|ить, ю, ⁓ишь *pf.* (*of* **~ивать**) to paste in.

вкле́йк|а, и *f.* **1.** pasting in. **2.** inset (*in a book*).

вкли́нива|ть(ся), ю(сь) *impf. of* **вклини́ть(ся)**

вкли́н|и́ть, ю́, ⁓и́шь *pf.* to wedge in; **в. сло́во** (*fig., coll.*) to put a word in.

вкли́н|и́ться, ю́сь, ⁓и́шься *pf.* **1.** *pass. of* **~и́ть. 2.** (**в**+*a.*) to edge one's way into; (*mil.*) to drive a wedge (into).

включ|а́ть(ся), а́ю(сь) *impf. of* **~и́ть(ся)**

включа́|я *pres. ger. of* **~ть;** *as prep.+a.* including.

включе́ни|е, я *nt.* **1.** inclusion, insertion; **со ~ем** (*+g.*) including, with the inclusion of. **2.** (*tech.*) switching on, turning on.

включи́тельно *adv.* inclusive; **с пя́того по девя́тое в.** from the 5th to the 9th inclusive.

включ|и́ть, у́, и́шь *pf.* (*of* **~а́ть**) **1.** (**в**+*a.*) to include (in); to insert (in); **в. в себя́** to include, comprise, take in; **в. в спи́сок** to enter on a list. **2.** (*tech.*) to switch on, turn on.

включ|и́ться, у́сь, и́шься *pf.* (*of* **~а́ться**) **1.** (**в**+*a.*) to join (in), enter (into); **в. в за́говор** to enter into a conspiracy. **2.** *pass. of* **~и́ть**

вкола́чива|ть, ю *impf. of* **вколоти́ть**

вкол|оти́ть, очу́, ~о́тишь *pf.* (*of* **~а́чивать**) to knock in, hammer in (*also fig.*); **в. в го́лову** (*+d.*; *coll.*) to knock into s.o.'s head.

вкол|о́ть, ю́, ⁓ешь *pf.* (*of* **вка́лывать**) (**в**+*a.*) to stick (in, into).

вкол|очу́, ~о́тишь *see* **~оти́ть**

вконе́ц *adv.* (*coll.*) completely, absolutely.

вко́пан|ный (~, ~а) *p.p.p. of* **вкопа́ть; как в.** rooted to the ground.

вкопа́|ть, ю *pf.* to dig in.

вкорен|и́ть, ю́, и́шь *pf.* (*of* **~я́ть**) to inculcate.

вкорен|и́ться, ю́сь, и́шься *pf.* (*of* **~я́ться**) to be inculcated; to take root.

вкореня́|ть(ся), ю(сь) *impf. of* **вкорени́ть(ся)**

вкось *adv.* obliquely; slantwise; **вкривь и в.,** *see* **вкривь**

вкрад|у́сь, ёшься *see* **вкра́сться**

вкра́дчив|ый (~, ~а) *adj.* insinuating, ingratiating.

вкра́дыва|ться, юсь *impf. of* **вкра́сться**

вкра́п|ить, лю, ишь *pf.* (*of* **~ливать**) to sprinkle (with); (*fig.*) to intersperse (with); **он ~ил в речь цита́ты** he interspersed his speech with quotations.

вкра́плива|ть, ю *impf. of* **вкра́пить**

вкрапл|я́ть, я́ю *impf.* = **⁓ивать**

вкра́|сться, ду́сь, дёшься, *past* **~лся** *pf.* (*of* **~дываться**) to steal in, creep in; **в. текст ~лось мно́го оши́бок** many mistakes have crept into the text; **в. в дове́рие к кому́-н.** to worm one's way into s.o.'s confidence.

вкра́тце *adv.* briefly; succinctly.

вкривь *adv.* aslant; (*fig.*) wrongly, perversely; **в. и вкось** all over the place; (*fig., coll.*) indiscriminately.

вкругову́ю *adv.* (*coll.*) round; **пусти́ть ча́шу в.** to send the cup round (*at banquets*).

вкруту́ю *adv.* (*coll.*): **яйцо́ в.** hard-boiled egg; **свари́ть яйцо́ в.** to hard-boil an egg.

вкус, а *m.* **1.** taste (*also fig.*); **на в. и цвет това́рища нет** (*prov.*) tastes differ; **челове́к со ⁓ом** a man of taste. **2.** (*coll.*) manner, style; **во ⁓е Ренесса́нса** in the Renaissance style.

вку|си́ть, шу́, ⁓сишь *pf.* (*of* **~ша́ть**) (*fig., poet.*) to taste, savour.

вку́с|ный (~ен, ~на́, ~но) *adj.* good, nice (*to taste*); appetizing, tasty.

вкусов|о́й *adj.* taste; gustatory; **~о́е веще́ство́** flavouring.

вкуша́|ть, ю *impf. of* **вкуси́ть**

вку|шу́, ⁓сишь *see* **~си́ть**

вла́г|а, и *no pl., f.* moisture, liquid.

влага́лищ|е, а *nt.* vagina.

влага́|ть, ю *impf. of* **вложи́ть**

владе́л|ец, ьца *m.* owner; proprietor.

владе́ни|е, я *nt.* **1.** ownership; possession; **в. иму́ществом** possession of property. **2.** *pl.* possessions; **колониа́льные ~я** colonial possessions.

владе́|ть, ю, ешь *impf.* (*+i.*) **1.** to own, possess. **2.** to control; **в. собо́й** to control o.s. **3.** (*fig.*) to have (a) command (of); to have the use (of); **она́ ~ет шестью́ языка́ми** she has a command of six languages; **он не ~ет пра́вой руко́й** he has not the use of his right arm.

влады́к|а, и *m.* master, sovereign.

влады́честв|о, а *nt.* dominion, sway.

влады́честв|овать, ую *impf.* (**над**+*i.*) to hold sway, exercise dominion (over).

вла́жност|ь, и *f.* humidity, dampness.

вла́ж|ный (~ен, ~на́, ~но) *adj.* humid, damp; moist.

вла́мыва|ться, юсь *impf. of* **вломи́ться**

вла́ств|овать, ую *impf.* (**над**+*i.*) to rule, hold sway (over).

властели́н, а *m.* (*usu. fig.*) ruler; lord, master.

власти́тел|ь, я *m.*: **в. дум** dominant influence.

вла́ст|ный (~ен, ~на) *adj.* **1.** imperious, commanding; masterful. **2.** (**в**+*p.*; *leg.*) authoritative, competent; **я не ~ен в э́том де́ле** I have no competence to deal with this matter.

властолю́б|ец, ца *m.* power-seeker.

властолюби́в|ый (~, ~а) *adj.* power-loving; power-seeking.

властолю́би|е, я *nt.* love of power; lust for power.

власт|ь, и, *pl.* **⁓и, ~е́й** *f.* **1.** power; **во ⁓и** (*+g.*) at the mercy (of); **прийти́ к ⁓и** to come to power; **у ⁓и** in power. **2.** power, authority; (*pl.*) authorities; **ме́стная в., в. на места́х** local authority; **сове́тская в.** Soviet rule. **3.: ва́ша в.** (*coll.*) as you like, please yourself.

власяни́ц|а, ы *f.* hair shirt.

влач|и́ть, у́, и́шь *impf.* (*obs., poet.*) to drag; **в. жа́лкое существова́ние** to drag out a miserable existence.

вле́во *adv.* to the left (*also fig., pol.*).

влеза́|ть, ю *impf. of* **влезть**

влез|ть, у, ешь, *past* **~, ⁓ла** *pf.* (*of* **~а́ть**) **1.** to climb in, into, up; to get in, into; **в. на де́рево** to climb up a tree; **в. в долги́** (*fig.*) to get into debt; **в. в ду́шу** (*+g.*) to worm one's way into s.o.'s confidence. **2.** (*coll.*) to get on, board; **в. в авто́бус** to get on the bus. **3.** (*coll.*) to fit in, go in, go on; **все э́ти ве́щи не ⁓ут в мою́ су́мку** these things will not all go into my bag.

влеп|и́ть, лю́, ⁓ишь *pf.* to stick in, fasten in; (*coll.*): **в. пощёчину кому́-н.** to slap s.o.'s face.

влепля́|ть, ю *impf. of* **влепи́ть**
влет|а́ть, а́ю *impf. of* **~е́ть**
вле|те́ть, чу́, ти́шь *pf.* (*of* **~та́ть**) to fly in, into; (*fig., coll.*) to rush in, into; **в. в исто́рию** to get into trouble; (*impers.*): **ему́ опя́ть ~те́ло** he's in trouble again.
влече́ни|е, я *nt.* **(к)** attraction (to); bent (for).
вле|чь, ку́, чёшь, ку́т, *past* **влёк, ~кла́** *impf.* to draw, drag; to attract; **в. за собо́й** to involve, entail.
влива́ни|е, я *nt.* infusion.
влива́ть, ю *impf. of* **влить**
влипа́ть, ю *impf. of* **вли́пнуть**
вли́п|нуть, ну, нешь, *past* **~, ла** *pf.* (*coll.*) to get into a mess; to put one's foot in it; to get caught.
вли|ть, волью́, вольёшь, *past* **~л, ~ла́, ~́ло** *pf.* (*of* **~ва́ть**) **1.** to pour in; **в. по ка́пле** to instil, administer drops; (*med.*) to infuse; (*fig.*) to instil; **в. наде́жду в кого́-н.** to instil hope into s.o. **2.** (*mil.*) to bring in; **в. пополне́ния в часть** to reinforce a unit.
влия́ни|е, я *nt.* influence; **по́льзоваться ~ем** to have influence, be influential.
влия́тел|ьный (~ен, ~ьна) *adj.* influential.
влия́|ть, ю *impf.* (*of* **по~**) **(на+*a.*)** to influence, have an influence on, affect.
вложе́ни|е, я *nt.* **1.** enclosure. **2.** (*fin.*) investment.
влож|и́ть, у́, ~́ишь *pf.* (*of* **вкла́дывать** *and* **влага́ть**) **1.** to put in, insert; to enclose; **он ~и́л всю свою́ ду́шу в рабо́ту** (*fig.*) he put his whole soul into his work. **2.** (*fin.*) to invest.
влом|и́ться, лю́сь, ~́ишься *pf.* (*of* **вла́мываться**) to break in, into.
вло́па|ться, юсь *pf.* (*coll.*) **1.** to get into an awkward situation. **2.** to fall in love.
влюб|и́ть, лю́, ишь *pf.* (*of* **~ля́ть**) **(в+*a.*)** to make fall in love (with).
влюб|и́ться, лю́сь, ~́ишься *pf.* (*of* **~ля́ться**) **(в+*a.*)** to fall in love (with).
влюблён|ный (~, ~а́) *p.p.p. of* **влюби́ть** *and adj.* **1.** (*p.p.p.*) in love; **в. по́ уши** head over ears in love. **2.** (*adj.*) loving; tender.
влюбля́|ть, ю *impf. of* **влюби́ть**
влюбля́|ться, юсь *impf. of* **влюби́ться**
влю́бчив|ый (~, ~а) *adj.* (*coll.*) amorous.
вмен|и́ть, ю́, и́шь *pf.* (*of* **~я́ть**) **(*d.*+в+*a.*) 1.** to regard (as); **в. в заслу́гу** to regard as a merit; **в. в обя́занность** to impose as a duty; **он ~и́л себе́ в обя́занность чте́ние всех газе́т** he imposed on himself the duty of reading all the newspapers. **2.** to impute.
вменя́емост|ь, и *f.* (*leg.*) responsibility; liability.
вменя́ем|ый (~, ~а) *adj.* (*leg.*) responsible, liable; of sound mind.
вменя́|ть, ю *impf. of* **вмени́ть**
вме́сте *adv.* together; at the same time; **в. с тем** at the same time, also.
вмести́лищ|е, а *nt.* receptacle.
вмести́мост|ь, и *f.* capacity.
вмести́тел|ьный (~ен, ~ьна) *adj.* capacious; spacious, roomy.
вме|сти́ть, щу́, сти́шь *pf. of* **~ща́ть**
вме́сто *prep.+g.* instead of; in place of.
вмеша́тельств|о, а *nt.* interference; (*mil., econ.*) intervention.
вмеша́|ть, ю *pf.* (*of* **вме́шивать**) **(в+*a.*) 1.** to mix in. **2.** (*coll., fig.*) to mix up (in), implicate (in).
вмеш|а́ться, а́юсь *pf.* (*of* **~́иваться**) **(в+*a.*)** to interfere (in), meddle (with); to intervene (in).
вме́шива|ть, ю *impf. of* **вмеша́ть**
вме́шива|ться, юсь *impf. of* **вмеша́ться**
вмеща́|ть, ю *impf.* (*of* **вмести́ть**) **1.** to contain; to hold; to accommodate; to seat; **э́та бо́чка ~ет пятьдеся́т ли́тров** this barrel holds fifty litres. **2.** (**в+*a.***) to put, place (in, into).
вмеща́|ться, юсь *impf.* (*of* **вмести́ться**) **1.** to fit, go in(to). **2.** *pass. of* **~ть 2.**
вмиг *adv.* in an instant; in a flash.
вмина́|ть, ю *impf. of* **вмять**
ВМФ *m. indecl.* (*abbr. of* ***вое́нно-морско́й флот***) Navy.
вмя́тин|а, ы *f.* dent.
вмять, вомну́, вомнёшь *pf.* (*of* **вмина́ть**) to press in.
внаём, внаймы́ *adv.*: **отда́ть в.** to let, hire out, rent; **взять в.** to hire, rent; **«сдаётся в.»** 'to let'.
внаки́дку *adv.* (*coll.*) over one's shoulders.
внакла́де *adv.* (*coll.*): **оста́ться в.** to be the loser, come off loser.
внакла́дку *adv.*: **пить чай в.** to drink tea with sugar.
внача́ле *adv.* at first, in the beginning.
вне *prep.+g.* outside; out of; **объяви́ть в. зако́на** to outlaw; **в. о́череди** out of turn; **в. себя́** beside o.s.; **в. вся́ких сомне́ний** beyond any doubt.
вне... *comb. form* extra-.
внебра́чный *adj.* extra-marital; **в. ребёнок** illegitimate child.
вневре́менный *adj.* timeless.
внедре́ни|е, я *nt.* introduction; inculcation; indoctrination.
внедр|и́ть, ю́, и́шь *pf.* (*of* **~я́ть**) **1.** to inculcate, instil. **2.** to introduce; **в. но́вые ме́тоды** to introduce new methods.
внедр|и́ться, ю́сь, и́шься *pf.* (*of* **~я́ться**) to take root.
внедря́|ть(ся), ю(сь) *impf. of* **внедри́ть(ся)**
внеза́пно *adv.* suddenly, all of a sudden.
внеза́пност|ь, и *f.* suddenness.
внеза́пный *adj.* sudden.
внеземля́н|ин, ина, *pl.* **~е, ~** *m.* = **инопланетя́нин**
внеземно́й *adj.* alien, extra-terrestrial.
внекла́ссн|ый *adj.* extra-curricular.
вне́мл|ю, ешь *see* **внима́ть**
внеочередн|о́й *adj.* **1.** out of turn; **зада́ть в. вопро́с** to ask a question out of order. **2.** extraordinary; extra; **в. съезд** extraordinary congress.
внесе́ни|е, я *nt.* **1.** bringing in, carrying in. **2.** paying in, deposit. **3.** entry, insertion. **4.** moving, submission.
внес|ти́, у́, ёшь, *past* **~̈, ~ла́** *pf.* (*of* **вноси́ть**) **1.** to bring in, carry in. **2.** (*fig.*) to introduce, put in; **в. я́сность в де́ло** to clarify a matter; **в. свой вклад в де́ло** to do one's bit. **3.** to pay in, deposit. **4.** to bring in; move, table; **в. законопрое́кт** to bring in a bill; **в. предложе́ние** to table a resolution. **5.** to insert, enter; **в. в спи́сок** to enter on a list. **6.** to bring about, cause; **в. раздо́ры** to cause strife.
внешко́льн|ый *adj.*: **~ое образова́ние** adult education.
вне́шне *adv.* outwardly.
вне́шн|ий *adj.* **1.** outer, exterior; outward, external; outside. **2.** foreign; **~яя поли́тика** foreign policy.
вне́шност|ь, и *f.* exterior; surface; appearance; **суди́ть по ~и** to judge by appearances.
внешта́тник, а *m.* (*coll.*) freelancer; casual.
внешта́тный *adj.* not on permanent staff; freelance; casual.
вниз *adv.* down, downwards; **в. голово́й** head first; **в. по тече́нию** downstream.
внизу́ *adv.* below; downstairs; *prep.+g.*; **в. страни́цы** at the foot of the page.
вник|а́ть, а́ю *impf. of* **~́нуть**
вни́к|нуть, ну, нешь, *past* **~, ~ла** *pf.* (*of* **~а́ть**) **(в+*a.*)** to go carefully (into), investigate thoroughly.
внима́ни|е, я *nt.* **1.** attention; heed; notice, note; **обраща́ть в. (на+*a.*)** (*i*) to pay attention (to) (*ii*) to draw attention (to); **он весь в.** he is all ears; **принима́я во в.** taking into account. **2.** kindness,

consideration; **оказа́ть в.** to do a kindness. **3.** (*int.*): **в.!** look out!; mind out!

внима́тельност|ь, и *f.* **1.** attentiveness. **2.** thoughtfulness, consideration.

внима́тел|ьный (~ен, ~ьна) *adj.* **1.** attentive. **2.** (**к**+*d.*) thoughtful, considerate (towards).

внима́|ть, ю *and* **вне́млю** *impf.* (*of* **внять**) (+*d.*; *poet.*, *obs.*) to hear (*fig.*); to heed; **в. моли́тве** to hear prayer.

вничью́ *adv.* (*sport*) drawn; **па́ртия око́нчилась в.** the game ended in a draw.

вно́ве *adv. as pred.* new, strange.

вновь *adv.* **1.** afresh, anew; again. **2.** newly; **в. при-бы́вший** newcomer.

вно|си́ть, шу́, ~сишь *impf. of* **внести́**

внук, а *m.* grandson; grandchild (*also fig.*).

вну́тренн|ий *adj.* **1.** inner, interior; internal; intrinsic. **2.** home, inland; **~ие дохо́ды** inland revenue.

вну́тренност|ь, и *f.* **1.** interior. **2.** (*pl. only*) entrails, intestines; internal organs.

внутри́ *adv. and prep.*+*g.* inside, within.

внутри́... *comb. form* intra-.

внутриве́нный *adj.* (*med.*) intravenous.

внутрима́точный *adj.* intra-uterine.

внутрь *adv. and prep.*+*g.* within, inside; inwards.

внуча́т|а, ~ *no sg.* grandchildren.

внуча́тный *adj.*: **в. брат** second cousin; **в. племя́н-ник** great-nephew.

внуча́т|ый = **~ный**

вну́чк|а, и *f.* granddaughter.

внуша́емост|ь, и *f.* suggestibility.

внуш|а́ть, а́ю *impf. of* **~и́ть**

внуше́ни|е, я *nt.* **1.** (*psych.*) suggestion. **2.** reproof, reprimand.

внуши́тел|ьный (~ен, ~ьна) *adj.* inspiring, impressive; (*coll.*) imposing, striking.

внуш|и́ть, у́, и́шь *pf.* (*of* **~а́ть**) (+*a.* and *d.*) to inspire (with); to instil; to suggest; **в. уве́ренность в себе́** to instil self-confidence.

вня́т|ный (~ен, ~на) *adj.* distinct.

вня|ть *fut. not used*, *past* **~л, ~ла́, ~ло,** *imper.* **вонми́(те),** *pf. of* **внима́ть**

во *prep.* = **в**

вобр|а́ть, вберу́, вберёшь, *past* **~а́л, ~ала́, ~а́ло** *pf.* (*of* **вбира́ть**) to absorb, suck in; to inhale.

во́ве́к(и) *adv.* (*obs.*) for ever; **в. веко́в** for ever and ever.

вовлека́|ть, ю *impf. of* **вовле́чь**

вовл|е́чь, еку́, ечёшь, еку́т, *past* **~ёк, ~екла́** *pf.* to draw in, involve; to inveigle.

вовне́ *adv.* outside.

во́время *adv.* at the proper time; in time; **говори́ть не в.** to speak out of turn.

во́все *adv.* (+*neg.*; *coll.*) at all; **он в. не бога́тый челове́к** he is not at all a rich man.

вовсю́ *adv.* to its (one's) utmost; **бежа́ть в.** to run as fast as one's legs will carry one.

во-вторы́х *adv.* secondly, in the second place.

вогна́|ть, вгоню́, вго́нишь, *past* **~л, ~ла́, ~ло** *pf.* (*of* **вгоня́ть**) to drive in; **в. в гроб** to be the death of; **в. в кра́ску** to make (*s.o.*) blush.

во́гнут|ый (~, ~а) *p.p.p. of* **~ь** *and adj.* concave.

вогн|у́ть, у́, ёшь *pf.* (*of* **вгиба́ть**) to bend, curve inwards.

вод|а́, ы́, *a.* **~у,** *pl.* **~ы, ~ам** (*obs.* **~а́м**) *f.* **1.** water; **выводи́ть на чи́стую ~у** to show up, unmask; **как две ка́пли ~ы́ похо́жи** as like as two peas; **как с гу́ся в.** like water off a duck's back; **он ~ы́ не заму́тит** he would not hurt a fly; **как в ~у опу́щенный** downcast, dejected. **2.** (*pl.*) the waters; watering-place, spa. **3.** (*coll.*) waffle; **~у лить** to waffle (on).

водвор|и́ть, ю́, и́шь *pf.* **1.** to settle, install, house. **2.** to establish; **в. мир и споко́йствие** to introduce peace and quiet.

водворя́|ть, ю *impf. of* **водвори́ть**

водеви́л|ь, я *m.* vaudeville; musical comedy.

води́тел|ь, я *m.* driver.

во|ди́ть, жу́, ~дишь *impf.* (*indet. of* **вести́**) **1.** (*see also* **вести́**) to lead; to conduct; to drive. **2.** (*see also* **вести́**) **в. дру́жбу** (**с**+*i.*) to be friends with. **3.** (+*i.*, **по**+*d.*; *see also* **вести́**) to pass (over, across); **в. глаза́ми** (**по**+*d.*) to cast one's eye (over) (*only* **в.** *used in this phr.*).

во|ди́ться, жу́сь, ~дишься *impf.* **1.** (**с**+*i.*) to associate (with); to play (with). **2.** to be, be found; **львы́ не ~дятся в Евро́пе** lions are not found in Europe; (*fig.*) **у него́ де́нег никогда́ не ~дится** he never has any money. **3.** to be the custom; to happen; **так у нас ~дится** it is the custom here.

во́дк|а, и *f.* vodka.

водноло́ыжник, а *m.* water-skier.

во́дн|ый *adj.* **1.** water; watery; **~ые лы́жи** (*i*) water-skiing, (*ii*) water-skis; **в. спорт** aquatic sports. **2.** (*chem.*) aqueous.

водобоя́знь, и *f.* (*med.*) hydrophobia.

водово́з, а *m.* water-carrier.

водоворо́т, а *m.* whirlpool; maelstrom (*also fig.*).

водоём, а *m.* reservoir (*natural or artificial*).

водоизмеще́ни|е, я *nt.* (*naut.*) displacementt.

водока́чк|а, и *f.* water-tower.

водола́з[1]**, а** *m.* diver; **в.-аквалангист** frogman.

водола́з[2]**, а** *m.* Newfoundland (dog).

водола́з|ный *adj. of* **~**[1]; **в. костю́м** diving-suit.

Водоле́|й, я *m.* Aquarius.

водоме́р, а *m.* (*tech.*) water-gauge.

водомёт, а *m.* water cannon.

водонапо́рн|ый *adj.*: **~ая ба́шня** water-tower.

водонепроница́ем|ый (~, ~а) *adj.* water-tight; waterproof.

водоно́с, а *m.* water-carrier.

водоотво́д, а *m.* drainage system.

водоотво́дн|ый *adj.* drainage; **~ая тру́бка** waste-pipe.

водопа́д, а *m.* waterfall.

водопла́вающ|ий *adj.*: **~ие пти́цы** waterfowl.

водопо́|й, я *m.* **1.** watering-place. **2.** watering (*of livestock*).

водопрово́д, а *m.* **1.** water-pipe; plumbing. **2.** water-supply; **дом с ~ом** house with running water.

водопрово́д|ный *adj. of* **~; ~ная магистра́ль** water-main; **~ная ста́нция** waterworks.

водопрово́дчик, а *m.* plumber.

водоразде́л, а *m.* (*geog.*; *fig.*) watershed.

водоро́д, а *m.* (*chem.*) hydrogen.

водоро́дн|ый *adj.* hydrogen; **~ая бо́мба** hydrogen bomb.

во́доросл|ь, и *f.* (*bot.*) alga; **морска́я в.** seaweed.

водосли́в, а *m.* (*tech.*) waste-gate; sluice.

водоснабже́ни|е, я *nt.* water-supply.

водосто́к, а *m.* drain; gutter.

водосто́|чный *adj. of* **~к; ~чная труба́** drain-pipe.

водоупо́р|ный (~ен, ~на) *adj.* waterproof.

водоусто́йчивый *adj.* water-repellant.

водохрани́лищ|е, а *nt.* reservoir; cistern, tank.

во́д|очный *adj. of* **~ка**

водружа́|ть, ю *impf. of* **водрузи́ть**

водру|зи́ть, жу́, зи́шь *pf.* (*of* **~жа́ть**) to hoist, erect.

водяни́ст|ый (~, ~а) *adj.* watery; (*fig.*, *coll.*) wishy-washy.

водя́нк|а, и *f.* (*med.*) dropsy.

водян|о́й[1] *adj.* **1.** *adj. of* **вода́. 2.** water, aquatic. **3.** water-driven, water-operated; **~а́я ме́льница** water-mill. **4.: в. знак** watermark.

водян|о́й[2]**, о́го** *m.* water-sprite.

во|ева́ть, ю́ю, ю́ешь *impf.* (**с**+*i.*) **1.** to be at war

(with). **2.** (*coll.*) to quarrel (with).
воево́д|а, ы *m.* (*hist.*) voivode (*commander of an army in medieval Russia*; *also*, *in Muscovite period*, *governor of a town or province*).
воеди́но *adv.* together; **собра́ть в.** to bring together.
воен... *comb. form*, *abbr. of* **вое́нный**
военача́льник, а *m.* commander; leader in war.
военизаци|я, и *f.* militarization.
военизи́р|овать, ую *impf. and pf.* to militarize.
военко́р, а *m.* (*abbr. of* **вое́нный корреспонде́нт**) war correspondent.
вое́нно-... *comb. form*, *abbr. of* **вое́нный**
вое́нно-возду́шн|ый *adj.*: **~ые си́лы** Air Force(s).
вое́нно-морско́й *adj.* naval; **в. флот** the Navy.
военнообя́занн|ый, ого *m.* man liable for call-up (*including reservists*).
военнопле́нн|ый, ого *m.* prisoner of war.
военнослу́жащ|ий, его *m.* serviceman.
военн|ый *adj.* military; war; army; **в. врач** (army) medical officer; **~ое вре́мя** wartime; **в. заво́д** munitions factory; **~ое положе́ние** martial law; **~ое учи́лище** military college; *as n.* **в., ~ого** *m.* soldier, serviceman; **~ые** (*collect.*) the military.
вое́нщин|а, ы *f.* (*coll.*, *pej.*) (*collect.*) militarists, military clique.
вожа́к, а́ *m.* **1.** guide. **2.** leader.
вожа́т|ый, ого *m.* **1.** leader (*of youth organization*). **2.** (*coll.*) tram-driver.
вожделе́ни|е, я *nt.* desire, lust (*also fig.*).
вожделе́нный *adj.* (*poet.*, *obs.*) desired, longed-for.
вожде́ни|е, я *nt.* leading; driving; **в. корабля́** navigation; **в. самолёта** flying, piloting; **в. в нетре́звом состоя́нии** drink driving.
вожд|ь, я́ *m.* leader; chief.
во́жж|и, е́й *pl.* (*sg.* **~а́, ~и́** *f.*) reins.
во|жу́ [1], **~дишь** *see* **~ди́ть**
во|жу́ [2], **~зишь** *see* **~зи́ть**
воз, а, о ~е, на ~у́, *pl.* **~ы́** *m.* **1.** cart, wagon; **что с ~а упа́ло, то пропа́ло** (*prov.*) it is no use crying over spilt milk. **2.** cartload.
возбуди́мост|ь, и *f.* excitability.
возбуди́м|ый (~, ~а) *adj.* excitable.
возбуди́тел|ь, я *m.* agent; stimulus; (*fig.*) instigator.
возбу|ди́ть, жу́, ди́шь *pf.* (*of* **~жда́ть**) **1.** to excite, rouse, arouse; **в. аппети́т** to whet the appetite. **2.** (**про́тив**+*g.*) to stir up (against), incite (against). **3.** (*leg.*) to institute; **в. де́ло (про́тив**+*g.*) to institute proceedings (against), bring an action (against); **в. иск (про́тив**+*g.*) to bring a suit (against).
возбужда́емост|ь, и *f.* excitability.
возбужда́|ть, ю *impf. of* **возбуди́ть**
возбужда́|ющий *pres. part. act. of* **~ть; ~ющее сре́дство** (*med.*) stimulant.
возбу|жу́, ди́шь *see* **~ди́ть**
возбужде́ни|е, я *nt.* excitement.
возбу|жде́нный *p.p.p. of* **~ди́ть** *and adj.* excited.
возведе́ни|е, я *nt.* **1.** raising; erection. **2.** (*math.*) raising. **3.**: **в. обвине́ния** bringing of an accusation.
возвед|у́, ёшь *see* **возвести́**
возвели́чива|ть, ю *impf. of* **возвели́чить**
возвели́ч|ить, у, ишь *pf.* (*of* **~ивать**) (*obs.*) to extol.
возве|сти́, ду́, дёшь, *past* **~л, ~ла́** *pf.* (*of* **возводи́ть**) **1.** to elevate; **в. в сан патриа́рха** to elect to the patriarchate. **2.** to raise, erect; **в. высо́тный дом** to erect a skyscraper **3.** (*math.*) to raise. **4.** to bring, level (*a charge*, *an accusation. etc.*); **в. клевету́ на кого́-н.** to cast aspersions on s.o. **5.** (**к**+*d.*) to trace back (to).
возве|сти́ть, щу́, сти́шь *pf.* (*of* **~ща́ть**) to proclaim, announce; **в. побе́ду** to proclaim a victory.
возвеща́|ть, ю *impf. of* **возвести́ть**
возве|щу́, сти́шь *see* **~сти́ть**
возво|ди́ть, жу́, ~дишь *impf. of* **возвести́**
возво|жу́, ~дишь *see* **~ди́ть**
возвра́т, а *m.* return; repayment, reimbursement; **в. боле́зни** relapse.
возвра|ти́ть, щу́, ти́шь *pf.* (*of* **~ща́ть**) **1.** to return, give back; to pay back; **в. иму́щество** to restore property. **2.** to recover, retrieve.
возвра|ти́ться, щу́сь, ти́шься *pf.* (*of* **~ща́ться**) to return; (*fig.*) to revert.
возвра́т|ный *adj.* **1.** *adj. of* **~; на ~ном пути́** on the way back. **2.** (*med.*) recurring. **3.** (*gram.*) reflexive.
возвраща́|ть(ся), ю(сь) *impf. of* **возврати́ть(ся)** *and* **верну́ть(ся)**
возвраще́ни|е, я *nt.* return; home-coming.
возвра|щу́, ти́шь *see* **~ти́ть**
возвы́|сить, шу, сишь *pf.* (*of* **~ша́ть**) **1.** to raise, elevate. **2.**: **в. го́лос** to raise one's voice.
возвы́|ситься, шусь, сишься *pf.* (*of* **~ша́ться**) (*in var. senses*) to rise, go up.
возвыша́|ть, ю *impf.* **1.** *impf. of* **возвы́сить. 2.** (*impf. only*) to elevate, ennoble.
возвыша́|ться, юсь *impf.* **1.** *impf. of* **возвы́ситься. 2.** (*impf. only*) (**над**+*i.*) to tower (above) (*also fig.*).
возвыше́ни|е, я *nt.* **1.** rise; raising. **2.** eminence; raised place.
возвы́шенност|ь, и *f.* **1.** (*geog.*) height; eminence. **2.** loftiness, sublimity.
возвы́шен|ный *p.p.p. of* **возвы́сить** *and adj.* **1.** high; elevated. **2.** lofty, sublime, elevated.
возвы́|шу, сишь *see* **~сить**
возгла́в|ить, лю, ишь *pf.* (*of* **~ля́ть**) to head, be at the head of.
возглавля́|ть, ю *impf. of* **возгла́вить**
во́зглас, а *m.* cry, exclamation.
возгла|си́ть, шу́, си́шь *pf.* (*of* **~ша́ть**) to proclaim.
возглаша́|ть, ю *impf. of* **возгласи́ть**
возгна́|ть, возгоню́, возго́нишь, *past* **~л, ~ла́, ~ло** *pf. of* **возгоня́ть**
возго́нк|а, и *f.* (*chem.*) sublimation.
возгон|ю́, ~ишь *see* **возгна́ть**
возгоня́|ть, ю *impf.* (*chem.*) to sublimate.
возгора́емост|ь, и *f.* inflammability.
возгора́емый *adj.* inflammable.
возгора́|ться, юсь *impf. of* **возгоре́ться**
возгор|ди́ться, жу́сь, ди́шься *pf.* to become proud; (+*i.*) to begin to pride o.s. (on).
возгор|е́ться, ю́сь и́шься *pf.* **1.** to flare up (*also fig.*). **2.** (+*i.*) to be inflamed (with); **она́ ~е́лась стра́стью к кино́** she was seized with a passion for the cinema.
возда|ва́ть, ю́, ёшь *impf. of* **возда́ть**
возда́|м, шь, ст *see* **~ть**
возда́|ть, м, шь, ст, ди́м, ди́те, ду́т, *past* **~л, ~ла́, ~ло** *pf.* (*of* **~ва́ть**) to render; **в. кому́-н. до́лжное** to give s.o. his due.
воздвига́|ть, ю *impf.* to raise, erect.
воздви́г|нуть, ну, нешь, *past* **~, ~ла** *pf. of* **~а́ть**
воздева́|ть, ю *impf. of* **возде́ть**
возде́йстви|е, я *nt.* influence; **оказа́ть мора́льное в.** (**на**+*a.*) to bring moral pressure to bear (upon).
возде́йств|овать, ую *impf. and pf.* (**на**+*a.*) to influence, affect; to bring pressure to bear (upon).
возде́л|ать, аю *pf.* (*of* **~ывать**) to cultivate, till.
возде́лыва|ть, ю *impf. of* **возде́лать**
воздержа́вш|ийся *p.p. of* **воздержа́ться**; *as n.* **в., ~егося** *m.* abstention.
воздержа́ни|е, я *nt.* **1.** abstinence. **2.** abstention.
возде́ржанност|ь, и *f.* abstemiousness; temperance.
возде́ржан|ный (~, ~на) *adj.* abstemious; temperate.
воздерж|а́ться, у́сь *pf.* (*of* **~иваться**) (**от**+*g.*) **1.** to keep o.s. (from); to abstain (from); to refrain (from); **в. от мя́са** to abstain from meat. **2.** to abstain (*from voting*).

возде́ржива|ться, юсь *impf. of* **воздержа́ться**
во́здух, а *no pl., m.* air; **на (откры́том) ~е** out of doors; **вы́йти на в.** to go out of doors.
воздухопла́вани|е, я *nt.* aeronautics.
воздухопла́вател|ь, я *m.* **1.** aeronaut. **2.** balloonist.
воздухопла́вательный *adj.* aeronautic(al).
возду́ш|ный *adj.* **1.** air, aerial; **в. змей** kite; **~ная прово́дка** overhead cable; **~ная трево́га** air-raid warning; **в. шар** balloon. **2.** air-driven, air-operated; **в. насо́с** air-pump.
воззва́ни|е, я *nt.* appeal.
возз|ва́ть, ову́, овёшь, *past* **~ва́л, ~вала́, ~ва́ло** *pf.* (*of* **взыва́ть**) (**к**+*d.*, **о**+*p.*) to appeal (to), call (for); **он ~ва́л к избира́телям о подде́ржке** he appealed to the electors for their support.
возз|ову́, овёшь *see* **~ва́ть**
воззре́ни|е, я *nt.* view, outlook.
воззр|и́ться, ю́сь, и́шься *pf.* (**на**+*a.*; *coll.*) to stare (at).
во|зи́ть, жу́, ~́зишь *impf.* (*indet. of* **везти́**) **1.** to cart, convey; to carry; to draw. **2.** (+*i.*, **по**+*d.*; *coll.*) to pass (over), run (over).
во|зи́ться, жу́сь, ~́зишься *impf.* **1.** to romp (*of children*). **2.** (**с**+*i.*, **над**+*i.*) to take trouble (over), busy o.s. (with); (*coll.*) to potter; to tinker (with), fiddle about (with); **он лю́бит в. в саду́** he likes pottering about in the garden.
возлага́|ть, ю *impf. of* **возложи́ть**
во́зле *adv. and prep.*+*g.* by, near; past; **он стоя́л в.** he was standing nearby.
возлия́ни|е, я *nt.* libation.
возлож|и́ть, у́, ~́ишь *pf.* (*of* **возлага́ть**) **1.** to lay (on) (*also fig.*); **в. вено́к на моги́лу** to lay a wreath on a grave. **2.** to place, pin; **он ~и́л все наде́жды на но́вого президе́нта** he pinned all his hopes on the new president.
возлю́бленн|ый *adj.* beloved; *as n.* (*i*) **в., ~ого** *m.* boy-friend; (*ii*) **~ая, ~ой** *f.* girl-friend, sweetheart.
возме́зди|е, я *nt.* retribution; requital.
возме|сти́ть, щу́, сти́шь *pf.* (*of* **~ща́ть**) to compensate, make up (for); **в. поте́рянное вре́мя** to make up for lost time; **в. расхо́ды** to refund expenses.
возмеща́|ть, ю *impf. of* **возмести́ть**
возмеще́ни|е, я *nt.* **1.** compensation, indemnity; (*leg.*) **в. убы́тков** damages. **2.** replacement; refund, reimbursement.
возме|щу́, сти́шь *see* **~сти́ть**
возмо́жно *adv.* **1.** possibly; (+*comp.*) as … as possible; **в. лу́чше** as well as possible. **2.** *as pred.* it is possible.
возмо́жност|ь, и *f.* **1.** possibility; **по (ме́ре) ~и** as far as possible. **2.** opportunity; **при пе́рвой ~и** at the first opportunity. **3.** (*pl.*) means, resources; **у него́ больши́е ~и** he has great potentialities.
возмо́ж|ный (~ен, ~на) *adj.* possible; **врач сде́лал для неё всё ~ное** the doctor did all in his power for her.
возмужа́лост|ь, и *f.* maturity; manhood.
возмужа́лый *adj.* mature; grown up.
возмужа́|ть, ю *pf.* **1.** to mature. **2.** to gain in strength, become stronger.
возмути́тел|ьный (~ен, ~ьна) *adj.* disgraceful, scandalous.
возму|ти́ть, щу́, ти́шь *pf.* to anger, rouse the indignation (of).
возму|ти́ться, щу́сь, ти́шься *pf.* (+*i.*) to be indignant (at).
возмуща́|ть, ю *impf. of* **возмути́ть**
возмуща́|ться, юсь *impf. of* **возмути́ться**
возмуще́ни|е, я *nt.* indignation.
возмущён|ный (~, ~а́) *p.p.p. of* **возмути́ть** *and adj.* (+*i.*) indignant (at).
возму|щу́, ти́шь *see* **~ти́ть**
вознагра|ди́ть, жу́, ди́шь *pf.* to reward; to recompense; to compensate, make up (for).
вознагражда́|ть, ю *impf. of* **вознагради́ть**
вознагражде́ни|е, я *nt.* **1.** reward, recompense; compensation. **2.** fee, remuneration.
вознаме́рива|ться, юсь *impf. of* **вознаме́риться**
вознаме́р|иться, юсь, ишься *pf.* (+*inf.*) to conceive the idea (of).
возненави́|деть, жу, дишь *pf.* to come to hate.
Вознесе́ни|е, я *nt.* (*eccl.*) Ascension (Day).
вознес|ти́, у́, ёшь, *past* **~̈, ~ла́** *pf.* (*of* **возноси́ть**) (*poet.*) to raise, lift up; **в. моли́тву** to offer up a prayer.
вознес|ти́сь, у́сь, ёшься, *past* **~̈ся, ~ла́сь** *pf.* (*of* **возноси́ться**) (*poet.*) to rise; to ascend.
возник|а́ть, а́ю *impf.* (*of* **~́нуть**) to arise, spring up; **у меня́ ~а́ет мысль** the thought occurs to me.
возникнове́ни|е, я *m.* rise, beginning, origin.
возни́к|нуть, ну, нешь, *past* **~, ~ла** *pf. of* **~а́ть**
возни́ц|а, ы *m.* coachman, driver.
возно|си́ть, шу́, ~́сишь *impf. of* **вознести́**
возно|си́ться, шу́сь, ~́сишься *impf. of* **вознести́сь**
возно|шу́, ~́сишь *see* **~си́ть**
возн|я́, и́ *no pl., f.* (*coll.*) **1.** row, noise; **мыши́ная в.** (*fig.*) petty intrigues. **2.** bother, trouble.
возоблада́|ть, ю *pf.* (**над**+*i.*) to prevail (over).
возобнов|и́ть, лю́, и́шь *pf.* (*of* **~ля́ть**) **1.** to renew, resume. **2.** to restore.
возобновле́ни|е, я *nt.* renewal, resumption.
возобновля́|ть, ю *impf. of* **возобнови́ть**
возомн|и́ть, ю́, и́шь *pf.*: **в. о себе́** (*iron.*) to get a false idea of one's own importance; **в. себя́ авторите́том** to consider o.s. an authority.
возража́|ть, ю *impf. of* **возрази́ть; не ~ю** I have no objection.
возраже́ни|е, я *nt.* objection; retort.
возра|зи́ть, жу́, зи́шь *pf.* (*of* **~жа́ть**) (**про́тив**+*g. or* **на**+*a.*) to object (to); to take issue (with). **2.** (*pf. only*) to retort.
во́зраст, а *m.* age; **одного́ ~а** of the same age; **в. совершенноле́тия** age of majority; **преклóнный в.** declining years.
возраста́ни|е, я *nt.* growth, increase; increment.
возраст|а́ть, а́ю *impf. of* **~и́**
возраст|и́, у́, ёшь, *past* **возро́с, возросла́** *pf.* (*of* **~а́ть**) to grow, increase.
возраст|но́й *adj. of* **во́зраст**
возро|ди́ть, жу́, ди́шь *pf.* (*of* **~жда́ть**) to regenerate; to revive.
возро|ди́ться, жу́сь, ди́шься *pf.* (*of* **~жда́ться**) to revive (*intrans.*).
возрожда́|ть, ю *impf. of* **возроди́ть**
возрожда́|ться, юсь *impf. of* **возроди́ться**
возрожде́ни|е, я *nt.* rebirth; revival; **эпо́ха Возрожде́ния** Renaissance.
во́зчик, а *m.* carter, carrier.
возыме́|ть, ю, ешь *pf.* to conceive (*wish, intention, etc.*); **в. де́йствие** to take effect; **в. си́лу** to come into force.
возьм|у́(сь), ёшь(ся) *see* **взя́ть(ся)**
во́ин, а *m.* warrior; fighter.
во́инск|ий *adj.* **1.** military; **~ая пови́нность** liability for military service; **в. по́езд** troop-train. **2.** martial, warlike.
вои́нствен|ный (~, ~на) *adj.* warlike; bellicose.
во́инств|о, а *nt.* (*collect.*; *obs.*) host, army.
вои́нствующ|ий *adj.* militant; (*pol.*, *mil.*) hawkish.
вои́стину *adv.* (*obs.*) indeed; verily; **(Христо́с) в. воскре́с!** (*response at Orthodox Easter service*) He (Christ) is risen indeed!
во|й, я *no pl., m.* howl, howling; wail, wailing.
вой|ду́, дёшь *see* **~ти́**
во́йлок, а *m.* felt; strip of felt.

во́йлочный *adj.* felt.
войн|а́, ы́, *pl.* **~ы** *f.* war; warfare; **агресси́вная в.** war of aggression; **вести́ ~у́** to wage war.
войск|а́, ~ *pl.* (*sg.* **~о, ~а** *nt.*) troops; forces; **наёмные в.** mercenaries.
войсково́й *adj.* troop; military.
во|йти́, йду́, йдёшь, *past* **~шёл, ~шла́** *pf.* (*of* **входи́ть**) (**в.**+*a.*) to enter; to go in(to); to come in(to); **в. в исто́рию** to go down in history; **в. в мо́ду** to become fashionable.
вокали́ст, а *m.* (*mus.*) singing teacher.
вока́льный *adj.* vocal.
вокза́л, а *m.* station; **железнодоро́жный в.** railway station.
вокза́л|ьный *adj. of* ~; station.
вокру́г *adv. and prep.*+*g.* round, around, about; **верте́ться в. да о́коло** (*coll.*) to beat about the bush.
вол, а́ *m.* ox, bullock.
вола́н, а *m.* **1.** flounce (*on skirt*). **2.** shuttlecock.
волды́р|ь, я́ *m.* blister.
волево́й *adj.* **1.** (*psych.*) volitional. **2.** strong-willed.
волеизъявле́ни|е, я *nt.* will, pleasure; command; **по короле́вскому ~ю** by royal command.
волейбо́л, а *m.* (*sport*) volley-ball.
волейболи́ст, а *m.* volley-ball player.
во́лей-нево́лей *adv.* (*coll.*) willy-nilly.
волк, а, *pl.* **~и, ~о́в** *m.* wolf; **морско́й в.** (*coll.*) old salt; **смотре́ть ~ом** (*fig.*) to scowl; **с ~а́ми жить, по-во́лчьи выть** (*prov.*) when in Rome do as the Romans do.
волкода́в, а *m.* wolf-hound.
волн|а́, ы́, *pl.* **~ы, ~а́м** *f.* (*in var. senses*) wave; breaker.
волне́ни|е, я *nt.* **1.** choppiness (*of water*). **2.** (*fig.*) agitation, disturbance; emotion; **прийти́ в в.** to become agitated, excited. **3.** (*usu. pl.*; *pol.*) disturbance(s); unrest.
волни́ст|ый (~, ~а) *adj.* wavy; watered (*of stuffs*); **~ое желе́зо** corrugated iron; **~ая ме́стность** undulating ground.
волн|ова́ть, у́ю, *impf.* (*of* **вз~**) to disturb, agitate (*also fig.*); to excite; to worry.
волн|ова́ться, у́юсь *impf.* **1.** (*of water, etc.*) to be agitated, choppy. **2.** to be disturbed, agitated; to worry, be nervous; to be excited.
волноло́м, а *m.* breakwater.
волнообра́з|ный (~ен, ~на) *adj.* wavy, undulating.
волноре́з, а *m.* breakwater.
волн|у́ющий *pres. part. act. of* **~ова́ть** *and adj.* disturbing, worrying; exciting, thrilling, stirring.
вол|о́вий *adj. of* ~; (*fig.*) very strong; **~о́вья шку́ра** oxhide; **у него́ ~о́вья си́ла** he is as strong as an ox.
во́лок, а *m.* portage; **перепра́вить ~ом** to portage.
воло́к(ся), ла́(сь) *see* **воло́чь(ся)**
волоки́т|а, ы *f.* (*coll.*) red tape.
волокни́ст|ый (~, ~а) *adj.* fibrous; stringy.
волок|но́, на́, *pl.* **~на, ~он, ~нам** *nt.* fibre, filament.
волок|о́нный *adj. of* **~но́**; **~о́нная о́птика** fibre optics.
волонтёр, а *m.* (*obs.*) volunteer.
во́лос, а, *pl.* **~ы** (*and coll.* **~а́**), **воло́с, ~а́м** *m.* hair; (*pl.*) hair (*of the head*); **рвать на себе́ ~ы** to tear one's hair; **схвати́ть за́ ~ы** to take by the hair; **при ви́де тру́па ~ы у меня́ ста́ли ды́бом** the sight of the corpse made my hair stand on end; **ни на́ волос** not a bit.
волоса́т|ый (~, ~а) *adj.* hairy; hirsute.
волос|о́к, ка́ *m.* **1.** *dim. of* **во́лос; на в.** (**от**+*g.*) within a hairbreadth (of); **висе́ть, держа́ться на ~ке́** to hang by a thread. **2.** hair-spring. **3.** (*elec.*) filament.
во́лост|ь, и, *pl.* **~и, ~е́й** *f.* (*hist.*) volost (*smallest administrative division of tsarist Russia*).
волосяно́й *adj.* hair, of hair; **в. покро́в** (*anat.*) scalp.
волоч|и́ть, у́, ~ишь *impf.* to drag; **в. де́ло** to drag out an affair.
волоч|и́ться, у́сь, ~ишься, *impf.* **1.** *pass. of* **~и́ть.** **2.** to drag (*intrans.*), trail. **3.** (**за**+*i.*; *coll.*) to run after; **уже́ три ме́сяца он ~ится за ней** he has been running after her for three months (now).
вол|о́чь, оку́, очёшь, оку́т, *past* **~о́к, ~окла́** *impf.* (*coll.*) to drag.
вол|о́чься, оку́сь, очёшься, оку́тся, *past* **~о́кся, ~окла́сь** *impf.* (*coll.*) **1.** to drag (*intrans.*), trail. **2.** to drag (o.s.) along; to shuffle.
волхв, а́ *m.* sorcerer; soothsayer; **три ~а́** the Magi.
волч|е́ц, ца́ *m.* (*bot.*) thistle.
во́лч|ий *adj. of* **волк;** wolf, lupine; **в. аппети́т** (*coll.*) voracious appetite; **~ья пасть** cleft palate.
волчи́ц|а, ы *f.* she-wolf.
волч|о́к, ка *m.* top; **верте́ться ~ко́м** to spin like a top.
волч|о́нок, о́нка, *pl.* **~а́та, ~а́т** *m.* wolf-cub.
волше́бник, а *m.* magician; wizard.
волше́бниц|а, ы *f.* enchantress.
волше́б|ный (~ен, ~на) *adj.* **1.** magic; magical; **~ное ца́рство** fairyland. **2.** (*fig.*) bewitching; enchanting.
волшебств|о́, а́ *nt.* magic.
волы́н|ить, ю, ишь *impf.* (*coll.*) to dawdle, delay, be dilatory, slack.
волы́нк|а[1], **и** *f.* bagpipes.
волы́нк|а[2], **и** *f.* dawdling, delay; hold-up; **тяну́ть ~у** to dawdle.
волы́нщик[1], **и** *m.* piper.
волы́нщик[2], **и** *m.* (*coll.*) dawdler, slacker.
вольго́тный *adj.* (*coll.*) free, free-and-easy.
волье́р, а *m.* cage; enclosure.
волье́р|а, и *f.* = **волье́р**
во́льнича|ть, ю *impf.* (*pej.*) to take liberties.
во́льн|о *adv. of* **~ый**; (*as mil. command*) **в.!** stand at ease!
вольноду́м|ец, ца *m.* (*hist.*) free-thinker.
вольноду́м|ный (~ен, ~на) *adj.* (*hist.*) free-thinking.
вольноду́мств|о, а *nt.* (*hist.*) free-thinking.
вольнолюби́в|ый (~, ~а) *adj.* freedom-loving.
вольнонаёмн|ый *adj.* **1.** civilian (*employed in or for mil. establishment*). **2.** (*obs.*) hired; free-lance.
во́льност|ь, и *f.* **1.** freedom; liberty; **поэти́ческая в.** poetic license; **позволя́ть себе́ ~и** to take liberties. **2.** (*usu. pl.*; *hist.*) liberties, rights.
во́л|ьный *adj.* **1.** free; **в. го́род** free city. **2.** (*econ.*) free, unrestricted; **в. ры́нок** free market. **3.** (*of clothing*) free, loose. **4.: в. перево́д** (*liter.*) free translation. **5.** (*sport*) free, free-style; **~ьная борьба́** free-style wrestling; **в. уда́р** free-kick. **6.: (~ен, ~ьна́)** free(-and-easy), familiar (*in behaviour*). **7. (~ен, ~ьна́,** *pl.* **~ьны́)** (*full form not used*) free, at liberty; **ты ~ен де́лать, что хо́чешь** you are free to do as you wish.
вольт, а, *g. pl.* **в.** *m.* (*elec.*) volt.
вольта́ж, а *m.* (*elec.*) voltage.
вольтме́тр, а *m.* (*elec.*) voltmetre.
вольфра́м, а *m.* (*chem.*) tungsten.
вольфра́мовый *adj. of* ~
воль|ю́, ёшь *see* **влить**
во́л|я, и *no pl., f.* **1.** (*in var. senses*) will; volition; wish(es); **после́дняя в.** last will; **свобо́дная в.** free will; **в. к жи́зни** will to live; **си́ла ~и** will-power; **в. ва́ша** (*coll.*) as you please, as you like; **по до́брой ~е** of one's own free will; **не по свое́й ~е** against one's will. **2.** freedom, liberty; **вы́пустить, отпусти́ть на ~ю** to set free; **на ~е** at liberty; at large; **дать ~ю** (+*d.*) to give free rein (to).

вон[1] *adv.* out; off, away; **вы́йти в.** to go away; **в. отсю́да!** get out!; **из рук в. пло́хо** abysmally; **у меня́ э́то из ума́ в.** (*coll.*) it completely slipped my mind.

вон[2] *particle* there; over there; **в. он идёт** there he goes.

вон|жу́, зи́шь *see* **~зи́ть**

вонза́|ть, ю *impf. of* **вонзи́ть**

вонза́|ться, юсь 1. *impf. of* **вонзи́ться. 2.** *pass. of* **~ть**

вон|зи́ть, жу́, жи́шь *pf.* (*of* **~за́ть**) (**в**+*a.*) to plunge, thrust (into)

вон|зи́ться, жу́сь, зи́шься *pf.* (*of* **~за́ться**) **1.** to pierce, penetrate. **2.** *pass. of* **~зи́ть**

вонми́ *see* **внять**

вон|ь, и *no pl., f.* stink, stench.

воню́ч|ий (~, ~а) *adj.* stinking, fetid.

воню́чк|а, и *f.* (*zool.*) skunk.

воня́|ть, ю *impf.* (+*i.*) to stink, reek (of).

вообража́|емый *pres. part. pass. of* **~ть** *and adj.* imaginary; fictitious.

вообража́л|а, ы *c.g.* (*coll.*) show-off.

вообража́|ть, ю *impf.* (*of* **вообрази́ть**) **1.** to imagine; **в. жизнь в ка́менном ве́ке** to imagine life in the Stone Age; **~ю, как вы чу́вствуете себя́** I can imagine how you feel. **2.** (*coll.*): **в. о себе́** to fancy o.s.

воображе́ни|е, я *nt.* imagination; **у неё живо́е в.** she has a lively imagination.

вообрази́м|ый (~, ~а) *pres. part. pass of* **вообрази́ть** *and adj.* imaginable.

вообра|зи́ть, жу́, зи́шь *pf. of* **~жа́ть; ~зи́(те)!** fancy!; (just) imagine!

вообще́ *adv.* **1.** in general; on the whole; **в. говоря́** generally speaking. **2.** always; **она́ вы́глядит бле́дной в., а не то́лько сего́дня** she always looks pale, not just today.

воодушев|и́ть, лю́, и́шь *pf.* (*of* **~ля́ть**) to inspire, rouse; to hearten, cheer.

воодушевле́ни|е, я *nt.* animation; enthusiasm; fervour; **говори́ть с больши́м ~ем** to speak with great fervour.

воодушевлён|ный (~, ~а́) *p.p.p. of* **воодушеви́ть** *and adj.* animated; enthusiastic; fervent.

воодушевля́|ть, ю *impf. of* **воодушеви́ть**

вооруж|а́ть(ся), а́ю(сь) *impf. of* **~и́ть(ся)**

вооруже́ни|е, я *nt.* **1.** arming. **2.** arms, armament; **го́нка вооруже́ний** arms race.

вооружён|ный (~, ~а́) *p.p.p. of* **вооружи́ть** *and adj.* armed; **в. до зубо́в** armed to the teeth; **~ные си́лы** armed forces.

вооруж|и́ть, у́, и́шь *pf.* (*of* **~а́ть**) **1.** (+*i.*) to arm; to equip (with) (*also fig.*). **2.** (**про́тив**+*g.*) to set (against).

вооруж|и́ться, у́сь, и́шься *pf.* (*of* **~а́ться**) **1.** to arm o.s.; (*fig.*) to equip o.s. **2.** *pass. of* **~и́ть**

воо́чию *adv.* **1.** with one's own eyes, for o.s.; **я в. убеди́лся в том, что он небре́жно пра́вил маши́ной** I could see for myself that he was driving carelessly. **2.** clearly, plainly; **показа́ть в.** to show clearly.

во-пе́рвых *adv.* first, first of all, in the first place.

воп|и́ть, лю́, и́шь *impf.* (*coll.*) to cry out; to howl; to wail.

вопи|ю́щий *pres. part. act. of* **~я́ть** *and adj.* scandalous; crying; **~ю́щее безобра́зие** crying shame; **~ю́щее противоре́чие** glaring contradiction.

вопло|ти́ть, щу́, ти́шь *pf.* (*of* **~ща́ть**) to embody; to personify; **в. в себе́** to be the embodiment (of).

воплоща́|ть, ю *impf. of* **воплоти́ть**

воплоще́ни|е, я *nt.* embodiment, incarnation; **он — в. здоро́вья** he is the picture of health.

воплощён|ный (~, ~а́) *p.p.p. of* **воплоти́ть** *and adj.* incarnate; personified; **он — ~ная добросо́вестность** he is conscientiousness personified.

вопл|ь, я *m.* cry, wail; wailing, howling.

вопреки́ *prep.*+*d.* despite, in spite of; against, contrary to; **он встал с посте́ли в. предписа́нию врача́** he got out of bed against doctor's orders.

вопро́с, а *m.* **1.** question; **зада́ть в.** to put a question. **2.** question, problem; matter; **поста́вить под в.** to call into question; **в. жи́зни и сме́рти** matter of life and death; **спо́рный в.** moot point; **что за в.!** of course!

вопроси́тельный *adj.* interrogative; interrogatory; **в. знак** question-mark; **в. взгляд** inquiring look.

вопро́сник, а *m.* questionnaire.

вопь|ю́, ёшь *see* **впить**

вор, а, *pl.* **∠ы, ~о́в** *m.* thief; **карма́нный в.** pickpocket; **магази́нный в.** shoplifter.

во́рван|ь, и *f.* train-oil; blubber.

ворв|а́ться, у́сь, ёшься, *past* **~а́лся, ~ала́сь** *pf.* (*of* **врыва́ться**) to burst (into).

вори́шк|а, и *m.* petty thief.

ворк|ова́ть, у́ю *impf.* (*of pigeons*) to coo; (*fig.*) to bill and coo.

воркотн|я́, и́ *f.* (*coll.*) grumbling.

вороб|е́й, ья́ *m.* sparrow; **стре́ляный в.** (*fig.*) old hand.

вороб|ьи́ный *adj. of* **~е́й**

воро́ванный *adj.* stolen.

ворова́т|ый (~, ~а) *adj.* thievish; furtive; **в. взгляд** furtive glance.

вор|ова́ть, у́ю *impf.* (*pf.* **с~**) to steal.

воро́вк|а, и *f. of* **вор**

воровски́ *adv.* (*coll.*) furtively.

воровск|о́й *adj.* of thieves; **в. язы́к, ~о́е арго́** thieves' cant.

воровств|о́, а́ *nt.* stealing; theft.

ворожб|а́, ы *no pl., f.* sorcery; fortune-telling.

вороже|я́, и́ *f.* sorceress; fortune-teller.

ворож|и́ть, у́, и́шь *impf.* (*of* **по~**) to practise sorcery; to tell fortunes.

во́рон, а *m.* raven.

воро́н|а, ы *f.* crow.

воро́н|ий *adj. of* **~а**

ворон|и́ть, ю́, и́шь *impf.* (*tech.*) to burnish.

воро́нк|а, и *f.* **1.** funnel (*for pouring liquids*). **2.** (*mil.*) crater.

ворон|о́й *adj.* black (*of horses*).

во́рот[1], **а,** *pl.* **~ы** *m.* collar (*of garment*); neckband; **схвати́ть за́ в.** to seize by the collar, collar.

во́рот[2], **а** *m.* (*tech.*) winch; windlass.

воро́т|а (*coll.* **~а́), ~** *no sg.* **1.** gate, gates; gateway; **пришла́ беда́, отворя́й ~а́** (*prov.*) misfortunes never come singly. **2.** (*sport*) goal, goal-posts.

вороти́л|а, ы *m.* (*coll.*) bigwig.

воро|ти́ть, чу́, ∠тишь *pf.* (*coll.*) to bring back; **сде́ланного не ∠тишь** what's done can't be undone.

воро|ти́ться, чу́сь, ∠тишься *pf.* (*coll.*) to return.

воротни́к, а́ *m.* collar.

воротнич|о́к, ка́ *m.* collar.

во́рох, а, *pl.* **~а́** *m.* heap, pile; (*fig., coll.*) heaps, masses, stacks.

воро́ча|ть, ю *impf.* (*coll.*) **1.** to turn, move; **в. глаза́ми** to roll one's eyes. **2.** (+*i.*; *fig.*) to have control (of).

воро́ча|ться, юсь *impf.* to turn, move (*intrans.*); **в. с бо́ку на́ бок** to toss and turn.

воро|чу́(сь), ∠тишь(ся) *see* **~ти́ть(ся)**

ворош|и́ть, у́, и́шь *impf.* (*of* **раз~**) **1.: в. се́но** to turn, ted hay **2.** (*fig., coll.*) to stir up.

ворош|и́ться, у́сь и́шься *impf.* (*coll.*) to move about, stir.

ворс, а, *no pl., m.* pile; nap.

ворси́нк|а, и *f.* **1.** (*text.*) hair. **2.** (*physiol., bot.*) fibre.

ворча́ни|е, я *nt.* grumbling; growling.

ворч|а́ть, у́, и́шь *impf.* (**на**+*a.*) to grumble (at); to growl (at).

ворчли́в|ый (~, ~а) *adj.* querulous.
ворчу́н, а́ *m.* (*coll.*) grumbler.
восвоя́си *adj.* (for) home.
восемна́дцатый *adj.* eighteenth.
восемна́дцат|ь, и *num.* eighteen.
во́с|емь, ьми́, ьмью́, *and* **емью́** *num.* eight.
во́с|емьдесят, ьми́десяти *num.* eighty.
вос|емьсо́т, ьмисо́т, емьюста́ми (*coll.* **ьмиста́ми**) *num.* eight hundred.
во́семью *adv.* eight times (*in multiplication*).
воск, а *m.* wax.
воскли́кн|уть, у, ешь *pf.* to exclaim.
восклица́ни|е, я *nt.* exclamation.
восклица́тельный *adj.* exclamatory; **в. знак** exclamation mark.
восклица́|ть, ю *impf.* (*of* **воскли́кнуть**) to exclaim.
восков|о́й *adj.* wax; waxen.
воскрес|а́ть, а́ю *impf.* (*of* **~нуть**) to rise again, rise from the dead; (*fig.*) to revive.
воскресе́ни|е, я *nt.* resurrection.
воскресе́нь|е, я *nt.* Sunday.
воскре|си́ть, шу́, си́шь, *pf.* (*of* **~ша́ть**) to raise from the dead, resurrect; (*fig.*) to resurrect, revive.
воскре́с|нуть, ну, нешь, *past* **~, ~ла** *pf. of* **~а́ть**
воскре́сн|ый *adj.* Sunday.
воскреша́|ть, ю *impf. of* **воскреси́ть**
воскреше́ни|е, я *nt.* raising from the dead, resurrection; (*fig.*) revival.
воспале́ни|е, я *nt.* (*med.*) inflammation; **в. лёгких** pneumonia; **в. по́чек** nephritis.
воспалён|ный (~, ~а́) *p.p.p. of* **воспали́ть** *and adj.* sore; inflamed (*also fig.*).
воспали́тельный *adj.* (*med.*) inflammatory; **в. проце́сс** inflammation.
воспал|и́ться, ю́сь, и́шься *pf.* (*of* **~я́ться**) to become inflamed.
воспал|я́ть(ся), я́ю(сь) *impf. of* **~и́ть(ся)**
воспева́|ть, ю *impf. of* **воспе́ть**
восп|е́ть, ою́, оёшь *pf.* (*of* **~ева́ть**) (*poet.*) to sing (of), extol (in song).
воспита́ни|е, я *nt.* **1.** education; upbringing. **2.** (good) breeding.
воспи́танник, а *m.* **1.** pupil. **2.** ward (*a minor*).
воспи́танност|ь, и *f.* (good) breeding.
воспи́танный *p.p.p. of* **воспита́ть** *and adj.* well brought up.
воспита́тел|ь, я *m.* tutor, educator.
воспита́тельниц|а, ы *f.* governess.
воспита́тельный *adj.* educational; **в. дом** foundling hospital.
воспит|а́ть, а́ю *pf.* (*of* **~ывать**) **1.** to educate, bring up. **2.** to cultivate, foster. **3.** (**из**+*g.*) to make (of); **в. солда́т из сбро́да** to make an army of a rabble.
воспи́тыва|ть, ю *impf. of* **воспита́ть**
воспламене́ни|е, я *nt.* ignition.
воспламен|и́ть, ю́, и́шь *pf.* (*of* **~я́ть**) to kindle, ignite; (*fig.*) to fire, inflame.
воспламен|и́ться, ю́сь, и́шься *pf.* (*of* **~я́ться**) to catch fire, ignite; (*fig.*) to take fire, flare up.
воспламеня́емост|ь, и *f.* inflammability.
воспламеня́емый *adj.* inflammable.
воспламеня́|ть(ся), ю(сь) *impf. of* **воспламени́ть(ся)**
воспо́лн|ить, ю, ишь *pf.* to fill in.
восполня́|ть, ю *impf. of* **воспо́лнить**
воспо́льз|оваться, уюсь *pf. of* **по́льзоваться**
воспомина́ни|е, я *nt.* **1.** recollection, memory; **жить ~ями** to live on memories. **2.** *pl.* (*liter.*) memoirs; reminiscences.
восп|ою́, оёшь *see* **~е́ть**
воспрепя́тств|овать, ую *pf. of* **препя́тствовать**
воспре|ти́ть, щу́, ти́шь *pf.* (*of* **~ща́ть**) (+*a. or inf.*) to forbid, prohibit.
воспреща́|ть, ю *impf. of* **воспрети́ть**
воспреща́|ться, юсь *impf.* to be prohibited; **«кури́ть ~ется»** 'No Smoking'; **«посторо́нним вход ~ется»** 'Unauthorized Persons Not Admitted'.
воспреще́ни|е, я *nt.* prohibition.
восприи́мчив|ый (~, ~а) *adj.* **1.** receptive; impressionable. **2.** susceptible.
восприм|у́, ~ешь *see* **восприня́ть**
воспринима́|ть, ю *impf. of* **восприня́ть**
воспри|ня́ть, му́, ~мешь, *past* **~нял, ~няла́, ~няло** *pf.* (*of* **~нима́ть**) **1.** to perceive, apprehend; to grasp, take in. **2.** to take (for), interpret.
восприя́ти|е, я *nt.* (*phil., psych.*) perception.
воспроизведе́ни|е, я *nt.* **1.** reproduction. **2.** playback, replay; **заме́дленное в.** slow-motion replay.
воспроизве|сти́, ду́, дёшь, *past* **~л, ~ла́** *pf.* (*of* **воспроизводи́ть**) (*in var. senses*) to reproduce; **в. в па́мяти** to recall.
воспроизводи́тельный *adj.* reproductive.
воспроизво|ди́ть, жу́, ~дишь *impf. of* **воспроизвести́**
воспроти́в|иться, люсь, ишься *pf. of* **проти́виться**
воспря́н|уть, у, ешь *pf.* **1.** to leap up. **2.** (*coll.*) to cheer up; **в. ду́хом** to take heart.
восседа́|ть, ю *impf. of* **воссе́сть**
воссоедине́ни|е, я *nt.* reunion, reunification.
воссоедин|и́ть, ю́, и́шь *pf.* (*of* **~я́ть**) to reunite.
воссоединя́|ть, ю *impf. of* **воссоедини́ть**
воссозда|ва́ть, ю́, ёшь *impf. of* **~ть**
воссозда́ни|е, я *nt.* reconstruction.
воссоз|да́ть, да́м, да́шь да́ст, дади́м, дади́те, даду́т, *past* **~да́л, ~дала́, ~да́ло** *pf.* (*of* **~дава́ть**) to reconstruct; to reconstitute.
восста|ва́ть, ю́, ёшь *impf. of* **~ть**
восстана́влива|ть, ю *impf. of* **восстанови́ть**
восста́ни|е, я *nt.* rising, insurrection.
восстанови́тел|ь, я *m.* renovator, restorer.
восстанови́тельн|ый *adj.* restorative; **в. перио́д** period of reconstruction; **~ые рабо́ты** restoration work.
восстанов|и́ть, лю́, ~ишь *pf.* (*of* **восстана́вливать**) **1.** to restore, renew; to rehabilitate; **в. мир** to restore peace; **в. в па́мяти** to recall, recollect; **в. кого́-н. в. права́х** to restore s.o.'s rights; **его́ ~и́ли в (пре́жней) до́лжности** he has been reinstated. **2.** (**про́тив**+*g.*) to set (against), antagonize.
восстановле́ни|е, я *nt.* restoration, renewal; rehabilitation; **в. в до́лжности** reinstatement.
восстановля́|ть, ю *impf.* **1.** *impf. of* **восстанови́ть. 2.** (*chem.*) to reduce.
восста́|ть, ну, нешь, *imper.* **~нь,** *pf.* (*of* **~ва́ть**) (**на**+*a.*, **про́тив**+*g.*) to rise (against); (*fig.*) to be up in arms (against).
восто́к, а *m.* **1.** east; **на в., с ~а** to, from the east. **2. В.** the East; the Orient; **Бли́жний В.** the Middle East.
востокове́д, а *m.* orientalist.
востокове́дени|е, я *nt.* oriental studies.
восто́рг, а *m.* delight; rapture; **быть в ~е** (**от**+*g.*) to be delighted (with).
восторга́|ть, ю *impf.* to delight, enrapture.
восторга́|ться, юсь *impf.* (+*i.*) to be delighted (with); to go into, be in raptures (over).
восто́рженност|ь, и *f.* **1.** enthusiasm. **2.** proneness to enthusiasm.
восто́ржен|ный (~, ~на) *adj.* enthusiastic, rapturous.
восторжеств|ова́ть, у́ю *pf. of* **торжествова́ть**
восто́чн|ый *adj.* east, eastern; oriental.
востре́бовани|е, я *nt.* claiming, demand; **посла́ть паке́т до ~я** to send a parcel poste restante.
востре́б|овать, ую *pf.* to claim.
востро́ *adv.* (*coll.*): **держа́ть у́хо в.** to keep a sharp

look-out.
восхвале́ни|е, я *nt.* eulogy.
восхвал|и́ть, ю́, ∠ишь *pf.* (*of* **~я́ть**) to laud, extol, eulogize.
восхваля́|ть, ю *impf. of* **восхвали́ть**
восхити́тел|ьный (~ен, ~ьна) *adj.* entrancing, ravishing; delightful; delicious.
восхи|ти́ть, щу́, ти́шь *pf.* (*fig.*) to carry away, delight, captivate.
восхи|ти́ться, щу́сь, ти́шься *pf.* (+*i.*) to be carried away (by); to admire.
восхища́|ть(ся), ю(сь) *impf. of* **восхити́ть(ся)**
восхище́ни|е, я *nt.* delight, rapture; admiration.
восхищён|ный (~, ~а́) *p.p.p. of* **восхити́ть** *and adj.* rapt; admiring.
восхи́|щу, тишь *see* **~тить**
восхи|щу́(сь), ти́шь(ся) *see* **~ти́ть(ся)**
восхо́д, а *m.* rising; **в. со́лнца** sunrise.
восхо|ди́ть, жу́, ∠дишь *impf.* **1.** *impf. of* **взойти́. 2.** (*impf. only*) **(к)** to go back (to), date (from).
восход|я́щий *pres. part. of* **~и́ть** *and adj.* **~я́щая звезда́** (*fig.*) rising star.
восхожде́ни|е, я *nt.* ascent; **в. на Монбла́н** the ascent of Mont Blanc.
восше́стви|е, я *nt.* **(на престо́л)** accession (to the throne).
восьм|а́я *see* **~о́й**
восьмёрк|а, и *f.* **1.** (*coll.*) eight; number eight (*of buses, etc.*). **2.** (*cards*) eight.
во́сьмер|о, ы́х *num.* eight; **нас бы́ло в.** there were eight of us.
восьмигра́нник, а *m.* (*math.*) octahedron.
восьмидеся́тый *adj.* eightieth.
восьмиле́тний *adj.* **1.** eight-year. **2.** eight-year-old.
восьмисо́тый *adj.* eight-hundredth.
восьмиуго́льник, а *m.* (*math.*) octagon.
восмиуго́льный *adj.* octagonal.
восьмичасово́й *adj.* eight-hour; **в. рабо́чий день** eight-hour (working-)day.
восьм|о́й *adj.* eighth; *as n.* **~а́я, ~о́й** *f.* an eighth.
восьму́шк|а, и *f.* octavo; **писа́ть на ~е** to write on octavo.
вот *particle* **1.** here (is), there (is); this is; **в. мой дом** here is my house, this is my house; **в. авто́бус идёт** here comes the bus; **в. мы пришли́** here we are; **в. где я живу́** this is where I live. **2.** (*emph. prons.*; *unstressed*): **в. э́ти ту́фли ей нра́вились** *these* are the shoes she liked. **3.** (*in excl.*; *always stressed*) here's a …, there's a … (for you)!; **во́т так исто́рия!** here's a pretty kettle of fish!; (*expr. surprise*) **во́т как!; во́т что!** really? you don't say!; **в. так та́к!; в. тебе на́!** well!; well, I never!; (*surprise and disapproval*) **в. ещё!** indeed!; what(ever) next!; (*approval and/or encouragement*) **в. та́к!; в.-в.!** that's right!; that's it!; (*accompanying blows*) **во́т тебе!** take that!; **вот тебе́ и...** so much for …; **вот тебе́ и пое́здка в Пари́ж!** so much for the trip to Paris!
вот-во́т *adv.* just, on the point of; **по́езд в.-в. придёт** the train is just coming.
воткн|у́ть, у́, ёшь *pf.* (*of* **втыка́ть**) **(в**+*a.*) to stick (into); drive (into).
вотр|у́, ёшь *see* **втере́ть**
во́тум, а *no pl.*, *m.* vote; **в. (не)дове́рия** (+*d.*) vote of (no) confidence (in).
во́тчин|а, ы *f.* (*hist.*) inherited estate, lands.
воцаре́ни|е, я *nt.* accession (to the throne).
воцар|и́ться, ю́сь, и́шься *pf.* (*of* **~я́ться**) **1.** to come to the throne. **2.** (*fig.*) to set in.
воцаря́|ться, юсь *impf. of* **воцари́ться**
вош|ёл, ла́ *see* **войти́**
вошь, вши, *i.* **∠ю,** *pl.* **вши, вшей** *f.* louse.
вощанк|а, и *f.* wax-paper.
вощёный *adj.* waxed.
вощ|и́ть, у́, и́шь *impf.* (*of* **на~**) to wax.
во́|ю, ешь *see* **выть**
вою́|ю, ешь *see* **воева́ть**
воя́к|а, и *m.* (*coll.*, *iron.*) warrior.
впада́|ть, ю *impf.* **1.** *impf. of* **впасть. 2.** *impf. only* (*of rivers*) to fall (into), flow (into).
впаде́ни|е, я *nt.* confluence.
впа́дин|а, ы *f.* cavity, hollow; socket.
впад|у́, ёшь *see* **впасть**
впа́л|ый *adj.* hollow, sunken.
впа|сть, ду́, дёшь *pf.* (*of* **~да́ть**) **1. (в**+*a.*) to fall (into), lapse (into), sink (into); **в. в бе́дность** to fall into penury. **2.** (*of eyes, cheeks*) to fall in, sink.
впервы́е *adv.* for the first time; first.
вперева́лку *adv.* (*coll.*): **ходи́ть в.** to waddle.
вперёд *adv.* **1.** forward(s), ahead; (*of clocks and watches*) fast; **взад и в.** back and forth. **2.** (*coll.*) in future, from now on; **в. будь осторо́жнее** be more careful in future. **3.** in advance; **заплати́ть в.** to pay in advance.
впереди́ 1. *adv.* in front, ahead. **2.** *adv.* in (the) future; ahead. **3.** *prep.*+*g.* in front of, ahead of.
вперемёжку *adv.* (*coll.*) alternately.
вперемёшку *adv.* (*coll.*) pell-mell, higgledy-piggledy; in confusion.
впечатле́ни|е, я *nt.* impression; **произвести́ в.** (**на**+*a.*) to make an impression (upon).
впечатли́тел|ьный (~ен, ~ьна) *adj.* impressionable.
впечатля́ющий *adj.* impressive.
впива́|ть, ю *impf.* **1.** *impf. of* **впить. 2.** *impf. only* to drink in (*esp. olfactory sensations*).
впива́|ться, юсь *impf. of* **впи́ться**
впи|са́ть, шу́, ∠шешь *pf.* (*of* **∠сывать**) **1.** to enter; to insert. **2.** (*math.*) to inscribe.
впи|са́ться, шу́сь, ∠шешься *pf.* (*of* **∠сываться**) (*coll.*) to be enrolled, join.
впи́ск|а, и *f.* (*coll.*) **1.** entry. **2.** insertion.
впи́сыва|ть(ся), ю(сь) *impf. of* **вписа́ть(ся)**
впит|а́ть, а́ю *pf.* (*of* **∠ывать**) to absorb; (*fig.*) to absorb, take in.
впи́тыва|ть, ю *impf. of* **впита́ть**
впи|ть, вопью́, вопьёшь, *past* **~л, ~ла́, ∠ло** *pf.* (*of* **~ва́ть**) to imbibe, absorb.
впи́|ться, вопью́сь, вопьёшься, *past* **~лся, ~ла́сь** *pf.* (*of* **~ва́ться**) **(в**+*a.*) **1.** to stick (into); to bite; to sting. **2.: в. взо́ром, глаза́ми** to fix, fasten one's eyes (upon).
впих|а́ть, а́ю *pf.* (*coll.*) = **~ну́ть**
впи́хива|ть, ю *impf. of* **впиха́ть** *and* **впихну́ть**
впих|ну́ть, ну́, нёшь *pf.* (*of* **∠ивать**) to stuff in, cram in; to shove.
вплавь *adv.* by swimming.
впле|сти́, ту́, тёшь, *past* **~̈л, ~ла́** *pf.* (*of* **~та́ть**) **(в**+*a.*) to plait (into), intertwine.
вплета́|ть, ю *impf. of* **вплести́**
впле|ту́, тёшь *see* **~сти́**
вплотну́ю *adv.* close; (*fig.*) in earnest; **поста́вить стол в. к стене́** to put the table right up against the wall.
вплоть *adv.* **1.: в. до** (right) up to; until. **2. в. (к**+*d.*) right up against, right up to.
вплыва́|ть, ю *impf. of* **вплыть**
вплы|ть, ву́, вёшь, *past* **~л, ~ла́, ∠ло** *pf.* (*of* **~ва́ть**) to swim in; to sail in, steam in.
впова́лку *adv.* (*coll.*) side by side.
вполго́лоса *adv.* in an undertone; under one's breath.
вполз|а́ть, а́ю *impf. of* **~ти́**
вполз|ти́, у́, ёшь, *past* **~, ~ла́** *pf.* (*of* **~а́ть**) to creep in, crawl in; to creep up, crawl up.
вполне́ *adv.* fully, completely; quite.
вполоборо́та *adv.* half-turned; half-face.
впольяна́ *adv.* (*coll.*) half seas over.
впопа́д *adv.* (*coll.*) to the point; opportunely.

впопыха́х *adv.* (*coll.*) **1.** in a hurry, hastily. **2.** in one's haste; **в. я оста́вил мой зо́нтик в по́езде** in my haste I left my umbrella on the train.
впо́ру *adv.* (*coll.*) just right, exactly; **э́тот костю́м мне соверше́нно в.** this suit fits me perfectly; **бе́дному да во́ру вся́кое пла́тье в.** (*prov.*) beggars cannot be choosers.
впорхн|у́ть, у́, ёшь *pf.* (*of birds or butterflies*) to flit in(to), flutter in(to); (*fig.*) to fly (into).
впосле́дствии *adv.* subsequently; afterwards.
впотьма́х *adv.* (*coll.*) in the dark.
впра́вду *adv.* (*coll.*) really, in reality.
впра́ве *as pred.*: **быть в.** (+*inf.*) to have a right (to); **он был в. серди́ться на вас** he had a right to be angry with you.
впра́в|ить, лю, ишь *pf.* (*of* **~ля́ть**) **1.** (*med.*) to set (*fractured or dislocated bone*). **2.** to tuck in.
вправля́|ть, ю *impf. of* **впра́вить**
впра́во *adv.* (**от**+*g.*) to the right (of).
впредь *adv.* in future, henceforth; **в. до** (+*g.*) until.
вприку́ску *adv.* (*coll.*) *only in phr.* **пить чай в.** to drink (unsweetened) tea while holding a lump of sugar in the mouth.
вприпры́жку *adv.* (*coll.*) skipping; hopping.
вприся́дку *adv.*: **пляса́ть в.** to dance squatting.
впро́голодь *adv.* half-starving.
впрок *adv.* **1.** for future use; **загото́вить в.** to lay in, stock up on. **2.** to advantage; **э́то не пойдёт ему́ в.** it will not do him any good.
впроса́к *adv.* (*coll.*): **попа́сть в.** to put one's foot in it.
впросо́нках *adv.* (*coll.*) (while) half asleep.
впро́чем *adv. and conj.* **1.** however; but. **2.** or rather; **приезжа́йте за́втра, в. лу́чше бы́ло бы послеза́втра** come tomorrow, or better still the day after.
впры́гива|ть, ю *impf. of* **впры́гнуть**
впры́г|нуть, ну, нешь *pf.* (*of* **~ивать**) (**в, на**+*a.*) to jump (into, on).
впры́скивани|е, я *nt.* injection.
впры́скива|ть, ю *impf. of* **впры́снуть**
впры́сн|уть, у, ешь *pf.* (*of* **впры́скивать**) to inject.
впрямь *adv.* (*coll.*) really, indeed.
впря|чь, гу́, жёшь, гу́т, *past* **впряг, ~гла́, ~гло́** *pf.* (*of* **~га́ть**) (**в**+*a.*) to harness (to), put (to).
впу́ск, а *m.* admission, admittance.
впуска́|ть, ю *impf. of* **впусти́ть**
впу|сти́ть, щу́, ~́стишь *pf.* (*of* **~ска́ть**) to admit, let in.
впусту́ю *adv.* (*coll.*) for nothing, to no purpose.
впу́т|ать, аю *pf.* (*of* **~ывать**) to entangle, involve.
впу́т|аться, аюсь *pf.* (*of* **~ываться**) *pass. of* **~ать;** (*fig.*) to get mixed up (in).
впу́тыва|ть(ся), ю(сь) *impf. of* **впу́тать(ся)**
впу|щу́, ~́стишь *see* **~сти́ть**
впя́теро *adv.* five times; **в. бо́льше** five times as much.
впятеро́м *adv.* five (together).
враг, а́ *m.* enemy; (*collect*) the enemy.
вражд|а́, ы́ *f.* enmity, hostility.
вражде́б|ный (~ен, ~на) *adj.* hostile.
вражд|ова́ть, у́ю *impf.* (**с**+*i. and* **ме́жду собо́ю**) to be at odds (with).
вра́жеский *adj.* (*mil.*) enemy; hostile.
вразби́вку *adv.* (*coll.*) at random.
вразбро́д *adv.* (*coll.*) separately; in disunity.
вразбро́с *adv.* (*coll.*) separately.
вразва́лку *adv.* (*coll.*): **ходи́ть в.** to waddle.
вразно́с *adv.* (*coll.*): **торгова́ть в.** to peddle.
вразре́з *adv.*, *only in phr.* **идти́ в.** (**с**+ *i.*) to go against.
вразуми́тел|ьный (~ен, ~ьна) *adj.* **1.** intelligible; perspicuous. **2.** instructive.
вразум|и́ть, лю́, и́шь *pf.* (*of* **~ля́ть**) to make understand; **ниче́м их не ~и́шь** they will never learn.
вразумля́|ть, ю *impf. of* **вразуми́ть**
вра́к|и, ~ *no sg.* (*coll.*) nonsense, rubbish.
врал|ь, я́ *m.* (*coll.*) liar; chatterbox.
вран|ьё, я́ *nt.* (*coll.*) lies; nonsense.
врасплóх *adv.*: **заста́ть, засти́гнуть в.** to take unawares; to catch off guard.
врассыпну́ю *adv.* in all directions; helter-skelter.
враст|а́ть, а́ю *impf.* (*of* **~и́**) to grow in(to); **~а́ющий но́готь** ingrowing nail.
враст|и́, у́, ёшь, *past* **врос, вросла́** *pf. of* **~а́ть**
врастя́жку *adv.* (*coll.*) **1.** at full length; **упа́сть в.** to fall flat. **2. говори́ть в.** to drawl.
врата́р|ь, я́ *m.* (*sport*) goalkeeper.
вр|ать, у, ёшь, *past* **~ал, ~ала́, ~а́ло** *impf.* (*of* **на~** *and* **со~**) (*coll.*) **1.** to lie, tell lies. **2.** to talk nonsense.
врач, а́ *m.* doctor, physician; **зубно́й в.** dentist.
враче́бный *adj.* medical.
враща́тельный *adj.* rotary.
враща́|ть, ю *impf.* to revolve, rotate; **в. глаза́ми** to roll one's eyes.
враща́|ться, юсь *impf.* to revolve, rotate (*intrans.*); **он ~ется в худо́жественных круга́х** he moves in artistic circles.
враще́ни|е, я *nt.* rotation; revolution.
вред, а́ *no pl.*, *m.* harm; injury; damage; **без ~а́** (**для**+*g.*) without detriment (to).
вреди́тел|ь, я *m.* **1.** (*agric.*) pest; vermin. **2.** (*pol.*) (economic) saboteur.
вреди́тель|ский *adj. of* **~ 2.**
вреди́тельств|о, а *nt.* **1.** (economic) sabotage. **2.** act of sabotage.
вре|ди́ть, жу́, ди́шь *impf.* (*of* **по~**) (+*d.*) to injure, harm, hurt; **в. здоро́вью** to be injurious to health.
вре́дно *adv. as pred.* it is harmful, it is injurious; **в. для здоро́вья** bad for one's health.
вре́д|ный (~ен, ~на́, ~но) *adj.* harmful, injurious; unhealthy.
вре́|жу(сь), жешь(ся) *see* **~зать(ся)**
вре|жу́, ди́шь *see* **~ди́ть**
вре́|зать, жу, жешь *pf.* (*of* **~за́ть**) to cut in; to set in.
врез|а́ть, а́ю *impf. of* **~́ать**
вре́|заться, жусь, жешься *pf.* (*of* **~за́ться**) (**в**+*a.*) **1.** to cut (into); to plunge, plough (into). **2.** to be engraved (on); **черты́ её лица́ ~зались в его́ па́мять** her features were engraved on his memory.
врез|а́ться, а́юсь *impf. of* **~́аться**
вре́зыва|ть(ся), ю(сь) *impf.* = **вреза́ть(ся)**
временно́й *adj.* **1.** (*phil.*) temporal. **2.** (*gram.*) tense. **3.** (*tech.*) time.
вре́менн|ый *adj.* temporary; provisional; interim.
вре́м|я, ени, енем, ени, *pl.* **~ена́, ~ён, ~ена́м** *nt.* **1.** time; times; **в да́нное в.** at the present moment; **в ми́рное в.** in peace-time **(в) пе́рвое в.** at first; **(в) после́днее в.** lately; **в своё в.** (*i*) (*in ref. to past*) in one's time, once, at one time, (*ii*) (*in ref. to future*) in due course; in one's own time; **в ско́ром ~ени** shortly, before long; **в то же (са́мое) в.** at the same time; **до поры́ до ~ени** for the time being; **за после́днее в.** lately; **на в.** for a while; **с тече́нием ~ени** in the course of time; **всё в.** all the time, continually; **ра́ньше ~ени** prematurely; **ско́лько ~ени?** what is the time?; **тем ~енем** meanwhile. **2.** (*gram.*) tense. **3.: в то в. как** while, whereas. **4.: во в.** (+*g.*) during, in.
время́нк|а, и *f.* temporary structure or fitting.
времяпрепровожде́ни|е, я *nt.* way of spending one's time.
вро́вень *adv.* (**с**+*i.*) level (with).
вро́де 1. *prep.*+*g.* like; **не́что в.** (*coll.*) a sort of, a kind of. **2.** *particle* such as, like.
врождён|ный (~, ~а́) *adj.* innate; congenital.
врозь *adv.* separately, apart.
вро́|ю(сь), ~ешь(ся) *see* **врыть(ся)**

вруб, а *m.* (*mining*) cut.
вруб|áть(ся), áю(сь) *impf. of* **~и́ть(ся)**
вруб|и́ть, лю́, ~ишь *pf.* (*of* **~áть**) to cut in(to).
вруб|и́ться, лю́сь, ~ишься *pf.* (*of* **~áться**) (**в**+*a.*) to cut one's way (into), hack one's way (through).
врукопáшную *adv.*: **схвати́ться в.** to engage in hand-to-hand combat.
врун, á *m.* (*coll.*) liar.
врýн|ья, ьи *f. of* **~**
вруч|áть, áю *impf. of* **~и́ть**
вручéни|е, я *nt.* handing, delivery; presentation; (*leg.*) service (*of summons, etc.*).
вруч|и́ть, ý, и́шь *pf.* (*of* **~áть**) to hand, deliver; to present; to entrust; **в. судéбную повéстку** to serve a subpoena.
вручнýю *adv.* by hand.
врывá|ть, ю *impf. of* **врыть**
врывá|ться, юсь *impf. of* **ворвáться**
вр|ыть, óю, óешь *pf.* (*of* **~ывáть**) to dig in(to), bury (in).
вряд ли *adv. coll.* it is unlikely; hardly; **они́ ужé в. придýт** I doubt whether they will come now.
вса|ди́ть, жý, ~дишь, *pf.* (*of* **~живать**) **1.** to thrust, plunge (into); **в. нож в спи́ну** (+*d.*) to stab in the back (*also fig.*). **2.** (*coll.*) to put, sink (into).
всáдник, а *m.* rider, horseman.
всáдниц|а, ы *f.* horsewoman.
всáжива|ть, ю *impf. of* **всади́ть**
вса|жý, ~дишь *see* **~ди́ть**
всáсывани|е, я *nt.* suction; absorption.
всáсыва|ть(ся), ю(сь), *impf. of* **всосáть(ся)**
все... *comb. form* all-, omni-, pan-.
всё 1. *pron. see* **весь. 2.** *adv.* always; all the time; **он в. ругáется** he swears all the time. **3. в. (ещё)** still; **дождь в. (ещё) идёт** it is still raining. **4.** *as particle*: **в. бóлее и бóлее** more and more; **он в. толстéет** he is getting fatter and fatter.
всевéдени|е, я *nt.* omniscience.
всевéдущий *adj.* omniscient.
всевлáсти|е, я *nt.* absolute power.
всевлáстный *adj.* all-powerful.
всевозмóжный *adj.* various; all kinds of; every possible; **в. товáр** goods of all kinds.
Всевы́шний *n.* (*relig.*) the Almighty.
всегдá *adv.* always; **как в.** as ever.
всегдáшний *adj.* usual, customary.
всегó *adv.* **1.** in all, all told. **2.** only; **в.-нáвсего** all in all; **нас бы́ло в. пя́теро** there were only five of us. **3.** (good)bye!; see you!
вседозвóленност|ь, и *f.* permissiveness; **óбщество ~и** the permissive society.
всезнáйк|а, и *c.g.* (*coll., iron.*) know-all.
вселéни|е, я *nt.* installation, quartering; moving in.
вселéнн|ая, ой *no pl., f.* universe.
вселéнский *adj.* universal; (*eccl.*) ecumenical.
всел|и́ть, ю́, и́шь *pf.* (*of* **~я́ть**) **1.** to install, quarter (in) **2.** (*fig., rhet.*) to inspire (in); **в. страх (в**+*a.*) to strike fear (into).
всел|и́ться, ю́сь, и́шься *pf.* (*of* **~я́ться**) (**в**+*a.*) **1.** to move in(to). **2.** (*fig.*) to be implanted (in); to seize.
вселя́|ть(ся), ю(сь) *impf. of* **всели́ть(ся)**
всемéрный *adj.* utmost.
всеми́рный *adj.* world; world-wide.
всемогýществ|о, а *nt.* omnipotence.
всемогýщ|ий (~, ~а) *adj.* omnipotent, all-powerful; Almighty.
всенарóдн|ый *adj.* national; nationwide.
всéнощн|ая, ой *f.* (*eccl.*) night service (vespers and matins).
всеóбщ|ий *adj.* general; universal; across-the-board.
всеобъéмлющ|ий (~, ~а) *adj.* all-embracing, comprehensive.
всеорýжи|е, я *nt. only in phr.* **во ~и** fully armed.
всепоглощáющий *adj.* all-consuming (*also fig.*).
всепожирáющий *adj.* all-consuming.
всеросси́йский *adj.* All-Russian.
всерьёз *adv.* seriously, in earnest.
всесезóнный *adj.* (*coll.*) year-round.
всеси́л|ьный (~ен, ~ьна) *adj.* all-powerful.
всесторóнний *adj.* all-round; thorough, detailed.
всё-таки *conj. and particle* still, all the same.
всеуслы́шани|е, я *nt. only in phr.* **во в.** publicly, for all to hear.
всецéло *adv.* completely; exclusively.
всея́дный *adj.* omnivorous.
вскáкива|ть, ю *impf. of* **вскочи́ть**
вскáпыва|ть, ю *impf. of* **вскопáть**
вскарáбк|аться, аюсь *pf.* (*of* **карáбкаться** *and* **~иваться**) (**на**+*a.*; *coll.*) to scramble (up, on to) clamber (up, on to).
вскарáбкива|ться, юсь *impf. of* **вскарáбкаться**
вскáрмлива|ть, ю *impf. of* **вскорми́ть**
вскачь *adv.* at a gallop.
вски́дыва|ть(ся), ю(сь) *impf. of* **вски́нуть(ся)**
вски́|нуть, ну, нешь *pf.* (*of* **~дывать**) to throw up; **в. на плéчи** to shoulder; **в. глазá** to look up suddenly.
вски́|нуться, нусь, нешься *pf.* (*of* **~дываться**) (**на**+*a.*; *coll.*) **1.** to leap up (on to). **2.** (*fig.*) to turn (on), go (for).
вскипá|ть, ю *impf. of* **вскипéть**
вскип|éть, лю́, и́шь *pf.* (*of* **~áть**) **1.** to boil up. **2.** (*fig.*) to flare up; fly into a rage.
вскипя|ти́ть, чý, ти́шь *pf. of* **кипяти́ть**
вскипя|ти́ться, чýсь, ти́шься *pf.* **1.** *pass. of* **вскипяти́ть 2.** (*coll.*) to flare up; fly into a rage.
всклокóчен|ный (~, ~а) *p.p.p. of* **всклокóчить** *and adj.* (*coll.*) dishevelled, tousled
всклокóчива|ть, ю *impf. of* **всклокóчить**
всклокóч|ить, у, ишь *pf.* (*of* **~ивать**) (*coll.*) to dishevel, tousle.
всклóчива|ть, ю *impf. of* **всклóчить**
всклóч|ить, у, ишь *pf.* (*of* **~ивать**) (*coll.*) to dishevel, tousle.
всколыхн|ýть, ý, ёшь *pf.* to stir; to rock; (*fig.*) to stir up.
всколыхн|ýться, ýсь, ёшься *pf.* to rock (*intrans.*); (*fig.*) to be roused.
вскользь *adv.* slightly; in passing; **упомянýть в.** to mention in passing.
вскопá|ть, ю *pf.* (*of* **вскáпывать**) to dig up.
вскóре *adv.* soon, shortly after.
вскорм|и́ть, лю́, ~ишь *pf.* (*of* **вскáрмливать**) to rear; raise.
вскоч|и́ть, ý, ~ишь *pf.* (*of* **вскáкивать**) **1.** (**в, на**+*a.*, **с**+*g.*) to leap up (into, on to; from). **2.** (*coll.*) to come up (*of bumps, boils, etc.*).
вскри́кива|ть, ю *impf. of* **вскри́кнуть**
вскри́к|нуть, ну, нешь *pf.* (*of* **~ивать**) to cry out.
вскрич|áть, ý, и́шь *pf.* to exclaim.
вскрó|ю, ешь *see* **вскрыть**
вскруж|и́ть, ý, ~и́шь *pf. only in phr.* **в. гóлову комý-н.** to turn s.o.'s head.
вскрывá|ть(ся), ю(сь) *impf. of* **вскры́ть(ся)**
вскры́ти|е, я *nt.* **1.** opening, unsealing. **2.** (*fig.*) revelation, disclosure. **3.** (*geog.*) opening (*of rivers after break-up of ice*). **4.** (*med.*) lancing. **5.** (*med.*) autopsy; dissection; post-mortem.
вскр|ыть, óю, óешь *pf.* (*of* **~ывáть**) **1.** to open, unseal. **2.** (*fig.*) to reveal, disclose. **3.** (*med.*) to lance. **4.** (*med.*) to dissect.
вскр|ы́ться, óюсь, óешься *pf.* (*of* **~ывáться**) **1.** to come to light, be revealed. **2.** (*geog.*) to become clear (of ice; *of rivers*); become open. **3.** (*med.*) to break, burst.
всласть *adv.* (*coll.*) to one's heart's content.

вслед 1. *adv.* (**за**+*i.*) after; **посла́ть письмо́ в.** to forward a letter. **2.** *prep.*+*d.* after; **смотре́ть в.** to follow with one's eyes.
всле́дствие *prep.*+*g.* on account of, owing to.
вслепу́ю *adv.* **1.** blindly. **2.** blindfold; **печа́тать в.** to touch-type.
вслух *adv.* aloud, out loud.
вслу́ш|аться, аюсь *pf.* (*of* **~иваться**) (**в**+*a*) to listen attentively (to).
вслу́шива|ться, юсь *impf. of* **вслу́шаться**
всма́трива|ться, юсь *impf. of* **всмотре́ться**
всмотр|е́ться, ю́сь, ~ишься *pf.* (*of* **всма́триваться**) (**в**+*a*) to peer (at); to scrutinize.
всмя́тку *adv.*: **яйцо́ в.** soft-boiled, lightly-boiled egg.
вс|ова́ть, ую́, уёшь *pf.* (*of* **~о́вывать**) (*coll.*) to put in, stick in; to slip in.
всо́выва|ть, ю *impf. of* **всова́ть** *and* **всу́нуть**
всос|а́ть, у́, ёшь *pf.* (*of* **вса́сывать**) to suck in; (*fig.*) to absorb, imbibe.
всос|а́ться, у́сь, ёшься *pf.* (*of* **вса́сываться**) (**в**+*a*) **1.** to fasten upon (*with mouth, lips, etc.*) **2.** to soak through (into).
вспа́ива|ть, ю *impf. of* **вспои́ть**
вспа́рхива|ть, ю *impf. of* **вспорхну́ть**
вспа́рыва|ть, ю *impf. of* **вспоро́ть**
вспа|ха́ть, шу́, ~шешь *pf.* (*of* **~хивать**) to plough up
вспа́хива|ть, ю *impf. of* **вспаха́ть**
вспа́шк|а, и *f.* ploughing.
вспаш|у́, ~ешь *see* **вспаха́ть**
вспе́нива|ть(ся), ю, (~ется) *impf. of* **вспе́нить(ся)**
вспе́н|ить, ю, ишь *pf.* (*of* **~ивать**) to make foam, make lather; **в. коня́** get one's horse into a lather.
вспе́н|иться, ится *pf.* (*of* **~иваться**) to froth; to lather (*intrans.*).
вспетуш|и́ться, у́сь, и́шься *pf. of* **петуши́ться**
всплакн|у́ть, у́, ёшь *pf.* to shed a few tears, have a little cry.
всплеск, а *m.* splash.
всплёскива|ть, ю *impf. of* **всплесну́ть**
всплес|ну́ть, ну́, нёшь *pf.* (*of* **~кивать**) to splash; **в. рука́ми** to throw up one's hands.
всплыва́|ть, ю *impf. of* **всплыть**
всплы|ть, ву́, вёшь, *past* **~л, ~ла́, ~ло** *pf.* (*of* **~ва́ть**) to rise to the surface, surface; (*fig.*) to come to light.
вспо|и́ть, ю́, и́шь *pf.* (*of* **вспа́ивать**) to nurse; to rear; **в.-вскорми́ть** (*fig., coll.*) to bring up.
всполош|и́ть, у́, и́шь *pf.* (*of* **полоши́ть**) (*coll.*) to rouse; to alarm.
всполош|и́ться, у́сь, и́шься *pf.* (*of* **полоши́ться**) (*coll.*) to be alarmed.
вспомина́|ть(ся), ю(сь) *impf. of* **вспо́мнить(ся)**
вспо́м|нить, ню, нишь *pf.* (*of* **~ина́ть**) to remember, recall, recollect.
вспо́м|ниться, нюсь, нишься *pf.* (*of* **~ина́ться**) (*impers.*, +*d.*): **мне,** *etc.*, **~нилось** I, *etc.*, remembered.
вспомога́тельн|ый *adj.* auxiliary; subsidiary; (*gram.*) auxiliary.
вспор|о́ть, ю́, ~ешь *pf.* (*of* **вспа́рывать**) (*coll.*) to rip open.
вспорхн|у́ть, у́, ёшь *pf.* to take wing.
вспоте́|ть, ю *pf.* (*of* **поте́ть**) to break out in a sweat; to mist over (*of spectacles, etc.*).
вспры́гива|ть, ю *impf. of* **вспры́гнуть**
вспры́г|нуть, ну, нешь *pf.* (*of* **~ивать**) (**на**+*a.*) to jump up (on to), spring up (on to).
вспры́скива|ть, ю *impf. of* **вспры́снуть**
вспры́с|нуть, ну, нешь *pf.* (*of* **~кивать**) to sprinkle; (*fig., coll.*) to celebrate; **в. сде́лку** to wet a bargain.
вспу́гива|ть, ю *impf. of* **вспугну́ть**
вспуг|ну́ть, ну́, нёшь *pf.* (*of* **~ивать**) to scare away.
вспух|а́ть, а́ю *impf. of* **~нуть**
вспу́х|нуть, ну, нешь *pf.* (*of* **~а́ть**) to swell up.
вспу́чива|ть, ю *impf. of* **вспу́чить**
вспу́ч|ить, у, ишь *pf.* (*of* **~ивать**) (*usu. impers.*) to distend; **у него́ живо́т ~ило** his abdomen is distended.
вспыл|и́ть, ю́, и́шь *pf.* to flare up; **в.** (**на**+*a.*) to fly into a rage (with).
вспы́льчив|ый (~, ~а) *adj.* hot-tempered; irascible.
вспы́хива|ть, ю *impf. of* **вспы́хнуть**
вспы́х|нуть, ну, нешь *pf.* (*of* **~ивать**) **1.** to burst into flames, blaze up; (*fig.*) to flare up; to break out. **2.** to blush.
вспы́шк|а, и *f.* flash; (*phot.*) flash (attachment); **электро́нная в.** flashgun; (*astron.*) flare; (*fig.*) outburst, burst; outbreak (*of epidemic, etc.*).
вспять *adv.* back(wards).
встава́ни|е, я *nt.*: **почти́ть ~ем** to stand in honour (of).
вста|ва́ть, ю́, ёшь *impf. of* **~ть**
вста́в|ить, лю, ишь *pf.* (*of* **~ля́ть**) to put in, insert; **в. себе́ зу́бы** to have a set of (false) teeth made.
вста́вк|а, и *f.* **1.** insertion; framing, mounting. **2.** inset. **3.** interpolation.
вставля́|ть, ю *impf. of* **вста́вить**
вставн|о́й *adj.* inserted; **~ы́е зу́бы** false teeth.
встарь *adv.* of old, in olden time(s).
вста|ть, ну, нешь *pf.* (*of* **~ва́ть**) **1.** to get up, rise; to stand up; **в. с ле́вой ноги́** to get out of bed on the wrong side; **в. из-за стола́** to rise from table; (*fig.*) **в. на свои́ но́ги** to stand on one's own feet. **2.** to stand; **в. на рабо́ту** to start work. **3.** (**в**+*a.*) to go (into), fit (into). **4.** (*fig.*) to arise, come up.
встрево́жен|ный (~, ~на) *p.p.p. of* **встрево́жить** *and adj.* anxious.
встрево́ж|ить, у, ишь *pf. of* **трево́жить**
встрёпанный *adj.* (*coll.*) dishevelled.
встрепен|у́ться, у́сь, ёшься *pf.* **1.** to rouse o.s., start (up). **2.** to begin to beat faster (*of heart*).
встре́|тить, чу, тишь *pf.* (*of* **~ча́ть**) **1.** to meet (with), encounter. **2.** to greet, receive; **в. аплодисме́нтами** to greet with cheers; **в. Но́вый год** to see the New Year in.
встре́|титься, чусь, тишься *pf.* (*of* **~ча́ться**) (**с**+*i.*) **1.** to meet (with), encounter, come across. **2.** to be found, occur.
встре́ч|а, и *f.* **1.** meeting, encounter; reception; **в. в верха́х** (*pol.*) summit; **в. выпускнико́в** old boys' *or* old girls' reunion; **в. Но́вого го́да** New Year's Eve party. **2.** (*sport*) match, meeting.
встреча́|ть, ю *impf. of* **встре́тить**
встреча́|ться, юсь *impf.* **1.** *impf. of* **встре́титься. 2.** *impf. only* to be found, be met with.
встре́чный *adj.* **1.** approaching; oncoming; **в. ве́тер** head wind; *as n.* **пе́рвый в.** the first person you meet, anyone; **(ка́ждый) в. и попере́чный** every Tom, Dick, and Harry. **2.** counter; **в. иск** (*leg.*) counterclaim.
встро́енн|ый *adj.* built-in.
встря́ск|а, и *f.* (*coll.*) **1.** shaking; shock. **2.** dressing-down; telling off.
встря́хива|ть(ся), юсь *impf. of* **встряхну́ть(ся)**
встрях|ну́ть, ну́, нёшь *pf.* (*of* **~ивать**) to shake; (*fig.*) to shake up, rouse.
встрях|ну́ться, ну́сь, нёшься *pf.* (*of* **~иваться**) **1.** to shake o.s. **2.** (*fig.*) to rouse o.s.; to cheer up; **~ни́тесь!** pull yourself together.
вступа́|ть(ся), ю(сь) *impf. of* **вступи́ть(ся)**
вступи́тельн|ый *adj.* introductory; **в. взнос** entrance fee; **~ая ле́кция** inaugural lecture.
вступ|и́ть, лю́, ~ишь *pf.* (*of* **~а́ть**) **1.** (**в**+*a.*) to enter (into), join (in); **в. в бой** to join battle; **в. в**

де́йствие to come into force; **в. в брак** to marry; **в. в свои́ права́** to come into one's own. **2.** (**на**+*a.*) to mount, go up; **в. на престо́л** to ascend the throne.
вступ|и́ться, лю́сь, ∠ишься *pf.* (*of* **~а́ться**) **1.** (**за**+*a.*) to stand up (for), take (s.o.'s) part. **2.** (*coll.*) to intervene.
вступле́ни|е, я *nt.* **1.** entry, joining. **2.** prelude, introduction.
всу́н|уть, у, ешь *pf.* (*of* **всо́вывать**) to stick in; to slip in.
всухомя́тку *adv.* (*coll.*): **есть в.** to live on, eat cold food without liquids.
всу́чива|ть, ю *impf. of* **всучи́ть**
всуч|и́ть, у́, ∠ишь *pf.* (*of* **∠ивать**) (+*d.*; *fig.*, *coll.*, *pej.*) to foist (on), palm off (on).
всхли́п|нуть, ну, нешь *pf.* (*of* **∠ывать**) to sob.
всхли́пывань|е, я *nt.* sobbing; sobs.
всхли́пыва|ть, ю *impf. of* **всхли́пнуть**
всхо|ди́ть, жу́, ∠дишь *impf. of* **взойти́**
всхо́д|ы, ов *no sg.* (cereal-)shoots.
всхрап|ну́ть, ну́, нёшь *pf.* **1.** *pf. of* **∠ывать. 2.** (*coll.*) to have a nap.
всхра́пыва|ть, ю *impf.* (*of* **всхрапну́ть**) to snore; to snort (*of a horse*).
всып|ать, лю, лешь *pf.* (*of* **~а́ть**) **1.** (**в**+*a.*) to pour (into). **2.** (+*d.*; *coll.*) to give what for; to thrash; **в. по пе́рвое число́** to give a drubbing.
всыпа́|ть, ю *impf. of* **вы́сыпать**
вы́пк|а, и *f.* rating; beating, drubbing.
всю́ду *adv.* everywhere.
вся *see* **весь**[1]
вся́к|ий *adj.* **1.** any; **во ~ом слу́чае** in any case; at any rate; *as pron.* anyone. **2.** all sorts of; every; **на в. слу́чай** just in case.
вся́чески *adv.* (*coll.*) in every way possible.
вся́ческ|ий *adj.* (*coll.*) all kinds of.
вся́чин|а, ы *f.* (*coll.*): **вся́кая в.** all kinds of things; odds and ends.
Вт (*abbr. of* **ва́тт**) W, watt.
вта́йне *adv.* secretly, in secret.
вта́лкива|ть, ю *impf. of* **втолкну́ть**
вта́птыва|ть, ю *impf. of* **втопта́ть**
вта́скива|ть, ю *impf. of* **втащи́ть**
втащ|и́ть, у́, ∠ишь *pf.* (*of* **вта́скивать**) (**в**+*a.* **на**+*a.*) to drag (into, on to).
втека́|ть, ю *impf. of* **втечь**
втер|е́ть, вотру́, вотрёшь, *past* **∸, ∸ла** *pf.* (*of* **втира́ть**) (**в**+*a.*) to rub in(to); **в. очки́ кому́-н.** (*fig.*, *coll.*) to bluff, pull the wool over s.o.'s eyes.
втер|е́ться, вотру́сь, вотрёшься, *past* **∸ся, ∸лась** *pf.* (*of* **втира́ться**) **1.** (**в**+*a.*; *coll.*) to insinuate *or* worm o.s. into; **ему́ удало́сь в. в дове́рие к премье́р-мини́стру** he succeeded in worming his way into the confidence of the Prime Minister. **2.** to sink in(to), soak in(to).
вте|чь, ку́, чёшь, ку́т, *past* **∸к, ~кла́** *pf.* (*of* **~ка́ть**) to flow in(to).
втира́ни|е, я *nt.* **1.** rubbing in. **2.** liniment.
втира́|ть(ся), ю(сь) *impf. of* **втере́ть(ся)**
вти́скива|ть(ся), ю(сь) *impf. of* **вти́снуть(ся)**
вти́с|нуть, ну, нешь *pf.* (*of* **~кивать**) (**в**+*a.*) to squeeze in(to).
вти́с|нуться, нусь, нешься *pf.* (*of* **~киваться**) (*coll.*) to squeeze (o.s.) in(to).
втихомо́лку *adv.* (*coll.*) surreptitiously; on the quiet, on the sly.
втолкн|у́ть, у́, ёшь *pf.* (*of* **вта́лкивать**) (**в**+*a.*; *coll.*) to push in(to), shove in(to).
втолк|ова́ть, у́ю *pf.* (*of* **~о́вывать**) (+*d.*; *coll.*) to din (into), ram (into).
втолко́выва|ть, ю *impf. of* **втолкова́ть**
втоп|та́ть, чу́, ∠чешь *pf.* (*of* **вта́птывать**) to trample in; **в. в грязь** (*fig.*) to drag in the mire.
вторг|а́ться, а́юсь *impf. of* **∠нуться**
вто́рг|нуться, нусь, нешься, *past* **~ся, ~лась** *pf.* (*of* **~а́ться**) (**в**+*a.*) to invade; to encroach (upon), trespass (on), intrude (in) (*also fig.*).
вторже́ни|е, я *nt.* invasion; intrusion.
вто́р|ить, ю, ишь *impf.* (+*d.*) **1.** (*mus.*) to play, sing second part (to). **2.** (*fig.*, *pej.*) to echo, repeat.
втори́чн|ый *adj.* **1.** second. **2.** secondary.
вто́рник, а *m.* Tuesday.
второго́дник, а *m.* pupil remaining in same form for second year.
Второзако́ни|е, я *nt.* (*bibl.*) Deuteronomy.
втор|о́й *adj.* **1.** second; **в. час** (it is) past one; **из ~ы́х рук** (at) second hand. **2.** *as n.* **~о́е, ~ого** *nt.* main course (*of meal*). **3.** *as particle* **~о́е** (*coll.*) in the second place.
второкла́ссник, а *m.* second-year (boy).
второкла́ссниц|а, ы *f.* second-year (girl).
второку́рсник, а *m.* second-year student.
второпя́х *adv.* **1.** hurriedly, in haste. **2.** in one's haste.
второразря́дный *adj.* second-rate.
второсо́ртный *adj.* second-rate; inferior.
второстепе́нный *adj.* secondary; minor.
в-тре́тьих *adv.* thirdly; in the third place.
втри́дорога *adv.* (*coll.*) triple the price; **плати́ть в.** to pay through the nose.
втро́е *adv.* three times; treble.
втроём *adv.* three (together); **мы в.** the three of us.
втройне́ *adv.* three times as much; treble.
вту́лк|а, и *f.* **1.** (*tech.*) bush. **2.** plug; bung.
вту́не *adv.* (*obs.*) in vain.
втык, а *m.* (*coll.*) dressing-down, rocket; **сде́лать в.** (+*d.*) to tear s.o. off a strip.
втыка́|ть, ю *impf. of* **воткну́ть**
вты́чк|а, и *f.* (*coll.*) **1.** sticking in. **2.** plug, bung.
втя́гива|ть(ся), ю(сь) *impf. of* **втяну́ть(ся)**
втя|ну́ть, ну́, ∠нешь *pf.* (*of* **∠гивать**) **1.** to draw (in, into, up), pull (in, into, up); to absorb, take in; **в. живо́т** to pull in one's stomach. **2.** (*fig.*) to draw (into), involve (in).
втя|ну́ться, ну́сь, ∠нешься *pf.* (*of* **∠гиваться**) (**в**+*a.*) **1.** to draw (into), enter. **2.** (*of cheeks*) to sag, fall in. **3.** (*coll.*) to get accustomed (to), used (to). **4.** to become keen (on).
вуа́л|ь, и *f.* veil.
вуз, а *m.* (*abbr. of* **вы́сшее уче́бное заведе́ние**) institution of higher education.
ву́зов|ец, ца *m.* student (*at any institution of higher education*).
ву́зов|ка, ки *f. of* **~ец**
ву́з|овский *adj. of* **~**
вулка́н, а *m.* volcano; **де́йствующий, поту́хший в.** active, extinct volcano.
вулканиза́ци|я, и *f.* (*tech.*) vulcanization.
вулканизи́р|овать, ую *impf. and pf.* (*tech.*) to vulcanize.
вулкани́ческий *adj.* volcanic (*also fig.*).
вульгаризи́р|овать, ую *impf. and pf.* to vulgarize.
вульгари́зм, а *m.* (*ling.*) vulgarism.
вульга́рност|ь, и *f.* vulgarity.
вульга́р|ный (~ен, ~на) *adj.* vulgar.
вундерки́нд, а *m.* child prodigy.
вурдала́к, а *m.* vampire.
вход, а *m.* **1.** entry. **2.** entrance.
вхо|ди́ть, жу́, ∠дишь *impf. of* **войти́**
вход|но́й *adj. of* **∠**; **~на́я пла́та** entrance fee.
вход|я́щий *pres. part. of* **~и́ть** *and adj.* incoming.
вхожде́ни|е, я *nt.* entry.
вхо́ж|ий (~, ~а) *adj.* (*coll.*): **быть ~им** (**в**+*a.*, **к**) to be (well) received (at); to be well in (with).
вхолосту́ю *adv.* (*tech.*): **рабо́тать в.** to idle.
вцеп|и́ться, лю́сь, ∠ишься *impf.* (*of* **~ля́ться**) (**в**+*a.*) to seize hold of (by).

вцепля́|ться, юсь *impf. of* **вцепи́ться**
вчера́ *adv.* yesterday.
вчера́|шний *adj. of* ~
вчерне́ *adv.* in rough; **я написа́л свою́ ле́кцию в.** I have made a rough draft of my lecture.
вче́тверо *adv.* four times; fourfold; **сложи́ть в.** to fold in four.
вчетверо́м *adv.* four (together).
в-четвёртых *adv.* fourthly; in the fourth place.
вчит|а́ться, а́юсь *pf.* (*of* ~ываться) (**в**+*a.*) to get a grasp (of) (*a text*).
вчи́тыва|ться, юсь *impf.* **1.** *impf. of* **вчита́ться. 2.** *impf. only* to try to grasp the meaning (of).
вшива́|ть, ю *impf. of* **вшить**
вши́вк|а, и *f.* (*coll.*) **1.** sewing in. **2.** patch.
вшивно́й *adj.* sewn-in.
вши́в|ый (~, ~а) *adj.* lousy, lice-ridden.
вширь *adv.* in breadth.
вшить, вошью́, вошьёшь *pf.* (*of* **вшива́ть**) (**в**+*a.*) to sew in(to).
въеда́|ться, юсь *impf. of* **въе́сться**
въе́длив|ый (~, ~а) *adj.* (*coll.*) corrosive; (*fig.*) acid; **~ое замеча́ние** acid remark.
въезд, а *m.* **1.** entry; **«В. запрещён»** 'No entry'. **2.** entrance.
въезд|но́й *adj. of* ~; **~на́я ви́за** entry visa.
въезжа́|ть, ю *impf. of* **въе́хать**
въе́|сться, мся, шься, стся, ди́мся, ди́тесь дя́тся, *past* **~лся** *pf.* (*of* **~да́ться**) (**в**+*a.*) to eat (into).
въе́|хать, ду, дешь *pf.* (*of* **~зжа́ть**) (**в**+*a.*) to enter, ride in(to), drive in(to); to ride, drive up.
вы, вас, вам, ва́ми, вас *pron.* (*pl. and formal mode of address to one person*) you; **быть на в.** (**с**+*i.*) to be on formal terms (with).
вы... *pref. indicating* **1.** motion outwards. **2.** action directed outwards. **3.** acquisition (*as outcome of a series of actions*). **4.** completion of a process.
выба́лтыва|ть, ю *impf. of* **вы́болтать**
выбега́|ть, ю *impf. of* **вы́бежать**
вы́бе|жать, гу, жишь, гут *pf.* (*of* **~га́ть**) to run out.
вы́бел|ить, ю, ишь *pf. of* **бели́ть 3.**
вы́бер|у, ешь *see* **вы́брать**
выбива́|ть(ся), ю(сь) *impf. of* **вы́бить(ся)**
выбира́|ть(ся), ю(сь) *impf. of* **вы́брать(ся)**
вы́б|ить, ью, ьешь *pf.* (*of* **~ива́ть**) **1.** to knock out; to dislodge. **2.** to beat (clean); **в. ковёр** to beat a carpet. **3.** to beat; to stamp; to print (*fabrics*); **в. меда́ль** to strike a medal.
вы́б|иться, ьюсь, ьешься *pf.* (*of* **~ива́ться**) **1.** to get out; to break loose (from); **в. в лю́ди** to make one's way in the world; **в. из сил** to wear o.s. out. **2.** to come out, show.
вы́боин|а, ы *f.* **1.** rut, pot-hole. **2.** dent; groove.
вы́болта|ть, ю *pf.* (*of* **выба́лтывать**) (*coll.*) to let out, blurt out.
вы́бор, а *m.* **1.** choice; option. **2.** selection; assortment. **3.** (*pl. only*) election(s); **дополни́тельные ~ы** by-election.
вы́борк|а, и *f.* **1.** selection; sample. **2.** (*coll.*) excerpt.
вы́борност|ь, и *f.* appointment by election.
вы́борн|ый *adj.* **1.** elective. **2.** electoral; **в. бюллете́нь** ballot-paper. **3.** elected; *as n.* **в., ~ого** *m.* delegate.
вы́борочный *adj.* selective.
вы́борщик, а *m.* elector; **колле́гия ~ов** electoral college.
вы́бор|ы, ов *see* ~
вы́бран|ить, ю, ишь *pf. of* **брани́ть**
выбра́сыва|ть(ся), ю(сь) *impf. of* **вы́бросить(ся)**
вы́б|рать, еру, ерешь *pf.* (*of* **~ира́ть**) **1.** to choose, select, pick out. **2.** to elect. **3.** to take (everything) out. **4.** (*naut.*) to haul in.
вы́б|раться, ерусь, ерешься *pf.* (*of* **~ира́ться**) **1.** to get out; **в. из затрудне́ний** to get out of a difficulty. **2.** to move (house). **3.** (*coll.*) (**в**+*a.*) to (manage to) get to.
выбрива́|ть(ся), ю(сь) *impf. of* **вы́брить(ся)**
вы́бр|ить, ею, еешь *pf.* (*of* **~ива́ть**) to shave.
вы́бр|иться, еюсь, еешься *pf.* (*of* **~ива́ться**) to shave, have a shave.
вы́брос, а *m.* **1.** ejection. **2.** (*mil.*) landing. **3.** *pl.* emissions, discharges.
вы́бро|сить, шу, сишь *pf.* (*of* **выбра́сывать**) to throw out. **2.** to reject, discard, throw away; **в. зря** to waste; **в. из головы́** to dismiss from one's thoughts. **3.** (*in var. senses*) to put out; **в. флаг** to hoist a flag; **в. ло́зунг** to launch a slogan.
вы́бро|ситься, шусь, сишься *pf.* (*of* **выбра́сываться**) to jump out; (*naut.*) **в. на мель, на́ берег** to run aground; **в. с парашю́том** to bale out.
вы́броск|а, и *f.* (*mil.*) (air)drop.
выбыва́|ть, ю *impf. of* **вы́быть**
выбы́ти|е, я *nt.* departure.
вы́б|ыть, уду, удешь *pf.* (*of* **~ыва́ть**) (**из**) to leave, quit; **в. из стро́я** (*mil.*) (*i*) to leave the ranks (*ii*) to become a casualty.
выва́лива|ть(ся), ю(сь) *impf. of* **вы́валить(ся)**
вы́вал|ить, ю, ишь *pf.* (*of* ∸ивать) **1.** to throw out. **2.** (*coll.*) to pour out (*intrans.*; *of a crowd*).
вы́вал|иться, юсь, ишься *pf.* (*of* ∸иваться) to fall out, tumble out.
вы́валя|ть, ю *pf.* (*of* **валя́ть 2.**) to drag (in, through) (*mud, snow, etc.*).
выва́рива|ть, ю *impf. of* **вы́варить**
вы́вар|ить, ю, ишь *pf.* (*of* ∸ивать) **1.** to boil down; to extract by boiling. **2.** to boil thoroughly. **3.** to remove (*stains, etc.*) by boiling.
вы́вед|ать, аю *pf.* (*of* ∸ывать) to find out; **в. секре́т у кого́-н.** to worm a secret out of s.o.
выведе́ни|е, я *nt.* **1.** leading out, bringing out. **2.** deduction, conclusion. **3.** hatching (out); growing (*of plants*); breeding, raising. **4.** erection. **5.** removal (*of stains*); extermination (*of pests*).
выве́дыва|ть, ю *impf.* **1.** *impf. of* **вы́ведать. 2.** *impf. only* to investigate, try to find out.
вы́вез|ти, у, ешь, *past* **~, ~ла** *pf.* (*of* **вывози́ть**) **1.** to take out, remove; to bring out. **2.** (*econ.*) to export. **3.** (*coll.*) to save, rescue.
вы́вер|ить, ю, ишь *pf.* (*of* **~я́ть**) to adjust; to regulate.
вы́верк|а, и *f.* adjustment; regulation.
вы́вер|нуть, ну, нешь *pf.* (*of* ∸тывать) **1.** to unscrew; to pull out. **2.** (*coll.*) to twist, wrench. **3.** to turn (inside) out.
вы́вер|нуться, нусь, нешься *pf.* (*of* ∸тываться) **1.** to come unscrewed. **2.** (*coll.*) to slip out. **3.** (*coll.*) to get out (of), extricate o.s. (from).
вы́верт, а *m.* (*coll.*) **1.** caper. **2.** mannerism; affectation; **челове́к с ~ом** eccentric.
вывёртыва|ть(ся), ю(ст) *impf. of* **вы́вернуть(ся)**
выверя́|ть, ю *impf. of* **вы́верить**
вы́ве|сить[1]**, шу, сишь** *pf.* (*of* ∸шивать) **1.** to put up; to post up. **2.** to hang out (*linen, flags, etc.*).
вы́ве|сить[2]**, шу, сишь** *pf.* (*of* ∸шивать) to weigh.
вы́веск|а, и *f.* **1.** sign, signboard. **2.** (*fig.*) screen, mask.
вы́ве|сти, ду, дешь, *past* **~л, ~ла** *pf.* (*of* **выводи́ть**) **1.** to lead out, bring out; **в. кого́-н. в лю́ди** to help s.o. on in life; **в. кого́-н. из себя́** to drive s.o. out of his wits; **в. из стро́я** to disable, put out of action (*also fig.*); **в. из терпе́ния** to exasperate; **в. кого́-н. на доро́гу** (*fig.*) to set s.o. on the right path; **в. на чи́стую во́ду** bring out into the open. **2.** to turn out, force out; **в. из соста́ва президиума**

to remove from the presidium. **3.** to remove (*stains*); to exterminate (*pests*). **4.** to deduce, conclude. **5.** to hatch (out); to grow (*plants*); to breed, raise. **6.** to put up, erect. **7.** to depict, portray (*in a liter. work*). **8.** to write, draw, trace out painstakingly. **9.: в. балл, в. отме́тку** to give a mark.

вы́ве|стись, дусь, дешься *pf.* (*of* **выводи́ться**) **1.** to go out of use; to lapse. **2.** to disappear; to come out (*of stains*); to become extinct. **3.** to hatch out (*intrans.*).

выве́тривани|е, я *nt.* **1.** airing. **2.** (*geol.*) weathering.

выве́трива|ть(ся), ю(сь) *impf. of* **вы́ветрить(ся)**

вы́ветр|ить, ю, ишь *pf.* (*of* **~ивать**) **1.** to air; to ventilate; to remove (by ventilation); **в. дурно́й за́пах** to remove a bad smell. **2.** (*fig.*) to remove. **3.** (*impers.*; *geol.*) to weather.

вы́ветр|иться, юсь, ишься *pf.* (*of* **~иваться**) **1.** (*geol.*) to weather. **2.** to disappear (*by action of wind or fresh air*; *also fig.*); **в. из па́мяти** to be effaced from memory.

выве́шива|ть, ю *impf. of* **вы́весить**

вы́вин|тить, чу, тишь *pf.* (*of* **~чивать**) to unscrew.

вы́вин|титься, чусь, тишься *pf.* (*of* **~чиваться**) to come unscrewed.

выви́нчива|ть(ся), ю(сь) *impf. of* **вы́винтить(ся)**

вы́вих, а *m.* dislocation.

выви́хива|ть, ю *impf. of* **вы́вихнуть**

вы́вих|нуть, ну, нешь *pf.* (*of* **~ивать**) to dislocate; **он ~нул себе́ но́гу** he has dislocated his foot.

вы́вод, а *m.* **1.** deduction; conclusion. **2.** withdrawal; pull-out.

выво|ди́ть(ся), жу́(сь), ~дишь(ся) *impf. of* **вы́вести(сь)**

выводно́й *adj.* **1.** (*tech.*) discharge. **2.** (*anat.*) excretory.

вы́вод|ок, ка *m.* brood (*also fig.*); hatch; litter.

выво|жу́[1], **~дишь** *see* **~ди́ть**

выво|жу́[2], **~зишь** *see* **~зи́ть**

вы́воз, а *m.* **1.** export. **2.** removal.

выво|зи́ть, жу́, ~зишь *impf. of* **вы́везти**

вы́возк|а, и *f.* (*coll.*) carting out; removal.

вывозно́й *adj.* export.

вывола́кива|ть, ю *impf. of* **вы́волочь**

вы́волочк|а, и *f.* (*coll.*) **1.** beating. **2.** dressing-down.

вы́воло|чь, ку, чешь, кут, *past* **~к, ~кла** *pf.* (*of* **вывола́кивать**) (*coll.*) to drag out.

вывора́чива|ть, ю *impf. of* **вы́воротить**

вы́воро|тить, чу, тишь *pf.* (*of* **вывора́чивать**) (*coll.*) **1.** to pull out, shake loose. **2.** to twist, wrench. **3.** to turn (inside) out. **4.** to overturn.

вы́гад|ать, аю *pf.* (*of* **~вывать**) to gain; to save; **что вы ~али на э́том?** what did you gain by it?

выга́дыва|ть, ю *impf. of* **вы́гадать**

вы́гиб, а *m.* curve; curvature.

выгиба́|ть(ся), ю(сь) *impf. of* **вы́гнуть(ся)**

вы́гла|дить, жу, дишь *pf. of* **гла́дить 1.**

вы́гля|деть, жу, дишь *impf.* to look (like); **он ~дит о́чень молоды́м** he looks very young; **она́ пло́хо ~дит** she does not look well.

выгля́дыва|ть, ю *impf. of* **вы́глянуть**

вы́гля|нуть, ну, нешь *pf.* (*of* **~дывать**) **1.** to look out. **2.** to peep out, emerge; **из-за туч ~нуло со́лнце** the sun peeped out from behind the clouds.

вы́г|нать, оню, онишь *pf.* (*of* **~оня́ть**) **1.** to drive out; to expel; **в. со слу́жбы** (*coll.*) to sack. **2.** to distil. **3.** (*coll.*) to make (*a sum of money, etc.*).

вы́гнут|ый (~, ~а) *p.p.p. of* **~ь** *and adj.* curved; convex.

вы́гн|уть, у, ешь *pf.* (*of* **выгиба́ть**) to bend; **в. спи́ну** to arch the back.

вы́гн|уться, усь, ешься *pf.* (*of* **выгиба́ться**) to bend (*intrans.*).

выгова́рива|ть, ю *impf.* **1.** *impf. of* **вы́говорить. 2.** *impf. only* (*+d.*; *coll.*) to reprimand, tell off.

вы́говор, а *m.* **1.** accent; pronunciation. **2.** reprimand; rebuke.

вы́говор|ить, ю, ишь *pf.* (*of* **выгова́ривать**) to articulate, speak.

вы́говор|иться, юсь, ишься *pf.* (*coll.*) to speak out; to speak one's mind.

вы́год|а, ы *f.* advantage, benefit; profit, gain.

вы́годно *adv.* **1.** advantageously. **2.** *as pred.* it is profitable, it pays.

вы́год|ный (~ен, ~на) *adj.* advantageous, beneficial; profitable.

вы́гон, а *m.* pasture; common.

выгоня́|ть, ю *impf. of* **вы́гнать**

выгора́жива|ть, ю *impf. of* **вы́городить**

выгора́|ть, ет *impf. of* **вы́гореть**

вы́гор|еть[1], **ит** *pf.* (*of* **~а́ть**) **1.** to burn down, burn out (*intrans.*). **2.** to fade.

вы́гор|еть[2], **ит** *pf.* (*of* **~а́ть**) (*3rd pers. only or impers.*; *coll.*) to succeed, come off.

вы́горо|дить, жу, дишь *pf.* (*of* **выгора́живать**) **1.** to fence off. **2.** (*fig.*, *coll.*) to shield, screen.

вы́гравир|овать, ую *pf. of* **гравирова́ть**

вы́гре|б *see* **~сти**

выгреба́|ть, ю *impf. of* **вы́грести**

выгребн|о́й *adj.* refuse; **~а́я я́ма** cesspool.

вы́гре|сти[1], **бу, бешь,** *past* **~б, ~бла** *pf.* (*of* **~ба́ть**) to rake out; to clear away.

вы́гре|сти[2], **бу, бешь,** *past* **~б, ~бла** *pf.* (*of* **~ба́ть**) to row (out).

выгружа́|ть(ся), ю(сь) *impf. of* **вы́грузить(ся)**

вы́гру|зить, жу, зишь *pf.* (*of* **~жа́ть**) to unload.

вы́гру|зиться, жусь, зишься *pf.* (*of* **~жа́ться**) to disembark.

вы́грузк|а, и *f.* unloading.

выгрыза́|ть, ю *impf. of* **вы́грызть**

вы́грыз|ть, у, ешь, *past* **~, ~ла** *pf.* (*of* **~а́ть**) to gnaw out.

выгу́лива|ть, аю *impf. of* **вы́гулять**

вы́гуля|ть, ю *pf.* (*of* **выгу́ливать**) to walk (*a dog*).

выда|ва́ть(ся), ю́(сь), ёшь(ся) *impf. of* **вы́дать(ся)**

вы́дав|ить, лю, ишь *pf.* (*of* **~ливать**) **1.** to press out, squeeze out (*also fig.*); **в. улы́бку** to force a smile. **2.** to break, knock out.

выда́влива|ть, ю *impf. of* **вы́давить**

выда́лблива|ть, ю *impf. of* **вы́долбить**

вы́да|ть, м, шь, ст, дим, дите, дут *pf.* (*of* **~ва́ть**) **1.** to give (out), issue, produce; **в. зарпла́ту** to pay out wages; **в. кого́-н. за́муж** (**за**+*a.*) to give s.o. in marriage (to); **в. у́голь на-гора́** to produce coal. **2.** to give away, betray; to extradite. **3.** (**за**+*a.*) to pass off (as); **(себя́)** to pose (as).

вы́да|ться, мся, шься, стся, димся, дитесь, дутся *pf.* (*of* **~ва́ться**) **1.** to protrude, project, jut out; (*fig.*) to stand out, be conspicuous. **2.** (*coll.*) to happen; **как то́лько ~лся хоро́ший денёк, мы пое́хали в дере́вню** on the first fine day that came along we went into the country.

вы́дач|а, и *f.* **1.** issuing. **2.** issue; payment. **3.** extradition.

выдаю́щийся *pres. part. of* **выдава́ться** *and adj.* prominent, salient; (*fig.*) eminent, outstanding; prominent.

выдвига́|ть(ся), ю(сь) *impf. of* **вы́двинуть(ся)**

выдвиже́н|ец, ца *m.* worker promoted to an administrative post.

выдвиже́ни|е, я *nt.* **1.** nomination. **2.** promotion.

выдвиже́н|ка, ки *f. of* **~ец**

выдвижно́й *adj.* sliding; (*tech.*) telescopic.

вы́дви|нуть, ну, нешь *pf.* (*of* **~га́ть**) **1.** to move out, pull out. **2.** (*fig.*) to bring forward, advance; **в. обвине́ние** to level an accusation. **3.** to promote. **4.**

to nominate, propose.
вы́дви|нуться, нусь, нешься *pf.* (*of* **~га́ться**) **1.** to move forward, move out; to slide. **2.** to rise, get on (in the world). **3.** *pass. of* **~нуть**
вы́двор|ить, ю, ишь *pf.* (*of* **~я́ть**) (*coll. and leg.*; *obs.*) to evict; (*fig.*) to throw out.
выдворя́|ть, ю *impf. of* **вы́дворить**
вы́дел|ать, аю *pf.* (*of* **~ывать**) **1.** to manufacture; to process. **2.** to dress, curry (*leather*).
выделе́ни|е, я *nt.* **1.** (*physiol.*) secretion; excretion. **2.** apportionment.
выдели́тельный *adj.* (*physiol.*) secretory; excretory.
вы́дел|ить, ю, ишь *pf.* (*of* **~я́ть**) **1.** to pick out, single out; (*mil.*) to detach, detail; (*typ.*) **в. курси́вом** to italicize. **2.** to assign, earmark; to allot. **3.** (*physiol.*) to secrete; to excrete. **4.** to emit.
вы́дел|иться, юсь, ишься *pf.* (*of* **~я́ться**) **1.** to take one's share (*of a legacy*). **2.** (+*i.*) to stand out (for); **он ~ился остроу́мием** he was noted for his wit. **3.** to ooze out, exude. **4.** *pass. of* **~ить**
вы́делк|а, и *f.* **1.** manufacture. **2.** workmanship. **3.** dressing, currying.
выде́лыва|ть, ю *impf. of* **вы́делать; что ты тепе́рь ~ешь?** (*coll.*) what are you up to now?
выделя́|ть(ся), ю(сь) *impf. of* **вы́делить(ся)**
выдёргива|ть, ю *impf. of* **вы́дернуть**
вы́держанност|ь, и *f.* **1.** consistency. **2.** self-possession; firmness.
вы́держа|нный (~н, ~на) *p.p.p. of* **~ть** *and adj.* **1.** consistent; **~нная поли́тика** consistent policy. **2.** self-possessed; firm. **3.** mature; seasoned (*of wine, cheese, wood, etc.*)
вы́держ|ать, у, ишь *pf.* (*of* **~ивать**) **1.** to bear, support. **2.** (*fig.*) to bear, stand (up to), endure; to contain o.s.; **не в.** to break down; **я не мог э́того бо́льше в.** I could stand it no longer; **ва́ше поведе́ние не ~ит кри́тики** your conduct will not stand up to criticism. **3.: в. экза́мен** to pass an examination. **4.: в. не́сколько изда́ний** to run into several editions. **5.** to keep, lay up; to mature; to season. **6.: в. под аре́стом** to keep in custody. **7.** to maintain, sustain; **в. хара́ктер** to stand firm; **в. па́узу** to pause.
выде́ржива|ть, ю *impf. of* **вы́держать**
вы́держк|а[1]**, и** *f.* **1.** endurance; self-possession. **2.** (*phot.*) exposure.
вы́держк|а[2]**, и** *f.* excerpt, quotation.
вы́дер|нуть, ну, нешь *pf.* (*of* **~гивать**) to pull out.
выдира́|ть, ю *impf. of* **вы́драть**[1]
вы́долб|ить, лю, ишь *pf.* (*of* **выда́лбливать**) to hollow out.
вы́дох, а *m.* exhalation.
вы́дохн|уть, у, ешь *pf.* (*of* **выдыха́ть**) to breathe out.
вы́дохн|уться, усь, ешься *pf.* (*of* **выдыха́ться**) to have lost fragrance, smell; (*of wines, etc.*) to be flat; (*fig.*) to be past one's best, be played out.
вы́др|а, ы *f.* otter.
вы́д|рать[1]**, еру, ерешь** *pf.* (*of* **~ира́ть**) to tear out.
вы́д|рать[2]**, еру, ерешь** *pf.* (*of* **драть 4.**) (*coll.*) to thrash, flog.
вы́дрессир|овать, ую *pf. of* **дрессирова́ть**
вы́дуб|ить, лю, ишь *pf. of* **дуби́ть**
вы́думан|ный (~, ~а) *p.p.p. of* **вы́думать** *and adj.* made-up, fabricated; **~ная исто́рия** fabrication, fiction.
вы́дум|ать, аю *pf.* (*of* **~ывать**) to invent; to make up, fabricate
вы́думк|а, и *f.* **1.** invention; **голь на ~и хитра́** (*prov.*) necessity is the mother of invention. **2.** (*coll.*) inventiveness. **3.** (*coll.*) invention, fabrication (*lie*).
вы́думщик, а *m.* (*coll.*) **1.** inventor. **2.** fabricator (*liar*).
выду́мыва|ть, ю *impf. of* **вы́думать**
вы́ду|ть, ю, ешь *pf.* (*of* **~ва́ть**) to blow out.
выдыха́ни|е, я *nt.* exhalation.
выдыха́|ть(ся), ю(сь) *impf. of* **вы́дохнуть(ся)**
выеда́|ть, ю *impf. of* **вы́есть**
вы́еденн|ый *p.p.p. of* **вы́есть; не сто́ит ~ого яйца́** it is not worth a brass farthing.
вы́езд, а *m.* **1.** departure. **2.** exit.
вы́ез|дить, жу, дишь *pf.* (*of* **~жа́ть**) to break (in); to train (*horses*).
вы́ездк|а, и *f.* **1.** breaking-in; training (*of horses*). **2.** (*equestrian event*) dressage.
выезд|но́й *adj. of* **вы́езд; ~на́я се́ссия суда́** assizes; **в. матч** (*sport*) away match.
выезжа́|ть, ю *impf. of* **вы́ездить** *and* **вы́ехать**
вы́емк|а, и *f.* **1.** taking out; collection (*of letters from letter-box*); **в. докуме́нтов** seizure of documents. **2.** hollow; groove.
вы́е|сть, м, шь, ст, дим, дите, дят *pf.* (*of* **~да́ть**) to eat away; (*coll.*) to corrode.
вы́е|хать, ду, дешь *pf.* (*of* **~зжа́ть**) **1.** to go out, depart (*in or on a vehicle or on an animal*); to drive out; to ride out. **2.** to move (*from dwelling-place*). **3.** (**на**+*p.*) (*fig., coll.*) to exploit, take advantage (of).
вы́ж|ать, му, мешь *pf.* (*of* **~има́ть**) to wring (out); to squeeze out; **~атый лимо́н** (*fig.*) a has-been.
вы́жд|ать, у, ешь *pf.* (*of* **выжида́ть**) (+*g.*) to wait (for); to bide one's time.
вы́ж|ечь, гу, жешь *pf.* (*of* **~ига́ть**) **1.** to burn down; to burn out; to scorch. **2.** (*med.*) to cauterize. **3.** to burn in; **в. клеймо́** (**на**+*p.*) to brand.
вы́жжен|ный *p.p.p. of* **вы́жечь** *and adj.* **~ная земля́** scorched earth.
выжива́ни|е, я *nt.* survival; **в. наибо́лее приспосо́бленных** (*biol.*) survival of the fittest.
выжива́|ть, ю *impf. of* **вы́жить**
выжига́ни|е, я *nt.* **1.** scorching; **в. по де́реву** poker-work. **2.** (*med.*) cauterization.
выжига́|ть, ю *impf. of* **вы́жечь**.
выжида́ни|е, я *nt.* waiting; temporizing.
выжида́тельн|ый *adj.* waiting; temporizing; **занима́ть ~ую пози́цию** to play a waiting game.
выжида́|ть, ю *impf. of* **вы́ждать**
выжима́|ть, ю *impf. of* **вы́жать**[1]
вы́жи|ть, ву, вешь *pf.* (*of* **~ва́ть**) **1.** to survive; to pull through; to live through. **2.: в. из ума́** to lose possession of one's faculties. **3.** (*coll.*) to drive out, hound out.
вы́з|вать, ову, овешь *pf.* (*of* **~ыва́ть**) **1.** to call (out); to send for; to summon; **в. врача́** to send for a doctor; **в. ученика́** to call out a pupil; **в. в суд** (*leg.*) to summons, subpoena. **2.** to challenge; **в. на дуэ́ль** to challenge to a duel. **3.** to call forth, provoke; to cause; to arouse; **в. пожа́р** to cause a fire.
вы́з|ваться, овусь, овешься *pf.* (*of* **~ыва́ться**) (+*inf. or* **в**+*a.*) to volunteer; to offer.
вы́звол|ить, ю, ишь *pf.* (*of* **~я́ть**) (*coll.*) to help out; **в. из беды́** to get out of trouble.
вызволя́|ть, ю *impf. of* **вы́зволить**
выздора́влива|ть, ю *impf. of* **вы́здороветь**
вы́здорове|ть, ю, ешь *pf.* (*of* **выздора́вливать**) to recover, get better.
выздоровле́ни|е, я *nt.* recovery; convalescence.
вы́зов, а *m.* **1.** call; **в. по телефо́ну** telephone call. **2.** summons. **3.** challenge.
вы́золо|тить, чу, тишь *pf. of* **золоти́ть**
вы́золочен|ный (~, ~а) *p.p.p. of* **вы́золотить** *and adj.* gilt.
вызрева́|ть, ю *impf. of* **вы́зреть**
вы́зре|ть, ю, ешь *pf.* (*of* **~ва́ть**) to ripen.
вы́зубр|ить, ю, ишь *pf.* (*of* **зубри́ть**[2]) (*coll.*) to learn by heart.
вызыва́|ть(ся), ю(сь) *impf. of* **вы́звать(ся)**
вызыва́|ющий *pres. part. act. of* **~ть** *and adj.* de-

fiant; provocative.

вы́игр|ать, аю *pf.* (*of* **∠ывать**) to win; to gain; **в. вре́мя** to gain time.

выи́грыва|ть, ю *impf. of* **вы́играть**

вы́игрыш, а *m.* **1.** win; winning. **2.** gain, winnings; prize; **быть в ~е** to be winner; (*fig.*) to be the gainer; stand to gain.

вы́игрышн|ый *adj.* **1.** winning; **в. ход** winning move. **2.** advantageous.

вы́и|скать, щу, щешь *pf.* to light upon, track down.

вы́и|скаться, щусь, щешься *pf.* (*coll.*, *iron.*) to turn up, put in an appearance.

выи́скива|ть, ю *impf.* to search for, seek out.

вы́|йти, йду, йдешь, *past* **~шел, ~шла** *pf.* (*of* **~ходи́ть**) **1.** to go out; to come out; **в. в отста́вку** to retire; **в. в офице́ры** to get a commission; **в. в фина́л** (*sport*) to reach the final; **в. из берего́в** to overflow its banks; **в. из бо́я** (*mil.*) to disengage; **в. из ваго́на** to alight from a carriage; **в. из себя́** to lose one's temper; **в. из терпе́ния** to lose patience; **в. на прогу́лку** to go out for a walk. **2. (в свет)** (*of publications*) to come out, appear. **3.** (*of photographs or persons photographed*) to come out. **4.: в., в. за́муж (за**+*a.*) (*of a woman*) to marry. **5.** to come (out); to turn out (*also impers.*); to ensue; **не в.** (+*i. of n.*; *coll.*) to be lacking (in); **в. победи́телем** to emerge the victor; **из э́того ничего́ не ~йдет** nothing will come of it; **~шло, (что) он ни одного́ сло́ва не по́нял** it turned out that he did not understand a single word; **как бы чего́ не ~шло** (*coll.*) it will come to no good; **умо́м не ~шел** (*coll.*) he is not too bright. **6.** to be by origin; **она́ ~шла из крестья́н** she comes of peasant stock. **7.** to be used up; (*of a period of time*) to have expired; **горчи́ца вся ~шла** the mustard is used up; **срок уже́ ~шел** time is up. **8.: года́ ~шли** (+*d.* or *g.*; *coll.*) (*i*) to be of age, (*ii*) to be over the age (for).

вы́ка|зать, жу, жешь *pf.* (*of* **∠зывать**) (*coll.*) to manifest, display.

выка́зыва|ть, ю *impf. of* **вы́казать**

выка́лыва|ть, ю *impf. of* **вы́колоть**

выка́пыва|ть, ю *impf. of* **вы́копать**

вы́карабк|аться, аюсь *pf.* (*of* **∠иваться**) to scramble out; (*fig.*, *coll.*) to get (o.s.) out; **в. из боле́зни** to get over an illness.

выкара́бкива|ться, юсь *impf. of* **вы́карабкаться**

выка́рмлива|ть, ю *impf. of* **вы́кормить**

вы́кат|ать, аю *pf.* (*of* **∠ывать**[1]) **1.** to roll out. **2.** (*impf.* **ката́ть**) to smooth out; to mangle (*linen*). **3.** (*coll.*) to roll (in).

вы́ка|тить, чу, тишь *pf.* (*of* **∠тывать**) to roll out; to wheel out.

вы́ка|титься, чусь, тишься *pf.* (*of* **∠тываться**) to roll out (*intrans.*).

выка́тыва|ть(ся), ю(сь) *impf. of* **вы́катить(ся)**

вы́кач|ать, аю *pf.* (*of* **∠ивать**) to pump out.

выка́чива|ть, ю *impf. of* **вы́качать**

выка́шива|ть, ю *impf. of* **вы́косить**

выка́шлива|ть(ся), ю(сь) *impf. of* **вы́кашлять(ся)**

вы́кашл|ять, яю *pf.* (*of* **∠ивать**) to cough up.

вы́кашл|яться, яюсь *pf.* (*of* **∠иваться**) to clear one's throat.

выки́дыва|ть, ю *impf. of* **вы́кинуть**

вы́кидыш, а *m.* (*med.*) **1.** miscarriage; abortion. **2.** foetus (*after miscarriage or abortion*).

вы́ки|нуть, ну, нешь *pf.* (*of* **∠дывать**) **1.** to throw out, reject. **2.** to put out; **в. флаг** to hoist a flag. **3.** (*coll.*): **в. но́мер, штý ку, фо́кус** to play a trick.

выкипа́|ть, ет *impf. of* **вы́кипеть**

вы́кип|еть, ит *pf.* (*of* **~а́ть**) to boil away.

вы́кладк|а, и *f.* **1.** laying-out; lay-out. **2.** (*mil.*) kit. **3.** (*math.*) computation.

выкла́дыва|ть, ю *impf. of* **вы́ложить**

вы́кл|евать, юю, юешь *pf.* (*of* **~ёвывать**) **1.** to peck out. **2.** to peck up.

выклёвыва|ть, ю *impf. of* **вы́клевать**

выклика́|ть, ю *impf. of* **вы́кликнуть**

вы́клик|нуть, ну, нешь *pf.* (*of* **~а́ть**) to call out.

выключа́тел|ь, я *m.* switch.

выключа́|ть, ю *impf. of* **вы́ключить**

вы́ключ|ить, у, ишь *pf.* (*of* **~а́ть**) **1.** to turn off, switch off. **2.** to remove, exclude.

выкля́нчива|ть, ю *impf.* **1.** *impf. of* **вы́клянчить. 2.** *impf. only* **в. что-н. у кого́-н.** to try to get sth. out of s.o.

вы́клянч|ить, у, ишь *pf.* (*of* **∠ ивать**) (**у**+*g.*; *coll.*) to cadge (from, off), get (out of).

вы́к|овать, ую, уешь *pf.* (*of* **~о́вывать**) to forge.

выко́выва|ть, ю *impf. of* **вы́ковать**

выкола́чива|ть, ю *impf. of* **вы́колотить**

вы́коло|тить, чу, тишь *pf.* (*of* **выкола́чивать**) **1.** to knock out, beat out. **2.** to beat (*a carpet, etc.*). **3.** (*coll.*) to extort, wring out.

вы́кол|оть, ю, ешь *pf.* (*of* **выка́лывать**) to thrust out; **в. глаза́ кому́-н.** to put out s.o.'s eyes.

вы́копа|ть, ю *pf.* (*of* **выка́пывать**) **1.** to dig. **2.** (*impf. also* **копа́ть**) to dig up, dig out; to exhume; (*fig.*, *coll.*) to unearth.

вы́корм|ить, лю, ишь *pf.* (*of* **выка́рмливать**) to rear, bring up.

вы́корч|евать, ую *pf.* (*of* **~ёвывать**) to uproot; (*fig.*) to root out, extirpate.

выкорчёвыва|ть, ю *impf. of* **вы́корчевать**

вы́ко|сить, шу, сишь *pf.* (*of* **выка́шивать**) to mow clean.

выкра́дыва|ть, ю, *impf. of* **вы́красть**

выкра́ива|ть, ю *impf. of* **вы́кроить**

вы́кра|сить, шу, сишь *pf.* (*of* **∠шивать**) to paint; to dye.

вы́кра|сть, ду, дешь, *past* **~л** *pf.* (*of* **∠дывать**) to steal; (*fig.*) to plagiarize.

выкра́шива|ть, ю *impf. of* **вы́красить**

вы́крик, а *m.* cry, shout; yell.

выкри́кива|ть, ю *impf. of* **вы́крикнуть**

вы́крик|нуть, ну, нешь *pf.* (*of* **∠ивать**) to cry out; to yell.

вы́кро|ить, ю, ишь *pf.* (*of* **выкра́ивать**) **1.** to cut out. **2.** (*fig.*) to find; **в. вре́мя** to find time.

вы́кройк|а, и *f.* pattern.

выкрута́с|ы, ов *no sg.* (*coll.*) intricate movements, figures; flourishes.

вы́кру|тить, чу, тишь *pf.* (*of* **∠чивать**) **1.** to unscrew. **2.** (*tech.*) to twist; (*coll.*) **ему́ ~тили ру́ку** they twisted his arm.

вы́кру|титься, чусь, тишься *pf.* (*of* **∠чиваться**) **1.** to come unscrewed. **2.** (*fig.*, *coll.*) to extricate o.s., get o.s. out (of).

выкру́чива|ть(ся), ю(сь) *impf. of* **вы́крутить(ся)**

вы́куп, а *m.* **1.** (*leg.*) redemption. **2.** ransom.

вы́купа|ть(ся), ю(сь) *pf. of* **купа́ть(ся)**

выкуп|а́ть, а́ю *impf. of* **вы́купить**

вы́куп|ить, лю, ишь *pf.* (*of* **~а́ть**) **1.** to ransom. **2.** to redeem; **в. из-под зало́га** to get out of pawn.

выку́рива|ть, ю *impf. of* **вы́курить**

вы́кур|ить, ю, ишь *pf.* (*of* **∠ивать**) **1.** to smoke; to finish smoking. **2.** to smoke out; (*fig.*, *coll.*) to drive out.

вы́ку|ю, ешь *see* **вы́ковать**

выла́влива|ть, ю *impf. of* **вы́ловить**

вы́лазк|а, и *f.* **1.** (*mil.*) sally, sortie (*also fig.*). **2.** ramble, excursion, outing.

вы́лака|ть, ю *pf.* (*of* **лака́ть**) to lap up.

выла́мыва|ть, ю *impf. of* **вы́ломать** *and* **вы́ломить**

выла́щива|ть, ю *impf. of* **вы́лощить**

вы́леж|ать, у, ишь *pf.* (*of* **∠ивать**) (*coll.*) to remain lying down; to stay in bed.

вы́леж|аться, усь, ишься *pf.* (*of* **~́иваться**) (*coll.*) **1.** to have a thorough rest. **2.** to ripen; to mature.
вылёжива|ть(ся), ю(сь) *impf. of* **вы́лежать(ся)**
вылеза́|ть, ю *impf. of* **вы́лезть**
вы́лезт|и = ~ь
вы́лез|ть, у, ешь, *past* **~, ~ла** *pf.* (*of* **~а́ть**) **1.** to crawl out; to climb out; (*coll.*) to get out, alight. **2.** to fall out, come out.
вы́леп|ить, лю, ишь *pf. of* **лепи́ть**
вы́лет, а *m.* flight (*of birds*); (*aeron.*) take-off; commencement of flight; sortie.
вылета́|ть, ю *impf. of* **вы́лететь**
вы́ле|теть, чу, тишь *pf.* (*of* **~та́ть**) **1.** to fly out; (*aeron.*) to take off; (*fig., coll.*) to rush out, dash out; **в. из головы́** to slip one's mind. **2.: в. со слу́жбы** (*fig., coll.*) to be given the sack.
вылечива|ть(ся), ю(сь) *impf. of* **вы́лечить(ся)**
вы́леч|ить, у, ишь *pf.* (*of* **~́ивать**) **(от)** to cure (of) (*also fig.*)
вы́леч|иться, усь, ишься *pf.* (*of* **~́иваться**) **(от)** to be cured (of); to get over.
вы́леч|у[1], **ишь** *see* **~ить**
вы́ле|чу[2], **тишь** *see* **~теть**
вылива́|ть(ся), ю(сь) *impf. of* **вы́лить(ся)**
вы́ли|зать, жу, жешь *pf.* (*of* **~́зывать**) to lick clean, lick up.
вылизыва|ть, ю *impf. of* **вы́лизать**
вы́линя|ть, ю *pf. of* **линя́ть**
вы́лит|ый (~, ~а) *p.p.p. of* **~ь**; (*fig., coll.*; *long form only*) **он — в. оте́ц** he is the image of his father.
вы́л|ить, ью, ьешь *pf.* (*of* **~ива́ть**) **1.** to pour out; to empty (out). **2.** (*tech.*) to cast, found; to mould.
вы́л|иться, ьюсь, ьешься *pf.* (*of* **~ива́ться**) **1.** to run out, flow out; (*fig.*) to flow (from), spring (from). **2.** (**в**+*a. or* **в фо́рму** +*g.*) to take the form (of); to be expressed, express itself (in).
вы́лов|ить, лю, ишь *pf.* (*of* **выла́вливать**) to fish out.
вы́лож|ить, у, ишь *pf.* (*of* **выкла́дывать**) **1.** to lay out, spread out; (*fig., coll.*) to tell; to reveal, make an exposé (of). **2.** (+*i.*) to cover, lay (with); **в. дёрном** to turf; **в. ка́мнем** to face with masonry.
вы́лома|ть, ю *pf.* (*of* **выла́мывать**) to break open; to break off.
вы́лощен|ный (~, ~а) *p.p.p. of* **вы́лощить** *and adj.* **1.** glossy. **2.** (*coll., fig.*) polished, smooth.
вы́лощ|ить, у, ишь *pf.* (*of* **выла́щивать**) to polish.
вы́луп|иться, люсь, ишься *pf.* (*of* **~ля́ться**) to hatch (out).
вылупля́|ться, юсь *impf. of* **вы́лупиться**
вы́л|ью, ьешь *see* **~ить**
вы́ма|зать, жу, жешь *pf.* (*of* **ма́зать 2.** *and* **~́зывать**) (+*i.*) to smear (with), daub (with); (*coll.*) to dirty; **в. свои́ па́льцы в черни́лах** to make one's fingers inky.
вы́ма|заться, жусь, жешься *pf.* (*of* **ма́заться 1.** *and* **~́зываться**) (*coll.*) to get dirty, make o.s. dirty.
вымазыва|ть(ся), ю(сь) *impf. of* **вы́мазать(ся)**
выма́лива|ть, ю *impf.* **1.** *impf. of* **вы́молить. 2.** *impf. only* to beg for.
выма́нива|ть, ю *impf. of* **вы́манить**
вы́ман|ить, ю, ишь *pf.* (*of* **~́ивать**) **1.** (**у**+*g.*) to cheat (out of); to wheedle (out of). **2.** (**из**+*g.*) to entice (from), lure (out of, from).
вы́мар|ать, аю *pf.* (*of* **~́ывать**) (*coll.*) **1.** to soil, dirty. **2.** to strike out, cross out.
выма́рива|ть, ю *impf. of* **вы́морить**
выма́рыва|ть, ю *impf. of* **вы́марать**
выма́тыва|ть(ся), ю(сь) *impf. of* **вы́мотать(ся)**
выма́чива|ть, ю *impf. of* **вы́мочить**
выма́щива|ть, ю *impf. of* **вы́мостить**
вы́м|ени, енем *see* **~я**
выме́нива|ть, ю *impf. of* **выменять**

вы́мен|ять, яю *pf.* (*of* **~́ивать**) (**на**+*a.*) to receive in exchange, barter (for).
вы́м|ереть, ру, решь, *past* **~ер, ~ерла** *pf.* (*of* **~ира́ть**) **1.** to die out, become extinct. **2.** to become desolate, deserted.
вымерз|а́ть, а́ю *impf. of* **вы́мерзнуть**
вы́мерз|нуть, ну, нешь, *past* **~, ~ла** *pf.* (*of* **~а́ть**) **1.** to be killed by frost. **2.** to freeze (right through).
выме́рива|ть, ю *impf. of* **вы́мерить**
вы́мер|ить, ю, ишь *pf.* (*of* **~́ивать**) to measure.
вы́мер|ший *p.p. of* **~еть** *and adj.* extinct.
вымеря́|ть, ю = выме́ривать
вы́ме|сти, ту, тешь, *past* **~л** *pf.* (*of* **~та́ть**) to sweep out; to sweep clean.
вы́ме|стить, щу, стишь *pf.* (*of* **~ща́ть**) **1.** (+*d.*) to retaliate (against). **2.** (**на**+*p.*) to vent; **в. зло́бу на ком-н.** to vent one's anger on s.o.
вы́мет|ать[1], **аю** *pf.* (*of* **~́ывать**) **1.** to put out, cast out (*a net, etc.*). **2.: в. икру́** to spawn.
вы́мет|ать[2], **аю** *pf.* (*of* **~́ывать**) **в. пе́тли** to make buttonholes.
вымета́|ть, ю *impf. of* **вы́мести**
вымета́|ться, юсь *impf.* (*coll.*) to clear out, clear off (*intrans.*).
вымётыва|ть, ю *impf. of* **вы́метать**
вымеща́|ть, ю *impf. of* **вы́местить**
вы́ме|щу, стишь *see* **~стить**
вымира́|ть, ю *impf. of* **вы́мереть**
вымога́тел|ь, я *m.* extortioner.
вымога́тельский *adj.* extortionate.
вымога́тельств|о, а *nt.* extortion.
вымога́|ть, ю *impf.* to extort.
вымока́|ть, ю *impf. of* **вы́мокнуть**
вы́мок|нуть, ну, нешь, *past* **~, ~ла** *pf.* (*of* **~а́ть**) to get drenched, be soaked; **мы ~ли до ни́тки** we are soaked to the skin.
вы́молв|ить, лю, ишь *pf.* to say, utter.
вы́мол|ить, ю, ишь *pf.* (*of* **выма́ливать**) to obtain by entreaties; to beg (for) and obtain.
вымора́жива|ть, ю *impf. of* **вы́морозить**
вы́мор|ить, ю, ишь *pf.* (*of* **мори́ть**[1] *and* **выма́ривать**) to exterminate.
вы́моро|зить, жу, зишь *pf.* (*of* **вымора́живать**) **1.** to cool; to air. **2.** to freeze to death (*trans.*).
вы́мо|стить, щу, стишь *pf.* (*of* **мости́ть** *and* **выма́щивать**) to pave.
вы́мота|ть, ю *pf.* (*of* **выма́тывать**) (*coll.*) to use up; to exhaust; **в. ду́шу** to wear out; **они́ ~ли не́рвы друг дру́гу** they got on one another's nerves.
вы́мота|ться, юсь *pf.* (*of* **выма́тываться**) (*coll.*) **1.** *pass. of* **~ть. 2.** to be worn out.
вы́моч|ить, у, ишь *pf.* (*of* **выма́чивать**) **1.** to soak, drench. **2.** to steep, macerate.
вы́мо|щу, стишь *see* **~стить**
вы́м|ою, оешь *see* **~ыть**
вы́мпел, а *m.* pennant.
вы́мр|у, ешь *see* **вы́мереть**
вы́мучен|ный (~, ~а) *p.p.p. of* **вы́мучить** *and adj.* forced; (*liter.*) laboured.
вымучива|ть, ю *impf. of* **вы́мучить**
вы́муч|ить, у, ишь *pf.* (*of* **~́ивать**) (**из**+*g.*) to wring (from), force (out of).
вы́муштр|овать, ую *pf. of* **муштрова́ть**
вымыва́|ть(ся), ю(сь) *impf. of* **вы́мыть(ся)**
вы́мыс|ел, ла *m.* **1.** invention, fabrication. **2.** fantasy.
вы́м|ыть, ою, оешь *pf.* (*of* **мыть** *and* **~ыва́ть**) **1.** to wash; to wash out, off; **в. го́лову кому́-н.** to give s.o. a dressing-down. **2.** to wash away.
вы́м|ыться, оюсь, оешься *pf.* (*of* **мы́ться** *and* **~ыва́ться**) to wash o.s.
вы́мышлен|ный (~, ~а) *adj.* fictitious, imaginary.
вы́м|я, ени, ени, енем, ени, *pl.* **~ена́, ~ён, ~ена́м** *nt.* udder.

вына́шива|ть, ю *impf. of* **вы́носить**
вынесе́ни|е, я *nt.*: **в. пригово́ра** (*leg.*) pronouncement of sentence.
вы́нес|ти, у, ешь *pf.* (*of* **выноси́ть**) **1.** to carry out, take out; to take way; to carry away; **в. на бе́рег** to wash ashore; **в. на поля́** to enter in the margin (*of a book*); **в. сор из избы́** to wash one's dirty linen in public. **2.** (*fig.*) to take away, carry away, derive; **в. прия́тное впечатле́ние** to be favourably impressed. **3.**: **в. вопро́с (на собра́ние, на обсужде́ние)** to put, submit a question (to a meeting, for discussion). **4.**: **в. на свои́х плеча́х** (*fig.*) to shoulder, bear the full brunt (of). **5.** to bear, stand, endure. **6.**: **в. благода́рность** to express gratitude; **в. пригово́р** (+*d.*) to pass sentence (on).
вы́нес|тись, усь, ешься, *past* **~ся, ~лась** *pf.* (*of* **выноси́ться**) (*coll.*) to fly out, rush out.
вынима́|ть, ю *impf. of* **вы́нуть**
вы́нос, а *m.* **(из це́ркви)** bearing-out, carrying-out.
вы́но|сить, шу, сишь *pf.* (*of* **вына́шивать**) to bear, bring forth (*a child at full term*); **в. мысль** (*fig.*) to give birth to an idea.
выно|си́ть, шу́, ~́сишь *impf.* **1.** *impf. of* **вы́нести. 2.** *impf. only* (+*neg.*) to be unable to bear, be unable to stand; **я его́ не ~шу́** I can't stand him.
выно́сливост|ь, и *f.* endurance; staying-power.
выно́слив|ый (~, ~а) *adj.* hardy; robust, sturdy.
вы́но|шу, сишь *see* **~сить**
выно|шу́, ~́сишь *see* **~си́ть**
вы́ну|дить, жу, дишь *pf.* (*of* **~жда́ть**) **1.** (+*inf.*) to force, compel. **2.** (**у**+*g.*) to extract, force (from, out of); **они́ ~дили у него́ призна́ние в свое́й вине́** they have extracted an admission of guilt from him.
вынужда́|ть, ю *impf. of* **вы́нудить**
вы́нужден|ный (~, ~а) *p.p.p. of* **вы́нудить** *and adj.* forced; **~ная поса́дка** (*aeron.*) forced landing.
вы́н|уть, у, ешь *pf.* (*of* **~има́ть**) **1.** to take out; to pull out, extract; to draw out (*money from bank, etc.*). **2.**: **~ь да поло́жь** (*coll.*) (right) here and now, on the spot.
выны́рива|ть, ю *impf. of* **вы́нырнуть**
вы́ныр|нуть, ну, нешь *pf.* (*of* **~́ивать**) to come to the surface; (*fig., coll.*) to turn up.
вы́нюх|ать, аю *pf.* (*of* **~́ивать**) (*coll.*) to sniff up; (*fig.*) to sniff out; to uncover.
вынюхива|ть, ю *impf. of* **вы́нюхать**
выня́нчива|ть, ю *impf. of* **вы́нянчить**
вы́нянч|ить, у, ишь *pf.* (*of* **~́ивать**) (*coll.*) to bring up, nurse.
вы́пад, а *m.* **1.** (*fig.*) attack. **2.** (*sport*) lunge, thrust.
выпада́|ть, ю *impf. of* **вы́пасть**
выпаде́ни|е, я *nt.* **1.** falling out. **2.** (*med.*) prolapse.
выпа́лива|ть, ю *impf. of* **вы́палить**
вы́пал|ить, ю, ишь *pf.* (*of* **~́ивать**) (*coll.*) **1.** (**в**+*a.*) to shoot, fire (at). **2.** (*fig.*) to blurt out.
выпа́рива|ть, ю *impf. of* **вы́парить**
вы́пар|ить, ю, ишь *pf.* (*of* **~́ивать**) to steam; to clean, disinfect (by steaming).
выпа́рхива|ть, ю *impf. of* **вы́порхнуть**
выпа́рыва|ть, ю *impf. of* **вы́пороть 1.**
вы́па|сть, ду, дешь, *past* **~л** *pf.* (*of* **~да́ть**) **1.** to fall out. **2.** to fall (*of rain, snow, etc.*). **3.** to befall, fall (to); **ему́ ~л жре́бий стоя́ть на карау́ле в день Рождества́** it fell to his lot to be on guard on Christmas Day. **4.** to turn out; **ночь ~ла звёздная** it turned out to be a starry night.
вы́пачка|ть, ю *pf.* to soil, dirty; to stain.
вы́пачка|ться, юсь *pf.* to make o.s. dirty.
вы́пе|к *see* **~чь**
выпека́|ть, ю *impf. of* **вы́печь**
вы́п|ереть, ру, решь, *past* **~ер, ~ерла** *pf.* (*of* **~ира́ть**) **1.** to push out, shove out. **2.** to stick out, bulge out, protrude. **3.** (*sl.*) to throw out, sling out.
вы́пест|овать, ую *pf. of* **пе́стовать**
вы́печк|а, и *f.* **1.** baking. **2.** batch (*of loaves, etc.*).
вы́пе|чь, ку, чешь, кут, *past* **~к, ~кла** *pf.* (*of* **~ка́ть**) to bake.
выпива́|ть, ю *impf.* **1.** *impf. of* **вы́пить. 2.** (*impf. only*; *coll.*) to be fond of the bottle.
вы́пивк|а, и *f.* (*coll.*) **1.** drinking-bout. **2.** (*collect.*) drinks.
выпи́лива|ть, ю *impf. of* **вы́пилить**
вы́пил|ить, ю, ишь *pf.* (*of* **~́ивать**) to saw, saw up, saw off.
выпира́|ть, ю *impf. of* **вы́переть**
вы́пи|сать, шу, шешь *pf.* (*of* **~́сывать**) **1.** to copy out; to excerpt. **2.** to delineate scrupulously; to trace out. **3.** to write out; **в. квита́нцию** to write out a receipt. **4.** to order; to subscribe (to); to send for (*in writing*). **5.** to strike off the list; to discharge.
вы́пи|саться, шусь, шешься *pf.* (*of* **~́сываться**) to leave (*on discharge*); to be discharged.
вы́писк|а, и *f.* **1.** copying, excerpting. **2.** writing out. **3.** extract, excerpt. **4.** ordering; subscription. **5.** discharge.
выпи́сыва|ть(ся), ю(сь) *impf. of* **вы́писать(ся)**
вы́п|ить, ью, ьешь *pf.* (*of* **выпива́ть** *and* **пить**) to drink; to drink up, off.
выпи́хива|ть, ю *impf. of* **вы́пихнуть**
вы́пих|нуть, ну, нешь *pf.* (*of* **~́ивать**) (*coll.*) to shove out, bundle out.
вы́пи|шу, шешь *see* **~сать**
вы́плав|ить, лю, ишь *pf.* (*of* **~ля́ть**) to smelt.
вы́плавк|а, и *f.* **1.** smelting. **2.** smelted metal.
выплавля́|ть, ю *impf. of* **вы́плавить**
вы́пла|кать, чу, чешь *pf.* **1.** (*coll., folk poet.*) to sob out. **2.** (*coll.*) to obtain by tearful entreaties. **3.** (*coll., folk poet.*): **в. (все) глаза́** to cry one's eyes out.
вы́пла|каться, чусь, чешься *pf.* (*coll.*) to have a good cry.
вы́плат|а, ы *f.* payment.
вы́пла|тить, чу, тишь *pf.* (*of* **~́чивать**) **1.** to pay (out). **2.** to pay off (*debts*).
выпла́чива|ть, ю *impf. of* **вы́платить**
вы́пла|чу[1], тишь *see* **~тить**
вы́пла|чу[2], чешь *see* **~кать**
выплёвыва|ть, ю *impf. of* **вы́плюнуть**
вы́пле|скать, щу, щешь *pf.* (*of* **~̈скивать**) to splash out.
выплёскива|ть, ю *impf. of* **вы́плескать** *and* **вы́плеснуть**
вы́плес|нуть, ну, нешь *pf.* (*of* **~̈кивать**) to splash out.
выплыва́|ть, ю *impf. of* **вы́плыть**
вы́плы|ть, ву, вешь *pf.* (*of* **~ва́ть**) **1.** to swim out; (*fig.*) to sail out. **2.** to come to the surface; (*fig., coll.*) to emerge; to appear; to crop up.
вы́плюн|уть, у, ешь *pf.* (*of* **выплёвывать**) to spit out
выпола́скива|ть, ю *impf. of* **вы́полоскать**
выполза́|ть, ю *impf. of* **вы́ползти**
вы́полз|ти, у, ешь, *past* **~, ~ла** *pf.* (*of* **~а́ть**) (**из**+*g.*) to crawl out, creep out (from).
выполне́ни|е, я *nt.* execution, carrying-out; fulfilment.
выполни́м|ый (~, ~а) *pres. part. pass. of* **вы́полнить** *and adj.* practicable, feasible.
вы́полн|ить, ю, ишь *pf.* (*of* **~я́ть**) to execute, carry out; to fulfil; **в. свои́ обя́занности** to discharge one's obligations; **в. приказа́ние** to carry out an order.
выполня́|ть, ю *impf. of* **вы́полнить**
вы́поло|скать, щу, щешь *pf.* (*of* **выпола́скивать**) to rinse out.
вы́пол|оть, ю, ешь *pf.* (*of* **поло́ть**) to weed.
вы́пор|оть[1], ю, ешь *pf.* (*of* **выпа́рывать**) (*coll.*)

to rip out, rip up.

вы́пор|оть[2], **ю ешь** *pf. of* **поро́ть**[2]

вы́порхн|уть, у, ешь *pf.* (*of* **выпа́рхивать**) to flit out (*of birds*); (*fig., coll.*) to dart out.

вы́потрош|ить, у, ишь *pf. of* **потроши́ть**

вы́прав|ить, лю, ишь *pf.* (*of* **~ля́ть**) **1.** to straighten (out). **2.** to correct; to improve.

вы́прав|иться, люсь, ишься *pf.* (*of* **~ля́ться**) **1.** to become straight. **2.** to improve (*intrans.*).

вы́правк|а, и *f.* bearing.

выправля́|ть(ся), ю(сь) *impf. of* **вы́править(ся)**

выпра́стыва|ть, ю *impf. of* **вы́простать**

выпра́шива|ть, ю *impf.* **1.** *impf. of* **вы́просить. 2.** *impf. only* to solicit, try to get; **он всё ~ет разреше́ние на вы́езд** he is always trying to get permission to go abroad.

выпрова́жива|ть, ю *impf. of* **вы́проводить**

вы́прово|дить, жу, дишь *pf.* (*of* **выпрова́живать**) (*coll.*) to send packing; to show the door (to).

вы́про|сить, шу, сишь *pf.* (*of* **выпра́шивать**) (**у**+*g.*) to get (out of), obtain, elicit (by begging).

вы́проста|ть, ю *pf.* (*of* **выпра́стывать**) (*coll.*) **1.** to free, work loose. **2.** to empty.

вы́про|шу, сишь *see* **~сить**

вы́п|ру, решь *see* **~ереть**

выпры́гива|ть, ю *impf. of* **вы́прыгнуть**

вы́прыг|нуть, ну, нешь *pf.* (*of* **≃ивать**) to jump out, spring out.

выпряга́|ть, ю *impf. of* **вы́прячь**

вы́прям|ить, лю, ишь *pf.* (*of* **~ля́ть**) to straighten (out).

вы́прям|иться, люсь, ишься *pf.* (*of* **~ля́ться**) to become straight; **в. во весь рост** to draw o.s. up to one's full height.

выпрямля́|ть(ся), ю(сь) *impf. of* **вы́прямить(ся)**

вы́пря|чь, гу, жешь, гут, *past* **~г, ~гла** *pf.* (*of* **~га́ть**) to unharness.

вы́пуклост|ь, и *f.* **1.** protuberance; bulge. **2.** (*phys.*) convexity.

вы́пуклый *adj.* **1.** protuberant; prominent, bulging. **2.** (*phys.*) convex. **3.** in relief. **4.** (*fig.*) clear, distinct.

вы́пуск, а *m.* **1.** output; issue; discharge (*of steam, gases, etc.*). **2.** part, number, instalment (*of serial publication*); **дебю́тный в.** launch issue; **сери́йный в.** mass production. **3.** leavers; graduates.

выпуска́|ть, ю *impf. of* **вы́пустить**

выпускни́к, а́ *m.* **1.** graduate; **бы́вший в.** old boy. **2.** final-year student.

выпускни́|ца, цы *f. of* **~к**

выпуск|но́й *adj. of* **вы́пуск**; (*tech.*) exhaust; discharge; **в. экза́мен** final examination; finals.

вы́пу|стить, щу, стишь *pf.* (*of* **~ска́ть**) **1.** to let out; to release; **в. (пулемётную) о́чередь** (*mil.*) to fire a burst. **2.** to put out, issue; to turn out, produce; **в. в прода́жу** to put on the market; **в. кинокарти́ну** to release a film. **3.** to cut (out), omit. **4.** (*tailoring*) to let out, let down. **5.** to show; **в. свой ко́гти** to show one's claws.

вы́пут|ать, аю *pf.* (*of* **≃ывать**) to disentangle.

вы́пут|аться, аюсь *pf.* (*of* **≃ываться**) to disentangle o.s., extricate o.s. (*also fig.*).

выпу́тыва|ть(ся), ю(сь) *impf. of* **вы́путать(ся)**

вы́пуч|енный *p.p.p. of* **~ить** *and adj.* (*coll.*): **с ~енными глаза́ми** wide-eyed, goggle-eyed.

выпу́чива|ть, ю *impf. of* **вы́пучить**

вы́пуч|ить, у, ишь *pf.* (*of* **≃ивать**) **в. глаза́** (*coll.*) to open one's eyes wide.

вы́пушк|а, и *f.* edging, braid, piping.

вы́пыт|ать, аю *pf.* (*of* **≃ывать**) (**у**+*g.*) to elicit, extract (*information, secrets, etc., from*).

выпы́тыва|ть, ю *impf.* **1.** *impf. of* **вы́пытать. 2.** *impf. only* to try to discover (*by interrogation*); **в. секре́т у кого́-н.** to try to get a secret out of s.o.

вып|ь, и *f.* (*zool.*) bittern.

вы́пя|тить, чу, тишь *pf.* (*of* **≃чивать**) (*coll.*) **1.** to stick out; **в. грудь** to stick out one's chest. **2.** (*fig.*) to over-emphasize.

вы́пя|титься, чусь, тишься *pf.* (*of* **≃чиваться**) (*coll.*) to stick out (*intrans.*), protrude.

выпя́чива|ть(ся), ю(ся) *impf. of* **вы́пятить(ся)**

вырaба́тыва|ть, ю *impf. of* **вы́работать**

вы́работа|ть, ю *pf.* (*of* **выраба́тывать**) **1.** to manufacture; to produce, make. **2.** to work out, draw up. **3.** to develop; **в. хоро́ший стиль** to develop a good style. **4.** (*coll.*) to earn, make.

вы́работк|а, и *f.* **1.** manufacture; production, making. **2.** working-out, drawing-up. **3.** output, yield. **4.** (*coll.*) workmanship; **хоро́шей ~и** well-made.

выра́внивани|е, я *nt.* smoothing-out, levelling; alignment.

выра́внива|ть(ся), ю(сь) *impf. of* **вы́ровнять(ся)**

выража́|ть, ю *impf. of* **вы́разить**

выража́|ться, юсь *impf.* **1.** *impf. of* **вы́разиться; мя́гко ~ясь** to put it mildly. **2.** (*coll.*) to swear.

выраже́ни|е, я *nt.* (*in var. senses*) expression.

вы́ражен|ный (~, ~а) *p.p.p. of* **вы́разить** *and adj.* pronounced, marked.

вырази́тел|ь, я *m.* spokesperson; exponent.

вырази́тел|ьный (~ен, ~ьна) *adj.* expressive.

вы́ра|зить, жу, зишь *pf.* (*of* **~жа́ть**) to express; to convey; to voice.

вы́ра|зиться, жусь, зишься *pf.* (*of* **~жа́ться**) **1.** to express o.s. **2.** (**в**+*p.*) to manifest itself (in.). **3.** (**в**+*p.*) to amount to, come to; **изде́ржки ~зились в шести́ рубля́х** the costs came to six roubles.

выраста́|ть, ю *impf. of* **вы́расти**

вы́р|асти, асту, астешь, *past* **~ос, ~осла** *pf.* (*of* **~аста́ть**) **1.** to grow (up). **2.** (**в**+*a.*) to grow (into), develop (into); **их дру́жба ~осла в любо́вь** their friendship grew into love. **3.** (**из**+*g.*) to outgrow (*clothing*). **4.** to increase; **населе́ние за пять лет ~осло на два́дцать проце́нтов** in five years the population had increased by twenty per cent. **5.** to appear, rise up; **пе́ред на́шими глаза́ми ~ос Арара́т** Mount Ararat rose up before our eyes. **6.: в. в чьих-н. глаза́х** to rise in s.o.'s estimation.

вы́ра|стить, щу, стишь *pf.* (*of* **≃щивать**) to bring up; to rear, breed; to grow, cultivate.

выра́щива|ть, ю *impf. of* **вы́растить**

вы́рв|ать[1], **у, ешь** *pf.* (*of* **вырыва́ть**[1]) **1.** to pull out, tear out; **в. зуб** to pull a tooth; **в. зуб (у врача́)** to have a tooth out; **он ~ал кни́гу у меня́ из рук** he snatched the book out of my hands. **2.** (*fig.*) to wring; **в. призна́ние у кого́-н.** to wring a confession out of s.o.

вы́рв|ать[2], **у, ешь** *pf. of* **рвать**[2]

вы́рв|аться, усь, ешься *pf.* (*of* **вырыва́ться**) **1.** (**из**+*g.*) to tear o.s. away (from); to break out (from), break loose (from), break free (from); to get away (from); **в. из чьих-н. объя́тий** to tear o.s. away from s.o.'s embrace; **едва́ ли мне уда́стся до ле́та в. из Москвы́** I shall hardly manage to get away from Moscow before the summer. **2.** to come loose, come out; **не́сколько страни́ц ~алось из э́той кни́ги** several pages have come out of this book. **3.** (*of a sound, a remark, etc.*) (**из, у**+*g.*) to burst (from), escape. **4.** to shoot up, shoot out; **четвёртая маши́на вдруг ~алась вперёд на пе́рвое ме́сто** the fourth car suddenly shot ahead into first place.

вы́рез, а *m.* cut; notch; **пла́тье с больши́м ~ом** low-necked dress.

вы́ре|зать, жу, жешь *pf.* (*of* **~за́ть**) **1.** to cut out; to excise. **2.** to carve; to engrave. **3.** (*fig.*) to slaughter, butcher.

выреза́|ть, ю *impf. of* **вы́резать**

вы́резк|а, и *f.* **1.** cutting-out, excision; carving;

engraving. **2. газе́тная в.** press-cutting. **3.** fillet steak.
вырезн|о́й *adj.* **1.** cut; cut-out; carved. **2.** low-necked.
выре́зыва|ть, ю *impf.* = **выреза́ть**
вы́рис|овать, ую *pf.* (*of* **~о́вывать**) to draw carefully, draw in detail.
вы́рис|оваться, уется *pf.* (*of* **~о́вываться**) to appear (in outline); to stand out; **на горизо́нте ~овалась го́рная цепь** a mountain chain stood out against the horizon.
вырисо́выва|ть(ся), ю(сь) *impf. of* **вы́рисовать(ся)**
вы́ровня|ть, ю *pf.* (*of* **выра́внивать**) **1.** to smooth (out), level; **в. доро́гу** to level a road. **2.** to equalize; to align. **3.** (*mil.*) to draw up in line; **в. ряды́** to dress ranks. **4.: в. самолёт** to straighten out an aeroplane.
вы́ровня|ться, юсь, *pf.* (*of* **выра́вниваться**) **1.** to become level; to become even; (*mil.*) to form up; to dress; (*sport*) to equalize. **2.** (*fig.*) to catch up, draw level. **3.** (*fig.*) to improve, get better.
вы́род|иться, ится *pf.* (*of* **вырожда́ться**) to degenerate.
вы́род|ок, ка *m.* (*coll.*) degenerate; **он — в. в на́шей семье́** he is the black sheep of our family.
вырожда́|ться, юсь *impf. of* **вы́родиться**
вырожде́н|ец, ца *m.* degenerate.
вырожде́ни|е, я *nt.* degeneration.
вы́рон|ить, ю, ишь *pf.* to drop.
вы́р|ою, оешь *see* **~ыть**
выруба́|ть, ю *impf. of* **вы́рубить**
вы́руб|ить, лю, ишь *pf.* (*of* **~а́ть**) **1.** to cut down, fell; to hew out. **2.** to cut out. **3.** to carve (out).
вы́рубк|а, и *f.* **1.** cutting down, felling; hewing out; **в. лесо́в** deforestation. **2.** clearing, glade.
вы́руга|ть(ся), ю(сь) *pf. of* **руга́ть(ся)**
выру́лива|ть, ю *impf. of* **вы́рулить**
вы́рул|ить, ю, ишь *pf.* (*of* **~ивать**) (*aeron.*) to taxi.
выруча́|ть, ю *impf. of* **вы́ручить**
вы́руч|ить, у, ишь *pf.* (*of* **~а́ть**) **1.** to rescue; to come to the aid (of). **2.** to make (*coll.*); **он ~ил мно́го де́нег от прода́жи свои́х карти́н** he has made a lot of money from the sale of his pictures.
вы́ручк|а, и *f.* **1.** rescue; **прийти́ на ~у** to come to the rescue. **2.** proceeds, receipts; earnings.
вырыва́|ть[1]**, ю** *impf. of* **вы́рвать**[1]
вырыва́|ть[2]**, ю** *impf. of* **вы́рыть**
вырыва́|ться, юсь *impf. of* **вы́рваться**
вы́р|ыть, ою, оешь *pf.* (*of* **~ыва́ть**[2]) to dig up, dig out, unearth; **в. труп** to exhume a corpse.
вы́ря|дить, жу, дишь *pf.* (*coll.*) to dress up (*trans.*).
вы́ря|диться, жусь, дишься *pf.* (*coll.*) to dress up (*intrans.*).
выряжа́|ть(ся), ю(сь) *impf. of* **вы́рядить(ся)**
вы́са|дить, жу, дишь *pf.* (*of* **~живать**) **1.** to set down; to help down; to make alight; **в. на бе́рег** to put ashore; **пья́ницу ~дили из авто́буса** the drunk was put off the bus. **2.** (*hort.*) to transplant.
вы́са|диться, жусь, дишься *pf.* (*of* **~живаться**) (**из, с**+*g.*) to alight (from), get off; **в. (с су́дна)** to land, disembark; **в. (с самолёта)** to land.
вы́садк|а, и *f.* **1.** debarkation, disembarkation; landing. **2.** (*hort.*) transplanting.
выса́жива|ть(ся), ю(сь) *impf. of* **вы́садить(ся)**
вы́са|жу, дишь *see* **~дить**
выса́сыва|ть, ю *impf. of* **вы́сосать**
высве́рлива|ть, ю *impf. of* **вы́сверлить**
вы́сверл|ить, ю, ишь *pf.* to drill, bore.
вы́све|тить, чу, тишь *pf.* (*of* **высве́чивать**) **1.** to light up, illuminate. **2.** (*fig.*) to highlight.
высве́чива|ть, ю *impf. of* **вы́светить**
вы́свобо|дить, жу, дишь *pf.* **1.** to free, liberate; to disentangle, disengage. **2.** to release; **в. сре́дства** to release funds.
высвобожда́|ть, ю *impf. of* **вы́свободить**
высева́|ть, ю *impf.* = **высе́ивать**
высе́ива|ть, ю *impf. of* **вы́сеять**
высека́|ть, ю *impf. of* **вы́сечь**[2]
вы́се|ку, чешь *see* **~чь**
выселе́ни|е, я *nt.* eviction.
вы́сел|ить, ю, ишь *pf.* (*of* **~я́ть**) **1.** to evict. **2.** to evacuate, move.
вы́сел|иться, юсь, ишься *pf.* (*of* **~я́ться**) to move.
выселя́|ть(ся), ю(сь) *impf. of* **вы́селить(ся)**
вы́се|чь[1]**, ку, чешь, кут,** *past* **~к, ~кла** *pf.* (*of* **сечь**[1]) to beat, flog.
вы́се|чь[2]**, ку, чешь, кут,** *past* **~к, ~кла** *pf.* (*of* **~ка́ть**) to cut (out); to carve, sculpture; to hew; **в. ого́нь** to strike; ignite.
вы́се|ять, ю *pf.* (*of* **~ва́ть** *and* **~ивать**) (*agric.*) to sow.
вы́си|деть, жу, дишь *pf.* (*of* **~живать**) **1.** to hatch (out). **2.** to stay; to sit out, through.
выси́жива|ть, ю *impf. of* **вы́сидеть**
вы́|ситься, шусь, сишься *impf.* to tower (up), rise.
выска́блива|ть, ю *impf. of* **вы́скоблить**
вы́ска|зать, жу, жешь *pf.* (*of* **~зывать**) to express; to state; **в. мне́ние** to advance an opinion; **в. предположе́ние** to come out with a suggestion.
вы́ска|заться, жусь, жешься *pf.* (*of* **~зываться**) **1.** to speak out; to have one's say. **2.** to speak (for *or* against); **никто́ не ~зался про́тив законопрое́кта** no one spoke against the bill.
выска́зывани|е, я *nt.* **1.** utterance. **2.** pronouncement; opinion.
выска́зыва|ть(ся), ю(сь) *impf. of* **вы́сказать(ся)**
выска́кива|ть, ю *impf. of* **вы́скочить**
выска́льзыва|ть, ю *impf. of* **вы́скользнуть**
вы́скобл|ить, ю, ишь *pf.* (*of* **выска́бливать**) to scrape out; to erase; (*med.*) to remove.
вы́скользн|уть, у, ешь *pf.* (*of* **выска́льзывать**) to slip out (*also fig.*); **ры́ба ~ула из его́ рук** the fish slipped out of his hands.
вы́скоч|ить, у, ишь *pf.* (*of* **выска́кивать**) **1.** to jump out; to leap out, spring out; (*fig., coll.*) to come out (with); **он ~ил с кра́йне неуме́стным замеча́нием** he came out with an extremely uncalled-for remark. **2.** (*of a boil, etc.*) (*coll.*) to come up. **3.** (*coll.*) to fall out.
вы́скочк|а, и *c.g.* (*coll.*) upstart.
вы́|слать, шлю, шлешь *pf.* (*of* **~сыла́ть**) **1.** to send, send out, dispatch. **2.** (*pol.*) to exile; to deport.
вы́сле|дить, жу, дишь *pf.* to trace; to track down.
высле́жива|ть, ю *impf.* **1.** *impf. of* **вы́следить. 2.** *impf. only* to be on the track of; to shadow.
вы́сле|жу, дишь *see* **~дить**
вы́слуг|а, и *f.* period of service; **за ~у лет** for long service.
выслу́жива|ть(ся), ю(сь) *impf. of* **вы́служить(ся)**
вы́служ|ить, у, ишь *pf.* to qualify for, obtain (*as result of service*); **он ~ил повыше́ние** he has qualified for promotion.
вы́служ|иться, усь, ишься *pf.* **1.** to gain promotion, be promoted. **2.** (*coll., pej.*) to gain favour (with), get in (with); **он ~ился пе́ред бригади́ром** he is well in with the foreman.
вы́слуша|ть, ю *pf.* (*of* **выслу́шивать**) **1.** to hear out. **2.** (*med.*) to sound; to listen to.
выслу́шивани|е, я *nt.* (*med.*) auscultation.
выслу́шива|ть, ю *impf. of* **вы́слушать**
высма́трива|ть, *impf. of* **вы́смотреть**
высме́ива|ть, ю *impf. of* **вы́смеять**
вы́сме|ять, ю, ешь *pf.* (*of* **~ивать**) to deride, ridicule.
вы́смол|ить, ю, ишь *pf. of* **смоли́ть**
вы́сморка|ть(ся), ю(сь) *pf. of* **сморка́ть(ся)**

вы́смотр|еть, ю, ишь *pf.* (*of* **высма́тривать**) **1.** to scrutinize, look through. **2.** to spy out; to locate (*by eye*).

высо́выва|ть(ся), ю(сь) *impf. of* **вы́сунуть(ся)**

высо́к|ий (~, ~а́, ~о́) *adj.* (*in var. senses*) high; tall; lofty; elevated, sublime; (*mus.*) high, high-pitched; **~ая вода́** high tide; **в. гость** distinguished visitor.

высо́ко́ *adv.* **1.** high (up); **лежа́ть в. над у́ровнем мо́ря** to be high above sea level. **2.** *as pred.* it is high (up); it is a long way up; **окно́ бы́ло в. от земли́** the window was high up off the ground.

высоко... *comb. form* high-, highly-.

высокого́рный *adj.* Alpine, mountain.

высокока́чественный *adj.* high-quality.

высококвалифици́рованный *adj.* (highly-)skilled.

высокоме́ри|е, я *nt.* haughtiness, arrogance.

высокоме́р|ный (~ен, ~на) *adj.* haughty, arrogant.

высокопа́р|ный (~ен, ~на) *adj.* (*liter.*) high-flown; bombastic.

высокопоста́вленный *adj.* high-ranking.

вы́сос|ать, у, ешь *pf.* (*of* **выса́сывать**) to suck out, suck dry; **в. из па́льца** to invent, fabricate; **всё э́то из па́льца ~ано** it is a complete fabrication.

высот|а́, ы́, *pl.* **~ы, ~** *f.* **1.** height, altitude; (*mus.*) pitch; **набра́ть ~у́** (*aeron.*) to gain altitude. **2.** height, eminence (*concr.*). **3.** (*fig.*): **на до́лжной ~е́** up to the mark; **быть на ~е́ положе́ния** to be equal to the occasion.

высо́тный *adj.* **1.** high-altitude. **2.** high-rise.

высотоме́р, а *m.* altimeter.

вы́сох|нуть, ну, нешь, *past* **~, ~ла** *pf.* (*of* **высыха́ть**) **1.** to dry (out); to dry up. **2.** to wither, fade; (*fig.*) to waste away, fade away.

вы́сох|ший *p.p. act. of* **~нуть** *and adj.* dried-up; shrivelled; wizened.

высоча́йш|ий *adj.* **1.** *superl. of* **высо́кий. 2.** (*epithet of tsar or emperor*) imperial, royal; **проше́ние на ~ее и́мя** petition to His Imperial Majesty.

высоче́нный *adj.* (*coll.*) very high, very tall.

высо́честв|о, а *nt.* **(ва́ше) в.** (your) Highness.

вы́сп|аться, люсь, ишься *pf.* (*of* **высыпа́ться**[2]) (*coll.*) to have a good sleep.

выспра́шива|ть, ю *impf. of* **вы́спросить**

вы́спренний *adj.* high-flown; bombastic.

вы́спро|сить, шу, сишь *pf.* (*of* **выспра́шивать**) (*coll.*) **1.** to inquire. **2.** to inquire of, interrogate; to pump.

вы́став|ить, лю, ишь *pf.* (*of* **~ля́ть**) **1.** to bring out, bring forward; to display, exhibit; **в. на свет** to expose to the light. **2.** (*mil.*) to post (*guard, etc.*). **3.** (*+i.*) to represent (as), make out (as); **в. в плохо́м све́те** to present in an unfavourable light; **его́ ~или тру́сом** he was made out to be a coward. **4.** to put forward; to adduce; **в. свою́ кандидату́ру** to come forward as a candidate; **в. до́воды** to adduce arguments. **5.** to put down, set down (*in writing*); **в. отме́тки** to put down marks **6.** (*coll.*) to send out, turn out, throw out; to order out; **в. из ко́мнаты** to send out of the room; **в. со слу́жбы** to sack.

вы́став|иться, люсь, ишься *pf.* (*of* **~ля́ться**) **1.** (*coll.*) to lean out; to thrust o.s. forward; (*fig., pej.*) to show off.

вы́ставк|а, и *f.* exhibition, show; display.

выставля́|ть, ю *impf. of* **вы́ставить**

выставля́|ться, юсь *impf. of* **вы́ставиться**

вы́став|очный *adj. of* **~ка**

выста́ива|ть(ся), ю(сь) *impf. of* **вы́стоять(ся)**

вы́стега|ть, ю *pf. of* **стега́ть**[2]

вы́ст|елю, елешь *see* **~лать**

выстила́|ть, ю *impf. of* **вы́стлать**

вы́стира|ть, ю *pf. of* **стира́ть**[2]

вы́ст|лать, елю, елешь *pf.* to cover; to pave.

вы́сто|ять, ю, ишь *pf.* (*of* **выста́ивать**) **1.** to stand; **нам пришло́сь в. весь путь** we had to stand the whole way. **2.** to stand one's ground.

вы́сто|яться, юсь, ишься *pf.* (*of* **выста́иваться**) to mature, ripen.

выстра́гива|ть, ю *impf. of* **вы́строгать**

вы́страда|ть, ю *pf.* **1.** to suffer; to go through. **2.** to gain, achieve through suffering.

выстра́ива|ть(ся), ю(сь) *impf. of* **вы́строить(ся)**

вы́стрел, а *m.* shot; report; **произвести́ в.** to fire a shot; **разда́лся в.** a shot rang out; **на в. (от+** *g.***)** (*coll.*) within gunshot (of).

вы́стрел|ить, ю, ишь *pf.* to shoot, fire; **я ~ил в него́ три ра́за** I fired three shots at him.

вы́стри|г, гу, жешь *see* **~чь**

выстрига́|ть, ю *impf. of* **вы́стричь**

вы́стри|чь, гу, жешь, гут, *past* **~г, ~гла** *pf.* to cut, clip out; to shear.

вы́строга|ть, ю *pf.* (*of* **строга́ть** *and* **выстра́гивать**) (*tech.*) to plane, shave.

вы́стро|ить, ю, ишь *pf.* (*of* **выстра́ивать**) **1.** to build. **2.** to draw up, order, arrange; (*mil.*) to form up.

вы́стро|иться, юсь, ишься *pf.* (*of* **выстра́иваться**) **1.** (*mil.*) to form up (*intrans.*). **2.** *pass. of* **~ить**

вы́стука|ть, ю *pf.* (*of* **высту́кивать**) (*coll.*) to tap out.

высту́кива|ть, ю *impf. of* **вы́стукать**

вы́ступ, а *m.* projection; ledge; **в. фро́нта** (*mil.*) salient.

выступа́|ть, ю *impf.* **1.** *impf. of* **вы́ступить. 2.** (*impf. only*) to project, jut out, stick out. **3.** (*impf. only*) to strut, pace.

вы́ступ|ить, лю, ишь *pf.* **1.** to come forward; to come out; **в. в похо́д** (*mil.*) to take the field. **2.** (**из**+*g.*) to go beyond; **в. из берего́в** to overflow its banks. **3.** to appear (*publicly*); to come out (with, as); **в. в печа́ти** to appear in print; **в. за предложе́ние** to come out in favour of a proposal; **в. с ре́чью** to make a speech; **в. по телеви́дению** to appear on television.

выступле́ни|е, я *nt.* **1.** appearance (*in public*); speech. **2.** setting out.

вы́сун|уть, у, ешь *pf.* (*of* **высо́вывать**) to put out, thrust out; **в. язы́к** to stick one's tongue out.

вы́сун|уться, усь, ешься *pf.* (*of* **высо́вываться**) to show o.s., thrust o.s. forward; **в. в окно́** to lean out of the window.

высу́шива|ть, ю *impf. of* **вы́сушить**

вы́суш|ить, у, ишь *pf.* **1.** to dry (out). **2.** (*coll.*) to emaciate. **3.** (*coll., fig.*) to make callous, make hard.

вы́счита|ть, ю *pf.* to calculate, compute.

высчи́тыва|ть, ю *impf. of* **вы́считать**

вы́с|ший *adj.* (*comp. and superl. of* **высо́кий**) highest; supreme; high; higher; **~шего ка́чества** of the highest quality; **~шая ме́ра наказа́ния** (*leg.*) capital punishment; the death penalty; **суд ~шей инста́нции** High Court; **~шее образова́ние** higher education; **~шее о́бщество** (high) society; **~шее уче́бное заведе́ние** higher education establishment; **в ~шей сте́пени** in the highest degree.

высыла́|ть, ю *impf. of* **вы́слать**

вы́сылк|а, и *f.* **1.** sending, dispatch. **2.** expulsion; exile.

вы́сып|ать, лю, лешь *pf.* **1.** to pour out; to empty (out); to spill; (*fig., coll.*) to pour out; **в. все свои́ забо́ты** to pour out all one's troubles. **2.** (*coll.*) to pour out (*intrans.*). **3.** to break out (*of a rash, etc.*); (*impers.*): **у него́ ~ало на всем те́ле** he has come out in a rash all over.

высыпа́|ть, ю *impf. of* **вы́сыпать**

вы́сып|аться, люсь, лешься *pf.* **1.** *pass. of* **~ать.**

2. to pour out; to spill (*intrans.*).
высыпа́|ться[1], **юсь** *impf. of* **вы́сыпаться**
высыпа́|ться[2], **юсь,** *impf. of* **вы́спаться**
высыха́|ть, ю *impf. of* **вы́сохнуть**
выс|ь, и *f.* height; (*usu. pl.*) summit.
выта́лкива|ть, ю *impf. of* **вы́толкать** *and* **вы́толкнуть**
выта́плива|ть, ю *impf. of* **вы́топить**
выта́птыва|ть, ю *impf. of* **вы́топтать**
вытара́щива|ть, ю *impf. of* **вы́таращить**
вы́таращ|ить, у, ишь *pf.* (*coll.*): **в. глаза́** to open one's eyes wide.
выта́скива|ть, ю *impf. of* **вы́тащить**
вы́тача|ть, ю *pf. of* **тача́ть**
выта́чива|ть, ю *impf. of* **вы́точить**
вы́тачк|а, и *f.* tuck, dart.
вы́тащ|ить, у, ишь *pf.* (*of* **выта́скивать**) to drag out; to pull out, extract; (*coll.*) **в. кого́-н.** to drag s.o. out, drag s.o. off; **они́ ~или его́ в. кино́** they have dragged him off to the cinema.
вы́твер|дить, жу, дишь *pf.* (*coll.*) to get by heart.
вытве́ржива|ть, ю *impf. of* **вы́твердить**
вытворя́|ть, ю *impf.* (*coll.*) to get up to, be up to; **что ты тепе́рь ~ешь?** what are you up to now?
вытека́|ть, ю *impf.* **1.** *impf. of* **вы́течь. 2.** (*impf. only*) to flow (from, out of) (*of a river*). **3.** (*impf. only*) (*fig.*) to result, follow (from).
вы́те|ку, чешь, кут *see* **~чь**
вы́т|ереть, ру, решь, *past* **~ер, ~ерла** *pf.* (*of* **~ира́ть**) **1.** to wipe (up); to dry, rub dry; **в. но́ги** to wipe one's feet; **в. посу́ду** dry the crockery. **2.** (*coll.*) to wear out, wear threadbare.
вы́терп|еть, лю, ишь *pf.* to bear, endure; to suffer; **я е́ле ~ел, когда́ он сказа́л э́то** I could hardly stand it when he said that.
вы́терт|ый (~, ~а) *p.p.p. of* **вы́тереть** *and adj.* threadbare.
вы́те|сать, шу, шешь *pf.* to square off.
вытесне́ни|е, я *nt.* **1.** ousting; supplanting. **2.** (*phys.*) displacement.
вы́тесн|ить, ю, ишь *pf.* **1.** to crowd out; to force out; (*fig.*) to oust; to supplant. **2.** (*phys.*) to displace.
вытесня́|ть, ю *impf. of* **вы́теснить**
вытёсыва|ть, ю *impf. of* **вы́тесать**
вы́те|чь, ку, чешь, кут, *past* **~к, ~кла** *pf.* (*of* **~ка́ть**) to flow out, run out.
вы́те|шу, шешь *see* **~сать**
вытира́|ть, ю *impf. of* **вы́тереть**
вы́тисн|ить, ю, ишь *pf.* to stamp, imprint, impress.
вытисня́|ть, ю *impf. of* **вы́тиснить**
вы́тк|ать, у, ешь *pf.* to weave, finish weaving; **в. ковёр** to weave a carpet.
вы́толка|ть, ю *pf.* (*of* **выта́лкивать**) (*coll.*) to throw out; **его́ ~ли в ше́ю** (*sl.*) he was thrown out on his ear.
вы́толкн|уть, у, ешь *pf.* (*of* **выта́лкивать**) **1.** to throw out. **2.** (*coll.*) to push out, force out.
вы́топ|ить, лю, ишь *pf.* (*of* **выта́пливать**) **1.** (*coll.*) to heat. **2.** to melt (down).
вы́топ|тать, чу, чешь *pf.* (*of* **выта́птывать**) to trample down.
вы́торг|овать, ую *pf.* **1.** to obtain (*by bargaining, haggling*); to get a reduction (of); **он ~овал де́сять рубле́й из цены́ э́тих сапо́г** he got a reduction of ten roubles on the price of these boots; (*fig., coll.*) to manage to get. **2.** (*coll.*) to make, clear.
выторго́выва|ть, ю *impf.* **1.** *impf. of* **вы́торговать. 2.** to try to get (*by bargaining*); to haggle over.
вы́точен|ный (~, ~а) *p.p.p. of* **вы́точить** *and adj.* **сло́вно в.** chiselled (*of facial features*); perfect, perfectly-formed (*of bodies*).
вы́точ|ить, у, ишь *pf.* (*of* **выта́чивать**) **1.** to turn (*tech.*). **2.** (*coll.*) to sharpen.
вы́трав|ить, лю, ишь *pf.* (*of* **трави́ть**[1] *and* **~ля́ть**) **1.** to exterminate. **2.** to remove (*by chemical action*). **3.** to etch. **4.** (*of cattle, etc.*) to trample down.
вытра́влива|ть, ю *impf.* (*coll.*) = **вытравля́ть**
вытравля́|ть, ю *impf. of* **вы́травить**
вы́треб|овать, ую *pf.* **1.** to obtain on demand. **2.** to send for, summon; **в. кого́-н. в суд пове́сткой** to summons s.o.
вытрезви́тел|ь, я *m.* detoxification centre.
вы́трезв|ить, лю, ишь *pf.* to sober.
вы́трезв|иться, люсь, ишься *pf.* (*coll.*) to sober up (*intrans.*).
вытрезвля́|ть(ся), ю(сь) *impf. of* **вы́трезвить(ся)**
вы́т|ру, решь *see* **~ереть**
вытряса́|ть, ю *impf. of* **вы́трясти**
вы́тряс|ти, у, ешь, *past* **~, ~ла** *pf.* to shake out.
вытря́хива|ть, ю *impf. of* **вы́тряхнуть**
вы́тряхн|уть, у, ешь *pf.* to shake out.
выть, во́ю, во́ешь *impf.* to howl; wail.
выть|ё, я́ *no pl., nt.* (*coll.*) howling; wailing.
вытя́гива|ть(ся), ю(сь) *impf. of* **вы́тянуть(ся)**
вытяже́ни|е, *nt.* stretching.
вы́тяжк|а, и *f.* **1.** drawing out, extraction. **2.** (*chem., med.*) extract. **3.** stretching, extension.
вытяжн|о́й *adj.* for extracting, for drawing out; **в. трос** rip cord (*of parachute*); **~а́я труба́** ventilating pipe.
вы́тянут|ый (~, ~а) *p.p.p. of* **~ь** *and adj.* stretched; **~ое лицо́** (*fig.*) a long face.
вы́тян|уть, у, ешь *pf.* (*of* **вытя́гивать**) **1.** to stretch (out); to extend. **2.** to draw out, extract (*also fig.*). **3.** (*coll.*) to endure, stick; **он до́лго не ~ет при тако́м кли́мате** he won't stick it for long in a climate like that.
вы́тян|уться, усь, ешься *pf.* (*of* **вытя́гиваться**) **1.** to stretch (*intrans.*); to stretch o.s. (out); **он засну́л ~увшись на полу́** he fell asleep stretched out on the floor; **лицо́ у неё ~улось** (*coll.*) her face fell. **2.** (*coll.*) to grow, shoot up. **3.** to stand erect; **в. в стру́нку, в. во фронт** (*mil.*) to stand at attention.
вы́у|дить, жу, дишь *pf.* **1.** to catch. **2.** (*fig., pej.*) to extract, dig up.
выу́жива|ть, ю *impf. of* **вы́удить**
вы́утюж|ить, у, ишь *pf. of* **утю́жить**
вы́ученик, а *m.* pupil; disciple, follower.
выу́чива|ть, ю *impf. of* **вы́учить**
вы́уч|ить, у, ишь *pf.* (*of* **учи́ть** *and* **~ивать**) **1.** to learn. **2.** (*+a. and d. or +inf.*) to teach; **он ~ил нас испа́нскому языку́** he taught us Spanish.
вы́уч|иться, усь ишься *pf.* (*of* **учи́ться**) (*+d. or inf.*) to learn.
вы́учк|а, и *f.* teaching, training; **отда́ть на ~у** (*+d.*) to apprentice (to); **он прошёл хоро́шую ~у** he has had a sound schooling.
выха́жива|ть, ю *impf. of* **вы́ходить**
вы́хва|тить, чу, тишь *pf.* **1.** to snatch; to grab. **2.** to pull out, draw; **в. нож** to draw a knife. **3.** to pull out, pick up (*at random*).
выхва́тыва|ть, ю *impf. of* **вы́хватить**
вы́хва|чу, тишь *see* **~тить**
вы́хлоп, а *m.* (*tech.*) exhaust.
выхлопа́тыва|ть, ю *impf. of* **вы́хлопотать**
выхлопн|о́й *adj.* (*tech.*) exhaust.
вы́хлопо|тать, чу, чешь *pf.* (*of* **выхлопа́тывать**) to obtain (*after much trouble*).
вы́ход, а *m.* **1.** going out; leaving, departure; **в. за́муж** marriage (*of woman*); **в. в отста́вку** retirement. **2.** way out, exit; outlet; **из э́того положе́ния ~а не́ было** (*fig.*) there was no way out of this situation; **дать в.** (*+d.*) to give vent (to). **3.** appearance (*of a publication*); (*theatr.*) entrance. **4.** (*econ.*) output; yield.

вы́ход|ец, ца *m.* **1.** emigrant; immigrant; **в. с того́ све́та** apparition. **2.** person springing from different social group; **он — в. из крестья́н** he is of peasant origin.
вы́хо|дить[1], **жу, дишь** *pf.* (*of* **выха́живать**) (*coll.*) **1.** to nurse. **2.** to rear, bring up; to grow (*plants*).
вы́хо|дить[2], **жу, дишь** *pf.* (*of* **выха́живать**) (*coll.*) to pass (through); go all over.
выхо|ди́ть, жу́, ∠дишь *impf.* **1.** *impf. of* **вы́йти. 2.** (*impf. only*) to look out (on), give (on), face; **его́ ко́мната ∠дит о́кнами на у́лицу** his room looks onto the street. **3.: не в. из головы́, из ума́** to stick in one's mind. **4.** *as pred.* **∠дит** (*coll.*) it turns out.
вы́ходк|а, и *f.* (*pej.*) trick; escapade.
выходн|о́й *adj.* **1.** exit; **~а́я дверь** street door. **2.: в. день** day off, rest-day; **~а́я оде́жда** 'best' clothes; **~о́е пла́тье** party dress; *as n.* **в., ~о́го** *m.* = **в. день. 3.: ~о́е посо́бие** (*also as n.* **~ы́е, ~ы́х**) severance pay. **4.** (*theatr.*): **~а́я роль** bit part.
вы́хо|жу, дишь *see* **~дить**
выхо|жу́, ∠дишь *see* **~ди́ть**
выхола́щива|ть, ю *impf. of* **вы́холостить**
вы́хол|енный *p.p.p. of* **~ить** *and adj.* well-cared-for; well-groomed.
вы́хол|ить, ю, ишь *pf.* to care for, tend.
вы́холо|стить, щу, стишь *pf.* (*of* **выхола́щивать**) to castrate, geld; (*fig.*) to emasculate.
вы́хухолевый *adj.* musquash.
вы́хухол|ь, я *m.* **1.** desman, musk-rat. **2.** (*fur*) musquash.
вы́царапа|ть, ю *pf.* (*coll.*) **1.** to scratch; (+*a. and d.*) to scratch out. **2.** (*fig.*) to extract, get (out of).
выцара́пыва|ть, ю *impf. of* **вы́царапать**
вы́цве|сти (*coll.* **~сть**)**, ту, тешь,** *past* **~л** *pf.* to fade.
выцвета́|ть, ю *impf. of* **вы́цвести**
вы́цве|тший *p.p. of* **~сти** *and adj.* faded.
вычека́нива|ть, ю *impf. of* **вы́чеканить**
вы́чекан|ить, ю, ишь *pf.* to mint; **в. меда́ль** to strike a medal.
вы́ч|ел, ла *see* **~есть**
вычёркива|ть, ю *impf. of* **вы́черкнуть**
вы́черкн|уть, у, ешь *pf.* to cross out, strike out; to expunge, erase.
вы́черпа|ть, ю *pf.* (**из**+*g.*) to take out (*fluids*); to bail (out); **в. во́ду из ло́дки** bail out a boat.
выче́рпыва|ть, ю *impf. of* **вы́черпать**
вы́чер|тить, чу, тишь *pf.* to draw; to trace.
вы́черчен|ный (~, ~а) *p.p.p. of* **вы́чертить** *and adj.* finely-drawn; **~ные бро́ви** pencilled eyebrows.
выче́рчива|ть, ю *impf. of* **вы́чертить**
вы́чер|чу, тишь *see* **~тить**
вы́че|сать, шу, шешь *pf.* (*of* **∸сывать**) to comb out.
вы́ч|есть, ту, тешь, *past* **~ел, ~ла,** *pres. ger.* **~тя** *pf.* (*of* **~ита́ть**) **1.** (*math.*) to subtract. **2.** to deduct, keep back.
вычёсыва|ть, ю *impf. of* **вы́чесать**
вы́чет, а *m.* deduction; **за ~ом** (+*g.*) except; less; minus.
вы́че|шу, шешь *see* **~сать**
вычисле́ни|е, я *nt.* calculation.
вычисли́тел|ь, я *m.* calculator.
вычисли́тельн|ый *adj.* calculating, computing; **~ая маши́на** computer.
вы́числ|ить, ю, ишь *pf.* to calculate, compute.
вычисля́|ть, ю *impf. of* **вы́числить**
вы́чи|стить, щу, стишь *pf.* (*of* **чи́стить** *and* **~ща́ть**) **1.** to clean (up, out). **2.** (*fig.*) to purge; to expel.
вычита́ем|ое, ого *nt.* (*math.*) subtrahend.
вычита́ни|е, я, *nt.* (*math.*) subtraction.
вы́чита|ть, ю *pf.* (*of* **вычи́тывать**) **1.** (*coll.*) to find (*by reading*); **я ~л сообще́ние о его́ сме́рти в газе́те** I found a report of his death in the newspaper. **2.** (*typ.*) to read, proofread.
вычита́|ть, ю *impf. of* **вы́честь**
вычи́тыва|ть, ю *impf.* **1.** *impf. of* **вы́читать. 2.** *impf. only* to reprimand, tell off.
вычища́|ть, ю *impf. of* **вы́чистить**
вы́чи|щу, стишь *see* **~стить**
вы́ч|ту, тешь *see* **~есть**
вычу́р|ный (~ен, ~на) *adj.* fanciful; mannered; precious.
вышвы́рива|ть, ю *impf. of* **вы́швырнуть**
вы́швырн|уть, у, ешь *pf.* to throw out, hurl out (*fig., coll.*) to chuck out.
вы́ше 1. *comp. of* **высо́кий** *and* **высо́ко́**; higher, taller. **2.** *prep.*+*g.* above, beyond; over; **э́то в. моего́ понима́ния** it is beyond my comprehension; **зада́ча оказа́лась в. его́ сил** the task proved to be beyond him. **3.** *adv.* (*liter.*) above.
выше... *comb. form* above-, afore-.
вышеизло́женный *adj.* foregoing.
вы́|шел, шла *see* **~йти**
вышена́званный *adj.* aforenamed.
вышеозна́ченный *adj.* aforesaid, above-mentioned.
вышеприведённый *adj.* above-cited; **в. приме́р** the example above.
вышеска́занный *adj.* aforesaid.
вышестоя́щ|ий *adj.* higher; (*pol.*) **~ие о́рганы вла́сти** the higher organs of power.
вышеука́занный *adj.* foregoing.
вышеупомя́нутый *adj.* afore-mentioned.
вышиба́л|а, ы *m.* (*sl.*) chucker-out; bouncer.
вышиба́|ть, ю *impf. of* **вы́шибить**
вы́шиб|ить, у, ешь, *past* **~, ~ла** *pf.* (*coll.*) **1.** to knock out. **2.** to chuck out.
вышива́ни|е, я *nt.* embroidery, needle-work.
вышива́|ть, ю *impf. of* **вы́шить**
вы́шивк|а, и *f.* embroidery, needle-work.
вышивно́й *adj.* embroidered.
вышин|а́, ы́, *pl.* **∠ы** *f.* height; **в ~е́** aloft, high up; **~о́й в ты́сячу ме́тров** a thousand metres high, up.
вы́ш|ить, ью, ьешь, *imper.* **~ей** *pf.* (*of* **~ива́ть**) to embroider.
вы́шк|а, и *f.* **1.** turret. **2.** tower; **сторожева́я в.** watch-tower; **бурова́я в.** derrick. **3.** (*sport*) high board.
вы́школ|ить, ю, ишь *pf. of* **шко́лить**
вы́|шлю, шлешь *see* **~слать**
вышмы́гива|ть, ю *impf. of* **вы́шмыгнуть**
вы́шмыгн|уть, у, ешь *pf.* (*coll.*) to slip out.
выштукату́рива|ть, ю *impf. of* **вы́штукатурить**
вы́штукатур|ить, ю, ишь *pf.* to stucco.
вы́шу|тить, чу, тишь *pf.* to laugh at, make fun of; to poke fun at.
вышу́чива|ть, ю *impf. of* **вы́шутить**
вы́щип|ать, лю, лешь *pf.* to pull out; to pluck.
выщи́пыва|ть, ю *impf. of* **вы́щипать**
вы́яв|ить, лю, ишь *pf.* (*of* **~ля́ть**) **1.** to display, reveal. **2.** to bring out; to make known. **3.** (*pej.*) to show up, expose.
выявле́ни|е, я *nt.* revelation; exposure.
выясне́ни|е, я *nt.* elucidation; explanation.
вы́ясн|ить, ю, ишь *pf.* to elucidate; to clear up, explain.
вы́ясн|иться, ится *pf.* to become clear; to turn out, prove (*intrans.*); **~илось, что...** it turned out that ...
выясн|я́ть(ся), я́ю(сь) *impf. of* **вы́яснить(ся)**
Вьетна́м, а *m.* Vietnam.
вьетна́м|ец, ца *m.* Vietnamese.
вьетна́м|ка, ки *f. of* **~ец**
вьетна́мский *adj.* Vietnamese.
вью, вьёшь *see* **вить**
вью́г|а, и *f.* snow-storm, blizzard.
вьюк, а *m.* pack; load.

вьюн|о́к, ка́ *m.* (*bot.*) bindweed, convolvulus.
вью́ч|ить, у, ишь *impf.* (*of* **на~**) to load (up).
вью́чн|ый *adj.* pack; **~ое живо́тное** pack animal; beast of burden.
вью́шк|а, и *f.* damper.
вью́щ|ийся *pres. part. of* **ви́ться** *and adj.*: **~иеся во́лосы** curly hair; **~ееся расте́ние** (*bot.*) creeper.
вя|жу́, ̃жешь *see* **~за́ть**
вя́жущий *pres. part. act. of* **вяза́ть** *and adj.* astringent.
вяз, а *m.* elm(-tree).
вяза́льн|ый *adj.* knitting; **~ая спи́ца** knitting-needle.
вяза́льщик, а *m.* **1.** knitter. **2.** binder.
вяза́ни|е, я *nt.* **1.** knitting. **2.** binding, tying.
вя́занк|а, и *f.* (*coll.*) knitted garment (*jumper etc.*).
вяза́нк|а, и *f.* bundle; truss.
вя́заный *adj.* knitted.
вяза́нь|е, я *nt.* knitting (*object being knitted*).
вя|за́ть, жу́, ̃жешь *impf.* **1.** (*pf.* **с~**) to tie, bind; (*tech.*) to tie, clamp; **в. кому́-н. ру́ки** to tie s.o.'s hands. **2.** (*pf.* **с~**) to knit. **3.** (*impf. only*) to be astringent; (*impers.*): **у меня́ ̃жет во рту** my mouth feels constricted.
вя|за́ться, жу́сь, ̃жешься *impf.* **1.** (**с**+*i.*) to accord, agree (with); to be in keeping (with); tally (with). **2.** to work out (well); **де́ло не ~жется** things are not going well.
вя́зк|а, и *f.* **1.** tying, binding. **2.** knitting. **3.** bunch.
вя́з|кий (~ок, ~ка́, ~ко) *adj.* **1.** viscous, sticky; boggy. **2.** (*tech.*) ductile, malleable; tough. **3.** (*coll.*) astringent.
вя́зкост|ь, и *f.* **1.** viscosity, stickiness; bogginess. **2.** (*tech.*) ductility, malleability; toughness.
вя́зн|уть, у, ешь *impf.* (**в**+*p.*) to stick, get stuck (in); to sink (into).
вя́з|че *comp. of* **~кий** *and* **~ко**
вя́леный *adj.* dried.
вя́л|ить, ю, ишь *impf.* (*of* **про~**) to dry (*in the sun*); to dry-cure, jerk (*meat, fish, etc.*).
вя́лост|ь, и *f.* flabbiness; limpness; (*fig.*) sluggishness; inertia; slackness.
вя́л|ый *adj.* **1.** faded. **2. (~, ~а́, ~о)** flabby, flaccid; limp; (*fig.*) sluggish, inert; slack; **в. ры́нок** (*econ.*) slack market.
вя́н|уть, у, ешь, *past* **~ул, ~ула** *and* **вял, вя́ла** *impf.* (*of* **за~**) to fade, wither; (*fig.*) to droop, flag; **у́ши ~ут от тако́го разгово́ра** it makes one sick to listen to such talk.
вя́щ|ий *adj.* (*obs. or joc.*) greater; **к ~ему несча́стью** to crown the misfortune; **для ~ей предосторо́жности** as an extra precaution.

Г

г (*abbr. of* **грамм**) g, gr, gram(me)(s).
г. *abbr. of* **1. год** year. **2. гора́** mountain; Mount, Mt. **3. го́род** city, town. **4. господи́н** Mr.
га (*abbr. of* **гекта́р**) ha, hectare(s).
габарди́н, а *m.* gaberdine.
габари́т, а *m.* size, dimensions.
гава́йский *adj.* Hawaiian.
га́вань|ь, и *f.* harbour.
га́г|а, и *f.* eider-duck.
гага́р|а, ы *f.* (*zool.*) loon, diver.
гага́рк|а, и *f.* (*zool.*) auk, razorbill.
гага́т, а *m.* (*min.*) jet.
гага́чий *adj. of* **га́га; г. пух** eider-down.
гад, а *m.* **1.** (*obs.*) amphibian, reptile. **2.** (*fig.*, *coll.*) rat, reptile (*pers.*); (*pl.*) vermin.
гада́лк|а, и *f.* fortune-teller.
гада́ни|е, я *nt.* **1.** fortune-telling; **г. по руке́** palmistry. **2.** guess-work.
гада́тел|ьный (~ен, ~ьна) *adj.* problematic, conjectural, hypothetical.
гада́|ть, ю *impf.* **1.** (*pf.* **по~**) (**на**+*p. or* **по**+*d.*) to tell fortunes (by). **2.** *impf. only* (**о**+*p.*) to guess, conjecture, surmise.
га́дин|а, ы *f.* (*fig.*) reptile; (*coll.*) repulsive person; (*pl.*) vermin.
га́|дить, жу, дишь *impf.* (*of* **на~**) **1.** (*of animals*) to defecate. **2.** (**на**+*a. or p.*, **в**+*p.*) to foul, defile.
га́д|кий (~ок, ~ка́, ~ко) *adj.* nasty, vile, repulsive; **г. утёнок** ugly duckling.
га́дк|о[1] *adv. of* **~ий**
га́дко[2] *as pred.* **мне,** *etc.*, **г.** I, *etc.*, loathe (it); I, *etc.*, am repelled.
гадли́вост|ь, и *f.* aversion, disgust.
гадли́в|ый (~, ~а) *adj.*: **~ое чу́вство** (feeling of) disgust.
га́дост|ь, и *f.* **1.** (*coll.*) filth, muck. **2.** dirty trick; **он спосо́бен на вся́кую г.** he is capable of the lowest trick; **говори́ть ~и** to say foul things.
гадю́к|а, и *f.* adder, viper.
га́ечный *adj. of* **га́йка; г. ключ** spanner, wrench.
га́же *comp. of* **га́дкий**
газ[1]**, а** *m.* **1.** gas; *pl.* fumes; **~ (не́рвно)паралити́ческого де́йствия** nerve gas. **2.** (*coll.*): **на по́лном ~у́** at top speed; **дать г.** to step on the gas, step on it; **педа́ль** (*f.*) **га́за** accelerator, gas pedal; **сба́вить г.** to reduce speed; **быть под ̃ом** to be tipsy. **3.** (*pl.*; *med.*) wind; **скопле́ние ̃ов** flatulence, wind.
газ[2] *no pl.*, *m.* gauze.
газе́л|ь, и *f.* (*zool.*) gazelle.
газе́т|а, ы *f.* newspaper.
газе́т|ный *adj. of* **~а; ~ная бума́га** news-print; **г. коро́ль** *or* **магна́т** press baron; **г. стиль** journalese.
газе́тчик, а *m.* **1.** newspaper-seller; newspaper-boy. **2.** (*coll.*) journalist.
газиро́ванный *adj.* carbonated.
гази́р|овать, ую (*and* **газир|ова́ть, у́ю)** *impf.* to carbonate.
га́зов|ый[1] *adj. of* **газ**[1]; **~ая коло́нка** geyser; **~ая плита́** gas-cooker; **г. счётчик** gas-meter.
га́зовый[2] *adj. of* **газ**[2]
газоли́н, а *m.* gasoline.
газоме́р, а *m.* gas-meter.
газо́н, а *m.* grass-plot, lawn; **«по ~ам ходи́ть воспреща́ется»** 'Keep off the grass'.
газонокоси́лка, и *f.* lawn-mower.
газообра́з|ный (~ен, ~на) *adj.* (*phys.*) gaseous.
газопрово́д, а *m.* gas pipeline; gas-main.
газопровод|ный *adj. of* **~**
ГАИ *f. indecl.* (*abbr. of* ***госуда́рственная автомоби́льная инспе́кция***) State Motor-Vehicle Inspectorate.
Гаи́ти *m. indecl.* Haiti.
гаитя́н|ин, ина, *pl.* **~е, ~** *m.* Haitian.
гаитя́н|ка, ки *f. of* **~ин**
гаитя́нский *adj.* Haitian.
га́йк|а, и *f.* nut, female screw; **бара́шковая г.** wing-nut; **закрути́ть ~и** (*fig.*) put the screws on.
гала́ *adj. indecl.* gala; **г.-представле́ние** gala performance.
гала́ктик|а, и *f.* (*astron.*) galaxy.
галантере́|йный *adj. of* **~я; ~йная ко́жа** fancy leather; **г. магази́н** haberdashery, fancy-goods shop.
галантере́|я, и *f.* haberdashery, fancy goods.

гала́нтност|ь, и *f.* gallantry (= *courtliness*).
гала́нт|ный (~ен, ~на, ~но) *adj.* gallant (= *courtly*).
гал|дёж, а́ *m.* (*coll.*) din, racket.
галд|е́ть, *1st pers. not used,* **и́шь** *impf.* (*coll.*) to make a din, racket.
гале́р|а, ы *f.* galley.
галере́|я, и *f.* gallery.
галёрк|а, и *f.* (*theatr.*; *coll.*) gallery, 'the gods'.
гале́р|ный *adj. of* **~а**
гале́т|а, ы *f.* (ship's) biscuit.
га́лечный *adj.* pebble, shingle; pebbly, shingly.
галимать|я́, и́ *f.* (*coll.*) rubbish, nonsense.
галифе́ *nt. pl. indecl.* riding-breeches, jodhpurs.
га́лк|а, и *f.* daw, jackdaw.
галл, а *m.* Gaul.
га́лли|й, я *m.* (*chem.*) gallium.
галлици́зм, а *m.* Gallicism.
галлома́ни|я, и *f.* Gallomania.
галло́н, а *m.* gallon.
га́лльский *adj.* Gallic.
галлюцина́ци|я, и *f.* hallucination.
галлюцини́р|овать, ую *impf.* to have hallucinations.
галлюциноге́н, а *m.* hallucinogen.
галлюциноге́нный *adj.* hallucinogenic.
галоге́н, а *m.* (*chem.*) halogen.
гало́п, а *m.* gallop; **~ом** at a gallop; **лёгкий г.** canter; **скака́ть ~ом** to gallop.
галопи́р|овать, ую *impf.* to gallop.
гало́ш|а, и *f.* galosh; **сесть в ~у** (*coll.*) to get into a fix, into a spot.
галс, а *m.* (*naut.*) tack; **пра́вым (ле́вым) ~ом** on the starboard (port) tack.
га́лстук, а *m.* (neck)tie, cravat; **г.-ба́бочка** bow-tie, dicky bow.
галу́н, а́ *m.* lace, galloon.
галу́шк|а, и *f.* (*cul.*) dumpling.
гальванизи́р|овать, ую *impf. and pf.* (*phys.*) to galvanize.
гальвани́ческий *adj.* (*phys.*) galvanic.
га́л|ька, ьки *f.* **1.** (*g. pl.* **~ек**) pebble. **2.** (*collect.*) pebble, shingle.
гам, а *m.* (*coll.*) din, uproar.
гама́к, а́ *m.* hammock.
гама́ш|а, и *f.* gaiter, legging.
га́мм|а[1]**, ы** *f.* (*mus.*) scale; gamut (*also fig.*); **г. кра́сок** colour range.
га́мм|а[2]**, ы** *f.* gamma (*letter of Greek alphabet*); **г.-лучи́** (*phys.*) gamma-rays.
га́нгли|й, я *m.* (*anat.*) ganglion.
гангре́н|а, ы *f.* gangrene.
гангрено́зный *adj.* gangrenous.
га́нгстер, а *m.* gangster.
гандбо́л, а *m.* handball.
гандболи́ст, а *m.* handball-player.
гандика́п, а *m.* (*sport*) handicap.
ганте́л|ь, и *f.* (*sport*) dumb-bell.
гара́ж, а́ *m.* garage.
гара́нт, а *m.* (*leg.*) guarantor.
гаранти́йный *adj.* guarantee.
гаранти́р|овать, ую *impf. and pf.* **1.** to guarantee, vouch for. **2.** (**от**+*g.*) to guarantee (against).
гара́нти|я, и *f.* guarantee; safeguard.
гардеро́б, а *m.* **1.** wardrobe (*article of furniture*). **2.** cloakroom. **3.** (*collect.*) wardrobe (*clothes*).
гардеро́бщик, а *m.* cloakroom attendant.
гардеро́бщи|ца, цы *f. of* **~к**
гарди́н|а, ы *f.* curtain.
га́р|евый *adj. of* **~ь; ~евая доро́жка** cinder path.
гаре́м, а *m.* harem.
га́рк|ать, аю *impf. of* **~нуть**
га́рк|нуть, ну, нешь *pf.* (*of* **~ать**) (*coll.*) to bark (out), bawl (out); **г. на кого́-н.** to bark at s.o.
гармонизи́р|овать, ую *impf. and pf.* (*mus.*) to harmonize (*trans.*).
гармо́ник|а, и *f.* accordion; **губна́я г.** harmonica, mouth organ.
гармони́р|овать, ую *impf.* (**с**+*i.*) to harmonize (*intrans.*) (with); to tone (with).
гармони́ст, а *m.* accordionist.
гармони́ческий *adj.* **1.** (*mus.*) harmonic. **2.** harmonious
гармони́ч|ный (~ен, ~на, ~но) *adj.* harmonious.
гармо́ни|я, и *f.* **1.** (*mus.*) harmony. **2.** (*fig.*) harmony, concord.
гармо́н|ь, и *f.* (*coll.*) accordion.
гармо́шк|а, и *f.* = **гармо́нь**
гарнизо́н, а *m.* garrison.
гарнизо́н|ный *adj. of* **~**
гарни́р, а *m.* (*cul.*) trimmings, garnish.
гарниту́р, а *m.* set; suite.
гарпу́н, а́ *m.* harpoon.
гарпу́н|ный *adj. of* **~; ~ная пу́шка** harpoon-gun.
га́рус, а *m.* worsted.
гарц|ева́ть, у́ю *impf.* to prance.
гар|ь, и *f.* **1.** burning; **па́хнет ~ью** there's a smell of burning. **2.** cinders, ashes.
га|си́ть, шу́, ~сишь *impf.* (*of* **по~**) **1.** (*pf. also* **за~**) to put out, extinguish; **г. свет** to turn off the light. **2.: г. и́звесть** to slake lime. **3.** (*fig.*) to suppress, stifle. **4.** to cancel; **г. долг** to liquidate a debt; **г. почто́вую ма́рку** to frank a postage stamp.
га́с|нуть, ну, нешь, *past* **~, ~ла** *impf.* (*of* **по~**) to be extinguished, go out; to grow feeble.
гастри́т, а *m.* gastritis.
гастри́ческий *adj.* gastric.
гастролёр, а *m.* **1.** artiste on tour. **2.** (*coll.*) casual worker.
гастроли́р|овать, ую *impf.* to tour, be on tour (*of an artiste*).
гастро́л|ь, и *f.* tour; temporary engagement (*of artiste*).
гастро́льный *adj.* touring (*of artistes*).
гастроно́м[1]**, а** *m.* gourmet.
гастроно́м[2]**, а** *m.* grocer's (shop).
гастрономи́ческий *adj.* **1.** gastronomical. **2.: г. магази́н** grocer's (shop).
гастроно́ми|я, и *f.* **1.** gastronomy. **2.** groceries, provisions.
гат|ь, и *f.* road of brushwood; **бреве́нчатая г.** corduroy road.
га́убиц|а, ы *f.* (*mil.*) howitzer.
гауптва́хт|а, ы *f.* (*mil.*) guardhouse.
гаше́ни|е, я *nt.* extinguishing; slaking.
гашён|ый *p.p.p. of* **гаси́ть** *and adj.*: **~ая и́звесть** slaked lime.
гаше́тк|а, и *f.* trigger.
гаши́ш, а *m.* hashish.
гвалт, а *m.* (*coll.*) row, uproar, rumpus.
гварде́|ец, йца *m.* (*mil.*) guardsman.
гварде́йский *adj.* (*mil.*) Guards'.
гва́рди|я, и *f.* (*mil.*) Guards.
гвоздево́й *adj.* feature, main; (*journ.*): **г. материа́л** feature item; **г. но́мер** main attraction, star turn.
гво́здик, а *m.* tack (*small nail*).
гвозди́к|а[1]**, и** *f.* (*bot.*) pink(s); **пе́ристая г.** carnation(s); **туре́цкая г., борода́тая г.** sweet william.
гвозди́к|а[2]**, и** *f.* (*collect.*) cloves.
гвозди́|чный[1] *adj. of* **~ка**[1]
гвозди́|чный[2] *adj. of* **~ка**[2]**; ~чное ма́сло** oil of cloves.
гвозд|ь, я́, *pl.* **~и, ~е́й** *m.* **1.** nail; tack; peg; **пове́сить шля́пу на г.** to hang one's hat on a peg. **2.** (+*g.*; *fig., coll.*) the highlight (of); **г. сезо́на** the hit of the season.
гг. *abbr. of* **1.** ***го́ды*** years. **2.** ***города́*** cities, towns. **3.** ***господа́*** Messrs.; Mr and Mrs.

где *adv.* **1.** (*interrog. and rel. adv.*) where; **г. бы ни** wherever; **г. бы то ни́ было** no matter where. **2.** (*coll.*) somewhere; anywhere. **3.: г...., г....** (*coll.*) in one place ..., in another .... **4. г. (уж)** (+*d. and inf.*) (*coll.*) how is one to; **г. мне знать?** how should I know?
где́-либо *adv.* anywhere.
где́-нибудь *adv.* somewhere; anywhere.
где́-то *adv.* somewhere.
геби́ст, а *m.* (*coll.*) KGB man *or* agent.
гегемо́ни|я, и *f.* hegemony, supremacy.
гедони́зм, а *m.* hedonism.
гедони́ст, а *m.* hedonist.
гедонисти́ческий *adj.* hedonistic.
гей *int.* hi!
ге́йзер, а *m.* geyser.
гекко́н, а *m.* (*zool.*) gecko.
гекта́р, а *m.* hectare.
ге́ли|й, я *m.* (*chem.*) helium.
гелио́граф, а *m.* heliograph.
гелиотро́п, а *m.* (*bot. and min.*) heliotrope.
гемоглоби́н, а *m.* (*physiol.*) haemoglobin.
геморро́|й, я *m.* (*med.*) haemorrhoids, piles.
гемофи́лик, а *m.* haemophiliac.
гемофили́|я, и *f.* (*med.*) haemophilia.
ген, а *m.* (*physiol.*) gene.
ген... *comb. form, abbr. of* **генера́льный**
генеалоги́ческий *adj.* genealogical.
генеало́ги|я, и *f.* genealogy.
ге́незис, а *m.* origin, genesis.
генера́л, а *m.* general; **г.-майо́р** major-general; **г.-лейтена́нт** lieutenant-general; **г.-полко́вник** colonel-general; **г.-губерна́тор** governor-general.
генерали́ссимус, а *m.* generalissimo.
генералите́т, а *m.* (*collect.*) the generals; the top brass.
генера́льн|ый *adv.* general; **г. констру́ктор** chief designer; **~ая репети́ция** dress rehearsal; **~ое сраже́ние** pitched battle.
генера́льский *adj.* general's; **г. чин** rank of general.
генера́тор, а *m.* (*tech.*) generator; **г. колеба́ний** oscillator; **г. то́ка** current generator.
генера́тор|ный *adj. of* **~**; **г. газ** producer gas.
гене́тик, а *m.* geneticist.
гене́тик|а, и *f.* genetics.
генети́ческий *adj.* genetic.
гениа́льност|ь, и *f.* genius.
гениа́л|ьный (~ен, ьна) *adj.* of genius; brilliant; **~ьная иде́я** a stroke of genius.
ге́ни|й, я *m.* genius; a genius; **злой г.** evil genius.
ге́н|ный *adj. of* **~**; **~ная инжене́рия** genetic engineering; **~ная дактилоско́пия** genetic fingerprinting.
генсе́к, а *m.* (*abbr. of* ***генера́льный секрета́рь***) General-Secretary; Secretary-General.
гео... *comb. form, abbr. of* **географи́ческий**
гео́граф, а *m.* geographer.
географи́ческий *adj.* geographical.
геогра́фи|я, и *f.* geography.
геодези́ст, а *m.* land-surveyor.
геодези́ческий *adj.* geodesic, geodetic.
геоде́зи|я, и *f.* geodesy, (land-)surveying.
гео́лог, а *m.* geologist.
геологи́ческий *adj.* geological.
геоло́ги|я, и *f.* geology.
гео́метр, а *m.* geometrician.
геометри́ческий *adj.* geometric(al).
геоме́три|я, и *f.* geometry.
георги́н, а *m.* (*bot.*) dahlia.
георги́н|а, ы *f.* = **~**
геофи́зик|а, и *f.* geophysics.
геофизи́ческий *adj.* geophysical.
гепа́рд, а *m.* cheetah.
гепати́т, а *m.* hepatitis.
гера́льдик|а, и *f.* heraldry.
геральди́ческий *adj.* heraldic.
гера́н|ь, и *f.* geranium.
герб, а́ *m.* arms, coat of arms.
герба́ри|й, я *m.* herbarium.
гербици́д, а *m.* herbicide, weed-killer.
ге́рбов|ый *adj.* **1.** heraldic. **2.** bearing a coat of arms.
геркуле́с, а *m.* **1.** (a) Hercules (*strong man*). **2.** (*sg. only*) rolled oats.
геркуле́совский *adj.* Herculean.
герма́н|ец, ца *m.* **1.** Teuton; ancient German; **~цы** the Germanic, Nordic peoples. **2.** (*coll.*) German..
герма́ни|й, я *m.* (*chem.*) germanium.
Герма́ни|я, и *f.* Germany.
герма́нск|ий *adj.* **1.** Germanic; Teutonic; **~ие языки́** Germanic languages. **2.** (*coll.*) German.
гермафроди́т, а *m.* hermaphrodite.
гермети́чески *adv.*: **г. закры́тый** hermetically sealed.
гермети́ческ|ий *adj.* air-tight; water-tight; **~ая каби́на** (*aeron.*) pressurized cabin.
герои́зм, а *m.* heroism.
геро́ик|а, и *f.* heroics; heroic spirit; heroic style.
герои́н|я, и *f.* heroine.
герои́ческ|ий *adj.* heroic.
геро́|й, я *m.* hero; (*liter.*) character.
геро́йский *adj.* heroic.
геро́йств|о, а *nt.* heroism.
геро́льд, а *m.* (*hist.*) herald.
геру́нди|й, я *m.* (*gram.*) gerund.
герц, а, *g. pl.* **г.** *m.* (*phys.*) hertz, cycle per second.
ге́рцог, а *m.* duke.
герцоги́н|я, и *f.* duchess.
ге́рцогский *adj.* ducal.
ге́рцогств|о, а *nt.* duchy.
геста́по *nt. indecl.* Gestapo.
геста́пов|ец, ца *m.* Gestapo agent.
гетеросексуали́ст, а *m.* heterosexual.
гетеросексуа́льный *adj.* heterosexual.
ге́тман, а *m.* (*hist.*) hetman.
ге́тр|ы, гетр *pl.* (*sg.* **~а, ~ы** *f.*) gaiters.
ге́тто *nt. indecl.* ghetto.
г-жа (*abbr. of* **госпожа́**) Mrs; Miss; Ms.
гиаци́нт, а *m.* (*bot.*) hyacinth.
ги́бел|ь, и *f.* death; destruction, ruin; loss; wreck; downfall.
ги́бел|ьный (~ен, ~ьна) *adj.* disastrous, fatal.
ги́б|кий (~ок, ~ка́, ~ко) *adj.* flexible; supple; lithe; floppy; **г. диск** (*comput.*) floppy disk.
ги́бкост|ь, и *f.* flexibility; suppleness.
ги́бл|ый *adj.* (*coll.*) God-forsaken; hopeless; **~ое де́ло** a lost cause.
ги́б|нуть, ну, нешь, *past* **~, ~ла** *impf.* (*of* **по~**) to perish.
гибри́д, а *m.* hybrid.
гигаба́йт, а *m.* (*comput.*) gigabyte.
гига́нт, а *m.* giant; **(пласти́нка-)г.** LP, long-player.
гига́нтский *adj.* gigantic.
гигие́н|а, ы *f.* hygiene.
гигиени́ческ|ий *adj.* hygienic, sanitary; **~ая повя́зка** sanitary towel; **~ая бума́га** toilet paper.
гид, а *m.* guide.
ги́др|а, ы *f.* (*myth., zool.; fig.*) hydra.
гидра́влик|а, и *f.* hydraulics.
гидравли́ческий *adj.* hydraulic.
гидра́нт, а *m.* hydrant.
гидра́т, а *m.* (*chem.*) hydrate.
гидро... *comb. form* hydro-.
гидродина́мик|а, и *f.* hydrodynamics.
гидрокостю́м, а *m.* wet suit.
гидро́лиз, а *m.* (*chem.*) hydrolysis.
гидроло́ги|я, и *f.* hydrology.
гидролока́тор, а *m.* sonar.

гидроо́кис|ь, и *f.* hydroxide.
гидросамолёт, а *m.* hydroplane.
гидроста́нци|я, и *f.* = **гидроэлектроста́нция**
гидроста́тик|а, и *f.* hydrostatics.
гидротерапи́|я, и *f.* hydrotherapy.
гидроте́хник, а *m.* hydraulic engineer.
гидроте́хник|а, и *f.* hydraulic engineering.
гидроэлектри́ческий *adj.* hydro-electric.
гидроэлектроста́нци|я, и *f.* hydro-electric power-station.
гие́н|а, ы *f.* hyena.
ги́к|ать, аю *impf.* (*of* **~нуть**) (*coll.*) to whoop.
ги́к|нуть, ну, нешь *pf.* (*of* **~ать**) to whoop.
ги́льди|я, и *f.* (*hist.*) guild.
ги́льз|а, ы *f.* case, empty; **патро́нная г.** cartridge-case; **папиро́сная г.** cigarette-paper.
гильоти́н|а, ы *f.* guillotine.
гильотини́р|овать, ую *impf. and pf.* to guillotine.
гимн, а *m.* hymn; **госуда́рственный г.** national anthem.
гимнази́ст, а *m.* grammar-school boy.
гимнази́стк|а, и *f.* grammar-school girl.
гимна́зи|я, и *f.* grammar school, high school.
гимна́ст, а *m.* gymnast; **г. на трапе́ции** trapeze artist.
гимнастёрк|а, и *f.* soldier's blouse.
гимна́стик|а, и *f.* gymnastics; **худо́жественная г.** eurhythmics, rhythmic gymnastics.
гимнасти́ческ|ий *adj.* gymnastic; **г. зал** gymnasium.
гинеко́лог, а *m.* gynaecologist.
гинекологи́ческий *adj.* gynaecological.
гинеколо́ги|я, и *f.* gynaecology.
гине́|я, и *f.* guinea.
гипе́рбол|а, ы *f.* **1.** hyperbole. **2.** (*math.*) hyperbola.
гиперболи́ческий *adj.* **1.** hyperbolical. **2.** (*math.*) hyperbolic.
гиперпростра́нств|о, а *nt.* hyperspace.
гиперто́ник, а *m.* hypertensive.
гипертони́|я, и *f.* (*med.*) hypertension; high blood-pressure.
гипно́з, а *m.* hypnosis.
гипнотизёр, а *m.* hypnotist.
гипнотизи́р|овать, ую *impf.* (*of* **за~**) to hypnotize.
гипноти́зм, а *m.* hypnotism.
гипноти́ческий *adj.* hypnotic.
гипо́тез|а, ы *f.* hypothesis.
гипотену́з|а, ы *f.* (*math.*) hypotenuse.
гипотети́ческий *adj.* hypothetical.
гиппопота́м, а *m.* hippopotamus.
гипс, а *m.* **1.** (*min.*) gypsum; plaster of Paris. **2.** plaster cast.
ги́псовый *adj.* **1.** gypsum. **2.** plaster.
гиреви́к, а́ *m.* (*sport*) weight-lifter.
гирля́нд|а, ы *f.* garland, wreath.
гироко́мпас, а *m.* gyrocompass.
гироско́п, а *m.* gyroscope.
гироскопи́ческий *adj.* gyroscopic.
ги́р|я, и *f.* weight; **г. для гимна́стики** dumb-bells.
гистерэктоми́|я, и *f.* hysterectomy.
гистогра́мм|а, ы *f.* histogram.
гисто́лог, а *m.* histologist.
гистологи́ческий *adj.* histological.
гистоло́ги|я, и. *f.* histology.
гита́р|а, ы *f.* guitar; **г.-ритм** rhythm guitar.
гитари́ст, а *m.* guitarist.
гитлери́зм, а *m.* Nazism.
ги́тлеров|ец, ца *m.* Nazi.
ги́тлеровский *adj.* Nazi.
ги́чк|а, и *f.* (*naut.*) gig.
глав|а́[1], **ы́,** *pl.* **˟ы** *f. and c.g.* **1.** *f.* (*obs. or rhet.*) head. **2.** *c.g.* head, chief; **г. делега́ции** head of a delegation; **быть во ~е́** (+*g.*) to be at the head (of), lead; **во ~е́ (с**+*i.*) under the leadership (of), led (by). **3.: поста́вить во ~у́ угла́** to regard as of paramount importance. **4.** *f.* (*archit.*) cupola (*of a church*).
глав|а́[2], **ы́,** *pl.* **˟ы** *f.* chapter.
глава́р|ь, я́ *m.* leader; ringleader.
главе́нств|о, а *nt.* supremacy.
главе́нств|овать, ую *impf.* (**в**+*p.*, **над**+*i.*) to have command (over), hold sway (over).
главнокома́ндующ|ий, его *m.* Commander-in-Chief (*abbr.* C.-in-C.); **верхо́вный г.** Supreme Commander.
гла́вн|ый *adj.* chief, main principal; head, senior; **г. врач** head physician; **г. инжене́р** chief engineer; **~ым о́бразом** chiefly, mainly, for the most part; *as n.* **~ое, ~ого** *nt.* the main thing; the essentials.
глаго́л, а *m.* verb.
глаго́лиц|а, ы *f.* (*ling.*) the Glagolitic alphabet.
глаголи́ческий *adj.* (*ling.*) Glagolitic.
глаго́льный *adj.* verbal.
гладиа́тор, а *m.* gladiator.
гладиа́торский *adj.* gladiatorial.
глади́льн|ый *adj.* ironing; **~ая доска́** ironing-board.
гла́|дить, жу, дишь *impf.* (*of* **по~**[1]) **1.** (*pf. also* **вы́~**) to iron, press. **2.** to stroke; **г. по голо́вке** (*coll.*) to pat on the back.
гла́д|кий (~ок, ~ка́, ~ко) *adj.* **1.** smooth; (*of hair*) straight; (*of fabrics*) plain, self-coloured.
гла́д|ко *adv. of* **~кий;** smoothly, swimmingly; **де́ло сошло́ г.** the affair went off smoothly; **г. вы́бритый** clean-shaven.
гладкоство́льный *adj.* (*of firearms*) smooth-bore.
глад|ь[1], **и** *f.* smooth surface (*of water*); **тишь да г.** (*coll.*) peace and quiet.
глад|ь[2], **и** *f.* satin-stitch; **вышива́ть ˟ью** to satin-stitch.
гла́же, *comp. of* **гла́дкий, гла́дко**
гла́жень|е, я *nt.* ironing.
глаз, а, о ˟е, в ~у́, *pl.* **~а́, ~, ~а́м** *m.* eye; eyesight; **дурно́й г.** evil eye; **невооружённый г.** naked eye; **в ~а́** to one's face; **я его́ в ~а́ не вида́л** I have never seen him; **в ~а́х** (+*g.*) in the eyes (of); **ни в одно́м ~у́** (*coll.*) not at all drunk; **за ~а́** (*i*) in absence; **руга́ть кого́-н. за ~а́** to abuse s.o. behind his back, (*ii*) (*coll.*) enough, more than enough; **на ~а́, на ~а́х** before one's eyes; **дитя́ вы́росло на её ~а́х** the child grew up before her eyes; **на г.** approximately, by eye; **с ~у на́ г.** tête-à-tête, cheek-by -jowl; **с г. доло́й** out of sight; **с г. доло́й — из се́рдца вон** out of sight, out of mind; **не спуска́ть г. с**+*g.* not to let out of one's sight; **смотре́ть во все ~а́** to be all eyes; **закрыва́ть ~а́ (на**+*a.*) to close one's eyes (to), connive (at); **идти́ куда́ ~а́ глядя́т** to follow one's nose.
глаза́ст|ый (~, ~а) *adj.* (*coll.*) big-eyed; quick-sighted.
глазе́|ть, ю *impf.* (*of* **по~**) (**на**+*a.*; *coll.*) to stare (at), gawk (at).
глазир|о́ванный *p.p.p. of* **~ова́ть** *and adj.* glazed; glossy; (*cul.*) iced, glacé.
глазир|ова́ть, у́ю *impf. and pf.* to glaze; (*cul.*) to ice.
глазиро́вк|а, и *f.* glazing; icing; **торт с ~ой** iced cake.
глазни́к, а́ *m.* (*coll.*) oculist.
глазни́ц|а, ы *f.* eye-socket.
глазн|о́й *adj. of* **глаз; г. врач** oculist; **г. нерв** optic nerve; **~о́е я́блоко** eyeball.
глаз|о́к, ка́, *pl.* **˟ки, ˟ок** *and* **~ки́, ~ко́в** *m.* **1.** (*pl.* **˟ки**) *dim. of* **˟; одни́м ~ко́м** with half an eye; **де́лать, стро́ить ˟ки кому́-н.** to make eyes at s.o.; **аню́тины ˟ки** (*bot.*) pansy. **2.** (*pl.* **~ки́**) (*coll.*) peephole; inspection hole; head (*of periscope*). **3.** (*pl.* **~ки́**) bud; eye (*of potato*).
глазоме́р, а *m.* **1.** measurement by eye. **2.** ability to judge by eye; **хоро́ший г.** good eye.

глазу́н|ья, ьи, *g. pl.* **~ий** *f.* fried eggs.
глазу́р|ь, и *f.* **1.** glaze (*on pottery*). **2.** (*cul.*) icing.
гла́нд|а, ы *f.* (*anat.*) tonsil; **удали́ть ~ы** to take out tonsils.
глас, а *m.* (*obs.*) voice; **г. вопию́щего в пусты́не** a voice in the wilderness.
гла|си́ть, шу́, си́шь *impf.* to say, run; **докуме́нт ~си́т сле́дующее** the paper runs as follows; **как ~си́т погово́рка** as the saying goes.
гла́сно *adv.* openly, publicly.
гла́сност|ь, и *f.* **1.** publicity; **преда́ть ~и** to make public, publicize. **2.** openness; *glasnost.*
гла́сный[1] *adj.* open, public; **г. суд** public trial.
гла́сн|ый[2] *adj.* vowel, vocalic; *as n.* **г., ~ого** *m.* vowel.
глаша́та|й, я *m.* **1.** (*hist.*) town crier. **2.** (*fig., rhet.*) herald.
гле́тчер, а *m.* glacier.
гли́н|а, ы *f.* clay; **фарфо́ровая г.** china clay; **ма́зать ~ой** to clay.
гли́нист|ый *adj.* clayey; **~ая по́чва** loam.
глинобы́тный *adj.* adobe; mud.
гли́нян|ый *adj.* **1.** clay; earthenware; **~ая посу́да** earthenware crockery. **2.** clayey.
гли́ссер, а *m.* (*naut.*) speed-boat.
глист, а́ *m.* (intestinal) worm.
глицери́н, а *m.* glycerine.
гл. об. (*abbr. of* **гла́вным о́бразом**) mostly, chiefly.
глоба́льный *adj.* global; (*fig.*) extensive, in-depth.
гло́бус, а *m.* globe.
гло|да́ть, жу́, ~́жешь *impf.* to gnaw (*also fig.*).
гло́кеншпил|ь, я *m.* glockenspiel.
глосса́ри|й, я *m.* glossary.
глота́|ть, ю *impf.* to swallow.
гло́тк|а, и *f.* **1.** (*anat.*) gullet. **2.** (*coll.*) throat.
глот|о́к, ка́ *m.* gulp, mouthful; drink.
гло́х|нуть, ну, нешь, *past* **~, ~ла** *impf.* **1.** (*pf.* **о~**) to become deaf. **2.** (*pf.* **за~**) to die away, subside (*of noise*). **3.** (*pf.* **за~**) to go to seed.
глу́б|же *comp. of* **~о́кий** *and* **~око́**
глубин|а́, ы́, *pl.* **~́ы** *f.* **1.** depth. **2.** (*pl.*) (the) depths. **3.** heart, interior (*also fig.*); **в ~е́ ле́са** in the heart of the forest; **в ~е́ души́** at heart, in one's heart of hearts; **от ~ы́ души́** with all one's heart.
глуби́нк|а, и *f.* (*coll.*) the sticks, the back of beyond; **жить в ~е** to live (way) out in the sticks.
глуби́нн|ый *adj.* **1.** deep; deep-sea; **~ая бо́мба** depth charge. **2.** remote, out-of-the-way.
глубо́к|ий (~, ~а́, ~́о) *adj.* **1.** (*in var. senses*) deep; in-depth; **~ая таре́лка** soup-plate. **2.** profound; thorough; serious; **~ие зна́ния** thorough knowledge; **~ая оши́бка** serious error. **3.** (*of time, age, seasons*) late; advanced; extreme; **до ~ой но́чи** (until) far into the night; **~ая ста́рость** extreme old age. **4.** (*fig.; of feelings, etc.*) deep, profound; **с ~им прискорбием** with deep regret.
глубоко́[1] *adv.* deep; (*fig.*) deeply, profoundly.
глубо́ко́[2] *as pred.* it is deep.
глубоково́д|ный (~ен, ~на) *adj.* **1.** deep-water. **2.** deep-sea.
глубокомы́сленный *adj.* thoughtful; serious.
глубокомы́сли|е, я *nt.* profundity.
глубокоуважа́емый *adj.* much-esteemed; (*in formal letters*) dear.
глубоча́йший *superl. of* **глубо́кий**
глуб|ь, и *f.* depth; **г. реки́** the river-bottom.
глум|и́ться, лю́сь, и́шься *impf.* (**над**+*i.*) to mock (at); to desecrate.
глумле́ни|е, я *nt.* mockery; desecration.
глумли́вый *adj.* (*coll.*) mocking.
глупе́|ть, ю *impf.* (*of* **по~**) to grow stupid.
глуп|е́ц, ца́ *m.* fool, blockhead.
глуп|и́ть, лю́, и́шь *impf.* (*of* **с~**) to make a fool of o.s.; to do sth. foolish.
глупова́т|ый (~, ~а) *adj.* silly; rather stupid.
глу́пост|ь, и *f.* **1.** foolishness, stupidity. **2.** foolish action; foolish thing. **3.** (*usu. pl.*) nonsense; **~и!** (stuff and) nonsense!
глу́п|ый (~, ~а́, ~о) *adj.* foolish, stupid; silly.
глупы́ш, а́ *m.* (*coll.*) silly; silly little thing.
глуха́р|ь, я́ *m.* **1.** (*zool.*) capercailzie, woodgrouse. **2.** (*coll.*) deaf person.
глу́хо[1] *adj. of* **глухо́й**; (*coll.*) = **на́глухо**
глу́хо[2] *as pred.* it is lonely, deserted.
глухова́т|ый (~, ~а) *adj.* hard of hearing.
глух|о́й (~́, ~а́, ~́о) *adj.* **1.** deaf (*also fig.*); **он был ~ к на́шим мольба́м** he was deaf to our entreaties; *as n.* **г., ~о́го** *m.* deaf person. **2.** (*of sound*) muffled, indistinct. **3.** (*ling.*) voiceless; **4.** thick, dense; **г. лес** dense forest. **5.** remote, out-of-the-way; **в ~о́й прови́нции** in the depths of the country. **6.** sealed; blank, blind; **~а́я стена́** blank wall. **7.** (*of clothing*) buttoned-up, done up. **8.** (*of times or seasons*) dead; late; **~а́я ночь** dead of night; **~а́я пора́** slack period.
глухома́н|ь, и *f.* (*coll.*) out-of-the-way place, backwoods.
глухонем|о́й *adj.* deaf-and-dumb; *as n.* **г., ~о́го** *m.* deaf mute; **язы́к (для) ~ы́х** sign language.
глухот|а́, ы́ *f.* deafness.
глу́|ше *comp. of* **~хо́й** *and* **~хо**
глуши́тел|ь, я *m.* silencer, muffler.
глуш|и́ть, у́, ~и́шь *impf.* **1.** (*pf.* **о~**) to stun. **2.** (*pf.* **за~**) to muffle (*sounds*); **г. мото́р** to stop the engine; **г. радиопереда́чи** to jam radio broadcasts. **3.** (*pf.* **за~**) to choke, stifle (*growth*). **4.** (*pf.* **за~**) (*fig.*) to suppress, stifle.
глуш|ь, и́ *f.* overgrown part (*of forest or garden*); backwoods (*also fig.*); **жить в ~и́** to live in the back of beyond.
глы́б|а, ы *f.* clod; lump, block.
глюко́з|а, ы *f.* glucose.
гля|де́ть, жу́, ди́шь *impf.* (*of* **по~**) **1.** (**на**+*a.*) to look (at); to peer (at); to gaze (upon); **г. сквозь па́льцы (на**+*a.*) to shut one's eyes (to), turn a blind eye (to); **идти́ куда́ глаза́ ~дя́т** to follow one's nose. **2.** (**на**+*a.*; *coll.*) to look to (= *to take as an example*). **3.** (*impf. only*) to show, appear. **4.** (*impf. only*) (**на**+*a.*) to look (on to), face, give (on to). **5.** (*impf. only*) (+*i. or adv.*; *coll.*) to look (like); appear. **6.** (**за**+*i.*; *coll.*) to look after, keep an eye on. **7.: ~ди́(те)** (*expr. warning or threat*) mind (out); **~ди́ не** (+*imper.*) mind you don't .... **8.: того́ и ~ди́** (*coll.*) it looks as if; **того́ и ~ди́ начнётся бу́ря** it looks as if we're in for a storm. **9.: ~́дя** (**по**+*d.*, *coll.*) depending (on).
гля|де́ться, жу́сь, ди́шься *impf.* (*of* **по~**) (**в**+*a.*) to look at o.s. (in).
гля́н|ец, ца *m.* gloss, lustre.
гля́|нуть, ну, нешь *pf.* (**на**+*a.*) glance (at).
глянцеви́т|ый (~, ~а) *adj.* glossy, lustrous.
гля́нцев|ый *adj.* glossy, lustrous.
гм *int.* hm!
г-н (*abbr. of* **господи́н**) Mr; Master; (*on envelope*) **~у** (+*d.*) Mr ...; ... Esq.; **~у Т. Джо́нсу** T. Jones, Esq.
гна|ть, гоню́, го́нишь, *past* **~л, ~ла́, ~́ло** *impf.* **1.** (*det. of* **гоня́ть**) to drive. **2.** to urge (on); (*coll.*) to drive (*a vehicle*) hard. **3.** (*coll.*) to dash, tear. **4.** to hunt, chase; (*fig.*) to persecute. **5.** to turn out, turf out. **6.** to distil.
гна́|ться, гоню́сь, го́нишься, *past* **~лся, ~ла́сь, ~́ло́сь** *impf.* (*det. of* **гоня́ться**) (**за**+*i.*) to pursue; to strive (for, after); (*fig.*) to keep up with.
гнев, а *m.* anger, rage, wrath.
гне́в|ный (~ен, ~на́, ~но) *adj.* angry, irate.

гнедо́й *adj.* bay (*colour of horse*).

гнез|ди́ться, жу́сь, ди́шься *impf.* **1.** to nest; to roost. **2.** (*fig.*) to have its seat; to be lodged.

гнезд|о́, а́, *pl.* **гнёзда** *nt.* **1.** nest; eyrie. **2.** den, lair (*also fig.*); **г. сопротивле́ния** (*mil.*) pocket of resistance. **3.** (*tech.*) socket; seat; housing.

гнездово́й *adj. of* **гнездо́**

гнездо́вь|е, я *nt.* nesting-site.

гнейс, а *m.* (*min.*) gneiss.

гне|сти́, ту́, тёшь *impf.* to oppress, weigh down; to press; **его́ ~ту́т забо́ты** he is weighed down by cares.

гнёт, а *m.* **1.** (*obs.*) press; weight. **2.** oppression, yoke (*fig.*).

гнету́щий *pres. part. act. of* **гнести́** *and adj.* oppressive.

гни́д|а, ы *f.* nit.

гние́ни|е, я *nt.* decay, putrefaction, rot.

гнил|о́й (~, ~а́, ~о) *adj.* **1.** rotten (*also fig.*); decayed; putrid. **2.** (*of weather*) damp, muggy.

гни́лостный *adj.* putrid.

гни́лост|ь, и *f.* rottenness (*also fig.*); putridity.

гнил|ь, и *f.* **1.** rotten stuff. **2.** mould.

гни|ть, ю́, ёшь *impf.* (*of* **с~**) to rot, decay; to decompose.

гное́ни|е, я *nt.* suppuration.

гно|и́ть, ю́, и́шь *impf.* (*of* **с~**) to let rot, allow to decay; **г. наво́з** to ferment manure; **г. в тюрьме́** to leave to rot in prison.

гно|и́ться, ю́сь, и́шься *impf.* to suppurate, fester.

гно|й, я, в ~е *or* **в ~ю́** *m.* pus.

гнойни́к, а́, *m.* abscess; ulcer.

гно́йный *adj.* purulent.

гном, а *m.* gnome.

гно́стик, а *m.* gnostic.

гностици́зм, а *m.* gnosticism.

гнус, а *m.* (*collect.*) midges.

гнуса́в|ить, лю, ишь *impf.* to speak through one's nose.

гнуса́вост|ь, и *f.* twang; nasal intonation.

гнуса́в|ый (~, ~а) *adj.* nasal.

гну́сност|ь, и *f.* **1.** vileness, foulness. **2.** vile, foul action.

гну́с|ный (~ен, ~на́, ~но) *adj.* vile, foul.

гну́т|ый *p.p.p. of* **гнуть** *and adj.* bent; **~ая ме́бель** bent-wood furniture.

гнуть, гну, гнёшь *impf.* (*of* **со~**) **1.** to bend, bow (*trans.*); **г. спи́ну, ше́ю (пе́ред+*i.*)** (*coll.*) to kowtow (to); **г. свою́ ли́нию** to have it one's own way. **2.** (*coll.*) to drive at; **я не понима́ю, куда́ ты гнёшь** I don't know what you are driving at.

гну́ться, гнусь, гнёшься *impf.* (*of* **со~**) to bend (*intrans.*), be bowed; to stoop.

гнуш|а́ться, а́юсь *impf.* (*of* **по~**) **1.** (+*g. or i.*) to abhor, have an aversion (to). **2.** (+*inf.*) to disdain (to).

гобеле́н, а *m.* tapestry.

гобои́ст, а *m.* (*mus.*) oboist.

гобо́|й, я *m.* oboe.

гов|е́ть, е́ю, е́ешь *impf.* (*eccl.*) to prepare for Communion (*by fasting*); (*coll.*) to fast, go without food.

говн|о́, а́ *nt.* (*vulg.*) shit.

го́вор, а *m.* **1.** sound of voices (*usu. human, but also fig.*); **г. волн** the murmur of the waves. **2.** mode of speech, accent. **3.** dialect.

говор|и́ть, ю́, и́шь *impf.* **1.** (*impf. only*) to (be able to) speak, talk; **он ещё не ~и́т** he can't speak yet; **г. по-францу́зски** to speak French. **2.** (*pf.* **сказа́ть**) to say; to tell; to speak, talk; **г. пра́вду** to tell the truth; **г. де́ло** to talk sense; **~я́т** they say, it is said; **(да) что вы ~и́те?** (*expr. incredulity*) you don't say!; **~и́т Москва́!** (*introducing radio programme*) this is Radio Moscow!; **не́чего (и) г.** it goes without saying, needless to say; **что и г.** (*coll.*) it cannot be denied; **что ни ~и́** say what you like; **и не ~и́!** certainly!; of course!; **ина́че ~я́** in other words; **со́бственно ~я́** strictly speaking; **не ~я́ уже́ (о+*p.*)** not to mention. **3.** (*pf.* **по~**) (**о**+*p.*) to talk (about), discuss. **4.** (*impf. only*) to mean, convey; **э́то и́мя мне ничего́ не ~и́т** this name means nothing to me. **5.** (*impf. only*) (**о**+*p.*) to point (to), indicate, testify (to); **всё ~и́т о том, что он ко́нчил самоуби́йством** everything points to his having committed suicide. **6.** (*impf. only*) **г. в по́льзу** (+*g.*) to tell in favour (of); to support, back.

говор|и́ться, и́тся *impf. pass. of* **~и́ть; как ~и́тся** as they say; as the saying goes.

говорли́вост|ь, и *f.* garrulity, talkativeness.

говорли́в|ый (~, ~а) *adj.* garrulous, talkative.

говору́н, а́ *m.* (*coll.*) chatterbox.

говору́н|ья, ьи, *g. pl.* **~ий** *f. of* **~**

говя́дин|а, ы *f.* beef.

говя́жий *adj.* beef.

го́гол|ь, я *m.* (*zool.*) golden-eye (*Clangula bucephala*); **ходи́ть ~ем** to strut.

го́гот, а *m.* cackle.

гогота́нь|е, я *nt.* cackling.

гого|та́ть, чу́, ~чешь *impf.* to cackle.

год, а, в ~у́, о ~е, *pl.* **~ы** *and* **~а́,** *g.* **~о́в** *and* **лет** *m.* **1.** (*g. pl.* **лет**) year; **високо́сный г.** leap year; **кру́глый г.** (*as adv.*) the whole year round; **в бу́дущем, про́шлом ~у́** next, last year; **в г.** a year, per annum; **из ~а в г.** year in, year out; **г. о́т ~у** every year; **спустя́ три ~а** three years later; **че́рез три ~а** in three years' time; **бе́з ~у неде́ля** (*coll.*) only a few days; **мы ~ы не вида́лись** we have not met for years; **встреча́ть Но́вый г.** to see the New Year in; **ей пошёл пятна́дцатый г.** she is in her fifteenth year. **2. двадца́тые, тридца́тые,** *etc.*, **~ы** (*g.* **~о́в**) the twenties, the thirties etc. **3. ~а́** *and* **~ы, ~о́в** (*pl. only*) years, age, time; **шко́льные ~ы** schooldays; **в ~ы** (+*g.*) in the days (of); during; **в те ~ы** in those days; **в ~а́х** advanced in years; **не по ~а́м** beyond one's years, precocious(ly).

года́ми *adv.* for years (*on end*).

го|ди́ться, жу́сь, ди́шься *impf.* **1.** (**на**+*a.*, **для**+*g.*, *or* +*d.*) to be fit (for), be suited (for), do (for), serve (for); **не ~ди́тся** it's no good; it won't do. **2.** (**в**+*nom.-a.*) to be suited to be; **он не ~ди́тся в офице́ры** he is not cut out to be an officer. **3.** (**в**+*nom.-a.*) to be old enough to be; **она́ ~ди́тся тебе́ в ма́тери** she is old enough to be your mother. **4.: не ~ди́тся** (+*inf.*) it does not do (to), one should not.

годи́чн|ый *adj.* **1.** lasting a year; **~ое путеше́ствие** a year's journey. **2.** annual, yearly; **г. съезд** annual conference.

го́дност|ь, и *f.* fitness, suitability; validity.

го́д|ный (~ен, ~на́, ~но) *adj.* fit, suitable, valid; **г. к вое́нной слу́жбе** fit for military service; **г. к пла́ванию** seaworthy; **биле́т го́ден три ме́сяца** the ticket is valid for three months.

годова́лый *adj.* one year old, yearling.

годово́й *adj.* annual, yearly.

годовщи́н|а, ы *f.* anniversary.

го|й, я *m.* goy, gentile.

гол, а *m.* (*sport*) goal; **заби́ть г.** to score a goal.

голени́щ|е, а *nt.* top (*of a boot*).

го́лен|ь, и *f.* shin.

голки́пер, а *m.* (*sport*) goalkeeper.

голла́нд|ец, ца *m.* Dutchman.

Голла́нди|я, и *f.* Holland.

голла́ндк|а, и *f.* Dutchwoman; Dutch girl.

голла́ндск|ий *adj.* Dutch; **~ая печь** tiled stove; **~ое полотно́** holland (*cloth*).

голли́зм, а *m.* (*pol.*) Gaullism.

голли́стский *adj.* (*pol.*) Gaullist.
голов|а́, ы́, *a.* **го́лову,** *pl.* **го́ловы, голо́в, ~а́м** *f. and c.g.* **1.** *f.* head (*also fig.*); **г. в го́лову** (*mil.*) shoulder to shoulder; **на све́жую го́лову** while one is fresh; **быть ~о́й, на́ голову вы́ше кого́-н.** (*fig.*) to be head and shoulders above s.o.; **с ~ы́ до ног** from head to foot; **с ~о́й погрузи́ться, окуну́ться, уйти́ (во что-н.)** (*fig.*) to throw o.s. (into sth.), plunge (into sth.); **свали́ть с больно́й ~ы́ на здоро́вую** to lay the blame on s.o. else; **че́рез чью-н. го́лову** (*fig.*) behind s.o.'s back; **у неё г. шла кру́гом** her head was going round and round; **у меня́ г. кру́жится** I feel dizzy; **намы́лить кому́-н. го́лову** to give s.o. a dressing-down. **2.** *f.* head (*of cattle*). **3.** *f.* (*fig.*) head (*as unit of calculation*); **с ~ы́** per head. **4.** *f.* (*fig.*) head; brain, mind; wits; **он па́рень с ~о́й** he's a bright lad; **лома́ть го́лову** to rack one's brains; **не теря́ть ~ы́** to keep one's head; **ей пришла́ в го́лову мысль** it occurred to her, it struck her. **5.** *f.* (*fig.*) head (= *person*); **горя́чая г.** hothead; **сме́лая г.** bold spirit. **6.** *f.* (*fig.*) head, life; **на свою́ го́лову** to one's cost; **заплати́ть, поплати́ться за что-н. ~о́й** to pay for sth. with one's life; **отвеча́ть, руча́ться ~о́й за что-н.** to stake one's life on sth. **7.** *c.g.* (*fig.*) head; pers. in charge; **сам себе́ г.** one's own master. **8.** *f.* **г. са́хару** sugar-loaf; **г. сы́ру** a cheese; **г. капу́сты** head of cabbage. **9.** *idiomatic phrr.*: **в пе́рвую го́лову** in the first place; first and foremost; **в ~а́х** at the head of the bed.
голова́стик, а *m.* tadpole.
голове́шк|а, и *f.* brand, smouldering piece of wood.
голо́вк|а, и *f.* **1.** *dim. of* **голова́. 2.** head, cap; tip; **боева́я г.** warhead; **г. лу́ка** an onion, onion bulb; **спи́чечная г.** match-head. **3.** (*collect.*; *coll.*) heads; the brass. **4.** (*pl.*) vamp (*of boot*).
головн|о́й *adj.* **1.** *adj. of* **голова́; ~а́я боль** headache. **2.** (*anat.*): **г. мозг** cerebrum. **3.** (*fig.*) head, leading.
головн|я́[1]**, и́,** *g. pl.* **~е́й** *f.* charred log.
головн|я́[2]**, и́,** *g. pl.* **~е́й** *f.* blight, smut, rust (*disease of crops*).
головокруже́ни|е, я *nt.* dizziness (*also fig.*); vertigo.
головокружи́тельн|ый *adj.* dizzy; vertiginous (*also fig.*); **~ая высота́** dizzy height; **~ые перспекти́вы** breath-taking prospects.
головоло́мк|а, и *f.* puzzle, conundrum.
головоло́мный *adj.* puzzling; baffling; **г. вопро́с** puzzler.
головомо́йк|а, и *f.* (*coll.*) reprimand, dressing-down.
головоре́з, а *m.* (*coll.*) **1.** cutthroat; bandit; desperado. **2.** blackguard, rascal.
голо́вушк|а, и *f. affectionate dim. of* **голова́; пропа́ла моя́ г.** I've had it; I'm done for.
гологра́мм|а, ы *f.* hologram.
го́лод, а (у) *m.* **1.** hunger; starvation; **умира́ть с ~у** to die of starvation; **мори́ть ~ом** to starve (*trans.*). **2.** famine. **3.** dearth, acute shortage; **шерстяно́й г.** wool shortage.
голода́ни|е, я *nt.* starvation.
голод|а́ть, а́ю *impf.* to go hungry, starve.
голода́|ющий *pres. part. act. of* **~ть** *and adj.* starving, hungry; *as n.* **г., ~ющего** *m.*, **~ющая, ~ющей** *f.* starving person.
голо́д|ный (го́лоден, ~на́, ~но) *adj.* **1.** hungry; **сексуа́льно г.** sex-starved. **2.** (*caused by*) hunger, starvation; **~ные бо́ли** hunger-pangs; **г. похо́д** hunger-march. **3.** (*of food, food supplies*) meagre, poor; **г. год** lean year; **г. край** barren country; **г. паёк** starvation rations.
голодо́вк|а, и *f.* **1.** starvation. **2.** hunger-strike; **объяви́ть ~у** to go on hunger-strike.
гололёд, а *m.* = **гололе́дица**
гололе́диц|а, ы *f.* black ice.
го́лос, а, *pl.* **~а́** *m.* **1.** voice; **во весь г.** at the top of one's voice; **с ~а** by ear. **2.** (*mus.*) voice, part; **фу́га на четы́ре ~а** four-part fugue. **3.** (*fig.*) voice, word, opinion; **в оди́н г.** with one accord, unanimously; **име́ть свой г.** to have one's say. **4.** vote; **пра́во ~а** the vote, suffrage, franchise; **пода́ть г. (за+***a.***)** to vote (for), cast one's vote (for).
голоси́ст|ый (~, ~а) *adj.* loud-voiced; vociferous; loud.
голо|си́ть, шу́, си́шь *impf.* **1.** (*coll.*) to sing loudly; to cry. **2.** (*obs.*) to wail; to keen; **г. по поко́йнику** to keen a dead person.
голосло́вно *adv.* without adducing any proof.
голосло́в|ный (~ен, ~на) *adj.* unsubstantiated, unfounded.
голосова́ни|е, я *nt.* voting; poll; **всео́бщее г.** universal suffrage; **поста́вить на г.** to put to the vote.
голос|ова́ть, у́ю *impf.* (*of* **про~**) **1. (за+***a.***, про́тив+***g.***)** to vote (for; against); **г. нога́ми** to vote with one's feet. **2.** to put to the vote, vote on. **3.** (*sl.*) to thumb a lift.
голосов|о́й *adj.* vocal; **~а́я щель** glottis.
голу́беньк|ий, ого *m.* = **голубо́й** *as n.*
голубе́|ть, ю *impf.* (*of* **по~**) to show blue; to turn blue.
голуб|е́ц, ца́ *m.* (*usu. pl.*) golubets (*rissole rolled in cabbage-leaves*).
голубизн|а́, ы́ *f.* blueness.
голуби́н|ый *adj.* **1.** *adj. of* **го́лубь; ~ая по́чта** pigeon post. **2.** (*fig.*) dove-like.
голу́бк|а, и *f.* **1.** female pigeon; dove **2.** (*fig.*; *as term of endearment*) (my) dear, (my) darling.
голубогла́з|ый (~, ~а) *adj.* blue-eyed.
голуб|о́й *adj.* pale blue, sky-blue; **~а́я кровь** (*fig.*) blue blood; **~о́е то́пливо** 'blue fuel' (= *natural gas*); **г. экра́н** the small screen (*i.e. TV*); *as n.* **голуб|о́й, о́го** *m.* gay (= *homosexual*).
голуб|о́к, ка́ *m. dim. of* **го́лубь**
голу́бчик, а *m.* (*coll.*; *as mode of address*) my dear fellow; my friend.
го́луб|ь, я, *g. pl.* **~е́й** *m.* pigeon; dove; **г. свя́зи** (*mil.*) carrier-pigeon.
голубя́тник, а *m.* pigeon-fancier.
голубя́т|ня, ни, *g. pl.* **~ен** *f.* dovecot(e), pigeon loft.
го́л|ый (~, ~а́, ~о) *adj.* **1.** naked, bare (*also fig.*); **~ая голова́** (*i*) bare head, (*ii*) bald head; **~ыми рука́ми** with one's bare hands. **2.** (*coll.*) poor; **~ как соко́л** poor as a church mouse.
голы́ш, а́ *m.* **1.** (*coll.*) naked child; naked person. **2.** (*obs.*) pauper. **3.** round flat stone.
гол|ь, и *no pl.*, *f.* **1.** (*collect.*) the poor; **г. на вы́думки хитра́** necessity is the mother of invention. **2.** (*obs.*) bare place, barren place.
гольф, а *m.* **1.** golf; **игро́к в г.** golfer. **2. ~ы** (*coll.*) plus-fours; knee-length stockings.
гольфи́ст, а *m.* golfer.
гомеопа́т, а *m.* homoeopath(ist).
гомеопати́ческий *adj.* homoeopathic.
гомеопа́ти|я, и *f.* homoeopathy.
го́мик, а *m.* (*coll., pej.*) fairy, queer, poof(ter).
гоминьда́н, а *m.* (*pol.*) Kuomintang
гоминьда́нов|ец, ца *m.* member of Kuomintang.
гоминьда́новский *adj.* Kuomintang.
гомоге́нный *adj.* homogeneous.
го́мон, а *m.* (*coll.*) hubbub.
гомон|и́ть, ю́, и́шь *impf.* (*coll.*) to talk noisily, shout (*of large number of people*).
гомосе́к = **го́мик**
гомосексуали́зм, а *m.* homosexuality.
гомосексуали́ст, а *m.* homosexual; gay.
гомосексуа́льный *adj.* homosexual; gay.
гонг, а *m.* gong.
гондо́л|а, ы *f.* **1.** gondola. **2.** (*aeron.*) car (*of balloon*).

гондолье́р, а *m.* gondolier.
гоне́ни|е, я *nt.* persecution.
гон|е́ц, ца́ *m.* courier; (*fig.*) herald, harbinger.
гони́тел|ь, я *m.* persecutor.
го́нк|а, и *f.* **1.** (*coll.*) haste, hurry, rush. **2.** (*sport, usu pl.*) race; **гребны́е ~и** boat race; **г. вооруже́ний** arms race.
Гонко́нг, а *m.* Hong Kong.
гоноко́кк, а *m.* gonococcus.
го́нор, а *m.* (*coll.*) arrogance, conceit.
гонора́р, а *m.* fee, honorarium; **а́вторский г.** royalties.
гоноре́|я, и *f.* gonorrhoea.
го́ночный *adj. of* **го́нка; г. автомоби́ль** racing car.
гонт, а *m.* (*collect.*; *tech.*) shingles.
гонтов|о́й *adj. of* **гонт; ~а́я кры́ша** shingle roof.
гонча́р, а́ *m.* potter.
гонча́рн|ый *adj.* potter's; **~ые изде́лия** pottery.
го́нч|ая, ей *f.* hound.
го́нщик, а *m.* racer; **велосипеди́ст-г.** racing cyclist.
гоню́(сь), го́нишь(ся) *see* **гна́ть(ся)**
гоня́|ть, ю *impf.* **1.** (*indet. of* **гнать**) to drive. **2.** (*coll.*) to make run errands. **3.** (**по**+*d.*; *coll.*) to make run over, grill (on) (*sth. learnt, read, etc.*). **4.: г. голубе́й** to race pigeons. **5.: г. ло́дыря** (*coll.*) to kick one's heels.
гоня́|ться, юсь *impf.* (*indet. of* **гна́ться**) (**за**+*i.*) to chase, pursue, hunt.
гопа́к, а́ *m.* gopak (*Ukrainian dance*).
гор... *comb. form, abbr. of* **1. городско́й. 2. го́рный**
гор|а́, ы́, *a.* **~́у,** *pl.* **~́ы,** *a.* **~а́м** *f.* **1.** mountain; hill; **г. Эвере́ст** Mount Everest; **г. с плеч** a load off one's mind; **ката́ться с ~ы́** to toboggan; **в ~́у** uphill; **идти́ в ~́у** to go uphill; (*fig.*) to go up in the world; **не за ~а́ми** (*fig.*) not far off; **по́д ~у** downhill (*also fig.*); **пир ~о́й** lavish feast; **наде́яться на кого́-н. как на ка́менную ~́у** to place implicit faith in s.o.; **стоя́ть за кого́-н. ~о́й** to be solidly behind s.o. **2.** (*fig.*) heap, pile, mass.
гора́зд (~а, ~о) *pred. adj.* (+*inf.* or **на**+*a.*; *coll.*) good (at); **он на всё г.** he's a Jack of all trades; **кто во что г.** each in his own way; **он г. вы́пить** he is no mean drinker.
гора́здо *adv.* (+*comp. adjs. and advs.*) much, far, by far; **г. лу́чше** far better.
горб, а́, о ~е́, на ~у́ *m.* hump; **свои́м ~о́м** by the sweat of one's brow.
горба́т|ый (~, ~а) *adj.* humpbacked, hunchbacked; **г. нос** hooked nose.
горби́нк|а, и *f.*: **нос с ~ой** aquiline nose.
го́рб|ить, лю, ишь *impf.* (*of* **с~**) to arch, hunch; **г. спи́ну** to arch one's back.
го́рб|иться, люсь, ишься *impf.* (*of* **с~**) to stoop, become bent.
горбоно́с|ый (~, ~а) *adj.* hook-nosed.
горбу́н, а́ *m.* hunchback.
горбу́шк|а, и *f.* crust (*of loaf*).
гордели́в|ый (~, ~а) *adj.* haughty, proud.
горде́ц, а *m.* arrogant man.
го́рдиев *adj.*: **г. у́зел** Gordian knot.
гор|ди́ться, жу́сь, ди́шься *impf.* (+*i.*) to be proud (of), pride o.s. (on).
го́рдост|ь, и *f.* pride.
го́рд|ый (~, ~а́, ~о, ~ы́) *adj.* proud.
го́р|е, я *nt.* **1.** grief, sorrow, woe; **на своё г.** to one's sorrow. **2.** misfortune, trouble; **г. в том, что...** the trouble is that .... **3.** *as pred.* (+*d.*; *coll.*) woe (unto), woe betide.
гор|ева́ть, ю́ю, ю́ешь *impf.* (**о**+*p.*) to grieve (for).
горе́лк|а, а *f.* burner; **г. Бу́нзена** Bunsen burner; **при́мусная г.** Primus (*propr.*) stove.
горе́л|ки, ок *no sg.* (*game of*) catch.
горе́л|ый *adj.* burnt; **па́хло ~ым** there was a smell of burning.
горемы́к|а, и *c.g.* (*coll.*) unlucky individual, victim of misfortune.
горемы́ч|ный (~ен, ~на) *adj.* hapless, ill-starred.
горе́ни|е, я *nt.* burning, combustion; (*fig.*) enthusiasm.
го́рест|ный (~ен, ~на) *adj.* sorrowful; mournful.
го́рест|ь, и *f.* **1.** sorrow, grief. **2.** (*pl.*) misfortunes, troubles.
гор|е́ть, ю́, и́шь *impf.* **1.** to burn, be on fire. **2.** to burn, be alight; **в ку́хне у них ~е́л свет** the lights were burning in their kitchen; **~и́т ли пе́чка?** is the stove alight?; **де́ло ~и́т** things are going like a house on fire. **3.** (+*i.*; *fig.*) to burn (with); **г. жела́нием** (+*inf.*) to be itching (to), be impatient (to). **4.** to glitter, shine.
го́р|ец, ца *m.* mountain-dweller, highlander.
го́реч|ь, и *f.* **1.** bitter taste. **2.** something bitter. **3.** bitterness.
горже́тк|а, и *f.* boa, throat-wrap.
горизо́нт, а *m.* horizon (*also fig.*), skyline.
горизонта́л|ь, и *f.* **1.** horizontal; **по ~и** (*in crossword*) across. **2.** (*geog.*) contour line.
горизонта́л|ьный (~ен, ~ьна) *adj.* horizontal.
гори́лл|а, ы *f.* gorilla.
гори́ст|ый (~, ~а) *adj.* mountainous, hilly.
го́рк|а, и *f.* **1.** hillock. **2.** cabinet, stand. **3.** (*aeron.*) steep climb.
го́ркн|уть, у, ешь *impf.* (*of* **про~**) to turn rancid.
горла́н|ить, ю, ишь *impf.* (*coll.*) to bawl.
го́рлиц|а, ы *f.* turtle-dove.
го́рл|о, а *nt.* **1.** throat; **дыха́тельное г.** windpipe; **во всё г.** at the top of one's voice; **по г.** up to one's eyes; **сыт по г.** full up; (*fig.*) fed up; **промочи́ть г.** (*coll.*) to wet one's whistle. **2.** neck (*of a vessel*).
горлово́й *adj. of* **го́рло**; throat; guttural.
го́рлыш|ко, ка, *g. pl.* **~ек** *nt. dim. of* **го́рло**
гормо́н, а *m.* hormone.
горн[1]**, а** *m.* furnace, forge.
горн[2]**, а** *m.* bugle.
горни́л|о, а *nt.* crucible.
горни́ст, а *m.* bugler.
го́рничн|ая, ой *f.* (house)maid.
горнолы́жник, а *m.* alpine skier.
горнолы́жный *adj.*: **г. спорт** alpine skiing.
горнопромы́шленност|ь, и *f.* mining industry.
горнопромы́шленный *adj.* mining.
горнорабо́ч|ий, его *m.* miner.
горноста́евый *adj.* ermine.
горноста́|й, я *m.* **1.** (*zool.*) ermine; stoat. **2.** ermine (*fur*).
го́рн|ый *adj.* **1.** *adj. of* **гора́**; mountain; mountainous; **~ые лы́жи** alpine skis. **2.** mineral; **~ая поро́да** rock. **3.** mining; **~ое де́ло** mining. **4.: ~ое со́лнце** artificial sunlight.
горня́к, а́ *m.* (*coll.*) **1.** miner. **2.** mining engineer. **3.** mining student.
горня́|цкий *adj. of* **~к 1.**
го́род, а, *pl.* **~а́** *m.* **1.** town; city; **г.-побрати́м** twin city; **вы́ехать за́ г.** to go out of town; **жить за́ ~ом** to live out of town, in the suburbs; **ни к селу́, ни к ~у** (*coll.*) for no reason at all, inappropriate(ly).
гор|оди́ть, ожу́, о́ди́шь *impf.* to enclose, fence; **огоро́д г.** to make unnecessary fuss; **г. чепуху́, чушь** to talk nonsense.
городи́ш|ко, ка, *g. pl.* **~ек** *m.* small town.
город|ки́, ко́в *pl.* (*sg.* **~о́к, ~ка́** *m.*) gorodki (*game similar to skittles*).
город|о́к, ка́ *m.* small town; **вое́нный г.** cantonment; **г. ми́ра** peace camp; **университе́тский г.** campus.
городо́шник, а *m.* gorodki player.
городо́шни|ца, цы *f. of* **~к**

городско́й *adj.* urban; city; municipal.
горожа́н|ин, ина, *pl.* **~е, ~** *m.* city-dweller, town-dweller; townsman.
горожа́н|ка, ки *f. of* **~ин**; townswoman.
гороско́п, а *m.* horoscope.
горо́х, а (у) *no pl., m.* **1.** pea. **2.** (*collect.*) peas.
горо́хов|ый *adj.* **1.** pea. **2.** pea-green; **шут г.** buffoon.
горо́ш|ек, ка *m.* **1.** *dim. of* **горо́х; души́стый г.** (*bot.*) sweet peas. **2.** (*collect.*) polka dots.
горо́шин|а, ы *f.* a pea.
горсове́т, а *m.* town council.
го́рсточк|а, и *f.* handful.
горст|ь, и, *g. pl.* **~е́й** *f.* **1.** cupped hand; **держа́ть ру́ку ~ью** to cup one's hand. **2.** handful (*also fig.*).
горта́нный *adj.* **1.** (*anat.*) laryngeal. **2.** (*ling.*) guttural.
горта́н|ь, и *f.* larynx.
горте́нзи|я, и *f.* hydrangea.
го́рче *comp. of* **го́рький**
горч|и́ть, и́т *impf.* (*impers.*) to have a bitter taste.
горчи́ц|а, ы *f.* mustard.
горчи́чник, а *m.* mustard-poultice.
горчи́чниц|а, ы *f.* mustard-pot.
горчи́чн|ый *adj. of* **горчи́ца; г. газ** mustard gas.
го́рше *comp. of* **го́рький**
горше́чник, а *m.* potter.
горше́чный *adj.* pottery; **г. това́р** pottery, earthenware.
горш|о́к, ка́ *m.* pot; jug; vase; **ночно́й г.** chamber pot; (*infant's*) potty.
горшо́чн|ый *adj.*: **~ое расте́ние** pot plant.
го́рьк|ая, ой *f.* vodka; **пить ~ую** (*coll.*) to hit the bottle.
го́р|ький (~ек, ~ька́, ~ько) *adj.* **1.** (*comp.* **~че**) bitter; **~ькое ма́сло** rancid butter. **2.** (*comp.* **~ше, ~ший**) (*fig.*) bitter; hard; **~ькие слёзы** bitter tears; **~ьким о́пытом узна́ть** to learn by bitter experience. **3.** (*coll.*) hapless, wretched. **4.: г. пья́ница** (*coll.*) inveterate drunkard.
го́рько[1] *adv.* bitterly.
го́рько[2] *as pred.* **1.: у меня́ г. во рту** I have a bitter taste in my mouth. **2.** it is bitter; **мне г.** I am sorry, I am grieved.
горю́ч|ее, его *nt.* fuel.
горю́чест|ь, и *f.* combustibility; inflammability.
горю́чий *adj.* combustible, inflammable.
горя́ч|ий (~, ~а́, ~о́) *adj.* **1.** hot (*also fig.*); **по ~им следа́м** (*i*) (+*g.*) hot on the heels (of), (*ii*) (*fig.*) forthwith; **под ~ую ру́ку** in the heat of the moment. **2.** passionate; ardent, fervent. **3.** hot-tempered; mettlesome; **~ая голова́** hothead. **4.** heated; impassioned; **г. спор** heated argument. **5.** busy; **~ее вре́мя** busy season.
горяч|и́ть, у́, и́шь *impf.* (*of* **раз~**) to excite, arouse.
горяч|и́ться, у́сь, и́шься *impf.* (*of* **раз~**) to get excited, become impassioned.
горя́чк|а, и *f. and c.g.* **1.** *f.* fever (*also fig.*). **2.** *f.* feverish activity; feverish haste; **поро́ть ~у** (*coll.*) to act impetuously. **3.** *c.g.* (*coll.*) hothead; firebrand.
горя́чност|ь, и *f.* zeal, fervour, enthusiasm; impulsiveness.
горячо́[1] *adv.* hot.
горячо́[2] *as pred.* it is hot.
гос... *comb. form, abbr. of* **госуда́рственный**
Госду́м|а, ы *f.* State Duma.
го́спелз *m. indecl.* gospel music.
госпитализа́ци|я, и *f.* hospitalization.
го́спитал|ь, я *m.* hospital (*esp. mil.*).
госпита́льный *adj. of* **го́спиталь**
Госпо́д|ень, ня, не *adj.* (*eccl.*) the Lord's; **моли́тва ~ня** the Lord's Prayer.
Го́споди *int.* good heavens!; good Lord!; good gracious!
господ|и́н, и́на, *pl.* **~а́, ~, ~а́м** *m.* **1.** master; **сам себе́ г.** one's own master. **2.** gentleman. **3.** (*as style*) (*i*) Mr, (*ii*) Master; **~а́** (*as form of address*) (*i*) gentlemen, (*ii*) ladies and gentlemen; (*as style*) (*i*) Messrs, (*ii*) Mr and Mrs.
госпо́дств|о, а *nt.* **1.** supremacy, dominion, mastery. **2.** predominance.
госпо́дств|овать, ую *impf.* **1.** to hold sway, exercise dominion. **2.** to predominate, prevail. **3.** (**над**+*i.*) to command, dominate; to tower (above).
госпо́дств|ующий *pres. part. act. of* **~овать** *and adj.* **1.** ruling; **г. класс** ruling class. **2.** predominant, prevailing.
Госпо́дь, Го́спода, *voc.* **Го́споди** *m.* God, the Lord; **Г. его́ зна́ет** (the) Lord knows!
госпож|а́, и́ *f.* **1.** mistress. **2.** lady. **3.** (*as style*) Mrs.; Miss.
госсекрета́р|ь, я́ *m.* Secretary of State.
гостево́й *adj.* guest, guests'.
гостеприи́м|ный (~ен, ~на) *adj.* hospitable.
гостеприи́мств|о, а *nt.* hospitality.
гости́н|ая, ой *f.* drawing-room, sitting-room.
гости́ниц|а, ы *f.* hotel.
гости́н|ичный *adj. of* **~ица**
гости́ный *adj.*: **г. двор** arcade.
гости́ть, гощу́, гости́шь *impf.* **(у)** to stay (with), be on a visit (to).
гост|ь, я, *g. pl.* **~е́й** *m.* guest, visitor; **пойти́ в ~и** (**к**+*d.*) to visit; **быть в гостя́х (у)** to be a guest (at, of), be visiting; **в гостя́х хорошо́, а до́ма лу́чше** there's no place like home.
го́ст|ья, ьи, *g. pl.* **~ий** *f. of* **~ь**
госуда́рственност|ь, и *f.* State system; statehood.
госуда́рственн|ый *adj.* State, public; **г. переворо́т** coup d'état; **~ая изме́на** high treason; **~ое пра́во** public law; **~ая слу́жба** public service; **г. слу́жащий** civil servant; **Г. сове́т** (*hist.*) State Council; **~ые экза́мены** final examinations (*in higher education institutions*).
госуда́рств|о, а *nt.* State.
госуда́р|ь, я *m.* sovereign; **Г.** (*as form of address*) Your Majesty, Sire.
гот, а *m.* (*hist.*) Goth.
го́тик|а, и *f.* (*archit.*) Gothic style.
готи́ческий *adj.* (*art*) Gothic; **г. шрифт** Gothic script.
гото́в|ить, лю, ишь *impf.* **1.** to prepare; to train. **2.** to cook.
гото́в|иться, люсь, ишься *impf.* **1.** (**к**+*d. or* +*inf.*) to get ready (for, to); to prepare (o.s.) (for). **2.** to be at hand, in the offing; **~ятся кру́пные собы́тия** great events are in the offing.
гото́вност|ь, и *f.* **1.** readiness, preparedness; **в боево́й ~и** ready for action. **2.** readiness, willingness.
гото́в|ый (~, ~а) *adj.* **1.** (**к**+*d.*) ready (for), prepared (for); **г. к де́йствию** ready for action; **я не ~** I'm not ready. **2.** (**на**+*a. or* +*inf.*) ready (for, to), prepared (for, to); willing (to); **мы ~ы на всё** we are prepared for anything; **она́ не ~а идти́** she is not willing to go. **3.** (+*inf.*) on the point (of), on the verge (of). **4.** ready-made, finished; ready-to-wear; **~ое пла́тье** ready-made clothes; **~ые изде́лия** finished articles.
го́тский *adj.* Gothic.
гофриро́ванн|ый *p.p.p. of* **гофрирова́ть** *and adj.* **~ое желе́зо** corrugated iron; **~ые во́лосы** waved hair; **~ая ю́бка** pleated skirt.
гофрир|ова́ть, у́ю *impf. and pf.* **1.** to corrugate; to wave; to crimp. **2.** to goffer.
гофриро́вк|а, и *no pl., f.* **1.** corrugation; goffering; waving. **2.** waves (*of hair*).
гр. (*abbr. of* **граждани́н** *or* **гражда́нка**) citizen.
грабёж, а́ *m.* robbery (*also fig., coll.*).
граби́тел|ь, я *m.* robber; **у́личный г.** mugger.
граби́тельский *adj.* **1.** predatory. **2.** extortionate,

exorbitant (*of prices*).
гра́б|ить[1], **лю, ишь** *impf.* (*of* **о~**) to rob, pillage; (*fig.*) to rob.
гра́б|ить[2], **лю, ишь** *impf.* to rake.
гра́бленый *adj.* stolen.
гра́б|ли, лей *or* **~ель** *no sg.* rake.
гравёр, а *m.* engraver.
гравёр|ный *adj. of* **~; ное иску́сство** engraving.
гра́ви|й, я *m.* gravel.
гравирова́льн|ый *adj.* engraving; **~ая игла́** etching needle.
гравир|ова́ть, у́ю, у́ешь *impf.* (*of* **вы~**) to engrave.
гравиро́вк|а, и *f.* engraving.
гравитацио́нный *adj.* gravitation(al).
гравита́ци|я, и *f.* (*phys.*) gravitation.
гравю́р|а, ы *f.* engraving, print; etching; **г. на де́реве** woodcut.
град[1], **а** *m.* **1.** hail. **2.** (*fig.*) hail, shower, torrent; volley.
град[2], **а** *m.* (*arch. or poet.*) city, town.
града́ци|я, и *f.* gradation, scale.
градие́нт, а *m.* gradient.
гра́дин|а, ы *f.* (*coll.*) hailstone.
градово́й *adj. of* **град 1.**
гра́дом *adv.* thick and fast; **уда́ры посы́пались г.** blows rained down.
градострои́тел|ь, я *m.* town-planner.
градострои́тельств|о, а *nt.* town-planning.
градуи́р|овать, ую *impf. and pf.* **1.** to graduate (*to mark with lines to indicate degrees, etc.*) **2.** to grade.
гра́дус, а *m.* **1.** degree (*unit of measurement*); **у́гол в 40 ~ов** angle of 40 degrees; **сего́дня 20 ~ов тепла́, моро́за** it is twenty degrees above, below zero today. **2.: под ~ом** (*coll.*) tiddly; one over the eight.
гра́дусник, а *m.* thermometer.
гра́дус|ный *adj. of* **~; ~ная се́тка** (*geog.*) grid.
граждани́н, а, *pl.* **гра́ждане, гра́ждан** *m.* **1.** citizen. **2.** person.
гражда́н|ка[1], **ки** *f. of* **~и́н**
гражда́нк|а[2], **и** *f.* (*coll.*) civilian life; civvy street; **на ~е** in civvy street.
гражда́нск|ий *adj.* **1.** (*leg., etc.*) civil; citizen's; civic; **г. ко́декс** civil code. **2.** civil, secular (*opp. ecclesiastical*). **3.** civilian; **~ое пла́тье** civilian clothes. **4.** civic, befitting a citizen; **~ие доброде́тели** civic virtues. **5.** (*of poetry, etc.*) civic, having social content. **6.: ~ая война́** civil war.
гражда́нственност|ь, и *f.* **1.** civilization; civil society. **2.** civic spirit.
гражда́нств|о, а *nt.* citizenship, nationality; **права́ ~а** civic rights; **получи́ть права́ ~а** to be granted civic rights; (*fig.*) to achieve general recognition.
грамза́пис|ь, и *f.* gramophone recording.
грамм, а *m.* gramme, gram.
грамма́тик|а, и *f.* **1.** grammar. **2.** grammar(-book).
грамматист, а *m.* grammarian.
граммати́ческий *adj.* grammatical.
граммофо́н, а *m.* gramophone.
граммофо́н|ный *adj. of* **~; ~ная пласти́нка** gramophone record.
гра́мот|а, ы *f.* **1.** ability to read and write. **2.** official document; deed.
гра́мотност|ь, и *f.* **1.** literacy (*also fig.*). **2.** grammatical correctness. **3.** competence.
гра́мот|ный (~ен, ~на) *adj.* **1.** literate; educated. **2.** grammatically correct. **3.** competent.
грампласти́нк|а, и *f.* gramophone record.
гран, а *m.* grain (*unit of weight*).
грана́т[1], **а** *m.* **1.** pomegranate. **2.** pomegranate tree.
грана́т[2], **а** *m.* (*min.*) garnet.
грана́т|а, ы *f.* (*mil.*) grenade; **ручна́я г.** hand-grenade.
грана́т|ный *adj. of* **~а**
грана́товый[1] *adj.* pomegranate.
грана́т|овый[2] **1.** *adj. of* **~**[2]. **2.** rich red.
гранатомёт, а *m.* (*mil.*) grenade launcher.
грандио́зност|ь, и *f.* grandeur; immensity.
грандио́з|ный (~ен, ~на) *adj.* grandiose; mighty; vast.
гранён|ый *adj.* cut, faceted; **~ое стекло́** cut glass.
грани́льный *adj.* lapidary; diamond-cutting.
грани́л|ьня, ьни, *g. pl.* **~ен** *f.* lapidary workshop; **г. алма́зов** diamond-cutting shop.
грани́льщик, а *m.* lapidary; **г. алма́зов** diamond-cutter.
грани́т, а *m.* granite.
грани́тный *adj.* granite.
гран|и́ть, ю́, и́шь *impf.*, to cut, facet.
грани́ц|а, ы *f.* **1.** frontier, border; **за ~ей** abroad; **е́хать за ~у** to go abroad. **2.** (*fig.*) boundary, limit; **вы́йти из ~** to overstep the mark; **в ~ах прили́чия** within the bounds of decency.
грани́ч|ить, у, ишь *impf.* (**с**+*i.*) **1.** to border (upon), be contiguous (with). **2.** (*fig.*) to border (on), verge (on); **э́то ~ит с изме́ной** it borders on treason.
гра́нк|а, и *f.* (*typ.*) galley-proof.
грануи́р|овать, ую *impf. and pf.* to granulate.
грануля́ци|я, и *f.* granulation.
гран|ь, и *f.* **1.** border, verge; brink; **на ~и сумасше́ствия** on the verge of insanity; **«поли́тика на ~и войны́»** brinkmanship. **2.** side, facet; edge.
граф, а *m.* count.
граф|а́, ы́ *f.* column; section.
гра́фик[1], **а** *m.* **1.** graph, chart. **2.** schedule; **пло́тный г.** packed *or* heavy schedule.
гра́фик[2], **а** *m.* graphic artist.
гра́фик|а, и *f.* (*art*) drawing; (*comput.*) graphics.
графи́н, а *m.* carafe; decanter.
графи́н|я, и *f.* countess.
графи́т, а *m.* **1.** (*min.*) graphite. **2.** (pencil-)lead.
графи́т|ный *adj.* = **~овый**
графи́товый *adj.* graphite.
граф|и́ть, лю́, и́шь *impf.* (*of* **раз~**) to rule (*paper*).
графи́ческий *adj.* graphic.
графлёный *adj.* (vertically) ruled.
гра́фский *adj. of* **граф**
гра́фств|о, а *nt.* **1.** title of count. **2.** county, shire.
грацио́з|ный (~ен, ~на) *adj.* graceful.
гра́ци|я, и *f.* gracefulness.
грач, а́ *m.* (*zool.*) rook.
гребёнк|а, и *f.* comb; **стричь под ~у** to crop close; **стричь всех под одну́ ~у** to treat all alike, reduce all to the same level.
гре́б|ень, ня *m.* **1.** comb. **2.** (*tech.*) comb; (*text.*) hackle. **3.** (*of bird*) comb, crest; **петуши́ный г.** cock's comb. **4.** crest (*of hill or wave*). **5.** (*archit.*) ridge-piece. **6.** (*agric.*) ridge.
греб|е́ц, ца́ *m.* rower, oarsman.
гребеш|о́к[1], **ка́** *m.* = **гре́бень**
гребеш|о́к[2], **ка́** *m.* (*zool.*) scallop.
гре́бл|я, и *f.* rowing.
гребн|о́й *adj.* **1.** rowing; **г. спорт** rowing. **2.: г. вал** propeller shaft; **~о́е колесо́** paddle wheel.
греб|о́к, ка́ *m.* **1.** stroke (*in rowing*). **2.** blade; paddle.
грёз|а, ы *f.* day-dream, reverie.
гре́|жу *see* **~зить**
гре́|зить, жу, зишь *impf.* to dream; **г. наяву́** to day-dream.
гре́|зиться, жусь, зишься *impf.* (*of* **при~**) (*impers.*, +*d.*) to dream; **она́ мне ча́сто ~зилась** I often used to dream about her.
гре́йдер, а *m.* (*tech.*) **1.** grader. **2.** (*coll.*) earth road (*levelled but unmetalled*).
гре́йпфрут, а *m.* grapefruit.
грек, а *m.* Greek.

гре́ко-ки́прский *adj.* Greek-Cypriot.
гре́лк|а, и *f.* hot-water bottle; **электри́ческая г.** electric blanket.
грем|е́ть, лю́, и́шь *impf.* to thunder, roar; peal; rattle; (*fig.*) to resound, ring out; **и́мя его́ ~е́ло по всей Евро́пе** his name resounded throughout Europe.
гремýч|ий *adj.* roaring; **~ая змея́** rattlesnake; **~ая ртуть** (*chem.*) fulminate of mercury.
гренаде́р, а *m.* grenadier.
гренаде́р|ский *adj. of* **~; г. полк** Grenadiers.
грен|о́к, ка́ *m.* (finger of) toast; (*cul.*) croûton.
гре|сти́, бу́, бёшь, *past* **≃б, ~бла́** *impf.* **1.** to row. **2.** to rake.
гре́ть, гре́ю, гре́ешь *impf.* **1.** (*intrans.*) to give out warmth. **2.** (*trans.*) to warm, heat; **г. (себе́) ру́ки** to warm one's hands; (*fig.*, *coll.*, *pej.*) to be on to a good thing.
гре́|ться, юсь, ешься *impf.* **1.** to warm o.s. **2.** *pass. of* **греть**
грех, а́ *m.* **1.** (*relig. or fig.*) sin; **перво. ро́дный г.** original sin; **приня́ть на себя́ г.** to take the blame upon o.s; **пода́льше от ~а́** out of harm's way; **как на г.** as ill-luck would have it. **2.** *as pred.* (*+inf.*; *coll.*) it is a sin, it is sinful; **не г.** (*+inf.*) there is no harm (in); **не г. вы́пить рю́мочку-две** there is no harm in (drinking) a glass or two. **3.: с ~о́м попола́м** (only) just; barely; **мы с ~о́м попола́м расшифрова́ли твой по́черк** we barely managed to decipher your handwriting.
Гре́ци|я, и *f.* Greece.
гре́цкий *adj.*: **г. оре́х** walnut.
греча́нк|а, и *f. of* **грек**
гре́ческий *adj.* Greek; Grecian.
гречи́х|а, и *f.* buckwheat.
гре́чнев|ый *adj.* buckwheat; **~ая ка́ша** buckwheat porridge.
греш|и́ть, у́, и́шь *impf.* **1.** (*pf.* **со~**) to sin. **2.** (*pf.* **по~**) (**про́тив**+*g.*; *fig.*) to sin (against).
гре́шник, а *m.* sinner.
гре́шни|ца, цы *f. of* **~к**
гре́ш|ный (~ен, ~на́) *adj.* sinful; culpable; **~ным де́лом** (*parenth.*) much as I regret it; I am ashamed to say.
греш|о́к, ка́ *m.* peccadillo.
гриб, а́ *m.* fungus; mushroom; **съедо́бный г.** mushroom, edible fungus; **несъедо́бный г.** toadstool; **расти́ как ~ы́** to spring up like mushrooms.
грибко́вый *adj.* fungoid.
грибн|о́й *adj. of* **гриб**; fungoid; mushroom; **г. дождь** sun shower; **~а́я похлёбка** mushroom soup.
гриб|о́к, ка́ *m.* **1.** *dim. of* **гриб. 2.** (*biol.*) fungus.
гри́в|а, ы *f.* mane.
грива́ст|ый (~, ~а) *adj.* with a long mane.
гри́венник, а *m.* (*coll.*) ten-kopeck piece.
григориа́нск|ий *adj.* Gregorian; **г. календа́рь** Gregorian Calendar.
гри́зли *m. indecl.* grizzly (bear)
грим, а *m.* make-up (*theatr. only*); grease-paint.
грима́с|а, ы *f.* grimace; **де́лать ~ы** to make *or* pull faces.
грима́снича|ть, ю *impf.* to grimace; to make *or* pull faces.
гримёр, а *m.* (*theatr.*, *etc.*) make-up artist.
гримёрн|ая, ой *f.* (*theatr.*, *etc.*) make-up room.
гримёр|ша, ши (*coll.*) *f. of* **~**
гримир|ова́ть, у́ю, *impf.* **1.** (*theatr.*) (*pf.* **на~**) to make up. **2.** (*pf.* **за~**) (*+i.*) to make up (to look like); (*+i. or* **под**+*a.*; *fig.*): **г. Наполео́на геро́ем, под геро́я** to paint Napoleon as a hero.
гримир|ова́ться, у́юсь *impf.* (*of* **за~**) (*theatr.*) to make up (*intrans.*); (*+i. or* **под**+*a.*; *fig.*) to make o.s. out; **г. патрио́том, под патрио́та** to make o.s. out a patriot.
Гри́нвич, а *m.* Greenwich; **вре́мя по ~у** Greenwich (Mean) Time (*abbr. GMT*).
грипп, а *m.* influenza.
гриппо́зный *adj.* influenzal
гриф[1], а *m.* **1.** (*myth.*) griffin. **2.** (*zool.*) vulture.
гриф[2], а *m.* (*mus.*) finger-board.
гриф[3], а *m.* seal, stamp.
гри́фел|ь, я *m.* slate-pencil; (*pencil*) lead.
гри́фельн|ый *adj.* slate; **~ая доска́** slate.
грифо́н, а *m.* **1.** (*myth.*, *archit.*) griffin. **2.** griffon (*dog*).
гроб, а, о ≃е, в ~у́, *pl.* **~ы́** *and* **~а́** *m.* **1.** coffin. **2.** (*fig.*) the grave (= *death*); **вогна́ть в г.** to drive to the grave; **до ≃а, по г. жи́зни** (*coll.*) until the end of one's days.
гробни́ц|а, ы *f.* tomb, sepulchre.
гробов|о́й *adj.* **1.** *adj. of* **гроб; ~а́я доска́** (*fig.*) the grave; **ве́рный до ~о́й доски́** faithful unto death. **2.** sepulchral, funereal; **г. го́лос** sepulchral voice; **~о́е молча́ние** deathly silence.
гробовщи́к, а́ *m.* coffin-maker; undertaker.
грог, а *m.* grog.
гроз|а́, ы́, *pl.* **≃ы** *f.* (thunder)storm.
грозд|ь, и, *pl.* **≃и, ~е́й** *and* **≃ья, ≃ьев** *f.* cluster, bunch (*of fruit or flowers*)
гро|зи́ть, жу́, зи́шь *impf.* **1.** (*pf.* **при~**) (*+d. and i. or +inf.*) to threaten; **он ~зи́л мне револьве́ром** he was threatening me with a revolver; **г. уби́ть кого́-н.** to threaten to kill s.o. **2.** (*pf.* **по~**) (*+i.*) to make threatening gestures; **г. кулако́м кому́-н.** to shake one's fist at s.o. **3.** (*no pf.*) to threaten; **ему́ ~зи́т банкро́тство** he is threatened with bankruptcy.
гро|зи́ться, жу́сь, зи́шься *impf.* (*of* **по~**) (*coll.*) (*+inf.*) to threaten
гро́з|ный (~ен, ~на́, ~но) *adj.* **1.** menacing, threatening. **2.** dread, terrible; **~ная опа́сность** terrible danger. **3.** (*coll.*) stern, severe.
гроз|ово́й *adj. of* **~а́; ~ова́я ту́ча** storm-cloud, thundercloud.
гром, а, *pl.* **≃ы, ~о́в** *m.* thunder (*also fig.*); **уда́р ≃а** thunderclap; **г. среди́ я́сного не́ба** a bolt from the blue.
грома́д|а, ы *f.* mass, bulk, pile (*+g.*).
грома́д|ный (~ен, ~на) *adj.* huge, vast, enormous, colossal.
громи́л|а, ы *m.* (*coll.*) **1.** burglar. **2.** thug.
гром|и́ть, лю́, и́шь *impf.* (*of* **раз~**) **1.** to destroy; (*mil.*) to smash, rout. **2.** (*fig.*) to lambaste; to fulminate against.
гро́м|кий (~ок, ~ка́, ~ко) *adj.* **1.** loud. **2.** famous; notorious; **~кое поведе́ние** infamous conduct. **3.** fine-sounding; **~кие слова́** (*iron.*) big words.
гро́мко *adv.* loud(ly); aloud.
громкоговори́тел|ь, я *m.* loud-speaker.
громов|о́й *adj.* **1.** *adj. of* **гром; ~ы́е раска́ты** peals of thunder. **2.** thunderous, deafening; **~ы́е рукоплеска́ния** thunderous applause. **3.** crushing, devastating.
громогла́с|ный (~ен, ~на) *adj.* loud; loud-voiced.
громоз|ди́ть, жу́, ди́шь *impf.* (*of* **на~**) to pile up, heap up.
громоз|ди́ться, жу́сь, ди́шься *impf.* **1.** to tower. **2.** (*coll.*) to clamber up.
громо́зд|кий (~ок, ~ка) *adj.* cumbersome, unwieldy.
громоотво́д, а *m.* lightning-conductor.
громоподо́б|ный (~ен, ~на) *adj.* thunderous.
гро́м|че *comp. of* **~кий** *and* **~ко**
громыха́|ть, ю *impf.* (*coll.*) to rumble.
гросс, а *m.* gross.
гроссбу́х, а *m.* ledger.
гроссме́йстер, а *m.* grand master (*at chess*).
грот[1], а *m.* grotto.

грот[2], **а** *m.* mainsail.
грот-... *comb. form* (*naut.*) main-.
гроте́ск, а *m.* (*art*) grotesque.
гроте́скный *adj.* grotesque.
гро́х|ать(ся), аю(сь) *impf. of* **~нуть(ся)**
гро́хн|уть, у, ешь *pf.* (*coll.*) **1.** to crash, bang. **2.** (*trans.*) to drop with a crash, bang down.
гро́хн|уться, усь, ешься *pf.* (*coll.*) to fall with a crash.
гро́хот[1], **а** *m.* crash, din.
гро́хот[2], **а** *m.* (*tech.*, *agric.*) riddle, screen, sifter.
грох|ота́ть, очу́, о́чешь *impf.* **1.** to crash; rumble; roar. **2.** (*coll.*) to roar (*with laughter*).
грош, а́ *m.* **1.** half-kopeck piece. **2.** *pl.* **~и́, ~е́й** (*fig.*, *coll.*) penny, farthing; **э́то ~а́ ме́дного, ло́маного не сто́ит** it's not worth a brass farthing; **купи́ть за ~и́** to buy for a song; **рабо́тать за ~и́** work for a pittance.
грошо́вый *adj.* (*coll.*) **1.** dirt-cheap; (*fig.*) cheap, shoddy. **2.** insignificant, trifling.
грубе́|ть, ю, ешь *impf.* (*of* **о~**) to grow coarse, rude.
груб|и́ть, лю́, и́шь *impf.* (*of* **на~**) (+*d.*) to be rude (to).
грубия́н, а *m.* (*coll.*) boor.
гру́бо *adv.* **1.** coarsely, roughly. **2.** crudely. **3.** rudely. **4.** roughly (= *approximately*); **г. говоря́** roughly speaking.
гру́бост|ь, и *f.* **1.** rudeness; coarseness; grossness. **2.** rude remark; coarse action; **говори́ть ~и** to be rude.
гру́б|ый (~, ~а́, ~о) *adj.* **1.** coarse, rough; **~ое сукно́** coarse fabric; **г. го́лос** gruff voice. **2.** (*of workmanship etc.*) crude. **3.** gross, flagrant; **г. обма́н** gross deception. **4.** rude; coarse, crude; **~ое сло́во** coarse word. **5.** rough (= *approximate*); **в ~ых черта́х** in rough outline.
гру́д|а, ы *f.* heap, pile.
груди́н|а, ы *f.* (*anat.*) breastbone.
груди́нк|а, и *f.* brisket; breast (*of lamb, etc.*).
грудни́ц|а, ы *f.* (*med.*) mastitis.
грудн|о́й *adj.* **1.** breast; chest; **~а́я жа́ба** (*med.*) angina pectoris; **~а́я железа́** (*anat.*) mammary gland; **~а́я кле́тка** (*anat.*) thorax. **2.** at the breast; **г. ребёнок** baby.
грудобрю́шн|ый *adj.*: **~ая прегра́да** (*anat.*) diaphragm.
груд|ь, и́, о ~́и, в (на) ~и́, *pl.* **~́и ~е́й** *f.* **1.** breast, chest; **стоя́ть ~́ью (за**+*a.*) to stand up (for), champion; **г. с ~́ью, г. на́ г. би́ться** to fight hand to hand **2.** (*female*) breast; bosom, bust; **корми́ть ~́ью** to breast-feed; **отня́ть от ~и́** to wean.
гружёный *adj.* loaded, laden.
груз, а *m.* **1.** load; cargo, freight; **поле́зный г.** payload. **2.** (*fig.*) weight, burden.
грузд|ь, я́, *pl.* **~́и, ~́ей** *m.* milk-agaric (*mushroom*).
грузи́л|о, а *nt.* sinker.
грузи́н, а, *g. pl.* **г.** *m.* Georgian.
грузи́н|ка, ки *f. of* **~**
грузи́нский *adj.* Georgian.
гру|зи́ть, жу́, ~́зишь *impf.* **1.** (*pf.* **за~** *and* **на~**) to load; to lade, freight; **г. су́дно** to lade a ship. **2.** (*pf.* **по~**) (**в, на**+*a.*) to load; **г. това́р на су́дно** to put a cargo aboard a ship.
гру|зи́ться, жу́сь, ~́зишься *impf.* (*of* **по~**) to load (*intrans.*), take on cargo.
Гру́зи|я, и *f.* Georgia (*Transcaucasia*).
гру́з|ный (~ен, ~на́, ~но) *adj.* weighty, bulky; corpulent.
грузови́к, а́ *m.* lorry.
грузов|о́й *adj.* goods, cargo, freight; **~о́е движе́ние** goods traffic; **~о́е су́дно** cargo boat, freighter.
грузооборо́т, а *m.* turnover of goods.
грузоотправи́тел|ь, я *m.* shipper; consignor of goods.
грузоподъёмный *adj.*: **г. кран** (*loading*) crane.
грузополуча́тел|ь я *m.* consignee.
гру́зчик, а *m.* docker, stevedore.
грунт, а *m.* **1.** soil, earth. **2.** priming, prime coating (*of a picture*).
грунтов|о́й *adj. of* **грунт; ~ы́е во́ды** subsoil waters; **~а́я доро́га** dirt road.
гру́пп|а, ы *f.* group; club; **г. кро́ви** (*med.*) blood group; **г. люби́телей бе́га** jogging club; **дошко́льная г.** playgroup; **операти́вная г.** task force.
группир|ова́ть, у́ю *impf.* (*of* **с~**) to group; to classify.
группир|ова́ться, у́ется *impf.* (*of* **с~**) to group, form groups.
группиро́вк|а, и *f.* **1.** grouping, classification. **2.** group, grouping.
группов|о́й *adj.* group; **~ы́е и́гры** team games; **г. полёт** formation flying.
гру|сти́ть, щу́, сти́шь *impf.* to grieve, mourn; (**по**+*d.*) to pine (for).
гру́стно[1] *adv.* sadly, sorrowfully.
гру́стно[2] *as pred.* it is sad; **ей г.** she feels sad; **нам г. узна́ть, что...** we are sorry to hear that ....
гру́ст|ный (~ен, ~на́, ~но) *adj.* sad; melancholy.
груст|ь, и *f.* sadness; melancholy.
гру́ш|а, и *f.* **1.** pear. **2.** pear-tree. **3.: земляна́я г.** Jerusalem artichoke. **4.: боксёрская г.** punchball.
гру́шевый *adj.* pear; **г. компо́т** stewed pears.
гры́ж|а, и *f.* (*med.*) hernia, rupture.
грыжево́й *and* **гры́жевый** *adj.* hernial; **г. банда́ж** truss.
грызн|я́, и́ *f.* (*coll.*) **1.** fight (*between animals*). **2.** squabble.
гры́з|ть, у́, ёшь, *past* **~, ~́ла** *impf.* **1.** to gnaw; to nibble; **г. но́гти** to bite one's nails. **2.** (*coll.*) to nag (at). **3.** (*fig.*) to devour, consume; **нас ~́ло любопы́тство** we were consumed with curiosity.
гры́з|ться, у́сь, ёшься, *past* **~ся, ~лась** *impf.* **1.** to fight (*of animals*). **2.** (*coll.*) to squabble, bicker.
грызу́н, а́ *m.* rodent.
гряд|а́, ы́, *pl.* **~́ы, ~, ~а́м** *f.* **1.** ridge. **2.** bed (*in garden*). **3.** row, series.
гря́дк|а, и *f. dim. of* **гряда́**
гряду́щ|ий *pres. part. act. of* **грясти́** (*obs.*) *and adj.* (*rhet.*): coming, future; **~ие дни** days to come; **на сон г.** (*coll.*) at bedtime; *as n.* **~ее, ~его** *nt.* the future.
грязев|о́й *adj.* mud; **~а́я ва́нна** mud-bath.
грязн|и́ть, ю́, и́шь *impf.* (*of* **на~**) **1.** to make dirty, soil; (*fig.*) to sully, besmirch. **2.** to litter.
грязн|и́ться, ю́сь, и́шься *impf.* to get dirty.
гря́зн|о[1] *adv. of* **~ый**
гря́зно[2] *as pred.* it is dirty.
грязну́л|я, и *c.g.* (*coll.*) guttersnipe; slut.
гря́з|ный (~ен, ~на́, ~но) *adj.* **1.** muddy, mud-stained. **2.** dirty; **~ное бельё** dirty washing. **3.** untidy; slovenly; **~ная тетра́дь** untidy copy-book.
гряз|ь, и, о ~́и, в ~и́ *f.* **1.** mud (*also fig.*); **заброса́ть ~́ью** (*fig.*) to sling mud (at). **2.** (*pl.*) (*therapeutic*) mud; mud-baths; mud-cure. **3.** dirt, filth (*also fig.*).
гря́н|уть, у, ешь *pf.* **1.** (*of sounds*) to burst forth; **~ул гром** there was a clap of thunder; **~ул вы́стрел** a shot rang out. **2.** to burst out; to erupt.
гуа́но *nt. indecl.* guano.
гуа́шь, и *f.* (*art*) gouache.
губ|а́[1], **ы́,** *pl.* **~́ы, ~а́м** *f.* lip; **наду́ть ~́ы** to pout; **у него́ гу́ба не ду́ра** (*coll.*) he knows which side his bread is buttered; **молоко́ на ~а́х не обсо́хло** he is still green.
губ|а́[2], **ы́,** *pl.* **~́ы, ~а́м** *f.* bay, inlet (*in northern Russia*).
губа́ст|ый (~, ~а) *adj.* (*coll.*) thick-lipped.
губерна́тор, а *m.* governor.

губерна́торск|ий *adj.* of a governor.
губерна́торств|о, а *nt.* governorship.
губе́рни|я, и *f.* (*hist.*) guberniya, province.
губи́тел|ьный (~ен, ~ьна) *adj.* destructive, ruinous; baneful, pernicious.
губ|и́ть, лю́, ~́ишь *impf.* (*of* **по~**) to destroy; to be the undoing (of); to ruin, spoil.
гу́б|ка[1], **ки** *f. dim. of* **губа́**[1]
гу́бк|а[2], **и** *f.* sponge; **мыть ~ой** to sponge.
губн|о́й *adj.* **1.** lip; **~а́я пома́да** lipstick. **2.** (*ling.*) labial.
гу́бчат|ый *adj.* porous, spongy; **г. каучу́к** foam rubber.
гуверна́нтк|а, и *f.* governess.
гувернёр, а *m.* tutor.
гугено́т, а *m.* (*hist.*) Huguenot.
гугу́ *only in phr.* **(об э́том) ни г.!** mum's the word!
гуде́ни|е, я *nt.* buzzing; drone; hum; honk (*of a motor-car horn, etc.*).
гу|де́ть, жу́, ди́шь *impf.* **1.** to buzz; to drone; to hum; (*impers.*): **у меня́ ~де́ло в уша́х** there was a buzzing in my ears. **2.** (*of a factory whistle, steamer's siren, etc.*) to hoot; to honk. **3.** (*coll.*) to ache.
гуд|о́к, ка́ *m.* **1.** hooter, siren, horn, whistle. **2.** hoot(ing); honk; toot.
гудро́н, а *m.* tar.
гудрони́р|овать, ую *impf. and pf.* to tar.
гуж, а́ *m.*: **взя́лся за г., не говори́, что не дюж** (*prov.*) in for a penny in for a pound.
гул, а *m.* rumble; hum; boom.
гу́л|кий (~ок, ~ка́, ~ко) *adj.* **1.** resonant; echoing. **2.** booming, rumbling.
гу́льден, а *m.* guilder (*Dutch unit of currency*).
гуля́к|а, и *c.g.* (*coll.*) idler; playboy.
гуля́н|ье, ья, *g. pl.* **~ий** *nt.* **1.** walking; (going for a) walk. **2.** fête; outdoor party.
гуля́|ть, ю *impf.* (*of* **по~**) **1.** to walk, stroll; to take a walk, go for a walk. **2.** (*impf. only*) (*coll.*) not to be working; **мы сего́дня ~ем** we have got the day off today. **3.** (*coll.*) to make merry, live it up. **4.** (**с**+*i.*; *coll.*) to go (with) (= *have a sexual relationship with*).
гуля́ш, а *m.* (*cul.*) goulash.
гумани́зм, а *m.* humanism.
гумани́ст, а *m.* humanist.
гуманисти́ческий *adj.* humanist.
гуманита́рн|ый *adj.* **1.** pertaining to the humanities; **~ые нау́ки** the humanities. **2.** humane.
гума́нност|ь, и *f.* humanity, humaneness.
гума́н|ный (~ен, ~на) *adj.* humane.
гум|но́, на́, *pl.* **~́на, ~́ен** *and* **~ён, ~́нам** *nt.* threshing-floor.
гу́мус, а *m.* (*agric.*) humus.
гунн, а *m.* (*hist.*) Hun.
гурма́н, а *m.* gourmet.
гурт, а *m.* herd, drove; flock.
гуртовщи́к, а́ *m.* herdsman; drover.
гурто́м *adv.* (*coll.*) **1.** wholesale; in bulk. **2.** together; in a body, en masse.
гу́ру *m. indecl.* guru.
гурьб|а́, ы́ *f.* crowd.
гуса́к, а́ *m.* gander.
гуса́р, а *m.* hussar.
гу́сениц|а, ы *f.* **1.** (*zool.*) caterpillar. **2.** (caterpillar) track.
гу́сеничн|ый *adj.* (*zool., tech.*) caterpillar; **~ая ле́нта** (*tech.*) caterpillar track.
гус|ёнок, ёнка, *pl.* **~я́та** *m.* gosling.
гуси́н|ый *adj.* goose; **~ая ко́жа** goose-flesh; **~ые ла́пки** crow's feet.
гу́сл|и, ей *no sg.* (*mus.*) psaltery, gusli.
густе́|ть, ет *impf.* (*of* **по~**) to thicken, get thicker.
гу́сто[1] *adv.* thickly, densely.
гу́сто[2] *as pred.* (*coll.*) there is plenty; **у меня́ де́нег не г.** I'm a bit hard up, a bit pushed.
густ|о́й (~́, ~а́, ~́о) *adj.* **1.** (*in var. senses*) thick, dense; **~ы́е бро́ви** bushy eyebrows. **2.** (*of sound or colour*) deep, rich.
густонаселённый *adj.* densely populated.
густот|а́, ы́ *f.* **1.** thickness, density. **2.** (*of sound or colour*) deepness, richness.
гусы́н|я, и *f.* (female) goose.
гус|ь, я, *pl.* **~́и, ~́ей** *m.* goose; **как с ~́я вода́** like water off a duck's back.
гусько́м *adv.* in (single) file.
гуся́тин|а, ы *f.* goose(-meat).
гуся́тник, а *m.* goose-pen, goose-run.
гутали́н, а *m.* shoe-polish.
гуттапе́рч|а, и *f.* gutta percha.
гу́щ|а, и *f.* **1.** dregs; lees; sediment; **кофе́йная г.** coffee grounds. **2.** thicket; (*fig.*) thick, centre, heart; **в са́мой ~е собы́тий** in the thick of things.
гу́ще *comp. of* **густо́й, гу́сто**
гэ́льский *adj.* Gaelic.
ГЭС *f. indecl.* (*abbr. of* **гидроэлектроста́нция**) hydro-electric power-station.

д. (*abbr. of* **дом**) house.
да[1] *particle* **1.** yes. **2.** (*interrog*) is that so?, really?, indeed?; **он мно́го лет прожива́л в Пари́же. — Да? а я и не знал** he lived in Paris for many years. Really? I didn't know. **3.** (*emph.*) why; well; **да не мо́жет быть!** why, that's impossible!; **д. нет!** of course not!; not likely!; **да в чём де́ло?** well, what's it all about? **4. (вот) э́то да!** (*coll.*) splendid!; super!
да[2] *particle* (*+3rd pers. pres. or fut. of v.*) may, let; **да здра́вствует..!** long live ...!
да[3] *conj.* **1.** (*mainly in conventional phrr.*) and; **ко́жа да ко́сти** skin and bone. **2.: да (и** *or* **ещё)** and (besides); and what is more; **бы́ло за́ полночь, да и снег шёл** it was past midnight and (what is more) it was snowing. **3.: да и то́лько** and that's all; **она́ ворчи́т, да и то́лько** she does nothing but grouse. **4.** but; **я охо́тно проводи́л бы тебя́, да вре́мени не́ту** I would gladly come with you but I haven't the time.
дабы́ *conj.* (*obs.*) in order (to, that).
дава́й(те) *as particle* **1.** (*+inf. or 1st pers. pl. of fut.*) let's; **дава́йте приостано́вимся мину́точку-две** let's pause for a minute or two; **дава́йте заку́рим** let's light up. **2.** (*+imper.*; *coll.*) come on; **дава́й, расскажи́ что-н.** come on, tell us a story.
да|ва́ть, ю, ёшь *impf. of* **дать**
да|ва́ться, ю́сь, ёшься *impf.* (*of* **~́ться**) **1.** *pass. of* **дава́ть. 2.** to let o.s. be caught; **не д.** (*+d.*) to dodge, evade. **3.: легко́ д.** to come easily, naturally; **ру́сский язы́к ему́ легко́ даётся** Russian comes easily to him.
дави́льный *adj.*: **д. пресс** winepress.
дави́л|ьня, ьни, *g. pl.* **~ен** *f.* winepress.
дав|и́ть, лю́, ~́ишь *impf.* **1.** (*also* **на**+*a.*) to press (upon); (*fig.*) to oppress, weigh (upon), lie heavy (on); (*impers.*): **се́рдце ~ит** (my) heart is heavy. **2.** to crush; to trample. **3.** to squeeze (*juice out of fruit, etc*).

дав|и́ться, лю́сь, ⁓ишься *impf.* (*of* **по⁓**) **1.** (+*i. or* **от**) to choke (with); **д. от ка́шля** to choke with coughing. **2.** *pass. of* **⁓и́ть**

да́вка, и *f.* (*coll.*) **1.** crushing, squeezing. **2.** throng, crush.

давле́ни|е, я *nt.* pressure (*also fig.*); **под ⁓ем** (+*g.*) under pressure (of).

да́вленый *adj.* pressed, crushed.

да́вн|ий adj. **1.** ancient. **2.** of long standing; **с ⁓их пор, времён** of old, for a long time.

давни́шний *adj.* (*coll.*) = **да́вний**

давно́ *adv.* **1.** long ago; **он д. у́мер** he died long ago. **2.** for a long time; long since; **мы д. живём в дере́вне** we have been living in the country for a long time.

давнопроше́дш|ий *adj.*: **⁓ее вре́мя** (*gram.*) pluperfect tense.

да́вност|ь, и *f.* **1.** antiquity; remoteness. **2.** long standing. **3.** (*leg.*) prescription.

давны́м-давно́ *adv.* (*coll.*) long ago, ages ago.

да́же *particle* even; **е́сли д.** even if.

дактили́ческий *adj.* (*liter.*) dactylic.

дактилоскопи́|я, и *f.* dactyloscopy; **ге́нная д.** genetic fingerprinting.

да́ктил|ь, я *m.* (*liter.*) dactyl.

дакти́льн|ый *adj.*: **⁓ая а́збука** sign language.

дала́й-ла́м|а, ы *m.* Dalai Lama.

да́лее *adv.* further; **не д., как вчера́, он был здесь** he was here only yesterday; **и так д.** (*abbr.* **и т. д.**) and so on, etcetera.

далёк|ий (⁓, ⁓а́, ⁓о́ *and* ⁓о) *adj.* **1.** (*in var. senses*) distant, remote; far(away); **д. путь** long journey; **⁓ое про́шлое** distant past; **я ⁓ от того́, что́бы жела́ть** I am far from wishing. **2.** (*only with neg.*; *coll.*) clever, bright; **она́ не о́чень ⁓а́** she is not terribly bright.

далеко́ *and* **далёко**[1] *adv.* **1.** far, far off; **(от)** far (from); **д. зайти́** (*fig.*) to go too far, burn one's boats; **д. пойти́** (*fig.*) to go far (= *to be a success*). **2.** far, by a long way, by much; **д. за** (*of time*) long after; **д. не** far from; **она́ д. не краса́вица** she is far from beautiful.

далеко́ *and* **далёко**[2] *as pred.* it is far, it is a long way; (+*d.* **до** *fig.*) to be far (from), be much inferior (to); **ему́ д. до соверше́нства** he is far from perfect.

дал|ь, и, о ⁓и, в ⁓и́ *f.* **1.** distance. **2.** (*coll.*) distant spot. **3.: така́я д.!** (*coll.*) it is so far, such a long way!

дальневосто́чный *adj.* Far Eastern.

дальне́йш|ий *adj.* further, furthest; **в ⁓ем** (*i*) in future, henceforth, (*ii*) below, hereinafter.

да́льн|ий *adj.* **1.** distant, remote; **Д. Восто́к** the Far East (*of former USSR*); **⁓ее пла́вание** long voyage; **⁓его де́йствия** long-range. **2.** (*of kinship*) distant. **3.: без ⁓их слов** without further ado.

дальнобо́йный *adj.* (*mil.*) long-range.

дальнови́дност|ь, и *f.* foresight.

дальнови́д|ный (⁓ен, ⁓на) *adj.* far-sighted.

дальнозо́р|кий (⁓ок, ⁓ка) *adj.* long-sighted.

дальнозо́ркост|ь, и *f.* long sight.

дальноме́р, а *m.* range-finder.

да́льност|ь, и *f.* distance; range.

дальтони́зм, а *m.* colour-blindness.

дальто́ник, а *m.* colour-blind person.

да́льше *adj. and adv.* **1.** *comp. of* **далёкий. 2.** (*adv.*) farther; **ти́ше е́дешь, д. бу́дешь** (*prov.*) more haste, less speed. **3.** (*adv.*) further; **расска́зывать д.** to go on (telling a story); **д.!** go on! **4.** (*adv.*) then, next; **они́ не зна́ли, что д. де́лать** they did not know what to do next. **5.** (*adv.*) longer; **ждать д. нельзя́ бы́ло** it was impossible to wait any longer.

да́м|а, ы *f.* **1.** lady. **2.** partner (*in dancing*). **3.** (*cards*) queen.

да́мб|а, ы *f.* dike.

да́мк|а, и *f.* king (*at draughts*).

да́м|ский *adj. of* **⁓а; ⁓ская су́мка** ladies' handbag; **д. уго́дник** ladies' man.

дан, а *m.* (*judo*) dan.

Да́ни|я, и *f.* Denmark.

да́нн|ые, ых *no sg.* **1.** data; facts, information; **необрабо́танные д.** raw data. **2.** qualities, gifts, potentialities.

да́нн|ый *p.p.p. of* **дать** *and adj.* given; present; in question; **в д. моме́нт** at the present moment, at present; **в ⁓ом слу́чае** in this case.

дан|ь, и *f.* **1.** (*hist.*) tribute; **обложи́ть ⁓ью** to lay under tribute. **2.** (*fig.*) tribute; debt; **отда́ть д.** (+*d.*) to appreciate, recognize.

дар, а, *pl.* **⁓ы́** *m.* **1.** gift; donation; **посме́ртный д.** bequest. **2.** (+*g.*) gift (of); **д. сло́ва** (*i*) the gift of the gab, (*ii*) speech, ability to speak.

дарвини́зм, а *m.* Darwinism.

дарвини́ст, а *m.* Darwinist.

дарён|ый *adj.* received as a gift; **⁓ому коню́ в зу́бы не смо́трят** (*prov.*) one should not look a gift horse in the mouth.

дар|и́ть, ю́, ⁓ишь *impf.* (*of* **по⁓**) **1.** (+*d. of pers.*) to give, make a present. **2.** (+*a. of pers. and i.*) to favour (with), bestow (upon); **д. кого́-н. улы́бкой** to bestow a smile upon s.o.

дармое́д, а *m.* (*coll.*) parasite, sponger, scrounger.

дармое́днича|ть, ю *impf.* (*coll.*) to sponge, scrounge.

дармое́дств|о, а *nt.* (*coll.*) parasitism, sponging, scrounging.

дарова́ни|е, я *nt.* gift, talent

дар|ова́ть, у́ю *impf. and pf.* to grant, confer.

дарови́т|ый (⁓, ⁓а) *adj.* gifted, talented.

дарово́й *adj.* free (of charge), gratuitous.

да́ром *adv.* **1.** free (of charge), gratis; **э́то вам д. не пройдёт** you won't get away with this. **2.** in vain, to no purpose; **пропа́сть д.** to be wasted.

дароно́сиц|а, ы *f.* (*eccl.*) pyx.

дарохрани́тельниц|а, ы *f.* (*eccl.*) tabernacle.

да́рственн|ый *adj.* **1.** (*obs.*) received as a gift. **2.** confirming a gift; **⁓ая на́дпись** dedicatory inscription; **⁓ая за́пись** (*leg.*) settlement, deed.

да́т|а, ы *f.* date.

да́тельный *adj.* (*gram.*) dative.

дати́р|овать, ую *impf. and pf.* to date (= (*i*) *affix a date to*, (*ii*) *establish the date of*).

датиро́вк|а, и *f.* dating; **д. по углеро́ду** carbon dating.

да́тский *adj.* Danish.

датча́н|ин, ина, *pl.* **⁓е, ⁓** *m.* Dane.

датча́н|ка, ки *f. of* **⁓ин**

дать, дам, дашь, даст, дади́м, дади́те, даду́т, *past* **дал, дала́, да́ло, да́ли** *pf.* (*of* **дава́ть**) **1.** to give; **д. взаймы́** to lend (*money*). **2.** to give, administer; **д. лека́рство** to give medicine; **д. кому́-н. пощёчину** (*coll.*) to box s.o.'s ears. **3.** (**по**+*d.*, **в**+*a.*; *coll.*) to give (it); to hit; **д. кому́-н. по́ уху** to clip s.o. round the ear; **я те дам!** (*coll.*; *expr. vague threat*) I'll give you what-for! **4.** (*fig.*) to give; **д. кля́тву** to take an oath; **д. нача́ло** (+*d.*) to give rise (to); **д. сло́во** to pledge one's word; **д. себе́ труд** (+*inf.*) to put o.s. to the trouble (of). **5.** (*fig.*) to give, grant; **д. во́лю** (+*d.*) to give (free) rein (to), give vent (to); **д. газ** (*coll.*) to open the throttle; **д. доро́гу** (+*d.*) to make way (for); **не д. поко́я** (+*d.*) to give no peace; **д. кому́-н. сло́во** to give s.o. the floor (*at a meeting*); **д. ход** (+*d.*) to set in motion, get going; **д. ход кому́-н.** (*coll.*) to help s.o. on, give s.o. a leg-up. **6.** + *certain nn. expr. action related to meaning of n.*; **д. залп** to fire a volley; **д. звоно́к** to ring (*a bell*); **д. отбо́й** to ring off (*on telephone*); **д. отпо́р** (+*d.*) to repulse; **д. течь** to spring a leak; **д. тре́щину** to crack. **7.** (+*inf.*) to let; **д. поня́ть** to give to understand; **д. себя́ знать, д. себя́ почу́вствовать** to make o.s. (itself) felt; **да́йте ему́ говори́ть** let him speak. **8.: дай**+*1st pers. of fut. expr. decision to take some action*: **дай вы́купаюсь** I think I'll take a bath. **9.: ни д. ни взять** (*i*) exactly the same, (*ii*) as like as two peas.

да́ться, да́мся, да́шься *etc., past* **да́лся, дала́сь** *pf. of* **дава́ться**

дацзыба́о *nt. indecl.* wall posters (*in China*).

да́ч|а, и *f.* **1.** dacha; **д.-(авто)прице́п** mobile home. **2.: быть на ~е** to be in the country; **пое́хать на ~у** to go to the country.

да́чник, а *m.* (holiday) visitor (*in the country*).

да́ч|ный *adj. of* **~а; д. о́тдых** country holiday; **д. по́езд** suburban train.

два (*f.* две), двух, двум, двумя́, о двух *num.* two; **два-три, две-три** two or three, a couple; **ни д. ни полтора́** (*coll.*) neither one thing nor another; **в двух слова́х** briefly, in short; **в д. счёта** in no time, in two ticks; **в двух шага́х** a short step away; **ка́ждые д. дня** every other day, on alternate days.

двадцати... *comb. form* twenty-.

двадцатиле́ти|е, я *nt.* **1.** period of twenty years. **2.** twentieth anniversary.

двадцатиле́тний *adj.* **1.** twenty-year. **2.** twenty-year-old.

двадцатипятиле́ти|е, я *nt.* **1.** period of twenty-five years. **2.** twenty-fifth anniversary.

двадца́т|ый *adj.* twentieth; **одна́ ~ая** a twentieth; **~ое января́** the twentieth of January; **~ые го́ды** the twenties.

два́дцат|ь, и́, *i.* ью *num.* twenty; **д. оди́н**, etc., twenty-one, etc.

два́жды *adv.* twice; **я́сно как д. два четы́ре** as plain as a pikestaff.

двенадцатипе́рстн|ый *adj.*: **~ая кишка́** (*anat.*) duodenum.

двена́дцатый *adj.* twelfth.

двена́дцат|ь, и *num.* twelve.

двер|но́й *adj. of* **~ь; д. проём** doorway; **~на́я ру́чка** door-handle.

две́р|ца, ы, *g. pl.* **~ец** *f.* door (*of car, cupboard, etc.*).

двер|ь, и, о ~́и, в ~и́, *pl.* **~́и, ~е́й,** *i.* **~я́ми** *and* **~ьми́** *f.* door; **в ~я́х** in the doorway; **при закры́тых ~я́х** behind closed doors, in camera.

две́сти, двухсо́т, двумста́м, двумяста́ми, о двухста́х *num.* two hundred.

дви́гател|ь, я *m.* motor, engine; (*fig.*) mover, motive force.

дви́гательн|ый *adj.* **1.** motive; **~ая си́ла** moving force, impetus. **2.** (*anat.*) motor.

дви́га|ть, ю *and* **дви́жу** *impf.* (*of* **дви́нуть**) **1. (~ю)** to move. **2. (~ю)** (+*i.*) to move (*part of the body*); to make a movement (of). **3. (дви́жу)** to drive; to set in motion; **д. вперёд** (*fig.*) to advance, further.

дви́га|ться, юсь *and* **дви́жусь** *impf.* (*of* **дви́нуться**) **1.** to move (*intrans.*); **д. вперёд** to advance (*also fig.*). **2.** to start, get going. **3.** *pass. of* **~ть**

движе́ни|е, я *nt.* **1.** (*in var. senses*) movement; motion; **д. вперёд** forward movement, advance; **привести́ в д.** to set in motion; **д. сторо́нников ми́ра** peace movement. **2.** (*physical*) movement, exercise. **3.** traffic; **д. в одно́м направле́нии** one-way traffic; **пра́вила у́личного ~я** traffic regulations.

дви́жимост|ь, и *f.* movables, chattels; personal property.

дви́жим|ый *adj.* movable; **~ое иму́щество** movable, personal property.

движко́в|ый *adj.* slide; **~ые регуля́торы** slide controls.

дви́жущ|ий *pres. part. act. of* **дви́гать** *and adj.*: **~ие си́лы** driving force.

дви́|нуть, ну, нешь *pf. of* **~гать**

дви́|нуться, нусь, нешься *pf. of* **~гаться**

дво́е, двои́х *num.* **1.** (+*m. nn. denoting persons, pers. prons. in pl. or nn. used only in pl.*) two; **д. сынове́й** two sons; **нас бы́ло д.** there were two of us; **д. сане́й** two sledges; **д. су́ток** forty-eight hours. **2.** (+*nn. denoting objects usu. found in pairs*) two pairs; **д. чуло́к** two pairs of stockings; **на свои́х (на) двои́х** on Shanks's pony.

двоебо́рь|е, я *nt.* (*sport*) biathlon.

двоебра́чи|е, я *nt.* bigamy.

двоевла́сти|е, я *nt.* diarchy.

двоеже́н|ец, ца *m.* bigamist (*of a man*).

двоежёнств|о, а *nt.* bigamy (*of man*).

двоему́жи|е, я *nt.* bigamy (*of woman*).

двоему́жниц|а, ы *f.* bigamist (*of a woman*).

двоето́чи|е, я *nt.* (*gram.*) colon.

дво́ечник, а *m.* (*coll.*) low-achiever (*pupil receiving an 'unsatisfactory' mark*).

дво|и́ться, ю́сь, и́шься *impf.* **1.** to divide in two (*intrans.*). **2.** to appear double; **у него́ ~и́лось в глаза́х** he saw double.

двои́чн|ый *adj.* (*math.*) binary; **~ая ци́фра** binary digit, bit.

дво́йк|а, и *f.* **1.** (*figure*) two. **2.** (*coll.*) No. 2 (*bus, tram, etc.*). **3.** 'two' (*out of five, acc. to marking system used in Russ. educational establishments*). **4.** (*cards*) two; **д. треф** two of clubs.

двойни́к, а́ *m.* **1.** (*a person's*) double. **2.** (*coll.*) twin.

двойн|о́й *adj.* double, twofold, binary; **д. подборо́док** double chin; **~а́я бухгалте́рия** double-entry book-keeping; **~а́я фами́лия** double-barrelled surname; **вести́ ~у́ю игру́** to play a double game.

дво́|йня, йни, *g. pl.* **~ен** *f.* twins.

дво́йственност|ь, и *f.* **1.** duality. **2.** duplicity.

дво́йствен|ный (~, ~на) *adj.* **1.** dual; **~ное число́** (*gram.*) dual number. **2.** two-faced. **3.** bipartite.

двор, а́ *m.* **1.** yard, court, courtyard. **2.** (*peasant*) homestead. **3.: ско́тный д.** farmyard. **4.: на ~е́** out of doors, outside. **5.** (royal) court; **при ~е́** at court. **6.: быть ко ~у́** to be (found) suitable; **быть не ко ~у́** not to be wanted.

двор|е́ц, ца́ *m.* palace; **Д. бракосочета́ния** Wedding Palace.

дворе́цк|ий, ого *m.* butler, major-domo.

дво́рник, а *m.* **1.** caretaker, janitor. **2.** (*coll.*) windscreen-wiper.

дво́рницк|ий *adj. of* **дво́рник 1.**; *as n.* **~ая, ~ой** *f.* caretaker's lodge.

дворня́г|а, и *f.* (*coll.*) mongrel (dog).

дворня́жк|а, и *f.* = **дворня́га**

дворо́в|ый *adj. of* **двор 1., 2.; ~ые постро́йки** outbuildings, farm buildings; **~ая соба́ка** watch-dog.

дворцо́вый *adj. of* **дворе́ц; д. переворо́т** palace revolution.

дворян|и́н, и́на, *pl.* **~́е, ~́** *m.* noble(man).

дворя́н|ка, ки *f. of* **дворяни́н**

дворя́нск|ий *adj.* of the nobility; of the gentry; **~ое зва́ние** the rank of gentleman.

дворя́нств|о, а *nt.* (*collect.*) nobility, gentry.

двою́родный *adj.* related through grandparent; **д. брат** (first) cousin (*male*); **д. дя́дя** (first) cousin once removed.

двоя́кий *adj.* double, two-fold.

двоя́ко *adv.* in two ways.

двояково́гнутый *adj.* (*phys.*) concavo-concave.

двояковы́пуклый *adj.* (*phys.*) convexo-convex.

дву..., двух... *comb. form* bi-, di-, two-, double-.

двубо́ртный *adj.* double-breasted.

двувидово́й *adj.* (*gram.*) biaspectual.

двугла́в|ый *adj.* two-headed; **~ая мы́шца** (*anat.*)

biceps; **д. орёл** double-headed eagle.
двугла́сн|ый, ого *m.* (*gram.*) diphthong.
двуго́рбый *adj.* two-humped; **д. верблю́д** Bactrian camel.
двугра́нный *adj.* two-sided; dihedral.
двугри́венн|ый, ого *m.* (*coll.*) twenty-kopeck piece.
двудо́льный *adj.* two-part.
двужи́льный *adj.* **1.** (*coll.*) strong; hardy, tough. **2.** (*tech.*) twin-core.
двузна́чный *adj.* two-digit.
двуко́лк|а, и *f.* two-wheeled cart.
двукра́тный *adj.* twofold, double; reiterated.
двули́к|ий (~, ~а) *adj.* two-faced (*also fig.*).
двули́чи|е, я *nt.* double-dealing, duplicity.
двули́чност|ь, и *f.* duplicity.
двули́ч|ный (~ен, ~на) *adj.* (*fig.*) two-faced; duplicitous.
двуно́гий *adj.* two-legged, biped.
двуо́кис|ь, и *f.* (*chem.*) dioxide.
двупла́нный *adj.* two-dimensional.
двупо́лый *adj.* bisexual.
двуправору́кост|ь, и *f.* ambidextrousness.
двуру́чный *adj.* two-handed; two-handled.
двуру́шник, а *m.* double-dealer.
двуру́шнича|ть, ю *impf.* to play a double game.
двуру́шничеств|о, а *nt.* double-dealing.
двуска́тн|ый *adj.*: **~ая кры́ша** gable roof.
двусло́жный *adj.* disyllabic.
двусме́нный *adj.* two-shift.
двусмы́сленност|ь, и *f.* **1.** ambiguity. **2.** double entendre.
двусмы́слен|ный (~, ~на) *adj.* ambiguous.
двуспа́льный *adj.* double (*of beds*).
двуство́лк|а, и *f.* double-barrelled gun.
двуство́льный *adj.* double-barrelled.
двуство́рчат|ый *adj.* bivalve; **~ая две́рь** folding door.
двусторо́нн|ий *adj.* **1.** double-sided; **~ее воспале́ние лёгких** double pneumonia; **ку́ртка ~ей но́ски** reversible jacket. **2.** two-way. **3.** bilateral; **~ее соглаше́ние** bilateral agreement.
двууглеки́сл|ый *adj.* (*chem.*) bicarbonate; **~ая со́да** sodium bicarbonate.
двуутро́бк|а, и *f.* (*zool.*) marsupial.
двухгоди́чный *adj.* two-year.
двухгодова́лый *adj.* two-year-old.
двухдне́вный *adj.* two-day.
двухкварти́рный *adj.* containing two flats.
двухколёсный *adj.* two-wheeled.
двухкра́сочный *adj.* two-tone.
двухле́тний *adj.* **1.** two-year. **2.** two-year-old. **3.** (*bot.*) biennial.
двухле́тник, а *m.* (*bot.*) biennial.
двухма́чтовый *adj.* two-masted.
двухме́стн|ый *adj.* two-seater; **~ая каю́та** two-berth cabin; **д. но́мер** double room.
двухме́сячный *adj.* **1.** two-month. **2.** two-month-old. **3.** (*of periodicals, etc.*) bimonthly.
двухмото́рный *adj.* twin-engined.
двухнеде́льник, а *m.* (*coll.*) fortnightly, biweekly (*magazine, etc.*).
двухнеде́льный *adj.* **1.** two-week. **2.** two-week-old. **3.** (*of publications*) fortnightly, biweekly.
двухпала́тный *adj.* (*pol.*) bicameral, two-chamber.
двухпарти́йный *adj.* (*pol.*) two party; bipartisan.
двухсотле́ти|е, я *nt.* bicentenary.
двухсотле́тний *adj.* **1.** of two hundred year's duration. **2.** bicentenary.
двухсо́тый *adj.* two-hundredth.
двухстепе́нн|ый *adj.*: **~ые вы́боры** indirect elections.
двухсу́точный *adj.* forty-eight-hour.
двухта́ктный *adj.* (*tech.*) two-stroke.
двухто́мник, а *m.* (*coll.*) two-volume book, work.
двухты́сячный *adj.* **1.** two-thousandth. **2.** costing two thousand roubles.
двухцве́тный *adj.* two-coloured.
двухчасово́й *adj.* **1.** two-hour. **2.** (*coll.*) two o'clock.
двухъя́русный *adj.* two-tier(ed).
двухэта́жный *adj.* two-storeyed; double-decker.
двучле́н, а *m.* (*math.*) binomial.
двучле́нный *adj.* (*math.*) binomial.
двуязы́чи|е, я *nt.* bilingualism.
двуязы́ч|ный (~ен, ~на) *adj.* bilingual.
-де (*coll.*) *enclitic particle indicating attribution of utterance to another speaker*; **они́-де не мо́гут прийти́** (they say) they can't come.
дебаркаде́р, а *m.* landing-stage.
дебати́р|овать, ую *impf.* to debate.
деба́т|ы, ов *no sg.* debate.
дебе́л|ый (~, ~а) *adj.* (*coll.*) plump, corpulent.
де́бет, а *m.* debit.
дебет|ова́ть, у́ю *impf. and pf.* to debit.
деби́л, а *m.* moron.
деблоки́р|овать, ую *impf. and pf.* (*mil.*) to relieve, raise the blockade (of).
дебо́ш, а *m.* (*coll.*) riot; uproar, shindy.
дебоши́р, а *m.* (*coll.*) rowdy, brawler, hell-raiser.
дебоши́р|ить, ю, ишь *impf.* (*coll.*) to kick up a row, create a shindy.
дебоши́рств|о, а *nt.* (*coll.*) rowdyism, hell-raising.
де́бр|и, ей *no sg.* **1.** jungle; thickets. **2.** the wilds. **3.** (*fig.*) maze, labyrinth; **запу́таться в ~ях** (+*g.*) to get bogged down in.
дебю́т, а *m.* **1.** début. **2.** (*chess*) opening.
дебюта́нт, а *m.* débutant.
дебюта́нтк|а, и *f.* débutante.
дебюти́р|овать, ую *impf. and pf.* to make one's debut.
дебю́т|ный *adj. of* **~**; **д. спекта́кль** (*theatr.*) début, first performance; **д. ход** (*chess*) opening move.
де́в|а, ы *f.* **1.** (*obs.*) girl, maiden; unmarried girl; **ста́рая д.** (*coll.*) old maid. **2.** **Д.** (*relig.*) the Virgin. **3.** **Д.** (*astron.*) Virgo.
девальва́ци|я, и *f.* (*econ.*) devaluation.
дева́|ть, ю 1. *impf. of* **деть. 2.** (*in past tense* = **деть**) to put, do (with); **куда́ ты ~л письмо́ ?** what have you done with the letter?
дева́|ться, юсь 1. *impf. of* **де́ться; она́ не зна́ла, куда́ д. от смуще́ния** she did not know where to put herself for embarrassment. **2.** (*in past tense* = **де́ться**) to get to, disappear; **куда́ ~лись мои́ часы́?** where has my watch got to?
де́вер|ь, я, *pl.* **~ья́, ~е́й** *and* **~ьёв** (*coll.*) brother-in-law (*husband's brother*).
деви́з, а *m.* motto; device (*in heraldry*).
деви́ц|а, ы *f.* (*obs.*) maiden; damsel.
деви́ческий = **де́ви́чий**
деви́честв|о, а *nt.* girlhood; maidenhood.
де́вич|ий *adj.* girlish; maidenly; **~ья фами́лия** maiden name; **~ья па́мять** (*joc.*) a memory like a sieve.
де́вк|а, и *f.* **1.** (*coll. and dial.*) girl, wench, lass; **засиде́ться в ~ах** to remain on the shelf; **оста́ться в ~ах** to become an old maid. **2.** (*coll.*) tart, whore.
дево́н, а *m.* (*geol.*) Devonian period.
дево́нский *adj.* (*geol.*) Devonian.
де́вочк|а, и *f.* (little) girl.
де́вственник, а *m.* virgin.
де́вственниц|а, ы *f.* virgin.
де́вственност|ь, и *f.* virginity; chastity; **обе́т ~и** vow of chastity.
де́вствен|ный (~, ~на) *adj.* **1.** virgin; **~ная плева́** (*anat.*) hymen. **2.** virginal. **3.** (*fig.*) virgin; **д. лес** virgin forest.
де́вушк|а, и *f.* **1.** (unmarried) girl; young lady. **2.**

(*coll.*; *as mode of address to shop assistant*, *etc.*) miss.

девча́т|а, ~ *no sg.* (*coll.*) girls.

девчо́нк|а, и *f.* (*coll.*) girl.

девяно́ст|о *g.*, *d.*, *i. and p.* **а** *num.* ninety.

девяно́стый *adj.* ninetieth.

де́вятер|о, ы́х *num.* (*+m. nn. denoting persons*, *pers. prons. in pl. or nn. used only in pl.*) nine.

девятиле́тний *adj.* **1.** nine-year. **2.** nine-year-old.

девятисо́тый *adj.* nine-hundredth.

девя́тк|а, и *f.* **1.** (*figure*) nine. **2.** (*coll.*) No. 9 (*bus*, *tram*, *etc.*). **3.** (*coll.*) group of nine objects. **4.** (*cards*) nine.

девятна́дцатый *adj.* nineteenth.

девятна́дцат|ь, и *num.* nineteen.

девя́тый *adj.* ninth.

де́вят|ь, и́, *i.* **ью́** *num.* nine.

девятьсо́т, девятисо́т, девятиста́м, девятьюста́ми, о девятиста́х *num.* nine hundred.

де́вятью *adv.* nine times.

дегаза́тор, а *m.* decontaminator.

дегазацио́нн|ый *adj. of* **дегаза́ция; ~ая часть** decontamination unit.

дегаза́ци|я, и *f.* decontamination.

дегази́р|овать, ую *impf. and pf.* to decontaminate.

дегенера́т, а *m.* degenerate.

дегенерати́в|ный (~ен, ~на) *adj.* degenerate.

дегенера́ци|я, и *f.* degeneration.

дегенери́р|овать, ую *impf. and pf.* to degenerate.

дёг|оть, тя *no pl.*, *m.* tar; **ло́жка ~тя в бо́чке мёда** a fly in the ointment.

деграда́ци|я, и *f.* degradation.

деградир|овать, ую *impf. and pf.* to become degraded.

дегтя́рн|ый *adj.* tar; **~ое мы́ло** coal-tar soap.

дегуста́тор, а *m.* taster.

дегуста́ци|я, и *f.* tasting; **д. вин** wine-tasting.

дегусти́р|овать, ую *impf. and pf.* to carry out a tasting (of).

дед, а *m.* **1.** grandfather; (*pl.*; *fig.*) grandfathers, forefathers. **2.** (*coll.*; *as mode of address to an old man*) grand-dad. **3.: д.-моро́з** Father Christmas, Santa Claus.

де́довский *adj.* **1.** grandfather's. **2.** old-world; old-fashioned.

дедовщи́н|а, ы *f.* (*mil. sl.*) bullying, harassment (*of subordinates*).

дедукти́вный *adj.* deductive.

дедý́кци|я, и *f.* deduction.

дедуци́р|овать, ую *impf. and pf.* to deduce.

де́душк|а, и *m.* grandfather.

дееприча́сти|е, я *nt.* (*gram.*) gerund.

дееприча́ст|ный *adj. of* **~ие**

дееспосо́бност|ь, и *f.* **1.** energy, activity. **2.** (*leg.*) capability.

дееспосо́б|ный (~ен, ~на) *adj.* **1.** energetic, active. **2.** (*leg.*) capable.

дежу́р|ить, ю, ишь *impf.* **1.** to be on duty. **2.** to be in constant attendance, not to leave one's post.

дежу́рн|ый *adj.* **1.** duty; on duty; **д. офице́р** (*mil.*) orderly officer; **д. пункт** (*mil.*) guard-room. **2.: ~ое блю́до** plat du jour. **3.** *as n.* **д., ~ого** *m.*, **~ая, ~ой** *f.* person on duty; **кто д.?** who is on duty? **д. по шко́ле** teacher on duty. **4.** *as n.* **~ая, ~ой** *f.* duty room.

дежу́рств|о, а *nt.* duty; **расписа́ние ~а** rota, (*mil.*) roster; **смени́ться с ~а** to come off duty, be relieved.

дезавуи́р|овать, ую *impf. and pf.* to repudiate, disavow.

дезерти́р, а *m.* deserter.

дезерти́р|овать, ую *impf. and pf.* to desert.

дезерти́рств|о, а *nt.* desertion.

дезинсекцио́нн|ый *adj. of* **дезинсе́кция; ~ые сре́дства** insecticides

дезинсе́кци|я, и *f.* insecticide.

дезинфекта́нт, а *m.* disinfectant.

дезинфекцио́нный *adj. of* **дезинфе́кция**

дезинфе́кци|я, и *f.* disinfection.

дезинфици́р|овать, ую *impf. and pf.* to disinfect.

дезинформа́ци|я, и *f.* disinformation.

дезинформи́р|овать, ую *impf. and pf.* to misinform.

дезодора́нт, а *m.* deodorant.

дезорганиза́ци|я, и *f.* disorganization; disruption.

дезорганиз|ова́ть, у́ю *impf. and pf.* to disorganize; to disrupt.

дезориента́ци|я, и *f.* disorientation.

дезориенти́р|овать, ую *impf. and pf.* to disorient; to confuse.

дезориенти́р|оваться, уюсь *impf. and pf.* to lose one's bearings.

деи́зм, а *m.* deism.

деи́ст, а *m.* deist.

де́йственност|ь, и *f.* efficacy; effectiveness.

де́йствен|ный (~, ~на) *adj.* efficacious; effective.

де́йстви|е, я *nt.* **1.** action, operation; activity; **ввести́ в д.** to put into effect, bring into force. **2.** functioning (*of a machine etc.*). **3.** effect; action; **под ~ем** (*+g.*) under the influence (of); **не ока́зывать никако́го ~я** to have no effect. **4.** action (*of a story*, *etc.*). **5.** act (*of a play*). **6.** (*math.*) operation.

действи́тельно *adv.* really; indeed.

действи́тельност|ь, и *f.* **1.** reality. **2.** realities; conditions, life; **совреме́нная кита́йская д.** present-day conditions in China; **в ~и** in reality, in fact. **3.** validity (*of a document*). **4.** efficacy (*of a medicine*, *etc.*).

действи́тел|ьный (~ен, ~ьна) *adj.* **1.** real, actual; true, authentic; **~ьное положе́ние веще́й** the true state of affairs; **э́то бы́ли его́ ~ьные слова́** these were his actual words; **~ьная слу́жба** (*mil.*) active service; **д. член Акаде́мии нау́к** (full) member of the Academy of Sciences. **2.** valid; **удостовере́ние ~ьно на шесть ме́сяцев** the licence is valid for six months. **3.** efficacious (*of a medicine*, *etc.*). **4.: д. зало́г** (*gram.*) active voice.

де́йств|овать, ую *impf.* **1.** (*impf. only*) to act; to work, function; to operate; **телефо́н не ~ует** the telephone is not working, is out of order. **2.** (*pf.* **по~**) (**на**+*a.*) to have an effect (upon), act (upon); **лека́рство ~ует** the medicine is taking effect; **д. кому́-н. на не́рвы** to get on s.o.'s nerves. **3.** (*impf. only*) (*+i.*; *coll.*) to work, operate; to use.

де́йствующ|ий *pres. part. act. of* **де́йствовать** *and adj.*: **~ая а́рмия** army in the field; **д. вулка́н** active volcano; **~ее лицо́** (*theatr.*, *liter.*) character; **~ие ли́ца** (*theatr.*) dramatis personae.

де́к|а, и *f.* (*mus.*) sounding-board.

декабри́ст, а *m.* (*hist.*) Decembrist.

декабри́ст|ский *adj. of* **~**

дека́бр|ь, я́ *m.* December.

дека́брь|ский *adj. of* **~**

дека́д|а, ы *f.* ten days; ten-day period.

декаде́нт, а *m.* decadent.

декаде́нтский *adj.* decadent.

декаде́нтств|о, а *nt.* decadence.

дека́дник, а *m.* (*pol.*) ten-day campaign.

дека́д|ный *adj. of* **~а**

дека́н, а *m.* dean (*of university*).

декана́т, а *m.* **1.** office of dean (*of university*). **2.** dean's office (*building*).

дека́нств|о, а *nt.* (*of university*) duties of dean, deanship.

деклама́тор, а *m.* reciter, declaimer.

деклама́ци|я, и *f.* recitation, declamation.

деклами́р|овать, ую *impf.* (*of* **про~**) to recite, declaim.
декларати́в|ный (~ен, ~на) *adj.* declaratory; solemn.
деклара́ци|я, и *f.* declaration; **нало́говая д.** tax return.
деклари́р|овать, ую *impf. and pf.* to declare; to proclaim.
деклассиро́ванный *adj.* déclassé.
декольте́ *nt. indecl.* décolleté (*also as adj.*); décolletage.
декольтиро́ванный *adj.* **1.** décolleté. **2.** bare(d).
деко́р, а *m.* décor.
декорати́в|ный (~ен, ~на) *adj.* decorative, ornamental.
декора́тор, а *m.* decorator; scene-painter.
декора́ци|я, и *f.* **1.** scenery, décor. **2.** (*fig.*) window-dressing.
декори́р|овать, ую *impf. and pf.* to decorate.
деко́рум, а *m.* decorum.
декре́т, а *m.* decree.
декрети́р|овать, ую *impf. and pf.* to decree.
декре́тниц|а, ы *f.* (*coll.*) woman on maternity leave.
декре́т|ный *adj. of* **~**; **д. о́тпуск** maternity leave.
де́ланност|ь, и *f.* artificiality; affectation.
де́ланный *p.p.p. of* **де́лать** *and adj.* artificial, forced, affected.
де́ла|ть, ю *impf.* (*of* **с~**) **1.** to make (= *to construct, produce*). **2.** to make (= *to cause to become*); **д. кого́-н. несча́стным** to make s.o. unhappy; **д. из кого́-н. посме́шище** to make a laughing-stock of s.o. **3.** to do; **д. не́чего** it can't be helped; **от не́чего д.** for want of anything better to do. **4.** (+*var. nn.*) to make, do, give; **д. вид** to pretend, feign; **д. вы́воды** to draw conclusions; **д. вы́говор** (+*d.*) to reprimand; **д. гла́зки** (+*d.*; *coll.*) to make eyes (at); **д. комплиме́нт** (+*d.*) to pay a compliment; **д. предложе́ние** (+*d.*) to propose (*marriage*) (to); **д. честь** (+*d.*) (*i*) to honour, (*ii*) to do credit. **5.** (*of distance covered*) to do, make; **д. два́дцать узло́в** (*naut.*) to make twenty knots.
де́ла|ться, юсь *impf.* (*of* **с~**) **1.** to become, get, grow. **2.** to happen; **что там ~ется?** what is going on? **что с ней ~ется?** what is the matter with her? **3.** (*coll.*) to break out, appear.
делега́т, а *m.* delegate.
делега́т|ский *adj. of* **~**
делега́ци|я, и *f.* delegation; group.
делеги́р|овать, ую *impf. and pf.* to delegate.
делёж, а́ *m.* sharing, division; partition.
делёж|ка, ки *f.* (*coll.*) = **~**
деле́ни|е, я *nt.* **1.** (*in var. senses*) division; **д. кле́ток** (*biol.*) cell-fission; **знак ~я** (*math.*) division sign. **2.** (*on graduated scale*) point, degree, unit.
дел|е́ц, ьца́ *m.* (*pej.*) smart operator.
деликате́с, а *m.* delicacy.
делика́тнича|ть, ю *impf.* (*coll.*) to be overnice; (**с**+*i.*) to be too soft with s.o.
делика́тност|ь, и *f.* (*in var. senses*) delicacy.
делика́т|ный (~ен, ~на) *adj.* (*in var. senses*) delicate.
дели́м|ое, ого *nt.* (*math.*) dividend.
дели́мост|ь, и *f.* divisibility.
дели́тел|ь, я *m.* divisor.
дел|и́ть, ю́, ~́ишь *impf.* **1.** (*pf.* **раз~**) to divide; **д. по́ровну** to divide into equal parts; **д. шесть на́ три** to divide six by three. **2.** (*pf.* **по~**) (**с**+*i.*) to share (with); **д. с кем-н. го́ре и ра́дость** to share s.o.'s sorrows and joys.
дел|и́ться, ю́сь ~́ишься *impf.* **1.** (*pf.* **раз~**) (**на**+*a.*) to divide (into). **2.** (*impf. only*) (**на**+*a.*) to be divisible (by). **3.** (*pf.* **по~**) (+*i.*, **с**+*i.*) to share (with); to communicate (to), impart (to); **д. куско́м хле́ба с кем-н.** to share a crust of bread with s.o.; **д. ве́стью с кем-н.** to impart news to s.o.; **д. впечатле́ниями с кем-н.** to compare notes with s.o.
де́л|о, а, *pl.* **~а́, ~, ~а́м** *nt.* **1.** business, affair(s); **ме́жду ~ом** (*coll.*) at odd moments, between times; **по ~у, по ~а́м** on business; **э́то моё д.** that is my affair; **име́ть д.** (**с**+*i.*) to have to do (with), deal (with); **не вме́шивайтесь не в своё д.** mind your own business; **как (ва́ши) ~а́?** how are you getting on?; **за чем д. ста́ло?** what's holding things up?; **привести́ свой ~а́ в поря́док** to put one's affairs in order; **д. в шля́пе** (*coll.*) it's in the bag; **говори́ть д.** to talk sense; **вот э́то д.!** (*coll.*) now you're talking; **д. за ва́ми** it's up to you; **како́е мне до э́того д.?** what has this to do with me?; **пе́рвым ~ом** first of all. **2.** cause; **д. ми́ра** the cause of peace; **э́то д. его́ жи́зни** it's his life's work. **3.** (+*adj.*) occupation; (*obs.*) business, concern; **печа́тное д.** printing; **го́рное д.** mining. **4.** matter point; **д. вку́са** matter of taste; **д. че́сти** point of honour; **д. в том, что...** the point is that ...; **в то́м-то и д.** that's (just) the point; **не в э́том д.** that's not the point; **совсе́м друго́е д.** quite another matter; **д. идёт о** (+*p.*) it is a matter of .... **5.** fact, deed; thing; **на са́мом ~е** in actual fact, as a matter of fact; **и на слова́х и на ~е** in word and deed; **на слова́х..., на ~е же** in theory, nominally ... but actually; **в са́мом ~е** really, indeed. **6.** (*leg.*) case; cause; **вести́ д.** to plead a cause; **возбуди́ть д.** (**про́тив**) to bring an action (against), institute proceedings (against). **7.** file, dossier; **ли́чное д.** personal file. **8.** *idiomatic phrr.*: **то и д.** continually, constantly.
делови́тост|ь, и *f.* business-like character; efficiency.
делови́т|ый (~, ~а) *adj.* business-like; efficient.
делов|о́й *adj.* **1.** business; work; professional; **~а́я пое́здка** business trip. **2.** business-like.
делопроизво́дств|о, а *nt.* office work, clerical work.
де́льн|ый *adj.* **1.** business-like, efficient. **2.** sensible, practical; **~ое предложе́ние** sensible suggestion.
де́льт|а, ы *f.* delta.
дельтапла́н, а *m.* hang-glider (*craft*).
дельтапланери́ст, а *m.* hang-glider (*pers.*).
дельтапланери́ст|ка, ки *f. of* **~**
дельтапла́нер|ный *adj. of* **~и́зм**; **д. спорт** hang-gliding.
дельтапланери́зм, а *m.* hang-gliding.
дельтови́дн|ый *adj.* deltoid; **д. самолёт** delta-wing aircraft.
дельфи́н, а *m.* dolphin.
дельфина́ри|й, я *m.* dolphinarium.
деля́г|а, и *m.* (*coll.*) person pursuing his own interests.
демаго́г, а *m.* demagogue.
демагоги́ческий *adj.* demagogic.
демаго́ги|я, и *f.* demagogy.
демаркацио́нн|ый *adj.*: **~ая ли́ния** line of demarcation.
демарка́ци|я, и *f.* demarcation.
демилитариза́ци|я, и *f.* demilitarization.
демилитаризи́р|овать ую *impf. and pf.* to demilitarize.
демисезо́нн|ый *adj.*: **~ое пальто́** light overcoat (*for spring and autumn wear*).
демобилизацио́нный *adj.* demobilization.
демобилиза́ци|я, и *f.* demobilization.
демобилиз|ова́ть у́ю *impf. and pf.* to demobilize.
демограф|и́ческий *adj. of* **~́ия**; **д. взрыв** population explosion.
демогра́фи|я, и *f.* demography.
демокра́т, а *m.* democrat.
демократиза́ци|я, и *f.* democratization.
демократизи́р|овать, ую *impf. and pf.* to democratize
демократи́ческий *adj.* democratic.

демокра́ти|я, и *f.* democracy; **стра́ны наро́дной ~и** the People's Democracies.
де́мон, а *m.* demon.
демони́ческий *adj.* demonic, demoniacal.
демонстра́нт, а *m* (*pol.*) demonstrator.
демонстрати́в|ный (~ен, ~на) *adj.* **1.** demonstrative, done for effect. **2.** demonstration; **~ная ле́кция** demonstration lecture. **3.** (*mil.*) feint, decoy.
демонстра́тор, а *m.* demonstrator.
демонстра́ци|я, и *f.* **1.** (*in var. senses*) demonstration; **д. му́скулов** (*pol.*) muscle-flexing. **2.** (*public*) showing (*of a film, etc.*); **повто́рная д.** repeat, rerun. **3.** (*mil.*) feint, manœuvre.
демонстри́р|овать, ую *impf. and pf.* **1.** to demonstrate. **2.** (*pf. also* **про~**) to show, display; to give a demonstration (of); **д. но́вый кинофи́льм** to show a new film.
демонта́ж, а *m.* (*tech.*) dismantling.
демонти́р|овать, ую *impf. and pf.* (*tech.*) to dismantle.
деморализа́ци|я, и *f.* demoralization.
деморализ|ова́ть, у́ю *impf. and pf.* to demoralize.
де́мпинг, а *m.* (*econ.*) dumping.
денатура́т, а *m.* methylated spirits.
денатури́р|овать, ую *impf. and pf.* (*chem.*) to denature.
де́нди *m. indecl.* dandy.
дендри́т, а *m.* (*anat.*, *min.*) dendrite.
дендроло́ги|я, и *f.* dendrology.
де́нежный *adj.* **1.** monetary; money; **д. автома́т** cash dispenser; **д. знак** bank-note; **д. перево́д** money order; **д. я́щик** strong-box. **2.** (*coll.*) moneyed; affluent; **д. челове́к** a man of means.
ден|ёк, ька́ *m., dim. of* **день**
де́нно *adv.*: **д. и но́щно** day and night.
деномина́ци|я, и *f.* (*econ.*) denomination.
денонси́р|овать, ую *impf. and pf.* (*dipl.*) to denounce.
денщи́к, а́ *m.* (*mil.*, *obs.*) batman.
де́нь, дня *m.* **1.** day; afternoon; **в 4 ч. дня** at 4 p.m.; **днём** in the afternoon; **д.-деньско́й** all day long; **д. рожде́ния** birthday; **д. откры́тых двере́й** open day; **д. в д.** to the day; **д. ото дня** with every passing day, day by day; **в оди́н прекра́сный д.** one fine day; **изо дня в д.** day after day; **на друго́й, сле́дующий д.** next day; **на днях** (*i*) the other day, (*ii*) one of these days; any day now; **не по дням, а по часа́м** hourly, fast, rapidly; **со дня на́ д.** daily, from day to day; **че́рез д.** every other day; **Д. сме́ха** April Fool's Day; **Д. поминове́ния** Remembrance Day; **второ́й д. Рождества́** Boxing Day. **2.** (*pl.*) days (= (*i*) *time, period*, (*ii*) *life*); **его́ дни сочтены́** his days are numbered.
де́н|ьги, ег, ьга́м *pl.* money; **кро́вные д.** hard-earned money; **ме́лкие д.** small change; **нали́чные д.** cash, ready money; **при ~ьга́х** in funds; **не при ~ьга́х** hard up; **не за каки́е д.** not for all the tea in China.
департа́мент, а *m.* department.
депе́ш|а, и *f.* dispatch
депо́ *nt. indecl.* (*rail.*) depot; shed, roundhouse; **пожа́рное д.** fire-station.
депози́т, а *m.* (*fin.*) deposit.
депозита́ри|й, я *m.* depository.
депози́тор, а *m.* (*fin.*) depositor.
депоне́нт, а *m* (*fin.*) depositor.
депони́р|овать, ую *impf. and pf.* (*fin.*, *leg.*) to deposit.
депорта́ци|я, и *f.* deportation.
депорти́р|овать, ую *impf. and pf.* to deport.
депресси́вн|ый *adj. of* **депре́ссия; д. пери́од** (*econ.*) depression, slump; **~ое состоя́ние** (*econ. and psych.*) depression.
депре́сси|я, и *f.* **1.** (*econ.*) depression, slump. **2.** (*psych.*) depression.
депута́т, а *m.* deputy; delegate; **пала́та ~ов** Chamber of Deputies.
депута́ци|я, и *f.* deputation.
де́рвиш, а *m.* dervish.
дёрга|ть, ю *impf.* (*of* **дёрнуть**) **1.** to pull, tug; **д. кого́-н. за рука́в** to tug at s.o.'s sleeve. **2.** to pull out; **д. зу́бы** (*i*) to extract teeth, (*ii*) to have teeth out (*at the dentist's*). **3.** (*impf. only*) to harass, pester. **4.** (*impf. only*) (*coll.*) to cause to twitch; (*impers.*) to twitch; **его́ всего́ ~ло** he was twitching all over. **5.** (*impf. only*) (*+i.*; *coll.*) to jerk; **д. плеча́ми** to shrug one's shoulders.
дёрга|ться, юсь *impf.* (*of* **дёрнуться**) **1.** *pass. of* **~ть. 2.** to twitch.
дерга́ч, а́ *m.* (*zool.*) landrail, corncrake.
деревене́|ть, ю *impf.* (*of* **о~**) to grow stiff, numb.
дереве́нский *adj.* **1.** village. **2.** rural, country.
дереве́нщин|а, ы *c.g.* (*coll.*) (country) bumpkin.
дере́в|ня, ни, *g. pl.* **~е́нь** *f.* **1.** village. **2.** (the) country (*opp. the town*).
де́рев|о, а, *pl.* **∠ья, ∠ьев** *nt.* **1.** tree; **за ∠ьями ле́са не ви́деть** not to see the wood for the trees. **2.** (*sg. only*) wood (*as material*).
деревообде́лочник, а *m.* woodworker.
деревообде́лочный *adj.* wood-working.
дереву́шк|а, и *f.* hamlet.
де́ревц|е, а *and* **деревц|о́, а́** *nt.* sapling.
деревяни́ст|ый (~, ~а) *adj.* **1.** ligneous. **2.** hard (*of fruit, etc.*).
деревя́нн|ый *adj.* **1.** wood; wooden. **2.** (*fig.*) wooden; expressionless; dull; **~ое выраже́ние лица́** wooden expression; **д. го́лос** expressionless voice.
деревя́шк|а, и *f.* **1.** piece of wood. **2.** (*coll.*) wooden leg; peg leg.
держа́в|а, ы *f.* (*pol.*) power; **вели́кие ~ы** the Great Powers.
держа́лк|а, и *f.* (*coll.*) handle.
держа́тел|ь, я *m.* **1.** (*fin.*) holder. **2.** bracket; socket; holder.
держ|а́ть, у́, ∠ишь *impf.* **1.** to hold; to hold on to; **~и́те во́ра!** stop thief! **2.** to hold up, support. **3.** (*in var. senses*) to keep, hold; **д. в посте́ли** to keep in bed; **д. курс** (**на**+*a.*) to head (for); (*fig.*) to be working (for); **д. путь** (**к, на**+*a.*) to head (for), make (for); **д. чью-н. сто́рону** to take s.o.'s side; **д. язы́к за зуба́ми** to hold one's tongue; **д. в ку́рсе** to keep posted; **д. в неве́дении** to keep in the dark; **д. в плену́** to hold prisoner. **4.** to keep (= *to own, possess*); **д. лошаде́й** to keep horses. **5. д. себя́** to behave. **6.** + *certain nn.* = *to carry out*; **д. ре́чь** to make a speech; **д. экза́мен** to sit, take an examination.
держ|а́ться, у́сь, ∠ишься *impf.* **1.** (**за**+*a.*) to hold (on to); **~и́тесь за пери́ла** hold on to the banister. **2.** (**на**+*p.*) to be held up (by), be supported (by); **д. на ни́точке** to hang by a thread (*also fig.*). **3.** to keep, stay, be; **д. вме́сте** to stick together; **д. в стороне́** to hold aloof. **4.** to hold o.s.; (*fig.*) to behave. **5.** to last; to hold together; **э́тот стол у вас е́ле ∠ится** this table of yours is on its last legs. **6.** to hold out, stand firm. **7.** (+*g.*) to keep (to); **д. ле́вой стороны́** to keep to the left; **д. бе́рега** to hug the shore. **8.** (+*g.*) to adhere (to), stick (to); **д. те́мы** to stick to the subject.
дерза́ни|е, я *nt.* daring.
дерз|а́ть, а́ю *impf.* (*of* **~ну́ть**) to dare.
дерз|и́ть, (у́), и́шь *impf.* (*of* **на~**) (+*d.*; *coll.*) to be impertinent (to), cheek.
де́рз|кий (~ок, ~ка́, ~ко) *adj.* **1.** impertinent, cheeky. **2.** daring, audacious.
дерзнове́ни|е, я *nt.* (*obs.*) audacity.
дерзнове́н|ный (~ен, ~на) *adj.* daring, audacious.

дерзн|у́ть, у́, ёшь *pf. of* **дерза́ть**
де́рзост|ь, и *f.* **1.** impertinence; cheek; rudeness; **говори́ть ~и** to be impertinent, cheeky, rude. **2.** daring, audacity.
дерива́т, а *m.* (*tech.*) derivative.
дермати́н, а *m.* leatherette.
дермати́т, а *m.* dermatitis.
дермато́лог, а *m.* dermatologist.
дерматоло́ги|я, и *f.* dermatology.
дёрн, а *m.* turf.
дерни́ст|ый (~, ~а) *adj.* turfy.
дерн|ова́ть, у́ю *impf.* to cover with turf; to make a turf edging round.
дёрн|уть, у, ешь *pf.* **1.** *pf. of* **дёргать; чёрт ~ет (~ул), нелёгкая ~ет (~ула)** *or* (*impers.*) **~ет (~уло) кого́-н.** (*+inf.*; *coll.*) to be possessed (to do sth.); **чёрт меня́ ~ул дать сло́во** I don't know what possessed me to promise. **2.** to get going, get cracking. **3.** (*coll.*) to go off. **4.** (*coll.*) to drink up; to take a swig. **5.** (*coll.*) to start vigorously to do sth.; **д. пля́сову́ю** to strike up a (dance) tune.
дёрн|уться, усь, ешься *pf.* (*of* **дёргаться**) to start up (with a jerk), to dart.
дер|у́, ёшь *see* **драть**
дерьм|о́, а́ *nt.* (*vulg.*) dung, muck (*also fig.*).
дерьмо́вый *adj.* (*coll.*) crappy (= *inferior*).
дерю́г|а, и *f.* sackcloth, sacking.
дерю́жный *adj.* sackcloth.
деса́нт, а *m.* (*mil.*) **1.** landing. **2.** landing force.
деса́нтник, а *m.* paratrooper.
деса́нтный *adj.* (*mil.*) landing.
десе́рт, а *m.* dessert.
десе́рт|ный *adj. of* **~**; **~ная ло́жка** dessert spoon.
де́скать *particle indicating reported speech* (*coll.*): **она́, д., ничего́ подо́бного не хоте́ла сказа́ть** she said she had not meant anything of the kind.
десн|а́, ы́, *pl.* **~ы, дёсен** *f.* (*anat.*) gum.
десни́ц|а, ы *f.* (*obs. or poet.*) right hand.
де́спот, а *m.* despot.
деспоти́зм, а *m.* despotism.
деспоти́ческий *adj.* despotic.
деспоти́ч|ный (~ен, ~на) *adj.* despotic.
деспоти́|я, и *f.* despotism.
дестабилизи́р|овать, ую *impf. and pf.* (*pol.*) to destabilize.
дест|ь, и, *g. pl.* **~е́й** *f.* quire (*of paper*) (**ру́сская д.** = 24 sheets; **метри́ческая д.** = 50 sheets).
де́сятер|о, ы́х *num.* (*+m. nn. denoting persons, pers. prons. in pl. or nn. used only in pl.*) ten.
десятибо́р|ец, ца *m.* decathlete.
десятибо́рь|е, я *nt.* (*sport*) decathlon.
десятигра́нник, а *m.* decahedron.
десятизу́б|ый *adj.*: **~ые ко́шки** (*mountaineering*) crampons.
десятикра́тный *adj.* tenfold.
десятиле́ти|е, я *nt.* **1.** decade. **2.** tenth anniversary.
десятиле́тк|а, и *f.* ten-year (secondary) school.
десятиле́тний *adj.* **1.** ten-year. **2.** ten-year-old.
десяти́н|а, ы *f.* **1.** dessiatine, desyatin (*old Russ. land measure, equivalent to 1.09 hectares*). **2.** tithe.
десятирублёвк|а, и *f.* (*coll.*) ten-rouble note.
десятиуго́льник, а *m.* (*math.*) decagon.
десяти́чн|ый *adj.* decimal; **~ая дробь** decimal fraction.
деся́тка, и *f.* **1.** (*figure*) ten. **2.** (*coll.*) No. 10 (*bus, tram, etc.*). **3.** (*coll.*) group of ten objects. **4.** (*cards*) ten. **5.** (*coll.*) ten-rouble note.
деся́тник, а *m.* (*obs.*) foreman.
деся́т|ок, ка *m.* **1.** ten. **2.** ten years, decade (*of life*). **3.** (*pl.*) (*math.*) tens. **4.** (*pl.*) tens. **5.: не ро́бкого ~ка** plucky.
деся́т|ый *num.* tenth; **э́то де́ло ~ое** (*coll.*) it is of no consequence.
де́сят|ь, и́, ью́ *num.* ten.
де́сятью *adv.* ten times (*in multiplication*).
дет... *comb. form, abbr. of* **де́тский**
детализа́ци|я, и *f.* working out in detail.
детализи́р|овать, ую *and* **детализ|ова́ть, у́ю** *impf. and pf.* to work out in detail.
дета́л|ь, и *f.* **1.** detail. **2.** part, component.
дета́л|ьный (~ен, ~ьна) *adj.* detailed; minute.
детвор|а́, ы́ *no pl., f.* (*collect.*; *coll.*) children.
детдо́м, а *m.* children's home.
детдо́мов|ец, ца *m.* (*coll.*) resident of a children's home.
детекти́в, а *m.* **1.** detective. **2.** detective story; whodunit.
детекти́вный *adj.*: **д. рома́н** detective story.
дете́ктор, а *m.* (*tech.*) detector; spark indicator.
детёныш, а *m.* young (*of animals*).
детерміни́зм, а *m.* determinism.
детермини́ст, а *m.* determinist.
де́т|и, ~е́й, ~ям, ~ьми́, о ~ях *pl.* (*sg.* **дитя́** *nt.*) children.
дети́н|а, ы *m.* (*coll.*) big fellow, hefty chap.
де́тищ|е, а, *g. pl.* **~** *nt.* child, offspring; (*fig.*) child, creation; brainchild.
детона́тор, а *m.* (*tech.*) detonator.
детона́ци|я, и *f.* (*tech.*) detonation.
детони́р|овать[1], ую *impf.* (*tech.*) to detonate.
детони́р|овать[2], ую *impf.* to sing, play out of tune.
деторо́дный *adj.* genital.
деторожде́ни|е, я *nt.* procreation.
детоуби́йств|о, а *nt.* infanticide (*action*).
детоуби́йц|а, ы *c.g.* infanticide (*agent*).
детплоща́дк|а, и *f.* playground.
детса́д, а *m.* kindergarten, nursery school; **д.-я́сли** day nursery.
детса́дов|ец, ца *m.* (*coll.*) child attending kindergarten.
де́тск|ая, ой *f.* nursery.
де́тск|ий *adj.* **1.** child's, children's; **д. дом** children's home; **д. сад** kindergarten, nursery school; **~ая сме́ртность** infant mortality; **д. труд** child labour. **2.** childish; **д. язы́к** baby-talk. **3.: ~ое ме́сто** (*anat.*) placenta.
де́тств|о, а *nt.* childhood; **с ~а** from childhood, from a child; **впада́ть в д.** to lapse into dotage.
деть, де́ну, де́нешь *pf.* (*of* **дева́ть**) to put, do (with); **куда́ ты дел моё перо́?** what have you done with my pen?; **не знать, куда́ глаза́ д.** not to know where to look.
де́|ться, нусь, нешься *pf.* (*of* **дева́ться**) to get to, disappear.
де-фа́кто *adv.* de facto.
дефе́кт, а *m.* defect.
дефекти́в|ный (~ен, ~на) *adj.* defective; handicapped; **д. ребёнок** (mentally) defective *or* (physically) handicapped child.
дефе́ктный *adj.* imperfect, faulty.
дефекто́лог, а *m.* specialist in mental defects and physical handicaps (*in children*).
дефектол|оги́ческий *adj. of* **~о́гия**
дефектоло́ги|я, и *f.* study of mental defects and physical handicaps.
дефили́р|овать, ую *impf.* (*of* **про~**) to march past, go in procession.
дефи́с, а *m.* hyphen.
дефици́т, а *m.* **1.** (*econ.*) deficit; **д. торго́вого бала́нса** trade gap. **2.** shortage, deficiency; **д. в то́пливе** fuel shortage.
дефици́т|ный (~ен, ~на) *adj.* **1.** (*econ.*) loss-making. **2.** in short supply; scarce.
дефля́ция, и *f.* (*econ.*) deflation.
деформа́ци|я, и *f.* deformation.
деформи́р|овать, ую *impf. and pf.* to deform; to

transform.

деформи́р|оваться, уюсь *impf. and pf.* to change one's shape; to become deformed.

децентрализа́ци|я, и *f.* decentralization.

децентрализ|ова́ть, у́ю *impf. and pf.* to decentralize.

деци... *comb. form* deci-.

децили́тр, а *m.* decilitre.

децима́льный *adj.* decimal.

децимéтр, а *m.* decimetre.

дешевé|ть, ю *impf.* (*of* **по~**) to fall in price, become cheaper.

дешеви́зн|а, ы *f.* cheapness; low price.

дешёвк|а, и *f.* **1.** low price; **купи́ть по ~е** to buy cheap. **2.** (*fig.*) cheap stuff; worthless object.

дешéвле *comp. of* **дешёвый** *or* **дёшево; д. пáреной рéпы** dirt-cheap.

дёшево *adv.* cheap, cheaply; (*fig.*) cheaply, lightly; **д. и серди́то** cheap but good; **д. отдéлаться** to get off lightly; **э́то вам д. не пройдёт** this will cost you dear.

дешёв|ый (дёшев, дешевá, дёшево) *adj.* **1.** cheap, inexpensive. **2.** (*fig.*) cheap; worthless; **~ая остротá** cheap crack.

дешифри́р|овать, ую *impf. and pf.* to decipher; to decode.

дешифрóвк|а, и *f.* deciphering; decoding.

деэскалáци|я, и *f.* (*mil., pol.*) de-escalation.

де-ю́ре *adv.* de jure.

дея́ни|е, я *nt.* (*obs. or rhet.*) act; action; **Дея́ния апóстолов** the Acts of the Apostles.

дéятел|ь, я *m.* agent; **госудáрственный д.** statesman; **общéственный д.** public figure; **полити́ческий д.** politician.

дéятельност|ь, и *f.* **1.** activity, activities; work; **общéственная д.** public work; **педагоги́ческая д.** educational work. **2.** (*physiol, psych., etc.*) activity, operation; **д. сéрдца** operation of the heart.

дéятел|ьный (~ен, ~ьна) *adj.* active, energetic.

джаз, а *m.* jazz.

джаз-ансáмбл|ь, я *m.* jazz-combo.

джаз-бáнд, а *m.* jazz band.

джази́ст, а *m.* jazzman, jazz musician.

джазмéн, а *m.* = **джази́ст**

джаз-му́зык|а, и *f.* jazz.

джáзовый *adj.* jazz.

джем, а *m.* jam.

джéмпер, а *m.* jumper.

джентльмéн, а *m.* gentleman.

джентльмéнск|ий *adj.* gentlemanly; **~ое соглашéние** gentlemen's agreement.

джентльмéнств|о, а *nt.* gentlemanliness.

джерсé *nt. indecl.* = **джéрси́**

джéрси́ *nt. indecl.* jersey (*material*).

джерсóвый *adj. of* **джéрси́**

джи́г|а, и *f.* jig.

джиги́т, а *m.* Dzhigit (*Caucasian horseman*).

джиги́тóвк|а, и *f.* trick riding (*originally by Caucasian horsemen*).

джин, а *m.* gin (*liquor*); **д. с тóником** gin and tonic.

джинн, а *m.* genie.

джинсóвый *adj.* denim.

джи́нс|ы, ов *no sg.* jeans.

джип, а *m.* jeep.

джи́у-джи́тсу *nt. indecl.* ju-jitsu.

джóггинг, а *m.* jogging, fun-running; jog, fun-run.

джóйстик, а *m.* (*comput.*) joystick.

джóнк|а, и *f.* junk (*Chinese sailing vessel*).

джóул|ь, я, *g. pl.* **~ей** *m.* (*phys.*) joule.

джу́нгл|и, ей *no sg.*, jungle; **«шкóльные д.»** 'blackboard jungle'.

джут, а *m.* jute.

джу́т|овый *adj. of* **~**

ДЗУ *nt. indecl.* (*abbr. of* **долговрéменное запоминáющее устрóйство**) (*comput.*) ROM (*read-only memory*).

дзэн-будди́зм, а *m.* Zen-Buddhism.

дзю(-)дó *nt. indecl.* judo.

дзюдои́ст, а *m.* judoist, judoka.

диабéт, а *m.* diabetes.

диабéтик, а *nt.* diabetic.

диáгноз, а *nt.* diagnosis.

диагнóст, а *m.* diagnostician.

диагнóстик|а, и *f.* diagnostics.

диагности́р|овать, ую *impf. and pf.* to diagnose.

диагонáл|ь, и *f.* diagonal; **по ~и** diagonally.

диагонáл|ьный (~ен, ~ьна) *adj.* diagonal.

диагрáмм|а, ы *f.* diagram; chart; **круговáя д.** pie chart.

диадéм|а, ы *f.* diadem.

диакрити́ческий *adj.*: **д. знак** (*ling.*) diacritical mark.

диалéкт, а *m.* dialect.

диалéктик, а, *m.* (*phil.*) dialectician.

диалéктик|а, и *f.* (*phil.*) dialectics.

диалекти́ческий *adj.* (*phil.*) dialectical.

диалéктный *adj.* (*ling.*) dialectal.

диалектологи́ческий *adj.* (*ling.*) dialectological.

диалектолóги|я, и *f.* (*ling.*) dialectology.

диалóг, а *m.* dialogue.

диалоги́ческий *adj.* having dialogue form.

диалóговый *adj.* (*comput.*) interactive.

диамáт, а *m.* (*abbr. of* **диалекти́ческий материали́зм**) dialectical materialism.

диáметр, а *m.* diameter.

диаметрáльно *adv.*: **д. противополóжный** diametrically opposite.

диаметрáльный *adj.* diametrical.

диапазóн, а *m.* **1.** (*mus.*) range. **2.** (*fig.*) range, compass; **у негó óчень большóй д. интерéсов** he has a very wide range of interests. **3.** (*tech.*; *fig.*) range; **д. волн** (*radio*) wave band.

диапозити́в, а *m.* (*phot.*) slide, transparency.

диафрáгм|а, ы *f.* diaphragm.

ди́в|а, ы *f.* (*obs.*) diva, prima donna.

диван, а *m.* divan (*couch*); sofa; **д.-кровáть** sofa bed.

ди́вáн|ный *adj. of* **~**.

диверсáнт, а *m.* saboteur.

дивéрси|я, и *f.* **1.** (*mil.*) diversion. **2.** sabotage.

дивидéнд, а *m.* dividend.

дивизиóн, а *m.* (*mil.*) battalion.

дивизиóн|ный *adj.* **1.** *adj. of* **диви́зия; д. комáндный пункт** division command post. **2.** *adj. of* **~**

диви́зи|я, и *f.* (*mil.*) division.

див|и́ть, лю́, и́шь *impf.* (*coll.*) to amaze.

див|и́ться, лю́сь, и́шься *impf.* (*of* **по~**) (*+d.*) to wonder, marvel (at); (**на**+*a.*) to look upon with wonder.

ди́в|ный (~ен, ~на) *adj.* **1.** amazing; remarkable. **2.** marvellous, wonderful.

ди́в|о, а *nt.* wonder, marvel; **~у дáться** to wonder, marvel; **что за д.!** how extraordinary!; **на д.** marvellously; *as pred.* it is amazing; **не д.** it is no wonder.

дидакти́ческий *adj.* didactic.

диéз, а *m.* (*and as indecl. adj.*) (*mus.*) sharp; **ре-д.** D sharp.

диéт|а, ы *f.* diet; **посади́ть на ~у** to put on a diet; **соблюдáть ~у** to keep to a diet.

диетéтик|а, и *f.* dietetics.

диетети́ческий *adj.* dietetic.

диетóлог, а *m.* nutritionist.

дизáйн, а *m.* design.

дизáйнер, а *m.* designer.

ди́зел|ь, я *m.* diesel engine.

ди́зельный *adj.* diesel

дизентери́|я, и *f.* dysentery.
дика́р|ский *adj. of* **~ь**
дика́рств|о, а *nt.* shyness.
дика́р|ь, я́ *m.* **1.** savage; (*fig.*) barbarian. **2.** (*fig., coll.*) unsociable person; loner.
ди́к|ий (~, ~а́, ~о) *adj.* **1.** wild (*opp. tame, cultivated*); **~ая ко́шка** wild cat; **~ое я́блоко** crab-apple. **2.** savage (= *pertaining to primitive society*; *also as n.* **д., ~ого** *m.*). **3.** wild (= *unrestrained*); **~ие кри́ки** wild cries; **д. восто́рг** wild delight. **4.** absurd; preposterous. **5.** shy; unsociable. **6.: ~ое мя́со** (*med.*) proud flesh.
ди́к|о[1] *adv.* **1.** *adv. of* **~ий. 2.** in fright; startled; **д. озира́ться** to look around wildly.
ди́ко[2] *as pred.* it is absurd, it is ridiculous; **д. задава́ть таки́е вопро́сы** it is ridiculous to ask such a question.
дикобра́з, а *m.* porcupine.
дико́вин|а, ы *and* **~ка, ~ки** *f.* (*coll.*) marvel, wonder; **э́то мне не в ~(к)у** I see nothing remarkable about it.
дико́винный *adj.* strange, unusual, remarkable.
дикорасту́щий *adj.* wild.
ди́кост|ь, и *f.* **1.** wildness; savagery. **2.** shyness; unsociableness. **3.** absurdity; **э́то соверше́нная д.** it is quite absurd.
дикта́нт, а *m.* dictation.
дикта́т, а *m.* (*pol.*) diktat.
дикта́тор, а *m.* dictator.
дикта́торский *adj.* dictatorial.
дикта́торств|о, а *nt.* **1.** dictatorship. **2.** (*coll.*) dictatorial attitude.
диктату́р|а, ы *f.* dictatorship.
дикт|ова́ть, у́ю, у́ешь *impf.* (*of* **про~**) to dictate.
дикто́вк|а, и *f.* dictation; **под чью-н. ~у** to s.o.'s dictation; (*fig.*) at s.o.'s bidding.
ди́ктор, а *m.* (radio-)announcer.
диктофо́н, а *m.* Dictaphone (*propr.*).
ди́кци|я, и *f.* diction; enunciation.
диле́мм|а, ы *f.* dilemma.
ди́лер, а *m.* dealer.
дилета́нт, а *m.* dilettante, dabbler.
дилета́нтств|о, а *nt.* dilettantism.
дилижа́нс, а *m.* stage-coach.
динами́зм, а *m.* dynamism.
дина́мик, а *m.* loudspeaker.
дина́мик|а, и *f.* dynamics.
динами́т, а *m.* dynamite.
динами́ческий *adj.* dynamic.
дина́мо *nt. indecl.* dynamo.
дина́р, а *m.* dinar.
династи́ческий *adj.* dynastic.
дина́сти|я, и *f.* dynasty; **д. Тюдо́ров** the House of Tudor.
ди́нго *m. indecl.* (*zool.*) dingo.
диноза́вр, а *m.* dinosaur.
дио́д, а *m.*: **светоизлуча́ющий д.** light-emitting diode, LED.
дип... *comb. form, abbr. of* **дипломати́ческий**
дипло́м, а *m.* diploma; degree (*certificate*).
диплома́нт, а *m.* diploma-winner.
диплома́т, а *m.* **1.** diplomat (*lit. and fig.*). **2.** (*coll.*) attaché case.
диплома́тик|а, и *f.* (*palaeog.*) diplomatic(s).
дипломати́ческий *adj.* diplomatic; **д. курье́р** diplomatic courier; Queen's Messenger.
дипломати́ч|ный (~ен, ~на) *adj.* (*fig.*) diplomatic.
диплома́ти|я, и *f.* diplomacy; **д. каноне́рок** gunboat diplomacy.
дипломи́рованный *adj.* graduate; professionally qualified.
дипло́м|ный *adj. of* **~; ~ная рабо́та** degree work, degree thesis.
директи́в|а, ы *f.* directive; instruction.
дире́ктор, а, *pl.* **~а́** *m.* director, manager; **д. шко́лы** head (master, mistress); principal.
дире́кци|я, и *f.* management; board (of directors).
дирижа́бл|ь, я *m.* airship, dirigible.
дирижёр, а *m.* conductor (*of band or orchestra*).
дирижёр|ский *adj. of* **~; ~ская па́лочка** conductor's baton.
дирижи́р|овать, ую *impf.* (*+i.*; *mus.*) to conduct.
дисгармони́р|овать, ую *impf.* **1.** (*mus.*) to be out of tune. **2.** (*fig.*) to clash, jar.
дисгармо́ни|я, и *g.* (*mus. and fig.*) disharmony; discord.
диск, а *m.* **1.** disk; dial. **2.** (*sport*) discus. **3.** disc, record.
ди́скант, а *m.* (*mus.*) treble.
дисквалифика́ци|я, и *f.* disqualification.
дисквалифици́р|овать, ую *impf. and pf.* to disqualify.
диске́т, а *m.* (*comput.*) diskette; **пусто́й д.** blank diskette.
диске́т|а, ы *f.* = **диске́т**
диск-жоке́|й, я *m.* disc-jockey.
дискобо́л, а *m.* discus-thrower.
дискове́чер, а *m.* disco(thèque) (*event*).
дисково́д, а *m.* (*comput.*) disk drive.
ди́сков|ый *adj.* disc-shaped; **~ая борона́** disc-harrow.
дискоте́к|а, и *f.* disco(thèque) (*place*).
дискоте́|чный *adj. of* **~ка**
дискредити́р|овать, ую *impf. and pf.* to discredit.
дискриминацио́нный *adj.* discriminatory.
дискримина́ци|я, и *f.* discrimination; **д. же́нщин** sexism; **д. по во́зрасту** ageism.
дискримини́р|овать, ую *impf. and pf.* to discriminate (against); **д. национа́льные меньшинства́** to discriminate against national minorities.
дискуссио́нн|ый *adj.* **1.** *adj. of* **диску́ссия; д. клуб** debating club; **в ~ом поря́дке** as a basis for discussion. **2.** debatable, open to question.
диску́сси|я, и *f.* discussion.
дискути́р|овать, ую *impf. and pf.* (*+a. or* **о**+*p.*) to discuss.
дислока́ци|я, и *f.* **1.** (*mil.*) stationing, distribution (*of troops*). **2.** (*med.*) dislocation.
дислоци́р|овать, ую *impf. and pf.* (*mil.*) to station (*troops*).
диспансе́р, а *m.* (*med.*) clinic, (health) centre.
диспепси́|я, и *f.* dyspepsia.
диспе́тчер, а *m.* controller (*of movement of transport, etc.*).
диспе́тчер|ский *adj. of* **~;** (*aeron.*): **~ская вы́шка** control tower; *as n.* **~ская, ~ской** *f.* controller's office; (*aeron.*) control tower.
диспле́|й, я *m.* (*comput.*) display, VDU (*visual display unit*).
ди́спут, а *m.* (public) debate.
диссерта́нт, а *m.* author of dissertation.
диссерта́ци|я, и *f.* dissertation, thesis.
диссиде́нт, а *m.* (*relig.*) nonconformist.
диссона́нс, а *m.* (*mus. and fig.*) dissonance, discord.
диссони́р|овать, ую *impf.* to strike a discordant note, be discordant.
дистанцио́нн|ый *adj.*: **~ое управле́ние** remote control.
диста́нци|я, и *f.* **1.** distance; **на большо́й, ма́лой ~и** at a great, short distance. **2.** (*sport*) distance; **сойти́ с ~и** to withdraw, scratch.
дистилли́р|овать, ую *impf. and pf.* to distil.
дистилля́ци|я, и *f.* distillation.
дистрофи́|я, и *f.* (*med.*) dystrophy.
дисципли́н|а, ы *f.* (*in var. senses*) discipline.
дисциплина́рный *adj.* disciplinary; **д. батальо́н**

penal battalion.

дисциплини́рова|нный *p.p.p. of* **~ть** *and adj.* disciplined.

дисциплини́р|овать, ую *impf. and pf.* to discipline.

дитя́, *g. and d.* **~ти,** *i.* **~тею,** *p.* **о ~ти,** *pl.* **де́ти** *nt.* child; baby.

дифира́мб, а *m.*: **петь ~ы** (+*d.*) to sing the praises (of), extol, eulogize.

дифтер|и́йный *adj. of* **~и́я**; diphtheritic.

дифтер|и́т, а *m.* = **~и́я**

дифтери́|я, и *f.* diphtheria.

дифто́нг, а *m.* diphthong.

диффама́ци|я, и *f.* (*leg.*) defamation, libel.

дифференциа́л, а *m.* **1.** (*math.*) differential. **2.** (*tech.*) differential gear.

дифференциа́льн|ый *adj.* differential; **~ое исчисле́ние** (*math.*) differential calculus.

дифференци́р|овать, ую *impf. and pf.* to differentiate.

growth

дича́|ть, ю *impf.* (*of* **о~**) to run wild, become wild; (*fig.*) to become unsociable.

дич|и́ться, у́сь, и́шься *impf.* (+*g.*; *coll.*) to be shy (of); to avoid.

дич|ь, и *f.* **1.** (*collect.*) game; wildfowl. **2.** wilderness, wilds. **3.** (*coll.*) nonsense; **поро́ть д.** to talk nonsense.

длин|а́, ы́ *f.* length; **в ~у́** lengthwise; **~о́й в шесть ме́тров** six metres long.

длинно... *comb. form* long-.

длинново́лновый *adj.* (*radio*) long-wave.

длиннот|а́, ы́, *pl.* **~́ы** *f.* **1.** (*obs or coll.*) length. **2.** (*pl.*) longueurs, prolixities.

длиннофо́кусный *adj.*: **д. объекти́в** telephoto lens.

дли́н|ный (~ен, ~на́, ~но) *adj.* long; lengthy; **д. рубль** (*coll.*) easy money; **у него́ д. язы́к** he has a long tongue.

дли́тельност|ь, и *f.* duration.

дли́тел|ьный (~ен, ~ьна) *adj.* long, protracted, long-drawn-out; **~ьная боле́знь** lingering illness.

дл|и́ться, и́тся *impf.* (*of* **про~**) to last.

для *prep.*+*g.* **1.** for (the sake of); **э́то д. тебя́** this is for you. **2.** (*expr. purpose*) for; **маши́на д. выка́чивания воды́** machine for pumping out water; **д. того́, что́бы...** in order to .... **3.** for, to (= *in relation to, in respect of*); **д. нас не сто́ит** for us it is not worth while; **вре́дно д. дете́й** bad for children; **непроница́емый д. воды́** waterproof. **4.** for, of (= *in relation to a stated norm*); **он о́чень высо́к д. свои́х лет** he is very tall for his age; **э́то поведе́ние типи́чно д. них** such behaviour is typical of them.

днева́л|ить, ю, ишь *impf.* (*coll.*) to be on duty.

днева́льн|ый, ого *m.* (*mil.*) orderly, fatigue man.

днева́ть, дню́ю, дню́ешь *impf.* to spend the day; **д. и ночева́ть** to spend all one's time.

дневни́к, а́ *m.* diary, journal; **вести́ д.** to keep a diary.

дневн|о́й *adj.* **1.** day; **в ~о́е вре́мя** during daylight hours; **д. свет** daylight; **~а́я сме́на** day shift. **2.** day's; **~а́я зарпла́та** day's pay.

днём *adv.* **1.** in the day-time, by day. **2.** in the afternoon; **сего́дня д.** this afternoon.

дни́щ|е, а *nt.* bottom (*of vessel or barrel*).

ДНК *f. indecl.* (*abbr. of* **дезоксирибонуклеи́новая кислота́**) (*chem.*) DNA (*deoxyribonucleic acid*).

дно, дна, *pl.* **до́нья, до́ньев** *nt.* **1.** bottom (*of sea, river, etc.*); **идти́ ко дну** to go to the bottom, sink; **золото́е д.** (*fig.*) gold-mine. **2.** bottom (*of vessel*); **вверх дном** upside down; **пить до дна** to empty one's glass; **(пей) до дна!** bottoms up!

до *prep.*+ *g.* **1.** (*of place or indicating length, etc.*) to, up to; as far as; **от Ло́ндона до Москвы́** from London to Moscow; **дое́хать до Пари́жа** to go as far as Paris; **ю́бка до коле́н** knee-length skirt. **2.** (*of time*) to, up to; until, till; **до шести́ часо́в** till six o'clock; **до сих пор** up to now, till now, hitherto; **до тех пор** till then, before; **до тех пор, пока́** until; **до свида́ния!** good-bye! **3.** before; **до войны́** before the war; **до на́шей э́ры (до н. э.)** before Christ (*abbr.* BC); **до того́, как** before. **4.** (*expr. degree or limiting point*) to, up to, to the point of; **до бо́ли** until it hurt(s); **до того́..., что** to the point where; **мы до того́ уста́ли, что и засну́ть не удало́сь** we were too tired even to be able to sleep. **5.** under, up to (= *not over, not more than*); **де́ти до пяти́ лет** children under five; under-fives; **зараба́тывать до ты́сячи рубле́й** to earn up to a thousand roubles. **6.** around; **у нас в больни́це до двух ты́сяч ко́ек** in our hospital there are around two thousand beds. **7.** with regard to, concerning; **что до меня́** as far as I am concerned; **у меня́ до тебя́ де́ло** (*coll.*) I want to have a word with you; **мне,** *etc.*, **не до** (*coll.*) I, *etc.*, don't feel like, am not in the mood for; **мне не до разгово́ра** I am not in a mood for talk.

до...[1] *vbl. pref.* **1.** *expr. completion of action*: **дочита́ть кни́гу** to finish (reading) a book. **2.** *indicates that action is carried to a certain point*: **дочита́ть до страни́цы 270** to read as far as page 270. **3.** *expr. supplementary action*: **докупи́ть** to buy in addition. **4.** (+*refl. vv.*) *expr. eventual attainment of object*: **дозвони́ться** to ring until one gets an answer.

до...[2] *pref. of nn. and adjs., used to indicate priority in chronological sequence* (pre-).

доба́в|ить, лю, ишь *pf.* (*of* **~ля́ть**) (+*a. or g.*) to add.

доба́вк|а, и *f.* **1.** addition. **2.** second helping.

добавле́ни|е, я *nt.* addition; appendix, addendum.

добавля́|ть, ю *impf. of* **доба́вить**

доба́вочн|ый *adj.* additional, extra; (*teleph.*) extension; **~ое вре́мя** (*sport*) extra time; **д. нало́г** surtax; **д. три́дцать** extension 30.

добега́|ть, ю *impf. of* **добежа́ть**

добе|жа́ть, гу́, жи́шь, гу́т *pf.* (*of* **~га́ть**) (**до**+*g.*) to run (to, as far as); to reach (*also fig.*).

добела́ *adv.* **1.** to white heat; **раскалённый д.** white-hot. **2.** clean, white; **чёрного кобеля́ не отмо́ешь д.** (*prov.*) the leopard can't change his spots.

добива́|ть, ю *impf. of* **доби́ть**

добива́|ться, юсь *impf.* **1.** *impf. of* **доби́ться. 2.** (+*g.*) to seek, strive (for), aim (at).

добира́|ться, юсь *impf. of* **добра́ться**

до|би́ть, бью́, бьёшь *pf.* (*of* **~бива́ть**) to finish off, do for (*also in var. senses corresponding to meanings of pref. and simple v.*).

до|би́ться, бью́сь, бьёшься *pf.* (*of* **добива́ться**) (+*g.*) to get, obtain, secure; **д. своего́** to get one's way.

до́блест|ный (~ен, ~на) *adj.* valiant, valorous.

до́блест|ь, и *f.* valour, gallantry.

до|бра́ться, беру́сь, берёшься, *past* **~бра́лся, ~брала́сь, ~бра́ло́сь** *pf.* (*of* **~бира́ться**) **1.** (**до**+*g.*) to get (to), reach. **2.** (*coll.*) to get (one's hands on); **я до тебя́ ~беру́сь!** I'll get you!

добра́чн|ый *adj.* pre-marital; **~ая фами́лия** maiden name.

добре|сти́, ду́, дёшь, *past* **~̈л, ~ла́** *pf.* (**до**+*g.*) to get (to), reach (*slowly or with difficulty*).

добре́|ть[1]**, ю, ешь** *impf.* (*of* **по~**) to become kinder.

добре́|ть[2]**, ю, ешь** *impf.* (*of* **раз~**) (*coll.*) to put on weight.

добр|о́[1]**, а́** *nt.* **1.** good; **жела́ю вам ~а́** I wish you well; **от ~а́ ~а́ не и́щут** let well alone; **нет ху́да без ~а́** every cloud has a silver lining; **э́то не к ~у́** it is a bad sign, it bodes ill; **помина́ть ~о́м** to speak well (of), remember kindly. **2.** (*collect.*; *coll.*) goods, property. **3.: дать/получи́ть добро́** to give/get the go-ahead.

добро́[2] *particle* (*coll.*) good; all right.
добро́[3]**: д. пожа́ловать!** welcome!
добро́[4] *as conj.* (+**бы**) it would be a different matter if; there would be some excuse if.
доброво́л|ец, ьца *m.* volunteer.
доброво́льно *adv.* voluntarily.
доброво́л|ьный (~ен, ~ьна) *adj.* voluntary.
доброво́льческий *adj.* volunteer.
доброде́тел|ь, и *f.* virtue.
доброде́тел|ьный (~ен, ~ьна) *adj.* virtuous.
доброду́ши|е, я *nt.* good-nature.
доброду́ш|ный (~ен, ~на) *adj.* good-natured; genial.
доброжела́тел|ь, я *m.* well-wisher.
доброжела́тел|ьный (~ен, ~ьна) *adj.* benevolent.
доброка́чествен|ный (~, ~на) *adj.* **1.** of good quality. **2.** (*med.*) benign.
добро́м *adv.* (*coll.*) voluntarily.
добросерде́ч|ный (~ен, ~на) *adj.* good-hearted.
добросо́вест|ный (~ен, ~на) *adj.* conscientious.
добрососе́дский *adj.* (good-)neighbourly; friendly.
добрососе́дств|о, а *nt.* (good-)neighbourliness.
доброт|а́, ы́ *f.* goodness, kindness.
добро́т|ный (~ен, ~на) *adj.* of good, high quality; durable.
до́бр|ый (~, ~а́, ~о, ~́ы) *adj.* **1.** (*in var. senses*) good; **~ое и́мя** good name; **д. ма́лый** decent chap; **~ое у́тро!** good morning!; **всего́ ~ого!** good-bye!; all the best!; **в д. час!** good luck!; **по ~у́ по здоро́ву** while the going is (was) good. **2.** kind, good; **бу́дьте ~ы** (+*imper.*) please, would you be so kind as to. **3.** (*coll.*) a good (= *fully, not less than*); **д. час** a good hour. **4.: чего́ ~ого** (*introducing expr. of anticipation of unpleasant eventuality*) who knows; it may be.
добря́к, а́ *m.* (*coll.*) good-natured person.
добу|ди́ться, жу́сь, ~́дишься *pf.* (*coll.*) to wake, succeed in waking.
добыва́|ть, ю *impf. of* **добы́ть**
до|бы́ть, бу́ду, бу́дешь, *past* **~́был, ~была́, ~́было** *pf.* (*of* **~быва́ть**) **1.** to get, obtain, procure. **2.** to extract, mine, quarry.
добы́ч|а, и *f.* **1.** extraction, mining, quarrying. **2.** booty, spoils, loot. **3.** (*hunting*) bag; catch (*of fish*). **4.** mineral products; output.
дова́рив|ать, аю *impf. of* **довари́ть**
довар|и́ть, ю́, ~́ишь *pf.* (*of* **~́ивать**) to finish cooking; to do to a turn.
довез|ти́, у́, ёшь, *past* **~̈, ~ла́** *pf.* (*of* **довози́ть**) to take (to).
дове́ренност|ь, и *f.* warrant; power of attorney; **получи́ть де́ньги по ~и** to obtain money by proxy.
дове́р|енный *p.p.p. of* **~ить** *and adj.* trusted; **~енное лицо́**; *also as n.* **д., ~енного** *m.* agent, proxy; person empowered to act for s.o.
дове́ри|е, я *nt.* trust, confidence; **ме́ры ~я** confidence-building measures; **по́льзоваться чьим-н. ~ем** to enjoy s.o.'s confidence.
довери́тельный *adj.* confiding; trusting.
дове́р|ить, ю, ишь *pf.* (*of* **~я́ть**) (+*d.*) to entrust (to).
дове́р|иться, юсь, ишься *pf.* (*of* **~я́ться**) (+*d.*) to trust (in), confide (in).
до́верху *adv.* to the top; to the brim.
дове́рчивост|ь, и *f.* trusting nature; gullibility.
дове́рчив|ый (~, ~а) *adj.* trusting, credulous; gullible.
доверш|а́ть, а́ю *impf. of* **~и́ть**
доверше́ни|е, я *nt.* completion; **в д. всего́** to crown all; on top of it all.
доверш|и́ть, у́, и́шь *pf.* (*of* **~а́ть**) to complete.
довер|я́ть, я́ю *impf.* **1.** *impf. of* **~́ить. 2.** (*impf. only*) (+*d.*) to trust, confide (in).
довер|я́ться, я́юсь *impf. of* **~́иться**
дове́с|ок, ка *m.* makeweight.
дове|сти́, ду́, дёшь, *past* **~̈л, ~ла́** *pf.* (*of* **доводи́ть**) **1.** (**до**+*g.*) to lead (to), take (to), accompany (to). **2.** (**во**+*g.*) to bring (to); to drive (to), reduce (to); **д. до соверше́нства** to perfect; **д. до сумасше́ствия** to drive mad; **д. до слёз** to reduce to tears; **д. до све́дения** (+*g.*) to inform, bring to the attention (of).
дове|сти́сь, дётся, *past* **~ло́сь** *pf.* (*of* **доводи́ться**) (*impers., +d.; coll.*) to have occasion (to); to manage (to); to happen (to); **нам ~ло́сь заста́ть его́ до́ма** we happened to catch him in.
довле́|ть, ет *impf.* (**над**+*i.*) to dominate, prevail over.
до́вод, а *m.* argument.
дово|ди́ть, жу́, ~́дишь *impf. of* **довести́**
дово|ди́ться, жу́сь, ~́дишься *impf.* **1.** *impf. of* **довести́сь. 2.** (+*d. and i.*) to be related (to as); **он ~́дится ей племя́нником** he is her nephew.
дово́енный *adj.* pre-war.
дово|зи́ть, жу́, ~́зишь *impf. of* **довезти́**
дово́льно[1] *adv.* **1.** enough; *as pred.* it is enough; **с нас э́того д.** we've had enough of this; **д. спо́рить!** stop arguing! **2.** rather, pretty **д. хоро́ший фильм** a rather good film.
дово́льно[2] *adv.* contentedly.
дово́л|ьный (~ен, ~ьна) *adj.* **1.** contented, satisfied; **д. вид** contented expression. **2.** (+*i.*) satisfied (with), pleased (with); **д. собо́й** pleased with o.s.
дово́льстви|е, я *nt.* (*mil.*) allowance.
дово́льств|о, а *nt.* **1.** contentment. **2.** (*coll.*) ease, prosperity.
дово́льств|оваться, уюсь *impf.* (*of* **у~**) (+*i.*) to be content (with), be satisfied (with).
довы́бор|ы, ов *no sg.* by-election.
дог, а *m.* mastiff; **да́тский д.** Great Dane; **далма́тский д.** Dalmatian.
догад|а́ться, а́юсь *pf.* (*of* **~́ываться**) to guess; to have the sense to.
дога́дк|а, и *f.* guess, conjecture; (*pl.*) guesswork; **теря́ться в ~ах** to be stumped.
дога́длив|ый (~, ~а) *adj.* quick-witted; bright.
дога́дыва|ться, юсь *impf.* **1.** *impf. of* **догада́ться. 2.** (*impf. only*) to suspect.
до́гм|а, ы *f.* dogma.
до́гмат, а *m.* **1.** (*relig.*) doctrine, dogma; **д. непогреши́мости Па́пы** the doctrine of Papal infallibility. **2.** tenet, foundation; **~ы христиа́нства** the foundations of Christianity.
догмати́зм, а *m.* dogmatism.
догма́тик, а *m.* dogmatist.
догмати́ческий *adj.* dogmatic.
до|гна́ть, гоню́, го́нишь, *past* **~гна́л, ~гнала́, ~гна́ло** *pf.* (*of* **~гоня́ть**) to catch up (with) (*also fig.*).
догова́рива|ть, ю *impf. of* **договори́ть**
догова́рива|ться, юсь *impf.* **1.** *impf. of* **договори́ться. 2.** (*impf. only*) (**о**+*p.*) to negotiate (about); **Высо́кие ~ющиеся сто́роны** (*dipl.*) the High Contracting Parties.
догово́р, а *and* (*coll.*) **до́говор,** *pl.* **~а́** *m.* agreement; (*pol.*) treaty, pact; **заключи́ть ми́рный д.** to conclude a peace treaty.
договорённост|ь, и *f.* agreement, understanding; (*pol.*) accord.
договор|и́ть, ю́, и́шь *pf.* (*of* **догова́ривать**) to finish saying; to finish telling.
договор|и́ться, ю́сь, и́шься *pf.* (*of* **догова́риваться**) **1.** (**о**+*p.*) to come to an agreement, understanding (about); to arrange; **~и́лись!** agreed!; it's settled. **2.** (**до**+*g.*) to come (to); to talk (to the point of).
догово́рн|ый *adj.* **1.** agreed; contractual; **~ая цена́**

agreed price. **2.** (fixed by) treaty.

догола́ *adv.* naked; **разде́ться д.** to strip to the skin.

догоня́|ть, ю *impf. of* **догна́ть**

догор|а́ть, а́ю *impf. of* **~е́ть**

догор|е́ть, ю́, и́шь *pf.* (*of* **~а́ть**) to burn down, burn out.

дода|ва́ть, ю́, ёшь *impf. of* **~́ть**

дода́|ть, м, шь, ст, ди́м, ди́те, ду́т, *past* **до́да́л, ~ла́, до́дало** *pf.* (*of* **~ва́ть**) to make up (the rest of); to pay up.

доде́л|ать, аю *pf.* (*of* **~ывать**) to finish.

доде́лыва|ть, ю *impf. of* **доде́лать**

доду́м|аться, аюсь *pf.* (*of* **~ываться**) (**до**+*g.*) to hit (upon) (*afterthought*).

доду́мыва|ться, юсь *impf. of* **доду́маться**

доеда́|ть, ю *impf. of* **дое́сть**

доезжа́|ть, ю *impf. of* **дое́хать**

дое́ни|е, я *nt.* milking.

до|е́сть, е́м, е́шь, е́ст, еди́м, еди́те, едя́т *pf.* (*of* **~еда́ть**) to eat up, finish eating.

до|е́хать, е́ду, е́дешь *pf.* (*of* **~езжа́ть**) (**до**+*g.*) to reach, arrive (at).

дож, а *m.* (*hist.*) doge.

дожд|а́ться, у́сь, ёшься, *past* **~а́лся ~ала́сь, ~ало́сь** *pf.* (+*g.*) to wait (for, until).

дождева́льный *adj.*: **д. аппара́т** (*agric.*) water-sprinkler.

дождева́ни|е, я *nt.* (*agric.*) sprinkling.

дождеви́к, а́ *m.* (*coll.*) raincoat.

дождев|о́й *adj. of* **дожд; ~о́е о́блако** rain-cloud.

до́ждик, а *m.* shower.

дождли́в|ый (~, ~а) *adj.* rainy.

дожд|ь, я́ *m.* **1.** rain (*also fig.*); **под ~ём** in the rain; **ме́лкий д.** drizzle; **проливно́й д.** downpour; **кисло́тные ~и́** acid rain; **д. идёт** it is raining; **д. льёт как из ведра́** it's raining cats and dogs. **2.** (*fig.*) rain, hail, cascade; **д. руга́тельств** torrent of abuse; **сы́паться ~ём** to rain down, cascade.

дожива́|ть, ю *impf.* **1.** *impf. of* **дожи́ть. 2.** (*impf. only*) to live out; **д. свой век** to live out one's days.

дожида́|ться, юсь *impf.* (*of* **дожда́ться**) (+*g.*) to wait (for).

до|жи́ть, живу́, живёшь, *past* **~́жил, ~лила́, ~́жило** *pf.* (*of* **~жива́ть**) **1.** (**до**+*g.*) to live (till); to attain the age (of); **она́ ~жила́ до конца́ войны́** she lived to see the end of the war. **2.** (**до**+*g.*) to come (to), be reduced (to); **до чего́ мы ~́жили!** what have we come to! **3.** (*coll.*) to spend (the rest of); **я доживу́ ле́то в Пари́же** I shall spend the rest of the summer in Paris.

до́з|а, ы *f.* dose.

дозапра́вк|а, и *f.* refuelling.

до|зва́ться, зову́сь, зовёшься, *past* **~зва́лся, ~звала́сь, ~зва́ло́сь** *pf.* (*coll.*) to call until one gets an answer; **его́ не ~зовёшься** he never comes when he is called.

дозво́л|енный *p.p.p. of* **~ить** *and adj.* permitted.

дозво́л|ить, ю, ишь *pf.* (*of* **~я́ть**) (*obs. or coll.*) to permit, allow.

дозвол|я́ть, я́ю, *impf. of* **~́ить**

дозвон|и́ться, ю́сь и́шься *pf.* (*coll.*) (**до**+*g.*, **к**+*d.*) to ring until one gets an answer; to get through (*on telephone*); **я не мог к тебе́ д.** I rang you but could not get through.

дозвуково́й *adj.* subsonic.

дозиро́вк|а, и *f.* dosage.

дозна|ва́ться, ю́сь, ёшься *impf.* **1.** *impf. of* **~́ться. 2.** (*only impf.*) (**о**+*p.*) to inquire (about).

дозна́ни|е, я *nt.* (*leg.*) inquiry; inquest.

дозн|а́ться, а́юсь *pf.* (*of* **~ава́ться**) to find out, ascertain.

дозо́р, а *m.* patrol.

дозо́р|ный *adj. of* **~; ~ная шлю́пка** patrol boat; *as n.* **д., ~ного** *m.* (*mil.*) scout.

дозрева́|ть, ю *impf. of* **дозре́ть**

дозре́лый *adj.* fully ripe.

дозр|е́ть, е́ю *pf.* (*of* **~ева́ть**) to ripen.

доигр|а́ть, а́ю *pf.* (*of* **~́ывать**) to finish (playing).

доигр|а́ться, а́юсь *pf.* (*of* **~́ываться**) (**до**+*g.*) to play (until); (*fig.*) to get o.s. (into), land o.s. (in); **вот и ~а́лся!** now you've (he's, *etc.*) done it!

дои́грыва|ть(ся), ю(сь) *impf. of* **доигра́ть(ся)**

до́ильн|ый *adj.*: **~ая маши́на** milking machine.

до|иска́ться, ищу́сь, и́щешься *pf.* (*of* **~и́скиваться**) (*coll.*) **1.** (+*g.*) to find, discover. **2.** to find out, ascertain.

дои́скива|ться, юсь *impf.* **1.** *impf. of* **доиска́ться. 2.** (*impf. only*) to try to find out.

доистори́ческий *adj.* prehistoric.

доисто́ри|я, и *f.* prehistory.

до|и́ть, ю́, ~́ишь *impf.* (*of* **по~**) to milk.

до|и́ться, ~́ится *impf.* **1.** to give milk; **хорошо́ д.** to be a good milker. **2.** *pass. of* **~и́ть**

до́йк|а, и *f.* milking.

до́йн|ый *adj.* milch; **~ая коро́ва** milch cow.

до|йти́, йду́, йдёшь, *past* **~шёл, ~шла́** *pf.* (*of* **~ходи́ть**) **1.** (**до**+*g.*) (*in var. senses*) to reach; **слух ~шёл до нас** a rumour reached us; **д. до све́дения** (+*g.*) to come to the attention (of); **д. до того́, что...** to reach a point where ...; **ру́ки не ~шли́** (**до**+*g.*) I, *etc.*, had no time (for). **2.** (*coll.*) (**до**+*g.*) to make an impression (upon), get through (to); **его́ выступле́ние про́сто не ~шло́ до слу́шателей** his speech made no impression whatever on the audience. **3.** (*impers.*; *also* **де́ло ~йдёт, ~шло́ до**+*g.*) to come (to); **де́ло ~шло́ до проце́сса** it came to a court case. **4.** (*coll.*) to be done (= *to be cooked*); to be ripe.

док, а *m.* dock.

до́к|а, и *c.g.* (*coll.*) expert, authority.

доказа́тел|ьный (~ен, ~ьна) *adj.* demonstrative, conclusive.

доказа́тельств|о, а *nt.* proof, evidence.

док|аза́ть, ажу́, а́жешь *pf.* (*of* **~а́зывать**) to demonstrate, prove.

доказу́ем|ый (~, ~а) *adj.* demonstrable.

дока́зыва|ть, ю *impf.* **1.** *impf. of* **доказа́ть. 2.** (*impf. only*) to argue, try to prove.

дока́нчива|ть, ю *impf. of* **доко́нчить**

дока́пыва|ться, юсь *impf. of* **докопа́ться**

док|ати́ться, ачу́сь, а́тишься *pf.* (*of* **~а́тываться**) **1.** (**до**+*g.*) to roll (to). **2.** (*of sounds*) to thunder, boom. **3.** (*fig., coll.*) (**до**+*g.*) to sink (to), come (to); **д. до преступле́ния** to sink to crime.

дока́тыва|ться, юсь *impf. of* **докати́ться**

до́кер, а *m.* docker.

докла́д, а *m.* **1.** report; lecture; paper; talk, address; **чита́ть д.** to give a report, read a paper. **2.** announcement (*of arrival of guest, etc.*); **войти́ без ~а** to enter unannounced.

докладн|о́й *adj.*: **~а́я запи́ска** report, memorandum; *as n.* **~а́я, ~о́й** *f.* = **~а́я запи́ска.**

докла́дчик, а *m.* speaker, lecturer; reader of a report.

докла́дыва|ть(ся), ю(сь) *impf. of* **доложи́ть(ся)**

доко́ле *adv.* (*obs.*) **1.** (*interrog.*) how long? **2.** (*rel.*) as long as; until.

доколу́мбов *adj.* pre-Columbian; **~о иску́сство** pre-Columbian art.

докона́|ть, ю *pf.* (*coll.*) to finish off, be the end (of).

доко́нч|ить, у, ишь *pf.* (*of* **дока́нчивать**) to finish, complete.

докопа́|ться, юсь *pf.* (*of* **дока́пываться**) (**до**+*g.*) **1.** to dig down (to). **2.** (*fig.*) to get to the bottom (of); to find out, discover.

до́красна́ *adv.* to redness; to red heat; **раскалённый д.** red-hot.

докрич|а́ться, у́сь, и́шься *pf.* **1.** to shout until one is heard. **2.: д. до хрипоты́** to shout o.s. hoarse.

до́ктор, а, *pl.* **~а́** *m.* doctor.

доктора́нт, а *m.* person working for degree of doctor.

до́ктор|ский *adj. of* **~; ~ская диссерта́ция** doctoral thesis.

доктри́н|а, ы *f.* doctrine.

доктринёр, а *m.* doctrinaire.

доктринёрский *adj.* doctrinaire

доктринёрств|о, а. *nt.* doctrinaire attitude.

докуме́нт, а *m.* **1.** document, paper. **2.** (*leg.*) deed; instrument.

документали́ст, а *m.* documentary film-maker.

документа́льный *adj.* documentary; **д. фильм** documentary (film).

документа́ци|я, и *f.* **1.** documentation. **2.** (*collect.*) documents, papers.

документи́р|овать, ую *impf. and pf.* to document.

докуп|а́ть, а́ю *impf. of* **~и́ть**

докуп|и́ть, лю́, ~́ишь *pf.* (*of* **~а́ть**) to buy in addition.

докуча́|ть, ю *impf.* (*+d. and i.*; *coll.*) to bother (with), pester (with), plague (with).

доку́члив|ый (~, ~а) *adj.* (*coll.*) tiresome, importunate.

дол, а *m.* (*poet.*) dale, vale; **за гора́ми, за ~а́ми** far and wide; **по гора́м, по ~а́м** up hill and down dale.

долбёжк|а, и *f.* (*sl.*) swotting.

долб|и́ть, лю́, и́шь *impf.* **1.** to hollow; to chisel, gouge. **2.** (*coll.*) to repeat, say over and over. **3.** (*sl.*) to swot (up); to learn by rote.

долг, а, о ~́е, в ~у́, *pl.* **~и́** *m.* **1.** duty; **по ~́у слу́жбы** in the performance of one's duty. **2.** debt; **в д.** on credit; **войти́, влезть в ~и́** to get into debt; **быть у кого́-н. в ~у́** to be indebted to s.o.; **отда́ть после́дний д.** to pay one's last respects; **д. платежо́м кра́сен** one good turn deserves another.

до́л|гий (~ог, ~га́, ~го) *adj.* long; **~гая пе́сня** (*fig.*) a long story; **отложи́ть в д. я́щик** to shelve, put off.

до́лго *adv.* long, (for) a long time.

долгове́ч|ный (~ен, ~на) *adj.* lasting; long-lived.

долгов|о́й *adj. of* **долг 2.; ~о́е обяза́тельство** promissory note.

долговре́менный *adj.* of long duration.

долговя́з|ый (~, ~а) *adj.* (*coll.*) lanky.

долгогри́вый *adj.* shaggy-maned.

долгожи́тел|ь, я *m.* old-timer, senior citizen.

долгоигра́ющ|ий *adj.*: **~ая пласти́нка** long-playing (gramophone) record.

долголе́ти|е, я *nt.* longevity.

долголе́тний *adj.* of many years; of many years' standing, long-standing.

долгоно́сик, а *m.* weevil.

долгосро́чный *adj.* long-term; of long duration.

долгот|а́, ы́, *pl.* **~́ы** *f.* **1.** (*sg. only*) duration. **2.** longitude.

долготерпели́в|ый (~, ~а) *adj.* long-suffering.

долготерпе́ни|е, я *nt.* long-suffering.

долево́й *adj. of* **до́ля**

до́лее *comp. of* **до́лго**

долет|а́ть, а́ю *impf. of* **~е́ть**

доле|те́ть, чу́, ти́шь, *pf.* (*of* **~та́ть**) (**до**+*g.*) **1.** to fly (to, as far as). **2.** to reach (*also fig.*).

до́лж|ен (~на́, ~но́) *pred. adj.* **1.** owing; **он д. мне три рубля́** he owes me three roubles. **2.** (*+inf.*) *expr. obligation*; **я д. идти́** I must go, I have to go; **он д. был отказа́ться** he had to refuse. **3.** (*+inf.*) *expr. probability or expectation*; **она́ ~на́ ско́ро прийти́** she should be here soon; **~но́ быть** probably; **вы с ним, ~но́ быть, уже́ знако́мы** you probably know each other.

должни́к, а́ *m.* debtor.

должностн|о́й *adj.* official; **~о́е лицо́** official, functionary; **~о́е преступле́ние** malfeasance in office.

до́лжност|ь, и, *g. pl.* **~е́й** *f.* post, position; office.

до́лжн|ый *adj.* due, fitting, proper; **~ым о́бразом** properly; *as n.* **~ое, ~ого** due; **воздава́ть д.** (*+d.*) to pay tribute (to).

долива́|ть, ю *impf. of* **доли́ть**

доли́н|а, ы *f.* valley.

доли́н|ный *adj. of* **~а**

дол|и́ть, ью́, ьёшь, *past* **~́ил, ~ила́, ~́ило** *pf.* (*of* **~ива́ть**) **1.** to add; to pour in addition. **2.** to fill (up); to refill.

до́ллар, а *m.* dollar.

долож|и́ть[1], у́, ~́ишь *pf.* (*of* **докла́дывать**) **1.** (*+a. or* **о**+*p.*) to report; to give a report (on). **2.** (**о**+*p.*) to announce (*a visitor, etc.*).

долож|и́ть[2], у́, ~́ишь *pf.* (*of* **докла́дывать**) to add.

долож|и́ться, у́сь, ~́ишься *pf.* (*of* **докла́дываться**) to announce one's arrival.

доло́й *adv.* (*+a.*; *coll.*) down (with); **д. изме́нников!** down with the traitors!; **уйди́ с глаз д.!** out of my sight! **2.** off (with); **ша́пки д.!** hats off!

долот|о́, а́, *pl.* **~́а, ~́** *nt.* chisel.

до́льк|а, и *f.* segment; clove.

до́льше *adv.* longer.

до́л|я, и, *g. pl.* **~е́й** *f.* **1.** part, portion; share; quota, allotment; **войти́ в ~ю** (**с**+*i.*) to go shares (with); **в его́ слова́х не́ было и ~и и́стины** there was not a grain of truth in his words. **2.** (*anat., bot.*) lobe. **3.** lot, fate; **вы́пасть на чью́-н. ~ю** to fall to s.o.'s lot.

дом, а (у), *pl.* **~а́** *m.* **1.** (*in var. senses*) building, house; block (of flats); **д. о́тдыха** rest home, holiday home; **Д. учёных** Scientists' Club; **д.-музе́й...** ... House; **д.-музе́й Пу́шкина** Pushkin House. **2.** home; house, household; **вести́ д.** to keep house, run the house; **на ~у́** at home; **брать рабо́ту на́ д.** to take work home; **тоска́ по ~́у** homesickness. **3.** house (= *dynasty*), lineage; **д. Рома́новых** the House of Romanov.

дом... *comb. form, abbr. of* **1. домо́вый. 2. дома́шний**

до́ма *adv.* at home, in; **быть как д.** to feel at home; **бу́дьте как д.** make yourself at home; **у него́ не все д.** he's not all there.

домаркси́стский *adj.* pre-Marxist.

дома́шн|ий *adj.* **1.** house; home; domestic; **д. а́дрес** home address; **~ие забо́ты** household chores; **~яя рабо́тница** domestic servant; **~яя хозя́йка** housewife; **под ~им аре́стом** under house arrest. **2.** home-made. **3.** tame (*opp. wild*); domestic; **~ие живо́тные** domestic animals; **~ие пти́цы** poultry. **4.** *as n.* **~ие, ~их** (members of) one's family.

до́менн|ый *adj. of* **до́мна; ~ая печь** blast furnace.

до́менщик, а *m.* blast-furnace operator.

до́мик, а *m. dim. of* **дом**; **охо́тничий д.** hunting lodge.

домина́нт|а, ы *f.* **1.** (*mus.*) dominant. **2.** (*fig.*) leitmotif.

доминика́н|ец, ца *m.* Dominican (monk).

доминио́н, а *m.* dominion.

домини́р|овать, ую *impf.* **1.** to dominate, prevail (*fig.*). **2.** (*geog.*) (**над**+*i.*) to dominate, command.

домино́ *nt. indecl.* **1.** dominoes (*game*). **2.** domino (*costume*).

доми́ш|ко, ~ка, *pl.* **~ки, ~ек, ~кам** *m.* (*coll.*) tiny, wretched house; hovel.

домкра́т, а *m.* (*tech.*) jack.

до́мн|а, ы *f.* blast furnace.

домови́т|ый (~, ~а) *adj.* thrifty, economical; **~ая**

хозя́йка good housewife.
домовладе́л|ец, ьца *m.* home-owner.
домово́дств|о, а *nt.* housekeeping; household management; home economics.
домов|о́й, о́го *m.* (*folklore*) brownie, house-sprite.
домо́в|ый *adj.* **1.** house; household; **~ая кни́га** register of tenants; **~ая конто́ра** house-manager's office; **д. пау́к** house-spider. **2.** housing; **д. трест** housing trust.
домога́тельств|о, а *nt.* **1.** solicitation. **2.** demand, bid; **д. госпо́дства** bid for power.
домога́|ться, юсь *impf.* (+*g.*) to seek (after), solicit, covet.
домо́й *adv.* home, homewards; **нам пора́ д.** it's time for us to go home.
доморо́щенный *adj.* **1.** home-bred. **2.** (*fig.*) crude; primitive; homespun.
домосе́д, а *m.* stay-at-home.
домострое́ни|е, я *nt.* house-building.
домостро́ительный *adj.* house-building.
домотка́ный *adj.* home-spun.
домоуправле́ни|е, я *nt.* house management (committee).
домохозя́|ин, ина, *pl.* **~ева, ~ев** *m.* **1.** householder. **2.** househusband.
домохозя́йк|а, и *f.* housewife.
до́мр|а, ы *f.* (*mus.*) domra (*Russ. stringed instrument similar to mandolin*).
домрабо́тниц|а, ы *f.* domestic (servant), maid; **приходя́щая д.** home help; daily.
домри́ст, а *m.* domra-player.
дому́шник, а *m.* (*sl.*) burglar, housebreaker.
домч|а́ть, у́, и́шь *pf.* (*coll.*) to rush, bring quickly (*in a vehicle, etc.*).
домч|а́ться, у́сь, и́шься *pf.* (*coll.*) to reach quickly (*at a run or gallop*).
до́мыс|ел, ла *m.* conjecture.
донага́ *adv.* naked; to the skin.
дона́шива|ть, ю *impf. of* **доноси́ть**[1]
доне́льзя *adv.* to the utmost; in the extreme; **он д. упря́м** he is obstinate in the extreme.
донесе́ни|е, я *nt.* dispatch, report, message; **д. о боевы́х поте́рях** casualty report.
донес|ти́[1], **у́, ёшь,** *past* **~́, ~ла́** *pf.* (*of* **доноси́ть**[2]) (**до**+*g.*) to carry (to, as far as); to carry, bear (*a sound or smell*).
донес|ти́[2], **у́, ёшь,** *past* **~́, ~ла́** *pf.* (*of* **доноси́ть**[3]) **1.** to report, announce; (+*d.*) to inform. **2.** (**на**+*a.*) to inform (on, against), denounce.
донес|ти́сь, у́сь, ёшься, *past* **~́ся, ~ла́сь** *pf.* (*of* **доноси́ться**[2]) (*of sounds or smells, also of news, etc.*) to reach; **до нас уже́ ~́ся слух** a rumour had already reached us.
дон|е́ц, ца́ *m.* Don Cossack.
донжуа́н, а *m.* Don Juan, philanderer.
донжуа́нств|о, а *nt.* philandering.
до́низу *adv.* to the bottom.
донима́|ть, ю *impf. of* **доня́ть**
донкихо́тский *adj.* quixotic.
донкихо́тств|о, а *adj.* quixotic behaviour.
до́нный *adj. of* **дно; д. лёд** ground ice.
до́нор, а *m.* (blood-)donor.
до́нор|ский *adj. of* **~; д. пункт** blood donation centre.
доно́с, а *m.* denunciation.
дон|оси́ть[1], **ошу́, ~о́сишь** *pf.* (*of* **дона́шивать**) **1.** to wear out. **2.: д. ребёнка** to carry a baby to full term.
дон|оси́ть[2,3], **ошу́, ~о́сишь** *impf. of* **донести́**[1,2]
дон|оси́ться[1], **~о́сится** *pf.* to wear out, be worn out.
дон|оси́ться[2], **~о́сится** *impf. of* **донести́сь**
доно́счик, а *m.* informer.
донско́й *adj.* (of the river) Don; **д. каза́к** Don Cossack.
доны́не *adv.* (*rhet.*) hitherto.
до|ня́ть, йму́, йме́шь, *past* **~́нял, ~няла́, ~́няло** *pf.* (*of* **~нима́ть**) (*coll.*) to weary, tire out, exasperate.
дообе́денный *adj.* pre-prandial.
дооктя́брьский *adj.* pre-October (*before the Russ. Revolution of October 1917*).
допека́|ть, ю *impf. of* **допе́чь**
допетро́вский *adj.* pre-Petrine.
допе́|чь, ку́, чёшь, ку́т, *past* **~́к, ~кла́** *pf.* (*of* **~ка́ть**) **1.** to bake until done; to finish baking. **2.** (*fig., coll.*) to wear out, plague, pester.
допива́|ть, ю *impf. of* **допи́ть**
до́пинг, а *m.* **1.** stimulant. **2.** (*fig.*) **(психологи́ческий) д.** boost, shot in the arm.
до́пинговый *adj.*: **д. контро́ль** dope test; dope testing.
допи|са́ть, шу́, ~́шешь *pf.* (*of* **~́сывать**) **1.** to finish writing. **2.** to add.
допи́сыва|ть, ю *impf. of* **дописа́ть**
доп|и́ть, ью́, ьёшь, *past* **~́ил, ~ ила́, ~́ило** *pf.* (*of* **~ива́ть**) to drink (up).
допла́т|а, ы *f.* additional payment; excess fare.
допл|ати́ть, ачу́, ~а́тишь *pf.* (*of* **~а́чивать**) to pay in addition, in excess.
допла́чива|ть, ю *impf. of* **доплати́ть**
доплыва́|ть, ю *impf. of* **доплы́ть**
доплы́|ть, ву́, вёшь, *past* **~л, ~ла́, ~ло** *pf.* (*of* **~ва́ть**) (**до**+*g.*) to swim (to, as far as); to sail (to, as far as); (*fig.*) to reach.
допо́длинно *adv.* (*coll.*) for certain.
допо́длинный *adj.* (*coll.*) authentic, genuine.
дополне́ни|е, я *nt.* **1.** supplement, addition; addendum. **2.** (*gram.*) object; **прямо́е д.** direct object; **ко́свенное д.** indirect object.
дополни́тельно *adv.* in addition.
дополни́тельн|ый *adj.* **1.** supplementary, additional, extra; **~ое вре́мя** (*sport*) extra time; **д. окла́д** extra pay. **2.** complementary; **~ые цвета́** complementary colours.
допо́лн|ить, ю, ишь *pf.* (*of* **~я́ть**) to supplement, add to; **д. друг дру́га** to complement one another.
дополн|я́ть, я́ю, *impf. of* **~́ить**
допото́пный *adj.* antediluvian.
допра́шива|ть, ю *impf. of* **допроси́ть**
допро́с, а *m.* (*leg.*) interrogation, examination; **перекрёстный д.** cross-examination.
допр|оси́ть, ошу́, о́сишь *pf.* (*of* **~а́шивать**) (*leg.*) to interrogate, question.
до́пуск, а *m.* **1.** right of entry, admittance. **2.** (*tech.*) tolerance.
допуска́|ть, ю *impf. of* **допусти́ть**
допусти́м|ый (~, ~а) *adj.* permissible, admissible; **~ая нагру́зка** permissible load.
допу|сти́ть, щу́, ~́стишь *pf.* (*of* **~ска́ть**) **1.** (**до**+*g.* **к**+*d.*) to admit (to); **д. к ко́нкурсу** to allow to compete. **2.** to allow, permit; to tolerate. **3.** to grant, assume; **~́стим** let us suppose, let us assume. **4.** to commit.
допуще́ни|е, я *nt.* assumption.
допыт|а́ться, а́юсь *pf.* (*of* **~́ываться**) to find out.
допы́тыва|ться, юсь *impf. of* **допыта́ться;** (*impf. only*) to try to find out, try to elicit.
до́пьяна́ *adv.* (*coll.*) dead drunk; **напои́ть д.** to make dead drunk.
дораст|а́ть, а́ю *impf. of* **~и́**
дораст|и́, у́, ёшь, *past* **доро́с, доросла́** *pf.* (*of* **дорасти́ть**) **1.** (**до**+*g.*) to grow (to); (fig.) to attain (to), come up (to). **2. не д. что́бы** (+*inf.*) not to be old enough (to); **она́ ещё не доросла́, что́бы е́здить на велосипе́де** she is not old enough yet to ride a bicycle.

дореволюцио́нный *adj.* pre-revolutionary.
дорефо́рменный *adj.* pre-reform.
доро́г|а, и *f.* **1.** road, way (*also fig.*); **желе́зная д.** railway(s); **д. госуда́рственного значе́ния** national highway; **дать, уступи́ть кому́-н. ~у** to let s.o. pass, make way for s.o. (*also fig.*); **идти́ свое́й ~ой** to go one's own way; **пойти́ по плохо́й ~е** to be on the downward path; **стать кому́-н. попере́к ~и** to stand in s.o.'s way; **туда́ ему́ и д.** (*coll.*) it serves him right; **ска́тертью д.!** good riddance! **2.** journey; **отпра́виться в ~у** to set out; **в ~е** on the journey, en route; **с ~и** after the journey, from the road. **3.** (the) way, route; **показа́ть ~у** to show the way, direct; **сби́ться с ~и** to lose one's way; **нам с ни́ми бы́ло по ~е** we went the same way.
до́рого *adv.* dear, dearly; **д. обойти́сь** (*+d.*) to cost one dear; **д. бы я дал, что́бы...** (*coll.*) I would give anything to ....
дороговизн|а, ы *f.* high prices.
доро́гой *adv.* on the way, en route.
дорог|о́й (до́рог, дорога́, до́рого) *adj.* **1.** dear, expensive; costly; **по ~о́й цене́** at a high price. **2.** dear; precious; *as n.* **д., ~о́го** *m.*, **~а́я, ~о́й** *f.* (my) dear.
доро́д|ный (~ен, ~на) *adj.* portly, stout.
дородово́й *adj.* antenatal.
дорожа́|ть, ет *impf.* (*of* **вз~** *and* **по~**) to rise (in price), go up.
доро́же *comp. of* **дорого́й** *and* **до́рого**
дорож|и́ть, у́, и́шь *impf.* (*+i.*) to value; to prize, set store (by).
доро́жк|а, и *f.* **1.** path, walk; **велосипе́дная д.** cycle-path. **2.** (*sport*) track; lane. **3.** strip (*of carpet, linoleum or fabric*); runner. **4.** (*of tape recorder*) track.
доро́жно-тра́нспортн|ый *adj.*: **~ое происше́ствие** road accident.
доро́жн|ый *adj.* **1.** *adj. of* **доро́га; д. знак** road sign; **~ая поли́ция** traffic police; **~ое строи́тельство** road-building. **2.** travel, travelling; **д. буди́льник** travel alarm; **~ые расхо́ды** travelling expenses.
доса́д|а, ы *f.* vexation; annoyance, irritation; **кака́я д.!** what a nuisance!
доса|ди́ть, жу́, ди́шь *pf.* (*of* **~жда́ть**) (*+d.*) to annoy, vex.
доса́длив|ый (~, ~а) *adj.* expressing vexation, irritation; **д. жест** gesture of vexation.
доса́дно *as pred.* it is vexing, annoying.
доса́д|ный (~ен, ~на) *adj.* vexing, annoying.
доса́д|овать, ую *impf.* (**на**+*a.*) to be annoyed (with), be vexed (with).
досажда́|ть, ю *impf. of* **досади́ть**
доси|де́ть, жу́, ди́шь *pf.* (*of* **~́живать**) (**до**+*g.*) to sit (until), stay (until).
дoff́жива|ть, ю *impf. of* **досиде́ть**
доск|а́, и́, *a.* **~́у,** *pl.* **~́и,** *g.* **досо́к,** *d.* **~а́м** *f.* **1.** board, plank; **д. объявле́ний** notice-board; bulletin board; **д. почёта** board of honour; **ро́ликовая** *or* **ро́ллинговая д.** skateboard; **как д. (худо́й)** thin as a rake; **проче́сть от ~и́ до ~и́** to read from cover to cover; **ста́вить на одну́ ~́у** (**с**+*i.*) to equate, put on a level (with); **пьян в ~́у** (*sl.*) dead drunk. **2.** slab; plaque, plate.
доскона́л|ьный (~ен, ~ьна) *adj.* thorough.
до|сла́ть, шлю́, шлёшь *pf.* (*of* **~сыла́ть**) to send in addition; to send the remainder.
досло́вно *adv.* verbatim, word for word.
досло́вный *adj.* literal, verbatim; **д. перево́д** literal translation.
дослу́жива|ть(ся), ю(сь) *impf. of* **дослужи́ть(ся)**
дослуж|и́ть, у́, ~́ишь *pf.* (*of* **~́ивать**) (**до**+*g.*) to serve (until); to finish a period of service.
дослуж|и́ться, у́сь, ~́ишься *pf.* (*of* **~́иваться**) to obtain as a result of service; **д. до чи́на майо́ра** to rise to the rank of major; **д. до пе́нсии** to qualify for a pension.
досма́трива|ть, ю, *impf. of* **досмотре́ть**
досмо́тр, а *m.* examination; inspection.
досмотр|е́ть, ю́, ~́ишь *pf.* (*of* **досма́тривать**) **1.** (**до**+*g.*) to watch, look at (to, as far as); **мы ~е́ли пье́су до тре́тьего а́кта** we watched the play as far as the third act. **2. не д.** to overlook, to allow to escape one's notice.
досмо́трщик, а *m.* inspector, examiner.
досове́тский *adj.* pre-Soviet.
доспева́|ть, ю *impf. of* **доспе́ть**
доспе́|ть, ю, ешь *pf.* (*of* **~ва́ть**) to ripen, mature.
доспе́х|и, ов *pl.* (*sg.* **~, ~а** *m.*) armour.
досро́чный *adj.* ahead of schedule, early.
доста|ва́ть(ся), ю́(сь), ёшь(ся) *impf. of* **~́ть(ся)**
доста́в|ить, лю, ишь *pf.* (*of* **~ля́ть**) **1.** to deliver, convey; to supply, furnish. **2.** to give, cause; **д. слу́чай** to afford an opportunity; **д. удово́льствие** to give pleasure.
доста́вк|а, и *f.* delivery.
доставля́|ть, ю *impf. of* **доста́вить**
доста́вщик, а *m.* delivery man.
доста́ива|ть, ю *impf. of* **достоя́ть**
доста́т|ок, ка *m.* **1.** sufficiency. **2.** prosperity; **жить в ~ке** to be comfortably off; **сре́днего ~ка** middle-income. **3.** (*pl. only*) income.
доста́точно[1] *adv.* sufficiently, enough.
доста́точно[2] *as pred.* it is enough; **д. сказа́ть** suffice it to say; **д. бы́ло одного́ взгля́да** one glance was enough.
доста́точност|ь, и *f.* sufficiency.
доста́точ|ный (~ен, ~на) *adj.* sufficient.
доста́|ть, ну, нешь *pf.* (*of* **~ва́ть**) (*+d.*) **1.** to fetch; to take out; **д. плато́к из карма́на** to take a handkerchief out of one's pocket. **2.** (*+g. or* **до**+*g.*) to touch; to reach; **д. руко́й до потолка́** to touch the ceiling. **3.** to get, obtain. **4.** (*impers.*, *+g.*; *coll.*) to suffice.
доста́|ться, нусь, нешься *pf.* (*of* **~ва́ться**) (*+d.*) **1.** to pass (to) (by inheritance); **ему́ ~лось большо́е име́ние** he came into a large estate. **2.** to fall to one's lot. **3.** (*impers.*; *coll.*): **ему́** *etc.*, **~нется** he, *etc.*, will catch it.
достига́|ть, ю *impf. of* **дости́гнуть** *and* **дости́чь**
дости́г|нуть, ну, нешь, *past* **~, ~ла** *pf.* (*of* **~а́ть**) **1.** (*+g. or* **до**+*g.*) to reach; **д. ста́рости** to reach old age; **слух ~ до на́ших уше́й** a rumour had come to our ears. **2.** (*+g.*) to attain, achieve.
достиже́ни|е, я *nt.* achievement, attainment.
достижи́м|ый (~, ~а) *adj.* accessible; attainable.
дости́чь = дости́гнуть
достове́рност|ь, и *f.* authenticity; trustworthiness.
достове́р|ный (~ен, ~на) *adj.* authentic; trustworthy; reliable.
досто́инств|о, а *nt.* **1.** merit, virtue. **2.** (*sg. only*) dignity; **чу́вство со́бственного ~а** self-respect. **3.** (*econ.*) value; **моне́ты ма́лого ~а** coins of small denomination.
досто́йно *adv.* suitably, fittingly.
досто́|йный (~ин, ~йна) *adj.* **1.** (*+g.*) worthy (of), deserving; **д. внима́ния** worthy of note; **д. похвалы́** praiseworthy. **2.** (well-)deserved; fitting, adequate; **~йная награ́да** deserved reward. **3.** suitable, fit. **4.** worthy.
достопа́мят|ный (~ен, ~на) *adj.* memorable.
достопримеча́тельност|ь, и *f.* sight; place, object of note; **осма́тривать ~и** to see the sights.
достопримеча́тел|ьный (~ен, ~ьна) *adj.* remarkable, notable.
достоя́ни|е, я *nt.* property.
досту́ка|ться, юсь *pf.* (*coll.*) to get one's comeuppance.

до́ступ, а *m.* access.
досту́п|ный (~ен, ~на) *adj.* **1.** accessible; easy of access. **2.** (**для**+*g*) open (to); available (to). **3.** easily understood; intelligible. **4.** (*of prices*) moderate, reasonable; **~ные це́ны** affordable prices. **5.** affable, approachable.
достуч|а́ться, у́сь, и́шься *pf.* (*coll.*) to knock until one is heard.
досу́г, а *m.* **1.** leisure, leisure-time; **на ~е** at leisure, in one's spare time. **2.** *as pred.* (+*d. and inf.*; *coll.*) to have time (to, for); **где мне д. чита́ть?** what time have I for reading?
досу́ж|ий *adj.* (*coll.*) **1.** leisure; **~ее вре́мя** leisure-time, spare time. **2.** idle; **~ие разгово́ры** idle talk.
до́суха *adv.* (until) dry; **вы́тереть д.** to rub dry.
досчита́|ть, ю *pf.* (*of* **досчи́тывать**) **1.** to finish counting. **2.** (**до**+*g.*) to count (up to); **д. до ста** to count up to a hundred.
досчи́тыва|ть, ю *impf. of* **досчита́ть**
досыла́|ть, ю *impf. of* **досла́ть**
досы́п|ать, лю, лешь *pf.* (*of* **~а́ть**) to pour in, fill up.
досып|а́ть, а́ю *impf. of* **~́ать**
до́сыта *adv.* (*coll.*) to satiety.
досье́ *nt. indecl.* dossier, file.
досю́да *adv.* (*coll.*) as far as here, up to here.
досяга́емост|ь, и *f.* reach; (*mil.*) range; **вне преде́лов ~и** beyond reach; out of range.
досяга́ем|ый (~, ~а) *adj.* attainable, accessible.
дота́скива|ть(ся), ю(сь) *impf. of* **дотащи́ть(ся)**
дота́ци|я, и *f.* grant, subsidy.
дотащ|и́ть, у́, ~́ишь *pf.* (*of* **дота́скивать**) (*coll.*) (**до**+*g.*) to carry, drag (to).
дотащ|и́ться, у́сь, ~́ишься *pf.* (*of* **дота́скиваться**) (*coll.*) to drag o.s.
дотемна́ *adv.* until it gets (got) dark.
дотла́ *adv.* utterly, completely; **сгоре́ть д.** to burn to the ground.
дото́шный *adj.* (*coll.*) meticulous.
дотра́гива|ться, юсь *impf. of* **дотро́нуться**
дотро́н|уться, усь, ешься *pf.* (*of* **дотра́гиваться**) (**до**+*g.*) to touch.
дотя́гива|ть(ся), ю(сь), ешь(ся) *impf. of* **дотяну́ть(ся)**
дотян|у́ть, у́, ~́ешь *pf.* (*of* **дотя́гивать**) (**до**+*g.*) **1.** to draw, drag, haul (to, as far as). **2.** (*coll.*) to reach. **3.** to stretch out (to, as far as). **4.** (*coll.*) to hold out (till); to live (till); **он до утра́ не ~́ет** he won't last till morning. **5.** (*coll.*) to put off (till).
дотян|у́ться, у́сь, ~́ешься *pf.* (*of* **дотя́гиваться**) (**до**+*g.*) **1.** to reach; to touch. **2.** (*coll.*) to stretch (to), reach; **о́чередь ~у́лась до конца́ у́лицы** the queue stretched to the end of the street.
доу́чива|ть(ся), ю(сь) *impf. of* **доучи́ть(ся)**
доуч|и́ть, у́, ~́ишь *pf.* (*of* **~́ивать**) **1.** to finish teaching; (**до**+*g.*) to teach (up to). **2.** to finish learning; (**до**+*g.*) to learn (up to, as far as).
доуч|и́ться, у́сь, ~́ишься *pf.* (*of* **~́иваться**) **1.** to complete one's studies, finish one's education. **2.** (**до**+*g.*) to study (up to, till).
дох|а́, и́, *pl.* **~́и** *f.* fur-coat (*with fur on both sides*).
до́хлый *adj.* **1.** dead (*of animals*). **2.** (*coll.*) sickly (*of human beings*).
дохля́тин|а, ы *f.* (*coll.*) (*collect.*) carrion.
до́х|нуть, ну, нешь, *past* **~, ~ла** *impf.* (*of* **по~**) to die (*of animals*).
дохн|у́ть, у́, ёшь *pf.* to breathe, take a breath; **тут д. не́где** there is no room to breathe here.
дохо́д, а *m.* income; receipts; revenue.
доходи́ть, жу́, ~́дишь *impf. of* **дойти́**
дохо́дност|ь, и *f.* profitability; income.
дохо́д|ный (~ен, ~на) *adj.* **1.** profitable, lucrative, paying. **2.** *adj. of* **~**
дохо́дчив|ый (~, ~а) *adj.* intelligible, easy to understand.
дохристиа́нский *adj.* pre-Christian.
доце́нт, а *m.* senior lecturer, (university) reader.
до́чери, до́черью *see* **дочь**
доче́рн|ий *adj.* **1.** daughter's. **2.** subsidiary; branch; **~ее предприя́тие** (*comm.*) branch (*establishment*).
до́чиста *adv.* **1.** clean; **вы́мыть д.** to wash clean. **2.** (*fig.*, *coll.*) clean, completely; **его́ обыгра́ли д.** they cleaned him out (*at cards*).
дочит|а́ть, а́ю *pf.* (*of* **~́ывать**) **1.** to finish reading. **2.** (**до**+*g*) to read (to, as far as).
до́чк|а, и *f.* (*coll.*) = **дочь**
дочу́рк|а, и *f.* (*coll.*) *dim. of* **дочь**
доч|ь, ~́ери, *i.* **~́ерью,** *pl.* **~́ери, ~ере́й, ~еря́м, ~ерьми́, о ~еря́х** *f.* daughter.
дошко́льник, а *m.* child of preschool age; preschooler.
дошко́льни|ца, ы *f. of* **~к**
дошко́льный *adj.* preschool.
до́шлый *adj.* (*coll.*) cunning, shrewd.
доща́тый *adj.* made of planks, boards; **д. насти́л** duckboards.
доще́чк|а, и *f.* **1.** *dim. of* **доска́. 2.** door-plate, name-plate.
доя́рк|а, и *f.* milkmaid.
д-р *abbr. of* **1. до́ктор** Dr, Doctor. **2.** Director.
др.: и ~ (*abbr. of* **и други́е**) & co.; *et al.*
дра́г|а, и *f.* (*tech.*) dredge.
драги́р|овать *impf. and pf.* (*tech.*) to drag, dredge.
драгоце́нност|ь, и *f.* **1.** jewel; gem; (*pl.*) jewellery. **2.** object of great value; (*pl.*) valuables.
драгоце́н|ный (~ен, ~на) *adj.* precious (*also fig.*); **~ные ка́мни** precious stones.
драгу́н, а, *g. pl.* **~** *m.* dragoon.
дража́йш|ий *superl. of* **дорого́й; ~ая полови́на** 'better half'.
драже́ *nt. indecl.* dragée; **шокола́дное д.** chocolate drop(s).
дразн|и́ть, ю́, ~́ишь *impf.* **1.** to tease; **его́ ~и́ли тру́сом** they used to mock him by calling him a coward. **2.** to excite; to tantalize.
дра́|ить, ю, ишь *impf.* (*naut.*) to polish; to swab.
дра́к|а, и *f.* fight; **у них дошло́ до ~и** they came to blows.
драко́н, а *m.* **1.** dragon. **2.** (*heraldry*) wyvern.
драко́новский *adj.* Draconian.
дра́м|а, ы *f.* drama.
драматиза́ци|я, и *f.* dramatization.
драматизи́р|овать, ую *impf. and pf.* to dramatize.
драмати́зм, а *m.* **1.** (*theatr.*) dramatic effect. **2.** (*fig.*) dramatic character, quality; tension.
драмати́ческ|ий *adj.* **1.** dramatic; drama, theatre; **~ое иску́сство** dramatic art; **д. теа́тр** theatre. **2.** dramatic, theatrical; **~им то́ном** in a dramatic tone. **3.** (*fig.*) dramatic; tense.
драмати́ч|ный (~ен, ~на) *adj.* (*fig.*) dramatic.
драмату́рг, а *m.* playwright, dramatist.
драматурги́|я, и *f.* **1.** dramaturgy; dramatic art. **2.** (*collect.*) plays, drama; **д. Че́хова** the plays of Chekhov.
драмкруж|о́к, ка́ *m.* dramatic circle.
драндуле́т, а *m.* (*coll.*, *joc.*) jalopy, old banger.
дра́нк|а, и *f.* (*tech.*) **1.** lathing, shingle. **2.** lath.
дра́ный *adj.* (*coll.*) tattered, ragged.
драп, а *m.* thick woollen cloth.
драпир|ова́ть, у́ю *impf.* to drape.
драпиро́вк|а, и *f.* **1.** draping. **2.** curtain; hangings.
драпиро́вщик, а *m.* upholsterer.
дра́п|овый *adj. of* **~**
дра|ть, деру́, дерёшь, *past* **~л, ~ла́, ~́ло** *impf.* **1.** (*impf. only*) to tear (up, to pieces); **д. го́рло** (*coll.*) to bawl; **д. нос** (*coll.*) to put on airs; **д. на**

себе́ во́лосы (*fig.*) to tear one's hair. **2.** (*pf.* **со~**) to tear, strip off; **д. шку́ру** to flay. **3.** (*pf.* **за~**) to kill (*of wild animals*). **4.** (*pf.* **вы́~**) (*coll.*) to flog, thrash. **5.** (*pf.* **со~**) (**с**+*g.*; *fig.*, *coll.*) to fleece. **6.** (*pf.* **по~**): **чёрт его́ (по)дери́!** damn him! **7.** (*impf. only*) (*coll.*) to sting, irritate; **д. у́ши** (+*d.*) to jar (on); (*impers.*): **у меня́ в го́рле дерёт** I have a sore throat.

дра́|ться, деру́сь, дерёшься, *past* **~лся, ~ла́сь, ~ло́сь** *impf.* **1.** (**с**+*i.*) to fight (with); **д. на дуэ́ли** to fight a duel. **2.** (*fig.*) (**за**+*a.*) to fight, struggle (for).

дра́хм|а, ы *f.* drachma (*Greek unit of currency*).

драчли́вост|ь, и *f.* pugnacity.

драчли́в|ый (~, ~а) *adj.* pugnacious.

драчу́н, а́ *m.* (*coll.*) pugnacious, quarrelsome fellow.

драчу́н|ья, и, *g. pl.* **~ий** (*coll.*) *f. of* **~**

дребеде́н|ь, и *f.* (*coll.*) nonsense; **сплошна́я д.** absolute rubbish.

дре́безг, а *m.* (*coll.*) **1.** tinkling sound (*as of breaking glass, etc.*). **2.** (*pl. only*) **разби́ть(ся) в (ме́лкие) ~и** to smash to smithereens.

дребезж|а́ть, и́т *impf.* to jingle, tinkle.

древеси́н|а, ы *f.* **1.** wood. **2.** timber.

древесноволокни́ст|ый *adj.*: **~ая плита́** fibreboard.

древесностру́жечн|ый *adj.*: **~ая плита́** chipboard.

древе́сн|ый *adj. of* **де́рево; ~ая ма́сса** wood-pulp; **д. спирт** wood alcohol; **д. у́голь** charcoal.

дре́вк|о, а, *pl.* **~и, ~ов** *nt.* pole, staff; shaft (*of spear, etc.*); **д. зна́мени** flagstaff.

древнегре́ческий *adj.* ancient, classical Greek.

древнееврéйский *adj.* ancient, classical Hebrew.

древнеру́сский *adj.* Old Russian.

древнецерко́внославя́нский *adj.* (*ling.*) Old Church Slavonic.

дре́в|ний (~ен, ~ня) *adj.* ancient; **~няя исто́рия** ancient history; **~ние языки́** classical languages; *as n.* **~ние, ~них** the ancients.

дре́вност|ь, и *f.* **1.** (*sg. only*) antiquity. **2.** (*pl.*; *archaeol.*) antiquities.

дре́в|о, а, *pl.* **~еса́, ~е́с, ~еса́м** *nt.* (*poet.*) tree.

дрези́н|а, ы *f.* (*rail.*) trolley, hand car.

дрейф, а *m.* (*naut.*) drift, leeway; **лечь в д.** to heave to; **лежа́ть в ~е** to lie to.

дре́йф|ить, лю, ишь *impf.* (*of* **с~**) (*coll.*) to be a coward.

дрейф|ова́ть, у́ю *impf.* (*naut.*) to drift; **~у́ющий лёд** drift ice.

дрел|ь, и *f.* (*tech.*) drill.

дрем|а́ть, лю́, ~лешь *impf.* to doze; to slumber; **не д.** (*also fig.*) to be watchful; to be wide awake.

дрем|а́ться, ~лется *impf.* (*impers.*, +*d.*) to feel sleepy, drowsy.

дремо́т|а, ы *f.* drowsiness.

дремо́тный *adj.* drowsy.

дрему́ч|ий (~, ~а) *adj.* (*poet.*) thick, dense.

дрена́ж, а *m.* drainage.

дренажи́р|овать, ую *impf. and pf.* (*med.*) to drain.

дрена́ж|ный *adj. of* **~; ~ная труба́** drain-pipe.

дрени́р|овать, ую *impf. and pf.* to drain.

дрессиро́ванн|ый *p.p.p. of* **дрессирова́ть** *and adj.*: **~ые живо́тные** performing animals.

дрессир|ова́ть, у́ю *impf.* (*of* **вы́~**) to train (*animals*); (*fig.*) to school.

дрессиро́вк|а, и *f.* training.

дрессиро́вщик, а *m.* trainer.

дриа́д|а, ы *f.* (*myth.*) dryad.

дри́блинг, а *m.* (*sport*) dribbling.

дроби́лк|а, и *f.* (*tech.*) crusher.

дроби́льн|ый *adj.* (*tech.*) crushing; **~ая маши́на** crusher.

дроби́н|а, ы *f.* pellet.

дроб|и́ть, лю́, и́шь *impf.* (*of* **раз~**) **1.** to break up, crush, smash (to pieces). **2.** (*fig.*) to subdivide, split up.

дроб|и́ться, и́тся *impf.* (*of* **раз~**) **1.** to break into pieces, smash (into pieces). **2.** to divide, split up.

дробле́ни|е, я *nt.* **1.** crushing, breaking up. **2.** (*fig.*) subdivision, splitting up.

дроблёный *adj.* crushed.

дро́б|ный (~ен, ~на) *adj.* **1.** separate; subdivided, split up. **2.** staccato; **д. стук** staccato knocking; **д. дождь** fine rain. **3.** (*math.*) fractional.

дробови́к, а́ *m.* shotgun.

дроб|ь, и, *pl.* **~и, ~е́й** *f.* **1.** (*collect.*) (small) shot. **2.** drumming; tapping; patter. **3.** (*math.*) fraction. **4.** oblique stroke, slash.

дров|а́, ~, ~а́м *no sg.* firewood.

дро́вн|и, ~е́й *no sg.* sledge.

дров|яно́й *adj. of* **~а́; д. сара́й** woodshed; **д. склад** woodyard.

дро́г|и, ~ *no sg.* **1.** dray cart. **2.** hearse.

дро́г|нуть[1]**, ну, нешь,** *past* **~, ~ла** *impf.* to be chilled, freeze.

дро́гн|уть[2]**, у, ешь,** *past* **~ул, ~ула** *pf.* **1.** to shake, move; to quaver; to flicker. **2.** to waver, falter; **у меня́ рука́ не ~ет** (+*inf.*) I shall not hesitate to ….

дрожа́ни|е, я *nt.* trembling, vibration.

дрож|а́ть, у́, и́шь *impf.* **1.** to tremble; to shiver, shake; **д. от хо́лода, испу́га** to shiver with cold, with fright. **2.** (**за**+*a. or* **пе́ред** *i.*; *fig.*) to tremble (for; before). **3.** (**над**+*i.*) to grudge; **д. над ка́ждой копе́йкой** to count every penny.

дро́жж|и, е́й *no sg.* yeast, leaven; **ста́вить на ~а́х** to leaven; **пивны́е д.** brewer's yeast.

дро́ж|ки, ~ек, ~кам *no sg.* droshky.

дрож|ь, и *f.* shivering, trembling; tremor, quaver.

дрозд, а́ *m.* thrush; **чёрный д.** blackbird; **дать ~а́** (+*d.*) to tear s.o. off a strip.

дрок, а *m.* (*bot.*) gorse.

дромаде́р, а *m.* (*zool.*) dromedary.

дро́ссел|ь, я *m.* (*tech.*) throttle, choke.

дро́тик, а *m.* javelin.

друг[1]**, а,** *pl.* **друзья́, друзе́й** *m.* friend; **д. до́ма** friend of the family; **д. по перепи́ске** pen-friend, pen-pal.

друг[2] (*short form of* **~о́й**) **д. ~а** each other, one another; **д. за ~ом** one after another; **д. с ~ом** with each other.

друг|о́й *adj.* **1.** other, another; different; **и тот и д.** both; **ни тот ни д.** neither; **никто́ д.** none other; **э́то ~о́е де́ло** that is another matter; **~и́ми слова́ми** in other words; **с ~о́й стороны́** on the other hand; **на д. день** the next day; *as n.* **~и́е, ~и́х** others. **2.** second.

дру́жб|а, ы *f.* friendship; **не в слу́жбу, а в ~у** out of friendship.

дружелю́би|е, я *nt.* friendliness.

дружелю́б|ный (~ен, ~на) *adj.* friendly, amicable.

дру́жеск|ий *adj.* friendly; **быть на ~ой ноге́** (**с**+*i.*) to be on friendly terms (with).

дру́жественн|ый *adj.* friendly, amicable; **~ая держа́ва** friendly power.

дружи́н|а, ы *f.* **1.** (*hist.*) (*prince's*) bodyguard. **2.** militia unit, detachment (*in tsarist Russia*). **3.** squad, team; **наро́дная д.** people's patrol (*in former USSR, voluntary civilian organization assisting police in maintaining public order*).

дружи́нник, а *m.* **1.** (*hist.*) member of (*prince's*) bodyguard. **2.** (*hist.*) member of militia unit. **3.** member of people's patrol, vigilante.

друж|и́ть, у́, ~ишь *impf.* (**с**+*i.*) to be friends (with), on friendly terms (with).

друж|и́ться, у́сь, ~ишься *impf.* (*of* **по~**) (**с**+*i.*) to make friends (with).

дру́жно *adv.* **1.** harmoniously. **2.** (all) together, in concert; **раз, два, ~!** heave-ho!; all together!
дру́ж|ный (~ен, ~на́, ~но) *adj.* **1.** amicable; harmonious. **2.** simultaneous, concerted; **~ные уси́лия** concerted efforts.
друж|о́к, ка́ *m.* (*coll.*) pal; (*as mode of address*) my dear.
друзья́ *see* **друг**
дры́г|ать, аю *impf.* (*of* **~нуть**) (+*i.*; *coll.*) to jerk, twitch.
дры́г|нуть, ну, нешь *pf. of* **~ать**
дря́бл|ый (~, ~а́, ~о) *adj.* flabby (*also fig.*); flaccid; sluggish.
дря́бн|уть, у, ешь *impf.* (*coll.*) to become flabby.
дря́зг|и, ~ *no sg.* (*coll.*) squabbles.
дрян|но́й (~́ен, ~на́, ~́но) *adj.* (*coll.*) worthless, rotten; good-for-nothing.
дрян|ь, и *f.* (*coll.*) **1.** trash, rubbish. **2.** *as pred.* it is rotten, it is no good; **пого́да — д.** the weather is awful. **3.** (*of a pers.*) good-for-nothing.
дряхле́|ть, ю *impf.* (*of* **о~**) to grow decrepit.
дря́хлост|ь, и *f.* decrepitude.
дря́хл|ый (~, ~а́, ~о) *adj.* decrepit.
дуайе́н, а *m.* (*dipl.*) doyen.
дуали́зм, а *m.* (*phil.*) dualism.
дуб, а, *pl.* **~ы́** *m.* oak; **дать ~а** (*coll.*) to snuff it; to kick the bucket.
дуба́|сить, шу, сишь *impf.* (*of* **от~**) (*coll.*) **1.** to cudgel. **2.** (**по**+*d.* **в**+*a.*) to bang (on).
дуби́льн|ый *adj.* tanning, tannic; **~ая кислота́** tannic acid.
дуби́л|ьня, ьни, *g. pl.* **~ен** *f.* tannery.
дуби́льщик, а *m.* tanner.
дуби́н|а, ы *f.* **1.** club, cudgel. **2.** (*coll.*) blockhead, numskull.
дуби́нк|а, и *f.* truncheon, baton.
дуб|и́ть, лю́, и́шь *impf.* (*of* **вы~**) to tan.
дублёнк|а, и *f.* (*coll.*) sheepskin coat.
дублёный *adj.* tanned; (*fig.*) leathery, weather-beaten.
дублёр, а *m.* (*theatr.*) understudy; (*cin.*) stand-in.
дубле́т, а *m.* duplicate.
дублика́т, а *m.* duplicate.
дубли́р|овать, ую *impf.* **1.** to duplicate; **д. роль** (*theatr.*) to understudy a part. **2.** (*cinema*) to dub.
дубня́к, а́ *nt.* oak forest.
дубова́т|ый (~, ~а) *adj.* (*coll.*) coarse; stupid, thick.
дубо́в|ый *adj.* **1.** oak; **д. гроб** oak coffin. **2.** (*fig., coll.*) coarse; thick; **~ая голова́** blockhead, numskull.
дуб|о́к, ка́ *m.* young oak.
дубра́в|а, ы *f.* oak forest.
дуг|а́, и́, *pl.* **~́и** *f.* **1.** shaft-bow (*part of harness*). **2.** arc, arch; **бро́ви ~о́й** arched brows.
дуг|ово́й *adj. of* **~а́**; **~ова́я ла́мпа** arc-lamp; **~ова́я сва́рка** arc welding.
дугообра́з|ный (~ен, ~на) *adj.* arched.
дуд|е́ть, *1st pers. not used,* **и́шь** *impf.* (*coll.*) to play the pipes, fife.
ду́дк|а, и *f.* pipe, fife; **пляса́ть под чью-н. ~у** (*fig.*) to dance to s.o.'s tune.
ду́дки *int.* (*coll.*) not if I know it!; not on your life!
ду́жк|а, и *f.* **1.** *dim. of* **дуга́**. **2.** hoop (*at croquet*). **3.** handle.
дука́т, а *m.* ducat.
ду́л|о *nt.* muzzle, barrel (*of firearm*); **под ~ом пистоле́та** at gunpoint.
ду́л|ьце, ьца, *g. pl.* **~ец** *nt.* **1.** *dim. of* **~о**. **2.** (*mus.*) mouthpiece (*of wind instruments*).
ду́м|а, ы *f.* **1.** thought. **2.** Duma; **Госуда́рственная Д.** the State Duma.
ду́ма|ть, ю *impf.* (*of* **по~**) **1.** (**о**+*p. or* **над**+*i.*) to think (about); to be concerned (about); **мно́го о себе́ д.** to have a high opinion of o.s. **2.** (*impf. only*) **д. что...** to think, suppose that ...; **я ~ю!** of course!; I should think so! **3.** (+*inf.*) to think of, plan to; **он ~ет пое́хать в Ло́ндон** he is thinking of going to London; **и не ~ю** (+*inf.*) I would not dream (of).
ду́ма|ться, ется *impf.* (*impers.*, +*d.*) to seem; **мне ~ется** I think, I fancy; **~ется** it seems.
ду́м|ец, ца *m.* member of Duma.
ду́мк|а, и *f.* **1.** *dim. of* **ду́ма 1.**. **2.** (*coll.*) small pillow.
дунове́ни|е, я *nt.* puff, breath.
ду́н|уть, у, ешь *pf.* to blow.
ду́пел|ь, я *pl.* **~я́** *m.* (*zool.*) great snipe.
дупли́ст|ый (~, ~а) *adj.* hollow.
дупл|о́, а́, *pl.* **~́а, ду́пел** *nt.* **1.** hollow. **2.** cavity.
-дур *adj. indecl.* (*mus.*) major.
ду́р|а, ы *f. of* **дура́к**
дура́к, а́ *m.* **1.** (*hist.*) jester, fool. **2.** fool, ass; **д. ~о́м** an utter fool; **оста́вить в ~а́х** to make a fool of; **оста́ться в ~а́х** to be fooled, make a fool of o.s.; **валя́ть, лома́ть ~а́** the play the fool; to make a fool of o.s.; **на ~а́** for fun, for a joke; **~а́м зако́н не пи́сан** (*prov.*) fools rush in where angels fear to tread; **нашёл ~а́!** not likely!; no thanks!
дурале́|й, я *m.* = **дура́к 2.**
дура́цкий *adj.* (*coll.*) stupid, foolish, idiotic; **д. колпа́к** dunce's cap.
дура́честв|о, а *nt.* (*coll.*) prank.
дура́ч|ить, у, ишь *impf.* (*of* **о~**) to fool, dupe.
дура́ч|иться, усь, ишься *impf.* to play the fool.
дурач|о́к, ка́ *m.* **1.** *affectionate dim. of* **дура́к. 2.** (*coll.*) idiot, imbecile.
дура́шлив|ый (~, ~а) *adj.* (*coll.*) stupid.
ду́р|ень, ня *m.* (*coll.*) fool, simpleton.
дуре́|ть, ю *impf.* (*of* **о~**) to become stupid.
дур|и́ть, ю́, и́шь *impf.* (*coll.*) to be naughty (*of children*); to play tricks.
дурма́н, а *m.* **1.** (*bot.*) thorn-apple. **2.** (*coll.*) drug, narcotic.
дурма́н|ить, ю, ишь *impf.* (*of* **о~**) to stupefy.
дурне́|ть, ю *impf.* (*of* **по~**) to grow ugly.
ду́рно *adv. of* **дурно́й**
ду́рно *as pred.* (*impers.*, +*d.*): **мне,** *etc.*, **д.** I, *etc.*, feel faint.
дур|но́й (~́ен, ~на́, ~́но) *adj.* **1.** (*in var. senses*) bad, evil; nasty; **д. вкус** nasty taste; **д. глаз** the evil eye; **~ны́е мы́сли** evil thoughts; **~ны́е привы́чки** bad habits; **д. сон** bad dream. **2. (собо́ю)** ugly.
дурнот|а́, ы́ *f.* (*coll.*) faintness; nausea; **у́тренняя д.** morning sickness; **чу́вствовать ~у́** to feel faint, sick.
дурну́шк|а, и *f.* (*coll.*) plain girl, plain Jane.
дуршла́г, а *m.* (*cul.*) colander.
дур|ь, и *f.* (*coll.*) foolishness, stupidity.
ду́т|ый *p.p.p. of* **~ь** *and adj.* **1.** hollow. **2.** inflated; **~ые ши́ны** pneumatic tyres. **3.** (*fig.*) inflated, exaggerated.
дуть, ду́ю, ду́ешь *impf.* **1.** (*pf.* **по~**) to blow. **2.** (*impers.*) to be draughty; **от окна́ ду́ет** there is a draught coming from the window.
дуть|ё, я́ *nt.* **1.** blowing. **2.** (*tech.*) blast.
ду́|ться, юсь, ешься *impf.* (*coll.*) (**на**+*a.*) to grumble (at), pout (at).
дух, а *m.* **1.** (*relig., phil., and fig.*) spirit; **свято́й д.** the Holy Spirit, the Holy Ghost; **д. ве́ка** Zeitgeist (*spirit of the age*). **2.** spirit(s); heart; mind; **расположе́ние ~́а** mood, frame of mind; **быть в ~́е** to be in good (high) spirits; **не в ~́е** in low spirits; **па́дать ~́ом** to lose heart; **собра́ться с ~́ом** to pluck up one's courage; **прису́тствие ~́а** presence of mind; **у меня́ ~́у не хвата́ет** (+*inf.*) I have not the heart (to); **э́то не в моём ~́е** it is not to my taste; **что́-то в э́том ~́е** something of the sort. **3.**

breath; (*coll.*) air; **перевести́ д.** to catch one's breath; **испусти́ть д.** (*fig.*) to give up the ghost; **во весь д.** (*coll.*) at full tilt; **одни́м ~́ом** in one breath; (*fig.*) at one go, at a stretch; **о нём ни слу́ху ни ~́у** nothing is heard of him. **4.** spectre, ghost.

дух|и́, о́в *no sg.* perfume, scent.

ду́хов *adj.*: **Д. день** (*eccl.*) Whit Monday.

духове́нств|о, а *nt.* (*collect.*) clergy.

духови́д|ец, ца *m.* clairvoyant; medium.

духо́вк|а, и *f.* oven.

духовни́к, а́ *m.* (*eccl.*) confessor.

духо́вност|ь, и *f.* spirituality.

духо́вн|ый *adj.* **1.** spiritual; inner; **~ые запро́сы** spiritual demands; **д. мир** inner world. **2.** ecclesiastical, church; religious; **~ое лицо́** ecclesiastic; **~ая му́зыка** sacred music; **д. сан** holy orders. **3.: ~ое завеща́ние** last will and testament. **4.: ~ое о́ко** (the) mind's eye.

духов|о́й *adj.* **1.** (*mus.*) wind; **д. инструме́нт** wind instrument; **д. орке́стр** brass band. **2.** (hot-)air; **~а́я печь** oven; **~о́е ружьё** air-gun; blowpipe.

духот|а́, ы́ *f.* stuffiness, closeness; stuffy heat.

душ, а *m.* shower; **приня́ть д.** to take a shower.

душ|а́, и́, *a.* **~́у,** *pl.* **~́и** *f.* **1.** soul; (*fig.*) heart; **д. в ~́у** at one, in harmony; **в ~е́** (*i*) inwardly, secretly, (*ii*) at heart; **для ~и́** for one's private satisfaction; **за ~о́й** to one's name; **у него́ за ~о́й ни гроша́** he hasn't a penny to his name; **от ~и́** from the heart; **от всей ~и́** with all one's heart; **по ~е́** (+*d.*) to one's liking; **по ~а́м говори́ть** (**с**+*i.*) to have a heart-to-heart talk (with); **вложи́ть ~́у** (**в**+*a.*) to put one's heart (into); **изли́ть, отвести́ ~́у** to pour out one's heart; **~и́ не ча́ять** (**в**+*p.*) to think the world of; to dote on; **ско́лько ~е́ уго́дно** to one's heart content; **~о́й и те́лом** heart and soul. **2.** feeling, spirit; **говори́ть с ~о́й** to speak with feeling. **3.** (*fig.*) (the) soul; moving spirit; inspiration; **д. о́бщества** the life and soul of the party. **4.** (*fig.*) spirit (= *person*); **сме́лая д.** a bold spirit. **5.** (*fig.*) soul (= *person*); **на ~́у** per head; **потребле́ние на ~́у населе́ния** per-capita consumption; **ни (живо́й) ~и́** not a (living) soul. **6.: душа́ моя́!** (*coll.*; *affectionate mode of address*) my dear, darling.

душев|а́я, о́й *f.* shower-room.

душевнобольн|о́й *adj.* insane; mentally ill; *as n.* **д., ~о́го** *m.*, **~а́я, ~о́й** *f.* insane person; mental case.

душе́вн|ый *adj.* **1.** mental; **~ая боле́знь** mental illness. **2.** sincere, heartfelt; **~ая бесе́да** friendly chat; **д. челове́к** understanding person.

душев|о́й[1] *adj.* per-capita; **~о́е потребле́ние** per-capita consumption.

душево́й[2] *adj. of* **душ**

душегре́йк|а, и *f.* (*woman's*) sleeveless jacket (*usu. wadded or fur-lined*).

душегу́б, а *m.* (*coll.*) murderer.

душегу́б|ка, ки *f.* **1.** *f. of* **~. 2.** dugout (canoe). **3.** (*hist.*) mobile gas-chamber.

душегу́бств|о, а *nt.* (*coll.*) murder.

душераздира́ющий *adj.* heart-rending.

ду́шечк|а, и *c.g.* = **ду́шенька**

душещипа́тельный *adj.*: **д. фильм** tear-jerker, weepie.

души́ст|ый (~, ~а) *adj.* fragrant, sweet-smelling.

душ|и́ть[1], **у́, ~́ишь** *impf.* (*of* **за~**) **1.** to strangle; to smother, suffocate; (*fig.*) to stifle, suppress; **д. поцелу́ями** to smother with kisses. **2.** (*impf. only*) to choke; **его́ ~и́л гне́в** he choked with rage.

душ|и́ть[2], **у́, ~́ишь** *impf.* (*of* **на~**) to scent, perfume.

душ|и́ться[1], **у́сь, ~́ишься** *impf.*, *pass. of* **~и́ть**[1]

душ|и́ться[2], **у́сь, ~́ишься** *impf.* (*of* **на~**) (+*i.*) to perfume o.s. (with); **она́ всегда́ ~́ится францу́зскими духа́ми** she always uses French perfume.

ду́шк|а, и *c.g.* (*coll.*) dear (person); **он тако́й д., она́ така́я д.** he, she is such a dear.

душни́к, а́ *m.* vent.

ду́шно *as pred.* it is stuffy; it is stifling; **мне ста́ло д.** I felt suffocated.

ду́ш|ный (~ен, ~на́, ~но) *adj.* stuffy, close, sultry; stifling.

душ|о́к, ка́ *m.* (*coll.*) **1.** smell (*esp. of decaying matter*); **с ~ко́м** high, tainted. **2.** (*fig.*) smack, taint; tinge; **газе́та с либера́льным ~ко́м** (*pej.*) newspaper with a liberal tinge.

дуэли́ст, а *m.* duellist.

дуэ́л|ь и *f.* duel; **вы́звать на д.** to challenge; **дра́тся на ~и** to fight a duel.

дуэля́нт, а *m.* = **дуэли́ст**

дуэ́т, а *m.* duet.

ды́б|а, ы *f.* (*hist.*) rack (*instrument of torture*).

ды́б|иться, ится *impf.* **1.** to stand on end. **2.** (*of a horse*) to rear, prance.

ды́бом *adv.* on end; **во́лосы у него́ вста́ли д.** his hair stood on end.

дыбы́: на д. on to the hind legs; **станови́ться на д.** to rear, prance; (*fig.*) to kick, resist.

ды́лд|а, ы *c.g.* (*coll.*) lanky person, beanpole.

дым, а (у), о ~́е, в ~у́, *pl.* **~ы́** *m.* smoke; **в д.** (*coll.*) completely.

дым|и́ть, лю́, и́шь *impf.* (*of* **на~**) to smoke (*intrans.*), emit smoke.

дым|и́ться, и́тся *impf.* to smoke (*intrans.*); (*of fog*) to billow.

ды́мк|а, и *f.* haze.

ды́мный *adj.* smoky.

дымов|о́й *adj. of* **дым; ~а́я заве́са** (*mil.*) smoke-screen; **~а́я труба́** flue, chimney; funnel, smoke-stack.

дым|о́к, ка́ *m.* puff of smoke.

дымохо́д, а *m.* flue.

ды́мчат|ый (~, ~а) *adj.* smoke-coloured.

ды́нный *adj. of* **ды́ня**

ды́н|я, и *f.* melon.

дыр|а́, ы́, *pl.* **~́ы** *f.* **1.** hole; **заткну́ть ~у́** (*fig.*) to plug a gap. **2.** (*fig., coll.*) hole (= *remote place*).

дыроко́л, а *m.* hole-punch.

дыря́в|ить, лю, ишь *impf.* (*coll.*) to make a hole (in).

дыря́в|ый (~, ~а) *adj.* full of holes.

дыха́ни|е, я *nt.* breathing; breath; **второ́е д.** (*fig.*) second wind; **иску́сственное д.** artificial respiration.

дыха́тельн|ый *adj.* respiratory; **~ое го́рло** (*anat.*) windpipe; **~ые пути́** respiratory tract.

дыш|а́ть, у́, ~́ишь *impf.* (+*i.*) to breathe; **е́ле д.** to be at one's last gasp; (*fig.*) to be on one's last legs.

ды́шл|о, а *nt.* shaft, pole, beam.

дья́вол, а *m.* devil.

дьявол|ёнок, ёнка, *pl.* **~я́та, ~я́т** *m.* (*coll.*) imp.

дья́вольский *adj.* devilish, diabolical.

дья́кон, а, *pl.* **~а́, ~о́в** *m.* (*eccl.*) deacon.

дья́конств|о, а *nt.* (*eccl.*) diaconate.

дьяч|о́к, ка́ *m.* (*eccl.*) sacristan, sexton; reader.

дю́же *adv.* (*coll. or dial.*) terribly, awfully.

дю́ж|ий (~, ~а́, ~е) *adj.* (*coll.*) hefty; strapping.

дю́жин|а, ы *f.* dozen; **чёртова д.** baker's dozen.

дю́жинный *adj.* ordinary, commonplace.

дюйм, а *m.* inch.

дюймо́вый *adj.* one-inch.

дю́н|а, ы *f.* dune.

дюра́л|ь, я *m.* = **~юми́ний**

дюралюми́ни|й, я *m.* (*tech.*) duralumin.

дя́гил|ь, я *m.* (*bot.*) angelica.

дя́деньк|а, и *m. affectionate form of* **дя́дя**

дя́дьк|а, и *m.* **1.** *pej. form of* **дя́дя. 2.** (*coll.*) = **дя́дя 2.**

дя́дюшк|а, и *m.* (*coll.*) *affectionate form of* **дя́дя**; (*fig.*): **д. Сэм** Uncle Sam.
дя́д|я, и, *pl.* **~и, ~ей** *and* **~ья́, ~ьёв** *m.* **1.** uncle. **2.** (*coll.*) mister (*as term of address by child to any mature male*).
дя́т|ел, ла *m.* woodpecker.

Е

еб|а́ть, у́, ёшь *impf.* (*of* **уе́ть**) (*vulg.*) to fuck; **ёб твою́ мать! 1.** fuck you! **2.** *int.* fuck!; fucking hell!
Ева́нгели|е, я *nt.* (*collect.*) the Gospels; **е.** gospel (*also fig.*).
евангели́ст, а *m.* **1.** Evangelist. **2.** (an) evangelical.
евангели́ческ|ий *adj.* evangelical; **~ая це́рковь** Evangelical Church.
ева́нгельский *adj.* gospel
евге́ник|а, и *f.* eugenics.
е́внух, а *m.* eunuch.
евразийский *adj.* Eurasian.
евре́|й, я *m.* Jew; Hebrew; **ве́рующий е.** Orthodox Jew.
евре́йк|а, и *f.* Jewess.
евре́йский *adj.* Jewish.
евре́йств|о, и *nt.* Jewry.
евро... *comb. form* Euro-.
Евро́п|а, ы *f.* Europe.
Европарла́мент, а *m.* Europarliament.
европе́|ец, йца *m.* European.
европеиза́ци|я, и *f.* Europeanization.
европеизи́р|овать, ую *impf. and pf.* to Europeanize.
европе́|йка, йки *f. of* **~ец**
европе́йск|ий *adj.* European.
евхари́сти|я, и *f.* (*eccl.*) Eucharist.
е́гер|ь, я, *pl.* **~и, ~ей** *and* **~я́, ~е́й** *m.* huntsman.
Еги́пет, а *m.* Egypt.
еги́петский *adj.* Egyptian.
египто́лог, а *m.* Egyptologist.
египтоло́ги|я, и *f.* Egyptology.
египтя́н|ин, ина, *pl.* **~е, ~** *m.* Egyptian.
египтя́н|ка, ки *f. of* **~ин**
его́ 1. *g. and a. sg. of* **он**; *g. sg. of* **оно́. 2.** (*possessive adj.*) his; its.
егоз|а́, ы́ *m.and f.* (*coll.*) fidget.
его|зи́ть, жу́, зи́шь *impf.* (*coll.*) **1.** to fidget. **2.** (**пе́ред**+*i.*) to fawn (upon).
егозли́в|ый (~, ~а) *adj.* (*coll.*) fidgety.
ед|а́, ы *f.* **1.** food. **2.** meal; **во вре́мя ~ы́** at mealtimes, while eating.
едва́ *adv. and conj.* **1.** (*adv.*) hardly, barely, only just (= *with difficulty*); **мы е. попа́ли на по́езд** we only just caught the train. **2.** (*adv.*) hardly, scarcely, barely, only just (= *only slightly*); **печь е. гори́т** the fire is barely alight. **3. едва́-едва́** *emph. variant of* **е. 1., 2.. 4.: е. ли** (*adv.*) hardly, scarcely (*in judgements of probability*); **е. ли он отка́жется от тако́го соблазни́тельного предложе́ния** he will hardly refuse such a tempting offer. **5.: е. (ли) не** (*adv.*) nearly, almost, practically; **я е. не по́мер со́ смеху** I nearly died laughing. **6.** (*conj.*) hardly, scarcely, barely; **е...., как** scarcely ... when; no sooner ... than.
еди́м *see* **есть**[1]
едине́ни|е, я *nt.* unity.
едини́ц|а, ы *f.* **1.** one; figure 1. **2.** (*in var. senses*) unit; **е. мо́щности** unit of power; **~ы вое́нно-морско́го фло́та** naval units. **3.** 'one' (*lowest mark in Russ. university and school marking system*). **4.** individual; **(то́лько) ~ы** only a few, only a handful.
едини́чн|ый *adj.* single; **е. слу́чай** solitary instance; **~ые слу́чаи** isolated cases.
единобо́жи|е, я *nt.* monotheism.
единобо́рств|о, а *nt.* single combat.
единобра́чи|е, я *nt.* monogamy.
единобра́чный *adj.* monogamous.
единове́р|ец, ца *m.* coreligionist.
единове́р|ный (~ен, ~на) *adj.* (+*d. or* **с**+*i.*) of the same faith (as).
единовла́сти|е, я *nt.* autocracy, absolute rule.
единовла́ст|ный (~ен, ~на) *adj.* autocractic; **е. прави́тель** absolute ruler.
единовре́менно *adv.* **1.** but once, once only. **2.** simultaneously.
единовре́менн|ый *adj.* **1.** extraordinary; one-time; **~ое посо́бие** extraordinary grant. **2.** (+*d. or* **с**+*i.*) simultaneous (with).
единогла́си|е, я *nt.* unanimity.
единогла́сно *adv.* unanimously.
единогла́сный *adj.* unanimous.
единоду́ши|е, я *nt.* unanimity.
единоду́ш|ный (~ен, ~на) *adj.* unanimous.
единокро́в|ный (~ен, ~на) *adj.* **1.** (*obs.*) consanguineous; **е. брат** half-brother. **2.** of the same stock.
единоли́чн|ый *adj.* individual; personal; **~ое реше́ние** individual decision; **~ое хозя́йство** individual peasant holding.
единомы́сли|е, я *nt.* like-mindedness.
единомы́шленник, а *m.* **1.** person who holds the same views; like-minded person; **мы с ним ~и по вопро́сам вне́шней поли́тики** we think the same way on matters of foreign policy. **2.** confederate, accomplice.
единонасле́ди|е, я *nt.* (*leg.*) primogeniture.
единообра́зи|е, я *nt.* uniformity.
единообра́з|ный (~ен, ~на) *adj.* uniform.
единоро́г, а *m.* unicorn.
единоро́дный *adj.* (*obs.*) only-begotten; **е. сын** only son.
единоутро́б|ный (~ен, ~на) *adj.* (*obs.*) uterine; **е. брат** half-brother, uterine brother.
еди́нственно *adv.* only, solely; **е. возмо́жный ход** the only possible move; **она́ прису́тствовала е. из любопы́тства** she came solely out of curiosity.
еди́нственн|ый *adj.* only, sole; one and only; **е. сын** only son; **он е. оста́лся в живы́х** he was the sole survivor; **е. в своём ро́де** the only one of its kind, unique; **~ое число́** (*gram.*) the singular.
еди́нств|о, а *nt.* (*in var. senses*) unity.
еди́н|ый (~, ~а) *adj.* **1.** one; single, sole; **не́ было там ни ~ой души́** there was not a soul there; **всё ~о** (*coll.*) it's all one; **все до ~ого** to a man; one and all. **2.** united, unified; **~ая сре́дняя шко́ла** comprehensive school. **3.** common, single; **~ая во́ля** single will, purpose.
еди́те *see* **есть**[1]
е́д|кий (~ок, ~ка́, ~ко) *adj.* **1.** caustic; acrid, pungent; **е. натр** (*chem.*) caustic soda; **е. за́пах** pungent smell. **2.** caustic, sarcastic.
е́дкост|ь, и *f.* **1.** causticity; pungency; (*fig.*) sarcasm. **2.** sarcastic remark.
едо́к, а́ *m.* **1.** mouth; head; **у него́ в семье́ де́сять ~о́в** he has ten mouths to feed; **на ~а́** per head. **2.** (*coll.*) (big) eater; **плохо́й е.** a poor eater.
е́д|у, ешь *see* **е́хать**
е́дучи *pres. ger.* (*coll.*) *of* **е́хать**
е́д|че *comp. of* **~кий**

едя́т *see* **есть**[1]
её 1. *g. and a. of* **она́. 2.** (*possessive adj.*) her.
ёж, ежа́ *m.* hedgehog; **~у поня́тно** (*coll.*) it's as plain as can be.
ежеви́к|а, и *f.* **1.** (*collect.*) blackberries. **2.** bramble, blackberry bush.
ежеви́|чный *adj. of* **~ка; ~чное варе́нье** bramble preserve.
ежего́дник, а *m.* annual, year-book.
ежего́дный *adj.* annual, yearly.
ежедне́вн|ый *adj.* daily; everyday.
е́жели *conj.* (*obs. or coll.*) if.
ежеме́сячник, а *m.* monthly.
ежеме́сячный *adj.* monthly.
ежемину́тный *adj.* **1.** occurring every minute, at intervals of a minute; **у нас есть е. авто́бусный рейс в го́род** we have a one-minute bus service to town. **2.** incessant, continual.
еженеде́льник, а *m.* weekly.
еженеде́льный *adj.* weekly.
ежено́щный *adj.* nightly.
ежесеку́ндный *adj.* **1.** occurring every second. **2.** (*coll.*) incessant, continual.
ежесу́точный *adj.* daily (= *occurring every 24 hours*).
ежеча́сный *adj.* hourly.
ёжик, а *m.* **1.** *dim. of* **ёж. 2.: стри́чься ~ом** to have a crew cut.
ёж|иться, усь, ишься *impf.* (*of* **съ~**) **1.** to shiver, huddle o.s. up (*from cold, fever, etc.*). **2.** (*fig., coll.*) to shrink (*from fear, shyness, etc.*).
ежи́х|а, и *f.* female hedgehog.
ежо́в|ый *adj. of* **ёж; держа́ть в ~ых рукави́цах** (*coll.*) to rule with a rod of iron.
езд|а́, ы́ *f.* **1.** ride, riding; drive, driving; **е. на велосипе́де** bicycling. **2.** *in phrr. indicating distance from one point to another*; journey; **отсю́да до о́зера — до́брых три часа́ ~ы́** from here to the lake is a good three hours' journey.
е́з|дить, жу, дишь *impf.* **1.** (*indet. of* **е́хать**) to go (*in or on a vehicle or on an animal*); to ride, drive; **е. верхо́м** to ride (on horseback). **2.** **(к)** to visit (*habitually*).
езд|ово́й *adj. of* **~а́; ~овы́е соба́ки** draught-dogs; *as n.* **е., ~ово́го** *m.* (*mil.*) driver.
ездо́к, а́ *m.* **1.** rider; horseman. **2.: туда́ я бо́льше не е.** I am not going there again.
езжа́|ть *no pres., past* **~л, ~ла** (*coll.*), *freq. of* **е́здить; ~й(те)** (*as imper. of* **е́хать**) go!; get going!
е́зжен|ый *adj.*: **~ая доро́га** well-trodden track.
ей *d. and i. of* **она́**
ей-Бо́гу *int.* (*coll.*) truly!; really and truly!
ёк|ать, аю *impf.* (*of* **~нуть**) (**+се́рдце**) (*coll.*) to miss a beat; to go pit-a-pat.
ёкн|уть, у, ешь *pf. of* **ёкать**
ел, е́ла *see* **есть**[1]
е́ле *adv.* **1.** hardly, barely, only just (= *with difficulty*); **его́ речь была́ е. слышна́** his speech was barely audible. **2.** hardly, scarcely, barely, only just (= *only slightly*); **по́езд е. дви́гался** the train was scarcely moving. **3.: е́ле-е́ле** *emph. variant of* **е.; он е.-е. спа́сся** he had a very narrow escape.
е́левый *adj.* (*bot.*) fir, spruce.
еле́|й, я *m.* (*eccl.*) anointing oil; unction; (*fig.*) unction; balm.
еле́й|ный *adj.* **1.** (*eccl.*) *adj. of* **~. 2.** unctuous.
елизаве́тинский *adj.* Elizabethan.
ёлк|а, и *f.* fir(-tree), spruce; **рожде́ственская е.** Christmas-tree; **быть на ~е** (*coll.*) to be at a Christmas, New Year's party.
ел|о́вый *adj. of* **~ь; ~о́вые ши́шки** fir-cones.
ело́|зить, жу, зишь *impf.* (*coll.*) to crawl.
ёлочк|а, и *f.* **1.** *dim. of* **ёлка. 2.** herring-bone (pattern); **он но́сит зелёный пиджа́к ~ой, в ~у** he wears a green herring-bone jacket.
ёлочн|ый *adj. of* **ёлка; ~ые украше́ния** Christmas-tree decorations.
ел|ь, и *f.* spruce; fir(-tree).
е́льник, а *m.* fir-grove.
ем *see* **есть**[1]
ём|кий (~ок, ~ка) *adj.* capacious.
ёмкост|ь, и *f.* capacity, cubic content.
ему́ *d. of* **он, оно́**
ено́т, а *m.* **1.** (*zool.*) raccoon. **2.** raccoon (fur).
ено́т|овый *adj. of* **~; ~овая шу́ба** coonskin coat.
епархиа́льн|ый *adj.* (*eccl.*) diocesan.
епа́рхи|я, и *f.* (*eccl.*) diocese.
епи́скоп, а *m.* bishop.
епископа́льный *adj.* (*eccl.*) episcopalian.
епи́скопский *adj.* episcopal.
епи́скопств|о, а *nt.* episcopate.
ерала́ш, а *m.* (*coll.*) jumble, muddle.
е́рес|ь, и, *pl.* **~и, ~ей** *f.* heresy.
ерети́к, а́ *m.* heretic.
ерети́ческий *adj.* heretical.
ёрза|ть, ю *impf.* (*coll.*) to fidget.
ермо́лк|а, и *f.* skull-cap.
еро́ш|ить, у, ишь *impf.* (*coll.*) to rumple, ruffle; to dishevel.
ерунд|а́, ы́ *f.* (*coll.*) **1.** nonsense, rubbish; **говори́ть ~у́** to talk nonsense; **е. на по́стном ма́сле** twaddle, poppycock. **2.** trifle, trifling matter; child's play.
ерундо́вый *adj.* (*coll.*) **1.** foolish. **2.** trifling.
ёрш[1], **ерша́** *m.* **1.** (*fish*) ruff. **2.** brush. **3.** hair sticking up; **~о́м** (*as adv.*) sticking up, on end.
ёрш[2], **ерша́** *m.* (*coll.*) mixture of beer and vodka.
ерши́ст|ый (~, ~а) *adj.* (*coll.*) **1.** bristling; sticking up. **2.** (*fig.*) obstinate; unyielding.
ерш|и́ться, у́сь, и́шься *impf.* (*coll.*) **1.** to stick up. **2.** to grow heated, fly into a rage.
е́сли *conj.* if; **е. не** unless; **е. то́лько** provided; **е. бы не** but for, if it were not for; **е. бы не ты, он мог бы ко́нчить самоуби́йством** but for you he might have committed suicide; **е. бы** (*in exclamations*) if only; **что е...?** what if ...?; **что, е. бы** (*introducing suggestion of course of action*) what about, how about.
ессе́|й, я *m.* (*relig.*) Essene.
ессенту́к|и́, о́в *no sg.* Essentuki (*mineral water*).
ест *see* **есть**[1]
есте́ственник, а *m.* (natural) scientist.
есте́ственно[1] *adv.* **1.** naturally. **2.** *as particle* naturally, of course.
есте́ственно[2] *as pred.* it is natural.
есте́ствен|ный (~, ~на) *adj.* (*in var. senses*) natural; **~ные бога́тства** natural resources; **~ные нау́ки** natural sciences; **е. отбо́р** (*biol.*) natural selection.
естеств|о́, а́ *nt.* essence.
естествозна́ни|е, я *nt.* (natural) science.
естествоиспыта́тел|ь, я *m.* (natural) scientist.
есть[1], **ем, ешь, ест, еди́м, еди́те, едя́т,** *past* **ел, е́ла,** *imper.* **ешь,** *impf.* (*of* **съ~**) to eat; **е. глаза́ми** to devour with one's eyes.
есть[2] **1.** *3rd pers. sg.* (*also, rarely, substituted for all persons*) *pres. of* **быть; и е.** (*coll.*) yes, indeed; **как е.** (*coll.*) entirely, completely. **2.** there is; there are; **у меня́, него́** *etc.*, **е.** I have, he has, *etc.*; **е. тако́е де́ло** (*coll.*) all right; agreed!
есть[3] *int.* (*mil.*; *in acknowledgement of a superior's order*) yes, sir!; (*naut.*) aye-aye!
ефре́йтор, а *m.* (*mil.*) lance-corporal.
е́хать, е́ду, е́дешь *impf.* (*of* **по~**) (*det. of* **е́здить**) to go (*in or on a vehicle or on an animal*); to ride, drive; **е. верхо́м** to ride (*on horseback*); **е. по́ездом, на по́езде** to go by train.
ехи́дн|а, ы *f.* **1.** (*zool.*) echidna. **2.** (*fig., coll.*) viper, snake.

ехи́д|ный (~ен, ~на) *adj.* (*coll.*) malicious, spiteful; venomous (*fig.*).

ехи́дств|о, а *nt.* (*coll.*) malice, spite.

ешь *see* **есть**[1]

ещё *adv.* **1.** still; yet; **е. не, нет е.** not yet; **всё е.** still; **пока́ е.** for the time being; **э́то е. ничего́!** that's nothing! **2.** (some) more; any more; further; again; **мо́жно нали́ть е. (вина́** *etc.*)? may I pour you some more (wine, *etc.*)?; **есть ли е. хлеб?** is there any more bread?; **е. оди́н** one more, yet another; **е. раз** (*i*) once more, again, (*ii*) *as int.* encore!; **наде́юсь, е. приду́** I hope I shall come again. **3.** already; as long ago as; **е. в 1900-ом году́** in 1900 already; as long ago as 1900. **4.** (+*comp.*) still, yet, even; **е. гро́мче** even louder; **е. и е.** more and more. **5.** (+*prons. and advs.*) *as emph. particle*; **ты ви́дел инду́са? — како́го е. инду́са?** have you seen the Indian? — What Indian, for heaven's sake? **6.: е. бы** I'll say!; you can say that again! **7.: а е.** *expr. reproach or sarcastic criticism*: **тепе́рь ворчи́шь, а е. сам предложи́л** you grumble now, but it was you who suggested it.

ЕЭС *nt. indecl.* (*abbr. of* **Европе́йское экономи́ческое соо́бщество**) EEC (*European Economic Community*).

е́ю *i. of* **она́**

Ж (*abbr. of* **Же́нская (убо́рная)**) Ladies (*lavatory*).

ж = же

жа́б|а[1], **ы** *f.* (*zool.*) toad.

жа́б|а[2], **ы** *f.* (*med.*) quinsy; **грудна́я ж.** angina pectoris.

жабо́ *nt. indecl.* jabot.

жа́бр|ы, ~ *pl.* (*sg.* **~а, ~ы** *f.*) (*zool.*) gills.

жа́ворон|ок, ка *m.* (*zool.*) lark; **полево́й ж.** skylark.

жа́днича|ть, ю *impf.* (*coll.*) to be greedy; to be mean.

жа́дност|ь, и *f.* **1.** greed; greediness. **2.** avarice, meanness.

жа́д|ный (~ен, ~на́, ~но) *adj.* **1.** (**к**+*d.*) greedy (for); avid (for); **он всегда́ был ~ным к но́вым ощуще́ниям** he was always greedy for new sensations. **2.** avaricious, mean.

жа́жд|а, ы *no pl., f.* thirst; (+*g.*; *fig.*) thirst, craving (for); **ж. зна́ний** thirst for knowledge.

жа́жд|ать, у *impf.* (+*g. or inf.*; *fig.*) to thirst (for, after), crave.

жаке́т, а *m.* (*ladies'*) jacket.

жаке́тк|а, и *f.* = **жаке́т**

жале́|ть, ю *impf.* (*of* **по~**) **1.** to pity, feel sorry (for). **2.** (**о**+*p. or* +*g.*; **что**) to regret, be sorry (for, about); **~ю об утра́ченном вре́мени** I regret the waste of time; **~ю, что не оста́лся до конца́ ма́тча** I am sorry I did not stay till the end of the match. **3.** (+*a. or g.*) to spare; to grudge; **не ~я сил** unsparingly.

жа́л|ить, ю, ишь *impf.* (*of* **у~**) to sting; to bite.

жа́л|иться, юсь, ишься *impf.* (*coll.*) to sting; to bite.

жа́л|кий (~ок, ~ка́, ~ко) *adj.* pitiful, pathetic; wretched; miserable; **име́ть ж. вид** to be a sorry sight.

жа́лк|о[1] *adv. of* **~ий**

жа́лко[2] *as pred.* (*impers.*) **1.** (+*d. and g.*) to pity, feel sorry (for); **ей ж. бы́ло себя́** she felt sorry for herself. **2.** (it is) a pity, a shame; (+*d. and g. or a.*) it grieves (me, *etc.*); to regret, feel sorry. **3.** (+*g. or* +*inf.*) to grudge.

жа́л|о, а *nt.* **1.** sting (*also fig.*). **2.** point (*of needle, etc.*).

жа́лоб|а, ы *f.* complaint; **пода́ть ~у (на**+*a.*) to make, lodge a complaint (about).

жа́лоб|ный (~ен, ~на) *adj.* **1.** plaintive; mournful. **2.** *adj. of* **~а; ~ная кни́га** complaints book.

жа́лобщик, а *m.* **1.** person lodging complaint. **2.** (*leg.*) plaintiff.

жа́лова|нный *p.p.p. of* **~ть** *and adj.* (*hist.*) granted, received as grant; **~нная гра́мота** letters patent, charter.

жа́ловань|е, я *nt.* salary.

жа́л|овать, ую *impf.* (*of* **по~**) **1.** (+*a. and i. or* +*d. and a.*) to grant (to); to bestow, confer (on); to reward (with). **2.** (*coll.*) to favour, regard with favour.

жа́л|оваться, уюсь *impf.* (*of* **по~**) (**на**+*a.*) to complain (of, about); **ж. в суд** to go to law.

жа́лостлив|ый (~, ~а) *adj.* (*coll.*) **1.** compassionate, sympathetic. **2.** pitiful.

жа́лост|ный (~ен, ~на) *adj.* (*coll.*) **1.** plaintive, mournful. **2.** compassionate, sympathetic.

жа́лост|ь, и *f.* pity, compassion; **из ~и (к)** out of pity (for); **кака́я ж.!** what a pity!; **ж. к себе́** self-pity.

жаль *as pred.* (*impers.*) **1.** (+*d. and a. or g.*) to pity, feel sorry (for); **мне ж. тебя́** I pity you. **2.** (it is) a pity, shame; (+*d.*) it grieves (me, *etc.*); to regret, feel sorry; **ж., что вас там не бу́дет** it is a pity you will not be there; **нам ж. бы́ло расстава́ться** it grieved us to part. **3.** (+*g. or* +*inf.*) to grudge.

жалюзи́ *nt. indecl.* Venetian blind(s), jalousie.

жанда́рм, а *m.* gendarme.

жандарме́ри|я, и *f.* (*collect.*) gendarmerie.

жанда́рм|ский *adj. of* **~**

жанр, а *m.* **1.** genre. **2.** genre-painting.

жанри́ст, а *m.* genre-painter.

жа́нр|овый *adj. of* **~**

жар, а (у), о ~́е, в ~у́ *no pl., m.* **1.** heat; heat of the day; hot place; **в ~у́** (+*g.*) in the heat (of). **2.** (*coll.*) embers; **как ж. горе́ть** to gleam, glitter; **чужи́ми рука́ми ж. загреба́ть** to use others to pull one's chestnuts out of the fire. **3.** fever; (high) temperature. **4.** (*fig.*) heat, ardour; **с ~́ом приня́ться за что-н.** to set about sth. with a will.

жар|а́, ы́ *f.* heat; hot weather.

жарго́н, а *m.* jargon; slang, cant.

жарго́н|ный *adj. of* **~**

жа́реный *adj.* roast, broiled; fried; grilled.

жа́р|ить, ю, ишь *impf.* **1.** (*pf.* **за~** *or* **из~**) **(на огне́)** to roast, broil; **(на сковороде́)** to fry; **(на решётке)** to grill. **2.** (*of the sun*) to burn, scorch.

жа́р|иться, юсь ишься *impf.* **1.** (*pf.* **за~** *or* **из~**) to roast, fry (*intrans.*). **2.: ж. на со́лнце** (*coll.*) to bask in the sun, sun o.s. **3.** *pass. of* **~ить**

жа́р|кий (~ок, ~ка́,~ко) *adj.* **1.** hot; torrid; **ж. по́яс** (*geog.*) torrid zone. **2.** (*fig.*) heated; ardent; passionate; **ж. спор** heated argument.

жа́р|ко[1] *adv. of* **~кий**

жа́рко[2] *as pred.* it is hot; **мне,** *etc.*, **ж.** I am, *etc.*, hot.

жарк|о́е, о́го *nt.* roast (meat).

жаро́в|ня, ни, *g. pl.* **~ен** *f.* brazier.

жарово́й *adj.* **1.** *adj. of* **жар 1.**. **2.** caused by heat.

жаропро́чн|ый *adj.* ovenproof; **~ая кастрю́ля** casserole (dish).

жаросто́йкий *adj.* (*tech.*) heat-resisting, heatproof.

жароупо́рный = жаросто́йкий

жар-пти́ц|а, ы *f.* (*folklore*) the Fire-bird.
жа́р|че *comp. of* **~кий** *and* **~ко**
жасми́н, а *m.* jasmine.
жа́тв|а, ы *no pl., f.* reaping, harvesting; harvest (*also fig.*).
жа́тв|енный *adj. of* **~а; ~енная маши́на** harvester, reaping-machine.
жа́тк|а, и *f.* harvester, reaping-machine.
жать[1], жму, жмёшь *impf.* (*no pf.*) **1.** to press, squeeze; **ж. ру́ку** to shake (s.o.) by the hand. **2.** to pinch, be tight (*of shoes or clothing*); (*impers.*): **в плеча́х жмёт** it is tight on the shoulders.
жать[2], жну, жнёшь *impf.* (*of* **с~**) to reap, cut, mow.
жа́ться, жму́сь, жмёшься *impf.* **1.** to huddle up. **2. (к)** to press close (to), draw closer (to). **3.** (*coll.*) to hesitate, vacillate. **4.** (*coll.*) to stint, be stingy.
жбан, а *m.* (wooden) jug.
жва́чк|а, и *f.* **1.** chewing, rumination. **2.** cud; **жева́ть ~у** to chew the cud, ruminate. **3.** (*coll.*) chewing-gum
жва́чн|ый *adj.* (*zool.*) ruminant; *as n.* **~ое, ~ого** *nt.* ruminant.
жгу, жжёшь, жгут *see* **жечь**
жгут, а́ *m.* **1.** plait; braid; wisp. **2.** (*med.*) tourniquet.
жгу́чест|ь, и *f.* burning heat.
жгу́ч|ий (~, ~а, ~е) *adj.* burning hot (*also fig.*); **~ая боль** smarting pain; **ж. вопро́с** burning question.
ж. д. (*abbr. of* ***желе́зная доро́га***) railway.
ждать, жду, ждёшь, *past* **ждал, ждала́, жда́ло** *impf.* **1.** (*+g.*) to wait (for); to await; **заста́вить ж.** to keep waiting; **не заста́вить себя́ ж.** to come quickly; **ж. не дожда́ться** (*coll.*) to wait impatiently, be on tenterhooks; **что нас ждёт?** what is in store for us?; **того́ и жди** (*coll.*) at any moment. **2.** (*+g.*) to expect (= *to hope for*). **3.** (**+что**) to expect; **мы жда́ли, что вы появи́тесь на ми́тинге** we expected you to come to the meeting.
же[1] *conj.* **1.** but; **иди́, е́сли тебе́ охо́та, я же оста́нусь здесь** you go, if you feel like it, but I shall stay here. **2.** (*introducing clause elucidating or modifying preceding clause*) and; **Ока́ впада́ет в Во́лгу, Во́лга же в Каспи́йское мо́ре** the Oka flows into the Volga, and the Volga flows into the Caspian Sea. **3.** after all; **расскажи́ ей — она́ же твоя́ мать** tell her — she's your mother, after all.
же[2] *emph. particle*: **когда́ же они́ прие́дут?** whenever will they come?; **что же ты де́лаешь?** whatever are you doing, what *are* you doing?
же[3] *particle expr. identity*: **тот же, тако́й же** the same, idem; **тогда́ же** at the same time; **там же** in the same place, ibidem; **Петрося́н, он же Петро́в** Petrosyan, alias Petrov.
жева́ни|е, я *nt.* mastication; rumination.
жёваный *adj.* (*coll.*) chewed up; crumpled.
жева́тельн|ый *adj.* masticatory; **~ая рези́нка** chewing gum.
жева́ть, жую́, жуёшь *impf.* to chew, masticate; to ruminate; (*fig.*) **ж. жва́чку,** *see* **жва́чка**
жёг, жгла *see* **жечь**
жезл, а́ *m.* rod; staff (*of office*).
жела́ни|е, я *nt.* (*+g.*) wish (for), desire (for); **бу́дет по ва́шему ~ю** it shall be as you wish; **при всём ~и** with the best will in the world; much as I would like to.
жела́|нный *p.p.p. of* **~ть** *and adj.* wished-for, desired; beloved; **ж. гость** welcome visitor.
жела́тельно[1] *adv.* preferably.
жела́тельно[2] *as pred.* it is desirable; it is advisable; **ж., что́бы вы прису́тствовали** it is desirable that you should be present.
жела́тел|ьный (~ен, ~ьна) *adj.* desirable; advisable.
желати́н, а *no pl., m.* gelatin(e).
желати́новый *adj.* gelatinous.
жела́|ть, ю *impf.* (*of* **по~**) **1.** (*+g.*) to wish (for), desire. **2.** (**что́бы** *or +inf.*) to wish, want; **я ~ю, что́бы вы при́няли уча́стие в игре́** I want you to join in the game. **3.** (*+d. and g. or inf.*) to wish (*s.o. sth.*); **~ю вам вся́ких благ** (*coll.*) I wish you every happiness; **~ю вам успе́ха** good luck!; **э́то оставля́ет ж. лу́чшего, мно́гого** it leaves much to be desired.
жела́|ющий *pres. part. act. of* **~ть; ~ющие** persons interested, those who so desire.
желва́к, а́ *m.* (*med.*) tumour.
желе́ *nt. indecl.* jelly.
желез|а́, ы́, *pl.* **же́лезы, ~̈, ~а́м** *f.* (*anat.*) gland *pl.*; (*coll.*) tonsils.
желе́зистый[1] *adj.* (*anat.*) glandular.
желе́зист|ый[2] (~, ~а) *adj.* (*chem.*) ferrous, ferriferous; **ж. прера́т** iron preparation.
желе́зк|а, и *f.* (*coll.*) piece of iron.
желёзк|а, и *f.* (*anat.*) glandule.
железнодоро́жник, а *m.* railwayman.
железнодоро́жн|ый *adj.* rail, railway; **~ая перево́зка** rail transport; **~ое полотно́** permanent way; **ж. путь** (railway) track; **ж. у́зел** (railway) junction.
желе́зн|ый *adj.* **1.** iron (*also fig.*); (*chem.*) ferric, ferrous; **ж. блеск** (*min.*) haematite; **ж. век** the Iron Age; **ж. за́навес** the 'Iron Curtain'; **ж. лом** scrap iron; **за ~ой решёткой** (*coll.*) behind bars; **~ая руда́** (*min.*) iron-ore; **~ые това́ры** ironmongery. **2.: ~ая доро́га** railway(s); **по ~ой доро́ге** by rail.
железня́к, а́ *m.* (*min.*) iron-stone.
желе́з|о, а, *pl.* (*obs. or poet.*) **~ы** *nt.* iron; **ж. в болва́нках** pig-iron; **о́кись ~а** (*chem.*) ferric oxide.
желе́зо... *comb. form* iron-, ferro-.
железобето́н, а *m.* (*tech.*) reinforced concrete, ferroconcrete.
железобето́н|ный *adj. of* **~**
железоплави́льный *adj.*: **ж. заво́д** (*tech.*) iron foundry.
железопрока́тный *adj.*: **ж. заво́д** (*tech.*) rolling mill.
жёлоб, а, *pl.* **~а́, ~о́в** *m.* gutter; trough; chute.
желоб|о́к, ка́ *m.* (*tech.*) groove, channel, flute.
желте́|ть, ю *impf.* **1.** (*pf.* **по~**) to turn yellow. **2.** (*impf. only*) to be yellow, show up yellow.
желтизн|а́, ы́ *f.* yellowness; yellow spot; sallow complexion.
жел|ти́ть, чу́, ти́шь *impf.* to colour yellow.
желтова́т|ый (~, ~а) *adj.* yellowish; sallow.
желт|о́к, ка́ *m.* yolk.
желтоко́жий *adj.* yellow-skinned.
желтоли́ц|ый (~, ~а) *adj.* sallow.
желторо́т|ый (~, ~а) *adj.* **1.** yellow-beaked. **2.** (*fig.*) inexperienced, green.
желтофио́л|ь, и *f.* (*bot.*) wallflower.
желт|о́чный *adj. of* **~о́к**
желту́х||а, и *f.* (*med.*) jaundice.
желту́|шный *adj. of* **~ха**; jaundiced.
жёлт|ый (~, ~а́, ~о *and* **~о́)** *adj.* yellow.
желудёвый *adj. of* **жёлудь; ж. ко́фе** acorn coffee.
желу́д|ок, ка *m.* stomach; **несваре́ние ~ка** indigestion.
желу́доч|ек, ка *m.* (*anat.*) ventricle.
желу́дочно-кише́чный *adj.* gastro-intestinal.
желу́дочный *adj.* stomach; gastric; **ж. сок** gastric juice.
жёлуд|ь, я, *g. pl.* **~е́й** *m.* acorn.
жёлч|ный (~ен, ~на) *adj.* **1.** bilious; **ж. ка́мень** gall-stone; **ж. пузы́рь** gall-bladder. **2.** (*fig.*) peevish, irritable.
жёлч|ь, и *no pl., f.* bile, gall (*also fig.*).
жема́н|иться, юсь, ишься *impf.* (*coll.*) to put on

airs, behave affectedly.
жема́н|ный (~ен, ~на) *adj.* affected.
жема́нств|о, а *nt.* affectedness.
же́мчуг, а, *pl.* **~а́** *m.* pearl(s).
жемчу́жин|а, ы *f.* (single) pearl (*also fig.*).
жемчу́жниц|а, ы *f.* pearl-oyster.
жемчу́жн|ый *adj. of* **же́мчуг;** (*fig.*) pearly(-white); **~ое ожере́лье** pearl necklace.
жен... *comb. form, abbr. of* **же́нский**
жен|а́, ы́, *pl.* **~ы, ~, ~ам** *f.* wife; **быть у ~ы́ под башмако́м** to be henpecked.
жена́т|ый (~) *adj.* married; **ж. (на**+*p.*) married (to; *of man*).
Жене́в|а, ы *f.* Geneva.
жен|и́ть, ю́, ~ишь *impf. and pf.* (*pf. also* **по~**) to marry (off); **без меня́ меня́ ~и́ли** (*fig., coll.*) I was roped in without being consulted.
жени́тьб|а, ы *no pl., f.* marriage.
жен|и́ться, ю́сь, ~ишься *impf. and pf.* (**на**+*p.*) (*of man*) to marry, get married (to).
жени́х, а́ *m.* **1.** fiancé; **смотре́ть ~о́м** (*coll.*) to look happy. **2.** (bride)groom. **3.** suitor. **4.** eligible bachelor.
женолю́б, а *nt.* ladies' man.
женолюби́в|ый (~) *adj.*: **ж. челове́к** ladies' man.
женолю́би|е, я *nt.* fondness for women.
женоненави́стник, а *m.* misogynist.
женоненави́стнический *adj.* misogynous.
женоненави́стничеств|о, а *nt.* misogyny.
женоподо́б|ный (~ен, ~на) *adj.* effeminate.
же́нск|ий *adj.* **1.** woman's; female; feminine; **ж. вопро́с** the question of women's rights; **~ое ца́рство** petticoat government. **2.** (*gram.*) feminine.
же́нственност|ь, и *f.* femininity.
же́нствен|ный (~, ~на) *adj.* feminine, womanly.
же́нщин|а, ы *f.* woman.
женьше́н|ь, я *m.* (*bot., med.*) ginseng.
жёрдочк|а, *f.* (*coll.*) pole; perch.
жерд|ь, и, *pl.* **~и, ~е́й** *f.* pole; stake; **худо́й, как ж.** (*coll.*) thin as a lath.
жереб|ёнок, ёнка, *pl.* **~я́та, ~я́т** *m.* foal, colt.
жереб|е́ц, ца́ *m.* stallion.
жереб|и́ться, и́тся *impf.* (*of* **о~**) to foal.
жеребьёвк|а, и *f.* casting of lots; (*sport*) draw (*for play-off*).
жереб|я́чий *adj. of* **~ёнок; ж. смех** (*coll.*) horse-laugh.
жерл|о́, а́, *pl.* **~а, ~** *nt.* mouth, orifice; muzzle (*of gun*); **ж. вулка́на** crater.
жёрнов, а, *pl.* **~а́, ~о́в** *m.* millstone.
же́ртв|а, ы *f.* **1.** sacrifice (*also fig.*); **принести́ ~у** (+*d.*) to make a sacrifice (to); **принести́ в ~у** to sacrifice. **2.** victim; (*pl.*) casualties; **пасть ~ой** (+*g.*) to fall victim (to.).
же́ртвенник, а *m.* sacrificial altar.
же́ртвенный *adj.* sacrificial.
же́ртвовател|ь, я *m.* donor.
же́ртв|овать, ую, *impf.* (*of* **по~**) **1.** to make a donation (of), present. **2.** (+*i.*) to sacrifice, give up.
жертвоприноше́ни|е, я *nt.* sacrifice; oblation.
жест, а *m.* gesture (*also fig.*).
жестикули́р|овать, ую *impf.* to gesticulate.
жестикуля́ци|я, и *f.* gesticulation.
жёст|кий (~ок, ~ка́, ~ло) *adj.* hard; tough; stiff; (*fig.*) rigid, strict; **ж. ваго́н** hard-seated carriage, 'hard' carriage; **~кая вода́** hard water; **~кие во́лосы** wiry hair.
жёст|ко[1] *adj. of* **~кий**
жёстко[2] *as pred.* it is hard.
жесто́к|ий (~, ~а́, ~о) *adj.* cruel; brutal; (*fig.*) severe, sharp.
жестокосе́рд|ный (~ен, ~на) *adj.* hard-hearted.
жесто́кост|ь, и *f.* cruelty, brutality.
жесто|ча́йший *superl. of* **~кий**
жёст|че *comp. of* **~кий** *and* **~ко**
жест|ь, и *f.* tin-plate.
жестя́нк|а, и *f.* tin, can; **ж. из-под сарди́нок** sardine tin.
жест|яно́й *adj. of* **~ь; ~яна́я посу́да** tinware.
жестя́нщик, а *m.* tin-smith.
жето́н, а *m.* **1.** medal. **2.** counter. **3.** token; **проездно́й ж.** travel token.
жечь, жгу, жжёшь, жгут, *past* **жёг, жгла** *impf.* **1.** (*pf.* **с~**) to burn (up, down); **ж. му́сор** to burn up refuse. **2.** (*impf. only*) to burn, sting; (*impers.*): **от э́того ликёра жжёт го́рло** this liqueur burns one's throat.
же́чься, жгусь, жжёшься, жгу́тся, *past* **жёгся, жгла́сь** *impf.* **1.** to burn, sting (*intrans.*) **2.** (*coll.*) to burn o.s.
жже́ни|е, я *nt.* **1.** burning. **2.** burning pain; heartburn.
жжёнк|а, и *f.* hot punch.
жжёный *adj.* burnt, scorched; **ж. ко́фе** roasted coffee.
жжёшь *see* **жечь**
жив|е́й, *see* **~о 5.**
жив|е́ц, ца́ *m.* live bait, sprat.
живи́тел|ьный (~ен, ~ьна) *adj.* life-giving; bracing; **~ьная вла́га** (*coll.*) intoxicating liquor.
жи́вност|ь, и *no pl., f.* (*collect.; coll.*) poultry, fowl.
жи́в|о *adj.* **1.** vividly. **2.** with animation. **3.** keenly; deeply; **он ж. чу́вствовал оскорбле́ние** he felt deeply insulted. **4.** (*coll.*) quickly, promptly. **5. ж.!; ~е́й!** (*coll.*) get a move on!; look lively!
живодёр, а *m.* knacker; (*fig.*) fleecer; profiteer.
живодёр|ня, ни, *g. pl.* **~ен** *f.* (*coll.*) knacker's yard.
живодёрств|о, а *nt.* (*coll.*) cruelty.
жив|о́й (~, ~а́, ~о) *adj.* **1.** living, live, alive; **он ещё в ~ы́х** he is still alive; **оста́ться в ~ы́х** to survive; **~ (и) здоро́в** (*coll.*) safe and sound; **ни ~ ни мёртв** (*coll.*) petrified (*with fright, astonishment*); **ж. вес** live weight; **ж. инвента́рь** livestock; **ж. портре́т** (+*g.*) the living image (of); **ж. уголо́к** nature corner (*in a school*); **~ые цветы́** natural flowers; **не́ было ви́дно ни (одно́й) ~о́й души́** there was not a living soul to be seen; **заде́ть за ~о́е** to cut to the quick. **2.** lively; keen; active; **ж. ум** lively mind; **проявля́ть ж. интере́с (к)** to take a keen interest (in). **3.** lively, vivacious; bright; **~ые глаза́** bright eyes. **4.** keen, poignant. **5.** (*short form only*; +*i.*) *expr. raison d'être*: **он ~ одни́ми ша́хматами** he lives for chess alone; **чем она́ ~а́?** what makes her tick?
жи́вокост|ь, и *f.* (*bot.*) larkspur.
живопи́с|ец, ца *m.* painter.
живопи́с|ный (~ен, ~на) *adj.* picturesque; **~ное ме́сто** beauty spot.
жи́вопис|ь, и *f.* **1.** painting. **2.** (*collect.*) paintings; **стенна́я ж.** murals.
живородя́щий *adj.* (*zool.*) viviparous.
жи́вост|ь, и *f.* liveliness, vivacity; animation.
живо́т, а *m.* abdomen, belly; stomach.
животво́р|ный (~ен, ~на) *adj.* life-giving.
животворя́щий *adj.* (*poet.*) = **животво́рный**
живо́тик, а *m.* (*coll.*) tummy.
животново́д, а *m.* cattle-breeder.
животново́дств|о, а *nt.* stock-raising, animal husbandry.
животново́дческий *adj.* cattle-breeding, stock-raising.
живо́тно|е, го *nt.* animal; **ко́мнатное ж.** pet.
живо́тный *adj.* **1.** animal; **ж. жир** animal fat. **2.** bestial, brute.
животрепе́щущий *adj.* **1.** topical; stirring, exciting. **2.** lively, full of life.

живу́чест|ь, и *f.* **1.** vitality, tenacity of life. **2.** (*fig.*) firmness, stability.
живу́ч|ий (~, ~а) *adj.* **1.** tenacious of life; (*bot.*) hardy; **он ~ как ко́шка** he has nine lives like a cat. **2.** (*fig.*) firm, stable.
жи́вчик, а *m.* **1.** (*coll.*) lively person. **2.** (*biol.*) spermatozoon. **3.** (*coll.*) perceptible pulsing of artery (*as on temple*).
живьём *adv.* (*coll.*) alive; **постара́йтесь схвати́ть его́ ж.** try to take him alive.
жи́голо *m. indecl.* gigolo.
жид, а́ *m.* (*pej. and vulg.*) Yid.
жи́дкий (~ок, ~ка́, ~ко) *adj.* **1.** liquid; fluid. **2.** watery; (*of liquids*) weak, thin; **ж. чай** weak tea. **3.** sparse, scanty; **~кая борода́** straggly beard. **4.** (*coll.*; *of voice or sound*) weak, thin. **5.** (*fig.*) weak, feeble.
жидкокристалли́ческий *adj.*: **ж. индика́тор** liquid-crystal display, LCD.
жи́дкостный *adj.* (*tech.*) liquid; fluid.
жи́дкост|ь, и *f.* **1.** liquid; fluid. **2.** wateriness; weakness, thinness (*also fig.*).
жи́ж|а, и *no pl.*, *f.* liquid; swill; slush.
жи́|же *comp. of* **~дкий**
жи́зненност|ь, и *f.* **1.** vitality. **2.** closeness to life; (*art*) lifelikeness.
жи́знен|ный (~, ~на) *adj.* **1.** life; (*biol.*) vital; **~ные отправле́ния** vital functions; **ж. путь** life; **ж. у́ровень** standard of living. **2.** close to life; lifelike. **3.** (*fig.*) vital, vitally important; **~ные це́нтры страны́** nerve-centres of a country.
жизнеобеспе́чени|е, я *nt.*: **систе́ма ~я** life-support system.
жизнеописа́ни|е, я *nt.* biography.
жизнера́достност|ь, и *f.* joie de vivre; vivacity.
жизнера́дост|ный (~ен, ~на) *adj.* vivacious.
жизнеспосо́бност|ь, и *f.* (*biol.*) viability; (*fig.*) vitality.
жизнеспосо́б|ный (~ен, ~на) *adj.* (*biol.*) viable; (*fig.*) vigorous, flourishing.
жизнесто́|йкий (~ек, ~йка) *adj.* tenacious of life; tough, durable.
жизн|ь, и *f.* life; existence; **ж. моя́!** my dear!; **зарабо́тать на ж.** to earn one's living; **как ж.?** (*coll.*) how are things?; how's life?; **лиши́ть себя́ ~и** to take one's life; **не на ж., а на смерть** to the death; **ни в ж.** never; **о́браз ~и** way of life; **вести́ широ́кий о́браз ~и** to live in style; **провести́ что-н. в ж.** to put sth. into practice.
жиклёр, а *m.* (*tech.*) (carburettor) jet.
жи́л|а[1], **ы** *f.* **1.** vein; tendon, sinew; **тяну́ть ~ы (из**+*g.*; *coll.*) to torment, rack. **2.** (*min.*) vein, lode. **3.** filament, strand (*of cable*).
жи́л|а[2], **ы** *c.g.* (*coll.*, *pej.*) skinflint.
жиле́т, а *m.* waistcoat; **пуленепробива́емый ж.** bulletproof vest; **спаса́тельный ж.** life-jacket.
жиле́тк|а, и *f.* (*coll.*) waistcoat; **пла́кать в ~у** (+*d.*) to cry on s.o.'s shoulders.
жиле́т|ный *adj. of* **~**; **ж. карма́н** waistcoat pocket, vest-pocket.
жил|е́ц, ьца́ *m.* lodger; tenant; **он не ж. на бе́лом све́те** (*coll.*) he is not long for this world.
жи́лист|ый (~, ~а) *adj.* **1.** having prominent veins. **2.** sinewy; (*fig.*) wiry; **~ое мя́со** stringy meat.
жил|и́ца, и́цы *f. of* **~е́ц**
жили́щ|е, а *nt.* **1.** dwelling, abode; habitation. **2.** lodging; (living) quarters.
жили́щно-строи́тельн|ый *adj.*: **ж. кооперати́в** building society.
жили́щ|ный *adj. of* **~е**; **~ные усло́вия** housing conditions; **~но-бытовы́е усло́вия** living conditions.
жи́лк|а, и *f.* **1.** (*anat.*, *geol.*) vein; (*zool.*, *bot.*) fibre, rib (*of insect's wing or of leaf*). **2.** (*fig.*) vein, streak; bent; **артисти́ческая ж.** artistic streak.
жилмасси́в, а *m.* housing estate.
жилова́т|ый (~, ~а) *adj.* (*coll.*) with prominent veins.
жил|о́й *adj.* **1.** dwelling; residential; inhabited; **ж. дом** block of flats (*opp. office block, etc.*); **ж. кварта́л** residential area; **~ы́е ко́мнаты** rooms lived in; **~а́я пло́щадь = жилпло́щадь. 2.** habitable, fit to live in.
жилотде́л, а *m.* housing department (*of local council*).
жилпло́щад|ь, и *f.* **1.** floor space. **2.** housing, accommodation (= *available dwelling space*).
жилстрои́тельств|о, а *nt.* house building.
жилфо́нд, а *m.* housing, accommodation.
жиль|ё, я́ *nt.* **1.** habitation; dwelling; **мы не нашли́ никако́го при́знака ~я́** we could find no sign of life. **2.** lodging; (living) accommodation.
жим, а *m.* (*sport*) press (*in weight-lifting*).
жи́молост|ь, и *f.* (*bot.*) honeysuckle.
жир, а (у), о ~е, в ~у́, *pl.* **~ы́** *m.* fat; grease.
жира́ф, а *m.* giraffe.
жира́ф|а, ы *f.* = **~**
жире́|ть, ю *impf.* (*of* **о~** *and* **раз~**) to grow fat, stout, plump.
жи́р|ный (~ен, ~на́, ~го) *adj.* **1.** fatty; rich (*of food*); greasy; **~ная кислота́** fatty acid; **~ное пятно́** grease stain. **2.** fat, plump. **3.** rich (*of soil*); lush (*of vegetation*); **~ная земля́** loam. **4.** (*typ.*) bold, heavy; **ж. шрифт** bold(-face) type.
жи́ро *nt. indecl.* (*fin.*) endorsement.
жирови́к, а́ *m.* (*med.*) fatty tumour, lipoma.
жиров|о́й *adj.* fatty; (*anat.*) adipose; **~а́я ткань** adipose tissue.
жите́йск|ий *adj.* **1.** worldly; **~ая му́дрость** worldly wisdom; **~ое мо́ре** the ups and downs of life. **2.** everyday; **де́ло ~ое** (*coll.*) there's nothing extraordinary in that.
жи́тел|ь, я *m.* inhabitant; dweller; **ми́рные ~и** civilians; civilian population.
жи́тельств|о, а *nt.* residence; **вид на ж.** residence permit; **ме́сто ~а** domicile; **ме́сто постоя́нного ~а** permanent address.
жи́тниц|а, ы *f.* granary (*also fig.*).
жить, живу́, живёшь, *past* **жил, жила́, жи́ло (не́ жил, не жила́, не́ жило)** *impf.* **1.** to live; **ж. в Москве́** to live in Moscow; **ж. ве́село** to have a good time; **ж. припева́ючи** to be in clover; **ж. на широ́кую но́гу** to live in style; **ж. со дня на́ день** to live from hand to mouth; **жил-был** once upon a time there lived ... **2.** (+*i. or* **на**+*a.*) to live (on); (+*i.*; *fig.*) to live (in, for); **нам не́чем ж.** we have nothing to live on; **ж. на свои́ сре́дства** to support o.s.; **ж. наде́ждами** to live in hopes; **ж. иску́сством** to live for art.
жить|ё, я́ *nt.* (*coll.*) **1.** life; existence; **~я́ тут нет от мух** the flies make life here impossible. **2.** habitation, occupancy; **кварти́ра гото́ва для ~я́** the flat is ready for habitation.
житьё-бытьё, житья́-бытья́ *nt.* (*coll.*) life; existence.
жи́ться, живётся, *past* **жило́сь** *impf.* (*impers.*, +*d.*; *coll.*) to live, get on; **ей ве́село живётся** she enjoys her life; **как вам жило́сь в Аме́рике?** how did you get on in America?
жмот, а *m.* (*coll.*) miser, skinflint.
жму, жмёшь *see* **жать**[1]
жму́р|ить, ю, ишь *impf.* (*of* **за~**): **ж. глаза́** to screw up one's eyes; to squint.
жму́р|иться, юсь, ишься *impf.* (*of* **за~**) to screw up one's eyes; to squint.
жму́р|ки, ок *no sg.* blind man's buff.
жне́йк|а, и *f.* (*agric.*) harvester, reaping-machine.
жнец, а́ *m.* harvester, reaper.

живь|ё, я́, *pl.* **∼я** *nt.* **1.** stubble-field. **2.** (*sg. only*) stubble.
жни́ц|а, ы *f. of* **жнец**
жну, жнёшь *see* **жать 2.**
жоке́|й, я *m.* jockey.
жоке́й|ский *adj. of* **∼**
жонглёр, а *m.* juggler.
жонглёрств|о, а *nt.* sleight-of-hand; juggling (*also fig.*).
жонгли́р|овать, ую *impf.* (+*i.*) to juggle (with) (*also fig.*).
жо́п|а, ы *f.* (*vulg.*) arse; **ну ты и ж.!** you arsehole!; **иди́** *or* **пошёл в ∼у!** fuck off!
жополи́з, а *m.* (*vulg.*) arse-licker.
жратв|а́, ы́ *f.* (*vulg.*) grub, nosh.
жр|ать, у́, ёшь, *past* **∼а́л, ∼ала́, ∼а́ло** *impf.* (*of* **со∼**) **1.** (*of animals*) to eat. **2.** (*vulg.*) to guzzle, gobble.
жре́би|й, я *m.* **1.** lot; **броса́ть ж.** to cast lots; **тяну́ть ж.** to draw lots. **2.** (*fig.*) lot, fate, destiny; **ж. бро́шен** the die is cast.
жрец, а́ *m.* (*pagan*) priest; (*fig.*) devotee.
жре́ческий *adj.* priestly.
жре́честв|о, а *nt.* priesthood.
жри́ц|а, ы *f.* priestess.
жу́желиц|а, ы *f.* (*zool.*) ground beetle.
жужжа́ни|е, я *nt.* hum, buzz, drone; humming, buzzing, droning.
жужж|а́ть, у́, и́шь *impf.* to hum, buzz, drone; to whiz (*of projectiles*).
жуи́р, а *m.* playboy.
жук, а́ *m.* **1.** beetle; **ма́йский ж.** may-bug, cockchafer. **2.** (*coll.*) rogue, twister.
жу́лик, а *m.* crook; cheat, swindler.
жуликова́т|ый (∼, ∼а) *adj.* (*coll.*) crooked.
жу́льнича|ть, ю *impf.* (*of* **с∼**) (*coll.*) to cheat; to swindle.
жу́льнический *adj.* (*coll.*) crooked; underhand(ed), dishonest.
жу́льничеств|о, а *nt.* (*coll.*) **1.** cheating (*at games*). **2.** underhand, dishonest action; sharp practice.
жу́пел, а *m.* bugbear, bogy.
журавл|и́ный *adj. of* **∼ь; ∼и́ные но́ги** spindleshanks.
жура́вл|ь, я́ *m.* **1.** (*zool.*) crane; **не сули́ ∼я в не́бе, а дай сини́цу в ру́ки** (*prov.*) a bird in the hand is worth two in the bush. **2.** well sweep, shadoof.
жур|и́ть, ю́, и́шь *impf.* (*coll.*) to reprove, take to task.
журна́л, а *m.* **1.** magazine; journal. **2.** journal, diary; register; **ж. заседа́ний** minutes, minute-book.
журнали́ст, а *m.* journalist.
журнали́стик|а, и *f.* **1.** journalism; **ж. с че́ковой кни́жкой** chequebook journalism. **2.** (*collect.*) periodical press.
журнали́стский *adj.* journalistic.
журна́л|ьный *adj. of* **∼; ∼ьная статья́** magazine article.
журча́ни|е, я *nt.* purling, babbling, murmur.
журч|а́ть, у́, и́шь *impf.* to purl, babble, murmur (*of water; also fig., poet.*).
жу́т|кий (∼ок, ∼ка́, ∼ко) *adj.* terrible, terrifying; awe-inspiring, eerie.
жу́тко[1] *adv.* terrifyingly; (*coll.*) terribly, awfully.
жу́тко[2] *as pred.* (*impers.*, +*d.*): **мне,** *etc.*, **ж.** I, *etc.*, am terrified.
жут|ь, и *f.* **1.** terror; awe; **воспомина́ния о де́тстве для него́ — пря́мо ж.** memories of childhood simply terrify him. **2.** *as pred.* = **∼ко**[2]
жу́хл|ый (∼, ∼а) *adj.* withered, dried-up; hardened; tarnished.
жу́х|нуть, нет, *past* **∼, ∼ла** *impf.* to dry up; to become hard; to become tarnished.
жу́чк|а, и *f.* (*coll.*) house-dog.
жуч|о́к, ка́ *m. dim. of* **жук**
жу|ю́, ёшь *see* **жева́ть**
жюри́ *indecl.* **1.** *nt.* (*collect.*) judges (*of competition, etc.*). **2.** *m.* (*obs.*) umpire, referee.

З

З (*abbr. of* **за́пад**) W, West.
за *prep.* **I.** +*a. and i.* (+*a.*: *indicates motion or action*; +*i.*: *indicates rest or state*). **1.** behind; **за крова́ть, за крова́тью** behind the bed. **2.** beyond; across, the other side of; **за боло́то, за боло́том** beyond the marsh; **за́ борт, за бо́ртом** overboard; **за́ угол, за угло́м** round the corner; **за́ городом** out of town; **за рубежо́м** abroad. **3.** at; **сесть за роя́ль** to sit down at the piano; **сиде́ть за роя́лем** to be at the piano. **4.** (*denoting occupation*) at, to (*or translated by part.*); **приня́ться за рабо́ту** to set to work; **заста́ть кого́-н. за рабо́той** to find s.o. at work, working; **сесть за кни́гу** to sit down with a book; **проводи́ть всё своё вре́мя за чте́нием** to spend all one's time reading. **5.: вы́йти за́муж за** (+*a.*) (*of a woman*) to marry; **(быть) за́мужем за** (+*i.*) (to be) married (to).
II. +*a.* **1.** after (*of time*); over (*of age*); **далеко́ за́ полночь** long after midnight; **ему́ уже́ за со́рок** he is already over forty. **2.** *expr. distance in space or time*: **самолёт разби́лся за ми́лю от дере́вни** the aeroplane crashed a mile from the village; **за два дня до его́ сме́рти** two days before his death. **3.** during, in the space of; **за́ ночь** during the night, overnight; **за су́тки** in the space of twenty-four hours; **за после́днее вре́мя** recently, lately, of late. **4.** (+*vv. having sense of to take hold of, etc.*) by; **вести́ за́ руку** to lead by the hand. **5.** (*in var. senses*) for; **плати́ть за биле́т** to pay for a ticket; **подписа́ть за дире́ктора** to sign for the director; **боя́ться, ра́доваться за кого́-н.** to fear, be glad for s.o.; **есть за трои́х** to eat (enough) for three; **за ва́ше здоро́вье!** your health!; cheers!
III. +*i.* **1.** after; **друг за дру́гом** one after another; **год за го́дом** year after year; **сле́довать за кем-н.** to follow s.o. **2.** (*fig.*) after; **следи́ть за детьми́** to look after children; **уха́живать за больны́м** to look after a sick person. **3.** for (= *in order to fetch, obtain*); **идти́ за молоко́м** to go for milk; **посла́ть за до́ктором** to send for a doctor; **зайти́ за кем-н.** to call for s.o. **4.** at, during; **за за́втраком** at breakfast. **5.** for, on account of, because of; **за неиме́нием, недоста́тком** (+*g.*) for want of; **за чем де́ло ста́ло?** what's up? **6.** (+*prons.*) (*i*) *ascribes habits, qualities*, (*ii*) *imputes responsibility*: **за ним во́дятся стра́нности** he has his peculiarities; **за тобо́й пять рубле́й** you are owing five roubles; **о́чередь за ва́ми** it is your turn. **7.** *indicates provenance of a document, etc.*: **письмо́ за по́дписью гла́вного реда́ктора** a letter signed by the editor-in-chief.
за... *pref.* **I.** (*of vv.*) **1.** *indicates commencement of action*: **зала́ять** to start barking. **2.** *indicates direction of action beyond given point*: **заверну́ть за́ угол** to turn a corner. **3.** *indicates continuation of action to excess*: **закорми́ть** to overfeed. **4.** *forms pf. aspect of some vv.*

II. (*of nn. and adjs.*) trans-; **Закавка́зье** Transcaucasia; **заатланти́ческий** transatlantic.

заадрес|ова́ть, у́ю *pf.* (*coll.*) to address, write the address (on).

заале́|ть, ет *pf. of* **але́ть**

зааплоди́р|овать, ую *pf.* to break out into applause, start clapping.

зааренд|ова́ть у́ю *pf.* (*of* **~о́вывать**) to rent, lease.

заарендо́выва|ть, ю *impf. of* **заарендова́ть**

заарка́н|ить, ю, ишь *pf. of* **арка́нить**

заарта́ч|иться, усь, ишься *pf.* (*coll.*) to become restive, stubborn.

заасфальти́р|овать ую *pf. of* **асфальти́ровать**

заатланти́ческий *adj.* transatlantic.

зaа́xa|ть, ю *pf.* (*coll.*) to begin to sigh, begin to groan.

заба́в|а, ы *f.* **1.** game; pastime. **2.** amusement, fun; **он э́то сде́лал для ~ы** he did it for fun.

забавля́|ть, ю *impf.* to amuse, entertain.

забавля́|ться, юсь *impf.* to amuse o.s.

заба́вник, а *m.* (*coll.*) amusing *or* entertaining person; humorist.

заба́вн|о[1] *adv. of* **~ый**

заба́вно[2] *as pred.* it is amusing, funny; **мне з.** I find it amusing, funny; **з.!** how funny!

заба́в|ный (~ен, ~на) *adj.* amusing; funny.

забаллоти́р|овать, ую *pf.* to blackball, reject.

заба́лтыва|ть, ю *impf. of* **заболта́ть**[1] **2.**

забараба́н|ить, ю, ишь *pf.* to begin to drum.

забаррикади́р|овать, ую *pf. of* **баррикади́ровать**

забаст|ова́ть, у́ю *pf.* to go, come out on strike.

забасто́вк|а, и *f.* strike; **всео́бщая з.** general strike; **голо́дная з.** hunger strike.

забасто́в|очный *adj. of* **~ка**

забасто́вщик, а *m.* striker.

забве́ни|е, я *nt.* oblivion; **преда́ть ~ю** to consign to oblivion.

забе́г, а *m.* (*sport*) heat, race.

забега́ловк|а, и *f.* (*coll.*) snack bar.

забе́га|ть, ю *pf.* to start running.

забега́|ть, ю *impf. of* **забежа́ть**

забе́га|ться, юсь *pf.* (*coll.*) to run o.s. to a standstill.

забе|жа́ть, гу́, жи́шь, гу́т *pf.* (*of* **~га́ть**) **1.** to run up. **2.** (**к**; *coll.*) to drop in (on). **3.** to run off; to stray. **4.: з. вперёд** to run ahead; (*fig., coll.*) to anticipate.

забел|и́ть, ю́, ~и́шь *pf.* **1.** to whiten, paint white. **2.** (*coll.*) to add milk, cream (to); **з. чай молоко́м** to put milk in tea.

забере́мене|ть, ю *pf.* (*of* **бере́менеть**) to become pregnant.

забеспоко́|иться, юсь, ишься *pf.* to begin to worry, become anxious.

забива́|ть(ся), ю(сь) *impf. of* **заби́ть(ся)**

забинт|ова́ть, у́ю *pf.* (*of* **~о́вывать**) to bandage.

забира́ть(ся), ю(сь) *impf. of* **забра́ть(ся)**

заби́т|ый (~, ~а) *p.p.p. of* **~ь** *and adj.* cowed; downtrodden.

заб|и́ть[1]**, ью́, ьёшь** *pf.* (*of* **~ива́ть**) **1.** to drive in, hammer in; **з. себе́ в го́лову** to get (it) firmly fixed in one's head. **2.** (*sport*) to score; **з. гол** to score a goal. **3.** to seal, stop up. **4.** to obstruct; (*of plants*) to choke. **5.** (*+i.*; *coll.*) to cram, stuff (with). **6.** to beat up, knock senseless; (*fig.*) to render defenceless. **7.** (*coll.*) to beat (*at sth.*); to outdo, surpass. **8.** to slaughter (*cattle*).

заб|и́ть[2]**, ью, ьёшь** *pf.* (*in var. senses*; *trans. and intrans.*) to begin to beat (*in some cases forms pf. aspect of* **бить**); **з. трево́гу** to sound the alarm; **у нас из сква́жины ~и́ла нефть** we have struck oil.

заб|и́ться, ью́сь, ьёшься *pf.* (*of* **~ива́ться**) **1.** (**в**+*a.*) to hide (in), take refuge (in). **2.** (**в**+*a.*) to get (into), penetrate. **3.** (*+i.*) to become cluttered (with), clogged (with).

забия́к|а, и *c.g.* (*coll.*) trouble-maker; bully.

заблаговре́менно *adv.* in good time; well in advance; **з. предупреди́ть** to warn in advance.

заблаговре́менный *adj.* timely, done in good time.

заблагорассу́д|иться, ится *pf.* (*impers.*) to like, see fit; to come into one's head; **он придёт, когда́ ему́ ~ится** he will come when he sees fit to do so.

забле|сте́ть, щу́, сти́шь *and* **~щешь** *pf.* to begin to shine, glitter.

заблу|ди́ться, жу́сь ~дишься *pf.* to lose one's way, get lost.

заблу́дш|ий *adj.* (*obs.*) lost, stray; **~ая овца́** a lost sheep.

заблужда́|ться, юсь *impf.* to be mistaken.

заблужде́ни|е, я *nt.* error; delusion; **ввести́ в з.** to delude, mislead; **впасть в з.** to be deluded.

забода́|ть, ю *pf. of* **бода́ть**

забо́|й[1]**, я** *m.* (*mining*) (pit-)face.

забо́|й[2]**, я** *m.* slaughter(ing).

забо́йщик, а *m.* face-worker (*in mine*).

заболева́емост|ь, и *f.* incidence; number of cases; **з. полиомиели́том утро́илась за про́шлую неде́лю** the number of polio cases has tripled during the last week.

заболева́ни|е, я *nt.* sickness, illness.

заболева́|ть[1]**, ю** *impf. of* **заболе́ть**[1]

заболева́|ть[2]**, ет** *impf. of* **заболе́ть**[2]

заболе́|ть[1]**, ю, ешь** *pf.* (*of* **~ва́ть**[1]) to fall ill, fall sick; (*+i.*) to be taken ill (with), go down (with).

забол|е́ть[2]**, ит** *pf.* (*of* **~ева́ть**[2]) to (begin to) ache, hurt; **у меня́ ~е́л зуб** I have toothache.

за́болон|ь, и *f.* (*bot.*) alburnum, sap-wood.

заболта́|ть[1]**, ю** *pf.* **1.** (*+i.*) to begin to swing. **2.** (*impf.* **заба́лтывать**) to mix (in).

заболта́|ться, юсь *pf.* (*coll.*) to become engrossed in conversation.

забо́р, а *m.* fence.

забо́рист|ый (~, ~а) *adj.* (*coll.*) **1.** strong (*of liquor, tobacco, etc.*). **2.** (*fig.*) **з. анекдо́т** risqué story; **з. моти́в** racy tune.

забо́р|ный *adj.* **1.** *adj. of* **~. 2.** coarse, indecent; risqué.

забо́ртный *adj.* (*naut.*) outboard; **з. дви́гатель** outboard engine.

забо́т|а, ы *f.* **1.** cares, trouble(s); **без ~** carefree; without a care; **ему́ ма́ло ~ы** what does he care? **2.** care, attention(s); concern; **з. о челове́ке** concern for people.

забо́|тить, чу, тишь *impf.* to trouble, worry, cause anxiety.

забо́|титься, чусь, тишься *impf.* (*of* **по~**) (**о**+*p.*) **1.** to worry, be troubled (about). **2.** to take care (of); to look after; to care (about); **он ни о чём не ~тится** he does not care about anything.

забо́тливост|ь, и *f.* solicitude; thoughtfulness.

забо́тлив|ый (~, ~а) *adj.* solicitous; thoughtful; caring.

забрако́в|анный *p.p.p. of* **~а́ть; з. това́р** rejects.

забрак|ова́ть, у́ю *pf. of* **бракова́ть**

забра́л|о, а *nt.* visor; **с откры́тым ~ом** openly, frankly.

забра́сыва|ть, ю *impf. of* **заброса́ть** *and* **забро́сить**

забра́|ть[1]**, заберу́, заберёшь,** *past* **~л, ~ла́, ~ло** *pf.* (*of* **забира́ть**) **1.** to take (*in one's hands*); to take (with one); **з. во́жжи** to take the reins; **з. с собо́й ве́щи** to take one's things with one; **з. себе́ в го́лову** to take it onto one's head; **з. за живо́е** to touch to the quick. **2.** to take away; to seize, appropriate. **3.** (*of emotions*; *coll.*) to come over, seize; **его́ ~ла́ охо́та пое́хать в Аме́рику** he was seized with a desire to go to America. **4.** to take in (*part of* *a garment, etc.*). **5.** to turn off, aside. **6.** (*tech.*) to catch; (*of an anchor*) to bite.

забра́|ть[2], **заберу́, заберёшь,** *past* **~л, ~ла́, ~ло** *pf.* (*of* **забира́ть**) to stop up, block up.

забра́|ться, заберу́сь, заберёшься, *past* **~лся, ~ла́сь, ~ло́сь** *pf.* (*of* **забира́ться**) **1.** (**в**+*a.*) to get (into); (**в, на**+*a.*) to climb (into, on to); **з. в чужо́й дом** to get into s.o. else's home. **2.** to get to; to hide out, go into hiding; **куда́ они́ ~лись?** where have they got to?

забре́|дить, жу, дишь *pf.* to become delirious.

забре|сти́, ду́, дёшь, *past* **~л, ~ла́** *pf.* (*coll.*) **1.** to drop in. **2.** to go astray, wander off.

заброни́р|овать, ую *pf.* (*of* **брони́ровать**) to reserve.

забронир|ова́ть, у́ю *pf.* (*of* **бронирова́ть**) to armour.

забро́с, а *m.*: **в ~е** (*coll.*) in a state of neglect.

заброса́|ть, ю *pf.* (*of* **забра́сывать**) (+*i.*) **1.** to fill (up) (with); **з. я́му золо́й** to fill up a hole with ashes. **2.** to shower (with), bespatter (with); **з. кого́-н. гря́зью** to sling mud at s.o. (*also fig.*); **з. кого́-н. бла́нками** to deluge s.o. with forms.

забро́|сить, шу, сишь *pf.* (*of* **забра́сывать**) **1.** to throw (*with force or to a distance*); to cast (*also fig.*); **кто ~сил мя́чик в окно́?** who threw a ball through the window?; **вое́нная слу́жба ~сила его́ на Да́льний Восто́к** military service took him to the Far East. **2.** to throw (*a part of the body, etc.*); **з. го́лову наза́д** to throw one's head back. **3.** (*pf. only*) to mislay. **4.** to throw up, give up, abandon; to neglect, let go; **з. иссле́дования** to throw up one's research; **з. дете́й** to neglect children. **5.** to take, bring (*to a certain place*). **6.** to leave behind (*somewhere*).

забро́шенност|ь, и *f.* **1.** neglect. **2.** desertion.

забро́|шенный *p.p.p. of* **~сить** *and adj.* **1.** neglected. **2.** deserted, desolate.

забры́зг|ать, аю *pf.* (*of* **~ивать**) (+*i.*) to splash; to bespatter (with).

забры́згива|ть, ю *impf. of* **забры́згать**

заб|у́ду, у́дешь *see* **~ыть**

забукси́р|овать, ую *pf.* to take in tow.

забыва́|ть(ся), ю(сь) *impf. of* **забы́ть(ся)**

забы́вчив|ый (~, ~а) *adj.* forgetful; absent-minded.

заб|ы́ть, у́ду, у́дешь *pf.* (*of* **~ыва́ть**) **1.** (+*a.*, **о**+*p. or inf.*) to forget; **себя́ не з.** to take care of o.s. **2.** to leave behind, forget (to bring); **вы опя́ть ~ы́ли биле́ты** you have forgotten the tickets again.

забыть|ё, я́, в ~и́ *nt.* **1.** drowsy state. **2.** half-conscious state, oblivion. **3.** (state of) distraction; **в ~и́** distractedly.

заб|ы́ться, у́дусь, у́дешься *pf.* (*of* **~ыва́ться**) **1.** to doze off, drop off. **2.** to become unconscious, lose consciousness. **3.** to sink into a reverie. **4.** to forget o.s. **5.** *pass. of* **~ы́ть**

зав, а *m.* (*coll.*) *abbr. of* **~е́дующий**

зав. (*abbr. of* **заве́дующий**) manager.

зав... *comb. form, abbr. of* **1. заве́дующий. 2. заводско́й, заво́дский**

зава́л, а *m.* obstruction, blockage.

зава́лива|ть(ся), ю(сь) *impf. of* **завали́ть(ся)**

завал|и́ть, ю́, ~ишь *pf.* (*of* **~ивать**) **1.** to block up, obstruct; to fill; **з. вход мешка́ми с песко́м** to block up the entrance with sandbags. **2.** (+*i.*; *coll.*) to pile (with); to fill cram-full (with); (*fig.*) to overload with; **прила́вок ~ен коро́бками** the stall is piled high with boxes. **3.** (*coll.*) to throw back; to tip up, cant. **4.** (*coll.*) to knock down, demolish. **5.** (*fig.*, *coll.*) to make a mess (of), muck up. **6.** (*impers.*; *coll.*) to block (up); **доро́гу ~и́ло обва́лом** the road has been blocked by a landslide.

завал|и́ться, ю́сь, ~ишься *pf.* (*of* **~иваться**) **1.** to fall; to collapse; **нож ~и́лся за шкаф** the knife has fallen behind the cupboard. **2.** (*coll.*) to lie down; **з. спать** to flop into bed. **3.** (*coll.*) to overturn, tip up. **4.** (*fig.*, *coll.*) to miscarry, come to grief.

заваля́|ться, ется *pf.* (*coll.*) **1.** to be still on hand; **э́тот това́р ~ется** these goods will not sell. **2.** to remain without attention; to be shelved.

заваля́щий *adj.* (*coll.*) worthless, useless.

зава́рива|ть(ся), ет(ся) *impf. of* **завари́ть(ся)**

завар|и́ть, ю́, ~ишь *pf.* (*of* **~ивать**) to make (*drinks, etc.*); **з. чай** to brew tea; **з. ка́шу** (*fig.*) to start trouble; **ну и ~и́л ка́шу!** now the fat's in the fire.

завар|и́ться, ~ится *pf.* (*of* **~иваться**) **1.** (*of drinks*) to have brewed. **2.** (*coll.*) to start; **~и́лось бо́льшое де́ло** there's big trouble brewing.

зава́рк|а, и *f.* **1.** brewing (*of tea, etc.*). **2.** (*coll.*) enough tea for one brew.

заварно́й *adj.* (*cul.*) boiled.

завару́х|а, и *f.* (*coll.*) commotion, stir.

заведе́ни|е, я *nt.* establishment, institution.

заве́д|овать, ую *impf.* (+*i.*) to manage, superintend; to be in charge (of).

заве́домо *adv.* wittingly; (+*adj.*) known to be; **з. зна́я** being fully aware; **переда́ть з. необосно́ванный слух** to pass on a rumour known to be unfounded.

заве́домый *adj.* notorious; undoubted.

заве|ду́, дёшь *see* **~сти́**

заве́дующ|ий, его *m.* (+*i.*) manager; head; **з. уче́бной ча́стью** director of studies; **з. отде́лом** head of a department.

завез|ти́, у́, ёшь, *past* **~, ~ла́** *pf.* (*of* **завози́ть**) **1.** to deliver, drop off; **з. запи́ску по доро́ге домо́й** to deliver a note on the way home. **2.** to take (to a distance *or* out of one's way).

заверб|ова́ть, у́ю *pf. of* **вербова́ть**

завере́ни|е, я *nt.* assurance.

завери́тел|ь, я *m.* witness (*to a signature, etc.*).

заве́р|ить, ю, ишь *pf.* (*of* **~я́ть**) **1.** (**в**+*p.*) to assure (of). **2.** to certify; **з. по́дпись** to witness a signature.

заве́рк|а, и *f.* certification.

заверн|у́ть, у́, ёшь *pf.* (*of* **завёртывать**) **1.** (**в**+*a.*) to wrap (in); **~и́те его́ в одея́ло** wrap him in a blanket. **2.** to tuck up, roll up (*sleeve, etc.*). **3.** to turn (*intrans.*); **з. напра́во** to turn to the right. **4.** (*coll.*) to drop in, call in. **5.** to screw tight; to tighten; to turn off (*by screwing*); **з. га́йку** to screw a nut tight; **з. кран** to turn off a tap.

заверн|у́ться, у́сь, ёшься *pf.* (*of* **завёртываться**) **1.** (**в**+*a.*) to wrap o.s. up (in), muffle o.s. (in). **2.** *pass. of* **~у́ть**

завер|те́ть, чу́, ~тишь *pf.* **1.** to begin to twirl. **2.: з. кого́-н.** (*fig.*, *coll.*) to turn s.o.'s head.

завер|те́ться, чу́сь, ~тишься *pf.* **1.** to begin to turn, begin to spin. **2.** (*coll.*) to become flustered; to lose one's head.

завёртыва|ть(ся), ю(сь) *impf. of* **заверну́ть(ся)**

заверш|а́ть, а́ю *impf. of* **~и́ть**

заверше́ни|е, я *nt.* completion; end; **в з.** in conclusion.

заверш|и́ть, у́, и́шь *pf.* (*of* **~а́ть**) to complete, conclude, crown.

завер|я́ть, я́ю *impf. of* **~ить**

заве́с|а, ы *f.*: **дымова́я з.** (*mil.*) smoke-screen; (*fig.*) veil, screen; **приподня́ть ~у** to lift the veil.

заве́|сить, шу, сишь *pf.* (*of* **~шивать**) to curtain (off.).

заве|сти́, ду́, дёшь, *past* **~л, ~ла́** *pf.* (*of* **заводи́ть**) **1.** to take, bring (*to a place*); to leave, drop of (*at a place*). **2.** to take (to a distance *or* out of one's way). **3.** to set up; to start; **з. де́ло** (*coll.*) to set up in business; **з. перепи́ску** to start up a correspondence. **4.** to acquire. **5.** to institute, introduce (*as a custom*); **з. привы́чку** (*+inf.*) to get into the habit (of). **6.** to wind (up), start (*a mechanism*); **з. часы́** to wind up a clock; **з. мото́р** to crank an engine.

заве|сти́сь, ду́сь, дёшься, *past* **~лся, ~ла́сь** *pf.* (*of* **заводи́ться**) **1.** to be; to appear; **в по́гребе ~ли́сь кры́сы** there are rats in the cellar. **2.** to be established, be set up; **~ло́сь обыкнове́ние** it has become a habit. **3.** (*of a mechanism*) to start (*intrans.*).

заве́т, а *m.* **1.** (*rhet.*) behest, bidding, ordinance. **2.**: **Ве́тхий, Но́вый з.** the Old, the New Testament.

заве́тн|ый *adj.* cherished; intimate; secret, hidden; **стать кинозвездо́й — её ~ая мечта́** her secret ambition is to become a film-star.

заве́ш|ать, аю *pf.* (*of* **~ивать**) (*+a. and i.*) to hang (all over); **он ~ал сте́ны своего́ кабине́та фотогра́фиями** he has hung the walls of his study with photographs.

заве́шива|ть, ю *impf. of* **заве́сить** *and* **заве́шать**

завеща́ни|е, я *nt.* will, testament.

завеща́тел|ь, я *m.* (*leg.*) testator.

завеща́тельниц|а, ы *f.* (*leg.*) testatrix.

завеща́|ть, ю *impf. and pf.* (*+a. and d.*) to leave (to), bequeath (to).

завзя́тый *adj.* (*coll.*) inveterate, out-and-out, downright; incorrigible.

завива́|ть(ся), ю(сь) *impf. of* **зави́ть(ся)**

зави́вк|а, и *f.* **1.** waving; curling; **сде́лать себе́ ~у** to have one's hair waved. **2.** (hair-)wave.

зави́|деть, жу, дишь *pf.* (*coll.*) to catch sight of.

зави́дно *as pred.* (*impers.*, *+d.*) to feel envious.

зави́д|ный (~ен, ~на) *adj.* enviable.

зави́д|овать, ую *impf.* (*of* **по~**) (*+d.*) to envy.

завиду́щий *adj.* (*coll.*) envious, covetous.

завизи́р|овать, ую *pf. of* **визи́ровать**[1]

завин|ти́ть, чу́, ти́шь *pf.* (*of* **~чивать**) to screw up.

завин|ти́ться, чу́сь, ти́шься *pf.* (*of* **~чиваться**) to screw up (*intrans.*).

зави́нчива|ть(ся), ю(сь) *impf. of* **завинти́ть(ся)**

завира́|ться, юсь *impf. of* **завра́ться**

зави́|сеть, шу, сишь *impf.* **(от) 1.** to depend (on). **2.** to lie in the power (of); **я сде́лаю для тебя́ всё, что от меня́ ~сит** I will help you as far as it is in my power to do so.

зави́симость *f.* dependence; **в ~и (от)** depending (on), subject (to).

зави́сим|ый (~, ~а) *adj.* **(от)** dependent (on).

зави́стлив|ый (~, ~а) *adj.* envious.

зави́стник, а *m.* envious person.

за́вист|ь, и *f.* envy.

завит|о́й *and* **~ый (зави́т, ~а́, зави́то)** *adj.* curled; waved.

завит|о́к, ка́ *m.* **1.** curl, lock. **2.** flourish (*in handwriting*).

зав|и́ть, ью́, ьёшь, *past* **~и́л, ~ила́, ~и́ло** *pf.* (*of* **~ива́ть**) to curl, to wave; to twist, wind.

зав|и́ться, ью́сь, ьёшься, *past* **~и́лся, ~ила́сь** *pf.* (*of* **~ива́ться**) **1.** to curl, wave; to twine. **2.** to curl, wave one's hair; to have one's hair curled, waved.

завко́м, а *m.* (*abbr. of* ***заводско́й комите́т***) factory committee.

завладева́|ть, ю *impf. of* **завладе́ть**

завладе́|ть, ю *pf.* (*of* **~ва́ть**) (*+i.*) to take possession (of); to seize, capture (*also fig.*); **свои́м красноре́чием он ~л внима́нием слу́шателей** he gripped the audience with his eloquence.

завлека́тел|ьный (~ен, ~ьна) *adj.* (*coll.*) alluring; captivating.

завлека́|ть, ю *impf. of* **завле́чь**

завле́|чь, ку́, чёшь, ку́т, *past* **~к, ~кла́** *pf.* (*of* **~ка́ть**) **1.** to lure, entice. **2.** to fascinate, captivate.

заво́д[1]**, а** *m.* **1.** factory, mill; works; **нефтеочисти́тельный з.** oil refinery. **2.** **(ко́нский) з.** stud(-farm).

заво́д[2]**, а** *m.* winding mechanism; **игру́шка с ~ом** clockwork toy.

заво|ди́ть, жу́, ~дишь *impf. of* **завести́**

завод|и́ться, ~ится *impf. of* **завести́сь**

заводн|о́й *adj.* **1.** clockwork. **2.** (*tech.*) winding. starting; **~а́я рукоя́тка, ру́чка** starting crank.

заво́д|ский *adj. of* **~**[1]; **~ская ло́шадь** stud-horse.

завод|ско́й = **~ский**

заво́дчик, а *m.* **1.** factory-owner, mill-owner.

за́вод|ь, и *f.* creek, backwater.

завоева́ни|е, я *nt.* **1.** winning. **2.** conquest; (*fig.*) achievement, attainment; **нове́йшие ~я те́хники** the latest achievements of technology.

завоева́тел|ь, я *m.* conqueror.

завоева́тельн|ый *adj.*: **~ая война́** war of conquest.

заво|ева́ть, ю́ю, ю́ешь *pf.* (*of* **~ёвывать**) to conquer; (*fig.*) to win, gain; **з. о́бщие симпа́тии** to gain general sympathy.

завоёвыва|ть, ю *impf. of* **завоева́ть**; to try to get.

заво́з, а *m.* delivery; carriage.

заво|зи́ть, жу́, ~зишь *impf. of* **завезти́**

заво́зный *adj.* brought in; imported.

завола́кива|ть(ся), ю(сь) *impf. of* **заволо́чь(ся)**

заволн|ова́ться, у́юсь *pf.* to become agitated.

заволо́|чь, ку́, чёшь, ку́т, *past* **~к, ~кла́** *pf.* (*of* **завола́кивать**) to cloud; to obscure; **тума́н ~к со́лнце** the sun was obscured by fog; **её глаза́ ~кло́ слеза́ми** her eyes were clouded with tears.

заволо́|чься, чётся, ку́тся, *past* **~кся, ~кла́сь** *pf.* (*of* **завола́киваться**) to cloud over, become clouded.

завора́жива|ть, ю *impf. of* **заворожи́ть**

завора́чива|ть[1]**, ю** *impf.* = **завёртывать**

завора́чива|ть[2]**, ю** *impf.* **1.** *impf. of* **заворoти́ть. 2.** (*impf. only*) (*+i.*; *coll.*) to be boss (of).

заворож|и́ть, у́, и́шь *pf.* (*of* **завора́живать**) to cast a spell (over), bewitch; (*fig.*) to fascinate.

заворо́т, а *m.* (*coll.*) **1.** turn, turning. **2.** bend (*in road, river, etc.*).

завор|оти́ть, очу́, о́тишь *pf.* (*of* **завора́чивать**[2]) **1.** to turn. **2.** to turn in; to drop in. **3.** to roll up; to tuck up.

завр|а́ться, у́сь, ёшься, *past* **~а́лся, ~ала́сь** *pf.* (*of* **завира́ться**) (*coll.*) to become entangled in lies; to become an inveterate liar.

завсегда́та|й, я *m.* habitué; regular; **театра́льный з.** regular theatre-goer; **з. ба́ров** barfly.

за́втра *adv.* tomorrow; **до з.!** see you tomorrow!

за́втрак, а *m.* breakfast; lunch(eon); **второ́й з.** elevenses, mid-morning snack.

за́втрака|ть, ю *impf.* (*of* **по~**) to (have) breakfast; to (have) lunch.

за́втрашн|ий *adj.* tomorrow's; **з. день** tomorrow; (*poet.*) the morrow.

за́вуч, а *m.* (*abbr. of* ***заве́дующий уче́бной ча́стью***) director of studies.

завхо́з, а *m.* (*abbr. of* ***заве́дующий хозя́йством***) bursar, steward.

завыва́|ть, ю *impf.* to howl; to wail.

завы́|сить, шу, сишь *pf.* (*of* **~ша́ть**) to raise too high; **з. отме́тку на экза́мене** to give too high a mark in an examination.

завыша́|ть, ю *impf. of* **завы́сить**

завя|за́ть[1]**, жу́, ~жешь** *pf.* (*of* **~зывать**) **1.** to tie (up); to knot; **з. шну́рки боти́нок** to tie up one's shoe-laces. **2.** to bind (up). **3.** (*fig.*) to start; **з. бой** to join battle; **з. перепи́ску** to start a correspondence; **з. разгово́р** to strike up a conversation.

завяза́|ть[2]**, ю** *impf. of* **завя́знуть**

завя|за́ться, ~жется *pf.* (*of* **~зываться**) **1.** *pass.*

of **~за́ть. 2.** to start; to arise.
завя́зк|а, и *f.* **1.** string, lace, band. **2.** beginning, start; opening (*of novel, etc.*).
завя́з|нуть, ну, нешь, *past* **~, ~ла** *pf.* (*of* **~а́ть**[2]) to get stuck; **з. в долга́х** to be steeped in debt.
завя́зыва|ть(ся), ет(ся) *impf. of* **завяза́ть(ся)**
за́вяз|ь, и *f.* (*bot.*) ovary.
завя́лый *adj.* (*obs.*) withered, faded.
завя́|нуть, ну, нешь, *past* **~л** *pf. of* **вя́нуть**
загад|а́ть, а́ю *pf.* (*of* **∠ывать**) **1.: з. зага́дки** to pose riddles. **2.** to guess one's fortune; to decide, settle (*by tossing a coin, etc.*). **3.** to think of (= *to select arbitrarily, at random*); **~а́йте число́** think of a number. **4.** to plan ahead, look ahead.
зага́|дить, жу, дишь *pf.* (*of* **~живать**) (*coll.*) to soil, dirty, foul.
зага́дк|а, и *f.* riddle; enigma; mystery.
зага́доч|ный (~ен, ~на) *adj.* enigmatic; mysterious.
зага́дыва|ть, ю *impf. of* **загада́ть**
зага́жива|ть, ю *impf. of* **зага́дить**
зага́р, а *m.* sunburn; (sun-)tan.
зага|си́ть, шу́, ∠сишь *pf. of* **гаси́ть 1.**
загво́здк|а, и *f.* (*coll.*) snag, obstacle; **вот в чём з.!** there's the rub!
заги́б, а *m.* **1.** fold; bend. **2.** (*pol.*; *coll.*) deviation.
загиба́|ть(ся), ю(сь) *impf. of* **загну́ть(ся)**
заги́бщик, а *m.* (*pol.*; *coll.*) deviationist.
загипнотизи́р|овать, ую *pf. of* **гипнотизи́ровать**
загла́ви|е, я *nt.* title; heading; **под ~ем** entitled, headed.
загла́в|ный *adj. of* **~ие; з. лист** title-page; **~ная бу́ква** capital letter; **~ные бу́квы** initials; **~ная роль** (*theatr.*) title-role; **~ное сло́во** headword.
загла́|дить, жу, дишь *pf.* (*of* **~живать**) **1.** to iron (out), press. **2.** (*fig.*) to make up (for), make amends (for); **з. грехи́** to expiate one's sins.
загла́жива|ть, ю *impf. of* **загла́дить**
загла́зно *adv.* (*coll.*) behind s.o.'s back.
загла́зн|ый *adj.* (*coll.*) done, said in s.o.'s absence, behind s.o.'s back; **∠ая клевета́** scandal uttered about s.o. behind his back; backbiting.
загла́тыва|ть, ю *impf. of* **заглота́ть**
заглота́|ть, ю *pf.* (*of* **загла́тывать**) to swallow.
загло́хн|уть, у, ешь *pf. of* **гло́хнуть 2., 3.**
заглуш|а́ть, а́ю *impf. of* **~и́ть**
заглуш|и́ть, у́, и́шь *pf.* (*of* **глуши́ть** *and* **~а́ть**) **1.** to drown (out), deaden, muffle (*sound*). **2.** to jam (*radio transmissions*). **3.** (*of weeds*) to choke. **4.** (*fig.*) to suppress, stifle.
загляде́нь|е, я *nt.* (*coll.*) lovely sight; sight for sore eyes.
загля|де́ться, жу́сь, ди́шься *pf.* (*of* **∠дываться**) (**на**+*a.*; *coll.*) to stare (at); to be lost in admiration (of).
загля́дыва|ть, ю *impf. of* **загляну́ть**
загля́дыва|ться, юсь *impf. of* **загляде́ться**
заглян|уть, у́, ∠ешь *pf.* (*of* **загля́дывать**) **1.** to peep; to glance; **она́ ~у́ла в окно́ и уви́дела, что де́ти засну́ли** she peeped in at the window and saw that the children were asleep; **з. в газе́ты** to glance at the newspapers. **2.** (*coll.*) to look in, drop in; **~и́те к нам, пожа́луйста!** please look in on us!
загна́ива|ть(ся), ю(сь) *impf. of* **загнои́ть(ся)**
за́гнанный *p.p.p. of* **загна́ть** *and adj.* **1.** tired out, exhausted; **как з. зверь** at the end of one's tether. **2.** down-trodden, cowed.
загна́|ть, загоню́, заго́нишь, *past* **~л, ~ла́, ~ло** *pf.* (*of* **загоня́ть**) **1.** to drive in; **з. коро́в в хлев** to drive the cows into the shed, get the cows in; **з. мяч в воро́та** (*sport*) to score, shoot a goal. **2.** to drive (off). **3.** to tire out, exhaust; to drive to exhaustion. **4.** (*coll.*) to drive in, home; **з. сва́и в зе́млю** to drive piles into the ground.
загнива́ни|е, я *nt.* rotting, putrescence; (*fig.*) decay; (*med.*) suppuration.
загнива́|ть, ю *impf. of* **загни́ть**
загни́|ть, ю́, ёшь, *past* **~л, ~ла́, ~ло** *pf.* (*of* **~ва́ть**) to begin to rot; to rot, decay (*also fig.*); (*med.*) to fester.
загно|и́ть, ю́, и́шь *pf.* (*of* **загна́ивать**) (*coll.*) **1.** to allow to fester. **2.** to allow to rot, allow to decay.
загно|и́ться, и́тся *pf.* (*of* **загна́иваться**) to fester.
загн|у́ть, у́, ёшь *pf.* (*of* **загиба́ть**) **1.** to turn up, turn down; to bend, fold; to crease; **з. страни́цу** to dog-ear a page. **2.** to turn (*intrans.*); **з. за́ угол** to turn a corner. **3.** (*coll.*) to utter, come out with (*a swear-word or vulgarism*); **ну и слове́чко ~у́л!** (*iron.*) what language! **4.** (*coll.*) to ask (*an exorbitant price*).
загн|у́ться, у́сь, ёшься *pf.* (*of* **загиба́ться**) **1.** to turn up, stick up; to turn down. **2.** (*sl.*) to turn up one's toes, kick the bucket.
загова́рива|ть, ю *impf. of* **заговори́ть**[1]
загова́рива|ться, юсь *impf.* (*of* **заговори́ться**) **1.** to be carried away by a conversation. **2.** (*impf. only*) to rave; to ramble (*in speech*).
за́говор, а *m.* **1.** plot, conspiracy. **2.** charm, spell.
заговор|и́ть[1]**, ю́, и́шь** *pf.* (*of* **загова́ривать**) **1.** (*coll.*) to talk s.o.'s head off. **2.** to cast a spell (over); (**от**) to put on a spell (against); to exorcize; **з. зу́бы кому́-н.** (*coll.*) to distract s.o. with smooth talk.
заговор|и́ть[2]**, ю́, и́шь** *pf.* **1.** to begin to speak. **2.** to (be able to) speak; to learn to speak.
заговор|и́ться, ю́сь, и́шься *pf. of* **загова́риваться**
загово́рщик, а *m.* conspirator, plotter.
загово́рщицкий *adj.* conspiratorial.
загово́рщический *adj.* = **загово́рщицкий**
за́годя *adv.* (*coll.*) in good time.
заголо́в|ок, ка *m.* **1.** title; heading. **2.** headline.
заго́н, а *m.* **1.** driving in; rounding-up. **2.** enclosure (*for cattle*); pen. **3.** strip (of ploughed land). **4.: быть в ~е** (*fig.*) to be kept down; **у кого́-н. в ~е** under s.o.'s thumb. **5.: в ~е** (*sl.*) to one's credit, 'chalked up'; **у него́ в ~е три дня** he had three days' (work) to his credit.
за|гоню́, го́нишь *see* **~гна́ть**
загоня́|ть, ю *impf. of* **загна́ть**
загора́жива|ть(ся), ю(сь) *impf. of* **загороди́ть(ся)**
загора́|ть(ся), ю(сь) *impf. of* **загоре́ть(ся)**
загоре́лый *adj.* sunburnt; (sun)tanned.
загор|е́ть, ю́, и́шь *pf.* (*of* **~а́ть**) to become sunburnt; to acquire a tan.
загор|е́ться, ю́сь, и́шься *pf.* (*of* **~а́ться**) **1.** to catch fire; to begin to burn; (*impers.*): **в библиоте́ке ~е́лось** a fire broke out in the library. **2.** (+*i.*; **от**) to blaze (with), burn (with) (*fig.*); **его́ глаза́ ~е́лись от гне́ва** his eyes blazed with anger. **3.** (*impers.*, +*d.*; *coll.*) to have a burning desire; **ей ~е́лось уви́деть Рим** she had a burning desire to see Rome. **4.** (*fig.*) to break out; **~е́лась дра́ка** a fight broke out.
загоро|ди́ть, жу́, ∠ди́шь *pf.* (*of* **загора́живать**) **1.** to enclose, fence in. **2.** to barricade; to obstruct; **з. кому́-н. свет** to stand in s.o.'s light.
загоро|ди́ться, жу́сь, ∠ди́шься *pf.* (*of* **загора́живаться**) **1.** to barricade o.s.; **з. ши́рмой** to screen o.s. off. **2.** *pass. of* **~ди́ть**
загоро́дк|а, и *f.* (*coll.*) **1.** fence. **2.** enclosure.
за́городн|ый *adj.* out-of-town; country; **~ая экску́рсия** excursion into the country.
заго|сти́ться, щу́сь, сти́шься *pf.* (*coll.*) to outstay one's welcome.
заготов|и́тельный *adj. of* **∠ка**
загото́в|ить, лю, ишь *pf.* (*of* **~ля́ть**) **1.** to lay in; to make a stock (of), stockpile, store. **2.** to prepare.
загото́вк|а, и *f.* **1.** (State) procurement (*of agricult-*

ural products, timber, etc.). **2.** laying in; stocking up, stockpiling.

заготовля́|ть, ю *impf. of* **загото́вить**

загради́тел|ь я *m.* (*naut.*) minelayer.

загради́тельный *adj.* (*mil.*) barrage; (*naut.*) minelaying; **з. аэроста́т** barrage balloon.

загра|ди́ть, жу́, ди́шь *pf.* (*of* **~жда́ть**) to block, obstruct; **з. путь** to bar the way.

загражда́|ть, ю *impf. of* **загради́ть**

загражде́ни|е, я *nt.* obstacle, barrier, obstruction.

грани́ц|а, ы *f.* (*coll.*) foreign countries (*see also* **грани́ца**).

загранú́чный *adj.* foreign.

загреба́|ть, ю *impf. of* **загрести́; чужи́ми рука́ми жар з.**, *see* **жар**

загрем|е́ть[1], **лю́, и́шь** *pf.* (*coll.*) to crash down.

загрем|е́ть[2], **лю́, и́шь** *pf.* to begin to thunder.

загре|сти́, бу́, бёшь, *past* **~̈б, ~бла́** *pf.* (*of* **~ба́ть**) (*coll.*) to rake up, gather; (*fig.*) to rake in; **з. жар** to bank up the fire; **з. де́ньги** to rake in the shekels.

загри́в|ок, ка *m.* **1.** withers. **2.** (*coll.*) nape (of the neck).

загримир|ова́ть(ся), у́ю(сь) *pf. of* **гримирова́ть(ся)**

загрипп|ова́ть, у́ю *pf.* (*coll.*) to catch flu, go down with the flu.

загро́бн|ый *adj.* **1.** beyond the grave; **~ая жизнь** life after death. **2.** sepulchral (*of voice*).

загроможда́|ть, ю *impf. of* **загромозди́ть**

загромоз|ди́ть, жу́, ди́шь *pf.* (*of* **загроможда́ть**) to block up, encumber; (*fig.*) to pack, cram; **з. расска́з подро́бностями** to pack a story with detail.

загрубе́лый *adj.* calloused; callous.

загрубе́|ть, ю *pf.* to become calloused; to become callous.

загружа́|ть, ю *impf. of* **загрузи́ть 2.**

загр|узи́ть, ужу́, у́зишь *pf.* **1.** (*impf.* **грузи́ть**) to load. **2.** (*impf.* **~ужа́ть**) (*coll.*) to keep fully occupied, provide with a full-time job; to fill out (*a period of time*) with occupations.

загру|зи́ться, жу́сь, зи́шься *pf.* (*of* **~жа́ться**) **1.** (*+i.*) to load up (with), take on. **2.** (*coll.*) to take on a job, a commitment.

загру́зк|а, и *f.* **1.** loading. **2.** workload; capacity; **заво́д рабо́тает при по́лной ~е** the factory is working at full capacity.

загру́з|очный *adj. of* **~ка; з. ковш, я́щик** hopper.

загрунт|ова́ть, у́ю *pf. of* **грунтова́ть**

загру|сти́ть, щу́, сти́шь *pf.* to grow sad.

загрыза́|ть, ю *impf. of* **загры́зть**

загры́з|ть, у́, ёшь *past* **~, ~ла** *pf.* (*of* **~а́ть**) **1.** to kill; to bite to death; (*fig.*) to worry the life out of. **2.** to tear to pieces.

загрязне́ни|е, я *nt.* soiling; pollution; contamination.

загрязни́тел|ь, я *m.* pollutant.

загрязн|и́ть, ю́, и́шь *pf.* (*of* **~я́ть**) to soil, dirty; to pollute.

загрязн|и́ться, ю́сь, и́шься *pf.* (*of* **~я́ться**) to make o.s. dirty, become dirty.

загрязня́|ть(ся), ю(сь) *impf. of* **загрязни́ть(ся)**

ЗАГС, а *or* **загс, а** *m.* (*abbr. of* **(отде́л) за́писи а́ктов гражда́нского состоя́ния**) registry office.

загуб|и́ть, лю́, ~ишь *pf.* **1.** to ruin; **з. чей-н. век, з. чью-н. жизнь** to make s.o.'s life a misery. **2.** (*coll.*) to squander.

загуля́|ть, ю *pf.* (*coll.*) to take to drink, start drinking.

зад, а, о ~е, на ~у́, *pl.* **~ы́** *m.* **1.** back; **~ом напере́д** back to front. **2.** rear; hind quarters; buttocks; rump; **бить ~ом** to kick (*of animal*).

зада́брива|ть, ю *impf. of* **задо́брить**

задава́к|а, и *c.g.* (*coll.*) snob, big-head.

задава́ла = задава́ка

зада|ва́ть, ю, ёшь *impf. of* **~ть**

зада|ва́ться[1], **ю́сь, ёшься** *impf. of* **~ться**

зада|ва́ться[2], **ю́сь, ёшься** *impf.* (*coll.*) to give o.s. airs, put on airs.

задав|и́ть, лю́, ~ишь *pf.* to crush; to run over, knock down.

зада́ни|е, я *nt.* task, job.

зада́рива|ть, ю *impf. of* **задари́ть**

задар|и́ть, ю́, ~ишь *pf.* (*of* **~ивать**) **1.** to load with presents. **2.** to bribe.

зада́ром *adv.* (*coll.*) **1.** for nothing; very cheaply; **купи́ть з.** to buy for a song. **2.** in vain, to no purpose.

зада́тк|и, ов *no sg.* aptitude; ability.

зада́т|ок, ка *m.* deposit, advance.

за|да́ть, да́м, да́шь, *past* **~дал, ~дала́, ~дало** *pf.* (*of* **~дава́ть**) to set; to give; **з. уро́к** to set a lesson; **з. вопро́с** to ask, put a question; **з. тон** to set the tone; **з. стра́ху** (*+d.*) to strike terror (into); **я ему́ ~да́м!** (*coll.*) I'll give him what-for!

за|да́ться, да́мся, да́шься, *past* **~да́лся, ~дала́сь** *pf.* (*of* **~дава́ться**[1]) **1.: з. це́лью, мы́слью** (*+inf.*) to set o.s. (to), make up one's mind (to); **з. вопро́сом** to ask o.s. the question. **2.** (*coll.*) to turn out (well); to work out, succeed; **пое́здка не ~дала́сь** the trip was not a success.

зада́ч|а, и *f.* **1.** (*math., etc.*) problem. **2.** task; mission.

зада́чник, а *m.* book of (mathematical) problems.

задвига́|ть, ю *impf. of* **задви́нуть**

задвига́|ться, юсь *impf.* **1.** *impf. of* **задви́нуться. 2.** (*impf. only*) to move, slide.

задви́жк|а, и *f.* bolt; catch, fastening.

задвижно́й *adj.* sliding.

задви́н|уть, у, ешь *pf.* (*of* **задвига́ть**) **1.** to push; **з. задви́жку** to shoot a bolt. **2.** to bolt; to bar; to close; **з. за́навес** to draw a curtain (across).

задви́н|уться, усь, ешься *pf.* (*of* **задвига́ться**) to shut; to slide (*intrans.*)

задво́р|ки, ок *no sg.* **1.** backyard; (*fig.*) out-of-the-way place, backwoods. **2.: быть на ~ках** (*fig.*) to take a back seat.

задева́|ть[1], **ю** *impf. of* **заде́ть**

задева́|ть[2], **ю** *pf.* (*coll.*) to mislay; **куда́ ~л мой очки́?** where did I put my spectacles?

задева́|ться[1], **юсь** *impf., pass. of* **~ть**[1]

задева́|ться[2], **юсь** *pf.* (*coll.*) to disappear; **куда́ ты ~лся?** where did you get to?

заде́л, а *m.* (*coll.*) work already done; reserve; stock.

заде́л|ать, аю *pf.* (*of* **~ывать**) to do up; to block up, close up; **з. посы́лку** to do up a parcel; **з. течь** to stop up a leak.

заде́ла|ться[1], **юсь** *pf., pass. of* **~ть**

заде́л|аться[2], **аюсь** *pf.* (*of* **~ываться**) (*coll.*) to become; to turn; **он ~ался литературове́дом** he has turned literary critic.

заде́лыва|ть(ся), ю(сь) *impf. of* **заде́лать(ся)**

задёрга|ть[1], **ю** *pf.* (*+a. or i.*) to begin to tug.

задёрга|ть[2], **ю** *pf.* to wear out; (*fig., coll.*) to wear down.

задёргива|ть, ю *impf. of* **задёрнуть**

задеревене́лый *adj.* numb(ed), stiff.

задеревене́|ть, ю *pf.* (*coll.*) to become numb, become stiff.

задержа́ни|е, я *nt.* **1.** detention; arrest. **2.** (*med.*): **з. мочи́** retention of urine.

заде́ржанн|ый, ого *m.* detainee.

задерж|а́ть, у́ ~ишь *pf.* (*of* **~ивать**) **1.** to detain; to delay; to hold up; **до́ждик ~а́л нача́ло ма́тча** the start of the match was delayed by a shower. **2.** to withhold, keep back; **з. зарпла́ту** to stop wages. **3.** to detain, arrest.

задерж|а́ться, у́сь ~ишься *pf.* (*of* **~иваться**) **1.** to stay too long; to linger. **2.** *pass. of* **~а́ть**

задéржива|ть(ся), ю(сь) *impf. of* **задержáть(ся)**
задéржк|а, и *f.* delay; hold-up.
задёрн|уть, у, ешь *pf.* (*of* **задёргивать**) **1.** to pull; to draw; **з. зáнавески** to draw the curtains. **2.** to cover; to curtain off.
задéт|ый (~, ~а) *p.p.p. of* **~ь; з. насмéшками** stung by taunts.
задé|ть, ну, нешь *pf.* (*of* **~вáть**[1]) **1.** to touch, brush (against), graze; (*fig.*) to offend, wound; **егó ~ло за живóе** he was cut to the quick. **2.** to catch (on, against).
задúр|а, ы *c.g.* (*coll.*) bully; trouble-maker.
задирá|ть(ся)[1], **ю(сь)** *impf. of* **задрáть(ся)**
задирá|ться[2], **юсь** *impf.* (*coll.*) to pick a quarrel.
задненёбный *adj.* (*ling.*) velar.
заднепрохóдный *adj.* (*anat.*) anal.
зáдн|ий *adj.* back, rear; hind; **~яя мысль** ulterior motive; **з. план** background; **з. прохóд** (*anat.*) anus; **~им умóм крéпок** (*coll.*) wise after the event; **з. фонáрь** tail-light; **з. ход** (*tech.*) backward movement; **дать з. ход** to go into reverse; to back up; **~им числóм** later; with hindsight; **помéтить ~им числóм** to antedate; **быть без ~их ног** (*coll.*) to be falling off one's feet; **ходúть на ~их лáпках (пéред)** (*coll.*) to dance attendance (on).
зáдник, а *m.* **1.** back, counter (*of shoe*). **2.** (*theatr.*) backdrop.
зáдниц|а, ы *f.* (*vulg.*) arse, backside.
задóбр|ить, ю, ишь *pf.* (*of* **задáбривать**) to cajole; to coax; to win over.
зад|óк, кá *m.* back.
задóлго *adv.* long before; **он кóнчил рабóту з. до вéчера** he finished the work long before evening.
задóлженност|ь, и *f.* debts; **погасúть з.** to pay off one's debts.
зáдом *adv.* backwards; **éхать з.** to reverse, back up.
задóр, а *m.* fervour, ardour; passion.
задóринк|а, и *f.* (*coll.*): **без сучкá, без ~и** *or* **ни сучкá, ни ~и** without a hitch.
задóр|ный (~ен, ~на) *adj.* **1.** fervent, ardent; impassioned. **2.** provocative; quick-tempered.
задох|нýться, нýсь, нёшься, *past* **ˊ~ся, ˊ~лась** *and* **~нýлся, ~нýлась** *pf.* (*of* **задыхáться**) **1.** to suffocate; to choke; (*fig.*): **з. от гнéва** to choke with anger. **2.** to pant; to gasp for breath.
задрáзнива|ть, ю *impf. of* **задразнúть**
задразн|úть, ю́, ˊ~ишь *pf.* (*coll.*) to tease unmercifully.
задрáива|ть, ю *impf. of* **задрáить**
задрá|ить, ю, ишь *pf.* (*naut.*) to batten down.
задрапир|овáть, ýю *pf.* (+*a. and i.*) to drape (with).
задрапир|овáться, ýюсь *pf.* (+*a. or* **в**+*a.*) to drape o.s. (with), wrap o.s. up (in).
задрапирóвыва|ть(ся), ю(сь) *impf. of* **задрапировáть(ся)**
зад|рáть, ерý, ерёшь, *past* **~рáл, ~ралá, ~рáло** *pf.* (*of* **~ирáть**) **1.** to tear to pieces; to kill (*of wolves, etc.*). **2.** (*coll.*) to lift up; to pull up; **з. гóлову** to crane one's neck; **з. нос** (*fig.*) to turn up one's nose. **3.** to break (*finger-nail, etc.*). **4.** (*coll.*) to insult; to provoke.
зад|рáться, ерётся, *past* **~рáлся, ~ралáсь, ~рáлóсь** *pf.* (*of* **~ирáться**) **1.** to break (*intrans.*; *finger-nail, etc.*); to split (*intrans.*). **2.** (*coll.*) to ride up (*of clothing*). **3.** *pass. of* **~рáть**
задрем|áть, лю́, ˊ~лешь *pf.* to doze off, begin to nod.
задрúпан|ный (~, ~а) *adj.* (*coll.*) bedraggled.
задрож|áть, ý, úшь *pf.* to begin to tremble; to begin to shiver.
задувá|ть, ю *impf. of* **задýть**
задýма|ть, ю *pf.* (*of* **задýмывать**) **1.** (+*a. or inf.*) to plan; to intend; to conceive the idea (of). **2.**: **з. числó** to think of a number.
задýма|ться, юсь *pf.* to become thoughtful, pensive; to fall to thinking; **о чём вы ~лись?** what are you thinking about?
задýмчивост|ь, и *f.* thoughtfulness, pensiveness; reverie.
задýмчив|ый (~, ~а) *adj.* thoughtful, pensive.
задýмыва|ть, ю *impf. of* **задýмать**
задýмыва|ться, юсь *impf.* to be thoughtful, be pensive; to meditate; to ponder; **не ~ясь, он соглаcúлся** he agreed without a moment's hesitation.
задý|ть, ю, ешь *pf.* (*of* **~вáть**) **1.** to blow out. **2.** (*tech.*): **з. дóмну** to blow in a blast-furnace. **3.** to begin to blow.
задушéв|ный (~ен, ~на) *adj.* sincere; cordial; intimate.
задуш|úть, ý, ˊ~ишь *pf. of* **душúть**[1]
зад|ы́ *see* **~**
задым|úть, лю́, úшь *pf.* **1.** to begin to (emit) smoke. **2.** to blacken with smoke.
задымля́|ть, ю *impf. of* **задымúть 2.**
задыхá|ться, юсь *impf. of* **задохнýться**
заедáни|е, я *nt.* (*tech.*) jamming.
заедá|ть(ся), ю(сь) *impf. of* **заéсть(ся)**
заéзд, а *m.* **1.** visit; call (*en route*). **2.** (*sport*) lap, round, heat.
заéз|дить, жу, дишь *pf.* to override (*a horse*); (*fig.*) to wear out; to work too hard.
заезжá|ть, ю *impf. of* **заéхать**
заéзженный *adj.* (*coll.*) **1.** hackneyed, trite. **2.** worn out.
заéзж|ий *adj.* visiting; **~ая трýппа** touring company; **он здесь з. человéк** he is just passing through.
заём, зáйма *m.* loan.
заёмщик, а *m.* borrower.
заé|сть[1], **м, шь, ст, дúм, дúте, дя́т,** *past* **~л** *pf.* (*of* **~дáть**) **1.** to bite to death; (*fig.*) to torment, oppress; **егó ~ла тоскá** he fell a prey to melancholy. **2.** (*impers.*; *tech.*) to jam; (*naut.*) to foul; **канáт ~ло** the cable has fouled.
заé|сть[2], **м, шь, ст, дúм, дúте, дя́т,** *past* **~л** *pf.* (*of* **~дáть**) (+*a. and i.*) to take (with); **он ~л пилю́лю сáхаром** he took the pill with sugar.
заé|хать, ду, дешь *pf.* (*of* **~зжáть**) **1. (к)** to call in (at); to drop in (on); **(в**+*a.***)** to enter, ride into, drive into; **(за**+*a.***)** to go beyond, past; **(за**+*i.***)** to call for; to fetch, pick up.
зажáр|ить(ся), ю(сь), ишь(ся) *pf. of* **жáрить(ся)**
заж|áть, мý, мёшь *pf.* (*of* **~имáть**) to squeeze; to press; to clutch; **з. в рукé** to grip; **з. рот комý-н.** (*fig.*) to stop s.o.'s mouth; **з. крúтику** to suppress criticism.
заж|гý, жёшь, гýт *see* **~éчь**
зажд|áться, ýсь, ёшься, *past* **~áлся, ~алáсь, ~áлóсь** *pf.* (*coll.*) to be tired of waiting (for).
заж|éчь, гý, жёшь, гýт, *past* **~ёг, ~глá** *pf.* (*of* **~игáть**) to set fire to; to kindle, light; to ignite; **з. спúчку** to strike a match; (*fig., rhet.*) to kindle; to inflame.
заж|éчься, гýсь, жёшься, гýтся, *past* **зажёгся, зажглáсь** *pf.* (*of* **~игáться**) to catch fire; to light up; (*fig.*) to flame up.
заживá|ть(ся), ю(сь) *impf. of* **зажúть(ся)**
зажив|úть, лю́, úшь *pf.* to heal.
заживля́ть, ю *impf. of* **заживúть**
зáживо *adv.* alive; **з. погребённый** buried alive.
зажигáлк|а, и *f.* (cigarette) lighter.
зажигáни|е, я *nt.* ignition; **ключ (от) зажигáния** ignition key.
зажигáтел|ьный (~ен, ~ьна) *adj.* **1.** incendiary; **~ьная бóмба** fire bomb, incendiary (device); **бутылка с ~ьной смéсью** petrol bomb. **2.** stirring, rousing; **~ьная речь** rousing speech.

зажига́|ть(ся), ю(сь) *impf. of* **заже́чь(ся)**
зажи́м, а *m.* **1.** (*tech.*) clamp; clutch; clip. **2.** (*elec.*) terminal. **3.** (*fig.*) suppression; clamping down.
зажима́|ть, ю *impf. of* **зажа́ть**
зажи́точност|ь, и *f.* prosperity; affluence.
зажи́точ|ный (~ен, ~на) *adj.* well-to-do; affluent; prosperous.
зажи́|ть, ву́, вёшь, *past* **за́жил, ~ла́, за́жило** *pf.* (*of* **~ва́ть**) **1.** to heal (*intrans.*); to close up (*of wound*). **2.** to begin to live; **з. по-но́вому** to begin a new life; **з. семе́йной жи́знью** to settle down; **з. трудово́й жи́знью** to begin to earn one's own living.
зажи́|ться, ву́сь, вёшься, *past* **~лся, ~ла́сь** *pf.* (*of* **~ва́ться**) (*coll.*) to live to a great age; to exceed one's allotted span.
зажму́р|ить(ся), ю(сь), ишь(ся) *pf. of* **жму́рить(ся)**
заз|ва́ть, ову́, овёшь, *past* **~ва́л, ~вала́, ~ва́ло** *pf.* (*of* **~ыва́ть**) (*coll.*) to press (to come); to press an invitation on.
зазвон|и́ть, ю́, и́шь *pf.* to begin to ring.
заздра́вный *adj.* to the health (of), in honour (of); **они́ вы́пили з. тост за посла́** they drank the ambassador's health.
зазева́|ться, юсь *pf.* (**на**+*a.*; *coll.*) to stand gaping (at); to gape (at).
зазелене́|ть, ю *pf.* to turn green.
заземле́ни|е, я *nt.* (*elec.*) **1.** earthing. **2.** earth.
заземл|и́ть, ю́, и́шь *pf.* (*elec.*) to earth.
заземл|я́ть, я́ю *impf. of* **~и́ть**
зазим|ова́ть, у́ю *pf.* to winter; to pass the winter.
зазна|ва́ться, ю́сь, ёшься *impf. of* **~́ться**
зазна́вшийся *adj.* (*coll.*) stuck-up, hoity-toity.
зазна́йка = задава́ка
зазна́йств|о, а *nt.* (*coll.*) conceit.
зазна́|ться, юсь *pf.* (*of* **~ва́ться**) (*coll.*) to give o.s. airs, become conceited.
зазно́б|а, ы *f.* (*coll.*) sweetheart.
заз|ову́, овёшь *see* **~ва́ть**
зазо́р, а *m.* gap; (*tech.*) clearance; (*mil.*) windage.
зазо́р|ный (~ен, ~на) *adj.* (*coll.*) shameful, disgraceful.
зазре́ни|е, я *nt.*: **без ~я (со́вести)** (*coll.*) without a twinge of conscience.
зазу́брен|ный (~, ~а) *p.p.p. of* **зазубри́ть**[1] *and adj.* notched, jagged, serrated.
зазу́брива|ть, ю *impf. of* **зазубри́ть**
зазу́брин|а, ы *f.* notch, jag.
зазубр|и́ть[1], **ю́, и́шь** *pf.* (*of* **зубри́ть**[1] *and* **~́ивать**) to notch, serrate.
зазубр|и́ть[2], **ю́, ~́ишь** *pf.* (*of* **зубри́ть**[2] *and* **~́ивать**) (*sl.*) **1.** to learn by rote. **2.** to start cramming.
зазыва́|ть, ю *impf. of* **зазва́ть**
заигра́|ть, ю *pf.* **1.** to begin to play; **з. весёлый моти́в** to strike up a lively tune. **2.** to begin to sparkle. **3.** to wear out (*cards, etc.*); **з. пье́су** to do a play to death.
заи́грыва|ть[1], **ю** *impf. of* **заигра́ть**
заи́грыва|ть[2], **ю** *impf.* (**с**+*i.*; *coll.*) to flirt (with); to make advances (to) (*also fig.*).
за́ик|а, и *c.g.* stammerer, stutterer.
заика́ни|е, я *nt.* stammer(ing), stutter(ing).
заика́|ться, юсь *impf.* **1.** to stammer, stutter; to falter (*in speech*). **2.** (**о**+*p.*; *coll.*) to hint (at), to mention (in passing); **он никогда́ не ~ется о свое́й про́шлой жи́зни** he never mentions his past life.
заикн|у́ться, у́сь, ёшься *pf. of* **заика́ться 2.**
заи́мствовани|е, я *nt.* borrowing.
заи́мствован|ный (~, ~а) *p.p.p. of* **заи́мствовать; ~ное сло́во** (*ling.*) loan-word.
заи́мств|овать, ую *impf.* (*of* **по~**) to borrow.
заи́ндеве|ть, ет *pf.* (*of* **и́ндеветь**) (*coll.*) to be covered with hoar-frost.
заинтересо́ван|ный (~, ~а) *p.p.p. of* **заинтересова́ть** *and adj.* (**в**+*p.*) interested (in); **он ~ в возмо́жности торго́вых сноше́ний с Да́льним Восто́ком** he is interested in the possibility of trade relations with the Far East; **~ная сторона́** interested party.
заинтерес|ова́ть, у́ю *pf.* to interest; to excite the curiosity (of).
заинтерес|ова́ться, у́юсь *pf.* (+*i.*) to become interested; to take an interest (in).
заинтриг|ова́ть, у́ю *pf. of* **интригова́ть 2.**
заи́скива|ть, ю *impf.* (**у** *or* **пе́ред**) to try to ingratiate o.s. (with); to curry favour (with).
заи́скива|ющий *pres. part. act. of* **~ть** *and adj.* ingratiating.
зай|ду́, дёшь *see* **~ти́**
займ|у́, ёшь *see* **заня́ть**
за|йти́, йду́, йдёшь, *past* **~шёл, ~шла́** *pf.* (*of* **~ходи́ть**[1]) **1.** (**к, в**+*a.*) to call (on); to look in (at); **по пути́ домо́й я ~шёл к Ивано́вым** I dropped in at the Ivanovs on the way home. **2.** (**за**+*i.*) to call for, fetch. **3.** (**в**+*a.*) to get (*to a place*); to find o.s. (*in a place*); **мы ~шли́ в во́ду по го́рло** we got up to our necks in water; **разгово́р ~шёл о выступле́нии президе́нта по ра́дио** the conversation turned to the President's broadcast. **4.** (**за**+*a.*) to go behind; to turn; to go on, continue (after); to set (*of sun, etc.*); **з. за́ угол** to turn a corner; **з. сли́шком далеко́** (*fig.*) to go too far.
за́йчик, а *m.* (*coll.*) **1.** *affectionate dim. of* **за́яц. 2.** reflection of a sunray.
зайчи́х|а, *f.* doe-hare.
зайч|о́нок, о́нка, *pl.* **~а́та, ~а́т** *m.* leveret.
закабал|и́ть, ю́, и́шь *pf.* to enslave.
закавка́зский *adj.* Transcaucasian.
Закавка́зь|е, я *nt.* Transcaucasia.
закавы́чк|а, и *f.* (*coll.*) **1.** obstacle, hitch. **2.** innuendo.
зака́дровый *adj.*: **з. го́лос** (*TV, cinema*) voice-over.
закады́чный *adj.*: **з. друг** (*coll.*) bosom friend.
зака́з, а *m.* order; **ваш з. ещё не гото́в** your order is not ready yet; **на з.** to order; **мне де́лают костю́м на з.** I am having a suit made to measure.
зака|за́ть, жу́, ~́жешь *pf.* (*of* **~́зывать**) to order; to reserve.
зака́зник, а *m.* (*game*) reserve.
заказн|о́й *adj.* **1.** made to order; made to measure. **2.**: **~о́е письмо́** registered letter; **посла́ть письмо́ ~ы́м** to send a letter registered.
зака́зчик, а *m.* customer, client.
зака́зыва|ть, ю *impf. of* **заказа́ть**
зака́ива|ться, юсь *impf. of* **зака́яться**
зака́л, а *m.* **1.** (*tech.*) temper; (*fig.*) stamp, cast; **он челове́к ста́рого ~а** he is a man of the old school. **2.** (*fig.*) strength of character; guts, backbone.
закалён|ный (~, ~а́) *p.p.p. of* **закали́ть** *and adj.* hardened, hard; **з. в боя́х** battle-hardened.
зака́лива|ть, ю *impf. of* **закали́ть**
закал|и́ть, ю́, и́шь *pf.* (*of* **~́ивать** *and* **~я́ть**) (*tech.*) to temper; to case-harden; (*fig.*) to temper, harden; to make hard, hardy.
зака́лк|а, и *f.* tempering; hardening; (*sport*) conditioning.
зака́лыва|ть, ю *impf. of* **заколо́ть**
закаля́|ть, ю *impf. of* **закали́ть**
зака́нчива|ть, ю *impf. of* **зако́нчить**
зака́п|ать, аю *pf.* **1.** to begin to drip; **дождь ~ал** it began to spot with rain. **2.** (*impf.* **~ывать**) to spot, stain; **вот ты ~ала себе́ пла́тье черни́лами** look, you have spotted your dress with ink.
зака́пыва|ть(ся), ю(сь) *impf. of* **закопа́ть(ся)** *and* **зака́пать 2.**

зака́рмлива|ть, ю *impf. of* **закорми́ть**
закаспи́йский *adj.* Trans-Caspian.
зака́т, а *m.* setting; **з. (со́лнца)** sunset; **он пришёл на ~е** he came at sunset; (*fig.*) decline; **на ~е дней** in one's declining years.
заката́|ть, ю *pf.* (*of* **зака́тывать**) **1.** to begin to roll. **2.** (**в**+*a.*) to roll up (in). **3.** to roll out.
зака|ти́ть, чу́, ∸тишь *pf.* (*of* **∸тывать**) (*coll.*) to roll; **она́ ~ти́ла ему́ пощёчину** she slapped his face; **з. исте́рику** to go into hysterics; **з. сце́ну** to make a scene.
зака|ти́ться, чу́сь, ∸тишься *pf.* (*of* **∸тываться**) **1.** to roll (*intrans.*). **2.** to set (*of heavenly bodies*); (*fig.*) to wane; to vanish, disappear; **его́ сла́ва давно́ ~ти́лась** his fame had long since waned; **моя́ звезда́ ~ти́лась** my luck is out. **3.: з. сме́хом** to go off into peals of laughter.
зака́тный *adj.* sunset.
зака́тыва|ть, ю *impf. of* **заката́ть** *and* **закати́ть**
зака́тыва|ться, юсь *impf. of* **закати́ться**
закача́|ть, ю *pf.* **1.** to begin to shake, begin to swing; **он ~л голово́й** he began shaking his head. **2.** to rock (to sleep). **3.** (*impers.*) to make feel sick by rocking; **я собира́юсь в каю́ту: меня́ ~ло** I am going to my cabin; I feel sick.
зака́шля|ться, юсь *pf.* to have a fit of coughing.
зака́|яться, юсь, ешься *pf.* (*of* **~иваться**) (+*inf.*; *coll.*) to forswear; to swear to give up; **он ~ялся кури́ть** he has sworn that he will give up smoking.
заква́|сить, шу, сишь *pf.* (*of* **~шивать**) to ferment; to leaven.
заква́ск|а, и *f.* ferment; leaven; starter; (*fig., coll.*) **у него́ хоро́шая з.** he's made of good stuff.
заква́шива|ть, ю *impf. of* **заква́сить**
закида́|ть, ю *pf.* (*coll.*) **1.** (+*a. and i.*) to bespatter (with); to shower (with); **з. камня́ми** to stone; **кандида́тов ~ли вопро́сами** the candidates were plied with questions; **з. гря́зью** (*fig.*) to sling mud (at). **2.** to fill up (with); to cover (with).
заки́дыва|ть, ю *impf. of* **закида́ть** *and* **заки́нуть**
заки́дыва|ться, юсь *impf. of* **заки́нуться**
заки́н|уть, у, ешь *pf.* to throw (out, away); to cast, toss; **з. но́гу на́ ногу** to cross one's legs; **з. винто́вку за́ спину** to sling a rifle on one's back; **з. у́дочку** (*fig., coll.*) to put out a feeler; **~ьте слове́чко за меня́** put in a word for me.
закипа́|ть, ю *impf. of* **закипе́ть**
закип|еть, лю́, и́шь *pf.* to begin to boil; to be on the boil; (*fig.*) to be in full swing.
закиса́|ть, ю *impf. of* **заки́снуть**
заки́с|нуть, ну, нешь, *past* **~, ~ла** *pf.* **1.** to turn sour. **2.** (*fig., coll.*) to become apathetic.
за́кис|ь, и *f.* (*chem.*) protoxide; **з. желе́за** ferrous oxide.
закла́д, а *m.* (*obs.*) **1.** pawning; mortgaging; **мои́ часы́ в ~е** my watch is in pawn. **2.** bet, wager; **би́ться об з.** to bet, wager.
закла́дк|а[1]**, и** *f.* laying (*of bricks, etc.*).
закла́дк|а[2]**, и** *f.* bookmark.
закладн|а́я, о́й *f.* (*leg., obs.*) mortgage(-deed).
заклад|но́й *adj. of* **∸**; **~на́я квита́нция** pawn-ticket.
закла́дыва|ть, ю *impf. of* **заложи́ть**
закла́ни|е, я *nt.* sacrifice; **идти́ (как) на з.** to go to the slaughter.
закл|ева́ть, юю́, юёшь *pf.* **1.** to begin to peck; to begin to bite (*of fish*). **2.** to peck to death; (*fig., coll.*) to go for.
заклёвыва|ть, ю *impf. of* **заклева́ть**
закле́ива|ть(ся), ю(сь) *impf. of* **закле́ить(ся)**
закле́|ить, ю, ишь *pf.* to glue up; to stick up; **з. конве́рт** to seal an envelope.
закле́|иться, ится *pf.* to stick (*intrans.*).
заклейм|и́ть, лю́, и́шь *pf. of* **клейми́ть**
заклепа́|ть, ю *pf.* (*of* **заклёпывать**) (*tech.*) to rivet.
заклёпк|а, и *f.* (*tech.*) rivet.
заклёпыва|ть, ю *impf. of* **заклепа́ть**
заклина́ни|е, я *nt.* **1.** incantation; spell. **2.** exorcism.
заклина́тел|ь, я *m.* exorcist; **з. змей** snake-charmer.
заклина́|ть, ю *impf.* (*of* **закля́сть**) **1.** to conjure; to invoke. **2.** to exorcize. **3.** to enchant. **4.** to entreat.
закли́нива|ть, ю *impf. of* **заклини́ть**
заклин|и́ть, ю́, и́шь *pf.* **1.** to wedge, fasten with a wedge. **2.** to jam.
заключа́|ть, ю *impf. of* **заключи́ть**
заключ|а́ться, а́юсь *impf.* (*of* **~и́ться**) **1.** *pass. of* **~а́ть. 2.** (*impf. only*) (**в**+*p.*) to consist (of); to lie (in); **затрудне́ние ~а́ется в недоста́тке де́нежных средств** the difficulty lies in the lack of funds.
заключе́ни|е, я *nt.* **1.** conclusion, end; **в з.** in conclusion. **2.** conclusion, inference. **3.: з. догово́ра** conclusion of a treaty. **4.** confinement, detention; **тюре́мное з.** imprisonment.
заключён|ный (~, ~а́, ~о) *p.p.p. of* **заключи́ть;** *as n.* **з., ~ного** *m., and* **~ная, ~ной** *f.* (*leg.*) prisoner.
заключи́тельн|ый *adj.* final, concluding; **з. акко́рд** (*mus.*) finale; **~ое сло́во** concluding remarks.
заключ|и́ть, у́, и́шь *pf.* (*of* **~а́ть**) **1.** (+*i.*) to conclude, end (with). **2.** to conclude, infer. **3.** to conclude, enter into; **з. брак** to contract marriage; **з. догово́р** to conclude a treaty; **з. сде́лку** to strike a bargain. **4.: з. в себе́** to contain, enclose; to comprise; **з. в ско́бки** to enclose in brackets. **5.** to confine; **з. в тюрьму́** to imprison.
заключ|и́ться, у́сь, и́шься *pf. of* **~а́ться**
закля́|сть, ну́, нёшь, *past* **~л, ~ла́, ~ло** *pf. of* **заклина́ть**
закля́ти|е, я *nt.* (*obs.*) **1.** incantation. **2.** oath, pledge.
закля́тый *adj.* (*coll.*) passionate; inveterate; **з. враг** sworn enemy.
зак|ова́ть, ую́, уёшь *pf.* to chain; **з. в кандалы́** to shackle, put in irons.
зако́выва|ть, ю *impf. of* **закова́ть**
закові́рист|ый (~, ~а) *adj.* (*coll.*) subtle, complicated; odd.
закола́чива|ть, ю *impf. of* **заколоти́ть**
заколдо́ван|ный (~, ~а) *p.p.p. of* **заколдова́ть** *and adj.* bewitched, enchanted; spellbound; (*fig.*) **з. круг** vicious circle.
заколд|ова́ть, у́ю *pf.* to bewitch, enchant; to cast a spell (on).
заколдо́выва|ть, ю *impf. of* **заколдова́ть**
зако́лк|а, и *f.* hairpin.
заколо|ти́ть, чу́, ∸тишь *pf.* (*of* **закола́чивать**) (*coll.*) **1.** to board up; to nail up. **2.** to knock in, drive in. **3.** to beat the life out of; to knock senseless. **4.** to begin to knock; **в дверь ~ти́ли** there was a knocking on the door.
заколо|ти́ться, чу́сь, ∸тишься *pf.* (*coll.*) **1.** *pass. of* **~ти́ть. 2.** to begin to beat; **се́рдце у неё ~ти́лось** her heart began to thump.
закол|о́ть, ю́, ∸ешь *pf.* (*of* **зака́лывать** *and* **коло́ть**[2]) **1.** to stab (to death), spear; to slaughter, stick. **2.** to pin (up). **3.** (*impers.*): **у меня́,** *etc.*, **~о́ло в боку́** I, *etc.*, have a stitch in my side.
закольц|ева́ть, у́ю, у́ешь *pf. of* **кольцева́ть**
зако́н, а *m.* law; **свод ~ов** code, statute book; **объяви́ть вне ~а** to outlaw; **з. по́длости** Sod's Law.
зако́нник, а *m.* (*coll.*) **1.** one versed in law; lawyer. **2.** one who keeps to letter of the law.
законнорождённый *adj.* legitimate (*child*).
зако́нност|ь, и *f.* lawfulness, legality.
зако́н|ный (~ен, ~на, ~но) *adj.* lawful, legal; legitimate, rightful; **з. брак** lawful wedlock; **з. владе́лец** rightful owner.
законове́д, а *m.* jurist.
законове́дени|е, я *nt.* jurisprudence, law.

законода́тел|ь, я *m.* legislator; lawgiver; **з. мо́ды** trendsetter.
законода́тельный *adj.* legislative.
законода́тельств|о, а *nt.* legislation.
закономе́рност|ь, и *f.* regularity; conformity with a law; normality.
закономе́р|ный (~ен, ~на) *adj.* **1.** regular, natural. **2.** *as pred.* **~но** it is in order.
законопа́|тить, чу, тишь *pf.* to caulk.
законоположе́ни|е, я *nt.* (*leg.*) statute.
законопослу́шный *adj.* (*obs.*) law-abiding.
законопрое́кт, а *m.* (*pol., leg.*) bill.
законсерви́р|овать, ую *pf. of* **консерви́ровать**
законспири́р|овать, ую *pf.* (*of* **конспири́ровать**) to keep secret, keep dark.
закронтракт|ова́ть, у́ю *pf.* (*of* **контрактова́ть**) to contract (for), enter into a contract (for).
законтракт|ова́ться, у́юсь *pf.* (*of* **контрактова́ться**) to contract to work (for); to hire o.s. out (to).
зако́нченност|ь, и *f.* finish; completeness.
зако́нчен|ный (~, ~а) *p.p.p. of* **зако́нчить** *and adj.* finished; complete; (*coll.*) consummate; accomplished; **он явля́ется ~ным проза́иком** he is an accomplished prose-writer; **з. лгун** consummate liar.
зако́нч|ить, у, ишь *pf.* (*of* **зака́нчивать**) to end, finish.
зако́нч|иться, усь, ишься *pf.* (*of* **зака́нчиваться**) to end, finish (*intrans.*).
закопа́|ть, ю *pf.* (*of* **зака́пывать**) **1.** to begin to dig. **2.** to bury.
закопа́|ться, юсь *pf.* (*of* **зака́пываться**) (*coll.*) **1.** to begin to rummage. **2.** to bury o.s. **3.** (*mil.*) to dig in.
закопте́лый *adj.* (*coll.*) sooty; smutty.
закопт|е́ть, и́т *pf.* (*of* **копте́ть**[1]) to become covered with soot.
закоп|ти́ть, чу́, ти́шь *pf.* (*of* **копти́ть**) **1.** to smoke. **2.** to blacken with smoke.
закоп|ти́ться, чу́сь, ти́шься *pf.* **1.** to be smoked. **2.** to become covered with soot.
закорене́лый *adj.* deep-rooted; ingrained; inveterate.
закорене́|ть, ю, ешь *pf.* **1.** (*fig.*) to take root. **2.** (**в**+*p.*) to become steeped (in); **он ~л в греха́х** he became an inveterate sinner.
зако́р|ки, ок *no sg.* (*coll.*) back, shoulders; **он перенёс де́вочку че́рез ре́ку́ на ~ках** he carried the little girl across the river on his shoulders.
закорм|и́ть, лю́, ~ишь *pf.* (*of* **зака́рмливать**) to overfeed; to stuff.
закорю́чк|а, и *f.* (*coll.*) **1.** hook; flourish (*in handwriting*). **2.** (*fig., dial.*) hitch, snag.
закосне́лый *adj.* incorrigible, inveterate.
закосне́|ть, ю *pf. of* **косне́ть**
закостене́лый *adj.* ossified; stiff.
закостене́|ть, ю *pf.* to ossify; (*fig.*): **он ~л от хо́лода** he became stiff with cold.
закоу́л|ок, ка *m.* **1.** back street, (dark) alley. **2.** (*coll.*) secluded corner; **обыска́ть все углы́ и ~ки** to search in every nook and cranny; **знать все ~ки** (*fig.*) to know all the ins and outs.
закоченелый *adj.* numb with cold.
закочене́|ть, ю, ешь *pf. of* **кочене́ть**
закра́дыва|ться, юсь *impf. of* **закра́сться**
закра́ива|ть, ю *impf. of* **закрои́ть**
закра́па|ть, ю *pf.* **1.** to begin to fall (*of raindrops*). **2.** to spot.
закра́пыва|ть, ю *impf. of* **закра́пать 2.**
закра́|сить, шу, сишь *pf.* (*of* **~шивать**) to paint over, paint out.
закра́|сться, ду́сь, дёшься, *past* **~лся** *pf.* (*of* **~дываться**) to steel in, creep in; (*fig.*): **у меня́ ~лось подозре́ние** a suspicion crept into my mind.
закра́шива|ть, ю *impf. of* **закра́сить**
закрепи́тел|ь, я *m.* (*chem., phot.*) fixing agent, fixer.
закреп|и́ть, лю́, и́шь *pf.* **1.** to fasten, secure; (*naut.*) to make fast; (*phot.*) to fix. **2.** (*fig.*) to consolidate. **3.** (+*a.* **за**+*i.*) to allot, assign (to); to appoint, attach (to); **з. за собо́й** to secure; **за на́ми ~и́ли одну́ из но́вых кварти́р** we have been assigned one of the new flats; **он ~и́л за собо́й места́ на за́втрашнее представле́ние** he has secured seats for tomorrow's performance.
закреп|и́ться, лю́сь, и́шься *pf.* **1.** *pass. of* **~и́ть. 2.** (**на**+*a.*) to consolidate one's hold (on).
закрепля́|ть(ся), ю(сь) *impf. of* **закрепи́ть(ся)**
закрепо|сти́ть, щу́, сти́шь *pf.* to enserf; to enslave.
закрепоща́|ть, ю *impf. of* **закрепости́ть**
закрепоще́ни|е, я *nt.* enslavement.
закристаллиз|ова́ться, у́юсь *pf. of* **кристаллизова́ться**
закрич|а́ть, у́, и́шь *pf.* **1.** to cry out. **2.** to begin to shout; to give a shout.
закро|и́ть, ю́, и́шь *pf.* (*of* **закра́ивать**) to cut out.
закро́|й, я *m.* cut; style (*of dress*).
закро́йны|й *adj.* for cutting clothes; **~е но́жницы** cutting-out scissors.
закро́йщик, а *m.* cutter.
за́кром, а, *pl.* **~а́** *m.* corn-bin; (*fig., rhet.*) granary.
закругле́ни|е, я *nt.* **1.** rounding, curving. **2.** curve; curvature.
закруглён|ный (~, ~а́) *p.p.p. of* **закругли́ть** *and adj.* rounded; (*liter.*) well-rounded.
закругл|и́ть, ю́, и́шь *pf.* to make round; **з. фра́зу** to round off a sentence.
закругл|и́ться, ю́сь, и́шься *pf.* to become round.
закруж|и́ть, у́, ~и́шь *pf.* **1.** to begin to whirl (*trans. and intrans.*); **з. кому́-н. го́лову** (*fig., coll.*) to turn s.o.'s head. **2.** to make giddy, make dizzy; **она́ его́ совсе́м ~и́ла** (*fig., coll.*) she has swept him off his feet.
закруж|и́ться, у́сь, ~и́шься *pf.* **1.** to begin to whirl, begin to go round; **у меня́ голова́ ~и́лась** my head began to swim. **2.** *pf. of* **кружи́ться**
закру|ти́ть, чу́, ~тишь *pf.* **1.** to twist; to twirl; to wind round; **они́ ~ти́ли ему́ ру́ки за́ спину** they twisted his arms behind his back. **2.** to turn; to screw in. **3.** (*fig., coll.*) to turn s.o.'s head.
закру|ти́ться, чу́сь, ~тишься *pf.* **1.** to twist; to twirl; to wind round (*intrans.*). **2.** to begin to whirl.
закру́чива|ть(ся), ю(сь) *impf. of* **закрути́ть(ся)**
закрыва́|ть(ся), ю(сь) *impf. of* **закры́ть(ся)**
закры́ти|е, я *nt.* **1.** closing; shutting. **2.** (*mil.*) cover.
закры́т|ый (~, ~а) *p.p.p. of* **~ь** *and adj.* closed, shut; private; **с ~ыми глаза́ми** (*fig.*) blindly; **~ое голосова́ние** secret ballot; **при ~ых дверя́х** behind closed doors; **~ое заседа́ние** private meeting; **~ое мо́ре** inland sea; **~ое пла́тье** high-necked dress; **в ~ом помеще́нии** indoors.
закр|ы́ть, о́ю, о́ешь *pf.* (*of* **~ыва́ть**) **1.** to close, shut; **з. глаза́** to pass away; **я ему́ ~ы́л глаза́** I attended him on his deathbed; **з. глаза́ (на**+*a.*) to shut one's eyes (to); **з. ско́бки** to close brackets; **з. счёт** to close an account. **2.** to shut off, turn off. **3.** to close down, shut down. **4.** to cover.
закр|ы́ться, о́юсь, о́ешься *pf.* (*of* **~ыва́ться**) **1.** to close, shut; to end; to close down; (*intrans.*). **2.** to cover o.s.; to take cover; **они́ ~лись от дождя́** they took cover from the rain. **3.** *pass. of* **~ы́ть**
закули́сный *adj.* (occurring) behind the scenes; (*fig.*) secret; underhand, undercover.
закупа́|ть, ю *impf. of* **закупи́ть**
закуп|и́ть, лю́, ~ишь *pf.* (*of* **~а́ть**) **1.** to buy up (wholesale). **2.** to lay in; to stock up with.
заку́пк|а, и *f.* purchase.
заку́порива|ть, ю *impf. of* **заку́порить**

заку́пор|ить, ю, ишь *pf.* **1.** to cork; to stop up. **2.** (*fig., coll.*) to shut up; coop up.
заку́порк|а, и *f.* **1.** corking. **2.** (*med.*) embolism, thrombosis.
заку́п|очный *adj. of* **~ка; ~очная цена́** purchase price.
заку́пщик, а *m.* purchaser; buyer.
заку́рива|ть(ся), ю(сь) *impf. of* **закури́ть(ся)**
закур|и́ть, ю́, ~́ишь *pf.* **1.** to light up (*cigarette, pipe, etc.*). **2.** to begin to smoke; to take up smoking; **ещё не ко́нчив шко́лу он ~и́л** he began to smoke before he had left school.
заку|си́ть[1]**, шу́, ~́сишь** *pf.* (*of* **~́сывать**) to bite; (*fig.*): **з. удила́** to take the bit between the teeth; **з. язы́к** to hold one's tongue.
заку|си́ть[2]**, шу́, ~́сишь** *pf.* (*of* **~́сывать**) **1.** to have a snack, have a bite; **з. на́скоро** to snatch a quick bite. **2.** (*+a. and i.*) to take (with); **з. во́дку ры́бкой** to drink vodka with fish hors-d'œuvres.
заку́ск|а, и *f.* (*usu. pl.*) hors-d'œuvre; snack; **на ~у** for a titbit; (*fig., coll.*) as a special treat.
заку́с|очный *adj. of* **~ка**; *as n.* **~очная, ~очной** *f.* snack bar.
заку́сыва|ть, ю *impf. of* **закуси́ть**
заку́та|ть, ю *pf.* (*of* **заку́тывать**) to wrap up, muffle; **з. в одея́ло** to tuck up (in bed).
заку́та|ться, юсь *pf.* (*of* **заку́тываться**) to wrap o.s. up, muffle o.s.
заку́тыва|ть(ся), ю(сь) *impf. of* **заку́тать(ся)**
зал, а *m.* hall; **з. ожида́ния** waiting room; **демонстрацио́нный з.** showroom.
зала́|дить, жу, дишь *pf.* (*coll.*) **1.** (*+inf.*) to take to; **он ~дил заходи́ть к нам по вечера́м** he has taken to calling in on us in the evening. **2.: з. одно́ и то́ же** to harp on the same string.
зала́мыва|ть, ю *impf. of* **заломи́ть**
залата́|ть, ю *pf. of* **лата́ть**
залега́|ть, ю *impf. of* **зале́чь**
заледене́лый *adj.* **1.** covered with ice; ice-bound. **2.** ice-cold, icy.
заледене́|ть, ю *pf.* (*of* **леденеть**) (*coll.*) **1.** to be covered with ice; to freeze up, ice up. **2.** to become cold as ice; to become numb.
залежа́лый *adj.* (*coll.*) **1.** stale. **2.** long unused.
залеж|а́ться, у́сь, и́шься *pf.* **1.** to lie too long; to lie idle a long time. **2.** become stale.
залёжива|ться, юсь *impf. of* **залежа́ться**
за́леж|ь, и *f.* **1.** (*geol.*) deposit, bed, seam. **2.** (*agric.*) fallow land. **3.** (*sg. only; collect.; coll.*) stale goods.
залеза́|ть, ю *impf. of* **зале́зть**
зале́з|ть, у, ешь, *past* **~, ~ла** *pf.* **1.** (**на**+*a.*) to climb (up, on to). **2.** (**в**+*a.*; *coll.*) to get (into); to creep (into); **з. кому́-н. в карма́н** to pick s.o.'s pocket; **з. в во́ду по го́рло** to get up to one's neck in water; **з. в долги́** to run into debt.
зален|и́ться, ю́сь, ~́ишься *pf.* (*coll.*) to grow lazy.
залеп|и́ть, лю́, ~́ишь *pf.* (*+a. and i.*) to paste up, paste over; to glue up; **всю сте́ну ~и́ли афи́шами** the whole wall had been plastered with bills; **глаза́ у него́ ~и́ло сне́гом** his eyes were stuck up with snow; **з. кому́-н. пощёчину** (*vulg.*) to slap s.o.'s face.
залепля́|ть, ю *impf. of* **залепи́ть**
залета́|ть, ю *impf. of* **залете́ть**
зале|те́ть, чу́, ти́шь *pf.* **1.** (**в**+*a.*) to fly (into); (**за**+*a.*) to fly (over, beyond); **пти́ца ~те́ла в ко́мнату** a bird flew into the room; **мы ~те́ли за Се́верный по́люс** we flew over the North Pole. **2.** (**в**+*a.*) to make a stopover (at), call in (at); **нам пришло́сь з. в Стокго́льм за горю́чим** we had to make a stopover at Stockholm to refuel. **3.** (*fig., coll.*): **з. высоко́, з. далеко́** to go up in the world.
залётн|ый *adj.* (*coll.*): **~ая пти́ца** bird of passage (*also fig.*); **з. гость** unexpected visitor.
зале́чива|ть, ю *impf. of* **залечи́ть**
залеч|и́ть, у́, ~́ишь *pf.* **1.** to heal; to remedy **2.** (*coll.*): **з. до́ смерти** to doctor to death; to murder (*by unskilful treatment*).
залеч|и́ться, ~́ится *pf.* (*coll.*) to heal (up).
зал|е́чь, я́гу, я́жешь, я́гут, *past* **~ёг, ~егла́** *pf.* (*of* **~ега́ть**) **1.** to lie down; to lie low; to lie in wait. **2.** (*geol.*) to lie, be deposited; **здесь руда́ ~егла́ на глубине́ ста ме́тров** there is a deposit of ore here at a depth of a hundred metres. **3.** (*fig.*) to take root; to become ingrained.
зали́в, а *m.* bay; gulf; creek, cove.
залива́|ть[1]**, ю** *impf.* (*coll.*) to lie, tell lies.
залива́|ть[2]**(ся), ю(сь)** *impf. of* **зали́ть(ся)**
заливн|о́е, о́го *nt.* aspic.
заливн|о́й *adj.* **1.: з. луг** water-meadow. **2.** for pouring; **~а́я труба́** funnel. **3.** jellied; **~а́я ры́ба** fish in aspic.
зали|за́ть, жу́, ~́жешь *pf.* **1.** to lick clean. **2.: з. себе́ во́лосы** to slick down one's hair.
зали́зыва|ть, ю *impf. of* **зализа́ть**
зал|и́ть, ью́, ьёшь, *past* **~́ил, ~ила́, ~́ило** *pf.* (*of* **~ива́ть**) **1.** to flood, inundate; (*fig.*): **ко́мнату ~́ило све́том** the room was flooded with light; **толпа́ ~ила́ у́лицы** the crowd filled the streets. **2.** (*+a. and i.*) to pour (over); to spill (on); **з. но́вую ска́терть черни́лами** to spill ink on the new table-cloth; **з. кра́ской** to give a wash of paint; **з. ту́шью** to ink in. **3.** to quench, extinguish (*with water*); **з. пожа́р** to put out a fire; **з. го́ре (вино́м)** to drown one's sorrows.
зал|и́ться, ью́сь, ьёшься, *past* **~и́лся́, ~ила́сь** *pf.* (*of* **ива́ться**) **1.** to be flooded, inundated. **2.** to pour; to spill (*intrans.*); **вода́ ~ила́сь мне за воротни́к** water has gone down my neck. **3.** to spill on o.s.; **ты весь ~и́лся́ су́пом** you have spilled soup all over yourself. **4.** (*+i.*) to break into, burst into; **соба́ка ~ила́сь ла́ем** the dog began to bark furiously; **з. пе́сней** to break into a song; **з. слеза́ми** to burst into tears, dissolve in tears. **5.** to set (*of jellies*).
залихва́тск|ий *adj.* (*coll.*) devil-may-care; **~ая пе́сня** rollicking song.
зало́г[1]**, а** *m.* **1.** deposit; pledge; security; (*leg.*) bail; **под з.** (*+g.*) on the security of; **отда́ть в з.** to pawn; to mortgage; **вы́купить из ~а** to redeem; to pay off mortgage (on); **усе́рдие — з. успе́ха** hard work is the key to success. **2.** (*fig.*) pledge, token.
зало́г[2]**, а** *m.* (*gram.*) voice.
зало́г|овый *adj. of* **~; ~овое свиде́тельство** mortgage-deed.
залогода́тел|ь, я *m.* depositor; mortgagor.
залогодержа́тел|ь, я *m.* pawnbroker.
залож|и́ть, у́, ~́ишь *pf.* (*of* **закла́дывать**) **1.** to put (behind); **он ~и́л ру́ки за́ спину** he put his hands behind his back. **2.** to lay (the foundation of). **3.** (*coll.*) to mislay. **4.** (*+i.*) to pile up, heap up (with); to block up (with); (*impers., +d.*): **мне нос ~́ило** my nose is blocked, is stuffed up. **5.** to mark, put a marker in; **я ~и́л страни́цу девяно́сто** I have put a marker in at page ninety. **6.** to pawn; to mortgage. **7.** to harness. **8.** to lay in, store, put by.
зало́жник, а *m.* hostage.
залом|и́ть, лю́, ~́ишь *pf.* (*of* **зала́мывать**) **1.** to break off. **2.** (*coll.*): **з. це́ну** to ask an exorbitant price; **з. ша́пку** to cock one's hat.
залп, а *m.* volley; salvo; **вы́стрелить ~́ом** to fire a volley, salvo; **~́ом** (*fig., coll.*) without pausing for breath; **вы́пить ~́ом** to drink in one (gulp).
залуча́|ть, ю *impf. of* **залучи́ть**
залуч|и́ть, у́, и́шь *pf.* (*coll.*) to entice, lure.
залюб|ова́ться, у́юсь *pf.* (*+i.*) to be lost in contemplation (of).

заля́па|ть, ю *pf.* (*coll.*) to make dirty.
зам, а *m.*(*coll.*) *abbr. of* **~ести́тель**
зам. (*abbr. of* **замести́тель**) deputy.
зам... *comb. form, abbr. of* **замести́тель**
зама́|зать, жу, жешь *pf.* (*of* **ма́зать** *and* **~зывать**) **1.** to paint over; to efface; (*fig.*) to slur over. **2.** to putty. **3.** to daub, smear, to soil.
зама́зк|а, и *f.* putty.
зама́лчива|ть, ю *impf. of* **замолча́ть**
зама́нива|ть, ю *impf. of* **замани́ть**
заман|и́ть, ю́, ~ишь *pf.* to entice, lure; to decoy.
зама́нчив|ый (~, ~а) *adj.* tempting, alluring.
замара́|ть, ю *pf.* (*of* **мара́ть 1.**) **1.** to soil, dirty; (*fig.*) to disgrace; **з. свою́ репута́цию** to sully one's reputation. **2.** to blot out, efface.
замара́|ться, юсь *pf. of* **мара́ться 1.**
замара́шк|а, и *c.g.* (*coll.*) slut, sloven; grubby child.
зама́рива|ть, ю *impf. of* **замори́ть**
замарин|ова́ть, у́ю *pf. of* **мариnова́ть**
замаскир|ова́ть, у́ю *pf.* to mask; to disguise; to camouflage; **з. свои́ чу́вства** (*fig.*) to conceal one's feelings.
замаскир|ова́ться, у́юсь *pf.* to disguise o.s.
замаскиро́выва|ть(ся), ю(сь) *impf. of* **замаскирова́ть(ся)**
зама́слива|ть(ся), ю(сь) *impf. of* **зама́слить(ся)**
зама́сл|ить, ю, ишь *pf.* **1.** to oil, grease. **2.** to make oily, make greasy. **3.** (*fig., sl.*) to butter up.
зама́сл|иться, юсь, ишься *pf.* to become oily, become greasy.
зама́тыва|ть(ся), ю(сь) *impf. of* **замота́ть(ся)**
зама|ха́ть, шу́, ~шешь *pf.* to begin to wave.
зама́хива|ться, юсь *impf. of* **замахну́ться**
замахн|у́ться, у́сь, ёшься *pf.* (+*i.*) to raise threateningly; **он да́же ~у́лся руко́й на беззащи́тную стару́ху** he even raised his hand against a defenceless old woman.
зама́чива|ть, ю *impf. of* **замочи́ть**
зама́шк|а, и *f.* (*coll., pej.*) way, manner.
зама́щива|ть, ю *impf. of* **замости́ть**
замая́ч|ить, у, ишь *pf.* to loom; **вдали́ ~или огни́ га́вани** the lights of the harbour loomed up in the distance.
замедле́ни|е, я *nt.* **1.** slowing down, deceleration. **2.** delay; **без ~я** without delay, at once.
заме́дленн|ый *p.p.p. of* **заме́длить** *and adj.* slow; delayed; **бо́мба ~ого де́йствия** delayed-action bomb; **~ое воспроизведе́ние** slow-motion replay.
заме́дл|ить, ю, ишь *pf.* **1.** to slow down; **з. шаг** to slacken one's pace; **з. ход** to reduce speed. **2.** (+*inf. or* +*i. or* **с**+*i.*) to delay (in); to be long (in); **отве́т не ~ил прийти́** the answer was not long in coming; **з. (с) отве́том** to delay in answering.
заме́дл|иться, ится *pf.* **1.** to slow down; to slacken, become slower. **2.** *pass. of* **~ить**
замедля́|ть(ся), ет(ся) *impf. of* **заме́длить(ся)**
заме́н|а, ы *f.* **1.** substitution; replacement; **з. сме́ртной ка́зни тюре́мным заключе́нием** commutation of death sentence to imprisonment. **2.** substitute.
замени́|мый *pres. part. pass. of* **~ть** *and adj.* replaceable.
замени́тел|ь, я *m.* (+*g.*) substitute; **з. ко́жи** leather substitute; **з. са́хара** sweetener.
замен|и́ть, ю́, ~ишь *pf.* **1.** (+*a. and i.*) to replace (by), substitute (for); **мы ~и́ли кероси́н электри́чеством** we have replaced oil with electricity; **з. ма́сло маргари́ном** to use margarine instead of butter. **2.** to take the place of; **она́ ~и́ла ребёнку мать** she was (like) a mother to the child; **тру́дно бу́дет з. его́** it will be hard to replace him.
замен|я́ть, я́ю *impf. of* **~и́ть**
зам|ере́ть, ру́, рёшь, *past* **~ер, ~ерла́, ~ерло** *pf.* (*of* **~ира́ть**) **1.** to stand still; to freeze, be rooted to the spot; to die (*fig.*); **се́рдце моё ~ерло, когда́ дверь откры́лась** my heart stopped beating when the door opened. **2.** to die down, die away; **к полу́ночи стрельба́ ~ерла́** towards midnight firing died down.
замерза́ни|е, я *nt.* freezing; **то́чка ~я** freezing point.
замерза́|ть, ю *impf. of* **замёрзнуть**
замёрз|нуть, ну, нешь, *past* **~, ~ла** *pf.* (*of* **~а́ть**) to freeze (up); to freeze to death; to be killed by frost.
за́мертво *adv.* like one dead; **она́ упа́ла з.** she collapsed in a dead faint.
заме|си́ть, шу́, ~сишь *pf.* (*of* **~шивать**) to mix; **з. те́сто** to knead dough.
заме|сти́, ту́, тёшь, *past* **~л, ~ла́** *pf.* (*of* **~та́ть**) **1.** to sweep up. **2.** to cover (up); (*impers.*): **доро́гу ~ло́ сне́гом** the road is covered with snow; (*fig.*): **з. следы́** to cover up one's tracks.
замести́тел|ь, я *m.* substitute; deputy; **з. дире́ктора** deputy director; **з. председа́теля** vice-chairman; **быть ~ем** (+*g.*) to stand proxy (for), substitute (for).
заме|сти́ть, щу́, сти́шь *pf.* (*of* **~ща́ть**) **1.** (+*a. and i.*) to replace (by); to substitute (for). **2.** (+*a. and i.*) to appoint (to); **они́ ~сти́ли ка́федру психоло́гии не́мцем** they have appointed a German to the chair of psychology. **3.** to deputize for, act for; to serve in place of.
замета́|ть[1], ю *impf. of* **замести́**
замета́|ть[2], ю *pf.* (*of* **замётывать**) to tack, baste.
заме|та́ться, чу́сь, ~чешься *pf.* to begin to rush about; to begin to toss.
заме́|тить, чу, тишь *pf.* (*of* **~ча́ть**) **1.** to notice; **~тили ли вы, что он ча́сто повторя́ется?** have you noticed that he often repeats himself? **2.** to take notice (of); to make a note (of). **3.** to remark, observe; **«соверше́нно ве́рно» — ~тил он** 'perfectly true', he remarked.
заме́тк|а, и *f.* **1.** mark. **2.** note; **~и на поля́х** marginal notes; **взять на ~у** (*coll.*) to make a note (of). **3.** notice; paragraph; **ни одна́ газе́та не удосто́ила вы́ставки ~ой** not a single newspaper gave the exhibition a notice.
заме́т|ный (~ен, ~на) *adj.* noticeable; appreciable; marked; **ме́жду ни́ми есть ~ная ра́зница в во́зрасте** there is an appreciable difference in age between them; **~но** (*as pred.*) it is noticeable; **~но, как он не лю́бит говори́ть о де́тстве** it is noticeable that he does not like talking about his childhood.
замётыва|ть, ю *impf. of* **замета́ть[2]**
замеча́ни|е, я *nt.* **1.** remark, observation. **2.** reprimand; reproof.
замеча́тел|ьный (~ен, ~ьна) *adj.* remarkable; splendid, wonderful.
замеча́|ть, ю *impf. of* **заме́тить**
заме́чен|ный (~, ~а) *p.p.p. of* **заме́тить; з. (в**+*p.*) discovered, noticed, detected (in); **он был неоднокра́тно ~ во взя́точничестве** he was several times discovered taking bribes.
замечта́|ться, юсь *pf.* to give o.s. up to day-dreaming; **он опя́ть ~лся** he is day-dreaming again.
замеша́тельств|о, а *nt.* confusion; embarrassment; **привести́ в з.** to throw into confusion; **прийти́ в з.** to be confused, be embarrassed.
замеша́|ть, ю *pf.* (**в**+*a.*) to mix up, entangle (in).
замеша́|ться, юсь *pf.* (**в**+*a.*) **1.** to become mixed up, entangled (in). **2.** to mix (with), mingle (in, with); **з. в толпу́** to mingle with the crowd.
заме́шива|ть(ся), ю(сь) *impf. of* **замеси́ть** *and* **замеша́ть(ся)**
заме́шка|ться, юсь *pf.* (*coll.*) to linger, tarry.
замеща́|ть, ю *impf. of* **замести́ть**
замеще́ни|е, я *nt.* **1.** substitution. **2.** appointment;

бу́дет ко́нкурс на з. вака́нтной до́лжности there will be a competition to fill the vacancy.

замза́в, а *m.* (*abbr. of* **замести́тель заве́дующего**) assistant manager.

замина́|ть, ю *impf. of* **замя́ть**

зами́нк|а, и *f.* (*coll.*) **1.** hitch. **2.** hesitation (*in speech*).

замира́ни|е, я *nt.* dying out, dying down; **он ждал с ~ем се́рдца** he waited with a sinking heart.

замира́|ть, ю *impf. of* **замере́ть**

замире́ни|е, я *nt.* peace-making.

за́мкнут|ый (~, ~а) *adj.* **1.** exclusive. **2.** reserved; **адмира́л — о́чень з. челове́к** the admiral is a very reserved person; **вести́ ~ую жизнь** to lead an unsociable life.

замкн|у́ть, у́, ёшь *pf.* (*of* **замыка́ть**) to close; **з. ше́ствие, з. коло́нну** to bring up the rear.

замкн|у́ться, у́сь, ёшься *pf.* (*of* **замыка́ться**) **1.** *pass. of* **~у́ть. 2.** to shut o.s. up; **з. в круг** to form a circle; (*fig.*) **з. в себе́** to withdraw into o.s.

зам|ну́, нёшь *see* **~я́ть**

замоги́льный *adj.* sepulchral (*of voice*).

за́м|ок, ка *m.* castle; **возду́шные ~ки** castles in the air.

зам|о́к, ка́ *m.* **1.** lock; **америка́нский з.** Yale (*propr.*) lock; **вися́чий з.** padlock; **секре́тный з.** combination lock; **под ~ко́м** under lock and key; **за семью́ ~ка́ми** well and truly hidden. **2.** (*archit.*) keystone. **3.** bolt (*of fire-arm*). **4.** clasp (*of necklace, etc.*); clip (*of ear-ring*).

замо́лв|ить, лю, ишь *pf.* (*coll.*): **з. слове́чко за** (+*a.*) to put in a word (for); **прошу́ вас з. слове́чко за меня́ у нача́льства** please put in a word for me with the authorities.

замолка́|ть, ю *impf. of* **замо́лкнуть**

замо́лк|нуть, ну, нешь, *past* **~, ~ла** *pf.* to fall silent; to stop, cease (*speaking, etc.*); **внеза́пно пе́ние ~ло** suddenly the singing ceased.

замолч|а́ть[1], у́, и́шь *pf.* to fall silent; (*fig.*), to cease corresponding.

замолч|а́ть[2], у́, и́шь *pf.* (*of* **зама́лчивать**) (*coll.*) to keep silent about; to hush up.

замора́живани|е, я *nt.* freezing.

замора́жива|ть, ю *impf. of* **заморо́зить**

замор|и́ть, ю́, и́шь *pf.* (*of* **зама́ривать**) (*coll.*) **1.** to overwork. **2.** to underfeed; **з. червячка́** to have a bite, have a snack.

заморо́|женный *p.p.p. of* **~зить** *and adj.* frozen; iced; **~женное мя́со** frozen meat; **~женное шампа́нское** iced champagne.

заморо́|зить, жу, зишь *pf.* (*of* **замора́живать**) to freeze; to ice.

за́морозк|и, ов *no sg.* (light) frosts.

замо́рский *adj.* oversea(s).

замо́рыш, а *m.* (*coll.*) weakling; runt.

замо|сти́ть, щу́, сти́шь *pf.* (*of* **мости́ть** *and* **зама́щивать**) to pave.

замо́тан|ный (~, ~а) *adj.* (*coll.*) fagged- *or* worn-out.

замота́|ть, ю *pf.* (*of* **зама́тывать**) **1.** to wind, twist; to roll up. **2.** (*fig.*) to tire out.

замота́|ться, юсь *pf.* (*of* **зама́тываться**) (*coll.*) **1.** to wind round. **2.** to be tired out, be fagged out.

замоч|и́ть, у́, ~́ишь *pf.* (*of* **зама́чивать**) to wet; to soak.

замо́чн|ый *adj. of* **замо́к; ~ая сква́жина** keyhole.

зампре́д, а *m.* (*abbr. of* **замести́тель председа́теля**) vice-chairman; deputy chairman.

за́муж *adv.*: **вы́йти з. за кого́-н.** to marry s.o. (*of woman*); **вы́дать кого́-н. з.** (**за**+*a.*) to give s.o. in marriage (to); to marry off (to).

за́мужем *adv.*: **быть з.** (**за**+*i.*) to be married (to) (*of woman*).

заму́жеств|о, а *nt.* marriage (*of woman*); **у неё о́чень счастли́вое з.** she is very happily married.

заму́жняя *adj.* married (*of woman*).

замур|ова́ть, у́ю *pf.* to brick up; to immure.

замуро́выва|ть, ю *impf. of* **замурова́ть**

замусо́лива|ть, ю *impf. of* **замусо́лить**

замусо́л|ить, ю, ишь *pf.* to beslobber.

заму|ти́ть, чу́, ~ти́шь *pf. of* **мути́ть; он воды́ не ~ти́т** he won't cause any trouble.

заму́чива|ть, ю *impf. of* **заму́чить**

заму́ч|ить, у, ишь *pf.* (*of* **му́чить** *and* **~ивать**) to torment; to wear out; to plague the life out of.

заму́ч|иться, усь, ишься *pf.* (*of* **му́читься**) to be worn out.

за́мш|а, и *f.* chamois (leather); suede.

замшеви́дный *adj.* suedette.

за́мш|евый *adj. of* **~а**

замше́лый *adj.* mossy, moss-covered.

замше́|ть, ет *pf.* to be overgrown with moss.

замыва́|ть, ю *impf. of* **замы́ть**

замыка́ни|е, я *nt.* locking; **коро́ткое з.** (*elec.*) short circuit.

замыка́|ть(ся), ю(сь) *impf. of* **замкну́ть(ся)**

за́мыс|ел, ла *m.* project, plan; design, scheme; idea; **его́ но́вая пье́са осно́вана на о́чень оригина́льном ~ле** his new play is based on a very original idea; **злы́е ~лы** evil designs.

замы́сл|ить, ю, ишь *pf.* (*of* **замышля́ть**) (+*a. or inf.*) to plan; to contemplate; **он ~ил самоуби́йство** he contemplated suicide; **они́ ~или убежа́ть под покро́вом темноты́** they had planned to escape under cover of darkness.

замыслова́т|ый (~, ~а) *adj.* intricate, complicated.

зам|ы́ть, о́ю, о́ешь *pf.* (*of* **~ыва́ть**) to wash off, wash out.

замышля́|ть, ю *impf. of* **замы́слить**

зам|я́ть, ну́, нёшь *pf.* (*of* **~ина́ть**) (*coll.*) to put a stop to; **з. разгово́р** to change the subject.

зам|я́ться, ну́сь, нёшься *pf.* (*coll.*) to stumble; to stop short (*in speech*).

за́навес, а *m.* curtain; **под з.** (*theatr.*) near the end of an act.

занаве́|сить, шу, сишь *pf.* (*of* **~шивать**) to curtain; to cover.

занаве́с|ка, ки *f.* curtain (*of light material*).

занаве́шива|ть, ю *impf. of* **занаве́сить**

зана́шива|ть, ю *impf. of* **заноси́ть[2]**

занес|ти́, у́, ёшь, *past* **~̈, ~ла́** *pf.* (*of* **заноси́ть[1]**) **1.** to bring, import. **2.** to raise, lift; **з. но́гу в стре́мя** to raise one's foot into the stirrup. **3.** to note down; **з. в протокол** to enter in the minutes. **4.** (*coll.*) to carry (away); **куда́ его́ нелёгкая ~ла́?** where the devil has he got to?; (*impers.*): **каки́м ве́тром вас сюда́ ~ло́?** what wind blows you here? **5.** (*impers.*): **з. сне́гом** to cover with snow; **доро́гу ~ло́ сне́гом** the road is snowed up.

занес|ти́сь, у́сь, ёшься, *past* **~̈ся, ~ла́сь** *pf.* (*of* **заноси́ться[1]**) (*coll., pej.*) to be carried away (*fig.*).

занима́тел|ьный (~ен, ~ьна) *adj.* entertaining, diverting; absorbing.

занима́|ть[1], ю *impf.* (*of* **заня́ть**) **1.** to occupy; **з. го́род** to occupy a city; **з. кварти́ру** to occupy a flat; **крова́ть ~ет мно́го ме́ста** the bed takes up a lot of room; **он ~ет высо́кое положе́ние** (*fig.*) he occupies a high post. **2.** to occupy; to interest; **она́ ника́к не могла́ з. дете́й** she simply could not keep the children occupied; **его́ ~ют бо́льше всего́ вопро́сы филосо́фии** his chief interest is in philosophy. **3.** to take (*of time*); **э́то ~ет мно́го вре́мени** this takes a lot of time.

занима́|ть[2], ю *impf.* (*of* **заня́ть**) to borrow.

занима́|ться[1], юсь *impf.* (*of* **заня́ться**) (+*i.*) **1.** to be occupied (with), be engaged (in); to work (at, on); to study; **чем вы ~лись вчера́?** what were you doing yesterday?; **он ~ется подгото́вкой но́вой экспеди́ции** he is engaged in preparations for a new expedition; **до заму́жества она́ ~лась му́зыкой** before her marriage she was studying music. **2.** to busy o.s. (with); to devote o.s. (to); **з. собо́й** to devote attention to one's appearance. **3.** (**с**+*i.*) to assist; to attend to.

занима́|ться[2] *impf.* (*of* **заня́ться**) to catch fire.

за́ново *adv.* anew.

зано́з|а, ы *f.* splinter.

зано́зист|ый (~, ~а) *adj.* (*coll.*) splintery.

зано|зи́ть, жу́, зи́шь *pf.* to get a splinter in.

зано́с, а *m.* snow-drift.

зано|си́ть[1], **шу́, ∠сишь** *impf. of* **занести́**

зано|си́ть[2], **шу́, ∠сишь** *pf.* (*of* **зана́шивать**) to wear out.

зано|си́ться[1], **шу́сь, ∠сишься** *impf. of* **занести́сь**

зано|си́ться[2], **∠сится** *pf.* to be worn out; to wear out (*intrans.*).

зано́счив|ый (~, ~а) *adj.* arrogant, haughty.

заноч|ева́ть, у́ю *pf.* (*coll.*) to stay for the night.

зану́д|а, ы *c.g.* (*coll.*) tiresome person, pain in the neck.

зану́дливый = зану́дный

зану́д|ный (~ен, ~на) *adj.* (*coll.*) tiresome.

занумер|ова́ть, у́ю *pf.* (*of* **нумерова́ть**) to number.

заня́ти|е, я *nt.* **1.** occupation; pursuit. **2.** (*pl.*) studies; work; **часы́ ~й** working hours.

заня́т|ный (~ен, ~на) *adj.* (*coll.*) entertaining, amusing.

занято́й *adj.* busy.

за́нятост|ь, и *f.* (*econ.*) employment; **по́лная з.** full employment.

за́нят|ый (~, ~а́, ~о) *p.p.p. of* **∠ь** *and adj.* **1.** occupied; **здесь ~о** this place is taken; **~о** engaged (*of telephone number*); **на э́том заво́де ~о свы́ше ты́сячи рабо́чих** over a thousand people are employed in this factory; **быть ~ым собо́й** to be self-centred. **2.** busy.

зан|я́ть(ся), займу́(сь), займёшь(ся), *past* **∠ял(ся), ~яла́(сь), ∠яло(сь)** *pf. of* **занима́ть(ся)**; (*impers.*; *coll.*): **у кого́-н. дух ∠яло** to be out of breath; (*fig.*) to be (left) breathless; **от э́того у меня́ дух ∠яло** it took my breath away.

заодно́ *adv.* **1.** in concert, at one; **де́йствовать з.** to act in concert; **насчёт э́того мужчи́ны — з. с же́нщинами** on this the men are in agreement with the women. **2.** (*coll.*) at the same time; **купи́те з. и апельси́нов** buy some oranges at the same time.

заозёрный *adj.* situated on the other side of the lake.

заокеа́нский *adj.* transoceanic.

заострённый *p.p.p. of* **заостри́ть** *and adj.* pointed, sharp.

заостр|и́ть, ю́, и́шь *pf.* to sharpen; (*fig.*) to stress, emphasize; **з. внима́ние** (**на**+*a.*) to focus attention (on).

заостр|и́ться, и́тся *pf.* to become sharp; to become pointed.

заостр|я́ть(ся), я́ет(ся) *impf. of* **~и́ть(ся)**

заочник, а *m.* student taking correspondence course; external student.

зао́чно *adv.* **1.** in one's absence; in absentia. **2.** by correspondence course, externally.

зао́чн|ый *adj.* **1.** (*leg.*): **з. пригово́р** judgment by default. **2.:** **з. курс** correspondence course; **~ое обуче́ние** postal tuition.

за́пад, а *m.* **1.** west. **2.** the West.

запада́|ть, ю *impf. of* **запа́сть**

за́падничеств|о, а *nt.* Westernism.

за́падный *adj.* west, western; westerly.

западн|я́, и́, *g. pl.* **~е́й** *f.* trap, snare; **попа́сть в ~ю́** to fall into a trap (*also fig.*).

запа́здывани|е, я *nt.* **1.** lateness, being late. **2.** (*tech.*) lag.

запа́здыва|ть, ю *impf. of* **запозда́ть** (*impf. only*; *tech.*) to be late, lag.

запа́ива|ть, ю *impf. of* **запая́ть**

запа́йк|а, и *f.* soldering.

запак|ова́ть, у́ю *pf.* to pack (up); to wrap up, do up.

запако́выва|ть, ю *impf. of* **запакова́ть**

запа́ко|стить, щу, стишь *pf. of* **па́костить 1.**

запа́л[1], **а** *m.* fuse; touchhole.

запа́л[2], **а** *m.* heaves.

запа́лива|ть, ю *impf. of* **запали́ть**[1]

запал|и́ть[1], **ю́, и́шь** *pf.* (*coll.*) to set fire to, kindle; to light.

запал|и́ть[2], **ю́, и́шь** *pf.* (*coll.*) **1.** to open fire. **2.** (+*i.*) to hurl.

запа́л|ьный *adj. of* **~**[1]; **~ьная свеча́** sparking plug.

запа́льчивост|ь, и *f.* (quick) temper.

запа́льчив|ый (~а) *adj.* quick-tempered.

запанибра́та *adv.* (*coll.*): **быть з. с кем-н.** to be hail-fellow-well-met with s.o.

запанибра́тский *adj.* (*coll.*) hail-fellow-well-met.

запа́рива|ть(ся), ю(сь) *impf. of* **запа́рить(ся)**

запа́р|ить, ю, ишь *pf.* **1.** (*coll.*) to put into a sweat. **2.** to stew; to bake.

запа́р|иться, юсь, ишься *pf.* **1.** (*coll.*) to get into a sweat. **2.** to be worn out.

запарк|ова́ть, у́ю *pf. of* **паркова́ть**

запарк|ова́ться, у́юсь *pf. of* **паркова́ться**

запарши́ве|ть, ю *pf. of* **парши́веть**

запа́рыва|ть, ю *impf. of* **запоро́ть**

запа́с, а *m.* **1.** supply, stock; reserve; **прове́рить з.** to take stock; **про з.** for emergency; **отложи́ть про з.** to put by; **истощи́ть з. терпе́ния** (*fig.*) to exhaust one's reserves of patience; **з. слов** vocabulary. **2.** (*mil.*) reserve; **его́ уво́лили в з.** he has been transferred to the reserve. **3.** hem; **вы́пустить з.** to let out.

запаса́|ть(ся), ю(сь) *impf. of* **запасти́(сь)**

запа́слив|ый (~, ~а) *adj.* thrifty; provident.

запа́сни́к[1], **а** *m.* (*coll.*) reservist.

запа́сник[2], **а** *m.* repository, depository; storeroom.

запасн|о́й *adj.* **1.** spare; reserve; **з. вы́ход** emergency exit; **з. путь** siding; **з. сте́ржень** refill (*for pen*); **~а́я часть** spare part. **2.** *as n.* **з., ~о́го** *m.* reservist.

запа́сн|ый *adj.* = **~о́й**

запас|ти́, у́, ёшь, *past* **∠, ~ла́** *pf.* (*of* **~а́ть**) (+*a. or g.*) to stock, store; to lay in a stock of.

запас|ти́сь, у́сь, ёшься, *past* **∠ся, ~ла́сь** *pf.* (*of* **~а́ться**) (+*i.*) to provide o.s. (with); to stock up (on, with); **з. терпе́нием** (*fig.*) to arm o.s. with patience.

запа́|сть, ду́, дёшь, *past* **~л** *pf.* (*of* **~да́ть**) to fall (behind); to sink down; **слова́ его́ ~ли мне в ду́шу** (*fig.*) his words are etched in my memory.

запат|ова́ть, у́ю *pf. of* **патова́ть**

за́пах, а *m.* smell, odour.

запа|ха́ть, шу́, ∠шешь *pf.* (*agric.*) **1.** to plough in. **2.** to begin to plough.

запа́хива|ть[1] **(ся), ю(сь)** *impf. of* **запахну́ть(ся)**

запа́хива|ть[2], **ю** *impf. of* **запаха́ть**

запа́хн|уть, у, ешь *pf.* to begin to (emit a) smell.

запахн|у́ть, у́, ёшь *pf.* (*of* **запа́хивать**[1]) **1.** to wrap over (*folds of a garment*). **2.** (*coll.*) **з. за́навеску** to draw the curtain.

запахн|у́ться, у́сь, ёшься *pf.* (**в**+*a.*) to wrap o.s. tighter (into).

запа́чка|ть, ю *pf. of* **па́чкать 1.**

запаш|о́к, ка́ *m.* (*coll.*) faint smell.

запая́|ть, ю *pf.* (*of* **запа́ивать**) to solder.

запева́л|а, ы *m.* leader (of choir); precentor; (*fig., coll.*) leader, instigator.
запева́|ть, ю *impf.* (*of* **запе́ть**) to lead the singing, set the tune.
запека́нк|а, и *f.* **1.** baked pudding; casserole; **ри́совая з.** rice pudding; **карто́фельная з.** shepherd's pie. **2.** spiced brandy.
запека́|ть(ся), ю(сь) *impf. of* **запе́чь(ся)**
запелена́|ть, ю *pf. of* **пелена́ть**
запе́н|иться, юсь, ишься *pf.* to begin to froth up, begin to foam (*intrans.*).
зап|ере́ть, ру́, рёшь, *past* **∸ер, ерла́, ∸ерло** *pf.* (*of* **~ира́ть**) **1.** to lock; **з. на засо́в** to bolt. **2.** to lock in; to shut up. **3.** to bar; to block up.
зап|ере́ться, ру́сь, рёшься, *past* **∸ерся́, ~ерла́сь, ∸ерлось** *pf.* (*of* **~ира́ться**) **1.** to lock o.s. in. **2.** (**в**+*p.*; *coll.*) to refuse to admit; to refuse to speak (about); to shut up (*intrans.*).
зап|е́ть, ою́, оёшь *pf.* **1.** *pf. of* **~ева́ть. 2.** to begin to sing; **з. пе́сню** to break into song; **з. друго́е** (*fig.*) to change one's tune. **3.** (*coll.*): **з. пе́сню** to plug a song.
запеча́т|ать, аю *pf.* (*of* **~ывать**) to seal.
запечатлева́|ть(ся) *impf. of* **запечатле́ть(ся)**
запечатле́ни|е, я *nt.* (*biol.*) imprinting.
запечатле́|ть, ю *pf.* to imprint, etch, engrave; **з. что-н. в па́мяти** (*fig.*) to imprint sth. on one's memory.
запечатле́|ться, юсь *pf.* (*fig.*) to imprint itself, stamp itself, etch itself; **черты́ его́ лица́ ~лись у неё в па́мяти** his features etched themselves in her memory.
запеча́тыва|ть, ю *impf. of* **запеча́тать**
запе́|чь, ку́, чёшь, ку́т, *past* **∸к, ~кла́** *pf.* (*of* **~ка́ть**) to bake.
запе́|чься, чётся, ку́тся, *past* **∸кся, ~кла́сь** *pf.* (*of* **~ка́ться**) **1.** to bake (*intrans.*). **2.** to clot, coagulate. **3.** to become parched.
запива́|ть, ю *impf. of* **запи́ть**
запина́|ться, юсь *impf.* (*of* **запну́ться**) to hesitate; to stumble, halt (*in speech*); to stammer; **з. ного́й** to trip up; **з. о ка́мень** to strike against a stone.
запи́нк|а, и *f.* hesitation (*in speech*).
запира́тельств|о, а *nt.* (*pej.*) denial, disavowal.
запира́|ть(ся), ю(сь) *impf. of* **запере́ть(ся)**
запи|са́ть, шу́, ∸шешь *pf.* (*of* **∸сывать**) **1.** to note, make a note (of); to take down (in writing); to record (*with apparatus*); **(на плёнку)** to tape; **(на ви́део)** to video; **з. ле́кцию** to take notes of a lecture. **2.** to enter, register, enrol; **~ши́те меня́ пожа́луйста на приём к врачу́** please, make an appointment with the doctor for me. **3.** (+*a.* **на**+*a.*; *leg.*) to make over (to); **он ~са́л всю со́бственность на свою́ племя́нницу** he made over all his property to his niece.
запи|са́ться, шу́сь, ∸шешься *pf.* (*of* **∸сываться**) **1.** to register, enter one's name, enrol; **з. в клуб** to join a club; **з. к врачу́** to make an appointment with the doctor. **2.** *pass. of* **~са́ть**
запи́ск|а, и *f.* **1.** note; **делова́я з.** memorandum, minute. **2. ~и** (*pl.*) notes; memoirs; (*as title of learned journals*) transactions.
записн|о́й[1] *adj.*: **~а́я кни́жка** notebook.
записно́й[2] *adj.* (*coll.*) inveterate; regular.
запи́сыва|ть(ся), ю(сь) *impf. of* **записа́ть(ся)**
за́пис|ь, и *f.* **1.** writing down; recording. **2.** entry; record; (*leg.*) deed.
зап|и́ть, ью́, ьёшь, *past* **∸и́л, ~ила́, ∸и́ло** *pf.* (*of* **~ива́ть**) **1.** (*coll.*; *past* **∸ил**) to take to drink; to go on a blind. **2.** (*past* **~и́л**; +*a. and i.*) to wash down (with); to take (with, after); **з. пилю́лю водо́й** to take a pill with water.
запиха́|ть, ю *pf.* (*coll.*) to cram into.
запи́хива|ть, ю *impf. of* **запиха́ть**
запих|ну́ть, ну́, нёшь *pf.* (*coll.*) = **~а́ть**
запи́чка|ть, ю *pf.* (*coll.*) to stuff, cram.
запи|шу́, ∸шешь *see* **~са́ть**
запла́кан|ный (~, ~а) *adj.* tear-stained; in tears.
запла́|кать, чу, чешь *pf.* to begin to cry.
заплани́р|овать, ую *pf. of* **плани́ровать**[1]
запла́т|а, ы *f.* patch (*in garments*); **наложи́ть ~у (на**+*a.*) to patch.
заплата́|ть, ю *pf.* (*of* **плата́ть**) (*coll.*) to patch.
запла|ти́ть, чу́, ∸тишь *pf. of* **плати́ть**
запла́|чу, чешь *see* **~кать**
запла|чу́, ∸тишь *see* **~ти́ть**
запл|ева́ть, юю́, юёшь *pf.* (*coll.*) to spit on; to spit at; (*fig.*) to rain curses on.
заплёвыва|ть, ю *impf. of* **заплева́ть**
запле́сневелый *adj.* mouldy, mildewed.
запле́сневе|ть, ю *pf. of* **пле́сневеть**
запле|сти́, ту́, тёшь, *past* **∸̈л, ~ла́** *pf.* to braid, plait.
запле|сти́сь, ту́сь, тёшься, *past* **∸̈лся, ~ла́сь** *pf.* **1.** (*coll.*) to stumble, be unsteady on one's legs; to falter (*in speech*). **2.** *pass. of* **~сти́**
заплета́|ть(ся), ю(сь) *impf. of* **заплести́(сь)**
запле́чный *adj.* over the shoulder; **з. мешо́к** rucksack.
запле́ч|ье, ья, *g. pl.* **~ий** *nt.* shoulder-blade.
запломбир|ова́ть, у́ю *pf.* (*of* **пломбирова́ть** *and* **~о́вывать**) **1.**: **з. зуб** to stop, fill a tooth. **2.** to seal.
запломбиро́выва|ть, ю *impf. of* **запломбирова́ть**
заплута́|ться, юсь *pf.* (*coll.*) to lose one's way, stray.
заплы́в, а *m.* round, heat (*of water sports*).
заплыва́|ть, ю *impf. of* **заплы́ть**
заплы́|ть[1]**, ву́, вёшь,** *past* **~л, ~ла́, ~ло** *pf.* to swim far out; to sail away.
заплы́|ть[2]**, ву́, вёшь,** *past* **~л, ~ла́, ~ло** *pf.* to be swollen; to be bloated.
запн|у́ться, у́сь, ёшься *pf. of* **запина́ться**
запове́дник, а *m.* reserve; preserve; sanctuary; **госуда́рственный з.** national park.
запове́дн|ый *adj.* **1.** prohibited; **з. лес** forest reserve. **2.** (*poet.*) precious.
за́поведь, и *f.* precept; (*relig. and fig.*) commandment; **де́сять ~ей** the Ten Commandments.
запода́зрива|ть, ю *impf. of* **заподо́зрить**
заподо́зр|ить, ю, ишь *pf.* (+*a.* **в**+*p.*) to suspect (of); **его́ ~или в прича́стности к за́говору** he was suspected of complicity in the plot.
запо́ем *adv.*: **пить з.** to drink like a fish; (*fig., coll.*) heavily, without restraint; **чита́ть з.** to read avidly; **кури́ть з.** to smoke like a chimney.
запозда́лый *adj.* belated, tardy.
запозда́|ть, ю *pf.* (*of* **запа́здывать**) (**с**+*i.*) to be late (with); **он ~л с упла́той аре́нды** he is late in paying his rent.
запо́|й, я *m.* hard drinking; **пить ~ем,** *see* **~ем; страда́ть ~ем** to be addicted to the bottle.
запо́й|ный *adj. of* **~**; **з. пери́од** drunken bout; **з. пья́ница** chronic drunkard.
запола́скива|ть, ю *impf. of* **заполоска́ть** *and* **заполосну́ть**
заполза́|ть, ю *impf. of* **заползти́**
запол|зти́, у́, ёшь, *past* **∸, ~ла́** *pf.* (**в, под**+*a.*) to creep, crawl (into, under).
запо́лн|ить, ю, ишь *pf.* (*of* **~я́ть**) to fill in, fill up; **чем вы ~или вре́мя?** how did you fill in the time? **з. бланк** to fill in a form; **з. пробе́л** to fill a gap.
заполня́|ть, ю *impf. of* **запо́лнить**
заполо|ска́ть, щу́, ∸щешь *pf.* (*of* **запола́скивать**) (*coll.*) **1.** to begin to rinse. **2.** to rinse out.
заполосн|у́ть, у́, ёшь *pf.* (*of* **запола́скивать**) (*coll.*) to rinse out.
заполуч|а́ть, а́ю *impf. of* **~и́ть**
заполуч|и́ть, у́, ∸ишь *pf.* (*of* **~а́ть**) (*coll.*) to get

hold of, pick up; **я мог бы з. биле́ты на представле́ние в суббо́ту** I could get tickets for Saturday's performance; **з. на́сморк** to pick up a cold.

заполя́рный *adj.* (*geog.*) **1.** polar (*situated within one or other of the polar circles*). **2.** trans-polar; **з. возду́шный путь** trans-polar air route.

заполя́рь|е, я *nt.* (*geog.*) polar regions.

запомина́|ть(ся), ю(сь) *impf. of* **запо́мнить(ся)**

запо́мн|ить, ю, ишь *pf.* (*of* **запомина́ть**) **1.** to memorize. **2.** (*pf. only*) (*+neg.*; *coll.*) to remember; **никто́ не ~ит тако́й жары́** no one remembers such heat.

запо́мн|иться, юсь ишься *pf.* (*of* **запомина́ться**) to stick, be etched in one's memory; **ему́ ~ился день землетрясе́ния** the day of the earthquake is etched in his memory.

за́понк|а, и *f.* cuff-link; stud.

запо́р[1]**, а** *m.* bolt; lock; **на ~(е)** locked; bolted (and barred)

запо́р[2]**, а** *m.* constipation.

запора́шива|ть. ен *impf. of* **запороши́ть**

запоро́ж|ец, ца *m.* (*hist.*) Zaporozhian Cossack.

запор|о́ть, ю́, ~ешь *pf.* (*of* **запа́рывать**) (*coll.*) to flog to death.

запорош|и́ть, и́т *pf.* (*of* **запора́шивать**) (*+i.*) to powder (with); (*impers.*): **доро́гу ~и́ло сне́гом** the road was powdered with snow; **глаза́ мои́ ~и́ло пы́лью** there is dust in my eyes.

запотева́|ть, ю *impf. of* **запоте́ть**

запоте́лый *adj.* misted; steamed-up.

запоте́|ть, ю *pf.* (*of* **поте́ть** *and* **~ва́ть**) to mist over.

зап|ою́, ое́шь *see* **~е́ть**

заправи́л|а, ы *m.* (*coll.*) boss; ringleader.

запра́в|ить, лю, ишь *pf.* (*of* **~ля́ть**) **1.** to insert; **з. брю́ки в сапоги́** to tuck one's trousers into one's boots. **2.** to prepare; to adjust; **з. автомоби́ль бензи́ном** to fill a car up with petrol. **3.** (*+i.*) to mix in; to season (with); **з. со́ус муко́й** to thicken a sauce with flour.

запра́в|иться, люсь, ишься *pf.* (*of* **~ля́ться**) **1.** (*coll.*) to satisfy hunger; to eat one's fill. **2. з. (горю́чим)** to refuel (*intrans.*).

запра́вк|а, и *f.* **1.** seasoning; **з. для сала́та** salad dressing. **2.** refuelling.

заправля́|ть(ся), ю(сь) *impf. of* **запра́вить(ся)**

запра́вочн|ый *adj.*: **з. пункт, ~ая ста́нция** petrol station.

запра́вский *adj.* (*coll.*) real, true; thorough; **он — з. моря́к** he is a real sailor.

запра́вщик, а *m.* petrol station attendant.

запра́шива|ть, ю *impf. of* **запроси́ть**

запресто́льн|ый *adj.* (*eccl.*) situated behind the altar; **з. о́браз** altar-piece.

запре́т, а *m.* prohibition, ban; **наложи́ть з.** (**на**+*a.*) to place a ban (on).

запрети́тельн|ый *adj.* prohibitive; prohibitory.

запре|ти́ть, щу́, ти́шь *pf.* (*of* **~ща́ть**) to prohibit, forbid, ban; **врач ~ти́л мне кури́ть, врач ~ти́л мне куре́ние** the doctor has forbidden me to smoke; **з. пье́су** to ban a play.

запре́тн|ый *adj.* forbidden; **~ая зо́на** (*mil.*) restricted area; **~ая те́ма** taboo subject.

запреща́|ть, ю *impf. of* **запрети́ть**

запреща́|ться, ется *impf.* to be forbidden, to be prohibited; (*in official notices, etc.*): **«кури́ть ~ется»** 'No Smoking'.

запреще́ни|е, я *nt.* prohibition; (*leg.*): **з. на иму́щество** distraint, arrest on property; **суде́бное з.** injunction.

запримé|тить, чу, тишь *pf.* (*coll.*) **1.** to notice, perceive. **2.** to recognize, spot; **я ~тил его́ в толпе́ по кра́сной руба́шке** I spotted him in the crowd by his red shirt.

заприхо́д|овать, ую *pf. of* **прихо́довать**

запрограмми́р|овать, ую *pf. of* **программи́ровать**

запроекти́р|овать, ую *pf. of* **проекти́ровать**[1] **1.**

запроки́дыва|ть, ю *impf. of* **запроки́нуть**

запроки́н|уть, у, ешь *pf.* (*coll.*) to throw back; **он захохота́л, ~ув го́лову** he threw back his head and guffawed.

запроки́н|уться, усь, ешься *pf.* (*coll.*) to lean back, slump back.

запропа|сти́ть, щу́, сти́шь *pf.* (*coll.*) to mislay.

запропа|сти́ться, щу́сь, сти́шься *pf.* (*coll.*) to get lost, disappear; **куда́ ты ~сти́лся?** where on earth did you get to?

запро́с, а *m.* **1.** inquiry; (*pol.*) question. **2.** overcharging; **це́ны без ~а** fixed prices. **3.** (*pl. only*) needs, requirements.

запро|си́ть, шу́, ~сишь *pf.* (*of* **запра́шивать**) **1.** (**о**+*p.*) to inquire (about); (*+a.*) to inquire (of), question; **мини́стра ~си́ли о его́ расхо́дах** the Minister was questioned about his expenditure. **2.: з. сли́шком высо́кую це́ну** to ask an exorbitant price.

за́просто *adv.* (*coll.*) without ceremony, without formality.

запро|шу́, ~сишь *see* **~си́ть**

зап|ру́, рёшь *see* **~ере́ть**

запру́д|а, ы *f.* **1.** dam, weir. **2.** mill-pond.

запру|ди́ть, жу́, ~ди́шь *pf.* **1.** (**~дишь**) to dam. **2.** (**~ди́шь**) (*fig.*, *coll.*) to block (up); to fill to overflowing.

запружа́|ть, ю *impf. of* **запруди́ть**

запру́жива|ть, ю *impf.* = **запружа́ть**

запры́га|ть, ю *pf.* to begin to jump; (*coll.*): **се́рдце у неё ~ло** her heart began to thump.

запры́гива|ть, ю *impf. of* **запры́гнуть**

запры́гн|уть, у, ешь *pf.* (**за**+*a.*; *coll.*) to leap (over).

запряга́|ть, ю *impf. of* **запря́чь**

запря́жк|а, и *f.* **1.** harnessing. **2.** equipage.

запря́|тать, чу, чешь *pf.* (*coll.*) to hide.

запря́|таться, чусь, чешься *pf.* (*coll.*) to hide o.s.

запря́тыва|ть(ся), ю(сь) *impf. of* **запря́тать(ся)**

запря́|чь, гу́, жёшь, гу́т, *past* **~г, ~гла́** *pf.* (*of* **~га́ть**) to harness (*also fig.*); **з. воло́в** to yoke oxen.

запря́|чься, гу́сь, жёшься, гу́ться, *past* **~гся, ~гла́сь** *pf.* **1.** *pass. of* **~чь. 2.** (*fig.*, *coll.*) to harness o.s.; to buckle down to, get down to.

запу́ганный *p.p.p. of* **запуга́ть** *and adj.* broken-spirited.

запуга́|ть, ю *pf.* to intimidate, cow.

запу́гива|ть, ю *impf. of* **запуга́ть**

запу́дрива|ть, ю *impf. of* **запу́дрить**

запу́др|ить, ю, ишь *pf.* to powder.

за́пуск, а *n.* starting; launch, launching.

запус|ка́ть, ка́ю *impf. of* **~ти́ть**

запусте́лый *adj.* neglected; desolate.

запусте́ни|е, я *nt.* neglect; desolation.

запусте́|ть, ет *pf.* to fall into neglect; to become desolate.

запу|сти́ть[1]**, щу́, ~стишь** *pf.* (*of* **~ска́ть**) **1.** (*+i.* **в**+*a.*; *coll.*) to throw (at), fling (at), hurl (at); **он ~сти́л кирпичо́м в окно́** he hurled a brick at the window. **2.** (**в**+*a.*) to thrust (*hands*, *etc.*, into); **ко́шка ~сти́ла ко́гти в мышь** the cat dug its claws into the mouse; **з. ко́гти, ла́пы, ру́ки** (**в**+*a.*; *fig.*) to get one's hands on. **3.** to start (up) (*mechanism*); **з. мото́р** to start up the engine; **з. раке́ту** to launch a rocket. **4.** (**в**+*a.*) (*coll.*) to put (into), let loose (in); **з. коро́в на луг** to let cows loose in a meadow.

запу|сти́ть[2]**, щу́, ~стишь** *pf.* (*of* **~ска́ть**) **1.** to neglect, allow to fall into neglect; **з. дела́** to neglect one's affairs; **з. сад** to neglect a garden. **2.** to allow to develop unchecked; **он ~сти́л на́сморк и тепе́рь**

заболе́л бронхи́том he neglected his cold and now he is ill with bronchitis.
запу́тан|ный *p.p.p. of* **запу́тать** *and adj.* tangled; (*fig.*) intricate, involved; **з. вопро́с** knotty question.
запу́та|ть, ю *pf.* **1.** to tangle (up). **2.** (*fig.*) to confuse; to complicate; to muddle; **его́ сообще́ние ~ло де́ло** his statement has complicated matters; **тако́го ро́да вопро́сы то́лько ~ют кандида́тов** questions of this kind will only confuse the candidates. **3.** (**в**+*a.*; *fig.*) to involve, embroil (in).
запу́та|ться, юсь *pf.* **1.** to become entangled; to foul (*intrans.*); (**в**+*p.*; *fig.*) to entangle o.s. (in), be caught (in). **2.** (**в**+*p.*; *fig.*) to become entangled (in), become involved (in); to become complicated; **з. в долга́х** to become involved in debts; **докла́дчик ~лся в слова́х** the lecturer got tied up in knots.
запу́тыва|ть(ся), ю(сь) *impf. of* **запу́тать(ся)**
запуш|и́ть, и́т *pf.* to cover lightly (*of snow or frost*).
запу́щен|ный *p.p.p. of* **запусти́ть**[2] *and adj.* neglected.
запча́ст|и, е́й *pl.* (*sg.* **~ь, ~и** *f.*; *abbr. of* ***запасны́е ча́сти***) spare parts; spares.
запыла́|ть, ю *pf.* to blaze up, flare up.
запыл|и́ть, ю́, и́шь *pf.* (*of* **пыли́ть**) to cover with dust, make dusty.
запыл|и́ться, ю́сь, и́шься *pf.* (*of* **пыли́ться**) to become dusty.
запыха́|ться, юсь *impf.* (*coll.*) to puff, pant.
запьяне́|ть, ю *pf.* (*coll.*) to get drunk.
запья́нств|овать, ую *pf.* to take to drink.
запя́сть|е, я *nt.* wrist.
запят|а́я, о́й *f.* comma.
запятна́|ть, ю *pf. of* **пятна́ть**
зараба́тыва|ть(ся), ю(сь) *impf. of* **зарабо́тать(ся)**
зарабо́та|ть, ю *pf.* **1.** to earn. **2.** to begin to work; to start (up).
зарабо́та|ться, юсь *pf.* (*coll.*) **1.** to overwork, tire o.s. out with work. **2.** to work late; **он вчера́ ~лся далеко́ за́ полночь** he went on working long after midnight last night.
за́работн|ый *adj.*: **~ая пла́та** wages, pay, salary.
за́работ|ок, ка *m.* earnings; **лёгкий з.** easy money.
зара́внива|ть, ю *impf. of* **заровня́ть**
заража́емост|ь, и *f.* susceptibility to infection.
заража́|ть(ся), ю(сь) *impf. of* **зарази́ть(ся)**
зараже́ни|е, я *nt.* infection.
зара|жу́, зи́шь *see* **~зи́ть**
зара́з *adv.* (*coll.*) at once; at a sitting; in one fell swoop.
зара́з|а, ы *f.* infection, contagion.
зарази́тел|ьный (~ен, ~ьна) *adj.* infectious; catching; **з. смех** infectious laughter.
зара|зи́ть, жу́, зи́шь *pf.* (*of* **~жа́ть**) (+*i.*) to infect (with); (*also fig.*) **з. свои́м приме́ром** to inspire by one's example.
зара|зи́ться, жу́сь, зи́шься *pf.* (*of* **~жа́ться**) (+*i.*) to be infected (with); catch (*also fig.*).
зара́з|ный (~ен, ~на) *adj.* **1.** infectious; contagious. **2.** of *or* for infectious diseases; **з. бара́к** infectious diseases ward; **з. больно́й** infectious case; *as n.* **з., ~ного** *m.*, **~ная, ~ной** *f.* infectious case.
зара́нее *adv.* beforehand; in good time; **заплати́ть з.** to pay in advance; **преступле́ние с з. обду́манным наме́рением** premeditated crime; **ра́доваться з.** (+*d.*) to look forward (to).
зарапорт|ова́ться, у́юсь *pf.* (*coll.*) to let one's tongue run away with one.
зараста́|ть, ю *impf. of* **зарасти́**
зараст|и́, у́, ёшь, *past* **заро́с, заросла́** *pf.* **1.** (+*i.*) to be overgrown (with). **2.** (*of a wound*) to heal.
зарв|а́ться, у́сь, ёшься, *past* **~а́лся, ~ала́сь, ~ало́сь** *pf.* (*of* **зарыва́ться**) (*coll.*) to go too far; to overstep the mark.
зарде́|ться, юсь *pf.* **1.** (*poet.*) to redden, grow red. **2.** to blush.
за́рев|о, а *nt.* glow; **з. (от) пожа́ра** the glow of a fire.
зарегистри́р|овать, ую *pf.* (*of* **регистри́ровать**) to register.
зарегистри́р|оваться, уюсь *pf.* (*of* **регистри́роваться**) **1.** to register o.s. **2.** (*coll.*) to register one's marriage. **3.** *pass. of* **~овать**
зарегистр|ова́ть(ся), у́ю(сь) *pf.* = **~и́ровать(ся)**
заре́з, а *m.* (*coll.*) disaster; **до ~у** extremely, badly, urgently; **мне до ~у нужны́ пять рубле́й** I badly need five roubles.
заре́|зать, жу, жешь *pf.* **1.** to murder; to knife; **з. свинью́** to stick a pig; (*of a wolf*) to devour, kill; **хоть заре́жь** (*coll.*) extremely, urgently; come what may. **2.** (*fig.*) to undo, be the undoing of; to do for; **без ножа́ з.** to do for; to make mincemeat of.
зареза́|ть(ся), ю(сь) *impf. of* **заре́зать(ся)**
заре́|заться, жусь, жешься *pf.* (*coll.*) to cut one's throat.
зарека́|ться, юсь *impf. of* **заре́чься**
зарекоменд|ова́ть, у́ю *pf. only in phr.* **з. себя́** (+*i.*) to prove o.s., show o.s. (to be); **хорошо́ з. себя́** to show to advantage.
зарекомендо́выва|ть, ю *impf. of* **зарекомендова́ть**
заре|ку́сь, чёшься, ку́тся *see* **~́чься**
заре́чный *adj.* situated on the other side of the river.
заре́чь|е, я *nt.* area on the other side of a river.
заре́|чься, ку́сь, чёшься, ку́тся, *past* **~́кся, ~кла́сь** *pf.* (*of* **~ка́ться**) (+*inf.*; *coll.*) to swear off; to promise to give up, vow to give up; **он ~́кся кури́ть** he has promised to give up smoking.
заржа́ве|ть, ет *pf.* (*of* **ржа́веть**) to rust; to have got rusty.
заржа́влен|ный (~, ~а) *adj.* rusty.
зарис|ова́ть, у́ю *pf.* (*of* **~о́вывать**) to sketch.
зарис|ова́ться, у́юсь *pf.* (*of* **~о́вываться**) (*coll.*) to spend too much time drawing.
зарисо́вк|а, и *f.* **1.** sketching. **2.** sketch.
зарисо́выва|ть(ся), ю(сь) *impf. of* **зарисова́ть(ся)**
за́р|иться, юсь, ишься *impf.* (*of* **по~**) (**на**+*a.*; *coll.*) to hanker (after).
зарни́ц|а, ы *f.* summer lightning.
заровня́|ть, ю *pf.* (*of* **зара́внивать**) to level, even up; **з. я́му** to fill up a hole.
заро|ди́ть, жу́, ди́шь *pf.* (*of* **~жда́ть**) to generate, engender (*also fig.*).
заро|ди́ться, жу́сь, ди́шься *pf. pass. of* **~ди́ть;** (*fig.*) to arise; **у него́ ~ди́лось сомне́ние** a doubt arose in his mind.
заро́дыш, а *m.* (*biol.*) foetus; (*bot.*) bud; (*fig.*) embryo, germ; **подави́ть в ~е** to nip in the bud.
заро́дышевый *adj.* embryonic.
зарожда́|ть(ся), ю(сь) *impf. of* **зароди́ть(ся)**
зарожде́ни|е, я *nt.* conception; (*fig.*) origin.
заро|жу́, ди́шь *see* **~ди́ть**
заро́к, а *m.* (solemn) promise, vow, pledge, undertaking; **дать з.** to pledge o.s., give an undertaking.
зарон|и́ть, ю́, ~́ишь *pf.* **1.** (*coll.*) to drop (behind); to let fall. **2.** (*fig.*) to excite, arouse; **з. сомне́ния** to give rise to doubts.
зароня́|ть, ю *impf. of* **зарони́ть**
за́росл|ь, и *f.* brake; thicket.
зар|о́ю, о́ешь *see* **~ы́ть**
зарпла́т|а, ы *f.* (*abbr. of* ***за́работная пла́та***) wages, pay, salary.
заруба́|ть, ю *impf. of* **заруби́ть**
зарубе́жный *adj.* foreign.
зарубе́жь|е, я *nt.* foreign countries; **стра́ны бли́жнего ~я** the 'near abroad', former Soviet republics.
заруб|и́ть, лю́, ~́ишь *pf.* (*of* **~а́ть**) **1.** to hack to

death. **2.** to notch, make an incision (on); **~и́ э́то себе́ на носу́** (*coll.*) put that in your pipe and smoke it. **3.** (*tech.*) to hew.

зару́бк|а, и *f.* **1.** notch; incision. **2.** (*tech.*) hewing.

зарубц|ева́ться, у́ется *pf.* (*of* **рубцева́ться** *and* **~о́вываться**) to form a scar.

зарубцо́выва|ться, ется *impf. of* **зарубцева́ться**

зару́бщик, а *m.* (coal-)hewer.

заруми́нива|ть(ся), ю(сь) *impf. of* **заруми́нить(ся)**

заруми́н|ить, ю, ишь *pf.* to redden.

заруми́н|иться, юсь, ишься *pf.* **1.** to redden (*intrans.*); to blush, colour. **2.** (*coll.*) to brown, bake brown.

заруч|а́ться, а́юсь *impf. of* **~и́ться**

заруч|и́ться, у́сь, и́шься *pf.* (*+i.*) to secure; **з. подде́ржкой** to enlist support; **з. согла́сием** to obtain consent.

зару́чк|а, и *f.* (*coll.*) pull, influence.

зарыва́|ть, ю *impf. of* **зары́ть**

зарыва́|ться[1], юсь *impf. of* **зары́ться**

зарыва́|ться[2], юсь *impf. of* **зарва́ться**

зар|ы́ть, о́ю, о́ешь *pf.* (*of* **~ыва́ть**) to bury; **з. тала́нт в зе́млю** (*fig.*) to hide one's light under a bushel.

зар|ы́ться, о́юсь, о́ешься *pf.* (*of* **~ыва́ться**) **1.** to bury o.s.; **з. лицо́м в поду́шку** to bury one's head in the pillow; **з. в дере́вне** (*fig.*, *coll.*) to bury o.s. in the country; **з. в кни́ги** to bury o.s. in one's books. **2.** (*mil.*) to dig in.

зар|я́, и́, *a.* **~ю́** *and* (*rare*) **зо́рю,** *pl.* **зо́ри, зорь, ~я́м** *and* **зо́рям** *f.* **1. (***a.* **~ю́)** dawn, daybreak; **на ~е́** at dawn, at daybreak; **встать с ~е́й** to rise at the crack of dawn; **что ты встал ни свет ни з.?** what made you get up at this unearthly hour? **2. (***a.* **~ю́) (вече́рняя) з.** sunset, evening glow; **от ~и́ до ~и́** from dawn till dusk; all night long. **3. (***a.* **~ю́)** (*fig.*) start, outset; dawn, threshold. **4. (***a.* **зо́рю,** *d. pl.* **зо́рям)** (*mil.*) reveille; retreat; **бить зо́рю** to beat retreat.

заря́д, а *m.* **1.** charge (*also elec.*), cartridge; **холосто́й з.** blank cartridge. **2.** (*fig.*) fund, supply.

заря|ди́ть[1], жу́, ∸ди́шь *pf.* (*of* **~жа́ть**) **1.** to load (*gun, camera, etc.*). **2.** (*elec.*) to charge.

заря|ди́ть[2], жу́, ди́шь *pf.* (*coll.*) to keep on, persist in; **с утра́ ~ди́л дождь** it has been raining non-stop since morning; **он ~ди́л одно́ и то же** he keeps saying the same thing over and over again.

заря́дк|а, и *f.* **1.** loading (*of fire-arms*); (*elec.*) charging. **2.** exercises; drill.

заря́д|ный *adj. of* **~; з. я́щик** ammunition wagon.

заряжа́|ть, ю *impf. of* **заряди́ть**

заря|жу́, ∸ди́шь *see* **~ди́ть**

заса́д|а, ы *f.* ambush.

заса|ди́ть, жу́, ∸дишь *pf.* (*of* **∸живать**) **1.** (*+a. and i.*) to plant (with); **з. сад плодо́выми дере́вьями** to plant a garden with fruit-trees. **2.** (*+a.* **в***+a.*; *coll.*) to plant (into), plunge (into), drive (into). **3.** (*coll.*) to shut in, confine; to keep in; **з. (в тюрьму́)** to put in prison, lock up; **боле́знь на це́лый ме́сяц ~ди́ла меня́ в го́спиталь** illness kept me in hospital for a whole month. **4.** (*+a.* **за***+a.*; *coll.*) to set (to); **его́ ~ди́ли за изуче́ние ру́сского языка́** he was set to learn Russian

заса́дк|а, и *f.* planting.

заса́жива|ть, ю *impf. of* **засади́ть**

заса́жива|ться, юсь *impf.* **1.** *impf. of* **засе́сть. 2.** *pass. of* **~ть**

заса|жу́, ∸дишь *see* **~ди́ть**

заса́лива|ть[1], ю *impf. of* **заса́лить**

заса́лива|ть[2], ю *impf. of* **засоли́ть**

заса́л|ить, ю, ишь *pf.* (*of* **~ивать[1]**) to soil, make greasy.

заса́сыва|ть, ю *impf. of* **засоса́ть**

заса́харен|ный *p.p.p. of* **заса́харить** *and adj.* candied; **~ные фру́кты** crystallized fruits, candied fruits.

заса́харива|ть, ю *impf. of* **заса́харить**

заса́хар|ить, ю, ишь *pf.* (*of* **~ивать**) to candy.

засве|ти́ть, чу́, ∸тишь *pf.* **1.** to light. **2.** (*+d.* **в***+a.*; *coll.*) to strike, hit; **з. кому́-н. в физионо́мию кулако́м** to stick one's fist in s.o.'s face.

засве|ти́ться, ∸тится *pf.* to light up (*also fig.*).

за́светло *adv.* (*coll.*) before nightfall, before dark.

засве|чу́, ∸тишь *see* **~ти́ть**

засвиде́тельств|овать, ую *pf. of* **свиде́тельствовать 2.**

засе́в, а *m.* **1.** sowing. **2.** sown area.

засева́|ть, ю *impf. of* **засе́ять**

заседа́ни|е, я *nt.* meeting; conference; session, sitting.

заседа́тел|ь, я *m.* assessor; **прися́жный з.** juryman.

заседа́|ть, ю *impf.* to sit; to meet.

засе́ива|ть, ю = засева́ть

засе́|к, кла *see* **~чь**

за́се́к|а, и *f.* abat(t)is.

засека́|ть, ет *impf. of* **засе́чь**

засекре́|тить, чу, тишь *pf.* **1.** to place on secret list; to classify (as secret), restrict. **2.** to give access to classified documents; to admit to secret work.

засекре́ченный *p.p.p. of* **засекре́тить** *and adj.* hush-hush; secret, classified.

засекре́чива|ть, ю *impf. of* **засекре́тить**

засе|ку́, чёшь, ку́т *see* **∸чь**

засе́|л, ла *see* **~сть**

заселе́ни|е, я *nt.* settlement; colonization.

заселённый *p.p.p. of* **засели́ть** *and adj.* populated; inhabited; **ре́дко з.** sparsely populated.

засел|и́ть, ю́, и́шь *pf.* (*of* **~я́ть**) to settle; to colonize; to populate; **з. но́вый дом** to occupy a new house.

засел|я́ть, я́ю *impf. of* **~и́ть**

зас|е́сть, я́ду, я́дешь, *past* **~е́л** *pf.* (*of* **~а́живаться**) (*coll.*) **1.** (**за***+a. or +inf.*) to sit down (to). **2.** to sit firm, sit tight; to ensconce o.s.; **з. в тюрьму́** to go to prison. **3.** (**в***+p.*) to lodge (in), stick (in); **пу́ля ~е́ла у него́ в боку́** a bullet had lodged in his side; **моти́в ~е́л у меня́ в голове́** (*fig.*) the tune has stuck in my head.

засе́чк|а, и *f.* **1.** notch, mark. **2.** (*typ.*) serif.

засе́|чь, ку́, чёшь, ку́т, *past* **~к, ~кла** *pf.* (*of* **~ка́ть**) **1.** to flog to death. **2.** to notch. **3.** (*geog.*) to determine by intersection.

засе́|ять, ю, ешь *pf.* (*of* **~ва́ть** *and* **~ивать**) to sow.

заси|де́ться, жу́сь, ди́шься *pf.* (*of* **∸живаться**) (*coll.*) to sit too long, stay too long; to sit up late; to stay late; **з. за рабо́той** to sit up late working; **з. в де́вках,** *see* **де́вка**

заси́женный *adj.* (*coll.*): **з. (му́хами)** fly-blown.

заси́жива|ться, юсь *impf. of* **засиде́ться**

заси́ль|е, я *no pl.*, (*pej.*) domination, sway.

засия́|ть, ю *pf.* **1.** to begin to shine, begin to beam. **2.** to appear, come out; **ме́сяц ~л из-за туч** the moon appeared from behind the clouds.

заска́кива|ть, ю *impf. of* **заскочи́ть**

заско́к, а *m.* (*coll.*) **1.** leap, jump. **2.** crazy idea; **э́то у тебя́ з.?** have you gone crazy?; are you out of your mind?

заскору́злый *adj.* **1.** hardened, calloused. **2.** (*fig.*) coarsened, callous.

заскору́з|нуть, ну, нешь, *past* **~, ~ла** *pf.* **1.** to harden, coarsen, become callous; (*also fig.*). **2.** (*fig.*) to stagnate; to become retarded.

заскоч|и́ть, у́, ∸ишь *pf.* (*of* **заска́кивать**) **1.** (**за***+a.*, **на***+a.*) to jump, spring (behind, onto). **2.** (**в***+a.*; *fig.*) to drop in (to, at).

засла|сти́ть, щу́, сти́шь *pf.* (*of* **∠щивать**) **1.** to take (*medicine*, *etc.*) with sth. sweet. **2.** to sweeten, put sugar into.
за|сла́ть, шлю́, шлёшь *pf.* (*of* **~сыла́ть**) to send, dispatch; **з. не по а́дресу** to send to the wrong address; **з. шпио́на** to send out a spy.
засла́щива|ть, ю *impf. of* **засласти́ть**
заслеп|и́ть, лю́, и́шь *pf.* (*of* **~ля́ть**) (*coll.*) to blind.
заслепля́|ть, ю *impf. of* **заслепи́ть**
засло́н, а *m.* **1.** screen, barrier. **2.** (*mil.*) covering force.
заслон|и́ть, ю́, и́шь *and* (*coll.*) **∠ишь** *pf. and* (*of* **~я́ть**) **1.** to hide, cover; to shield, screen. **2.** (*fig.*) to push into the background.
заслон|и́ться, ю́сь, и́шся *and* (*coll.*) **∠ишься** *pf.* (*of* **~я́ться**) **1. (от)** to shield o.s., screen o.s. (from). **2.** *pass. of* **~и́ть**
засло́нк|а, и *f.* oven-door; stove-door.
заслон|я́ть(ся), я́ю(сь) *impf. of* **~и́ть(ся)**
заслу́г|а, и *f.* merit, desert; service; contribution; **их наказа́ли по ~ам** they have been punished according to their deserts; **у него́ больши́е ~и пе́ред родны́м го́родом** he has rendered great services to his home town.
заслу́женно *adv.* deservedly.
заслу́жен|ный (*and* **∸ный**) *p.p.p. of* **заслужи́ть** *and adj.* **1.** deserved, merited. **2.** meritorious, of merit; (*as honorific in former USSR*) Honoured. **3.: ∸ный профе́ссор** professor emeritus.
заслу́жива|ть, ю *impf.* (*of* **заслужи́ть**) (*+g.*) to deserve, merit.
заслу́жива|ться, юсь *impf.* **1.** *impf. of* **заслужи́ться**. **2.** *pass. of* **~ть**
заслуж|и́ть, у́, ∠ишь *pf.* (*of* **∠ивать**) (*+a.*) to deserve, merit; win, earn.
заслуж|и́ться, у́сь, ∠ишься *pf.* (*of* **∠иваться**) (*coll.*) to serve for too long.
заслу́ш|ать, аю *pf.* (*of* **~ивать**) to hear, listen to (*a public or official pronouncement*).
заслу́ш|аться, аюсь *pf.* (*of* **~иваться**) (*+g.*) to listen spellbound (to).
заслу́шива|ть(ся), ю(сь) *impf. of* **заслу́шать(ся)**
заслы́ш|ать, у, ишь *pf.* **1.** to hear, catch. **2.** (*coll.*) to smell; **з. за́пах** to detect a smell.
заслю́нива|ть, ю *impf. of* **заслюни́ть**
заслюн|и́ть, ю́, и́шь *pf.* (*of* **слюни́ть** *and* **∠ивать**) (*coll.*) to slobber over.
засма́лива|ть, ю *impf. of* **засмоли́ть**
засма́трива|ть, ю *impf.* (**в**+*a.*; *coll.*) to look (into); to peep (into); **з. в окно́ к кому́-н.** to look in at s.o.'s window.
засма́трива|ться, юсь *impf. of* **засмотре́ться**
засме|я́ться, ю́сь, ёшься *pf.* to begin to laugh.
засмол|и́ть, ю́, и́шь *pf.* to tar; to caulk.
засмо́рканный *adj.* (*coll.*) snotty.
засмотр|е́ться, ю́сь, ∠ишься *pf.* (*of* **засма́триваться**) (**на**+*a.*) to be lost in contemplation (of), be carried away (by the sight of).
засне́женный *adj.* snow-covered, snow-clad.
заснима́|ть, ю *impf. of* **засня́ть**
засн|иму́, и́мешь *see* **~я́ть**
засн|у́ть, у́, ёшь *pf.* (*of* **засыпа́ть**[1]) to go to sleep. fall asleep; (*rhet.*): **з. ве́чным сном** to go to one's eternal rest.
засн|я́ть, иму́, и́мешь, *past* **~я́л, ~яла́, ~я́ло** *pf.* (*of* **~има́ть**) to photograph, snap (*coll.*); (*cinema sl.*) to shoot.
засо́в, а *m.* bolt, bar.
засо́выва|ть, ю *impf. of* **засу́нуть**
засо́л, а *m.* salting; pickling.
засол|и́ть, ю́, ∠и́шь *pf.* (*of* **заса́ливать**[2]) to salt; to pickle.
засо́льщик, а *m.* salter, pickler.
засоре́ни|е, я *nt.* littering; obstruction, clogging up.
засор|и́ть, ю́, и́шь *pf.* (*of* **~я́ть**) **1.** to clog, block up, stop. **2.** to litter; to get dirt into; (*fig.*): **з. чью-н. ду́шу** to poison s.o.'s mind.
засор|и́ться, ю́сь, и́шься *pf.* (*of* **~я́ться**) to become obstructed, blocked up.
засоря́|ть(ся), ю(сь) *impf. of* **засори́ть(ся)**
засо́с, а *m.* sucking in.
засос|а́ть, у́, ёшь *pf.* (*of* **заса́сывать**) to suck in, engulf, swallow up (*also fig.*).
засо́х|нуть, ну, нешь, *past* **~, ~ла** *pf.* (*of* **засыха́ть**) **1.** to dry (up). **2.** to wither.
засп|а́ться, лю́сь, и́шься, *past* **~а́лся, ~ала́сь, ~а́лось** *pf.* (*of* **засыпа́ться**[1]) (*coll.*) to oversleep.
заспирт|ова́ть, у́ю *pf.* (*of* **~о́вывать**) to preserve in alcohol.
заспирто́выва|ть, ю *impf. of* **заспиртова́ть**
заста́в|а, ы *f.* **1.** gate (*of town*). **2.** (*hist.*, *mil.*) barrier. **3.** (*mil.*) picket; outpost.
заста|ва́ть, ю́, ёшь *impf. of* **∠ть**
заста́в|ить[1]**, лю, ишь** *pf.* (*of* **~ля́ть**[1]) **1.** to cram, fill; **з. ко́мнату ме́белью** to cram a room with furniture. **2.** to block up, obstruct.
заста́в|ить[2]**, лю, ишь** *pf.* (*of* **~ля́ть**[2]) (*+a. and inf.*) to force, make, oblige; **он ~ил нас ждать себя́ два часа́** he kept us waiting for two hours.
заста́вк|а, и *f.* (*typ.*) headpiece.
заставля́|ть[1,2]**, ю** *impf. of* **заста́вить**[1,2]
заста́ива|ться, юсь *impf. of* **застоя́ться**
заста́|ну, нешь *see* **~ть**
застаре́лый *adj.* inveterate; chronic.
заста́|ть, ну, нешь *pf.* (*of* **~ва́ть**) to find; **~ли ли вы его́ до́ма?** did you find him in?; **я ~л его́ ещё спя́щим** I found him still asleep; **з. враспло́х** to catch napping; **з. на ме́сте преступле́ния** to catch red-handed.
заста|ю́, ёшь *see* **~ва́ть**
застёгива|ть, ю *impf. of* **застегну́ть**
застёгива|ться, юсь *impf.* **1.** *impf. of* **застегну́ться**. **2.** *pass. of* **~ть**. **3.** to fasten, do up (*intrans.*); **во́рот ~ется на пу́говицу** the collar buttons up.
застег|ну́ть, ну́, нёшь *pf.* (*of* **∸ивать**) to fasten, do up; **з. (на пу́говицы)** to button up.
застег|ну́ться, ну́сь, нёшься *pf.* (*of* **∸иваться**) to button o.s. up; **з. на все пу́говицы** to do up all one's buttons.
застёжк|а, и *f.* fastener; clasp; **з.-мо́лния** zip fastener.
застекл|и́ть, ю́, и́шь *pf.* (*of* **~я́ть**) to glaze, fit with glass; **з. портре́т** to frame a portrait.
застекл|я́ть, я́ю *impf. of* **~и́ть**
засте́н|ок, ка *m.* torture-chamber; prison.
засте́нчив|ый (~, ~а) *adj.* shy; bashful.
засти́|г, гла *see* **~чь**
засти|га́ть, га́ю *impf. of* **∠гнуть** *and* **∠чь**
засти́|гнуть = ~чь
застила́|ть, ю *impf. of* **застла́ть**
застир|а́ть, а́ю *pf.* (*of* **∠ывать**) (*coll.*) **1.** to wash off, out. **2.** to ruin by washing.
засти́рыва|ть, ю *impf. of* **застира́ть**
засти́|чь, гну, гнешь, *past* **~г, ~гла** *pf.* (*of* **~га́ть**) to catch; to take unawares; **нас ~гла гроза́** we were caught by the storm.
заст|ла́ть, елю́, е́лешь *pf.* (*of* **~ила́ть**) **1.** (*+i*) to cover (with); **з. ковро́м** to carpet, lay a carpet (over). **2.** (*fig.*) to hide from view; to cloud; **облака́ ~ла́ли со́лнце** clouds obscured the sun; **слёзы ~ла́ли её глаза́** tears dimmed her eyes.
засто́|й, я *m.* stagnation (*fig.*); **в ~е** at a standstill; (*econ.*) depression.
засто́йный *adj.* stagnant (*fig.*).
засто́льн|ый *adj.* table-, occurring at table; **~ая бесе́да** table-talk; **~ая пе́сня** drinking-song.

застóпорива|ть(ся), ю(сь) *impf. of* **застóпорить(ся)**

застóпор|ить, ю, ишь, *pf.* (*of* **~ивать**) (*tech.*) to stop; (*fig., coll.*) to bring to a standstill.

застóпор|иться, юсь, ишься *pf.* (*of* **~иваться**) (*tech.*) to stop (*of a machine*); (*fig., coll.*) to come to a standstill.

засто|я́ться, ю́сь, и́шься *pf.* (*of* **застáиваться**) **1.** to stand too long. **2.** to stagnate.

застрáива|ть, ю *impf. of* **застрóить**

застрахóван|ный *p.p.p. of* **застраховáть** *and adj.* insured; *as n.* **з., ~ного** *m.* insured person.

застрах|овáть, ýю *pf.* (*of* **страховáть** *and* **~óвывать**) (**от**) to insure (against).

застрах|овáться, ýюсь *pf.* (*of* **страховáться** *and* **~óвываться**) to insure o.s.

застрахóвыва|ть(ся), ю(сь) *impf. of* **застраховáть(ся)**

застрáчива|ть, ю *impf. of* **застрочи́ть**

застращá|ть, ю *pf.* (*coll.*) to frighten, intimidate.

застрáщива|ть, ю *impf. of* **застращáть**

застревá|ть, ю *impf. of* **застря́ть**

застрéлива|ть(ся), ю(сь) *impf. of* **застрели́ть(ся)**

застрел|и́ть, ю́, ~́ишь *pf.* (*of* **~́ивать**) to shoot (dead).

застрел|и́ться, ю́сь, ~́ишься *pf.* (*of* **~́иваться**) to shoot o.s.; to blow one's brains out.

застрéльщик, а *m.* pioneer, leader; **з. нóвых мод** trendsetter.

застрó|ить, ю, ишь *pf.* (*of* **застрáивать**) to build (over, on, up).

застрóйк|а, и *f.* building; **прáво ~и** building permit.

застроч|и́ть, ý, ~́ишь *pf.* **1.** (*impf.* **застрáчивать**) to sew up, stitch up. **2.** (*coll.*) to dash off (*a letter, etc.*). **3.** (*coll.*) to blaze, rattle away (*of or with automatic weapon*).

застря́|ну, нешь *see* **~ть**

застря́|ть, ну, нешь *pf.* (*of* **застревáть**) **1.** to stick; **з. в грязи́** to get stuck in the mud; **словá ~ли у негó в гóрле** the words stuck in his throat. **2.** (*fig., coll.*) to be held up; to become bogged down.

засту|ди́ться, жýсь, ~́дишься *pf.* (*of* **~́живаться**) (*coll.*) to catch cold, catch a chill.

застýжива|ться, юсь *impf. of* **застуди́ться**

зáступ, а *m.* spade.

заступá|ться, ю(сь) *impf. of* **заступи́ться**

заступ|и́ться, лю́сь, ~́ишься *pf.* (**за**+*a.*) to stand up for; to take s.o.'s part; to plead (for).

застýпник, а *m.* defender; intercessor.

застýпничеств|о, а *nt.* intercession.

застывá|ть, ю *impf. of* **засты́ть**

засты|ди́ть, жý, ди́шь *pf.* (*coll.*) to shame, cause to feel shame.

засты|ди́ться, жýсь, ди́шься *pf.* (*coll.*) to feel shame; to become confused.

засты|жý, ди́шь *see* **~ди́ть**

засты́|ну, нешь *see* **~ть**

засты́|нуть = **~ть**

засты́|ть *and* **~нуть, ну, нешь** *pf.* (*of* **~вáть**) **1.** to thicken, set; to harden; to congeal, coagulate. **2.** (*coll.*) to become stiff; (*fig.*): **з. от ýжаса** to be paralysed with fright. **3.** (*coll.*) to freeze (*also fig.*).

засýн|уть, у, ешь *pf.* (*of* **засóвывать**) to stick in, shove in; to tuck in; **з. рýки в кармáн** to thrust one's hands into one's pockets.

зáсух|а, и *f.* drought.

засухоустóйчив|ый (~, ~а) *adj.* (*agric.*) drought-resistant.

засýчива|ть, ю *impf. of* **засучи́ть**

засуч|и́ть, ý, ~́ишь *pf.* (*of* **~́ивать**) (**рукавá,** *etc.*) to roll up (*sleeves, etc.*).

засýшива|ть(ся), ю(сь) *impf. of* **засуши́ть(ся)**

засуш|и́ть, ý, ~́ишь *pf.* (*of* **~́ивать**) to dry up (*plants; also fig.*).

засуш|и́ться, ýсь, ~́ишься *pf.* (*of* **~́иваться**) to dry up (*intrans.*), shrivel.

засýшлив|ый (~, ~а) *adj.* parched, arid.

засчит|áть, áю *pf.* (*of* **~́ывать**) to take into consideration; **з. в уплáту дóлга** to reckon towards payment of a debt.

засчи́тыва|ть, ю *impf. of* **засчитáть**

засылá|ть, ю *impf. of* **заслáть**

засы́п|ать, лю, лешь *pf.* (*of* **~áть**[2]) **1.** to fill up. **2.** (+*i.*) to cover (with), strew (with); **дорóжка былá ~ана опáвшими ли́стьями** the path was strewn with fallen leaves. **3.** (+*i.*; *fig., coll.*) **з. вопрóсами** to bombard with questions; **з. поздравлéниями** to shower congratulations (on). **4.** (+*a. or g.* **в**+*a.*; *coll.*) to put (into), add (to); **з. овсá в я́сли** to pour oats into the manger.

засыпá|ть[1]**, ю** *impf. of* **заснýть**

засыпá|ть[2]**, ю** *impf. of* **засы́пать**

засы́п|аться, люсь, лешься *pf.* (*of* **~áться**[2]) **1.** to get into; **песóк ~ался мне в башмаки́** I have got sand in my shoes. **2.** (+*i.*) *pass. of* **~ать**

засыпá|ться[1]**, юсь** *impf. of* **заспáться**

засыпá|ться[2]**, юсь** *impf. of* **засы́паться**

засыхá|ть, ю *impf. of* **засóхнуть**

зас|я́ду, я́дешь *see* **~éсть**

заавр|и́ть, ю́, и́шь *pf.* (*of* **таври́ть**) to brand (*cattle, etc.*).

затаён|ный *p.p.p. of* **затаи́ть** *and adj.* secret; suppressed; **~ная мечтá** secret dream.

затáива|ть(ся), ю(сь) *impf. of* **затаи́ть(ся)**

зата|и́ть, ю́, и́шь *pf.* (*of* **~́ивать**) **1.** to conceal; to suppress; **з. дыхáние** to hold one's breath. **2.** to harbour, cherish; **з. оби́ду (на**+*a.*) to nurse a grievance (against).

зата|и́ться, ю́сь, и́шься *pf.* (*of* **~́иваться**) (*coll.*) to hide (*intrans.*); **з. в себé** (*fig.*) to become reserved, withdraw into o.s.

затáлкива|ть, ю *impf. of* **затолкáть** *and* **затолкнýть**

затáплива|ть[1,2]**, ю** *impf. of* **затопи́ть**[1,2]

затáптыва|ть, ю *impf. of* **затоптáть**

затáсканный *p.p.p. of* **затаскáть** *and adj.* worn; threadbare; (*fig.*) hackneyed, trite.

затаск|áть, áю *pf.* (*of* **~́ивать**[1]) (*coll.*) **1.** to wear out; to make dirty (with wear); (*fig.*) to make hackneyed, make trite. **2.** to drag about; **з. по судáм** to drag through the courts.

затáскива|ть[1]**, ю** *impf. of* **затаскáть**

затáскива|ть[2]**, ю** *impf. of* **затащи́ть**

затáчива|ть, ю *impf. of* **заточи́ть**[1]

затащ|и́ть, ý, ~́ишь *pf.* (*of* **затáскивать**[2]) (*coll.*) to drag off, drag away; (*fig.*): **они́ ~и́ли егó в теáтр** they have dragged him off to the theatre.

затвердевá|ть, ю *impf. of* **затвердéть**

затвердéлый *adj.* hardened.

затвердéни|е, я *nt.* **1.** hardening. **2.** (*med.*) callus.

затвердé|ть, ю *pf.* (*of* **~вáть**) to harden, become hard; to set.

затвер|ди́ть, жý, ди́шь *pf.* (*of* **~́живать**) (*coll.*) **1.** to learn by rote; to memorize. **2.: з. однó и то же** to harp on one string.

затвéржива|ть, ю *impf. of* **затверди́ть**

затвóр, а *m.* **1.** bolt, bar; breech-block (*of fire-arm*); **2.** (*phot.*) shutter.

затвор|и́ть, ю́, ~́ишь *pf.* (*of* **~я́ть**) to shut, close.

затвор|и́ться, ю́сь ~́ишься *pf.* (*of* **~я́ться**) **1.** to shut, close (*intrans.*). **2.** to shut o.s. in, lock o.s. in. **3.** (*eccl.*): **з. в монасты́рь, в монастырé** to go into a monastery.

затвóрник, а *m.* hermit, recluse; **он живёт совершéнным ~ом** (*fig.*) he is a complete recluse.

затво́рни|ческий *adj.* *of* **~к**; solitary; **~ческая жизнь** the life of a recluse.
затво́рничеств|о, а *nt.* (*eccl.*) seclusion, solitary life.
затвор|я́ть(ся), я́ю(сь) *impf. of* **~и́ть(ся)**
затева́|ть, ю *impf. of* **зате́ять**
зате́йлив|ый (~, ~а) *adj.* **1.** intricate, involved; **~ая речь** involved discourse. **2.** ingenious; inventive; **~ая игру́шка** ingenious toy.
зате́йник, а *m.* **1.** practical joker; humorist. **2.** entertainer; organizer (*of entertainments*).
зате́йщик, а *m.* (*coll.*) instigator.
затёк, ла́ *see* **зате́чь**
затека́|ть, ю́ *impf. of* **зате́чь**
зате|ку́, чёшь, ку́т *see* **~́чь**
зате́м *adv.* **1.** then, next. **2.** for that reason; **з. что** because, since, as; **заче́м ты прие́хала? з., что слыха́ла, что ты заболе́л** why have you come? because I heard that you had been taken ill; **з. что́бы** in order that; in order to; **она́ прие́хала з., что́бы уха́живать за тобо́й** she has come (in order) to look after you.
затемне́ни|е, я *nt.* **1.** darkening; obscuring (*also fig.*). **2.** (*mil.*) black-out. **3.** (*psych.*) black-out.
затемн|и́ть, ю́, и́шь *pf.* (*of* **~я́ть**) **1.** to darken; to obscure (*also fig.*). **2.** (*mil.*) to black-out.
за́темно *adv.* (*coll.*) before daybreak.
затемн|я́ть, я́ю *impf. of* **~и́ть**
затен|и́ть, ю́, и́шь *pf.* (*of* **~я́ть**) to shade.
затен|я́ть, я́ю *impf. of* **~и́ть**
зат|ере́ть, ру́, рёшь, *past* **~ёр, ~ёрла** *pf.* (*of* **~ира́ть**) **1.** to rub out. **2.** to block, jam; (*impers.*): **су́дно ~ёрло льда́ми** the ship was ice-bound.
зат|ере́ться, ру́сь, рёшься, *past* **~ёрся, ~ёрлась** *pf.* (*of* **~ира́ться**) (*coll.*) (**в**+*a.*) to get (into), worm one's way (into).
зате́рива|ть(ся), ю(сь) *impf. of* **затеря́ть(ся)**
зате́рпн|уть, ет *pf. of* **те́рпнуть**
зате́рянный *p.p.p. of* **затеря́ть** *and adj.* forgotten, forsaken.
затер|я́ть, я́ю *pf.* (*of* **~́ивать**) (*coll.*) to lose, mislay.
затер|я́ться, я́юсь *pf.* (*of* **~́иваться**) to be lost, be mislaid; (*fig.*) to become forgotten; **моё перо́ ~я́лось** (*coll.*) my pen has vanished; **з. в толпе́** to be lost in a crowd.
зате|са́ть, шу́, ~́шешь *pf.* (*of* **~́сывать**) to rough-hew; to sharpen (*stake, etc.*).
зате|са́ться, шу́сь, ~́шешься *pf.* (*of* **~́сываться**) (*coll.*) to worm one's way in, intrude.
затесн|и́ть, ю́, и́шь *pf.* (*of* **~я́ть**) (*coll.*) **1.** to jostle, press. **2.** (*fig.*) to oppress, persecute.
затесн|и́ться, ю́сь, и́шься *pf.* (*of* **~я́ться**) (*coll.*) to begin to crowd.
затесн|я́ть(ся), я́ю(сь) *impf. of* **~и́ть(ся)**
затёсыва|ть(ся), ю(сь) *impf. of* **затеса́ть(ся)**
зате́|чь, ку́, чёшь, ку́т, *past* **~́к, ~кла́** *pf.* (*of* **~ка́ть**) **1.** (**в**+*a.*; **за**+*a.*) to pour, flow, leak (into; behind). **2.** to swell up. **3.** to become numb; **у меня́ нога́ ~кла́** my foot has gone numb.
зате́|я, и *f.* **1.** undertaking, enterprise, venture. **2.** (*usu. pl.*) amusement; escapade; practical joke; **жить без ~й** to live simply, unpretentiously.
зате́|ять, ю *pf.* (*of* **~ва́ть**) (*coll.*) to undertake, venture; to organize; **з. дра́ку** to start a fight.
затира́|ть(ся), ю(сь) *impf. of* **затере́ть(ся)**
зати́ск|ать, аю *pf.* (*of* **~ивать**) (*coll.*) to smother with caresses.
зати́скива|ть(ся), ю(сь) *impf. of* **зати́скать** *and* **зати́снуть(ся)**
зати́с|нуть, ну, нешь *pf.* (*of* **~кивать**) (*coll.*) to squeeze in.
зати́с|нуться, нусь, нешься *pf.* (*of* **~киваться**) (*coll.*) to squeeze (o.s.) in.
затих|а́ть, а́ю *impf. of* **~́нуть**
зати́х|нуть, ну, нешь, *past* **~, ~ла** *pf.* (*of* **~а́ть**) to die down, abate; to die away, fade (*of noise*).
зати́ш|е, я *nt.* calm; lull.
заткн|у́ть, у́, ёшь *pf.* (*of* **затыка́ть**) **1.** (+*a. and i.*) to stop up; to plug; **з. буты́лку про́бкой** to cork a bottle; **з. рот, гло́тку кому́-н.** (*coll.*) to shut s.o. up; **~й гло́тку!** shut up! **2.** to stick, thrust; **з. кого́-н. за по́яс** (*fig., coll.*) to outdo s.o.
заткн|у́ться, у́сь, ёшься *pf.* (*coll.*) to shut up; **~и́сь!** shut up!
затмева́|ть, ю *impf. of* **затми́ть**
затме́ни|е, я *nt.* (*astron.*) eclipse.
затм|и́ть, и́шь *pf.* (*of* **~ева́ть**) **1.** to darken. **2.** (*fig.*) to eclipse; to overshadow.
зато́ *conj.* (*coll.*) but then, but on the other hand; but to make up for it; **до́рого, з. хоро́шая вещь** it is expensive, but then it is good.
затова́ренност|ь, и *f.* (*econ.*) glut.
затова́ренный *p.p.p. of* **затова́рить** *and adj.* (*econ.*) surplus.
затова́ривани|е, я *nt.* glutting; overstocking.
затова́рива|ть(ся), ю(сь) *impf. of* **затова́рить(ся)**
затова́р|ить, ю, ишь *pf.* (*of* **~ивать**) (*econ.*) to accumulate (excess stock of), overstock.
затова́р|иться, юсь, ишься *pf.* (*of* **~иваться**) (*econ.*) **1.** to be over-stocked. **2.** (*coll.*) to have a surplus.
затолка́|ть, ю *pf.* (*of* **зата́лкивать**) to jostle.
затолкн|у́ть, у́, ёшь *pf.* (*of* **зата́лкивать**) (*coll.*) to shove in.
зато́н, а *m.* **1.** backwater. **2.** boat-yard.
затон|у́ть, у́, ~́ешь *pf.* to sink (*intrans.*).
затоп|и́ть[1]**, лю́, ~́ишь** *pf.* (*of* **зата́пливать**) to light (*a stove*); to turn on the heating.
затоп|и́ть[2]**, лю́, ~́ишь** *pf.* (*of* **~ля́ть**) **1.** to flood; to submerge. **2.** to sink; **з. кора́бль** to scuttle a ship.
затопля́ть, ю *impf. of* **затопи́ть**[2]
затоп|та́ть, чу́, ~́чешь *pf.* (*of* **зата́птывать**) to trample (down, in); to trample underfoot.
затоп|чу́, ~́чешь *see* **~та́ть**
зато́р, а *m.* blocking, obstruction; **з. у́личного движе́ния** traffic-jam.
затормо|зи́ть, жу́, зи́шь *pf. of* **тормози́ть**
заточ|а́ть, а́ю *impf. of* **~и́ть**[2]
заточе́ни|е, я *nt.* confinement; incarceration, captivity.
заточ|и́ть[1]**, у́, ~́ишь** *pf.* (*of* **зата́чивать**) to sharpen.
заточ|и́ть[2]**, у́, ~и́шь** *pf.* (*of* **~а́ть**) to confine, shut up; to incarcerate.
затрав|и́ть, лю́, ~́ишь *pf.* (*of* **трави́ть**[1] *and* **~́ливать**) to hunt down, bring to bay; (*fig., coll.*) to persecute; to badger; to worry the life out of.
затра́влива|ть, ю *impf. of* **затрави́ть**
затра́гива|ть, ю *impf. of* **затро́нуть**
затрапе́зный *adj.* **1.** working-, every-day (*of clothing*). **2.** shabby.
затра́т|а, ы *f.* expense; outlay.
затра́|тить, чу, тишь *pf.* (*of* **~чивать**) to expend, spend.
затра́чива|ть, ю *impf. of* **затра́тить**
затре́б|овать, ую *pf.* to request, require; to ask for.
затреп|а́ть, лю́, ~́лешь *pf.* (*of* **~́ывать**) to wear out; to make dirty (with wear).
затреп|а́ться, лю́сь, ~́лешься *pf.* (*of* **~́ываться**) **1.** to wear out (*intrans.*), be worn out. **2.** (*fig.*): **я совсе́м ~а́лся** (*coll.*) I have stayed gossiping too long.
затрёпыва|ть(ся), ю(сь) *impf. of* **затрепа́ть(ся)**
затре́щин|а, ы *f.* (*coll.*) box on the ears.
затро́н|уть, у, ешь *pf.* (*of* **затра́гивать**) **1.** to affect; to touch, graze. **2.** (*fig.*) to touch (on); **з. вопро́с** to broach a question; **з. чьё-н. самолю́бие** to wound

s.o.'s self-esteem.
затруднéни|е, я *nt.* difficulty.
затруднённый *p.p.p. of* **затрудни́ть** *and adj.* laboured.
затрудни́тельност|ь, и *f.* difficulty; straits.
затрудни́тел|ьный (~ен, ~ьна) *adj.* difficult; embarrassing.
затрудн|и́ть, ю́, и́шь *pf.* (*of* **~я́ть**) **1.** to trouble; to cause trouble (to); to embarrass. **2.** to make difficult; to hamper.
затрудн|и́ться, ю́сь, и́шся *pf.* (*of* **~я́ться**) (*+inf. or i.*) to have difficulty (in); **з. отвéтом** to find difficulty in replying.
затрудн|я́ть(ся), я́ю(сь) *impf. of* **~и́ть(ся)**
затумáн|ивать(ся), иваю(сь), иваешь(ся) *impf. of* **~ить(ся)**
затумáн|ить, ю, ишь *pf.* (*of* **~ивать**) **1.** to befog; to cloud, dim; (*impers.*): **~ило горизóнт** the horizon was obscured by fog; **слёзы ~или её глазá** tears dimmed her eyes. **2.** (*fig.*) to obscure.
затумáн|иться, юсь, ишься *pf.* (*of* **~иваться**) **1.** to grow foggy, become clouded (with). **2.** (*fig.*) to become obscure.
затуп|и́ть, лю́, ~ишь *pf.* (*of* **~ля́ть**) to blunt; to dull.
затуп|и́ться, лю́сь, ~ишься *pf.* (*of* **~ля́ться**) to become blunt(ed).
затупля́|ть(ся), ю(сь) *impf. of* **затупи́ть(ся)**
затух|áть, áет *impf. of* **~нуть**
затýх|нуть, нет, *past* **~, ~ла** *pf.* (*of* **~áть**) **1.** to go out, be extinguished. **2.** (*fig., coll.*) to die away (*of sounds*).
затуш|евáть, ýю *pf.* (*of* **~ёвывать**) **1.** to shade. **2.** (*fig., coll.*) to conceal; to draw a veil over.
затушёвыва|ть, ю *impf. of* **затушевáть**
затуш|и́ть, ý, ~ишь *pf.* to put out, extinguish; (*fig.*) to suppress.
зáтхлый *adj.* mouldy, musty; stuffy; (*fig.*) stagnant.
затыкá|ть, ю *impf. of* **заткнýть**
заты́л|ок, ка *m.* **1.** back of the head; (*anat.*) occiput. **2.: станови́ться в з.** to form up in file.
заты́лочный *adj.* (*anat.*) occipital.
заты́чк|а, и *f.* (*coll.*) stopper; plug.
затя́гива|ть(ся), ю(сь) *impf. of* **затянýть(ся)**
затя́жк|а, и *f.* **1.** inhaling (*in smoking*). **2.** prolongation; (*coll.*) dragging out. **3.** delaying, putting off.
затяжн|óй, *adj.* long drawn-out, protracted; **~áя болéзнь** lingering illness.
затя|нýть, нý, ~нешь *pf.* (*of* **~гивать**) **1.** to tighten; to draw, pull tight; (*naut.*) to haul taut. **2.** to cover; to close; (*impers.*): **нéбо ~нýло тýчами** it has clouded over; **рáну ~нýло** the wound has closed. **3.** (*coll.*) to drag down, drag in; (*fig.*) to inveigle. **4.** (*coll.*) to drag out, spin out. **5.: з. пéсню** (*coll.*) to strike up a song.
затя|нýться, нýсь, ~нешься *pf.* (*of* **~гиваться**) **1.** to lace o.s. up; **з. пóясом** to tighten one's belt. **2.** to be covered; to close (*intrans.*), heal over (of a wound). **3.** (*coll.*) to be delayed; to linger; to drag on (*intrans.*); **вечери́нка ~нýлась до пóлночи** the party dragged on till midnight. **4.** to inhale (*in smoking*).
заýмн|ый *adj.* abstruse, esoteric; nonsensical.
зауны́в|ный (~ен, ~на) *adj.* doleful, plaintive.
заупокóйн|ый *adj.* for the repose of the soul (*of the dead*); **~ая слýжба** requiem.
зауря́м|иться, люсь, ишься *pf.* to turn obstinate.
заурéд|ный (~ен, ~на) *adj.* ordinary, commonplace; mediocre.
заусéниц|а, ы *f.* **1.** agnail, hangnail. **2.** (*tech.*) burr.
заýтрен|я, и *f.* (*eccl.*) prime.
заýченный *p.p.p. of* **заучи́ть** *and adj.* studied.
заýчива|ть(ся), ю(сь) *impf. of* **заучи́ть(ся)**
зау|чи́ть, чý, ~чишь *pf.* (*of* **~чивать**) **1.** to learn by heart. **2.** (*coll.*) to din learning into.
зауч|и́ться, ýсь, ~ишься *pf.* (*of* **~иваться**) (*coll.*) to study too hard.
заушáтельский *adj.* disparaging, abusive.
заушáтельств|о, а *nt.* disparagement, abuse.
заýшниц|а, ы *f.* (*med.*) mumps.
зафарши|ровáть, ýю *pf. of* **фаршировáть**
зафикси́р|овать, ую *pf. of* **фикси́ровать**
зафрахт|овáть, ýю *pf.* (*of* **фрахтовáть** *and* **~óвывать**) to charter, freight.
зафрахтóвыва|ть, ю *impf. of* **зафрахтовáть**
захáжива|ть, ю *freq. of* **заходи́ть**[1]**; он чáсто к нам ~л** he often used to drop in on us.
захвáлива|ть, ю *impf. of* **захвали́ть**
захвал|и́ть, ю́, ~ишь *pf.* (*coll.*) to praise to excess; to spoil by flattery.
захвáт, а *m.* **1.** seizure, capture. **2.** (*tech.*) claw.
захвáтанный *p.p.p. of* **захватáть** *and adj.* soiled by handling, thumbed; (*fig., coll.*) trite, hackneyed.
захват|áть, áю *pf.* (*of* **~ывать**[2]) (*coll.*) to soil by handling; to thumb.
захва|ти́ть, чý, ~тишь *pf.* (*of* **~тывать**[1]) **1.** to take; **з. горсть ви́шен** to take a handful of cherries; **они́ ~ти́ли с собóй детéй** they have taken the children with them. **2.** to seize; to capture; **з. власть** to seize power; **мы ~ти́ли три́ста плéнных** we took three hundred prisoners. **3.** (*fig.*) to carry away; to thrill, excite; **кни́га меня́ ~ти́ла** I was thrilled by the book. **4.** (*coll.*) to catch; **з. послéдний пóезд** to catch the last train; **я успéл з. егó в кабинéте** I managed to catch him in his office; **~ти́ла ли тебя́ грозá?** were you caught by the storm? **5.** to stop, check (*an illness, etc.*) in time. **6.** (*impers.*): **от э́того у меня́ дух ~ти́ло** it took my breath away.
захвáтнический *adj.* (*pej.*) predatory; expansionist.
захвáтчик, а *m.* invader; aggressor.
захвáтыва|ть[1]**, ю** *impf. of* **захвати́ть**
захвáтыва|ть[2]**, ю** *impf. of* **захватáть**
захвáтыва|ющий *pres. part. act. of* **~ть**[1] *and adj.* (*fig.*) gripping; **слýшать нóвости с ~ющим интерéсом** to listen to news with keen interest.
захворá|ть, ю *pf.* (*coll.*) to be taken ill.
захилé|ть, ю *pf. of* **хилéть**
захирéлый *adj.* faded; ailing.
захирé|ть, ю *pf. of* **хирéть**
захлеб|нýться, нýсь, нёшься *pf.* (*of* **~ываться**) **1.** to choke (*intrans.*); to swallow the wrong way. **2.** (*fig., coll.*): **з. от востóрга** to be transported with delight; **атáка ~нýлась** (*mil.*) the attack misfired.
захлёбыва|ться, юсь *impf.* (*of* **захлебнýться**) to choke (*intrans.*); (*fig.*): **з. от смéха** to choke with laughter; **говори́ть ~ющимся гóлосом** to speak in a voice choked with emotion.
захлест|нýть, нý, нёшь *pf.* (*of* **~ывать**) **1.** to fasten, secure. **2.** to flow over, swamp, overwhelm; (*fig.*): **её ~нýла волнá счáстья** a wave of happiness flowed over her.
захлёстыва|ть, ю *impf. of* **захлестнýть**
захлóп|нуть, ну, нешь *pf.* (*of* **~ывать**) **1.** to slam. **2.** to shut in.
захлóп|нуться, нусь, нешься *pf.* (*of* **~ываться**) to slam to; to close with a bang.
захлóпыва|ть(ся), ю(сь) *impf. of* **захлóпнуть(ся)**
захмелé|ть, ю *pf. of* **хмелéть**
захóд, а *m.* **1. (сóлнца)** sunset. **2.** call (at), putting in (at); **э́тот парохóд пришёл из Амéрики без ~а в Шербýр** this ship has arrived from America without calling at Cherbourg.
захо|ди́ть[1]**, жý, ~дишь** *impf. of* **зайти́**
захо|ди́ть[2]**, жý, ~дишь** *pf.* to begin to walk; **он ~ди́л по кóмнате** he began to pace up and down the room.

захо|жу́, ⁓дишь *see* **⁓ди́ть**
захолоде́|ть, ю *pf.* (*coll.*) to become cold; (*impers.*) to turn cold.
захолу́стный *adj.* remote; out-of-the-way.
захолу́ст|ье, ья, *g. pl.* **⁓ий** (*coll.* **⁓ьев**) *nt.* out-of-the-way place.
захороне́ни|е, я *nt.* burial.
захорон|и́ть, ю́, ⁓ишь *pf.* (*of* **хорони́ть**) to bury.
захо|те́ть(ся), чу́(сь) ⁓чешь(ся), ти́м(ся), ти́те(сь), тя́т(ся) *pf. of* **хоте́ть(ся)**
захуда́лый *adj.* impoverished; run-down.
заца́п|ать, аю *pf.* (*of* **⁓ывать**) (*coll.*) to grab; to lay hold of.
заца́пыва|ть, ю *impf. of* **заца́пать**
зацве|сти́, ту́, тёшь, *past* **⁓л, ⁓ла́** *pf.* (*of* **⁓та́ть**) to break into blossom.
зацвета́|ть, ю *impf. of* **зацвести́**
зацве|ту́, тёшь *see* **⁓сти́**
зацел|ова́ть, у́ю *pf.* (*coll.*) to smother with kisses, rain kisses on.
зацеп|и́ть, лю́, ⁓ишь *pf.* (*of* **⁓ля́ть**) **1.** to hook. **2.** (**за**+ *a.*) to catch (on); **з. ного́й за ка́мень** to catch one's foot on a stone.
зацеп|и́ться, лю́сь, ⁓ишься *pf.* (*of* **⁓ля́ться**) (**за**+*a.*) to catch (on), get caught (on); **чуло́к у неё ⁓и́лся за гвоздь** her stocking caught on a nail.
заце́пк|а, и *f.* (*coll.*) **1.** peg, hook. **2.** (*fig.*) pull, connections. **3.** hitch, catch (*fig.*).
зацепля́|ть(ся), ю(сь) *impf. of* **зацепи́ть(ся)**
зачаро́ванный *p.p.p. of* **зачарова́ть** *and adj.* spellbound.
зачар|ова́ть, у́ю *pf.* (*of* **⁓о́вывать**) to bewitch, enchant, captivate.
зачаро́выва|ть, ю *impf. of* **зачарова́ть**
зача|сти́ть, щу́, сти́шь *pf.* (*coll.*) **1.** (+ *inf.*) to take (to); **он ⁓сти́л игра́ть в те́ннис по вечера́м** he has taken to playing tennis in the evening; **они́ ⁓сти́ли к нам в го́сти** they have become regular visitors at our house. **2.** to begin to go fast; **докла́дчик ⁓сти́л так, что переводи́ть его́ слова́ ста́ло невозмо́жно** the speaker began to go so fast that it was impossible to translate; **дождь ⁓сти́л** it began to rain cats and dogs.
зачасту́ю *adv.* (*coll.*) often, frequently.
зача́ти|е, я *nt.* (*physiol.*) conception.
зача́т|ок, ка *m.* **1.** embryo. **2.** (*usu. pl.*; *fig.*) beginning, germ.
зача́точн|ый *adj.* rudimentary; **в ⁓ом состоя́нии** in embryo.
зач|а́ть, ну́, нёшь, *past.* **⁓а́л, ⁓ала́, ⁓а́ло** *pf.* (*of* **⁓ина́ть**) to conceive (*trans. and intrans.*).
зача́х|нуть, ну, нешь, *past* **⁓нул** *and* **⁓, ⁓ла** *pf. of* **ча́хнуть**
зача|щу́, сти́шь *see* **⁓сти́ть**
зач|ёл, ла́ *see* **⁓е́сть**
заче́м *interrog. and rel. adv.* why; what for; **з. ты пришла́?** why did you come? **вот з. пришла́** that's why I came.
заче́м-то *adv.* for some reason or other.
зачёркива|ть, ю *impf. of* **зачеркну́ть**
зачерк|ну́ть, ну́, нёшь *pf.* (*of* **⁓ивать**) to cross out, strike out.
зачерн|и́ть, ю́, и́шь *pf.* (*of* **черни́ть 1.** *and* **⁓я́ть**) to blacken, paint black.
зачерн|я́ть, я́ю *impf. of* **⁓и́ть**
зачерп|ну́ть, ну́, нёшь *pf.* (*of* **⁓ывать**) to draw up, scoop; to ladle.
заче́рпыва|ть, ю *impf. of* **зачерпну́ть**
зачерстве́лый *adj.* stale; (*fig.*) hard-hearted.
зачерстве́|ть, ю *pf. of* **черстве́ть 1.**
заче|са́ть, шу́, ⁓шешь *pf.* **1.** to begin to scratch. **2.** (*impf.* **⁓сывать**) to comb back.
заче|са́ться, шу́сь, ⁓шешься *pf.* (*coll.*) **1.** to begin to scratch o.s. **2.** to begin to itch.
зач|е́сть, ту́, тёшь, *past* **⁓ёл, ⁓ла́** *pf.* (*of* **⁓иты-вать**[1]) **1.** to take into account, reckon as, credit; **з. де́сять рубле́й в упла́ту до́лга** to account ten roubles towards payment of a debt; **з. проведённый на вое́нной слу́жбе год за два го́да** to reckon a year spent on war service as two years. **2.** (*+d. and a.*) to pass (*trans.*); **мы ⁓ли́ ему́ перево́д с францу́зского** we passed him in French translation.
зачёсыва|ть, ю *impf. of* **зачеса́ть**
зачёт, а *m.* **1.** reckoning. **2.** test (*in school, etc.*); **получи́ть з., сдать з.** (**по**+ *d.*) to pass a test (in); **поста́вить** (+ *d.*) **з.** (**по**+ *d.*) to pass (in); **поста́вили мне з. по исто́рии** they have passed me in history.
зачёт|ный *adj. of* **⁓. 1.: ⁓ная квита́нция** receipt. **2.: ⁓ная кни́жка** (student's) record book; **⁓ная се́ссия** test period.
зачехл|и́ть, ю́, и́шь *pf. of* **чехли́ть**
зач|ешу́, ⁓е́шешь *see* **⁓еса́ть**
зачина́тел|ь, я *m.* (*rhet.*) author, founder.
зачина́|ть, ю *impf. of* **зача́ть**
зачи́нива|ть, ю *impf. of* **зачини́ть**
зачин|и́ть, ю́, ⁓ишь *pf.* (*of* **⁓ивать**) (*coll.*) to mend; to patch; to sharpen (*a pencil*).
зачи́нщик, а *m.* (*pej.*) instigator, ring-leader.
зачисле́ни|е, я *nt.* enrolment.
зачи́сл|ить, ю, ишь *pf.* (*of* **⁓я́ть**) **1.** to include; **з. в счёт** to enter in an account. **2.** to enrol, enlist; **з. в штат** to take on the staff, on the strength.
зачи́сл|иться, юсь, ишься *pf.* (*of* **⁓я́ться**) (**в**+ *a.*) **1.** to join, enter. **2.** *pass. of* **⁓ить**
зачисл|я́ть(ся), я́ю(сь) *impf. of* **⁓ить(ся)**
зачит|а́ть, а́ю *pf.* (*of* **⁓ывать**[2]) (*coll.*) **1.** to read out. **2.** to fail to return (*a borrowed book*).
зачит|а́ться, а́юсь *pf.* (*of* **⁓ываться**) to become engrossed in reading; to go on reading; **я ⁓а́лся далеко́ за́ полночь** I went on reading until way past midnight.
зачи́тыва|ть[1]**, ю** *impf. of* **заче́сть**
зачи́тыва|ть[2]**, ю** *impf. of* **зачита́ть**
зачи́тыва|ться, юсь *impf.* **1.** *impf. of* **зачита́ться.** **2.** *pass. of* **⁓ть**[2]
зач|ну́, нёшь *see* **⁓а́ть**
зачтён|ный (⁓, ⁓а́) *p.p.p. of* **заче́сть**
зач|ту́, тёшь *see* **⁓е́сть**
зашварт|ова́ть, у́ю *pf.* (*of* **⁓о́вывать**) (*naut.*) to moor, tie up.
зашварт|ова́ться, у́юсь *pf.* (*of* **⁓о́вываться**) (*naut.*) to moor, tie up (*intrans.*).
зашварто́выва|ть(ся), ю(сь) *impf. of* **зашварто-ва́ть(ся)**
зашвы́рива|ть, ю *impf. of* **зашвырну́ть** *and* **за-швыря́ть**
зашвыр|ну́ть, ну́, нёшь *pf.* (*of* **⁓ивать**) (*coll.*) to throw, fling (away).
зашвыр|я́ть, я́ю *pf.* (*of* **⁓ивать**) (*+a. and i.*; *coll.*) to shower (with); **з. кого́-н. ка́мнями** to throw stones at s.o.
зашиб|а́ть, а́ю *impf.* (*coll.*) **1.** *impf. of* **⁓и́ть.** **2.** to drink (*intrans.*).
зашиб|а́ться, а́юсь *impf. of* **⁓и́ться**
зашиб|и́ть, у́, ёшь, *past* **⁓, ⁓ла** *pf.* (*of* **⁓а́ть**) (*coll.*) **1.** to bruise, knock, hurt; **он ⁓ себе́ коле́но** he has bruised his knee. **2.: з. деньгу́** (*sl.*) to coin money.
зашиб|и́ться, у́сь, ёшься, *past* **⁓ся, ⁓лась** *pf.* (*of* **⁓а́ться**) (*coll.*) to bruise o.s., knock o.s.
зашива́ть, ю *impf. of* **заши́ть**
заш|и́ть, ью́, ьёшь *pf.* (*of* **⁓ива́ть**) **1.** to mend. **2.** to sew up; **з. посы́лку в холст** to sew up a parcel in sacking. **3.** (*med.*) to put (a) stitch(es) in.
зашифр|ова́ть, у́ю *pf.* (*of* **шифрова́ть** *and* **⁓о́вы-вать**) to encipher, put into code.
зашифро́выва|ть, ю *impf. of* **зашифрова́ть**

за|шлю́, шлёшь *see* **~сла́ть**

зашнур|ова́ть, у́ю *pf.* (*of* **шнурова́ть** *and* **~о́вывать**) to lace up.

зашнуро́выва|ть, ю *impf. of* **зашнурова́ть**

зашпакл|ева́ть, ю́ю *pf.* (*of* **шпаклева́ть** *and* **~ёвывать**) to putty.

зашпаклёвыва|ть, ю *impf. of* **зашпаклева́ть**

зашпи́л|ить, ю, ишь *pf.* (*of* **~ивать**) to pin up, fasten with a pin.

зашпи́лива|ть, ю *impf. of* **зашпи́лить**

заштемпелева́|ть, ю *pf.* (*of* **штемплева́ть**) to stamp, postmark.

зашто́па|ть, ю *pf.* (*of* **што́пать**) to darn.

заштрих|ова́ть, у́ю *pf. of* **штрихова́ть**

заштукату́рива|ть, ю *impf. of* **заштукату́рить**

заштукату́р|ить, ю, ишь *pf.* (*of* **~ивать**) to plaster.

защёлк|а, и *f.* latch (*of lock*); catch.

защёлкива|ть, ю *impf. of* **защёлкнуть**

защёлк|нуть, ну, нешь *pf.* (*of* **~ивать**) (*coll.*) to latch.

защем|и́ть, лю́, и́шь *pf.* (*of* **~ля́ть**) **1.** to pinch, jam, nip; **з. па́лец** to pinch one's finger. **2.** (*impers.*; *coll.*): **у неё ~и́ло се́рдце** her heart aches.

защемля́|ть, ю *impf. of* **защеми́ть**

защи́т|а, ы *no pl., f.* defence; protection; **в ~у** (*+g.*) in defence (of); **под ~ой** (*+g.*) under the protection (of); **свиде́тели ~ы** witnesses for the defence; **з. окружа́ющей среды́** environmentalism.

защи|ти́ть(ся), щу́(сь), ти́шь(ся) *pf. of* **~ща́ть(ся)**

защи́тник, а *m.* **1.** defender, protector; (*leg.*) counsel for the defence; **колле́гия ~ов** the Bar; **з. окружа́ющей среды́** environmentalist. **2.** (*sport*) (full-)back; **ле́вый, пра́вый з.** left, right back.

защи́тн|ый *adj.* protective; **~ые очки́** goggles; **з. цвет** khaki.

защища́|ть, ю *impf.* **1.** (*impf. of* **защити́ть**) to defend, protect. **2.** (*no pl.*) to defend (*leg.*); to stand up for; **з. диссерта́цию** to defend a thesis (*before examiners*).

защища́|ться, юсь *impf.* (*of* **защити́ться**) **1.** to defend o.s., protect o.s. **2.** *pass. of* **~ть**

заяв|и́ть, лю́, ~́ишь *pf.* (*of* **~ля́ть**) (*+a.*, **о***+p. or* **что**) to announce, declare; **з. свои́ права́** (**на***+a.*) to claim one's rights (to); **з. об ухо́де со слу́жбы** to announce one's retirement.

заяв|и́ться, лю́сь, ~́ишься *pf.* (*coll.*) to appear, turn up.

зая́вк|а, и *f.* (**на***+a.*) claim (for); demand (for).

заявле́ни|е, я *nt.* **1.** statement, declaration. **2.** application; **пода́ть з.** to put in an application.

заявля́|ть, ю *impf. of* **заяви́ть**

зая́длый *adj.* (*coll.*) inveterate.

за́|яц, йца *m.* **1.** hare; (*prov.*) **одни́м уда́ром уби́ть двух ~йцев** to kill two birds with one stone. **2.** (*coll.*) stowaway; fare-dodger; **е́хать ~йцем** to travel without paying for a ticket.

за́я|чий *adj. of* **~ц; ~чья губа́** (*med.*) harelip.

зва́ни|е, я *nt.* rank; title; **ры́царское з.** knighthood.

зва́ный *adj.* **1.** invited. **2.** with invited guests; **з. ве́чер** guest-night; **з. обе́д** dinner-party.

зва́тельный *adj.* (*gram.*): **з. паде́ж** vocative case.

зва|ть, зову́, зовёшь, *past* **~л, ~ла́, ~́ло** *impf.* (*of* **по~́**) **1.** to call; **з. на по́мощь** to call for help. **2.** to ask, invite. **3.** (*impf. only*) to call; **как вас зову́т?** what is your name? **меня́ зову́т Влади́мир** my name is Vladimir.

зва́|ться, зову́сь, зовёшься, *past* **~́лся́, ~ла́сь, ~ло́сь** *impf.* (*+i.*; *coll.*) to be called; **её сестра́ ~ла́сь Татья́ной** her sister was called Tatyana.

звезд|а́, ы́, *pl.* **≃ы, ≃, ≃ам** *f.* **1.** star; **но́вая з.** (*astron.*) nova; (*fig.*): **з. экра́на** film star; **ве́рить в свою́ ~у́** to believe in one's lucky star; **роди́ться под счастли́вой ~о́й** to be born under a lucky star; **он ≃ с не́ба не хвата́ет** (*coll.*, *iron.*) he won't set the Thames on fire. **2.** (*zool.*): **морска́я з.** starfish.

звёздно-полоса́тый *adj.*: **з. флаг** the Stars and Stripes, the Star-Spangled Banner (= *national flag of USA*).

звёзд|ный *adj. of* **~а́; ~ная ка́рта** celestial map; **~ная ночь** starlit night; **з. час** finest hour.

звездообра́з|ный (~ен, ~на) *adj.* star-shaped.

звёздочк|а, и *f.* **1.** *dim. of* **звезда́**. **2.** asterisk.

звен|е́ть, ю́, и́шь *impf.* **1.** to ring; **у неё ~е́ло в уша́х** there was a ringing in her ears. **2.** (*+i.*) **з. моне́тами** to jingle coins; **з. стака́нами** to clink glasses.

звен|о́, а́, *pl.* **~́ья, ~́ьев** *nt.* **1.** link (*of a chain*; *also fig.*). **2.** (*fig.*) team, section (*in agriculture, etc.*); (*aeron.*) flight. **3.** row (*of logs*).

звен|ьево́й *adj. of* **~о́**

звер|ёк, ька́ *m. dim. of* **~ь**

зверёныш, а *m.* (*coll.*) young of wild animal; cub.

звере́|ть, ю, ешь *impf.* (*of* **о~**) to become brutalized.

звери́н|ец, ца *m.* menagerie.

звер|и́ный *adj. of* **~ь**; animal; savage.

зверобо́|й[1], я *m.* hunter, trapper.

зверобо́|й[2], я *m.* (*bot.*) St John's wort.

зверово́д, а *m.* fur farmer.

зверово́дств|о, а *nt.* fur farming.

зверово́д|ческий *adj. of* **~ство**

зверол́ов, а *m.* hunter, trapper.

зверол́ов|ный *adj. of* **~; з. про́мысел** hunting, trapping.

звероподо́б|ный (~ен, ~на) *adj.* bestial.

зверофе́рм|а, ы *f.* fur farm.

зве́рски *adv.* **1.** brutally, bestially. **2.** (*coll.*) terribly, awfully; **я з. уста́л** I am terribly tired.

зве́рский *adj.* **1.** brutal, bestial. **2.** (*coll.*) terrific, tremendous; **у него́ з. аппети́т** he has a tremendous appetite.

зве́рств|о, а *nt.* brutality; bestiality; (*pl.*) atrocities.

зве́рств|овать, ую *impf.* to behave with brutality; to commit atrocities.

звер|ь, я, *pl.* **~́и, ~е́й** *m.* **1.** (wild) animal; beast; **пушно́й з.** fur-bearing animal. **2.** (*fig.*) brute, beast; **смотре́ть ~́ем** to glare, glower.

зверь|ё, я́ *no pl., nt.* (*collect.*) wild animals, wild beasts; (*fig.*) brutes, beasts.

звон, а *m.* ringing (sound), peal; **з. моне́т** chinking of coins; **з. стака́нов** clinking of glasses.

звона́р|ь, я́ *m.* bell-ringer.

звон|и́ть, ю́, и́шь *impf.* (*pf. of* **по~**) (**в***+a.*) to ring; **з. кому́-н. (по телефо́ну)** to telephone s.o., ring s.o. up; **вы не туда́ ~и́те** you've got the wrong number.

зво́н|кий (~ок, ~ка́, ~ко) *adj.* **1.** ringing, clear; **~кая моне́та** hard cash, coin. **2.** (*ling.*) voiced.

звон|ко́вый *adj. of* **~о́к**

зво́нниц|а, ы *f.* belfry (*of old Russ. churches*).

звон|о́к, ка́ *m.* bell; **дать з.** to ring; **з. по телефо́ну** phone call; **встава́ть по ~ку́** to get up when the bell goes.

зво́н|че *comp. of* **~кий** *and* **~ко**

звук, а *m.* sound; **пусто́й звук** (*fig.*) (mere) name, empty phrase; **я звал её, а она́ ни ~́а** I kept calling her but she never uttered a sound; (*ling.*) **гла́сный з.** vowel; **согла́сный з.** consonant.

звук|ово́й *adj. of* **~; з. барье́р** sound barrier; **~ова́я волна́** sound wave; **з. фильм** sound-film, talkie.

звукоза́пис|ь, и *f.* sound recording.

звуконепроница́емый *adj.* sound-proof.

звукоопера́тор, а *m.* (*cin.*) sound recordist, sound man.

звукоподража́ни|е, я *nt.* onomatopoeia.

звукоподража́тельный *adj.* onomatopoeic.
звуча́ни|е, я *nt.* **1.** sound(s). **2.** resonance; significance **3.** (*ling.*) phonation.
звуч|а́ть, у́, и́шь *impf.* (*of* **про~**) **1.** to be heard; to (re)sound; **вдали́ ~а́ли голоса́** voices could be heard in the distance; **э́тот пасса́ж ~и́т прекра́сно** (*mus.*) this passage sounds splendid. **2.** (*+adv. or i.*; *fig.*) to sound; to express, convey; **з. трево́гой** to sound a note of alarm; **з. и́скренно** to ring true.
зву́ч|ный (~ен, ~на́, ~но) *adj.* sonorous.
звя́кань|е, я *nt.* jingling; tinkling.
звя́к|ать, аю *impf. of* **~нуть**
звя́к|нуть, ну, нешь *pf.* (*of* **~ать**) (*+i.*) to jingle; to tinkle.
зга *only in phr.* **ни зги не ви́дно** it is pitch dark.
зда́ни|е, я *nt.* building, edifice; premises.
здесь *adv.* **1.** here. **2.** (*coll.*) here, at this point; in this; **з. мы засмея́лись** at this point we burst out laughing; **з. нет ничего́ смешно́го** there is nothing funny in this.
зде́шний *adj.* local; of this place; **з. жи́тель** local (resident).
здоро́ва|ться, юсь *impf.* (*of* **по~**) (**с**+*i.*) to greet; to say hello (to); **з. за́ руку** to shake hands (*in greeting*).
здорове́нн|ый *adj.* (*coll.*) burly, strapping; **~ая ба́ба** strapping woman; **з. го́лос** powerful voice.
здорове́|ть, ю, ешь *impf.* (*of* **по~**) (*coll.*) to become stronger.
здо́рово (*coll.*) **1.** (*adv.*) splendidly, magnificently; **ты з. порабо́тал** you have worked splendidly. **2.** (*adv.*) very, very much; **вчера́ они́ з. вы́пили** they had a great deal to drink yesterday. **3.** (*int.*) well done!
здоро́во[1] *int.* (*coll.*) hullo.
здоро́в|о[2] *adv. of* **~ый**[1]; healthily, soundly; **(за) з. живёшь** for no reason (at all).
здоро́в|ый[1] **(~, ~а)** *adj.* **1.** healthy; **бу́дь(те) ~(ы)!** (*on parting*) look after yourselves!; take care!; (*to s.o. sneezing*) bless you! **2.** health-giving, wholesome; (*fig.*) sound, healthy; **з. кли́мат** healthy climate.
здоро́в|ый[2] **(~, ~а́, ~о́)** *adj.* (*coll.*) **1.** robust, sturdy. **2.** strong, powerful; sound; **з. моро́з** sharp frost; **~ая трёпка** sound thrashing. **3.** (*short form +inf.*) clever (at), good (at), expert; **он ~ льстить же́нщинам** he is expert at flattering women.
здоро́вь|е, я *no pl.*, *nt.* health; **пить за чьё-н. з.** to drink s.o.'s health; **за ва́ше з.!** your health!; **как ва́ше з.?** how are you?; **на з.** to your heart's content, as you please; **гру́ппа ~я** keep-fit group.
здоровя́к, а́ *m.* (*coll.*) person in the pink of health.
здрав... *comb. form*, *abbr. of* **здравоохрани́тельный**
здра́виц|а, ы *f.* toast; **провозгласи́ть ~у за** (*+a.*) to propose a toast to.
здра́вниц|а, ы *f.* sanatorium.
здравомы́слящий *adj.* sensible.
здравоохране́ни|е, я *nt.* public health; **Министе́рство ~я** Ministry of Health; **о́рганы ~я** (public) health services.
здравоохрани́тельный *adj.* public health.
здравпу́нкт, а *m.* first-aid station.
здра́вств|овать, ую *impf.* to be well; to be healthy; to thrive, prosper; **~уй(те)!** hello!; **да ~ует!** long live!
здра́в|ый (~, ~а) *adj.* sensible; sound; **з. смысл** common sense; **~ и невреди́м** safe and sound; **быть в ~ом уме́** to be in one's right mind.
зе́бр|а, ы *f.* zebra.
зе́бр|овый *adj. of* **~а**
зев, а *m.* (*anat.*) pharynx.
зева́к|а, и *c.g.* idler, gaper.
зев|а́ть, а́ю *impf.* **1.** (*pf.* **~ну́ть**) to yawn. **2.** (*no pf.*) (*coll.*) to gape, stand gaping; **не ~а́й!** keep your wits about you! **3.** (*pf.* **про~**) (*coll.*) to miss one's chance.
зев|ну́ть, ну́, нёшь *pf. of* **~а́ть 1.**
зев|о́к, ка́ *m.* yawn.
зево́т|а, ы *f.* (fit of) yawning.
зелене́|ть, ю *impf.* **1.** (*pf.* **по~**) to turn green, come out green. **2.** to show green.
зелен|и́ть, ю́, и́шь *impf.* (*of* **по~**) to make green, paint green.
зеленова́т|ый (~, ~а) *adj.* greenish.
зеленогла́з|ый (~, ~а) *adj.* green-eyed.
зеленщи́к, а́ *m.* greengrocer.
зелён|ый (зе́лен, ~а́, зе́лено) *adj.* green (*also fig.*); **з. горо́шек** green peas; **~ая ску́ка** utter boredom; **~ое я́блоко** green apple; **з. юне́ц** greenhorn; **~ая у́лица** 'go' (*of traffic signals*); **дать ~ую у́лицу** (*fig.*) to give the go-ahead, green-light (to).
зе́лен|ь, и *no pl.*, *f.* **1.** green colour. **2.** (*collect.*) verdure. **3.** (*collect.*) greens (*green vegetables*).
зе́л|ье, ья, *g. pl.* **~ий** *nt.* **1.** potion. **2.** (*fig.*) poison.
зельц, а *m.* (*cul.*) brawn.
зе́мельн|ый *adj.* land; **з. наде́л** allotment; **~ая ре́нта** ground-rent.
землеве́дени|е, я *nt.* physical geography.
землевладе́л|ец, ьца *m.* landowner.
землевладе́л|ьческий *adj. of* **~ец**
землевладе́ни|е, я *nt.* land-ownership.
земледе́л|ец, ьца *m.* farmer.
земледе́ли|е, я *nt.* agriculture, farming.
земледе́льческий *adj.* agricultural, farming.
землеко́п, а *m.* navvy.
землеме́р, а *m.* land-surveyor.
землеме́рный *adj.* geodetic; **з. шест** Jacob's staff.
землеро́йк|а, и *f.* (*zool.*) shrew.
землетрясе́ни|е, я *nt.* earthquake.
землечерпа́лк|а, и *f.* (*tech.*) dredger, excavator.
землечерпа́ни|е, я *nt.* (*tech.*) dredging.
земли́ст|ый (~, ~а) *adj.* earthy; sallow (*of complexion*).
зем|ля́, ли́, *a.* **´~лю**, *pl.* **´~ли, ~е́ль, ´~лям** *f.* **1.** earth; (dry) land; **увидеть ´~лю** to sight land; **упа́сть на ´~лю** to fall to the ground. **2.** land; soil (*fig.*); **поме́щичья з.** (*collect.*) landed estates; **на чужо́й ~ле́** on foreign soil. **3.** earth, soil. **4.** (*in Germany*) Land, state; (*in Austria*) province.
земля́к, а́ *m.* compatriot, fellow-countryman.
земляни́к|а, и *no pl.*, *f.* (*collect.*) wild strawberries.
земля́н|ин, ина, *pl.* **~е, ~** *m.* **1.** (*hist.*) landholder. **2.** earthling.
земляни́|чный *adj. of* **~ка**
земля́нк|а, и *f.* dug-out; mud hut.
землян|о́й *adj.* **1.** earthen, of earth; **~ые рабо́ты** excavations. **2.** earth-; **~а́я гру́ша** Jerusalem artichoke; **з. оре́х** peanut; **з. червь** earth-worm.
земля́честв|о, а *nt.* **1.** friendly society of persons coming from same district. **2.** national group (*of foreign students at Russian universities*).
земля́чк|а, и *f. of* **земля́к**
земново́дн|ый *adj.* amphibious; *as n.* (*zool.*) **~ые, ~ых** amphibia; *sg.* **~ое, ~ого** *nt.* amphibian.
земн|о́й *adj.* **1.** earthly; terrestrial; **з. шар** the globe. **2.** (*fig.*) mundane.
зе́м|ский *adj.* **1.** *of* **~ля́ 2.**; (*hist.*): **з. нача́льник** land captain (*holder of office established in 1889*); **~ское ополче́ние** militia; **3. собо́р** Assembly of the Land (*in Muscovite Russia*). **2.** *of* **~ство**
зе́мств|о, а *nt.* zemstvo (*elective district council in Russia, 1864–1917*).
зени́т, а *m.* zenith (*also fig.*)
зени́тк|а, и *f.* (*mil*; *coll.*) anti-aircraft gun.
зени́тн|ый *adj.* **1.** (*astron.*) zenithal; **~ое расстоя́ние** zenith-distance. **2.** (*mil.*) anti-aircraft.

зени́тчик, а *m.* (*mil.*) anti-aircraft gunner.
зени́ц|а, ы *f.* (*arch.*) pupil (*of the eye*); **бере́чь как ~у о́ка** to keep as the apple of one's eye.
зе́ркал|о, а, *pl.* **~á, зерка́л, ~áм** *nt.* looking-glass, mirror (*also fig.*); **криво́е з.** distorting mirror.
зерка́льн|ый *adj. of* **зе́ркало**; (*fig.*) smooth; **~ое стекло́** plate glass; **~ое окно́** plate-glass window; **з. фотоаппара́т** reflex camera; **~ая пове́рхность** smooth surface; **з. карп** (*zool.*) mirror carp.
зерни́ст|ый (~, ~а) *adj.* granular; **~ая икра́** unpressed caviar(e).
зер|но́, на́, *pl.* **~на, ~ен, ~нам** *nt.* **1.** grain; seed; (*fig.*) grain; kernel, core; **горчи́чное з.** mustard seed; **жемчу́жное з.** pearl; **ко́фе в ~нах** coffee beans; **з. и́стины** grain of truth. **2.** (*collect., sg. only*) grain, cereal.
зернобобо́в|ые, ых *no sg.* (*agric.*) grain legumes.
зернови́д|ный (~ен, ~на) *adj.* granular.
зернов|о́й *adj.* grain, cereal; **~ы́е зла́ки** cereals; **~а́я торго́вля** grain trade.
зернохрани́лищ|е, а *nt.* granary.
зефи́р, а *m.* **1. 3.** (*poet.*) Zephyr. **2.** zephyr (*material*).
зигза́г, а *m.* zigzag.
зижди́тел|ь, я *m.* (*relig.*) the Creator.
зи́жд|иться, ется *impf.* (**на**+*p.*; *obs. or rhet.*) to be founded (on), based (on).
зим|а́, ы́, *a.* **~у,** *pl.* **~ы,** *d.* **~ам** *f.* winter; **на́ ~у** for the winter; **всю ~у** all winter; **ско́лько лет, ско́лько ~,** *see* **ле́то**
Зимба́бве *nt. indecl.* Zimbabwe.
зимбабви́|ец, йца *m.* Zimbabwean.
зимбабви́|йка, йки *f. of* **~ец**
зимбабви́йский *adj.* Zimbabwean.
зи́м|ний *adj. of* **~а́**; winter; wintry.
зим|ова́ть, у́ю *impf.* (*of* **пере~** *and* **про~**) to winter, pass the winter; to hibernate; **знать, где ра́ки ~у́ют,** *see* **рак**
зимо́вк|а, и *f.* **1.** wintering, hibernation; **оста́ться на ~у** to stay for the winter. **2.** winter camp.
зимо́вщик, а *m.* winterer.
зимо́вь|е, я *nt.* winter quarters, winter hut.
зимо́й *adv.* in winter.
зимоpo̍д|ок, ка *m.* (*zool.*) kingfisher.
зипу́н, а́ *m.* homespun coat.
зия́ни|е, я *nt.* (*ling.*) hiatus.
зия́|ть, ю *impf.* to gape, yawn; **~ющая бе́здна** yawning abyss.
злак, а *m.* (*bot.*) grass; **хле́бные ~и** cereals.
зла́т|о, а *nt.* (*arch.*; *poet.*) gold.
Златовла́ск|а, и *f.* Goldilocks.
златогла́вый *adj.* gold-domed; with gold cupolas.
златоку́дрый *adj.* (*poet.*) golden-haired.
зле́йший *superl. of* **злой**
зл|ить, ю, ишь *impf.* (*of* **обо~** *and* **разо~**) to anger; to vex; to irritate.
зл|и́ться, юсь, и́ься *impf.* (*of* **обо~** *and* **разо~**) **1.** (**на**+*a.*) to be in a bad temper; to be angry (with). **2.** (*fig., poet.*) to rage (*of a storm*).
зло[1], **зла,** *no pl. except g.* **зол** *nt.* **1.** evil; harm; **отплати́ть ~м за добро́** to repay good with evil. **2.** evil, misfortune, disaster; **из двух зол вы́брать ме́ньшее** to choose the lesser of two evils; **жела́ть кому́-н. зла** to bear s.o. malice. **3.** (*sg. only*) malice, spite; vexation; **он э́то сде́лал то́лько со зла** he did it purely from malice, out of spite.
зло[2] *adv. of* **~й**
зло́б|а, ы *f.* malice; spite; anger; **по ~е** out of spite; **со ~ой** maliciously; **з. дня** topic of the day.
зло́б|ный (~ен, ~на) *adj.* malicious, spiteful; bad-tempered.
злободне́вност|ь, и *f.* topical interest, topical character.
злободне́вн|ый *adj.* topical; **~ые вопро́сы** burning topics of the day.
зло́бств|овать, ую *impf.* to bear malice; (**на**+*a.*) to have it in (for).
злове́щ|ий (~, ~а) *adj.* ominous, ill-omened; sinister.
злово́ни|е, я *nt.* stink, stench.
злово́н|ный (~ен, ~на) *adj.* stinking, fetid.
зловре́д|ный (~ен, ~на) *adj.* pernicious; noxious.
злоде́|й, я *m.* villain, scoundrel (*also joc.*).
злоде́йский *adj.* villainous.
злоде́йств|о, а *nt.* **1.** villainy. **2.** crime, evil deed.
злодея́ни|е, я *nt.* crime, evil deed.
злой (зол, зла, зло) *adj.* **1.** evil; bad; **з. ге́ний** evil genius. **2.** wicked; malicious; malevolent; vicious; **зла́я улы́бка** malevolent smile; **со злым у́мыслом** with malicious intent. **3.** (*short form only*) angry; **быть злым (на**+*a.*) to be angry (with). **4.** (*of animals*) ferocious; **«зла́я соба́ка»** 'beware of the dog!' **5.** dangerous; severe; **з. моро́з** severe frost. **6.** (*coll.*) bad, nasty; **з. ка́шель** bad cough.
злока́чественн|ый *adj.* (*med.*) malignant; **~ая о́пухоль** malignant tumour; **~ое малокро́вие** pernicious anaemia.
злоключе́ни|е, я *nt.* mishap, misadventure.
злонаме́рен|ный (~, ~на) *adj.* ill-intentioned.
злопа́мятност|ь, и *f.* = **злопа́мятство**
злопа́мят|ный (~ен, ~на) *adj.* rancorous.
злопа́мятств|о, а *nt.* rancour.
злополу́ч|ный (~ен, ~на) *adj.* unlucky, ill-starred.
злопыха́тел|ь, я *m.* (*coll.*) spiteful critic.
злопыха́тельский *adj.* (*coll.*) spiteful, malevolent; ranting.
злопыха́тельств|о, а *nt.* (*coll.*) malevolence; ranting.
злора́дный *adj.* gloating.
злора́дств|о, а *nt.* malicious pleasure.
злора́дств|овать, ую *impf.* to gloat.
злосло́ви|е, я *nt.* scandal, backbiting.
злосло́в|ить, лю, ишь *impf.* to say spiteful things.
зло́ст|ный (~ен, ~на) *adj.* **1.** malicious. **2.** conscious, intentional; **~ное банкро́тство** fraudulent bankruptcy; **з. неплате́льщик** persistent defaulter (*in payment of debt*). **3.** inveterate, hardened.
злост|ь, и *f.* malice; fury; **их з. берёт на него́** they are furious with him.
злосча́ст|ный (~ен, ~на) *adj.* ill-fated, ill-starred.
зло́т|ый, ого *m.* zloty (*Polish currency*).
злоупотреб|и́ть, лю́, и́шь *pf.* (*of* **~ля́ть**) (+*i.*) to abuse; to indulge in to excess; to overdo; **з. вла́стью** to abuse power; **з. чьим-н. внима́нием** to take up too much of s.o.'s time.
злоупотребле́ни|е, я *nt.* (+*i.*) abuse (of); **з. дове́рием** breach of confidence.
злоупотреб|ля́ть, ля́ю *impf. of* **~и́ть**
злю́к|а, и *c.g.* (*coll.*) curmudgeon, crosspatch; (*used of woman only*) shrew.
злю́чк|а, и *c.g.* = **злю́ка**
змееви́д|ный (~ен, ~на) *adj.* serpentine; sinuous.
змеёныш, а *m.* young snake.
зме|и́ный *adj. adj. of* **~я́**; **~и́ная ко́жа** snake-skin.
змеи́ст|ый (~, ~а) *adj.* serpentine; sinuous.
зме|и́ться, и́ся *impf.* to wind, coil; (*fig., poet. pej.*) to glide; **по её лицу́ ~и́лась улы́бка** a smile stole across her face.
змей, зме́я *m.* **1.** dragon. **2. (бума́жный) з.** kite; **запусти́ть зме́я** to fly a kite.
зме́йк|а, и *f. dim. of* **змея́; бежа́ть ~ой** to glide.
зме|я́, и́, *pl.* **~и, ~й** *f.* snake (*also fig.*); **отогре́ть, пригре́ть ~ю на свое́й груди́** to cherish a snake in one's bosom.
зми|й, я *m.* (*arch.*) serpent, dragon; **напи́ться до зелёного ~я** (*coll.*) to get blind drunk.

знава́ть *pres. not used, impf.* (*coll.*) *freq. of* **знать**
знак, а *m.* **1.** (*in var. senses*) sign; mark; token, symbol; (*comput.*) character; **номерно́й з.** licence plate; **па́мятный з.** plaque; **~́и препина́ния** punctuation marks; **~́и отли́чия** decorations (and medals); **в з.** (+*g.*) as a mark (of), as a token (of), to show. **2.** signal; **пода́ть з.** to give a signal.
знако́м|ить, лю, ишь *impf.* (*of* **по~**) (+*a.* **с**+*i.*) to acquaint (with); to introduce (to).
знако́м|иться, люсь, ишься *impf.* (*of* **по~**) (**с**+*i.*) **1.** to meet, make the acquaintance (*of a pers.*). **2.** to introduce o.s.; **~ьтесь!** (*informal mode of introduction*) may I introduce you? **3.** to become acquainted (with), familiarize o.s. (with); to study, investigate; **з. с ме́стностью** to get to know a locality; **з. с тео́рией относи́тельности** to go into the theory of relativity.
знако́мств|о, а *nt.* **1.** (**с**+*i.*) acquaintance (with). **2.** acquaintances; (*collect.*) acquaintance; **у него́ большо́е з.** he has a wide circle of acquaintances; **по ~у** by pulling strings. **3.** (**с**+*i.*) knowledge (of).
знако́м|ый (~, ~а) *adj.* **1.** familiar; **его́ лицо́ мне ~о** his face is familiar. **2.** (**с**+*i.*) familiar (with); **быть ~ым** (**с**+*i.*) to be acquainted (with), know; **я с ней ~ с де́тства** I have known her since childhood. **3.** *as n.* **з., ~ого** *m.*, **~ая, ~ой** *f.* acquaintance.
знамена́тел|ь, я *m.* (*math.*) denominator; **о́бщий з.** common denominator; **привести́ к одному́ ~ю** (*fig.*) to reduce to a common denominator.
знамена́тел|ьный (~ен, ~ьна) *adj.* significant, important.
зна́м|ени, енем, *etc., see* **~я**
зна́мени|е, я *nt.* sign; **~я вре́мени** signs of the times.
знамени́тост|ь, и *f.* celebrity.
знамени́т|ый (~, ~а) *adj.* celebrated, famous, renowned; **печа́льно з.** infamous, notorious.
знамен|ова́ть, у́ю *impf.* to signify, mark.
знамено́с|ец, ца *m.* standard-bearer (*also fig.*).
знамёнщик, а *m.* (*mil.*) colour bearer.
зна́м|я, *g., d., and p.* **~ени,** *i.* **~енем,** *pl.* **~ёна, ~ён** *nt.* banner; standard; **под ~енем** (+*g.*; *fig., rhet.*) in the name of; **высо́ко держа́ть з. свобо́ды** to keep the flag of freedom flying.
зна́ни|е, я *nt.* **1.** knowledge; **у него́ хоро́шее з. сце́ны** he has a good knowledge of the stage; **со ~ем де́ла** capably, competently. **2.** (*pl. only*) learning; accomplishments.
зна́т|ный (~ен, ~на́, ~но) *adj.* **1.** (*adj. of* **~ь**[2]) in an exalted station. **2.** outstanding, distinguished; **~ные лю́ди** notables. **3.** (*coll.*) splendid; **~ные бли́нчики** splendid pancakes.
знато́к, а́ *m.* expert; connoisseur.
зна|ть[1]**, ю** *impf.* to know, have a knowledge of; **~́ете ли вы Алекса́ндрова?** do you know Alexandrov?; **з. в лицо́** to know by sight; **з. своё де́ло** to know one's job; **з. своё ме́сто** to know one's place; **з. ме́ру** to know when to stop; **не з. поко́я** to know no peace; **з. толк** (**в**+*p.*) to be knowledgeable (about); **з. себе́ це́ну** to know one's own value; **они́ не ~́ли о на́ших наме́рениях** they were unaware of our intentions; **дать кому́-н. з.** to let s.o. know; **да́йте мне з. о вас** let me hear from you; **дать себя́ з.** to make itself felt; **он з. не хо́чет** he won't listen; **~й (себе́)** quite unconcerned; **она́ ~й себе пе́ла** she was singing away quite unconcerned; **то и ~й** (*coll.*) continually; **как з., почём з.?** who can tell?, how should I know?; **кто его́ ~́ет, Бог его́ ~́ет** (*coll.*) God knows!; **~́ешь (ли), ~́ете (ли)** (*coll.*) you know, do you know what.
знат|ь[2]**, и** *no pl., f.* (*collect.*) the nobility, the aristocracy.
зна́|ться, юсь *impf.* (**с**+*i.*; *coll.*) to associate (with).
зна́хар|ка, ки *f. of* **~ь**
зна́хар|ь, я *m.* sorcerer, witch-doctor; quack(-doctor).
зна́ч|ащий *pres. part. act. of* **~ить** *and adj.* significant, meaningful.
значе́ни|е, я *nt.* **1.** meaning, significance. **2.** importance, significance; **придава́ть большо́е з.** (+*d.*) to attach great importance (to); **э́то не име́ет ~я** it is of no importance. **3.** (*math.*) value.
зна́чимост|ь, и *f.* significance.
зна́чимый *adj.* significant.
зна́чит (*coll.*) so, then; **он у́мер до войны́? з., вы не́ бы́ли с ним знако́мы** he died before the war? so you didn't know him.
значи́тел|ьный (~ен, ~ьна) *adj.* **1.** considerable, sizeable; **в ~ьной сте́пени** to a considerable extent. **2.** important; **игра́ть ~ьную роль** to play an important part. **3.** significant, meaningful.
зна́ч|ить, у, ишь *impf.* **1.** to mean, signify. **2.** to mean, be of importance; **ничего́ не ~ит** it is of no importance; **получи́ть приглаше́ние на бал о́чень мно́го ~ит для неё** to be invited to a dance means a great deal to her.
зна́ч|иться, усь, ишься *impf.* to be; to be mentioned, appear; **з. в отпуску́** to be on leave; **з. в спи́ске** to appear on a list, be listed.
знач|о́к, ка́ *m.* **1.** badge. **2.** mark.
зна́|ющий *pres. part. act. of* **~ть** *and adj.* expert; learned, erudite.
зноб|и́ть, и́т *impf.* (*impers.*): **меня́,** *etc.*, **~и́т** I, *etc.*, feel shivery, feverish.
зно|й, я *m.* intense heat; sultriness.
зно́|йный (~ен, ~йна) *adj.* hot, sultry; torrid; burning (*also fig.*).
зоб, а, *pl.* **~ы́, ~о́в** *m.* **1.** crop, craw (*of birds*). **2.** (*med.*) goitre.
зов, а *m.* **1.** call, summons. **2.** (*coll.*) invitation.
зов|у́, ёшь *see* **звать**
зодиа́к, а *m.* (*astron.*) zodiac; **зна́ки ~а** signs of the zodiac.
зодиака́льный *adj.* (*astron.*) zodiacal, of the zodiac.
зо́дчес|кий *adj. of* **~тво**
зо́дчеств|о, а *nt.* architecture.
зо́дч|ий, его *m.* architect.
зол[1] *see* **злой**
зол[2] *g. pl. of* **зло**[1]
зол|а́, ы́ *no pl., f.* ashes, cinders.
зо́ло́вк|а, и *f.* sister-in-law (*husband's sister*).
золота́рник, а *m.* (*bot.*) golden rod.
золоти́льщик, а *m.* gilder.
золоти́ст|ый (~, ~а) *adj.* golden (*of colour*).
золо|ти́ть, чу́, ти́шь *impf.* (*of* **вы́~** *and* **по~**) to gild.
золо|ти́ться, ти́тся *impf.* **1.** to become golden. **2.** to shine (*of sth. golden*).
золотни́к, а́ *m.* zolotnik (*old Russ. measure of weight, equivalent to 4.26 grams*); **мал з., да до́рог** (*coll.*) good things come in small packages.
зо́лот|о, а *no pl., nt.* gold; (*collect.*) gold (*coins, ware*); **«бе́лое з.»** 'white gold' (= *cotton*); **«голубо́е з.»** 'blue gold' (= *natural gas*); **«чёрное з.»** 'black gold' (= *oil*); **плати́ть ~ом** to pay in gold; **есть на ~е** to eat off gold plate; (*fig.*) **она́ настоя́щее з.** she is pure gold, a treasure; **не всё то з., что блести́т** (*prov.*) all is not gold that glitters; **на вес ~а** worth its weight in gold.
золотоволо́сый *adj.* golden-haired.
золотоиска́тел|ь, я *m.* gold-prospector; gold-digger.
золот|о́й *adj.* gold; golden (*also fig.*); **~ы́х дел ма́стер** goldsmith; **з. песо́к** gold-dust; **з. запа́с** (*econ.*) gold reserves; **~а́я ры́бка** goldfish; **~о́е руно́** (*myth.*) golden fleece; **з. век** the Golden Age; **~о́е дно** (*fig.*) gold-mine; **~а́я молодёжь** gilded

youth; **~ые ру́ки** skilful fingers; **~ая середи́на** golden mean.

золотоно́сный *adj.* gold-bearing; **з. райо́н** gold-field.

золотопромы́шленност|ь, и *f.* gold-mining.

золоту́х|а, и *f.* (*med.*) scrofula.

золоту́шный *adj.* (*med.*) scrofulous.

золоче́ни|е, я *nt.* gilding.

золочёный *adj.* gilded, gilt.

Зо́лушк|а, и *f.* Cinderella.

зо́н|а, ы *f.* **1.** zone; area, belt; **з. де́йствий** (*mil.*) zone of operations; **з. безопа́сности** (*mil.*) safe area. **2.** (*geol.*) stratum, layer.

зона́льный *adj.* zone; regional.

зонд, а *m.* **1.** (*med.*) probe. **2.** weather-balloon.

зонди́р|овать, ую *impf.* (*med. and fig.*) to sound, probe; **з. по́чву** (*fig.*) to explore the ground.

зо́н|ный *adj. of* **~а**; (*rail.*) regional.

зонт, а́ *m.* **1.** umbrella. **2.** awning.

зо́нтик, а *m.* umbrella; sunshade, parasol.

зо́нти|чный *adj. of* **~к**; (*bot.*) umbellate, umbelliferous.

зоо... *comb. form, abbr. of* **зоологи́ческий**

зоо́лог, а *m.* zoologist.

зоологи́ческий *adj.* **1.** zoological; **з. парк, з. сад** zoological garden(s). **2.** (*fig.*) brutish, bestial.

зооло́ги|я, и *f.* zoology.

зоомагази́н, а *m.* pet-shop.

зоопа́рк, а *m.* zoo; **«сафа́ри» з.** safari park.

зооте́хник, а *m.* livestock specialist.

зооте́хник|а, и *f.* animal science.

зоофе́рм|а, ы *f.* fur farm.

зо́ри *see* **заря́**

зо́р|кий (~ок, ~ка́, ~ко) *adj.* **1.** sharp-sighted. **2.** (*fig.*) perspicacious, penetrating; vigilant.

зо́рю *see* **заря́**

зра́з|ы, ~ *pl.* (*cul.*) zrazy (*meat cutlets stuffed with rice, kasha, etc.*).

зрач|о́к, ка́ *m.* pupil (*of the eye*).

зре́лищ|е, а *nt.* **1.** sight. **2.** spectacle; show; pageant.

зре́лищ|ный *adj. of* **~е**; **~ные предприя́тия** places of entertainment.

зре́лост|ь, и *f.* ripeness; maturity (*also fig.*); **полова́я з.** puberty; **аттеста́т ~и** school-leaving certificate.

зре́л|ый (~, ~а́, ~о) *adj.* ripe; mature (*also fig.*); **дости́гнуть ~ого во́зраста** to reach maturity; **з. ум** mature mind; **по ~ом размышле́нии** on reflection, on second thoughts.

зре́ни|е, я *nt.* (eye)sight; **по́ле ~я** (*phys.*) field of vision; **обма́н ~я** optical illusion; **то́чка ~я** point of view, viewpoint; **под э́тим угло́м ~я** from this standpoint.

зре|ть[1], **ю, ешь** *impf.* (*of* **со~́**) to ripen; to mature (*also fig.*); **у нас ~́ет план** our plans are maturing.

зреть[2], **зрю, зришь** *impf.* (*of* **у~́**) (*obs.*) **1.** to behold. **2.** (**на**+*a.*) to gaze (upon).

зри́м|ый (~, ~а) *p.p.p. of* **зреть**[2] *and adj.* visible.

зри́тел|ь, я *m.* spectator, observer; (*pl.*) audience; **быть ~ем** to look on.

зри́тельн|ый *adj.* **1.** visual; optic; **з. нерв** optic nerve; **~ая па́мять** visual memory; **~ая труба́** telescope. **2.: з. зал** hall, auditorium.

зря *adv.* (*coll.*) to no purpose, for nothing; **болта́ть з.** to chatter idly; **рабо́тать з.** to work in vain.

зря́чий *adj.* sighted (*opp. blind*).

зуб, а *m.* **1.** (*pl.* **~́ы, ~о́в**) tooth; **з. му́дрости** wisdom tooth; **вооружённый до ~о́в** armed to the teeth; **име́ть з. (про́тив), точи́ть ~́ы (на**+*a.*; *coll.*) to have it in for s.o.; **положи́ть ~́ы на по́лку** (*coll.*) to tighten one's belt; **не по ~а́м** beyond one('s capacity); **э́то пробле́ма мне не по ~а́м** (*coll.*) this problem has me stumped; **э́то у меня́ в ~а́х навя́зло** (*coll.*) I am sick and tired of it; **~́ы загово-ри́ть** *see* **заговори́ть**[1]; **держа́ть язы́к за ~а́ми** to hold one's tongue. **2.** (*pl.* **~́ья, ~́ьев**) tooth, cog.

зуба́ст|ый (~, ~а) *adj.* (*coll.*) sharp-toothed; (*fig.*) sharp-tongued.

зуб|е́ц, ца́ *m.* tooth, cog; **з. ви́лки** prong.

зуби́л|о, а *nt.* (*tech.*) point-tool, chisel.

зубн|о́й *adj.* dental; **~а́я боль** tooth-ache; **з. врач** dentist; **~а́я щётка** tooth-brush.

зубовраче́бн|ый *adj. of* **зубно́й врач; з. кабине́т** dental surgery; **~ая шко́ла** dental school.

зуб|о́к, ка́, *pl.* **~ки́** *m.* (*g. pl.* **~о́к**) *dim. of* **~**; **подари́ть на з.** (*coll.*) to bring a present for a (newborn) baby; **попа́сть на з. кому́-н.** (*coll., fig.*) to be torn to shreds by s.o.

зубоска́л|ить, ю, ишь *impf.* (*coll.*) to scoff, mock.

зубоска́льств|о, а *nt.* (*coll.*) scoffing, mocking.

зуботы́чин|а, ы *f.* (*vulg.*) sock on the jaw.

зубочи́стк|а, и *f.* toothpick.

зубр, а *m.* (*zool.*) (European) bison.

зубрёжк|а, и *f.* (*coll.*) cramming.

зубри́л|а, ы *c.g.* (*coll.*) crammer.

зубр|и́ть[1], **ю, ~́ишь** *impf.* (*of* **за~**) to notch, serrate.

зубр|и́ть[2], **ю, ~́ишь** *impf.* (*of* **вы́~** *and* **за~**) (*coll.*) to cram.

зубча́т|ый *adj.* **1.** (*tech.*) toothed, cogged; **~ое колесо́** cogwheel; **~ая ре́йка** rack. **2.** jagged, indented.

зуд, а *m.* itch; (*fig.*) itch, urge.

зуд|е́ть, и́т *impf.* **1.** (*coll.*) to itch (*intrans.*). **2.** (*fig.*) to itch, feel an itch (*to do sth.*).

зу|ди́ть, жу́, ди́шь *impf.* (*coll.*) **1.** to nag at. **2.** to cram.

зу|ёк, йка́ *m.* (*zool.*) plover.

зулу́с, а *m.* Zulu.

зулу́с|ка, ки *f. of* **~**

зулу́сский *adj.* Zulu.

зу́ммер, а *m.* (*tech.*) buzzer; tone; **з. за́нятости** engaged tone.

ЗУПВ *nt. indecl.* (*abbr. of* ***запомина́ющее устро́йство с произво́льной вы́боркой***) (*comput.*) RAM (*random-access memory*).

зы́б|кий (~ок, ~ка́, ~ко) *adj.* unsteady, shaky; (*fig.*) vacillating.

зыбу́ч|ий *adj.* unsteady, unstable; **~ие пески́** quicksands.

зыб|ь, и, *pl.* **~́и, ~е́й** *f.* (*on water*) ripple; **мёртвая з.** swell.

зы́ч|ный (~ен, ~на) *adj.* (*coll.*) loud, shrill.

зюйд, а *m.* (*naut.*) **1.** south. **2.** southerly wind.

зюйдве́стк|а, и *f.* sou'wester (hat).

зэк, а *m.* (*sl.*) prisoner, convict.

зя́б|кий (~ок, ~ка́, ~ко) *adj.* sensitive to the cold.

зя́б|левый *adj. of* **~ь; ~левая вспа́шка** autumn ploughing.

зя́блик, а *m.* chaffinch.

зя́б|нуть, ну, нешь, *past* **~, ~ла** *impf.* to suffer from cold, feel the cold.

зяб|ь, и *f.* (*agric.*) land ploughed in autumn for spring sowing.

зят|ь, я, *pl.* **~ья́, ~ьёв** *m.* **1.** son-in-law. **2.** brother-in-law (*sister's husband or husband's sister's husband*).

И

и[1] *conj.* **1.** and; **добро́ и зло** good and evil; *indicating temporal sequence*: **я встал и вы́мылся и побри́лся** I got up and washed and shaved; *intro-*

ducing narrative: **и настáло ýтро** and then came the morning; *emph. questions*: **и рáзве э́то не прáвда?** and is it not the truth?; *adversative*: **мужчи́на, и плáчет!** a man, and crying!; **и так дáлее, и прóчее** (*abbr.* **и т. д., и пр.**) etcetera, and so on, and so forth. **2.: и... и** both ... and; **и тот и другóй** both. **3.** too, as well; (*with negation*) either; **онá сказáла, что и муж придёт** she said that her husband would come too; **и он не знал** he did not know either. **4.** even; **и знатóк ошибáется** even an expert may be mistaken; **я не мог бы и подýмать об э́том** I would not (even) think of it. **5.** (*emph.*): **в тóм-то и дéло** that is the whole point..

и[2] *int.* (*expr. disagreement*; *coll.*) oh!; **и, пóлно!** that's quite enough!; (*iron.*) you don't say (so)!

ибери́йский *adj.* Iberian.

и́бис, а *m.* (*zool.*) ibis.

и́бо *conj.* for.

и́в|а, ы *f.* willow; **корзи́ночная и.** osier; **плакýчая и.** weeping willow.

ивáновск|ий *adj. only in phr.* **во всю ~ую** (*coll.*) with all one's might; extremely loudly; **кричáть во всю ~ую** to shout at the top of one's voice; **скакáть во всю ~ую** to go hell-for-leather.

ивáн-чай, ивáн-чáя *no pl.*, *m.* (*bot.*) rose-bay, willow-herb.

ивня́к, á *no pl.*, *m.* **1.** osier-bed. **2.** (*collect.*) osier(s).

и́в|овый *adj. of* **~а**

и́волг|а, и *f.* (*zool.*) oriole.

иври́т, а *m.* (modern) Hebrew.

игл|á, ы́, *pl.* **ˊ~ы, ~** *f.* **1.** needle. **2.** (*bot.*) needle; thorn, prickle; **елóвая и.** fir-needle. **3.** quill, spine (*of porcupine, etc.*).

игли́ст|ый (~, ~а) *adj.* prickly; covered with quills.

игловáт|ый (~, ~а) *adj.* (*coll.*) prickly.

иглови́д|ный (~ен, ~на) *adj.* needle-shaped.

иглодержáтел|ь, я *m.* needle-holder.

иглообрáз|ный (~ен, ~на) *adj.* needle-shaped.

иглотерапéвт, а *m.* acupuncturist.

иглотерапи́|я, и *f.* acupuncture.

иглоукáлывани|е, я *nt.* = **иглотерапи́я**

игнори́р|овать, ую *impf. and pf.* to ignore; to disregard.

и́г|о, а *nt.* yoke (*fig.*); **татáрское и.** (*hist.*) the Tatar yoke.

игóлк|а, и *f.* needle; **сидéть как на ~ах** to be on thorns, on tenterhooks; **каблуки́ на ~ах** stiletto heels.

игóлочк|а, и *f. dim. of* **игóлка**; (*coll.*) **одéтый с ~и** spick and span; **костю́м с ~и** brand-new suit.

игóльник, а *m.* needle-case; pin-cushion.

игóльн|ый *adj. of* **иглá; ~ое ýшко** eye of a needle.

игóльчат|ый *adj.* **1.** needle-shaped; **~ые каблуки́** stiletto heels. **2.:** (*comput.*) **и. при́нтер** dot-matrix printer.

игóрный *adj.* playing, gaming; **и. дом** gaming-house; **и. притóн** gambling-den.

игр|á, ы́, *pl.* **ˊ~ы** *f.* **1.** play (*action*), playing; **гря́зная и.** foul play; **у скрипачá былá блестя́щая и.** the violinist's performance was brilliant; **и. свéта на стенé** the play of light on the wall; **и. слов** play on words; **и. прирóды** freak, sport of nature. **2.** game; **азáртная и.** game of chance; **кóмнатные ˊ~ы** indoor games, party games; **одинóчные ˊ~ы** (*tennis*) singles; **пáрные ˊ~ы** (*tennis*) doubles; **олимпи́йские ˊ~ы** Olympic games; (*fig.*) **опáсная и.** dangerous game; **и. не стóит свеч** the game is not worth the candle; **игрáть, вести́ большýю, крýпную ~ý** to play for high stakes; **раскры́ть чью-н. ~ý** to uncover s.o.'s game. **3.** (*sport, cards*) game (*part of set, match*, etc.). **4.** (*cards*) hand; **сдать хорóшую ~ý** to deal a good hand. **5.** turn (*to play*); **сейчáс твоя́ и.** it is your turn now.

игрáльн|ый *adj.* playing; **~ые кáрты** playing cards; **~ые кóсти** dice.

игрá|ть, ю *impf.* (*of* **сыгрáть**) **1.** to play; **и. пьéсу** to put on a play; **и. роль** to play a part; **и. Лéди Макбéт** to play Lady Macbeth; **э́то не ~ет рóли** it is of no importance; **и. симфóнию** to play a symphony; **и. пéрвую, вторýю скри́пку** (*fig.*) to play first, second fiddle; **и. комý-н. нá руку** (*fig.*) to play into s.o.'s hands; **и. глазáми** to flash one's eyes; **и. ферзём** to move the queen (*at chess*); **и. в кáрты, футбóл, шáхматы** *etc.*, to play cards, football, chess, *etc.*; **и. в пря́тки** to play hide-and-seek; (*fig.*) to be secretive; **и. в скрóмность** to feign modesty; **и. на роя́ле, скри́пке** *etc.*, to play the piano, the violin, etc.; **и. на бильярде** to play billiards; **и. на би́рже** to speculate on the Stock Exchange; **и. на** (*+p.*) to play on (*fig.*); **и. на чýвствах толпы́** to play on the emotions of a crowd. **2.** (*impf. only*) (*+i. or* **с***+i.*) to play with, toy with, trifle with (*also fig.*); **и. чьи́ми-н. чýвствами** to trifle with s.o.; **и. с огнём** (*fig.*) to play with fire. **3.** (*impf. only*) to play; to sparkle (*of wine, jewellery, etc.*); **улы́бка ~ла на её лицé** a smile played on her face.

и́грек, а *m.* (the letter) **y**.

игрéневый *adj.* skewbald.

игри́в|ый (~, ~а) *adj.* playful; (*coll.*) naughty, ribald.

игри́ст|ый (~, ~а) *adj.* sparkling (*of wine*).

игр|овóй *adj. of* **~á; и. автомáт** fruit machine; one-armed bandit.

игрóк, á *m.* **1.** (**в***+a.*, **на***+p.*) player (of); **и. в футбóл** football-player; **хорóший и. на балалáйке** a good balalaika player. **2.** gambler.

игрýшечный *adj.* **1.** toy; **и. паровóз** toy-engine. **2.** (*coll.*) tiny, miniature.

игрýшк|а, и *f.* toy; (*fig.*) plaything.

игуáн|а, ы *f.* (*zool.*) iguana.

игýмен, а *m.* (*eccl.*) Father Superior (*of monastery*).

игýмен|ья, ьи, *g. pl.* **~ий** *f.* (*eccl.*) Mother Superior (*of a convent*).

идеáл, а *m.* ideal.

идеализи́р|овать, ую *impf. and pf.* to idealize.

идеали́зм, а *m.* idealism.

идеали́ст, а *m.* idealist.

идеалисти́ческий *adj.* (*phil.*) idealist(ic).

идеалисти́ч|ный (~ен, ~на) *adj.* idealistic.

идеáл|ьный (~ен, ~ьна) *adj.* **1.** (*phil.*) ideal. **2.** (*coll.*) ideal, perfect; **~ьное состоя́ние** perfect *or* mint condition.

идéйност|ь, и *f.* **1.** ideological content. **2.** progressive character. **3.** high-mindedness.

идé|йный (~ен, ~йна) *adj.* **1.** ideological. **2.** expressing an idea *or* ideas; **~йная пьéса** play of ideas. **3.** progressive; **~йное искýсство** progressive art. **4.** high-minded.

идентификáци|я, и *f.* identification.

идентифици́р|овать, ую *impf. and pf.* to identify.

иденти́ч|ный (~ен, ~на) *adj.* identical.

идеогрáмм|а, ы *f.* (*ling.*) ideogram.

идеогрáфи|я, и *f.* (*ling.*) ideography.

идеóлог, а *m.* ideologist.

идеологи́ческий *adj.* ideological.

идеолóги|я, и *f.* ideology.

идёт (*3rd pers. sg. pres. of* **идти́**) *as int.* (*coll.*) (all) right!

идé|я, и *f.* **1.** idea (*also coll.*); notion, concept; **борóться за ~ю** to fight for an idea; **навя́зчивая и.** obsession, idée fixe; **счастли́вая и.** happy thought. **2.** point, purport (*of a work of art, of fiction, etc.*).

идилли́ческий *adj.* idyllic.

иди́лли|я, и *f.* idyll (*liter. and fig.*).

идиóм|а, ы *f.* idiom.

идиомати́ческий *adj.* idiomatic.

идиóт, а *m.* idiot, imbecile.

идиоти́зм, а *m.* idiocy, imbecility.
идиоти́ческий *adj.* idiotic, imbecile.
идио́тский *adj.* idiotic, imbecile.
и́диш *m. indecl.* Yiddish (*language*).
и́дол, а *m.* idol (*also fig.*); **стоя́ть, сиде́ть ~ом** to stand, sit like a stuffed dummy.
идолопокло́нник, а *m.* idolater.
идолопокло́ннический *nt.* idolatrous.
идолопокло́нств|о, а *nt.* idolatry.
ид|ти́, у́, ёшь, *past* **шёл, шла** *impf.* (*of* **пойти́**; *det. of* **ходи́ть**) **1.** to go; (*impf. only*) to come; **и. в го́ру** to go uphill; **авто́бус ~ёт** the bus is coming; **кто ~ёт?** who goes there?; **и. гуля́ть** to go for a walk; **и. в но́гу** to keep in step (*also fig.*); **и. на охо́ту** to go hunting; **и. на сме́ну** (+*d.*) to take the place (of), succeed. **2.** (**на**+*a.*) to enter; (**в**+*nom.-a.*) to become; **и. на госуда́рственную слу́жбу** to enter Government service; **и. в лётчики** to become an airman. **3.** (**в**+*a.*) to be used (for); (**на**+*a.*) to go to make; **и. в корм** to be used for fodder; **и. в лом** to go for scrap; **и. на ю́бку** to go to make a skirt. **4.** **(из, от)** to come (from), proceed (from); **из трубы́ шёл чёрный дым** black smoke was coming from the chimney. **5.** (*of news, etc.*) to go round; **шла мо́лва, что...** rumour had it that .... **6.** (*coll.*) to sell, be sold; **хорошо́ и.** to be selling well; **и. за бесцéнок** to go for a song. **7.** (*of machines, machinery, etc.*) to go, run, work. **8.** (*of rain, etc.*) to fall; **дождь, снег ~ёт** it is raining, snowing. **9.** (*of time*) to pass; **шли го́ды** years passed; **ей ~ёт тридца́тый год** she is in her thirtieth year. **10.** to go on, be in progress; (*of entertainments*) to be on, be showing; **перегово́ры ~у́т** are in progress; **сего́дня ~ёт «Ревизо́р»** 'The Government Inspector' is on tonight. **11.** (+*d.* or **к**) to suit, become; **э́та шля́па ей не ~ёт** this hat does not become her. **12.** (**в, на**+*a.*; *coll.*) to go (in, on). **13.** (+*i*, or **с**+*g.*) to play, lead, move (*at chess, cards, etc.*); **и. ферзём** to move one's queen; **и. с черве́й** to lead a heart. **14.** (**о**+*p.*; *of a discussion, etc.*) to be (about); **речь ~ёт о том, что...** it is a question of ....
и́д|ы, ~ *no sg.* (*hist.*) Ides.
иегови́ст, а *m.* (*relig.*) Jehovah's witness.
иезуи́т, а *m.* (*eccl.*) Jesuit.
иезуи́тский *adj.* (*eccl.*) Jesuit; (*fig.*) Jesuitical.
ие́н|а, ы *f.* yen (*Japanese currency*).
иерархи́ческий *adj.* hierarchic(al).
иера́рхи|я, и *f.* hierarchy.
иеро́глиф, а *m.* hieroglyph; ideogram, ideograph.
иероглифи́ческий *adj.* hieroglyphic.
иждиве́н|ец, ца *m.* dependant.
иждиве́ни|е, я *nt.* maintenance; **на чьём-н. ~и** at s.o.'s expense.
иждиве́нчеств|о, а *nt.* dependence.
и́же *rel. pron.*: **и и́же с ним(и)** (and others) of that ilk, and company.
из (изо) *prep.*+*g.* from, out of; of. **1.** *indicates place of origin of action, source, etc.*: **прие́хать из Ло́ндона** to come from London; **пить из ча́шки** to drink out of a cup; **узна́ть из газе́т** to learn from the newspapers; **из достове́рных исто́чников** from reliable sources; on good authority; **вы́йти из себя́** to be beside o.s.; **вы́йти из употребле́ния** to pass out of use, become obsolete; **он из крестья́н** he is of peasant origin. **2.** *with numeral or in partitive sense*: **оди́н из её покло́нников** one of her admirers; **ни оди́н из ста** not one in a hundred; **мла́дший из всех** the youngest of all; **главне́йшие собы́тия из исто́рии Росси́и** the principal events in the history of Russia. **3.** *indicates material*: **из чего́ э́то сде́лано?** what is it made of?; **варе́нье из абрико́сов** apricot jam; **обе́д из трёх блюд** a three-course dinner; **ло́жки из серебра́** silver spoons; **буке́т из кра́сных гвозди́к** bouquet of red carnations; (*fig.*; *of human potential*) **из него́ вы́йдет хоро́ший труба́ч** he will make a good trumpet-player. **4.** *indicates agency*: **изо всех сил** with all one's might. **5.** *indicates cause, motive*: **из благода́рности** out of gratitude; **из ли́чных вы́год** for private gain; **из ре́вности** from jealousy; **мно́го шу́му из ничего́** a lot of fuss about nothing.
из... (*also* **изо..., изъ...** *and* **ис...**) *vbl. pref. indicating*: **1.** motion outwards. **2.** action over entire surface of object, in all directions. **3.** expenditure of instrument *or* object in course of action; continuation *or* repetition of action to extreme point; exhaustiveness of action.
изб|а́, ы́, *a.* **~у́,** *pl.* **~ы** *f.* izba, (*peasant's*) hut.
избави́тел|ь, я *m.* deliverer.
изба́в|ить, лю, ишь *pf.* (*of* **~ля́ть**) **(от)** to save, deliver (from); **~ьте меня́ от ва́ших замеча́ний** spare me your remarks; **~ьте меня́!** leave me alone!; **~и Бог!** God forbid!
изба́в|иться, люсь, ишься *pf.* (*of* **~ля́ться**) **(от)** to be saved (from), escape; to get out (of); to get rid (of); **и. от привы́чки** to get out of a habit.
избавле́ни|е, я *nt.* deliverance.
избавля́|ть(ся), ю(сь) *impf. of* **изба́вить(ся)**
избало́ванный *p.p.p. of* **избалова́ть** *and adj.* spoilt.
избал|ова́ть, у́ю *pf.* (*of* **балова́ть** *and* **~о́вывать**) to spoil (*a child, etc.*).
избал|ова́ться, у́юсь *pf.* (*of* **~о́вываться**) to become spoilt.
избало́выва|ть(ся), ю(сь) *impf. of* **избалова́ть(ся)**
избе́га|ть, ю *pf.* (*coll.*) to run about, run all over.
избег|а́ть, а́ю *impf.* (*of* **~нуть** *and* **избежа́ть**) (+*g. or inf.*) to avoid; (*impf. only*) to shun; to escape, evade; **и. встреча́ться с кем-н.** to avoid meeting s.o.; **и. штра́фа** to evade a penalty.
избе́га|ться, юсь *pf.* (*coll.*) to exhaust o.s. by running (about).
избе́г|нуть, ну, нешь, *past* **~нул** *and* **~, ~ла** *pf. of* **~а́ть**
избежа́ни|е, я *nt.*: **во и.** (+*g.*) in order to avoid.
избе|жа́ть, гу́, жи́шь, гу́т *pf. of* **~га́ть**
избива́|ть, ю *impf. of* **изби́ть**
избие́ни|е, я *nt.* **1.** slaughter, massacre; **и. младе́нцев** (*bibl.*; *also fig. of persecutions*) Slaughter of the Innocents. **2.** (*leg.*) assault and battery; **и. гомосексуали́стов** gay-bashing.
избира́тел|ь, я *m.* elector, voter; **колеблющийся и.** floating voter.
избира́тельн|ый *adj.* **1.** electoral; **и. бюллете́нь** voting-paper; **~ая кампа́ния** election campaign; **и. о́круг** electoral district; **~ое пра́во** suffrage; franchise; **и. спи́сок** electoral; roll, register of voters; **~ая у́рна** ballot-box; **и. уча́сток** polling station. **2.** (*tech.*) selective.
избира́|ть, ю *impf. of* **избра́ть**
изби́т|ый *p.p.p. of* **~ь** *and adj.*; (*fig.*) hackneyed, trite.
из|би́ть, обью́, обьёшь *pf.* (*of* **~бива́ть**) **1.** to beat up. **2.** to slaughter, massacre.
избо́рник, а *m.* (*hist., liter.*) miscellany, anthology.
избороз|ди́ть, жу́, ди́шь *pf. of* **борозди́ть 2.**
избра́ни|е, я *nt.* election.
избра́нник, а *m.* (*rhet.*) chosen one.
избра́нн|ица, ицы *f. of* **~ик**
и́збран|ный *p.p.p. of* **избра́ть** *and adj.* **1.** selected; **~ные сочине́ния Пу́шкина** selected works of Pushkin; **вновь и.** ... elect; **вновь и. президе́нт** president elect. **2.** select; *as n.* **~ные, ~ных** *no sg.*, élite.
из|бра́ть, беру́, берёшь, *past* **~бра́л, ~брала́, ~бра́ло** *pf.* (*of* **~бира́ть**) (+*a. and i.*) to elect (as, for); to choose; **его́ ~бра́ли чле́ном парла́мента**

he has been elected a Member of Parliament.

избу́шк|а, и *f. dim. of* **изба́**

избы́т|ок, ка *m.* surplus, excess; abundance, plenty; **в ~ке** in abundance.

избы́точ|ный (~ен, ~на) *adj.* **1.** surplus. **2.** abundant, plentiful.

изваяни|е, я *nt.* statue, sculpture; graven image.

изваяя́|ть, ю *pf. of* **вая́ть**

изве́д|ать, аю *pf.* (*of* **~ывать**) to experience, learn the meaning of; **и. го́ре** to experience grief.

изве́дыва|ть, ю *impf. of* **изве́дать**

и́зверг, а *m.* monster, fiend.

изверг|а́ть, а́ю *impf.* (*of* **~нуть**) to throw out, disgorge; (*physiol.*) to excrete; (*fig.*) to eject, expel.

изверг|а́ться, а́юсь *impf.* (*of* **~нуться**) **1.** to erupt (*of volcanoes*). **2.** *pass. of* **~а́ть**

изве́рг|нуть(ся), ну(сь), нешь(ся), *past* **~(ся)** *and* **~нул(ся), ~ла(сь)** *pf. of* **~а́ть(ся)**

изверже́ни|е, я *nt.* **1.** eruption (*of volcano*). **2.** ejection, expulsion; (*physiol.*) excretion.

изве́рженный *p.p.p. of* **изве́ргнуть** *and adj.* (*geol.*) igneous, volcanic.

изве́рива|ться, юсь *impf. of* **изве́риться**

изве́р|иться, юсь, ишься *pf.* (*of* **~иваться**) (**в**+*a. or p.*) to lose faith (in), lose confidence (in); **и. в лю́дях** to lose faith in people.

извер|ну́ться, ну́сь, нёшься *pf.* (*of* **~тываться** *and* **извора́чиваться**) (*coll.*) to dodge, take evasive action (*also fig.*); **и. при отве́те** to give an evasive answer.

извёртыва|ться, юсь *impf. of* **изверну́ться**

изве|сти́, ду́, дёшь, *past* **~л, ~ла́** *pf.* (*of* **изводи́ть**) (*coll.*) **1.** to spend, use up; to waste. **2.** to destroy, exterminate. **3.** to vex, exasperate; to torment.

изве́сти|е, я *nt.* **1.** (**о**+*p.*) news (of); intelligence; information; **после́дние ~я** the latest news. **2.** (*pl. only*; *as title of periodicals*) proceedings, transactions; **~я Акаде́мии нау́к** Proceedings of the Academy of Sciences.

изве|сти́сь, ду́сь, дёшься, *past* **~лся, ~ла́сь** *pf.* (*of* **изводи́ться**) (*coll.*) **1.** to consume o.s., eat one's heart out; to exhaust o.s., wear o.s. out; **и. от за́висти** to be consumed with envy. **2.** to perish, disappear. **3.** *pass. of* **~сти́**

изве|сти́ть, щу́, сти́шь *pf.* (*of* **~ща́ть**) to inform, notify.

извёстк|а, и *f.* (slaked) lime.

известко́вый *adj. of* **и́звесть**

изве́стно 1. *as pred.* it is (well) know; **как и.** as is well known; **наско́лько мне и.** as far as I know. **2.** (*as particle*; *coll.*) of course, certainly.

изве́стност|ь, и *f.* **1.** fame; renown; notoriety; **приноси́ть и.** (+*d.*) to bring fame (to). **2.** publicity; **привести́ в и.** to make known, make public; **поста́вить кого́-н. в и.** to inform, notify. **3.** (*coll.*) celebrity, prominent figure.

изве́ст|ный (~ен, ~на) *adj.* **1.** (+*d.*) well-known (to); (+*i.*) (well-)known (for); (**за**+*a.*) (well-)known (as); **он ~ен свое́й бо́дростью** he is renowned for his cheerfulness; **челове́к, и. как пья́ница.** a well-known drunkard. **2.: печа́льно и.** infamous, notorious. **3.** (a) certain; **~ным о́бразом** in a certain way; **в ~ных слу́чаях** in certain cases; **до ~ной сте́пени, в ~ной ме́ре** to a certain extent.

известня́к, а́ *m.* limestone.

известняко́вый *adj.* limestone.

и́звест|ь, и *f.* lime; **гашёная и.** slaked lime; **негашёная и.** quicklime; **хло́рная и.** chloride of lime; bleaching powder.

извеща́|ть, ю *impf. of* **извести́ть**

извеще́ни|е, я *nt.* notification, notice; (*comm.*) advice.

изви́в, а *m.* winding, bend.

извива́|ть, ю *impf. of* **изви́ть**

извива́|ться, юсь *impf.* (*of* **изви́ться**) **1.** to coil (*intrans.*); to wriggle. **2.** (*impf. only*) to twist, wind (*intrans.*); to meander.

изви́лин|а, ы *f.* bend, twist; **~ы мо́зга** (*anat.*) convolutions of the brain.

изви́лист|ый (~, ~а) *adj.* winding; tortuous; sinuous; (*of river*) meandering.

извине́ни|е, я *nt.* **1.** excuse. **2.** apology; **приня́ть ~я** to accept an apology. **3.** pardon; **прошу́ ~я** I beg your pardon.

извини́тел|ьный (~ен, ~ьна) *adj.* **1.** excusable, pardonable. **2.** apologetic.

извин|и́ть, ю́, и́шь *pf.* (*of* **~я́ть**) **1.** to excuse (= *to pardon*); **~и́те (меня́)!** I beg your pardon; excuse me!; (I'm) sorry!; **~и́те, что я опозда́л** sorry I'm late; **прошу́ и. меня́ за беста́ктное замеча́ние** I apologize for my tactless remark; **~и́те за выраже́ние** (*coll.*) if you will excuse the expression. **2.** to excuse (= *to justify*); **э́то ниче́м нельзя́ и.** this is inexcusable.

извин|и́ться, ю́сь, и́шься *pf.* (*of* **~я́ться**) **1.** (**пе́ред**) to apologize (to); **~и́тесь за меня́** offer my apologies; make my excuses. **2.** (+*i.*) to excuse o.s. (on the ground of); to make excuses.

извин|я́ть, я́ю *impf. of* **~и́ть**

извин|я́ться, я́юсь *impf. of* **~и́ться; ~я́юсь** (*coll.*) I apologize; (I'm) sorry!

извиня́|ющийся *pres. part. of* **~ться** *and adj.* apologetic.

из|ви́ть, овью́, овьёшь, *past* **~ви́л, ~вила́, ~ви́ло** *pf.* (*of* **~вива́ть**) to coil, twist, wind (*trans.*).

из|ви́ться, овью́сь, овьёшься, *past* **~ви́лся, ~вила́сь** *pf. of* **~вива́ться**

извлека́|ть, ю *impf. of* **извле́чь**

извлече́ни|е, я *nt.* **1.** extraction. **2.** extract, excerpt.

извле́|чь, ку́, чёшь, ку́т, *past* **~к, ~кла́** *pf.* (*of* **~ка́ть**) to extract; (*fig.*) to extricate; to derive, elicit; **и. уро́к (из)** to learn a lesson (from); **и. дохо́д, по́льзу, удово́льствие (из)** to derive profit, benefit, pleasure (from).

извне́ *adv.* from without.

изво|ди́ть(ся), жу́(сь), ~дишь(ся) *impf. of* **извести́(сь)**

изво́зчик, а *m.* carrier; **(легково́й) и.** cabman, cabby; **(ломово́й) и.** carter, drayman.

изво́л|ить, ю, ишь *impf.* (+*inf.*; *expr. ironical disapproval*) to deign, be pleased; **~ь(те)** kindly, please (be so good as to); **~ьте молча́ть!** kindly be quiet!

извора́чива|ться, юсь *impf. of* **изверну́ться**

изворо́т, а *m.* **1.** bend, twist. **2.** (*pl.*; *fig.*) tricks, wiles.

изворо́тлив|ый (~, ~а) *adj.* versatile, resourceful; wily, shrewd.

извра|ти́ть, щу́, ти́шь *pf.* (*of* **~ща́ть**) **1.** to pervert. **2.** to misinterpret, misconstrue; **и. и́стину** to distort, misrepresent the truth; **и. чью-н. мысль** to misinterpret s.o.

извраща́|ть, ю *impf. of* **изврати́ть**

извраще́ни|е, я *nt.* **1.** perversion. **2.** misinterpretation, misrepresentation, distortion (*fig.*).

извращённый *p.p.p. of* **изврати́ть** *and adj.* perverted; unnatural.

изги́б, а *m.* bend, twist.

изгиба́|ть(ся), ю(сь) *impf. of* **изогну́ть(ся)**

изгла́|дить, жу, дишь *pf.* (*of* **~живать**) to efface, wipe out (*also fig.*); **и. из па́мяти** to blot out of one's memory.

изгла́жива|ть, ю *impf. of* **изгла́дить**

изгна́ни|е, я *nt.* **1.** banishment; expulsion. **2.** exile.

изгна́нник, а *m.* exile (*pers.*).

из|гна́ть, гоню́, го́нишь, *past* **~гна́л, ~гнала́, ~гна́ло** *pf.* (*of* **~гоня́ть**) to banish, expel; to exile; **и. из употребле́ния** to prohibit the use of, ban.

изгó|й, я *m.* outcast.
изголóвь|е, я *nt.* head of the bed; **сидéть у ~я** to sit at the bedside; **служи́ть ~ем** to serve as a pillow.
изголодá|ться, юсь *pf.* **1.** to be famished, starve. **2.** (**по**+*d.*) to yearn for.
из|гоню́, гóнишь *see* **~гнáть**
изгоня́|ть, ю *impf. of* **изгнáть**
и́згород|ь, и *f.* fence; **живáя и.** hedge.
изготáвлива|ть, ю *impf.* = **изготовля́ть**
изготови́тел|ь, я *m.* manufacturer, producer.
изготóв|ить, лю, ишь *pf.* (*of* **~ля́ть**) to manufacture.
изготовлéни|е, я *nt.* manufacture.
изда|вá|ть, ю́, ёшь, *impf. of* **∠ть**
и́здавна *adv.* for a long time; from time immemorial.
издал|екá (*more rarely* **~ёка**) *adv.* from afar; from a distance; **гóрод ви́ден и.** the town is visible from afar; **приéхать и.** to come from a distance.
и́здал|и *adv.* = **~екá**
издáни|е, я *nt.* **1.** publication; promulgation (*of law*). **2.** edition; **пéрвое и.** first edition; **репри́нтное и.** reprint.
издáтел|ь, я *m.* publisher.
издáтель|ский *adj. of* **~** *and* **~ство; ~ское дéло** publishing; **~ская фи́рма** publishing house.
издáтельств|о, а *nt.* publishing house.
издá|ть, м, шь, ст, ди́м, ди́те, дýт, *past* **~л, ~лá, ~ло** *pf.* (*of* **~вáть**) **1.** to publish; **и. закóн** to promulgate a law; **и. укáз** to issue an edict. **2.** to emit, give off (*a smell*); to utter, let out (*a sound*); **и. крик** to let out a cry.
изд-во (*abbr. of* **издáтельство**) publishing house.
издевáтельский *adj.* mocking.
издевáтельств|о, а *nt.* **1.** mocking, scoffing. **2.** mockery; taunt, insult.
издевá|ться, юсь *impf.* **(над)** to mock (at), scoff (at).
издёвк|а, и *f.* (*coll.*) taunt, insult.
издéли|е, я *nt.* **1.** (*sg. only*) make; **кустáрного ~я** hand-made; **фáбричного ~я** factory-made. **2.** (manufactured) article; (*pl.*) wares.
издёрган|ный *p.p.p. of* **издёргать** *and adj.* harassed; overstrained; **~ные нéрвы** shattered nerves.
издёрг|ать, аю *pf.* (*of* **~ивать**) (*coll.*) **1.** to pull to pieces. **2.** to harass; to overstrain.
издёрг|аться, аюсь *pf.* (*of* **~иваться**) (*coll.*) **1.** *pass. of* **~ать. 2.** to become overwrought, become unhinged.
издёргива|ть(ся), ю(сь) *impf. of* **издёргать(ся)**
издерж|áть, ý, ∠ишь *pf.* (*of* **∠ивать**) to spend; to expend.
издерж|áться, ýсь, ∠ишься *pf.* (*of* **∠иваться**) (*coll.*) **1.** to have spent all one has, be spent up. **2.** *pass. of* **~áть**
издéржива|ть(ся), ю(сь) *impf. of* **издержáть(ся)**
издéрж|ки, ек *f. pl.* expenses; **судéбные и.** (*leg.*) costs; **и. произвóдства** production costs.
издирá|ть, ю *impf. of* **изодрáть**
издóльщин|а, ы *f.* (*hist., econ.*) share-cropping.
издóх|нуть, ну, нешь *past* **~, ~ла** *pf.* (*of* **издыхáть**) to die (*of animals*); (*sl.; of human beings*) to peg out, kick the bucket.
издрéвле *adv.* from the earliest times.
издыхáни|е, я *nt.* (one's) last breath; **до послéднего ~я** to one's last breath; **при послéднем ~и** at one's last gasp.
издыхá|ть, ю *impf. of* **издóхнуть**
изжáр|ить(ся), ю(сь) ишь(ся) *pf. of* **жáрить(ся) 1., 2.**
изживá|ть, ю *impf. of* **изжи́ть**
изжи́ти|е, я *nt.* elimination.
изжи́|ть, вý, вёшь, *past* **~л, ~лá, ~ло** *pf.* (*of* **~вáть**) **1.** to eliminate. **2.: и. себя́** to become obsolete.
изжóг|а, и *f.* heartburn.
из-за *prep.+g.* **1.** from behind; **из-за двéри** from behind the door; **встать из-за столá** to rise from the table; **приéхать из-за мóря** to come from oversea(s); (*fig.*): **сплéтничать о ком-н. из-за углá** to gossip about s.o. behind his back. **2.** because of, through; **не засыпáть из-за шýма** to be unable to get to sleep because of the noise; **ссóриться из-за пустякóв** to fall out over trifles; **тóлько из-за тебя́ мы опоздáли** it was all because of you that we were late. **3.** for; **жени́ться из-за дéнег** to marry for money.
изя́б|нуть, ну, нешь, *past* **~, ~ла** *pf.* (*coll.*) to feel frozen, feel chilled to the marrow.
излагá|ть, ю *impf. of* **изложи́ть**
излáмыва|ть(ся), ю(сь) *impf. of* **изломáть(ся)**
излéнива|ться, юсь *impf. of* **излени́ться**
излен|и́ться, ю́сь, ∠ишься *pf.* (*of* **∠иваться**) (*coll.*) to grow incorrigibly lazy.
излёт, а *m.*: **пýля на ~е** spent bullet.
излечéни|е, я *nt.* **1.** medical treatment; **он был на ~и в Москвé** he was undergoing medical treatment in Moscow; **отпрáвить в гóспиталь на и.** to send to hospital for treatment. **2.** recovery.
излéчива|ть(ся), ю(сь) *impf. of* **излечи́ть(ся)**
излечи́м|ый (~, ~а) *adj.* curable.
излеч|и́ть, ý, ∠ишь *pf.* (*of* **∠ивать**) to cure.
излеч|и́ться, ýсь, ∠ишься *pf.* (*of* **∠иваться**) **(от)** to make a complete recovery (from); to be cured (of); (*fig.*) to rid o.s. (of), shake off.
изливá|ть(ся), ю(сь) *impf. of* **изли́ть(ся)**
из|ли́ть, олью́, ольёшь, *past* **~ли́л, ~лилá, ~ли́ло** *pf.* (*of* **~ливáть**) to pour out, give vent to; **и. свой гнев на** (+*a.*) to vent one's anger (on); **и. дýшу** to unbosom o.s.
из|ли́ться, олью́сь, ольёшься, *past* **~ли́лся, ~лилáсь, ~ли́лóсь** *pf.* (*of* **~ливáться**) **1.** (**в**+*p.*) to find expression (in). **2.** (**в**+*p.*) to give vent to one's feelings (in); (**на**+*a.*) to vent itself (on); **егó гнев ~ли́лся на всех окружáющих** his anger vented itself on all about him.
изли́ш|ек, ка *m.* **1.** surplus; remainder. **2.** excess; **нам э́того хвáтит с ~ком** we have more than enough, enough and to spare.
изли́шеств|о, а *nt.* excess; over-indulgence.
изли́шне *adv.* excessively; unnecessarily, superfluously.
изли́ш|ний (~ен, ~ня, ~не) *adj.* excessive; unnecessary, superfluous.
излия́ни|е, я *nt.* outpouring, effusion (*fig.*).
излов|и́ть, лю́, ∠ишь *pf.* (*coll.*) to catch.
изловч|и́ться, ýсь, и́шься *pf.* (*coll.*) to manage, succeed (in); **он ~и́лся попáсть в цель** he managed to hit the target.
изложéни|е, я *nt.* exposition, account; **крáткое и.** synopsis, outline.
излож|и́ть, ý, ∠ишь *pf.* (*of* **излагáть**) to expound, state; to set forth; **и. на бумáге** to commit to paper.
излóм, а *m.* **1.** break, fracture. **2.** sharp bend.
излóман|ный *p.p.p. of* **изломáть** *and adj.* **1.** broken. **2.** winding, tortuous. **3.** (*fig.*) unbalanced, unhinged; warped.
изломá|ть, ю *pf.* (*of* **излáмывать**) **1.** to break, smash. **2.** (*coll.*) to break (*in health*); (*impers.*) to have (crippling) rheumatism; **всю спи́ну у неё ~ло** she is crippled with rheumatism in her back. **3.** (*fig., coll.*) to warp, corrupt.
изломá|ться, юсь *pf.* (*of* **излáмываться**) to be broken, be smashed.
излуч|áть, áю *impf.* (*of* **~и́ть**) to radiate (*also fig.*); **её глазá ~áли нéжность** her face radiated tenderness.

излуч|а́ться, а́ется *impf.* (*of* **~и́ться**) **1.** **(из)** to emanate (from). **2.** *pass. of* **~а́ть**
излуче́ни|е, я *nt.* radiation; emanation.
излу́чин|а, ы *f.* bend, wind.
излуч|и́ть(ся), у́(сь), шь(ся) *pf. of* **~а́ть(ся)**
излю́бленный *adj.* favourite; pet.
изма́|зать, жу, жешь, *pf.* (*of* **ма́зать 3.** *and* **~зывать**) (*coll.*) to make dirty, smear; **и. пальто́ кра́ской** to get paint all over one's coat.
изма́|заться, жусь, жешься *pf.* (*of* **ма́заться 1.** *and* **~зываться**) (*coll.*) **1.** to get dirty; **он ~зался в кра́ске** he has got paint all over himself. **2.** *pass. of* **~зать**
изма́зыва|ть(ся), ю(сь) *impf. of* **изма́зать(ся)**
изма́тыва|ть(ся), ю(сь) *impf. of* **измота́ть(ся)**
изма́|ять, ю *pf.* (*coll.*) to exhaust, tire out.
изма́|яться, юсь *pf.* (*coll.*) to be exhausted, tired out.
измельча́|ть, ю *pf. of* **мельча́ть**
измельч|и́ть, у́, и́шь *pf. of* **мельчи́ть**
изме́н|а, ы *f.* betrayal; treachery; **госуда́рственная и.** high treason; **супру́жеская и.** unfaithfulness, (conjugal) infidelity.
измене́ни|е, я *nt.* change, alteration; (*gram.*) inflexion.
измен|и́ть[1], ю́, ~́ишь *pf.* (*of* **~я́ть**) to change, alter; (*pol.*) **и. законопрое́кт** to amend a bill.
измен|и́ть[2], ю́, ~́ишь *pf.* (*of* **~я́ть**) (*+d.*) to betray; to be unfaithful (to); (*fig.*) **зре́ние ~и́ло ему́** his eyesight had failed him; **сча́стье нам ~и́ло** our luck is out.
измен|и́ться, ю́сь, ~́ишься *pf.* (*of* **~я́ться**) **1.** to change, alter (*intrans.*); to vary (*intrans.*); **и. к лу́чшему, к ху́дшему** to change for the better, for the worse.
изме́нник, а *m.* traitor.
изме́ннический *adj.* treacherous, traitorous.
изме́нчивост|ь, и *f.* **1.** changeableness; mutability; inconstancy, fickleness. **2.** (*biol.*) variability.
изме́нчив|ый (~, ~а) *adj.* changeable; inconstant, fickle; **~ая пого́да** changeable weather.
измен|я́ть(ся), я́ю(сь) *impf. of* **~и́ть(ся)**
измере́ни|е, я *nt.* **1.** measurement, measuring; sounding; taking (*of temperature*). **2.** (*math.*) dimension; **двух, трёх ~й** two-, three-dimensional.
измери́м|ый (~, ~а) *adj.* measurable.
измери́тел|ь, я *m.* **1.** measuring instrument; gauge. **2.** (*econ.*) index.
измери́тельный *adj.* (for) measuring.
изме́р|ить, ю, ишь *pf.* (*of* **~я́ть**) to measure; **и. кому́-н. температу́ру** to take s.o.'s temperature.
измер|я́ть, я́ю *impf. of* **~́ить**
изможде́н|ный (~, ~а́) *adj.* emaciated; worn out.
измок|а́ть, а́ю *impf. of* **~́нуть**
измо́к|нуть, ну, нешь *past* **~, ~ла** *pf.* (*of* **~а́ть**) (*coll.*) to get soaked, get drenched.
измо́р, а *no pl., m.*: **взять ~ом** to starve into submission, starve out; (*fig., coll.*): **взять кого́-н. ~ом** to wear s.o. down.
измор|и́ть, ю́, и́шь *pf.* (*coll.*) to wear out, exhaust.
и́зморoз|ь, и *f.* hoar-frost; rime.
и́зморос|ь, и *f.* drizzle.
измота́|ть, ю *pf.* (*of* **изма́тывать**) (*coll.*) to exhaust, wear out.
измота́|ться, юсь *pf.* (*of* **изма́тываться**) (*coll.*) to be exhausted, worn out.
измоча́лива|ть, ю *impf. of* **измоча́лить**
измоча́л|ить, ю, ишь *pf.* (*of* **~ивать**) (*coll.*) **1.** to shred; to reduce to shreds. **2.** to exhaust, wear out.
изму́ченный *p.p.p. of* **изму́чить** *and adj.* worn out, tired out; **у вас и. вид** you look worn out.
изму́чива|ть(ся), ю(сь) *impf. of* **изму́чить(ся)**
изму́ч|ить, у, ишь *pf.* **1.** (*pf. of* **~ивать**) to torment; to tire out, exhaust. **2.** *pf. of* **му́чить**
изму́ч|иться, усь, ишься *pf.* **1.** *pf.* (*of* **~иваться**) to be tired out, be exhausted. **2.** *pf. of* **му́читься**
измыва́|ться, юсь *impf.* (**над**; *coll.*) to mock (at), scoff (at).
измы́сл|ить, ю, ишь *pf.* (*of* **измышля́ть**) **1.** to fabricate, invent. **2.** to contrive.
измышле́ни|е, я *nt.* fabrication; invention.
измышля́|ть, ю *impf. of* **измы́слить**
измя́т|ый *p.p.p. of* **~ь** *and adj.* **1.** crumpled, creased. **2.** (*fig.*) haggard, jaded.
из|мя́ть(ся), омну́, омнёт(ся) *pf. of* **мя́ть(ся)[1]**
изна́нк|а, и *f.* the wrong, reverse side (*of material, clothing*); **вы́вернуть на ~у** to turn inside out; **и. жи́зни** the seamy side of life.
изнаси́ловани|е, я *nt.* rape.
изнаси́л|овать, ую *pf.* (*of* **наси́ловать 2.**) to rape.
изнача́льный *adj.* primordial.
изна́шивани|е, я *nt.* wear; wear and tear.
изна́шива|ть(ся), ю(сь) *impf. of* **износи́ть(ся)**
изне́женный *p.p.p. of* **изне́жить** *and adj.* **1.** pampered; delicate. **2.** soft, effete.
изне́жива|ть(ся), ю(сь) *impf. of* **изне́жить(ся)**
изне́ж|ить, у, ишь *pf.* (*of* **~ивать**) to pamper, coddle.
изне́ж|иться, усь, ишься *pf.* (*of* **~иваться**) to go soft, become effete.
изнемога́|ть, ю *impf. of* **изнемо́чь**
изнеможе́ни|е, я *nt.* exhaustion; **быть в ~и** to be utterly exhausted; **рабо́тать до ~я** to work to the point of exhaustion.
изнеможён|ный (~, ~а́) *adj.* exhausted.
изнемо́|чь, гу́, ~́жешь, ~́гут, *past* **~г, ~гла́** *pf.* (*of* **~га́ть**) **(от)** to be exhausted (from), worn out (from).
изне́рвнича|ться, юсь *pf.* (*coll.*) to get into a state of nerves.
изно́с, а (у) *m.* (*coll.*) wear; wear and tear; **не знать ~у (а)** to wear well; (*+d.*) **э́тим боти́нкам нет ~у (а)** these boots will stand any amount of hard wear.
изно|си́ть, шу́, ~́сишь *pf.* (*of* **изна́шивать**) to wear out.
изно|си́ться, шу́сь, ~́сишься *pf.* (*of* **изна́шиваться**) to wear out (*intrans.*); (*fig., coll.*) to be used up, be played out.
износосто́йкий *adj.* hard-wearing, wear-resistant.
изно́шенный *p.p.p. of* **износи́ть** *and adj.* worn out; **и. костю́м** threadbare suit.
изнуре́ни|е, я *nt.* exhaustion.
изнурённый *p.p.p. of* **изнури́ть** *and adj.* exhausted, worn out; **у него́ был и. вид** he looked worn out; **и. го́лодом** faint with hunger.
изнури́тел|ьный (~ен, ~ьна) *adj.* exhausting; gruelling; **~ьная боле́знь** wasting disease.
изнур|и́ть ю́, и́шь *pf.* (*of* **~я́ть**) to exhaust, wear out.
изнур|я́ть, я́ю *impf. of* **~и́ть**
изнутри́ *adv.* from within; **дверь запира́ется и.** the door fastens on the inside.
изныва́|ть, ю *impf. of* **изны́ть**
изн|ы́ть, о́ю, о́ешь *pf.* (*of* **~ыва́ть**) to languish, be exhausted; **и. от жа́жды** to be tormented by thirst; **и. от тоски́** (**по**+*d.*; *poet.*) to pine (for).
изо *prep.* = **из**
изо...[1] *pref.* = **из...**
изо...[2] *comb. form* **1.** = iso-. **2.** = *abbr. of* **изобрази́тельный**
изоба́р|а, ы *f.* (*meteor.*) isobar.
изоби́ли|е, я *nt.* abundance, plenty, profusion; **рог ~я** cornucopia.
изоби́л|овать, ую *impf.* (*+i.*) to abound (in), be rich (in).
изоби́л|ьный (~ен, ~ьна) *adj.* **1.** abundant. **2.** (*+i.*)

abounding in.
изoблич|áть, áю *impf.* **1.** *impf. of* **~и́ть. 2.** (*no pl.*) (*+a.* **в**+*p.*) to show (to be), point to (as being); **все его́ посту́пки ~áли в нём моше́нника** his every action pointed to his being a swindler; **его́ похо́дка ~áет в нём моряка́** his gait gives him away as a sailor.
изобличе́ни|е, я *nt.* exposure; conviction.
изобличи́тельный *adj.* damning.
изoблич|и́ть, у́, и́шь *pf.* (*of* **~áть**) (*+a.* **в**+*p.*) to expose (as), convict (of); to unmask; **его́ ~и́ли во лжи** he stands convicted as a liar.
изобража́|ть, ю *impf. of* **изобрази́ть**
изображе́ни|е, я *nt.* **1.** (*artistic*) representation. **2.** representation, portrayal; image; imprint; effigy; **и. в зе́ркале** reflection.
изобрази́тельн|ый *adj.* graphic; decorative; **~ые иску́сства** fine arts.
изобра|зи́ть, жу́, зи́шь *pf.* (*of* **~жа́ть**) **1.** (*+i.*) to depict, portray, represent (as); **и. из себя́** (*+a.*; *coll.*) to make o.s. out (to be); **и. Га́млета сла́бым челове́ком** to portray Hamlet as a weak character (*of actor or producer*); **и. из себя́ хоро́шего певца́** to make o.s. out to be a good singer. **2.** to imitate, take off.
изобре|сти́, ту́, тёшь *past* **~́л, ~ла́** *pf.* (*of* **~та́ть**) to invent; to devise, contrive.
изобрета́тел|ь, я *m.* inventor.
изобрета́тельност|ь, и *f.* inventiveness.
изобрета́тел|ьный (~ен, ~ьна) *adj.* inventive; resourceful.
изобрета́|ть, ю *impf. of* **изобрести́**
изобрете́ни|е, я *nt.* invention.
изо́гнут|ый *p.p.p. of* **~́ь** *and adj.* bent, curved, winding.
изогн|у́ть, у́, ёшь *pf.* (*of* **изгиба́ть**) to bend, curve.
изогн|у́ться, у́сь, ёшься *pf.* (*of* **изгиба́ться**) to bend, curve (*intrans.*).
изо́дранный *p.p.p. of* **изодра́ть** *and adj.* tattered.
из|одра́ть, деру́, дерёшь, *past* **~одра́л, ~одрала́, ~одра́ло** *pf.* (*of* **~дира́ть**) (*coll.*) to tear to pieces; to tear in several places.
изо|йти́, йду́, йдёшь, *past* **~шёл, ~шла́** *pf. of* **исходи́ть**[2]
изол|га́ться, гу́сь, жёшься, гу́тся, *past* **~га́лся, ~гала́сь, ~га́лось** *pf.* to become an inveterate, hardened liar.
изоли́рованный *p.p.p. of* **изоли́ровать** *and adj.* **1.** isolated; separate. **2.** (*tech.*) insulated.
изоли́р|овать, ую *impf. and pf.* **1.** to isolate; to quarantine. **2.** (*tech.*) to insulate.
изоля́тор[1], **а** *m.* (*tech.*) insulator.
изоля́тор[2], **а** *m.* **1.** (*med.*) isolation ward. **2.** solitary confinement cell.
изоляциони́зм, а *m.* (*pol.*) isolationism.
изоляциони́ст, а *m.* (*pol.*) isolationist.
изоля|цио́нный *adj. of* **~́ция; ~цио́нная ле́нта** (*tech.*) insulating tape.
изоля́ци|я, и *f.* **1.** isolation; (*med.*) quarantine. **2.** (*tech.*) insulation.
изо́рванный *p.p.p. of* **изорва́ть** *and adj.* tattered, torn.
изорв|а́ть, у́, ёшь, *past* **~а́л, ~ала́, ~а́ло** *pf.* (*of* **изрыва́ть**[1]) to tear (to pieces).
изорв|а́ться, ётся, *past* **~а́лся, ~ала́сь, ~а́лось** *pf.* (*coll.*) to be in tatters.
изоте́рм|а, ы *f.* (*geog.*) isotherm.
изото́п, а *m.* (*chem.*) isotope.
изошу́тк|а, и *f.* (*coll.*) cartoon, humorous drawing.
изощре́ни|е, я *nt.* sharpening (*fig.*); refinement.
изощрённый *p.p.p. of* **изощри́ть** *and adj.* refined; keen, acute.
изощр|и́ть, ю́, и́шь *pf.* (*of* **~я́ть**) to sharpen (*fig.*); to cultivate, refine; **и. слух** to train one's ear; **и. ум** to cultivate one's mind.
изощр|и́ться, ю́сь, и́шься *pf.* (*of* **~я́ться**) **1.** to acquire refinement. **2.** (**в**+*p.*) to excel (in); **и. в приду́мывании каламбу́ров** to excel in devising puns.
изощр|я́ть(ся), я́ю(сь) *impf. of* **~и́ть(ся)**
из-под *prep.+g.* **1.** from under; **у него́ укра́ли бума́жник из-под но́су** he had his wallet stolen from under his nose; **из-под полы́** on the sly; under the counter. **2.** from near; **мы прие́хали из-под Москвы́** we have come from near Moscow. **3.** (for) (*indicates purpose of object*); **ба́нка из-под варе́нья** jam-jar.
изра|зе́ц, зца́ *m.* tile.
израз|цо́вый *adj. of* **~е́ц**
Изра́ил|ь, я *m.* Israel.
изра́ильский *adj.* Israeli.
израильтя́н|ин, ина, *pl.* **~е, ~** *m.* **1.** (*hist.*) Israelite. **2.** Israeli.
израильтя́н|ка, ки *f. of* **~ин**
изра́н|ить, ю, ишь *pf.* to cover with wounds.
израсхо́д|овать(ся), ую(сь) *pf. of* **расхо́довать(ся)**
и́зредка *adv.* now and then; from time to time.
изре́занный *p.p.p. of* **изре́зать** *and adj.*: **и. бе́рег** indented coastline.
изре́|зать, жу, жешь *pf.* (*of* **~зывать** *and* **~за́ть**) **1.** to cut to pieces; to cut up. **2.** (*geog.*) to indent.
изрез|а́ть, а́ю *impf.* (*coll.*) *of* **~́ать**
изре́зыва|ть, ю *impf. of* **изре́зать**
изрека́|ть, ю *impf. of* **изре́чь**
изрече́ни|е, я *nt.* dictum, saying.
изре́|чь, ку́, чёшь, ку́т, *past* **~́к, ~кла́** *pf.* (*of* **~ка́ть**) (*obs. or iron.*) to speak (solemnly); to utter; **так ~́к** thus he spake; **и. му́дрое сло́во** to utter a word of wisdom.
изреше|ти́ть, чу́, ти́шь *pf.* (*of* **~́чивать**) to pierce with holes; **и. пу́лями** to riddle with bullets.
изреше́чива|ть, ю *impf. of* **изрешети́ть**
изрис|ова́ть, у́ю *pf.* (*of* **~о́вывать**) to cover with drawings.
изрисо́выва|ть, ю *impf. of* **изрисова́ть**
изруб|а́ть, а́ю *impf. of* **~и́ть**
изруб|и́ть, лю́, ~́ишь *pf.* (*of* **~а́ть**) to chop up; to hack to pieces; to mince (*meat*).
изруга́|ть, ю *pf.* to revile, curse violently.
изрыва́|ть[1], **ю** *impf. of* **изорва́ть**
изрыва́|ть[2], **ю** *impf. of* **изры́ть**
изрыг|а́ть, а́ю *impf.* (*of* **~ну́ть**) to vomit, throw up; **пу́шки ~а́ли дым и пла́мень** the cannon were belching forth smoke and flames; (*fig.*): **и. руга́тельства** to let forth a stream of oaths.
изрыг|ну́ть, ну́, нёшь *pf. of* **~а́ть**
изры́т|ый *p.p.p. of* **~ь** pitted; **и. о́спой** pock-marked.
изр|ы́ть, о́ю, о́ешь *pf.* (*of* **~ыва́ть**[2]) to dig up; to dig through.
изря́дно *adv.* (*coll.*) fairly, pretty; tolerably; **я и. уста́л** I am pretty tired; **они́ вчера́ ве́чером и. вы́пили** they had a fair amount to drink last night.
изря́д|ный (~ен, ~на) *adj.* (*coll.*) fair; fairly large, tolerable; **~ое коли́чество** a fair amount; **и. пья́ница** a pretty heavy drinker.
изуве́р, а *m.* **1.** bigot, fanatic, zealot. **2.** fiend, monster.
изуве́рский *adj.* **1.** bigoted, fanatical. **2.** fiendish.
изуве́рств|о, а *nt.* **1.** bigotry, fanaticism; (fanatical) cruelty; zealotry. **2.** fiendishness.
изуве́чива|ть, ю *impf. of* **изуве́чить**
изуве́ч|ить, у, ишь *pf.* (*of* **~ивать**) to maim, mutilate.
изукра́|сить, шу, сишь *pf.* (*of* **~шивать**) to decorate (lavishly); **и. дом фла́гами** to bedeck a house with flags.
изукра́шива|ть, ю *impf. of* **изукра́сить**

изуми́тел|ьный (~ен, ~ьна) *adj.* amazing, astounding.
изум|и́ть, лю́, и́шь *pf.* (*of* **~ля́ть**) to amaze, astound.
изум|и́ться, лю́сь, и́шься *pf.* (*of* **~ля́ться**) to be amazed, astounded.
изумле́ни|е, я *nt.* amazement.
изумлённый *p.p.p. of* **изуми́ть** *and adj.* amazed, astounded; dumbfounded.
изумля́|ть(ся), ю(сь) *impf. of* **изуми́ть(ся)**
изумру́д, а *m.* emerald.
изумру́дный *adj.* **1.** emerald. **2.** emerald(-green).
изуро́дованный *p.p.p. of* **изуро́довать** *and adj.* maimed, mutilated; disfigured.
изуро́д|овать, ую *pf. of* **уро́довать**
изуч|а́ть, а́ю *impf.* (*of* **~и́ть**) to learn; (*impf. only*) to study; **он два го́да ~а́ет гре́ческий язы́к** he has been studying Greek for two years.
изуче́ни|е, я *nt.* study, studying.
изуч|и́ть, у́, ~́ишь *pf.* (*of* **~а́ть**) **1.** to learn; **за шесть ме́сяцев она ~и́ла и испа́нский и италья́нский языки́** in six months she had learned both Spanish and Italian. **2.** to come to know (very well), come to understand; **он кра́йне за́мкнут, но я всё-таки ~и́л его́** he is extremely reserved, but I came to understand him in the end.
изъ... *pref.* = **из...**
изъеда́|ть, ю *impf. of* **изъе́сть**
изъе́денный *p.p.p. of* **изъе́сть** *and adj.*: **и. мо́лью** moth-eaten.
изъе́з|дить, жу, дишь *pf.* (*of* **~живать**) to travel all over, traverse; **мы ~дили весь свет** we have been all round the world.
изъе́зжива|ть, ю *impf. of* **изъе́здить**
изъе́|сть, ст, дя́т, *past* **~л, ~ла** *pf.* (*of* **~да́ть**) **1.** to eat away. **2.** to corrode.
изъяви́тельн|ый *adj.*: **~ое наклоне́ние** (*gram.*) indicative mood.
изъяв|и́ть, лю́, ~́ишь *pf.* (*of* **~ля́ть**) to indicate, express; **и. своё согла́сие** to give one's consent.
изъявле́ни|е, я *nt.* expression.
изъявля́|ть, ю *impf. of* **изъяви́ть**
изъязв|и́ть, лю́, и́шь *pf.* (*of* **~ля́ть**) (*med.*) to ulcerate.
изъязвле́ни|е, я *nt.* (*med.*) ulceration.
изъязвлённый *p.p.p. of* **изъязви́ть** *and adj.* ulcerated.
изъязвля́|ть, ю *impf. of* **изъязви́ть**
изъя́н, а *m.* defect, flaw; **това́р с ~ом** defective goods; **у него́ мно́го ~ов** he has many defects.
изъясн|и́ться, ю́сь, и́шься *pf.* (*of* **~я́ться**) (*obs.*) to express o.s.; **и. в любви́** to declare one's love.
изъясн|я́ться, я́юсь *impf. of* **~и́ться**
изъя́ти|е, я *nt.* **1.** withdrawal; removal. **2.** exception; **без вся́кого ~я** without exception; **в и. из пра́вил** as an exception to the rule.
из|ъя́ть, ыму́, ы́мешь *pf.* (*of* **~ыва́ть**) to withdraw; to remove; **и. из обраще́ния** to withdraw from circulation; **и. в по́льзу госуда́рства** to confiscate.
изыма́|ть, ю *impf. of* **изъя́ть**
из|ыму́, ы́мешь *see* **~ъя́ть**
изыска́ни|е, я *nt.* (*usu. pl.*) investigation, research; prospecting; survey.
изы́сканност|ь, и *f.* refinement.
изы́скан|ный 1. (~, ~а) *p.p.p. of* **изыска́ть. 2. (~, ~на)** *adj.* refined; exquisite; recherché.
изыска́тел|ь, я *m.* prospector.
изы|ска́ть, щу́, ~́щешь *pf.* (*of* **~́скивать**) to find; to search out; **и. сре́дства на постро́йку домо́в** to find funds for house-building.
изы́скива|ть, ю *impf.* (*of* **изыска́ть**) to search out; to try to find.
изю́м, а (у) *no pl., m.* raisins; sultanas; **э́то не фунт ~у!** (*joc.*) it is no light matter, it is no joke.
изю́мин|а, ы *f.* raisin.
изю́мин|ка, ки *f., dim. of* **~а**; (*fig.*) pep, go, spirit; **с ~кой** spirited; **в ней нет ~ки** she has no go in her.
изя́ществ|о, а *nt.* elegance, grace.
изя́щ|ный (~ен, ~на) *adj.* elegant, graceful; (*obs.*) **~ные иску́сства** fine arts.
ика́ни|е, я *nt.* hiccupping.
ик|а́ть, а́ю *impf.* (*of* **~ну́ть**) to hiccup.
ик|ну́ть, ну́, нёшь *pf. of* **~а́ть**
ико́н|а, ы *f.* icon.
ико́н|ный *adj. of* **~а**
иконобо́р|ец, ца *m.* (*hist.*) iconoclast.
иконобо́рческий *adj.* (*hist.*) iconoclastic.
иконобо́рчеств|о, а *nt.* (*hist.*) iconoclasm.
иконопи́с|ец, ца *m.* icon-painter.
иконопи́сный *adj.* **1.** *adj. of* **и́конопись. 2.** (*fig.*) icon-like (*severe, severely beautiful*).
и́конопис|ь, и *f.* icon-painting.
иконоста́с, а *m.* (*eccl.*) iconostasis.
ико́рный *adj. of* **икра́[1]**
ико́т|а, ы *f.* hiccups.
икр|а́[1], ы́ *no pl. f.* **1.** (hard) roe; spawn; **мета́ть ~у́** to spawn; (*fig., coll.*) to rage. **2.** caviar(e); pâté; **баклажа́нная и.** aubergine pâté.
икр|а́[2], ы́, *pl.* **~́ы** *f.* (*anat.*) calf.
икри́нк|а, и *f.* (*coll.*) grain of roe.
икри́ст|ый (~, ~а) *adj.* containing much roe.
икромета́ни|е, я *nt.* spawning.
икс, а *m.* (*the letter*) x; (*math*) x (*unknown quantity*).
ил, а *m.* silt.
и́ли *conj. or*; **и.... и.** either ... or.
и́лист|ый (~, ~а) *adj.* covered in silt; containing silt.
иллю́зи|я, и *f.* illusion.
иллюзо́р|ный (~ен, ~на) *adj.* illusory.
иллюмина́тор, а *m.* (*naut.*) porthole; window.
иллюмина́ци|я, и *f.* illumination.
иллюмини́р|овать, ую *impf. and pf.* to illuminate.
иллюстрати́в|ный (~ен, ~на) *adj.* illustrative; **и. материа́л** illustration(s).
иллюстра́тор, а *m.* illustrator.
иллюстра́ци|я, и *f.* illustration.
иллюстри́р|ованный *p.p.p. of* **~овать** *and adj.* illustrated.
иллюстри́р|овать, ую *impf. and pf.* (*pf. also* **про~**) to illustrate (*also fig.*).
и́льк|а, и *f.* **1.** (*zool.*) fisher. **2.** fisher (*fur*).
и́льк|овый *adj. of* **~а**
ильм, а *m.* (*bot.*) elm (*Ulmus scabra*).
и́льм|овый *adj. of* **~**
им 1. *i. of prons.* **он, оно́. 2.** *d. of pron.* **они́**
им. (*abbr. of* **и́мени**) named after; **стадио́н им. Ле́нина** Lenin Stadium.
имби́р|ный *adj. of* **~ь**
имби́р|ь, я́ *m.* ginger.
и́м|ени, енем *see* **~я**
име́ни|е, я *nt.* estate.
имени́нник, а *m.* one whose name-day it is.
имени́н|ный *adj. of* **~ы; и. пиро́г** name-day cake.
имени́н|ы, ~ *no sg.* **1.** name-day (*day of saint after whom person is named*); **спра́вить и.** to celebrate one's name-day. **2.** name-day celebration; **пойти́ на и. к кому́-н.** to go to s.o.'s name-day party.
имени́тельный *adj.* (*gram.*) nominative.
имени́т|ый (~, ~а) *adj.* distinguished, eminent.
и́менно *adv.* **1. (а) и.** namely; to wit; **нас там бы́ло тро́е, а и.: Петро́в, Ивано́в и я** there were three of us there, namely Petrov, Ivanov, and myself. **2.** just, exactly; to be exact; **где и. она́ живёт?** where exactly does she live?; **в то вре́мя я был в Росси́и, а и. в Оде́ссе** I was in Russia then, in Odessa to be

exact; **вот и. э́то я и говори́л** that's just what I was saying; **вот и.!** exactly!; precisely!
именн|о́й *adj.* **1.** nominal; **~ы́е а́кции** (*fin.*) inscribed stock; **~о́е кольцо́** ring engraved with owner's name; **и. спи́сок** nominal roll; **и. чек** cheque payable to person named; **и. экземпля́р** autographed copy. **2.** *adj. of* **имя 3.**
имено́ван|ный *p.p.p. of* **именова́ть** *and adj.*; (*math.*): **~ное число́** concrete number.
имен|ова́ть, у́ю *impf.* (*of* **на~**) to name.
имен|ова́ться, у́юсь *impf.* **1.** (+*i.*) to be called; to be termed. **2.** *pass. of* **~ова́ть**
имену́емый *pres. part. pass. of* **именова́ть; царь Ива́н, и. Гро́зным** Tsar Ivan, called the Terrible.
име́|ть, ю, ешь *impf.* to have; **и. возмо́жность** (+*inf.*) to have an opportunity (to), be in a position (to); **и. де́ло (с**+*i.*) to have dealings (with); **и. значе́ние (для)** to matter (to), be important (to); **и. ме́сто** to take place; **и. на́глость, несча́стье** etc. (+*inf.*) to have the effrontery, the misfortune, *etc.* (to); **и. в виду́** to bear in mind, think of, mean; **ничего́ не и. про́тив** (+*g.*) to have no objection(s) (to); **и. сто ме́тров в высоту́** to be 100 metres high.
име́|ться, ется *impf.* to be; to be present, be available; **в на́шем го́роде ~ется два кинотеа́тра** there are two cinemas in our town; **бана́нов у нас не ~ется** we have no bananas; **и. налицо́** to be available, be on hand.
име́|ющийся *pres. part. of* **~ться** *and adj.* available; present.
и́ми *i. of pron.* **они́**
и́мидж, а *m.* image.
имита́тор, а *m.* **1.** mimic; impressionist. **2.** simulator; **и. полёта** flight simulator.
имита́ци|я, и *f.* **1.** mimicry; mimicking. **2.** imitation (*artefact*); **и. же́мчуга** imitation pearl.
имити́р|овать, ую *impf.* to imitate; to mimic.
иммигра́нт, а *m.* immigrant.
иммигра|цио́нный *adj. of* **~ция; ~цио́нные зако́ны** immigration laws.
иммигра́ци|я, и *f.* **1.** immigration. **2.** (*collect.*) immigrants.
иммигри́р|овать, ую *impf. and pf.* to immigrate.
иммуниза́ци|я, и *f.* (*med.*) immunization.
иммунизи́р|овать, ую *impf. and pf.* (*med.*) to immunize.
иммуните́т, а *m.* (*med., leg.*) immunity.
иммун|ный (~ен, ~на) *adj.* **(к)** immune (to).
императи́в, а *m.* (*phil., gram.*) imperative.
императи́в|ный (~ен, ~на) *adj.* imperative.
импера́тор, а *m.* emperor.
импера́торский *adj.* imperial.
императри́ц|а, ы *f.* empress.
империали́зм, а *m.* imperialism.
империали́ст, а *m.* imperialist.
империалисти́ческий *adj.* imperialist(ic).
импе́ри|я, и *f.* empire.
импе́рский *adj.* imperial.
импи́чмент, а *m.* impeachment.
импоза́нт|ный (~ен, ~на) *adj.* imposing, striking.
импони́р|овать, ую *impf.* (+*d.*) to impress, strike (*fig.*); **его́ зна́ния ~овали всем знако́мым** everyone he knew was impressed by his learning.
и́мпорт, а *m.* **1.** import. **2.** (*coll.*) imported goods.
импортёр, а *m.* importer.
импорти́р|овать, ую *impf. and pf.* (*econ.*) to import.
и́мпорт|ный *adj. of* **~; ~ные по́шлины** import duties; **~ные това́ры** imported goods.
импоте́нт, а *m.* impotent man.
импоте́нт|ный (~ен, ~на) *adj.* (*med.*) impotent.
импоте́нци|я, и *f.* (*med.*) impotence.
импреса́рио *m. indecl.* impresario.
импрессиони́зм, а *m.* (*art*) impressionism.
импрессиони́ст, а *m.* (*art*) impressionist.
импрессионисти́ческий *adj.* (*art*) impressionistic.
импрессиони́ст|ский *adj.* = **~и́ческий**
импровиза́тор, а *m.* improviser.
импровиза́торский *adj.* improvisational.
импровиза́ци|я, и *f.* improvisation.
импровизи́рова|нный *p.p.p. of* **~ть** *and adj.* improvised; impromptu.
импровизи́р|овать, ую *impf.* (*of* **сымпровизи́ровать**) to improvize.
и́мпульс, а *m.* impulse, impetus.
импульси́в|ный (~ен, ~на) *adj.* impulsive.
иму́ществ|енный *adj. of* **~о; и. ценз** property qualification.
иму́ществ|о, а *nt.* property, belongings; stock; **дви́жимое и.** (*leg.*) personalty, personal estate; **недви́жимое и.** realty, real estate.
иму́щий *adj.* propertied; well-off; **власть иму́щие** the powers that be.
и́м|я, *g., d., and p.* **~ени,** *i.* **~енем,** *pl.* **~ена́, ~ён, ~ена́м** *nt.* **1.** first, Christian name; name; **вы́мышленное и.** alias, false name; **по ~ени О́льга** Olga by name; **во и.** (+*g.*) in the name of; **посла́ть на и.** (+*g.*) to address to; **запиши́те счёт на моё и.** put it down to my account; **от ~ени** (+*g.*) on behalf of; **то́лько по ~ени** only in name, only nominally; **он тепе́рь изве́стен под други́м ~енем** he now goes by, under another name; **~енем зако́на** in the name of the law; **~ени** (+*g.*) named in honour of (*usu. not translated*); **Вое́нная акаде́мия ~ени Фру́нзе** the Frunze Military Academy; **называ́ть ве́щи свои́ми ~ена́ми** to call a spade a spade. **2.** (*fig.*) name, reputation; **челове́к с больши́м ~енем** a man with a big name; **у него́ европе́йское и.** he has a European reputation; **приобрести́ и.** to make a name; **замара́ть своё и.** to ruin one's good name; **кру́пные ~ена́ в о́бласти фи́зики** great names in the field of physics. **3.** (*gram.*) noun, nomen (*any part of speech declined, as opposed to conjugated*); **и. прилага́тельное** adjective; **и. существи́тельное** noun, substantive; **и. числи́тельное** numeral.
имяре́к, а *m.* (*joc.*) so-and-so.
ин... *comb. form, abbr. of* **иностра́нный**
инакомы́сли|е, я *nt.* dissidence; nonconformism; heterodoxy.
инакомы́слящ|ий *adj.* dissident; nonconformist; heterodox; *as n.* **и., ~его** *m.* dissident.
и́наче 1. (*adv.*) differently, otherwise; **так и́ли и.** one way or another; **не и́наче (как)** (*coll.*) precisely, of course; **не и́наче как полко́вник** none other than the colonel. **2.** (*conj.*) otherwise, or (else); **спеши́те, и. вы опозда́ете** hurry up, or you will be late.
инвали́д, а *m.* invalid; **и. войны́** disabled serviceman; **и. труда́** industrial invalid.
инвали́дност|ь, и *f.* disablement; invalidity; **посо́бие по ~и** invalidity allowance; **уво́литься по ~и** (*mil.*) to be invalided out.
инвали́д|ный *adj. of* **~; и. дом** home for invalids.
инвалю́т|а, ы *f.* foreign currency.
инвентариза́ци|я, и *f.* inventory making, stock-taking.
инвентариз|ова́ть, у́ю *impf. and pf.* to inventory.
инвента́р|ный *adj. of* **~ь; ~ная о́пись** inventory.
инвента́р|ь, я́ *m.* **1.** stock; equipment, appliances; **живо́й и.** livestock; **сельскохозя́йственный и.** agricultural implements. **2.** inventory.
инве́рси|я, и *f.* inversion.
инвести́р|овать, ую *impf. and pf.* to invest.
инвеститу́р|а, ы *f.* investiture.
инвести́ци|я, и *f.* investment.
инве́стор, а *m.* (*fin.*) investor.
ингаля́тор, а *m.* (*med.*) inhaler.
ингаля́ци|я, и *f.* (*med.*) inhalation.

ингредие́нт, а *m.* ingredient.
ингу́ш, á, *g. pl.* **~е́й** *m.* Ingush.
ингу́ш|ка, ки *f. of* ~
ингу́шский *adj.* Ingush.
и́ндеве|ть, ет *impf.* (*of* **за~**) to become covered with hoar-frost.
инде́|ец, йца, *pl.* **~йцы, ~йцев** *m.* (American) Indian.
инде́йк|а, и *f.* turkey(-hen).
инде́|йский *adj. of* **~ец**
и́ндекс, а *m.* index; **и. цен** (*econ.*) price index; **почто́вый и.** post-code.
инд|иа́нка, иа́нки *f. of* **~е́ец** *and* **~и́ец**
индиви́д, а *m.* individual.
индивидуализа́ци|я, и *f.* individualization.
индивидуализи́р|овать, ую *impf. and pf.* to individualize.
индивидуали́зм, а *m.* individualism.
индивидуали́ст, а *m.* individualist.
индивидуалисти́ческий *adj.* individualistic.
индивидуалисти́ч|ный (~ен, ~на) *adj.* individualistic
индивидуа́льност|ь, и *f.* individuality.
индивидуа́л|ьный (~ен, ~ьна) *adj.* individual; **в ~ьном поря́дке** individually; **и. слу́чай** single case.
индиви́дуум, а *m.* individual.
инди́го *nt. indecl.* indigo (*colour*).
инди́|ец, йца, *pl.* **~йцы, ~йцев** *m.* Indian.
инди́йский *adj.* Indian.
Инди́йск|ий океа́н, ~ого ~а *m.* the Indian Ocean.
индика́тор, а *m.* (*tech.*) indicator; (*comput.*) display; **жидко-кристалли́ческий и.** liquid-crystal display, LCD; **светово́й и.** indicator light.
индифферéнтност|ь, и *f.* indifference.
индифферéнт|ный (~ен, ~на) *adj.* **(к)** indifferent (to).
И́нди|я, и *f.* India.
индоевропе́йский *adj.* Indo-European.
Индокита́|й, я *m.* Indo-China.
индокита́йский *adj.* Indo-Chinese.
индонези́|ец, йца, *pl.* **~йцы, ~йцев** *m.* Indonesian.
индонези́|йка, йки *f. of* **~ец**
индонези́йский *adj.* Indonesian.
Индоне́зи|я, и *f.* Indonesia.
индоссаме́нт, а *m.* (*fin.*) endorsement.
индосса́нт, а *m.* (*fin.*) endorser.
индосса́т, а *m.* (*fin.*) endorsee.
индосси́р|овать, ую *impf. and pf.* (*fin.*) to endorse.
индуи́зм, а *m.* Hinduism.
индуи́стский *adj.* Hindu.
индукти́вный *adj.* (*phil., phys.*) inductive.
инду́ктор, а *m.* (*elec.*) inductor.
индукци|о́нный *adj. of* **~я; ~о́нная кату́шка** induction coil.
инду́кци|я, и *f.* (*phil., phys.*) induction.
индульге́нци|я, и *f.* (*eccl.*) indulgence.
инду́с, а *m.* Hindu.
инду́с|ка, ки *f. of* ~
инду́сский *adj.* Hindu.
индустриализа́ци|я, и *f.* industrialization.
индустриализи́р|овать, ую *impf. and pf.* to industrialize.
индустриа́льный *adj.* industrial.
инду́стри|я, и *f.* industry.
индю́к, á *m.* turkey(-cock); **наду́лся как и.** (*coll.*) he got on his high horse.
индю́шк|а, и *f.* turkey(-hen).
индюш|о́нок, о́нка, *pl.* **~а́та, ~а́т** *m.* (turkey-)poult.
и́не|й, я *no pl., m.* hoar-frost, rime.
ине́ртност|ь, и *f.* inertness, sluggishness, inaction.
ине́рт|ный (~ен, ~на) *adj.* inert (*phys. and fig.*); sluggish, inactive.
ине́рци|я, и *f.* (*phys. and fig.*) inertia; momentum; **дви́гаться по ~и** to move under its own momentum; (*fig.*): **де́лать что-н. по ~и** to do sth. from force of inertia.
инжене́р, а *m.* engineer; **и.-строи́тель** civil engineer.
инжене́ри|я, и *f.* engineering; **ге́нная и.** genetic engineering.
инжене́рн|ый *adj.* engineering; **~ые войска́** (*mil.*) Engineers; **~ое де́ло** engineering.
инжи́р, а *m.* **1.** fig tree. **2.** fig.
инжи́рный *adj.* fig.
и́нист|ый (~, ~а) *adj.* rimy, frost-covered.
инициа́л|ы, ов *pl.* (*sg.* **~, ~а** *m.*) initials.
инициати́в|а, ы *f.* initiative; **по со́бственной ~е** on one's own initiative.
инициати́в|ный *adj.* **1.** initiating, originating; **~ная гру́ппа** action committee. **2. (~ен, ~на)** enterprising; dynamic, go-getting.
инквизи́тор, а *m.* inquisitor.
инквизи́торский *adj.* inquisitorial.
инквизи́ци|я, и *f.* inquisition.
и́нк|и, ов *no sg.* the Incas.
инко́гнито *adv.* incognito.
инкорпора́ци|я, и *f.* incorporation.
инкорпори́р|овать, ую *impf. and pf.* to incorporate.
инкримини́р|овать ую *impf. and pf.* (*+a. and d.*) to charge (with); **ему́ ~уют поджо́г** he is being charged with arson.
инкруста́ци|я, и *f.* inlaid work, inlay.
инкрусти́р|овать ую *impf. and pf.* to inlay.
и́нкский *adj.* Incan.
инкуба́тор, а *m.* incubator.
инкубацио́нный *adj.* incubation.
инкуба́ци|я, и *f.* incubation.
инкуна́бул|ы, ~ *pl.* (*sg.* **~а, ~ы** *f.*) (*liter.*) incunabula.
иногда́, *adv.* sometimes.
иногоро́дн|ий *adj.* of, from another town; **~яя по́чта** mail for, from other towns.
инозе́м|ец, ца *m.* (*obs.*) foreigner.
инозе́мный *adj.* (*obs.*) foreign.
ин|о́й *adj.* **1.** different; other; **~ы́ми слова́ми** in other words; **не кто и., как; не что ~о́е, как** none other than; **тот и́ли и.** one or other. **2.** some; **и. раз** sometimes; **и. (челове́к) мог и согласи́ться** some might agree.
инокули́р|овать, ую *impf. and pf.* to inoculate.
инокуля́ци|я, и *f.* inoculation.
инопланета́рный *adj.* alien, extraterrestrial.
инопланетя́н|ин, а, *pl.* **~е, ~** *m.* alien, extraterrestrial.
иноро́дн|ый *adj.* heterogeneous; **~ое те́ло** (*med. or fig.*) foreign body.
иносказа́ни|е, я *nt.* allegory.
иносказа́тел|ьный (~ен, ~ьна) *adj.* allegorical.
иностра́н|ец, ца *m.* foreigner.
иностра́нный *adj.* foreign.
инотде́л, а *m.* foreign department (*of Russian institutions*).
инофи́рм|а, ы *f.* foreign company.
инохо́д|ец, ца *m.* ambler (*horse*).
и́ноход|ь, и *f.* amble.
иноязы́чн|ый *adj.* **1.** speaking another language. **2.** belonging to another language; foreign; **~ое сло́во** loan-word.
инсинуа́ци|я, и *f.* insinuation.
инсинуи́р|овать, ую *impf. and pf.* to insinuate.
инспекти́р|овать, ую *impf.* to inspect.
инспе́ктор, а, *pl.* **~а́, ~о́в** *m.* inspector; **и. мане́жа** ringmaster; **порто́вый и.** harbourmaster.
инспе́ктор|ский *adj. of* ~
инспе́кци|я, и *f.* **1.** inspection; **и. на ме́сте** (*mil.*)

on-site inspection. **2.** inspectorate.
инспири́р|овать, ую *impf. and pf.* to incite; to inspire; **и. слу́хи** to start rumours.
инста́нци|я, и *f.* (*leg.*) instance; (*pol.*) level of authority; **суд пе́рвой ~и** court of first instance; (*mil.*) **кома́ндная и.** chain of command.
инсти́нкт, а *m.* instinct.
инстинкти́в|ный (~ен, ~на) *adj.* instinctive.
институ́т, а *m.* **1.** institution; **и. бра́ка** the institution of marriage. **2.** institute, institution; school; **медици́нский и.** medical school; **педагоги́ческий и.** teacher training college.
институ́т|ский *adj. of* **~ 2.**
инструкта́ж, а *m.* instructing; (*mil., aeron.*) briefing.
инструкти́в|ный (~ен, ~на) *adj.* instructional.
инструкти́р|овать, ую *impf. and pf.* (*pf. also* **про~**) to instruct; to brief.
инстру́ктор, а *m.* instructor.
инстру́ктор|ский *adj. of* **~**
инстру́кци|я, и *f.* instructions, directions.
инструме́нт, а *m.* instrument; tool, implement; (*sg.*; *collect.*) tools.
инструментали́ст, а *m.* (*mus.*) instrumentalist.
инструмента́льн|ый *adj.* **1.** (*mus.*) instrumental. **2.** (*tech.*) tool-making; **~ая сталь** tool steel.
инструмента́льщик, а *m.* tool-maker, instrument-maker.
инструмента́ри|й, я *m.* (*collect.*) instruments, tools.
инструмент|ова́ть, у́ю *impf. and pf.* (*mus.*) to orchestrate.
инструменто́вк|а, и *f.* (*mus.*) orchestration.
инсули́н, а *m.* (*med.*) insulin.
инсу́льт, а *m.* (*med.*) stroke.
инсцени́р|овать, ую *impf. and pf.* **1.** to dramatize, adapt for stage *or* screen. **2.** (*fig.*) to feign, stage; **и. о́бморок** to stage a faint.
инсцениро́вк|а, и *f.* **1.** dramatization, adaptation for stage *or* screen. **2.** (*fig.*) pretence; act.
интегра́л, а *m.* (*math.*) integral.
интегра́льн|ый *adj.* (*math.*) integral; **~ое исчисле́ние** integral calculus.
интегра́ци|я, и *f.* (*math.*) integration.
интегри́р|овать, ую *impf. and pf.* (*math.*) to integrate.
интелле́кт, а *m.* intellect; **иску́сственный и.** (*comput.*) artificial intelligence.
интеллектуа́л|ьный (~ен, ~на) *adj.* intellectual.
интеллиге́нт, а *m.* intellectual.
интеллиге́нт|ный (~ен, ~на) *adj.* cultured, educated.
интеллиге́нци|я, и *f.* **1.** (*hist.*) intelligentsia. **2.** (*collect.*) professional class(es).
интенда́нт, а *m.* (*mil.*) quartermaster.
интенда́нтств|о, а *nt.* (*mil.*) quartermaster service, commissariat.
интенси́в|ный (~ен, ~на) *adj.* intensive.
интенсифици́р|овать, ую *impf. and pf.* to intensify.
интерва́л, а *m.* (*in var. senses*) interval; space; **и. строк** (*typ.*) line spacing.
интерве́нт, а *m.* (*pol.*) interventionist.
интерве́нци|я, и *f.* (*pol.*) intervention.
интервью *nt. indecl.* interview.
интервьюе́р, а *m.* (*press*) interviewer.
интервьюи́р|овать, ую *impf. and pf.* to interview.
интере́с, а *m.* **1.** interest (= *attention*); **представля́ть и.** to be of interest; **прояви́ть и. (к)** to show interest (in). **2.** interest (= *advantage*); (*pl.*) interests; **како́й мне и.?** how do I stand to gain?; **в ва́ших ~ах пое́хать** it is in your interest to go.
интере́сно *as pred.* it is, would be interesting; **и. знать, кто э́тот высо́кий иностра́нец** it would be interesting to know who the tall foreigner is; **и., что из него́ вы́йдет** I wonder how he will turn out.
интере́с|ный (~ен, ~на) *adj.* **1.** interesting; **в ~ном положе́нии** (*euph.*) in the family way. **2.** striking, attractive.
интерес|ова́ть, у́ю *impf.* to interest.
интерес|ова́ться, у́юсь *impf.* (*+i.*) to be interested (in).
интерлю́ди|я, и *f.* (*mus.*) interlude.
интерме́ццо *nt. indecl.* (*mus.*) intermezzo.
интерна́т, а *m.* boarding school.
интернациона́л, а *m.* **1.** international (*organization*); **Пе́рвый И.** (*hist.*) the First International. **2. И.** the 'Internationale'.
интернационализа́ци|я, и *f.* internationalization.
интернационализи́р|овать, ую *impf. and pf.* to internationalize.
интернационали́зм, а *m.* internationalism.
итнернационали́ст, а *m.* internationalist.
интернациона́льный *adj.* international.
интерни́ровани|е, я *nt.* internment.
интерни́рова|нный *p.p.p. of* **~ть**; *as n.* **и., ~нного** *m.* internee.
интерни́р|овать, ую *impf. and pf.* to intern.
интерполи́р|овать, ую *impf. and pf.* to interpolate.
интерполя́ци|я, и *f.* interpolation.
интерпрета́тор, а *m.* interpreter (*expounder*).
интерпрета́ци|я, и *f.* interpretation.
интерпрети́р|овать, ую *impf. and pf.* to interpret.
интерье́р, а *m.* interior.
инти́мност|ь, и *f.* intimacy.
инти́м|ный (~ен, ~на) *adj.* intimate.
интона́ци|я, и *f.* intonation.
интони́р|овать, ую *impf.* to intone.
интри́г|а, и *f.* **1.** intrigue. **2.** plot.
интрига́н, а *m.* intriguer, schemer.
интрига́н|ка, ки *f. of* **~**
интриг|ова́ть, у́ю *impf.* **1.** (*no pf.*) to intrigue, carry on an intrigue. **2.** (*pf.* **за~**) to intrigue, fascinate.
интроду́кци|я, и *f.* (*mus.*) introduction.
интроспе́кци|я, и *f.* introspection.
интуити́в|ный (~ен, ~на) *adj.* intuitive.
интуи́ци|я, и *f.* intuition.
интури́ст, а *m.* foreign tourist.
инфа́ркт, а *m.* heart attack.
инфекцио́нн|ый *adj.* infectious; **~ая больни́ца** isolation hospital.
инфе́кци|я, и *f.* infection.
инфинити́в, а *m.* (*gram.*) infinitive.
инфля́ци|я, и *f.* (*econ.*) inflation.
информа́тик, а *m.* information scientist.
информа́тик|а, и *f.* information science.
информа́тор, а *m.* informant; **полити́ческий и.** political information officer.
информ|ацио́нный *adj. of* **~а́ция**
информа́ци|я, и *f.* information; news item.
информи́р|овать, ую *impf. and pf.* to inform.
инфракра́сный *adj.* infrared.
инфраструкту́р|а, ы *f.* infrastructure.
инциде́нт, а *m.* incident; **пограни́чный и.** frontier incident.
инъекти́р|овать, ую, уешь *impf. and pf.* to inject.
инъе́кци|я, и *f.* injection.
и. о. (*abbr. of* **исполня́ющий обя́занности**) *+g.* acting ...
ио́н, а *m.* (*phys.*) ion.
иониза́ци|я, и *f.* (*phys., med.*) ionization.
иорда́нский *adj.* Jordanian.
иподья́кон, а *m.* (*eccl.*) subdeacon.
ипоме́|я, и *f.* (*bot.*) morning glory.
ипоста́с|ь, и *f.* (*theol.*) hypostasis; **в ипоста́си**+*g.* in the role of.
ипоте́к|а, *f.* mortgage.
ипоте́|чный *adj. of* **~ка**

ипохо́ндрик, а *m.* hypochondriac.
ипохо́ндри|я, и *f.* hypochondria.
ипподро́м, а *m.* hippodrome; racecourse.
ипри́т, а *m.* mustard gas.
Ира́к, а *m.* Iraq.
ира́к|ец, ца *m.* Iraqi.
ира́кский *adj.* Iraqi.
Ира́н, а *m.* Iran.
ира́н|ец, ца *m.* Iranian.
ира́н|ка, ки *f. of* **~ец**
ира́нский *adj.* Iranian.
ира́|чка, чки *f. of* **~кец**
ири́ди|й, я *m.* (*chem.*) iridium.
иридодиагно́стик|а, и *f.* iridology.
иридо́лог, а *m.* iridologist.
и́рис, а *m.* (*bot.*) iris.
ири́с, а *m.* toffee.
ири́ск|а, и (*coll.*) *f.* (a) toffee.
ирла́нд|ец, ца *m.* Irishman.
Ирла́нди|я, и *f.* Ireland.
ирла́нд|ка, ки *f. of* **~ец**
ирла́ндский *adj.* Irish.
иронизи́р|овать, ую *impf.* **(над)** to speak ironically (about).
ирони́ческий *adj.* ironic(al).
иро́ни|я, и *f.* irony.
иррациона́л|ьный (~ен, ~ьна) *adj.* irrational; **~ьное число́** (*math.*) irrational number, surd.
иррегуля́рн|ый *adj.* irregular; **~ые войска́** (*mil.*) irregulars.
ирригáци|я, и *f.* irrigation.
ис... *pref.* = **из...**
иск, а *m.* (*leg.*) suit, action; **предъяви́ть и. (к) кому́-н.** to sue, bring an action against s.o.; **отказа́ть в ~́е** to reject a suit; **и. за клевету́** libel action.
искажа́|ть, ю *impf. of* **искази́ть**
искаже́ни|е, я *nt.* distortion, perversion.
искажённый *p.p.p. of* **искази́ть** *and adj.* distorted, perverted.
иска|зи́ть, жу́, зи́шь *pf.* (*of* **~жа́ть**) to distort, pervert, twist; to misrepresent; **боль ~зи́ла черты́ её лица́** pain has distorted her features; **и. чьи-н. слова́** to twist s.o.'s words; **и. фа́кты** to misrepresent the facts.
искале́ч|енный *p.p.p. of* **~ить** *and adj.* crippled, maimed.
искале́чива|ть, ю *impf. of* **искале́чить**
искале́ч|ить, у, ишь *pf.* (*of* **~ивать** *and* **кале́чить**) to cripple, maim.
иска́лыва|ть, ю *impf. of* **исколо́ть**
иска́ни|е, я *nt.* **1.** (+*g.*) search (for), quest (of). **2.** (*pl.*) strivings.
иска́пыва|ть, ю *impf. of* **ископа́ть**
иска́тел|ь, я *m.* seeker, searcher; **и. же́мчуга** pearl-diver.
иска́тел|ьный (~ен, ~ьна) *adj.* ingratiating.
иска́ть, ищу́, и́щешь *impf.* **1.** (+*a.*) to look for, search for; to seek (*sth. concr.*); **и. иго́лку, кварти́ру** to be looking for a needle, for a flat. **2.** (+*g.*) to seek, look for (*sth. abstr.*); **и. ме́ста** to look for a job; **и. слу́чая, сове́та** to seek an opportunity, seek advice.
исключ|а́ть, а́ю *impf. of* **~и́ть**
исключа́|я *pres. ger. of* **~ть** *and prep.*+*g.* excepting, with the exception of; **и. прису́тствующих** the present company excepted.
исключе́ни|е, я *nt.* **1.** exception; **за ~ем** (+*g.*) with the exception (of). **2.** exclusion; expulsion; **по ме́тоду ~я** by process of elimination.
исключи́тельно *adv.* **1.** exceptionally. **2.** exclusively, solely.
исключи́тел|ьный (~ен, ~ьна) *adj.* **1.** exceptional; **и. слу́чай** exceptional case; **~ьной ва́жности** of exceptional importance. **2.** exclusive; **~ьное пра́во** exclusive right, sole right.
исключ|и́ть, у́, и́шь *pf.* (*of* **~а́ть**) **1.** to exclude; to eliminate; **и. из спи́ска** to strike off a list. **2.** to expel; to dismiss. **3.** to rule out; **не ~ено́, что́ на́ши проигра́ют** the possibility of our side losing cannot be ruled out.
исковéрка|нный *p.p.p. of* **~ть** *and adj.* (*coll.*) corrupt(ed); **~нное сло́во** corrupted word, corruption.
исковéрка|ть, ю *pf. of* **коверка́ть**
иск|ово́й *adj. of* **~**; **~ово́е заявле́ние** (*leg.*) statement of claim.
исколáчива|ть, ю *impf. of* **исколоти́ть**
исколе|си́ть, шу́, си́шь *pf.* (*coll.*) to travel all over.
исколо|ти́ть, чу́, ~́тишь *pf.* (*of* **исколáчивать**) (*coll.*) to beat up; **и. кого́-н. до полусме́рти** to beat s.o. to within an inch of his life.
искол|о́ть, ю́, ~́ешь *pf.* (*of* **иска́лывать**) to prick all over, cover with pricks.
иско́мка|ть, ю *pf. of* **ко́мкать**
иско́м|ый *adj.* sought for; *as n.* **~ое, ~ого** *nt.* (*math.*) unknown quantity.
исконú, *adv.* (*rhet.*) from time immemorial.
иско́нный *adj.* primordial; immemorial.
ископа́ем|ое, ого *nt.* **1.** mineral. **2.** fossil.
ископа́емый *adj.* fossilized.
ископа́|ть, ю *pf.* (*of* **иска́пывать**) to dig up.
искорёж|ить(ся), у(сь), ишь(ся) *pf. of* **корёжить(ся)**
искорене́ни|е, я *nt.* eradication.
искорен|и́ть, ю́, и́шь *pf.* (*of* **~я́ть**) to eradicate.
искорен|я́ть, я́ю *impf. of* **~и́ть**
и́скорк|а, и *f. dim. of* **и́скра**
и́скоса *adv.* (*coll.*) aslant, sideways; **взгляд и.** sidelong glance.
и́скр|а, ы *f.* spark; (*fig.*) flash; **промелькну́ть, как и.** to flash by; **и. наде́жды** glimmer of hope; **у меня́ ~ы из глаз посы́пались** (*coll.*) I saw stars.
и́скренн|е = ~о
и́скрен|ний (~ен, ~на) *adj.* sincere, candid.
и́скренно *adv.* sincerely, candidly; **и. ваш, и. пре́данный вам** (*epistolary formula*) Yours sincerely; Yours faithfully.
и́скренност|ь, и *f.* sincerity, candour.
искрив|и́ть, лю́, и́шь *pf.* (*of* **~ля́ть**) to bend; (*fig.*) to distort.
искривле́ни|е, я *nt.* bend; (*fig.*) distortion; **и. позвоно́чника** curvature of the spine.
искривля́|ть, ю *impf. of* **искриви́ть**
искри́ст|ый (~, ~а) *adj.* sparkling.
искр|и́ть, и́т *impf.* (*tech.*) to spark.
и́скр|иться, ~́ится *impf.* to sparkle; to scintillate (*also fig.*).
искр|ово́й *adj. of* **~́а; и. зазо́р, и. промежу́ток** (*elec.*) spark-gap.
искромётный *adj.* sparkling; (*fig.*) **и. взгляд** flashing glance.
искромса́|ть, ю *pf. of* **кромса́ть**
искрош|и́ть, у́, ~́ишь *pf.* (*of* **кроши́ть**) to crumble; to mince; (*fig.*) to cut to pieces (*with sabres*).
искрош|и́ться, ~́ится *pf.* (*of* **кроши́ться**) to crumble (*intrans.*).
искуп|а́ть, аю *impf. of* **~и́ть**
искупа́|ться, юсь *pf.* (*coll.*) to bathe; to take a bath.
искупи́тел|ь, я *m.* (*theol.*) redeemer.
искупи́тел|ьный (~ен, ~ьна) *adj.* expiatory, redemptive.
искуп|и́ть, лю́, ~́ишь *pf.* (*of* **~а́ть**) **1.** (*theol. and fig.*) to redeem; to expiate, atone for. **2.** to make up for, compensate for.
искупле́ни|е, я *nt.* redemption, expiation, atonement.
иску́с, а *m.* test, ordeal.

искус|а́ть, а́ю *pf.* (*of* **∠ывать**) to bite badly, all over; to sting badly, all over.
искуси́тел|ь, я *m.* tempter.
иску|си́ть, шу́, си́шь *pf. of* **~ша́ть**
иску|си́ться, шу́сь, си́шься *pf.* **1.** (**в**+*p.*) to become expert (at), become a past master (in, of). **2.** *pass. of* **~си́ть**
иску́сник, а *m.* (*coll.*) expert, past master.
иску́с|ный (~ен, ~на) *adj.* skilful; expert.
иску́сственност|ь, и *f.* artificiality.
иску́сствен|ный *adj.* **1.** artificial, synthetic; man-made; **~ное пита́ние (младе́нца)** bottle feeding. **2.** (**~, ~на**) (*fig.*) artificial, feigned.
иску́сств|о, а *nt.* **1.** art; **изобрази́тельные, изя́щные ~а** fine arts. **2.** craftsmanship, skill; **и. верхово́й езды́** horsemanship; **де́лать что-н. из любви́ к ~у** to do sth. for its own sake.
искусствове́д, а *m.* art historian.
искусствове́дени|е, я *nt.* history of art.
иску́сыва|ть, ю *impf. of* **искуса́ть**
искуша́|ть, ю *impf.* (*of* **искуси́ть**) to tempt; to seduce; **и. судьбу́** to tempt fate, tempt Providence.
искуше́ни|е, я *nt.* temptation; seduction; **ввести́ в и.** to lead into temptation; **подда́ться ~ю, впасть в и.** to yield to temptation.
искушённый *p.p.p. of* **искуси́ть** *and adj.* experienced; tested.
исла́м, а *m.* Islam.
исла́нд|ец, ца *m.* Icelander.
Исла́нди|я, и *f.* Iceland.
исла́нд|ка, ки *f. of* **~ец**
исла́ндский *adj.* Icelandic.
испа́ко|стить, щу, стишь *pf. of* **па́костить**
испа́н|ец, ца *m.* Spaniard.
Испа́ни|я, и *f.* Spain.
испа́нк|а[1]**, и** *f.* Spanish woman.
испа́нк|а[2]**, и** *f.* (*coll.*) Spanish 'flu.
испа́нский *adj.* Spanish.
испаре́ни|е, я *nt.* **1.** evaporation. **2.** exhalation; fumes.
испа́рин|а, ы *f.* perspiration.
испар|и́ть, ю́, и́шь *pf.* (*of* **~я́ть**) to evaporate (*trans.*).
испар|и́ться, ю́сь, и́шься *pf.* (*of* **~я́ться**) to evaporate; (*fig., joc.*) to vanish.
испар|я́ть(ся), я́ю(сь) *impf. of* **~и́ть(ся)**
испа́чка|ть, ю *pf. of* **па́чкать**
испепел|и́ть, ю́, и́шь *pf.* (*of* **~я́ть**) to reduce to ashes, incinerate.
испепел|я́ть, я́ю *impf. of* **~и́ть**
испестр|ённый *p.p.p. of* **~и́ть** *and adj.* speckled, mottled; variegated.
испестр|и́ть, ю́, и́шь *pf.* (*of* **~я́ть**) to speckle; to mottle; to make variegated.
испестр|я́ть, я́ю *impf. of* **~и́ть**
испечённый *p.p.p. of* **испе́чь; вновь и.** (*coll.*) new-fledged.
испе́|чь, ку́, чёшь, ку́т, *past* **∴к, ~кла́** *pf. of* **печь**
испещр|и́ть, ю́, и́шь *pf.* (*of* **~я́ть**) (+*a. and i.*) to spot (with); to mark all over (with); **и. сте́ну на́дписями** to cover a wall with inscriptions.
испещр|я́ть, я́ю *impf. of* **~и́ть**
испи|са́ть, шу́, ∠шешь *pf.* (*of* **∠сывать**) **1.** to cover with writing; **он уже́ ~са́л два́дцать тетра́дей** he has already filled up twenty exercise books. **2.** to use up (*pencil, paper, etc.*).
испи|са́ться, шу́сь, ∠шешься *pf.* (*of* **∠сываться**) (*coll.*) **1.** to be used up (*of writing instrument*). **2.** to write o.s. out (*of a writer*).
испи́сыва|ть(ся), ю(сь) *impf. of* **исписа́ть(ся)**
испито́й *adj.* (*coll.*) haggard, gaunt; hollow-cheeked.
исповеда́л|ьня, ьни, *g. pl.* **~ен** *f.* (*eccl.*) confessional.
испове́дани|е, я *nt.* creed; confession (*of faith*).
испове́д|ать, аю *pf.* (*coll.*) = **~овать**[1]
испове́д|аться, аюсь *pf.* (*coll.*) = **~оваться**[1]
испове́д|овать[1]**, ую** *impf. and pf.* **1.** (*eccl.*) to hear the confession (of). **2.** (*coll.*) to draw out. **3.** to confess.
испове́д|овать[2]**, ую** *impf.* to profess (*a faith*).
испове́д|оваться[1]**, уюсь** *impf. and pf.* **1.** (+*d. or* **у**; *eccl.*) to confess, make one's confession (to). **2.** (+*d. or* **пе́ред**; *fig., coll.*) to confess; to unburden o.s. of; **он мне ~овался в свои́х сомне́ниях** he confessed his doubts to me.
испове́д|оваться[2]**, уюсь** *impf. and pf., pass. of* **~овать**[2]
и́споведь|ь, и *f.* (*eccl.*) confession; **быть на ~и** to be at confession.
и́сподволь *adv.* (*coll.*) in leisurely fashion; by degrees.
исподло́бья *adv.* from under the brows (*distrustfully, sullenly*).
исподтишка́ *adv.* (*coll., pej.*) in an underhand way; on the quiet, on the sly; **смея́ться и.** to laugh in one's sleeve.
испоко́н *adv.*; *only in phrr.* **и. ве́ку, и. веко́в** from time immemorial.
исполи́н, а *m.* giant.
исполи́нский *adj.* gigantic.
исполко́м, а *m.* (*abbr. of* **исполни́тельный комите́т**) executive committee.
исполне́ни|е, я *nt.* **1.** fulfilment (*of wish*); execution (*of order*); discharge (*of duties*); **привести́ в и.** to carry out, execute. **2.** performance (*of play, etc.*); execution (*of music*); (*theatr., mus.*) **в ~и** (+*g.*) (as) played (by), (as) performed (by).
испо́лненный *p.p.p. of* **испо́лнить** *and adj.* (+*g.*) full (of).
исполни́м|ый (~, ~а) *adj.* feasible, practicable.
исполни́тел|ь, я *m.* **1.** executor; **суде́бный и.** bailiff. **2.** (*theatr., mus., etc.*) performer; **и. поп-му́зыки** pop musician; **соста́в ~ей** cast.
исполни́тельност|ь, и *f.* assiduity; expedition.
исполни́тел|ьный *adj.* **1.** executive; **и. лист** (*leg.*) writ, court order. **2.** (**~ен, ~ьна**) efficient; industrious; assiduous.
испо́лн|ить, ю, ишь *pf.* (*of* **~я́ть**) **1.** to carry out, execute (*orders, etc.*); to fulfil (*a wish*); **и. обеща́ние** to keep a promise; **и. про́сьбу** to grant a request. **2.** to perform; **и. роль** (+*g.*) to take the part (of).
испо́лн|иться, юсь, ишься *pf.* (*of* **~я́ться**) **1.** to be fulfilled. **2.** (*impers.*, +*d.*; *expr. passage of time*): **ему́ ~илось семь лет** he is seven; **~илось пять лет с тех пор, как он уе́хал в Аме́рику** it is five years since he went to America.
исполн|я́ть(ся), я́ю(сь) *impf. of* **∠ить(ся)**; **~я́ющий обя́занности** (+*g.*) acting.
исполос|ова́ть, у́ю *pf. of* **полосова́ть**
испо́льзовани|е, я *nt.* utilization; use; **повто́рное и.** recycling.
испо́льз|овать, ую *impf. and pf.* to make use of, utilize; to turn to account.
испо́льщик, а *m.* sharecropper.
испо́льщин|а, ы *f.* sharecropping.
испо́р|тить(ся), чу(сь), тишь(ся) *pf. of* **по́ртить(ся)**
испо́рченност|ь, и *f.* depravity.
испо́рчен|ный *p.p.p. of* **испо́ртить** *and adj.* **1.** depraved; corrupted. **2.** (*of perishable goods, etc.*) spoiled; bad, rotten; **~ные зу́бы** rotten teeth; **~ное мя́со** tainted meat. **3.** (*coll.*) spoiled (*child*).
исправи́м|ый (~, ~а) *adj.* remediable.
исправи́тельный *adj.* correctional; corrective; **и. дом** reformatory.
испра́в|ить, лю, ишь *pf.* (*of* **~ля́ть**) **1.** to correct,

emend. **2.** to repair, mend. **3.** to reform.
испра́в|иться, люсь, ишься *pf.* (*of* **~ля́ться**) **1.** to improve (*intrans.*); to reform (*intrans.*), turn over a new leaf. **2.** *pass. of* **~ить**
исправле́ни|е, я *nt.* **1.** correcting; repairing. **2.** improvement; correction.
испра́влен|ный *p.p.p. of* **испра́вить** *and adj.* improved, corrected; **~ное изда́ние** revised edition; **и. хара́ктер** reformed character.
исправля́|ть, ю *impf. of* **испра́вить**
исправля́|ться, юсь *impf. of* **испра́виться**
испра́вност|ь, и *f.* **1.** good condition; **в (по́лной) ~и** in good working order, in good repair. **2.** punctuality; preciseness; meticulousness.
испра́в|ный (~ен, ~на) *adj.* **1.** in good order. **2.** punctual; precise; meticulous.
испражне́ни|е, я *nt.* **1.** defecation. **2.** faeces.
испражн|и́ться, ю́сь, и́шься *pf. of* **~я́ться**
испражн|я́ться, я́юсь *impf.* (*of* **~и́ться**) to defecate.
испра́шива|ть, ю *impf.* (*of* **испроси́ть**) to` beg, solicit; **и. ми́лость** to ask a favour.
испро́б|овать, ую *pf.* **1.** to test. **2.** to try out; **и. все возмо́жности** to try everything, leave no stone unturned.
испро|си́ть, шу́, ~́сишь *pf.* (*of* **испра́шивать**) to obtain (by asking).
испу́г, а (у) *m.* fright; alarm; **с ~у** from fright.
испу́ганный *p.p.p. of* **испуга́ть** *and adj.* frightened, scared.
испуга́|ть(ся), ю(сь) *pf. of* **пуга́ть(ся)**
испуска́|ть, ю *impf. of* **испусти́ть**
испу|сти́ть, щу́, ~́стишь *pf.* (*of* **~ска́ть**) to emit, let out; **и. вздох** to heave a sigh; **и. дух** to breathe one's last; **и. крик** to utter a cry.
испыта́ни|е, я *nt.* **1.** test, trial; (*fig.*) ordeal; **быть на ~и** to be on trial, be on probation. **2.** examination; **вступи́тельные ~я, приёмные ~я** entrance examination.
испы́т|анный *p.p.p. of* **~а́ть** *and adj.* tried, well-tried; proven.
испыта́тел|ь, я *m.* tester; **лётчик-и.** test pilot.
испыта́тельн|ый *adj.* test, trial; probationary; **~ая коми́ссия** examining board; **и. полёт** test-flight; **и. пробе́г** trial run; **и. срок** period of probation; **~ая ста́нция** experimental station.
испыт|а́ть, а́ю *pf.* (*of* **~́ывать**) **1.** to test, put to the test; **и. чьё-н. терпе́ние** to try s.o.'s patience. **2.** to feel, experience.
испыту́ющий *adj.*: **и. взгляд** searching look.
испы́тыва|ть, ю *impf. of* **испыта́ть**
иссека́|ть, ю *impf. of* **иссе́чь**
иссече́ни|е, я *nt.* (*med.*) excision, removal.
иссе́|чь[1]**, ку́, чёшь, ку́т,** *past* **~к, ~кла́** *pf.* (*of* **~ка́ть**) **1.** to carve (*in stone, etc.*). **2.** (*med.*) to excise, remove.
иссе́|чь[2]**, ку́, чёшь, ку́т,** *past* **~к, ~кла** *pf.* (*of* **~ка́ть**) to cut up, cleave.
иссле́довани|е, я *nt.* **1.** investigation; research; exploration; **и. больно́го** examination of a patient; **и. кро́ви** blood test; **он занима́ется ~ями по ру́сской исто́рии** he is engaged in research on Russian history. **2.** (*scientific*) paper; study.
иссле́довател|ь, я *m.* researcher; investigator; explorer.
иссле́довательский *adj.* research.
иссле́д|овать ую *impf. and pf.* to investigate, examine; to research into; to explore; to analyse.
иссо́х|нуть, ну, нешь, *past* **~, ~ла** *pf.* (*of* **иссыха́ть**) **1.** to dry up. **2.** to wither; (*fig., coll.*) to fade away.
и́сстари *adv.* from of old, of yore; **так и. ведётся** it is an old custom.
исстрада́|ться, юсь *pf.* to become worn out (with suffering).
исступле́ни|е, и *nt.* frenzy; **и. восто́рга** ecstasy, transport; **гне́вное и.** rage.
исступлённый *adj.* frenzied; ecstatic.
иссуш|а́ть, а́ю *impf. of* **~и́ть**
иссуш|и́ть, у́, ~́ишь *pf.* (*of* **~а́ть**) to dry up; (*fig.*) to consume, waste.
иссыха́|ть, ю *impf. of* **иссо́хнуть**
иссяк|а́ть, а́ю *impf. of* **~́нуть**
исся́к|нуть, ну, нешь, *past* **~, ~ла** *pf.* (*of* **~а́ть**) to run dry, dry up; (*fig.*) to run low, fail.
иста́плива|ть, ю *impf. of* **истопи́ть**
иста́ск|анный *p.p.p. of* **~а́ть** *and adj.* **1.** worn out; threadbare. **2.** (*fig., coll.*) worn; haggard.
истаск|а́ть, а́ю *pf.* (*of* **~́ивать**) to wear out.
иста́скива|ть, ю *impf. of* **истаска́ть**
иста́чива|ть, ю *impf. of* **источи́ть**[1]
истека́|ть, ю *impf. of* **исте́чь**
исте́|кший *p.p. of* **~чь** *and adj.* past; **в тече́ние ~кшего го́да** during the past year.
истер|е́ть, изотру́, изотрёшь, *past* **~̈, ~̈ла** *pf.* (*of* **истира́ть**) **1.** to grate. **2.** to wear out, use up (*by rubbing*); **и. в порошо́к** to reduce to powder.
истер|е́ться, изотрётся, *past* **~̈ся, ~̈лась** *pf.* (*of* **истира́ться**) to wear out (*intrans.*).
исте́рз|анный *p.p.p. of* **~а́ть** *and adj.* tattered; lacerated; (*fig.*) tormented.
истерза́|ть, ю *pf.* **1.** to tear in pieces; to mutilate. **2.** to torment.
исте́рик, а *m.* hysterical man.
исте́рик|а, и *f.* hysterics.
истери́ческий *adj.* hysterical; **и. припа́док** fit of hysterics.
истери́чк|а, и *f.* hysterical woman.
истери́ч|ный (~ен, ~на) *adj.* hysterical.
истери́|я, и *f.* (*med.*) hysteria; (*fig.*): **вое́нная и.** war hysteria.
истёртый *p.p.p. of* **истере́ть** *and adj.* worn; old.
ист|е́ц, ца́ *m.* (*leg.*) plaintiff; petitioner.
истече́ни|е, я *nt.* **1.** outflow; **и. кро́ви** haemorrhage. **2.** expiry, expiration; **по ~и сро́ка каранти́на** on the expiry of the quarantine period.
исте́|чь, ку́, чёшь, ку́т, *past* **~̈к, ~кла́** *pf.* (*of* **~ка́ть**) **1.: и. кро́вью** to bleed profusely. **2.** to expire, elapse; **вре́мя ~кло́** time is up.
и́стин|а, ы *f.* truth; **изби́тая и.** truism; **свята́я и.** God's truth; gospel truth.
и́стин|ный (~ен, ~на) *adj.* true, veritable.
истира́ни|е, я *nt.* abrasion.
истира́|ть(ся), ю(сь) *impf. of* **истере́ть(ся)**
истле|ва́ть, ва́ю *impf. of* **~́ть**
истле́|ть, ю *pf.* (*of* **~ва́ть**) **1.** to rot, decay. **2.** to smoulder to ashes.
и́стов|ый (~, ~а) *adj.* (*obs.*) proper; devout; assiduous, punctilious.
исто́к, а *m.* source.
истолкова́ни|е, я *nt.* interpretation, commentary.
истолкова́тел|ь, я *m.* interpreter, commentator.
истолк|ова́ть, у́ю *pf.* (*of* **~о́вывать**) to interpret; to comment upon; **и. замеча́ние в дурну́ю сто́рону** to put a nasty construction on a remark.
истолко́выва|ть, ю *impf. of* **истолкова́ть**
истол|о́чь, ку́, чёшь, ку́т, *past* **~о́к, ~кла́** *pf.* to pound, crush.
исто́м|а, ы *f.* lassitude; languor.
истом|и́ть, лю́, и́шь *pf.* (*of* **томи́ть** *and* **~ля́ть**) to exhaust, weary.
истом|и́ться, лю́сь, и́шься *pf.* (*of* **~ля́ться**) **(от)** to be exhausted, worn out (with, from); to be weary (of); **и. от жа́жды** to be faint with thirst.
истом|лённый *p.p.p. of* **~и́ть** *and adj.* exhausted, worn out.

истомля́|ть(ся), ю(сь) *impf. of* **истоми́ть(ся)**
истоп|и́ть, лю́, ~́ишь *pf.* (*of* **иста́пливать**) **1.** to heat up. **2.** (*coll.*) to consume, use up (*fuel*). **3.** to melt down.
истопни́к, а́ *m.* stoker, boiler-man.
истоп|та́ть, чу́, ~́чешь *pf.* **1.** to trample (down, over). **2.** (*coll.*) to wear out (*footwear*).
исторг|а́ть, а́ю *impf. of* **~́нуть**
исто́рг|нуть, ну, нешь, *past* **~, ~ла** *pf.* (*of* **~а́ть**) **1.** (*rhet.*) to banish, expel; **и. из свое́й среды́** to ostracize. **2.** (**у** *or* **из;** *obs.*) to rest, wrench (from); (*fig.*) to force (from), extort; **и. обеща́ние** to extort a promise.
истори́зм, а *m.* historical method.
исто́рик, а *m.* historian.
историо́граф, а *m.* historiographer.
историогра́фи|я, и *f.* historiography.
истори́ческий *adj.* **1.** historical. **2.** historic.
исто́ри|я, и *f.* **1.** history; **войти́ в ~ю** to go down in history. **2.** (*coll.*) story. **3.** (*coll.*) incident, event; **вчера́ случи́лась со мной заба́вная и.** a funny thing happened to me yesterday; **ве́чная** (*or* **обы́чная**) **и.!** it's the same old story!
истоск|ова́ться, у́юсь *pf.* (**по**+*d.*) to yearn (for); to be wearied with longing (for).
источ|а́ть, а́ю *impf.* (*of* **~и́ть**[2]) to give off, impart.
источ|и́ть[1]**, у́, ~́ишь** *pf.* (*of* **иста́чивать**) **1.** to grind down. **2.** to eat away, gnaw through.
источ|и́ть[2]**, у́, ~́ишь** *pf. of* **~а́ть**
исто́чник, а *m.* **1.** spring. **2.** (*fig.*) source; **и. информа́ции** source of information; **ве́рный и.** reliable source; **и. све́та** source of light; **служи́ть ~ом** (+*g.*) to be a source (of).
исто́шный *adj.* (*coll.*) heart-rending.
истощ|а́ть(ся), а́ю(сь) *impf. of* **~и́ть(ся)**
истоще́ни|е, я *nt.* emaciation; exhaustion; depletion; **война́ на и.** war of attrition.
истощ|ённый *p.p.p. of* **~и́ть** *and adj.* emaciated; exhausted.
истощ|и́ть, у́, и́шь *pf.* (*of* **~а́ть**) to emaciate; to exhaust; to drain, sap; **и. ко́пи** to work out mines.
истощ|и́ться, у́сь, и́шься *pf.* (*of* **~а́ться**) to become emaciated; to become exhausted (*also fig.*); **все на́ши запа́сы ~и́лись** all our supplies had run out.
истра́|тить, чу, тишь *pf. of* **тра́тить**
истра́|титься, чусь, тишься *pf.* **1.** *pass. of* **~тить.** **2.** (*coll.*) to overspend.
истреби́тел|ь, я *m.* **1.** destroyer. **2.** fighter (*aircraft*); **и.-бомбардиро́вщик** fighter bomber.
истреби́тель|ный *adj.* **1.** destructive. **2.** *adj. of* **~ 2.**; **~ная авиа́ция** fighters (*collect.*).
истреб|и́ть, лю́, и́шь *pf.* (*of* **~ля́ть**) to destroy; to exterminate.
истребле́ни|е, я *nt.* destruction; extermination.
истребля́|ть, ю *impf. of* **истреби́ть**
истрёп|анный *p.p.p. of* **~а́ть** *and adj.* torn, frayed; worn.
истреп|а́ть, лю́, ~́лешь *pf.* (*of* **~́ывать**) to tear, fray; to wear to rags; **и. не́рвы** (*coll.*) to fray one's nerves.
истрёпыва|ть, ю *impf. of* **истрепа́ть**
истука́н, а *m.* idol; statue.
и́стый *adj.* true, genuine; **и. учёный** a true scholar; **и. люби́тель живо́тных** a genuine animal-lover.
истяза́ни|е, я *nt.* torture.
истяза́тел|ь, я *m.* torturer.
истяза́|ть, ю *impf.* to torture.
исхо́д, а *m.* **1.** outcome, issue; end; **быть на ~е** to be nearing the end, be coming to an end; **на ~е дня** towards evening; **день был на ~е** the day was drawing to a close. **2.** (*bibl.*) **И.** (*the Book of*) Exodus.
исхо|ди́ть[1]**, жу́, ~́дишь** *pf.* (*coll.*) to go, walk all over.
исхо|ди́ть[2]**, жу́, ~́дишь** *impf.* (*of* **изойти́**) **1.** (*impf. only*) (**из**) to issue (from), come (from); to emanate (from); **отку́да ~ди́л э́тот слух?** where did this rumour come from? **2.** (*impf. only*) (**из**) to proceed (from), base o.s. (on); **и. из необосно́ванных предположе́ний** to proceed from unfounded assumptions. **3.: и. слеза́ми** to cry one's heart out.
исхо́дн|ый *adj.* initial; **~ая то́чка, ~ое положе́ние** point of departure; **~ая ста́дия** initial phase.
исхуда́лый *adj.* emaciated, wasted.
исхуда́ни|е, я *nt.* emaciation.
исхуда́|ть, ю *pf.* to become emaciated, become wasted.
исцара́п|ать, аю *pf.* (*of* **~ывать**) to scratch badly; to scratch all over.
исцара́пыва|ть, ю *impf. of* **исцара́пать**
исцеле́ни|е, я *nt.* **1.** healing, cure. **2.** recovery.
исцел|и́мый *pres. part. pass. of* **~и́ть** *and adj.* curable.
исцели́тел|ь, я *m.* healer.
исцел|и́ть, ю́, и́шь *pf.* (*of* **~я́ть**) to heal, cure.
исцел|я́ть, я́ю *impf. of* **~и́ть**
исча́ди|е, я *nt.* (*rhet.*) offspring, progeny; *esp. in phr.* **и. а́да** fiend, devil incarnate.
исча́х|нуть, ну, нешь, *past* **~, ~ла** *pf.* to waste away.
исчез|а́ть, а́ю *impf.* (*of* **~́нуть**) to disappear, vanish.
исчезнове́ни|е, я *nt.* disappearance.
исчёз|нуть, ну, нешь, *past* **~, ~ла** *pf. of* **~а́ть**
исчёрк|ать, аю (*and* **~а́ть, ~а́ю**) *pf.* **1.** to cover with crossings-out. **2.** to scribble all over.
исче́рп|ать, аю *pf.* (*of* **~ывать**) **1.** to exhaust, drain; **и. все свои́ сре́дства** to exhaust all one's resources; (*fig.*): **и. терпе́ние** to exhaust s.o.'s patience. **2.** to settle, conclude; **и. вопро́с** to settle a question; **и. пове́стку дня** to conclude the agenda.
исче́рпыва|ть, ю *impf. of* **исче́рпать**
исче́рпыва|ющий *pres. part. act. of* **~ть** *and adj.* exhaustive.
исчер|ти́ть, чу́, ~́тишь *pf.* (*of* **~́чивать**) to cover with lines.
исче́рчив|ать, ю *impf. of* **исчерти́ть**
исчисле́ни|е, я *nt.* calculation; (*math.*) calculus.
исчи́сл|ить, ю, ишь *pf.* (*of* **~я́ть**) to calculate, compute; to estimate.
исчисл|я́ть, я́ю *impf. of* **~́ить**
исчисля́|ться, ется *impf.* (+*i. or* **в**+*a.*) to amount to, come to; to be estimated (at); **убы́тки ~лись в сто рубле́й** the damages came to one hundred roubles; **поте́ри ~ются ты́сячами** the casualties are estimated at thousands.
ита́к *conj.* thus; so then.
Ита́ли|я, и *f.* Italy.
италья́н|ец, ца *nt.* Italian.
италья́н|ка, ки *f. of* **~ец**
италья́нск|ий *adj.* Italian; **~ая забасто́вка** sit-down strike; work-to-rule.
и т. д. (*abbr. of* ***и так да́лее***) etc., etcetera, and so on.
ито́г, а *m.* **1.** sum, total; **о́бщий и.** grand total. **2.** (*fig.*) result; **подвести́ и.** to sum up; **в ~е** as a result; **в коне́чном ~е** in the end.
итого́ *adv.* in all, altogether.
ито́говый *adj.* total, final.
ито́ж|ить, у, ишь *impf.* to sum up, add up.
и т. п. (*abbr. of* ***и тому́ подо́бное***) etc., etcetera, and so on.
итте́рби|й, я *m.* (*chem.*) ytterbium.
и́ттри|й, я *m.* (*chem.*) yttrium.
иудаи́зм, а *m.* Judaism.
иуде́|й, я *m.* Jew.

иуде́й|ка, ки *f. of* ~
иуде́йский *adj.* Judaic.
их[1] *a. and g. of* **они́**
их[2] *possessive adj.* their(s); **их маши́на ме́ньше, чем на́ша** their car is smaller than ours.
ихневмо́н, а *m.* (*zool.*) ichneumon.
и́хний *possessive adj.* (*coll.*) their(s).
ихтио́лог, а *m.* ichthyologist.
ихтиологи́ческий *adj.* ichthyological.
ихтиоло́ги|я, и *f.* ichthyology.
иша́к, а́ *m.* donkey, ass (*also fig.*).
иша́|чий *adj. of* ~**к**
и́шиас, а *m.* (*med.*) sciatica.
ишь *int.* (*coll.*) *expr. surprise or disgust*: look!; **и. ты!** = **и.!** *or expr. disagreement or objection.*
ище́йк|а, и *f.* bloodhound, tracker dog (*also fig., pej.*).
и́щущий *pres. part. act. of* **иска́ть** *and adj.*: **и. взгляд** searching, wistful look.
ию́л|ь, я *m.* July.
ию́ль|ский *adj. of* ~
ию́н|ь, я *m.* June.
ию́нь|ский *adj. of* ~

Йе́мен, а *m.* Yemen.
йе́менский *adj.* Yemeni.
йе́ти *m. indecl.* yeti, abominable snowman.
йог, а *m.* yogi.
йо́г|а, и *f.* yoga.
йогу́рт, а *m.* yog(h)urt.
йод, а *m.* iodine.
йо́дист|ый *adj.* (*chem.*) containing iodine; **й. ка́лий** potassium iodide; ~**ая соль** iodized salt.
йо́д|ный *adj. of* ~; **и. раство́р** tincture of iodine.
йо́т|а, ы *f.* iota; **ни на** ~**у** not a jot, not an iota.
Йоха́ннесбург, а *m.* Johannesburg.

К

°К (*abbr. of* ***гра́дусов по Ке́львину***) K., degrees Kelvin; **273°К** 273K.
к, ко *prep.+d.* **1.** (*of space and fig.*) to, towards; **мы приближа́лись к Берли́ну** we were nearing Berlin; **прислони́те его́ к стене́** place it against the wall; **лицо́м к лицу́** face to face; **к лу́чшему** for the better; **моли́тва к Бо́гу** prayer to God; **любо́вь к де́тям** love of children; **к о́бщему удивле́нию** to everyone's surprise; **к (не)сча́стью** (un)fortunately; **к чёрту его́!** to hell with him!; **шля́па ей к лицу́** her hat becomes her; **к ва́шим услу́гам** at your service; (*in addition to*) **приба́вить три к пяти́** to add three and five; **к тому́ же** besides, moreover. **2.** (*of time*) to, towards; by; **зима́ подходи́ла к концу́** winter was drawing to a close; **к утру́** towards morning; by morning; **к пе́рвому января́** by the first of January; **я приду́ к восьми́ (часа́м)** I will be there by eight (o'clock); **к тому́ вре́мени** by then, by that time; **к сро́ку** on time. **3.** for; **к чему́?** what for?; **э́то ни к чему́** it is no good, no use; **к обе́ду, к у́жину** *etc.*, for dinner, for supper, *etc.* **4.** (*in titles of pamphlets, articles in newspapers and periodicals, etc.*) on; on the occasion of; **к столе́тию со дня рожде́ния Льва Толсто́го** on (the occasion of) the centenary of the birth of Lev Tolstoy; **к вопро́су о...** *oft. requires no translation.*
-ка *particle* (*coll.*) *modifying force of imper.*: **скажи́-ка мне** come on now, tell me; **да́й-ка мне посмотре́ть** come on, let me take a look; **ну́-ка** well; **ну́-ка спо́йте что-н.!** come on, give us a song!
каба́к, а́ *m.* (*obs.*) tavern; (*coll., fig.*) pigsty.
кабал|а́, ы́ *f.* servitude, bondage.
к. (*abbr. of* **копе́йка**) k, kopeck(s).
каба́л|ьный (~ен, ~ьна) *adj.* imposing bondage, enslaving; **к. догово́р** one-sided treaty.
каба́н, а́ *m.* **1.** wild boar. **2.** hog, boar.
каба́н|ий *adj. of* ~
кабар|га́, ги́, *g. pl.* ~**о́г** *f.* (*zool.*) musk-deer.
кабаре́ *nt. indecl.* cabaret.
каба́|цкий *adj. adj. of* ~**к**
кабач|о́к[1]**, ка́** *m.* **1.** *dim. of* **каба́к. 2.** (*coll.*) small restaurant.
кабач|о́к[2]**, ка́** *m.* vegetable marrow.
ка́бел|ь, я *m.* cable; **возду́шный к.** overhead cable.
ка́бель|ный *adj. of* ~; ~**ное телеви́дение** cable television.
кабеста́н, а *m.* (*tech.*) capstan.
каби́н|а, ы *f.* cabin; cockpit; cab (*of a lorry*); cubicle; booth; **(для купа́льщиков)** bathing-hut.
кабине́т[1]**, а** *m.* **1.** study; consulting-room, surgery; **физи́ческий к.** physics laboratory; **лингафо́нный к.** language laboratory; **отде́льный к.** private room (*in restaurant*); **к. красоты́** beauty parlour. **2.** suite (*of furniture*).
кабине́т[2]**, а** *m.* (*pol.*) cabinet.
кабине́т|ный *adj.* **1.** *adj. of* ~[1]. **2.**: **к. портре́т** cabinet photograph. **3.** (*fig.*) theoretical; **к. страте́г** armchair strategist.
каби́н|ка, ки *f. dim. of* ~**а**
каблогра́мм|а, ы *f.* cable(gram).
каблу́к, а́ *m.* heel (*of footwear*); **быть под** ~**о́м у кого́-н.** (*fig., coll.*) to be under s.o.'s thumb.
каблуч|о́к, ка́ *m. dim. of* **каблу́к**
кабриоле́т, а *m.* cabriolet.
кабы́ *conj.* (*coll. and folk poet.*) if; if only.
кавале́р[1]**, а** *m.* **1.** partner (*at dance*); (*in mixed company on social occasions*) escort; (gentle-)man; **была́ весёлая вечери́нка, но** ~**ов не хвата́ло** it was a good party but there were not enough men. **2.** (*coll.*) admirer.
кавале́р[2]**, а** *m.* **(о́рдена)** knight, holder (of an order); **гео́ргиевский к.** holder of the St George Cross.
кавалер|и́йский *adj. of* ~**ия**
кавалери́ст, а *m.* cavalryman.
кавале́ри|я, и *f.* cavalry.
кавалька́д|а, ы *f.* cavalcade.
каварда́к, а́ *m.* (*coll.*) mess, muddle.
ка́верз|а, ы *f.* (*coll.*) **1.** chicanery. **2.** mean trick, dirty trick; **устро́ить** ~**у кому́-н.** to play a mean trick on s.o.
ка́верзный *adj.* (*coll.*) **1.** (*pej.*) given to playing mean, dirty tricks; scheming. **2.** tricky, ticklish.
каве́рн|а, ы *f.* (*med. and geol.*) cavity.
Кавка́з, а *m.* Caucasus.
кавка́з|ец, ца *m.* Caucasian.
кавка́з|ка, ки *f. of* ~**ец**
кавка́зский *adj.* Caucasian.

кавы́ч|ки, ек *no sg.* inverted commas, quotation marks; **в ~ках** in inverted commas, in quotes; (*fig., coll.*) so-called; **демокра́тия в ~ках** so-called 'democracy'.

кагебе́шник, а *m.* (*coll.*) KGB agent.

кагеби́ст = кагебе́шник

кагэбэ́шник = кагебе́шник

каде́нци|я, и *f.* **1.** (*mus. and liter.*) cadence. **2.** (*mus.*) cadenza.

каде́т[1]**, а** *m.* cadet.

каде́т[2]**, а** *m.* (*abbr. of* **конституцио́нный демокра́т**) (*pol., hist.*) Constitutional Democrat (*abbr.* Cadet).

каде́т|ский[1] *adj. of* ~[1]; **к. ко́рпус** (*hist.*) military school.

каде́т|ский[2] *adj. of* ~[2]

кади́л|о, а *nt.* (*eccl.*) thurible, censer.

кади́л|ьный *adj.* **1.** *adj. of* **~о. 2.** of incense; **к. за́пах** smell of incense.

ка́дк|а, и *f.* tub, vat.

ка́дми|й, я *m.* (*chem.*) cadmium.

ка́дочник, а *m.* cooper.

ка́д|очный *adj. of* **~ка**

кадр[1]**, а** *m.* **1.** (*mil.*) cadre; **он слу́жит в ~ах** he is a regular (soldier). **2.** (*pl. only*) personnel; **отде́л ~ов** personnel department. **3.** (*pl. only*) (*pol.*) cadres.

кадр[2]**, а** *m.* (*cin.*) **1.** frame, still. **2.** close-up.

кадри́л|ь, и *f.* quadrille (dance).

ка́дровый *adj.* **1.** (*mil.*) regular; career. **2.** skilled; trained.

кады́к, а́ *m.* (*coll.*) Adam's apple.

каёмк|а, и *f.* (*coll.*) *dim. of* **кайма́**

каждодне́вный *adj.* daily.

ка́жд|ый *adj.* **1.** every, each; **к. день** every day; **~ые два дня** every two days; **~ую весну́** every spring; **к. из них получи́л по пять фу́нтов** they received five pounds each; **на ~ом шагу́** at every step. **2.** *as n.* everyone; **всех и ~ого** (*coll.*) all and sundry.

каза́к, а́, *pl.* **~и́** *m.* Cossack.

каза́рм|а, ы *f.* barracks (*also fig.*; *coll. of ugly buildings*).

каза́рм|енный *adj. of* **~а**; (*fig., pej.*): **к. вид** barrack-like appearance; **~енная остро́та** barrack-room humour.

ка|за́ть, жу́, ~шешь *impf.* (*coll.*) to show; **не к. глаз, но́су** not to show up.

ка|за́ться, жу́сь, ~жешься *impf.* (*of* **показа́ться**) **1.** to seem, appear; **он ~жется у́мным** he appears clever; **она́ ~жется ста́рше свои́х лет** she looks older than she is. **2.** (*impers.*): (**мне,** *etc.*) **~жется, ~за́лось** it seems, seemed (to me, *etc.*); apparently; **мне ~жется, что он был прав** I think he was right; **за́втра, ~жется, начина́ются его́ кани́кулы** apparently his holidays begin tomorrow; **вы, ~жется, из Москвы́?** you are from Moscow, I believe?; **~за́лось бы** it would seem; one would think.

каза́х, а *m.* Kazakh.

каза́хский *adj.* Kazakh.

Казахста́н, а *m.* Kazakhstan.

каза́цкий *adj.* Cossack.

каза́честв|о, а *nt.* (*collect.*) the Cossacks.

каза́чий *adj.* Cossack.

каза́|чка, чки *f. of* **~к**

казач|о́к[1]**, ка́** *m.* **1.** (*coll.*) *affectionate dim. of* **каза́к. 2.** (*hist.*) page, boy-servant.

казач|о́к[2]**, ка́** *m.* kazachok (*Ukrainian dance*).

каза́|шка, шки *f. of* **~х**

казеи́н, а *m.* (*chem.*) casein.

казеи́н|овый *adj. of* **~**

казема́т, а *m.* casemate.

казённ|ый *adj.* **1.** (*hist.*) fiscal; of State, of Treasury; **~ое иму́щество** State property; **на к. счёт** at public expense. **2.** (*fig.*) bureaucratic, formal; **к. язы́к** language of officialdom, official jargon. **3.: ~ая часть = казна́ 3.**

казино́ *nt. indecl.* casino.

казн|а́, ы́ *no pl., f.* **1.** (*hist.*) Exchequer, Treasury; public purse. **2.** the State (*as a legal person*); **перейти́ из ча́стных рук в ~у́** to pass from private ownership to the State. **3.** (*mil.*) breech, breech end.

казначе́|й, я *m.* **1.** treasurer, bursar. **2.** (*mil.*) paymaster; (*naut.*) purser.

казначе́й|ский *adj.* **1.** *of* **~. 2.** *of* **~ство; к. биле́т** treasury note.

казначе́йств|о, а *nt.* Treasury, Exchequer.

казн|и́ть, ю́, и́шь *impf. and pf.* to execute, put to death.

казн|и́ться, ю́сь, и́шься *impf.* **1.** *pass. of* **~и́ть. 2.** (*coll.*) to blame o.s.; to torment o.s. (*with remorse*).

казнокра́д, а *m.* embezzler of public funds.

казнокра́дств|о, а *nt.* embezzlement of public funds.

казн|ь, и *f.* execution, capital punishment; **сме́ртная к.** death penalty.

казуи́ст, а *m.* casuist.

казуи́стик|а, и *f.* casuistry.

казуисти́ческий *adj.* casuistic(al).

ка́зус, а *m.* **1.** (*leg.*) exceptional case. **2.** (*coll.*) extraordinary occurrence; **вот так к.!** here's an amazing thing. **3.: к. бе́лли** casus belli.

ка́зусный *adj.* involved, complex.

кайл|а́, ы́ *f.* (miner's) hack.

кайл|о́, а́ *nt.* = **~а́**

ка|йма́, ймы́, *pl.* **~ймы́, ~ём, ~йма́м** *f.* edging, border; hem, selvedge.

кайма́н, а *m.* (*zool.*) cayman.

ка́йр|а, ы *f.* (*zool.*) guillemot.

кайф, а *m.* (*sl.*) kicks, 'high'; turn-on; buzz; **быть под ~ом** (*sl.*) to be spaced out; **лови́ть к.** (*sl.*) to get stoned.

кайф|ова́ть, у́ю *impf.* (*sl.*) **1.** to get stoned (*on drugs* or *alcohol*). **2.** to enjoy o.s.

кайфо́вый *adj.* (*sl.*) cool, far-out, mind-blowing.

кайфоло́м, а *m.* (*sl.*) killjoy.

как[1] *adv. and particle* **1.** how; **к. вам нра́вится Москва́?** how do you like Moscow?; **к. чу́дно!** how wonderful! **к. вы пожива́ете?** how do you do?; **к. (ва́ши) дела́?** how are you getting on?; **забы́л, к. э́то де́лается** I have forgotten how to do this; **к. вам не сты́дно!** you ought to be ashamed!; **к. его́ фами́лия, к. его́ зову́т?** what is his name?; **к. называ́ется э́тот цвето́к?** what is this flower called?; **к. вы ду́маете?** what do you think?; *expr. surprise and/or displeasure*; **к.! ты опя́ть здесь** what! are you here again?; **к. же так?** how is that?; (*coll.*): **к. знать?** who knows?; (*coll.*): **к. есть** completely, utterly; **он к. есть дура́к** he is a complete fool; (*coll.*): **к.-ника́к** nevertheless; **к.-ника́к, но мы попа́ли во́ вре́мя** nevertheless, we managed to arrive in time; **к. же** (*coll. or iron.*) naturally, of course. **2.** *with fut. tense of pf. vv. expr. suddenness of action*: (*coll.*): **мы споко́йно слу́шали ра́дио, а — он к. вскочи́т!** we were listening quietly to the wireless when all of a sudden he jumped up; **она́ к. закричи́т!** she suddenly cried out. **3.: к. ни, к.... ни** however; **к. ни по́здно** however late it is; **к. он ни умён** clever as he is; **к. ни стара́йтесь** however hard you may try, try as you may. **4.** (*following* **беда́, пре́лесть, страх, ужа́сно,** *etc., in elliptical construction*; *coll.*) terribly, awfully, wonderfully, etc.; **она́ пре́лесть к. оде́та** she is beautifully dressed.

как[2] *conj.* **1.** as; like; **бе́лый, к. снег** white as snow; **сове́тую тебе́ э́то к. друг** I give this advice as a friend; **он говори́т по-ру́сски к. настоя́щий ру́сский** he speaks Russian like a native; **бу́дьте к. до́ма** make yourself at home; **к. наприме́р** as, for instance; **к. наро́чно** as luck would have it; **к. попа́ло** anyhow, at sixes and sevens; (*with comp.*) **к.**

мо́жно, к. нельзя́ as ... as possible; **к. мо́жно, скоре́е** as soon as possible; **к. нельзя́ лу́чше** as well as possible. **2.: к...., так и** both ... and; **к. ма́льчики, так и де́вочки** both the boys and the girls. **3.** *following vv. of perceiving not translated*: **я ви́дел, к. она́ ушла́** I saw her go out. **4.** (*coll.*) when; since; **к. пойдёшь, зайди́ за мной** when you go, call for me; **прошло́ два го́да, к. мы встре́тились** it is two years since we met; **к. то́лько** as soon as, when; **к. вдруг** when suddenly. **5.** (*+neg.*) but, except, than; **что ему́ остава́лось де́лать, к. не созна́ться?** what could he do but confess? **6.: в то вре́мя к.; до того́ к.; ме́жду тем к.; тогда́ к.**, *see* **вре́мя, до, ме́жду, тогда́. 7.: к. бу́дто, к. бы, к.-либо, к.-нибудь, к. ра́з, к.-то** *see separate entries.*

какаду́ *m. indecl.* (*zool.*) cockatoo.

кака́о *nt. indecl.* **1.** cocoa. **2.** cacao(-tree).

кака́о|вый *adj. of* ~; **~вые бобы́** cocoa-beans.

как бу́дто 1. *conj.* as if, as though; **она́ побледне́ла, к. б. уви́дела при́зрак** she turned pale as if she had seen a ghost. **2.** *particle* (*coll.*) apparently; **они́ к. б. за́втра прие́дут** apparently they are coming tomorrow.

как бы 1. (*+inf.*) how; **к. б. э́то сде́лать?** how is it to be done, I wonder. **2.: к. б. ни** however; **к. б. то ни́ было** be that as it may. **3.** as if, as though; **к. б. в шу́тку** as if in jest. **4.: к. б. не** (*expr. anxious expectation*) what if; (*following v.*) (that, lest); **к. б. он не был в дурно́м настрое́нии!** what if he is in a bad temper!; **бою́сь, к. б. он не был в дурно́м настрое́нии!** I am afraid (that) he may be in a bad temper. **5.** (*coll.*): **к. б. не так!** not likely, certainly not.

ка́к-либо *adv.* somehow.

ка́к-нибудь *adv.* **1.** somehow (or other). **2.** (*coll.*) anyhow; **он всё де́лает к.-н.** he does things all anyhow. **3.** (*coll.*) some time; **загляни́те к.-н.** look in some time.

как-ника́к *adv.* (*coll.*) nevertheless, for all that.

како́в (~а́, ~о́, ~ы́) *pron.* (*interrog., and in exclamations expr. strong feeling*) what; of what sort; **к. результа́т?** what is the result?; **к. он?** what is he like?; **к. он собо́й?** what does he look like?

какова́ *adv.* (*coll.*) how; **к. ему́ живётся?** how is he getting on?

как|о́й *pron.* **1.** (*interrog. and rel.; and in exclamations*) what; **~и́е у вас впечатле́ния о Ло́ндоне?** what are your impressions of London?; **~о́е сего́дня число́?** what is today's date?; **~и́м о́бразом?** how?; **не зна́ю, ~у́ю кни́гу ему́ дать** I don't know what book to give him; **~а́я беда́!** how unfortunate!;**~а́я на́глость!** what impudence!; **~а́я хоро́шенькая де́вушка!** what a pretty girl! **2. (тако́й) к.** such as; **гнев, ~о́го он никогда́ не испы́тывал** anger such as he had never felt. **3.: к. ни** whatever, whichever; **к. есть, к. ни на есть** (*coll.*): whatever you please, any you please; **дай мне ~у́ю ни на есть кни́гу** give me any book you please. **4.** *expr. negation*: (*in rhet., questions*) **к. он учёный?** what sort of scholar is that?; **~о́е там** nothing of the kind, quite the contrary; **ты хорошо́ спал? ~о́е там!** did you sleep well? I most certainly did not! **5.: к. тако́й?** which (exactly)?; **пришёл Ивано́в. — К. тако́й Ивано́в?** Ivanov is here. Which Ivanov? **6.** (*coll.*) any; **нет ли у вас ~о́го вопро́са?** have you any questions?

како́й-либо *pron.* = **како́й-нибудь 1.**

как|о́й-нибудь *pron.* **1.** some; any; **мы э́то сде́лаем ~и́м-н. спо́собом** we shall do it somehow; **да́йте мне кни́гу хоть ~у́ю-н.** give me a book, any one at all. **2.** (*with numerals*) some (*and not more*), only; **за́мок нахо́дится в ~и́х-н. трёх киломе́трах отсю́да** the castle is some three kilometres from here; **~и́е-н. пять рубле́й** some five roubles.

как|о́й-то *pron.* **1.** some, a. **2.** a kind of; **э́то ~а́я-то боле́знь** it is a kind of disease.

какофони́ческий *adj.* cacophonous.

какофо́ни|я, и *f.* cacophony.

как ра́з *adv.* just, exactly; **к. р. то, что мне ну́жно** just what I need; **к. р. вас я иска́л** you are the very person I was looking for; *as pred.*: **э́ти ту́фли мне к. р.** these shoes are just right.

ка́к-то *adv.* **1.** somehow; **он к.-то ухитри́лся сде́лать э́то** he managed to do it somehow; **в э́том до́ме к.-то всегда́ хо́лодно** somehow it is always cold in this house. **2.** how; **посмотрю́, к.-то он вы́вернется из э́того положе́ния** I wonder how he will get himself out of this situation. **3.** (*coll.*): **к.-то (раз)** once. **4.** namely, as for example.

ка́ктус, а *m.* (*bot.*) cactus.

кал, а *m.* faeces, excrement.

каламбу́р, а *m.* pun.

каламбури́ст, а *m.* punster.

каламбу́р|ить, ю, ишь *impf.* (*of* **с~**) to pun.

каламбу́рный *adj.* punning.

каланч|а́, и́, *g. pl.* **~е́й** *f.* watch-tower; **пожа́рная к.** fire observation tower; (*fig., coll.*) bean-pole.

кала́ч, а́ *m.* kalach (*kind of white, wheatmeal loaf*); **меня́ ~о́м туда́ не зама́нишь** (*coll.*) nothing will induce me to go there; (*fig., coll.*) **тёртый к.** person who has been around; old hand.

кала́чиком *adv.* (*coll.*) in the shape of a kalach; **лежа́ть к.** to lie curled up.

кала́ч|ный *adj. of* ~

калейдоско́п, а *m.* kaleidoscope.

калейдоскопи́ческий *adj.* kaleidoscopic.

кале́к|а, и *c.g.* cripple.

календа́р|ный *adj. of* **~ь**

календа́р|ь, я́ *m.* calender; (*sport*) fixture list.

кале́ни|е, я *nt.* incandescence; **бе́лое к.** white heat; **довести́ до бе́лого ~я** (*fig., coll.*) to rouse to fury.

калён|ый *adj.* **1.** red-hot. **2.: ~ые оре́хи** roasted nuts.

кале́ч|ить, у, ишь *impf.* (*of* **искале́чить**) to cripple, maim, mutilate; (*fig.*) to twist, pervert.

кали́бр, а *m.* **1.** calibre. **2.** (*tech.*) gauge.

калибр|ова́ть, у́ю *impf.* (*tech.*) to calibrate.

калибро́вк|а, и *f.* (*tech.*) calibration.

ка́лиевый *adj.* (*chem.*) potassic, potassium.

ка́ли|й, я *m.* (*chem.*) potassium.

кали́йн|ый *adj.* (*chem.*) potassium; **~ое удобре́ние** potash fertilizer.

кали́льн|ый *adj.* (*tech.*): **к. жар** temperature of incandescence; **~ая се́тка** (incandescent) mantle.

кали́н|а, ы *no pl., f.* (*bot.*) viburnum; guelder rose.

кали́н|овый *adj. of* **~а**

кали́тк|а, и *f.* (wicket-)gate.

кал|и́ть, ю́, и́шь *impf.* **1.** (*tech.*) to heat. **2.** to roast (*chestnuts, etc.*).

кали́ф, а *m.* caliph; **к. на час** (*iron.*) king for a day.

каллиграфи́ческий *adj.* calligraphic.

каллигра́фи|я, и *f.* calligraphy.

калмы́к, а́ *m.* Kalmuck, Kalmyk.

калмы́цкий *adj.* Kalmuck, Kalmyk.

калмы́|чка, чки *f. of* **~к**

ка́л|овый *adj. of* ~

калори́йност|ь, и *f.* calorie content.

калори́йный *adj.* high-calorie; fattening.

калори́метр, а *m.* (*phys.*) calorimeter.

калориме́три|я, и *m.* (*phys.*) calorimetry.

калори́фер, а *m.* (*tech.*) heater, radiator.

кало́ри|я, и *f.* calorie.

кало́ш|а, и *f.* = **гало́ша**

калу́жниц|а, ы *f.* (*bot.*) king-cup, marsh marigold.

калы́м, а *no pl., m.* **1.** (*ethnol.*) bride-money. **2.** (*coll.*) earnings on the side.

калы́м|ить, лю, ишь *impf.* (*coll.*) to moonlight, do

work on the side.
калы́мщик, а *m.* (*coll.*) moonlighter.
кальвини́зм, а *m.* Calvinism.
кальвини́ст, а *m.* Calvinist.
кальвинисти́ческий *adj.* Calvinistic(al).
ка́л|ька, ьки, *g. pl.* **~ек** *f.* **1.** tracing-paper. **2.** tracing, copy. **3.** (*ling.*) loan translation, calque.
кальки́р|овать, ую *impf.* (*of* **с~**) **1.** to trace. **2.** (*ling.*) to make a loan translation of.
калькули́р|овать, ую *impf.* (*of* **с~**) (*comm.*) to calculate.
калькуля́тор, а *m.* (*comm.*) calculator.
калькуля|цио́нный *adj. of* **~ция; ~цио́нная ве́домость** cost sheet; cost record.
калькуля́ци|я, и *f.* (*comm.*) calculation.
кальма́р, а *m.* (*zool.*) squid.
кальсо́н|ы, ~ *no sg.* (*men's*) drawers, long johns.
ка́льциевый *adj.* (*chem.*) calcium, calcic.
ка́льци|й, я *m.* (*chem.*) calcium.
калья́н, а *m.* hookah.
каля́ка|ть, ю *impf.* (*of* **по~**) (*coll.*) to chat.
кама́ринск|ая, ой *f.* kamarinskaya (*Russ. folk-dance*).
ка́мбал|а, ы *f.* **1.** flat-fish (*generic term*). **2.** plaice; flounder.
ка́мби|й, я *m.* (*bot.*) cambium.
камбоджи́йский *adj.* Cambodian.
ка́мбуз, а *m.* (*naut.*) galley.
камво́льный *adj.* (*text.*) worsted.
каме́дистый *adj.* gummy.
каме́д|ь, и *f.* gum.
камел|ёк, ька́ *m.* fire-place.
каме́ли|я, и *f.* (*bot.*) camellia.
камене́|ть, ю *impf.* (*of* **о~**) to become petrified, turn to stone; (*fig.*) to harden (*intrans.*).
камени́ст|ый (~, ~а) *adj.* stony.
ка́менк|а, и *f.* stove (*in bath-house in rural Russia*).
каменноуго́льн|ый *adj.* coal; **к. бассе́йн** coal-field; **~ые ко́пи** coal-mine.
ка́менн|ый *adj.* **1.** stone-; stony; **к. век** the Stone Age; **~ая кла́дка** stone-work; **~ая соль** rock-salt; **к. у́голь** coall. **2.** (*fig.*) stony; hard, immovable; **~ое се́рдце** stony heart.
каменоло́м|ня, ни, *g. pl.* **~ен** *f.* quarry.
каменотёс, а *m.* (stone)mason.
ка́менщик, а *m.* mason; bricklayer.
ка́м|ень, ня, *pl.* **~ни, ~не́й** *m.* stone; tartar; **зубно́й к.** dental tartar; **па́дать ~нем** to fall like a stone; **~ня на ~не не оста́вить** to raze to the ground; to not leave a stone standing; (*fig.*): **броса́ть ~нем (в**+*a.*) to cast stones (at); **держа́ть к. за па́зухой (на**+*a.*, **про́тив)** to harbour a grudge (against); **к. с души́ мое́й свали́лся** a load has been taken off my mind.
ка́мер|а, ы *f.* **1.** chamber (*in var. senses*); **морози́льная к.** freezer compartment (*of refrigerator*); **тюре́мная к.** prison cell; **к. хране́ния (багажа́)** cloak-room. **2. (фотографи́ческая) к.** camera. **3.** inner tube (*of tyre*); bladder (*of football*).
камерге́р, а *m.* chamberlain.
камерди́нер, а *m.* valet.
камери́стк|а, и *f.* lady's maid.
ка́мер|ный[1] *adj. of* **~а**
ка́мерн|ый[2] *adj.* (*mus.*): **~ая му́зыка** chamber music.
камерто́н, а *m.* tuning-fork.
ка́меш|ек, ка *m. dim. of* **ка́мень**; pebble; (*fig., coll.*): **бро́сить к. в чей-н. огоро́д** to make digs at s.o.
каме́|я, и *f.* cameo.
камзо́л, а *m.* camisole.
камика́дзе *m. indecl.* kamikaze pilot.
ками́н, а *m.* fire-place; (open) fire.
ками́н|ный *adj. of* **~; ~ная по́лка** mantelpiece; **~ная решётка** fireguard.
камко́рдер, а *m.* camcorder.
камнедроби́лк|а, и *f.* stone-breaker, stone-crusher.
камнело́мк|а, и *f.* (*bot.*) saxifrage.
камнепа́д, а *m.* rockfall.
камо́рк|а, и *f.* (*coll.*) closet, tiny room; box room.
кампа́ни|я, и *f.* campaign.
камуфля́ж, а *no pl., m.* camouflage.
камфар|а́, ы́ *f.* camphor.
камфа́р|ный *adj. of* **~а́**
камф|ора́ = **~ара́**
камы́ш, а́ *m.* reed, rush (*also collect.*).
камы́ш|евый *adj. of* **~**
камыш|о́вый *adj. of* **~; ~о́вое кре́сло** cane chair.
кана́в|а, ы *f.* ditch; **сто́чная к.** gutter.
Кана́д|а, ы *f.* Canada.
кана́д|ец, ца, *g. pl.* **~цев** *m.* Canadian.
кана́д|ка, ки *f. of* **~ец**
кана́дск|ий *adj.* Canadian; **~ая пи́хта** balsam fir.
кана́л, а *m.* **1.** canal. **2.** channel; **дипломати́ческие ~ы** diplomatic channels. **3.** (*anat.*) duct, canal; **мочеиспуска́тельный к.** urethra. **4.** bore (*of barrel of gun*).
канализа|цио́нный *adj. of* **~ция; ~цио́нная труба́** sewer(-pipe).
канализа́ци|я, и *f.* **1.** sewerage. **2.** sewerage system.
канализи́р|овать, ую *impf. and pf.* to provide with sewerage system.
канапе́ *nt. indecl.* canapé.
канаре́|ечный *adj.* **1.** *adj. of* **~йка. 2.** canary-yellow.
канаре́йк|а, и *f.* canary.
кана́т, а *m.* rope; cable, hawser.
кана́т|ный *adj. of* **~; ~ная желе́зная доро́га** funicular railway; **к. плясу́н** rope-dancer.
канатохо́д|ец, ца *m.* tightrope-walker.
канв|а́, ы́ *no pl., f.* canvas; (*fig.*) groundwork; outline, design; **к. рома́на** the outline of a novel.
канв|о́вый *adj. of* **~а́**
кандал|ы́, о́в *no sg.* shackles, fetters; **ручны́е к.** manacles; **закова́ть в к.** to put into irons.
канда́л|ьный *adj. of* **~ы́**
канделя́бр, а *m.* candelabrum.
кандида́т, а *m.* **1.** candidate; **к. в чле́ны коммунисти́ческой па́ртии** candidate-member of the Communist Party. **2.** kandidat (*in former USSR, holder of first higher degree, awarded on dissertation*).
кандида́тск|ая, ой *f.* (*coll.*) doctoral thesis.
кандида́т|ский *adj. of* **~**
кандидату́р|а, ы *f.* candidature; **вы́ставить чью-н. ~у** to nominate s.o. for election.
кани́кул|ы, ~ *no sg.* (*school*) holidays; (*university, etc.*) vacation.
кани|куля́рный *adj. of* **~кулы**
кани́стр|а, ы *f.* jerrycan.
каните́л|ить, ю, ишь *impf.* (*of* **про~**) (*coll., pej.*) to drag out; **к. кого́-н.** to waste s.o.'s time.
каните́л|иться, юсь, ишься *impf.* (*of* **про~**) (*coll., pej.*) to waste time; to mess about.
каните́л|ь, и *f.* **1.** gold thread, silver thread. **2.** (*fig., coll.*) long-drawn-out proceedings; **тяну́ть, разводи́ть к.** to drag out proceedings, procrastinate; **дово́льно ~и!** this has dragged on long enough!
каните́л|ьный (~ен, ~ьна) *adj.* (*coll.*) **1.** long-drawn out; tedious. **2.: к. челове́к** procrastinator. **3.** *adj. of* **~ь 1.**
каните́льщик, а *m.* (*coll.*) time-waster.
канифо́л|ить, ю, ишь *impf.* (*of* **на~**) to rosin.
канифо́л|ь, и *f.* rosin.
канка́н, а *m.* cancan.
канниба́л, а *m.* cannibal.
каннибали́зм, а *m.* cannibalism.
кано́ист, а *m.* canoeist.

кано́н, а *m.* canon.
канона́д|а, ы *f.* cannonade.
канонe’рк|а, и *f.* gunboat.
канонe’рск|ий *adj.*: **~ая ло́дка** gunboat.
канониза́ци|я, и *f.* (*eccl.*) canonization.
канонизи́р|овать, ую *impf. and pf.* (*eccl. and fig.*) to canonize.
кано́ник, а *m.* (*eccl.*) canon.
канони́ческ|ий *adj.* (*eccl.*) canonical; **~ое пра́во** canon law.
канотье́ *nt. indecl.* boater (*hat*).
кано́э *nt. indecl.* canoe.
кант, а *m.* edging, piping.
канта́т|а, ы *f.* (*mus.*) cantata.
кант|ова́ть[1], **у́ю** *impf.* (*of* **о~**) to border; to mount (*picture, etc.*).
кант|ова́ть[2], **у́ю** *impf.* (*tech.*) to cant.
канто́н, а *m.* canton.
кантона́льный *adj.* cantonal.
ка́нтор, а *m.* cantor.
кану́н, а *m.* eve; **к. Но́вого го́да** New Year's eve.
ка́н|уть, у, ешь *pf.* (*obs.*) to drop, sink; **к. в ве́чность, к. в Ле́ту** (*fig.*) to sink into oblivion; **как в во́ду к.** to vanish into thin air.
канцеляри́ст, а *m.* clerk.
канцеля́ри|я, и *f.* **1.** office. **2.** chancellery.
канцеля́р|ский *adj. of* **~**; **~ские принадле́жности** stationery; **~ская рабо́та** clerical work; **к. стол** office desk; **к. слог** officialese.
канцеля́рщин|а, ы *f.* (*coll.*) red tape.
канцероге́н, а *m.* carcinogen.
канцероге́нн|ый *adj.* carcinogenic; **~ое вещество́** carcinogen.
ка́нцлер, а *m.* chancellor.
канцтова́р|ы, ов *no sg.* (*abbr. of* ***канцеля́рские това́ры***) office supplies.
каньо́н, а *m.* (*geog.*) canyon.
каню́к, а́ *m.* (*zool.*) buzzard.
каоли́н, а m. china clay, kaolin.
кап... *comb. form, abbr. of* **капиталисти́ческий**
ка́п|ать, аю (*obs.* **~плю, ~лешь**) *impf.* (*of* **~нуть**) **1.** (*3rd pers. only*) to drip, drop; to trickle; to dribble; to fall (in drops); **из глаз у неё ~али слёзы** tear-drops were falling from her eyes; **дождь ~ает** it is spotting with rain; **с потолка́ ~ало** there was a drip from the ceiling; **над на́ми не ~лет** (*fig., coll.*) we can take our time; there is no hurry. **2.** to pour (a drop at a time); to pipette. **3.** (*+i.*; *coll.*) to spill; **ты ~аешь водо́й на ска́терть** you are spilling water on the tablecloth.
капе́лл|а, ы *f.* **1.** choir. **2.** chapel.
капелла́н, а *m.* chaplain.
ка́пельк|а, и *f.* **1.** (small) drop, droplet; **к. росы́** dew-drop; **вы́пить всё до ~и** to drink to the last drop. **2.** (*sg. only*; *fig.*) grain, minute quantity; **в нём нет ни ~и здра́вого смы́сла** he has not a grain of common sense; **она́ ни ~и не смути́лась** she was not the least bit put out; *as adv.* **~у** (*coll.*) a little; **подожди́ ~у!** wait a moment.
капельме́йстер, а *m.* (*mus.*) conductor, bandmaster.
капельме́йстер|ский *adj. of* **~**; **~ская па́лочка** conductor's baton.
ка́пельниц|а, ы *f.* (*medicine*) dropper.
ка́перс, а *m.* **1.** (*bot.*) caper. **2.** (*pl. only*; *cul.*) capers.
капилля́р, а *m.* (*phys., anat.*) capillary.
капилля́рный *adj.* (*phys., anat.*) capillary.
капита́л, а *m.* (*fin.*) capital.
капитализа́ци|я, и *f.* (*fin.*) capitalization.
капитализи́р|овать, ую *impf. and pf.* (*fin.*) to capitalize.
капитали́зм, а *m.* capitalism.
капитали́ст, а *m.* capitalist.
капиталисти́ческий *adj.* capitalist(ic).
капиталовложе́ни|е, я *nt.* capital investment.
капита́льн|ый *adj.* capital; main, fundamental; **к. вопро́с** fundamental question; **к. ремо́нт** major repairs, renovation; **~ая стена́** main wall.
капита́н, а *m.* captain.
капита́н|ский *adj. of* **~**; **к. мо́стик** captain's bridge.
капитули́р|овать, ую *impf. and pf.* **(пе́ред)** to capitulate (to).
капитуля́нт, а *m.* capitulationist.
капитуля́нтств|о, а *nt.* capitulationism.
капитуля́ци|я, и *f.* capitulation.
ка́пищ|е, а *nt.* (*pagan*) temple.
капка́н, а *m.* trap; **попа́сться в к.** to fall into a trap (*also fig.*).
капка́н|ный *adj. of* **~**; **к. про́мысел** trapping.
капли́ц|а, ы *f.* (*Roman Catholic*) chapel.
каплу́н, а́ *m.* capon.
ка́п|ля, ли, *g. pl.* **~ель** *f.* **1.** drop; **по ~ле, к. за ~лей** drop by drop; **до ~ли** to the last drop; **похо́жи как две ~ли воды́** as like as two peas; (*fig.*): **к. в мо́ре** a drop in the ocean; **после́дняя к.** the last straw; **би́ться до после́дней ~ли кро́ви** to fight to the last. **2.** (*pl.*; *med.*) drops. **3.: ни ~ли** (*as adv.*) not a bit; **у него́ (нет) ни ~ли благоразу́мия** he hasn't an ounce of sense.
ка́п|нуть, ну, нешь *pf. of* **~ать**
кап|о́к, ка́ *no pl., m.* (*text.*) kapok.
ка́пор, а *m.* hood; bonnet.
капо́т, а *m.* (*tech.*) hood; **к. мото́ра** (*aeron.*) engine cowling.
капра́л, а *m.* (*mil.*) corporal.
капри́з, а *m.* caprice, whim; vagary; **к. судьбы́** twist of fate.
капри́зник, а *m.* capricious person; capricious child.
капри́знича|ть, ю *impf.* to behave capriciously; (*of a child*) to play up.
капри́з|ный (~ен, ~на) *adj.* capricious; (*of a child*) wilful.
капро́н, а *nt.* kapron (*kind of nylon*).
капро́н|овый *adj. of* **~**
ка́псул|а, ы *f.* capsule.
ка́псюл|ь, я *m.* (percussion) cap.
капу́ст|а, ы *f.* cabbage; **кормова́я к.** kale; **спа́ржевая к.** broccoli; **цветна́я к.** cauliflower.
капу́стник, а *m.* **1.** cabbage patch. **2.** (satirical) revue.
капу́стниц|а, ы *f.* cabbage butterfly.
капу́ст|ный *adj. of* **~а**
капу́т *m. indecl.* (*coll.*) end, destruction; *used as adj. or adv.* done for, kaput; **ему́ к.** he's done for; he's finished.
капуци́н, а *m.* **1.** Capuchin (friar). **2.** (*zool.*) capuchin (monkey).
капюшо́н, а *m.* hood, cowl.
ка́р|а, ы *f.* (*rhet.*) punishment, retribution.
караби́н, а *m.* carbine.
кара́бка|ться, юсь *impf.* (*of* **вс~**) (*coll.*) to clamber.
карава́|й, я *m.* cottage loaf.
карава́н, а *m.* **1.** caravan. **2.** convoy (*of ships, etc.*).
Кар(а)и́бск|ое мо́р|е, ~ого ~я *m.* the Caribbean Sea; the Caribbean.
карака́тиц|а, ы *f.* (*zool.*) cuttlefish.
кара́ковый *adj.* dark-bay.
кара́кул|евый *adj. of* **~ь**
кара́кул|ь, я *no pl., m.* Persian lamb; astrakhan.
каракульч|а́, и́ *f.* astrakhan (fur); broadtail.
кара́кул|я, и *f.* scrawl, scribble.
карамбо́л|ь, я *m.* (*in billiards*) cannon.
караме́л|ь, и *no pl., f.* **1.** (*collect.*) caramels. **2.** caramel.

карамéльк|а, и *f.* (*coll.*) caramel.
карамéль|ный *adj. of* ~
карандáш, á *m.* pencil.
карандáш|ный *adj. of* ~; **к. рисýнок** pencil drawing.
карантúн, а *m.* quarantine; **подвéргнуть ~у** to place in quarantine.
карантúн|ный *adj. of* ~
карапýз, а *m.* (*coll.*) chubby lad.
карáс|ь, я́ *m.* (*fish*) crucian; **серéбряный к.** Prussian carp.
карáт, а *m.* carat.
каратé *nt. indecl.* karate.
каратейст, а *m.* = **каратúст**
карáтел|ь, я *m.* member of punitive expedition.
карáтельный *adj.* punitive.
каратúст, а *m.* karate enthusiast, karateka.
карá|ть, ю *impf.* (*of* **по~**) to punish, chastise.
караýл, а *m.* **1.** guard; **почётный к.** guard of honour. **2.** guard duty; sentry duty; **нестú к.** to be on guard. **3.** *word of command*: **на к.!** present arms!; **взять на к.** to present arms.
караýл|ить, ю, ишь *impf.* **1.** to guard. **2.** (*coll.*) to lie in wait for, watch out for.
караýл|ьный *adj. of* ~; **~ьная бýдка** sentry-box; *as n.* **к., ~ьного** *m.* sentry, guard.
караýл|ьня, ьни, *g. pl.* **~ен** *f.* guardroom.
караýльщик, а *m.* (*coll.*) sentry, guard; watchman
карáч|ки, ек *no sg.* (*coll.*): **на к., на ~ках** on all fours; **стать на к.** to get on all fours.
карбúд, а *m.* (*chem.*) carbide.
карбóван|ец, ца *m.* **1.** karbovanets (*Ukrainian unit of currency*). **2.** (*pl.*) money.
карбóлк|а, и *f.* (*coll.*) carbolic acid.
карбóловый *adj.* (*chem.*) carbolic.
карбонáт, а *m.* (*chem.*) carbonate.
карборýнд, а *m.* carborundum.
карбýнкул, а *m.* (*min., med.*) carbuncle.
карбюрáтор, а *m.* (*tech., chem*) carburettor.
карбюрúр|овать, ую *impf. and pf.* (*chem.*) to carburet.
карг|á, и́, *pl.* **~и́, ~, ~áм** *f.* (*coll.*): **стáрая к.** hag, old crow.
кардамóн, а *m.* (*bot.*) cardamom.
кардинáл, а *m.* (*eccl.*) cardinal.
кардинáльный *adj.* cardinal.
кардинáл|ьский *adj. of* ~
кардиогрáмм|а, ы *f.* cardiogram.
кардиóлог, а *m.* cardiologist.
кардиостимулятор, а *m.* (*med.*) pacemaker (*artificial*).
карéт|а, ы *f.* carriage, coach; **почтóвая к.** stagecoach.
карéтк|а, и *f.* (*tech.*) carriage, frame.
кариатúд|а, ы *f.* (*archit.*) caryatid.
кáрий *adj.* (*of colour of eyes*) brown, hazel; (*of colour of horses*) chestnut, dark-chestnut.
карикатýр|а, ы *f.* **1.** caricature. **2.** cartoon.
карикатурúст, а *m.* cartoonist.
карикатýр|ный *adj. of* **~а; ~ная фигýра** ludicrous figure.
кариóз, а *m.* (*med.*) caries, decay.
кариóзный *adj.* (*med.*) carious.
каркáс, а *m.* (*tech.*) frame; (*fig.*) framework.
каркáс|ный *adj. of* ~; **к. дом** framehouse.
кáрк|ать, аю *impf.* (*of* **~нуть**) to caw, croak.
кáрк|нуть, ну, нешь *pf. of* **~ать**
кáрлик, а *m.* dwarf; pygmy.
кáрликов|ый *adj.* (*anthrop., bot., and fig.*) dwarf; pygmean; **~ые племенá** the Pygmies.
кáрли|ца, цы *f. of* **~к**
кармáн, а *m.* pocket; (*fig., coll.*): **э́то мне не по ~у** I can't afford it; **бить по ~у** to cost a packet; **набúть себé к.** to fill one's pockets; **тóщий к.** empty pocket; **не лезть за слóвом в к.** to have a ready tongue.
кармáнник, а *m.* pickpocket.
кармáн|ный *adj. of* ~; **к. вор** pickpocket; **~ные дéньги** pocket money.
кармáнщик = **кармáнник**
кармúн, а *m.* carmine.
кармúнный *adj.* carmine.
карнавáл, а *m.* carnival.
карнúз, а *m.* (*archit.*) cornice.
карп, а *m.* carp.
карт, а *m.* go-cart.
кáрт|а, ы *f.* **1.** (*geog.*) map. **2.** (playing-)card; **игрáть в ~ы** to play cards; **имéть хорóшие ~ы** to have a good hand; **егó кáрта бúта** (*fig.*) his game is up; **постáвить на ~у** to stake, risk; **на ~е** at stake; **раскры́ть свой ~ы** to show one's hand.
картáв|ить, лю, ишь *impf.* to burr.
картáвост|ь, и *f.* (*ling.*) burr.
картáвый *adj.* **1.** pronounced gutturally. **2.** having a burr.
картёжник, а *m.* (*coll.*) card-player.
картёжный *adj.* (*coll.*) card-playing.
картéл|ь, я *m.* (*fin.*) cartel.
кáртер, а *m.* (*tech.*) crank case.
картéч|ный *adj. of* **~ь**
картéч|ь, и *f.* **1.** (*mil.*) case-shot; grape-shot. **2.** buck-shot.
картúн|а, ы *f.* **1.** picture. **2.** (*theatr.*) scene; **живáя к.** tableau vivant.
кáртинг, а *m.* go-carting.
картúнк|а, и *f.* picture; illustration; **к.-загáдка** jigsaw puzzle; **мóдная к.** fashion-plate; **переводны́е ~и** transfers.
картúн|ный (~ен, ~на) *adj.* **1.** *adj. of* **~а; ~ная галерéя** art gallery. **2.** picturesque.
картóграф, а *m.* cartographer.
картографúр|овать, ую *impf.* to map, draw a map of.
картографúческий *adj.* cartographic.
картогрáфи|я, и *f.* cartography.
картóн, а *m.* cardboard; pasteboard.
картонáж, а *m.* cardboard article; cardboard box.
картонáж|ный *adj of* ~; **~ная фáбрика** cardboard box factory.
картóнк|а, и *f.* cardboard box; carton; **к. для шля́пы** hat-box, bandbox.
картóн|ный *adj. of* ~
картотéк|а, и *f.* card-index.
картофелечúстк|а, и *f.* potato peeler.
картóфелин|а, ы *f.* (*coll.*) potato.
картóфел|ь, я *no pl., m.* **1.** (*collect.*) potatoes; **к. в мундúре** jacket potatoes; **молодóй к.** new potatoes. **2.** potato plant.
картóфель|ный *adj. of* ~; **~ное пюрé** mashed potatoes.
кáрточк|а, и *f.* **1.** card; **визúтная к.** business card; **к. вин** wine-list; **к. кýшаний** bill of fare; **продовóльственная к.** ration card. **2.** season ticket. **3.** (*coll.*) photo, snap.
кáрточ|ный *adj.* **1.** *adj. of* **кáрта; к. долг** gambling-debt; **к. стол** card-table; (*coll.*): **к. дóмик** house of cards (*also fig.*); **к. фóкус** card trick. **2.** *adj. of* **~ка; к. каталóг** card index; **~ная систéма** rationing (system).
картóшк|а, и *f.* (*coll.*) **1.** (*collect.*) potatoes. **2.** potato; **нос ~ой** bulbous nose.
картýз, á *m.* (peaked) cap.
карусéл|ь, и *f.* merry-go-round.
кáрцер, а *m.* cell, lock-up.
карьéр[1]**, а** *m.* full gallop; **во весь к.** at full speed; **пустúть лóшадь в к., ~ом** to put a horse into full gallop; (*fig., coll.*) **с мéста в к.** straight away, with-

out further ado.
карье́р[2], **а** *m.* quarry; sand-pit.
карье́р|а, ы *f.* career; **сде́лать ~у** to make good, get on.
карьери́зм, а *m.* careerism.
карьери́ст, а *m.* careerist.
карье́р|ный *adj. of* **1. ~**[1,2]. **2. ~а**
каса́ни|е, я *nt.* contact; (*math.*): **то́чка ~я** point of contact.
каса́тельн|ая, ой *f.* (*math.*) tangent.
каса́тельно *prep.+g.* touching, concerning.
каса́тельств|о, а *nt.* **(к)** connection (with); **я не име́л никако́го ~а к э́тому заявле́нию** I had nothing to do with this statement.
каса́т|ка, ки *f.* (*zool.*) **1.** swallow. **2.** killer whale.
каса́|ться, юсь *impf.* (*of* **косну́ться**) **1.** (*+g.*) to touch. **2.** (*+g.*; *fig.*) to touch (on, upon); **к. больно́го вопро́са** to touch on a sore subject. **3.** (*+g. or* **до**; *fig.*) to concern, relate (to); **э́то тебя́ не ~ется** it is no concern of yours; **что ~ется** as to, as regards, with regard to.
ка́ск|а, и *f.* helmet.
каска́д, а *m.* cascade; **к. красноре́чия** (*fig.*) flood of eloquence.
каскадёр, а *m.* stunt man.
Каспи́йск|ое мо́р|е, ~ого ~я *nt.* the Caspian Sea.
ка́сс|а, ы *f.* **1.** cash-box; cash register; cash-desk; **уплати́ть в ~у** to pay at the cash-desk; **несгора́емая к.** safe. **2.** cash. **3.** booking-office; box-office; **сберега́тельная к.** savings bank. **4.** (*typ.*) case.
касса|цио́нный *adj. of* **≁ция; ~цио́нная жа́лоба** appeal; **к. суд** Court of Appeal, Court of Cassation.
касса́ци|я, и *f.* (*leg.*) **1.** cassation. **2.** (*coll.*) **пода́ть ~ю** to appeal.
кассе́т|а, ы *f.* cassette.
кассе́т|ный *adj. of* **~а; к. магнитофо́н** cassette recorder.
касси́р, а *m.* cashier.
касси́р|овать, ую *impf. and pf.* (*leg.*) to annul, quash.
касси́р|ша, ши *f. of* **~**
ка́сс|овый *adj. of* **~а; ~овая кни́га** cash-book.
ка́ст|а, ы *f.* caste.
кастанье́т|ы, ~ *pl.* (*sg.* **~а, ~ы** *f.*) castanets.
кастеля́нш|а, и *f.* linen-keeper (*in institution*).
касте́т, а *m.* knuckleduster.
касто́р, а *m.* (*text.*) beaver, castor (cloth).
касто́рк|а, и *f.* (*coll.*) castor oil.
касто́ров|ый[1] *adj.*: **~ое ма́сло** castor oil.
касто́р|овый[2] *adj. of* **~**
кастра́т, а *m.* eunuch.
кастра́ци|я, и *f.* castration.
кастри́р|овать, ую *impf. and pf.* to castrate; to geld.
кастрю́л|я, и *f.* saucepan.
катава́си|я, и *f.* (*coll.*) confusion, muddle.
катаклизм, а *m.* cataclysm.
катако́мб|а, ы *f.* catacomb.
ката́лиз, а *m.* (*chem.*) catalysis.
катализа́тор, а *m.* (*chem.*) catalyst.
ката́лк|а, и *f.*: **де́тская к.** baby buggy, pushchair.
катало́г, а *m.* catalogue.
каталогиза́тор, а *m.* cataloguer.
каталогизи́р|овать, ую *impf. and pf.* to catalogue.
катало́жн|ая, ой *f.* catalogue room.
катало́|жный *adj. of* **~г**
катало́нский *adj.* Catalan; Catalonian.
катамара́н, а *m.* catamaran.
ката́ни|е, я *nt.* **1.** rolling. **2.**: **к. в экипа́же** driving; **к. верхо́м** riding; **к. на ло́дке** boating; **к. на конька́х** skating; **к. на ро́ликах** roller skating; **фигу́рное к.** figure skating; **к. с гор** tobogganing.
ка́тань|е, я *nt.*, *only in phr.* **не мытьём, так ~ем** (*coll.*) by hook or by crook.
катапу́льт|а, ы *f.* catapult.
ката́р, а *m.* catarrh.
катара́кт, а *m.* (*geog.*) cataract.
катара́кт|а, ы *f.* (*med.*) cataract.
катара́льный *adj.* catarrhal.
ка́тарсис, а *m.* catharsis.
катастро́ф|а, ы *f.* catastrophe, disaster; accident.
катастрофи́ческий *adj.* catastrophic.
кат|а́ть, а́ю *impf.* **1.** (*indet. of* **~и́ть**) to roll; to wheel, trundle. **2.** to take for a drive, ride. **3.** to roll (*dough etc.*). **4.** (*pf.* **вы~**) **к. бельё** to mangle linen.
кат|а́ться, а́юсь *impf.* **1.** (*indet. of* **~и́ться**) to roll (*intrans.*); (*coll.*) **к. от бо́ли** to roll in pain; **к. со́ смеху** to split one's sides with laughter. **2.** to go for a drive; **к. верхо́м** to ride, go riding; **к. на велосипе́де** to cycle, go cycling; **к. на конька́х** to skate, go skating; **к. на ло́дке** to go boating.
катафа́лк, а *m.* **1.** catafalque. **2.** hearse.
катафо́т, а *m.* cat's eye (*on road*); reflector.
категори́чески *adv.* categorically; **к. отказа́ться** to refuse flatly.
категори́ческий *adj.* categorical.
катего́ри|я, и *f.* category.
ка́тер, а, *pl.* **~а́** *m.* (*naut.*) cutter; **мото́рный к.** motor-launch; **сторожево́й к.** patrol boat.
ка́тер|ный *adj. of* **~**
кате́тер, а *m.* (*med.*) catheter.
катехи́зис, а *m.* catechism.
ка|ти́ть, чу́, ≁тишь *impf.* (*of* **по~**) **1.** *det. of* **~та́ть. 2.** (*coll.*) to bowl along, rip, tear.
ка|ти́ться, чу́сь, ≁тишься *impf.* (*of* **по~**) **1.** *det. of* **~та́ться; к. с горы́** to slide downhill. **2.** to flow, stream; (*fig.*) to roll; **слёзы ~ти́лись по её щека́м** tears were rolling down her cheeks. **3.** (*coll.*): **~ти́сь; ~ти́тесь отсю́да!** get out!; clear off!
като́д, а *m.* (*phys.*) cathode.
като́дн|ый *adj.* (*phys.*) cathodic; **~ые лучи́** cathode rays; **~ая тру́бка** cathode-ray tube.
кат|о́к[1], **ка́** *m.* skating-rink.
кат|о́к[2], **ка́** *m.* **1.** roller. **2. (для белья́)** mangle.
като́лик, а *m.* Catholic.
католици́зм, а *m.* Catholicism.
католи́ческий *adj.* Catholic.
католи́честв|о, а *nt.* Catholicism.
католи́чк|а, и *f. of* **като́лик**
ка́торг|а, и *no pl.*, *f.* penal servitude, hard labour.
ка́торжник, а *m.* convict.
ка́тор|жный *adj. of* **~га; ~жные рабо́ты** hard labour; (*fig.*) drudgery; **~жная тюрьма́** convict prison.
кату́шк|а, и *f.* **1.** reel, bobbin; (*text.*) spool. **2.** (*elec.*) coil.
катю́ш|а, и *f.* (*mil.*; *coll.*) Katyusha (*lorry-mounted multiple rocket launcher*).
кау́рый *adj.* (*of colour of horses*) light-chestnut.
кausти́ческий *adj.* (*chem.*) caustic.
каучу́к, а *m.* (india-)rubber, caoutchouc.
каучу́к|овый *adj. of* **~**; rubber.
каучуконо́с, а *m.* (*bot.*) rubber plant.
кафе́ *nt. indecl.* café; **к.-моро́женое** ice-cream parlour.
ка́федр|а, ы *f.* **1.** pulpit; rostrum, platform; **говори́ть с ~ы** to speak from the platform. **2.** (*fig.*; *at a university*) chair; **получи́ть ~у** to obtain a chair. **3.** (*fig.*; *at a university*) department, sub-faculty; **заседа́ние ~ы** sub-faculty meeting.
кафедра́льный *adj.*: **к. собо́р** cathedral.
ка́фел|ь, я *m.* Dutch tile.
ка́фель|ный *adj. of* **~**; **~ная печь** tiled stove.
кафете́ри|й, я *m.* cafeteria.
кафта́н, а *m.* caftan.
кача́лк|а, и *f.* rocking-chair; **конь-к.** rocking-horse.
кача́ни|е, я *nt.* **1.** rocking, swinging; **к. ма́ятника** swing of pendulum. **2.** pumping.

кач|а́ть, а́ю *impf.* (*of* **~ну́ть**) **1.** (*+a. or i.*) to rock, swing; to shake; **к. колыбе́ль** to rock a cradle; **к. голово́й** to shake one's head; (*impers.*): **его́ ~а́ло из стороны́ в сто́рону** he was reeling; **ло́дку ~а́ет** the boat is rolling. **2.** to lift up, chair (*as mark of esteem or congratulation*). **3.** to pump.

кач|а́ться, а́юсь *impf.* (*of* **~ну́ться**) **1.** to rock, swing (*intrans.*); (*of vessel*) to roll, pitch. **2.** to reel, stagger.

каче́л|и, ей *no sg.* (*child's*) swing; see-saw.

ка́чественный *adj.* **1.** qualitative. **2.** high-quality.

ка́честв|о, а *nt.* **1.** quality; **ни́зкого ~а** poor quality; low-grade; **в ~е** (*+g.*) in the capacity (of); **в ~е преподава́тельницы она́ отли́чна** (in her capacity) as a teacher she is excellent. **2.** (*chess*): **вы́играть, проигра́ть к.** to gain, lose an exchange.

ка́чк|а, и *f.* rocking; tossing; (*naut.*): **бортова́я к.** rolling; **килева́я к.** pitching.

кач|ну́ть(ся), ну́(сь), нёшь(ся) *pf. of* **~а́ть(ся)**

ка|чу́, ~тишь *see* **~ти́ть**

качу́рк|а, и *f.* (*zool.*) petrel.

ка́ш|а, и *f.* **1.** kasha (*dish of cooked grain or groats*); **ма́нная к.** semolina; **ри́совая к.** boiled rice. **2.** (*fig., coll.*): **у него́ к. во рту** he mumbles; **завари́ть ~у** to start sth., stir up trouble.

кашало́т, а *m.* (*zool.*) sperm-whale.

кашева́р, а *m.* (*mil.*) cook.

ка́ш|ель, ля *m.* cough.

кашеми́р, а *m.* (*text.*) cashmere.

каши́ц|а, ы *f.* (*coll.*) gruel.

ка́ш|ка, ки *f. dim. of* **~а**; pap.

ка́шлян|уть, у, ешь *pf.* to give a cough.

ка́шля|ть, ю *impf.* **1.** to cough. **2.** to have a cough.

кашне́ *nt. indecl.* scarf, muffler.

кашта́н, а *m.* **1.** chestnut; **таска́ть ~ы из огня́** (*fig.*) to pull the chestnuts out of the fire. **2.** chestnut-tree; **ко́нский к.** horse-chestnut.

кашта́н|овый *adj.* **1.** *adj. of* **~**. **2.** chestnut(-coloured).

каю́т|а, ы *f.* cabin, stateroom.

каю́т-компа́ни|я, и *f.* **1.** (*on warships*) wardroom. **2.** (*on passenger vessels*) passengers' lounge.

ка́|ющийся *pres. part. of* **~яться** *and adj.* repentant, contrite, penitent.

ка́|яться, юсь, ешься *impf.* **1.** (*pf.* **рас~**) (**в**+*p.*) to repent (of); **он сам тепе́рь ~ется** he is sorry himself now. **2.** (*pf.* **по~**) (**в**+*p.*) to confess. **3.** (*coll.*): **~юсь** I am sorry to say; I (must) confess; **я, ~юсь, совсе́м об э́том забы́л** I am sorry to say I had forgotten all about it.

кв. (*abbr. of* **кварти́ра**) flat, apartment.

квадра́нт, а *m.* quadrant.

квадра́т, а *m.* (*math.*) square; **возвести́ в к.** to square; **в ~е** squared.

квадра́тн|ый *adj.* square; quadratic; **к. ко́рень** square root; **~ое уравне́ние** quadratic equation.

квадрату́р|а, ы *f.* (*math.*) quadrature; (*fig.*): **к. кру́га** squaring the circle.

квадриллио́н, а *m.* (*math.*) quadrillion.

ква́зи... *comb. form* quasi-.

ква́кань|е, я *nt.* croaking.

ква́ка|ть, ю *impf.* to croak.

ква́кн|уть, у, ешь *pf.* to give a croak.

ква́кушк|а, и *f.* (*coll.*) frog.

квалификац|ио́нный *adj. of* **~ия**; **~ио́нная коми́ссия** board of experts.

квалифика́ци|я, и *f.* qualification.

квалифици́рова|нный (~н, ~на) *p.p.p. of* **~ть** *and adj.* qualified, skilled.

квалифици́р|овать, ую *impf. and pf.* **1.** to check, test. **2.** to qualify (as); **как к. тако́е поведе́ние?** how should one qualify such conduct?

квант, а *m. and* **~а, ~ы** *f.* (*phys.*) quantum.

ква́нт|овый *adj. of* **~**; **~овая тео́рия** quantum theory.

ква́рт|а, ы *f.* **1.** quart. **2.** (*mus.*) fourth.

кварта́л, а *m.* **1.** block (*of buildings*). **2.** quarter (*of a city*); district; neighbourhood; **к. кра́сных фонаре́й** red-light district; **кита́йский к.** Chinatown. **3.** quarter (*of year*).

кварта́льный *adj.* quarterly; **к. отчёт** quarterly account.

кварте́т, а *m.* (*mus.*) quartet(te).

кварти́р|а, ы *f.* **1.** flat; lodging; apartment(s); **к. и стол** board and lodging; **«сдаётся к.»** 'flat to let'. **2.** *pl.* (*mil.*) quarters, billets; **зи́мние ~ы** winter quarters.

квартира́нт, а *m.* lodger, tenant.

квартира́нт|ка, ки *f. of* **~**

квартирме́йстер, а *m.* quartermaster.

кварти́р|ный *adj. of* **~а**; **~ная пла́та** rent; **~ное расположе́ние** (*mil.*) billeting.

квартир|ова́ть, у́ю *impf.* **1.** (*coll.*) to lodge. **2.** (*mil.*) to be billeted, be quartered.

квартпла́т|а, ы *f.* (*abbr. of* ***кварти́рная пла́та***) rent.

кварц, а *m.* (*min.*) quartz.

ква́рц|евый *adj. of* **~**

кварци́т, а *m.* (*min.*) quartzite.

квас, а, *pl.* **~ы́** *m.* kvass.

ква́|сить, шу, сишь *impf.* to pickle; to make sour.

квас|но́й *adj. of* **~**; **к. патриоти́зм** (*fig.*) jingoism.

квас|о́к, ка́ *m* **1.** *dim. of* **~**. **2.** (*coll.*) sour tang.

квасцо́вый *adj.* (*chem.*) aluminous.

квасц|ы́, о́в *no sg.* (*chem.*) alum.

ква́шен|ый *adj.* sour, fermented; **~ая капу́ста** sauerkraut.

квашн|я́, и́, *g. pl.* **~е́й** *f.* kneading trough.

кве́рху *adv.* up, upwards.

квинте́т, а *m.* (*mus.*) quintet(te).

квинтэссе́нци|я, и *f.* quintessence.

квит, ~ы *as pred.* (*coll.*) quits; **мы с тобо́й ~ы** we are quits.

квита́нци|я, и *f.* receipt; **бага́жная к.** luggage-ticket.

кво́рум, а *m.* quorum.

кво́т|а, ы *f.* quota.

кг (*abbr. of* **кило́**) k, kg, kilo(s), kilogram(me)(s).

КГБ *m. indecl.* (*abbr. of* ***Комите́т госуда́рственной безопа́сности***) KGB, State Security Committee.

кеба́б, а *m.* kebab.

кеба́бн|ая, ой *f.* kebab house.

кегельба́н, а *m.* bowling alley; skittle alley.

ке́гл|и, ей *pl.* (*sg.* **~я, ~и** *f.*) **1.** skittles, ninepins; **спорти́вные к.** bowls. **2.** (*sg.*) skittle; pin.

кегл|ь, я *m.* (*typ.*) point; **к. 8** 8 point.

кедр, а *m.* cedar; **гимала́йский к.** deodar; **лива́нский к.** cedar of Lebanon; **сиби́рский к.** Siberian pine

кедро́вк|а, и *f.* (*zool.*) nutcracker.

кедр|о́вый *adj. of* **~**

ке́д|ы, ов *or* **~** *pl.* (*sg.* **кед, а** *m. or* **ке́д|а, ы** *f.*) baseball boots, tennis shoes.

кекс, а *m.* fruit-cake.

келе́йно *adv.* in secret, privately.

келе́йный *adj.* **1.** *adj. of* **ке́лья**. **2.** (*fig., pej.*) secret, private.

кельт, а *m.* Celt.

ке́льтский *adj.* Celtic.

ке́л|ья, ьи, *g. pl.* **~ий** *f.* (*eccl.*) cell.

кем *i. of* **кто**

кема́р|ить, ю, ишь *impf.* (*sl.*) to kip, grab some shut-eye.

ке́мпинг, а *m.* camp-site.

кенгуру́ *m. indecl.* kangaroo.

Ке́ни|я, и *f.* Kenya.

кенота́ф, а *m.* cenotaph.

кента́вр, а *m.* (*myth.*) centaur.

ке́пк|а, и *f.* (*coll.*) cloth cap.

кера́мик|а, и *f.* ceramics.
керами́ческий *adj.* ceramic.
ке́рвел|ь, я *m.* (*bot.*) chervil; **ди́кий к.** cow-parsley.
керога́з, а *m.* paraffin stove.
кероси́н, а *m.* paraffin, kerosene.
кероси́нк|а, и *f.* (*coll.*) paraffin stove.
кероси́н|овый *adj. of* **~**; **~овая ла́мпа** oil lamp.
ке́сарев *adj.* (*med.*): **~о сече́ние** Caesarean section.
кессо́н, а *m.* (*tech.*) caisson.
кессо́н|ный *adj. of* **~**; **~ная боле́знь** caisson disease; the bends.
ке́т|а, ы *f.* Siberian salmon.
ке́т|овый *adj. of* **~а**
ке́тч, а *m.* (*coll.*) all-in wrestling.
кетчи́ст, а *m.* (*coll.*) all-in wrestler.
кефа́л|ь, и *f.* grey mullet.
кефи́р, а *m.* kefir.
киберне́тик|а, и *f.* cybernetics.
кибернети́ческий *adj.* cybernetic.
киберпростра́нств|о, а *nt.* cyberspace.
киби́тк|а, и *f.* **1.** kibitka, covered wagon. **2.** nomad tent.
кибу́ц, а *m.* kibbutz.
кив|а́ть, а́ю *impf.* (*of* **~ну́ть**) **1. (голово́й)** to nod (one's head); to nod assent. **2.** (**на**+*a.*) to motion (to); (*fig.*) refer (to), put the blame (on to).
ки́вер, а, *pl.* **~а́** *m.* shako.
ки́ви *f.* & *nt. indecl.* **1.** (*f.*) (*zool.*) kiwi. **2.** (*nt.*) kiwi fruit.
кив|ну́ть, ну́, нёшь *pf. of* **~а́ть**
кив|о́к, ка́ *m.* nod.
ки|да́ть, да́ю *impf.* (*of* **~нуть**) to throw, fling, cast (*usage as for* **броса́ть**).
ки|да́ться, да́юсь *impf.* (*of* **~нуться**) **1.** to throw o.s., fling o.s.; to rush. **2.** (+*i.*) to throw, fling. **3.** *pass. of* **~да́ть**
Ки́ев, а *m.* Kiev.
киевля́н|ин, ина, *pl.* **~е, ~** *m.* Kievan.
киевля́н|ка, ки *f. of* **~ин**
ки́евский *adj.* Kiev; Kievan.
кизи́л, а *m.* (*bot.*) cornel.
ки|й, я́, *pl.* **~и́, ~ёв** *m.* (*billiard*) cue.
кики́мор|а, ы *f.* (*folklore*) kikimora (*hobgoblin in female form*).
кил|ево́й *adj. of* **~ь**; **~ева́я ка́чка** pitching.
ки́ллер, а *m.* contract killer, hit-man.
кило́ *nt. indecl.* kilogram(me).
килоба́йт, а *m.* (*comput.*) kilobyte.
килова́тт, а *m.* (*elec.*) kilowatt.
килогра́мм, а *m.* kilogram(me).
киломе́тр, а *m.* kilometre.
километра́ж, а *m.* kilometres (*travelled, flown etc.*), distance.
кил|ь, я *m.* (*naut.*) keel.
кильва́тер, а *m.* (*naut.*) wake; **идти́ в к.** (+*d.*) to follow in the wake (of).
ки́льк|а, и *f.* sprat.
кимоно́ *nt. indecl.* kimono.
кинемато́граф, а *m.* **1.** cinematography. **2.** cinema.
кинематографи́ст, а *m.* cinematographer, film-maker.
кинематографи́ческий *adj.* cinematographic.
кинематогра́фи|я, и *f.* cinematography.
кинеско́п, а *m.* television tube.
кине́тик|а, и *f.* (*phys.*) kinetics.
кинети́ческий *adj.* (*phys.*) kinetic.
кинжа́л, а *m.* dagger.
кинжа́л|ьный *adj. of* **~**
кино́ *nt. indecl.* (*abstr. and concr.*) cinema.
кино... *comb. form, abbr. of* **кинематографи́ческий**
киноаппара́т, а *m.* cine-camera.
киноарти́ст, а *m.* film actor.
киноарти́стк|а, и *f.* film actress.
киноателье́ *nt. indecl.* film studio.
ки́новар|ь, и *f.* cinnabar, vermilion.
кинове́д, а *m.* student of film, film historian.
кинове́дени|е, я *nt.* film studies.
кинове́дческий *adj.*: **к. факульте́т** department of film studies.
кинодел|е́ц, ьца́ *m.* movie mogul.
кинодрамату́рг, а *m.* screenwriter.
киножурна́л, а *m.* newsreel.
кинозвезд|а́, ы́, *pl.* **~ы, ~, ~ам** *f.* film star.
кинозри́тел|ь, я *m.* cinema-goer.
кинока́мер|а, ы *f.* cine-camera.
кинокарти́н|а, ы *f.* film; motion picture; movie.
кинокоме́ди|я, и *f.* comedy.
киноле́нт|а, ы *f.* reel (of film).
кинолюби́тел|ь, я *m.* amateur film-maker, cineast(e).
кинома́н, а *m.* cinephile.
киномеха́ник, а *m.* projectionist.
кинообозрева́тел|ь, я *m.* film critic.
кинооперáтор, а *m.* camera-man.
киноплёнк|а, и *f.* film.
кинопро́б|а, ы *f.* screen test.
кинопросмо́тр, а *m.* film screening.
кинорежиссёр, а *m.* film director.
кинорепорта́ж, а *m.* news film.
киносту́ди|я, и *f.* film studio.
киносцена́ри|й, я *m.* screenplay.
киносценари́ст, а *m.* scriptwriter.
киносъёмк|а, и *f.* filming, shooting.
киносъём|очный *adj. of* **~ка**; **~очная кома́нда** film crew; **к. аппара́т** film *or* movie camera.
кинотеа́тр, а *m.* cinema.
кинофи́льм, а *m.* film; **комеди́йный к.** comedy (*film*).
кинохро́ник|а, и *f.* newsreel.
ки́|нуть(ся), ну(сь), нешь(ся) *pf. of* **~да́ть(ся)**
кио́ск, а *m.* kiosk, stall; **газе́тный к.** news-stand.
киоскёр, а *m.* stall-holder.
кио́т, а *m.* icon-case.
ки́п|а, ы *f.* **1.** pile, stack. **2.** (*measure*) bale; **к. хло́пка** bale of cotton.
кипари́с, а *m.* (*bot.*) cypress.
кипе́ни|е, я *nt.* boiling; **то́чка ~я** boiling point.
кип|е́ть, лю́, ишь *impf.* (*of* **вс~**) to boil, seethe; **к. ключо́м** to gush up; **к. негодова́нием** (*fig.*) to seethe with indignation; **рабо́та ~е́ла** work was in full swing.
кипре́|й, я *m.* (*bot.*) willow-herb.
кипу́чест|ь, и *f.* ebullience; turbulence.
кипу́ч|ий (~, ~а) *adj.* **1.** boiling, seething. **2.** (*fig.*) ebullient; turbulent; **~ая де́ятельность** feverish activity.
кипя|ти́ть, чу́, ти́шь *impf.* (*of* **вс~**) to boil.
кипя|ти́ться, чу́сь, ти́шься *impf.* **1.** to boil (*intrans.*). **2.** (*fig., coll.*) to get excited. **3.** *pass. of* **~ти́ть**
кипят|о́к, ка́ *m.* boiling water.
кипячёный *adj.* boiled.
кира́с|а, ы *f.* (*mil., hist.*) cuirass.
кираси́р, а *m.* (*mil., hist.*) cuirassier.
кирги́з, а *m.* Kirghiz.
кирги́з|ка, ки *f. of* **~**
кирги́зский *adj.* Kirghiz.
кири́ллиц|а, ы *f.* Cyrillic alphabet.
ки́рк|а, и *f.* (Protestant) church.
кирк|а́, и́ *f.* pick(axe).
кирк|о́вый *adj. of* **~а́**
кирпи́ч, а́ *m.* **1.** brick. **2.** (*collect.*) bricks; **необожжённый, сама́нный к.** adobe. **3.** (*coll.*) no-entry sign.
кирпи́ч|ик, а *m.* **1.** *dim. of* **~**. **2.** (*pl.*) bricks (*as child's plaything*).
кирпи́ч|ный *adj. of* **~**; **к. заво́д** brickworks; **к. чай** brick-tea.

кúс|а, ы *f.* = **~ка**
кисé|йный *adj. of* **~я́**.
кисéл|ь, я́ *m.* kissel (*kind of blancmange*).
кисéт, а *m.* tobacco pouch.
кисе|я́, и́ *f.* muslin.
кúск|а, и *f.* (*coll.*) pussy(-cat).
кис-кúс *int.* puss-puss! (*when calling cat*).
кúсленький *adj.* (*coll.*) slightly sour.
кислé|ть, ю *impf.* (*coll.*) to become sour.
кислúнк|а, *f., only in phr.* **с ~ой** (*coll.*) slightly sour, sourish.
кислорóд, а *m.* oxygen.
кислорóдно-ацетилéновый *adj.* oxy-acetylene.
кислорóдный *adj.* (*chem.*) oxygen.
кúсло-слáдкий *adj.* sweet-and-sour..
кислот|á, ы́, *pl.* **~́ы** *f.* **1.** sourness; acidity. **2.** (*chem.*) acid.
кислóтност|ь, и *f.* (*chem.*) acidity.
кислóтный *adj.* (*chem.*) acid.
кúс|лый (~ел, ~лá, ~ло) *adj.* **1.** sour; (*fig.*): **~лое настроéние** sour mood. **2.** fermented; **~лая капу́ста** sauerkraut. **3.** (*chem.*) acid.
кúс|нуть, ну, нешь, *past* **~, ~ла** *impf.* **1.** to turn sour. **2.** (*fig., coll.*) to mope; to look sour.
кист|á, ы́ *f.* (*med.*) cyst.
кистéн|ь, я́ *m.* bludgeon, flail.
кúсточк|а, и *f.* **1.** brush; **к. для бритья́** shaving-brush. **2.** tassel.
кист|ь[1], и, *pl.* **~́и, ~éй** *f.* **1.** (*bot.*) cluster, bunch; **к. виногрáда** bunch of grapes. **2.** brush; **маля́рная к.** paintbrush. **3.** tassel.
кист|ь[2], и, *pl.* **~́и, ~éй** *f.* hand.
кит, á *m.* whale.
китаевéд, а *m.* sinologist.
китаевéдени|е, я *nt.* sinology.
китá|ец, йца, *pl.* **~йцы, ~йцев** *m.* Chinese.
китаúст, а *m.* sinologist.
Китá|й, я *m.* China.
китáйск|ий *adj.* Chinese; **~ая грáмота** double Dutch; **~ая тушь** India(n) ink.
китáйско-... *comb. form* Sino-.
китайч|óнок, óнка, *pl.* **~áта, ~áт** *m.* Chinese child.
китая́нк|а, и *f. of* **китáец**
кúтел|ь, я, *pl.* **~я́, ~éй** *m.* tunic, jacket (*with high collar*).
китобó|ец, йца *m.* whaler (*ship*).
китобó|й, я *m.* **1.** whaler (*pers.*). **2.** whaler (*ship*).
китобóйн|ый *adj.* whaling; **к. прóмысел** whaling; **~ое су́дно** whaler.
кит|óвый *adj. of* **~**; **к. жир** blubber; **к. ус** whalebone, baleen.
китолóв = китобóй 1.
кито|лóвный *adj.* = **~бóйный**
кич|úться, у́сь, úшься *impf.* (*+i.*) to plume o.s. (on); to strut.
кичлúвост|ь, и *f.* conceit; arrogance.
кичлúв|ый (~, ~а) *adj.* conceited, arrogant; strutting.
киш|éть, у́, úшь *impf.* (*+i.*) to swarm (with), teem (with).
кишéчник, а *m.* (*anat.*) bowels, intestines.
киш|éчный *adj. of* **~éчник** *and* **~кá**; intestinal.
киш|кá, кú, *g. pl.* **~óк** *f.* **1.** (*anat.*) gut, intestine; **пря́мая к.** rectum; **слепáя к.** caecum; **тóнкая, тóлстая к.** small, large intestine. **2.** hose; **полúть ~кóй** to hose.
кишлáк, á *m.* kishlak (*village in Central Asia*).
кишлá|чный *adj. of* **~к**
кишмúш, á *no pl., m.* raisins, sultanas.
кишмя́ *adv., only in phr.* **к. кишéть** to swarm.
клавесúн, а *m.* (*mus.*) harpsichord.
клавиату́р|а, ы *f.* keyboard.
клавикóрд|ы, ов *no sg.* (*mus.*) clavichord.
клáвиш, а *m.* = **клáвиша**
клáвиш|а, и *f.* key (*of piano, typewriter, etc.*); **к. пробéла** space-bar.
клáвиш|ный *adj. of* **~**; **~ные инструмéнты** keyboard instruments.
клад, а *m.* treasure; (*fig., coll.*) treasure(-house); **моя́ секретáрша — настоя́щий к.** my secretary is a real treasure.
клáдбищ|е, а *nt.* cemetery, graveyard; churchyard.
кладбúщенский *adj. of* **клáдбище; к. стóрож** sexton.
клáдез|ь, я *m.*: **к. прему́дрости** mine of information.
клáдк|а, и *f.* laying; **кáменная к.** masonry; **кирпúчная к.** brickwork.
кладов|áя, óй *f.* pantry, larder; storeroom.
кладóвк|а, и *f.* (*coll.*) pantry, larder.
кладовщúк, á *m.* storeman.
кла|ду́, дёшь *see* **~сть**
клад|ь, и *f.* load; **ручнáя к.** hand luggage.
клáк|а, и *no pl., f.* (*collect.*) claque.
клакёр, а *m.* (*theatr.*) claqueur.
клан, а *m.* clan.
клáня|ться, юсь *impf.* (*of* **поклонúться**) **1.** (*+d. or* **с***+i.*) to bow (to); to greet; **к. в пóяс** to bow from the waist; (*fig.*): **мы с ним не ~емся** I am not on speaking terms with him. **2.** to send, convey greetings; **~йтесь ему́ от меня́** give him my regards. **3.** (*+d. or* **пéред**; *coll.*) to cringe (before); to humiliate o.s. (before).
клáпан, а *m.* **1.** (*tech.*) valve; **предохранúтельный к.** safety valve. **2.** (*mus.*) vent. **3.** (*on clothing, etc.*) flap.
кларнéт, а *m.* clarinet.
кларнетúст, а *m.* clarinettist.
класс, а *m.* **1.** class; **госпóдствующий, прáвящий к.** ruling class; **к. млекопитáющих** (class of) mammalia; **игрá высóкого ~́а** high-class play. **2.** class-room.
клáссик, а *m.* **1.** classic; classic(al) author. **2.** classical scholar; classicist.
клáссик|а, и *f.* the classics.
классификáтор, а *m.* classifier.
классификáци|я, и *f.* classification.
классифицúр|овать, ую *impf. and pf.* to classify.
классицúзм, а *m.* **1.** (*liter., art*) classicism. **2.** classical education.
классúческий *adj.* classic(al).
клáсс|ный *adj.* (*of* **~**) **1.**: **~ная доскá** blackboard; **~ная кóмната** classroom; **~ная рабóта** class work. **2.**: **к. вагóн** passenger coach. **3.** (*sport*) first-class; top-flight.
клáссовост|ь, и *f.* (*pol.*) class character.
клáссов|ый *adj.* (*pol.*) class; **~ая борьбá** class struggle; **~ое сознáние** class-consciousness.
клáсс|ы, ов *no sg.* hopscotch.
кла|сть, ду́, дёшь, *past* **~л, ~́ла** *impf.* (*of* **положúть**) **1.** to lay; to put (*into prone position or fig.*); to place; **к. больнóго на носúлки** to lay a patient on a stretcher; **к. сáхар в чай** to put sugar in one's tea; **к. на мéсто** to replace; **к. не на мéсто** to mislay; **к. на му́зыку** to set to music; **к. я́йца** to lay eggs; **к. начáло, к. конéц чему́-н.** to start sth., put an end to sth.; (*fig.*): **к. под сукнó** to shelve. **2.** (*pf.* **сложúть**) to build. **3.** to assign, set aside; **мы ~дём ты́сячу фу́нтов на э́ту поéздку** we are setting aside a thousand pounds for this trip.
клаустрофóби|я, и *f.* claustrophobia.
клёв, а *m.* biting, bite; **сегóдня хорóший к.** the fish are biting well today.
кл|евáть, юю́, юёшь *impf.* (*of* **~ю́нуть**) **1.** to peck. **2.** (*of fish*) to bite; to take the bait; **вчерá ры́ба не**

~ева́ла the fish were not biting yesterday. **3.** (*coll.*): **к. но́сом** to nod (*from drowsiness*).
кл|ева́ться, ~юётся *impf.* (*of birds*) to peck (one another).
кле́вер, а *m.* (*bot.*) clover.
кле́вер|ный *adj. of* ~
клевет|а́, ы́ *f.* slander; libel; **возвести́ на кого́-н. ~у́** to slander s.o., cast aspersions on s.o.
клеве|та́ть, щу́, ~щешь *impf.* (*of* **на~**) (**на**+*a.*) to slander; to libel.
клеветни́к, а́ *m.* slanderer.
клеветн|и́ца, и́цы *f. of* **~и́к**
клеветни́ческ|ий *adj.* slanderous; libellous, defamatory; **~ая кампа́ния** smear campaign.
клеве|щу́, ~щешь *see* **~та́ть**
клев|о́к, ка́ *m.* (*coll.*) peck.
клевре́т, а *m.* minion, follower.
клёвый *adj.* (*sl.*) brill, knockout, fantastic.
клеёнк|а, и *f.* oil-cloth.
клеёнчатый *adj.* oilskin.
кле́|ить, ю, ишь *impf.* **1.** (*pf.* **с~**) to glue; to gum; to paste. **2.** (*pf.* **под~**): **к. де́вушку** (*sl.*) to pick up a girl.
кле́|иться, ится *impf.* (*coll.*) **1.** to become sticky. **2.** (*fig.*; *usu. with neg.*) to get on, go well; **моя́ рабо́та что́-то пло́хо ~ится** my work is not going too well somehow; **разгово́р не ~ился** the conversation was sticky. **3.** *pass. of* **~ить**
кле|й, я, о ~е, на ~ю́ *m.* glue; **мучно́й к.** paste; **пти́чий к.** bird-lime; **ры́бий к.** isinglass.
кле́йк|ий *adj.* sticky; **~ая бума́га (для мух)** fly-paper; **~ая ле́нта** adhesive tape.
клейкови́н|а, ы *f.* gluten.
кле́йкост|ь, и *f.* stickiness.
клеймёный *adj.* branded.
клейм|и́ть, лю́, и́шь *impf.* (*of* **за~**) to brand, stamp; (*fig.*) to brand, stigmatize; **к. позо́ром** to hold up to shame.
клеймле́ни|е, я *nt.* branding, stamping.
клейм|о́, а́, *pl.* **~а** *nt.* brand, stamp; **проби́рное к.** hall-mark; **фабри́чное к.** trade-mark; **к. позо́ра** (*fig.*) stigma.
кле́йстер, а *m.* paste.
клёкот, а *m.* screech.
клеко|та́ть, чу́, ~чешь *impf.* to screech.
клема́тис, а *m.* clematis.
клён, а *m.* maple.
клено́вый *adj. of* **клён**
клепа́льн|ый *adj.* riveting; **~ая маши́на** riveter, riveting machine.
клепа́льщик, а *m.* riveter (*operator*).
клепа́|ть, ю *impf.* (*tech.*) to rivet.
клёпк|а[1]**, и** *f.* riveting.
клёпк|а[2]**, и** *f.* stave, lag; (*fig., coll.*): **у него́ како́й-то ~и не хвата́ет** he has got a screw loose.
клептома́н, а *m.* kleptomaniac.
клептома́ни|я, и *f.* kleptomania.
клёст, а́ *m.* (*zool.*) crossbill.
кле́тк|а, и *f.* **1.** cage; coop; hutch. **2.** (*on paper, chess-board, etc.*) square; **бума́га в ~у** graph paper; (*on material*) check. **3.** (*anat.*): **грудна́я к.** thorax. **4.** (*biol.*) cell.
клету́шк|а, и *f.* (*coll.*) tiny room; cubicle.
клетча́тк|а, и *f.* cellulose.
кле́тчатый *adj.* checked; **к. плато́к** checked head-scarf.
клёцк|а, и *f.* (*cul.*) dumpling.
клёш, а *m.* (*and indecl. adj.*) flare; **брю́ки-к.** flared trousers; bell-bottomed trousers; **ю́бка-к.** flared skirt.
клешн|я́, и́, *g. pl.* **~е́й** *f.* claw, pincer.
клещ, а́ *m.* (*zool.*) tick.
кле́щ|и, е́й *no sg.* **1.** pincers, tongs; (*fig., coll.*): **э́того из меня́ ~а́ми не вы́тянешь** wild horses shall not drag it from me. **2.** (*mil.*; *fig.*) pincer-movement.
кли́вер, а *m.* (*naut.*) jib.
клие́нт, а *m.* client.
клиенту́р|а, ы *f.* (*collect.*) clientèle.
кли́зм|а, ы *f.* (*med.*) enema; **ста́вить ~у** (+*d.*) to give an enema.
клик, а *m.* (*poet.*) cry, call.
кли́к|а, и *f.* clique.
кли́|кать, чу, чешь *impf.* (*of* **~кнуть**) **1.** (*coll.*) to call, hail. **2.** (*of geese and swans*) to honk.
кли́к|нуть, ну, нешь *pf. of* **~ать**
кли́макс, а *m.* = **климакте́рий**
климакте́ри|й, я *m.* menopause.
климактери́ческий *adj.* menopausal; **к. пери́од** menopause.
кли́мат, а *m.* climate.
климати́ческий *adj.* climatic.
клин, а, *pl.* **~ья, ~ьев** *m.* **1.** wedge; **загна́ть к.** (**в**+*a.*) to drive a wedge (into); (*fig.*) **вбить к.** (**ме́жду**) to drive a wedge (between); **свет не ~ом сошёлся** there are plenty more fish in the sea. **2.** gore (*in skirt*); gusset (*in underwear*).
кли́ник|а, и *f.* clinic.
клиници́ст, а *m.* clinician.
клини́ческий *adj.* clinical.
клинови́дный *adj.* wedge-shaped.
клин|о́к, ка́ *m.* blade.
клинообра́з|ный (~ен, ~на) *adj.* wedge-shaped; **~ные письмена́** cuneiform characters.
клинопи́сный *adj.* cuneiform.
кли́нопис|ь, и *f.* cuneiform.
кли́ныш|ек, ка *m.*: **боро́дка ~ком** goatee.
кли́пер, а *m.* (*naut.*) clipper.
кли́пс|ы, ~ *or* **ов** *pl.* (*sg.* **~, ~а** *m. or* **~а, ~ы** *f.*) clip-on earrings.
кли́рос, а *m.* choir (*part of church*).
кли́тор, а *m.* (*anat.*) clitoris.
клич, а *m.* (*rhet.*) call; **боево́й к.** war-cry; **кли́кнуть к.** to issue a call.
кли́чк|а, и *f.* **1.** name (*of domestic animal, pet*). **2.** nickname.
клише́ *nt. indecl.* cliché.
клоа́к|а, и *f.* cesspit, sewer.
клок, а́ *pl.* **кло́чья, кло́чьев** *and* **~и́, ~о́в** *m.* **1.** rag, shred; **разорва́ть в кло́чья** to tear to shreds. **2.** tuft; **к. се́на** wisp of hay.
клокота́ни|е, я *nt.* bubbling; gurgling.
клоко|та́ть, чу́, ~чешь *impf.* to bubble; to gurgle; to boil up (*also fig.*); **в нём всё ~та́ло от гне́ва** he was seething with rage.
клон, а *m.* (*biol.*) clone.
клони́р|овать, ую *impf. and pf.* to clone.
клон|и́ть, ю́, ~ишь *impf.* **1.** to bend; to incline; (*impers.*): **ло́дку ~и́ло на́ бок** the boat was listing; **старика́ уже́ ~и́ло ко сну́** the old man was already nodding off. **2.** (*fig., coll.*) to steer, lead (*conversation*); **куда́ ты ~ишь?** what are you driving at?
клон|и́ться, ю́сь, ~ишься *impf.* **1.** to bow, bend (*intrans.*). **2.** (**к**+*d., fig.*): to be nearing; to be leading up (to), be heading (for); **де́ло ~ится к разва́зке** the affair is coming to a head; **к чему́ всё э́то ~ится?** what is all this leading up to?
клоп, а́ *m.* bedbug.
клопо́вник, а *m.* (*coll.*) bug-infested place.
клоп|о́вый *adj. of* ~
кло́ун, а *m.* clown.
клоуна́д|а, ы *f.* clowning; clown acts.
кло́ун|ский *adj. of* **~; к. колпа́к** fool's cap.
клох|та́ть, чу́, ~чешь *impf.* (*coll.*) to cluck.
клоч|о́к, ка́ *m. dim. of* **клок; разорва́ть в ~ки́** to tear to shreds, tatters; **к. бума́ги** scrap of paper; **к.**

землѝ plot of land; **к. лазýри средѝ облакóв** a patch of blue sky between the clouds.

клуб[1], **а** *m.* **1.** club; **к. любѝтелей бéга** jogging club; **к. здорóвья** keep-fit club; **к. одинóких сердéц** Lonely Hearts Club. **2.** club-house; **офицéрский к.** officers' mess.

клуб[2], **а**, *pl.* **~ы́, ~óв** *m.* puff; **~ы́ пы́ли** clouds of dust.

клу́б|ень, ня *m.* (*bot.*) tuber.

клуб|ѝть, ѝт *impf.* to blow up, puff out; **к. пыль** to raise clouds of dust.

клуб|ѝться, ѝтся *impf.* to swirl; to curl, wreathe.

клубневóй *adj.* (*bot.*) tuberose.

клубнѝк|а, и *f.* **1.** (cultivated) strawberry. **2.** (*collect.*) (cultivated) strawberries.

клубнѝ|чный *adj. of* **~ка; ~чное варéнье** strawberry preserve.

клу́б|ный *adj. of* **~**[1]

клуб|óк, кá *m.* **1.** ball; **свернýться ~кóм, в к.** to roll o.s. up into a ball. **2.** (*fig.*) tangle, mass; **к. интрѝг** network of intrigue; **к. противорéчий** mass of contradictions. **3.** (*fig.*) lump (in the throat); **слёзы у неё подступѝли ~кóм к гóрлу** a lump rose in her throat.

клу́мб|а, ы *f.* (flower-)bed.

клык, á *m.* **1.** canine (tooth). **2.** fang; tusk.

клюв, а *m.* beak; bill.

клюк|á, ѝ *f.* walking-stick, cane.

клю́кв|а, ы *f.* cranberry; (*collect.*) cranberries.

клю́кв|енный *adj. of* **~а; к. кисéль** cranberry jelly; **к. морс** cranberry drink.

клю́н|уть, у, ешь *pf. of* **клевáть**

ключ[1], **á** *m.* **1.** key; clue; **заперéть на к.** to lock; **гáечный к.** spanner, wrench; **францýзский к.** monkey-wrench; **к. к шѝфру** key to a cipher. **2.** (*mus.*) key, clef; **басóвый к.** bass clef.

ключ[2], **á** *m.* spring; source; **кипéть ~óм** to bubble over; **бить ~óм** to spout, jet; (*fig.*) to be in full swing.

ключ|евóй[1] *adj. of* **~**[1]; **~евы́е óтрасли промы́шленности** key industries; (*mil.*): **~евы́е позѝции** key positions; (*mus.*): **к. знак** clef.

ключ|евóй[2] *adj. of* **~**[2]; **~евáя водá** spring water.

ключѝц|а, ы *f.* (*anat.*) clavicle, collar-bone.

клю́шк|а, и *f.* (*sport*) (golf-)club; (hockey) stick; (*coll.*) walking-stick.

кл|юю́, юёшь *see* **~евáть**

кля́кс|а, ы *f.* blot, smudge.

кля|нý, нёшь *see* **~сть**

кля́нч|ить, у, ишь *impf.* **(у)** (*coll.*) to beg (of).

кляп, а *m.* gag; **засýнуть к. в рот** (+*d.*) to gag.

кля|сть, нý, нёшь, *past* **~л, ~лá, ~́ло** *impf.* to curse.

кля́|сться, нýсь, нёшься, *past* **~лся, ~лáсь** *impf.* (*of* **по~**) (**в**+*p.*, +*inf. or* +**что**) to swear, vow; **к. в вéрности** to swear allegiance.

кля́тв|а, ы *f.* oath, vow; **гиппокрáтова к.** Hippocratic oath; **лóжная к.** perjury; **дать ~у** to take an oath.

кля́тв|енный *adj. of* **~а; дать ~енное обещáние** to promise on oath.

клятвопреступлéни|е, я *nt.* perjury.

клятвопрестýпник, а *m.* perjurer.

кляу́з|а, ы *f.* (*coll.*) slander, scandal; tale-bearing.

кляу́зник, а *m.* (*coll.*) scandalmonger; tale-bearer.

кляу́знича|ть, ю *impf.* (*of* **на~**) (*coll.*) to spread slander; to tell tales.

кляу́зн|ый *adj.* (*coll.*) captious, pettifogging; **случѝлось ~ое дéло** a tiresome thing happened.

кля́ч|а, и *f.* (*pej.*; *of horse*) (old) nag.

км (*abbr. of* **киломéтр**) km, kilometre(s).

кнѝг|а, и *f.* book; **тебé и ~и в рýки** (*coll.*) you know best.

книговéдени|е, я *nt.* bibliography.

книголю́б, а *m.* bibliophile.

книготоргóв|ец, ца *m.* bookseller.

книгохранѝлищ|е, а *nt.* (book-)stack.

кнѝжк|а, и *f.* **1.** *dim. of* **кнѝга; записнáя к.** notebook; **к.-календáрь** pocket diary. **2.** (*document*) book, card; **расчётная к.** pay-book; **чéковая к.** cheque-book. **3. (сберегáтельная) к.** savings-bank book; **положѝть дéньги на ~у** to deposit money at a savings bank.

кнѝжник, а *m.* **1.** (*bibl.*) scribe. **2.** bibliophile. **3.** bookseller.

кнѝжн|ый *adj.* **1.** *adj. of* **кнѝга; к. знак** book-plate; **~ая пóлка** bookshelf; **к. шкаф** bookcase. **2.** bookish; **~ая учёность** book-learning; **к. червь** bookworm.

кнѝзу *adv.* downwards.

кнѝксен, а *m.* curts(e)y.

кнóпк|а, и *f.* **1.** drawing-pin; **прикрепѝть ~ой** to pin. **2.** press-button, snap fastener. **3.** (*elec.*) button; knob; **нажáть все ~и** (*fig.*, *coll.*) to do all in one's power, pull out all the stops.

кнóп|очный *adj. of* **~ка; к. телефóн** push-button telephone.

КНР *f. indecl.* (*abbr. of* ***Китáйская Нарóдная Респýблика***) People's Republic of China.

кнут, á *m.* whip; (*hist.*) knout; **щёлкать ~óм** to crack a whip; **полѝтика ~а и пря́ника** (*pol.*) carrot and stick policy.

кнутовѝщ|е, а *nt.* whip-handle.

княгѝн|я, и *f.* princess (*wife of prince*).

кня́жеств|о, а *nt.* principality.

кня́ж|ить, у, ишь *impf.* (*hist.*) to reign.

кня́жич, а *m.* prince (*prince's unmarried son*).

княж|нá, ны́, *g. pl.* **~óн** *f.* princess (*prince's unmarried daughter*).

княз|ь, я, *pl.* **~ья́, ~éй** *m.* prince; **велѝкий к.** grand duke.

К° (*abbr. of* **компáния**) Co., Company.

ко *see* **к**

коагуля́ци|я, и *f.* coagulation.

коалиц|иóнный *adj. of* **~́ия**

коалѝци|я, и *f.* (*pol.*) coalition.

кóбальт, а *m.* (*chem.*) cobalt.

кóбальт|овый *adj. of* **~**

кобéл|ь, я́ *m.* **1.** (*male*) dog. **2.** (*coll.*) lech(er).

кóбз|á, ~́ы *f.* kobza (*Ukrainian mus. instrument similar to guitar*).

кобзáр|ь, я́ *m.* kobza-player.

кóбр|а, ы *f.* cobra.

кобур|á, ы́ *f.* holster.

кобы́л|а[1], **ы** *f.* mare.

кобы́л|а[2], **ы** *f.* vaulting-horse.

кобы́л|ий *adj. of* **~а**[1]

кобы́лк|а[1], **и** *f.* filly.

кобы́лк|а[2], **и** *f.* bridge (*of stringed instruments*).

кóваный *adj.* **1.** forged; hammered. **2.** (*fig.*) terse.

ковáр|ный (~ен, ~на) *adj.* insidious, crafty; perfidious.

ковáрств|о, а *nt.* insidiousness, craftiness; perfidy.

ковáть, кую́, куёшь *impf.* **1.** (*pf.* **вы́~**) to forge (*also fig.*); to hammer (*iron*); **к. побéду** to forge victory; **куй желéзо, покá горячó** (*prov.*) strike while the iron is hot. **2.** (*pf.* **под~**) to shoe (*horses*).

ковбó|й, я *m.* cowboy.

ковбóй|ский *adj. of* **~; к. фильм** western (*film*).

ковбóйк|а, и *f.* (*coll.*) (*man's*) checked shirt.

ков|ёр, рá *m.* carpet; rug; mat; **к.-самолёт** magic carpet.

ковéрка|ть, ю *impf.* (*of* **ис~**) **1.** to spoil, ruin (*concr. and abstr.*). **2.** (*fig.*) to distort; to mangle, mispronounce; **к. чужýю мысль** to distort s.o. else's ideas **к. словá** to mangle words; **он ~ет францýзский язы́к** he murders the French language.

ко́вк|а, и *f.* **1.** forging. **2.** shoeing.
ко́в|кий (~ок, ~ка́, ~ко) *adj.* malleable, ductile.
ко́вкост|ь, и *f.* malleability, ductility.
коври́г|а, и *f.* loaf.
коври́жк|а, и *f.* gingerbread; **ни за каки́е ~и** (*coll.*) not for love nor money; not for all the tea in China.
ко́врик, а *m.* rug; **к. для ва́нной** bath mat.
коврочи́стк|а, и *f.* carpet sweeper.
ковче́г, а *m.* ark; **Но́ев к.** Noah's ark.
ковш, а́ *m.* **1.** scoop, ladle, dipper. **2.** (*tech.*) bucket.
ковы́л|ь, я́ *m.* (*bot.*) feather-grass.
ковыля́|ть, ю *impf.* (*coll.*) to hobble; (*of child*) to toddle.
ковыр|ну́ть, ну́, нёшь *pf. of* **~я́ть**
ковыр|я́ть, я́ю *impf.* (*of* **~ну́ть**) (*coll.*) **1.** to dig into; (**в**+*p.*) to pick (at); **к. в зуба́х** to pick one's teeth. **2.** to tinker (up), potter.
ковыря́|ться, юсь *impf.* (*coll.*) **1.** (**в**+*p.*) to rummage (in). **2.** to tinker.
когда́[1] *adv.* **1.** (*interrog. and rel.*) when; (*coll.*): **есть к.!** there's no time for it!; **есть к. мне болта́ть!** I've no time for talk! **2.: к. (бы) ни** whenever; **к. бы вы ни пришли́, к. (вы) ни придёте** whenever you come. **3.** (*coll.*): **к...., к.** sometimes ... sometimes; **я занима́юсь к. у́тром, к. ве́чером** sometimes I work in the morning, sometimes in the evening. **4.** (*coll.*): **к. как** it depends. **5.** (*coll.*) = **когда́-нибудь.**
когда́[2] *conj.* **1.** when; while, as; **я её встре́тил, к. шёл домо́й** I met her as I was going home. **2.** (*coll.*) if; **к. так, согла́сен с тобо́й** if that is the case, I agree.
когда́-либо *adv.* = **когда́-нибудь**
когда́-нибудь *adv.* **1.** (*in future*) some time, some day. **2.** ever; **вы бы́ли к.-н. в Кита́е?** have you ever been to China?
когда́-то *adv.* **1.** (*in past*) once; some time; formerly. **2.** (*in future*) some day (*indefinitely distant*); **к.-то ещё бу́дет тако́й прия́тный ве́чер** it will be a long time before we have such a pleasant evening again.
кого́ *a. and g. of* **кто**
кого́рт|а, ы *f.* cohort.
ко́г|оть, тя, *pl.* **~ти, ~те́й** *m.* claw; talon; **показа́ть свой ~ти** (*fig.*) to show one's teeth; **попа́сть в ~ти (к кому́-н.)** to fall into the clutches (of s.o.).
когти́ст|ый (~, ~а) *adj.* sharp-clawed.
код, а *m.* code.
ко́д|а, ы *f.* (*mus.*) coda.
кодеи́н, а *m.* (*pharm.*) codeine.
ко́декс, а *m.* (*leg. and fig.*) code; **мора́льный к.** moral code; **уголо́вный к.** criminal code.
кодифика́ци|я, и *f.* codification.
кодифици́р|овать, ую *impf. and pf.* (*leg.*) to codify.
ко́дов|ый *adj. of* **код; ~ое назва́ние** code-name.
ко́е-где́ (*and* **кой-где́**) *adv.* here and there, in places.
ко́е-ка́к (*and* **кой-ка́к**) *adv.* (*coll.*) **1.** anyhow (*badly, carelessly*). **2.** somehow (or other), just (*with great difficulty*); **к.-к. мы доплы́ли до того́ бе́рега** somehow we managed to swim to the other side.
ко́е-како́й (*and* **кой-како́й**) *pron.* some.
ко́е-кто́ (*and* **кой-кто́**), **ко́е-кого́** *pron.* somebody; some people.
ко́ечный *adj. of* **ко́йка; к. больно́й** in-patient.
ко́е-что́ (*and* **кой-что́**), **ко́е-чего́** *pron.* something; a little.
ко́ж|а, и *f.* **1.** skin; hide; **гуси́ная к.** goose-flesh; (*fig., coll.*) **из ~и (вон) лезть** to go all out, do one's utmost; **к. да ко́сти** skin and bone. **2.** leather; **свина́я к.** pig-skin; **теля́чья к.** calf.
ко́жаный *adj.* leather.
кожгалантере́|я, и *f.* leather goods.
коже́венный *adj.* leather; tanning; **к. заво́д** tannery; **к. това́р** leather goods.
коже́вник, а *m.* currier; tanner.
кожзамени́тел|ь, я *m.* imitation leather, leatherette.
кожими́т, а *m.* imitation leather, leatherette.
ко́жиц|а, ы *f.* **1.** thin skin, film. pellicle; **к. колбасы́** sausage-skin. **2.** peel, skin (*of fruit*).
ко́жный *adj.* skin; (*med.*) cutaneous.
кожур|а́, ы́ *f.* rind, peel, skin (*of fruit*).
кожу́х, а́ *m.* **1.** sheepskin jacket. **2.** (*tech.*) housing, casing, jacket.
коз|а́, ы́, *pl.* **∠ы** *f.* **1.** goat. **2.** she-goat. **3.** (*coll.*) tomboy.
коз|ёл, ла́ *m.* (billy) goat; **к. отпуще́ния** scapegoat.
козеро́г, а *m.* **1.** (*zool.*) ibex. **2. К.** (*astrol., astron.*) Capricorn; **тро́пик К~а** (*geog.*) Tropic of Capricorn.
ко́з|ий *adj. of* **~а́; к. пасту́х** goatherd.
козл|ёнок, ёнка, *pl.* **~я́та, ~я́т** *m.* kid.
коз|ли́ный *adj. of* **~ёл; ~ли́ная боро́дка** goatee.
козло́вый *adj.* goatskin.
ко́з|лы, ел, лам *no sg.* **1.** (coach-)box. **2.** trestle(s); saw-horse.
козл|я́та, я́т *see* **~ёнок**
ко́зн|и, ей *pl.* machinations, intrigues.
козово́д, а *m.* goat breeder.
козово́дств|о, а *nt.* goat-breeding.
козодо́|й, я *m.* (*zool.*) nightjar, goatsucker.
косу́л|я, и *f.* roe(buck).
козыр|ёк, ька́ *m.* (cap) peak; visor; **взять под к.** (+*d.*) to salute.
козыр|но́й *adj. of* **ко́зырь**
козыр|ну́ть, ну́, нёшь *pf. of* **~я́ть**
ко́зыр|ь, я, *pl.* **~и, ~е́й** *m.* (*cards and fig.*) trump; **откры́ть свой ~и** (*fig.*) to lay one's cards on the table; **покры́ть ~ем** to trump; **ходи́ть с ~я** to lead trumps; (*fig.*) to play a trump card; **гла́вный к.** (one's) trump card.
козыр|я́ть[1], **я́ю** *impf.* (*of* **~ну́ть**) (*coll.*) **1.** (*cards*) to lead trumps, play a trump; (*fig.*) to play one's trump card. **2.** (+*i.*) to show off, flaunt.
козыр|я́ть[2], **я́ю** *impf.* (*of* **~ну́ть**) (+*d.*; *coll.*) to salute.
козя́вк|а, и *f.* (*coll.*) small insect, bug.
ко́итус, а *m.* coition, coitus; **к. прерыва́емый** coitus interruptus.
кой *interrog. and rel. pron.* (*obs.*) which; **до ко́их пор?** how long?; **ни в ко́ем слу́чае** under no circumstances; (*coll.*): **на к. чёрт?** why in the world; what the devil for?
ко́йк|а, и *f.* **1.** berth, bunk (*on board ship*). **2.** bed (*in hospital*).
койо́т, а *m.* coyote.
кок, а *m.* **1.** (ship's) cook. **2.** quiff.
ко́к|а, и *f.* (*bot.*) coca.
кокаи́н, а *m.* cocaine.
кокаини́ст, а *m.* cocaine addict.
кока́рд|а, ы *f.* cockade.
коке́тк|а, и *f.* coquette, flirt.
коке́тлив|ый (~, ~а) *adj.* coquettish, flirtatious.
коке́тнича|ть, ю *impf.* **1.** (**с**+*i.*) to coquet(te), flirt (with). **2.** (+*i.*) to show off, flaunt.
коке́тств|о, а *nt.* coquetry, flirting.
кокк, а *m.* (*med.*) coccus.
коклю́ш, а *m.* whooping-cough.
ко́кон, а *m.* cocoon.
коко́с, а *m.* **1.** coconut palm. **2.** coconut.
коко́с|овый *adj. of* **~; ~овое волокно́** coir; **~овое ма́сло** coconut oil; **к. оре́х** coconut; **~овая па́льма** coconut palm.
коко́тк|а, и *f.* courtesan, cocotte.
коко́шник, а *m.* kokoshnik (*Russ. peasant woman's head-dress*).
кокс, а *m.* coke.
ко́кс|овый *adj. of* **~; ~овая печь** coke oven; **~овое число́** coking value.
кокс|у́ющийся *adj.*: **к. у́голь** coking coal.

кокте́йл|ь, я *m.* cocktail; cocktail party; **моло́чный к.** milk shake.
кол, а́ *m.* **1.** (*pl.* **∠ья, ∠ьев**) stake, picket; **сажа́льный к.** dibber; **посади́ть на́ к.** to impale; (*coll.*): **стоя́ть ~о́м в го́рле** to stick in one's throat; **у него́ нет ни ~а́ ни двора́** he has neither house nor home. **2.** (*pl.* **~ы́, ~о́в**) (*coll.*) a 'very poor' (*lowest possible acad. mark*).
кол... *comb. form, abbr. of* **коллекти́вный**
ко́лб|а, ы *f.* (*chem.*) retort.
колбас|а́, ы́, *pl.* **∠ы** *f.* sausage; **кровяна́я к.** black pudding.
колба́сник, а *m.* sausage-maker.
колба́с|ный *adj. of* **~а́**
колго́т|ки, ок *no sg.* tights.
колдо́бин|а, ы *f.* (*coll.*) rut, pothole (*in road*).
колд|ова́ть, у́ю *impf.* to practise witchcraft.
колдовско́й *adj.* magical; (*fig.*) magical, bewitching.
колдовств|о́, а́ *nt.* witchcraft, sorcery, magic.
колду́н, а́ *m.* sorcerer, magician, wizard.
колду́н|ья, ьи, *g. pl.* **~ий** *f.* witch, sorceress.
колеба́ни|е, я *nt.* **1.** (*phys.*) oscillation, vibration. **2.** fluctuation, variation. **3.** (*fig.*) hesitation, wavering, vacillation.
колеб|а́ть, ∠лю, ∠лешь *impf.* (*of* **по~**) to shake; (*fig.*): **к. обще́ственные усто́и** to shake the foundations of society.
колеб|а́ться, ∠люсь, ∠лешься *impf.* (*of* **по~**) **1.** to shake to and fro, sway; (*phys.*) to oscillate. **2.** to fluctuate, vary. **3.** (*fig.*) to hesitate; to waver, vacillate.
коле́нк|а, и *f.* (*coll.*) knee.
коленко́р, а *m.* (*text.*) calico; (*coll.*): **э́то совсе́м друго́й к.** that's quite another matter.
коленко́р|овый *adj. of* **~**
коле́н|ный *adj. of* **~о**; (*anat.*): **~ная ча́шка** patella, knee-cap.
коле́н|о, а *nt.* **1.** (*pl.* **~и, ~ей, ~ям**) knee; **преклони́ть ~и** to genuflect; **стать на ~и (пе́ред)** to kneel (to); **стоя́ть на ~ях** to be kneeling, be on one's knees; **по к., по ~и** knee-deep, up to one's knees; (*coll.*): **ему́ мо́ре по к.** he couldn't care less; **поста́вить кого́-н. на ~и** to bring s.o. to his knees. **2.** (*pl. only*; **~и, ~ей, ~ям**) lap; **сиде́ть у кого́-н. на ~ях** to sit on s.o.'s lap. **3.** (*pl.* **~ья, ~ьев**) (*tech.*) knee, joint; **к. трубы́** knee pipe, elbow pipe. **4.** (*pl.* **~а, ~, ~ам**) bend (*of river, etc.*). **5.** (*pl.* **~а, ~, ~ам**) (*obs.*) generation; **ро́дственники до пя́того ~а** cousins five times removed. **6.** (*pl.* **~а, ~, ~ам**) (*coll.*) figure (*in dance, song, etc.*); **выде́лывать к.** to execute a figure.
коленопреклоне́ни|е, я *nt.* genuflection.
коле́нчат|ый *adj.* (*tech.*) elbow-shaped, cranked; **к. вал** crankshaft.
колёсик|о, а *nt.* **1.** *dim. of* **колесо́. 2.** castor.
коле|си́ть, шу́, си́шь *impf.* (*coll.*) **1.** to go in a roundabout way. **2.** to go all over, travel about.
коле́сник, а *m.* wheelwright.
колесни́ц|а, ы *f.* chariot; **погреба́льная к.** hearse.
колёс|ный *adj.* **1.** *adj. of* **~о́. 2.** wheeled, on wheels.
колес|о́, а́, *pl.* **∸а** *nt.* wheel; **запасно́е к.** spare wheel; **к. обозре́ния** Big Wheel (*fairground attraction*); **рулево́е к.** driving wheel; **цепно́е к.** sprocket; **вста́вить кому́-н. па́лки в ∸а** to put a spoke in s.o.'s wheel; **кружи́ться, как бе́лка в ~е́** to run round in circles; **но́ги ~о́м** bandy legs; **кувырка́нье «~о́м»** cartwheel (*acrobatics*); **ходи́ть ~о́м** to cartwheel.
колес|ова́ть, у́ю *impf. and pf.* to break on the wheel.
коле́ч|ко, ка, *pl.* **~ки, ~ек, ~кам** *nt.* (*coll.*) ringlet.
коле|я́, и́ *f.* **1.** rut; (*fig.*): **войти́ в ~ю** to settle down (again); **вы́битый из ~и** unsettled. **2.** (*rail.*) track; gauge.
ко́ли (*and* **коль)** (*obs. or dial.*) if; (*coll.*): **к. на то пошло́** while we are about it; **коль ско́ро** if, as soon as.
коли́бри *c.g. indecl.* (*zool.*) humming-bird.
ко́лик|и, ~ *no sg.* (*med.*) colic.
коли́т, а *m.* (*med.*) colitis.
коли́чественный *adj.* quantitative; **~ое числи́тельное** cardinal number.
коли́честв|о, а *nt.* quantity, amount; number.
ко́л|кий[1] (~ок, ~ка́ ~ко) *adj.* easily split.
ко́л|кий[2] (~ок, ~ка́ ~ко) *adj.* prickly; (*fig.*) sharp, biting, caustic.
ко́лкост|ь, и *f.* **1.** (*fig.*) sharpness. **2.** sharp, caustic remark.
коллаборациони́ст, а *m.* (*pol.*; *pej.*) collaborator.
коллаборациони́ст|ский *adj. of* **~**
колла́ж, а *m.* collage.
колле́г|а, и *c.g.* colleague.
коллегиа́л|ьный (~ен, ~ьна) *adj.* joint, collective; corporate; **~ьное реше́ние** collective decision.
колле́ги|я, и *f.* **1.** board, collegium. **2.** college; **к. адвока́тов, к. правозасту́пников** the Bar; **к. вы́борщиков** electoral college.
колле́дж, а *m.* college.
колле́жский *adj.* (*in titles of officials in tsarist Russia*) collegiate; **а. сове́тник** collegiate counsellor.
коллекти́в, а *m.* collective; team; group, body; **нау́чный к.** (the) scientists; **парти́йный к.** Party members.
коллективиза́ци|я, и *f.* collectivization.
коллективизи́р|овать, ую *impf. and pf.* to collectivize.
коллективи́зм, а *m.* collectivism.
коллективи́ст, а *m.* collectivist.
коллекти́вн|ый *adj.* collective; joint; **~ое владе́ние** joint ownership; **~ое хозя́йство** collective farm.
коллекционе́р, а *m.* collector.
коллекциони́р|овать, ую *impf.* to collect.
колле́кци|я, и *f.* collection.
ко́лли *c.g. indecl.* collie (*dog*).
колли́зи|я, и *f.* clash, conflict.
колло́ди|й, я *m.* (*chem.*) collodion.
колло́ид, а *m.* (*chem.*) colloid.
колло́идный *adj.* (*chem.*) colloidal.
колло́квиум, а *m.* oral examination; colloqium.
колоб|о́к, ка́ *m.* small round loaf.
колобро́|дить, жу, дишь *impf.* (*coll.*) **1.** to roam, wander; to loaf. **2.** to make a noise; to get up to mischief.
коловоро́т, а *m.* (*tech.*) brace.
коло́д|а[1], ы *f.* **1.** block; log. **2.** (water-)trough.
коло́д|а[2], ы *f.* pack (*of cards*).
коло́де|зный *adj. of* **~ц**
коло́д|ец, ца *m.* well.
коло́дк|а, и *f.* **1.** boot-tree; last. **2.** (*tech.*) shoe. **3.** (*pl.*; *hist.*) stocks; **наби́ть ~и на́ ноги кому́-н.** to put s.o. in stocks.
кол|о́к, ка́ *m.* (*mus.*) peg.
ко́локол, а, *pl.* **~а́, ~о́в** *m.* bell.
колоко́льный *adj. of* **ко́локол; к. звон** peal, chime.
колоко́л|ьня, ьни, *g. pl.* **~ен** *f.* steeple, bell-tower, church-tower; (*coll.*): **смотре́ть со свое́й ~ьни на что-н.** to take a narrow, parochial view of sth.
колоко́льчик, а *m.* **1.** small bell; handbell. **2.** (*bot.*) bluebell.
колониа́льный *adj.* colonial.
колониза́тор, а *m.* colonizer.
колониза́ци|я, и *f.* colonization.
колониз|ова́ть, у́ю *impf. and pf.* to colonize.
колони́ст, а *m.* colonist.
коло́ни|я, и *f.* colony; settlement.
коло́нк|а, и *f.* **1.** geyser. **2.** (*street*) water fountain.

3.: бензи́новая к. petrol pump. **4.** (*typ.*) column; **газéтная полосá в шесть колóнок** newspaper page with six columns; **к. цифр** column of figures. **5.** (*coll.*) (loud)speaker.

колóнн|а, ы *f.* column; (*mil.*) **тáнковая к.** tank column.

колоннáд|а, ы *f.* colonnade.

колóнный *adj.* columned.

колон|óк, кá *m.* (*zool.*) Siberian weasel.

колонти́тул, а *m.* (*typ.*) running title.

колонци́фр|а, ы *f.* (*typ.*) folio, page number.

колорáдский *adj.*: **к. жук** Colorado beetle.

колоратýр|а, ы *f.* (*mus.*) coloratura.

колоратýр|ный *adj. of* **~а**

колори́ст, а *m.* (*art*) colourist.

колори́т, а *m.* colouring, colour; (*fig.*): **мéстный к.** local colour; **он придáл расскáзу о встрéче я́ркий к.** he painted a glowing picture of the encounter.

колори́т|ный (~ен, ~на) *adj.* colourful.

кóлос, а, *pl.* **∸ья, ∸ьев** *m.* (*agric.*) ear, spike.

колóсс, а *m.* colossus.

колоссáльный *adj.* colossal; (*coll.*) terrific, great.

коло|ти́ть, чý, ∸тишь *impf.* (*of* **поколоти́ть**) **1.** (**по**+*d.*, **в**+*a.*) to strike (on); to batter (on), pound (on); **к. в двéрь** to bang on the door. **2.** (*coll.*) to thrash, drub. **3.** (*impf. only*): **к. лён** to scutch flax. **4.** (*impf. only*) (*coll.*) to break, smash. **5.** (*impf. only*) (*coll.*) to shake; (*impers.*): **егó ~ти́ла лихорáдка** he was shaking with fever.

коло|ти́ться, чýсь, ∸тишься *impf.* (*of* **поколоти́ться**) **1.** (**о**+*a.*) to beat (against); to strike (against); **к. головóй об стéну** to beat one's head against a wall. **2.** (*impf. only*) (*coll.*) to pound; to shake; **сéрдце у неё ~ти́лось** her heart was pounding. **3.** *pass. of* **~ти́ть**

колотýшк|а, и *f.* **1.** beetle (*tech.*). **2.** (*wooden*) rattle (*used by night watchman*).

кóлот|ый[1] (~, ~а) *p.p.p. of* **∸ь[1]** *and adj.*; **к. сáхар** chipped sugar.

кóлот|ый[2] (~, ~а) *p.p.p. of* **∸ь[2]** *and adj.*; **~ая рáна** stab(-wound).

кол|óть[1], ю́, ∸ешь *impf.* (*of* **расколóть**) to break, chop, split; **к. дровá** to chop wood; **к. орéхи** to crack nuts.

кол|óть[2], ю́, ∸ешь *impf.* (*of* **заколóть**) **1.** to prick; (*impers.*): **у меня́ ∸ет в бокý** I have a stitch in my side. **2.** to stab. **3.** to slaughter (*cattle*). **4.** (*fig.*) to taunt; **к. глазá комý-н.** (+*i.*) to cast a thing in s.o.'s teeth; **прáвда глазá ∸ет** (*prov.*) home truths are unpalatable.

кóлоть|е, я (*and* **колоть|ё, я́**) *nt.* (*coll.*) stitch.

кол|óться[1], ю́сь, ∸ешься *impf., pass. of* **~óть[1]**

кол|óться[2], ю́сь, ∸ешься *impf.* to prick (*intrans.*).

колпáк, á *m.* **1.** cap; **ночнóй к.** nightcap; **шутовскóй к.** fool's cap; **к. колесá** hubcap. **2.** lamp-shade; (*tech.*) cowl; **стекля́нный к.** bell-glass.

колпач|óк, кá *m.* **1.** *dim. of* **колпáк. 2.** (gas) mantle.

колумби́йский *adj.* Colombian.

колýн, á *m.* (wood-)chopper, hatchet.

колхóз, а *m.* (*abbr. of* ***коллекти́вное хозя́йство***) collective farm.

колхóзник, а *m.* member of collective farm.

колхóзн|ица, ицы *f. of* **~ик**

колхóз|ный *adj. of* **~**; **к. строй** collective farm system.

колчáн, а *m.* quiver.

колчедáн, а *m.* (*min.*) pyrites.

колыбéл|ь, и *f.* cradle; (*fig.*): **к. наýки** the cradle of learning; **с ~и** from the cradle; **от ~и до моги́лы** from the cradle to the grave.

колыбéль|ный *adj. of* **~**; **~ная пéсня** lullaby; **~ная смерть** cot death.

колымáг|а, и *f.* (*obs.*) heavy, unwieldy carriage; (*iron.*) rattletrap.

колы|хáть, ∸шу, ∸шешь *impf.* (*of* **~хнýть**) to sway, rock.

колы|хáться, ∸шется *impf.* (*of* **~хнýться**) to sway, heave; to flutter; to flicker.

колых|нýть(ся), нý(сь), нёшь(ся) *pf. of* **~áть(ся)**

кóлыш|ек, ка *m.* peg.

коль *see* **кóли**

кольé *m. indecl.* necklace.

кол|ьнýть, ьнý, ьнёшь *inst. pf. of* **~óть[2]**

кольрáби *f. indecl.* (*bot.*) kohlrabi.

кольц|евáть, ýю *impf.* **1.** (*of* **закольцевáть**) to girdle, ring-bark (*a tree*). **2.** (*of* **окольцевáть**) to ring (*bird's leg., etc.*).

кольцев|óй *adj.* annular; circular; **~áя дорóга** ring road; **~áя развя́зка** roundabout.

кольцеобрáз|ный (~ен, ~на) *adj.* ring-shaped.

кол|ьцó ~ьцá, *pl.* **∸ьца, ~ец, ∸ьцам** *nt.* **1.** ring; **свернýться ~ьцóм** to coil up; **годи́чное к.** (*bot.*) ring; **обручáльное к.** wedding ring. **2.** (*tech.*) ring; collar; hoop.

кóльчат|ый *adj.* ring-shaped; annulate(d).

кольчýг|а, и *f.* shirt of mail, hauberk.

колю́ч|ий (~, ~а) *adj.* prickly; thorny; (*fig.*) sharp, biting; **~ая и́згородь** prickly hedge; **~ая прóволока** barbed wire; **к. язы́к** sharp tongue.

колю́чк|а, и *f.* (*coll.*) prickle; thorn.

кóлюшк|а, и *f.* (*fish*) stickleback.

кóл|ющий *pres. part. act. of* **~óть[2]** *and adj.*; **~ющая боль** shooting pain.

коляд|á, ы́ *f.* kolyada (*custom of house-to-house Christmas carol-singing*).

коляд|овáть, ýю *impf.* to go round carol-singing.

коля́ск|а, и *f.* **1.** carriage. **2.** **(дéтская** *or* **прогýлочная) к.** pram; pushchair; **инвали́дная к.** wheelchair. **3.** (*motor-cycle*) side-car.

ком[1], а, *pl.* **∸ья, ∸ьев** *m.* lump; ball; clod; **снéжный к.** snow-ball; (*fig.*): **к. в гóрле** lump in the throat; **пéрвый блин ∸ом** (*prov.*) practice make perfect.

ком[2] *p. of* **кто**

ком... *comb. form, abbr. of* **1. коммунисти́ческий. 2. комáндный. 3. команди́р**

...ком *comb. form, abbr. of* **1. комитéт. 2. комиссáр. 3. комиссариáт**

кóм|а, ы *f.* (*med.*) coma.

комáнд|а, ы *f.* **1.** command, order; **подáть ~у** to give a command. **2.** command; **приня́ть ~у (над)** to take command (of). **3.** (*mil.*) party, detachment, crew; (*naut.*) crew, ship's company; **пожáрная к.** fire-brigade. **4.** (*sport*) team.

команди́р, а *m.* (*mil.*) commander, commanding officer; (*naut.*) captain.

командир|овáть, ýю *impf. and pf.* to post; to dispatch, send on a mission.

командирóвк|а, и *f.* **1.** posting, dispatching (*on official business*). **2.** mission; assignment; (official business) trip; **он в ~е** he is away on business; **я получи́л ~у в Казахстáн** I have been posted to Kazakhstan; **наýчная к.** scientific mission.

командирóв|очный *adj. of* **~ка; ~очные дéньги** travel allowance; **~очное удостоверéние** warrant, authority (*for travelling on official business*); *as n.* **~очные, ~очных** travel allowance.

комáнд|ный *adj.* **1.** *adj. of* **~а; к. пункт** command post; **к. состáв** the officers (*of a military unit*). **2.** (*fig.*) commanding; **~ные высóты** commanding heights.

комáндовани|е, я *nt.* **1.** commanding, command; **приня́ть к. (над)** to take command (of, over). **2.** (*collect.*) command.

комáнд|овать ую *impf.* (*of* **с~**) **1.** to give orders. **2.** (+*i.*) to command, be in command (of). **3.** (*fig.*,

coll.) (+*i.* *or* **над**) to order about. **4.** (*fig.*) (**над**) to command (*terrain*).
кома́ндующ|ий, его *m.* commander.
кома́р, а́ *m.* mosquito.
комар|и́ный *adj. of* ~; **к. уку́с** mosquito bite.
комато́зный *adj.* (*med.*) comatose.
комба́йн, а *m.* (*tech.*) combine; **зерново́й к.** combine harvester; **ку́хонный к.** food processor.
комба́йнер, а *m.* (*agric.*) combine operator.
комбина́т, а *m.* industrial complex; combine; **к. бытово́го обслу́живания** service centre.
комбина́тор, а *m.* (*pej.*) schemer; wheeler-dealer.
комбинац|ио́нный *adj. of* ~**ия**
комбина́ци|я[1], **и** *f.* **1.** combination; (*econ.*) merger. **2.** (*fig.*) scheme; (*pol.*, *sport*) manœuvre.
комбина́ци|я[2], **и** *f.* (*underwear*) slip.
комбинезо́н, а *m.* **1.** overalls; dungarees. **2.** jumpsuit.
комбини́рованный *adj.* combined.
комбини́р|овать, ую *impf.* (*of* **с**~) to combine.
комбри́г, а *m.* (*abbr. of* **команди́р брига́ды**) brigade commander.
комди́в, а *m.* (*abbr. of* **команди́р диви́зии**) division commander.
комеди́йный *adj.* (*liter.*, *theatr.*) comic; comedy; **к. актёр** comedy actor, comedian.
коме́ди|я, *f.* comedy; **лома́ть** ~**ю, разы́грывать** ~**ю** to put on an act.
ко́м|ель, ля *m.* butt, butt-end (*of tree, etc.*).
коменда́нт, а *m.* **1.** (*mil.*) commandant. **2.** manager; warden; **к. теа́тра** theatre manager; **к. общежи́тия** warden of a hostel.
коменда́нт|ский *adj. of* ~; **к. час** (*mil.*) curfew.
комендату́р|а, ы *f.* commandant's office.
коме́т|а, ы *f.* comet.
коми́зм, а *m.* comedy; humour; **к. положе́ния** the funny side of a situation.
ко́мик, а *m.* **1.** comic actor. **2.** (*fig.*) comedian.
ко́микс, а *m.* comic(-book); comic strip.
комисса́р, а *m.* commissar, commissioner; **верхо́вный к.** high commissioner.
комиссариа́т, а *m.* commissariat.
комисса́р|ский *adj. of* ~
комиссионе́р, а *m.* agent, broker.
комисс|ио́нный *adj. of* ~**ия 2.**; *as n.* ~**ио́нные,** ~**ио́нных** (*comm.*) commission.
коми́сси|я, и *f.* **1.** commission, committee; **к. по разоруже́нию** disarmament commission; **сле́дственная к.** committee of investigation. **2.** (*comm.*) commission; **брать на** ~**ю** to take on commission.
комите́т, а *m.* committee; **специа́льный к.** select committee; ad hoc committee.
коми́ческ|ий *adj.* **1.** comic; ~**ая о́пера** comic opera. **2.** comical, funny.
коми́ч|ный (~**ен,** ~**на)** *adj.* comical, funny.
ко́мка|ть, ю *impf.* (*of* **с**~) **1.** (*pf. also* **иско́мкать**) to crumple. **2.** (*fig.*, *coll.*) to make a hash of, muff.
коммента́ри|й, я *m.* **1.** commentary. **2.** (*pl.*) comment; ~**и изли́шни** comment is superfluous.
коммента́тор, а *m.* commentator.
коммента́р|овать, ую *impf. and pf.* to comment (upon).
коммерса́нт, а *m.* merchant; business man.
комме́рци|я, и *f.* commerce, trade.
комме́рческ|ий *adj.* commercial; mercantile; **к. флот** mercantile marine.
коммивояжёр, а *m.* commercial traveller, travelling salesman.
комму́н|а, ы *f.* commune.
коммуна́лк|а, и *f.* (*coll.*) communal flat.
коммуна́льн|ый *adj.* **1.** communal; municipal; ~**ая кварти́ра** communal flat; ~**ые услу́ги** public utilities; ~**ое хозя́йство** municipal economy. **2.** *adj. of* **комму́на**
коммуни́зм, а *m.* communism.
коммуникацио́нн|ый *adj.*: ~**ая ли́ния** line of communication.
коммуника́ци|я, и *f.* communication; (*mil.*) line of communication.
коммуни́ст, а *m.* communist.
коммунисти́ческ|ий *adj.* communist.
коммута́тор, а *m.* (*elec.*) **1.** commutator. **2.** switchboard.
коммюнике́ *nt. indecl.* communiqué.
ко́мнат|а, ы *f.* room; **тёмная к.** (*phot.*) darkroom.
ко́мнатн|ый *adj.* **1.** of a room. **2.** indoor; pet; ~**ые и́гры** indoor games; ~**ые расте́ния** indoor plants; ~**ая соба́чка** lap-dog; ~**ая температу́ра** room temperature.
комо́д, а *m.* chest of drawers.
ком|о́к, ка́ *m. dim. of* ~; **сверну́ться в к.** to roll o.s. up into a ball; (*fig.*) **к. в го́рле** lump in the throat; **к. не́рвов** bundle of nerves.
комо́лый *adj.* polled, hornless.
компа́кт-ди́ск, а *m.* compact disk, CD; **проигрыватель** (*m.*) ~**ов** compact disk player.
компа́кт|ный (~**ен,** ~**на)** *adj.* compact, solid.
компане́йск|ий *adj.* (*coll.*) **1.** sociable, outgoing.
компа́ни|я, и *f.* (*in var. senses*) company; **доче́рняя к.** subsidiary; **води́ть** ~**ю с кем-н.** (*coll.*) to keep company with s.o.; **расстро́ить** ~**ю** to break up a party; **соста́вить кому́-н.** ~**ю** to keep s.o. company; **я провёл ве́чер в** ~**и с Воло́дей** I spent the evening in Volodya's company; **он тебе́ не к.** he is not suitable company for you; **пойти́ це́лой** ~**ей** to go all together; **гуля́ть** ~**ей** to go about in a group.
компаньо́н, а *m.* **1.** (*comm.*) partner. **2.** companion.
компаньо́н|ка, ки *f.* **1.** *f. of* ~. **2.** (female) companion; chaperon(e).
компа́рти|я, и *f.* Communist Party.
ко́мпас, а *m.* compass; **морско́й к.** mariner's compass.
ко́мпас|ный *adj. of* ~; ~**ная стре́лка** compass needle.
компатрио́т, а *m.* compatriot.
компе́ндиум, а *m.* compendium, digest.
компенсацио́нный *adj.* compensatory.
компенса́ци|я, и *f.* compensation.
компенси́р|овать, ую *impf. and pf.* **1.** to compensate, indemnify (for). **2.** (*tech.*) to compensate, equilibrate.
компете́нт|ный (~**ен,** ~**на)** *adj.* competent.
компете́нци|я, и *f.* competence; jurisdiction; **э́то не в мое́й** ~**и** it is outside my competence.
компили́ровать, ую *impf.* (*of* **с**~) (*pej.*) to rehash.
компиляти́в|ный (~**ен,** ~**на)** *adj. of* **компиля́ция; к. труд** rehash.
компиля́тор, а *m.* (*pej.*) hack.
компиля́ци|я, и *f.* (*pej.*) rehash.
ко́мплекс, а *m.* complex; set; **к. неполноце́нности** inferiority complex; **к. мероприя́тий** package of measures.
ко́мплексн|ый *adj.* **1.** (*math.*) complex; ~**ое число́** complex number. **2.** all-embracing, all-in; **к. обе́д** table d'hôte dinner.
компле́кт, а *m.* **1.** complete set; kit; outfit; **к. белья́** bedding, bed-clothes; **к. спорти́вного сти́ля** casual outfit; **шрифтово́й к.** (*typ.*) fo(u)nt. **2.** complement; specified number; **у нас ещё не хвата́ет двух челове́к до по́лного** ~**а** we are still two short of the full complement.
компле́ктный *adj.* complete.
комплект|ова́ть, у́ю *impf.* (*of* **у**~) **1.** to complete; to replenish; **к. журна́л** to acquire a complete set of a periodical. **2.** (*mil.*) to bring up to (full) strength.
компле́кци|я, и *f.* build; constitution.

комплиме́нт, а *m.* compliment; **сде́лать к.** (*+d.*) to pay a compliment (to).
компози́тор, а *m.* (*mus.*) composer.
компози́ци|я, и *f.* composition.
компоне́нт, а *m.* component.
компон|ова́ть, у́ю *impf.* (*of* **скомпонова́ть**) to put together, arrange; to group; **к. статью́** to put together an article.
компоно́вк|а, и *f.* arrangement; grouping.
компо́ст, а *m.* (*hort.*) compost.
компо́стер, а *m.* punch (*for bus tickets etc.*).
компости́р|овать, ую *impf.* (*of* **про~**) to punch (*bus tickets, etc.*).
компо́ст|ный *adj. of* ~; **~ная я́ма** compost pit.
компо́т, а *m.* compote, stewed fruit.
компре́сс, а *m.* (*med.*) compress; **согрева́ющий к.** hot compress; **поста́вить к.** to apply a compress.
компре́ссор, а *m.* (*tech., med.*) compressor.
компромети́р|овать, ую *impf.* (*of* **с~**) to compromise.
компроми́сс, а *m.* compromise; **идти́ на к.** to make a compromise, meet half-way.
компроми́сс|ный *adj. of* ~; **~ное реше́ние** compromise settlement.
компью́тер, а *m.* computer; **ИБМ-совмести́мый к.** IBM-compatible computer; **к.-калькуля́тор** scientific calculator.
компью́тер|ный *adj. of* ~; computerized.
комсомо́л, а *m.* (*abbr. of* ***коммунисти́ческий сою́з молодёжи***) Komsomol (*Young Communist League*).
комсомо́л|ец, ьца *m.* Komsomol (member).
комсомо́л|ка, ки *f. of* **~ец**
комсомо́л|ьский *adj. of* ~
кому́ *d. of* **кто**
комфо́рт, а *m.* comfort.
комфорта́бельный *adj.* comfortable.
кон, а, о ~е, на ~у́ *m.* kitty; **поста́вить (де́ньги) на́ к.** to put (money) in the kitty; **быть, стоя́ть на ~у́** (*fig.*) to be at stake.
конве́йер, а *m.* (*tech.*) conveyor; **сбо́рочный к.** assembly line.
конве́йер|ный *adj. of* ~; **~ная систе́ма** conveyor (belt) system.
конве́кци|я, и *f.* (*phys.*) convection.
конве́нт, а *m.* (*pol.*) convention.
конве́нци|я, и *f.* (*leg.*) convention, agreement.
конверге́нци|я, и *f.* convergence.
конве́рси|я, и *f.* (*econ.*) conversion.
конве́рт, а *m.* **1.** envelope. **2.** (*gramophone record*) sleeve.
конверти́р|овать, ую *impf. and pf.* (*econ.*) to convert.
конве́ртор, а *m.* (*tech.*) converter.
конво́ир, а *m.* escort.
конвои́р|овать, ую *impf.* to escort, convoy.
конво́|й, я *m.* escort, convoy; **вести́ под ~ем** to conduct under escort.
конво́й|ный *adj. of* ~; **~ное су́дно** escort vessel; *as n.* **к., ~ного** *m.* escort.
конвульси́в|ный (~ен, ~на) *adj.* (*med.*) convulsive.
конву́льси|я, и *f.* (*med.*) convulsion.
конгломера́т, а *m.* **1.** conglomeration. **2.** (*geol.*) conglomerate.
конгре́сс, а *m.* congress.
конденса́тор, а *m.* condenser.
конденсацио́нн|ый *adj.* condensing, obtained by condensation; **~ая вода́** condensation water; **к. горшо́к** condensing vessel.
конденса́ци|я, и *f.* condensation.
конденси́р|овать, ую *impf. and pf.* to condense.
конди́тер, а *m.* confectioner, pastry-cook.
конди́терск|ая, ой *f.* confectioner's.
конди́терск|ий *adj.*: **~ие изде́лия** confectionery; **к. магази́н = ~ая**
кондиционе́р, а *m.* air-conditioner.
кондициони́ровани|е, я *nt.* conditioning; **к. во́здуха** air conditioning.
кондициони́р|овать, ую *impf.* to condition; to air-condition.
ко́ндор, а *m.* (*zool.*) condor.
кондотье́р, а *m.* (*hist.*) soldier of fortune.
конду́ктор[1], а, *pl.* **~а́, ~о́в** *m.* (*bus, tram*) conductor; (*rail.*) guard.
конду́ктор[2], а, *pl.* **~ы, ~ов** *m.* (*elec.*) conductor.
конду́кторш|а, и *f.* (*coll.*) conductress.
конево́д, а *m.* horse-breeder.
конево́дств|о, а *nt.* horse-breeding.
конево́д|ческий *adj. of* **~ство**
кон|ёк, ька́ *m.* **1.** *dim. of* **~ь; морско́й к.** (*zool.*) sea-horse. **2.** (*fig., coll.*) hobby-horse; hobby; **сесть на своего́ ~ька́** to mount one's hobby-horse. **3.** *see* **~ьки́**
кон|е́ц, ца́ *m.* **1.** end; **о́стрый к.** point; **то́нкий к.** tip; **в к.** (*coll.*) completely; **в ~це́ ~цо́в** in the end, after all; **и де́ло с ~цо́м** and there's an end to it; **из ~ца́ в к.** from end to end, all over; **~цы́ с ~ца́ми своди́ть** (*coll.*) to make both ends meet; **на э́тот (тот) к.** to this (that) end; **на худо́й к.** (*coll.*) if the worst comes to the worst; **оди́н к.** (*coll.*) it comes to the same thing in the end; **со всех ~цо́в** from all quarters; **хорони́ть ~цы́** (*coll.*) to bury, remove traces; **и ~цы́ в во́ду** and none will be the wiser; **пришёл ему́ к.** that's the end of him; **отда́ть ~цы́** (*coll.*) to kick the bucket. **2.** (*coll.*) distance, way (*from one place to another*); **в оди́н к.** one way; **в о́ба ~ца́** there and back.
коне́чно *adv.* of course, certainly.
коне́чност|ь, и *f.* (*anat.*) extremity.
коне́ч|ный (~ен, ~на) *adj.* **1.** final, last; ultimate; **~ная ста́нция** terminus; **~ная цель** ultimate aim; **в ~ном ито́ге, счёте** ultimately, in the final analysis. **2.** finite.
кони́н|а, ы *no pl., f.* horse-flesh.
кони́ческ|ий *adj.* conic(al).
конкистадо́р, а *m.* (*hist.*) conquistador.
конкла́в, а *m.* conclave.
конкорда́т, а *m.* concordat.
конкретизи́р|овать, ую *impf. and pf.* to give concrete expression to.
конкре́т|ный (~ен, ~на) *adj.* concrete; specific.
конкуре́нт, а *m.* competitor; rival.
конкурентоспосо́бный *adj.* competitive.
конкуре́нци|я, и *f.* competition.
конкури́р|овать, ую *impf.* (**с**+*i.*) to compete (with).
ко́нкурс, а *m.* competition; contest; **к. красоты́** beauty contest; **уча́стник ~а** contestant.
конкурса́нт, а *m.* competitor; contestant.
ко́нкурс|ный *adj. of* ~; **к. экза́мен** competitive examination.
ко́нник, а *m.* cavalryman.
ко́нниц|а, ы *f.* cavalry.
конногварде́|ец, йца *m.* (*mil.*) horse-guardsman.
коннозаво́дств|о, а *nt.* horse-breeding.
коннозаво́дчик, а *m.* stud-farm owner.
коннокаскадёр, а *m.* trick rider.
конноспорти́вн|ый *adj.* equestrian; **~ая шко́ла** riding school.
ко́н|ный *adj. of* **~ь**; horse; mounted; equestrian; **~ная а́рмия** cavalry army; **к. двор** stables; **к. заво́д** stud farm; **к. спорт** equestrianism; **~ная ста́туя** equestrian statue; **на ~ной тя́ге** horse-drawn.
конова́л, а *m.* horse-doctor.
ко́новяз|ь, и *f.* tether; tethering-post.
конокра́д, а *m.* horse-thief.
конокра́дств|о, а *nt.* horse-stealing.
конопа́|тить, чу, тишь *impf.* (*of* **законопа́тить**) to caulk.

конопа́тчик, а *m.* caulker.
конопа́|чу, тишь *see* **~тить**
конопл|я́, и́ *f.* (*bot.*) hemp.
конопля́нк|а, и *f.* (*zool.*) linnet.
конопля́|ный *adj. of* **~**; **~ное ма́сло** hempseed oil.
коносаме́нт, а *m.* (*comm.*) bill of lading.
консе́нсус, а *m.* consensus.
консерва́нт, а *m.* preservative.
консервати́в|ный (~ен, ~на) *adj.* conservative.
консервати́зм, а *m.* conservatism.
консерва́тор, а *m.* (*esp. pol.*) conservative.
консервато́ри|я, и *f.* conservatoire, academy of music.
консерва́торский *adj.* conservative.
консервато́р|ский *adj. of* **~ия**
консерва́ци|я, и *f.* **1.** conservation. **2.** temporary shut-down.
консерви́рован|ный (~, ~а) *p.p.p. of* **консерви́ровать** *and adj.*; **~ные фру́кты** bottled fruit; tinned fruit.
консерви́р|овать, ую *impf. and pf.* (*pf. also* **за~**) **1.** to preserve; to can; to bottle. **2.: к. предприя́тие** to close down an enterprise temporarily.
консе́рв|ный *adj. of* **~ы; ~ная ба́нка** tin, can; **к. нож** tin-opener; **~ная фа́брика** cannery.
консе́рв|ы, ов *no sg.* canned food.
конси́лиум, а *m.* (*med.*) consultation.
консисте́нци|я, и *f.* (*phys., med.*) consistence.
ко́н|ский *adj. of* **~ь; ~ские бобы́** broad beans; **к. во́лос** horse-hair; **~ские состяза́ния** horse-races; **к. хвост** 'pony-tail' (*hairstyle*).
консолида́ци|я, и *f.* consolidation.
консо́л|ь, и *f.* (*archit.*) **1.** console, cantilever. **2.** pedestal.
консоме́ *nt. indecl.* (*cul.*) consommé.
консона́нс, а *m.* (*mus.*) consonance.
консонанти́зм, а *m.* (*ling.*) system of consonants.
консо́рциум, а *m.* (*fin.*) consortium.
конспе́кт, а *m.* synopsis, summary, abstract.
конспекти́в|ный (~ен, ~на) *adj.* concise, brief.
конспекти́р|овать, ую *impf.* (*of* **за~** *and* **проконспекти́ровать**) to make an abstract of.
конспирати́в|ный (~ен, ~на) *adj.* secret, clandestine.
конспира́тор, а *m.* conspirator.
конспира́ци|я, и *f.* secrecy.
конста́нт|а, ы *f.* (*math., phys.*) constant.
констата́ци|я, и *f.* ascertaining; verification, establishment.
констати́р|овать, ую *impf. and pf.* to ascertain; to verify, establish; **к. смерть** to certify death; **к. факт** to establish a fact.
конституционали́зм, а *m.* (*pol.*) constitutionalism.
конституцио́нный *adj.* (*pol.*) constitutional.
конститу́ци|я, и *f.* (*pol., med.*) constitution.
конструи́р|овать, ую *impf. and pf.* (*pf. also* **с~**) **1.** to construct; to design. **2.** to form (*a government, etc.*).
конструкти́вный *adj.* **1.** structural; constructional. **2.** constructive.
констру́ктор, а *m.* designer.
констру́ктор|ский *adj. of* **~; ~ское бюро́** design office.
констру́кци|я, и *f.* **1.** construction; design. **2.** structure. **3.** (*gram.*) construction.
ко́нсул, а *m.* consul.
ко́нсульский *adj.* consular.
ко́нсульств|о, а *nt.* consulate.
консульта́нт, а *m.* consultant; tutor.
консультати́вный *adj.* consultative, advisory.
консультац|ио́нный *adj. of* **~ия; ~ио́нное бюро́** advice bureau; **~ио́нная пла́та** consultation fee.
консульта́ци|я, и *f.* **1.** consultation; expert advice. **2.** advice bureau; **де́тская к.** children's clinic; **же́нская к.** ante-natal clinic; **юриди́ческиая к.** legal advice centre. **3.** tutorial.
консульти́р|овать, ую *impf.* **1.** (**с**+*i.*) to consult. **2.** (*pf.* **про~**) to advise; to act as tutor (to).
консульти́р|оваться, уюсь *impf.* (*of* **про~**) (**с**+*i.*) to consult.
конта́кт, а *m.* **1.** contact; **вступи́ть в к. с кем-н.** to come into contact, get in touch with s.o.; **быть в ~е** (**с**+*i.*) to be in touch (with). **2.** (*elec.*) **к. приёмный** socket; **к. штыково́й** plug.
конта́ктн|ый *adj.* **1.** (*tech.*) contact; **к. рельс** contact rail, live rail; **~ая сва́рка** point welding; **~ные ли́нзы** (*med.*) contact lenses. **2.** (*coll.*) outgoing.
конте́йнер, а *m.* container.
контейнерово́з, а *m.* container ship.
конте́кст, а *m.* context.
континге́нт, а *m.* **1.** (*econ.*) quota. **2.** contingent; batch; **к. войск** a military force; **к. новобра́нцев** batch, squad of recruits.
контине́нт, а *m.* continent.
континента́льный *adj.* continental.
конто́р|а, ы *f.* office, bureau.
конто́рк|а, и *f.* (writing-)desk, bureau.
конто́р|ский *adj. of* **~а**
ко́нтр|а, ы *c.g.* (*coll.*) counter-revolutionary.
контраба́нд|а, ы *f.* **1.** smuggling; **занима́ться ~ой** to smuggle. **2.** contraband.
контрабанди́ст, а *m.* smuggler.
контраба́ндный *adj.* contraband; bootleg.
контраба́с, а *m.* (*mus.*) double-bass.
контраге́нт, а *m.* contractor.
контр-адмира́л, а *m.* rear-admiral.
контра́кт, а *m.* contract.
контракт|ова́ть, у́ю *impf.* (*of* **за~**) to contract (for); **к. рабо́тников** to engage workmen.
контракт|ова́ться, у́юсь *impf.* (*of* **за~**) **1.** to contract, undertake. **2.** *pass. of* **~ова́ть**
контра́льто *nt. indecl.* (*mus.*) contralto.
контра́льто|вый *adj. of* **~**
контрама́рк|а, и *f.* complimentary ticket; free pass.
контрапу́нкт, а *m.* (*mus.*) counterpoint.
контрапункти́ческий *adj.* (*mus.*) contrapuntal.
контра́ст, а *m.* contrast; **по ~у** (**с**+*i.*) by contrast (with).
контрасти́р|овать, ую *impf.* (**с**+*i.*) to contrast (with).
котнра́стный *adj.* contrasting.
контрата́к|а, и *f.* (*mil.*) counter-attack.
контратак|ова́ть, у́ю *impf. and pf.* to counter-attack.
контрацепти́в, а *m.* contraceptive; **внутрима́точный к.** intrauterine (contraceptive) device, IUD.
контрибу́ци|я, и *f.* war indemnity.
контркульту́р|а, ы *f.* counterculture.
контрме́р|а, ы *f.* countermeasure.
контрнаступле́ни|е, я *nt.* counter-offensive.
контролёр, а *m.* inspector; ticket-collector.
контроли́р|овать, ую *impf.* (*of* **про~**) to check; **к. биле́ты** to inspect tickets; (*mil.*) to monitor, verify.
контро́л|ь, я *m.* **1.** control. **2.** check(ing); inspection; **предста́вить ци́фры ~ю** to check one's figures; (*tech., mil.*) monitoring; (*mil.*) verification; **ме́ры по ~ю** verification measures.
контро́льно-пропускно́й *adj.*: **к. пу́нкт** checkpoint.
контро́ль|ный *adj. of* **~; ~ная вы́шка** (*naut.*) conning tower; **~ная коми́ссия** control commission; **~ная рабо́та** test.
контрразве́дк|а, и *f.* counter-espionage; counter-intelligence.
контрразве́дчик, а *m.* counter-intelligence agent.
контрреволюционе́р, а *m.* counter-revolutionary.
контрреволюцио́нный *adj.* counter-revolutionary.
контрреволю́ци|я, и *f.* counter-revolution.
контруда́р, а *m.* (*mil.*) counter-blow.
контрфо́рс, а *m.* (*archit.*) buttress.

контýжен|ный (~, ~а) *p.p.p. of* **контýзить** *and adj.*; **~ные** (*mil.*) shell-shock cases.
контý|зить, жу, зишь *pf.* to contuse; to shell-shock.
контýзи|я, и *f.* contusion, bruising; shell-shock.
кóнтур, а *m.* **1.** contour. **2.** (*elec.*) circuit.
кóнтурный *adj. of* **~**; **~ная карта** contour map.
конур|á, ы́ *f.* kennel; (*fig.*) hovel, dump.
кóнус, а *m.* cone.
конусообрáз|ный (~ен, ~на) *adj.* conical.
конфедерáт, а *m.* (*hist.*) confederate.
конфедерати́вный *adj.* confederative.
конфедерáци|я, и *f.* confederation.
конферансьé *m. indecl.* compère, master of ceremonies.
конферéнц-зáл, а *m.* conference hall.
конферéнци|я, и *f.* conference.
конфéт|а, ы *f.* sweet; **шоколáдная к.** chocolate; **корóбка шоколáдных ~** box of chocolates.
конфéт|ка, ки *f.* = **~а**
конфéтниц|а, ы *f.* sweet dish *or* bowl.
конфéт|ный *adj.* **1.** *adj. of* **~а**; **~ная бумáжка** sweet wrapper. **2.** (*coll., pej.*) sugary, treacly.
конфетти́ *nt. indecl.* confetti.
конфигурáци|я, и *f.* configuration, conformation.
конфиденциáл|ьный (~ен, ~ьна) *adj.* confidential.
конфирмáци|я, и *f.* (*eccl.*) confirmation.
конфирм|овáть, ýю *impf. and pf.* (*eccl.*) to confirm.
конфискáци|я, и *f.* confiscation, seizure.
конфиск|овáть, ýю *impf. and pf.* to confiscate.
конфли́кт, а *m.* conflict.
конфли́кт|ный *adj. of* **~**; **~ная коми́ссия** arbitration tribunal.
конфликт|овáть, ýю *impf.* (**с**+*i.*) (*coll.*) to clash (with), come up (against).
конфóрк|а, и *f.* ring (*on cooker*).
конфронтáци|я, и *f.* (*pol.*) confrontation.
конфýз, а *m.* embarrassment; **привести́ в к.** to place in an embarrassing position.
конфý|зить, жу, зишь *impf.* (*of* **с~**) to embarrass.
конфý|зиться, жусь, зишься *impf.* (*of* **с~**) **1.** to be embarrassed. **2.** (+*g.*) to be shy (in front of).
конфýзлив|ый (~, ~а) *adj.* bashful; shy.
конфýзный *adj.* (*coll.*) awkward, embarrassing.
концентрáт, а *m.* concentrate.
концентрациóнный *adj.*: **к. лáгерь** concentration camp.
концентрáци|я, и *f.* concentration.
концентри́рова|нный *p.p.p. of* **~ть** *and adj.* concentrated.
концентри́р|овать, ую *impf.* (*of* **с~**) to concentrate; (*mil.*) to mass; (*fig.*): **к. внимáние на вопрóсе** to concentrate one's attention on a question.
концентри́р|оваться, уюсь *impf.* (*of* **с~**) **1.** to mass, collect (*intrans.*). **2.** (*fig.*; **на**+*p.*) to concentrate.
концентри́ческий *adj.* concentric.
концéпци|я, и *f.* conception.
концéрн, а *m.* (*econ.*) concern.
концéрт, а *m.* (*mus.*) **1.** concert; recital; **симфони́ческий к.** symphony concert; **быть на ~е** to be at a concert. **2.** concerto.
концертáнт, а *m.* (concert) performer.
концерти́но *nt. indecl.* concertina.
концерти́р|овать, ую *impf.* to give concerts.
концертмéйстер, а *m.* (*mus.*) **1.** leader (*of orchestra*). **2.** accompanist.
концéрт|ный *adj. of* **~**; **к. роя́ль** concert grand (piano).
концессионéр, а *m.* concessionaire.
концéсси|я, и *f.* (*econ.*) concession.
концлáгер|ь, я *m.* (*abbr. of* **концентрациóнный лáгерь**) concentration camp.
конч|áть(ся), áю(сь) *impf. of* **~ить(ся)**
кóнч|енный *p.p.p. of* **~ить**; *as int.* **~ено!** enough!; **всё ~ено!** it's all over!; **с ним всё ~ено** he's finished.
кóнчен|ый *adj.* (*coll.*) decided, settled; **э́то дéло ~ое** the matter is settled; **к. человéк** (*coll.*) goner.
кóнчик, а *m.* tip; point; **на ~е языкá** on the tip of one's tongue.
кончи́н|а, ы *f.* (*rhet.*) decease, demise.
кóнч|ить, у, ишь *pf.* (*of* **~áть**) **1.** to finish, end; **к. речь выражéнием благодáрности** to conclude a speech with thanks; **на э́том он ~ил** here he stopped; **к. шкóлу** to finish school; **к. университéт** to graduate; **к. самоуби́йством** to commit suicide; **к. плóхо, дýрно, сквéрно** to come to a bad end. **2.** (**с**+*i.*) to be finished (with), give up. **3.** (+*inf.*) to stop. **4.** (*coll.*) to come (= *experience orgasm*).
кóнч|иться, усь, ишься *pf.* (*of* **~áться**) (+*i.*) to end (in), finish (by); to come to an end; **дéло ~илось ничéм** it came to nothing.
конъюнктиви́т, а *m.* (*med.*) conjunctivitis.
конъюнктýр|а, ы *f.* situation; state of affairs; climate; **междунарóдная к.** international situation; **ры́ночная к.** (*econ.*) state of the market; market conditions.
конъюнктýр|ный *adj. of* **~а**; **~ные цéны** market prices.
конъюнктýрщик, а *m.* (*coll., pej.*) opportunist.
кон|ь, я́, *pl.* **~́и, ~éй** *m.* **1.** horse; **боевóй к.** warhorse, charger; (*prov.*) **дарёному ~ю в зýбы не смóтрят** never look a gift horse in the mouth. **2.** (vaulting-)horse; **к. с рýчками** pommel-horse. **3.** (*chess*) knight.
кон|ьки́,ькóв *pl.* (*sg.* **~ёк, ~ькá** *m.*) skates; **к. на рóликах** roller skates; **катáться на ~ькáх** to skate.
конькобéж|ец, ца *m.* skater.
конькобéжный *adj.* skating.
конья́к, á (ý) *m.* brandy.
конья́|чный *adj. of* **~к**
кóнюх, а *m.* groom, stable-boy.
конюш|ня, ни, *g. pl.* **~ен** *f.* stable.
кооперати́в, а *m.* **1.** cooperative society. **2.** (*coll.*) cooperative store.
кооперати́вн|ый *adj.* cooperative; **~ое движéние** (*econ., pol.*) the cooperative movement; **~ое товáрищество** cooperative society.
кооперáтор, а *m.* member of a cooperative.
кооперáци|я, и *f.* **1.** cooperation. **2.** (*collect.*) cooperative; **жили́щная к.** housing cooperative.
кооптáци|я, и *f.* co-option.
коопти́р|овать, ую *impf. and pf.* to co-opt.
координáт|а, ы *f.* (*math.*) coordinate; *pl.* (*coll.*) contact details.
координáтный *adj.* (*math.*) coordinate.
координáтор, а *m.* coordinator.
координáци|я, и *f.* coordination.
координи́р|овать, ую *impf. and pf.* to coordinate.
копáл, а *m.* copal.
копáни|е, я *nt.* digging.
коп|áть, áю *impf.* **1.** (*pf.* **~нýть**) to dig. **2.** (*pf.* **вы́~**) to dig up, dig out.
копá|ться, юсь *impf.* **1.** (**в**+*p.*) to rummage (in); to root (in); (*fig.*): **к. в душé** to be given to soul-searching. **2.** (*coll.*; **с**+*i.*) to dawdle (over). **3.** *pass. of* **~ть**
копéечк|а, и *f. dim. of* **копéйка**; (*coll.*): **э́то влети́т тебé в ~у** it will cost you a pretty penny.
копéечн|ый *adj.* **1.** one-kopeck; worth one kopeck. **2.** minor, trifling; **~ые расхóды** trifling expenses. **3.** (*fig., coll.*) petty; twopenny-halfpenny.
копéйк|а, и, *g. pl.* **копéек** *f.* kopeck; **к. в ~у** exactly; **до послéдней ~и** to the last farthing; **зашиби́ть, сколоти́ть ~у** to turn an honest penny; **к. рубль бережёт** (*prov.*) take care of the pence, the pounds will take care of themselves.

Копенга́ген, а *m.* Copenhagen.
коп|ёр, ра́ *m.* (*tech.*) pile-driver.
ко́п|и, ей *pl.* (*sg.* **~ь, ́~и** *f.*) mines.
копи́лк|а, и *f.* money-box.
копи́рк|а, и *f.* (*coll.*) carbon paper; **писа́ть под ~у** to make a carbon copy.
копирова́льн|ый *adj.* copying; **~ая бума́га** carbon paper.
копи́р|овать, ую *impf.* (*of* **с~**) to copy; to imitate, mimic.
копиро́вк|а, и *f.* copying.
копиро́вщик, а *m.* copyist.
коп|и́ть, лю́, ́~ишь *impf.* (*of* **на~**) to accumulate, amass; to store up; **к. де́ньги** to save up; (*fig.*): **к. си́лы** to save one's strength.
коп|и́ться, лю́сь, ́~ишься, *impf.* (*of* **на~**) to accumulate (*intrans.*).
ко́пи|я, и *f.* copy; duplicate; replica; **резе́рвная к.** (*comput.*) backup; **заве́ренная к.** (*leg.*) attested copy; **снять ~ю (с**+*g.*) to copy, make a copy (of); (*fig.*): **он то́чная к. своего́ отца́** he is the very image of his father.
коп|на́, ны́, *pl.* **́~ны, ~ён, ~на́м** *f.* shock, stook (*of corn*); **к. се́на** haycock; **к. воло́с** shock of hair.
коп|ну́ть, ну́, нёшь *pf. of* **~а́ть**
ко́пот|ь, и *f.* soot.
копош|и́ться, у́сь, и́шься *impf.* **1.** to swarm. **2.** (*fig., coll.*) to stir, creep in; **у меня́ в голове́ ~и́лось сомне́ние** a doubt was beginning to stir in my head. **3.** (*coll.*) to potter about.
ко́пр|а, ы *f.* copra.
копт|е́ть[1]**, и́т** *impf.* (*of* **за~**) (*coll.*) to be blackened (*from smoke, with soot*).
коп|те́ть[2]**, чу́, ти́шь** *impf.* **(над)** (*coll.*) **1.** to swot (at), plug away (at). **2.** to vegetate, rot away (*fig.*).
копти́лк|а, и *f.* (*coll.*) oil-lamp (*of primitive design*).
копти́льный *adj.* for smoking.
копти́л|ьня, ьни, *g. pl.* **~ен** *f.* smoking-shed.
коп|ти́ть, чу́, ти́шь *impf.* **1.** (*pf.* **за~**) to smoke, cure in smoke. **2.** (*pf.* **за~**) to blacken (*with smoke*); **к. стекло́** to smoke glass; **к. не́бо** (*coll.*) to idle one's life away. **3.** (*pf.* **на~**) to smoke (*intrans.*).
копу́н, а́ *m.* (*coll.*) dawdler.
копче́ни|е, я *nt.* smoking.
копчён|ый *adj.* smoked, smoke-dried; **~ая селёдка** bloater.
ко́пчик, а *m.* (*anat.*) coccyx.
коп|чу́[1]**, ти́шь** *see* **~те́ть**[2]
коп|чу́[2]**, ти́шь** *see* **~ти́ть**
копы́тн|ый *adj.* **1.** hoof. **2.** (*zool.*) hoofed, ungulate; *as n.* **~ые, ~ых** ungulates.
копы́т|о, а *nt.* hoof.
коп|ь *see* **́~и**
коп|ьё[1]**, ья́,** *pl.* **́~ья, ́~ий, ́~ьям** *nt.* spear, lance; **мета́ние ~ья́** (*sport*) javelin throwing; **би́ться на ́~ьях** to joust; (*fig., iron.*): **́~ья лома́ть (из-за)** to do battle (over).
копь|ё[2]**, я́** *nt.*: **у меня́ ни ~я́** (*coll.*) I haven't a penny.
копьемета́тел|ь, я *m.* javelin-thrower.
...кор *comb. form, abbr. of* **корреспонде́нт**
кор|а́, ы́ *f.* **1.** (*bot.*) bark. **2.** (*anat.*): **к. головно́го мо́зга** cerebral cortex. **3.** crust; **земна́я к.** the earth's crust; (*fig.*): **под ~о́й его́ суро́вости бы́ло до́брое се́рдце** he had a kind heart beneath his crusty exterior.
кораб|е́льный *adj. of* **́~ль; к. инжене́р** naval architect; **к. ма́стер** shipwright.
кораблевожде́ни|е, я *nt.* navigation.
кораблекруше́ни|е, я *nt.* ship-wreck; **потерпе́ть к.** to be ship-wrecked.
кораблестрое́ни|е, я *nt.* ship-building.
кораблестро́ител|ь, я *m.* ship-builder.
кора́бл|ик, а *m.* **1.** *dim. of* **~ь. 2.** toy boat. **3.** (*zool.*) nautilus.
кора́бл|ь, я́ *m.* **1.** ship, vessel; **лине́йный к.** battleship; **фла́гманский к.** flagship; **косми́ческий к.** spaceship; **сади́ться на к.** to go on board (ship); **сжечь свои́ ~и́** (*fig.*) to burn one's boats. **2.** (*archit.*) nave.
кора́лл, а *m.* coral.
кора́лловый *adj.* coral.
Кора́н, а *m.* the Koran.
корве́т, а *m.* (*naut.*) corvette.
кордебале́т, а *m.* corps de ballet.
корди́т, а *m.* cordite.
кордо́н, а *m.* cordon.
кор|ево́й *adj. of* **~ь**
коре́|ец, йца *m.* Korean.
корёж|ить, у, ишь *impf.* (*of* **ис~**) (*coll.*) to bend, warp; (*impers.*): **его́ ~ило от бо́ли** he was writhing with pain.
корёж|иться, усь, ишься *impf.* (*of* **ис~**) (*coll.*) **1.** to bend, warp (*intrans.*). **2.: к. от бо́ли** to writhe with pain.
коре́йк|а, и *f.* brisket (*of pork or veal*).
коре́йский *adj.* Korean.
корена́ст|ый (~, ~а) *adj.* thickset, stocky.
корени́т|ься, ся *impf.* **(в**+*p.*) to be rooted (in).
коренни́к, а́ *m.* shaft-horse.
коренн|о́й *adj.* radical, fundamental; **к. зуб** molar (tooth); **к. жи́тель** native; **~о́е населе́ние** indigenous population; **~а́я ло́шадь = ~и́к**
ко́р|ень, ня, *pl.* **~ни, ~не́й** *m.* **1.** root; **в ~не** radically; **вы́рвать с ~нем** to uproot (*also fig.*); **красне́ть до ~не́й воло́с** to blush to the roots of one's hair; **пусти́ть ~ни** to take root (*also fig.*); **смотре́ть в к. чего́-н.** to get at the root of sth.; **хлеб на ~ню́** standing crop. **2.** (*math.*) root; radical; **знак ~ня** radical sign; **куби́ческий к.** cube root.
коре́нь|я, ев *no sg.* roots.
ко́реш, а *m.* (*sl.*) pal, mate.
кореш|о́к, ка́ *m.* **1.** spine (*of book*). **2.** counterfoil. **3.** *dim. of* **ко́рень. 4.** (*sl.*) = **ко́реш**
Коре́|я, и *f.* Korea.
коре|я́нка, я́нки *f. of* **́~ец**
корзи́н|а, ы *f.* basket.
корзи́нк|а, и *f.* small basket, punnet.
корзи́н|ный *adj. of* **~а; ~ное произво́дство** basket-making.
корзи́нщик, а *m.* basket-maker.
коридо́р, а *m.* corridor, hall.
коридо́р|ный *adj. of* **~**; *as n.* **к., ~ного** *m.* boots (*in hotel*).
кори́нк|а, и *no pl., f.* currants.
кори́нфский *adj.* (*archit.*) Corinthian.
кор|и́ть, ю́, и́шь *impf.* (+*a.* **за**) to upbraid (for); (+*a. and i.*) to reproach (with).
корифе́|й, я *m.* (*rhet.*) leading light.
кори́ц|а, ы *f.* cinnamon.
кори́чневый *adj.* brown.
ко́рк|а, и *f.* **1.** crust. **2.** peel, rind. **3.** (*fig.*): **прочита́ть от ~и до ~и** to read from cover to cover; **руга́ть, брани́ть кого́-н. на все ~и** (*coll.*) to tear s.o. off a strip.
корм, а, о ́~е, на ́~е *and* **на ~у́,** *pl.* **~а́, ~о́в** *m.* **1.** fodder; forage; **пти́чий к.** birdseed. **2.** feeding.
корм|а́, ы́ *f.* (*naut.*) stern, poop.
кормёжк|а, и *f.* (*coll.*) feeding.
корми́л|ец, ьца *m.* bread-winner.
корми́лиц|а, ы *f.* **1.** *f. of* **корми́лец. 2.** wet-nurse.
корми́л|о, а *nt.* (*naut. and fig.*) helm; (*fig., rhet.*): **быть у ~а правле́ния, вла́сти** to be at the helm of state.
корм|и́ть, лю́, ́~ишь *impf.* **1.** (*pf.* **на~** *and* **по~**) to feed; **к. гру́дью** to nurse, (breast-)feed, suckle. **2.** (*pf.* **про~**) keep, maintain.

корм|и́ться, лю́сь, ~́ишься *impf.* **1.** (*pf.* **по~**) to eat, feed (*intrans.*). **2.** (*pf.* **про~**) (+*i.*) to live (on); **к. уро́ками** to make a living by giving tuition.
кормле́ни|е, я *nt.* feeding; nursing, suckling.
корм|ово́й[1] *adj. of* **~а́; ~ово́е весло́** scull; **к. флаг** ensign; **~ова́я часть** after-part, stern-part; **~ова́я ру́бка** roundhouse.
корм|ово́й[2] *adj. of* **~**; fodder, forage; **~овы́е культу́ры, расте́ния** fodder crops.
корму́шк|а, и *f.* (feeding-)trough.
ко́рмч|ий, его *m.* (*fig., rhet.*) helmsman.
корневи́щ|е, а *nt.* (*bot.*) rhizome.
кор|нево́й *adj. of* **~́ень**
корнепло́д, а *m.* root vegetable.
ко́рнер, а, *pl.* **~ы** *or* **~а́** *m.* (*sport*) corner.
корне́т, а *m.* (*mil. and mus.*) cornet.
корнети́ст, а *m.* (*mus.*) cornet-player, cornetist.
корни́йский *adj.* = **корну́эльский**
корнишо́н, а *m.* (*cul.*) gherkin.
корну́эльский *adj.* Cornish.
ко́роб, а, *pl.* **~а́** *m.* basket (*of bast*); (*fig., coll.*): **це́лый к. новосте́й** heaps of news.
коробе́йник, а *m.* (*obs.*) pedlar.
коро́б|ить, лю, ишь *impf.* (*of* **по~**) **1.** to warp. **2.** (*fig.*) to jar upon, grate upon; (*impers.*): **меня́ ~ит от его́ акце́нта** his accent jars upon me.
коро́б|иться, люсь, ишься *impf.* (*of* **по~** *and* **с~**) to warp, buckle.
коро́бк|а, и *f.* box; **дверна́я к.** door-frame; **к. скоросте́й** (*tech.*) gear-box; **черепна́я к.** (*anat.*) cranium.
короб|о́к, ка́ *m.* small box.
коро́бочк|а, и *f.* **1.** *dim. of* **коро́бка. 2.** (*bot.*) boll.
коро́в|а, ы *f.* cow; **морска́я к.** sea-cow.
коро́в|ий *adj. of* **~а; ~ье ма́сло** butter.
коро́в|ка, ки *f. affectionate dim. of* **~а; бо́жья к.** lady-bird.
коро́вник, а *m.* cow-shed.
коро́вниц|а, ы *f.* dairy-maid.
короле́в|а, ы *f.* queen.
короле́вич, а *m.* king's son.
короле́в|на, ны, *g. pl.* **~ен** *f.* king's daughter.
короле́вск|ий *adj.* royal; king's; regal; **~ая ко́бра** king cobra; (*chess*): **к. слон** king's bishop.
короле́вств|о, а *nt.* kingdom.
корол|ёк, ька́ *m.* **1.** (*zool.*): **желтоголо́вый к.** goldcrest; **красноголо́вый к.** firecrest. **2.** blood-orange.
коро́л|ь, я́ *m.* king; (*fig.*) baron; **газе́тный к.** press baron
коромы́сл|о, а *nt.* yoke (*for carrying buckets*).
коро́н|а, ы *f.* **1.** crown (*also fig.*); coronet. **2.** (*astron.*) corona.
коронаротромбо́з, а *m.* (*med.*) coronary (thrombosis).
корона́рный *adj.* coronary.
корона|цио́нный *adj. of* **~́ция**
корона́ци|я, и *f.* coronation.
коро́нк|а, и *f.* crown (*of tooth*).
коро́нн|ый *adj.* crown, of state; (*theatr.*): **~ая роль** best part.
корон|ова́ть, у́ю *impf. and pf.* to crown.
коро́ст|а, ы *f.* scab.
коросте́л|ь, я́ *m.* (*zool.*) corncrake, landrail.
корота́|ть, ю *impf.* (*of* **с~**) (*coll.*) to pass, while away (time).
коро́т|кий (ко́роток, ~ка́, ко́ротко́, *pl.* **~́ки́)** *adj.* **1.** short; brief; **э́то пальто́ тебе́ ~ко́** this coat is too short for you; **рассказа́ть в ~ких слова́х** to tell in just a few words; (*coll.*): **ру́ки коротки́!** just (you) try!; you couldn't if you tried!; **у́м ~ок** limited intelligence. **2.** (*fig.*) close, intimate; (*coll.*): **быть на ~кой ноге́ с кем-н.** to be well in with s.o.
ко́ротк|о́[1] *see* **~ий**
ко́ротко[2] *adv.* **1.** briefly; **к. говоря́** in short. **2.** intimately.
коротковолнови́к, а́ *m.* radio ham.
коротково́лновый *adj.* (*radio*) short-wave.
короткометра́жк|а, и *f.* (*coll.*) short (film); **рекла́мная к.** commercial, ad(vert).
короткометра́жный *adj.*: **к. фильм** short (film).
коро́ткост|ь, и *f.* (*coll.*) intimacy, familiarity.
короты́шк|а, и *c.g.* (*coll.*) titch, shorty.
кор|о́че *comp. of* **~о́ткий** *and* **~́отко** shorter; **к. говоря́** in short, to cut a long story short.
ко́рочк|а, и *f. dim. of* **ко́рка**
корп|е́ть, лю́, и́шь *impf.* **(над, за+** *i.*) (*coll.*) to pore (over), sweat (over).
ко́рпи|я, и *f.* (*obs.*) lint.
корпорати́вный *adj.* corporate.
корпора́ци|я, и *f.* corporation.
ко́рпус[1]**, а,** *pl.* **~ы** *m.* **1.** body; trunk, torso. **2.** length (*as unit of measurement*); **на́ша ло́шадь опереди́ла други́х на три ~а** our horse won by three lengths. **3.** hull; (*tech.*) frame, body, case.
ко́рпус[2]**, а,** *pl.* **~а́, ~о́в** *m.* **1.** (*mil.*) corps; **диплома́тический к.** diplomatic corps. **2.** building; block.
корректи́в, а *m.* amendment, correction.
корректи́р|овать, ую *impf.* (*of* **про~**) to correct.
корректиро́вщик, а *m.* (*mil.*) **1.** spotter. **2.** spotter plane.
корре́кт|ный (~ен, ~на) *adj.* correct, proper.
корре́ктор, а *m.* proof-reader; **к. орфогра́фии** (*comput.*) spell-checker.
корректу́р|а, ы *f.* **1.** proof-reading. **2.** proof(-sheet); **держа́ть ~у** to read, correct proofs; **к. в гра́нках** galley proof(s); **к. в листа́х** page proof(s). **3.** (*mil.*) correction, adjustment (*of fire*).
корректу́р|ный *adj. of* **~а; ~ные зна́ки** proof symbols.
корреспонде́нт, а *m.* correspondent.
корреспонде́нци|я, и *f.* **1.** correspondence; **заказна́я, проста́я к.** registered, non-registered mail. **2.** dispatch, report.
корреспонди́р|овать, ую *impf.* to correspond.
корро́зи|я, и *f.* (*chem.*) corrosion.
коррумпи́ров|анный (~ан, ~ана) *adj.* corrupt.
корру́пци|я, и *f.* (*pol.*) corruption.
корса́ж, а *m.* bodice.
корса́р, а *m.* corsair.
корсе́т, а *m.* corset.
корт, а *m.* (tennis-)court.
корте́ж, а *m.* cortège; motorcade.
кортизо́н, а *m.* cortisone.
ко́ртик, а *m.* dagger.
ко́рточ|ки, ек *no sg.*: **сиде́ть на ~ках, сесть на к.** to squat.
кору́нд, а *m.* (*min.*) corundum.
корч|ева́ть, у́ю *impf.* to uproot, root out.
ко́рч|и, ей *pl.* (*sg.* **~а, ~и** *f.*) (*coll.*) convulsions, spasm; **му́читься в ~ах** to writhe with pain.
ко́рч|ить, у, ишь *impf.* (*of* **с~**) **1.** to contort; (*coll.*): **к. грима́сы, ро́жи** to make, pull faces. **2.** (*impf. only*) (*coll.*): **к. из себя́** to pose (as); **к. дурака́** to play the fool.
ко́ршун, а *m.* (*zool.*) kite; (*fig.*): **налете́ть, набро́ситься ~ом** (**на**+*a.*) to pounce (on), swoop (onto).
коры́ст|ный (~ен, ~на) *adj.* mercenary, selfish.
корыстолю́б|ец, ца *m.* mercenary-minded person.
корыстолюби́в|ый (~, ~а) *adj.* mercenary.
корыстолю́би|е, я *nt.* self-interest.
коры́ст|ь, и *f.* (*coll.*) **1.** profit, gain; **кака́я тебе́ в э́том к.?** what are you getting out of it? **2.** self-interest.
коры́т|о, а *nt.* wash-tub; trough; **оста́ться у разби́того ~а** to be no better off than before, be back where one started.

кор|ь, и *f.* measles.
ко́рюшк|а, и *f.* smelt (*fish*).
коря́в|ый (~, ~а) *adj.* (*coll.*) **1.** rough, uneven; gnarled. **2.** (*fig.*) clumsy, uncouth. **3.** (*coll.*) pock-marked.
коря́г|а, и *f.* snag (*tree or boughs impeding navigation*).
кос|а́[1], **ы́,** *a.* **~у́,** *pl.* **~ы** *f.* plait, pigtail, braid.
кос|а́[2], **ы́,** *a.* **~у́,** *pl.* **~ы** *f.* scythe; **нашла́ к. на ка́мень** he (has) met his match; he ran (has run) into a brick wall.
кос|а́[3], **ы́,** *a.* **~у́,** *pl.* **~ы** *f.* (*geog.*) spit.
коса́р|ь[1], **я́** *m.* mower (*agent*).
коса́р|ь[2], **я́** *m.* chopper (*tool*).
коса́тк|а, и *f.* killer whale.
ко́свенн|ый *adj.* indirect, oblique; **~ые ули́ки** circumstantial evidence; (*gram.*): **к. паде́ж** oblique case; **~ая речь** indirect speech.
косе́канс, а *m.* (*math.*) cosecant.
коси́лк|а, и *f.* mowing-machine, mower; **газо́нная к.** lawn mower.
ко́синус, а *m.* (*math.*) cosine.
ко|си́ть[1], **шу́, ~сишь** *impf.* (*of* **с~**) to mow; to cut; (*fig.*) to mow down; **~си́ ~са́ пока́ роса́** (*prov.*) make hay while the sun shines.
ко|си́ть[2], **шу́, си́шь** *impf.* (*of* **с~**) **1.** to squint; **к. на о́ба глаза** to have a squint in both eyes. **2.** (*+a. or i.*) to twist, slant (*mouth, eyes*). **3.** to be crooked.
ко|си́ться, шу́сь, си́шься *impf.* (*of* **по~**) **1.** to slant. **2.** (*coll.*) (**на**+ *a.*) to cast a sidelong glance (at); (*fig.*) to look askance (at).
косма́т|ый (~, ~а) *adj.* shaggy.
косме́тик|а, и *f.* cosmetics, make-up.
космети́ческ|ий *adj.* cosmetic; **к. кабине́т** beauty parlour; **~ая ма́ска** face-pack; **~ая су́мочка** vanity bag *or* case.
космети́чк|а, и *f.* (*coll.*) **1.** beautician. **2.** vanity bag *or* case.
косми́ческ|ий *adj.* cosmic; space; **к. кора́бль** spaceship.
космого́ни|я, и *f.* cosmogony.
космогра́фи|я, и *f.* cosmography.
космодро́м, а *m.* cosmodrome, space centre.
космона́вт, а *m.* astronaut, cosmonaut, spaceman.
космона́втик|а, и *f.* astronautics, space exploration.
космополи́т, а *m.* cosmopolite.
космополити́зм, а *m.* cosmopolitanism.
космополити́ческий *adj.* cosmopolitan.
ко́смос, а *m.* cosmos; outer space.
космоте́хник|а, и *f.* space technology.
ко́см|ы, ~ *no sg.* (*coll.*) locks, mane.
косне́|ть, ю *impf.* (*of* **за~**) **1.** (**в**+ *p.*) to stagnate (in). **2.** to stick.
косноязы́чи|е, я *nt.* confused articulation.
косноязы́ч|ный (~ен, ~на) *adj.* speaking thickly.
косн|у́ться, у́сь, ёшься *pf. of* **каса́ться**
ко́с|ный (~ен, ~на) *adj.* inert, sluggish; stagnant.
ко́со *adv.* slantwise, askew; obliquely; **смотре́ть к.** to look askance.
кособо́к|ий (~, ~а) *adj.* (*coll.*) crooked, lop-sided.
косоворо́тк|а, и *f.* (*man's*) blouse (*with collar fastening at side*).
косогла́зи|е, я *nt.* squint, cast in the eye.
косогла́з|ый (~, ~а) *adj.* cross-eyed.
косого́р, а *m.* slope, hill-side.
кос|о́й[1] **(~, ~а́. ~о)** *adj.* **1.** slanting; oblique; **к. по́черк** sloping handwriting; **к. у́гол** (*math.*) oblique angle; **~а́я черта́** oblique stroke. **2.** cross-eyed. **3.: к. взгляд** (*fig.*) sidelong glance.
кос|о́й[2], **о́го** *m.* (*folk poet.*) hare.
косола́п|ый (~, ~а) *adj.* pigeon-toed; (*fig.*) clumsy.
костёл, а *m.* (Roman Catholic) church.
костене́|ть, ю *impf.* (*of* **о~**) to grow stiff; to grow numb.
кост|ёр, ра́ *m.* bonfire; camp-fire; **сжечь на ~ре́** to burn at the stake.
кости́ст|ый (~, ~а) *adj.* bony.
ко|сти́ть, щу́, сти́шь *impf.* (*coll.*) to abuse.
костля́в|ый (~, ~а) *adj.* bony.
ко́стный *adj.* osseous; (*anat.*): **к. мозг** (bone) marrow.
костое́д|а, ы *f.* (*med.*) caries.
ко́сточк|а, и *f.* **1.** *dim. of* **кость; перемыва́ть ~и** (+ *d.*) to gossip about, pull to pieces; **разбира́ть по ~ам** to go through (a thing, matter) with a fine comb. **2.** stone, pit (*of fruit*). **3.** ball (*of abacus*). **4.** bone (*of corset, etc.*).
косты́л|ь, я́ *m.* **1.** crutch; **ходи́ть на ~я́х** to walk on crutches. **2.** (*tech.*) spike.
кост|ь, и, *pl.* **~и, ~е́й** *f.* **1.** bone; **слоно́вая к.** ivory; **язы́к без ~е́й** loose tongue; **лечь ~ьми́** (*rhet.*) to fall in battle; **пересчита́ть кому́-н. ~и** to give s.o. a drubbing. **2.** *pl.* dice; **игра́ть в ~и** to dice.
костю́м, а *m.* **1.** dress, clothes; **в ~е Ада́ма, Е́вы** (*joc.*) in one's birthday suit; **маскара́дный к.** fancy-dress. **2.** suit; costume; **англи́йский к.** tailor-made coat and skirt; **вече́рний к.** dress suit; **купа́льный к.** swimsuit.
костюме́р, а *m.* (*theatr.*) wardrobe master.
костюме́р|ный *adj. of* **~**; *as n.* **~ная, ~ной** *f.* (*theatr.*) wardrobe (room).
костюме́рш|а, и *f.* (*coll., theatr.*) wardrobe mistress.
костюмиро́ва|нный *p.p.p. of* **~ть** *and adj.* **1.** in costume; in fancy-dress. **2.: к. бал** fancy-dress ball.
костю́м|ный *adj. of* **~**; **~ная пье́са** period play.
костя́к, а́ *m.* skeleton; (*fig.*) backbone.
костян|о́й *adj.* bone; **~а́я мука́** bone-meal.
костя́шк|а, и *f.* **1.** *dim. of* **кость. 2.** knuckle. **3.** ball (*of abacus*).
косу́л|я, и *f.* roe deer.
косы́нк|а, и *f.* (triangular) kerchief, scarf.
косьб|а́, ы́ *f.* mowing.
кося́к[1], **а́** *m.* door-post; jamb.
кося́к[2], **а́** *m.* herd (*of horses*); shoal, school (*of fish*); flock (*of birds*).
кот, а́ *m.* **1.** tom-cat; (*coll.*): **к. напла́кал** nothing to speak of; practically nothing; **купи́ть ~а́ в мешке́** to buy a pig in a poke. **2.** (*sl.*) pimp.
кота́нгенс, а *m.* (*math.*) cotangent.
кот|ёл, ла́ *m.* **1.** copper, cauldron. **2.** (*tech.*) boiler.
котел|о́к, ка́ *m.* **1.** pot. **2.** mess-tin. **3.** bowler (hat).
коте́льн|ая, ой *f.* boiler-house.
коте́л|ьный *adj. of* **~ 2.; ~ьное желе́зо** boiler plate.
коте́льщик, а *m.* boiler-maker.
кот|ёнок, ёнка, *pl.* **~я́та, ~я́т** *m.* kitten.
ко́тик, а *m.* **1.** fur-seal. **2.** sealskin. **3.** *affectionate dim. of* **кот.**
ко́тик|овый *adj. of* **~ 1., 2.; к. про́мысел** sealing; sealskin trade; **~овая ша́пка** sealskin cap.
котильо́н, а *m.* cotillion.
коти́р|овать, ую *impf. and pf.* (*fin.*) to quote.
котиро́вк|а, и *f.* (*fin.*) quotation.
ко|ти́ться, чу́сь, ти́шься *impf.* (*of* **о~**) to have kittens; to have young.
котле́т|а, ы *f.* cutlet; rissole, patty; **отбивна́я к.** chop.
котлова́н, а *m.* (*tech.*) foundation pit.
котлови́н|а, ы *f.* (*geog.*) hollow, basin.
кото́мк|а, и *f.* knapsack.
кото́р|ый *pron.* **1.** *interrog. and rel.* which; **к. час?** what time is it?; **в ~ом часу́ он зашёл?** what time did he call?; **к. раз?** how many times?; (*coll.*): **к. раз я тебе́ э́то говорю́?** how many times have I told you! **2.** *rel.* who. **3.** (*coll.*): **к.... к.** some ... some (others); **~ые бы́ли в чулка́х, ~ые с го́лыми нога́ми** some were wearing stockings and some were bare-legged.
кото́рый-либо *pron.* = **кото́рый-нибудь**

кото́рый-нибудь *pron.* some; one or other.
котте́дж, а *m.* cottage.
кот|я́та, я́т *see* **~ёнок**
ко́фе *m. indecl.* coffee; **раствори́мый к.** instant coffee; **к. в зёрнах** coffee beans.
кофева́рк|а, и *f.* coffee-maker.
кофеи́н, а *m.* caffeine.
кофе́йник, а *m.* coffee-pot.
кофе́йниц|а, ы *f.* coffee-grinder.
коф|е́йный *adj. of* **~е**
кофе́|йня, йни, *g. pl.* **~ен** *f.* (*obs.*) coffee-house.
ко́фт|а, ы *f.* (*woman's*) jacket.
ко́фточк|а, и *f.* blouse.
коча́н, а́ (*and coll.* **кочна́**) *m.*: **к. капу́сты** head of cabbage.
коч|ева́ть, у́ю *impf.* **1.** to be a nomad, to roam from place to place. **2.** (*of birds and animals*) to migrate.
коче́вник, а *m.* nomad.
кочево́й *adj.* **1.** nomadic. **2.** migratory.
коче́в|ье, ья, *g. pl.* **~ий** *nt.* **1.** nomad encampment. **2.** nomad territory.
кочега́р, а *m.* stoker, fireman.
кочене́|ть, ю *impf.* (*of* **за~** *and* **о~**) to become numb; to stiffen.
кочер|га́, ги́, *g. pl.* **~ёг** *f.* poker.
кочеры́жк|а, и *f.* cabbage-stump.
ко́чк|а, и *f.* hummock; tussock.
кочкова́т|ый (~, ~а) *adj.* hummocky, tussocky.
ко|чу́сь, ти́шься *see* **~ти́ться**
кош|а́чий *adj. of* **~ка**; feline; **к. конце́рт** caterwauling; (*fig.*) hooting, barracking.
кошел|ёк, ька́ *m.* purse.
кошени́л|ь, и *f.* cochineal.
коше́рный *adj.* kosher.
ко́шк|а, и *f.* **1.** cat; **(к.-)манкс, бесхво́стая к.** Manx cat; (*fig., coll.*) **игра́ть в ~и-мы́шки** to play cat-and-mouse; **жить как к. с соба́кой** to be at each other's throats; **чёрная к. пробежа́ла ме́жду ни́ми** they have fallen out; **у него́ ~и скребу́т на се́рдце** he is heavy-hearted. **2.** (*tech., naut.*) grapnel, drag. **3.** (*pl.*) crampons; climbing-irons. **4.** (*pl.*) cat-o'-nine tails.
кошма́р, а *m.* nightmare.
кошма́р|ный (~ен, ~на) *adj.* nightmarish.
ко|шу́, си́шь *see* **~си́ть**
каще́|й, я *m.* **1.** Koshchey (*an evil being in Russ. folk-lore*). **2.** (*fig., coll.*) skinflint.
кощу́нствен|ный (~, ~на) *adj.* blasphemous.
кощу́нств|о, а *nt.* blasphemy.
кощу́нств|овать, ую *impf.* to blaspheme.
коэффицие́нт, а *m.* (*math.*) coefficient, factor; **к. поле́зного де́йствия** efficiency; **к. у́мственных спосо́бностей** intelligence quotient, IQ.
КП *f. indecl.* (*abbr. of* **Коммунисти́ческая па́ртия**) Communist Party.
КПСС *f. indecl.* (*abbr. of* **Коммунисти́ческая па́ртия Сове́тского Сою́за**) CPSU (*Communist Party of the Soviet Union*).
кр. (*abbr. of* **край**) kray, krai.
краб, а *m.* (*zool.*) crab.
кра́г|и, ~ *pl.* (*sg.* **~а, ~и** *f.*) leggings.
кра́ден|ый *adj.* stolen; **~ое** (*collect.*) stolen goods.
кра|ду́, дёшь *see* **~сть**
кра́дучись *adv.* stealthily; **идти́ к.** to creep, slink.
краеве́д, а *m.* student of local lore; history and economy.
краеве́дени|е, я *nt.* study of local lore, history and economy.
краеве́д|ческий *adj. of* **~ение; к. музе́й** folk museum.
краево́й *adj. of* **край 4.**
краеуго́льный *adj.*: **к. ка́мень** corner-stone.
кра́ж|а, и *f.* theft; larceny; **к. со взло́мом** burglary; **магази́нная к.** shoplifting.
кра|й, я, о ~е, в ~ю́, *pl.* **~я́, ~ёв** *m.* **1.** edge; brim; brink (*also fig.*); **~ем у́ха слу́шать** to overhear; **на к. све́та** to the ends of the earth; **че́рез к.** in abundance; **хлебну́ть че́рез к.** (*coll.*) to have one too many (*sc.* to drink). **2.** side (*of meat*); **то́лстый к.** rib-steak. **3.** land, country; **в на́ших ~я́х** in these parts; **в чужи́х ~я́х** in foreign parts. **4.** (*administrative division of former USSR*) kray, krai.
край... *comb. form, abbr. of* **краево́й**
крайко́м, а *m.* (*abbr. of* **краево́й комите́т**) kray *or* krai committee.
кра́йне *adv.* extremely.
кра́йн|ий *adj.* **1.** extreme; last; **К. Се́вер** the Far North; **в ~ем слу́чае** if the worst comes to the worst; as a last resort; **по ~ей ме́ре** at least; **~яя плоть** (*anat.*) foreskin. **2.** complete, utter. **3.** (*sport*) outside, wing; **к. напада́ющий** winger; wing forward.
кра́йност|ь, и *f.* **1.** extreme; **до ~и** in the extreme, extremely. **2.** extremity; **быть в ~и** to be reduced to extremity.
крал, а *see* **красть**
крамо́л|а, ы *f.* (*obs.*) sedition.
крамо́льник, а *m.* (*obs.*) seditionary
крамо́льный *adj.* (*obs.*) seditious.
кран[1], а *m.* tap; (*tech.*) cock; **запо́рный к.** stopcock; **к.-смеси́тель** mixer tap.
кран[2], а *m.* crane.
краниоло́ги|я, и *f.* craniology.
крановщи́к, а́ *m.* crane operator.
кра́н|овый *adj. of* **~[1,2]**
крап, а *no pl., m.* spots; specks.
кра́п|ать, ает *and* **лет** *impf.* to spatter; **дождь ~лет** it is spitting with rain.
крапи́в|а, ы *f.* (stinging-)nettle; (*collect.*) nettles.
крапи́вник, а *m.* (*zool.*) wren.
крапи́вниц|а, ы *f.* nettle-rash.
крапи́в|ный *adj. of* **~а; ~ная лихора́дка** nettle-rash.
кра́пин|а, ы *f.* speck; spot.
кра́пин|ка, ки *f.* = **~а**
краплёный *adj.* (*of cards*) marked.
крас|а́, ы́ *f.* **1.** (*obs.*) beauty; (*iron.*): **во всей свое́й ~е́** in all one's glory. **2.** (*rhet.*) ornament.
краса́в|ец, ца *m.* handsome man; good-looker (*male*).
краса́виц|а, ы *f.* beauty (*beautiful woman*); good-looker (*female*).
краси́в|ый (~, ~а) *adj.* beautiful; handsome; fine.
краси́льный *adj.* appertaining to dyes.
краси́л|ьня, ьни, *g. pl.* **~ен** *f.* dye-works.
краси́льщик, а *m.* dyer.
краси́тел|ь, я *m.* dye(-stuff); **пищево́й к.** food colouring.
кра́|сить, шу, сишь *impf.* (*of* **по~**) **1.** to paint; to colour; **он кра́сит ло́дку в бе́лое с голубы́м** he is painting the boat white and blue. **2.** to dye; to stain (*wood, glass*). **3.** (*impf. only*) to adorn.
кра́|ситься, шусь, сишься *impf.* **1.** (*pf.* **на~**) to make up, apply one's make-up. **2.** *pass. of* **~сить**
кра́ск|а, и *f.* **1.** painting; colouring; dyeing. **2.** paint; dye; **акваре́льная к.** water-colour; **ма́сляная к.** oil-colour; **типогра́фская к.** printer's ink; **писа́ть ~ами** to paint; **к. для ресни́ц** mascara. **3.** (*pl., fig.*) colours; **сгуща́ть ~и** (*coll.*) to lay it on thick. **4.** blush; **вогна́ть кого́-н. в ~у** (*coll.*) to make s.o. blush.
краскопу́льт, а *m.* = **краскораспыли́тель**
краскораспыли́тел|ь, я *m.* spray-gun.
красне́|ть, ю *impf.* (*of* **по~**) **1.** to redden, become red. **2.** to blush, colour; (*fig.*): **к. за**+*a.* to blush for. **3.** (*impf. only*) to show red.
красноарме́|ец, йца *m.* Red Army man.
красноарме́|йский *adj. of* **~ец**; Red Army.
краснoба́|й, я *m.* (*coll.*) phrase-monger.

краснобáйств|о, а *nt.* (*coll.*) phrase-mongering.
красновáт|ый (~, ~а) *adj.* reddish.
красногвардé|ец, йца *m.* (*hist.*) Red Guard.
красногвардé|йский *adj. of* **~ец**
краснодерéв|ец, ца *m.* cabinet-maker.
краснодерéв|щик, щика *m.* = **~ец**
краснозвёздный *adj.* bearing the Red Star (*emblem of the former USSR and Soviet Army*).
краснознамённый *adj.* holding the order of the Red Banner (*decoration in former USSR*); **к. полк** Red Banner regiment.
краснокóж|ий (~, ~а) *adj.* red-skinned; *as n.* **к., ~его** *m.* redskin.
краснокрéстный *adj.* Red Cross.
краснолéсь|е, я *nt.* pine forest.
краснолицый *adj.* ruddy-faced.
красноречи́в|ый (~, ~а) *adj.* eloquent.
краснорéчи|е, я *nt.* eloquence.
краснот|á, ы́ *f.* redness.
краснощёкий *adj.* ruddy-cheeked.
краснýх|а, и *f.* (*med.*) German measles, rubella.
крáс|ный (~ен, ~нá, ~но) *adj.* **1.** red (*also fig., pol.*); **~ное дéрево** mahogany; **~ная шáпочка** Little Red Riding Hood; (*fig.*): **~ная строкá** new paragraph; **проходи́ть ~ной ни́тью** to stand out, run through (*of theme*). **2.** (*folk poet. or coll.*) beautiful; (*fig.*) fine; **~ная дéвица** bonny lass; (*prov.*) **долг платежóм ~ен** one good turn deserves another.
крас|овáться, ýюсь *impf.* **1.** to stand out (vividly). **2.** (+*i.*) (*coll.*) to flaunt, show off.
красот|á, ы́, *pl.* **∠ы** *f.* beauty.
красóтк|а, и *f.* (*coll.*) good-looking girl; beauty.
крáс|очный *adj.* **1.** *adj. of* **~ка. 2. (~очен, ~очна)** colourful, highly coloured.
кра|сть, дý, дёшь, *past* **~л, ∠ла** *impf.* (*of* **у∠**) to steal.
крá|сться, дýсь, дёшься, *past* **~лся, ~лась** *impf.* to steal, creep, sneak.
крат *only in phr.* **вó сто к.** hundredfold.
крáтер, а *m.* crater.
крáт|кий (~ок, ~кá, ~ко) *adj.* short; brief; concise; **в ~ких словáх** in short, briefly.
крáтко *adv.* briefly.
кратковрéменный *adj.* of short duration, brief.
краткосрóч|ный (~ен, ~на) *adj.* short-term.
крáтн|ое, ого *nt.* (*math.*) multiple; **óбщее наимéньшее к.** least common multiple.
крáт|ный (~ен, ~на) *adj.* (+*d.*) divisible without remainder (by); **дéвять — числó ~ное трём** nine is a multiple of three.
крат|чáйший *superl. of* **∠кий**
крáт|че *comp. of* **~кий** *and* **~ко**
крах, а *m.* (*fin. and fig.*) crash; failure.
крахмáл, а *m.* starch.
крахмáлист|ый (~, ~а) *adj.* containing starch.
крахмáл|ить, ю, ишь *impf.* (*of* **на~**) to starch.
крахмáл|ьный *adj. of* **~**; starched.
крáше (*coll.*) *comp. of* **краси́в|ый** *and* **~о**
крáшени|е, я *nt.* dyeing.
крáшен|ый *adj.* **1.** painted; coloured; **~ое яйцó** (decorated) Easter egg. **2.** dyed. **3.** made-up, wearing make-up.
краю́х|а, и *f.* (*coll.*) hunk.
кревéтк|а, и *f.* (*zool.*) shrimp; prawn.
крéдит, а *m.* (*book-keeping*) credit.
креди́т, а *m.* credit.
кредит|овáть, ýю *impf. and pf.* (*fin.*) to grant credit (to).
кредитóр, а *m.* creditor.
кредитоспосóб|ный (~ен, ~на) *adj.* creditworthy.
крéдо *nt. indecl.* credo.
крéйсер, а, *pl.* **~ы** *and* **~á** (*naut.*) cruiser; **линéйный к.** battle cruiser.
крéйсер|ский *adj. of* **~**; **~ская скóрость** cruising speed.
крейси́р|овать, ую *impf.* (*naut.*) to cruise.
крем, а *m.* cream; **сапóжный к.** shoe-polish; **увлажня́ющий к.** moisturizer; **защи́тный к.** sunblock.
крематóри|й, я *m.* crematorium.
кремáци|я, и *f.* cremation.
крем|éнь, ня́ *m.* flint.
кремлевéд, а *m.* Kremlinologist.
кремлевéдени|е, я *nt.* Kremlinology.
кремл|ёвский *adj. of* **~ь**
кремл|ь, я́ *m.* citadel; **(москóвский) К.** the Kremlin.
кремнёв|ый *adj.* flint; **~ое ружьё** flint-lock.
кремнезём, а *m.* (*min., chem.*) silica.
крéмниевый *adj.* (*chem.*) silicic.
крéмни|й, я *m.* (*chem.*) silicon.
кремни́стый *adj.* **1.** (*min.*) siliceous. **2.** stony.
крéм|овый *adj.* **1.** *adj. of* **~. 2.** cream(-coloured).
крен, а *m.* (*naut.*) list, heel; (*aeron.*) bank; **дать к.** (*naut.*) to list, heel (over); (*aeron.*) to bank.
крéндел|ь, я, *pl.* **~и** *and* **~я́, ~éй** *m.* (*cul.*) pretzel; **выпи́сывать ~я́** to stagger, lurch.
крен|и́ть, ю́, и́шь *impf.* (*of* **на~**) to cause to heel, list.
крен|и́ться, ю́сь, и́шься *impf.* (*of* **на~**) (*naut.*) to list, heel (over); (*aeron.*) to bank.
креóл, а *m.* creole.
креóл|ьский *adj. of* **~**
креп, а *m.* crêpe.
крепи́тельный *adj.* **1.** (*tech.*) strengthening. **2.** (*med.*) astringent.
креп|и́ть, лю́, и́шь *impf.* **1.** (*tech. and fig.*) to strengthen. **2.** (*naut.*) to make fast, hitch, lash; **к. парусá** to furl sails. **3.** (*med.*) to constipate.
креп|и́ться, лю́сь, и́шся *impf.* **1.** to hold out. **2.** *pass. of* **~и́ть**
крéп|кий (~ок, ~кá, ~ко) *adj.* strong; sound; sturdy, robust; (*fig.*) firm; **к. морóз** hard frost; **к. сон** sound sleep; **к. чай** strong tea.
крéпко *adv.* strongly; firmly; soundly; (*coll.*): **к.-нáкрепко** very firmly; **к.-нáкрепко завязáть** to tie really tight.
крепколóб|ый (~, ~а) *adj.* (*coll.*) pig-headed.
креплéни|е, я *nt.* **1.** strengthening; fastening. **2.** (*naut.*) lashing; furling.
креплёный *adj.* (*of wines*) fortified.
крéпн|уть, у, ешь *impf.* (*of* **о~**) to get stronger.
крепостни́|ческий *adj. of* **~чество**
крепостни́честв|о, а *nt.* serfdom.
крепостн|óй[1]**, и** *adj.* serf; **~óе прáво** serfdom; *as n.* **к., ~óго** *m.* serf.
крепостнóй[2] *adj. of* **крéпость**[2]
крéпост|ь[1]**, и** *f.* strength.
крéпост|ь[2]**, и** *f.* fortress.
крепчá|ть, ет *impf.* to grow stronger, get up (*of wind*); to get harder (*of frost*).
крéп|че *comp. of* **~кий** *and* **~ко**
крепы́ш, á *m.* (*coll.*) brawny fellow; sturdy child.
крéс|ло, ла, *g. pl.* **~ел** *nt.* arm-chair, easy-chair; **высóкое к.** high chair; **инвали́дное к.** wheelchair; **к.-качáлка** rocking chair.
кресс-салáт, а *m.* cress.
крест, á *m.* **1.** cross; **постáвить к.** (**на**+*p.*) to give up for lost. **2.** the sign of the cross; **осени́ть себя́ ~óм** to cross o.s.
крест|éц, цá *m.* (*anat.*) sacrum.
крести́льный *adj.* baptismal.
крести́н|ы, ~ *no sg.* christening.
крести́тел|ь, я *m.*: **Иоáнн К.** (*relig.*) John the Baptist.
кре|сти́ть, щý, ∠стишь *impf.* **1.** (*pf.* **к.** *or* **о~**) to baptize, christen. **2.** (*no pf.*) (+*a.* **у**) to be godfather, godmother (*to the child of*). **3.** (*pf.* **пере~**) to make

the sign of the cross over.

кре|сти́ться, щу́сь, ∼стишься *impf.* **1.** (*pf.* **к.** *or* **о∼**) to be baptized, be christened. **2.** (*pf.* **пере∼**) to cross o.s.

крест-на́крест, *adv.* crosswise.

кре́стник, а *m.* god-son, god-child.

кре́стниц|а, ы *f.* god-daughter, god-child.

кре́ст|ный *adj. of* **∼**; **∼ное зна́мение** sign of the cross; **к. ход** (religious) procession.

крёстн|ый *adj.*: **к. оте́ц** (*also as n.* **к., ∼ого** *m.*) god-father; **∼ая мать** (*also as n.* **∼ая ∼ой** *f.*) god-mother; **∼ые де́ти** god-children.

крестови́н|а, ы *f.* (*rail.*) frog.

крест|о́вый *adj. of* **∼**; **к. похо́д** crusade.

крестоно́с|ец, ца *m.* crusader.

крестообра́з|ный (∼ен, ∼на) *adj.* cruciform.

крестья́н|ин, ина, *pl.* **∼е, ∼** *m.* peasant.

крестья́нк|а, и *f.* peasant (woman).

крестья́нский *adj.* peasant.

крестья́нств|о, а *nt.* (*collect.*) peasantry.

крети́н, а *m.* cretin; (*fig., coll.*) idiot, imbecile.

кретини́зм, а *m.* cretinism; (*fig., coll.*) idiocy.

крето́н, а *m.* (*text.*) cretonne.

кре́чет, а *m.* (*zool.*) gyrfalcon.

креще́ндо *nt. indecl.* & *adv.* (*mus.*) crescendo.

креще́ни|е, я *nt.* **1.** baptism, christening; **боево́е к.** baptism of fire. **2.** Epiphany.

крещёный *adj.* baptized.

кре|щу́, ∼стишь *see* **∼сти́ть**

крив|а́я, о́й *f.* (*math., econ., etc.*) curve.

кривизн|а́, ы́ *f.* crookedness; curvature.

крив|и́ть, лю́, и́шь *impf.* (*of* **с∼**) to bend, distort; (*coll.*): **к. гу́бы, рот** to twist one's mouth, curl one's lip; **к.** (*pf.* **по∼**) **душо́й** to violate one's conscience.

крив|и́ться, лю́сь, и́шься *impf.* **1.** (*pf.* **по∼**) to become crooked, bent. **2.** (*pf.* **с∼**) (*coll.*) to make a wry face; to grimace.

кривля́к|а, и *c.g.* (*coll.*) poseur.

кривля́нь|е я *nt.* affectation.

кривля́|ться, юсь *impf.* (*coll.*) to put on airs, behave in an affected manner.

кривобо́к|ий (∼, ∼а) *adj.* lop-sided.

крив|о́й (∼, ∼а́, ∼о) *adj.* **1.** crooked; **∼о́е зе́ркало** distorting mirror; **∼а́я улы́бка** wry smile; (*fig.*): **∼ые пути́** crooked ways. **2.** (*coll.*) one-eyed.

криволине́йный *adj.* (*math.*) curvilinear.

кривоно́г|ий (∼, ∼а) *adj.* bandy-legged, bow-legged.

кривото́лк|и, ов *no sg.* false rumours.

кривоши́п, а *m.* (*tech.*) crank; crankshaft.

кри́зис, а *m.* crisis.

крик, а *m.* cry, shout; *pl.* clamour, outcry; **после́дний к. мо́ды** the last word in fashion.

кри́кет, а *m.* cricket; **игро́к в к.** cricketer.

крикли́в|ый (∼, ∼а) *adj.* **1.** clamorous, bawling. **2.** loud, penetrating. **3.** (*fig., coll.*) loud; blatant.

кри́кн|уть, у, ешь *inst. pf. of* **крича́ть**

крику́н, а́ *m.* (*coll.*) **1.** shouter, bawler. **2.** babbler.

кримина́л, а *m.* (*coll.*) **1.** foul play. **2.** crime.

кримина́лист, а *m.* (*leg.*) specialist in crime detection.

кримина́листик|а, и *f.* (*science of*) crime detection.

кримина́льный *adj.* criminal.

кримино́лог, а *m.* criminologist.

криминоло́ги|я, и *f.* criminology.

кри́нка = кры́нка

кринол́ин, а *m.* crinoline (*skirt*).

криоге́ник|а, и *f.* cryogenics.

криптогра́мм|а, ы *f.* cryptogram.

криптогра́фи|я, и *f.* cryptography.

криста́лл, а *m.* **1.** crystal. **2.** (*comput.*) (silicon) chip.

кристаллиза́ци|я, и *f.* crystallization.

кристаллиз|ова́ть, у́ю *impf. and pf.* (*pf. also* **за∼**) to crystallize (*trans.*).

кристаллиз|ова́ться, у́юсь *impf.* (*of* **вы∼** *and* **за∼**) to crystallize (*intrans.*; *also fig.*).

криста́л|ьный *adj.* **1.** crystalline. **2. (∼ен, ∼ьна)** (*fig.*) crystal-clear.

крите́ри|й, я *m.* criterion.

кри́тик, а *m.* critic.

кри́тик|а, и *f.* **1.** criticism. **2.** critique.

критика́н, а *m.* (*coll., pej.*) fault-finder, carper.

критика́нств|о, а *nt.* (*coll., pej.*) fault-finding; carping.

критик|ова́ть, у́ю *impf.* to criticize.

крити́ческий *adj.* critical; **к. моме́нт** (*fig.*) crucial moment.

кри|ча́ть, чу́, чи́шь *impf.* (*of* **∼кнуть**) **1.** to cry, shout; to yell, scream; **к.** (**на**+*a.*) to shout (at); **к. о по́мощи** to call for help. **2.** (**о**+*p.*) (*coll., pej.*) to cry out (against).

крича́|щий *pres. part. act. of* **∼ть** *and adj.* (*fig., coll.*) loud; blatant.

кришнаи́т, а *m.* Hare Krishna (follower).

кришнаи́тский *adj.* Hare Krishna.

кров, а *m.* roof; shelter; **оста́ться без ∼а** to be left without a roof over one's head.

крова́в|ый *adj.* **1.** bloody; (*fig.*): **∼ая ба́ня** blood-bath. **2.** blood-stained.

крова́тк|а, и *f.*: **перено́сная де́тская к.** carry-cot.

крова́т|ь, и *f.* bed; **двухъя́русная к.** bunk bed.

кро́в|ельный *adj. of* **∼ля**

кро́вельщик, а *m.* roofer.

кровено́сн|ый *adj.* appertaining to the circulation of the blood; **∼ая систе́ма** circulatory system; **к. сосу́д** blood-vessel.

крови́нк|а, и *f.* (*coll.*) drop of blood; **у него́ ни ∼и в лице́** he is as white as a sheet.

кро́в|ля, ли, *g. pl.* **∼ель** *f.* roof.

кро́вн|ый *adj.* **1.** blood; **∼ая месть** vendetta. **2.** (*of animals*) thorough-bred. **3.** (*fig.*) vital, deep, intimate; **моё ∼ое де́ло** an affair which concerns me closely; **∼ые интере́сы** vital interests; **∼ые де́ньги** hard-earned money. **4.** (*fig.*) grievous, deadly; **∼ая оби́да** deadly insult.

кровожа́д|ный (∼ен, ∼на) *adj.* blood-thirsty.

кровоизлия́ни|е, я *nt.* (*med.*) haemorrhage.

кровообраще́ни|е, я *nt.* circulation of the blood.

кровоостана́вливающ|ий *adj.*: **∼ее сре́дство** styptic.

кровопи́йц|а, ы, *g. pl.* **∼** *c.g.* blood-sucker.

кровоподтёк, а *m.* bruise.

кровопроли́ти|е, я *nt.* bloodshed.

кровопроли́тный *adj.* bloody.

кровопуска́ни|е, я *nt.* (*med.*) blood-letting, phlebotomy.

кровосмеси́тельный *adj.* incestuous.

кровосмеше́ни|е, я *nt.* incest.

кровосо́с, а *m.* vampire bat.

кровотече́ни|е, я *nt.* haemorrhage; bleeding.

кровоточи́вост|ь, и *f.* (*med.*) haemophilia.

кровоточи́т|ь, ∼, *impf.* to bleed.

кров|ь, и, о ∼и, в ∼и́, *g. pl.* **∼е́й** *f.* blood (*also fig.*); **в к., до ∼и** till it bleeds; **пусти́ть к.** (+*d.*) to bleed (*trans.*); (*fig.*): **по ∼и** by birth; **к. с молоко́м** (*coll.*) the very picture of health; **у него́ к. кипи́т** his blood is up; **страсть к игре́ у него́ в ∼и́** gambling is in his blood; **се́рдце у меня́ облива́ется ∼ью** my heart bleeds.

кров|яно́й *adj. of* **∼ь**

кро|и́ть, ю́, и́шь *impf.* (*of* **с∼**) to cut (out).

кро́йк|а, и *f.* cutting (out).

кроке́т, а *m.* croquet.

кроки́ *nt. indecl.* sketch-map; rough sketch.

крокоди́л, а *m.* crocodile.

крокоди́л|ов *and* **∼овый** *adj. of* **∼**

кро́кус, а *m.* (*bot.*) crocus.

кро́лик, а *m.* rabbit.
кро́ли|ковый *and* **~чий** *adj. of* **~к; ~чий мех** rabbit-skin.
крол|ь, я *m. (sport)* crawl (stroke).
крольча́тник, а *m.* rabbit-hutch.
крольчи́х|а, и *f.* doe-rabbit.
кро́ме *prep.+g.* **1.** except. **2.** besides, in addition to; **к. того́** besides, moreover, furthermore; *(coll.)*: **к. шу́ток** joking apart.
кроме́шн|ый *adj.*: **ад к.** inferno; **тьма ~ая** pitch darkness.
кро́мк|а, и *f.* edge; *(of material)* selvage.
кромса́|ть, ю *impf. (of* **ис~***) (coll.)* to cut up carelessly.
кро́н|а[1]**, ы** *f.* crown *(of a tree)*.
кро́н|а[2]**, ы** *f. (unit of currency)* crown.
кронпри́нц, а *m.* crown prince.
кронци́ркул|ь, я *m. (tech.)* calipers.
кро́ншнеп, а *m. (zool.)* curlew.
кронште́йн, а *m. (tech.)* bracket; corbel.
кроп|и́ть, лю́, и́шь *impf. (of* **о~***)* **1.** to besprinkle. **2.** *(intrans.; of rain)* to trickle, spot.
кропотли́в|ый (~, ~а) *adj.* **1.** laborious. **2.** painstaking, precise.
кросс, а *m. (sport)* cross-country (race).
кроссво́рд, а *m.* crossword.
кроссме́н, а *m.* cross-country runner.
кроссови́к, а́ *m.* = **кроссме́н**
кроссо́в|ки, ок *pl. (sg.* **~ка, ~ки** *f.)* trainers.
крот, а́ *m.* **1.** mole. **2.** moleskin.
кро́т|кий (~ок, ~ка́, ~ко) *adj.* gentle; mild, meek.
крот|о́вый *adj.* **1.** *of* **~; ~о́вая нора́** mole-hill. **2.** moleskin.
кро́тост|ь, и *f.* gentleness; mildness, meekness.
крох|а́, и́, *pl.* **∠и, ~а́м** *f.* crumb *(pl. also fig.)*.
крохобо́р, а *m.* quibbler, hair-splitter.
крохобо́рств|о, а *nt.* quibbling, hair-splitting.
кро́хотный *adj. (coll.)* tiny.
кро́шечк|а, и *f. dim. of* **кро́шка**
кро́шечный *adj. (coll.)* tiny.
крош|и́ть, у́, ∠ишь *impf.* **1.** *(pf.* **ис~, на~** *or* **рас~***)* to crumble; to chop, hack; *(fig.)* to hack to pieces. **2.** *(pf.* **на~***) (+i.)* to spill crumbs (of); **к. хле́бом на́ пол** to spill breadcrumbs on the floor.
крош|и́ться, ∠ится *impf. (of* **ис~** *and* **рас~***)* to crumble, disintegrate.
кро́шк|а, и *f.* **1.** crumb. **2.** *(fig.)* a tiny bit; **ни ~и** not a bit.
круг, а, *pl.* **~и́** *m.* **1.** *(p. sg.* **в, на ~у́** *= circular area;* **в, на ~е** *= circumference)* circle; **движе́ние по ∠у** movement in a circle; **~и́ (на воде́)** ripples (on water); **стать в к.** to form a circle. **2.** *(sport; p. sg.* **на ~у́***)* **бегово́й к.** race-course; **к. почёта** lap of honour. **3.** *(fig.; p. sg.* **в ~у́***)* sphere, range; compass; **вне ∠а свои́х обя́занностей** outside one's province. **4.** *(fig.; p. sg.* **в ~у́***)* circle *(of persons)*; **деловы́е ~и́** business circles.
кру́гленьк|ий *adj. (coll.)* **1.** *dim. of* **кру́глый; ~ая су́мма** a tidy sum. **2.** rotund, portly.
кругле́|ть, ю *impf. (of* **по~***)* to become round.
круглоли́ц|ый (~, ~а) *adj.* moon-faced, chubby-faced.
круглосу́точный *adj.* round-the-clock, twenty-four-hour.
кру́гл|ый (~, ~а́, ~о) *adj.* **1.** round; **к. год** all year round; **~ые су́тки** day and night; **к. по́черк** round hand; **в ~ых ци́фрах** in round figures. **2.** *(coll.)* complete, utter; **к. дура́к** absolute fool; **к., ~ая сирота́** orphan *(having neither father nor mother)*
кругов|о́й *adj.* circular; **~а́я пору́ка** mutual responsibility, guarantee; **~а́я ча́ша** loving-cup; **~а́я доро́га** roundabout route.
круговоро́т, а *m.* rotation, circulation.
кругозо́р, а *m.* **1.** prospect. **2.** *(fig.)* horizon, range of interests.
круго́м[1] *adv.* **1.** round, around; **он обошёл маши́ну к.** he walked around the car. **2.** (all) round, round about; **к. всё бы́ло ти́хо** all around was still. **3.** *(coll.)* completely, entirely; **вы к. винова́ты** you are entirely to blame.
круго́м[2] *prep.+g.* round, around.
кругообра́з|ный (~ен, ~на) *adj.* circular.
кругосве́тный *adj.* round-the-world.
круж|ева́, ∠ев, ~ева́м = **∠ево**
кружев|но́й *adj. of* **~а́** *and* **кру́жево**
кру́жев|о, а *nt.* lace
круж|и́ть, у́, ∠и́шь *impf.* **1.** to whirl, spin round; *(fig.)*: **к. кому́-н. го́лову** to turn s.o.'s head. **2.** to circle. **3.** *(coll.)* to wander.
круж|и́ться, у́сь, ∠и́шься *impf. (of* **за~***)* to whirl, spin round; to circle; **у меня́ ∠ится голова́** my head is going round.
кру́жк|а, и *f.* **1.** mug; tankard; *(measure)*: **к. пи́ва** glass of beer; **ме́рная к.** *(cul.)* measuring cup. **2.** collecting-box.
кружковщи́н|а, ы *f.* clannishness, cliquishness.
круж|ко́вый *adj. of* **~о́к 2.**
кру́жный *adj.* roundabout, circuitous.
круж|о́к, ка́ *m.* **1.** *dim. of* **круг. 2.** circle, club, study group.
круи́з, а *m.* cruise.
круп[1]**, а** *m. (med.)* croup.
круп[2]**, а** *m.* croup, crupper *(of horse)*.
круп|а́, ы́, *pl.* **∠ы** *f.* **1.** *(collect.)* groats; **гре́чневая к.** buckwheat; **ма́нная к.** semolina; **овся́ная к.** oatmeal; **перло́вая к.** pearl-barley. **2.** *(fig.)* sleet.
крупи́нк|а, ы *f.* grain.
крупи́ц|а, ы *f.* grain; ounce; **у него́ нет ни ~ы́ здра́вого смы́сла** he hasn't an ounce of common sense.
крупне́|ть, ю *impf. (of* **по~***)* to grow larger.
кру́пн|о *adv. of* **~ый; к. наре́зать** to cut into large pieces; **к. писа́ть** to write large; **к. поспо́рить (с+***i.***)** to have a slanging-match (with).
крупномасшта́б|ный (~ен, ~на) *adj.* large-scale.
кру́п|ный (~ен, ~на́, ~но) *adj.* **1.** large, big; large-scale; *(fig.)* prominent; **к. рога́тый скот** cattle; **к. план** *(cin.)* close-up. **2.** coarse; **к. песо́к** coarse sand. **3.** important; serious; **~ная неприя́тность** serious trouble; **к. разгово́р** *(fig.)* row, slanging-match.
крупча́тый *adj.* granular.
крупье́ *m. indecl.* croupier.
крутизн|а́, ы́ *f.* **1.** steepness. **2.** steep slope.
кру|ти́ть, чу́, ∠тишь *impf. (of* **за~** *and* **с~***)* **1.** to twist; to twirl; **к. верёвку** to twist a rope; **к. папиро́су** to roll a cigarette; **к. усы́** to twirl one's moustache; *(coll.; +i.)* **она́ ∠тит им, как хо́чет** she twists him round her little finger. **2.** to turn, wind *(tap, handle, etc.)*. **3.** to whirl *(trans.)*. **4.** *(coll.;* **с***+i.)* to go out (with), knock about (with).
кру|ти́ться, чу́сь, ∠тишься *impf.* **1.** to turn, spin, revolve. **2.** to whirl. **3.** *(fig., coll.)* to be in a whirl.
кру́то *adv.* **1.** steeply. **2.** abruptly, sharply; **к. поверну́ть** to turn round sharply. **3.** *(coll.)* harshly; **к. распра́виться с кем-н.** to give s.o. short shrift. **4.** thoroughly; **к. отжа́ть** to wring out thoroughly; **к. посоли́ть** to put (too) much salt (into).
крут|о́й (~, ~а́, ∠о) *adj.* **1.** steep; **к. вира́ж** *(aeron.)* steep turn. **2.** abrupt, sharp. **3.** *(coll.)* severe; drastic; **~ы́е ме́ры** drastic measures. **4.** *(cul.)* thick; well-done; **к. кипято́к** fiercely boiling water; **~о́е яйцо́** hard-boiled egg.
кру́ч|а, и *f.* steep slope.
кру́|че *comp. of* **~то́й** *and* **~то**
круче́ни|е, я *nt.* **1.** *(text.)* twisting. **2.** *(tech.)* torsion.
кручи́н|а, ы *f. (folk poet.)* sorrow, woe.
кру|чу́, ∠тишь *see* **~ти́ть**

круше́ни|е, я *nt.* **1.** wreck; ruin; **к. по́езда** derailment. **2.** (*fig.*) ruin; collapse; downfall.
круши́н|а, ы *f.* (*bot.*) buckthorn.
круш|и́ть, у́, и́шь *impf.* to shatter, destroy.
крыжо́венный *adj.* gooseberry.
крыжо́вник, а *m.* **1.** gooseberry bush(es). **2.** (*collect.*) gooseberries.
крыла́т|ый *adj.* winged (*also fig.*): **~ые слова́** pithy saying(s); (*tech.*): **~ая га́йка** wing nut.
крыл|е́чко, е́чка *nt. dim. of* **~ьцо́**
крыл|о́, а́, *pl.* **~ья, ~ьев** *nt.* wing; sail, vane; splash-board, mud-guard.
кры́лыш|ко, ка, *pl.* **~ки, ~ек, ~кам** *nt. dim. of* **крыло́**; (*fig.*): **под ~ком** under the wing (*of*).
крыл|ьцо́, ьца́, *pl.* **~ьца, ~ец, ~ьца́м** *nt.* porch.
Крым, а *m.* the Crimea.
кры́мский *adj.* Crimean.
крымча́к, а́ *m.* inhabitant of the Crimea.
кры́нк|а, и *f.* (milk-)jug; pitcher.
кры́с|а, ы *f.* rat.
крыс|и́ный *adj. of* **~а**; **к. яд** rat poison.
крысоло́в, а *m.* rat-catcher.
крысоло́вк|а, и *f.* rat-trap.
кры́т|ый *p.p.p. of* **~ь** *and adj.* covered; sheltered; **к. ры́нок** covered market.
крыть, кро́ю, кро́ешь *impf.* (*of* **по~**) to cover; to roof; to coat (*with paint*).
кры́ться, кро́юсь, кро́ешься *impf.* **1.** (**в**+*p.*) to be, lie (in). **2.** to be concealed.
кры́ш|а, и *f.* roof.
кры́шк|а, и *f.* lid; cover; cap.
крэк, а *m.* crack (*drug*).
крю|к, ка́ *m.* **1.** (*pl.* **~ки́, ~ко́в**) hook; **(альпини́стский) к.** piton; (*pl.* **~чья, ~чьев**) hook (*for supporting load*). **2.** (*coll.*) detour.
крючкова́т|ый (~, ~а) *adj.* hooked.
крюч|о́к, ка́ *m.* hook; **спусково́й к.** trigger.
крюшо́н, а *m.* cup, punch (*beverage*).
кря́ду *adv.* (*coll.*) running; in a row.
кряж, а *m.* **1.** (mountain-)ridge. **2.** block, log.
кря́жист|ый (~, ~а) *adj.* thick; (*fig.*) thick-set.
кря́к|ать, аю *impf.* (*of* **~нуть**) **1.** to quack. **2.** (*coll.*) to wheeze.
кря́кв|а, ы *f.* wild duck, mallard.
кря́к|нуть, ну, нешь *inst. pf. of* **~ать**
крях|те́ть, чу́, ти́шь *impf.* to groan; to wheeze, grunt.
ксе́р|ить, ю, ишь *impf.* (*of* **откс́ерить**) (*coll.*) to xerox.
ксерокопи́р|овать, ую *impf. and pf.* to xerox.
ксероко́пи|я, и *f.* Xerox (*propr.*) (copy).
ксилогра́фи|я, и *f.* wood-engraving.
ксилофо́н, а *m.* (*mus.*) xylophone.
кста́ти *adv.* **1.** to the point, apropos **2.** opportunely; **как раз к.** at just the right moment. **3.** (*coll.*) at the same time; while you are at it; **к. зайди́те пожа́луйста в апте́ку** will you please call at the chemist's at the same time. **4.: к. (сказа́ть)** by the way.
кто, кого́, кому́, кем, ком *pron.* **1.** (*interrog.*) who; **к. э́то тако́й?** who is that?; **к. из вас э́то сде́лал?** which of you did it? **к. идёт?** (*mil.*) who goes there? **2.** (*rel.*) who (*normally after pron. antecedent*); **тот, к.** he who; **те, к.** those who. **3.** (*indef.*): **к. (бы) ни** who(so)-ever; **к. ни придёт** whoever comes; **к. бы то ни́ был** whoever it may be. **4.** (*indef.*) some ... others; **разбежа́лись к. куда́** they scattered in all directions. **5.** (*coll., indef.*) anyone; **е́сли к. позвони́т, дай мне знать** if anyone rings, let me know.
кто́-либо, кого́-либо *pron.* = **кто́-нибудь**
кто́-нибудь, кого́-нибудь *pron.* anyone, anybody; someone, somebody.
кто́-то, кого́-то *pron.* someone, somebody.
куб[1]**, а,** *pl.* **~ы́** *m.* **1.** (*math.*) cube; **два в ~е** two cubed. **2.** (*coll.*) cubic metre.
куб[2]**, а,** *pl.* **~ы́** *m.* boiler; still.
Ку́б|а, ы *f.* Cuba.
куба́н|ец, ца *m.* Kuban Cossack.
куба́нский *adj.* (*geog.*) (of the) Kuban.
ку́барем *adv.* (*coll.*) head over heels; **скати́ться к.** to roll head over heels.
куба́р|ь, я́ *m.* peg-top.
кубату́р|а, ы *f.* cubic content.
куби́зм, а *m.* (*art*) cubism.
ку́бик, а *m.* **1.** *dim. of* **куб. 2.** (*pl.*) blocks, bricks (*as children's toy*). **3.** (*coll.*) cubic centimetre.
куби́н|ец, ца *m.* Cuban.
куби́н|ка, ки *f. of* **~ец**
куби́нский *adj.* Cuban.
куби́ческий *adj.* cubic; **к. ко́рень** (*math.*) cube root.
кубови́д|ный (~ен, ~на) *adj.* cube-shaped, cuboid.
куб|ово́й *adj. of* **~**[2]
ку́бовый *adj.* indigo.
ку́б|ок, ка *m.* goblet; **переходя́щий к.** (*sport etc.*) (challenge) cup; **встре́ча на к.** cup-tie.
кубоме́тр, а *m.* cubic metre.
ку́брик, а *m.* (*naut.*) crew's quarters.
кубы́шк|а, и *f.* (*coll.*) **1.** money-box. **2.** (*joc.*) dumpy woman, girl; roly-poly.
кува́лд|а, ы *f.* sledge-hammer.
Куве́йт, а *m.* Kuwait.
куве́йтский *adj.* Kuwaiti.
кувши́н, а *m.* jug; pitcher.
кувши́нк|а, и *f.* (*bot.*) water-lily.
кувырк|а́ться, а́юсь *impf.* (*of* **~ну́ться**) to somersault, turn somersaults, tumble.
кувырк|ну́ться, ну́сь, нёшься *inst. pf. of* **~а́ться**
кувырко́м *adv.* (*coll.*) head over heels.
кугуа́р, а *m.* (*zool.*) cougar.
куда́ *adv.* **1.** (*interrog. and rel.*) where (*expr. motion*); **к. ты идёшь?** where are you going? **2.: к. (бы) ни** wherever; **к. бы то ни́ было** anywhere; (*coll.*): **к. ни кинь** wherever one looks; **к. ни шло** come what may. **3.** (*coll.*) what for; **к. вам сто́лько багажа́?** what do you want so much luggage for? **4.** (+*comp.*; *coll.*) much, far; **сего́дня мне к. лу́чше** I am much better today. **5.** (*coll.*): **хоть к.** fine, excellent. **6.** (*expr. doubt, incredulity*; *coll.*): **к ча́су я наме́рен дочита́ть до страни́цы 200 — к. тебе́!** I intend to reach page 200 by one o'clock — you'll never do it!; **узна́ли ли тебя́ они́? к. им** did they recognize you? how could they?
куда́-либо *adv.* = **куда́-нибудь**
куда́-нибудь *adv.* anywhere; somewhere.
куда́-то *adv.* somewhere.
куда́хтань|е, я *nt.* cackling, clucking.
куда́х|тать, чу, чешь *impf.* to cackle, cluck.
куде́л|ь, и *f.* (*text.*) tow.
куде́сник, а *m.* magician, sorcerer.
кудла́тый *adj.* (*coll.*) shaggy.
ку́др|и, е́й *no sg.* curls.
кудря́в|ый (~, ~а) *adj.* **1.** curly; curly-headed. **2.** leafy, bushy. **3.** (*fig.*) florid; flowery.
кудря́ш|ки, ек *no sg.* (*coll.*) ringlets.
кузе́н, а *m.* (male) cousin.
кузи́н|а, ы *f.* (female) cousin.
кузне́ц, а́ *m.* (black)smith.
кузне́чик, а *m.* grasshopper.
кузне́чный *adj.* blacksmith's; **к. мех** bellows.
ку́зниц|а, ы *f.* forge, smithy.
ку́зов, а, *pl.* **~ы** *and* **~а́** *m.* **1.** basket. **2.** body (*of carriage, etc.*).
кукаре́ка|ть, ю *impf.* to crow.
кукареку́ cock-a-doodle-doo.
ку́киш, а *m.* (*coll.*) fig (*gesture of derision or contempt with thumb between two fingers*); **показа́ть кому́-н. к.** to cock a snook at s.o.
ку́к|ла, лы, *g. pl.* **~ол** *f.* doll; puppet.

ку-клукс-кла́н, а *m.* Ku Klux Klan.
куклуксклáнов|ец, ца *m.* Ku Klux Klaner.
кук|ова́ть, у́ю *impf.* to (cry) cuckoo.
ку́колк|а, и *f.* **1.** (*affectionate dim. of* **ку́кла**) dolly. **2.** (*zool.*) chrysalis, pupa.
ку́кол|ь, я *m.* (*bot.*) cockle.
ку́кольник, а *m.* (*coll.*) puppeteer.
ку́кольн|ый *adj.* doll's; **к. теа́тр** puppet-theatre.
ку́к|ситься, шусь, сишься *impf.* (*coll.*) to sulk; to be in the dumps.
кукуру́з|а, ы *f.* maize; sweetcorn.
кукуру́з|ный *adj. of* **~а**
куку́шк|а, и *f.* cuckoo; **часы́ с ~ой** cuckoo-clock.
кула́к[1], **а́** *m.* fist; **дойти́ до ~о́в** to come to blows; **смея́ться в ~** to laugh up one's sleeve.
кула́к[2], **а́** *m.* kulak.
кула́к[3], **а́** *m.* (*tech.*) cam.
кула́|цкий *adj. of* **~к**[2]
кула́честв|о, а *nt.* (*collect.*) the kulaks.
кула́чк|а, и *f. of* **кула́к**[2]
кула́чк|и *only in phrr.* **идти́ на к.** to come to blows; **би́ться на ~ах** to engage in fisticuffs.
кулач|ко́вый *adj. of* **~о́к**[2]; **к. вал** camshaft.
кула́|чный *adj. of* **~к**[1,3]; **к. бой** fisticuffs.
кула|чо́к[1], **чка́** *m. dim. of* **∠к**[1]
кулач|о́к[2], **ка́** *m.* (*tech.*) cam.
кулебя́к|а, и *f.* kulebyaka (*pie*).
кул|ёк, ька́ *m.* (*paper*) bag.
ку́ли *m. indecl.* coolie.
кули́к, а́ *m.* (*zool.*) stint; sandpiper.
кулинáри́|я, и *f.* cookery.
кулина́рный *adj.* culinary.
кули́с|ы, ~ *pl.* (*sg.* **~а, ~ы** *f.*) (*theatr.*) wings; **за ~ами** backstage; behind the scenes (*also fig.*).
кули́ч, а́ *m.* Easter cake.
кули́чк|и *only in phrr.* (*coll.*): **у чёрта на ~ах** in the middle of nowhere; **к чёрту на к.** to the back of beyond.
куло́н[1], **а** *m.* pendant.
куло́н[2], **а** *m.* (*elec.*) coulomb.
кулуа́р|ный *adj. of* **~ы**
кулуа́р|ы, ов *sg. not used* lobby (*in Parliament*; *also fig.*).
кул|ь, я́ *m.* sack.
кульминацио́нный *adj.* climactic; **к. пункт** culmination, climax.
кульмина́ци|я, и *f.* culmination.
культ, а *m.* cult; **к. ли́чности** personality cult.
культ... *comb. form, abbr. of* **культу́рный**
культиви́р|овать, ую *impf.* to cultivate (*also fig.*).
культу́р|а, ы *f.* **1.** culture. **2.** standard, level; **к. ре́чи** standard of speech. **3.** (*agric.*) crop; **зерновы́е ~ы** cereals; **кормовы́е ~ы** forage crops. **4.** (*agric.*) cultivation; **к. карто́феля** potato-growing.
культури́зм, а *m.* body-building.
культури́ст, а *m.* body-builder.
культу́рност|ь, и *f.* (level of) culture; cultivation; (*fig.*): **он отлича́лся ~ью** he was exceptionally cultivated.
культу́р|ный (~ен, ~на) *adj.* **1.** cultured, cultivated. **2.** cultural. **3.** (*agric., hort.*) cultured; cultivated.
культ|я́, и́ *f.* stump (*of limb*).
кум, а, *pl.* **~овья́, ~овьёв** *m.* god-father of one's child; father of one's god-child.
кум|а́, ы́ *f.* god-mother of one's child; mother of one's god-child.
кума́ч, а́ *m.* red calico.
куми́р, а *m.* idol (*also fig.*)
кумовств|о́, а́ *nt.* nepotism.
кумуляти́вн|ый *adj.* cumulative.
ку́мушк|а, и *f.* **1.** *affectionate of* **кума́**. **2.** (*coll.*) gossip, scandal-monger.
кумы́с, а *m.* koumiss (*fermented mare's milk*).
кунжу́т, а *m.* (*bot.*) sesame.
кунжу́т|ный *adj. of* **~**
куни́ц|а, ы *f.* (*zool.*) marten.
кун-фу́ *nt. indecl.* kung fu.
ку́п|а, ы *f.* group, clump (*of trees*).
купа́льник, а *m.* bathing costume.
купа́льный *adj.* bathing, swimming; **к. костю́м** swimming costume.
купа́л|ьня, ьни, *g. pl.* **~ен** *f.* (*enclosed*) bathing-place.
купа́льщик, а *m.* bather.
купа́|ть, ю *impf.* (*of* **вы́~**) to bathe; to bath.
купа́|ться, юсь *impf.* (*of* **вы́~**) to bathe; to have, take a bath; (*coll.*): **к. в зо́лоте** to be rolling in money.
купе́ *nt. indecl.* compartment (*of rail. carriage*).
купе́л|ь, и *f.* (*eccl.*) font.
куп|е́ц, ца́ *m.* merchant.
купе́ческ|ий *adj.* merchant, mercantile; **~ое сосло́вие** the merchant class.
купе́честв|о, а *nt.* (*collect.*) the merchants.
куп|и́ть, лю́, ∠ишь *pf.* (*of* **покупа́ть**) to buy, purchase.
купле́т, а *m.* **1.** stanza, strophe. **2.** (*pl.*) satirical ballad(s), song(s).
куплети́ст, а *m.* singer of satirical songs, ballads.
ку́пл|я, и *f.* purchase.
ку́пол, а, *pl.* **~а́** *m.* cupola, dome.
купо́н, а *m.* coupon.
купоро́с, а *m.* (*chem.*) vitriol.
купчи́х|а, и *f.* **1.** *f. of* **купе́ц**. **2.** merchant's wife.
купю́р|а, ы *f.* **1.** cut. **2.** (*fin.*) denomination.
кураг|а́, и́ *f.* (*collect.*) dried apricots.
кура́ж|иться, усь, ишься *impf.* (*coll.*) to swagger, boast; **(над)** to bully.
кура́нт|ы, ов *no sg.* chimes.
кура́тор, а *m.* (academic) supervisor, tutor.
курга́н, а *m.* burial mound.
кургу́з|ый (~, ~а) *adj.* (*coll.*) **1.** too short and/or tight. **2.** bob-tailed.
курд, а *m.* Kurd.
ку́рдский *adj.* Kurdish.
курдя́нк|а, и *f.* Kurdish woman.
ку́рев|о, а *nt.* (*coll.*) tobacco; sth. to smoke; **у меня́ нет ~а** I haven't got a smoke.
куре́ни|е, я *nt.* **1.** smoking. **2.** incense.
кури́лк|а[1], **и** *f.* (*coll.*) smoking-room.
кури́лка[2] *only in phr.* **жив к.!** there's life in the old dog yet.
кури́льниц|а, ы *f.* censer; incense-burner.
кури́л|ьня, ни, *g. pl.* **~ен** *f.*: **к. о́пиума** opium-den.
кури́льщик, а *m.* smoker.
кури́н|ый *adj.* hen's; chicken's; **~ая слепота́** (*med.*) night-blindness.
кури́р|овать, ую *impf.* to supervise.
кури́тельн|ый *adj.* smoking; **~ая бума́га** cigarette paper.
кур|и́ть, ю́, ∠ишь *impf.* (*of* **по~**) **1.** to smoke; **к. тру́бку** to smoke a pipe. **2.** (*+a. or i.*) to burn; **к. ла́даном** to burn incense.
кур|и́ться, ∠ится *impf.* **1.** to smoke (*intrans.*). **2.** (*+i.*) to emit. **3.** *pass. of* **~и́ть**
ку́р|ица, ицы, *pl.* **~ы, ~** *f.* hen; (*fig., coll.*): **мо́края к.** milksop.
курку́м|а, ы *f.* turmeric.
курно́с|ый (~, ~а) (*coll.*) snub-nosed.
куроводство|о, а *nt.* poultry-breeding.
кур|о́к, ка́ *m.* cocking-piece; **взвести́ к.** to cock; **спусти́ть к.** to pull the trigger.
куропа́тк|а, и *f.* (*zool.*) **(се́рая)** partridge; **бе́лая к.** willow grouse.
куро́рт, а *m.* (holiday) resort; spa.
куро́ртник, а *m.* holidaymaker.
куро́рт|ный *adj. of* **~**; **~ное лече́ние** spa treatment.

куросле́п, а *m.* (*bot.*) buttercup.
ку́рочк|а, и *f.* **1.** pullet. **2.** moor-hen.
курс, а *m.* **1.** course; **но́вый к.** (*pol.*) new policy; **ускóренный к.** crash course; **быть на тре́тьем ∼е** to be in the third year (*of a course of studies*); **держа́ть к.** (**на**+*a.*) to head (for); **быть в ∼е де́ла** to be fully informed. **2.** (*fin.*) rate (of exchange).
курса́нт, а *m.* **1.** student. **2.** cadet.
курси́в, а *m.* italics; **∼ом** in italics.
курси́вный *adj.* (*typ.*) italic.
курси́р|овать, ую *impf.* **(ме́жду)** to ply, run (between).
курсо́вк|а, и *f.* board and treatment authorization (*at health resort*).
ку́рсор, а *m.* (*comput.*) cursor.
куртиза́нк|а, и *f.* courtesan.
ку́ртк|а, и *f.* (*man's*) jacket.
курча́в|иться, ится *impf.* to curl.
курча́в|ый (∼, ∼а) *adj.* (*coll.*) curly; curly-headed.
ку́р|ы *see* **∼ица**
курьёз, а *m.* curious, amusing incident; **для, ра́ди ∼а** for fun.
курьёз|ный (∼ен, ∼на) *adj.* curious; funny.
курье́р, а *m.* messenger; courier.
курье́р|ский *adj.* **1.** *adj. of* **∼**. **2.** fast; **к. по́езд** express.
куря́тин|а, ы *f.* chicken (*as meat*).
куря́тник, а *m.* hen-house, hen-coop.
куса́|ть, ю *impf.* to bite; to sting.
куса́|ться, юсь *impf.* **1.** to bite (= *to be given to biting*). **2.** to bite one another.
куса́ч|ки, ек *no sg.* pliers; wire-cutters.
кусково́й *adj.* broken in lumps; **к. са́хар** lump sugar.
кус|óк, ка́ *m.* lump; piece, bit; slice; cake (*of soap*); **зарабо́тать к. хле́ба** to earn a crust.
куст, а́ *m.* bush, shrub.
куста́рник, а *m.* (*collect.*) bush(es), shrub(s); shrubbery.
куста́рн|ый *adj.* **1.** handicraft; **∼ые изде́лия** craftwork. **2.** (*fig., pej.*) crude, primitive.
куста́р|ь, я́ *m.* handicraftsman.
ку́та|ть, ю *impf.* (*of* **за∼**) (**в**+*a.*) to muffle up (in).
ку́та|ться, юсь *impf.* (*of* **за∼**) (**в**+*a.*) to muffle o.s. up (in).
кутёж, а́ *m.* drinking-bout; binge.
кутерьм|а́, ы́ *f.* (*coll.*) commotion.
кути́л|а, ы *m.* fast liver; hard drinker.
ку|ти́ть, чу́, ∼тишь *impf.* (*of* **∼тну́ть**) to carouse; to go on the booze.
кут|ну́ть, ну́, нёшь *inst. pf. of* **∼и́ть**
кутýзк|а, и *f.* (*coll.*) jail, lock-up.
куха́рк|а, и *f.* cook.
кухми́стерск|ая, ой *f.* (*obs.*) eating-house, cook-shop.
ку́х|ня, ни, *g. pl.* **∼онь** *f.* **1.** kitchen; cook-house. **2.** cooking, cuisine.
ку́хонн|ый *adj.* kitchen; **∼ая плита́** kitchen-range.
ку́ц|ый (∼, ∼а) *adj.* **1.** tailless; bob-tailed. **2.** (*of clothing*) skimpy; (*fig.*) limited, abbreviated.
ку́ч|а, и *f.* **1.** heap, pile; (*coll.*): **вали́ть в одну́ ∼у** to lump together. **2.** (*coll.*; +*g.*) heaps (of), piles (of); **у него́ к. де́нег** he has stacks of money.
кучево́й *adj.* (*meteor.*) cumulous.
ку́чер, а, *pl.* **∼а́, ∼о́в** *m.* coachman.
ку́ч|ка, ки *f. dim. of* **∼а; к. люде́й** small group of people.
ку|чу́, ∼тишь *see* **∼ти́ть**
куш, а *m.* (*coll.*) large sum (*of money*).
куша́к, а́ *m.* sash, girdle.
ку́шань|е, я *nt.* food; dish.
ку́ша|ть, ю *impf.* (*of* **по∼** *and* **с∼**) to eat, have.
куше́тк|а, и *f.* couch.
ку|ю́, ёшь *see* **кова́ть**

кхме́р|ы, ов *pl.* (*sg.* **∼, а** *m.*) the Khmers; **кра́сные к.** the Khmer Rouge.
кюве́т, а *m.* ditch (*at side of road*).

Л

Л. (*abbr. of* **Ленингра́д**) Leningrad.
л (*abbr. of* **литр**) l, litre(s).
лабири́нт, а *m.* (*in var. senses*) labyrinth, maze.
лабора́нт, а *m.* laboratory assistant.
лаборато́ри|я, и *f.* laboratory.
лаборато́р|ный *adj. of* **∼ия**
ла́в|а, ы *f.* lava.
лава́нд|а, ы *f.* (*bot.*) lavender.
лави́н|а, ы *f.* avalanche.
лави́р|овать, ую *impf.* **1.** (*naut.*) to tack. **2.** (*fig.*) to manœuvre.
ла́вк|а¹, и *f.* bench.
ла́вк|а², и *f.* shop; store.
ла́вочк|а¹, и *f. dim. of* **ла́вка¹**
ла́вочк|а², и *f. dim. of* **лавка²**
ла́вочник, а *m.* shop-keeper.
лавр, а *m.* **1.** (*bot.*) laurel; bay(-tree). **2.** (*pl., fig.*) laurels; **почи́ть на ∼ах** to rest on one's laurels.
ла́вр|а, ы *f.* monastery (*of highest rank*).
ла́вр|óвый *adj. of* **∼; ∼о́вый вено́к** laurel wreath, (*fig.*) laurels; **∼о́вый лист** bay leaf.
ла́вр|ский *adj. of* **∼а**
лавса́н, а *m.* lavsan (*Terylene(propr.)-like synthetic fibre*).
ла́гер|ный *adj. of* **∼ь**
ла́гер|ь, я *m.* **1.** (*pl.* **∼я́, ∼е́й**) camp; (*mil.*): **располага́ться, стоя́ть ∼ем** to camp, be encamped; **снять л.** to strike camp. **2.** (*pl.* **∼и, ∼ей**) (*fig.*) camp.
лагу́н|а, ы *f.* lagoon.
лад, а, о ∼е, в ∼у́, *pl.* **∼ы, ∼о́в** *m.* **1.** (*mus. and fig.*) harmony, concord; **петь в л., не в л.** to sing in, out of tune; **запе́ть на друго́й л.** (*fig.*) to change one's tune; **жить в ∼у́ (с**+*i.*) to live in harmony (with); **быть не в ∼а́х (с**+*i.*) to be at odds (with); (*coll.*) **идти́, пойти́ на л.** to go well; **де́ло не идёт на л.** things are not going well. **2.** manner, way; **на ра́зные ∼ы́** in various ways; **на свой л.** in one's own way; **на ста́рый л.** in the old style. **3.** (*mus.*) stop; fret (*of stringed instrument*).
ла́дан, а *m.* incense; **дыша́ть на л.** (*fig., coll.*) to have one foot in the grave.
ла́данк|а, и *f.* amulet.
ла́|дить, жу, дишь *impf.* (**с**+*i.*) to get on (with), be on good terms (with).
ла́д|иться, ится *impf.* (*coll.*) to go well, succeed.
ла́дно *adv.* (*coll.*) **1.** harmoniously. **2.** well. **3.** *particle* **л.!** all right!; okay!
ла́д|ный (∼ен, ∼на́, ∼но) *adj.* (*coll.*) **1.** fine, excellent. **2.** harmonious.
ладо́н|ь, и *f.* palm (*of hand*).
ладо́ши *only in phrr.* **бить, ударя́ть, хло́пать в л.** to clap one's hands.
лад|ья́, ьи́, *g. pl.* **∼е́й** *f.* (*chess*) castle, rook.
ла́|жу¹, дишь *see* **∼дить**
ла́|жу², зишь *see* **∼зить**
лаз, а *m.* manhole.
лазаре́т, а *m.* (*mil.*) field hospital; (*naut.*) sick-bay.
лазе́йк|а, и *f.* hole, gap; (*fig., coll.*) loophole; **оста́-**

вить себе́ ~у to leave o.s. a loophole.
ла́зер, а *m.* (*phys.*, *tech.*) laser.
ла́зер|ный *adj. of* ~; **л. при́нтер** laser printer.
ла́|зить, жу, зишь *impf.* (*indet. of* **лезть**) **1.** (**на**+*a.*, **по**+*d.*) to climb, clamber (on to, up); **л. на сте́ну** to climb a wall; **л. по дере́вьям** to climb trees; **л. по кана́ту** to swarm up a rope. **2.** (**в**+*a.*) to climb (into), get (into); **л. в окно́** to climb through a window.
лазу́р|ный (~ен, ~на) *adj.* sky-blue, azure.
лазу́р|ь, и *f.* azure; **берли́нская л.** Prussian blue.
лазу́тчик, а *m.* (*mil.*, *obs.*) spy, scout.
ла|й, я *m.* bark(ing).
ла́йк|а[1], и *f.* husky (*dog*).
ла́йк|а[2], и *f.* kid-skin.
ла́йк|овый *adj. of* **~а[2]**; **~овые перча́тки** kid gloves.
ла́йнер, а *m.* (*naut.*, *aeron.*) liner.
лак, а *m.* varnish, lacquer; **л. для воло́с** hair spray.
лака́|ть, ю *impf.* (*of* **вы́~**) to lap (up).
лаке́|й, я *m.* footman; lackey, flunkey (*also fig.*, *pej.*).
лаке́й|ский *adj. of* ~; (*fig.*) servile.
лаке́йств|о, а *nt.* servility.
лакиро́в|анный *p.p.p. of* **~а́ть** *and adj.* varnished, lacquered; **~анная ко́жа** patent leather; **~анные ту́фли** patent-leather shoes.
лакир|ова́ть, у́ю *impf.* (*of* **от~**) to varnish, lacquer; (*fig.*, *pej.*) to varnish, embellish.
лакиро́вк|а, и *f.* varnishing, lacquering (*also fig.*, *pej.*).
ла́кмус, а *m.* (*chem.*) litmus.
ла́кмус|овый *adj. of* ~; **~овая бума́га** litmus paper.
ла́к|овый *adj. of* ~; varnished, lacquered.
ла́ком|ить, лю, ишь *impf.* (*of* **по~**) (*coll.*) to regale (with), treat (to).
ла́ком|иться, люсь, ишься *impf.* (*of* **по~**) (+*i.*) to treat o.s. (to), feast (on).
ла́комк|а, и *c.g.* gourmand; **быть ~ой** to have a sweet tooth.
ла́комств|о, а *nt.* dainty, delicacy.
ла́ком|ый (~, ~а) *adj.* **1.** tasty; **л. кусо́к** titbit, tasty morsel (*also fig.*). **2.** (*coll.*) **(до)** fond (of), partial (to).
лакони́зм, а *m.* laconicism; brevity.
лакони́ческий *adj.* laconic.
лакони́ч|ный (~ен, ~на) *adj.* = **~еский**
лакри́ц|а, ы *f.* (*bot.*) liquorice.
лакро́сс, а *m.* lacrosse.
лакта́ци|я, и *f.* lactation.
лактобацилли́н, а *m.* yoghurt.
лакто́з|а, ы *f.* (*chem.*) lactose.
ла́м|а[1], ы *f.* (*zool.*) llama.
ла́м|а[2], ы *m.* (*relig.*) lama.
ламаи́зм, а *m.* (*relig.*) Lamaism.
Ла-Ма́нш, а *m.* the (English) Channel.
ла́мп|а, ы *f.* **1.** lamp; **л. дневно́го све́та** fluorescent lamp. **2.** (*radio*) valve; tube.
лампа́д|а, ы *f.* icon-lamp.
лампа́дн|ый *adj.*: **~ое ма́сло** lamp-oil.
лампа́с, а *m.* stripe (*on side of trousers*).
ла́мп|овый *adj. of* **~а**
ла́мпочк|а, и *f.* **1.** *dim. of* **ла́мпа**. **2.** (*electric light*) bulb. **3.**: **э́то мне до ~и** (*sl.*) I couldn't care less.
ланге́т, а *m.* breaded cutlet.
лангу́ст, а *m.* (*also* **лангу́ст|а, ~ы** *f.*) spiny lobster; rock lobster.
ландша́фт, а *m.* landscape.
ла́ндыш, а *m.* lily of the valley.
ланоли́н, а *m.* (*pharm.*) lanolin.
ланце́т, а *m.* (*med.*) lancet; **вскрыть ~ом** to lance.
лан|ь, и *f.* fallow deer; doe (*of fallow deer*).
лао́сский *adj.* Laotian.
ла́п|а, ы *f.* **1.** paw; (*fig.*, *coll.*): **попа́сть в ~ы к кому́-н.** to fall into s.o.'s clutches. **2.** (*tech.*) tenon, dovetail. **3.** (*naut.*) fluke (*of anchor*).
ла́п|ка, ки *f. dim. of* **~а**; (*fig.*, *coll.*): **стоя́ть ходи́ть на за́дних ~ках (перед)** to dance attendance (upon).
ла́п|оть тя, *pl.* **~ти, ~те́й** *m.* bast shoe; **ходи́ть в ~тя́х** to wear bast shoes.
лапт|а́, ы́ *f.* **1.** (*Russ. ball game*) lapta. **2.** lapta bat.
лапш|а́, и́ *f.* **1.** noodles. **2.** noodle soup.
лар|ёк,ька́ *m.* stall.
лар|е́ц, ца́ *m.* casket, small chest.
ларинги́т, а *m.* laryngitis
ла́рчик, а *m.* small box; (*coll.*): **а л. про́сто открыва́лся** the explanation was quite simple.
лар|ь, я́ *m.* bin.
ла́ск|а[1], и *f.* **1.** caress; (*pl.*) petting. **2.** kindness.
ла́с|ка[2], и, *g. pl.* **~ок** *f.* (*zool.*) weasel.
ласка́тельн|ый *adj.* **1.** caressing; **~ое и́мя** pet name. **2.** (*gram.*) affectionate, expressing endearment.
ласка́|ть, ю *impf.* to caress, fondle, pet.
ласка́|ться, юсь *impf.* **1.** **(к)** to make up to; to snuggle up to; to coax. **2.** (*coll.*) to exchange caresses.
ла́сковый *adj.* affectionate, tender; (*fig.*) gentle.
лассо́ *nt. indecl.* lasso.
ласт, а *m.* flipper.
ла́стик[1], а *m.* (*material*) lasting.
ла́стик[2], а *m.* (*coll.*) rubber.
ла́сточк|а, и *f.* swallow; **городска́я л.** house martin; **пе́рвая л.** (*fig.*) the first signs; **одна́ л. весны́ не де́лает** (*prov.*) one swallow does not make a summer.
лата́|ть, ю *impf.* (*of* **за~**) (*coll.*) to patch.
латви́|ец, йца *m.* Latvian.
латви́|йка, йки *f. of* **~ец**
латви́йский *adj.* Latvian.
Ла́тви|я, и *f.* Latvia.
ла́текс, а *m.* latex.
лати́нский *adj.* Latin.
лату́к, а *m.* (*bot.*) lettuce.
лату́нный *adj.* brass.
лату́н|ь, и *f.* brass.
ла́т|ы, ~ *no sg.* (*hist.*) armour.
латы́н|ь, и *f.* (*coll.*) Latin.
латы́ш, а́, *pl.* **~и́, ~е́й** *m.* Lett.
латы́ш|ка, ки *f. of* ~
латы́шский *adj.* Lettish, Latvian.
лауреа́т, а *m.* prize-winner; laureate; **л. Но́белевской пре́мии** Nobel prize-winner.
лафе́т, а *m.* (*mil.*) gun-carriage.
ла́цкан, а, *pl.* **~ы, ~ов** *m.* lapel.
лачу́г|а, и *f.* hovel; shack.
ла́|ять, ю, ешь *impf.* to bark; to bay.
лба, лбу *etc.*, *see* **лоб**
лгать, лгу, лжёшь, лгут, *past* **лгал, лгала́, лга́ло** *impf.* **1.** (*pf.* **со~**) to lie; to tell lies. **2.** (*pf.* **на~**) (**на**+*a.*) to slander.
лгун, а́ *m.* liar.
лебед|ёнок, ёнка, *pl.* **~я́та, ~я́т** *m.* cygnet.
лебеди́н|ый *adj. of* **ле́бедь; ~ая по́ступь** graceful gait; (*fig.*) **~ая пе́сня** swan-song.
лебёдк|а[1], и *f.* (female) swan, pen.
лебёдк|а[2], и *f.* (*tech.*) winch, windlass.
ле́бед|ь, я, *pl.* **~и, ~е́й** *m.* swan, cob.
лебе|зи́ть, жу́, зи́шь *impf.* (*coll.*) **(пе́ред)** to fawn (upon), cringe (to).
леб|я́жий *adj. of* **~́едь; л. пух** swansdown.
лев, льва *m.* lion; **морско́й л.** sea-lion.
лева́к, а́ *m.* **1.** (*pol.*) leftist. **2.** (*coll.*) moonlighter.
лева́цкий *adj.* (*pol.*, *pej.*) ultra-left.
леве́|ть, ю *impf.* (*of* **по~**) (*pol.*) to move to the left.
левиафа́н, а *m.* leviathan.
левко́|й, я *m.* (*bot.*) stock, gilly-flower.
левре́тк|а, и *f.* Italian greyhound.
левш|а́, и́, *i.* **~о́й**, *g. pl.* **~е́й** *c.g.* left-hander.
ле́в|ый *adj.* **1.** left; left-hand; (*naut.*) port; **л. борт**

port side; **~ая сторонá** left-hand side, (*of horse, carriage, etc.*) near side; (*of material*) wrong side; (*fig.*): **встать с ~ой ноги́** to get out of bed on the wrong side. **2.** unofficial; **~ая рабóта** work on the side. **3.** (*pl.*) left-wing; *as n.* **л., ~ого** *m.* left-winger; (*pl.*; *collect.*) the left.
легáв|ая, ой *f.* setter; pointer.
легализáци|я, и *f.* legalization.
легализ|и́ровать, и́рую = **~овáть**
легализ|овáть, у́ю *impf. and pf.* to legalize.
легáл|ьный (~ен, ~ьна) *adj.* legal.
легáто *mus.* **1.** *adv.* legato. **2.** *n.*; *nt. indecl.* slur.
легéнд|а, ы *f.* legend.
легендáр|ный (~ен, ~на) *adj.* legendary.
легиóн, а *m.* legion.
легионéр, а *m.* legionary.
легислату́р|а, ы *f.* term of office.
лёг|кий (~ок, ~кá, ~кó, *pl.* **~ки́** *or* **~ки)** *adj.* **1.** light (*in weight*). **2.** easy; **л. слог** simple style; **у негó л. харáктер** he is easy to get on with; **~кó сказáть!** easier said than done! **3.** light; slight; **~кая атлéтика** (*sport*) athletics; **~кая простýда** slight cold; **л. слу́чай (заболевáния)** mild case; **~кое чтéние** light reading; (*coll.*): **~ок на поми́не, вы ~ки́ на поми́не!** talk of the devil!; (*coll.*): **у негó ~кая рукá** he is lucky; **жéнщина лёгкого поведéния** woman of easy virtue.
легкó *adv.* easily, lightly, slightly; **э́то емý л. даётся** it comes easily to him; **л. коснýться** to touch lightly.
легкоатлéт, а *m.* athlete.
легковéри|е, я *nt.* credulity, gullibility.
легковéр|ный (~ен, ~на) *adj.* credulous, gullible.
легковéс, а *m.* (*sport*) light-weight.
легковéс|ный (~ен, ~на) *adj.* **1.** light-weight; light. **2.** (*fig., pej.*) superficial.
легковóй *adj.*: **л. автомоби́ль** (motor) car.
лёгк|ое, ого *nt.* lung.
легкомы́слен|ный (~, ~на) *adj.* thoughtless; flippant, frivolous; **л. постýпок** thoughtless action.
легкомы́сли|е, я *nt.* thoughtlessness; flippancy, frivolity.
лёгкост|ь, и *f.* **1.** lightness. **2.** ease.
лёгочный *adj.* (*med.*) pulmonary.
легчá|ть, ет *impf.* (*of* **по~**) **1.** to lessen, abate. **2.** (*impers.*, *+d.*) to feel better.
лéг|че *comp. of* **~́кий** *and* **~кó**; **больнóму л.** the invalid is feeling better; (*coll.*): **час óт часу не л.** things are getting worse by the minute; **л. на поворóтах!** mind what you say!
лёд, льда, о льдé, на льдý *m.* ice.
леденé|ть, ю *impf.* (*of* **за~** *and* **о~**) (*intrans.*) **1.** to freeze. **2.** to become numb with cold; (*fig.*): **кровь ~ет** (one's) blood runs cold.
леден|éц, цá *m.* fruit-drop.
леден|и́ть, и́т *impf.* (*of* **о~**) (*trans.*) to freeze; (*fig.*) to chill.
леден|я́щий *pres. part. of* **~и́ть** *and adj.* chilling, icy.
ледери́н, а *m.* leatherette.
лéди *f. indecl.* lady.
лéдник, а *m.* **1.** ice-house. **2.** ice-box.
ледни́к, á *m.* glacier.
ледникóвый *adj.* glacial; **л. периóд** ice age.
ледóв|ый *adj.* ice; **~ые плáвания** Arctic voyages; **~ое побóище** (*hist.*) Battle on the Ice.
ледокóл, а *m.* ice-breaker.
ледорýб, а *m.* ice-axe.
ледостáв, а *m.* freeze-up, freezing-over (*of river*).
ледохóд, а *m.* drifting of ice.
леды́шк|а, и *f.* (*coll.*) piece of ice.
лед|янóй *adj.* **1.** *adj. of* **~̈**; **~янáя горá** ice slope (*for tobogganing*). **2.** icy (*also fig.*); ice-cold.
лёжа *adv.* lying down, in lying position.
лежáлый *adj.* stale, old.
лежáнк|а, и *f.* stove-bench.
леж|áть, ý, и́шь *impf.* to lie; to be (situated); **л. в больни́це** to be in hospital; **л. больны́м** to be laid up; **врач велéл мне л.** the doctor told me to stay in bed; **л. на бокý, на печи́** (*fig., coll.*) to idle, loaf; **у меня́ душá не ~и́т (к)** I have no appetite (for).
лежáч|ий *adj.* lying, recumbent; **л. больнóй** bed-case.
лéжбищ|е, а *nt.* breeding ground; rookery.
лежебóк|а, и *c.g.* (*coll.*) loafer, lie-abed.
лежмя́ *adv.* (*coll.*): **лежáть л.** to lie without getting up; to lie helpless.
лéзви|е, я *nt.* blade.
лезги́нк|а, и *f.* lezginka (*Caucasian dance*).
лез|ть, у, ешь, *past* **~, ~́ла** *impf.* (*of* **по~**) **1.** (**на**+*a.*, **по**+*d.*) to climb (up, on to). **2.** (**в**+*a.*, **под**+*a.*) to clamber, crawl (through, into, under). **3.** to sneak. **4.** (**в**+*a.*) to reach (into). **5.** (**в**+*a.*) to fit, go (into). **6.** to fall out (*of hair, fur*); **л. нá стену** (*fig., coll.*) to hit the roof; **не л. в кармáн за слóвом** never to be at a loss for a word; **л. в пéтлю** (*coll.*) to stick one's neck out.
лейбори́ст, а *m.* (*pol.*) Labourite.
лейбори́стск|ий *adj.* (*pol.*) Labour; **~ая пáртия** Labour Party.
лéйк|а, и *f.* **1.** watering-can. **2.** (*naut.*) bail. **3.** funnel.
лейкеми́|я, и *f.* (*med.*) leukaemia.
лейкоплáстыр|ь, я *m.* sticking plaster.
лейкоци́т, а *m.* (*physiol.*) leucocyte.
лейтенáнт, а *m.* lieutenant.
лейтмоти́в, а *m.* (*mus. and fig.*) leitmotif.
лекáл|о, а *nt.* French curve.
лекáрственный *adj.* medicinal.
лекáрств|о, а *nt.* medicine.
лéкар|ь, я, *pl.* **~и, ~éй** *m.* (*obs. or pej.*) physician.
лéксик|а, и *f.* vocabulary; lexis.
лексикóграф, а *m.* lexicographer.
лексикографи́ческий *adj.* lexicographical.
лексикогрáфи|я, и *f.* lexicography.
лексикóлог, а *m.* lexicologist.
лексиколóги|я, и *f.* lexicology.
лекси́ческий *adj.* lexical.
лéктор, а *m.* lecturer.
лекциóнный *adj. of* **лéкция; л. зал** lecture-room.
лéкци|я, и *f.* lecture.
лелé|ять, ю *impf.* **1.** to coddle, pamper. **2.** (*fig.*) to cherish, foster; **л. мечтý** to cherish a hope.
лéмех, а (*and* **лемéх, á**) *m.* ploughshare.
лéмминг, а *m.* (*zool.*) lemming.
лемýр, а *m.* (*zool.*) lemur.
лён, льна *m.* (*bot.*) flax.
лени́в|ец, ца *m.* **1.** idler; sluggard. **2.** (*zool.*) sloth.
лени́в|ый (~, ~а) *adj.* lazy, idle; sluggish.
Ленингрáд, а *m.* Leningrad.
лéнин|ец, ца *m.* Leninist.
ленини́зм, а *m.* Leninism.
лéнинский *adj.* of Lenin; Leninist.
лен|и́ться, ю́сь, ~́ишься *impf.* **1.** to be lazy. **2.** (*+inf.*) to be too lazy (to).
лéност|ь, и *f.* laziness, idleness; sloth.
лéнт|а, ы *f.* ribbon, band; tape; film; **изоляциóнная л.** insulating tape; **патрóнная л.** cartridge belt; **ви́ться ~ой** to twist, meander.
лéнт|очный *adj. of* **~а; л. червь** tape-worm; **~очная пилá** band-saw; **л. транспортёр** conveyor belt.
лентя́|й, я *m.* idler, sluggard.
лентя́йнича|ть, ю *impf.* (*coll.*) to loaf, idle.
ленц|á, ы́ *f.* (*coll.*) disposition to laziness; **он с ~óй** he is inclined to be lazy.
лен|ь, и *f.* **1.** laziness. **2.** *as pred.* (*+d. and inf.*; *coll.*) to feel too lazy (to), not to feel like; **емý бы́ло л. вы́ключить рáдио** he was too lazy to turn the wire-

less off; **на́до бы пойти́, да л.** I ought to go, but I don't feel like it.
леопа́рд, а *m.* leopard.
лепест|о́к, ка́ *m.* petal.
ле́пет, а *m.* babble (*also fig.*); prattle.
лепе|та́ть, чу́, ~́чешь *impf.* to babble; to prattle.
лепёшк|а, и *f.* **1.** (flat) cake. **2.** (*medicinal*) tablet, lozenge.
леп|и́ть, лю́, ~́ишь *impf.* **1.** (*pf.* **вы́~** *and* **с~**) to model, fashion; to mould; **л. гнездо́** to build a nest. **2.** (*pf.* **на~**) (*coll.*) to stick (on).
леп|и́ться, лю́сь, ~́ишься *impf.* **1.** (**по**+*d.*) to cling (to).
ле́пк|а, и *f.* modelling.
лепн|о́й *adj.* modelled, moulded; **~о́е украше́ние** stucco moulding.
ле́пт|а, ы *f.* (small) contribution; **внести́ свою́ ~у** to do one's bit.
лес, а(у), *pl.* **~а́** *m.* **1. (в ~у́)** forest, wood(s); **вы́йти из ~́а (и́з ~у)** to come out of the wood; **тропи́ческий л.** rainforest; **быть как в ~у́** (*fig., coll.*) to be all at sea. **2. (в ~́е)** (*sg. only; collect.*) timber.
лес|а́[1] *pl. of* **~**
лес|а́[2], **о́в** scaffolding.
ле́са́[3], **ле́сы,** *pl.* **ле́сы, лес** *f.* fishing-line.
лесби́йск|ий *adj.* lesbian; **~ая любо́вь** lesbianism.
лесбия́нк|а, и *f.* lesbian.
ле́сенк|а, и *f.* (*coll.*) *dim. of* **ле́стница**; short flight of stairs; short ladder.
леси́ст|ый (~, ~а) *adj.* wooded.
лесни́к, а́ *m.* forester.
лесни́честв|о, а *nt.* forest area.
лесни́ч|ий, его *m.* forestry officer; forest warden.
лес|но́й *adj. of* **~**; **л. двор, склад** timber-yard; **~но́е де́ло** timber industry; **л. институ́т** forestry institute.
лесово́д, а *m.* forestry specialist.
лесово́дств|о, а *nt.* forestry.
лесозаво́д, а *m.* timber mill.
лесоматериа́л, а *m.* timber.
лесонасажде́ни|е, я *nt.* **1.** afforestation. **2.** (forest) plantation.
лесопа́рк, а *m.* forest park.
лесопи́лк|а, и *f.* saw-mill.
лесопи́льн|ый *adj.* sawing; **л. заво́д** saw-mill.
лесопромы́шленност|ь, и *f.* timber industry.
лесору́б, а *m.* woodcutter; lumberjack.
ле́стниц|а, ы *f.* stairs, staircase; ladder; **пожа́рная л.** fire-escape; **складна́я л.** step-ladder.
ле́стни|чный *adj. of* **~ца**; **~чная кле́тка** stairwell.
ле́ст|ный (~ен, ~на) *adj.* **1.** complimentary. **2.** flattering.
лест|ь, и *f.* flattery; adulation.
лёт, а, на ~у́, о ~́е *m.* flight, flying; **стреля́ть в пти́цу в л.** to shoot at a bird in flight; **на ~у́** in the air, on the wing; (*fig., coll.*) in passing; **хвата́ть на ~у́** to be quick to grasp.
Ле́т|а, ы *f.* (*myth.*): **ка́нуть в ~у** to sink into oblivion.
лет|а́, ~ *pl.* **1.** years; age; **ско́лько вам ~?** how old are you?; **с де́тских лет** from childhood; **мы одни́х лет** we are the same age; **сре́дних лет** middle-aged; **быть в ~а́х** to be getting on (in years); **на ста́рости ~** in one's old age. **2.** *g. pl.* (*as g. pl. of* **год**) years; **мно́го ~** many years. **3.** *pl. of* **ле́то.**
летарги́ческий *adj.* lethargic.
летарги́|я, и *f.* lethargy.
лета́тельн|ый *adj.* flying; **л. аппара́т** aircraft.
лет|а́ть, а́ю *indet. of* **~е́ть**
ле|те́ть, чу́, ти́шь *impf.* (*of* **по~**) **1.** to fly. **2.** (*fig.*) to fly; to rush, tear. **3.** (*fig., coll.*) to fall, drop (*intrans.*); **ли́стья ~тя́т** the leaves are falling; **а́кции ~тя́т вниз** shares are plummeting.
ле́тний *adj.* summer; **л. сад** pleasure garden(s).
лётн|ый *adj.* flying; **~ое по́ле** airfield; **л. соста́в** aircrew.
ле́т|о, а, *pl.* **~а́** *nt.* summer; **ба́бье л.** Indian summer; (*coll.*): **ско́лько ~, ско́лько зим** it's been ages!
ле́том *adv.* in summer.
летопи́с|ец, ца *m.* chronicler, annalist.
ле́топис|ь, и *f.* chronicle, annals.
летосчисле́ни|е, я *nt.* chronology.
лету́н, а́ *m.* **1.** flyer, flier. **2.** (*fig., coll.*) drifter; job-hopper.
лету́чест|ь, и *f.* (*chem.*) volatility.
лету́ч|ий *adj.* **1.** flying; **~ая мышь** bat. **2.** (*fig.*) fleeting, ephemeral; brief. **3.** (*chem.*) volatile.
лету́чк|а, и *f.* (*coll.*) **1.** leaflet. **2.** emergency meeting. **3.** mobile unit.
лётчик, а *m.* pilot; aviator, flyer; **л.-испыта́тель** test-pilot; **л.-истреби́тель** fighter pilot.
лече́бниц|а, ы *f.* clinic.
лече́бн|ый *adj.* **1.** medical. **2.** medicinal.
лече́ни|е, я *nt.* (medical) treatment.
леч|и́ть, у́, ~́ишь *impf.* to treat (*medically*); **его́ ~́ат от шо́ка** he is being treated for shock.
леч|и́ться, у́сь, ~́ишься *impf.* **1. (от)** to receive, undergo treatment (for). **2.** *pass. of* **~и́ть**
ле|чу́[1], **ти́шь** *see* **~те́ть**
леч|у́[2], **~́ишь** *see* **~и́ть**
лечь, ля́гу, ля́жешь, ля́гут, *past* **лёг, легла́,** *imper.* **ляг, ля́гте** *pf.* (*of* **ложи́ться**) **1.** to lie (down); **л. в больни́цу** to go (in) to hospital; **л. спать** to go to bed; **л. в осно́ву** (+*g.*) to underlie. **2. (на**+*a.*) to fall (on); (*fig.*): **отве́тственность ля́жет на вас** it will be your responsibility; **подозре́ние легло́ на иностра́нцев** suspicion fell upon the foreigners; **л. на со́весть** to weigh on one's conscience.
ле́ш|ий, его *m.* wood-goblin.
лещ, а́ *m.* (*fish*) bream.
лещи́н|а, ы *f.* (*bot.*) hazel.
лже... *comb. form* pseudo-, false-, mock-.
лжесвиде́тел|ь, я *m.* false witness; perjurer.
лжесвиде́тельств|о, а *nt.* false evidence; perjury.
лжесвиде́тельств|овать, ую *impf.* to give false evidence, commit perjury.
лжец, а́ *m.* liar.
лжёшь *see* **лгать**
лжи́вост|ь, и *f.* mendacity, falseness; untruthfulness.
лжи́в|ый (~, ~а) *adj.* lying; mendacious; false; untruthful.
ли (ль) 1. *interrog. particle* **возмо́жно ли?** is it possible?; **придёт ли он?** is he coming? **2.** *conj.* whether, if; **посмотри́, идёт ли по́езд** go and see if the train is coming. **3.: ли... ли** whether ... or; **сего́дня ли, за́втра ли** whether today or tomorrow.
либера́л, а *m.* liberal.
либерали́зм, а *m.* liberalism.
либера́льнича|ть, ю *impf.* (*of* **с~**) (**с**+*i.*; *coll., pej.*) to be too easy-going (with).
либера́л|ьный (~ен, ~ьна) *adj.* **1.** liberal. **2.** over-tolerant.
ли́бо *conj.* or; **л.... л.** (either) ... or.
либретти́ст, а *m.* librettist.
либре́тто *nt. indecl.* libretto.
Лива́н, а *m.* (the) Lebanon.
лива́н|ец, ца *m.* Lebanese.
лива́н|ка, ки *f. of* **~ец**
лива́нский *adj.* Lebanese.
ли́в|ень, ня *m.* heavy shower, downpour; cloud-burst.
ли́вер, а *m.* (*cul.*) pluck.
ли́вер|ный *adj. of* **~**[1]; **~ная колбаса́** liver sausage.
ливи́йский *adj.* Libyan.
Ли́ви|я, и *f.* Libya.
ливмя́ *adv.* (*coll.*): **л. лить** (*of rain*) to come down in torrents.
ливре́|я, и *f.* livery.
ли́г|а, и *f.* league.

лигату́р|а, ы *f.* (*ling. and med.*) ligature.
лигни́т, а *m.* (*min.*) lignite.
ли́дер, а *m.* leader.
ли́дерств|о, а *nt.* **1.** leadership. **2.** lead; **занима́ть л.** to be in the lead.
лиди́р|овать, ую *impf.* to lead, be in the lead.
ли|за́ть, жу́, ∠жешь *impf.* (*of* **∼зну́ть**) to lick; (*fig., coll.*): **л. ру́ки (но́ги, пя́тки) кому́-н.** to lick s.o.'s boots.
лиз|ну́ть, ну́, нёшь *inst. pf. of* **∼а́ть**
лизоблю́д, а *m.* (*coll., pej.*) lickspittle; bootlicker.
лик[1]**, а** *m.* **1.** (*obs.*) face. **2.** representation of face (*on icon*). **3.: л. луны́** face of the moon.
лик[2]**, а** *m.* (*eccl.*) assembly; **причи́слить к ∠у святы́х** to canonize.
ликвида́ци|я, и *f.* **1.** (*comm.*) liquidation. **2.** elimination, abolition.
ликвиди́р|овать, ую *impf. and pf.* **1.** (*comm.*) to liquidate, wind up. **2.** to eliminate, abolish.
ликви́дн|ый *adj.* (*fin.*) liquid; **∼ые сре́дства** liquid assets.
ликёр, а *m.* liqueur.
ликова́ни|е, я *nt.* rejoicing, jubilation, exultation.
лик|ова́ть, у́ю *impf.* to rejoice, exult.
лик|у́ющий *pres. part. of* **∼ова́ть** *and adj.* jubilant, exultant, triumphant.
лилипу́т, а *m.* Lilliputian.
ли́ли|я, и *f.* lily.
лилове́|ть, ю *impf.* (*of* **по∼**) to turn violet.
лило́вый *adj.* lilac, violet.
лима́н, а *m.* **1.** estuary. **2.** flood plain.
лими́т, а *m.* quota; limit.
лимити́р|овать, ую *impf. and pf.* (*comm.*) to limit.
лимо́н, а *m.* **1.** lemon. **2.** lemon-tree.
лимона́д, а *m.* **1.** lemonade; lemon squash. **2.** fruit squash.
лимо́нн|ый *adj.* lemon; **∼ая кислота́** (*chem.*) citric acid.
лимузи́н, а *m.* limousine.
ли́мф|а, ы *f.* (*physiol.*) lymph.
лимфати́ческий *adj.* (*physiol.*) lymphatic.
лингафо́нный *adj.*: **л. кабине́т** language laboratory.
лингви́ст, а *m.* linguist.
лингви́стик|а, и *f.* linguistics.
лингвисти́ческий *adj.* linguistic.
лине́йк|а, и *f.* **1.** (ruled) line (*on paper etc.*); **писа́ть по ∼ам** to write on the lines; **но́тные ∼и** (*mus.*) staves. **2.** ruler; **логарифми́ческая л.** slide-rule. **3.** line; parade.
лине́йн|ый *adj.* **1.** (*math.*) linear. **2.** (*mil., naut.*) of the line; **л. кора́бль** battleship.
ли́нз|а, ы *f.* lens.
ли́ни|я, и *f.* line; (*fig.*) policy; **по ∼и** (*+g.*) through; under the auspices of.
линко́р, а *m.* (*abbr. of* ***лине́йный кора́бль***) battleship.
лино́ваный *adj.* lined, ruled.
лин|ова́ть, у́ю *impf.* (*of* **на∼**) to rule.
лино́леум, а *m.* linoleum.
линч|ева́ть, у́ю *impf. and pf.* to lynch.
ли́ньк|а, и *f.* moult(ing).
линю́ч|ий (∼, ∼а) *adj.* (*coll.*) liable to fade.
линя́лый *adj.* (*coll.*) faded, discoloured.
линя́|ть, ет *impf.* **1.** (*pf.* **по∼**) to fade; (*of paint*) to run. **2.** (*pf.* **вы́∼**) (*of animals*) to shed hair; (*of birds*) to moult; (*of snakes*) to slough.
ли́п|а[1]**, ы** *f.* lime(-tree).
ли́п|а[2]**, ы** *f.* (*sl.*) forgery.
ли́п|ка, ки *f. dim. of* **∼а**[1]; (*coll.*): **ободра́ть как ∼ку** to fleece.
ли́п|кий (∼ок, ∼ка́, ∼ко) *adj.* sticky, adhesive; **л. пла́стырь** sticking plaster.
ли́п|нуть, ну, нешь, *past* **∼, ∼ла** *impf.* **(к)** to stick (to), adhere (to).
ли́п|овый[1] *adj. of* **∼а**[1]
ли́повый[2] *adj.* (*sl.*) sham, fake, forged.
ли́р|а[1]**, ы** *f.* lyre.
ли́р|а[2]**, ы** *f.* (*monetary unit*) lira.
лири́зм, а *m.* lyricism.
ли́рик, а *m.* lyric poet.
ли́рик|а, и *f.* lyric poetry; lyrics.
лири́ческ|ий *adj.* lyric; lyrical.
лис|а́, ы́, *pl.* **∠ы** *f.* fox; **черно-бу́рая л.** silver fox.
лис|ёнок, ёнка, *pl.* **∼я́та, ∼я́т** *m.* fox-cub.
ли́с|ий *adj. of* **∼а́**
лиси́ц|а, ы *f.* fox; vixen.
лиси́чк|а, и *f.* (*mushroom*) chanterelle.
Лиссабо́н, а *m.* Lisbon
лист[1]**, а́,** *pl.* **∠ья, ∠ьев** *m.* leaf (*of plant*).
лист[2]**, а́,** *pl.* **∼ы́, ∼о́в** *m.* **1.** leaf, sheet (*of paper, etc.*); (*metal*) plate; **в л.** in folio; **корректу́ра в ∼а́х** page-proofs; **игра́ть с ∼а́** (*mus.*) to play at sight. **2.: опро́сный л.** questionnaire; **охра́нный л.** safe-conduct.
листа́|ть, ю *impf.* (*coll.*) to leaf through.
листв|а́, ы́ *f.* (*collect.*) leaves, foliage.
ли́ственниц|а, ы *f.* (*bot.*) larch.
ли́ственный *adj.* (*bot.*) deciduous.
листо́вк|а, и *f.* leaflet.
лист|ово́й *adj. of* **∼; ∼ово́е желе́зо** sheet iron.
лист|о́к, ка́ *m.* **1.** *dim. of* **∼**[1]. **2.** sheet.
листопа́д, а *m.* (*autumn*) fall of the leaves.
лит... *comb. form, abbr. of* **литерату́рный**
лита́вр|ы, ∼ *pl.* (*sg.* **∼а, ∼ы** *f.*) kettledrum.
Литв|а́, ы́ *f.* Lithuania.
лите́йный *adj.* founding, casting.
лите́йщик, а *m.* founder, caster.
литера́тор, а *m.* man of letters.
литерату́р|а, ы *f.* literature.
литерату́р|ный (∼ен, ∼на) *adj.* literary.
литературове́д, а *m.* literary critic.
литературове́дени|е, я *nt.* literary criticism.
ли́ти|й, я *m.* (*chem.*) lithium.
лито́в|ец, ца *m.* Lithuanian.
лито́в|ка, ки *f. of* **∼ец**
лито́вский *adj.* Lithuanian.
лито́граф, а *m.* lithographer.
литографи́р|овать, ую *impf. and pf.* to lithograph.
литогра́фи|я, и *f.* **1.** lithograph. **2.** lithography.
литогра́фск|ий *adj.* lithographic.
лит|о́й *adj.* cast.
литр, а *m.* litre.
литро́вый *adj.* litre (*of one litre capacity*).
литурги́ческий *adj.* liturgical.
литурги́|я, и *f.* liturgy.
литфа́к, а *m.* (*abbr. of* **литерату́рный факульте́т**) literature department.
лить, лью, льёшь, *past* **лил, лила́, ли́ло,** *imper.* **лей** *impf.* **1.** to pour (*trans. and intrans.*); to shed, spill; **л. слёзы** to shed tears; **дождь льёт как из ведра́** it is raining cats and dogs; **л. во́ду на чью-н. ме́льницу** to play into s.o.'s hands. **2.** (*tech.*) to found, cast, mould.
лить|ё, я́ *no pl., nt.* (*tech.*) **1.** casting. **2.** (*collect.*) castings.
ли́|ться, льётся, *past* **∠лся, ∼ла́сь, ∠ло́сь** *impf.* **1.** to flow; to stream, pour. **2.** *pass. of* **∼ть**
лиф, а *m.* bodice.
лифт, а *m.* lift, elevator.
лифтёр, а *m.* lift operator.
ли́фчик, а *m.* **1.** brassière. **2.** (*child's*) bodice.
лиха́ч, а́ *m.* **1.** reckless driver; road-hog. **2.** daredevil.
лиха́честв|о, а *nt.* **1.** reckless driving. **2.** recklessness, daredevilry.
лихв|а́, ы́ *f.* interest; **отплати́ть с ∼о́й** to repay with interest.

ли́х|о[1], **а** *nt.* (*poet.*) evil, ill; **не помина́йте ~ом** (*coll.*) remember me (us) kindly; **узна́ть, почём фунт ~а** (*coll.*) to fall on hard times.
ли́х|о[2], **а** *adv. of* **~о́й**[2]; **л. заломи́ть ша́пку** to cock one's hat at a jaunty angle.
лих|о́й[1] **(~, ~á, ~о)** *adj.* (*dial. and folk poet.*) evil; **~á беда́ нача́ло** (*coll.*) the first step is the hardest.
лих|о́й[2] **(~, ~á, ~о)** *adj.* (*coll.*) dashing, spirited; jaunty.
лихора́|дить, жу, дишь *impf.* **1.** to have a fever. **2.** (*impers.*): **меня́ ~дит** I feel feverish.
лихора́дк|а, и *f.* fever (*also fig.*); **сенна́я л.** hay fever.
лихора́доч|ный (~ен, ~на) *adj.* feverish (*also fig.*).
ли́хост|ь, и *f.* (*coll.*) spirit, mettle; swagger.
ли́хтер, а *m.* (*naut.*) lighter.
лицев|о́й *adj.* **1.** (*anat.*) facial. **2.** exterior; **~áя сторона́** (*of building*) front; (*of material*) right side; (*of coin, etc.*) obverse. **3.: ~áя ру́копись** illuminated manuscript. **4.** (*book-keeping*): **л. счёт** personal account.
лицезр|е́ть, ю́, и́шь *impf.* (*obs. and iron.*) to behold with one's own eyes.
лице́|й, я *m.* lycée.
лице́й|ский *adj. of* **~**
лицеме́р, а *m.* hypocrite.
лицеме́ри|е, я *nt.* hypocrisy.
лицеме́р|ить, ю, ишь *impf.* to play the hypocrite.
лицеме́р|ный (~ен, ~на) *adj.* hypocritical.
лице́нзи|я, и *f.* (*econ.*) licence.
лиц|о́, á, *pl.* **~а** *nt.* **1.** face; **черты́ ~á** features; **сказа́ть в л. кому́-н.** to say to s.o.'s face; **знать кого́-н. в л.** to know s.o. by sight; **на нём ~á нет** he looks awful; **быть к ~у́** (*+d.*) to suit, become; (*fig.*) to become, befit; **~о́м к ~у́** face to face; **поста́вить ~о́м к ~у́** to confront; **они́ на одно́ л.** (*coll.*) they are as like as two peas; **ра́дость была́ напи́сана у неё на ~е́** joy was written all over her face; **показа́ть своё (настоя́щее) л.** to show one's true colours; **пе́ред ~о́м** (*+g.*) in the face (of); **(исче́знуть) с ~á земли́** (to vanish) from the face of the earth. **2.** exterior; (*of material*) right side; (*fig.*): **показа́ть това́р ~о́м** to show sth. to advantage; to make the best of sth. **3.** person; **гражда́нское л.** civilian; **де́йствующее л.** (*theatr., liter.*) character; **должностно́е л.** official; **духо́вное л.** clergyman; **в ~е́** (*+g.*) in the person (of); **невзира́я на ~а** without respect of persons; **от ~á** (*+g.*) on behalf (of). **4.** identity.
личи́н|а, ы *f.* mask; (*fig.*) guise; **под ~ой** (*+g.*) in the guise (of).
личи́нк|а[1], **и** *f.* larva, grub; maggot.
ли́чно *adv.* personally, in person.
личн|о́й *adj.* face; **~ой крем** face cream.
ли́чност|ь, и *f.* **1.** personality. **2.** person, individual; **тёмная л.** shady character; **удостовере́ние ~и** identity card; **установи́ть чью-н. л.** to establish s.o.'s identity. **3.** (*pl.*) personal remarks; **переходи́ть на ~и** to get personal, resort to personalities.
ли́чн|ый *adj.* personal, individual; private; **~ое местоиме́ние** (*gram.*) personal pronoun; **~ая охра́на** body-guard; **л. секрета́рь** private secretary; **~ая со́бственность** personal property; **л. соста́в** personnel, staff.
лиша́|й, я́ *m.* **1.** (*bot.*) lichen. **2.** (*med.*) herpes; **опоя́сывающий л.** shingles.
лиша́йник, а *m.* (*bot.*) lichen.
лиш|а́ть(ся), а́ю(сь) *impf. of* **~и́ть(ся)**
лише́ни|е, я *nt.* **1.** deprivation. **2.** privation, hardship.
лишён|ный (~, ~á, ~о́) *p.p.p. of* **лиши́ть** *and adj.* (*+g.*) lacking (in), devoid (of).
лиш|и́ть, у́, и́шь *pf.* (*of* **~а́ть**) (*+g.*) to deprive (of); **л. кого́-н. насле́дства** to disinherit s.o.; **л. себя́ жи́зни** to take one's (own) life.
лиш|и́ться, у́сь, и́шься *pf.* (*of* **~а́ться**) (*+g.*) to lose, be deprived (of); **л. зре́ния** to lose one's sight.
ли́шн|ий *adj.* **1.** superfluous; unnecessary; unwanted; **бы́ло бы не ~е** (*+inf.*) it would not be out of place. **2.** spare, odd; **л. раз** once more; **с ~им** (*coll.*) and more, odd; **со́рок фу́нтов с ~им** forty pounds odd.
лишь *adj. and conj. only*; **не хвата́ет л. одного́** one thing only is lacking; **л. то́лько** as soon as; **л. бы** as long as, provided that; **л. бы он мог прие́хать** provided that he can come.
лоб, лба, о лбе́, во (на) лбу́, *pl.* **лбы, лбов** *m.* forehead, brow; **стреля́ть в л.** to fire point-blank; **ата́ка в л.** frontal attack; **пусти́ть себе́ пу́лю в л.** to blow one's brains out; (*coll.*): **на лбу́ напи́сано** written all over one's face; **что в л., что по́ лбу** it comes to the same thing.
ло́бби *nt. indecl.* (*pol.*) lobby.
лобби́зм, а *m.* (*pol.*) lobbyism.
лобби́ст, а *m.* (*pol.*) lobbyist.
ло́бзик, а *m.* fret-saw.
ло́бн|ый *adj.* (*anat.*) frontal; **~ое ме́сто** (*hist.*) place of execution.
лобов|о́й *adj.* frontal, front; **~áя ата́ка** (*mil.*) frontal attack; **л. фона́рь** headlight.
лоботря́с, а *m.* (*coll.*) lazy-bones, idler.
лов, а *m.* **1.** = **~ля. 2.** = **уло́в**
ловела́с, а *m.* (*coll.*) ladies' man, lady-killer.
лов|е́ц, ца́ *m.* fisherman; hunter.
лов|и́ть, лю́, ~ишь *impf.* (*of* **пойма́ть**) to (try to) catch; (*fig.*) **л. ры́бу в му́тной воде́** to fish in troubled waters; **л. чей-н. взгляд** to try to catch s.o.'s eye; **л. (удо́бный) моме́нт, слу́чай** to seize an opportunity; **л. ка́ждое сло́во** to hang on every word; **л. себя́ на чём-н.** to catch o.s. at sth.; **л. кого́-н. на сло́ве** to take s.o. at his word; **л. ста́нцию** (*radio*) to try to pick up a station.
ловка́ч, á *m.* (*coll.*) dodger.
ло́в|кий (~ок, ~ка́, ~ко) *adj.* **1.** adroit, dexterous, deft. **2.** cunning, smart.
ло́вкост|ь, и *f.* **1.** adroitness, dexterity, deftness; **л. рук** sleight of hand. **2.** cunning, smartness.
ло́в|ля, ли *f.* catching; hunting, trapping; **ры́бная л.** fishing; **л. силка́ми** snaring.
лову́шк|а, и *f.* snare, trap.
ло́в|че (*and* **~че́е**) *comp. of* **~кий** *and* **~ко**
ло́вчий *adj.* **1.** hunting. **2.** serving as snare, trap.
лог, а, в ~е *or* **в ~у́,** *pl.* **~á, ~о́в** *m.* ravine.
логари́фм, а *m.* (*math.*) logarithm.
логарифми́ческ|ий *adj.* (*math.*) logarithmic; **~ая лине́йка** slide-rule.
ло́гик|а, и *f.* logic.
логи́ческий *adj.* logical.
логи́чност|ь, и *f.* logicality.
логи́ч|ный (~ен, ~на) *adj.* = **~еский**
ло́говищ|е, а *nt.* den, lair.
ло́гов|о, а *nt.* = **~ище**
логопе́д, а *m.* speech therapist.
логопе́ди|я, и *f.* speech therapy.
ло́дк|а, и *f.* boat; **подво́дная л.** submarine; **ката́ться на ~е** to go boating.
ло́дочк|а, и *f. dim. of* **ло́дка**
ло́дочник, а *m.* boatman.
ло́д|очный *adj. of* **~ка**
лоды́жк|а, и *f.* (*anat.*) ankle-bone.
ло́дырнича|ть, ю *impf.* (*coll.*) to loaf, idle.
ло́дыр|ь, я *m.* (*coll.*) loafer, idler.
ло́ж|а[1], **и** *f.* (*theatr.*) box.
ло́ж|а[2], **и** *f.* (gun-)stock.
ложби́н|а, ы *f.* (*geog.*) narrow, shallow gully.
ло́ж|е, а *nt.* bed (*of river*).
ло́жечк|а[1], **и** *f. dim. of* **ло́жка**

ло́жечк|а², и *f.*: **под ~ой** in the pit of the stomach.
лож|и́ться, у́сь, и́шься *impf. of* **лечь**
ло́жк|а, и *f.* **1.** spoon; **ча́йная л.** tea-spoon; **че́рез час по ча́йной ~е** (*fig.*) in dribs and drabs. **2.** spoonful; **л. дёгтя в бо́чке мёда** a fly in the ointment.
ложно... *comb. form* pseudo-.
ло́жност|ь, и *f.* falsity, error.
ло́ж|ный (~ен, ~на) *adj.* false, erroneous; sham, dummy; **~ная трево́га** false alarm.
ложь, лжи *f.* lie, falsehood.
лоз|а́, ы́, *pl.* **∸ы** *f.* **1.** rod; **«волше́бная л.»** dowsing rod. **2.** withe. **3.** vine.
лозня́к, а́ *m.* willow-bush.
лозоиска́тел|ь, я *m.* dowser, water diviner.
ло́зунг, а *m.* slogan, catchword; watch-word.
локализа́ци|я, и *f.* localization.
локализ|ова́ть, у́ю *impf. and pf.* to localize.
лока́льный *adj.* local.
лока́ут, а *m.* (*pol.*) lock-out.
локомоти́в, а *m.* locomotive.
ло́кон, а *m.* lock, curl, ringlet.
ло́к|оть, тя, *pl.* **~ти, ~те́й** *m.* elbow; **с про́дранными ~тя́ми** out at the elbow(s); **чу́вство ~тя** (*fig.*) feeling of comradeship; **бли́зок л., да не уку́сишь** (*prov.*) so near and yet so far.
локтев|о́й *adj.* (*anat.*): **~а́я кость** ulna; funny-bone.
лом, а, *pl.* **∸ы, ~о́в** *m.* **1.** crow-bar. **2.** (*sg. only*; *collect.*) scrap, waste; **желе́зный л.** scrap-iron.
лома́к|а, и *c.g.* (*coll.*) poseur.
ло́ман|ый *adj.* broken; **л. англи́йский язы́к** broken English.
лома́|ть, ю *impf.* (*of* **с~**) **1.** to break; to fracture. **2.** (*no pl.*) (*fig.*): **л. себе́ го́лову (над)** to rack one's brains (over); **л. ру́ки** to wring one's hands; **л. ша́пку (пе́ред)** to bow obsequiously (to). **3.** (*no pf.*): **л. ка́мень** to quarry stone. **4.** (*no pl.*; *of pain, sickness*) (*coll.*) to rack; to cause to ache; (*impers.*): **меня́ всего́ ~ло** I was aching all over.
лома́|ться, юсь *impf.* **1.** (*pf.* **с~**) to break (*intrans*). **2.** (*no pl.*) (*of voice*) to crack, break. **3.** (*pf.* **по~**) (*coll.*) to put on airs.
ломба́рд, а *m.* pawn-shop; **заложи́ть в л.** to pawn.
ломба́рд|ный *adj. of* **~; ~ная квита́нция** pawn ticket.
ло́мберный *adj.*: **л. стол** card-table.
лом|и́ть, лю́, ∸ишь *impf.* (*coll.*) **1.** to break. **2.** to break through. **3.** (*impers.*) to cause to ache; **у меня́ ∸ит спи́ну** my back aches.
лом|и́ться, лю́сь, ∸ишься *impf.* **1.** to be (near to) breaking; **(от)** to burst (with), be crammed (with); **ве́тви ~ятся от плодо́в** the boughs are groaning with fruit. **2.** (*coll.*) to force one's way; **л. в откры́тую дверь** (*fig.*) to force an open door.
ло́мк|а, и *f.* breaking (*also fig.*).
ло́м|кий (~ок, ~ка́, ~ко) *adj.* fragile, brittle.
ломови́к, а́ *m.* drayman, carter.
ломов|о́й *adj.* dray, draught; **л. изво́зчик = ломови́к; ~а́я ло́шадь** cart-horse; **~а́я подво́да** dray; *as n.* **л., ~о́го** *m.* **= ломови́к**
ломоно́с, а *m.* (*bot.*) clematis.
ломо́т|а, ы *f.* (*coll.*) ache.
лом|о́ть, тя́, *pl.* **~ти́, ~те́й** *m.* hunk; chunk.
ло́мтик, а *m.* slice; **ре́зать ~ами** to slice.
Ло́ндон, а *m.* London.
ло́ндон|ец, ца *m.* Londoner.
ло́ндон|ка, ки *f. of* **~ец**
ло́ндонский *adj.* London.
лонжеро́н, а *m.* (*aeron.*) spar.
ло́н|о, а *no pl., nt.* (*obs.*) bosom, lap; **на ~е приро́ды** in the bosom of nature.
ло́паст|ь, и, *pl.* **~и, ~е́й** *f.* blade; vane (*of propeller, etc.*); (wheel) paddle.
лопа́т|а, ы *f.* spade; shovel.
лопа́тк|а, и *f.* **1.** shovel; trowel, scoop; (*cul.*) spatula; blade (*of turbine*). **2.** (*anat.*) shoulder-blade; (*part of joint of meat*) shoulder; **положи́ть на о́бе лопа́тки** to throw (*in wrestling*); (*fig.*) to best, get the better of; **бежа́ть во все ~и** (*coll.*) to run for all one's worth.
ло́па|ть, ю *impf.* (*of* **с~**) (*coll.*) to eat; to gobble (up).
ло́п|аться, аюсь *impf. of* **~нуть**
ло́п|нуть, ну, нешь *pf.* (*of* **~аться**) **1.** to break, burst; to split, crack; **чуть не л. от сме́ха** to split one's sides with laughter; (*fig.*): **у меня́ терпе́ние ~нуло** my patience is exhausted. **2.** (*fig., coll.*) to fail, be a failure; (*fin.*) to go bankrupt, crash.
лопо|та́ть, чу́, ∸чешь *impf.* (*coll.*) to mutter, mumble.
лопоу́х|ий (~, ~а) *adj.* lop-eared.
лопу́х, а́ *m.* (*bot.*) burdock.
лорд, а *m.* lord; **пала́та ∸ов** House of Lords.
лорне́т, а *m.* lorgnette.
лоси́н|а, ы *f.* **1.** elk-skin. **2.** (*pl.*; *hist.*) buckskin breeches. **3.** (*meat*) elk.
лос|и́ный *adj. of* **~ь**
лоск, а *m.* lustre, gloss, shine (*also fig.*).
лоску́т, а́, *pl.* **~ы́, ~о́в** *and* **~ья, ~ьев** *m.* rag, shred, scrap.
лоску́тн|ый *adj.* **1.** scrappy. **2.** made of scraps; **~ое одея́ло** patchwork quilt.
лосн|и́ться, ю́сь, и́шься *impf.* to be glossy, shine.
лососи́н|а, ы *f.* salmon (flesh).
ло́сос|ь, я, *pl.* **ло́соси, ло́сосей** *m.* salmon.
лос|ь, я, *pl.* **∸и, ~е́й** *m.* elk; moose.
лосьо́н, а *m.* lotion; aftershave.
лот, а *m.* (*naut.*) (sounding-)lead, plummet.
лотере́|йный *adj. of* **~я; л. биле́т** lottery-ticket.
лотере́|я, и *f.* lottery, raffle.
лото́ *nt. indecl.* lotto; bingo.
лот|о́к, ка́ *m.* **1.** tray. **2.** chute; **ме́льничный л.** mill-race.
ло́тос, а *m.* (*bot.*) lotus.
лото́чник, а *m.* hawker.
леха́нк|а, и *f.* **= моха́нь**
лоха́н|ь, и *f.* (wash-)tub.
лохма́т|ый (~, ~а) *adj.* **1.** shaggy(-haired). **2.** dishevelled.
лохмо́ть|я, ев *no sg.* rags, tatters.
ло́ци|я, и *f.* (*naut.*) sailing directions.
ло́цман, а *m.* **1.** (*naut.*) pilot. **2.** pilot-fish.
лошади́н|ый *adj.* of horses; equine; **~ая си́ла** horse-power.
лоша́дк|а, и *f. dim. of* **ло́шадь**
ло́шад|ь, и, *pl.* **~и, ~е́й, ~я́м, ~ьми́, ~я́х** *f.* horse; **бегова́я, скакова́я л.** race-horse; **вью́чная л.** pack-horse; **чистокро́вная л.** thoroughbred; **сади́ться на л.** to mount; **ходи́ть за ~ью** to groom a horse.
лоша́к, а́ *m.* hinny.
лощён|ый *adj.* glossy; (*fig.*) polished.
лощи́н|а, ы *f.* (*geog.*) hollow, depression.
лощ|и́ть, у́, и́шь *impf.* (*of* **на~**) to polish, buff.
лоя́льност|ь, и *f.* loyalty.
лоя́л|ьный (~ен, ~ьна) *adj.* loyal.
луб, а, *pl.* **∸ья, ∸ьев** *m.* (*bot.*) (lime) bast.
луб|о́к¹, ка́ *m.* **1.** (*med.*) splint. **2.** strip of bast.
луб|о́к², ка́ *m.* popular print.
луг, а, о ∸е, на ~у́, *pl.* **~а́, ~о́в** *m.* meadow.
луди́льщик, а *m.* tinsmith, tinman.
лу|ди́ть, жу́, ∸дишь *impf.* (*of* **по~**) (*tech.*) to tin.
лу́ж|а, и *f.* puddle, pool; **сесть в ~у** (*fig., coll.*) to get into a mess; to slip up.
лужа́йк|а, и *f.* (forest)glade; lawn; **л. для игры́ в шары́** bowling green.
лужён|ый *adj.* tinned, tin-plate(d).

луж|óк, кá *m. dim. of* **луг**
лу́з|а, ы *f.* (billiard-)pocket.
лук[1], **а** *m.* (*collect.*) onions; **голóвка ∠а** (*a single*) onion; **зелёный л.** spring onions; **л.-порéй** leek.
лук[2], **а** *m.* bow; **натянýть л.** to bend, draw a bow.
лук|á, и́, *pl.* **∠и** *f.* **1.** bend (*of river, road, etc.*). **2.** pommel (*of saddle*).
лукáв|ец, ца *m.* (*coll.*) crafty person; (*joc.*) slyboots.
лукáв|ить, лю, ишь *impf.* (*of* **с~**) to be cunning.
лукáвств|о, а *nt.* craftiness, guile.
лукáв|ый (~, ~а) *adj.* crafty, cunning.
лу́ковиц|а, ы *f.* **1.** an onion. **2.** (*bot.*) bulb. **3.** 'onion' dome.
лу́кови|чный *adj. of* **~ца**; bulbous.
лукомóрь|е, я *nt.* (*poet.*) cove, creek.
лукóш|ко, ка, *pl.* **~ки, ~ек** *nt.* basket; punnet.
лун|á, ы́, *pl.* **∠ы** *f.* moon; the Moon.
лу́на-пáрк, а *m.* funfair.
лунати́зм, а *m.* sleep-walking, somnambulism.
лунáтик, а *m.* sleep-walker, somnambulist.
лунати́ческий *adj.* somnambulistic.
лу́нк|а, и *f.* hole; (*anat.*) alveolus, socket.
лу́нник, а *m.* lunar probe.
лу́н|ный *adj. of* **~á**; (*astron.*) lunar; **~ное затмéние** lunar eclipse; **л. свет** moonlight.
лунохóд, а *m.* lunar rover, Moon buggy.
лун|ь, я́ *m.* (*zool.*) harrier; **седóй, бéлый, как л.** white as snow (*of hair*).
лу́п|а, ы *f.* magnifying glass.
луп|и́ть[1], **лю́, ∠ишь** *impf.* **1.** (*pf.* **об~**) to peel; to bark. **2.** (*pf.* **с~**) (*coll.*) to fleece; to take to the cleaners.
луп|и́ть[2], **лю́, ∠ишь** *impf.* (*of* **от~**) (*coll.*) to thrash, flog.
луп|и́ться, ∠ится *impf.* (*of* **об~**) to peel (off); (*coll.*) to come off (*of paint, plaster, etc*).
луч, á *m.* ray; beam; **рентгéновы ~и́** X-rays; **л. надéжды** (*fig.*) ray of hope.
луч|евóй *adj.* **1.** *adj. of* **~**. **2.** radial. **3.** (*med.*): **~евáя болéзнь** radiation sickness.
лучезáр|ный (~ен, ~на) *adj.* (*poet.*) radiant, resplendent.
лучи́н|а, ы *f.* splinter, chip (*of kindling wood; also collect.*).
лучи́ст|ый (~, ~а) *adj.* radiant.
луч|и́ться, и́тся *impf.* (*poet.*) to shine brightly, sparkle.
лучкóв|ый *adj.* bow-shaped; **~ая пилá** frame-saw.
лу́чник, а *m.* (*hist.*) archer.
лу́чше *adj. and adv.* (*comp. of* **хорóший** *and* **хорошó**) better; **тем л.** so much the better; **л. всегó, л. всех** best of all; **как мóжно л.** as well as possible; *as pred.* it is better; **л. ли вам сегóдня?** are you better today?; **л. не спрáшивай** better not ask; **нам л. вернýться** we had better go back.
лу́чш|ий *adj.* (*comp. and superl. of* **хорóший**) better; best; **к ~ему** for the better; **в ~ем слу́чае** at best; **всегó ~его!** all the best!
лущ|и́ть, у́, и́шь *impf.* (*pf.* **об~**) to shell, hull; to pod (*peas, etc.*).
лы́ж|а, и *f.* ski; **ходи́ть на ~ах** to ski.
лы́жник, а *m.* skier.
лы́ж|ный *adj. of* **~а; л. спуск** ski-run.
лыжн|я́, и́ *f.* ski-track.
лы́к|о, а, *pl.* **~и** *nt.* bast; **я не ~ом шит** I was not born yesterday.
лысé|ть, ю *impf.* (*of* **об~** *and* **по~**) to grow bald.
лы́син|а, ы *f.* bald spot, bald patch.
лысу́х|а, и *f.* (*zool.*) coot.
лы́с|ый (~, ~á, ~о) *adj.* bald.
ль = ли
льв|ёнок, ёнка, *pl.* **~я́та, ~я́т** *m.* lion cub.
льви́н|ый *adj. of* **лев**[1]; **~ая дóля** (*fig.*) the lion's share; (*bot.*): **л. зев, ~ая пасть** snap-dragon.
льви́ц|а, ы *f.* lioness.
льв|я́та *see* **~ёнок**
льгóт|а, ы *f.* privilege; advantage.
льгóтн|ый *adj.* privileged; favourable; **л. билéт** concessionary ticket; **~ые дни** (*comm.*) days of grace; **на ~ых услóвиях** on preferential terms.
льда *g. sg. of* **лёд**
льди́н|а, ы *f.* block of ice; ice-floe.
льна, льну *see* **лён**
льнуть, льну, льнёшь *impf.* (*of* **при~**) **(к) 1.** to cling (to), stick (to). **2.** (*fig., coll.*) to have a weakness (for). **3.** (*fig., coll.*) to make up (to), (*sl.*) try to get in (with).
льнян|óй *adj.* **1.** flax; **~óе мáсло** linseed-oil; **~óго цвéта** flaxen. **2.** linen; **~áя промы́шленность** linen industry.
льстец, á *m.* flatterer.
льсти́в|ый (~, ~а) *adj.* flattering; (*of a pers.*) smooth-tongued.
льстить, льщу, льстишь *impf.* (*of* **по∠**) **1.** (*+d.*) to flatter. **2.** (*+a., with refl. pron. only*) to delude; **л. себя́ надéждой** to live in hope.
лью, льёшь *see* **лить**
любвеоби́л|ьный (~ен, ~ьна) *adj.* loving; full of love.
любéзнича|ть, ю *impf.* **(с**+*i.*) (*coll.*) to pay compliments (to).
любéзност|ь, и *f.* **1.** courtesy; politeness, civility. **2.** kindness; **оказáть, сдéлать комý-н. л.** to do s.o. a kindness. **3.** compliment; **говори́ть ~и комý-н.** to pay s.o. compliments.
любéз|ный (~ен, ~на) *adj.* **1.** courteous; polite; obliging. **2.** kind, amiable; **л. читáтель** gentle reader; **бу́дьте ~ны...** be so kind as ...
люби́м|ец, ца *m.* favourite, darling.
люби́мчик, а *m.* (*pej.*) pet, blue-eyed boy.
люби́м|ый (~, ~а) *adj.* **1.** beloved. **2.** favourite.
люби́тел|ь, я *m.* **1.** (*+g. or +inf.*) lover; **л. му́зыки** music-lover; **л. собáк** dog-fancier. **2.** amateur.
люби́тельский *adj.* amateur; **л. спектáкль** amateur performance.
люби́тельств|о, а *nt.* amateurishness.
люб|и́ть, лю́, ∠ишь *impf.* **1.** to love. **2.** to like, be fond (of).
люб|овáться, у́юсь *impf.* (*of* **по~**) (*+i.*, **на**+*a.*) to admire; **л. на себя́ в зéркало** to admire o.s. in the mirror.
любóвник, а *m.* lover.
любóвниц|а, ы *f.* lover; mistress.
любóвн|ый *adj.* **1.** love-; **~ое письмó** love-letter. **2.** loving.
люб|óвь, ви́, *i.* **~óвью** *f.* **(к)** love (for, of).
любознáтел|ьный (~ен, ~ьна) *adj.* inquisitive.
любóй 1. *adj.* any; either (*of two*); **л. ценóй** at any price. **2.** *as n.* anyone.
любопы́т|ный (~ен, ~на) *adj.* curious; interesting; (*impers.*; *+d. and inf.*): **~но знать, что с ним стáло** it would be interesting to know what became of him; **~но, придёт ли онá?** I wonder if she will come?
любопы́тств|о, а *nt.* curiosity.
любопы́тств|овать, ую *impf.* (*of* **по~**) to be curious.
лю́б|ящий *pres. part. act. of* **~и́ть** *and adj.* loving, affectionate; **л. Вас** (*in letters*) yours affectionately.
люд, а *m.* (*collect.; coll.*) people.
лю́д|и, éй, ∠ям, ~ьми́, о ∠ях *no sg.* (*pl. of* **человéк**) people; **вы́биться, вы́йти в л.** to get on (in life); **вы́вести когó-н. в л.** to put s.o. on his feet; **уйти́ в л.** to go out into the world; **на ~ях** in company.
лю́д|ный (~ен, ~на) *adj.* **1.** populous. **2.** crowded.
людоéд, а *m.* cannibal; **тигр-л.** man-eating tiger.
людоéдств|о, а *nt.* cannibalism.

людск|о́й *adj.* **1.** human. **2.** (*mil.*): **л. соста́в** personnel, effectives.
люк, а *m.* **1.** (*naut.*) hatch, hatchway; manhole. **2.** (*theatr.*) trap. **3.: светово́й л.** sky-light.
люкс *adj. indecl.* de luxe, luxury.
лю́льк|а, и *f.* cradle.
люмба́го *nt. indecl.* lumbago.
люминесце́нтн|ый *adj.* luminescent; **~ая ла́мпа** fluorescent lamp.
люминесце́нци|я, и *f.* (*phys.*) luminescence.
лю́стр|а, ы *f.* chandelier.
лютера́н|ин, ина, *pl.* **~е, ~** *m.* (*relig.*) Lutheran.
лютера́нский *adj.* (*relig.*) Lutheran.
лютера́нств|о, а *nt.* (*relig.*) Lutheranism.
лю́тик, а *m.* (*bot.*) buttercup.
лю́т|ня, ни, *g. pl.* **~ен** *f.* (*mus.*) lute.
лю́т|ый (~, ~а́, ~о) *adj.* ferocious, fierce, cruel (*also fig.*).
люце́рн|а, ы *f.* (*bot.*) lucerne.
ля *nt. indecl.* (*mus.*) A; **ля бемо́ль** A flat.
ляг(те) *imper. of* **лечь**
ляг|а́ть, а́ю *impf.* (*of* **~ну́ть**) to kick.
ляга́|ться, юсь *impf.* to kick (*intrans*); to kick one another.
ляг|ну́ть, ну́, нёшь *inst. pf. of* **~а́ть**
ля́|гу, жешь, гут *see* **лечь**
лягуш|а́чий (*and* **~ечий**) *adj. of* **~ка**
лягу́шк|а, и *f.* frog.
ля́жк|а, и *f.* thigh, haunch.
лязг, а *no pl., m.* clank, clang.
ля́зга|ть, ю *impf.* (+*i.*) to clank, clang; **он ~л зуба́ми** his teeth were chattering; **л. це́пью** to rattle a chain.
ля́мк|а, и *f.* strap; **тяну́ть ~у** (*fig., coll.*) to toil, sweat.
ляп, а *m.* (*coll.*) blunder, gaffe.
ля́п|ать, аю *impf.* (*coll.*) **1.** (*pf.* **на~**) to make hastily *or* any old how. **2.** *impf. of* **~нуть**
ля́пис-лазу́р|ь, и *f.* lapis lazuli.
ля́п|нуть, ну, нешь *pf.* (*of* **~ать**) (*coll.*) to blurt out.
ля́псус, а *m.* blunder; slip (*of tongue, pen*).

M

М *abbr. of* **1. метро́** Metro, Underground. **2. Мужска́я (убо́рная)** Gents, Gentlemen (*lavatory*).
М. (*abbr. of* **Москва́**) Moscow.
м (*abbr. of* **метр**) m, metre(s).
м. (*abbr. of* **мину́та**) min., minute(s).
мавзоле́|й, я *m.* mausoleum.
мавр, а *m.* Moor.
маврита́нский *adj.* Moorish.
маг[1], **а** *m.* magician, wizard.
магази́н, а *m.* **1.** shop; **гастрономи́ческий м.** grocer's (shop); **универса́льный м.** department store. **2.** (*in fire-arm*) magazine.
магази́н|ный *adj. of* **~**; **м. вор** shoplifter; **~ная коро́бка** magazine (*of fire-arm*).
магара́дж|а, и *m.* Maharaja(h).
маги́ст|ерский *adj. of* **~р 3.**
магист|е́рский *adj. of* **~р 1., 2.**
маги́стр, а *m.* **1.** holder of a master's degree. **2.** master's degree.
магистра́л|ь, и *f.* main; main line; **га́зовая м.** gas main; **железнодоро́жная м.** main (railway) line.
магистра́ль|ный *adj. of* **~**
магистра́т, а *m.* city, town council.
магистрату́р|а, ы *f.* magistracy.
маги́ческий *adj.* magic(al).
ма́ги|я, и *f.* magic.
магна́т, а *m.* magnate, tycoon.
магне́зи|я, и *f.* (*chem.*) magnesia.
магнети́зм, а *m.* **1.** magnetism. **2.** (*phys.*) magnetics.
магнети́т, а *m.* (*min.*) magnetite.
магнети́ческий *adj.* magnetic.
магне́то *nt. indecl.* (*tech.*) magneto.
магнетро́н, а *m.* magnetron.
ма́гниевый *adj.* magnesium.
ма́гни|й, я *m.* (*chem.*) magnesium.
магни́т, а *m.* magnet.
магни́тный *adj.* magnetic; **м. железня́к** magnetite.
магнито́л|а, ы *f.* radio cassette (player).
магнитофо́н, а *m.* tape-recorder.
магнитофо́н|ный *adj. of* **~**; **~ная за́пись** tape-recording.
магнито-электри́ческий *adj.* electromagnetic.
магно́ли|я, и *f.* (*bot.*) magnolia.
магомета́н|ин, ина, *pl.* **~е, ~** *m.* Mohammedan.
магомета́нств|о, а *nt.* Mohammedanism.
мада́м *f. indecl.* madam(e).
мадемуазе́л|ь, и *f.* mademoiselle.
маде́р|а, ы *f.* Madeira (wine).
мадо́нн|а, ы *f.* madonna.
мадрига́л, а *m.* madrigal.
Мадри́д, а *m.* Madrid.
мадья́р, а, *pl.* **~ы, ~** *m.* Magyar.
мадья́рский *adj.* Magyar.
мает|а́, ы́ *f.* (*coll.*) trouble, bother.
мажо́р, а *m.* **1.** (*mus.*) major key. **2.** (*fig.*) a cheerful mood; **быть в ~е** to be in high spirits.
мажордо́м, а *m.* major-domo.
мажо́рный *adj.* **1.** (*mus.*) major. **2.** (*fig.*) cheerful.
ма́|зать, жу, жешь *impf.* **1.** (*pf.* **на~, по~**) to oil, grease, lubricate. **2.** (*pf.* **вы́~, на~, по~**) to smear (with), anoint (with); **м. хлеб ма́слом** to butter bread. **3.** (*pf.* **за~, из~**; *coll.*) to soil, stain. **4.** (*pf.* **на~**; *coll.*) to daub. **5.** (*pf.* **про~**[2]; *coll.*) to miss (*target*).
ма́|заться, жусь, жешься *impf.* **1.** (*pf.* **вы́~, за~, из~**) to soil o.s., stain o.s. **2.** (*coll.*) to soil, stain (*of objects; intrans.*). **3.** (*pf.* **на~, по~**) to make up; **она́ си́льно ~жется** (*coll.*) she makes up heavily.
мазн|я́, и́ *f.* (*coll.*) poor painting, daub.
маз|о́к, ка́ *m.* **1.** dab; stroke (*of paint-brush*); **класть после́дние ~ки́** (*fig.*) to put the finishing touches. **2.** (*med.*) smear (*for microscopic examination*). **3.** (*coll.*) miss.
мазохи́зм, а *m.* (*med.*) masochism.
мазохи́ст, а *m.* masochist.
мазу́рк|а, и *f.* mazurka.
мазу́т, а *m.* (*tech.*) fuel oil
маз|ь, и *f.* **1.** ointment. **2.** grease; **де́ло на ~и́** (*fig., coll.*) things are going swimmingly.
маис, а *m.* maize.
ма|й, я *m.* May.
ма́йк|а, и *f.* T-shirt.
майоне́з, а *m.* (*cul.*) mayonnaise.
майо́р, а *m.* major.
майора́н, а *m.* (*bot.*) marjoram.
майо́р|ский *adj. of* **~**
ма́й|ский *adj. of* **~**; **м. жук** may-bug, cockchafer.
ма́йя *c.g. indecl. and adj. indecl.* Maya.
мак, а *m.* **1.** poppy. **2.** (*collect.*) poppy-seed.
мака́к|а, и *f.* (*zool.*) macaque.
мака́о *m. indecl.* (*zool.*) macaw.
макаро́н|ы, ~ *pl.* macaroni.

мак|áть, áю *impf.* (*of* **~нýть**) to dip.
македóн|ец, ца *m.* Macedonian.
Македóни|я, и *f.* Macedonia.
македóн|ка, ки *f. of* **~ец**
македóнский *adj.* Macedonian; **Алексáндр ~** Alexander the Great.
макéт, а *m.* **1.** model. **2.** dummy.
макинтóш, а *m.* mackintosh.
мáклер, а *m.* (*comm.*) (stock)broker.
мáклерств|о, а *nt.* (*comm.*) brokerage.
мак|нýть, нý, нёшь *pf. of* **~áть**
мáковк|а, и *f.* **1.** poppy-head. **2.** (*coll.*) crown (*of head*). **3.** (*coll.*) cupola, dome.
мáк|овый *adj. of* **~**
макрéл|ь, и *f.* mackerel.
макрокомáнд|а, ы *f.* (*comput.*) macro.
макрокóсм, а *m.* macrocosm.
максимáльный *adj.* maximum.
мáксимум, а *m.* **1.** maximum. **2.** *as adv.* at most; **м. сто рублéй** a hundred roubles at most.
макулатýр|а, ы *f.* **1.** (*typ.*) spoilage. **2.** (*fig.*) pulp literature.
макýшк|а, и *f.* **1.** top, summit. **2.** crown (*of head*); **у нас ýшки на ~е** (*fig.*) we are on our guard.
малá|ец, йца *m.* Malay.
Малáйзи|я, и *f.* Malaysia.
малá|йка, йки *f. of* **~ец**
малáйский *adj.* Malay, Malayan.
малахи́т, а *m.* (*min.*) malachite.
мал|евáть, ю́ю, ю́ешь *impf.* (*of* **на~**) (*coll.*) to paint.
малéйший *adj.* (*superl. of* **мáлый**) least, slightest.
мал|ёк, ькá *m.* young fish; (*collect.*) fry.
мáленьк|ий *adj.* **1.** little, small; **~ие лю́ди** humble folk; **идти́ по ~ому** (*baby talk*) to do a wee-wee. **2.** slight; diminutive **3.** young; *as n.* **м., ~ого** *m.*, **~ая, ~ой** *f.* the baby, the little one.
малéнько *adv.* (*coll.*) a little, a bit.
мали́н|а, ы *no pl.*, *f.* **1.** (*collect.*) raspberries. **2.** raspberry-bush; raspberry-cane.
мали́новк|а, и *f.* (*zool.*) robin (redbreast).
мали́новый *adj.* **1.** raspberry. **2.** crimson.
мáло *adv.* little; few; not enough; **у нас м. врéмени** we don't have much time; **э́того мáло** this is not enough; **об э́том м. кто знáет** few people know about it; **я м. где бывáл** I have been hardly anwhere; **м. ли что!** what does it matter!; **м. ли что мóжет случи́ться** anything may happen; **м. тогó** moreover; **м. тогó, что...** not only ...; it is not enough that ...
маловáж|ный (~ен, ~на) *adj.* insignificant.
маловáт (~а, ~о) *adj.* (*coll.*) on the small side; **м. рóстом** undersized.
маловáто *adv.* (*coll.*) not quite enough; not very much.
маловéр, а *m.* sceptic.
маловероя́т|ный (~ен, ~на) *adj.* unlikely, improbable.
маловóдный *adj.* shallow; arid, dry (*of land*).
маловóдь|е, я *nt.* **1.** shortage of water. **2.** low water-level, shallowness.
маловы́год|ный (~ен, ~на) *adj.* unprofitable, unrewarding.
малогрáмот|ный (~ен, ~на) *adj.* **1.** semiliterate. **2.** crude, ignorant.
малодохóд|ный (~ен, ~на) *adj.* unprofitable.
малодýши|е, я *nt.* faint-heartedness.
малодýш|ный (~ен, ~на) *adj.* faint-hearted.
маложи́р|ный (~ен, ~нá, ~но) *adj.* low-fat.
малозамéт|ный (~ен, ~на) *adj.* **1.** barely visible, barely noticeable. **2.** ordinary, undistinguished.
малознакóм|ый (~, ~а) *adj.* little-known, unfamiliar.
малозначи́тел|ьный (~ен, ~ьна) *adj.* insignificant.
малоимýщ|ий (~, ~а) *adj.* needy, indigent.
малокали́берный *adj.* small-calibre; (*of fire-arm*) small-bore.
малокалори́йный *adj.* low-calorie.
малокрóви|е, я *nt.* anaemia.
малокрóв|ный (~ен, ~на) *adj.* anaemic.
малолéтн|ий *adj.* **1.** young; juvenile. **2.** *as n.* **м., ~его** *m.* infant; juvenile, minor.
малолéтств|о, а *nt.* infancy; minority.
малолитрáжк|а, и *f.* (*coll.*) compact (car); mini.
малолитрáжный *adj.* of small (*cylinder*) capacity; **м. автомоби́ль** compact (car); mini.
малолю́д|ный (~ен, ~на) *adj.* **1.** uncrowded; **~ное собрáние** poorly attended meeting. **2.** thinly, sparsely populated.
мало-мáльски *adv.* (*coll.*) in the slightest degree, at all.
малометрáжн|ый *adj.*: **~ая кварти́ра** small flat.
маломóщный *adj.* low-power(ed).
малонадёжный *adj.* unreliable.
малонаселённый *adj.* thinly, sparsely populated.
малоплáчиваемый *adj.* low-paid (*of work*).
мало-помáлу *adv.* (*coll.*) little by little, bit by bit.
малопоня́т|ный (~ен, ~на) *adj.* hard to understand; obscure.
малопри́был|ьный (~ен, ~ьна) *adj.* barely profitable.
малорáзвит|ый (~, ~а) *adj.* **1.** undeveloped. **2.** underdeveloped. **3.** uneducated.
малоразговóрчив|ый (~, ~а) *adj.* taciturn.
малорóсл|ый (~, ~а) *adj.* undersized, stunted.
малосвéдущ|ий (~, ~а) *adj.* ill-informed.
малосемéйный *adj.* having a small family.
малоси́л|ьный (~ен, ~ьна) *adj.* **1.** weak, feeble. **2.** (*tech.*) low-powered.
малосодержáтел|ьный (~ен, ~ьна) *adj.* uninteresting; (*fig.*) empty, shallow.
малосóл|ьный (~ен, ~ьна) *adj.* lightly salted.
малосостоя́тел|ьный (~ен, ~ьна) *adj.* unconvincing.
мáлост|ь, и *f.* (*coll.*) **1.** a bit; trifle. **2.** *as adv.* a little, a bit; **м. поспáть** to take a little nap.
малосущéствен|ный (~, ~на) *adj.* of little importance, immaterial.
малотирáжн|ый *adj.* small-circulation; **~ое издáние** limited edition.
малоубеди́тел|ьный (~ен, ~ьна) *adj.* unconvincing.
малоупотреби́тел|ьный (~ен, ~ьна) *adj.* little, rarely used.
малоцéн|ный (~ен, ~на) *adj.* of little value.
малочи́сленност|ь, и *f.* small number; paucity.
малочи́слен|ный (~, ~на) *adj.* small (in numbers); scanty.
мáл|ый[1] **(~, ~á, ~ó)** *adj.* little, (too) small; **м. рóстом** short; **м. ход!** (*naut.*) slow speed (ahead)!; **э́ти сапоги́ мне ~ы́** these boots are too small for me; **от ~а до вели́ка** young and old alike; **с ~ых лет** from childhood; *as n.* **~ое, ~ого** *nt.* little; **сáмое ~ое** (*coll.*) at the least; **без ~ого** almost, nearly; **за ~ым дéло стáло** (*frequently iron.*) one small thing is lacking.
мáл|ый[2]**, ого** *m.* (*coll.*) fellow, chap, bloke.
малы́ш, á *m.* (*coll.*) child, kid; little boy.
мáльв|а, ы *f.* (*bot.*) mallow, hollyhock.
Мальóрк|а, и *f.* Majorca.
Мáльт|а, ы *f.* Malta.
мальти́|ец, йца *m.* Maltese.
мальти́|йка, йки *f. of* **~ец**
мальти́йский *adj.* Maltese.
мáльчик, а *m.* boy, lad; (male) child.
мальчи́шеский *adj.* **1.** boyish. **2.** (*pej.*) childish, puerile.
мальчи́шеств|о, а *nt.* boyishness; (*pej.*) childishness.

мальчи́шк|а, и *m.* (*coll.*) urchin, lad.
мальчи́шник, а *m.* stag-party.
мальчуга́н, а *m.* (*coll., affectionate*) little fellow.
малю́сенький *adj.* (*coll.*) tiny, wee.
малю́тк|а, и *c.g.* baby, tot.
маля́р, а́ *m.* (house-)painter, decorator.
маляри́йный *adj.* malarial.
маляри́|я, и *f.* (*med.*) malaria.
маля́р|ный *adj. of* ~; **~ная кисть** paintbrush.
ма́м|а, ы *f.* mum(my), mamma.
мама́ш|а, и *f.* (*coll.*) = **ма́ма**
ма́менькин *adj.* mother's; **м. сыно́к** (*coll., iron.*) mummy's boy
ма́мин *adj.* mother's.
ма́монт, а *m.* mammoth.
ма́монт|овый *adj. of* ~
ма́мочк|а, и *f.* (*coll.*) = **ма́ма**
мана́т|ки, ок *no sg.* (*sl.*) possessions, one's bits and pieces.
мангани́т, а *m.* (*min.*) manganite.
ма́нго *nt. indecl.* (*bot.*) mango.
ма́нго|вый *adj. of* ~
мангу́ст|а, ы *f.* (*zool.*) mongoose.
мандари́н[1], а *m.* mandarin (*Chinese official*).
мандари́н[2], а *m.* mandarin(e), tangerine.
мандари́н|ный *adj. of* ~[2]
мандари́н|овый *adj.* = **~ный**
мандари́н|ский *adj. of* ~[1]
манда́т, а *m.* **1.** warrant. **2.** (*pol.*) mandate; credentials.
манда́т|ный *adj. of* ~; **~ная коми́ссия** credentials committee; **~ная террито́рия** mandated territory.
мандоли́н|а, ы *f.* (*mus.*) mandolin(e).
мандолини́ст, а *m.* mandolin(e)-player.
мандрагóр|а, ы *f.* (*bot.*) mandrake.
мандри́л, а *m.* (*zool.*) mandrill.
манёвр, а *m.* manœuvre; (*pl.*; *mil.*) manœuvres.
манёвренност|ь, и *f.* manœuvrability; (*mil.*) mobility.
манёвр|енный *adj. of* ~; **~енная война́** mobile warfare; **~енный самолёт** manœuvrable aircraft.
маневри́р|овать, ую *impf.* (*of* **с~**) **1.** to manœuvre. **2.** (*+i.*) to make good use (of), use to advantage.
мане́ж, а *m.* **1.** riding-school. **2.** (*circus*) ring; **инспе́ктор ~а** ringmaster. **3. спорти́вный м.** sports hall. **4. (де́тский) м.** play-pen.
манеке́н, а *m.* mannequin; dummy.
манеке́нщик, а *m.* (male) model.
манеке́нщиц|а, ы *f.* model.
мане́р, а *m.* (*coll.*) manner; **таки́м ~ом** in this manner, in this way; **на англи́йский м.** in the English manner.
мане́р|а, ы *f.* **1.** manner, style; **м. вести́ себя́** way of behaving; **м. держа́ть себя́** bearing, carriage; **петь в ~е Кару́зо** to sing in the style of Caruso. **2.** (*pl.*) manners; **у него́ плохи́е ~ы** he has no manners.
мане́рност|ь, и *f.* affectation.
мане́р|ный (~ен, ~на) *adj.* affected.
манже́т|а, ы *f.* cuff.
маниака́льный *adj.* maniacal; manic.
маникю́р, а *m.* manicure.
маникю́рш|а, и *f.* manicurist.
манипули́р|овать, ую *impf.* to manipulate.
манипуля́ци|я, и *f.* manipulation.
ман|и́ть, ю́, ~ишь *impf.* **1.** (*pf.* **по~**) to beckon. **2.** (*pf.* **вз~**) (*fig.*) to attract; to lure, allure.
манифе́ст, а *m.* manifesto; proclamation.
манифеста́нт, а *m.* (*pol., etc.*) demonstrator.
манифеста́ци|я, и *f.* (*street*) demonstration.
манифести́р|овать, ую *impf. and pf.* to demonstrate, take part in a demonstration.
мани́шк|а, и *f.* (*false*) shirt-front, dicky.
ма́ни|я, и *f.* mania; **м. вели́чия** delusions of grandeur; megalomania.
манки́р|овать, ую *impf. and pf.* (*+i.*) to neglect.
ма́нн|а, ы *f.* manna.
ма́нн|ый *adj.*: **~ая крупа́** semolina.
манове́ни|е, я *nt.* (*obs.*) beck, nod; **~ем руки́** with a wave of one's hand.
мано́метр, а *m.* (*tech.*) pressure-gauge, manometer.
манометри́ческий *adj.* (*tech.*) manometric.
манса́рд|а, ы *f.* attic, garret.
манти́ль|я, и *f.* mantilla.
ма́нти|я, и *f.* cloak, mantle; robe, gown.
манто́ *nt. indecl.* (*lady's*) coat.
мануфакту́р|а, ы *f.* (*sg. only*; *collect.*) cotton textiles.
маньчжу́рский *adj.* Manchu.
манья́к, а *m.* maniac.
маои́зм, а *m.* Maoism.
маои́стский *adj.* Maoist.
ма́ори *c.g. indecl.* Maori.
маори́йский *adj.* Maori.
марабу́ *nt. indecl.* (*zool.*) marabou.
мара́зм, а *m.* (*med.*) marasmus; **ста́рческий м.** senility; (*fig.*) decay.
мара́л, а *m.* (*zool.*) Siberian deer.
мараски́н, а *m.* maraschino (*liqueur*).
мара́|ть, ю *impf.* (*coll.*) **1.** (*pf.* **за~**) to soil, dirty; (*fig.*) to sully; **м. ру́ки (о+а.)** to soil one's hands (on). **2.** (*pf.* **на~**) to daub; to scribble. **3.** (*pf.* **вы́~**) to cross out, strike out.
мара́|ться, юсь *impf.* (*coll.*) **1.** (*pf.* **за~**) to soil o.s., get (o.s.) dirty. **2.** (*no pf.*; *fig.*) to soil one's hands. **3.** *pass. of* **~ть**
марафо́н|ец, ца *m.* marathon runner.
марафо́нский *adj.*: **м. бег** (*sport*) Marathon race.
ма́рган|ец, ца *m.* (*chem.*) manganese.
ма́рган|цевый *adj. of* **~ец**
маргари́н, а *m.* margarine.
маргари́тк|а, и *f.* (*bot.*) daisy.
маргина́ли|и, ев *and* **ий** *no sg.* marginalia.
ма́рев|о, а *nt.* **1.** mirage. **2.** heat haze.
маре́н|а, ы *f.* (*bot.*) madder.
мари́н|а, ы *f.* (*art*) seascape.
марина́д, а *m.* marinade.
марини́ст, а *m.* painter of seascapes.
марино́в|анный *p.p.p. of* **~а́ть** *and adj.* (*cul.*) marinated; pickled.
марин|ова́ть, у́ю *impf.* **1.** (*pf.* **за~**) to marinate; to pickle. **2.** (*pf.* **про~**) (*fig., coll.*) to put off, shelve.
марионе́т|ка, ки *f.* marionette; puppet (*also fig.*).
марионе́т|очный *adj. of* **~ка; ~очное госуда́рство** puppet state.
марихуа́н|а, ы *f.* marijuana, marihuana.
ма́рк|а, и *f.* **1.** (postage-)stamp. **2.** (*monetary unit*) mark. **3.** mark; brand; **фабри́чная м.** trade-mark; **како́й ма́рки?** what make? **4.** counter. **5.** grade, quality; **това́р вы́сшей ~и** goods of the highest quality. **6.** (*fig.*) name, reputation; **держа́ть ~у** to uphold one's reputation.
ма́ркетинг, а *m.* (*econ.*) marketing.
марки́з, а *m.* marquis, marquess.
марки́з|а[1], ы *f.* marchioness.
марки́з|а[2], ы *f.* sun-blind; awning; marquee.
ма́р|кий (~ок, ~ка) *adj.* easily soiled.
маркир|ова́ть, у́ю *impf. and pf.* to mark; to brand.
маркси́зм, а *m.* Marxism.
маркси́зм-ленини́зм, а-а *m.* Marxism-Leninism.
маркси́ст, а *m.* Marxist.
маркси́стский *adj.* Marxist, Marxian.
маркси́стско-ле́нинский *adj.* Marxist-Leninist.
ма́рл|евый *adj. of* **~я; м. бинт** gauze bandage.
ма́рл|я, и *f.* gauze; cheesecloth.
мармела́д, а *m.* fruit jellies (*sweets*).
маро́дёр, а *m.* marauder; (*coll.*) profiteer.
мародёрск|ий *adj.* marauding; **~ие це́ны** (*fig., coll.*)

exorbitant prices.
мародёрств|о, а *nt.* marauding, pillage.
мародёрств|овать, ую *impf.* to maraud.
мáр|очный *adj. of* **~ка**[1]; **~очное винó** fine wine.
Марс, а *m.* (*astron., myth.*) Mars.
мáрсел|ь, я *m.* (*naut.*) topsail.
Марсельéз|а, ы *f.* Marseillaise.
марсиáн|ин, ина, *pl.* **~е, ~** *m.* Martian.
март, а *m.* March.
мартéн, а *m.* (*tech.*) open-hearth furnace.
мартéновский *adj.* (*tech.*) open-hearth.
мáрт|овский *adj. of* **~**
мартышк|а, и *f.* marmoset; (*fig., coll.*) monkey.
марципáн, а *m.* marzipan.
марш[1]**, а** *m.* march; **м. протéста** protest march.
марш[2] *int.* (*as word of command*) forward!; **шáгом м.!** quick march!; (*coll.*) off you go!
марш[3]**, а** *m.* flight of stairs.
мáршал, а *m.* marshal.
мáршал|ьский *adj. of* **~**
марширов|áть, ýю *impf.* to march.
марширóвк|а, и *f.* marching.
маршрýт, а *m.* route, itinerary.
маршрýт|ный *adj. of* **~**; **м. пóезд** through goods-train; **~ное такси** fixed-route taxi.
мáск|а, и *f.* mask; **противогáзовая м.** gas-mask; (*fig.*): **сбрóсить с себя́ ~у** to throw off the mask.
маскарáд, а *m.* masquerade.
маскарáд|ный *adj. of* **~**; **м. костюм** fancy dress.
маскир|овáть, ýю *impf.* (*of* **за~**) to mask, disguise; (*mil.*) to camouflage.
маскирóвк|а, и *f.* masking, disguise; (*mil.*) camouflage.
мáслениц|а, ы *f.* Shrove-tide; carnival.
маслёнк|а, и *f.* **1.** butter-dish. **2.** oil-can.
масл|ёнок, ёнка, *pl.* **~я́та, ~я́т** *m. Boletus lutens* (*variety of edible mushroom*).
мáслен|ый *adj.* **1.** buttered; oiled, oily, **~ая недéля = ~ица. 2.** (*fig., coll.*) oily, unctuous.
маслин|а, ы *f.* **1.** olive-tree. **2.** olive.
мáсл|ить, ю, ишь *impf.* (*of* **на~** *and* **по~**) **1.** to butter. **2.** to oil; to grease.
мáсл|иться, ится *impf.* **1.** to leave greasy marks. **2.** (*coll.*) to shine; to glisten. **3.** *pass. of* **~ить**
мáсличный *adj.* (*of plants*) oil-yielding.
масли́|чный *adj. of* **~на**
мáс|ло, ла, *pl.* **~лá, ~ел, ~лáм** *nt.* **1. (сли́вочное)** butter. **2.** oil; **как по ~лу** (*fig., coll.*) swimmingly. **3.** oil (paints); **писáть ~лом** to paint in oils.
маслобóйк|а, и *f.* churn.
маслобóйн|ый *adj.*: **м. завóд = ~я**
маслобó|йня, йни, *g. pl.* **~ен** *f.* creamery.
маслодéли|е, я *nt.* butter manufacturing.
маслозавóд, а *m.* creamery.
масляни́ст|ый (~, ~а) *adj.* oily.
мáсл|яный *adj. of* **~о**; **~яная кислотá** (*chem.*) butyric acid; **~яные крáски** oil paints.
масóн, а *f.* Freemason, Mason.
масóнский *adj.* Masonic.
масóнств|о, а *nt.* Freemasonry.
мáсс|а, ы *f.* **1.** mass; *pl.* (*pol.*) the masses; **в ~е** on the whole. **2.: древéсная м.** wood-pulp. **3.** (*coll.*) a lot, lots.
массáж, а *m.* massage.
массажи́ст, а *m.* masseur.
массажи́стк|а, и *f.* masseuse.
масси́в, а *m.* (*geog.*) massif, mountain-mass; (*fig.*) expanse; **жилóй м.** housing development; **леснóй м.** forest tract.
масси́в|ный (~ен, ~на) *adj.* massive.
масси́р|овать[1]**, ую** *impf. and pf.* (*mil.*) to mass, concentrate.
масси́р|овать[2]**, ую** *impf. and pf.* to massage.
массóвк|а, и *f.* (*coll.*) **1.** mass meeting. **2.** group excursion. **3.** crowd scene (*in play, film*).
мáссов|ый *adj.* **1.** mass; **~ые арéсты** mass arrests; **~ое произвóдство** mass production. **2.** popular; **м. читáтель** the general reader.
мастáк, á *m.* (*coll.*) expert, past master.
мáстер, а, *pl.* **~á** *m.* **1.** foreman. **2.** craftsman, skilled workman; **золоты́х дел м.** goldsmith. **3.** (**на**+*a., or* +*inf.*) expert, master (at, of); **м. (по ремóнту)** repairman; **телевизиóнный м.** TV repairman; **м. на все рýки** jack-of-all-trades.
мастер|и́ть, ю́, и́шь *impf.* (*of* **с~**) (*coll.*) to make, build.
мастерск|áя, óй *f.* workshop; studio; (*in factory*) shop; **авторемóнтная м.** car repair garage.
мастерски́ *adv.* skilfully; in masterly fashion.
мастерскóй *adj.* masterly.
мастерств|ó, á *nt.* **1.** trade, craft. **2.** skill, craftsmanship.
масти́к|а, и *f.* **1.** mastic. **2.** floor-polish.
масти́к|овый *adj. of* **~а.**
масти́т, а *m.* (*med.*) mastitis.
масти́т|ый (~, ~а) *adj.* venerable.
мастодóнт, а *m.* mastodon.
маст|ь, и, *pl.* **~и, ~éй** *f.* **1.** colour (*of animal's hair or coat*). **2.** (*cards*) suit; **ходи́ть в м.** to follow suit.
масштáб, а *m.* scale; (*fig.*): **в большóм, мáленьком ~е** on a large, small scale; **конфли́кт большóго ~а** large-scale conflict.
масштáб|ный (~ен, ~на) *adj.* **1.** scale; **~ная модéль** scale model. **2.** large-scale.
мат[1]**, а** *m.* (*chess*) checkmate, mate; **объяви́ть м.** (+*d.*) to mate.
мат[2]**, а** *m.* (floor-, door-)mat.
мат[3]**, а** *m.* (*coll.*) *only in phr.* **благи́м ~ом** at the top of one's voice.
мат[4]**, а** *m.* foul language, obscenities; **ругáться ~ом** to use foul language.
матемáтик, а *m.* mathematician.
матемáтик|а, и *f.* mathematics.
математи́ческ|ий *adj.* mathematical; **~ое обеспéчение** (*comput.*) software.
матереуби́йств|о, а *nt.* matricide.
материáл, а *m.* material; stuff; **м. (для печáтания)** copy; **гвоздевóй м.** feature (item).
материали́зм, а *m.* materialism.
материализ|овáть(ся), ýю(сь) *impf. and pf.* to materialize (*trans. and intrans.*).
материали́ст, а *m.* materialist.
материалисти́ческий *adj.* (*phil.*) materialist.
материáльно-техни́ческий *adj.* (*mil.*) logistical.
материáл|ьный (~ен, ~ьна) *adj.* material; **~ьная заинтересóванность** material incentive(s); **~ьные затруднéния** financial difficulties; **~ьная часть** (*tech., mil.*) matériel.
матери́к, á *m.* continent, mainland.
материкóвый *adj.* continental.
матери́нский *adj.* maternal, motherly.
матери́нств|о, а *nt.* maternity, motherhood.
матéри|я[1]**, и** *f.* **1.** (*phil.*) matter. **2..** (*fig., coll.*) subject, topic.
матéри|я[2]**, и** *f.* (*text.*) material, cloth.
мáтерный *adj.* (*coll.*) obscene, abusive.
матéрчатый *adj.* (*coll.*) (made of) cloth.
матёрый *adj.* (*coll.*) **1.** experienced, practised. **2.** inveterate, out-and-out.
мáтк|а, и *f.* **1.** (*anat.*) uterus, womb. **2.** female (*of animals*); queen (bee).
мáтов|ый *adj.* mat(t); dull; suffused (*of light*); **~ое стеклó** frosted glass.
мáточн|ый *adj.* (*anat.*) uterine.
матрáс, а *m.* mattress; **надувнóй м.** air bed, inflatable mattress.

матрá|ц = **~с**
матрёшк|а, и *f.* matrioshka, (set of) nested Russian dolls.
матриархáльный *adj.* matriarchal.
матриархáт, а *m.* matriarchy.
мáтриц|а, ы *f.* **1.** (*typ.*) matrix. **2.** (*tech.*) die, mould.
матрóс, а *m.* sailor, seaman.
матрóск|а, и *f.* sailor's jacket.
мáтушк|а, и *f.* (*coll.*) **1.** mother; **~и (мой)!** *excl. of surprise or fright.* **2.** priest's wife. **3.** (*as familiar form of address to an elderly woman*) gran(ny), ma.
матч, а *m.* (*sport*) match; **междунарóдный м.** (*cricket, rugby*) test (match); **повтóрный м.** return match.
мат|ь, *g., d., p.* **´~ери, ´~ерью,** *pl.* **´~ери, ~ерéй** *f.* **1.** mother; **бýдущая м.** expectant mother; **м.-одинóчка** single mother. **2.** (*coll.*) *familiar term of address to a woman.*
мáузер, а *m.* Mauser (*automatic pistol or rifle*).
мафиóзи *m. indecl.* Mafioso, Mafia member.
мафиóзо = **мафиóзи**
мáфи|я, и *f.* Mafia.
мах, а (у) *m.* swing, stroke; (*coll.*): **дать ´~у** to commit a blunder; **одни́м ´~ом** at one stroke, in a trice; **с ´~у** rashly, without thinking.
ма|хáть, шý, ´~шешь *impf.* (*of* **~хнýть**) (+*i.*) to wave; to brandish; to wag; to flap.
махи́н|а, ы *f.* (*coll.*) bulky and cumbersome object.
махинáци|я, и *f.* machination, intrigue.
мах|нýть, нý, нёшь *pf. of* **~áть; м. рукóй (на**+*a.*) (*fig., coll.*) to give up as a bad job.
махови́к, á *m.* fly-wheel.
махов|óй *adj.* (*tech.*): **~óе колесó** fly-wheel.
махóрк|а, и *f.* makhorka (*inferior variety of tobacco*).
махрóв|ый *adj.* **1.** (*bot.*) double. **2.** dyed-in-the-wool, out-and-out; **~ая порногрáфия** hard-core pornography. **3.** (*text.*) terry.
мац|á, ы́ *no pl., f.* matzo.
мáчех|а, и *f.* stepmother.
мáчт|а, ы *f.* mast.
маши́н|а, ы *f.* **1.** machine, mechanism (*also fig.*); **кýхонная м.** food processor; **(посудо)мóечная м.** dishwasher. **2.** vehicle; car; **м. «скóрой пóмощи»** ambulance; **служéбная м.** company car.
машинáл|ьный (~ен, ~ьна) *adj.* mechanical (*fig.*); **м. отвéт** an automatic response.
машинизáци|я, и *f.* mechanization.
машинизи́р|овать, ую *impf. and pf.* to mechanize.
машини́ст, а *m.* **1.** machinist, engineer. **2.** (*rail.*) engine-driver. **3.** (*theatr.*) scene-shifter.
машини́стк|а, и *f.* typist; **м.-стенографи́стка** shorthand-typist.
маши́н|ка, ки *f. dim. of* **~а; (пи́шущая) м.** typewriter.
маши́н|ный *adj. of* **~а; ~ая грáфика** computer graphics; **~ное обучéние** computer-aided learning.
машинопи́сный *adj.* typewritten; **м. текст** typescript.
маши́нопис|ь, и *f.* typing.
машинострoéни|е, я *nt.* mechanical engineering; machine building.
машинострo|и́тельный *adj. of* **~éние**
маэ́стро *m. indecl.* maestro; master.
мая́к, á *m.* lighthouse; beacon (*also fig.*).
мáятник, а *m.* pendulum.
мá|яться, юсь, ешься *impf.* (*coll.*) **1.** (**с**+*i.*) to toil (with, over). **2.** to pine, suffer.
мая́ч|ить, у, ишь *impf.* (*coll.*) to loom (up), appear indistinctly.
м. б. (*abbr. of* **мóжет быть**) maybe, perhaps.
МВФ *m. indecl.* (*abbr. of* **Междунарóдный валю́тный фонд**) IMF (*International Monetary Fund*).
мг (*abbr. of* **миллигрáмм**) mg, milligram(s).
мгл|а, ы *f.* **1.** haze; mist. **2.** gloom, darkness.
мгли́ст|ый (~, ~а) *adj.* hazy.
мгновéни|е, я *nt.* instant, moment; **в м. óка** in the twinkling of an eye.
мгновéн|ный (~ен, ~на) *adj.* instantaneous.
мéбель, и *f.* furniture.
мéбель|ный *adj. of* **~**
мéбельщик, а *m.* furniture-maker.
меблирó|ванный *p.p.p. of* **~вáть** *and adj.* furnished.
меблир|овáть, ýю *impf. and pf.* to furnish.
меблирóвк|а, и *f.* **1.** furnishing. **2.** furniture, furnishings.
мегабáйт, а *m.* (*comput.*) megabyte.
мегагéрц, а *m.* (*radio*) megahertz.
мегафóн, а *m.* megaphone.
мегéр|а, ы *f.* (*coll.*) shrew, termagant.
мёд, а, о ´~е, в ~ý, *pl.* **~ы́, ~óв** *m.* **1.** honey. **2.** mead.
мед... *comb. form, abbr. of* **медици́нский**
медали́ст, а *m.* medallist; medal winner.
медáл|ь, и *f.* medal.
медальóн, а *m.* medallion, locket.
медбрáт, а *m.* male nurse.
медвéдиц|а, ы *f.* she-bear; (*astron.*): **Большáя М.** the Great Bear (Ursa Major); **Мáлая М.** the Little Bear (Ursa Minor).
медвéд|ь, я *m.* bear (*also fig.*); **бамбýковый м.** giant panda; **бéлый м.** polar bear.
медвеж|áта *pl. of* **~óнок**
медвé|жий *adj. of* **~дь; м. ýгол** (*coll.*) god-forsaken place; **~жья услýга** well-meant action having opposite effect.
медвеж|óнок, óнка, *pl.* **~áта, ~áт** *m.* bear-cub; **плю́шевый м.** teddy (bear).
медвя́н|ый *adj.* **1.** (*poet.*) honeyed. **2.** smelling of honey. **3.: ~ая росá** honey-dew.
медиáн|а, ы *f.* (*math.*) median.
мéдик, а *m.* **1.** physician, doctor. **2.** medical student, medic.
медикамéнт, а *m.* medicine.
медитáци|я, и *f.* meditation.
медити́р|овать, ую *impf.* to meditate.
медици́н|а, ы *f.* medicine.
медици́нский *adj.* medical.
мед|и́чка, и́чки *f.* (*coll.*) *of* **´~ик 2.**
мéдленно *adv.* slowly.
мéдлен|ный (~, ~на) *adj.* slow.
медли́тел|ьный (~ен, ~ьна) *adj.* sluggish; slow, tardy.
мéдл|ить, ю, ишь *impf.* to linger; to tarry; (**с**+*i.*) to be slow (in); **он ~ит с отвéтом** he is a long time replying.
мéдник, а *m.* copper-smith.
мéдно-крáсный *adj.* copper-coloured.
меднолитéйный *adj.* copper-smelting.
мéдн|ый *adj.* **1.** copper; **м. лоб** (*fig., coll.*) blockhead. **2.** (*chem.*) cupric, cuprous; **м. купорóс** copper sulphate.
медóвый *adj. of* **мёд; м. мéсяц** honeymoon.
медонóсн|ый *adj.*: **пчелá ~ая** honey-bee.
медосмóтр, а *m.* medical (examination), checkup.
медпýнкт, а *m.* first-aid station.
медсестр|á, ы́ *f.* (*medical*) nurse.
медýз|а, ы *f.* (*zool.*) jellyfish.
мед|ь, и *f.* copper.
медя́к, á *m.* (*coll.*) copper (coin).
медя́нк|а¹, и *f.* grass-snake.
медя́нк|а², и *f.* (*chem.*) verdigris.
меж = **мéжду**
меж... *comb. form* inter-.
меж|á, и́, *pl.* **~и, ~, ~áм** *f.* boundary.
межгородскóй *adj.* inter-city.
междомéти|е, я *nt.* (*gram.*) interjection.

междоусо́би|е, я *nt.* civil strife; intestine strife.
междоусо́б|ица, ицы *f.* (*obs.*) = **~ие**
междоусо́бный *adj.* intestine.
ме́жду *prep.+i.* (*+g. pl., obs.*) **1.** between; **м. де́лом** at odd moments; **м. на́ми (говоря́)** between ourselves; between you and me; **м. про́чим** incidentally; **м. тем** meanwhile; **м. тем, как** while, whereas. **2.** among, amongst.
междугоро́дный *adj.* inter-city, inter-urban; long-distance.
междунаро́дный *adj.* international.
междуца́рстви|е, я *nt.* interregnum.
межева́ни|е, я *nt.* surveying.
меж|ева́ть, у́ю *impf.* to survey; to establish the boundaries (of).
меж|ево́й *adj. of* **~а́; м. знак** landmark, boundary-mark.
меже́н|ь, и *f.* lowest water-level (*in river or lake*).
межеу́м|ок, ка *m.* (*coll.*) person of limited intelligence; a mediocrity.
межеу́мочный *adj.* (*coll.*) mediocre; ill-defined.
межконтинента́льный *adj.* inter-continental; **м. баллисти́ческий снаря́д** intercontinental ballistic missile.
межли́чностный *adj.* interpersonal.
межнациона́льный *adj.* interethnic.
межплане́тн|ый *adj.* interplanetary.
межра́совый *adj.* interracial.
межсезо́нь|е, я *nt.* (*sport*) off-season.
мезозо́йский *adj.* (*geol.*) Mesozoic.
мезолити́ческий *adj.* (*archaeol.*) mesolithic.
мезони́н, а *m.* **1.** attic story. **2.** mezzanine (floor).
Ме́ксик|а, и *f.* Mexico.
мексика́н|ец, ца *m.* Mexican.
мексика́н|ка, ки *f. of* **~ец**
мексика́нский *adj.* Mexican.
мел, а, о ~е, в ~у́ *m.* chalk.
меланхо́лик, а *m.* melancholic (*pers.*).
меланхоли́ческий *adj.* melancholy.
меланхоли́ч|ный (~ен, ~на) *adj.* = **~еский**
меланхо́ли|я, и *f.* melancholy; (*med.*) melancholia.
меле́|ть, ет *impf.* (*of* **об~**) to grow shallow.
мелиора́ци|я, и *f.* (land) reclamation.
мелиори́р|овать, ую *impf. and pf.* (*agric.*) to reclaim.
ме́л|кий (~ок, ~ка́, ~ко) *adj.* **1.** small, petty. **2.** shallow. **3.** (*of rain, sand, etc.*) fine. **4.** (*fig.*) petty, small-minded.
ме́лко *adv.* fine, into small particles.
мелкобуржуа́з|ный (~ен, ~на) *adj.* petit-bourgeois.
мелково́д|ный (~ен, ~на) *adj.* shallow.
мелково́дь|е, я *nt.* shallow water.
мелкозерни́ст|ый (~, ~а) *adj.* fine-grained.
мелкот|а́, ы́ *f.* **1.** smallness. **2.** (*collect.*; *coll.*) small fry.
мелово́й *adj.* **1.** (consisting of) chalk. **2.** white as chalk. **3.** (*geol.*) cretaceous.
мело́дик|а, и *f.* melodics.
мелоди́ческий *adj.* melodious, tuneful.
мелоди́ч|ный (~ен, ~на) *adj.* = **~еский**
мело́ди|я, и *f.* melody, tune.
мелодра́м|а, ы *f.* melodrama.
мелодрамати́ческий *adj.* melodramatic.
мел|о́к, ка́ *m.* piece of chalk; **игра́ть на м.** (*cards, billiards, etc.*) to play on credit.
мелома́н, а *m.* music-lover.
мелочно́й = **ме́лочный**
ме́лочност|ь, и *f.* pettiness, small-mindedness.
ме́лоч|ный (~ен, ~на) *adj.* **1.** petty, trifling. **2.** (*pej.*) petty, small-minded.
ме́лоч|ь, и, *pl.* **~и, ~е́й** *f.* **1.** (*collect.*) small items; small fry. **2.** (*collect.*) (small) change. **3.** (*pl.*) trifles, trivialities.
мел|ь, и, о ~и, на ~и́ *f.* shoal; bank; **песча́ная м.** sandbank; **на ~и́** aground; (*fig.*) on the rocks, high and dry; **сесть на м.** to run aground.
мельк|а́ть, а́ю *impf.* (*of* **~ну́ть**) to glimmer, twinkle.
мельк|ну́ть, ну́, нёшь, *inst. pf. of* **~а́ть; у меня́ ~ну́ла мысль** a thought flashed through my mind.
ме́льком *adv.* in passing, cursorily.
ме́льник, а *m.* miller.
ме́льниц|а, ы *f.* mill; **э́то вода́ на на́шу ~у** (*fig., coll.*) it's grist to our mill.
ме́льни|чный *adj. of* **~ца**
мельхио́р, а *m.* cupro-nickel, German silver.
мельча́йший *superl. of* **ме́лкий**
мельча́|ть, ю *impf.* (*of* **из~**) **1.** to grow shallow. **2.** to become small; to grow smaller.
ме́л|ьче *comp. of* **~кий** *and* **~ко**
мельч|и́ть, у́, и́шь *impf.* (*of* **из~** *and* **раз~**) to crush, crumble.
мелю́, ме́лешь *see* **моло́ть**
мелюзг|а́, и́ *f.* (*collect.*; *coll.*) small fry.
мембра́н|а, ы *f.* (*tech.*) diaphragm.
мемора́ндум, а *m.* (*dipl.*) memorandum.
мемориа́л, а *m.* memorial.
мемориа́льный *adj.* memorial.
мемуа́р|ы, ов *no sg.* memoirs.
ме́неджер, а *m.* manager; **м. по сбы́ту** sales manager.
ме́нее *adv.* (*comp. of* **ма́ло**) less; **тем не м.** none the less.
менестре́л|ь, я *m.* (*hist.*) minstrel.
мензу́рк|а, и *f.* (*pharm.*) measuring-glass.
менинги́т, а *m.* (*med.*) meningitis.
менов|о́й *adj.* (*econ.*) exchange; **~а́я торго́вля** barter.
менструа́льный *adj.* (*physiol.*) menstrual.
менструа́ци|я, и *f.* (*physiol.*) menstruation.
менструи́р|овать, ую *impf.* (*physiol.*) to menstruate.
менто́л, а *m.* (*chem.*) menthol.
менуэ́т, а *m.* minuet.
ме́ньше *comp. of* **ма́ленький** *and* **ма́ло** smaller, less.
меньшеви́зм, а *m.* (*pol.*) Menshevism.
меньшеви́к, а́ *m.* (*pol.*) Menshevik.
меньшеви́стский *adj.* (*pol.*) Menshevik, Menshevist.
ме́ньш|ий *adj.* (*comp. of* **ма́ленький, ма́лый**) lesser, smaller; younger; **по ~ей ме́ре** at least; **са́мое ~ее** at the least.
меньшинств|о́, а́ *nt.* minority.
меню́ *nt. indecl.* menu, bill of fare.
меня́ *a. and g. of* **я**
меня́л|а, ы *m.* (*coll.*) money-changer.
меня́льный *adj.* (*comm.*) money-changing.
меня́|ть, ю *impf.* **1.** (*no pf.*) to change. **2.** (*+a.* **на***+a.*; *pf.* **об~, по~**) to exchange (for).
меня́|ться, юсь *impf.* **1.** (*no pf.*) to change. **2.** (*+i.*; *pf.* **об~, по~**) to exchange; **м. с кем-н. ко́мнатами** to exchange rooms with s.o.
ме́р|а, ы *f.* measure; **вы́сшая м. наказа́ния** capital punishment; **~ы по укрепле́нию дове́рия** (*pol.*) confidence-building measures; **в ~у** (*+g.*) to the extent (of); **по ~е возмо́жности, по ~е сил** as far as possible; **по ~е того́, как** as, (in proportion) as; **по кра́йней, ма́лой, ме́ньшей ~е** at least; **в ~у** fairly; **сверх ~ы, че́рез ~у, не в ~у** excessively, immoderately.
ме́ргел|ь, я *m.* (*geol.*) marl.
мере́жк|а, и *f.* hem-stitch, open work.
мере́нг|а, и *f.* meringue.
мере́ть, мру, мрёшь, *past* **мёр, мёрла** *impf.* (*coll.*) to die (*in large numbers*); **мрут, как му́хи** they are dropping like flies.

мерéщ|иться, усь, ишься *impf.* (*of* **по~**) (*coll.*; +*d.*) **1.** to seem (to), appear (to); **онá мне ~ится** her image haunts me; **э́то тебé ~ится** you only imagine you see it. **2.** (*obs.*) to appear dimly.
мерзáв|ец, ца *m.* (*coll.*) swine, bastard.
мéрз|кий (~ок, ~кá, ~ко) *adj.* vile, loathsome; abominable, foul.
мерзлот|á, ы *f.* frozen ground; **вéчная м.** permafrost.
мёрзлый *adj.* frozen.
мёрз|нуть, ну, нешь, *past* **~, ~ла** *impf.* (*of* **за~**) to freeze.
мéрзост|ь, и *f.* **1.** vileness, loathsomeness. **2.** abomination.
меридиáн, а *m.* meridian.
мери́л|о, а *nt.* standard, criterion.
мéрин, а *m.* gelding; **врёт как си́вый м.** (*coll.*) he's a barefaced liar.
мерино́с, а *m.* **1.** merino (sheep). **2.** merino (wool).
мерино́совый *adj.* merino.
мéр|ить, ю, ишь *impf.* **1.** (*pf.* **с~**) to measure; **м. взгля́дом** to look up and down. **2.** (*pf.* **по~, при~**) to try on (*clothing, footwear*).
мéр|иться, юсь, ишься *impf.* (*of* **по~**) (+*i.*) to measure (against); **м. ро́стом с кем-н.** to compare heights with s.o.
мéрк|а, и *f.* measure; yardstick; **подходи́ть ко всему́ с одно́й ~ой** (*fig.*) to apply the same standard to all alike.
меркантили́зм, а *m.* (*econ.*) mercantilism.
меркантíл|ьный *adj.* (*econ.*) mercantile.
мéрк|нуть, нет, *past* **~нул** *and* **~, ~ла** *impf.* (*of* **по~**) to grow dark, grow dim; (*fig.*) to fade.
Меркýри|й, я *m.* (*myth., astron.*) Mercury.
мерлýшк|а, и *f.* lambskin.
мéрный *adj.* measured; rhythmical.
мероприя́ти|е, я *nt.* measure; event.
мéртвенный *adj.* deathly, ghastly.
мертвé|ть, ю *impf.* **1.** (*pf.* **о~**) to grow numb; (*med.*) to mortify. **2.** (*pf.* **по~**) to be numb (*with fright, grief, etc.*).
мертвéц, á *m.* corpse, dead man.
мертвéцк|ая, ой *f.* (*coll.*) mortuary, morgue.
мертвéцки *adv.* (*coll.*) *only in phrr.* **м. пьян** dead drunk; **напи́ться м.** to become dead drunk.
мертвечи́н|а, ы *f.* (*collect.*) carrion.
мертв|и́ть, лю́, и́шь *impf.* to deaden.
мертворождённый *adj.* still-born.
мёртв|ый (~, ~á, ~о, *pl.* **~ы;** *in fig. senses* **~ó, ~ы́)** *adj.* dead; **ни жив ни ~** more dead than alive; **пить ~ую** (*coll.*) to drink hard; **спать ~ым сном** (*coll.*) to be dead to the world; **быть на ~ой то́чке** to be at a standstill; to be deadlocked; **~ая хвáтка** mortal grip; **м. час** quiet time (*in sanatoria, etc.*).
мерцá|ть, ю *impf.* to twinkle, glimmer, flicker.
мéсив|о, а *nt.* **1.** mash. **2.** (*fig., coll.*) medley; jumble.
ме|си́ть, шý, ∠сишь *impf.* (*of* **с~**) to knead; **м. грязь** (*coll., joc.*) to wade through mud.
мéсс|а, ы *f.* (*relig., mus.*) mass.
мессиáнский *adj.* Messianic.
мессиáнств|о, а *nt.* Messianism.
месси́|я, и *m.* Messiah.
местáми *adj.* (*coll.*) here and there, in places.
местéч|ко[1]**, ка,** *pl.* **~ки, ~ек, ~кам** *nt.* small town.
местéч|ко[2]**, ка,** *pl.* **~ки, ~ек, ~кам** *nt. dim. of* **мéсто; тёплое м.** (*coll.*) cushy job.
ме|сти́, тý, тёшь, *past* **мёл, ~лá** *impf.* **1.** to sweep. **2.** to whirl; (*impers.*): **~тёт** there is a snow-storm.
мéстност|ь, и *f.* **1.** locality, district; area. **2.** (*mil.*) ground, country, terrain.
мéстный *adj.* **1.** local; **м. колори́т** local colour. **2.** (*gram.*) locative.
-мéстный *comb. form* -seated, -seater.
мéст|о, а, *pl.* **~á, ~, ~áм** *nt.* **1.** place; site; **больнóе м.** (*fig.*) tender spot, sensitive point; **дéтское м.** (*anat.*) after-birth, placenta; **óбщее м.** platitude; **пустóе м.** blank (space); (*fig.*) a nobody, a nonentity; **слáбое м.** (*fig.*) weakness, weak spot; **ýзкое м.** bottleneck; **м. дéйствия, м. происшéствия** scene (of action); **на ~е преступлéния** in the act, red-handed; **знать своё м.** (*fig.*) to know one's place; **имéть м.** to take place; **постáвить на своё м.** (*fig.*) to put s.o. in his place; **не к ~у** (*fig.*) out of place; **по ~áм!** to your places!; **ни с ~а!** don't move!; stay put! **2.** (*in theatre, etc.*) seat; (*on ship or train*) berth, seat. **3.** space; room; **нет ~а** there is no room. **4.** post, situation; job; **быть без ~а** to be out of work. **5.** passage (*of book or mus. work*). **6.** piece (*of luggage*). **7.** (*pl.*) the provinces, the country; **на ~áх** in the provinces.
местожи́тельств|о, а *nt.* (place of) residence; **без определённого ~а** of no fixed abode.
местоимéни|е, я *nt.* (*gram.*) pronoun.
местоимéнный *adj.* (*gram.*) pronominal.
местонахождéни|е, я *nt.* location, the whereabouts.
местоположéни|е, я *nt.* site, situation, position.
местопребывáни|е, я *nt.* abode, residence.
месторождéни|е, я *nt.* (*geol.*) deposit.
мест|ь, и *f.* vengeance, revenge.
мéсяц, а *m.* **1.** month; **медóвый м.** honeymoon. **2.** moon; **молодóй м.** new moon.
мéсячник, а *m.* month (*marked by special observances or devoted to some special cause*).
мéсячный *adj.* monthly.
метаболи́зм, а *m.* metabolism.
метáлл, а *m.* metal; **презрéнный м.** filthy lucre.
металли́ст, а *m.* metal-worker.
металли́ческий *adj.* metal; metallic (*also fig.*).
металлоискáтел|ь, я *m.* metal-detector.
металлонóс|ный (~ен, ~на) *adj.* metalliferous.
металлообрабáтывающий *adj.* metal-working.
металлоплави́льный *adj.* smelting.
металлýрг, а *m.* metallurgist.
металлурги́ческий *adj.* metallurgical; **м. завóд** iron and steel works.
металлýрги|я, и *f.* metallurgy.
метаморфóз, а *m.* = **~а**
метаморфóз|а, ы *f.* metamorphosis (*also fig.*).
метáн, а *m.* (*chem.*) methane.
метáни|е, я *nt.* **1.** throwing, casting. **2.: м. икры́** spawning.
метанóл, а *m.* (*chem.*) methanol.
метáтел|ь, я *m.* (*sport*) thrower; **м. ди́ска** discus thrower.
метáтельный *adj.* missile; **м. снаря́д** projectile.
ме|тáть[1]**, чý, ∠чешь** *impf.* (*of* **~нýть**) **1.** to throw, cast, fling; **м. грóмы и мóлнии** (*fig., coll.*) to rage, fulminate; **рвать и м.** (*coll.*) to be in a rage; **м. жрéбий** to cast lots; **м. сéно** to stack hay. **2.: м. икрý** to spawn. **3.** (*cards*): **м. банк** to keep the bank.
метá|ть[2]**, ю** *impf.* (*of* **на~, с~**) to baste, tack; **м. пéтли** to edge buttonholes.
ме|тáться, чýсь, ∠чешься *impf.* to rush about; to toss (*in bed*).
метафи́зик, а *m.* metaphysicist.
метафи́зик|а, и *f.* metaphysics.
метафизи́ческий *adj.* metaphysical.
метáфор|а, ы *f.* metaphor.
метафори́ческий *adj.* metaphorical.
метéл|ица, ицы *f.* (*poet.*) = **~ь**
метёлк|а, и *f.* **1.** *dim. of* **метлá.** **2.** (*bot.*) panicle.
метéл|ь, и *f.* snow-storm; blizzard.
метео... *comb. form, abbr. of* **метеорологи́ческий**
метеопрогнози́ровани|е, я *nt.* weather forecasting.
метеóр, а *m.* **1.** meteor. **2.** hydrofoil (*vessel*).

метеори́зм, а *m.* (*med.*) flatulence.
метеори́т, а *m.* (*astron.*) meteorite.
метео́р|ный *adj. of* ~
метеоро́лог, а *m.* meteorologist; (*coll.*) weatherman.
метеорологи́ческ|ий *adj.* meteorological; **~ая ста́нция** weather station.
метеороло́ги|я, и *f.* meteorology.
метеосво́дк|а, и *f.* weather report.
метиза́ци|я, и *f.* (*biol.*) cross-breeding.
мети́л, а *m.* (*chem.*) methyl.
мети́с, а *m.* **1.** (*biol.*) mongrel. **2.** (*anthrop.*) mestizo.
ме́|тить[1]**, чу, тишь** *impf.* (*of* **на~** *and* **по~**) to mark.
ме́|тить[2]**, чу, тишь** *impf.* (*of* **на~**) **1.** (**в**+*a*) to aim at; (*fig., coll.*; **в**+*nom.-a. pl.*) to aim (at), aspire (to); **он всегда́ ~тил в профессора́** he had always had his sights set on becoming a professor. **2.** (*fig.*; **в**+*a.*, **на**+*a.*) to drive (at), mean.
ме́тк|а, и *f.* **1.** marking. **2.** mark.
ме́т|кий (~ок, ~ка́, ~ко) *adj.* well-aimed, accurate; **м. стрело́к** a good shot; (*fig.*): **~кое замеча́ние** apt remark.
ме́ткост|ь, и *f.* marksmanship; accuracy; (*fig.*) aptness.
мет|ла́, лы́, *pl.* **~́лы, ~́ел, ~́лам** *f.* broom.
мет|ну́ть, ну́, нёшь *inst. pf. of* **~а́ть**[1]
ме́тод, а *m.* method; **печа́тать слепы́м ~ом** to touch-type.
мето́д|а, ы *f.* (*obs.*) method.
методи́зм, а *m.* (*relig.*) Methodism.
мето́дик|а, и *f.* method(s); principles; **м. преподава́ния ру́сского языка́** methods of teaching Russian; **м. пожа́рного де́ла** principles of fire-fighting.
методи́ст[1]**, а** *m.* methodologist.
методи́ст[2]**, а** *m.* (*relig.*) Methodist.
методи́ст|ский *adj. of* ~[2]
метод|и́ческий *adj.* **1.** methodical, systematic. **2.** *adj. of* **~́ика; м. приём** procedure.
методи́ч|ный (~ен, ~на) *adj.* methodical, orderly.
методологи́ческий *adj.* methodological.
методоло́ги|я, и *f.* methodology..
метр, а *m.* (*unit of measurement and liter.*) metre.
метра́ж, а *m.* **1.** metric area. **2.** length in metres.
метранпа́ж, а *m.* (*typ.*) maker-up.
метрдоте́л|ь, я *m.* head waiter.
ме́трик|а[1]**, и** *f.* (*liter.*) metrics.
ме́трик|а[2]**, и** *f.* birth-certificate.
метри́ческий[1] *adj.* metric.
метри́ческ|ий[2] *adj.* (*liter.*) metrical.
метри́ческ|ий[3] *adj.*: **~ая кни́га** register of births; **~ое свиде́тельство** birth-certificate.
метро́ *nt. indecl.* (*abbr. of* **~полите́н**) **1.** the underground; the tube. **2.** (*coll.*) tube station.
метро... *comb. form, abbr. of* **метрополите́нный**
метроно́м, а *m.* (*phys., mus.*) metronome.
метрополите́н, а *m.* the underground (railway).
метрополите́н|ный *adj. of* ~
метропо́ли|я, и *f.* mother country, centre (*of empire*).
ме|ту́, тёшь *see* **~сти́**
ме́т|че *comp. of* **~кий** *and* **~ко**
ме́тчик, а *m.* (*tech.*) **1.** punch, stamp. **2.** marker.
мех[1]**, а о ~́е, в ~у́ (~́е), на ~у́,** *pl.* **~а́, ~о́в** *m.* fur; **на ~у́** fur-lined.
мех[2]**, а,** *pl.* **~и́, ~о́в** *m.* **1.** (*pl.*) bellows. **2.** wine-skin; water-skin.
механиза́тор, а *m.* **1.** specialist in mechanization. **2.** (*agric.*) machine operator, machine servicer.
механиза́ци|я, и *f.* mechanization.
механизи́р|овать, ую *impf. and pf.* to mechanize.
механи́зм, а *m.* mechanism, gear(ing); (*pl.*; *collect.*) machinery (*also fig.*).
меха́ник, а *m.* **1.** mechanic. **2.** mechanical engineer.
меха́ник|а, и *f.* mechanics.
механи́ческий *adj.* **1.** mechanical; power(-driven); **м. моме́нт** momentum; **м. тка́цкий стано́к** power loom; **м. цех** machine shop. **2.** of mechanics.
мехово́й *adj. of* **мех**[1]
меховщи́к, а́ *m.* furrier.
мецена́т, а *m.* patron.
ме́ццо-сопра́но *indecl.* (*mus.*) **1.** *nt.* mezzo-soprano (*voice*). **2.** *f.* mezzo-soprano (*singer*).
ме́ццо-ти́нто *nt. indecl.* (*art*) mezzotint.
меч, а́ *m.* sword; **дамо́клов м.** sword of Damocles.
ме́ченый *adj.* marked.
мече́т|ь, и *f.* mosque.
меч-ры́б|а, ы *f.* sword-fish.
мечт|а́, ы́ (*g. pl. not used*) *f.* **1.** dream, day-dream. **2.** dream, ambition.
мечта́ни|е, я *nt.* day-dreaming, reverie.
мечта́тел|ь, я *m.* dreamer; day-dreamer.
мечта́тел|ьный (~ен, ~ьна) *adj.* dreamy.
мечта́|ть, ю *impf.* (**о**+*p.*) to dream (of, about); **м. мно́го, высоко́** *etc.*, **о себе́** (*coll.*) to think much of o.s.
ме́|чу, тишь *see* **~тить**
ме|чу́, ~́чешь *see* **~та́ть**[1]
меша́лк|а, и *f.* (*coll.*) mixer, stirrer.
мешани́н|а, ы *f.* (*coll.*) medley, jumble.
меша́|ть[1]**, ю** *impf.* (*of* **по~**) **1.** (+*d.* +*inf.*) to prevent (from); to hinder, impede, hamper; **что ~ет вам прие́хать в Москву́?** what prevents you from coming to Moscow? **2.** (+*d.*) to disturb; **вам не ~ет, что я игра́ю на пиани́но?** does my playing the piano disturb you?; **не ~ло бы** (+*inf.*) (*coll.*) it wouldn't hurt (to).
меша́|ть[2]**, ю** *impf.* **1.** (*pf.* **по~**) to stir, agitate; **м. у́голь в пе́чке** to poke the fire; **м. в котле́** to stir the cauldron. **2.** (*pf.* **с~**) (**с**+*i.*) to mix (with), blend (with). **3.** (*pf.* **с~**) to confuse, mix up.
меша́|ться, юсь *impf.* **1.** (*coll.*; **в**+*a.*) to interfere (in), meddle (with); **не ~йтесь не в своё де́ло!** mind your own business! **2.** (*pf.* **с~**) *pass. of* **~ть**[2]
ме́шка|ть, ю *impf.* (*coll.*; **с**+*i.*) to linger, tarry (over); to loiter.
мешкова́т|ый (~, ~а) *adj.* **1.** (*of clothing*) baggy. **2.** awkward, clumsy.
мешкови́н|а, ы *f.* sacking, hessian.
ме́шкот|ный (~ен, ~на) *adj.* (*coll.*) **1.** sluggish, slow. **2.** long (*of a job*).
меш|о́к, ка́ *m.* bag; sack; **вещево́й м.** haversack, knapsack; kit-bag; **~ки́ под глаза́ми** bags under the eyes.
мешо́ч|ек, ка *m. dim. of* **мешо́к**; sac; **м. с ча́ем** tea bag.
мещан|и́н, и́на, *pl.* **~́е, ~́** *m.* **1.** (*hist.*) petit bourgeois. **2.** (*fig.*) Philistine.
меща́н|ский *adj. of* **~и́н**; (*fig.*) Philistine; bourgeois, narrow-minded.
меща́нств|о, а *nt.* **1.** (*collect.*) petite bourgeoisie, lower middle class. **2.** (*fig.*) philistinism, narrow-mindedness.
мзд|а, ы *no pl., f.* (*arch., now joc.*) recompense, payment (*iron.* = *bribe*).
ми *nt. indecl.* (*mus.*) me (mi); E.
миг, а *m.* moment, instant.
мига́лк|а, и *f.* (*coll.*) **1.** flashing light. **2.** blinker.
мига́ни|е, я *nt.* **1.** wink; twinkling. **2.** blinking.
миг|а́ть, а́ю *impf.* (*of* **~ну́ть**) **1.** to blink. **2.** (+*d.*) to wink (at); (*fig.*) to twinkle.
миг|ну́ть, ну́, нёшь *inst. pf. of* **~а́ть**
ми́гом *adv.* (*coll.*) in a flash; in a jiffy.
мигра́ци|я, и *f.* migration.
мигре́н|ь, и *f.* migraine.
мигри́р|овать, ую *impf.* to migrate.
ми́ди|я, и *f.* mussel.
мизансце́н|а, ы *f.* (*theatr.*) mise en scène, staging.
мизантро́п, а *m.* misanthrope.

мизантропи́ческий *adj.* misanthropic.
мизантро́пи|я, и *f.* misanthropy.
ми́зе́р|ный (~ен, ~на) *adj.* scanty, wretched.
мизи́н|ец, ца *m.* little finger; little toe.
микро... *comb. form* micro-
микроавто́бус, а *m.* minibus.
микро́б, а *m.* microbe.
микробио́лог, а *m.* microbiologist.
микробиоло́ги|я, и *f.* microbiology.
микрово́лнов|ый *adj.*: **~ая пе́чка** microwave (oven).
микрокомпью́тер, а *m.* microcomputer.
микроко́см, а *m.* microcosm.
микро́метр, а *m.* micrometer.
микро́н, а *m.* (*phys.*) micron.
микроорганизм, а *m.* (*biol.*) micro-organism.
микроплёнк|а, и *f.* microfilm.
микропроце́ссор, а *m.* microprocessor.
микрорайо́н, а *m.* **1.** micro-district (*administrative subdivision of urban district in former USSR*). **2.: м. шко́лы** school catchment area.
микроско́п, а *m.* microscope.
микроскопи́ческий *adj.* microscopic.
микросхе́м|а, ы *f.* microcircuit.
микрофи́льм, а *m.* microfilm.
микрофи́ш|а, и *f.* (micro)fiche.
микрофо́н, а *m.* microphone.
микрохирурги́|я, и *f.* microsurgery.
микроэлектро́ник|а, и *f.* microelectronics.
микроэлеме́нт, а *m.* **1.** (*tech.*) microelement, micro-component. **2.** trace element.
ми́ксер, а *m.* (*cul.*) blender, liquidizer.
миксту́р|а, ы *f.* (liquid) medicine, mixture.
ми́ленький *adj.* **1.** pretty; nice; sweet; dear. **2.** (*as form of address*) darling.
милитариза́ци|я, и *f.* militarization.
милитари́зм, а *m.* militarism.
милитариз|ова́ть, у́ю *impf. and pf.* to militarize.
милитари́ст, а *m.* militarist.
милитаристи́ческий *adj.* militaristic.
милиц|е́йский *adj. of* **∠ия**
милиционе́р, а *m.* **1.** policeman (*in former USSR*). **2.** militiaman.
мили́ци|я, и *f.* police (*in former USSR*).
миллиа́рд, а *m.* billion.
миллиарде́р, а *m.* billionaire; multimillionaire.
миллиа́рдный *adj.* **1.** billionth. **2.** worth billions.
миллигра́мм, а *m.* milligram(me).
миллиме́тр, а *m.* millimetre.
миллиметро́вк|а, и *f.* (*coll.*) graph paper.
миллио́н, а *m.* million.
миллионе́р, а *m.* millionaire.
миллио́нный *adj.* **1.** millionth. **2.** worth millions. **3.** million-strong.
ми́л|овать, ую *impf.* (*of* **по~**) to pardon, spare.
милови́д|ный (~ен, ~на) *adj.* pretty, nice-looking.
милосе́рди|е, я *nt.* mercy, charity.
милосе́рд|ный (~ен, ~на) *adj.* merciful, charitable.
ми́лостив|ый (~, ~а) *adj.* (*obs.*) gracious, kind; **м. госуда́рь** (*form of address*) sir; (*in letters*) (Dear) Sir; **~ая госуда́рыня** madam; (*in letters*) (Dear) Madam.
ми́лостын|я, и *no pl.*, *f.* alms.
ми́лост|ь, и *f.* **1.** favour, grace; *pl.* favours; **~и про́сим!** (*coll.*) welcome!; **скажи́(те) на м.!** (*coll.*, *iron.*) you don't say (so)! **2.** mercy; charity; **сда́ться на м. победи́теля** to surrender unconditionally. **3.** (*form of address to superior*): **ва́ша м.** your worship.
ми́лочк|а, и *f.* (*coll.*) dear(est), darling.
ми́л|ый (~, ~а́, ~л) *adj.* **1.** nice, sweet; **э́то о́чень ~о с ва́шей стороны́** it is very nice of you. **2.** dear; *as n.* **м., ~ого** *m.*, **~ая, ~ой** *f.* dear, darling.
ми́л|я, и *f.* mile.
мим, а *m.* (*theatr.*) mime.
ми́мик|а, и *f.* mimicry.
мимикри́|я, и *f.* (*biol.*) mimicry.
мими́ст, а *m.* mimic.
мими́ческий *adj.* mimic.
ми́мо *adv. and prep.+g.* by, past; **пройти́, прое́хать м.** to pass by, to pass.
мимое́здом *adv.* (*coll.*) in passing.
мимо́з|а, ы *f.* (*bot.*) mimosa.
мимолёт|ный (~ен, ~на) *adj.* fleeting, transient.
мимохо́дом *adv.* in passing; **м. упомяну́ть** (*fig.*, *coll.*) to mention in passing.
мин. (*abbr. of* **мину́та**) min., minute(s).
ми́н|а[1]**, ы** *f.* **1.** (*mil.*, *naut.*) mine. **2.** (*mil.*) mortar shell.
ми́н|а[2]**, ы** *f.* mien, expression; **сде́лать весёлую (хоро́шую) ~у при плохо́й игре́** to put a brave face on a sorry business.
минаре́т, а *m.* minaret.
миндалеви́дн|ый *adj.* almond-shaped; **~ая железа́** (*anat.*) tonsil.
минда́лин|а, ы *f.* (*anat.*) tonsil.
минда́л|ь, я́ *m.* **1.** almond-tree. **2.** (*collect.*) almonds.
минда́ль|ный *adj. of* **~**
минёр, а *m.* (*mil.*) mine-layer.
минера́л, а *m.* mineral.
минералоги́ческий *adj.* mineralogical.
минерало́ги|я, и *f.* mineralogy.
минера́льный *adj.* mineral.
Минздра́в, а *m.* (*abbr. of* ***Министе́рство здравоохране́ния***) Ministry of Health.
миниатю́р|а, ы *f.* (*art*) miniature.
миниатю́р|ный (~ен, ~на) *adj.* **1.** *adj. of* **~а. 2.** (*fig.*) tiny.
мини(-)компью́тер, а *m.* minicomputer.
минима́л|ьный (~ен, ~ьна) *adj.* minimum.
ми́нимум, а *m.* **1.** minimum; **м. за́работной пла́ты** minimum wage; **прожи́точный м.** living wage. **2.** (*as adv.*) at the least, at the minimum.
мини́р|овать, ую *impf. and pf.* (*mil.*, *naut.*) to mine.
министе́рский *adj.* ministerial.
министе́рств|о, а *nt.* (*pol.*) ministry.
мини́стр, а *m.* (*pol.*) minister.
мини-футбо́л, а *m.* ≃ five-a-side.
миниЭВМ *f. indecl.* = **мини(-)компью́тер**
ми́нн|ый *adj.* (*mil.*) mine; **~ое по́ле** minefield.
мин|ова́ть, у́ю *impf. and pf.* **1.** to pass (by); **~у́я подро́бности** omitting details. **2.** (*pf. only*) to be over, be past; **опа́сность ~ова́ла** the danger is past. **3.** (*only with* **не**+*g.*) to escape; **не м. тебе́ тюрьмы́** you cannot escape being sent to prison.
мино́г|а, и *f.* (*zool.*) lamprey.
миниска́тел|ь, я *m.* (*mil.*) mine-detector.
миномёт, а *m.* (*mil.*) mortar.
миномёт|ный *adj. of* **~**
миноно́с|ец, ца *m.* (*naut.*) torpedo-boat; **эска́дренный м.** destroyer.
мино́р, а *m.* **1.** (*mus.*) minor key. **2.** (*fig.*): **быть в ~е** to be down in the dumps.
мино́рн|ый *adj.* **1.** (*mus.*) minor. **2.** (*fig.*) gloomy, depressed.
мину́вш|ий *adj.* past; *as n.* **~ее, ~его** *nt.* the past.
ми́нус, а *m.* **1.** (*math.*) minus. **2.** (*fig.*, *coll.*) defect, shortcoming.
ми́нусовый *adj.* sub-zero; (*elec.*) negative.
мину́т|а, ы *f.* minute.
мину́т|ный *adj.* **1.** *adj. of* **~а**; **~ная стре́лка** minute-hand. **2.** momentary; **~ная встре́ча** brief encounter.
мин|у́ть, ∠ешь *pf.* **1.** (*past* **~у́л, ~у́ла**) = **минова́ть. 2.** (*past* **∠ул, ∠ула**) (+*d.*) to pass (*only in expressions of age*); **ему́ ∠уло два́дцать лет** he has turned twenty.
миопи́|я, и *f.* (*med.*) myopia.
мир[1]**, а** *m.* peace; **про́чный м.** lasting peace; **заключи́ть м.** to make peace; **иди́те с ∠ом** go in peace.

мир[2], **а**, *pl.* **~ы́** *m.* world (*also fig.*); universe; **живо́тный м.** fauna; **расти́тельный м.** flora; **престу́пный м.** the underworld; **не от ~а сего́** (*coll.*) other-worldly; **ходи́ть по́ ~у** to live by begging; **пусти́ть по́ ~у** to bankrupt, ruin utterly.
мир[3], **а** *m.* (*hist.*) mir (*Russ. village community*).
мира́ж, а *m.* mirage (*also fig.*); optical illusion.
мир|и́ть, ю́, и́шь *impf.* **1.** (*pf.* **по~**) to reconcile. **2.** (*pf.* **при~**) (**с**+*i.*) to reconcile (to).
мир|и́ться, ю́сь, и́шься *impf.* (**с**+*i.*) **1.** (*pf.* **по~**) to be reconciled (with), make up (with). **2.** (*pf.* **при~**) to reconcile o.s. (to); **м. со свои́м положе́нием** to accept the situation.
ми́р|ный (~ен, ~на) *adj.* **1.** *adj. of* **~**[1]; **2.** peaceful; **~ное сосуществова́ние** (*pol.*) peaceful co-existence.
миров|а́я, о́й *f.* amicable agreement.
мировоззре́ни|е, я *nt.* (world-)outlook, (one's) philosophy.
мир|ово́й[1] *adj. of* **~**[2]; **~ова́я война́** world war.
мирово́й[2] *adj.* (*obs.*) conciliatory; (*hist.*): **м. посре́дник** arbitrator **м. судья́** Justice of the Peace.
мирозда́ни|е, я *nt.* the universe.
миролюби́в|ый (~, ~а) *adj.* peace-loving, peaceable.
миролю́би|е, я *nt.* peaceableness.
миропома́зани|е, я *nt.* (*eccl.*) anointing.
миротво́р|ец, ца *m.* peace-maker.
ми́рр|а, ы *f.* (*bot.*) myrrh.
мирско́й[1] *adj.* secular, lay; mundane, worldly.
мир|ско́й[2] *adj. of* **~**[3]
мирт, а *m.* (*bot.*) myrtle.
ми́рт|овый *adj. of* **~**
ми́ск|а, и *f.* basin, bowl.
ми́сс *f. indecl.* Miss.
миссионе́р, а *m.* missionary.
миссионе́р|ский *adj. of* **~**
миссионе́рств|о, а *nt.* missionary work.
ми́ссис *nt. indecl.* missis, Mrs.
ми́сси|я, и *f.* **1.** mission. **2.** legation.
ми́стер, а *m.* mister, Mr.
мисте́ри|я, и *f.* (*hist.*, *theatr.*) mystery, miracle-play.
ми́стик, а *m.* mystic.
ми́стик|а, и *f.* mysticism.
мистифика́ци|я, и *f.* hoax, leg-pull.
мистици́зм, а *m.* mysticism.
мисти́ческий *adj.* mystic(al).
ми́тинг, а *m.* mass-meeting; rally.
митинг|ова́ть, у́ю *impf.* (*coll.*) to hold a rally.
митка́л|ь, я́ *m.* (*text.*) calico.
ми́тр|а, ы *f.* (*eccl.*) mitre.
митрополи́т, а *m.* (*eccl.*) metropolitan.
миф, а *m.* myth (*also fig.*).
мифи́ческий *adj.* mythic(al).
мифологи́ческий *adj.* mythological.
мифоло́ги|я, и *f.* mythology.
ми́чман, а, *pl.* (*in naval usage*) **~а́, ~о́в** *m.* (*naut.*) warrant officer.
мише́н|ь, и *f.* target (*also fig.*).
ми́шк|а, и *m.* (*coll.*) bear; teddy bear.
мишур|а́, ы́ *f.* **1.** tinsel. **2.** (*fig.*) trumpery.
мишу́рный *adj.* tinsel, tawdry (*also fig.*).
мл (*abbr. of* **миллили́тр**) ml, millilitre(s).
младе́н|ец, ца *m.* baby; infant.
младе́нческий *adj.* infant; infantile.
младе́нчеств|о, а *nt.* infancy, babyhood.
млад|о́й (~, ~а́, ~́о) *adj.* (*arch. or poet.*) young; **стар и ~** young and old (alike), one and all.
младопи́сьменный *adj.*: **м. язы́к** language having recently acquired a written form.
мла́дший *adj.* (*comp. and superl. of* **молодо́й**) **1.** younger. **2.** the youngest. **3.** junior; **м. лейтена́нт** second lieutenant.
млекопита́ющ|ее, его *nt.* (*zool.*) mammal.
мле|ть, ю *impf.* **1.** to grow numb. **2.** (**от**) to be overcome (*with an emotion*).
мле́чный *adj.* milk; lactic; **м. сок** (*bot.*) latex; **М. Путь** (*astron.*) the Milky Way.
млн. (*abbr. of* **миллио́н**) m, million(s).
млрд. (*abbr. of* **миллиа́рд**) b., billion(s) (= *thousand million*).
мм (*abbr. of* **миллиме́тр**) mm, millimetre(s).
мне *d. and p. of* **я**
мне́ни|е, я *nt.* opinion.
мни́мый *adj.* **1.** imaginary. **2.** sham, feigned.
мни́тел|ьный (~ен, ~ьна) *adj.* **1.** hypochondriac. **2.** mistrustful, suspicious.
мн|ить, ю, ишь *impf.* **1.** (*obs.*) to think, imagine. **2.**: **м. мно́го о себе́** to think a lot of o.s.
мно́г|ие, их *adj. and n.* many; **во ~их отноше́ниях** in many respects.
мно́го *adv.* (+*g.*) much; many; a lot (of); **м. вре́мени** much time; **м. лет** many years; **о́чень м. знать** to know a great deal; **м. лу́чше** much better; **ни м., ни ма́ло** (*coll.*) neither more nor less.
много... *comb. form* many-, poly-, multi-.
многобо́жи|е, я *nt.* polytheism.
многобра́чи|е, я *nt.* polygamy.
многобра́ч|ный (~ен, ~на) *adj.* polygamous.
многова́то *adv.* (*coll.*) a bit too much.
многовеково́й *adj.* centuries-old.
многогра́нник, а *m.* (*math.*) polyhedron.
многогра́нный *adj.* (*math.*) polyhedral; (*fig.*) multi-faceted.
многоде́т|ный (~ен, ~на) *adj.* having many children.
мно́г|ое, ого *nt.* much, a great deal; **во ~ом** in many respects.
многожё́н|ец, ца *m.* polygamist.
многожё́нств|о, а *nt.* polygamy.
многозада́чный *adj.*: **м. режи́м (рабо́ты)** (*comput.*) multitasking.
многозначи́тел|ьный (~ен, ~ьна) *adj.* significant.
многокра́сочный *adj.* multicoloured, polychromatic.
многокра́тный *adj.* **1.** repeated; frequent. **2.** (*gram.*) frequentative.
многоле́тний *adj.* **1.** lasting *or* living many years; of many years' standing. **2.** (*bot.*) perennial.
многолю́д|ный (~ен, ~на) *adj.* populous; crowded.
многомиллио́нный *adj.* of many millions.
многому́жи|е, я *nt.* polyandry.
многонациона́л|ьный (~ен, ~ьна) *adj.* multinational.
многоно́жк|а, и *f.* (*zool.*) myriapod.
многообеща́ющий *adj.* **1.** promising, hopeful. **2.** significant.
многообра́зи|е, я *nt.* variety, diversity.
многообра́з|ный (~ен, ~на) *adj.* varied, diverse.
многопо́ль|е, я *nt.* (*agric.*) crop-rotation system involving seven or eight fields.
многора́совый *adj.* multiracial.
многоречи́в|ый (~, ~а) *adj.* loquacious, verbose, prolix.
многосеме́|йный (~ен, ~йна) *adj.* having a large family.
многосло́в|ный (~ен, ~на) *adj.* verbose, prolix.
многосло́жный *adj.* polysyllabic.
многосторо́н|ний (~ен, ~ня) *adj.* **1.** (*math.*) multilateral (*also fig.*). **2.** (*fig.*) many-sided, versatile.
многострада́л|ьный (~ен, ~ьна) *adj.* long-suffering.
многоступе́нчатый *adj.* (*tech.*) multi-stage.
многотира́жк|а, и *f.* (*coll.*) factory newspaper; house organ.
многотира́жный *adj.* large-circulation.
многото́мный *adj.* multivolume.
многото́чи|е, я *nt.* (*typ.*) ellipsis; suspension points.
многоуважа́емый *adj.* respected; (*in letters*) dear.
многоуго́льник, а *m.* (*math.*) polygon.
многоуго́льный *adj.* (*math.*) polygonal.

многоцве́тный *adj.* **1.** multicoloured. **2.** (*typ.*) polychromatic.
многочи́слен|ный (~, ~на) *adj.* numerous.
многочле́н, а *m.* (*math.*) multinomial.
многоэта́жный *adj.* multi-storey.
мно́жественност|ь, и *f.* plurality.
мно́жественн|ый *adj.* plural; **~ое число́** (*gram.*) plural (number).
мно́жеств|о, а *nt.* a great number, a quantity; multitude; (*math.*) set.
мно́жим|ое, ого *nt.* (*math.*) multiplicand.
мно́жител|ь, я *m.* multiplier, factor.
мно́ж|ить, у, ишь *impf.* **1.** (*pf.* **по~, у~**) (*math.*) to multiply. **2.** (*pf.* **у~**) to increase, augment.
мно́ж|иться, усь, ишься *impf.* (*of* **у~**) **1.** to multiply, increase (*intrans.*). **2.** *pass. of* **~ить**
мной, мно́ю *i. of* **я**
мобилиза|цио́нный *adj. of* **~ция**
мобилиза́ци|я, и *f.* mobilization.
мобилиз|ова́ть, у́ю *impf. and pf.* (**на**+*a.*) to mobilize (for).
моби́льный *adj.* mobile.
моги́л|а, ы *f.* grave; **свести́ в ~у** to be the death of.
моги́льный *adj.* **1.** *adj. of* **моги́ла. 2.** sepulchral.
моги́льщик, а *m.* grave-digger.
мо|гу́, ~гут *see* **мочь**
могу́ч|ий (~, ~а) *adj.* mighty, powerful.
могу́ществен|ный (~, ~на) *adj.* powerful; potent.
могу́честв|о, а *nt.* power, might.
мо́д|а, ы *f.* fashion, vogue; **выходи́ть из ~ы** to go out of fashion.
мода́льный *adj.* modal.
моделир|ова́ть, у́ю *impf. and pf.* (*pf. also* **с~**) to design.
моде́л|ь, и *f.* model, pattern.
моделье́р, а *m.* (fashion) designer, couturier.
моде́ль|ный *adj.* **1.** *adj. of* **~. 2.** fashionable.
моде́льщик, а *m.* (*tech.*) modeller, pattern maker.
моде́м, а *m.* (*comput.*) modem.
моде́рн, а *m.* modernist style; *as indecl. adj.* modern; **м.-бале́т** modern dance.
модерниза́ци|я, и *f.* modernization; updating.
модернизи́р|овать, ую *impf. and pf.* to modernize; to update.
модерни́зм, а *m.* (*art*) modernism.
модерни́ст, а *m.* (*art*) modernist.
моди́стк|а, и *f.* milliner, modiste.
модифика́ци|я, и *f.* modification.
модифици́р|овать, ую *impf. and pf.* to modify.
мо́дник, а *m.* (*coll.*) trendy dresser.
мо́днича|ть, ю *impf.* (*coll.*) to dress in the latest fashions.
мо́дниц|а, ы *f. of* **мо́дник**
мо́д|ный (~ен, ~на́, ~но) *adj.* **1.** fashionable, stylish. **2.** *adj. of* **~а; м. журна́л** fashion magazine.
модули́р|овать, ую *impf.* to modulate.
мо́дул|ь, я *m.* (*math.*) modulus.
модуля́ци|я, и *f.* modulation.
моёвк|а, и *f.* (*orn.*) kittiwake.
мо́жет *see* **мочь**
можжеве́льник, а *m.* (*bot.*) juniper.
мо́жно *pred.* (*impers.*+ *inf.*) **1.** it is possible; **м. бы́ло э́то предви́деть** it could have been foreseen; **как м.**+*comp.* as ... as possible; **как м. скоре́е** as soon as possible. **2.** one may; **м. идти́?** may I (we) go?
моза́ик|а, и *f.* mosaic; inlay.
моза́ичный *adj.* inlaid, mosaic.
мозг, а, в ~у́, *pl.* **~и́, ~о́в** *m.* **1.** brain (*also fig.*); **головно́й м.** brain, cerebrum; **спинно́й м.** spinal cord. **2.** (*anat.*) marrow; **до ~а косте́й** (*fig., coll.*) to the core.
мозгови́т|ый (~, ~а) *adj.* (*coll.*) brainy.
мозгово́й *adj.* (*anat.*) cerebral; (*fig.*) brain.
мозжеч|о́к, ка́ *m.* (*anat.*) cerebellum.
мозо́лист|ый (~, ~а) *adj.* calloused.
мозо́л|ить, ю, ишь *impf.* (*of* **на~**) to make callous; **м. глаза́** (+*d.*; *fig., coll.*) to plague.
мозо́л|ь, и *f.* corn; callus; **ру́ки в ~ях** calloused hands.
мозо́ль|ный *adj. of* **~; м. пла́стырь** corn-plaster.
мой *poss. adj.* my; mine; *as n.* **мои́, мои́х** my people; **по-мо́ему** in my opinion; as I think right.
мо́йк|а, и *f.* **1.** washing. **2.** (*tech.*) washer.
мо́йщик, а *m.* washer; **м. о́кон** window-cleaner.
мо́к|нуть, ну, нешь, *past* **~, ~ла** *impf.* **1.** (*pf.* **вы́~**) to become wet, become soaked. **2.** to soak (*intrans.*).
мокри́ц|а, ы *f.* wood-louse.
мокрова́тый *adj.* moist, damp.
мокро́т|а, ы *f.* (*med.*) phlegm.
мокрот|а́, ы́ *f.* humidity, moistness.
мо́кр|ый (~, ~а́, ~о) *adj.* wet, damp; soggy; (*impers., pred.*) **~о** it is wet; **у неё глаза́ на ~ом ме́сте** (*coll.*) she is easily moved to tears.
мол[1]**, а** *m.* mole, pier.
мол[2] *parenthesis* he says (said), they say (said), *etc.* (*indicating reported speech*); **он, м., никогда́ там не́ был** he said he had never been there.
молв|а́, ы́ *f.* (*obs.*) rumour, talk; **идёт м.** it is rumoured, rumour has it.
мо́лв|ить, лю, ишь *pf.* (*obs.*) to say.
молдава́н|ин, ина, *pl.* **~е, ~** *m.* Moldovan.
молдава́н|ка, ки *f. of* **~ин**
молда́вский *adj.* Moldovan.
Молдо́в|а, ы *f.* Moldova.
моле́б|ен, на *m.* (*eccl.*) service; public prayer.
моле́кул|а, ы *f.* (*phys.*) molecule.
молекуля́рный *adj.* molecular.
моле́л|ьня, ьни, *g. pl.* **~ен** *f.* chapel, meeting-house.
моле́ни|е, я *nt.* **1.** praying. **2.** entreaty, supplication.
молески́н, а *m.* (*text.*) moleskin.
молибде́н, а *m.* (*chem.*) molybdenum.
молибде́н|овый *adj. of* **~**
моли́тв|а, ы *f.* prayer.
моли́твенник, а *m.* prayer-book.
мол|и́ть, ю́, ~ишь *impf.* (*a. and* **о**+*p.*) to pray (for), entreat (for), beseech; **~ю́ вас о по́мощи** I beg you to help me.
мол|и́ться, ю́сь, ~ишься *impf.* **1.** (*pf.* **по~; о**+*p.*) to pray (for); **он ~ится Бо́гу** he is saying his prayers. **2.** (*fig.*; **на**+*a.*) to idolize.
моллю́ск, а *m.* mollusc; shell-fish.
молниено́с|ный (~ен, ~на) *adj.* lightning-fast; **~ная война́** blitzkrieg.
молниеотво́д, а *m.* lightning-conductor.
мо́лни|я, и *f.* **1.** lightning. **2. (телегра́мма-)м.** express telegram. **3. (застёжка-)м.** zip-fastener.
молодёж|ный *adj. of* **~ь**
молодёж|ь, и *f.* (*collect.*) youth; young people.
молоде́|ть, ю, ешь *impf.* (*of* **по~**) to grow young again.
молод|е́ц, ца́ *m.* fine fellow; *as int.* **м.!** well done!
молоде́цкий *adj.* (*coll.*) dashing, spirited.
молоде́честв|о, а *nt.* spirit, dash.
моло|ди́ть, жу́, ди́шь *impf.* to make look younger.
молодня́к, а́ *m.* (*collect.*) **1.** saplings. **2.** young animals; cubs. **3.** (*coll.*) the younger generation.
молодожён|ы, ов *pl.* newly-weds.
молод|о́й (мо́лод, ~а́, мо́лодо) *adj.* **1.** young; youthful; **м. ме́сяц** new moon. **2.** *as n.* (*coll.*) **м., ~о́го** *m.* bridegroom; **~а́я, ~о́й** *f.* bride.
мо́лодост|ь, и *f.* youth; youthfulness.
молодцева́т|ый (~, ~а) *adj.* dashing.
моло́дчик, а *m.* (*coll.*) thug.
молодчи́н|а, ы *m.* (*coll.*) = **молоде́ц**
моложа́в|ый (~, ~а) *adj.* young-looking; youthful.
моло́|же *comp. of* **~до́й**

моло́к|и, ~ *no sg.* soft roe, milt.
молок|о́, а́ *no pl., nt.* milk.
молокосо́с, а *m.* (*coll.*) greenhorn, raw youth.
мо́лот, а *m.* hammer; **кузне́чный м.** sledge-hammer.
молоти́лк|а, и *f.* threshing-machine.
молоти́льщик, а *m.* thresher.
моло|ти́ть, чу́, ~́тишь *impf.* (*of* **с~**) to thresh.
молот|о́к, ка́ *m.* hammer; gavel; **прода́ть с ~ка́** to auction (off).
мо́лот|ый (~, ~а) *p.p.p. of* **моло́ть** *and adj.* ground.
моло́ть, мелю́, ме́лешь *impf.* (*of* **с~**) to grind, mill; **м. вздор** (*fig., coll.*) to talk nonsense.
молотьб|а́, ы́ *f.* threshing.
моло́чн|ая, ой *f.* dairy; creamery.
моло́чник[1]**, а** *m.* milk-can.
моло́чник[2]**, а** *m.* milkman.
моло́чниц|а[1]**, ы** *f.* dairy-maid.
моло́чниц|а[2]**, ы** *f.* (*med.*) thrush.
моло́чн|ый *adj.* **1.** *adj. of* **молоко́; м. брат** foster-brother; **~ое хозя́йство** dairy-farm(ing). **2.** milky; lactic; **~ая кислота́** (*chem.*) lactic acid.
мо́лча *adv.* silently, in silence.
молчали́в|ый (~, ~а) *adj.* **1.** taciturn. **2.** tacit.
молча́ни|е, я *nt.* silence.
молч|а́ть, у́, и́шь *impf.* to be silent, keep silence.
молчо́к *m. indecl.* (*coll.*) silence; **об э́том — м.!** not a word of (about) this!
мол|ь, и *f.* (clothes-)moth.
мольб|а́, ы́ *f.* entreaty, supplication.
мольбе́рт, а *m.* easel.
моля́щ|ийся, егося *m.* worshipper.
моме́нт, а *m.* **1.** moment; instant; **лови́ м.!** now's your chance!; go for it! **2.** feature, element, factor (*of process, situation, etc.*). **3.** (*phys.*) moment.
моментáльно *adv.* immediately, instantly.
момента́льный *adj.* instantaneous.
мона́рх, а *m.* monarch.
монархи́зм, а *m.* monarchism.
монархи́ст, а *m.* monarchist.
монархи́ческ|ий *adj.* monarchic(al).
мона́рхи|я, и *f.* monarchy.
монасты́рский *adj.* monastic.
монасты́р|ь, я́ *m.* monastery; **(же́нский)** convent.
мона́х, а *m.* monk; friar; **постри́чься в ~и** to take the monastic vows.
мона́хин|я, и *f.* nun; **постри́чся в ~и** to take the veil.
мона́шеский *adj.* monastic; (*fig., joc.*) monkish.
мона́шеств|о, а *nt.* **1.** monasticism. **2.** (*collect.*) monks.
монго́л, а *m.* Mongol, Mongolian.
Монго́ли|я, и *f.* Mongolia.
монго́л|ка, ки *f. of* **~**
монго́льский *adj.* Mongolian.
моне́т|а, ы *f.* coin; **разме́нная м.** small change; **ходя́чая м.** currency; **плати́ть кому́-н. той же ~ой** (*fig.*) to give s.o. a dose of his own medicine; **приня́ть за чи́стую ~у** (*fig., coll.*) to take at face value, take in good faith.
монетари́ст, а *m.* (*econ.*) monetarist.
монетари́ст|ский *adj. of* **~**
моне́тный *adj.* monetary; **м. двор** mint.
мони́ст|о, а *nt.* necklace.
монито́р, а *m.* (*tech.*) monitor.
монога́ми|я, и *f.* monogamy.
монога́мный *adj.* monogamous.
моногра́мм|а, ы *f.* monogram.
моногра́фи|я, и *f.* monograph.
моно́кл|ь, я *m.* monocle.
моноли́т, а *m.* monolith.
моноли́тност|ь, и *f.* monolithic character.
моноли́т|ный (~ен, ~на) *adj.* monolithic.
моноло́г, а *m.* monologue, soliloquy.
монома́н, а *m.* (*med.*) monomaniac.
монома́ни|я, и *f.* (*med.*) monomania.
монопла́н, а *m.* monoplane.
монополиза́ци|я, и *f.* monopolization.
монополизи́р|овать, ую *impf. and pf.* to monopolize.
монополи́ст, а *m.* monopolist.
монополисти́ческий *adj.* monopolistic.
монопо́ли|я, и *f.* (*econ. and fig.*) monopoly.
монопо́л|ьный *adj. of* **~ия; ~ьное пра́во** exclusive rights.
моноспекта́кл|ь, я *m.* one-man show.
монотеи́зм, а *m.* monotheism.
монотеисти́ческий *adj.* monotheistic.
моноти́п, а *m.* (*typ.*) monotype.
моното́нный *adj.* monotonous.
монта́ж, а *m.* **1.** (*tech.*) assembling, installation. **2.** (*cin.*) montage; (*art, mus., liter.*) arrangement.
монта́жник, а *m.* rigger, fitter.
монтёр, а *m.* **1.** fitter. **2.** electrician.
монти́р|овать, ую *impf.* (*of* **с~**) **1.** (*tech.*) to assemble. **2.** (*art, cin., etc.*) to mount; to arrange.
монуме́нт, а *m.* monument.
монумента́льный *adj.* monumental (*also fig.*).
мопс, а *m.* pug(-dog).
морализи́р|овать, ую *impf.* to moralize.
морали́ст, а *m.* moralist.
мора́л|ь, и *f.* **1.** (code of) morals, ethics. **2.** (*coll.*) moralizing; **чита́ть м.** to moralize, preach. **3.** moral (*of a story, etc.*).
мора́льный *adj.* moral; ethical.
морато́ри|й, я *m.* (*leg., comm.*) moratorium.
морг, а *m.* morgue, mortuary.
морганати́ческий *adj.* morganatic.
морг|а́ть, а́ю *impf.* (*of* **~ну́ть**) to blink; to wink.
морг|ну́ть, ну́, нёшь *pf. of* **~а́ть; гла́зом не ~ну́в** (*coll.*) without batting an eyelid.
мо́рд|а, ы *f.* **1.** snout, muzzle. **2.** (*coll.*) face, mug.
мо́р|е, я, *pl.* **~я́, ~е́й** *nt.*: **за́ ~ем** oversea(s); **из-за ~я** from overseas; **на́ м.** at sea; **у ~я** by the sea; **ему́ м. по коле́но** (*coll.*) he doesn't care a damn.
море́н|а, ы *f.* (*geol.*) moraine.
морёный *adj.* stained.
морепла́вани|е, я *nt.* navigation, seafaring.
морепла́вател|ь, я *m.* navigator, seafarer.
морепла́вательный *adj.* nautical, navigational.
морехо́д, а *m.* = **морепла́ватель**
морехо́дност|ь, и *f.* seaworthiness.
морехо́дный *adj.* nautical.
морж, а́ *m.* walrus; (*coll.*) (*open-air*) winter bather.
моржи́х|а, и *f. of* **морж**
морж|о́вый *adj. of* **~**
Мо́рзе *indecl.* Morse; **а́збука М.** Morse code.
мори́лк|а, и *f.* (*tech.*) stain.
мор|и́ть[1]**, ю́, и́шь** *impf.* **1.** (*pf.* **вы́~** *and* **по~**) to exterminate. **2.** (*pf.* **у~**) to exhaust, wear out; **м. го́лодом** to starve.
мор|и́ть[2]**, ю́, и́шь** *impf.* to stain (*wood*).
морко́вк|а, и *f.* (*coll.*) a carrot.
морко́в|ный *adj. of* **~ь**
морко́в|ь, и *f.* carrots.
мормо́н, а *m.* (*relig.*) Mormon.
моро́жен|ое, ого *nt.* ice(-cream); **м. в шокола́де** choc-ice.
моро́женщик, а *m.* ice-cream vendor.
моро́женщи|ца, ы *f. of* **~к**
моро́жен|ый *adj.* frozen, chilled; **~ое мя́со** chilled meat.
моро́з, а *m.* **1.** frost; **у меня́ м. по ко́же подира́ет (пошёл)** it makes (made) my flesh creep. **2.** (*usu. in pl.*) freezing cold weather.
морози́лк|а, и *f.* (*coll.*) freezer (compartment).
морози́льник, а *m.* deep-freezer.

морози́льщик, а *m.* (*coll.*) refrigerator ship.
моро́|зить, жу, зишь *impf.* (*of* **по~**) **1.** to freeze. **2.** (*impers.*): **~зит** it is freezing.
моро́зн|ый *adj.* frosty; (*impers., pred.*) **~о** it is freezing.
морозосто́йкий *adj.* (*bot.*) frost-resistant.
морос|и́ть, и́т *impf.* to drizzle.
моро́ч|ить, у, ишь *impf.* (*of* **об~**) (*coll.*) to fool, pull the wool over the eyes of; **м. го́лову кому́-н.** to take s.o. in.
моро́шк|а, и *f.* cloudberry.
морс, а *m.* fruit drink.
морск|о́й *adj.* **1.** sea; maritime; marine, nautical; **м. волк** (*coll.*) old salt; **~а́я звезда́** starfish; **м. ёж** (*zool.*) sea-urchin; **м. конёк** (*zool.*) sea-horse; **м. разбо́йник** pirate; **~а́я сви́нка** guinea-pig; **~а́я свинья́** porpoise. **2.** naval; **~а́я пехо́та** marines; **м. флот** navy, fleet.
морти́р|а, ы *f.* (*mil.*) mortar.
морти́р|ный *adj. of* **~а**
морфе́м|а, ы *f.* (*ling.*) morpheme.
мо́рфи|й, я *m.* (*pharm.*) morphine.
морфини́зм, а *m.* addiction to morphine.
морфини́ст, а *m.* morphine addict.
морфологи́ческий *adj.* morphological.
морфоло́ги|я, и *f.* morphology.
морщи́н|а, ы *f.* wrinkle; crease.
морщи́нист|ый (~, ~а) *adj.* wrinkled, lined; creased.
мо́рщ|ить, у, ишь *impf.* **1.** (*pf.* **на~**) **м. лоб** to knit one's brow. **2.** (*pf.* **с~**) to wrinkle, pucker; **м. гу́бы** to purse one's lips.
морщ|и́ть, и́т *impf.* to crease, ruck up (*intrans.*).
мо́рщ|иться, усь, ишься *impf.* **1.** (*pf.* **на~**) to knit one's brow. **2.** (*pf.* **по~** *and* **с~**) to make a wry face, wince. **3.** (*pf.* **с~**) to crease, wrinkle.
моря́к, а́ *m.* sailor.
москате́л|ь, и *f.* (*collect.*) dry-salter's wares (*paints, oil, gum, etc.*).
москате́ль|ный *adj. of* **~**; **~ная торго́вля** dry-saltery.
москате́льщик, а *m.* dry-salter.
Москв|а́, ы́ *f.* **1.** Moscow; **М. не сра́зу стро́илась** (*prov.*) Rome wasn't built in a day. **2.** the Moskva (*river*).
москви́ч, а́ *m.* **1.** Muscovite. **2.** Moskvich (*trade name of Russian-made motor car*).
москви́ч|ка, ки *f. of* **~ 1.**
моски́т, а *m.* mosquito.
моски́т|ный *adj. of* **~**; **~ная се́тка** mosquito net.
Моско́ви|я, и *f.* (*hist.*) Muscovy.
моско́вск|ий *adj.* (of) Moscow; **~ая Русь** (*hist.*) Muscovy.
мост, ~а́, о ~е, на ~у́, *pl.* **~ы́** *m.* bridge.
мо́стик, а *m.* **1.** *dim. of* **мост. 2.: капита́нский м.** (*naut.*) bridge.
мо|сти́ть, щу́, сти́шь *impf.* **1.** (*pf.* **вы́~, за~**) to pave. **2.** (*pf.* **на~**) to lay (*a floor*).
мостк|и́, о́в *no sg.* **1.** planked walkway. **2.** wooden platform.
мостов|а́я, о́й *f.* road(way), carriage way.
мост|ово́й *adj. of* **~**
мо́ськ|а, и *f.* (*coll.*) pug-dog.
мот, а *m.* prodigal, spendthrift.
мота́льный *adj.* (*tech.*) winding.
мот|а́ть[1]**, а́ю** *impf.* **1.** (*pf.* **за~, на~**) to wind, reel; **м. себе́ что-н. на ус** (*fig., coll.*) to make a mental note of sth. **2.** (*pf.* **~ну́ть**) (+*i.*; *coll.*) to shake (*head, etc.*).
мота́|ть[2]**, ю** *impf.* (*of* **про~**) (*coll.*) to squander.
мота́|ться[1]**, ется** *impf.* (*coll.*) to dangle.
мота́|ться[2]**, юсь** *impf.* (*coll.*) to rush about; **м. по́ свету** to knock about the world.
моте́л|ь, я *m.* motel.
моти́в[1]**, а** *m.* **1.** motive. **2.** reason.
моти́в[2]**, а** *m.* **1.** (*mus.*) tune. **2.** (*mus. and fig.*) motif.
мотиви́р|овать, ую *impf. and pf.* to give reasons (for), justify.
мотивиро́вк|а, и *f.* reason(s), justification.
мот|ну́ть, ну́, нёшь *pf. of* **~а́ть**[1]
мото... *comb. form, abbr. of* **1. мото́рный**[1]**. 2. моторизо́ванный. 3. мотоцикле́тный**
мото́вк|а, и *f.* (*coll.*) *of* **мот**
мотовско́й *adj.* wasteful, extravagant.
мотовств|о́, а́ *nt.* wastefulness, extravagance.
мотого́н|ки, ок *no sg.* motor-cycle races.
мотого́нщик, а *m.* motor cycle racer.
мотодро́м, а *m.* motor-cycle racing track.
мот|о́к, ка́ *m.* skein, hank.
мотоклу́б, а *m.* motorcycle club.
мотокро́сс, а *m.* moto-cross, scramble.
мотокроссме́н, а *m.* moto-cross competitor.
мотопехо́т|а, ы *f.* motorized infantry.
мотопил|а́, ы́ *f.* power saw.
мото́р, а *m.* motor, engine.
моторизо́в|анный *p.p.p. of* **~а́ть** *and adj.* (*mil.*) motorized.
моториз|ова́ть, у́ю *impf. and pf.* to motorize.
мото́р|ный *adj. of* **~**; **~ная устано́вка** power plant, power unit.
мотоaccess
моторо́ллер, а *m.* (motor-)scooter.
мотоспо́рт, а *m.* motorcycle racing.
мототрюка́ч, а́ *m.* motorcycle stunt rider.
мотоци́кл, а *m.* motor-cycle.
мотоцикле́т, а *m.* = **мотоци́кл**
мотоцикле́т|ный *adj. of* **~**
мотоцикли́ст, а *m.* motor-cyclist; biker.
мотошле́м, а *m.* crash helmet.
моты́г|а, и *f.* hoe, mattock.
моты́ж|ить, у, ишь *impf.* to hoe.
мотыл|ёк, ька́ *m.* moth.
мох, мха *and* **мо́ха, о мхе** *and* **о мо́хе, во (на) мху́,** *pl.* **мхи, мхов** *m.* moss.
мохна́т|ый (~, ~а) *adj.* hairy, shaggy; **~ое полоте́нце** Turkish towel.
моцио́н, а *m.* exercise; constitutional; **де́лать, соверша́ть м.** to take exercise.
моч|а́, и́ *f.* urine.
моча́лк|а, и *f.* loofah; washing-up mop.
моча́л|о, а *nt.* bast.
мочеви́н|а, ы *f.* (*chem.*) urea.
мочево́й *adj.* urinary, uric; **м. пузы́рь** (*anat.*) bladder.
мочего́нн|ый *adj.* (*med.*) diuretic; **~ое сре́дство** diuretic (*n.*).
мочеиспуска́ни|е, я *nt.* urination.
мочеиспуска́тельный *adj.* urinary; **м. кана́л** (*anat.*) urethra.
мочёный *adj.* soaked.
мочеполово́й *adj.* (*anat.*) urino-genital.
моч|и́ть, у́, ~ишь *impf.* (*of* **на~**) **1.** to wet, moisten. **2.** to soak; to steep, macerate; **м. селёдку** to souse herring.
моч|и́ться, у́сь, ~ишься *impf.* (*of* **по~**) (*coll.*) to urinate.
мо́чк|а[1]**, и** *f.* soaking, macerating; retting.
мо́чк|а[2]**, и** *f.* ear lobe.
мочь[1]**, могу́, мо́жешь, мо́гут,** *past* **мог, могла́** *impf.* (*of* **с~**) to be able; **мо́жет быть** perhaps, maybe; **не мо́жет быть!** impossible!; **как живёте-мо́жете?** (*coll.*) how are things with you?
моч|ь[2]**, и** *f.* (*coll.*) power, might; **во всю м., изо всей ~и, что есть ~и** with all one's might; with might and main; **~и нет (как)** it is unendurable, unbearable; **~и нет, как хо́лодно** it's so cold, I can stand it no longer.
моше́нник, а *m.* swindler, crook.

мошéннича|ть, ю *impf.* (*of* **с~**) to perpetrate swindles.
мошéннический *adj.* fraudulent, crooked.
мошéнничеств|о, а *nt.* swindling; cheating; swindle, fraud.
мóшк|а, и *f.* midge.
мошкар|á, ы́ *f.* (*collect.*) (swarm of) midges.
мошóнк|а, и *f.* (*anat.*) scrotum.
мощéни|е, я *nt.* paving.
мощённый *p.p.p. of* **мости́ть**
мощёный *adj.* paved.
мóщ|и, éй *no sg.* (*relig.*) relics.
мóщност|ь, и *f.* power; (*tech.*) capacity, rating; output; **дви́гатель ~ью в сто лошади́ных сил** hundred horsepower engine.
мóщ|ный (~ен, ~нá, ~но) *adj.* powerful, mighty.
мо|щý, сти́шь *see* **~сти́ть**
мощ|ь, и *f.* power, might.
мó|ю, ешь *see* **мыть**
мóющ|ий *pres. part. act. of* **мыть** *and adj.* detergent; **~ие срéдства** detergents.
мóющ|ийся *adj.* washable; **~иеся обóи** washable wallpaper.
мраз|ь, и *no pl., f.* (*coll.*) dregs, scum.
мрак, а *m.* darkness, gloom; **покры́то ~ом неизвéстности** shrouded in mystery.
мракобéс, а *m.* obscurantist.
мракобéси|е, я *nt.* obscurantism.
мрáмор, а *m.* marble.
мрáморный *adj.* marble.
мрачнé|ть, ю *impf.* (*of* **по~**) to grow dark/gloomy.
мрáч|ный (~ен, ~нá, ~но) *adj.* **1.** dark, sombre. **2.** (*fig.*) gloomy, dismal.
мсти́тел|ь, я *m.* avenger.
мсти́тел|ьный (~ен, ~ьна) *adj.* vindictive.
мсти́ть, мщу, мстишь *impf.* (*of* **ото~**) (*+d.* **за**+*a.*) to take revenge (on for); (**за**+*a.*) to avenge; **м. врагý** to take revenge on an enemy; **м. за дрýга** to avenge a friend.
муáр, а *m.* moire, watered silk.
муáровый *adj.* moiré.
мудрён|ый (~, ~á) *adj.* (*coll.*) **1.** strange, queer, odd; **не ~ó, что...** it is no wonder that .... **2.** abstruse, complicated.
мудрéц, á *m.* (*rhet.*) sage, wise man.
мудр|и́ть, ю́, и́шь *impf.* (*of* **на~**) (*coll.*) to complicate matters unduly.
мýдрост|ь, и *f.* wisdom.
мýдр|ый (~, ~á, ~о) *adj.* wise.
муж, а *m.* **1.** (*pl.* **~ья́, ~éй, ~ья́м**) husband. **2.** (*pl.* **~и́, ~éй, ~áм**) (*rhet.*) man; **госудáрственный м.** statesman; **учёный м.** scholar.
мужá|ть, ю *impf.* to reach manhood.
мужá|ться, юсь *impf.* to take heart, have courage; **~йтесь!** courage!
мужелóж|ец, ца *m.* sodomite.
мужелóжств|о, а *nt.* sodomy.
мужененави́стниц|а, ы *f.* misandrist.
мужененави́стничеств|о, а *nt.* misandry.
мужеподóб|ный (~ен, ~на) *adj.* mannish.
мýжествен|ный (~, ~на) *adj.* manly.
мýжеств|о, а *nt.* courage.
мужи́к, á *m.* **1.** muzhik, moujik (*Russ. peasant*). **2.** (*coll.*) bloke, guy.
мужиковáт|ый (~, ~а) *adj.* (*coll.*) loutish, boorish.
мужи́цкий *adj. of* **мужи́к 1.**
мужск|óй *adj.* masculine; male; **м. род** (*gram.*) masculine gender; **~áя шкóла** boys' school.
мужчи́н|а, ы *m.* man.
мýз|а, ы *f.* muse.
музé|й, я *m.* museum.
музéй|ный *adj. of* **~**
мýзык|а, и *f.* **1.** music. **2.** (*coll.*) band; **воéнная м.** military band. **3.: блатнáя м.** thieves' cant.
музыкáл|ьный (~ен, ~ьна) *adj.* music; musical.
музыкáнт, а *m.* musician; **ýличный м.** busker.
музыковéд, а *m.* musicologist.
музыковéдени|е, я *nt.* musicology.
мýк|а, и *f.* torment; torture; (*pl.*) pangs, throes; **родовы́е ~и** birth-pangs.
мук|á, и́ *f.* meal; flour.
мукомóльный *adj.* flour-milling.
мул, а *m.* mule.
мулáт, а *m.* mulatto.
мулл|á, ы́ *m.* mullah.
мýльтик, а *m.* (*coll.*) = **мультфи́льм**
мультимéдиа *f. indecl.* (*comput.*) multimedia.
мультим|еди́йный *adj. of* **~éдиа**
мультипликáтор, а *m.* animator, cartoonist.
мультипликáци|я, и *f.* (film) animation.
мультфи́льм, а *m.* cartoon, animation.
мультя́шк|а, и *f.* (*coll.*) = **мультфи́льм**
мýми|я, и *f.* mummy.
мунди́р, а *m.* full-dress uniform; **картóфель в ~е** jacket potatoes.
мундштýк, á *m.* **1.** mouth-piece. **2.** cigarette-holder.
муниципалитéт, а *m.* municipality; town council; **здáние ~а** town hall.
муниципáльн|ый *adj.* municipal; **~ая кварти́ра** council flat.
мур|á, ы́ *f.* (*coll.*) mess; nonsense.
мурав|éй, ья́ *m.* ant.
муравéйник, а *m.* ant-hill.
муравьéд, а *m.* (*zool.*) ant-eater.
мурав|ьи́ный *adj.* **1.** *adj. of* **~éй. 2.** (*chem.*) formic.
мурáшк|а, и *f.* (*coll.*) small insect; **~и по спинé бéгают** it gives one the creeps.
мурлы́|кать, чу, чешь *impf.* **1.** to purr. **2.** (*coll.*) to hum.
мускáт, а *m.* **1.** nutmeg. **2.** (*kind of grape*) muscat. **3.** muscatel, muscat (*wine*).
мускáт|ный *adj. of* **~; м. орéх** nutmeg.
мýскул, а *m.* muscle; **у негó ни оди́н м. не дрóгнул** (*fig.*) he didn't move a muscle.
мускулатýр|а, ы *f.* (*collect.*) muscular system.
мýскулист|ый (~, ~а) *adj.* muscular, brawny.
мýскульный *adj.* muscular.
мýскус, а *m.* musk.
мýскусн|ый *adj.* musky; **~ая кры́са** musk-rat, musquash.
мусли́н, а *m.* muslin.
мусли́н|овый *adj. of* **~**
мýсл|ить, ю, ишь *impf.* (*of* **на~**) (*coll.*) **1.** to wet moisten (*with saliva*). **2.** to beslobber; to soil (*with wet or sticky hands*); **м. кни́гу** to soil a book.
мусóл|ить, ю, ишь *impf.* (*of* **за~, на~**) **1.** = **мýслить. 2.** (*fig.*) to spend much time (over); **м. вопрóс** to drag out a question.
мýсор, а *m.* rubbish, refuse, garbage.
мýсор|ный *adj. of* **~; ~ная повóзка** dust cart; **м. я́щик** dustbin.
мусоропровóд, а *m.* refuse chute.
мусоросжигáтельн|ый *adj.*: **~ая печь** incinerator.
мусороубóрочный *adj.* refuse collection.
мýсорщик, а *m.* dustman.
мусс, а *m.* (*cul.*) mousse.
мусси́р|овать, ую *impf.* to blow up, inflate (*reports, significance of sth.*).
муссóн, а *m.* (*geog.*) monsoon.
мусульмáн|ин, ина, *pl.* **~е, ~** *m.* Muslim, Moslem.
мусульмáнский *adj.* Muslim, Moslem.
мусульмáнств|о, а *nt.* Islam, Mohammedanism.
мутáнт, а *m.* (*biol.*) mutant.
мутáци|я, и *f.* (*biol.*) mutation.
му|ти́ть, чý, ти́шь *impf.* **1.** (*pf.* **вз~, за~**) (*pres. also* **~тишь** *etc.*) to cloud (*liquids*). **2.** (*pf.* **по~**)

(*fig.*) to stir up, upset. **3.** (*pf.* **по~**) (*fig.*) to dull. **4.** (*impers.*): **меня́,** *etc.*, **~ти́т** I *etc.* feel sick.
му|ти́ться, чу́сь, ти́шься *impf.* **1.** (*pf.* **за~**) (*pres. also* **~тишься** *etc.*) to cloud (*of liquids*). **2.** (*pf.* **по~**) (*fig.*) to grow dull, dim. **3.** (*impers.*; *coll.*): **у меня́ ~ти́тся в голове́** my head is going round.
мутне́|ть, ет *impf.* (*of* **по~**) to cloud; (*fig.*) to grow dull.
му́тност|ь, и. *f.* **1.** turbidity. **2.** dullness.
му́т|ный (~ен, ~на́, ~но) *adj.* **1.** cloudy; turbid; **в ~ной воде́ ры́бу лови́ть** (*fig.*) to fish in troubled waters. **2.** (*fig.*) dull(ed); confused; **~ные глаза́** lack-lustre eyes; **~ное созна́ние** dulled consciousness.
муто́вк|а¹, и *f.* whisk.
муто́вк|а², и *f.* (*bot.*) whorl.
му́тор|ный (~ен, ~на) *adj.* (*coll.*) dreary, sombre.
му́т|ь, и *f.* **1.** lees, sediment. **2.** murk.
му́фт|а, ы *f.* **1.** muff. **2.** (*tech.*) coupling; (*elec.*) connecting box; **м. сцепле́ния** clutch.
му́фти|й, я *m.* (*relig.*) mufti.
му́х|а, и *f.* fly; **кака́я м. его́ укуси́ла** (*fig., coll.*) what's eating him?; **де́лать из ~и слона́** (*fig.*) to make a mountain out of a mole-hill; **быть под ~ой, с ~ой** (*coll.*) to be three sheets in the wind.
мухоло́вк|а, и *f.* **1.** fly-paper. **2.** (*bot.*) Venus's fly-trap. **3.** (*zool.*) fly-catcher.
мухомо́р, а *m.* fly agaric.
муче́ни|е, я *nt.* torment, torture.
му́ченик, а *m.* martyr.
му́чени|ца, цы *f. of* **~к**
му́чени|ческий *adj. of* **~к**
му́ченичеств|о, а *nt.* martyrdom.
мучи́тел|ь, я *m.* torturer; tormenter.
мучи́тел|ьный (~ен, ~ьна) *adj.* excruciating; agonizing.
му́ч|ить, у, ишь *impf.* (*of* **за~, из~**) to torment; to worry, harass.
му́ч|иться, усь, ишься *impf.* (*of* **за~, из~**) **1.** (*+i.,* **от**) *pass. of* **~ить; м. от бо́ли** to be racked with pain. **2.** (**из-за**) to worry (about), feel unhappy. **3.** (**над**) to torment o.s. (over, about).
мучни́ст|ый (~, ~а) *adj.* farinaceous.
мучн|о́е, о́го *nt.* farinaceous foods.
мучно́й *adj. of* **мука́**
му́шк|а¹, и *f.* **1.** *dim. of* **му́ха. 2.** beauty-spot.
му́шк|а², и *f.* foresight (*of fire-arm*); **взять на ~у** to take aim (at).
мушке́т, а *m.* musket.
мушкетёр, а *m.* musketeer.
муштр|а́, ы́ *f.* **1.** drill. **2.** regimentation.
муштр|ова́ть, у́ю *impf.* (*of* **вы́~**) to drill.
муэдзи́н, а *m.* muezzin.
мха, мху *see* **мох**
мчать, мчу, мчишь *impf.* to rush, speed along (*trans.*; *coll. also intrans.*).
мч|а́ться, усь, и́шься *impf.* to rush, race, tear along; **м. во весь опо́р** to go at full speed; **вре́мя ~и́тся** time flies.
мши́ст|ый (~, ~а) *adj.* mossy.
мще́ни|е, я *nt.* vengeance, revenge.
мы, *a., g., p.* **нас,** *d.* **нам,** *i.* **на́ми** *pron.* we; **мы с ва́ми** you and I.
мы́ка|ться, юсь *impf.* (*coll.*) to roam, wander.
мы́л|ить, ю, ишь *impf.* (*of* **на~**) to soap; to lather.
мы́л|иться, юсь, ишься *impf.* (*of* **на~**) **1.** to soap o.s. **2.** to lather, form a lather.
мы́л|кий (~ок, ~ка́, ~ко) *adj.* freely lathering.
мы́л|о, а, *pl.* **~а́, ~, ~а́м** *nt.* **1.** soap. **2.** (*of horse*) lather.
мыловаре́ни|е, я *nt.* soap-making.
мылова́р|енный *adj. of* **~е́ние; м. заво́д** soap works.
мы́льниц|а, ы *f.* soap-dish; soap-box.
мы́л|ьный *adj. of* **~о; м. ка́мень** soapstone; **~ьные хло́пья** soap-flakes.
мыс, а *m.* (*geog.*) cape, promontory.
мы́сик, а *m.* **1.** (*coll.*) protuberance; jutting out part. **2.** widow's peak.
мы́сленн|ый *adj.* mental; **~ое пожела́ние** unspoken wish.
мы́слим|ый (~, ~а) *adj.* conceivable, thinkable.
мысли́тел|ь, я *m.* thinker.
мы́сл|ить, ю, ишь *impf.* to think; to reason.
мысл|ь, и *f.* (**о**+*p.*) thought (of, about); idea; **за́дняя м.** ulterior motive; **о́браз ~ей** way of thinking, views; **у него́ э́того и в ~ях не́ было** it never even crossed his mind; **быть с кем-н. одни́х ~ей** to be of the same opinion as s.o.; **собира́ться с ~ями** to collect one's thoughts.
мыта́р|ить, ю, ишь *impf.* (*of* **за~**) (*coll.*) to harass, torment, try.
мыта́р|иться, юсь, ишься *impf.* (*of* **за~**) (*coll.*) to be harassed; to have a hard time of it.
мыта́рств|о, а *nt.* ordeal, hardship.
мыть, мо́ю, мо́ешь *impf.* (*of* **вы́~, по~**) to wash.
мыть|ё, я́ *nt.* wash, washing; **не ~ём, так ка́таньем** by hook or by crook.
мы́ть|ся, мо́юсь, мо́ешься *impf.* (*of* **вы́~, по~**) **1.** to wash (o.s.). **2.** *pass. of* **~**
мыч|а́ть, у́, и́шь *impf.* **1.** to low, moo; to bellow. **2.** (*fig., coll.*) to mumble.
мышело́вк|а, и *f.* mouse-trap.
мы́шечный *adj.* muscular.
мыш|и́ный *adj. of* **~ь; ~и́ная возня́ (суета́)** fussing over trifles.
мы́шк|а¹, и *f. dim. of* **мышь**
мы́шк|а², и *f.*: **под ~у, под ~ой** under one's arm; **нести́ под ~ой** to carry under one's arm.
мы́шле́ни|е, я *nt.* thinking, thought.
мыш|о́нок, о́нка, *pl.* **~а́та, ~а́т** young mouse.
мы́шц|а, ы *f.* muscle.
мыш|ь, и, *pl.* **~и, ~е́й** *f.* **1.** mouse. **2.: лету́чая м.** bat.
мышья́к, а́ *m.* (*chem., pharm.*) arsenic.
мышьяко́вый *adj.* (*chem.*) arsenic.
мэ́нский *adj.*: **м. язы́к** Manx (*language*).
мэр, а *m.* mayor.
мэ́ри|я, и *f.* **1.** town council. **2.** town hall.
мю́зикл, а *m.* musical.
мюзик-хо́лл, а *m.* music-hall.
мя́г|кий (~ок, ~ка́, ~ко) *adj.* soft; (*fig.*) mild, gentle; **м. ваго́н** (*rail.*) soft-(seated) carriage; **м. знак** (*ling.*) soft sign (*name of Russ. letter* **'ь'**); **~кое кре́сло** easy chair; **м. хлеб** new bread.
мя́гко *adv.* softly; (*fig.*) mildly, gently; **м. выража́ясь** (*iron.*) to put it mildly, to say the least.
мягкосерде́чи|е, я *nt.* soft-heartedness.
мягкосерде́ч|ный (~ен, ~на) *adj.* soft-hearted.
мягкоте́лый *adj.* soft; (*fig.*) spineless.
мя́г|че *comp. of* **~кий** *and* **~ко**
мягч|и́ть, у́, и́шь *impf.* (*of* **с~**) to soften.
мяки́н|а, ы *f.* chaff.
мя́киш, а *m.* inside, soft part (*of loaf*).
мя́к|нуть, ну, нешь, *past* **~, ~ла** *impf.* (*of* **раз~**) to soften; to become soft (*also fig.*).
мя́кот|ь, и *f.* **1.** flesh. **2.** pulp.
мя́мл|ить, ю, ишь *impf.* (*coll.*) **1.** (*pf.* **про~**) to mumble. **2.** (*no pf.*) to vacillate, dither; to procrastinate.
мя́мл|я, и, *g. pl.* **~ей** *c.g.* (*coll.*) **1.** mumbler. **2.** ditherer.
мяси́ст|ый (~, ~а) *adj.* fleshy; meaty.
мясн|а́я, о́й *f.* butcher's (shop).
мясни́к, а́ *m.* butcher.
мяс|но́й *adj. of* **~о; ~ные консе́рвы** tinned meat.
мя́с|о, а *nt.* **1.** flesh; **сла́дкое м.** (*anat.*) sweetbread. **2.** meat; **пу́шечное м.** (*fig.*) cannon fodder.

мясое́д, а *m.* meat-eater.
мясору́бк|а, и *f.* mincing-machine.
мя́т|а, ы *f.* (*bot.*) mint; **пе́речная м.** peppermint.
мяте́ж, а́ *m.* mutiny, revolt.
мяте́жник, а *m.* mutineer, rebel.
мяте́жный *adj.* **1.** rebellious, mutinous. **2.** (*fig.*) restless; stormy.
мя́тн|ый *adj.* mint; **~ые леденцы́** peppermints.
мя́т|ый *p.p.p. of* **~ь**
мять, мну, мнёшь *impf.* **1.** (*pf.* **раз~**) to work, knead. **2.** (*pf.* **из~, с~**) to crumple; to rumple (*a dress, etc.*); **м. траву́** to trample grass.
мя́ться[1], **мнётся** *impf.* (*of* **из~, по~** *and* **с~**) to become crumpled; to rumple up easily.
мя́ться[2], **мнусь, мнёшься** *impf.* (*coll.*) to vacillate.
мя́ука|ть, ю, *impf.* to mew, miaow.
мяч, а́ *m.* ball.
мя́чик, а *m. dim. of* **мяч**

Н

на́[1] *int.* (*coll.*) here; here you are; here, take it; **на́ кни́гу!** here, take the book!; **вот тебе́ на́!** well, I never!; well, how d'you like that?
на[2] *prep.* **I.** *+a.* **1.** on (to); to; into; over, through; **положи́те кни́гу на стол** put the book on the table; **сесть на авто́бус, по́езд** to board a bus, a train; **на Украи́ну** to (the) Ukraine; **на Се́вер** to the North; **на се́вер от** (to the) north of; **на заво́д** to the factory; **на конце́рт** to a concert; **перевести́ на англи́йский** to translate into English; **сла́ва его́ греме́ла на весь мир** his fame resounded throughout the world. **2.** (*of time*) at; on; until, to (*or untranslated*); **на сле́дующий день** (the) next day; **на Но́вый год** on New Year's day; **на Рождество́** at Christmas; **отложи́ть на бу́дущую неде́лю** to put off until the following week. **3.** for; **на два дня** for two days; **на́ зиму** for the winter; **на э́тот раз** this time; **на чёрный день** (*fig.*) for a rainy day; **ко́мната на двои́х** a room for two; **уро́к на за́втра** the lesson for tomorrow; **учи́ться на инжене́ра** (*coll.*) to study engineering; **на беду́** unfortunately. **4.** by (*or untranslated*); **коро́че на дюйм** shorter by an inch; **купи́ть на вес** to buy by weight; **опозда́ть на час** to be an hour late; **четы́ре ме́тра (в длину́) на два (в ширину́)** four metres (long) by two (broad); **дели́ть на два** to divide into two. **5.** worth (*of sth.*); **на рубль ма́рок** a rouble's worth of stamps.
II. *+p.* **1.** on, upon; in; at; **на столе́** on the table; **на бума́ге** on paper (*also fig.*); **на Украи́не** in (the) Ukraine; **на Се́вере** in the North; **на заво́де** at the factory; **на конце́рте** at a concert; **на со́лнце** in the sun; **на чи́стом во́здухе** in the open air; **на дворе́, на у́лице** out of doors; **на рабо́те** at work; **на мо́ре** at sea; **игра́ть на роя́ле** to play the piano; **жа́рить на ма́сле** to fry; **на свои́х глаза́х** before one's eyes; **на его́ па́мяти** within his recollection; **писа́ть на неме́цком языке́** to write in German. **2.** (*of time*) in (*or untranslated*); during; **на э́той неде́ле** this week; **на лету́** in flight, during the flight; **на кани́кулах** during the holidays. **3.** (*made, prepared with, of*); on (= *operated by means of*); **на ва́те** padded; **матра́ц на рессо́рах** sprung mattress; **э́тот дви́гатель рабо́тает на не́фти** this engine runs on oil.
на... *as vbl. pref.* **I.** *forms pf. aspect.*
II. *indicates* **1.** action continued to sufficiency, to point of satisfaction or exhaustion. **2.** action relating to determinate quantity or number of objects.
наб. (*abbr. of* **на́бережная**) Embankment.
наба́в|ить, лю, ишь *pf.* (*of* **~ля́ть**) to add (to), increase; **н. ша́гу** to quicken one's pace.
набавля́|ть, ю, *impf. of* **наба́вить**
набалда́шник, а *m.* knob; handle.
набальзами́р|овать, ую *pf. of* **бальзами́ровать**
наба́т, а *m.* alarm (bell); **бить (ударя́ть) (в) н.** to sound the alarm (*also fig.*).
наба́т|ный *adj. of* **~**
набе́г, а *m.* raid; foray, incursion.
набега́|ть, ю, *impf.* **1.** *impf. of* **набежа́ть. 2.** (*impers., coll.*) to ruck up.
набе́га|ться, юсь *pf.* to be tired out with running about; to have one's fill of running.
набе|гу́, жи́шь, гу́т *see* **~жа́ть**
набедоку́р|ить, ю, ишь *pf. of* **бедоку́рить**
набе|жа́ть, гу́, жи́шь, гу́т *pf.* (*of* **~га́ть**) **1.** (**на**+*a.*) to run against, run into. **2.** (*coll.*) to come running (*together*). **3.** (*of liquids*) to run into; to fill up; (*fig.*; *of money, etc.*) to accumulate. **4.** (*of wind*) to spring, blow up.
набекре́нь *adv.* (*coll.*) (*of hats*) aslant, at an angle.
набел|и́ть(ся), ю́(сь), ~́ишь(ся) *pf. of* **бели́ть(ся) 2.**
на́бело *adv.* clean, without corrections and erasures; **переписа́ть н.** to make a fair copy of.
на́бережн|ая, ой *f.* embankment.
набива́|ть(ся), ю(сь) *impf. of* **наби́ть(ся)**
наби́вк|а, и *f.* **1.** (*action and substance*) stuffing, padding, packing. **2.** (*text.*) printing.
набивно́й *adj.* (*text.*) printed.
набира́|ть(ся), ю(сь) *impf. of* **набра́ть(ся)**
наби́т|ый (~, ~а) *p.p.p. of* **~ь** *and adj.* packed, crowded; **зал ~ битко́м** the hall is crowded out; **н. дура́к** complete fool.
наб|и́ть[1], **ью, ьёшь** *pf.* (*of* **~ива́ть**) **1.** (*+a. and i.*) to stuff (with), pack (with), fill (with); **н. тру́бку** to fill one's pipe; **н. це́ны** to jack up prices; **н. ру́ку на чём-н.** (*fig., coll.*) to become a dab hand at sth. **2.** (*text.*) to print.
наб|и́ть[2], **ью, ьёшь** *pf.*: **н. гвозде́й в сте́ну** to drive (*a number of*) nails into a wall; **н. у́ток** to bag (*a number of*) duck.
наб|и́ться, ью́сь, ьёшься *pf.* (*of* **~ива́ться**) **1.** to crowd (*into a place*); **битко́м н.** to be crowded out. **2.** (*coll.*; *+d.*) to impose o.s. (upon), force o.s. (upon); **н. к кому́-н. в го́сти** to invite o.s. to s.o's house (*etc.*).
наблюда́тел|ь, я *m.* observer, spectator.
наблюда́тельност|ь, и *f.* powers of observation.
наблюда́тел|ьный *adj.* **1.** **(~ен, ~ьна)** observant. **2.** observation; **н. пункт** (*mil.*) observation post.
наблюда́|ть, ю *impf.* **1.** to observe; to watch. **2.** (**за**+*i.*) to look after. **3.** (**за**+*i.*) to supervise, superintend; **н. за у́личным движе́нием** to control traffic; **н. за поря́дком** to be responsible for keeping order.
наблюде́ни|е, я *nt.* **1.** observation. **2.** supervision, superintendence.
набо́б, а *m.* nabob.
на́божност|ь, и *f.* piety.
на́бож|ный (~ен, ~на) *adj.* devout, pious.
набо́йк|а, и *f.* **1.** (*text.*) printed cloth. **2.** printed pattern on cloth. **3.** heel (*of foot-wear*).
на́бок *adv.* on one side, awry.
наболе́|вший *p.p. of* **~ть** *and adj.* sore, painful (*also fig.*).

набол|е́ть, е́ет *pf.* to become painful.

наболта́|ть, ю *pf.* (*coll.*) (*+a. or g.*) to talk a lot (*of nonsense, etc.*).

набо́р, а *m.* **1.** recruitment. **2.** levy. **3.** (*typ.*) composition, (type)setting. **4.** (*typ.*) composed matter. **5.** set, collection; **н. слов** mere verbiage.

набо́рн|ый *adj.* typesetting; **~ая маши́на** typesetter (*machine*).

набо́рщик, а *m.* compositor, typesetter.

набра́сыва|ть(ся), ю(сь) *impf. of* **наброса́ть(ся)** *and* **набро́сить(ся)**

набра́|ть, наберу́, наберёшь, *past* **~л, ~ла́, ~ло** *pf.* (*of* **набира́ть**) **1.** (*+g. or a.*) to gather; to collect, assemble; **н. у́гля** to take on coal; **н. но́мер** to dial a (*telephone*) number; **н. ско́рость** to pick up, gather speed; **н. высоту́** (*aeron.*) to climb. **2.** to recruit, enrol, engage. **3.** (*typ.*) to compose, set (in type).

набра́|ться, наберу́сь, наберёшься, *past* **~лся, ~ла́сь ~́ло́сь** *pf.* (*of* **набира́ться**) **1.** (*usu. impers.*) to assemble, collect; to accumulate; **~ло́сь мно́го наро́ду** a large crowd collected. **2.** (*+g.; coll.*) to find, collect; to acquire; (*pej.*) to pick up; **н. хра́брости** to take courage; **н. блох** to pick up fleas.

набре|сти́, ду, дёшь, *past* **~̈л, ~ла́** *pf.* **1.** (**на**+*a.*) to come across; to happen upon; **я ~̈л на интере́сную мысль** I have hit on an interesting idea. **2.** to collect, gather; **~ло́ мно́го наро́ду** a large crowd gathered.

наброса́|ть[1]**, ю** *pf.* (*of* **набра́сывать**) **1.** to sketch, outline; **н. план** to outline a plan. **2.** to jot down.

наброса́|ть[2]**, ю** *pf.* to throw about; to throw, toss.

набро́|сить, шу, сишь *pf.* (*of* **набра́сывать**) to throw (on, over); **н. шаль на пле́чи** to throw a shawl over one's shoulders.

набро́|ситься, шусь, сишься *pf.* (*of* **набра́сываться**) to set upon; to go for; **соба́ка ~силась на меня́** the dog went for me; **н. на кого́-н. с вопро́сами** to deluge s.o. with questions.

набро́с|ок, ка *m.* sketch, draft.

набры́зга|ть, ю *pf.* (*+i. or g.*) to splash.

набрю́шник, а *m.* abdominal band.

набрю́шный *adj.* abdominal

набух|а́ть, а́ю *impf. of* **~́нуть**

набу́х|нуть, ну, нешь, *past* **~, ~ла** *pf.* (*of* **~а́ть**) to swell.

наб|ью́, ьёшь *see* **~и́ть**

нава́г|а, и *f.* (*zool.*) navaga (*a variety of cod*).

наважде́ни|е, я *nt.* delusion; hallucination.

нава́к|сить, шу, сишь *pf. of* **ва́ксить**

нава́лива|ть(ся), ю(сь) *impf. of* **навали́ть(ся)**

навал|и́ть, ю́, ~́ишь *pf.* (*of* **~́ивать**) to heap, pile; to load (*also fig.*); *impers.*: **сне́гу ~и́ло по коле́но** the snow had piled up knee deep.

навал|и́ться, ю́сь, ~́ишься *pf.* (*of* **~́иваться**) (**на**+*a.*) **1.** (*coll.*) to pounce (upon). **2.** to lean (on, upon); to bring all one's weight to bear (on).

нава́лом *adv.* piled up; **фру́ктов н.** loads of fruit.

нава́р, а *m.* **1.** fat (*on the surface of soup*). **2.** (*coll.*) profit; **соли́дный н.** a fat profit.

нава́рива|ть, ю *impf. of* **навари́ть**[1]

нава́рист|ый (~, ~а) *adj.* rich (*of soup*).

навар|и́ть[1]**, ю́, ~́ишь** *pf.* (*of* **~́ивать**) to weld on.

навар|и́ть[2]**, ю́, ~́ишь** *pf.* to cook, boil (*a quantity of*).

навева́|ть, ю *impf. of* **наве́ять**

наве́д|аться, аюсь *pf.* (*of* **~ываться**) (**к**; *coll.*) to call (on).

наведе́ни|е, я *nt.* laying; placing; «**н. мосто́в**» (*pol.*) bridge-building.

наве|ду́, дёшь *see* **~сти́**

наве́дыва|ться, юсь, *impf. of* **наве́даться**

навез|ти́[1]**, у́, ёшь,** *past* **~̈, ~ла́** *pf.* (*of* **навози́ть**[1]) (**на**+*a.*; *coll.*) to drive (on, against).

навез|ти́[2]**, у́, ёшь,** *past* **~̈, ла́** *pf.* (*of* **навози́ть**[2]) to bring (*a quantity of*).

наве́к, *adv.* for ever.

наве́к|и = ~

наверб|ова́ть, у́ю *pf. of* **вербова́ть**

наве́рно *adv.* probably, most likely.

наве́рно|е *adv.* = **~**

наверн|у́ть, у́, ёшь *pf.* (*of* **навёртывать**) **1.** to screw (on). **2.** to wind (round).

наверн|у́ться, у́сь, ёшься *pf.* (*of* **навёртываться**) **1.** (*coll.*) to turn up; (*of tears*) to well up. **2.** *pass. of* **~у́ть**

наверняка́ *adv.* (*coll.*) **1.** for sure, certainly. **2.** safely, without taking risks; **бить н.** to take no chances; **держа́ть пари́ н.** to bet on a certainty.

наверста́|ть, ю *pf.* (*of* **навёрстывать**) to make up (for); **н. поте́рянное вре́мя** to make up for lost time; **н. упу́щенное** to repair an omission.

навёрстыва|ть, ю *impf. of* **наверста́ть**

навер|те́ть[1]**, чу́, ~́тишь** *pf.* (*of* **~̈тывать**) to wind (round), twist (round).

навер|те́ть[2]**, чу́, ~́тишь** *pf.* (*of* **~́чивать**) to drill (*a number of*) (*holes, etc.*).

навёртыва|ть, ю *impf. of* **наверну́ть** *and* **наверте́ть**[1]

навёртыва|ться, юсь *impf. of* **наверну́ться**

наве́рх *adv.* up, upward; upstairs; to the top.

наверху́ *adv.* above; upstairs.

наве́рчива|ть, ю *impf. of* **наверте́ть**[2]

наве́с, а *m.* **1.** penthouse; awning. **2.** overhang, jutting-out part. **3.** (*sport*) lob.

навеселе́ *adv.* (*coll.*) tipsy.

наве́|сить, шу, сишь *pf.* (*of* **~шивать**[1]) **1.** (*+a. or g.*) to hang (up), suspend; **н. карти́н** to hang (*a number of*) pictures. **2.** (*sport*) to lob.

навесн|о́й *adj.*: **~а́я дверь** door on hinges; **~а́я пе́тля** hinge.

наве|сти́[1]**, ду́, дёшь,** *past* **~̈л, ~ла́** *pf.* (*of* **наводи́ть**) (**на**+*a.*) **1.** to direct (at); to aim (at); to train (on); **н. кого́-н. на мысль** to suggest an idea to s.o.; **н. на след** to put on the track. **2.** to apply (*a coat of*); **н. лоск, гля́нец** to polish, gloss, glaze. **3.** to lay, put, make; **н. поря́док** to introduce order, establish order; **н. спра́вку** to make an inquiry; **н. ску́ку** to bore; **н. страх** to inspire fear.

наве|сти́[2]**, ду́, дёшь,** *past* **~̈л, ~ла́** *pf.* (*of* **наводи́ть**) to bring (*a quantity of*).

наве|сти́ть, щу́, сти́шь *pf.* (*of* **~ща́ть**) to visit, call on.

наве́т, а *m.* (*obs.*) slander, calumny.

наве́тренный *adj.* windward.

наве́чно *adv.* for ever; in perpetuity.

наве́ш|ать[1]**, аю** *pf.* (*of* **~ивать**[1]) (*+a. or g.*) to hang (up), suspend.

наве́ш|ать[2]**, аю** *pf.* (*of* **~ивать**[2]) to weigh out (*a quantity of*).

наве́шива|ть[1]**, и** *impf. of* **наве́сить** *and* **наве́шать**[1]

наве́шива|ть[2]**, ю** *impf. of* **наве́шать**[2]

навеща́|ть, ю *impf. of* **навести́ть**

наве́|ять[1]**, ю, ешь** *pf.* (*of* **~ва́ть**) to blow; (*fig.*; *+a.* **на**+*a.*) to cast (on, over), plunge (into); **его́ расска́з ~ял грусть на слу́шателей** his story plunged the audience into gloom.

наве́|ять[2]**, ю, ешь** *pf.* (*of* **~ва́ть**) to winnow (*a quantity of*).

на́взничь *adv.* backwards, (flat) on one's back.

навзры́д *adv.*: **пла́кать н.** to sob.

навига́тор, а *m.* navigator.

навигац|ио́нный *adj. of* **~́ия**

навига́ци|я, и *f.* navigation.

навин|ти́ть, чу́, ти́шь *pf.* (*of* **~́чивать**) (**на**+*a.*) to screw (on).

нави́нчива|ть, ю *impf. of* **навинти́ть**

навис|а́ть, а́ю *impf.* (*of* **~́нуть**) (**на**+*a.*, **над**) to hang

(over), overhang; (*fig.*) to impend, threaten; **над на́ми ~а́ет опа́сность** danger threatens us.
нави́с|нуть, ну, нешь, *past* **~, ~ла** *pf. of* **~а́ть**
нави́с|ший *p.p. act. of* **~нуть** *and adj.*: **~шие бро́ви** beetling brows.
навлека́|ть, ю *impf. of* **навле́чь**
навле|ку́, чёшь, ку́т *see* **~чь**
навле́|чь, ку́, чёшь, ку́т, *past* **~к, ~кла́** *pf.* (*of* **~ка́ть**) (**на**+*a.*) to bring (on); to draw (on); **н. на себя́ гнев** to incur anger.
наво|ди́ть, жу́, ~дишь *impf. of* **навести́; наводя́щие вопро́сы** leading questions; **наводя́щий, наводи́вший** 'it' (*in children's games*).
наво́дк|а, и *f.* (*mil.*) laying, training.
наводне́ни|е, я *nt.* flood, inundation.
наводн|и́ть, ю́, и́шь *pf.* (*of* **~я́ть**) (+*a. and i.*) to flood (with), inundate (with); (*fig.*): **н. ры́нок дешёвыми това́рами** to flood the market with cheap goods.
наводн|я́ть, я́ю *impf. of* **~и́ть**
наво́дчик, а *m.* **1.** gun-layer. **2.** (*sl.*) inside man (*thieves' informant*).
наво́|жу, зишь *see* **~зить**
наво|жу́[1], **~дишь** *see* **~ди́ть**
наво|жу́[2], **~зишь** *see* **~зи́ть**
наво́з, а *m.* manure, dung.
наво́|зить, жу, зишь *impf.* (*of* **у~**) to manure.
наво|зи́ть[1,2], **жу́, ~зишь** *impf. of* **навезти́**[1,2]
наво|зи́ть[3], **жу́, ~зишь** *pf.* (*coll.*) to get in (*a supply of*).
наво́зник, а *m.* dung-beetle.
наво́з|ный *adj. of* **~; н. жук** dung-beetle; **гром не из ту́чи, а из ~ной ку́чи** (*coll.*) his bark is worse than his bite.
на́волок|а, и *f.* pillow-case, pillow-slip.
на́воло|чка = ~ка
навора́чива|ть, ю *impf. of* **наворотить**
навор|ова́ть, у́ю *pf.* (*coll.*) to steal (*a quantity of*).
наворо|ти́ть, чу́, ~тишь *pf.* (*of* **навора́чивать**) (*coll.*; +*a. or g.*) to heap up, pile up.
наворо|чу́, ~тишь *see* **~ти́ть**
навостр|и́ть, ю́, и́шь *pf.* (*coll.*) to sharpen; **н. у́ши** to prick up one's ears; **н. лы́жи** to take to one's heels.
навостр|и́ться, ю́сь, и́шься *pf.* (**в**+*p. or* +*inf.*; *coll.*) to become good (at), become adept (at); **он ~и́лся пляса́ть** he has become a good dancer.
навощ|и́ть, у́, и́шь *pf. of* **вощи́ть**
навр|а́ть[1], **у́, ёшь,** *past* **~а́л, ~ала́, ~а́ло** *pf.* (*coll.*) **1.** (*pf. of* **врать**) to romance, tell yarns. **2.** (**в**+*p.*) to make a mistake (in); **н. в расска́зе** to get the story wrong. **3.** (**на**+*a.*) to slander.
навр|а́ть[2], **у́. ёшь** *pf.* (*coll.*; +*a. or g.*) to tell (*a lot of*) (*sc. lies*); **н. вся́ких небыли́ц** to tell all manner of tales.
навре|ди́ть, жу́, ди́шь *pf.* (+*d.*) to do a great deal of harm (to).
навря́д (ли) *adv.* scarcely, hardly.
навсегда́ *adv.* for ever, for good; **раз (и) н.** once and for all.
навстре́чу *adv.* to meet; towards; **пойти́ н. кому́-н.** to go to meet s.o.; (*fig.*) to meet s.o. halfway.
навы́ворот *adv.* (*coll.*) **1.** inside out, wrong side out. **2.** (*fig.*) the wrong way round.
на́вык, а *m.* skill.
навы́кат(е) *adv.*: **глаза́ н.** bulging eyes.
навы́лет *adv.* (right) through; **он был ра́нен н. в ру́ку** he was wounded by a bullet passing right through his arm.
навы́нос *adv.* for consumption off the premises; takeaway.
навы́пуск *adv.* worn outside; **брю́ки н.** trousers worn over boots; **руба́ха н.** shirt worn outside of trousers.
навы́тяжку *adv.*: **стоя́ть н.** to stand at attention.
навью́чива|ть, ю *impf. of* **навью́чить**
навью́ч|ить, у, ишь *pf.* (*of* **вью́чить** *and* **~ивать**) to load (up).
навя|за́ть[1], **жу́, ~жешь** *pf.* (*of* **~зывать**) **1.** (**на**+*a.*) to tie on (to), fasten (to). **2.** (*fig.*; +*d. and a.*) to thrust (on); to foist (on); **н. кому́-н. сове́т** to thrust advice on s.o.
навя|за́ть[2], **жу́, ~жешь** *pf.* (*of* **~зывать**) (+*a. or g.*) to knit (*a number of*).
навяз|а́ть[3], **а́ет** *impf. of* **~нуть**
навя|за́ться, жу́сь, ~жешься *pf.* (*of* **~зываться**) (*coll.*; +*d.*) **1.** to thrust o.s. (upon), intrude (upon). **2.** *pass. of* **~за́ть**[1]
навя́з|нуть, нет, *past* **~, ~ла** *pf.* (*of* **~а́ть**) to stick; **э́то ~ло у нас в зуба́х** (*fig.*) we are sick and tired of it.
навя́зчив|ый (~, ~а) *adj.* **1.** importunate; obtrusive. **2.** persistent; **~ая иде́я** obsession.
навя́зыва|ть(ся), ю(сь) *impf. of* **навяза́ть(ся)**
нага́|дить, жу, дишь *pf. of* **га́дить**
нага́йк|а, и *f.* whip.
нага́н, а *m.* revolver.
нага́р, а *m.* (candle-)snuff.
нагиба́|ть(ся), ю(сь) *impf. of* **нагну́ть(ся)**
нагишо́м *adv.* (*coll.*) stark naked.
нагла́|дить[1], **жу, дишь** *pf.* (*of* **~живать**) to smooth (out).
нагла́|дить[2], **жу, дишь** *pf.* (*of* **~живать**) to iron (*a quantity of*).
нагла́жива|ть, ю *impf. of* **нагла́дить**
нагла́зник, а *m.* **1.** eye-shade. **2.** blinker.
нагле́|ть, ю *impf.* (*of* **об~**) to become impudent, become insolent.
нагле́ц, а́ *m.* impudent fellow, insolent fellow.
на́глост|ь, и *f.* impudence, insolence, effrontery, impertinence.
наглота́|ться, юсь *pf.* (+*g.*) to swallow (*a large quantity of*).
на́глухо *adv.* tight(ly), securely; **застегну́ться н.** to do up all one's buttons.
на́гл|ый (~, ~а́, ~о) *adj.* impudent, insolent, impertinent.
нагля|де́ться, жу́сь, ди́шься *pf.* (**на**+*a.*) to see enough (of); **на э́тот вид гляжу́ — не ~жу́сь** I never tire of looking at this view.
нагля́дно *adv.* clearly, graphically.
нагля́дност|ь, и *f.* **1.** clarity. **2.** use of visual aids.
нагля́д|ный (~ен, ~на) *adj.* **1.** clear; graphic, obvious. **2.** visual; **~ные посо́бия** visual aids; **н. уро́к** object-lesson.
наг|на́ть[1], **оню́, о́нишь,** *past* **~на́л, ~нала́, ~на́ло** *pf.* (*of* **~оня́ть**) **1.** to overtake, catch up (with). **2.** to make up (for). **3.** (*fig., coll.*) to inspire, arouse, occasion.
наг|на́ть[2], **оню́, о́нишь** *pf.* (+*a. or g.*) to herd together (*a number of*).
нагне|сти́, ту́, тёшь *pf.* (*of* **~та́ть**) to compress, force; (*tech.*) to supercharge.
нагнета́тел|ь, я *m.* (*tech.*) supercharger.
нагнета́тельн|ый *adj.* (*tech.*): **н. кла́пан** pressure valve; **~ая труба́** force pipe.
нагнета́|ть, ю *impf. of* **нагнести́**
нагне|ту́, тёшь *see* **~сти́**
нагное́ни|е, я *nt.* (*med.*) **1.** fester. **2.** suppuration.
нагно|и́т|ься, и́тся *pf.* (*med.*) to fester, suppurate.
нагн|у́ть, у́, ёшь *pf.* (*of* **нагиба́ть**) to bend.
нагн|у́ться, у́сь, ёшься *pf.* (*of* **нагиба́ться**) to bend (down), stoop.
нагова́рива|ть, ю *impf. of* **наговори́ть**[1]
наговóр, а *m.* **1.** slander, calumny. **2.** incantation.
наговор|и́ть[1], **ю́, и́шь** *pf.* (*of* **нагова́ривать**) **1.** (*coll.*; **на**+*a.*) to slander. **2.: н. пласти́нку** to record (one's voice).

наговор|и́ть², **ю́, и́шь** *pf.* (*+a. or g.*) to talk, say a lot (of); **н. чепухи́** to talk a lot of nonsense.
наговор|и́ться, ю́сь, и́шься *pf.* to talk o.s. out; **они́ не мо́гут н.** they cannot talk enough.
наг|о́й (~, ~а́, ~́о) *adj.* naked, nude, bare.
на́голо *adv.* bare; **остри́чь на́голо** to crop close.
наголо́ *adv.*: **с ша́шками н.** with drawn swords.
на́голову *adv.*: **разби́ть н.** to rout, smash.
наголода́|ться, юсь *pf.* to be half-starved.
нагоня́|й, я *m.* (*coll.*) scolding, dressing-down.
нагоня́|ть, ю, *impf. of* **нагна́ть**
на-гора́ *adv.* (*mining*) to the surface, to the top.
нагора́жива|ть, ю *impf. of* **нагороди́ть**
нагор|а́ть, а́ю *impf. of* **~е́ть**
нагор|е́ть¹, и́т *pf.* (*of* **~а́ть**) **1.** to need snuffing (*of a candle*). **2.** (*+g.*) to be used up (*of fuel*).
нагор|е́ть², и́т *pf.* (*of* **~а́ть**) (*impers., +d.; coll.*): **тебе́ за э́то ~и́т** you'll catch it for this.
наго́рн|ый *adj.* **1.** mountainous, hilly. **2.** (*of river bank*) high. **3.: Н~ая про́поведь** (*bibl.*) Sermon on the Mount.
нагоро|ди́ть, жу́, ~́дишь *pf.* (*of* **нагора́живать**) **1.** to build, erect (*in large quantity*). **2.** (*coll.*) to pile up, heap up. **3.** (*fig.*) to come out with; **н. вздо́ра, чепухи́** to talk a lot of nonsense.
наго́рь|е, я *nt.* table-land, plateau.
нагот|а́, ы́ *f.* nakedness, nudity.
наготове *adv.* in readiness; ready to hand; **быть н.** to hold o.s. in readiness, be on call.
нагото́в|ить, лю, ишь *pf.* (*+a. or g.*) **1.** to lay in, stock up with. **2.** to cook (*a large quantity of*).
награ́б|ить, лю, ишь *pf.* (*+a. or g.*) to amass by robbery.
награ́д|а, ы *f.* **1.** reward, recompense. **2.** award; decoration; (*in schools*) prize.
навра|ди́ть, жу́, ди́шь *pf.* (*of* **~жда́ть**) (*+a. and i.*) **1.** to reward (with). **2.** to decorate (with); to award, confer; (*fig.*) to endow (with); **н. кого́-н. о́рденом** to confer a decoration upon s.o.; **приро́да ~ди́ла его́ вели́кими тала́нтами** nature has endowed him with great talent.
наград|но́й *adj. of* **~́а**
наградн|ы́е, ы́х *pl. only* bonus.
награжда́|ть, ю *impf. of* **награди́ть**
награждённ|ый *p.p.p. of* **награди́ть**; *as n.* **н., ~ого** *m.* recipient (*of an award*).
нагре́в, а *m.* (*tech.*) heat, heating.
нагрева́тел|ь, я *m.* (*tech.*) heater.
нагрева́тельный *adj.* (*tech.*) heating.
нагрева́|ть(ся) ю(сь) *impf. of* **нагре́ть(ся)**
нагре́|ть, ю *pf.* (*of* **~ва́ть**) to warm, heat; **н. ру́ки** (*fig.*) to feather one's nest; to line one's pockets.
нагре́|ться¹, юсь, *pf.* (*of* **нагрева́ться**) to become warm, become hot; to warm up, heat up.
нагримир|ова́ть, у́ю *pf. of* **гримирова́ть**
нагроможда́|ть, ю *impf. of* **нагромозди́ть**
нагромоз|ди́ть, жу́, ди́шь *pf.* (*of* **громозди́ть** *and* **нагроможда́ть**) to pile up, heap up.
нагруб|и́ть, лю́, и́шь *pf. of* **груби́ть**
нагру́дник, а *m.* **1.** bib. **2.** breastplate.
нагру́дный *adj.* breast.
нагружа́|ть(ся), ю(сь) *impf. of* **нагрузи́ть(ся)**
нагру|зи́ть, жу́, ~́зишь *pf.* (*of* **грузи́ть** *and* **~жа́ть**) (*+a. and i.*) **1.** to load (with). **2.** (*fig.*) to burden (with).
нагру|зи́ться, жу́сь, ~́зишься *pf.* (*of* **~за́ться**) (*+i.*) to load o.s. (with), burden o.s. (with).
нагру́зк|а, и *f.* **1.** loading. **2.** load; **поле́зная н.** (*tech.*) payload. **3.** (*fig.*) work(load); commitments; **преподава́тельская н.** teaching load.
нагрязн|и́ть, ю́, и́шь *pf. of* **грязни́ть**
нагря́н|уть, у, ешь *pf.* (*coll.*) to appear unexpectedly; (**на**+*a.*) to descend (on).
нагу́л, а *m.* (*agric.*) fattening.
нагу́лива|ть, ю *impf. of* **нагуля́ть**
нагул|я́ть, я́ю *pf.* (*of* **~́ивать**) to acquire, develop (*as result of feeding, exercise, etc.*); **н. жи́ру** (*agric.*) to fatten, put on weight; **н. брюшко́** (*fig., joc.*) to develop a paunch; **н. аппети́т** to work up an appetite.
нагуля́|ться, юсь *pf.* to have had a long walk.
над *prep.+i.* **1.** over, above. **2.** on; at; **рабо́тать над диссерта́цией** to work on a dissertation; **смея́ться над** to laugh at.
над... *comb. form* super-, over-.
нада|ва́ть, ю́, ёшь *pf.* (*coll.; +d. and a. or g.*) to give (*a large quantity of*).
надав|и́ть, лю́, ~́ишь *pf.* (*of* **~́ливать**) (**на**+*a.*) to press (on).
нада́влива|ть, ю *impf. of* **надави́ть**
нада́ива|ть, ю *impf. of* **надои́ть**
нада́рива|ть, ю *impf. of* **надари́ть**
надар|и́ть, ю́, и́шь *pf.* (*of* **~́ивать**) (*coll.; +a. or g. and d.*) to present (*a large quantity of*).
надба́в|ить, лю, ишь *pf.* = **наба́вить**
надба́вк|а, и *f.* = **наба́вка**
надбавля́|ть, ю *impf. of* **надба́вить**
надбив|а́ть, ю *impf. of* **надби́ть**
надби́т|ый *p.p.p. of* **~ь** *and adj.* cracked; chipped.
над|би́ть, обью́, обьёшь *pf.* (*of* **~бива́ть**) to crack; to chip.
надвига́|ть(ся), ю(сь) *impf. of* **надви́нуть(ся)**
надви́н|уть, у, ешь *pf.* (*of* **надвига́ть**) to move, pull (up to, over).
надви́н|уться, усь, ешься *pf.* (*of* **надвига́ться**) to approach, draw near.
надво́дный *adj.* above-water; **н. кора́бль** surface vessel.
на́двое *adv.* **1.** in two. **2.: ба́бушка н. сказа́ла** (*coll.*) I wouldn't be too sure about that.
надво́рн|ый *adj.* situated outside; **~ая постро́йка** outbuilding.
надгорта́нник, а *m.* (*anat.*) epiglottis.
надгро́би|е, я *nt.* gravestone.
надгро́бн|ый *adj.* grave; funeral, graveside; **~ое сло́во** funeral oration.
надгрыз|а́ть, а́ю *impf. of* **~́ть**
надгры́з|ть, у́, ёшь, *past* **~, ~ла** *pf.* (*of* **~а́ть**) to nibble (at).
надева́|ть, ю *impf. of* **наде́ть**
наде́жд|а, ы *f.* hope, prospect; **подава́ть ~у** to hold out hope; **подава́ть ~ы** to promise well.
надёж|ный (~ен, ~на) *adj.* reliable, trustworthy; safe.
наде́л, а *m.* allotment; land holding.
наде́ла|ть, ю *pf.* (*+a. or g.*) **1.** to make (*a quantity of*). **2.** (*coll.; +g.*) to cause (*a lot of*), make (*a lot of*). **3.** (*coll.*) to do (*sth. wrong*); **что ты ~л?** what have you done?
надел|ённый *p.p.p of* **~и́ть; он ~ён больши́ми спосо́бностями** he is richly talented.
надел|и́ть, ю́, и́шь *pf.* (*of* **~я́ть**) (*+a. and i.*) to provide (with); (*fig.*) to endow (with).
наде́|ну, нешь *see* **~ть**
надёрг|ать, аю *pf.* (*of* **~ивать**) (*+a. or g.*) to pull, pluck (*a quantity of*).
надёргива|ть, ю *impf. of* **надёргать** *and* **надёрнуть**
надёр|нуть, ну, нешь *pf.* (*of* **~гивать**) (**на**+*a.*) to pull (on, over).
над|еру́, ерёшь *see* **~ра́ть**
наде́|ть, ну, нешь *pf.* (*of* **~ва́ть**) to put on (*clothes, etc.*).
наде́|яться, юсь, ешься *impf.* (*of* **по~**) **1.** (**на**+*a.*) to hope (for). **2.** (**на**+*a.*) to rely (on).
надзе́мный *adj.* overground.
надзира́тел|ь, я *m.* overseer, supervisor; guard.

надзира́|ть, ю *impf.* (**за**+*i.*) to oversee, supervise.
надзо́р, а *m.* **1.** supervision, surveillance. **2.** (*collect.*) inspectorate; **прокуро́рский н.** Directorate of Public Prosecutions.
надив|и́ться, лю́сь, и́шься *pf.* (*coll.*; +*d. or* **на**+*a.*) to admire sufficiently; **не мо́жешь н. на его́ му́жество** one cannot sufficiently admire his courage.
надира́|ть, ю *impf. of* **надра́ть**
надка́лыва|ть, ю *impf. of* **надколо́ть**
надколе́нн|ый *adj.*: **~ая ча́шка** knee-cap; (*anat.*) patella.
надкол|о́ть, ю́, ∠ешь *pf.* (*of* **надка́лывать**) **1.** to crack. **2.** to score.
надку|си́ть, шу́, ∠сишь *pf.* (*of* **∠сывать**) to take a bite (out) of.
надку́сыва|ть, ю *impf. of* **надкуси́ть**
надла́мыва|ть(ся), ю(сь) *impf. of* **надломи́ть(ся)**
налдежа́щий *adj.* fitting, proper; appropriate.
надлеж|и́т, *past* **~а́ло** (*impers.*, +*d. and inf.*) it is required; **вам н. яви́ться в де́сять часо́в** you are to present yourself at ten o'clock.
надло́м, а *m.* **1.** break; crack. **2.** (*fig.*) breakdown; crack-up.
надлом|и́ть, лю́, ∠ишь *pf.* (*of* **надла́мывать**) to break partly; to crack; (*fig.*) to overtax.
надлом|и́ться, лю́сь, ∠ишься *pf.* (*of* **надла́мываться**) **1.** to crack (*also fig.*); **здоро́вье у него́ ~и́лось** he has had a breakdown. **2.** *pass. of* **~и́ть**
надло́м|ленный *p.p.p. of* **~и́ть** *and adj.* broken (*also fig.*).
надме́нност|ь, и *f.* haughtiness, arrogance.
надме́н|ный (~ен, ~на) *adj.* haughty, arrogant.
на́до[1] = **над**
на́до[2] +*d. and inf.* it is necessary; one must, one ought; (+*a. or g.*) there is need of; **не н.** (*i*) one need not, (*ii*) one must not; (*iii*) *as int.* don't (do that)!; **мне н. идти́** I have to go; **мне н. вина́** I need some wine; **так ему́ и н.** serves him right!; **что н.** (*as pred.*; *coll.*) the best there is.
на́добност|ь, и *f.* necessity, need; **име́ть н. в чём-н.** to require sth.
надое́д|а, ы *c.g.* (*coll.*) pain (in the neck), nuisance.
надоеда́ла = **надое́да**
надоеда́|ть, ю *impf. of* **надое́сть**
надое́длив|ый (~, ~а) *adj.* annoying; boring, tiresome.
надое́|сть, м, шь, ст, ди́м, ди́те, дя́т *pf.* (*of* **~да́ть**) **1.** (+*d. and i.*) to get on the nerves (of), to pester (with), plague (with); to bore (with); **он мне до чёртиков ~л** I'm sick to death of him. **2.** (*impers.*, +*d. and inf.*): **мне,** *etc.*, **~ло** I, *etc.*, am tired (of), sick (of); **нам ~ло игра́ть в чехарду́** we are tired of playing leapfrog.
надо́|й, я *m.* (*agric.*) yield (*of milk*).
на́долб|а, ы *f.* stake; **противота́нковые ~ы** anti-tank obstacles.
надо́лго *adv.* for a long time.
надо́мник, а *m.* homeworker.
надорв|а́ть, у́, ёшь, *past* **~а́л, ~ала́, ~а́ло** *pf.* (*of* **надрыва́ть**) to tear slightly; (*fig.*) to (over)strain, overtax.
надорв|а́ться, у́сь, ёшься, *past* **~а́лся, ~ала́сь, ~а́лось** *pf.* (*of* **надрыва́ться**) **1.** to tear slightly (*intrans.*); to overexert o.s. **2.** to let o.s. go, let rip.
надоу́м|ить, лю, ишь *pf.* (*of* **~ливать**) (*coll.*) to advise, to give the (*required*) idea.
надоу́млива|ть, ю *impf. of* **надоу́мить**
надпа́рыва|ть, ю *impf. of* **надпоро́ть**
надпи́лива|ть, ю *impf. of* **надпили́ть**
надпил|и́ть, ю́, ∠ишь *pf.* (*of* **∠ивать**) to make an incision in (*by sawing*).
надпи|са́ть, шу́, ∠шешь *pf.* (*of* **∠сывать**) to inscribe.
надпи́сыва|ть, ю *impf. of* **надписа́ть**
на́дпис|ь, и *f.* inscription.
надпор|о́ть, ю́, ∠ешь *pf.* (*of* **надпа́рывать**) (*coll.*) to unstitch, unpick (*a few stitches*).
надпо́чечный *adj.* (*anat.*) adrenal.
над|ра́ть, еру́, ерёшь, *past* **~ра́л, ~рала́, ~ра́ло** *pf.* (*of* **~ира́ть**) (+*a. or g.*) to tear off, strip (*a quantity of*); **н. у́ши кому́-н.** to pull s.o.'s ears.
надре́з, а *m.* cut, incision; notch.
надре́|зать, жу, жешь *pf.* (*of* **~за́ть** *and* **~зывать**) to make an incision (in).
надрез|а́ть, а́ю *impf. of* **∠ать**
надре́зыва|ть, ю *impf.* = **надреза́ть**
надруга́тельств|о, а *nt.*: **(над)** outrage (upon).
надруга́|ться, юсь *pf.*: **(над)** to commit an outrage (against).
надры́в, а *m.* **1.** slight tear, rent. **2.** strain. **3.** (*fig.*) breakdown; crack-up. **4.** emotional outburst.
надрыва́|ть(ся), ю(сь) *impf. of* **надорва́ть(ся)**
надры́в|ный (~ен, ~на) *adj.* **1.** hysterical. **2.** heart-rending.
надса́д|а, ы *f.* (*coll.*) strain; effort.
надса́д|ный (~ен, ~на) *adj.* (*coll.*) back-breaking; heavy; **н. ка́шель** hacking cough.
надсма́трива|ть, ю *impf.* (**за**+*i. or* **над**) to oversee, supervise; to inspect.
надсмо́тр, а *m.* supervision; surveillance.
надсмо́трщик, а *m.* overseer, supervisor; jailer.
надста́в|ить, лю, ишь *pf.* (*of* **~ля́ть**) to lengthen (*garment or part of garment*).
надста́вк|а, и *f.* added piece, extension.
надставля́|ть, ю *impf. of* **надста́вить**
надстра́ива|ть, ю *impf. of* **надстро́ить**
надстро́|ить, ю, ишь *pf.* (*of* **надстра́ивать**) **1.** to build on. **2.** to raise the height (of).
надстро́йк|а, и *f.* **1.** building on; raising. **2.** superstructure (*also phil.*).
надстро́чный *adj.* superscript.
надтре́снут|ый (~, ~а) *adj.* cracked (*also fig.*).
надува́л|а, ы *c.g.* (*coll.*) swindler, cheat.
надува́тельский *adj.* (*coll.*) swindling, underhanded.
надува́тельств|о, а *nt.* (*coll.*) swindling, cheating.
надува́|ть(ся), ю(сь) *impf. of* **наду́ть(ся)**
надувн|о́й *adj.* inflatable; pneumatic; **н. матра́ц** air bed.
наду́манный *adj.* far-fetched, forced.
наду́м|ать, аю *pf.* (*coll.*) **1.** (+*inf.*) to decide (to). **2.** (*impf.* **~ывать**) to think up, make up.
наду́мыва|ть, ю *impf. of* **наду́мать**
наду́т|ый (~, ~а) *p.p.p. of* **~ь** *and adj.* (*coll.*) **1.** swollen. **2.** haughty; puffed up. **3.** sulky. **4.** (*liter.*) inflated, turgid.
наду́|ть, ю, ешь *pf.* (*of* **~ва́ть**) **1.** to inflate, blow up; to puff out; **н. велосипе́дную ка́меру** to blow up a bicycle tyre; (*impers.*; *pf. only*): **ве́тром ~ло пы́ли** the wind blew the dust up; **мне ~ло в у́хо** I have ear-ache from the draught; **н. гу́бы** (*coll.*) to pout one's lips. **2.** (*coll.*) to dupe; to swindle.
наду́|ться, юсь, ешься *pf.* (*of* **~ва́ться**) **1.** to fill out, swell out; **паруса́ ~лись** the sails filled out. **2.** (*fig., coll.*) to be puffed up. **3.** (*fig., coll.*) to pout; to sulk.
надуш|и́ть(ся), у́(сь), ∠ишь(ся) *pf. of* **души́ть(ся)**[2]
надшива́|ть, ю *impf. of* **надши́ть**
над|ши́ть, ошью́, ошьёшь *pf.* (*of* **~шива́ть**) **1.** to lengthen (*a garment*). **2.** to stitch on (to).
надым|и́ть, лю́, и́шь *pf. of* **дыми́ть**
наеда́|ться, юсь *impf. of* **нае́сться**
наедине́ *adv.* privately, in private; **н. с** (+*i.*) alone (with).
нае́|ду, дешь *see* **~хать**
нае́зд, а *m.* flying visit; **быва́ть ~ом** to pay short, infrequent visits.

нае́з|дить, жу, дишь *pf.* (*of* **~живать**) **1.** to cover (*driving or riding*); **мы ~дили сто миль за два часа́** we covered a hundred miles in two hours. **2.** (**доро́гу,** *etc.*) to use (a road, *etc.*) a good deal. **3.** to break in (*a horse*).

нае́здник, а *m.* horseman, rider.

нае́здничеств|о, а *nt.* horsemanship.

наезжа́|ть, ю *impf.* **1.** (*coll.*) to pay occasional visits. **2.** *impf. of* **нае́хать**

нае́з|женный *p.p.p. of* **~дить** *and adj.* well-trodden, beaten; worn.

нае́зжива|ть, ю *impf. of* **нае́здить**

нае́з|жу, дишь *see* **~дить**

на|ём, ~́йма *m.* hire; renting; **взять в н.** to rent; **сдать в н.** to let.

наёмник, а *m.* **1.** (*hist.*) mercenary. **2.** hireling (*also fig.*).

наёмный *adj.* hired; rented.

нае́|сться, мся, шься, стся, ди́мся, ди́тесь, дя́тся, *past* **~лся, ~лась** *pf.* (*of* **~да́ться**) **1.** to eat one's fill. **2.** (*+g. or i.*) to gorge o.s. (on), stuff o.s. (with).

нае́|хать, ду, дешь *pf.* (*of* **~зжа́ть**) **1.** (**на**+*a.*) to run (into, over), collide (with); **на нас ~хал авто́бус** a bus ran into us. **2.** (*coll.*) to come, arrive (*unexpectedly or in numbers*).

нажа́р|ить, ю, ишь *pf.* to roast, fry (*a quantity of*).

наж|а́ть[1], му́, мёшь *pf.* (*of* **~има́ть**) **1.** (*+a. or* **на**+*a.*) to press (on); **н. (на) кно́пку** to press the button. **2.** (*fig., coll.*; **на**+*a.*) to put pressure (upon). **3.** (*fig., coll.*) to press on, press ahead; **~мём и вы́полним э́ту рабо́ту!** let us press on and finish this job!

наж|а́ть[2], ну́, нёшь *pf.* (*of* **~ина́ть**) (*+a. or g.*) to reap, harvest (*a quantity of*).

нажда́к, а́ *m.* emery.

нажда́|чный *adj. of* **~к; ~чная бума́га** emery paper.

наж|е́чь, гу́, жёшь, гу́т, *past* **~ёг, ~гла́** *pf.* (*of* **~ига́ть**) (*+a. or g.*) to burn (*a quantity of*).

нажи́в|а[1], ы *f.* gain, profit.

нажи́в|а[2], ы *f.* = **~ка**

нажива́|ть(ся), ю(сь) *impf. of* **нажи́ть(ся)**

нажив|и́ть, лю́, и́шь *pf.* (*of* **~ля́ть**) to bait.

нажи́вк|а, и *f.* bait.

наживля́|ть, ю *impf. of* **наживи́ть**

наживн|о́й *adj. only in phr.* **э́то де́ло ~о́е** (*coll.*) it'll come (with time).

нажи|ву́, вёшь *see* **~́ть**

нажига́|ть, ю *impf. of* **наже́чь**

нажи́м, а *m.* **1.** pressure (*also fig.*) **2.** (*tech.*) clamp.

нажима́|ть, ю *impf. of* **нажа́ть[1]**

нажина́|ть, ю *impf. of* **нажа́ть[2]**

наж|и́ть, иву́, ивёшь, *past* **~́ил, ~ила́, ~́ило** *pf.* (*of* **~ива́ть**) to acquire, gain; (*fig.*) to contract (*disease*), incur.

наж|и́ться, иву́сь, ивёшься, *past* **~и́лся́, ~ила́сь** *pf.* (*of* **~ива́ться**) to become rich, make a fortune.

наж|му́, мёшь *see* **~а́ть[1]**

наж|ну́, нёшь *see* **~а́ть[2]**

наза́втра *adv.* (*coll.*) (the) next day.

наза́д *adv.* **1.** back, backwards; **н.!** back!; stand back! **2. (тому́) н.** ago.

назва́нива|ть, ю *impf.* (*coll.*) to keep ringing.

назва́ни|е, я *nt.* name; title (*book*).

назва́ный *adj.* sworn; adopted; (*fig.*): **он мой н. брат** he is my sworn brother.

наз|ва́ть[1], ову́, овёшь, *past* **~ва́л, ~вала́, ~ва́ло** *pf.* (*of* **~ыва́ть**) (*+i.*) to call; to name; **они́ ~ва́ли дочь Татья́ной** they have called their daughter Tatyana; **он ~ва́л себя́ Никола́ем** he gave his name as Nicholas.

наз|ва́ть[2], ову́, овёшь, *past* **~ва́л, ~вала́, ~ва́ло** *pf.* (*coll.*; *+g.*) to invite (*a number of*).

наз|ва́ться[1], ову́сь, овёшься, *past* **~ва́лся, ~вала́сь** *pf. of* **~ыва́ться**

наз|ва́ться[2], ову́сь, овёшься, *past* **~ва́лся, ~вала́сь** *pf.* (*coll.*) to invite o.s.

назе́мн|ый *adj.* ground, surface; terrestrial; **~ые войска́** (*mil.*) ground troops; **~ая (по́чта)** surface mail.

на́земь *adv.* (down) to the ground.

назида́ни|е, я *nt.* (*iron.*) edification; **сказа́ть что-н. в н. кому-н.** to say sth. for s.o.'s edification.

назида́тел|ьный (~ен, ~ьна) *adj.* edifying.

на́зло́ 1. *adv.* out of spite. **2.** *prep.* (*+d.*) to spite.

назнач|а́ть, а́ю *impf. of* **~́ить**

назначе́ни|е, я *nt.* **1.** fixing, setting. **2.** appointment. **3.** (*med.*) prescription. **4.** purpose. **5.** destination.

назна́ч|ить, у, ишь *pf.* (*of* **~а́ть**) **1.** to fix, set, appoint; **н. день встре́чи** to fix, appoint a day for a meeting; **н. опла́ту** to fix a rate of pay. **2.** (*+i.*) to appoint, nominate; **его́ ~или команди́ром ро́ты** he has been appointed company commander. **3.** (*med.*) to prescribe.

назо́йливост|ь, и *f.* importunity.

назо́йлив|ый (~, ~а) *adj.* importunate.

назрева́|ть, ю *impf.* (*of* **назре́ть**) **1.** to ripen, mature; to come to a head. **2.** (*fig.*) to become imminent; **кри́зис ~л** a crisis was brewing.

назре́|ть, ю, ешь, *pf. of* **~ва́ть**

назубо́к *adv.* (*coll.*): **знать н.** to know by heart.

называ́|емый *pres. part. pass. of* **~ть; так н.** so-called.

называ́|ть, ю *impf. of* **назва́ть[1]**

называ́|ться, юсь *impf.* (*of* **назва́ться[1]**) (*+i.*) **1.** to call o.s. **2.** to be called; **как ~ется э́то село́?** what is the name of this village?; **что ~ется** (*coll.*) as they say. **3.** to give one's name.

наибо́лее *adv.* (the) most.

наибо́льший *adj.* the greatest; the largest.

наи́вност|ь, и *f.* naïvety.

наи́в|ный (~ен, ~на) *adj.* naïve.

наивы́сш|ий *adj.* the highest; **в ~ей сте́пени** to the utmost.

наи́гранн|ый 1. *p.p.p. of* **наигра́ть. 2.** *adj.* (*fig.*) put on, assumed; forced; **~ая весёлость** false gaiety.

наигра́|ть, ю *pf.* (*of* **наи́грывать**) **1.** (*coll.*) to win, make (*by playing*). **2.** (*coll.*) to strum. **3.: н. пласти́нку** to make a recording.

наигра́|ться, юсь *pf.* (*coll.*) to play for a long time, for long enough.

наи́грыва|ть, ю *impf. of* **наигра́ть**

наизна́нку *adv.* inside out; **вы́вернуть н.** to turn inside out.

наизу́сть *adv.* by heart; from memory.

наилу́чший *adj.* (the) best.

наиме́нее *adv.* (the) least.

наименова́ни|е, я *nt.* appellation, designation.

наимен|ова́ть, у́ю *pf. of* **именова́ть**

наиме́ньш|ий *adj.* (the) least.

наискосо́к *adv.* = **на́искось**

на́искось *adv.* obliquely, slantwise.

найти́|е, я *nt.* inspiration; **по ~ю** instinctively, intuitively.

наиху́дший *adj.* (the) worst.

найдёныш, а *m.* foundling.

найми́т, а *m.* hireling.

на|йти́[1], ~йду́, ~йдёшь, *past* **~шёл, ~шла́** *pf.* (*of* **~ходи́ть**) to find; to discover; **н. себе́ моги́лу, смерть** (*rhet.*) to meet one's death.

на|йти́[2], йду́, йдёшь, *past* **~шёл, ~шла́** *pf.* (*of* **~ходи́ть**) **1.** (**на**+*a.*) to come (across, over, upon); to come (up against); **что э́то на неё ~шло́?** what has come over her? **2.** (*impers., coll.*) to gather, collect; **~шло́ мно́го наро́ду** a large crowd collected.

на|йти́сь, йду́сь, йдёшься, *past* **~шёлся, ~шла́сь**

pf. (*of* **~ходи́ться**[1]) **1.** to be found; to turn up. **2.** not to be at a loss; **я не ~шёлся, что сказа́ть** I was at a loss for what to say.
нака́з, а *m.* **1.** (*obs.*) order; instructions. **2.** (*pol.*) mandate.
наказа́ни|е, я *nt.* **1.** punishment. **2.** (*fig., coll.*) nuisance; **мне с ним (су́щее, пря́мо, про́сто) н.** he is a (perfect) nuisance to me.
нака|за́ть, жу́, ~жешь *pf.* (*of* **~зывать**) to punish.
наказу́емый *adj.* (*leg.*) punishable.
нака́л, а *m.* **1.** incandescence. **2.** (*fig.*) tension.
накал|ённый *p.p.p. of* **~и́ть** *and adj.* **1.** incandescent; white-hot. **2.** (*fig.*) strained, tense; **~ённая междунаро́дная обстано́вка** tense international situation.
нака́лива|ть(ся), ю(сь) *impf. of* **накали́ть(ся)**
накал|и́ть, ю́, и́шь *pf.* (*of* **~ивать**) to heat, incandesce.
накал|и́ться, ю́сь, и́шься *pf.* (*of* **~иваться**) to glow, incandesce.
нака́лыва|ть(ся), ю(сь) *impf. of* **наколо́ть(ся)**
наканифо́л|ить, ю, ишь *pf. of* **канифо́лить**
накану́не 1. (*adv.*) the day before. **2.** (*prep.+g.*) on the eve (of); **н. Рождества́ Христо́ва** on Christmas Eve.
нака́п|ать, аю *pf.* (*of* **~ывать**[1]) **1.** (*+a. or g.*) to pour by drops; **н. лека́рства** to pour out some medicine. **2.** (*+g. or i.*) to spill; **он ~ал на столе́ черни́лами (черни́л)** he has spilled ink on the table.
нака́пливать(ся) *impf.* = **накопля́ть(ся)**
нака́пыва|ть[1]**, ю** *impf. of* **нака́пать**
нака́пыва|ть[2]**, ю** *impf. of* **накопа́ть**
накат|а́ть[1]**, а́ю** *pf.* (*of* **~ывать**) **1.** to roll out; to roll smooth. **2.** (*coll.*) to write hurriedly; **н. письмо́** to dash off a letter.
накат|а́ть[2]**, а́ю** *pf.* (*of* **~ывать**) (*+a. or g.*) to roll (*a quantity of*).
нака|ти́ть, чу́, ~тишь *pf.* (*of* **~тывать**) (**на**+*a.*) to roll up (onto).
нака́тыва|ть, ю *impf. of* **наката́ть** *and* **накати́ть**
накач|а́ть[1]**, а́ю** *pf.* (*of* **~ивать**) to pump up, pump full.
накача́|ть[2]**, а́ю** *pf.* to pump (*a quantity of*).
накач|а́ться, а́юсь *pf.* (*of* **~иваться**) **1.** (*coll.*) to become sozzled. **2.** *pass. of* **~а́ть**
нака́чива|ть(ся), ю(сь) *impf. of* **накача́ть(ся)**
накид|а́ть, а́ю *pf.* (*of* **~ывать**) = **наброса́ть**[2]
наки́дк|а, и *f.* **1.** cloak, mantle; wrap. **2.** pillow-cover. **3.** increase; extra charge.
наки́дыва|ть(ся), ю(сь) *impf. of* **накида́ть** *and* **наки́нуть(ся)**
наки́|нуть, ну, нешь *pf.* (*of* **~дывать**) **1.** to throw on, throw over. **2.** (**на**+*a.*) to add (*to the price of*).
наки́|нуться, нусь, нешься *pf.* (*of* **~дываться**) (**на**+*a.*) to attack; to pounce (on, upon).
накип|а́ть, а́ет *impf. of* **~е́ть**
накип|е́ть, и́т *pf.* (*of* **~а́ть**) to form a scum; to form a scale; (*fig., impers.*) to swell, boil; **в нём ~е́ла зло́ба** he is boiling with resentment.
на́кип|ь, и *f.* **1.** scum. **2.** scale, fur, coating, deposit.
накла́дк|а, и *f.* **1.** hair-piece. **2.** (*sl.*) blunder, clanger.
накладн|а́я, о́й *f.* invoice, way-bill.
накла́дно *adv.* (*coll.*) to one's disadvantage, to one's cost.
накладн|о́й *adj.* **1.** superimposed; **~о́е зо́лото** rolled gold; **н. карма́н** patch pocket; **~ы́е расхо́ды** overheads. **2.** false; **~а́я борода́** false beard.
накла́дыва|ть, ю *impf. of* **наложи́ть**
наклеве|та́ть, щу́, ~щешь *pf. of* **клевета́ть**
накле́ива|ть, ю *impf. of* **накле́ить**
накле́|ить, ю, ешь *pf.* (*of* **~ивать**) to stick on, paste on.
накле́йк|а, и *f.* **1.** sticking on, pasting on. **2.** sticker.
наклепа́|ть, ю *pf.* (*of* **наклёпывать**) to rivet.
наклёпыва|ть, ю *impf. of* **наклепа́ть**
наклик|а́ть, а́ю *impf. of* **~ать**
накли́|кать, чу, чешь *pf.* (*of* **~ка́ть**); **н. на себя́** to bring upon o.s.; **н. беду́ (на**+*a.*) to bring disaster (upon).
накло́н, а *m.* slope, incline; declivity.
наклоне́ни|е[1]**, я** *nt.* inclination.
наклоне́ни|е[2]**, я** *nt.* (*gram.*) mood.
наклон|и́ть, ю́, ~ишь *pf.* (*of* **~я́ть**) to incline, bend; to bow.
наклон|и́ться, ю́сь, ~ишься *pf.* (*of* **~я́ться**) to stoop, bend.
накло́нност|ь, и *f.* **1. (к)** leaning (towards), penchant (for). **2.** inclination, propensity, proclivity; **дурны́е ~и** evil propensities.
накло́нн|ый *adj.* inclined, sloping; **~ая пло́скость** inclined plane; **кати́ться по ~ой пло́скости** (*fig.*) to go downhill, go to the dogs.
наклон|я́ть(ся), я́ю(сь) *impf. of* **~и́ть(ся)**
накля́узнича|ть, ю *pf. of* **кля́узничать**
накова́л|ьня, ьни, *g. pl.* **~ен** *f.* anvil.
нако́жный *adj.* (*med.*) cutaneous; skin.
наколе́нник, а *m.* knee-pad.
накол|о́ть[1]**, ю́, ~ешь** *pf.* (*of* **нака́лывать**) (*+a. or g.*) to split (*a quantity of*); **н. дров** to chop (*a quantity of*) wood.
накол|о́ть[2]**, ю́, ~ешь** *pf.* (*of* **нака́лывать**) **1.** to prick; **н. узо́р** to prick out a pattern. **2.** to pin down; **н. ба́бочку на була́вку** to pin down a butterfly. **3.** to slaughter, kill (*a number of*).
накол|о́ться, ю́сь, ~ешься *pf.* (*of* **нака́лываться**) to prick o.s.
наконе́ц *adv.* at last; finally; **н.-то!** at long last!; (and) about time too!
наконе́чник, а *m.* tip, point; **н. стрелы́** arrow-head.
наконе́чн|ый *adj.* final; **~ое ударе́ние** (*gram.*) end-stress.
накопа́|ть, ю *pf.* (*of* **нака́пывать**) (*+a. or g.*) to dig up (*a number of*).
накопи́тел|ь, я *m.* (*comput.*) storage; **н. на ди́сках** disk drive.
накоп|и́ть, лю́, ~ишь *pf.* (*of* **копи́ть; ~ля́ть** *and* **нака́пливать**) (*+a. or g.*) to accumulate, amass.
накоп|и́ться, лю́сь, ~ишься *pf.* (*of* **~ля́ться** *and* **нака́пливаться**) to accumulate.
накопле́ни|е, я *nt.* accumulation.
накопля́|ть(ся), ю(сь) *impf. of* **накопи́ть(ся)**
накоп|ти́ть, чу́, ти́шь *pf. of* **копти́ть 3.**
накорм|и́ть, лю́, ~ишь *pf. of* **корми́ть**
накоротке́ *adv.*: **произвести́ ата́ку н.** to carry out an attack at close range.
нако́стн|ый *adj.* (*situated on*) bone; **~ая о́пухоль** bone tumour.
накра́пыва|ть, ет *impf.* (*impers. or* +**дождь**) to trickle, drizzle; **ста́ло н.** it began to drizzle (*with rain*).
накра́|сить, шу, сишь *pf.* (*of* **~шивать**) **1.** to paint. **2.** to make up.
накра́|ситься, шусь, сишься *pf. of* **кра́ситься**
накра́|сть, ду́, дёшь, *past* **~л** *pf.* (*of* **~дывать**) (*+a. or g.*) to steal (*a number of*).
накрахма́л|ить, ю, ишь *pf. of* **крахма́лить**
накра́шива|ть, ю *impf. of* **накра́сить**
накрен|и́ть, ю́, и́шь *pf.* **1.** *pf. of* **крени́ть. 2.** (*impf.* **~я́ть**) to tilt to one side, tilt.
накрен|и́ться, ю́сь, и́шься *pf.* **1.** *pf. of* **крени́ться. 2.** (*impf.* **~я́ться**) to tilt, list.
накрен|я́ть(ся), я́ю(сь) *impf. of* **~и́ть(ся)**
на́крепко *adv.* **1.** fast, tight; **закры́ть н.** to shut fast. **2.** (*coll.*) categorically; strictly; **приказа́ть н.** to give a strict injunction.
на́крест *adv.* crosswise; **сложи́ть ру́ки крест-н.** to

cross one's arms.

накрич|áть, ý, и́шь *pf.* (**на**+*a.*) to shout (at).

накро|и́ть, ю́, и́шь *pf.* (+*a. or g.*) to cut out (*a quantity of*).

накрош|и́ть, ý, ∸ишь *pf.* (*of* **кроши́ть**) **1.** to crumble, shred (*a quantity of*). **2.** to spill crumbs.

накр|óю, óешь *see* **~ы́ть**

накро|ю́, и́шь *see* **~и́ть**

накру|ти́ть, чý, ∸тишь *pf.* (*of* **~чивать**) to wind, turn.

накрýчива|ть, ю *impf. of* **накрути́ть**

накрывá|ть(ся), ю(сь) *impf. of* **накры́ть(ся)**

накр|ы́ть, óю, óешь *pf.* (*of* **~ывáть**) **1.** to cover; **н. (на) стол** to lay the table; **н. к ýжину** to lay supper. **2.** (*fig., coll.*) to catch (in the act); **н. на мéсте преступлéния** to catch red-handed.

накр|ы́ться, óюсь, óешься *pf.* (*of* **~ывáться**) (+*i.*) to cover o.s. (with).

накуп|áть, áю *impf. of* **~и́ть**

накуп|и́ть, лю́, ∸ишь *pf.* (*of* **~áть**) (+*a. or g.*) to buy up (*a number or quantity of*).

накýр|енный *p.p.p. of* **~и́ть** *and adj.* smoky, smoke-filled; **в. кóмнате ~ено** the room is full of (tobacco) smoke.

накур|и́ть, ю́, ∸ишь *pf.* (+*i.*) to fill with smoke, with fumes.

накур|и́ться, ю́сь, ∸ишься *pf.* (*coll.*) to smoke to one's heart's content.

налáвлива|ть, ю *impf. of* **налови́ть**

налагá|ть, ю *impf. of* **наложи́ть**

налá|дить, жу, дишь *pf.* (*of* **~живать**) **1.** to regulate, adjust; to repair, put right. **2.** to set going, arrange; **н. делá** to get things going.

налá|диться, жусь, дишься *pf.* (*of* **~живаться**) **1.** to go right; **рабóта ~дилась** the work is well in hand. **2.** *pass. of* **~дить**

налáдчик, а *m.* (*tech.*) adjuster.

налáжива|ть(ся), ю(сь) *impf. of* **налáдить(ся)**

на|лгáть, лгý, лжёшь, лгýт, *past* **~лгáл, ~лгалá, ~лгáло** *pf.* **1.** to lie, tell lies. **2.** (*impf.* **лгать 2.**) (**на**+*a.*) to slander.

налéво *adv.* **1. (от)** to the left (of); **н.!** (*mil.*) left turn! **2.** (*coll.*) on the side (= *illicitly*); **рабóтать н.** to moonlight.

налегá|ть, ю *impf. of* **налéчь**

налегкé *adv.* (*coll.*) **1.** without luggage; **путешéствовать н.** to travel light. **2.** lightly clad.

налез|áть[1,2], áю *impf. of* **∸ть[1,2]**

налéз|ть[1], у, ешь, *past* **~, ~ла** *pf.* (*of* **~áть[1]**) to get in, get on (*in large numbers, in quantities*).

налéз|ть[2], ет *pf.* (*of* **~áть[2]**) (*of clothing or footwear*) (**на**+*a.*) to fit, go on.

налеп|и́ть[1], лю́, ∸ишь *pf.* (*of* **лепи́ть 2.** *and* **~ля́ть**) to stick on.

налеп|и́ть[2], лю́, ∸ишь *pf.* (+*a. or g.*) to model (*a number of*).

налеп|ля́ть, ля́ю, *impf. of* **~и́ть[1]**

налёт[1], а *m.* raid; **воздýшный н.** air-raid; **с ~а** (*fig.*) suddenly, without warning; **бить с ~а** to swoop down on.

налёт[2], а *m.* deposit; thin coating; (*on bronze*) patina; **зубнóй н.** dental plaque; (*fig.*) touch, tinge; **с ~ом ирóнии** with a touch of irony.

налет|áть[1], áю *impf. of* **~éть**

налет|áть[2], áю *pf.* to have flown (so many hours *or* miles).

нале|тéть[1], чý, ти́шь *pf.* (*of* **~тáть[1]**) **1.** (**на**+*a.*) to fall (upon); to swoop down (on); to fly (upon, against); to run (into) (*of vehicles*). **2.** (*of wind, storm*) to spring up.

нале|тéть[2], чý, ти́шь *pf.* (*of* **~тáть[1]**) to fly in, drift in (*in quantities, in large numbers*).

налётчик, а *m.* burglar, robber; raider.

на|лéчь, ля́гу, ля́жешь, ля́гут, *imper.* **~ля́г,** *past* **~лёг, ~леглá** *pf.* (*of* **~легáть**) (**на**+*a.*) **1.** to lean (on); to weigh down (on); to lie (upon); **н. плечóм на дверь** to try to force the door with one's shoulder; **н. на подчинённых** (*fig.*) to come down upon one's subordinates. **2.** to apply o.s. (to), throw o.s. (into); **н. на вёсла** to ply one's oars.

наливá|ть(ся), ю(сь) *impf. of* **нали́ть(ся)**

нали́вк|а, и *f.* fruit liqueur; **вишнёвая н.** cherry brandy.

наливн|óй *adj.* **1.** (*tech.*) worked by water; for conveying liquids; **~óе колесó** overshot wheel; **~óе сýдно** (*naut.*) tanker. **2.** ripe; juicy.

нали́м, а *m.* (*zool.*) burbot.

налин|овáть, ýю *pf. of* **линовáть**

налип|áть, áет *impf. of* **∸нуть**

нали́п|нуть, нет, *past* **~, ~ла** *pf.* (*of* **~áть**) (**на**+*a.*) to stick (to).

налитóй *adj.* **1.** ripe. **2.** fleshy, well-fleshed.

нал|и́ть, ью́, ьёшь, *past* **∸и́л, ~илá, ∸и́ло** *pf.* (*of* **~ивáть**) to pour out; (+*i.*) to fill (with); **н. бóчку водóй** to fill a barrel with water.

нал|и́ться, ью́сь, ьёшься, *past* **~и́лся, ~илáсь, ~илóсь** *pf.* (*of* **~ивáться**) **1.** (+*i.*) to fill (with); **н. крóвью** to become bloodshot. **2.** to ripen. **3.** *pass. of* **~и́ть**

налицó *adv.* present, available, on hand.

нали́честв|овать, ую *impf.* to be present, be on hand.

нали́чи|е, я *nt.* presence; **быть, оказáться в ~и** to be present, be available; **при ~и** (+*g.*) in the presence (of), given.

нали́чност|ь, и *f.* **1.** amount on hand; cash-in-hand; **н. товáров в магази́не** stock-in-trade. **2.** = **нали́чие**

нали́чн|ый *adj.* on hand, available; **~ые (дéньги)** ready money, cash; **плати́ть ~ыми** to pay in cash; **за н. расчёт** for cash.

налов|и́ть, лю́, ∸ишь *pf.* (+*a or g.*) to catch (*a number of*).

наловч|и́ться, ýсь, и́шься *pf.* (+*inf.*) to become proficient (in), become good (at).

налóг, а *m.* tax; **добáвочный подохóдный н.** surtax; **н. на добáвленную стóимость** value added tax, VAT; **необлагáемый ~ом** tax-deductible.

налóг|овый *adj. of* **~**

налогоплатéльщик, а *m.* tax-payer.

наложéни|е, я *nt.* imposition; **н. арéста** (*leg.*) seizure; **н. швов** (*med.*) suture, stitching.

налóж|енный *p.p.p. of* **~и́ть; ~енным платежóм** cash on delivery (*abbr.* C.O.D.).

налож|и́ть[1], ý, ∸ишь *pf.* **1.** (*impf.* **наклáдывать**) to lay in, on; to put in, on; to superimpose; to apply; **н. повя́зку** to apply a bandage. **2.** (*impf.* **наклáдывать**) to load, pack; **н. корзи́ну бельём, н. белья́ в корзи́ну** to load a basket with linen. **3.** (*impf.* **налагáть**) (**на**+*a.*) to lay (on), impose; **н. на себя́ брéмя** to undertake a burden; **н. штраф** to impose a fine; **н. арéст на чьё-н. имýщество** (*leg.*) to seize s.o.'s property.

налож|и́ть[2], ý, ∸ишь *pf.* (*of* **наклáдывать**) to put, lay (*a quantity of*).

налóжниц|а, ы *f.* (*obs.*) concubine.

наломá|ть, ю *pf.* (+*a. or g.*) to break (*a quantity of*); **н. бокá комý-н.** (*coll.*) to give s.o. a sound thrashing; **н. дров** (*coll., joc.*) to commit follies.

налощ|и́ть, ý, и́шь *pf. of* **лощи́ть**

нал|ью́, ьёшь *see* **~и́ть**

налюб|овáться, ýюсь *pf.* (+*i. or* **на**+*a.*) to gaze to one's heart's content (at) (*usu. with neg.*).

нал|я́гу, я́жешь, я́гут *see* **~éчь**

наля́па|ть, ю *pf. of* **ля́пать**

нам *d. of* **мы**

намагни́|тить, чу, тишь *pf.* (*of* **~чивать**) to magnetize.

намагни́чива|ть, ю *impf. of* **намагни́тить**
нама́|зать, жу, жешь *pf. of* **ма́зать** *and* **~зывать**
нама́|заться, жусь, жешься *pf.* **1.** (*impf.* **~зываться**) (*+i.*) to rub o.s. (with). **2.** *pf. of* **ма́заться**
нама́зыва|ть(ся), ю(сь) *impf. of* **нама́зать(ся)**
намал|ева́ть, ю́ю, ю́ешь *pf. of* **малева́ть**
намара́|ть, ю *pf. of* **мара́ть 2.**
намарин|ова́ть, у́ю *pf.* (*+a. or g.*) to pickle (*a quantity of*).
нама́сл|ить, ю, ишь *pf. of* **ма́слить**
наматра́цник, а *m.* mattress cover.
нама́тыва|ть, ю *impf. of* **намота́ть**[2]
нама́чива|ть, ю *impf. of* **намочи́ть**
намёк, а *m.* hint, allusion; **то́нкий н.** gentle hint; **ко́свенный н.** innuendo; **сде́лать н.** to drop a hint; **с ~ом** (**на**+*a.*) with a suggestion (of).
намек|а́ть, а́ю *impf.* (*of* **~ну́ть**) (**на**+*a.*, **о**+*p.*) to hint (at), allude (to).
намек|ну́ть, ну́, нёшь *pf. of* **~а́ть**
наменя́|ть, ю *pf.* (*+a. or g.*) to obtain (*a quantity of*) by exchange.
намерева́|ться, юсь *impf.* (*+inf.*) to intend (to), mean (to).
наме́рен (~а, ~о) *adj. as pred.* **быть н.** (*+inf.*) to intend; **я н. за́втра е́хать** I intend to go tomorrow; **что вы ~ы сде́лать?** what do you intend to do?
наме́рени|е, я *nt.* intention; purpose.
наме́ренный *adj.* intentional, deliberate.
намерз|а́ть, а́ю *impf. of* **~нуть**
намёрз|нуть, ну, нешь, *past* **~, ~ла** *pf.* (*of* **~а́ть**) to freeze (on); **на ступе́ньках ~ло мно́го льда** a thick layer of ice had formed on the steps.
намёрз|нуться, нусь, нешься, *past* **~ся, ~лась** *pf.* (*coll.*) to get frozen.
на́мертво *adv.* tightly, fast.
наме|сти́, ту́, тёшь, *past* **~л, ~ла́** *pf.* (*of* **~та́ть**[1]) (*+a. or g.*) **1.** to sweep together (*a quantity of*). **2.** to cause to drift; **~ло́ мно́го сне́гу** big snow-drifts have formed.
намета́|ть[1]**, ю** *impf. of* **намести́**
намета́|ть[2]**, ю** *pf. of* **мета́ть**[2]
наме|та́ть[3]**, чу́, ~чешь** *pf.* (*+a. or g.*) to throw together (*a quantity of*).
наме|та́ть[4]**, чу́, ~чешь** *pf.* (*of* **~тывать**) (*coll.*) to train; **н. глаз** to acquire a (good) eye; **н. ру́ку** (**на**+*a.*) to become proficient (at).
наме́|тить[1]**, чу, тишь** *pf. of* **ме́тить**[1] *and* **~ча́ть**[1]
наме́|тить[2]**, чу, тишь** *pf.* **1.** (*impf.* **~ча́ть**[2]) to plan, project; to have in view; **н. пое́здку в Росси́ю** to plan a visit to Russia. **2.** (*impf.* **~ча́ть**[2]) to nominate; to select; **его́ ~тили кандида́том в председа́тели** he has been nominated for chairman; **н. зда́ние к сно́су** to designate a building for demolition. **3.** *pf. of* **ме́тить**[2]
наме́|титься, чусь, тишься *pf.* (*of* **~ча́ться**) to be outlined; to take shape.
намётк|а[1]**, и** *f.* **1.** basting, tacking. **2.** basting thread, tacking thread.
намётк|а[2]**, и** *f.* rough draft, preliminary outline.
намётыва|ть, ю *impf. of* **намета́ть**[4]
намеча́|ть[1]**, ю** *impf.* = **ме́тить**
намеча́|ть[2]**, ю** *impf. of* **наме́тить**[2]
намеча́|ться, юсь *impf. of* **наме́титься**
наме́|чу, тишь *see* **~тить**
наме|чу́, чешь *see* **~та́ть**
намеш|а́ть, а́ю *pf.* (*of* **~ивать**) (*+a. or g.* **в**+*a.*) to add (to), mix in(to).
наме́шива|ть, ю *impf. of* **намеша́ть**
на́ми *i. of* **мы**
намина́|ть, ю *impf. of* **namя́ть**
намно́го *adv.* much, far (*with comparatives*); **н. лу́чше** much better.
нам|ну́, нёшь *see* **~я́ть**
намозо́л|ить, ю, ишь *pf. of* **мозо́лить**
намок|а́ть, а́ю *impf.* (*of* **~нуть**) to become wet, get wet.
намо́к|нуть, ну, нешь, *past* **~, ~ла** *pf. of* **~а́ть**
нам|оло́ть, елю́, е́лешь *pf.* (*+a. or g.*) to grind, mill (*a quantity of*); **н. вздо́ру, чепухи́** (*coll.*) to talk a lot of nonsense.
намо́рдник, а *m.* muzzle.
намо́рщ|ить(ся), у(сь) ишь(ся) *pf. of* **мо́рщить(ся)**
намо|сти́ть, щу́, сти́шь *pf. of* **мости́ть 2.**
намота́|ть[1]**, ю** *pf. of* **мота́ть**[1]
намота́|ть[2]**, ю** *pf.* (*of* **нама́тывать**) (*+a. or g.*) to wind (*a quantity of*).
намоч|и́ть, у́, ~ишь *pf.* (*of* **нама́чивать**) **1.** to wet, moisten. **2.** to soak, steep. **3.** (*intrans.*; *coll.*) to spill water (on the floor, *etc.*).
намудр|и́ть, ю́, и́шь *pf. of* **мудри́ть**
наму́сл|ить, ю, ишь *pf. of* **му́слить**
намус|о́лить *pf.* = **~лить**
наму́ч|иться, усь, ишься *pf.* (*coll.*) to be worn out; to have had a hard time.
намы́ливать(ся) *impf.* = **мы́лить(ся)**
намы́л|ить(ся), ю(сь), ишь(сь) *pf. of* **~ивать(ся)** *and* **мы́лить(ся)**
нам|ы́ть, о́ю, о́ешь *pf.* (*+a. or g.*) **1.** to wash (*a quantity of*). **2.** (*of a river*) to deposit.
нам|я́ть[1]**, ну́, нёшь** *pf.* (*of* **~ина́ть**) to hurt (*by pressure or friction*); to crush; **н. кому́-н. бока́, ше́ю** to give s.o. a sound thrashing.
нам|я́ть[2]**, ну́, нёшь** *pf.* (*+a. or g.*) **1.** to mash (*a quantity of*). **2.** to trample down (*a certain area of*).
нанесе́ни|е, я *nt.* **1.** drawing, plotting (*on a map*). **2.** infliction; **н. уда́ров** assault and battery.
нанес|ти́[1]**, у́, ёшь,** *past* **~, ~ла́** *pf.* (*of* **наноси́ть**) **1.** (**на ка́рту**) to draw, plot, (on a map). **2.** to cause; to inflict; **н. оскорбле́ние** to insult; **н. визи́т** to pay a visit. **3.** (*+a.* **на**+*a.*) to dash (against); (*impers.*): **ло́дку ~ло́ на мель** the boat struck a shoal.
нанес|ти́[2]**, у́, ёшь,** *past* **~, ~ла́** *pf.* (*+a. or g.*) **1.** to bring (*a quantity of*). **2.** to pile up (*a quantity of*); (*of sand, snow, etc.*) to drift.
нани|за́ть, жу́, ~жешь *pf. of* **низа́ть** *and* **~зывать**
нани́зыва|ть, ю *impf.* = **низа́ть**
нанима́тел|ь, я *m.* **1.** tenant. **2.** (*obs.*) employer.
нанима́|ть(ся), ю(сь) *impf. of* **наня́ть(ся)**
на́ново *adv.* (*coll.*) anew, afresh.
нано́с, а *m.* (*geol.*) alluvium.
нано|си́ть[1]**, шу́, ~сишь** *impf. of* **нанести́**
нано|си́ть[2]**, шу́, ~сишь** *pf.* (*+a. or g.*) to bring (*a quantity of*).
нано́сный *adj.* **1.** (*geol.*) alluvial. **2.** (*fig., coll.*) alien; borrowed.
на́н|ятый *p.p.p. of* **~я́ть**
на|ня́ть, найму́, наймёшь, *past* **~нял, ~няла́, ~няло** *pf.* (*of* **~нима́ть**) to rent; to hire; **н. на рабо́ту** to engage, employ; to take on.
на|ня́ться, найму́сь, наймёшься, *past* **~нялся́, ~няла́сь** *pf.* (*of* **~нима́ться**) (*coll.*) to get a job, be taken on.
наобеща́|ть, ю *pf.* (*+a. or g.*) to promise (too much); **н. с три ко́роба** to promise the earth.
наоборо́т *adv.* **1.** back to front; **проче́сть сло́во н.** to read a word backwards. **2.** the other way round; the wrong way (round); **он всё понима́ет н.** he take everything the wrong way. **3.** on the contrary; **как раз н.** quite the contrary; **и н.** and vice versa; **я не сержу́сь, а, н., рад был, что вы пришли́** I am not angry; on the contrary, I was glad that you came.
наобу́м *adv.* without thinking; at random.
наор|а́ть, у́, ёшь *pf.* (**на**+*a.*; *coll.*) to shout (at).
нао́тмашь *adv.* **1.** with the back of the hand; **уда́рить н.** to strike a swinging blow. **2.** out from the body.
наотре́з *adv.* flatly, point-blank.

напа́да|ть, ет *pf.* to fall (*in a certain quantity*); **в тече́ние но́чи ~ло мно́го сне́га** there was a heavy fall of snow during the night.
напада́|ть, ю *impf. of* **напа́сть**
напада́ющ|ий, его *m.* (*sport*) forward.
нападе́ни|е, я *nt.* **1.** attack, assault. **2.** (*sport*) forward-line.
напа́д|ки, ок, кам *no sg.* (*verbal*) attacks.
напа|ду́, дёшь *see* **⌐сть**
напа́ива|ть[1], ю *impf. of* **напои́ть**
напа́ива|ть[2], ю *impf. of* **напая́ть**
напа́ко|стить, щу, стишь *pf. of* **па́костить**
напа́лм, а *m.* (*chem.*; *mil.*) napalm.
напа́лм|овый *adj. of* **~**
напа́рник, а *m.* fellow worker, mate.
напа́рыва|ть(ся), ю(сь) *impf. of* **напоро́ть(ся)**
напа́|сть[1], ду́, дёшь, *past* **~л** *pf.* (*of* **~да́ть**) (**на**+*a.*) **1.** to attack; to descend (on). **2.** to come (over); to grip, seize; **на нас всех ~л страх** we were all gripped with fear. **3.** to come (upon, across); **я ~л на мысль** the thought occurred to me.
напа́ст|ь[2], и *f.* (*coll.*) misfortune, disaster.
напая́|ть, ю, ешь *pf.* (*of* **напа́ивать[2]**) to solder (onto).
напе́в, а *m.* tune, melody.
напева́|ть, ю *impf.* **1.** *impf. of* **напе́ть. 2.** to hum; to croon.
напе́в|ный (~ен, ~на) *adj.* melodious.
напека́|ть, ю *impf. of* **напе́чь[1]**
наперебо́й *adv.* vying with one another.
напереве́с *adv.* in a horizontal position.
наперего́нки́ *adv.* racing one another; **бе́гать н.** to race one another.
наперёд *adv.* (*coll.*) **1.** in front. **2.** in advance.
напереко́р *adv. and prep.* (+*d.*) in defiance (of), counter (to).
наперере́з *adv.* (*and prep.*+*d.*) so as to cross one's path; **бежа́ть кому́-н. н.** to run to head s.o. off.
напереры́в *adv.* = **наперебо́й**
на|пере́ть, пру́, прёшь, *past* **~пёр, ~пёрла** *pf.* (*of* **~пира́ть**) (*coll.*; **на**+*a.*) to press; to put pressure (upon).
напере|хва́т *adv.* (*dial.*) **1.** = **~ре́з. 2.** = **~бо́й.**
наперечёт *adv.* **1.** through and through; every single one. **2.** *as pred.* very few, not many.
напе́рсник, а *m.* (*obs.*) confidant.
напе́рсниц|а, ы *f.* (*obs.*) **1.** confidante. **2.** mistress.
напе́рсный *adj.* (*eccl.*) pectoral.
напёрст|ок, ка *m.* thimble.
наперстя́нк|а, и *f.* (*bot.*) foxglove.
напе́рч|ить, у, ишь *pf. of* **пе́рчить**
нап|е́ть, ою́, оёшь *pf.* (*of* **~ева́ть**) **1.** to sing (*air, melody*). **2.: н. пласти́нку** to make a record(ing of one's voice). **3.** (*coll.*; +*d. or* **в у́ши** +*d.*) to give s.o. a piece of one's mind.
напеча́та|ть(ся), ю(сь) *pf. of* **печа́тать(ся)**
напе́|чь[1], чёт, *past* **~кло́** *pf.* (*of.* **~ка́ть**) (*impers.*; *coll.*) to burn, scorch (*with the sun*); **го́лову у меня́ ~кло́** my head got scorched.
напе́|чь[2], ку́, чёшь, ку́т, *past* **⌐̈к, ~кла́** *pf.* (+*a. or g.*) to bake (*a number of*); **н. расска́зов** (*fig., coll.*) to concoct stories.
напива́|ться, юсь *impf. of* **напи́ться**
напи́лива|ть, ю *impf. of* **напили́ть**
напил|и́ть, ю́, ⌐ишь *pf.* (*of* **⌐ивать**) (+*a. or g.*) to saw (*a quantity of*).
напи́л|ок, ка *m.* (*coll.*) = **~ьник**
напи́льник, а *m.* (*tech.*) file.
напира́|ть, ю *impf.* (*coll.*; **на**+*a.*) **1.** *impf. of* **напе-ре́ть. 2.** to emphasize, stress.
написа́ни|е, я *nt.* **1.** (way of) writing. **2.** spelling.
напи|са́ть, шу́, ⌐шешь *pf. of* **писа́ть**
напит|а́ть, а́ю *pf.* **1.** (*impf.* **пита́ть**) to sate, satiate. **2.** (*impf.* **⌐ывать**) (+*i.*) to impregnate (with).
напит|а́ться, а́юсь *pf.* **1.** (*coll.*) to sate o.s.; to take one's fill. **2.** (*impf.* **⌐ываться**) (+*i.*) to be impregnated (with).
напи́т|ок, ка *m.* drink, beverage; **тонизи́рующий н.** tonic, pick-me-up.
напи́тыва|ть(ся), ю(сь) *impf. of* **напита́ть(ся)**
нап|и́ться, ью́сь, ьёшься, *past* **~и́лся, ~ила́сь, ~и́ло́сь** *pf.* (*of* **~ива́ться**) **1.** (+*g.*) to slake one's thirst (with, on); to have a drink (of). **2.** to get drunk.
напих|а́ть, а́ю *pf.* (*of* **⌐ивать**) (**в**+*a.*) to cram (into), stuff (into).
напи́хива|ть, ю *impf. of* **напиха́ть**
напи́чка|ть, ю *pf. of* **пи́чкать**
напи|шу́, ⌐шешь *see* **~са́ть**
напла́канный *adj.* tear-stained.
напла́|каться, чусь, чешься *pf.* **1.** to have a good cry. **2.** (*coll.*) to have trouble; **он ещё ~чется** there is trouble in store for him yet.
напластова́ни|е, я *nt.* (*geol.*) bedding, stratification.
напла́|чу, чешь *see* **~кать**
наплева́тельский *adj.* (*coll.*) devil-may-care.
напл|ева́ть, юю́, юёшь *pf.* **1.** (+*g.*) to spit (out). **2.** (*fig., coll.*; **на**+*a.*) to wash one's hands (of); **н.!** to hell with it!; who cares!; **н. на него́!** to hell with him!; **мне н.!** I couldn't care less!
напле|сти́, ту́, тёшь, *past* **⌐̈л, ~ла́** *pf.* (+*a. or g.*) to make by weaving (*a number of*); **н. вздо́ру** (*fig., coll.*) to talk a lot of nonsense.
напле́чник, а *m.* shoulder strap; (*sport*) shoulder pad.
напле́чный *adj.* (worn on the) shoulder.
напло|ди́ть, жу́, ди́шь *pf.* (*coll.*) to produce (*in great numbers*); to breed.
напло|ди́ться, жу́сь, ди́шься *pf.* (*coll.*) to multiply; to breed.
наплы́в| а *m.* **1.** influx. **2.** (*med., bot.*) canker; excrescence.
наплыва́|ть, ю *impf. of* **наплы́ть**
наплы́|ть, ву́, вёшь, *past* **~л, ~ла́, ~ло** *pf.* (*of* **~ва́ть**) **1.** (**на**+*a.*) to run (against), dash (against). **2.** (*of incrustation, etc.*) to form.
напова́л *adv.* outright, on the spot.
наподо́бие *prep.* (+*g.*) like, resembling, in the likeness of.
напо́|енный *p.p.p. of* **~и́ть 1., 2.**
напо|и́ть, ю́, и́шь *pf.* (*of* **пои́ть** *and* **напа́ивать[1]**) **1.** to give to drink; to water (*an animal*). **2.** to make drunk.
напока́з *adv.* for show; **вы́ставить н.** to show off (*also fig.*).
наполз|а́ть, а́ю *impf. of* **~ти́**
наполз|ти́[1], у́, ёшь, *past* **⌐, ~ла́** *pf.* (*of* **~а́ть**) (**на**+*a.*) to crawl (over, against).
наполз|ти́[2], у́, ёшь, *past* **⌐, ~ла́** *pf.* to crawl in (*in great numbers*).
наполне́ни|е, я *nt.* filling.
наполни́тел|ь, я *m.* (*tech.*) filler.
напо́лн|ить, ю, ишь *pf.* (*of* **~я́ть**) to fill.
напо́лн|иться, юсь, ишься *pf.* (*of* **~я́ться**) (+*i.*) to fill (with) (*intrans.*)
наполн|я́ть(ся), я́ю(сь) *impf. of* **⌐ить(ся)**
наполови́ну *adv.* half; **зал ещё н. пуст** the hall is still half empty; **де́лать де́ло н.** to do a thing by halves.
напома́|дить, жу, дишь *pf. of* **пома́дить**
напомина́ни|е, я *nt.* **1.** reminding. **2.** reminder.
напомина́|ть, ю *impf. of* **напо́мнить**
напо́мн|ить, ю, ишь *pf.* (*of* **напомина́ть**) **1.** (+*d.* **о**+*p. or* +*d. and a.*) to remind (of); **портре́т ~ил мне о про́шлом** *or* **~ил мне про́шлое** the portrait reminded me of the past. **2.** to remind (of), recall (= *to resemble*); **он ~ил мне моего́ де́да** he reminded me of my grandfather.

напо́р, а *m.* pressure (*also fig.*); (*of water, steam, etc.*) head; **он подде́рживал меня́ с ~ом** (*coll.*) he supported me vigorously.
напо́ристост|ь, и *f.* (*coll.*) energy; push, go.
напо́рист|ый (~, ~а) *adj.* (*coll.*) energetic; pushy.
напо́р|ный *adj. of* ~ (*tech.*); **н. бак** pressure tank; **н. кла́пан** pressure valve; **н. насо́с** force pump; **~ная труба́** rising pipe, rising main.
напор|о́ть[1], ю́ ~ешь *pf.* (*of* **напа́рывать**) (*coll.*) to tear, cut; **н. ру́ку на гвоздь** to cut one's hand on a nail.
напор|о́ть[2], ю́, ~ешь *pf.* to rip (*a quantity of*); (*coll.*): **н. вздо́ру, чепухи́** to talk a lot of nonsense.
напор|о́ться, ю́сь, ~ешься *pf.* (*of* **напа́рываться**) (**на**+*a.*) **1.** to cut o.s. (on). **2.** to run (upon, against); (*fig.*) to run (into, up against).
напо́р|тить[1], чу, тишь *pf.* (+*a. or g.*) to spoil (*a quantity of*).
напо́р|тить[2], чу, тишь *pf.* (+*d.*) to injure, harm.
напосле́док *adv.* (*coll.*) in the end, finally, after all.
нап|ою́[1], оёшь *see* **~е́ть**
напо|ю́[2], и́шь *see* **~и́ть**
напр. (*abbr. of* **наприме́р**) e.g., for example.
напра́в|ить, лю, ишь *pf.* (*of* **~ля́ть**) **1.** (**на**+*a.*) to direct (to, at); **н. внима́ние** to direct one's attention (to); **н. свой путь** to make one's way (towards); **н. уда́р** to aim a blow (at). **2.** to send; **н. заявле́ние** to send in an application. **3.** to sharpen; **н. бри́тву** to set a razor. **4.** (*coll.*): **н. рабо́ту** to organize work.
напра́в|иться, люсь, ишься *pf.* (*of* **~ля́ться**) **1.** (**к, в**+*a.*, **на**+*a.*) to make (for). **2.** (*coll.*) to get going, get under way (*fig.*). **3.** *pass. of* **~ить**
напра́вк|а, и *f.* setting (*of razor, etc.*)
направле́ни|е, я *nt.* **1.** direction; **по ~ю (к)** in the direction (of), towards; **взять н. на се́вер** to make for, head for the north. **2.** (*mil.*) sector. **3.** (*fig.*) trend, tendency; **н. ума́** turn of mind; **либера́льное н.** liberal tendency. **4.** (*official*) order, warrant; directive; **н. в санато́рий** warrant for stay at a sanatorium.
напра́вленност|ь, и *f.* **1.** direction, tendency, trend. **2.** purposefulness.
напра́в|ленный *p.p.p. of* **~ить** *and adj.* **1.** (*radio*) directional. **2.** purposeful; unswerving.
направля́|ть, ю *impf. of* **напра́вить**
направля́|ться, юсь *impf. of* **напра́виться; ~емся в Му́рманск** we are bound for Murmansk.
направля́|ющий *pres. part. act. of* **~ть** *and adj.* (*tech.*) guiding, guide; leading; **н. ва́лик, н. ро́лик** guide roller.
напра́во *adv.* to the right; on the right.
напрактик|ова́ться, у́юсь *pf.* (**в**+*p.*; *coll.*) to acquire skill (in).
напра́слин|а, ы *f.* (*coll.*) wrongful accusation, slander.
напра́сно *adv.* **1.** vainly, in vain; to no purpose. **2.** wrong, unjustly, mistakenly; **н. вы пришли́ без де́нег** it was a mistake for you to come without money.
напра́с|ный (~ен, ~на) *adj.* **1.** vain, idle; **~ная наде́жда** vain hope. **2.** unfounded, wrongful.
напра́шива|ться, юсь *impf. of* **напроси́ться**; (*impf. only*) to arise, suggest itself; **~ется вопро́с** the question inevitably arises.
наприме́р for example, for instance.
напрока́|зить, жу, зишь *pf. of* **прока́зить**
напрока́знича|ть, ю *pf. of* **прока́зничать**
напрока́т *adv.* for hire, on hire; **взять н.** to hire; **дать, отда́ть н.** to hire out, let.
напролёт *adv.* (*coll.*) through, without a break; **рабо́тать всю ночь н.** to work the whole night through.
напроло́м *adv.* straight, regardless of obstacles (*also fig.*).
напропалу́ю *adv.* (*coll.*) regardless of the consequences; all out.
напроро́ч|ить, у, ишь *pf. of* **проро́чить**
напро|си́ться, шу́сь, ~сишься *pf.* (*of* **напра́шиваться**) (*coll.*) to thrust o.s. upon; **н. на комплиме́нты** to fish for compliments.
напро́тив *adv. and prep.*+*g.* **1.** opposite; **он живёт н. (на́шего до́ма)** he lives opposite (our house). **2.** (+*d.*) in defiance (of); to contradict; **она́ всё де́лает мне н.** she does everything to spite me. **3.** on the contrary.
на́прочь *adv.* (*coll.*) completely.
нап|ру́, рёшь *see* **~ере́ть**
напру́жива|ть(ся), ю(сь) *impf. of* **напру́житься**
напру́ж|ить, у, ишь *pf.* (*of* **~ивать**) (*coll.*) to strain; to tense, tauten.
напру́ж|иться, усь, ишься *pf.* (*of* **~иваться**) (*coll.*) to become tense, become taut.
напряга́|ть(ся), ю(сь) *impf. of* **напря́чь(ся)**
напря|гу́, жёшь *see* **~чь**
напряже́ни|е, я *nt.* **1.** tension; effort, exertion. **2.** (*phys., tech.*) strain; stress; (*elec.*) tension; voltage.
напряжённост|ь, и *f.* tenseness; intensity; tension.
напряжён|ный (~, ~на) *adj.* tense, strained; intense; intensive; all-out; **~ные отноше́ния** strained relations; **~ная рабо́та** intensive work.
напрями́к *adv.* (*coll.*) **1.** straight. **2.** (*fig.*) straight out, bluntly.
напря́|чь, гу́, жёшь, гу́т, *past* **~г, ~гла́** *pf.* (*of* **~га́ть**) to tense, strain (*also fig.*); **н. все си́лы** to strain every nerve.
напря́|чься, гу́сь, жёшься, гу́ться, *past* **~гся, ~гла́сь** *pf.* **1.** to become tense. **2.** to exert o.s., strain o.s.
напу́др|ить(ся), ю(сь), ишь(ся) *pf. of* **пу́дрить(ся)**
напу́льсник, а wrist-band.
напуска́|ть(ся), ю(сь) *impf. of* **напусти́ть(ся)**
напускно́й *adj.* assumed, feigned.
напу|сти́ть, щу́, ~стишь *pf.* (*of* **~ска́ть**) **1.** (+*g.*) to let in; **н. воды́ в ва́нну** to fill a bath. **2.** to let loose, slip, set on (*hounds, etc.*). **3.** (**на себя́**+*a.*) to affect, put on; **н. на себя́ ва́жность** to assume an air of importance. **4.:** **н. стра́ху на кого́-н.** (*coll.*) to strike fear into s.o.
напу|сти́ться, щу́сь, ~стишься *pf.* (*of* **~ска́ться**) (*coll.*; **на**+*a.*) to fly at, go for.
напу́та|ть, ю *pf.* (*coll.*, **в**+*p.*) to make a mess (of), make a hash (of); to confuse, get wrong; **вы ~ли в а́дресе** you got the address wrong.
напу́тственн|ый *adj.* parting, farewell; **~ое сло́во** parting words.
напу́тстви|е, я *nt.* parting words, farewell speech.
напу́тств|овать, ую *impf. and pf.* to address (at parting); **н. до́брыми пожела́ниями** to bid farewell.
напух|а́ть, а́ет *impf. of* **~нуть**
напу́х|нуть, нет, *past* **~, ~ла** *pf.* (*of* **~а́ть**) to swell.
напу|щу́, ~стишь *see* **~сти́ть**
напы́ж|иться, усь, ишься *pf. of* **пы́житься**
напыл|и́ть, ю́, и́шь *pf. of* **пыли́ть**
напы́щенност|ь, и *f.* **1.** pomposity. **2.** bombast.
напы́щен|ный (~, ~на) *adj.* **1.** pompous. **2.** bombastic, high-flown.
напя́лива|ть, ю *impf. of* **напя́лить**
напя́л|ить, ю, ишь *pf.* (*of* **~ивать**) **1.** to stretch on. **2.** (*coll.*) to pull on, struggle into (*a tight-fitting garment*).
нар... *comb. form, abbr. of* **наро́дный 4.**
нараба́тыва|ть, ю *impf. of* **нарабо́тать[2]**
нарабо́та|ть[1], ю *pf.* (+*a. or g.*) to make, turn out (*a quantity of*).
нарабо́та|ть[2], ю *pf.* (*of* **нараба́тывать**) to make, earn.
нарабо́та|ться, юсь *pf.* (*coll.*) to have worked

enough; to have tired o.s. with work.

наравнé *adv.* (**с**+*i.*) **1.** on a level (with); **мáльчик шёл н. с солдáтами** the small boy kept pace with the soldiers. **2.** equally (with); on an equal footing (with).

нарáд|оваться, уюсь *pf.* (+*d. or* **на**+*a.*; *usu.* +*neg.*) to rejoice, delight sufficiently (in); **онá на сы́на не ~уется** she dotes on her son.

нараспáшку *adv.* (*coll.*) unbuttoned; **у негó душá н.** (*fig.*) he wears his heart upon his sleeve.

нараспéв *adv.* in a sing-song voice; drawlingly.

нарастáни|е, я *nt.* growth, accumulation.

нараст|áть, áю *impf. of* **~и́**

нарас|ти́, тý, тёшь, *past* **нарóс, нарослá** *pf.* (*of* **~тáть**) **1.** (**на**+*p.*) to grow (on), form (on); **мох нарóс на камня́х** moss has grown on the stones. **2.** to increase; (*of sound*) to swell. **3.** to accumulate.

нара|сти́ть, щý, сти́шь *pf.* (*of* **∸щивать**) **1.** to graft (on). **2.** to lengthen; (*fig.*) to increase, augment.

нарасхвáт *adv.*: **продавáться, раскупáться н.** to sell like hot cakes.

нарáщивани|е, я *nt.* increase; build-up; **н. вооружéний** arms build-up.

нарáщива|ть, ю *impf. of* **нарасти́ть**

нарвáл, а *m.* (*zool.*) narwhal.

нарв|áть[1]**, ý, ёшь,** *past* **~áл, ~алá, ~áло** *pf.* (+*a. or g.*) **1.** to pick (*a quantity of*). **2.** to tear (*a quantity of*).

нарв|áть[2]**, ёт,** *past* **~áл, ~алá, ~áло** *pf.* (*of* **нарывáть**) to gather, come to a head.

нарв|áться, ýсь, ёшься, *past* **~áлся, ~алáсь, ~áлóсь** *pf.* (*of* **нарывáться**) (*coll.*; **на**+*a.*) to run into, run up (against).

нард, а *m.* spikenard, nard.

нарé|жу, жешь *see* **~зать**

нарé|зать[1]**, жу, жешь** *pf.* (*of* **~зáть**) **1.** to cut into pieces; to slice; to carve. **2.** (*tech.*) to thread; to rifle.

нарé|зать[2]**, жу, жешь** *pf.* (+*a. or g.*) to cut, slice (*a quantity of*).

нарез|áть, áю *impf. of* **∸ать**[1]

нарé|заться, жусь, жешься *pf.* (*of* **~зáться**) **1.** (*coll.*) to get drunk. **2.** *pass. of* **~зать**[1]

нарез|áться, áюсь *impf. of* **∸аться**

нарéзк|а, и *f.* **1.** cutting, slicing. **2.** (*tech.*) thread; rifling.

нарезнóй *adj.* (*tech.*) threaded; rifled.

нарекáни|е, я *nt.* censure; reprimand.

нарекá|ть, ю *impf. of* **нарéчь**

нарéчи|е[1]**, я** *nt.* dialect.

нарéчи|е[2]**, я** *nt.* adverb.

нарéчный *adj.* adverbial.

нарé|чь, кý, чёшь, кýт, *past* **∸̈к, ~клá** *pf.* (*of* **~кáть**) (*obs.*) (+*a. and i. or d. and a.*) to name; **мáльчика ~кли́ Сергéем, мáльчику ~кли́ и́мя Сергéй** they named the boy Sergei.

нарзáн, а *m.* Narzan (*kind of mineral water*).

нарис|овáть, ýю *pf. of* **рисовáть**

нарицáтельн|ый *adj.* **1.** (*econ.*) nominal; **~ая стóимость** nominal cost. **2.** (*gram.*): **и́мя ~ое** common noun.

наркоби́знес, а *m.* drug trafficking.

наркодел|éц, ьцá *m.* drug trafficker *or* pusher.

наркóз, а *m.* **1.** narcosis, anaesthesia. **2.** anaesthetic; **мéстный н.** local anaesthetic.

наркологи́ческий *adj.*: **н. диспансéр** drug-abuse clinic.

наркóм, а *m.* (*abbr. of* **нарóдный комиссáр**) (*hist.*) people's commissar.

наркомáн, а *m.* drug addict.

наркомáни|я, и *f.* drug addiction.

наркомáт, а *m.* (*abbr. of* **нарóдный комиссариáт**) (*hist.*) people's commissariat.

наркосиндикáт, а *m.* drug ring.

наркотизи́р|овать, ую *impf. and pf.* to anaesthetize.

наркóтик, а *m.* narcotic; drug; **торгóвля ~ами** drug trafficking.

наркоти́ческ|ий *adj.* narcotic; **~ие срéдства** narcotics, drugs.

нарóд, а (у) *m.* people; **англи́йский н.** the English people; **человéк из ~а** a man of the people; **мáло бы́ло ~у на ми́тинге** there were not many people at the meeting; **как говоря́т в ~е** as the expression goes; as they say.

наро|ди́ть, жý, ди́шь *pf.* (+*a. or g.*) to give birth to (*a number of*).

наро|ди́ться, жýсь, ди́шься *pf.* (*of* **~ждáться**) **1.** (*coll.*) to be born. **2.** (*fig.*) to come into being, arise.

нарóдник, а *m.* (*hist.*) narodnik; populist.

нарóдничес|кий *adj. of* **~тво**

нарóдничеств|о, а *nt.* (*hist.*) narodnik movement; populism.

нарóдност|ь, и *f.* **1.** nationality. **2.** (*sg. only*) national character; national traits.

народнохозя́йственный *adj.* pertaining to the national economy.

нарóдн|ый *adj.* **1.** national; **~ое хозя́йство** national economy; **н. поэ́т** national poet. **2.** folk; **~ое искýсство** folk art. **3.** (*pol.*) of the people, popular; **~ая вóля** (*hist.*) Narodnaya volya ('The People's Will') **Н. фронт** Popular Front. **4.** *forms part of the official designation of certain Communist and former Communist states, also of certain organs of power and offices in the former USSR*; **стрáны ~ой демокрáтии** 'the People's Democracies'; **Китáйская Н~ая Респýблика** the People's Republic of China; **н. заседáтель** assessor (*in courts*); **н. слéдователь** examining magistrate; **н. суд** 'People's Court' (*court of first instance*).

народовлáсти|е, я *nt.* 'people's power', government by the people..

народонаселéни|е, я *nt.* population.

нарождá|ться, юсь *impf. of* **народи́ться**

нарождéни|е, я *nt.* birth, springing up; **н. мéсяца** appearance of new moon.

нарóст, а *m.* outgrowth, excrescence; tumour.

нарочи́то *adv.* deliberately, intentionally.

нарочи́т|ый (~, ~а) *adj.* deliberate, intentional.

нарóчно *adv.* **1.** on purpose, purposely. **2.** for fun, pretending.

нáрочн|ый, ого *m.* courier; special messenger.

нарсýд, а *m.* People's Court.

нáрт|ы, ~ *pl.* (*sg.* **~а, ~ы** *f.*) sledge (*drawn by reindeer or dogs*).

наруб|и́ть, лю́, ∸ишь *pf.* (+*a. or g.*) to chop (*a quantity of*); to cut (*a quantity of*).

нарýбк|а, и *f.* notch.

нарýжно *adv.* outwardly.

нарýжност|ь, и *f.* exterior; appearance; **н. обмáнчива** appearances are deceptive.

нарýжн|ый *adj.* external, exterior, outward; **~ое лекáрство** medicine to be taken externally; **~ое спокóйствие** outward calm.

нарýжу *adv.* outside, on the outside; **вы́йти н.** to come out; (*fig.*) to come to light, transpire.

нарукáвник, а *m.* oversleeve; armlet.

нарукáвн|ый *adj.* (worn on the) sleeve; **~ая повя́зка** arm-band.

нарумя́н|ить(ся), ю(сь), ишь(ся) *pf. of* **румя́нить(ся)**

нарýчник, а *m.* handcuff; manacle.

нарýчн|ый *adj.* worn on the arm; **~ые часы́** wristwatch.

наруш|áть, áю *impf. of* **∸ить**

нарушéни|е, я *nt.* breach; infringement, violation;

offence; **н. суточного ритма** jet lag.
нарушител|ь, я *m.* transgressor, infringer.
нару́ш|ить, у, ишь *pf.* (*of* **~а́ть**) **1.** to break, disturb (*sleep, quiet, etc.*). **2.** to break, infringe (upon), violate, transgress.
нарци́сс, а *m.* narcissus; daffodil.
на́р|ы, ~ *no sg.* plank-bed; bunk.
нары́в, а *m.* abscess; boil.
нарыва́|ть(ся), ю(сь) *impf. of* **нарва́ть²(ся)**
нар|ы́ть, о́ю, о́ешь *pf.* (+*a. or g.*) to dig (*a quantity of*).
наря́д¹, а *m.* attire, apparel, costume.
наря́д², а *m.* **1.** order, warrant. **2.** (*mil.*) detail. **3.** (*mil.*) duty; **расписа́ние ~ов** roster; duty detail.
наря|ди́ть¹, жу́, ⁓ди́шь *pf.* (*of* **~жа́ть**) **1.** (**в**+*a.*) to dress (in), array (in). **2.** (+*i.*) to dress up (as).
наря|ди́ть², жу́, ⁓ди́шь *pf.* (*of* **~жа́ть**) to detail, appoint; **н. в карау́л** to put on guard; **н. сле́дствие** to set up, order an inquiry.
наря|ди́ться¹, жу́сь, ⁓ди́шься *pf.* (*of* **~жа́ться**) **1.** (**в**+*a.*) to array o.s. (in). **2.** to dress up. **3.** *pass. of* **~ди́ть¹**
наря|ди́ться², жу́сь, ⁓ди́шься *pf.* (*of* **~жа́ться**) *pass. of* **~ди́ть¹**
наря́дност|ь, и *f.* elegance, smartness.
наря́д|ный (~ен, ~на) *adj.* well-dressed; elegant; smart (*also of items of dress*).
наряду́ *adv.* (**с**+*i.*) side by side (with), equally (with); **де́ти н. со взро́слыми** grown-ups and children alike; **н. с э́тим** at the same time.
наряжа́|ть(ся), ю(сь) *impf. of* **наряди́ть(ся)**
нас *a., g., and p. of* **мы**
НАСА *nt. indecl.* NASA (*abbr. of* National Aeronautics and Space Administration).
наса|ди́ть¹, жу́, ⁓дишь *pf.* (*of* **⁓живать**) (+*a. or g.*) **1.** to plant (*a quantity of*). **2.** to sit (*a number of*).
наса|ди́ть², жу́, ⁓дишь *pf.* (*of* **⁓живать**) to put; to stick, pin; **н. червяка́ на крючо́к** to fix a worm on to a hook.
наса|ди́ть³, жу́, ⁓дишь *pf.* (*of* **~жда́ть**) (*fig.*) to implant, inculcate; to propagate.
наса́дк|а, и *f.* **1.** setting, fixing, putting on. **2.** attachment; **набо́р ⁓ок** set of attachments. **3.** bait.
насажа́|ть, ю *pf.* = **насади́ть¹**
насажда́|ть, ю *impf. of* **насади́ть³**
насажде́ни|е, я *nt.* **1.** planting, plantation; (*fig.*) spreading, propagation. **2.** (*forest*) stand; wood.
наса|ждённый *p.p.p. of* **~ди́ть³**
наса́|женный *p.p.p. of* **~ди́ть¹,²**
наса́жива|ть, ю *impf. of* **насади́ть¹,²**
наса́жива|ться, юсь *impf. of* **насе́сть¹**
наса́лива|ть, ю *impf. of* **насоли́ть**
наса́сыва|ть, ю *impf. of* **насоса́ть**
наса́харива|ть, ю *impf. of* **наса́харить**
наса́хар|ить, ю, ишь *pf.* (*of* **~ивать**) to sugar, sweeten (*with sugar*).
насви́стыва|ть, ю *impf.* (*coll.*) to whistle (*a tune*); (*of birds*) to twitter.
наседа́|ть, ю *impf.* (*of* **насе́сть²**) (**на**+*a.*) **1.** to press (*of mil. forces, crowds, etc.*). **2.** (*of dust, etc.*) to settle, collect.
насе́дк|а, и *f.* brood-hen, sitting hen.
насека́|ть, ю *impf. of* **насе́чь**
насеко́м|ое, ого *nt.* insect.
насекомоя́дный *adj.* insectivorous.
населе́ни|е, я *nt.* **1.** population; inhabitants. **2.** peopling, settling.
населённост|ь, и *f.* population density.
насел|ённый *p.p.p. of* **~и́ть** *and adj.* **1.** populated; **н. пункт** (*official designation*) locality, place; built-up area. **2.** populous, densely populated.
насел|и́ть, ю́, и́шь *pf.* (*of* **~я́ть**) to people, settle.
насел|я́ть, я́ю *impf.* **1.** to inhabit. **2.** *impf. of* **~и́ть**
насе́ст, а *m.* roost, perch.
нас|е́сть¹, я́дет, *past* **~е́л** *pf.* (*of* **~а́живаться**) to sit down (*in numbers*).
нас|есть², я́ду, я́дешь, *past* **~е́л** *pf. of* **~еда́ть**
насе́чк|а, и *f.* **1.** cut, incision; notch. **2.** inlay.
насе́|чь, ку́, чёшь, ку́т, *past* **~к, ~кла́** *pf.* (*of* **~ка́ть**) **1.** to make incisions (in, on); to notch. **2.** to emboss; to damascene.
насе́|ять, ю, ешь *pf.* (+*a. or g.*) to sow (*a quantity of*).
наси|де́ть, жу́, ди́шь *pf.* (*of* **⁓живать**) **1.** to hatch. **2.** to warm (*by sitting*).
наси|де́ться, жу́сь, ди́шься *pf.* (*coll.*) to sit long enough.
наси́|женный *p.p.p. of* **~де́ть; ~женное яйцо́** fertilized egg; **~женное ме́сто** (*fig.*) familiar spot, old haunt.
наси́жива|ть, ю *impf. of* **насиде́ть**
наси|жу́, ди́шь *see* **~де́ть**
наси́ли|е, я *nt.* violence, force.
наси́л|овать, ую *impf.* **1.** to coerce, constrain. **2.** (*pf.* **из~**) to rape, violate.
наси́лу *adv.* (*coll.*) with difficulty, hardly.
наси́льник, а *m.* **1.** aggressor. **2.** rapist.
наси́льно *adv.* by force, forcibly.
наси́льственный *adj.* violent; forcible.
наска|за́ть, жу́, ⁓жешь *pf.* (*coll.*; +*a. or g.*) to say, talk a lot (of); **н. новосте́й** to have a lot of news to tell.
наска|ка́ть, чу́, ⁓чешь *pf.* (*of* **⁓кивать**) **1.** (**на**+*a.*) to ride (into); to run (against), collide (with). **2.** to ride up, gallop up.
наска́кива|ть, ю *impf. of* **наскака́ть** *and* **наскочи́ть**
наскандал|ить, ю, ишь *pf. of* **сканда́лить**
насквозь *adv.* through (and through); throughout; **промо́кнуть н.** to get wet through; **ви́деть кого́-н. н.** (*fig.*) to see through s.o.
наско́к, а *m.* **1.** swoop; lunge; **де́йствовать ~ом** to act on impulse; **с ~а** (*fig., coll.*) hurriedly, on the spur of the moment. **2.** (*fig., coll.*) attack.
наско́лько *adv.* **1.** (*interrog.*) how much?; how far? **2.** (*rel.*) as far as; **н. мне изве́стно** as far as I know, to the best of my knowledge.
на́скоро *adv.* (*coll.*) hastily, hurriedly.
наскоч|и́ть, у́, ⁓ишь *pf.* (*of* **наска́кивать**) **1.** to run (against), collide (with); **н. на неприя́тность** (*fig.*) to get into trouble. **2.** (*fig., coll.*) to fly (at).
наскреба́|ть, ю *impf. of* **наскрести́**
наскре|сти́, бу́, бёшь, *past* **⁓б, ~бла́** *pf.* (*of* **~ба́ть**) to scrape up, scrape together; (*fig.*): **н. де́нег на пое́здку** to scrape up some money for an outing.
наску́ч|ить, у, ишь *pf.* (*coll.*) (+*d.*) to bore; **мне э́то ~ило** I am sick of it.
насла|ди́ть, жу́, ди́ть *pf.* (*of* **~жда́ть**) to delight, please.
насла|ди́ться, жу́сь, ди́шься *pf.* (*of* **~жда́ться**) (+*i.*) to enjoy; to take pleasure (in), delight (in).
наслажда́|ть(ся), ю(сь) *impf. of* **наслади́ть(ся)**
наслажде́ни|е, я *nt.* enjoyment, delight.
насла́ива|ться, юсь *impf. of* **наслои́ться**
на|сла́ть¹, шлю́, шлёшь *pf.* (*of* **~сыла́ть**) to send down (*calamities, etc.*).
на|сла́ть², шлю́, шлёшь *pf.* (+*a. or g.*) to send (*a quantity of*).
насле́ди|е, я *nt.* legacy; heritage.
насле|ди́ть, жу́, ди́шь *pf.* (*of* **следи́ть²**) to leave (dirty) marks, traces.
насле́дник, а *m.* heir; legatee; (*fig.*) successor.
насле́дниц|а, ы *f.* heiress.
насле́дный *adj.*: **н. принц** Crown prince.
насле́довани|е, я *nt.* inheritance.

наслéд|овать, ую *impf. and pf.* **1.** (*pf. also* **у~**) to inherit. **2.** (*+d.*) to succeed (to).
наслéдственность, и *f.* heredity.
наслéдственный *adj.* hereditary, inherited.
наслéдств|о, а *nt.* **1.** inheritance, legacy; **получи́ть в н., по ~у** to inherit. **2.** (*fig.*) heritage.
наслоéни|е, я *nt.* **1.** (*geol.*) stratification. **2.** layer, deposit.
насло|и́ться, ю́сь, и́шься *pf.* (*of* **наслáиваться**) (**на**+*a.*) to be deposited (on), accumulate (on).
наслуж|и́ться, у́сь ~ишься *pf.* (*coll.*) to have served for long enough.
наслу́ша|ться, юсь *pf.* (*+g.*) **1.** to hear (a lot of). **2.** to hear enough, listen to long enough; **я не ~юсь э́тих пéсен** I never tire of listening to these songs.
насль́ıшан *adj. as pred.* (*coll.*; **о**+*p.*) familiar (with) by hearsay; **мы о вас мно́го ~ы** we have heard a lot about you.
наслы́ш|аться, усь, ишься *pf.* (**о**+*p.*) to have heard a lot (about).
наслы́шк|а, и *f.*: **по ~е** (*coll.*) by hearsay.
насмáрку *adv.* (*coll.*): **пойти́ н.** to come to nothing.
нáсмерть *adv.* to death; **сражáться н.** to fight to the death; **испугáть н.** to frighten to death.
насмехá|ться, юсь *impf.* **(над)** to mock, ridicule.
насмеш|и́ть, у́, и́шь, *pf.* (*of* **смеши́ть**) (**когó-н.**) to make (s.o.) laugh.
насмéшк|а, и *f.* mockery, ridicule; gibe.
насмéшлив|ый (~, ~) *adj.* **1.** mocking, derisive. **2.** sarcastic.
насмéшник, а *m.* (*coll.*) mocker, scoffer.
насме|я́ться, ю́сь, ёшься *pf.* **1.** (*coll.*) to have a good laugh. **2. (над)** to laugh (at); **н. над чьи́ми-н. чу́вствами** to insult s.o.'s feelings.
нáсморк, а *m.* (*head*) cold; **схвати́ть, получи́ть н.** to catch a cold; **у меня́ сдéлался нáсморк** I have caught a cold.
насмотр|éться, ю́сь, ~ишься *pf.* **1.** (*+g.*) to see a lot (of). **2.** (**на**+*a.*) to have looked enough (at), to see enough (of); **не н.** not to tire of looking (at).
насобáч|иться, усь, ишься *pf.* (*coll.*; *+inf.*) to become adept (at), become a good hand (at).
нас|овáть, ую́ уёшь *pf.* (*of* **~о́вывать**) (*coll.*; *+g. or a.*) to shove in, stuff in (*a quantity of*); **н. конфéт в кармáны** to stuff sweets into one's pockets.
насо́выва|ть, ю *impf. of* **насовáть**
насол|и́ть¹, ю́, ~и́шь *pf.* (*of* **насáливать**) **1.** to salt; to put much salt (into). **2.** (*fig.*; *+d.*) to spite, injure; to do a bad turn (to).
насол|и́ть², ю́, ~и́шь *pf.* (*+a. or g.*) to salt, pickle (*a quantity of*).
насоло|ди́ть, жу́, ди́шь *pf. of* **солоди́ть**
насор|и́ть, ю́, и́шь *pf. of* **сори́ть**
насо́с, а *m.* pump.
насос|áть, у́, ёшь, *pf.* (*of* **насáсывать**) (*+a. or g.*) **1.** to suck (*a quantity of*). **2.** to pump.
насос|áться, у́сь, ёшься *pf.* **1.** (*+g.*) to have sucked one's fill. **2.** (*coll.*) to get drunk.
насо́с|ный *adj. of* **~¹**; **н. агрегáт** pumping unit; **~ная стáнция** pumping station.
насочин|и́ть, ю́, и́шь *pf.* (*coll.*) (*+a. or g.*) to talk a lot of nonsense; to make up (a lot of falsehoods).
нáспех *adv.* hastily; carelessly.
насплéтнича|ть, ю *pf. of* **сплéтничать**
наср|áть, у, ёшь *pf. of* **срáть**
наст, а *m.* thin crust of ice over snow.
наста|вáть, ю́, ёшь *impf. of* **~ть**
наставúтел|ьный (~ен, ~ьна) *adj.* edifying, instructive; **н. тон** didactic tone.
настáв|ить¹, лю, ишь *pf.* (*of* **~ля́ть**) **1.** to lengthen; to put on, add on; **н. нос комý-н.** to fool, dupe s.o. **2.** (**на**+*a.*) to aim (at), point (at); **н. револьвéр на когó-н.** to point a revolver at s.o.
настáв|ить², лю, ишь *pf.* (*of* **~ля́ть**) to edify; to exhort, admonish; **н. на путь и́стинный** to set on the right path.
настáв|ить³, лю, ишь *pf.* (*+a. or g.*) to set up, place (*a quantity of*).
настáвк|а, и *f.* addition.
наставлéни|е, я *nt.* **1.** exhortation, admonition. **2.** directions, instructions; (*mil.*) manual.
наставля́|ть, ю *impf. of* **настáвить**
настáвник, а *m.* **1.** mentor; **клáссный н.** form-master. **2.** instructor (*of apprentices*).
настáвни|ческий *adj. of* **~к**; **н. тон** edifying tone.
наставно́й *adj.* lengthened; added.
настáива|ть¹,², ю, *impf. of* **настоя́ть¹,²**
настáива|ться, юсь *impf. of* **настоя́ться²**
настá|ть, ну, нешь *pf.* (*of* **~вáть**) (*of times or seasons*) to come, begin.
наста|ю́, ёшь *see* **~вáть**
нáстежь *adv.* wide open; **откры́ть н.** to open wide.
настели́ть = настлáть
наст|елю́, éлешь *see* **~лáть**
настéнный *adj.* wall.
настиг|áть, áю *impf. of* **~нуть** *and* **насти́чь**
насти́гн|уть, у, ешь *pf.* = **насти́чь**
насти́л, а *m.* flooring; planking.
настилá|ть, ю *impf. of* **настлáть**
насти́лк|а, и *f.* **1.** laying, spreading. **2. = насти́л**
настирá|ть, ю *pf.* (*+a. or g.*) to wash, launder (*a quantity of*).
насти́|чь, гну, гнешь, *past.* **~г, ~гла** *pf.* (*of* **~гáть**) to overtake (*also fig.*).
наст|лáть, елю́, ~éлешь *pf.* (*of* **~илáть**) to lay, spread; **н. пол** to lay a floor; **н. соло́му** to spread straw.
насто́|й, я *m.* infusion.
насто́йк|а, и *f.* **1.** liqueur. **2.** (*pharm.*) tincture.
насто́йчив|ый (~, ~а) *adj.* **1.** persistent. **2.** urgent, insistent.
насто́лько *adv.* so; so much; **н., наско́лько** as much as.
насто́льно-издáтельский *adj.* desktop publishing; DTP.
насто́льн|ый *adj.* **1.** table, desk; desktop; **~ая полигрáфия** desktop publishing; **~ая игрá** board game; **н. тéннис** table tennis. **2.** (*fig.*) for constant reference, in constant use; **~ая кни́га, ~ое руково́дство** reference book; handbook, manual.
насторáжива|ть(ся), ю(сь) *impf. of* **насторожи́ть(ся)**
насторожé *adv.*: **быть н.** to be on one's guard; to be on the qui vive.
насторо|жённый (*and* **~женный**) *p.p.p. of* **~жи́ть** *and adj.* guarded, suspicious.
насторож|и́ть, у́, и́шь *pf.* (*of* **насторáживать**) to put on one's guard; **н. у́ши** to prick up one's ears (*also fig.*).
насторож|и́ться, у́сь, и́шься *pf.* (*of* **насторáживаться**) to prick up one's ears.
настоя́ни|е, я *nt.* insistence.
настоя́тел|ь, я *m.* (*eccl.*) prior; dean.
настоя́тельниц|а, ы *f.* (*eccl.*) prioress, mother superior.
настоя́тел|ьный (~ен, ~ьна) *adj.* **1.** persistent; insistent. **2.** urgent, pressing.
насто|я́ть¹, ю́, и́шь *pf.* (*of* **настáивать**) (**на**+*p.*) to insist (on); **н. на своём** to insist on having one's own way; **он ~я́л на том, что́бы пойти́ самомý** he insisted on going himself.
насто|я́ть², ю́, и́шь *pf.* (*of* **настáивать**) to draw, infuse; **н. чай** to let tea draw.
насто|я́ться¹, ю́сь, и́шься *pf.* (*coll.*) to stand a long time.
насто|я́ться², ю́сь, и́шься *pf.* (*of* **настáиваться**)

1. to draw, brew (*of tea, etc.*). **2.** *pass. of* **~я́ть**[2]
настоя́щ|ий *adj.* **1.** present; this; **в ~ее вре́мя** at present, now; **~ее вре́мя** (*gram.*) the present tense; *as n.* **~ее, ~его** *nt.* the present (time); **жить ~им** to live in the present. **2.** real, genuine; veritable; **~ая цена́** fair price. **3.** (*coll., pej.*) complete, utter, absolute; **он н. дура́к** he is an absolute fool.
настрада́|ться, юсь *pf.* to suffer much.
настра́ива|ть(ся), ю(сь) *impf. of* **настро́ить(ся)**
настра́чива|ть, ю *impf. of* **настрочи́ть**[2]
настреля́|ть, ю *pf.* (+*a. or g.*) to shoot (*a quantity of*).
настри́г, а *m.* (*agric.*) **1.** shearing, clipping. **2.** clip.
настри́|чь, гу́, жёшь, гу́т, *past* **~г, ~гла** *pf.* (+*a. or g.*) (*agric.*) to shear, clip (*a number of*).
на́строго *adv.* (*coll.*) strictly.
настрое́ни|е, я *nt.* **1.** (*also* **н. ду́ха**) mood, temper, humour; **припо́днятое/пода́вленное н.** high/low spirits; **челове́к ~я** a man of moods; **быть в плохо́м** *etc.*, **~и** to be in a bad, *etc.*, mood; **н. умо́в** state of opinion, public mood. **2.** (+*inf.*) mood (for); **у меня́ нет ~я танцева́ть, я не в ~и танцева́ть** I am not in the mood for dancing; I don't feel like dancing.
настро́енност|ь, и *f.* mood, humour.
настро́|ить[1]**, ю, ишь** *pf.* (*of* **настра́ивать**) **1.** (*mus.*) to tune; to tune up, attune; **н. приёмник на сре́днюю волну́** to tune in to medium wave. **2.** (*fig.*; **на**+*a.*) to dispose (to), incline (to); to incite; **н. кого́-н. на весёлый лад** to make s.o. happy, cheer s.o. up; **н. кого́-н. (про́тив)** to incite s.o. (against).
настро́|ить[2]**, ю, ишь** *pf.* (+*a. or g.*) to build (*a quantity of*)
настро́|иться, юсь, ишься *pf.* (*of* **настра́иваться**) **1.** (**на**+*a.*) to dispose o.s. (to); (+*inf.*) to make up one's mind (to); **я ~ился е́хать в Москву́** I made up my mind to go to Moscow. **2.** *pass. of* **~ить**[1]
настро́|й, я *m.* (*coll.*) = **настрое́ние**
настро́йк|а, и *f.* (*mus., radio*) tuning.
настро́йщик, а *m.* tuner.
настроч|и́ть[1]**, у́, и́шь** *pf. of* **строчи́ть**
настроч|и́ть[2]**, у́, и́шь** *pf.* (*of* **настра́чивать**) (*coll.*) to incite, set on.
настря́па|ть, ю *pf.* **1.** (+*a. or g.*) to cook (*a quantity of*). **2.** (*fig., coll.*) to cook up.
насту́к|ать, аю *pf.* (*of* **~ивать**) (*coll.*) to knock out, bash out (*on typewriter*).
насту́кива|ть, ю *impf. of* **насту́кать**
наступа́тельный *adj.* (*mil.*) offensive.
наступ|а́ть[1]**, а́ю** *impf. of* **~и́ть**
наступа́|ть[2]**, ю** *adj.* (*mil.*) to advance, be on the offensive.
наступа́|ющий[1] *pres. part. act. of* **~ть**[1] *and adj.* coming.
наступа́|ющий[2] *pres. part. act. of* **~ть**[2]; *as n.* **н., ~ющего** *m.* attacker.
наступ|и́ть[1]**, лю́, ~ишь** *pf.* (*of* **~а́ть**[1]) (**на**+*a.*) to tread (on); **медве́дь (***or* **слон) наступи́л ему́ на у́хо** he has absolutely no ear for music.
наступ|и́ть[2]**, ~ит** *pf.* (*of* **~а́ть**[1]) (*of times or seasons*) to come, begin; to ensue; to set in (*also fig.*); **~ит вре́мя, когда́...** there will come a time, when ...
наступле́ни|е[1]**, я** *nt.* (*mil.*) offensive; **перейти́ в н.** to assume the offensive.
наступле́ни|е[2]**, я** *nt.* coming, approach; onset.
насту́рци|я, и *f.* (*bot.*) nasturtium.
насул|и́ть, ю́, и́шь *pf.* (+*a. or g.*) (*coll.*) to promise (much.)
насу́п|ить(ся), лю(сь), ишь(ся) *pf. of* **су́пить(ся)** *and* **~ливать(ся)**
насу́пливать(ся) = **су́пить(ся)**
насурьм|и́ть(ся), лю́(сь), и́шь(ся) *pf. of* **сурьми́ть(ся)**
на́сухо *adv.* dry; **вы́тереть н.** to wipe dry.
насуш|и́ть, у́, ~ишь *pf.* (+*a. or g.*) to dry (*a quantity of*).
насу́щност|ь, и *f.* urgency.
насу́щ|ный (~ен, ~на) *adj.* vital, urgent; **хлеб н.** daily bread (*also fig.*).
нас|у́ю, уёшь *see* **~ова́ть**
насчёт *prep.*+*g.* about; as regards, concerning.
насчит|а́ть, а́ю *pf.* (*of* **~ывать**) to count, number.
насчи́тыва|ть, ю *impf.* **1.** *impf. of* **насчита́ть. 2.** (*no pf.*) to number (= *to contain*); **э́тот го́род ~ет свы́ше ста ты́сяч жи́телей** this city has over one hundred thousand inhabitants.
насчи́тыва|ться, ется *impf.* (*impers.*) to number (= *to be, be contained*); **в на́шем селе́ ~ется не бо́лее двухсо́т жи́телей** the population of our village numbers no more than two hundred.
насыла́|ть, ю *impf. of* **насла́ть**[1]
насы́п|ать, лю, лешь *pf.* (*of* **~а́ть**) **1.** (+*a. or g.*) to pour (in, into); to fill (with); **н. муки́ в мешо́к** to pour flour into a bag; **н. мешо́к муко́й** to fill up a bag with flour. **2.** (+*a. or g.* **на**+*a.*) to spread (on); **н. песку́ на доро́жку** to spread sand on the path. **3.** to raise (*a heap or pile of sand, etc.*)
насып|а́ть, а́ю *impf. of* **~ать**
на́сып|ь, и *f.* embankment (*of rail. or road*).
насы́|тить, щу, тишь *pf.* (*of* **~ща́ть**) **1.** to sate, satiate. **2.** (*chem.*) to saturate, impregnate.
насы́|титься, щусь, тишься *pf.* (*of* **~ща́ться**) **1.** to be full; to be sated. **2.** (*chem.*) to become saturated.
насыща́|ть(ся), ю(сь) *impf. of* **насы́тить(ся)**
насыще́ни|е, я *nt.* **1.** satiety, satiation. **2.** (*chem.*) saturation.
насы́щенност|ь, и *f.* **1.** saturation. **2.** (*fig.*) richness.
насы́|щенный *p.p.p. of* **~тить** *and adj.* **1.** saturated. **2.** (*fig.*) rich.
ната́лкива|ть(ся), ю(сь) *impf. of* **натолкну́ть(ся)**
ната́плива|ть, ю *impf. of* **натопи́ть**[1]
ната́птыва|ть, ю *impf. of* **натопта́ть**
ната́ск|анный *p.p.p. of* **~а́ть**
натаск|а́ть[1]**, а́ю** *pf.* (*of* **~ивать**) to train (*hounds*); (*fig., coll.*) to coach, cram.
натаск|а́ть[2]**, а́ю** *pf.* (+*a. or g.*) **1.** to bring, lay (*a quantity of*). **2.** (*coll.*) to fish out, hook (*a quantity of*).
ната́скива|ть, ю *impf. of* **натаска́ть**[1] *and* **натащи́ть**[1]
натащ|и́ть[1]**, у́, ~ишь** *pf.* (*of* **ната́скивать**) to pull (on, over).
натащ|и́ть[2]**, у́, ~ишь** *pf.* (+*a. or g.*) to bring (*a quantity of*); to pile up (*a quantity of*).
натвор|и́ть, ю́, и́шь *pf.* (+*g.*; *coll., pej.*) to do, get up to; **н. вся́ких глу́постей** to get up to every sort of stupid trick; **что ты ~и́л!** what ever have you done?
на́те *int.* (*coll., addressed to more than one person or, politely, to one*) here (you are)!; there (you are)!
натека́|ть, ет *impf. of* **нате́чь**
нате́льн|ый *adj.* worn next to the skin; **~ое бельё** (*collect.*) underwear.
на|тере́ть[1]**, тру́, трёшь,** *past* **~тёр, ~тёрла** *pf.* (*of* **~тира́ть**) **1.** to rub (in, on); **н. ру́ки вазели́ном** to rub vaseline into one's hands. **2.** to polish (*floors, etc.*). **3.** to rub sore; to chafe; **н. себе́ мозо́ль** to get a corn.
на|тере́ть[2]**, тру́, трёшь,** *past.* **~тёр, ~тёрла** *pf.* (+*a. or g.*) to grate, rasp (*a quantity of*).
на|тере́ться, тру́сь, трёшься, *past* **~тёрся, ~тёрлась** *pf.* (*of* **~тира́ться**) **1.** (+*i.*) to rub o.s. (with). **2.** *pass. of* **~тере́ть**
натерп|е́ться, лю́сь, ~ишься *pf.* (+*g.*; *coll.*) to have endured much; to have gone through much.
натёр|тый *p.p.p. of* **~е́ть**

натé|чь, чёт, кýт, *past.* **~́к, ~клá** *pf.* (*of* **~кáть**) (*of liquids*) to accumulate.
натéш|иться, усь, ишься *pf.* (*coll.*) **1.** to enjoy o.s., have a good time. **2. (над)** to have a good laugh (at).
натирá|ть(ся), ю(сь) *impf. of* **натерéть(ся)**
нáтиск, а *m.* **1.** onslaught, charge. **2.** pressure. **3.** (*typ.*) impress.
нати́ска|ть, ю *pf.* (+*a. or g.*) **1.** (*coll.*) to cram in, stuff in (*a quantity of*). **2.** (*coll.*) to shove (s.o.) about. **3.** (*typ.*) to impress (*a quantity of*).
натк|áть, ý, ёшь, *past* **~áл, ~алá, ~áло** *pf.* (+*a. or g.*) to weave (*a quantity of*).
наткн|ýть, ý, ёшь *pf.* (*of* **наты́кать**) **1.** to stick, pin. **2.** to stick, pin (*a quantity of*).
наткн|ýться, ýсь, ёшься *pf.* (*of* **натыкáться**) (**на**+*a.*) **1.** to run (against), strike; to stumble (upon); **н. на гвоздь** to run against a nail; **н. на неожи́данное сопротивлéние** (*fig.*) to meet with unexpected resistance. **2.** (*fig.*) to stumble (upon, across), come (across); **н. на интерéсную мысль** to stumble across an interesting idea.
НАТО *nt. indecl.* NATO (*abbr. of* North Atlantic Treaty Organization — *Организáция Сéвероатланти́ческого договóра*).
нáтов|ец, ца *m.* NATO member.
нáтовский *adj. of* **НАТО**
натолкн|ýть, ý, ёшь *pf.* (*of* **натáлкивать**) (+*a.* **на**+*a.*) **1.** to push (against), shove (against). **2.** (*fig.*) to direct, lead (into, onto); **он меня́ ~ýл на мысль** he suggested the idea to me; **н. на грех** to lead into sin.
натолкн|ýться, ýсь ёшься *pf.* (*of* **натáлкиваться**) **на**+*a.*) to run (against); (*fig.*) to run across.
натол|óчь, кý, чёшь, кýт, *past* **~óк, ~клá** *pf.* (+*a. or g.*) to pound, crush (*a quantity of*).
натоп|и́ть[1]**, лю́, ~́ишь** *pf.* (*of* **натáпливать**) to heat well, heat up.
натоп|и́ть[2]**, лю́, ~́ишь** *pf.* (+*a. or g.*) **1.** to melt (*a quantity of*). **2.** to heat (*a quantity of*).
натоп|тáть, чý, ~́чешь *pf.* (*of* **натáптывать**) (*coll.*; **в, на**+*p.*) to make dirty footmarks (in, on).
наторé|ть, ю *pf.* (**в**+*p.*; *coll.*) to become skilled (at, in), become expert (at, in).
наточ|и́ть, ý, ~́ишь *pf. of* **точи́ть**[1]
натощáк *adv.* on an empty stomach.
натр, а *m.*: **éдкий н.** caustic soda.
натрав|и́ть[1]**, лю́, ~́ишь** *pf.* (*of* **~́ливать**) (**на**+*a.*) to set (*dog*) (on); (*fig.*) to stir up (against).
натрав|и́ть[2]**, лю́, ~́ишь** *pf.* (*of* **~́ливать**) to etch.
натрáвлива|ть, ю *impf. of* **натрави́ть**[1,2]
натравл|я́ть = **~́ивать**
натрениро́ванный *adj.* trained.
натренир|овáть(ся), ýю(сь) *pf. of* **тренировáть(ся)**
нáтри|евый *adj. of* **~й**
нáтри|й, я *m.* (*chem.*) sodium.
нáтрое *adv.* in three.
натрóнн|ый *adj.* (*chem.*) sodium; **~ая и́звесть** sodium carbonate.
нат|рý, рёшь *see* **~ерéть**
натру|ди́ть, жý, ~́ди́шь *pf.* (*of* **~́живать**) to tire out, overwork.
натру|ди́ться, жýсь, ~́ди́шься *pf.* (*coll.*) **1.** to become tired out. **2.** to have worked long enough; to have overworked.
натрýжива|ть, ю *impf. of* **натруди́ть**
натýг|а, и *f.* effort, strain.
нáтуго *adv.* (*coll.*) tightly; **тýго-нáтуго** very tightly.
натýжива|ть(ся), ю(сь) *impf. of* **натýжить(ся)**
натýж|ить, у, ишь *pf.* (*of* **~ивать**) (*coll.*) to tense, tighten.
натýж|иться, усь, ишься *pf.* (*of* **~иваться**) (*coll.*) to exert all one's strength; to strain.
натýжный *adj.* (*coll.*) strained, forced.
натýр|а, ы *f.* **1.** nature. **2.** (artist's) model, sitter; **рисовáть с ~ы** to paint from life. **3.** (*econ.*) kind; **плати́ть ~ой** to pay in kind. **4.: на ~е** (*coll.*) on the spot; (*cin.*) on location.
натурализáци|я, и *f.* naturalization.
натурали́зм, а *m.* naturalism.
натурализ|овáть, ýю *impf. and pf.* to naturalize.
натурали́ст, а *m.* naturalist.
натуралисти́ческий *adj.* naturalistic.
натурáльност|ь, и *f.* genuineness; naturalness.
натурáл|ьный (~ен, ~ьна) *adj.* **1.** natural; **в ~ьную величинý** life-size. **2.** real; genuine; **н. смех** unforced laughter. **3.** (*econ.*) in kind; **н. обмéн** barter.
натуропáт, а *m.* naturopath.
натуропáти|я, и *f.* naturopathy.
натýрщик, а *m.* (artist's) model, sitter.
натýрщи|ца, цы *f. of* **~к**
наты́кать = **наткнýть**
натыкá|ть(ся), ю(сь) *impf. of* **наткнýть(ся)**
натюрмóрт, а *m.* (*art*) still life.
натюрмóрт|ный *adj. of* **~**
натя́гива|ть(ся), ю(сь) *impf. of* **натянýть(ся)**
натяжéни|е, я *nt.* pull, tension.
натя́жк|а, и *f.* (*coll.*) **1.** strained interpretation; **допусти́ть ~у** to stretch a point; **с ~ой** (*fig.*) at a stretch. **2.** = **натяжéние**
натя́нутост|ь, и *f.* tension (*also fig.*)
натя́н|утый *p.p.p. of* **~ýть** *and adj.* **1.** tight. **2.** (*fig.*) strained; forced; **~утые отношéния** strained relationse.
натя|нýть, нý, ~́нешь *pf.* (*of* **~́гивать**) **1.** to stretch; to draw (tight); **н. лук** to draw a bow; **н. верёвку** (*naut.*) to haul a rope taut. **2.** to pull on; **н. шáпку нá уши** to pull a cap over one's ears.
натя|нýться, нýсь, ~́нешься *pf.* (*of* **~́гиваться**) to stretch (*intrans.*).
наугáд *adv.* at random, by guess-work.
наугóльник, а *m.* (*tech.*) (try-)square, back square; bevel, bevel square.
наудáчу *adv.* at random; by guesswork.
нау|ди́ть, жý, ~́дишь *pf.* (+*a. or g.*) to hook, catch (*a number of*).
наýк|а, и *f.* **1.** science; learning; study; scholarship; **общéственные ~и** social sciences; **прикладны́е ~и** applied science; **тóчные ~и** exact science. **2.** (*coll.*) lesson; **э́то тебé н.!** let this be a lesson to you!
наýськ|ать, аю *pf.* (*of* **~ивать**) (**на**+*a.*) to set (*dogs on*).
наýськива|ть, ю *impf. of* **наýськать**
наутёк *adv.*: **пусти́ться н.** (*coll.*) to take to one's heels.
наýтро *adv.* next morning.
науч|и́ть, ý, ~́ишь *pf.* (*of* **учи́ть**) (+*a. and d. or* +*inf.*) to teach; **н. когó-н. рýсскому языкý** to teach s.o. Russian; **н. когó-н. води́ть маши́ну** to teach s.o. to drive (a car).
науч|и́ться, ýсь, ~́ишься *pf.* (*of* **учи́ться**) (+*d. or inf.*) to learn.
наýчно-исслéдовательск|ий *adj.* scientific research; **~ая рабóта** (scientific) research work.
наýчно-фантасти́ческий *adj.* science fiction.
наýч|ный (~ен, ~на) *adj.* scientific; **н. рабóтник** researcher; **~ная фантáстика** science fiction.
наýшник[1]**, а** *m.* **1.** ear-flap; ear-muff. **2.** ear-phone, head-phone.
наýшник[2]**, а** *m.* (*pej.*) informer, slanderer.
наýшнича|ть, ю *impf.* (+*d.* **на**+*a.*) to tell tales (about), inform (on, about).
наýшничеств|о, а *nt.* tale-bearing, informing.
нафтали́н, а *m.* (*chem.*) naphthalene.
нафтали́н|ный *adj. of* **~**

нафтали́н|овый = **~ный; н. ша́рик** moth-ball.
наха́л, а *m.* impudent, insolent fellow; smart alec(k).
наха́лк|а, и *f.* impudent, insolent woman.
наха́льнича|ть, ю *impf.* to be impudent, insolent.
наха́л|ьный (~ен, ~ьна) *adj.* impudent, impertinent; cheeky, brazen.
наха́льств|о, а *nt.* impudence, impertinence, effrontery; **име́ть н.** (+*inf.*) to have the cheek (to).
нахва́лива|ть, ю *impf. of* **нахвали́ть**
нахвал|и́ть, ю́, ~́ишь *pf.* (*of* **~́ивать**) (*coll.*) to praise (highly).
нахвал|и́ться, ю́сь, ~́ишься *pf.* (*coll.*) **1.** to boast much. **2.** (+*i.*; *usu.* +*neg.*) to praise sufficiently; **я не могу́ им н.** I cannot speak too highly of him.
нахват|а́ть, а́ю *pf.* (*of* **~́ывать**) (*coll.*; +*a.* *or* *g.*) to pick up, get hold (of), come by.
нахват|а́ться, а́юсь *pf.* (*of* **~́ываться**) (*coll.*, *fig.*; +*g.*) to pick up, come by; **в солда́тах он нахвата́лся ара́бских слов** in the army he picked up a few words of Arabic.
нахле́бник, а *m.* parasite, hanger-on.
нахле|ста́ть, щу́, ~́щешь *pf.* (*of* **~́стывать**) (*coll.*) to whip.
нахлёстыва|ть, ю *impf. of* **нахлеста́ть**
нахлобу́чива|ть, ю *impf. of* **нахлобу́чить**
нахлобу́ч|ить, у, ишь *pf.* (*of* **~ивать**) (*coll.*) to pull down (over one's head *or* eyes).
нахлобу́чк|а, и *f.* (*coll.*) dressing-down; scolding.
нахлы́н|уть, ет *pf.* (**на**+*a.*) to flow, gush (over, into); (*fig.*) to surge, crowd; **~ули слёзы** tears welled (in my, her, *etc.*, eyes); **на меня́ ~ули мы́сли** thoughts crowded into my mind.
нахму́р|енный *p.p.p. of* **~ить** *and adj.* frowning, scowling.
нахму́р|ить(ся), ю(сь), ишь(ся) *pf. of* **хму́рить(ся)**
нахо|ди́ть, жу́, ~́дишь *impf. of* **найти́**
нахо|ди́ться[1]**, жу́сь, ~́дишься** *impf. of* **найти́сь**
нахо|ди́ться[2]**, жу́сь ~́дишься** *impf.* to be (situated); **где ~́дится ста́нция?** where is the station?
нахо́дк|а, и *f.* **1.** find. **2.** (*fig.*, *coll.*) godsend.
нахо́дчивост|ь, и *f.* **1.** resourcefulness. **2.** quick-wittedness.
нахо́дчив|ый (~, ~а) *adj.* **1.** resourceful. **2.** quick-witted.
нахожде́ни|е, я *nt.* **1.** finding. **2.: ме́сто ~я** the whereabouts.
нахоло|ди́ть, жу́, ди́шь *pf. of* **холоди́ть 1.**
нахо́хл|иться, юсь, ишься *pf.* (*of* **хо́хлиться**) (*fig.*, *coll.*) to bristle (up).
нахохо|та́ться, чу́сь, ~́чишься *pf.* (*coll.*) to have had a good laugh.
нахра́пист|ый (~, ~а) *adj.* (*coll.*, *pej.*) high-handed.
нахра́пом *adv.* (*coll.*) high-handedly.
нацара́п|ать, аю *pf.* (*of* **~ывать**) **1.** to scratch. **2.** (*fig.*, *coll.*) to scrawl, scribble.
нацара́пыва|ть, ю *impf. of* **нацара́пать**
наце|ди́ть, жу́, ~́дишь *pf.* (+*a.* *or* *g.*) **1.** to fill (*a vessel*) through a strainer. **2.** to strain (*a quantity of*).
наце́лива|ть(ся), ю(сь) *impf. of* **наце́лить(ся)**
наце́л|ить, ю, ишь *pf.* **1.** (*impf.* **це́лить** *and* **~ивать**) to aim, level. **2.** (*impf.* **~ивать**) (*fig.*) to aim, direct.
наце́л|иться, юсь, ишься *pf.* (*of* **~иваться**) **1.** (**в**+*a.*) to aim (at), take aim (at). **2.** (*fig.*, *coll.*; **на**+*a.*) to aim (at, for).
на́цело *adv.* (*coll.*) entirely, without remainder.
наце́нива|ть, ю *impf. of* **наце́ни́ть**
нацен|и́ть, ю́, ~́ишь *pf.* (*of* **~́ивать**) (*comm.*) to raise the price of.
наце́нк|а, и *f.* mark-up.
нацеп|и́ть, лю́, ~́ишь *pf.* (*of* **~ля́ть**) to fasten on; to attach (*by means of hook or pin*).
нацеп|ля́ть, ля́ю *impf. of* **~ить**
наци́зм, а *m.* Nazism.
национализа́ци|я, и *f.* nationalization.
национализи́р|овать, ую *impf. and pf.* to nationalize.
национали́зм, а *m.* nationalism.
национали́ст, а *m.* nationalist.
националисти́ческий *adj.* nationalist(ic).
национа́льност|ь, и *f.* **1.** nationality. **2.** national character.
национа́льн|ый *adj.* national; **~ые словари́** minority-language dictionaries.
наци́ст, а *m.* Nazi.
наци́стский *adj.* Nazi.
на́ци|я, и *f.* nation.
нацме́н, а *m.* (*coll.*) member of a national minority.
нацме́н|ка, ки *f. of* **~**
нач... *comb. form, abbr. of* **1. нача́льник. 2. нача́льствующий**
нача|ди́ть, жу́, ди́шь *pf. of* **чади́ть**
нача́л|о, а *nt.* beginning; commencement; **для ~а** to start with, for a start; **положи́ть н.** (+*d.*) to begin, commence. **2.** origin, source; **вести́ н. (от), взять н.** (**в**+*p.*) to originate (from, in). **3.** principle, basis; **рабо́тать на но́вых ~ах** to work on a new basis; **~а матема́тики** the elements of mathematics. **4.: быть под ~ом у кого́-н.** to be under s.o.; **отда́ть под н., под ~а** (+*d.*) to put under, place in the charge (of).
нача́льник, а *m.* head, chief; superior; **н. свя́зи** chief signal officer; **н. отде́ла** head of a department.
нача́льн|ый *adj.* **1.** initial, first. **2.** elementary; **~ая шко́ла** primary school.
нача́льственный *adj.* overbearing, domineering.
нача́льств|о, а *nt.* **1.** (*collect.*) (the) authorities. **2.** command, direction. **3.** (*coll.*) head, boss.
нача́льствовани|е, я *nt.* command.
нача́льств|овать, ую *impf.* **(над)** to command, be in command (of).
нача́льствующий *adj.*: **н. соста́в** command personnel.
нача́тк|и, ов *no sg.* rudiments, elements.
нач|а́ть, ну́, нёшь, *past* **~́ал, ~ала́, ~́ало** *pf.* (*of* **~ина́ть**) to begin, start, commence; **н. с нача́ла** to begin at the beginning; **н. всё снача́ла** to start all over again, start afresh; **н. с того́, что он ни одного́ сло́ва не по́нял** to begin with, he did not understand a single word; **он на́чал моли́твой** (*or* **с моли́твы)** he began with a prayer.
нач|а́ться, ну́сь, нёшься, *past* **~ался́, ~ала́сь** *pf.* (*of* **~ина́ться**) to begin, start; to break out.
начди́в, а *m.* (*abbr. of* **нача́льник диви́зии**) division commander.
начеку́ *adv.* on the alert, on the qui vive.
начерн|и́ть, ю́, и́шь *pf. of* **черни́ть 1.**
на́черно *adv.* roughly; **написа́ть н.** to make a rough copy.
начерта́ни|е, я *nt.* tracing; outline.
начерта́тельн|ый *adj. only in phr.* **~ая геоме́трия** descriptive geometry.
начерта́|ть, ю *pf.* to trace (*also fig.*); to inscribe.
начер|ти́ть, чу́, ~́чишь *pf. of* **черти́ть**[1]
начёс, а *m.* nap (*of cloth*).
начётничеств|о, а *nt.* (*pej.*) dogmatism.
начётчик, а *m.* (*pej.*) dogmatist.
начина́ни|е, я *nt.* undertaking.
начина́тел|ь, я *m.* originator, initiator.
начина́тельный *adj.* (*gram.*): **н. глаго́л** inceptive *or* inchoative verb.
начина́|ть(ся), ю(сь) *impf. of* **нача́ть(ся)**
начина́|ющий *pres. part. act. of* **~ть**; *as n.* **н., ~ющего** *m.* beginner.
начина́я *as prep.* (**с**+*g.*) as (from), starting (with).

начин|и́ть, ю́, ~́ишь *pf.* (*+a. or g.*) **1.** to mend (*a quantity of*). **2.:** **н. карандаше́й** to sharpen (*a number of*) pencils.
начи́нк|а, и *f.* (*cul.*) stuffing, filling.
начи́|стить¹, щу, стишь *pf.* (*of* **~ща́ть**) to polish, shine (*trans.*).
начи́|стить², щу, стишь *pf.* (*+a. or g.*) to peel (*a quantity of*); to clean (*a quantity of*).
на́чисто *adv.* **1.** clean, fair; **переписа́ть н.** to make a fair copy (of). **2.** (*coll.*) completely, thoroughly; **н. отказа́ться** to refuse flatly. **3.** (*coll.*) openly, without equivocation.
начистоту́ *adv.* openly, without equivocation.
начи́танност|ь, и *f.* (wide) reading; erudition.
начи́тан|ный (~, ~на) *adj.* well-read, widely-read.
начита́|ть, ю *pf.* (*+a. or g.*) to read (*a number of*).
начита́|ться, юсь *pf.* **1.** (*+g.*) to have read (*much of*). **2.** to have read one's fill.
начища́|ть, ю *impf. of* **начи́стить**
нач|ну́, нёшь *see* **~а́ть**
наш, ~́его, *f.* **~́а, ~́ей;** *nt.* **~́е, ~́его;** *pl.* **~́и, ~́их** *possessive pron.* our(s); **(служи́ть) и ~́им и ва́шим** (*coll.*) to run with the hare and hunt with the hounds; *as n.* **~́и, ~́их** our people, people on our side; **его́ счита́ют одни́м из ~́их** they regard him as one of us.
нашал|и́ть, ю́, и́шь *pf.* to be naughty.
нашаты́р|ный *adj. of* **~ь; н. спирт** liquid ammonia.
нашаты́р|ь, я́ *m.* (*chem.*) sal ammoniac, ammonium chloride.
нашеп|та́ть, чу́, ~́чешь *pf.* (*of* **~́тывать**) (*+a. or g.*) to whisper (*a number of*) (*also fig.*).
нашёптыва|ть, ю *impf. of* **нашепта́ть**
наше́стви|е, я *nt.* invasion, descent.
нашива́|ть, ю *impf. of* **наши́ть¹**
наши́вк|а, и *f.* (*mil.*) stripe, chevron (*on sleeve*); tab.
нашивно́й *adj.* sewed (sewn) on.
наш|и́ть¹, ью́, ьёшь *pf.* (*of* **~ива́ть**) to sew on.
наш|и́ть², ью́, ьёшь *pf.* (*+a. or g.*) to sew (*a quantity of*).
на|шлю́, шлёшь *see* **~сла́ть**
нашпиг|ова́ть, у́ю *pf. of* **шпигова́ть**
нашпи́лива|ть, ю *impf. of* **нашпи́лить**
нашпи́л|ить, ю, ишь *pf.* (*of* **~ивать**) (*coll.*) to pin on.
нашум|е́ть, лю́, и́шь *pf.* to make a lot of noise; (*fig.*) to cause a sensation.
нащип|а́ть, лю́, ~́лешь *pf.* (*+a. or g.*) to pluck, pick (*a quantity of*).
нащу́п|ать, аю *pf.* (*of* **~ывать**) to find, discover (*by groping*).
нащу́пыва|ть, ю *impf.* (*of* **нащу́пать**) to grope (for, after); to fumble (for, after); to feel about (for) (*also fig.*); **н. по́чву** (*fig.*) to feel one's way, see how the land lies.
наэлектриз|ова́ть, у́ю *pf.* (*of* **~о́вывать**) to electrify (*also fig.*).
наэлектризо́выва|ть, ю *impf. of* **наэлектризова́ть**
ная́беднича|ть, ю *pf. of* **я́бедничать**
наяву́ *adv.* waking; in reality; **гре́зить н.** to daydream.
ная́д|а, ы *f.* (*myth.*) naiad.
не¹ not; **не..., не** neither ... nor.
не² *separable component of prons.* **не́кого** *and* **не́чего; мне не́ с кем разгова́ривать** I have no one to talk to; **не́ о чем бы́ло говори́ть** there was nothing to talk about.
не... *pref.* un-, in-, non-, mis-, dis-.
неавтоно́мный *adj.* (*comput.*) on-line.
неаккура́тност|ь, и *f.* **1.** carelessness; inaccuracy. **2.** unpunctuality. **3.** untidiness.
неаккура́т|ный (~ен, ~на) *adj.* **1.** careless; inaccurate. **2.** unpunctual. **3.** untidy.
неандерта́л|ец, ьца *m.* (*anthrop.*) Neanderthal man.
неандерта́льский *adj.* (*anthrop.*) Neanderthal.
неаппети́т|ный (~ен, ~на) *adj.* unappetizing (*also fig.*).
небезопа́с|ный (~ен, ~на) *adj.* unsafe, insecure.
небезоснова́тел|ьный (~ен, ~ьна) *adj.* not unfounded.
небезразли́ч|ный (~ен, ~на) *adj.* not indifferent.
небезрезульта́т|ный (~ен, ~на) *adj.* not fruitless, not futile.
небезупре́ч|ный (~ен, ~на) *adj.* not irreproachable.
небезуспе́ш|ный (~ен, ~на) *adj.* not unsuccessful.
небезызве́ст|ный (~ен, ~на) *adj.* not unknown; **~но, что...** it is no secret that ....
небезынтере́с|ный (~ен, ~на) *adj.* not without interest.
небелёный *adj.* unbleached.
небережли́в|ый (~, ~а) *adj.* thriftless, improvident.
неб|еса́ *pl. of* **~́о**
небе́сн|ый *adj.* heavenly, celestial; **~ые свети́ла** heavenly bodies; **н. свод** firmament; **Ца́рство ~ое** the Kingdom of Heaven; **~ого цве́та** sky-blue.
небесполе́з|ный (~ен, ~на) *adj.* of some use.
неблагови́д|ный (~ен, ~на) *adj.* unseemly, improper.
неблагода́рност|ь, и *f.* ingratitude.
неблагода́р|ный (~ен, ~на) *adj.* **1.** ungrateful. **2.** thankless.
неблагожела́тел|ьный (~ен, ~ьна) *adj.* malevolent, ill-disposed.
неблагозву́чи|е, я *nt.* disharmony, dissonance.
неблагозву́ч|ный (~ен, ~на) *adj.* inharmonious, disharmonious.
неблагонадёж|ный (~ен, ~на) *adj.* (*hist.*) unreliable (*esp. politically*).
неблагополу́чи|е, я *nt.* trouble.
неблагополу́чно *adv.* unsuccessfully, badly; **дела́ у них обстоя́т н.** their affairs are in a bad way.
неблагополу́ч|ный (~ен, ~на) *adj.* unfavourable, bad; **де́ло име́ло н. исхо́д** the affair had a bad ending; (*impers.*): **у нас ~но** we are in a bad way.
неблагопристо́йност|ь, и *f.* indecency.
неблагопристо́|йный (~ен, ~йна) *adj.* indecent, improper.
неблагоприя́т|ный (~ен, ~на) *adj.* unfavourable, inauspicious.
неблагоразу́м|ный (~ен, ~на) *adj.* imprudent, ill-advised, unwise.
неблагоро́д|ный (~ен, ~на) *adj.* ignoble, base; **н. мета́лл** base metal.
неблагоскло́н|ный (~ен, ~на) *adj.* unfavourable; **(к)** ill-disposed (towards).
неблагоустро́ен|ный (~, ~на) *adj.* uncomfortable; badly planned.
нёбн|ый *adj.* (*ling.*) palatal; **~ая занаве́ска** uvula.
не́б|о, а, *pl.* **~еса́, ~е́с, ~еса́м** *nt.* sky; heaven; **попа́сть па́льцем в н.** (*coll.*) to be wide of the mark; **жить ме́жду ~ом и землёй** not to have a roof over one's head; **под откры́тым ~ом** in the open (air); **с ~а свали́ться** (*fig., coll.*) to fall from the moon; **упа́сть с ~а на зе́млю** (*fig.*) to come down to earth.
нёб|о, а *nt.* (*anat.*) palate.
небога́т|ый (~, ~а) *adj.* **1.** of modest means. **2.** (*fig.*) modest.
небольш|о́й *adj.* small; not great; **о́чень ~ое расстоя́ние** a very short distance; **с ~и́м** a little over; a little after; **ты́сяча с ~и́м** a thousand odd; **де́ло ста́ло за ~и́м** one small thing is lacking.
небосво́д, а *m.* firmament; the vault of heaven.
небоскло́н, а *m.* horizon (*strictly*, sky immediately

over the horizon).
небоскрёб, а *m.* skyscraper.
небо́сь *adv.* (*coll.*) probably, I dare say; **ты, н., мно́го книг чита́л** I suppose you've read lots of books.
небре́жност|ь, и *f.* carelessness, negligence.
небре́ж|ный (~ен, ~на) *adj.* careless, negligent; slipshod; offhand.
небри́т|ый (~, ~а) *adj.* unshaven.
небыва́лый *adj.* **1.** unprecedented. **2.** fantastic.
небыли́ц|а, ы *f.* fable; cock-and-bull story.
небыти|е́, я́ *nt.* non-existence.
небьющийся *adj.* unbreakable.
Нев|а́, ы́ *f.* the Neva (*river*).
нева́жно *adv.* not too well, poorly; **дела́ иду́т н.** things are not going too well.
нева́ж|ный (~ен, ~на́, ~но) *adj.* **1.** unimportant. **2.** poor.
невдалеке́ *adv.* not far away, not far off.
невдомёк *adv.* (+*d.*) (*coll.*): **мне бы́ло н.** it never occurred to me, I never thought of it.
неве́дени|е, я *nt.* ignorance; **пребыва́ть в блаже́нном ~и** (*iron.*) to be in a state of blissful ignorance.
неве́домо *adv.* (*coll.*; +**что, как, когда́, куда́** *etc.*) God knows, no one knows; **он так и появи́лся, н. отку́да** he just turned up, God knows where from.
неве́дом|ый (~, ~а) *adj.* **1.** unknown. **2.** (*fig.*) mysterious.
неве́ж|а, и *c.g.* boor, lout.
неве́жд|а, ы *c.g.* ignoramus.
неве́жествен|ный (~, ~на) *adj.* ignorant.
неве́жеств|о, а *nt.* ignorance.
неве́жливост|ь, и *f.* rudeness, impoliteness.
неве́жлив|ый (~, ~а) *adj.* rude, impolite.
невезе́ни|е, я *nt.* (*coll.*) bad luck.
невезу́ч|ий (~, а) *adj.* (*coll.*) unlucky.
невели́к|ий (~, ~а́, ~́о) *adj.* **1.** small, short. **2.** slight, insignificant.
неве́ри|е, я *nt.* unbelief; lack of faith.
неве́рност|ь, и *f.* **1.** incorrectness. **2.** disloyalty; infidelity, unfaithfulness.
неве́р|ный (~ен, ~на́, ~но) *adj.* **1.** incorrect; **~ная но́та** false note. **2.** unsteady, uncertain; **~ная похо́дка** unsteady gait; **Фома́ н.** (*coll.*) a doubting Thomas. **3.** faithless, disloyal; unfaithful; **н. друг** false friend. **4.** dim, flickering (*of light*). **5.** *as n.* **н., ~ного** *m.* (*relig.*) infidel.
невероя́тно *adv.* incredibly, unbelievably.
невероя́тност|ь, и *f.* **1.** improbability. **2.** incredibility; **до ~и** incredibly, unbelievably.
невероя́т|ный (~ен, ~на) *adj.* **1.** improbable, unlikely. **2.** incredible, unbelievable (*also fig.*); (*impers., as pred.*): **~но** it is incredible, it is unbelievable; it is beyond belief.
неве́рующ|ий *adj.* (*relig.*) unbelieving; **Фома́ н.** (*coll.*) a doubting Thomas; *as n.* **н., ~его** *m.*, **~ая, ~ей** *f.* unbeliever;
невес|ёлый (~́ел, ~ела́, ~́ело) *adj.* joyless, mirthless; melancholy, sombre.
невесо́мост|ь, и *f.* weightlessness.
невесо́мый *adj.* weightless (*also fig.*).
неве́ст|а, ы *f.* fiancée; bride.
неве́стк|а, и *f.* **1.** daughter-in-law (*son's wife*). **2.** sister-in-law (*brother's wife*).
неве́сть *adv.* (*col.*; +**кто, что, ско́лько** *etc.*) God knows, goodness knows, heaven knows.
невеще́ственный *adj.* immaterial.
невзго́д|а, ы *f.* adversity, misfortune.
невзира́я *prep.* (**на**+*a.*) in spite of, regardless of; **н. на ли́ца** without respect of persons.
невзнача́й *adv.* (*coll.*) by chance; unexpectedly.
невзно́с, а *m.* non-payment (*of fees, etc.*).
невзра́ч|ный (~ен, ~на) *adj.* unprepossessing, unattractive; plain.
невзыска́тел|ьный (~ен, ~ьна) *adj.* modest, undemanding.
не́видал|ь, и *f.* (*coll.*) wonder, prodigy; **вот н.!; э́ка(я) н.!** (*iron.*) that's nothing.
неви́дан|ный (~, ~а) *adj.* unprecedented.
невиди́мк|а, и *c.g and f.* **1.** *c.g.* invisible being; **сде́латься ~ой** to become invisible; **челове́к-н.** invisible man. **2.** *f.* invisible hairpin.
неви́димост|ь, и *f.* invisibility.
неви́дим|ый (~, ~а) *adj.* invisible.
неви́д|ный (~ен, ~на) *adj.* **1.** invisible. **2.** (*coll.*) insignificant.
неви́дящ|ий *adj.* unseeing; **смотре́ть ~им взгля́дом** to look vacantly.
неви́нност|ь, и *f.* innocence; **де́вичья н.** virginity.
неви́н|ный (~ен, ~на) *adj.* innocent; virgin(al); **~ная же́ртва** innocent victim; **~ные удово́льствия** innocent pleasures.
невино́в|ный (~ен, ~на) *adj.* (**в**+*p.*) innocent (of); (*leg.*) not guilty; **призна́ть ~ным** to acquit.
невку́с|ный (~ен, ~на) *adj.* unpalatable.
невменя́емост|ь, и *f.* (*leg.*) irresponsibility.
невменя́ем|ый (~, ~а) *adj.* (*leg.*) irresponsible.
невмеша́тельств|о, а *m.* (*pol.*) non-intervention, non-interference; **поли́тика ~а** (*pol.*) hands-off policy.
невмоготу́ *adv.* (*coll.*; +*d.*) unbearable (to, for), unendurable (to, for); **э́то мне н.** I can't stand it; this is more than I can stand; **ста́ло н.** it became unbearable; it became too much.
невнима́ни|е, я *nt.* **1.** inattention; carelessness. **2.** (**к**) lack of consideration (for).
невнима́тельност|ь, и *f.* inattention, thoughtlessness.
невнима́тел|ьный (~ен, ~ьна) *adj.* inattentive, thoughtless.
невня́т|ный (~ен, ~на) *adj.* indistinct, incomprehensible.
не́вод, а, *pl.* **~а́, ~о́в** *m.* seine, sweep-net.
невозвра́т|ный (~ен, ~на) *adj.* irrevocable, irretrievable.
невозвраще́н|ец, ца *m.* (*pol.*) defector.
невозвраще́ни|е, я *nt.* failure to return.
невозде́ланн|ый *adj.* uncultivated, untilled.
невозде́ржанност|ь, и *f.* intemperance; incontinence; (*fig.*) lack of self-control, lack of self-restraint.
невозде́ржан|ный (~, ~на) *adj.* intemperate; incontinent; (*fig.*) uncontrolled, unrestrained.
невозде́ржност|ь, и *f.* = **невозде́ржанность**
невозде́рж|ный (~ен, ~на) *adj.* = **невозде́ржанный**
невозмо́жност|ь, и *f.* impossibility; **до ~и** (*coll.*) to the last degree; **за ~ью** (+*g. or inf.*) owing to the impossibility (of).
невозмо́ж|ный (~ен, ~на) *adj.* **1.** impossible; (*impers., pred.*): **~но** it is impossible; *as n.* **~ное, ~ного** *nt.* the impossible. **2.** insufferable.
невозмути́м|ый (~, ~а) *adj.* **1.** imperturbable; unflappable. **2.** calm, unruffled.
невознагради́м|ый (~, ~а) *adj.* **1.** irreparable. **2.** that can never be repaid.
невозобновля́емый *adj.* non-renewable.
нево́л|ить, ю, ишь *impf.* (*of* **при~**) (*coll.*) to force, compel.
нево́льник, а *m.* slave.
нево́льн|ица, ицы *f. of* **~ик**
нево́льничеств|о, а *nt.* slavery.
нево́льн|ичий *adj. of* **~ик; н. ры́нок** slave market; **н. труд** slave labour.
нево́льно *adv.* involuntarily; unintentionally, unwittingly.
нево́льн|ый *adj.* **1.** involuntary; unintentional. **2.** forced; **~ая поса́дка** forced landing.

нево́л|я, и *f.* **1.** bondage; captivity. **2.** (*coll.*) necessity.
невообрази́м|ый (~, ~а) *adj.* unimaginable, inconceivable; **н. шум** (*fig.*) unimaginable din.
невооружённ|ый *adj.* unarmed; **~ым гла́зом** with the naked eye.
невоспи́танност|ь, и *f.* lack of breeding; bad manners.
невоспи́танный *adj.* ill-bred; ill-mannered.
невоспламеня́ем|ый (~, ~а) *adj.* non-inflammable.
невосполни́м|ый (~, ~а) *adj.* irreplaceable.
невосприи́мчивост|ь, и *f.* (*med.*) immunity.
невосприи́мчив|ый (~, ~а) *adj.* **1.** unreceptive. **2.** (*med.*) (**к**) immune (to).
невостре́бованный *adj.* unclaimed.
невпопа́д *adv.* (*coll.*) out of place, inopportunely; **отвеча́ть н.** to answer irrelevantly.
невпроворо́т *adv.* (*coll.*) a lot, a great deal; **у нас дел н.** we are up to our eyes (in work).
невразуми́тел|ьный (~ен, ~ьна) *adj.* unintelligible, incomprehensible.
невралги́ческий *adj.* neuralgic.
невралги́|я, и *f.* neuralgia; **н. седа́лищного не́рва** sciatica.
неврасте́ник, а *m.* neurasthenic.
неврастени́|я, и *f.* neurasthenia.
невреди́м|ый (~, ~а) *adj.* unharmed, intact; **цел и ~** safe and sound.
неври́т, а *m.* neuritis.
невро́з, а *m.* neurosis.
неврологи́ческий *adj.* neurological
невроло́ги|я, и *f.* neurology.
невропато́лог, а *m.* neuropathologist.
невропатоло́ги|я, и *f.* neuropathology.
невро́тик, а *m.* neurotic.
невроти́ческий *adj.* neurotic.
невы́год|а, ы *f.* **1.** disadvantage. **2.** loss.
невы́год|ный (~ен, ~на) *adj.* **1.** disadvantageous, unfavourable; **ста́вить в ~ное положе́ние** to place at a disadvantage. **2.** unprofitable, unremunerative; (*impers., pred.*): **~но** it does not pay.
невы́держанност|ь, и *f.* **1.** lack of self-control. **2.** inconsistency.
невы́держанный *adj.* **1.** lacking self-control. **2.** inconsistent; **н. стиль** uneven style. **3.** (*of cheese, wine, etc.*) unmatured.
невыла́з|ный (~ен, ~на) *adj.* such that one cannot emerge from it; **~ная грязь** a veritable quagmire; **быть в ~ных долга́х** (*fig.*) to be up to the eyes in debt.
невыноси́м|ый (~, ~а) *adj.* unbearable, insufferable, intolerable.
невыполне́ни|е, я *nt.* non-fulfilment; failure to carry out.
невыполни́м|ый (~, ~а) *adj.* impracticable; unrealizable.
невырази́м|ый (~, ~а) *adj.* inexpressible.
невырази́тел|ьный (~ен, ~ьна) *adj.* inexpressive, expressionless.
невы́сказанный *adj.* unexpressed, unspoken.
невысо́к|ий (~, ~а́, ~о) *adj.* rather low; rather short; **~ого ка́чества** of poor quality; **быть ~ого мне́ния** (**о**+*p.*) to have a low opinion (of).
невы́ход, а *m.* failure to appear; **н. на рабо́ту** absence (from work).
не́г|а, и *f.* **1.** comfort; abundance. **2.** voluptuousness, languor.
негаси́м|ый (~, ~а) *adj.* (*rhet.*) ever-burning, eternal (*of flame, etc.*); unquenchable (*also fig.*).
негати́в, а *m.* (*phot.*) negative.
негати́вный *adj.* negative.
негашён|ый *adj.*: **~ая и́звесть** quick-lime.
не́где *adv.* (+*inf.*) there is nowhere; **н. доста́ть э́ту кни́гу** this book is nowhere to be had; **я́блоку н. упа́сть** there's no room to move.
неги́бкий *adj.* inflexible.
негла́сный *adj.* secret.
неглиже́ *nt. indecl.* negligée.
неглубо́кий *adj.* rather shallow; (*fig.*) superficial.
неглу́п|ый (~, ~а́, ~л) *adj.* quite intelligent; **он о́чень ~** he is no fool.
него́ *a. and g. of* **он** *when governed by preps.*
него́дник, а *m.* reprobate, scoundrel; ne'er-do-well.
него́дност|ь, и *f.* worthlessness; **привести́ в н.** to put out of commission.
него́д|ный (~ен, ~на) *adj.* **1.** unfit, unsuitable. **2.** worthless, good-for-nothing; **н. чек** dud cheque.
негодова́ни|е, я *nt.* indignation.
негод|ова́ть, у́ю *impf.* (**на**+*a.*, **про́тив**) to be indignant (with).
негод|у́ющий *pres. part. act. of* **~ова́ть** *and adj.* indignant.
негодя́|й, я *m.* scoundrel, rascal.
негостеприи́мный *adj.* inhospitable.
негр, а *m.* black (man), Negro; **америка́нский н.** Afro-American.
негра́мотност|ь, и *f.* illiteracy (*also fig.*).
негра́мот|ный (~ен, ~на) *adj.* **1.** illiterate (*also fig.*); *as n.* **н., ~ного** *m.*, **~ная, ~ной** *f.* illiterate (*pers.*). **2.** (*fig.*) crude, inexpert.
негрит|ёнок, ёнка, *pl.* **~я́та, ~я́т** *m.* black child, Negro child.
негритя́нк|а, и *f.* black woman, Negress.
негритя́нский *adj.* Negro.
негро́мкий *adj.* low.
неда́вний *adj.* recent.
неда́вно *adv.* recently.
недалёк|ий (~, ~а́, ~л *or* **~о́)** *adj.* **1.** not far off, near; short; **на ~ом расстоя́нии** at a short distance. **2.** (*fig.*) dim, dull-witted.
недалеко́ (*and* **недалёко**) *adv.* not far, near; **за приме́ром идти́ н.** one does not have to search far for an example.
недальнови́дност|ь, и *f.* short-sightedness (*fig.*).
недальнови́д|ный (~ен, ~на) *adj.* short-sighted (*fig.*).
неда́ром *adv.* not for nothing; for good reason.
недви́жимост|ь, и *f.* (*leg.*) property, real estate.
недви́жим|ый[1] *adj.* immovable; **~ое иму́щество** = **~ость**
недвижи́м|ый[2] **(~, ~а)** *adj.* motionless.
недвусмы́сленный *adj.* unequivocal, unambiguous.
недееспосо́б|ный (~ен, ~на) *adj.* **1.** (*leg.*) incapable. **2.** unable to function.
недействи́тельност|ь, и *f.* **1.** ineffectiveness. **2.** (*leg.*) invalidity; nullity.
недействи́тел|ьный (~ен, ~ьна) *adj.* **1.** (*obs.*) ineffective, ineffectual. **2.** (*leg.*) invalid; null and void.
неделика́т|ный (~ен, ~на) *adj.* indelicate, indiscreet.
недели́мост|ь, и *f.* indivisibility.
недели́м|ый (~, ~а) *adj.* indivisible.
неде́льный *adj.* of a week's duration; **я вы́полню э́ту рабо́ту в н. срок** I will finish this work in a week's time; **н. о́тпуск** week's leave.
неде́л|я, и *f.* week; **~ями** for weeks (at a time); **на э́той ~е** this week.
недёшево *adv.* (*coll.*) at a considerable price, rather dear (*also fig.*).
недисциплини́рованност|ь, и *f.* indiscipline.
недисциплини́рованный *adj.* undisciplined.
недобо́р, а *m.* arrears; shortage.
недоброжела́тел|ь, я *m.* ill-wisher.
недоброжела́тельност|ь, и *f.* malevolence, ill-will.
недоброжела́тел|ьный (~ен, ~ьна) *adj.* malevolent, ill-disposed.

недоброжела́тель|ство = **~ность**
недоброка́чественност|ь, и *f.* poor quality.
недоброка́чествен|ный (~, ~на) *adj.* poor-quality, low-grade.
недобросо́вестност|ь, и *f.* **1.** bad faith; unscrupulousness. **2.** carelessness.
недобросо́вест|ный (~ен, ~на) *adj.* **1.** unscrupulous. **2.** lackadaisical; careless.
недо́бр|ый *adj.* **1.** unkind; unfriendly. **2.** bad, evil; **~ая весть** bad news.
недове́ри|е, я *nt.* distrust; mistrust; **во́тум ~я** vote of no confidence.
недове́рчив|ый (~, ~а) *adj.* distrustful; mistrustful.
недове́с, а *m.* short weight.
недово́л|ьный (~ен, ~ьна) *adj.* (*+i.*) dissatisfied, discontented, displeased (with); *as n.* **н., ~ьного** *m.* malcontent.
недово́льств|о, а *nt.* dissatisfaction, discontent, displeasure.
недога́длив|ый (~, ~а) *adj.* slow(-witted).
недогля|де́ть, жу́, ди́шь *pf.* **1.** (*+g.*) to overlook, miss. **2.** (**за**+*i.*) fail to take sufficient care (of), not to look after properly.
недоговорённост|ь, и *f.* **1.** reticence. **2.** lack of agreement.
недода|ва́ть, ю́, ёшь *impf. of* **∠ть**
недо|да́ть, да́м, да́шь, да́ст, дади́м, дади́те, даду́т, *past* **∠дал, ~дала́, ∠дало** *pf.* (*of* **~дава́ть**) to give short; to deliver short; **он мне ∠дал три рубля́** he gave me three roubles short.
недода́ч|а, и *f.* deficiency in payment *or* supply.
недоде́ланный *adj.* unfinished.
недоде́лк|а, и *f.* incompleteness.
недодерж|а́ть, у́, ∠ишь *pf.* (*phot.*) to under-expose.
недоде́ржк|а, и *f.* (*phot.*) under-exposure.
недоеда́ни|е, я *nt.* malnutrition.
недоеда́|ть, ю *impf.* to be malnourished, be underfed.
недозво́лен|ный (~, ~а) *adj.* illicit, unlawful.
недозре́лый *adj.* unripe, immature (*also fig.*).
недои́мк|а, и *f.* arrears.
недои́мщик, а *m.* person in arrears.
недока́зан|ный (~, ~а) *adj.* unproven.
недоказу́емый *adj.* unprovable.
недолга́ *only in phr.* **(вот) и вся н.** (*coll.*) and that is all there is to it.
недо́л|гий (~ог, ~га́, ~го) *adj.* short, brief.
недо́лго *adv.* **1.** not long; **н. ду́мая** without hesitation. **2.** (*coll.*): **н. и** (*+inf.*) one can easily; it is easy (to); **тут и потону́ть н.** one could easily drown here.
недолгове́ч|ный (~ен, ~на) *adj.* short-lived, ephemeral.
недолю́блива|ть, ю *impf.* (*+a. or g.*; *coll.*) not to be overfond of; **они́ ~ли друг дру́га** there was no love lost between them.
недоме́рива|ть, ю *impf. of* **недоме́рить**
недомога́ни|е, я *nt.* indisposition.
недомога́|ть, ю *impf.* to be indisposed, be unwell.
недомо́лвк|а, и *f.* innuendo; reservation, omission.
недомы́сли|е, я *nt.* thoughtlessness, inability to think things out.
недоно́с|ок, ка *m.* premature baby.
недоно́шен|ный (~, ~а) *adj.* (*med.*) premature, preterm.
недооце́нива|ть, ю *impf. of* **недооцени́ть**
недооцен|и́ть, ю́, ∠ишь *pf.* (*of* **∠ивать**) to underestimate, underrate.
недооце́нк|а, и *f.* underestimation, underestimate.
недопечённый *adj.* half-baked.
недополуч|а́ть, а́ю *impf. of* **~и́ть**
недополуч|и́ть, у́, ∠ишь *pf.* (*of* **~а́ть**) to receive less (than one's due).
недопусти́м|ый (~, ~а) *adj.* inadmissible, intolerable.
недора́звитост|ь, и *f.* under-development, backwardness.
недора́звит|ый *adj.* under-developed, backward.
недоразуме́ни|е, я *nt.* misunderstanding.
недо́рого *adv.* not dear, cheaply.
недор|ого́й (∠ог, ~ога́, ∠ого) *adj.* inexpensive; reasonable (*of price*).
недоро́д, а *m.* crop failure.
не́доросл|ь, я *m.* **1.** (*hist.*) minor. **2.** (*fig.*, *coll.*) young ignoramus, young oaf.
недоска́занност|ь, и *f.* understatement.
недослы́ш|ать, у, ишь *pf.* **1.** (*+a. or g.*) to fail to hear all of. **2.** (*intrans.*; *coll.*) to be hard of hearing.
недосмо́тр, а *m.* oversight.
недосмотр|е́ть, ю́, ∠ишь *pf.* **1.** (*+g.*) to overlook, miss. **2.** (**за**+*i.*) not to look after properly.
недос|па́ть, плю́, пи́шь *pf.* (*of* **~ыпа́ть**) not to get enough sleep.
недоста|ва́ть, ёт, *impf.* (*of* **∠ть**) (*impers.*, *+g.*) to be missing, be lacking, be wanting; **ему́ ~ёт о́пыта** he lacks experience; **мне о́чень ~ва́ло вас** I missed you very much.
недоста́т|ок, ка *m.* **1.** (*+g. or* **в**+*p.*) shortage (of), lack (of), deficiency (in); **за ~ком** (*+g.*) for want (of); **име́ть н. в рабо́чей си́ле** to be short-handed. **2.** shortcoming, imperfection; defect; **н. зре́ния** defective eyesight.
недоста́точно *adv.* **1.** insufficiently. **2.** not enough.
недоста́точност|ь, и *f.* insufficiency; inadequacy; **витами́нная н.** vitamin deficiency.
недоста́точ|ный (~ен, ~на) *adj.* insufficient; inadequate.
недоста́|ть, нет *pf. of* **~ва́ть**
недоста́ч|а, и *f.* (*coll.*) lack, shortage.
недостаю́щий *adj.* missing.
недостижи́м|ый (~, ~а) *adj.* unattainable.
недостове́р|ный (~ен, ~на) *adj.* unreliable.
недосто́|йный (~ин, ~йна) *adj.* unworthy.
недосту́пност|ь, и *f.* inaccessibility.
недосту́п|ный (~ен, ~на) *adj.* inaccessible (*also fig.*); **э́то ~но моему́ понима́нию** it is beyond my comprehension.
недосу́г, а *m.* (*coll.*) lack of time; **придёт он на конце́рт? нет, ему́, мол, н.** is he coming to the concert? No, he says he hasn't the time.
недосчит|а́ться, а́юсь *pf.* (*of* **∠ываться**) (*+g.*) to find missing, miss; to be out (in one's accounts); **он ~а́лся десяти́ рубле́й** he found he was ten roubles short.
недосчи́тыва|ться, юсь *impf. of* **недосчита́ться**
недосыпа́|ть, ю *impf. of* **недоспа́ть**
недосяга́ем|ый (~, ~а) *adj.* unattainable.
недотёп|а, ы *c.g.* (*coll.*) duffer.
недотро́г|а, и *c.g.* (*coll.*) touchy person.
недоумева́|ть, ю *impf.* to be perplexed, be at a loss.
недоуме́ни|е, я *nt.* perplexity, bewilderment; **быть в ~и** to be in a quandary.
недоуме́нный *adj.* puzzled, perplexed.
недоу́чк|а, и *c.g.* (*coll.*) half-educated person.
недочёт, а *m.* **1.** deficit; shortage. **2.** defect, shortcoming.
не́др|а, ~ *no sg.* **1.** depths (*of the earth*); **н. земли́** bowels of the earth; **разве́дка ~** prospecting of mineral wealth. **2.** (*fig.*) depths, heart.
недре́млющий *adj.* vigilant, watchful.
не́друг, а *m.* enemy, foe.
недружелю́б|ный (~ен, ~на) *adj.* unfriendly.
недру́жный *adj.* disunited; disjointed.
неду́г, а *m.* ailment, disease.
неду́рно *adv.* not badly; **н.!** not bad!

недур|но́й (~ён, ~на́, ~но) *adj.* **1.** not bad. **2.** **(собо́й)** not bad-looking.
недю́жинный *adj.* outstanding, exceptional.
неё *a. and g. of* **она́** *when governed by preps.*
неесте́ствен|ный (~, ~на) *adj.* unnatural.
нежда́нно *adv.* (*coll.*) unexpectedly.
нежда́нный *adj.* (*coll.*) unexpected.
нежела́ни|е, я *nt.* unwillingness, disinclination.
нежела́тел|ьный (~ен, ~ьна) *adj.* undesirable.
не́женк|а, и *c.g.* (*coll.*) mollycoddle.
нежив|о́й *adj.* **1.** lifeless; **роди́ться ~ы́м** to be still-born. **2.** inanimate, inorganic. **3.** (*fig.*) dull, lifeless.
нежи́знен|ный (~, ~на) *adj.* **1.** impracticable; inapplicable. **2.** weird.
нежило́й *adj.* **1.** uninhabited. **2.** not fit for habitation; uninhabitable.
не́ж|ить, у, ишь *impf.* to pamper, coddle; caress.
не́ж|иться, усь, ишься *impf.* to luxuriate; **н. на со́лнце** to bask in the sun.
не́жнича|ть, ю *impf.* (*coll.*) **1.** to bill and coo, canoodle. **2.** (*fig.*) to be over-indulgent.
не́жност|ь, и *f.* **1.** tenderness. **2.** delicacy. **3.** (*pl. only*) endearments; compliments, flattery.
не́ж|ный (~ен, ~на́, ~но) *adj.* **1.** tender; **~ные взгля́ды** tender glances. **2.** delicate; **н. пол** the weaker sex.
незабве́н|ный (~, ~на) *adj.* unforgettable.
незабу́дк|а, и *f.* (*bot.*) forget-me-not.
незабыва́ем|ый (~, ~а) *adj.* unforgettable.
незави́д|ный (~ен, ~на) *adj.* unenviable; poor.
незави́симо *adv.* independently; **н. от** irrespective of.
незави́симост|ь, и *f.* independence.
незави́сим|ый (~, ~а) *adj.* independent.
незави́сящ|ий *only in phr.* **по ~им от нас,** *etc.*, **обстоя́тельствам** owing to circumstances beyond our, *etc.*, control.
незада́ч|а, и *f.* (*coll.*) ill-luck.
незада́члив|ый (~, ~а) *adj.* (*coll.*) unlucky, luckless.
незадо́лго *adv.* **(до, пе́ред)** shortly (before), not long (before).
незаконнорождённост|ь, и *f.* illegitimacy.
незаконнорождённый *adj.* illegitimate.
незако́нност|ь, и *f.* illegality, unlawfulness.
незако́нн|ый *adj.* illegal, illicit, unlawful; illegitimate; **~ая жена́** common-law wife.
незакономе́р|ный (~ен, ~на) *adj.* exceptional.
незако́нчен|ный (~, ~а) *adj.* incomplete, unfinished.
незамедли́тельно *adv.* without delay.
незамедли́тел|ьный (~ен, ~ьна) *adj.* immediate.
незамени́м|ый (~, ~а) *adj.* **1.** irreplaceable. **2.** indispensable.
незаме́тно *adv.* imperceptibly; **н., что́бы...** you cannot tell that ...
незаме́т|ный (~ен, ~на) *adj.* **1.** imperceptible. **2.** inconspicuous, insignificant.
незаму́жняя *adj.* unmarried, single; **н. же́нщина** (*leg.*) spinster.
незамыслова́т|ый (~, ~а) *adj.* simple, uncomplicated.
незапа́мятн|ый *adj.* immemorial; **с ~ых времён** from time immemorial.
незапя́тнанный *adj.* unsullied, stainless.
незарабо́танный *adj.* unearned.
незара́зный *adj.* non-contagious.
незаслу́жен|ный (~, ~на) *adj.* undeserved.
незате́йлив|ый (~, ~а) *adj.* simple, plain; modest.
незауря́д|ный (~ен, ~на) *adj.* outstanding, exceptional.
не́зачем *adv.* (*+inf.*) there is no point (in), it is pointless; there is no need (to); **н. бо́льше ждать** there is no point in waiting any longer.
незва́ный *adj.* uninvited.
незде́шний *adj.* **1.** (*coll.*) not of these parts; **я н.** I am a stranger here. **2.** unearthly, supernatural; **н. мир** the other world.
нездоро́вит|ься, ~ся *impf.* (*impers.*, *+d.*) to feel unwell.
нездоро́в|ый (~, ~а) *adj.* **1.** unhealthy, morbid (*also fig.*); sickly; unwholesome; **~ая обстано́вка** unhealthy environment. **2.** *as pred.* unwell, poorly.
нездоро́вь|е, я *nt.* indisposition; ill-health.
неземно́й *adj.* unearthly.
незло́би́в|ый (~, ~а) *adj.* mild, forgiving.
незлопа́мят|ный (~ен, ~на) *adj.* forgiving.
незнако́м|ец, ца *m.* stranger.
незнако́м|ка, ки *f. of* **~ец**
незнако́м|ый (~, ~а) *adj.* **1.** unknown, unfamiliar. **2.** **(с+*i.*)** unacquainted (with).
незна́ни|е, я *nt.* ignorance.
незна́чащий *adj.* insignificant.
незначи́тел|ьный (~ен, ~ьна) *adj.* insignificant, negligible; unimportant.
незре́лост|ь, и *f.* unripeness; (*fig.*) immaturity.
незре́л|ый (~, ~а) *adj.* unripe (*also fig.*); (*fig.*) immature.
незри́м|ый (~, ~а) *adj.* invisible.
незы́блем|ый (~, ~а) *adj.* unshakeable; stable.
неизбе́жност|ь, и *f.* inevitability.
неизбе́ж|ный (~ен, ~на) *adj.* inevitable, unavoidable; inescapable.
неизбы́в|ный (~ен, ~на) *adj.* unescapable, permanent.
неизве́дан|ный (~, ~на) *adj.* unexplored; new, not experienced before.
неизве́стност|ь, и *f.* **1.** uncertainty; **быть в ~и** **(о+*p.*)** to be uncertain (about), be in the dark (about). **2.** obscurity; **жить в ~и** to live in obscurity.
неизве́ст|ный (~ен, ~на) *adj.* unknown; uncertain; **~но где, когда́** etc., no one knows where, when, *etc.* (= *somewhere*, *at some time*, *etc.*); *as n.* **н., ~ного** *m.*, **~ная, ~ной** *f.* unknown person; **~ное, ~ного** *nt.* (*math.*) unknown (quantity).
неизвини́тел|ьный (~ен, ~ьна) *adj.* inexcusable.
неизглади́м|ый (~, ~а) *adj.* indelible.
неи́зданный *adj.* unpublished.
неизлечи́м|ый (~, ~а) *adj.* incurable.
неизме́н|ный (~ен, ~на) *adj.* **1.** invariable, immutable. **2.** (*rhet.*) devoted, true.
неизменя́ем|ый (~, ~а) *adj.* unalterable.
неизмери́мо *adv.* immeasurably.
неизмери́мост|ь, и *f.* immeasurability; immensity.
неизмери́м|ый (~, ~а) *adj.* immeasurable; immense.
неизъясни́м|ый (~, ~а) *adj.* inexplicable; ineffable, indescribable.
неиме́ни|е, я *nt.* absence; lack, want; **за ~ем лу́чшего** for want of sth. better.
неимове́р|ный (~ен, ~на) *adj.* incredible, unbelievable.
неиму́щий *adj.* indigent, poor.
неискорени́м|ый (~, ~а) *adj.* ineradicable.
неи́скрен|ний (~ен, ~на) *adj.* insincere.
неи́скренност|ь, и *f.* insincerity.
неискушённост|ь, и *f.* inexperience.
неискушён|ный (~, ~а) *adj.* inexperienced; unsophisticated.
неисповеди́м|ый (~, ~а) *adj.* inscrutable.
неисполне́ни|е, я *nt.* non-execution, non-performance; **н. зако́на** failure to observe a law.
неисполни́м|ый (~, ~а) *adj.* impracticable; unrealizable.
неиспо́рчен|ный (~, ~а) *adj.* (*fig.*) unspoiled, innocent.
неиспо́рченност|ь, и *f.* (*fig.*) innocence.

неисправи́м|ый (~, ~а) *adj.* **1.** incorrigible. **2.** irreparable.
неиспра́вност|ь, и *f.* **1.** disrepair. **2.** carelessness.
неиспра́в|ный (~ен, ~на) *adj.* **1.** out of order; faulty, defective. **2.** careless.
неиспы́танный *adj.* untried, untested.
неиссяка́ем|ый (~, ~а) *adj.* inexhaustible.
нейстовств|о, а *nt.* **1.** fury, frenzy. **2.** brutality, savagery; (*pl.*) atrocities.
нейстовств|овать, ую *impf.* **1.** to rage, rave. **2.** to commit brutalities.
нейстов|ый (~, ~а) *adj.* furious, frenzied; **~ые аплодисме́нты** tempestuous applause.
неистощи́м|ый (~, ~а) *adj.* inexhaustible.
неистреби́м|ый (~, ~а) *adj.* ineradicable; undying.
неисчерпа́ем|ый (~, ~а) *adj.* inexhaustible.
неисчисли́м|ый (~, ~а) *adj.* innumerable; incalculable.
ней *d., i., and p. of* **она́** *when governed by preps.*
нейло́н, а *m.* nylon.
нейло́новый *adj.* nylon, made of nylon.
нейро́н, а *m.* neuron.
нейтрализа́тор, а *m.*: **каталисти́ческий н.** catalytic converter.
нейтрализа́ци|я, и *f.* neutralization.
нейтрализ|ова́ть, у́ю *impf. and pf.* to neutralize.
нейтралите́т, а *m.* (*pol.*) neutrality.
нейтра́л|ьный (~ен, ~ьна) *adj.* neutral.
нейтро́н, а *m.* (*phys.*) neutron.
неказѝст|ый (~, ~а) *adj.* (*coll.*) unprepossessing, ill-favoured.
неквалифици́рованный *adj.* unqualified; unskilled.
не́кий *pron.* a certain; s.o. by the name of; **вас спра́шивал н. господи́н Па́влов** a Mr Pavlov was asking for you.
не́когда[1] *adv.* once, formerly; in the old days.
не́когда[2] *adv.* there is no time; **мне сего́дня н. разгова́ривать с ва́ми** I have no time to chat today.
не́кого, не́кому, не́кем, не́ о ком *pron.* (*+inf.*) there is nobody (to); **н. вини́ть** nobody is to blame; **ей не́ с кем пойти́** she has nobody to go with (her).
неколеби́мый = непоколеби́мый
некомпете́нт|ный (~ен, ~на) *adj.* not competent, unqualified.
некомпле́кт|ный (~ен, ~на) *adj.* incomplete; not up to strength.
некороно́ванный *adj.* uncrowned.
некорре́ктност|ь, и *f.* discourtesy, impoliteness.
некорре́кт|ный (~ен, ~на) *adj.* discourteous, impolite.
не́котор|ый *pron.* some; **он ~ое вре́мя не дви́гался с ме́ста** for a while he did not budge; **мы с ~ых пор живём здесь** we have been living here for some time (now); **в, до ~ой сте́пени** to some extent, to a certain extent; *as n.* **~ые, ~ых** some; some people.
некраси́в|ый (~, ~а) *adj.* **1.** plain; unsightly. **2.** (*coll.*; *of conduct, actions, etc.*) unseemly, indecorous.
некро́з, а *m.* (*med.*) necrosis.
некроло́г, а *m.* obituary (notice).
некрома́нти|я, и *f.* necromancy.
некста́ти *adv.* inopportunely.
некта́р, а *m.* nectar.
не́кто *pron.* someone; **н. Петро́в** s.o. by the name of Petrov, a certain Petrov.
не́куда *adv.* (*+inf.*) there is nowhere (to); **мне н. пойти́** I have nowhere to go.
некульту́рност|ь, и *f.* **1.** low level of civilization; uncivilized ways. **2.** bad manners, boorishness.
некульту́р|ный (~ен, ~на) *adj.* **1.** uncivilized; backward. **2.** rough(-mannered), boorish. **3.** (*bot.*) uncultivated.
некуря́щ|ий *adj.* non-smoking; *as n.* **н., ~его** *m.* non-smoker; **ваго́н для ~их** non-smoking carriage.
нела́д|ный (~ен, ~на) *adj.* (*coll.*) wrong, bad; **у него́ ~но с гру́дью** he has sth. wrong with his chest.
нелад|ы́, о́в *no sg.* (*coll.*) discord, disagreement; **у них н.** they don't get on.
нела́сковый *adj.* cold; unfriendly.
нелега́льност|ь, и *f.* illegality.
нелега́л|ьный (~ен, ~ьна) *adj.* illegal.
нелёг|кий (~ок, ~ка́) *adj.* **1.** difficult, not easy. **2.** heavy, not light (*also fig.*).
неле́пост|ь, и *f.* absurdity, nonsense.
неле́п|ый (~, ~а) *adj.* absurd, ridiculous.
неле́ст|ный (~ен, ~на) *adj.* unflattering, uncomplimentary.
нели́шний *adj.* not superfluous; not out of place.
нело́в|кий (~ок, ~ка́, ~ко) *adj.* **1.** awkward; gauche; clumsy. **2.** uncomfortable. **3.** (*fig.*) awkward; embarrassing; **~кое молча́ние** awkward silence.
нело́вко *adv.* awkwardly; uncomfortably; **чу́вствовать себя́ н.** to feel ill at ease, feel awkward, feel uncomfortable.
нело́вкост|ь, и *f.* **1.** awkwardness, clumsiness (*also fig.*); **чу́вствовать н.** to feel awkward, feel uncomfortable. **2.** gaffe.
нелоги́чност|ь, и *f.* illogicality.
нелоги́ч|ный (~ен, ~на) *adj.* illogical.
нельзя́ *adv.* (*+inf.*) **1.** it is impossible; **н. не призна́ть** one cannot but admit. **2.** it is not allowed; **здесь н. кури́ть** smoking is not allowed here. **3.** one ought not, one should not; **н. ложи́ться (спать) так по́здно** you ought not to go to bed so late. **4.: как н.** (*+comp. adv.*) as ... as possible; **как н. лу́чше** in the best possible way.
нелюбе́зност|ь, и *f.* ungraciousness; discourtesy.
нелюбе́з|ный (~ен, ~на) *adj.* ungracious, unobliging; discourteous.
нелюби́м|ый (~, ~а) *adj.* unloved.
нелюб|о́вь, ви́ *f.* **(к)** dislike (for).
нелюди́м, а *m.* unsociable person.
нелюди́м|ый (~, ~а) *adj.* unsociable.
нём *p. of* **он, оно́**
нема́ло *adv.* **1.** not a little; not a few. **2.** a good deal; considerably.
немалова́ж|ный (~ен, ~на) *adj.* of no small importance; significant.
нема́лый *adj.* no small; considerable.
неме́дленно *adv.* immediately, forthwith.
неме́дленный *adj.* immediate.
неме́ркнущий *adj.* (*fig., rhet.*) unfading.
неме́|ть, ю *impf.* (*of* **о~**) **1.** to become dumb, grow dumb. **2.** (*pf. also* **за~**) to become numb, grow numb.
не́м|ец, ца *m.* German.
неме́цк|ий *adj.* German; **~ая овча́рка** Alsatian (dog).
немилосе́рд|ный (~ен, ~на) *adj.* merciless, unmerciful (*also fig.*).
неми́лостив|ый (~, ~а) *adj.* ungracious; harsh.
неми́лост|ь, и *f.* disgrace, disfavour; **впасть в н.** to fall into disgrace.
немину́ем|ый (~, ~а) *adj.* inevitable, unavoidable.
не́м|ка, ки *f. of* **~ец**
немно́г|ие *adj.* few, a few; *as n.* **н., ~их** few.
немно́го *adv.* **1.** (*+g.*) a little, some, not much; a few, not many; **вре́мени оста́лось н.** time is short. **2.** a little, somewhat, rather; **я н. уста́л** I am a little tired; **н. спустя́** not long after.
немно́г|ое, ого *nt.* few things, little.
немногосло́в|ный (~ен, ~на) *adj.* laconic, terse.
немно́жко *adv.* (*coll.*) a little; a trifle, a bit.
немну́щийся *adj.* (*text.*) crease-resistant; 'non-iron'.
нем|о́й (~, ~а́, ~о) *adj.* **1.** dumb; **~а́я а́збука** deaf-and-dumb alphabet; *as n.* **н., ~о́го** *m.* mute. **2.** (*fig.*) silent; **н. фильм** silent film. **3.** (*ling.*) mute.

немот|а́, ы́ *f.* dumbness; muteness.
не́моч|ь, и *f.* (*coll.*) illness, sickness.
не́мощ|ный (~ен, ~на) *adj.* sick; feeble, sickly.
не́мощ|ь, и *f.* (*coll.*) sickness; feebleness.
нему́ *d. of* **он, оно́** *after preps.*
немудрён|ый (~, ~а́) *adj.* (*coll.*) simple, easy; **э́то де́ло ~ое** it is a simple matter; (*impers., as pred.*): **~о́** it is no wonder.
немы́слим|ый (~, ~а) *adj.* (*coll.*) unthinkable, inconceivable.
ненави́|деть, жу, дишь *impf.* to hate, detest, loathe.
ненави́стник, а *m.* hater.
ненави́ст|ный (~ен, ~на) *adj.* hated; hateful.
не́навист|ь, и *f.* hatred, detestation.
ненагля́дный *adj.* (*coll.*) beloved.
ненадёж|ный (~ен, ~на) *adj.* unreliable, untrustworthy; insecure.
нена́добност|ь, и *f.* uselessness; **за ~ью** as not wanted.
ненадо́лго *adv.* for a short while, not for long.
ненаме́ренно *adv.* unintentionally, unwittingly, accidentally.
ненаме́рен|ный (~, ~а) *adj.* unintentional, accidental.
ненападе́ни|е, я *nt.* non-aggression; **пакт о ~и** non-aggression pact.
ненаро́ком *adv.* (*coll.*) unintentionally; by chance.
ненаруши́м|ый (~, ~а) *adj.* inviolable.
нена́ст|ный (~ен, ~на) *adj.* (*of weather*) bad, inclement.
ненастоя́щий *adj.* artificial; counterfeit.
нена́сть|е, я *nt.* bad, inclement weather.
ненасы́т|ный (~ен, ~на) *adj.* insatiable (*also fig.*).
ненатура́л|ьный (~ен, ~ьна) *adj.* **1.** affected; not natural. **2.** artificial, imitation.
ненау́ч|ный (~ен, ~на) *adj.* unscientific.
ненорма́льност|ь, и *f.* abnormality.
ненорма́л|ьный (~ен, ~ьна) *adj.* **1.** abnormal. **2.** deranged.
нену́ж|ный (~ен, ~на́, ~но) *adj.* unnecessary; superfluous; needless.
необду́ман|ный (~, ~на) *adj.* rash, precipitate.
необеспе́ченн|ый *adj.* **1.** without means; unprovided for; **~ая жизнь** precarious existence. **2.** (*+i.*) not provided (with).
необита́ем|ый (~, ~а) *adj.* uninhabited; **н. о́стров** desert island.
необозри́м|ый (~, ~а) *adj.* boundless, immense.
необосно́ван|ный (~, ~на) *adj.* unfounded, groundless.
необрабо́тан|ный (~, ~а) *adj.* **1.** (*of land*) uncultivated, untilled. **2.** (*of minerals*) raw, crude. **3.** (*fig.*) unpolished; untrained.
необразо́ванност|ь, и *f.* lack of education.
необразо́ван|ный (~, ~на) *adj.* uneducated.
необрати́м|ый (~, ~а) *adj.* irreversible.
необу́здан|ный (~, ~на) *adj.* unbridled; ungovernable.
необходи́мост|ь, и *f.* necessity; **по ~и** perforce, out of necessity; **това́ры пе́рвой ~и** essential goods.
необходи́м|ый (~, ~а) *adj.* necessary, essential; (*impers., as pred.*): **~о** it is necessary *or* imperative.
необщи́тел|ьный (~ен, ~ьна) *adj.* unsociable.
необъясни́м|ый (~, ~а) *adj.* inexplicable, unaccountable.
необъя́т|ный (~ен, ~на) *adj.* immense, unbounded.
необыкнове́н|ный (~ен, ~на) *adj.* unusual, uncommon.
необыча́|йный (~ен, ~йна) *adj.* extraordinary, exceptional.
необы́ч|ный (~ен, ~на) *adj.* unusual; **~ные ви́ды вооруже́ний** unconventional weapons.
необяза́тел|ьный (~, ~на) *adj.* **1.** non-obligatory, optional. **2.** unobliging.
неограни́чен|ный (~, ~на) *adj.* unlimited, unbounded; **~ная мона́рхия** absolute monarchy.
неоднозна́ч|ный (~ен, ~на) *adj.* **1.** ambiguous, equivocal. **2.** complex, complicated.
неоднокра́тно *adv.* repeatedly.
неоднокра́тный *adj.* repeated.
неоднoро́дност|ь, и *f.* heterogeneity.
неоднoро́д|ный (~ен, ~на) *adj.* heterogeneous; dissimilar.
неодобре́ни|е, я *nt.* disapproval.
неодобри́тел|ьный (~ен, ~на) *adj.* disapproving.
неодоли́м|ый (~, ~а) *adj.* invincible, insuperable.
неодушевлён|ный (~, ~на) *adj.* inanimate.
неожи́данност|ь, и *f.* **1.** unexpectedness, suddenness. **2.** surprise.
неожи́дан|ный (~, ~на) *adj.* unexpected, sudden.
неоклассици́зм, а *m.* neoclassicism.
неоконча́тел|ьный (~ен, ~на) *adj.* inconclusive.
неоко́нченный *adj.* unfinished.
неоли́т, а *m.* (*archaeol.*) the neolithic period.
неолити́ческий *adj.* (*archaeol.*) neolithic.
неологи́зм, а *m.* neologism.
нео́н, а *m.* (*chem.*) neon.
нео́н|овый *adj. of* **~**; **~овая ла́мпа** neon lamp.
неопа́с|ный (~ен, ~на) *adj.* safe; harmless.
неопера́бельный *adj.* (*med.*) inoperable.
неопери́вшийся *adj.* unfledged; (*fig.*) callow.
неопису́ем|ый (~, ~а) *adj.* indescribable.
неопла́тн|ый *adj.* that cannot be repaid; **я у вас в ~ом долгу́** (*fig.*) I am forever indebted to you.
неопо́знан|ный (~, ~а) *adj.* unidentified.
неопра́вданный *adj.* unjustified, unwarranted.
неопределённост|ь, и *f.* vagueness, uncertainty.
неопределён|ный (~ен, ~на) *adj.* **1.** indefinite; **~ная фо́рма глаго́ла** (*gram.*) infinitive; **н. член** (*gram.*) indefinite article. **2.** indeterminate; vague, uncertain.
неопредели́м|ый (~, ~а) *adj.* indefinable.
неопровержитм|ый (~, ~а) *adj.* irrefutable.
неопря́тност|ь, и *f.* slovenliness; untidiness, sloppiness.
неопря́т|ный (~ен, ~на) *adj.* slovenly; untidy, sloppy.
нео́пытност|ь, и *f.* inexperience.
нео́пыт|ный (~ен, ~на) *adj.* inexperienced.
неорганизо́ванност|ь, и *f.* lack of organization; disorganization.
неорганизо́ван|ный (~, ~на) *adj.* unorganized; disorganized.
неоргани́ческий *adj.* inorganic.
неосведомлённый *adj.* ill-informed.
неосе́длый *adj.* nomadic.
неосла́б|ный (~ен, ~на) *adj.* unremitting, unabated.
неосмотри́тельност|ь, и *f.* imprudence.
неосмотри́тел|ьный (~ен, ~ьна) *adj.* imprudent, incautious.
неоснова́тел|ьный (~ен, ~ьна) *adj.* **1.** unfounded, groundless. **2.** (*coll.*) frivolous.
неоспори́мост|ь, и *f.* indisputability.
неоспори́м|ый (~, ~а) *adj.* indisputable; undeniable.
неосторо́жност|ь, и *f.* carelessness; imprudence.
неосторо́ж|ный (~ен, ~на) *adj.* careless; imprudent, incautious.
неосуществи́м|ый (~, ~а) *adj.* impracticable, unrealizable.
неосяза́ем|ый (~, ~а) *adj.* intangible.
неотврати́мост|ь, и *f.* inevitability.
неотврати́м|ый (~, ~а) *adj.* inevitable.
неотвя́з|ный (~ен, ~на) *adj.* importunate; obsessive.

неотвя́зчив|ый (~, ~а) *adj.* = **неотвя́зный**
неотдели́м|ый (~, ~а) *adj.* inseparable.
неотёсан|ный (~, ~на) *adj.* **1.** unpolished. **2.** (*fig.*) uncouth.
не́откуда *adv.* there is nowhere; **мне н. э́то доста́ть** there is nowhere I can get it from.
неотло́жк|а, и *f.* (*coll.*) emergency medical service.
неотло́жност|ь, и *f.* urgency.
неотло́ж|ный (~ен, ~на) *adj.* urgent, pressing; **~ная по́мощь** first aid.
неотлу́чно *adv.* constantly, permanently.
неотлу́ч|ный (~ен, ~на) *adj.* ever-present; permanent.
неотрази́м|ый (~, ~а) *adj.* irresistible (*also fig.*); **~ые до́воды** incontrovertible arguments.
неотсту́пност|ь, и *f.* persistence; importunity.
неотсту́п|ный (~ен, ~на) *adj.* persistent; importunate.
неотчётлив|ый (~, ~а) *adj.* vague, indistinct.
неотъе́млем|ый (~, ~а) *adj.* inalienable; **~ое пра́во** inalienable right; **~ая часть** integral part.
неофициа́л|ьный (~ен, ~ьна) *adj.* unofficial.
неохо́т|а, ы *f.* **1.** reluctance. **2.** (*+d., as pred.*): **мне,** *etc.*, **н. идти́** I, *etc.*, have no wish to go.
неохо́тно *adv.* reluctantly; unwillingly.
неоцени́м|ый (~, ~а) *adj.* inestimable, priceless, invaluable.
неощути́м|ый (~, ~а) *adj.* imperceptible.
непа́рный *adj.* odd (*not forming a pair*).
непарти́йный *adj.* (*pol., in former USSR*) non-Party; unbefitting a member of the (Communist) Party.
непереводи́м|ый (~, ~а) *adj.* untranslatable.
непередава́ем|ый (~, ~а) *adj.* inexpressible, indescribable.
непереходный *adj.* (*gram.*) intransitive.
непеча́тный *adj.* (*coll.*) unprintable.
непи́сан|ый *adj.* unwritten.
неплатёж, а́ *m.* non-payment.
неплатёжеспосо́бност|ь, и *f.* (*fin.*) insolvency.
неплатёжеспосо́б|ный (~ен, ~на) *adj.* (*fin.*) insolvent.
неплате́льщик, а *m.* defaulter; person in arrears with payment (*of taxes, etc.*)
неплодоро́д|ный (~ен, ~на) *adj.* barren, sterile; infertile.
непло́хо *adv.* not badly, quite well.
неплох|о́й (~́, ~а́, ~́о) *adj.* not bad, quite good.
непобеди́м|ый (~, ~а) *adj.* invincible.
непова́дно *as pred.* (*impers., +d. and inf.; coll.*): **что́бы н. бы́ло** to teach (s.o.) not (to do sth. again); **мальчи́шку вы́пороли, что́бы ему́ н. бы́ло кра́сть я́блоки** they gave the boy a thrashing to teach him not to steal apples again.
непови́н|ный (~ен, ~на) *adj.* innocent.
неповинове́ни|е, я *nt.* insubordination, disobedience.
неповоро́тлив|ый (~, ~а) *adj.* clumsy, awkward.
неповтори́м|ый (~, ~а) *adj.* unique.
непого́д|а, ы *f.* bad weather.
непогреши́мост|ь, и *f.* infallibility.
непогреши́м|ый (~, ~а) *adj.* infallible.
неподалёку *adv.* not far off.
непода́тлив|ый (~, ~а) *adj.* stubborn, intractable; unyielding, tenacious.
неподве́домствен|ный (~, ~на) *adj.* (*+d*) not subject to the authority (of), beyond the jurisdiction (of).
неподви́жност|ь, и *f.* immobility.
неподви́ж|ный (~ен, ~на) *adj.* motionless, immobile, immovable (*also fig.*); fixed, stationary.
неподде́льност|ь, и *f.* genuineness; sincerity.
неподде́л|ьный (~ен, ~ьна) *adj.* genuine; unfeigned, sincere.
неподку́пност|ь, и *f.* incorruptibility, integrity.
неподку́п|ный (~ен, ~на) *adj.* incorruptible.
неподоба́ющий *adj.* unseemly, improper.
неподража́ем|ый (~, ~а) *adj.* inimitable.
неподсу́д|ный (~ен, ~на) *adj.* (*+d.*) not under the jurisdiction (of).
неподходя́щий *adj.* unsuitable, inappropriate.
неподчине́ни|е, я *nt.* insubordination; **н. суде́бному постановле́нию** (*leg.*) contempt of court.
непозволи́тел|ьный (~ен, ~ьна) *adj.* inadmissible, impermissible.
непокла́дист|ый (~, ~а) *adj.* obstinate, uncompromising.
непоколеби́м|ый (~, ~а) *adj.* steadfast, unshakeable.
непоко́рност|ь, и *f.* recalcitrance; unruliness.
непоко́р|ный (~ен, ~на) *adj.* recalcitrant; unruly.
непокры́т|ый (~, ~а) *adj.* uncovered, bare.
непола́дк|а, и *f.* **1.** defect, fault. **2.** (*in pl.*) disagreement, quarrel.
неполнопра́вный *adj.* not possessing full rights.
неполнот|а́, ы́ *f.* incompleteness.
неполноце́нност|ь, и *f.* inferiority; **ко́мплекс ~и** inferiority complex; **психи́ческая н.** mental deficiency.
неполноце́н|ный (~ен, ~на) *adj.* inferior; substandard; **у́мственно н.** mentally deficient; **физи́чески н.** physically handicapped.
непо́л|ный (~он, ~на́, ~но) *adj.* not full; incomplete; **с тех пор прошло́ непо́лных два́дцать лет** since then not quite twenty years had passed; **рабо́тать ~ную неде́лю** to work part-time.
непоме́р|ный (~ен, ~на) *adj.* excessive, inordinate.
непонима́ни|е, я *nt.* incomprehension.
непоня́тливост|ь, и *f.* slowness, dimness.
непоня́тлив|ый (~, ~а) *adj.* slow (to grasp things), dim.
непоня́т|ный (~ен, ~на) *adj.* unintelligible, incomprehensible; (*impers., as pred*): **~но** it is incomprehensible; **мне ~но, как он мог э́то сде́лать** I cannot understand how he could do it.
непопада́ни|е, я *nt.* miss (*in shooting*).
непоправи́м|ый (~, ~а) *adj.* irreparable, irremediable; irretrievable.
непоро́ч|ный (~ен, ~на) *adj.* pure, chaste; **~ное зача́тие** (*relig.*) the Immaculate Conception.
непоря́д|ок, ка *m.* disorder; violation of order.
непоря́доч|ный (~ен, ~на) *adj.* dishonourable.
непосвящён|ный (~, ~а́) *adj.* uninitiated.
непосе́д|а, ы *c.g.* (*coll.*) fidget; rolling stone.
непосе́дливост|ь, и *f.* restlessness.
непосе́длив|ый (~, ~а) *adj.* fidgety, restless.
непосеще́ни|е, я *nt.* (*+g.*) non-attendance (at).
непоси́л|ьный (~ен, ~ьна) *adj.* beyond one's strength; excessive.
непосле́довательност|ь, и *f.* inconsistency.
непосле́довател|ьный (~ен, ~ьна) *adj.* inconsistent.
непослуша́ни|е, я *nt.* disobedience.
непослу́ш|ный (~ен, ~на) *adj.* disobedient; naughty.
непосре́дственност|ь, и *f.* spontaneity.
непосре́дствен|ный (~, ~на) *adj.* **1.** immediate, direct. **2.** (*fig.*) direct; spontaneous.
непостижи́м|ый (~, ~а) *adj.* incomprehensible, inscrutable; **уму́ ~о** it passes understanding.
непостоя́н|ный (~ен, ~на) *adj.* inconstant, changeable; non-permanent.
непостоя́нств|о, а *nt.* inconstancy.
непоти́зм, а *m.* nepotism.
непотопля́ем|ый (~, ~а) *adj.* unsinkable.
непотре́б|ный (~ен, ~на) *adj.* (*obs.*) obscene, indecent; **~ные слова́** obscenities.

непоча́тый *adj.* (*coll.*) untouched, entire; **н. край** (+*g.*) a wealth (of), a whole host (of).
непочте́ни|е, я *nt.* disrespect.
непочти́тел|ьный (~ен, ~ьна) *adj.* disrespectful.
непра́вд|а, ы *f.* untruth, falsehood, lie; **все́ми пра́вдами и ~ами** by fair means or foul; by hook or by crook.
неправдоподо́би|е, я *nt.* improbability, unlikelihood.
неправдоподо́б|ный (~ен, ~на) *adj.* improbable, unlikely; implausible.
непра́вильно *adv.* **1.** irregularly. **2.** incorrectly, erroneously; *in conjunction with vv. frequently* = mis-; *e.g.*, **н. истолкова́ть** to misinterpret.
непра́вильност|ь, и *f.* **1.** irregularity; anomaly. **2.** incorrectness.
непра́вил|ьный (~ен, ~ьна) *adj.* **1.** irregular; anomalous; **н. глаго́л** irregular verb; **~ьная дробь** (*math.*) improper fraction; **~ьные черты́ лица́** irregular features. **2.** incorrect, wrong.
неправоме́рност|ь, и *f.* illegality.
неправоме́р|ный (~ен, ~на) *adj.* illegal.
неправомо́чност|ь, и *f.* (*leg.*) incompetence.
неправомо́ч|ный (~ен, ~на) *adj.* (*leg.*) not competent; lacking the necessary authority.
неправот|а́, ы́ *f.* **1.** error. **2.** wrongness; injustice.
непра́в|ый (~, ~а́, ~о) *adj.* **1.** wrong, mistaken. **2.** unjust.
непревзойдённый *adj.* unsurpassed; matchless.
непредви́денный *adj.* unforeseen.
непреднаме́рен|ный (~, ~на) *adj.* unpremeditated.
непредубеждённый *adj.* unprejudiced, unbiased.
непредумы́шленный *adj.* unpremeditated.
непредусмотри́тельност|ь, и *f.* improvidence, short-sightedness.
непредусмотри́тел|ьный (~ен, ~ьна) *adj.* improvident, short-sighted.
непреклóнност|ь, и *f.* inflexibility; inexorability.
непреклóн|ный (~ен, ~на) *adj.* inflexible, unbending; inexorable, adamant.
непрелóж|ный (~ен, ~на) *adj.* **1.** immutable, unalterable. **2.** indisputable.
непреме́нно *adv.* **1.** without fail; certainly; **они́ н. приду́т за́втра** they are sure to come tomorrow. **2.** absolutely; **мне н. ну́жно поговори́ть с ним** it is absolutely essential that I speak to him.
непреме́н|ный (~ен, ~на) *adj.* indispensable.
непреобори́м|ый (~, ~а) *adj.* insuperable; irresistible.
непреодоли́м|ый (~, ~а) *adj.* insuperable, insurmountable; irresistible; **~ая си́ла** (*leg.*) force majeure.
непререка́ем|ый (~, ~а) *adj.* unquestionable, indisputable; **н. тон** peremptory tone.
непреры́вно *adv.* uninterruptedly, continuously.
непреры́вност|ь, и *f.* continuity.
непреры́в|ный (~ен, ~на) *adj.* uninterrupted, unbroken; continuous.
непреста́нно *adv.* incessantly, continually.
непреста́н|ный (~ен, ~на) *adj.* incessant, continual.
неприве́тлив|ый (~, ~а) *adj.* unfriendly, ungracious; bleak, forbidding.
непривы́чк|а, и *f.* want of habit; **с ~и он бы́стро захмеле́л** being unaccustomed to strong drink, he quickly became drunk.
непривы́ч|ный (~ен, ~на) *adj.* unaccustomed, unwonted; unusual.
непригля́д|ный (~ен, ~на) *adj.* unattractive, unsightly.
неприго́д|ный (~ен, ~на) *adj.* unfit, useless; unserviceable; ineligible.
неприе́млем|ый (~, ~а) *adj.* unacceptable.
непри́знанный *adj.* unrecognized, unacknowledged.
неприкаса́ем|ый, ого *m.* untouchable, Harijan.
неприка́янный *adj.* (*coll.*) restless, unable to find anything to do; **ходи́ть, броди́ть,** *etc.*, **как н.** to go about, wander about, *etc.*, like a lost soul.
неприкоснове́нност|ь, и *f.* inviolability; **дипломати́ческая н.** diplomatic immunity.
неприкоснове́н|ный (~ен, ~на) *adj.* inviolable; **н. запа́с** (*mil.*) emergency ration, iron ration; **н. капита́л** reserve capital.
неприкра́шенный *adj.* plain, unvarnished.
неприкры́т|ый *adj.* undisguised; **~ая ложь** barefaced lie.
неприли́чи|е, я *nt.* indecency, impropriety, unseemliness.
неприли́ч|ный (~ен, ~на) *adj.* indecent, improper; unseemly, unbecoming.
неримени́м|ый (~, ~а) *adj.* inapplicable.
неприме́т|ный (~ен, ~на) *adj.* **1.** imperceptible. **2.** (*fig.*) unremarkable, undistinguished.
непримири́мост|ь, и *f.* irreconcilability; intransigence.
непримири́м|ый (~, ~а) *adj.* irreconcilable; intransigent, uncompromising.
непринуждённост|ь, и *f.* unconstraint; naturalness, ease.
непринуждён|ный (~, ~на) *adj.* unconstrained; natural, relaxed, easy; spontaneous; laid-back.
неприсоедине́ни|е, я *nt.*: **поли́тика ~я** (*pol.*) policy of non-alignment.
неприсоедини́вш|ийся *adj.*: **~иеся стра́ны** non-aligned countries.
неприспосо́блен|ный (~, ~на) *adj.* **(к)** unadapted (to); maladjusted.
непристо́йност|ь, и *f.* obscenity; indecency.
непристо́|йный (~ен, ~йна) *adj.* obscene; indecent.
непристу́п|ный (~ен, ~на) *adj.* **1.** inaccessible; unassailable, impregnable. **2.** (*fig.*) unapproachable.
непритво́р|ный (~ен, ~на) *adj.* unfeigned, genuine.
неприхотли́вост|ь, и *f.* **1.** unpretentiousness; modesty. **2.** simplicity, plainness.
неприхотли́в|ый (~, ~а) *adj.* **1.** unpretentious; modest, undemanding. **2.** simple, plain.
неприча́ст|ный (~ен, ~на) *adj.* **(к)** not implicated (in), not involved (in).
неприя́знен|ный (~, ~на) *adj.* hostile, inimical.
неприя́зн|ь, и *f.* hostility, enmity.
неприя́тел|ь, я *m.* enemy; (*mil.*) the enemy.
неприя́тельский *adj.* hostile; (*mil.*) enemy
неприя́тност|ь, и *f.* unpleasantness; nuisance, annoyance, trouble.
неприя́т|ный (~ен, ~на) *adj.* unpleasant, disagreeable; annoying, troublesome.
непробу́дный *adj.* from which there is no waking; **н. сон** deep sleep; **н. пья́ница** inveterate drunkard.
непроводни́к, а́ *m.* (*phys.*) non-conductor.
непрогля́д|ный (~ен, ~на) *adj.* (*of darkness, fog. etc.*) impenetrable; pitch-dark.
непродолжи́тел|ьный (~ен, ~ьна) *adj.* of short duration, short-lived.
непродукти́в|ный (~ен, ~на) *adj.* unproductive.
непрое́зжий *adj.* impassable.
непрозра́чност|ь, и *f.* opacity.
непрозра́ч|ный (~ен, ~на) *adj.* opaque.
непроизводи́тел|ьный (~ен, ~ьна) *adj.* unproductive; wasteful.
непроизво́л|ьный (~ен, ~ьна) *adj.* involuntary.
непроло́з|ный (~ен, ~на) *adj.* (*coll.*) impassable.
непромока́ем|ый (~, ~а) *adj.* waterproof; **н. плащ** raincoat.
непроница́емост|ь, и *f.* impenetrability; impermeability.
непроница́ем|ый (~, ~а) *adj.* **1.** impenetrable, im-

permeable; **(для)** impervious (to); **н. для зву́ка** sound-proof. **2.** inscrutable, impassive.
непропорциона́льност|ь, и *f.* disproportion.
непропорциона́л|ьный (~ен, ~ьна) *adj.* disproportionate.
непрости́тел|ьный (~ен, ~ьна) *adj.* unforgivable, unpardonable, inexcusable.
непротивле́ни|е, я *nt.* non-resistance.
непроходи́м|ый (~, ~а) *adj.* **1.** impassable. **2.** (*fig., coll.*) complete, utter; **н. дура́к** utter fool.
непро́ч|ный (~ен, ~на) *adj.* fragile, flimsy; (*fig.*) precarious, unstable.
непро́шеный *adj.* (*coll.*) uninvited; unsolicited.
непрям|о́й (~́, ~а́, ~́о) *adj.* **1.** indirect; circuitous. **2.** (*fig., coll.*) evasive.
непутёвый *adj.* (*coll.*) good-for-nothing, useless.
непью́щий *adj.* temperate, abstemious (*in relation to alcoholic liquor*).
неработоспосо́б|ный (~ен, ~на) *adj.* incapacitated; disabled.
нерабо́ч|ий *adj.* non-working; **~ее вре́мя** time off, free time.
нера́венств|о, а *nt.* inequality, disparity.
неравноду́ш|ный (~ен, ~на) *adj.* **(к)** not indifferent (to).
неравноме́р|ный (~ен, ~на) *adj.* uneven, irregular.
неравнопра́в|ный (~ен, ~на) *adj.* not enjoying equal rights.
нера́в|ный (~ен, ~на́, ~но) *adj.* unequal.
нерадíвост|ь, и *f.* negligence, carelessness.
нерадíв|ый (~, ~а) *adj.* negligent, careless.
неразбери́х|а, и *f.* (*coll.*) muddle, confusion.
неразбо́рчив|ый (~, ~а) *adj.* **1.** illegible, indecipherable. **2.** (*fig.*) undiscriminating; **н. в сре́дствах** unscrupulous; **сексуа́льно н.** promiscuous.
неразвит|о́й (нера́звит, ~а́, ~о) *adj.* undeveloped; backward, retarded.
нера́звитост|ь, и *f.* lack of development; **у́мственная н.** backwardness.
неразга́данн|ый *adj.* unsolved.
неразгово́рчив|ый (~, ~а) *adj.* taciturn.
неразделённ|ый *adj.*: **~ая любо́вь** unrequited love.
неразделíм|ый (~, ~а) *adj.* indivisible, inseparable.
неразде́л|ьный (~ен, ~ьна) *adj.* indivisible, inseparable; **~ьное иму́щество** (*leg.*) common estate.
неразличи́м|ый (~, ~а) *adj.* indistinguishable; indiscernible.
неразлу́ч|ный (~ен, ~на) *adj.* inseparable.
неразрешённый *adj* **1.** unsolved. **2.** prohibited, banned.
неразреши́м|ый (~, ~а) *adj.* insoluble.
неразры́в|ный (~ен, ~на) *adj.* indissoluble.
неразу́м|ный (~ен, ~на) *adj.* unreasonable; unwise; foolish.
нерасположе́ни|е, я *nt.* **(к)** dislike (of), disinclination (to).
нерасполо́женный *adj.* **(к)** ill-disposed (towards); unwilling (to), disinclined (to).
нераспоряди́тел|ьный (~ен, ~ьна) *adj.* inefficient, incompetent.
нераспростране́ни|е, я *nt.* non-proliferation.
нерассуди́тельност|ь, и *f.* irrationality; lack of common sense.
нерассуди́тел|ьный (~ен, ~ьна) *adj.* irrational, unreasoning; lacking common sense.
нерастворíм|ый (~, ~а) *adj.* insoluble.
нерастoржи́м|ый (~, ~а) *adj.* indissoluble.
нерасторо́п|ный (~ен, ~на) *adj.* sluggish, slow.
нерасчётливост|ь, и *f.* **1.** extravagance, wastefulness. **2.** improvidence.
нерасчётлив|ый (~, ~а) *adj.* **1.** extravagant, wasteful. **2.** improvident.
нерациона́л|ьный (~ен, ~ьна) *adj.* irrational.
нерв, а *m.* nerve; **де́йствовать кому́-н. на ~́ы** to get on s.o.'s nerves.
нерви́р|овать, ую *impf.* to get on s.o.'s nerves, irritate.
нерви́ческий *adj.* nervous.
не́рвнича|ть, ю *impf.* to be *or* become fidgety, fret, be *or* become irritable.
нервнобольн|о́й, о́го *m.* person suffering from a nervous disorder.
не́рвно-паралити́ческ|ий *adj.* (*mil.*): **ОВ ~ого ти́па** nerve gas.
не́рвност|ь, и *f.* irritability, edginess.
не́рв|ный (~ен, ~на́, ~но) *adj.* **1.** nervous; neural; **н. припа́док** fit of nerves; **~ная систе́ма** the nervous system; **н. у́зел** (*anat.*) ganglion; **н. центр** nerve-centre. **2.** irritable, highly strung.
нерво́з|ный (~ен, ~на) *adj.* nervy, irritable.
нереа́л|ьный (~ен, ~ьна) *adj.* **1.** unreal. **2.** impracticable.
нерегуля́р|ный (~ен, ~на) *adj.* irregular.
нере́д|кий (~ок, ~ка́, ~ко) *adj.* not infrequent; not uncommon.
нере́дко *adv.* not infrequently, quite often.
не́рест, а *m.* (*zool.*) spawning.
нерести́лищ|е, а *nt.* spawning-ground.
нереши́мост|ь, и *f.* indecision.
нереши́тельност|ь, и *f.* indecision; indecisiveness; **быть в ~и** to be undecided.
нереши́тел|ьный (~ен, ~ьна) *adj.* indecisive, irresolute.
нержаве́ющ|ий *adj.* non-rusting; **~ая сталь** stainless steel.
неро́б|кий (~ок, ~ка́, ~ко) *adj.* not timid; **он челове́к ~кого деся́тка** he is no coward.
неро́вност|ь, и *f.* **1.** unevenness, roughness. **2.** inequality; irregularity.
неро́в|ный (~ен, ~на́, ~но) *adj.* **1.** uneven, rough; **н. грунт** rough country. **2.** unequal; irregular; **н. пульс** irregular pulse.
неро́вн|я, и (*and* **неровн|я́, и́**) *c.g.* (*coll.*): **он её н.** he is not her equal.
не́рп|а, ы *f.* (*zool.*) ringed seal.
нерукотво́рный *adj.* (*relig. and poet.*) not made by hands.
неруши́м|ый (~, ~а) *adj.* inviolable, indissoluble.
неря́х|а, и *c.g.* sloven; (*coll.*) scruff; (*used of woman only*) slattern.
неря́шеств|о, а *nt.* = **неря́шливость**
неря́шливост|ь, и *f.* slovenliness, untidiness; (*coll.*) scruffiness; (*used of woman only*) sluttishness.
неря́шлив|ый (~, ~а) *adj.* **1.** slovenly, untidy; (*coll.*) scruffy; (*used of woman only*) sluttish. **2.** careless, slipshod.
несваре́ни|е, я *nt. only in phr.* **н. желу́дка** indigestion.
несве́дущ|ий (~, ~а) *adj.* **(в+*p.*)** ignorant (about), not well-informed (about).
несве́ж|ий (~, ~а́, ~е) *adj.* **1.** not fresh, stale; tainted. **2.** (*fig.*) weary, wan.
несвоевре́мен|ный (~ен, ~на) *adj.* inopportune, untimely.
несвя́з|ный (~ен, ~на) *adj.* disconnected, incoherent.
несгиба́емый *adj.* unbending, inflexible.
несгово́рчив|ый (~, ~а) *adj.* intractable.
несгора́емый *adj.* fire-proof, incombustible; **н. шкаф** safe.
несде́ржанный *adj.* unrestrained.
несе́ни|е, я *nt.* performance, execution.
несессе́р, а *m.* toilet-case.
несказа́нный *adj.* unspeakable, ineffable.

нескла́диц|а, ы *f.* (*coll.*) nonsense.
нескла́д|ный (~ен, ~на) *adj.* **1.** incoherent. **2.** ungainly, awkward. **3.** absurd.
несклоня́ем|ый (~, ~а) *adj.* (*gram.*) indeclinable.
не́скольк|о[1], **их** *num.* some, several; a few; **в ~их слова́х** in a few words; **н. челове́к** several people.
не́сколько[2] *adv.* somewhat, rather, slightly; **они́ н. разочаро́ваны** they are rather disillusioned.
несконча́ем|ый (~, ~а) *adj.* interminable, never-ending.
нескро́мност|ь, и *f.* **1.** immodesty. **2.** indelicacy; indiscretion. **3.** indiscreetness.
нескро́м|ный (~ен, ~на́, ~но) *adj.* **1.** immodest; vain. **2.** indiscreet.
несло́ж|ный (~ен, ~на́, ~но) *adj.* simple, uncomplicated.
несль́ıхан|ный (~, ~на) *adj.* unheard-of, unprecedented.
несль́ıш|ный (~ен, ~на) *adj.* inaudible.
несменя́емост|ь, и *f.* irremovability (from office).
несменя́ем|ый (~, ~а) *adj.* irremovable.
несме́т|ный (~ен, ~на) *adj.* countless, incalculable.
несмолка́ем|ый (~, ~а) *adj.* ceaseless, unremitting.
несмотря́ *prep.* (**на**+*a.*) in spite of, despite; notwithstanding; **н. ни на что** in spite of everything.
несмыва́ем|ый (~, ~а) *adj.* indelible.
несно́с|ный (~ен, ~на) *adj.* intolerable.
несоблюде́ни|е, я *nt.* non-observance.
несовершенноле́ти|е, я *nt.* minority.
несовершенноле́тн|ий *adj.* under-age; *as n.* **н., ~его** *m.* minor.
несоверше́н|ный (~ен, ~на) *adj.* **1.** imperfect. **2.** (*gram.*) imperfective.
несовмести́м|ый (~, ~а) *adj.* incompatible.
несогла́си|е, я *nt.* **1.** disagreement; **н. в мне́ниях** difference of opinion; **н. ме́жду двумя́ ве́рсиями** discrepancy between two versions. **2.** discord. **3.** (*sg. only*) refusal.
несогла́с|ный (~ен, ~на) *adj.* **1.** (**с**+*i.*) not agreeing (with) **2.** (**с**+*i.*) inconsistent (with), incompatible (with). **3.** (**на**+*a. or* +*inf.*) not consenting (to), not agreeing (to); **я на э́то ~ен** I cannot agree to this. **4.** discordant.
несогласо́ванност|ь, и *f.* lack of co-ordination.
несогласо́ванный *adj.* uncoordinated.
несозна́тельност|ь, и *f.* thoughtlessness; irresponsibility.
несозна́тел|ьный (~ен, ~ьна) *adj.* irresponsible.
несоизмери́мост|ь, и *f.* incommensurability.
несоизмери́м|ый (~, ~а) *adj.* incommensurable.
несокруши́м|ый (~, ~а) *adj.* indestructible; unconquerable.
несоли́д|ный (~ен, ~на) *adj.* unimpressive, lightweight.
несо́лоно *adv. only in phr.* (*coll.*): **уйти́ н. хлеба́вши** to accomplish nothing, come away empty-handed.
несомне́нно *adv.* undoubtedly, doubtless.
несомне́н|ный (~ен, ~на) *adj.* undoubted, indubitable, unquestionable.
несообрази́тел|ьный (~ен, ~ьна) *adj.* slow(-witted).
несообра́зност|ь, и *f.* **1.** incongruity. **2.** absurdity.
несообра́з|ный (~ен, ~на) *adj.* **1.** (**с**+*i.*) incongruous (with). **2.** absurd.
несоотве́тствен|ный (~, ~на) *adj.* (+*d.*) not corresponding (to).
несоотве́тстви|е, я *nt.* lack of correspondence, disparity.
несоразме́рност|ь, и *f.* disproportion.
несоразме́р|ный (~ен, ~на) *adj.* disproportionate.
несостоя́тельност|ь, и *f.* **1.** insolvency, bankruptcy. **2.** modest means. **3.** groundlessness.
несостоя́тел|ьный (~ен, ~ьна) *adj.* **1.** insolvent, bankrupt. **2.** of modest means. **3.** groundless, unsupported.
неспе́л|ый (~, ~а́, ~о) *adj.* unripe.
неспе́ш|ный (~ен, ~на) *adj.* unhurried.
неспоко́|йный (~ен, ~йна) *adj.* restless; uneasy.
неспосо́бност|ь, и *f.* inability.
неспосо́б|ный (~ен, ~на) *adj.* dull, not able; (**к**+*d.*, **на**+*a.*) incapable (of); **она́ ~на к му́зыке** she has no aptitude for music; **н. на ложь** incapable of a lie.
несправедли́вост|ь, и *f.* injustice, unfairness.
несправедли́в|ый (~, ~а) *adj.* **1.** unjust, unfair. **2.** incorrect, unfounded.
неспровоци́рованный *adj.* unprovoked.
неспроста́ *adv.* (*coll.*) for a (definite) reason.
несравне́нно *adv.* **1.** incomparably, matchlessly. **2.** far, by far; **н. лу́чше** far better.
несравне́н|ный (~ен, ~на) *adj.* incomparable, matchless.
несравни́м|ый (~, ~а) *adj.* **1.** incomparable; unmatched. **2.** not comparable.
нестерпи́м|ый (~, ~а) *adj.* unbearable, unendurable.
нес|ти́[1], **у́, ёшь,** *past* **~̈, ~ла́** *impf.* (*of* **по~**), *det.* **1.** to carry. **2.** to bear; to support. **3.** (*fig.*) to bear; to suffer; to incur; **н. убы́тки** (*fin.*) to incur losses. **4.** to perform; **н. дежу́рство** to be on duty. **5.** (*fig.*) to bear, bring; **н. ги́бель** to bring destruction. **6.** (*impers.*, *coll.*; +*i.*) to stink (of), reek (of); **от него́ ~ёт чесноко́м** he reeks of garlic. **7.** (*coll.*) (**вздор, чепуху́**, *etc.*) to talk (nonsense).
нес|ти́[2], **ёт,** *past* **~̈, ~ла́** *impf.* (*of* **с~**) to lay (*eggs*).
нес|ти́сь[1], **у́сь, ёшься,** *past* **~̈ся, ~ла́сь** *impf.* (*of* **по~**), *det.* **1.** to rush, tear, fly; (*on water, in the air*) to float, drift; (**по**+*d.*, **вдоль; над**) to skim (along; over). **2.** (*of sounds, smells, etc.*) to spread, be diffused.
нес|ти́сь[2], **ётся,** *past* **~̈ся, ~ла́сь** *impf.* (*of* **с~**) to lay (eggs) (*intrans.*).
несто́ящий *adj.* (*coll.*) worthless, good-for-nothing.
нестроево́й[1] *adj.* unfit for building purposes.
нестроево́й[2] *adj.* (*mil.*) non-combatant.
нестро́|йный (~ен, ~йна́, ~йно) *adj.* **1.** clumsily built. **2.** discordant, dissonant. **3.** disorderly.
несть (*obs.*) there is not.
несура́зност|ь, и *f.* **1.** absurdity, senselessness. **2.** awkwardness.
несура́з|ный (~ен, ~на) *adj.* **1.** absurd, senseless. **2.** awkward.
несусве́т|ный (~ен, ~на) *adj.* (*coll.*) extreme, utter; unimaginable; **~ная чепуха́** utter nonsense.
несу́шк|а, и *f.* (*coll.*) laying hen, layer.
несуще́ствен|ный (~, ~на) *adj.* inessential, immaterial.
несхо́д|ный (~ен, ~на) *adj.* unlike, dissimilar.
несчастли́в|ец, ца *m.* unlucky person.
несчастли́в|ый (~, ~а) *adj.* **1.** unfortunate; unlucky. **2.** unhappy.
несча́ст|ный (~ен, ~на) *adj.* **1.** unhappy; unfortunate, unlucky; **н. слу́чай** accident; mishap. **2.** *as n.* **н., ~ного** *m.* unfortunate.
несча́сть|е, я *nt.* misfortune; **к ~ю** unfortunately.
несчёт|ный (~ен, ~на) *adj.* innumerable, countless.
несъедо́бный *adj.* **1.** uneatable. **2.** inedible; **н. гриб** toadstool.
нет[1] **1.** no; not; **вы его́ ви́дели? н.** you saw him? — No; **вы не ви́дели его́? н., ви́дел** you didn't see him? Yes, I did; **н. да н., н. как н.** (*coll.*; *emph.*) absolutely not, absolutely nothing; **н.-н. да и взгля́нет на меня́** he glanced at me from time to time. **2.** nothing, naught; **свести́ на н.** to negate, nullify; **свести́сь (сойти́) на н.** to come to naught.
нет[2] (+*g.*) (there) is not, (there) are not; **здесь н. собо́ра** there isn't a cathedral here; **у меня́ н. вре́мени** I have no time.

нетакти́ч|ный (~ен, ~на) *adj.* tactless.
нетвёрдо *adv.* **1.** unsteadily, not firmly. **2.** not definitely; **знать н.** to have a shaky knowledge of.
нетвёрд|ый (~, ~á, ~о) *adj.* unsteady; shaky (*also fig.*).
нетерпели́в|ый (~, ~а) *adj.* impatient.
нетерпе́ни|е, я *nt.* impatience.
нетерпи́мост|ь, и *f.* intolerance.
нетерпи́м|ый (~, ~а) *adj.* **1.** intolerable. **2.** intolerant.
нетле́н|ный (~ен, ~на) *adj.* imperishable.
нетороплив|ый (~, ~а) *adj.* leisurely, unhurried.
нето́чност|ь, и *f.* **1.** inaccuracy, inexactitude. **2.** error, slip.
нето́ч|ный (~ен, ~нá, ~но) *adj.* inaccurate, inexact.
нетрадицио́н|ный (~ен, ~на) *adj.* unconventional.
нетре́бовател|ьный (~ен, ~ьна) *adj.* not exacting, undemanding; unpretentious.
нетре́зв|ый (~, ~á, ~о) *adj.* not sober, drunk; **в ~ом ви́де** in a state of intoxication.
нетро́нут|ый (~, ~а) *adj.* untouched; (*fig.*) unsullied, virginal.
нетрудово́й *adj.* **1.** not derived from labour; **н. дохо́д** unearned income. **2.** not engaged in labour.
нетрудоспосо́бност|ь, и *f.* disablement, disability.
нетрудоспосо́б|ный (~ен, ~на) *adj.* disabled; incapacitated.
не́тто *adj. indecl.* (*comm.*) net.
не́ту (*coll.*) = **нет**[2]
неубеди́тел|ьный (~ен, ~ьна) *adj.* unconvincing.
неу́бранный *adj.* **1.** untidy. **2.** unharvested.
неуваже́ни|е, я *nt.* disrespect, lack of respect; (*leg.*) **н. к суду́** contempt of court.
неуважи́тел|ьный (~ен, ~ьна) *adj.* **1.** (*of excuse etc.*) inadequate; not acceptable. **2.** disrespectful.
неуве́ренност|ь, и *f.* uncertainty; **н. в себе́** diffidence.
неуве́рен|ный *adj.* **1. (~, ~а)** uncertain; **н. в себе́** diffident. **2. (~, ~на)** hesitating; vacillating.
неувяда́|емый (~ем, ~ема) *adj.* = **~ющий**
неувяда́ющий *adj.* (*rhet.*) unfading, undying.
неувя́зк|а, и *f.* (*coll.*) lack of co-ordination; misunderstanding.
неугаси́м|ый (~, ~а) *adj.* inextinguishable, unquenchable (*also fig.*).
неугомо́н|ный (~ен, ~на) *adj.* (*coll.*) indefatigable, irrepressible.
неуда́ч|а, и *f.* failure; setback.
неуда́члив|ый (~, ~а) *adj.* unlucky.
неуда́чник, а *m.* unlucky person, failure.
неуда́ч|ный (~ен, ~на) *adj.* unsuccessful; unfortunate; **~ное нача́ло** bad start.
неудержи́м|ый (~, ~а) *adj.* irrepressible.
неудо́б|ный (~ен, ~на) *adj.* **1.** uncomfortable. **2.** (*fig.*) inconvenient; awkward; embarrassing.
неудобовари́м|ый (~, ~а) *adj.* indigestible (*also fig.*).
неудобопроизноси́м|ый (~, ~а) *adj.* unpronounceable.
неудобочита́емый *adj.* difficult to read, obscure.
неудо́бств|о, а *nt.* **1.** discomfort; inconvenience. **2.** embarrassment.
неудовлетворе́ни|е, я *nt.* **1.** non-compliance; **н. жа́лобы** failure to act on a complaint. **2.** dissatisfaction.
неудовлетворённост|ь, и *f.* dissatisfaction, discontent.
неудовлетворён|ный *adj.* **1. (~, ~на)** dissatisfied, discontented. **2. (~, ~á)** unsatisfied.
неудовлетвори́тел|ьный (~ен, ~ьна) *adj.* unsatisfactory.
неудово́льстви|е, я *nt.* displeasure.
неуём|ный (~ен, ~на) *adj.* (*coll.*) irrepressible; **~ная печа́ль** uncontrollable grief.
неуже́ли *interrog. particle* really? is it possible?; **н. он так ду́мает?** does he really think that?
неужи́вчивост|ь, и *f.* quarrelsome disposition.
неужи́вчив|ый (~, ~а) *adj.* difficult (to get on with); quarrelsome.
неу́жто *interrog. particle* (*coll.*) = **неуже́ли**
неузнава́емост|ь, и *f.* unrecognizability; **он похуде́л до ~и** he has become so thin that you would not recognize him.
неузнава́ем|ый (~, ~а) *adj.* unrecognizable.
неукло́н|ный (~ен, ~на) *adj.* steady, steadfast; undeviating.
неуклю́жест|ь, и *f.* clumsiness, awkwardness.
неуклю́ж|ий (~, ~а, ~е) *adj.* clumsy; awkward.
неукосни́тел|ьный (~ен, ~ьна) *adj.* strict, rigorous.
неукроти́м|ый (~, ~а) *adj.* indomitable.
неулови́м|ый (~, ~а) *adj.* **1.** elusive. **2.** (*fig.*) imperceptible.
неуме́л|ый (~, ~а) *adj.* clumsy; unskilful.
неуме́ни|е, я *nt.* inability; lack of skill.
неуме́ренност|ь, и *f.* **1.** immoderation. **2.** intemperance.
неуме́рен|ный (~, ~на) *adj.* **1.** immoderate; excessive. **2.** intemperate.
неуме́ст|ный (~ен, ~на) *adj.* **1.** inappropriate; misplaced, uncalled-for. **2.** irrelevant.
неу́м|ный (~ён, ~нá, ~нó) *adj.* foolish, silly.
неумоли́м|ый (~, ~а) *adj.* implacable; inexorable.
неумолка́ем|ый (~, ~а) *adj.* incessant, unceasing.
неумо́л|чный (~чен, ~чна) *adj.* = **~ка́емый**
неумы́шлен|ный (~, ~на) *adj.* unpremeditated; unintentional, inadvertent.
неупла́т|а, ы *f.* non-payment.
неупотреби́тел|ьный (~ен, ~ьна) *adj.* not in use.
неуравнове́шен|ный (~, ~на) *adj.* (*psych.*) unbalanced.
неурожа́|й, я *m.* bad harvest; crop failure.
неурожа́й|ный *adj. of* **~; н. год** lean year, bad harvest year.
неуро́чный *adj.* untimely.
неуря́диц|а, ы *f.* (*coll.*) **1.** disorder, mess. **2.** (*pl.*) squabbling.
неуси́дчив|ый (~, ~а) *adj.* restless, not persevering.
неуспева́емост|ь, и *f.* poor progress (*in studies*).
неуспева́ющий *adj.* backward, not making satisfactory progress.
неуста́н|ный (~ен, ~на) *adj.* tireless, unwearying.
неусто́йк|а, и *f.* **1.** (*leg.*) forfeit. **2.** (*coll.*) failure.
неусто́йчивост|ь, и *f.* instability, unsteadiness.
неусто́йчив|ый (~, ~а) *adj.* unstable, unsteady.
неустрани́м|ый (~, ~а) *adj.* irremovable; **~ое препя́тствие** insurmountable obstacle.
неустраши́м|ый (~, ~а) *adj.* fearless, intrepid.
неустро́ен|ный (~, ~на) *adj.* unsettled; badly organized.
неустро́йств|о, а *nt.* disorder.
неусту́пчив|ый (~, ~а) *adj.* unyielding, uncompromising.
неусы́п|ный (~ен, ~на) *adj.* vigilant; indefatigable.
неутеши́тел|ьный (~ен, ~ьна) *adj.* not comforting, depressing; **~ьные ве́сти** distressing news.
неуте́ш|ный (~ен, ~на) *adj.* inconsolable; disconsolate.
неутоли́м|ый (~, ~а) *adj.* unquenchable; (*fig.*) insatiable.
неутоми́м|ый (~, ~а) *adj.* tireless, indefatigable.
не́уч, а *m.* (*coll.*) ignoramus.
неучти́вост|ь, и *f.* discourtesy, impoliteness, incivility.

неучти́в|ый (~, ~а) *adj.* discourteous, impolite.
неую́т|ный (~ен, ~на) *adj.* bleak, comfortless.
неуязви́м|ый (~, ~а) *adj.* **1.** invulnerable. **2.** unassailable.
нефри́т[1], **а** *m.* (*med.*) nephritis.
нефри́т[2], **а** *m.* (*min.*) nephrite, jade.
нефте... *comb. form* oil-, petro-.
нефтево́з, а *m.* oil-tanker (*lorry*).
нефтеналивн|о́й *adj.* equipped for carrying oil in bulk; **~о́е су́дно** oil-tanker.
нефтено́с|ный (~ен, ~на) *adj.* oil-bearing.
нефтепереro´нный *adj.* oil-refining; **н. заво́д** oil refinery.
нефтеперераба́тывающий *adj.* oil-refining.
нефтепрово́д, а *m.* oil pipe-line.
нефтета́нкер, а *m.* oil-tanker (*ship*).
нефт|ь, и *f.* oil, petroleum; **н.-сыре́ц** crude oil.
нефтя́ник, а *m.* oil(-industry) worker.
нефтян|о́й *adj.* oil; **~а́я вы́шка** derrick; **н. платфо́рма** oil rig.
нехва́тк|а, и *f.* (*coll.*) shortage.
нехи́т|рый (~ёр, ~ра́, ~́ро) *adj.* **1.** artless, guileless. **2.** (*coll.*) simple; uncomplicated.
нехоро́ш|ий (~, ~а́, ~о́) *adj.* bad.
нехорошо́ *adv.* badly; **чу́вствовать себя́ н.** to feel unwell.
не́хотя *adv.* **1.** reluctantly, unwillingly. **2.** inadvertently, unintentionally.
нецелесообра́з|ный (~ен, ~на) *adj.* inexpedient; pointless.
нецензу́р|ный (~ен, ~на) *adj.* unprintable; **~ные слова́** swear words, obscenities.
нечая́нност|ь, и *f.* **1.** unexpectedness. **2.** surprise. **3.** unexpected event.
нечая́нный *adj.* **1.** unexpected. **2.** accidental; unintentional.
не́чего, не́чему, не́чем, не́ о чем 1. *pron.* (+*inf.*) there is nothing (to); **мне н. чита́ть** I have nothing to read; **не́ о чем бы́ло говори́ть** there was nothing to talk about; **от н. де́лать** for want of sth. better to do; **н. сказа́ть!** (*coll., iron.*) indeed!; well, I declare! **2.** *as pred.* (*impers.*; +*inf.*) it's no good, it's no use; **н. жа́ловаться** it's no use complaining; **н. и говори́ть, что...** it goes without saying that ....
нечелове́ческий *adj.* **1.** superhuman. **2.** inhuman.
нечести́в|ый (~, ~а) *adj.* impious, profane.
нече́стност|ь, и *f.* dishonesty.
нече́ст|ный (~ен, ~на́) *adj.* **1.** dishonest. **2.** dishonourable; crooked; **~ная игра́** (*sport*) foul play.
не́чет, а *m.* (*coll.*) odd number.
нечёт|кий (~ок, ~ка́) *adj.* illegible; indistinct; inaccurate, slipshod.
нечётный *adj.* odd.
нечистопло́т|ный (~ен, ~на) *adj.* **1.** dirty; untidy, slovenly. **2.** (*fig.*) unscrupulous.
нечистот|а́, ы́, *pl.* **~́ы, ~́** *f.* **1.** dirtiness. **2.** *pl. only* sewage; garbage.
нечи́ст|ый (~, ~а́, ~о) *adj.* **1.** unclean, dirty (*also fig.*); **~ое де́ло** shady affair. **2.** impure, adulterated; **~ая поро́да** impure breed. **3.** careless, inaccurate. **4.** dishonourable; dishonest; **быть ~ым на́ руку** to be light-fingered.
не́чист|ь, и *f.* (*collect.*; *coll.*) **1.** evil spirits. **2.** (*fig., pej.*) scum, vermin.
нечленоразде́л|ьный (~ен, ~на) *adj.* inarticulate.
не́что *pron.* (*nom. and a. cases only*) something.
нечувстви́тел|ьный (~ен, ~ьна) *adj.* **(к)** insensitive (to).
нешу́точ|ный (~ен, ~на) *adj.* grave, serious; **де́ло ~ное** it is no joke; it is no laughing matter.
неща́д|ный (~ен, ~на) *adj.* merciless.
нея́вк|а, и *f.* non-appearance, failure to appear.
неядови́тый *adj.* non-poisonous; (*chem.*) non-toxic.
нея́сност|ь, и *f.* vagueness, obscurity.
нея́с|ный (~ен, ~на́, ~но) *adj.* vague, obscure.
нея́сыт|ь, и *f.* tawny owl.
ни 1. *correlative conj.* **ни... ни** neither ... nor; **ни тот ни друго́й** neither (one); **ни то ни сё** neither one thing nor the other; **ни с того́, ни с сего́** all of a sudden. **2.** *particle* not a; **ни оди́н, ни одна́, ни одно́** not a, not one, not a single; **на у́лице не́ было ни (одно́й) души́** there was not a soul about. **3.** *separable component of prons.* **никако́й, никто́, ничто́** *following preps.*; **ни в како́м (ни в ко́ем) слу́чае** on no account; **ни за что на све́те!** not for the world! **4.** (*particle, in comb. with* **как, кто, куда́** *etc.*) = -ever; **как бы мы ни стара́лись** however hard we tried; **что бы он ни говори́л** whatever he might say.
ни́в|а, ы *f.* (corn-)field; **на ~е просвеще́ния** (*fig.*) in the field of education.
нивели́р, а *m.* (*tech.*) level.
нивели́р|овать, ую *impf. and pf.* (*tech. and fig.*) to level.
нивелиро́вк|а, и *f.* levelling.
нигде́ *adv.* nowhere.
нигили́зм, а *m.* nihilism.
нигили́ст, а *m.* nihilist.
нигилисти́ческий *adj.* nihilistic.
нидерла́нд|ец, ца *m.* Dutchman.
нидерла́ндский *adj.* Dutch, Netherlands.
Нидерла́нд|ы, ов *no sg.* the Netherlands.
ни́же 1. *comp. of* **ни́зкий** *and* **ни́зко. 2.** *prep.* (+*g.*) *and adv.* below, beneath.
нижеподписа́вшийся *adj.* (the) undersigned.
нижесле́дующий *adj.* following.
нижеупомя́нутый *adj.* undermentioned.
ни́жн|ий *adj.* lower; **~ее бельё** underclothes, underwear; **~яя пала́та** Lower Chamber, Lower House; **~яя ю́бка** slip; **н. эта́ж** ground floor.
ни|жу́, ~́жешь *see* **~за́ть**
низ, а, *pl.* **~ы́** *m.* **1.** bottom; ground floor. **2.** (*pl.*) lower classes. **3.** (*pl.*; *mus.*) low notes.
ни|за́ть, жу́, ~́жешь *impf.* (*of* **на~**) to string, thread.
низверг|а́ть, а́ю *impf.* (*of* **~́нуть**) to precipitate; (*fig.*) to overthrow.
низверг|а́ться, а́юсь *impf.* (*of* **~́нуться**) **1.** to crash down. **2.** *pass. of* **~а́ть**
низве́рг|нуть(ся), ну(сь), нешь(ся), *past* **~(ся), ~ла(сь),** *pf. of* **~а́ть(ся)**
низверже́ни|е, я *nt.* overthrow.
низве|сти́, ду́, дёшь, *past* **~́л, ~ла́** *pf.* (*of* **низводи́ть**) to bring down; (*fig.*) to bring low; to reduce.
низво|ди́ть, жу́, ~́дишь *impf. of* **низвести́**
низи́н|а, ы *f.* low-lying area.
ни́з|кий (~ок, ~ка́, ~ко) *adj.* **1.** low; **~кого происхожде́ния** of humble origin. **2.** base, mean; **н. посту́пок** shabby act.
низкоопла́чиваемый *adj.* poorly-paid.
низкопокло́нник, а *m.* toady, crawler.
низкопокло́ннича|ть, ю *impf.* **(пе́ред)** to grovel (before).
низкопокло́нств|о, а *nt.* servility.
низкопро́б|ный (~ен, ~на) *adj.* **1.** base, low-grade (*of precious metals*). **2.** (*fig.*) base; inferior; trashy.
низкоро́сл|ый (~, ~а) *adj.* undersized, stunted.
низкосо́рт|ный (~ен, ~на) *adj.* low-grade; poor-quality.
низлага́|ть, ю *impf. of* **низложи́ть**
низложе́ни|е, я *nt.* deposition, dethronement.
низлож|и́ть, у́, ~́ишь *pf.* (*of* **низлага́ть**) to depose, dethrone.
ни́зменност|ь, и *f.* **1.** (*geog.*) lowland. **2.** baseness.
ни́змен|ный (~, ~на) *adj.* **1.** low-lying. **2.** low; base.
низово́й[1] *adj.* (*geog.*) lower; situated down stream.

низово́й[2] *adj.* local; (*pol.*) grass-roots.
низо́в|ье, ья, *g. pl.* **~ьев** *nt.* the lower reaches (*of a river*).
ни́зом *adv.* (*coll.*) along the bottom; **е́хать н.** to take the lower road.
ни́зост|ь, и *f.* lowness; baseness, meanness.
ни́зш|ий *superl. of* **ни́зкий**; lowest; **~ее образова́ние** primary education.
ника́к *adv.* by no means, in no way; **он н. не мог узна́ть её а́дрес** he simply couldn't discover her address; **н. нельзя́** it is quite impossible; **н. нет** *respectful reply in negative to question.*
никак|о́й *pron.* no; **не... ~о́го, ~о́й, ~и́х** no ... whatever; **я не име́ю ~о́го представле́ния** I have no idea; **учёный он н.** (*coll.*) he is no scholar.
ни́келевый *adj.* nickel.
никелиро́в|анный *p.p.p of* **~а́ть** and nickel-plated.
никелир|ова́ть, у́ю *impf. and pf.* to plate with nickel, nickel(-plate).
никелиро́вк|а, и *f.* nickel-plating.
ни́кел|ь, я *m.* nickel.
ни́к|нуть, ну, нешь, *past* **~, ~ла** *impf.* (*of* **по~** *and* **с~**) to droop, flag (*also fig.*).
никогда́ *adv.* never; **как н.** as never before.
нико́|й *pron.* (*obs.*) no; *now only in phrr.* **~им о́бразом** by no means, in no way; **ни в ко́ем слу́чае** on no account, under no circumstances.
никоти́н, а *m.* nicotine.
никоти́н|ный *adj. of* **~**
никоти́н|овый *adj.* = **~ный**
никто́, никого́, никому́, нике́м, ни о ком *pron.* nobody, no one; **там никого́ не́ было** there was nobody there; **н. друго́й** nobody else.
никуда́ *adv.* nowhere; **э́то н. не годи́тся** (*fig.*) this won't do; it is no good at all; **н. не го́дный** good-for-nothing, worthless, useless.
никуд|ы́шный *adj.* (*coll.*) = **~а́ не го́дный.**
никчёмный *adj.* (*coll.*) useless, good-for-nothing; worthless.
Нил, а *m.* the Nile (*river*).
ним *i. of* **он, оно́**; *d. of* **они́** *after preps.*
нима́ло *adv.* not in the least, not at all.
нимб, а *m.* halo, nimbus.
ни́ми *i. of* **они́** *after preps.*
ни́мф|а, ы *f.* nymph.
нимфома́ни|я, и *f.* nymphomania.
нимфома́нк|а, и *f.* nymphomaniac.
ниотку́да *adv.* from nowhere; **н. не сле́дует, что...** it in no way follows that ....
нипочём *adv.* (*coll.*) **1.** (*+d.*) it is nothing (to); **ему́ н. провести́ це́лую ночь на заня́тиях** he thinks nothing of spending a whole night working. **2.** for nothing, dirt-cheap; **прода́ть н.** to sell for a song.
ни́ппел|ь, я, *pl.* **~я́, ~е́й** *m.* (*tech.*) nipple.
нирва́н|а, ы *f.* nirvana.
ниско́лько *adv.* not a bit, not in the least; **ей от э́того бы́ло н. не лу́чше** she was none the better for it.
ниспада́|ть, ет *impf. of* **ниспа́сть**
ниспа́|сть, ду́, дёшь, *past* **~л, ~ла** *pf.* (*of* **~да́ть**) (*obs.*) to fall, drop.
ниспроверг|а́ть, а́ю *impf.* (*of* **~́нуть**) to overthrow.
ниспрове́рг|нуть, ну, нешь, *past* **~, ~ла** *pf. of* **~а́ть**
ниспроверже́ни|е, я *nt.* overthrow.
нисход|я́щий *pres. part. act. of* **~и́ть** *and adj.* descending; **по ~я́щей ли́нии** in the line of descent, in a descending line.
ни́тк|а, и *f.* thread; **н. же́мчуга** string of pearls; **на живу́ю ~у** (*fig., coll.*) hastily, anyhow; **ши́то бе́лыми ~ами** (*fig., coll.*) transparent, obvious; **до (после́дней) ~и обобра́ть** (*fig., coll.*) to fleece, leave without a shirt to one's back; **промо́кнуть до ~и** (*fig.*) to get soaked to the skin.
ни́точк|а, и *f. dim. of* **ни́тка; по ~е разобра́ть** (*fig.*) to analyse minutely; **ходи́ть по ~е** (*fig.*) to toe the line.
нитра́т, а *m.* (*chem.*) nitrate.
нитри́т, а *m.* (*chem.*) nitrite.
нитроглицери́н, а *m.* (*chem.*) nitroglycerine.
нит|ь, и *f.* **1. ~́и дру́жбы** bonds of friendship; **проходи́ть кра́сной ~́ью** (*fig.*) to run through (*of theme, motif*). **2.** (*bot., elec.*) filament. **3.** (*med.*) suture.
них *a. and g. of* **они́** *when governed by preps.*
ниц *adv.* (*obs.*) face downwards; **пасть н.** to prostrate o.s., kiss the ground.
ничего́[1] *g. of* **ничто́**
ничего́[2] *adv.* **1.** (*also* **н. себе́**) so-so; passably, not (too) badly; all right; **ко́рмят здесь н.** the food here is not too bad; **как вы чу́вствуете себя́? — н.** how do you feel? all right. **2.** *as indecl. adj.* not (too) bad, passable, tolerable; **на́ша кварти́ра н.** our flat is not too bad; **па́рень он н.** he is not a bad chap.
нич|е́й (~ья́, ~ьё) *pron.* nobody's, no one's; **~ья́ земля́** no man's land; *as n.* **~ья́, ~ье́й** *f.* (*sport*) draw, drawn game; **сыгра́ть в ~ью́** to draw.
ниче́йный *adj.* (*coll.*) **1.** no man's. **2.** (*sport*) drawn.
ничко́м *adv.* prone, face down(wards).
ничто́, ничего́, ничему́, ниче́м, ни о чём *pron.* **1.** nothing; **э́то ничего́ не зна́чит** it means nothing; **ничего́ подо́бного!** nothing of the kind!; **э́то ничего́!** it's nothing!; it doesn't matter!; **ничего́!** (*coll.*) that's all right!; never mind! **2.** nought; nil.
ничто́же *pron.* **н. сумня́ся, н. сумня́шеся** (*iron.*) without a moment's hesitation.
ничто́жеств|о, а *nt.* **1.** nothingness. **2.** a nonentity, a nobody.
ничто́жност|ь, и *f.* **1.** insignificance. **2.** a nonentity, a nobody.
ничто́ж|ный (~ен, ~на) *adj.* insignificant; worthless.
ничу́ть *adv.* (*coll.*) not at all, not in the least, not a bit; **н. не быва́ло** not at all.
ничь|я́, е́й *f. see* **ниче́й**
ни́ш|а, и *f.* niche, recess; (*archit.*) bay.
нища́|ть, ю *impf.* (*of* **об~**) to be reduced to beggary.
ни́щенк|а, и *f.* beggar-woman.
ни́щенский *adj.* beggarly.
ни́щенств|о, а *nt.* **1.** begging. **2.** beggary.
ни́щенств|овать, ую *impf.* **1.** to beg, go begging. **2.** to live in poverty; to be destitute.
нищет|а́, ы́ *f.* poverty.
ни́щ|ий *adj.* **1.** destitute; poverty-stricken; **н. ду́хом** poor in spirit. **2.** *as n.* **н., ~его** *m.* beggar; pauper.
НЛО *m. indecl.* (*abbr. of* **неопо́знанный лета́ющий обье́кт**) UFO (*unidentified flying object*).
но *conj.* **1.** but; *after concessive clause not translated or* still, nevertheless; **хотя́ он и бо́лен, но наме́рен прийти́** although he is ill, he (still) intends to come. **2.** (*coll.*) *as n.* a 'but'; snag, difficulty; **тут есть одно́ «но»** there is just one snag in it.
нова́тор, а *m.* innovator.
нова́тор|ский *adj. of* **~** *and* **~ство**
нова́торств|о, а *nt.* innovation.
Но́в|ая Гвине́|я, ~ой ~и *f.* New Guinea.
Но́в|ая Зела́нди|я, ~ой ~и *f.* New Zealand.
Но́в|ая Шотла́нди|я, ~ой ~и *f.* Nova Scotia.
нове́йший *superl. of* **но́вый**; newest; latest.
нове́лл|а, ы *f.* short story; novella.
новелли́ст, а *m.* short story-writer.
но́веньк|ий *adj.* **1.** brand-new. **2.** *as n.* **н., ~ого** *m.* new boy; **~ая, ~ой** *f.* new girl.
новизн|а́, ы́ *f.* novelty; newness.
нови́нк|а, и *f.* novelty; **мне в ~у лете́ть самолётом** it is a new experience for me to travel by plane.
нович|о́к, ка́ *m.* **1.** (**в**+*p.*) novice (at), beginner (at).

2. (*in school*) new boy; new girl.
новобра́н|ец, ца *m.* recruit.
новобра́чн|ая, ой *f.* bride.
новобра́чн|ые, ых *pl.* newly-weds.
новобра́чн|ый, ого *m.* bridegroom.
нововведе́ни|е, я *nt.* innovation.
нового́дний *adj.* new year's.
новогре́ческий *adj.*: **н. язы́к** Modern Greek.
новозаве́тный *adj.* of the New Testament.
новозела́нд|ец, ца *m.* New Zealander.
новозела́нд|ка, ки *f. of* **~ец**
новозела́ндский *adj.* New Zealand.
новоиспечённый *adj.* (*coll., joc.*) newly made; newly fledged.
новокаи́н, а *m.* (*pharm.*) novocaine.
новолу́ни|е, я *nt.* new moon.
новомо́д|ный (~ен, ~на) *adj.* in the latest fashion, up-to-date; (*fig., pej.*) newfangled.
новообразова́ни|е, я *nt.* new growth; new formation; (*med.*) neoplasm.
новообращённый *adj.* (*relig. and fig.*) newly converted.
новопреста́вленный *adj.* (*relig.*) the late, the late-lamented.
новоприбы́вш|ий *adj.* newly-arrived; *as n.* **н., ~его** *m.* new-comer.
новорождённ|ый *adj.* new-born; *as n.* **н., ~ого** *m.* (new-born) baby; (*med.*) neonate.
новосёл, а *m.* new settler; new occupant.
новосе́лье, я *nt.* **1.** new home. **2.** house-warming; **справля́ть н.** to give a house-warming party.
новостро́йк|а, и *f.* **1.** erection of new buildings. **2.** newly-erected building; **шко́ла-н.** new school.
но́вост|ь, и, *g. pl.* **~е́й** *f.* **1.** news. **2.** novelty.
новоя́вленный *adj.* (*relig. or iron.*) newly brought to light.
но́вшеств|о, а *nt.* innovation, novelty.
но́в|ый (~, ~а́, ~о) *adj.* **1.** new; novel; fresh; **соверше́нно н.** brand-new; **Н. год** new year's day; **Н. заве́т** the New Testament; **Н. свет** the New World; **что ~ого?** what's new? **2.** modern; recent; **~ая исто́рия** modern history; **~ые языки́** modern languages.
нов|ь, и *f.* virgin soil.
ног|а́, и́, *a.* **∸у,** *pl.* **∸и, ног, ~а́м** *f.* foot; leg; **вверх ~а́ми** head over heels; **без (за́дних) ног** (*coll.*) dead on one's feet; **в ~а́х посте́ли** at the foot of the bed; **идти́ в ∸у (с+*i.*)** to keep step (with), keep pace (with) (*also fig.*); **идти́ н. за́ ~у** (*coll.*) to amble along; **к ~е́!** (*mil.*) order arms!; **положи́ть ∸у на́ ~у** to cross one's legs; **стать на́ ~и** (*fig.*) to stand on one's own feet; **жить на широ́кую (большу́ю, ба́рскую) ∸у** to live in (grand) style; **быть на коро́ткой ~е́ (с+*i.*)** to be on a good terms (with); **сбить с ног** to knock down; **встать с ле́вой ~и́** to get out of bed on the wrong side; **со всех ног** (*coll.*) as fast as one's legs will carry one; **ног под собо́й не чу́ять (от ра́дости)** (*coll.*) to be beside o.s. (*with joy*); **мое́й ~и́ у вас не бу́дет** (*coll.*) I shall not set foot in your house again; **мы — ни ~о́й туда́** (*coll.*) we never go near the place; **стоя́ть одно́й ~о́й в моги́ле** to have one foot in the grave; **протяну́ть ~и** (*coll.*) to turn up one's toes.
ноготк|и́, о́в (*bot.*) marigold.
но́г|оть, тя, *pl.* **~ти, ~те́й** *m.* (finger-, toe-) nail.
ног|тево́й *adj. of* **∸оть**
нож, а́ *m.* knife; **перочи́нный н.** penknife; **садо́вый н.** pruning-knife; **н. в спи́ну** (*fig.*) stab in the back; **быть на ~а́х (с+*i.*)** to be at daggers drawn (with).
нож|ево́й *adj. of* **~**; **н. ма́стер** cutler; **~евы́е това́ры** cutlery.
но́жик, а *m.* (small) knife.
но́жк|а, и *f.* **1.** *dim. of* **нога́; подста́вить ~у** (+*d.*) to trip up. **2.** leg (*of furniture, utensils, etc*); stem (of wine-glass). **3.** (*bot.*) stalk; stem (*of mushroom*).
но́жниц|ы, ~ *pl.* (pair of) scissors; shears.
ножн|о́й *adj. of* **нога́; н. то́рмоз** foot brake.
но́ж|ны ~ен, ~нам (*and* **нож|ны́, ~о́н, ~на́м**) *pl.* sheath; scabbard.
ножо́вк|а, и *f.* hacksaw.
ноздрева́тост|ь, и *f.* porosity.
ноздрева́т|ый (~, ~а) *adj.* porous.
ноздр|я́, и́, *pl.* **∸и, ~е́й** *f.* nostril
нока́ут, а *m.* (*sport*) knock-out.
нокаути́р|овать, ую *impf. and pf.* (*sport*) to knock out.
нокда́ун, а *m.* (*sport*) knock-down.
ноктю́рн, а *m.* (*mus.*) nocturne.
нолево́й = нулево́й
нол|ь, я́ *m.* **= нуль**
номенклату́р|а, ы *f.* **1.** nomenclature. **2.** list. **3.** nomenklatura.
номенклату́р|ный *adj. of* **~а**
но́мер, а, *pl.* **~а́** *m.* **1.** number; number, issue (*of newspaper, magazine, etc.*). **2.** size. **3.** room (*in hotel*). **4.** act (*on a programme*), number, turn. **5.** (*coll.*) trick; ploy; **вы́кинуть н.** to play a trick.
номерн|о́й 1. *adj. of* **но́мер**; numbered. **2.** *as n.* **н., ~о́го** *m.* boots (*in a hotel*).
номер|о́к, ка́ *m.* **1.** tally; label, ticket (*in cloakroom, etc.*). **2.** small room (*in a hotel*).
номина́л, а *m.* (*econ.*) face-value; **по ~у** at face-value.
номина́льн|ый *adj.* **1.** nominal; **~ая цена́** face value. **2.** (*tech.*) rated, indicated, nominal.
нор|а́, ы́, *pl.* **∸ы, ~, ∸ам** *f.* burrow, hole; lair; (*of hare*) form.
Норве́ги|я, и *f.* Norway.
норве́ж|ец, ца *m.* Norwegian.
норве́ж|ка, ки *f. of* **~ец**
норве́жский *adj.* Norwegian.
норд, а *m.* (*naut.*) **1.** north. **2.** north wind.
норд-ве́ст, а *m.* (*naut.*) **1.** north-west. **2.** northwester, north-westerly wind.
норд-о́ст, а *m.* (*naut.*) **1.** north-east. **2.** north-easter, north-easterly wind.
но́рк|а¹, и *f. dim. of* **нора́**
но́рк|а², и *f.* mink.
но́рк|овый *adj. of* **~а²**
но́рм|а, ы *f.* **1.** standard, norm. **2.** rate; **н. вы́работки** rate of output; **сверх ~ы** in excess of planned rate.
нормализа́ци|я, и *f.* standardization.
нормализ|ова́ть, у́ю *impf. and pf.* to standardize.
норма́л|ь, и *f.* (*math., phys.*) normal.
норма́льно *as pred.* (*coll.*) it is all right, OK.
норма́льност|ь, и *f.* normality.
норма́л|ьный (~ен, ~ьна) *adj.* normal.
норма́нд|ец, ца *m.* Norman.
норма́нд|ка, ки *f. of* **~ец**
Норма́ндск|ие остров|а́, ~их ~о́в *no sg.* the Channel Islands.
норма́ндский *adj.* Norman.
норма́нн, а *m.* (*hist.*) Northman, Norseman.
норма́ннский *adj.* (*hist.*) Norse.
нормати́в, а *m.* (*econ.*) norm.
нормати́в|ный (~ен, ~на) *adj.* **1.** *adj. of* **~**; corresponding to norm. **2.** normative.
нормирова́ни|е, я *nt.* **1.** regulation, normalization; **н. труда́** norm-fixing, norm-setting (*in production*). **2.** rationing.
нормиро́в|анный *p.p.p. of* **~а́ть; н. рабо́чий день** fixed working hours; **~анное снабже́ние** rationing.
нормир|ова́ть, у́ю *impf. and pf.* **1.** to regulate, normalize; **н. за́работную пла́ту** to fix wages. **2.** to ration.
но́ров, а *m.* **1.** (*coll.*) obstinacy, capriciousness; **челове́к с ~ом** difficult person. **2.** (*of horses*) restiveness.

норови́ст|ый (~, ~а) *adj.* (*coll.*) restive; jibbing.
норов|и́ть, лю́, и́шь *impf.* (*coll.*) **1.** (+*inf.*) to strive (to), aim (at). **2.** (**в**+*nom.-a.*) to strive to become; **он ~и́т в писа́тели** he has literary aspirations.
нос, а, о ~е, на ~у́, *pl.* **~ы́** *m.* **1.** nose; **у меня́ идёт кровь ~ом (и́з ~у)** my nose is bleeding; **говори́ть в н.** to speak through one's nose; **~ом к ~у** (*coll.*) face to face; **на ~у́** (*coll.*) near at hand, just around the corner; **оста́вить с ~ом** (*coll.*) to dupe, make a fool of; **оста́ться с ~ом** (*coll.*) to be duped, be left looking a fool; **н. вороти́ть (от)** (*coll.*) to turn up one's nose (at); **сова́ть н. не в своё де́ло** (*coll.*) to poke one's nose into other people's affairs. **2.** beak. **3.** (*naut.*) bow, head; prow.
носа́ст|ый (~, ~а) *adj.* big-nosed.
носа́т|ый (~, ~а) *adj.* = **носа́стый**
но́сик, а *m.* **1.** *dim. of* **нос. 2.** toe (*of a shoe*). **3.** spout.
носи́л|ки, ок *no sg.* **1.** stretcher. **2.** sedan(-chair).
носи́льщик, а *m.* porter.
носи́тел|ь, я *m.* **1.** (*fig.*) bearer; repository. **2.: н. зара́зы** (*biol., med.*) carrier. **3.: н. языка́** native speaker.
но|си́ть, шу́, ~сишь *impf.* **1.** *indet. of* **нести́. 2.** (*indet. only*) to carry; to bear (*also fig.*); **н. свою́ де́ви́чью фами́лию** to use one's maiden name; **н. кого́-н. на рука́х** (*indet. only*) to make a fuss of s.o., dote on s.o. **3.** (*indet. only*) to wear; to carry.
но|си́ться, шу́сь, ~сишься *impf.* **1.** *indet. of* **нести́сь; э́то ~сится в во́здухе** (*fig.*) it is in the air, it is rumoured. **2.** (**с**+*i.*) to make a fuss (of); **н. с мы́слью** to nurse an idea. **3.** (*intr.*) to wear; **э́та мате́рия хорошо́ ~сится** this stuff wears well.
но́ск|а[1], и *f.* **1.** carrying; bearing. **2.** wearing.
но́ск|а[2], и *f.* laying.
но́с|кий[1] (~ок, ~ка) *adj.* (*of clothing, footwear*, etc.) hard-wearing, durable.
но́ск|ий[2] *adj.*: **~ая ку́рица** a good layer.
носов|о́й *adj.* **1.** *adj. of* **нос; н. плато́к** handkerchief. **2.** (*ling.*) nasal.
нос|о́к[1], ка́ *m.* **1.** toe (*of boot, stocking*). **2.** *dim.of* **~**
нос|о́к[2], ка́, *pl.* **~ки́, ~ко́в** *m.* sock.
носоро́г, а *m.* rhinoceros.
носо́|чный *adj. of* **~к[2]**
ностальги́|я, и *f.* homesickness.
но́счик, а *m.* carrier, porter.
но́т|а[1], ы *f.* **1.** (*mus.*) note. **2.** (*pl.*) (sheet) music; **игра́ть по ~ам (без нот)** to play from music (without music); **как по ~ам** (*fig.*) without a hitch, according to plan.
но́т|а[2], ы *f.* (diplomatic) note.
нотариа́льный *adj.* notarial.
нота́риус, а *m.* notary.
нота́ци|я[1], и *f.* (*coll.*) lecture, reprimand; **прочита́ть кому́-н. ~ю** to give s.o. a talking-to.
нота́ци|я[2], и *f.* notation.
но́т|ка, ки *f. dim. of* **~а[1]**
но́тный *adj. of* **но́ты**
но́утбук, а *m.* notebook (computer).
но́у-ха́у *nt. indecl.* know-how.
ноч|ева́ть, у́ю *impf.* (*of* **пере~**) to spend, pass the night.
ночёвк|а, и *f.* spending the night, passing the night.
ночле́г, а *m.* **1.** lodging for the night. **2. = ночёвка**
ночле́жк|а, и *f.* (*coll.*) doss-house.
ночле́жник, а *m.* **1.** (*coll.*) (overnight) visitor, guest. **2.** dosser.
ночле́|жный *adj. of* **~г; н. дом** doss-house.
ночни́к, а́ *m.* night-light.
ночн|о́й *adj.* night; nocturnal; **~а́я ба́бочка** moth; **н. горшо́к** chamber-pot; **~ы́е ту́фли** bedroom slippers.
ноч|ь, и, о ~и, в ~и́, *pl.* **~и, ~е́й** *f.* night; **споко́йной ~и!** good-night!; **по ~а́м** by night, at night.
но́чью *adv.* by night.
но́ш|а, и, *f.* burden.
ноше́ни|е, я *nt.* **1.** carrying. **2.** wearing.
но́щно *adv. only in phr.* **де́нно и н.** (*coll.*) day and night.
но́|ю, ешь *see* **ныть**
но́ющ|ий *pres. part. act. of* **ныть; ~ая боль** ache.
ноя́бр|ь, я́ *m.* November.
ноя́брь|ский *adj. of* **~**
нрав, а *m.* **1.** disposition, temperament; **быть** (+*d.*) **по ~у** to please. **2.** (*pl.*) manners, customs, ways.
нра́в|иться, люсь, ишься *impf.* (*of* **по~**) (+*d.*) to please; **мне, ему́,** *etc.*, **~ится** I like, he likes, *etc.*; **мне о́чень ~ится э́та пье́са** I like this play very much; **мы стара́емся н. вам** we try to please you; (*impers.*): **ей не ~ится ката́ться на ло́дке** she does not like going in boats.
нравоуче́ни|е, я *nt.* moralizing; moral admonition.
нравоучи́тельный *adj.* moralistic; moralizing.
нра́вственност|ь, и *f.* morality; morals.
нра́вствен|ный (~, ~на) *adj.* moral.
н. ст. (*abbr. of* **но́вый стиль**) NS, New Style (*of calendar*).
НТР *f. indecl.* (*abbr. of* **нау́чно-техни́ческая револю́ция**) scientific and technological revolution.
ну *int. and particle* **1.** well!; well … then!; come on!; **ну, ну!** come now! **2. (да) ну!** you don't say so! **3.** *expr. surprise and pleasure or displeasure* well; what; why; **ну и…** what (a) …!; here's … (for you)!; there's … (for you)!; **ну и денёк!** what a day! **4.** *indicating resumption of talk*; *expr. concession, resignation, relief, qualified recognition of point* well; **ну вот** (*in narration*) well, well then; **ну что ж, ну́ так** well then; **ну хорошо́** all right then, very well then. **5.: а ну́** (+*g.*) to hell (with)!; **а ну́ тебя́!** to hell with you!
нуди́зм, а *m.* nudism, naturism.
нуди́ст, а *m.* nudist, naturist.
ну́д|ный (~ен, ~на) *adj.* (*coll.*) tedious, boring.
нужд|а́, ы́, *pl.* **~ы** *f.* **1.** want; poverty. **2.** need; necessity; **в слу́чае ~ы́** if necessary, if need be; **н. всему́ нау́чит** necessity is the mother of invention; **~ы́ нет, нет ~ы́** (*coll.*) no matter!; never mind.
нужда́|ться, юсь *impf.* **1.** to be in need; to be hard-up. **2.** (**в**+*p.*) to need, require; to be in need (of).
ну́жно (+*d.*) **1.** (*impers.*; +*inf. or* +**что́бы**) it is necessary; (one) ought, (one) should, (one) must, (one) need(s); **н. бы́ло (бы) взять такси́** you should have taken a taxi. **2.** (*impers.*, +*a. or g.*; *coll.*) I, *etc.*, need; **мне н. пять рубле́й** I need five roubles. **3.** *see* **ну́жный**
ну́ж|ный (~ен, ~на́, ~но, ~ны́) *adj.* necessary; requisite; (*pred. forms* +*d.*) I, *etc.*, need; **мне нужны́ де́ньги** I need money; **о́чень (мне) ~но!** (*coll., iron.*) a fat lot of good that is!
ну́-ка *int.* now!; now then!; come on!
нул|ево́й *adj. of* **~ь**; (*math.*) zero; **н. вариа́нт** (*pol.*) zero option.
нул|ь, я́ *m.* **1.** nought; zero; nil; cipher; **своди́ться к ~ю** (*fig.*) to come to nought. **2.** (*fig.*) nonentity, nobody.
нумера́тор, а *m.* numerator.
нумера́ци|я, и *f.* numeration; numbering.
нумер|ова́ть, у́ю *impf.* (*of* **за~** *and* **пере~**) to number.
нумизма́т, а *m.* numismatist.
нумизма́тик|а, и *f.* numismatics.
нумизмати́ческий *adj.* numismatic.
ну́нци|й, я *m.* nuncio.
ну́три|я, и *f.* (*zool.*) coypu; (*fur*) nutria.
нутр|о́, а́ *nt.* (*coll.*) **1.** inside, interior. **2.** (*fig.*) core, kernel. **3.** (*fig.*) instinct(s), intuition; **~о́м понима́ть** to understand intuitively; **всем ~о́м** with one's whole being; **э́то мне не по ~у́** it goes against the grain with me.
нутряно́й *adj.* internal.

ны́не *adv.* today.
ны́нешн|ий *adj.* present; present-day; incumbent; **н. президе́нт** the incumbent president; **в ~ие времена́** nowadays.
ны́нче *adv.* (*coll.*) now; nowadays; **не н. за́втра** any day now.
ныр|ну́ть, ну́, нёшь *pf. of* **~я́ть**
ныр|о́к[1], **ка́** *m.* (*coll.*) dive.
ныр|о́к[2], **ка́** *m.* (*zool.*) pochard.
ныря́льщик, а *m.* diver.
ныр|я́ть, я́ю *impf.* (*of* **~ну́ть**) to dive.
ны́тик, а *m.* (*coll.*) (*coll.*) moaner, whinger.
ныть, но́ю, но́ешь *impf.* **1.** to ache. **2.** (*coll., pej.*) to moan, whinge.
нытьё, я́ *nt.* (*coll., pej.*) moaning, whining.
Нью-Йо́рк, а *m.* New York.
Ньюфа́ундле́нд, а *m.* Newfoundland.
н. э. (*abbr. of* **на́шей э́ры**) AD; **до н. э.** (*abbr. of* **до на́шей э́ры**) BC.
НЭП, а *or* **нэп, а** *m.* (*abbr. of* **но́вая экономи́ческая поли́тика**) (*hist.*) NEP (*New Economic Policy*).
нэ́п|овский *adj. of* **~**
нюа́нс, а *m.* nuance.
ню́ни *only in phr.* **распусти́ть н.** (*coll.*) to snivel, whimper.
ню́н|я, и *c.g.* (*coll.*) sniveller, cry-baby.
нюх, а *m.* scent; (*fig.*) flair.
ню́хательный *adj.*: **н. таба́к** snuff.
ню́ха|ть, ю *impf.* (*of* **по~**) to smell (at); **н. таба́к** to take snuff; **не ~л** (*+g.*) to have no experience (of); **по́роха не ~л** (*fig.*) he's still wet behind the ears.
ня́нч|ить, у, ишь *impf.* to nurse.
ня́нч|иться, усь, ишься *impf.* (**с**+*i.*) **1.** to nurse. **2.** (*fig.*) to fuss (over).
ня́ньк|а, и *f.* (*coll.*) = **ня́ня; у семи́ ня́нек дитя́ без гла́зу** (*prov.*) too many cooks spoil the broth.
ня́н|я, и *f.* **1.** (dry-)nurse; **приходя́щая н.** babysitter; child-minder. **2.** (*coll.*) auxiliary (*nurse*).

о[1] **(об, обо)** *prep.* **1.** (*+p.*) of, about, concerning; on; **о чём вы ду́маете?** what are you thinking about?; **ле́кция о Пу́шкине** a lecture on Pushkin. **2.** (*+p.*) with, having; **стол о трёх но́жках** three-legged table; **па́лка о двух конца́х** a two-edged weapon. **3.** (*+a.*) against; on, upon; **опере́ться о сте́ну** to lean against the wall; **споткну́ться о ка́мень** to stumble on a stone; **бок о́ бок** side by side; **рука́ о́б руку** hand in hand.
о[2] *int.* oh!
о. (*abbr. of* **о́стров**) I., Island, Isle.
о... (*also* **об..., обо...** *and* **объ...**) *vbl. pref. indicating*: **1.** transformation; process of becoming sth. **2.** action applied to entire surface of object *or* to series of objects.
оа́зис, а *m.* oasis (*also fig.*).
об *prep. see* **о**[1]
об... (*also* **обо...** *and* **объ...**) *vbl. pref.* **1.** = **о... . 2.** indicating action *or* motion about an object.
о́ба, обо́их *m. and nt.*; **о́бе, обе́их** *f. num.* both; **гляде́ть в о., смотре́ть в о.** (*coll.*) to be on one's guard; **обе́ими рука́ми** with both hands (*fig., coll.*); very willingly, readily.
обагр|и́ть, ю́, и́шь *pf.* (*of* **~я́ть**) to crimson; **о. кро́вью** to stain with blood; **о. ру́ки в крови́ (кро́вью)** to steep one's hands in blood.
обагр|я́ть(ся), я́ю(сь) *impf. of* **~и́ть(ся)**
обалдева́|ть, ю *impf. of* **обалде́ть**
обалде́лый *adj.* (*coll.*) crazed; stunned.
обалде́|ть, ю *pf.* (*of* **~ва́ть**) (*coll.*) to become dulled, become crazed; to be stunned (*by surprise, etc.*).
обанкро́|титься, чусь, тишься *pf. of* **банкро́титься**
обая́ни|е, я *nt.* fascination, charm.
обая́тел|ьный (~ен, ~на) *adj.* fascinating, charming.
обва́л, а *m.* **1.** collapse; cave-in. **2.** landslide; avalanche.
обва́лива|ть[1]**(ся), ю(сь)** *impf. of* **обвали́ть(ся)**
обва́лива|ть[2], **ю** *impf. of* **обваля́ть**
обвал|и́ть, ю́, ~ишь *pf.* (*of* **~ивать**[1]) to cause to fall, cause to collapse; to crumble (*trans.*).
обвал|и́ться, ю́сь, ~ишься *pf.* (*of* **~иваться**) to fall, collapse, cave in; to crumble.
обвал|я́ть, я́ю *pf.* (*of* **~ивать**[2]) (*+a.*, **в**+*p.*) to roll (in).
обва́рива|ть(ся), ю(сь) *impf. of* **обвари́ть(ся)**
обвар|и́ть, ю́, ~ишь *pf.* (*of* **~ивать**) **1.** to pour boiling water over. **2.** to scald.
обвар|и́ться, ю́сь, ~ишься *pf.* (*of* **~иваться**) **1.** to scald o.s. **2.** *pass. of* **~и́ть**
обвева́|ть, ю *impf. of* **обве́ять**
обве|ду́, дёшь *see* **~сти́**
обвенча́|ть(ся), ю(сь) *pf. of* **венча́ть(ся)**[1]
обверн|у́ть, у́, ёшь *pf.* (*of* **обвёртывать**) (*+i.*) to wrap up (in).
обвер|те́ть, чу́, ~тишь *pf.* (*of* **~тывать**) (*+i.*) to wrap up (in); **о. ше́ю ша́рфом** to wrap a scarf about one's neck.
обвёртыва|ть, ю *impf. of* **оберну́ть** *and* **оберте́ть**
обве́|сить, шу, сишь *pf.* (*of* **~шивать**[1]) to give short weight to; to cheat (*in weighing goods*).
обве|сти́, ду́, дёшь, *past* **~л, ~ла́** *pf.* (*of* **обводи́ть**) **1.** to lead, take round; **о. вокру́г па́льца** (*fig., coll.*) to twist round one's little finger. **2.** (*+i.*) to encircle (with); to surround (with); **о. взо́ром, глаза́ми** to look round (at), take in. **3.** to outline; **о. чертёж ту́шью** to outline a sketch in ink. **4.** (*sport*) to dodge; to get past.
обве́тр|енный *p.p.p. of* **~ить** *and adj.* weather-beaten; chapped.
обвре́трива|ть(ся), ю(сь) *impf. of* **обве́трить(ся)**
обве́тр|ить, ю, ишь *pf.* (*of* **~ивать**) to expose to the wind; (*impers.*): **мне ~ило гу́бы** my lips are chapped.
обве́тр|иться, юсь, ишься *pf.* (*of* **~иваться**) to become weather-beaten.
обветша́лый *adj.* decrepit, decayed; dilapidated.
обветша́|ть, ю *pf. of* **ветша́ть**
обве́ш|ать, аю *pf.* (*of* **~ивать**[2]) (*coll.*; *+i.*) to hang round (with), cover (with).
обве́шива|ть[1], **ю** *impf. of* **обве́сить**
обве́шива|ть[2], **ю** *impf. of* **обве́шать**
обве́|ять, ю, ешь *pf.* (*of* **~ва́ть**) **1.** (*+i.*) to fan (with). **2.** (*agric.*) to winnow.
обвива́|ть(ся), ю(сь) *impf. of* **обви́ть(ся)**
обвине́ни|е, я *nt.* **1.** charge, accusation; **возвести́ на кого́-н. о.** (**в**+*p.*) to charge s.o. (with); **вы́нести о.** to find guilty. **2.** (*leg.*) the prosecution.
обвини́тел|ь, я *m.* accuser; (*leg.*) prosecutor; **госуда́рственный о.** public prosecutor.
обвини́тельн|ый *adj.* accusatory; **о. акт** (bill of) indictment; **о. пригово́р** verdict of 'guilty'.
обвин|и́ть, ю́, и́шь *pf.* (*of* **~я́ть**) **1.** (**в**+*p.*) to accuse (of), charge (with). **2.** (*leg.*) to prosecute, indict.

обвиня́ем|ый, ого *m.* (*leg.*) the accused; defendant.
обвин|я́ть, я́ю *impf. of* **~и́ть**
обвис|а́ть, а́ет *impf.* (*of* **~́нуть**) to hang, droop; to sag.
обви́сл|ый *adj.* (*coll.*) flabby; hanging; **~ые усы́** drooping moustache.
обви́с|нуть, нет, *past* **~, ~ла** *pf. of* **~а́ть**
обви́|ть, обовью́, обовьёшь, *past* **~л, ~ла́ ~ло** *pf.* (*of* **~ва́ть**) to wind around, entwine.
обви́|ться, обовью́сь, обовьёшься, *past* **~лся, ~ла́сь** *pf.* (*of* **~ва́ться**) to wind (around), twine (around).
об-во (*abbr. of* **о́бщество**) Soc., Society.
обво|ди́ть, жу́, ~́дишь *impf. of* **обвести́**
обводне́ни|е, я *nt.* irrigation.
обводн|и́ть, ю́, и́шь *pf.* (*of* **~я́ть**) to irrigate.
обводн|я́ть, я́ю *impf. of* **~и́ть**
обвола́кива|ть(ся), ю(сь) *impf. of* **обволо́чь(ся)**
обволо́|чь, ку́, чёшь, ку́т, *past* **~к, ~кла́** *pf.* (*of* **обвола́кивать**) to cover; to envelop (*also fig.*).
обволо́|чься, ку́сь, чёшься, ку́тся, *past* **~кся, ~кла́сь** *pf.* (*of* **обвола́киваться**) (*+i.*; *coll.*) to become covered (with), enveloped (by, in).
обвора́жива|ть, ю *impf. of* **обворожи́ть**
обвор|ова́ть, у́ю *pf.* (*of* **~о́вывать**) (*coll.*) to rob.
обворо́выва|ть, ю *impf. of* **обворова́ть**
обворожи́тел|ьный (~ен, ~ьна) *adj.* fascinating, charming, enchanting.
обворож|и́ть, у́, и́шь *pf.* (*of* **обвора́живать**) to fascinate, charm, enchant.
обвя|за́ть[1]**, жу́, ~́жешь** *pf.* (*of* **~́зывать**) to tie round; **о. го́лову платко́м** to tie a scarf round one's head.
обвя|за́ть[2]**, жу́, ~́жешь** *pf.* (*of* **~́зывать**) to edge in chain-stitch.
обвя|за́ться, жу́сь, ~́зешься *pf.* (*of* **~́зываться**) **1.** (*+i.*) to tie round o.s.; **о. верёвкой** to tie a rope round o.s. **2.** *pass. of* **~за́ть**
обвя́зыва|ть(ся), ю(сь) *impf. of* **обвяза́ть(ся)**
обго́н, а *m.* passing.
обгон|ю́, ~́ишь *see* **обогна́ть**
обгоня́|ть, ю *impf. of* **обогна́ть**
обгор|а́ть, а́ю *impf. of* **~е́ть**
обгоре́лый *adj.* charred; scorched; sunburnt.
обгор|е́ть, ю́, и́шь *pf.* to be scorched; to get sunburnt.
обгрыз|а́ть, а́ю *impf. of* **~́ть**
обгры́з|ть, у́, ёшь, *past* **~, ~ла** *pf.* (*of* **~а́ть**) to gnaw round.
обда|ва́ть(ся), ю́(сь), ёшь(ся) *impf. of* **обда́ть(ся)**
обд|а́ть, а́м, а́шь, а́ст, ади́м, ади́те, аду́т, *past* **~́ал, ~ала́, ~́ало** *pf.* (*of* **~ава́ть**) (*+i.*) **1.** to pour over; **о. кого́-н. кипятко́м** to pour boiling water over s.o. **2.** (*impers.*): **меня́ ~́ало хо́лодом** I came over cold.
обд|а́ться, а́мся, а́шься, а́стся, ади́мся, ади́тесь, аду́тся, *past* **~а́лся, ~ала́сь** *pf.* (*of* **~ава́ться**) (*+i.*) to pour over o.s.; **о. кипятко́м** to scald o.s.
обде́л|ать, аю *pf.* (*of* **~ывать**) **1.** to finish; to dress (*leather, stone, etc.*); **о. драгоце́нные ка́мни** to set precious stones. **2.** (*fig.*) to manage, arrange; **о. те́му** (*coll.*) to treat, handle a subject.
обдел|и́ть, ю́, ~́ишь *pf.* (*of* **~я́ть**) (*+a. and i.*) to do out of one's share (of); **он ~и́л сестёр насле́дством** he did his sisters out of their share of the legacy.
обде́лыва|ть, ю *impf. of* **обде́лать**
обдел|я́ть, я́ю *impf. of* **~и́ть**
обдер|у́, ёшь *see* **ободра́ть**
обдира́л|а, ы *m.* (*coll.*) fleecer.
обдира́|ть, ю *impf. of* **ободра́ть**
обдува́л|а, ы *m.* (*coll.*) cheat, trickster.
обдува́|ть, ю *impf. of* **обду́ть**
обду́манност|ь, и *f.* deliberation; deliberateness; careful planning.
обду́ман|ный 1. (~, ~а) *p.p.p. of* **обду́мать. 2. (~, ~на)** *adj.* well-considered, well-weighed, carefully thought out; **с зара́нее ~ным наме́рением** deliberately; (*leg.*) of malice prepense.
обду́м|ать, аю *pf.* (*of* **~ывать**) to consider, think over, weigh.
обду́мыва|ть, ю *impf. of* **обду́мать**
обду́|ть[1]**, ю, ешь** *pf.* (*of* **~ва́ть**) to blow (on, round).
обду́|ть[2]**, ю, ешь** *pf.* (*of* **~ва́ть**) (*coll.*) to cheat; to fool, dupe.
о́бе *see* **о́ба**
обе́га|ть, ю *pf.* (*of* **обега́ть**) **1.** to run (all over, all round). **2.** to run round (to see); **нам удало́сь о. всех знако́мых** we managed to look in on all our acquaintances.
обега́|ть, ю *impf. of* **обе́гать** *and* **обежа́ть**
обе́д, а *m.* **1.** dinner; **зва́ный о.** dinner-party. **2.** dinner-time (= *midday*); **пе́ред ~ом** before dinner.
обе́да|ть, ю *impf.* (*of* **по~**) to have dinner, dine.
обе́д|енный[1] *adj. of* **~**; **~енное вре́мя** dinner time; **о. переры́в** lunch hour, lunch break.
обе́д|енный[2] *adj. of* **~ня**
обедне́|вший *p.p. act. of* **~ть** *and adj.* impoverished.
обедне́|лый *adj.* (*coll.*) = **~вший**
обедне́ни|е, я *nt.* impoverishment.
обедне́|ть, ю *pf. of* **бедне́ть**
обедн|и́ть, ю́, и́шь *pf.* (*of* **~я́ть**) to impoverish.
обе́д|ня, ни, *g. pl.* **~ен** *f.* (*eccl.*) mass.
обедн|я́ть, я́ю *impf. of* **~и́ть**
обе|жа́ть, гу́, жи́шь, гу́т *pf.* (*of* **~га́ть**) **1.** to run (over, round). **2.** to run (past). **3.** (*sport*) to outrun, pass.
обезбо́ливани|е, я *nt.* anaesthetization.
обезбо́лива|ть, ю *impf. of* **обезбо́лить**
обезбо́лива|ющий *pres. part. act. of* **~ть; ~ющее сре́дство** anaesthetic.
обезбо́л|ить, ю, ишь *pf.* (*of* **~ивать**) to anaesthetize.
обезво́|дить, жу, дишь *pf.* (*of* **~живать**) to dehydrate.
обезво́|женный *p.p.p. of* **~дить** *and adj.* dehydrated.
обезво́жива|ть, ю *impf. of* **обезво́дить**
обезвре́|дить, жу, дишь *pf.* (*of* **~живать**) to neutralize; to defuse; to deactivate.
обезвре́жива|ть, ю *impf. of* **обезвре́дить**
обезгла́в|ить, лю, ишь *pf.* (*of* **~ливать**) to behead, decapitate.
обезгла́влива|ть, ю *impf. of* **обезгла́вить**
обезде́неже|ть, ю *pf.* (*coll.*) to run short of money.
обездо́л|енный *p.p.p. of* **~ить** *and adj.* unfortunate, hapless.
обездо́лива|ть, ю *impf. of* **обездо́лить**
обездо́л|ить, ю, ишь *pf.* (*of* **~ивать**) to deprive of one's share.
обезжи́р|енный *p.p.p. of* **~ить** *and adj.* fat-free; skimmed.
обезжи́рива|ть, ю *impf. of* **обезжи́рить**
обезжи́р|ить, ю, ишь *pf.* (*of* **~ивать**) to remove fat (from); to skim.
обеззара́жива|ть, ю *impf. of* **обеззара́зить**
обеззара́жива|ющий *p.p.p of* **~ть** *and adj.* disinfectant.
обеззара́|зить, жу, зишь *pf.* (*of* **~живать**) to disinfect.
обезземе́л|енный *p.p.p. of* **~ить** *and adj.* landless.
обезземе́лива|ть, ю *impf. of* **обезземе́лить**
обезземе́л|ить, ю, ишь *pf.* (*of* **~ивать**) to dispossess of land.
обезле́сени|е, я *nt.* deforestation.
обезле́си|ть, шь *pf.* to deforest.

обезли́чени|е, я *nt.* **1.** depersonalization. **2.** depriving of personal responsibility.
обезли́чива|ть, ю *impf. of* **обезли́чить**
обезли́ч|ить, у, ишь *pf.* (*of* **~ивать**) **1.** to depersonalize. **2.** to deprive of personal responsibility.
обезлю́де|ть, ю *pf.* to become depopulated.
обезобра́жива|ть, ю *impf. of* **обезобра́зить**
обезобра́|зить, жу, зишь *pf.* (*of* **~живать** *and* **безобра́зить**) to disfigure.
обезопа́|сить, шу, сишь *pf.* **(от)** to secure (against).
обезору́жива|ть, ю *impf. of* **обезору́жить**
обезору́ж|ить, у, ишь *pf.* (*of* **~ивать**) to disarm (*also fig.*).
обезу́ме|ть, ю *pf.* to lose one's senses, lose one's head; **о. от испу́га** to become panic-stricken.
обезья́н|а, ы *f.* monkey; ape.
обезья́н|ий *adj. of* **~а**; (*zool.*) simian; (*fig.*) ape-like.
обезья́нник, а *m.* monkey-house.
обезья́ннича|ть, ю *impf.* (*of* **с~**) (*coll.*) to ape.
обел|и́ть, ю́, и́шь *pf.* (*of* **~я́ть**) (*fig.*) to whitewash; to vindicate; to prove the innocence (of).
обел|я́ть(ся), я́ю(сь) *impf. of* **~и́ть(ся)**
оберега́|ть(ся), ю(сь) *impf. of* **оберéчь(ся)**
оберé|чь, гу́, жёшь, гу́т, *past* **~г, ~гла́** *pf.* (*of* **~га́ть**) **(от)** to guard (against), protect (from).
оберé|чься, гу́сь, жёшься, гу́тся, *past* **~гся, ~гла́сь** *pf.* (*of* **~га́ться**) **1. (от)** to guard o.s. (from, against), protect o.s. (from) **2.** *pass. of* **~чь**
оберн|у́ть, у́, ёшь *pf.* (*of* **обора́чивать**) **1.** (*impf. also* **обёртывать**) to wind (round), twist (round); **о. вокру́г па́льца** (*coll.*) to twist round one's little finger. **2.** (*impf. also* **обёртывать**) to wrap up. **3.** (*impf. also* **обёртывать**) to turn; **о. лицо́ (к)** to turn one's face (towards). **4.** (*coll.*) to overturn, upturn. **5.** (*comm.*) to turn over. **6.** (*coll.*) to work through, go through.
оберн|у́ться, у́сь, ёшься *pf.* (*of* **обора́чиваться**) **1.** (*impf. also* **обёртываться**) to turn; **о. лицо́м** to turn one's head. **2.** (*impf. also* **обёртываться**) to turn out. **3.** (*coll.*) to (go and) come back; **я ~у́сь за два часа́** I shall be back in two hours. **4.** (*coll.*) to manage, get by. **5.** (*impf. also* **обёртываться**) (+*i. or* **в**+*a.*) to turn into, become (*also fig.*); **о. вампи́ром** to turn into a vampire.
обёртк|а, и *f.* wrapper; envelope.
оберто́н, а *m.* (*mus.*) overtone.
обёрт|очный *adj. of* **~ка**; **~очная бума́га** wrapping paper.
обёртыва|ть(ся), ю(сь) *impf. of* **оберну́ть(ся)**
обескро́в|ить, лю, ишь *pf.* (*of* **~ливать**) to drain of blood; to bleed white; (*fig.*) to render lifeless.
обескро́влива|ть, ю *impf. of* **обескро́вить**
обескура́жива|ть, ю *impf. of* **обескура́жить**
обескура́ж|ить, у, ишь *pf.* (*coll.*) to discourage, dishearten; to dismay.
обеспа́мяте|ть, ю *pf.* **1.** to lose one's memory. **2.** to lose consciousnesst.
обеспéчени|е, я *nt.* **1.** securing, guaranteeing; ensuring. **2.** (+*i.*) providing (with), provision (of, with). **3.** guarantee; security (= *pledge*). **4.** security (= *material maintenance*); safeguard(s); **социа́льное о.** social security. **5.** (*mil.*) security; protection. **6.: програ́ммное о.** (*comput.*) software.
обеспéченност|ь, и *f.* **1.** (+*i.*) being provided (with), provision (of, with); **о. школ учéбниками** the provision of schools with text-books. **2.** (*material*) security.
обеспéч|енный *p.p.p. of* **~ить** *and adj.* well-to-do.
обеспéчива|ть, ю *impf. of* **обеспéчить**
обеспéч|ить, у, ишь *pf.* (*of* **~ивать**) **1.** to provide for. **2.** (+*i.*) to provide (with); **о. экспеди́цию обору́дованием** to provide an expedition with equipment. **3.** to secure, guarantee; to ensure, assure.
обеспоко́|ить(ся), ю(сь) *pf. of* **беспоко́ить(ся) 1.**
обесси́ле|ть, ю *pf.* to grow weak, lose one's strength.
обесси́лива|ть, *impf. of* **обесси́лить**
обесси́л|ить, ю, ишь *pf.* (*of* **~ивать**) to weaken.
обесслáв|ить, лю, ишь *pf.* (*of* **бесслáвить**) to defame.
обессмéр|тить, чу, тишь *pf.* to immortalize.
обесцвé|тить, чу, тишь *pf.* (*of* **~чивать**) to discolour; to decolo(u)rize; (*fig.*) to tone down.
обесцвé|титься, чусь, тишься *pf.* (*of* **~чиваться**) to discolour; to become colourless (*also fig.*).
обесцвéчива|ть(ся), ю(сь) *impf. of* **обесцвéтить(ся)**
обесцéнени|е, я *nt.* depreciation.
обесцéн|енный *p.p.p. of* **~ить** *and adj.* depreciated.
обесцéнива|ть(ся), ю(сь) *impf. of* **обесцéнить(ся)**
обесцéн|ить, ю, ишь *pf.* (*of* **~ивать**) to depreciate, cheapen.
обесцéн|иться, юсь, ишься *pf.* (*of* **~иваться**) **1.** (*intrans.*) to depreciate. **2.** *pass. of* **~ить**
обесчé|стить, щу, стишь *pf. of* **бесчéстить**
обéт, а *m.* (*rhet.*) vow, promise.
обетова́нн|ый *adj.*: **~ая земля́, о. край** the Promised Land.
обеща́ни|е, я *nt.* promise; **дать, сдержа́ть о.** to give, keep a promise (*or* one's word).
обеща́|ть, ю *impf. and pf.* to promise.
обжа́ловани|е, я *nt.* (*leg.*) appeal.
обжа́л|овать, ую *pf.* (*leg.*) to appeal (against).
обжа́рива|ть, ю *impf. of* **обжа́рить**
обжа́р|ить, ю, ишь *pf.* (*of* **~ивать**) (*cul.*) to fry on both sides, all over.
обжéчь, обожгу́, обожжёшь, обожгу́т, *past* **обжёг, обожгла́** *pf.* (*of* **обжига́ть**) **1.** to burn; to scorch; **о. себé па́льцы** to burn one's fingers (*also fig.*). **2.** to bake (*bricks, etc.*).
обжéчься, обожгу́сь, обожжёшься, обожгу́тся, *past.* **обжёгся, обожгла́сь** *pf.* **1.** (+*i. or* **на**+*p.*) to burn o.s. (on, with); **о. горя́чим ча́ем** to scald o.s. with hot tea. **2.** (*fig., coll.*) to burn one's fingers.
обжива́|ть(ся), ю(сь) *impf. of* **обжи́ть(ся)**
обжига́|ть(ся), ю(сь) *impf. of* **обжéчь(ся)**
обжира́|ться, юсь *impf. of* **обожра́ться**
обжит|о́й (*and* **~ый)** *p.p.p. of* **~ь**
обж|и́ть, иву́, ивёшь, *past* **~ил, ~ила́, ~ило** *pf.* (*of* **~ива́ть**) (*coll.*) to render habitable.
обж|и́ться, иву́сь, ивёшься, *past* **~ился́, ~ила́сь** *pf.* (*of* **~ива́ться**) (*coll.*) to make o.s. at home, feel at home.
обжо́р|а, ы *c.g.* (*coll.*) glutton.
обжо́рлив|ый (~, ~а) *adj.* gluttonous.
обжо́рств|о, а *nt.* gluttony.
обжу́лива|ть, ю *impf. of* **обжу́лить**
обжу́л|ить, ю, ишь *pf.* (*coll.*) to cheat, swindle.
обзаве|сти́сь, ду́сь, дёшься, *past* **~лся, ~ла́сь** *pf.* (*of* **обзаводи́ться**) (+*i.*; *coll.*) to acquire; to get o.s.; to set up; **о. семьёй** to start a family; **о. хозя́йством** to set up home.
обзаво|ди́ться, жу́сь, ~дишься *impf. of* **обзавести́сь**
обзо́р, а *m.* **1.** survey, review. **2.** (*mil.*) field of view.
обзо́р|ный *adj. of* **~**; **~ная лéкция, ~ная статья́** survey.
обзыва́|ть, ю *impf. of* **обозва́ть**
обива́|ть, ю *impf. of* **оби́ть; о. (все) поро́ги** (*fig.*) to leave no stone unturned.
оби́вк|а, и *f.* **1.** upholstering. **2.** upholstery.
оби́д|а, ы *f.* **1.** offence, injury, insult; (sense of) grievance, resentment; **быть на кого́-н. в оби́де** to bear a grudge against s.o.; **затаи́ть ~у** to nurse a grievance; **не дава́ть себя́ в ~у** to stick up for o.s.; **не в ~у будь ска́зано** no offence meant. **2.** (*coll.*) annoying thing, nuisance; **кака́я о.!** what a nuisance!

оби|деть, жу, дишь *pf.* (*of* **~жа́ть**) **1.** to offend; to hurt (the feelings of), wound. **2.** to hurt; to do damage (to); **му́хи не ~дит** (*fig.*) he would not harm a fly. **3.** (*+i.*; *following* **Бог, приро́да** *etc.*) to stint; **приро́да не ~дела его́ тала́нтом** he has plenty of natural ability.

оби|деться, жусь, дишься *pf.* (*of* **~жа́ться**) (**на** *+a.*) to take offence (at); to feel hurt (by), resent.

оби́д|ный (~ен, ~на) *adj.* **1.** offensive; **мне ~но** I feel hurt; I am offended. **2.** (*coll.*) annoying; **~но** (*impers.*) it is a pity, it is a nuisance; **~но, что мы опозда́ли** it is a pity that we were late.

оби́дчивост|ь, и *f.* touchiness; sensitivity.

оби́дчив|ый (~, ~а) *adj.* touchy; sensitive.

оби́дчик, а *m.* (*coll.*) offender.

обижа́|ть, ю *impf. of* **оби́деть**

обижа́|ться, юсь *impf. of* **оби́деться; не ~йтесь** don't be offended.

оби|женный *p.p.p of* **~деть** *and adj.* offended, hurt, aggrieved; **быть ~жен (на**+*a.*) to have a grudge (against); **у него́ был о. вид** he had an aggrieved air; **о. Бо́гом, о. приро́дой** (*joc.*) not over-blessed (with talents); ill-starred.

оби́ли|е, я *nt.* abundance, plentyt.

оби́л|ьный (~ен, ~ьна) *adj.* abundant, plentiful; (*+i.*) rich (in); **о. урожа́й** bumper crop.

обиня́к, а́ *m. only in phrr.* **говори́ть ~о́м, ~а́ми** to beat about the bush; **говори́ть без ~о́в** to speak plainly; to be direct.

обира́л|а, ы *c.g.* (*coll.*) extortionist.

обира́|ть, ю *impf. of* **обобра́ть**

обита́ем|ый (~, ~а) *adj.* inhabited; **~ая косми́ческая ста́нция** manned space station.

обита́тел|ь, я *m.* inhabitant; denizen.

обита́|ть, ю *impf.* (**в**+*p.*) to live (in), inhabit.

оби́|ть, обобью́, обобьёшь *pf.* (*of* **~ва́ть**) **1.** (**с**+*g.*) to knock (off, down from). **2.** (*+i.*) to upholster (with), cover (with). **3.** to wear out (*the surface of, at the edges*); **о. подо́л ю́бки** to wear the hem of a skirt.

обихо́д, а *m.* **1.** everyday life. **2.** use; **предме́ты дома́шнего ~а** household articles; **войти́ в о.** to come into use; **вы́йти из ~а** to go out of use.

обихо́д|ный (~ен, ~на) *adj.* everyday; **~ное выраже́ние** colloquial expression.

обка́п|ать, аю *pf.* (*of* **~ывать**[1]) (*+i.*) to let drops (of) fall on; to cover with drops (of).

обка́пыва|ть[1]**, ю** *impf. of* **обка́пать**

обка́пыва|ть[2]**, ю** *impf. of* **обкопа́ть**

обка́рмлива|ть, ю *impf. of* **обкорми́ть**

обкат|а́ть, а́ю *pf.* (*of* **~́ывать**) **1.** to roll. **2.** to roll smooth (*a road surface, etc.*). **3.** (*tech.*) to run in (*a new vehicle, etc.*).

обка́тк|а, и *f.* (*tech.*) running in.

обка́тыва|ть, ю *impf. of* **обката́ть**

обкла́дк|а, и *f.* facing; **о. дёрном** turfing.

обкла́дыва|ть, *impf. of* **обложи́ть**

обко́м, а *m.* (*abbr. of* ***областно́й комите́т***) oblast committee; regional committee.

обкопа́|ть, ю *pf.* (*of* **обка́пывать**[2]) (*coll.*) to dig round.

обкорм|и́ть, лю́, ~́ишь *pf.* (*of* **обка́рмливать**) to overfeed.

обкра́дыва|ть, ю *impf. of* **обокра́сть**

обку́р|енный *p.p.p. of* **~ить** *and adj.*; **~енные па́льцы** tobacco-stained fingers.

обку́рива|ть, ю *impf. of* **обкури́ть**

обкур|и́ть, ю́, ~́ишь *pf.* (*of* **~́ивать**) (*coll.*) to fill with (tobacco) smoke; to stain with tobacco.

обкус|а́ть, а́ю *pf.* (*of* **~́ывать**) to bite round; to nibble.

обку́сыва|ть, ю *impf. of* **обкуса́ть**

обл. *abbr. of* **1. о́бласть** oblast. **2. областно́й** dial., dialectal.

обл... *comb. form, abbr. of* **областно́й 1.**

обла́в|а, ы *f.* **1.** (*hunting*) battue; beating up. **2.** (*fig.*) (*police*) raid, swoop; round-up.

облага́|ть, ю *impf. of* **обложи́ть**

облага́|ться, юсь *impf.* (*of* **обложи́ться**): **о. нало́гом** to be liable to tax, be taxable.

облагоде́тельств|овать, ую *pf.* (*iron.*) to do a great favour.

облагора́жива|ть, ю *impf. of* **облагоро́дить**

облагоро́|дить, жу, дишь *pf.* (*of* **облагора́живать**) to ennoble.

облада́ни|е, я *nt.* possession.

облада́тел|ь, я *m.* possessor.

облада́|ть, ю *impf.* (*+i.*) to possess, have; **о. хоро́шим здоро́вьем** to enjoy good health; **о. пра́вом** to have the right.

обла́|зить, жу, зишь *pf.* (*coll.*) to climb all over; to travel all round.

о́блак|о, а, *pl.* **~а́, ~о́в** *nt.* cloud; **быть, носи́ться в ~а́х** (*fig.*) to have one's head in the clouds; **свали́ться с ~о́в** (*fig.*) to turn up out of the blue.

обла́мыва|ть(ся), ю(сь) *impf. of* **облома́ть(ся)**

облапо́шива|ть, ю *impf. of* **облапо́шить**

облапо́ш|ить, у, ишь *pf.* (*of* **~ивать**) (*coll.*) to cheat, swindle.

обласка́|ть, ю *pf.* to be kind to.

областно́й *adj.* **1.** oblast; provincial; regional. **2.** (*ling.*) dialectal; regional.

о́бласт|ь, и, *g. pl.* **~е́й** *f.* **1.** (*administrative division of former USSR*) oblast; province. **2.** region, district; belt; **о. вечнозелёных расте́ний** evergreen belt; **озёрная о.** lake district; (*in Germany*) -land; **Ре́йнская о.** the Rhineland. **3.** (*fig.*) field, sphere, realm, domain; **о. микробиоло́гии** the field of microbiology; **о. мифоло́гии** the realm of mythology.

обла́тк|а, и *f.* **1.** (*eccl.*) wafer, host. **2.** (*pharm.*) capsule.

облач|а́ть(ся), а́ю(сь) *impf. of* **~и́ть(ся)**

облаче́ни|е, я *nt.* **1.** (**в**+*a.*) robing (in). **2.** (*eccl.*) vestments, robes.

облач|и́ть, у́, и́шь *pf.* (*of* **~а́ть**) (**в**+*a.*) **1.** (*eccl.*) to robe (in). **2.** (*rhet. or coll., joc.*) to deck out (in).

облач|и́ться, у́сь, и́шься *pf.* (*of* **~а́ться**) **1.** (*eccl.*) to robe. **2.** (*rhet. or coll., joc.*) to deck o.s. out.

о́блачк|о, а, *pl.* **~а́, ~о́в** *nt. dim. of* **о́блако**

о́блачност|ь, и *f.* cloudiness.

о́блач|ный (~ен, ~на) *adj.* cloudy.

облега́|ть, ю *impf.* **1.** *impf. of* **обле́чь**[1]. **2.** (*of clothes*) to fit tightly; to cling to.

облега́|ющий *pres. part. act. of* **~ть** *and adj.* tight-fitting.

облегч|а́ть(ся), а́ю(сь) *impf. of* **~и́ть(ся)**

облегче́ни|е, я *nt.* **1.** facilitation. **2.** relief; **вздохну́ть с ~ем** to heave a sigh of relief.

облегч|и́ть, у́, и́шь *pf.* (*of* **~а́ть**) **1.** to facilitate. **2.** to lighten. **3.** to relieve; to alleviate; to mitigate; (*leg.*) to commute; **о. ду́шу** to ease one's mind.

облегч|и́ться, у́сь, и́шься *pf.* (*of* **~а́ться**) **1.** to be relieved. **2.** to become easier; to become lighter. **3.** (*coll., euph.*) to relieve o.s.

обледене́лый *adj.* ice-covered.

обледене́ни|е, я *nt.* icing(-over); **пери́од ~я** Ice Age.

обледене́|ть, ю *pf.* to ice over, become covered with ice.

облез|а́ть, а́ет *impf. of* **~́ть**

обле́зл|ый *adj.* (*coll.*) shabby, bare; **~ая ко́шка** mangy cat.

обле́з|ть, ет, *past* **~, ~ла** *pf.* (*of* **~а́ть**) (*coll.*) **1.** (*of fur, etc.*) to come out, come off. **2.** to grow bare (*of fur, feathers, etc.*); to grow mangy. **3.** (*of paintwork, etc.*) to peel off.

облека́|ть(ся), ю(сь) *impf. of* **обле́чь²(ся)**
обле́нива|ться, юсь *impf. of* **обленИ́ться**
облен|И́ться, ю́сь, ∸ишься *pf.* (*of* **∸иваться**) to grow lazy.
облеп|И́ть, лю́, ∸ишь *pf.* (*of* **~ля́ть**) **1.** to stick (to); (*fig.*) to cling (to); to surround, throng; **нас ~и́ла ку́ча мальчи́шек** we were surrounded by a swarm of small boys. **2.** (+*a. and i.*) to cover (with), plaster (with); **о. сте́ну объявле́ниями** to plaster a wall with notices.
облепля́|ть, ю *impf. of* **облепи́ть**
облет|а́ть¹, а́ю *impf. of* **~е́ть**
облет|а́ть², а́ю *pf.* (*of* **∸ывать**) **1.** to fly (all round, all over); **мы ~а́ли всю Евро́пу** we have flown all over Europe. **2.** to test(-fly) (*an aircraft*).
обле|те́ть, чу́, ти́шь *pf.* (*of* **~та́ть¹**) **1.** (+*a. or* **вокру́г**) to fly (round). **2.** (*of news, rumours, etc.*) to spread (round, all over); **за полчаса́ весть о побе́де ~те́ла го́род** in half an hour the news of the victory had spread round the town. **3.** (*of leaves*) to fall.
облётыва|ть, ю *impf. of* **облета́ть²**
облеч|ённый *p.p.p. of* **∸ь²** *and adj.*: **о. вла́стью** invested with power.
обл|е́чь¹, я́гу, я́жешь, я́гут, *past* **~ёг, ~егла́** *pf.* (*of* **~ега́ть**) to cover, surround, envelop (*also fig.*); **ту́чи ~егли́ го́ру** rain-clouds enveloped the mountain.
обле́|чь², ку́, чёшь, ку́т, *past* **∸к, ~кла́** *pf.* (*of* **~ка́ть**) (+*a.* **в**+*a. or* +*a. and i.*) to invest (with), vest (in); (*fig.*) to shroud (in); **о. полномо́чиями** to invest with authority; **о. та́йной** to shroud in mystery; **о. свою́ мысль непоня́тными слова́ми** to wrap one's idea in unintelligible words; **о. кого́-н. дове́рием** to express confidence in s.o.
обле́|чься, ку́сь, чёшься, ку́тся, *past* **∸кся, ~кла́сь** *pf.* (*of* **~ка́ться**) (**в**+*a.*) to clothe o.s. (in), dress o.s. (in); (*fig.*) to take the form (of), assume the shape (of).
облива́ни|е, я *nt.* **1.** spilling (over), pouring (over). **2.** shower-bath; sponge-down.
облива́|ть, ю *impf. of* **обли́ть**
облива́|ться, юсь *impf. of* **обли́ться; се́рдце у меня́ кро́вью ~ется** my heart bleeds.
облигац|ио́нный *adj. of* **∸ия**
облига́ци|я, и *f.* (*fin.*) bond, debenture.
обли|за́ть, жу́, ∸жешь *pf.* (*of* **∸зывать**) to lick (all over); to lick clean; **па́льчики ∸жешь** (*fig., coll.*) (*sc.* it is, it will be) a real treat.
обли|за́ться, жу́сь, ∸жешься *pf.* (*of* **∸зываться**) **1.** to smack one's lips (*also fig.*). **2.** (*of an animal*) to lick itself.
обли́зыва|ть, ю *impf. of* **облиза́ть; о. гу́бы** (*fig., coll.*) to smack one's lips.
обли́зыва|ться, юсь *impf. of* **облиза́ться**
о́блик, а *m.* **1.** look, aspect, appearance. **2.** (*fig.*) cast of mind, temper.
облиня́|ть, ю *pf.* (*coll.*) **1.** to fade (*also fig.*). **2.** to moult, lose hair *or* feathers.
облиспълко́м, а *m.* (*abbr. of* ***областно́й исполни́тельный комите́т***) oblast executive committee.
о́блит|ый (~, ~а́, ~о) *and* **обли́тый (~, ~а́, ~о)** *p.p.p. of* **обли́ть**; (*fig.*; +*i.*) covered (by), enveloped (in); **о. све́том луны́** bathed in moonlight.
обл|И́ть, оболью́, обольёшь, *past* **∸ил, ~ила́, ∸ило** *and* **~и́л, ~ила́, ~и́ло** *pf.* (*of* **~ива́ть**) (*p.p.p.* **∸итый**) to pour (over), sluice (over); to spill (over); **о. ска́терть вино́м** to spill wine over the table-cloth; **о. презре́нием** (*fig.*) to pour contempt (on); **о. гря́зью, о. помо́ями** (*fig., coll.*) to vilify.
обли́|ться, оболью́сь, обольёшься, *past* **~лся, ~ла́сь, ~ло́сь** *and* **~лось** *pf.* (*of* **~ва́ться**) **1.** to have a shower-bath; to sponge down; **о. холо́дной водо́й** to have a cold shower. **2.** to pour over o.s., spill over o.s.; **о. по́том** to be bathed in sweat; **о. слеза́ми** to melt into tears. **3.** *pass. of* **~ть**
облиц|ева́ть, у́ю, у́ешь *pf.* (*of* **~о́вывать**) (+*a. and i.*) to face (with).
облицо́вк|а, и *f.* facing, revetment.
облицо́выва|ть, ю *impf. of* **облицева́ть**
облич|а́ть, а́ю *impf.* (*of* **~и́ть**) **1.** to expose, unmask, denounce. **2.** (*impf. only*) to reveal, display; to point (to).
обличе́ни|е, я *nt.* exposure, unmasking, denunciation.
обличи́тел|ь, я *m.* exposer, unmasker, denouncer.
обличи́тельн|ый *adj.* denunciatory; **~ая речь, ~ая статья́** diatribe, tirade.
облич|И́ть, у́, и́шь *pf. of* **~а́ть**
обли́чь|е, я *nt.* **1.** (*coll.*) face. **2.** aspect, appearance (*also fig.*).
облобыза́|ть, ю *pf.* (*obs., joc.*) to kiss.
обложе́ни|е, я *nt.* taxation; assessment, rating.
облож|И́ть, у́, ∸ишь *pf.* **1.** (*impf.* **обкла́дывать**) to put (round); to edge; **о. больно́го поду́шками** to surround a patient with pillows; **о. сте́ну мра́мором** to face a wall with marble. **2.** (*impf.* **обкла́дывать**) to cover; (*impers.*): **круго́м ~и́ло (не́бо)** the sky is completely overcast. **3.** (*impf.* **обкла́дывать**) to surround; to besiege. **4.** (*impf.* **облага́ть**) to assess; **о. нало́гом** to tax.
облож|И́ться, у́сь, ∸ишься *pf.* **1.** (*impf.* **обкла́дываться**) (+*i.*) to surround o.s. (with). **2.** *pass. of* **~и́ть**
обло́жк|а, и *f.* (dust-)cover; folder.
обложно́й *adj.*: **о. дождь** (*coll.*) incessant rain.
облока́чиваться, юсь *impf. of* **облокоти́ться**
облоко|ти́ться, чу́сь, ~ти́шься *pf.* (*of* **облока́чиваться**) (**на**+*a.*) to lean one's elbow(s) (on, against).
облома́|ть, ю, *pf.* (*of* **обла́мывать**) **1.** to break off. **2.** (*fig., coll.*) to talk into, cajole.
облома́|ться, юсь, *pf.* (*of* **обла́мываться**) to break off, snap.
облом|И́ть, лю́, ∸ишь *pf.* to break off.
облом|И́ться, лю́сь, ∸ишься *pf.* = **~а́ться**
обло́мовщин|а, ы *f.* sluggishness, lethargy.
обло́м|ок, ка *m.* **1.** fragment. **2.** (*pl.*) débris, wreckage.
облуп|И́ть, лю́, ∸ишь *pf. of* **лупи́ть¹** *and* **∸ливать**
облуп|И́ться, лю́сь, ∸ишься *pf. of* **лупи́ться** *and* **∸ливаться**
облу́плива|ть, ю *impf.* (*of* **облупи́ть**) **1.** to peel; to shell (*eggs*). **2.** (*fig., coll.*) to fleece.
облу́плива|ться, юсь *impf.* (*of* **облупи́ться**) to peel (off), scale; to come off, chip.
облуч|а́ть, а́ю *impf. of* **~и́ть**
облуче́ни|е, я *nt.* (*med.*) irradiation.
облуч|И́ть, у́, и́шь *pf.* (*of* **~а́ть**) to irradiate.
облуч|о́к, ка́ *m.* coachman's seat.
облущ|И́ть, у́, и́шь *pf. of* **лущи́ть**
облысе́|ть, ю, ешь *pf. of* **лысе́ть**
облюб|ова́ть, у́ю *pf.* (*of* **~о́вывать**) to pick, choose, select.
облюбо́выва|ть, ю *impf. of* **облюбова́ть**
обл|я́гу, я́жешь, я́гут *see* **~е́чь¹**
обма́|зать, жу, жешь *pf.* (*of* **~зывать**) **1.** to coat (with). **2.** to smear (with); **о. себе́ ру́ки ма́слом** to cover one's hands with oil.
обма́|заться, жусь, жешься *pf.* (*of* **~зываться**) **1.** (+*i.*) to get o.s. covered (with). **2.** *pass. of* **~зать**
обма́зыва|ть(ся), ю(сь) *impf. of* **обма́зать(ся)**
обма́кива|ть, ю *impf. of* **обмакну́ть**
обмак|ну́ть, ну́, нёшь, *past* **~ну́л** *pf.* (*of* **∸ивать**) to dip.
обма́н, а *m.* fraud, deception; **о. зре́ния** optical illusion; **ввести́ в о.** to deceive.

обма́нк|а, и *f.* (*min.*) blende; **смоляна́я о.** pitchblende.
обма́нны|й *adj.* fraudulent; **~м путём** fraudulently.
обман|у́ть, у́, ∠ешь *pf.* (*of* **∠ывать**) to deceive; to cheat, swindle; **о. чьё-н. дове́рие** to betray s.o.'s trust; **о. чьи-н. наде́жды** to fail to live up to s.o.'s hopes.
обман|у́ться, у́сь, ∠ешься *pf.* (*of* **∠ываться**) to be deceived; **о. в свои́х ожида́ниях** to be disappointed in one's expectations.
обма́нчив|ый (~, ~а) *adj.* deceptive, delusive; **нару́жность ~а** appearances are deceptive.
обма́нщик, а *m.* deceiver; cheat, fraud.
обма́нывa|ть(ся), ю(сь) *impf. of* **обману́ть(ся)**
обма́тыва|ть(ся), ю(сь) *impf. of* **обмота́ть(ся)**
обма́хива|ть(ся), ю(сь) *impf. of* **обмахну́ть(ся)**
обмах|ну́ть, ну́, нёшь *pf.* (*of* **∠ивать**) **1.** to fan. **2.** to dust (off); to brush (off); **о. сор со ска́терти** to brush crumbs off the cloth.
обмах|ну́ться, ну́сь, нёшься *pf.* (*of* **∠иваться**) **1.** to fan o.s. **2.** *pass. of* **~ну́ть**
обма́чива|ть, ю *impf. of* **обмочи́ть**
обмеле́|ть, ет *pf.* (*of* **меле́ть**) **1.** to become shallow. **2.** (*naut.*) to run aground.
обме́н, а *m.* (*+i.*) exchange (of); **о. мне́ниями** exchange of opinions; **о. веще́ств** (*biol.*) metabolism; **в о.** (**за**+*a.*) in exchange (for).
обме́нива|ть(ся), ю(сь) *impf. of* **обмени́ть(ся)** *and* **обменя́ть(ся)**
обмен|и́ть, ю́, ∠ишь *pf.* (*of* **∠ивать**) (*coll.*) to exchange; to barter; to swap.
обмен|и́ться, ю́сь, ∠ишься *pf.* (*of* **∠иваться**) (*+i.*) (*coll.*) to exchange.
обме́н|ный *adj. of* **~**
обмен|я́ть, я́ю *pf.* (*of* **меня́ть 2.** *and* **∠ивать**) (*+a.* **на**+*a.*) to exchange (for).
обмен|я́ться, я́юсь *pf.* (*of* **меня́ться 2.** *and* **∠иваться**) (*+i.*) to exchange; to swap; **о. взгля́дами** to exchange looks; **о. впечатле́ниями** to compare notes.
обме́р[1]**, а** *m.* measurement.
обме́р[2]**, а** *m.* false measure.
об|мере́ть, омру́, омрёшь, *past* **∠мер, ~мерла́, ∠мерло** *pf.* (*of* **~мира́ть**) (*coll.*) to faint; **о. от у́жаса** to be horror-struck; **я ∠мер** my heart stood still.
обме́рива|ть, ю *impf. of* **обме́рить**
обме́р|ить[1]**, ю, ишь** *pf.* (*of* **~ивать**) to measure.
обме́р|ить[2]**, ю, ишь** *pf.* (*of* **~ивать**) to cheat in measuring; to give short measure (to).
обме|сти́, ту́, тёшь, *past* **∸л, ~ла́** *pf.* (*of* **~та́ть**[1]) to sweep off; to dust.
обмета́|ть[1]**, ю** *impf. of* **обмести́**
обме|та́ть[2]**, чу́, ∠чешь** *pf.* (*of* **∸тывать**) **1.** to overstitch, oversew. **2.** (*impers.*; *coll.*): **у меня́ ~та́ло гу́бы** my lips are cracked (with cold sores).
обмётыва|ть, ю *impf. of* **обмета́ть**[2]
обмина́|ть, ю *impf. of* **обмя́ть**
обмира́|ть, ю *impf. of* **обмере́ть**
обмозг|ова́ть, у́ю *pf.* (*of* **~о́вывать**) (*coll.*) to think over, mull over.
обмозго́выва|ть, ю *impf. of* **обмозгова́ть**
обмола́чива|ть, ю *impf. of* **обмолоти́ть**
обмо́лв|иться, люсь, ишься *pf.* (*coll.*) **1.** to make a slip in speaking. **2.** (*+i.*) to say; to utter; **не о. ни сло́вом** (**о**+*p.*) to say not a word (about).
обмо́лвк|а, и *f.* slip of the tongue.
обмоло́т, а *m.* (*agric.*) threshing.
обмоло|ти́ть, чу́, ∠тишь *pf.* (*of* **обмола́чивать**) (*agric.*) to thresh.
обмора́жива|ть(ся), ю(сь) *impf. of* **обморо́зить(ся)**
обморо́же́ни|е, я *nt.* frost-bite.
обморо́|женный *p.p.p. of* **~зить** *and adj.* frost-bitten.
обморо́|зить, жу, зишь *pf.* (*of* **обмора́живать**); **я ~зил себе́ нос, ру́ки** *etc.* my nose is, hands, *etc.*, are frost-bitten.
обморо́|зиться, жусь, зишься *pf.* (*of* **обмора́живаться**) to suffer frost-bite, be frost-bitten.
о́бморок, а *m.* fainting-fit; swoon; **упа́сть в о.** to faint; to swoon.
обморо́ч|ить, у, ишь *pf. of* **моро́чить**
о́бморо|чный *adj. of* **~к; ~чное состоя́ние** (*med.*) syncope.
обмота́|ть, ю *pf.* (*of* **обма́тывать**) (*+a. and i. or a.* **вокру́г**) to wind (round); to wrap (round) **о. ше́ю ша́рфом, о. шарф вокру́г ше́и** to wind a scarf round one's neck.
обмота́|ться, юсь *pf.* (*of* **обма́тываться**) **1.** (*+i.*) to wrap o.s. (in). **2.** *pass. of* **~ть**
обмо́т|ки, ок *no sg.* puttees, leg-wrappings.
обмоч|и́ть, у́, ∠ишь *pf.* (*of* **обма́чивать**) to wet.
обм|о́ю, о́ешь *see* **~ы́ть**
обмундирова́ни|е, я *nt.* **1.** fitting out (with uniform). **2.** uniform.
обмундир|ова́ть, у́ю *pf.* (*of* **~о́вывать**) to fit out (with uniform).
обмундиро́в|очный *adj. of* **~ка; ~очные де́ньги** uniform allowance.
обмундиро́выва|ть, ю *impf. of* **обмундирова́ть**
обмыва́|ть(ся), ю(сь) *impf. of* **обмы́ть(ся)**
обмы́л|ок, ка *m.* (*coll.*) remnant of a bar of soap.
обм|ы́ть, о́ю, о́ешь *pf.* (*of* **~ыва́ть**) **1.** to bathe, wash; **о. ра́ну** to bathe a wound. **2.** (*coll.*) to celebrate, drink to.
обм|ы́ться, о́юсь, о́ешься *pf.* (*of* **~ыва́ться**) **1.** to bathe, wash. **2.** *pass. of* **~ы́ть**
обмяк|а́ть, а́ю *impf.* (*of* **∠нуть**) (*coll.*) to become soft; (*fig.*) to become flabby.
обмя́к|нуть, ну, нешь, *past* **~, ~ла** *pf. of* **~а́ть**
об|мя́ть, омну́, омнёшь, *pf.* (*of* **~мина́ть**) to press down; to trample down.
обнагле́|ть, ю, ешь *pf. of* **нагле́ть**
обнадёжива|ть, ю *impf. of* **обнадёжить**
обнадёж|ить, у, ишь *pf.* (*of* **~ивать**) to give hope (to), reassure.
обнаж|а́ть(ся), а́ю(сь) *impf. of* **~и́ть(ся)**
обнаж|ённый *p.p.p. of* **~и́ть** *and adj.* naked, bare; nude.
обнаж|и́ть, у́, и́шь *pf.* (*of* **~а́ть**) **1.** to bare, uncover; **о. го́лову** to bare one's head; **о. шпа́гу** to draw a sword. **2.** (*fig.*) to lay bare, reveal.
обнаж|и́ться, у́сь, и́шься *pf.* (*of* **~а́ться**) **1.** to bare o.s., uncover o.s. **2.** *pass. of* **~и́ть**
обнаро́довани|е, я *nt.* publication, promulgation.
обнаро́д|овать, ую *pf. and impf.* (*liter.*) to publish, promulgate.
обнару́же́ни|е, я *nt.* **1.** disclosure; displaying, revealing. **2.** discovery; detection.
обнару́жива|ть(ся), ю(сь) *impf. of* **обнару́жить(ся)**
обнару́ж|ить, у, ишь *pf.* (*of* **~ивать**) **1.** to disclose; to display, reveal. **2.** to discover, bring to light; to detect.
обнару́ж|иться, усь, ишься *pf.* (*of* **~иваться**) **1.** to be revealed; to come to light. **2.** *pass. of* **~иваться**
обна́шива|ть, ю *impf. of* **обноси́ть**[1]
обнес|ти́[1]**, у́, ёшь,** *past* **∸, ~ла́** *pf.* (*of* **обноси́ть**[2]) (*+i.*) to enclose (with); **о. и́згородью** to fence (in).
обнес|ти́[2]**, у́, ёшь,** *past* **∸, ~ла́** *pf.* (*of* **обноси́ть**[3]) (*+i.*) to serve round; **~ли́ ли вы всех госте́й шампа́нским?** have you served all of the guests with champagne?
обнес|ти́[3]**, у́, ёшь,** *past* **∸, ~ла́** *pf.* (*of* **обноси́ть**[4]) (*+a. and i.*) to pass over (*in serving sth.*); **меня́ ~ли́ вино́м** I have not had (= *been offered*) wine.

обнима́|ть(ся), ю(сь) *impf. of* **обня́ть(ся)**
обни́мк|а, и *f. only in phr.* **в ~у** (*coll.*) in an embrace, embracing one another.
обнища́лый *adj.* impoverished; beggarly.
обнища́ни|е, я *nt.* impoverishment.
обнища́|ть, ю *pf. of* **нища́ть**
обнов|и́ть, лю́, и́шь *pf.* (*of* **~ля́ть**) **1.** to renovate; to renew; to reform; to update. **2.** to repair, restore; **о. свои́ зна́ния** (*fig.*) to refresh one's knowledge. **3.** (*coll., fig.*) to christen; to use *or* wear for the first time.
обнов|и́ться, лю́сь, и́шься *pf.* (*of* **~ля́ться**) **1.** to revive, be restored. **2.** *pass. of* **~и́ть**
обно́вк|а, и *f.* (*coll.*) new acquisition.
обновле́ни|е, я *nt.* renovation, renewal; **вне́шнее о.** face-lift.
обновля́|ть(ся), ю(сь) *impf. of* **обнови́ть(ся)**
обно|си́ть[1], шу́, ~сишь *pf.* (*of* **обна́шивать**) (*coll.*) to wear in (*new clothing or footwear*).
обно|си́ть[2,3,4], шу́, ~сишь *impf. of* **обнести́[1,2,3]**
обно|си́ться, шу́сь, ~сишься *pf.* (*coll.*) **1.** to have worn out all one's clothes. **2.** to become worn in (*of new clothes*).
обно́с|ки, ков *pl.* (*sg.* **~ок, ~ка** *m.*) (*coll.*) old clothes.
обн|я́ть, иму́, и́мешь, *past* **~ял, ~яла́, ~яло** *pf.* (*of* **~има́ть**) to embrace; to clasp in one's arms; (*fig.*) to envelop; **он шёл, ~я́в её за та́лию** he was walking with his arm round her waist; **о. взгля́дом** to survey; **о. умо́м** (*fig.*) to comprehend, take in.
обн|я́ться, иму́сь, и́мешься, *past* **~ялся́, ~яла́сь, ~яло́сь** *pf.* (*of* **~има́ться**) to embrace; to hug (one another).
обо *prep.* = **о[1]**
обо... *vbl. pref.* = **о...** *and* **об...**
обобра́|ть, оберу́, оберёшь, *past* **~л, ~ла́ ~ло** *pf.* (*of* **обира́ть**) (*coll.*) **1.** to pick, gather; **о. кусты́ мали́ны** to pick raspberries. **2.** to rob; (*sl.*) to clean out.
обобщ|а́ть, а́ю *impf. of* **~и́ть**
обобще́ни|е, я *nt.* generalization.
обобществ|и́ть, лю́, и́шь *pf.* (*of* **~ля́ть**) to socialize; to collectivize.
обобществле́ни|е, я *nt.* socialization; collectivization.
обобществля́|ть, ю *impf. of* **обобществи́ть**
обобщ|и́ть, у́, и́шь *pf.* (*of* **~а́ть**) to generalize.
обобь|ю́, ёшь *see* **оби́ть**
обога|ти́ть, щу́, ти́шь *pf.* (*of* **~ща́ть**) to enrich.
обога|ти́ться, щусь, ти́шься *pf.* (*of* **~ща́ться**) **1.** to become rich; (+*i.*) to enrich o.s. (with). **2.** *pass. of* **~ти́ть**
обогаща́|ть(ся), ю(сь) *impf. of* **обогати́ть(ся)**
обогаще́ни|е, я *nt.* enrichment.
обогна́|ть, обгоню́, обго́нишь, *past* **~л, ~ла́, ~ло** *pf.* (*of* **обгоня́ть**) to pass; to outstrip, outdistance (*also fig.*).
обогн|у́ть, у́, ёшь *pf.* (*of* **огиба́ть**) **1.** to round; to skirt. **2.** to bend round.
обоготворе́ни|е, я *nt.* deification.
обоготвор|и́ть, ю́, и́шь *pf.* (*of* **~я́ть**) to deify.
обоготвор|я́ть, я́ю *impf. of* **~и́ть**
обогре́в, а *m.* (*tech.*) heating.
обогрева́тел|ь, я *m.* (*tech.*) heater.
обогрева́|ть(ся), ю(сь) *impf. of* **обогре́ть(ся)**
обогре́|ть, ю, ешь *pf.* (*of* **~ва́ть**) to heat, warm.
обогре́|ться, юсь, ешься *pf.* (*of* **~ва́ться**) **1.** to warm o.s.; to warm up. **2.** *pass. of* **~ть**
о́бод, а, *pl.* **~ья, ~ьев** *m.* rim; felloe.
обод|о́к, ка́ *m.* thin rim, thin border, fillet.
ободо́|чный *adj. of* **~к; ~чная кишка́** (*anat.*) colon.
ободра́н|ец, ца *m.* (*coll.*) ragamuffin.
обо́др|анный *p.p.p. of* **~а́ть** *and adj.* ragged.
ободра́ть, обдеру́, обдерёшь *pf.* (*of* **обдира́ть**) **1.** to strip; to skin, flay; to peel. **2.** (*fig., coll.*) to fleece.
ободре́ни|е, я *nt.* encouragement, reassurance.
ободри́тел|ьный (~ен, ~ьна) *adj.* encouraging, reassuring.
ободр|и́ть, ю́, и́шь *pf.* (*of* **~я́ть**) to cheer up; to encourage, reassure.
ободр|и́ться, ю́сь, и́шься *pf.* (*of* **~я́ться**) **1.** to cheer up, take heart. **2.** *pass. of* **~и́ть**
ободр|я́ть(ся), я́ю(сь) *impf. of* **~и́ть(ся)**
обо́его, обо́ему (*no nom. or a.*), *m. and nt. num.* both; **обо́его по́ла** of both sexes.
обожа́ни|е, я *nt.* adoration.
обожа́тел|ь, я *m.* (*coll.*) admirer.
обожа́|ть, ю *impf.* to adore, worship.
обож|гу́, жёшь, гу́т *see* **обже́чь**
обожд|а́ть, у́, ёшь, *past* **~а́л, ~ала́, ~а́ло** *pf.* (*coll.*) to wait (for a while).
обожеств|и́ть, лю́, и́шь *pf.* (*of* **~ля́ть**) to deify.
обожествле́ни|е, я *nt.* deification.
обожествля́|ть, ю *impf. of* **обожестви́ть**
обожжённый *p.p.p. of* **обже́чь**
обожр|а́ться, у́сь, ёшься, *past* **~а́лся, ~ала́сь** *pf.* (*of* **обжира́ться**) (*coll.*) to guzzle, stuff o.s.
обо́з, а *m.* **1.** string of carts; string of sledges. **2.** (*mil.*) (*unit*) transport; **быть в ~е** (*fig.*) to bring up the rear.
обозва́|ть, обзову́, обзовёшь, *past* **л, ~ла́, ~ло** *pf.* (*of* **обзыва́ть**) (+*a. and i.*) to call; **о. кого́-н. дурако́м** to call s.o. a fool.
обозл|ённый *p.p.p. of* **~и́ть** *and adj.* embittered.
обозл|и́ть, ю́, и́шь *pf.* **1.** *pf. of* **зли́ть. 2.** to embitter.
обозл|и́ться, ю́сь, и́шься *pf. of* **зли́ться**
обозна|ва́ться, ю́сь, ёшься *impf. of* **~ться**
обозна́|ться, юсь, ешься *pf.* (*of* **~ва́ться**) (*coll.*) to take s.o. for s.o. else; to be mistaken.
обознач|а́ть, а́ю *impf.* **1.** (*no pf.*) to mean. **2.** (*pf.* **~ить**) to mark, designate; **о. на ка́рте грани́цу** to mark a frontier on a map.
обознач|а́ться, а́юсь *impf.* (*of* **~иться**) **1.** to appear; to reveal o.s. **2.** *pass. of* **~а́ть 2.**
обозначе́ни|е, я *nt.* **1.** marking, designation. **2.** sign, symbol.
обозна́ч|ить, у, ишь *pf. of* **~а́ть 2.**
обозна́ч|иться, усь, ишься *pf. of* **~а́ться**
обозрева́тел|ь, я *m.* commentator; columnist; **полити́ческий о.** political correspondent (*of newspaper*).
обозрева́|ть, ю *impf. of* **обозре́ть**
обозре́ни|е, я *nt.* **1.** surveying, viewing. **2.** survey; overview. **3.** review (*periodical journal*). **4.** (*theatr.*) revue.
обозр|е́ть, ю́, и́шь *pf.* (*of* **~ева́ть**) **1.** to survey, view; to look round. **2.** (*fig.*) to survey, review.
обозри́м|ый (~, ~а) *adj.* visible; **в ~ом бу́дущем** in the foreseeable future.
обо́|и, ев *no sg.* wall-paper; **окле́ить ~ями** to paper.
обо́йм|а, ы, *g. pl.* **~** *f.* (*mil.*) cartridge clip, charger.
обо|йти́, йду́, йдёшь, *past* **~шёл, ~шла́** *pf.* (*of* **обходи́ть[1]**) **1.** to go round, pass; **о. фланг проти́вника** (*mil.*) to turn the enemy's flank. **2.** to make the rounds (of), go (all) round; (*of doctor, sentry, etc.*) to make (go) one's round(s); **слух ~шёл весь го́род** the rumour spread all over the town. **3.** to avoid; to leave out; to pass over; **о. молча́нием** to pass over in silence; **о. зако́н** to get round a law.
обо|йти́сь, йду́сь, йдёшься, *past* **~шёлся, ~шла́сь** *pf.* (*of* **обходи́ться**) **1.** (**с**+*i.*) to treat; **пло́хо о. с кем-н.** to treat s.o. badly. **2.** (*coll.*) to cost, come to; **во ско́лько ~шёлся ваш костю́м?** how much did

your suit come to? **3.** (*+i.*) to manage (with, on), make do (with, on); **о. ста рубля́ми** to make do with one hundred roubles; **без ва́шей по́мощи мы бы не ~шли́сь** without your aid we could not have managed. **4.** to turn out, end; **всё ~шло́сь благополу́чно** everything turned out all right; **как-н. ~йдётся!** things will sort themselves out!
обо́йщик, а *m.* paper-hanger; upholsterer.
о́бок *adv. and prep. +g. or d.* (*coll.*) close by; near.
обокра́|сть, обкраду́, обкрадёшь, *past* **~л, ~ла** *pf.* (*of* **обкра́дывать**) to rob.
оболва́нива|ть, ю *impf. of* **оболва́нить**
оболва́н|ить, ю, ишь *pf.* (*of* **~ивать**) (*coll.*) to make a fool of.
обо|лга́ть, лгу́, лжёшь, *past* **~лга́л, ~лгала́, ~лга́ло** *pf.* to slander.
оболо́чк|а, и *f.* **1.** cover, envelope, jacket; shell; (*tech.*) casing. **2.** (*anat.*) membrane; **ра́дужная о.** iris; **рогова́я о.** cornea; **сли́зистая о.** mucous membrane. **3.** (*bot.*) coat.
обо́лтус, а *m.* (*coll.*) blockhead, booby.
обольсти́тел|ь, я *m.* seducer.
обольсти́тел|ьный (~ен, ~ьна) *adj.* seductive, captivating.
оболь|сти́ть, щу́, сти́шь *pf.* (*of* **~ща́ть**) **1.** to captivate. **2.** to seduce.
оболь|сти́ться, щу́сь, сти́шься *pf.* (*of* **~ща́ться**) to be (labour) under a delusion; (*+i.*) to flatter o.s. (with).
обольща́|ть(ся), ю(сь) *impf. of* **обольсти́ть(ся)**
обольще́ни|е, я *nt.* **1.** seduction. **2.** delusion.
оболь|ю́, ёшь *see* **обли́ть**
обомле́|ть, ю, ешь *pf.* (*coll.*) to be stupefied.
обомн|у́, ёшь *see* **обмя́ть**
обомр|у́, ёшь *see* **обмере́ть**
обомше́лый *adj.* moss-grown.
обоня́ни|е, я *nt.* (sense of) smell; **име́ть то́нкое о.** to have a fine sense of smell.
обоня́тельный *adj.* (*anat.*) olfactory.
обоня́|ть, ю *impf.* to smell.
обора́чиваемост|ь, и *f.* (*fin., econ.*) turnover.
обора́чива|ть(ся), ю(сь) *impf. of* **оберну́ть(ся)** *and* **оборoти́ть(ся)**
оборва́н|ец, ца *m.* ragamuffin.
обо́рв|анный *p.p.p. of* **~а́ть** *and adj.* torn, ragged.
оборв|а́ть, у́, ёшь, *past* **~а́л, ~ала́, ~а́ло** *pf.* (*of* **обрыва́ть**) **1.** to tear off, pluck; to strip. **2.** to break; to snap. **3.** (*fig.*) to cut short, interrupt.
оборв|а́ться, у́сь, ёшься, *past* **~а́лся, ~ала́сь, ~а́ло́сь** *pf.* (*of* **обрыва́ться**) **1.** to break; to snap. **2.** to slip; to fall. **3.** to stop suddenly, stop short.
обо́рвыш, а *m.* (*coll.*) ragamuffin.
обо́рк|а, и *f.* frill, flounce.
оборо́н|а, ы *no pl., f.* **1.** defence. **2.** (*mil.*) defences.
оборони́тельный *adj.* defensive.
оборон|и́ть, ю́, и́шь *pf.* (*of* **~я́ть**) to defend.
оборон|и́ться, ю́сь, и́шься *pf.* (*of* **~я́ться**) **(от)** to defend o.s. (from).
оборо́н|ный *adj. of* **~а**; **~ная промы́шленность** defence industry.
обороноспосо́бност|ь, и *f.* defensive capability.
обороноспосо́б|ный (~ен, ~на) *adj.* prepared for defence.
оборон|я́ть(ся), я́ю(сь) *impf. of* **~и́ть(ся)**
оборо́т, а *m.* **1.** turn; (*tech.*) revolution, rotation; **приня́ть дурно́й о.** (*fig.*) to take a turn for the worse. **2.** circulation; (*fin., comm., rail.*) turnover; **ввести́, пусти́ть в о.** to put into circulation. **3.** back (= *reverse side*); **смотри́ на ~е** please turn over; **взять кого́-н. в о.** (*fig., coll.*) to get at s.o. **4.** turn (of speech); **о. ре́чи** phrase, locution.
о́борот|ень, ня *m.* werewolf.
оборо́тист|ый (~, ~а) *adj.* (*coll.*) resourceful.
оборо|ти́ть, чу́, ~тишь *pf.* (*of* **обора́чивать**) (*coll.*) to turn.
оборо|ти́ться, чу́сь, ~тишься *pf.* (*of* **обора́чиваться**) (*coll.*) **1.** to turn (round). **2.** **(в**+*a. or* +*i.*) to turn (into).
оборо́тлив|ый (~, ~а) *adj.* (*coll.*) resourceful.
оборо́т|ный *adj. of* **~**; **о. капита́л** (*fin., comm.*) working capital; **~ная сторона́** verso; reverse side (*also fig.*).
обору́довани|е, я *nt.* **1.** equipping. **2.** equipment; **вспомога́тельное о.** (*comput.*) peripherals.
обору́д|овать, ую *impf. and pf.* to equip, fit out.
обосновáни|е, я *nt.* **1.** basing. **2.** basis, ground.
обосно́в|анный *p.p.p. of* **~а́ть** *and adj.* well-founded, well-grounded.
обосн|ова́ть, ую́, уёшь *pf.* (*of* **~о́вывать**) to ground, base; to substantiate.
обосн|ова́ться, ую́сь, уёшься *pf.* (*of* **~о́вываться**) **1.** to settle down. **2.** *pass. of* **~ова́ть**
обосно́выва|ть(ся), ю(сь) *impf. of* **обоснова́ть(ся)**
обосо́б|ить, лю, ишь *pf.* (*of* **~ля́ть**) to isolate.
обосо́б|иться, люсь, ишься *pf.* (*of* **~ля́ться**) to stand apart, remain aloof.
обособле́ни|е, я *nt.* isolation.
обосо́бленно *adv.* apart; aloof.
обосо́б|ленный *p.p.p. of* **~ить** *and adj.* isolated, solitary.
обособля́|ть(ся), ю(сь) *impf. of* **обосо́бить(ся)**
обостре́ни|е, я *nt.* aggravation, exacerbation.
обостр|ённый *p.p.p. of* **~и́ть** *and adj.* **1.** sharp, pointed. **2.** of heightened sensitivity; **о. слух** a keen ear. **3.** strained, tense.
обостр|и́ть, ю́, и́шь *pf.* (*of* **~я́ть**) **1.** to sharpen, intensify. **2.** to strain; to aggravate, exacerbate.
обостр|и́ться, ю́сь, и́шься *pf.* (*of* **~я́ться**) **1.** to become sharp, become pointed. **2.** (*of the senses, etc.*) to become keener. **3.** to become strained; to become aggravated, become exacerbated; to worsen. **4.** *pass. of* **~и́ть**
обостр|я́ть(ся), я́ю(сь) *impf. of* **~и́ть(ся)**
оботр|у́, ёшь *see* **обтере́ть**
обо́чин|а, ы *f.* edge; side (*of road, etc.*).
обою́дност|ь, и *f.* mutuality, reciprocity.
обою́д|ный (~ен, ~на) *adj.* mutual, reciprocal; **по ~ному согла́сию** by mutual consent.
обоюдоо́стрый *adj.* double-edged, two-edged (*also fig.*).
обраба́тыва|ть, ю *impf. of* **обрабо́тать**
обраба́тыва|ющий *pres. part. act. of* **~ть** *and adj.*; **~ющая промы́шленность** manufacturing industry.
обрабо́та|ть, ю *pf.* (*of* **обраба́тывать**) **1.** to work (up); to treat, process; (*tech.*) to machine; **о. зе́млю** to work the land; **о. ра́ну** to dress a wound. **2.** to polish (*a liter. production, etc.*). **3.** (*fig., coll.*) to work upon.
обрабо́тк|а, и *f.* working (up); treatment, processing; (*tech.*) machining; **о. земли́** cultivation of land.
обра́д|овать(ся), ую(сь) *pf. of* **ра́довать(ся)**
о́браз¹**, а** *m.* **1.** shape, form; appearance. **2.** (*liter.*) image; **мы́слить ~ами** to think in images. **3.** (*liter.*) type; figure; **о. Га́млета** the Hamlet type. **4.** mode, manner; way; **о. жи́зни** way of life; **о. правле́ния** form of government; **каки́м ~ом?** how?; **таки́м ~ом** thus; **гла́вным ~ом** mainly, chiefly, largely; **ра́вным ~ом** equally.
о́браз²**, а,** *pl.* **~а́** *m.* icon.
образ|е́ц, ца́ *nt.* **1.** model, pattern (*also fig.*); **ста́вить в о.** to set up as a model. **2.** specimen, sample; (*of material*) pattern.
о́бразност|ь, и *f.* picturesqueness; (*liter.*) figurativeness; imagery.
о́браз|ный (~ен, ~на) *adj.* picturesque, graphic;

(*liter.*) figurative; employing images.
образова́ни|е[1], **я** *nt.* formation; **о. слов** word-formation.
образова́ни|е[2], **я** *nt.* education.
образо́ванност|ь, и *f.* education (= *educated state*).
образо́в|анный *p.p.p. of* **~а́ть** *and adj.*; **о. челове́к** an educated person
образова́тел|ьный (~ен, ~ьна) *adj.* educational.
образ|ова́ть, у́ю *impf.* (*in pres. tense*) *and pf.* (*of* **~о́вывать**) to form; to make up.
образ|ова́ться, у́ется *pf.* (*of* **~о́вываться**) **1.** to form; to arise. **2.** (*coll.*) to turn out well; **не беспоко́йтесь, всё ~у́ется!** don't worry, everything will be all right! **3.** *pass. of* **~ова́ть**
образо́выва|ть(ся), ю(сь) *impf. of* **образова́ть(ся)**
образу́м|ить, лю, ишь *pf.* (*coll.*) to bring to one's senses, make listen to reason.
образу́м|иться, люсь, ишься *pf.* (*coll.*) to come to one's senses, see reason.
образцо́в|ый *adj.* model; exemplary; **~ое хозя́йство** model farm.
обра́зчик, а *m.* specimen, sample; (*of material*) pattern.
обра́м|ить, лю, ишь *pf.* (*of* **~ля́ть**) to frame.
обрамле́ни|е, я *nt.* **1.** framing. **2.** frame; (*fig.*) setting.
обрамля́|ть, ю, *impf. of* **обра́мить**
обраста́ни|е, я *nt.* **1.** overgrowing. **2.** (*fig.*) accumulation, acquisition.
обраст|а́ть, а́ю *impf. of* **~и́**
обраст|и́, у́, ёшь, *past* **обро́с, обросла́** *pf.* (*of* **~а́ть**) (*+i.*) **1.** to become (be) overgrown (with); **о. гря́зью** (*coll.*) to be covered in mud. **2.** (*fig.*) to become (be) surrounded (by), become (be) cluttered (with); to acquire, accumulate.
обрати́мост|ь, и *f.* reversibility.
обрати́м|ый (~, ~а) *adj.* reversible.
обра|ти́ть, щу́, ти́шь *pf.* (*of* **~ща́ть**) to turn; **(в+*a.*)** to turn (into); **о. внима́ние (на+*a.*)** to pay attention (to), take notice (of), notice; **о. чьё-н. внима́ние (на+*a.*)** to call, draw s.o.'s attention (to); **о. на себя́ внима́ние** to attract attention (to o.s.); **о. в бе́гство** to put to flight; **о. в свою́ ве́ру** to convert (to one's faith); **о. в шу́тку** to turn into a joke.
обра|ти́ться, щу́сь, ти́шься *pf.* (*of* **~ща́ться**) **1.** to turn; to revert; **о. лицо́м к стене́** to turn towards the wall; **о. в бе́гство** to take flight. **2. (к)** to turn (to), appeal (to); to apply (to); to accost; **она́ не зна́ла, к кому́ о. за по́мощью** she did not know to whom to turn for help; **о. с призы́вом к кому́-н.** to appeal to s.o.; **о. к юри́сту** to take legal advice. **3. (в+*a.*)** to turn (into), become; **о. в ци́ника** to become a cynic; **о. в слух** (*fig.*) to be all ears; to prick up one's ears. **4. (в+*a.*)** to be converted (to).
обра́тно *adv.* **1.** back; backwards; **туда́ и о.** there and back; **пое́здка туда́ и о.** round trip; **взять о.** to take back; **идти́ о., е́хать о.** to go back; to return, retrace one's steps. **2.** conversely; inversely; **о. пропорциона́льный** inversely proportional.
обра́тн|ый *adj.* **1.** reverse; **о. а́дрес** return address; **о. биле́т** return ticket; **име́ющий ~ую си́лу** (*leg.*) retroactive, retrospective; **о. уда́р** backfire; **~ая связь** (*elec.*) feed-back. **2.** opposite; **в ~ую сто́рону** in the opposite direction. **3.** (*math.*) inverse; **~ое отноше́ние** inverse ratio.
обраща́|ть, ю *impf. of* **обрати́ть**
обраща́|ться, юсь *impf.* **1.** *impf. of* **обрати́ться. 2.** (*physiol., econ., etc.*) to circulate. **3. (с+*i.*)** to treat; **пло́хо о. с кем-н.** to treat s.o. badly, maltreat s.o. **4. (с+*i.*)** to handle, manage (*an inanimate object*); **он не уме́ет о. с автома́том** he does not know how to handle a sub-machine-gun; **«о. осторо́жно!»** 'handle with care!'.
обраще́ни|е, я *nt.* **1. (к)** appeal (to), address (to). **2. (в+*a.*)** conversion (to, into); **о. в ве́ру** conversion to faith. **3.** circulation; **изъя́ть из ~я** to withdraw from circulation. **4. (с+*i.*)** treatment (of); **плохо́е о.** ill-treatment. **5. (с+*i.*)** handling (of), use (of). **6.** manner.
обревиз|ова́ть, у́ю *pf. of* **ревизова́ть**
обре́з[1], **а** *m.* edge; **в о.** (*coll.*; *+g.*) only just enough; **де́нег у меня́ в о.** I haven't a penny to spare.
обре́з[2], **а** *m.* sawn-off shotgun.
обре́зани|е, я *nt.* circumcision.
обреза́ни|е, я *nt.* **1.** cutting. **2.** trimming.
обре́|зать, жу, жешь *pf.* (*of* **~зывать** *and* **~за́ть**) **1.** to clip, trim; to prune; **о. кому́-н. кры́лья** (*fig.*) to clip s.o.'s wings. **2.** to cut; **о. себе́ па́лец** to cut one's finger. **3.** to circumcise. **4.** (*coll.*) to cut short; to snub.
обрез|а́ть, а́ю *impf. of* **~́ать**
обре́|заться, жусь, зешься *pf.* (*of* **~за́ться** *and* **~зываться**) **1.** to cut o.s. **2.** *pass. of* **~зать**
обрез|а́ться, а́юсь *impf. of* **~́аться**
обре́з|ок, ка *m.* scrap.
обре́зыва|ть(ся), ю(сь) *impf. of* **обре́зать(ся)**
обрека́|ть, ю *impf. of* **обре́чь**
обре|ку́, чёшь, ку́т *see* **~́чь**
обремени́тел|ьный (~ен, ~ьна) *adj.* burdensome, onerous.
обремен|и́ть, ю́, и́шь *pf.* (*of* **~я́ть**) to burden.
обремен|я́ть, я́ю *impf. of* **~и́ть**
обре|сти́, ту́, тёшь, *past* **~̈л, ~ла́** *pf.* (*of* **~та́ть**) (*rhet.*) to find.
обрета́|ть, ю *impf. of* **обрести́**
обречённост|ь, и *f.* doom; **чу́вство ~и** feeling of doom.
обреч|ённый *p.p.p. of* **~́ь** *and adj.* doomed.
обре́|чь, ку́, чёшь, ку́т, *past* **~̈к, ~кла́** *pf.* (*of* **~ка́ть**) to condemn, doom.
обрис|ова́ть, у́ю *pf.* (*of* **~о́вывать**) to outline, delineate, depict (*also fig.*).
обрис|ова́ться, у́юсь *pf.* (*of* **~о́вываться**) **1.** to appear (in outline); to take shape. **2.** *pass. of* **~ова́ть**
обрисо́выва|ть(ся), ю(сь) *impf. of* **обрисова́ть(ся)**
обр|и́ть, е́ю, е́ешь *pf.* to shave (off).
обр|и́ться, е́юсь, е́ешься *pf.* to shave one's head.
обро́к, а *m.* (*hist.*) quit-rent.
оброн|и́ть, ю́, ~́ишь *pf.* **1.** to drop (*sc. and lose*). **2.** to let drop, let fall (*a remark, etc.*).
обруб|а́ть, а́ю *impf. of* **~и́ть**
обруб|и́ть[1], **лю́, ~́ишь** *pf.* (*of* **~а́ть**) to chop off; to lop off; to dock.
обруб|и́ть[2], **лю́, ~́ишь** *pf.* (*of* **~а́ть**) to hem.
обру́б|ок, ка *m.* stump.
обруга́|ть, ю *pf.* to curse; to call names; (*coll.*) to tear to pieces; to pan.
обрусе́ни|е, я *nt.* Russification.
обрусе́|ть, ю *pf.* to become Russified.
обруси́|ть, шь *pf.* to Russify.
о́бруч, а, *pl.* **~и, ~е́й** *m.* hoop.
обруча́льн|ый *adj.*: **~ое кольцо́** wedding ring; **о. обря́д** betrothal.
обруч|а́ть(ся), а́ю(сь) *impf. of* **~и́ть(ся)**
обруче́ни|е, я *nt.* betrothal.
обруч|и́ть, у́, и́шь *pf.* (*of* **~а́ть**) to betrothe.
обруч|и́ться, у́сь, и́шься *pf.* (*of* **~а́ться**) **(с+*i.*)** to become engaged (to).
обру́шива|ть(ся), ю(сь) *impf. of* **обру́шить(ся)**
обру́ш|ить, у, ишь *pf.* (*of* **~ивать**) to bring down, rain down.
обру́ш|иться, усь, ишься *pf.* (*of* **~иваться**) **1.** to come down, collapse, cave in. **2.** (*fig.*) to come down (upon), fall (upon).

обры́в, а *m.* precipice.
обрыва́|ть(ся), ю(сь) *impf. of* **оборва́ть(ся)**
обры́вист|ый (~, ~а) *adj.* steep, precipitous.
обры́в|ок, ка *m.* scrap; snatch (*of tune, song, etc.*).
обры́зг|ать, аю *pf.* (*of* **~ивать**) (+*i.*) to sprinkle (with); to splash; to spatter (with).
обры́згива|ть, ю *impf. of* **обры́згать**
обры́ска|ть, ю *pf.* (*coll.*) to go through (in search of), hunt through.
обрю́зглый *adj.* flabby, flaccid.
обрю́зг|нуть, ну, нешь, *past* **~, ~ла** *pf.* to become flabby, become flaccid.
обрю́зг|ший = ~лый
обря́д, а *m.* rite, ceremony.
обря́дност|ь, и *f.* (*collect.*) rites, ritual, ceremonial.
обря́довый *adj.* ritual, ceremonial.
обса|ди́ть, жу́, ~дишь *pf.* (*of* **~живать**) to plant round.
обса́жива|ть, ю *impf. of* **обсади́ть**
обсервато́ри|я, и *f.* observatory.
обска|ка́ть, чу́, ~чешь *pf.* (*of* **~кивать**) **1.** to gallop round. **2.** (*pf. only*) to outgallop.
обска́кива|ть, ю *impf. of* **обскака́ть 1.**
обскура́нт, а *m.* obscurant, obscurantist.
обскуранти́зм, а *m.* obscurantism.
обскуранти́стский *adj.* obscurantist.
обсле́довани|е, я *nt.* (+*g.*) inspection (of), inquiry (into); investigation (of); observation, tests (*in hospital*).
обсле́д|овать, ую *impf. and pf.* to inspect; to investigate; **о. больно́го** to examine a patient.
обслу́живани|е, я *nt.* service; (*tech.*) servicing, maintenance; **бытово́е о.** consumer service; **медици́нское о.** health care.
обслу́жива|ть, ю *impf. of* **обслужи́ть; о. стано́к** to mind a machine; (*naut.*): **о. ору́дия** to man the guns; **~ющий персона́л** ancillary staff.
обслуж|и́ть, у́, ~ишь *pf.* (*of* **~ивать**) to attend (to), serve; (*tech.*) to serve; to mind, operate; **о. потреби́теля** to serve a customer.
обсо́х|нуть, ну, нешь, *past* **~, ~ла** *pf.* (*of* **обсыха́ть**) to dry (off); **у него́ молоко́ на губа́х не ~ло** (*fig.*) he is still green.
обста́в|ить, лю, ишь *pf.* (*of* **~ля́ть**) **1.** (+*i.*) to surround (with). **2.** (+*i.*) to furnish (with). **3.** (*fig.*) to arrange; to organize.
обставля́|ть, ю *impf. of* **обста́вить**
обстано́вк|а, и *f.* **1.** furniture; décor; (*theatr.*) set. **2.** situation, climate; environment.
обстир|а́ть, а́ю *pf.* (*of* **~ывать**) (*coll.*) to do the washing (*for a number of*).
обсти́рыва|ть, ю *impf. of* **обстира́ть**
обстоя́тел|ьный (~ен, ~ьна) *adj.* **1.** thorough, detailed. **2.** (*coll.*; *of a person*) solid, reliable.
обстоя́тельств|о, а *nt.* circumstance; **по незави́сящим от меня́ ~ам** for reasons beyond my control; **ни при каки́х ~ах** under no circumstances.
обсто|я́ть, и́т *impf.* to be; to get on; **как ~и́т де́ло?** how is it going?; **как ~я́т ва́ши дела́?** how are you getting on?; **вот как ~и́т де́ло** that's how matters stand.
обстра́ива|ть(ся), ю(сь) *impf. of* **обстро́ить(ся)**
обстре́л, а *m.* firing, fire; **артиллери́йский о.** bombardment, shelling; **попа́сть под о.** to come under fire.
обстре́лива|ть, ю *impf. of* **обстреля́ть**
обстре́л|янный *p.p.p. of* **~я́ть** *and adj.* seasoned, battle-hardened (*also fig.*); **~янная пти́ца** (*coll.*) old hand.
обстрел|я́ть, я́ю *pf.* (*of* **~ивать**) to fire (at, on); to bombard; to shell.
обстро́|ить, ю, ишь *pf.* (*of* **обстра́ивать**) to build (up).
обстро́|иться, юсь, ишься *pf.* (*of* **обстра́иваться**) **1.** to be built (up); (*coll.*) to spring up. **2.** to build for o.s.
обструкциони́зм, а *m.* (*pol.*) obstructionism.
обструкциони́ст, а *m.* (*pol.*) obstructionist.
обстру́кци|я, и *f.* (*pol.*) obstruction; filibustering.
обступ|а́ть, а́ю *impf. of* **~и́ть**
обступ|и́ть, лю́, ~ишь *pf.* (*of* **~а́ть**) to surround; to cluster (round).
обсу|ди́ть, жу́, ~дишь *pf.* (*of* **~жда́ть**) to discuss; to consider.
обсужда́|ть, ю *impf. of* **обсуди́ть**
обсужде́ни|е, я *nt.* discussion.
обсу́шива|ть(ся), ю(сь) *impf. of* **обсуши́ть(ся)**
обсуш|и́ть, у́, ~ишь *pf.* (*of* **~ивать**) to dry (out).
обсуш|и́ться, у́сь, ~ишься *pf.* (*of* **~иваться**) to dry o.s., get dry.
обсчит|а́ть, а́ю *pf.* (*of* **~ывать**) to shortchange.
обсчит|а́ться, а́юсь *pf.* (*of* **~ываться**) to make a mistake (*in counting*); **вы ~а́лись на шесть копе́ек** you were six kopecks out.
обсчи́тыва|ть(ся), ю(сь) *impf. of* **обсчита́ть(ся)**
обсы́п|ать, лю, лешь *pf.* (*of* **~а́ть**) (+*i.*) to strew; to sprinkle.
обсып|а́ть, а́ю *impf. of* **~ать**
обсыха́|ть, ю *impf. of* **обсо́хнуть**
обта́чива|ть, ю *impf. of* **обточи́ть**
обтека́ем|ый *adj.* (*tech.*) streamlined.
обтека́|ть, ю *impf. of* **обте́чь**
обтер|е́ть, оботру́, оботрёшь, *past* **~, ~ла** *pf.* (*of* **обтира́ть**) **1.** to wipe; to wipe dry. **2.** (+*i.*) to rub (with).
обтер|е́ться, оботру́сь, оботрёшься, *past* **~ся, ~лась** *pf.* (*of* **обтира́ться**) **1.** to dry o.s. **2.** to sponge o.s. down. **3.** (*coll.*) to wear thin (*as result of friction*).
обте|са́ть, шу́, ~шешь *pf.* (*of* **~сывать**) to square; to rough-hew; to dress, trim. **2.** (*fig., coll.*) to teach manners (to), lick into shape.
обтёсыва|ть *impf. of* **обтеса́ть**
обте́|чь, ку́, чёшь, ку́т, *past* **~к, ~кла́** *pf.* (*of* **~ка́ть**) **1.** to flow round. **2.** (*mil.*) to by-pass.
обтира́ни|е, я *nt.* sponge-down.
обтира́|ть(ся), ю(сь) *impf. of* **обтере́ть(ся)**
обточ|и́ть, у́, ~ишь *pf.* (*of* **обта́чивать**) to grind; (*tech.*) to turn, machine, round off.
обтрёп|анный *p.p.p. of* **~а́ть** *and adj.* **1.** frayed. **2.** shabby.
обтреп|а́ть, лю́, ~лешь *pf.* to fray.
обтреп|а́ться, лю́сь, ~лешься *pf.* **1.** to become frayed, fray. **2.** to become shabby.
обтя́гива|ть, ю *impf. of* **обтяну́ть**
обтя́гивающий *adj.* skin-tight, figure-hugging.
обтя́жк|а, и *f.* **1.** cover (*for furniture*). **2.: пла́тье в ~у** close-fitting dress.
обтя|ну́ть, ну́, ~нешь *pf.* (*of* **~гивать**) **1.** (+*i.*) to cover (*furniture*) (with). **2.** to fit tightly; to hug.
обува́|ть(ся), ю(сь) *impf. of* **обу́ть(ся)**
обувн|о́й *adj. of* **о́бувь; о. магази́н** shoe shop; **~а́я промы́шленность** boot and shoe industry.
о́був|ь, и *no pl., f.* footwear; boots, shoes.
обу́глива|ть, ю *impf. of* **обу́глить**
обу́гл|ить, ю, ишь *pf.* (*of* **~ивать**) to char; to carbonize.
обу́з|а, ы *f.* burden; **быть ~ой для кого́-н.** to be a burden to s.o.
обузд|а́ть, а́ю *pf.* (*of* **~ывать**) to bridle; (*fig.*) to restrain, control; **о. свои́ стра́сти** to curb one's passions.
обу́здыва|ть, ю *impf. of* **обузда́ть**
обурева́|ть, ет *impf.* to grip; **его́ ~ют сомне́ния** he is a prey to doubts.
обусло́в|ить, лю, ишь *pf.* (*of* **~ливать**) **1.** to condition; (+*i.*) to make conditional (upon); **он ~ил**

своё согла́сие предоставле́нием маши́ны he made his consent conditional upon the provision of a car. **2.** to cause, bring about.
обусло́в|иться, люсь, ишься *pf. of* **~ливаться**
обусло́влива|ть, ю *impf. of* **обусло́вить**
обусло́влива|ться, юсь *impf.* (*of* **обусло́виться**) (+*i.*) to be conditional (upon); to depend (on).
обу́т|ый *p.p.p. of* **~ь; оде́тый и о.** clothed and shod.
обу́|ть, ю, ешь *pf.* (*of* **~ва́ть**) **1.: о. кого́-н.** to put on s.o.'s boots (shoes) for him. **2.** to provide with boots *or* shoes.
обу́|ться, юсь, ешься *pf.* (*of* **~ва́ться**) to put on one's boots, shoes.
о́бух, а (*and* **обу́х, а́**) *m.* butt (*of an axe*); **меня́ то́чно ~ом по голове́** (*coll.*) you could have knocked me down with a feather.
обуч|а́ть(ся), а́ю(сь) *impf. of* **~и́ть(ся)**
обуче́ни|е, я *nt.* teaching; instruction, training; **совме́стное о. (лиц обо́его по́ла)** co-education; **о. по ме́сту рабо́ты** on-the-job *or* in-service training.
обуч|и́ть, у́, ~́ишь *pf.* (*of* **учи́ть** *and* **~а́ть**) (**кого́-н. чему́-н.**) to teach (s.o. sth.); to instruct, train (in).
обуч|и́ться, у́сь, ~́ишься *pf.* (*of* **учи́ться** *and* **~а́ться**) (+*d. or* +*inf.*) to learn.
обуя́|ть, ет *pf.* to seize; to grip; **его ~л страх** fear had seized him.
обха́жива|ть, ю *impf.* (*coll.*) to cajole, try to get round.
обхва́т, а *m.* (*measurement of circumference*) girth; **в ~е** in circumference; **ме́рить в ~е** to girth.
обхва|ти́ть, чу́, ~́тишь *pf.* (*of* **~́тывать**) to encompass (with outstretched arms); to clasp.
обхва́тыва|ть, ю *impf. of* **обхвати́ть**
обхо́д, а *m.* **1.** (*doctor's, postman's, etc.*) round; (*guard's, policeman's*) beat; **пойти́ в о.** to go round, make one's round(s). **2.** detour; by-pass. **3.** (*mil.*) turning movement. **4.** evasion, circumvention (*of law, etc.*).
обходи́тел|ьный (~ен, ~ьна) *adj.* pleasant; courteous; well-mannered.
обхо|ди́ть[1]**, жу́, ~́дишь** *impf. of* **обойти́**
обхо|ди́ть[2]**, жу́, ~́дишь** *pf.* to go all round.
обхо|ди́ться, жу́сь, ~́дишься *impf. of* **обойти́сь**
обхо́дн|ый *adj.* roundabout, circuitous; **о. путь** detour; **~ым путём** in a roundabout way; **~ое движе́ние** (*mil.*) turning movement.
обхо́дчик, а *m.* (*rail.*) trackman.
обхожде́ни|е, я *nt.* manners; (**с**+*i.*) treatment (of), behaviour (towards).
обче́сться, обочту́сь, обочтёшься, *past* **обчёлся, обочла́сь** *pf.* (*coll.*) = **обсчита́ться; (их) раз, два и обчёлся** (they) can be counted on the fingers of one hand.
обчи́|стить, щу, стишь *pf.* (*of* **~ща́ть**) **1.** to clean. **2.** (*fig., coll.*) to clean out (= *to rob*).
обчища́|ть, ю *impf. of* **обчи́стить**
обша́рива|ть, ю *impf. of* **обша́рить**
обша́р|ить, ю, ишь *pf.* (*of* **~ивать**) to rummage; to ransack.
обша́рпанный *adj.* dilapidated, run-down.
обшива́|ть, ю *impf. of* **обши́ть**[1,2]
обши́вк|а, и *f.* **1.** edging, bordering. **2.** trimming, facing. **3.** boarding, panelling; **о. фане́рой** veneering; (*tech.*) sheathing; (*naut.*) planking; **стальна́я о.** plating.
обши́в|очный *adj. of* **~ка**
обши́р|ный (~ен, ~на) *adj.* extensive (*also fig.*) spacious; vast.
об|ши́ть[1]**, ошью́, ошьёшь** *pf.* (*of* **~шива́ть**) **1.** to edge. **2.** to trim, face. **3.** to plank.
об|ши́ть[2]**, ошью́, ошьёшь** *pf.* (*of* **~шива́ть**) to make clothes for; **она́ сама́ ~ши́ла всю семью́** she has made all the family's clothes herself.
обшла́г, а́, *pl.* **~а́** *m.* cuff.
обща́|ться, юсь *impf.* (**с**+*i.*) to associate (with), mix (with).
общедосту́п|ный (~ен, ~на) *adj.* **1.** of moderate price. **2.** (*of book, etc.*) popular.
общежите́йский *adj.* everyday, ordinary.
общежи́ти|е, я *nt.* **1.** hostel. **2.** society, community; communal life.
общеизве́ст|ный (~ен, ~на) *adj.* well-known, generally known; notorious.
общенаро́дный *adj.* national; public; **о. пра́здник** public holiday.
обще́ни|е, я *nt.* intercourse; relations, links; **ли́чное о.** personal contact.
общеобразова́тельны|й *adj.* of general education; **~е предме́ты** general subjects.
общепоня́т|ный (~ен, ~на) *adj.* comprehensible to all.
общепри́знан|ный (~, ~а) *adj.* universally recognized.
общепри́нят|ый (~, ~а) *adj.* generally accepted.
общесою́зн|ый *adj.* All-Union (*in former USSR, common to or valid for the entire Union*).
обще́ственник, а *m.* social activist; person actively engaging in public life.
обще́ственност|ь, и *f.* **1.** (*collect.*) (the) public; **англи́йская о.** the British public. **2.** public opinion.
обще́ственн|ый *adj.* **1.** social, public; **~ая жизнь** public life; **~ое мне́ние** public opinion; **~ые нау́ки** social sciences. **2.** voluntary, unpaid; **на ~ых нача́лах** on a voluntary basis; **~ые организа́ции** voluntary organizations.
о́бществ|о, а *nt.* **1.** society; association; **нау́чное о.** learned body; **первобы́тное о.** primitive society. **2.** (*econ.*) company; **акционе́рное о.** joint-stock company. **3.** company, society; **в ~е кого́-н.** in s.o.'s company; **попа́сть в дурно́е о.** to fall into bad company.
общеупотреби́тел|ьный (~ен, ~ьна) *adj.* in general use.
общечелове́ческий *adj.* common to all mankind.
о́бщ|ий *adj.* general; common; **о. враг** common enemy; **о. знако́мый** mutual acquaintance; **~ее собра́ние** general meeting; **~ая су́мма** sum total; grand total; **в ~ем** on the whole, in general; **не име́ть ничего́ ~его (с**+*i.*) to have nothing in common (with).
о́бщи́н|а, ы *f.* community; commune.
общи́нн|ый *adj.* communal; **~ая земля́** common (land).
общип|а́ть, лю́, ~́лешь *pf.* (*of* **щипа́ть 4.** *and* **~́ывать**) to pluck.
общи́пыва|ть, ю *impf. of* **общипа́ть**
общи́тельност|ь, и *f.* sociability.
общи́тел|ьный (~ен, ~ьна) *adj.* sociable.
о́бщност|ь, и *f.* commonality; **о. интере́сов** commonality of interests.
объ... *vbl. pref.* = **о...** *and* **об...**
объего́рива|ть, ю *impf. of* **объего́рить**
объего́р|ить, ю, ишь, *pf.* (*of* **~ивать**) (*coll.*) to cheat, swindle.
объеда́|ть(ся), ю(сь) *impf. of* **объе́сть(ся)**
объеде́ни|е, я *nt.* **1.** overeating. **2.** (*as prep., coll.*) sth. delicious; **то́рты э́ти — пря́мо о.** these cakes are simply delicious.
объедине́ни|е, я *nt.* **1.** unification. **2.** union, association.
объедин|ённый *p.p.p. of* **~и́ть** *and adj.* united; **Организа́ция Объединённых На́ций** United Nations (Organization).
объедин|и́ть, ю́, и́шь *pf.* (*of* **~я́ть**) to unite; to join; **о. ресу́рсы** to pool resources; **о. уси́лия** to combine efforts.

объедин|и́ться, ю́сь, и́шься *pf.* (*of* **~я́ться**) (**с**+*i.*) to unite (with).
объедин|я́ть(ся), я́ю(сь) *impf. of* **~и́ть(ся)**
объе́д|ки, ков *pl.* (*sg.* **~ок, ~ка** *m.*) (*coll.*) leftovers, scraps.
объе́зд, а *m.* **1.** riding round, going round. **2.** circuit, detour.
объе́з|ди́ть[1], **жу, дишь** *pf.* (*of* **~жа́ть**[1]) to travel over.
объе́з|дить[2], **жу, дишь** *pf.* (*of* **~жа́ть**[2]) to break in (*horses*).
объе́здк|а, и *f.* breaking in (*of horses*).
объе́здчик[1], **а** *m.* mounted patrol; **лесно́й о.** forest warden.
объе́здчик[2], **а** *m.* horse-breaker.
объезжа́|ть[1], **ю** *impf. of* **объе́здить**[1] *and* **объе́хать**
объезжа́|ть[2], **ю** *impf. of* **объе́здить**[2]
объе́зжий *adj.* roundabout, circuitous; **о. путь** detour.
объе́кт, а *m.* **1.** object. **2.** (*mil.*) objective. **3.** establishment; works; **строи́тельный о.** building site.
объекти́в, а *m.* (*opt.*) lens.
объекти́вност|ь, и *f.* objectivity.
объекти́в|ный (~ен, ~на) *adj.* objective.
объе́кт|ный *adj. of* **~ 1.**
объе́кт|овый *adj. of* **~ 3.**
объём, а *m.* volume (*also fig.*); bulk, size, capacity.
объёмист|ый (~, ~а) *adj.* (*coll.*) voluminous, bulky.
объёмн|ый *adj.* by volume, volumetric.
объе́|сть, м, шь, ст, ди́м, ди́те, дя́т, *past* **~л** *pf.* (*of* **~да́ть**) **1.** to eat round; to nibble. **2.** (*coll.*): **о. кого́-н.** to eat s.o. out of house and home.
объе́|сться, мся, шься, стся, ди́мся, ди́тесь, дя́тся, *past* **~лся** *pf.* (*of* **~да́ться**) to overeat.
объе́|хать, ду, дешь *pf.* (*of* **~зжа́ть**[1]) **1.** to go round, skirt. **2.** to overtake, pass. **3.** to travel over.
объяв|и́ть, лю́, ~́ишь *pf.* (*of* **~ля́ть**) to declare, announce; **о. войну́** to declare war; **о. ко́нкурс** to announce a competition; **о. собра́ние откры́тым** to declare a meeting open; **о. вне зако́на** to outlaw.
объяв|и́ться, лю́сь, ~́ишься *pf.* (*of* **~ля́ться**) **1.** (*coll.*) to turn up, appear. **2.** (+*i.*) to declare o.s. (to be). **3.** *pass. of* **~и́ть**
объявле́ни|е, я *nt.* **1.** declaration, announcement; notice; **о. войны́** declaration of war. **2.** advertisement; **дать о. в газе́ту, помести́ть о. в газе́те** to put an advertisement in a paper.
объявля́|ть(ся), ю(сь) *impf. of* **объяви́ть(ся)**
объясне́ни|е, я *nt.* explanation; **о. в любви́** declaration of love.
объясни́м|ый (~, ~а) *adj.* explicable, explainable.
объясни́тельный *adj.* explanatory.
объясн|и́ть, ю́, и́шь *pf.* (*of* **~я́ть**) to explain.
объясн|и́ться, ю́сь, и́шься *pf.* (*of* **~я́ться**) **1.** to explain o.s.; (**с**+*i.*) to have a talk (with); to have it out (with); **о. в любви** (+*d.*) to make a declaration of love (to). **2.** to become clear, be explained; **тепе́рь всё ~и́лось** everything is now clear.
объясн|я́ть, я́ю *impf. of* **~и́ть**
объясн|я́ться, я́юсь *impf.* **1.** *impf. of* **~и́ться. 2.** to speak; to make o.s. understood; **уме́ете ли вы о. по-францу́зски?** can you make yourself understood in French?; **о. же́стами и зна́ками** to use sign language. **3.** (+*i.*) to be explained (by), be accounted for (by); **э́тим ~я́ется его́ стра́нное поведе́ние** that accounts for his strange behaviour.
объя́ти|е, я *nt.* embrace; **с распростёртыми ~ями** with open arms; **бро́ситься кому́-н. в ~я** to fall into s.o.'s arms.
объя́т|ый *p.p.p. of* **~ь; о. пла́менем** enveloped in flames; **о. стра́хом** terror-stricken.
объя́|ть, обойму́, обоймёшь *pf.* (*obs.*) to seize, grip, come over; **у́жас ~л его́** terror seized him.
обыва́тел|ь, я *m.* **1.** (*obs.*) inhabitant, resident. **2.** (*fig.*) philistine.
обыва́тельский *adj.* philistine; narrow-minded.
обыгр|а́ть, а́ю *pf.* (*of* **~́ывать**) **1.** to beat (*at a game*); to win; **о. кого́-н. на что-н.** to win sth. of s.o. **2.** to turn to advantage, turn to account. **3.** (*mus.*) to break in (*an instrument by playing*).
обы́грыва|ть, ю *impf. of* **обыгра́ть**
обы́денн|ый *adj.* ordinary; everyday; **~ое происше́ствие** everyday occurrence.
обыкнове́ни|е, я *nt.* habit; **по ~ю** as usual; **име́ть о.** (+*inf.*) to be in the habit (of).
обыкнове́нно *adv.* usually; as a rule.
обыкнове́н|ный (~ен, ~на) *adj.* usual; ordinary; commonplace; **~ная исто́рия** everyday occurrence; **бо́льше ~ного** more than usual.
о́быск, а *m.* search; **о́рдер на пра́во ~а** search warrant.
обы|ска́ть, щу́, ~щешь *pf.* (*of* **~́скивать**) to search.
обы́скива|ть, ю *impf. of* **обыска́ть**
обы́ча|й, я *m.* custom; **э́то у нас в ~е** it is our custom.
обы́чно *adv.* usually; as a rule.
обы́чн|ый *adj.* usual; ordinary; conventional.
обя́занност|ь, и *f.* duty; responsibility; **во́инская о.** military service; **исполня́ть ~и дире́ктора** to act as director; **исполня́ющий ~и дире́ктора** acting director.
обя́зан|ный (~, ~а) *adj.* **1.** (+*inf.*) obliged, bound; **он ~ верну́ться** he is obliged to go back. **2.** (+*d.*) obliged, indebted (to); **я вам о́чень ~** I am very much obliged to you; **она́ вам ~а свое́й жи́знью** she owes her life to you.
обяза́тельно *adv.* without fail; **я о. приду́** I shall come without fail; **он о. там бу́дет** he is sure to be there.
обяза́тел|ьный (~ен, ~ьна) *adj.* **1.** obligatory; compulsory; binding; **~ьное обуче́ние** compulsory education; **~ьное постановле́ние** binding decree. **2.** obliging.
обяза́тельств|о, а *nt.* **1.** obligation; **долгово́е о.** promissory note; **взять на себя́ о.** (+*inf.*) to pledge o.s. (to), undertake (to). **2.** (*pl.*; *leg.*) liabilities.
обя|за́ть, жу́, ~́жешь *pf.* (*of* **~́зывать**) **1.** to bind, oblige, commit; **о. кого́-н. яви́ться в определённое вре́мя** to bind s.o. to appear at a stated time. **2.** to oblige; **вы меня́ о́чень ~́жете** I shall be greatly indebted to you.
обя|за́ться, жу́сь, ~́жешься *pf.* (*of* **~́зываться**) to bind o.s., pledge o.s., undertake.
обя́зыва|ть, ю *impf. of* **обяза́ть**
обя́зыва|ться, юсь *impf. of* **обяза́ться**
ОВ *nt. indecl.* (*abbr. of* **отравля́ющее вещество́**) (*mil.*) toxic chemical agent; **ОВ не́рвно-паралити́ческого ти́па** nerve gas.
о-в (*abbr. of* **о́стров**) I., Island, Isle.
о-ва́ (*abbr. of* **острова́**) Is, Islands, Isles.
ова́л, а *m.* **1.** oval. **2.** balloon (*in comic strip, etc.*).
ова́льный *adj.* oval.
ова́ци|я, и *f.* ovation.
овдове́|вший *p.p. of* **~ть** *and adj.* widowed.
овдове́|ть, ю *pf.* to become a widow(er).
овева́|ть, ю *impf. of* **ове́ять**
ов|е́н, на́ *m.* **1.** (*obs.*) ram. **2.** (*astron.*) Aries.
ов|ёс, са́ *m.* oats.
ов|е́чий *adj. of* **~ца́; волк в ~е́чьей шку́ре** a wolf in sheep's clothing.
ове́чк|а, и *f. dim. of* **овца́**
ове́я|нный *p.p.p of* **~ть; о. сла́вой** covered with glory.
ове́|ять, ю, ешь *pf.* (*of* **~ва́ть**) (+*i.*) **1.** to fan. **2.** (*fig.*) to surround (with), cover (with).
овладева́|ть, ю *impf. of* **овладе́ть**

овладе́ни|е, я *nt.* (+*i.*) mastery; mastering.
овладе́|ть, ю *pf.* (*of* **~ва́ть**) (+*i.*) **1.** to seize; to take possession (of); **о. собо́й** to regain one's composure; **мно́ю ~ла ра́дость** I was overcome with joy. **2.** (*fig.*) master.
о-во (*abbr. of* **о́бщество**) Soc., Society.
о́вод, а, *pl.* **~ы, ~ов** (*and* **~а́, ~о́в**) gadfly.
овощево́дств|о, а *nt.* vegetable-growing.
о́вощ|и, е́й *pl.* (*sg.* **~, ~а** *m.*) vegetables.
овощно́й *adj.* vegetable; **о. магази́н** greengrocer's (shop).
овра́г, а *m.* ravine, gully.
овся́нк|а[1], **и** *f.* **1.** oatmeal. **2.** (oatmeal) porridge.
овся́нк|а[2], **и** *f.* (*zool.*) yellow-hammer.
овсян|о́й *adj. of* **овёс; ~о́е по́ле** field of oats.
овся́н|ый *adj.* made of oats; oatmeal; **~ая ка́ша** (oatmeal) porridge; **~ая крупа́** oatmeal.
овуля́ци|я, и *f.* (*biol.*) ovulation.
овц|а́, ы́, *pl.* **<́ы, ове́ц, <́ам** *f.* sheep; ewe; **заблу́дшая о.** (*fig.*) lost sheep.
овцебы́к, а *m.* musk-ox.
овцево́д, а *m.* sheep-breeder.
овцево́дств|о, а *nt.* sheep-breeding.
овча́рк|а, и *f.* sheep-dog; **неме́цкая о.** German shepherd (*dog*), Alsatian.
овча́р|ня, ни, *g. pl.* **~ен** *f.* sheep-fold.
овчи́н|а, ы *f.* sheepskin.
овчи́н|ка, ки *f. dim. of* **~а; ей не́бо с ~ку показа́лось** she was frightened out of her wits.
овчи́нный *adj.* sheepskin.
ога́р|ок, ка *m.* candle-end; *pl.* cinders.
огиба́|ть, ю *impf. of* **обогну́ть**
оглавле́ни|е, я *nt.* table of contents.
огла|си́ть, шу́, си́шь *pf.* (*of* **~ша́ть**) **1.** to proclaim, announce; **о. резолю́цию** to read out a resolution; **о. жениха́ и неве́сту** to publish banns of marriage. **2.** to divulge, make public. **3.** to fill (*with loud cries, etc.*).
огла|си́ться, шу́сь, си́шься *pf.* (*of* **~ша́ться**) **1.** (+*i.*) to resound (with). **2.** *pass. of* **~си́ть**
огла́ск|а, и *f.* publicity; **избега́ть ~и** to shun publicity; **преда́ть ~е** to make public, make known.
оглаша́|ть(ся), ю(сь) *impf. of* **огласи́ть(ся)**
оглаше́ни|е, я *nt.* proclaiming, publication; **не подлежи́т ~ю** confidential (*classification of document*); (*eccl.*) (publication of) banns.
огло́б|ля, ли, *g. pl.* **~ель** *f.* shaft.
огло́х|нуть, ну, нешь, *past* **~, ~ла** *pf. of* **гло́хнуть 1.**
оглуш|а́ть, а́ю *impf. of* **~и́ть**
оглуши́тел|ьный (~ен, ~ьна) *adj.* deafening.
оглуш|и́ть, у́, и́шь *pf.* **1.** *pf. of* **глуши́ть 1.. 2.** (*impf.* **~а́ть**) to deafen; to stun (*also fig.*).
огля|де́ть, жу́, ди́шь *pf.* (*of* **<́дывать**) to look round; to examine, inspect.
огля|де́ться, жу́сь, ди́шься *pf.* (*of* **~дываться**) **1.** to look round. **2.** to get used to things around one; (*fig.*) to adapt o.s., become acclimatized; **о. в темноте́** to become accustomed to the darkness.
огля́дк|а, и *f.* **1.** looking back; **бежа́ть без ~и** to run as fast as one's legs will carry one. **2.** care, caution; **без ~и** without a second thought; **де́йствовать с ~ой** to act circumspectly.
огля́дыва|ть(ся), ю(сь) *impf. of* **огляде́ть(ся)** *and* **огляну́ть(ся)**
огля|ну́ть, ну́, <́нешь *inst. pf.* (*of* **<́дывать**) to take a look over.
огля|ну́ться, ну́сь, <́нешься *pf.* (*of* **<́дываться**) to turn (back) to look at sth.; to glance back.
огнев|о́й *adj. of* **ого́нь;** (*fig.*) fiery; **о. вал** (*mil.*) barrage; **~а́я то́чка** (*mil.*) emplacement.
огнемёт, а *m.* (*mil.*) flame-thrower.
о́гненный *adj.* fiery (*also fig.*).
огнеопа́с|ный, (~ен, ~на) *adj.* inflammable.
огнепокло́нник, а *m.* fire-worshipper.
огнепокло́нничеств|о, а *nt.* fire-worship.
огнесто́|йкий (~ек, ~йка) *adj.* fire-proof.
огнестре́льн|ый *adj.*: **~ое ору́жие** fire-arm(s); **~ая ра́на** bullet wound.
огнетуши́тел|ь, я *m.* fire-extinguisher.
огнеупо́р|ный (~ен, ~на) *adj.* fire-proof; refractory; **~ная гли́на** fire-clay; **о. кирпи́ч** fire-brick.
ого́ *int.* oho!; my!
огова́рива|ть(ся), ю(сь) *impf. of* **оговори́ть(ся)**
огово́р, а *m.* slander.
оговор|и́ть[1], **ю, и́шь** *pf.* (*of* **огова́ривать**) to slander.
оговор|и́ть[2], **ю́, и́шь** *pf.* (*of* **огова́ривать**) **1.** to stipulate (for); to fix, agree (on); **мы ~и́ли усло́вия рабо́ты** we have fixed the conditions of work. **2.** to make a reservation, make a proviso (concerning); to specify; **он ~и́л своё несогла́сие** he specified his disagreement.
оговор|и́ться, ю́сь, и́шься *pf.* (*of* **огова́риваться**) **1.** to make a reservation, make a proviso. **2.** to make a slip in speaking. **3.** *pass. of* **~и́ть**
огово́р|ка, ки *f.* **1.** reservation, proviso; **без ~ок** without reservation; **он согласи́лся, но с не́которыми ~ками** he agreed but made certain reservations. **2.** slip of the tongue.
огол|ённый *p.p.p. of* **~и́ть** *and adj.* bare, nude; uncovered, exposed.
огол|и́ть, ю́, и́шь *pf.* (*of* **~я́ть**) to bare; to strip, uncover; **о. фланг** (*mil.*) to expose one's flank.
огол|и́ться, ю́сь, и́шься *pf.* (*of* **~я́ться**) **1.** to strip (o.s.). **2.** to become exposed. **3.** *pass. of* **~и́ть**
оголте́лый *adj.* (*coll.*) unbridled; frenzied.
огол|я́ть(ся), я́ю(сь) *impf. of* **~и́ть(ся)**
огон|ёк, ька́ *m.* **1.** (small) light; **блужда́ющий о.** will o' the wisp; **зайти́ к кому́-н. на о.** (*coll.*) to drop in on s.o. **2.** (*fig.*) zest, spirit.
ог|о́нь, ня́ *m.* **1.** fire (*also fig.*); **говори́ть с ~нём** to speak with fervour; **между двух ~не́й** between the devil and the deep blue sea; **пройти́ о. и во́ду** to go through fire and water. **2.** (*mil.*) fire; firing; **отвеча́ть ~нём** to fire back. **3.** light; **хвостово́й о.** (*aeron.*) tail light; **опознава́тельный о.** recognition lights; **тако́го челове́ка днём с ~нём не найдёшь** (*coll.*) you'll not find another like him in a month of Sundays.
огора́жива|ть, ю *impf. of* **огороди́ть**
огоро́д, а *m.* kitchen-garden; **бро́сить ка́мешек в чей-н. о.** (*fig., coll.*) to make disparaging remarks about s.o.
огоро|ди́ть, жу́, <́ди́шь *pf.* (*of* **огора́живать**) to fence in, enclose.
огоро́дник, а *m.* market-gardener.
огоро́дничеств|о, а *nt.* market-gardening.
огоро́д|ный *adj. of* **~; ~ное хозя́йство** market-gardening; market-garden.
огоро́ш|ить, у, ишь *pf.* (*coll.*) to take aback.
огорч|а́ть(ся), а́ю(сь) *impf. of* **~и́ть(ся)**
огорче́ни|е, я *nt.* grief, affliction; chagrin; **быть в ~и** to be in distress.
огорчи́тел|ьный (~ен, ~ьна) *adj.* distressing.
огорч|и́ть, у́, и́шь *pf.* (*of* **~а́ть**) to grieve, distress, pain.
огорч|и́ться, у́сь, и́шься *pf.* (*of* **~а́ться**) to grieve; to be distressed.
огра́б|ить, лю, ишь *pf. of* **гра́бить**[1]
ограбле́ни|е, я *nt.* robbery; burglary; **у́личное о.** mugging.
огра́д|а, ы *f.* fence.
огра|ди́ть, жу́, ди́шь *pf.* (*of* **~жда́ть**) **(от)** to guard (against, from), protect (against).
огражда́|ть, ю *impf. of* **огради́ть**

ограниче́ни|е, я *nt.* limitation, restriction.
ограни́ченност|ь, и *f.* limited nature; (*fig.*) narrowness, narrow-mindedness.
ограни́ч|енный *p.p.p. of* **~ить** *and adj.* limited; **о. челове́к** (*fig.*) narrow(-minded) person.
ограни́чива|ть(ся), ю(сь) *impf. of* **ограни́чить(ся)**
ограничи́тельный *adj.* restrictive, limiting.
ограни́ч|ить, у, ишь *pf.* (*of* **~ивать**) to limit, restrict; **о. себя́ в расхо́дах** to restrict one's expenditure.
ограни́ч|иться, усь, ишься *pf.* (*of* **~иваться**) (*+i.*) **1.** to limit o.s. (to), confine o.s. (to); **он ~ился кра́ткой ре́чью** he confined himself to a short speech. **2.** to be limited (to), be confined (to).
огре́|ть, ю *pf.* (*coll.*) to whack.
огре́х, а *m.* (*coll.*) fault, imperfection.
огро́м|ный (~ен, ~на) *adj.* huge; vast; enormous.
огрубе́лый *adj.* coarse, hardened.
огрубе́|ть, ю *pf. of* **грубе́ть.**
огрыз|а́ться, а́юсь *impf.* (*of* **~ну́ться**) (**на**+*a.*) to snap (at) (*of a dog*; *also fig.*).
огрыз|ну́ться, ну́сь, нёшься *pf. of* **~а́ться**
огры́з|ок, ка *m.* bit, end; remnant; **о. карандаша́** (*coll.*) pencil stub, stump.
огу́лом *adv.* (*coll.*) wholesale, indiscriminately.
огу́льно *adv.* without grounds; **о. обвиня́ть** to make a groundless accusation.
огу́л|ьный (~ен, ~ьна) *adj.* **1.** wholesale, indiscriminate; **~ьное оха́ивание** wholesale disparagement. **2.** unfounded, groundless.
огур|е́ц, ца́ *m.* cucumber.
огуре́|чный *adj. of* **~ц**
огу́рчик, а *m. affectionate dim. of* **огуре́ц**
о́д|а, ы *f.* ode.
ода́лжива|ть, ю *impf. of* **одолжи́ть**
одарённост|ь, и *f.* endowments, (natural) gifts, talent.
одар|ённый *p.p.p. of* **~и́ть** *and adj.* gifted, talented.
ода́рива|ть, ю *impf. of* **одари́ть**
одар|и́ть, ю́, и́шь *pf.* **1.** (*impf.* **~ивать**) to give presents (to); **она́ ~и́ла всех дете́й игру́шками** she has given all the children toys. **2.** (*impf.* **~я́ть**) (*+i.*) to endow (with); **приро́да ~и́ла его́ разнообра́зными спосо́бностями** nature has endowed him with a variety of talents.
одар|я́ть, я́ю *impf. of* **~и́ть**
одева́|ть(ся), ю(сь) *impf. of* **оде́ть(ся)**
оде́жд|а, ы *f.* clothes; clothing; **ве́рхняя о.** outer clothing, overcoat; **мужска́я о.** menswear; **фо́рменная о.** uniform.
одеколо́н, а *m.* eau-de-Cologne.
одел|и́ть, ю́, и́шь *pf.* (*of* **~я́ть**) (*+i.*) to present (with).
одел|я́ть, я́ю *impf. of* **~и́ть**
одёргива|ть, ю *impf. of* **одёрнуть**
одеревене́лый *adj.* numb; (*fig.*) lifeless.
одеревене́|ть, ю *pf. of* **деревене́ть**
одерж|а́ть, у́, ~ишь *pf.* (*of* **~ивать**) to gain; **о. верх (над)** to gain the upper hand (over), prevail (over); **о. побе́ду** to score a victory, carry the day.
оде́ржива|ть, ю *impf. of* **одержа́ть**
одержи́м|ый (~, ~а) *adj.* (*+i.*) possessed (by); **о. стра́хом** consumed with fear; **о. навя́зчивой иде́ей** obsessed by an idée fixe.
одёр|нуть, ну, нешь *pf.* (*of* **~гивать**) **1.** to pull down, straighten (*article of clothing*). **2.** (*fig., coll.*) to call to order; to silence; to snub.
оде́т|ый *p.p.p. of* **~ь** *and adj.* (*+i. or* **в**+*a.*) dressed (in), clothed (in); with one's clothes on; **о. сне́гом** snow-clad; **хорошо́ о.** well-dressed.
оде́|ть, ну, нешь *pf.* (*of* **~ва́ть**) (*+i. or* **в**+*a.*) to dress (in), clothe (in).
оде́|ться, нусь, нешься *pf.* (*of* **~ва́ться**) **1.** to dress (o.s.); to clothe o.s.; **о. в вече́рнее пла́тье** to put on an evening dress. **2.** *pass. of* **~ть**
одея́л|о, а *nt.* blanket; coverlet; **о-гре́лка** electric blanket; **стёганое о.** counterpane, quilt.
одея́ни|е, я *nt.* garb, attire.
оди́н, одного́ *m.*; **одна́, одно́й** *f.*; **одно́, одного́** *nt.*; *pl.* **одни́, одни́х** *num. and pron.* **1.** one; **о. стол** one table; **одно́** one thing; **одно́ де́ло..., друго́е де́ло...** it is one thing ..., another thing ...; **о. за други́м** one after the other; one by one; **одни́... други́е** some ..., (while) others; **с одно́й стороны́... с друго́й (стороны́)** on the one hand ... on the other hand; **о. раз** once; **одни́м сло́вом** in a word; **о.-два** one or two; **о. из ты́сячи** one in a thousand; **в о. го́лос** with one voice, with one accord; **в о. прекра́сный день** one fine day, once upon a time; **все до одного́** all to a man; **все, как о.** one and all; **о. на о.** in private; face to face; **по одному́** one at a time; in single file. **2.** a, an; a certain; **я встре́тил одного́ моего́ бы́вшего колле́гу** I met an old colleague of mine. **3.** alone; by o.s.; **да́йте ей сде́лать э́то одно́й** let her do it by herself; **я живу́ о.** I live alone. **4.** only; **он о. зна́ет доро́гу** only he knows the way; **она́ чита́ет одни́ детекти́вные рома́ны** she reads nothing but detective stories. **5.: о., о. и тот же** the same, one and the same; **мы с ней одного́ во́зраста** she and I are the same age; **э́то одно́ и то же** it is the same thing.
одина́ково *adv.* equally, alike.
одина́ковост|ь, и *f.* identity (*of views, etc.*)
одина́ков|ый (~, ~а) *adj.* (**с**+*i.*) identical (with), the same (as).
одина́рный *adj.* single.
оди́ннадцатый *adj.* eleventh.
оди́ннадцат|ь, и *num.* eleven.
одино́к|ий (~, ~а) *adj.* **1.** solitary; lonely; lone. **2.** *as n.* **о., ~ого** *m.* single man, bachelor; **~ая, ~ой** *f.* single woman.
одино́ко *adv.* lonely; **чу́вствовать себя́ о.** to feel lonely.
одино́честв|о, а *nt.* solitude; loneliness.
одино́чк|а, и *c.g and f.* **1.** *c.g.* lone person; **мать-о.** unmarried mother; **оте́ц-о.** single father; **жить ~ой** to live alone; **в ~у** alone, on one's own; **по ~е** one by one. **2.** *f.* (*coll.*) one-man cell, solitary confinement.
одино́чн|ый *adj.* **1.** individual; one-man; solo; **~ое заключе́ние** solitary confinement. **2.** single; **о. вы́стрел** single shot.
одио́з|ный (~ен, ~на) *adj.* odious, offensive.
одиссе́|я, и *f.* (*fig.*) odyssey.
одича́лый *adj.* wild.
одича́|ть, ю *pf. of* **дича́ть**
одна́жды *adv.* once; one day; **о. у́тром** one morning.
одна́ко 1. *adv. and conj.* however; but; though. **2.** *int.* you don't say so!; not really!
однобо́к|ий (~, ~а) *adj.* one-sided (*also fig.*).
однобо́ртный *adj.* single-breasted.
одновре́ме́нно *adv.* simultaneously, at the same time.
одновре́ме́нност|ь, и *f.* simultaneity.
одновре́ме́нный *adj.* simultaneous.
одногла́зый *adj.* one-eyed.
одногоди́чный *adj.* one-year.
одного́д|ок, ка *m.* (**с**+*i.*; *coll.*) of the same age (as).
однодне́вный *adj.* one-day.
однозна́ч|ный (~ен, ~на) *adj.* **1.** synonymous. **2.** (*ling.*) monosemantic. **3.** (*math.*) simple; **~ное число́** simple number, digit. **4.** (*fig.*) simple, straightforward.
одноимён|ный (~ен, ~на) *adj.* of the same name.
однокла́ссник, а *m.* classmate.
однокле́точный *adj.* (*biol.*) singe-cell, unicellular.
одноклу́бник, а *m.* (*coll.*) fellow-member of club.

одноколе́йный *adj.* single-track.
одноко́лк|а, и *f.* (*coll.*) gig.
однокра́тный *adj.* single; (*gram.*): **о. глаго́л** semelfactive verb.
однoку́рсник, а *m.* fellow-member of course.
одноле́тний *adj.* **1.** one-year. **2.** (*bot.*) annual.
одноле́т|ок, ка *m.* (**с**+*i.*) (*coll.*) of the same age (as).
одноме́стный *adj.* single-seated, single-seater.
одномото́рный *adj.* single-engine.
одноно́гий *adj.* one-legged.
однообра́зи|е, я *nt.* monotony.
однообра́з|ный (~ен, ~на) *adj.* monotonous.
однопала́тный *adj.* (*pol.*) unicameral, single-chamber.
однополча́н|ин, ина, *pl.* **~е, ~** *m.* comrade-in-arms (*one serving in same regiment*).
однопо́лый *adj.* (*bot.*) unisexual.
однора́зовый *adj.* disposable; temporary.
одноро́дност|ь, и *f.* homogeneity, uniformity.
одноро́д|ный (~ен, ~на) *adj.* **1.** homogeneous, uniform. **2.** similar.
однору́кий *adj.* one-handed, one-armed.
односельча́н|ин, ина, *pl.* **~е, ~** *m.* fellow-villager.
односло́жно *adv.*: **говори́ть о.** to speak in monosyllables.
односло́ж|ный *adj.* **1.** monosyllabic. **2. (~ен, ~на)** (*fig.*) terse, abrupt.
односпа́льн|ый *adj.*: **~ая крова́ть** single bed.
односторо́нн|ий *adj.* **1.** one-sided (*also fig.*); unilateral. **2.** one-way; **~ее движе́ние** one-way traffic; **о. ум** (*fig.*) one-track mind.
одноти́п|ный (~ен, ~на) *adj.* of the same type, of the same kind; **о. кора́бль** sister-ship.
однoто́мник, а *m.* single-volume edition.
однoто́мный *adj.* one-volume.
однофами́л|ец, ьца *m.* (**с**+*i.*) person bearing the same surname (as), namesake.
одноцве́тный *adj.* one-colour; (*typ.*) monochrome.
одноэта́жный *adj.* single-storey, one-storey.
одноязы́ч|ный (~ен, ~на) *adj.* monolingual.
одобре́ни|е, я *nt.* approval.
одобри́тел|ьный (~ен, ~ьна) *adj.* approving.
одо́бр|ить, ю, ишь *pf.* (*of* **~я́ть**) to approve (of); **не о.** to disapprove (of).
одобр|я́ть, я́ю *impf. of* **~ить**
одолева́|ть, ю *impf. of* **одоле́ть**
одоле́|ть, ю *pf.* (*of* **~ва́ть**) **1.** to overcome, conquer; **его́ ~л сон** he was overcome by sleepiness; **нас ~ло злово́ние** the stench overpowered us. **2.** (*fig.*) to master; to cope (with); to get through.
одолж|а́ть, а́ю *impf. of* **~и́ть**
одолже́ни|е, я *nt.* favour, service; **сде́лайте мне о.** do me a favour.
одолж|и́ть, у́, и́шь *pf.* (*of* **ода́лживать** *and* **~а́ть**) **1.** (+*d.*) to lend. **2.** (*coll.*; **у**) to borrow (from).
одома́шнени|е, я *nt.* domestication.
одома́шн|енный *p.p.p. of* **~ить** *and adj.* domesticated.
одома́шнива|ть, ю *impf. of* **одома́шнить**
одома́шн|ить, ю, ишь *pf.* (*of* **~ивать**) to domesticate.
одр, а́ *m.* (*arch.*; *now only in certain phrr.*) bed; **на сме́ртном ~е́** on one's death-bed.
одряхле́|ть, ю *pf. of* **дряхле́ть**
одува́нчик, а *m.* (*bot.*) dandelion.
оду́м|аться, аюсь *pf.* (*of* **~ываться**) to change one's mind; to think better of it.
оду́мыва|ться, юсь *impf. of* **оду́маться**
одура́чива|ть, ю *impf. of* **одура́чить**
одура́ч|ить, у, ишь *pf.* (*of* **дура́чить** *and* **~ивать**) (*coll.*) to make a fool (of), fool.
одуре́лый *adj.* (*coll.*) dulled, besotted.
одуре́ни|е, я *nt.* stupefaction, torpor.
одуре́|ть, ю *pf. of* **дуре́ть**
одурма́нива|ть, ю *impf. of* **одурма́нить**
одурма́н|ить, ю, ишь *pf.* (*of* **дурма́нить** *and* **~ивать**) to stupefy; to drug.
о́дур|ь, и *f.* (*coll.*) stupefaction, torpor.
одуря́|ть, ю *impf.* (*coll.*) to stupefy; **~ющий за́пах** heavy scent.
одутлова́т|ый (~, ~а) *adj.* puffy.
одухотворённост|ь, и *f.* spirituality.
одухотворённый *p.p.p. of* **одухотвори́ть** *and adj.* inspired.
одухотвор|и́ть, ю́, и́шь *pf.* (*of* **~я́ть**) **1.** to inspire; to animate. **2.** to attribute soul (to).
одухотвор|я́ть, я́ю *impf. of* **~и́ть**
одушев|и́ть, лю́, и́шь *pf.* (*of* **~ля́ть**) to animate.
одушевле́ни|е, я *nt.* animation.
одушевлённый *p.p.p. of* **одушеви́ть** *and adj.* animated.
одушевля́|ть, ю *impf. of* **одушеви́ть**
оды́шк|а, и *f.* short breath; **страда́ть ~ой** to be short-winded.
ожереб|и́ться, лю́сь, и́шься *pf. of* **жереби́ться**
ожере́ль|е, я *nt.* necklace.
ожесточ|а́ть(ся), а́ю(сь) *impf. of* **~и́ть(ся)**
ожесточе́ни|е, я *nt.* bitterness.
ожесточённый *p.p.p. of* **ожесточи́ть** *and adj.* bitter; embittered; hardened.
ожесточ|и́ть, у́, и́шь *pf.* (*of* **~а́ть**) to embitter; to harden.
ожесточ|и́ться, у́сь, и́шься *pf.* (*of* **~а́ться**) to become embittered; to become hardened.
ожива́|ть, ю *impf. of* **ожи́ть**
ожив|и́ть, лю́, и́шь *pf.* (*of* **~ля́ть**) **1.** to revive. **2.** (*fig.*) to enliven, vivify, animate.
ожив|и́ться, лю́сь, и́шься *pf.* (*of* **~ля́ться**) **1.** to become animated, liven (up). **2.** *pass. of* **~и́ть**
оживле́ни|е, я *nt.* **1.** animation, gusto. **2.** reviving; enlivening.
оживлённый *p.p.p. of* **оживи́ть** *and adj.* animated; lively.
оживля́|ть(ся), ю(сь) *impf. of* **оживи́ть(ся)**
ожида́ни|е, я *nt.* expectation; waiting; **обману́ть ~я** to disappoint; **в ~и** (+*g.*) pending.
ожида́|ть, ю *impf.* (+*g.*) to wait (for); to expect, anticipate; **мы э́того не ~ли** we were not expecting that; **как я и ~л** just as I expected.
ожире́ни|е, я *nt.* obesity.
ожире́|ть, ю *pf. of* **жире́ть**
ож|и́ть, иву́, ивёшь, *past* **~ил, ~ила́, ~ило** *pf.* (*of* **~ива́ть**) to come to life, revive (*also fig.*).
ожо́г, а *m.* burn; scald.
оз. (*abbr. of* **о́зеро**) L., Lake.
озабо́|тить, чу, тишь *pf.* (*of* **~чивать**) to trouble, worry, cause anxiety.
озабо́|титься, чусь, тишься *pf.* (*of* **~чиваться**) (+*i.*) to attend (to).
озабо́ченност|ь, и *f.* preoccupation; anxiety.
озабо́|ченный *p.p.p. of* **~тить** *and adj.* preoccupied; anxious, worried.
озабо́чива|ть(ся), ю(сь) *impf. of* **озабо́тить(ся)**
озагла́в|ить, лю, ишь *pf.* (*of* **~ливать**) to entitle; to head (*a chapter, etc.*).
озагла́влива|ть, ю *impf. of* **озагла́вить**
озада́ченност|ь, и *f.* perplexity, puzzlement.
озада́ч|енный *p.p.p. of* **~ить** *and adj.* perplexed, puzzled.
озада́чива|ть, ю *impf. of* **озада́чить**
озада́ч|ить, у, ишь *pf.* (*of* **~ивать**) to perplex, puzzle, take aback.
озар|и́ть, ю́, и́шь *pf.* (*of* **~я́ть**) to light up, illuminate, illumine; **улы́бка ~и́ла её лицо́** a smile lit up her face; **их ~и́ло** (*fig.*) it dawned upon them.

озар|и́ться, ю́сь, и́шься *pf.* (*of* **~я́ться**) **1.** (+*i.*) to light up (with); **её лицо́ ~и́лось ра́достью** her face lit up with joy. **2.** *pass. of* **~и́ть**
озар|я́ть(ся), я́ю(сь) *impf. of* **~и́ть(ся)**
озвере́лый *adj.* brutal; brutalized.
озвере́|ть, ю *pf. of* **звере́ть**
озву́ч|енный *p.p.p. of* **~ить; о. фильм** sound film.
оздорови́тел|ьный (~ен, ~ьна) *adj.* **1.** sanitary. **2.** fitness, keep-fit; **о. бег** jogging; **о. ла́герь** health camp.
оздоров|и́ть, лю́, и́шь *pf.* (*of* **~ля́ть**) to render (more) healthy (*also fig.*).
оздоровля́|ть, ю *impf. of* **оздорови́ть**
озелене́ни|е, я *nt.* planting with trees and gardens.
озелен|и́ть, ю́, и́шь *pf.* (*of* **~я́ть**) to plant with trees and gardens.
озелен|я́ть, я́ю *impf. of* **~и́ть**
о́земь *adv.* (*coll.*) to the ground, down.
озёрный *adj. of* **о́зеро; о. райо́н** lake district.
о́зер|о, а, *pl.* **озёра, озёр** *nt.* lake; **о. Лох-Не́сс** Loch Ness.
ози́м|ый *adj.* winter; **~ая культу́ра** winter crop; *as n.* **~ые, ~ых** winter crops.
о́зим|ь, и *f.* winter crop.
озира́|ть, ю *impf.* (*obs.*) to view.
озира́|ться, юсь *impf.* to look round; to look back.
озло́б|ить, лю, ишь *pf.* (*of* **~ля́ть**) to embitter.
озло́б|иться, люсь, ишься *pf.* (*of* **~ля́ться**) to become embittered.
озлобле́ни|е, я *nt.* bitterness, animosity.
озло́б|ленный *p.p.p. of* **~ить** *and adj.* embittered.
озлобля́|ть(ся), ю(сь) *impf. of* **озло́бить(ся)**
ознако́м|ить, лю, ишь *pf.* (*of* **~ля́ть**) (**с**+*i.*) to acquaint (with).
ознако́м|иться, люсь, ишься *pf.* (*of* **~ля́ться**) (**с**+*i.*) to familiarize o.s. with.
ознакомля́|ть(ся), ю(сь) *impf. of* **ознако́мить(ся)**
ознаменова́ни|е, я *nt.* marking, commemoration; **в о.** (+*g.*) to mark, to commemorate, in commemoration (of).
ознамен|ова́ть, у́ю *pf.* (*of* **~о́вывать**) to mark, commemorate; to celebrate.
означа́|ть, ю *impf.* to mean, signify, stand for; **что ~ют э́ти бу́квы?** what do these letters stand for?
озно́б, а *m.* shivering; chill; **почу́вствовать о.** to feel shivery.
озоло|ти́ть, чу́, ти́шь *pf.* **1.** to gild. **2.** (*coll.*) to load with money.
озо́н, а *m.* ozone.
озо́н|овый *adj. of* **~; о. слой** ozone layer.
озорни́к, а́ *m.* (*coll.*) **1.** scallywag, mischievous child. **2.** mischief-maker.
озорнича́|ть, ю *impf.* (*of* **с~**) (*coll.*) **1.** (*of a child*) to get up to mischief. **2.** (*of an adult*) to make mischief.
озорно́й *adj.* (*coll.*) mischievous.
озорств|о́, а́ *nt.* (*coll.*) mischief.
озя́б|нуть, ну, нешь, *past* **~, ~ла** *pf.* to be cold; **я ~!** I'm frozen!
ой (*or* **ой-ой-ой**) *int. expr. surprise, fright or pain* o; oh; ow, ouch!; oops!
ок. (*abbr. of* **о́коло**) approx., c., circa.
ока|за́ть, жу́, ∠жешь *pf.* (*of* **∠зывать**) to render, show; **о. влия́ние (на**+*a.*) to influence, exert influence (upon); **о. внима́ние** (+*d.*) to pay attention (to); **о. давле́ние (на**+*a.*) to put pressure (upon); **о. де́йствие (на**+*a.*) to have an effect (upon); to take effect; **о. по́мощь** (+*d.*) to help, give help; **о. предпочте́ние** (+*d.*) to prefer; **о. соде́йствие** (+*d.*) to render assistance; **о. сопротивле́ние** (+*d.*) to offer, put up resistance (to); **о. услу́гу** (+*d.*) to render a service; to do a good turn; **о. честь** (+*d.*) to do an honour.
ока|за́ться, жу́сь, ∠жешься *pf.* (*of* **∠зываться**) **1.** to turn out (to be), prove (to be); to be found (to be); **он ~за́лся отли́чным расска́зчиком** he proved to be a first-rate story-teller; **~за́лось, что она́ всё вре́мя лгала́** it turned out that she had been lying all the time. **2.** to find o.s.; to be found; **я ~за́лся в больни́це** I found myself in hospital; **трёх экземпля́ров не ~за́лось** three copies were missing.
ока́зи|я, и *f.* **1.** opportunity; **посла́ть письмо́ с ~ей** to make use of an opportunity to send a letter. **2.** unexpected happening; **что за о.!** how odd!
ока́зыва|ть(ся), ю(сь) *impf. of* **оказа́ть(ся)**
окайм|и́ть, лю́, и́шь *pf.* (*of* **~ля́ть**) (+*i.*) to border (with), edge (with).
окаймля́|ть, ю *impf. of* **окайми́ть**
ока́лин|а, ы *f.* cinder; (*tech.*) scale; slag, dross.
окамене́лост|ь, и *f.* fossil.
окамене́лый *adj.* fossilized; petrified.
окамене́|ть, ю *pf. of* **камене́ть**
окант|ова́ть, у́ю *pf. of* **кантова́ть**[1]
ока́нчива|ть(ся), ю(сь) *impf. of* **око́нчить(ся)**
о́кань|е, я *nt.* okanie (*pronunciation of unstressed* 'o' *as* 'o').
ока́пыва|ть(ся), ю(сь) *impf. of* **окопа́ть(ся)**
ока|ти́ть, чу́, ∠тишь *pf.* (*of* **∠чивать**) to pour (over); **о. холо́дной водо́й** to pour cold water (over) (*also fig.*).
ока|ти́ться, чу́сь, ∠тишься *pf.* (*of* **∠чиваться**) to pour over o.s.
о́ка|ть, ю *impf.* to pronounce unstressed Russian 'o' as 'o' rather than 'a'.
ока́чива|ть(ся), ю(сь) *impf. of* **окати́ть(ся)**
океа́н, а *m.* ocean.
океаногра́фи|я, и *f.* oceanography.
океанографи́ческий *adj.* oceanographic.
океа́нский *adj.* ocean; oceanic; ocean-going.
оки́дыва|ть, ю *impf. of* **оки́нуть**
оки́|нуть, ну, нешь *pf.* (*of* **~дывать**) to cast round; **о. взгля́дом, о. взо́ром** to take in at a glance; to glance over.
о́кис|ел, ла *m.* (*chem.*) oxide.
окисле́ни|е, я *nt.* (*chem.*) oxidation.
окисл|и́ть, ю́, и́шь *pf.* (*of* **~я́ть**) (*chem.*) to oxidize.
окисл|и́ться, ю́сь, и́шься *pf.* (*of* **~я́ться**) (*chem.*) **1.** to oxidize. **2.** *pass. of* **~и́ть**
окисл|я́ть(ся), я́ю(сь) *impf. of* **~и́ть(ся)**
о́кис|ь, и *f.* (*chem.*) oxide; **о. желе́за** ferric oxide; **о. углеро́да** carbon monoxide.
окказионали́зм, а *m.* (*ling.*) nonce-word.
оккульти́зм, а *m.* occultism.
окку́льтный *adj.* occult.
оккупа́нт, а *m.* invader, occupier.
оккупа|цио́нный *adj. of* **∠ция; ~цио́нная а́рмия** army of occupation.
оккупа́ци|я, и *f.* (*mil.*) occupation.
оккупи́р|овать, ую *impf. and pf.* (*mil.*) to occupy.
окла́д, а *m.* salary scale; salary.
окла́дист|ый (~, ~а) *adj.* (*of beard*) broad and thick.
оклеве|та́ть, щу́, ∠шешь *pf.* to slander, defame.
окле́ива|ть, ю *impf. of* **окле́ить**
окле́|ить, ю, ишь *pf.* (*of* **~ивать**) (+*i.*) to cover (with); to paste over (with); **о. ко́мнату обо́ями** to paper a room.
о́клик, а *m.* hail, call.
оклик|а́ть, а́ю *impf. of* **∠нуть**
окли́к|нуть, ну, нешь *pf.* (*of* **~а́ть**) to hail, call (to).
окн|о́, а́, *pl.* **∠а, о́кон, ∠ам** *nt.* window; **ко́мната в три ~а́** room with three windows; **о. вы́дачи** serving-hatch.
о́к|о, а, *pl.* **о́чи, оче́й** *nt.* (*arch. or poet.*) eye; **в мгнове́ние ~а** in the twinkling of an eye; **о. за о.** an eye for an eye.
ок|ова́ть, ую́, уёшь *pf.* (*of* **~о́вывать**) to bind

(*with metal*); (*fig.*) to fetter, shackle.
око́в|ы, ~ *no sg.* fetters (*also fig.*).
око́выва|ть, ю *impf. of* **окова́ть**
окола́чива|ться, юсь *impf.* (*coll.*) to lounge about, kick one's heels.
околд|ова́ть, у́ю *pf.* (*of* **~о́вывать**) to bewitch, entrance, enchant (*also fig.*).
околдо́выва|ть, ю *impf. of* **околдова́ть**
околева́|ть, ю *impf. of* **околе́ть**
околёсиц|а, ы *f.* (*coll.*) nonsense, rubbish; **нести́ ~у** to talk stuff and nonsense.
околе́|ть, ю *pf.* (*of* **~ва́ть**) (*of animals and pej. of persons*) to die.
око́лиц|а, ы *f.* outskirts (of a village); **вы́ехать за ~у** to leave the confines of a village; **на ~е** on the outskirts.
околи́чност|ь, и *f.*: **говори́ть без ~ей** to speak plainly.
о́коло *prep.+g. and adv.* **1.** by; close (to), near; around, about; **он сиде́л о. меня́** he was sitting by me; **никого́ нет о.** there is nobody about; **где́-н. о. (э́того ме́ста)** hereabouts; **(что́-н.) о. э́того, о. того́** thereabouts. **2.** about; **о. полу́ночи** about midnight; **о. шести́ ме́тров** about six metres.
околопло́дник, а *m.* (*bot.*) pericarp.
околосерде́чн|ый *adj.*: **~ая су́мка** (*anat.*) pericardium.
околпа́чива|ть, ю *impf. of* **околпа́чить**
околпа́ч|ить, у, ишь *pf.* (*of* **~ивать**) (*coll.*) to fool, dupe.
око́лыш, а *m.* cap-band.
око́льны|й *adj.* roundabout; **вы́ведать ~м путём** (*fig.*) to find out in a roundabout way.
окольц|ева́ть, у́ю *pf. of* **кольцева́ть 2.**
оконе́чност|ь, и *f.* extremity.
око́нн|ый *adj. of* **окно́**; **~ое стекло́** window-pane.
оконча́ни|е, я *nt.* **1.** end; conclusion, termination; **о. сро́ка** expiration; **по ~и университе́та** on graduating; **о. сле́дует** (*note to serial article, story, etc.*) to be concluded. **2.** (*gram.*) ending.
оконча́тельно *adv.* finally, definitively; completely.
оконча́тельный *adj.* final, definitive.
око́нч|ить, у, ишь *pf.* (*of* **ока́нчивать**) to finish, end; **о. шко́лу** to leave school; **о. университе́т** to graduate.
око́нч|иться, ится *pf.* (*of* **ока́нчиваться**) **1.** to finish, end, terminate; to be over. **2.** *pass. of* **~ить**
око́п, а *m.* (*mil.*) trench; entrenchment.
окопа́|ть, ю *pf.* (*of* **ока́пывать**) to dig round.
окопа́|ться, юсь *pf.* (*of* **ока́пываться**) **1.** (*mil.*) to entrench o.s., dig in. **2.** *pass. of* **~ть**
око́п|ный *adj. of* **~**; **~ная война́** trench warfare.
о́коро|к, ка, *pl.* **~ка́** *m.* ham, gammon; (*of mutton, veal*) leg.
окостенева́|ть, ю *impf. of* **окостене́ть**
окостене́лый *adj.* ossified (*also fig.*).
окостене́|ть, ю *pf.* (*of* **костене́ть** *and* **~ва́ть**) to ossify (*also fig.*); to stiffen.
око|ти́ться, чу́сь, ти́шься *pf. of* **коти́ться**
окочене́лый *adj.* stiff with cold.
окочене́|ть, ю *pf. of* **кочене́ть**
око́ш|ко, ка, *pl.* **~ки, ~ек, ~кам** *nt. dim. of* **окно́**
окра́ин|а, ы *f.* **1.** outskirts; outlying districts. **2.** (*obs.*) *pl.* borders, marches (*of a country*).
окра́|сить, шу, сишь *pf.* (*of* **~шивать**) to paint, colour; to dye; to stain; **слегка́ о.** to tinge, tint.
окра́ск|а, и *f.* **1.** painting, colouring; dyeing; staining. **2.** colouring, coloration; colour; **защи́тная о.** (*zool.*) protective coloration. **3.** (*fig.*) tinge, tint; (*pol.*) slant; **ирони́ческая о.** ironic tinge; **стилисти́ческая о.** stylistic nuance; **прида́ть чему́-н. другу́ю ~у** to put a different complexion on sth.
окра́шива|ть, ю *impf. of* **окра́сить**
окре́п|нуть, ну, нешь, *past* **~, ~ла** *pf. of* **кре́пнуть**
окре|сти́ть, щу́, ∠стишь *pf.* **1.** (*impf.* **крести́ть**) to baptize, christen. **2.** (*coll.*; *+a. and i.*) to nickname; **его́ ~сти́ли «медве́дем»** he was nicknamed 'the bear'.
окре|сти́ться, щу́сь, ∠стишься *pf. of* **крести́ться 1.**
окре́стност|ь, и *f.* **1.** environs. **2.** neighbourhood, vicinity.
окре́стный *adj.* **1.** neighbouring. **2.** surrounding.
о́крик, а *m.* shout, cry.
окри́кива|ть, ю *impf. of* **окри́кнуть**
окри́к|нуть, ну, нешь *pf.* (*of* **~ивать**) to hail, shout (to).
окрова́в|ить, лю, ишь *pf.* (*of* **~ливать**) to stain with blood.
окрова́в|ленный *p.p.p. of* **~ить** *and adj.* bloodstained; bloody.
окрова́влива|ть, ю *impf. of* **окрова́вить**
окроп|и́ть, лю́, и́шь *pf.* (*of* **кропи́ть** *and* **~ля́ть**) to sprinkle.
окропля́|ть, ю *impf. of* **окропи́ть**
окро́шк|а, и *f.* **1.** okroshka (*cold kvass soup with chopped vegetables and meat or fish*). **2.** (*fig., coll.*) hodgepodge, jumble.
о́круг, а, *pl.* **~а́** *m.* (*in former USSR, territorial division for administrative, legal, military, etc., purposes*) okrug; region, district; **избира́тельный о.** electoral district.
окру́г|а, и *f.* (*coll.*) neighbourhood.
округл|ённый *p.p.p. of* **~и́ть** *and adj.* rounded (*also fig.*).
округле́|ть, ю *pf. of* **кругле́ть**
округл|и́ть, ю́, и́шь *pf.* (*of* **~я́ть**) **1.** to round (off) (*also fig.*). **2.** to express in round numbers.
округл|и́ться, ю́сь, и́шься *pf.* (*of* **~я́ться**) **1.** to become rounded. **2.** to fill out.
окру́гл|ый (~, ~а) *adj.* rounded, roundish.
округл|я́ть(ся), я́ю(сь) *impf. of* **~и́ть(ся)**
окруж|а́ть, а́ю *impf. of* **~и́ть**
окружа́|ющий *pres. part. act. of* **~ть** *and adj.* surrounding; **~ющая обстано́вка** surroundings; *as n.* **~ющее, ~ющего** *nt.* environment; **~ющие, ~ющих** one's associates; entourage.
окруже́ни|е, я *nt.* **1.** encirclement; **попа́сть в о.** (*mil.*) to be encircled, be surrounded. **2.** surroundings; environment; milieu; **в ~и** (*+g.*) surrounded (by), in the midst (of); **он появи́лся в ~и боле́льщиков** he appeared surrounded by fans.
окруж|и́ть, у́, и́шь *pf.* (*of* **~а́ть**) to surround; to encircle; **о. кого́-н. забо́тами** to lavish attentions on s.o.
окружн|о́й *adj.* **1.** *adj. of* **о́круг**; **о. суд** circuit court. **2.** operating (situated) about a circle; **~а́я желе́зная доро́га** circle line.
окру́жност|ь, и *f.* circumference; circle; **име́ть де́сять ме́тров в ~и** to be ten metres in circumference; **на три ми́ли в ~и** within a radius of three miles.
окру|ти́ть, чу́, ∠тишь *pf.* (*of* **∠чивать**) (*+i.*) to wind round.
окру́чива|ть, ю *impf. of* **окрути́ть**
окрыл|и́ть, ю́, и́шь *pf.* (*of* **~я́ть**) to inspire, encourage.
окрыл|я́ть, я́ю *impf. of* **~и́ть**
окры́с|иться, ишься *pf.* (**на**+*a.*; *coll.*) to snap (at).
окта́в|а, ы *f.* (*mus. and liter.*) octave.
окта́н, а *m.* (*chem.*) octane.
окте́т, а *m.* (*mus.*) octet.
октябр|ёнок, ёнка, *pl.* **~я́та, ~я́т** *m.* Little Octobrist (*in former USSR, child aged 7–11 preparing for entry into Pioneers*).
октя́бр|ь, я́ *m.* October (*fig. = Russ. revolution of October 1917*).

октя́брь|ский *adj. of* ~
окули́ст, а *m.* oculist.
окуля́р, а *m.* eye-piece.
окун|а́ть(ся), а́ю(сь) *impf. of* **~у́ть(ся)**
окун|у́ть, у́, ёшь, *pf.* (*of* **~а́ть**) to dip.
окун|у́ться, у́сь, ёшься, *pf.* (*of* **~а́ться**) **1.** to dip (o.s.). **2.** (*fig.*; **в**+*a.*) to plunge (into), become (utterly) absorbed (in), engrossed (in); **о. в спор** to plunge into an argument.
о́кун|ь, я, *pl.* **~и, ~е́й** *m.* (*zool.*) perch.
окуп|а́ть(ся), а́ю(сь) *impf. of* **~и́ть(ся)**
окуп|и́ть, лю́, ~́ишь *pf.* (*of* **~а́ть**) to compensate, repay, make up (for); **о. расхо́ды** to cover one's outlay.
окуп|и́ться, лю́сь, ~́ишься *pf.* (*of* **~а́ться**) to be compensated, be repaid; (*fig.*) to pay; to be justified, be rewarded; **затра́ченные на́ми уси́лия ~и́лись** our efforts were rewarded.
оку́ривани|е, я *nt.* fumigation.
оку́рива|ть, ю *impf. of* **окури́ть**
окур|и́ть, ю́, ~́ишь *pf.* (*of* **~́ивать**) to fumigate.
оку́р|ок, ка *m.* cigarette-end; cigar-butt.
оку́т|ать, аю *pf.* (*of* **~ывать**) **1.** (+*i.*) to wrap up (in). **2.** (*fig.*) to shroud, cloak; **о. та́йной** to shroud in mystery.
оку́тыва|ть, ю *impf. of* **оку́тать**
ола́д|ья, ьи, *pl.* **~ий** *f.* fritter; **карто́фельная о.** potato cake.
олеа́ндр, а *m.* oleander.
оледене́лый *adj.* frozen.
оледене́|ть, ю *pf. of* **леденеть**
оледен|и́ть, ю́, и́шь *pf. of* **леденить**
оленево́д, а *m.* reindeer-breeder.
оленево́дств|о, а *nt.* reindeer-breeding.
оле́н|ий *adj. of* **~ь; ~ьи рога́** antlers; **о. лиша́й, о. мох** (*bot.*) reindeer moss.
оле́нин|а, ы *f.* venison.
оле́н|ь, я *m.* deer; **благоро́дный о.** red deer; **се́верный о.** reindeer.
оли́в|а, ы *f.* olive; olive-tree.
оливи́н, а *m.* (min.) olivine, chrysolite.
оли́вк|а, и *f.* = **оли́ва**
оли́вков|ый *adj.* **1.** olive; **~ая ветвь** olive branch (*fig.*); **~ое ма́сло** olive oil. **2.** olive(-green).
олига́рх, а *m.* oligarch.
олигархи́ческий *adj.* oligarchical.
олига́рхи|я, и *f.* oligarchy.
олимпиа́д|а, ы *f.* **1.** Olympics. **2.** Olympiad.
олимпи́|ец, йца *m.* (*myth. and fig.*) Olympian.
олимпи́йски|й[1] *adj.* Olympic; **~е и́гры** Olympic Games.
олимпи́йск|ий[2] *adj.* of Olympus; **~ое споко́йствие** (*fig.*) Olympian calm.
оли́ф|а, ы *f.* drying oil.
олицетворе́ни|е, я *nt.* personification; embodiment.
олицетвор|ённый *p.p.p. of* **~и́ть; он — ~ённая хи́трость** he is cunning personified.
олицетвор|и́ть, ю́, и́шь *pf.* (*of* **~я́ть**) to personify; to embody.
олицетвор|я́ть, я́ю *impf. of* **~и́ть**
о́лов|о, а *nt.* tin.
оловя́нн|ый *adj.* tin; **~ая посу́да** tinware; pewter; **~ая фо́льга** tin foil.
о́лух, а *m.* (*coll.*) blockhead, dolt, oaf.
олу́ш|а, и *f.* (*zool.*): **се́верная о.** gannet.
ольх|а́, и́, *pl.* **~́и** *f.* alder(-tree).
оля́пк|а, и *f.* (*zool.*) dipper.
ом, а *m.* (*elec.*) ohm.
ома́р, а *m.* lobster.
оме́г|а, и *f.* omega.
оме́л|а, ы *f.* mistletoe.
омерзе́ни|е, я *nt.* loathing; **внуши́ть о.** (+*d.*) to inspire loathing (in).
омерзи́тел|ьный (~ен, ~ьна) *adj.* loathsome, sickening.
омертве́л|ый *adj.* stiff, numb; (*med.*) necrotic; **~ая ткань** dead tissue.
омертве́|ть, ю *pf. of* **мертве́ть 1.**
омёт, а *m.* stack (of straw).
омле́т, а *m.* omelette.
омове́ни|е, я *nt.* ablution(s).
омола́жива|ть, ю *impf. of* **омолоди́ть**
омоло|ди́ть, жу́, ди́шь *pf.* (*of* **омола́живать**) to rejuvenate.
омоложе́ни|е, я *nt.* rejuvenation.
ОМОН *m. indecl.* (*abbr. of* ***отря́д мили́ции осо́бого назначе́ния***) special forces unit; (unit of) 'black berets'; riot squad.
омо́ним, а *m.* (*ling.*) homonym.
омо́нов|ец, ца *m.* member of 'black berets'.
омрач|а́ть, а́ю *impf. of* **~и́ть**
омрач|и́ть, у́, и́шь *pf.* (*of* **~а́ть**) to darken, cloud.
о́мут, а *m.* **1.** whirlpool; (*fig.*) whirl, maelstrom. **2.** deep place (*in river or lake*); **в ти́хом ~е че́рти во́дятся** (*prov.*) still waters run deep.
омыва́|ть, ю 1. *impf. of* **омы́ть. 2.** *impf.* (*geog.*) to wash (*of seas*).
ом|ы́ть, о́ю, о́ешь *pf.* (*of* **~ыва́ть**) (*rhet., obs.*) to wash; **о. кро́вью** to steep in blood.
он, его́, ему́, им, о нём *pron.* he.
она́, её, ей, ей (е́ю), о ней *pron.* she.
онани́зм, а *m.* masturbation.
онани́р|овать, ую *impf.* to masturbate.
онани́ст, а *m.* masturbator.
онда́тр|а, ы *f.* (*animal*) musk-rat, musquash; (*fur*) musquash.
онда́тр|овый *adj. of* **~а**
онеме́лый *adj.* **1.** dumb. **2.** numb.
онеме́|ть, ю *pf. of* **неме́ть**
они́, их, им, и́ми, о них *pron.* they.
о́никс, а *m.* onyx.
онколо́ги|я, и *f.* (*med.*) oncology.
оно́, его́, ему́, им, о нём *pron.* **1.** it. **2.** (= **э́то**) this, that; **о. и ви́дно** that is evident. **2.** *as emph. particle* **вот о. что!** oh, I see!
онома́стик|а, и *f.* (*ling.*) onomastics.
онтологи́ческий *adj.* (*phil.*) ontological.
отноло́ги|я, и *f.* (*phil.*) ontology.
ону́ч|а, и *f.* onucha (*foot cloth worn with bast-shoe in place of stocking*).
о́ный *pron.*: **во вре́мя о́но** in those days; (*joc.*) in days of old.
ООН *f. indecl.* (*abbr. of* ***Организа́ция Объединён-ных На́ций***) UN (*United Nations Organization*).
оо́новский *adj.* (*coll.*) UN (*United Nations*).
опада́|ть, ю *impf. of* **опа́сть**
опа́здыва|ть, ю *impf.* **1.** *impf. of* **опозда́ть. 2.** (*impf. only*) (*coll.*) to be slow (*of clocks and watches*).
опа́ива|ть, ю *impf. of* **опои́ть**
опа́л, а *m.* opal.
опа́л|а, ы *f.* disgrace, disfavour; **быть в ~е** to be in disgrace, be out of favour.
опа́лива|ть, ю *impf. of* **опали́ть**
опал|и́ть, ю́, и́шь *pf.* (*of* **пали́ть**[1] *and* **~́ивать**) to singe.
опа́ловый *adj.* opal; opaline.
опа́льный *adj.* disgraced; in disgrace, out of favour.
опа́р|а, ы *f.* **1.** leavened dough. **2.** leaven.
опарши́ве|ть, ю *pf. of* **парши́веть**
опаса́|ться, юсь *impf.* **1.** (+*g.*) to fear, be afraid (of). **2.** (+*g. or inf.*) to beware (of); to avoid, keep off; **он ~ется алкого́ля** he does not touch alcohol.
опасе́ни|е, я *nt.* fear; apprehension; misgiving(s).
опа́ск|а, и *f.*: **с ~ой** (*coll.*) with caution, cautiously; warily.
опа́слив|ый (~, ~а) *adj.* (*coll.*) cautious; wary.

опа́сност|ь, и *f.* danger; peril; **вне ~и** out of danger.
опа́с|ный (~ен, ~на) *adj.* dangerous, perilous.
опа́|сть, ду́, дёшь *pf.* (*of* **~да́ть**) **1.** (*of leaves*) to fall (off). **2.** to subside; (*of a swelling, etc.*) to go down.
опаха́л|о, а *nt.* fan.
опе́к|а, и *f.* **1.** guardianship, wardship, tutelage (*also fig.*); trusteeship; **быть под ~ой кого́-н.** to be under s.o.'s guardianship; **взять под ~у** to take as ward; (*fig.*) to take charge (of), take under one's wing. **2.** (*collect.*) guardians, board of guardians; **Междунаро́дная о.** International Trusteeship. **3.** (*fig.*) care; surveillance.
опека́|емый *pres. part. pass. of* **~ть;** *as n.* **о., ~емого** *m.* ward.
опека́|ть, ю *impf.* **1.** to be guardian (to). **2.** (*fig.*) to take care (of), watch (over).
опеку́н, а́ *m.* (*leg.*) guardian.
опеку́н|ский *adj. of* **~**
опеку́нств|о, а *nt.* guardianship.
о́пер|а, ы *f.* opera; **из друго́й ~ы, не из той ~ы** (*coll.*) quite a different matter.
операти́вност|ь, и *f.* drive; energy (*in getting things done*).
операти́в|ный *adj.* **1. (~ен, ~на)** energetic; efficient. **2.** executive. **3.** (*med.*) operative; surgical; **~ное вмеша́тельство** surgical interference. **4.** (*mil.*) operation(s), operational.
опера́тор, а *m.* **1.** operator. **2.** cameraman.
опера|цио́нный *adj. of* **~́ция; ~цио́нное отделе́ние** (*in hospital*) surgical wing; **о. стол** operating-table; *as n.* **~цио́нная, ~цио́нной** *f.* operating-theatre.
опера́ци|я, и *f.* (*med., mil., etc.*) operation; **перенести́ ~ю** to have, undergo an operation; **сде́лать ~ю** to perform an operation.
опере|ди́ть, жу́, ди́шь *pf.* (*of* **~жа́ть**) **1.** to outstrip, leave behind. **2.** to forestall.
опережа́|ть, ю *impf. of* **опереди́ть**
опере́ни|е, я *nt.* plumage.
оперённый *adj.* feathered.
опере́т|очный *adj. of* **~та**
опере́тт|а, ы *f.* musical comedy, operetta.
опере́ть, обопру́, обопрёшь, *past* **опёр, оперла́** *pf.* (*of* **опира́ть**) (**о**+*a.*) to lean (against).
опере́ться, обопру́сь, обопрёшься, *past* **опёрся, оперла́сь** *pf.* (*of* **опира́ться**) (**на**+*a.*; **о**+*a.*) **1.** to lean (on; against); **о. о подоко́нник** to lean against the window-sill. **2.** to rely on; to depend on.
опери́р|овать, ую *impf. and pf.* **1.** (*med.*) to operate (on). **2.** (*mil.*) to operate, act. **3.** (+*i.*; *fin., etc.*) to operate (with), execute operations (with); (*fig.*) to use, handle; **о. недоста́точными да́нными** to operate with inadequate data.
опер|и́ться, ю́сь, и́шься *pf.* (*of* **~я́ться**) **1.** (*of birds*) to be fledged. **2.** (*fig.*) to stand on one's own feet.
о́перн|ый *adj.* opera; operatic; **о. певе́ц, ~ая певи́ца** opera singer; **о. теа́тр** opera-house.
опёрт|ый (~, ~а́, ~о) *p.p.p. of* **опере́ть**
опер|ши́сь *past ger. of* **~е́ться; о.** (**на**+*a.*) leaning (on).
опер|я́ться, я́юсь *impf. of* **~и́ться**
опеча́л|ить(ся), ю(сь), ишь(ся) *pf. of* **печа́лить(ся)**
опеча́т|ать, аю *pf.* (*of* **~ывать**) to seal up.
опеча́т|ка, ки *f.* misprint; **спи́сок ~ок** (list of) errata.
опе́ш|ить, у, ишь *pf.* (*coll.*) to be taken aback.
опива́|ться, юсь *impf. of* **опи́ться**
о́пи|й, я *m.* opium.
о́пий|ный *adj. of* **~**
опи́лива|ть, ю *impf. of* **опили́ть**
опил|и́ть, ю́, ~́ишь *pf.* (*of* **~́ивать**) to saw; to file.
опи́л|ки, ок *no sg.* sawdust; (metal) filings.
опира́|ть(ся), ю(сь) *impf. of* **опере́ть(ся)**
описа́ни|е, я *nt.* description; account; **э́то не поддаётся ~ю** it beggars description.
описа́тельный *adj.* descriptive.
описа́тельств|о, а *nt.* (*pej.*) (bare) description.
опи|са́ть, шу́, ~́шешь *pf.* (*of* **~́сывать**) **1.** to describe. **2.** to list, inventory. **3.** (*math.*) to describe, circumscribe.
опи|са́ться, шу́сь, ~́шешься *pf.* to make a slip of the pen.
опи́ск|а, и *f.* slip of the pen.
опи́сыва|ть, ю *impf. of* **описа́ть**
о́пис|ь, и *f.* list, schedule; inventory.
опи́|ться, обопью́сь, обопьёшься, *past* **~́лся, ~ла́сь, ~́ло́сь** *pf.* (*of* **~ва́ться**) (*coll.*) to drink to excess; to have too much to drink.
о́пиум, а *m.* opium.
о́пиум|ный *adj. of* **~**
опла́|кать, чу, чешь *pf.* (*of* **~кивать**) to mourn (over); to bewail, bemoan.
опла́кива|ть, ю *impf. of* **опла́кать**
опла́т|а, ы *f.* pay, payment; **почасова́я о.** payment by the hour; **сде́льная о.** piece work payment.
опла|ти́ть, чу́, ~́тишь *pf.* to pay (for); **о. счёт** to settle the account, pay the bill; **о. убы́тки** to pay damages.
опла́чива|ть, ю *impf. of* **оплати́ть**
опла́|чу, чешь *see* **~кать**
опла|чу́, ~́тишь *see* **~ти́ть**
опл|ева́ть, юю́, юёшь *pf.* (*of* **~ёвывать**) **1.** (*coll.*) to cover with spittle. **2.** (*fig.*) to spit upon, humiliate.
оплёвыва|ть, ю *impf. of* **оплева́ть**
опле|сти́, ту́, тёшь, *past* **~̈л, ~ла́** *pf.* (*of* **~та́ть**) to twine (round); to braid.
оплета́|ть, ю *impf. of* **оплести́**
оплеу́х|а, и *f.* (*coll.*) slap in the face.
оплеши́ве|ть, ю *pf. of* **плеши́веть**
оплодотворе́ни|е, я *nt.* impregnation; fertilization.
оплодотвор|и́ть, ю́, и́шь *pf.* (*of* **~я́ть**) to impregnate (*also fig.*); to fertilize.
оплодотвор|я́ть, я́ю *impf. of* **~и́ть**
опломбир|ова́ть, у́ю *pf. of* **пломбирова́ть**
оплo̓т, а *m.* (*rhet.*) stronghold, bulwark.
оплоша́|ть, ю *pf.* (*coll.*) to blunder.
опло́шност|ь, и *f.* blunder.
оплыва́|ть, ю *impf. of* **оплы́ть**
оплы́|ть[1], ву́, вёшь *pf.* (*of* **~ва́ть**) **1.** to become swollen, swell up. **2.** (*of a candle*) to gutter. **3.** to fall (*as a result of a landslide*).
оплы́|ть[2], ву́, вёшь *pf.* (*of* **~ва́ть**) to sail round; to swim round; **о. о́стров** to sail round an island.
опове|сти́ть, щу́, сти́шь *pf.* (*of* **~ща́ть**) to notify, inform.
оповеща́|ть, ю *impf. of* **оповести́ть**
оповеще́ни|е, я *nt.* notification.
опога́н|ить, ю, ишь *pf. of* **пога́нить**
оподле́|ть, ю *pf. of* **подле́ть**
опо́|ек, йка *m.* calf(-leather).
опо́ечный *adj.* calf(-skin).
опозда́|вший *p.p. act. of* **~ть;** *as n.* **о., ~вшего** *m.* late-comer.
опозда́ни|е, я *nt.* lateness; delay; **с ~ем на де́сять мину́т** ten minutes late.
опозда́|ть, ю *pf.* (*of* **опа́здывать**) to be late; **о. на ле́кцию** to be late for the lecture; **о. на полчаса́** to be half an hour late; **о. с упла́той нало́гов** to be late in paying taxes.
опознава́ни|е, я *nt.* identification; **о. самолётов** aircraft recognition.
опознава́тельный *adj.* distinguishing; **о. знак** landmark, (*naut.*) beacon; (*on wings of aircraft*) marking.

опозна|ва́ть, ю́, ёшь *impf. of* ∠**ть**
опозна́ни|е, я *nt.* (*leg.*) identification.
опозна́|ть, ю *pf.* (*of* ~**ва́ть**) to identify.
опозо́р|ить(ся), ю(сь), ишь(ся) *pf. of* **позо́рить(ся)**
опо|и́ть, ю́, и́шь *pf.* (*of* **опа́ивать**) to give too much to drink.
опо́йковый *adj.* calf(-skin).
ополáскива|ть, ю *impf. of* **ополоска́ть** *and* **ополосну́ть**
ополз|а́ть, а́ю *impf. of* ~**ти́**[1,2]
о́полз|ень, ня *m.* landslide, landslip.
о́полз|невый *adj. of* ~**ень**
ополз|ти́[1], **у́, ёшь,** *past* ∠, ~**ла́** *pf.* (*of* ~**а́ть**) to crawl round.
ополз|ти́[2], **ёт,** *past* ∠, ~**ла́** *pf.* (*of* ~**а́ть**) to slip.
ополо|ска́ть, щу́, ∠**шешь** *pf.* (*of* **ополáскивать**) = ~**сну́ть**
ополосн|у́ть, у́, ёшь, *pf.* (*of* **ополáскивать**) to rinse; to swill.
ополч|а́ть(ся), а́ю(сь) *impf. of* ~**и́ть(ся)**
ополче́н|ец, ца *m.* militiaman; home guard.
ополче́ни|е, я *nt.* **1.** militia; home guard. **2.** (*collect.*; *hist.*) irregulars; levies.
ополч|и́ться, у́сь, и́шься *pf.* (*of* ~**а́ться**) (**на**+*a.* *or* **про́тив**) to take up arms (against); (*fig.*) to be up in arms (against); to turn (against).
опо́мн|иться, юсь, ишься *pf.* to come to one's senses; to collect o.s.
опо́р, а *m. only in phr.* **во весь о.** at top speed, full tilt.
опо́р|а, ы *f.* support (*also fig.*); (*tech.*) bearing; pier (*of a bridge*); (*fig.*) buttress; **то́чка** ~**ы** (*phys.*, *tech.*) fulcrum.
опора́жнива|ть, ю *impf. of* **опоро́жнить**
опо́р|ки, ков *pl.* (*sg.* ~**ок,** ~**ка** *m.*) down-at-heel shoes.
опо́р|ный *adj. of* ~**а**; (*tech.*) bearing, supporting; **о. ка́мень** abutment stone; **о. пункт** (*mil.*) strong point; ~**ная сва́я** bridge pile.
опоро́жн|ить, ю, ишь *pf.* (*of* **опора́жнивать**) to empty; to drain.
опорожня́|ть, ю *impf.* = **опора́жнивать**
опоро́с, а *m.* farrow (*of sow*).
опоро́ч|ить, у, ишь *pf. of* **поро́чить**
опо́ссум, а *m.* (*zool.*) opossum.
опосты́ле|ть, ю *pf.* (*coll.*; +*d.*) to become hateful (to).
опохмел|и́ться, ю́сь, и́шься *pf.* (*of* ~**я́ться**) (*coll.*) to take a hair of the dog that bit you.
опохмел|я́ться, я́юсь, *impf. of* ~**и́ться**
опочива́|ть, ю *impf. of* **опочи́ть**
опочи́|ть, ю, ешь *pf.* (*of* ~**ва́ть**) (*obs.*) **1.** to go to sleep. **2.** (*fig.*, *poet.*) to pass to one's rest.
опо́шл|ить, ю, ишь *pf.* (*of* ~**я́ть**) to vulgarize, debase.
опошля́|ть, ю *impf. of* **опо́шлить**
опоя́|сать, шу, шешь *pf.* (*of* ~**сывать**) **1.** to gird, engird(le). **2.** (*fig.*) to girdle.
опоя́|саться, шусь, шешься *pf.* (*of* ~**сываться**) **1.** (+*i.*) to gird o.s. (with), gird on. **2.** *pass. of* ~**сать**
опоя́сыва|ть(ся), ю(сь) *impf. of* **опоя́сать(ся)**
оппози|цио́нный *adj. of* ∠**ция**
оппози́ци|я, и *f.* opposition.
оппоне́нт, а *m.* opponent.
оппони́р|овать, ую *impf.* (+*d.*) to oppose.
оппортуни́зм, а *m.* opportunism.
оппортуни́ст, а *m.* opportunist.
оппортунисти́ческий *adj.* opportunist.
опра́в|а, ы *f.* setting, mounting; frame; **очки́ без** ~**ы** rimless spectacles.
оправда́ни|е, я *nt.* **1.** justification. **2.** excuse. **3.** (*leg.*) acquittal, discharge.
оправда́тельный *adj.*: **о. пригово́р** verdict of 'not guilty'.
оправд|а́ть, а́ю *pf.* (*of* ∠**ывать**) **1.** to justify; **о. ожида́ния** to come up to expectations; **о. себя́** to justify o.s.; **о. расхо́ды** to authorize expenses. **2.** to excuse; **о. посту́пок боле́знью** to excuse an action by reason of sickness. **3.** (*leg.*) to acquit, discharge.
оправд|а́ться, а́юсь *pf.* (*of* ∠**ываться**) **1.** to justify o.s.; to vindicate o.s.; **о. незна́нием** (*leg.*) to plead ignorance. **2.** to be justified; **моё предсказа́ние** ~**а́лось** my prediction has come true; **расхо́ды** ~**а́лись** the expense was worth it.
опра́вдыва|ть, ю *impf. of* **оправда́ть**
опра́вдыва|ться, юсь *impf.* **1.** *impf. of* **оправда́ться. 2.** to try to justify *or* vindicate o.s.
опра́в|ить, лю, ишь *pf.* (*of* ~**ля́ть**) **1.** to put in order, adjust (*dress*, *coiffure*, *etc.*). **2.** to set, mount.
опра́в|иться, люсь, ишься *pf.* (*of* ~**ля́ться**) **1.** to put (one's dress, *etc.*) in order. **2.** (**от**) to recover (from).
опра́вк|а, и *f.* **1.** (*tech.*) mandrel, chuck; (riveting) drift. **2.** setting, mounting.
оправля́|ть(ся), ю(сь) *impf. of* **опра́вить(ся)**
опра́шива|ть, ю *impf. of* **опроси́ть**
определе́ни|е, я *nt.* **1.** definition; (*chem.*, *phys.*, *etc.*) determination. **2.** (*leg.*) decision. **3.** (*gram.*) attribute.
определён|ный (~**ен,** ~**на)** *adj.* **1.** definite; fixed; **о. за́работок** fixed wage; **о. член** (*gram.*) definite article. **2.** certain; **в** ~**ных слу́чаях** in certain cases.
определи́тел|ь, я *m.* (*math.*) determinant.
определ|и́ть, ю́, и́шь *pf.* (*of* ~**я́ть**) to define; to determine; to fix, appoint; **о. боле́знь** to diagnose a disease; **о. ме́ру наказа́ния** to fix a punishment; **о. расстоя́ние** to judge a distance.
определ|и́ться, ю́сь, и́шься *pf.* (*of* ~**я́ться**) **1.** to be formed; to take shape; to be determined. **2.** (*aeron.*) to obtain a fix, find one's position. **3.** *pass. of* ~**и́ть**
определ|я́ть(ся), я́ю(сь) *impf. of* ~**и́ть(ся)**
опресне́ни|е, я *nt.* desalination.
опресн|и́ть, ю́, и́шь *pf.* (*of* ~**я́ть**) to desalinate.
опресн|я́ть, я́ю *impf. of* ~**и́ть**
опри́чнин|а, ы *f.* (*hist.*) oprichnina (*special administrative élite established in Russia by Ivan IV, also the territory assigned to this élite*).
опро́б|овать, ую *pf.* **1.** (*tech.*) to test. **2.** to sample, try.
опроверг|а́ть, а́ю *impf. of* ∠**нуть**
опрове́рг|нуть, ну, нешь, *past* ~, ~**ла** *pf.* (*of* ~**а́ть**) to refute, disprove.
опроверже́ни|е, я *nt.* refutation; disproof; denial.
опрокидн|о́й *adj.*: **грузови́к с** ~**ы́м я́щиком** tip-up lorry.
опроки́дыва|ть(ся), ю(сь) *impf. of* **опроки́нуть(ся)**
опроки́|нуть, ну, нешь *pf.* (*of* ~**дывать**) **1.** to overturn; to topple over. **2.** (*mil.*) to overthrow; to overrun. **3.** (*fig.*) to upset; to refute.
опроки́|нуться, нусь, нешься *pf.* (*of* ~**дываться**) **1.** to overturn; to topple over, tip over; to capsize. **2.** *pass. of* ~**нуть**
опроме́тчив|ый (~, ~**а)** *adj.* precipitate, rash, hasty.
о́прометью *adv.* headlong.
опро́с, а *m.* (*mil.*, *etc.*) interrogation; (*leg.*, *etc.*) (cross-)examination; poll; **о. обще́ственного мне́ния** opinion poll.
опро|си́ть, шу́, ∠**сишь** *pf.* (*of* **опра́шивать**) to interrogate; to (cross-)examine.
опро́с|ный *adj. of* ~; **о. лист** questionnaire.
опроста́|ть, ю *pf.* (*of* **опра́стывать**) (*coll.*) to empty; to remove the contents (of).
опростоволо́|ситься, шусь, сишься *pf.* (*coll.*) to make a gaffe, blunder.
опротест|ова́ть, у́ю *pf.* (*of* ~**о́вывать**) **1.: о. ве́ксель** (*fin.*) to protest a bill. **2.** (*leg.*) to appeal (against).

опротестóвыва|ть, ю *impf. of* **опротестовáть**
опротúве|ть, ю *pf.* to become loathsome, become repulsive.
опры́ск|ать, *pf.* (*of* **~ивать**) to sprinkle; to spray.
опры́скива|ть, ю *impf. of* **опры́скать**
опря́тност|ь, и *f.* neatness, tidiness.
опря́т|ный (~ен, ~на) *adj.* neat, tidy.
óптик, а *m.* optician.
óптик|а, и *f.* optics.
оптимáльный *adj.* optimum, optimal.
оптимúзм, а *m.* optimism.
оптимúст, а *m.* optimist.
оптимистúческий *adj.* optimistic.
óптимум, а *m.* (*biol., etc.*) optimum.
оптúческ|ий *adj.* optic, optical; **о. обмáн** optical illusion.
оптовúк, á *m.* wholesaler.
оптóвый *adj.* wholesale.
óптом *adv.* wholesale.
опубликовáни|е, я *nt.* publication; **о. закóна** promulgation of a law.
опублик|овáть, ýю *pf.* (*of* **публиковáть** *and* **~óвывать**) to publish; **о. закóн** to promulgate a law.
опубликóвыва|ть, ю *impf. of* **опубликовáть**
óпус, а *m.* (*mus.*) opus.
опускá|ть(ся), ю(сь) *impf. of* **опустúть(ся)**
опустéлый *adj.* deserted.
опустé|ть, ю *pf. of* **пустéть**
опу|стúть, щý, ~́стишь *pf.* (*of* **~скáть**) **1.** to lower; to let down; **о. штóры** to draw the blinds; **о. глазá** to look down; **о. гóлову** (*fig.*) to hang one's head; **о. рýки** (*fig.*) to lose heart. **2.** to turn down (*collar, etc.*). **3.** to omit.
опу|стúться, щýсь, ~́стишься *pf.* (*of* **~скáться**) **1.** to lower o.s. **2.** to sink; to fall; to go down; **о. в крéсло** to sink into a chair; **о. на колéни** to go down on one's knees; **у негó рýки ~стúлись** (*fig.*) he has lost heart. **3.** (*fig.*) to sink; to let o.s. go; to go to pieces.
опустош|áть, áю *impf. of* **~úть**
опустошéни|е, я *nt.* devastation.
опустошúтел|ьный (~ен, ~ьна) *adj.* devastating.
опустош|úть, ý, úшь *pf.* (*of* **~áть**) to devastate, lay waste, ravage.
опýт|ать, аю *pf.* (*of* **~ывать**) to enmesh, entangle (*also fig.*); (*fig.*) to ensnare.
опýтыва|ть, ю *impf. of* **опýтать**
опух|áть, áю *impf. of* **~́нуть**
опýхлый *adj.* (*coll.*) swollen.
опýх|нуть, ну, нешь, *past* **~, ~ла** *pf.* (*of* **~áть**) to swell (up).
óпухол|ь, и *f.* swelling; (*med.*) tumour.
опуш|áть, áю *impf. of* **~úть**
опуш|úть, ý, úшь *pf.* (*of* **~áть**) **1. (мéхом)** to edge, trim (with fur). **2.** (*of hoar-frost or snow*) to powder; to cover; **бóроду у негó ~úло снéгом** his beard was powdered with snow.
опýшк|а[1], и *f.* edging, trimming.
опýшк|а[2], и *f.* edge (*of a forest, of a wood*).
опущéни|е, я *nt.* **1.** lowering; letting down; **о. мáтки** (*med.*) prolapse of the uterus. **2.** omission.
опý|щенный *p.p.p. of* **~стúть; как в вóду о.** (*fig.*) crestfallen, downcast.
опылéни|е, я *nt.* (*bot.*) pollination; **перекрёстное о.** cross-pollination.
опы́лива|ть, ю *impf. of* **опылúть 2.**
опыл|úть, ю́, úшь *pf.* (*impf.* **~я́ть**) **1.** (*bot.*) to pollinate. **2.** (*impf.* **~́ивать**) (*agric.*) to dust.
опыл|я́ть, я́ю *impf. of* **~úть 1.**
óпыт, а *m.* **1.** experience; **на сóбственном ~е** from (one's own) experience. **2.** experiment; test, trial; attempt.
óпыт|ный *adj.* **1. (~ен, ~на)** experienced. **2.** experimental; **узнáть ~ным путём** to learn by means of experiment; **~ная стáнция** experimental station.
опьянéлый *adj.* intoxicated.
опьянéни|е, я *nt.* intoxication.
опьянé|ть, ю *pf. of* **пьянéть**
опьян|úть, ю́, úшь *pf.* (*of* **пьянúть** *and* **~я́ть**) to intoxicate, make drunk; **успéх ~úл егó** success has gone to his head.
опьян|я́ть, я́ю *impf. of* **~úть**
опьяня́|ющий *pres. part. act. of* **~ть** *and adj.* intoxicating.
опя́ть *adv.* again.
опя́ть-таки *adv.* (*coll.*) **1.** (and) what is more; **он холостя́к, о.-т. богáтый человéк** he is a bachelor, and what is more he is a rich man. **2.** but (yet) again; **я постучáл ещё раз, о.-т. ничегó не послы́шалось** I knocked again, but again there was nothing to be heard.
орáв|а, ы *f.* (*coll.*) crowd, horde.
орáкул, а *m.* oracle.
орáл|о, а *nt.* (*obs. and dial.*) plough.
орáнжевый *adj.* orange (*colour*).
оранжерé|йный *adj. of* **~я; ~йное растéние** hothouse plant (*also fig.*)
оранжерé|я, и *f.* hothouse, greenhouse, conservatory.
орáтор, а *m.* orator, (public) speaker.
оратóри|я, и *f.* (*mus.*) oratorio.
орáтор|ский *adj. of* **~**; oratorical; **~ское искýсство** oratory.
орáторств|овать, ую *impf.* to orate, speechify.
ор|áть, ý, ёшь *impf.* (*coll.*) to bawl, yell.
орбúт|а, ы *f.* **1.** (*astron. and fig.*) orbit; **вы́вести на ~у** to put into orbit. **2.** (*anat.*) eye-socket; **глазá у негó вы́шли из ~** (*fig.*) his eyes leaped from their sockets.
орг... *comb. form, abbr. of* **организациóнный**
...орг *comb. form, abbr. of* **организáтор**
оргáзм, а *m.* (*physiol.*) orgasm.
óрган, а *m.* (*biol., pol., etc.*) organ; **исполнúтельный о.** agency; **~ы влáсти** organs of government; **половы́е ~ы** genitals.
оргáн, а *m.* (*mus.*) organ.
организáтор, а *m.* organizer.
организáтор|ский *adj. of* **~; о. талáнт** talent for organization.
организа|циóнный *adj. of* **~́ция**
организáци|я, и *f.* organization; agency; **о. по оказáнию пóмощи** aid *or* relief agency.
органúзм, а *m.* organism.
организóванност|ь, и *f.* (good) organization.
организóванный *p.p.p. of* **организовáть** *and adj.* organized; well-organized.
организ|овáть, ýю *impf. and pf.* (*pf. also* **с~**) to organize.
организ|овáться, ýюсь *impf. and pf.* **1.** to be organized. **2.** to organize (*intrans.*).
органúст, а *m.* organist.
органúческ|ий *adj.* organic; **~ая хúмия** organic chemistry.
оргáн|ный *adj. of* **~; о. концéрт** concerto for organ.
óрги|я, и *f.* orgy.
оргпрестýпност|ь, и *f.* organized crime.
оргтéхник|а, и *f.* (*abbr. of* ***организациóнная тéхника***) office equipment.
орд|á, ы́, *pl.* **~́ы, ~, ~́ам** *f.* (*hist. and fig.*) horde; **Золотáя о.** the Golden Horde.
óрден[1], а, *pl.* **~á, ~óв** *m.* order; decoration; **о. Подвя́зки** Order of the Garter.
óрден[2], а, *pl.* **~ы, ~ов** *m.* order; **масóнский о.** Masonic Order.
орденонóс|ец, ца *m.* holder of an order.
орденонóсный *adj.* decorated with an order.

о́рден|ский *adj. of* ~; **~ская ле́нта** ribbon.
о́рдер, а, *pl.* **~а́, ~о́в** *m.* order, warrant; (*leg.*) writ; **о. на о́быск** search warrant; **о. на поку́пку** coupon; **о. на кварти́ру** authorization to an apartment.
ордина́р|ец, ца *m.* (*mil.*) orderly; batman.
ордина́р|ный (~ен, ~на) *adj.* ordinary.
ордина́т|а, ы *f.* (*math.*) ordinate.
ор|ёл, ла́, *m.* eagle; **о. и́ли ре́шка?** heads or tails?
орео́л, а *m.* halo, aureole.
оре́х, а *m.* **1.** nut; **америка́нский о.** Brazil nut; **гре́цкий о.** walnut; **коко́совый о.** coconut; **лесно́й о.** hazel-nut; **разде́лать (отде́лать) кого́-н. под о.** (*coll.*) to give it s.o. hot. **2.** nut-tree. **3.** (*wood*) walnut; **шкаф из ~а** walnut cupboard.
оре́х|овый *adj. of* ~; **~овое де́рево** nut-tree; (*wood*) walnut; **о. шокола́д** nut chocolate.
оре́ш|ек, ка *m. dim. of* **оре́х; черни́льный о.** nut-gall.
оре́шник, а *m.* **1.** (hazel) nut-tree. **2.** hazel-grove.
оригина́л, а *m.* **1.** original. **2.** character, oddball.
оригина́льнича|ть, ю *impf.* (*of* **с~**) (*coll.*) to put on an act, try to be clever.
оригина́л|ьный (~ен, ~ьна) *adj.* original; offbeat, oddball.
ориента́ци|я, и *f.* **1.** (**на**+*a.*) orientation (toward). **2.** (*fig.*) (**в**+*p.*) understanding (of), grasp (of); **у него́ хоро́шая о. в ю́жно-америка́нских дела́х** he has a firm grasp of South American affairs.
ориенти́р, а *m.* (*mil.*) reference point; guiding line; **(есте́ственный) о.** landmark.
ориенти́р|овать, ую *impf. and pf.* **1.** to orient, orientate; (**в**+*p.*) to enlighten (concerning); **он не ~овал меня́ в экономи́ческом положе́нии** he did not put me in the picture about the economic position. **2.** (**на**+*a.*) to direct (toward).
ориенти́р|оваться, уюсь *impf. and pf.* **1.** to orient o.s.; to find one's bearings (*also fig.*); **я пло́хо ~уюсь** I have a poor sense of direction; **она́ бы́стро ~овалась в но́вой обстано́вке** (*fig.*) she quickly found her feet in her new surroundings. **2.** (**на**+*a.*) to head (for), make (for); (*fig.*) to direct one's attention (to, toward); **о. на рабо́чих слу́шателей** to cater for a working-class audience.
ориентиро́вк|а, и *f.* = **ориента́ция**
ориентиро́вочно *adv.* tentatively; approximately; **гру́бо о.** as a rough guide.
ориентиро́воч|ный *adj.* **1.** position-finding. **2.** **(~ен, ~на)** tentative; rough, approximate.
орке́стр, а *m.* **1.** orchestra; band. **2.** orchestra-pit.
оркестр|ова́ть, у́ю *impf. and pf.* to orchestrate.
оркестро́вк|а, и *f.* orchestration.
оркестро́вый *adj.* **1.** *adj. of* **орке́стр. 2.** orchestral.
орла́н, а *m.* sea eagle.
орл|ёнок, ёнка, *pl.* **~я́та, ~я́т** *m.* eaglet.
орли́ный *adj. of* **орёл; о. нос** aquiline nose.
орли́ц|а, ы *f.* female eagle.
орна́мент, а *m.* ornament; ornamental design.
орнамента́льный *adj.* ornamental.
орнамента́ци|я, и *f.* ornamentation.
орнаменти́р|овать, ую *impf. and pf.* to ornament.
орнито́лог, а *m.* ornithologist; **о.-люби́тель** bird-watcher.
орнитологи́ческий *adj.* ornithological.
орнитоло́ги|я, и *f.* ornithology.
оробе́лый *adj.* timid; frightened.
оробе́|ть, ю *pf. of* **робе́ть**
ороси́тельный *adj.* irrigation; irrigating; **о. кана́л** irrigation canal.
оро|си́ть, шу́, си́шь *pf.* (*of* **~ша́ть**) to irrigate.
оро|ша́ть, ша́ю *impf. of* **~си́ть**
ороше́ни|е, я *nt.* irrigation; **поля́ ~я** sewage-farm.
ортодо́кс, а *m.* conformist.
ортодокса́л|ьный (~ен, ~ьна) *adj.* orthodox.
ортодо́кси|я, и *f.* orthodoxy.
ортопе́д, а *m.* orthopaedist.
ортопеди́ческий *adj.* orthopaedic.
ортопе́ди́|я, и *f.* orthopaedics.
ору́ди|е, я *nt.* **1.** instrument; implement; tool (*also fig.*); **сельскохозя́йственные ~я** agricultural implements. **2.** gun; **зени́тное о.** anti-aircraft gun.
оруд|и́йный *adj. of* **∸ие 2.; о. ого́нь** gun-fire; **о. око́п** gun-entrenchment; **о. расчёт** gun crew.
ору́д|овать, ую *impf.* (*coll.*; +*i.*) **1.** to handle. **2.** (*fig.*, *pej.*) to be active; **он там всем ~ует** he bosses the whole show.
оруже́йник, а *m.* gunsmith, armourer.
оруж|е́йный *adj. of* **∸ие; ~е́йная пала́та** armoury; **~е́йная блока́да** arms embargo; **о. ма́стер** armourer.
ору́жи|е, я *nt.* arm(s); weapons; **огнестре́льное о.** fire-arm(s); **стрелко́вое о.** small arms; **я́дерное о.** nuclear weapons; **бра́ться за о.** to take up arms; **положи́ть о., сложи́ть о.** to lay down one's arms; **бить кого́-н. его́ же ~ем** (*fig.*) to beat s.o. at his own game.
орфографи́ческ|ий *adj.* orthographic(al); **~ая оши́бка** spelling mistake.
орфогра́фи|я, и *f.* orthography, spelling.
орфоэпи́ческий *adj.*: **о. слова́рь** pronouncing dictionary.
орхиде́|я, и *f.* (*bot.*) orchid.
ос|а́, ы́, *pl.* **∸ы** *f.* wasp.
оса́д|а, ы *f.* siege; **снять ~у** to raise a siege.
оса|ди́ть[1], жу́, ди́шь *pf.* (*of* **~жда́ть**) to besiege, lay siege to; to beleaguer; **о. вопро́сами** to ply with questions; **о. про́сьбами** to bombard with requests.
оса|ди́ть[2], жу́, ∸дишь *pf.* (*of* **∸живать**) **1.** to check, halt; to force back; **о. ло́шадь** to rein in a horse. **2.** (*fig.*): **о. кого́-н.** to put s.o. in his place, take s.o. down a peg.
оса́дк|а, и *f.* **1.** set, settling (*of soil, etc.*). **2.** (*naut.*) draught; **су́дно с небольшо́й ~ой** vessel of shallow draught.
оса́д|ный *adj. of* **~а; ~ная война́** siege warfare; **~ное положе́ние** state of siege.
оса́д|ок, ка *m.* **1.** (*pl.*) precipitation. **2.** sediment, deposition. **3.** (*fig.*) after-taste.
оса́д|очный *adj. of* **~ок; ~очные поро́ды** (*geol.*) sedimentary rocks.
осажда́|ть, ю *impf. of* **осади́ть[1]**
осаждённый *p.p.p. of* **осади́ть[1]**
оса́женный *p.p.p. of* **осади́ть[2]**
оса́жива|ть, ю *impf. of* **осади́ть[2]**
оса́нист|ый (~, ~а) *adj.* portly.
оса́нк|а, и *f.* carriage, bearing.
оса́нн|а, ы *f.* hosanna; **восклица́ть, петь ~у кому́-н.** (*fig.*) to sing s.o.'s praises.
ОСВ *nt. indecl.* (*abbr. of* ***ограниче́ние стратеги́ческих вооруже́ний***): **перегово́ры по ОСВ** SALT (*Strategic Arms Limitation Treaty*) talks.
осва́ива|ть(ся), ю(сь) *impf. of* **осво́ить(ся)**
осведоми́тел|ь, я *m.* informant.
осведоми́тельн|ый *adj.* **1.** informative. **2.** (*giving, conveying*) information; **~ая рабо́та** information work, publicity work.
осве́дом|ить, лю, ишь *pf.* (*of* **~ля́ть**) to inform.
осве́дом|иться, люсь, ишься *pf.* (*of* **~ля́ться**) (**о**+*i.*) to inquire (about).
осведомле́ни|е, я *nt.* notification.
осведомлённост|ь, и *f.* knowledge, (possession of) information; **у него́ хоро́шая о. в исла́ндских са́гах** he is very knowledgeable about the Icelandic sagas.
осведомлённый *p.p.p. of* **осве́домить** *and* (**в**+*p.*) well-informed (about), knowledgeable (about).
осведом|ля́ть(ся), ля́ю(сь) *impf. of* **∸ить(ся)**
освеж|а́ть, а́ю *impf. of* **~и́ть**

освеж|ева́ть, у́ю *pf. of* **свежева́ть**
освежи́тельный *adj.* refreshing.
освеж|и́ть, у́, и́шь *pf.* (*of* **~а́ть**) **1.** to refresh; to freshen; **о. ко́мнату** to give a room an airing. **2.** (*fig.*) to refresh, revive; **о. свои́ зна́ния** to brush up one's knowledge.
освети́тельн|ый *adj.* lighting, illuminating; **~ая ракéта** (*aeron.*) flare.
осве|ти́ть, щу́, ти́шь *pf.* (*of* **~ща́ть**) to light up; to illuminate, illumine; (*fig.*) to shed light on; to cover, report (*in the press*).
осве|ти́ться, щу́сь, ти́шься *pf.* (*of* **~ща́ться**) **1.** to light up; to brighten; **её лицо́ ~ти́лось улы́бкой** (*fig.*) a smile lit up her face. **2.** *pass. of* **~ти́ть**
освеща́|ть(ся), ю(сь) *impf. of* **освети́ть(ся)**
освеще́ни|е, я *nt.* lighting, illumination; **иску́сственное о.** artificial lighting.
освещённост|ь, и *f.* (*degree of, area of*) illumination.
осве|щённый *p.p.p. of* **~ти́ть; о. звёздами** star-lit; **о. луно́й** moonlit; **о. свеча́ми** candle-lit.
освиде́тельств|овать, ую *pf. of* **свиде́тельствовать 3.**
осви|ста́ть, щу́, ∠щешь *pf.* (*of* **∠стывать**) to hiss (off), catcall; **о. актёра** to hiss an actor off the stage.
осви́стыва|ть, ю *impf. of* **освиста́ть**
освободи́тел|ь, я *m.* liberator.
освободи́тельн|ый *adj.* liberation, emancipation; **~ая война́** war of liberation.
освобо|ди́ть, жу́, ди́шь *pf.* (*of* **~жда́ть**) **1.** to free, liberate; to release, set free; to emancipate; **о. от вое́нной слу́жбы** to exempt from military service. **2. (от до́лжности)** to dismiss. **3.** to vacate; to clear, empty.
освобо|ди́ться, жу́сь, ди́шься *pf.* (*of* **~жда́ться**) **1. (от)** to free o.s. (of, from); to become free. **2.** *pass. of* **~ди́ть**
освобожда́|ть(ся), ю(сь) *impf. of* **освободи́ть(ся)**
освобожде́ни|е, я *nt.* **1.** liberation; release; emancipation; discharge. **2.** dismissal. **3.** vacation (*of premises, etc.*).
освобо|ждённый *p.p.p. of* **~ди́ть; о. от нало́га** tax-free.
освое́ни|е, я *nt.* assimilation, mastery, familiarization; **о. но́вой те́хники** learning to handle new machinery; **о. кра́йнего се́вера** the opening up of the Far North.
осво́|ить, ю, ишь *pf.* (*of* **осва́ивать**) **1.** to assimilate, master; to cope (with); to become familiar (with). **2.** (*bot.*) to acclimatize.
осво́|иться, юсь, ишься *pf.* (*of* **осва́иваться**) **1.** (**с**+*i.*) to familiarize o.s. (with). **2.** to feel at home; **о. в но́вой среде́** to get the feel of new surroundings.
освя|ти́ть, щу́, ти́шь *pf.* **1.** (*impf.* **святи́ть**) (*eccl.*) to consecrate; to bless, sanctify. **2.** (*impf.* **~ща́ть**) (*fig.*) to sanctify, hallow.
освяща́|ть, ю *impf. of* **освяти́ть**
освя|щённый *p.p.p. of* **~ти́ть; обы́чай, о. века́ми** time-honoured custom.
ос|ево́й *adj. of* **~ь**; axial.
осе́да́|ть, ю *impf. of* **осе́сть**
оседла́|ть, ю *pf.* **1.** (*impf.* **седла́ть**) to saddle. **2.** (*mil.*; *fig.*) to gain control (of).
осе́длост|ь, и *f.* settled (way of) life; **черта́ ~и** (*hist.*) the Pale of Settlement.
осе́длый *adj.* settled.
осека́|ться, юсь *impf. of* **осе́чься**
ос|ёл, ла́ *m.* donkey; ass (*also fig.*).
осел|о́к, ка́ *m.* **1.** touchstone (*also fig.*). **2.** whetstone.
осемене́ни|е, я *nt.* insemination.
осемен|и́ть, ю́, и́шь *pf.* (*of* **~я́ть**) to inseminate.
осемен|я́ть, я́ю *impf. of* **~и́ть**
осен|и́ть, ю́, и́шь *pf.* (*of* **~я́ть**) **1.** to overshadow; (*fig.*) to shield; **о. кре́стом** to make the sign of the cross (over). **2.** (*fig.*) to dawn upon, strike; **его́ ~и́ла мысль** it dawned upon him; (*impers.*): **меня́ внеза́пно ~и́ло** it suddenly occurred to me.
осе́нний *adj. of* **о́сень**; autumnal.
о́сен|ь, и *f.* autumn.
о́сенью *adv.* in autumn.
осен|я́ть, я́ю *impf. of* **~и́ть**
осерча́|ть, ю *pf. of* **серча́ть**
ос|е́сть, я́ду, я́дешь, *past* **~е́л, ~е́ла** *pf.* (*of* **~еда́ть**) **1.** to settle, subside; to sink; to form a sediment. **2.** (*of human beings*) to settle.
осётр, а́ *m.* sturgeon.
осетри́н|а, ы *f.* (flesh of) sturgeon.
осетро́вый *adj. of* **осётр**
осе́чк|а, и *f.* misfire; **дать ~у** to misfire (*also fig.*).
осе́|чься, ку́сь, чёшься, ку́тся, *past* **~кся, ~клась** *pf.* (*of* **~ка́ться**) (*coll.*) **1.** to misfire (*also fig.*). **2.** to stop short (*in speaking*).
оси́лива|ть, ю *impf. of* **оси́лить**
оси́л|ить, ю, ишь *pf.* (*of* **~ивать**) **1.** to overpower. **2.** (*coll.*) to master; to manage; **о. гре́ческий алфави́т** to master the Greek alphabet; **я е́ле ~ил ещё оди́н стака́н** I was hardly able to manage another glass.
оси́н|а, ы *f.* asp(en).
оси́н|овый *adj. of* **~а; дрожа́ть как о. лист** to shake like a leaf.
ос|и́ный *adj. of* **~а́; ~и́ное гнездо́** (*fig.*) hornets' nest; **потрево́жить ~и́ное гнездо́** to stir up a hornets' nest.
оси́плый *adj.* hoarse, husky.
оси́п|нуть, ну, нешь, *past* **~, ~ла** *pf.* to go hoarse.
осироте́лый *adj.* orphaned.
осироте́|ть, ю *pf.* to become an orphan, be orphaned.
оска́л, а *m.* bared teeth; grin.
оска́лива|ть(ся), ю(сь) *impf. of* **оска́лить(ся)**
оска́л|ить, ю, ишь *pf.* (*of* **ска́лить** *and* **~ивать**): **о. зу́бы** to bare one's teeth.
оска́л|иться, юсь, ишься *pf.* (*of* **ска́литься** *and* **~иваться**) to bare one's teeth.
оскальпи́р|овать, ую *pf. of* **скальпи́ровать**
осканда́л|ить(ся), ю(сь), ишь(ся) *pf. of* **сканда́лить(ся)**
оскверне́ни|е, я *nt.* defilement; profanation.
оскверн|и́ть, ю́, и́шь *pf.* (*of* **~я́ть**) to defile; to profane.
оскверн|и́ться, ю́сь, и́шься *pf.* (*of* **~я́ться**) **1.** to defile o.s. **2.** *pass. of* **~и́ть**
оскверн|я́ть(ся), я́ю(сь) *impf. of* **~и́ть(ся)**
оскла́б|иться, люсь, ишься *pf.* to grin.
оско́л|ок, ка *m.* splinter, sliver; fragment.
оско́ло|чный *adj. of* **~к; ~чная бо́мба** fragmentation bomb.
оско́мин|а, ы *f.* bitter taste (in the mouth); **наби́ть ~у** to set the teeth on edge (*also fig.*).
оскоп|и́ть, лю́, и́шь *pf.* (*of* **~ля́ть**) to castrate.
оскопля́|ть, ю *impf. of* **оскопи́ть**
оскорби́тел|ьный (~ен, ~ьна) *adj.* insulting, abusive.
оскорб|и́ть, лю́, и́шь *pf.* (*of* **~ля́ть**) to insult, offend.
оскорб|и́ться, лю́сь, и́шься *pf.* (*of* **~ля́ться**) to take offence; to be offended.
оскорбле́ни|е, я *nt.* insult; **о. де́йствием** (*leg.*) assault and battery; **переноси́ть ~я** to bear insults.
оскорб|лённый *p.p.p. of* **~и́ть; ~лённая неви́нность** outraged innocence.
оскорбля́|ть, ю *impf. of* **оскорби́ть**
оскудева́|ть, ю *impf. of* **оскуде́ть**
оскуде́ни|е, я *nt.* scarcity; impoverishment.

оскуде́|ть, ю *pf.* (*of* **скуде́ть** *and* **~ва́ть**) to grow scarce.
ослабева́|ть, ю *impf. of* **ослабе́ть**
ослабе́лый *adj.* weakened, enfeebled.
ослабе́|ть, ю *pf.* (*of* **слабе́ть** *and* **~ва́ть**) to weaken, become weak; to slacken; to abate.
осла́б|ить, лю, ишь *pf.* (*of* **~ля́ть**) **1.** to weaken. **2.** to slacken, relax; to loosen; **о. внима́ние** to relax one's attention; **о. нажи́м** to slacken pressure; **о. по́яс** to loosen a belt.
ослабле́ни|е, я *nt.* weakening; slackening, relaxation; **о. напряже́ния** slackening of tension.
ослабля́|ть, ю *impf. of* **осла́бить**
осла́б|нуть, ну, нешь, *past* **~, ~ла** *pf.* = **~е́ть**
осла́в|ить, лю, ишь *pf.* (*of* **~ля́ть**) (*coll.*) to defame, decry; to give a bad name.
осла́в|иться, люсь, ишься *pf.* (*of* **~ля́ться**) (*coll.*) to get a bad name.
ославля́|ть(ся), ю(сь) *impf. of* **осла́вить(ся)**
осл|ёнок, ёнка, *pl.* **~я́та** *m.* foal (*of ass*).
ослепи́тел|ьный (~ен, ~ьна) *adj.* blinding, dazzling.
ослеп|и́ть, лю́, и́шь *pf.* (*of* **~ля́ть**) to blind, dazzle (*also fig.*).
ослепле́ни|е, я *nt.* **1.** blinding, dazzling. **2.** (*fig.*) blindness; **де́йствовать в ~и** to act blindly.
ослепля́|ть, ю *impf. of* **ослепи́ть**
осле́п|нуть, ну, нешь, *past* **~, ~ла** *pf. of* **сле́пнуть**
осли́ный *adj. of* **осёл**; ass's; (*fig.*) asinine.
осли́ц|а, ы *f.* she-ass.
осложне́ни|е, я *nt.* complication.
осложн|и́ть, ю́, и́шь *pf.* (*of* **~я́ть**) to complicate.
осложн|и́ться, ю́сь, и́шься *pf.* (*of* **~я́ться**) to become complicated.
осложн|я́ть(ся), я́ю(сь) *impf. of* **~и́ть(ся)**
ослуша́ни|е, я *nt.* disobedience.
ослу́ш|аться, аюсь *pf.* (*of* **~иваться**) to disobey.
ослу́шива|ться, юсь *impf. of* **ослу́шаться**
ослы́ш|аться, усь, ишься *pf.* to mishear.
ослы́шк|а, и *f.* mishearing.
осма́трива|ть(ся), ю(сь) *impf. of* **осмотре́ть(ся)**
осме́ива|ть, ю *impf. of* **осмея́ть**
осмеле́|ть, ю *pf. of* **смеле́ть**
осме́лива|ться, юс, *impf. of* **осме́литься**
осме́л|иться, юсь, ишься *pf.* (*of* **~иваться**) (+*inf.*) to dare; to take the liberty (of).
осме|я́ть, ю́, ёшь *pf.* (*of* **∸ивать**) to mock, ridicule.
осмол|и́ть, ю́, и́шь *pf. of* **смоли́ть**
о́смос, а *m.* (*phys.*) osmosis.
осмо́тр, а *m.* examination, inspection; **медици́нский о.** medical (examination); checkup.
осмотр|е́ть, ю́, ∸ишь *pf.* (*of* **осма́тривать**) to examine, inspect; to look round, look over.
осмотр|е́ться, ю́сь, ∸ишься *pf.* (*of* **осма́триваться**) **1.** to look round. **2.** (*fig.*) to take one's bearings, see how the land lies. **3.** *pass. of* **~е́ть**
осмотри́тельност|ь, и *f.* circumspection.
осмотри́тел|ьный (~ен, ~ьна) *adj.* circumspect.
осмо́трщик, а *m.* inspector.
осмы́сл|енный *p.p.p. of* **~ить** *and adj.* intelligent, sensible.
осмы́слива|ть, ю *impf. of* **осмы́слить**
осмы́сл|ить, ю, ишь *pf.* (*of* **~ивать** *and* **~я́ть**) to interpret; to comprehend.
осмысл|я́ть, я́ю *impf.* = **∸ивать**
осна|сти́ть, щу́, сти́шь *pf.* (*of* **~ща́ть**) (*naut.*) to rig; (*fig.*) to fit out, equip.
осна́стк|а, и *f.* (*naut.*) rigging.
оснаща́|ть, ю *impf. of* **оснасти́ть**
оснаще́ни|е, я *nt.* **1.** rigging; fitting out. **2.** equipment.
осне́женный *adj.* snow-covered.
оснежённый *adj.* = **осне́женный**
осно́в|а, ы *f.* **1.** base, basis, foundation; *pl.* fundamentals; **лежа́ть в ~е** (+*g.*) to be the basis (of). **2.** (*gram.*) stem. **3.** (*text.*) warp.
основа́ни|е, я *nt.* **1.** founding, foundation. **2.** (*chem., math., etc.*) base; foundation (*of building*); **о. горы́** foot of a mountain; **разру́шить до ~я** to raze to the ground; **изучи́ть до ~я** (*fig.*) to study from A to Z. **3.** (*fig.*) foundation, basis; ground, reason; **на како́м ~и вы э́то утвержда́ете?** on what grounds do you assert this?; **не без ~я** not without reason; **име́ть о. предполага́ть** to have reason to suppose; **с по́лным ~ем** with good reason.
основа́тел|ь, я *m.* founder.
основа́тел|ьный (~ен, ~ьна) *adj.* **1.** well-founded; just; **~ьная жа́лоба** reasonable complaint. **2.** solid, sound (*also fig.*); thorough; **~ьные до́воды** sound arguments. **3.** (*coll.*) bulky.
осн|ова́ть, ую́, уёшь *pf.* (*of* **~о́вывать**) **1.** to found. **2.** (**на**+*p.*) to base (on).
осн|ова́ться, ую́сь, уёшься *pf.* (*of* **~о́вываться**) **1.** to settle. **2.** *pass. of* **~ова́ть**
основн|о́й *adj.* fundamental, basic; principal; **~о́е значе́ние** primary meaning; **о. капита́л** (*fin.*) fixed capital; **~а́я мысль** keynote; **~ы́е цвета́** primary colours; **в ~о́м** for the most part; on the whole.
основополо́жник, а *m.* founder, initiator.
осно́выва|ть, ю *impf. of* **основа́ть**
осно́выва|ться, юсь *impf.* **1.** *impf. of* **основа́ться.** **2.** *impf. only* (**на**+*p.*) to base o.s. (on); to be based, founded (on); **о. на дога́дках** to base o.s. on conjecture.
осо́б|а, ы *f.* person, personage; **ва́жная о.** (*iron.*) big-wig.
осо́бенно *adv.* especially; particularly; unusually; **не о.** not very, not particularly; **она́ сего́дня ве́чером о. болтли́ва** she is unusually talkative this evening; **Вы лю́бите соба́к? — не о.** Do you like dogs? Not much.
осо́бенност|ь, и *f.* peculiarity; **в ~и** especially, in particular.
осо́бенн|ый *adj.* special, particular, peculiar; **ни́чего ~ого** nothing in particular; nothing much.
особня́к, а́ *m.* private residence; detached house.
особняко́м *adv.* by oneself; **держа́ться о.** to remain aloof.
осо́б|ый *adj.* special; particular; peculiar; **оста́ться при ~ом мне́нии** to reserve one's own opinion; (*leg.*) to dissent; **удели́ть ~ое внима́ние** (+*d.*) to give special attention (to).
о́соб|ь, и *f.* individual.
осовреме́нива|ть, ю *impf. of* **осовреме́нить**
осовреме́н|ить, ю, ишь *pf.* (*of* **~ивать**) to bring up to date; to modernize.
осозна|ва́ть, ю́, ёшь *impf. of* **∸ть**
осозна́|ть, ю *pf.* (*of* **~ва́ть**) to realize.
осо́к|а, и *f.* (*bot.*) sedge.
осоко́р|ь, я *m.* (*bot.*) black poplar.
осолове́лый *adj.* (*coll.*) dazed, dreamy.
осолове́|ть, ю, ешь *pf. of* **солове́ть**
о́сп|а, ы *f.* **1.** smallpox; **ве́тряная о.** chicken-pox; **чёрная о.** smallpox. **2.** (*coll.*) pock-marks; **лицо́ в ~е** pock-marked face.
оспа́рива|ть, ю *impf.* **1.** *impf. of* **оспо́рить.** **2.** *impf. only* to contend (for); **он ~ет зва́ние чемпио́на ми́ра** he is contending for the title of world champion.
о́сп|енный *adj. of* **~а**; **о. знак** pock-mark.
о́спин|а, ы *f.* pock-mark.
оспопривива́ни|е, я *nt.* vaccination.
оспо́р|ить, ю, ишь *pf.* (*of* **оспа́ривать**) to dispute, question; **о. завеща́ние** to dispute a will.
осрам|и́ть(ся), лю́(сь), и́шь(ся) *pf. of* **срами́ть(ся)**

ост, а *m.* (*naut.*) east.
оста|ва́ться, ю́сь, ёшься *impf. of* **оста́ться**
оста́в|ить, лю, ишь *pf.* (*of* **~ля́ть**) **1.** to leave; to abandon, give up; **о. в поко́е** to leave alone; **о. на второ́й год** (*in schools*) to keep back; to make repeat a year; **~ь(те)!** stop that!; lay off! **2.** to reserve; to keep; **о. за собо́й пра́во** to reserve the right.
оставля́|ть, ю *impf. of* **оста́вить; ~ет жела́ть мно́гого (*or* лу́чшего)** it leaves much to be desired.
остальн|о́й *adj.* the rest (of); **в ~о́м** in other respects; *as n.* **~ы́е** *pl.* the others; **~о́е** *nt.* the rest; **всё ~о́е** everything else.
остана́влива|ть(ся), ю(сь) *impf. of* **останови́ть(ся)**
оста́нк|и, ов *no sg.* remains.
останов|и́ть, лю́, ~́ишь *pf.* (*of* **остана́вливать**) **1.** to stop. **2.** to stop short, restrain. **3.** (**на**+*p.*) to direct (to), concentrate (on); **о. взгляд** to rest one's gaze (on); **о. внима́ние** to concentrate one's attention (on).
останов|и́ться, лю́сь, ~́ишься *pf.* (*of* **остана́вливаться**) **1.** to stop; to come to a stop, come to a halt; **ни пе́ред чем не о.** (*fig.*) to stop at nothing. **2.** to stay, put up; **о. у знако́мых** to stay with friends. **3.** (**на**+*p.*) (*fig.*) to dwell (on) (*in a speech, lecture, etc.*); to settle (on), rest (on); **взор ма́льчика ~и́лся на но́вой игру́шке** the boy's gaze rested on the new toy.
остано́вк|а, и *f.* **1.** stop; stoppage; hold-up. **2.** (*bus, tram*) stop; **коне́чная о.** terminus; **мне на́до прое́хать ещё одну́ ~у** I have to go one stop further.
остано́в|очный *adj. of* **~ка; о. пункт** stop, stopping place.
оста́т|ок, ка *m.* **1.** remainder; rest; residue; remnant (*of material*); *pl.* remains; leavings, leftovers; **распрода́жа ~ков** clearance sale. **2.** (*fin., comm.*) rest, balance.
оста́то|чный *adj. of* **~к;** (*chem., tech.*) residual.
оста́|ться, нусь, нешься *pf.* (*of* **~ва́ться**) to remain; to stay; to be left (over); **о. в живы́х** to survive, come through; **о. на́ ночь** to stay the night; **о. при своём мне́нии** to remain of the same opinion; **о. на второ́й год (в том же кла́ссе)** to repeat a year; **по́сле него́ ~лись жена́ и тро́е дете́й** he left a wife and three children; (*impers.*): **~ётся, ~лось** (+*d.*) it remains (remained), it is (was) necessary; **нам не ~лось ничего́ друго́го, как согласи́ться** we had no choice but to consent; **~лось то́лько заплати́ть** it remained only to pay.
остеклене́|ть, ю *pf. of* **стеклене́ть**
остео́лог, а *m.* osteologist.
остеологи́ческий *adj.* osteological.
остеоло́ги|я, и *f.* osteology.
остеомиэли́т, а *m.* (*med.*) osteomyelitis.
остепен|и́ть, ю́, и́шь *pf.* (*of* **~я́ть**) to calm, mellow.
остепен|и́ться, ю́сь, и́шься *pf.* (*of* **~я́ться**) to settle down; to mellow.
остепеня́|ть(ся), ю(сь) *impf. of* **остепени́ть(ся)**
остервене́лый *adj.* frenzied.
остервене́ни|е, я *nt.* frenzy; **рабо́тать с ~ем** to work like a maniac.
остервен|е́ть, ю *pf. of* **стервене́ть**
остервен|и́ться, ю́сь, и́шься *pf.* to be frenzied.
остерега́|ть, ю *impf. of* **остере́чь**
остерега́|ться, юсь *impf.* (*of* **остере́чься**) (+*g. or inf.*) to beware (of); to be careful (of); **~йтесь соба́ки!** beware of the dog!; **~йся, что́бы не упа́сть!** mind you don't fall!
остере́|чь, гу́, жёшь, гу́т, *past* **~̈г, ~гла́** *pf.* (*of* **~га́ть**) to warn, caution.
остере́|чься, гу́сь, жёшься, гу́тся, *past* **~̈гся, ~гла́сь** *pf. of* **~га́ться**
о́стов, а *m.* **1.** frame, framework (*also fig.*); shell; hull. **2.** (*anat.*) skeleton.
остолбене́лый *adj.* (*coll.*) dumbfounded.
остолбене́|ть, ю *pf. of* **столбене́ть**
остоло́п, а *m.* (*coll.*) blockhead.
осторо́жно *adv.* carefully; cautiously; guardedly; gingerly; **о.!** look out! mind out!; (*on package*) 'with care'.
осторо́жност|ь, и *f.* care; caution.
осторо́ж|ный (~ен, ~на) *adj.* careful; cautious; **бу́дьте ~ны!** take care!; be careful!
осточерте́|ть, ю *pf.* (+*d.*; *coll.*) to bore; to repel; **мне э́то ~ло** I am fed up with it.
остраки́зм, а *m.* ostracism; **подве́ргнуть ~у** to ostracize.
остра́стк|а, и *f.* (*coll.*) warning, caution; **для ~и** as a warning.
острига́|ть(ся), ю(сь) *impf. of* **остри́чь(ся)**
остри|ё, я́ *nt.* **1.** point; spike; **о. кли́на** (*mil.*) spearhead of the attack. **2.** (cutting) edge; **о. кри́тики** (*fig.*) the edge of a criticism.
остр|и́ть[1], ю́, и́шь *impf.* to sharpen, whet.
остр|и́ть[2], ю́, и́шь *impf.* (*of* **с~**) to be witty; to crack jokes.
остри́|чь, гу́, жёшь, гу́т, *past* **~г, ~гла** *pf.* (*of* **стричь** *and* **~га́ть**) to cut; to clip.
остри́|чься, гу́сь, жёшься, гу́ться, *past* **~гся, ~глась** *pf.* (*of* **стри́чься** *and* **~га́ться**) to cut one's hair; to have one's hair cut.
о́стров, а, *pl.* **~а́** *m.* island; isle.
островитя́н|ин, ина, *pl.* **~е, ~** *m.* islander.
островно́й *adj.* island; insular.
остров|о́к, ка́ *m.* islet; **о. безопа́сности** island (*in road*).
острог|а́, и́ *f.* fish-spear, harpoon.
острогла́з|ый (~, ~а) *adj.* (*coll.*) sharp-eyed.
острогу́бц|ы, ев (*tech.*) cutting nippers.
остроконе́чный *adj.* pointed.
остроли́ст, а *m.* (*bot.*) holly.
острonóс|ый (~, ~а) *adj.* sharp-nosed; (*fig.*) pointed, tapered.
остросюже́т|ный (~ен, ~на) *adj.* gripping, tense.
остро́т|а, ы *f.* witticism, joke; **зла́я о.** sarcasm; **пло́ская о.** stupid joke.
острот|а́, ы́ *f.* sharpness; keenness; acuteness; pungency, poignancy.
остроуго́л|ьный (~ен, ~ьна) *adj.* (*math.*) acute-angled.
остроу́ми|е, я *nt.* wit; wittiness.
остроу́м|ный (~ен, ~на) *adj.* witty.
о́стр|ый (~ *and* остёр, ~а́, ~о) *adj.* sharp (*also fig.*); pointed (*also fig.*); acute; keen; **~ое воспале́ние** (*med.*) acute inflammation; **~ое замеча́ние** pointed remark; **о. за́пах** acrid smell; **~ое зре́ние** keen eyesight; **о. интере́с (к)** keen interest (in); **о. недоста́ток** acute shortage; **~ое положе́ние** critical situation; **о. со́ус** spicy sauce; **о. сыр** strong cheese; **о. у́гол** (*math.*) acute angle; **он остёр на язы́к** (*coll.*) he has a sharp tongue.
остря́к, а́ *m.* wit.
осту|ди́ть, жу́, ~́дишь *pf.* (*of* **студи́ть** *and* **~жа́ть**) to cool.
остужа́|ть, ю *impf. of* **остуди́ть**
оступ|а́ться, а́юсь *impf. of* **~и́ться**
оступ|и́ться, лю́сь, ~́ишься *pf.* (*of* **~а́ться**) to stumble.
остыва́|ть, ю *impf. of* **осты́ть**
осты́|ть, ну, нешь *pf.* (*of* **~ва́ть**) to get cold; (*fig.*) to cool (down); **у вас чай ~л** your tea is cold.
осу|ди́ть, жу́, ~́дишь *pf.* (*of* **~жда́ть**) **1.** to censure, condemn. **2.** (*leg.*) to condemn, sentence; to convict.

осужда́|ть, ю *impf. of* **осуди́ть**
осужде́ни|е, я *nt.* **1.** censure, condemnation. **2.** (*leg.*) conviction.
осуждённ|ый *p.p.p. of* **осуди́ть** *and adj.* condemned; convicted; *as n.* **о., ~ого** *nt.* convict.
осу́н|уться, усь, ешься *pf.* (*coll.*) (*of the face*) to grow thin, get pinched(-looking).
осуш|а́ть, а́ю *impf. of* **~и́ть**
осуше́ни|е, я *nt.* drainage.
осуш|и́тельный *adj. of* **~е́ние; о. кана́л** drainage canal.
осуш|и́ть, у́, ~ишь *pf.* (*of* **~а́ть**) to drain; to dry; **о. глаза́** to dry one's eyes; **о. луга́** to drain meadows; **о. слёзы кому́-н.** to console s.o.; **о. стака́н пи́ва** to drain a glass of beer.
осуществи́м|ый (~, ~а) *adj.* practicable, feasible.
осуществ|и́ть, лю́, и́шь *pf.* (*of* **~ля́ть**) to realize, bring about; to accomplish, carry out; to implement.
осуществ|и́ться, и́тся *pf.* (*of* **~ля́ться**) **1.** to be fulfilled, come true; **её де́тская мечта́ ~и́лась** her childhood dream has come true. **2.** *pass. of* **~и́ть**
осуществле́ни|е, я *nt.* realization; accomplishment; implementation.
осуществля́|ть(ся), ю(сь) *impf. of* **осуществи́ть**
осцилло́граф, а *m.* (*phys.*) oscillograph.
осцилля́тор, а *m.* (*phys.*) oscillator.
осчастли́в|ить, лю, ишь *pf.* (*of* **~ливать**) to make happy; to grace (*iron.*).
осчастли́влива|ть, ю *impf. of* **осчастли́вить**
осы́па|нный *p.p.p. of* **~ть; о. звёздами** star-studded, star-spangled.
осы́п|ать, лю, лешь *pf.* (*of* **~а́ть**) (*+a. and i.*) to strew (with); to shower (on); (*fig.*) to heap (on); **о. кого́-н. бра́нью** to heap abuse on s.o.; **о. поцелу́ями** to smother with kisses; **о. кого́-н. уда́рами** to rain blows on s.o.
осы́п|аться, люсь, лешься *pf.* (*of* **~а́ться**) to crumble; (*of leaves, etc.*) to fall.
осып|а́ть(ся), а́ю(сь) *impf. of* **~ать(ся)**
ос|ь, и, *pl.* **~и, ~е́й** *f.* **1.** axis; **име́ющий о́бщую о.** coaxial. **2.** axle.
осьмино́г, а *m.* (*zool.*) octopus.
осяза́ем|ый (~, ~а) *adj.* tangible; palpable.
осяза́ние, я *nt.* touch; **чу́вство ~я** a sense of touch.
осяза́тел|ьный (~ен, ~ьна) *adj.* **1.** tactile; **~ьные о́рганы** tactile organs. **2.** (*fig.*) tangible, palpable; **~ьные результа́ты** tangible results.
осяза́|ть, ю *impf.* to feel.
от (ото) *prep.+g.* from; of; for **1.** (*indicates initial point, point of origin of action, prior of pair of termini, source, etc.*) **от це́нтра го́рода** from the centre of the town; **от нача́ла до конца́** from beginning to end; **от Пу́шкина до Маяко́вского** from Pushkin to Mayakovsky; **де́ти в во́зрасте от пяти́ до десяти́ лет** children aged from five to ten; **це́ны от рубля́ и вы́ше** prices from a rouble upward; **бли́зко от го́рода** near the town; **на се́вер от Москвы́** to the north of Moscow; **вре́мя от вре́мени** from time to time; **день ото дня** from day to day; **от всей души́** with all one's heart; **от и́мени** (*+g.*) on behalf (of); **узна́ть от дру́га** to learn from a friend; **я получи́л письмо́ от до́чери** I have received a letter from my daughter; **сын от пре́жнего бра́ка** a son by a previous marriage. **2.** (*indicates cause or instrumentality*) **вскри́кнуть от ра́дости** to cry out for joy; **дрожа́ть от стра́ха** to tremble with fear; **умере́ть от го́лода** to die of hunger; **глаза́, кра́сные от слёз** eyes red with weeping. **3.** (*indicates date of document*) **ва́ше письмо́ от пе́рвого а́вгуста** your letter of the first of August. **4.** (*indicates use, purpose, or assignment*) **ключ от две́ри** door key; **пу́говица от пиджака́** coat button; **цепо́чка от часо́в** watch-chain. **5.** for; against; **миксту́ра от ка́шля** cough mixture; **защища́ть глаза́ от со́лнца** to shield one's eyes from the sun; **застрахова́ть от огня́** to insure against fire.
от... (*also* **ото...** *and* **отъ...**) *vbl. pref. indicating* **1.** completion of action *or* task assigned. **2.** action *or* motion away from given point. **3.** (*vv. in form refl.*) action of negative character.
ота́плива|ть, ю *impf. of* **отопи́ть**
ота́р|а, ы *f.* flock (*of sheep*).
отба́в|ить, лю, ишь *pf.* (*of* **~ля́ть**) to pour off.
отбавля́|ть, ю *impf. of* **отба́вить; хоть ~й** (*coll.*) more than enough.
отбараба́н|ить, ю, ишь *pf.* (*coll.*) to rattle off.
отбега́|ть, ю *impf. of* **отбежа́ть**
отбе|жа́ть, гу́, жи́шь, гу́т *pf.* (*of* **~га́ть**) to run off.
отбе́лива|ть, ю *impf. of* **отбели́ть**
отбел|и́ть, ю́, ~ишь *pf.* (*of* **~ивать**) to bleach.
отбива́|ть(ся), ю(сь) *impf. of* **отби́ть(ся)**
отбивн|о́й *adj.*: **~а́я котле́та** (*cul.*) chop.
отбира́|ть, ю *impf. of* **отобра́ть**
отби́|ть, отобью́, отобьёшь *pf.* (*of* **~ва́ть**) **1.** to beat off, repulse, repel; **о. ата́ку** to beat off an attack; **о. мяч** (*sport*) to return a ball; **о. уда́р** to parry a blow. **2.** to take (*by force*); to win over; (*coll.*): **о. у кого́-н.** to take off s.o., do s.o. out of; **о. пле́нных** to liberate prisoners; **он ~л у това́рища его́ де́вушку** he has taken his friend's girl. **3.** to remove, dispel; **о. у кого́-н. охо́ту к чему́-н.** to discourage s.o. from sth. **4.** to break off, knock off; **о. но́сик у ча́йника** to knock the spout off a tea-pot. **5.** to hone, sharpen. **6.: о. такт** to beat time. **7.** to knock up; to injure; **о. ру́ку нело́вким уда́ром** to injure one's hand with a clumsy blow.
отби́|ться, отобью́сь, отобьёшься *pf.* (*of* **~ва́ться**) **1. (от)** to defend o.s. (against); to repulse, beat off. **2.** to drop behind, straggle; **о. от ста́да** to stray from the herd; **о. от рук** (*coll.*) to get out of hand. **3.** to break off. **4.** *pass. of* **~ть**
отбла́гове|стить, щу, стишь *pf. of* **бла́говестить 1.**
отблагодар|и́ть, ю́, и́шь *pf.* to show one's gratitude (to).
о́тблеск, а *m.* reflection.
отбо́|й, я *m.* **1.** repulse; repelling; **о. мяча́** (*sport*) return; **~ю нет (от;** *coll.*) no end (of); a whole stream (of). **2.** (*mil.*) retreat; **о. возду́шной трево́ги** all-clear signal; **бить о.** to beat a retreat (*also fig.*). **3.** ringing off (*on telephone*); **дать о.** to ring off.
отбо́й|ный *adj.* **1.: о. молото́к** miner's pick; **пневмати́ческий о. молото́к** pneumatic drill (*for coal-cutting*). **2.** *adj. of* **~ 3.**
отбо́р, а *m.* selection; **есте́ственный о.** (*biol.*) natural selection.
отбо́рн|ый *adj.* choice, select(ed); **~ые войска́** crack troops; **~ая ру́гань** choice swear-words.
отбо́рочн|ый *adj.*: **~ая коми́ссия** selection board; **~ое соревнова́ние** (*sport*) knock-out competition.
отбоя́рива|ться, юсь *impf.* (*of* **отбоя́риться**) (*coll.*) to try to escape, get out of.
отбоя́р|иться, юсь, ишься *pf.* (*of* **~иваться**) (*coll.*; **от**) to escape (from), give the slip (to).
отбра́сыва|ть, ю *impf. of* **отбро́сить**
отбро́|сить, шу, сишь *pf.* (*of* **отбра́сывать**) **1.** to throw off; to cast away; **о. тень** to cast a shadow. **2.** (*mil.*) to throw back, hurl back. **3.** to give up, reject, discard; **о. мысль** to give up an idea.
отбро́с|ы, ов *pl.* (*sg.* **~, ~а** *m.*) garbage, refuse; offal; **о. произво́дства** industrial waste; **о. о́бщества** (*fig.*) dregs of society.
отбыва́|ть, ю *impf. of* **отбы́ть**
отбы́ти|е, я *nt.* departure.
от|бы́ть[1], бу́ду, бу́дешь, *past* **~был, ~была́, ~было** *pf.* (*of* **~быва́ть**) to depart, leave.

от|бы́ть[2], **бу́ду, бу́дешь,** *past* **∠был, ~была́, ∠было** *pf.* (*of* **~быва́ть**) to serve (a period of); **о. наказа́ние** to serve one's sentence; **о. во́инскую пови́нность** to do (one's) military service.

отва́г|а, и *f.* courage, bravery.

отва́|дить, жу, дишь *pf.* (*of* **~живать**) **1.** (*+a.* **от**) to break (of), make to stop;**о. кого́-н. от пья́нства** to break s.o. of drunkenness. **2.** to scare away, drive off.

отва́жива|ть, ю *impf. of* **отва́дить**

отва́ж|иться, усь, ишься *pf.* (*+inf.*) to dare, venture; to have the courage (to).

отва́ж|ный (~ен, ~на) *adj.* courageous, brave.

отва́л[1], **а** *m.*: **до ~а** (*coll.*) to satiety; **нае́сться до ~а** to stuff o.s.

отва́л[2], **а** *m.* dump; heap.

отва́л[3], **а** *m.* (*naut.*) putting off, casting off.

отва́лива|ть(ся), ю(сь) *impf. of* **отвали́ть(ся)**

отвал|и́ть, ю́, ∠ишь *pf.* (*of* **∠ивать**) **1.** to heave off; to push aside. **2.** (*naut.*) to put off, cast off. **3.** (*coll.*) to fork out, stump up (*a sum of money*).

отвал|и́ться, ю́сь, ∠ишься *pf.* (*of* **∠иваться**) **1.** to fall off, slip. **2.** *pass. of* **~и́ть**

отва́льн|ая, ой *f.* (*coll.*) farewell party.

отва́р, а *m.* broth; decoction; **ячме́нный о.** barley-water.

отва́рива|ть, ю *impf. of* **отвари́ть**

отвар|и́ть, ю́ ∠ишь *pf.* (*of* **∠ивать**) to boil.

отварно́й *adj.* (*cul.*) boiled.

отве́д|ать, аю *pf.* (*of* **~ывать**) (*+a. or g.*) to taste; to try.

отве|дённый *p.p.p of* **~сти́**

отве́дыва|ть, ю *impf. of* **отве́дать**

отвез|ти́, у́, ёшь, *past* **∸, ~ла́** *pf.* (*of* **отвози́ть**) to take (away); to cart away.

отверг|а́ть, а́ю *impf. of* **∠нуть**

отве́рг|нуть, ну, нешь, *past* **~, ~ла** *pf.* (*of* **~а́ть**) to reject, turn down; to repudiate; to spurn.

отвердева́|ть, ю *impf. of* **отверде́ть**

отверде́лый *adj.* hardened.

отверде́|ть, ю *pf.* (*of* **~ва́ть**) to harden.

отве́р|женный *p.p.p.* (*obs.*) *of* **~гнуть** *and adj.* outcast; *as n.* **~женный, женного** *m.* outcast.

отвер|ну́ть, ну́, нёшь, *pf.* (*of* **∸тывать**) **1.** (*impf. also* **отвора́чивать**) to turn away, turn aside; **о. лицо́** to turn one's face away. **2.** to turn on (*a tap, etc.*). **3.** to unscrew. **4.** (*coll.*) to screw off, twist off; **он едва́ не ~ну́л мне ру́ку** he almost twisted my arm off.

отвер|ну́ться, ну́сь, нёшься *pf.* (*of* **∸тываться**) **1.** (*impf. also* **отвора́чиваться**) to turn away, turn aside; **о. от кого́-н.** (*fig.*) to turn one's back upon s.o. **2.** (*of a tap, etc.*) to come on. **3.** to come unscrewed.

отве́рсти|е, я *nt.* opening, aperture, orifice; hole; slot; **входно́е о.** inlet; **выходно́е о., выпускно́е о.** outlet; **заднепрохо́дное о.** (*anat.*) anus.

отвер|те́ть, чу́, ∠тишь *pf.* (*of* **∸тывать**) **1.** to unscrew. **2.** to screw off, twist off.

отверт|е́ться[1], **∠ится** *pf.* (*of* **∸ываться**) to come unscrewed.

отвер|те́ться[2], **чу́сь, ∠тишься** *pf.* (*coll.*; **от**) to get off; to get out (of), wriggle out (of); **нам удало́сь о.** we managed to get out of it.

отвёртк|а, и *f.* screwdriver.

отвёртыва|ть(ся), ю(сь) *impf. of* **отверну́ть(ся)** *and* **отверте́ть(ся)**

отве́с, а *m.* **1.** (*tech.*) plumb. **2.** (*vertical*) face, slope; **по ~у** plumb, perpendicularly.

отве́|сить, шу, сишь *pf.* (*of* **~шивать**) to weigh out; **о. фунт са́хару** to weigh out a pound of sugar; **о. покло́н** (*+d*) to make a low bow (to); **о. пощёчину** (*+d.*) (*fig., coll.*) to give s.o. a slap in the face.

отве́сно *adv.* plumb; sheer.

отве́с|ный (~ен, ~на) *adj.* perpendicular; steep.

отве|сти́, ду́, дёшь, *past* **∸л, ~ла́** *pf.* (*of* **отводи́ть**) **1.** to lead, take; **о. ло́шадь в коню́шню** to lead a horse to the stable. **2.** to draw aside, take aside; **о. от собла́зна** to lead out of temptation's way. **3.** to deflect; to draw off; **о. войска́** (*mil.*) to draw off one's troops; **о. во́ду (из)** to drain; **о. ду́шу** to unburden o.s.; **о. уда́р** to parry a blow; **он не мог о. глаз от неё** he could not take his eyes off her; **о. глаза́ кому́-н.** (*fig.*) to delude s.o.; to pull the wool over s.o.'s eyes. **4.** to reject. **5.** to allot, assign.

отве́т, а *m.* **1.** answer, reply, response; **в о.** (**на**+*a.*) in reply (to), in response (to). **2.** (*obs.*) responsibility; **быть в ~е** (**за**+*a.*) to be answerable (for); **призва́ть к ~у** to call to account.

ответв|и́ться, лю́сь, и́шься *pf.* (*of* **~ля́ться**) to branch off.

ответвле́ни|е, я *nt.* branch, offshoot (*also fig.*).

ответвля́|ться, юсь *impf. of* **ответви́ться**

отве́|тить, чу, тишь *pf.* (*of* **~ча́ть**) **1.** (**на**+*a.*) to answer, reply (to); **о. на письмо́** to answer a letter; **о. уро́к** to repeat one's lesson. **2.** (**на**+*a.* +*i.*) to answer (with), return; **о. на чьё-н. чу́вство** to return s.o.'s feelings. **3.** (**за**+*a.*) to answer (for), pay (for); **вы ~тите за э́ти слова́!** you will pay for these words!

отве́тн|ый *adj.* given in reply; return; retaliatory.

отве́тственност|ь, и *f.* responsibility; **снять о. с кого́-н.** to relieve s.o. of responsibility; **привле́чь к ~и** (**за**+*a.*) to call to account, bring to book.

отве́тствен|ный (~, ~на) *adj.* **1.** responsible; senior; **о. рабо́тник** executive. **2.** crucial; **о. моме́нт** crucial point.

отве́тств|овать, ую *impf. and pf.* (*obs.*) to answer, reply.

отве́тчик, а *m.* **1.** (*leg.*) defendant, respondent. **2.** (*coll.*) bearer of responsibility. **3.: телефо́нный о.** answerphone.

отвеча́|ть, ю *impf.* **1.** *impf. of* **отве́тить. 2.** (**за**+*a.*) to answer (for), be answerable (for). **3.** (*+d.*) to answer (to), meet; **о. тре́бованиям** to meet requirements.

отве́шива|ть, ю *impf. of* **отве́сить**

отви́лива|ть, ю *impf. of* **отвильну́ть**

отвильн|у́ть, у́, ёшь *pf.* (*of* **отви́ливать**) (*coll., pej.*; **от**) to dodge.

отвин|ти́ть, чу́, ти́шь *pf.* (*of* **∠чивать**) to unscrew.

отвис|а́ть, а́ю *impf.* (*of* **∠нуть**) to hang down, sag.

отви́слы|й *adj.* loose-hanging, baggy; **с ~ми уша́ми** lop-eared.

отви́с|нуть, ну, нешь, *past* **~, ~ла** *pf. of* **~а́ть**

отвлека́|ть(ся), ю(сь) *impf. of* **отвле́чь(ся)**

отвлече́ни|е, я *nt.* **1.** abstraction. **2.** distraction; **для ~я внима́ния** to distract attention.

отвлечён|ный (~, ~на) *adj.* abstract; **~ное и́мя существи́тельное** abstract noun.

отвле́|чь, ку́, чёшь, ку́т, *past* **∸к, ~кла́** *pf.* (*of* **~ка́ть**) to distract, divert; **о. чьё-н. внима́ние** to divert s.o.'s attention.

отвле́|чься, ку́сь, чёшься, ку́тся, *past* **∸кся, ~кла́сь** *pf.* (*of* **~ка́ться**) to be distracted; **о. от те́мы** to digress; **его́ мы́сли ~кли́сь далеко́** his thoughts were far away.

отво́д, а *m.* **1.** leading, taking, conducting. **2.** taking aside; deflection; diversion; **о. воды́** draining off of water; **о. войск** withdrawal of troops; **для ~а глаз** (*coll.*) as a blind. **3.** rejection; (*leg.*) challenge; **дать о. кандида́ту** to reject a candidate. **4.** allotment, allocation.

отво|ди́ть, жу́, ∠дишь *impf. of* **отвести́**

отво́дн|ый *adj.* (*tech.*) branch; drain, outlet; **о. кана́л**

drain; **о. кран** drain cock.
отво|ева́ть[1], **ю́ю, ю́ешь** *pf.* (*of* **~ёвывать**) (**у**) to win back (from), retake (from).
отво|ева́ть[2], **ю́ю, ю́ешь** *pf.* (*coll.*) **1.** to fight, spend in fighting; **мы де́сять лет ~ева́ли** we have fought for ten years. **2.** to finish fighting.
отвоёвыва|ть, ю *impf. of* **отвоева́ть**[1]
отво|зи́ть, жу́, ∠зишь *impf. of* **отвезти́**
отвора́чива|ть(ся), ю(сь) *impf. of* **отверну́ть(ся)** *and* **отвороти́ть(ся)**
отвор|и́ть, ю́, ∠ишь *pf.* (*of* **~я́ть**) to open.
отвор|и́ться, ю́сь, ∠ишься *pf.* (*of* **~я́ться**) to open.
отворо́т, а *m.* lapel; flap; top (*of boot*).
отворо|ти́ть, чу́, ∠тишь *pf.* (*of* **отвора́чивать**) to turn away, turn aside; **о. взгляд** to avert one's gaze.
отворо|ти́ться, чу́сь, ∠тишься *pf.* (*of* **отвора́чиваться**) to turn away, turn aside; **о. от кого́-н.** to look away from s.o.; (*fig.*) to turn one's back on s.o.
отвор|я́ть(ся), я́ю(сь) *impf. of* **~и́ть(ся)**
отврати́тел|ьный (~ен, ~ьна) *adj.* disgusting, revolting; abominable, rotten.
отвра|ти́ть, щу́, ти́шь *pf.* (*of* **~ща́ть**) to avert, stave off.
отвра́т|ный (~ен, ~на) *adj.* (*coll.*) = **~и́тельный**
отвра|ща́ть,ща́ю *impf. of* **~ти́ть**
отвраще́ни|е, я *nt.* aversion, disgust, repugnance; loathing, revulsion; **внуши́ть о.** (*+d.*) to disgust, repel; **пита́ть о. (к)** to have an aversion (for), be repelled (by), loathe.
отвык|а́ть, а́ю *impf. of* **∠нуть**
отвы́к|нуть, ну, нешь, *past* **~, ~ла** *pf.* (*of* **~а́ть**) (**от** *or* *+inf.*) to break o.s. (of the habit of), give up; to get out of the habit of; to grow out (of); **о. от куре́ния, о. кури́ть** to give up smoking; **о. от дурно́й привы́чки** to break o.s. of a bad habit.
отвя|за́ть, жу́, ∠жешь *pf.* (*of* **∠зывать**) to untie, unfasten; to untether.
отвя|за́ться, жу́сь, ∠жешься *pf.* (*of* **∠зываться**) **1.** to come untied, come loose. **2.** (*fig., coll.*; **от**) to get rid (of), shake off, get shot (of). **3.** (*fig., coll.*; **от**) to leave alone, leave in peace; **~жи́сь от меня́!** leave me alone!
отвя́зыва|ть(ся), ю(сь) *impf. of* **отвяза́ть(ся)**
отгад|а́ть, а́ю *pf.* (*of* **∠ывать**) to guess.
отга́дк|а, и *f.* answer, solution (*to a riddle*).
отга́дчик, а *m.* (*coll.*) guesser, diviner.
отга́дыва|ть, ю *impf. of* **отгада́ть**
отгиба́|ть, ю *impf. of* **отогну́ть**
отглаго́льный *adj.* (*gram.*) verbal.
отгла́|дить, жу, дишь *pf.* (*of* **~живать**) to iron (out).
отгла́жива|ть, ю *impf. of* **отгла́дить**
отгова́рива|ть(ся), ю(сь) *impf. of* **отговори́ть(ся)**
отговор|и́ть, ю́, и́шь *pf.* (*of* **отгова́ривать**) (**от** *or* *+inf.*) to dissuade (from); **я ~и́л его́ е́хать** I have talked him out of going.
отговор|и́ться, ю́сь, и́шься *pf.* (*of* **отгова́риваться**) (*+i.*) to excuse o.s. (on the ground of); to plead; **о. нездоро́вьем** to plead ill-health.
отгово́рк|а, и *f.* excuse; pretext; **пуста́я о.** lame excuse.
отголо́с|ок, ка *m.* echo (*also fig.*).
отгоня́|ть, ю *impf. of* **отогна́ть**
отгора́жива|ть(ся), ю(сь) *impf. of* **отгороди́ть(ся)**
отгоро|ди́ть, жу́, ∠и́шь *pf.* (*of* **отгора́живать**) to fence off, partition off; **о. ши́рмой** to screen off.
отгоро|ди́ться, жу́сь, ∠ди́шься *pf.* (*of* **отгора́живаться**) to fence o.s. off; (*fig., coll.*; **от**) to shut *or* cut o.s. off (from).
отгреба́|ть, ю *impf. of* **отгрести́**
отгре|сти́[1], **бу́, бёшь,** *past* **∸б, ~бла́** *pf.* (*of* **~ба́ть**) to rake away.
отгре|сти́[2], **бу́, бёшь,** *past* **∸б, ~бла́** *pf.* (*of* **~ба́ть**) to row off.
отгружа́|ть, ю *impf. of* **отгрузи́ть**
отгру|зи́ть, жу́, ∠зи́шь *pf.* (*of* **~жа́ть**) to ship, dispatch.
отгру́зк|а, и *f.* shipment, dispatching.
отгрыз|а́ть, а́ю *impf. of* **∠ть**
отгры́з|ть, у́, ёшь, *past* **~, ~ла** *pf.* (*of* **~а́ть**) to bite off, gnaw off.
отгу́лива|ть, ю *impf. of* **отгуля́ть 2.**
отгул|я́ть, я́ю *pf.* (*coll.*) **1.** to have spent, to have finished (*holidays, leave, etc.*); **мы ~я́ли о́тпуск** our holidays are over. **2.** (*impf.* **∠ивать**) to take (time) off; **о. день** to take a day off.
отда|ва́ть[1]**(ся), ю́(сь), ёшь(ся)** *impf. of* **отда́ть(ся)**
отда|ва́ть[2], **ёт** *impf.* (*impers.+i.*; *coll.*) to taste (of); to smell (of); (*fig.*) to smack (of); **от него́ ~ёт во́дкой** he reeks of vodka.
отдав|и́ть, лю́, ∠ишь *pf.* to crush; **о. кому́-н. но́гу** to tread on s.o.'s foot.
отдале́ни|е, я *nt.* **1.** removal; (*fig.*) estrangement. **2.** distance; **в ~и** in the distance.
отдалённост|ь, и *f.* remoteness.
отдалён|ный (~, ~на) *adj.* distant, remote; **о. ро́дственник** distant relative; **~ное схо́дство** remote likeness.
отдал|и́ть, ю́, и́шь *pf.* (*of* **~я́ть**) **1.** to remove; (*fig.*) to estrange, alienate. **2.** to postpone, put off.
отдал|и́ться, ю́сь, и́шься *pf.* (*of* **~я́ться**) **1. (от)** to move away (from) (*also fig.*). **2.** (*fig.*) to digress; **о. от те́мы** to stray from the subject. **3.** *pass. of* **~и́ть**
отдал|я́ть(ся), я́ю(сь) *impf. of* **~и́ть(ся)**
отда́ни|е, я *nt.*: **о. че́сти** (*mil.*) salute; saluting.
отда́рива|ть, ю *impf. of* **отдари́ть**
отдар|и́ть, ю́, и́шь *pf.* (*of* **∠ивать**) (*coll.*) to give in return.
отд|а́ть, а́м, а́шь, а́ст, ади́м, ади́те, аду́т, *past* **∠ал, ~ала́, ∠ало** *pf.* (*of* **~ава́ть**) **1.** to give back, return; **о. до́лжное кому́-н.** to render s.o. his due; **о. после́дний долг** (*+d.*) to pay one's last respects; **о. себе́ отчёт (в+*p.*)** to be aware (of), realize; **не о. себе́ отчёта (в+*p.*)** to fail to realize. **2.** to devote; **о. жизнь нау́ке** to devote one's life to learning. **3.** (*+a. and d. or +a.* **за**+*a.*) to give in marriage (to), give away. **4.** (**в**+*a.*, **под**+*a.*) to give, put, place (= *hand over for certain purpose*); **о. кни́гу в переплёт** to have a book bound; **о. ма́льчика в шко́лу** to send a boy to school; **о. под стра́жу** to give into custody; **о. под суд** to prosecute. **5.** (*in comb. with certain nn.*) to give; to make (*or not requiring separate translation*); **о. прика́з** (*+d.*) to issue an order, give orders (to); **о. распоряже́ние** to give instructions; **о. честь** (*+d.*) to salute. **6.** (*coll.*) to sell, let have; **он мне э́то ∠ал за бесце́нок** he let me have it for a song. **7.** (*of a fire-arm*) to kick, recoil.
отд|а́ться, а́мся, а́шься, а́стся, ади́мся, ади́тесь, аду́тся, *past* **~а́лся, ~ала́сь** *pf.* (*of* **~ава́ться**) **1.** (*+d.*) to give o.s. up (to), to devote o.s. (to); (*of a woman*) to give o.s. (to). **2.** to resound; to reverberate; to ring (*in one's ears*).
отда́ч|а, и *f.* **1.** return; payment, reimbursement. **2.** (*tech.*) efficiency; output. **3.** (*mil.*) recoil, kick.
отде́л, а *m.* **1.** department; **о. ка́дров** personnel department. **2.** section, part (*of book, periodical, etc.*).
отде́л|ать, аю *pf.* (*of* **~ывать**) **1.** to finish, put the finishing touches (to); to decorate; **о. пла́тье кружева́ми** to trim a dress with lace. **2.** (*coll.*) to give a dressing down.
отде́л|аться, аюсь *pf.* (*of* **~ываться**) **1. (от)** to get rid (of), get shot (of). **2.** (*+i.*) to escape (with), get off (with); **сча́стливо о.** to have a lucky escape; **о. цара́пиной** to get off with a scratch.

отделе́ни|е, я *nt.* **1.** separation. **2.** department, branch; **о. мили́ции** local police-station; **о. свя́зи** local post office. **3.** compartment, section; part (*of concert programme, etc.*); **о. шка́фа** pigeon-hole; **маши́нное о.** (*naut.*) engine-room. **4.** (*mil.*) section.

отдел|ённый[1] *p.p.p. of* **~и́ть**

отделён|ный[2] *adj. of* **~ие 3.; о. команди́р** section commander.

отдел|и́ть, ю́, ~ишь *pf.* (*of* **~я́ть**) **1.** to separate, part; to detach. **2.** to separate off; **о. перегоро́дкой** to partition off.

отдел|и́ться, ю́сь, ~ишься *pf.* (*of* **~я́ться**) to separate, part; to get detached; to come apart; to come off.

отде́лк|а, и *f.* **1.** finishing; trimming. **2.** finish, decoration; décor.

отде́лыва|ть(ся), ю(сь) *impf. of* **отде́лать(ся)**

отде́льно *adv.* separately.

отде́льност|ь, и *f.*: **в ~и** taken separately, individually.

отде́льный *adj.* separate, individual.

отдел|я́ть(ся), я́ю(сь) *impf. of* **~и́ть(ся)**

отдёргива|ть, ю *impf. of* **отдёрнуть**

отдёр|нуть, ну, нешь *pf.* (*of* **~гивать**) **1.** to draw aside, pull aside; **о. занаве́ску** to draw back the curtain. **2.** to jerk back, withdraw.

отдира́|ть, ю *impf. of* **отодра́ть**

отдохн|у́ть, у́, ёшь *pf.* (*of* **отдыха́ть**) to rest; to have (take) a rest.

отдуба́|сить, шу, сишь *pf. of* **дуба́сить**

отдува́|ть, ю *impf. of* **отду́ть**

отдува́|ться, юсь *impf.* **1.** to pant, puff. **2.** (*fig., coll.*; **за**+*a.*) to carry the can (for).

отду́м|ать, аю *pf.* (*of* **~ывать**) (*coll.*) to change one's mind; **мы ~али перее́хать** we have changed our mind about moving.

отду́мыва|ть ю *impf. of* **отду́мать**

отду́|ть, ю, ешь *pf.* (*of* **~ва́ть**) (*coll.*) to blow away.

отду́шин|а, ы *f.* air-hole, (air) vent; (*fig.*) safety-valve.

о́тдых, а *m.* rest; relaxation; **день ~а** rest day.

отдыха́|ть, ю *impf.* (*of* **отдохну́ть**) to be resting; to (be on) holiday.

отдыха́|ющий *pres. part. of* **~ть**; *as n.* **о., ~ющего** *m.*; **~ющая, ~ющей** *f.* holiday-maker.

отдыш|а́ться, у́сь, ~ишься *pf.* to catch, recover one's breath.

отёк, а *m.* (*med.*) oedema; **о. лёгких** emphysema.

отека́|ть, ю *impf. of* **отёчь**

отел|и́ться, ю́сь, ~ишься *pf. of* **тели́ться**

оте́л|ь, я *m.* hotel.

отепл|и́ть, ю́, и́шь *pf.* (*of* **~я́ть**) to protect against the cold; to winterize.

отепл|я́ть, я́ю *impf. of* **~и́ть**

от|е́ц, ца́ *m.* father (*also fig.*); **О. небе́сный** (*relig.*) the heavenly Father.

оте́ческий *adj.* fatherly, paternal.

оте́честв|енный *adj. of* **~о**; **~енная промы́шленность** home industry; **Вели́кая ~енная война́** the Great Patriotic War (*in former USSR, official designation of war of 1941–45 against Germany and her allies*).

оте́честв|о, а *nt.* native land, fatherland, homeland.

оте́|чь, ку́, чёшь, ку́т, *past* **~к, ~кла́** *pf.* (*of* **~ка́ть**) **1.** to swell, become swollen. **2.** (*of a candle*) to gutter.

от|жа́ть, отожму́, отожмёшь *pf.* (*of* **~жима́ть**) **1.** to wring out. **2.** (*coll.*) to push back.

от|же́чь, отожгу́, отожжёшь, *past* **~жёг, ~ожгла́** *pf.* (*of* **~жига́ть**) (*tech.*) to anneal.

отжива́|ть, ю *impf. of* **отжи́ть**

отжива́|ющий *pres. part. act. of* **~ть** *and adj.* moribund.

отжи́|вший *past part. act. of* **~ть** *and adj.* obsolete; outmoded.

отжига́|ть, ю *impf. of* **отже́чь**

отжима́|ть, ю *impf. of* **отжа́ть**

от|жи́ть, живу́, живёшь, *past* **~жил, ~жила́, ~жило** *pf.* (*of* **~жива́ть**) to become obsolete, die out; **о. свой век** to have had one's day; to go out of fashion.

отзвон|и́ть, ю́, и́шь *pf.* to stop ringing; to stop striking (*of a clock*).

о́тзвук, а *m.* echo (*also fig.*).

о́тзыв, а *m.* **1.** opinion, judgement; **похва́льный о.** honourable mention. **2.** reference; testimonial; **дать хоро́ший о. о ко́м-н.** to give s.o. a good reference. **3.** review. **4.** (*mil.*) reply (*to password*).

отзы́в, а *m.* recall (*of diplomatic representative*).

отзыва́|ть, ю *impf.* **1.** *impf. of* **отозва́ть. 2.** (+*i.*) to taste (of); **о. го́речью** to have a bitter taste.

отзыва́|ться, юсь *impf.* **1.** *impf. of* **отозва́ться. 2.** (+*i.*) = **~ть**

отзы́вчив|ый (~, ~а) *adj.* responsive.

оти́т, а *m.* (*med.*) otitis.

отка́з, а *m.* **1.** refusal; denial; repudiation; **получи́ть о.** to be refused, be turned down; **до ~а** to overflowing; **по́лный до ~а** cram-full, jam-packed. **2.** **(от)** renunciation (of), giving up (of). **3.** (*tech.*) failure; **де́йствовать без ~а** to run smoothly.

отка|за́ть, жу́, ~жешь *pf.* (*of* **~зывать**) **1.** (+*d.* **в**+*p.*) to refuse, deny; **она́ ~за́ла ему́ в про́сьбе** she refused his request; **ему́ нельзя́ о. в тала́нте** there is no denying that he has talent; **не ~жи́те в любе́зности...** be so kind as .... **2.** (*tech.*) to fail, break down.

отка|за́ться, жу́сь, ~жешься *pf.* (*of* **~зываться**) **1.** (**от** *or* +*inf.*) to refuse, decline; to turn down; **о. от предложе́ния** to turn down a proposal; **о. от упла́ты до́лга** to repudiate a debt; **о. служи́ть** (*fig., coll.*) to be out of order; **мой часы́ ~за́лись служи́ть** my watch would not go; **не ~жу́сь** (*coll.*) I don't mind if I do; **не ~за́лся бы** (*coll.*) I wouldn't say no. **2.** to renounce, give up; to relinquish, abdicate; **о. от борьбы́** to give up the struggle.

отка́зни|к, а *m.* refusenik.

отка́зни|ца, ~цы *f. of* **~к**

отка́зыва|ть(ся), ю(сь) *impf.* (*of* **отказа́ть(ся)**): **ни в чём себе́ не о.** to deny o.s. nothing.

отка́лыва|ть(ся), ю(сь) *impf. of* **отколо́ть(ся)**

отка́пыва|ть, ю *impf. of* **откопа́ть**

отка́рмлива|ть, ю *impf. of* **откорми́ть**

отка́т, а *m.* (*mil.*) recoil.

отка|ти́ть, чу́, ~тишь *pf.* (*of* **~тывать**) to roll away.

отка|ти́ться, чу́сь, ~тишься *pf.* (*of* **~тываться**) **1.** to roll away. **2.** (*mil.*; *fig., coll.*) to roll back, fall back.

откач|а́ть, а́ю *pf.* (*of* **~ивать**) **1.** to pump out. **2.** to resuscitate.

отка́чива|ть, ю *impf. of* **откача́ть**

откачн|у́ться, у́сь, ёшься *pf.* (*coll.*) **1.** to swing to one side. **2.** (*of a pers.*) to reel back; to slump back.

отка́шл|иваться, иваюсь *impf. of* **~яться**

отка́шл|яться, яюсь *pf.* (*of* **~иваться**) to clear one's throat.

откидно́й *adj.* folding, collapsible.

отки́дыва|ть(ся), ю(сь) *impf. of* **отки́нуть(ся)**

отки́|нуть, ну, нешь *pf.* (*of* **~дывать**) **1.** to throw away; to cast away (*also fig.*). **2.** to turn back, fold back.

отки́|нуться, нусь, нешься *pf.* (*of* **~дываться**) **1.** to lean back; to recline, settle back. **2.** *pass. of* **~нуть**

откла́дыва|ть, ю *impf. of* **отложи́ть**

откла́нива|ться, юсь *impf. of* **откла́няться**

отклáн|яться, яюсь, *pf.* (*of* **~иваться**) (*obs.*) to take one's leave.
отклéива|ть(ся), ю(сь) *impf. of* **отклéить(ся)**
отклé|ить, ю, ишь *pf.* (*of* **~ивать**) to unstick.
отклé|иться, ится *pf.* (*of* **~иваться**) **1.** to come unstuck. **2.** *pass. of* **~ить**
óтклик, а *m.* **1.** response; (*fig.*) comment. **2.** (*fig.*) echo; repercussion.
отклик|áться, áюсь *impf.* (*of* **∸нуться**) (**на**+*a.*) to answer, respond (to) (*also fig.*).
отклúк|нуться, нусь, нешься *pf. of* **~áться**
отклонéни|е, я *nt.* **1.** deviation; divergence; **о. от тéмы** digression. **2.** declining, refusal. **3.** (*phys.*) deflection, declination; error; diffraction; **вероя́тное о.** probable error; **магнúтное о.** deflection of the needle; **ýгол ~я** angle of deviation.
отклон|úть, ю́, ∸ишь *pf.* (*of* **~я́ть**) **1.** to deflect. **2.** to decline; **о. попрáвку** to vote down an amendment; **о. предложéние** to decline an offer.
отклон|úться, ю́сь, ∸ишься *pf.* (*of* **~я́ться**) **1.** to deviate; to diverge; to swerve; **о. от тéмы** to digress. **2.** *pass. of* **~úть**
отключ|áть, áю *impf. of* **~úть**
отключ|úть, ý, úшь *pf.* (*of* **~áть**) (*elec.*) to cut off, disconnect; **о. телефóнный аппарáт** to cut off a telephone.
откозыря́|ть, ю *pf.* (*coll.*; +*d.*) to salute.
отколо|тúть, чý, ∸тишь *pf.* **1.** to knock off. **2.** to beat up.
откол|óть, ю́, ∸ешь *pf.* (*of* **откáлывать**) **1.** to break off; to chop off. **2.** to unpin. **3.** (*coll.*, *pej.*): **о. глýпость** to play a stupid trick; **о. словцó** to make a wisecrack.
откол|óться, ю́сь, ∸ешься *pf.* (*of* **откáлываться**) **1.** to break off. **2.** to come unpinned *or* undone. **3.** (*fig.*) to break away; to cut o.s. off.
откомандир|овáть, ýю *pf.* (*of* **~óвывать**) **1.** to detach; to post (*to new duties or establishment*). **2.** (**за**+*i.*) (*coll.*) to send (*to fetch*).
откомандирóвыва|ть, ю *impf. of* **откомандировáть**
откопá|ть, ю *pf.* (*of* **откáпывать**) **1.** to dig out; to exhume, disinter. **2.** (*fig.*, *coll.*) to dig up, unearth.
откóрм, а *m.* fattening (up).
откорм|úть, лю́, ∸ишь *pf.* (*of* **откáрмливать**) to fatten (up).
откóс, а *m.* slope, side (*of embankment etc.*); **о. холмá** hillside; **пустúть пóезд под о.** to derail a train.
откреп|úть, лю́, úшь *pf.* (*of* **~ля́ть**) **1.** to unfasten, untie. **2.** to strike off the register.
открепля́|ть, ю *impf. of* **открепúть**
открéщива|ться, юсь *impf.* (*coll.*; **от**) to disown; to refuse to have anything to do (with).
откровéни|е, я *nt.* revelation.
откровéннича|ть, ю *impf.* (*coll.*; **с**+*i.*) to be candid (with), be frank (with).
откровéнност|ь, и *f.* candour, frankness; outspokenness.
откровéн|ный (~ен, ~на) *adj.* **1.** candid, frank; outspoken. **2.** open, unconcealed; **~ная неприя́знь** unconcealed hostility. **3.** (*coll.*; *of dress*) revealing.
откру|тúть, чý, ∸тишь *pf.* (*of* **∸чивать**) to untwist; **о. кран** to turn off a tap.
открýчива|ть, ю *impf. of* **открутúть**
открывáлк|а, и *f.* **1.** tin- *or* can-opener. **2.** corkscrew.
открывá|ть(ся), ю(сь) *impf. of* **откры́ть(ся)**
откры́ти|е, я *nt.* **1.** opening. **2.** discovery.
откры́тк|а, и *f.* post-card; **о. с вúдом** picture postcard.
откры́то *adv.* openly.
откры́т|ый *p.p.p. of* **~ь** *and adj.* open; **в ~ую** (*cards and fig.*) showing one's hand; **на ~ом вóздухе** out of doors, in the open air; **о. дом** (*fig.*) open house; **~ое заседáние** public sitting; **~ое мóре** the open sea; **~ое письмó** open letter; **~ое плáтье** low-necked dress; **~ые гóрные рабóты** opencast mining; **~ая сцéна** open-air stage.
откр|ы́ть, óю, óешь *pf.* (*of* **~ывáть**) **1.** to open; **о. комý-н. глазá на что-н.** (*fig.*) to open s.o.'s eyes to sth.; **о. мúтинг** to open a meeting; **о. огóнь** (*mil.*) to open fire; **о. пáмятник** to unveil a monument; **о. счёт** to open an account. **2.** to uncover, reveal (*also fig.*); **о. дýшу** to lay bare one's heart; **о. кáрты** (*fig.*) to show one's hand; **о. секрéт** to reveal a secret. **3.** to discover. **4.** to turn on (*gas, water, etc.*).
откр|ы́ться, óюсь, óешься *pf.* (*of* **~ывáться**) **1.** to open. **2.** to come to light, be revealed; **пéред нáми ~ы́лся великолéпный вид** a magnificent view unfolded before us. **3.** (+*d.*) to confide (in, to). **4.** *pass. of* **~ы́ть**
отксéр|ить, ю, ишь *pf. of* **ксéрить**
откýда *adv.* (*interrog.*) where from; (*rel.*) whence, from which; **о. вы?** where are you from?; **о. вы об э́том знáете?** how come you know about it?; **о. ни возьмúсь** (*coll.*) from (right) out of the blue.
откýда-либо *adv.* from somewhere or other.
откýда-нибудь *adv.* = **откýда-либо**
откýда-то *adv.* from somewhere.
óткуп, а, *pl.* **~á** *m.* (*hist.*) farming (*of revenues, etc.*); **взять на о.** to farm; **отдáть на о.** to farm out (*also fig.*).
откуп|áть(ся), áю(сь) *impf. of* **~úть(ся)**
откуп|úть, лю́, ∸ишь *pf.* (*of* **~áть**) to pay up.
откуп|úться, лю́сь, ∸ишься *pf.* (*of* **~áться**) (**от**) to pay off.
откýпорива|ть, ю *impf. of* **откýпорить**
откýпор|ить, ю, ишь *pf.* (*of* **~ивать**) to uncork; to open (*a bottle*).
откупщúк, á *m.* tax-farmer.
отку|сúть, шý, ∸сишь *pf.* (*of* **∸сывать**) to bite off; to snap off (*with pincers, etc.*).
откýсыва|ть, ю *impf. of* **откусúть**
отлагáтельств|о, а *nt.* delay; procrastination; **дéло не тéрпит ~а** the matter is urgent.
отлакир|овáть, ýю *pf. of* **лакировáть**
отлáмыва|ть(ся), ю(сь) *impf. of* **отломáть(ся)** *and* **отломúть(ся)**
отлегá|ть, ю *impf. of* **отлéчь**
отлеж|áть, ý, úшь *pf.* (*of* **∸ивать**): **я ~áл нóгу** my foot has gone to sleep.
отлеж|áться, ýсь, úшься *pf.* **1.** to lie up; to rest (*in bed*). **2.** to lie, be stored (*in order to season, ripen, etc.*).
отлёжива|ть(ся), ю(сь) *impf. of* **отлежáть(ся)**
отлёт, а *m.* flying away; departure (*of aircraft*); **быть на ~е** to be about to leave; **держáть на ~е** to hold in one's outstretched hand; **дом на ~е** house standing by itself.
отлетá|ть[1], ю *pf.* **1.** to have completed a flight. **2.** (*coll.*) to have been flying (*for a given period*); **он ~л двáдцать лет** he has twenty years' flying experience.
отлет|áть[2], áю *impf. of* **~éть**
отле|тéть, чý, тúшь *pf.* (*of* **~тáть[2]**) **1.** to fly (away, off); (*fig.*) to fly, vanish. **2.** to rebound, bounce back. **3.** (*coll.*; *of buttons, etc.*) to come off.
отл|éчь, я́гу, я́жешь, я́гут, *past* **~ёг, ~eглá** *pf.* (*of* **~егáть**) (*coll.*; *impers.*): **у неё ~еглó от сéрдца** she felt relieved.
отлúв[1], а *m.* ebb, ebb-tide.
отлúв[2], а *m.* tint; play of colours; **с золоты́м ~ом** shot with gold.
отливá|ть[1], ю *impf. of* **отлúть**
отливá|ть[2], ет *impf.* (+*i.*) to be shot (*with a colour*).

отли́вк|а, и *f.* (*tech.*) **1.** casting, founding. **2.** cast, ingot.
отлип|а́ть, а́ет *impf. of* **∠нуть**
отли́п|нуть, нет, *past* **~, ~ла** *pf.* (*of* **~а́ть**) to come off, come unstuck.
отли́ть, отолью́, отольёшь, *past* **о́тли́л, отлила́, о́тли́ло** *pf.* (*of* **отлива́ть**[1]) **1.** (*+a. or g.*) to pour off; to pump out. **2.** (*tech.*) to cast, found.
отлич|а́ть, а́ю *impf. of* **~и́ть**
отлич|а́ться, а́юсь *impf.* **1.** (*pf.* **~и́ться**) to distinguish o.s., excel (*also joc., iron.*). **2.** (*impf. only*) **(от)** to differ (from). **3.** (*impf. only*) (*+i.*) to be notable (for).
отли́чи|е, я *nt.* **1.** difference, distinction; **знак ~я** distinguishing feature; (*mil.*) order, decoration; **в о. от** unlike; in contrast to. **2.** distinction (*as grade of merit*); distinguished services; **получи́ть дипло́м с ~ем** to graduate with honours.
отличи́тельный *adj.* distinctive; distinguishing; **о. при́знак** distinguishing feature.
отлич|и́ть, у́, и́шь *pf.* (*of* **~а́ть**) **1.** to distinguish; **о. одно́ от друго́го** to tell one thing from another. **2.** to single out.
отлич|и́ться, у́сь, и́шься *pf. of* **~а́ться**
отли́чник, а *m.* **1.** pupil *or* student obtaining 'excellent' marks. **2.: о. произво́дства** exemplary worker.
отли́чно 1. *adv.* excellently; perfectly; extremely well; **о. знать** to know perfectly well. **2.** *n.*; *nt. indecl.* 'excellent' mark (*in school, etc.*).
отли́ч|ный (~ен, ~на) *adj.* **1.** (*obs.*) **(от)** different (from). **2.** excellent; **~но!** excellent!; great!
отло́г|ий (~, ~а) *adj.* (gently) sloping.
отло́гост|ь, и *f.* (gentle) slope.
отложе́ни|е, я *nt.* sediment, precipitation; (*geol.*) deposit.
отлож|и́ть, у́, и́шь *pf.* **1.** (*impf.* **откла́дывать**) to put aside, set aside; to put by; **о. на чёрный день** to put by for a rainy day. **2.** (*impf.* **откла́дывать** *and* **отлага́ть**) to put off, postpone; **о. па́ртию** to adjourn a game; **о. реше́ние** to suspend judgement; **о. в до́лгий я́щик** to shelve. **3.** (*impf.* **откла́дывать**) (*of insects*) to lay. **4.** (*impf.* **откла́дывать**) to unharness. **5.** (*impf.* **отлага́ть**) (*geol.*) to deposit.
отложно́й *adj.*: **о. воротни́к** turn-down collar.
отлома́|ть, ю *pf.* (*of* **отла́мывать**) to break off.
отлома́|ться, юсь *pf.* (*of* **отла́мываться**) to break off.
отлом|и́ть(ся), лю́(сь), ∠ишь(ся) *pf.* = **~а́ть(ся)**
отлуп|и́ть, лю́, ∠ишь *pf. of* **лупи́ть**[2]
отлуч|а́ть(ся), а́ю(сь) *impf. of* **отлучи́ть(ся)**
отлуче́ни|е, я *nt.* (*eccl. and fig.*) excommunication.
отлуч|и́ть, у́, и́шь *pf.* (*of* **~а́ть**) (*obs.*; **от**) to separate *or* remove (from); **о. (от це́ркви)** (*eccl.*) to excommunicate.
отлуч|и́ться, у́сь, и́шься *pf.* (*of* **~а́ться**) **1.** to absent o.s. **2.** *pass. of* **~и́ть**
отлу́чк|а, и *f.* absence; **самово́льная о.** (*mil.*) absence without leave (*abbr.* AWOL); **быть в ~е** to be absent, be away.
отлы́нива|ть, ю *impf.* (*coll.*; **от**) to shirk.
отма́лчива|ться, юсь *impf. of* **отмолча́ться**
отма́тыва|ть, ю *impf. of* **отмота́ть**
отма|ха́ть[1]**, шу́, ∠шешь** *pf.* (*of* **∠хивать**) **1.** to stop waving. **2.: о. ру́ки** to tire one's arms by waving.
отмаха́|ть[2]**, ю** *pf.* (*coll.*) to cover (*a distance*); **за день мы ~ли свы́ше тридцати́ миль** in the day we covered more than thirty miles.
отма́хива|ть(ся), ю(сь) *impf. of* **отмаха́ть**[1] *and* **отмахну́ть(ся)**
отмах|ну́ть, ну́, нёшь *pf.* (*of* **∠ивать**) (*coll.*) to wave away, brush off (*with one's hand*).
отмах|ну́ться, ну́сь, нёшься *pf.* (*of* **∠иваться**) **(от) 1.** = **~ну́ть; о. от комаро́в** to brush mosquitoes off. **2.** (*fig.*) to brush aside.
отма́чива|ть, ю *impf. of* **отмочи́ть**
отмеж|ева́ть, у́ю *pf.* (*of* **~ёвывать**) to mark off, draw a boundary line (between).
отмеж|ева́ться, у́юсь *pf.* (*of* **~ёвываться**) **1. (от)** to dissociate o.s. (from); to refuse to acknowledge. **2.** *pass. of* **~ева́ть**
отмежёвыва|ть(ся), ю(сь) *impf. of* **отмежева́ть(ся)**
о́тмел|ь, и *f.* (sand-)bar, (sand-)bank.
отме́н|а, ы *f.* abolition; repeal; cancellation; **о. крепостно́го пра́ва** abolition of serfdom; **о. зако́на** repeal of a law; **о. спекта́кля** cancellation of a show.
отмен|и́ть, ю́, ∠ишь *pf.* (*of* **~я́ть**) to abolish; to repeal, revoke, rescind; to cancel.
отме́н|ный (~ен, ~на) *adj.* excellent.
отмен|я́ть, я́ю *impf. of* **~и́ть**
отмер|е́ть, отомрёт, *past* **о́тмер, ~ла́, о́тмерло** *pf.* (*of* **отмира́ть**) to die off; (*fig.*) to die out, die away.
отмерз|а́ть, а́ет *impf. of* **∠нуть**
отмёрз|нуть, нет, *past* **~, ~ла** *pf.* (*of* **~а́ть**) to freeze; **ру́ки у меня́ ~ли** my hands are frozen.
отме́рива|ть, ю *impf. of* **отме́рить**
отме́р|ить, ю, ишь *pf.* (*of* **~ивать** *and* **~я́ть**) to measure off.
отмер|я́ть, я́ю *impf.* = **∠ивать**
отме|сти́, ту́, тёшь, *past* **∠л, ~ла́** *pf.* (*of* **~та́ть**) to sweep aside (*also fig.*).
отме́стк|а, и *f.* (*coll.*) revenge; **в ~у** in revenge.
отмета́|ть, ю *impf. of* **отмести́**
отме́тин|а, ы *f.* mark; (*on forehead of horse, etc.*) star.
отме́|тить, чу, тишь *pf.* (*of* **~ча́ть**) **1.** to mark, note; to make a note (of); **о. пти́чкой** to tick off. **2.** to point to, mention, record; **о. чьи-н. по́двиги** to point to s.o.'s feats. **3.** to register (out), sign out (*departing tenant, etc.*). **4.** to celebrate.
отме́|титься, чусь, тишься *pf.* (*of* **~ча́ться**) **1.** to sign one's name (*on a list*). **2.** to register (out), sign out (*on departure*).
отме́тк|а, и *f.* **1.** note. **2.** (*in school or examinations*) mark.
отмеча́|ть(ся), ю(сь) *impf. of* **отме́тить(ся)**
отмобилиз|ова́ть, у́ю *pf.* (*coll.*) to mobilize totally.
отмок|а́ть, а́ет *impf. of* **∠нуть**
отмо́к|нуть, нет, *past* **~, ~ла** *pf.* (*of* **~а́ть**) **1.** to grow wet. **2.** to soak off.
отмолч|а́ться, у́сь, и́шься *pf.* (*of* **отма́лчиваться**) (*coll.*) to keep silent, say nothing.
отмора́жива|ть, ю *impf. of* **отморо́зить**
отморо́жени|е, я *nt.* frost-bite.
отморо́|женный *p.p.p of* **~зить** *and adj.* frost-bitten.
отморо́|зить, жу, зишь *pf.* (*of* **отмора́живать**) to injure by frost-bite; **я ~зил себе́ у́ши** my ears are frost-bitten.
отмота́|ть, ю *pf.* (*of* **отма́тывать**) to unwind.
отмоч|и́ть, у́, ∠ишь *pf.* (*of* **отма́чивать**) to soak off.
отмыва́|ть(ся), ю(сь) *impf. of* **отмы́ть(ся)**
отмы́вщик, а *m.*: **о. де́нег** money launderer.
отмыка́|ть, ю *impf. of* **отомкну́ть**
отм|ы́ть, о́ю, о́ешь *pf.* (*of* **~ыва́ть**) **1.** to wash clean. **2.** to wash off, wash away. **3.** (*fig.*): **о. де́ньги** to launder money.
отм|ы́ться, о́юсь, о́ешься *pf.* (*of* **~ыва́ться**) **1.** to wash o.s. clean. **2.** (*of dirt, etc.*) to come out, come off.
отмы́чк|а, и *f.* pass key, master key; lock-pick.
отне́кива|ться, юсь *impf.* (*coll.*) to refuse.
отнес|ти́, у́, ёшь, *past* **∠, ~ла́** *pf.* (*of* **относи́ть**) **1.** **(в+a., к)** to take (to). **2.** to carry away, carry off; (*impers.*): **ло́дку ~ло́ тече́нием** the boat was carried away by the current. **3.** (*coll.*) to cut off. **4. (к)**

to ascribe (to), attribute (to), refer (to); **ру́копись ~ли́ к пя́тому ве́ку** the manuscript was believed to date from the fifth century; **мы ~ли́ его́ раздражи́тельность на счёт глухоты́** we put his irritability down to his deafness.

отнес|ти́сь, у́сь, ёшься, *past* **∸ся, ~ла́сь** *pf.* (*of* **относи́ться**) (**к**) to treat; to regard; **хорошо́ о. к кому́-н.** to treat s.o. well, be nice to s.o.; **скепти́чески о. к предположе́нию** to be sceptical about an hypothesis; **как вы ~ли́сь к э́той ле́кции?** what did you think of the lecture?

отнима́|ть(ся), ю(сь) *impf. of* **отня́ть(ся)**

относи́тельно 1. *adv.* relatively. **2.** *prep.* (+*g.*) concerning, about, with regard to.

относи́тельност|ь, и *f.* relativity; **тео́рия ~и Эйнште́йна** Einstein's Theory of Relativity.

относи́тел|ьный (~ен, ~ьна) *adj.* relative; **~ьное местоиме́ние** (*gram.*) relative pronoun.

относ|и́ть, шу́, ∸сишь *impf. of* **отнести́**

отно|си́ться, шу́сь, ∸сишься *impf.* **1.** *impf. of* **отнести́сь. 2.** *impf. only* (**к**) to concern, have to do (with), relate (to); **э́то к де́лу не ∸сится** that's beside the point, that is irrelevant. **3.** *impf. only* (**к**) to date (from); **храм э́тот ∸сится к двена́дцатому ве́ку** this church dates from the twelfth century.

отноше́ни|е, я *nt.* **1.** (**к**) attitude (to); treatment (of); **внима́тельное о. к ста́рым** consideration for the old; **у него́ стра́нное о. к же́нщинам** he has a strange attitude to women. **2.** relation; respect; **име́ть о. к чему́-н.** to bear a relation to sth., have a bearing on sth.; **не име́ть ~я (к)** to have nothing to do (with); **в ~и** (+*g.*), **по ~ю (к)** with respect (to), with regard (to); **в не́которых ~ях** in some respects. **3.** (*pl.*) relations; terms; **дипломати́ческие ~я** diplomatic relations; **быть в дру́жеских ~ях** (**с**+*i.*) to be on friendly terms (with). **4.** (*math.*) ratio; **в прямо́м (обра́тном) ~и** in direct (inverse) ratio. **5.** (*official*) letter, memorandum.

отны́не *adv.* (*obs.*) henceforth, henceforward.

отню́дь *adv.* by no means, not at all.

отня́ти|е, я *nt.* taking away; **о. руки́** amputation of an arm; **о. от груди́** weaning.

от|ня́ть, ниму́, ни́мешь, *past* **∸нял, ~няла́, ∸няло** *pf.* (*of* **~нима́ть**) **1.** to take (away); **о. от груди́** to wean; **о. жизнь у кого́-н.** to take s.o.'s life; **от шести́ о. три** to take away three from six; **э́то ∸няло у меня́ три часа́** it took me three hours. **2.** to amputate.

от|ня́ться, ни́мется, *past* **~ня́лся, ~няла́сь** *pf.* (*of* **~нима́ться**) to be paralyzed; **у него́ ~няла́сь пра́вая рука́** he has lost the power of his right arm; **у неё ~ня́лся язы́к** she has lost the power of speech.

ото *prep.* = **от**

ото... *vbl. pref.* = **от...**

отобе́да|ть, ю *pf.* to have finished dinner.

отобража́|ть, ю *impf. of* **отобрази́ть**

отображе́ни|е, я *nt.* reflection; representation.

отобра|зи́ть, жу́, зи́шь *pf.* (*of* **~жа́ть**) to reflect; to represent.

от|обра́ть, беру́, берёшь, *past* **~обра́л, ~обрала́, ~обра́ло** *pf.* (*of* **отбира́ть**) **1.** to take (away); to seize. **2.** to select, pick out.

отова́рива|ть, ю *impf. of* **отова́рить**

отова́р|ить, ю, ишь *pf.* (*of* **~ивать**) to pledge goods in support of; **о. чек** to issue goods against a sale receipt.

отовсю́ду *adv.* from everywhere, from every quarter.

от|огна́ть, гоню́, го́нишь, *past* **~огна́л, ~огнала́, ~огна́ло** *pf.* (*of* **~гоня́ть**) to drive off; to keep off; (*fig.*) to suppress.

отогн|у́ть, у́, ёшь *pf.* (*of* **отгиба́ть**) to bend back; to flange.

отогрева́|ть(ся), ю(сь) *impf. of* **отогре́ть(ся)**

отогре́|ть, ю *pf.* (*of* **~ва́ть**) to warm.

отогре́|ться, юсь *pf.* (*of* **~ва́ться**) to warm o.s.

отодвига́|ть(ся), ю(сь) *impf. of* **отодви́нуть(ся)**

отодви́|нуть, ну, нешь *pf.* (*of* **~га́ть**) **1.** to move aside. **2.** (*fig.*) to put off, put back.

отодви́|нуться, нусь, нешься *pf.* (*of* **~га́ться**) **1.** to move aside. **2.** *pass. of* **~нуть**

от|одра́ть, деру́, дерёшь, *past* **~одра́л, ~одрала́, ~одра́ло** *pf.* (*of* **~дира́ть**) **1.** to tear off, rip off. **2.** (*coll.*) to flog, thrash.

отож(д)еств|и́ть, лю́, и́шь *pf.* (*of* **~ля́ть**) to identify.

отож(д)ествля́|ть, ю *impf. of* **отож(д)естви́ть**

от|озва́ть, зову́, зовёшь, *past* **~озва́л, ~озвала́, ~озва́ло** *pf.* (*of* **~зыва́ть**) **1.** to take aside. **2.** to recall (*a diplomatic representative*).

от|озва́ться, зову́сь, зовёшься, *past* **~озва́лся, ~озвала́сь, ~озва́ло́сь** *pf.* (*of* **~зыва́ться**) **1.** (**на**+*a.*) to answer; to respond (to). **2.** (**о**+*p.*) to speak (of); **рецензе́нты хорошо́ ~озва́ли́сь о его́ второ́й кни́ге** his second book was well received by the reviewers. **3.** (**на**+*a.*) to tell (on, upon); **деторожде́ние ~озвало́сь на её здоро́вье** child-bearing has told on her health.

ото|йти́, йду́, йдёшь, *past* **~шёл, ~шла́** *pf.* (*of* **отходи́ть**[1]) **1.** to move away; to move off; (*of trains, etc.*) to leave, depart. **2.** to withdraw; to recede; (*mil.*) to withdraw, fall back; (*fig.*; **от**) to move away (from); to digress (from), diverge (from); **он далеко́ ~шёл от пре́жних взгля́дов** he has moved a long way from his earlier views. **3.** (*of stains, etc.*) to come out; (**от**) to come away (from), come off; **обо́и ~шли́ от стены́** the paper has come off (the wall). **4.** to recover (normal state); to come to o.s.; to come round; (*impers., coll.*): **у меня́ ~шло́ от се́рдца** I felt better; I felt relieved. **5.** (**к**) to pass (to), go (to) (= *pass into the possession of, by inheritance, etc.*). **6.** to be lost (*in processing*). **7. о. в ве́чность** (*rhet.*) to pass away.

отомкн|у́ть, у́, ёшь *pf.* (*of* **отмыка́ть**) to unlock, unbolt.

отом|сти́ть, щу́, сти́шь *pf. of* **мстить**

отопи́тельный *adj.* heating; **о. сезо́н** cold season.

отоп|и́ть, лю́, ∸шь *pf.* (*of* **ота́пливать** *and* **отопля́ть**) to heat.

отопле́ни|е, я *nt.* heating.

отопля́|ть, ю *impf. of* **отопи́ть**

ото́рванност|ь, и *f.* isolation; loneliness; **чу́вствовать о. от цивилиза́ции** to feel cut off from civilization.

оторв|а́ть, у́, ёшь, *past* **~а́л, ~ала́, ~а́ло** *pf.* (*of* **отрыва́ть**[1]) to tear off; to tear away (*also fig.*); **о. кого́-н. от рабо́ты** to tear s.o. away from his work; **с рука́ми о.** (*coll.*) to seize with both hands.

оторв|а́ться, у́сь, ёшься, *past* **~а́лся, ~ала́сь, ~а́ло́сь** *pf.* (*of* **отрыва́ться**) **1.** to come off, be torn off. **2.** (*aeron.*): **о. от земли́** to take off. **3.** (*fig.*; **от**) to be cut off (from), lose touch (with); to break away (from); **о. от проти́вника** to lose contact with the enemy. **4.** (*fig.*; **от**) to tear o.s. away (from); **от э́той кни́ги я не мог о.** I could not tear myself away from this book.

оторопе́лый *adj.* (*coll.*) dumb-founded.

оторопе́|ть, ю *pf.* (*coll.*) to be struck dumb.

о́тороп|ь, и *f.* (*coll.*) confusion, fright.

оторо́чк|а, и *f.* edging, trimming.

ото|сла́ть, шлю́, шлёшь *pf.* (*of* **отсыла́ть**) **1.** to send off, dispatch; **о. де́ньги** to send a remittance. **2.** (**к**) to refer (to).

отосп|а́ться, лю́сь, и́шься, *past* **~а́лся, ~ала́сь** *pf.* (*of* **отсыпа́ться**) to have a (good) long sleep;

о. по́сле доро́ги to sleep off a journey.
ото|шёл, шла́ *see* **~йти́**
ото|шлю́, шлёшь *see* **~сла́ть**
отоща́лый *adj.* (*coll.*) emaciated.
отоща́|ть, ю *pf. of* **тоща́ть**
отпада́|ть, ю *impf. of* **отпа́сть**
отпари́р|овать, ую *pf. of* **пари́ровать**
отпа́рыва|ть, ю *impf. of* **отпоро́ть**[1]
отпа́|сть, ду́, дёшь, *past* **~л** *pf.* (*of* **~да́ть**) **1.** to fall off, drop off; to fall away. **2.** (*fig.*; **от**) to drop out (of); **мно́гие чле́ны ~ли от па́ртии** many members have dropped out of the party. **3.** (*fig.*) to pass, fade; **у него́ ~ла охо́та к путеше́ствию по А́фрике** his desire to travel in Africa has passed; **вопро́с об э́том ~л** the question no longer arises.
отпева́ни|е, я *nt.* burial service.
отпева́|ть, ю *impf. of* **отпе́ть**
от|пере́ть, опру́, опрёшь, *past* **∠пер, ~перла́, ∠перло** *pf.* (*of* **~пира́ть**) to unlock; to open.
от|пере́ться[1]**, опрётся,** *past* **~пёрся, ~перла́сь** *pf.* (*of* **~пира́ться**) to open.
от|пере́ться[2]**, опру́сь, опрёшься,** *past* **~пёрся, ~перла́сь** *pf.* (*of* **~пира́ться**) (*coll.*; **от**) to deny; to disown.
отпе́т|ый *p.p.p. of* **~ь** *and adj.* (*coll.*) out-and-out, inveterate.
отп|е́ть, ою́, оёшь *pf.* (*of* **~ева́ть**) to read the burial service (for, over).
отпеча́т|ать, аю *pf.* **1.** (*impf.* **печа́тать**) to print (off). **2.** (*impf.* **~ывать**) to imprint; **о. па́льцы на стекле́** to leave finger-prints on glass. **3.** (*impf.* **~ывать**) to open (up).
отпеча́т|ок, ка *m.* imprint, impress (*also fig.*); **о. па́льца** finger-print.
отпеча́тыва|ть, ю *impf. of* **отпеча́тать**
отпива́|ть, ю *impf. of* **отпи́ть**
отпи́лива|ть, ю *impf. of* **отпили́ть**
отпил|и́ть, ю́, ∠ишь *pf.* (*of* **∠ивать**) to saw off.
отпира́тельств|о, а *nt.* denial, disavowal.
отпира́|ть(ся), ю(сь) *impf. of* **отпере́ть(ся)**
отпи|са́ть, шу́, ∠шешь *pf.* (*of* **∠сывать**) **1.** (*obs.*) to bequeath, leave. **2.** (*obs.*) to confiscate.
отпи|са́ться, шу́сь, ∠шешься *pf.* (*of* **∠сываться**) to make a (purely) formal reply.
отпи́сыва|ть(ся), ю(сь) *impf. of* **отписа́ть(ся)**
от|пи́ть, опью́, опьёшь, *past* **∠пил, ~пила́, ∠пило** *pf.* (*of* **~пива́ть**) (+*a. or g.*) to take a sip (of).
отпи́хива|ть, ю *impf. of* **отпихну́ть**
отпих|ну́ть, ну́, нёшь *pf.* (*of* **∠ивать**) (*coll.*) to push off; to shove aside.
отпла́т|а, ы *f.* repayment.
отпла|ти́ть, чу́, ∠тишь *pf.* (*of* **∠чивать**) (+*d.*) to pay back (to); repay; **о. кому́-н. той же моне́той** to pay s.o. in his own coin.
отпла́чива|ть, ю *impf. of* **отплати́ть**
отплёвыва|ть, ю *impf. of* **отплю́нуть**
отплёвыва|ться, юсь *impf.* to spit (*also fig., to express disgust*).
отплыва́|ть, ю *impf. of* **отплы́ть**
отплы́ти|е, я *nt.* sailing, departure.
отплы́|ть, ву́, вёшь, *past* **~л, ~ла́, ~ло** *pf.* (*of* **~ва́ть**) to sail, set sail; to swim off.
отплю́н|уть, у, ешь *pf.* (*of* **отплёвывать**) to spit (out), expectorate.
о́тповед|ь, и *f.* reproof, rebuke.
отполз|а́ть, а́ю *impf. of* **~ти́**
отполз|ти́, у́, ёшь, *past* **∠, ~ла́** *pf.* (*of* **~а́ть**) to crawl away.
отполир|ова́ть, у́ю *pf. of* **полирова́ть**
отпо́р, а *m.* repulse; rebuff; **дать о.** (+*d.*) to repulse; **встре́тить о.** to be repulsed; to meet with a rebuff.
отпор|о́ть[1]**, ю́, ∠ешь** *pf.* (*of* **отпа́рывать**) to rip off.
отпор|о́ть[2]**, ю́, ∠ешь** *pf.* (*of* **поро́ть**) (*coll.*) to flog, thrash.
отправи́тел|ь, я *m.* sender.
отпра́в|ить, лю, ишь *pf.* (*of* **~ля́ть**) to send, forward, dispatch; **о. на тот свет** to send to kingdom come.
отпра́в|иться, люсь, ишься *pf.* (*of* **~ля́ться**) to set out, set off, start; to leave, depart; **о. на бокову́ю** (*coll.*) to turn in, hit the sack.
отпра́вк|а, и *f.* sending off, forwarding, dispatch.
отправле́ни|е, я *nt.* **1.** sending. **2.** departure (*of trains, ships*). **3.** function (*of the organism*). **4.** exercise, performance; **о. обя́занностей** exercise of one's duties.
отправля́|ть, ю *impf.* **1.** *impf. of* **отпра́вить. 2.** (*impf. only*) to exercise, perform (*duties, functions*).
отправля́|ться, юсь *impf.* **1.** *impf. of* **отпра́виться. 2.** (*fig.*; **от**) to proceed (from).
отправн|о́й *adj.*: **о. пункт, ~а́я то́чка** starting-point.
отпра́здн|овать, ую *pf. of* **пра́здновать**
отпра́шива|ться, юсь *impf.* (*of* **отпроси́ться**) to ask (for) leave.
отпро|си́ться, шу́сь, ∠сишься *pf.* (*of* **отпра́шиваться**) **1.** to ask (for) leave. **2.** to obtain leave.
отпры́гива|ть, ю *impf. of* **отпры́гнуть**
отпры́г|нуть, ну, нешь *pf.* (*of* **~ивать**) to jump back, spring back; to jump aside, spring aside; to bounce back.
о́тпрыск, а *m.* (*bot. and fig.*) offshoot, scion.
отпряга́|ть, ю *impf. of* **отпря́чь**
отпря́|нуть, ну, нешь *pf.* to recoil, start back.
отпря́|чь, гу́, жёшь, гу́т, *past* **~г, ~гла́** *pf.* (*of* **~га́ть**) to unharness.
отпу́гива|ть, ю *impf. of* **отпугну́ть**
отпуг|ну́ть, ну́, нёшь, *pf.* (*of* **∠ивать**) to frighten off, scare away.
о́тпуск, а, в ~е *or* **в ~у́,** *pl.* **~а́, ~о́в** *m.* leave, holiday(s); (*mil.*) leave, furlough; **в ~е, в ~у́** on leave; **о. по боле́зни** sick-leave.
отпуска́|ть, ю *impf. of* **отпусти́ть**
отпускни́к, а́ *m.* person on leave; holiday-maker.
отпускн|о́й *adj.* **1.** *adj. of* **о́тпуск; ~ы́е де́ньги** holiday pay; **~о́е свиде́тельство** authorization of leave (*of absence*); (*mil.*) leave pass. **2.** (*econ.*): **~а́я цена́** selling price.
отпу|сти́ть, щу́, ∠стишь *pf.* (*of* **~ска́ть**) **1.** to let go, let off; to let out; to set free; to release; to give leave (of absence); **~сти́ мою́ ру́ку!** let go of my arm!; **о. на пра́здник** to release for the holiday; **о. шу́тку** (*coll.*) to crack a joke. **2.** to relax, slacken; (*impers., coll.*): **боль ~сти́ло** the pain has eased. **3.** to (let) grow; **о. (себе́) бо́роду** to grow a beard. **4.** to issue, give out; (*in a shop, etc.*) to serve. **5.** to assign, allot. **6.** to remit; to forgive; **о. кому́-н. грехи́** (*eccl.*) to give s.o. absolution.
отпуще́ни|е, я *nt.* remission; **о. грехо́в** (*eccl.*) absolution; **козёл ~я** (*coll.*) scapegoat.
отраба́тыва|ть, ю *impf. of* **отрабо́тать**
отрабо́та|нный *p.p.p. of* **~ть** *and adj.* (*tech.*) worked out; waste, spent, exhaust; **о. газ** waste gas, exhaust gas.
отрабо́та|ть, ю *pf.* (*of* **отраба́тывать**) **1.** to work off (*a debt, etc.*). **2.** (*coll.*) to work (*a given length of time*).
отра́в|а, ы *f.* poison.
отрави́тел|ь, я *m.* poisoner.
отрав|и́ть, лю́, ∠ишь *pf.* (*of* **~ля́ть**) to poison (*also fig.*).
отрав|и́ться, лю́сь, ∠ишься *pf.* (*of* **~ля́ться**) **1.** to poison o.s. **2.** *pass. of* **~и́ть**
отравля́|ть(ся), ю(сь) *impf. of* **отрави́ться**
отра́д|а, ы *f.* joy, delight; comfort.
отра́дный *adj.* gratifying, pleasing; comforting.

отража́тел|ь, я *m.* (*phys.*) reflector; (*radar*) scanner.

отража́|ть(ся), ю(сь) *impf. of* **отрази́ть(ся)**

отраже́ни|е, я *nt.* **1.** reflection; reverberation. **2.** repulse, parry; warding off.

отра|зи́ть, жу́, зи́шь *pf.* (*of* **~жа́ть**) **1.** to reflect (*also fig.*). **2.** to repulse, repel, parry; to ward off.

отра|зи́ться, жу́сь, зи́шься *pf.* (*of* **~жа́ться**) **1.** to be reflected; to reverberate. **2.** (*fig.*; **на**+*p.*) to affect; to tell (on); **пое́здка в го́ры благоприя́тно ~зи́лась на его́ рабо́те** the mountain trip had a beneficial effect on his work.

отрапорт|ова́ть, у́ю *pf.* to report.

отраслево́й *adj. of* **о́трасль**

о́трасл|ь, и *f.* branch; **о. промы́шленности** branch of industry.

отраст|а́ть, а́ю *impf. of* **~и́**

отраст|и́, у́, ёшь, *past* **отро́с, отросла́** *pf.* (*of* **~а́ть**) to grow.

отра|сти́ть, щу́, сти́шь *pf.* (*of* **~щивать**) to (let) grow; **о. во́лосы** to grow one's hair long; **о. брю́хо** (*coll.*) to develop a paunch.

отра́щива|ть, ю *impf. of* **отрасти́ть**

отреаги́р|овать, ую *pf.* (*coll.*) *of* **реаги́ровать 2.**

отре́бь|е, я *nt.* (*collect.*) rabble.

отрегули́р|овать, ую *pf. of* **регули́ровать**

отредакти́р|овать, ую *pf. of* **редакти́ровать**

отре́з, а *m.* **1.** cut; **ли́ния ~а** line of the cut. **2.** perforated line. **3.** length (*of material*); **о. на пла́тье** dress length.

отрез|а́ть, а́ю *impf. of* **~ать**

отре́|зать, жу, жешь *pf.* (*of* **~за́ть**) **1.** to cut off (*also fig.*); to divide, apportion (land); **проти́вник ~зал нам отступле́ние** the enemy had cut off our retreat. **2.** (*coll.*) to snap out.

отрезве́|ть, ю *pf. of* **трезве́ть**

отрезв|и́ть, лю́, и́шь *pf.* (*of* **~ля́ть**) to sober (*also fig.*).

отрезв|и́ться, лю́сь, и́шься *pf.* (*of* **~ля́ться**) to become sober, sober up.

отрезвле́ни|е, я *nt.* sobering (up).

отрезвля́|ть(ся), ю(сь) *impf. of* **отрезви́ть(ся)**

отрезно́й *adj.* perforated; **о. тало́н** tear-off coupon.

отре́з|ок, ка *m.* piece, cut; section; (*hist.*) portion (*of land*); (*math.*) segment; **о. вре́мени** stretch of time.

отрека́|ться, юсь *impf. of* **отре́чься**

отрекоменд|ова́ть, у́ю *pf.* to introduce.

отрекоменд|ова́ться, у́юсь *pf.* to introduce o.s.

отремонти́р|овать, ую *pf. of* **ремонти́ровать**

отре́пь|е, я, *pl.* **~я, ~ев** *nt.* (*collect.*) rags; **ходи́ть в о., в ~ях** to be in rags.

отрече́ни|е, я *nt.* **(от)** renunciation (of); **о. от престо́ла** abdication.

отре́|чься, ку́сь, чёшься, ку́тся, *past* **~кся, ~кла́сь** *pf.* (*of* **~ка́ться**) **(от)** to renounce, disavow, give up; **о. от престо́ла** to abdicate.

отреш|а́ться, а́юсь *impf. of* **~и́ться**

отрешённост|ь, и *f.* estrangement, aloofness.

отреш|и́ться, у́сь, и́шься *pf.* (*of* **~а́ться**) **(от)** to renounce, give up; **я не мог о. от мы́сли** I could not get rid of the idea.

отрица́ни|е, я *nt.* denial; negation.

отрица́тел|ьный (~ен, ~ьна) *adj.* negative; (*fig.*) bad, unfavourable; **~ьное электри́чество** negative electricity; **~ьная сторона́** bad side, drawback.

отрица́|ть, ю *impf.* to deny; to disclaim; **о. вино́вность** (*leg.*) to plead not guilty.

отро́г, а *m.* (*geog.*) spur.

о́троду *adv.* (*coll.*) **не ... о.** never in one's life; never in one's born days; **я о. не вида́л ничего́ подо́бного** I have never seen the like.

отро́дь|е, я *nt.* (*pej.*) spawn, offspring.

отродя́сь *adv.* (*coll.*) = **о́троду**

отро́ст|ок, ка *m.* **1.** (*bot.*) shoot, sprout. **2.** (*tech.*) branch, extension. **3.** (*anat.*) appendix.

о́троческий *adj.* adolescent.

о́трочеств|о, а *nt.* adolescence.

о́труб|и, е́й *no sg.* bran.

отруб|а́ть, а́ю *impf. of* **~и́ть**

отруб|и́ть, лю́, ~ишь *pf.* (*of* **~а́ть**) **1.** to chop off. **2.** (*fig., coll.*) to snap back.

отрубно́й *adj. of* **о́труб**

о́труб|ный *adj. of* **~и**

отру́гива|ться, юсь *impf.* (*coll.*) to return abuse.

отры́в, а *m.* **1.** tearing off. **2.** (*fig.*) alienation, isolation; loss of contact; **в ~е (от)** out of touch (with); **учи́ться без ~а от произво́дства** to study while continuing (normal) work; **о. от земли́** (*aeron.*) take-off; **о. от проти́вника** (*mil.*) disengagement.

отрыва́|ть[1], ю *impf. of* **оторва́ть**

отрыва́|ть[2], ю *impf. of* **отры́ть**

отрыва́|ться, юсь *impf. of* **оторва́ться**

отры́вист|ый (~, ~а) *adj.* jerky, abrupt; curt.

отрывно́й *adj.* perforated; **о. календа́рь** tear-off calendar.

отры́в|ок, ка *m.* fragment, excerpt; passage (*of book, etc.*); **о. из фи́льма** film clip.

отры́воч|ный (~ен, ~на) *adj.* fragmentary, scrappy.

отры́гива|ть, ю *impf. of* **отрыгну́ть**

отрыг|ну́ть, ну́, нёшь *pf.* (*of* **~ивать**) (+*a. or g.*) to belch.

отры́жк|а, и *f.* **1.** belch; belching. **2.** (*fig.*) survival, throw-back.

отр|ы́ть, о́ю, о́ешь *pf.* (*of* **~ыва́ть[2]**) to dig out; to unearth (*also fig.*).

отря́д, а *m.* **1.** detachment; group; **передово́й о.** (*fig.*) vanguard. **2.** (*biol.*) order.

отря|ди́ть, жу́, ди́шь *pf.* (*of* **~жа́ть**) to dispatch, send; (*mil.*) to detail.

отряжа́|ть, ю *impf. of* **отряди́ть**

отряс|а́ть, а́ю *impf. of* **~ти́**

отряс|ти́, у́, ёшь, *past* **~, ~ла́** *pf.* (*of* **~а́ть**) (*obs.*) to shake off; **о. прах от ног свои́х** (*fig.*) to shake off the dust from one's feet.

отря́хива|ть(ся), ю(сь) *impf. of* **отряхну́ть(ся)**

отрях|ну́ть, ну́, нёшь *pf.* (*of* **~ивать**) to shake down, shake off; **о. снег с воротника́** to shake snow off one's collar.

отрях|ну́ться, ну́сь, нёшься *pf.* (*of* **~иваться**) to shake o.s. down.

отса|ди́ть, жу́, ~дишь *pf.* (*of* **~живать**) **1.** (*hort.*) to transplant, plant out. **2.** to seat apart.

отса́дк|а, и *f.* (*hort.*) transplanting, planting out.

отса́жива|ть, ю *impf. of* **отсади́ть**

отса́жива|ться, юсь *impf. of* **отсе́сть**

отсалют|ова́ть, у́ю *pf. of* **салютова́ть**

отса́сыва|ть, ю *impf. of* **отсоса́ть**

отсве́т, а *m.* reflection; reflected light.

отсве́чива|ть, ю *impf.* to be reflected; (+*i.*) to shine (with); **в ко́мнате ~л с у́лицы фона́рь** the light of the street-lamp was reflected in the room.

отсебя́тин|а, ы *f.* (*coll.*) words of one's own; sth. of one's own devising; (*theatr.*) ad-libbing.

отсе́в, а *m.* **1.** sifting, selection. **2.** siftings, residue.

отсе́ива|ть(ся), ю(сь) *impf. of* **отсе́ять(ся)**

отсе́к, а *m.* **1.** compartment; bay; carrel (*in library*). **2.** (*astronautics*) module.

отсека́|ть, ю *impf. of* **отсе́чь**

отс|е́сть я́ду, я́дешь, *past* **~е́л** *pf.* (*of* **~а́живаться**) to seat o.s. apart; **(от)** to move away (from).

отсече́ни|е, я *nt.* cutting off, severance; **дать го́лову на о.** (*coll.*) to stake one's life.

отсе́|чь, ку́, чёшь, ку́т, *past* **~к, ~кла́** *pf.* (*of* **~ка́ть**) to cut off, chop off, sever.

отсе́|ять, ю, ешь *pf.* (*of* **~ивать**) **1.** to sift, screen.

2. (*fig.*) to eliminate.

отсе́|яться, юсь, ешься *pf.* (*of* **~иваться**) **1.** *pass. of* **~ять. 2.** (*fig.*) to fall off, fall away.

отси|де́ть, жу́, ди́шь *pf.* (*of* **~́живать**) **1.** to stay (for); to sit out. **2.** to make numb by sitting; **я ~де́л себе́ но́гу** I have pins and needles in my leg.

отси|де́ться, жу́сь, ди́шься *pf.* (*of* **~́живаться**) (*coll.*) to sit out (a siege); (*fig., pej.*) to sit on the fence.

отси́жива|ть(ся), ю(сь) *impf. of* **отсиде́ть(ся)**

отска́блива|ть, ю *impf. of* **отскобли́ть**

отска́кива|ть, ю *impf. of* **отскочи́ть**

отскобл|и́ть, ю́, ~́ишь *pf.* (*of* **отска́бливать**) to scratch off.

отско́к, а *m.* rebound.

отскоч|и́ть, у́, ~́ишь *pf.* (*of* **отска́кивать**) **1.** to jump aside, jump away; to rebound, bounce back. **2.** (*coll.*) to come off, break off.

отсла́ива|ться, ется *impf. of* **отслои́ться**

отслое́ни|е, я *nt.* (*geol.*) exfoliation.

отсло|и́ться, и́тся *pf.* (*of* **отсла́иваться**) (*geol.*) to exfoliate; to scale off.

отслу́жива|ть, ю *impf. of* **отслужи́ть**

отслуж|и́ть, у́, ~́ишь *pf.* (*of* **~́ивать**) **1.** to serve; to serve one's time. **2.** (*coll.*) (*of implements, etc.*) to be worn out. **3.** (*eccl.*) to conduct (*a service*).

отсове́т|овать, ую *pf.* (*+d. and inf.*) to dissuade (from).

отсос|а́ть, у́, ёшь *pf.* (*of* **отса́сывать**) (*+a. or g.*) to suck off; to filter by suction.

отсо́х|нуть, нет, *past* **~, ~ла** *pf.* (*of* **отсыха́ть**) to dry up, to wither.

отсро́чива|ть, ю *impf. of* **отсро́чить**

отсро́ч|ить, у, ишь *pf.* (*of* **~ивать**) **1.** to postpone, delay, defer; (*leg.*) to adjourn. **2.** (*coll.*) to extend (*period of validity of a document*).

отсро́чк|а, и *f.* **1.** postponement, delay, deferment; (*leg.*) adjournment. **2.** (*coll.*) extension (*of period of validity of document*).

отстава́ни|е, я *nt.* lag.

отста|ва́ть, ю́, ёшь *impf. of* **~́ть**

отста́в|ить, лю, ишь *pf.* (*of* **~ля́ть**) **1.** to set aside, put aside. **2.: о.!** (*mil. word of command*) as you were!

отста́вк|а, и *f.* resignation; retirement; **вы́йти в ~у** to resign; to retire; **пода́ть в ~у** to tender one's resignation; **в ~е** retired, in retirement.

отставля́|ть, ю *impf. of* **отста́вить**

отставно́й *adj.* retired.

отста́ива|ть, ю *impf. of* **отстоя́ть**[1]

отста́ива|ться, юсь *impf. of* **отстоя́ться**

отста́лост|ь, и *f.* (*fig.*) backwardness.

отста́лый *adj.* (*fig.*) backward; **у́мственно о.** mentally retarded; **физи́чески о.** physically handicapped.

отста́|ть, ну, нешь *pf.* (*of* **~ва́ть**) **1. (от)** to fall behind; to lag behind; (*fig.*) to be backward, be retarded; to be behind(hand); **о. в рабо́те** to be behind in (with) one's work; **о. от ве́ка, о. от совреме́нности** to be behind the times. **2. (от)** to become detached (from); **о. от гру́ппы** to become detached from a group; **о. от по́езда** to be left behind by the train (*sc., at a station en route*). **3. (от)** to lose touch (with). **4.** (*coll.*; **от**) to give up; **о. от привы́чки** to break o.s. of a habit. **5.** (*of a clock or watch*) to be slow; **о. на полчаса́** to be half an hour slow. **6.** (*of plaster, wall-paper, etc.*) to come off; to peel off. **7.** (*coll.*; **от**) to leave alone; **~нь от меня́!** leave me alone!

отста|ю́щий *pres. part. of* **~ва́ть**; *as n.* **о., ~ю́щего** *m.* backward pupil; **рабо́та с ~ю́щими** remedial work.

отстега́|ть, ю *pf.* (*of* **стега́ть**[1]) to beat, lash.

отстёгива|ть(ся), ю(сь) *impf. of* **отстегну́ть(ся)**

отстег|ну́ть, ну́, нёшь *pf.* (*of* **~̈ивать**) to unfasten, undo; to unbutton.

отстег|ну́ться, нётся *pf.* (*of* **~̈иваться**) to come unfastened, come undone.

отстир|а́ть, а́ю *pf.* (*of* **~́ывать**) to wash off.

отстир|а́ться, а́юсь *pf.* (*of* **~́ываться**) to wash off, come out in the wash.

отсти́рыва|ть(ся), ю(сь) *impf. of* **отстира́ть(ся)**

отсто|я́ть[1]**, ю́, и́шь** *pf.* (*of* **отста́ивать**) to defend, save; to stand up for; **о. свои́ права́** to assert one's rights.

отсто|я́ть[2]**, ю́, и́шь** *pf.* to stand through; **мы ~я́ли весь спекта́кль** we stood through the entire show.

отсто|я́ть[3]**, ю́, и́шь** *impf.* **(от)** to be ... distant (from); **ста́нция ~и́т от це́нтра го́рода на два киломе́тра** the station is two kilometres from the centre of the town.

отсто|я́ться, и́тся *pf.* (*of* **отста́иваться**) **1.** (*chem.*) to settle. **2.** (*fig.*) to settle, become stabilized.

отстра́ива|ть, ю *impf. of* **отстро́ить**

отстране́ни|е, я *nt.* **1.** pushing aside. **2.** dismissal, discharge.

отстран|и́ть, ю́, и́шь *pf.* (*of* **~я́ть**) **1.** to push aside; **о. от себя́ все забо́ты** to lay aside all one's cares. **2.** to dismiss, discharge.

отстран|и́ться, ю́сь, и́шься *pf.* (*of* **~я́ться**) **1. (от)** to move away (from); (*fig.*) to keep out of the way (of), keep aloof (from); **о. от уда́ра** to dodge a blow; **о. от до́лжности** to relinquish a post. **2.** *pass. of* **~и́ть**

отстран|я́ть(ся), я́ю(сь) *impf. of* **~и́ть(ся)**

отстре́лива|ть[1]**, ю** *impf. of* **отстрели́ть**

отстре́лива|ть[2]**, ю** *impf. of* **отстреля́ть**

отсре́лива|ться, юсь *impf. of* **отстреля́ться**

отстрел|и́ть, ю́, ~́ишь *pf.* (*of* **~́ивать**[1]) to shoot off.

отстрел|я́ть, я́ю *pf.* (*of* **~́ивать**[2]) to shoot (*for commercial purposes, etc.*).

отстрел|я́ться, я́юсь *pf.* (*of* **~́иваться**) **1.** to defend o.s. (by shooting). **2.** to return fire, fire back.

отстрига́|ть, ю *impf. of* **отстри́чь**

отстри́|чь, гу́, жёшь, гу́т, *past* **~г, ~гла** *pf.* (*of* **~га́ть**) to cut off, clip.

отстр|о́ить, о́ю, о́ишь *pf.* (*of* **~а́ивать**) to complete construction (of), finish building.

о́тступ, а *m.* (*typ.*) indention; indentation.

отступ|а́ть(ся), а́ю(сь) *impf. of* **~и́ть(ся)**

отступ|и́ть, лю́, ~́ишь *pf.* (*of* **~а́ть**) **1.** to step back; to recede. **2.** (*mil.*) to retreat, fall back. **3.** (*fig.*) to back down; **(от)** to go back (on); to give up; **о. от реше́ния** to go back on a decision. **4.** (*fig.*; **от**) to deviate (from); **о. от обы́чая** to depart from custom; **о. от те́мы** to digress. **5.** (*typ.*) to indent.

отступ|и́ться, лю́сь, ~́ишся *pf.* (*of* **~а́ться**) (*coll.*; **от**) to give up, renounce; **о. от своего́ сло́ва** to go back on one's word; **они́ все ~и́лись от него́** they have all given him up.

отступле́ни|е, я *nt.* **1.** (*mil. and fig.*) retreat. **2.** deviation; digression.

отсту́пник, а *m.* apostate.

отсту́пничеств|о, а *nt.* apostasy.

отступн|о́й *adj.*: **~ы́е де́ньги** (*or as n.* **~о́е, ~о́го** *nt.*) indemnity, compensation.

отступ|я́ *ger. of* **~и́ть,** *as adv.* **(от)** off, away (from); **о. два-три ме́тра** two or three metres off; **немно́го о. от до́ма** a short distance away from the house.

отсу́тстви|е, я *nt.* absence; (*+g.*) lack (of); **в его́ о.** in his absence; **находи́ться в ~и** to be absent.

отсу́тств|овать, ую *impf.* to be absent; to be lacking

отсу́тств|ующий *pres. part. of* **~овать** *and adj.* absent (*also fig.*); **о. вид** blank expression; *as n.* **о., ~ующего** *m.* absentee.

отсчёт, а *m.* reading (*on an instrument*).
отсчит|ать, аю *pf.* (*of* **∼ывать**) **1.** to count out, count off; **о. десять рублей** to count out ten roubles. **2.** to read off, take a reading.
отсчитыва|ть, ю *impf. of* **отсчитать**
отсыла|ть, ю *impf. of* **отослать**
отсылк|а, и *f.* **1.** dispatch; **о. денег** remittance. **2.** reference.
отсып|ать, лю, лешь *pf.* (*of* **∼ать**) (*+a. or g.*) to pour off; to measure off.
отсып|ать, аю *impf. of* **∼ать**
отсып|аться, аюсь *impf. of* **отоспаться**
отсырелый *adj.* damp.
отсыре|ть, ю *pf. of* **сыреть**
отсыха|ть, ю *impf. of* **отсохнуть**
отсюда *adv.* from here; hence (*also fig.*); (*fig.*) from this; **о. следует, что...** from this it follows that ....
оттаива|ть, ю *impf. of* **оттаять**
отталкива|ть, ю *impf. of* **оттолкнуть**
отталкива|ющий *pres. part. act. of* **∼ть** *and adj.* repulsive, repellent.
оттаска|ть, ю *pf.* (*of* **таскать 2.**) to pull; **о. кого-н. за волосы** to pull s.o.'s hair.
оттаскива|ть, ю *impf. of* **оттащить**
оттачива|ть, ю *impf. of* **отточить**
оттащ|ить, у, ∼ишь *pf.* (*of* **оттаскивать**) to drag aside (away), pull aside (away).
отта|ять, ю, ешь *pf.* (*of* **∼ивать**) (*trans. and intrans.*) to thaw out.
оттен|ить, ю, ишь *pf.* (*of* **∼ять**) **1.** to shade (in). **2.** (*fig.*) to set off, make more prominent.
оттен|ок, ка *m.* shade, nuance (*also fig.*); tint, hue; **о. значения** shade of meaning; **он говорил с ∼ком иронии** there was a note of irony in his voice.
оттен|ять, яю *impf. of* **∼ить**
оттепел|ь, и *f.* thaw.
оттер|еть, ототру, ототрёшь, *past* **∼, ∼ла** *pf.* (*of* **оттирать**) **1.** to rub off, rub out. **2.** to restore sensation (*to parts of the body*) by rubbing. **3.** (*coll.*) to press back, push aside.
оттесн|ить, ю, ишь *pf.* (*of* **∼ять**) to drive back; press back; to push aside, shove aside (*also fig.*); **о. противника** (*mil.*) to force the enemy back; **о. конкурента** (*fig.*) to edge a competitor out.
оттесн|ять, яю *impf. of* **∼ить**
оттиск, а *m.* **1.** impression. **2.** off-print.
оттискива|ть, ю *impf. of* **оттиснуть**
оттис|нуть, ну, нешь *pf.* (*of* **∼кивать**) **1.** (*coll.*) to push aside. **2.** to print.
оттого *adv.* that is why; **о. мы и не могли приехать** that's why we couldn't come; **о... что** because; **я о. опоздал, что мотор не заводился** I was late because the engine would not start.
оттолкн|уть, у, ёшь *pf.* (*of* **отталкивать**) **1.** to push away, push aside. **2.** (*fig.*) to antagonize, alienate.
оттолкн|уться, усь, ёшься *pf.* (*of* **отталкиваться**) **1. (от)** to push off (from). **2.** (*fig.*; **от**) to take as a starting-point.
оттоманк|а, и *f.* ottoman.
оттопыр|енный *p.p.p. of* **∼ить** *and adj.* protruding, sticking out.
оттопырива|ть(ся), ю(сь) *impf. of* **оттопырить(ся)**
оттопыр|ить, ю, ишь *pf.* (*of* **∼ивать**) (*coll.*) to stick out; **о. локти** to stick out one's elbows.
оттопыр|иться, ится *pf.* (*of* **∼иваться**) to protrude, stick out; to bulge.
отторг|ать, аю *impf. of* **∼нуть**
отторг|нуть, ну, нешь, *past* **∼, ∼ла** *pf.* (*of* **∼ать**) to tear away, seize.
отторжени|е, я *nt.* tearing away; (*med.*) rejection (*of a transplanted organ*).
отточ|ить, у, ∼ишь *pf.* (*of* **оттачивать**) to sharpen, whet.
оттуда *adv.* from there.
оттягива|ть, ю *impf. of* **оттянуть**
оттяжк|а, и *f.* delay, procrastination.
оття|нуть, ну, ∼нешь *pf.* (*of* **∼гивать**) **1.** to draw out, pull away. **2.** (*mil.*) to draw off. **3.** (*coll.*) to delay; **чтобы о. время** to gain time.
отуманива|ть, ю *impf. of* **отуманить**
отуман|ить, ю, ишь *pf.* (*of* **∼ивать**) **1.** to blur; to dim; **её глаза ∼ило слезами** her eyes were dimmed with tears. **2.** (*fig.*) to cloud, dull; **моё сознание ∼ило вином** wine had clouded my reason.
отупелый *adj.* (*coll.*) stupefied, dulled.
отупени|е, я *nt.* stupefaction, dullness, torpor.
отупе|ть, ю *pf.* (*coll.*) to grow dull, sink into torpor.
отутюжива|ть, ю *impf. of* **отутюжить**
отутюж|ить, у, ишь *pf.* (*of* **∼ивать**) to iron (out).
отуч|ать(ся), аю(сь) *impf. of* **∼ить(ся)**
отуч|ить, у, ∼ишь *pf.* (*of* **∼ать**) (**от** *or +inf.*) to break (of); **о. от груди** to wean.
отуч|иться, усь, ∼ишься *pf.* (*of* **∼аться**) (**от** *or +inf.*) to break o.s. (of).
отхажива|ть, ю *impf. of* **отходить**[2]
отхарк|ать, аю *pf.* (*of* **∼ивать**) to expectorate.
отхаркива|ть, ю *impf. of* **отхаркать**
отхаркива|ться, юсь *impf. of* **отхаркнуться**
отхаркива|ющий *pres. part. act. of* **∼ть; ∼ющее (средство)** (*med.*) expectorant.
отхаркн|уть, у, ешь *pf.* to hawk up.
отхарк|нуться, нусь, нешься *pf.* (*of* **∼иваться**) (*coll.*) to clear one's throat.
отхва|тить, чу, ∼тишь *pf.* (*of* **∼тывать**) (*coll.*) to snip off; to chop off; **он ∼тил себе палец топором** he chopped his finger off with an axe.
отхватыва|ть, ю *impf. of* **отхватить**
отхлеб|нуть, ну, нёшь *pf.* (*of* **∼ывать**) (*coll.*; *+a. or g.*) to take a sip (of); to take a mouthful (of).
отхлёбыва|ть, ю *impf. of* **отхлебнуть**
отхле|стать, щу, ∼щешь *pf.* (*coll.*) to give a lashing.
отхлын|уть, у, ешь *pf.* to rush back, flood back (*also fig.*).
отход, а *m.* **1.** departure; sailing. **2.** (*mil.*) withdrawal. **3. (от)** deviation (from), break (with). **4.** *see* **∼ы**
отхо|дить[1]**, жу, ∼дишь** *impf. of* **отойти**
отхо|дить[2]**, жу, ∼дишь** *pf.* (*of* **отхаживать**) (*coll.*) to nurse back to health.
отходн|ая, ой *f.* prayer for the dying.
отходчив|ый (∼, ∼а) *adj.* not bearing grudges.
отход|ы, ов (*tech.*) waste (products).
отхож|ий *adj.*: **∼ее место** (*coll.*) latrine, earth closet.
отцве|сти, ту, тёшь, *past* **∼л, ∼ла** *pf.* (*of* **∼тать**) to finish blossoming, fade (*also fig.*); **она ∼ла** she has lost her bloom.
отцве|тать, таю *impf. of* **∼сти**
отцеп|ить, лю, ∼ишь *pf.* (*of* **∼лять**) to unhook; to uncouple.
отцеп|иться, люсь, ∼ишься *pf.* (*of* **∼ляться**) **1.** to come unhooked; to come uncoupled. **2.** (*fig., coll.*) to leave alone; **∼ись ты от меня!** leave me alone!
отцепля|ть(ся), ю(сь) *impf. of* **отцепить(ся)**
отцеубийств|о, а *nt.* patricide (*act*).
отцеубийц|а, ы *c.g.* patricide (*agent*).
отцов *adj.* one's father's.
отцовский *adj.* one's father's; paternal.
отцовств|о, а *nt.* paternity.
отчаива|ться, юсь *impf. of* **отчаяться**
отчалива|ть, ю *impf. of* **отчалить; ∼й!** (*coll.*) clear off!; beat it!
отчал|ить, ю, ишь *pf.* (*of* **∼ивать**) (*naut.*) to cast off.
отчасти *adv.* partly.
отчаяни|е, я *nt.* despair.
отчаян|ный (∼, ∼а) *adj.* despairing; (*fig.*) desperate; **о. взор** despairing look; **о. дурак** (*coll.*) awful fool; **∼ное положение** desperate plight.

отчá|яться, юсь, ешься *pf.* (*of* **~иваться**) (*+inf. or* **в**+*p.*) to despair (of).
óтче (*obs.*) *voc. of* **отéц; О. наш** Our Father (*prayer*).
отчегó *adv.* why; **вот о.** that's why.
отчегó-либо *adv.* for some reason or other.
отчегó-то *adv.* for some reason.
отчекáнива|ть, ю *impf. of* **отчекáнить**
отчекáн|ить, ю, ишь *pf.* (*of* **чекáнить** *and* **~ивать**) **1.** to coin, mint. **2.** (*fig.*) to articulate.
отчёркива|ть, ю *impf. of* **отчеркнýть**
отчерк|нýть, нý, нёшь *pf.* (*of* **∸ывать**) to mark off.
óтчеств|о, а *nt.* patronymic; **как егó по ~у** what is his patronymic?
отчёт, а *m.* account; report; **отдавáть себé о.** (**в**+*p.*) to be aware (of), realize.
отчётливост|ь, и *f.* **1.** distinctness; precision. **2.** intelligibility, clarity.
отчётлив|ый (~, ~а) *adj.* **1.** distinct; precise. **2.** intelligible, clear.
отчётност|ь, и *f.* **1.** book-keeping. **2.** accounts.
отчёт|ный *adj. of* **~**; **о. год** financial year, current year; **о. доклáд** report.
отчи́зн|а, ы *f.* (*poet.*) native land; fatherland.
óтчий *adj.* (*obs., poet.*) paternal.
óтчим, а *m.* step-father.
óтчина, ы *f.* = **вóтчина**
отчислéни|е, я *nt.* **1.** deduction. **2.** dismissal.
отчи́сл|ить, ю, ишь *pf.* (*of* **~я́ть**) **1.** to deduct. **2.** to dismiss.
отчисл|я́ть, я́ю *impf. of* **∸ить**
отчи́|стить, щу, стишь *pf.* (*of* **~щáть**) **1.** to clean off; to brush off. **2.** to clean up.
отчит|áть, áю *pf.* (*of* **∸ывать**) (*coll.*) to read a lecture (to), tell off.
отчит|áться, áюсь *pf.* (*of* **∸ываться**) (**в**+*p.*) to give an account (of), report (on); **о. пéред избирáтелями** to report back to the electors.
отчи́тыва|ть(ся), ю(сь) *impf. of* **отчитáть(ся)**
отчищá|ть, ю *impf. of* **отчи́стить**
отчу|ди́ть, жý, ди́шь *pf.* (*of* **~ждáть**) (*leg.*) to alienate; to estrange.
отчуждá|ть, ю *impf. of* **отчуди́ть**
отчуждéни|е, я *nt.* **1.** (*leg.*) alienation. **2.** estrangement.
отчуждённост|ь, и *f.* estrangement.
отшагá|ть, ю *pf.* (*coll.*) to walk.
отшагн|ýть, ý, ёшь *pf.* (*coll.*) to step aside, step back.
отшвы́рива|ть, ю *impf. of* **отшвырнýть**
отшвыр|нýть, нý, нёшь *pf.* (*of* **∸ивать**) to fling away; to throw off.
отшéльник, а *m.* hermit, anchorite; (*fig.*) recluse.
отшéльни|ческий *adj. of* **~к**
отшéльничеств|о, а *nt.* a hermit's life, a recluse's life (*also fig., iron.*).
отши́б, а *m. only in phr.* **на ~е** at a distance (*from a settlement*); **жить на ~е** (*fig.*) to live in seclusion, live a recluse's life.
отшиб|áть, áю *impf. of* **~и́ть**
отшиб|и́ть, ý, ёшь, *past* **∸, ∸ла** *pf.* (*of* **~áть**) (*coll.*) **1.** to hurt; **о. себé рýку** to hurt one's arm. **2.: у меня́ ∸ло пáмять** my memory has failed me.
отшлёп|ать, аю *pf.* (*of* **~ывать**) (*coll.*) to spank.
отшлёпыва|ть, ю *impf. of* **отшлёпать**
отшлиф|овáть, ýю *pf.* (*of* **~óвывать**) to grind; to polish (*also fig.*).
отштукатýр|ить, ю, ишь *pf. of* **штукатýрить**
отшу|ти́ться, чýсь, ∸тишься *pf.* (*of* **∸чиваться**) to laugh off; to make a joke in reply.
отшýчива|ться, юсь *impf. of* **отшути́ться**
отщепéн|ец, ца *m.* renegade.
отщеп|и́ть, лю́, и́шь *pf.* (*of* **~ля́ть**) to chip off.
отщепля́|ть, ю *impf. of* **отщепи́ть**
отщип|áть, лю́, ∸лешь *pf.* (*of* **∸ывать**) to pinch off, nip off.
отщи́пыва|ть, ю *impf. of* **отщипáть**
отъ... *vbl. pref.* = **от...**
отъедá|ть(ся), ю(сь) *impf. of* **отъéсть(ся)**
отъéзд, а *m.* departure.
отъéз|дить, жу, дишь *pf.* (*coll.*) to have driven; to have covered (*driving, riding.*)
отъезжá|ть, ю *impf. of* **отъéхать**
отъé|сть, м, шь, ст, ди́м, ди́те, дя́т, *past* **~л, ~ла** *pf.* (*of* **~дáть**) to eat off.
отъé|сться, мся, шься, стся, ди́мся, ди́тесь, дя́тся, *past* **~лся, ~лась** *pf.* (*of* **~дáться**) to put on weight; to feed well.
отъé|хать, ду, дешь *pf.* (*of* **~зжáть**) to depart.
отъя́вленный *adj.* (*coll., pej.*) thorough, inveterate, out-and-out.
отыгр|áть, áю *pf.* (*of* **∸ывать**) to win back.
отыгр|áться, áюсь *pf.* (*of* **∸ываться**) **1.** to win back, get back what one has lost. **2.** (*fig., coll.*) to get out (*of an awkward situation*).
оты́грыва|ть(ся), ю(сь) *impf. of* **отыгрáть(ся)**
оты|скáть, щý, ∸щешь *pf.* (*of* **∸скивать**) to find; to track down, run to earth.
оты|скáться, щýсь, ∸щешься *pf.* (*of* **∸скиваться**) to turn up, appear.
оты́скива|ть, ю *impf.* **1.** *impf. of* **отыскáть. 2.** (*impf. only*) to look for, try to find.
оты́скива|ться, юсь *impf. of* **отыскáться**
отяго|ти́ть, щý, ти́шь *pf.* (*of* **~щáть**) to burden.
отягощá|ть, ю *impf. of* **отяготи́ть**
отягч|áть, áю *impf. of* **~и́ть; ~áющие (винý) обстоя́тельства** aggravating circumstances.
отягч|и́ть, ý, и́шь *pf.* (*of* **~áть**) to aggravate.
отяжелé|ть, ю *pf.* to become heavy.
офицéр, а *m.* officer.
офицéр|ский *adj. of* **~**
офицéрств|о, а *nt.* **1.** (*collect.*) the officers. **2.** commissioned rank.
официáльн|ый *adj.* official; **~ое лицó** an official.
официáнт, а *m.* waiter.
официáнтк|а, и *f.* waitress.
официóз, а *m.* semi-official organ (*of press*).
официóз|ный (~ен, ~на) *adj.* semi-official.
оформи́тел|ь, я *m.* decorator, stage-painter.
офóрм|ить, лю, ишь *pf.* (*of* **~ля́ть**) **1.** to design; **о. пьéсу** to design the sets for a play. **2.** to make official; to legalize; **о. вступлéние в брак** to register a marriage; **о. доку́мéнт** to draw up a paper. **3.** to enrol, take on the staff.
офóрм|иться, люсь, ишься *pf.* (*of* **~ля́ться**) **1.** to take shape. **2.** to be registered; to legalize one's position. **3.** to be taken on (the staff).
оформлéни|е, я *nt.* **1.** design; **сцени́ческое о.** staging. **2.** registration, legalization.
оформля́|ть(ся), ю(сь) *impf. of* **офóрмить(ся)**
офóрт, а *m.* etching.
офсáйд, а *m.* (*sport*) offside.
офсéт, а *m.* (*typ.*) offset (process).
офтальмóлог, а *m.* ophthalmologist.
офтальмолóги|я, и *f.* ophthalmology.
ох *int.* oh!; ah!
охáива|ть, ю *impf. of* **охáять**
óхань|е, я *nt.* (*coll.*) moaning, groaning.
охáпк|а, и *f.* armful; **взять в ~у** (*coll.*) to take in one's arms.
охарактериз|овáть, ýю *pf.* to characterize, describe.
óх|ать, аю *impf.* (*of* **~нуть**) to moan, groan; to sigh.
охá|ять, ю *pf.* (*of* **хáять** *and* **~ивать**) (*coll.*) to slate, censure.
охвáт, а *m.* **1.** scope, range. **2.** inclusion. **3.** (*mil.*) outflanking, envelopment.
охва|ти́ть, чý, ∸тишь *pf.* (*of* **∸тывать**) **1.** to envelop; to enclose; **дом ~ти́ло плáменем** the house

was enveloped in flames. **2.** to grip, seize; **их ~тúл ýжас** they were seized with panic. **3.** (+*i.*) (*coll.*) to draw (in), involve (in); **о. молодёжь общéственной рабóтой** to draw young people into social work. **4.** (*fig.*) to comprehend, take in. **5.** (*mil.*) to outflank.

охвáтн|ый *adj.*: **~ое движéние** (*mil.*) flanking movement.

охвáтыва|ть, ю *impf. of* **охватúть**

охвá|ченный *p.p.p. of* **~тúть; о. ýжасом** terror-stricken.

охладевá|ть, ю *impf. of* **охладéть**

охладé|ть, ю *pf.* (*of* **~вáть**) to grow cold; (*fig.*; **к**) to grow cold (towards).

охла|дúть, жý, дúшь *pf.* (*of* **~ждáть**) to cool, cool off (*also fig.*); **о. чей-н. пыл** to damp s.o.'s ardour.

охла|дúться, жýсь, дúшься *pf.* (*of* **~ждáться**) to become cool, cool down (*also fig.*).

охлаждá|ть(ся), ю(сь) *impf. of* **охладúть(ся)**

охлаждá|ющий *pres. part. act. of* **~ть** *and adj.* cooling; **~ющая жúдкость** coolant.

охлаждéни|е, я *nt.* **1.** cooling (off); **с воздýшным ~ем** air-cooled. **2.** (*fig.*) coolness.

охмелé|ть, ю *pf.* (*of* **хмелéть**) (*coll.*) to become tight.

óх|нуть, ну, нешь *pf. of* **~ать**

охóт|а[1], ы *f.* hunt, hunting; **о. с ружьём** shooting; **псóвая о.** riding to hounds.

охóт|а[2], ы *f.* **1.** (**к** *or* +*inf.*) desire, wish; **по своéй ~е** of one's own accord; **о. тебé спóрить с ним!** (*coll.*) what's the use of arguing with him? **2.** heat (*in female animals*).

охó|титься, чусь, тишься *impf.* (**на**+*a.* *or* **за**+*i.*) to hunt; (*fig.*; **за**+*i.*) to hunt for.

охóтник[1], а *m.* hunter.

охóтник[2], а *m.* **1.** (**до** *or* +*inf.*) lover (of); enthusiast (for); **он большóй о. до грибóв** he is a great mushroom lover. **2.** volunteer; **есть ли ~и пойтú?** are there any volunteers to go?

охóтнич|ий *adj.* hunting; shooting; **о. билéт** hunting permit; **~ья собáка** hound, gun-dog; **о. расскáз** (*joc.*) tall story.

охóтно *adv.* willingly, gladly, readily.

охóч|ий (~, ~а) *adj.* (+*inf.*; *coll.*) inclined (to), keen (to), having an urge (to).

óхр|а, ы *f.* ochre.

охрáн|а, ы *f.* **1.** guarding; protection. **2.** guard; **лúчная о.** body-guard; **пограничная о.** frontier guard.

охранéни|е, я *nt.* safeguarding; (*mil.*) protection.

охран|úть, ю́, úшь *pf.* (*of* **~я́ть**) to guard, protect.

охрáнк|а, и *f.* (*coll.*) Okhranka (*Secret Police Department in tsarist Russia*).

охрáнник, а *m.* (*coll.*) **1.** guard. **2.** secret police agent; member of Okhranka.

охрáн|ный *adj. of* **~а; ~ная грáмота, о. лист** safe-conduct, pass; **~ная зóна** (*mil.*) restricted area.

охран|я́ть, я́ю *impf. of* **~úть**

охрúплый *adj.* (*coll.*) hoarse.

охрúп|нуть, ну, нешь, *past* **~, ~ла** *pf.* (*of* **хрúпнуть**) to become hoarse.

охромé|ть, ю *pf.* (*of* **хромéть**) (*coll.*) to go lame.

оцарáпа|ть, ю *pf.* (*of* **царáпать**) to scratch.

оцелóт, а *m.* (*zool.*) ocelot.

оцéнива|ть, ю *impf. of* **оценúть**

оцен|úть, ю́, ∠ишь *pf.* (*of* **∠ивать**) **1.** to estimate, evaluate; to appraise; **о. в дéсять рублéй** to estimate at ten roubles. **2.** to appreciate; **о. что-н. по достóинству** to appreciate sth. at its true value.

оцéнк|а, и *f.* **1.** estimation, evaluation; appraisal; estimate; **о. имýщества** valuation of property; **о. обстанóвки** (*mil.*) estimate of the situation. **2.** appreciation; **дать настоя́щую ~у чемý-н.** to give sth. a proper appreciation.

оцéн|очный *adj. of* **~ка**

оцéнщик, а *m.* valuer.

оцепенéлый *adj.* torpid; benumbed.

оцепенé|ть, ю *pf. of* **цепенéть**

оцеп|úть, лю́, ∠ишь *pf.* (*of* **~ля́ть**) to surround; to cordon off.

оцеплéни|е, я *nt.* **1.** surrounding; cordoning off. **2.** cordon.

оцепля́|ть, ю *impf. of* **оцепúть**

очáг, á *m.* **1.** hearth (*also fig.*); **кýхонный о.** kitchen range; **домáшний о.** (*fig.*) hearth, home. **2.** (*fig.*) centre, seat; **о. войны́** seat of war; **о. землетрясéния** earthquake centre.

очаровáни|е, я *nt.* charm, fascination.

очаровáтел|ьный (~ен, ~ьна) *adj.* charming, fascinating.

очар|овáть, ýю *pf.* (*of* **~óвывать**) to charm, fascinate.

очарóвыва|ть, ю *impf. of* **очаровáть**

очевúд|ец, ца *m.* eye-witness.

очевúдно *adv.* obviously, evidently; **вы, о., не соглáсны** you obviously do not agree.

очевúд|ный (~ен, ~на) *adj.* obvious, evident.

очеловéчива|ть, ю *impf. of* **очеловéчить**

очеловéч|ить, у, ишь *pf.* (*of* **~ивать**) to humanize.

óчень *adv.* very; very much.

очервúве|ть, ю *pf. of* **червúветь**

очередн|óй *adj.* **1.** next; next in turn; **о. вопрóс** the next question; **о. вы́пуск** latest issue (*of a journal, etc.*); **~áя задáча** the immediate task. **2.** usual; ordinary; (just) another; **~ы́е неприя́тности** the usual trouble; **о. óтпуск** regular holidays.

очерёдност|ь, и *f.* regular succession; order of priority.

óчеред|ь, и, *pl.* **~и, ~éй** *f.* **1.** turn; **пропустúть свою́ о.** to miss one's turn; **о. за вáми** it is your turn; **в свою́ о.** in one's turn; **на ~и** next (in turn); **по ~и** in turn, in order, in rotation; **в пéрвую о.** in the first place, in the first instance. **2.** queue, line; **стоя́ть в ~и** (**за**+*i.*) to queue (for), stand in line (for). **3.** (*mil.*): **(пулемётная) о.** burst; **батарéйная о.** (battery) salvo.

óчерк, а *m.* essay, sketch, study; outline; **~и рýсской истóрии** studies in Russian history.

очеркúст, а *m.* essayist.

очерн|úть, ю́, úшь *pf. of* **чернúть 2.**

очерствéлый *adj.* hardened, callous.

очерствé|ть, ю *pf. of* **черствéть 2.**

очертáни|е, я *nt.* outline.

очер|тúть, чý, ~тишь *pf.* (*of* **∠чивать**) to outline; **~тя́ гóлову** (*coll.*) without thinking, headlong.

очéрчива|ть, ю *impf. of* **очертúть**

очёс|ки, ков *pl.* (*sg.* **~ок, ~ка** *m.*) combings; flocks; **льняны́е о.** flax tow.

óчи *pl. of* **óко**

очúнива|ть, ю *impf. of* **очинúть**

очин|úть, ю́, ∠ишь *pf.* (*of* **∠ивать** *and* **чинúть[2]**) to sharpen.

очúнк|а, и *f.* sharpening; **машúнка для ~и карандашéй** pencil-sharpener.

очистúтельн|ый *adj.* purifying, cleansing; **о. завóд** refinery; **~ое срéдство** cleanser.

очú|стить, щу, стишь *pf.* (*of* **~щáть**) **1.** to clean; to cleanse, purify; (*tech.*) to refine; to rectify. **2.** **(от)** to clear (of); to free; **о. почтóвый я́щик** to clear a letter-box.

очú|ститься, щусь, стишься *pf.* (*of* **~щáться**) **1.** to clear o.s. **2.** **(от)** to become clear (of). **3.** *pass. of* **~стить**

очúстк|а, и *f.* **1.** cleaning; cleansing, purification; (*tech.*) refinement; rectification; **для ~и сóвести** (*coll.*) to clear one's conscience. **2.** clearance; freeing; (*mil.*) mopping-up.

очúстк|и, ов *no sg.* peelings.

очищá|ть(ся), ю(сь) *impf. of* **очи́стить(ся)**
очищéни|е, я *nt.* cleansing; purification.
очк|и́, óв *no sg.* spectacles; goggles; **защи́тные о.** protective goggles.
очк|ó[1], **á**, *pl.* **~и́, ~óв** *nt.* **1.** (*on cards or dice*) pip. **2.** (*in scoring*) point. **3.** hole; **смотровóе о.** peephole.
очк|ó[2], **á** *nt.*: **втерéть кому́-н. ~и́** (*coll.*) to pull the wool over s.o.'s eyes.
очковтирáтельств|о, а *nt.* (*coll.*) deception.
очкó|вый[1] *adj. of* **~**[1]; **~вая систéма** points system (of scoring).
очкóв|ый[2] *adj.*: **~ая змея́** cobra.
очн|у́ться, у́сь, ёшься *pf.* **1.** to wake. **2.** to come to, regain consciousness.
óчн|ый *adj.* **1.** (*opp.* **заóчный**) internal (*instruction, student, etc., as opposed to* external, extra-mural). **2.: ~ая стáвка** (*leg.*) confrontation.
очумéлый *adj.* (*coll.*) mad, off one's head; **бежáть, как о.** to run like mad.
очумé|ть, ю *pf.* (*coll.*) to go mad, go off one's head.
очут|и́ться, ⁓ишься *pf.* to find o.s.; to come to be; **о. в нелóвком положéнии** to find o.s. in an awkward position.
очу́ха|ться, юсь *pf.* (*coll.*) to come to, regain consciousness.
ошалéлый *adj.* (*coll.*) crazy, crazed.
ошалé|ть, ю *pf. of* **шалéть**
ошарáшива|ть, ю *impf. of* **ошарáшить**
ошарáш|ить, у, ишь *pf.* (*of* **~ивать**) (*coll.*) to strike dumb, flabbergast.
ошéйник, а *m.* (*animal's*) collar; **собáчий о.** dog-collar.
ошеломи́тельный *adj.* stunning.
ошелом|и́ть, лю́, и́шь *pf.* (*of* **~ля́ть**) to stun.
ошеломлéни|е, я *nt.* stupefaction.
ошеломля́|ть, ю *impf. of* **ошеломи́ть**
ошельм|овáть, у́ю *pf. of* **шельмовáть**
ошиб|áться, áюсь *impf. of* **~и́ться**
ошиб|и́ться, у́сь, ёшься, *past* **~ся, ⁓лась** *pf.* (*of* **~áться**) to make a mistake; to be mistaken.
оши́бк|а, и *f.* mistake; error; **по ~е** by mistake.
оши́боч|ный (~ен, ~на) *adj.* erroneous, mistaken.
оши́ка|ть, ю *pf.* (*of* **ши́кать 2.**) (*coll.*) to boo (off the stage).
ошпáрива|ть, ю *impf. of* **ошпáрить**
ошпáр|ить, ю, ишь *pf.* (*of* **~ивать**) to scald.
оштраф|овáть, у́ю *pf. of* **штрафовáть**
оштукату́р|ить, ю, ишь *pf. of* **штукату́рить**
ощен|и́ться, и́тся *pf. of* **щени́ться**
ощети́нива|ться, юсь *impf. of* **ощети́ниться**
ощети́н|иться, юсь, ишься *pf.* (*of* **~иваться** *and* **щети́ниться**) to bristle up (*also fig.*).
ощип|áть, лю́, ⁓лешь *pf.* (*of* **щипáть 4.** *and* **⁓ывать**) to pluck.
ощи́пыва|ть, ю *impf. of* **ощипáть**
ощу́п|ать, аю *pf.* (*of* **~ывать**) to feel; to grope about (in).
ощу́пыва|ть, ю *impf. of* **ощу́пать**
óщуп|ь, и *f.*: **на о.** to the touch; by touch; **идти́ на о.** to grope one's way.
óщупью *adv.* **1.** by groping one's way; by touch; **искáть о.** to grope for; **пробрáться о.** to grope one's way. **2.** (*fig.*) blindly.
ощут|и́мый (~и́м, ~и́ма) *adj.* = **~и́тельный**
ощути́тел|ьный (~ен, ~ьна) *adj.* **1.** perceptible, tangible, palpable. **2.** (*fig.*) appreciable.
ощу|ти́ть, щу́, ти́шь *pf.* (*of* **~щáть**) to feel, sense; **о. гóлод** to feel hunger; **он ~ти́л её отсу́тствие** he felt her absence.
ощущá|ть, ю *impf. of* **ощути́ть**
ощущéни|е, я *nt.* **1.** (*physiol.*) sensation. **2.** feeling.
оягн|и́ться, и́тся *pf. of* **ягни́ться**

П

па *nt. indecl.* (*dance*) step.
пабли́сити *nt. indecl.* publicity.
пáв|а, ы *f.* peahen.
павиáн, а *m.* baboon.
павильóн, а *m.* **1.** pavilion. **2.** film studio.
павли́н, а *m.* peacock.
павли́н|ий *adj. of* **~**
пáвод|ок, ка *m.* flood (*esp. resulting from melting of snow*); freshet.
пагинáци|я, и *f.* pagination.
пáгод|а, ы *f.* pagoda.
пáгуб|а, ы *f.* ruin, destruction.
пáгуб|ный (~ен, ~на) *adj.* pernicious, ruinous; fatal.
пáдал|ь, и *f.* (*usu. collect.*) carrion.
пáда|ть, ю *impf.* **1.** (*pf.* **пасть** *and* **упáсть**) to fall; to sink; to drop; to decline; **барóметр ~л** the barometer was falling; **~ет снег** it is snowing; **цéны ~ют** prices are dropping; **п. ду́хом** to lose heart; **п. в óбморок** to faint. **2.** (*pf.* **пасть**) (*fig.*; **на**+*a.*) to fall (on, to); **отвéтственность ~ет на вас** the responsibility falls on you. **3.** (*impf. only*) (*ling.*; *of stress or accent*) to fall, be; **ударéние ~ет на пéрвый слог** the stress is on the first syllable. **4.** (*impf. only*) (*of hair, teeth, etc.*) to fall out, drop out. **5.** (*pf.* **пасть**; *of cattle*) to die.
пáда|ющий *pres. part. of* **~ть** *and adj.*: **~ющие звёзды** shooting stars.
падéж, á *m.* (*gram.*) case.
падёж, á *m.* murrain, cattle plague.
падéж|ный *adj. of* **~**; **~ное окончáние** case ending.
падéни|е, я *nt.* **1.** fall; drop, sinking; **морáльное п.** degradation; **п. цен** slump in prices. **2.** (*phys.*) incidence; **у́гол ~я** angle of incidence. **3.** (*geol.*) dip.
пáд|кий (~ок, ~ка) *adj.* (**на**+*a. or* **до**) having a weakness (for); susceptible (to); **п. на дéньги** mercenary; **он ~ок до слáдкого** he has a sweet tooth.
пáдуб, а *m.* holly.
паду́ч|ий *adj.* (*obs.*) falling; **~ая болéзнь** epilepsy.
пáдчериц|а, ы *f.* step-daughter.
паевóй *adj. of* **пай**[1]; **п. взнос** share.
па|ёк, йкá *m.* ration.
паж, á *m.* (*hist.*) page.
паз, а, о ⁓е, в ~у́, *pl.* **~ы́, ~óв** *m.* (*tech.*) groove, slot, mortise, rabbet.
пáзух|а, и *f.* **1.** bosom; **за ~ой** in one's bosom; **держáть кáмень за ~ой** (*fig.*) to bear a grudge. **2.** (*anat.*) sinus. **3.** (*bot.*) axil.
пáин|ька, ьки, *g. pl.* **~ек** *c.g.* (*coll.*) good child; **будь п.!** be a good boy (girl)!; **п.-мáльчик** good (little) boy.
па|й, я, *pl.* **~и́, ~ёв** *m.* share; **товáрищество на ~я́х** joint-stock company; **на ~я́х** (*fig., coll.*) on an equal footing, going shares.
пáйк|а, и *f.* solder(ing).
пайкóвый *adj. of* **паёк**; rationed.
пáйщик, а *m.* shareholder.
пакгáуз, а *m.* warehouse; **тамóженный п.** bonded warehouse.
пакéт, а *m.* **1.** parcel, package; packet. **2.** (official)

letter. **3.** paper bag.
Пакиста́н, а *m.* Pakistan.
пакиста́н|ец, ца *m.* Pakistani.
пакиста́н|ка, ки *f. of* **~ец**
пакиста́нский *adj.* Pakistani.
па́кл|я, и *f.* tow; oakum.
пак|ова́ть, у́ю *impf.* (*of* **у~**) to pack.
па́ко|стить, щу, стишь *impf.* (*coll.*) **1.** (*pf.* **за~** *and* **на~**) to soil, dirty. **2.** (*pf.* **ис~**) to spoil, mess up. **3.** (*pf.* **на~**) (*+d.*) to play dirty tricks (on).
па́кост|ный (~ен, ~на) *adj.* dirty, mean, foul; nasty.
па́кост|ь, и *f.* **1.** dirty trick; **де́лать ~и** (*+d.*) to play dirty tricks (on). **2.** obscenity, filthy word.
пакт, а *m.* pact; **п. о ненападе́нии** non-aggression pact.
пала́нти́н, а *m.* (fur) stole.
пала́т|а, ы *f.* **1.** (*pl. only*; *obs.*) palace. **2.** (*obs.*) chamber, hall; **Оруже́йная п.** Armoury Museum (*in Moscow*); **у него́ ума́ п.** (*coll.*) he is as wise as Solomon. **3.** (*hospital*) ward. **4.** (*pol.*) chamber, house; **ве́рхняя, ни́жняя п.** Upper, Lower Chamber; **п. ло́рдов** House of Lords; **п. о́бщин** House of Commons. **5.** *as name of State institutions*; **П. мер и весо́в** Weights and Measures Office; **Торго́вая п.** Chamber of Commerce.
палатализа́ци|я, и *f.* (*ling.*) palatalization.
палатализ|ова́ть, у́ю *impf. and pf.* (*ling.*) to palatalize.
палата́льный *adj.* (*ling.*) palatal.
пала́тк|а, и *f.* **1.** tent; marquee; **в ~ах** under canvas. **2.** stall, booth.
пала́ч, а́ *m.* hangman; executioner; (*fig.*) butcher.
пала́ш, а́ *m.* broadsword.
па́левый *adj.* straw-coloured, pale yellow.
палёны|й *adj.* singed, scorched; **па́хнет ~м** there is a smell of burning.
палео́граф, а *m.* palaeographer.
палеографи́ческий *adj.* palaeographic.
палеогра́фи|я, и *f.* palaeography.
палеозо́йский *adj.* (*geol.*) Palaeozoic.
палеоли́т, а *m.* (*archaeol.*) palaeolithic period.
палеолити́ческий *adj.* (*archaeol.*) palaeolithic.
палеонто́лог, а *m.* palaeontologist.
палеонтологи́ческий *adj.* palaeontological.
палеонтоло́ги|я, и *f.* palaeontology.
палести́н|ец, ца *m.* Palestinian.
палести́н|ка, ки *f. of* **~ец**
палести́нский *adj.* Palestinian.
па́л|ец, ьца *m.* **1.** finger; **п. ноги́** toe; **большо́й п.** thumb; (*fig.*): **п. о п. не уда́рить, ~ьцем не шевельну́ть** (*coll.*) not to lift a finger; **ему́ ~ьца в рот не клади́** (*coll.*) be on your guard with him; **~ьцы лома́ть** to tear one's hair; **смотре́ть сквозь ~ьцы на что-н.** (*coll.*) to shut one's eyes to sth.; **знать что-н., как свой пять ~ьцев** (*coll.*) to know sth. like the back of one's hand; **вы́сосать из ~ьца** (*coll.*) to fabricate, concoct; **он ~ьцем никого́ не тро́нет** he wouldn't hurt a fly; **попа́сть ~ьцем в не́бо** (*coll.*) to be wide of the mark. **2.** (*tech.*) pin, peg; cam, cog, tooth.
палиса́д, а *m.* palisade, stockade.
палиса́дник, а *m.* front garden.
палиса́ндр, а *m.* rosewood.
палиса́ндр|овый *adj. of* **~**
пали́тр|а, ы *f.* palette.
пал|и́ть[1]**, ю́, и́шь** *impf.* **1.** (*pf.* **с~**) to burn, scorch. **2.** (*pf.* **о~**) to singe.
пал|и́ть[2]**, ю́, и́шь** *impf.* (*coll.*) to fire (*from gun*); **~и́!** (*word of command*) fire!
па́лк|а, и *f.* stick; cane, staff; **вста́вить кому́-н. ~и в колёса** to put a spoke in s.o.'s wheel; **из-под ~и** under the lash; **п. о двух конца́х** two-edged weapon; **э́то п. о двух конца́х** it cuts both ways.
паллиати́в, а *m.* palliative.
паллиати́вный *adj.* palliative.
пало́мник, а *m.* pilgrim (*also fig.*).
пало́мнича|ть, ю *impf.* to go on a pilgrimage.
пало́мничеств|о, а *nt.* pilgrimage (*also fig.*).
па́лочк|а, и *f.* **1.** *dim. of* **па́лка; бараба́нная п.** drumstick; **волше́бная п.** magic wand; **дирижёрская п.** conductor's baton; **ры́бная п.** fish finger. **2.** (*med.*) bacillus.
па́л|очный *adj. of* **~ка; ~очные уда́ры** strokes of the cane; **~очная дисципли́на** discipline of the rod.
па́лтус, а *m.* halibut, turbot.
па́луб|а, ы *f.* deck; **полётная п.** flight deck.
па́луб|ный *adj. of* **~а; п. груз** deck cargo.
па́лый *adj.* (*dial.*; *of cattle*) dead.
пальб|а́, ы́ *f.* firing; **пу́шечная п.** cannonade.
па́льм|а, ы *f.* palm(-tree).
пал|ьну́ть, ьну́, ьнёшь *inst. pf.* (*of* **~и́ть**[2]) to fire a shot; to discharge a volley.
пальто́ *nt. indecl.* (over)coat.
па́льчик, а *m. dim. of* **па́лец**
пал|я́щий *pres. part. act. of* **~и́ть**[1] *and adj.* burning, scorching.
пампа́с|овый *adj. of* **~ы; ~овая трава́** pampas grass.
пампа́с|ы, ов *no sg.* (*geog.*) pampas.
памфле́т, а *m.* lampoon.
памфлети́ст, а *m.* lampoonist.
па́мятк|а, и *f.* (list of) instructions, guidelines; **п. по ухо́ду** care-label.
па́мятлив|ый (~, ~а) *adj.* (*coll.*) having a retentive memory, retentive.
па́мятник, а *m.* monument; memorial; tombstone; **~и пи́сьменности** literary monuments.
па́мят|ный (~ен, ~на) *adj.* **1.** memorable. **2.** serving to assist the memory; **~ная доска́** memorial plate, plaque; **~ная кни́жка** notebook.
па́мят|ь, и *f.* **1.** memory; **у него́ кури́ная п.** he has a memory like a sieve; **на моей ~и** within my memory; **говори́ть на п.** to speak from memory; **вдруг мне пришло́ на п., что...** suddenly I remembered that ...; **по ~и** from memory; **по ста́рой ~и** from force of habit. **2.** memory, recollection, remembrance; **ве́чная п. ему́!** may his memory live for ever! **оста́вить по себе́ до́брую п.** to leave fond memories of o.s.; **в п.** (*+g.*) in memory (of); **подари́ть на п.** to give as a keepsake. **3.** mind, consciousness; **быть без ~и** to be unconscious; **быть от кого́-н. без ~и** (*coll.*) to be head over heels in love with s.o. **4.** (*eccl.*; *+g.*) commemoration of death (of), feast (of).
Пана́м|а, ы *f.* Panama.
пана́м|а, ы *f.* panama (hat).
пана́мский *adj.* Panamanian.
панаце́|я, и *f.* panacea; **п. от всех зол** (*fig.*) universal panacea.
па́нд|а, ы *f.* panda.
панеги́рик, а *m.* panegyric, eulogy.
панегири́ст, а *m.* panegyrist, eulogist.
панегири́ческий *adj.* panegyrical, eulogistic.
пане́л|ь, и *f.* **1.** pavement, footpath. **2.** panel(ling), wainscot(ting). **3.: п. прибо́ров** instrument panel; dashboard.
панибра́тский *adj.* (*coll.*) (over-)familiar.
панибра́тств|о, а *nt.* (*coll.*) (undue) familiarity.
па́ник|а, и *f.* panic; **впасть в ~у** to panic.
паникёр, а *m.* panic-monger, scaremonger, alarmist.
паникёр|ский *adj. of* **~**
паникёрств|о, а *nt.* alarmism.
паник|ова́ть, у́ю *impf.* (*no pf.*) (*coll.*) to panic.
панихи́д|а, ы *f.* funeral service; requiem; **гражда́нская п.** civil funeral.
панихи́д|ный *adj. of* **~а**; (*fig.*) funereal.
пани́ческий *adj.* **1.** panic. **2.** (*coll.*) panicky.
панк, а *m.* (*also as indecl. adj.*) punk.

па́нков|ский *adj.* = **~ый**
па́нк|овый *adj. of* **~**
панно́ *nt. indecl.* panel.
пано́птикум, а *m.* waxworks.
панора́м|а, ы *f.* panorama.
панора́мный *adj.* panoramic.
пансио́н, а *m.* **1.** boarding school. **2.** boarding-house. **3.** (full) board and lodging; **ко́мната с ~ом** room and board; **жить на ~е** to have full board and lodging, live en pension.
пансиона́т, а *m.* holiday hotel, guest-house.
пансионе́р, а *m.* **1.** boarder (*in school*). **2.** guest (*in boarding-house*).
панслави́зм, а *m.* (*hist.*) Pan-Slavism.
пантало́н|ы, ~ *no sg.* **1.** (*obs.*) trousers. **2.** (*woman's*) drawers, knickers.
панталы́к, а (у) *m.* (*coll.*) *only in phrr.* **сбить с ~у** to drive demented; **сби́ться с ~у** to be at one's wit's end.
пантеи́зм, а *m.* pantheism.
пантеи́ст, а *m.* pantheist.
пантеисти́ческий *adj.* pantheistic.
пантео́н, а *m.* pantheon.
панте́р|а, ы *f.* panther.
пантоми́м|а, ы *f.* pantomime.
пантомими́ческий *adj.* pantomimic.
пантоми́м|ный *adj.* = **~и́ческий**
па́нцирн|ый *adj.* **1.** armour-clad, iron-clad. **2.** (*zool.*) testaceous.
па́нцир|ь, я *m.* **1.** (*hist.*) coat of mail, armour. **2.** (*zool.*) shell; test; armour.
па́п|а[1], ы *m.* (*coll.*) papa, daddy.
па́п|а[2], ы *m.*: **п. ри́мский** (the) Pope.
папа́й|я, и *f.* papaya, paw-paw.
папа́х|а, и *f.* papakha (*Caucasian fur hat*).
папа́ш|а, и *m.* (*coll.*) = **па́па**
па́перт|ь, и *f.* church-porch, parvis.
папи́зм, а *m.* papism.
папилько́тк|а, и *f.* curling-paper.
папиро́с|а, ы *f.* cigarette.
папиро́сниц|а, ы *f.* cigarette-case.
папиро́с|ный *adj. of* **~а; ~ная бума́га** rice-paper.
папи́рус, а *m.* papyrus.
папи́рус|ный *adj*; *of* **~**
папи́ст, а *m.* papist.
па́пк|а, и *f.* folder, file; document case.
па́поротник, а *m.* fern.
па́прик|а, и *f.* paprika.
па́пский *adj.* papal.
па́пств|о, а *nt.* papacy.
папье́-маше́ *nt. indecl.* papier-mâché.
пар[1], а, о ~е, в ~у́, *pl.* **~ы́** *m.* **1.** steam; **быть под ~а́ми** to be under steam, have steam up; **на всех ~а́х** (*fig.*) full steam ahead, at full speed; **очи́стить ~а́ми** to fumigate. **2.** exhalation.
пар[2], а, *pl.* **~ы́** *m.* (*agric.*) fallow; **находи́ться под ~ом** to lie fallow.
па́р|а, ы *f.* **1.** pair; couple; **супру́жеская п.** married couple; **ходи́ть ~ами** to walk in pairs; **е́хать на ~е** to drive a pair (*of horses*); **на ~у мину́т** for a couple of minutes; **п. пустяко́в!** it's child's play!; **на ~у слов** for a few words; **она́ ему́ не п.** she is no match for him; **два сапога́ п.** (*coll., pej.*) they make a pair. **2.** suit (*of clothes*). **3.** (*school sl.*) a 'two' (*out of five*).
пара́бол|а, ы *f.* parabola.
параболи́ческий *adj.* parabolic.
пара́граф, а *m.* paragraph.
пара́д, а *m.* **1.** parade; (*mil.*) review; **возду́шный п.** air display; fly-past. **2.** (*coll., joc.*) ceremonial get-up; **быть в по́лном ~е** to be in one's best bib and tucker.
паради́гм|а, ы *f.* (*gram.*) paradigm.
пара́дност|ь, и *f.* magnificence; ostentation.
пара́д|ный (~ен, ~на) *adj.* **1.** *adj. of* **~ 1.**; **п. костю́м** ceremonial dress; **~ная фо́рма** full dress (uniform). **2.** gala; **п. спекта́кль** gala night. **3.** main, front; **~ная дверь** front door; **п. подъе́зд** main entrance; *as n.* **~ное, ~ного** *nt. and* **~ная, ~ной** *f.* front door.
парадо́кс, а *m.* paradox.
парадокса́л|ьный (~ен, ~ьна) *adj.* paradoxical.
парази́т, а *m.* (*biol. and fig.*) parasite.
паразити́зм, а *m.* (*biol. and fig.*) parasitism.
паразити́р|овать, ую *impf.* to parasitize.
паразити́ческий *adj.* (*biol. and fig.*) parasitic(al).
парази́тный *adj.* (*biol.*) parasitic.
парализо́в|анный *p.p.p. of* **~а́ть** *and adj.* paralysed.
парализ|ова́ть, у́ю *impf. and pf.* to paralyse (*also fig.*).
парали́тик, а *m.* paralytic.
паралити́ческий *adj.* paralytic.
парали́ч, а́ *m.* paralysis; palsy.
парали́чный *adj.* paralytic; **п. больно́й** paralytic.
паралла́кс, а *m.* (*astron.*) parallax.
параллели́зм, а *m.* parallelism.
параллелогра́мм, а *m.* (*math.*) parallelogram.
паралле́л|ь, и *f.* parallel; **провести́ п. (ме́жду)** to draw a parallel (between).
паралле́льно *adv.* (c+*i.*) **1.** parallel (with). **2.** simultaneously (with), at the same time(as).
паралле́л|ьный (~ен, ~ьна) *adj.* parallel; **~ьные бру́сья** (*sport*) parallel bars.
пара́метр, а *m.* (*math.*) parameter.
парандж|а́, и́ *f.* yashmak.
парано́ик, а *m.* (*med.*) paranoiac.
параноических
парано́йческий *adj.* (*med.*) paranoid; paranoiac.
парано́й|я, и *f.* (*med.*) paranoia.
парапе́т, а *m.* parapet.
парати́ф, а *m.* paratyphoid.
парафи́н, а *m.* paraffin (wax).
парафи́н|овый *adj. of* **~**
парафи́р|овать, ую *impf. and pf.* (*dipl.*) to initial.
парашю́т, а *m.* parachute; **на ~е** by parachute; **прыжо́к с ~ом** parachute jump.
парашюти́зм, а *m.* parachute jumping (*as sport*); sky-diving.
парашюти́ст, а *m.* parachutist; sky-diver; **п.-деса́нтник** paratrooper.
парашю́т|ный *adj. of* **~**; **п. спорт** parachute jumping; sky-diving.
пардо́н *int.* (I beg your) pardon.
па́рен|ый *adj.* stewed; **деше́вле ~ой ре́пы** dirt-cheap.
па́р|ень, ня, *pl.* **~ни, ~не́й** *m.* **1.** boy, lad. **2.** (*coll.*) chap, fellow.
пари́ *nt. indecl.* bet; **держа́ть п., идти́ на п.** to bet, lay a bet; **п. держу́, что...** I bet that ....
Пари́ж, а *m.* Paris.
парижа́н|ин, ина, *pl.* **~е, ~** *m.* Parisian.
парижа́н|ка, ки *f. of* **~ин**; Parisienne.
пари́жск|ий *adj.* Parisian.
пари́к, а́ *m.* wig.
парикма́хер, а *m.* barber; hairdresser.
парикма́херск|ая, ой *f.* barber's (shop), hairdresser's.
пари́л|ьня, ьни, *g. pl.* **~ен** *f.* steam-room.
пари́р|овать, ую *impf. and pf.* (*pf. also* **от~**) to parry, counter.
парите́т, а *m.* parity.
парите́т|ный *adj. of* **~**; **на ~ных нача́лах** (c+*i.*) on a par (with), on an equal footing(with).
па́р|ить, ю, ишь *impf.* (*no pf.*) **1.** to steam. **2.** to steam out, sweat out (*in baths*). **3.** (*cul.*) to stew. **4.** (*impers.*): **~ит** it is sultry.
пар|и́ть, ю́, и́шь *impf.* (*no pf.*) to soar, swoop, hover;

п. в облака́х (*fig.*) to live in the clouds.

па́р|иться, юсь, ишься *impf.* **1.** (*pf.* **по~**) to steam, sweat (*in baths*). **2.** (*cul.*) to stew.

па́ри|я, и, *g. pl.* **~й** *c.g.* pariah, outcast.

парк, а *m.* **1.** park **2.** yard, depot; (*mil.*) park, depot; **трамва́йный п.** tram depot. **3.** fleet; stock; pool; **автомоби́льный п.** fleet of motor vehicles; **ваго́нный п.** rolling-stock; **мирово́й п. персона́льных компью́теров** the total number of personal computers in the world.

па́рк|а, и *f.* parka.

парке́т, а *m.* parquet; parquetry.

парке́т|ный *adj. of* **~; п. пол** parquet floor.

парк|ова́ть, у́ю *v.t. impf.* (*of* **запаркова́ть**) to park.

парк|ова́ться, у́юсь *v.i. impf.* (*of* **запаркова́ться**) to park.

парко́вочный *adj.*: **п. автома́т** *or* **счётчик** parking meter.

парла́мент, а *m.* parliament.

парламентари́зм, а *m.* parliamentarism.

парламента́ри|й, я *m.* parliamentarian.

парламента́рный *adj.* parliamentarian.

парламентёр, а *m.* (*mil.*) envoy; bearer of a flag of truce.

парламентёр|ский *adj. of* **~; п. флаг** flag of truce.

парла́ментский *adj.* parliamentary; **п. зако́н** Act of Parliament.

парни́к, а́ *m.* hotbed, seed-bed; forcing bed; **в ~е́** under glass.

парник|о́вый *adj. of* **~; ~о́вые расте́ния** hothouse plants.

парни́шк|а, и *m.* (*coll.*) boy, lad.

парн|о́й *adj.* **1.** fresh; **~о́е молоко́** milk fresh from the cow; **~о́е мя́со** fresh meat. **2.** (*coll.*) steamy.

па́рн|ый *adj.* pair; forming a pair; twin; **п. носо́к, п. сапо́г,** *etc.*, pair, fellow (*other one of pair of socks, boots, etc.*); **~ая гре́бля** sculling.

парово́з, а *m.* (steam-)engine, locomotive.

парово́з|ный *adj. of* **~; ~ная брига́да** engine crew; **~ное депо́** engine-shed.

паров|о́й[1] *adj.* **1.** *adj. of* **пар**[1]; **~а́я маши́на** steam-engine; **~а́я пра́чечная** steam laundry. **2.** (*cul.*) steamed.

парово́й[2] *adj.* lying fallow.

парод|и́йный *adj. of* **~ия**

пароди́р|овать, ую *impf. and pf.* to parody.

пароди́ст, а *m.* mimic, impressionist.

паро́ди|я, и *f.* **1.** parody. **2.** skit. **3.** travesty, caricature.

парокси́зм, а *m.* paroxysm.

паро́л|ь, я *m.* password, countersign.

паро́м, а *m.* ferry(-boat); **перепра́вить на ~е** to ferry.

паро́мщик, а *m.* ferryman.

парообра́зный *adj.* vaporous.

парообразова́ни|е, я *nt.* (*phys., tech.*) steam-generation, vaporization.

парохо́д, а *m.* steamer; steamship; **колёсный п.** paddle-boat *or* steamer; **океа́нский п.** ocean liner.

парохо́д|ный *adj. of* **~; ~ное о́бщество** steamship company.

парохо́дств|о, а *nt.* **1.** steam-navigation. **2.** steamship-line.

парт... *comb. form, abbr. of* **парти́йный**

па́рт|а, ы *f.* (school) desk.

партакти́в, а *m.* (*pol.*) Party activists.

партбиле́т, а *m.* (*pol.*) party(-membership) card.

партеногене́з, а *m.* (*zool.*) parthenogenesis.

парте́р, а *m.* (*theatr.*) the pit; the stalls.

парти́|ец, йца *m.* (*Soviet Communist*) Party-member.

партиза́н, а, *pl.* **~ы** *m.* partisan; guerrilla.

партиза́н|ский *adj. of* **~; ~ская война́** guerrilla warfare; **~ское движе́ние** the Resistance (movement); **п. отря́д** partisan detachment.

партиза́нств|о, а *nt.* guerrilla warfare.

парти́йк|а, и *f. of* **парти́ец**

парти́йност|ь, и *f.* **1.** Party spirit. **2.** party membership.

парти́йн|ый *adj.* (*pol.*) **1.** party; **п. стаж** length of (Communist) Party membership; **~ая яче́йка** Party cell. **2.** Party (*in accordance with the spirit of the CPSU*); **п. дух** Party spirit. **3.** *as n.* **п., ~ого** *m.* (*Communist*) Party member.

партиту́р|а, ы *f.* (*mus.*) score.

па́рти|я[1], **и** *f.* (*pol.*) party; the Party.

па́рти|я[2], **и** *f.* **1.** party, group. **2.** batch; lot; consignment (*of goods*). **3.** (*sport*) game; set. **4.** (*mus.*) part.

партко́м, а *m.* Party committee.

партнёр, а *m.* partner.

партнёрств|о, а *nt.* partnership; **войти́ в п. (с+*i.*)** to go into partnership (with).

парто́рг, а *m.* (*abbr. of* **парти́йный организа́тор**) Party organizer.

партсъе́зд, а *m.* Party congress.

па́рус, а, *pl.* **~а́** *m.* sail; **идти́ под ~а́ми** to sail, be under sail; **подня́ть ~а́, поста́вить ~а́** to make sail, set sail; **на всех ~а́х** in full sail (*also fig.*).

паруси́н|а, ы *f.* canvas, sail-cloth.

па́русник, а *m.* sailing vessel.

па́рус|ный *adj. of* **~; п. спорт** sailing.

парфюме́р, а *m.* perfumer.

парфюме́ри|я, и *f.* (*collect.*) perfumery.

парфюме́р|ный *adj. of* **~ия; п. магази́н** perfumer's shop; **~ная фа́брика** perfumery.

парч|а́, и́, *g. pl.* **~е́й** *f.* brocade.

парч|о́вый *adj. of* **~а́**

парш|а́, и́ *f.* mange.

парши́ве|ть, ю *impf.* (*of* **за~** *and* **о~**) to become mangy; to be covered with scabs.

парши́в|ый (~, ~а) *adj.* **1.** mangy; **~ая овца́** (*fig.*) black sheep. **2.** (*coll.*) nasty; rotten, lousy.

пас[1], **а** *m.* (*cards*) pass; *as int.* **я п.** (I) pass; **в э́том де́ле я п.** (*fig., coll.*) I'm no good at this; this is not in my line.

пас[2], **а** *m.* (*sport*) pass; *as int.* **п. сюда́!** pass!

па́сек|а, и *f.* apiary.

па́сечник, а *m.* bee-keeper.

па́сквил|ь, я *m.* libel, lampoon; squib.

па́сквильный *adj.* libellous.

пасквиля́нт, а *m.* lampoonist, slanderer.

паску́д|ный (~ен, ~на) *adj.* (*coll.*) foul, filthy.

паслён, а *m.* (*bot.*) solanum; morel; **чёрный п.** deadly nightshade.

па́смур|ный (~ен, ~на) *adj.* **1.** dull, cloudy; overcast. **2.** (*fig.*) gloomy, sullen.

пас|ова́ть[1], **у́ю** *impf.* (*of* **с~**) **1.** (*also pf. in past tense*) (*cards*) to pass. **2.** (*fig., coll.*) to give up, give in; **п. пе́ред тру́дностями** to give in to difficulties.

пас|ова́ть[2], **у́ю** *impf. and pf.* (*sport*) to pass.

паспарту́ *nt. indecl.* mount.

па́спорт, а, *pl.* **~а́** *m.* **1.** passport. **2.** registration certificate.

па́спорт|ный *adj. of* **~; п. стол** passport office.

пасса́ж, а *m.* **1.** passage; arcade. **2.** (*mus.*) passage.

пассажи́р, а *m.* passenger; **попу́тный п.** hitchhiker.

пассажи́р|ский *adj. of* **~**

пасса́т, а *m.* (*meteor.*) trade wind.

пасса́т|ный *adj. of* **~; п. ве́тер** trade wind.

пасси́в, а *m.* **1.** (*comm.*) liabilities. **2.** (*gram.*) passive voice.

пасси́вност|ь, и *f.* passivity.

пасси́в|ный (~ен, ~на) *adj.* **1.** passive. **2.** (*econ.*): **п. бала́нс** unfavourable balance.

па́ст|а, ы *f.* paste; purée; **зубна́я п.** toothpaste.

па́стбищ|е, а *nt.* pasture.

пáстбищный *adj.* pasture; grazing.
пáств|а, ы *f.* (*eccl.*) flock, congregation.
пастéл|ь, и *f.* **1.** pastel, crayon. **2.** pastel (drawing).
пастéльный *adj.* pastel.
пастеризáци|я, и *f.* pasteurization.
пастеризóв|анный *p.p.p. of* **~áть** *and adj.* pasteurized.
пастериз|овáть, ýю *impf. and pf.* to pasteurize.
пастернáк, а *m.* parsnip.
пас|тú, ý, ёшь, *past* **~, ~лá** *impf.* (*no pf.*) to graze, pasture; to shepherd, tend.
пастил|á, ы́, *pl.* **∠ы** *f.* fruit fudge.
пас|тúсь, ётся, *past* **∠ся, ~лáсь** *impf.* (*no pf.*) to graze, pasture; to browse.
пáстор, а *m.* (*Protestant*) minister, pastor.
пасторáл|ь, и *f.* **1.** (*liter.*) pastoral. **2.** (*mus.*) pastorale.
пасторáльный *adj.* pastoral, bucolic.
пастýх, á *m.* herdsman; shepherd.
пастý|шеский *adj. of* **~х; п. пóсох** shepherd's crook.
пастý|ший *adj. of* **~х; ~шья сýмка** (*bot.*) shepherd's purse.
пастýшк|а, и *f.* shepherdess.
пастуш|óк, кá *m.* **1.** *affectionate dim. of* **пастýх. 2.** (*poet.*) swain. **3.** (*zool.*): **водянóй п.** water-rail.
пáстыр|ский *adj. of* **~ь;** (*eccl.*) pastoral.
пáстыр|ь, я *m.* **1.** (*obs.*) shepherd. **2.** (*eccl.*) pastor.
па|сть[1], дý, дёшь, *past* **~л, ∠ла** *pf. of* **∠дать**
паст|ь[2], и *f.* mouth (*of animal*); jaws.
пастьб|á, ы́ *f.* pasturage.
Пáсх|а, и *f.* **1.** Passover. **2.** Easter. **3. п.** (*cul.*) paskha (*sweet cream-cheese dish eaten at Easter*).
пáсын|ок, ка *m.* stepson, stepchild.
пасьянс, а *m.* (*card-game*) patience; **раскладывать п.** to play patience.
пат, а *m.* (*in chess*) stalemate.
патéнт, а *m.* (**на**+*a.*) patent (for); **владéлец ~а** patentee.
патентóв|анный *p.p.p. of* **~áть** *and adj.* patent; **~анное лекáрство** patent medicine.
патент|овáть, ýю *impf.* (*of* **за~**) to patent.
патетúческий *adj.* **1.** enthusiastic; passionate. **2.** emotional.
патефóн, а *m.* (*small, portable*) gramophone.
пáтл|ы, ~ *pl.* (*sg.* **~а, ~ы** *f.*) (*coll.*) locks (*of hair*).
пат|овáть, ýю *impf.* (*of* **за~**) (*in chess*) to stalemate.
пáток|а, и *f.* treacle; syrup; **свéтлая п.** golden syrup; **чёрная п.** molasses.
патóлог, а *m.* pathologist.
патологúческий *adj.* pathological.
патолóги|я, и *f.* pathology.
пáто|чный *adj. of* **~ка;** treacly.
патриáрх, а *m.* (*ethnol. and eccl.*) patriarch.
патриархáл|ьный (~ен, ~ьна) *adj.* (*ethnol. and fig.*) patriarchal.
патриархáт, а *m.* (*ethnol.*) patriarchy.
патриáрхи|я, и *f.* (*eccl.*) patriarchate.
патриóт, а *m.* patriot.
патриотúзм, а *m.* patriotism.
патриотúческий *adj.* patriotic.
патрициáнский *adj. of* **патрúций**
патрúци|й, я *m.* (*hist.*) patrician.
патрóн[1], а *m.* patron.
патрóн[2], а *m.* **1.** cartridge. **2.** (*tech.*) chuck (*of drill, lathe*), holder. **3.** lamp socket, lamp holder.
патронáж, а *m.* home visiting (*by health service worker*).
патронáж|ный *adj. of* **~; ~ная сестрá** district nurse, health visitor.
патрóнник, а *m.* (*mil.*) (cartridge-)chamber.
патрóн|ный *adj. of* **~[2]; ~ная гúльза** cartridge case; **~ная сýмка** cartridge pouch.
патронтáш, а *m.* bandolier, ammunition belt.
патрулúр|овать, ую *impf.* (*no pf.*) (*mil.*) to patrol.
патрýл|ь, я́ *m.* patrol.
патрýль|ный *adj. of* **~;** *as n.* **п., ~ного** *m.* patrol.
пáуз|а, ы *f.* pause; interval; (*mus.*) rest.
паýк, á *m.* spider.
паутúн|а, ы *f.* cobweb, spider's web; (*fig.*) web; **п. лжи** tissue of lies.
паý|чий *adj. of* **~к**
пáфос, а *m.* **1.** pathos. **2.** (+*g.*) enthusiasm (for), zeal (for); **п. коммунистúческого строúтельства** enthusiasm for the building of Communism. **3.** spirit; emotional content; **п. ромáна** the spirit of a novel.
пах, а, о ∠е, в ~ý *m.* (*anat.*) groin.
пáханы|й *adj.* ploughed (up); **~е зéмли** ploughland.
пáхар|ь, я *m.* ploughman.
па|хáть, шý, ∠шешь *impf.* to plough, till.
пáх|нуть, ну, нешь, *past* **~** *or* **~нул, ~ла** *impf.* (*no pf.*) (+*i.*) to smell (of); to reek (of); **~нет лýком** there is a smell of onions; (*fig.*) to savour (of), smack (of); **~нет бедóй** this means trouble; **~ло ссóрой** a quarrel was in the air.
пахн|ýть, ёт *pf.* (*no impf.*) (+*i.*; *coll.*) to puff, blow; **~ýл вéтер** there was a gust of wind; (*impers.*): **~ýло хóлодом** there came a cold blast.
пáхот|а, ы *f.* ploughing.
пáхотный *adj.* arable.
пáхт|а, ы *f.* buttermilk; **жир ~ы** butterfat.
пáхта|ть, ю *impf.* to churn.
пахýч|ий (~, ~а) *adj.* strong-smelling.
пацáн, а *m.* (*coll.*) boy, lad.
пациéнт, а *m.* patient.
пацифúзм, а *m.* pacifism.
пацифúст, а *m.* pacifist.
пáче *adv.* (*arch.*) more; *now only in phrr.* **тем п.** the more so, the more reason; **п. чáяния** contrary to expectations.
пáчк|а, и *f.* **1.** bundle; batch; packet, pack; **п. пúсем** bundle of letters; **п. папирóс** packet of cigarettes; **п. книг** parcel of books. **2.** tutu.
пáчка|ть, ю *impf.* (*pf.* **за~** *and* **ис~**) to dirty, soil, stain, sully (*also fig.*); **п. рýки** (*fig.*) to soil one's hands; **п. чьё-н. дóброе úмя** to sully s.o.'s good name.
пáчка|ться, юсь *impf.* (*of* **за~, ис~,** *and* **на~**) **1.** to make o.s. dirty; to soil o.s. **2.** to become dirty.
пачкотн|я́, ú *f.* (*coll.*) daub.
пачкýн, а *m.* (*coll.*) **1.** sloven. **2.** dauber.
паш|á, ú, *g. pl.* **~éй** *m.* pasha.
пáш|ня, ни, *g. pl.* **~ен** *f.* ploughed field.
паштéт, а *m.* pâté.
пáюсн|ый *adj.*: **~ая икрá** pressed caviar(e).
пая́льник, а *m.* soldering iron.
пая́льн|ый *adj.* soldering; **~ая лáмпа** blow lamp; **~ая трýбка** blowpipe.
пая́льщик, а *m.* solderer.
пая́снича|ть, ю *impf.* (*no pf.*) (*coll.*) to clown, play the fool.
пая́|ть, ю *impf.* (*no pf.*) to solder.
пая́ц, а *m.* **1.** (*circus*) clown. **2.** (*fig., pej.*) clown.
пев|éц, цá *m.* singer.
певúц|а, ы *f. of* **певéц**
певýн, á *m.* (*coll.*) songster.
певýч|ий (~, ~а) *adj.* melodious.
пéвч|ий 1. *adj.* singing; **~ая птúца** songbird. **2.** *as n.* **п., ~его** *m.* chorister, choirboy.
пегáнк|а, и *f.* (*zool.*) shelduck.
пéг|ий (~, ~а) *adj.* skewbald.
пед... *comb. form, abbr. of* **педагогúческий**
педагóг, а *m.* teacher; pedagogue.
педагóгик|а, и *f.* pedagogy.
педагогúческий *adj.* pedagogic(al); educational; **п. институт** teachers' training college.
педáл|ь, и *f.* pedal; treadle; **брать п., нажáть п.** to

pedal; рабо́тать ~ью to treadle; нажа́ть на все ~и (*fig., coll.*) to go flat out.
педа́ль|ный *adj. of* ~
педа́нт, а *m.* pedant.
педанти́зм, а *m.* pedantry.
педанти́чност|ь, и *f.* pedantry.
педанти́ч|ный (~ен, ~на) *adj.* pedantic.
педву́з, а *m.* = **пединститу́т**
педера́ст, а *m.* p(a)ederast, sodomite.
педера́сти|я, и *f.* p(a)ederasty, sodomy.
педиа́тр, а *m.* p(a)ediatrician.
педиатри́|я, и *f.* p(a)ediatrics.
педикю́р, а *m.* chiropody.
педикю́рш|а, и *f.* chiropodist.
пединститу́т, а *m.* teacher training college.
педо́метр, а *m.* pedometer.
педофи́л, а *m.* paedophile.
пейза́ж, а *m.* **1.** landscape; scenery. **2.** (*art*) landscape.
пейзажи́ст, а *m.* landscape painter.
пейза́ж|ный *adj. of* ~; **~ная жи́вопись** landscape painting.
пёк, пекла́ *see* **печь**[1]
пека́рн|ый *adj.* baking; **~ое ремесло́** bakery trade.
пека́р|ня, ни, *g. pl.* **~ен** *f.* bakery.
пе́кар|ский *adj. of* **~ь; ~ские дро́жжи** baker's yeast.
пе́кар|ь, я, *pl.* **~я́, ~е́й** *and* **~и, ~ей** *m.* baker.
Пеки́н, а *m.* Beijing; Peking.
пеклева́нн|ый *adj.* finely ground; **~ая мука́** rye flour (of the best quality); **п. хлеб** fine rye bread.
пе́кл|о, а *nt.* **1.** scorching heat; **попа́сть в са́мое п.** (*fig., coll.*) to get into the thick of it. **2.** (*coll.*) hell.
пеку́, пеку́т *see* **печь**[1]
пелен|а́, ы́, *pl.* **~ы́, ~̈, ~а́м** *f.* shroud; **с ~̈** (*obs., fig.*) from the cradle; **у него́ (сло́вно) п. (с глаз) упа́ла** the scales fell from his eyes.
пелена́|ть, ю *impf.* (*of* **за~** *and* **с~**) to swaddle.
пе́ленг, а *m.* (*naut., aeron.*) bearing.
пеленга́тор, а *m.* (*naut., aeron.*) direction finder.
пеленг|ова́ть, ую́ *impf. and pf.* (*naut., aeron.*) to take the bearings (of).
пелён|ка, ки *f.* nappy; (*pl.*) swaddling clothes; **с пелёнок** (*fig.*) from the cradle.
пелери́н|а, ы *f.* cape.
пелика́н, а *m.* pelican.
пельме́н|и, ей *pl.* (*sg.* **~ь, ~я** *m.*) (*cul.*) pelmeni (*kind of ravioli*).
пе́мз|а, ы *f.* pumice(-stone).
пе́н|а, ы *f.* **1.** foam; scum; froth, head (*on liquids*); **мы́льная п.** soapsuds; **говори́ть с ~ой у рта, с ~ой на уста́х** (*fig.*) to foam at the mouth. **2.** lather (*on horses*).
пена́л, а *m.* pencil-box.
пе́ни|е, я *nt.* singing; **п. (птиц)** (birds') song; **п. петуха́** cock's crow.
пе́нист|ый (~, ~а) *adj.* foamy; frothy; **~ое вино́** sparkling wine.
пе́н|ить, ю, ишь *impf.* to froth.
пе́н|иться, ится *impf.* to foam; to froth (*intrans.*).
пеницилли́н, а *m.* penicillin.
пе́нк|а, и *f.* (*on milk, etc.*) skin; **снять ~и (с**+*g.*) to skim; (*fig.*) to take the pickings (of).
пе́нни *nt. indecl.* penny.
пенопла́ст, а *m.* foam plastic.
пенопласт|и́ческий *adj. of* ~́
пеностекл|о́, а́ *nt.* glass fibre.
пеностек|о́льный *adj. of* **~ло́**
пенс, а *m.* penny.
пенсионе́р, а *m.* pensioner.
пенсио́нн|ый *adj. of* **пе́нсия; ~ая кни́жка** pension book; **п. во́зраст** retirement age.
пе́нси|я, и *f.* pension.
пенсне́ *nt. indecl.* pince-nez.
пента́метр, а *m.* (*liter.*) pentameter.
пень, пня *m.* stump, stub; **стоя́ть как п.** (*coll.*) to be rooted to the ground.
пеньк|а́, и́ *f.* hemp.
пенько́вый *adj.* hempen.
пеньюа́р, а *m.* peignoir, negligée.
пе́н|я, и *f.* fine.
пеня́|ть, ю *impf.* (*of* **по~**) (+*d. or* **на**+*a.*; *coll.*) to blame, reproach; **~й на себя́!** you have only yourself to blame!
пео́н, а *m.* peon.
пе́п|ел, ла *m.* ash(es).
пепели́щ|е, а *nt.* site of fire.
пе́пельниц|а, ы *f.* ash-tray.
пе́пельно-се́рый *adj.* ash-grey.
пе́пельн|ый *adj.* ashy; **~ого цве́та** ash-grey.
пепси́н, а *m.* (*physiol.*) pepsin.
пепси́новый *adj.* peptic.
пепто́н, а *m.* (*physiol.*) peptone.
пер. (*abbr. of* **переу́лок**) Lane.
перве́йший *adj.* (*coll.*) primary; very best.
пе́рвен|ец, ца *m.* first-born.
пе́рвенств|о, а *nt.* first place; (*sport*) championship.
пе́рвенств|овать, ую *impf.* (*no pf.*) to take first place; **(над)** to take precedence (over).
перви́чн|ый *adj.* primary; initial; **п. пери́од боле́зни** initial period of illness; **~ые поро́ды** (*geol.*) primary rocks.
первобы́тный *adj.* (*ethnol. and fig.*) primitive; primordial; primeval.
пе́рв|ое, ого *nt.* first course (*of a meal*).
перво́зда́нный *adj.* primordial; (*geol.*) primitive, primary; **п. хаос** primordial chaos (*also fig., iron.*).
первоисто́чник, а *m.* primary source; origin.
первокла́ссник, а *m.* first-former.
первокла́ссный *adj.* first-class, first-rate.
первоку́рсник, а *m.* first-year student, freshman.
Первома́|й, я *m.* (*coll.*) May Day.
первома́й|ский *adj. of* ~
первонача́льно *adv.* originally.
первонача́льн|ый *adj.* **1.** original. **2.** primary; initial; **~ое накопле́ние** (*econ.*) primary accumulation; **~ая причи́на** (*phil.*) first cause. **3.** elementary. **4.: ~ые чи́сла** (*math.*) prime numbers.
первоо́браз, а *m.* prototype.
первообра́зный *adj.* prototypal.
первооткрыва́тел|ь, я *m.* discoverer.
первоочередн|о́й *adj.* immediate; **~а́я зада́ча** immediate task.
первопрохо́д|ец, ца *m.* (*fig., rhet.*) pioneer; pacemaker; trailblazer.
первопрохо́дческий *adj.* trail-blazing, pioneering.
первоpазря́дный *adj.* first-class, first-rank.
первоpо́дный *adj.* (*obs.*) **1.** first-born. **2.** primal; **п. грех** (*eccl.*) original sin.
первоpо́дств|о, а *nt.* primogeniture.
первоpождённый *adj.* first-born.
первосвяще́нник, а *m.* high priest; pontiff.
первосо́ртный *adj.* **1.** of the best quality. **2.** (*coll.*) first-class, first-rate.
первостате́йный *adj.* (*coll.*) first-rate, first-class.
первостепе́нный *adj.* paramount.
первоцве́т, а *m.* (*bot.*) primrose.
пе́рв|ый *adj.* first; former; earliest; **~ое (число́ ме́сяца)** the first (of the month); **~ого января́** on the first of January; **полови́на ~ого** half past twelve; **в ~ом часу́** between twelve and one; **он п. вошёл** he was the first to enter; **быть ~ым, идти́ ~ым** to come first, lead; **~ое вре́мя** at first; **~ое де́ло, ~ым де́лом** (*coll.*) first of all, first thing; **не ~ой мо́лодости** not in one's first youth; **~ая по́мощь** first aid; **п. рейс** maiden voyage; **не ~ой**

свéжести not quite fresh; **п. этáж** ground floor; **в ~ую óчередь** in the first place; **из ~ых рук** first-hand; **на п. взгляд** at first sight; **при ~ой возмóжности** at the first opportunity.

пергáмент, а *m.* parchment.

пергáмент|ный *adj. of* ~

пер|дéть, жý, дúшь *impf.* (*vulg.*) to fart.

пере... *vbl. pref. indicating* **1.** *action across or through sth.* (trans-). **2.** *repetition of action* (re-). **3.** *superiority, excess, etc.* (over-, out-). **4.** *extension of action to encompass many or all objects or cases of a given kind.* **5.** *division into two or more parts.* **6.** (*reflexives*) reciprocity of action.

переадрес|овáть, ýю *pf.* (*of* **~óвывать**) to re-address; to foward.

переадресóвыва|ть, ю *impf. of* **переадресовáть**

перебазúр|овать, ую *pf.* (*no impf.*) to shift.

перебаллотирóвк|а, и *f.* second ballot.

перебáрщива|ть, ю *impf. of* **переборщúть**

перебегá|ть, ю *impf. of* **перебежáть**

перебе|жáть, гý, жúшь, гýт *pf.* (*of* **~гáть**) **1.** (**чéрез**) to cross (running); **п. (чéрез) ýлицу** to run across the street; **п. комý-н. дорóгу** to cross s.o.'s path. **2.** (*fig., coll.*; **к**) to go over (to), desert (to).

перебéжк|а, и *f.* (*mil.*) bound, rush.

перебéжчик, а *m.* deserter; (*fig.*) turncoat.

перебéлива|ть, ю *impf. of* **перебелúть**

перебел|úть, ю́, úшь *pf.* (*of* **~ивать**) **1.** to whitewash again. **2.** to make a fair copy (of).

перебе|сúться, шýсь, ~сишься *pf.* **1.** to go mad, run mad. **2.** (*coll.*) to have sown one's wild oats.

перебивá|ть(ся), ю(сь) *impf. of* **перебúть(ся)**[1,2]

перебинт|овáть[1], **ýю** *pf.* (*of* **~óвывать**) to change the dressing (on), put a new dressing (on).

перебинт|овáть[2], **ýю** *pf.* (*of* **~óвывать**) to dress, bandage (*all, a quantity of*).

перебинтóвыва|ть, ю *impf. of* **перебинтовáть**

перебирá|ть[1]**(ся), ю(сь)** *impf. of* **перебрáть(ся)**

перебирá|ть[2], **ю** *impf.* **1.** to finger; **п. стрýны** to run one's fingers over the strings. **2.** (+*i.*) to move, advance (*in turn or in a regular manner*).

переб|úть[1], **ью́, ьёшь** *pf.* (*of* **~ивáть**) **1.** to reupholster. **2.** to beat up again (*pillow, feather-bed, etc.*).

переб|úть[2], **ью́, ьёшь** *pf.* (*of* **~ивáть**) **1.** to interrupt. **2.** to intercept; **п. комý-н. дорóгу** to cross s.o.'s path.

переб|úть[3], **ью́, ьёшь** *pf.* **1.** to slay, slaughter. **2.** to beat. **3.** to break.

переб|úться[1], **ью́сь, ьёшься** *pf.* (*of* **~ивáться**) to break.

переб|úться[2], **ью́сь, ьёшься** *pf.* (*of* **~ивáться**) (*coll.*) to make ends meet.

перебó|й, я *m.* interruption; stoppage; irregularity; misfire (*of engine*); **пульс с ~ями** irregular pulse.

переболé|ть[1], **ю** *pf.* (+*i.*) to have had, have been down (*with an illness*); **дéти все ~ли коклю́шем** the children have all been down with whooping-cough.

перебол|éть[2], **úт** *pf.* to recover.

перебóрк|а[1], **и** *f.* **1.** sorting out. **2.** (*tech.*) re-assembly.

перебóрк|а[2], **и** *f.* partition; (*naut.*) bulk-head.

перебор|óть, ю́, ~ешь *pf.* (*no impf.*) to master.

переборщ|úть, ý, úшь *pf.* (*of* **перебáрщивать**) (**в**+*p.*; *coll.*) to go too far; to overdo it; to go over the top.

перебрáнива|ться, юсь *impf.* (**с**+*i.*; *coll.*) to have words (with).

перебран|úться, ю́сь, úшься *pf.* (**с**+*i.*; *coll.*) to quarrel (with), fall out (with).

перебрáнк|а, и *f.* (*coll.*) wrangle, squabble; slanging match.

перебрáсыва|ть(ся), ю(сь) *impf. of* **перебрóсить(ся)**

пере|брáть, берý, берёшь, *past* **~брáл, ~бралá, ~брáло** *pf.* (*of* **~бирáть**) **1.** to sort out (*also fig.*); to look through. **2.** (*fig.*) to turn over (in one's mind). **3.** to take too much.

пере|брáться, берýсь, берёшься, *past* **~брáлся, ~бралáсь, ~брáлóсь** *pf.* (*coll.*) **1.** to get over, cross. **2.** to move; **п. на нóвую квартúру** to move to a new flat.

перебр|одúть, óдит *pf.* to have fermented; to have risen.

перебрó|сить, шу, сишь *pf.* (*of* **перебрáсывать**) **1.** to throw over; **п. мост чéрез рéку** to throw a bridge across a river. **2.** to transfer (*troops, etc.*).

перебрó|ситься, шусь, сишься *pf.* (*of* **перебрáсываться**) **1.** (+*i.*) to throw one to another; **п. нéсколькими словáми** (*fig.*) to exchange a few words. **2.** (*of fire, disease, etc.*) to spread.

перебрóск|а, и *f.* transfer.

перебывá|ть, ю *pf.* to have visited, have been; **он вездé ~л** he has been all over the world.

перевáл, а *m.* **1.** passing, crossing. **2.** (*geog.*) pass.

перевáлива|ть, ю *impf. of* **перевалúть**

перевáлива|ться[1], **юсь** *impf. of* **перевалúться**

перевáлива|ться[2], **юсь** *impf.* (*no pf.*) to waddle.

перевал|úть, ю́, ~ишь *pf.* (*of* **~ивать**) **1.** to transfer, shift. **2.** to cross; (*impers.*; *coll.*): **~úло за пóлночь** it is past midnight; **ей ~úло зá сорок (лет)** she has turned forty.

перевал|úться, ю́сь, ~ишься *pf.* (*of* **~иваться**[1]) to roll over; to fall over.

перевáлк|а, и *f.* **1.** transshipment. **2.** transshipment point.

перевáл|очный *adj. of* **~ка**; **п. пункт** staging post.

перевáрива|ть, ю *impf. of* **переварúть**

переварúм|ый (~, ~а) *adj.* digestible.

перевар|úть[1], **ю́, ~ишь** *pf.* (*of* **~ивать**) **1.** to cook again; to boil again. **2.** to overcook.

перевар|úть[2], **ю́, ~ишь** *pf.* (*of* **~ивать**) **1.** to digest. **2.** (*fig.*) to swallow; to bear, stand.

перевез|тú, ý, ёшь, *past* **~̈, ~лá** *pf.* (*of* **перевозúть**) **1.** to take across, put across. **2.** to transport, convey; to (re)move (*furniture, etc.*).

переверн|ýть, ý, ёшь *pf.* (*of* **перевёртывать** *and* **перевора́чивать**) to turn over; to invert; **п. наизнáнку** to turn inside out.

переверн|ýться, ýсь, ёшься *pf.* (*of* **перевёртываться** *and* **перевора́чиваться**) to turn over; **~ётся в гробý** (*joc.*) he would turn in his grave.

перевер|тéть, чý, ~тишь *pf.* (*of* **~̈тывать** *and* **~чивать**) (*coll.*) to overwind.

перевёртыва|ть(ся), ю(сь) *impf. of* **перевернýть(ся)** *and* **перевертéть**

перевéрчива|ть, ю *impf. of* **перевертéть**

перевéс, а *m.* preponderance; advantage; **числéнный п.** numerical superiority; **взять п.** to gain the upper hand.

перевé|сить[1], **шу, сишь** *pf.* (*of* **~шивать**) to hang somewhere else.

перевé|сить[2], **шу, сишь** *pf.* (*of* **~шивать**) **1.** to weigh again. **2.** to outweigh (*also fig.*); (*fig.*) to tip the scales.

перевé|ситься, шусь, сишься *pf.* (*of* **~шиваться**) to lean over.

переве|стú[1], **дý, дёшь,** *past* **~̈л, ~лá** *pf.* (*of* **переводúть**) **1.** to take across. **2.** to transfer, move, switch, shift; **п. на другýю рабóту** to transfer to another post; **п. стрéлку** to shunt, switch; **п. стрéлку часóв вперёд (назáд)** to put a clock on (back). **3.** (**с**+*g.* **на**+*a.*) to translate (from into); (**в, на**+*a.*) to convert (to), express (as, in); **п. с рýсского языкá на английский** to translate from Russian into English; **п. в метри́ческие ме́ры** to convert to metric units. **4.: п. дух** to catch one's breath. **5.** (*art*) to transfer, copy.

переве|сти́², **ду́, дёшь**, *past* **∸л, ~ла́** *pf.* (*of* **переводи́ть**) (*coll.*) **1.** to exterminate. **2.** to spend, use up.

переве|сти́сь¹, **ду́сь, дёшься**, *past* **∸лся, ~ла́сь** *pf.* (*of* **переводи́ться**) **1.** to move, be transferred. **2.** *pass. of* **~сти́¹,²**

переве|сти́сь², **ду́сь, дёшься**, *past* **∸лся, ~ла́сь** *pf.* (*of* **переводи́ться**) (*coll.*) to come to an end; **де́ньги у меня́ ~ли́сь** my money was all gone.

переве́шива|ть, ю *impf. of* **переве́сить**

переве́шива|ться, юсь *impf. of* **переве́ситься**

перевива́|ть, ю *impf. of* **переви́ть**

перевида́|ть, ю *pf.* (*coll.*) to have seen (*also fig.*).

перевира́|ть, ю *impf. of* **перевра́ть**

перев|и́ть, ью́, ьёшь, *past* **~и́л, ~ила́, ~и́ло** *pf.* (*of* **~ива́ть**) (+*i.*) to interweave (with), intertwine (with).

перево́д, а *m.* **1.** transfer, move, switch, shift; **п. де́нег** remittance; **почто́вый п.** postal order. **2.** translation; **п. мер** conversion of measures; **синхро́нный п.** simultaneous interpreting.

перево|ди́ть(ся), жу́(сь), ∸дишь(ся) *impf. of* **перевести́(сь)**

переводн|о́й *adj. of* **перево́д; ~а́я бума́га** carbon paper; **~а́я карти́нка** transfer.

перево́д|ный *adj. of* **~; п. рома́н** novel in translation; **п. бланк** postal order form.

перево́дчик, а *m.* translator; interpreter.

перево́з, а *m.* **1.** transportation. **2.** ferry.

перево|зи́ть, жу́, ∸зишь *impf. of* **перевезти́**

перево́зк|а, и *f.* transportation.

перево́з|очный *adj. of* **~ка; ~очные сре́дства** means of conveyance.

перево́зчик, а *m.* **1.** ferryman; boatman; removal man. **2.** (*zool.*) common sandpiper.

перевооруж|а́ть(ся), а́ю(сь) *impf. of* **~и́ть(ся)**

перевооруже́ни|е, я *nt.* re-armament.

перевооруж|и́ть, у́, и́шь *pf.* (*of* **~а́ть**) to re-arm.

перевооруж|и́ться, у́сь, и́шься *pf.* (*of* **~а́ться**) to re-arm (*intrans.*).

перевопло|ти́ть, щу́, ти́шь *pf.* (*of* **~ща́ть**) to reincarnate; to transform.

перевопло|ти́ться, щу́сь, ти́шься *pf.* (*of* **~ща́ться**) to be reincarnated; to undergo a transformation.

перевоплоща́|ть(ся), ю(сь) *impf. of* **перевоплоти́ть(ся)**

перевора́чива|ть(ся), ю(сь) *impf. of* **переверну́ть(ся)**

переворо́т, а *m.* **1.** revolution; **госуда́рственный п.** coup d'état. **2.** (*geol.*) cataclysm.

перворош|и́ть, у́, и́шь *pf.* (*coll.*) **1.** to turn (over) (*also fig.*); **п. се́но** to turn hay. **2.** (*fig.*) to turn upside down.

перевоспита́ни|е, я *nt.* re-education; rehabilitation.

перевоспит|а́ть, а́ю *pf.* (*of* **∸ывать**) to re-educate; to rehabilitate.

перевоспи́тыва|ть, ю *impf. of* **перевоспита́ть**

переврр|а́ть, у́, ёшь, *past* **~а́л, ~ала́, ~а́ло** *pf.* (*of* **перевира́ть**) (*coll.*) to garble, confuse; to misinterpret; **п. цита́ту** to misquote.

перевы́бор|ы, ов *no sg.* re-election.

перевыполне́ни|е, я *nt.* over-fulfilment.

перевы́полн|ить, ю, ишь *pf.* (*of* **~я́ть**) to over-fulfil.

перевыполн|я́ть, я́ю *impf. of* **∸ить**

перевя|за́ть¹, жу́, ∸жешь *pf.* (*of* **∸зывать**) **1.** to dress, bandage. **2.** to tie up, cord.

перевя|за́ть², жу́, ∸жешь *pf.* (*of* **∸зывать**) to knit again.

перевя́зк|а, и *f.* dressing, bandage.

перевя́з|очный *adj. of* **~ка; п. материа́л** dressing; **п. пункт** dressing station.

перевя́зыва|ть, ю *impf. of* **перевяза́ть**

пе́ревяз|ь, и *f.* **1.** (*mil., hist.*) shoulder-belt. **2.** (*med.*) sling.

перега́р, а *m.* (*coll.*) reek of alcohol; **от него́ несло́ ~ом** he reeked of alcohol

переги́б, а *m.* **1.** bend, twist; fold. **2.** (*fig.*) excess; **допусти́ть п. в чём-н.** to carry sth. too far.

перегиба́|ть(ся), ю(сь) *impf. of* **перегну́ть(ся)**

переглaсо́вк|а, и *f.* (*ling.*) mutation.

перегля́дыва|ться, юсь *impf. of* **перегляну́ться**

перегля|ну́ться, ну́сь, ∸нешься *pf.* (*of* **∸дываться**) (**с**+*i.*) to exchange glances (with).

перегн|а́ть, перегоню́, перего́нишь, *past* **~а́л, ~ала́, ~а́ло** *pf.* (*of* **перегоня́ть**) **1.** to outdistance, leave behind; (*fig.*) to overtake, surpass. **2.** to drive (*somewhere else*) **3.** (*chem., tech.*) to distil.

перегнива́|ть, ю *impf. of* **перегни́ть**

перегн|и́ть, иёт, *past* **~и́л, ~ила́, ~и́ло** *pf.* (*of* **~ива́ть**) to rot through.

перегно́|й, я *m.* humus.

перег|ну́ть, ну́, нёшь *pf.* (*of* **~иба́ть**) to bend; **п. па́лку** (*fig., coll.*) to go too far.

перег|ну́ться, ну́сь, нёшься *pf.* (*of* **~иба́ться**) **1.** to bend. **2.** to lean over.

перегова́рива|ть, ю *impf. of* **переговори́ть²**

перегова́рива|ться, юсь *impf.* (**с**+*i.*) to exchange remarks (with).

переговор|и́ть¹, ю́, и́шь *pf.* (**о**+*p.*) to talk (about); to talk over.

переговор|и́ть², ю́, и́шь *pf.* (*of* **перегова́ривать**) to silence; to out-talk.

перегово́р|ы, ов *no sg.* negotiations; talks; **вести́ п.** (**с**+*i.*) to negotiate (with).

перего́н¹, а *m.* driving.

перего́н², а *m.* stage (*between two rail. stations*).

перего́нк|а, и *f.* (*tech., chem.*) distillation.

перего́н|ный *adj. of* **~ка; п. заво́д** distillery.

перегоня́|ть, ю *impf. of* **перегна́ть**

перегора́жива|ть, ю *impf. of* **перегороди́ть**

перегор|а́ть, а́ю *impf. of* **~е́ть**

перегор|е́ть, и́т *pf.* (*of* **~а́ть**) **1.** to burn out. **2.** to burn through. **3.** to rot through.

перегоро|ди́ть, жу́, ∸ди́шь *pf.* (*of* **перегора́живать**) to partition off.

перегоро́дк|а, и *f.* **1.** partition. **2.** (*fig.*) barrier.

перегре́в, а *m.* overheating.

перегрева́|ть(ся), ю(сь) *impf. of* **перегре́ть(ся)**

перегре́|ть, ю *pf.* (*of* **~ва́ть**) to overheat.

перегре́|ться, юсь *pf.* (*of* **~ва́ться**) to burn (out), get burned.

перегружа́|ть, ю *impf. of* **перегрузи́ть**

перегру|зи́ть¹, жу́, ∸зи́шь *pf.* (*of* **~жа́ть**) to overload; **п. рабо́той** to overwork.

перегру|зи́ть², жу́, ∸зи́шь *pf.* (*of* **~жа́ть**) to load (*from A to B*); to transship; **п. с по́езда на парохо́д** to load from a train on to a ship.

перегру́зк|а¹, и *f.* overload; overloading; **п. рабо́той** overwork.

перегру́зк|а², и *f.* reloading; shifting; transfer, transshipping.

перегруппир|ова́ть, у́ю *pf.* (*of* **~о́вывать**) to regroup.

перегруппиро́вк|а, и *f.* re-grouping.

перегруппир|о́вывать, о́вываю *impf. of* **~ова́ть**

перегры́з|ть, у́, ёшь, *past* **~, ~ла** *pf.* (*of* **~а́ть**) to gnaw through, bite through.

перегры́з|ться, у́сь, ёшься, *past* **~ся, ~лась** *pf.* (*no impf.*) (**из-за**; *coll.*; *of dogs*) to fight (over); (*fig.*) to quarrel (over), wrangle (about).

пе́ред *and* **пе́редо** *prep.*+*i.* **1.** (*of place*; *also fig.*) before; in front of; in the face of; **п. дворцо́м** in front of the palace; **п. опа́сностью** in the face of danger. **2.** (*in relation to, as compared with*) to; **извини́ться п. кем-н.** to apologize to s.o.; **ва́ша исто́рия ничто́ п. на́шей** your story is nothing compared to ours. **3.** (*of time*) before; **п. обе́дом** before dinner; **п. тем, как** (*conj.*) before.

перёд, пе́реда, *pl.* **~а́, ~о́в** *m.* front, fore-part.

переда|ва́ть(ся), ю(сь), ёшь(ся) *impf. of* **переда́ть(ся)**

переда́|точный *adj. of* **~ча; п. вал** (*tech.*) countershaft; **п. механи́зм** driving gear, drive; **~точное число́** (*tech.*) gear ratio.

переда́тчик, а *m.* (*radio*) transmitter.

переда́|ть[1], **м, шь, ст, ди́м, ди́те, ду́т,** *past* **пе́редал, ~ла́, пе́редало** *pf.* (*of* **~ва́ть**) **1.** to pass; to hand; to hand over; to transfer; **п. де́ло в суд** to take a matter to law. **2.** to tell; to communicate; to transmit, convey; **п. по ра́дио** to broadcast; **п. благода́рность** to convey thanks; **п. зара́зу** to communicate infection; **п. поруче́ние** to deliver a message; **п. приве́т** to convey greetings; **~й(те) им (мой) приве́т** give them my regards. **3.** to reproduce (*a sound, a thought, etc.*).

переда́|ть[2], **м, шь, ст, ди́м, ди́те, ду́т,** *past* **пе́редал, ~ла́, пе́редало** *pf.* (*of* **~ва́ть**) to pay too much, give too much.

переда́|ться, стся, ду́тся, *past* **~лся, ~ла́сь** *pf.* (*of* **~ва́ться**) **1.** to pass; to be transmitted, be communicated; to be inherited. **2.** (*+d.*; *coll.*) to go over (to).

переда́ч|а, и *f.* **1.** passing; transmission; communication; transfer; **без пра́ва ~и** not transferable; **Петро́ву для ~и Ивано́вой** (*form of address on letter*) (Mrs., Miss) Ivanova, c/o (Mr.) Petrov. **2.** parcel (*delivered to person in hospital or prison*). **3.** broadcast; programme; **пряма́я п.** live broadcast. **4.** (*tech.*) drive; gear(ing); transmission; **реме́нная п.** belt drive.

передвига́|ть(ся), ю(сь) *impf. of* **передви́нуть(ся)**

передвиже́ни|е, я *nt.* movement; **сре́дства ~я** means of conveyance.

передви́ж|ка, ки *f.* **1.** = **~е́ние. 2.** *as adj.* travelling, mobile; **библиоте́ка-р.** travelling library.

передвижн|о́й *adj.* **1.** movable. **2.** mobile; travelling.

передви́|нуть, ну, нешь *pf.* (*of* **~га́ть**) to move, shift (*also fig.*); **п. сро́ки экза́менов** to alter the date of examinations.

передви́|нуться, нусь, нешься *pf.* (*of* **~га́ться**) to move, shift.

переде́л, а *m.* repartition; redistribution.

переде́л|ать[1], **аю** *pf.* (*of* **~ывать**) to do anew; to alter; (*fig.*) to re-fashion, recast; **п. пла́тье** to alter a dress.

переде́л|ать[2], **аю** *pf.* (*coll.*) to do; **я ~ал все дела́** I have done all I had to do.

передел|и́ть, ю́, ~ишь *pf.* (*of* **~я́ть**) to re-divide.

переде́лк|а, и *f.* **1.** alteration; **отда́ть что-н. в ~у** to have sth. altered; **попа́сть в ~у** (*coll.*) to get into a mess. **2.** adaptation (*of liter. work, etc.*).

переде́лыва|ть, ю *impf. of* **переде́лать**[1]

передел|я́ть, я́ю *impf. of* **~и́ть**

передёргива|ть, ю *impf. of* **передёрнуть**

передерж|а́ть[1], **у́, ~ишь** *pf.* (*of* **~ивать**) **1.** to overdo; to overcook. **2.** (*phot.*) to over-expose.

передерж|а́ть[2], **у́, ~ишь** *pf.* (*of* **~ивать**) (*coll.*): **п. экза́мен** to retake an examination.

переде́ржива|ть, ю *impf. of* **передержа́ть**

переде́ржк|а[1], **и** *f.* (*phot.*) over-exposure.

переде́ржк|а[2], **и** *f.* (*coll.*) re-examination.

переде́ржк|а[3], **и** *f.* (*coll.*) cheating (*at cards*), juggling (*with facts*).

передёр|нуть, ну, нешь *pf.* (*of* **~гивать**) **1.** to pull aside. **2.** (*impers.*): **его́ ~нуло от бо́ли** he was convulsed with pain. **3.** to cheat (*at cards*). **4.** (*fig.*): **п. фа́кты** to juggle with facts.

пере́дн|ий *adj.* front; anterior; **~ие коне́чности** fore-legs; **п. план** foreground.

пере́дник, а *m.* apron; pinafore.

пере́дн|яя, ей *f.* (entrance) hall, lobby.

пе́редо = пе́ред

передова́я, ~о́й *f.* **1.** lead article, leader; editorial. **2.** (*mil.*) forward position.

передове́р|ить, ю, ишь *pf.* (*of* **~я́ть**) (*+d.*) to transfer trust (to); (*leg.*) to transfer power of attorney (to); **п. догово́р** to sub-contract (to).

передовер|я́ть, я́ю *impf. of* **~ить**

передови́к, а́ *m.* leading worker.

передов|о́й *adj.* forward; foremost, advanced (*also fig.*); **~ы́е взгля́ды** advanced views; **п. отря́д** (*mil.*) advanced detachment; (*fig.*) vanguard; **~а́я статья́** lead article, leader; editorial.

передозиро́вк|а, и *f.* (*med.*) overdose.

перед|о́к, ка́ *m.* front (*of carriage, etc.*).

передо́х|нуть, нет, *past* **~, ~ла** *pf.* (*no impf.*) to die off (*usu. of animals*).

передохн|у́ть, у́, ёшь *pf.* (*of* **передыха́ть**) (*coll.*) to pause for breath, take a short rest.

передра́знива|ть, ю *impf. of* **передразни́ть**

передразн|и́ть, ю́, ~ишь *pf.* (*of* **~ивать**) to take off, mimic.

пере|дра́ться, деру́сь, дерёшься, *past* **~дра́лся, ~драла́сь, ~дра́ло́сь** *pf.* (*no impf.*) (*coll.*) to fight, brawl (*of many people, etc.*).

передро́г|нуть, ну, нешь, *past* **~, ~ла** *pf.* (*no impf.*) (*coll.*) to get chilled through

передря́г|а, и *f.* (*coll.*) row, scrape.

переду́м|ать, аю *pf.* (*of* **~ывать**) **1.** to change one's mind. **2.** to do a great deal of thinking.

переду́мыва|ть, ю *impf. of* **переду́мать**

передыха́|ть, ю *impf. of* **передохну́ть**

переды́шк|а, и *f.* respite, breathing-space; breather.

перееда́ни|е, я *nt.* overeating.

перееда́|ть, ю *impf. of* **перее́сть**

перее́зд[1], **а** *m.* crossing.

перее́зд[2], **а** *m.* move, removal.

переезжа́|ть, ю *impf. of* **перее́хать**

перее́|сть[1], **м, шь, ст, ди́м, ди́те, дя́т,** *past* **~л** *pf.* (*of* **~да́ть**) to overeat.

перее́|сть[2], **м, шь, ст, ди́м, ди́те, дя́т,** *past* **~л** *pf.* (*of* **~да́ть**) to corrode, eat away.

перее́|хать[1], **ду, дешь** *pf.* (*of* **~зжа́ть**) **1.** to cross. **2.** to run over, knock down.

перее́|хать[2], **ду, дешь** *pf.* (*of* **~зжа́ть**) to move (*to a new place of residence*).

пережа́рива|ть, ю *impf. of* **пережа́рить**

пережа́р|ить, ю, ишь *pf.* (*of* **~ивать**) to overdo, overcook.

пережд|а́ть, у́, ёшь, *past* **~а́л, ~ала́, ~а́ло** *pf.* (*of* **пережида́ть**) to wait through; **мы ~а́ли грозу́** we waited till the storm was over.

переж|ева́ть, ую́, уёшь *pf.* (*of* **~ёвывать**) to masticate, chew.

пережёвыва|ть, ю *impf.* **1.** *impf. of* **пережева́ть. 2.** (*fig.*) to repeat over and over again.

пережен|и́ться, ~ится *pf.* (*coll.*) to marry; **все её бра́тья ~и́лись** all her brothers have married.

переж|е́чь, гу́, жёшь, гу́т, *past* **~ёг, ~гла́** *pf.* (*of* **~ига́ть**) **1.** to burn more than one's quota (*of fuel, etc.*). **2.** to burn through.

пережива́ни|е, я *nt.* experience; feeling.

пережива́|ть, ю *impf.* **1.** *impf. of* **пережи́ть. 2.** (*impf. only*) (*coll.*) to be upset, worry.

пережида́|ть, ю *impf. of* **пережда́ть**

пережит|о́е, о́го *nt.* one's past.

пережи́т|ок, ка *m.* relic, vestige, survival.

пережи́|ть, ву́, вёшь, *past* **пе́режил, ~ла́, пе́режило** *pf.* (*of* **~ва́ть**) **1.** to live through; **п. жизнь**

to live one's life through. **2.** to experience; to go through; to endure, suffer; **тяжело́ п. что-н.** to take sth. hard. **3.** to outlive, survive.

перезаб|ы́ть, у́ду, у́дешь *pf.* (*no impf.*) (*coll.*) to forget.

перезаключ|а́ть, а́ю *impf. of* **~и́ть**

перезаключ|и́ть, у́, и́шь *pf.* (*of* **~а́ть**) to renew; **п. догово́р** to renew a contract.

перезаря|ди́ть, жу́, ~ди́шь *pf.* (*of* **~жа́ть**) **1.** to re-charge; to re-load. **2.** (*elec.*) to overcharge.

перезаряжа́|ть, ю *impf. of* **перезаряди́ть**

перезво́н, а *m.* ringing, chime.

перезим|ова́ть, у́ю *pf.* (*of* **зимова́ть**) to winter, pass the winter.

перезрева́|ть, ю *impf. of* **перезре́ть**

перезре́|ть, ю *pf.* (*of* **~ва́ть**) to become overripe.

переигр|а́ть[1], **а́ю** *pf.* (*of* **~ывать**) to play again.

переигр|а́ть[2], **а́ю** *pf.* (*of* **~ывать**) (*theatr.*; *coll.*) to overact, overdo.

переигр|а́ть[3], **а́ю** *pf.* to play, act, perform (*all or a number of*).

переи́грыва|ть, ю *impf. of* **переигра́ть**[1,2]

переизбира́|ть, ю *impf. of* **переизбра́ть**

переизбра́ни|е, я *nt.* re-election.

переиз|бра́ть, беру́, берёшь, *past* **~бра́л, ~бра-ла́, ~бра́ло** *pf.* (*of* **~бира́ть**) to re-elect.

переизда|ва́ть, ю́, ёшь *impf. of* **~ть**

переизда́ни|е, я *nt.* **1.** re-publication. **2.** reprint.

переизда́|ть, м, шь, ст, ди́м, ди́те, ду́т, *past* **~л, ~ла́, ~ло** *pf.* (*of* **~ва́ть**) to re-publish, reprint.

переимен|ова́ть, у́ю *pf.* (*of* **~о́вывать**) (**в**+*a.*) to rename.

переимено́выва|ть, ю *impf. of* **переименова́ть**

переи́мчив|ый (~, ~а) *adj.* (*coll.*) imitative.

переина́чива|ть, ю *impf. of* **переина́чить**

переина́ч|ить, у, ишь *pf.* (*of* **~ивать**) to alter, to modify.

пере|йти́, йду́, йдёшь, *past* **~шёл, ~шла́** *pf.* (*of* **~ходи́ть**) **1.** (+*a. or* **че́рез**) to cross; to get across, get over, go over. **2.** (**в, на**+*a. or* **к**) to pass (to); **п. в наступле́ние** to switch to the offensive; **п. в ру́ки** (+*g.*) to pass into the hands (of); **п. в сосе́днюю ко́мнату** to go into the next room; **п. к друго́му владе́льцу** to change hands; **п. на другу́ю рабо́ту** to change one's job; **п. на сто́рону проти́вника** to go over to the enemy. **3.** (**в**+*a.*) to turn (into).

перека́лыва|ть, ю *impf. of* **переколо́ть**

перека́пыва|ть, ю *impf. of* **перекопа́ть**

перека́рмлива|ть, ю *impf. of* **перекорми́ть**

перека́т[1], **а** *m.* shoal.

перека́т[2], **а** *m.* roll, peal (*of thunder*).

перекати́-по́л|е, я *nt.* (*of pers.*) rolling stone.

перека|ти́ть, чу́, ~тишь *pf.* (*of* **~тывать**) to roll (*somewhere else*).

перека|ти́ться, чу́сь, ~тишься *pf.* (*of* **~тывать-ся**) to roll (*somewhere else*).

перека́шива|ть(ся), ю(сь) *impf. of* **перекоси́ть(ся)**

переквалифика́ци|я, и *f.* retraining.

переквалифици́р|овать, ую *impf. and pf.* to retrain.

переквалифици́р|оваться, уюсь *impf. and pf.* to retrain.

перекид|а́ть, а́ю *pf.* (*of* **~ывать**) to throw (one after another).

перекидно́й *adj.*: **п. мо́стик** footbridge; **п. кален-да́рь** desk calendar.

переки́дыва|ть(ся), ю(сь) *impf. of* **перекида́ть** *and* **переки́нуть(ся)**

переки́|нуть, ну, нешь *pf.* (*of* **~дывать**) to throw (over).

переки́|нуться, нусь, нешься *pf.* (*of* **~дываться**) **1.** to leap (over). **2.** (*of fire, disease, etc.*) to spread. **3.** (+*i.*) to throw (one to another).

пе́рекис|ь, и *f.* (*chem.*) peroxide.

перекла́дин|а, ы *f.* **1.** cross-beam, cross-piece, transom; joist. **2.** (*sport*) horizontal bar, crossbar.

перекла́дыва|ть, ю *impf. of* **переложи́ть**

перекле́ива|ть, ю *impf. of* **перекле́ить**

перекле́|ить[1], **ю, ишь** *pf.* (*of* **~ивать**) to re-stick; to glue again, paste again.

перекле́|ить[2], **ю, ишь** *pf.* (*of* **~ивать**) to stick (*a number of*).

переклик|а́ться, а́юсь *impf.* (**с**+*i.*) **1.** (*pf.* **~нуться**) to call to one another. **2.** (*fig.*) to have sth. in common (with).

перекли́чк|а, и *f.* roll-call.

переключа́тел|ь, я *m.* (*tech.*) switch.

переключ|а́ть(ся), а́ю(сь) *impf. of* **~и́ть(ся)**

переключ|и́ть, у́, и́шь *pf.* (*of* **~а́ть**) (*tech. and fig.*; **на**+*a.*) to switch (over to); **п. ско́рость** to change gear.

переключ|и́ться, у́сь и́шься *pf.* (*of* **~а́ться**) (*tech. and fig.*; **на**+*a.*) to switch (over to); **п. на бли́жний свет** to dip one's headlights.

перек|ова́ть, ую́, уёшь *pf.* (*of* **~о́вывать**) **1.** to re-forge; to hammer again; **п. коня́** to re-shoe a horse. **2.** to hammer out, beat out; **п. мечи́ на ора́ла** to beat swords into ploughshares (*also fig.*).

переко́выва|ть, ю *impf. of* **перекова́ть**

перекол|о́ть[1], **ю́, ~ешь** *pf.* (*of* **перека́лывать**) **1.** to pin (*somewhere else*). **2.** to prick all over.

перекол|о́ть[2], **ю́, ~ешь** *pf.* (*of* **перека́лывать**) to chop, hew.

перекопа́|ть, ю *pf.* (*of* **перека́пывать**) **1.** to dig over again. **2.** to dig (*all of*). **3.** to dig across.

перекорм|и́ть, лю́, ~ишь *pf.* (*of* **перека́рмли-вать**) **1.** to overfeed. **2.** (*pf. only*) to feed (*all of, many*).

переко́р|ы, ов *no sg.* (*coll.*) squabble.

переко|си́ть[1], **шу́, ~сишь** *pf.* (*of* **перека́шивать**) to warp; (*fig.*) to distort; (*impers.*): **~си́ло око́нную ра́му** the window-frame has warped; **от зло́бы его́ ~си́ло** his face was distorted with malice.

переко|си́ть[2], **шу́, ~сишь** *pf.* to mow (*all of, a large area of*).

переко|си́ться, шу́сь, ~сишься *pf.* (*of* **перека́ши-ваться**) to warp, be warped; (*fig.*) to become distorted.

перекоч|ева́ть, у́ю *pf.* (*of* **~ёвывать**) to migrate; to move on (*of nomads, also coll.*).

перекочёвыва|ть, ю *impf. of* **перекочева́ть**

переко́|шенный *p.p.p. of* **~си́ть** *and adj.* distorted, twisted.

перекра́ива|ть, ю *impf. of* **перекрои́ть**

перекра́|сить[1], **шу, сишь** *pf.* (*of* **~шивать**) to repaint; to paint a different colour.

перекра́|сить[2], **шу, сишь** *pf.* (*of* **~шивать**) to colour, paint; to dye.

перекра́|ситься, шусь, сишься *pf.* (*of* **~шивать-ся**) **1.** to change colour. **2.** (*fig.*) to become a turncoat.

перекра́шива|ть(ся), ю(сь) *impf. of* **перекра́сить-(ся)**

перекре|сти́ть[1], **щу́, ~стишь** *pf.* (*of* **крести́ть 3.**) to make the sign of the cross over.

перекре|сти́ть[2], **щу́, ~стишь** *pf.* (*of* **~щивать**) to cross.

перекре|сти́ть[3], **щу́, ~стишь** *pf.* (*of* **~щивать**) to baptize (*all of, a large number of*).

перекре|сти́ться[1], **щу́сь, ~стишься** *pf.* (*of* **кре-сти́ться 2.**) to cross o.s.

перекре|сти́ться[2], **щу́сь, ~стишься** *pf.* (*of* **~щи-ваться**) to cross, intersect.

перекрёстн|ый *adj.* cross; **п. допро́с** cross-examination; **п. ого́нь** (*mil.*) cross-fire; **~ая ссы́лка** cross-reference.

перекрёст|ок, ка *m.* cross-roads, crossing; **крича́ть**

на всех ~ках (*coll.*) to shout from the house-tops.
перекрéщива|ть(ся), ю(сь) *impf. of* **перекрестить**[2,3]**(ся)**[2]
перекри́кива|ть, ю *impf. of* **перекрича́ть**
перекри|ча́ть, чу́, чи́шь *pf.* (*of* **∠кивать**) to shout down.
перекро|и́ть, ю́, и́шь *pf.* (*of* **перекра́ивать**) to cut out again; (*fig.*) to rehash; to re-shape; **п. ка́рту ми́ра** to re-draw the map of the world.
перекрыва́|ть, ю *impf. of* **перекры́ть**
перекр|ы́ть[1]**, о́ю, о́ешь** *pf.* (*of* **~ыва́ть**) to re-cover.
перекр|ы́ть[2]**, о́ю, о́ешь** *pf.* (*of* **~ыва́ть**) **1.** (*coll.*) to exceed; **п. реко́рд** to break a record. **2.** (*cards*) to beat; to trump. **3.** to close, cut off; to dam (*a river*).
перекувы́ркива|ть(ся), ю(сь) *impf. of* **перекувыр-ну́ть(ся)**
перекувыр|ну́ть, ну́, нёшь *pf.* (*of* **∠кивать**) (*coll.*) to upset, overturn.
перекувыр|ну́ться, ну́сь, нёшься *pf.* (*of* **∠киваться**) (*coll.*) **1.** to topple over. **2.** to turn a somersault.
перекуп|а́ть[1]**, а́ю** *impf. of* **~и́ть**
перекупа́|ть[2]**, ю** *pf.* to bath.
перекупа́|ть[3]**, ю** *pf.* (*coll.*) to bathe too long.
перекупа́|ться, юсь *pf.* (*coll.*) to bathe too long, stay in (the water) too long.
перекуп|и́ть, лю́, ∠ишь *pf.* (*of* **~а́ть**) to buy up (*sth. sought by others*); to outbid for.
переку́пщик, а *m.* (second-hand) dealer.
переку́р, а *m.* (*coll.*) smoke break.
переку́рива|ть, ю *impf. of* **перекури́ть**
перекур|и́ть, ю́, ∠ишь *pf.* (*of* **∠ивать**) (*coll.*) to break for a smoke.
переку|си́ть, шу́, ∠сишь *pf.* (*of* **∠сывать**) **1.** to bite through. **2.** (*coll.*) to have a bite (to eat).
переку́сыва|ть *impf. of* **перекуси́ть**
перелага́|ть, ю *impf. of* **переложи́ть**
перела́мыва|ть(ся), ю(сь) *impf. of* **переломи́ть(ся)**
перележ|а́ть, у́, и́шь *pf.* to lie too long.
перелез|а́ть, а́ю *impf. of* **∠ть**
переле́з|ть, у, ешь, *past* **~, ~ла** *pf.* (*of* **~а́ть**) to climb over.
переле́с|ок, ка *m.* copse, coppice.
перелёт, а *m.* **1.** flight (*of aircraft*). **2.** migration (*of birds*). **3.** shot over the target.
перелет|а́ть, а́ю *impf. of* **~е́ть**
переле|те́ть, чу́, ти́шь *pf.* (*of* **~та́ть**) **1.** (+*a. or* **че́рез**) to fly over. **2.** to fly too far; to overshoot (the mark).
перелётн|ый *adj.*: **~ая пти́ца** bird of passage (*also fig.*); migratory bird.
пере|ле́чь, ля́гу, ля́жешь, ля́гут, *past* **~лёг, ~легла́** *pf.* (*no impf.*) to lie somewhere else; to move; **п. с дива́на на крова́ть** to move from the sofa to the bed.
перели́в, а *m.* tint, tinge; play (of colours); modulation (*of voice*).
переливá́ни|е, я *nt.* **1.** decantation. **2.** (*med.*) transfusion.
перелива́|ть[1]**, ю** *impf. of* **перели́ть**
перелива́|ть[2]**, ет** *impf.* (*of colours*) to play.
перелива́|ться[1]**, юсь** *impf. of* **перели́ться**
перелива́|ться[2]**, ется** *impf.* (*of colours*) to play; (*of voices*) to modulate.
перели́вчат|ый (~, ~а) *adj.* iridescent; (*of voice*) modulating; (*of silk*) shot.
перелист|а́ть, а́ю *pf.* (*of* **∠ывать**) **1.** to turn over, leaf. **2.** to look through.
перели́стыва|ть, ю *impf. of* **перелиста́ть**
перел|и́ть[1]**, ью́, ьёшь,** *past* **~и́л, ~ила́, ~и́ло** *pf.* (*of* **~ива́ть**) **1.** to pour (*from one vessel to another*); to decant; **п. молоко́ из кастрю́ли в кувши́н** to pour milk from a saucepan into a jug. **2.** (*med.*) to transfuse; **п. кровь** (+*d.*) to give a blood transfusion (to).
перел|и́ть[2]**, ью́, ьёшь,** *past* **~и́л, ~ила́, ~и́ло** *pf.* (*of* **~ива́ть**) **1.** to re-cast. **2.** to melt down; **п. колокола́ на пу́шки** to melt down bells for guns.
перел|и́ться, ью́сь, ьёшься, *past* **~и́лся, ~ила́сь, ~и́ло́сь** *pf.* (*of* **~ива́ться**) **1.** to flow (*from one place to another*). **2.** to overflow.
перелиц|ева́ть, у́ю *pf.* (*of* **~о́вывать**) to turn (*an article of clothing*); to have turned.
перелицо́выва|ть, ю *impf. of* **перелицева́ть**
перелов|и́ть, лю́, ∠ишь *pf.* to catch (*all or a number of*).
переложе́ни|е, я *nt.* (*mus.*) arrangement; transposition; **п. в стихи́** versification.
перелож|и́ть, у́, ∠ишь *pf.* **1.** (*impf.* **перекла́дывать** *and* **перелага́ть**) to put somewhere else; to shift, move; (*fig.*) to shift; **п. отве́тственность на кого́-н.** to shift the responsibility on to s.o. **2.** (*impf.* **перекла́дывать**) (+*a. and i.*) to interlay, pack (with); **п. посу́ду соло́мой** to interlay crockery with straw. **3.** (*impf.* **перекла́дывать**) to re-set, re-lay. **4.** (*impf.* **перелага́ть**) **(в, на**+*a.*) to set (to), arrange (for); to transpose; to put (into); **п. на му́зыку** to set to music; **п. в стихи́** to put into verse. **5.** (*impf.* **перекла́дывать**) (+*g.*) to put in too much; **вы ~и́ли со́ли в суп** you have put too much salt in the soup.
перело́м, а *m.* **1.** break, breaking; fracture. **2.** (*fig.*) turning point, crisis, sudden change.
перелома́|ть, ю *pf.* to break (*all or a number of*).
перелома́|ться, юсь *pf.* (*coll.*) to break, be broken.
перелом|и́ть, лю́, ∠ишь *pf.* (*of* **перела́мывать**) **1.** to break in two; to break *or* fracture. **2.** (*fig.*) to break *or* master; **п. себя́** to master o.s.; to restrain one's feelings; **п. кому́-н. во́лю** to break s.o.'s will.
перелом|и́ться, ∠ится *pf.* (*of* **перела́мываться**) to break in two; to be fractured.
перело́м|ный *adj. of* **~**; **п. моме́нт** critical moment, crucial moment.
перема́|зать, жу, жешь *pf.* (*of* **~зывать**) (*coll.*; +*i.*) to soil (with), make dirty (with).
перема́|заться, жусь, жешься *pf.* (*of* **~зываться**) (*coll.*) to soil o.s., besmear o.s.
перема́зыва|ть(ся), ю(сь) *impf. of* **перема́зать(ся)**
перема́лыва|ть, ю *impf. of* **перемоло́ть**
перема́нива|ть, ю *impf. of* **перемани́ть**
переман|и́ть, ю́, ∠ишь *pf.* (*of* **∠ивать**) to entice; **п. на свою́ сто́рону** to win over.
перема́тыва|ть, ю *impf. of* **перемота́ть**
перема́хива|ть, ю *impf. of* **перемахну́ть**
перемах|ну́ть, ну́, нёшь *pf.* (*of* **∠ивать**) (*coll.*) to jump over, leap over.
перемежа́|ть, ю *impf.* (*no pf.*) (+*a. and i.* or **с**+*i.*) to alternate; **он ~л угро́зы (с) ле́стью** he alternated threats and blandishments.
перемежа́|ться, ется *impf.* (*no pf.*) **(с**+*i.*) to alternate; **снег ~лся с гра́дом** snow alternated with hail.
переме́н|а, ы *f.* **1.** change, alteration. **2.** change (of clothes). **3.** (*school*) break.
перемен|и́ть, ю́, ∠ишь *pf.* (*of* **~я́ть**) to change; **п. пози́цию** to shift one's ground (*also fig.*); **п. тон** (*fig.*) to change one's tune.
перемен|и́ться, ю́сь, ∠ишься *pf.* (*of* **~я́ться**) to change; **п. места́ми** to change places; **п. к кому́-н.** to change one's attitude towards s.o.
переме́нн|ый *adj.* variable; **~ая величина́** (*math.*) variable; **п. ток** (*elec.*) alternating current.
переме́нчив|ый (~, ~а) *adj.* (*coll.*) changeable.
перемен|я́ть(ся), я́ю(сь) *impf. of* **~и́ть(ся)**
перемерз|а́ть, а́ю *impf. of* **∠нуть**
перемёрз|нуть, ну, нешь *pf.* (*of* **~а́ть**) (*coll.*) **1.** to

get chilled, freeze. **2.** (*of plants*) to be nipped by the frost.
перемéрива|ть, ю *impf. of* **перемéрить**
перемéр|ить[1], **ю, ишь** *pf.* (*of* **~ивать**) to re-measure.
перемéр|ить[2], **ю, ишь** *pf.* to try on.
переме|сти́ть, щу́, сти́шь *pf.* (*of* **~щáть**) to move (*somewhere else*); to transfer.
переме|сти́ться, щу́сь, сти́шься *pf.* (*of* **~щáться**) **1.** to move. **2.** *pass. of* **~сти́ть**
перемé|тить[1], **чу, тишь** *pf.* (*of* **~чáть**) to mark again.
перемé|тить[2], **чу, тишь** *pf.* (*no impf.*) to mark (*a quantity of*).
переметн|у́ться, у́сь, ёшься *pf.* (*no impf.*) (*coll.*) to go over (to the enemy), desert.
перемётн|ый *adj.*: **~ая сумá** saddle bag.
перемеш|áть, áю *pf.* (*of* **∸ивать**) **1.** to mix, intermingle; **п. кáрты** to shuffle cards. **2.** (*coll.*) to mix up; (*fig.*) to confuse; **он, по-ви́димому, ~áл нáши фами́лии** he evidently got our names mixed up.
перемеш|áться, áюсь *pf.* (*of* **∸иваться**) **1.** to get mixed (up); **всё у негó в головé ~áлось** he has got everything mixed up. **2.** *pass. of* **~áть**
перемéшива|ть(ся), ю(сь) *impf. of* **перемешáть(ся)**
перемещá|ть(ся), ю(сь) *impf. of* **перемести́ть(ся)**
перемещéни|е, я *nt.* **1.** transference, shift; displacement. **2.** (*geol.*) dislocation, displacement.
переме|щённый *p.p.p. of* **~сти́ть; ~щённые ли́ца** (*pol.*) displaced persons.
переми́гива|ться, юсь *impf. of* **перемигну́ться**
перемиг|ну́ться, ну́сь, нёшься *pf.* (*of* **∸иваться**) (*coll.*; **с**+*i.*) to wink (at); **п. мéжду собóй** to wink at each other.
переминá|ться, юсь *impf.* (*no pf.*): **п. с ноги́ нá ногу** (*coll.*) to shift from one foot to the other.
переми́ри|е, я *nt.* armistice, truce.
перемнож|áть, áю *impf. of* **∸ить**
перемнóж|ить, у, ишь *pf.* (*of* **~áть**) to multiply.
перемогá|ть, ю *impf.* (*coll.*) **1.** (*pf.* **перемóчь**) to overcome (*an illness, etc.*). **2.** to try to overcome (*an illness, etc.*).
перемогá|ться, юсь *impf.* (*coll.*) to try to overcome an illness.
перемок|áть, áю *impf. of* **∸нуть**
перемóк|нуть, ну, нешь, *past* **~, ~ла** *pf.* (*of* **~áть**) (*coll.*) to get drenched.
перемóлв|ить, лю, ишь *pf.* (*no impf.*): **п. слóво** (**с**+*i.*; *coll.*) to have a word (with).
перемóлв|иться, люсь, ишься *pf.* (*no impf.*) (+*i.*; **с**+*i.*; *coll.*) to have a word (with); **п. нéсколькими словáми с сосéдом** to pass the time of day with a neighbour.
перем|олóть, елю́, éлешь *pf.* (*of* **~áлывать**) to grind, mill; (*fig.*) to pulverize.
перем|олóться, éлется *pf.* (*of* **~áлываться**) *pass. of* **~олóть; ~éлется — мукá бу́дет** (*prov.*) it will all come right in the end.
перемотá|ть, ю *pf.* (*of* **перемáтывать**) **1.** to wind; to reel. **2.** to re-wind.
перемó|чь, гу́, ∸жешь *pf. of* **~гáть**
перемывá|ть, ю *impf. of* **перемы́ть**
перем|ы́ть[1], **óю, óешь** *pf.* (*of* **~ывáть**) to wash up again.
перем|ы́ть[2], **óю, óешь** *pf.* to wash (up) (*all or a quantity of*).
перемы́чк|а, и *f.* (*tech.*) **1.** straight arch. **2.** cross piece; tie plate. **3.** bulkhead; dam.
перенапрягá|ть(ся), ю(сь) *impf. of* **перенапря́чь(ся)**
перенапря́|чь, гу́, жёшь, *past* **~г, ~глá** *pf.* (*of* **~гáть**) to overstrain.
перенапря́|чься, гу́сь, жёшься, *past* **~гся, ~глáсь** *pf.* (*of* **~гáться**) to overexert o.s.
перенаселéни|е, я *nt.* overpopulation.
перенаселённост|ь, и *f.* overpopulation; overcrowding.
перенасел|ённый *p.p.p. of* **~и́ть** *and adj.* overpopulated; overcrowded.
перенасел|и́ть, ю́, и́шь *pf.* (*of* **~я́ть**) to overpopulate.
перенасел|я́ть, я́ю *impf. of* **~и́ть**
перенесéни|е, я *nt.* transference, transportation.
перенес|ти́[1], **у́, ёшь,** *past* **∸, ~лá** *pf.* (*of* **переноси́ть**) **1.** to carry (*somewhere else*); to transport; to transfer; **п. столи́цу в Москву́** to move the capital to Moscow. **2.: п. слóво** (*typ.*) to carry over (*part of word*) to the next line. **3.** to put off, postpone; to carry over.
перенес|ти́[2], **у́, ёшь,** *past* **∸, ~лá** *pf.* (*of* **переноси́ть**) to endure, bear, stand; **п. болéзнь** to have an illness; **я э́того не мог п.** I couldn't stand that.
перенес|ти́сь, у́сь, ёшься, *past* **∸ся, ~лáсь** *pf.* (*of* **переноси́ться**) **1.** to be carried, be borne; (*fig.*) to be carried away (*in thought*). **2.** *pass. of* **~ти́**[1]
перенимá|ть, ю *impf. of* **переня́ть**
перенóс, а *m.* **1.** transfer; transportation. **2.** (*typ.*) word division; **знак ~а** hyphen.
перено|си́ть(ся), шу́(сь), ∸сишь(ся) *impf. of* **перенести́(сь)**
перенóсиц|а, ы *f.* bridge of the nose.
переносно́й = перенóсный 1.
перенóсный *adj.* **1.** portable. **2.** (*ling.*) figurative.
перенóсчик, а *m.* carrier.
переноч|евáть, у́ю *pf.* (*of* **ночевáть**) to spend the night.
перенумер|овáть, у́ю *pf.* (*of* **нумеровáть**) to number.
пере|ня́ть, йму́, ймёшь, *past* **пéренял, ~нялá, пéреняло** *pf.* (*of* **~нимáть**) (*coll.*) to imitate, copy; **п. привы́чку** to acquire a habit.
переобору́д|овать, ую *impf. and pf.* to re-equip; to refit.
переобремен|и́ть, ю́, и́шь *pf.* (*of* **~я́ть**) to overburden.
переобремен|я́ть, я́ю *impf. of* **~и́ть**
переобувá|ть(ся), ю(сь) *impf. of* **переобу́ть(ся)**
переобу́|ть, ю, ешь *pf.* (*of* **~вáть**) to change s.o.'s shoes; **п. боти́нки** to change one's shoes.
переобу́|ться, юсь, ешься *pf.* (*of* **~вáться**) to change one's shoes, boots, *etc.*
переодевá|ть(ся), ю(сь) *impf. of* **переодéть(ся)**
переодé|ть, ну, нешь *pf.* (*of* **~вáть**) **1.** to change s.o.'s clothes; **п. бельё ребёнку** (*coll.*) to change a baby; **п. плáтье** to change one's dress. **2.** (+*i.*; **в**+*a.*) to dress up, disguise (as); **п. дéвочку мáльчиком** to dress up a little girl as a boy.
переодé|ться, нусь, нешься *pf.* (*of* **~вáться**) **1.** to change (one's clothes). **2.** (+*i.*, **в**+*a.*) to disguise o.s. (as); **она ~лась в мáльчика** she disguised herself as a boy.
переоцéнива|ть, ю *impf. of* **переоцени́ть**
переоцен|и́ть, ю́, ∸ишь *pf.* (*of* **∸ивать**) **1.** to overestimate, overrate. **2.** to revalue, reappraise.
переоцéнк|а, и *f.* **1.** overestimation. **2.** reappraisal, reassessment.
перепáд, а *m.* (*tech.*) overfall; differential; drop.
перепадá|ть, ю *impf. of* **перепáсть**
перепáива|ть, ю *impf. of* **перепои́ть**
перепáлк|а, и *f.* (*coll.*) exchange of fire, skirmish (*also fig.*).
перепá|сть, дёт, *past* **~л** *pf.* (*of* **~дáть**) (*coll.*) **1.** to fall intermittently. **2.** (*impers.*; +*d.*) to fall to one's lot.
перепáчка|ть, ю *pf.* to make all dirty.

перепа́чка|ться, юсь *pf.* to get o.s. all dirty.
перепе́в, а *m.* repetition, rehash.
пе́репел, а, *pl.* **~а́** *m.* (*zool.*) quail.
перепелен|а́ть, а́ю *pf.* (*of* **~ывать**): **п. ребёнка** to change a baby.
перепелёныва|ть, ю *impf. of* **перепелена́ть**
перепёлк|а, и *f.* (*zool.*) female quail.
перепеля́тник, а *m.* sparrow-hawk.
перепе́рчива|ть, ю *impf. of* **перепе́рчить**
перепе́рч|ить, у, ишь *pf.* (*of* **~ивать**) to put too much pepper into.
перепеча́т|ать, аю *pf.* (*of* **~ывать**) **1.** to reprint. **2.** to type (out).
перепеча́тк|а, и *f.* **1.** reprinting. **2.** reprint.
перепеча́тыва|ть, ю *impf. of* **перепеча́тать**
перепива́|ть(ся), ю(сь) *impf. of* **перепи́ть(ся)**
перепи́лива|ть, ю *impf. of* **перепили́ть**
перепил|и́ть¹**, ю́, ~ишь** *pf.* (*of* **~ивать**) to saw in two.
перепил|и́ть²**, ю́, ~ишь** *pf.* to saw (*all or a number of*).
перепи|са́ть¹**, шу́, ~шешь** *pf.* (*of* **~сывать**) **1.** to re-write; **п. на́бело** to make a fair copy (of). **2.** to re-copy.
перепи|са́ть²**, шу́, ~шешь** *pf.* (*of* **~сывать**) to make a list (of), list; **п. всех прису́тствующих** to take the names of all those present.
перепи́ск|а, и *f.* **1.** copying. **2.** correspondence; **быть в ~е (с**+*i.*) to be in correspondence (with). **3.** (*collect.*) correspondence, letters.
перепи́счик, а *m.* copyist.
перепи́сыва|ть, ю *impf. of* **переписа́ть**
перепи́сыва|ться, юсь *impf.* (**с**+*i.*) to correspond (with).
пе́репис|ь, и *f.* **1.** census. **2.** inventory.
переп|и́ть, ью́, ьёшь, *past* **~и́л, ~ила́, ~и́ло** *pf.* (*of* **~ива́ть**) (*coll.*) **1.** to drink excessively. **2.** to out-drink; to drink under the table.
переп|и́ться, ью́сь, ьёшься, *past* **~и́лся, ~ила́сь, ~и́ло́сь** *pf.* (*of* **~ива́ться**) (*coll.*) to get completely drunk.
перепла́в|ить¹**, лю, ишь** *pf.* (*of* **~ля́ть**) to smelt.
перепла́в|ить²**, лю, ишь** *pf.* (*of* **~ля́ть**) to float; to raft.
переплавля́|ть, ю *impf. of* **перепла́вить**
перепла́т|а, ы *f.* surplus payment.
перепла|ти́ть, чу́, ~тишь *pf.* (*of* **~чивать**) to overpay; to pay excessively.
перепла́чива|ть, ю *impf. of* **переплати́ть**
переплёвыва|ть, ю *impf. of* **переплю́нуть**
перепле|сти́¹**, ту́, тёшь,** *past* **~ёл, ~ла́** *pf.* (*of* **~та́ть**) **1.** to bind (*books*). **2.** (+*i.*) to interlace (with), interknit (with).
перепле|сти́¹**, ту́, тёшь,** *past* **~ёл, ~ла́** *pf.* (*of* **~та́ть**) to braid again, plait again.
перепле|сти́сь, тётся, *past* **~ёлся, ~ла́сь** *pf.* (*of* **~та́ться**) **1.** to interlace, interweave. **2.** (*fig.*) to get mixed up.
переплёт, а *m.* **1.** binding; **отда́ть кни́гу в п.** to have a book bound. **2.** binding, cover. **3.** transom (*of door or window*); **око́нный п.** window-sash. **4.** (*coll.*) mess, scrape; **попа́сть в п.** to get into a mess, get into trouble.
переплета́|ть(ся), ю(сь) *impf. of* **переплести́(сь)**
переплётн|ая, ой *f.* bindery.
переплётчик, а *m.* bookbinder.
переплыва́|ть, ю *impf. of* **переплы́ть**
переплы́|ть, ву́, вёшь, *past* **~л, ~ла́, ~ло** *pf.* (*of* **~ва́ть**) to swim (across); to sail (across).
переплю́н|уть, у, ешь *pf.* (*of* **переплёвывать**) (*coll.*) to spit further than; (*fig.*) to outdo.
переподгота́влива|ть, ю *impf. of* **переподгото́вить**
переподгото́в|ить, лю, ишь *pf.* (*of* **переподгота́вливать**) to retrain.
переподгото́вк|а, и *f.* further training; retraining; **ку́рсы по ~е** refresher courses.
перепо|и́ть, ю́, ~и́шь *pf.* (*of* **перепа́ивать**) **1.** to give too much to drink (*to an animal*). **2.** (*coll.*) to make drunk.
переполз|а́ть, а́ю *impf. of* **~ти́**
переполз|ти́, у́, ёшь, *past* **~, ~ла́** *pf.* (*of* **~а́ть**) to crawl across; to creep across.
переполне́ни|е, я *nt.* overfilling; overcrowding.
перепо́лн|ить, ю, ишь *pf.* (*of* **~я́ть**) to overfill; to overcrowd.
перепо́лн|иться, ится *pf.* (*of* **~я́ться**) to overfill; to be overcrowded; **её се́рдце ~илось ра́достью** her heart overflowed with joy.
переполн|я́ть(ся), я́ю(сь) *impf. of* **~ить(ся)**
перепо́лох, а *m.* alarm; commotion, rumpus.
переполош|и́ть, у́, и́шь *pf.* (*coll.*) to alarm.
перепо́нк|а, и *f.* membrane; web (*of bat or waterfowl*); **бараба́нная п.** (*anat.*) ear-drum.
перепо́нчатый *adj.* membraneous, membranous; webbed; web-footed.
перепоруч|а́ть, а́ю *impf. of* **~и́ть**
перепоруч|и́ть, у́, ~ишь *pf.* (*of* **~а́ть**) (+*d.*) to turn over (to), reassign (to).
перепра́в|а, ы *f.* passage, crossing; ford.
перепра́в|ить¹**, лю, ишь** *pf.* (*of* **~ля́ть**) **1.** to convey, transport to; take across. **2.** to forward (*mail*).
перепра́в|ить²**, лю, ишь** *pf.* (*of* **~ля́ть**) (*coll.*) to correct.
перепра́в|иться, люсь, ишься *pf.* (*of* **~ля́ться**) to cross, get across; to swim across; to sail across.
переправля́|ть(ся), ю(сь) *impf. of* **перепра́вить(ся)**
перепрева́|ть, ю *impf. of* **перепре́ть**
перепре́|ть, ю *pf.* (*of* **~ва́ть**) **1.** to rot. **2.** (*coll.*) to be overdone, overcooked.
перепро́б|овать, ую *pf.* to taste (*all or a quantity of*); (*fig.*) to try.
перепрода|ва́ть, ю́, ёшь *impf. of* **~ть**
перепрода́ж|а, и *f.* re-sale.
перепрода́|ть, м, шь, ст, ди́м, ди́те, ду́т, *past* **перепро́дал, ~ла́, перепро́дало** *pf.* (*of* **~ва́ть**) to re-sell.
перепроизво́дств|о, а *nt.* overproduction.
перепры́гива|ть, ю *impf. of* **перепры́гнуть**
перепры́г|нуть, ну, нешь *pf.* (*of* **~ивать**) to jump (over).
перепу́г, а (у) *m.* (*coll.*): **с ~у, от ~у** in one's fright.
перепуга́|ть, ю *pf.* (*no impf.*) to give a fright.
перепуга́|ться, юсь *pf.* (*no impf.*) to get a fright.
перепу́т|ать, аю *pf.* (*of* **~ывать**) **1.** to entangle. **2.** (*fig.*) to confuse, mix up, muddle up.
перепу́т|аться, аюсь *pf.* (*of* **~ываться**) **1.** to get entangled. **2.** (*fig.*) to get confused, get mixed up.
перепу́тыва|ть(ся), ю(сь) *impf. of* **перепу́тать(ся)**
перепу́ть|е, я *nt.* cross-roads; **быть на п.** (*fig.*) to be at the cross-roads.
перераба́тыва|ть(ся), ю(сь) *impf. of* **перерабо́тать(ся)**
перерабо́та|ть¹**, ю** *pf.* (*of* **перераба́тывать**) **1.** to process; (**в, на**+*a.*) to make (into); to convert (to); **п. свёклу в са́хар** to convert beet to sugar; **п. пи́щу** to digest food. **2.** to re-make; (*fig.*) to rework, revise; **п. статью́** to rework an article.
перерабо́та|ть²**, ю** *pf.* (*of* **перераба́тывать**) (*coll.*) **1.** to work overtime. **2.** to overwork.
перерабо́тк|а¹**, и** *f.* **1.** processing; treatment. **2.** remaking; (*fig.*) reworking.
перерабо́тк|а²**, и** *f.* overtime work.
перераспределе́ни|е, я *nt.* re-distribution.
перераспредел|и́ть, ю́, и́шь *pf.* (*of* **~я́ть**) to re-distribute.

перераспредел|я́ть, я́ю *impf. of* **~и́ть**
перераста́ни|е, я *nt.* **1.** outgrowing. **2.** (**в**+*a.*) growing (into), development (into). **3.** (*mil.*) escalation.
перераст|а́ть, а́ю *impf. of* **~и́**
перераст|и́, у́, ёшь, *past* **перербс, переросла́** *pf.* (*of* **~а́ть**) **1.** to outgrow. **2.** (*fig.*; **в**+*a.*) to grow (into), develop (into), turn (into).
перерасхо́д, а *m.* **1.** over-expenditure. **2.** (*fin.*) overdraft.
перерасхо́д|овать, ую *pf.* (*no impf.*) **1.** to spend to excess. **2.** (*fin.*) to overdraw.
перерв|а́ть, у́, ёшь, *past* **~а́л, ~ала́, ~а́ло** *pf.* (*of* **перерыва́ть**[1]) to break, tear asunder.
перере́|зать[1]**, жу, жешь** *pf.* (*of* **~за́ть** *and* **~зывать**) **1.** to cut. **2.** (*fig.*) to cut off; **п. путь неприя́телю** to bar the enemy's way.
перере́|зать[2]**, жу, жешь** *pf.* to kill, slaughter (*all or a number of*).
перерез|а́ть, а́ю *impf. of* **^ать**[1]
перере́зыва|ть, ю *impf.* = **перереза́ть**
перереш|а́ть[1]**, а́ю** *impf. of* **~и́ть**
перереш|а́ть[2]**, а́ю** *pf.* to solve (*all or a number of problems*).
перереш|и́ть, у́, и́шь *pf.* (*of* **~а́ть**[1]) **1.** to decide, settle in a different way. **2.** to change one's mind.
переро|ди́ть, жу́, ди́шь *pf.* (*of* **~жда́ть**) to regenerate.
переро|ди́ться, жу́сь, ди́шься *pf.* (*of* **~жда́ться**) **1.** (*coll.*) to be re-born. **2.** (*fig.*) to be regenerated. **3.** (*biol. and fig.*) to degenerate.
перерожде́ни|е, я *nt.* **1.** regeneration. **2.** degeneration.
переро́ст|ок, ка *m.* (*coll.*) slow developer.
переруб|а́ть, а́ю *impf. of* **~и́ть**
переруб|и́ть, лю́, ^ишь *pf.* (*of* **~а́ть**) to chop in two.
переруга́|ться, юсь *pf.* (*coll.*; **с**+*i.*) to fall out (with).
переры́в, а *m.* interval, break, intermission; **обе́денный п.** lunch break; **с ~ами** off and on.
перерыва́|ть[1]**, ю** *impf. of* **перерва́ть**
перерыва́|ть[2]**, ю** *impf. of* **переры́ть**
перер|ы́ть, о́ю, о́ешь *pf.* (*of* **~ыва́ть**[2]) **1.** to dig up. **2.** (*fig., coll.*) to rummage (in).
переря|ди́ть, жу́, ^ди́шь *pf.* (*of* **^живать**) (+*i.*; *coll.*) to disguise (as), dress up (as).
переря|ди́ться, жу́сь, ^ди́шься *pf.* (*of* **^живаться**) (+*i.*; *coll.*) to disguise o.s. *or* dress up (as).
переря́жива|ть(ся), ю(сь) *impf. of* **переряди́ть(ся)**
переса|ди́ть, жу́, ^дишь *pf.* (*of* **^живать**) **1.** to make s.o. change his seat. **2.: п. кого́-н. че́рез что-н.** to help s.o. across sth. **3.** (*bot.*) to transplant. **4.** (*med.*) to graft.
переса́дк|а, и *f.* **1.** (*bot.*) transplantation. **2.** (*med.*) transplant; grafting; **опера́ция по ~е се́рдца** heart transplant operation. **3.** (*on rail.*) change.
переса́жива|ть, ю *impf. of* **пересади́ть**
переса́жива|ться, юсь *impf. of* **пересе́сть**
переса́лива|ть, ю *impf. of* **пересоли́ть**
пересда|ва́ть, ю́, ёшь *impf. of* **^ть**
пересда́|ть, м, шь, сь, ди́м, ди́те, ду́т, *past* **~л, ~ла́, ^ло** *pf.* (*of* **~ва́ть**) **1.** to re-let; to sub-let. **2.** (*cards*) to re-deal. **3.** (*coll.*) to re-sit (*an examination*).
пересека́|ть(ся), ю(сь) *impf. of* **пересе́чь(ся)**
переселе́н|ец, ца *m.* **1.** migrant, emigrant; immigrant. **2.** settler.
переселе́ни|е, я *nt.* **1.** migration, emigration; immigration, re-settlement. **2.** move (*to new place of residence*).
переселе́н|ческий *adj. of* **~ец; ~ческая организа́ция** re-settlement organization.
пересел|и́ть, ю́, и́шь *pf.* (*of* **~я́ть**) to move; to transplant; to resettle.
пересел|и́ться, ю́сь, и́шься *pf.* (*of* **~я́ться**) to move; to migrate.
пересел|я́ть(ся), я́ю(сь) *impf. of* **~и́ть(ся)**
перес|е́сть, я́ду, я́дешь *pf.* (*of* **~а́живаться**) **1.** to change one's seat. **2.** to change (*trains, etc.*).
пересече́ни|е, я *nt.* crossing, intersection; **то́чка ~я** point of intersection.
перес|ечённый *p.p.p. of* **~е́чь**[1]; **~ечённая ме́стность** (*geog.*) broken terrain.
пересе́|чь, ку́, чёшь, ку́т, *past* **~к, ~кла́** *pf.* (*of* **~ка́ть**) **1.** to cross; to traverse; **п. у́лицу** to cross the road; **п. путь неприя́телю** (*fig.*) to cut the enemy off. **2.** to cross, intersect.
пересе́|чься, чётся, ку́тся, *past* **~кся, ~кла́сь** *pf.* (*of* **~ка́ться**) to cross, intersect.
переси|де́ть, жу́, ди́шь *pf.* (*of* **^живать**) **1.** (*coll.*) to out-sit; **он ~де́л всех други́х госте́й** he out-stayed all the other guests. **2.** to sit too long.
переси́жива|ть, ю *impf. of* **пересиде́ть**
переси́лива|ть, ю *impf. of* **переси́лить**
переси́л|ить, ю, ишь *pf.* (*of* **~ивать**) to overpower; (*fig.*) to overcome, master.
переска́з, а *m.* **1.** retelling. **2.** exposition.
переска|за́ть, жу́, ^жешь *pf.* (*of* **^зывать**) to re-tell, narrate; **~жи́(те) мне содержа́ние э́того рома́на** tell me the story of this novel (in your own words).
переска́зыва|ть, ю *impf. of* **пересказа́ть**
переска́кива|ть, ю *impf. of* **перескочи́ть**
перескоч|и́ть, у́, ^ишь *pf.* (*of* **переска́кивать**) **1.** (+*a. or* **че́рез**) to jump (over); (*fig.*; *in reading*) to skip (over). **2.** (*fig.*) to skip; **п. с одно́й те́мы на другу́ю** to skip from one topic to another.
пересла|сти́ть, щу́, сти́шь *pf.* (*of* **^щивать**) to oversweeten, put too much sugar (into).
пере|сла́ть, шлю́, шлёшь *pf.* (*of* **~сыла́ть**) to send; to remit; to forward.
пересла́щива|ть, ю *impf. of* **пересласти́ть**
пересма́трива|ть, ю *impf. of* **пересмотре́ть**
пересме́ива|ться, юсь *impf.* (*coll.*; **с**+*i.*) to exchange smiles (with).
пересме́шк|а, и *f.* (*coll.*) mockery, banter.
пересме́шник, а *m.* **1.** (*coll.*) mocker. **2.** (*zool.*) mocking-bird.
пересмо́тр, а *m.* **1.** revision. **2.** reconsideration; review.
пересмотр|е́ть[1]**, ю́, ^ишь** *pf.* (*of* **пересма́тривать**) **1.** to revise; to go over again. **2.** to re-consider; to review. **3.** to go through (*in search of sth.*).
пересмотр|е́ть[2]**, ю́, ^ишь** *pf.* to have seen (*all or a quantity of*); to have gone all through.
переснима́|ть, ю *impf. of* **пересня́ть**
пересн|я́ть, иму́, и́мешь, *past* **~я́л, ~яла́, ~я́ло** *pf.* (*of* **~има́ть**) **1.** to photograph again, take another photo (of). **2.** to make a copy.
пересозда|ва́ть, ю́, ёшь *impf. of* **^ть**
пересозда́|ть, м, шь, ст, ди́м, ди́те, ду́т, *past* **~л, ~ла́, ~ло** *pf.* (*of* **~ва́ть**) to re-create.
пересо́л, а *m.* excess of salt.
пересол|и́ть, ю́, ^ишь *pf.* (*of* **переса́ливать**) **1.** to put too much salt (into). **2.** (*fig., coll.*) to go too far.
пересо́х|нуть, нет, *past* **~, ~ла** *pf.* (*of* **пересыха́ть**) to dry out; to dry up, become parched.
пересп|а́ть, лю́, и́шь, *past* **~а́л, ~ала́, ~а́ло** *pf.* (*coll.*) **1.** to oversleep. **2.** to spend the night. **3.** (**с**+*i.*; *euph.*) to sleep (with).
переспе́лый *adj.* overripe.
переспо́р|ить, ю, ишь *pf.* to defeat in an argument.
переспра́шива|ть, ю *impf. of* **переспроси́ть**
переспро|си́ть[1]**, шу́, ^сишь** *pf.* (*of* **переспра́шивать**) to ask again; to ask to repeat.
переспро|си́ть[2]**, шу́, ^сишь** *pf.* to question (*all or a number of*).
перессо́р|ить, ю, ишь *pf.* (*coll.*) to set at odds.

пересcóр|иться, юсь, ишься *pf.* (*coll.*; **с**+*i.*) to quarrel (with), fall out (with).
переста|вáть, ю́, ёшь *impf. of* **∸ть**
перестáв|ить, лю, ишь *pf.* (*of* **~ля́ть**) to move, shift; **п. мéбель** to re-arrange the furniture; **п. словá во фрáзе** to transpose the words in a sentence.
переставля́|ть, ю *impf. of* **перестáвить**
перестáива|ть, ю *impf. of* **перестоя́ть**
перестанóвк|а, и *f.* **1.** re-arrangement, transposition. **2.** (*math.*) permutation.
перестарá|ться, юсь *pf.* (*coll.*) to overdo it.
перестá|ть, ну, нешь *pf.* (*of* **~вáть**) (+*inf.*) to stop, cease.
перестел|и́ть, ю́, ∸ешь *pf.* (*coll.*) = **перестлáть**
перестилá|ть, ю *impf. of* **перестели́ть** *and* **перестлáть**
перестир|áть[1], **áю** *pf.* (*of* **∸ывать**) to wash again.
перестир|áть[2], **áю** *pf.* (*no impf.*) to wash (*all or a number of*).
перести́рыва|ть, ю *impf. of* **перестирáть**[1]
перест|лáть, елю́, éлешь *pf.* (*of* **~илáть**) to re-lay; **п. пол** to re-lay a floor; **п. постéль** to re-make a bed.
пересто|я́ть, ю́, и́шь *pf.* (*of* **перестáивать**) stand too long.
перестрадá|ть, ю *pf.* (*no impf.*) to have suffered, have gone through.
перестрáива|ть(ся), ю(сь) *impf. of* **перестрóить(ся)**
перестрах|овáть, ýю *pf.* (*of* **~óвывать**) to re-insure.
перестрах|овáться, ýюсь *pf.* (*of* **~óвываться**) **1.** to re-insure o.s. **2.** (*fig.*, *pej.*) to play safe.
перестрахóвк|а, и *f.* **1.** re-insurance. **2.** (*fig.*, *pej.*) playing safe.
перестрахóвыва|ть(ся), ю(сь) *impf. of* **перестраховáть(ся)**
перестрéлива|ть, ю *impf. of* **перестреля́ть**
перестрéлива|ться, юсь *impf.* to exchange fire, to shoot it out.
перестрéлк|а, и *f.* exchange of fire; shootout.
перестрел|я́ть, я́ю *pf.* (*of* **∸ивать**) **1.** to shoot (down). **2.** to use up, expend (*in shooting*).
перестрó|ить, ю, ишь *pf.* (*of* **перестрáивать**) **1.** to rebuild, reconstruct. **2.** to re-design, re-fashion, re-shape; to reorganize; **п. фрáзу** to rejig a sentence. **3.** (*mil.*) to re-form. **4.** (*mus.*, *radio*) to re-tune.
перестрó|иться, юсь, ишься *pf.* (*of* **перестрáиваться**) **1.** to re-form; to reorganize o.s.; to restructure. **2.** (*mil.*) to re-form. **3.** (*radio*) (**на**+*a.*) to re-tune, switch over (to); **п. на корóткую волнý** to switch over to short wave.
перестрóйк|а, и *f.* **1.** rebuilding, reconstruction; (*pol.*, *econ.*) perestroika. **2.** reorganization. **3.** (*mil.*) re-formation. **4.** (*mus.*, *radio*) re-tuning.
переступ|áть, áю *impf.* **1.** *impf. of* **~и́ть**. **2.** (*impf. only*) to move slowly; **он éле ~áл (ногáми)** his feet would hardly carry him; **п. с ноги́ нá ногу** to shift from one foot to the other.
переступ|и́ть, лю́, ∸ишь *pf.* (*of* **~áть**) (+*a. or* **чéрез**) to step over; (*fig.*) to overstep; **п. порóг** to cross the threshold; **п. закóн** to break the law.
пересýд, а *m.* (*coll.*) re-trial.
пересýд|ы, ов *no sg.* (*coll.*) gossip.
пересýшива|ть, ю *impf. of* **пересуши́ть**[1]
пересуш|и́ть[1], **ý, ∸ишь** *pf.* (*of* **∸ивать**) to overdry.
пересуш|и́ть[2], **ý, ∸ишь** *pf.* (*no impf.*) to dry (*all or a quantity of*).
пересчит|áть[1], **áю** *pf.* (*of* **∸ывать**) **1.** to re-count. **2.** (**на**+*a.*) to convert (to).
пересчит|áть[2], **áю** *pf.* (*no impf.*) to count.
пересчи́тыва|ть, ю *impf. of* **пересчитáть**[1]
пересылá|ть, ю *impf. of* **переслáть**
пересы́лк|а, и *f.* sending; forwarding; remittance; **стóимость ~и** postage.
пересы́льн|ый *adj.* transit; **~ая тюрьмá** transit prison.
пересы́п|ать[1], **лю, лешь** *pf.* (*of* **~áть**) to pour (*dry substance*) into another container; **п. зернó в мешки́** to pour off grain into bags.
пересы́п|ать[2], **лю, лешь** *pf.* (*of* **~áть**) (+*i.*) **1.** to powder (with). **2.** (*fig.*) to intersperse, lard (with).
пересып|áть, áю *impf. of* **∸ать**
пересыхá|ть, ет *impf. of* **пересóхнуть**
перетáплива|ть, ю *impf. of* **перетопи́ть**[1]
перетаск|áть, áю *pf.* (*of* **∸ивать**) to carry away.
перетáскива|ть, ю *impf. of* **перетаскáть** *and* **перетащи́ть**
перетас|овáть, ýю *pf.* (*of* **~óвывать**) to re-shuffle (*cards, also fig.*).
перетасóвыва|ть, ю *impf. of* **перетасовáть**
перетащ|и́ть, ý, ∸ишь *pf.* (*of* **перетáскивать**) to drag over; to carry over; to move, shift; **п. сундýк на чердáк** to drag a trunk into the attic.
пере|терéть, трý, трёшь, *past* **~тёр, ~тёрла** *pf.* (*of* **~тирáть**) **1.** to wear out, wear down. **2.** (**в**+*a.*) to grind (into).
пере|терéться, трётся, *past* **~тёрся, ~тёрлась** *pf.* (*of* **~тирáться**) **1.** to wear out, wear through. **2.** *pass. of* **~терéть**
перетерп|éть, лю́, ∸ишь *pf.* (*coll.*) to suffer, endure.
перетирá|ть(ся), ю(сь) *impf. of* **перетерéть(ся)**
перетóлк|и, ов *no sg.* (*coll.*) tittle-tattle.
перетолк|овáть[1], **ýю** *pf.* (*no impf.*) (*coll.*) to talk over, discuss; **нáдо нам с тобóй об э́том п.** we must talk it over.
перетолк|овáть[2], **ýю** *pf.* (*of* **~óвывать**) (*coll.*) to misinterpret.
перетолкóвыва|ть, ю *impf. of* **перетолковáть**[2]
перетоп|и́ть[1], **лю́, ∸ишь** *pf.* (*of* **перетáпливать**) to melt.
перетоп|и́ть[2], **лю́, ∸ишь** *pf.* (*coll.*) to heat; to kindle.
пере|трý, трёшь, тёр, тёрла *see* **~терéть**
перетряс|áть, áю *impf. of* **~ти́**
перетряс|ти́, ý, ёшь, *past* **∸, ~лá** *pf.* (*of* **~áть**) to shake up.
перéть, пру, прёшь, *past* **пёр, пёрла** *impf.* (*coll.*) **1.** to go, make one's way. **2.** to push, press. **3.** to drag. **4.** to come out; to appear, show.
перетя́гивани|е, я *nt.*: **п. канáта** (*sport*) tug-of-war.
перетя́гива|ть(ся), ю(сь) *impf. of* **перетянýть(ся)**
перетя|нýть[1], **нý, ∸нешь** *pf.* (*of* **∸гивать**) **1.** to pull (*somewhere else*; *from A to B*). **2.** (*fig.*, *coll.*) to pull over, attract; **п. на свою стóрону** to win over. **3.** to pull in too tight. **4.** to outbalance, outweigh.
перетя|нýть[2], **нý, ∸нешь** *pf.* (*of* **∸гивать**) to stretch again.
перетя|нýться, нýсь, ∸нешься *pf.* (*of* **∸гиваться**) to lace o.s. too tight.
переубе|ди́ть, ди́шь *pf.* (*of* **~ждáть**) to make change one's mind.
переубе|ди́ться, ди́шься *pf.* (*of* **~ждáться**) to change one's mind.
переубеждá|ть(ся), ю(сь) *impf. of* **переубеди́ть(ся)**
переýл|ок, ка *m.* lane, side-street.
переустрóйств|о, а *nt.* reconstruction.
переутом|и́ть, лю́, и́шь *pf.* (*of* **~ля́ть**) to tire out; to overwork.
переутом|и́ться, лю́сь, и́шься *pf.* (*of* **~ля́ться**) to tire o.s. out; to overwork; (*pf. only*) to be run down.
переутомлéни|е, я *nt.* exhaustion; overwork.
переутомля́|ть(ся), ю(сь) *impf. of* **переутоми́ть(ся)**
переуч|éсть, тý, тёшь, *past* **~ёл, ~лá** *pf.* (*of* **~и́тывать**) to take stock.

переучёт, а *m.* stock-taking.
переу́чива|ть(ся), ю(сь) *impf. of* **переучи́ть(ся)**
переучи́тыва|ть, ю *impf. of* **переуче́сть**
переуч|и́ть, у́, ~ишь *pf.* (*of* **~ивать**) to teach again.
переуч|и́ться, у́сь ~ишься *pf.* (*of* **~иваться**) **1.** to relearn. **2.** (*coll.*) to study too much.
переформир|ова́ть, у́ю *pf.* (*of* **~о́вывать**) (*mil.*) to re-form.
переформиро́выва|ть, ю *impf. of* **переформирова́ть**
перефрази́р|овать, ую *impf. and pf.* to paraphrase.
перефразиро́вк|а, и *f.* paraphrase.
перехва́лива|ть, ю *impf. of* **перехвали́ть**
перехвал|и́ть, ю́, ~ишь *pf.* (*of* **~ивать**) to over-praise.
перехва́т, а *m.* interception.
перехва|ти́ть, чу́, ~тишь *pf.* (*of* **~тывать**) **1.** to intercept; to catch. **2.** to take in. **3.** (*coll.*) to grab a bite to eat. **4.** (*coll.*) to borrow (*for a short time*). **5.** (*coll.*) to overshoot the mark.
перехва́тчик, а *m.* (*aeron.*) interceptor.
перехва́тыва|ть, ю *impf. of* **перехвати́ть**
перехитр|и́ть, ю́, и́шь *pf.* to outwit.
перехо́д, а *m.* **1.** passage, transition; crossing; switch; **подзе́мный п.** underpass, subway. **2.** (*mil.*) (day's) march. **3.** (*relig.*) going over, conversion.
перехо|ди́ть[1], **жу́, ~дишь** *impf. of* **перейти́**
перехо|ди́ть[2], **жу́, ~дишь** *pf.* (*no impf.*) (*coll.*) to go all over.
перехо|ди́ть[3], **жу́, ~дишь** *pf.* (*no impf.*) (*coll.*; *at games*) to have one's turn again, make one's move again.
перехо́дный *adj.* **1.** transitional. **2.** (*gram.*) transitive. **3.** (*tech.*) transient.
переход|я́щий *pres. part. of* **~и́ть** *and adj.* **1.** transient, transitory; **п. ку́бок** (*sport*) challenge cup. **2.** intermittent. **3.** (*fin.*) brought forward, carried over.
пе́р|ец, ца *m.* pepper; **стручко́вый п.** capsicum.
перецара́па|ться, юсь *pf.* **1.** to scratch o.s. **2.** to scratch each other.
пе́реч|ень, ня *m.* list; enumeration.
перечёркива|ть, ю *impf. of* **перечеркну́ть**
перечерк|ну́ть, ну́, нёшь *pf.* (*of* **~ивать**) to cross (out), cancel.
перечер|ти́ть, чу́, ~тишь *pf.* (*of* **~чивать**) **1.** to draw again. **2.** to copy, trace.
перече́рчива|ть, ю *impf. of* **перечерти́ть**
пере|че́сть[1], **чту́, чтёшь,** *past* **~чёл, ~ла́** *pf.* = **~счита́ть**[2]; **их мо́жно по па́льцам п.** you could count them on the fingers of one hand.
пере|че́сть[2], **чту́, чтёшь,** *past* **~чёл, ~ла́** *pf.* = **~чита́ть**
перечи́нива|ть, ю *impf. of* **перечини́ть**[1]
перечин|и́ть[1], **ю́, ~ишь** *pf.* (*of* **~ивать**) to mend again, repair again.
перечин|и́ть[2], **ю́, ~ишь** *pf.* to mend, repair (*all or a number of*).
перечисле́ни|е, я *nt.* **1.** enumeration. **2.** (*fin.*) transfer.
перечи́сл|ить, ю, ишь *pf.* (*of* **~я́ть**) **1.** to enumerate. **2.** to transfer.
перечисл|я́ть, я́ю *impf. of* **~ить**
перечит|а́ть[1], **а́ю** *pf.* (*of* **~ывать**) to re-read.
перечит|а́ть[2], **а́ю** *pf.* to read (*all or a quantity of*).
пере́ч|ить, у, ишь *impf.* (*no pf.*) (+*d.*; *coll.*) to contradict; to go against.
пе́речниц|а, ы *f.* pepper-pot.
пе́ре|чный *adj. of* **~ц**
перечу́вств|овать, ую *pf.* (*no impf.*) to feel, experience.
переша́гива|ть, ю *impf. of* **перешагну́ть**
перешаг|ну́ть, ну́, нёшь *pf.* (*of* **~ивать**) to step over; **п. (че́рез) поро́г** to cross the threshold.
переше́|ек, йка *m.* isthmus.
перешёптыва|ться, юсь *impf.* to whisper to one another.
перешиб|а́ть, а́ю *impf. of* **~и́ть**
перешиб|и́ть, у́, ёшь, *past* **~, ~ла** *pf.* (*of* **~а́ть**) (*coll.*) to break, fracture.
перешива́|ть, ю *impf. of* **переши́ть**
переши́вк|а, и *f.* alteration (*of clothes*).
переш|и́ть, ью́, ьёшь *pf.* (*of* **~ива́ть**) to alter; to have altered.
перещеголя́|ть, ю *pf.* (*no impf.*) (*coll.*) to outdo, surpass.
переэкзамен|ова́ть, у́ю *pf.* (*of* **~о́вывать**) to re-examine.
переэкзамен|ова́ться, у́юсь *pf.* (*of* **~о́вываться**) to resit an examination.
переэкзамено́вк|а, и *f.* re-examination, resit.
переэкзамено́выва|ть(ся), ю(сь) *impf. of* **переэкзаменова́ть(ся)**
периге́|й, я *m.* (*astron.*) perigee.
периге́ли|й, я *m.* (*astron.*) perihelion.
перика́рд, а *m.* (*anat.*) pericardium.
пери́л|а, ~ *no sg.* rail(ing); handrail; banisters.
пери́метр, а *m.* (*math.*) perimeter.
пери́н|а, ы *f.* feather-bed.
пери́од, а *m.* period; **леднико́вый п.** (*geol.*) ice age.
перио́дик|а, и *f.* (*collect.*) periodicals.
периоди́ческ|ий *adj.* periodic; recurring; **~ая дробь** recurring decimal; **~ое изда́ние** periodical; **~ое явле́ние** recurrent phenomenon.
периоди́ч|ный (~ен, ~на) *adj.* periodic.
перипате́тик, а *m.* (*hist. phil.*) peripatetic.
перипат|ети́ческий *adj. of* **~е́тик**
перипети́|я, и *f.* reversal of fortune, upheaval.
периско́п, а *m.* periscope.
пе́ристо-кучево́й *adj.* (*meteor.*) cirro-cumulus.
пе́ристы|й *adj.* **1.** (*zool.*, *bot.*) pinnate. **2.** feather-like, plumose; **~е облака́** fleecy clouds; cirri.
перитони́т, а *m.* (*med.*) peritonitis.
перифери́йный *adj.* provincial.
перифери́ческий *adj.* peripheral.
перифери́|я, и *f.* **1.** periphery. **2.** (*collect.*) the provinces; the outlying districts. **3.** (*comput.*) peripherals, peripheral devices.
перифра́з|а, ы *f.* periphrasis.
перифрасти́ческий *adj.* periphrastic.
пёрк|а, и *f.* (*tech.*) (drill) bit.
перка́л|ь, и *f.* (*and* **~я,** *m.*) (*text.*) percale.
перколя́тор, а *m.* (coffee) percolator.
перку́сси|я, и *f.* (*med.*) percussion.
перл, а *m.* pearl (*fig.*).
перламу́тр, а *m.* mother-of-pearl.
перламу́тр|овый *adj. of* **~**
пе́рлин|ь, я *m.* (*naut.*) hawser.
перло́в|ый *adj.*: **~ая крупа́** pearl barley.
перлюстра́ци|я, и *f.* censorship (*opening and inspection of correspondence*).
пермане́нт, а *m.* permanent wave.
пермане́нтный *adj.* permanent.
перна́т|ый (~, ~а) *adj.* feathered, feathery.
пёр|нуть, нет (*inst. pf. of* **~де́ть**) (*vulg.*) to fart.
пер|о́, а́, *pl.* **~ья, ~ьев** *nt.* **1.** feather; **ни пу́ха, ни ~а́!** good luck! **2.** pen; **взя́ться за п.** (*fig.*) to take up the pen; **владе́ть ~о́м** to wield a skilful pen; **про́ба ~а́** (*fig.*) first attempt at writing.
перочи́нный *adj.*: **п. нож** pen-knife.
перпендикуля́р, а *m.* (*math.*) perpendicular.
перпендикуля́р|ный (~ен, ~на) *adj.* perpendicular.
перро́н, а *m.* platform (*at rail. station*).
перро́н|ный *adj. of* **~**; **п. биле́т** platform ticket.
перс, а *m.* Persian.
перси́дский *adj.* Persian.

Перси́дск|ий зали́в, ~ого ~а *m.* the Persian Gulf.
пе́рсик, а *m.* **1.** peach. **2.** peach-tree.
пе́рсик|овый *adj. of* ~; peachy; **~овое де́рево** peach-tree.
Пе́рси|я, и *f.* Persia.
перс|ия́нка, ия́нки *f. of* ~
персо́н|а, ы *f.* person; **яви́ться со́бственной ~ой** (*iron.*) to appear in person; **п. гра́та** persona grata; **обе́д на́ шесть ~** dinner for six.
персона́ж, а *m.* (*liter.*) character; (*fig.*) personage.
персона́л, а *m.* personnel, staff.
персона́льный *adj.* personal; individual.
перспекти́в|а, ы *f.* **1.** (*art*) perspective. **2.** vista, prospect. **3.** (*fig.*) prospect, outlook; **име́ть ~у** to have prospects, have a future (before one).
перспекти́в|ный *adj.* **1.** (*art*) perspective. **2.** long-term, long-range; **~ное плани́рование** (*econ.*) long-term planning. **3.** (**~ен, ~на**) promising; **~ная молода́я балери́на** a promising young ballerina.
перст, а́ *m.* (*obs.*) finger; **оди́н, как п.** all alone.
пе́рст|ень, ня *m.* ring.
Перу́ *f. indecl.* Peru.
перуа́н|ец, ца *m.* Peruvian.
перуа́н|ка, ки *f. of* **~ец**
перуа́нский *adj.* Peruvian.
перфе́кт, а *m.* (*gram.*) perfect (tense).
перфока́рт|а, ы *f.* punched card.
перфоле́нт|а, ы *f.* punched tape.
перфора́тор, а *m.* (*tech.*) **1.** perforator; punch. **2.** drill, boring machine.
перфора́ци|я, и *f.* (*tech.*) **1.** perforation, punching. **2.** drilling, boring.
перфори́р|овать, ую *impf. and pf.* (*tech.*) **1.** to perforate, punch. **2.** to drill, bore.
перха́|ть, ю *impf.* (*no pf.*) (*coll.*) to cough (*in order to clear the throat*).
перхо́т|а, ы *f.* (*coll.*) tickling in the throat.
пе́рхот|ь, и *f.* dandruff.
перцо́вк|а, и *f.* pepper-brandy.
перцо́вый *adj. of* **пе́рец**
перча́тк|а, и *f.* glove; gauntlet; **бро́сить ~у** (*fig.*) to throw down the gauntlet.
пе́рч|ить, у, ишь *impf.* (*of* **на~** *and* **по~**) (*coll.*) to pepper.
перш|и́ть, и́т *impf.* (*coll.*; *impers.*): **у меня́ в го́рле ~и́т** I have a tickle in my throat.
пёрыш|ко, ка, *pl.* **~ки, ~ек, ~кам** *nt.* (*coll.*) *dim. of* **перо́; лёгкий, как п.** light as a feather.
пёс, пса *m.* (*coll.*) dog.
пе́сенк|а, и *f.* song; **его́ п. спе́та** (*coll.*) he is done for; he has had it.
пе́сенник, а *m.* **1.** song-book. **2.** (chorus) singer. **3.** song-writer.
пе́с|енный *adj. of* **~ня**
песе́т|а, ы *f.* peseta.
пес|е́ц, ца́ *m.* polar fox; **голубо́й п.** blue fox (fur).
пёсик, а *m.* (*coll.*) *dim. of* **пёс**; doggie.
песка́р|ь, я́ *m.* gudgeon (*fish*).
песнопе́ни|е, я *nt.* **1.** (*eccl.*) psalm; canticle. **2.** (*poet.*) poetry, poesy.
песн|ь, и, *g. pl.* **~́ей** *f.* **1.** (*obs.*) song; **П. ~́ей** the Song of Songs. **2.** (*liter.*) canto, book.
пе́с|ня, ни, *g. pl.* **~ен** *f.* song; air; **до́лгая п.** (*fig.*, *coll.*) a long story; **э́то п. стара́** (*coll.*) it's the same old story; **тяну́ть всё ту же ~ню** (*coll.*) to harp on one string.
пес|о́к, ка́ *m.* **1.** sand; **золото́й п.** gold dust; **са́харный п.** granulated sugar; **стро́ить на ~ке́** (*fig.*) to build on sand. **2.** (*pl.*) sands; **зыбу́чие ~ки́** quicksands.
песо́чник, а *m.* (*zool.*) sand-piper.
песо́чниц|а, ы *f.* sand-pit.
песо́чн|ый *adj.* **1.** *adj. of* **песо́к**; sandy; **~ые часы́** hour-glass. **2.** (*cul.*) short; **~ое пече́нье** shortbread.
пессими́зм, а *m.* pessimism.
пессими́ст, а *m.* pessimist.
пессимисти́ческий *adj.* pessimistic.
пест, а́ *m.* pestle.
пе́стик[1], **а** *m.* (*bot.*) pistil.
пе́стик[2], **а** *m. dim. of* **пест**
пе́ст|овать, ую *impf.* (*of* **вы́~**) **1.** (*obs.*) to nurse. **2.** (*fig.*) to cherish, foster.
пестр|е́ть[1], **е́ет** *impf.* (*no pf.*) **1.** to become many-coloured. **2.** (*+i.*) to be gay (with); **корабли́ ~е́ли фла́гами** the ships were gay with bunting. **3.** to show colourfully (*of objects of different colours*).
пестр|е́ть[2], **и́т** *impf.* (*no pf.*) **1.** (*of many-coloured objects*) to strike the eye (*also fig.*); **его́ и́мя ~и́т в газе́тах** (*coll.*) he is always getting his name in the papers. **2.** (*coll.*) to be too gaudy, be flashy. **3.** (*+i.*) to abound (in); **письмо́ ~и́т оши́бками** the letter bristles with mistakes.
пестр|и́ть, ю́, и́шь *impf.* (*no pf.*) **1.** to make gaudy; to make colourful. **2.** (*impers.*): **у меня́ ~и́ло в глаза́х** I was dazzled (*sc.* by the colours).
пестрот|а́, ы́ *no pl.*, *f.* diversity of colours; (*fig.*) mixed character.
пёстр|ый (~, ~а́, ~о *and* **~о́)** *adj.* **1.** motley, variegated, multi-coloured. **2.** (*fig.*, *coll.*) mixed; **п. соста́в населе́ния** mixed population. **3.** (*fig.*) florid; pretentious, mannered; **п. слог** florid style.
песча́ник, а *m.* (*geol.*) sandstone.
песча́нк|а, и *f.* (*zool.*) sanderling.
песча́н|ый *adj.* sandy; **~ая коса́** sandbar; **п. холм** dune.
песчи́нк|а, и *f.* grain of sand.
пета́рд|а, ы *f.* **1.** (*hist. mil.*) petard. **2.** fire-cracker.
петербу́ргский = санкт-петербу́ргский
петербуржа́нка = санкт-петербуржа́нка
петербу́ржец = санкт-петербу́ржец
пети́ци|я, и *f.* petition.
петли́ц|а, ы *f.* **1.** buttonhole. **2.** tab (*on uniform collar*).
пе́т|ля, ли, *g. pl.* **~ель** *f.* **1.** loop; **мёртвая п.** (*aeron.*) loop; **сде́лать мёртвую ~лю** to loop the loop. **2.** (*fig.*) noose; **лезть в ~лю** to risk one's neck. **3.** buttonhole. **4.** stitch; **спусти́ть ~лю** to drop a stitch. **5.** hinge; **дверь соскочи́ла с ~ель** the door has come off its hinges.
петля́|ть, ю *impf.* (*coll.*) to dodge.
петру́шк|а[1], **и** *f.* parsley.
петру́шк|а[2], **и** *m.* **1.** Punch. **2.** Punch-and-Judy show.
пету́н|ия, ии *f.* (*bot.*) petunia.
пету́н|ья, ьи, *g. pl.* **~ий** *f.* = **~ия**
пету́х, а́ *m.* cock; **до ~о́в** before cock-crow; **встать с ~а́ми** to rise with the lark; **пусти́ть кра́сного ~а́** to start a fire, commit an act of arson.
пету́|ший *adj. of* **~х; п. гре́бень** cockscomb.
петуши́ный *adj. of* **пету́х; п. бой** cockfight(-ing).
петуш|и́ться, у́сь, и́шься *impf.* (*of* **вс~**) (*coll.*) to get on one's high horse; to take umbrage.
петуш|о́к, ка́ *m.* cockerel.
пе́т|ый *p.p.p. of* **~ь**; (*coll.*): **п. дура́к** perfect fool.
петь пою́, поёшь *impf.* (*of* **про~́** *and* **с~**) to sing; to chant, intone; **п. вполго́лоса** to hum; **п. другу́ю пе́сню** to sing another tune; **п. сла́ву** (*+d.*) to sing the praises (of).
пехо́т|а, ы *f.* infantry; **морска́я п.** (the) marines.
пехоти́н|ец, ца *m.* infantryman.
пехо́тный *adj.* infantry.
печа́л|ить, ю, ишь *impf.* (*of* **о~**) to grieve, sadden.
печа́л|иться, юсь, ишься *impf.* (*of* **о~**) to grieve, be sad.
печа́л|ь, и *f.* grief, sorrow.
печа́л|ьный (~ен, ~ьна) *adj.* sad; doleful.
печа́тани|е, я *nt.* printing.
печа́та|ть, ю *impf.* (*of* **на~**) to print; to type.

печа́та|ться, юсь *impf.* (*of* **на~**) **1.** to have (*literary compositions, etc.*) published; **он ещё нигде́ не ~лся** he had not yet had anything published. **2.** to be at the printer's.
печа́тк|а, и *f.* signet.
печа́тник, а *m.* printer.
печа́тн|ый *adj.* **1.** printing; **~ое де́ло** printing; **п. лист** printer's sheet. **2.** printed. **3.: писа́ть по ~ому, ~ыми бу́квами** to write in block capitals.
печа́т|ь¹, и *f.* seal, stamp (*also fig.*); **наложи́ть п.** (**на**+*a.*) to affix a seal (to); **носи́ть п.** (+*g.*) to bear the stamp (of); **на мои́х уста́х п. молча́ния** my lips are sealed.
печа́ть², и *f.* **1.** print(ing); **вы́йти из ~и** to appear, come out, be published. **2.** print, type; **ме́лкая п.** small print; **кру́пная п.** large print. **3.** (the) press; **свобо́да ~и** freedom of the press.
пече́ни|е, я *nt.* baking.
печёнк|а, и *f.* liver (*of animal, as food*); (*coll.*) **сиде́ть (у кого́-н.) в ~ах** to get on s.o.'s nerves.
печёночник, а *m.* (*bot.*) liverwort.
печён|очный *adj. of* **~ка** *and* **пе́чень**; hepatic.
печёный *adj.* (*cul.*) baked.
пе́чен|ь, и *f.* liver.
пече́нь|е, я *nt.* biscuit.
пе́чк|а, и *f.* stove; **танцева́ть от ~и** (*coll.*, *iron.*) to begin again from the beginning.
печ|но́й *adj. of* **~ь²**; **~на́я труба́** chimney, flue.
печь¹, пеку́, печёшь, пеку́т, *past* **пёк, пекла́** *impf.* (*of* **ис~**) to bake; **со́лнце пекло́** the sun beat down.
печь², и, о ~и, в ~и́, *pl.* **~и, ~е́й** *f.* **1.** stove; oven; **сверхвысокочасто́тная п.** microwave oven. **2.** (*tech.*) furnace, kiln; **до́менная п.** blast-furnace.
пе́чься¹, печётся, пеку́тся, *past* **пёкся, пекла́сь** *impf.* (*of* **ис~**) to bake; to broil (*in the sun*).
пе́чься², пеку́сь, печёшься, пеку́тся, *past* **пёкся, пекла́сь** *impf.* (*no pf.*) (**о**+*p.*) to take care (of), look after.
пешехо́д, а *m.* pedestrian.
пешехо́дн|ый *adj.* pedestrian; **п. мост** foot-bridge.
пе́ш|ий *adj.* **1.** pedestrian. **2.** (*mil.*) unmounted, foot.
пе́шк|а, и *f.* (*in chess, also fig.*) pawn.
пешко́м *adv.* on foot.
пеще́р|а, ы *f.* cave, cavern; grotto.
пеще́рист|ый (~, ~а) *adj.* with many caves.
пеще́р|ный *adj. of* **~а**; **п. челове́к** cave-dweller, cave-man.
ПЗУ *nt. indecl.* (*abbr. of* ***постоя́нное запомина́ющее устро́йство***) (*comput.*) ROM (*read-only memory*).
пиани́но *nt. indecl.* (upright) piano.
пиани́ссимо *adv.* (*mus.*) pianissimo.
пиани́ст, а *m.* pianist.
пиа́но *adv.* (*mus.*) piano.
пиано́л|а, ы *f.* (*mus.*) pianola.
пиа́стр, а *m.* piastre.
пивн|а́я, о́й *f.* alehouse; pub.
пив|но́й *adj. of* **~о; ~ные дро́жжи** brewer's yeast.
пи́в|о, а *nt.* beer.
пивова́р, а *m.* brewer.
пивоваре́ни|е, я *nt.* brewing.
пивова́ренн|ый *adj.*: **п. заво́д** brewery.
пи́галиц|а, ы *f.* (*zool.*) lapwing, peewit; (*fig.*, *coll.*) pipsqueak.
пигме́|й, я *m.* pygmy (*also fig.*).
пигме́нт, а *m.* pigment.
пигмента́ци|я, и *f.* pigmentation.
пиджа́к, а́ *m.* jacket, coat.
пиджа́|чный *adj. of* **~к; п. костю́м, ~чная па́ра** (lounge-)suit.
пиете́т, а *m.* reverence.
пижа́м|а, ы *f.* pyjamas.
пижо́н, а *m.* (*coll.*) fop; show-off; (*sl.*, *pej.*) twit.
пизд|а́, ы́ *f.* (*vulg.*) cunt.
пик¹, а *m.* (*geog.*) peak; pinnacle.
пик², а 1. *m.* peak (*of work, traffic, etc.*); **п. нагру́зки** (*elec.*) peak load. **2.** *adj. indecl.* **часы́ пик** rush-hour.
пи́к|а¹, и *f.* pike, lance.
пи́к|а², и *f.* (*cards*) spade; **да́ма ~** the queen of spades; **пойти́ ~ой** to play a spade.
пи́к|а³, и *f. only in phr.* **сде́лать что-н. в ~у кому́-н.** to do a thing to spite s.o.
пика́нтност|ь, и *f.* piquancy; spiciness.
пика́нт|ный (~ен, ~на) *adj.* piquant (*also fig.*); (*fig.*) juicy; spicy; **п. анекдо́т** risqué story.
пика́п, а *m.* pick-up (van).
пике́ *nt. indecl.* (*aeron.*) dive; **перейти́ в п.** to go into a dive.
пике́т¹, а *m.* picket.
пике́т², а *m.* (*card-game*) piquet.
пикети́р|овать, ую *impf.* to picket.
пике́тчик, а *m.* picket (*pers.*).
пики́ровани|е, я *nt.* (*aeron.*) dive, diving.
пики́р|овать, ую *impf. and pf.* (*pf. also* **с~**) (*aeron.*) to dive.
пики́р|оваться, уюсь *impf.* (*no pf.*) (**с**+*i.*) to trade insults.
пикиро́вк|а, и *f.* (*coll.*) slanging-match.
пикиро́вщик, а *m.* dive-bomber.
пики́р|ующий *pres. part of* **~овать** *and adj.*; **п. бомбардиро́вщик** dive-bomber.
пи́кколо *nt. indecl.* piccolo.
пикни́к, а́ *m.* picnic.
пи́кн|уть, у, ешь *pf.* (*coll.*) to let out a squeak; (*fig.*) to make a sound (of protest); **попро́буй то́лько п.** (*with implied threat*) one sound out of you!; **п. не сметь** not to dare utter a word.
пи́к|овый *adj.* **1.** *adj. of* **~а²**; **~овая да́ма** queen of spades. **2.** (*fig.*, *coll.*) awkward; **~овое положе́ние** sticky situation; **оста́ться при ~овом интере́се** to get nothing for one's pains.
пикт, а *m.* (*hist.*) Pict.
пиктографи́ческий *adj.* pictographic.
пиктогра́фи|я, и *f.* pictography.
пи́кул|и, ей *no sg.* pickles.
пи́кш|а, и *f.* haddock.
пил|а́, ы́, *pl.* **~ы, ~** *f.* saw.
пила́в, а *m.* (*cul.*) pilaff, pilau.
пила́-ры́ба, пилы́-ры́бы *f.* saw-fish.
пилёный *adj.* sawn; **п. са́хар** lump sugar.
пилигри́м, а *m.* pilgrim.
пили́ка|ть, ю *impf.* (*coll.*) to scrape, strum (*on a fiddle, etc.*).
пил|и́ть, ю́, ~ишь *impf.* **1.** to saw. **2.** (*fig.*, *coll.*) to nag (at).
пи́лк|а, и *f.* **1.** sawing. **2.** fret-saw. **3.** nail-file.
пи́ллерс, а *m.* (*naut.*) deck stanchion.
пиломатериа́л|ы, ов *no sg.* saw-timber.
пило́н, а *m.* (*archit.*) pylon.
пило́т, а *m.* pilot; **п.-сме́ртник** suicide pilot.
пилота́ж, а *m.* pilotage; **вы́сший п.** aerobatics.
пилоти́р|овать, ую *impf.* to pilot; to man.
пило́тк|а, и *f.* (*mil.*) forage cap.
пи́льщик, а *m.* sawyer, wood-cutter.
пилю́л|я, и *f.* pill.
пиля́стр|а, ы *f.* (*archit.*) pilaster.
пина́|ть, ю *impf. of* **пнуть**
пингви́н, а *m.* penguin.
пинг-по́нг *m.* ping-pong.
пине́тк|а, и *f.* (*baby's*) bootee.
пин|о́к, ка́ *m.* (*coll.*) kick.
пи́нт|а, ы *f.* pint.
пинце́т, а *m.* pincers, tweezers.
пио́н, а *m.* (*bot.*) peony.
пионе́р, а *m.* pioneer; **(ю́ный) пионе́р** (Young) Pioneer (*in former USSR, member of Communist children's organization*).

пионе́р|ский *adj. of* ~
пиоре́|я, и *f.* (*med.*) pyorrhoea.
пипе́тк|а, и *f.* pipette; medicine dropper.
пи-пи́ (*baby talk*): **сде́лать п.** to do a wee(-wee).
пир, а, о ~**е, в** ~**у́,** *pl.* ~**ы** *m.* feast, banquet; **п. горо́й, п. на весь мир** sumptuous feast.
пирами́д|а, ы *f.* pyramid.
пирамида́льный *adj.* pyramidal.
пира́нь|я, и *f.* (*zool.*) piranha.
пира́т, а *m.* pirate.
пира́тский *adj.* piratic(al).
пира́тств|о, а *nt.* piracy.
пири́т, а *m.* (*min.*) pyrites.
пир|ова́ть, у́ю *impf.* to feast, banquet.
пиро́г, а́ *m.* pie; tart; **п. с мя́сом** meat pie; **возду́шный п.** soufflé; **сва́дебный п.** wedding cake.
пиро́жн|ое, ого *nt.* (*collect.*) pastries; (fancy) cake, pastry
пирож|о́к, ка́ *m.* pasty, patty, (*small*) pie.
пироксили́н, а *m.* pyroxylin, gun-cotton.
пироте́хник|а, и *f.* pyrotechnics.
пиротехни́ческий *adj.* pyrotechnic.
пи́рров *adj.*: ~**а побе́да** Pyrrhic victory.
пиру́шк|а, и *f.* (*coll.*) carousal; binge.
пиру́эт, а *m.* pirouette.
пи́ршеств|о, а *nt.* feast, banquet.
писа́к|а, и *m.* (*coll.*) hack writer, scribbler.
писа́ни|е, я *nt.* **1.** writing. **2.** writing, screed; **(свяще́нное) п.** Holy Scripture, Holy Writ.
пи́сан|ый *adj.* written; ~**ая краса́вица** a picture of beauty; **носи́ться с чем-н. как (дура́к) с** ~**ой то́рбой** to fuss over sth. like a child with a new toy.
пи́сар|ь, я, *pl.* ~**я́** *m.* clerk.
писа́тел|ь, я *m.* writer, author.
писа́тель|ский *adj. of* ~
пи́са|ть, ю *impf.* (*vulg.*) to piss.
пи|са́ть, шу́, ~**шешь** *impf.* (*of* **на**~) **1.** to write; **п. на маши́нке** to type; **п. стиха́ми** to write verse; **п. дневни́к** to keep a diary; **п. под дикто́вку** to take dictation; ~**ши́ пропа́ло** it is as good as lost. **2.** (*+i.*) to paint (in); **п. портре́ты ма́слом** to paint portraits in oils.
пи|са́ться, шу́сь, ~**шешься** *impf.* **1.** to be spelled; **как** ~**шется э́то сло́во?** how do you spell this word? **2.** (*impers.*; *+d.*) to feel an inclination for writing; **мне сего́дня не** ~**шется** I don't feel like writing today. **3.** *pass. of* ~**са́ть**
пис|е́ц, ца́ *m.* (*hist.*) scribe.
писк, а *m.* peep; chirp; squeak; (*of chicks*) cheep.
пискли́в|ый (~**,** ~**а)** *adj.* squeaky.
пи́скн|уть, у, ешь *inst. pf.* (*of* **пища́ть**) (*coll.*) to give a squeak; **то́лько** ~**и у меня́!** (*with implied threat*) one squeak out of you!
писсуа́р, а *m.* urinal.
пистоле́т, а *m.* pistol; **п.-пулемёт** sub-machine-gun.
писто́н, а *m.* **1.** (percussion) cap. **2.** (*mus.*) piston.
писчебума́жны|й *adj.*: ~**е принадле́жности** stationery.
пи́сч|ий *adj.*: ~**ая бума́га** writing paper.
письмена́, письмён, ~**м** *no sg.* characters, letters; **дре́вние еги́петские п.** ancient Egyptian characters.
пи́сьменно *adv.* in writing.
пи́сьменност|ь, и *f.* **1.** literature; (*collect.*) literary texts. **2.** the written language.
пи́сьменн|ый *adj.* **1.** writing; **п. стол** writing-table, desk. **2.** written; **в** ~**ом ви́де, в** ~**ой фо́рме** in writing; **п. знак** letter; **п. экза́мен** written examination.
письм|о́, а́, *pl.* ~**а, пи́сем,** ~**ам** *nt.* **1.** letter; **заказно́е п.** registered letter. **2.** writing; **иску́сство** ~**а́** art of writing. **3.** script; hand(-writing); **ара́бское п.** Arabic script.
письмоно́с|ец, ца *m.* postman.
пита́ни|е, я *nt.* **1.** nourishment, nutrition; feeding; **недоста́точное п.** malnutrition. **2.** (*tech.*) feed, feeding; **резервуа́р** ~**я** feed tank. **3.** (*elec.*) power supply.
пита́тельност|ь, и *f.* nutritiousness.
пита́тел|ьный (~**ен,** ~**ьна)** *adj.* **1.** nourishing, nutritious; ~**ьная среда́** (*biol.*) culture medium; (*fig.*) breeding-ground; ~**ьное вещество́** nutrient. **2.** (*anat.*) alimentary. **3.** (*tech.*) feed; ~**ьная труба́** feed pipe.
пита́|ть, ю *impf.* (*of* **на**~) **1.** to feed; to nourish (*also fig.*); to sustain; **п. больно́го** to feed a patient; **п. наде́жду** to nourish the hope; **п. отвраще́ние (к)** to have an aversion (for). **2.** (*tech.*) to supply; **п. го́род электроэне́ргией** to supply a city with electricity.
пита́|ться, юсь *impf.* (*+i.*) to feed (on), live (on); **хорошо́ п.** to eat well; **п. наде́ждами** to live on hope.
Пи́тер, а *m.* (*coll.*) St. Petersburg.
пи́тер|ский *adj. of* **П**~
пито́м|ец, ца *m.* **1.** foster-child, nursling; charge. **2.** pupil; alumnus.
пито́мник, а *m.* nursery.
пито́н, а *m.* python.
пить, пью, пьёшь, *past* **пил, пила́, пи́ло** *impf.* (*of* **вы́**~) to drink; to take (*liquids*); **мне п. хо́чется** I am thirsty; **п. за** (*+a.*), **за здоро́вье** (*+g.*) to drink to, to the health (of); **как п. дать** (*coll.*) for sure; **как п. дать придёт** he will come for sure.
пить|ё, я́ *nt.* **1.** drinking. **2.** drink, beverage.
питьев|о́й *adj.* drinkable; ~**а́я вода́** drinking water.
пифаго́ров *adj.*: ~**а теоре́ма** Pythagoras' theorem.
пих|а́ть, а́ю *impf.* (*of* ~**ну́ть**) (*coll.*) **1.** to push, shove; to elbow, jostle. **2.** to stuff, cram; **п. ве́щи в чемода́н** to cram things into a suitcase.
пих|ну́ть, ну́, нёшь *pf. of* ~**а́ть**
пи́хт|а, ы *f.* fir(-tree).
пи́хт|овый *adj. of* ~**а**
пи́цц|а, ы *f.* pizza.
пиццери́|я, и *f.* pizza parlour, pizzeria.
пиццика́то = пиччика́то
пи́чка|ть, ю *impf.* (*of* **на**~) (*coll.*) to stuff, cram (*also fig.*)
пичу́г|а, и *f.* (*coll.*) bird.
пичу́жк|а, и *f.* (*coll.*) = **пичу́га**
пиччика́то (*mus.*) **1.** *adv.* **2.** *n*: *indecl. nt.* pizzicato.
пи́шущ|ий *pres. part. act. of* **писа́ть** *and adj.*; ~**ая маши́нка** typewriter.
пи́щ|а, и *no pl., f.* food; **п. для ума́** food for thought.
пища́л|ь, и *f.* (*hist.*) (h)arquebus.
пищ|а́ть, у́, и́шь *impf.* (*of* **пи́скнуть**) to squeak; (*of chicks, etc.*) to cheep, peep.
пище... *comb. form, abbr. of* **пищево́й**
пищеваре́ни|е, я *nt.* digestion; **расстро́йство** ~**я** indigestion, dyspepsia.
пищевари́тельный *adj.* digestive; **п. кана́л** alimentary canal.
пищево́д, а *m.* (*anat.*) oesophagus, gullet.
пищ|ево́й *adj. of* ~**а;** ~**евы́е проду́кты** foodstuffs.
пия́вк|а, и *f.* leech.
пл. (*abbr. of* **пло́щадь**) Sq., Square.
плав, а *m.*: **на** ~**у́** afloat.
пла́вани|е, я *nt.* **1.** swimming; **худо́жественное п.** synchronized swimming. **2.** sailing; navigation; **су́дно да́льнего** ~**я** ocean-going ship.
пла́вательн|ый *adj.* swimming; **п. бассе́йн** swimming pool.
пла́ва|ть, ю *impf.* **1.** *indet. of* **плыть. 2.** to float.
плавба́з|а, ы *f.* (*abbr. of* **плаву́чая ба́за**) factory ship.
пла́в|ень, ня *m.* (*tech.*) flux.
плавико́в|ый *adj.*: ~**ая кислота́** (*chem.*) hydrofluoric

acid; **п. шпат** (*min.*) fluorspar.
плави́льн|ый *adj.* (*tech.*) melting, smelting; **~ая печь** smelting furnace.
плави́л|ьня, ьни, *g. pl.* **~ен** *f.* foundry, smeltery.
плави́льщик, а *m.* smelter.
пла́в|ить, лю, ишь *impf.* to melt, smelt; to fuse.
пла́в|иться, ится *impf.* to melt; to fuse (*intrans.*).
пла́вк|а, и *f.* fusing; fusion.
пла́в|ки, ок *no sg.* swimming trunks.
пла́вк|ий *adj.* fusible; **~ая про́волока** fuse wire.
плавле́ни|е, я *nt.* melting, fusion; **то́чка ~я** melting point.
пла́вленый *adj.*: **п. сыр** processed cheese.
плавни́к, а́ *m.* fin; flipper; **спинно́й п.** dorsal fin.
пла́вност|ь, и *f.* smoothness; facility.
пла́в|ный (~ен, ~на) *adj.* smooth; **~ная речь** flowing speech.
плаву́чест|ь, и *f.* buoyancy.
плаву́ч|ий *adj.* **1.** floating; **~ая льди́на** ice-floe. **2.** buoyant.
плагиа́т, а *m.* plagiarism.
плагиа́тор, а *m.* plagiarist.
пла́зм|а, ы *f.* (*biol. and phys.*) plasma.
плака́т, а *m.* placard; poster, bill.
пла́|кать, чу, чешь *impf.* to weep, cry; **п. навзры́д** to sob.
пла́|каться, чусь, чешься *impf.* (*of* **по~**) (**на**+*a.*) to complain (of), lament; **п. на свою́ судьбу́** to bemoan one's fate.
пла́кс|а, ы *c.g.* (*coll.*) cry-baby.
плакси́в|ый (~, ~а) *adj.* (*coll.*) whining.
плаку́ч|ий *adj.* weeping; **~ая и́ва** weeping willow.
пламене́|ть, ю *impf.* (*poet.*) to flame, blaze; **п. стра́стью** to burn with passion.
пла́менност|ь, и *f.* ardour.
пла́менн|ый *adj.* **1.** flaming, fiery; (*fig.*) ardent, burning. **2.** (*tech.*) **~ая труба́** flue; **п. у́голь** bituminous coal.
пла́м|я, ени *nt.* flame; fire, blaze.
план, а *m.* **1.** plan; scheme; **уче́бный п.** curriculum; **по ~́у** according to plan. **2.** plane (*also fig.*); **пере́дний п.** foreground; **за́дний п.** background; **кру́пный п.** close-up (*in filming*); (*fig.*): **вы́двинуть на пе́рвый п.** to bring to the forefront.
планёр, а *m.* (*aeron.*) glider.
планери́зм, а *m.* gliding.
планери́ст, а *m.* glider-pilot.
планёр|ный *adj.* *of* **~**; **п. спорт** gliding.
плане́т|а, ы *f.* **1.** planet. **2.** (the) planet (= *Earth*)
планета́ри|й, я *m.* planetarium.
плане́т|ный *adj.* *of* **~а**; planetary.
планиме́тр, а *m.* (*surveying*) planimeter.
планиметр|и́ческий *adj.* **1.** *of* **~́**. **2.** *of* **~́ия**
планиме́три|я, и *f.* (*math.*) plane geometry.
плани́ровани|е[1], **я** *nt.* planning; **п. городо́в** town-planning.
плани́ровани|е[2], **я** *nt.* (*aeron.*) gliding; glide.
плани́р|овать[1], **ую** *impf.* (*of* **за~**) to plan.
плани́р|овать[2], **ую** *impf.* (*of* **с~**) (*aeron.*) to glide (down).
планир|ова́ть, у́ю *impf.* (*of* **рас~**) to lay out.
планиро́вк|а, и *f.* laying out; lay-out.
планиро́вщик, а *m.* planner (*designer*).
пла́нк|а, и *f.* lath, slat.
планкто́н, а *m.* (*biol.*) plankton.
планови́к, а́ *m.* (*econ.*) planner.
пла́нов|ый *adj.* **1.** planned; **~ое хозя́йство** planned economy. **2.** planning; **~ая коми́ссия** planning commission.
планоме́рност|ь, и *f.* systematic character, planned character.
планоме́р|ный (~ен, ~на) *adj.* systematic, planned.
планта́тор, а *m.* planter.
планта́ци|я, и *f.* plantation.
планше́т, а *m.* map-case.
планши́р, а *m.* (*naut.*) gunwale.
пласт, а́ *m.* layer; sheet; (*archit.*) course; (*geol.*) stratum, bed; **лежа́ть ~о́м** to be flat on one's back.
пла́стик, а *m.* plastic (*material*).
пла́стик|а, и *f.* **1.** (*collect.*) the plastic arts. **2.** eurhythmics.
пластили́н, а *m.* Plasticine (*propr.*).
пласти́н|а, ы *f.* plate.
пласти́нк|а, и *f.* **1.** plate; **граммофо́нная п.** gramophone record; **чувстви́тельная п.** (*phot.*) sensitive plate. **2.** (*bot.*) blade, lamina.
пласти́ческ|ий *adj.* plastic; **~ая ма́сса** plastic; **~ая хирурги́я** plastic surgery.
пласти́ч|ный *adj.* **1.** plastic; supple, pliant. **2.** **(~ен, ~на)** rhythmical; fluent, flowing; **~ное движе́ние те́ла** rhythmical movement of the body.
пластма́сс|а, ы *f.* (*abbr. of* ***пласти́ческая ма́сса***) plastic.
пластма́сс|овый *adj.* *of* **~а**
пла́стыр|ь, я *m.* **1.** (*med.*) plaster.
пла́т|а, ы *f.* **1.** pay; salary; **за́работная п.** wages. **2.** payment, charge; fee; **входна́я п.** entrance fee; **кварти́рная п.** rent; **п. за прое́зд** fare.
плата́н, а *m.* plane(-tree).
плата́|ть, ю *impf.* (*of* **за~**) (*coll.*) to patch.
платёж, а *m.* payment; **нало́женным ~о́м** cash on delivery, C.O.D.
платёжеспосо́бност|ь, и *f.* solvency.
платёжеспосо́б|ный (~ен, ~на) *adj.* solvent.
платёж|ный *adj.* *of* **~**; **п. бала́нс** balance of payments; **~ная ве́домость** pay-roll.
плате́льщик, а *m.* payer.
пла́тин|а, ы *f.* (*min.*) platinum.
пла́тин|овый *adj.* *of* **~а**
пла|ти́ть, чу́, ~́тишь *impf.* (*of* **за~**) **1.** to pay; **п. нали́чными** to pay in cash; **п. нату́рой** to pay in kind. **2.** (*fig.*; +*i.* **за**+*a.*) to pay back, repay; **п. кому́-н. услу́гой за услу́гу** to make it up to s.o.
пла|ти́ться, чу́сь, ~́тишься *impf.* (*of* **по~**) (+*i.* **за**+*a.*) to pay (with for); **п. жи́знью за свои́ оши́бки** to pay for one's mistakes with one's life.
пла́тн|ый *adj.* **1.** paid; chargeable; **~ая доро́га** toll road. **2.** paying; fee-paying; private; **п. посети́тель** paying guest.
плато́ *nt. indecl.* plateau.
плат|о́к, ка́ *m.* shawl; kerchief; **носово́й п.** handkerchief.
платони́ческий *adj.* (*phil.*) Platonic; (*fig.*) platonic.
платфо́рм|а, ы *f.* **1.** platform (*of rail. station*). **2.** (open) goods truck. **3.** (*fig., pol.*) platform.
пла́ть|е, я, *g. pl.* **~ев** *nt.* **1.** clothes, clothing; **ве́рхнее п.** outer garments. **2.** dress, gown, frock; **вече́рнее п.** evening dress.
плат|яно́й *adj.* *of* **~́ье**; **п. шкаф** wardrobe.
плафо́н, а *m.* **1.** decorated ceiling. **2.** shade (*for lamp suspended from ceiling*).
пла́х|а, и *f.* block; (*hist.*) executioner's block.
плац, а, о ~́е, на ~у́ *m.* (*mil.*) parade-ground.
плацда́рм, а *m.* **1.** (*mil.*) bridgehead; beachhead. **2.** (*pol.*; *fig.*) base.
плаце́нт|а, ы *f.* (*anat.*) placenta.
плацка́рт|а, ы *f.* reserved seat *or* berth ticket.
плацка́рт|ный *adj.* *of* **~а**; **~ное ме́сто** reserved seat.
плач, а *m.* weeping, crying.
плаче́в|ный (~ен, ~на) *adj.* **1.** mournful, sad. **2.** (*fig.*) lamentable, deplorable, sorry; **в ~ном состоя́нии** in a sorry state.
плашмя́ *adv.* flat; **лежа́ть п.** to lie flat.
плащ, а́ *m.* **1.** cloak. **2.** raincoat.
плебе́|й, я *m.* (*hist.*) plebeian.
плебе́йский *adj.* plebeian.

плебисци́т, а *m.* plebiscite.
плебс, а *m.* (*collect.*; *hist.*) plebs.
плев|á, ы́ *f.* (*anat.*) membrane; **де́вственная п.** hymen.
плева́тельниц|а, ы *f.* spittoon.
плева́ть, плюю́, плюёшь *impf.* (*of* **плю́нуть**) **1.** to spit; to expectorate. **2.** (**на**+*a.*; *coll.*) to spit (upon); not to care a rap about; **им п. на всё** they don't give a damn about anything.
плева́ться, плюю́сь, плюёшься *impf.* (*coll.*) to spit.
пле́вел, а *m.* (*bot.*) darnel; weed.
плев|о́к, ка́ *m.* **1.** spit(tle). **2.** (*med.*) sputum.
пле́вр|а, ы *f.* (*anat.*) pleura.
плеври́т, а *m.* (*med.*) pleurisy.
плёв|ый *adj.* (*coll.*) **1.** worthless; rubbishy. **2.** trivial, trifling.
плед, а *m.* rug; plaid.
плеер, а *m.* personal stereo, Walkman (*propr.*).
пле́йер = пле́ер
плейстоце́н, а *m.* (*geol.*) Pleistocene.
плейстоце́н|овый *adj. of* **~**
племенно́й *adj.* **1.** tribal. **2.** pedigree; **п. скот** pedigree cattle, bloodstock.
пле́м|я, ени, *pl.* **~ена́, ~ён, ~ена́м** *nt.* **1.** tribe. **2.** breed; **на п.** for breeding. **3.** (*fig.*) tribe; breed, stock.
племя́нник, а *m.* nephew.
племя́нниц|а, ы *f.* niece.
плен, а, о ~е, в ~у́ *m.* captivity; **быть в ~у́** to be in captivity; **взять в п.** to take prisoner; **попа́сть в п. (к)** to be taken prisoner (by).
плена́рный *adj.* plenary.
плене́ни|е, я *nt.* capture; captivity.
плени́тел|ьный (~ен, ~ьна) *adj.* captivating, charming.
плен|и́ть, ю́, и́шь *pf.* (*of* **~я́ть**) **1.** (*obs.*) to take prisoner. **2.** (*fig.*) to captivate, charm.
плен|и́ться, ю́сь, и́шься *pf.* (*of* **~я́ться**) (+*i.*) to be captivated (by), be fascinated (by).
плёнк|а, и *f.* film; pellicle.
пле́нник, а *m.* (*fig.*) prisoner, captive.
пле́нн|ый *adj.* captive; *as n.* **п., ~ого** *m.* captive, prisoner.
плён|очный *adj. of* **~ка**; filmy.
пле́нум, а *m.* plenum, plenary session.
плен|я́ть(ся), я́ю(сь) *impf. of* **~и́ть(ся)**
плёс, а *m.* reach (*of river*); stretch (*of river or lake*).
пле́сенный *adj.* mouldy, musty.
пле́сен|ь, и *f.* mould.
плеск, а *m.* splash; **п. волн** lapping of waves.
пле|ска́ть, щу́, ~щешь *impf.* (*of* **~сну́ть**) to splash; to lap; **п. о бе́рег** to lap against the shore; **п. на кого́-н. водо́й** to splash s.o. (with water).
пле|ска́ться, щу́сь, ~щешься *impf.* to splash; to lap.
пле́снев|еть, еет *impf.* (*of* **за~**) to grow mouldy, grow musty.
плес|ну́ть, ну́, нёшь *pf. of* **~ка́ть**
пле|сти́, ту́, тёшь, *past* **~л, ~ла́** *impf.* (*of* **с~**) to braid, plait; to weave; **п. корзи́ну** to make a basket; **п. небыли́цы** (*coll., pej.*) to spin yarns; **п. вздор, п. чепуху́** (*coll., pej.*) to talk rubbish.
пле|сти́сь, ту́сь, тёшься, *past* **~лся, ~ла́сь** *impf.* (*coll.*) to trudge, plod (along).
плете́ни|е, я *nt.* **1.** braiding, plaiting; **п. слове́с** (*iron.*) verbiage. **2.** wicker-work.
плетёнк|а, и *f.* **1.** (wicker) basket. **2.** twist (*of bread*).
плетён|ый *adj.* wattled, wicker; **~ая корзи́нка** wicker basket.
плет|ёнь, ня́ *m.* wattle fencing.
плётк|а *f.* lash.
плет|ь, и, *pl.* **~и, ~е́й** *f.* lash.
плечев|о́й *adj.* (*anat.*): **~а́я кость** humerus.
пле́чик|и, ов *no sg.* (*coll.*) (coat-)hanger.
пле́чик|о, а, *pl.* **~и, ~ов** *nt.* **1.** shoulder-strap. **2.** *dim. of* **плечо́**
плечи́ст|ый (~, ~а) *adj.* broad-shouldered.
плеч|о́, а́, *pl.* **~и, ~, ~а́м** *nt.* shoulder; **всё э́то у меня́ за ~а́ми** (*fig.*) all that is behind me; **~о́м к ~у́** shoulder to shoulder; **име́ть го́лову на ~а́х** to have a good head on one's shoulders; **вы́нести на свои́х ~а́х** to bear (the full brunt of); **э́то ему́ не по ~у́** he is not up to it; **(сло́вно) гора́ с мои́х ~ свали́лась** that's a weight off my mind; **с ~ доло́й!** that's done, thank goodness; **пожа́ть ~а́ми** to shrug one's shoulders.
плеши́ве|ть, ю *impf.* (*of* **о~**) to grow bald.
плеши́в|ый (~, ~а) *adj.* bald.
плеш|ь, и *f.* bald patch; bare patch.
плея́д|ы, ~ *pl.* (*sg.* **~а, ~ы** *f.*) **1. П.** (*astron.*) Pleiades. **2.** (*sg.*; *fig.*) Pleiad; galaxy.
пли́нтус, а *m.* **1.** plinth. **2.** skirting board.
плиоце́н, а *m.* (*geol.*) Pl(e)iocene.
плис, а *m.* velveteen.
пли́с|овый *adj. of* **~**
плиссе́ *indecl.* **1.** *adj.* pleated; **ю́бка п.** pleated skirt. **2.** *n.*; *nt.* pleat(s).
плиссир|ова́ть, у́ю *impf.* (*no pf.*) to pleat.
плит|á, ы́, *pl.* **~ы** *f.* **1.** plate, slab; flag-(stone); **моги́льная п.** gravestone. **2.** stove; cooker.
пли́тк|а, и *f.* **1.** *dim. of* **плита́**; tile, (thin) slab; **п. шокола́да** bar of chocolate. **2.** stove; cooker.
плитня́к, а́ *m.* flagstone.
пли́т|очный *adj. of* **~ка**; **п. пол** tiled floor.
плов, а *m.* (*cul.*) = **пила́в**
плов|е́ц, ца́ *m.* swimmer.
плод, а́ *m.* **1.** fruit (*also fig.*); **приноси́ть п.** to bear fruit. **2.** (*biol.*) foetus.
пло|ди́ть, жу́, ди́шь *impf.* (*of* **рас~**) to produce, procreate; to engender (*also fig*).
пло|ди́ться, жу́сь, ди́шься *impf.* (*of* **рас~**) to multiply; to propagate.
пло́дный *adj.* **1.** (*biol.*) fertile. **2.** fertilized.
плодови́тост|ь, и *f.* fertility, fecundity.
плодови́т|ый (~, ~а) *adj.* fruitful, prolific (*also fig.*); fertile, fecund; **п. писа́тель** prolific writer.
плодово́дств|о, а *nt.* fruit-growing.
плодо́в|ый *adj. of* **плод**; **~ое де́рево** fruit-tree; **п. сад** orchard.
плодоно|си́ть, ~сит *impf.* (*no pf.*) to bear fruit.
плодоно́с|ный (~ен, ~на) *adj.* fruit-bearing.
плодоо́вощ|и, е́й *no sg.* fruit and vegetables.
плодоовощно́й *adj.* fruit and vegetable.
плодоро́ди|е, я *nt.* fertility, fecundity.
плодоро́д|ный (~ен, ~на) *adj.* fertile.
плодотво́р|ный (~ен, ~на) *adj.* fruitful.
плодоя́д|ный (~ен, ~на) *adj.* frugivorous.
пло́мб|а, ы *f.* **1.** (*lead*) seal. **2.** filling (*for tooth*); **ста́вить ~у в зуб** to fill a tooth.
пломби́р, а *m.* 'plombières' (*ice cream with candied fruit*).
пломбир|ова́ть, у́ю *impf.* **1.** (*pf.* **о~**) to seal. **2.** (*pf.* **за~**) to fill (*a tooth*).
пло́с|кий (~ок, ~ка́, ~ко) *adj.* **1.** flat; plane; **~кая грудь** flat chest; **~кая пове́рхность** plane surface. **2.** (*fig.*) trivial, tame; **~кая шу́тка** feeble joke.
плоского́рь|е, я *nt.* plateau; tableland.
плоскогру́д|ый (~, ~а) *adj.* flat-chested.
плоскогу́бц|ы, ев *no sg.* pliers.
плоскодо́нк|а, и *f.* flat-bottomed boat; punt.
плоскодо́нный *adj.* flat-bottomed.
плоскостно́й *adj.* plane.
плоскосто́пи|е, я *nt.* (*med.*) flat feet.
пло́скост|ь, и, *pl.* **~и, ~е́й** *f.* **1.** flatness. **2.** plane (*also fig.*). **3.** platitude.
плот, а́ *m.* raft.
плотв|á, ы́ *f.* (*fish*) roach.
плоти́н|а, ы *f.* dam.

плóтник, а *m.* carpenter.
плóтнича|ть, ю *impf.* to work as a carpenter.
плóтничеств|о, а *nt.* carpentry.
плóтно *adv.* **1.** close(ly), tightly. **2.: п. поéсть** to eat heartily.
плóтност|ь, и *f.* **1.** thickness; solidity; **п. населéния** density of population. **2.** (*phys.*) density.
плóт|ный (~ен, ~нá, ~но) *adj.* **1.** thick; compact; dense (*also phys.*). **2.** solid, strong; (*of a pers.*; *coll.*) thick-set. **3.** tightly-filled. **4.** (*coll.*; *of a meal*) hearty.
плотоя́д|ный (~ен, ~на) *adj.* carnivorous; **~ное живóтное** carnivore.
плóтский *adj.* (*arch.*) carnal, fleshly.
плот|ь, и *f.* flesh; **во ~и́** in the flesh; **п. от ~́и** flesh of one's flesh; **п. и кровь** (one's) flesh and blood; **крáйняя п.** (*anat.*) foreskin.
плóхо 1. *adv.* bad(ly); ill; **п. вести́ себя́** to behave badly; **п. обращáться (с+*i.*)** to ill-treat; **чу́вствовать себя́ п.** to feel unwell; **п. кóнчить** (*coll.*) to come to a bad end. **2.** *n.*; *nt. indecl.* bad mark; **я опя́ть получи́л п. по áлгебре** I have got a bad mark in algebra again.
плох|óй (~, ~á, ~́о) *adj.* bad; poor; **~áя погóда** bad weather; **~óе пищеварéние** poor digestion; **с ним шу́тки ~́и** he is not one to be trifled with; *as pred.* **ему́ óчень ~́о** he is in a very bad way.
плошá|ть, ю *impf.* (*of* **с~**) (*coll.*) to make a mistake, slip up.
площáдк|а, и *f.* **1.** ground, area; **дéтская п.** children's playground; **спорти́вная п.** sports ground; **строи́тельная п.** building site; **тéннисная п.** tennis court; **киносъёмочная п.** (*film*) set; **п. для игры́ в гóльф** golf course. **2.** landing (*on staircase*). **3.** platform; **пусковáя п.** launching pad (*of rocket*).
площаднóй *adj.* vulgar, coarse.
плóщад|ь, и, *pl.* **~и, ~éй** *f.* **1.** (*math.*) area. **2.** area; space; **жилáя п.** living space. **3.** square; **базáрная п.** market-place.
плó|ще *comp. of* **~ский** *and* **~ско**
плуг, а, *pl.* **~и́** *m.* plough.
плу́нжер, а *m.* (*tech.*) plunger.
плут, á *m.* **1.** cheat, swindler. **2.** (*joc.*) rogue.
плутá|ть, ю *impf.* (*coll.*) to stray.
плути́шк|а, и *m.* (*coll.*) (little) rascal, imp.
плу́тн|и, ей *pl.* (*sg.* **~я, ~и** *f.*) (*coll.*) tricks.
плутовáт|ый (~, ~а) *adj.* cunning.
плут|овáть, у́ю *impf.* (*of* **на~** *and* **с~**) (*coll.*) to cheat.
плутовск|óй *adj.* **1.** knavish. **2.** (*coll.*) roguish, mischievous. **3.** (*liter.*) picaresque.
плутовств|ó, á *nt.* cheating; trickery, knavery.
плутокрáт, á *m.* plutocrat.
плутократи́ческий *adj.* plutocratic.
плутокрáти|я, и *f.* plutocracy.
плы|ть, ву́, вёшь, *past* **~л, ~лá, ~́ло** *impf.* (*det. of* **плáвать**) **1.** to swim; to float; **п. стóя** to tread water. **2.** to sail; **п. на вёслах** to row; **п. под парусáми** to sail; **п. по вóле волн** to drift.
плюгáв|ый (~, ~а) *adj.* (*coll.*) unprepossessing.
плюмáж, а *m.* plume (*on hat*).
плю́н|уть, у, ешь *pf. of* **плевáть**
плюрали́зм, а *m.* (*phil. & pol.*) pluralism.
плюралисти́ческий *adj.* (*phil. & pol.*) pluralistic.
плюс, а *m.* **1.** plus; *as connective in math. expressions* **два п. два равнó четырём** two plus two equals four. **2.** (*fig.*, *coll.*) advantage; **э́тот проéкт не без ~́ов** this scheme has some advantages.
плюс|нá, ны́, *pl.* **~́ны, ~́ен, ~́нам** *f.* (*anat.*) metatarsus.
плю́х|аться, аюсь *impf. of* **~нуться**
плю́х|нуться, нусь, нешься *pf.* (*of* **~аться**) (*coll.*) to flop (down); **п. в крéсло** to flop into an armchair.
плюш, а *m.* plush.
плю́ш|евый *adj. of* **~**
плю́шк|а, и *f.* (*coll.*) bun.
плющ, á *m.* ivy.
пляж, а *m.* beach.
пляс, а *no pl.*, *m.* (*coll.*) dance.
пля́ск|а, и *f.* dance; dancing (*esp. folk-dancing*); **п. святóго Ви́та** (*med.*) St. Vitus's dance, chorea.
пля|сáть, шу́, ~́шешь *impf.* (*of* **с~**) to dance.
плясов|óй *adj.* dancing; *as n.* **~áя, ~óй** *f.* dance tune.
плясу́н, á *m.* (*coll.*) dancer.
пневмати́ческий *adj.* pneumatic.
пневмони́|я, и *f.* pneumonia.
пнуть, пну, пнёшь *pf.* (*of* **пинáть**) (*coll.*) to kick.
по *prep.* **I.** *+d.* **1.** on; along; **идти́ по травé** to walk on the grass; **éхать по у́лице** to go along the street; **идти́ по следáм** (*+g.*) to follow in the tracks (of); **хлóпнуть по спинé** to slap on the back; **по всему́, по всей** all over. **2.** round, about (*or not translated*); **ходи́ть по магази́нам** to go round the shops; **ходи́ть по кóмнате** to pace the room. **3.** by, on, over (*sc. some means of communication*); **по вóздуху** by air; **по желéзной дорóге** by rail; **по пóчте** by post; **по рáдио** over the radio; **по телефóну** on, over the telephone. **4.** according to; by; in accordance with; **по прáву** by right(s); **по расписáнию** according to schedule; **жени́ться по люби́** to marry for love; **звать по и́мени** to call by first name; **су́дя по результáтам** judging by results; **по мне** as far as I am concerned; **жить по срéдствам** to live within one's means; **по Платóну** according to Plato. **5.** by, in (= *in respect of*); **по профéссии** by profession; **по происхождéнию он армяни́н** he is of Armenian origin; **лу́чший по кáчеству** better in quality; **товáрищ по ору́жию** comrade-in-arms; **товáрищ по шкóле** school-mate; **рóдственник по мáтери** a relative on one's mother's side. **6.** at, on, in (= *in the field of*); **лéкции по европéйской истóрии** lectures on European history; **специали́ст по я́дерной фи́зике** specialist in nuclear physics. **7.** by (reason of); on account of; from; **по болéзни** on account of sickness; **по рассéянности** from absent-mindedness; **егó прости́ли по мóлодости лет** he was pardoned by reason of his youth. **8.** (*indicating the object of an action or feeling*) at, for (*or not translated*); **стреля́ть по проти́внику** to fire at the enemy; **охóта по кру́пному звéрю** big game hunting; **скучáть по дéтям** to miss one's children; **тоскá по дóму, по рóдине** homesickness; **по áдресу** (*+g.*) to the address (of); **э́то по егó áдресу** (*fig.*) this is meant for him. **9.** (*in temporal phrr.*) on; in; **по понедéльникам** on Mondays; **по прáздникам** on holidays; **онá рабóтает по утрáм** she works (in the) mornings.

II. *+d. or a. of cardinal num. forms distributive num.* (*+d.*, *but also +a.*, *esp. in coll. usage*) **по одномý (однóй); по пяти́, по шести́,** *etc.*; **по оди́ннадцати,** *etc.*; **по двадцати́,** *etc.*; **по ста; по пятисóт,** *etc.*; **по полторá (полторы́)**; (*+a.*) **пó два (две), пó три, по четы́ре, по двéсти, по три́ста, по четы́реста; дáйте им по** (*sc.* **одномý**) **я́блоку** give them an apple each; **мы получи́ли по три фу́нта** we received three pounds each; **по рублю́ шту́ка** one rouble each; **по дéсять (десяти́) рублéй шту́ка** ten roubles each; **пó два, пó двое** in twos, two by two.

III. *+a.* **1.** to, up to; **по пóяс в водé** up to the waist in water; **зáнят по гóрло** up to one's eyes in work; **пó уши влюблён** head over heels in love; **по сегóдня** up to today; **по пéрвое мáя** up to (and including) the first of May; **по сю (ту) стóрону** on this (that) side. **2.** (*following vv. of motion*; *coll.*) for (= *to fetch, to get*); **идти́ пó воду** to go for water.

IV. *+p.* **1.** on, after; **по окончáнии рабóты** after work; **по прибы́тии** on arrival; **по рассмотре́нии** on examination. **2.** (*after vv. of grieving, mourning, etc.*) for; **пла́кать по му́же** to mourn (for) one's husband; **носи́ть тра́ур по ком-н.** to be in mourning for s.o. **3.: по нём,** *etc.*, as he, *etc.*, likes, is used.

по- *+d. of adj. or ending* **...ски** *forms adv. indicating* **1.** *manner of action, conduct, etc., as* **жить по-ста́рому** to live in the old style; **рабо́тать по-това́рищески** to work in a comradely fashion. **2.** *use of given language, as* **говори́ть по-ру́сски** to speak Russian. **3.** *accordance with opinion or wish, as* **по-мо́ему** in my opinion; **пусть бу́дет по-ва́шему** as you wish.

по...[1] *as vbl. pref.* **1.** *forms pf. aspect.* **2.** *indicates action of short duration or of incomplete character, as* **порабо́тать** to do a little work; **поспа́ть** to have a sleep. **3.** (*+suff.* **...ыва..., ...ива...**) *indicates action repeated at intervals or of indet. duration, as* **позва́нивать** to keep ringing.

по...[2] *pref. modifying comp. adj. or adv., as* **погро́мче** a little louder.

п. о. (*abbr. of* **почто́вое отделе́ние**) PO, Post Office.

побагрове́|ть, ю *pf. of* **багрове́ть**

поба́ива|ться, юсь *impf.* (*+g. or inf.; coll.*) to be rather afraid.

поба́лива|ть, ю *impf.* (*coll.*) to ache a little; to ache on and off.

побасёнк|а, и *f.* (*coll.*) tale, story.

побе́г[1]**, а** *m.* flight; escape.

побе́г[2]**, а** *m.* (*bot.*) sprout, shoot.

побе́га|ть, ю *pf.* to have a run.

побегу́шк|и: быть у кого́-н. на ~ах (*coll.*) to run errands for s.o.; (*fig.*) to be at s.o.'s beck and call.

побе́д|а, ы *f.* victory.

победи́тел|ь, я *m.* victor; (*sport*) winner.

побед|и́ть, и́шь *pf.* (*of* **побежда́ть**) to conquer, vanquish; to defeat; (*fig.*) to master, overcome.

побе́дный *adj.* victorious, triumphant; **п. гол** winning goal.

победоно́с|ный (~ен, ~на) *adj.* victorious, triumphant.

побе|жа́ть, гу́, жи́шь, гу́т *pf.* **1.** *pf. of* **бежа́ть. 2.** to break into a run.

побежда́|ть, ю *impf. of* **победи́ть**

побеле́|ть, ю *pf. of* **беле́ть**

побел|и́ть, ю́, ~́ишь *pf. of* **бели́ть 1.**

побе́лк|а, и *f.* whitewashing.

побере́жный *adj.* coastal.

побере́жь|е, я *nt.* coast, seaboard.

побере́|чь, гу́, жёшь, гу́т, *past* **~̈г, ~гла́** *pf.* (*coll.*) to take care (of); to look after; **п. здоро́вье** to take care of one's health; **~ги́ мой ве́щи до моего́ возвраще́ния** look after my things until I return.

побере́|чься, гу́сь, жёшься, гу́ться, *past* **~̈гся, ~гла́сь** *pf.* to take care of o.s.; **~ги́сь!** mind out!

побесе́д|овать, ую *pf.* to have a chat.

побеспоко́|ить, ю, ишь *pf. of* **беспоко́ить 2.; позво́льте вас п.** may I trouble you?

побеспоко́|иться, юсь, ишься *pf.* **1.** *pf. of* **беспоко́иться 2.. 2.** to be rather worried.

побира́|ться, юсь *impf.* (*coll.*) to beg, live by begging.

поб|и́ть, ью́, ьёшь *pf.* **1.** *pf. of* **бить 1., 2.; п. реко́рд** to break a record. **2.** (*of rain, hail, etc.*) to beat down; (*of frost*) to nip. **3.** to break, smash (*a number of*). **4.** to kill (*a number of*).

поб|и́ться, ьётся *pf.* **1.** *pf. of* **би́ться. 2.** to break.

поблагодар|и́ть, ю́, и́шь *pf. of* **благодари́ть**

побла́жк|а, и *f.* indulgence; allowance(s); **де́лать ~у** (*+d.*) to indulge, make allowance(s) (for).

побледне́|ть, ю *pf. of* **бледне́ть**

поблёклый *adj.* faded; withered.

поблёк|нуть, ну, нешь, *past* **~, ~ла** *pf. of* **блёкнуть**

побли́зости *adv.* nearby; **п. (от)** near (to).

побож|и́ться, у́сь, и́шься *pf. of* **божи́ться**

побо́|и, ев *no sg.* beating; **терпе́ть п.** to take a beating.

побо́ищ|е, а *nt.* slaughter, carnage; bloody battle.

поболта́|ть, ю *pf.* (*coll.*) to have a chat.

побо́рник, а *m.* champion, upholder.

побор|о́ть, ю́, ~́ешь *pf.* to overcome; to beat (*in wrestling*).

побо́р|ы, ов *pl.* (*sg.* **~, ~а** *m.*) requisitions; extortion.

побо́чн|ый *adj.* side; secondary; **п. эффе́кт** side effect; **п. проду́кт** by-product; **~ая рабо́та** side-line; **п. сын** natural son.

побо|я́ться, ю́сь, и́шься *pf.* (*+g. or inf.*) to be afraid.

побран|и́ть, ю́, и́шь *pf.* to give a scolding, tick off.

побран|и́ться, ю́сь, и́шься *pf.* (**с**+*i.*; *coll.*) to have a quarrel (with).

побрата́|ться, юсь *pf. of* **брата́ться**

побрати́м, а *m.*: **го́род-п.** twin(ned) town.

по-бра́тски *adv.* like a brother; fraternally.

по|бра́ть, беру́, берёшь, *past* **~бра́л, ~брала́, ~бра́ло** *pf.* (*coll.*) to take (a quantity of).

побре́зга|ть, ю *pf. of* **бре́згать**

побре|сти́, ду́, дёшь, *past* **~̈л, ~ла́** *pf.* to plod.

побр|и́ть(ся), е́ю(сь) *pf. of* **бри́ть(ся)**

побро|ди́ть, жу́, ~́дишь *pf.* to wander for some time.

поброса́|ть, ю *pf.* **1.** to throw up; to throw about. **2.** to desert, abandon.

побря́к|ать, аю *pf.* (*of* **~ивать**) (*+i.*; *coll.*) to rattle.

побря́кива|ть, ю *impf. of* **побря́кать**

побряку́шк|а, и *f.* (*coll.*) trinket; rattle.

побуди́тельн|ый *adj.* stimulating; **~ая причи́на** motive, incentive; **~ые сре́дства** stimulants.

побу|ди́ть, жу́, ~ди́шь *pf.* (*of* **~жда́ть**) (**к** *or +inf.*) to induce (to), impel (to), prompt (to), spur (to).

побу́дк|а, и *f.* (*mil.*) reveille.

побужда́|ть, ю *impf. of* **побуди́ть**

побужде́ни|е, я *nt.* motive; inducement; incentive; **по со́бственному ~ю** of one's own accord.

побуре́|ть, ю *pf. of* **буре́ть**

побыва́льщин|а, ы *f.* (*obs.*) narration; true story.

побыва́|ть, ю *pf.* **1.** to have been to; to visit; **он ~л всю́ду** he has been everywhere; **в про́шлом году́ мы ~ли в Норве́гии и в Шве́ции** last year we visited Norway and Sweden. **2.** (*coll.*) to look in, call in; **мне на́до п. в конто́ре** I have to look in at the office.

побы́вк|а, и *f.* leave; **прие́хать домо́й на ~у** to come home on leave.

по|бы́ть, бу́ду, бу́дешь, *past* **~́был, ~была́, ~́было** *pf.* to stay (*for a short time*); **мы ~́были в Ло́ндоне два дня** we stayed in London for two days.

пова́|дить, жу, дишь *pf.* (*of* **~живать**) (*coll.*) to accustom; to train.

пова́|диться, жусь, дишься *pf.* (*+inf.*; *coll., pej.*) to get into the habit (of); to take to going (*somewhere*).

пова́дк|а, и *f.* (*coll.*) habit.

пова́дно *only in phr.* **что́бы не́ было п.** (*+d.*) (in order) to teach not to do so (again).

пова́жива|ть, ю *impf. of* **пова́дить**

повал|и́ть[1]**, ю́, ~́ишь** *pf. of* **вали́ть**[1]

повал|и́ть[2]**, ю́, ~́ишь** *pf.* to begin to throng, begin to pour; **дым ~и́л из трубы́** smoke began to belch from the chimney; **снег ~и́л хло́пьями** snow began to fall in flakes.

пова́льно *adv.* without exception.

пова́льн|ый *adj.* general, mass; **п. о́быск** general search; **~ая боле́знь** epidemic.

пова́нива|ть, ет *impf.* (*coll.*) to smell slightly.

по́вар, а, *pl.* **~а́** *m.* cook; **п.-ма́стер** master chef.

пова́ренн|ый *adj.* culinary; **~ая кни́га** cookery-book; **~ая соль** table salt.

поварёшк|а, и *f.* (*coll.*) ladle, strainer.

повари́х|а, и *f. of* **по́вар**
по-ва́шему *adv.* **1.** in your opinion. **2.** as you wish.
пове́д|ать, аю *pf.* (*of* **~ывать**) to relate, communicate; **п. та́йну** to disclose a secret.
поведе́ни|е, я *nt.* conduct, behaviour.
пове́дыва|ть, ю *impf. of* **пове́дать**
повез|ти́, у́, ёшь, *past* **~̈,** **~ла́** *pf. of* **везти́**
повелева́|ть, ю *impf.* **1.** (+*i.*) to command, rule. **2.** (+*d. and inf.*) to enjoin; **так ~ет мне со́весть** thus my conscience enjoins.
повеле́ни|е, я *nt.* command, injunction.
повел|е́ть, ю́, и́шь *pf.* to order, command.
повели́тел|ь, я *m.* (*rhet.*) sovereign, master.
повели́тел|ьный (~ен, ~ьна) *adj.* imperious, peremptory; **п. тон** peremptory tone; **~ьное наклоне́ние** (*gram.*) imperative mood.
повенча́|ть(ся), ю(сь) *pf. of* **венча́ть(ся)**[1]
поверг|а́ть, а́ю *impf. of* **~́нуть**
пове́рг|нуть, ну, нешь, *past* **~,** **~ла** *pf.* (*of* **~а́ть**) **1.** (*obs.*) to lay low; **боле́знь ~ла его́ в посте́ль** the illness has prostrated him. **2.** (**в**+*a.*) to plunge (into); **п. в отча́яние** to plunge into despair.
пове́р|енный *p.p.p. of* **~ить**[2]; *as n.* **п., ~енного** *m.* **1.** (*also* **~енная, ~енной** *f.*) confidant(e). **2.** attorney; **п. в дела́х** chargé d'affaires.
пове́р|ить[1]**, ю, ишь** *pf. of* **ве́рить**
пове́р|ить[2]**, ю, ишь** *pf.* (*of* **~я́ть**) **1.** to check (up); to verify. **2.** (+*d.*) to confide (to), entrust (to); **п. кому́-н. та́йну** to confide a secret to s.o.
пове́рк|а, и *f.* **1.** check; verification. **2.** (*mil.*) roll-call.
повер|ну́ть, ну́, нёшь *pf.* (*of* **~̈тывать**) to turn; (*fig.*) to change; **п. разгово́р** to change the subject.
повер|ну́ться, ну́сь, нёшься *pf.* (*of* **~̈тываться**) to turn; **п. круго́м** to turn round; **п. спино́й (к)** to turn one's back (upon); **п. к лу́чшему** to take a turn for the better.
повёртыва|ть(ся), ю(сь) *impf. of* **поверну́ть(ся)**
пове́рх *prep.*+*g.* over, above; on top of; **смотре́ть п. очко́в** to look over the top of one's spectacles.
пове́рхностност|ь, и *f.* superficiality.
пове́рхност|ный *adj.* **1.** surface, superficial; **~ное натяже́ние** (*tech.*) surface tension; **~ная ра́на** superficial injury; **~ное унаво́живание** (*agric.*) top dressing. **2. (~ен, ~на)** (*fig.*) superficial; shallow.
пове́рхност|ь, и *f.* surface.
по́верху *adv.* on the surface, on top.
пове́р|ье, ья, *g. pl.* **~ий** *nt.* popular belief, superstition.
повер|я́ть, я́ю *impf. of* **~́ить**
пове́с|а, ы *m.* (*coll.*) rake, scapegrace.
повеселе́|ть, ю *pf.* to cheer up, become cheerful.
повесел|и́ть(ся), ю́(сь), и́шь(ся) *pf. of* **весели́ть(ся)**
пове́|сить(ся), шу(сь), сишь(ся) *pf. of* **ве́шать(ся)**[1]
повествова́ни|е, я *nt.* narrative, narration.
повествова́тельный *adj.* narrative.
повеств|ова́ть, у́ю *impf.* (**о**+*p.*) to narrate, recount, relate.
пове|сти́[1]**, ду́, дёшь,** *past* **~̈л, ~ла́** *pf. of* **вести́ 1.**
пове|сти́[2]**, ду́, дёшь,** *past* **~̈л, ~ла́** *pf.* (*of* **поводи́ть**[1]) (+*i.*) to move; **п. бровя́ми** to raise one's eyebrows; **он и бро́вью не ~̈л** he did not turn a hair.
пове|сти́сь, ду́сь, дёшься, *past* **~̈лся, ~ла́сь** *pf. of* **вести́сь; уж так ~ло́сь** (*coll.*) such is the custom.
пове́стк|а, и *f.* notice, notification; **п. на заседа́ние** notice of meeting; **п. в суд** summons, writ, subpoena; **п. дня** agenda, order of the day.
по́вест|ь, и, *pl.* **~и, ~е́й** *f.* story, tale.
пове́три|е, я *nt.* (*coll.*) epidemic, infection (*also fig.*); **п. на дифтери́т** diphtheria epidemic.
пове́шени|е, я *nt.* hanging.
пове́|ять, ет *pf.* **1.** to begin to blow; to blow softly. **2.** (*impers.*, +*i.*) to breathe (of); (*fig.*) to begin to be felt; **~яло весно́й** spring was in the air.
повздо́р|ить, ю, ишь *pf. of* **вздо́рить**
повзросле́|ть, ю *pf.* to grow up.
повива́льн|ый *adj.* (*obs.*) obstetric; **~ая ба́бка** midwife; **~ое иску́сство** midwifery.
повида́|ть, ю *pf.* (*coll.*) to see.
повида́|ться, юсь *pf. of* **вида́ться**
по-ви́димому *adv.* apparently, seemingly.
пови́дл|о, а *nt.* jam.
пови́нн|ая, ой *f.* confession, acknowledgement of guilt; **принести́ ~ую** to acknowledge one's guilt, own up; **яви́ться с ~ой** to give o.s. up.
пови́нност|ь, и *f.* duty, obligation; **во́инская п.** compulsory military service, conscription.
пови́н|ный (~ен, ~на) *adj.* guilty.
повин|ова́ться, у́юсь *impf.* (*in past tense also pf.*) (+*d.*) to obey.
повинове́ни|е, я *nt.* obedience.
повис|а́ть, а́ю *impf. of* **~́нуть**
пови́с|нуть, ну, нешь, *past* **~,** **~ла** *pf.* (*of* **~а́ть**) **1.** (**на**+*p.*) to hang (by). **2.** to hang down, droop; **п. в во́здухе** (*fig.*) to hang in mid-air; (*of a joke*) to fall flat.
повиту́х|а, и *f.* (*coll.*) midwife.
повле́|чь, ку́, чёшь, ку́т, *past* **~̈к, ~кла́** *pf.* **(за собо́й)** to entail, result in; **п. за собо́й неприя́тные после́дствия** to have unpleasant consequences.
повлия́|ть, ю *pf. of* **влия́ть**
по́вод[1]**, а,** *pl.* **~ы** *m.* **(к)** cause, ground (for, of); **п. к войне́** casus belli; **дать п.** (+*d.*) to give occasion (to), give cause (for); **без вся́кого ~а** without cause; **по ~у** (+*g.*) apropos (of), as regards, concerning; **по како́му ~у?** in what connection?; why?
по́вод[2]**, а, о ~е, на ~у́,** *pl.* **~́ья, ~́ьев** *m.* rein; **быть у кого́-н. на ~у́** (*fig.*) to be under s.o.'s thumb.
пово|ди́ть[1]**, жу́, ~́дишь** *impf. of* **повести́**[2]
пово|ди́ть[2]**, жу́, ~́дишь** *pf.* to make go; **п. ло́шадь** to walk a horse.
повод|о́к, ка́ *m.* lead, leash.
поводы́р|ь, я́ *m.* (*coll.*) leader, guide.
пово́зк|а, и *f.* cart.
пово́лжский *adj.* situated on the Volga.
повора́чива|ть(ся), ю(сь) *impf. of* **повороти́ть(ся); ~йся!; ~йтесь!** (*coll.*) get a move on!; look sharp!
поворож|и́ть, у́, и́шь *pf. of* **ворожи́ть**
поворо́т, а *m.* turn(ing); **огни́ ~а** indicator lights (*of motor vehicle*); (*fig.*) turning-point; **п. реки́** bend in a river; **пе́рвый п. напра́во** the first turning to the right; **на ~е доро́ги** at the turn of the road; **п. к лу́чшему** turn for the better.
поворо|ти́ть(ся), чу́(сь), ~́тишь(ся) *pf. of* **повора́чивать(ся)** to turn.
поворо́тливост|ь, и *f.* **1.** nimbleness, agility. **2.** (*tech., naut.*) manoeuvrability.
поворо́тлив|ый (~, ~а) *adj.* **1.** nimble, agile. **2.** (*tech., naut.*) manoeuvrable.
поворо́тн|ый *adj.* rotary, rotating, revolving; (*fig.*) turning; **п. круг** turn-table; **п. мост** swing bridge; **~ое сиде́нье** swivel seat; **п. пункт** turning-point.
повре|ди́ть, жу́, ди́шь *pf.* **1.** *pf. of* **вреди́ть. 2.** (*pf. of* **~жда́ть**) to damage; to injure, hurt; **п. себе́ но́гу** to hurt one's leg.
повре|ди́ться, жу́сь, ди́шься *pf.* (*of* **~жда́ться**) to be damaged; to be injured; **п. в уме́** (*coll.*) to become mentally deranged.
поврежда́|ть(ся), ю(сь) *impf. of* **повреди́ть(ся)**
поврежде́ни|е, я *nt.* damage, injury.
повре|ждённый *p.p.p. of* **~ди́ть; п. в уме́** (*coll.*) mentally deranged.
повремен|и́ть, ю́, и́шь *pf.* (*coll.*) to wait a little; (**с**+*i.*) to delay (over).
повреме́нн|ый *adj.* **1.** periodic(al). **2.** reckoned on

time basis; **~ая опла́та** payment by time (*by the hour, etc.*).
повседне́вно *adv.* daily, every day.
повседне́вн|ый *adj.* daily; everyday.
повсеме́стно *adv.* everywhere.
повсеме́ст|ный (~ен, ~на) *adj.* universal, general.
повста́н|ец, ца *m.* insurgent, rebel.
повста́нческий *adj.* insurgent, rebel.
повстреча́|ть, ю *pf.* (*coll.*) to meet, run into.
повстреча́|ться, юсь *pf.* (*+d.* or **с***+i.*) to meet, run into; **мне ~лся знако́мый** I met an acquaintance.
повсю́ду *adv.* everywhere.
повто́р, а *m.* replay.
повторе́ни|е, я *nt.* **1.** repetition; reiteration. **2.** recurrence. **3.** revision (*of school work*).
повтори́тельный *adj.* repeat; recapitulatory; **п. курс** refresher course.
повтор|и́ть, ю́, и́шь *pf.* (*of* **~я́ть**) **1.** to repeat; to reiterate. **2.** to revise (*school work*).
повтор|и́ться, ю́сь, и́шься *pf.* (*of* **~я́ться**) **1.** to repeat o.s. **2.** to recur. **3.** *pass. of* **~и́ть**
повто́рный *adj.* repeated; recurring.
повтор|я́ть(ся), я́ю(сь) *impf. of* **~и́ть(ся)**
повы́|сить, шу, сишь *pf.* (*of* **~ша́ть**) **1.** to raise, heighten; **п. вдво́е, втро́е** to double, treble; **п. давле́ние** to increase pressure; **п. го́лос** to raise one's voice (*also fig., in anger*). **2.** to promote, advance; **п. кого́-н. по слу́жбе** to give s.o. promotion.
повы́|ситься, шусь, сишься *pf.* (*of* **~ша́ться**) **1.** to rise; to improve; **п. в чьём-н. мне́нии** to rise in s.o.'s estimation. **2.** to be promoted.
повыша́|ть(ся), ю(сь) *impf. of* **повы́сить(ся)**
повы́ше *comp. adj. and adv.* a little higher (up); a little taller.
повыше́ни|е, я *nt.* rise, increase; **п. по слу́жбе** promotion.
повы́|шенный *p.p.p. of* **~сить** *and adj.* heightened; increased; **~шенная температу́ра** a (raised) temperature.
повя|за́ть, жу́, ~жешь *pf.* (*of* **~зывать**) to tie; **п. га́лстук** to tie a tie.
повя|за́ться, жу́сь, ~жешься *pf.* (*of* **~зываться**) (*+i.*) to tie o.s. (with); **п. (платко́м)** to tie a scarf around one's head.
повя́зк|а, и *f.* **1.** band; fillet. **2.** bandage.
повя́зыва|ть(ся), ю(сь) *impf. of* **повяза́ть(ся)**
погада́|ть, ю *pf. of* **гада́ть**
пога́н|ка, ки *f.* **1.** = **~ый гриб. 2.** grebe.
пога́н|ый (~, ~а) *adj.* **1.** foul, unclean; **п. гриб** toadstool; **~ая пи́ща** (*relig.*) unclean food; **~ое ведро́** refuse pail. **2.** (*coll.*) foul, vile; **~ое настрое́ние** foul mood.
погаса́|ть, ю *impf.* to go out, be extinguished.
пога|си́ть, шу́, ~сишь *pf.* (*of* **гаси́ть** *and* **~ша́ть**) to liquidate; to cancel; **п. ма́рку** to cancel a stamp.
пога́с|нуть, ну, нешь, *past* **~, ~ла** *pf. of* **га́снуть**
погаша́|ть, ю *impf. of* **погаси́ть**
погиб|а́ть, а́ю *impf. of* **~нуть**
поги́бел|ь, и *f.* (*obs.*) ruin, perdition; **согну́ться в три ~и** to be hunched up; (*fig.*) to be cowed.
поги́б|нуть, ну, нешь, *past* **~, ~ла** *pf.* (*of* **ги́бнуть** *and* **~а́ть**) to perish; (*naut. and fig.*) to be lost; to go down.
погла́|дить, жу, дишь *pf. of* **гла́дить**
погла́жива|ть, ю *impf.* to stroke (*every so often, from time to time*).
поглазе́|ть, ю *pf. of* **глазе́ть**
погло|ти́ть, щу́, ~тишь *pf.* (*of* **~ща́ть**) to soak up, absorb (*also fig.*); **п. во́ду** to absorb water; **п. чьё-н. внима́ние** to engross s.o.; **п. рома́н** to devour a novel.
поглоща́|ть, ю *impf. of* **поглоти́ть**
поглупе́|ть, ю *pf. of* **глупе́ть**
погля|де́ть, жу́, ди́шь *pf.* **1.** *pf. of* **гляде́ть. 2.** to have a look. **3.** to look for a while.
погля|де́ться, жу́сь, ди́шься *pf. of* **гляде́ться**
погля́дыва|ть, ю *impf.* **1.** (**на***+a.*) to glance from time to time (at). **2.** (**за***+i.*; *coll.*) to keep an eye (on).
по|гна́ть, гоню́, го́нишь, *past* **~гна́л, ~гнала́, ~гна́ло** *pf.* to drive; to begin to drive.
по|гна́ться, гоню́сь, го́нишься, *past* **~гна́лся, ~гнала́сь, ~гна́ло́сь** *pf.* (**за***+i.*) to run (after); to give chase; (*fig.*) to strive (after, for); **п. за эффе́ктами** to strive for effect.
погн|у́ть, у́, ёшь *pf.* to bend.
погн|у́ться, ётся *pf.* to bend (*intrans.*).
погнуша́|ться, юсь *pf. of* **гнуша́ться**
погова́рива|ть, ю *impf.* (**о***+p.*) to talk (of); **~ют** there is talk (of); it is rumoured; **~ют о его́ жени́тьбе** there is talk of his marrying.
поговор|и́ть, ю́, и́шь *pf.* to have a talk.
погово́рк|а, и *f.* saying.
пого́д|а, ы *f.* weather; **кака́я бы ни была́ п.** rain or shine; **э́то не де́лает ~ы** that is not what counts; **ждать у мо́ря ~ы** to wait for sth. to turn up.
пого|ди́ть, жу́, ди́шь *pf.* (*coll.*) to wait a little; **~ди́те!** wait a moment!; **немно́го ~дя́** a little later.
пого́д|ки, ков *pl.* (*sg.* **~ок, ~ка** *m.*) brothers or sisters born a year apart; **мы с ней п.** there is a year's difference between us.
пого́дный[1] *adj.* annual, yearly.
пого́д|ный[2] *adj. of* **~а**
пого́жий *adj.* fine, lovely (*of weather*).
поголо́вно *adv.* one and all; (all) to a man.
поголо́вн|ый *adj.* general, universal; **п. нало́г** poll-tax; **~ая пе́репись** universal census.
поголо́вь|е, я *nt.* (total) number, head (*of live-stock*).
поголубе́|ть, ю *pf. of* **голубе́ть**
пого́н, а *m.* (*mil.*) shoulder-strap.
пого́нный *adj.* linear.
пого́нщик, а *m.* driver; **п. му́лов** muleteer.
пого́н|я, и *f.* pursuit, chase.
погоня́|ть, ю *impf.* to urge on, drive (*also fig.*).
погор|а́ть, а́ю *impf. of* **~е́ть**[1]
погор|е́ть[1]**, ю́, и́шь** *pf.* (*of* **~а́ть**) **1.** to lose all one's possessions in a fire. **2.** to burn down; to be burnt out.
погор|е́ть[2]**, ю́, и́шь** *pf.* to burn for a while.
погоряч|и́ться, у́сь, и́шься *pf.* to get heated (*fig.*), get worked up.
пого́ст, а *m.* (*obs.*) country churchyard.
пого|сти́ть, щу́, сти́шь *pf.* (**у**) to stay for a while (at, with).
погран... *comb. form* frontier(-).
пограни́чник, а *m.* border-guard.
пограни́чно-пропускно́й *adj.*: **п. пункт** border control post.
пограни́чн|ый *adj.* border; frontier; boundary; **п. столб** boundary post; **~ая стра́жа** border-guards.
по́греб, а, *pl.* **~а́** *m.* cellar (*also fig.*); **ви́нный п.** wine-cellar.
погреба́льн|ый *adj.* funeral; **~ое пе́ние** dirge.
погреба́|ть, ю *impf. of* **погрести́**[1]
погребе́ни|е, я *nt.* burial, interment.
погрему́шк|а, и *f.* rattle.
погре|сти́[1]**, бу́, бёшь,** *past* **~̈б, ~бла́** *pf.* (*of* **~ба́ть**) to bury, inter.
погре|сти́[2]**, бу́, бёшь,** *past* **~̈б, ~бла́** *pf.* to row a little.
погре́|ть, ю *pf.* to warm.
погре́|ться, юсь *pf.* to warm o.s.
погреш|а́ть, а́ю *impf. of* **~и́ть**
погреш|и́ть, у́, и́шь *pf.* (*of* **~а́ть**) (**про́тив**) to sin (against); to err.
погре́шност|ь, и *f.* error, mistake.
погро|зи́ть, жу́, зи́шь *pf. of* **грози́ть 2.**

погро|зи́ться, жу́сь, зи́шься *pf. of* **грози́ться**
погро́м, а *m.* pogrom, massacre.
погро́мщик, а *m.* person organizing *or* taking part in a pogrom; thug.
погружа́|ть(ся), ю(сь) *impf. of* **погрузи́ть(ся)**
погруже́ни|е, я *nt.* sinking, submergence; immersion; (*of a submarine*) dive, diving.
погру́|женный *and* **~жённый** *p.p.p. of* **~зи́ть; п. в во́ду** immersed (in water); **п. в размышле́ния** deep in thought; **п. в себя́** wrapped up in o.s.
погру|зи́ть, жу́, ≁зи́шь *pf.* (*of* **~жа́ть**) **1.** (**в**+*a.*) to dip (into), plunge (into), immerse; to submerge; to duck. **2.** *pf. of* **грузи́ть 2.**
погру|зи́ться, жу́сь, ≁зи́шься *pf.* **1.** (**в**+*a.*) to sink (into), plunge (into); (*of a submarine*) to submerge, dive; (*fig.*) to be plunged (in); to be absorbed (in), be lost (in); **п. в темноту́** to be plunged into darkness; **п. в чте́ние** to be absorbed in reading; **п. в размышле́ния** to be deep in thought. **2.** *pf. of* **грузи́ться**
погру́зк|а, и *f.* loading.
погру́зочный *adj.* loading; **п. жёлоб** loading chute.
погряз|а́ть, а́ю *impf. of* **≁нуть**
погря́з|нуть, ну, нешь, *past* **~, ~ла** *pf.* (*of* **~а́ть**) (**в**+*p.*) to be stuck (in); to be bogged down (in); to wallow (in) (*also fig.*).
погуб|и́ть, лю́, ≁ишь *pf. of* **губи́ть**
погу́дк|а, и *f.* (*coll.*) tune, melody; **ста́рая п. на но́вый лад** (*fig.*) the (same) old story.
погу́лива|ть, ю *impf.* (*coll.*) **1.** to walk up and down. **2.** to go on the spree from time to time.
погуля́|ть, ю *pf. of* **гуля́ть**
погусте́|ть, ет *pf. of* **густе́ть**
под[1]**, а, о ≁е, на ~у́** *m.* hearth(-stone); sole (of furnace).
под[2] (*also* **подо**) *prep.* **1.** (+*a. and i.*) under; **поста́вить п. стол** to put under the table; **находи́ться п. столо́м** to be under the table; **п. аре́стом** under arrest; **п. ви́дом** (+*g.*) in the guise (of); **п. влия́нием** (+*g.*) under the influence (of); **п. вопро́сом** open to question; **по́д гору** downhill; **п. замко́м** under lock and key; **п. землёй** underground; **быть п. ружьём** to be under arms; **взять кого́-н. по́д руку** to take s.o.'s arm; **п. руко́й** (close) at hand, to hand; **отда́ть п. суд** to prosecute; **п. усло́вием** on condition. **2.** (+*a. and i.*) near; **жить п. Москво́й** to live near Moscow; **би́тва п. Бородино́м** the battle of Borodino. **3.** (+*i.*) occupied by, used as; (+*a.*) for; (to serve) as; **помеще́ние под шко́лой** premises occupied by a school; **отвести́ помеще́ние п. шко́лу** to earmark premises for a school; **ба́нка п. варе́нье** jam-jar; **по́ле п. пшени́цей** wheat-field. **4.** (+*a.*) towards (*of time*); on the eve of; **п. ве́чер** towards evening; **п. Но́вый год** on New Year's Eve; **ему́ п. пятьдеся́т (лет)** he is getting on for fifty. **5.** (+*a.*) to (the accompaniment of); **танцева́ть п. му́зыку** to dance to music. **6.** (+*a.*) in imitation of; **э́то сде́лано п. оре́х** it is imitation walnut; **он пи́шет п. Турге́нева** he writes in imitation of (*the style of*) Turgenev. **7.** (+*a.*) on (= *in exchange for*); **п. зало́г** on security; **п. распи́ску** on receipt. **8.** (+*i.*) (*meant, etc.*) by; **что на́до понима́ть п. э́тим выраже́нием?** what is meant by this expression? **9.** (+*i.*; *cul.*) in, with; **ры́ба п. бешаме́лью** fish cooked in white sauce; **говя́дина п. хре́ном** beef with horse-radish.
под...[1] (*also* **подо...** *and* **подъ...**) *as vbl. pref. indicates* **1.** *action from beneath or affecting lower part of sth., as* **подчеркну́ть** to underline. **2.** *motion upwards, as* **подня́ть** to raise. **3.** *motion towards, as* **подъе́хать** to approach. **4.** *action carried out or event occurring in slight degree, as* **подкра́сить** to touch up; **поджи́ть** to begin to heal up. **5.** *supplementary action, as* **подрабо́тать** to earn additionally. **6.** *underhand action, as* **подкупи́ть** to bribe.
под...[2] (*also* **подо...** *and* **подъ...**) *as pref. of nn. and adjs.* under-, sub-.
подава́льщик, а *m.* **1.** waiter. **2.** supplier.
подава́льщиц|а, ы *f.* waitress.
пода|ва́ть(ся), ю́(сь), ёшь(ся) *impf. of* **пода́ть(ся)**
подав|и́ть[1]**, лю́, ≁ишь** *pf.* (*of* **~ля́ть**) **1.** to suppress, put down; to repress; **п. стон** to stifle a groan. **2.** (*fig.*) to depress; to crush, overwhelm. **3.** (*mil.*) to neutralize.
подав|и́ть[2]**, лю́, ≁ишь** *pf.* (*no impf.*) **1.** (*coll.*) to press, trample (*a quantity of*). **2.** to press, squeeze for a time.
подав|и́ться, лю́сь, ≁ишься *pf. of* **дави́ться**
подавле́ни|е, я *nt.* **1.** suppression; repression. **2.** (*mil.*) neutralization.
пода́вленност|ь, и *f.* depression; blues.
пода́в|ленный *p.p.p. of* **~и́ть** *and adj.* **1.** suppressed. **2.** depressed, dispirited.
подавля́|ть, ю *impf. of* **подави́ть**[1]
подавля́|ющий *pres. part. act. of* **~ть** *and adj.* overwhelming.
пода́вно *adv.* even more so.
пода́гр|а, ы *f.* gout.
пода́грик, а *m.* gout sufferer.
пода́льше *adv.* (*coll.*) a little farther.
подар|и́ть, ю́, ≁ишь *pf. of* **дари́ть**
пода́р|ок, ка *m.* present, gift; **получи́ть в п.** to receive as a present.
пода́тел|ь, я *m.* bearer (*of a letter, etc.*).
пода́тлив|ый (~, ~а) *adj.* **1.** pliant, pliable. **2.** (*fig.*) complaisant.
по́дат|ь, и, *pl.* **~и, ~ей** *f.* (*hist.*) tax, duty.
по|да́ть, да́м, да́шь, да́ст, дади́м, дади́те, даду́т *past* **≁дал, ~дала́, ≁дало** *pf.* (*of* **~дава́ть**) **1.** to give; to proffer; **п. го́лос** to cast a vote; **п. знак** to give a sign; **п. по́мощь** to lend a hand; **п. приме́р** to set an example; **п. ру́ку** (+*d.*) to offer one's hand; **п. сигна́л** to give the signal; **~да́йте ей пальто́** help her on with her coat. **2.** to serve (*food*); **п. на стол** to serve up; **обе́д ≁дан** dinner is served. **3.** (*sport*): **п. мяч** to serve. **4.** to serve, forward, present, hand in (*application etc.*); **п. апелля́цию** to appeal; **п. жа́лобу** to lodge a complaint; **п. заявле́ние** to hand in an application; **п. телегра́мму** to send a telegram; **п. в отста́вку** to tender one's resignation; **п. в суд** (**на**+*a.*) to bring an action (against). **5.** (*liter., theatr.*) to present, display.
по|да́ться, да́мся, да́шься, да́стся, дади́мся, дади́тесь, даду́тся, *past* **~да́лся, ~дала́сь, ~дало́сь** *pf.* (*of* **~дава́ться**) **1.** to move; **п. наза́д** to draw back; **п. в сто́рону** to move aside. **2.** (*coll.*) to give way, yield (*also fig.*); to cave in, collapse. **3.** (**на**+*a.*; *coll.*) to make (for), set out (for).
пода́ч|а, и *f.* **1.** giving, presenting; **п. го́лоса** voting. **2.** (*sport*) service, serve. **3.** (*tech.*) feeding, supply.
пода́чк|а, и *f.* (*coll.*) **1.** sop; crumb. **2.** (*fig.*) tip.
подая́ни|е, я *nt.* charity, alms; dole.
подба́в|ить, лю, ишь *pf.* (*of* **~ля́ть**) (+*a. or g.*) to add.
подбавля́|ть, ю *impf. of* **подба́вить**
подбега́|ть, ю *impf. of* **подбежа́ть**
подбе|жа́ть, гу́, жи́шь, гу́т *pf.* (*of* **~га́ть**) (**к**) to run up (to), come running up (to).
подбива́|ть, ю *impf. of* **подби́ть**
подбира́|ть(ся), ю(сь) *impf. of* **подобра́ть(ся)**
под|би́ть, обью́, обьёшь *pf.* (*of* **~бива́ть**) **1.** (+*i.*) to line (with). **2.** to re-sole. **3.** to injure; to bruise; **п. кому́-н. глаз** to give s.o. a black eye. **4.** (*mil.*) to knock out; **п. самолёт** to (shoot) down a plane. **5.** (+*inf. or* **на**+*a.*; *coll.*) to incite (to), instigate (to).
подбодр|и́ть, ю́, и́шь *pf.* (*of* **~я́ть**) (*coll.*) to cheer up.

подбодр|и́ться, ю́сь, и́шься *pf.* (*of* **~я́ться**) to cheer up, take heart.
подбодр|я́ть(ся), я́ю(сь) *impf. of* **~и́ть(ся)**
подбо́р, а *m.* selection, assortment; **(как) на п.** choice.
подбо́рк|а, и *f.* set, selection.
подборо́д|ок, ка *m.* chin.
подбоче́нива|ться, юсь *impf. of* **подбоче́ниться**
подбоче́нившись *adv.* with arms akimbo, with one's hands on one's hips.
подбоче́н|иться, юсь, ишься *pf.* (*of* **~иваться**) to place one's arms akimbo.
подбра́сыва|ть, ю *impf. of* **подбро́сить**
подбро́|сить, шу, сишь *pf.* (*of* **подбра́сывать**) **1.** to throw up, toss up; **(под)** to throw (under); **п. моне́ту** to toss up. **2.** (*+a. or g.*) to throw in, throw on; **п. резе́рвы** (*mil.*) to throw in one's reserves; **п. дров в печь** to throw more wood on the fire. **3.: п. младе́нца** to abandon a baby.
подва́л, а *m.* cellar; basement.
подва́л|ьный *adj. of* **~**
подве́домствен|ный (~, ~на) *adj.* (*+d.*) dependent (on), within the jurisdiction (of).
подвез|ти́, у́, ёшь, *past* **~̈, ~ла́** *pf.* (*of* **подвози́ть**) **1.** to bring, take (with one); to give a lift. **2.** (*+a. or g.*) to bring up, transport.
подвене́чн|ый *adj.*: **~ое пла́тье** wedding dress.
подверг|а́ть(ся), а́ю(сь) *impf. of* **~́нуть(ся)**
подве́рг|нуть, ну, нешь, *past* **~, ~ла** *pf.* (*of* **~а́ть**) (*+d.*) to subject (to); to expose (to); **п. испыта́нию** to put to the test; **п. опа́сности** to endanger; **п. сомне́нию** to question, challenge.
подве́рг|нуться, нусь, нешься, *past* **~ся, ~лась** *pf.* (*of* **~а́ться**) **1.** (*+d.*) to undergo. **2.** *pass. of* **~нуть**
подве́рженност|ь, и *f.* (*+d.*) susceptibility (to).
подве́ржен|ный (~, ~а) *adj.* (*+d.*) subject (to), liable (to); susceptible (to).
подвер|ну́ть, ну́, нёшь *pf.* (*of* **~̈тывать**) **1.** to screw up a little; **п. винт** to tighten a screw. **2.** to tuck in, tuck up; **п. одея́ло** to tuck in a blanket. **3.** to twist, sprain; **п. но́гу** to sprain one's ankle.
подвер|ну́ться, ну́сь, нёшься *pf.* (*of* **~̈тываться**) **1.** to be twisted, sprained; **нога́ у меня́ ~ну́лась** I have sprained my ankle. **2.** (*fig., coll.*) to turn up, show up; **он кста́ти ~ну́лся** he turned up just at the right moment. **3.** *pass. of* **~ну́ть**
подвёртыва|ть(ся), ю(сь) *impf. of* **подверну́ть(ся)**
подве́|сить, шу, сишь *pf.* (*of* **~шивать**) to hang up, suspend.
подве́ск|а, и *f.* **1.** hanging up, suspension. **2.** pendant.
подвесн|о́й *adj.* hanging, suspended; overhead; **п. конве́йер** overhead conveyer; **п. мост** suspension bridge; **п. мото́р** outboard motor.
подве|сти́, ду́, дёшь, *past* **~̈л, ~ла́** *pf.* (*of* **подводи́ть**) **1.** to lead up, bring up; to extend; **п. резе́рвы** to bring up reserves. **2. (под**+*a.*) to place (under); **п. ми́ну под мост** to mine a bridge; **п. про́чную ба́зу под свои́ до́воды** to place one's arguments on a sound footing; **п. бро́ви** to pencil one's eyebrows. **3.** to subsume; to put together; **п. бала́нс** (*+g.*) to balance; **п. ито́ги** to reckon up; to sum up (*also fig.*). **4.** (*coll.*) to let down. **5.** (*impers.; coll.*): **у меня́ живо́т от го́лода ~ло́** I'm absolutely famished.
подве́тренн|ый *adj.* leeward.
подве́шива|ть, ю *impf. of* **подве́сить**
подвива́|ть, ю *impf. of* **подви́ть**
по́двиг, а *m.* exploit, feat; heroic deed.
подви́га|ть, ю *pf.* (*+i.*) to move a little.
подвига́|ть(ся), ю(сь) *impf. of* **подви́нуть(ся)**
подви́д, а *m.* (*biol.*) subspecies.
подви́жник, а *m.* **1.** (*relig.*) ascetic; zealot. **2.** (*fig.*) zealot, devotee.
подвижн|о́й *adj.* **1.** mobile; movable; (*tech.*) travelling; **п. го́спиталь** mobile hospital; **~ы́е и́гры** outdoor games; **п. кран** travelling crane; **п. соста́в** (*rail.*) rolling stock. **2.** lively; agile; **~о́е лицо́** mobile features.
подви́жност|ь, и *f.* **1.** mobility. **2.** liveliness; agility.
подви́жный *adj.* mobile; lively; agile.
подвиза́|ться, юсь *impf.* (*rhet. or iron.*) to work; to pursue an occupation; **п. на юриди́ческом по́прище** to follow the law; **п. на сце́не** to tread the boards.
подвин|ти́ть, чу́, ти́шь *pf.* (*of* **~́чивать**) to screw up, tighten.
подви́|нуть, ну, нешь *pf.* (*of* **~га́ть**) **1.** to move; to push. **2.** (*fig.*) to advance, push forward.
подви́|нуться, нусь, нешься *pf.* (*of* **~га́ться**) **1.** to move. **2.** (*fig.*) to advance, progress.
подви́нчива|ть, ю *impf. of* **подвинти́ть**
под|ви́ть, овью́, овьёшь, *past* **~ви́л, ~вила́, ~ви́ло** *pf.* (*of* **~вива́ть**) to curl slightly, frizz.
подвла́ст|ный (~ен, ~на) *adj.* (*+d.*) subject to, under the control of.
подво́д|а, ы *f.* cart.
подво|ди́ть, жу́, ~́дишь *impf. of* **подвести́**
подво́дник, а *m.* (*naut.*) submariner.
подво́дн|ый *adj.* submarine; under-water; **п. ка́мень** reef, rock; **~ая ло́дка** submarine; **~ое тече́ние** undercurrent.
подво́з, а *m.* transport; supply.
подво|зи́ть, жу́, ~́зишь *impf. of* **подвезти́**
подворо́т|ня, ни, *g. pl.* **~ен** *f.* **1.** space between gate and ground. **2.** board attached to bottom of gate.
подво́х, а *m.* (*coll.*) dirty trick.
подвы́пи|вший *p.p. of* **~ть** *and adj.* (*coll.*) tipsy.
подвя|за́ть, жу́, ~́жешь *pf.* (*of* **~́зывать**) to tie up; to keep up.
подвя́зк|а, и *f.* garter; (*stocking*) suspender.
подвя́зыва|ть, ю *impf. of* **подвяза́ть**
подгиба́|ть(ся), ю(сь) *impf. of* **подогну́ть(ся)**
подгля|де́ть, жу́, ди́шь *pf.* (*of* **~́дывать**) **(в**+*a.*; *coll.*) to peep (at); to spy (on), watch furtively.
подгля́дыва|ть, ю *impf. of* **подгляде́ть**
подгнива́|ть, ю *impf. of* **подгни́ть**
подгни́|ть, ю́, ёшь, *past* **~л, ~ла́, ~ло** *pf.* (*of* **~ва́ть**) to begin to rot, rot slightly.
подгова́рива|ть, ю *impf. of* **подговори́ть**
подговор|и́ть, ю́, и́шь *pf.* (*of* **подгова́ривать**) **(на**+*a. or +inf.*) to put up (to), incite (to).
подголо́вник, а *m.* head-rest.
подголо́с|ок, ка *m.* **1.** (*mus.*) second part, supporting voice. **2.** (*coll., pej.*) yes-man.
подгоня́|ть, ю *impf. of* **подогна́ть**
подгор|а́ть, а́ю *impf. of* **~е́ть**
подгоре́лый *adj.* slightly burnt.
подгор|е́ть, и́т *pf.* (*of* **~а́ть**) to burn slightly.
подгота́влива|ть(ся), ю(сь) *impf. of* **подгото́вить(ся)**
подготови́тельн|ый *adj.* preparatory.
подгото́в|ить, лю, ишь *pf.* (*of* **подгота́вливать** *and* **~ля́ть**) **(для, к)** to prepare (for).
подгото́в|иться, люсь, ишься *pf.* (*of* **подгота́вливаться** *and* **~ля́ться**) **(к)** to prepare (for), get ready (for).
подгото́вк|а, и *f.* **1. (к)** preparation (for), training (for). **2. (в**+*p. or* **по**+*d.*) grounding (in).
подгото́вленност|ь, и *f.* preparedness.
подготовля́|ть(ся), ю(сь) *impf. of* **подгото́вить(ся)**
подгреба́|ть, ю *impf. of* **подгрести́**
подгре|сти́[1], бу́, бёшь, *past* **~̈б, ~бла́** *pf.* (*of* **~ба́ть**) to rake up.
подгре|сти́[2], бу́, бёшь, *past* **~̈б, ~бла́** *pf.* (*of* **~ба́ть**) **(к)** to row up (to).
подгру́д|ок, ка *m.* dewlap.
подгру́пп|а, ы *f.* sub-group.
подгу́зник, а *m.* nappy.

подгуля́|ть, ю *pf.* (*coll.*) to have a little too much to drink.
подда|ва́ть(ся), ю́(сь), ёшь(ся) *impf. of* **подда́ть-(ся)**
подда́кива|ть, ю *impf.* (*of* **подда́кнуть**) (+*d.*; *coll.*) to say yes (to), assent (to) (*also pej.*).
подда́к|нуть, ну, нешь *pf. of* **~ивать**
по́дданн|ый *p.p.p. of* **подда́ть**; *as n.* **п., ~ого** *m.*, *and* **~ая, ~ой** *f.* subject, national.
по́дданств|о, а *nt.* citizenship, nationality.
под|да́ть, да́м, да́шь, да́ст, дади́м, дади́те, даду́т, *past* **∠дал, ~дала́, ∠дало** *pf.* (*of* **~дава́ть**) **1.** to strike; to kick. **2.** (*at cards, draughts, etc.*) to give away. **3.** (+*g.*; *coll.*) to add, increase; **п. жа́ру** to add fuel to the fire; **п. па́ру** to increase steam.
под|да́ться, да́мся, да́шься, да́стся, дади́мся, дади́тесь, даду́тся, *past* **~да́лся, ~дала́сь** *pf.* (*of* **~дава́ться**) (+*d.*) to yield (to), give way (to), give in (to); **дверь не ~дала́сь** the door would not give; **п. искуше́нию** to yield to temptation; **не п. описа́нию** to beggar description; **п. отча́янию** to give way to despair; **п. угро́зам** to give in to threats.
поддева́|ть, ю *impf. of* **подде́ть**
подде́л|ать, аю *pf.* (*of* **~ывать**) to forge; to counterfeit.
подде́л|аться, аюсь *pf.* (*of* **~ываться**) **1.** (**под**+*a.*) to imitate. **2.** (**к**; *coll.*) to ingratiate o.s. (with).
подде́лк|а, и *f.* forgery; counterfeit; fake.
подде́лывател|ь, я *m.* forger; counterfeiter.
подде́лыва|ть(ся), ю(сь) *impf. of* **подде́лать(ся)**
подде́льн|ый *adj.* forged, counterfeit; sham; **~ые драгоце́нности** imitation jewellery.
поддержа́ни|е, я *nt.* maintenance; **п. ми́ра** peace-keeping; **войска́ по ~ю ми́ра** peacekeeping force.
поддерж|а́ть, у́, ∠ишь *pf.* (*of* **∠ивать**) **1.** to support (*also fig.*); to back (up), second; **п. резолю́цию** to second a resolution. **2.** to keep up, maintain; **п. разгово́р** to keep up a conversation; **п. регуля́рное сообще́ние** to maintain a regular service; **п. отноше́ния** (**с**+*i.*) to keep in touch (with).
подде́ржива|ть, ю *impf.* **1.** *impf. of* **поддержа́ть. 2.** (*impf. only*) to bear, support.
подде́ржк|а, и *f.* **1.** support; backing; seconding. **2.** support, prop, stay.
подде́|ть, ну, нешь *pf.* (*of* **~ва́ть**) **1.** (**под**+*a.*; *coll.*) to put on under, wear under; **~нь(те) сви́тер под ку́ртку** put a sweater on under your jacket. **2.** to hook; to catch up. **3.** (*fig.*, *coll.*) to catch out.
поддра́знива|ть, ю *impf. of* **поддразни́ть**
поддразн|и́ть, ю́, ∠ишь *pf.* (*of* **∠ивать**) (*coll.*) to tease.
поддува́л|о, а *nt.* ash-pit (*of stove, furnace*).
поддува́|ть, ю *impf.* **1.** to blow (*from underneath*). **2.** to blow slightly.
поде́йств|овать, ую *pf. of* **де́йствовать 2.**
поде́ла|ть, ю *pf.* (*no impf.*) (*coll.*) **1.** to do; **ничего́ не ~ешь** it can't be helped; **ничего́ не могу́ с ни́ми п.!** I can't do anything with them. **2.** to make, build.
подел|и́ть(ся), ю́(сь), ∠ишь(ся) *pf. of* **дели́ть(ся)**
поде́лк|а, и *f.* **1.** odd job. **2.** article; **~и из де́рева** wood articles.
подело́м *adv.* (*coll.*): **п. ему́,** *etc.*, it serves him, *etc.*, right.
поде́лыва|ть *impf.* (*coll.*) *only used in question* **что ~ешь?; что ~ете?** how are you getting on?
подёнк|а, и *f.* (*zool.*) mayfly.
подённо *adv.* by the day.
подённ|ый *adj.* by the day; **~ая опла́та** pay by the day; **~ая рабо́та** day-labour, time-work.
подёнщик, а *m.* day-labourer.
подёнщин|а, ы *f.* day-labour.
подёрг|ать, аю *pf. of* **~ивать**
подёргивани|е, я *nt.* twitch(ing).
подёргива|ть, ю *impf.* **1.** (*impf. of* **подёргать**) (+*a. or* **за**+*a.*) to pull (at), tug (at). **2.** (*impf. only*) (+*i.*) to twitch.
подёргива|ться, юсь *impf.* to twitch.
поде́ржанный *adj.* second-hand.
подерж|а́ть, у́, ∠ишь *pf.* to hold for some time; to keep for some time.
подерж|а́ться, у́сь, ∠ишься *pf.* **1.** (**за**+*a.*) to hold (on to) for some time. **2.** to hold (out), last.
подёрн|уть, ет *pf.* to cover, coat; (*impers.*): **реку́ ~уло льдом** the river was coated with ice.
подёрн|уться, ется *pf.* (+*i.*) to be covered (with).
подешеве́|ть, ет *pf. of* **дешеве́ть**
поджа́рива|ть(ся), ю(сь) *impf. of* **поджа́рить(ся)**
поджа́рист|ый (~, ~а) *adj.* brown, browned; crisp.
поджа́р|ить, ю, ишь *pf.* (*of* **~ивать**) to fry, roast, grill (slightly); **п. хлеб** to toast bread.
поджа́р|иться, юсь, ишься *pf.* (*of* **~иваться**) **1.** to fry, roast (slightly). **2.** *pass. of* **~ить**
поджа́р|ый (~, ~а) *adj.* (*coll.*) lean, wiry.
под|жа́ть, ожму́, ожмёшь *pf.* (*of* **~жима́ть**) to draw in; **п. гу́бы** to purse one's lips; **п. хвост** to have one's tail between one's legs (*also fig.*).
поджелу́дочн|ый *adj.*: **~ая железа́** (*anat.*) pancreas.
под|же́чь, ожгу́, ожжёшь, ожгу́т, *past* **~жёг, ~ожгла́** *pf.* (*of* **~жигать**) **1.** to set fire (to), set on fire. **2.** (*coll.*) to burn slightly.
поджига́тел|ь, я *m.* **1.** incendiary. **2.** (*fig.*) instigator; **п. войны́** warmonger.
поджига́тельский *adj.* inflammatory.
поджига́|ть, ю *impf. of* **подже́чь**
поджида́|ть, ю *impf.* to wait (for); to lie in wait (for).
поджи́л|ки, ок *no sg.* knee tendons; **у меня́ от стра́ха п. затрясли́сь** (*fig.*, *coll.*) I was quaking in my shoes.
поджима́|ть, ю *impf. of* **поджа́ть**
поджо́г, а *m.* arson.
подзаб|ы́ть, у́ду, у́дешь *pf.* (*coll.*) to forget partially; **я ~ы́л ру́сский язы́к** my Russian is a little rusty.
подзаголо́в|ок, ка *m.* sub-title, sub-heading.
подзадо́рива|ть, ю *impf. of* **подзадо́рить**
подзадо́р|ить, ю, ишь *pf.* (*of* **~ивать**) (*coll.*) to egg on.
подзаты́льник, а *m.* (*coll.*) clip round the ear.
подзащи́тн|ый, ого *m.* (*leg.*) client.
подземе́л|ье, ья, *g. pl.* **~ий** *nt.* cave; dungeon.
подзе́мк|а, и *f.* (*coll.*) underground (railway), tube.
подзе́мн|ый *adj.* underground, subterranean; **п. толчо́к** earth tremor.
подзерка́льник, а *m.* pier-glass table.
подзо́рн|ый *adj.*: **~ая труба́** spy-glass, telescope.
подзыва́|ть, ю *impf. of* **подозва́ть**
поди́[1] (*coll.*) = **пойди́** (*imper. of* **пойти́**); **п. сюда́!** come here!
поди́[2] (*coll.*) **1.** probably; I dare say; *or translated* must (be), is sure (to be); **ты, п., уста́ла** you must be tired; **он, п., забы́л** he has probably forgotten. **2.** *particle+imper.* just try; **п. удержи́ его́** just try to stop him.
подив|и́ться, лю́сь, и́шься *pf. of* **диви́ться**
подира́|ть, ет *impf.*: **моро́з по ко́же ~ет** (*coll.*) it makes one's flesh creep; it gives one the creeps.
подка́лыва|ть, ю *impf. of* **подколо́ть**
подка́пыва|ть(ся), ю(сь) *impf. of* **подкопа́ть(ся)**
подкарау́лива|ть, ю *impf.* (*of* **подкарау́лить**) **1.** to catch. **2.** (*impf. only*) to be on the watch (for).
подкарау́л|ить, ю, ишь *pf. of* **подкарау́ливать**
подка́рмлива|ть, ю *impf. of* **подкорми́ть**
подка|ти́ть, чу́, ∠тишь *pf.* (*of* **∠тывать**) **1.** to roll. **2.** (*coll.*; *of a carriage, etc.*) to roll up, drive up. **3.** (*coll.*): **у меня́ ком ~ти́л к го́рлу** I felt a lump in my throat.

подка|ти́ться, чу́сь, ∠тишься *pf.* (*of* **∠тываться**) (**под**+*a.*) to roll (under).
подка́тыва|ть(ся), ю(сь) *impf. of* **подкати́ть(ся)**
подка́шива|ть(ся), ю(сь) *impf. of* **подкоси́ть(ся)**
подки́дыва|ть, ю *impf. of* **подки́нуть**
подки́дыш, а *m.* foundling.
подки́|нуть, ну, нешь *pf.* (*of* **~дывать**) = **подбро́сить**
подкла́дк|а, и *f.* lining.
подкладно́|й *adj.*: **~е су́дно** bed-pan.
подкла́д|очный *adj. of* **~ка**
подкла́дыва|ть, ю *impf. of* **подложи́ть**
подкла́сс, а *m.* (*biol.*) sub-class.
подкле́ива|ть, ю *impf. of* **подкле́ить**
подкле́|ить, ю, ишь *pf.* (*of* **~ивать**) **1.** (**под**+*a.*) to glue (under), paste (under). **2.** to glue up, paste up. **3.** *pf. of* **кле́ить 2.**
подключ|а́ть(ся), а́ю(сь) *impf. of* **~и́ть(ся)**
подключ|и́ть, у́, и́шь *pf.* (*of* **~а́ть**) (*coll.*) **1.** (*tech.*) to link up, connect up. **2.** (*fig.*) to attach; **его́ ~и́ли ко второ́му ку́рсу** he has been attached to the second year.
подключ|и́ться, у́сь, и́шься *pf.* (*of* **~а́ться**) (*coll.*) **1.** (*tech. and fig.*) *pass. of* **~и́ть. 2.** (*fig.*) to settle down; to get the hang of things.
подко́в|а, ы *f.* (horse-)shoe.
подк|ова́ть, ую́, уёшь *pf.* (*of* **кова́ть** *and* **~о́вывать**) **1.** to shoe. **2.** (**в**+*p.*; *fig.*, *coll.*) to ground (in), give a grounding (in).
подко́выва|ть, ю *impf. of* **подкова́ть**
подко́жный *adj.* subcutaneous; hypodermic.
подколо́дн|ый *adj.*: **змея́ ~ая** (*fig.*, *coll.*) snake in the grass.
подкол|о́ть, ю́, ∠ешь *pf.* (*of* **подка́лывать**) **1.** to pin up. **2.** to chop up. **3.** to attach, append.
подкоми́сси|я, и *f.* sub-committee.
подкомите́т, а *m.* sub-committee.
подконтро́льный *adj.* under control.
подко́п, а *m.* **1.** undermining. **2.** underground passage. **3.** (*fig.*, *coll.*) intrigue(s), machinations.
подкопа́|ть, ю *pf.* (*of* **подка́пывать**) to dig under; (*fig.*) to undermine.
подкопа́|ться, юсь *pf.* (*of* **подка́пываться**) (**под** +*a.*) **1.** to dig, tunnel under; (*of animals*) to burrow (under). **2.** (*fig.*, *coll.*) to intrigue (against).
подкорм|и́ть, лю́, ∠ишь *pf.* (*of* **подка́рмливать**) to feed up; to fatten (up).
подко́рмк|а, и *f.* feeding; fattening.
подко́с, а *m.* (*tech.*) strut, brace, angle brace.
подко|си́ть, шу́, ∠сишь *pf.* (*of* **подка́шивать**) **1.** to cut down. **2.** to fell (*also fig.*); **э́то оконча́тельно ~си́ло (меня́, его́, *etc.*)** that was the last straw.
подкос|и́ться, ∠ится *pf.* (*of* **подка́шиваться**) to give way, buckle.
подкра́дыва|ться, юсь *impf. of* **подкра́сться**
подкра́|сить, шу, сишь *pf.* (*of* **~шивать**) to tint, colour; to touch up (*make-up, etc.*).
подкра́|ситься, шусь, сишься *pf.* (*of* **~шиваться**) to touch up one's make-up.
подкра́|сться, ду́сь, дёшься *pf.* (*of* **~дываться**) (**к**) to steal up (to), sneak up (to, on).
подкра́шива|ть(ся), ю(сь) *impf. of* **подкра́сить(ся)**
подкреп|и́ть, лю́, и́шь *pf.* (*of* **~ля́ть**) **1.** to support (*also fig.*). **2.** to fortify (*with food and/or drink*); **п. себя́ пе́ред доро́гой** to fortify o.s. for a journey. **3.** (*mil.*) to reinforce.
подкреп|и́ться, лю́сь, и́шься *pf.* (*of* **~ля́ться**) **1.** to fortify o.s. **2.** *pass. of* **~и́ть**
подкрепле́ни|е, я *nt.* **1.** confirmation, corroboration. **2.** sustenance. **3.** (*mil.*) reinforcement.
подкрепля́|ть(ся), ю(сь) *impf. of* **подкрепи́ть(ся)**
по́дкуп, а *m.* bribery; graft.
подкуп|а́ть, а́ю *impf. of* **~и́ть**
подкуп|и́ть, лю́, ∠ишь *pf.* (*of* **~а́ть**) **1.** to bribe. **2.** (*fig.*) to win over.
подла́|диться, жусь, дишься *pf.* (*of* **~живаться**) (**к**; +*coll.*) **1.** to adapt o.s. (to), fit in (with). **2.** to humour; to make up (to).
подла́жива|ться, юсь *impf. of* **подла́диться**
подла́мыва|ться, ется *impf. of* **подломи́ться**
по́дле *prep.*+*g.* by the side of, beside.
подлеж|а́ть, у́, и́шь *impf.* (+*d.*) to be liable (to), be subject (to); **э́тот дом ~и́т сно́су** this house is to be pulled down; **«не ~и́т оглаше́нию»** 'Confidential'; **не ~и́т сомне́нию** it is beyond doubt.
подлежа́щ|ее, его *nt.* (*gram.*) subject.
подлежа́|щий *pres. part. act. of* **~ть** *and adj.* (+*d.*) liable (to), subject (to); **п. обложе́нию сбо́ром** dutiable; **не п. обложе́нию сбо́ром** duty-free; **не п. оглаше́нию** confidential; off-the-record.
подлез|а́ть, а́ю *impf. of* **∠ть**
подле́з|ть, у, ешь *pf.* (*of* **~а́ть**) (**под**+*a.*) to crawl (under), creep (under).
подле́с|ок, ка *m.* undergrowth.
подлет|а́ть, а́ю *impf. of* **~е́ть**
подле|те́ть, чу́, ти́шь *pf.* (*of* **~та́ть**) (**к**) to fly up (to); (*fig.*) to rush up (to).
подле́ц, а́ *m.* scoundrel, villain, rascal.
подлива́|ть, ю *impf. of* **подли́ть**
подли́вк|а, и *f.* sauce, dressing; gravy.
подли́з|а, ы *c.g.* (*coll.*) lickspittle, toady.
подли|за́ться, жу́сь, ∠жешься *pf.* (*of* **∠зываться**) (**к**; *coll.*) to lick s.o.'s boots; to suck up (to).
подли́зыва|ть(ся), ю(сь) *impf. of* **подлиза́ть(ся)**
по́длинник, а *m.* original.
по́длинно *adv.* really; genuinely; **п. хоро́ший фильм** a really good film.
по́длинност|ь, и *f.* authenticity.
по́длин|ный (~ен, ~на) *adj.* **1.** genuine; authentic; original. **2.** true, real; **п. учёный** a true scholar.
под|ли́ть, олью́, ольёшь, *past* **~ли́л, ~лила́, ~ли́ло** *pf.* (*of* **~лива́ть**) (+*a. or g.* **в**+*a.*) to add (to); **п. ма́сла в ого́нь** (*fig.*) to add fuel to the fire.
по́длича|ть, ю *impf.* to act meanly.
подло́г, а *m.* forgery.
подло́дк|а, и *m.* submarine; sub.
подлож|и́ть, у́, ∠ишь *pf.* (*of* **подкла́дывать**) **1.** (**под**+*a.*) to lay under; to line; **п. ва́ту** to wad. **2.** (+*a. or g.*) to add; **~и́те дрова́** *or* **дров** put some more wood on. **3.** to put furtively; **п. свинью́ кому́-н.** to play a dirty trick on s.o.
подло́ж|ный (~ен, ~на) *adj.* counterfeit, forged.
подлоко́тник, а *m.* elbow-rest; arm (*of chair*).
подлом|и́ться, ∠ится *pf.* (*of* **подла́мываться**) (**под**+*i.*) to break (under).
по́длост|ь, и *f.* **1.** meanness, baseness. **2.** mean trick, low-down trick.
по́дл|ый (~, ~а́, ~л) *adj.* mean, base, despicable.
подма́|зать, жу, жешь *pf.* (*of* **~зывать**) to grease, oil; (*fig.*, *coll.*) to grease s.o.'s palm.
подма́|заться, жусь, жешься *pf.* (*of* **~зываться**) **1.** to touch up one's make-up. **2.** (**к**) to curry favour (with), make up (to).
подма́зыва|ть(ся), ю(сь) *impf. of* **подма́зать(ся)**
подманда́тн|ый *adj.* (*pol.*) mandated; **~ая террито́рия** mandated territory.
подмасте́рь|е, я, *g. pl.* **~ев** *m.* apprentice.
подма́хива|ть, ю *impf. of* **подмахну́ть**
подмах|ну́ть, ну́, нёшь *pf.* (*of* **∠ивать**) (*coll.*) to scribble a signature on.
подма́чива|ть, ю *impf. of* **подмочи́ть**
подме́н, а *m.* substitution (*of sth. false for sth. real*).
подме́н|а, ы *f.* = **~**
подме́нива|ть, ю *impf. of* **подмени́ть**
подмен|и́ть, ю́, ∠ишь *pf.* (*of* **∠ивать** *and* **~я́ть**) (+*a. and i.*) to substitute (for) (*intentionally*); **кто́-**

то на вечери́нке ~и́л мне шля́пу s.o. at the party took my hat (and left his own instead).

подмен|я́ть, я́ю *impf. of* **~и́ть**

подмерз|а́ть, а́ет *impf. of* **≃нуть**

подмёрз|нуть, нет, *past* **~, ~ла** *pf.* (*of* **~а́ть**) to freeze slightly.

подме|си́ть, шу́, ≁сишь *pf.* (*of* **≁шивать**[1]) to add, mix in.

подме|сти́, ту́, тёшь, *past* **≃л, ~ла́** *pf.* (*of* **~та́ть**) to sweep.

подмета́|ть, ю *impf. of* **подмести́**

подме́|тить, чу, тишь *pf.* (*of* **~ча́ть**) to notice, spot.

подмётк|а, и *f.* sole; **в ~и кому́-н. не годи́ться** (*coll.*) not to be fit to hold a candle to s.o.

подмеча́|ть, ю *impf. of* **подме́тить**

подмеш|а́ть, а́ю *pf.* (*of* **≁ивать**[2]) to stir in.

подме́шива|ть[1]**, ю** *impf. of* **подмеси́ть**

подме́шива|ть[2]**, ю** *impf. of* **подмеша́ть**

подми́гива|ть, ю *impf. of* **подмигну́ть**

подмиг|ну́ть, ну́, нёшь *pf.* (*of* **≁ивать**) (+*d.*) to wink (at).

подмина́|ть, ю *impf. of* **подмя́ть**

подмо́г|а, и *f.* (*coll.*) help.

подмок|а́ть, а́ю *impf. of* **≁нуть**

подмо́к|нуть, ну, нешь, *past* **~, ~ла** *pf.* (*of* **~а́ть**) to get slightly wet.

подмора́жива|ть, ет *impf. of* **подморо́зить**

подморо́з|ить, ит *pf.* (*of* **подмора́живать**) to freeze; **к ве́черу ~ило** towards evening it began to freeze.

подмоско́вный *adj.* (situated) near Moscow.

подмо́стк|и, ов *no sg.* **1.** scaffolding, staging. **2.** (*theatr.*) stage; boards.

подмо́ч|енный *p.p.p. of* **~и́ть** *and adj.* **1.** moist; damp. **2.** damaged (*also fig.*); **~енная репута́ция** tarnished reputation.

подмоч|и́ть, у́, ≁ишь *pf.* (*of* **подма́чивать**) **1.** to moisten, dampen. **2.** (*fig.*) to tarnish.

подмыва́|ть, ю *impf.* **1.** *impf. of* **подмы́ть. 2.** (*impers.*) to urge; **меня́ так и ~ет** (+*inf.*) I feel an urge (to).

подм|ы́ть, о́ю, о́ешь *pf.* (*of* **~ыва́ть**) **1.** to wash. **2.** to wash away, undermine.

подмы́шк|а, и *f.* arm-pit (*of article of clothing*).

подмы́ш|ки, ек *no sg.* arm-pits.

подмы́шник, а *m.* dress-preserver *or* -shield.

под|мя́ть, омну́, омнёшь *pf.* (*of* **~мина́ть**) to crush; to trample down.

поднадзо́р|ный (~ен, ~на) *adj.* under surveillance.

поднебе́сь|е, я *nt.* (*folk poet.*) the heavens.

поднево́л|ьный (~ен, ~ьна) *adj.* **1.** dependent; subordinate. **2.** forced; **п. труд** forced labour.

поднес|ти́, у́, ёшь, *past* **≃, ~ла́** *pf.* (*of* **подноси́ть**) **1. (к)** to take (to), bring (to). **2.** (+*d. and a.*) to present (with); to treat (to); **п. кому́-н. буке́т цвето́в** to present s.o. with a bouquet.

поднима́|ть(ся), ю(сь) *impf. of* **подня́ть(ся)**

поднов|и́ть, лю́, и́шь *pf.* (*of* **~ля́ть**) to renew, renovate.

подновля́|ть, ю *impf. of* **поднови́ть**

подного́тн|ая, ой *f.* (*coll.*) the whole truth, all there is to know; **он зна́ет про них всю ~ую** he knows all about them.

подно́жи|е, я *nt.* **1.** foot (*of mountain, etc.*). **2.** pedestal.

подно́жк|а[1]**, и** *f.* step, footboard.

подно́жк|а[2]**, и** *f.* (*in wrestling*) backheel; **дать кому́-н. ~у** to trip s.o. up.

подно́жн|ый *adj.*: **п. корм** pasture, pasturage.

подно́с, а *m.* tray; salver; **ча́йный п.** tea-tray.

подно|си́ть, шу́, ≁сишь *impf. of* **поднести́**

подно́счик, а *m.* **1.** carrier; **п. патро́нов** ammunition carrier. **2.** innkeeper's assistant, drinks server.

подноше́ни|е, я *nt.* **1.** presenting, giving. **2.** present, gift; **цвето́чные ~я** floral tributes.

подня́ти|е, я *nt.* raising; rising; **голосова́ть ~ем рук** to vote by show of hands.

под|ня́ть, ниму́, ни́мешь, *past* **≁нял, ~няла́, ≁няло** *pf.* (*of* **~нима́ть**) **1.** to raise; to lift; to hoist; **п. настрое́ние** (+*g.*) to lift the spirits (of); **п. ору́жие** to take up arms; **п. ру́ку (на**+*a.*) to raise a hand (against); **п. флаг** to hoist a flag; **п. целину́** to open up virgin lands; **п. я́корь** to weigh anchor; **п. на во́здух** to blow up; **п. на́ смех** to make a laughing-stock (of). **2.** to pick up; **п. пе́тли** to pick up stitches. **3.** to rouse, stir up; **п. восста́ние** to stir up rebellion; **п. ссо́ру** to pick a quarrel; **п. на́ ноги** to rouse. **4.** (*fig.*) to improve; to enhance.

под|ня́ться, ниму́сь, ни́мешься, *past* **~ня́лся́, ~няла́сь** *pf.* (*of* **~нима́ться**) **1.** to rise; to go up; to get up; **н. на́ ноги** to rise to one's feet. **2. (на**+*a.*) to climb, ascend, go up. **3.** to arise; to break out, develop; **~няла́сь ссо́ра** a quarrel arose; **~няла́сь дра́ка** a fight started. **4.** (*econ.*; *fig.*) to improve; to recover.

подо *prep.* = **под**[2]

подо...[1] *as vbl. pref.* = **под...**[1]

подо...[2] *as pref. of nn. and adjs.* = **под...**[2]

подоба́|ть, ет *impf.* (*impers.*; +*d. and inf.*) to become, befit.

подоба́|ющий *pres. part. act. of* **~ть** *and adj.* proper, fitting.

подо́би|е, я *nt.* **1.** likeness; **по своему́ о́бразу и ~ю** in one's own image. **2.** (*math.*) similarity.

подо́бно *adv.* (+*d.*) like; **п. тому́, как** just as.

подо́б|ный (~ен, ~на) *adj.* like; similar; **~ное поведе́ние** such behaviour; **~ные треуго́льники** (*math.*) similar triangles; **ничего́ ~ного!** (*coll.*) nothing of the kind!; **и тому́ ~ное** (*abbr.* **и т. п.**) and so on, and such like.

подобостра́сти|е, я *nt.* servility.

подобостра́ст|ный (~ен, ~на) *adj.* servile.

подо́бранност|ь, и *f.* neatness, tidiness.

подо́бр|анный *p.p.p. of* **~а́ть** *and adj.* neat, tidy.

под|обра́ть, беру́, берёшь, *past* **~обра́л, ~обрала́, ~обра́ло** *pf.* (*of* **~бира́ть**) **1.** to pick up. **2.** to tuck up; to take up; **п. во́лосы** to put up one's hair. **3.** to select, choose, pick; **п. дже́мпер под цвет костю́ма** to choose a jumper to match a suit.

под|обра́ться, беру́сь, берёшься, *past* **~обра́лся, ~обрала́сь, ~обра́ло́сь** *pf.* (*of* **~бира́ться**) **1. (к)** to steal up (to), approach stealthily. **2.** to make o.s. tidy. **3.** *pass. of* **~обра́ть**

подобре́|ть, ю *pf. of* **добре́ть**[1]

по-добрососе́дски: жить п. (с+*i.*) to have good-neighbourly relations (with ...).

под|огна́ть, гоню́, го́нишь, *past* **~огна́л, ~огнала́, ~огна́ло** *pf.* (*of* **~гоня́ть**) **1. (к)** to drive (to). **2.** (*coll.*) to drive on, urge on, hurry. **3. (к)** to adjust (to), fit (to).

под|огну́ть, огну́, огнёшь *pf.* (*of* **~гиба́ть**) to tuck in; to bend under.

под|огну́ться, огну́сь, огнёшься *pf.* (*of* **~гиба́ться**) to bend.

подогрева́|ть, ю *impf. of* **подогре́ть**

подогре́|ть, ю *pf.* (*of* **~ва́ть**) to warm up, heat up; (*fig.*) to rouse.

пододвига́|ть, ю *impf. of* **пододви́нуть**

пододви́|нуть, ну, нешь *pf.* (*of* **~га́ть**) **(к)** to move up (to), push up (to).

пододея́льник, а *m.* quilt cover, blanket cover.

подожд|а́ть, у́, ёшь, *past* **~а́л, ~ала́, ~а́ло** *pf.* (+*a. or g.*) to wait (for).

под|озва́ть, зову́, зовёшь, *past* **~озва́л, ~озвала́, ~озва́ло** *pf.* (*of* **~зыва́ть**) to call up; to beckon.

подозрева́|емый *pres. part. pass. of* **~ть** *and adj.* suspected; suspect.

подозрева́|ть, ю *impf.* (*no pf.*) to suspect; **я ~ю его́ в преступле́нии** I suspect him of a crime.
подозре́ни|е, я *nt.* suspicion; **оста́ться вне ~й** to remain above suspicion; **по ~ю (в+*p.*)** on suspicion (of); **быть под ~ем, на ~и** to be under suspicion.
подозри́тельно *adv.* suspiciously; **вести́ себя́ п.** to behave suspiciously; **смотре́ть п. (на+*a.*)** to regard with suspicion.
подозри́тельност|ь, и *f.* suspiciousness.
подозри́тел|ьный (~ен, ~ьна) *adj.* **1.** suspicious; suspect; shady; **п. субъе́кт** shady character. **2.** suspicious (= *mistrustful*).
подо|и́ть, ю́, ⁓и́шь *pf. of* **дои́ть**
подо́йник, а *m.* milk-pail.
подо|йти́, йду́, йдёшь, *past* **~шёл, ~шла́** *pf.* (*of* **подходи́ть**) **1. (к)** to approach (*also fig.*); to come up (to), go up (to); **по́езд ~шёл к ста́нции** the train pulled in to the station. **2.** (+*d.*) to do (for); to fit; to suit; **э́тот пиджа́к о́чень мне ~йдёт** this coat will suit me very well.
подоко́нник, а *m.* window-sill.
подо́л, а *m.* hem (*of skirt*); **держа́ться за чей-н. п.** to cling to s.o.'s skirts.
подо́лгу *adv.* for a long time; for hours on end.
подоль|сти́ться, щу́сь, сти́шься *pf.* (**к**; *coll.*) to ingratiate o.s. (with).
подольща́|ться, юсь *impf. of* **подольсти́ться**
подо́н|ки, ков *pl.* (*sg.* **~ок, ~ка** *m.*) dregs (*also fig.*); (*fig.*) scum; riff-raff.
подопе́чн|ый *adj.* under wardship; **~ая террито́рия** (*pol.*) trust territory.
подоплёк|а, и *f.* (*coll.*) true cause; underlying cause.
подо́пытный *adj.* experimental; **п. кро́лик** (*fig.*) guinea-pig.
подорв|а́ть, у́, ёшь, *past* **~а́л, ~ала́, ~а́ло** *pf.* (*of* **подрыва́ть**[1]) **1.** to blow up. **2.** (*fig.*) to undermine; to sap; **п. чей-н. авторите́т** to undermine s.o.'s authority; **п. здоро́вье** to sap one's health.
подорожа́|ть, ю *pf. of* **дорожа́ть**
подоро́жник, а *m.* (*bot.*) plantain.
подоро́жный *adj.* roadside; **п. столб** milestone.
подо|сла́ть, шлю, шлёшь *pf.* (*of* **подсыла́ть**) to send, dispatch (*secretly, on a secret mission*).
подосно́в|а, ы *f.* true cause; underlying cause.
подоспева́|ть, ю *impf. of* **подоспе́ть**
подоспе́|ть, ю *pf.* (*of* **~ва́ть**) (*coll.*) to arrive, appear (in time).
под|остла́ть, стелю́, сте́лешь *pf.* (*of* **~стила́ть**) (**под**+*a.*) to lay (under), stretch (under).
подоткн|у́ть, у́, ёшь *pf.* (*of* **подтыка́ть**) to tuck in, tuck up; **п. простыню́** to tuck in a sheet.
подотчёт|ный (~ен, ~на) *adj.* **1.** (+*d.*) accountable (to). **2.** (*fin.*) on account.
подо́хн|уть, у, ешь *pf.* (*of* **до́хнуть** *and* **подыха́ть**) **1.** (*of animals*) to die. **2.** (*coll.*; *of human beings*) to kick the bucket.
подохо́дный *adj.*: **п. нало́г** income tax.
подо́шв|а, ы *f.* **1.** sole. **2.** foot (*of slope*).
подпада́|ть, ю *impf. of* **подпа́сть**
подпа́ива|ть, ю *impf. of* **подпои́ть**
подпа́лин|а, ы *f.* scorch-mark; **ло́шадь с ~ой** dappled horse.
подпал|и́ть, ю, и́шь *pf.* (*of* **⁓ивать**) (*coll.*) **1.** to singe, scorch. **2.** to set on fire.
подпа́с|ок, ка *m.* shepherd boy.
подпа́|сть, ду́, дёшь, *past* **~л** *pf.* (*of* **~да́ть**) (**под**+*a.*) to fall (under); **п. под чьё-н. влия́ние** to fall under s.o.'s influence.
подпева́л|а, ы *c.g.* (*coll.*) yes-man.
подпева́|ть, ю *impf.* (+*d.*) to join (in singing); to take up a song; (*fig.*) to echo.
под|пере́ть, опру́, опрёшь, *past* **~пёр, ~пёрла** *pf.* (*of* **~пира́ть**) to prop up.
подпи́лива|ть, ю *impf. of* **подпили́ть**
подпил|и́ть, ю́, ⁓ишь *pf.* (*of* **⁓ивать**) **1.** to saw; to file. **2.** to saw a little off; to file down.
подпира́|ть, ю *impf. of* **подпере́ть**
подписа́вш|ий, его *m.* signatory.
подписа́ни|е, я *nt.* signing.
подпи|са́ть, шу́, ⁓шешь *pf.* (*of* **⁓сывать**) **1.** to sign. **2.** to add (*to sth. written*). **3.: п. кого́-н. на журна́л** to take out a magazine subscription for s.o.
подпи|са́ться, шу́сь, ⁓шешься *pf.* (*of* **⁓сываться**) **1.** (**под**+*i.*) to sign, put one's name (to); (*fig.*) to subscribe (to). **2.** (**на**+*a.*) to subscribe (to).
подпи́ск|а, и *f.* **1.** subscription. **2.** written undertaking; signed statement.
подписн|о́й *adj.* subscription.
подпи́счик, а *m.* (**на**+*a.*) subscriber (to).
по́дпис|ь, и *f.* **1.** signature; **поста́вить свою́ п.** (**под**+*i.*) to put one's signature (to); **за ~ью** (+*g.*) signed (by). **2.** caption; inscription.
подплыва́|ть, ю *impf. of* **подплы́ть**
подплы́|ть, ву́, вёшь, *past* **~л, ~ла́ ~ло** *pf.* (*of* **~ва́ть**) (**к**) to swim up (to); to sail up (to).
подпо|и́ть, ю́, ⁓и́шь *pf.* (*of* **подпа́ивать**) (*coll.*) to make tipsy.
подполз|а́ть, а́ю *impf. of* **~ти́**
подполз|ти́, у́, ёшь, *past* **⁓, ~ла́** *pf.* (*of* **~а́ть**) (**к**) to creep up (to); (**под**+*a.*) to creep (under).
подполко́вник, а *m.* lieutenant-colonel.
подпо́ль|е, я *nt.* **1.** cellar. **2.** (*fig.*) underground (organization, activities); **уйти́ в п.** to go underground.
подпо́льный *adj.* underground; secret, clandestine.
подпо́льщик, а *m.* member of the underground.
подпо́р|а, ы *f.* prop, support; brace, strut.
подпо́рк|а, и *f.* = **подпо́ра**
подпо́р|ный *adj. of* **~а**; **~ная сте́нка** breast-wall; (*naut.*) bulkhead.
подпору́чик, а *m.* (*hist.*) second lieutenant.
подпо́чв|а, ы *f.* subsoil, substratum.
подпоя́|сать, шу, шешь *pf.* (*of* **~сывать**) to belt; to gird (on).
подпоя́|саться, шусь, шешься *pf.* (*of* **~сываться**) to belt o.s.; to gird o.s.; to put on a belt, girdle.
подпоя́сыва|ть(ся), ю(сь) *impf. of* **подпоя́сать(ся)**
подпра́в|ить, лю, ишь *pf.* (*of* **~ля́ть**) to rectify; to touch up, retouch.
подправля́|ть, ю *impf. of* **подпра́вить**
подпру́г|а, и *f.* saddle-girth, belly-band.
подпры́гива|ть, ю *impf. of* **подпры́гнуть**
подпры́г|нуть, ну, нешь *pf.* (*of* **~ивать**) to leap up, jump up; to bob up and down.
подпуска́|ть, ю *impf. of* **подпусти́ть**
подпу|сти́ть, шу́, ⁓стишь *pf.* (*of* **~ска́ть**) to allow to approach; **п. на расстоя́ние вы́стрела** to allow to come within range.
подраба́тыва|ть, ю *impf. of* **подрабо́тать**
подрабо́та|ть, ю *pf.* (*of* **подраба́тывать**) (*coll.*) **1.** (+*a. or g.*) to earn extra. **2.** to work up.
подра́внива|ть, ю *impf. of* **подровня́ть**
подра́гива|ть, ю *impf.* (*coll.*) to shake, tremble intermittently.
подража́ни|е, я *nt.* imitation.
подража́тел|ь, я *m.* imitator.
подража́тел|ьный (~ен, ~ьна) *adj.* imitative.
подража́|ть, ю *impf.* (*no pf.*) (+*d.*) to imitate.
подразделе́ни|е, я *nt.* **1.** subdivision. **2.** (*mil.*) subunit, element.
подраздел|и́ть, ю́, и́шь *pf.* (*of* **~я́ть**) to subdivide.
подраздел|я́ть, я́ю *impf. of* **~и́ть**
подразумева́|ть, ю *impf.* to imply, entail, mean.
подразумева́|ться, ется *impf.* to be implied, be entailed, be meant; **что ~ется под э́тим выраже́нием?** what is meant by this expression?
подраст|а́ть, а́ю *impf. of* **~и́; ~а́ющее поколе́ние**

the rising generation.

подраст|и́, у́, ёшь, *past* **подро́с, подросла́** *pf.* to grow (a little).

по|дра́ть(ся), деру́(сь), дерёшь(ся), *past* **~дра́л(ся), ~драла́(сь), ~дра́ло́(сь)** *pf. of* **дра́ть(ся)**

подре́|зать, жу, жешь *pf.* (*of* **~за́ть**) to cut; to clip, trim; to prune, lop; **п. кому́-н. кры́лья** (*fig.*) to clip s.o.'s wings.

подреза́|ть, ю *impf. of* **подре́зать**

подрис|ова́ть, у́ю *pf.* (*of* **~о́вывать**) **1.** to retouch, touch up. **2.** to add, put in (*on a painting etc.*).

подрисо́выва|ть, ю *impf. of* **подрисова́ть**

подро́бно *adv.* minutely, in detail; at (great) length.

подро́бност|ь, и *f.* detail; **вдава́ться в ~и** to go into detail.

подро́б|ный (~ен, ~на) *adj.* detailed, minute.

подровня́|ть, ю *pf.* (*of* **подра́внивать**) to level, even; to trim.

подро́ст|ок, ка *m.* adolescent, teenager.

подруб|а́ть, а́ю *impf. of* **~и́ть**

подруб|и́ть[1]**, лю́, ~́ишь** *pf.* (*of* **~а́ть**) to hew.

подруб|и́ть[2]**, лю́, ~́ишь** *pf.* (*of* **~а́ть**) to hem.

подру́г|а, и *f.* (*female*) friend; **п. жи́зни** helpmate.

по-дру́жески *adv.* in a friendly way; as a friend.

подруж|и́ться, у́сь, и́шься *pf. of* **дружи́ться**

подру́жк|а, и *f. affectionate dim. of* **подру́га; п. неве́сты** bridesmaid.

подру́лива|ть, ю *impf. of* **подрули́ть**

подрул|и́ть, ю́, и́шь *pf.* (*of* **~́ивать**) (**к**; *aeron.*) to taxi up (to).

подрумя́нива|ть(ся), ю(сь) *impf. of* **подрумя́нить(ся)**

подрумя́н|ить, ю, ишь *pf.* (*of* **~ивать**) **1.** to rouge; to touch up with rouge. **2.** to make ruddy, make rosy; **моро́з ~ил им щёки** the frost brought a flush to their cheeks. **3.** (*cul.*) to brown.

подрумя́н|иться, юсь, ишься *pf.* (*of* **~иваться**) **1.** to apply rouge. **2.** to flush, become flushed. **3.** (*cul.*) to brown.

подру́чн|ый *adj.* **1.** at hand, to hand; improvised, makeshift; **~ые сре́дства** improvised means. **2.** *as n.* **п., ~ого** *m.* assistant; mate.

подры́в, а *m.* undermining; (*fig.*) injury, detriment.

подрыва́|ть[1]**, ю** *impf. of* **подорва́ть**

подрыва́|ть[2]**, ю** *impf. of* **подры́ть**

подрывни́к, а́ *m.* (*mil.*) demolition man, engineer.

подрывн|о́й *adj.* blasting, demolition; (*fig.*) subversive.

подр|ы́ть, о́ю, о́ешь *pf.* (*of* **~ыва́ть**[2]) to undermine, sap.

подря́д[1] *adv.* in succession; in a row; running; on end; **три го́да п.** three years running; **не́сколько дней п. шёл дождь** it rained for days on end.

подря́д[2]**, а** *m.* contract; **сдать п. (на+***a.***), сдать с ~а** to put out to contract.

подря|ди́ть, жу́, ди́шь *pf.* (*of* **~жа́ть**) (*coll.*) to hire.

подря|ди́ться, жу́сь, ди́шься *pf.* (*of* **~жа́ться**) (*coll.*) **1.** to contract, undertake. **2.** *pass. of* **~ди́ть**

подря́д|ный *adj. of* **~**[2]

подря́дчик, а *m.* contractor.

подряжа́|ть(ся), ю(сь) *impf. of* **подряди́ть(ся)**

подса|ди́ть[1]**, жу́, ~́дишь** *pf.* (*of* **~́живать**) **1.** to help (to) sit down. **2.** (**к**) to seat next (to); **меня́ ~ди́ли к глухо́й да́ме** I was seated next to a deaf lady.

подса|ди́ть[2]**, жу́, ~́дишь** *pf.* (*of* **~́живать**) (*+a. or g.*) to plant some more.

подса́жива|ть, ю *impf. of* **подсади́ть**

подса́жива|ться, юсь *impf. of* **подсе́сть**

подса́лива|ть, ю *impf. of* **подсоли́ть**

подсве́чник, а *m.* candlestick.

подсева́|ть, ю *impf. of* **подсе́ять**

подсека́|ть, ю *impf. of* **подсе́чь**

подсе́кци|я, и *f.* sub-section.

под|се́сть, ся́ду, ся́дешь, *past* **~се́л** *pf.* (*of* **~са́живаться**) (**к**) to sit down (near, next to), take a seat (near, next to).

подсе́|чь, ку́, чёшь, ку́т, *past* **~к, ~кла́** *pf.* (*of* **~ка́ть**) to hew; to hack (down).

подсе́|ять, ю, ешь *pf.* (*of* **~ва́ть**) (*+a. or g.*) to sow (*in addition*); to undersow.

подси|де́ть, жу́, ди́шь *pf.* (*of* **~́живать**) **1.** lie in wait (for). **2.** (*fig., coll.*) to scheme, intrigue (against).

подси́жива|ть, ю *impf. of* **подсиде́ть**

подси́нива|ть, ю *impf. of* **подсини́ть**

подсин|и́ть, ю́, и́шь *pf.* (*of* **~́ивать**) to blue, apply blueing to.

подска́блива|ть, ю *impf. of* **подскобли́ть**

подска|за́ть, жу́, ~́жешь *pf.* (*of* **~́зывать**) (*+d.*) to prompt (*also fig.*); to suggest.

подска́зк|а, и *f.* prompting.

подска́зыва|ть, ю *impf. of* **подсказа́ть**

подска|ка́ть, чу́, ~́чешь *pf.* (*of* **~кивать**[1]) (**к**) to come galloping up (to).

подска́кива|ть[1]**, ю** *impf. of* **подскака́ть**

подска́кива|ть[2]**, ю** *impf. of* **подскочи́ть**

подскобл|и́ть, ю́, ~́ишь *pf.* (*of* **подска́бливать**) to scrape off.

подскоч|и́ть, у́, ~́ишь *pf.* (*of* **подска́кивать**[2]) **1.** (**к**) to run up (to), come running (to). **2.** to jump up, leap up; **п. от ра́дости** to jump with joy; **це́ны ~и́ли** prices soared.

подсла|сти́ть, щу́, сти́шь *pf.* (*of* **~́щивать**) to sweeten.

подсла́щива|ть, ю *impf. of* **подсласти́ть**

подсле́дственный *adj.* (*leg.*) under investigation.

подслепова́т|ый (~, ~а) *adj.* weak-sighted.

подслу́жива|ться, юсь *impf. of* **подслужи́ться**

подслуж|и́ться, у́сь, ~́ишься *pf.* (*of* **~́иваться**) (**к**; *coll.*) to fawn (upon); to worm o.s. into the favour (of).

подслу́ш|ать, аю *pf.* (*of* **~ивать**) to overhear; to eavesdrop (on).

подслу́шива|ть, ю *impf. of* **подслу́шать**

подсма́трива|ть, ю *impf. of* **подсмотре́ть**

подсме́ива|ться, юсь *impf.* (**над**) to make fun (of).

подсмотр|е́ть, ю́, ~́ишь *pf.* (*of* **подсма́тривать**) to spy.

подсне́жник, а *m.* (*bot.*) snowdrop.

подсо́бн|ый *adj.* subsidiary; secondary; auxiliary; ancillary; **~ое предприя́тие** subsidiary enterprise; **п. рабо́чий** ancillary worker.

подсо́выва|ть, ю *impf. of* **подсу́нуть**

подсозна́ни|е, я *nt.* the subconscious.

подсозна́тел|ьный (~ен, ~ьна) *adj.* subconscious.

подсол|и́ть, ю́, ~́ишь *pf.* (*of* **подса́ливать**) to add more salt (to).

подсо́лнечник, а *m.* sunflower.

подсо́лнечн|ый *adj. of* **~ик; ~ое ма́сло** sunflower oil.

подсо́лнух, а *m.* (*coll.*) **1.** sunflower. **2.** sunflower-seeds.

подсо́х|нуть, ну, нешь *pf.* (*of* **подсыха́ть**) to dry out a little.

подспо́рь|е, я *nt.* (*coll.*) help, support.

подспу́дн|ый *adj.* latent; secret, hidden.

подста́в|ить, лю, ишь *pf.* (*of* **~ля́ть**) **1.** (**под+***a.*) to put (under), place (under); **п. но́жку кому́-н.** to trip s.o. up (*also fig.*). **2.** (*+d.*) to bring up (to), put up (to); to hold up (to); **п. кому́-н. стул** to offer s.o. a seat. **3.** (*fig.*) to expose; **п. ферзя́ под уда́р** (*chess*) to expose one's queen. **4.** (*math.*) to substitute.

подста́вк|а, и *f.* stand; support, rest, prop; coaster.

подставля́|ть, ю *impf. of* **подста́вить**

подставн|о́й *adj.* false; substitute; **~о́е лицо́** dummy, figure-head.

подстака́нник, а *m.* glass-holder.
подстано́вк|а, и *f.* (*math.*) substitution.
подста́нци|я, и *f.* sub-station.
подстёгива|ть, ю *impf. of* **подстегну́ть**
подстег|ну́ть[1], **ну́, нёшь** *pf.* (*of* **∸ивать**) to fasten underneath.
подстег|ну́ть[2], **ну́, нёшь** *pf.* (*of* **∸ивать**) to whip; to urge forward, urge on (*also fig.*).
подстерега́|ть, ю *impf. of* **подстере́чь**
подстере́|чь, гу́, жёшь, гу́т, *past* **∸г, ~гла́** *pf.* (*of* **~га́ть**) to be on the watch (for), lie in wait (for).
подстила́|ть, ю *impf. of* **подостла́ть**
подсти́лк|а, и *f.* bedding; litter.
подстра́ива|ть, ю *impf. of* **подстро́ить**
подстрека́тел|ь, я *m.* instigator.
подстрека́тельств|о, а *nt.* instigation, incitement.
подстрек|а́ть, а́ю *impf. of* **~ну́ть**
подстрек|ну́ть, ну́, нёшь *pf.* (*of* **~а́ть**) **1.** (**к**) to incite (to). **2.** to excite; **п. любопы́тство** to excite one's curiosity.
подстре́лива|ть, ю *impf. of* **подстрели́ть**
подстрел|и́ть, ю́, ∸ишь *pf.* (*of* **∸ивать**) to wound (*by a shot*); to wing.
подстрига́|ть(ся), ю(сь) *impf. of* **подстри́чь(ся)**
подстри́|женный *p.p.p. of* **~чь; ко́ротко ~женные во́лосы** (closely) cropped hair.
подстри́|чь, гу́, жёшь, гу́т, *past* **~г, ~гла** *pf.* (*of* **~га́ть**) to cut; to clip, trim; to prune; **п. бо́роду** to trim one's beard.
подстри́|чься, гу́сь, жёшься, гу́ться, *past* **~гся, ~глась** *pf.* (*of* **~га́ться**) to get a trim.
подстро́|ить, ю, ишь *pf.* (*of* **подстра́ивать**) **1.** (**к**) to build on (to). **2.** to tune (up). **3.** (*fig., coll.*) to contrive; (*pej.*) to arrange; **п. шу́тку** (*+d.*) to play a trick (on); **э́то де́ло ~ено** it's a put-up job.
подстро́чник, а *m.* word-for-word translation.
подстро́чн|ый *adj.* word-for-word; **~ое примеча́ние** footnote.
по́дступ, а *m.* (*geog.; fig.*) approach; **к нему́ и ~а нет** he is quite inaccessible.
подступ|а́ть(ся), а́ю(сь) *impf. of* **~и́ть(ся)**
подступ|и́ть, лю́, ∸ишь *pf.* (*of* **~а́ть**) (**к**) to approach, come up (to), come near; **слёзы ~и́ли к её глаза́м** tears came to her eyes.
подступ|и́ться, лю́сь, ∸ишься *pf.* (*of* **~а́ться**) (**к**) to approach; **к нему́ не ∸ишься** he is quite inaccessible.
подсуди́м|ый, ого *m.* (*leg.*) defendant; the accused.
подсу́дност|ь, и *f.* jurisdiction.
подсу́д|ный (~ен, ~на) *adj.* (*+d.*) within the jurisdiction (of).
подсу́м|ок, ка *m.* (*mil.*) cartridge pouch.
подсу́н|уть, у, ешь *pf.* (*of* **подсо́вывать**) **1.** (**под**+*a.*) to shove (under). **2.** (*+d. and a.; coll.*) to slip (into); to palm off (on, upon).
подсу́шива|ть, ю *impf. of* **подсуши́ть**
подсуш|и́ть, у́, ∸ишь *pf.* (*of* **∸ивать**) to dry a little.
подсчёт, а *m.* calculation; count.
подсчит|а́ть, а́ю *pf.* (*of* **∸ывать**) to count up, reckon up; to calculate.
подсчи́тыва|ть, ю *impf. of* **подсчита́ть**
подсыла́|ть, ю *impf. of* **подосла́ть**
подсы́п|ать, лю, лешь *pf.* (*of* **~а́ть**) (*+a. or g.*) to add, pour in.
подсыха́|ть, ю *impf. of* **подсо́хнуть**
подта́ива|ть, ет *impf. of* **подта́ять**
подта́лкива|ть, ю *impf. of* **подтолкну́ть**
подта́плива|ть, ю *impf. of* **подтопи́ть**
подта́скива|ть, ю *impf. of* **подтащи́ть**
подтас|ова́ть, у́ю *pf.* (*of* **~о́вывать**) to shuffle unfairly; (*fig.*) to juggle (with); **п. фа́кты** to juggle with facts.
подтасо́вк|а, и *f.* unfair shuffling; (*fig.*) juggling.
подтасо́выва|ть, ю *impf. of* **подтасова́ть**
подта́чива|ть, ю *impf. of* **подточи́ть**
подтащ|и́ть, у́, ∸ишь *pf.* (*of* **подта́скивать**) (**к**) to drag up (to).
подта́|ять, ет *pf.* (*of* **~ивать**) to thaw a little, melt a little.
подтвер|ди́ть, жу́, ди́шь *pf.* (*of* **~жда́ть**) to confirm; to corroborate, bear out; **п. получе́ние чего́-н.** to acknowledge receipt of sth.
подтвержда́|ть, ю *impf. of* **подтверди́ть**
подтвержде́ни|е, я *nt.* confirmation; corroboration.
подтёк, а *m.* bruise.
подтека́|ть, ет *impf.* **1.** *impf. of* **подте́чь. 2.** (*impf. only*) to leak; to be leaking.
подте́кст, а *m.* subtext, concealed meaning; **угада́ть п.** to read between the lines.
под|тере́ть, отру́, отрёшь, *past* **~тёр, ~тёрла** *pf.* (*of* **~тира́ть**) to wipe (up).
подте́|чь, чёт, ку́т, *past* **∸к, ~кла́** *pf.* (*of* **~ка́ть**) (**под**+*a.*) to flow (under), run (under).
подтира́|ть, ю *impf. of* **подтере́ть**
подтолкн|у́ть, у́, ёшь *pf.* (*of* **подта́лкивать**) **1.** to push slightly; **п. ло́ктем** to nudge. **2.** (*fig.*) to urge on.
подтоп|и́ть, лю́, ∸ишь *pf.* (*of* **подта́пливать**) (*coll.*) to heat a little.
подточ|и́ть, у́, ∸ишь *pf.* (*of* **подта́чивать**) **1.** to sharpen slightly. **2.** to eat away, gnaw; to undermine (*also fig.*).
подтру́нива|ть, ю *impf. of* **подтруни́ть**
подтрун|и́ть, ю́, и́шь *pf.* (*of* **∸ивать**) (**над**) to tease.
подтыка́|ть, ю *impf. of* **подоткну́ть**
подтя́гива|ть(ся), ю(сь) *impf. of* **подтяну́ть(ся)**
подтя́ж|ки, ек *no sg.* braces, suspenders.
подтя́н|утый *p.p.p. of* **~у́ть** *and adj.* smart.
подтя|ну́ть, ну́, ∸нешь *pf.* (*of* **∸гивать**) **1.** to tighten. **2.** (**к**) to pull up (to), haul up (to). **3.** (*mil.*) to bring up, move up. **4.** (*fig., coll.*) to take in hand, pull up, chase up.
подтя|ну́ться, ну́сь, ∸нешься *pf.* (*of* **∸гиваться**) **1.** to gird o.s. more tightly; **п. по́ясом** to tighten one's belt. **2.** to pull o.s. up (*on gymnastic apparatus, etc.*). **3.** (*mil.*) to move up. **4.** (*fig., coll.*) to pull o.s. together.
поду́ма|ть, ю *pf.* **1.** *pf. of* **ду́мать; п. (то́лько)!** just think!; **~ешь** (*as iron. int.; coll.*) I say!; what do you know?; **~ешь, кака́я блестя́щая мысль!** I say, what a brain-wave!; **и не ~ю!** I wouldn't dream of it. **2.** to think a little, for a while.
поду́мыва|ть, ю *impf.* (**о**+*p. or +inf.; coll.*) to think (of, about).
по-дура́цки *adv.* (*coll.*) foolishly, like a fool.
подурне́|ть, ю *pf. of* **дурне́ть**
поду́|ть, ю, ешь *pf.* **1.** *pf. of* **дуть 1.. 2.** to begin to blow.
поду́чива|ть(ся), ю(сь) *impf. of* **подучи́ть(ся)**
подуч|и́ть, у́, ∸ишь *pf.* (*of* **∸ивать**) **1.** (*+a. and d.*) to teach, instruct (in). **2.** to learn. **3.** (*inf.; coll.*) to egg on (to), put up (to).
подуч|и́ться, у́сь, ∸ишься *pf.* to learn (a little more, a little better).
поду́шечк|а, и *f. dim. of* **поду́шка; п. для була́вок** pincushion.
подуш|и́ть, у́, ∸ишь *pf.* to spray with perfume.
подуш|и́ться, у́сь, ∸ишься *pf.* to put some perfume on.
поду́шк|а, и *f.* pillow; cushion; **п. для штемпеле́й** ink-pad.
поду́шн|ый *adj.*: **~ая по́дать** (*hist.*) poll-tax.
подфа́рник, а *m.* (*tech.*) sidelight.
подхали́м, а *m.* toady, lickspittle.
подхали́мнича|ть, ю *impf.* (*coll.*) to toady.
подхали́мств|о, а *nt.* toadyism.

подхва|ти́ть, чу́, ∽тишь *pf.* (*of* **∽тывать**) to catch (up); to pick up; **п. мяч** to catch a ball; **п. на́сморк** to catch, pick up a cold; **п. пе́сню** to join in a song.
подхва́тыва|ть, ю *impf. of* **подхвати́ть**
подхлест|ну́ть, ну́, нёшь *pf.* (*of* **∽ывать**) to whip up (*also fig., coll.*).
подхлёстыва|ть, ю *impf. of* **подхлестну́ть**
подхо́д, а *m.* approach.
подхо|ди́ть, жу́, ∽дишь *impf. of* **подойти́**
подход|я́щий *pres. part. of* **∽и́ть** *and adj.* suitable, proper, appropriate; **п. моме́нт** the right moment.
подцеп|и́ть, лю́, ∽ишь *pf.* (*of* **∽ля́ть**) to hook on, couple on; to attach; (*fig., joc.*) to pick up; **п. на́сморк** to pick up a cold.
подцепля́|ть, ю *impf. of* **подцепи́ть**
подча́с *adv.* sometimes, at times.
подчёркива|ть, ю *impf. of* **подчеркну́ть**
подчерк|ну́ть, ну́, нёшь *pf.* (*of* **∽ивать**) **1.** to underline. **2.** (*fig.*) to emphasize, stress.
подчине́ни|е, я *nt.* **1.** subordination; submission, subjection; **быть в ∽и (у)** to be subordinate (to). **2.** (*gram.*) subordination.
подчинённост|ь, и *f.* subordination.
подчин|ённый 1. *p.p.p. of* **∽и́ть**; (+*d.*) under, under the command (of). **2.** *adj.* subordinate; *as n.* **п., ∽ённого** *m.* subordinate.
подчин|и́ть, ю́, и́шь *pf.* (*of* **∽я́ть**) (+*d.*) to subordinate (to), subject (to); to place under the command (of); **п. свое́й во́ле** to bend to one's will.
подчин|и́ться, ю́сь, и́шься *pf.* (*of* **∽я́ться**) (+*d.*) to submit (to); **п. прика́зу** to obey an order.
подчин|я́ть(ся), я́ю(сь) *impf. of* **∽и́ть(ся)**
подчи́|стить, щу, стишь *pf.* (*of* **∽ща́ть**) to rub out, erase.
подчи́стк|а, и *f.* erasure.
подчисту́ю *adv.* (*coll.*) completely, without remainder; **мы съе́ли всё п.** we left our plates clean.
подчи́тчик, а *m.* (*typ.*) copy-holder.
подчища́|ть, ю *impf. of* **подчи́стить**
подше́фный *adj.* aided, assisted; (+*d.*) under the patronage (of), sponsored by, supported (by).
подшива́|ть, ю *impf. of* **подши́ть**
подши́вк|а, и *f.* **1.** hemming; lining; soling. **2.** hem. **3.** filing (*of papers*); **п. газе́ты** newspaper file.
подши́пник, а *m.* (*tech.*) bearing; **ша́риковый п.** ball bearing.
под|ши́ть, ошью́, ошьёшь *pf.* (*of* **∽шива́ть**) **1.** to sew underneath; to hem; to line; to sole. **2.** to file (*papers*).
подшта́нник|и, ов *no sg.* (*coll.*) (*men's*) drawers.
подшу|ти́ть, чу́, ∽тишь *pf.* (*of* **∽чивать**) **(над)** to make fun (of); to mock; to play a trick (on).
подшу́чива|ть, ю *impf. of* **подшути́ть**
подъ...[1] *as vbl. pref.* = **под...**[1]
подъ...[2] *as pref. of nn. and adjs.* = **под...**[2]
подъе́зд, а *m.* **1.** entrance, doorway. **2.** approach(es).
подъезд|но́й *adj. of* **∽ 2.**; **∽на́я алле́я** drive; **∽на́я доро́га** access road.
подъезжа́|ть, ю *impf. of* **подъе́хать**
подъём, а *m.* **1.** lifting; raising. **2.** ascent. **3.** (*aeron.*) climb. **4.** rise, upgrade slope. **5.** (*fig.*) development; rise; **круто́й п. произво́дства** a sharp rise in production; **на ∽е** on the up and up. **6.** (*fig.*) élan; enthusiasm, animation; **говори́ть с больши́м ∽ом** to speak with great animation; **лёгок на п.** quick off the mark; **тяжёл на п.** sluggish, slow to start. **7.** instep. **8.** rising time; (*mil.*) reveille.
подъёмник, а *m.* lift, elevator, hoist.
подъёмн|ый *adj.* **1.** lifting; **п. кран** crane; **∽ое окно́** sash window. **2.: п. мост** drawbridge. **3.: ∽ые (де́ньги)** relocation expenses.
подъе́|хать, ду, дешь *pf.* (*of* **∽зжа́ть**) **(к) 1.** to drive up (to), draw up (to). **2.** (*coll.*) to call (on).
подыгр|а́ть, а́ю *pf.* (*of* **∽ывать**) (+*d.*; *coll.*) **1.** (*mus.*) to accompany; to vamp. **2.** (*theatr.*) to play up (to).
подыгр|а́ться, а́юсь *pf.* (*of* **∽ываться**) **(к**; *coll.*) to get round.
поды́грыва|ть, ю *impf. of* **подыгра́ть**
поды́грыва|ться, юсь *impf.* **1.** *impf. of* **подыгра́ться. 2.** (*impf. only*) to try to get round.
подыма́|ть(ся), ю(сь) *impf.* (*coll.*) = **поднима́ть(ся)**
поды|ска́ть, щу́, ∽щешь *pf.* (*of* **∽скивать**) to seek out, find.
поды́скива|ть, ю *impf.* **1.** *impf. of* **подыска́ть. 2.** (*impf. only*) to seek, try to find.
подыто́жива|ть, ю *impf. of* **подыто́жить**
подыто́ж|ить, у, ишь *pf.* (*of* **∽ивать**) to sum up.
подыш|а́ть, у́, ∽ишь *pf.* to breathe; **вы́йти п. све́жим во́здухом** to go out for a breath of fresh air.
поеда́|ть, ю *impf. of* **пое́сть**
поеди́н|ок, ка *m.* duel.
поедо́м *adv.*: **п. есть кого́-н.** (*coll.*) to make s.o.'s life a misery (by nagging).
по́езд, а, *pl.* **∽а́** *m.* train; **∽ом** by train; **п. прямо́го сообще́ния** through train.
пое́з|дить, жу, дишь *pf.* to travel about.
пое́здк|а, и *f.* journey; trip, excursion, outing, tour.
поезд|но́й *adj. of* **по́езд**
поезжа́й(те): *used as imper. of* **е́хать** *and* **пое́хать**
по|е́сть, е́м, е́шь, е́ст, еди́м, еди́те, едя́т, *past* **∽е́л** *pf.* (*of* **∽еда́ть**) **1.** to eat (up). **2.** to eat a little; to have a bite (to eat). **3.** (*of rodents, insects, etc.*) to eat, devour.
пое́|хать, ду, дешь *pf.* (*of* **е́хать**) to go (*in or on a vehicle or on an animal*); to set off, depart; **∽хали!** (*coll.*) let's go!
пожале́|ть, ю *pf. of* **жале́ть**
пожа́л|овать, ую *pf. of* **жа́ловать; добро́ п.!** welcome!; **∽уйте** *formula of polite request*; **∽уйте сюда́!** this way, please!; **∽уйте в столо́вую!** dinner (supper, *etc.*) is served!
пожа́л|оваться, уюсь *pf. of* **жа́ловаться**
пожа́луй *adv.* perhaps; very likely; it may be; **мы, п., пое́дем** we shall very likely go; **п., ты прав** you may be right; **по мне п.** (*coll.*) it's all right by me.
пожа́луйста *particle* **1.** please; **сади́тесь, п.** please sit down. **2.** (*polite expr. of consent*) certainly!; by all means!; **мо́жно посмотре́ть э́ти сни́мки? — п.** may I look at these photos? Certainly; **переда́йте мне, п., кни́гу. — п.** would you mind passing me the book? — There you are. **3.** (*acknowledgement of thanks*) you're welcome!; don't mention it; not at all.
пожа́р, а *m.* fire; conflagration.
пожа́рищ|е[1]**, а** *m.* (*coll.*) big fire.
пожа́рищ|е[2]**, а** *nt.* site of a fire.
пожа́рник, а *m.* fireman.
пожа́р|ный *adj. of* **∽**; **∽ная кома́нда** fire-brigade; **∽ная маши́на** fire-engine; **в ∽ном поря́дке** (*coll., joc.*) hastily, in slapdash fashion; **на вся́кий п. слу́чай** (*coll., joc.*) in case of dire need; *as n.* **п., ∽ного** *m.* fireman.
пожа́ти|е, я *nt.*: **п. руки́** handshake.
по|жа́ть[1]**, жму́, жмёшь** *pf.* (*of* **∽жима́ть**) press, squeeze; **п. ру́ку** (+*d.*) to shake hands (with); **п. плеча́ми** to shrug one's shoulders.
по|жа́ть[2]**, жну́, жнёшь** *pf.* (*of* **∽жина́ть**) to reap (*also fig.*); **п. плоды́ чужо́го труда́** (*fig.*) to reap where one has not sown.
пож|ева́ть, ую́, уёшь *pf.* (*of* **∽ёвывать**) to chew.
пожёвыва|ть, ю *impf. of* **пожева́ть**
пожела́ни|е, я *nt.* wish, desire.
пожела́|ть, ю *pf. of* **жела́ть**
пожелте́лый *adj.* yellowed.
пожелте́|ть, ю *pf. of* **желте́ть**
пожен|и́ть, ю́, ∽ишь *pf. of* **жени́ть**

пожен|úться, ∠имся *pf.* (*pl. used only*; *of two people*) to get married.
пожéртвовани|е, я *nt.* donation.
пожéртв|овать, ую *pf. of* **жéртвовать**
пожúв|а, ы *f.* (*coll.*) gain, profit.
поживá|ть, ю *impf.* to live; **как (вы) ~ете?** how are you (getting on)?
пожив|úться, люсь, úшься *pf.* (*+i.*; *coll.*) to live (off), profit (by); **п. на счёт другóго** to profit at another's expense.
пожúзненн|ый *adj.* life(long); for life; **~ое заключéние** life imprisonment.
пожилóй *adj.* middle-aged; elderly.
пожимá|ть, ю *impf. of* **пожáть**[1]
пожинá|ть, ю *impf. of* **пожáть**[2]
пожирá|ть, ю *impf. of* **пожрáть**
пожúтк|и, ов *no sg.* (*coll.*) belongings; (one's) things; **со всéми ~ами** bag and baggage.
по|жúть, живý, живёшь, *past* **∠жил, ~жилá, ∠жило** *pf.* **1.** to live (*for a time*); to stay; **мы ∠жили три гóда в Кúеве** we lived for three years in Kiev. **2.** (*coll.*) to live it up; **~живём-увúдим** we shall see what we shall see.
пожм|ý, ёшь *see* **пожáть**[1]
пожн|ý, ёшь *see* **пожáть**[2]
пожр|áть, ý, ёшь, *past* **~áл, ~алá, ~áло** *pf.* (*of* **пожирáть**) to devour; (*coll.*) to gobble up.
пóз|а, ы *f.* pose, attitude, posture; (*fig.*) pose; **принять, какýю-н. ~у** to strike an attitude; **принять ~у велúкого учёного** to pose as a great scholar; **э́то тóлько п.** it is a mere pose.
позабáв|ить, лю, ишь *pf.* to amuse a little.
позабáв|иться, люсь, ишься *pf.* to have a bit of fun.
позабó|титься, чусь, тишься *pf. of* **заботиться**
позабывá|ть, ю *impf. of* **позабы́ть**
позаб|ы́ть, ýду, ýдешь *pf.* (*of* **~ывáть**) (*+a. or o+p.*; *coll.*) to forget (about).
позавúд|овать, ую *pf. of* **завúдовать**
позáвтрака|ть, ю *pf. of* **зáвтракать**
позавчерá *adv.* the day before yesterday.
позадú[1] *adv.* (*of place*; *fig. of time*) behind; **остáвить п.** to leave behind.
позадú[2] *prep.+g.* behind.
позаимств|овать, ую *pf. of* **заимствовать**
позапрóшлый *adj.* before last.
позáр|иться, юсь, ишься *pf. of* **зáриться**
по|звáть, зовý, зовёшь, *past* **~звáл, ~звалá, ~звáло** *pf. of* **звать**
по-звéрски *adv.* brutally, like a beast.
позволéни|е, я *nt.* permission, leave; **с вáшего ~я** with your permission; **с ~я сказáть** if I may say so; **э́тот, с ~я сказáть, вождь** (*iron.*) this, if one may so call him, leader.
позволúтел|ьный (~ен, ~ьна) *adj.* permissible.
позвóл|ить, ю, ишь *pf.* (*of* **~ять**) (*+d. of pers. and inf., +a. of inanimate object*) to allow, permit; **п. себé** (*+inf.*) to venture, take the liberty (of); (*+a.*) to allow o.s.; **п. себé сдéлать замечáние** to venture a remark; **п. себé поéздку в Парúж** to treat o.s. to a trip to Paris; **~ь(те)** (*i*) *polite form of request* **~ьте представить дóктора X.** allow me to introduce Doctor X., (*ii*) *expr. of disagreement or objection* **~ьте, что э́то знáчит?** excuse me, what does that mean?
позвол|ять, яю *impf. of* **∠ить**
позвон|úть, ю, úшь *pf. of* **звонúть**
позвон|óк, кá *m.* (*anat.*) vertebra.
позвонóчник, а *m.* (*anat.*) spine, backbone.
позвонóчн|ый *adj.* (*anat.*) vertebral; **п. столб** spinal column; *as n.* **~ые, ~ых** (*zool.*) vertebrates.
поздн|ée *comp. of* **∠ий** *and* **∠о** later.
пóздн|ий *adj.* late; tardy; **до ~ей нóчи** until late at night, late into the night; **~о** it is late.
пóздно *adv.* late.
поздорóва|ться, юсь *pf. of* **здорóваться**
поздоровé|ть, ю *pf. of* **здоровéть**
поздорóв|иться, ится *pf. only in phr.* (*coll.*): **не ~ится емý,** *etc.* (**от**) much good will it do him, *etc.*
поздравúтельн|ый *adj.* congratulatory; **~ая открытка** greetings card.
поздрáв|ить, лю, ишь *pf.* (*of* **~лять**) (**с**+*i.*) to congratulate (on, upon); **п. когó-н. с днём рождéния** to wish s.o. a happy birthday.
поздравлéни|е, я *nt.* congratulation.
поздравля|ть, ю *impf. of* **поздрáвить**
позеленé|ть, ю *pf. of* **зеленéть 1.**
позелен|úть, ю́, úшь *pf. of* **зеленúть**
позёр, а *m.* poseur; pseud (*coll.*).
пóз|же *comp. of* **~дний** *and* **~дно**; later (on).
по-зúмнему *adv.*: **одéт п.** (dressed) in winter clothes.
позúр|овать, ую *impf.* (*+d.*) to pose (for); (*fig.*) to pose.
позитúв, а *m.* (*phot.*) positive.
позитивúзм, а *m.* (*phil.*) positivism.
позитúв|ный (~ен, ~на) *adj.* positive.
позитрóн, а *m.* (*phys.*) positron.
позициóнный *adj.* positional.
позúци|я, и *f.* position; stand; **выжидáтельная п.** wait-and-see attitude; **занять ~ю** (*mil.*) to take up a position; (*fig.*) to take one's stand; **с ~и сúлы** from (a position of) strength.
познавáтельный *adj.* cognitive; **п. процéсс** cognition.
позна|вáть, ю́, ёшь *impf. of* **∠ть**
позна|вáться, ю́сь, ёшься *impf.* (*no pf.*) to become known; **друзья ~ю́тся в бедé** (*prov.*) a friend in need is a friend indeed.
познакóм|ить(ся), лю(сь), ишь(ся) *pf. of* **знакóмить(ся)**
познáни|е, я *nt.* **1.** (*phil.*) cognition; **теóрия ~я** epistemology. **2.** (*pl.*) knowledge.
познá|ть, ю *pf.* (*of* **~вáть**) to get to know; to become acquainted with; (*phil.*) to cognize; **п. гóре** to become acquainted with grief.
позолóт|а, ы *f.* gilding, gilt.
позоло|тúть, чý, тúшь *pf. of* **золотúть**
позóр, а *m.* shame, disgrace; **вы́ставить на п.** to put to shame; **покры́ть себя ~ом** to disgrace o.s.
позóр|ить, ю, ишь *impf.* (*of* **о~**) to disgrace.
позóр|иться, юсь, ишься *impf.* (*of* **о~**) to disgrace o.s.
позóрищ|е, а *nt.* (*coll.*) shameful event, disgrace.
позóр|ный (~ен, ~на) *adj.* shameful, disgraceful; ignominious; **п. столб** pillory; **постáвить к ~ному столбý** (*fig.*) to pillory.
позумéнт , а *m.* galoon, braid; **золотóй п.** gold braid.
позы́в, а *m.* urge; **п. на рвóту** (feeling of) nausea.
позывн|óй *adj.* **п. сигнáл** (*radio*) call sign; *as n.* **~ы́е, ~ы́х** call sign.
поигрá|ть, ю *pf.* to have a game, play a little.
поимённо *adv.* by name.
поимённый *adj.* nominal; **п. спúсок** list of names.
поимен|овáть, ýю *pf.* to name, call out by name.
пóимк|а, и *f.* capture.
по-инóму *adv.* differently.
поинтерес|овáться, ýюсь *pf.* (*+i.*) to be curious (about); to take an interest (in).
пóиск, а *m.* **1.** (*pl.*) search; **в ~ах** (*+g.*) in search (of). **2.** (*mil.*) (reconnaissance) raid.
пои|скáть, щý, ∠щешь *pf.* to look for, search for.
поистúне *adv.* indeed, in truth.
по|úть, ю́, ∠úшь *impf.* (*of* **на~**) to give to drink; to water (*cattle*).
по|ищý, úщешь *see* **~искáть**
пой|дý, дёшь *see* **~тú**

по́йл|о, а *nt.* swill, mash; **п. для свине́й** pig-swill.
по́йм|а, ы, *g. pl.* ~ *f.* flood-lands; water-meadow.
пойма́|ть, ю *pf. of* **лови́ть**
пойм|у́, ёшь *see* **поня́ть**
по́йнтер, а *m.* (*dog*) pointer.
пой|ти́, ду́, дёшь, *past* **пошёл, пошла́** *pf.* **1.** *pf. of* **идти́** *and* **ходи́ть; пошёл!** off you go!; **пошёл вон!** be off!; on your way!; **уж е́сли на то пошло́** if it comes to that; for that matter; **(так) не ~дёт** (*coll.*) that won't work. **2.** to begin to (be able to) walk. **3.** (*coll.*) to begin. **4. (в**+*a.*) to take after; **он пошёл в отца́** he takes after his father.
пока́[1] *adv.* for the present, for the time being; **п. что** (*coll.*) in the meanwhile; **п. ещё, п.-то ещё** (*coll.*) not for a while yet; **э́то п. всё** that is all for now; **ну, п.!** (*coll.*) cheerio!; bye!
пока́[2] *conj.* **1.** while; **нам на́до попроси́ть его́, п. он тут** we must ask him while he is here. **2.: п. не** until, till, before; **не на́до уходи́ть, п. она́ не придёт** we must not go until she comes; **п. ещё не по́здно** before it's too late.
пока́з, а *m.* showing, demonstration.
показа́ни|е, я *nt.* **1.** testimony, evidence. **2.** (*leg.*) deposition; affidavit; **дава́ть п.** to testify, give evidence. **3.** reading (*on an instrument*).
показа́тел|ь, я *m.* **1.** (*math.*) exponent, index. **2.** indicator; index.
показа́тел|ьный (~ен, ~ьна) *adj.* **1.** significant; instructive, revealing. **2.** model; demonstration; **п. проце́сс** show-trial; **~ьное хозя́йство** model farm.
пока|за́ть, жу́, ∠жешь *pf.* (*of* **∠зывать**) **1.** to show; to display, reveal; **п. себя́** to prove o.s. *or* one's worth; **он ~за́л себя́ хоро́шим ора́тором** he has shown himself to be a good speaker; **они́ ~за́ли де́вочку врачу́** they took the little girl to the doctor; **он ~за́л вид, что се́рдится** he feigned anger. **2.** (*of instruments*) to show, register, read. **3. (на**+*a.*) to point (at, to); **п. кому́-н. на дверь** (*fig., coll.*) to show s.o. the door. **4.** (*leg.*) to testify, give evidence.
пока|за́ться, жу́сь, ∠жешься *pf.* **1.** *pf. of* **каза́ться. 2.** (*pf. of* **∠зываться**) to show o.s.; to appear; to come in sight; **из-за облако́в ~за́лась луна́** the moon appeared from behind the clouds; **п. врачу́** to see a doctor. **3.** *pass. of* **~за́ть**
показно́й *adj.* for show; ostentatious.
показу́х|а, и *f.* (*coll.*) show; **э́то сплошна́я п.** it's all put on, just for show.
пока́зыва|ть(ся), ю(сь) *impf. of* **показа́ть(ся)**
пока́лыва|ть, ю *impf.* (*impers.*): **у меня́ ~ет в боку́** I have occasional stabbing pains in my side.
пока́мест *adv. and conj.* (*coll.*) = **пока́**
покара́|ть, ю *pf. of* **кара́ть**
íпоката́|ть, ю *pf.* to take for a drive; **п. дете́й** to take children out.
поката́|ться, юсь *pf.* to go for a drive; **п. на ло́дке** to go out boating.
пока|ти́ть, чу́, ∠тишь *pf. of* **кати́ть**
пока|ти́ться, чу́сь, ∠тишься *pf.* **1.** *pf. of* **кати́ться; п. со́ смеху** (*coll.*) to roar with laughter. **2.** to start rolling.
пока́тост|ь, и *f.* slope, incline; declivity.
пока́т|ый (~, ~а) *adj.* sloping; slanting; **п. лоб** receding forehead.
покача́|ть, ю *pf.* to rock, swing (for a time); **п. голово́й** to shake one's head.
покача́|ться, юсь *pf.* to rock, swing (for a time); to have a swing.
пока́чива|ться, юсь *impf.* to rock slightly; **идти́ ~ясь** to walk unsteadily.
покачн|у́ть, у́, ёшь *pf.* to shake.
покачн|у́ться, у́сь, ёшься *pf.* **1.** to sway, totter, give a lurch. **2.** (*fig., coll.*) to go downhill.
пока́шлива|ть, ю *impf.* to have a slight cough; to cough intermittently.
пока́шля|ть, ю *pf.* to cough.
покая́ни|е, я *nt.* **1.** (*eccl.*) confession. **2.** penitence, repentance; **принести́ п. (в**+*p.*) to repent (of).
покая́нный *adj.* penitential.
пока́|яться, юсь, ешься *pf. of* **ка́яться**
покварта́льно *adv.* quarterly.
поквита́|ться, юсь *pf.* (**с**+*i.*; *coll.*) to get even (with); **тепе́рь мы с ва́ми ~лись** now we're quits; **я ещё с ним ~юсь** I'll get even with him yet.
по́кер, а *m.* (*card-game*) poker.
по́кер|ный *adj. of* ~
покида́|ть, ю *impf. of* **поки́нуть**
поки́|нуть, ну, нешь *pf.* (*of* **~да́ть**) to leave; to desert, abandon, forsake.
поклада́я *only in phr.* **не п. рук** indefatigably.
покла́дист|ый (~, ~а) *adj.* complaisant, obliging.
покла́ж|а, и *f.* (*coll.*) load; luggage.
поклёп, а *m.* (*coll.*) slander, calumny; **в(о)звести́ п.** (**на**+a.) to slander, cast aspersions (on).
покло́н, а *m.* **1.** bow; **сде́лать п.** to bow; **идти́ на п., идти́ с ~ом к кому́-н.** to go cap in hand to s.o. **2.** (*fig.*) greeting; **посла́ть ~ы** to send one's compliments, send one's kind regards.
поклоне́ни|е, я *nt.* worship.
поклон|и́ться, ю́сь, ∠ишься *pf. of* **кла́няться**
покло́нник, а *m.* admirer; worshipper.
покло́ня́|ться, юсь *impf.* (+*d.*) to worship.
покля́|сться, ну́сь, нёшься *pf. of* **кля́сться**
поко́|иться, юсь, ишься *impf.* **1. (на**+*p.*) to rest (on, upon), be based (on, upon); **п. на дога́дке** to be based on conjecture. **2.** (*of the dead*) to lie; **здесь ~ится прах** (+*g.*) here lies (the body of).
поко́|й[1]**, я** *m.* rest, peace; **ве́чный п.** (*fig., poet.*) eternal rest; **оста́вить в ~е** to leave in peace; **уйти́ на п., удали́ться на п.** to retire.
поко́|й[2]**, я** *m.* room, chamber; office.
поко́йник, а *m.* the deceased.
поко́йницк|ая, ой *f.* mortuary.
поко́йн|ый *adj.* (the) late; **п. коро́ль** the late king; *as n.* **п., ~ого** *m.*, **~ая, ~ой** *f.* the deceased.
поколеб|а́ть, ∠лю, ∠лешь *pf. of* **колеба́ть**
поколеб|а́ться, ∠люсь, ∠лешься *pf.* **1.** *pf. of* **колеба́ться. 2.** to waver (for a time).
поколе́ни|е, я *nt.* generation.
поколо|ти́ть(ся), чу́(сь), ∠тишь(ся) *pf. of* **колоти́ть(ся)**
поко́нч|ить, у, ишь *pf.* **(с**+*i.*) **1.** to finish off; to finish (with). **2.** to put an end (to); to do away (with); **п. жизнь самоуби́йством, п. с собо́й** to commit suicide; to kill o.s.
покоре́ни|е, я *nt.* conquest.
покори́тел|ь, я *m.* conqueror; **п. серде́ц** lady-killer.
покор|и́ть, ю́, и́шь *pf.* (*of* **~я́ть**) to conquer, subdue; **п. чьё-н. се́рдце** to win s.o.'s heart.
покор|и́ться, ю́сь, и́шься *pf.* (*of* **~я́ться**) (+*d.*) to submit (to); to resign o.s. (to); **п. свое́й у́части** to resign o.s. to one's lot.
покорм|и́ть(ся), лю́(сь), ∠ишь(ся) *pf. of* **корми́ть(ся)**
поко́рно *adv.* humbly; submissively, obediently.
поко́рност|ь, и *f.* submissiveness, obedience.
поко́р|ный (~ен, ~на) *adj.* **1.** (+*d.*) submissive (to), obedient; **п. судьбе́** resigned to one's fate. **2.** (*in conventional expressions of politeness; obs.*) humble, obedient; **ваш п. слуга́** your obedient servant.
покоро́б|ить(ся), лю(сь), ишь(ся) *pf. of* **коро́бить(ся)**
покор|я́ть(ся), я́ю(сь) *impf. of* **~и́ть(ся)**
поко́с, а *m.* **1.** mowing; haymaking. **2.** meadow(-land).
поко|си́ться, шу́сь, си́шься *pf. of* **коси́ться**
покра́|сить, шу, сишь *pf. of* **кра́сить**
покрасне́|ть, ю *pf. of* **красне́ть 1.**

покрив|и́ть(ся), лю́(сь), и́шь(ся) *pf. of* **криви́ть(ся)**
покри́кива|ть, ю *impf.* (**на**+*a.*; *coll.*) to shout (at).
покро́в, а *m.* cover; covering; (*fig.*) cloak, shroud, pall; **по́чвенный п.** top-soil; **сне́жный п.** blanket of snow; **твёрдый п.** (*biol.*) crust, incrustation; **под ~ом но́чи** under cover of night.
покрови́тел|ь, я *m.* patron, protector.
покрови́тельниц|а, ы *f.* patroness, protectress.
покрови́тельственн|ый *adj.* **1.** protective; **~ая окра́ска** (*zool.*) protective colouring. **2.** patronizing.
покрови́тельств|о, а *nt.* protection, patronage; **О́бщество ~а живо́тным** Society for the Prevention of Cruelty to Animals; **под ~ом** (+*g.*) under the patronage (of), under the auspices (of).
покрови́тельств|овать, ую *impf.* (+*d.*) to protect, patronize.
покро́|й, я *m.* cut (*of garment*); **все на оди́н п.** (*fig.*) all in the same style.
покрош|и́ть, у́, ∠ишь *pf.* (+*a. or g.*) to crumble; to crumb; to mince, chop.
покругле́|ть, ю *pf. of* **кругле́ть**
покруж|и́ть, у́, ∠ишь *pf.* (*coll.*) **1.** to circle several times. **2.** to roam, wander (*for a while*).
покрупне́|ть, ю *pf. of* **крупне́ть**
покрыва́л|о, а *nt.* **1.** coverlet, bedspread, counterpane. **2.** shawl; veil. **3.** cover; **нефтяно́е п.** oil-slick.
покрыва́|ть(ся), ю(сь) *impf. of* **покры́ть(ся)**
покры́ти|е, я *nt.* **1.** covering; **п. доро́ги** road surfacing; **п. кры́ши** roofing. **2.** covering, payment; **п. расхо́дов** defrayal of expenses.
покр|ы́ть, о́ю, о́ешь *pf.* (*of* **крыть** *and* **~ыва́ть**) **1.** to cover; **п. кра́ской** to coat with paint; **п. ла́ком** to varnish, lacquer; **п. позо́ром** to cover with shame; **п. себя́ сла́вой** to cover o.s. with glory; **п. та́йной** to shroud in mystery. **2.** to cover, defray; **п. расхо́ды** to defray expenses. **3.** to drown out (*sound*). **4.** to shield, cover up (for); to hush up.
покр|ы́ться, о́юсь, о́ешься *pf.* (*of* **~ыва́ться**) to cover o.s.; to get covered.
покры́шк|а, и *f.* **1.** cover(ing). **2.** (outer) tyre.
поку́да *adv. and conj.* (*coll.*) = **пока́**
покупа́тел|ь, я *m.* buyer, purchaser; customer.
покупа́тельн|ый *adj.* purchasing; **~ая спосо́бность** (*econ.*) purchasing power.
покупа́тель|ский *adj. of* **~**
покупа́|ть, ю *impf. of* **купи́ть**
поку́пк|а, и *f.* **1.** buying; purchasing, purchase. **2.** (*object purchased*) purchase; **вы́годная п.** bargain; **де́лать ~и** to go shopping.
покуп|но́й *adj.* **1.** bought. **2.** = **~а́тельный; ~на́я цена́** purchase price.
покур|и́ть, ю́, ∠ишь *pf.* **1.** *pf. of* **кури́ть. 2.** to have a smoke; **дава́й ∠им** let's have a smoke.
покуса́|ть, ю *pf.* to bite; to sting.
поку|си́ться, шу́сь, си́шься *pf.* (*of* **~ша́ться**) (**на** +*a.*) **1.** to make an attempt (upon); **п. на свою́ жизнь, п. на самоуби́йство** to attempt suicide. **2.** to encroach (on, upon).
поку́ша|ть, ю *pf. of* **ку́шать**
покуша́|ться, юсь *impf. of* **покуси́ться**
покуше́ни|е, я *nt.* attempt; **п. на жизнь** (+*g.*) (*or* **на**+*a.*) attempt upon the life (of).
пол[1]**, а, о ∠е, на ~у́,** *pl.* **~ы́** *m.* floor.
пол[2]**, а** *m.* sex; **обо́его ∠а** of both sexes.
пол... *comb. form* (*abbr. of* **полови́на**) half (*as in* **полчаса́** half an hour; **полдеся́того** half past nine).
пол|а́, ы́, *pl.* **∠ы** *f.* skirt, flap, lap; **из-под ~ы́** on the sly, under cover; **торгова́ть из-под ~ы́** to sell under the counter.
полага́|ть, ю *impf.* to suppose, think; **~ют, что он умира́ет** he is believed to be dying; **на́до п.** it is to be supposed; one must suppose.
полага́|ться, юсь *impf.* **1.** *impf. of* **положи́ться. 2.** (*impers.*): **~ется** one is supposed (to); **так ~ется** it is the custom; **не ~ется** it is not done; **здесь ~ется снима́ть шля́пу** one is supposed to take off one's hat here. **3. ~ется** (+*d.*) to be due (to); **нам э́то ~ется** it is our due; we have a right to it.
пола́|дить, жу, дишь *pf.* (**с**+*i.*) to come to an understanding (with); to get on (with).
пола́ком|ить(ся), лю(сь), ишь(ся) *pf. of* **ла́комить(ся)**
полбеды́ *f.* (*coll.*): **э́то ещё п.** it is not so very serious.
полве́ка, полуве́ка *m.* half a century.
полго́да, полуго́да *m.* half a year, six months; **с п., о́коло полуго́да** for about six months.
по́лдень, полу́дня *and* **по́лдня** *m.* noon, midday.
полдне́вный *adj. of* **по́лдень**
по́лдник, а *m.* (afternoon) snack.
полдоро́г|и *f.* half-way (point); **встре́титься на ~е** to meet half-way.
по́л|е, я, *pl.* **~я́, ~е́й** *nt.* **1.** field; **спорти́вное п.** playing field; **п. би́твы, п. сраже́ния** battle-field; **п. зре́ния** field of vision. **2.** (*art*) ground; (*heraldry*) field. **3.** (*pl.*) margin; **заме́тки на ~я́х** notes in the margin. **4.** (*pl.*) brim (*of hat*).
полеве́|ть, ю *pf. of.* **леве́ть**
полёвк|а, и *f.* field-vole.
полево́дств|о, а *nt.* field-crop cultivation.
полев|о́й *adj.* field; **п. бино́кль** field glasses; **~а́я мышь** field-mouse; **~ы́е цветы́** wild flowers.
полего́ньку *adv.* (*coll.*) by easy stages.
полегча́|ть, ет *pf. of* **легча́ть; больно́му ~ло** the patient is feeling better; **у меня́ на душе́ ~ло** I feel a load off my mind.
полеж|а́ть, у́, и́шь *pf.* to lie down (*for a while*).
поле́з|ный (~ен, ~на) *adj.* useful; helpful; wholesome; **~ное де́йствие** efficiency (*of a machine*); **~ная жила́я пло́щадь** actual living space; **э́то лека́рство о́чень ~но от ка́шля** this medicine is very good for coughs; **чем могу́ быть ~ен?** can I help you?
поле́з|ть, у, ешь, *past* **~, ~ла** *pf.* **1.** *pf. of* **лезть. 2.** to start to climb.
полемизи́р|овать, ую *impf.* (**с**+*i.*) to engage in polemics (with).
поле́мик|а, и *f.* polemic(s); **вступи́ть в ~у** (**с**+*i.*) to enter into polemics (with).
полеми́ст, а *m.* polemicist.
полеми́ческий *adj.* polemic(al).
полен|и́ться, ю́сь, ∠ишься *pf.* (+*inf.*) to be too lazy to.
поле́нниц|а, ы *f.* pile (*of logs*); stack (*of firewood*).
поле́н|о, а, *pl.* **~ья, ~ьев** log.
поле́сь|е, я *nt.* wooded locality; woodlands.
полёт, а *m.* flight; flying; **бре́ющий п.** hedge-hopping; **фигу́рный п.** aerobatics; **вид с пти́чьего ~а** bird's-eye view; **п. фанта́зии** flight of fancy.
полета́|ть, ю *pf.* to fly (*for a while*), do some flying.
поле|те́ть, чу́, ти́шь *pf.* **1.** *pf. of* **лете́ть. 2.** to start to fly; to fly off. **3.** (*fig., coll.*) to fall, go headlong.
по-ле́тнему *adv.*: **оде́т п.** (dressed) in summer clothes.
полеч|и́ть, у́, ∠ишь *pf.* to treat (*for a while*).
полеч|и́ться, у́сь, ∠ишься *pf.* to undergo treatment (*for a while*).
пол|е́чь, я́гу, я́жешь, я́гут, *past* **~ёг, ~егла́** *pf.* **1.** to lie down (*in numbers*). **2.** (*fig.*) to be killed (*in numbers*).
по́лз|ать, аю *impf.*, *indet. of* **~ти́**
ползко́м *adv.* crawling, on all fours.
полз|ти́, у́, ёшь, *past* **~, ~ла́** *impf.* **1.** to crawl, creep (along); **по́езд ~** the train was crawling. **2.** to ooze (out). **3.** (*fig., coll.*; *of rumour, etc.*) to spread. **4.** (*coll.*; *of fabric*) to fray.
ползун|о́к, ка́ *m.* **1.** (*coll.*) toddler. **2.** *pl.* (*coll.*) rompers.

ползу́ч|ий *adj.* creeping; **~ее расте́ние** (*bot.*) creeper.
поли... *comb. form* poly-.
полиа́ндри|я, и *f.* polyandry.
полива́|ть(ся), ю(сь) *impf. of* **поли́ть(ся)**
поли́вк|а, и *f.* watering.
поли́в|очный *adj. of* **~ка**
полига́ми|я, и *f.* polygamy.
полигло́т, а *m.* polyglot.
полиго́н, а *m.* (*mil.*) (artillery *or* bombing) range; **испыта́тельный п.** proving ground; **уче́бный п.** training ground.
полиграфи́ст, а *m.* printing trades worker.
полиграфи́ческий *adj.* polygraphic; printing.
полиграфи́|я, и *f.* (*tech.*) polygraphy; printing trades.
поликли́ник|а, и *f.* clinic; health centre.
полилове́|ть, ю *pf. of* **лилове́ть**
полиме́р, а *m.* (*chem.*) polymer.
полинези́|ец, йца *m.* Polynesian.
полинези́|йка, йки *f. of* **~ец**
полинези́йский *adj.* Polynesian.
Полине́зи|я, и *f.* Polynesia.
полиненасы́щенный *adj.* polyunsaturated.
полиня́лый *adj.* faded, discoloured.
полиня́|ть, ет *pf. of* **линя́ть**
полиомиели́т, а *m.* (*med.*) polio(myelitis).
поли́п, а *m.* polyp.
полирова́льн|ый *adj.* polishing; **п. стано́к** buffing machine.
полир|ова́ть, у́ю *impf.* (*of* **от~**) to polish.
поliро́вк|а, и *f.* polishing; polish.
полиро́вочный *adj.* polishing.
полиро́вщик, а *m.* polisher.
по́лис, а *m.* policy; **страхово́й п.** insurance policy.
полисме́н, а *m.* policeman; constable.
полит... *comb. form, abbr. of* **полити́ческий**
политбюро́ *nt. indecl.* Politburo.
политеи́зм, а *m.* polytheism.
политеи́ст, а *m.* polytheist.
политеисти́ческий *adj.* polytheistic.
полите́хникум, а *m.* polytechnic (school).
политехни́ческий *adj.* polytechnic(al).
политзаключённ|ый, ого *m.* political prisoner.
поли́тик, а *m.* politician.
поли́тик|а, и *f.* **1.** policy; **п. на гра́ни войны́** 'brinkmanship'. **2.** politics; **п. си́лы** power politics.
политика́н, а *m.* (*pej.*) political intriguer.
политика́нств|о, а *nt.* politicking; intrigue.
политика́нств|овать, ую *impf.* to politick, intrigue.
полити́ческ|ий *adj.* political; **п. де́ятель** political figure, politician.
полити́ч|ный (~ен, ~на) *adj.* (*coll.*) politic.
полито́лог, а *m.* political scientist.
политу́р|а, ы *f.* polish, varnish.
пол|и́ть, ью́, ьёшь, *past* **~л, ~ила́, ~и́ло** *pf.* (*of* **~ива́ть**) **1.** (*+a. and i.*) to pour (on, upon); **п. что-н. водо́й** to pour water on sth.; **п. цветы́** to water the flowers. **2.** to begin to pour.
пол|и́ться, ью́сь, ьёшься, *past* **~и́лся, ~ила́сь, ~и́ло́сь** *pf.* (*of* **~ива́ться**) **1.** (*+i.*) to pour over o.s. **2.** to begin to flow.
политэмигра́нт, а *m.* political refugee.
полихлорвини́л, а *m.* PVC (*polyvinyl chloride*).
полице́йск|ий *adj.* police; **п. уча́сток** police-station; *as n.* **п., ~ого** *m.* policeman.
поли́ци|я, и *f.* police.
поли́чн|ое, ого *nt.*: **пойма́ть с ~ым** to catch red-handed.
полиэтиле́н, а *m.* polythene.
полк, а́, о ~е́, в ~у́ *m.* regiment; **на́шего ~у́ при́было** (*coll.*) our ranks have swollen.
по́лк|а, и *f.* **1.** shelf. **2.** berth.
полко́вник, а *m.* colonel.
полково́д|ец, ца *m.* commander; military leader.
полково́й *adj.* regimental.
полне́йший *adj.* sheer, utter(most).
полне́|ть, ю *impf.* (*of* **по~**) to grow stout, put on weight.
по́лно[1] *adv.* brim-full, full to the brim.
по́лно[2] *adv.* (*coll.*) **1.** enough (of that)!; that will do!; **п. ворча́ть!** stop grumbling! **2.** you don't mean that; you don't mean to say so.
полно́ *adv.* (*+g.*) (*coll.*) lots; **в ко́мнате полно́ наро́ду** the room is packed with people.
полнове́с|ный (~ен, ~на) *adj.* **1.** full-weight. **2.** (*fig.*) sound.
полновла́сти|е, я *nt.* sovereignty.
полновла́ст|ный (~ен, ~на) *adj.* sovereign; **п. хозя́ин** sole master.
полново́д|ный (~ен, ~на) *adj.* deep.
полново́дь|е, я *nt.* high water.
полнокро́ви|е, я *nt.* (*med.*) plethora.
полнокро́в|ный (~ен, ~на) *adj.* **1.** (*med.*) plethoric. **2.** (*fig.*) full-blooded.
полнолу́ни|е, я *nt.* full moon.
полнометра́жный *adj.* feature-length.
полномо́чи|е, я *nt.* authority, power; (*leg.*) proxy; **чрезвыча́йные ~я** emergency powers; **срок ~й** term of office; **дать ~я** (*+d.*) to empower.
полномо́ч|ный (~ен, ~на) *adj.* plenipotentiary; **п. представи́тель** plenipotentiary.
полнопра́ви|е, я *nt.* full rights; competency.
полнопра́в|ный (~ен, ~на) *adj.* enjoying full rights; competent; **п. член** full member.
по́лностью *adv.* fully, in full; completely.
полнот|а́, ы́ *no pl., f.* **1.** fullness, completeness; **п. вла́сти** absolute power. **2.** stoutness; corpulence.
полноце́н|ный (~ен, ~на) *adj.* **1.** of full value. **2.** (*fig.*) valuable; fully fledged.
полно́чный *adj.* midnight.
по́лночь, по́лночи *and* **полу́ночи** *f.* midnight; **за́ п.** after midnight.
по́л|ный (~он, ~на́, ~но́) *adj.* **1.** (*+g. or i.*) full (of); complete, total; absolute; **~ным го́лосом** at the top of one's voice; **~ное затме́ние** total eclipse; **п. карма́н** (*+g.*) a pocketful (of); **~ное собра́ние сочине́ний** complete works; **идти́ ~ным хо́дом** to be in full swing; **в ~ной ме́ре** fully, in full measure; **в ~ном расцве́те сил** in one's prime. **2.** stout; plump.
полны́м-полно́ *adv.* (*+g.*) chock-full (of), jam-packed (with).
по́ло *nt indecl.* (*sport*) polo; **во́дное п.** water polo.
поло́в|а, ы *f.* chaff.
полови́к, а́ *m.* mat; door-mat.
полови́н|а, ы *f.* half; **два с ~ой** two and a half; **п. шесто́го** half past five; **на ~е доро́ги** halfway; **п. две́ри** leaf of a door.
полови́нн|ый *adj.* half; **п. окла́д** half-pay; **заплати́ть за что-н. в ~ом разме́ре** to pay half-price for sth.
полови́нчат|ый (~, ~а) *adj.* **1.** halved; half-and-half; **п. кирпи́ч** half-brick. **2.** (*fig.*) half-hearted; undecided; **~ое реше́ние** compromise decision.
полови́ц|а, ы *f.* floor board.
поло́вник, а *m.* (*coll.*) ladle.
полово́дь|е, я *nt.* flood, high water.
полов|о́й[1] *adj.* floor; **~а́я тря́пка** floorcloth.
полов|о́й[2] *adj.* sexual; **~о́е бесси́лие** impotence; **~а́я зре́лость** puberty; **~а́я связь** sexual intercourse.
по́лог, а *m.* bed-curtain; **под ~ом но́чи** (*poet.*) under cover of night.
поло́гий *adj.* gently sloping.
положе́ни|е, я *nt.* **1.** position. **2.** position; state; situation; status; circumstances; **семе́йное п.** marital status; **вое́нное п.** martial law; **чрезвыча́йное п.** state of emergency; **п. веще́й** state of affairs; **при тако́м**

~и дел as things stand; **быть на высоте́ ~я** to be on top of the situation; **быть в (интере́сном) ~и** (*coll., euph.*) to be in the family way, be expecting. **4.** regulations, statute. **5.** thesis; tenet. **6.** clause, provision.

поло́ж|енный *p.p.p. of* **~и́ть** *and adj.* agreed, determined; **в п. час** at a time agreed.

поло́жим let us assume; **п., что вы пра́вы** let us assume that you are right.

положи́тельно *adv.* **1.** positively; favourably; **отнести́сь п. (к)** to take a favourable view (of). **2.** (*coll.*) positively, absolutely; **она́ п. ничего́ не понима́ет** she understands absolutely nothing.

положи́тел|ьный (~ен, ~ьна) *adj.* **1.** positive. **2.** affirmative; **п. отве́т** affirmative reply. **3.** favourable; **~ьная оце́нка** favourable reception. **4.** (*coll.*) complete, absolute; **п. дура́к** complete fool.

полож|и́ть, у́, ~́ишь *pf. of* **класть; п. жизнь** to lay down one's life; **п. ору́жие** to lay down one's arms.

полож|и́ться, у́сь, ~́ишься *pf.* (*of* **полага́ться**) (**на**+*a.*) to rely (upon), count (upon).

по́лоз, а, *pl.* **поло́зья, поло́зьев** *m.* runner.

полома́|ть, ю *pf.* to break.

полома́|ться, юсь *pf. of* **лома́ться**

поло́мк|а, и *f.* breakage; breakdown.

поломо́йк|а, и *f.* (*coll.*) char(woman).

полоне́з, а *m.* polonaise.

поло́ни|й, я *m.* (*chem.*) polonium.

полос|а́, ы́, *a.* **по́лосу́,** *pl.* **по́лосы, поло́с, ~а́м** *f.* **1.** stripe; streak. **2.** strip. **3.** weal. **4.** region; zone, belt; **чернозёмная п.** black-earth belt. **5.** period; spell; **п. хоро́шей пого́ды** spell of fine weather; **п. неуда́ч** run of bad luck. **6.** (*typ.*) page.

полоса́тик, а *m.* (*zool.*) rorqual.

полоса́т|ый (~, ~а) *adj.* striped.

поло́ск|а, и *f. dim. of* **полоса́; в ~у** striped.

полоска́ни|е, я *nt.* **1.** rinse, rinsing; gargling. **2.** gargle.

полоска́тельниц|а, ы *f.* slop-basin.

поло|ска́ть, щу́, ~́щешь *impf.* (*of* **вы́~**) to rinse; **п. го́рло** to gargle.

поло|ска́ться, щу́сь, ~́щешься *impf.* **1.** to paddle. **2.** (*of a flag, sail, etc.*) to flutter, flap.

полос|ова́ть, у́ю *impf.* (*of* **ис~**) (*coll.*) to flog.

по́лост|ь[1], и, *g. pl.* **~е́й** *f.* (*anat.*) cavity.

по́лост|ь[2], и, *g. pl.* **~е́й** *f.* travelling rug.

полоте́н|це, ца, *g. pl.* **~ец** *nt.* towel; **посу́дное п.** tea-towel; **п. на ва́лике** roller towel.

полотёр, а *m.* floor-polisher.

поло́тнищ|е, а *nt.* **1.** (*of material*) width; panel; **п. пала́тки** tent section; **па́рус в пять ~** sail of five panels. **2.** flat (part), blade.

полот|но́, на́, *pl.* **~́на, ~́ен, ~́нам** *nt.* **1.** linen; **бле́дный как п.** white as a sheet. **2.** (*art*) canvas (*fig. = painting*). **3.** (*tech.*) blade; **п. пилы́** saw blade.

полотня́ный *adj.* linen.

пол|о́ть, ю́, ~́ешь *impf.* (*of* **вы́~**) to weed.

полоу́ми|е, я *nt.* craziness.

полоу́м|ный (~ен, ~на) *adj.* (*coll.*) crazy.

полпре́д, а *m.* (*abbr. of* ***полномо́чный представи́тель***) (ambassador) plenipotentiary.

полпути́ *m. indecl.*: **на п.** half-way.

полсло́в|а, на ~е *nt.*: **п. от него́ не услы́шишь** you cannot get a word out of him; **мо́жно вас на п.?** may I have a word with you?

полтерге́йст, а *m.* poltergeist.

полти́н|а, ы *f.* (*coll.*) = **~ник; два с ~ой** two roubles fifty kopecks.

полти́нник, а *m.* **1.** fifty kopecks. **2.** fifty-kopeck piece.

полтора́, полу́тора *m. and nt.* one and a half; **в п. ра́за бо́льше** half as much again.

полтора́ста, полу́тораста *num.* a hundred and fifty.

полтор|ы́ *f.* = **~а́; п. ты́сячи** one and a half thousand.

полу... *comb. form* half-, semi-, demi-.

полубессозна́тельный *adj.* semi-unconscious.

полубо́г, а *m.* demigod.

полуботи́н|ки, ок *pl.* (*sg.* **~ок, ~ка** *m.*) shoes.

полувое́нный *adj.* paramilitary.

полуго́ди|е, я *nt.* half-year, six months.

полугоди́чный *adj.* half-yearly; six-month.

полугова́лый *adj.* six-month(s)-old.

полугодово́й *adj.* half-yearly, six-monthly; **п. отчёт** half-yearly report.

полугра́мотный *adj.* semi-literate.

полу́денный *adj.* midday.

полу|ди́ть, жу́, ~́дишь *pf. of* **луди́ть**

полужив|о́й (~́, ~а́, ~́о) *adj.* half dead; more dead than alive.

полузащи́тник, а *m.* (*sport*) half-back.

полукро́вк|а, и *f.* half-breed.

полукру́г, а *m.* semicircle.

полукру́глый *adj.* semicircular.

полулеж|а́ть, у́, и́шь *impf.* to recline.

полуме́р|а, ы *f.* half-measure.

полумёртв|ый (~, ~а́) *adj.* half-dead.

полуме́сяц, а *m.* half moon; crescent.

полуме́сячный *adj.* fortnightly; of a fortnight's duration.

полумра́к, а *m.* semi-darkness.

полуно́чни|к, а *m.* (*coll.*) night-owl.

полуно́чнича|ть, ю *impf.* (*coll.*) to burn the midnight oil.

полу́но́чный *adj.* midnight.

полуоборо́т, а *m.* half-turn.

полуо́стров, а *m.* peninsula.

полуостровно́й *adj.* peninsular.

полуотво́рен|ный (~, ~а) *adj.* half-open; ajar.

полуоткры́т|ый (~, ~а) *adj.* half-open; ajar.

полупальто́ *nt indecl.* (short) overcoat.

полупроводни́к, а́ *m.* (*phys.*) semi-conductor.

полуразру́шен|ный (~, ~а) *adj.* tumbledown, dilapidated.

полусве́т, а *m.* twilight.

полусло́в|о, а *nt.*: **оборва́ть кого́-н. на ~е** to cut s.o. short; **останови́ться на ~е** to stop short, stop in mid-sentence; **поня́ть с ~а** to be quick on the uptake.

полусме́рт|ь, и *f.*: **до ~и** (*fig., coll.*) to death; **изби́ть кого́-н. до ~и** to beat s.o. within an inch of his life; **испуга́ться до ~и** to be frightened to death.

полус|о́н, на́ *m.* half sleep; somnolence, drowsiness.

полусо́нный *adj.* half asleep; dozing.

полуста́н|ок, ка *m.* (*rail.*) halt.

полуте́н|ь, и, о ~и, в ~и́ *f.* penumbra.

полуто́н, а, *pl.* **~ы** *and* **~а́** *m.* **1.** (*mus.*) semitone. **2.** (*art*) half-tint.

полутьм|а́, ы́ *f.* semi-darkness.

полуфабрика́т, а *m.* semi-finished product; prepared raw material (*esp. of foodstuffs*).

полуфина́л, а *m.* (*sport*) semi-final.

полуфина́л|ьный *adj. of* **~; ~ьные встре́чи** semi-finals.

получасово́й *adj.* half-hour; half-hourly.

получа́тел|ь, я *m.* recipient.

получ|а́ть(ся), а́ю(сь) *impf. of* **~и́ть(ся)**

получе́ни|е, я *nt.* receipt; **распи́ска в ~и** receipt.

получ|и́ть, у́, ~́ишь *pf.* (*of* **~а́ть**) to get, receive, obtain; **п. на́сморк** to catch a cold; **п. обра́тно** to recover, get back; **п. паёк** to draw rations; **п. удово́льствие** to derive pleasure.

получ|и́ться, ~́ится *pf.* (*of* **~а́ться**) **1.** to come, arrive, turn up; **~и́лась посы́лка** a parcel has come. **2.** to turn out, prove, be; **результа́ты ~и́лись нева́жные** the results are poor; **~и́лось, что он был**

прав it turned out that he was right. **3.** *pass. of* **~и́ть**

полу́чк|а, и *f.* (*coll.*) **1.** receipt. **2.** pay (packet).

полуша́ри|е, я *nt.* hemisphere.

полушу́б|ок, ка *m.* (knee-length) sheepskin coat.

полушутя́ *adv.* half in joke.

полцены́ *f. indecl.*: **за п.** at half price.

полчаса́, получа́са *m.* half an hour.

по́лчищ|е, а *nt.* horde; (*fig.*) mass, flock.

по́л|ый *adj.* **1.** hollow. **2.**: **~ая вода́** flood-water.

по́лымя *nt.*: **из огня́ да в п.** (*prov.*) out of the frying-pan into the fire.

полы́н|ный *adj. of* **~ь**; **~ная во́дка** absinthe.

полы́н|ь, и *f.* wormwood.

полысе́|ть, ю *pf. of* **лысе́ть**

полыха́|ть, ет *impf.* to blaze.

по́льз|а, ы *f.* use; advantage, benefit; **кака́я от э́того п.?** what good will it do?; **извлека́ть из чего́-н. ~у** to benefit from sth.; **принести́ ~у** (*+d.*) to be of benefit (to); **для ~ы** (*+g.*) for the benefit (of); **в ~у** (*+g.*) in favour (of), on behalf (of); **э́то говори́т не в ва́шу ~у** it does not speak well for you; **два-ноль в ~у Дина́мо** (*sport*) 2–0 to Dynamo.

по́льзовани|е, я *nt.* use; **многокра́тного ~я** re-usable; **о́бщего ~я** in general use.

по́льзовател|ь, я *m.* user; **коне́чный п.** end-user.

по́льз|оваться, уюсь *impf.* (*+i.*) **1.** to make use (of), utilize. **2.** (*pf.* **вос~**) to profit (by); **п. слу́чаем** to take an opportunity. **3.** to enjoy; **п. дове́рием** (*+g.*) to enjoy the confidence (of); **п. права́ми** to enjoy rights; **п. успе́хом** to be a success.

по́льк|а[1], и Pole, Polish woman.

по́льк|а[2], и *f.* polka.

по́льск|ий *adj.* Polish.

поль|сти́ть, щу́, сти́шь *pf. of* **льсти́ть**

По́льш|а, и *f.* Poland.

полюб|и́ть, лю́, ~ишь *pf.* to come to like, grow fond (of); to fall in love (with).

полюб|и́ться, лю́сь, ~ишься *pf.* (*coll.*) (*+d.*) to catch the fancy (of); **она́ мне сра́зу же ~и́лась** I took an immediate liking to her.

полюб|ова́ться, у́юсь *pf. of* **любова́ться**

полюбо́вно *adv.* amicably; **реши́ть, ко́нчить де́ло п.** to come to an amicable agreement.

полюбо́вный *adj.* amicable.

полюбопы́тств|овать, ую *pf. of* **любопы́тствовать**

по́люс, а *m.* (*geog., phys., and fig.*) pole; **Се́верный п.** North Pole; **они́ — два ~а** they are poles apart.

поля́к, а *m.* Pole.

поля́н|а, ы *f.* glade, clearing.

поляриза́ци|я, и *f.* (*phys.*) polarization.

поляриз|ова́ть, у́ю *impf. and pf.* (*phys.*) to polarize.

поля́рник, а *m.* polar explorer.

поля́рност|ь, и *f.* (*phys.*) polarity.

поля́рн|ый *adj.* **1.** polar, arctic; **~ая звезда́** North star; **се́верный п. круг** Arctic Circle. **2.** (*fig.*) polar, diametrically opposed.

пома́д|а, ы *f.* pomade; **губна́я п.** lipstick.

пома́|дить, жу, дишь *impf.* (*of* **на~**) (*obs.*) to pomade; **п. во́лосы** to grease one's hair; **п. гу́бы** to put lipstick on.

пома́дк|а, и *f.* (*collect.*) fruit candy.

пома́зани|е, я *nt.* (*eccl.*) anointing.

пома́|зать, жу, жешь *pf.* **1.** *pf. of* **ма́зать[1]**. **2.** (*eccl.*) to anoint.

пома́|заться, жусь, жешься *pf. of* **ма́заться**

помаз|о́к, ка́ *m.* (*small*) brush.

помале́ньку *adv.* (*coll.*) **1.** gradually, gently; **рабо́тать п.** to take one's time over one's work. **2.** in a small way, modestly. **3.** tolerably, so-so.

пома́лкива|ть, ю *impf.* (*coll.*) to hold one's tongue, keep mum.

поман|и́ть, ю́, ~ишь *pf. of* **мани́ть**

пома́рк|а, и *f.* blot; pencil mark; correction.

пома|ха́ть, шу́, ~шешь *pf.* (*+i.*) to wave (*for a while, a few times*).

пома́хива|ть *impf.* (*+i.*) to wave, brandish, swing (*from time to time*); **соба́ка ~ла хвосто́м** the dog would wag its tail.

поме́дл|ить, ю, ишь *pf.* (**с**+*i.*; *coll.*) to linger (over).

помел|о́, а́, *pl.* **~ья, ~ьев** *nt.* mop; (*witch's*) broomstick.

поме́ньше *comp. of* **ма́ленький** *and* **ма́ло** a little smaller; a little less.

поменя́|ть(ся), ю(сь) *pf. of* **меня́ть(ся) 2.**

помера́н|ец, ца *m.* **1.** Seville *or* sour orange (*fruit*). **2.** sour orange (*tree*).

по|мере́ть, мру́, мрёшь, *past* **~мер, ~мерла́, ~мерло** *pf.* (*of* **~мира́ть**) (*coll.*) to die; **п. со́ смеху** to split one's sides (with laughing).

помере́щ|иться, усь, ишься *pf. of* **мере́щиться**

помёрз|нуть, ну, нешь, *past* **~, ~ла** *pf.* to be frost-bitten; (*of flowers, etc.*) to be killed by frost.

поме́р|ить(ся), ю(сь), ишь(ся) *pf. of* **ме́рить(ся)**

поме́рк|нуть, ну, нешь, *past* **~, ~ла** *pf. of* **ме́ркнуть**

помертве́лый *adj.* deathly pale; (*fig.*) lifeless.

помертве́|ть, ю *pf. of* **мертве́ть**

помести́тельност|ь, и *f.* spaciousness; capaciousness.

помести́тел|ьный (~ен, ~ьна) *adj.* spacious, roomy; capacious.

поме|сти́ть, щу́, сти́шь *pf.* (*of* **~ща́ть**) **1.** to lodge, accommodate; to put up. **2.** to place, locate; (*fin.*) to invest; **п. объявле́ние в газе́те** to put an advertisement in a paper; **п. на пе́рвой страни́це** to carry on the front page.

поме|сти́ться, щу́сь, сти́шься *pf.* (*of* **~ща́ться**) **1.** to find room; to put up; (*of things*) to go in; **в э́тот я́щик мои́ ве́щи не ~стя́тся** my things will not go into this drawer. **2.** *pass. of* **~сти́ть**

поме́стн|ый *adj.*: **~ое дворя́нство** landed gentry.

поме́ст|ье, ья, *g. pl.* **~ий** *nt.* (*hist.*) estate.

по́мес|ь, и *f.* **1.** hybrid; cross; **п. терье́ра и овча́рки, п. терье́ра с овча́ркой** a cross between a terrier and a sheepdog. **2.** (*fig.*) mixture, hotchpotch.

поме́сячно *adv.* by the month; monthly, per month.

поме́сячный *adj.* monthly.

помёт, а *m.* **1.** dung; droppings. **2.** litter, brood; (*of piglets*) farrow.

поме́т|а, ы *f.* mark, note.

поме́|тить, чу, тишь *pf.* (*of* **~ча́ть**) to mark; to date; **п. га́лочкой** to tick.

поме́х|а, и *f.* **1.** hindrance; obstacle; **быть ~ой** (*+d.*) to hinder, impede. **2.** (*pl. only*) (*radio*) interference.

помеча́|ть, ю *impf. of* **поме́тить**

поме́шан|ный (~, ~а) *adj.* **1.** mad, crazy; insane; *as n.* **п., ~ного** *m.* madman; **~ная, ~ной** *f.* madwoman. **2.** (**на**+*p.*; *fig., coll.*) mad (on, about); **они́ ~ы на бри́дже** they are mad about bridge.

помеша́тельств|о, а *nt.* madness; lunacy, insanity.

помеша́|ть[1,2], ю *pf. of* **меша́ть[1,2]**

помеша́|ться, юсь *pf.* **1.** to go mad, go crazy. **2.** (**на**+*p.*; *fig., coll.*) to become mad (on, about).

помеща́|ть, ю *impf. of* **помести́ть**

помеща́|ться, юсь *impf.* **1.** (*impf. only*) to be; to be located, be situated; to be housed; **где ~ется ваш кабине́т?** where is your office? **2.** (*impf. only*): **в э́том стадио́не ~ется се́мьдесят ты́сяч челове́к** this stadium holds seventy thousand people. **3.** *impf. of* **помести́ться**

помеще́ни|е, я *nt.* **1.** placing, location. **2.** room; accommodation; premises; **жило́е п.** housing.

поме́щик, а *m.* (*hist.*) landowner.

поме́щи|чий *adj. of* **~к**; **~п. дом** manor-house.

помидо́р, а, *g. pl.* **~ов** *m.* tomato.

помидо́р|ный *adj. of* **~**

поми́ловани|е, я *nt.* (*leg.*) pardon; forgiveness.
поми́л|овать, ую *pf.* to pardon, forgive; **Го́споди, ~уй!** Lord, have mercy!
поми́мо *prep.+g.* **1.** apart from; besides; **п. всего́ про́чего** apart from anything else. **2.** without the knowledge (of), unbeknown (to); **всё э́то реши́лось п. меня́** all this was decided without my knowledge.
поми́н, а *m.* (*coll.*) mention; **лёгок на ~е** talk of the devil; **его́ и в ~е нет** there is no trace of him.
помина́льны|й *adj.* funeral; **п. обе́д** funeral repast.
помина́|ть, ю *impf. of* **помяну́ть; не ~й(те) меня́ ли́хом!** remember me kindly!; **а его́ ~й, как зва́ли!** (*coll.*) he just vanished into thin air.
поми́н|ки, ок *no sg.* funeral repast.
помину́тно *adv.* (*coll.*) continually, constantly.
помину́тн|ый *adj.* **1.** occurring every minute; (*fig.*, *coll.*) continual, constant. **2.** by the minute.
помира́|ть, ю *impf. of* **помере́ть**
помир|и́ть(ся), ю́(сь), и́шь(ся) *pf. of* **мири́ть(ся)**
по́мн|ить, ю, ишь *impf.* (*+a. or* **о**+*p.*) to remember; **не п. себя́ (от)** to be beside o.s. (with).
по́мн|иться, ится *impf.* (*impers.+d.*) I, *etc.*, remember; **наско́лько мне ~ится** as far as I can remember; **~ится, э́то произошло́ в декабре́** as I remember, it happened in December.
помно́гу *adv.* (*coll.*) in plenty, in large quantities; in large numbers.
помнож|а́ть, а́ю *impf. of* **~ить**
помно́ж|ить, у, ишь *pf.* (*of* **мно́жить** *and* **~а́ть**) to multiply; **п. два на́ три** to multiply two by three.
помога́|ть, ю *impf. of* **помо́чь**
пом|огу́, о́жешь, о́гут *see* **~о́чь**
по-мо́ему *adv.* **1.** in my opinion. **2.** my way.
помо́|и, ев *no sg.* slops; **обли́ть кого́-н. ~ями** (*fig.*, *coll.*) to fling mud at s.o.
помо́й|ка, ки, *g. pl.* **помо́ек** *f.* rubbish dump; cesspit.
помо́|йный *adj. of* **~и; ~йное ведро́** slop-pail; **~йная я́ма** refuse pit; cesspit.
помо́л, а *m.* grinding; **мука́ кру́пного, ме́лкого ~а** coarse-ground, fine-ground flour.
помо́лв|ить, лю, ишь *pf.* (*+a.* **с**+*i.*, *or +a.* **за**+*a.*; *obs.*) to betrothe (to); **её ~или с Ива́ном** she is engaged to Ivan.
помо́лвк|а, и *f.* betrothal, engagement.
помо́лв|ленный *p.p.p. of* **~ить; быть ~ленным с кем-н.** to be engaged to s.o.
помол|и́ться, ю́сь, ~ишься *pf. of* **моли́ться**
помолоде́|ть, ю *pf. of* **молоде́ть**
помолч|а́ть, у́, и́шь *pf.* to be silent for a while.
помор|и́ть, ю́, и́шь *pf. of* **мори́ть**[1]
помо́рник, а *m.* (*zool.*) skua.
поморо́|зить, жу, зишь *pf. of* **моро́зить**
помо́рщ|иться, усь, ишься *pf. of* **мо́рщиться**
помо́рь|е, я *nt.* seaboard, coastal region; **се́верное п.** White Sea Coast.
помо́ст, а *m.* dais; platform, stage, rostrum; scaffold.
по́моч|и, ей *no sg.* **1.** leading strings; **быть, ходи́ть на ~а́х** (*fig.*) to be in leading strings. **2.** braces.
помоч|и́ться, у́сь, ~ишься *pf. of* **мочи́ться**
помо́|чь, гу́, жешь, гут, *past* **~г, ~гла́** *pf.* (*of* **~га́ть**) **1.** (*+d.*) to help, aid, assist. **2.** to relieve, bring relief; **инъе́кции ~гли́ от бо́ли** the injections relieved the pain.
помо́щник, а *m.* **1.** help, helper. **2.** assistant; aide; mate; **п. дире́ктора** assistant director; **п. капита́на** (*naut.*) mate; **п. судьи́** (*sport*) linesman.
по́мощ|ь, и *f.* help, aid, assistance; relief; **оказа́ть п.** to help, render assistance; **отказа́ть в ~и** to refuse aid; **пода́ть ру́ку ~и** (*+d.*) to lend a hand; **позва́ть на п.** to call for help; **прийти́ на п.** (*+d.*) to come to the aid (of); **на п.!** help!; **с ~ью** (*+g.*), **при ~и** (*+g.*) with the help (of), by means (of); **пе́рвая п.** first aid; **п. иностра́нным госуда́рствам** foreign aid.
по́мп|а[1]**, ы** *f.* pomp, state.
по́мп|а[2]**, ы** *f.* pump.
помпе́зност|ь, и *f.* pomposity.
помпе́зный *adj.* pompous.
помпо́н, а *m.* pompon.
помрач|а́ть(ся), а́ет(ся) *impf. of* **~и́ть(ся)**
помрач|и́ть, и́т *pf.* (*of* **~а́ть**) to darken, obscure, cloud.
помрач|и́ться, и́тся *pf.* (*of* **~а́тся**) to grow dark, become obscured, become clouded.
помрачне́|ть, ю *pf. of* **мрачне́ть**
пому|ти́ть(ся), чу́, ти́шь, ти́т(ся) *pf. of* **му́тить(ся)**
пому́ч|ить, у, ишь *pf.* to make suffer, torment.
пому́ч|иться, усь, ишься *pf.* to suffer (*for a while*).
помч|а́ть, у́, и́шь *pf.* **1.** to begin to whirl, rush. **2.** (*coll.*) = **~а́ться**
помч|а́ться, у́сь, и́шься *pf.* to begin to rush, begin to tear along.
помыка́|ть, ю *impf.* (*+i.*; *coll.*) to order about.
по́мыс|ел, ла *m.* thought; intention, design; **благи́е ~лы** good intentions.
помы́сл|ить, ю, ишь *pf.* (*of* **помышля́ть**) (**о**+*p.*) to think (of, about), contemplate.
пом|ы́ть(ся), о́ю(сь), о́ешь(ся) *pf. of* **мыть(ся)**
помышля́|ть, ю *impf. of* **помы́слить**
помян|у́ть, у́, ~ешь *pf.* (*of* **помина́ть**) **1.** to mention; **п. добро́м кого́-н.** to speak well of s.o.; **~и́ моё сло́во** (*coll.*) mark my words. **2.** to pray (for), remember in one's prayers. **3.** to give a funeral repast (in memory of).
помя́т|ый *p.p.p. of* **~ь** *and adj.* (*coll.*) flabby, baggy.
пом|я́ть, ну́, нёшь *pf.* to rumple slightly; to crumple slightly.
пом|я́ться, ну́сь, нёшься *pf. of* **мя́ться**[1]
понаде́|яться, юсь, ешься *pf.* (**на**+*a.*; *coll.*) to count (upon), rely (on).
пона́доб|иться, люсь, ишься *pf.* to be, become necessary; **е́сли ~ится** if necessary.
понапра́сну *adv.* (*coll.*) in vain.
понаслы́шке *adv.* (*coll.*) by hearsay.
по-настоя́щему *adv.* in the right way, properly.
поnача́лу *adv.* (*coll.*) at first, in the beginning.
по-на́шему *adv.* in our opinion.
поnево́ле *adv.* willy-nilly; against one's will.
понеде́льник, а *m.* Monday.
понеде́льно *adv.* by the week, per week; weekly.
понеде́льный *adj.* weekly.
понемно́гу *adv.* **1.** a little at a time. **2.** little by little.
понес|ти́, у́, ёшь, *past* **~̈, ~ла́** *pf.* **1.** *pf. of* **нести́. 2.** (*of horses*) to bolt.
понес|ти́сь, у́сь, ёшься, *past* **~̈ся, ~ла́сь** *pf.* **1.** *pf. of* **нести́сь. 2.** to rush off, tear off, dash off.
по́ни *m. indecl.* pony.
понижа́|ть(ся), ю(сь) *impf. of* **пони́зить(ся)**
пониже́ни|е, я *nt.* fall, drop; lowering; reduction; **п. давле́ния** drop in pressure; **п. по слу́жбе** demotion.
пони́|зить, жу, зишь *pf.* (*of* **~жа́ть**) to lower; to reduce; **п. по слу́жбе** to demote.
пони́|зиться, жусь, зишься *pf.* (*of* **~жа́ться**) to fall, drop, go down.
по́низу *adv.* low; along the ground.
поника́|ть, ю *impf. of* **пони́кнуть**
пони́к|нуть, ну, нешь, *past* **~, ~ла** *pf.* (*of* **ни́кнуть** *and* **~а́ть**) to droop; **п. голово́й** to hang one's head.
понима́ни|е, я *nt.* **1.** understanding, comprehension. **2.** interpretation; **в моём ~и** as I see it.
понима́|ть, ю *impf.* (*of* **поня́ть**) **1.** to understand; to comprehend; to realize; **~ю!** I see! **2.** to interpret; **непра́вильно п.** to misunderstand. **3.** (*impf. only*) (*+a. or* **в**+*p.*) to know (about); **я ничего́ не ~ю в му́зыке** I know nothing about music.
по-но́вому *adv.*: **нача́ть жить п.** to turn over a new leaf.

поножо́вщин|а, ы *f.* (*coll.*) knife-fight; knifing.
понома́р|ь, я́ *m.* sexton, sacristan.
поно́с, а *m.* diarrhoea.
поно|си́ть[1], **шу́, ~сишь** *impf.* to vilify, revile.
поно|си́ть[2], **шу́, ~сишь** *pf.* **1.** to carry (*for a while*). **2.** to wear (*for a while*).
поно́|шенный *p.p.p. of* **~си́ть**[2] *and adj.* worn, shabby, threadbare.
понра́в|иться, люсь, ишься *pf. of* **нра́виться**
понто́н, а *m.* **1.** pontoon. **2.** pontoon bridge.
понто́н|ный *adj. of* **~**; **~ный мост** pontoon bridge.
пону́|дить, жу, дишь *pf.* (*of* **~жда́ть**) to force, compel, coerce; **его́ ~дили к реше́нию** he was forced into a decision.
понужда́|ть, ю *impf. of* **пону́дить**
понука́|ть, ю *impf.* (*coll.*) to urge on, goad.
пону́р|ить, ю, ишь *pf.*: **п. го́лову** to hang one's head.
пону́р|иться, юсь, ишься *pf.* to hang one's head.
пону́рый *adj.* downcast.
по́нчик, а *m.* doughnut.
поны́не *adv.* up to the present, until now.
понюха|ть, ю *pf. of* **ню́хать**
поню́шк|а, и *f.*: **п. табаку́** pinch of snuff; **ни за ~у табаку́** (*fig.*, *coll.*) for nothing, to no purpose.
поня́ти|е, я *nt.* **1.** concept. **2.** notion, idea; **~я не име́ю!** (*coll.*) I've no idea!; I haven't a clue!; **не име́ю ни мале́йшего ~я!** I haven't the faintest idea!
поня́тлив|ый (~, ~а) *adj.* sharp, quick on the uptake.
поня́тност|ь, и *f.* clearness, intelligibility.
поня́т|ный (~ен, ~на) *adj.* **1.** understandable; **~но, что...** it is understandable that...; **~но** (*coll.*) of course, naturally; **я, ~но, не мог согласи́ться** of course, I could not consent. **2.** clear, intelligible; **~но?** (*coll.*) (do you) see?; is that clear?; **~но!** (*coll.*) I see!; I understand!
понят|о́й, о́го *m.* witness (*at an official search, etc.*).
пон|я́ть, пойму́, поймёшь, *past* **~ял, ~яла́, ~яло** *pf.* (*of* **~има́ть**) to understand; to comprehend; to realize; **дать п.** to give to understand.
пообе́да|ть, ю *pf. of* **обе́дать**
пообеща́|ть, ю *pf.* (*of* **обеща́ть**) to promise.
по́одаль *adv.* at a distance, a little way away.
поодино́чке *adv.* one at a time, one by one.
поочерёдно *adv.* in turn, by turns.
поочерёдный *adj.* alternating; taken in turn.
поощре́ни|е, я *nt.* encouragement; incentive, spur.
поощри́тел|ьный (~ен, ~ьна) *adj.* encouraging.
поощр|и́ть, ю́, и́шь *pf.* (*of* **~я́ть**) to encourage; to give an incentive (to), give a spur (to).
поощр|я́ть, я́ю *impf. of* **~и́ть**
поп, а́ *m.* (*coll.*) priest.
поп-... *comb. form* pop-.
по́п|а, ы *f.* (*coll.*) (*baby's*) bottom.
попада́ни|е, я *nt.* hit; **прямо́е п.** direct hit.
попада́|ть(ся), ю(сь) *impf. of* **попа́сть(ся)**
попадь|я́, и́ *f.* (*coll.*) priest's wife.
поп-анса́мбл|ь, я *m.* pop group.
попа́рно *adv.* in pairs, two by two.
попа́|сть, ду́, дёшь, *past* **~л** *pf.* (*of* **~да́ть**) **1.** (**в**+*a.*) to hit; **п. в цель** to hit the target; **не п. в цель** to miss; **пу́ля ~ла ему́ в лоб** the bullet hit him in the forehead. **2.** (**в**+*a.*) to get (to), find o.s. (in); (**на**+*a.*) to hit (upon), come (upon); **п. в Ло́ндон** to get to London; **п. на по́езд** to catch a train; **п. в плен** to be taken prisoner; **п. кому́-н. в ру́ки** to fall into s.o.'s hands; **не туда́ п.** to get the wrong number (*on telephone*); **п. на рабо́ту** to land a job; **п. впроса́к** to put one's foot into it; **п. в беду́** to get into trouble; **п. в са́мую то́чку** to hit the nail on the head; (*impers.*; *coll.*): **ему́ ~дёт!** he'll catch it! **3.** (*coll.*): **~ло** *gives indef. force to certain prons. and advs.*: **как ~ло** anyhow; helter-skelter; **что ~ло** any old thing; **где ~ло** anywhere.
попа́|сться, ду́сь, дёшься, *past* **~лся** *pf.* (*of* **~да́ться**) **1.** to find o.s.; **он мне ~лся навстре́чу на у́лице** I ran into him in the street; **п. кому́-н. на глаза́** to catch s.o.'s eye; **что ~дётся** anything; **пе́рвый ~вшийся** the first person one happens to meet. **2.** to be caught; (**в**+*a.*) to get (into); **п. в кра́же** to be caught stealing; **п. с поли́чным** to be caught red-handed; **п. на у́дочку** to swallow the bait (*also fig.*).
попа́хива|ть, ет *impf.* (*coll.*) (+*i.*) to smell slightly (of).
попеня́|ть, ю *pf. of* **пеня́ть**
попере́к *adv. and prep.*+*g.* across; **де́рево упа́ло п. доро́ги** the tree fell across the road; **стоя́ть у кого́-н. п. доро́ги** to be in s.o.'s way; **стать кому́-н. п. го́рла** to stick in s.o.'s throat; **знать что-н. вдоль и п.** to know sth. inside out.
попереме́нно *adv.* in turn, by turns.
попере́чин|а, ы *f.* cross-beam, cross-piece, cross-bar.
попере́чник, а *m.* diameter.
попере́чн|ый *adj.* transverse, cross-; **~ая пила́** cross-cut saw; **п. разре́з, ~ое сече́ние** cross-section; **(ка́ждый) встре́чный и п.** every Tom, Dick, and Harry.
поперхн|у́ться, у́сь ёшься *pf.* (+*i.*) to choke (over).
попе́рч|ить, у, ишь *pf. of* **пе́рчить**
попече́ни|е, я *nt.* care; charge; **быть на ~и** (+*g.*) to be in the charge (of).
попечи́тел|ь, я *m.* guardian, trustee.
попечи́тельств|о, а *nt.* guardianship, trusteeship.
попива́|ть, ю *impf.* (*coll.*) to have a little drink (of); **стать п.** to take to drink.
попира́|ть, ю *impf. of* **попра́ть**
попи́са|ть, ю *pf. of* **пи́сать**
попи́сыва|ть, ю *impf.* (*coll.*) to write (*from time to time*); (*of a literary man*; *iron.*) to do a bit of writing.
по|пи́ть, пью́, пьёшь, *past* **~пи́л, ~пила́, ~пи́ло** *pf.* to have a drink.
по́пк|а[1], **и** *m.* (*coll.*) parrot; Polly.
по́пк|а[2], **и** *f.* (*coll.*) = **по́па**
popла́ва|ть, ю *pf.* to have, take a swim.
поплав|о́к, ка́ *m.* **1.** float. **2.** (*coll.*) floating restaurant.
попла́|кать, чу, чешь *pf.* to cry (*a little, for a while*); to shed a few tears.
попла|ти́ться, чу́сь, ~тишься *pf. of* **плати́ться**
попле|сти́сь, ту́сь, тёшься, *past* **~лся, ~ла́сь** *pf.* (*coll.*) to push off; to trudge along.
попли́н, а *m.* (*text.*) poplin.
попли́н|овый *adj. of* **~**
поплы́|ть, ву́, вёшь, *past* **~л, ~ла́, ~ло** *pf.* to strike out, start swimming.
попля|са́ть, шу́, ~шешь *pf.* (*coll.*) to dance (*for a while*).
поп-му́зык|а, и *f.* pop (music).
попо́вич, а *m.* (*coll.*) priest's son.
попо́в|на, ны, *g. pl.* **~ен** *f.* (*coll.*) priest's daughter.
попо́вник, а *m.* (*bot.*) marguerite, white ox-eye.
попо́вский *adj. of* **поп**
попо́йк|а, и *f.* (*coll.*) drinking-bout.
попола́м *adv.* in two, in half; half-and-half; **раздели́ть п.** to divide in two, halve.
по́полз|ень, ня *m.* (*zool.*) nuthatch.
поползнове́ни|е, я *nt.* feeble impulse; half-formed intention; **я име́л п. вы́сказать своё мне́ние, но в конце́ концо́в сдержа́лся** I had half a mind to say what I thought but in the end I restrained myself.
попол|з|ти́, у́, ёшь, *past* **попо́лз, ~ла́** *pf.* to begin to crawl.
пополне́ни|е, я *nt.* **1.** replenishment; re-stocking; **п. горю́чим** re-fuelling. **2.** (*mil.*) reinforcement.
пополне́|ть, ю *pf. of* **полне́ть**
попо́лн|ить, ю, ишь *pf.* (*of* **~я́ть**) to replenish, supplement, fill up; to re-stock; (*mil.*) to reinforce; **п.**

горю́чим to re-fuel.
пополн|я́ть, я́ю, я́ет *impf. of* **∠ить**
пополу́дни *adv.* in the afternoon; **в два часа́ п.** at 2 p.m.
пополу́ночи *adv.* after midnight; **в два часа́ п.** at 2 a.m.
попо́мн|ить, ю, ишь *pf.* (*coll.*) to remember; **~и(те) моё сло́во** mark my words!
попо́н|а, ы *f.* horse-cloth.
попо́тч|евать, ую *pf. of* **по́тчевать**
поп-пев|е́ц, ца́ *m.* pop singer.
поправе́|ть, ю *pf. of* **праве́ть**
поправи́м|ый (~, ~а) *adj.* rectifiable, remediable.
попра́в|ить, лю, ишь *pf.* (*of* **~ля́ть**) **1.** to mend, repair. **2.** to correct, set right, put right. **3.** to adjust, set straight. **4.** to improve; **п. своё здоро́вье** to restore one's health.
попра́в|иться, люсь, ишься *pf.* (*of* **~ля́ться**) **1.** to correct o.s. **2.** to get better; **я совсе́м ~ился** I am completely recovered. **3.** to put on weight; to look better; **он о́чень ~ился** he has put on a lot of weight; he looks much better. **4.** to improve.
попра́вк|а, и *f.* **1.** mending, repairing. **2.** correction; amendment; **п. к резолю́ции** amendment to a resolution. **3.** adjustment. **4.** recovery; **де́ло идёт на ~у** things are on the mend.
поправле́ни|е, я *nt.* **1.** correction, correcting. **2.** recovery; improvement.
поправля́|ть(ся), ю(сь) *impf. of* **попра́вить(ся)**
попр|а́ть, у́, ёшь *pf.* (*of* **попира́ть**) to trample (upon); (*fig.*) to flout.
по-пре́жнему *adv.* as before; as usual.
попрёк, а *m.* reproach.
попрек|а́ть, а́ю *impf.* (*of* **~ну́ть**) (*+a. and i. or +a.* **за***+a.*) to reproach (with).
попрек|ну́ть, ну́, нёшь *pf. of* **~а́ть**
по́прищ|е, а *nt.* field; profession; **вое́нное п.** soldiering; **литерату́рное п.** the world of letters.
попро́б|овать, ую *pf. of* **про́бовать**
попро|си́ть(ся), шу́(сь), ∠сишь(ся) *pf. of* **проси́ть(ся)**
по́просту *adv.* (*coll.*) simply; **п. говоря́** to put it bluntly.
попроша́йк|а, и *c.g.* **1.** (*obs.*) beggar. **2.** (*coll., pej.*) cadger.
попроша́йнича|ть, ю *impf.* **1.** (*obs.*) to beg. **2.** (*coll., pej.*) to cadge.
попроша́йничеств|о, а *nt.* **1.** (*obs.*) begging. **2.** (*coll., pej.*) cadging.
попроща́|ться, юсь *pf.* (**с***+i.*) to take leave (of), say good-bye (to).
попру́ *see* **попра́ть**
попры́гива|ть, ю *impf.* (*coll.*) to hop about.
попрыгу́н (*oblique cases not used*) *m.* (*coll., joc.*) fidget.
попрыгу́н|ья, ьи *f. of* **~**
попря́|тать, чу, чешь *pf.* (*coll.*) to hide.
попря́|таться, чусь, чешься *pf.* (*coll.*) to hide (o.s.).
попуга́|й, я *m.* parrot.
попуга́йчик, а *m.* parakeet; **волни́стый п.** budgerigar; budgie.
попуга́|ть, ю *pf.* (*coll.*) to frighten a little.
попу́дно *adv.* (*obs.*) by the pood (*see* **пуд**) .
попу́др|ить, ю, ишь *pf.* to powder.
попу́др|иться, юсь, ишься *pf.* to powder one's face.
попули́ст, а *m.* populist.
попули́стский *adj.* populist.
популяриза́ци|я, и *f.* popularization.
популяризи́р|овать, ую *impf. and pf.* to popularize.
популяриз|ова́ть, у́ю *impf. and pf.* = **~и́ровать**
популя́рност|ь, я *f.* popularity.
популя́р|ный (~ен, ~на) *adj.* popular.
попурри́ *nt indecl.* (*mus.*) medley.
попусти́тельств|о, а *nt.* (*pej.*) tolerance; connivance; **при ~е** (*+g.*) with the connivance (of).
попусти́тельств|овать, ую *impf.* (*+d.*) (*pej.*) to tolerate, put up (with); to connive (at).
по-пусто́му *adv.* (*coll.*) in vain, to no purpose.
по́пусту *adv.* (*coll.*) = **по-пусто́му**
попу́тно *adv.* on one's way; at the same time; (*fig.*) in passing; **п. заме́тить, что...** to observe in passing that ....
попу́тн|ый *adj.* **1.** accompanying; following; passing; **п. ве́тер** favourable wind. **2.** (*fig.*) passing; **~ое замеча́ние** passing remark.
попу́тчик, а *m.* fellow-traveller (*also fig., pol.*).
попыта́|ть, ю *pf.* (*+a. or g.; coll.*) to try (out); **п. сча́стья** to try one's luck.
попыта́|ться, юсь *pf. of* **пыта́ться**
попы́тк|а, и *f.* attempt, try.
попы́хива|ть, ю *impf.* (*coll.*) to let out puffs; **п. тру́бкой, п. из тру́бки** to puff away at a pipe.
попя́|титься, чусь, тишься *pf. of* **пя́титься**
попя́тн|ый *adj.*: **идти́ на п.** *or* **на ~ую** (*coll.*) to go back on one's word.
по́р|а, ы *f.* pore.
пор|а́, ы́ *a.* **∠у** *f.* **1.** time, season; **весе́нняя п.** springtime; **осе́нняя п.** autumn; **в ∠у** at (just) the right time; **не в ∠у** at the wrong time; **в ту ∠у** then, at that time; **до ~ы́, до вре́мени** for the time being; **до каки́х ~?** until when?; **до каки́х ~ вы оста́нетесь здесь?** how long will you be here?; **до сих ~** till now, up to now; **на пе́рвых ~а́х** at first; **с да́вних ~** for a long time; **с каки́х ~?** since when?; **с тех ~, как...** (ever) since ...; **с э́тих ~** since then, since that time. **2.** *as pred.* it is time; **давно́ п.** it is high time; **п. спать!** (it is) bedtime!
порабо́та|ть, ю *pf.* to do some work.
поработи́тел|ь, я *m.* enslaver.
порабо|ти́ть, щу́, ти́шь *pf.* (*of* **~ща́ть**) to enslave.
порабоща́|ть, ю *impf. of* **поработи́ть**
порабоще́ни|е, я *nt.* enslavement.
поравня́|ться, юсь *pf.* (**с***+i.*) to pull alongside (of).
пора́д|овать, ую *pf. of* **ра́довать**
пора́д|оваться, уюсь *pf. of* **ра́доваться**
поража́|ть(ся), ю(сь) *impf. of* **порази́ть(ся)**
пораже́н|ец, ца *m.* defeatist.
пораже́ни|е, я *nt.* **1.** defeat. **2.** (*med.*) lesion. **3. п. в права́х** (*leg.*) disfranchisement.
пораже́нческий *adj.* defeatist.
пораже́нчеств|о, а *nt.* defeatism.
порази́тел|ьный (~ен, ~ьна) *adj.* striking; staggering, startling.
пора|зи́ть, жу́, зи́шь *pf.* (*of* **~жа́ть**) **1.** to defeat; to rout. **2.** (*mil.*) to hit, strike. **3.** (*med.*) to affect, strike. **4.** (*fig.*) to strike; to stagger; to startle; **меня́ ~зи́л её мра́чный вид** I was taken aback by her gloomy appearance.
пора|зи́ться, жу́сь, зи́шься *pf.* (*of* **~жа́ться**) **1.** to be staggered, be astounded. **2.** *pass. of* **~зи́ть**
по-ра́зному *adv.* differently, in different ways.
пора́н|ить, ю, ишь *pf.* to wound; to injure; to hurt.
пора́н|иться, юсь, ишься *pf.* to injure o.s.; to hurt o.s.
пораст|а́ть, а́ет *impf. of* **~и́**
пораст|и́, ёт, *past* **поро́с, поросла́** *pf.* (*+i.*) to become overgrown (with).
порв|а́ть, у́, ёшь, *past* **~а́л, ~ала́, ~а́ло** *pf.* **1.** to tear slightly. **2.** (*impf.* **порыва́ть**) (**с***+i.; fig.*) to break (with); to break off (with); **п. дипломати́ческие сноше́ния** to break off diplomatic relations.
порв|а́ться, ётся, *past* **~а́лся, ~ала́сь, ~а́ло́сь** *pf.* **1.** to break (off), snap. **2.** to tear slightly. **3.** (*impf.* **порыва́ться**[1]) (*fig.*) to be broken (off).
поре́де́|ть, ет *pf. of* **реде́ть**
поре́з, а *m.* cut.
поре́|зать, жу, жешь *pf.* **1.** to cut; **п. себе́ па́лец** to

cut one's finger. **2.** (+*a. or g.*) to cut (*a quantity of*).
порé|заться, жусь, жешься *pf.* to cut o.s.
порé|й, я *m.* leek.
порекоменд|овáть, ýю *pf. of* **рекомендовáть**
пóристост|ь, и *f.* porosity.
пóрист|ый (~, ~а) *adj.* porous.
порицáни|е, я *nt.* censure; reprimand; **достóйный ~я** reprehensible; **вы́разить п.** (+*d.*) to censure.
порицá|ть, ю *impf.* to censure; to reprimand.
пóрк|а[1], и *f.* unstitching, unpicking.
пóрк|а[2], и *f.* (*coll.*) flogging, thrashing; lashing.
порнографи́ческий *adj.* pornographic.
порногрáфи|я, и *f.* pornography.
порномагази́н, а *m.* sex shop.
порнофи́льм, а *m.* blue movie.
пóровну *adv.* equally, in equal parts.
порóг, а *m.* **1.** threshold (*also fig.*); **п. бéдности** poverty line; **стоя́ть на ~е смéрти** to be at death's door. **2.** (*geog.*) rapids.
порóд|а, ы *f.* **1.** breed, strain; (*fig.*) sort, type; **корóва джерсéйской ~ы** Jersey cow. **3.** (*geol.*) rock; **материкóвая п.** bed-rock.
порóдистост|ь, и *f.* (pure) breeding.
порóдист|ый (~, ~а) *adj.* thoroughbred, pedigree.
поро|ди́ть, жý, ди́шь *pf.* (*of* **~ждáть**) to give rise (to), spawn (*fig.*).
породн|и́ть(ся), ю́(сь), и́шь(ся) *pf. of* **родни́ть(ся)**
порождá|ть, ю *impf. of* **породи́ть**
порождéни|е, я *nt.* result, outcome.
порóжист|ый (~, ~а) *adj.* full of rapids.
порóжний *adj.* (*coll.*) empty.
порожня́к, á *m.* empties (*empty wagons on rail.*).
порожнякóм *adv.* (*coll.*) empty, without a load.
пóрознь *adv.* separately, apart.
порозовé|ть, ю *pf. of* **розовéть**
порóй (*and* **порóю**) *adv.* at times, now and then.
порóк, а *m.* **1.** vice. **2.** defect; flaw, blemish.
поролóн, а *m.* foam rubber.
поропла́ст, а *m.* foam plastic.
порос|ёнок, ёнка, *pl.* **~я́та, ~я́т** *m.* piglet; (*cul.*) sucking-pig.
пóросл|ь, и *f.* verdure, shoots.
порося́тин|а, ы *f.* sucking-pig (*meat*).
пор|óть[1], ю́, ∸ешь *impf.* (*of* **рас~**) to unstitch, unpick; **п. вздор** (*coll.*) to talk nonsense.
пор|óть[2], ю́, ∸ешь *impf.* (*of* **вы́~**) (*coll.*) to flog, thrash; to whip, lash.
пор|óться, ∸ется *impf.* (*of* **рас~**) **1.** to come unstitched, come undone; to rip. **2.** *pass. of* **~óть[1]**
пóрох, а (у), *pl.* **~á, ~óв** *m.* gun-powder; powder; **емý ~а не хватáет** (*coll.*) he has not got it in him, he is not up to it; **держáть п. сухи́м** (*fig.*) to keep one's powder dry; **~ом пáхнет** (*fig.*) there is trouble brewing.
порохов|óй *adj. of* **пóрох; ~áя бóчка** powder-keg.
порóч|ить, у, ишь *impf.* (*of* **о~**) **1.** to discredit. **2.** to bring into disrepute; to denigrate, blacken, smear; **п. чью-н. репутáцию** to blacken s.o.'s reputation.
порóчност|ь, и *f.* **1.** depravity. **2.** fallaciousness.
порóч|ный (~ен, ~на) *adj.* **1.** depraved; wanton **2.** faulty, defective; fallacious; **п. круг** vicious circle.
порóш|а, и *f.* newly-fallen snow.
порош|и́ть, и́т *impf.* (*of snow*) to fall in powdery form; (*impers.*): **~и́ло** it was snowing lightly.
порош|кóвый *adj. of* **~óк**
порошкообрáз|ный (~ен, ~на) *adj.* powdery.
порош|óк, кá *m.* powder; **стирáльный п.** washing-powder; **стерéть в п.** to grind into dust; (*fig., coll.*) to make mincemeat (of).
порóю = **порóй**
порт, а, о ∸е, в ~ý, *pl.* **∸ы, ~óв** *m.* port; **воздýшный п.** airport.
портáл, а *m.* (*archit.*) portal.
портати́в|ный (~ен, ~на) *adj.* portable; **п. телефóн** mobile phone.
портвéйн, а *m.* port (*wine*).
пóртик, а *m.* portico.
пóр|тить, чу, тишь *impf.* (*of* **ис~**) **1.** to spoil, mar; to damage; **п. своё зрéние** to ruin one's eyesight; **не ~тите себé нéрвы** don't take it to heart. **2.** to corrupt.
пóр|титься, чусь, тишься *impf.* (*of* **ис~**) **1.** to deteriorate; (*of foodstuffs*) to go bad; to go off; (*of teeth*) to decay; to rot. **2.** to get out of order. **3.** to become corrupt.
порт|ки́, óк-кóв *no sg.* (*coll.*) pants, trousers.
портни́х|а, и *f.* dressmaker.
портнóвский *adj.* tailor's, tailoring.
портн|óй, óго *m.* tailor.
портня́жн|ый *adj.* tailor's; **~ое дéло** tailoring.
портови́к, á *m.* docker.
портóвый *adj. of* **порт; п. гóрод** port; **п. рабóчий** docker.
портрéт, а *m.* portrait; **он — живóй п. своегó отцá** he is the image of his father.
портрети́ст, а *m.* portrait-painter, portraitist.
портрéт|ный *adj. of* **~**
портсигáр, а *m.* cigarette-case.
португáл|ец, ьца *m.* Portuguese.
Португáли|я, и *f.* Portugal.
португáл|ка, ки *f. of* **~ец**
португáльский *adj.* Portuguese.
портулáк, а *m.* (*bot.*) purslane.
портупé|я, и *f.* (*mil.*) sword-belt.
портфéл|ь, я *m.* **1.** brief-case; portfolio; **п.-дипломáт** attaché case. **2.** (*fig.*) portfolio; **мини́стр без ~я** Minister without Portfolio.
портшéз, а *m.* sedan(-chair).
портьé *m. indecl.* (*hotel*) porter, doorman.
портьéр|а, ы *f.* portière, door-curtain.
портя́нк|а, и *f.* foot binding; puttee.
поруб|и́ть, лю́, ∸ишь *pf.* **1.** to chop down (*all or a large number of*). **2.** to do a bit of chopping.
порýбк|а, и *f.* tree-felling, wood-chopping.
поругáни|е, я *nt.* profanation, desecration; **отдáть на п.** to profane, desecrate.
поругá|ть, ю *pf.* (*coll.*) to scold, swear (at).
поругá|ться, юсь *pf.* **1.** to swear, curse. **2.** (**с**+*i.*; *coll.*) to fall out (with).
порýк|а, и *f.* bail; guarantee; surety; **круговáя п.** collective guarantee; **взять на ~и** to go bail (for); **отпусти́ть на ~и** to release on bail.
по-рýсски *adv.* (in) Russian; **говори́ть п.** to speak Russian.
поруч|áть, áю *impf. of* **~и́ть**
поручéни|е, я *nt.* commission, errand; mission; **по ~ю** (+*g.*) on the instructions (of).
пóруч|ень, ня *m.* handrail.
порýчик, а *m.* (*obs.*) lieutenant.
поручи́тел|ь, я *m.* guarantor.
поручи́тельств|о, а *nt.* guarantee; bail.
поруч|и́ть, ý, ∸ишь *pf.* (*of* **~áть**) **1.** to charge, commission; to instruct; **он ~и́л мне передáть вам дéньги** he charged me to hand you the money. **2.** to entrust.
поруч|и́ться, ýсь, ∸ишься *pf. of* **ручáться**
порфи́р, а *m.* (*min.*) porphyry.
порх|áть, áю *impf.* (*of* **~нýть**) to flutter, fly about.
порх|нýть, нý, нёшь *pf. of* **~áть**
порциóнный *adj.* à la carte.
пóрци|я, и *f.* portion; (*of food*) helping.
пóрч|а, и *f.* spoilage; damage; **п. отношéний** deterioration of relations.
пóрш|ень, ня *m.* (*tech.*) piston.
порш|невóй *adj. of* **∸ень**
поры́в, а *m.* **1.** gust; rush. **2.** (*fig.*) fit; upsurge; **п.**

гне́ва fit of temper; **под влия́нием ~а** on an impulse, on the spur of the moment.

порыва́|ть, ю *impf. of* **порва́ть**

порыва́|ться[1], **юсь** *impf. of* **порва́ться**

порыва́|ться[2], **юсь** *impf.* **1.** to make jerky movements. **2.** (+*inf.*) to try, endeavour.

поры́вист|ый (~, ~а) *adj.* **1.** gusty. **2.** jerky. **3.** (*fig.*) impetuous; fitful.

порыже́|ть, ю *pf. of* **рыже́ть**

поря́дков|ый *adj.* ordinal; **~ое числи́тельное** ordinal numeral.

поря́дком *adv.* (*coll.*) **1.** pretty; **мне п. надое́л э́тот фильм** I found it a pretty boring film. **2.** properly, thoroughly; **он не объясни́л п., как туда́ попа́сть** he did not explain properly how to get there.

поря́д|ок, ка *m.* order. **1.** = *correct state or arrangement*; **привести́ в п.** to put in order; **следи́ть за ~ком** to keep order; **всё в ~ке!** everything is all right!; all correct!; OK!; **э́то в ~ке веще́й** it is in the order of things; **не в ~ке** out of order; not right; **для ~ка** (*i*) to maintain order, (*ii*) to preserve the conventions; **к ~ку!** (*at a meeting*) order! **2.** = *sequence*; **алфави́тный п.** alphabetical order; **де́ло идёт свои́м ~ком** things are taking their (normal) course; **по ~ку** in order, in succession; **п. дня** agenda. **3.** procedure; **в ~ке** (+*g.*) by way (of); **в обяза́тельном ~ке** without fail; **в спе́шном ~ке** quickly; **зако́нным ~ком** legally; **пресле́довать суде́бным ~ком** to prosecute; **п. голосова́ния** voting procedure. **4.** (*mil.*) = *formation*; **боево́й п.** battle order. **5.** (*pol.*) = *system*, *régime*; **ста́рый п.** the old order. **6.** (*pl.*) customs, usages, observances.

поря́дочно *adv.* **1.** decently; honestly; respectably. **2.** (*coll.*) fairly, pretty; a fair amount; **мы п. вы́пили** we had a fair amount to drink. **3.** (*coll.*) fairly well.

поря́дочност|ь, и *f.* decency; honesty, probity.

поря́доч|ный (~ен, ~на) *adj.* **1.** decent; honest. **2.** (*coll.*) fair, considerable; **они́ живу́т на ~ном расстоя́нии отсю́да** they live a fair way from here.

поса|ди́ть, жу́, ~́дишь *pf. of* **сади́ть** *and* **сажа́ть**

поса́дк|а, и *f.* **1.** planting. **2.** embarkation; boarding. **3.** (*aeron.*) landing; **вы́нужденная п.** forced landing.

поса́дочн|ый *adj.* **1.** planting. **2.** (*aeron.*) landing; **~ая фа́ра** landing light.

поса́|женный *p.p.p. of* **~ди́ть**

поса́пыва|ть, ю *impf.* (*coll.*) to snuffle; to breathe heavily (*in sleep*).

поса́сыва|ть, ю *impf.* (*coll.*) to suck (at).

посва́та|ть(ся), ю(сь) *pf. of* **сва́тать(ся)**

посвеже́|ть, ю *pf. of* **свеже́ть**

посве|ти́ть, чу́, ~́тишь *pf.* **1.** to shine for a while. **2.** (+*d.*) to hold a light (for).

посветле́|ть, ю *pf. of* **светле́ть**

по́свист, а *m.* whistle; whistling.

посви|ста́ть, щу́, ~́щешь *pf.* to whistle (to, up).

посви|сте́ть, щу́, сти́шь *pf.* to whistle.

посви́стыва|ть, ю *impf.* to whistle (*softly*, *from time to time*).

по-сво́ему *adv.* in one's own way.

по-сво́йски *adv.* (*coll.*) **1.** in one's own way. **2.** in a familiar way, as between friends.

посвя|ти́ть, щу́, ти́шь *pf.* (*of* **~ща́ть**) **1.** (+*a.* **в**+*a.*) to let (in on); **мы вас ~ти́м в на́шу та́йну** we will let you in on our secret. **2.** (+*a. and d.*) to devote (to); to dedicate (to). **3.** (+*a.* **в**+*nom.-a.*) to ordain, consecrate; **п. в ры́цари** to knight.

посвяща́|ть, ю *impf. of* **посвяти́ть**

посвяще́ни|е, я *nt.* **1.** initiation. **2.** dedication. **3.** ordination; consecration; **п. в ры́цари** knighting.

посе́в, а *m.* **1.** sowing. **2.** crops.

посевн|о́й *adj.* sowing; **~а́я пло́щадь** sown area; *as n.* **~а́я, ~о́й** *f.* sowing campaign.

поседе́лый *adj.* grown grey, grizzled.

поседе́|ть, ю *pf. of* **седе́ть**

посейча́с *adv.* (*coll.*) up to now, up to the present.

поселе́н|ец, ца *m.* **1.** settler. **2.** deportee.

поселе́ни|е, я *nt.* **1.** settling. **2.** settlement. **3.** deportation; **отпра́вить на п.** to deport.

посел|и́ть, ю́, и́шь *pf.* (*of* **~я́ть**) **1.** to settle; to lodge. **2.** to arouse, engender.

посел|и́ться, ю́сь, и́шься *pf.* (*of* **~я́ться**) to settle, take up residence.

посел|ко́вый *adj. of* **~́ок**

посёл|ок, ка *m.* village; settlement.

посел|я́ть(ся), я́ю(сь) *impf. of* **~и́ть(ся)**

посеребр|ённый *p.p.p. of* **~и́ть** *and adj.* silver-plated.

посеребр|и́ть, ю́, и́шь *pf. of* **серебри́ть**

посереди́не *adv. and prep.*+*g.* in the middle (of).

посере́|ть, ю *pf. of* **сере́ть**

посети́тел|ь, я *m.* visitor; caller; patron.

посе|ти́ть, щу́, ти́шь *pf.* (*of* **~ща́ть**) to visit, call on; **п. ле́кции** to attend lectures.

посе́т|овать, ую *pf. of* **се́товать**

посе́|чься, чётся, ку́тся *pf. of* **се́чься**

посеща́емост|ь, и *f.* attendance.

посеща́|ть, ю *impf. of* **посети́ть**

посеще́ни|е, я *nt.* visiting; visit.

посе́|ять, ю *pf. of* **се́ять**

поси|де́ть, жу́, ди́шь *pf.* to sit (*for a while*).

поси́л|ьный (~ен, ~ьна) *adj.* within one's powers, feasible; **~ьная зада́ча** feasible task; **оказа́ть ~ьную по́мощь** to do what one can to help.

посине́|ть, ю *pf. of* **сине́ть**

поска|ка́ть, чу́, ~́чешь *pf. of* **скака́ть**

поскользн|у́ться, у́сь, ёшься *pf.* to slip.

поско́льку *conj.* **1.** as far as; **п. мне изве́стно** as far as I know. **2.** since; so long as; **п. вы гото́вы подписа́ть, гото́в и я** so long as you are ready to sign, I am too.

поско́нный *adj.* hemp(en).

по́скон|ь, и *f.* hemp-plant.

поскоре́е *adv.* somewhat quicker; *int.* **~!** quick!

поскуп|и́ться, лю́сь, и́шься *pf. of* **скупи́ться**

послабле́ни|е, я *nt.* indulgence.

посла́н|ец, ца *m.* messenger, envoy.

посла́ни|е, я *nt.* **1.** message. **2.** (*liter.*) epistle.

посла́нник, а *m.* envoy, minister.

по́сл|анный *p.p.p. of* **~а́ть**; *as n.* **п., ~анного** *m.* messenger, envoy.

по|сла́ть, шлю́, шлёшь *pf.* (*of* **~сыла́ть**) to send; **п. за до́ктором** to send for the doctor; **п. по по́чте** to post.

по́сле *adv. and prep.*+*g.* after; afterwards, later (on); (*after a neg.*) since; **п. войны́** after the war; **мы с ним не вида́лись п. войны́** he and I have not seen one another since the war; **п. чего́** whereupon.

после... *comb. form* post-.

послевое́нный *adj.* post-war.

после́д, а *m.* (*anat.*) placenta.

после|ди́ть, жу́, ди́шь *pf.* (**за**+*i.*) to look (after), see (to).

после́дн|ий *adj.* **1.** last; final; **(в) ~ее вре́мя, за ~ее вре́мя** lately, of late, recently; **(в) п. раз** for the last time. **2.** (the) latest; **~ие изве́стия** the latest news. **3.** the latter. **4.** (*coll.*) worst, lowest; **э́то уже́ ~ее де́ло!** it's the end!; it's the very limit!; **~яя ка́пля** the last straw; **руга́ться ~ими слова́ми** to use foul language. **5.** *as n.* **~ее, ~его** *nt.* the last; the uttermost.

после́довател|ь, я *m.* follower.

после́довательност|ь, и *f.* **1.** succession, sequence. **2.** consistency.

после́довател|ьный (~ен, ~ьна) *adj.* **1.** successive, consecutive. **2.** consistent, logical.

послéд|овать, ую *pf. of* **слéдовать**
послéдстви|е, я *nt.* consequence; **остáвить жáлобу без ~й** to take no action on a complaint.
послéдующий *adj.* subsequent.
послéдыш, а *m.* **1.** (*coll.*) youngest child (*in a family*). **2.** (*fig., pej.*) belated follower.
послезáвтра *adv.* the day after tomorrow.
послеобéденный *adj.* after-dinner.
послереволюциóнный *adj.* post-revolutionary.
послеродовóй *adj.* post-natal.
послеслóви|е, я *nt.* afterword; concluding remarks.
послóвиц|а, ы *f.* proverb; **войти в ~у** to become proverbial.
послуж|ить[1], **ý, ~ишь** *pf. of* **служить**
послуж|ить[2], **ý, ~ишь** *pf.* to serve (*for a while*).
послужнóй *adj.*: **п. спúсок** service record.
послушáни|е, я *nt.* obedience.
послýша|ть(ся), ю(сь) *pf. of* **слýшать(ся)**
пóслушник, а *m.* novice, lay brother.
послýш|ный (~ен, ~на) *adj.* obedient, dutiful.
послы́ш|аться, усь, ишься *pf. of* **слы́шаться**
послюн|ить, ю́, и́шь *pf. of* **слюни́ть**
посмáтрива|ть, ю *impf.* (**на**+*a.*) to look (at) from time to time.
посмéива|ться, юсь *impf.* to chuckle.
посмéнно *adv.* in turns, by turns; by shifts.
посмéнн|ый *adj.* in shifts; **~ая рабóта** shift work.
посмéртный *adj.* posthumous.
посмé|ть, ю *pf. of* **сметь**
посмéшищ|е, а *nt.* laughing-stock.
посмотр|éть(ся), ю́(сь), ~ишь(ся) *pf. of* **смотрéть(ся)**
посóби|е, я *nt.* **1.** allowance; benefit; **п. безработным** unemployment benefit. **2.** textbook; (educational) aid; **нагля́дные ~я** visual aids.
посóбник, а *m.* accomplice; abettor.
посóбничеств|о, а *nt.* (+*g.*) complicity (in); aiding and abetting.
посóве|ститься, щусь, стишься *pf. of* **сóвеститься**
посовéт|овать(ся), ую(сь) *pf. of* **совéтовать(ся)**
посодéйств|овать, ую *pf. of* **содéйствовать**
пос|óл, лá *m.* ambassador.
посол|и́ть, ю́, ~и́шь *pf. of* **соли́ть**
посоловéлый *adj.* bleary, bleared.
посоловé|ть, ю *pf. of* **соловéть**
посóльс|кий *adj.* **1.** ambassadorial, ambassador's. **2.** *adj. of* **~тво; п. автомоби́ль** embassy car.
посóльств|о, а *nt.* embassy.
пóсох, а *m.* **1.** staff, crook. **2.** crozier.
посóх|нуть, ну, нешь, *past* **~, ~ла** *pf.* to wither.
посп|áть, лю́, и́шь, *past* **~áл, ~алá, ~áло** *pf.* to have a sleep, have a nap.
поспевá|ть[1], **ет** *impf. of* **поспéть**[1]
поспевá|ть[2], **ет** *impf. of* **поспéть**[2]
поспé|ть[1], **ет** *pf.* (*of* **~вáть**[1]) (*coll.*) **1.** to ripen. **2.** (*of food in preparation*) to be done.
поспé|ть[2], **ю** *pf.* (*of* **~вáть**[2]) (*coll.*) to have time; (**к, на**+*a.*) to be in time (for); (**за**+*i.*) to keep up (with), keep pace (with).
поспеш|и́ть, ý, и́шь *pf. of* **спеши́ть**
поспéшно *adv.* in a hurry, hurriedly, hastily.
поспéшност|ь, и *f.* haste.
поспéш|ный (~ен, ~на) *adj.* hasty, hurried.
поспóр|ить, ю, ишь *pf.* **1.** *pf. of* **спóрить. 2.** (**с**+*i.*) to contend (with). **3.** to bet, have a bet.
посрам|и́ть, лю́, и́шь *pf.* (*of* **~ля́ть**) to disgrace.
посрам|и́ться, лю́сь, и́шься *pf.* (*of* **~ля́ться**) to disgrace o.s.
посрамлéни|е, я *nt.* disgrace.
посрамля́|ть(ся), ю(сь) *impf. of* **посрами́ть(ся)**
посреди́ *adv. and prep.*+*g.* in the middle (of), in the midst (of).
посреди́не *adv.* = **посереди́не**
посрéдник, а *m.* **1.** mediator, intermediary; go-between. **2.** (*comm.*) middle-man.
посрéднича|ть, ю *impf.* to act as a go-between, mediate.
посрéднический *adj.* intermediary; mediation.
посрéдничеств|о, а *nt.* mediation.
посрéдственно 1. *adv.* fairly well; moderately well; **он п. игрáет в тéннис** he is fairly good at tennis. **2.** *n.*; *nt. indecl.* fair (*as examination mark*).
посрéдственност|ь, и *f.* mediocrity.
посрéдствен|ный (~, ~на) *adj.* **1.** mediocre; so-so. **2.** (*of school marks, etc.*) fair.
посрéдств|о, а *nt.* mediation; **при ~е, чéрез п.** (+*g.*) by means of; through the intercession of; thanks to.
посрéдством *prep.*+*g.* by means of; by dint of; with the aid of.
поссóр|ить(ся), ю(сь), ишь(ся) *pf. of* **ссóрить(ся)**
пост[1], **á, о ~é, на ~ý,** *pl.* **~ы́** *m.* post; **наблюдáтельный п.** observation post; **быть на своём ~ý, стоя́ть на ~ý** to be at one's post; **занимáть высóкий п.** to hold a high post.
пост[2], **á, о ~é, в ~ý** *m.* **1.** fasting; (*fig., coll.*) abstinence. **2.** (*eccl.*) fast; **Вели́кий п.** Lent.
постáв|ить[1],**лю, ишь** *pf. of* **стáвить**
постáв|ить[2], **лю, ишь** *pf.* (*of* **~ля́ть**) to supply.
постáвк|а, и *f.* supply; delivery.
поставщи́к, á *m.* supplier.
постамéнт, а *m.* pedestal, base.
постанов|и́ть, лю́, ~ишь *pf.* (*of* **~ля́ть**) to decide, resolve; to decree.
постанóвк|а, и *f.* **1.** erection. **2.** putting, placing, setting; arrangement, organization; **п. вопрóса** formulation of a question; **п. гóлоса** (*mus.*) voice training. **3.** (*theatr.*) staging, production.
постановлéни|е, я *nt.* **1.** decision, resolution. **2.** decree; **издáть п.** to issue a decree.
постанóв|очный *adj. of* **~ка 3.**
постанóвщик, а *m.* producer (*of play*), stage-manager; director (*of film*).
постарá|ться, юсь *pf. of* **старáться**
постарé|ть, ю *pf. of* **старéть**
по-стáрому *adv.* **1.** as before. **2.** as of old.
постéл|ь, и *f.* **1.** bed; **лежáть в ~и** to be in bed. **2.** (*geol., tech.*) bed; bottom.
постéль|ный *adj. of* **~; ~ное бельё** bed-clothes.
постепéнно *adv.* gradually, little by little.
постепéн|ный (~ен, ~на) *adj.* gradual.
постесня́|ться, юсь *pf. of* **стесня́ться**
постиг|áть, áю *impf. of* **~нуть** *and* **пости́чь**
пости́гнуть = **пости́чь**
постижéни|е, я *nt.* comprehension, grasp.
постижи́м|ый (~, ~а) *adj.* comprehensible.
постилá|ть, ю *impf. of* **постлáть**
по|сти́ться, щýсь, сти́шься *impf.* to fast.
пости́|чь, гну, гнешь, *past* **~г, ~гла** *pf.* (*of* **~гáть**) **1.** to comprehend, grasp. **2.** to befall, overtake.
пост|лáть, елю́, éлешь, *past* **~лáл, ~лалá, ~лáло** *pf.* (*of* **стлать** *and* **~илáть**) to spread, lay; **п. ковёр** to lay a carpet; **п. постéль** to make one's bed.
пóстник, а *m.* faster.
пóстнича|ть, ю *impf.* to fast.
пóстничеств|о, а *nt.* fasting.
пóст|ный (~ен, ~нá, ~но) *adj.* **1.** Lenten; **п. день** fast-day; **п. обéд** meatless dinner; **~ное мáсло** vegetable oil. **2.** (*coll.; of meat*) lean. **3.** (*fig., coll., joc.*) glum. **4.** (*fig., coll., joc.*) pious, sanctimonious.
постов|óй *adj. of* **пост**[1]; **~áя бýдка** sentry-box; **п. милиционéр** militia-man on point-duty; *as n.* **п., ~óго** *m.* = **п. милиционéр**
постóй[1], **~те** (*coll.*) stop!; wait!
постó|й[2], **я** *m.* billeting, quartering; **постáвить на п.** to billet, quarter.

постóльку *conj.* **п., поскóльку** in so far as ...
посторон|и́ться, ю́сь, ~ишься *pf. of* **сторони́ться**
посторóнн|ий *adj.* **1.** extraneous, outside; **без ~ей пóмощи** unaided; **~ее тéло** foreign body. **2.** strange; *as n.* **п., ~его** *m.* stranger; outsider.
постоя́л|ец, ьца *m.* lodger; (*in hotel, etc.*) guest.
постоя́лый *adj.*: **п. двор** (*obs.*) coaching inn.
постоя́нно *adv.* constantly, continually.
постоя́н|ный *adj.* **1.** constant, continual; **п. посети́тель** constant visitor. **2.** constant; permanent, invariable; **п. áдрес** permanent address; **~ная áрмия** regular army; **~ная величинá** (*math.*) constant; **п. ток** (*elec.*) direct current. **3. (~ен, ~на)** (*of personal, moral qualities, etc.*) constant.
постоя́нств|о, а *nt.* constancy; permanency.
посто|я́ть[1], **ю́, и́шь** *pf.* to stand (*for a while*).
посто|я́ть[2], **ю́, и́шь** *pf.* (**за**+*a.*) to stand up (for).
пострадá|вший *p.p. of* **~ть**; *as n.* **п., ~вшего** *m.* victim.
пострадá|ть, ю *pf. of* **страдáть**
постращá|ть, ю *pf. of* **стращáть**
пострéл, а *m.* (*coll.*) little imp, little rascal.
пострéлива|ть, ю *impf.* to fire intermittently.
постреля́|ть, ю *pf.* **1.** to do some shooting. **2.** (+*a. or g.*; *coll.*) to shoot, bag (*a number of*).
постригá|ть(ся), ю(сь) *impf. of* **пострúчь(ся)**
постри́|чь, гý, жёшь, гýт, *past* **~г, ~гла** *pf.* to clip, trim.
постри́|чься, гýсь, жёшься, гýтся, *past* **~гся, ~глась** *pf.* to have a (hair-)trim.
построéни|е, я *nt.* **1.** construction. **2.** (*mil.*) formation.
постро́|ить(ся), ю(сь), ишь(ся) *pf. of* **стрóить(ся)**
построй́к|а, и *f.* **1.** (*action*) building, erection, construction. **2.** (*edifice*) building. **3.** building-site.
пострóмк|а, и *f.* trace (*part of harness*).
пострóчный *adj.* by the line, per line.
постскри́птум, а *m.* postscript.
постýкива|ть, ю *impf.* to knock (*from time to time*), tap, patter.
постулáт, а *m.* (*math., phil.*) postulate.
постули́р|овать, ую *impf. and pf.* to postulate.
поступáтельн|ый *adj.* forward; **~ое движéние** forward movement; **п. ход** onward march.
поступ|áть(ся), áю(сь) *impf. of* **~и́ть(ся)**
поступ|и́ть, лю́, ~ишь *pf.* (*of* **~áть**) **1.** to act; **он прáвильно ~ил** he acted correctly; **они́ с ним плóхо ~или** they have treated him badly. **2.** (**в, на**+*a.*) to enter, join; **п. в шкóлу** to go to school; **п. в университéт** to enter the university; **п. на рабóту** to start work; **п. на воéнную слýжбу** to join up, enlist. **3.** to be received; to come through; **~ило ли егó заявлéние?** has his application come through?; **п. в продáжу** to go on sale; **п. в произвóдство** to go into production.
поступ|и́ться, лю́сь, ~ишься *pf.* (*of* **~áться**) (+*i.*) to waive, forgo; to give up.
поступлéни|е, я *nt.* **1.** entering, joining; **п. на воéнную слýжбу** enlisting. **2.** receipt; entry.
постýп|ок, ка *m.* act, deed.
пóступ|ь, и *f.* gait; step, tread.
постуч|áть(ся), ý(сь), и́шь(ся) *pf. of* **стучáть(ся)**
посты|ди́ться, жýсь, ди́шься *pf. of* **стыди́ться**
посты́д|ный (~ен, ~на) *adj.* shameful.
посты́л|ый (~, ~а) *adj.* (*coll.*) hateful, repellent.
посýд|а, ы *f.* **1.** (*collect.*) crockery; service; **гли́няная п., фая́нсовая п.** earthenware; **кýхонная п.** kitchen utensils; **фарфóровая п.** china; **чáйная п.** tea-service. **2.** (*coll.*) vessel, crock.
посýдин|а, ы *f.* **1.** vessel, crock. **2.** (*coll.*) (*naut.*) old tub.
посу|ди́ть, жý, ~дишь *pf.* to judge, consider; **~ди́ сам** judge for yourself.
посýд|ный *adj. of* **~а; п. магази́н** china-shop; **п. шкаф** dresser, china cupboard.
посудомóйк|а, и *f.* dishwasher.
посýл, а *m.* (*coll.*) promise.
посул|и́ть, ю, и́шь *pf. of* **сули́ть**
пóсуху *adv.* (*coll.*) on dry land.
посцáть (*vulg.*) *pf. of* **сцáть**
посчастли́в|иться, ится *pf.* (*impers.*+*d.*) to have the luck (to); to be lucky enough (to).
посчитá|ть, ю *pf.* to count (up).
посчитá|ться, юсь *pf.* **1.** (**с**+*i.*; *coll.*) to get even (with). **2.** *pf. of* **считáться**
посылá|ть, ю *impf. of* **послáть**
посы́лк|а[1], **и** *f.* **1.** sending. **2.** parcel. **3.** errand; **быть на ~ах (у)** to run errands (for).
посы́лк|а[2], **и** *f.* (*phil.*) premise.
посы́лочный *adj.* parcel; mail-order.
посы́льн|ый, ~ого *m.* messenger.
посып|áть, áю *impf. of* **~ать**
посы́п|ать, лю, лешь *pf.* (*of* **~áть**) (+*i.*) to strew (with); to sprinkle (with).
посы́п|аться, лется *pf.* to begin to fall; (*fig.*) to rain down.
посягáтельств|о, а *nt.* (**на**+*a.*) encroachment (on, upon), infringement (of).
посяг|áть, áю *impf. of* **~нýть**
посяг|нýть, нý, нёшь *pf.* (*of* **~áть**) (**на**+*a.*) to encroach (on, upon), infringe (on, upon); **п. на чью-н. жизнь** to make an attempt on s.o.'s life.
пот, а, о ~е, в ~ý, *pl.* **~ы́, ~óв** *m.* sweat, perspiration; **весь в ~ý** bathed in sweat; **в ~е лицá** by the sweat of one's brow; **~ом и крóвью** with blood and sweat; **труди́ться до седьмóго (четвёртого) ~а** (*coll.*) to sweat one's guts out.
потайнóй *adj.* secret; hidden.
потакá|ть, ю *impf.* (*no pf.*) (+*d.*; *coll.*) to indulge.
потанц|евáть, ýю *pf.* to have a dance.
потаскýх|а, и *f.* (*coll.*) strumpet, trollop.
потасóвк|а, и *f.* (*coll.*) brawl, fight.
потáчк|а, и *f.* indulgence.
потáш, á *m.* potash.
потащ|и́ть, ý, ~ишь *pf.* to begin to drag.
потащ|и́ться, ýсь, ~ишься *pf.* to begin slowly to make one's way.
по-твоéму *adv.* **1.** in your opinion. **2.** as you wish.
потвóрств|о, а *nt.* indulgence, pandering.
потвóрств|овать, ую *impf.* (+*d.*) to show indulgence (towards), pander (to).
потёк, а *m.* stain; damp patch.
потём|ки, ок *no sg.* darkness.
потемнéни|е, я *nt.* darkening; dimness.
потемнé|ть, ю *pf. of* **темнéть**
потéни|е, я *nt.* sweating, perspiration.
потенциáл, а *m.* potential.
потенциáл|ьный (~ен, ~ьна) *adj.* potential.
потенциóметр, а *m.* (*elec.*) potentiometer.
потéнци|я, и *f.* potentiality.
потеплéни|е, я *nt.* warm(er) spell.
потеплé|ть, ет *pf. of* **теплéть**
по|терéть, трý, трёшь, *past* **~тёр, ~тёрла** *pf.* to rub.
по|терéться, трýсь, трёшься, *past* **~тёрся, ~тёрлась** *pf. of* **терéться**
потерпé|вший *p.p. act. of* **~ть**; *as n.* **п., ~вшего** *m.* victim; survivor; **п. от пожáра** fire victim; **п. кораблекрушéние** shipwreck survivor.
потерп|éть, лю́, ~ишь *pf.* **1.** to be patient. **2.** to tolerate, stand (for). **3.** to suffer, undergo.
потёртост|ь, и *f.* sore spot.
потёр|тый *p.p.p. of* **~éть** *and adj.* (*coll.*) shabby, threadbare.
потéр|я, и *f.* loss; waste; *pl.*; (*mil.*) losses; **спи́сок ~ь** (*mil.*) casualty list.
потéр|янный *p.p.p. of* **~я́ть** *and adj.* (*fig.*) lost.

потеря́|ть(ся), ю(сь) *pf. of* **теря́ть(ся)**
потесн|и́ть, ю́, и́шь *pf. of* **тесни́ть**
потесн|и́ться, ю́сь, и́шься *pf.* to squeeze up, move closer together (*so as to make room for others*).
поте́|ть, ю *impf.* **1.** (*pf.* **вс~**) to sweat, perspire. **2.** (*pf.* **за~**) to mist over, steam up. **3.** (*impf. only*) (**над**; *fig.*) to sweat (over), toil (over).
поте́ха, и *f.* (*coll.*) fun, amusement; **устро́ить что-н. для ~и** to do sth. for fun.
поте́|чь, ку́, чёшь, ку́т, *past* **~к, ~кла́** *pf.* to begin to flow.
потеша́|ть, ю *impf.* to amuse.
потеша́|ться, юсь *impf.* **1.** to amuse o.s. **2.** **(над)** to make fun (of).
поте́ш|ить, у, ишь *pf.* **1.** *pf. of* **те́шить. 2.** to amuse (for a while).
поте́ш|иться, усь, ишься *pf.* **1.** *pf. of* **те́шиться. 2.** to have a bit of fun.
поте́ш|ный (~ен, ~на) *adj.* (*coll.*) funny, amusing.
потира́|ть, ю *impf.* to rub.
потихо́ньку *adv.* (*coll.*) **1.** slowly. **2.** softly, noiselessly. **3.** on the sly, secretly.
потни́к, а́ *m.* saddle-cloth.
по́т|ный (~ен, ~на́, ~но) *adj.* **1.** sweaty; damp with perspiration. **2.** (*of glass, etc.*) misted, steamed-up.
потов|о́й *adj. of* **пот; ~ы́е же́лезы** sweat glands.
потого́нн|ый *adj.*: **~ое (сре́дство)** (*med.*) sudorific; **~ая систе́ма труда́** sweated labour system.
пото́к, а *m.* **1.** stream; flow; **го́рный п.** mountain stream; **людско́й п.** stream of people; **лить ~и слёз** to shed floods of tears. **2.** production line. **3.** (*in education*) stream.
потолк|ова́ть, у́ю *pf.* **(с+***i.*; *coll.*) to have a talk (with).
потол|о́к, ка́ *m.* ceiling; **взять что-н. с ~ка́** (*joc.*) to make sth. up.
потолсте́|ть, ю *pf. of* **толсте́ть**
пото́м *adv.* afterwards; later (on); then, after that.
пото́м|ок, ка *m.* descendant; *pl.* offspring, progeny.
пото́мственный *adj.* hereditary; **он п. сере́бряных дел ма́стер** he comes of a family of silversmiths.
пото́мств|о, а *nt.* (*collect.*) posterity, descendants.
потому́ 1. *adv.* that is why; **я был в отпуску́, п. я и не знал об э́том** I was on leave, that is why I did not know about it. **2.** *conj.* **п. что** because, as.
потон|у́ть, у́, ~ешь *pf. of* **тону́ть**
пото́п, а *m.* flood, deluge; **всеми́рный п.** (*bibl.*) the Flood.
потоп|и́ть, лю́, ~ишь *pf.* (*of* **~ля́ть**) to sink.
потопле́ни|е, я *nt.* sinking.
потоп|та́ть, чу́, ~чешь *pf. of* **топта́ть**
потора́плива|ть, ю *impf.* (*coll.*) to hurry, urge on.
потора́плива|ться, юсь *impf.* (*coll.*) to hurry; **~йтесь!** get a move on!
потороп|и́ть(ся), лю́(сь), ~ишь(ся) *pf. of* **торопи́ть(ся)**
пото́|чный *adj. of* **~к; ~чная ли́ния** production line; **ма́ссовое ~чное произво́дство** mass production.
потра́в|а, ы *f.* damage (*caused to crops by cattle*).
потрав|и́ть, лю́, ~ишь *pf. of* **трави́ть**[1] **4.**
потра́|тить(ся), чу(сь), тишь(ся) *pf. of* **тра́тить(ся)**
потра́ф|ить, лю, ишь *pf.* (*of* **~ля́ть**) (+*d. or* **на**+*a.*; *coll.*) to please, satisfy.
потрафля́|ть, ю *impf. of* **потра́фить**
потреби́тел|ь, я *m.* consumer, user.
потреби́тель|ский *adj. of* **~; ~ская коопера́ция** (*collect.*) consumers' co-operatives.
потреб|и́ть, лю́, и́шь *pf. of* **~ля́ть**
потребле́ни|е, я *nt.* consumption, use; **това́ры широ́кого ~я** consumer goods.
потребля́|ть, ю *impf.* (*of* **потреби́ть**) to consume, use.
потре́бност|ь, и *f.* need, requirement; **жи́зненные ~и** the necessities of life.
потре́б|ный (~ен, ~на) *adj.* necessary, required, requisite.
потре́б|овать(ся), ую(сь) *pf. of* **тре́бовать(ся)**
потрево́ж|ить(ся), у(сь), ишь(ся) *pf. of* **трево́жить(ся)**
потрёп|анный *p.p.p. of* **~а́ть** *and adj.* **1.** shabby; ragged, tattered. **2.** battered. **3.** (*fig.*) worn, seedy.
потреп|а́ть(ся), лю́, ~лет(ся) *pf. of* **трепа́ть(ся)**
потре́ска|ться, ется *pf. of* **тре́скаться**
потре́скива|ть, ю *impf.* to crackle.
потро́га|ть, ю *pf.* to touch, run one's hand over; **п. па́льцем** to finger.
потрох|а́, о́в *no sg.* giblets.
потрош|и́ть, у́, и́шь *impf.* (*of* **вы́~**) to disembowel; to draw (*fowl*).
потру|ди́ться, жу́сь, ~дишься *pf.* to do some work; to take pains; **~ди́сь, ~ди́тесь** (+*inf.*) (*official or joc. injunction*) be so kind as (to).
потряс|а́ть, а́ю *impf. of* **~ти́**
потряса́|ющий *pres. part. act. of* **~ть** *and adj.* (*coll.*) staggering, stupendous, tremendous.
потрясе́ни|е, я *nt.* shock.
потряс|ти́, у́, ёшь, *past* **~, ~ла́** *pf.* (*of* **~а́ть**) **1.** to shake; to rock; **п. до основа́ния** to rock to its foundations. **2.** (+*i.*) to brandish, shake; **п. кулако́м** to shake one's fist. **3.** (*fig.*) to shake; to stagger, stun.
потря́хива|ть, ю *impf.* (+*i.*) to shake (*a little, from time to time*); to jolt.
поту́г|а, и *f.* **1.** contraction; **родовы́е ~и** labour pains. **2.** (*fig.*) (*vain, unsuccessful*) attempt; **~и на остроу́мие** attempts to be funny.
поту́п|ить, лю, ишь *pf.* (*of* **~ля́ть**) to lower, cast down; **~я взор** with downcast eyes.
поту́п|иться, люсь, ишься *pf.* (*of* **~ля́ться**) to look down, cast down one's eyes.
потупля́|ть(ся), ю(сь) *impf. of* **поту́пить(ся)**
по-туре́цки *adv.* in Turkish; in the Turkish fashion; **сиде́ть п.** to sit cross-legged.
потускне́лый *adj.* tarnished; (*fig.*) lack-lustre.
потускне́|ть, ю *pf. of* **тускне́ть**
потусторо́нний *adj.*: **п. мир** the other world.
потух|а́ть, а́ю *impf. of* **~нуть**
поту́х|нуть, ну, нешь, *past* **~, ~ла** *pf.* (*of* **ту́хнуть**[1] *and* **~а́ть**) to go out; (*fig.*) to die out.
поту́х|ший *p.p. act. of* **~нуть** *and adj.* extinct; (*fig.*) lifeless, lack-lustre; **п. вулка́н** extinct volcano.
потучне́|ть, ю *pf. of* **тучне́ть**
потуш|и́ть, у́, ~ишь *pf. of* **туши́ть**
по́тч|евать, ую *impf.* (*of* **по~**) (+*i.*; *coll.*) to regale (with), treat (to).
потяга́|ться, юсь *pf. of* **тяга́ться**
потя́гива|ть, ю *impf.* (*coll.*) **1.** to pull (at); to tug (at); **п. папиро́су** to draw on a cigarette. **2.** to sip.
потя́гива|ться, юсь *impf. of* **потяну́ться**
потян|у́ть, у́, ~ешь *pf.* to begin to pull.
потян|у́ться, у́сь, ~ешься *pf.* (*of* **тяну́ться** *and* **потя́гиваться**) to stretch o.s.
поу́жина|ть, ю *pf. of* **у́жинать**
поумне́|ть, ю *pf. of* **умне́ть**
поуро́чн|ый *adj.* **1.** by the piece; **~ая опла́та** piece-work payment. **2.** by the lesson.
поутру́ *adv.* (*coll.*) in the morning.
поуча́|ть, ю *impf.* **1.** (*obs.*) to teach, instruct. **2.** (*coll., iron.*) to preach (at), lecture.
поуче́ни|е, я *nt.* (*liter.*) exhortation, homily; (*coll., iron.*) preaching; sermon, sermonizing.
поучи́тел|ьный (~ен, ~ьна) *adj.* instructive.
поха́б|ный (~ен, ~на) *adj.* (*coll.*) dirty, smutty.
поха́бщин|а, ы *f.* (*coll.*) smut(tiness), filth.
поха́жива|ть, ю *impf.* (*coll.*) **1.** to pace; to stroll. **2.** to come, go (*from time to time*).
похвал|а́, ы́ *f.* praise.
похва́лива|ть, ю *impf.* (*coll.*) to praise.

похвал|и́ть(ся), ю́(сь), ~ишь(ся) *pf. of* **хвали́ть(ся)**
похвальб|á, ы́ *f.* (*coll.*) bragging, boasting.
похвáл|ьный (~ен, ~ьна) *adj.* **1.** praiseworthy, laudable, commendable. **2.** laudatory; **~ьная грáмота** certificate of merit.
похваля́|ться, юсь *impf.* (*+i.*; *coll.*) to boast (of, about), brag (about).
похвáста|ть(ся), ю(сь) *pf. of* **хвáстать(ся)**
похéр|ить, ю, ишь *pf.* (*coll.*) to cross out, cancel.
похити́тел|ь, я *m.* thief; kidnapper; abductor; hijacker.
похи́|тить, щу, тишь *pf.* (*of* **~щáть**) to steal; to kidnap; to abduct; to hijack.
похищá|ть, ю *impf. of* **похи́тить**
похищéни|е, я *nt.* theft; kidnapping; abduction; hijacking.
похлёбк|а, и *f.* soup, broth.
похлóпа|ть, ю *pf.* to slap, clap (a few times).
похлопо|тáть, чý, ~чешь *pf. of* **хлопотáть**
похмéль|е, я *nt.* hangover.
похóд, а *m.* **1.** march; (*naut.*) cruise; **на ~е** on the march. **2.** (*mil.*; *fig.*) campaign; **крестóвый п.** crusade. **3.** walking tour, hike.
походáтайств|овать, ую *pf. of* **ходáтайствовать**
похо|ди́ть¹, жý, ~дишь *impf.* (**на**+*a.*) to resemble, look like.
похо|ди́ть², жý, ~дишь *pf.* to walk (*for a while*).
похóдк|а, и *f.* gait, walk, step.
похóд|ный *adj. of* **~¹**; **п. гóспиталь** field hospital; **~ная кровáть** camp-bed; **~ная пéсня** marching song; **~ная рáция** walkie-talkie set.
пóходя *adv.* (*coll.*) **1.** as one goes along; **мы éли п.** we ate as we went along. **2.** (*fig.*) in passing; in an offhand manner.
похождéни|е, я *nt.* adventure, escapade.
похóж|ий (~, ~а) *adj.* resembling, alike; (**на**+*a.*) like; **он ~ на дéда** he is like his grandfather; **э́то на неё не ~е** (*fig.*) that's not like her; **э́то ни на чтó не ~е** (*fig.*, *pej.*) it is unheard of. **2.** (*coll.*): **~е** it appears, it would appear; **~е на то, что...** it looks as if ...; **он, ~е, бóлен** it would appear he is ill.
по-хозя́йски *adv.* thriftily.
похолодáни|е, я *nt.* drop in temperature, cold snap.
похолодá|ть *pf. of* **холодáть**
похолодé|ть, ю *pf. of* **холодéть**
похорон|и́ть, ю́, ~ишь *pf. of* **хорони́ть**
похорóнн|ый *adj.* **1.** funeral; **~ое бюрó** undertaker's. **2.** (*fig.*, *coll.*) funereal. **3.: п. мешóк** body bag.
пóхор|оны, óн, онáм *no sg.* funeral; burial.
похорошé|ть, ю *pf. of* **хорошéть**
похотли́вост|ь, и *f.* lewdness, lasciviousness.
похотли́в|ый (~, ~а) *adj.* lustful, lewd, lascivious.
похотни́к, á *m.* (*anat.*) clitoris.
пóхот|ь, и *f.* lust.
похрабрé|ть, ю *pf. of* **храбрéть**
похудé|ть, ю *pf. of* **худéть**
поцел|овáть(ся), ýю(сь) *pf. of* **целовáть(ся)**
поцелý|й, я *m.* kiss.
поцеремóн|иться, юсь, ишься *pf. of* **церемóниться**
почасовóй *adj.* by the hour.
почáт|ок, ка *m.* (*bot.*) ear; spadix.
пóчв|а, ы *f.* **1.** soil, ground. **2.** (*fig.*) foundation, basis; **на ~е** (*+g.*) owing (to), because (of); **вы́бить ~у из-под чьих-н. ног** to cut the ground from under s.o.'s feet; **подготóвить ~у** to prepare the ground, pave the way.
пóчв|енный *adj. of* **~а**
почвовéд, а *m.* soil scientist.
почвовéдени|е, я *nt.* soil science.
почём¹ *interrog. and rel. adv.* (*coll.*) how much; **п. сегóдня я́блоки?** how much are apples today?; **узнáть, п. фунт ли́ха** (*coll.*) to fall upon hard times.
почём² *interrog. adv.* (*only used with parts of v.* **знать** *coll.*) how?; **п. знать?** who knows?; how is one to know?; **п. я знáю?** how should I know?
почемý 1. *interrog. and rel. adv.* why; **п. вы так дýмаете?** why do you think that? **2.** *as conj.* (and) so; which is why; **онá простуди́лась, п. и остáлась дóма** she has caught a cold, which is why she has stayed at home.
почемý-либо = почемý-нибудь
почемý-нибудь *adv.* for some reason or other.
почемý-то *adv.* for some reason.
пóчерк, а *m.* handwriting.
почернéлый *adj.* darkened.
почернé|ть, ю *pf. of* **чернéть**
почерп|áть, áю *impf. of* **~нýть**
почерп|нýть, нý, нёшь *pf.* (*of* **~áть**) **1.** (*+a. or g.*) to draw. **2.** (*fig.*) to glean, pick up.
почерствé|ть, ю *pf. of* **черствéть**
поче|сáть(ся), шý(сь), ~шешь(ся) *pf. of* **чесáть(ся)**
пóчест|ь, и *f.* honour; **воздáть ~и, оказáть ~и** (*+d.*) to pay homage (to).
почёсыва|ть, ю *impf.* (*coll.*) to scratch (*from time to time*).
почёт, а *m.* honour; respect, esteem.
почёт|ный *adj.* **1.** honoured; **п. гость** guest of honour. **2.** honorary; **п. член** honorary member. **3. (~ен, ~на)** honourable; **п. караýл** guard of honour.
пóчечный *adj.* (*anat.*, *med.*) nephritic; renal.
почивá|ть, ю *impf.* (*obs.*) **1.** to sleep. **2.** *impf. of* **почи́ть**
почи́|вший *p.p. of* **~ть**; *as n.* **п., ~вшего** *m.*, **~вшая, ~вшей** *f.* the deceased.
почи́н, а *m.* **1.** initiative; **взять на себя́ п.** to take the initiative. **2.** beginning, start.
почин|и́ть, ю́, ~ишь *pf.* (*of* **чини́ть¹** *and* **~я́ть**) to repair, mend.
почи́нк|а, и *f.* repairing, mending; **отдáть чтó-н. в ~у** to have sth. repaired, mended.
почин|я́ть, я́ю *impf. of* **~и́ть**
почи́|стить(ся), щу(сь), стишь(ся) *pf. of* **чи́стить(ся)**
почитáй *adv.* (*coll.*) **1.** almost. **2.** it seems; very likely.
почитáни|е, я *nt.* **1.** honouring; (*+g.*) respect (for). **2.** reverence, worship.
почитáтел|ь, я *m.* admirer; worshipper.
почитá|ть¹, ю *impf.* **1.** to honour, respect, esteem. **2.** to revere.
почитá|ть², ю *pf.* **1.** to read (a little, for a while). **2.** (*coll.*) to read.
почи́тыва|ть, ю *impf.* (*coll.*) to read (now and then).
почи́|ть, ю, ешь *pf.* (*of* **~вáть**) (*rhet.*) to rest, take one's rest; (*fig.*) to pass away, pass to one's rest; **п. на лáврах** to rest on one's laurels.
пóчк|а¹, и *f.* (*bot.*) bud.
пóч|ка², ки *f.* (*anat.*) kidney; (*pl.*; *cul.*) kidneys.
пóчт|а, ы *f.* **1.** post; **воздýшная п.** air mail; **электрóнная п.** e-mail; **послáть по ~е, ~ой** to post. **2.** (the) post, (the) mail; **пришлá ли п.?** has the post come? **3.** post office.
почтальóн, а *m.* postman.
почтáмт, а *m.* main post office (*of city or town*).
почтéни|е, я *nt.* respect; deference; **относи́ться с ~ем (к)** to treat with respect; **с совершéнным ~ем** (*epistolary formula*) respectfully yours.
почтéн|ный (~ен, ~на) *adj.* **1.** worthy, estimable; venerable; **~ная рабóта** estimable work; **п. вóзраст** venerable age. **2.** (*fig.*, *coll.*) considerable.
почти́ *adv.* almost, nearly; **п. ничегó** next to nothing; **п. что = п.**
почти́тельност|ь, и *f.* respect, deference.
почти́тел|ьный (~ен, ~ьна) *adj.* respectful, deferential.

по|чти́ть, чту́, чти́шь *pf.* to honour.
почт|о́вый *adj. of* **~а; ~о́вая бума́га** note-paper; **п. ваго́н** mail-van; **п. го́лубь** carrier-pigeon, homing pigeon; **п. и́ндекс** post-code; **~о́вая откры́тка** postcard; **~о́вая ма́рка** postage stamp; postal order; **п. по́езд** mail train; **~о́вые расхо́ды** postage; **п. я́щик** pillar-box.
поч|ту́, ти́шь *see* **~ти́ть**
почу́вств|овать, ую *pf. of* **чу́вствовать**
почу́д|иться, ится *pf. of* **чу́диться**
почу́|ять, ю *pf. of* **чу́ять**
пошаба́ш|ить, у, ишь *pf. of* **шаба́шить**
поша́лива|ть, ю *impf.* (*coll.*) to be naughty; to act up; to play up (*from time to time*) (*also fig.*).
пошатн|у́ть, у́, ёшь *pf.* to shake (*also fig.*); (*impers.*): **меня́ ~у́ло** I was shaken.
пошатн|у́ться, у́сь, ёшься *pf.* **1.** to sway, totter, stagger. **2.** (*fig.*) to be shaken; **её здоро́вье ~у́лось** her health has suffered.
поша́тыва|ться, юсь *impf.* to sway, totter, stagger.
пошевел|и́ть(ся), ю́(сь), ~и́шь(ся) *pf. of* **шевели́ть(ся)**
пош|ёл, ла́ *see* **пойти́**
поши́б, а *m.* (*coll.*) manners; ways.
поши́вк|а, и *f.* sewing.
поши́вочн|ый *adj.* sewing; **~ая мастерска́я** (sewing) workshop.
по́шлин|а, ы *f.* duty; customs; **суде́бная п.** costs.
по́шлин|ный *adj. of* **~а**
по́шлост|ь, и *f.* **1.** vulgarity, commonness. **2.** trite remark, banality.
по́шл|ый (~, ~а́, ~о) *adj.* **1.** vulgar, common. **2.** commonplace, trivial; trite, banal.
пошля́к, а́ *m.* (*coll.*) vulgar person.
пошту́чно *adv.* by the piece.
пошту́чн|ый *adj.* by the piece; **~ая опла́та** piece-work payment.
пошум|е́ть, лю́, и́шь *pf.* to make a bit of a noise.
пошу|ти́ть, чу́, ~тишь *pf. of* **шути́ть**
поща́д|а, ы *f.* mercy; **не дать ~ы** to give no quarter.
поща|ди́ть, жу́, ди́шь *pf. of* **щади́ть**
пощеко|та́ть, чу́, ~чешь *pf. of* **щекота́ть**
пощёчин|а, ы *f.* slap in the face (*also fig.*); **дать ~у** (*+d.*) to slap in the face.
пощи́пыва|ть, ю *impf.* (*coll.*) to pinch (*from time to time*).
пощу́па|ть, ю *pf. of* **щу́пать**
по́эзи|я, и *f.* poetry.
поэ́м|а, ы *f.* (*usu. long*) poem.
поэ́т, а *m.* poet.
поэта́пный *adj.* phased.
поэте́сс|а, ы *f.* poetess.
поэти́ческ|ий *adj.* poetic(al).
поэ́тому *adv.* therefore, and so.
по|ю́[1], ёшь *see* **петь**
по|ю́[2], ~и́шь *see* **пои́ть**
появ|и́ться, лю́сь, ~ишься *pf.* (*of* **~ля́ться**) to appear.
появле́ни|е, я *nt.* appearance.
появля́|ться, юсь *impf. of* **появи́ться**
по́яс, а, *pl.* **~а́, ~о́в** *m.* **1.** belt; **спаса́тельный п.** lifebelt. **2.** (*fig.*) waist; **кла́няться в п.** to bow from the waist; **по п.** waist-high. **3.** (*pl.* **~ы**) (*geog., econ.*) zone, belt.
поясне́ни|е, я *nt.* explanation.
поясни́тельный *adj.* explanatory.
поясн|и́ть, ю́, и́шь *pf.* (*of* **~я́ть**) to explain, elucidate.
поясни́ц|а, ы *f.* small of the back; **боль, простре́л в ~е** lumbago.
поясни́чный *adj.* (*anat.*) lumbar.
поясн|о́й *adj.* **1.** *adj. of* **по́яс 1.**. **2.** to the waist, waist-high; **п. покло́н** bow from the waist; **п. портре́т** half-length portrait. **3.** (*geog., econ.*) zonal.
поясн|я́ть, я́ю *impf. of* **~и́ть**
пр. *abbr. of* **1. прое́зд** Passage. **2. проспе́кт** Avenue. **3. про́чее: и ~** etc., etcetera, and so on.
праба́б|ка, ки *f.* = **~ушка**
праба́бушк|а, и *f.* great-grandmother.
пра́вд|а, ы *f.* **1.** truth; the truth; **су́щая п.** the honest truth; **э́то п.** it is true; it is the truth; **по ~е сказа́ть, ~у говоря́** to tell the truth; **всеми ~ами и непра́вдами** by fair means or foul. **2.** justice; **иска́ть ~ы** to seek justice. **3.: п.?** is that so?; really?; **п. (ли)?** is it true?; **п. ли, что он умира́ет?** is it true that he is dying?; **не п. ли?** *in interrog. sentences indicates that affirmative answer is expected*; **вы погаси́ли свет, не п. ли?** you (did) put out the light, didn't you? **5.** (*as concessive conj.*) true; **п., я ему́ не написа́л, но я вот-во́т собира́лся позвони́ть** true I had not written to him, but I was on the point of ringing.
правди́вост|ь, и *f.* **1.** truth; veracity. **2.** truthfulness; uprightness.
правди́в|ый (~, ~а) *adj.* **1.** true; veracious; **п. расска́з** true story. **2.** truthful; upright; **п. отве́т** honest answer.
правдоподо́би|е, я *nt.* verisimilitude; probability, likelihood; plausibility.
правдоподо́б|ный (~ен, ~на) *adj.* probable, likely; plausible.
пра́ведник, а *m.* righteous man.
пра́ведн|ица, ицы *f. of* **~ик**
пра́вед|ный (~ен, ~на) *adj.* **1.** righteous; upright. **2.** just.
праве́|ть, ю *impf.* (*of* **по~**) (*pol.*) to swing to the right.
пра́вил|о, а *nt.* **1.** rule; regulation; **граммати́ческие ~а** grammatical rules; **~а у́личного движе́ния** Highway Code; **как п.** as a rule. **2.** rule, principle; **взять за п.** to make it a rule; **взять себе́ за п.** (*+inf.*) to make a point (of).
пра́вильно *adv.* **1.** rightly; correctly. **2.** regularly.
пра́вильност|ь, и *f.* **1.** rightness; correctness. **2.** regularity.
пра́вил|ьный (~ен, ~ьна) *adj.* **1.** right, correct; **п. отве́т** the right answer; **~ьная дробь** proper fraction; **~ьно** (*as pred.*) it is correct; **~ьно!** that's right! **2.** regular; **~ьное спряже́ние** (*gram.*) regular conjugation; **~ьные черты́ лица́** regular features.
прави́тел|ь, я *m.* ruler.
прави́тельственный *adj.* governmental; government.
прави́тельств|о, а *nt.* government.
пра́в|ить[1], лю, ишь *impf.* (*no pf.*) (*+i.*) **1.** to rule (over), govern. **2.** to drive; **п. маши́ной** to drive a car; **п. рулём** to steer.
пра́в|ить[2], лю, ишь *impf.* (*no pf.*) **1.** to correct; **п. корректу́ру** to read, correct proofs. **2.** to set (*metal tools*).
пра́вк|а, и *f.* **1.** correcting; **п. корректу́ры** proofreading. **2.** setting (*of metal tools*).
правле́ни|е, я *nt.* **1.** government; **о́браз ~я** form of government. **2.** board; governing body.
пра́внук, а *m.* great-grandson.
пра́внучк|а, и *f.* great-granddaughter.
пра́в|о[1], а, *pl.* **~а́** *nt.* **1.** law; **уголо́вное п.** criminal law. **2.** right; **(води́тельские) ~а́** driving licence; **п. ве́то** (right of) veto; **п. го́лоса, избира́тельное п.** the vote, suffrage; **п. убе́жища** asylum, right of sanctuary; **по ~у** by rights; **быть в ~е** (*+inf.*) to have the right (to), be entitled (to).
пра́во[2] *adv.* (*coll.*) really; **я, п., не зна́ю, куда́ она́ де́лась** I really do not know where she has got to.
правове́р|ный (~ен, ~на) *adj.* (*relig.*) **1.** orthodox. **2.** *as n.* **п., ~ного** *m.* true believer (*esp. of Moslems*); **~ные** the faithful.

правов|о́й *adj.* legal; lawful; **~о́е госуда́рство** (*pol.*) state based on the rule of law.
правозащи́тник, а *m.* human rights activist.
правозащи́тн|ый *adj.*: **~ое движе́ние** human rights movement.
правоме́р|ный (~ен, ~на) *adj.* lawful, rightful.
правомо́чи|е, я *nt.* competence.
правомо́ч|ный (~ен, ~на) *adj.* competent.
правонаруше́ни|е, я *nt.* offence.
правонаруши́тел|ь, я *m.* lawbreaker; offender.
правоохрани́тельн|ый *adj.* law-enforcement.
правописа́ни|е, я *nt.* spelling, orthography.
правопоря́д|ок, ка *m.* law and order.
правосла́ви|е, я *nt.* (*relig.*) Orthodoxy.
правосла́вн|ый *adj.* (*relig.*) orthodox; **~ая це́рковь** Orthodox Church; *as n.* **п., ~ого** *m.*, **~ая, ~ой** *f.* member of the Orthodox Church.
правоспосо́б|ный, (~ен, ~на) *adj.* (*leg.*) capable.
правосу́ди|е, я *nt.* justice.
правот|а́, ы́ *f.* rightness; (*leg.*) innocence.
пра́в|ый[1] *adj.* **1.** right; right-hand; (*naut.*) starboard; **~ая рука́** (*fig.*) right-hand man. **2.** (*pol.*) right-wing, rightist; **~а́я па́ртия** party of the right.
пра́в|ый[2] **(~, ~а́, ~о, ~ы́)** *adj.* **1.** right, correct; **вы не совсе́м ~ы** you are not quite right. **2.** righteous, just; **~ое де́ло** a just cause.
пра́в|ящий *pres. part. act. of* **~ить** *and adj.* ruling; **~ящие кла́ссы** the ruling classes.
прагмати́зм, а *m.* (*phil.*) pragmatism.
прагма́тик, а *m.* (*phil.*) pragmatist.
прагмати́ческ|ий *adj.* pragmatic.
пра́дед, а *m.* **1.** great-grandfather. **2.** (*pl.*) ancestors, forefathers.
пра́зднеств|о, а *nt.* festival; festivities.
пра́здник, а *m.* **1.** (public) holiday; **с ~ом!** compliments of the season; **бу́дет и на на́шей у́лице п.** (*fig.*) our day will come. **2.** festive occasion, occasion for celebration.
пра́здничный *adj.* holiday; festive.
пра́здновани|е, я *nt.* celebration.
пра́здн|овать, ую *impf.* (*of* **от~**) to celebrate.
пра́зднност|ь, и *f.* idleness.
пра́зд|ный (~ен, ~на) *adj.* idle; **~ная жизнь** a life of idleness.
пра́ктик, а *m.* **1.** practical worker. **2.** practical person.
пра́ктик|а, и *f.* **1.** practice; **на ~е** in practice. **2.** practical work.
практика́нт, а *m.* trainee.
практик|ова́ть, у́ю *impf.* **1.** to practise. **2.** (*intrans.*; *of a doctor or lawyer*) to practise.
практик|ова́ться, у́юсь *impf.* **1.** (*pf.* **на~**) (**в**+*p.*) to practise. **2.** *pass. of* **~ова́ть; э́тот приём бо́льше не ~у́ется** this method is no longer used.
пра́ктикум, а *m.* practical work.
практи́ческ|ий *adj.* practical; **~ая медици́на** applied medicine.
практи́чност|ь, и *f.* practicality.
практи́ч|ный (~ен, ~на) *adj.* practical.
пра́от|ец, ца *m.* forefather.
пра́порщик, а *m.* **1.** (*in tsarist army*) ensign. **2.** (*in Russian army*) warrant officer.
прах, а *no pl., m.* **1.** (*rhet.*) dust, earth; **обрати́ть в п., пове́ргнуть в п.** to reduce to dust, to ashes; **пойти́ ~ом** to go to rack and ruin. **2.** ashes, remains; **здесь поко́ится п.** (+*g.*) here lies; **мир ~у его́** may he rest in peace.
пра́чечн|ая, ой *f.* laundry; **п.-автома́т, автомати́ческая п.** launderette.
пра́чк|а, и *f.* laundress.
пращ|а́, и́, *g. pl.* **~е́й** *f.* sling (*weapon*).
пра́щур, а *m.* ancestor, forefather.
пре...[1] *adj. pref. indicating superl. degree* very, most, exceedingly.
пре...[2] *vbl. pref. indicating action in extreme degree or superior measure* sur-, over-, out- (*cf.* **пере...**).
преа́мбул|а, ы *f.* preamble.
пребыва́ни|е, я *nt.* stay; **п. в до́лжности** tenure in office.
пребыва́|ть, ю *impf.* **1.** to be; to abide, reside. **2.** to be (*in a state of*); **п. у вла́сти** to be in power.
превали́р|овать, ую *impf.* to prevail.
превенти́вн|ый *adj.* preventive.
превзо|йти́, йду́, идёшь, *past* **~шёл, ~шла́** *pf.* (*of* **превосходи́ть**) (**в**+*p. or* +*i.*) to surpass (in); to excel (in); **п. все ожида́ния** to exceed expectations; **п. самого́ себя́** to surpass o.s.; **п. чи́сленностью** to outnumber.
превозмога́|ть, ю *impf. of* **превозмо́чь**
превозмо́|чь, гу́, ~жешь, ~гут, *past* **~г, ~гла́** *pf.* (*of* **~га́ть**) to overcome, surmount.
превознес|ти́, у́, ёшь, *past* **~, ~ла́** *pf.* (*of* **превозноси́ть**) to extol.
превозно|си́ть, шу́, ~сишь *impf. of* **превознести́**
превосходи́тельств|о, а *nt.* (*as title*) Excellency.
превосхо|ди́ть, жу́, ~дишь *impf. of* **превзойти́**
превосхо́д|ный (~ен, ~на) *adj.* **1.** superb, outstanding. **2.: ~ная сте́пень** (*gram.*) superlative degree.
превосхо́дств|о, а *nt.* superiority.
превосход|я́щий *pres. part. of* **~и́ть** *and adj.* superior.
превра|ти́ть, щу́, ти́шь *pf.* (*of* **~ща́ть**) (**в**+*a.*) to convert (into), turn (to, into); to reduce (to); **п. в ка́мень** to turn to stone.
превра|ти́ться, щу́сь, ти́шься *pf.* (*of* **~ща́ться**) (**в**+*a.*) to turn (into), change (into).
превра́тно *adv.* wrongly; **п. истолкова́ть** to misinterpret.
превра́тност|ь, и *f.* **1.** wrongness, falsity. **2.** vicissitude, reversal; **~и судьбы́** vicissitudes of life.
превра́т|ный (~ен, ~на) *adj.* **1.** wrong, false. **2.** fickle, perverse; **~ная судьба́** perverse fate.
превраща́|ть(ся), ю(сь) *impf. of* **преврати́ть(ся)**
превраще́ни|е, я *nt.* transformation, conversion.
превы́|сить, шу, сишь *pf.* (*of* **~ша́ть**) to exceed.
превыша́|ть, ю *impf. of* **превы́сить**
превыше́ни|е, я *nt.* exceeding, excess.
прегра́д|а, ы *f.* bar, barrier; obstacle.
прегра|ди́ть, жу́, ди́шь *pf.* (*of* **~жда́ть**) to bar, obstruct, block; **п. путь кому́-н.** to bar s.o.'s way.
преграждá|ть, ю *impf. of* **прегради́ть**
прегреше́ни|е, я *nt.* sin, transgression.
пред *prep.* = **пе́ред**
пред...[1] *pref.* pre-, fore-, ante-.
пред...[2] *comb. form, abbr. of* **председа́тель**
преда|ва́ть(ся), ю́(сь), ёшь(ся) *impf. of* **преда́ть(ся)**
преда́ни|е[1]**, я** *nt.* legend, tradition.
преда́ни|е[2]**, я** *nt.* handing over, committing; **п. земле́** committing to the earth; **п. сме́рти** putting to death.
пре́данност|ь, и *f.* devotion.
пре́дан|ный (~, ~на) *p.p.p. of* **преда́ть** *and adj.* (+*d.*) devoted (to); **п. друг** staunch friend; **п. Вам** (*epistolary formula*) yours faithfully, yours truly.
преда́тел|ь, я *m.* traitor.
преда́тельниц|а, ы *f.* traitress.
преда́тельск|ий *adj.* traitorous; treacherous (*also fig.*); **~ая пого́да** treacherous weather.
преда́тельств|о, а *nt.* treachery, betrayal.
пре|да́ть, да́м, да́шь, да́ст, дади́м, дади́те, даду́т, *past* **~дал, ~дала́, ~дало** *pf.* (*of* **~дава́ть**) **1.** (+*d.*) to commit (to); **п. гла́сности** to make public; **п. земле́** to commit to the earth; **п. суду́** to bring to trial. **2.** to betray.
пре|да́ться, да́мся, да́шься, да́стся, дади́мся, дади́тесь, даду́тся, *past* **~да́лся, ~дала́сь** *pf.* (*of* **~дава́ться**) (+*d.*) to give o.s. up (to); **п. от-**

чая́нию to give way to despair; **п. поро́кам** to indulge in vices; **п. страстя́м** to abandon o.s. to one's passions.

предба́нник, а *m.* dressing-room (*in a bath-house*).

предвари́тельно *adv.* beforehand; as a preliminary.

предвари́тельн|ый *adj.* preliminary; prior; advance; **~ое сле́дствие** (*leg.*) preliminary investigation, inquest; **по ~ому соглаше́нию** by prior arrangement; **~ое усло́вие** precondition.

предвар|и́ть, ю́, и́шь *pf.* (*of* **~я́ть**) **1.** (*obs.*) to forewarn. **2.** to forestall, anticipate.

предвар|я́ть, я́ю *impf. of* **~и́ть**

предве́сти|е, я *nt.* presage, portent.

предве́стник, а *m.* forerunner, precursor; herald, harbinger; presage, portent.

предвеща́|ть, ю *impf.* (*no pf.*) to betoken, foreshadow, herald, presage, portend; **э́то ~ет хоро́шее** this bodes well, this augurs well.

предвзя́тост|ь, и *f.* prejudice, bias.

предвзя́т|ый (~, ~а) *adj.* prejudiced, biased.

предви́дени|е, я *nt.* foresight; foreknowledge.

предви́|деть, жу, дишь *impf.* (*no pf.*) to foresee.

предви́д|еться, ится *impf.* (*no pf.*) to be foreseen; to be expected.

предвку|си́ть, шу́, ~сишь *pf.* (*of* **~ша́ть**) to look forward (to), anticipate (with pleasure).

предвкуша́|ть, ю *impf. of* **предвкуси́ть**

предвкуше́ни|е, я *nt.* (pleasurable) anticipation.

предводи́тел|ь, я *m.* leader.

предводи́тельств|о, а *nt.* leadership.

предводи́тельств|овать, ую *impf.* (*+i.*) to lead, be the leader (of).

предвое́нный *adj.* pre-war.

предвосхи́|тить, щу́, тишь *pf.* (*of* **~ща́ть**) to anticipate.

предвосхища́|ть, ю *impf. of* **предвосхи́тить**

предвосхище́ни|е, я *nt.* anticipation.

предвы́борн|ый *adj.* (pre-)election; **~ая кампа́ния** election campaign.

предго́р|ье, ья, *g. pl.* **~ий** *nt.* foothills.

преддве́ри|е, я *nt.* threshold (*also fig.*); **в ~и** (*+g.*) on the threshold (of).

преде́л, а *m.* limit; bound; **в ~ах** (*+g.*) within; **за ~ами** (*+g.*) outside, beyond; **в ~ах го́рода** within the city; **в ~ах го́да** within the year; **за ~ами страны́** outside the country; **вы́йти за ~ы** (*+g.*) to exceed the bounds (of); **п. жела́ний** pinnacle of (one's) desires; **положи́ть п.** (*+d.*) to put an end (to), terminate.

преде́л|ьный *adj.* **1.** *adj. of* **~**; **н. во́зраст** age-limit; **~ьная ли́ния** boundary line; **п. срок** time-limit, deadline. **2.** maximum; utmost; **~ьная ско́рость** maximum speed; **с ~ьной я́сностью** with the utmost clarity.

предержа́щ|ий *only in phr.* **вла́сти ~ие** (*iron.*) the powers that be.

предзнаменова́ни|е, я *nt.* omen, augury.

предика́т, а *m.* (*gram.*) predicate.

предикати́вный *adj.* (*gram.*) predicative; **п. член** predicate.

предисло́ви|е, я *nt.* preface, foreword.

предлага́|ть, ю *impf. of* **предложи́ть**

предло́г[1]**, а** *m.* pretext; excuse; **под ~ом** (*+g.*) on the pretext (of).

предло́г[2]**, а** *m.* (*gram.*) preposition.

предложе́ни|е[1]**, я** *nt.* **1.** offer; proposition; proposal; **п. по́мощи** offer of assistance; **сде́лать п. кому́-н.** to propose (marriage) to s.o. **2.** (*at meeting*) proposal, motion; suggestion; **внести́ п.** to introduce a motion. **3.** (*econ.*) supply; **спро́с и ~е** supply and demand.

предложе́ни|е[2]**, я** *nt.* **1.** (*gram.*) sentence; **гла́вное п.** main clause; **прида́точное п.** subordinate clause. **2.** (*phil.*) proposition.

предлож|и́ть, у́, ~ишь *pf.* (*of* **предлага́ть**) **1.** to offer; **п. свои́ услу́ги** to offer one's services. **2.** to propose; to suggest; **п. резолю́цию** to move a resolution; **п. тост** to propose a toast; **п. кого́-н. в председа́тели** to propose s.o. for chairman; **мы ~и́ли ей обрати́ться к врачу́** we suggested that she should see a doctor. **3.** to put, set, propound; **п. вопро́с** to put a question; **п. зада́чу** to set a problem; **п. но́вую тео́рию** to propound a new theory. **4.** to order; **им ~и́ли освободи́ть кварти́ру** they have been ordered to vacate their apartment.

предло́жный *adj.* (*gram.*) prepositional; **п. паде́ж** prepositional case.

предме́ст|ье, ья, *g. pl.* **~ий** *nt.* suburb.

предме́т, а *m.* **1.** object; article, item; (*pl.*) goods; **~ы пе́рвой необходи́мости** necessities; **~ы широ́кого потребле́ния** consumer goods. **2.** subject, topic, theme; (*+g.*) object (of); **п. насме́шек** object of ridicule. **3.** (*school*) subject; **она́ сдала́ экза́мен по пяти́ ~ам** she passed the examination in five subjects. **4.** object (= *purpose*); **на п.** (*+g.*) with the object (of).

предме́т|ный *adj. of* **~**; **п. уро́к** object-lesson; **п. катало́г** subject catalogue.

предмо́стн|ый *adj.*: **п. плацда́рм, ~ое укрепле́ние** bridge-head.

предназнач|а́ть, а́ю *impf. of* **~ить**

предназначе́ни|е, я *nt.* **1.** earmarking. **2.** (*obs.*) destiny.

предназна́ч|ить, у, ишь *pf.* (*of* **~а́ть**) **(для,** *or* **на***+a.*) to destine (for), intend (for), mean (for); to earmark (for), set aside (for).

преднаме́ренно *adv.* deliberately.

преднаме́ренност|ь, и *f.* premeditation.

преднаме́рен|ный (~, на) *adj.* premeditated; deliberate.

предначерта́ни|е, я *nt.* outline, plan, design.

предначе́рт|анный *p.p.p. of* **~а́ть; п. судьбо́й** predestined.

предначерта́|ть, ю *pf.* to plan beforehand; to foreordain.

предо = пред

пре́д|ок, ка *m.* forefather, ancestor; (*pl.*) forbears.

предопределе́ни|е, я *nt.* **1.** predetermination. **2.** predestination.

предопредел|и́ть, ю́, и́шь *pf.* (*of* **~я́ть**) to predetermine; to predestine, foreordain.

предопредел|я́ть, я́ю *impf. of* **~и́ть**

предоста́в|ить, лю, ишь *pf.* (*of* **~ля́ть**) **1.** to let; to leave; **нам ~или сами́м реши́ть де́ло** we were left to decide the matter for ourselves; **п. кого́-н. самому́ себе́** to leave s.o. to his own devices. **2.** to give, grant, extend; **п. креди́т** to give credit; **п. пра́во** to concede a right; **п. возмо́жность** to afford an opportunity; **п. кому́-н. сло́во** to call upon s.o. to speak; **они́ ~или ко́мнату в на́ше распоряже́ние** they have put a room at our disposal.

предоставля́|ть, ю *impf. of* **предоста́вить**

предостерега́|ть, ю *impf. of* **предостере́чь**

предостереже́ни|е, я *nt.* warning, caution.

предостере́|чь, гу́, жёшь, гу́т, *past* **~г, ~гла́** *pf.* (*of* **~га́ть**) **(от)** to warn (against), caution (against).

предосторо́жност|ь, и *f.* **1.** (*no pl.*) caution; **ме́ры ~и** precautionary measures. **2.** precaution.

предосуди́тел|ьный (~ен, ~ьна) *adj.* reprehensible, blameworthy.

предотвра|ти́ть, щу́, ти́шь *pf.* (*of* **~ща́ть**) to prevent, avert.

предотвраща́|ть, ю *impf. of* **предотврати́ть**

предотвраще́ни|е, я *nt.* prevention, averting.

предохране́ни|е, я *nt.* **(от)** protection (against).

предохрани́тел|ь, я *m.* guard, safety device; safety catch; **(пла́вкий) п.** (*elec.*) fuse.

предохрани́тельн|ый *adj.* **1.** precautionary; preventive; **~ые ме́ры** precautions. **2.** (*tech.*) safety; **п. кла́пан** safety-valve.
предохран|и́ть, ю́, и́шь *pf.* (*of* **~я́ть**) **(от)** to protect (from, against).
предохран|я́ть, я́ю *impf. of* **~и́ть**
предписа́ни|е, я *nt.* order, injunction; (*pl.*) directions, instructions; (*med., etc.*) prescription.
предпи|са́ть, шу́, ~́шешь *pf.* (*of* **~́сывать**) **1.** (+*inf.*) to order, direct, instruct (to). **2.** to prescribe.
предпи́сыва|ть, ю *impf. of* **предписа́ть**
предпле́ч|ье, ья, *g. pl.* **~ий** *nt.* (*anat.*) forearm.
предплюс|на́, ны́, *pl.* **~́ны, ~́ен** *f.* (*anat.*) tarsus.
предполага́емый *pres. part. pass. of* **предполага́ть** *and adj.* proposed.
предполага́|ть, ю *impf.* **1.** *impf. of* **предположи́ть. 2.** (*impf. only*) to intend; to contemplate; **мы ~ем оста́вить дете́й у ба́бушки** we intend to leave the children at their grandmother's. **3.** (*impf. only*) to presuppose.
предполага́|ться, ется *impf.* **1.** *pass. of* **~ть. 2.** (*impers.*): **~ется** it is proposed, it is intended; **~ется проложи́ть отсю́да автостра́ду** it is proposed to build a motorway from here.
предположе́ни|е, я *nt.* **1.** supposition, assumption. **2.** intention.
предположи́тельно *adv.* **1.** supposedly, presumably. **2.** (*in parenthesis*) probably.
предлположи́тельн|ый *adj.* conjectural; hypothetical; estimated.
предполож|и́ть, у́, ~́ишь *pf.* (*of* **предполага́ть**) to suppose, assume; **~́им, что он опозда́л на по́езд** suppose he missed the train.
предпо|сла́ть, шлю́, шлёшь *pf.* (*of* **~сыла́ть**) (+*d. and a.*) to preface (with).
предпосле́дн|ий *adj.* penultimate, next to last.
предпосыла́|ть, ю *impf. of* **предпосла́ть**
предпосы́лк|а, и *f.* **1.** prerequisite, precondition. **2.** (*phil.*) premise.
предпоч|е́сть, ту́, тёшь, *past* **~ёл, ~ла́** *pf.* (*of* **~ита́ть**) to prefer.
предпочита́|ть, ю *impf. of* **предпоче́сть**
предпочте́ни|е, я *nt.* preference.
предпочти́тел|ьный (~ен, ~ьна) *adj.* preferable.
предприи́мчивост|ь, и *f.* enterprise.
предприи́мчив|ый (~, ~а) *adj.* enterprising.
предпринима́тел|ь, я *m.* entrepreneur; businessman.
предпринима́тель|ский *adj. of* **~**
предпринима́тельств|о, а *no pl., nt.* enterprise; **ча́стное п.** private enterprise.
предпринима́|ть, ю *impf. of* **предприня́ть**
предпри|ня́ть, му́, ~́мешь, *past* **~́нял, ~няла́, ~́няло** *pf.* (*of* **~нима́ть**) to undertake; to launch; **п. ата́ку** to launch an attack; **п. шаги́** to take steps.
предприя́ти|е, я *nt.* **1.** undertaking, enterprise; venture. **2.** (*econ.*) enterprise, concern, business; works; **ме́лкое п.** small business.
предрасполага́|ть, ю *impf. of* **предрасположи́ть**
предрасположе́ни|е, я *nt.* **(к)** predisposition (to).
предрасполо́ж|енный *p.p.p. of* **~и́ть; (к)** predisposed (to).
предрасполож|и́ть, у́, ~́ишь *pf.* (*of* **предрасполага́ть**) **(к)** to predispose (to).
предрассу́д|ок, ка *m.* prejudice.
предрека́|ть, ю *impf. of* **предре́чь**
предре́|чь, ку́, чёшь, ку́т, *past* **~̈к, ~кла́** *pf.* (*of* **~ка́ть**) (*obs.*) to foretell.
предреш|а́ть, а́ю *impf. of* **~и́ть**
предреш|и́ть, у́, и́шь *pf.* (*of* **~а́ть**) **1.** to decide beforehand. **2.** to predetermine.
предродово́й *adj.* antenatal.
председа́тел|ь, я *m.* chairman; president.
председа́тель|ский *adj. of* **~; заня́ть ~ское ме́сто** to take the chair.
председа́тельств|о, а *nt.* chairmanship; presidency.
председа́тельств|овать, ую *impf.* to preside.
предсе́рди|е, я *nt.* (*anat.*) auricle.
предсказа́ни|е, я *nt.* prediction.
предсказа́тел|ь, я *m.* forecaster; soothsayer.
предска|за́ть, жу́, ~́жешь *pf.* (*of* **~́зывать**) to foretell, predict.
предска́зыва|ть, ю *impf. of* **предсказа́ть**
предсме́ртн|ый *adj.* (occurring before) death; **~ое жела́ние** dying wish.
предста|ва́ть, ю́, ёшь *impf. of* **~́ть**
представи́тел|ь, я *m.* **1.** representative; (+*g.*) spokesman (for); **полномо́чный п.** plenipotentiary.
представи́тельный[1] *adj.* (*pol., leg.*) representative.
представи́тел|ьный[2] **(~ен, ~ьна)** *adj.* imposing.
представи́тельств|о, а *nt.* **1.** representation. **2.** (*collect.*) representation; **дипломати́ческое п.** diplomatic representatives; **торго́вое п.** trade mission.
предста́в|ить, лю, ишь *pf.* (*of* **~ля́ть**) **1.** to present; **п. интере́с** to be of interest. **2.** to produce, submit. **3.** (+*a. and d.*) to introduce (to), present (to). **4. (к)** to recommend (for), put forward (for). **5.: п. себе́** to imagine, picture; **~ь(те) себе́!** (just) imagine! **6.** to represent, display; **п. что́-то в смешно́м ви́де** to hold sth. up to ridicule.
предста́в|иться, люсь, ишься *pf.* (*of* **~ля́ться**) **1.** to present itself, arise. **2.** (*impers.*+*d.*) to seem (to); **э́то тебе́ то́лько ~илось** it was just your imagination. **3.** (+*d.*) to introduce o.s. (to). **4.** (+*i.*) to pretend (to be); **п. больны́м** to feign sickness.
представле́ни|е, я *nt.* **1.** presentation; introduction. **2.** statement; representation. **3.** (*theatr.*) performance. **4.** (*psych.*) representation. **5.** idea, notion; **дать п. (о**+*p.*) to give an idea (of); **я не име́ю ни мале́йшего ~я** I have not the faintest idea.
представля́|ть ю *impf.* **1.** *impf. of* **предста́вить. 2.** (*impf. only*) to represent; **он ~ет США в ООН** he represents the USA at the UN. **3.: п. собо́й** to represent, be; to constitute; **э́то ~ет собо́й исключе́ние** this constitutes an exception.
представля́|ться, юсь *impf. of* **предста́виться**
предста́тельн|ый *adj.*: **~ая железа́** (*anat.*) prostate (gland).
предста́|ть, ну, нешь *pf.* (*of* **~ва́ть**) **(пе́ред)** to appear (before); **п. пе́ред судо́м** to appear in court.
предсто|я́ть, и́т *impf.* to be in prospect, lie ahead; to be in store; **~я́ла суро́вая зима́** a hard winter lay ahead; **нам ~и́т мно́го неприя́тностей** we are in for a lot of trouble; **ему́ ~и́т предста́вить диссерта́цию к пе́рвому ию́ня** he has to submit his dissertation by the first of June.
предстоя́|щий *pres. part. of* **~ть** *and adj.* forthcoming; impending.
предте́ч|а, и *c.g.* forerunner, precursor.
предубежде́ни|е, я *nt.* prejudice, bias.
предубе|ждённый *p.p.p. of* **~ди́ть** (*obs.*) *and adj.* prejudiced, biased.
предугад|а́ть, а́ю *pf.* (*of* **~́ывать**) to guess (in advance).
предуга́дыва|ть, ю *impf. of* **предугада́ть**
предупреди́тельност|ь, и *f.* courtesy; attentiveness.
предупреди́тел|ьный *adj.* **1.** preventive, precautionary. **2. (~ен, ~ьна)** courteous; attentive; obliging.
предупре|ди́ть, жу́, ди́шь *pf.* (*of* **~жда́ть**) **1. (о**+*p.*) to notify (about), warn (about); to give notice (of, about). **2.** to prevent, avert. **3.** to anticipate; to forestall; **я как раз э́то хоте́л сказа́ть, но вы ~ди́ли меня́** that is just what I was about to say, but you took the words out of my mouth.
предупрежда́|ть, ю *impf. of* **предупреди́ть**

предупрежде́ни|е, я *nt.* **1.** notice; notification. **2.** prevention. **3.** anticipating; forestalling. **4.** warning.
предусма́трива|ть, ю *impf. of* **предусмотре́ть**
предусмотр|е́ть, ю́, ~ишь *pf.* (*of* **предусма́тривать**) to envisage, foresee; to stipulate (for), provide (for); **п. все возмо́жности** to provide for every eventuality.
предусмотри́тельност|ь, и *f.* foresight, prudence.
предусмотри́тел|ьный (~ен, ~ьна) *adj.* prudent; provident; far-sighted.
предчу́встви|е, я *nt.* presentiment; foreboding, misgiving, premonition.
предчу́вств|овать, ую *impf.* to have a premonition (of, about); **я ~овал, что вы сего́дня поя́витесь** I had a feeling that you would turn up today.
предше́ственник, а *m.* predecessor; forerunner, precursor.
предше́ств|овать, ую *impf.* (+*d.*) to precede.
предше́ствующий *adj.* previous; foregoing.
предъяви́тел|ь, я *m.* bearer; **п. и́ска** plaintiff.
предъяв|и́ть, лю́, ~ишь *pf.* (*of* **~ля́ть**) **1.** to show, produce, present; **п. биле́т** to show one's ticket. **2.** (*leg., etc.*) to bring (forward); **п. иск (к)** to bring a suit (against); **п. обвине́ние** (+*d.* **в**+*p.*) to charge (with); **ему́ ~или обвине́ние в поджо́ге** he is charged with arson; **п. пра́во (на**+*a.*) to lay claim (to); **п. тре́бование (к)** to lay claim (to); **п. высо́кие тре́бования (к)** to make big demands (of, on).
предъявле́ни|е, я *nt.* **1.** production, presentation. **2.** (*leg., etc.*) bringing; **п. и́ска** bringing of a suit.
предъявля́|ть, ю *impf. of* **предъяви́ть**
предыду́щ|ий *adj.* previous, preceding; *as n.* **~ее, ~его** *nt.* the foregoing.
предыстори́ческий *adj.* prehistoric.
предысто́ри|я, и *f.* prehistory.
прее́мник, а *m.* successor.
прее́мственност|ь, и *f.* succession; continuity.
прее́мствен|ный (~, ~на) *adj.* successive.
прее́мств|о, а *nt.* succession.
пре́жде 1. *adv.* (*opp.* **пото́м**) before; first; **п. чем** *as conj.* before. **2.** *adv.* (*opp.* **тепе́рь**) formerly, in former times; before; **п. он учи́л в интерна́те** he taught in a boarding-school before. **3.** *prep.*+*g.* before; ahead of; **они́ пришли́ п. нас** they arrived before us; **п. всего́** first of all; first and foremost.
преждевре́менно *adv.* prematurely; before one's time.
преждевре́менност|ь, и *f.* prematurity, untimeliness.
преждевре́мен|ный (~ен, ~на) *adj.* premature, untimely.
пре́жн|ий *adj.* previous, former; **в ~ее вре́мя** in the old days, in former times.
презента́бел|ьный (~ен, ~ьна) *adj.* presentable.
презента́ци|я, и *f.* presentation; launch.
презервати́в, а *m.* condom.
презерва́ци|я, и *f.* preservation.
президе́нт, а *m.* president.
президе́нтский *adj.* presidential.
президе́нтств|о, а *nt.* presidency.
прези́диум, а *m.* presidium.
презира́|ть, ю *impf.* **1.** (*impf. only*) to despise, hold in contempt. **2.** (*pf.* **презре́ть**) to disdain; **п. опа́сность** to scorn danger.
презре́ни|е, я *nt.* disdain, contempt, scorn.
презре́н|ный (~, ~на) *adj.* contemptible, despicable; **п. мета́лл** (*coll.*) filthy lucre.
презр|е́ть, ю́, и́шь *pf. of* **презира́ть**
презри́тел|ьный (~ен, ~ьна) *adj.* contemptuous, scornful, disdainful.
презу́мпци|я, и *f.* (*phil., leg.*) presumption.
преиму́щественно *adv.* mainly, chiefly, principally.
преиму́щественн|ый *adj.* **1.** primary, prime, principal. **2.** preferential, priority.
преиму́ществ|о, а *nt.* advantage; **получи́ть п. (пе́ред)** to gain an advantage (over); **по ~у** for the most part, chiefly.
преиспо́дн|яя, ей *f.* the nether regions, the underworld.
преиспо́лн|енный *p.p.p. of* **~ить** *and adj.* (+*g. or i.*) filled (with), full (of); **п. опа́сности** fraught with danger.
преиспо́лн|ить, ю, ишь *pf.* (*of* **~я́ть**) (+*g. or i.*) to fill (with).
преисполн|я́ть, я́ю *impf. of* **~ить**
прейскура́нт, а *m.* price-list; bill of fare.
преклоне́ни|е, я *nt.* **(пе́ред)** admiration (for), worship (of).
преклон|и́ть, ю́, и́шь *pf.* (*of* **~я́ть**) to incline, bend; **п. го́лову** to bow (one's head); **п. коле́на** to genuflect.
преклон|и́ться, ю́сь, и́шься *pf.* (*of* **~я́ться**) **(пе́ред) 1.** to bow down (before). **2.** (*fig.*) to admire, worship.
прекло́нный *adj.*: **п. во́зраст** old age, declining years.
преклон|я́ть(ся), я́ю(сь) *impf. of* **~и́ть(ся)**
прекосло́в|ить, лю, ишь *impf.* (+*d.*) to contradict.
прекра́сно *adv.* **1.** excellently; perfectly well; **они́ п. зна́ют, что э́то воспрещено́** they know perfectly well that it is forbidden. **2.** *as int.* excellent!; fine!
прекра́с|ный (~ен, ~на) *adj.* **1.** beautiful, fine; **п. пол** the fair sex; **в оди́н п. день** one fine day, once upon a time; *as n.* **~ное, ~ного** *nt.* (*phil.*) the beautiful. **2.** excellent, first-rate.
прекра|ти́ть, щу́, ти́шь *pf.* (*of* **~ща́ть**) to stop, cease, discontinue; to put a stop (to), put an end (to); to break off, sever; **п. войну́** to end the war; **п. знако́мство (с**+*i.*) to break (it off) (with); **п. ого́нь** (*mil.*) to cease fire; **п. рабо́ту** to down tools; **п. рабо́тать** to stop work(ing); **п. сноше́ния (с**+*i.*) to sever relations (with).
прекра|ти́ться, ти́тся *pf.* (*of* **~ща́ться**) **1.** to cease, end. **2.** *pass. of* **~ти́ть**
прекраща́|ть(ся), ю, ет(ся) *impf. of* **прекрати́ть(ся)**
прекраще́ни|е, я *nt.* halt, cessation, discontinuance; suspension; **п. вое́нных де́йствий** cessation of hostilities; **п. огня́** cease-fire.
прела́т, а *m.* prelate.
преле́ст|ный (~ен, ~на) *adj.* charming, delightful, lovely.
пре́лест|ь, и *f.* charm; delight; **кака́я п.!** how lovely!; **~и жи́зни в дере́вне** the delights of living in the country.
прелом|и́ть, лю́, ~ишь *pf.* (*of* **~ля́ть**) (*phys.*) to refract.
преломле́ни|е, я *nt.* (*phys.*) refraction.
преломля́|ть, ю, ет *impf. of* **преломи́ть**
пре́л|ый (~, ~а) *adj.* rotten, fusty.
прел|ь, и *f.* rot, mouldiness, mould.
прель|сти́ть, щу́, сти́шь *pf.* (*of* **~ща́ть**) **1.** to attract; **его́ ~сти́ла перспекти́ва повы́шенной зарпла́ты** he was attracted by the prospect of higher wages. **2.** to lure, entice; **п. обеща́ниями** to lure with promises.
прель|сти́ться, щу́сь, сти́шься *pf.* (*of* **~ща́ться**) (+*i.*) to be attracted (by); to be tempted (by), fall (for).
прельща́|ть(ся), ю(сь) *impf. of* **прельсти́ть(ся)**
прелюбоде́|й, я *m.* adulterer.
прелюбоде́йств|овать, ую *impf.* to commit adultery.
прелюбодея́ни|е, я *nt.* adultery.
прелю́ди|я, и *f.* (*mus. and fig.*) prelude.
премиа́льн|ый *adj. of* **пре́мия**; *as n.* (*pl.*) **~ые, ~ых** bonus.
преми́н|уть, у, ешь *pf. only with neg.* (+*inf.*) not to

fail (to).

премиро́в|анный *p.p.p. of* **~а́ть** *and adj.* prize-winning, prize; *as n.* **п., ~анного** *m.* prize-winner.

премир|ова́ть, у́ю *impf. and pf.* to award a prize (to); to give a bonus (to).

пре́ми|я, и *f.* **1.** prize; bonus; **Но́белевская п.** Nobel Prize; (*cin.*): **п. О́скара** Oscar. **2.** (*fin.*) premium.

прему́дрост|ь, и *f.* wisdom; **~и** (*iron.*) subtleties.

прему́др|ый (~, ~а) *adj.* (very) wise, sage.

премье́р, а *m.* **1.** premier. **2.** (*theatr.*) leading actor, lead.

премье́р|а, ы *f.* (*theatr.*) première, opening night.

премье́р-мини́стр, а *m.* prime minister.

премье́рш|а, и *f.* (*theatr.*) leading lady, lead.

пренебрега́|ть, ю *impf. of* **пренебре́чь**

пренебреже́ни|е, я *nt.* **1.** scorn, contempt, disdain. **2.** neglect, disregard.

пренебрежи́тел|ьный (~ен, ~ьна) *adj.* scornful, disdainful.

пренебре́|чь, гу́, жёшь, гу́т, *past* **~̈г, ~гла́** *pf.* (*of* **~га́ть**) (*+i.*) **1.** to scorn, despise; **п. опа́сностью** to scorn danger. **2.** to neglect, disregard.

пре́ни|я, й *no sg.* debate.

преоблада́ни|е, я *nt.* predominance.

преоблада́|ть, ет *impf.* to predominate; to prevail.

преоблада́|ющий *pres. part. act. of* **~ть** *and adj.* predominant; prevalent.

преобража́|ть, ю *impf. of* **преобрази́ть**

преображе́ни|е, я *nt.* **1.** transformation. **2.** (*relig.*) the Transfiguration.

преобра|зи́ть, жу́, зи́шь *pf.* (*of* **~жа́ть**) to transform, transfigure.

преобразова́ни|е, я *nt.* **1.** transformation. **2.** reform; reorganization.

преобразова́тел|ь, я *m.* **1.** reformer. **2.** (*phys., tech.*) transformer.

преобраз|ова́ть, у́ю *pf.* (*of* **~о́вывать**) **1.** to transform (*also phys., tech.*). **2.** to reform, reorganize.

преобразо́выва|ть, ю *impf. of* **преобразова́ть**

преодолева́|ть, ю *impf. of* **преодоле́ть**

преодоле́|ть, ю *pf.* (*of* **~ва́ть**) to overcome, surmount; **п. тру́дности** to get over difficulties.

преодоли́м|ый (~, ~а) *adj.* surmountable.

препара́т, а *m.* (*chem., pharm.*) preparation.

препина́ни|е, я *nt.*: **зна́ки ~я** (*gram.*) punctuation marks.

препира́тельств|о, а *nt.* wrangling, squabbling.

препира́|ться, юсь *impf.* (**с**+*i.*; *coll.*) to wrangle (with), squabble (with).

преподава́ни|е, я *nt.* teaching, tuition, instruction.

преподава́тел|ь, я *m.* teacher; lecturer.

преподава́тель|ский *adj. of* **~**; **п. соста́в** teaching staff.

препода|ва́ть, ю́, ёшь *impf.* to teach.

препода́|ть, м, шь, ст, ди́м, ди́те, ду́т, *past* **препо́дал, ~ла́, препо́дало** *pf.* to give (*advice, a lesson, etc.*).

преподнес|ти́, у́, ёшь, *past* **~̈, ~ла́** *pf.* (*of* **преподноси́ть**) (*+a. and d.*) to present (with); **он ~̈ нам неприя́тную но́вость** he brought us a piece of bad news.

преподно|си́ть, шу́, ~́сишь *impf. of* **преподнести́**

преподо́би|е, я *nt.*: **его́ п.** (*title of priest*) his Reverence, the Reverend.

преподо́бный *adj.* Saint; Venerable.

препо́н|а, ы *f.* (*obs.*) obstacle, impediment.

препрово|ди́ть, жу́, ди́шь *pf.* (*of* **~жда́ть**) to send, forward, dispatch.

препровожда́|ть, ю *impf. of* **препроводи́ть**

препровожде́ни|е¹, я *nt.* forwarding, dispatching.

препровожде́ни|е², я *nt.* passing; **для ~я вре́мени** to pass the time.

препя́тстви|е, я *nt.* **1.** obstacle, hindrance; **чини́ть кому́-н. ~я** to put obstacles in s.o.'s way. **2.** (*sport*) obstacle; hurdle.

препя́тств|овать, ую *impf.* (*of* **вос~**) (*+d.*) to hinder, impede.

прерв|а́ть, у́, ёшь, *past* **~а́л, ~ала́, ~а́ло** *pf.* (*of* **прерыва́ть**) to break off, sever; to interrupt, to cut short; **п. заня́тия** to interrupt one's studies; **п. молча́ние** to break a silence; **п. дипломати́ческие отноше́ния** to break off *or* sever diplomatic relations; **нас ~а́ли** (*of telephone conversation*) we have been cut off.

прерв|а́ться, ёшься, *past* **~а́лся, ~ала́сь, ~а́ло́сь** *pf.* (*of* **прерыва́ться**) **1.** to be interrupted. **2.** (*of a voice*) to break.

пререка́ни|е, я *nt.* wrangle, argument.

пререка́|ться, юсь *impf.* (**с**+*i.*) to argue (with).

пре́ри|я, и *f.* prairie.

прерогати́в|а, ы *f.* prerogative.

прерыва́тел|ь, я *m.* (*elec.*) circuit breaker, cut-out.

прерыва́|ть(ся), ю(сь) *impf. of* **прерва́ть(ся)**

преры́вист|ый (~, ~а) *adj.* broken; interrupted, intermittent.

пресви́тер, а *m.* (*eccl.*) **1.** presbyter. **2.** (*in Presbyterian Church*) elder.

пресвитериа́нский *adj.* (*relig.*) Presbyterian.

пресека́|ть(ся), ю, ет(ся) *impf. of* **пресе́чь(ся)**

пресе́|чь, ку́, чёшь, ку́т, *past* **~к, ~кла** *pf.* (*of* **~ка́ть**) to cut short, stop; **п. в ко́рне** to nip in the bud.

пресе́|чься, чётся, ку́тся, *past* **~кся, ~кла́сь** *pf.* (*of* **~ка́ться**) **1.** to stop. **2.** (*of a voice*) to break. **3.** *pass. of* **~чь**

пресле́довани|е, я *nt.* **1.** pursuit. **2.** persecution; **ма́ния ~я** persecution complex. **3.** (*leg.*): **суде́бное п.** prosecution.

пресле́довател|ь, я *m.* persecutor.

пресле́д|овать, ую *impf.* **1.** to pursue; (*fig.*) to haunt; **подозре́ние ~ует меня́** a suspicion haunts me. **2.** (*fig.*) to strive (for, after), pursue; **п. цель** to pursue an end. **3.** to persecute. **4.** (*leg.*) to prosecute.

преслову́тый *adj.* notorious; (*iron.*) celebrated.

пресмыка́|ться, юсь *impf.* (**пе́ред**) to grovel (before), cringe (before).

пресмыка́ющ|ееся, егося *nt.* reptile.

пресново́дный *adj.* freshwater.

пре́с|ный (~ен, ~на́, ~но) *adj.* **1.** (*of water*) fresh. **2.** unleavened. **3.** (*of food*) tasteless, bland; (*fig.*) insipid, vapid; **~ные остро́ты** feeble jokes.

пресс, а *m.* press; punch.

пре́сс|а, ы *f.* (*collect.*) the press.

пресс-конфере́нци|я, и *f.* press conference.

пресс|ова́ть, у́ю *impf.* (*of* **с~**) to press, compress.

прессо́вк|а, и *f.* pressing, compressing.

прессовщи́к, а́ *m.* presser, press operator.

пресс-папье́ *nt. indecl.* **1.** paper-weight. **2.** blotter.

преста́в|иться, люсь, ишься *pf.* (*obs.*) to pass away.

престаре́л|ый *adj.* aged; **дом ~ых** old people's home.

прести́ж, а *m.* prestige.

престо́л, а *m.* **1.** throne; **отре́чься от ~а** to abdicate. **2.** (*eccl.*): **Па́пский п.** Holy See, See of Rome.

престолонасле́ди|е, я *nt.* succession to the throne.

престо́л|ьный *adj. of* **~**; **п. го́род** capital (city).

преступ|а́ть, а́ю *impf. of* **~и́ть**

преступ|и́ть, лю́, ~́ишь *pf.* (*of* **~а́ть**) to transgress, trespass (against); **п. зако́н** to break the law.

преступле́ни|е, я *nt.* crime; **уголо́вное п.** criminal offence.

престу́пник, а *m.* criminal; **вое́нный п.** war criminal.

престу́пност|ь, и *f.* **1.** criminality. **2.** (*collect.*) crime;

рост ~и increase in crime.
престу́п|ный (~ен, ~на) *adj.* criminal.
пресы́|тить, щу, тишь *pf.* (*of* **~ща́ть**) (*obs.*) (+*i.*) to satiate (with); to surfeit (on), sate (with).
пресыща́|ть, ю *impf. of* **пресы́тить**
пресыще́ни|е, я *nt.* satiety; surfeit.
пресы́|щенный *p.p.p. of* **~тить** *and adj.* satiated; surfeited, sated, replete.
претворе́ни|е, я *nt.* conversion; **п. в жизнь** realization, putting into practice.
претвор|и́ть, ю́, и́шь *pf.* (*of* **~я́ть**) **1.** (**в**+*a.*) to turn (into), change (into), convert (into). **2.: п. в жизнь** to realize, carry out, put into practice.
претвор|я́ть, я́ю, я́ет *impf. of* **~и́ть**
претенде́нт, а *m.* (**на**+*a.*) **1.** claimant (to, upon), aspirant (to); candidate (for); contestant, challenger; **он п. на ру́ку принце́ссы** he aspires to the hand of the princess. **2.** pretender (to); **п. на престо́л** pretender to the throne.
претенд|ова́ть, у́ю *impf.* (**на**+*a.*) to have pretensions (to); to aspire (to); to lay claim (to); **он ~у́ет на до́лжность мини́стра иностра́нных дел** he aspires to the position of Minister of Foreign Affairs.
прете́нзи|я, и *f.* **1.** claim; **име́ть ~ю (на**+*a.*) to claim, lay claim (to), make claims (on). **2.** pretension; **челове́к с ~ями, без ~й** a pretentious, an unpretentious person; **у него́ нет никаки́х ~й на остро-у́мие** he has no pretensions to wit; **быть в ~и на кого́-н.** to have a grievance against s.o.
претенцио́зност|ь, и *f.* pretentiousness.
претенцио́з|ный (~ен, ~на) *adj.* pretentious.
претерпева́|ть, ю *impf. of* **претерпе́ть**
претерп|е́ть, лю́, ∻ишь *pf.* (*of* **~ева́ть**) to undergo; to suffer, endure.
прет|и́ть, и́т *impf.* (+*d.*) to sicken; to nauseate; **э́та пи́ща мне ~и́т** I am nauseated by this food.
преткнове́ни|е, я *nt.*: **ка́мень ~я** stumbling-block.
пре|ть, ю *impf.* **1.** (*pf.* **со∻**) to rot. **2.** (*impf. only*) to become damp.
преувеличе́ни|е, я *nt.* exaggeration; overstatement.
преувели́чива|ть, ю *impf. of* **преувели́чить**
преувели́ч|ить, у, ишь *pf.* (*of* **~ивать**) to exaggerate; to overstate.
преуменьш|а́ть, а́ю *impf. of* **∻и́ть**
преуменьше́ни|е, я *nt.* underestimation; understatement.
преуме́ньш|ить, ∻у́, ∻и́шь *pf.* (*of* **~а́ть**) to underestimate, minimize; to belittle; to understate.
преуспева́|ть, ю *impf.* **1.** *impf. of* **преуспе́ть. 2.** (*impf. only*) to thrive, prosper, flourish.
преуспева́|ющий *pres. part. act. of* **~ть** *and adj.* successful.
преуспе́|ть, ю *pf.* (*of* **~ва́ть**) (**в**+*p.*) to succeed (in), be successful (in); **п. в жи́зни** to get on in life.
префе́кт, а *m.* prefect.
префекту́р|а, ы *f.* prefecture.
префера́нс, а *m.* preference (*card-game*).
пре́фикс, а *m.* (*gram.*) prefix.
преходя́щий *adj.* transient.
прецеде́нт, а *m.* precedent.
при *prep.*+*p.* **1.** by, at; in the presence of; **при доро́ге** by the roadside; **би́тва при Бородине́** the battle of Borodino; **письмо́ бы́ло подпи́сано при мне** the letter was signed in my presence; **не на́до так выража́ться при де́тях** you should not use such language in front of the children. **2.** attached to, affiliated to, under the auspices of (*usu. not translated*); **он рабо́тает при университе́те** he is attached to the university. **3.** (*indicating possession, presence of object(s) mentioned*) by, with; about, on; **у него́ не́ было при себе́ де́нег** he had no money on him; **есть ли у вас при себе́ перочи́нный нож?** do you have a pen-knife about you?; **быть при ору́жии** to be armed. **4.** with (= *taking into account the attribute, etc., referred to*); for, notwithstanding; **при таки́х тала́нтах он должно́ быть далеко́ пойдёт** with such talent he ought to go far; **при всех его́ досто-и́нствах, он мне не нра́вится** for all his virtues, I do not like him; **при всём том** (*i*) with it all, moreover, (*ii*) for all that. **5.** in the time of, in the days of; under (*sc.* the rule of); during; **при Ива́не Гро́зном** in the time of Ivan the Terrible; **при Рома́новых** under the Romanovs. **6.** (*indicating accompanying circumstances*) by; **при све́те ла́мпы** by lamplight. **7.** (*referring to action on occasion unspecified*) when; on; in case of; **при перехо́де че́рез у́лицу** when crossing the street; **при ана́лизе** on analysis; **при маляри́и** in case of malaria; **при усло́вии** under the condition (that). **8.** with (= *by means of, thanks to*); **при по́мощи рыбако́в нам удало́сь оттолк-ну́ть ло́дку** with the aid of the fishermen we succeeded in pushing the boat off.
при...[1] *vbl. pref. indicating* **1.** *completion of action or motion up to given terminal point, as* **прие́хать** to arrive. **2.** *action of attaching, as* **пристро́ить** to build on. **3.** *direction of action towards speaker, as* **пригласи́ть** to invite. **4.** *direction of action from above downward, as* **придави́ть** to press down. **5.** *incompleteness or tentativeness of action, as* **при-откры́ть** to open slightly. **6.** *exhaustiveness of action, as* **приучи́ть** to train. **7.** (+*suffix.* **...ыва..., ...ива...**) *accompaniment, as* **припля́сывать** to dance (to a tune).
при...[2] *as pref. of nn. and adjs.* (*esp. geog.*) *indicates juxtaposition or proximity, as* **приозе́рье** lake-side; **прибре́жный, примо́рский** coastal.
приба́в|ить, лю, ишь *pf.* (*of* **~ля́ть**) **1.** (+*a. or g.*) to add; **п. (в ве́се)** to put on (weight). **2.** (+*g.*) to increase, augment; **п. жа́лованья** to increase a salary; **п. ша́гу** to hasten one's steps. **3.** (**в**+*p.*) to lengthen, widen (*part of an item of clothing*); **на́до п. в рукава́х** the sleeves need to be lengthened.
приба́в|иться, ится *pf.* (*of* **~ля́ться**) **1.** to increase; (*of water*) to rise; (*impers.*): **воды́ ~илось** the water has risen; **наро́ду ~илось** the crowd has grown. **2.** *pass. of* **~ить**
приба́вк|а, и *f.* **1.** addition. **2.** increase; rise.
прибавле́ни|е, я *nt.* **1.** addition; **п. семе́йства** addition to the family. **2.** supplement, appendix.
прибавля́|ть(ся), ю, ет(ся) *impf. of* **приба́вить(ся)**
приба́вочн|ый *adj.* **1.** additional. **2.** (*econ.*) surplus; **~ая сто́имость** surplus value.
приба́лт, а *m.* Balt.
прибалти́йский *adj.* Baltic.
Приба́лтик|а, и *f.* the Baltic States.
приба́лт|ка, ки *f. of* **~**
прибау́тк|а, и *f.* humorous catchphrase.
прибега́|ть[1]**, ю** *impf. of* **прибе́гнуть**
прибега́|ть[2]**, ю** *impf. of* **прибежа́ть**
прибе́г|нуть, ну, нешь, *past* **~, ~ла** *pf.* (*of* **~а́ть**[1]) (**к**) to resort (to), have resort (to).
прибедн|и́ться, ю́сь, и́шься *pf.* (*of* **~я́ться**) (*coll.*) **1.** to feign poverty. **2.** to show false modesty.
прибедн|я́ться, я́юсь *impf. of* **~и́ться**
прибе|жа́ть, гу́, жи́шь, гу́т *pf.* (*of* **~га́ть**[2]) to come running.
прибе́жищ|е, а *nt.* refuge.
приберега́|ть, ю *impf. of* **прибере́чь**
прибере́|чь, гу́, жёшь, гу́т, *past* **∻г, ~гла́** *pf.* (*of* **~га́ть**) to save up.
прибива́|ть, ю *impf. of* **приби́ть**[1]
прибира́|ть, ю *impf. of* **прибра́ть**
приб|и́ть[1]**, ью́, ьёшь** *pf.* (*of* **~ива́ть**) **1.** to nail; **п. флаг к дре́вку** to nail a flag to a pole. **2.** to flatten, beat down. **3.** (*usu. impers.*) to throw up; **труп ~и́ло к бе́регу** a body was washed ashore.

приб|и́ть², **ью́, ьёшь** *pf. of* **бить 1.**
прибл. (*abbr. of* **приблизи́тельно**) approx., approximately.
приближа́|ть, ю *impf. of* **прибли́зить**
приближа́|ться, юсь *impf.* **1.** *impf. of* **прибли́зиться. 2.** (*impf. only*) to approximate; **п. к и́стине** to approximate to the truth.
приближе́ни|е, я *nt.* **1.** approach; approaching, drawing near. **2.** (*math.*) approximation.
приближённост|ь, и *f.* proximity.
приближённый¹ *adj.* approximate, rough.
приближённ|ый², **ого** *m.* (*obs.*) retainer; (*pl.*) retinue.
приблизи́тельно *adv.* approximately, roughly.
приблизи́тел|ьный (~ен, ~ьна) *adj.* approximate, rough.
прибли́|зить, жу, зишь *pf.* (*of* **~жа́ть**) **1.** to bring nearer, move nearer. **2.** to hasten, bring forward.
прибли́|зиться, жусь, зишься *pf.* (*of* **~жа́ться**) (**к**) to approach, draw near; to draw nearer (to), come nearer (to).
прибо́|й, я *m.* surf, breakers.
прибо́р, а *m.* **1.** instrument, device, apparatus, appliance. **2.** set; **бри́твенный п.** shaving set; **ча́йный п.** tea-service. **3.** fittings; **печно́й п.** stove fittings.
прибо́р|ный *adj. of* **~**; **~ная доска́** dashboard; (*aeron.*) instrument panel.
при|бра́ть, беру́, берёшь, *past* **~бра́л, ~брала́, ~бра́ло** *pf.* (*of* **~бира́ть**) **1.** to clear up, tidy (up); **п. посте́ль** to make a bed; **п. на столе́** to clear the table; **п. кого́-н. к рука́м** to take s.o. in hand; **п. что-н. к рука́м** to lay one's hands on sth. **2.** to put away.
прибре́жн|ый *adj.* coastal; off-shore.
прибре́жь|е, я *nt.* coastal strip.
прибыва́|ть, ю *impf. of* **прибы́ть**
при́был|ь, и *f.* **1.** profit, gain (*also fig.*); return. **2.** increase, rise; **п. населе́ния** population increase; **вода́ идёт на п.** the water is rising.
при́быльност|ь, и *f.* profitability, lucrativeness.
при́быльный *adj.* profitable, lucrative.
прибы́ти|е, я *nt.* arrival.
при|бы́ть¹, **бу́ду, бу́дешь,** *past* **~был, ~была́, ~было** *pf.* (*of* **~быва́ть**) to arrive.
при|бы́ть², **бу́дет,** *past* **~был, ~была́, ~было** *pf.* (*of* **~быва́ть**) (*coll.*) to increase, grow; (*of water*) to rise, swell; (*of the moon*) to wax.
прива́л, а *m.* **1.** halt, stop. **2.** stopping-place.
прива́лива|ть, ю *impf. of* **привали́ть**
привал|и́ть, ю́, ~ишь *pf.* (*of* **~ивать**) **1.** to lean, rest; **п. дрова́ к забо́ру** to pile logs against the fence. **2.** (*fig., coll.*) to turn up; **на матч ~и́ло мно́го наро́ду** people flocked to the match; **сча́стье нам ~и́ло** fortune smiled on us.
приватиза́ци|я, и *f.* privatization.
приватизи́р|овать, ую *impf. & pf.* to privatize.
прива́тный *adj.* (*obs.*) private.
приведе́ни|е, я *nt.* **1.** bringing; **п. к прися́ге** administration of oath. **2.** putting; **п. в движе́ние** setting in motion; **п. в исполне́ние** putting into effect. **3.** adducing; **п. приме́ров** adducing of instances.
привез|ти́, у́, ёшь, *past* **~, ~ла́** *pf.* (*of* **привози́ть**) to bring (*not on foot*).
привере́длив|ый (~, ~а) *adj.* fussy, finicky.
приве́ржен|ец, ца *m.* adherent; follower.
приве́рженност|ь, и *f.* adherence; devotion.
приве́ржен|ный (~, ~а) *adj.* (**к**) dedicated (to), devoted (to).
приверн|у́ть, у́, ёшь *pf.* (*of* **привёртывать**) **1.** to screw tight, tighten, clamp. **2.** to turn down.
привер|те́ть, чу́, ~тишь *pf.* (*of* **~тывать**) to screw tight, tighten, clamp.
привёртыва|ть, ю *impf. of* **приверну́ть** *and* **привéрте́ть**
приве́|сить, шу, сишь *pf.* (*of* **~шивать**) to hang up.
приве|сти́, ду́, дёшь, *past* **~л, ~ла́** *pf.* (*of* **приводи́ть**) **1.** to bring; to lead, take; **п. кого́-н. к прися́ге** to swear s.o. in. **2.** (**к**; *fig.*) to lead (to), bring (to), result (in); **э́то к добру́ не ~дёт** no good will come of it. **3.** (**в**+*a.*) to put, set (*or translated by v. corresponding to n. governed by* **в**); **п. в бе́шенство** to drive mad; **п. в движе́ние, в де́йствие** to set in motion, set going; **п. в изумле́ние** to astound; **п. в исполне́ние** to carry out, put into effect; **п. в отча́яние** to reduce to despair; **п. в поря́док** to put in order, tidy (up); to arrange, fix; **п. в у́жас** to horrify; **п. в чу́вство** to bring round. **4.** to adduce, cite; **п. приме́р** to give an example.
приве|сти́сь, дётся, *past* **~ло́сь** *pf.* (*of* **приводи́ться**) (*impers.+d.*; *coll.*) to happen, chance; **мне ~ло́сь там быть тогда́, когда́ они́ проезжа́ли** I happened to be there when they drove past.
приве́т, а *m.* greeting(s); regards; **переда́ть п., слать п.** to send one's regards; **п. из Москвы́!** greetings from Moscow!; **он с~ом** (*coll.*) he's crackers.
приве́тливост|ь, и *f.* affability; cordiality.
приве́тлив|ый (~, ~а) *adj.* affable; cordial.
приве́тственн|ый *adj.* salutatory; welcoming; **~ая речь** speech of welcome.
приве́тстви|е, я *nt.* **1.** greeting, salutation. **2.** speech of welcome.
приве́тств|овать, ую *impf.* **1.** (*in past tense also pf.*) to greet, salute, hail; to welcome. **2.** (*fig.*) to welcome; **п. предложе́ние** to welcome a suggestion. **3.** (*also pf.*) (*mil.*) to salute.
приве́шива|ть, ю *impf. of* **приве́сить**
привива́|ть(ся), ю, ет(ся) *impf. of* **приви́ть(ся)**
приви́вк|а, и *f.* **1.** (**от, про́тив**; *med.*) inoculation (against); vaccination. **2.** (*bot.*) grafting.
привиде́ни|е, я *nt.* ghost, spectre; apparition.
приви́|деться, дится *pf. of* **ви́деться 2.**
привилегиро́ванн|ый *adj.* privileged.
привиле́ги|я, и *f.* privilege.
привин|ти́ть, чу́, ти́шь *pf.* (*of* **~чивать**) to screw on.
приви́нчива|ть, ю *impf. of* **привинти́ть**
привира́|ть, ю *impf. of* **приври́ть**
приви́ти|е, я *nt.* inculcation.
прив|и́ть, ью́, ьёшь, *past* **~и́л, ~ила́, ~и́ло** *pf.* (*of* **~ива́ть**) (+*a. and d.*) **1.** (*med.*) to inoculate (with); **п. кому́-н. о́спу** to vaccinate s.o. against smallpox. **2.** (*bot.*) to graft. **3.** (*fig.*) to inculcate (in); **п. кому́-н. вкус к стиха́м** to inculcate in s.o. a taste for poetry.
прив|и́ться, ьётся, *past* **~и́лся, ~ила́сь** *pf.* (*of* **~ива́ться**) **1.** to take. **2.** (*fig.*) to find acceptance, catch on.
при́вкус, а *m.* after-taste; smack (*also fig.*).
привлека́тельност|ь, и *f.* attractiveness.
привлека́тел|ьный (~ен, ~ьна) *adj.* attractive.
привлека́|ть, ю *impf. of* **привле́чь**
привлече́ни|е, я *nt.* attraction.
привле́|чь, ку́, ёшь, ку́т, *past* **~к, ~кла́** *pf.* (*of* **~ка́ть**) **1.** to attract; **п. внима́ние** to attract attention. **2.** to draw in; **п. на свою́ сто́рону** to win over. **3.** (*leg.*) to have up; **п. к суду́** to take to court; to put on trial; **п. к отве́тственности (за**+*a.*) to call to account (for).
привнес|ти́, у́, ёшь, *past* **~, ~ла́** *pf.* (*of* **привноси́ть**) to introduce.
привно|си́ть, шу́, ~сишь *impf. of* **привнести́**
приво́д¹, **а** *m.* (*leg.*) taking into custody; arrest.
при́вод², **а** *m.* (*tech.*) drive.
приво|ди́ть(ся), жу́(сь) ~дишь(ся) *impf. of* **привести́(сь)**
приводне́ни|е, я *nt.* splash-down.
приводн|и́ться, ю́сь, и́шься *pf.* (*of* **~я́ться**) to land on water, splash down.

приводн|о́й *adj.* (*tech.*) driving, drive; **п. вал** driving shaft; **п. механи́зм** driving gear.
приводн|я́ться, я́юсь *impf. of* **~и́ться**
приво|жу́[1], **∠дишь** *see* **~ди́ть**
приво|жу́[2], **∠зишь** *see* **~зи́ть**
приво́з, а *m.* **1.** delivery, supply; import, importation. **2.** (*coll.*) load.
приво|зи́ть, жу́, ∠зишь *impf. of* **привезти́**
привозно́й *adj.* imported.
приво́зн|ый = **~о́й**
привола́кива|ть, ю *impf. of* **приволо́чь**
приволо́|чь, ку́, чёшь, ку́т, *past* **~к, ~кла́** *pf.* (*of* **привола́кивать**) (*coll.*) to drag (over).
приво́ль|е, я *nt.* **1.** free space. **2.** freedom.
приво́льн|ый *adj.* free; **~ая жизнь** free and easy life.
привора́жива|ть, ю *impf. of* **приворожи́ть**
привórож|и́ть, у́, и́шь *pf.* (*of* **привора́живать**) (*fig.*) to bewitch, charm.
привра́тник, а *m.* doorman, porter.
привр|а́ть, у́, ёшь, *past* **~а́л, ~ала́, ~а́ло** *pf.* (*of* **привира́ть**) (*coll.*) to make up; to exaggerate.
привска́кива|ть, ю *impf. of* **привскочи́ть**
привскоч|и́ть, у́, ∠ишь *pf.* (*of* **привска́кивать**) to start, jump up.
привста|ва́ть, ю́, ёшь *impf. of* **∠ть**
привста́|ть, ну, нешь *pf.* (*of* **~ва́ть**) to rise, stand up (*for a moment*); to half-rise; **когда́ судья́ вошёл, все ~ли** when the judge entered everyone stood up.
привходя́щ|ий *adj.*: **~ие обстоя́тельства** attendant circumstances.
привык|а́ть, а́ю *impf. of* **∠нуть**
привы́к|нуть, ну, нешь, *past* **~, ~ла** *pf.* (*of* **~а́ть**) (**к** *or*+*inf.*) **1.** to get accustomed (to), get used (to). **2.** to get into the habit (of).
привы́чк|а, и *f.* habit; **войти́ в ~у** to become a habit; **име́ть ~у (к)** to be accustomed (to); to be in the habit (of); **приобрести́ ~у** (+*inf.*) to get into the habit (of), fall into the habit (of).
привы́ч|ный (~ен, ~на) *adj.* **1.** habitual, usual, customary. **2. (к)** accustomed (to), used (to); **он челове́к п.** he is a man of habit.
привя́занност|ь, и *f.* **(к)** attachment (to).
привя́з|анный *p.p.p. of* **~а́ть** *and adj.* **(к)** attached (to).
привя|за́ть, жу́, ∠жешь *pf.* (*of* **∠зывать**) **(к) 1.** to tie (to), bind (to), fasten (to), attach (to); **п. козу́** to tether a goat. **2. (к себе́;** *fig.*) to win over, endear o.s. to.
привя|за́ться, жу́сь, ∠жешься *pf.* (*of* **∠зываться**) **(к) 1.** to become attached (to). **2.** to attach o.s. (to); **на доро́ге како́й-то ни́щий ~за́лся к нам** a beggar attached himself to us on the road. **3.** (*coll.*) to pester, bother.
привязно́й *adj.* fastened, secured; **п. реме́нь** seat-belt.
привя́зчив|ый (~, ~а) *adj.* **1.** affectionate. **2.** annoying, bothersome.
при́вяз|ь, и *f.* lead, leash; tether; **на ~и** on a leash.
пригвожда́|ть, ю *impf. of* **пригвозди́ть**
пригвоз|ди́ть, жу́, ди́шь *pf.* (*of* **пригвожда́ть**) **(к)** to nail (to); **п. к ме́сту** to root to the spot.
пригиба́|ть(ся), ю(сь) *impf. of* **пригну́ть(ся)**
пригла́|дить, жу, дишь *pf.* (*of* **~живать**) to smooth.
пригла́жива|ть, ю *impf. of* **пригла́дить**
пригласи́тельный *adj.* invitation; **п. биле́т** invitation card.
пригла|си́ть, шу́, си́шь *pf.* (*of* **~ша́ть**) **1.** to invite, ask; **п. на обе́д** to invite, ask to dinner; **п. в го́сти** to invite, ask round. **2.** to call (*a doctor, etc.*). **3.** to offer; **его́ ~си́ли на рабо́ту в но́вой шко́ле** he has been offered a job in a new school.
приглаша́|ть, ю *impf. of* **пригласи́ть**
приглаше́ни|е, я *nt.* **1.** invitation; **по ~ю** by invitation. **2.** offer (*of employment*).
приглуш|а́ть, а́ю *impf. of* **~и́ть**
приглуш|и́ть, у́, и́шь *pf.* (*of* **~а́ть**) to damp down; to muffle, deaden (*sound*); to damp (a fire).
пригля|де́ть, жу́, ди́шь *pf.* (*of* **∠дывать**) (*coll.*) **1.** to find, look out. **2.** (**за**+*i.*) to look after.
пригля|де́ться, жу́сь, ди́шься *pf.* (*of* **∠дываться**) (*coll.*) **1. (к)** to stare (at), scrutinize. **2. (к)** to get used (to). **3.** (+*d.*) to tire, bore; **мне ~де́лись кинофи́льмы о вое́нных де́йствиях** I am tired of war-films.
пригля́дыва|ть(ся), ю(сь) *impf. of* **пригляде́ть(ся)**
приглян|у́ться, у́сь, ∠ешься *pf.* (+*d.*; *coll.*) to take one's fancy, attract.
при|гна́ть[1], **гоню́, го́нишь,** *past* **~гна́л, ~гнала́, ~гна́ло** *pf.* (*of* **~гоня́ть**) to drive home, bring in (*cattle*).
при|гна́ть[2], **гоню́, го́нишь,** *past* **~гна́л, ~гнала́, ~гна́ло** *pf.* (*of* **~гоня́ть**) to fit, adjust, joint.
пригн|у́ть, у́, ёшь *pf.* (*of* **пригиба́ть**) to bend down, bow.
пригн|у́ться, у́сь, ёшься *pf.* (*of* **пригиба́ться**) to bend down, bow.
пригова́рива|ть[1], **ю** *impf.* (*coll.*) to keep saying, keep repeating (*as accompaniment to given action*).
пригова́рива|ть[2], **ю** *impf. of* **приговори́ть**
пригово́р, а *m.* sentence; verdict.
приговор|и́ть, ю́, и́шь *pf.* (*of* **пригова́ривать**[2]) **(к)** to sentence (to), condemn (to).
приго|ди́ться, жу́сь, ди́шься *pf.* (+*d.*) to be useful, come in handy; to stand in good stead.
приго́дност|ь, и *f.* fitness, suitability.
приго́д|ный (~ен, ~на) *adj.* **(к)** fit (for), suitable (for), good (for).
приго́ж|ий (~, ~а) *adj.* (*folk poet.*) **1.** comely. **2.** (*of weather*) fine.
пригоня́|ть, ю *impf. of* **пригна́ть**
пригор|а́ть, а́ет *impf. of* **~е́ть**
пригоре́лый *adj.* burnt.
пригор|е́ть, и́т *pf.* (*of* **~а́ть**) to be burnt.
при́город, а *m.* suburb.
при́городн|ый *adj.* suburban.
приго́р|ок, ка *m.* hillock, knoll.
при́го́рш|ня, ни, *g. pl.* **~ен** *and* **~ней** *f.* handful.
пригота́влива|ть(ся), ю(сь) *impf.* = **приготовля́ть(ся)**
приготови́тельный *adj.* preparatory.
пригото́в|ить, лю, ишь *pf.* (*of* **пригота́вливать** *and* **~ля́ть**) to prepare; to cook; **п. роль** to learn a part.
пригото́в|иться, люсь, ишься *pf.* (*of* **пригота́вливаться** *and* **~ля́ться**) (+*inf.*) to prepare (to); **(к)** to prepare (o.s.) (for).
приготовле́ни|е, я *nt.* preparation.
приготовля́|ть(ся), ю(сь) *impf. of* **пригото́вить(ся)**
пригрева́|ть, ю *impf. of* **пригре́ть**
пригре́|зиться, жусь, зишься *pf. of* **гре́зиться**
пригре́|ть, ю *pf.* (*of* **~ва́ть**) **1.** to warm. **2.** (*fig.*) to give shelter (to).
пригро|зи́ть, жу́, зи́шь *pf. of* **грози́ть 1.**
пригу́б|ить, лю, ишь *pf.* to take a sip (of), taste.
прида|ва́ть, ю́, ёшь *impf. of* **прида́ть**
придав|и́ть, лю́, ∠ишь *pf.* (*of* **∠ливать**) to press; to press down, weigh down (*also fig.*); to squeeze.
прида́влива|ть, ю *impf. of* **придави́ть**
прида́ни|е, я *nt.* giving, imparting.
прида́н|ое, ого *nt.* **1.** dowry; trousseau. **2.** layette.
прида́т|ок, ка *m.* appendage, adjunct.
прида́точн|ый *adj.* (*gram.*) subordinate; **~ое предложе́ние** subordinate clause.
прида́|ть, м, шь, ст, ди́м, ди́те, ду́т, *past* **при́дал, ~ла́, при́дало** *pf.* (*of* **~ва́ть**) **1.** (*mil.*) to attach.

2. to increase, strengthen; **п. бóдрости** (*+d.*) to hearten; **п. дýху** (*+d.*) to inspire, encourage. **3.** (*+a. and d.*) to give (to), impart (to); (*fig.*) attach (to); **п. значéние** to attach importance (to).

придáч|а, и *f.* **1.** adding; (*mil.*) attaching. **2.** addition, supplement; **в ~у** into the bargain, in addition.

придвигá|ть(ся), ю(сь) *impf. of* **придвúнуть(ся)**

придвú|нуть, ну, нешь *pf.* (*of* **~гáть**) to move (up), draw (up); **~нь(те) крéсло к пéчке** draw your chair up to the stove.

придвú|нуться, нусь, нешься *pf.* (*of* **~гáться**) to move up, draw near.

придвóрн|ый *adj.* court; **п. шут** court jester; *as n.* **п., ~ого** *m.* courtier.

придéл|ать, аю *pf.* (*of* **~ывать**) (**к**) to fix (to), attach (to).

придéлыва|ть, ю *impf. of* **придéлать**

придерж|áть, ý, ~ишь *pf.* (*of* **~ивать**) to hold back (*also fig.*); **п. товáр** to hold back goods; **п. язы́к** to hold one's tongue.

придéржива|ть, ю *impf. of* **придержáть**

придéржива|ться, юсь *impf.* **1.** (**за**+*a.*) to hold on (to); **п. за пóручень** to hold on to the rail. **2.** (*+g.*) to hold (to), keep (to) (*also fig.*); (*fig.*) to stick (to), adhere (to); **п. прáвой стороны́** to keep to the right; **п. договóра** to adhere to an agreement; **п. мнéния** to be of the opinion; **п. тéмы** to stick to the subject.

придúр|а, ы *c.g.* (*coll.*) quibbler, fault-finder.

придирá|ться, юсь *impf. of* **придрáться**

придúрк|а, и *f.* (*coll.*) quibble; (*pl.*) fault-finding, quibbling, carping.

придúрчив|ый (~, ~а) *adj.* captious, fault-finding, carping.

придорóжный *adj.* roadside, wayside.

при|дрáться, дерýсь, дерёшься, *past* **~дрáлся, ~дралáсь, ~дрáлóсь** *pf.* (*of* **~дирáться**) (**к**) to find fault (with), carp (at); pick (on).

придýм|ать, аю *pf.* (*of* **~ывать**) to think (of), think up, devise, invent.

придýмыва|ть, ю *impf. of* **придýмать**

придуркoвáт|ый (~, ~а) *adj.* (*coll.*) dopey, daft, simple(-minded).

прúдур|ь, и *f.*: **с ~ью** (*coll.*) touched (in the head).

придуш|úть, ý, ~ишь *pf.* (*coll.*) to strangle, smother.

придыхáни|е, я *nt.* (*ling.*) aspiration.

придыхáтельн|ый *adj.* (*ling.*) aspirate; *as n.* **п., ~ого** *m.* aspirate.

при|дý *see* **~йтú**

приедá|ться, юсь *impf. of* **приéсться**

приéзд, а *m.* arrival; **с ~ом!** welcome!

приезжá|ть, ю *impf. of* **приéхать**

приéзж|ий *adj.* newly arrived; visiting; *as n.* **п., ~его** *m.*, **~ая, ~ей** *f.* newcomer; visitor.

приём, а *m.* **1.** receiving; reception. **2.** reception, welcome; **оказáть комý-н. радýшный п.** to accord s.o. a hearty welcome. **3.** admittance. **4.** reception (= *formal party*). **5.** dose. **6.** go; motion, movement; **в оди́н п.** at one go. **7.** method, way, mode; device, trick (*also pej.*); (*sport*) hold, grip; **лечéбный п.** method of treatment.

приéмлем|ый (~, ~а) *adj.* acceptable; admissible.

приёмн|ая, ой *f.* waiting-room; reception (room).

приёмник, а *m.* radio (set), receiver.

приёмн|ый *adj.* **1.** receiving; reception; **п. день** visiting day; **~ые часы́** (reception) hours; (*of a doctor*) surgery (hours). **2.** admission; selection; **п. экзáмен** entrance examination. **3.** foster, adoptive.

приёмыш, а *m.* adopted child, foster-child.

при|éсться, éстся, едя́тся, *past* **~éлся, ~éлась** *pf.* (*of* **~едáться**) (*+d.*; *coll.*) to pall (on), bore; **мне ~éлась э́та рабóта** I am fed up with this work.

приé|хать, ду, дешь *pf.* (*of* **~зжáть**) to arrive, come (*not on foot*).

приж|áть, мý, мёшь *pf.* (*of* **~имáть**) **1.** (**к**) to press (to), clasp (to); **п. к землé** (*mil.*) to pin down; **п. к груди́** to clasp to one's bosom; **п. к стенé** (*fig.*) to drive into a corner. **2.** (*fig.*) to put pressure on.

приж|áться, мýсь, мёшься *pf.* (*of* **~имáться**) **1.** (**к**) to press o.s. (against); to cuddle up (to), snuggle up (to), nestle up (to); **п. к стенé** to flatten o.s. against the wall. **2.** *pass. of* **~áть**

при|жéчь, жгý, жжёшь, жгýт, *past* **~жёг, ~жглá** *pf.* (*of* **~жигáть**) to cauterize, sear.

приживáл|ка, ки *f. of* **~ьщик**

приживáльщик, а *m.* hanger-on, sponger.

приживá|ться, юсь *impf. of* **прижи́ться**

прижигáни|е, я (*med.*) cauterization.

прижигá|ть, ю *impf. of* **прижéчь**

прижи́зненный *adj.* occurring during one's lifetime.

прижимá|ть(ся), ю(сь) *impf. of* **прижáть(ся)**

прижи́мист|ый (~, ~а) *adj.* (*coll.*) tight-fisted, stingy.

приж|и́ться, ивýсь, ивёшься, *past* **~и́лся, ~илáсь** *pf.* (*of* **~ивáться**) **1.** to settle down, get acclimatized. **2.** (*of plants*) to take root, strike root.

приз, а, *pl.* **~ы́** *m.* prize.

призадýм|аться, аюсь *pf.* (*of* **~ываться**) to become thoughtful, become pensive.

призадýмыва|ться, юсь *impf. of* **призадýматься**

приза|ня́ть, йму́, йме́шь, *past* **~нял, ~нялá, ~няло** *pf.* (*coll.*) to borrow.

призвáни|е, я *nt.* vocation, calling.

при|звáть, зовý, зовёшь, *past* **~звáл, ~звалá, ~звáло** *pf.* (*of* **~зывáть**) to call, summon; to call upon, appeal; **п. на пóмощь** to call for help; **п. на воéнную слýжбу** to call up (*for mil. service*); **п. к порядку** to call to order.

призéмист|ый (~, ~а) *adj.* stocky, squat; thickset.

приземлéни|е, я *nt.* (*aeron.*) landing, touch-down.

приземл|и́ть, ю́, и́шь *pf.* (*of* **~я́ть**) (*aeron.*) to land.

приземл|и́ться, ю́сь, и́шься *pf.* (*of* **~я́ться**) (*aeron.*) to land, touch down.

приземля́|ть(ся), ю(сь) *impf. of* **приземли́ть(ся)**

призёр, а *m.* prize-winner.

при́зм|а, ы *f.* prism.

призмати́ческий *adj.* prismatic.

призна|вáть(ся), ю́(сь), ёшь(ся) *impf. of* **признáть(ся)**

при́знак, а *m.* sign; indication; **п. болéзни** symptom; **служи́ть ~ом** (*+g.*) to be a sign (of).

признáни|е, я *nt.* **1.** confession; admission, acknowledgement; **п. в любви́** declaration of love. **2.** recognition; **получи́ть п.** to obtain, win recognition.

при́зн|анный *p.p.p. of* **~áть** *and adj.* acknowledged, recognized.

признáтельност|ь, и *f.* gratitude.

признáтел|ьный (~ен, ~ьна) *adj.* grateful.

признá|ть, ю *pf.* (*of* **~вáть**) **1.** to recognize; **вы меня́ не ~ли?** did you not recognize me? **2.** (*leg.*, *pol.*) to recognize; **п. прави́тельство** to recognize a government. **3.** to admit, acknowledge; **п. себя́ винóвным** (*leg.*) to plead guilty; **п. свою́ оши́бку** to admit one's mistake. **4.** to deem; **п. нýжным** to deem (it) necessary; **п. недействи́тельным** to declare invalid; **п. (не)винóвным** to find (not) guilty.

признá|ться, юсь *pf.* (*of* **~вáться**) (**в**+*p.*) to confess (to); **п. в любви́** to make a declaration of love; **п. в преступлéнии** to confess to a crime.

призов|óй *adj. of* **приз; ~ы́е дéньги** prize-money.

при́зрак, а *m.* spectre, ghost, apparition.

при́зрач|ный (~ен, ~на) *adj.* **1.** spectral, ghostly. **2.** (*fig.*) illusory, imagined.

призы́в, а *m.* **1.** call, appeal. **2.** slogan. **3.** (*mil.*) call-up, conscription.

призывá|ть, ю *impf. of* **призвáть**

призывни́к, á *m.* conscript.

призывнóй *adj.* call-up; **п. вóзраст** call-up age.

при́иск, а *m.* mine; **золоты́е ~и** gold-field(s).

при|иска́ть, ищу́, и́щешь *pf.* (*of* **~и́скивать**) to find.

прии́скива|ть, ю *impf.* (*coll.*) **1.** *impf. of* **прииска́ть. 2.** (*impf. only*) to look for, search for.

при|йти́, ду́, дёшь, *past* **~шёл, ~шла́** *pf.* (*of* **~ходи́ть**) to come; to arrive; **п. в восто́рг (от)** to go into raptures (over); **п. в у́жас** to be horrified; **п. в я́рость** to fly into a rage; **п. в го́лову кому́-н., на ум кому́-н.** to occur to s.o., cross one's mind; **п. в себя́** to come to, regain consciousness; (*fig.*) to come to one's senses; **п. к концу́** to come to an end; **п. к соглаше́нию** to come to an agreement.

при|йти́сь, ду́сь, дёшься, *past* **~шёлся, ~шла́сь** *pf.* (*of* **~ходи́ться**) **1.** (**по**+*d.*) to fit; **ковёр ~шёлся как раз по разме́рам спа́льни** the carpet fitted the bedroom floor just right; **п. кому́-н. по вку́су** to be to s.o.'s liking. **2.** (**на**+*a.*; *of dates, days or occasions*) to fall (on). **3.** (*impers.+d.*) to have (to); **нам ~шло́сь подожда́ть ещё два часа́** we had to wait another two hours. **4.** (*impers.+d.*) to happen (to); **мне ~шло́сь быть ря́дом в тот моме́нт, когда́ он упа́л в о́бморок** I happened to be standing by when he fainted; **им ту́го ~шло́сь** they had a rough time (of it); **как ~дётся** (*coll.*) anyhow. **5.** (*impers.*; **на**+*a. or* **с**+*g.*; *coll.*) to be owing (to, from); **с вас ~дётся де́сять рубле́й** you owe ten roubles.

прика́з, а *m.* order, command; **по ~у** by order.

приказа́ни|е, я *nt.* order, command.

прика|за́ть, жу́, ~́жешь *pf.* (*of* **~́зывать**) (+*d.*) to order, command; **п. до́лго жить** (*coll.*) to pass on, depart this life; **как ~́жете** as you wish; **как ~́жете понима́ть э́то?** how am I supposed to take this?; what do you mean by this?

прика́зчик, а *m.* (*obs.*) **1.** shop-assistant, salesman. **2.** steward, bailiff.

прика́зыва|ть, ю *impf. of* **приказа́ть**

прика́лыва|ть, ю *impf. of* **приколо́ть**

прика́нчива|ть, ю *impf. of* **прико́нчить**

прикарма́нива|ть, ю *impf. of* **прикарма́нить**

прикарма́н|ить, ю, ишь *pf.* (*of* **~ивать**) (*coll.*) to pocket.

прикаса́|ться, юсь *impf. of* **прикосну́ться**

прика|ти́ть, чу́, ~́тишь *pf.* (*of* **~́тывать**) **1. (к)** to roll up (to). **2.** (*coll.*) to roll up, turn up.

прика́тыва|ть, ю *impf. of* **прикати́ть**

прики́дыва|ть(ся), ю(сь) *impf. of* **прики́нуть(ся)**

прики́|нуть, ну, нешь *pf.* (*of* **~дывать**) **1.** to throw in, add. **2.** to estimate (approximately); **п. на веса́х** to weigh; **п. в уме́** (*fig.*) to weigh (up), ponder.

прики́|нуться, нусь, нешься *pf.* (*of* **~дываться**) (+*i.*; *coll.*) to pretend (to be), feign; **п. больны́м** to pretend to be ill, feign illness.

прикла́д[1]**, а** *m.* butt (*of firearm*).

прикла́д[2]**, а** *m.* findings.

прикладн|о́й *adj.* applied; **~а́я фи́зика** applied physics.

прикла́дыва|ть(ся), ю(сь) *impf. of* **приложи́ть(ся)**

прикле́ива|ть(ся), ю(сь) *impf. of* **прикле́ить(ся)**

прикле́|ить, ю, ишь *pf.* (*of* **~ивать**) to stick; to glue; to paste; **п. ма́рку** to stick on a stamp; **п. афи́шу к стене́** to stick (up) a bill on a wall.

прикле́|иться, ится *pf.* (*of* **~иваться**) **(к)** to stick (to), adhere (to).

приклеп|а́ть, а́ю *pf.* (*of* **~́ывать**) to rivet.

приклёпыва|ть, ю *impf. of* **приклепа́ть**

приклон|и́ть, ю́, ~́ишь *pf.* (*of* **~я́ть**): **п. го́лову** to lay one's head; **у него́ не́где п. го́лову** he has nowhere to lay his head.

приключ|а́ться, а́ю, а́ется *impf. of* **~и́ться**

приключе́ни|е, я *nt.* adventure.

приключе́нческий *adj.* adventure; **п. рома́н** adventure story.

приключ|и́ться, и́тся *pf.* (*of* **~а́ться**) (*coll.*) to happen, occur.

прико́в|анный *p.p.p. of* **~а́ть; п. к посте́ли** bedridden.

прик|ова́ть, ую́, уёшь *pf.* (*of* **~о́вывать**) **1. (к)** to chain (to). **2.** (*fig.*) to fix; to rivet; **на́ше внима́ние ~ова́ла к себе́ их блестя́щая фо́рма** our attention was riveted on their gorgeous uniforms; **страх ~ова́л нас к ме́сту** fear rooted us to the spot.

прико́выва|ть, ю *impf. of* **прикова́ть**

прико́л, а *m.*: **стоя́ть на ~е** (*naut.*) to be laid up.

прикола́чива|ть, ю *impf. of* **приколоти́ть**

приколо|ти́ть, чу́, ~́тишь *pf.* (*of* **прикола́чивать**) to nail, fasten with nails.

прикол|о́ть, ю́, ~́ешь *pf.* (*of* **прика́лывать**) **1.** to pin. **2.** (*coll.*) to stab; **п. штыко́м** to bayonet.

прикомандир|ова́ть, у́ю *pf.* (*of* **~о́вывать**) **(к)** to attach (to), second (to).

прикомандиро́выва|ть, ю *impf. of* **прикомандирова́ть**

прико́нч|ить, у, ишь *pf.* (*of* **прика́нчивать**) (*coll.*) **1.** to use up. **2.** (*fig.*) to finish off.

прикорн|у́ть, у́, ёшь *pf.* (*coll.*) to curl up.

прикоснове́ни|е, я *nt.* touch; **то́чка ~я** point of contact.

прикосн|у́ться, у́сь ёшься *pf.* (*of* **прикаса́ться**) **(к)** to touch (lightly).

прикра́с|а, ы *f.* (*usu. pl.*) (*coll.*) embellishment; **без ~** unvarnished.

прикра́|сить, шу, сишь *pf.* (*of* **~шивать**) to embellish, embroider (*in speech*).

прикра́шива|ть, ю *impf. of* **прикра́сить**

прикреп|и́ть, лю́, и́шь *pf.* (*of* **~ля́ть**) **(к) 1.** to fasten (to). **2.** (*fig.*) to attach (to); **п. де́тский сад к больни́це** to attach a kindergarten to a hospital.

прикреп|и́ться, лю́сь, и́шься *pf.* (*of* **~ля́ться**) **(к) 1.** to register (at, with). **2.** *pass. of* **~и́ть**

прикрепле́ни|е, я *nt.* **1.** fastening. **2.** (*fig.*) attachment. **3.** registration.

прикрепля́|ть(ся), ю(сь) *impf. of* **прикрепи́ть(ся)**

прикри́кива|ть, ю *impf. of* **прикри́кнуть**

прикри́к|нуть, ну, нешь *pf.* (*of* **~ивать**) **(на**+*a.*) to shout (at).

прикрыва́|ть(ся), ю(сь) *impf. of* **прикры́ть(ся)**

прикры́ти|е, я *nt.* cover; escort; (*fig.*) screen, cloak; **под ~ем** (+*g.*) under cover (of); **артиллери́йское п.** artillery cover.

прикр|ы́ть, о́ю, о́ешь *pf.* (*of* **~ыва́ть**) **1.** (+*i.*) to cover (with); to screen. **2.** to protect, shield. **3.** (*fig.*) to cover (up), conceal. **4.** (*coll.*) to close down.

прикр|ы́ться, о́юсь, о́ешься *pf.* (*of* **~ыва́ться**) **1.** (+*i.*) to cover o.s. (with); (*fig.*) to take refuge (in), shelter (behind); **он ~ы́лся положе́нием иностра́нца** he took refuge in the fact of being a foreigner. **2.** (*coll.*) to close down, go out of business. **3.** *pass. of* **~ы́ть**

прикуп|а́ть, а́ю *impf. of* **~и́ть**

прикуп|и́ть, лю́, ~́ишь *pf.* (*of* **~а́ть**) (+*a. or g.*) to buy (*some more*).

прику́рива|ть, ю *impf. of* **прикури́ть**

прикур|и́ть, ю́, ~́ишь *pf.* (*of* **~́ивать**) **(у кого́-н.)** to get a light (*from s.o.'s cigarette*).

прику́с, а *m.* bite.

прику|си́ть, шу́, ~́сишь *pf.* (*of* **~́сывать**) to bite; **п. (себе́) язы́к** to bite one's tongue; (*fig., coll.*) to hold one's tongue.

прику́сыва|ть, ю *impf. of* **прикуси́ть**

прила́в|ок, ка *m.* counter.

прилага́|емый *pres. part. pass. of* **~ть** *and adj.* accompanying; enclosed.

прилага́тельн|ый *adj.*: **и́мя ~ое** (*or as n.* **~ое, ~ого** *nt.*) adjective.

прилага́|ть, ю *impf. of* **приложи́ть**

прила́|дить, жу, дишь *pf.* (*of* **~живать**) (**к**) to fit (to), adjust (to).
прила́жива|ть, ю *impf. of* **прила́дить**
приласка́|ть, ю *pf.* to caress, fondle, pet.
приласка́|ться, юсь *pf.* (**к**) to snuggle up (to).
прилега́|ть, ет *impf.* (**к**) **1.** (*pf.* **приле́чь**[1]) to fit. **2.** (*no pf.*) to adjoin, be adjacent (to).
прилега́|ющий *pres. part. of* **~ть** *and adj.* **1.** close-fitting, tight-fitting. **2.** (**к**) adjoining, adjacent (to).
прилежа́ни|е, я *nt.* diligence, assiduousness.
приле́ж|ный (~ен, ~на) *adj.* diligent, assiduous.
прилеп|и́ть, лю́, ~́ишь *pf.* (*of* **~ля́ть**) (**к**) to stick (to, on).
прилеп|и́ться, лю́сь, ~́ишься *pf.* (*of* **~ля́ться**) **1.** (**к**) to stick (to, on). **2.** *pass. of* **~и́ть**
прилепля́|ть(ся), ю(сь) *impf. of* **прилепи́ть(ся)**
прилёт, а *m.* arrival (*by air*).
прилет|а́ть, а́ю *impf. of* **~е́ть**
приле|те́ть, чу́, ти́шь *pf.* (*of* **~та́ть**) **1.** to arrive (*by air*), fly in. **2.** (*fig., coll.*) to fly, come flying.
при|ле́чь[1]**, ля́жет, ля́гут,** *past* **~лёг, ~легла́** *pf. of* **~лега́ть**
при|ле́чь[2]**, ля́гу, ля́жешь, ля́гут,** *past* **~лёг, ~легла́** *pf.* to lie down (*for a short while*).
прили́в, а *m.* **1.** flow, flood (*of tide*); rising tide; (*fig.*) surge, influx; **п. и отли́в** ebb and flow. **2.** (*med.*) congestion; **п. кро́ви** rush of blood; (*fig.*) **п. эне́ргии** burst of energy.
прилива́|ть, ет *impf. of* **прили́ть**
прили́вный *adj.* tidal.
прили́з|анный *p.p.p. of* **~а́ть; ~анные во́лосы** slicked-down hair.
прили|за́ть, жу́, ~́жешь *pf.* (*of* **~́зывать**) to slick down.
прили́зыва|ть, ю *impf. of* **прилиза́ть**
прилип|а́ть, а́ет *impf. of* **~́нуть**
прили́п|нуть, нет, *past* **~, ~ла** *pf.* (*of* **~а́ть**) (**к**) to stick (to), adhere (to).
прили́пчив|ый (~, ~а) *adj.* (*coll.*) **1.** sticky. **2.** (*fig.*) tiresome. **3.** (*of diseases*) catching.
при|ли́ть, льёт, *past* **~ли́л, ~лила́, ~ли́ло** *pf.* (*of* **~лива́ть**) (**к**) to flow (to); (of blood) to rush (to).
прили́чи|е, я *nt.* decency, propriety; decorum; **соблюда́ть ~я** to observe the proprieties.
прили́ч|ный (~ен, ~на) *adj.* **1.** decent, proper; decorous. **2.** (*coll.*) decent, tolerable; **~ная зарпла́та** a decent wage.
приложе́ни|е, я *nt.* **1.** application. **2.** affixing; **п. печа́ти** affixing of a seal. **3.** enclosure. **4.** supplement. **5.** appendix. **6.** (*gram.*) apposition.
прилож|и́ть, у́, ~́ишь *pf.* **1.** (*impf.* **прикла́дывать**) (**к**) to put (to), hold (to); **п. ру́ку** to put one's hand (to), take a hand (in). **2.** (*impf.* **прикла́дывать** *and* **прилага́ть**) to add, join; to enclose; to affix. **3.** (*impf.* **прилага́ть**) to apply; **п. си́лу** to apply force; **п. все уси́лия** to make every effort.
прилож|и́ться, у́сь, ~́ишься *pf.* (*of* **прикла́дываться**) **1.** (*+i.,* **к**) to put (to); **п. гла́зом к замо́чной сква́жине** to put one's eye to the keyhole; **п. (губа́ми)** to kiss. **2.** to take aim. **3.** *pass. of* **~и́ть; остально́е ~́ится** the rest will come.
прилуне́ни|е, я *nt.* (*aeron.*) Moon landing, moonfall.
прилун|и́ться, ю́сь, и́шься *pf.* to land on the Moon.
прильн|у́ть, у́, ёшь *pf. of* **льнуть**
при́ма-балери́на, при́мы-балери́ны *f.* prima ballerina.
примадо́нн|а, ы *f.* prima donna.
прима́нива|ть, ю *impf. of* **промани́ть**
приман|и́ть, ю́, ~́ишь *pf.* (*of* **~́ивать**) (*coll.*) to lure; to decoy; to entice, allure.
прима́нк|а, и *f.* bait, lure; (*fig.*) enticement, allurement.
прима́с, а *m.* (*eccl.*) primate.
прима́т[1]**, а** *m.* (*phil.*) primacy; pre-eminence.
прима́т[2]**, а** *m.* (*zool.*) primate.
примелька́|ться, юсь *pf.* (*coll.*) to become familiar; **её лицо́ мне о́чень ~лось** her face is very familiar to me.
примене́ни|е, я *nt.* application; use; adoption; **на́ши ме́тоды получи́ли широ́кое п.** our methods have been widely adopted; **в ~и (к)** in application (to).
примени́мост|ь, и *f.* applicability.
примени́м|ый (~, ~а) *adj.* applicable.
примени́тельно *adv.* (**к**) in conformity (with); as applied (to).
примен|и́ть, ю, ~́ишь *pf.* (*of* **~я́ть**) to apply; to employ, use; **п. на пра́ктике** to put into practice.
примен|и́ться, ю́сь, ~́ишься *pf.* (*of* **~я́ться**) (**к**) to adapt o.s. (to), conform (to).
приме́р, а *m.* **1.** example, instance; **к ~у** (*coll.*) for example. **2.** example; model; **брать п. с кого́-н.** to follow s.o.'s example; **подава́ть п.** to set an example; **по ~у** (*+g.*) after the example (of), on the pattern (of); **не в п.** (*+d.; coll.*) unlike; (*+comp.*) far more, by far; **не в п. про́чим** unlike the others; **не в п. лу́чше** far better.
примерз|а́ть, а́ю *impf. of* **~́нуть**
примёрз|нуть, ну, нешь, *past* **~, ~ла** *pf.* (*of* **~а́ть**) (**к**) to freeze (to).
приме́р|ить, ю, ишь *pf.* (*of* **ме́рить 2.** *and* **~я́ть**) to try on.
приме́рк|а, и *f.* trying on; fitting.
приме́рно *adv.* **1.** in exemplary fashion; **п. вести́ себя́** to be an example. **2.** approximately, roughly.
приме́р|ный (~ен, ~на) *adj.* **1.** exemplary, model. **2.** approximate, rough.
приме́рочн|ая, ой *f.* fitting-room.
пример|я́ть, я́ю *impf. of* **~́ить**
при́мес|ь, и *f.* admixture; dash; (*fig.*) touch; **без ~ей** unadulterated.
приме́т|а, ы *f.* sign, token; mark; **име́ть на ~е** to have one's eye (on).
примет|а́ть, а́ю *pf.* (*of* **~́ывать**) to tack (on), stitch (on).
приме́|тить, чу, тишь *pf.* (*of* **~ча́ть**) to notice.
приме́тлив|ый (~, ~а) *adj.* (*coll.*) observant.
приме́т|ный (~ен, ~на) *adj.* **1.** perceptible, noticeable. **2.** conspicuous, prominent.
примётыва|ть, ю *impf. of* **примета́ть**
примеча́ни|е, я *nt.* **1.** note, footnote; **снабди́ть ~ями** to annotate. **2.** (*pl.*) commentary.
примеча́тел|ьный (~ен, ~ьна) *adj.* noteworthy, notable.
примеча́|ть, ю *impf.* **1.** *impf. of* **приме́тить. 2.** (*impf. only*) (**за***+i.; coll.*) to keep an eye (on).
примеш|а́ть, а́ю *pf.* (*of* **~́ивать**) (*+a. or g.*) to add, admix; (*tech.*) to alloy.
приме́шива|ть, ю *impf. of* **примеша́ть**
примина́|ть, ю *impf. of* **примя́ть**
примире́ни|е, я *nt.* reconciliation.
примири́тел|ь, я *m.* conciliator, peace-maker.
примири́тел|ьный (~ен, ~ьна) *adj.* conciliatory.
примир|и́ть, ю́, и́шь *pf.* (*of* **~я́ть**) to reconcile; **п. супру́гов** to reconcile a husband and wife.
примир|и́ться, ю́сь, и́шься *pf.* (*of* **~я́ться**) (**с***+i.*) **1.** to be(come) reconciled (with). **2.** to reconcile o.s. (to); **п. с неудо́бствами** to reconcile o.s. to discomforts.
примир|я́ть(ся), я́ю(сь) *impf. of* **~и́ть(ся)**
примити́в|ный (~ен, ~на) *adj.* primitive.
примкн|у́ть, у́, ёшь *pf.* (*of* **примыка́ть**) (**к**) **1.** to fix (to), attach (to); **п. штыки́!** fix bayonets! **2.** (*fig.*) to join; to side (with).
примо́лкн|уть, у, ешь *pf.* (*coll.*) to fall silent.
примо́рский *adj.* seaside; maritime.

примо́рь|е, я *nt.* seaside.
примо|сти́ться, щу́сь, сти́шься *pf.* (*coll.*) to perch o.s.
примо́чк|а, и *f.* wash, lotion.
при́мул|а, ы *f.* primula, primrose.
при́мус, а *m.* Primus (*propr.*)(-stove).
примч|а́ться, у́сь, и́шься *pf.* to come tearing along.
примыка́|ть, ю *impf.* **1.** *impf. of* **примкну́ть. 2.** (*impf. only*) (**к**) to adjoin, abut (upon).
при|мя́ть, мну́, мнёшь *pf.* (*of* **~мина́ть**) to crush, flatten; to trample down, tread down.
принадлеж|а́ть, у́, и́шь *impf.* **1.** (+*d.*) to belong (to); to appertain (to). **2.** (**к**) to belong (to), be a member (of); **п. к клу́бу** to belong to a club.
принадле́жност|ь, и *f.* **1.** (**к**) belonging (to), membership (of). **2.** (*pl.*) accessories; equipment; tackle; **туале́тные ~и** toiletries; **канцеля́рские ~и** office equipment. **3.** characteristic.
принa|ле́чь, ля́гу, ля́жешь, ля́гут, *past* **~лёг, ~легла́** *pf.* (**на**+*a.*; *coll.*) **1.** to rest lightly (upon). **2.** to apply o.s. (to).
принаря|ди́ть, жу́, ~ди́шь *pf.* (*of* **~жа́ть**) (*coll.*) to dress up, deck out.
принаря|ди́ться, жу́сь, ~ди́шься *pf.* (*of* **~жа́ться**) (*coll.*) to get dolled up.
принаряжа́|ть(ся), ю(сь) *impf. of* **принаряди́ть(ся)**
принево́лива|ть, ю *impf. of* **принево́лить**
принево́л|ить, ю, ишь *pf.* (*of* **~ивать**) (+*inf.*; *coll.*) to force (to), make.
принес|ти́, у́, ёшь, *past* **~, ~ла́** *pf.* (*of* **приноси́ть**) **1.** to bring (*also fig.*); to fetch; **п. обра́тно** to bring back; **п. благода́рность** to express thanks; **п. жа́лобу** (**на**+*a.*) to lodge a complaint (against); **п. в же́ртву** to sacrifice. **2.** to bear, yield; to bring in; **п. плоды́** to bear fruit, yield fruit; **п. по́льзу** to be of use.
принижа́|ть, ю *impf. of* **прини́зить**
приниже́ни|е, я *nt.* disparagement, belittling.
прини́|женный *p.p.p. of* **~зить** *and adj.* humbled, submissive.
прини́|зить, жу, зишь *pf.* (*of* **~жа́ть**) **1.** to humble, humiliate. **2.** to disparage, belittle, play down.
приник|а́ть, а́ю *impf. of* **~нуть**
прини́к|нуть, ну, нешь, *past* **~, ~ла** *pf.* (*of* **~а́ть**) (**к**) to press o.s. (against); to nestle up (against).
принима́|ть, ю *impf.* **1.** *impf. of* **приня́ть. 2.** (*impf. only*) to receive (*guests, visitors, patients*); **она́ ча́сто ~ет** she does a lot of entertaining; **до́ктор Петро́в сего́дня не ~ет** Doctor Petrov does not see patients today. **3.** to deliver (*at birth of child*).
принима́|ться, юсь *impf. of* **приня́ться**
принора́влива|ть(ся), ю(сь) *impf. of* **приноровить(ся)**
приноров|и́ть, лю́, и́шь *pf.* (*of* **принора́вливать**) (*coll.*) to adapt, adjust; to time to coincide (with).
приноров|и́ться, лю́сь, и́шься *pf.* (*of* **принора́вливаться**) (**к**; *coll.*) to adapt o.s. (to), accommodate o.s. (to).
прино|си́ть, шу́, ~сишь *impf. of* **принести́**
приноше́ни|е, я *nt.* gift, offering.
при́нтер, а *m.* (*comput.*) printer.
принуди́тел|ьный (~ен, ~ьна) *adj.* compulsory, forced; coercive; **~ьные рабо́ты** forced labour; **п. сбор** levy.
прину́|дить, жу, дишь *pf.* (*of* **~жда́ть**) to force, compel, coerce.
принужда́|ть, ю *impf. of* **прину́дить**
принужде́ни|е, я *nt.* compulsion, coercion; **по ~ю** under duress.
принуждённост|ь, и *f.* constraint; stiffness.
принуждённый *p.p.p. of* **прину́дить** *and adj.* constrained, forced; **п. смех** forced laughter.
принц, а *m.* prince.
принце́сс|а, ы *f.* princess.
при́нцип, а *m.* principle; **в ~е** in principle; **из ~а** on principle.
принципиа́льно *adv.* **1.** on principle; on a question of principle. **2.** in principle.
принципиа́льност|ь, и *f.* adherence to principle(s).
принципиа́л|ьный (~ен, ~ьна) *adj.* **1.** of principle; based on, guided by principle; **п. вопро́с** question of principle; **п. челове́к** man of principle. **2.** in principle; **они́ да́ли ~ьное согла́сие** they agreed in principle.
принюх|аться, аюсь *pf.* (*of* **~иваться**) (**к**; *coll.*) to get used to the smell (of).
принюхива|ться, юсь *impf. of* **принюхаться**
приня́ти|е, я *nt.* **1.** taking; taking up, assumption; **п. пи́щи** taking of food; **п. прися́ги** taking of the oath; **п. поста́** taking up a post. **2.** acceptance. **3.** admission, admittance.
при́нят|ый *p.p.p. of* **приня́ть; ~о** it is customary, it is usual; **не ~о** it is not done.
при|ня́ть, му́, ~мешь, *past* **~нял, ~няла́, ~няло** *pf.* (*of* **~нима́ть**) **1.** to take; to accept; **п. ва́нну** to have a bath; **п. реше́ние** to take, reach, come to a decision; **п. това́ры** to take receipt of goods; **~ми́те моё сочу́вствие** accept my condolences; **п. уча́стие** (**в**+*p.*) to take part (in); participate (in); **п. христиа́нство** to adopt Christianity; **п. за пра́вило** to make it a rule; **п. (бли́зко) к се́рдцу** to take to heart. **2.** to take up (*a post, etc.*); to take over; **п. но́вое назначе́ние** to take up a new appointment; **п. кома́ндование** (+*i.*) to take command (of); **п. духо́вный сан** to take holy orders; **п. дела́ (от)** to take over duties (from). **3.** to accept; **п. зако́н** to pass a law; **п. предложе́ние** to accept an offer; to accept a proposal; **п. резолю́цию** to pass, adopt, carry a resolution; **п. сове́т** to take advice. **4.** (**в, на**+*a.*) to admit (to); to accept (for); **п. в па́ртию** to admit to a party; **п. на слу́жбу** to accept for a job; **п. в гражда́нство** to grant citizenship. **5.** (*see also* **~нима́ть**) to receive; **они́ ~няли нас раду́шно** they gave us a warm welcome. **6.** to assume, take (on); **перегово́ры ~няли благоприя́тный оборо́т** the talks took a favourable turn. **7.** (+*a.* **за**+*a.*) to take (for); **я ~нял вас за шотла́ндца** I took you for a Scotsman.
при|ня́ться, му́сь, ~мешься, *past* **~нялся́, ~няла́сь** *pf.* (*of* **~нима́ться**) **1.** (+*inf.*) to begin; to start. **2.** (**за**+*a.*) to set (to), get down (to); **п. за рабо́ту** to set to work; **п. за чте́ние** to get down to reading. **3.** (*of plants*) to take root; (*of injections*) to take.
приободр|и́ть, ю́, и́шь *pf.* (*of* **~я́ть**) to cheer up, encourage, hearten.
приободр|и́ться, ю́сь, и́шься *pf.* (*of* **~я́ться**) to cheer up.
приободр|я́ть(ся), я́ю(сь) *impf. of* **~и́ть(ся)**
приобре|сти́, ту́, тёшь, *past* **~л, ~ла́** *pf.* (*of* **~та́ть**) **1.** to acquire, gain; **п. о́пыт** to gain experience. **2.** to take on, assume; **п. но́вое значе́ние** to take on new significance.
приобрета́|ть, ю *impf. of* **приобрести́**
приобрете́ни|е, я *nt.* **1.** acquisition. **2.** acquisition, gain; (*fig., coll.*) bargain, 'a find'.
приобщ|а́ть(ся), а́ю(сь) *impf. of* **~и́ть(ся)**
приобщ|и́ть, у́, и́шь *pf.* (*of* **~и́ть**) **1.** (**к**) to introduce (to), acquaint (with). **2.** to join, attach; **п. к де́лу** to file. **3.** (*eccl.*) to administer the sacrament (to).
приобщ|и́ться, у́сь, и́шься *pf.* (*of* **~а́ться**) (**к**) to join (in); **п. к обще́ственной жи́зни** to join in social life.
приоде́|ть, ну, нешь *pf.* (*coll.*) to dress up.

приоде́|ться, нусь, нешься *pf.* (*coll.*) to dress up, get dressed up
прио́р, а *m.* (*eccl.*) prior.
приорите́т, а *m.* priority.
приоса́нива|ться, юсь *impf. of* **приоса́ниться**
приоса́н|иться, юсь, ишься *pf.* (*coll.*) to assume a dignified air.
приостана́влива|ть(ся), ю(сь) *impf. of* **приостанови́ть(ся)**
приостанов|и́ть, лю́, ‿ишь *pf.* (*of* **приостана́вливать**) to halt; to suspend.
приостанов|и́ться, лю́сь, ‿ишься *pf.* (*of* **приостана́вливаться**) to halt, come to a halt; to pause.
приостано́вк|а, и *f.* halt; suspension.
приотвор|и́ть, ю́, ‿ишь *pf.* (*of* **~я́ть**) to open slightly; **п. дверь** to set a door ajar.
приотвор|и́ться, ‿ится *pf.* (*of* **~я́ться**) to open slightly.
приотвор|я́ть(ся), я́ю(сь) *impf. of* **~и́ть(ся)**
приоткрыва́|ть(ся), ю(сь) *impf. of* **приоткры́ть(ся)**
приоткр|ы́ть(ся), о́ю(сь), о́ешь(ся) *pf.* = **приотвори́ть(ся)**
приохо́|тить, чу, тишь *pf.* (**к**; *coll.*) to give a taste (for).
приохо́|титься, чусь, тишься *pf.* (**к**; *coll.*) to acquire a taste (for), take (to).
припада́|ть, ю *impf.* **1.** *impf. of* **припа́сть. 2.** (*impf. only*) to have a slight limp; **п. на ле́вую но́гу** to have a slight limp in the left leg.
припа́д|ок, ка *m.* fit; attack; **серде́чный п.** heart attack.
припа́дочн|ый *adj.* subject to fits; *as n.* **п., ~ого** *m.* epileptic.
припа́ива|ть, ю *impf. of* **припая́ть**
припа́йк|а, и *f.* soldering; brazing.
припа́рк|а, и *f.* (*med.*) poultice.
припас|а́ть, а́ю *impf. of* **~ти́**
припас|ти́, у́, ёшь, *past* **‿, ~ла́** *pf.* (*of* **~а́ть**) (+*a. or g.*; *coll.*) to store, lay in (a supply of).
припа́|сть, ду́, дёшь, *past* **~л** *pf.* (*of* **~да́ть**) (**к**) to press o.s. (to), fall down (before); **п. к чьим-н. нога́м** to prostrate o.s. before s.o.; **п. у́хом** to press one's ear (to).
припа́с|ы, ов *no sg.* stores, supplies; **боевы́е п.** ammunition; **вое́нные п.** munitions; **съестны́е п.** provisions, rations.
припая́|ть, ю *pf.* (*of* **припа́ивать**) (**к**) to solder (to).
припе́в, а *m.* refrain.
припева́|ть, ю *impf.* to hum; **жить ~ючи** (*coll.*) to be in clover; to live the life of Riley.
припёк, а *m.*: **на ~е** (*coll.*) right in the sun, exposed to the full heat of the sun.
припека́|ть, ет *impf.* (*coll.*) (*of the sun*) to be very hot, beat down.
при|пере́ть, пру́, прёшь, *past* **~пёр, ~пёрла** *pf.* (*of* **~пира́ть**) **1.** (**к**) to press (against); **п. стул к две́ри** to put a chair against the door; **п. кого́-н. к сте́нке** (*fig., coll.*) to drive s.o. into a corner. **2.** (*coll.*) to set ajar.
припира́|ть, ю *impf. of* **припере́ть**
припи|са́ть, шу́, ‿шешь *pf.* (*of* **~сывать**) **1.** to add (*to sth. written*). **2.** (**к**) to register (at). **3.** (+*d.*) to attribute (to); to ascribe (to); to put down (to).
припи́ск|а, и *f.* **1.** addition; postscript; **п. к завеща́нию** (*leg.*) codicil. **2.** registration.
припи́сыва|ть, ю *impf. of* **приписа́ть**
припла́т|а, ы *f.* additional payment; surcharge.
припла|ти́ть, чу́, ‿тишь *pf.* (*of* **‿чивать**) to pay in addition.
припла́чива|ть, ю *impf. of* **приплати́ть**
припло́д, а *m.* issue, increase (*of animals*).
приплыва́|ть, ю *impf. of* **приплы́ть**
приплы́|ть, ву́, вёшь, *past* **~л, ~ла́, ~ло** *pf.* (*of* **~ва́ть**) to swim up; to sail up.
приплю́снут|ый *p.p.p. of* **~ь** *and adj.*: **п. нос** flat nose.
приплю́сн|уть, у, ешь *pf.* (*of* **приплю́щивать**) to flatten.
приплюс|ова́ть, у́ю *pf.* (*of* **~о́вывать**) (*coll.*) to add on.
приплюсо́выва|ть, ю *impf. of* **приплюсова́ть**
приплю́щива|ть, ю *impf. of* **приплю́снуть**
припля́сыва|ть, ю *impf.* to trip, skip.
приподнима́|ть(ся), ю(сь) *impf. of* **приподня́ть(ся)**
припо́днятост|ь, и *f.* elation; animation.
припо́дн|ятый *p.p.p. of* **~я́ть** *and adj.* elated; animated; uplifted.
приподн|я́ть, иму́, и́мешь, *past* **‿ял, ~яла́, ‿яло** *pf.* (*of* **~има́ть**) to raise slightly; to lift slightly.
приподн|я́ться, иму́сь, и́мешься, *past* **~я́лся, ~яла́сь** *pf.* (*of* **~има́ться**) to raise o.s. (a little); **п. на цы́почках** to stand on tiptoe.
припо́|й, я *m.* solder.
securelyприполз|а́ть, а́ю *impf. of* **~ти́**
приполз|ти́, у́, ёшь, *past* **~, ~ла́** *pf.* (*of* **~а́ть**) to creep up, crawl up.
припомина́|ть, ю *impf. of* **припо́мнить**
припо́м|нить, ню, нишь *pf.* (*of* **~ина́ть**) to remember, recollect, recall.
припра́в|а, ы *f.* relish, condiment, flavouring, seasoning, dressing; **п. к сала́ту** salad dressing.
припра́в|ить, лю, ишь *pf.* (*of* **~ля́ть**) (+*i.*) to season (with), flavour (with), dress (with).
приправля́|ть, ю *impf. of* **припра́вить**
припря́|тать, чу, чешь *pf.* (*of* **~тывать**) (*coll.*) to secrete, put by (*for further use*).
припря́тыва|ть, ю *impf. of* **припря́тать**
припу́гива|ть, ю *impf. of* **припугну́ть**
припуг|ну́ть, ну́, нёшь *pf.* (*of* **‿ивать**) (*coll.*) to intimidate, scare.
припу́дрива|ть(ся), ю(сь) *impf. of* **припу́дрить(ся)**
припу́др|ить, ю, ишь *pf.* (*of* **~ивать**) to powder.
припу́др|иться, юсь, ишься *pf.* (*of* **~иваться**) to powder o.s.
припуска́|ть, ю *impf. of* **припусти́ть**
припу|сти́ть, щу́, ‿стишь *pf.* (*of* **~ска́ть**) **1.** (**к**) to put (to) (*for coupling or feeding*); **п. телёнка к коро́ве** to put a calf to the cow. **2.** (*tailoring*) to let out. **3.** (*coll.*) to urge on. **4.** (*coll.*) to quicken one's pace. **5.** (*coll.*; *of rain*) to come down harder.
припух|а́ть, а́ет *impf. of* **‿нуть**
припу́хлост|ь, и *f.* (slight) swelling.
припу́хлый *adj.* (slightly) swollen.
припу́х|нуть, нет, *past* **~, ~ла** *pf.* (*of* **~а́ть**) to swell up a little.
прирабатыва|ть, ю *impf. of* **прирабо́тать**
прирабо́та|ть, ю *pf.* (*of* **прираба́тывать**) to earn extra.
при́работ|ок, ка *m.* extra earnings.
прира́внива|ть, ю *impf. of* **приравня́ть**
приравн|я́ть, я́ю *pf.* (*of* **‿ивать**) (**к**) to equate (with).
прираст|а́ть, а́ю *impf. of* **~и́**
прираст|и́, у́, ёшь, *past* **приро́с, приросла́** *pf.* (*of* **~а́ть**) **1.** (**к**) to adhere (to); (*of a graft*) to take; (*fig.*) to become rooted (to). **2.** to increase; to accrue.
приращени|е, я *nt.* increase; increment.
приревн|ова́ть, у́ю *pf.* (**к**) to be jealous (of).
прирез|а́ть, а́ю *impf. of* **‿ать**[2]
прире́|зать[1]**, жу, жешь** *pf.* (*of* **~зывать**) (*coll.*) to kill; to cut the throat (of).
прире́|зать[2]**, жу, жешь** *pf.* (*of* **~за́ть** *and* **~зывать**) to add on.
прире́з|ок, ка *m.* additional piece.
прире́зыва|ть, ю *impf. of* **прире́зать**
приро́д|а, ы *f.* **1.** nature; **отда́ть долг ~е** (*i*) (*rhet.*) to pay the debt to nature, (*ii*) (*coll., euph.*) to an-

swer a call of nature. **2.** nature, character; **от ~ы** by nature, congenitally; **по ~е** by nature, naturally; **это в ~е вещей** it is in the nature of things.
приро́дн|ый *adj.* **1.** natural. **2.** born; **п. англича́нин** an Englishman by birth. **3.** inborn, innate.
природобезвре́д|ный (~ен, ~на) *adj.* environment-friendly.
природове́дени|е, я *nt.* natural history.
прирождённый *adj.* **1.** inborn, innate. **2.** a born; **п. лгун** a born liar.
приро́ст, а *m.* increase, growth.
прируч|а́ть, а́ю *impf. of* **~и́ть**
прируче́ни|е, я *nt.* taming; domestication.
прируч|и́ть, у́, и́шь *pf.* (*of* **~а́ть**) to tame (*also fig.*); to domesticate.
приса́жива|ться, юсь *impf. of* **присе́сть**
приса́лива|ть, ю *impf. of* **присоли́ть**
приса́сыва|ться, юсь *impf. of* **присоса́ться**
присва́ива|ть, ю *impf. of* **присво́ить**
при́свист, а *m.* whistle; whistling.
присви́стыва|ть, ю *impf.* to whistle.
присвое́ни|е, я *nt.* **1.** appropriation; **незако́нное п.** misappropriation. **2.** awarding, conferment.
присво́|ить, ю, ишь *pf.* (*of* **присва́ивать**) **1.** to appropriate; **незако́нно п.** to misappropriate. **2.** (*+a. and d.*) to give, award, confer; **п. и́мя** (*+d. and g.*) to name (after).
приседа́ни|е, я *nt.* squatting.
приседа́|ть, ю *impf. of* **присе́сть**
присе́ст, а *m.*: **в оди́н п., за оди́н п.** (*coll.*) at one sitting, at a stretch.
при|се́сть, ся́ду, ся́дешь, *past* **~се́л** *pf.* **1.** (*impf.* **~са́живаться**) to sit down, take a seat. **2.** (*impf.* **~седа́ть**) to squat; (*in fright*) to cower. **3.** (*impf.* **~седа́ть**) to curts(e)y.
при́сказк|а, и *f.* introduction; prelude.
приска|ка́ть, чу́, ~́чешь *pf.* to arrive at a gallop.
приско́рби|е, я *nt.* sorrow, regret; **к моему́ ~ю** to my regret.
приско́рб|ный (~ен, ~на) *adj.* lamentable, deplorable.
прискуч|ить, у, ишь *pf.* (*+d.*; *coll.*) to bore, tire.
при|сла́ть, шлю́, шлёшь *pf.* (*of* **~сыла́ть**) to send.
прислон|и́ть, ю́, ~́ишь *pf.* (*of* **~я́ть**) (**к**) to lean (against), rest (against).
прислон|и́ться, ю́сь, ~́ишься *pf.* (*of* **~я́ться**) (**к**) to lean (against), rest (against).
прислон|я́ть(ся), я́ю(сь) *impf. of* **~и́ть(ся)**
прислу́г|а, и *f.* **1.** maid, servant. **2.** (*collect.*; *obs.*) servants. **3.** (*mil.*) crew; **оруди́йная п.** gun crew.
прислу́жива|ть, ю *impf.* (*+d.*; *obs.*) to wait (upon), attend.
прислу́жива|ться, юсь *impf. of* **прислужи́ться**
прислуж|и́ться, у́сь, ~́ишься *pf.* (*of* **~́иваться**) (**к**; *obs.*) to worm o.s. into the favour (of), fawn (upon).
прислу́жник, а *m.* **1.** (*obs.*) servant. **2.** (*coll.*) lickspittle; underling.
прислу́жничеств|о, а *nt.* servility.
прислу́ш|аться, аюсь *pf.* (*of* **~иваться**) (**к**) **1.** to listen (to). **2.** (*fig.*) to listen (to); to heed; **п. к чьему́-н. сове́ту** to listen to s.o.'s advice. **3.** (*coll.*) to get used to the sound (of).
прислу́шива|ться, юсь *impf. of* **прислу́шаться**
присма́трива|ть(ся), ю(сь) *impf. of* **присмотре́ть(ся)**
присмире́|ть, ю *pf.* to grow quiet.
присмо́тр, а *m.* care; supervision; **п. за детьми́** child-minding.
присмотр|е́ть, ю́, ~́ишь *pf.* (*of* **присма́тривать**) **1.** (**за**+*i.*) to look after, keep an eye (on); **п. за ребёнком** to mind the baby. **2.** (*coll.*) to look for; **п. себе́ рабо́ту** to look for a job. **3.** *pf. only* to find.
присмотр|е́ться, ю́сь, ~́ишься *pf.* (*of* **присма́триваться**) (**к**) **1.** to look closely (at); **п. к кому́-н.** to size s.o. up, take s.o.'s measure. **2.** to get accustomed (to).
присн|и́ться, ю́сь, и́шься *pf. of* **сни́ться**
при́сн|ые, ~ых *no sg.* (*coll.*) associates.
присовокуп|и́ть, лю́, и́шь *pf.* (*of* **~ля́ть**) to add; to say in addition; **п. бума́гу к де́лу** to file a paper.
присовокупля́|ть, ю *impf. of* **присовокупи́ть**
присоедине́ни|е, я *nt.* **1.** addition. **2.** (*pol.*) annexation. **3.** (**к**) joining.
присоедин|и́ть, ю́, и́шь *pf.* (*of* **~я́ть**) **1.** to add; to join. **2.** (*pol.*) to annex.
присоедин|и́ться, ю́сь, и́шься *pf.* (*of* **~я́ться**) (**к**) **1.** to join. **2.** (*fig.*) to endorse, associate o.s. (with); **п. к мне́нию** to subscribe to an opinion.
присоедин|я́ть(ся), я́ю(сь) *impf. of* **~и́ть(ся)**
присол|и́ть, ю́, ~́ишь *pf.* (*of* **приса́ливать**) (*coll.*) to salt, add salt (to).
присос|а́ться, у́сь, ёшься *pf.* (*of* **приса́сываться**) (**к**) to stick (to), adhere (to) (*by suction*).
присосе́|диться, жусь, дишься *pf.* (**к**; *coll.*) to sit down next (to).
присо́ск|а, и *f.* (*biol., zool.*) sucker.
присо́х|нуть, нет, *past* **~, ~ла** *pf.* (*of* **присыха́ть**) (**к**) to adhere (*in drying*) (to); to stick (to), dry (on).
приспева́|ть, ю *impf. of* **приспе́ть**
приспе́|ть, ю *pf.* (*of* **~ва́ть**) (*coll.*; *of time*) to be ripe.
приспе́шник, а *m.* stooge, henchman.
приспоса́блива|ть(ся), ю(сь) *impf.* = **приспособля́ть(ся)**
приспосо́б|ить, лю, ишь *pf.* (*of* **~ля́ть**) to adapt, convert; **п. шко́лу под больни́цу** to convert a school into a hospital.
приспосо́б|иться, люсь, ишься *pf.* (*of* **~ля́ться**) **1.** (**к**) to adapt (o.s.) (to). **2.** *pass. of* **~ить**
приспособле́ни|е, я *nt.* **1.** adaptation; **п. к кли́мату** acclimatization. **2.** device; appliance.
приспосо́бленност|ь, и *f.* fitness, suitability.
приспособля́емост|ь, и *f.* adaptability.
приспособля́|ть(ся), ю(сь) *impf. of* **приспосо́бить(ся)**
приспуска́|ть, ю *impf. of* **приспусти́ть**
приспу|сти́ть, щу́, ~́стишь *pf.* (*of* **~ска́ть**) to lower a little; **п. флаг** to lower a flag to half-mast.
при́став, а, *pl.* **~а́** *m.* (*hist.*) police-officer; **суде́бный п.** bailiff.
пристава́ни|е, я *nt.* pestering; molestation; **сексуа́льные ~я** sexual harassment.
приста|ва́ть, ю́, ёшь *impf. of* **приста́ть**
приста́в|ить, лю, ишь *pf.* (*of* **~ля́ть**) **1.** (**к**) to place (to, against), lean (against); **п. ле́стницу к стене́** to put a ladder against the wall. **2.** to add. **3.** (**к**) to appoint to look after; **п. проводника́ к тури́стам** to appoint a guide to look after tourists.
приста́вк|а, и *f.* (*gram.*) prefix.
приставля́|ть, ю *impf. of* **приста́вить**
приставн|о́й *adj.* added, attached; **~а́я ле́стница** step ladder
приста́вочный *adj.* (*gram.*) **1.** of a prefix. **2.** prefixed.
при́стально *adv.* intently; **п. смотре́ть** (**на**+*a.*) to stare (at), gaze (at).
при́стал|ьный (~ен, ~ьна) *adj.* fixed; **п. взгляд** fixed look; stare, gaze.
приста́нищ|е, а *nt.* refuge, shelter, asylum.
при́стан|ь, и, *pl.* **~и, ~е́й** *f.* landing-stage, jetty; pier; wharf.
приста́|ть, ну, нешь *pf.* (*of* **~ва́ть**) **1.** (**к**) to stick (to), adhere (to). **2.** (**к**) to join. **3.** (**к**; *fig., coll.*; *of infectious disease*) to be passed on (to); **к де́тям ~ла ве́треная о́спа** the children have picked up chickenpox. **4.** (**к**) to pester, bother; **п. с предложе́ниями** to pester with suggestions. **5.** (**к**; *naut.*) to

put in (to), come alongside. **6.** *pf. only* (*impers.+d.*; *coll.*) to befit; **не ~ло тебé так говорить** you ought not to speak like that. **7.** *pf. only* (*+d.*; *coll.*) to become, suit.

пристёгива|ть, ю *impf. of* **пристегнýть**

пристег|нýть, нý, нёшь *pf.* (*of* **~́ивать**) to fasten; to button up.

пристó|йный (~ен, ~йна) *adj.* proper, decorous, seemly.

пристрáива|ть(ся), ю(сь) *impf. of* **пристрóить(ся)**

пристрáсти|е, я *nt.* **(к) 1.** passion (for); **у неё п. к верховóй ездé** she has a passion for riding. **2.** partiality (for, towards), bias (towards).

пристра|стить, щý, стишь *pf.* (**к**; *coll.*) to instil a passion (for); **егó доклáд ~стил меня к занятиям по истóрии Индии** his talk instilled in me a passion for studying the history of India.

пристра|ститься, щýсь, стишься *pf.* **(к)** to develop a passion (for).

пристрáстност|ь, и *f.* partiality, bias.

пристрáст|ный (~ен, ~на) *adj.* partial, biased.

пристрáчива|ть, ю *impf. of* **пристрочить**

пристрéлива|ть, ю *impf. of* **пристрелить** *and* **пристрелять**

пристрéлива|ться, юсь *impf. of* **пристреляться**

пристрел|ить, ю́, ~́ишь *pf.* (*of* **~́ивать**) to shoot (down).

пристрéлк|а, и *f.* (*mil.*) adjustment (of fire), ranging; **вести ~у** to find the range.

пристрел|ять, я́ю *pf.* (*of* **~́ивать**) (*mil.*) to adjust.

пристрел|яться, я́юсь *pf.* (*of* **~́иваться**) (*mil.*) to adjust fire; to find the range.

пристрó|ить, ю, ишь *pf.* (*of* **пристрáивать**) **1. (к)** to add (*to a building*), build on (to). **2.** (*coll.*) to place, settle, fix up; **п. когó-н. на слýжбу** to settle s.o. in a job.

пристрó|иться, юсь, ишься *pf.* (*of* **пристрáиваться**) **1.** (*coll.*) to get a job. **2.** (**к**; *mil.*) to form up (with).

пристрóйк|а, и *f.* annexe, extension; outhouse.

пристроч|ить, ý, ~́ишь *pf.* (*of* **пристрáчивать**) **(к)** to sew on (to).

пристрýнива|ть, ю *impf. of* **пристрýнить**

пристрýн|ить, ю, ишь *pf.* (*of* **~ивать**) (*coll.*) to take in hand.

пристýкива|ть, ю *impf. of* **пристýкнуть**

пристýк|нуть, ну, нешь *pf.* (*of* **~ивать**) (*+i.*; *coll.*) to tap; **п. каблукáми** to tap one's heels.

при́ступ, а *m.* **1.** (*mil.*) assault, storm; **взять ~ом** to (take by) storm. **2.** fit, attack; bout.

приступ|áть(ся), áю(сь) *impf. of* **~ить(ся)**

приступ|ить, лю́, ~́ишь *pf.* (*of* **~áть**) **(к)** to set about, get down (to), start; **п. к дéлу** to set to work, get down to business.

приступ|иться, лю́сь, ~́ишься *pf.* (*of* **~áться**) (**к**; *coll.*) to approach, accost, go up (to).

присты|дить, жý, ди́шь *pf. of* **стыдить**

прису|дить, жý, ~́дишь *pf.* (*of* **~ждáть**) **1. (к)** to sentence (to); **п. к штрáфу, п. штраф** (*+d.*) to fine. **2.** (*+d.*) to award (to); to confer (on).

присуждá|ть, ю *impf. of* **присудить**

присуждéни|е, я *nt.* awarding; conferment.

присýтстви|е, я *nt.* presence; **п. дýха** presence of mind.

присýтств|овать, ую *impf.* (**на**+*p.*) to be present (at), attend.

присýтств|ующий *pres. part. act. of* **~овать** *and adj.* present; *as n.* **~ующие, ~ующих** those present.

присýщ|ий (~, ~а) *adj.* (*+d.*) inherent (in); characteristic; **~ая ей щéдрость** her characteristic generosity.

присчит|áть, áю *pf.* (*of* **~́ывать**) to add on.

присчи́тыва|ть, ю *impf. of* **присчитáть**

присылá|ть, ю *impf. of* **прислáть**

присы́п|ать, лю, лешь *pf.* (*of* **~áть**) **1.** (*+a. or g.*) to pour some more. **2.** (*+a. and i.*) to sprinkle (with).

присып|áть, áю *impf. of* **~́ать**

присы́пк|а, и *f.* **1.** sprinkling. **2.** powder.

присыхá|ть, ю *impf. of* **присóхнуть**

присяг|а, и *f.* oath; **принять ~у** to take the oath; **привести к ~е** to swear in, administer the oath (to); **под ~ой** on oath, under oath.

присяг|áть, áю *impf.* (*of* **~нýть**) (**в**+*p.*) to swear (to); **п. в вéрности** (*+d.*) to swear allegiance (to).

присяг|нýть, нý, нёшь *pf. of* **~áть**

прися́жн|ый *adj.* **1. п. повéренный** barrister; **п. заседáтель** juror; *as n.* **п., ~ого** *m.* = **п. заседáтель; суд ~ых** jury. **2.** (*coll.*) inveterate.

прита|и́ться, ю́сь, и́шься *pf.* to hide; to conceal o.s.

притáптыва|ть, ю *impf. of* **притоптáть**

притáскива|ть, ю *impf. of* **притащить**

притащ|ить, ý, ~́ишь *pf.* (*of* **притáскивать**) to bring, drag.

притащ|иться, ýсь, ~́ишься *pf.* (*coll.*) to drag o.s.

притвор|ить, ю́, ~́ишь *pf.* (*of* **~я́ть**) to set ajar; to leave not quite shut.

притвор|иться[1], ~́ится *pf.* (*of* **~я́ться**) to be ajar, to be not quite shut.

притвор|иться[2], ю́сь, и́шься *pf.* (*of* **~я́ться**) (*+i.*) to pretend (to be); to feign; **п. больны́м** to feign illness.

притвóр|ный (~ен, ~на) *adj.* pretended, feigned; **~ные слёзы** crocodile tears.

притвóрств|о, а *nt.* pretence; sham.

притвóрщик, а *m.* sham, faker.

притвор|я́ть(ся), я́ю(сь) *impf. of* **~ить(ся)**

притекá|ть, ю *impf. of* **притéчь**

притерп|éться, лю́сь, ~́ишься *pf.* (**к**; *coll.*) to get accustomed (to), get used (to).

притёр|тый *p.p.p. of* **~éть** *and adj.*; **~тое стеклó** ground glass.

притеснéни|е, я *nt.* oppression.

притесни́тел|ь, я *m.* oppressor.

притесни́тел|ьный (~ен, ~ьна) *adj.* oppressive.

притесн|ить, ю́, и́шь *pf.* (*of* **~я́ть**) to oppress, keep down.

притесн|я́ть, я́ю *impf. of* **~ить**

притé|чь, чёт, кýт, *past* **~́к, ~клá** *pf.* (*of* **~кáть**) to flow in, pour in (*also fig.*).

прити́скива|ть, ю *impf. of* **прити́снуть**

прити́с|нуть, ну, нешь *pf.* (*of* **~кивать**) (*coll.*) to press, squeeze; **п. пáлец двéрью** to pinch one's finger in the door.

притих|áть, áю *impf. of* **~́нуть**

прити́х|нуть, ну, нешь, *past* **~, ~ла** *pf.* (*of* **~áть**) to quiet down, grow quiet.

приткн|ýть, ý, ёшь *pf.* (*of* **притыкáть**) (*coll.*) to stick.

приткн|ýться, ýсь, ёшься *pf.* (*coll.*) to perch o.s.; to find room for o.s.

притóк, а *m.* **1.** (*geog.*) tributary. **2.** inflow, influx (*also fig.*).

при́толок|а, и *f.* lintel.

притóм *conj.* (and) besides; and what's more.

притóн, а *m.* den; **воровскóй п.** den of thieves; **игóрный п.** gambling-den.

притóп|нуть, ну, нешь *pf.* (*of* **~ывать**) to stamp one's foot; **п. каблукáми** to tap one's heels.

притоп|тáть, чý, ~́чешь *pf.* (*of* **притáптывать**) to tread down.

притóпыва|ть, ю *impf. of* **притóпнуть**

при́тор|ный (~ен, ~на) *adj.* sickly sweet, cloying (*also fig.*); **~ная улы́бка** unctuous smile.

притрáгива|ться, юсь *impf. of* **притрóнуться**

притрóн|уться, усь, ешься *pf.* (*of* **притрáгиваться**) **(к)** to touch.

притуп|и́ть, лю́, ⁓ишь *pf.* (*of* **⁓ля́ть**) to blunt; (*fig.*) to dull, deaden.
притуп|и́ться, лю́сь, ⁓ишься *pf.* (*of* **⁓ля́ться**) to become blunt; (*fig.*) to become dull.
притупля́|ть(ся), ю(сь) *impf. of* **притупи́ть(ся)**
притуш|и́ть, у́, ⁓ишь *pf.* (*coll.*) to damp (*a fire*); **п. фа́ры** to dip lights.
при́тч|а, и *f.* parable; **что за п.?** (*coll.*) what an extraordinary thing!; **п. во язы́цех** (*joc.*) the talk of the town.
притыка́|ть, ю *impf. of* **приткну́ть**
притяга́тел|ьный (⁓ен, ⁓ьна) *adj.* attractive, magnetic.
притя́гива|ть, ю *impf. of* **притяну́ть**
притяжа́тельный *adj.* (*gram.*) possessive.
притяже́ни|е, я *nt.* (*phys.*) attraction; **зако́н земно́го ⁓я** law of gravity.
притяза́ни|е, я *nt.* claim, pretension; **име́ть ⁓я** (**на**+*a.*) to have claims (to, on).
притяза́тел|ьный (⁓ен, ⁓ьна) *adj.* demanding, exacting.
притя|ну́ть, ну́, ⁓нешь *pf.* (*of* **⁓гивать**) **1.** to drag (up), pull (up); **п. за́ уши доказа́тельства** to adduce far-fetched arguments. **2.** (*fig.*) to draw, attract. **3.** (*coll.*) to summon; **п. к отве́ту** to call to account.
приукра́|сить, шу, сишь *pf.* (*of* **⁓шивать**) (*coll.*) to adorn; (*fig.*) to embellish, embroider.
приукра́шива|ть, ю *impf. of* **приукра́сить**
приуменьш|а́ть, а́ю *impf. of* **⁓и́ть**
приуме́ньш|и́ть, ⁓у́, ⁓и́шь *pf.* (*of* **⁓а́ть**) to diminish, lessen, reduce.
приумнож|а́ть(ся), а́ю(сь) *impf. of* **⁓ить(ся)**
приумноже́ни|е, я *nt.* increase, augmentation.
приумно́ж|ить, у, ишь *pf.* (*of* **⁓а́ть**) to increase, augment, multiply.
приумно́ж|иться, ится *pf.* (*of* **⁓а́ться**) to increase, multiply.
приун|ы́ть, о́ю, о́ешь *pf.* (*coll.*) to become depressed, become gloomy.
приуро́чива|ть, ю *impf. of* **приуро́чить**
приуро́ч|ить, у, ишь *pf.* (*of* **⁓ивать**) (**к**) to time (for, to coincide with).
приуса́дебный *adj.*: **п. уча́сток** personal plot.
приуч|а́ть(ся), а́ю(сь) *impf. of* **⁓и́ть(ся)**
приуч|и́ть, у́, ⁓ишь *pf.* (*of* **⁓а́ть**) (**к** *or +inf.*) to train (to), teach (to, in); **п. кого́-н. к дисципли́не** to inculcate discipline in s.o.
приуч|и́ться, у́сь, ⁓ишься *pf.* (*of* **⁓а́ться**) (*+inf.*) to train o.s. (to); to accustom o.s. (to).
прифронтов|о́й *adj.* (*mil., pol.*) forward; front-line.
прихва́рыва|ть, ю *impf.* (*coll.*) to be unwell off and on.
прихвастн|у́ть, у́, ёшь *pf.* (*coll.*) to boast a little, brag a little.
прихва|ти́ть, чу́, ⁓тишь *pf.* (*of* **⁓тывать**) (*coll.*) **1.** to catch up, seize up (= *to take*; *to get*). **2.** to tie up, fasten. **3.** (*of frost*) to nip.
прихва́тыва|ть, ю *impf. of* **прихвати́ть**
прихворн|у́ть, у́, ёшь *pf.* (*coll.*) to be indisposed, be unwell.
при́хвост|ень, ня *m.* (*coll.*) hanger-on, stooge.
прихлеба́тел|ь, я *m.* (*coll.*) sponger.
прихлебн|у́ть, у́, ёшь *pf.* to take a sip.
прихлёбыва|ть, ю *impf.* (*coll.*) to sip.
прихло́п|нуть, ну, нешь *pf.* (*of* **⁓ывать**) (*coll.*) **1.** to slam. **2.** to squeeze, pinch; **п. па́лец две́рью** to pinch one's finger in the door.
прихло́пыва|ть, ю *impf.* **1.** *impf. of* **прихло́пнуть. 2.** *impf. only*to clap.
прихлы́н|уть, у, ешь *pf.* (**к**) to rush (towards), surge (towards).
прихо́д[1], **а** *m.* coming, arrival.
прихо́д[2], **а** *m.* receipts; **п. и расхо́д** credit and debit.
прихо́д[3], **а** *m.* (*eccl.*) parish.
прихо|ди́ть, жу́, ⁓дишь *impf. of* **прийти́**
прихо|ди́ться, жу́сь, ⁓дишься *impf.* **1.** *impf. of* **прийти́сь. 2.** *impf. only* (*+d. and i.*) to be (*in a given degree of relationship to*); **я ей ⁓жу́сь дя́дей** I am her uncle.
прихо́д|ный *adj. of* **⁓**[2]; **⁓ная кни́га** receipt-book.
прихо́д|овать, ую *impf.* (*of* **за⁓**) to enter (*in receipt-book*).
прихо́дский *adj.* parish; parochial.
приход|я́щий *pres. part. act. of* **⁓и́ть** *and adj.* non-resident; **п. больно́й** outpatient; **⁓я́щая домрабо́тница** daily, char(woman).
прихожа́н|ин, ина, *pl.* **⁓е** *m.* parishioner.
прихо́ж|ая, ей *f.* (entrance) hall, lobby.
прихора́шива|ться, юсь *impf.* (*coll.*) to spruce o.s. up.
прихотли́в|ый (⁓, ⁓а) *adj.* **1.** capricious, whimsical. **2.** fancy, intricate (*of pattern, etc.*).
при́хот|ь, и *f.* whim, caprice, fancy.
прихра́мыва|ть, ю *impf.* to limp, hobble.
прице́л, а *m.* (back-)sight; **п. для бомбомета́ния** bomb sight; **взять на п.** to take aim (at).
прице́лива|ться, юсь *impf. of* **прице́литься**
прице́л|иться, юсь, ишься *pf.* (*of* **⁓иваться**) to take aim.
прице́л|ьный *adj. of* **⁓**; **⁓ьная бомбардиро́вка** precision bombing; **⁓ьная ли́ния** line of sight.
прице́нива|ться, юсь *impf. of* **прицени́ться**
прицен|и́ться, ю́сь, ⁓ишься *pf.* (*of* **⁓иваться**) (**к**; *coll.*) to ask the price (of).
прице́п, а *m.* trailer.
прицеп|и́ть, лю́, ⁓ишь *pf.* (*of* **⁓ля́ть**) (**к**) **1.** to hitch (to), hook on (to); to couple (to). **2.** (*coll.*) to pin on (to), fasten (to).
прицеп|и́ться, лю́сь, ⁓ишься *pf.* (*of* **⁓ля́ться**) (**к**) **1.** to stick (to), cling (to). **2.** (*fig., coll.*) to pester; to nag (at).
прице́пк|а, и *f.* **1.** hitching, hooking on; coupling. **2.** (*coll.*) pestering; nagging.
прицепля́|ть(ся), ю(сь) *impf. of* **прицепи́ть(ся)**
прицепно́й *adj.*: **п. ваго́н** trailer.
прича́л, а *m.* **1.** mooring. **2.** mooring line. **3.** berth, moorage; **у ⁓ов** at its, her moorings.
прича́лива|ть, ю *impf. of* **прича́лить**
прича́л|ить, ю, ишь *pf.* (*of* **⁓ивать**) **1.** (**к**) to moor (to). **2.** (*intrans.*) to moor.
прича́л|ьный *adj. of* **⁓**; **п. кана́т** mooring line.
прича́сти|е[1], **я** *nt.* (*gram.*) participle.
прича́сти|е[2], **я** *nt.* (*eccl.*) communion; the Eucharist.
прича|сти́ть, щу́, сти́шь *pf.* (*of* **⁓ща́ть**) (*eccl.*) to give communion.
прича|сти́ться, щу́сь, сти́шься *pf.* (*of* **⁓ща́ться**) (*eccl.*) to receive communion.
прича́ст|ный[1] **(⁓ен, ⁓на)** *adj.* (**к**) connected (with), involved (in); **быть ⁓ным (к)** to be connected (with), be involved (in), a party (to).
прича́стный[2] *adj.* (*gram.*) participial.
причаща́|ть(ся), ю(сь) *impf. of* **причасти́ть(ся)**
причём *conj.* **1.** moreover, and; **бы́ло о́чень темно́, п. я пло́хо ориенти́руюсь в э́той ме́стности** it was very dark and I don't know this area well. **2.** while (*+participial clause*); **он реши́л пое́хать, п. отдава́л себе́ отчёт в опа́сности** he decided to go, while recognizing the danger.
приче|са́ть, шу́, ⁓шешь *pf.* (*of* **⁓сывать**) to comb; **п. кого́-н.** to brush, comb s.o.'s hair.
приче|са́ться, шу́сь, ⁓шешься *pf.* (*of* **⁓сываться**) to brush, comb one's hair; to have one's hair done.
причёск|а, и *f.* hair style, hair-do.
причёсыва|ть(ся), ю(сь) *impf. of* **причеса́ть(ся)**
причи́н|а, ы *f.* cause; reason; **по той просто́й ⁓е, что** for the simple reason that; **по ⁓е** (*+g.*) by rea-

son (of), on account (of), owing (to) because (of).

причин|и́ть, ю́, и́шь *pf.* (*of* **~я́ть**) to cause; to occasion.

причи́нност|ь, и *f.* causality.

причи́нн|ый *adj.* causal, causative.

причин|я́ть, я́ю *impf. of* **~и́ть**

причи́сл|ить, ю, ишь *pf.* (*of* **~я́ть**) (**к**) **1.** to add on (to). **2.** to number (among), rank (among); **его́ ~или к са́мым вы́дающимся матема́тикам** he was ranked among the foremost mathematicians.

причисл|я́ть, я́ю *impf. of* **~ить**

причита́ни|е, я *nt.* (ritual) lamentation.

причита́|ть, ю *impf.* (**по**+*p.*) to lament (for); to bewail.

причита́|ться, ется *impf.* (+*d.*; **с**+*g.*) to be due (to; from); **с вас ~ется два рубля́** you have two roubles to pay.

причмо́кива|ть, ю *impf. of* **причмо́кнуть**

причмо́к|нуть, ну, нешь *pf.* (*of* **~ивать**) to smack one's lips.

причу́д|а, ы *f.* caprice, whim, fancy.

причу́д|иться, ится *pf. of* **чу́диться**

причу́длив|ый (~, ~а) *adj.* **1.** odd, queer; quaint. **2.** (*coll.*) capricious, whimsical.

пришварт|ова́ть, у́ю *pf.* (*of* **~о́вывать**) (**к**) to moor (to), make fast (to).

пришварт|ова́ться, у́юсь *pf.* (*of* **~о́вываться**) (**к**) to moor (to), tie up (at).

пришварто́выва|ть(ся), ю(сь) *impf. of* **пришвартова́ть(ся)**

прише́л|ец, ьца *m.* newcomer, stranger.

прише́стви|е, я́ *nt.* (*obs.*) advent, coming; **до второ́го ~я** (*joc.*) till doomsday.

пришиб|и́ть, у́ ёшь, *past* **~, ~ла** *pf.* (*coll.*) **1.** to strike dead. **2.** (*fig.*) to crush, break (= *to dispirit*).

приши́б|ленный *p.p.p. of* **~и́ть** *and adj.* (*coll.*) crushed, broken; crest-fallen.

пришива́|ть, ю́ *impf. of* **приши́ть**

приш|и́ть, ью́, ьёшь *pf.* (*of* **~ива́ть**) **1.** to sew on. **2.** (+*a.* **к** *or* +*a. and d.*; *fig., coll.*) to pin (on).

пришко́льный *adj.* (adjoining a) school.

при́шлый *adj.* newly arrived; strange, alien.

пришпи́лива|ть, ю *impf. of* **пришпи́лить**

пришпи́л|ить, ю, ишь *pf.* (*of* **~ивать**) to pin.

пришпо́рива|ть, ю *impf. of* **пришпо́рить**

пришпо́р|ить, ю, ишь *pf.* (*of* **~ивать**) to spur; to put, set spurs (to).

прищёлкива|ть, ю *impf. of* **прищёлкнуть**

прищёлк|нуть, ну, нешь *pf.* (*of* **~ивать**): **п. кнуто́м** to crack the whip; **п. па́льцами** to snap one's fingers.

прищем|и́ть, лю́, и́шь *pf.* (*of* **~ля́ть**) to pinch, squeeze; **п. себе́ па́лец две́рью** to pinch one's finger in the door.

прищемля́|ть, ю *impf. of* **прищеми́ть**

прищеп|и́ть лю́, и́шь *pf.* (*of* **~ля́ть**) (*bot.*) to graft.

прищепля́|ть, ю *impf. of* **прищепи́ть**

прище́пк|а, и *f.* (clothes-)peg.

прищу́рива|ть(ся), ю(сь) *impf. of* **прищу́рить(ся)**

прищу́р|ить, ю, ишь *pf.* (*of* **~ивать**); **п. глаза́** = **~иться**

прищу́р|иться, юсь, ишься *pf.* (*of* **~иваться**) to screw up one's eyes.

приют, а *m.* **1.** shelter, refuge. **2.: де́тский п.** orphanage.

прию|ти́ть, чу́, ти́шь *pf.* to shelter, give refuge.

прию|ти́ться, чу́сь, ти́шься *pf.* to take shelter.

прия́тел|ь, я *m.* friend.

прия́тельниц|а, ы *f.* **1.** (female) friend. **2.** girl-friend, lady-friend.

прия́тельский *adj.* friendly.

прия́т|ный (~ен, ~на) *adj.* nice, pleasant, pleasing; **п. на вид** nice-looking; (*impers.*, *pred.*): **~но** it is pleasant; it is nice.

про *prep.*+*a.* **1.** about; **мы говори́ли про вас** we were talking about you. **2.: про себя́** to o.s.; **чита́ть про себя́** to read to o.s.

про...[1] *vbl. pref. indicating* **1.** *action through, across or past object, as* **простреля́ть** to shoot through; **прое́хать** to pass (by). **2.** *overall or exhaustive action, as* **прогре́ть** to warm thoroughly. **3.** *duration of action throughout given period of time, as* **просиде́ть всю ночь** sit up all night. **4.** *loss or failure, as* **проигра́ть** to lose (*a game*).

про...[2] *as pref. of nn. and adjs.* pro-.

проанализи́р|овать, ую *pf. of* **анализи́ровать**

про́б|а, ы *f.* **1.** trial, test; try-out; audition; **п. сил** trial of strength; **взять на ~у** to take on trial. **2.** sample. **3.** standard (*measure of purity of gold*); **зо́лото 56-о́й ~ы** 14 carat gold; **зо́лото 96-о́й ~ы** 24 carat gold. **4.** hallmark.

пробавля́|ться, юсь *impf.* (*coll.*) to subsist (on), make do (on).

проба́лтыва|ть(ся), ю(сь) *impf. of* **проболта́ть(ся)**

пробе́г, а *m.* **1.** (*sport*) run, race; **лы́жный п.** ski-run. **2.** mileage, distance covered.

пробе́га|ть, ю *pf.* (*coll.*) to run about (*for a certain time*).

пробега́|ть, ю *impf. of* **пробежа́ть**

пробе|жа́ть, гу́, жи́шь, гу́т *pf.* (*of* **~га́ть**) **1.** to run past; to run through; to run along; **п. па́льцами по клавиату́ре** to run one's fingers over the keyboard. **2.** (*fig.*) to run, flit (over, down, across); **хо́лод ~жа́л по её спине́** a chill ran down her spine. **4.** (*fig., coll.*) to glance over, skim.

пробе|жа́ться, гу́сь, жи́шься, гу́тся *pf.* to run, take a run.

пробе́л, а *m.* **1.** blank, gap; lacuna; **запо́лнить ~ы** to fill in the blanks. **2.** (*fig.*) gap; **~ы в зна́ниях** gaps in one's knowledge.

пробива́|ть(ся), ю(сь) *impf. of* **проби́ть(ся)**

пробивн|о́й *adj.* (*coll.*) go-ahead, go-getting.

пробира́|ть(ся), ю(сь) *impf. of* **пробра́ть(ся)**

проби́рк|а, и *f.* test-tube.

проби́рн|ый *adj.* testing; assaying; **п. ка́мень** touchstone; **~ая пала́та** assay office.

про|би́ть[1]**, бью́, бьёшь,** *past* **~би́л, ~би́ла, ~би́ло** *pf. of* **бить 9.**

про|би́ть[2]**, бью́, бьёшь,** *past* **~би́л, ~би́ла, ~би́ло** *pf.* (*of* **~бива́ть**) to make a hole (in); to pierce; to punch; **п. сте́ну** to breach a wall; **п. ши́ну** to puncture a tyre; **п. путь, доро́гу** to open the way (*also fig.*); **п. себе́ доро́гу** (*fig.*) to carve one's way.

про|би́ться, бью́сь, бьёшься *pf.* (*of* **~бива́ться**) **1.** to fight, force one's way through; to break, strike through. **2.** (*of plants*) to appear, push up.

про́бк|а, и *f.* **1.** cork (*substance*). **2.** cork; stopper; plug. **3.** (*elec.*) fuse. **4.** (*fig.*) traffic jam; congestion.

про́бков|ый *adj.* cork; **п. по́яс** cork jacket, lifejacket.

пробле́м|а, ы *f.* problem.

проблема́тик|а, и *f.* (*collect.*) problems.

проблемати́ческий *adj.* problematic(al).

проблемати́ч|ный (~ен, ~на) *adj.* = **~еский**

про́блеск, а *m.* flash; ray, gleam (*also fig.*); **п. наде́жды** ray of hope.

проблужда́|ть, ю *pf.* to wander (*for a certain time*).

про́бный *adj.* **1.** trial, test; **п. ка́мень** touchstone; **п. полёт** test flight; **п. экземпля́р** specimen copy. **2.** hallmarked.

про́б|овать, ую *impf.* (*of* **по~**) **1.** to test; **п. пи́щу** to taste, sample food. **2.** (+*inf.*) to try (to).

прободе́ни|е, я *nt.* (*med.*) perforation.

пробо́ин|а, ы *f.* hole (*esp. caused by missile*).

пробо|й, я *m.* clamp, hasp.

проболе́|ть[1]**, ю** *pf.* to be ill (*for a certain time*).

пробол|е́ть[2]**, и́т** *pf.* to hurt (*for a certain time*).

проболта́|ть, ю *pf.* (*of* **проба́лтывать**) (*coll.*) **1.** to play for time by talking. **2.** to blab (out).

проболта́|ться, юсь *pf.* (*of* **проба́лтываться**) (*coll.*) to shoot off one's mouth, let the cat out of the bag.

пробо́р, а *m.* parting (*of the hair*).

пробормо|та́ть, чу́, ∠чешь *pf. of* **бормота́ть**

про́бочник, а *m.* (*coll.*) corkscrew.

про|бра́ть, беру́, берёшь, *past* **~бра́л, ~брала́, ~бра́ло** *pf.* (*of* **~бира́ть**) **1.** to penetrate; to seize; **моро́з ~бра́л меня́ до косте́й** I was chilled to the marrow; **их ~бра́л страх** fear had struck them. **2.** (*coll.*) to scold.

про|бра́ться, беру́сь, берёшься, *past* **~бра́лся, ~брала́сь, ~бра́ло́сь** *pf.* (*of* **~бира́ться**) **1.** to fight, force one's way. **2.** to steal (through, past); **п. на цы́почках** to tiptoe (through).

пробро|ди́ть, жу́, ∠дишь *pf.* to wander (*for a certain time*).

пробу|ди́ть, жу́, ∠дишь *pf.* (*of* **буди́ть** *and* **~жда́ть**) to wake; to awaken, rouse, arouse (*also fig.*).

пробу|ди́ться, жу́сь, ∠дишься *pf.* (*of* **~жда́ться**) to wake up, awake (*also fig.*).

пробужда́|ть(ся), ю(сь) *impf. of* **пробуди́ть(ся)**

пробужде́ни|е, я *nt.* awakening.

пробура́в|ить, лю, ишь *pf.* (*of* **~ливать**) to bore, drill, perforate.

пробура́влива|ть, ю *impf. of* **пробура́вить**

пробурч|а́ть, у́, и́шь *pf. of* **бурча́ть**

проб|ы́ть, у́ду, у́дешь, *past* **∠ыл, ~ыла́** *pf.* to stay, remain; to be (*for a certain time*); **он ∠ыл у нас три неде́ли** he stayed with us for three weeks.

прова́л, а *m.* **1.** downfall. **2.** (*geog.*) gap; funnel. **3.** failure; **како́й п.!** what a flop!

прова́лива|ть, ю *impf.* **1.** *impf. of* **провали́ть. 2. ~й!** (*coll.*) clear off!; beat it!; hop it!

прова́лива|ться, юсь *impf. of* **провали́ться**

провал|и́ть, ю́, ∠ишь *pf.* (*of* **∠ивать**) **1.** to cause to collapse, knock down. **2.** (*fig., coll.*) to ruin, make a mess (of). **3.** (*fig.*) to reject; **п. кандида́та на экза́мене** to fail a candidate in an examination; **п. законопрое́кт** to kill a bill.

провал|и́ться, ю́сь, ∠ишься *pf.* (*of* **∠иваться**) **1.** to collapse, fall through. **2.** (*fig., coll.*) to fail, fall through; (*in an examination*) to fail. **3.** (*coll.*) to disappear, vanish; **он как сквозь зе́млю ~и́лся** he vanished into thin air.

провანса́л|ь, я *m.* mayonnaise, salad dressing.

прова́нск|ий *adj.*: **~ое ма́сло** olive oil.

прова́рива|ть *impf. of* **провари́ть**

провар|и́ть, ю́, ∠ишь *pf.* (*of* **∠ивать**) to boil thoroughly.

прове́д|ать, аю *pf.* (*of* **~ывать**) (*coll.*) **1.** to come to see, call on. **2.** (**о**+*p.*) to find out (about), learn (of, about).

проведе́ни|е, я *nt.* **1.** leading, taking, piloting. **2.** building; installation. **3.** carrying out; conducting; conduct; **п. в жизнь** implementation.

прове́дыва|ть, ю *impf. of* **прове́дать**

провез|ти́, у́, ёшь, *past* **∸, ~ла́** *pf.* (*of* **провози́ть**) **1.** to convey, transport; **п. контраба́ндой** to smuggle. **2.** to bring (with one).

провентили́р|овать, ую *pf. of* **вентили́ровать**

прове́р|енный *p.p.p. of* **~ить** *and adj.* proved, of proved worth.

прове́р|ить, ю, ишь *pf.* (*of* **~я́ть**) **1.** to check; to verify; **п. тетра́ди** to correct exercise-books. **2.** to test; **п. свои́ си́лы** to try one's strength.

прове́рк|а, и *f.* **1.** checking; examination; verification; check-up. **2.** testing.

провер|ну́ть, ну́, нёшь *pf.* (*of* **∸тывать**) (*coll.*) to bore, perforate, pierce.

прове́рочн|ый *adj.* checking, verifying; **~ая рабо́та** test paper.

провер|те́ть, чу́, ∠тишь *pf.* (*of* **∸тывать**) (*coll.*) to bore, perforate, pierce.

провёртыва|ть, ю *impf. of* **провернуть** *and* **провертеть**

провер|я́ть, я́ю *impf. of* **∠ить**

прове|сти́, ду́, дёшь, *past* **∸л, ~ла́** *pf.* (*of* **проводи́ть**[1]) **1.** to lead, take; **п. су́дно** (*naut.*) to pilot a vessel. **2.** to build; to install. **3.** to carry out, carry on; to conduct, hold; **п. о́пыты** to carry out tests; **п. заседа́ние** to hold a meeting. **4.** to carry through; to carry, pass (*a resolution, a bill, etc.*); to implement (*a decision, etc.*); **п. иде́ю в жизнь** to put an idea into effect. **5.** to advance, put forward (*an idea, etc.*). **6.** (*book-keeping*) to register. **7.** to draw (*a line, etc.*). **8.** (+*i.*) to pass over, run over; **она́ ~ла́ руко́й по лбу** she passed her hand over her forehead. **9.** to spend, pass (*time*); **как вы ~ли́ вре́мя?** what sort of time did you have? **10.** (*coll.*) to take in, fool; to trick.

прове́трива|ть(ся), ю(сь) *impf. of* **прове́трить(ся)**

прове́тр|ить, ю, ишь *pf.* (*of* **~ивать**) to air; to ventilate.

прове́тр|иться, юсь, ишься *pf.* (*of* **~иваться**) **1.** to have an airing; (*fig., coll.*) to have a change of scene. **2.** *pass. of* **~ить**

прови́дени|е, я *nt.* foresight, forecast.

провиде́ни|е, я *nt.* (*relig.*) Providence.

прови́|деть, жу, дишь *impf.* to foresee.

прови́д|ец, ца *m.* (*obs., rhet.*) seer, prophet.

прови́зи|я, и *no pl., f.* provisions.

прови́зор, а *m.* pharmacist.

провин|и́ться, ю́сь, и́шься *pf.* (**в**+*p.*) to be guilty (of); to commit an offence; **п. пе́ред кем-н.** to wrong s.o.; **в чём мы ~и́лись?** what have we done wrong?

прови́нност|ь, и *f.* (*coll.*) fault; offence.

провинциа́л, а *m.* provincial (*pers.*).

провинциали́зм, а *m.* provincialism.

провинциа́льност|ь, и *f.* provinciality.

провинциа́л|ьный (~ен, ~ьна) *adj.* provincial (*also fig.*).

прови́нци|я, и *f.* **1.** province. **2.** the provinces.

провис|а́ть, а́ет *impf. of* **∠нуть**

прови́с|нуть, нет *pf.* (*of* **~а́ть**) to sag.

про́вод, а, *pl.* **~а́** *m.* wire, lead; **заземля́ющий п.** earth(-wire).

проводи́мост|ь, и *f.* (*elec.*) conductivity.

прово|ди́ть[1], **жу́, ∠дишь** *impf.* **1.** *impf. of* **провести́. 2.** *impf. only* (*phys., elec.*) to conduct.

прово|ди́ть[2], **жу́, ∠дишь** *pf.* (*of* **~жа́ть**) to accompany; to see off; **п. кого́-н. домо́й** to walk, see s.o. home; **п. кого́-н. до двере́й** to see s.o. to the door; **п. глаза́ми** to follow with one's eyes.

прово́дк|а, и *f.* **1.** leading, taking. **2.** building; installation. **3.** (*collect.*; *elec.*) wiring.

проводни́к[1], **а́** *m.* **1.** guide. **2.** (*of train*) conductor; guard.

проводни́к[2], **а́** *m.* **1.** (*phys., elec.*) conductor. **2.** (*fig.*) bearer; transmitter.

проводни́|ца, цы *f. of* **~к**[1]

про́вод|ы, ов *no sg.* seeing-off; send-off.

провожа́т|ый, ого *m.* guide, escort.

провожа́|ть, ю *impf. of* **проводи́ть**[2]

прово́з, а *m.* carriage, conveyance, transport; **пла́та за п.** carriage charge.

провозгла|си́ть, шу́, си́шь *pf.* (*of* **~ша́ть**) to proclaim; **п. тост** to propose a toast; **его́ ~си́ли королём** he was proclaimed king.

провозглаша́|ть, ю *impf. of* **провозгласи́ть**

провозглаше́ни|е, я *nt.* proclamation; declaration.

прово|зи́ть, жу́, ∠зишь *impf. of* **провезти́**

прово|зи́ться[1], **жу́сь, ∠зишься** *pf.* **1.** (*coll.*) to play about (*for a certain time*). **2.** (**с**+*i.*) to spend (*a certain time*) (over, in seeing to).

прово|зи́ться[2], **жу́сь, ~зишься** *impf. pass., of* **~зи́ть**
провока́тор, а *m.* **1.** agent provocateur. **2.** (*fig.*) instigator.
провокацио́нный *adj.* provocative.
провока́ци|я, и *f.* provocation.
про́волок|а, и *f.* wire; **колю́чая п.** barbed wire.
про́волочк|а, и *f. dim. of* **про́волока**; short wire; fine wire.
проволо́чк|а, и *f.* (*coll.*) delay, procrastination.
про́воло|чный *adj. of* **~ка**
провоня́|ть, ет *pf.* (*+i.*; *coll.*) to stink (of).
прово́р|ный (~ен, ~на) *adj.* **1.** quick. swift, expeditious. **2.** agile, nimble, adroit, dexterous.
провор|ова́ться, у́юсь *pf.* (*coll.*) to be caught stealing, embezzling.
проворо́н|ить, ю, ишь *pf.* (*coll.*) to miss, let slip, lose; **п. свою́ о́чередь** to miss one's turn.
прово́рств|о, а *nt.* **1.** quickness, swiftness. **2.** agility, nimbleness, adroitness, dexterity.
проворч|а́ть, у́, и́шь *pf.* to mutter.
провоци́р|овать, ую *impf. and pf.* (*pf. also* **с~**) to provoke.
провя́л|ить, ю, ишь *pf. of* **вя́лить**
прогад|а́ть, а́ю *pf.* (*of* **~ывать**) (*coll.*) to miscalculate.
прога́дыва|ть, ю *impf. of* **прогада́ть**
прога́лин|а, ы *f.* glade.
проги́б, а *m.* sagging; sag.
прогиба́|ть(ся), ю(сь) *impf. of* **прогну́ть(ся)**
прогла́|дить[1], **жу, дишь** *pf.* (*of* **~живать**) to iron (out).
прогла́|дить[2], **жу, дишь** *pf.* to iron (*for a certain time*).
прогла́жива|ть, ю *impf. of* **прогла́дить**[1]
прогла́тыва|ть, ю *impf. of* **проглоти́ть**
прогло|ти́ть, чу́, ~тишь *pf.* (*of* **прогла́тывать**) to swallow (*also fig.*); **п. язы́к** to lose one's tongue; **п. кни́гу** to devour a book; **язы́к ~тишь** it makes your mouth water.
прогля|де́ть[1], **жу́, ди́шь** *pf.* (*of* **~дывать**) to look through, skim through.
прогля|де́ть[2], **жу́, ди́шь** *pf.* to overlook.
прогля́дыва|ть, ю *impf. of* **прогляде́ть** *and* **прогляну́ть**
прогля|ну́ть, ~нет *pf.* (*of* **~дывать**) to appear, peep (out, through); **со́лнце ~ну́ло из-за облако́в** the sun peeped out from behind the clouds.
про|гна́ть, гоню́, го́нишь, *past* **~гна́л, ~гнала́, ~гна́ло** *pf.* (*of* **~гоня́ть**) **1.** to drive away (*also fig.*); (*fig.*) to banish; **п. с глаз доло́й** to banish from one's sight. **2.** to drive (through); **п. коро́в в по́ле** to drive the cows into the field. **3.** (*coll.*) to sack, fire.
прогнива́|ть, ю *impf. of* **прогни́ть**
прогн|и́ть, ию́, иёшь, *past* **~и́л, ~ила́, ~и́ло** *pf.* (*of* **~ива́ть**) to rot through.
прогно́з, а *m.* prognosis; forecast.
прогн|у́ть, у́, ёшь *pf.* (*of* **прогиба́ть**) to weigh down, cause to sag.
прогн|у́ться, у́сь, ёшься *pf.* (*of* **прогиба́ться**) to cave in, sag.
прогова́рива|ть(ся), ю(сь) *impf. of* **проговори́ть(ся)**
проговор|и́ть, ю́, и́шь *pf.* (*of* **прогова́ривать**) **1.** to say, utter; **п. сквозь зу́бы** to mutter. **2.** to speak, talk (*for a certain time*).
проговор|и́ться, ю́сь, и́шься *pf.* (*of* **прогова́риваться**) to blab (out); to let the cat out of the bag.
проголода́|ть, ю *pf.* to starve, go hungry.
проголода́|ться, юсь *pf.* to grow hungry.
проголос|ова́ть, у́ю *pf. of* **голосова́ть**
прого́н[1], **а** *m.* **1.** (*archit.*) purlin; (*of a bridge*) bearer, baulk. **2.** (*archit.*) well(-shaft).
прогоня́|ть, ю *impf. of* **прогна́ть**
прогор|а́ть, а́ю *impf. of* **~е́ть**[1]
прогор|е́ть, ю́, и́шь *pf.* (*of* **~а́ть**) **1.** to burn through; to burn to a cinder. **2.** (*coll.*) to go bankrupt, go bust.
прого́рклый *adj.* rancid.
прого́рк|нуть, ну, нешь, *past* **~, ~ла** *pf. of* **го́ркнуть**
програ́мм|а, ы *f.* programme; (*comput.*) application, program; **уче́бная п.** syllabus; curriculum.
программи́р|овать, ую *impf.* (*of* **за~**) to programme.
программи́ст, а *m.* (computer) programmer.
програ́мм|ный *adj.* **1.** *adj. of* **~а**; **~ная му́зыка** programme music; **~ное обеспе́чение** (*comput.*) software. **2.** (*tech.*) programmed.
прогрева́|ть(ся), ю(сь) *impf. of* **прогре́ть(ся)**
прогре́сс, а *m.* progress.
прогресси́в|ный (~ен, ~на) *adj.* progressive.
прогресси́р|овать, ую *impf.* to progress, make progress; (*of an illness*) to grow progressively worse.
прогре́сси|я, и *f.* (*math.*) progression.
прогре́|ть, ю *pf.* (*of* **~ва́ть**) to heat, warm up.
прогре́|ться, юсь *pf.* (*of* **~ва́ться**) to warm up.
прогу́л, а *m.* absence; truancy.
прогу́лива|ть, ю *impf.* **1.** *impf. of* **прогуля́ть**[1]. **2.** *impf. only* to walk; **п. ло́шадь** to walk a horse.
прогу́лива|ться, юсь *impf.* **1.** *impf. of* **прогуля́ться**. **2.** *impf. only* to stroll, saunter.
прогу́лк|а, и *f.* **1.** walk; stroll. **2.** outing; drive; ride.
прогу́л|очный *adj. of* **~ка**; **~очная зо́на** pedestrian precinct; **~очная ло́дка** pleasure-boat.
прогу́льщик, а *m.* absentee; truant.
прогуля́|ть[1], **ю** *pf.* (*of* **прогу́ливать**) **1.** to be absent from; to play truant. **2.** to miss; **п. обе́д** to miss one's dinner; **п. уро́ки** to skip lessons.
прогуля́|ть[2], **ю** *pf.* to walk; to stroll.
прогуля́|ться, юсь *pf.* (*of* **прогу́ливаться**) to take a walk, go for a stroll.
прод... *comb. form, abbr. of* **продово́льственный**
прода|ва́ть, ю́, ёшь *impf. of* **~ть**
прода|ва́ться, ю́сь, ёшься *impf.* **1.** (*impf. only*) to be on sale, be for sale. **2.** (*impf. only*) to sell; **дёшево п.** to sell cheap, go cheap; **его́ но́вый рома́н хорошо́ ~ётся** his new novel is selling well. **3.** *impf. of* **~ться**
продав|е́ц, ца́ *m.* **1.** seller; vendor. **2.** salesman, shop-assistant.
продав|и́ть, лю́, ~ишь *pf.* (*of* **~ливать**) to break (through); to crush.
прода́влива|ть, ю *impf. of* **продави́ть**
продавщи́ц|а, ы *f.* **1.** seller; vendor. **2.** saleswoman, shop-assistant.
прода́ж|а, и *f.* sale; **опто́вая п.** wholesale; **нет в ~е** out of stock; sold out; **п. по телефо́ну** telesales.
прода́жност|ь, и *f.* corruption; venality.
прода́ж|ный *adj.* **1.** sale; selling; **~ная цена́** selling price. **2. (~ен, ~на)** (*fig.*) corrupt; venal; **~ная же́нщина** streetwalker.
прода́лблива|ть, ю *impf. of* **продолби́ть**
прода́|ть, м, шь, ст, ди́м, ди́те, ду́т, *past* **про́дал, ~ла́, про́дало** *pf.* (*of* **~ва́ть**) **1.** to sell; **п. о́птом** to sell wholesale; **п. с торго́в** to auction; **п. в креди́т** to sell on credit. **2.** (*fig., pej.*) to sell out.
прода́|ться, мся, шься, стся, ди́мся, ди́тесь, ду́тся, *past* **~лся, ~ла́сь** *pf.* (*of* **~ва́ться**) to sell o.s.
продвига́|ть(ся), ю(сь) *impf. of* **продви́нуть(ся)**
продвиже́ни|е, я *nt.* **1.** advancement. **2.** (*mil.*; *fig.*) progress, advance.
продви́|нуть, ну, нешь *pf.* (*of* **~га́ть**) **1.** to move forward. **2.** (*fig.*) to promote, advance; **п. по слу́жбе** to promote; **п. де́ло** to expedite a matter.
продви́|нуться, нусь, нешься *pf.* (*of* **~га́ться**) **1.** to advance (*also fig.*); to move on, move forward; to push on; to forge ahead. **2.** to be promoted. **3.** *pass. of* **~нуть**

продева́|ть, ю *impf. of* **проде́ть**

продеклами́р|овать, ую *pf. of* **деклами́ровать**

проде́л|ать, аю *pf.* (*of* **~ывать**) **1.** to make (*a hole, etc.*). **2.** to do, perform, accomplish.

проде́лк|а, и *f.* trick; prank.

проде́лыва|ть, ю *impf. of* **проде́лать**

продемонстри́р|овать, ую *pf. of* **демонстри́ровать**

продёргива|ть, ю *impf. of* **продёрнуть**

продерж|а́ть, у́, ~́ишь *pf.* to hold (*for a certain time*); to keep (*for a certain time*).

продерж|а́ться, у́сь, ~́ишься *pf.* to hold out.

продёр|нуть, ну, нешь *pf.* (*of* **~гивать**) (*coll.*) **1.** to pass, run; **п. ни́тку в иго́лку** to thread a needle. **2.** (*fig.*) to tear to shreds (= *to criticize severely*).

проде́|ть, ну, нешь *pf.* (*of* **~ва́ть**) to pass, run; **п. ни́тку в иго́лку** to thread a needle.

продефили́р|овать, ую *pf. of* **дефили́ровать**

продешев|и́ть, лю́, и́шь *pf.* (*coll.*) to sell too cheap.

продикт|ова́ть, у́ю *pf. of* **диктова́ть**

продира́|ть(ся), ю(сь) *impf. of* **продра́ть(ся)**

продлева́|ть, ю *impf. of* **продли́ть**

продле́ни|е, я *nt.* extension, prolongation

продл|ённый *p.p.p. of* **~и́ть; шко́ла с ~ённым днём** extended-day school.

продл|и́ть, ю́, и́шь *pf.* (*of* **~ева́ть**) to extend, prolong; **п. срок де́йствия ви́зы** to extend a visa.

продл|и́ться, ю́сь, и́шься *pf. of* **дли́ться**

продма́г, а *m.* (*abbr. of* **продово́льственный магази́н**) grocer's (shop).

продово́льств|енный *adj. of* **~ие; ~енная ка́рточка** ration book, ration card; **п. магази́н** grocery (store); **~енные райо́ны** food-producing areas; **~енные това́ры** food-stuffs.

продово́льстви|е, я *nt.* food(-stuffs), provisions; (*mil.*) rations; **но́рма ~я** ration scale.

продолб|и́ть, лю́, и́шь *pf.* (*of* **прода́лбливать**) to make a hole (in), chisel through.

продолгова́т|ый (~, ~а) *adj.* oblong; **п. мозг** (*anat.*) medulla oblongata.

продолжа́тел|ь, я *m.* continuer.

продолж|а́ть, а́ю *impf.* **1.** to continue, go on; **п. рабо́тать** to go on working. **2.** *impf. of* **~́ить**

продолж|а́ться, а́ется *impf.* (*of* **~́иться**) to continue, last, go on; **восста́ние ~а́ется уже́ второ́й год** the insurrection is now in its second year.

продолже́ни|е, я *nt.* **1.** continuation; sequel; **п. сле́дует** to be continued. **2.** extension, prolongation; continuation. **3.**: **в п.** (+*g.*) in the course (of), during, for, throughout.

продолжи́тельност|ь, и *f.* duration, length.

продолжи́тел|ьный (~ен, ~ьна) *adj.* long; prolonged, protracted.

продо́лж|ить, у, ишь *pf.* (*of* **~а́ть**) to extend, prolong.

продо́лж|иться, усь, ишься *pf. of* **~а́ться**

продо́льн|ый *adj.* longitudinal; (*naut.*) fore-and-aft; **~ая ось** longitudinal axis; **~ая пила́** rip-saw.

продохн|у́ть, у́, ёшь *pf.* (*coll.*) to breathe freely.

про|дра́ть, деру́, дерёшь, *past* **~дра́л, ~драла́, ~дра́ло** *pf.* (*of* **~дира́ть**) (*coll.*) to tear; to wear holes (in); **п. глаза́** to open one's eyes.

про|дра́ться, деру́сь, дерёшься, *past* **~дра́лся, ~драла́сь, ~дра́ло́сь** *pf.* (*of* **~дира́ться**) (*coll.*) **1.** to tear; to be worn through. **2.** to squeeze through, force one's way through.

продро́г|нуть, ну, нешь, *past* **~, ~ла** *pf.* to be chilled to the marrow.

продува́|ть, ю *impf.* **1.** *impf. of* **проду́ть. 2.** (*impf. only*) to blow (*from all sides*); **прия́тно ~л ветеро́к** there was a pleasant breeze.

продувно́й *adj.* (*coll.*) crafty, sly.

проду́кт, а *m.* **1.** product; **побо́чный п.** by-product. **2.** *pl.* produce; food(-stuffs); **моло́чные ~ы** dairy produce; **натура́льные ~ы** wholefoods; **~ы се́льского хозя́йства** farm produce.

продукти́вност|ь, и *f.* productivity.

продукти́в|ный (~ен, ~на) *adj.* productive.

продукто́вый *adj.* food; **п. магази́н** grocery (store).

проду́кци|я, и *f.* production, output.

проду́ма|нный *p.p.p. of* **~ть** *and adj.* well thought-out, considered.

проду́м|ать, аю *pf.* (*of* **~ывать**) to think over; to think out.

проду́мыва|ть, ю *impf. of* **проду́мать**

проду́|ть, ю, ешь *pf.* (*of* **~ва́ть**) **1.** to blow through; (*tech.*) to blow through, blow out. **2.** (*impers.*+*a.*) to be in a draught; **придви́ньте стул, а то вас ~ет** bring your chair up, or else you will be in a draught.

продыря́в|ить, лю, ишь *pf.* (*of* **~ливать**) to make a hole (in), pierce.

продыря́в|иться, люсь, ишься *pf.* (*of* **~ливаться**) to become full of holes.

продыря́влива|ть(ся), ю(сь) *impf. of* **продыря́вить(ся)**

проеда́|ть, ю *impf. of* **прое́сть**

прое́зд, а *m.* **1.** passage, thoroughfare; **«~а нет!»** 'no thoroughfare!' **2.** journey.

прое́з|дить[1]**, жу, дишь** *pf.* (*of* **~жа́ть**) **1.** to exercise (*a horse, etc.*). **2.** (*coll.*) to spend on a journey; **мы ~дили сто рубле́й** we got through a hundred roubles on the journey.

прое́з|дить[2]**, жу, дишь** *pf.* to spend (*a certain time*) driving, riding, travelling; **они́ ~дили тро́е су́ток** they had travelled for three days and nights.

проездн|о́й *adj.* travelling; **п. биле́т** ticket; **~а́я пла́та** fare.

прое́здом *adv.* en route, while passing through.

проезжа́|ть, ю *impf. of* **прое́здить** *and* **прое́хать**

прое́зж|ий *adj.*: **~ая доро́га** thoroughfare; **~ие лю́ди** passers-by; *as n.* **п., ~его** *m.* passer-by.

прое́кт, а *m.* **1.** project, scheme, design. **2.** draft; **п. догово́ра** draft treaty.

проекти́р|овать[1]**, ую** *impf.* **1.** (*pf.* **за~** *and* **с~**) to project, plan, design; **п. но́вый теа́тр** to design a new theatre. **2.** *impf. only* (*fig.*) to plan; **мы ~уем уе́хать весно́й** we plan to go away in the spring.

проекти́р|овать[2]**, ую** *impf.* (*math.*) to project.

проектиро́вщик, а *m.* planner, designer.

прое́ктн|ый *adj.* **1.** planning; **~ое бюро́** planning office. **2.** designed; **~ая мо́щность** (*tech.*) rated capacity.

проекцио́нный *adj.*: **п. фона́рь** projector.

прое́кци|я, и *f.* projection.

проём, а *m.* (*archit.*) aperture; embrasure; **дверно́й п.** doorway.

прое́|сть, м, шь, ст, ди́м, ди́те, дя́т, *past* **~л** *pf.* (*of* **~да́ть**) **1.** to eat through; to corrode. **2.** (*coll.*) to spend on food.

прое́|хать, ду, дешь *pf.* (*of* **~зжа́ть**) **1.** to pass (by, through); to drive (by, through), ride (by, through). **2.** to pass, go (right) past (*inadvertently or by mistake*). **3.** to cover (*a certain distance*).

прое́|хаться, дусь, дешься *pf.* (*coll.*) to go for a drive, ride.

прожа́р|енный *p.p.p. of* **~ить** *and adj.* (*cul.*) well-done.

прожа́рива|ть, ю *impf. of* **прожа́рить**

прожа́р|ить, ю, ишь *pf.* (*of* **~ивать**) to fry, roast thoroughly.

прожд|а́ть, у́, ёшь, *past* **~а́л, ~ала́, ~а́ло** *pf.* (+*a. or g.*) to wait (for), spend (*a certain time*) waiting (for).

прож|ева́ть, у́ю, уёшь *pf.* (*of* **~ёвывать**) to chew well, thoroughly

прожёвыва|ть, ю *impf. of* **прожева́ть**

проже́кт, а *m.* (*coll., iron.*) (hair-brained) scheme.

прожектёр, а *m.* (*iron.*) schemer.
прожектёрств|о, а *nt.* (*iron.*) (hair-brained) scheming.
прожéктор, а, *pl.* **~ы** *and* **~á** *m.* searchlight; floodlight.
про|жéчь, жгу́, жжёшь, жгу́т, *past* **~жёг, ~жглá** *pf.* (*of* **~жигáть**) to burn through; **п. дыру́ в чём-н.** to burn a hole in sth.
про|жжённый *p.p.p. of* **~жéчь** *and adj.* (*coll.*) arch, double-dyed; **п. плут** arch-scoundrel.
прожива́|ть, ю *impf.* **1.** to live, reside. **2.** *impf. of* **прожи́ть**
прожива́|ться, юсь *impf. of* **прожи́ться**
прожига́|ть[1], ю *impf. of* **прожéчь**
прожига́|ть[2], ю *impf.*: **п. жизнь** to lead a fast life.
прожи́лк|а, и *f.* vein.
прожи́ти|е, я *nt.*: **на п.** to live on; **хватáет ли у них дéнег на п.?** have they enough to live on?
прожи́точный *adj.* sufficient to live on; **п. ми́нимум** living wage, subsistence wage.
про|жи́ть, живу́, живёшь, *past* **~́жил, ~́жилá, ~́жило** *pf.* (*of* **~живáть**) **1.** to live; **он ~́жил сто лет** he lived to be a hundred. **2.** to spend; **мы ~́жили мéсяц áвгуст на берегу́ мóря** we spent the month of August at the seaside. **3.** to spend, run through (*money*).
про|жи́ться, живу́сь, живёшься, *past* **~жи́лся, ~жилáсь** *pf.* (*of* **~живáться**) (*coll.*) to have spent all one's money, be spent up.
прожóрлив|ый (~, ~а) *adj.* voracious, gluttonous.
прожужж|áть, у́, и́шь *pf.* to buzz, drone, hum; **п. у́ши кому́-н.** (*coll.*) to drone on at s.o.
прóз|а, ы *f.* prose.
прозáик, а *m.* prose-writer.
прозаи́ческий *adj.* **1.** prose; **п. перевóд** prose translation. **2.** prosaic; matter-of-fact.
прозаи́ч|ный (~ен, ~на) *adj.* **1.** prosaic; matter-of-fact. **2.** (*fig.*) common-place, humdrum.
прозвáни|е, я *nt.* nickname.
про|звáть, зову́, зовёшь, *past* **~звáл, ~звалá, ~́звáло** *pf.* (*of* **~зывáть**) to nickname.
прóзвищ|е, я *nt.* nickname.
прозвон|и́ть, ю́, и́шь *pf.* **1.** to ring out, peal. **2.** to announce by ringing; **~и́ли обéд, ~и́ли обéдать** the bell (gong, *etc.*) went for dinner.
прозвуч|áть, и́т *pf. of* **звучáть**
прозевá|ть, ю *pf. of* **зевáть 3.**; (*coll.*) to miss.
прозели́т, а *m.* proselyte.
прозим|овáть, у́ю *pf. of* **зимовáть**
прозорли́вост|ь, и *f.* sagacity, perspicacity.
прозорли́в|ый (~, ~а) *adj.* sagacious, perspicacious.
прозрáчност|ь, и *f.* transparency.
прозрáч|ный (~ен, ~на) *adj.* transparent (*also fig.*); clear, limpid; **п. намёк** broad hint.
прозревá|ть, ю *impf. of* **прозрéть**
прозрéни|е, я *nt.* **1.** recovery of sight. **2.** (*fig.*) insight.
прозр|éть, ю́, и́шь *pf.* (*of* **~евáть**) **1.** to recover one's sight. **2.** (*fig.*) to see the light.
прозывá|ть, ю *impf. of* **прозвáть**
прозябá|ть, ю *impf.* to vegetate (*also fig.*).
прозя́б|нуть, ну, нешь, *past* **~, ~ла** *pf.* (*coll.*) to be chilled.
проигр|áть[1], áю *pf.* (*of* **~́ывать**) to lose; **п. судéбный процéсс** to lose a case.
проигр|áть[2], áю *pf.* (*of* **~́ывать**) to play (through, over).
проигр|áть[3], áю *pf.* to play (*for a certain time*).
проигр|áться, áюсь *pf.* (*of* **~́ываться**) to lose all one's money (*at gambling*); to be cleaned out.
прои́грывател|ь, я *m.* record-player; **п. компакт-ди́сков** CD player.
прои́грыва|ть(ся), ю(сь) *impf. of* **проигрáть(ся)**
прóигрыш, а *m.* loss; **остáться в ~е** to be the loser, come off loser
произведéни|е, я *nt.* **1.** work; **и́збранные ~я Л. Н. Толстóго** selected works of L. N. Tolstoy. **2.** (*math.*) product.
произве|сти́, ду́, дёшь, *past* **~́л, ~лá** *pf.* (*of* **производи́ть**) **1.** to make; to carry out; to execute; **п. вы́стрел** to fire a shot; **п. смотр** (+*d.*) to review. **2.** to give birth (to); **п. на свет** to bring into the world. **3.** (*fig.*) to cause, produce; **п. впечатлéние (на+*a.*)** to make an impression (on, upon); **п. сенсáцию** to cause a sensation. **4.** (**в**+*nom.-a.*) to promote (to, to the rank of).
производи́тел|ь[1], я *m.* **1.** producer. **2.** sire; **бык-п.** breeding bull.
производи́тел|ь[2], я *m.*: **п. рабóт** clerk of the works.
производи́тельност|ь, и *f.* productivity.
производи́тел|ьный (~ен, ~ьна) *adj.* productive.
произво|ди́ть, жу́, ~́дишь *impf.* **1.** *impf. of* **произвести́**. **2.** *impf. only* to produce.
произвóдн|ый *adj.* derivative; **~ое слóво** derivative; *as n.* **~ая, ~ой** *f.* (*math.*) derivative.
произвóдственник, а *m.* production worker.
произвóдств|енный *adj. of* **~о**; production; industrial.
произвóдств|о, а *nt.* **1.** production, manufacture; **срéдства ~а** means of production; **япóнского ~а** Japanese-made. **2.** factory, works. **3.** carrying-out, execution. **4.** (**в**+*nom.-a.*) promotion (to, to the rank of).
произвóл, а *m.* **1.** arbitrariness; **остáвить на п. судьбы́** to leave to the mercy of fate. **2.** arbitrary rule.
произвóльно *adv.* **1.** arbitrarily. **2.** at will.
произвóл|ьный (~ен, ~ьна) *adj.* arbitrary.
произнесéни|е, я *nt.* pronouncing; utterance, delivery.
произнес|ти́, у́, ёшь, *past* **~́, ~лá** *pf.* (*of* **произноси́ть**) **1.** to pronounce; to articulate. **2.** to pronounce, utter; **п. речь** to deliver a speech; **он не ~́ ни слóва** he did not utter a word.
произно|си́ть, шу́, ~́сишь *impf. of* **произнести́**
произношéни|е, я *nt.* pronunciation.
произо|йти́, йду́, йдёшь, *past* **~шёл, ~шлá** *pf.* (*of* **происходи́ть**) **1.** to happen, occur, take place. **2. (от, из-за)** to result (from); **авáрия ~шлá от небрéжности** the crash resulted from carelessness. **3. (из, от)** to come (from, of), be descended (from).
произраст|áть, áет *impf. of* **~и́**
произраст|и́, ёт, *past* **произрóс, произрослá** *pf.* (*of* **~áть**) to grow, sprout, spring up.
проиллюстри́р|овать, ую *pf.* (*of* **иллюстри́ровать**) to illustrate.
проинструкти́р|овать, ую *pf.* (*of* **инструкти́ровать**) to instruct, give instructions (to).
проинтервьюи́р|овать, ую *pf.* (*of* **интервьюи́ровать**) to interview.
проинформи́р|овать, ую *pf.* (*of* **информи́ровать**) to inform.
прóиск|и, ов *no sg.* intrigues; machinations.
проистекá|ть, ю *impf. of* **проистéчь**
проистé|чь, ку́, чёшь, ку́т, *past* **~́к, ~клá** *pf.* (*of* **~кáть**) **(из, от)** to spring (from), result (from).
происхо|ди́ть, жу́, ~́дишь *impf.* **1.** *impf. of* **произойти́**. **2.** *impf. only* to go on, be going on; **что тут ~́дит?** what is going on here?
происхождéни|е, я *nt.* origin; provenance; parentage, descent, extraction, birth; **он по ~ю армяни́н** he is (an) Armenian by birth.
происшéстви|е, я *nt.* event, incident, occurrence; accident.
пройдóх|а, и *c.g.* (*coll.*) creeper; scoundrel, rascal.
прóйм|а, ы *f.* armhole.
про|йти́, йду́, йдёшь, *past* **~шёл, ~шлá** *pf.* (*of*

~ходи́ть[1]) **1.** to pass (by, through); to go (by, through); **п. ми́мо** to pass by, go by, go past; (+*g.*; *fig.*) to overlook, disregard; **п. торже́ственным ма́ршем** to march past; **п. молча́нием** to pass over in silence; **п. по мосту́** to cross a bridge. **2.** to pass, go (right) past (*inadvertently or by mistake*). **3.** to do, make, cover (*a certain distance*); **п. две ты́сячи миль за неде́лю** to do two thousand miles in a week. **4.** (*of news, rumours, etc.*) to travel, spread. **5.** (*of rain, etc.*) to fall. **6.** (*of time*) to pass, elapse, go by; **~шёл це́лый год** a whole year had passed. **7.** to be over; to pass (off), abate, let up; **~шло́ ле́то** summer was over; **боль ~шла́** the pain passed (off). **8.** (+*a. or* **че́рез**) to pass, get through; **пье́са не ~шла́ че́рез цензу́ру** the play did not pass the censorship. **9.** to go, go off; **как ~шёл ваш докла́д?** how did your lecture go?; **заседа́ние ~шло́ уда́чно** the meeting went off successfully. **10.** (*coll.*) to do, take; **п. хи́мию** to do chemistry; **п. ку́рс лече́ния** to take a course of treatment.

про|йти́сь, йду́сь, йдёшься, *past* **~шёлся, ~шла́сь** *pf.* (*of* **~ха́живаться**) **1.** to walk up and down, stroll; to take a stroll; **п. по ко́мнате** to pace up and down the room. **2.** (*coll.*) to dance. **3.** (**по**+*d.*; *coll.*) to run (over), go (over); **п. по кла́вишам** to run one's fingers over the keys. **4.: п. на чей-н. счёт, п. по чьему́-н. а́дресу** (*coll.*) to give s.o. a bad write-up.

прок, а (у) *m.* (*coll.*) use, benefit; **что в э́том ~у?** what is the good of it?

прокажённ|ый *adj.* leprous; *as n.* **п., ~ого** *m.*, **~ая, ~ой** *f.* leper.

прока́з|а[1], ы *f.* leprosy.

прока́з|а[2], ы *f.* mischief, prank, trick.

прока́|зить, жу, зишь *impf.* (*of* **на~**) (*coll.*) to be up to mischief, play pranks.

прока́злив|ый (~, ~а) *adj.* mischievous.

прока́зник, а *m.* mischief-maker, prankster.

прока́знича|ть, ю *impf.* (*of* **на~**) = **прока́зить**

прока́лыва|ть, ю *impf. of* **проколо́ть**

проканите́л|ить(ся), ю(сь), ишь(ся) *pf. of* **каните́лить(ся)**

прока́пыва|ть, ю *impf. of* **прокопа́ть**

прока́т[1], а *m.* (*tech.*) **1.** rolling. **2.** rolled iron.

прока́т[2], а *m.* hire.

прока|ти́ть, чу́, ~тишь *pf.* (*of* **~тывать**) **1.** to take out; to take for a drive, ride. **2.** to roll. **3.** to roll by, past. **4.** (*coll.*) to slate.

прока|ти́ться, чу́сь, ~тишься *pf.* (*of* **~тываться**) **1.** to roll (*also fig., of thunder, etc.*). **2.** to go for a drive, go for a spin.

прока́тк|а, и *f.* (*tech.*) rolling (*of metal*).

прока́тн|ый[1] *adj.* (*tech.*) rolling; **п. стан** rolling mill.

прока́тный[2] *adj.* hired, let out on hire.

прока́тыва|ть(ся), ю(сь) *impf. of* **прокати́ть(ся)**

прока́шлива|ть(ся), ю(сь) *impf. of* **прока́шлять(ся)**

прока́шл|яться, яюсь *pf.* (*of* **~иваться**) to clear one's throat.

прокипя|ти́ть, чу́, ти́шь *pf.* to boil thoroughly.

прокис|а́ть, а́ет *impf. of* **~нуть**

прокис|нуть, нет *pf.* (*of* **~а́ть**) to turn (sour).

прокла́дк|а, и *f.* **1.** laying; building; **п. доро́ги** road building; **п. трубопрово́да** pipe laying. **2.** (*tech.*) washer, gasket; packing, padding.

прокла́дыва|ть, ю *impf. of* **проложи́ть**

проклама́ци|я, и *f.* (political) leaflet.

проклами́р|овать, ую *impf. and pf.* to proclaim.

прокле́ива|ть, ю *impf. of* **прокле́ить**

прокле́|ить, ю, ишь *pf.* (*of* **~ивать**) to paste, glue; to size.

проклина́|ть, ю *impf.* **1.** *impf. of* **прокля́сть. 2.** (*coll.*) to curse, swear at.

прокл|я́сть, яну́, янёшь, *past* **~ял, ~яла́, ~яло** *pf.* (*of* **~ина́ть**) to curse, damn.

прокля́ти|е, я *nt.* **1.** damnation; perdition. **2.** curse; imprecation. **3.** *as int.* **п.!** damn it!; damnation!

про́кл|ятый *p.p.p. of* **~я́сть; будь я ~ят, е́сли...** I'll be damned if ...; **будь он ~ят!** damn him!

прокля́тый *adj.* accursed, damned; (*coll.*) damnable, confounded.

проко́л, а *m.* **1.** puncture. **2.** pricking, piercing.

прокол|о́ть, ю́, ~ешь *pf.* (*of* **прока́лывать**) to prick, pierce; to perforate; **п. нары́в** to lance a boil; **п. ши́ну** to puncture a tyre.

прокомменти́р|овать, ую *pf.* to comment (upon).

прокомпости́р|овать, ую *pf. of* **компости́ровать**

проконспекти́р|овать, ую *pf. of* **конспекти́ровать**

прокóнсул, а *m.* (*hist.*) proconsul.

проконсульти́р|овать(ся), ую(сь) *pf. of* **консульти́ровать(ся).**

проконтроли́р|овать, ую *pf. of* **контроли́ровать**

прокопа́|ть, ю *pf.* (*of* **прока́пывать**) **1.** to dig. **2.** to dig through.

прокопте́лый *adj.* (*coll.*) sooty, soot-covered.

прокóрм, а *m.* nourishment, sustenance.

прокорм|и́ть(ся), лю́(сь), ~ишь(ся) *pf. of* **корми́ть(ся)**

прокорректи́р|овать, ую *pf. of* **корректи́ровать**

прокóс, а *m.* swath.

прокра́дыва|ться, юсь *impf. of* **прокра́сться**

прокра́|сться, ду́сь, дёшься *pf.* (*of* **~дываться**) to steal; **п. ми́мо** to steal by, past.

прокрич|а́ть, у́, и́шь *pf.* **1.** to shout, cry; to give a shout, raise a cry. **2.** (**о**+*p.*; *coll.*) to trumpet.

прокурату́р|а, ы *f.* office of public prosecutor.

прокурóр, а *m.* public prosecutor; counsel for the prosecution (*in criminal cases*); **речь ~а** speech for the prosecution.

прокурóр|ский *adj. of* **~**

проку|си́ть, шу́, ~сишь *pf.* (*of* **~сывать**) to bite through.

проку́сыва|ть, ю *impf. of* **прокуси́ть**

проку|ти́ть, чу́, ~тишь *pf.* (*of* **~чивать**) (*coll.*) **1.** to squander, dissipate. **2.** to go on a binge.

проку́чива|ть, ю *impf. of* **прокути́ть**

прола́га|ть, ю *impf. of* **проложи́ть**

прола́мыва|ть(ся), ю(сь) *impf. of* **пролома́ть(ся)** *and* **проломи́ть(ся)**

пролега́|ть, ет *impf.* (*of road, path, etc.*) to lie, run, pass.

пролеж|а́ть, у́, и́шь *pf.* (*of* **~ивать**) to lie; to spend (*a certain time*) lying; **посы́лка неде́лю ~а́ла на по́чте** the parcel lay for a week in the post office.

про́леж|ень, ня *m.* (*med.*) bedsore.

пролёжива|ть, ю *impf. of* **пролежа́ть**

пролез|а́ть, а́ю *impf. of* **~ть**

проле́з|ть, у, ешь, *past* **~, ~ла** *pf.* (*of* **~а́ть**) **1.** to get through, climb through. **2.** (**в**+*a.*; *fig., coll., pej.*) to worm o.s. (into, on to); **он ~в чле́ны комите́та** he has wormed his way on to the committee.

пролёт[1], а *m.* flight.

пролёт[2], а *m.* **1.** (*archit.*) bay; **п. мо́ста** span. **2.** stairwell. **3.** (*coll.*) stage (*distance between stations on rail.*).

пролетариа́т, а *m.* proletariat.

пролета́ри|й, я *m.* proletarian; **~и всех стран, соединя́йтесь!** workers of the world, unite!

пролета́рский *adj.* proletarian.

пролет|а́ть[1], а́ю *impf. of* **~е́ть**

пролет|а́ть[2], а́ю *pf.* to fly (*for a certain time*).

проле|те́ть, чу́, ти́шь *pf.* (*of* **~та́ть[1]**) **1.** to fly, cover (*a certain distance*). **2.** to fly (by, through, past) (*also fig.*); **кани́кулы ~те́ли** the holidays flew by. **3.** (*fig.*) to flash, flit.

пролётк|а, и *f.* droshky, (horse-)cab.

проли́в, а *m.* (*geog.*) strait, sound.

пролива́|ть, ю *impf. of* **проли́ть**

проливно́й *adj.*: **п. дождь** pouring rain.

проли́ти|е, я *nt.* shedding; **п. кро́ви** bloodshed.

прол|и́ть, ью́, ьёшь, *past* **∸ил, ~ила́, ∸ило** *pf.* (*of* **~ива́ть**) to spill, shed; **п. чью-н. кровь** to shed s.o.'s blood; **п. слёзы** (**по**+*d. or p.*, **о**+*p.*) to shed tears (over); **п. свет** (**на**+*a.*; *fig.*) to shed light (on).

проло́г, а *m.* prologue.

пролож|и́ть, у́, ∸ишь *pf.* (*of* **прокла́дывать**) **1.** (*impf. also* **пролага́ть**) to lay; to build, construct; **п. доро́гу** to build; (*fig.*) to pave the way; **п. себе́ доро́гу че́рез толпу́** to hack one's way through the crowd; **п. путь** (*fig.*) to pave the way; **п. но́вые пути́** (*fig.*) to blaze new trails. **2.** (**ме́жду** *or* +*a. and i.*) to interlay; to insert (between); **п. кни́гу бе́лыми листа́ми** to interleave a book.

проло́м, а *m.* **1.** breach, break. **2.** (*med.*) fracture.

пролома́|ть, ю *pf.* (*of* **прола́мывать**) to break (through); **п. лёд** to break the ice.

пролома́|ться, ется *pf.* (*of* **прола́мываться**) to break.

пролом|и́ть, лю́, ∸ишь *pf.* (*of* **прола́мывать**) to break (through); **п. дыру́** to make a hole; **п. себе́ че́реп** to fracture one's skull.

пролом|и́ться, ∸ится *pf.* (*of* **прола́мываться**) to break (down); give way.

пром... *comb. form, abbr. of* **промы́шленный**

прома́|зать[1]**, жу, жешь** *pf.* (*of* **~зывать**) to smear thoroughly; to oil thoroughly.

прома́|зать[2]**, жу, жешь** *pf. of* **ма́зать 5.**

прома́ргива|ть, ю *impf. of* **проморга́ть**

промарин|ова́ть, у́ю *pf.* (*of* **марино́ва́ть**) (*coll.*) to delay, hold up, shelve.

прома́слива|ть, ю *impf. of* **прома́слить**

прома́сл|ить, ю, ишь *pf.* (*of* **~ивать**) to oil, treat with oil, grease.

прома́тыва|ть, ю *impf. of* **промота́ть**

про́мах, а *m.* miss; (*fig.*) slip, blunder; **он ма́лый не п.** (*coll.*) he's nobody's fool.

прома́хива|ться, юсь *impf. of* **промахну́ться**

промах|ну́ться, ну́сь, нёшься *pf.* (*of* **∸иваться**) to miss; (*fig., coll.*) to (make a) blunder.

прома́чива|ть, ю *impf. of* **промочи́ть**

промедле́ни|е, я *nt.* delay; procrastination.

проме́дл|ить, ю, ишь *pf.* to delay; to procrastinate.

проме́жност|ь, и *f.* (*anat.*) perineum.

промежу́т|ок, ка *m.* interval; space.

промежу́точный *adj.* intermediate (*also fig.*); intervening; interim.

промелькн|у́ть, у́, ёшь *pf.* **1.** to flash; (*of time*) to fly by; **п. в голове́** to flash through one's mind. **2.** to be faintly perceptible.

проме́нива|ть, ю *impf. of* **променя́ть**

промен|я́ть, я́ю *pf.* (*of* **∸ивать**) (**на**+*a.*) to exchange (for), trade (for), barter (for).

промерз|а́ть, а́ю *impf. of* **∸нуть**

промёрзлый *adj.* frozen.

промёрз|нуть, ну, нешь, *past* **~, ~ла** *pf.* (*of* **~а́ть**) to freeze through.

проме́рива|ть, ю *impf. of* **проме́рить**

проме́р|ить, ю, ишь *pf.* (*of* **~ивать** *and* **~я́ть**) to measure; to survey; to sound.

промер|я́ть, я́ю *impf.* = **∸ивать**

проме́шка|ть, ю *pf.* (*coll.*) to linger, dawdle.

промо́зглый *adj.* dank.

промока́тельн|ый *adj.*: **~ая бума́га** blotting-paper.

промок|а́ть[1]**, а́ю** *impf.* **1.** *impf. of* **∸нуть. 2.** *impf. only* to not be waterproof; **э́ти боти́нки ~а́ют** these boots are not waterproof. **3.** *impf. only* to absorb ink.

промок|а́ть[2]**, а́ю** *impf. of* **~ну́ть**

промока́шк|а, и *f.* (*coll.*) blotting-paper.

промо́к|нуть, ну, нешь *pf.* (*of* **~а́ть**[1]) to get soaked, get drenched.

промок|ну́ть, ну, нёшь *pf.* (*of* **~а́ть**[2]) (*coll.*) to blot.

промо́лв|ить, лю, ишь *pf.* to say, utter.

промолч|а́ть, у́, и́шь *pf.* to keep silent, say nothing.

проморга́|ть, ю *pf.* (*of* **прома́ргивать**) (*coll.*) to miss, overlook; **п. удо́бный слу́чай** to miss an opportunity, let a chance slip.

промота́|ть, ю *pf.* (*of* **мота́ть**[2] *and* **прома́тывать**) to squander.

промоч|и́ть, у́, ∸ишь *pf.* (*of* **прома́чивать**) to get wet (through); to soak, drench; **п. но́ги** to get one's feet wet; **п. го́рло** (*coll.*) to wet one's whistle.

промтова́р|ный *adj. of* **~ы; п. магази́н** shop selling manufactured goods.

промтова́р|ы, ов *no sg.* manufactured goods.

промч|а́ться, у́сь, и́шься *pf.* **1.** to tear (by, past, through); **п. стрело́й** to dart (by, past), flash (by, past). **2.** (*fig.*; *of time*) to fly (by).

промыва́ни|е, я *nt.* washing (out); (*med.*) bathing, irrigation.

промыва́|ть, ю *impf. of* **промы́ть**

про́мыс|ел, ла *m.* **1.** hunting, catching; **охо́тничий п.** hunting; game-shooting; **пушно́й п.** trapping; **ры́бный п.** fishing. **2.** trade, business; **го́рный п.** mining; **куста́рный п.** cottage industry; **пушно́й п.** fur trade. **3.** *pl.* fields; mines; **нефтяны́е ~лы** oil-fields; **соляны́е ~лы** salt-mines.

про́мысл, а *m.* (*relig.*) Providence.

промысло́в|ый *adj.* **1.** *adj. of* **про́мысел 1.; ~ые пти́цы** game-birds. **2.** *adj. of* **про́мысел 2., 3.; ~ая коопера́ция** producers' co-operative; **п. нало́г** business tax; **~ая ры́ба** marketable fish.

пром|ы́ть, о́ю, о́ешь *pf.* (*of* **~ыва́ть**) **1.** to wash well, thoroughly; **п. мозги́** (+*d.*) to brain-wash. **2.** (*med.*) to bathe. **3.** (*tech.*) to wash; to scrub (*gas*).

промы́шленник, а *m.* manufacturer, industrialist.

промы́шленност|ь, и *f.* industry.

промы́шленный *adj.* industrial.

промышля́|ть, ю *impf.* **1.** (+*i.*) to earn one's living (by). **2.** to hunt; to trade (in).

промя́мл|ить, ю, ишь *pf. of* **мя́млить 1.**

прона́шива|ть(ся), ю(сь) *impf. of* **пронос́ить(ся)**[1]

пронес|ти́, у, ёшь, *past* **∸̈, ~ла́** *pf.* (*of* **проноси́ть**[3]) to carry (by, past, through).

пронес|ти́сь, у́сь, ёшься, *past* **∸̈ся, ~ла́сь** *pf.* (*of* **проноси́ться**[2]) **1.** to rush (by, past, through). **2.** (*fig.*) to fly by. **3.** (*of rumours, etc.*) to spread.

пронз|а́ть, а́ю *impf. of* **~и́ть**

пронзи́тел|ьный (~ен, ~ьна) *adj.* piercing; (*of sounds*) shrill, strident; **п. взгляд** penetrating glance; **~ьным го́лосом** in a shrill voice.

прон|зи́ть, жу́, зи́шь *pf.* (*of* **~за́ть**) to pierce, run through; **п. взгля́дом** to pierce with a glance.

прони|за́ть, жу́, ∸жешь *pf.* (*of* **∸зывать**) to pierce; to permeate, penetrate; (*fig.*) to run through; **одна́ иде́я ~за́ла все его́ произведе́ния** one idea ran through all his works.

прони́зыва|ть, ю *impf. of* **прониза́ть**

прони́зыва|ющий *pres. part. act. of* **~ть** *and adj.* piercing, penetrating.

проник|а́ть, а́ю *impf. of* **∸нуть**

проникнове́ни|е, я *nt.* **1.** penetration. **2.** = **проникнове́нность**

проникнове́нност|ь, и *f.* feeling; heartfelt conviction; **говори́ть с ~ью** to speak with feeling.

проникнове́н|ный (~ен, ~на) *adj.* full of feeling; heartfelt.

прони́кнут|ый (~, ~а) *adj.* (+*i.*) imbued (with), full (of).

прони́к|нуть, ну, нешь, *past* **~, ~ла** *pf.* (*of* **~а́ть**) (**в**+*a.*) to penetrate (*also fig.*); (**че́рез**) to percolate (through); **п. в чьи-н. наме́рения** to fathom s.o.'s designs; **п. в суть де́ла** to get to the bottom of the matter.

пронима́|ть, ю *impf. of* **проня́ть**

проница́емост|ь, и *f.* permeability.
проница́ем|ый (~, ~а) *adj.* permeable.
проница́тельност|ь, и *f.* perspicacity; insight, acumen, shrewdness.
проница́тел|ьный (~ен, ~ьна) *adj.* perspicacious; astute, shrewd; penetrating, piercing.
проно|си́ть[1], шу́, ≁сишь *pf.* (*of* **прона́шивать**) to wear out, wear to shreds.
проно|си́ть[2], шу́, ≁сишь *pf.* to wear (*for a certain time*).
проно|си́ть[3], шу́, ≁сишь *impf. of* **пронести́**
проно|си́ться[1], ≁сится *pf.* (*of* **прона́шиваться**) to wear through, wear to shreds.
проно|си́ться[2], шу́сь, ≁сишься *impf. of* **пронести́сь**
проны́р|а, ы *c.g.* (*coll.*) string-puller.
проны́рлив|ый (~, ~а) *adj.* wily, sharp.
пронюх|ать, аю *pf.* (*of* **~ивать**) (*coll.*) to nose out, get wind (of).
пронюхива|ть, ю *impf. of* **пронюхать**
про|ня́ть, йму́, ймёшь, *past* **≁нял, ~няла́, ≁няло** *pf.* (*of* **~нима́ть**) (*coll.*) **1.** to penetrate. **2.** (*fig.*) to get at; **ничем не ~ймёшь** you can't get through to him.
прообраз, а *m.* prototype.
пропага́нд|а, ы *f.* propaganda; promotion.
пропаганди́р|овать, ую *impf.* to propagandize.
пропаганди́ст, а *m.* propagandist.
пропаганди́ст|ский *adj. of* **~**
пропада́|ть, ю *impf. of* **пропа́сть**
пропа́ж|а, и *f.* **1.** loss. **2.** lost object, missing object.
пропа́лыва|ть, ю *impf. of* **пропо́лоть**
пропа́н, а *m.* propane.
про́паст|ь, и *f.* **1.** precipice (*also fig.*); abyss; **на краю́ ~и** (*fig.*) on the brink of disaster. **2.** (*coll.*) loads (of), stacks (of); **у него́ п. де́нег** he has stacks of money.
пропа́|сть ду́, дёшь, *past* **~л** *pf.* (*of* **~да́ть**) **1.** to be missing; to be lost; **п. бе́з вести** (*mil.*) to be missing; **пиши́ ~ло** (*coll.*) it is as good as lost. **2.** to disappear, vanish; **куда́ вы ~ли?** where did you vanish to? **3.** to be lost, be done for; (*of flowers, etc.*) to die; **~ди́ про́падом!** (*coll.*) to hell with it! **4.** to be wasted; **п. да́ром** to go to waste.
пропа́х|нуть, ну, нешь, *past* **~, ~ла** *pf.* to become permeated with the smell (of).
пропа́щ|ий *adj.* (*coll.*) hopeless; good-for-nothing; **он п. челове́к** he's a hopeless case.
пропека́|ть(ся), ю(сь) *impf. of* **пропе́чь(ся)**
пропе́ллер, а *m.* propeller.
проп|е́ть[1], ою́, оёшь *pf. of* **петь**
проп|е́ть[2], ою́, оёшь *pf.* to sing (*for a certain time*).
пропе́|чь, ку́, чёшь, ку́т, *past* **≁к, ~кла́** *pf.* (*of* **~ка́ть**) to bake well, thoroughly.
пропе́|чься, ку́сь, чёшься, ку́тся, *past* **≁кся, ~кла́сь** *pf.* (*of* **~ка́ться**) to bake well, get baked through.
пропива́|ть, ю *impf. of* **пропи́ть**
пропи́лива|ть, ю *impf. of* **пропили́ть**
пропил|и́ть, ю́, ≁ишь *pf.* (*of* **≁ивать**) to saw through.
пропи|са́ть, шу́, ≁шешь *pf.* (*of* **≁сывать**) **1.** to prescribe. **2.** to register; **п. па́спорт** to stamp a passport.
пропи|са́ться, шу́сь, ≁шешься *pf.* (*of* **≁сываться**) to register (*intrans.*).
пропи́ск|а, и *f.* **1.** registration; **п. па́спорта** stamping of a passport. **2.** residence permit.
прописн|о́й *adj.* **1.** (*of letters of the alphabet*) capital; **писа́ться с п. бу́квы** to be written with a capital letter. **2.** commonplace, trivial; **~а́я и́стина** truism; **~а́я мора́ль** copy-book ethics.
пропи́сыва|ть(ся), ю(сь) *impf. of* **прописа́ть(ся)**
про́пис|ь, и *f.* **1.** *usu. pl.* sample(s) of writing. **2.** (*fig., pej.*) platitude.
про́писью *adv.* in words, in full.
пропита́ни|е, я *nt.* subsistence; sustenance; **зарабо́тать себе́ на п.** to earn one's living.
пропит|а́ть, а́ю *pf.* (*of* **≁ывать**) **1.** to keep, provide (for). **2.** (*+i.*) to impregnate (with), saturate (with), soak (in), steep (in); **п. ма́слом** to oil.
пропит|а́ться, а́юсь *pf.* (*of* **≁ываться**) **1.** (*+i.*) to become saturated (with). **2.** *pass. of* **~а́ть**
пропи́тыва|ть(ся), ю(сь) *impf. of* **пропита́ть(ся)**
про|пи́ть, пью́, пьёшь, *past* **≁пил, ~пила́, ≁пило** *pf.* (*of* **~пива́ть**) **1.** to spend on drink, squander on drink. **2.** (*coll.*) to ruin (*through excessive drinking*).
пропла́ва|ть, ю *pf.* to swim (*for a certain time*); to sail (*for a certain time*).
пропла́|кать, чу, чешь *pf.* to cry, weep (*for a certain time*); **п. глаза́** (*coll.*) to cry one's eyes out.
проплыва́|ть, ю *impf. of* **проплы́ть**
проплы́|ть, ву́, вёшь, *past* **~л, ~ла́, ~ло** *pf.* (*of* **~ва́ть**) **1.** to swim (by, past, through); to sail (by, past, through); to float, drift (by, past, through); (*fig., joc.*) to sail (by, past). **2.** to cover (*a certain distance*).
пропове́дник, а *m.* **1.** preacher. **2.** (*+g.; fig.*) advocate (of).
пропове́д|овать, ую *impf.* **1.** to preach. **2.** (*fig.*) to advocate, propagate.
про́поведь|ь, и *f.* **1.** sermon; homily. **2.** (*+g.; fig.*) advocacy (of), propagation (of).
пропо́йц|а, ы *m.* (*coll.*) drunkard.
пропола́скива|ть, ю *impf. of* **прополоска́ть**
прополз|а́ть, а́ю *impf. of* **~ти́**
прополз|ти́, у́, ёшь, *past* **~, ~ла́** *pf.* (*of* **~а́ть**) to creep, crawl (by, past, through).
пропо́лк|а, и *f.* weeding.
прополо|ска́ть, щу́, ≁щешь *pf.* (*of* **пропола́скивать**) to rinse, swill; **п. го́рло** to gargle.
пропол|о́ть, ю́, ≁ешь *pf.* (*of* **пропа́лывать**) to weed.
пропорциона́льност|ь, и *f.* proportionality; proportion; **обра́тная п.** inverse proportion.
пропорциона́л|ьный (~ен, ~ьна) *adj.* **1.** proportional; proportionate; **~ьное представи́тельство** proportional representation. **2.** well-proportioned.
пропо́рци|я, и *f.* proportion; ratio.
пропоте́|ть, ю *pf.* **1.** to sweat profusely. **2.** to be soaked in sweat.
про́пуск, а *m.* **1.** *no pl.* admission. **2.** (*pl.* **~а́**) pass, permit. **3.** (*pl.* **~а́**) (*mil.*) password. **4.** (*pl.* **~и**) (*+g.*) non-attendance (at), absence (from). **5.** (*pl.* **~и**) blank, gap.
пропуска́|ть, ю *impf.* **1.** *impf. of* **пропусти́ть. 2.** *impf. only* to let pass; **п. во́ду** to leak; **не п. воды́** to be waterproof.
пропускн|о́й *adj.*: **~а́я бума́га** blotting-paper; **~а́я спосо́бность** capacity.
пропу|сти́ть, щу́, ≁стишь *pf.* (*of* **~ска́ть**) **1.** to let pass, let through; to let in, admit; to take, have a capacity (of). **2.** **(че́рез)** to run (through), pass (through); **п. че́рез фильтр** to filter. **3.** to omit, leave out; (*in reading*) to skip. **4.** to miss; to let slip; **п. ле́кцию** to miss a lecture; **п. удо́бный слу́чай** to miss an opportunity.
пропылесо́с|ить, ю, ишь *pf. of* **пылесо́сить**
пропых|те́ть, чу́, ти́шь *pf. of* **пыхте́ть**
проpа́б, а *m.* (*abbr. of* ***производи́тель рабо́т***) clerk of the works, work superintendent.
прораба́тыва|ть, ю *impf. of* **прорабо́тать[1]**
прорабо́та|ть[1], ю *pf.* (*of* **прораба́тывать**) (*coll.*) **1.** to work (at), study; to mug up. **2.** to slate, pick holes (in).
прорабо́та|ть[2], ю *pf.* to work (*for a certain time*).
прорабо́тк|а, и *f.* **1.** study, studying. **2.** slating.
прораста́ни|е, я *nt.* germination; sprouting.
прораст|а́ть, а́ет *impf. of* **~и́**

прораст|и́, ёт, *past* **проро́с, проросла́** *pf.* (*of* **~а́ть**) to germinate, sprout, shoot (*of plant*).
про́рв|а, ы *f.* (*coll.*) **1.** (*+g.*) masses (of), heaps (of). **2.** glutton.
прорв|а́ть, у́, ёшь, *past* **~а́л, ~ала́, ~а́ло** *pf.* (*of* **прорыва́ть**) to break through; to tear, make a hole (in); **п. блока́ду** to run the blockade; (*impers.*): **~а́ло плоти́ну** the dam has burst; **я ~а́л носо́к** I have a hole in my sock.
прорв|а́ться, у́сь, ёшься, *past* **~а́лся, ~ала́сь, ~ало́сь** *pf.* (*of* **прорыва́ться**) **1.** to break, burst (open). **2.** to tear. **3.** to break (out, through); to force one's way (through).
проре́з, а *m.* cut; slit, notch; **ме́лкий п.** nick.
проре́|зать, жу, жешь *pf.* (*of* **~зывать** *and* **~за́ть**) to cut through (*also fig.*).
проре́|заться, жется *pf.* (*of* **ре́заться, ~зываться** *and* **~за́ться**) (*of teeth*) to cut, come through; **у неё уже́ ~зались зу́бы** she has already cut her teeth.
прорез|а́ть(ся), а́ю(сь) *impf. of* **∠ать(ся)**
прорези́нива|ть, ю *impf. of* **прорези́нить**
прорези́н|ить, ю, ишь *pf.* (*of* **~ивать**) to rubberize.
проре́зыва|ть(ся), ю(сь) *impf. of* **проре́зать(ся)**
про́рез|ь, и *f.* opening, aperture.
прорепети́р|овать, ую *impf. of* **репети́ровать**
проре́х|а, и *f.* **1.** tear. **2.** (*fig., coll.*) gap, deficiency.
прорецензи́р|овать, ую *pf. of* **рецензи́ровать**
проржа́ве|ть, ет *pf.* to rust through.
прорица́ни|е, я *nt.* soothsaying, prophecy.
прорица́тел|ь, я *m.* soothsayer, prophet.
прорица́|ть, ю *impf.* to prophesy.
проро́к, а *m.* prophet.
пророн|и́ть, ю́, ∠ишь *pf.* to utter; **он не ~и́л ни зву́ка** he did not utter a sound.
проро́ческий *adj.* prophetic, oracular.
проро́честв|о, а *nt.* prophecy, oracle.
проро́ч|ить, у, ишь *impf.* (*of* **на~**) to prophesy.
проруб|а́ть, а́ю *impf. of* **~и́ть**
проруб|и́ть, лю́, ∠ишь *pf.* (*of* **~а́ть**) to hack through, cut through, hew through.
про́руб|ь, и *f.* ice-hole.
проры́в, а *m.* **1.** break; (*mil.*) break-through, breach. **2.** (*fig.*) hitch, hold-up; **по́лный п.** breakdown.
прорыва́|ть[1]**, ю** *impf. of* **прорва́ть**
прорыва́|ть[2]**, ю** *impf. of* **проры́ть**
прорыва́|ться, юсь *impf. of* **прорва́ться**
прор|ы́ть, о́ю, о́ешь *pf.* (*of* **~ыва́ть**[2]) to dig through.
проса́лива|ть[1]**, ю** *impf. of* **проса́лить**
проса́лива|ть[2]**, ю** *impf. of* **просоли́ть**
проса́л|ить, ю, ишь *pf.* (*of* **~ивать**[1]) to grease.
проса́чивани|е, я *nt.* **1.** percolation; oozing, exudation. **2.** (*fig.*) leakage; infiltration.
проса́чива|ться, юсь *impf. of* **просочи́ться**
просве́рлива|ть, ю *impf. of* **просверли́ть**
просверл|и́ть, ю́, и́шь *pf.* (*of* **∠ивать**) to drill, bore; to perforate, pierce.
просве́т, а *m.* **1.** shaft of light; (*fig.*) ray of hope. **2.** (*archit.*) light; aperture, opening.
просвети́тельн|ый *adj.* educational.
просве|ти́ть[1]**, щу́, ти́шь** *pf.* (*of* **~ща́ть**) to educate; to enlighten.
просве|ти́ть[2]**, чу́, ∠тишь** *pf.* (*of* **∠чивать**[1]) (*med.*) to X-ray.
просветле́ни|е, я *nt.* **1.** (*of weather*) clearing up, brightening up. **2.** (*fig.*) lucid interval.
просветл|ённый *p.p.p. of* **~и́ть** *and adj.* (*fig.*) clear, lucid.
просветле́|ть, ю *pf.* **1.** (*of weather*) to brighten up. **2.** (*fig.*) to brighten; **п. от ра́дости** to light up with joy. **3.** (*fig.*; *of consciousness, etc.*) to become lucid.
просветл|и́ть, ю́, и́шь *pf.* (*of* **~я́ть**) to clarify.
просветл|я́ть, я́ю *impf. of* **~и́ть**
просве́чива|ть[1]**, ю** *impf. of* **просвети́ть**[2]
просве́чива|ть[2]**, ю** *impf.* **1.** to be translucent. **2.** **(че́рез, сквозь)** to show (through), appear (through); to shine (through); **шрам ~л че́рез её чуло́к** the scar showed through her stocking.
просвеща́|ть, ю *impf. of* **просвети́ть**[1]
просвеще́ни|е, я *nt.* **1.** education; **наро́дное п.** public education. **2.** enlightenment; **эпо́ха П~я** (*hist.*) the Age of the Enlightenment.
просве|щённый *p.p.p. of* **~ти́ть**[1] *and adj.* enlightened; educated, cultured.
просвир|а́, ы́, *pl.* **про́свиры, просви́р, просвира́м** *f.* (*eccl.*) (communion) bread; host.
просвирня́к, а́ *m.* (*bot.*) marsh mallow.
просви|сте́ть, щу́, сти́шь *pf.* **1.** to whistle; **п. мело́дию** to whistle a tune. **2.** to give a whistle; to whistle (by, past).
про́сед|ь, и *f.* streak(s) of grey.
просе́ива|ть, ю *impf. of* **просе́ять**
про́сек|а, и *f.* cutting (*in a forest*).
просёл|ок, ка *m.* country road, cart-track.
просе́|ять, ю, ешь *pf.* (*of* **~ивать**) to sift.
просигнализи́р|овать, ую *pf. of* **сигнализи́ровать**
проси|де́ть[1]**, жу́, ди́шь** *pf.* (*of* **∠живать**) to sit (*for a certain time*); **п. ночь у посте́ли больно́го** to sit up all night with a patient.
проси|де́ть[2]**, жу́, ди́шь** *pf.* (*of* **∠живать**) to wear out the seat (of); to wear into holes (*by sitting*).
проси́жива|ть, ю *impf. of* **просиде́ть**
про́син|ь, и *f.* (*coll.*) bluish tint.
проси́тел|ь, я *m.* applicant; petitioner.
проси́тельный *adj.* pleading.
про|си́ть, шу́, ∠сишь *impf.* (*of* **по~**) **1.** (*+a. of person asked*; *+a. or g. of thing sought, or* **о**+*p.*) to ask (for), beg; **~шу́ (вас)** please; **п. кого́-н. о по́мощи** to ask s.o. for help; **п. разреше́ния** to ask permission; **п. сове́та** to ask (for) advice; **п. извине́ния у кого́-н.** to apologize to s.o. **2.** **(за**+*a.*) to intercede (for). **3.** to invite; **вас ∠сят к столу́** please to take your places at the table; **«∠сят не кури́ть»** 'no smoking'.
про|си́ться, шу́сь, ∠сишься *impf.* (*of* **по~**) **1.** (*+inf. or* **в**+*a.*, **на**+*a.*) to ask (for); to apply (for); **п. в о́тпуск** to apply for leave. **2.** (*fig., coll.*) to ask (for); **п. с языка́** to be on the tip of one's tongue; **зака́т так и ~си́лся на карти́ну** the sunset was just asking to be painted.
просия́|ть, ю *pf.* **1.** (*of the sun*) to begin to shine. **2.** **(от)** to beam (with), light up (with); **она́ ~ла от сча́стья** she beamed with joy; **лицо́ у него́ ~ло** his face lit up.
проска|ка́ть, чу́, ∠чешь *pf.* to gallop (by, past).
проска́кива|ть, ю *impf. of* **проскочи́ть**
проска́льзыва|ть, ю *impf. of* **проскользну́ть**
просквоз|и́ть, и́т *pf.* (*impers.*; *coll.*): **меня́,** *etc.*, **~и́ло** I, *etc.*, have caught a chill from being in a draught.
проскло́ня|ть, ю *pf. of* **склоня́ть**[2]
проскользн|у́ть, у́, ёшь *pf.* (*of* **проска́льзывать**) (*coll.*) to slip in, creep in (*also fig.*); **~у́ло мно́го оши́бок** many errors have crept in.
проскоч|и́ть, у́, ∠ишь *pf.* (*of* **проска́кивать**) **1.** to rush by, tear by. **2.** **(че́рез)** to slip (through). **3.** **(сквозь, ме́жду)** to fall (through, between). **4.** (*fig., coll.*) to slip in, creep in; **~и́ло не́сколько оши́бок** a few errors crept in.
проскрип|е́ть, лю́, и́шь *pf.* **1.** *pf. of* **скрипе́ть. 2.** (*coll.*) to creak along.
проскурня́к, а́ *m.* (*bot.*) marsh mallow.
проскуча́|ть, ю *pf.* to have a dull, boring time; **мы ~ли всю неде́лю** we had a dull week.
просла́б|ить, ит *pf. of* **сла́бить**
просла́в|ить, лю, ишь *pf.* (*of* **~ля́ть**) to glorify; to bring glory (to); to make famous.

прослáв|иться, люсь, ишься *pf.* (*of* **~ля́ться**) (*+i.*) to become famous (for).
прославлéни|е, я *nt.* glorification; apotheosis.
прослáв|ленный *p.p.p. of* **~ить** *and adj.* renowned, celebrated.
прославля́|ть(ся), ю(сь) *impf. of* **прослáвить(ся)**
просле|ди́ть, жу́, ди́шь *pf.* (*of* **∸живать**) **1.** to track (down). **2.** to trace (through); to trace back.
прослéд|овать, ую *pf.* to proceed, go in state.
прослéжива|ть, ю *impf. of* **проследи́ть**
просле|зи́ться, жу́сь, зи́шься *pf.* to shed a few tears.
прослóйк|а, и *f.* **1.** layer, stratum (*also fig.*). **2.** (*geol.*) seam, streak.
прослуж|и́ть, у́, ∸ишь *pf.* **1.** to work, serve (*for a certain time*). **2.** to last (*for a certain time*).
прослу́ш|ать, аю *pf.* **1.** (*impf.* **слу́шать**) to hear (through); **п. курс лéкций** to attend a course of lectures. **2.** (*impf.* **~ивать**) (*med.*) to listen to; **п. чьё-н. сéрдце** to listen to s.o.'s heart. **3.** (*impf.* **~ивать**) (*coll.*) to miss, not to catch; **прости́те, я ~ал, что вы сказáли** I am sorry, I did not catch what you said.
прослу́шива|ть, ю *impf. of* **прослу́шать**
прослы́|ть, ву́, вёшь, *past* **~л, ~лá, ∸ло** *pf.* (*+i.*) to pass (for), be reputed.
прослы́ш|ать, у, ишь *pf.* (*coll.*) to find out, hear.
просмáтрива|ть, ю *impf. of* **просмотрéть**
просмóтр, а *m.* survey; viewing; **п. докумéнтов** examination of papers; **предвари́тельный п.** preview.
просмотр|éть, ю́, ∸ишь *pf.* (*of* **просмáтривать**) **1.** to survey; to view. **2.** to look over, look through; to glance over, glance through; **п. ру́копись** to glance through a manuscript. **3.** to overlook, miss.
прос|ну́ться, ну́сь, нёшься *pf.* (*of* **~ыпáться**[1]) to wake up, awake.
прóс|о, а *nt.* millet.
просóвыва|ть(ся), ю(сь) *impf. of* **просу́нуть(ся)**
просоди́ческий *adj.* (*liter.*) prosodic.
просóди|я, и *f.* (*liter.*) prosody.
просол|и́ть, ю́, ∸ишь *pf.* (*of* **просáливать**[2]) to salt; **п. мя́со** to corn meat.
просóх|нуть, ну, нешь, *past* **~, ~ла** *pf.* (*of* **просыхáть**) to get dry, dry out.
просоч|и́ться, и́тся *pf.* (*of* **просáчиваться**) **1.** to percolate; to filter; to leak; to seep out. **2.** (*fig.*) to filter through; to leak out; **~и́лись свéдения о поражéнии** news of the defeat filtered through.
просп|áть[1]**, лю́, и́шь,** *past* **~áл, ~алá, ~áло** *pf.* (*of* **просыпáть**[2]) **1.** to oversleep. **2.** to miss, pass (*due to being asleep*).
просп|áть[2]**, лю́, и́шь,** *past* **~áл, ~алá, ~áло** *pf.* to sleep (*for a certain time*).
просп|áться, лю́сь, и́шся, *past* **~áлся, ~алáсь, ~áлось** *pf.* (*coll.*) to sleep it off (*sc. one's drunkenness*).
проспéкт[1]**, а** *m.* avenue.
проспéкт[2]**, а** *m.* **1.** prospectus. **2.** summary, résumé.
проспóрива|ть, ю *impf. of* **проспóрить**[1]
проспóр|ить[1]**, ю, ишь** *pf.* (*of* **~ивать**) to lose (*in a bet*).
проспóр|ить[2]**, ю, ишь** *pf.* to argue (*for a certain time*).
проспрягá|ть, ю *pf. of* **спрягáть**
просрóч|енный *p.p.p. of* **~ить** *and adj.* overdue.
просрóчива|ть, ю *impf. of* **просрóчить**
просрóч|ить, у, ишь *pf.* (*of* **~ивать**) to exceed the time limit; **п. óтпуск** to overstay one's leave; **п. платёж** to fail to pay in time.
просрóчк|а, и *f.* delay; expiration of a time limit.
простáв|ить, лю, ишь *pf.* (*of* **~ля́ть**) to put down (*in writing*), state, fill in; **п. дáту (в, на+*p.*)** to date.
проставля́|ть, ю *impf. of* **простáвить**
простáива|ть, ю *impf. of* **простоя́ть**
простáк, á *m.* simpleton.
простáт|а, ы *f.* (*anat.*) prostate (gland).
простéйш|ий *superl. of* **простóй**; *pl. as n.* **~ие, ~их** (*zool.*) protozoa.
простéн|ок, ка *m.* (*archit.*) pier.
прос|терéть, тру́, трёшь, *past* **~тёр, ~тёрла** *pf.* (*of* **~тирáть**[1]) **1.** to extend, hold out; **п. ру́ку** to hold out one's hand. **2.** (*fig.*) to raise, stretch; **они́ сли́шком далекó ~тёрли свои́ трéбования** they raised their demands too high.
прос|терéться, трётся, *past* **~тёрся, ~тёрлась** *pf.* (*of* **~тирáться**[1]) to stretch, extend; **п. на сóтни миль** to stretch for hundreds of miles.
простирá|ть[1]**, ю** *impf. of* **простерéть**
простир|áть[2]**, áю** *pf.* (*of* **∸ывать**) (*coll.*) to wash thoroughly.
простирá|ться, юсь *impf. of* **простерéться**
прости́рыва|ть, ю *impf. of* **простирáть**[2]
прости́тел|ьный (~ен, ~ьна) *adj.* pardonable, excusable.
проститу́тк|а, и *f.* prostitute.
проститу́ци|я, и *f.* prostitution.
про|сти́ть, щу́, сти́шь *pf.* (*of* **~щáть**) **1.** to forgive, pardon; **~сти́те (меня́)!** excuse me! **2.** to remit; **п. долг комý-н.** to remit s.o.'s debt.
про|сти́ться, щу́сь, сти́шься *pf.* (*of* **~щáться**) (**с**+*i.*) to say good-bye (to), bid farewell (to).
прóсто *adv.* simply; purely out of habit; **п. так** for no particular reason; **э́то п. невероя́тно** it is simply incredible; **я п. не знáю** I really don't know.
простовáт|ый (~, ~а) *adj.* simple, simple-minded.
простоволóс|ый (~, ~а) *adj.* bare-headed.
простоду́ши|е, я *nt.* simple-heartedness; ingenuousness, artlessness.
простоду́ш|ный (~ен, ~на) *adj.* simple-hearted; ingenuous, artless.
прост|óй[1] **(~, ~á, ∸о)** *adj.* **1.** simple; easy. **2.** simple (= *unitary*); **~óе предложéние** (*gram.*) simple sentence; **~óе числó** (*math.*) prime number. **3.** simple; ordinary; **~ы́м глáзом** with the naked eye; **п. нарóд** the common people. **4.** simple, plain; unaffected, unpretentious. **5.** mere; **~óе любопы́тство** mere curiosity; **по той ~óй причи́не, что** for the simple reason that.
простó|й[2]**, я** *m.* downtime, idle time; stoppage; **плáта за п.** demurrage.
простоквáш|а, и *f.* thick soured milk.
прóсто-нáпросто *adv.* (*coll.*) simply.
простонарóд|ный (~ен, ~на) *adj.* of the common people.
простон|áть, у́, ∸ешь *pf.* **1.** to utter a groan, moan. **2.** to groan, moan (*for a certain time*).
простóр, а *m.* **1.** space, expanse. **2.** freedom, scope.
просторéчи|е, я *nt.* popular speech; **в ~и** in common parlance.
просторéч|ный (~ен, ~на) *adj. of* **~ие**
простóр|ный (~ен, ~на) *adj.* spacious, roomy; (*of clothing*) loose-fitting.
простосердéчи|е, я *nt.* simple-heartedness.
простосердéч|ный (~ен, ~на) *adj.* simple-hearted; frank; open.
простот|á, ы́ *f.* simplicity.
простофи́л|я, и *c.g.* (*coll.*) duffer, ninny.
просто|я́ть, ю́, и́шь *pf.* (*of* **простáивать**) **1.** to stay, stand (*for a certain time*). **2.** to stand idle, lie idle. **3.** to stand, last.
прострáн|ный (~ен, ~на) *adj.* **1.** extensive, vast. **2.** diffuse, prolix; verbose.
прострáнственный *adj.* spatial.
прострáнств|о, а *nt.* space; expanse; **возду́шное п.** air space; **безвозду́шное п.** (*phys.*) vacuum; **боя́знь ~а** (*med.*) agoraphobia.
прострáци|я, и *f.* prostration.

прострáчива|ть, ю *impf. of* **прострочи́ть**
прострéл, а *m.* (*coll.*) lumbago.
прострéлива|ть, ю *impf.* **1.** *impf. of* **прострели́ть. 2.** *impf. only* (*mil.*) to rake, sweep with fire.
простре|ли́ть, ю́, ∸ишь *pf.* (*of* **∸ивать**) to shoot through.
простроч|и́ть, у́, ∸ишь *pf.* (*of* **прострáчивать**) to stitch; to back-stitch.
простýд|а, ы *f.* (chest) cold; **схвати́ть ~у** (*coll.*) to catch (a) cold.
просту|ди́ть, жу́, ∸дишь *pf.* (*of* **~жáть**) to allow to catch cold.
просту|ди́ться, жу́сь, ∸дишься *pf.* (*of* **~жáться**) to catch (a) cold.
простýдный *adj.* catarrhal.
простужá|ть(ся), ю(сь) *impf. of* **простуди́ть(ся)**
простý|женный *p.p.p. of* **~ди́ть** *and adj.*; **я вновь ~жен** I have caught another cold.
простýк|ать, аю *pf.* (*of* **~ивать**) (*med.*) to tap.
простýкива|ть, ю *impf. of* **простýкать**
проступ|áть, áет *impf. of* **~и́ть**
проступ|и́ть, ∸ит *pf.* (*of* **~áть**) to appear, show through; **пот ~и́л у негó на лбу** perspiration stood out on his forehead.
простýп|ок, ка *m.* misdeed; (*leg.*) misdemeanour.
простывá|ть, ю *impf. of* **просты́ть**
простын|ный *adj. of* **~я́**; **~ное полотнó** sheeting.
простын|я́, и́, *pl.* **прóстыни, ∸ь, ~я́м** *f.* sheet.
просты́|ть, ну, нешь *pf.* (*of* **~вáть**) to get cold; to cool; **и след ~л** (*+g.*; *coll.*) not a trace (of).
просýн|уть, у, ешь *pf.* (*of* **просóвывать**) (**в**+*a.*) to push (through, in), shove (through, in), thrust (through, in).
просýн|уться, усь, ешься *pf.* (*of* **просóвываться**) to push through, force one's way through.
просýшива|ть(ся), ю(сь) *impf. of* **просуши́ть(ся)**
просуш|и́ть, у́, ∸ишь *pf.* (*of* **∸ивать**) to dry thoroughly, properly.
просуш|и́ться, у́сь, ∸ишься *pf.* (*of* **∸иваться**) to (get) dry.
просýшк|а, и *f.* drying.
просуществ|овáть, ýю *pf.* to exist (*for a certain time*); to last, endure.
просфор|á, ы́ *f.* (*eccl.*) (communion) bread; host.
просцéниум, а *m.* (*theatr.*) proscenium.
просчёт, а *m.* **1.** counting (up), reckoning (up). **2.** error (*in counting, reckoning*). **2.** (*fig.*) miscalculation.
просчит|áть, áю *pf.* (*of* **∸ывать**) **1.** to count (up), reckon (up). **2.** to miscount; **вы ~áли пятьдеся́т рублéй** you are out by fifty roubles.
просчит|áться, áюсь *pf.* (*of* **∸ываться**) **1.** to miscount; **мы ~áлись на двáдцать рублéй** we are out by twenty roubles. **2.** (*fig.*) to miscalculate.
просчи́тыва|ть(ся), ю(сь) *impf. of* **просчитáть(ся)**
прóсы́п, а *m.*: **без ~у** (*coll.*) without waking, without stirring.
просы́п|ать, лю, лешь *pf.* (*of* **~áть**[1]) to spill.
просып|áть[1]**, áю** *impf. of* **∸ать**
просып|áть[2]**, áю** *impf. of* **проспáть**
просып|áться, áюсь *impf. of* **проснýться**
просыхá|ть, ю *impf. of* **просóхнуть**
прóсьб|а, ы *f.* request; **обращáться с ~ой** to make a request; **у меня́ к вам п.** I have a favour to ask you; **«п. не кури́ть!»** 'no smoking, please!'
просянóй *adj.* millet.
протáлин|а, ы *f.* thawed patch (*of earth*).
протáлкива|ть, ю *impf. of* **протолкнýть**
протáлкива|ться, юсь *impf. of* **протолкáться** *and* **протолкнýться**
протанц|евáть, ýю *pf.* **1.** to dance; **п. вальс** to dance a waltz, do a waltz. **2.** to dance (*for a certain time*).
протáплива|ть, ю *impf. of* **протопи́ть**
протáптыва|ть, ю *impf. of* **протоптáть**
протарáн|ить, ю, ишь *pf.* (*of* **тарáнить**) **1.** (*mil.*) to ram. **2.** (*fig.*) to break through, smash.
протáскива|ть, ю *impf. of* **протащи́ть**
протáчива|ть, ю *impf. of* **проточи́ть**
протащ|и́ть, ý, ∸ишь *pf.* (*of* **протáскивать**) **1.** to pull (through, along), drag (through, along), trail. **2.** (*coll., pej.*) to insinuate, work in.
протá|ять, ю, ешь *pf.* to thaw through.
протежé *c.g. indecl.* protégé; protégée.
протéз, а *m.* prosthesis; artificial limb; **зубнóй п.** denture.
протéзн|ый *adj.* prosthetic; **~ая мастерскáя** orthopaedic workshop.
протеи́н, а *m.* (*chem.*) protein.
протекá|ть, ю *impf.* **1.** *impf. of* **протéчь. 2.** *impf. only* (*of a river or stream*) to flow, run. **3.** *impf. only* to leak, be leaky.
протéктор, а *m.* **1.** (*obs.*) protector, patron. **2.** (*tech.*) protector; tread (*of pneumatic tyre*).
протекторáт, а *m.* protectorate.
протекциони́зм, а *m.* **1.** (*pol., econ.*) protectionism. **2.** (*coll.*) favouritism.
протéкци|я, и *f.* patronage, influence.
про|терéть, трý, трёшь, *past* **~тёр, ~тёрла** *pf.* (*of* **~тирáть**) **1.** to rub a hole (in); to wear into holes. **2.** to rub through, grate; **п. чéрез си́то** to rub through a sieve. **3.** to rub over, wipe over. **4.: п. глазá** (*coll.*) to rub one's eyes.
про|терéться, трётся, *past* **~тёрся, ~тёрлась** *pf.* (*of* **~тирáться**) to wear through, wear into holes.
протéст, а *m* **1.** protest. **2.** (*leg.*) objection.
протестáнт[1]**, а** *m.* protester, objector.
протестáнт[2]**, а** *m.* (*relig.*) Protestant.
протестанти́зм, а *m.* = **протестáнтство**
протестáнтский *adj.* (*relig.*) Protestant.
протестáнтств|о, а *nt.* (*relig.*) Protestantism.
протест|овáть, ýю *impf.* **(прóтив)** to protest (against).
протé|чь, чёт, кýт, *past* **∸̈к, ~клá** *pf.* (*of* **~кáть**) **1.** to ooze, seep. **2.** (*of time*) to go by, pass. **3.** (*of an illness, etc.*) to take its course.
прóтив *prep.+g.* **1.** against; **п. течéния** against the current; **за и п.** pro and con; **имéть что-н. п.** to have sth. against; to mind, object; **вы ничегó не имéете п. тогó, что я курю́?** do you mind my smoking? **2.** opposite; facing; **друг п. дрýга** facing one another; **останови́тесь, пожáлуйста, п. цéркви** please stop opposite the church. **3.** contrary to; **п. нáших ожидáний** contrary to our expectations. **4.** (*coll.*) as against; according to; **в э́том годý п. прóшлого** this year as against last (year); **кáждому п. потрéбностей егó** to each according to his needs.
прóтив|ень, ня *m.* griddle.
проти́в|иться, люсь, ишься *impf.* (*of* **вос~**) (*+d.*) to oppose; to resist, stand up (against).
проти́вник, а *m.* **1.** opponent, adversary; **п. войны́** war resister; **п. коммуни́зма** anticommunist. **2.** (*collect.*; *mil.*) the enemy.
проти́вно[1] *adv.* in a disgusting way.
проти́вно[2] *prep.+d.* against; contrary to; **поступáть п. своéй сóвести** to go against one's conscience.
проти́вн|ый[1] *adj.* **1.** opposite; contrary; **~ое мнéние** a contrary opinion; **в ~ом слýчае** otherwise. **2.** opposing, opposed; **~ые стóроны** opposing sides.
проти́в|ный[2] **(~ен, ~на)** *adj.* nasty, disgusting; **п. зáпах** nasty smell; **он мне ~ен** I find him offensive.
противо... *comb. form* anti-, contra-, counter-.
противобóрств|о, а *nt.* struggle; (*pol.*) confrontation.
противобóрств|овать, ую *impf.* (*+d.*; *obs.*) to oppose; to fight (against).
противовéс, а *m.* (*tech. and fig.*) counterbalance, counterpoise.
противовоздýшн|ый *adj.* anti-aircraft; **~ая оборóна** air defence.

противога́з, а *m.* gas-mask.
противоде́йстви|е, я *nt.* opposition, counteraction.
противоде́йств|овать, ую *impf.* (+*d.*) to oppose, counteract.
противоесте́ствен|ный (~, ~на) *adj.* unnatural.
противозако́нност|ь, и *f.* illegality.
противозако́н|ный (~ен, ~на) *adj.* unlawful; (*leg.*) illegal.
противозача́точн|ый *adj.* contraceptive; **~ые сре́дства** contraceptives.
противолежа́щий *adj.* (*math.*) opposite; **п. у́гол** alternate angle.
противоло́дочный *adj.* (*naut.*) anti-submarine.
противообще́ственный *adj.* antisocial.
противопехо́тный *adj.* (*mil.*) antipersonnel.
противопожа́рн|ый *adj.* fire-prevention; **~ая дверь** fire door.
противопоказа́ни|е, я *nt.* (*med.*) contra-indication.
противопока́занный *adj.* (*med.*) contra-indicated.
противоположе́ни|е, я *nt.* opposition.
противополо́жност|ь, и *f.* **1.** opposition; contrast; **в п.** (+*d.*) as opposed (to), in contrast (to). **2.** opposite, antithesis; **по́лная п.** complete antithesis; **пряма́я п.** exact opposite.
противополо́ж|ный (~ен, ~на) *adj.* **1.** opposite. **2.** opposed, contrary; **диаметра́льно п.** diametrically opposed.
противопоста́в|ить, лю, ишь *pf.* (*of* **~ля́ть**) (+*d.*) **1.** to oppose (to). **2.** to contrast (with), set off (against).
противопоставле́ни|е, я *nt.* (+*d.*) **1.** opposition (to). **2.** contrasting (with), setting off (against).
противопоставля́|ть, ю *impf. of* **противопоста́вить**
противораке́тн|ый *adj.* (*mil.*) anti-missile; **~ая раке́та** anti-missile missile.
противоречи́в|ый (~, ~а) *adj.* contradictory; conflicting; **~ые сообще́ния** conflicting reports.
противоре́чи|е, я *nt.* **1.** contradiction; inconsistency; **~я в показа́ниях** contradictions in evidence. **2.** contrariness; defiance; **дух ~я** spirit of defiance, contrariness. **3.** conflict, clash; **находи́ться в ~и (с**+*i.*) to be at variance (with), conflict (with).
противоре́ч|ить, у, ишь *impf.* (+*d.*) **1.** to contradict; **он всё ~ил ма́тери** he was always contradicting his mother. **2.** to be at variance (with), conflict (with), be contrary (to); **их показа́ния ~ат одно́ друго́му** their evidence is conflicting.
противосамолётный *adj.* (*mil.*) anti-aircraft.
противостолбня́чный *adj.* (*med.*) anti-tetanus.
противостоя́ни|е, я *nt.* **1.** (*astron.*) opposition. **2.** (*pol.*) confrontation.
противосто|я́ть, ю, и́шь *impf.* (+*d.*) **1.** to resist, withstand. **2.** to countervail. **3.** (*astron.*) to be in opposition.
противота́нков|ый *adj.* anti-tank; **~ая лову́шка** tank trap.
противоуго́нный *adj.* anti-theft.
противоя́ди|е, я *nt.* antidote.
протира́|ть(ся), ю(сь) *impf. of* **протере́ть(ся)**
проти́ск|аться, аюсь *pf.* (*of* **~иваться**) to push one's way through, elbow one's way through.
проти́скива|ть, ю *impf. of* **проти́снуть**
проти́скива|ться, юсь *impf. of* **проти́скаться**
проти́с|нуть, ну, нешь *pf.* (*of* **~кивать**) to push through, shove through.
проти́с|нуться, нусь, нешься *pf.* = **~каться**
проткн|у́ть, у́, ёшь *pf.* (*of* **протыка́ть**) to pierce; to transfix; to spit, skewer.
протодья́кон, а *m.* (*eccl.*) archdeacon.
протоисто́ри|я, и *f.* prehistory.
прото́к, а *m.* **1.** channel. **2.** (*anat.*) duct.
протоко́л, а *m.* **1.** minutes; report; **вести́ п.** to take the minutes; **занести́ в п.** to enter in the minutes. **2.** (*leg.*) statement; charge-sheet; **п. дозна́ния, п. допро́са** examination record; **соста́вить п.** to draw up a report. **3.** (*dipl.*) protocol.
протоко́л|ьный *adj. of* **~**
протолка́|ться, юсь *pf.* (*of* **прота́лкиваться**) (*coll.*) to force, jostle one's way (through).
протолкн|у́ть, у́, ёшь *pf.* (*of* **прота́лкивать**) to push through, press through; (*fig.*): **п. де́ло** to push a matter forward.
протолкн|у́ться, у́сь, ёшься *pf.* = **протолка́ться**
прото́н, а *m.* (*phys.*) proton.
прото́н|ный *adj. of* **~**
протоп|и́ть, лю́, ~ишь *pf.* (*of* **прота́пливать**) to heat thoroughly.
протопла́зм|а, ы *f.* (*biol.*) protoplasm.
протоп|та́ть, чу́, ~чешь *pf.* (*of* **прота́птывать**) **1.** to beat, make (*by walking*); **п. тропи́нку** to make a path. **2.** to wear out (*footwear*).
протор|ённый *p.p.p. of* **~и́ть** *and adj.* beaten, well-trodden; **~ённая доро́жка** beaten track.
протор|и́ть, ю́, и́шь *pf.* (*of* **~я́ть**) to beat; **п. путь** to blaze a trail.
протор|я́ть, я́ю *impf. of* **~и́ть**
прототи́п, а *m.* prototype.
проточ|и́ть, у́, ~ишь *pf.* (*of* **прота́чивать**) **1.** to gnaw through, eat through. **2.** (*of running water*) to wash. **3.** to turn (*on a lathe*).
прото́чн|ый *adj.* flowing, running; **~ая вода́** running water; **п. пруд** pond fed by springs.
протра́в|а, ы *f.* (*chem.*) mordant.
протра́л|ить, ю, ишь *pf. of* **тра́лить**
протрезв|и́ть, лю́, и́шь *pf.* (*of* **~ля́ть**) to sober.
протрезв|и́ться, лю́сь, и́шься *pf.* (*of* **~ля́ться**) to sober up.
протрезвля́|ть(ся), ю(сь) *impf. of* **протрезви́ть(ся)**
протух|а́ть, а́ю *impf. of* **~нуть**
прото́х|нуть, ну, нешь *past* **~, ~ла** *pf.* (*of* **~а́ть**) to become foul, rotten; to go bad.
прото́х|ший *p.p. act. of* **~нуть** *and adj.* foul, rotten; (*of food*) bad, tainted.
протыка́|ть, ю *impf. of* **проткну́ть**
протя́гива|ть(ся), ю(сь) *impf. of* **протяну́ть(ся)**
протяже́ни|е, я *nt.* **1.** extent; expanse, area; **на всём ~и** (+*g.*) along the whole length (of). **2.** space (*of time*); **на ~и** (+*g.*) during, for the space (of).
протяжённост|ь, и *f.* extent, length.
протя́жност|ь, и *f.* slowness; **п. ре́чи** drawl.
протя́ж|ный (~ен, ~на) *adj.* long drawn-out; **~ное произноше́ние** drawl.
протя|ну́ть, ну́, ~нешь *pf.* (*of* **~гивать**) **1.** to stretch; to extend. **2.** to stretch out, extend, hold out; **п. ру́ку по́мощи** to extend a helping hand; **п. но́ги** (*fig., coll.*) to turn up one's toes. **3.** to protract. **4.** to drawl out. **5.** (*pf. only*) to last; **больно́й недо́лго ~нет** the patient won't last long.
протя|ну́ться, ну́сь, ~нешься *pf.* (*of* **~гиваться**) **1.** to stretch out; to reach out. **2.** to extend, stretch, reach. **3.** *pf. only* to last, go on.
проу́чива|ть, ю *impf. of* **проучи́ть**[1]
проуч|и́ть[1]**, у́, ~ишь** *pf.* (*of* **~ивать**) (*coll.*) to teach, give a good lesson; **я его́ ~у́!** I'll teach him!
проуч|и́ть[2]**, у́, ~ишь** *pf.* to study, learn up (*for a certain time*).
проуч|и́ться, у́сь, ~ишься *pf.* to spend (*a certain time*) in study.
проф... *comb. form, abbr. of* **1. профессиона́льный. 2. профсою́зный**
профа́н, а *m.* **1.** (*in relation to a given field of knowledge*) layman. **2.** ignoramus.
профана́ци|я, и *f.* profanation.
профани́р|овать, ую *impf. and pf.* to profane.
профессиона́л, а *m.* professional.

профессионали́зм, а *m.* professionalism.
профессиона́льн|ый *adj.* **1.** professional, occupational; **п. диплома́т** career diplomat; **~ое заболева́ние** occupational disease; **~ое образова́ние** vocational training; **~ая ориента́ция** career guidance; **п. риск** occupational hazard; **п. сою́з** trade union. **2.** professional (*opp. amateur*).
профе́сси|я, и *f.* profession, occupation, trade.
профе́ссор, а, *pl.* **~а́** *m.* professor.
профе́ссорск|ий *adj.* **1.** professorial. **2.** *as n.* **~ая ~ой** *f.* staff common room.
профе́ссорств|о, а *nt.* professorship, chair.
профессу́р|а, ы *f.* **1.** professorship, chair. **2.** (*collect.*) the professors.
профила́ктик|а, и *f.* **1.** (*med.*) prophylaxis. **2.** (*collect.*) preventive measures.
профилакти́ческий *adj.* **1.** (*med.*) prophylactic. **2.** preventive.
профилакто́ри|й, я *m.* dispensary.
про́фил|ь, я *m.* **1.** profile; side-view; **в п.** in profile. **2.** section; **попере́чный п.** cross-section. **3.** type; **шко́лы ра́зного ~я** schools of various types.
профильтр|ова́ть, у́ю *pf. of* **фильтрова́ть**
профко́м, а *m.* (*abbr. of* ***профсою́зный комите́т***) trade-union committee.
профконсульта́нт, а *m.* careers adviser.
профо́рм|а, ы *f.* form, formality; **чи́стая п.** pure, mere formality; **для ~ы** as a matter of form.
профсою́з, а *m.* trade union.
профсою́зный *adj.* trade-union.
проха́жива|ться, юсь *impf. of* **пройти́сь**
прохва|ти́ть, чу́, ~́тишь *pf.* (*of* **~́тывать**) (*coll.*) (*of cold, draught, etc.*) to penetrate; **меня́ ~ти́ло на сквозняке́** I caught a chill from being in a draught.
прохва́тыва|ть, ю *impf. of* **прохвати́ть**
прохво́ст, а *m.* (*coll.*) scoundrel.
прохла́д|а, ы *f.* cool, coolness.
прохла́д|ец, ца *m.*: **с ~цем** (*coll.*) without making much effort; listlessly.
прохлади́тельн|ый *adj.* refreshing, cooling; **~ые напи́тки** soft drinks.
прохла|ди́ться, жу́сь, ди́шься *pf.* (*coll.*) to cool off.
прохла́д|ный (~ен, ~на) *adj.* **1.** cool; fresh; (*impers., pred.*): **~но** it is cool. **2.** (*fig.*) cool.
прохла́д|ца, цы *f.* = **~ец**
прохлажда́|ться, юсь *impf.* (*coll.*) to take it easy.
прохо́д, а *m.* **1.** passage; **пра́во ~а** right of way; **не дава́ть ~а** (*+d.*) to give no peace, pester. **2.** passage(way), aisle. **3.** (*anat.*) duct; **за́дний п.** anus.
проходи́м|ец, ца *m.* rogue, rascal.
проходи́мост|ь, и *f.* **1.** (*of roads, etc.*) passability. **2.** (*of motor, etc., transport*) cross-country ability.
проходи́м|ый (~, ~а) *adj.* passable.
прохо|ди́ть[1], жу́, ~́дишь *impf.* **1.** *impf. of* **пройти́. 2.** *impf. only* **(че́рез)** to lie (through), go (through), pass (through); **кана́л ~́дит че́рез джу́нгли** the canal passes through jungle.
прохо|ди́ть[2], жу́, ~́дишь *pf.* to walk (*for a certain time*).
проходн|о́й *adj. of* **прохо́д**; passage; **~а́я бу́дка** check-point; **~а́я ко́мната** inter-communicating room; **п. балл** pass mark.
прохожде́ни|е, я *nt.* passing, passage; **п. торже́ственным ма́ршем** (*mil.*) march past.
прохо́ж|ий *adj.* passing, in transit; *as n.* **п., ~его** *m.*, **~ая, ~ей** *f.* passer-by.
процвета́ни|е, я *nt.* prosperity, well-being.
процвета́|ть, ю *impf.* to prosper, flourish, thrive.
проце|ди́ть, жу́, ~́дишь *pf.* (*of* **~́живать**) to filter, strain.
процеду́р|а, ы *f.* **1.** procedure. **2.** (*usu. pl.*) treatment.
проце́жива|ть, ю *impf. of* **процеди́ть**
проце́нт, а *m.* **1.** percentage; rate (per cent); **сто ~ов** one hundred per cent; **ба́нковский учётный п.** bank rate; **рабо́тать на ~ах** to work on a percentage basis. **2.** (*oft. pl.*) interest; **разме́р ~а** rate of interest; **просты́е, сло́жные ~ы** simple, compound interest.
проце́нт|ный *adj. of* **~**; interest-bearing; **~ное отноше́ние** percentage; **~ные облига́ции** interest-bearing bonds.
проце́сс, а *m.* **1.** process. **2.** (*leg.*) trial; legal action, legal proceedings; lawsuit. **3.** (*med.*) active condition; **п. в лёгких** active pulmonary tuberculosis.
проце́сси|я, и *f.* procession.
проце́ссор, а *m.* (*comput.*) processor.
процессуа́льн|ый *adj. of* **проце́сс 2.**; **~ые но́рмы** legal procedure.
процити́р|овать, ую *pf. of* **цити́ровать**
про́черк, а *m.* dash.
прочер|ти́ть, чу́, ~́тишь *pf.* (*of* **~́чивать**) to draw.
проче́рчива|ть, ю *impf. of* **прочерти́ть**
проче|са́ть, шу́, ~́шешь *pf.* (*of* **~́сывать**) **1.** to comb out thoroughly. **2.** (*mil.*; *fig.*) to comb.
прочёск|а, и *f.* screening (*as a security measure*).
про|че́сть, чту́, чтёшь, *past* **~чёл, ~чла́** *pf.* = **~чита́ть**
прочёсыва|ть, ю *impf. of* **прочеса́ть**
про́ч|ий *adj.* other; **и ~ее (***abbr.* **и пр., и проч.)** etcetera, and so on; **~ие** (the) others; **ме́жду ~им** by the way.
прочи́|стить, щу, стишь *pf.* (*of* **~ща́ть**) to clean; to cleanse thoroughly; **п. тру́бку** to clean a pipe.
прочита́|ть[1], ю *pf. of* **чита́ть**
прочита́|ть[2], ю *pf.* to read (*for a certain time*).
прочи́тыва|ть, ю *impf.* (*coll.*) to read through.
про́ч|ить, у, ишь *impf.* **(в**+*a.*) to intend (for), destine (for); **его́ ~или в свяще́нники** he was intended for the church.
прочища́|ть, ю *impf. of* **прочи́стить**
про́чно *adv.* firmly, soundly, solidly, well.
про́чност|ь, и *f.* firmness, soundness, solidity; durability; strength; **п. на уда́р** (*tech.*) shock resistance; **запа́с ~и, коэффицие́нт ~и** safety factor, safety margin.
про́ч|ный (~ен, ~на́, ~но) *adj.* firm, sound, solid; durable; enduring, lasting; **~ные зна́ния** sound knowledge; **~ная кра́ска** fast dye; **~ное сча́стье** lasting happiness; **~ная ткань** durable fabric.
прочте́ни|е, я *nt.* reading; perusal.
прочу́вствова|нный *p.p.p. of* **~ть** *and adj.* full of emotion; heart-felt.
прочу́вств|овать, ую *pf.* **1.** to feel deeply, keenly. **2.** to experience, go through.
прочь *adv.* **1.** away, off; **(поди́) п.!** go away!; **(пошёл) п. отсю́да!** get out of here!; **п. с глаз мои́х!** get out of my sight!; **п. с доро́ги!** (get) out of the way!; **ру́ки п.!** hands off! **2.** *as pred.* averse (to); **не п.** (*+inf.*, *coll.*) to have no objection (to); not to be averse (to); **он не п. вы́пить стака́нчик** he is not averse to taking a drop.
проше́дш|ий *p.p. act. of* **пройти́** *and adj.* past; last; **~им ле́том** last summer; **~ее вре́мя** (*gram.*) past tense; *as n.* **~ее, ~его** *nt.* the past.
проше́ни|е, я *nt.* application, petition; **пода́ть п.** to submit an application, forward a petition.
прошеп|та́ть, чу́, ~́чешь *pf. of* **шепта́ть**
проше́стви|е, я *nt.*: **по ~и** (*+g.*) after the lapse (of), after the expiration (of).
прошиб|а́ть, а́ю *impf. of* **~и́ть**
прошиб|и́ть, у́, ёшь, *past* **~́, ~́ла** *pf.* (*of* **~а́ть**) (*coll.*) **1.** to break through. **2.: его́ ~́ пот** he broke into a sweat; **её ~́ла слеза́** she shed a tear.
прошива́|ть, ю *impf. of* **проши́ть**
проши́вк|а, и *f.* trim, insertion (*on linen, etc.*).
прош|и́ть, ью́, ьёшь *pf.* (*of* **~ива́ть**) to sew, stitch.

прошлогóдний *adj.* last year's; of last year.
прóшл|ый *adj.* **1.** past; former; **э́то дéло ~ое** it's a thing of the past; *as n.* **~ое, ~ого** *nt.* the past; **отойти́ в ~ое** to become a thing of the past. **2.** last; **в ~ом годý** last year; **на ~ой недéле** last week.
прошмы́гива|ть, ю *impf. of* **прошмыгнýть**
прошмыг|нýть, нý, нёшь *pf.* (*of* **~ивать**) (*coll.*) to slip (by, past, through).
проштрáф|иться, люсь, ишься *pf.* (*coll.*) to be at fault.
проштуди́р|овать, ую *pf. of* **штуди́ровать**
прошум|éть, лю́, и́шь *pf.* **1.** to roar past. **2.** (*fig.*) to become famous.
прощáй(те) good-bye!; farewell!, adieu!
прощáльн|ый *adj.* farewell, parting; valedictory; **~ая пирýшка** farewell party; **~ые словá** parting words.
прощáни|е, я *nt.* farewell; parting, leave-taking; **на п.** at parting.
прощá|ть(ся), ю(сь) *impf. of* **прости́ть(ся)**
прóще *comp. of* **простóй** *and* **прóсто**; simpler; plainer; easier.
прощéни|е, я *nt.* forgiveness; pardon; **проси́ть ~я у когó-н.** to ask for s.o.'s forgiveness; **прошý ~я!** I beg your pardon!
прощýп|ать, аю *pf.* (*of* **~ывать**) **1.** to feel; to detect (*by feeling*). **2.** (*fig., coll.*) to sound (out).
прощýпыва|ть, ю *impf. of* **прощýпать**
проэкзамен|овáть(ся), ýю(сь) *pf. of* **экзаменовáть(ся)**
прояви́тел|ь, я *m.* (*phot.*) developer.
прояв|и́ть, лю́, ~ишь *pf.* (*of* **~ля́ть**) **1.** to show, display; **п. забóту (о+*p.*)** to show concern (for, about); **п. интерéс (к)** to show interest (in); **п. себя́** to show one's worth; **п. себя́** (+*i.*) to show o.s., prove (to be); **он ~и́л себя́ прéданным коллéгой** he proved to be a loyal colleague. **2.** (*phot.*) to develop.
прояв|и́ться, ~ится *pf.* (*of* **~ля́ться**) **1.** to show (itself), reveal itself, manifest itself. **2.** *pass. of* **~и́ть**
проявлéни|е, я *nt.* display, manifestation; **при пéрвом ~и** (+*g.*) at the first sign(s) of.
проявля́|ть(ся), ю(сь) *impf. of* **прояви́ть(ся)**
проя́сне|ть, ет *pf.* (*of the sky*) to clear; (*impers.*): **~ло** it cleared up.
прояснé|ть, ет *pf.* to brighten (up).
проясн|и́ться, и́тся *pf.* (*of* **~я́ться**) (*of weather and fig.*) to clear (up); **днём ~и́лось** in the afternoon it cleared up.
проясн|я́ться, я́ется *impf. of* **~и́ться**
пруд, á, в ~ý, *pl.* **~ы́** *m.* pond.
пру|ди́ть, жý, ~ди́шь *impf.* (*of* **за~**) to dam (up); **хоть пруд ~ди́** (*coll.*) in abundance; **дéнег у них — хоть пруд ~ди́** they are rolling in money.
пружи́н|а, ы *f.* spring; **глáвная п.** mainspring (*also fig.*); **п.-волосóк** hairspring.
пружи́нистост|ь, и *f.* springiness, elasticity.
пружи́нист|ый (~, ~а) *adj.* springy, elastic.
пружи́н|ить, ю, ишь *impf.* **1.** (*trans.*) to tense. **2.** (*intrans.*) to be elastic, possess spring.
пружи́н|ный *adj. of* **~а; ~ные весы́** spring balance; **п. матрáц** spring mattress.
прусáк, á *m.* (*coll.*) cockroach.
пруссáк, á *m.* Prussian.
пруссá|чка, чки *f. of* **~к**
прýсск|ий *adj.* Prussian.
прут, а-á *m.* **1.** (*pl.* **~ья, ~ьев**) twig; switch; **и́вовый п.** withe, withy. **2.** (*pl.* **~ы́, ~óв**) (*tech.*) bar.
прýтик, а *m. dim. of* **прут; волшéбный п.** dowsing rod.
пры́гани|е, я *nt.* jumping, leaping; skipping.
пры́г|ать, аю *impf.* (*of* **~нуть**) **1.** to jump, leap, spring; to bound; **п. на однóй ногé** to hop on one leg; **п. со скакáлкой** to skip; **п. от рáдости** to jump with, for joy. **2.** to bounce.
пры́г|нуть, ну, нешь *pf. of* **~ать**
прыгýн, á *m.* (*sport*) jumper; **п. в вóду** diver.
прыжкóв|ый *adj.*: **~ая вы́шка** diving board.
прыж|óк, кá *m.* **1.** jump, leap, spring. **2.** (*sport*) jump; **~ки́** jumping; **акробати́ческие ~ки́** tumbling; **~ки́ на батýте** trampolining; **~ки́ в вóду** diving; **~ки́ с парашю́том** parachute jumping; **п. в высотý** high jump; **п. в длинý** long jump; **п. с шестóм** pole-vault.
пры́ска|ть, ю *impf. of* **пры́снуть**
пры́с|нуть, ну, нешь *pf.* (*of* **~кать**) (*coll.*) **1.** (+*i.*) to sprinkle (with); to spray (with). **2.** to spurt, gush; **(có смеху)** (*fig.*) to burst out laughing.
пры́т|кий (~ок, ~кá, ~ко) *adj.* quick, lively, sharp.
пры́т|ь, и *f.* (*coll.*) **1.** speed; **во всю п.** at full speed. **2.** energy, liveliness, go; **откýда у негó такáя п.?** where does he get his energy from?
прыщ, á *m.* pimple; **лицó в ~áх** pimply face.
прыщáв|ый (~, ~а) *adj.* pimply, pimpled.
прядéни|е, я *nt.* spinning.
пря́деный *adj.* spun.
пряди́льн|ый *adj.* spinning; **п. станóк** spinning loom.
пряди́льщик, а *m.* spinner.
пряд|ь, и *f.* **1.** lock (*of hair*). **2.** strand.
пря́ж|а, и *no pl., f.* yarn; **шерстянáя п.** woollen yarn.
пря́жк|а, и *f.* buckle, clasp.
пря́лк|а, и *f.* distaff; spinning-wheel.
прям|áя, óй *f.* **1.** straight line; **расстоя́ние по ~óй** distance as the crow flies. **2.** (*sport*) straight; **фи́нишная п.** home straight (*athletics*); home stretch (*horse- or motor-racing*).
прямизн|á, ы́ *f.* straightness.
прямикóм *adv.* (*coll.*) straight; across country.
пря́мо *adv.* **1.** straight (on); **иди́те п.!** (go) straight on!; **держáться п.** to hold o.s. straight *or* erect. **2.** straight, directly; **попáсть п. в цель** to hit the bull's eye (*also fig.*); **смотрéть п. в глазá комý-н.** to look s.o. straight in the face. **3.** (*fig.*) straight; frankly, openly; **мы емý п. сказáли, что э́то емý не удáстся** we told him straight that he would not succeed. **4.** (*coll.*) real; really; **он п. идиóт** he is a real idiot; **я п. не знáю, что с ней стáло** I really don't know what has become of her.
прямодýши|е, я *nt.* directness, straightforwardness.
прямодýш|ный (~ен, ~на) *adj.* direct, straightforward.
прям|óй (~, ~á, ~о) *adj.* **1.** straight; upright, erect; **~áя кишкá** (*anat.*) rectum; **п. угóл** (*math.*) right angle. **2.** (*of means of communication, etc.*) through; direct; **пóезд ~óго сообщéния** through train; **п. прóвод** direct (*telephone*) line. **3.** direct; **~ы́е вы́боры** direct elections; **~óе дополнéние** (*gram.*) direct object; **п. налóг** direct tax; **п. начáльник** immediate superior; **~óе попадáние** (*mil.*) direct hit; **~áя речь** (*gram.*) direct speech; **п. смысл слóва** the literal sense of a word. **4.** (*of character*) straightforward. **5.** (*coll.*) real; **п. убы́ток** sheer loss; **п. расчёт пойти́ самомý** it is really worth while going o.s.
прямолинé|йный (~ен, ~на) *adj.* **1.** rectilinear. **2.** (*fig.*) straightforward; direct.
прямот|á, ы́ *f.* straightforwardness; plain dealing.
прямоугóльник, а *m.* (*math.*) rectangle.
прямоугóльный *adj.* right-angled; rectangular; **п. треугóльник** right-angled triangle.
пря́ник, а *m.* spice cake; gingerbread; **медóвый п.** honey-cake.
пря́ност|ь, и *f.* spice.
пря́ный *adj.* spicy (*also fig.*); (*of smells*) heady.
пря|сть[1]**, дý, дёшь,** *past* **~л, ~лá, ~ло** *impf.* (*of* **с~**) to spin.
пря́|тать, чу, чешь *impf.* (*of* **с~**) to hide, conceal.

пря́|таться, чусь, чешься *impf.* (*of* **с~**) to hide; to conceal o.s.; to take refuge.
пря́т|ки, ок *no sg.* hide-and-seek.
пря́х|а, и *f.* spinner.
псал|о́м, ма́ *m.* psalm.
псало́мщик, а *m.* (*eccl.*) (psalm-)reader; sexton.
псалты́р|ь, и *f. and* (*coll.*) **п., ~я́** *m.* (*eccl.*) Psalter.
пса́р|ня, ни, *g. pl.* **~ен** *f.* kennel.
псевдо... *comb. form* pseudo-.
псевдони́м, а *m.* pseudonym; pen-name; alias.
пси́н|а, ы *f.* (*coll.*) **1.** dogmeat. **2.** doggy smell.
псих, а *m.* (*abbr. of* **психопа́т**) (*coll.*) loony, nutcase.
психиа́тр, а *m.* psychiatrist.
психиатри́ческ|ий *adj.* psychiatric; **~ая лече́бница** mental hospital.
психиатри́|я, и *f.* psychiatry.
пси́хик|а, и *f.* psyche.
психи́чески *adv.* mentally; **п. больно́й** mentally ill; *as n.* **п. больно́й, п. больно́го** *m.* mental patient, mental case.
психи́ческ|ий *adj.* mental; **~ая боле́знь** mental illness.
психоана́лиз, а *m.* psychoanalysis.
психоанали́тик, а *m.* psychoanalyst.
психоаналити́ческий *adj.* psychoanalytic(al).
психо́з, а *m.* (*med.*) psychosis; **вое́нный п.** war hysteria.
психо́лог, а *m.* psychologist.
психологи́ческий *adj.* psychological.
психоло́ги|я, и *f.* psychology.
психопа́т, а *m.* psychopath.
психотерапе́вт, а *m.* psychotherapist.
психотерапи́|я, и *f.* psychotherapy.
псо́в|ый *adj.*: **~ая охо́та** the chase, hunting (*with hounds*).
псориа́з, а *m.* psoriasis.
пта́шк|а, и *f.* little bird; birdie; **ра́нняя п.** (*fig.*) early bird.
птен|е́ц, ца́ *m.* nestling; fledg(e)ling (*also fig.*).
птерода́ктил|ь, я *m.* pterodactyl.
пти́ц|а, ы *f.* bird; **дома́шняя п.** (*collect.*) poultry; **перелётная п.** bird of passage; **хи́щные ~ы** birds of prey.
птицево́д, а *m.* poultry farmer, poultry breeder.
птицево́дств|о, а *nt.* poultry farming, poultry-keeping.
птицево́дческий *adj.* poultry-farming, poultry-keeping.
птицело́в, а *m.* fowler.
птицело́вств|о, а *nt.* fowling.
птицефе́рм|а, ы *f.* poultry farm.
пти́ч|ий *adj. of* **пти́ца; п. двор** poultry-yard; **вид с ~ьего полёта** bird's-eye view; **жить на ~ьих права́х** to live from hand to mouth.
пти́чк|а[1], **и** *f. dim. of* **пти́ца**
пти́чк|а[2], **и** *f.* tick; **ста́вить ~у** to tick.
пти́чник, а *m.* poultry-yard, hen-run; hen-house.
пу́блик|а, и *f.* (*collect.*) (the) public; (*in theatres, etc.*) (the) audience.
публика́ци|я, и *f.* **1.** publication. **2.** advertisement, notice; **помести́ть ~ю в газе́те** to place an advertisement in a newspaper; **п. о сме́рти** obituary notice.
публик|ова́ть, у́ю *impf.* (*of* **о~**) to publish.
публици́ст, а *m.* publicist; commentator on current affairs.
публици́стик|а, и *f.* sociopolitical journalism.
публицисти́ческий *adj.* publicistic.
публи́чно *adv.* publicly; in public; openly.
публи́чн|ый *adj.* public; **п. дом** brothel
пу́гал|о, а *nt.* scarecrow.
пу́ган|ый *adj.* (*coll.*) scared; **~ая воро́на (и) куста́ бои́тся** (*prov.*) once bitten twice shy.
пуга́|ть, ю *impf.* (*of* **ис~**) **1.** to frighten, scare. **2.** to intimidate; (+*i.*) to threaten (with).
пуга́|ться, юсь *impf.* (*of* **ис~**) (+*g.*) to be frightened (of), be scared (of).
пуга́ч, а́ *m.* toy-pistol.
пугли́в|ый (~, ~а) *adj.* fearful, timorous; timid.
пу́говиц|а, ы *f.* button.
пуд, а, *pl.* **~ы́, ~о́в** *m.* pood (*old Russ. measure of weight, equivalent to 16.38 kilograms*).
пу́дел|ь, я, *pl.* **~и, ~ей** *or* **~я́, ~е́й** *m.* poodle.
пу́динг, а *m.* pudding.
пу́др|а, ы *f.* powder; **са́харная п.** castor sugar.
пу́дрениц|а, ы *f.* powder-case, compact.
пу́др|ить, ю, ишь *impf.* (*of* **на~**) to powder.
пу́др|иться, юсь, ишься *impf.* (*of* **на~**) to use powder, powder one's face.
пуза́т|ый (~, ~а) *adj.* (*coll.*) pot-bellied.
пу́з|о, а *nt.* (*coll.*) belly, paunch.
пузыр|ёк,ька́ *m.* **1.** phial, vial. **2.** bubble.
пузы́р|иться, ится *impf.* (*coll.*) to bubble; to effervesce.
пузы́р|ь, я́ *m.* **1.** bubble; **мы́льный п.** soap-bubble. **2.** blister. **3.** (*anat.*) bladder; **жёлчный п.** gall-bladder; **мочево́й п.** (urinary) bladder. **4.** air-bladder; **п. со льдом** ice-bag.
пук, а, *pl.* **~и́** *m.* bunch, bundle; tuft; wisp.
пу́к|ать, аю *impf.* (*of* **~нуть**) (*coll.*) to fart.
пу́к|нуть, ну, нешь *pf. of* **~ать**
пул|ево́й *adj. of* **~я**
пулемёт, а *m.* machine-gun.
пулемёт|ный *adj. of* **~**
пулемётчик, а *m.* machine-gunner.
пулесто́йкий *adj.* bullet-proof.
пуло́вер, а *m.* pullover.
пульвериза́тор, а *m.* atomizer, sprayer.
пу́льп|а, ы *f.* (*anat.*) pulp.
пульс, а *m.* pulse; pulse rate; **счита́ть п.** to take the pulse.
пульса́ци|я, и *f.* pulsation, pulse.
пульси́р|овать, ую *impf.* to pulsate; to beat, throb.
пульт, а *m.* **1.** desk, stand; **дирижёрский п.** conductor's stand. **2.** control panel.
пу́л|я, и *f.* bullet; **лить, отлива́ть ~и** (*fig., coll.*) to tell lies.
пуля́рк|а, и *f.* fatted fowl.
пу́м|а, ы *f.* puma.
пункт, а *m.* **1.** point; spot; **наблюда́тельный п.** observation post; **населённый п.** inhabited locality; **опо́рный п.** (*mil.*) strong point; **исхо́дный п., нача́льный п.** starting point; **коне́чный п.** terminus, terminal; **кульминацио́нный п.** culmination, climax. **2.** point; centre; **медици́нский п.** (*mil.*) dressing-station, aid post; **перегово́рный п.** (*collect.*) public (telephone) call-boxes; **призывно́й п.** recruiting centre. **3.** point; paragraph, item; **по ~ам** point by point; **соглаше́ние из трёх ~ов** a three-point agreement.
пункти́р, а *m.* dotted line.
пункти́рн|ый *adj.*: **~ая ли́ния** dotted line.
пунктуа́льност|ь, и *f.* punctuality.
пунктуа́л|ьный (~ен, ~ьна) *adj.* punctual.
пунктуа́ци|я, и *f.* punctuation.
пу́нкци|я, и *f.* (*med.*) puncture.
пу́ночк|а, и *f.* (*zool.*) snow-bunting.
пунцо́вый *adj.* crimson.
пунш, а *m.* punch (*drink*).
пуп, а́ *m.* (*coll.*) belly button, navel; **п. земли́** the hub of the universe.
пупови́н|а, ы *f.* (*anat.*) umbilical cord.
пуп|о́к, ка́ *m.* **1.** navel. **2.** (*of birds*) gizzard.
пупо́чный *adj.* (*anat.*) umbilical.
пупы́рыш|ек, ка *m.* (*coll.*) pimple.
пург|а́, и́ *no pl., f.* snow-storm, blizzard.

пури́зм, а *m.* purism.
пури́ст, а *m.* purist.
пурита́н|ин, ина, *pl.* **~е, ~** *m.* Puritan.
пурита́нский *adj.* Puritan; (*fig.*) puritanical.
пурита́нств|о, а *nt.* Puritanism.
пу́рпур, а *m.* purple.
пурпу́рный *adj.* purple.
пурпу́р|овый *adj.* = **~ный**
пуск, а *m.* starting (up); setting in motion.
пуска́й *particle and conj.* (*coll.*) = **пусть**
пуска́|ть(ся), ю(сь) *impf. of* **пусти́ть(ся)**
пусков|о́й *adj.* starting; **п. пери́од** initial phase (*of working of factory, etc.*); **~о́е устро́йство** starter; **~а́я площа́дка** (rocket) launching platform.
пустельг|а́, и́ *f.* (*zool.*) kestrel.
пусте́|ть, ет *impf.* (*of* **о~**) to (become) empty; to become deserted.
пу|сти́ть, щу́, ~́стишь *pf.* (*of* **~ска́ть**) **1.** to let go; **п. на во́лю** to set free. **2.** to let; to allow, permit; **нас не ~сти́ли в пала́ту** they would not let us into the ward; **~сти́те соба́ку на двор** let the dog out. **3.** to let in, allow to enter; **не п.** to keep out; **п. по предъявле́нии биле́та** to allow to enter on showing a ticket. **4.** to start, set in motion, set going; to set working; **п. во́ду** to turn on water; **п. заво́д** to start up a factory; **п. слух** to start a rumour; **п. фейерве́рк** to let off fireworks. **5.** to set, put; to send; **п. себе́ пу́лю в лоб** to put a bullet through one's head; **п. в обраще́ние** to put in circulation; **п. в прода́жу** to offer for sale; **п. в произво́дство** to put in production; **п. в ход** to start, launch, set going, set in train; **п. в ход все сре́дства** to move heaven and earth; **п. кора́бль ко дну** to send a ship to the bottom; **п. по́ миру** to ruin utterly. **6.** (*+a. or i.*) to throw, fling; **п. ка́мнем в окно́** to throw a stone at a window; **п. пыль в глаза́** to cut a dash, show off. **7.** (*bot.*) to put forth, put out; **п. ко́рни** to take root (*also fig.*); **п. ростки́** to shoot, sprout.
пу|сти́ться, щу́сь, ~́стишься *pf.* (*of* **~ска́ться**) (**в**+*a. or +inf.*; *coll.*) **1.** to set out, start; **п. в путь** to set out. **2.** to begin, start; **п. в оправда́ния** to start making excuses; **п. в пляс** to break into a dance.
пуст|ова́ть, у́ю *impf.* to be empty, stand empty.
пустоголо́в|ый (~, ~а) *adj.* empty-headed.
пустозво́н, а *m.* (*coll.*) windbag.
пуст|о́й (~, ~а́, ~́о) *adj.* **1.** empty; void; hollow; uninhabited; deserted; **~о́е ме́сто** blank space; **на п. желу́док** on an empty stomach; **с ~ы́ми рука́ми** empty-handed. **2.** (*fig.*) idle; shallow; futile; **~а́я болтовня́** idle talk; **п. челове́к** shallow person. **3.** (*fig.*) vain, ungrounded; **~а́я зате́я** vain enterprise; **~а́я отгово́рка** lame excuse; **~ы́е слова́** mere words; **~ы́е угро́зы** empty threats.
пустоме́л|я, и *c.g.* (*coll.*) windbag.
пустопоро́жний *adj.* (*coll.*) empty, vacant.
пустосло́в, а *m.* (*coll.*) windbag.
пустосло́ви|е, я *nt.* (*coll.*) idle talk, verbiage.
пустосло́в|ить, лю, ишь *impf.* (*coll.*) to engage in idle talk.
пустот|а́, ы́, *pl.* **~́ы** *f.* **1.** emptiness; void; (*phys.*) vacuum. **2.** (*fig.*) shallowness; futility.
пустоте́лый *adj.* hollow.
пустоцве́т, а *m.* barren flower (*also fig.*).
пу́стош|ь, и *f.* waste (plot of) land, waste ground.
пусты́нник, а *m.* hermit.
пусты́н|ный (~ен, ~на) *adj.* **1.** uninhabited; **п. о́стров** desert island. **2.** deserted.
пусты́н|я, и *f.* desert, wilderness.
пусты́р|ь, я́ *m.* waste land, vacant plot (of land).
пусты́шк|а, и *f.* (*coll.*) **1.** (*baby's*) dummy. **2.** (*fig.*) shallow person, hollow man.
пусть 1. *particle* let; **п. бу́дет так!** so be it!; **п. она́ сама́ реши́т** let her decide herself; **п.** x **ра́вен 3** (*math.*) let $x = 3$. **2.** *as conj.* though, even if; **п. им бу́дет проти́вно, но я до́лжен вы́сказать своё мне́ние** even if they don't like it, I must express my opinion.
пустя́к, а́ *m.* trifle; **спо́рить из-за ~о́в** to split hairs; **па́ра ~о́в!** (*coll.*) child's play!; **~и́!** (*i*) it's nothing!; never mind!; (*ii*) nonsense!; rubbish!
пустяко́вый *adj.* trifling, trivial.
пустя́чный *adj.* = **пустяко́вый**
пу́таник, а *m.* muddle-head (*pers.*)
пу́таниц|а, ы *f.* muddle, confusion; mess, tangle.
пу́таный *adj.* **1.** muddled, confused; confusing. **2.** (*coll.*) muddle-headed.
пу́та|ть, ю *impf.* (*of* **с~**) **1.** to tangle (*a thread, etc.*). **2.** to confuse, muddle. **3.** to mix up, get mixed up; **ты ещё ~ешь на́ши имена́** you are still mixing our names up. **4.** (*pf.* **в~**) (**в**+*a.*; *coll.*) to implicate (in), mix up (in).
пу́та|ться, юсь *impf.* (*of* **с~**) **1.** to get tangled. **2.** (*of thoughts*) to get confused. **3.** to get mixed up, get muddled. **4.** (*pf.* **в~**) (**в**+*a.*; *coll.*) to get mixed up (in); **п. в тёмные дели́шки** to get mixed up in shady business. **5.** (**с**+*i.*; *coll.*) to get mixed up (with), get entangled (with); to carry on (with) (*a person of the opposite sex*).
путёвк|а, и *f.* **1.** pass, authorization; **сде́лать зая́вку на ~у в санато́рий** to apply for a place in a sanatorium; **п. в жизнь** a start in life. **2.** place in a tourist group; **я купи́л ~у в Чехослова́кию** I have booked a place on a tour of Czechoslovakia.
путеводи́тел|ь, я *m.* guide, guide-book.
путево́дн|ый *adj.* guiding; **~ая звезда́** guiding star; (*fig.*) lodestar.
путев|о́й *adj.* railway; travel; **~ы́е заме́тки** travel notes; **~а́я ка́рта** road-map; **~а́я ско́рость** (*aeron.*) ground speed.
путе́|ец, йца *m.* (*coll.*) **1.** railway engineer. **2.** railwayman, railman.
путём *prep.* (*+g.*) by means of, by dint of.
путепрово́д, а *m.* overpass, flyover; underpass.
путеше́ственник, а *m.* traveller.
путеше́стви|е, я *nt.* **1.** journey; trip; voyage; cruise. **2.** *pl.* (*liter.*) travels.
путеше́ств|овать, ую *impf.* to travel; to voyage.
пу́тник, а *m.* traveller, wayfarer.
пу́тн|ый *adj.* (*coll.*) sensible; **из него́ ничего́ ~ого не вы́йдет** you'll never make a man of him.
путч, а *m.* (*pol.*) putsch; coup attempt.
путчи́ст, а *m.* (*pol.*) putschist; coup plotter.
пу́ты, пут *no sg.* **1.** hobble. **2.** (*fig.*) fetters, chains.
пут|ь, и́, *i.* **ём, о ~и́,** *pl.* **~и́, ~е́й, ~я́м** *m.* **1.** way, track, path; (*aeron.*) track; (*fig.*) road, course; **морски́е ~и́** shipping-routes, sea-lanes; **~и́ сообще́ния** communications; **жи́зненный п.** (*fig.*) life; **на пра́вильном ~и́** on the right track; **сби́ться с (ве́рного) ~и́** to lose one's way; (*fig.*) to go astray. **2.** (*rail.*) track; **запа́сный п.** siding. **3.** journey; voyage; **в ~и́** on one's way, en route; **в четырёх днях ~и́ (от)** four days' journey (from); **на обра́тном ~и́** on the way back; **по ~и́** on the way; **нам с ва́ми по ~и́** we are going the same way; **держа́ть п. (на**+*a.*) to head (for), make (for); **счастли́вого ~и́!** bon voyage! **4.** *pl.* (*anat.*) passage, duct; **дыха́тельные ~и́** respiratory tract. **5.** (*fig.*) way, means; **каки́м ~ём?** how?; in what way?; **ми́рным ~ём** amicably, peaceably; **око́льным ~ём, око́льными ~я́ми** in, by a roundabout way; **пойти́ по ~и́** (*+g.*) to take the path (of). **6.** (*coll.*) use, benefit; **без ~и́** in vain, uselessly.
пуф, а *m.* pouf(fe).
пух, а, о ~́е, в ~у́ *m.* down; fluff; **в п. и прах** (*coll.*) completely, utterly; **разряди́ться в п. и прах** to

put on all one's finery; **разби́ть в п. и прах** to put to complete rout; **ни ~а, ни пера́!** (*coll.*) good luck!
пу́хл|ый (~, ~а́, ~о) *adj.* chubby, plump.
пу́х|нуть, ну, нешь, *past* **~, ~ла** *impf.* to swell.
пухови́к, а́ *m.* feather-bed.
пухо́вк|а, и *f.* powder-puff.
пухо́вый *adj.* downy.
пучегла́з|ый (~, ~а) *adj.* goggle-eyed.
пучи́н|а, ы *f.* gulf, abyss (*also fig.*); the deep.
пуч|о́к, ка́ *m* **1.** bunch, bundle; (*bot.*) fascicle; (*phys.*) beam; **п. се́на** wisp of hay; **п. цвето́в** bunch of flowers. **2.** (*coll.*) bun (*hair-do*).
пу́ш|ечный *adj. of* **~ка**[1]; **~ечное мя́со** cannon-fodder.
пуши́нк|а, и *f.* bit of fluff; **п. сне́га** snow-flake.
пуши́ст|ый (~, ~а) *adj.* fluffy, downy.
пуш|и́ть, у́, и́шь *impf.* (*of* **рас~**) to fluff up.
пу́шк|а, и *f.* gun, cannon; **стреля́ть из пу́шек по воробья́м** (*prov.*) to swat a fly with a sledgehammer.
пушка́р|ь, я́ *m.* (*obs., coll.*) gunner.
пушкини́ст, а *m.* Pushkin scholar.
пушкинове́дени|е, я *nt.* Pushkin studies.
пушни́н|а, ы *f.* (*collect.*) furs, fur-skins, pelts.
пушно́й *adj.* **1.** fur-bearing. **2.** fur; **п. про́мысел** fur trade; **п. това́р** furs.
пуш|о́к, ка́ *m.* fluff.
пу́щ|а, и *f.* dense forest, virgin forest.
пу́ще *adv.* (*coll.*) more; **п. всего́** most of all.
пу́щ|ий *adj. only in phr.* **для ~ей ва́жности** for greater show.
пчел|а́, ы́, *pl.* **~ы** *f.* bee; **рабо́чая п.** worker bee.
пчел|и́ный *adj. of* **~а́; п. воск** beeswax; **~и́ная ма́тка** queen bee; **п. рой** swarm of bees.
пчелово́д, а *m.* bee-keeper, apiarist.
пчелово́дств|о, а *nt.* bee-keeping, apiculture.
пче́льник, а *m.* bee-garden, apiary.
пшени́ц|а, ы *f.* wheat; **ярова́я п.** spring wheat; **ози́мая п.** winter wheat.
пшени́чный *adj.* wheat(en).
пшен|о́, а́ *nt.* millet.
пыж, а́ *m.* wad (*used in loading fire-arm*).
пы́жик, а *m.* young deer; fur of young deer.
пы́ж|иться, усь, ишься *impf.* (*of* **на~**) (*coll.*) **1.** to be puffed up, strut. **2.** to go all out.
пыл, а, о ~е, в ~у́ *m.* **1.: с ~у** piping-hot. **2.** (*fig.*) heat, ardour; **ю́ный п.** youthful ardour; **в ~у́ сраже́ния** in the heat of the battle.
пыла́|ть, ю *impf.* **1.** to blaze, flame. **2.** (*fig.; of the face*) to glow. **3.** (*+i.; fig.*) to burn, be consumed (with).
пылесо́с, а *m.* vacuum cleaner, Hoover (*propr.*).
пылесо́с|ить, ю, ишь *impf.* (*of* **про~**) to vacuum-clean, hoover.
пыли́нк|а, и *f.* speck of dust.
пыл|и́ть, ю, и́шь *impf.* **1.** (*pf.* **на~**) to raise dust. **2.** (*pf.* **за~**) to cover with dust, make dusty.
пыл|и́ться, ю́сь, и́шься *impf.* (*of* **за~**) to get dusty, gather dust.
пы́л|кий (~ок, ~ка́, ~ко *adj.* ardent, passionate, fervent; **~кая речь** impassioned speech.
пы́лкост|ь, и *f.* ardour, passion, fervency.
пыл|ь, и, о ~и, в ~и́ *f.* dust; **у́гольная п.** coal-dust; slack; **смести́ п. (с+***g.***)** to dust.
пы́льник[1]**, а** *m.* (*bot.*) anther.
пы́льник[2]**, а** *m.* dust-coat.
пы́л|ьный (~ен, ~ьна́, ~ьно) *adj.* **1.** dusty; **~ная тря́пка** (*coll.*) duster. **2.: п. котёл** (*agric.*) dust bowl.
пыльц|а́, ы́ *f.* (*bot.*) pollen.
пырн|у́ть, у́, ёшь *pf.* (*coll.*) to jab; to stab; **п. ножо́м** to knife.
пыта́|ть, ю *impf.* to torture (*also fig.*); (*fig.*) to torment.
пыта́|ться, юсь *impf.* (*of* **по~**) to try, attempt, endeavour.
пы́тк|а, и *f.* torture, torment (*also fig.*); **ору́дие ~и** instrument of torture.
пытли́вост|ь, и *f.* inquisitiveness.
пытли́в|ый (~, ~а) *adj.* inquisitive.
пы́|хать, шу, шешь *impf.* **1. (жа́ром)** to blaze. **2.** (*fig.*): **п. гне́вом** to blaze with anger; **п. здоро́вьем** to be the picture of health.
пых|те́ть, чу́, ти́шь *impf.* to puff, pant.
пы́шк|а, и *f.* **1.** bun. **2.** (*fig., coll.*) chubby child; plump woman.
пы́шност|ь, и *f.* splendour, magnificence.
пы́ш|ный (~ен, ~на́, ~но) *adj.* **1.** splendid, magnificent. **2.** fluffy; light; luxuriant; **~ные во́лосы** fluffy hair; **п. пиро́г** light pie; **~ные рукава́** puffed sleeves.
пьедеста́л, а *m.* pedestal (*also fig.*).
пье́с|а, ы *f.* (*theatr.*) play.
пьяне́|ть, ю, ешь *impf.* (*of* **о~**) to get drunk.
пьян|и́ть, ю, и́шь *impf.* (*of* **о~**) to make drunk, intoxicate (*also fig.*); (*fig.*) to go to one's head.
пья́ниц|а, ы *c.g.* drunkard; **го́рький п.** hard drinker.
пья́нк|а, и *f.* (*coll.*) drinking-bout.
пья́нств|о, а *nt.* drunkenness.
пья́нств|овать, ую *impf.* to drink heavily.
пья́н|ый (~, ~а́, ~о) *adj.* drunk; drunken; intoxicated; **по ~ой ла́вочке, с ~ых глаз** (*coll.*) one over the eight; *as n.* **п., ~ого** *m.* (a) drunk.
пэр, а *m.* peer.
пюпи́тр, а *m.* reading-desk; **но́тный п.** music-stand.
пюре́ *nt. indecl.* (*cul.*) purée; **карто́фельное п.** mashed potatoes.
пяд|ь, и, *pl.* **~и, ~е́й** *f.* span; **ни ~и не уступи́ть** (*fig.*) not to yield an inch; **будь он семи́ ~е́й во лбу** (*fig.*) be he a Solomon.
пя́л|ить, ю, ишь *impf.*: **п. глаза́** (**на+***a.*; *coll.*) to stare (at).
пя́л|ьцы, ец *no sg.* tambour; lace-frame.
пяст|ь, и *f.* (*anat.*) metacarpus.
пят|а́, ы́, *pl.* **~ы, ~, ~а́м** *f.* **1.** heel; **ахилле́сова п.** Achilles' heel; **ходи́ть за кем-н. по ~а́м** to follow on s.o.'s heels; **под ~о́й** (*+g.; fig.*) under the heel (of); **с, от головы́ до́ ~** from top to toe. **2.** (*tech.*) abutment.
пята́к, а́ *m.* (*coll.*) five-copeck piece.
пятач|о́к[1]**, ка́** *m.* (*coll.*) = **пята́к; аэродро́м с п.** pocket handkerchief aerodrome.
пятач|о́к[2]**, ка́** *m.* (*coll.*) snout.
пятёрк|а, и *f.* **1.** (*number*) five. **2.** five, 'A' (*highest mark in Russ. educational marking system*). **3.** (*coll.*) five-rouble note. **4.** (*cards*) five.
пятерн|я́, и́, *g. pl.* **~е́й** *f.* (*coll.*) one's hand.
пя́тер|о, ы́х *num.* five.
пятибо́р|ец, ца *m.* pentathlete.
пятибо́рь|е, я *nt.* (*sport*) pentathlon.
пятигра́нник, а *m.* (*math.*) pentahedron.
пятидесятиле́ти|е, я *nt.* **1.** fifty years. **2.** fiftieth anniversary; fiftieth birthday.
пятидесятиле́тний *adj.* **1.** fifty-year. **2.** fifty-year-old.
Пятидеся́тниц|а, ы *f.* (*eccl.*) Pentecost.
пятидеся́т|ый *adj.* fiftieth; **~ые го́ды** the fifties.
пятикла́ссник, а *m.* fifth-form pupil, fifth-former.
Пятикни́жи|е, я *nt.* (*eccl., liter.*) Pentateuch.
пятиконе́чн|ый *adj.*: **~ая звезда́** five-pointed star.
пятикра́тный *adj.* fivefold.
пятиле́ти|е, я *nt.* **1.** five years. **2.** fifth anniversary.
пятиле́тк|а, и *f.* (*econ.*) five-year plan.
пятиле́тний *adj.* **1.** five-year. **2.** five-year-old.
пятио́кис|ь, и *f.* (*chem.*) pentoxide.
пятисотле́ти|е, я *nt.* **1.** five centuries. **2.** quincentenary.
пятисо́тый *adj.* five-hundredth.

пятисто́пный *adj.* (*liter.*) pentameter; **п. ямб** iambic pentameter.
пя́|титься, чусь, тишься *impf.* (*of* **по~**) to back, move backward(s); (*of a horse*) to jib.
пятиуго́льник, а *m.* (*math.*) pentagon.
пятиуго́льный *adj.* pentagonal.
пя́тк|а, и *f.* heel (*also of sock or stocking*); **лиза́ть кому́-н. ~и** to lick s.o.'s boots; **показа́ть ~и** to show a clean pair of heels; **у меня́ душа́ в ~и ушла́** my heart sank to my boots.
пятна́дцатый *adj.* fifteenth.
пятна́дцат|ь, и *num.* fifteen.
пятна́|ть, ю *impf.* (*of* **за~**) to spot, stain (*also fig.*).
пятна́ш|ки, ек *no sg.* (*coll.*) (*children's game*) tag.
пятни́ст|ый (~, ~а) *adj.* spotted, dappled.
пя́тниц|а, ы *f.* Friday; **у него́ семь ~ на неде́ле** he keeps changing his mind.
пят|но́, на́, *pl.* **~на, ~ен, ~нам** *nt.* **1.** spot; patch; blot; stain; **роди́мое п.** birth-mark; **со́лнечные ~на** (*astron.*) sun-spots. **2.** (*fig.*) blot, stain; blemish.
пя́тныш|ко, ка, *pl.* **~ки, ~ек, ~кам** *nt.* speck.
пят|о́к, ка́ *m.* (*+g.*; *coll.*) five (*similar objects*).
пя́т|ый *adj.* fifth; **глава́ ~ая** chapter five; **п. но́мер** number five; size five; **~ое число́ (ме́сяца)** the fifth (*day of the month*); **в ~ом часу́** after four (o'clock).
пят|ь, и́, ью *num.* five.
пятьдеся́т, пяти́десяти, пятью́десятью *num.* fifty.
пятьсо́т, пятисо́т, пятиста́м *num.* five hundred.
пя́тью *adv.* five times.

Р

р. *abbr. of* **1. река** R., River. **2. рубль** r., rouble(s).
раб, а́ *m.* slave (*also fig.*).
раб... *comb. form, abbr. of* **рабо́чий**, *adj.* **1.**
раб|а́, ы́ *f.* (*female*) slave.
рабовладе́л|ец, ьца *m.* slave-owner.
рабовладе́льческий *adj.* slave-owning.
раболе́пи|е, я *nt.* servility.
раболе́п|ный (~ен, ~на) *adj.* servile.
раболе́пств|о, а *nt.* servility.
раболе́пств|овать, ую *impf.* **(пе́ред)** to fawn (on), kowtow (to).
рабо́т|а, ы *f.* **1.** work, working; functioning, running; **обеспе́чить норма́льную ~у** (*+g.*) to ensure normal functioning (of). **2.** work; labour; **дома́шняя р.** homework; **принуди́тельные ~ы** forced labour; **сельскохозя́йственные ~ы** agricultural work; **совме́стная р.** collaboration; **взять в ~у** (*coll.*) to take to task. **3.** work, job; **постоя́нная р.** regular work; **случа́йная р.** casual work; **иска́ть ~у** to look for a job; **снять с ~ы** to lay off. **4.** work, workmanship.
рабо́та|ть, ю *impf.* **1.** **(на+*a.*; над)** to work (for; on); **вре́мя ~ет на нас** time is on our side; **он ~ет над но́вым рома́ном** he is working on a new novel. **2.** to work, run, function; **не р.** not to work, be out of order; **р. на не́фти** to run on oil. **3.** (*of an institution, etc.*) to be open; **галере́я не ~ет по воскресе́ньям** the gallery is not open on Sundays. **4.** (*+i.*) to work, operate; **р. вёслами** to ply the oars; **р. рычаго́м** to operate a lever.
рабо́та|ться, ется *impf.* (*impers.*; *coll.*): **сего́дня хорошо́ ~ется** work is going well today; **вчера́ мне не ~лось** I didn't feel like working yesterday.
рабо́тник, а *m.* worker; employee; **нау́чный р.** researcher; **р. иску́сства** person working in the arts; **р. физи́ческого труда́** manual worker.
рабо́тниц|а, ы *f.* (woman-)worker; **дома́шняя р.** domestic servant, (house)maid; home help.
рабо́тн|ый *adj.*: **р. дом** (*obs.*) workhouse.
работода́тел|ь, я *m.* employer.
работорго́в|ец, ца *m.* slave-trader, slaver.
работорго́вл|я, и *f.* slave-trade.
работоспосо́бност|ь, и *f.* capacity for work.
работоспосо́б|ный (~ен, ~на) *adj.* **1.** able-bodied. **2.** hardworking.
работя́г|а, и *c.g.* (*coll.*) hard worker; slogger.
работя́щий *adj.* (*coll.*) hard-working, industrious.
рабо́ч|ий[1]**, его** *m.* worker; working man; workman; **~ие** (*collect.*; *as social class*) the workers; **сезо́нный р.** seasonal worker; **сельскохозя́йственный р.** farm labourer, agricultural worker; **р. от станка́** factory worker.
рабо́ч|ий[2] *adj.* **1.** worker's, working-class; **~ее движе́ние** working-class movement; **р. класс** the working class. **2.** work, working; **~ая ло́шадь** draught-horse; **~ая пчела́** worker bee; **~ие ру́ки** hands; **~ая си́ла** (*i*) (*collect.*) manpower, labour force, (*ii*) labour; **р. скот** draught animals. **3.** working; **~ее вре́мя** working time, working hours; **р. день** working day; **р. костю́м, ~ее пла́тье** working clothes.
ра́б|ский *adj.* **1.** *adj. of* **~**; **р. труд** slave labour. **2.** (*fig.*) servile.
ра́бств|о, а *nt.* slavery, servitude.
рабы́н|я, и, *g. pl.* **~ь** *f.* slave, bondwoman.
равви́н, а *m.* rabbi.
ра́венств|о *nt.* equality; parity; **знак ~а** (*math.*) equals sign.
равне́ни|е, я *nt.* dressing, alignment; **р. нале́во!, р. напра́во!** (*mil. words of command*) left dress!, right dress!
равни́н|а, ы *f.* plain.
равни́н|ный *adj. of* **~а**; **р. жи́тель** plainsman; **~ная ме́стность** flat country.
равно́[1] *adv.* **1.** alike. **2.** *as conj.* **р. как (и), а р. и** as well as; (*after neg.*) nor.
равно́[2] *nt. pred. form of* **ра́вный. 1.** (*math.*) make(s), equals; **три плюс три р. шести́** three plus three equals six. **2.: всё р.** it is all the same, it makes no difference; *as adv.* all the same; **всё р., что** it is just the same as; **мне всё р.** I don't mind; it's all the same to me; **я всё р. вам позвоню́** I will ring you all the same.
равно... *comb. form* equi-, iso-.
равнобе́дренный *adj.* (*math.*) isosceles.
равнове́си|е, я *nt.* equilibrium (*also fig.*); balance, equipoise; **вы́вести из ~я** to disturb the equilibrium (of), upset the balance (of); **привести́ в р.** to balance; **сохраня́ть р.** to keep one's balance.
равноде́нстви|е, я *nt.* equinox.
равноду́ши|е, я *nt.* indifference.
равноду́ш|ный (~ен, ~на) *adj.* **(к)** indifferent (to).
равнозна́ч|ный (~ен, ~на) *adj.* equivalent.
равноме́рност|ь, и *f.* evenness; uniformity.
равноме́р|ный (~ен, ~на) *adj.* even; uniform.
равнопра́ви|е, я *nt.* equal rights.
равнопра́в|ный (~ен, ~на) *adj.* possessing, enjoying equal rights.
равноси́л|ьный (~ен, ~ьна) *adj.* **1.** of equal strength. **2.** (*+d.*) equivalent (to), tantamount (to).
равносторо́нний *adj.* (*math.*) equilateral.
равноуго́льный *adj.* (*math.*) equiangular.
равноце́н|ный (~ен, ~на) *adj.* of equal value, of equal worth; equivalent.
ра́в|ный (~ен, ~на́, ~но́) *adj.* equal; **~ным о́бразом** equally, likewise; **при про́чих ~ных усло́виях**

other things being equal; **ему́ нет ~ного** he has no equal.

равня́|ть, ю *impf.* (*of* **с~**) **1.** to make even; to treat equally; **р. счёт** (*sport*) to equalize. **2.** (**с**+*i.*; *coll.*) to compare (with), treat as equal (to).

равня́|ться, юсь *impf.* (*of* **с~**) **1.** (**по**+*d.*) (*mil.*) to dress; **~йсь!** (*word of command*) right dress! **2.** (**с**+*i.*; *coll.*) to compete (with), compare (with); match. **3.** *impf. only* (+*d.*) to equal, be equal (to); (*fig.*) to be equivalent (to), be tantamount (to), amount (to); **два́жды пять ~ется десяти́** twice five is ten.

рагу́ *nt. indecl.* (*cul.*) ragout; **кита́йское р.** chop suey.

рад (~а, ~о) *pred. adj.* (+*d.*; +*inf.*; **что**) glad (of; to; that); **я был о́чень р. слу́чаю поговори́ть с ни́ми** I was very glad of the opportunity to talk to them; **о́чень р. (познако́миться с ва́ми)!** pleased to meet you!; **и не р., сам не р.** (*coll.*) I, *etc.*, regret it; I, *etc.*, am sorry; **и не р., что пошёл** I'm sorry I went; **р. не р.** (*coll.*) willy-nilly; like it or not.

рада́р, а *m.* radar.

рада́р|ный *adj. of* ~

ра́дж|а, и *m.* rajah.

ра́ди *prep.+g.* for the sake of; **шу́тки р.** for fun; **р. Бо́га** (*coll.*) for God's sake, for goodness' sake.

радиа́льный *adj.* (*math.*, *tech.*) radial.

радиа́тор, а *m.* radiator.

радиацио́нный *adj.* radiation.

радиа́ци|я, и *f.* radiation.

ра́диев|ый *adj.* radium.

ра́ди|й, я *m.* (*chem.*) radium.

радика́л[1]**, а** *m.* (*math.*, *chem.*) radical.

радика́л[2]**, а** *m.* (*pol.*) radical.

радикали́зм, а *m.* (*pol.*) radicalism.

радика́л|ьный (~ен, ~ьна) *adj.* **1.** (*pol.*) radical. **2.** radical, drastic, sweeping; **~ьные измене́ния** sweeping changes; **~ьные ме́ры** drastic measures; **~ьное сре́дство** drastic remedy.

ра́дио *nt. indecl.* **1.** radio; **по р.** by radio, over the air; **переда́ть по р.** to broadcast; **слу́шать р.** to listen in. **2.** radio; **провести́ р.** to install a radio.

радиоакти́вност|ь, и *f.* radio-activity.

радиоакти́в|ный (~ен, ~на) *adj.* radio-active.

радиобесе́д|а, ы *f.* phone-in.

радиовеща́ни|е, я *nt.* broadcasting.

радиовеща́тельн|ый *adj.* broadcasting; **~ая ста́нция** transmitter.

радиогра́мм|а, ы *f.* radio-telegram.

радио́граф, а *m.* radiographer.

радиогра́фи|я, и *f.* radiography.

радио́л|а, ы *f.* radiogram.

радио́лог, а *m.* radiologist.

радиологи́ческий *adj.* radiological.

радиоло́ги|я, и *f.* radiology.

радиолока́тор, а *m.* radar set.

радиолок|ацио́нный *adj. of* **~а́ция**

радиолока́ци|я, и *f.* radar.

радиолюби́тел|ь, я *m.* radio amateur, 'ham'.

радиомая́к, а́ *m.* radio-beacon.

радиопеленга́тор, а *m.* radio direction finder.

радиопереда́тчик, а *m.* radio transmitter.

радиопереда́ча, и *f.* radio transmission, broadcast.

радиоперехва́т, а *m.* radio interception; radio intercept.

радиоприёмник, а *m.* radio.

радиосвя́з|ь, и *f.* radio communication.

радиослу́шател|ь, я *m.* (radio) listener.

радиоста́нци|я, и *f.* radio station.

радиотелегра́ф, а *m.* radio telegraph.

радиотелеграфи́|я, и *f.* radio-telegraphy.

радиотелефо́н, а *m.* radio-telephone.

радиотерапи́|я, и *f.* radio-therapy.

радиоте́хник, а *m.* radio mechanic.

радиоте́хник|а, и *f.* radio engineering.

радио|техни́ческий *adj. of* **~те́хника**

радиоуправля́емый *adj.* remote-controlled.

радиофици́рованный *adj.*: **р. автомоби́ль** radio car.

ради́р|овать, ую *impf. and pf.* to radio.

ради́ст, а *m.* radio operator.

ра́диус, а *m.* radius.

ра́д|овать, ую *impf.* (*of* **об~**) to gladden, make happy.

ра́д|оваться, уюсь *impf.* (*of* **об~**) (+*d.*) to be glad (at), be happy (at), rejoice (in).

ра́дост|ный (~ен, ~на) *adj.* glad, joyous, joyful; **~ное изве́стие** glad tidings, good news.

ра́дост|ь, и *f.* gladness, joy; **р. жи́зни** joie de vivre; **на ~ях** (+*g.*, *coll.*) in celebration (of), to celebrate; **с ~ью** with pleasure, gladly; **моя́ р., р. моя́** my darling.

ра́дуг|а, и *f.* rainbow.

ра́дужно *adv.* cheerfully; **р. смотре́ть** (**на**+*a.*) to look on the bright side (of).

ра́дужн|ый *adj.* **1.** iridescent, opalescent; **~ая оболо́чка (гла́за)** (*anat.*) iris. **2.** cheerful; optimistic; **~ые наде́жды** high hopes; **~ое настрое́ние** high spirits.

раду́ши|е, я *nt.* cordiality.

раду́ш|ный (~ен, ~на) *adj.* cordial.

ра|ёк, йка́ *m.* (*theatr.*; *obs.*) gallery; the gods.

раж, а *m.* (*coll.*) rage, passion; **войти́ в р., прийти́ в р.** to fly into a rage.

раз[1]**, а,** *pl.* **~ы́, ~** *m.* **1.** time; occasion; **оди́н р., ка́к-то р.** once; **два ~а** twice; **ещё р.** once again, once more; **не р.** more than once; **ни ~у** not once, never; **р. навсегда́** once (and) for all; **р. в день** once a day; **вся́кий р.** every time; **вся́кий р., когда́** whenever; **ино́й р.** now and again; **во второ́й р.** for the second time; **в друго́й р.** another time, some other time; **в са́мый р.** (*coll.*) at the right moment; just right; **р. за ~ом** time after time; **на э́тот р.** this time, on this occasion, for (this) once; **с пе́рвого ~а** from the very first; **во́т тебе (и) р.!** (*coll.*) well, I never!; **как р.** just, exactly; **как р. то** the very thing. **2.** (*num.*) one.

раз[2] *adv.* once, one day.

раз[3] *conj.* if; since; **р. вы бу́дете во Фра́нции, не смо́жете ли вы прие́хать и сюда́?** if you are going to be in France, can't you come here too?

раз... (*also* **разо..., разъ...** *and* **рас...)** *vbl. pref. indicating* **1.** *division into parts* (dis-, un-). **2.** *distribution, direction of action in different directions* (dis-). **3.** *action in reverse* (un-). **4.** *termination of action or state.* **5.** *intensification of action.*

разбави́тел|ь, я *m.* thinner.

разба́в|ить, лю, ишь *pf.* (*of* **~ля́ть**) to dilute.

разбавля́|ть, ю *impf. of* **разба́вить**

разбаза́рива|ть, ю *impf. of* **разбаза́рить**

разбаза́р|ить, ю, ишь *pf.* (*of* **~ивать**) (*coll.*) to squander.

разба́лива|ться, юсь *impf. of* **разболе́ться**

разба́лтыва|ть(ся), ю(сь) *impf. of* **разболта́ть(ся)**

разбе́г, а *m.* run, running start; **пры́гнуть с ~у** to take a running jump; **прыжо́к с ~у** running jump; **р. при взлёте** (*aeron.*) take-off run.

разбега́|ться, юсь *impf. of* **разбежа́ться**

разбе|жа́ться, гу́сь, жи́шься, гу́тся *pf.* (*of* **~га́ться**) **1.** to take a run, run up. **2.** to scatter, disperse. **3.** (*of thoughts*, *etc.*) to be scattered; **глаза́ у меня́ ~жа́лись** I was dazzled.

разбере|ди́ть, жу́, ди́шь *pf. of* **береди́ть**

разбива́|ть(ся), ю(сь) *impf. of* **разби́ть(ся)**

разби́вк|а, и *f.* laying out (*of a garden*, *etc.*).

разбинт|ова́ть, у́ю *pf.* (*of* **~о́вывать**) to remove a bandage (from).

разбинто́выва|ть, ю *impf. of* **разбинтова́ть**

разбира́тельств|о, а *nt.* (*leg.*) examination, investi-

gation; **суде́бное р.** court examination.
разбира́|ть, ю *impf.* **1.** *impf. of* **разобра́ть. 2.** (*impf. only*) to be fastidious; **не ~я** indiscriminately.
разбира́|ться, юсь *impf. of* **разобра́ться**
разбитно́й *adj.* (*coll.*) bright, sprightly; sharp.
разби́т|ый *p.p.p. of* **~ь** *and adj.* (*coll.*) jaded, down.
раз|би́ть, обью́, обьёшь *pf.* (*of* **~бива́ть**) **1.** (*impf. also* **бить**) to break, smash. **2.** to divide (up); to break up; **р. на гру́ппы** to divide up into groups. **3.** to lay out, mark out; **р. ла́герь** to pitch a camp. **4.** to damage severely; to fracture; **р. кому́-н. нос в кровь** to make s.o.'s nose bleed. **5.** to beat, defeat, smash (*also fig.*); **р. чьи-н. до́воды** to demolish s.o.'s arguments.
раз|би́ться, обью́сь, обьёшься *pf.* (*of* **~бива́ться**) **1.** to break, get broken, get smashed. **2.** to divide; to break up. **3.** to be badly hurt; to smash o.s. up.
разбогате́|ть, ю, ешь *pf. of* **богате́ть**
разбо́|й, я *m.* robbery; **морско́й р.** piracy.
разбо́йник, а *m.* **1.** robber; **морско́й р.** pirate; **р. с большо́й доро́ги** highwayman. **2.** (*joc.*; *affectionate form of address to child, etc.*) scamp!; scallywag!
разбо́йнича|ть, ю *impf.* to rob, plunder.
разбо́йни|чий *adj. of* **~к; р. прито́н** den of thieves.
разболе́|ться[1]**, юсь, ешься** *pf.* (*of* **разба́ливаться**) (*coll.*) to become ill; **он совсе́м ~лся** his health has completely cracked.
разбол|е́ться[2]**, и́тся** *pf.* (*of* **разба́ливаться**) to begin to ache badly.
разболта́|ть[1]**, ю** *pf.* (*of* **разба́лтывать**) **1.** to shake up, stir up. **2.** to loosen.
разболта́|ть[2]**, ю** *pf.* (*of* **разба́лтывать**) (*coll.*) to blab out, give away.
разболта́|ться, юсь *pf.* (*of* **разба́лтываться**) **1.** to mix (*as result of stirring*). **2.** to come loose, work loose. **3.** (*fig.*) to get out of hand; to come unstuck.
разбомб|и́ть, лю́, и́шь *pf.* (*no impf.*) to destroy by bombing.
разбо́р, а *m.* **1.** stripping, dismantling. **2.** buying up. **3.** sorting out. **4.** investigation; **р. де́ла** (*leg.*) trial, hearing (*of a case*). **5.** (*gram.*) parsing. **6.** critique. **7.** selectiveness; **без ~у** indiscriminately; **с ~ом** discriminatingly, fastidiously. **8.** sort, quality.
разбо́рк|а, и *f.* **1.** sorting out. **2.** stripping, dismantling, taking to pieces.
разбо́рный *adj.* collapsible.
разбо́рчивост|ь, и *f.* **1.** fastidiousness; scrupulousness. **2.** legibility.
разбо́рчив|ый (~, ~а) *adj.* **1.** fastidious, exacting; discriminating; scrupulous. **2.** legible.
разбран|и́ть, ю́, и́шь *pf.* (*coll.*) to berate; to blow up.
разбран|и́ться, ю́сь, и́шься *pf.* (**с**+*i.*; *coll.*) to fall out (with); to quarrel (with), squabble (with).
разбра́сыва|ть, ю *impf. of* **разброса́ть**
разбра́сыва|ться, юсь *impf.* **1.** *impf. of* **разброса́ться. 2.** (*fig.*) to dissipate one's energies; to try to do too much at once.
разбреда́|ться, юсь *impf. of* **разбрести́сь**
разбре|сти́сь, ду́сь, дёшься, *past* **~лся, ~ла́сь** *pf.* (*of* **~да́ться**) to disperse; **р. по дома́м** to disperse and go home.
разбро́д, а *m.* disorder.
разбро́с|анный *p.p.p. of* **~а́ть** *and adj.* **1.** sparse, scattered; straggling. **2.** (*fig.*) disconnected, incoherent.
разброса́|ть, ю *pf.* (*of* **разбра́сывать**) to scatter, spread, strew; **р. наво́з** to spread manure.
разброса́|ться, юсь *pf.* (*of* **разбра́сываться**) to throw o.s. *or* one's things about.
разбры́з|гать, жу, жешь *pf.* (*of* **~гивать**) to splash; to spray.
разбры́згивател|ь, я *m.* sprinkler.
разбры́згива|ть, ю *impf. of* **разбры́згать**
разбу|ди́ть, жу́, ~дишь *pf. of* **буди́ть**
разбух|а́ть, а́ет *impf. of* **~нуть**
разбу́х|нуть, нет, *past* **~, ~ла** *pf.* (*of* **~а́ть**) to swell (*also fig.*).
разбуш|ева́ться, у́юсь *pf.* **1.** (*of a storm*) to rage; to blow up; (*of the sea*) to run high. **2.** (*coll.*) to fly into a rage.
разва́л, а *m.* **1.** breakdown, disintegration; disorganization. **2.** flea market.
разва́л|ец, ьца *m.* (*coll.*): **ходи́ть с ~ьцем** to shamble; **рабо́тать с ~ьцем** to go slow.
разва́лива|ть(ся), ю(сь) *impf. of* **развали́ть(ся)**
разва́лин|а, ы *f.* **1.** *pl.* ruins; **лежа́ть в ~ах** to be in ruins; **преврати́ть в ~ы** to reduce to ruins. **2.** (*fig.*, *coll.*; *of a pers.*) wreck.
развал|и́ть, ю́, ~ишь *pf.* (*of* **~ивать**) **1.** to pull down (*a building, etc.*). **2.** (*fig.*) to mess up.
развал|и́ться, ю́сь, ~ишься *pf.* (*of* **~иваться**) **1.** to fall down, collapse. **2.** (*fig.*) to go to pieces, fall to pieces. **3.** (*coll.*) to sprawl.
разва́рива|ть, ю *impf. of* **развари́ть**
развар|и́ть, ю́, ~ишь *pf.* (*of* **~ивать**) to boil soft.
ра́зве 1. *interrog. particle, neutral or indicating that neg. answer is expected*; +*neg. indicates that affirmative answer is expected* **р. они́ все вместя́тся в э́ту маши́ну?** will they (really) all get in this car?; **р. ты не знал, что он ру́сский?** didn't you know that he is Russian?; surely you knew that he is Russian? **2.** *interrog. particle, expr. hesitation about course of action to be followed* (+*inf.*; *coll.*) **р. отложи́ть нам пое́здку?** perhaps we had better postpone the trip? **3. р. (что), р. (то́лько)** *as adv.* only; perhaps; *as conj.* except that, only; **он вы́глядит так же как всегда́, р. что похуде́л** he looks the same as ever, except that he has lost weight. **4.** *conj.* (*obs.*) unless.
развева́|ть, ю *impf.* **1.** *impf. of* **разве́ять. 2.** *impf. only* to blow about.
развева́|ться, юсь *impf.* **1.** *impf. of* **разве́яться. 2.** *impf. only* to fly, flutter.
разве́д|ать, аю *pf.* (*of* **~ывать**) **1.** (**о**+*p.*; *coll.*) to find out (about), ascertain. **2.** (*mil.*) to reconnoitre. **3.** (**на**+*a.*; *geol.*) to prospect (for); *pf. only* to locate; **р. на нефть** to prospect for oil.
разведе́ни|е, я *nt.* breeding, rearing; cultivation.
разведённ|ый *p.p.p. of* **развести́** *and adj.* divorced; *as n.* **р., ~ого** *m.*, **~ая, ~ой** *f.* divorcee.
разве́дк|а, и *f.* **1.** (*geol., etc.*) prospecting. **2.** (*mil.*) reconnaissance. **3.** (*mil.*) reconnaissance party. **4.** secret service, intelligence service.
разве́дочн|ый *adj.* (*geol.*) prospecting, exploratory; **~ая сква́жина** test well.
разве́дчик[1]**, а** *m.* **1.** (*mil.*) scout. **2.** secret-service agent; intelligence officer. **3.** (*geol.*) prospector.
разве́дчик[2]**, а** *m.* reconnaissance aircraft.
разве́дывательн|ый *adj.* (*mil.*) **1.** reconnaissance. **2.** intelligence; **р. отде́л** intelligence section.
разве́дыва|ть, ю *impf. of* **разве́дать**
развез|ти́[1]**, у́, ёшь,** *past* **~, ~ла́** *pf.* (*of* **развози́ть**) to convey, deliver.
развез|ти́[2]**, у́, ёшь,** *past* **~, ~ла́** *pf.* (*of* **развози́ть**) (*coll.*) **1.** to exhaust, wear out; (*impers.*): **от жары́ нас ~ло́** we were exhausted from the heat. **2.** to make impassable; (*impers.*): **доро́гу ~ло́ от дожде́й** the road was made impassable by rain.
разве́ива|ть, ю *impf. of* **разве́ять**
развенч|а́ть, а́ю *pf.* (*of* **~ивать**) **1.** to dethrone. **2.** (*fig.*) to debunk.
разве́нчива|ть, ю *impf. of* **развенча́ть**
развёрн|утый *p.p.p. of* **~у́ть** *and adj.* **1.** extensive, large-scale, all-out. **2.** detailed; comprehensive. **3.** (*mil.*) deployed.

развер|ну́ть, ну́, нёшь *pf.* (*of* **∸тывать** *and* **разворáчивать**) **1.** to unfold; to unroll; to unwrap; to unfurl; **р. ковёр** to unroll a carpet; **р. знáмя** to unfurl a banner. **2.** (*mil.*) to deploy. **3.** (**в**+*a.*; *mil.*) to expand (into); **р. батальóн в полк** to expand a battalion into a regiment. **4.** (*fig.*) to show, display. **5.** (*fig.*) to develop; to expand; **р. аргументáцию** to develop a line of argument; **р. торгóвлю** to expand trade. **6.** to turn; to swing (about, around).

развер|ну́ться, ну́сь, нёшься *pf.* (*of* **∸тываться** *and* **разворáчиваться**) **1.** to unfold; to unroll; to come unwrapped. **2.** (*mil.*) to deploy. **3.** (**в**+*a.*, *mil.*) to expand (into), be expanded (into). **4.** (*fig.*) to show *or* display o.s. **5.** (*fig.*) to develop; to spread; to expand. **6.** to turn, swing (about, around).

развёртк|а, и *f.* (*tech.*) reamer.

развёртывани|е, я *nt.* **1.** unfolding; unrolling; unwrapping. **2.** (*mil.*) deployment. **3.** (*fig.*) development, expansion.

развёртыва|ть(ся), ю(сь) *impf. of* **разверну́ть(ся)**

развесел|и́ть, ю́, и́шь *pf.* to cheer up, amuse.

развесел|и́ться, ю́сь, и́шься *pf.* to cheer up.

развесёлый *adj.* (*coll.*) merry, gay.

развéсист|ый (∼, ∼а) *adj.* branchy; **р. каштáн** spreading chestnut.

развé|сить[1], **шу, сишь** *pf.* (*of* **∼шивать**) to weigh out.

развé|сить[2], **шу, сишь** *pf.* (*of* **∼шивать**) **1.** to hang. **2.** to spread (*branches*); **р. у́ши** (*fig.*, *coll.*) to listen open-mouthed.

развé|сить[3], **шу, сишь** *pf.* (*of* **∼шивать**) to hang.

развеснóй *adj.* sold by weight.

разве|сти́[1], **ду́, дёшь**, *past* **∸л, ∼лá** *pf.* (*of* **разводи́ть**) **1.** to take, conduct; **р. детéй по домáм** to take the children to their homes; **р. часовы́х** to post sentries. **2.** to part, separate; **р. мост** to raise a bridge; **р. рукáми** to throw up one's hands (*in a gesture of helplessness*). **3.** to grant a divorce (to). **4.** to dilute, to dissolve.

разве|сти́[2], **ду́, дёшь**, *past* **∸л, ∼лá** *pf.* (*of* **разводи́ть**) **1.** to breed, rear; to cultivate; **р. сад** to plant a garden; **р. парк** to lay out a park. **2.** to start; **р. огóнь** to light a fire; **р. пáры** to raise steam, get up steam. **3.** (*fig.*, *coll.*; *pej.*) to start; **р. чепуху́** to start talking nonsense.

разве|сти́сь[1], **ду́сь, дёшься**, *past* **∸лся, ∼лáсь** *pf.* (*of* **разводи́ться**) (**с**+*i.*) to divorce, be divorced (from).

разве|сти́сь[2], **ду́сь, дёшься**, *past* **∸лся, ∼лáсь** *pf.* (*of* **разводи́ться**) to breed, multiply.

разветв|и́ться, и́тся *pf.* (*of* **∼ля́ться**) to branch; to fork; to ramify.

разветвлéни|е, я *nt.* **1.** branching; ramification; forking. **2.** branch; fork (*of road, etc.*).

разветвля́|ться, юсь *impf. of* **разветви́ться**

развéш|ать, аю *pf.* (*of* **∼ивать**) to hang.

развéшива|ть, ю *impf. of* **развéсить** *and* **развéшать**

развé|ять, ю, ишь *pf.* **1.** (*impf.* **∼ивать**) to scatter, disperse; (*fig.*) to dispel; **р. миф** to shatter a myth. **2.** (*impf.* **∼вáть**) to cause to flutter.

развивá|ть(ся), ю(сь) *impf. of* **разви́ть(ся)**

разви́лин|а, ы *f.* fork, bifurcation.

разви́лист|ый (∼, ∼а) *adj.* forked.

развин|ти́ть, чу́, ти́шь *pf.* (*of* **∸чивать**) to unscrew.

развин|ти́ться, чу́сь, ти́шься *pf.* (*of* **∸чиваться**) **1.** to come unscrewed. **2.** (*fig.*) to come unstuck.

разви́н|ченный *p.p.p. of* **∼ти́ть** *and adj.* (*coll.*) **1.** unstrung, unstuck. **2.** (*of gait*) unsteady, lurching.

разви́нчива|ть(ся), ю(сь) *impf. of* **развинти́ть(ся)**

разви́ти|е, я *nt.* development; evolution.

развит|óй (рáзвит, ∼á, рáзвито) *adj.* **1.** developed. **2.** (intellectually) mature; adult.

раз|ви́ть[1], **овью́, овьёшь**, *past* **∼ви́л, ∼вилá, ∼ви́ло** *pf.* (*of* **∼вивáть**) to unwind, untwist.

раз|ви́ть[2], **овью́, овьёшь**, *past* **∼ви́л, ∼вилá, ∼ви́ло** *pf.* (*of* **∼вивáть**) to develop; **р. мысль** to develop an idea; **р. скóрость** to gather speed.

раз|ви́ться[1], **овью́сь, овьёшься**, *past* **∼ви́лся, ∼вилáсь** *pf.* (*of* **∼вивáться**) to unwind, untwist.

раз|ви́ться[2], **овью́сь, овьёшься**, *past* **∼ви́лся, ∼вилáсь** *pf.* (*of* **∼вивáться**) to develop.

развлекáтел|ьный (∼ен, ∼ьна) *adj.* entertaining; **∼ьное чтéние** light reading.

развлекá|ть(ся), ю(сь) *impf. of* **развлéчь(ся)**

развлечéни|е, я *nt.* entertainment; amusement; diversion.

развлé|чь, ку́, чёшь, ку́т, *past* **∸к, ∼клá** *pf.* (*of* **∼кáть**) to entertain, amuse; to divert.

развлé|чься, ку́сь, чёшься, ку́тся, *past* **∸кся, ∼клáсь** *pf.* (*of* **∼кáться**) **1.** to amuse o.s. **2.** to be diverted, be distracted.

развóд[1], **а** *m.* divorce; **дать р. комý-н.** to give s.o. a divorce; **процéсс о ∼е** divorce proceedings; **они́ в ∼е** they are divorced.

развóд[2], **а** *m.* (*mil.*): **р. карау́лов** guard mounting; **р. часовы́х** posting of sentries.

развóд[3], **а** *m.* breeding.

разво|ди́ть(ся), жу́(сь), ∸дишь(ся) *impf. of* **развести́(сь)**

развóдк|а, и *f.* separation; **р. мóста** raising of a bridge.

разводнóй *adj.*: **р. ключ** adjustable spanner, monkey wrench; **р. мост** drawbridge.

развóд|ы, ов *no sg.* **1.** design, pattern. **2.** stains; **черни́льные р.** ink-stains.

развóз, а *m.* conveyance.

разво|зи́ть, жу́, ∸зишь *impf. of* **развезти́**

развóзк|а, и *f.* conveyance; delivery.

разволн|овáть, у́ю *pf.* to excite, agitate.

разволн|овáться, у́юсь *pf.* to get excited, get agitated.

разворáчива|ть, ю *impf. of* **разверну́ть** *and* **разворoти́ть**

разворáчива|ться, юсь *impf. of* **разверну́ться**

развор|овáть, у́ю *pf.* (*of* **∼óвывать**) to loot, clean out.

разворóвыва|ть, ю *impf. of* **разворовáть**

разворóт, а *m.* **1.** (*aeron.*, *etc.*) turn; (*of motor transport*) U-turn. **2.** (*coll.*) development; **р. торгóвли** growth of trade. **3.** double page; centrefold.

разворо|ти́ть, чу́, ∸тишь *pf.* (*of* **разворáчивать**) **1.** to make havoc (of); to knock to pieces. **2.** to smash up, break up.

разврáт, а *m.* debauchery, depravity, dissipation.

развра|ти́ть, щу́, ти́шь *pf.* (*of* **∼щáть**) **1.** to debauch, corrupt. **2.** (*fig.*) to deprave.

развра|ти́ться, щу́сь, ти́шься *pf.* (*of* **∼щáться**) to become corrupted, give o.s. up to debauchery.

разврáтник, а *m.* debauchee, profligate, libertine.

разврáтнича|ть, ю *impf.* to lead a depraved life.

разврáт|ный (∼ен, ∼на) *adj.* debauched, depraved, profligate.

развращá|ть(ся), ю(сь) *impf. of* **разврати́ть(ся)**

развращённост|ь, и *f.* corruptness; depravity.

развра|щённый *p.p.p. of* **∼ти́ть** *and adj.* corrupt; depraved.

развью́чива|ть, ю *impf. of* **развью́чить**

развью́ч|ить, у, ишь *pf.* (*of* **∼ивать**) to unload, unburden.

развя|зáть, жу́, ∸жешь *pf.* (*of* **∸зывать**) to untie, undo; to unleash; **р. комý-н. ру́ки** to untie s.o.'s hands (*also fig.*); **р. войну́** to unleash war.

развя|зáться, жу́сь, ∸жешься *pf.* (*of* **∸зываться**) **1.** to come untied, come undone; **у негó ∼зáлся язы́к** (*fig.*) his tongue has been loosened. **2.** (**с**+*i.*;

fig.) to have done (with), be through (with).
развя́зк|а, и *f.* **1.** (*liter.*) denouement. **2.** outcome, upshot; **счастли́вая р.** happy ending; **де́ло идёт к ~е** things are coming to a head. **3.: р. движе́ния, кольцева́я (тра́нспортная) р.** (traffic) roundabout.
развя́з|ный (~ен, ~на) *adj.* (unduly) familiar; free-and-easy.
развя́зыва|ть(ся), ю(сь) *impf. of* **развяза́ть(ся)**
разгад|а́ть, а́ю *pf.* (*of* **∸ывать**) **1.** to guess the meaning (of); **р. зага́дку** to solve a riddle; **р. сны** to interpret dreams; **р. шифр** to break a cipher. **2.** to guess, divine; **р. челове́ка** to size a person up.
разга́дк|а, и *f.* solution (*of a riddle, etc.*).
разга́дыва|ть, ю *impf. of* **разгада́ть**
разга́р, а *m.*: **в ~е** (*+g.*) at the height (of); **в по́лном ~е** in full swing.
разгиба́|ть(ся), ю(сь) *impf. of* **разогну́ть(ся)**; **не ~я спины́** without a let-up.
разгильдя́|й, я *m.* (*coll.*) sloven; sloppy individual.
разглаго́льствовани|е, я *nt.* (*coll.*) big talk.
разглаго́льств|овать, ую *impf.* (*coll.*) to hold forth, expatiate; to talk big.
разгла́|дить, жу, дишь *pf.* (*of* **~живать**) to smooth out; to iron out, press.
разгла́|диться, дится *pf.* (*of* **~живаться**) **1.** to become smoothed out. **2.** *pass. of* **~дить**
разгла́жива|ть(ся), ет(ся) *impf. of* **разгла́дить(ся)**
разгла|си́ть, шу́, си́шь *pf.* (*of* **~ша́ть**) **1.** to divulge, disclose. **2.** (**о**+*p.*; *coll.*) to trumpet, broadcast.
разглаша́|ть, ю *impf. of* **разгласи́ть**
разглаше́ни|е, я *nt.* divulging, (unauthorized) disclosure.
разгля|де́ть, жу́, ди́шь *pf.* to make out, discern.
разгля́дыва|ть, ю *impf.* to examine closely, scrutinize.
разгне́ва|ть, ю *pf.* to anger, incense.
разгне́ва|ться, юсь *pf. of* **гне́ваться**
разгова́рива|ть, ю *impf.* (**с**+*i.*) to talk (to, with), speak (to, with), converse (with); **они́ друг с дру́гом не ~ют** they are not on speaking terms.
разгов|е́ться, е́юсь, е́ешься *pf.* (*of* **~ля́ться**) to break a (period of) fast.
разговля́|ться, юсь *impf. of* **разгове́ться**
разгово́р, а (у) *m.* talk, conversation; **перемени́ть р.** to change the subject; **об э́том и ~у быть не мо́жет** there can be no question about it; **без ~ов!** and no argument!
разговор|и́ться, ю́сь, и́шься *pf.* **1.** (**с**+*i.*) to get into conversation (with). **2.** to warm to one's theme.
разгово́рник, а *m.* phrase-book.
разгово́р|ный *adj.* **1.** colloquial; conversational. **2.: ~ная бу́дка** telephone booth; **р. уро́к** conversation class.
разгово́рчивост|ь, и *f.* talkativeness, loquacity.
разгово́рчив|ый (~, ~а) *adj.* talkative, loquacious.
разго́н, а *m.* **1.** dispersal; dissolution. **2. быть в ~е** (*coll.*) to be out. **3.** (*sport*) run, running start; **прыжо́к с ~а** running jump.
разгоня́|ть(ся), ю(сь) *impf. of* **разогна́ть(ся)**
разгора́жива|ть, ю *impf. of* **разгороди́ть**
разгор|а́ться, а́ется *impf. of* **~е́ться**
разгор|е́ться, и́тся *pf.* (*of* **~а́ться**) **1.** to flare up. **2.** (*fig.*) to flare up; **~е́лся спор** a heated argument developed; **стра́сти ~е́лись** feeling ran high, passions rose. **3.** (*fig.*) to flush.
разгоро|ди́ть, жу́, ∸ди́шь *pf.* (*of* **разгора́живать**) to partition off.
разгоряч|и́ть, у́, и́шь *pf. of* **горячи́ть**
разгоряч|и́ться, у́сь, и́шься *pf.* (*of* **горячи́ться**) (**от**) to be flushed (with).
разгра́б|ить, лю, ишь *pf.* to plunder, pillage, loot.
разграбле́ни|е, я *nt.* plunder, pillage.
разграниче́ни|е, я *nt.* **1.** demarcation, delimitation. **2.** differentiation.
разграни́чива|ть, ю *impf. of* **разграни́чить**
разграничи́тельн|ый *adj.*: **~ая ли́ния** line of demarcation, dividing line.
разграни́ч|ить, у, ишь *pf.* (*of* **~ивать**) **1.** to delimit, demarcate. **2.** to differentiate, distinguish.
разграф|и́ть, лю́, и́шь *pf.* (*of* **графи́ть** *and* **~ля́ть**) to rule (*in squares, columns, etc.*).
разграфля́|ть, ю *impf. of* **разграфи́ть**
разгреба́|ть, ю *impf. of* **разгрести́**
разгре|сти́, бу́, бёшь, *past* **∸̈б, ~бла́** *pf.* (*of* **~ба́ть**) to rake (aside); to shovel (aside).
разгро́м, а *m.* **1.** crushing defeat, rout. **2.** (*coll.*) havoc, devastation; **в кварти́ре был по́лный р.** there was complete chaos in the flat.
разгром|и́ть, лю́, и́шь *pf. of* **громи́ть**
разгружа́|ть(ся), ю(сь) *impf. of* **разгрузи́ть(ся)**
разгру|зи́ть, жу́, ∸зи́шь *pf.* (*of* **~жа́ть**) **1.** to unload. **2.** (**от**; *fig., coll.*) to relieve (of).
разгру|зи́ться, жу́сь, ∸зи́шься *pf.* (*of* **~жа́ться**) **1.** to unload. **2.** (**от**; *fig., coll.*) to be relieved (of).
разгру́зк|а, и *f.* unloading.
разгрыза́|ть, ю *impf. of* **разгры́зть**
разгры́з|ть, у́, ёшь, *past* **~, ~ла** *pf.* (*of* **~а́ть**) to crack (*with one's teeth*); **р. оре́х** to crack a nut.
разгу́л, а *m.* **1.** revelry, debauch. **2.** (*+g.*; *fig.*) wave (of); outburst (of); **р. антисемити́зма** a wave of anti-semitism.
разгу́лива|ть, ю *impf.* **1.** to stroll about, walk about. **2.** *impf. of* **разгуля́ть**
разгу́лива|ться, юсь *impf. of* **разгуля́ться**
разгу́ль|е, я *nt.* (*coll.*) merry-making.
разгу́л|ьный (~ен, ~ьна) *adj.* (*coll.*) loose, wild; **вести́ ~ьную жизнь** to lead a wild life.
разгул|я́ть, я́ю *pf.* (*of* **∸ивать**) (*coll.*) **1.** to amuse so as to keep awake. **2.** to dispel; **р. чью-н. хандру́** to dispel s.o.'s gloom.
разгул|я́ться, я́юсь *pf.* (*of* **∸иваться**) (*coll.*) **1.** to spread o.s.; to have free scope. **2.** (*of children*) to wake up. **3.** (*of weather*) to clear up; **день ~я́лся** it has turned out a fine day.
разда|ва́ть(ся), ю́(сь), ёшь(ся) *impf. of* **разда́ть(ся)**
раздав|и́ть, лю́, ∸ишь *pf.* (*of* **∸ливать**) **1.** to crush; to squash. **2.** (*fig.*) to crush, overwhelm. **3.** (*coll.*) to down, sink (*alcoholic beverages*).
разда́влива|ть, ю *impf. of* **раздави́ть**
разда́рива|ть, ю *impf. of* **раздари́ть**
раздар|и́ть, ю́, ∸ишь *pf.* (*of* **∸ивать**) (*+d.*) to give away (to), make a present of.
разда́точный *adj.* distributing, distribution; **р. пункт** distribution centre.
разда́|ть, м, шь, ст, ди́м, ди́те, ду́т, *past* **ро́здал, ~ла́, ро́здало** *pf.* (*of* **~ва́ть**) to distribute, give out, serve out, dispense; **р. ми́лостыню** to dispense charity; **р. кни́ги** to give out books.
разда́|ться[1]**, мся, шься, стся, ди́мся, ди́тесь, ду́тся,** *past* **~лся, ~ла́сь, ~ло́сь** *pf.* (*of* **~ва́ться**) to be heard; to resound; to ring (out); **~лся вы́стрел** a shot rang out; **~лся стук в дверь** there was a knock at the door.
разда́|ться[2]**, мся, шься, стся, ди́мся, ди́тесь, ду́тся,** *past* **~лся, ~ла́сь, ~ло́сь** *pf.* (*of* **~ва́ться**) (*coll.*) **1.** to make way. **2.** to stretch, expand. **3.** to put on weight.
разда́ч|а, и *f.* distribution.
раздва́ива|ть(ся), ю(сь) *impf. of* **раздвои́ть(ся)**
раздвига́|ть(ся), ю(сь) *impf. of* **раздви́нуть(ся)**
раздвижно́й *adj.* expanding; sliding; **р. за́навес** (*theatr.*) draw curtain; **р. стол** expanding table.
раздви́|нуть, ну, нешь *pf.* (*of* **~га́ть**) to move apart, slide apart; **р. занаве́ски** to draw back the curtains; **р. стол** to extend a table.

раздви́|нуться, нется *pf.* (*of* **~га́ться**) to move apart, slide apart; **за́навес ~нулся** the curtain was drawn back; (*in theatre*) the curtain rose; **толпа́ ~нулась** the crowd made way.

раздвое́ни|е, я *nt.* division into two; bifurcation; **р. ли́чности** (*med.*) split personality.

раздво́|енный *p.p.p. of* **~и́ть** *and adj.* forked; bifurcated; **~енное копы́то** cloven hoof; **~енное созна́ние** split mind.

раздво|и́ть, ю́, и́шь *pf.* (*of* **раздва́ивать**) to divide into two; to bisect.

раздво|и́ться, ю́сь, и́шься *pf.* (*of* **раздва́иваться**) to bifurcate, fork, split, become double.

раздева́лк|а, и *f.* (*coll.*) cloak-room.

раздева́л|ьня, ьни, *g. pl.* **~ен** *f.* = **~ка**

раздева́ни|е, я *nt.* undressing.

раздева́|ть(ся), ю(сь) *impf. of* **разде́ть(ся)**

разде́л, а *m.* **1.** division; partition; allotment. **2.** section, part (*of book, etc.*).

разде́л|ать, аю *pf.* (*of* **~ывать**) to dress, prepare; **р. гря́дки** to prepare (flower-)beds (*for sowing*); **р. под дуб** to grain in imitation of oak; **р. кого́-н. под оре́х** (*coll.*) to give it s.o. hot.

разде́л|аться, аюсь *pf.* (*of* **~ываться**) (**с**+*i.*) **1.** to be through (with); to settle (accounts) (with); **р. с долга́ми** to pay off debts. **2.** (*fig.*) to settle accounts (with), get even (with).

разделе́ни|е, я *nt.* division.

раздели́м|ый (~, ~а) *adj.* divisible.

раздели́тельн|ый *adj.* **1.** dividing, separating; **~ая черта́** dividing line. **2.** (*phil.*, *gram.*) disjunctive; (*gram.*) distributive; **р. сою́з** disjunctive conjunction; **~ое местоиме́ние** distributive pronoun.

раздел|и́ть, ю́, ⁓ишь *pf.* (*of* **~я́ть**) **1.** to divide. **2.** to separate, part. **3.** to share.

раздел|и́ться, ю́сь, ⁓ишься *pf.* (*of* **~я́ться**) **1.** (**на**+*a.*) to divide (into); to be divided; **нам придётся р. на две гру́ппы** we shall have to divide into two groups; **мне́ния ~и́лись** opinions were divided. **2.** to separate, part company.

разде́льн|ый *adj.* **1.** separate. **2.** (*of pronunciation*) clear, distinct.

раздел|я́ть, я́ю *impf. of* **~и́ть; р. чьи-н. взгля́ды** to share s.o.'s views.

раздел|я́ться, я́юсь *impf. of* **~и́ться**

разде́|ть, ну, нешь *pf.* (*of* **~ва́ть**) to undress.

разде́|ться, нусь, нешься *pf.* (*of* **~ва́ться**) to undress, strip; to take off one's things.

раздира́|ть, ю *impf.* **1.** *impf. of* **разодра́ть. 2.** *impf. only* (*fig.*) to rend, tear, lacerate, harrow.

раздира́|ться, ю, ет(ся) *impf. of* **разодра́ться**

раздира́|ющий *pres. part. act. of* **~ть** *and adj.*; **р. (ду́шу)** heart-rending, heart-breaking, harrowing.

раздобре́|ть, ю *pf. of* **добре́ть**[2]

раздобыва́|ть, ю *impf. of* **раздобы́ть**

раздо|бы́ть, бу́ду, бу́дешь, *past* **~бы́л** *pf.* (*of* **~бывать**) (*coll.*) get, procure, get hold of.

раздо́ль|е, я *nt.* **1.** expanse. **2.** (*fig.*) freedom.

раздо́л|ьный (~ен, ~ьна) *adj.* free.

раздо́р, а *m.* discord, dissension; **я́блоко ~а** bone of contention; **се́ять р.** to breed strife.

раздоса́д|овать, ую *pf.* to vex.

раздраж|а́ть(ся), а́ю(сь) *impf. of* **~и́ть(ся)**

раздраже́ни|е, я *nt.* irritation.

раздражи́тел|ь, я *m.* (*med.*) irritant.

раздражи́тельност|ь, и *f.* irritability.

раздражи́тел|ьный (~ен, ~ьна) *adj.* irritable; short-tempered.

раздраж|и́ть, у́, и́шь *pf.* (*of* **~а́ть**) **1.** to irritate, annoy. **2.** (*med.*) to irritate.

раздраж|и́ться, у́сь, и́шься *pf.* (*of* **~а́ться**) **1.** to get irritated, get annoyed. **2.** (*med.*) to become inflamed.

раздразн|и́ть, ю, ⁓ишь *pf.* **1.** to tease. **2.** to stimulate; **р. чей-н. аппети́т** to whet s.o.'s appetite.

раздроб|и́ть, лю́, и́шь *pf.* **1.** *pf. of* **дроби́ть. 2.** (*impf.* **~ля́ть**) (**в**+*a.*; *math.*) to convert (to); to reduce (to); **р. гра́ммы в сантигра́ммы** to convert grams to centigrams.

раздроб|и́ться, и́тся *pf. of* **дроби́ться**

раздро́б|ленный (*and* **раздроблённый)** *p.p.p. of* **~и́ть** *and adj.* (*fig.*) fragmented.

раздробля́|ть, ю *impf. of* **раздроби́ть**

раздува́|ть(ся), ю(сь) *impf. of* **разду́ть(ся)**

разду́м|ать, аю *pf.* (*of* **~ывать**) to change one's mind; (+*inf.*) to decide against; **я ~ал подава́ть заявле́ние на э́то ме́сто** I decided against applying for that job.

разду́м|аться, аюсь *pf.* (**о**+*p.*; *coll.*) to be absorbed in thinking (about).

разду́мыва|ть, ю *impf.* **1.** *impf. of* **разду́мать. 2.** *impf. only* (**о**+*p.*) to ponder (on, over), consider; **не ~я** without a moment's thought.

разду́мь|е, я *nt.* **1.** meditation; thought; **в глубо́ком р.** deep in thought. **2.** hesitation; **меня́ взяло́ р.** I can't make up my mind.

разду́т|ый *p.p.p. of* **~ь** *and adj.* (*fig.*, *coll.*) exaggerated; inflated; excessive.

разду́|ть, ю, ешь *pf.* (*of* **~ва́ть**) **1.** to blow; to fan; **р. пла́мя** (*fig.*) to fan the flames. **2.** to blow (out); **р. щёки** to blow out one's cheeks; (*impers.*): **у него́ ~ло щёку** his cheek is swollen. **3.** (*fig.*, *coll.*) to exaggerate; to inflate, swell; **р. поте́ри** to exaggerate losses. **4.** to blow about; (*impers.*): **~ло бума́ги по́ полу** the papers had blown all over the floor.

разду́|ться, юсь, ешься *pf.* (*of* **~ва́ться**) to swell.

разева́|ть, ю *impf. of* **рази́нуть**

разжа́лоб|ить, лю, ишь *pf.* to move (to pity).

разжа́ловани|е, я *nt.* demotion.

разжа́л|овать, ую *pf.* (*mil.*) to demote; **р. в солда́ты** to reduce to the ranks.

раз|жа́ть, ожму́, ожмёшь *pf.* (*of* **~жима́ть**) to unclasp; to release, undo; **р. кула́к** to unclench one's fist; **р. ру́ки** to unclasp one's hands.

раз|жа́ться, ожмётся *pf.* (*of* **~жима́ться**) to come loose; to relax.

разж|ева́ть, ую́, уёшь *pf.* (*of* **~ёвывать**) to chew, masticate; (*fig.*, *coll.*) to chew over.

разжёвыва|ть, ю *impf. of* **разжева́ть**

раз|же́чь, ожгу́, ожжёшь, ожгу́т, *past* **~жёг, ~ожгла́** *pf.* (*of* **~жига́ть**) **1.** to kindle. **2.** (*fig.*) to kindle, rouse, stir up; **р. стра́сти** to arouse passion.

разжива́|ться, юсь *impf. of* **разжи́ться**

разжига́ни|е, я *nt.* kindling (*also fig.*).

разжига́|ть, ю *impf. of* **разже́чь**

разжи|ди́ть, жу́, ди́шь *pf.* (*of* **~жа́ть**) to dilute, thin.

разжижа́|ть, ю *impf. of* **разжиди́ть**

разжиже́ни|е, я *nt.* dilution, thinning.

разжима́|ть(ся), ет(ся) *impf. of* **разжа́ть(ся)**

разжире́|ть, ю *pf. of* **жире́ть**

разж|и́ться, иву́сь, ивёшься, *past* **~и́лся, ~ила́сь** *pf.* (*of* **~ива́ться**) (*coll.*) to get rich, make a pile.

раззадо́рива|ть, ю *impf. of* **раззадо́рить**

раззадо́р|ить, ю, ишь *pf.* (*of* **~ивать**) (*coll.*) to stir up, excite.

рази́н|уть, у, ешь *pf.* (*of* **разева́ть**) (*coll.*) to open wide (*the mouth*); to gape; **слу́шать, ~ув рот** to listen open-mouthed.

рази́н|я, и *c.g.* (*coll.*) scatter-brain.

рази́тел|ьный (~ен, ~ьна) *adj.* striking.

ра|зи́ть[1]**, жу́, зи́шь** *impf.* to strike, hit.

раз|и́ть[2]**, и́т** *impf.* (*impers.*+*i.*; *coll.*) to reek (of), stink (of); **из ко́мнаты ~и́ло чесноко́м** the room reeked of garlic.

разлага́|ть(ся), ю(сь) *impf. of* **разложи́ть(ся)**

разла́д, а *m.* **1.** disorder. **2.** discord, dissension.
разла́|дить, жу, дишь *pf.* (*of* **~живать**) to derange; (*coll.*) to mess up.
разла́|диться, дится *pf.* (*of* **~живаться**) to get out of order; (*coll.*) to go wrong.
разла́мыва|ть(ся), ю, ет(ся) *impf. of* **разлома́ть(ся)** *and* **разломи́ть(ся)**
разле́нива|ться, юсь *impf. of* **разлени́ться**
разлен|и́ться, ю́сь, ́ишься *pf.* (*of* **́иваться**) (*coll.*) to become sunk in sloth.
разлет|а́ться, а́юсь *impf. of* **~е́ться**
разле|те́ться, чу́сь, ти́шься *pf.* (*of* **~та́ться**) **1.** to fly away; to scatter (*in the air*). **2.** (*coll.*) to smash, shatter. **3.** (*fig., coll.*) to vanish, be shattered; **её мечта́ ~те́лась** her dream was shattered; **все на́ши наде́жды ~те́лись** all our hopes were dashed. **4.** (*coll.*) to rush.
разл|е́чься, я́гусь, я́жешься, *past* **~ёгся, ~егла́сь** *pf.* (*coll.*) to sprawl; to stretch o.s. out.
разли́в, а *m.* **1.** bottling. **2.** flood; overflow.
разлива́ни|е, я *nt.* pouring out.
разлива́тельн|ый *adj.*: **~ая ло́жка** ladle.
разлива́|ть(ся), ю, ет(ся) *impf. of* **разли́ть(ся)**
разливн|о́й *adj.* on tap, on draught.
разлин|ова́ть, у́ю *pf.* (*of* **~о́вывать**) to rule (*paper, etc.*).
разлино́выва|ть, ю *impf. of* **разлинова́ть**
раз|ли́ть, олью́, ольёшь, *past* **~ли́л, ~лила́, ~ли́ло** *pf.* (*of* **~лива́ть**) **1.** to pour out; **р. чай** to pour the tea. **2.** to spill; **р. водо́й** to pour water (over), douse, drench; **их водо́й не ~ольёшь** (*coll.*) they are thick as thieves. **3.** (*fig.*) to spread, broadcast.
раз|ли́ться, ольётся, *past* **~ли́лся, ~лила́сь** *pf.* (*of* **~лива́ться**) **1.** to spill; **суп ~ли́лся по ска́терти** the soup has spilled over the table-cloth. **2.** to overflow; to burst its banks. **3.** (*fig.*) to spread; **по её лицу́ ~лила́сь улы́бка** a smile spread across her face.
различ|а́ть, а́ю *impf. of* **~и́ть**
различа́|ться, юсь *impf.* to differ.
разли́чи|е, я *nt.* distinction; difference; **де́лать р. (ме́жду)** to make distinctions (between).
различи́тельный *adj.* distinctive; distinguishing.
различ|и́ть, у́, и́шь *pf.* (*of* **~а́ть**) **1.** to distinguish; to tell apart. **2.** to discern, make out.
разли́ч|ный (~ен, ~на) *adj.* **1.** different; differing. **2.** various, diverse; **по ~ным соображе́ниям** for various reasons.
разложе́ни|е, я *nt.* **1.** breaking down. **2.** decomposition, decay; putrefaction. **3.** (*fig.*) demoralization; disintegration.
разлож|и́ть[1], **у́, ́ишь** *pf.* (*of* **раскла́дывать**) **1.** to put away. **2.** to lay out, to spread (out); **р. ого́нь** to make a fire; **р. ска́терть** to spread a table-cloth; **р. складну́ю крова́ть** to put up a camp bed. **3.** to distribute, apportion; **р. при́быль** to distribute, share out profits.
разлож|и́ть[2], **у́, ́ишь** *pf.* (*of* **разлага́ть**) **1.** to break down; (*math.*) to expand; **р. вещество́ на составны́е ча́сти** to break a substance down into its component parts. **2.** (*fig.*) to break down, demoralize.
разлож|и́ться[1], **у́сь, ́ишься** *pf.* (*of* **раскла́дываться**) (*coll.*) to lay one's things out.
разлож|и́ться[2], **у́сь, ́ишься** *pf.* (*of* **разлага́ться**) **1.** (*chem.*) to decompose; (*math.*) to expand. **2.** to decompose, rot, decay; **труп уже́ ~и́лся** the body has already decomposed. **3.** (*fig.*) to become demoralized; to crack up, go to pieces.
разло́м, а *m.* **1.** breaking. **2.** break.
разлома́|ть, ю *pf.* (*of* **разла́мывать**) to break (in pieces); **р. дом** to pull down a house.
разлома́|ться, ется *pf.* (*of* **разла́мываться**) to break (in pieces); to break up.
разлом|и́ть, лю́, ́ишь *pf.* (*of* **разла́мывать**) **1.** to break (in pieces). **2.** (*impers.*; *coll.*): **меня́ всего́ ~и́ло** every bone in my body aches.
разлом|и́ться, ́иться *pf.* (*of* **разла́мываться**) to break in pieces.
разлу́к|а, и *f.* **1.** separation; **жить в ~е (с+***i.*) to be separated (from). **2.** parting; **час ~и** hour of parting.
разлуч|а́ть(ся), а́ю(сь) *impf. of* **~и́ть(ся)**
разлуч|и́ть, у́, и́шь *pf.* (*of* **~а́ть**) (*+a.* **с+***i.*) to separate (from), part (from).
разлуч|и́ться, у́сь, и́шься *pf.* (*of* **~а́ться**) (**с+***i.*) to separate, part (from).
разлюб|и́ть, лю́, ́ишь *pf.* to cease to love, stop loving; to cease to like.
размагни́|тить, чу, тишь *pf.* (*of* **~чивать**) (*tech.*) to demagnetize.
размагни́чива|ть, ю *impf. of* **размагни́тить**
разма́|зать, жу, жешь *pf.* (*of* **~зывать**) **1.** to spread, smear; **р. варе́нье по всему́ лицу́** to get jam all over one's face. **2.** (*coll.*) to pad out, amplify (*a narration*).
разма́|заться, жется *pf.* (*of* **~зываться**) to spread; to get smeared.
размазн|я́, и́, *g. pl.* **~е́й** *f. and c.g.* (*coll.*) **1.** *f.* gruel. **2.** *c.g.* (*fig.*) ninny, wishy-washy person.
разма́зыва|ть(ся), ю, ет(ся) *impf. of* **разма́зать(ся)**
разма́лыва|ть, ю *impf. of* **размоло́ть**
разма́тыва|ть(ся), ю, ет(ся) *impf. of* **размота́ть(ся)**
разма́х, а *m.* **1.** sweep; **со всего́ ~у** with all one's might. **2.** span; **р. кры́льев** (*aeron.*) wing-span. **3.** (*fig*) scope, range; **широ́кий р.** grand scale; **у них широ́кий р. жи́зни** they live on the grand scale.
разма́хива|ть, ю *impf.* (*+i.*) to swing; to brandish; **р. рука́ми** to gesticulate.
разма́хива|ться, юсь *impf. of* **размахну́ться**
размах|ну́ться, ну́сь, нёшься *pf.* (*of* **́иваться**) **1.** to draw back one's arm (*to strike or as if to strike*). **2.** (*fig., coll.*) to do things in a big way.
разма́чива|ть, ю *impf. of* **размочи́ть**
разма́шист|ый (~, ~а) *adj.* sweeping; **р. жест** sweeping gesture; **р. по́черк** bold hand.
размежева́ни|е, я *nt.* demarcation, delimitation.
размеж|ева́ть, у́ю, у́ешь *pf.* (*of* **~ёвывать**) to divide out, delimit (*also fig.*); **р. сфе́ры влия́ния** to delimit spheres of influence.
размеж|ева́ться, у́юсь, у́ешься *pf.* (*of* **~ёвываться**) **1.** to fix the boundaries. **2.** (*fig.*) to break off relations.
размежёвыва|ть(ся), ю(сь) *impf. of* **размежева́ть(ся)**
размельч|а́ть, а́ю *impf. of* **~и́ть**
размельч|и́ть, у́, и́шь *pf.* (*of* **~а́ть**) to divide into particles; to pulverize.
разме́н, а *m.* exchange; **р. де́нег** changing of money.
разме́нива|ть(ся), ю(сь) *impf. of* **разменя́ть(ся)**
разме́нн|ый *adj.*: **~ая моне́та** small change.
размен|я́ть, я́ю *pf.* (*of* **́ивать**) to change; **р. сторублёвку** to change a hundred-rouble note.
размен|я́ться, я́юсь *pf.* (*of* **́иваться**) (*coll.*) **1.** (*+i.*) to exchange. **2.** (*fig.*) to dissipate one's talents.
разме́р, а *m.* **1.** dimensions; **воро́нка ~ом в де́сять квадра́тных ме́тров** a crater measuring ten square metres. **2.** size; (*pl.*) measurements; **како́й ваш р.?** what size do you take? **3.** rate, amount; **получа́ть зарпла́ту в ~е десяти́ рубле́й в день** to be paid at the rate of ten roubles per day. **4.** scale, extent; (*pl.*) proportions; **в широ́ких ~ах** on a large scale; **увели́читься до огро́мных ~ов** to assume enormous proportions. **5.** metre (*of verse*); (*mus.*) measure.

разме́р|енный *p.p.p. of* **~ить** *and adj.* measured.
разме́р|ить, ю, ишь *pf.* (*of* **~я́ть**) to measure (off).
размер|я́ть, я́ю *impf. of* **~́ить**
разме|си́ть, шу́, ~́сишь *pf.* (*of* **~́шивать**) to knead.
разме|сти́, ту́, тёшь, *past* **~̈л, ~ла́** *pf.* (*of* **~та́ть**[1]) **1.** to sweep clean. **2.** to shovel, sweep away.
разме|сти́ть, щу́, сти́шь *pf.* (*of* **~ща́ть**) **1.** to place, accommodate; **р. делега́тов по гости́ницам** to accommodate the delegates in hotels; **р. войска́ по кварти́рам** to quarter troops. **2.** to distribute; **р. заём** to float a loan.
разме|сти́ться, щу́сь, сти́шься *pf.* (*of* **~ща́ться**) **1.** to take one's seat. **2.** *pass. of* **~сти́ть**
размета́|ть[1]**, ю** *impf. of* **размести́**
разме|та́ть[2]**, чу́, ~́чешь** *pf.* (*of* **~̈тывать**) to scatter, disperse.
разме|та́ться, чу́сь, ~́чешься *pf.* **1.** (*coll.*) to toss (*in sleep or delirium*). **2.** to sprawl.
разме́|тить, чу, тишь *pf.* (*of* **~ча́ть**) to mark.
размётыва|ть, ю *impf. of* **размета́ть**[2]
размеча́|ть, ю *impf. of* **разме́тить**
размеш|а́ть, а́ю *pf.* (*of* **~́ивать**) to stir.
разме́шива|ть, ю *impf. of* **размеси́ть** *and* **размеша́ть**
размеща́|ть(ся), ю(сь) *impf. of* **размести́ть(ся)**
размеще́ни|е, я *nt.* **1.** placing, accommodation; distribution, disposal, allocation; siting; **р. войск по кварти́рам** quartering, billeting of troops; **р. вооружённых сил** stationing of armed forces; **р. промы́шленности** location of industry. **2.** (*fin.*) placing, investment; **р. за́йма** floating a loan.
размина́|ть(ся), ю(сь) *impf. of* **размя́ть(ся)**
размини́р|овать, ую *pf.* to clear of mines.
рами́нк|а, и *f.* (*sport*) limbering-up; warm-up.
размин|у́ться, у́сь, ёшься *pf.* (*coll.*) **1.** (**с**+*i.*) to pass (*without meeting*); to miss; **мы, должно́ быть, ~у́лись с ним на доро́ге** we must have passed one another on the road. **2.** (*of letters*) to cross (in the post). **3.** to (be able to) pass; **на э́том уча́стке доро́ги маши́нам нельзя́ р.** it is impossible for cars to pass on this part of the road.
размнож|а́ть(ся), а́ю, ает(ся) *impf. of* **~́ить(ся)**
размноже́ни|е, я *nt.* **1.** duplicating; mimeographing. **2.** (*biol.*) reproduction, propagation.
размно́ж|ить, у, ишь *pf.* (*of* **~а́ть**) **1.** to duplicate; to mimeograph. **2.** to breed, rear.
размно́ж|иться, ится *pf.* (*of* **~а́ться**) **1.** (*biol.*) to propagate itself; to breed; to spawn. **2.** *pass. of* **~ить**
размозж|и́ть, у́, и́шь *pf.* to smash.
размок|а́ть, а́ет *impf. of* **~́нуть**
размо́к|нуть, нет, *past* **~, ~ла** *pf.* (*of* **~а́ть**) to get soaked; to get sodden.
размо́л, а *m.* **1.** grinding. **2.: мука́ ме́лкого ~а** finely ground flour.
размо́лвк|а, и *f.* tiff, disagreement.
раз|моло́ть, мелю́, ме́лешь *pf.* (*of* **разма́лывать**) to grind.
размора́жива|ть(ся), ю(сь) *impf. of* **разморо́зить(ся)**
разморо́|зить, жу, зишь *pf.* (*of* **размора́живать**) to unfreeze; to defrost.
разморо́|зиться, жусь, зишься *pf.* (*of* **размора́живаться**) to defrost.
размота́|ть, ю *pf.* (*of* **разма́тывать**) to unwind, uncoil, unreel.
размота́|ться, ется *pf.* (*of* **разма́тываться**) to unwind, uncoil, unreel; to come unwound.
размоч|и́ть, у́, ~́ишь *pf.* (*of* **разма́чивать**) to soak, steep.
размы́в, а *m.* wash-out, erosion.
размыва́|ть, ю *impf. of* **размы́ть**
размыка́|ть, ю *impf. of* **разомкну́ть**
размы́сл|ить, ю, ишь *pf.* (*of* **размышля́ть**) (**о**+*p.*) to reflect (on, upon), meditate (on, upon), ponder (over).
разм|ы́ть, о́ю, о́ешь *pf.* (*of* **~ыва́ть**) to wash away, (*geol.*) to erode.
размышле́ни|е, я *nt.* reflection, meditation, thought; **по зре́лом ~и** on second thoughts, on reflection.
размышля́|ть, ю *impf. of* **размы́слить**
размягч|а́ть(ся), а́ю(сь) *impf. of* **~и́ть(ся)**
размягче́ни|е, я *nt.* softening.
размягч|и́ть, у́, и́шь *pf.* (*of* **~а́ть**) to soften.
размягч|и́ться, у́сь, и́шься *pf.* (*of* **~а́ться**) to soften, grow soft.
размя́к|нуть, ну, нешь, *past* **~, ~ла** *pf. of* **мя́кнуть**
раз|мя́ть, омну́, омнёшь *pf.* (*of* **мять** *and* **~мина́ть**) **1.** to knead; to mash. **2.: р. но́ги** (*coll.*) to stretch one's legs.
раз|мя́ться, омну́сь, омнёшься *pf.* (*of* **~мина́ться**) (*coll.*) to stretch one's legs; (*sport*) to limber up.
разна́шива|ть(ся), ю, ет(ся) *impf. of* **разноси́ть(ся)**[1]
разнес|ти́, у́, ёшь, *past* **~̈, ~ла́** *pf.* (*of* **разноси́ть**[2]) **1.** to carry, convey; to take round; **р. газе́ты** to deliver newspapers; **р. слух** to spread a rumour. **2.** to enter, note down; **р. цита́ты на ка́рточки** to note down quotations on cards. **3.** to smash, break up. **4.** to scatter, disperse. **5.** (*coll.*) to cause to swell; (*impers.*): **его́ щёку ~ло́** his cheek is swollen. **6.** (*fig., coll.*) to slam, pan.
разнес|ти́сь, ётся, *past* **~̈ся, ~ла́сь** *pf.* (*of* **разноси́ться**[2]) **1.** to spread. **2.** to resound.
разнима́|ть, ю *impf. of* **разня́ть**
ра́зн|иться, юсь, ишься *impf.* to differ.
ра́зниц|а, ы *f.* difference; disparity; **кака́я р.?** (*coll.*) what difference does it make?
разнобо́|й, я *m.* lack of co-ordination; difference, disagreement.
разнови́дност|ь, и *f.* variety.
разновреме́нный *adj.* ocurring at different times.
разногла́си|е, я *nt.* **1.** difference, disagreement; **р. во взгля́дах** difference of opinion. **2.** discrepancy; **р. в показа́ниях** conflicting evidence.
разноголо́сиц|а, ы *f.* discordance, dissonance (*also fig., coll.*); **р. во мне́ниях** dissent.
разноголо́сый *adj.* discordant.
разнома́стный *adj.* **1.** of different colours. **2.** (*cards*) of different suits.
разнообра́зи|е, я *nt.* variety, diversity; **для ~я** for a change.
разнообра́|зить, жу, зишь *impf.* to vary, diversify.
разнообра́з|ный (~ен, ~на) *adj.* varied, diverse.
разнорабо́ч|ий, его *m.* unskilled labourer.
разноречи́в|ый (~, ~а) *adj.* contradictory, conflicting.
разноро́дност|ь, и *f.* heterogeneity.
разноро́д|ный (~ен, ~на) *adj.* heterogeneous.
разно́с, а *m.* **1.** carrying; delivery (*of mail, etc.*). **2.** (*fig., coll.*) dressing-down.
разно|си́ть[1]**, шу́, ~́сишь** *pf.* (*of* **разна́шивать**) to wear in (*footwear*).
разно|си́ть[2]**, шу́, ~́сишь** *impf. of* **разнести́**
разно|си́ться[1]**, ~́сится** *pf.* (*of* **разна́шиваться**) (*of footwear*) to become comfortable.
разно|си́ться[2]**, ~́сится** *impf. of* **разнести́(сь)**
разно́ск|а, и *f.* delivery.
разно́сн|ый *adj.* (*coll.*) abusive; **~ая реце́нзия** scathing review; **~ые слова́** swear-words.
разносторо́н|ний *adj.* **1.** (*math.*) scalene. **2.** (**~ен, ~ня**) (*fig.*) many-sided; versatile; **~нее образова́ние** all-round education.
разносторо́нност|ь, и *f.* versatility.
ра́зност|ь, и *f.* **1.** (*math.*) difference. **2.** difference, diversity; **ра́зные ~и** (*coll.*) this and that.
разно́счик, а *m.* pedlar, hawker; barrow boy.

разноцве́тный *adj.* of different colours; many-coloured, variegated, motley.
разночи́н|ец, ца *m.* (*hist.*) raznochinets (*in 19th century, Russ. intellectual of non-aristocatic descent*).
разночи́н|ный *adj. of* **~ец**
разношёрст|ный (~ен, ~на) *adj.* **1.** (*of animals*) with coats of different colour. **2.** (*fig., coll.*) motley.
разноязы́чный *adj.* polyglot.
разну́зд|анный *p.p.p. of* **~а́ть** *and adj.* unbridled, unruly.
разнузд|а́ть, а́ю *pf.* (*of* **~ывать**) to unbridle.
разну́здыва|ть, ю *impf. of* **разнузда́ть**
ра́зн|ый *adj.* **1.** different, differing. **2.** various, diverse; **~ого ро́да** of various kinds; *as n.* **~ое, ~ого** *nt.* (*on agenda of meeting, etc.*) any other business.
разню́х|ать, аю *pf.* (*of* **~ивать**) (*coll.*) to smell out (*also fig.*); (*fig.*) to nose out, ferret out.
разню́хива|ть, ю *impf. of* **разню́хать**
раз|ня́ть, ниму́, ни́мешь, *past* **~ня́л (***and* **ро́знял), ~няла́, ~ня́ло (***and* **ро́зняло)** *pf.* (*of* **~нима́ть**) **1.** to take to pieces, dismantle. **2.** to pull apart, separate (*persons fighting*).
разо... *vbl. pref.* = **раз...**
разоблач|а́ть, а́ю *impf. of* **~и́ть**
разоблаче́ни|е, я *nt.* exposure, unmasking.
разоблач|и́ть, у́, и́шь *pf.* (*of* **~а́ть**) to expose, unmask.
раз|обра́ть, беру́, берёшь, *past* **~обра́л, ~обрала́, ~обра́ло** *pf.* (*of* **~бира́ть**) **1.** to take apart, strip, dismantle; **р. дом** to pull down a house. **2.** to buy up, take. **3.** to sort out. **4.** to investigate, look into; **р. де́ло** (*leg.*) to hear a case. **5.** (*gram.*) to parse; to analyse. **6.** to make out, understand; **я не могу́ р. его́ по́черк** I cannot make out his handwriting. **7.** (*fig., coll.*) to fill (with), seize (with); **её ~обрала́ ре́вность** she was filled with jealousy.
раз|обра́ться, беру́сь, берёшься, *past* **~обра́лся, ~обрала́сь, ~обра́ло́сь** *pf.* (*of* **~бира́ться**) **1.** (*coll.*) to unpack. **2.** (**в**+*p.*) to investigate, look into; to understand; **р. в пчелово́дстве** to know about bee-keeping; **я в нём не ~обра́лся** I could not make him out.
разобщ|а́ть, а́ю *impf. of* **~и́ть**
разобщённо *adv.* apart, separately; **де́йствовать р.** to act independently.
разобщ|и́ть, у́, и́шь *pf.* (*of* **~а́ть**) to separate; (*fig.*) to estrange, alienate.
ра́зов|ый *adj.* valid for one occasion (only); **~ого по́льзования** disposable, throwaway.
раз|огна́ть, гоню́, го́нишь, *past* **~огна́л, ~огнала́, ~огна́ло** *pf.* (*of* **~гоня́ть**) **1.** to drive away; to disperse; (*fig.*) to dispel; **р. демонстра́цию** to break up a demonstration. **2.** (*coll.*) to drive at high speed, race.
раз|огна́ться, гоню́сь, го́нишься, *past* **~огна́лся, ~огнала́сь, ~огна́ло́сь** *pf.* (*of* **~гоня́ться**) to gather speed; to gather momentum.
разогн|у́ть, у́, ёшь *pf.* (*of* **разгиба́ть**) to unbend, straighten; **р. спи́ну** to straighten one's back.
разогн|у́ться, у́сь, ёшься *pf.* (*of* **разгиба́ться**) to straighten (o.s.) up.
разогрева́|ть(ся), ю(сь) *impf. of* **разогре́ть(ся)**
разогре́|ть, ю *pf.* (*of* **~ва́ть**) to warm up.
разогре́|ться, юсь *pf.* (*of* **~ва́ться**) to warm up, grow warm.
разоде́т|ый *p.p.p. of* **~ь** *and adj.* dressed up; **весь р.** all dressed up, in one's best bib and tucker.
разоде́|ть, ну, нешь *pf.* (*coll.*) to dress up.
разоде́|ться, нусь, нешься *pf.* (*coll.*) to dress up; **р. в пух и прах** to be dressed to kill.
раз|одра́ть, деру́, дерёшь, *past* **~одра́л, ~одрала́, ~одра́ло** *pf.* (*of* **~дира́ть**) to tear up.
раз|одра́ться, дерётся, *past* **~одра́лся, ~одрала́сь, ~одра́ло́сь** *pf.* (*of* **~дира́ться**) (*coll.*) to tear.
разозл|и́ть, ю́, и́шь *pf.* (*of* **зли́ть**) to anger, enrage.
разозл|и́ться, ю́сь, и́шься *pf.* (*of* **зли́ться**) to get angry, get in a rage.
раз|ойти́сь, ойду́сь, ойдёшься, *past* **~ошёлся, ~ошла́сь** *pf.* (*of* **расходи́ться**) **1.** to go away; to disperse. **2.** (**с**+*i.*) to part (from), separate (from), to get divorced (from); **мы ~ошли́сь друзья́ми** we parted friends; **он ~ошёлся с жено́й** he has separated from his wife. **3.** to branch off, diverge; to radiate. **4.** to pass (*without meeting*). **5.** (**с**+*i.*) to be at variance (with), conflict (with); **р. во мне́нии с кем-н.** to disagree with s.o. **6.** to dissolve; to melt. **7.** to be sold out; to be spent; (*of a book*) to be out of print; **все де́ньги ~ошли́сь** all the money has been spent. **8.** (*coll.*) to gather speed. **9.** (*coll.*) to let o.s. go; to fly off the handle; **бу́ря ~ошла́сь** the storm raged.
ра́зом *adv.* (*coll.*) at once, at one go.
разомкн|у́ть, у́, ёшь *pf.* (*of* **размыка́ть**) to open, unfasten; (*tech.*) to break, disconnect.
разорв|а́ть, у́, ёшь, *past* **~а́л, ~ала́, ~а́ло** *pf.* (*of* **разрыва́ть**[1]) **1.** to tear (to pieces). **2.** (*impers.*) to blow up, burst; **котёл ~а́ло** the boiler has burst. **3.** (*fig.*) to break (off), sever; **р. дипломати́ческие сноше́ния** to break off diplomatic relations.
разорв|а́ться, ётся, *past* **~а́лся, ~ала́сь, ~а́ло́сь** *pf.* (*of* **разрыва́ться**) **1.** to break, snap; to tear, become torn. **2.** to blow up, burst; to explode, go off. **3.** (*coll.; usu.+neg.*) to be everywhere at once; **я не могу́ р.** I can't be everywhere at once!
разоре́ни|е, я *nt.* destruction, ravage; ruin.
разори́тел|ьный (~ен, ~ьна) *adj.* ruinous; wasteful.
разор|и́ть, ю́, и́шь *pf.* (*of* **~я́ть**) **1.** to destroy, ravage. **2.** to ruin.
разор|и́ться, ю́сь, и́шься *pf.* (*of* **~я́ться**) to ruin o.s.; to be ruined.
разоруж|а́ть(ся), а́ю(сь) *impf. of* **~и́ть(ся)**
разоруже́ни|е, я *nt.* disarmament.
разоруж|и́ть, у́, и́шь *pf.* (*of* **~а́ть**) to disarm.
разоруж|и́ться, у́сь, и́шься *pf.* (*of* **~а́ться**) to disarm.
разор|я́ть(ся), я́ю(сь) *impf. of* **~и́ть(ся)**
разо|сла́ть, шлю́, шлёшь *pf.* (*of* **рассыла́ть**) **1.** to distribute, circulate; **р. листо́вки** to distribute leaflets. **2.** to send out, dispatch.
разосп|а́ться, лю́сь, и́шься, *past* **~а́лся, ~ала́сь, ~а́лось** *pf.* (*coll.*) to be fast asleep; to oversleep.
разостла́ть (*and* **расстели́ть), расстелю́, расстéлешь** *pf.* (*of* **расстила́ть**) to spread (out), lay.
разостла́|ться (*and* **расстели́ться), расстéлется** *pf.* (*of* **расстила́ться**) to spread
разохо́|титься, чусь, тишься *pf.* (*+inf.; coll.*) to take a liking (to), feel an inclination (for); **сперва́ он не хоте́л танцева́ть, а тепе́рь ~тился** he did not want to go to the dance at first, but now he is keen to go.
разочарова́ни|е, я *nt.* disappointment.
разочаро́в|анный *p.p.p. of* **~а́ть** *and adj.* disappointed, disillusioned.
разочар|ова́ть, у́ю *pf.* (*of* **~о́вывать**) to disappoint.
разочар|ова́ться, у́юсь *pf.* (*of* **~о́вываться**) (**в ком-н., в чём-н.**) to be disappointed (in s.o., with sth.).
разочаро́выва|ть(ся), ю(сь) *impf. of* **разочарова́ть(ся)**
разраба́тыва|ть, ю *impf. of* **разрабо́тать**
разрабо́та|ть, ю *pf.* (*of* **разраба́тывать**) **1.** (*agric.*) to cultivate. **2.** (*mining*) to work, exploit. **3.** to work out; to develop; to elaborate; **р. ме́тоды** to devise methods; **р. пла́ны** to work out plans.
разрабо́тк|а, и *f.* **1.** (*agric.*) cultivation. **2.** (*mining*)

working, exploitation; **откры́тая р.** open-cast mining. **3.** field; pit, working; **р. сла́нца** slate quarry. **4.** working out; elaboration.

разра́внива|ть, ю *impf. of* **разровня́ть**

разража́|ться, юсь *impf. of* **разрази́ться**

разра|зи́ться, жу́сь, зи́шься *pf.* (*of* **~жа́ться**) (*of a storm, etc.*) to break out; **р. слеза́ми** to burst into tears; **р. сме́хом** to burst out laughing.

разраст|а́ться, а́ется *impf. of* **~и́сь**

разраст|и́сь, ётся, *past* **разро́сся, разросла́сь** *pf.* (*of* **~а́ться**) to grow (up) (*also fig.*); to spread; to grow thickly.

разре|ди́ть, жу́, ди́шь *pf.* (*of* **~жа́ть**) **1.** to thin out, weed out. **2.** to rarefy.

разрежа́|ть, ю *impf. of* **разреди́ть**

разре́з, а *m.* **1.** cut; slit. **2.** section; **попере́чный р.** cross-section. **3.** (*fig., coll.*) point of view; **в ~е** (+*g.*) from the point of view (of), in the context (of).

разре́|зать, жу, жешь *pf.* (*of* **~за́ть**) to cut; to slit.

разрез|а́ть, а́ю *impf. of* **∠ать**

разреш|а́ть, а́ю *impf. of* **~и́ть**

разреш|а́ться, а́юсь *impf.* **1.** *impf. of* **~и́ться. 2.** *impf. only* to be allowed; to be permitted.

разреше́ни|е, я *nt.* **1.** permission; **с ва́шего ~я** with your permission. **2.** permit, authorization; **р. на въезд** entry permit. **3.** solution (*of a problem*). **4.** settlement (*of a dispute*).

разреши́м|ый (~, ~а) *adj.* solvable.

разреш|и́ть, у́, и́шь *pf.* (*of* **~а́ть**) **1.** (+*d.*) to allow, permit; **~и́те пройти́** allow me to pass. **2.** to authorize; **р. кни́гу к печа́ти** to authorize the printing of a book. **3.** to solve (*a problem*). **4.** to settle; **р. сомне́ния** to resolve doubts.

разреш|и́ться, у́сь, и́шься *pf.* (*of* **~а́ться**) **1.** to be solved. **2.** to be settled. **3. (от бре́мени)** (+*i.*; *obs.*) to be delivered (of); **она́ ~и́лась де́вочкой** she was delivered of a girl.

разрис|ова́ть, у́ю *pf.* (*of* **~о́вывать**) to cover with drawings.

разрисо́выва|ть, ю *impf. of* **разрисова́ть**

разровня́|ть, ю *pf.* (*of* **разра́внивать**) to level.

разро́зн|енный *p.p.p. of* **~ить** *and adj.* **1.** uncoordinated. **2.** odd; **р. компле́кт** broken set, set made up of odd parts; **~енные тома́** odd volumes.

разро́знива|ть, ю *impf. of* **разро́знить**

разро́зн|ить, ю, ишь *pf.* (*of* **~ивать**) to break a set (of).

разруб|а́ть, а́ю *impf. of* **~и́ть**

разруб|и́ть, лю́, ∠ишь *pf.* (*of* **~а́ть**) to cut, cleave.

разруга́|ть, ю *pf.* (*coll.*) to berate; to blow up.

разруга́|ться, юсь *pf.* (**с**+*i.*; *coll.*) to quarrel (with).

разру́х|а, и *f.* ruin, collapse.

разруш|а́ть(ся), а́ю, а́ет(ся) *impf. of* **∠ить(ся)**

разруше́ни|е, я *nt.* destruction; (*pl.*) havoc.

разруши́тел|ьный (~ен, ~ьна) *adj.* destructive.

разру́ш|ить, у, ишь *pf.* (*of* **~а́ть**) **1.** to destroy; to demolish, wreck; to ruin (*also fig.*). **2.** (*fig.*) to frustrate, blight; **р. чьи-н. наде́жды** to blight s.o.'s hopes.

разру́ш|иться, ится *pf.* (*of* **~а́ться**) **1.** to go to ruin, collapse. **2.** *pass. of* **~ить**

разры́в, а *m.* **1.** break; gap; rupture, severance; breach; **р. дипломати́ческих отноше́ний** severance of diplomatic relations; **р. ме́жду поколе́ниями** generation gap. **2.** (*shell*) burst, explosion.

разрыва́|ть¹, ю *impf. of* **разорва́ть**

разрыва́|ть², ю *impf. of* **разры́ть**

разрыва́|ться, юсь *impf. of* **разорва́ться**

разрывно́й *adj.* explosive.

разр|ы́ть, о́ю, о́ешь *pf.* (*of* **~ыва́ть²**) **1.** to dig up. **2.** (*fig., coll.*) to rummage through.

разрыхл|и́ть, ю́, и́шь *pf.* (*of* **~я́ть**) to loosen; to hoe.

разрыхл|я́ть, я́ю *impf. of* **~и́ть**

разря́д¹, а *m.* discharge.

разря́д², а *m.* category, rank; sort; (*sport*) class, rating; **пе́рвого ~а** first-class.

разря|ди́ть¹, жу́, ∠ди́шь *pf.* (*of* **~жа́ть**) (*coll.*) to dress up.

разря|ди́ть², жу́, ди́шь *pf.* (*of* **~жа́ть**) **1.** (*elec.*) to discharge; **р. атмосфе́ру** (*fig.*) to clear the air. **2.** to unload (*a fire-arm*).

разря|ди́ться¹, жу́сь, ∠ди́шься *pf.* (*of* **~жа́ться**) to dress up; to doll o.s. up.

разря|ди́ться², ди́тся *pf.* (*of* **~жа́ться**) **1.** (*elec.*) to run down; (*fig.*) to clear, ease; **атмосфе́ра ~ди́лась** the atmosphere has become less tense. **2.** *pass. of* **~ди́ть²**

разря́дк|а, и *f.* discharging; unloading; **р. напряжённости** (*pol.*) lessening of tension, détente.

разряжа́|ть(ся), ю(сь) *impf. of* **разряди́ть(ся)**

разубе|ди́ть, жу́, ди́шь *pf.* (*of* **~жда́ть**) (**в**+*p.*) to dissuade (from), argue (out of); **мы их ~ди́ли** we have made them change their mind.

разубе|ди́ться, жу́сь, ди́шься *pf.* (*of* **~жда́ться**) (**в**+*p.*) to change one's mind (about).

разубежда́|ть(ся), ю(сь) *impf. of* **разубеди́ть(ся)**

разува́|ть(ся), ю(сь) *impf. of* **разу́ть(ся)**

разуве́р|ить, ю, ишь *pf.* (*of* **~я́ть**) (**в**+*p.*) to undermine faith (in); to argue (out of).

разуве́р|иться, юсь, ишься *pf.* (*of* **~я́ться**) (**в**+*p.*) to lose faith (in).

разузна|ва́ть, ю́, ёшь *impf.* **1.** *impf. of* **разузна́ть. 2.** *impf. only* to make inquiries (about).

разузна́|ть, ю *pf.* (*of* **~ва́ть**) to find out.

разукра́|сить, шу, сишь *pf.* (*of* **~шивать**) to adorn; to decorate; to embellish.

разукра́шива|ть, ю *impf. of* **разукра́сить**

разукрупн|и́ть, ю́, и́шь *pf.* (*of* **~я́ть**) to break up into smaller units.

разукрупн|я́ть, я́ю, я́ет *impf. of* **~и́ть**

ра́зум, а *m.* reason; mind, intellect; **у него́ ум за р. зашёл** (*coll.*) he was at his wit's end.

разуме́ни|е, я *nt.* **1.** (*obs.*) understanding. **2.** opinion, viewpoint; **по моему́ ~ю** to my mind.

разуме́|ть, ю *impf.* **1.** (*obs.*) to understand. **2. (под)** to understand (by), mean (by).

разуме́|ться, ется *impf.* to be understood, be meant; **под э́тим ~ется...** by this is meant ...; **(са́мо собо́й) ~ется** it goes without saying.

разу́м|ный (~ен, ~на) *adj.* **1.** possessing reason. **2.** judicious, intelligent. **3.** reasonable; **э́то (вполне́) ~но** it is (perfectly) reasonable.

разу́|ть, ю, ешь *pf.* (*of* **~ва́ть**); **р. кого́-н.** to take s.o.'s shoes off.

разу́|ться, юсь, ешься *pf.* (*of* **~ва́ться**) to take one's shoes off.

разу́чива|ть(ся), ю(сь) *impf. of* **разучи́ть(ся)**

разуч|и́ть, у́, ∠ишь *pf.* (*of* **∠ивать**) to learn (up); **р. роль** to learn, study one's part.

разуч|и́ться, у́сь, ∠ишься *pf.* (*of* **∠иваться**) (+*inf.*) to forget (how to), lose the ability (to); **я ~и́лся ходи́ть на лы́жах** I have forgotten how to ski.

разъ... *vbl. pref.* = **раз...**

разъеда́|ть, ю *impf. of* **разъе́сть**

разъедине́ни|е, я *nt.* **1.** separation. **2.** (*elec.*) disconnection, breaking.

разъедин|и́ть, ю́, и́шь *pf.* (*of* **~я́ть**) **1.** to separate. **2.** (*elec.*) to disconnect, break; **нас ~и́ли** we were cut off (*on telephone*).

разъедин|и́ться, ю́сь, и́шься *pf.* (*of* **~я́ться**) **1.** to separate, part. **2.** *pass. of* **~и́ть**

разъедин|я́ть(ся), я́ю(сь) *impf. of* **~и́ть(ся)**

разъе́зд, а *m.* **1.** departure; dispersal. **2.** (*pl.*) travel, journeyings. **3.** (*mil.*) mounted patrol. **4.** section of double track; station, halt.

разъездн|о́й *adj.*: **~ы́е де́ньги** travelling expenses;

р. путь (*rail.*) siding.

разъезжа́|ть, ю *impf.* to drive (about, around), ride (about, around); to travel; **р. по дела́м слу́жбы** to travel about on business.

разъезжа́|ться, юсь *impf. of* **разъе́хаться**

разъе́|сть, ст, дя́т, *past* **~л** *pf.* (*of* **~да́ть**) to eat away; to corrode (*also fig.*).

разъе́|хаться, дусь, дешься *pf.* (*of* **~зжа́ться**) **1.** to depart; to disperse. **2.** to separate. **3.** to (be able to) pass; **тут грузовика́м нельзя́ р.** it is impossible for lorries to pass here. **4.** to pass one another (*without meeting*), miss one another. **5.** (*coll.*) to fall to pieces, fall apart.

разъяр|и́ть, ю́, и́шь *pf.* (*of* **~я́ть**) to infuriate.

разъяр|и́ться, ю́сь, и́шься *pf.* (*of* **~я́ться**) to become enraged, fly into a rage.

разъяр|я́ть(ся), я́ю(сь) *impf. of* **~и́ть(ся)**

разъясне́ни|е, я *nt.* explanation; interpretation.

разъясни́тельный *adj.* explanatory.

разъясн|и́ть, ю́, и́шь *pf.* (*of* **~я́ть**) to explain, elucidate; to interpret.

разъясн|и́ться, и́тся *pf.* (*of* **~я́ться**) to become clear, be cleared up.

разъясн|я́ть(ся), я́ю, я́ет(ся) *impf. of* **~и́ть(ся)**

разыгр|а́ть, а́ю *pf.* (*of* **~́ывать**) **1.** to play (through); to perform; **р. дурака́** to play the fool. **2.** to draw (*a lottery, etc.*); to raffle. **3.** (*coll.*) to play a trick (on), play a practical joke (on).

разыгр|а́ться, а́юсь *pf.* (*of* **~́ываться**) **1.** to be carried away by a game, by play. **2.** (*of a pianist etc.*) to warm up. **3.** (*of wind or sea*) to rise; to get up; (*of a storm*) to break; (*fig.*; *of feelings*) to run high.

разы́грыва|ть(ся), ю(сь) *impf. of* **разыгра́ть(ся) 2., 3.**

разы|ска́ть, щу́, ~́щешь *pf.* to find (after searching).

разы|ска́ться, щу́сь, ~́щешься *pf.* **1.** (*impf.* **~́скиваться**) to be sought for. **2.** to turn up, be found.

разы́скива|ть, ю *impf.* to hunt, search for.

разы́скива|ться, юсь *impf. of* **разыска́ться; р. поли́цией** to be wanted by the police.

ра|й, я, о ~́е, в ~ю́ *m.* paradise.

рай... *comb. form, abbr. of* **райо́нный**

райко́м, а *m.* (*abbr. of* **райо́нный комите́т**) district committee.

райо́н, а *m.* **1.** region; area; zone. **2.** (*designation of administrative division of former USSR*) rayon *or* raion; district.

райо́н|ный *adj. of* **~**

ра́й|ский *adj. of* **~**; (*fig.*) heavenly; **~ская пти́ца** bird of paradise.

рак, а *m.* **1.** (*zool.*) crawfish, crayfish; **кра́сный как р.** red as a lobster. **2.** (*med.*) cancer. **3. Р.** (*astrol.*, *astron.*) Cancer; **тро́пик ~́а** (*geog.*) Tropic of Cancer.

ра́к|а, и *f.* (*eccl.*) shrine (*of a saint*).

раке́т|а, ы *f.* **1.** (air-)rocket; flare. **2.** (*mil.*) missile; **межконтинента́льная р.** inter-continental ballistic missile (ICBM). **3.** (*outer-space*) rocket. **4.** (*coll.*) hydrofoil (*vessel*).

раке́т|ка, ки *f.* (*sport*) racket.

раке́тный *adj.* rocket(-powered); missile.

ракетодро́м, а *m.* rocket launch site.

ра́ковин|а, ы *f.* **1.** shell; **ушна́я р.** (*anat.*) aural cavity. **2.** sink; wash-basin.

ра́к|овый *adj. of* **~**; (*med.*) cancerous.

ракообра́зн|ые, ых *pl.* (*sg.* **~ое, ~ого** *nt.*) (*zool.*) Crustacea.

раку́рс, а *m.* (*art*) foreshortening; **в ~е** foreshortened.

раку́шк|а, и *f.* cockle-shell; mussel.

ра́лли *nt. indecl.* rally.

ралли́ст, а *m.* rallyist, rally driver.

ра́м|а, ы *f.* **1.** frame; **око́нная р.** window-frame; **вста́вить в ~у** to frame. **2.** chassis, carriage.

рамаза́н, а *m.* (*relig.*) Ramadan.

ра́мк|а, и *f.* frame.

ра́м|ки, ок (*pl. only*) framework; limits; **в ~ках** (*+g.*) within the framework (of); **вы́йти за р.** (*+g.*) to exceed the limits (of).

ра́м|очный *adj. of* **~ка**

ра́мп|а, ы *f.* (*theatr.*) footlights.

ра́н|а, ы *f.* wound.

ранг, а *m.* class, rank.

ранго́ут, а *m.* (*naut.*) masts and spars.

ранго́ут|ный *adj. of* **~**; **~ное де́рево** (*naut.*) spar.

ра́нее *adv.* = **ра́ньше**

ране́ни|е, я *nt.* **1.** wounding. **2.** wound; injury.

ра́нен|ый *adj.* wounded; injured; *as n.* **р., ~ого** *m.* injured man; wounded man; casualty; *pl.* the injured; the wounded.

ра́н|ец, ца *m.* knapsack, haversack; satchel; (*mil.*) pack.

ранжи́р, а *m.*: **по ~у** (*coll.*) in order of size.

ра́н|ить, ю, ишь *impf. and pf.* to wound; to injure.

ра́нн|ий *adj.* early; **~яя пти́чка** (*fig.*) early bird; **с ~их лет** from one's earliest years.

ра́но[1] *pred.* it is early; **ещё р. ложи́ться спать** it is too early for bed.

ра́но[2] *adv.* early; **р. и́ли по́здно** sooner or later.

рант, а, о ~́е, на ~у́ *m.* welt.

ран|ь, и *f.* (*coll.*) early hour; **куда́ ты направля́ешься в таку́ю р.?** where are you bound for at this ungodly hour?

ра́ньше *adv.* **1.** earlier; **как мо́жно р.** as early as possible; as soon as possible. **2.** before; **до Ло́ндона он не дое́дет р. ве́чера** he will not reach London before evening. **3.** before, formerly; **р. мы жи́ли в дере́вне** we used to live in the country.

рапи́р|а, ы *f.* foil.

ра́порт, а *m.* report.

рапорт|ова́ть, у́ю *impf. and pf.* to report.

рапс, а *m.* (*bot.*) rape.

рапсо́ди|я, и *f.* (*mus.*) rhapsody.

рас... *vbl. pref.* = **раз...**

ра́с|а, ы *f.* race.

раси́зм, а *m.* racism.

раси́ст, а *m.* racist.

раска́ива|ться, юсь *impf. of* **раска́яться**

раскал|ённый *p.p.p. of* **~и́ть** *and adj.* scorching, burning hot; **р. до́красна́** red-hot.

раскал|и́ть, ю́, и́шь *pf.* (*of* **~я́ть**) to bring to a great heat; **р. добела́** to make white-hot.

раскал|и́ться, ю́сь, и́шься *pf.* (*of* **~я́ться**) to glow, become hot; **р. добела́** to become white-hot.

раска́лыва|ть(ся), ю(сь) *impf. of* **расколо́ть(ся)**

раскал|я́ть(ся), я́ю(сь) *impf. of* **~и́ть(ся)**

раска́пыва|ть, ю *impf. of* **раскопа́ть**

раска́рмлива|ть, ю *impf. of* **раскорми́ть**

раска́т, а *m.* roll, peal; **р. гро́ма** peal of thunder.

раскат|а́ть, а́ю *pf.* (*of* **~́ывать**) **1.** to unroll. **2.** to roll (out); to smooth out; to level; **р. те́сто** to roll out dough.

раскат|а́ться, а́юсь *pf.* (*of* **~́ываться**) **1.** to unroll. **2.** to roll out.

раска́тист|ый (~, ~а) *adj.* rolling, booming; **р. смех** peal(s) of laughter.

раска|ти́ть, чу́, ~́тишь *pf.* (*of* **~́тывать**) **1.** to set rolling. **2.** to roll away.

раска|ти́ться, чу́сь, ~́тишься *pf.* (*of* **~́тываться**) **1.** to gather momentum. **2.** to roll away.

раска́тыва|ть, ю *impf.* **1.** *impf. of* **раската́ть** *and* **раскати́ть. 2.** (*coll.*) to drive (about, around), ride (about, around).

раска́тыва|ться, юсь *impf. of* **раската́ть(ся)** *and* **раскати́ть(ся)**

раскач|áть, áю *pf.* (*of* **⁓ивать**) **1.** to swing; to rock. **2.** to loosen, shake loose. **3.** (*fig., coll.*) to shake up, stir up.

раскач|áться, áюсь *pf.* (*of* **⁓иваться**) **1.** to swing (o.s.); to rock (o.s.). **2.** to shake loose. **3.** (*fig., coll.*) to bestir o.s., get into the swing of.

расќашля|ться, юсь *pf.* to have a fit of coughing.

раскáяни|е, я *nt.* repentance.

раскá|яться, юсь *pf.* (*of* **кáяться** *and* **~иваться**) (**в**+*p.*) to repent (of).

расквартировáни|е, я *nt.* quartering, billeting.

расквартир|овáть, ýю *pf.* (*of* **~óвывать**) to quarter, billet.

расквартирóвыва|ть, ю *impf. of* **расквартировáть**

расквá|сить, шу, сишь *pf.* (*of* **~шивать**) (*coll.*) to punch (*and draw blood from*); **р. комý-н. нос** to give s.o. a bloody nose.

расквáшива|ть, ю *impf. of* **расквáсить**

расквитá|ться, юсь *pf.* (**с**+*i.*; *coll.*) to settle accounts (with) (*also fig.*); (*fig.*) to get even (with).

раскидáть, áю *pf.* (*of* **⁓ывать**) to scatter; to throw about.

раски́дист|ый (~, ~а) *adj.* branchy, spreading.

раски́дыва|ть, ю *impf. of* **раскидáть** *and* **раски́нуть**

раски́дыва|ться, юсь *impf. of* **раски́нуться**

раски́|нуть, ну, нешь *pf.* (*of* **~дывать**) **1.** to stretch (out); **р. рýки** to stretch one's arms. **2.** to spread (out); to set up; **р. шатёр** to pitch a tent. **3.: р. умóм** to consider, think over.

раски́|нуться, нусь, нешься *pf.* (*of* **~дываться**) **1.** to spread out, stretch out. **2.** (*coll.*) to sprawl.

раскис|áть, áю *impf. of* **⁓нуть**

раски́с|нуть, ну, нешь, *past* **~, ~ла** *pf.* (*of* **~áть**) **1.** to rise (*from fermentation*). **2.** (*fig., coll.*) to become limp.

расклáдк|а, и *f.* apportionment; going shares.

раскладýшк|а, и *f.* (*coll.*) folding bed.

складн|óй *adj.* folding; **~áя кровáть** camp-bed.

расклáдыва|ть(ся), ю(сь) *impf. of* **разложи́ть(ся)**[1]

расклáнива|ться, юсь *impf. of* **расклáняться**

расклáн|яться, яюсь *pf.* (*of* **~иваться**) **1.** to exchange bows (*on meeting or leave-taking*). **2.** to take leave (of).

расклéива|ть(ся), ю(сь) *impf. of* **расклéить(ся)**

расклé|ить, ю, ишь *pf.* (*of* **~ивать**) **1.** to unstick. **2.** to stick, paste (*in various places*).

расклé|иться, юсь, ишься *pf.* (*of* **~иваться**) **1.** to come unstuck. **2.** (*fig., coll.*) to fall through; **сдéлка ~илась** the deal fell through. **3.** (*fig., coll.*) to be off colour; **он совсéм ~ился** he has gone to pieces.

расклéйк|а, и *f.* sticking, pasting.

расклéйщик, а *m.* bill-sticker.

раск|овáть, ую́, уёшь *pf.* (*of* **~óвывать**) **1.** to unchain, unfetter. **2.** to unshoe (*a horse*).

раскóвыва|ть, ю *impf. of* **расковáть**

расковыр|я́ть, я́ю *pf.* (*of* **⁓ивать**) to pick open; to scratch raw.

раскóл, а *m.* **1.** (*relig., hist.*) schism, dissent. **2.** (*pol., etc.*) split, division.

расколáчива|ть, ю *impf. of* **расколоти́ть**

расколо|ти́ть, чý, ⁓тишь *pf.* (*of* **расколáчивать**) (*coll.*) to break; to smash.

раскол|óть, ю́, ⁓ешь *pf.* **1.** *pf. of* **колóть**[1]. **2.** (*impf.* **раскáлывать**) (*fig.*) to disrupt, break up.

раскол|óться, ю́сь, ⁓ешься *pf.* (*of* **раскáлываться**) to split (*also fig.*).

раскóльник, а *m.* **1.** (*relig., hist.*) schismatic, dissenter. **2.** (*pol.; fig.*) splitter.

раскóльническ|ий *adj.* **1.** (*relig., hist.*) schismatic, dissenting. **2.: ~ая тáктика** (*pol.*) splitting tactics.

раскопá|ть, ю *pf.* (*of* **раскáпывать**) to dig up, unearth (*also fig.*); (*archaeol.*) to excavate.

раскóпк|а, и *f.* digging up; *pl.* (*archaeol.*) excavations.

раскорм|и́ть, лю́, ⁓ишь *pf.* (*of* **раскáрмливать**) to fatten.

раскоря́к|а, и *c.g.* (*coll.*) bow-legged person.

раскóсый *adj.* (*of eyes*) slanting.

раскошéлива|ться, юсь *impf. of* **раскошéлиться**

раскошéл|иться, юсь, ишься *pf.* (*of* **~иваться**) (*coll.*) to loosen one's purse-strings, to fork out.

раскрáдыва|ть, ю *impf. of* **раскрáсть**

раскрáива|ть, ю *impf. of* **раскрои́ть**

раскрá|сить, шу, сишь *pf.* (*of* **~шивать**) to paint, colour.

раскрáск|а, и *f.* **1.** painting, colouring. **2.** colours, colour scheme.

раскраснé|ться, юсь *pf.* to flush, go red (in the face).

раскрá|сть, дý, дёшь, *past* **~л** *pf.* (*of* **~дывать**) to loot, clean out.

раскрепо|сти́ть, щý, сти́шь *pf.* (*of* **~щáть**) to emancipate.

раскрепощá|ть, ю *impf. of* **раскрепости́ть**

раскрепощéни|е, я *nt.* emancipation.

раскритик|овáть, ýю *pf.* to criticize severely, slate.

раскрич|áться, ýсь, и́шься *pf.* **1.** to start shouting. **2.** (**на**+*a.*) to shout (at), bellow (at).

раскро|и́ть, ю́, и́шь *pf.* (*of* **раскрáивать**) **1.** to cut out (*material*). **2.** (*fig., coll.*) to cut open; **р. комý-н. чéреп** to split s.o.'s skull.

раскрош|и́ть(ся), ý(сь), ⁓ишь(ся) *pf. of* **кроши́ть(ся)**

раскру|ти́ть, чý, ⁓тишь *pf.* (*of* **⁓чивать**) to untwist, untwine, undo.

раскру|ти́ться, тится *pf.* (*of* **⁓чиваться**) to come untwisted, come undone.

раскрýчива|ть(ся), ю, ет(ся) *impf. of* **раскрути́ть(ся)**

раскрывá|ть(ся), ю(сь) *impf. of* **раскры́ть(ся)**

раскры́ти|е, я *nt.* **1.** opening. **2.** exposure; disclosure.

раскр|ы́ть, óю, óешь *pf.* (*of* **~ывáть**) **1.** to open (wide); **р. зóнтик** to put up an umbrella; **р. кни́гу** to open a book. **2.** to expose, bare. **3.** to reveal, disclose, lay bare; to discover; **р. секрéт** to disclose a secret; **р. свой кáрты** (*fig.*) to reveal one's hand.

раскр|ы́ться, óюсь, óешься *pf.* (*of* **~ывáться**) **1.** to open. **2.** to uncover o.s. **3.** to come out; to come to light.

раскуп|áть, áю *impf. of* **~и́ть**

раскуп|и́ть, лю́, ⁓ишь *pf.* (*of* **~áть**) to buy up.

раскýпорива|ть, ю, ет *impf. of* **раскýпорить**

раскýпор|ить, ю, ишь *pf.* (*of* **~ивать**) to uncork, open.

раскýрива|ть, ю, ет *impf. of* **раскури́ть**

раскур|и́ть, ю́, ⁓ишь *pf.* (*of* **⁓ивать**) **1.** to puff at (*a pipe or cigarette*). **2.** to light up.

раску|си́ть, шý, ⁓сишь *pf.* (*of* **⁓сывать**) **1.** to bite through. **2.** (*pf. only*) to get to the core, heart (of); **р. когó-н.** to see through s.o., rumble s.o.

раскýсыва|ть, ю *impf. of* **раскуси́ть**

раскýт|ать, аю *pf.* (*of* **~ывать**) to unwrap.

раскýтыва|ть, ю *impf. of* **раскýтать**

рáсовый *adj.* racial.

распáд, а *m.* disintegration, break-up; (*fig.*) collapse.

распадá|ться, ется *impf. of* **распáсться**

распáива|ть, ю, ет *impf. of* **распая́ть**

распак|овáть, ýю *pf.* (*of* **~óвывать**) to unpack.

распак|овáться, ýюсь *pf.* (*of* **~óвываться**) **1.** (*of a parcel, etc.*) to come undone. **2.** (*coll.*) to unpack.

распакóвыва|ть(ся), ю(сь) *impf. of* **распаковáть(ся)**

распал|и́ть, ю́, и́шь *pf.* (*of* **~я́ть**) **1.** to make burning hot. **2.** (*fig.*) to inflame; **р. гнéвом** to incense.

распал|и́ться, ю́сь, и́шься *pf.* (*of* **~я́ться**) **1.** to get burning hot. **2.** (+*i.*; *fig.*) to burn (with).

распал|я́ть(ся), я́ю(сь) *impf. of* **~и́ть(ся)**
распа́рива|ть, ю *impf. of* **распа́рить**
распа́р|ить, ю, ишь *pf.* (*of* **~ивать**) **1.** to steam out; to stew well. **2.** to cause to sweat.
распа́рыва|ть(ся), ю, ет(ся) *impf. of* **распоро́ть(ся)**
распа́|сться, дётся, *past* **~лся** *pf.* (*of* **~да́ться**) to disintegrate, fall to pieces; (*fig.*) to break up; to collapse; **коали́ция ~лась** the coalition broke up.
распа|ха́ть, шу́, ~́шешь *pf.* (*of* **~́хивать**) to plough up.
распа́хива|ть, ю *impf. of* **распаха́ть** *and* **распахну́ть**
распа́хива|ться, юсь *impf. of* **распахну́ться**
распах|ну́ть, ну́, нёшь *pf.* (*of* **~́ивать**) to open wide; to fling open, throw open; **широко́ р. две́ри** (+*d.*) to open wide the doors (to) (*also fig.*).
распах|ну́ться, ну́сь, нёшься *pf.* (*of* **~́иваться**) to open wide; to fly open, swing open.
распашо́нк|а, и *f.* (*baby's*) vest.
распа|я́ть, я́ю *pf.* (*of* **~́ивать**) to unsolder.
распева́|ть, ю *impf.* **1.** *impf. of* **распе́ть. 2.** to sing for a certain time.
распека́|ть, ю *impf. of* **распе́чь**
распере́ть, разопру́, разопрёшь, *past* **распёр, распёрла** *pf.* (*of* **распира́ть**) (*coll.*) to burst open, cause to burst.
расп|е́ть, ою́, оёшь *pf.* (*of* **~ева́ть**) **1.** to sing through. **2.** to practise (*one's voice*).
расп|е́ться, ою́сь, оёшься *pf.* (*coll.*) **1.** (*of a singer*) to warm up. **2.** to sing away.
распеча́т|ать, аю *pf.* (*of* **~ывать**) **1.** to unseal; **р. письмо́** to open a letter. **2.** to print out.
распеча́тк|а, и *f.* printout.
распеча́тыва|ть, ю, ет *impf. of* **распеча́тать**
распе́|чь, ку́, чёшь, ку́т, *past* **~̈к, ~кла́** *pf.* (*of* **~ка́ть**) (*coll.*) to tell off.
распива́|ть, ю *impf. of* **распи́ть**
распи́лива|ть, ю *impf. of* **распили́ть**
распил|и́ть, ю́, ~́ишь *pf.* (*of* **~́ивать**) to saw up.
распина́|ть, ю *impf. of* **распя́ть**
распина́|ться, юсь *impf.* (**за кого́-н.**; *coll.*) to put o.s. out (*sc. on s.o.'s behalf*).
распира́|ть, ю *impf. of* **распере́ть**
расписа́ни|е, я *nt.* time-table, schedule.
распи|са́ть, шу́, ~́шешь *pf.* (*of* **~́сывать**) **1.** to enter; to note down. **2.** to assign, allot. **3.** to paint. **4.** (*fig., coll.*) to paint a picture (of).
распи|са́ться, шу́сь, ~́шешься *pf.* (*of* **~́сываться**) **1.** to sign (one's name); (**в**+*p.*) to sign (for); **р. в получе́нии заказно́го паке́та** to sign for a registered letter. **2.** (*coll.*) to register one's marriage. **3.** (**в**+*p.*; *fig.*) to acknowledge, testify (to); **р. в со́бственном неве́жестве** to acknowledge one's own ignorance.
распи́ск|а, и *f.* receipt; **р. в получе́нии** (+*g.*) receipt (for); **сдать письмо́ под ~у** to make s.o. sign for a letter.
расписно́й *adj.* painted, decorated.
распи́сыва|ть(ся), ю(сь) *impf. of* **расписа́ть(ся)**
рас|пи́ть, разопью́, разопьёшь, *past* **~пи́л** (*and* **ро́спил**), **~пила́, ~пи́ло** (*and* **ро́спило**) *pf.* (*of* **~пива́ть**) (*coll.*) to drink up; **р. буты́лку (с кем-н.)** to split a bottle (with s.o.).
распих|а́ть, а́ю *pf.* (*of* **~́ивать**) (*coll.*) **1.** to push aside. **2.** to shove; **р. я́блоки по карма́нам** to stuff apples into one's pockets.
распи́хива|ть, ю *impf. of* **распиха́ть**
распла́в|ить, лю, ишь *pf.* (*of* **~ля́ть**) to melt, fuse.
расплавля́|ть, ю, ет *impf. of* **распла́вить**
распла́|каться, чусь, чешься *pf.* to burst into tears.
распланир|ова́ть, у́ю *pf. of* **планирова́ть**
распласт|а́ть, а́ю *pf.* (*of* **~́ывать**) **1.** to split, divide into layers. **2.** to spread; **р. кры́лья** to spread one's wings.
распласт|а́ться, а́юсь *pf.* (*of* **~́ываться**) to sprawl.
распла́стыва|ть(ся), ю(сь) *impf. of* **распласта́ть(ся)**
распла́т|а, ы *f.* payment; (*fig.*) retribution; **час ~ы** day of reckoning.
распла|ти́ться, чу́сь, ~́тишься *pf.* (*of* **~́чиваться**) **1.** (**с**+*i.*) to pay off; to settle accounts (with), get even (with) (*also fig.*); **р. с долга́ми** to pay off one's debts; **р. по ста́рым счета́м** to pay off old scores. **2.** (**за**+*a.*; *fig.*) to pay (for).
распла́чива|ться, юсь *impf. of* **расплати́ться**
расплe|ска́ть, щу́, ~́щешь *pf.* (*of* **~̈скивать**) to spill.
расплe|ска́ться, щу́сь, ~́щешься *pf.* (*of* **~̈скиваться**) **1.** to spill. **2.** *pass. of* **~ска́ть**
расплёскива|ть(ся), ю(сь) *impf. of* **расплеска́ть(ся)**
распле|сти́, ту́, тёшь, *past* **~̈л, ~ла́** *pf.* (*of* **~та́ть**) to untwine, untwist, undo.
расплета́|ть, ю, ет *impf. of* **расплести́**
распло|ди́ть(ся), жу́(сь), ди́шь(ся) *pf. of* **плоди́ть(ся)**
расплыва́|ться, ется *impf. of* **расплы́ться**
расплы́вчат|ый (~, ~а) *adj.* indistinct; blurred; diffuse, vague.
расплы́|ться, вётся, *past* **~лся, ~ла́сь** *pf.* (*of* **~ва́ться**) **1.** to run; **черни́ла ~лись** the ink has run. **2.** (*coll.*) to spread; to grow fat; **р. в улы́бку** to break into a smile.
расплю́щива|ть(ся), ю, ет(ся) *impf. of* **расплю́щить(ся)**
расплю́щ|ить, у, ишь *pf.* (*of* **~ивать**) to flatten out, hammer out.
расплю́щ|иться, ится *pf.* (*of* **~иваться**) to become flat.
распознава́ни|е, я *nt.* recognition, identification.
распозна|ва́ть, ю́, ёшь *impf. of* **~́ть**
распозна́|ть, ю, ешь *pf.* (*of* **~ва́ть**) to recognize, identify; **р. боле́знь** to diagnose an illness.
располага́|ть[1]**, ю** *impf.* (+*i.*) to dispose (of), have at one's disposal, have available; **р. вре́менем** to have time available; **р. больши́ми сре́дствами** to dispose of ample means.
располага́|ть[2]**, ю** *impf. of* **расположи́ть**
располага́|ться, юсь *impf. of* **расположи́ться**[1]
располага́|ющий *pres. part. act. of* **~ть** *and adj.* prepossessing.
располз|а́ться, а́юсь *impf. of* **~ти́сь**
располз|ти́сь, у́сь ёшься, *past* **~́ся, ~ла́сь** *pf.* (*of* **~а́ться**) **1.** to crawl (away). **2.** (*of clothing, etc.; coll.*) to come unravelled; to tear, give at the seams.
расположе́ни|е, я *nt.* **1.** disposition, arrangement; **р. по кварти́рам** (*mil.*) billeting. **2.** situation, location. **3.** favour; sympathies; **по́льзоваться чьим-н. ~ем** to enjoy s.o.'s favour, be liked by s.o.; **чу́вствовать к кому́-н. р.** to be favourably disposed towards s.o. **4. (к)** disposition (to), inclination (to, for); tendency (to), propensity (to). **5. р. (ду́ха)** mood, humour; **у меня́ нет ~я танцева́ть** I am not in the mood for dancing.
располо́жен|ный (~, ~а) *p.p.p. of* **расположи́ть** *and pred adj.* **1. (к)** well disposed (to, towards). **2.** (**к** *or* +*inf.*) disposed (to), inclined (to); in the mood (for); **я не о́чень ~ сего́дня рабо́тать** I don't feel much like working today.
располож|и́ть, у́, ~́ишь *pf.* (*of* **располага́ть**[2]) **1.** to dispose, arrange, set out; **р. свои́ войска́** to station one's troops. **2.** to win over, gain; **р. кого́-н. к себе́, в свою́ по́льзу** to gain s.o.'s favour.
располож|и́ться[1]**, у́сь, ~́ишься** *pf.* (*of* **располага́ться**) to take up position; to settle o.s.; to make

o.s. comfortable; **р. спать** to settle o.s. to sleep.
располож|и́ться[2], **у́сь**, **~ишься** *pf.* (*+inf.*; *obs.*) to resolve, make up one's mind.
распор|о́ть, ю́, ~ешь *pf.* (*of* **поро́ть**[1] *and* **распа́рывать**) to unstitch, unpick, undo, rip.
распор|о́ться, ~ется *pf.* (*of* **поро́тся** *and* **распа́рываться**) to come unstitched, come undone, rip.
распоряди́тел|ь, я *m.* manager; master of ceremonies.
распоряди́тел|ьный (~ен, ~ьна) *adj.* capable; efficient; **р. челове́к** a good organizer.
распоря|ди́ться, жу́сь, ди́шься *pf.* (*of* **~жа́ться**) **1.** (**о**+*p. or +inf.*) to order; to see (that); **я ~жу́сь возмести́ть вам расхо́ды** I will see that you are reimbursed for the expenses. **2.** (*+i.*) to manage; to deal (with); **разреши́ть кому́-н. р. по своему́ усмотре́нию** to give s.o. a free hand; **как р. э́тими деньга́ми?** what is to be done with this money?
распоря́д|ок, ка *m.* order; routine.
распоряжа́|ться, юсь *impf.* **1.** *impf. of* **распоряди́ться. 2.** *impf. only* to give orders, be in charge; **р. как у себя́ до́ма** to behave as though the place belongs to one.
распоряже́ни|е, я *nt.* **1.** order; instruction, direction; **до осо́бого ~я** until further notice. **2.** disposal; **име́ть в своём ~и** to have at one's disposal.
распоя́|сать, шу, шешь *pf.* (*of* **~сывать**) to ungird.
распоя́|саться, шусь, шешься *pf.* (*of* **~сываться**) **1.** to take off one's belt. **2.** (*fig.*, *coll.*, *pej.*) to throw aside all restraint; to let o.s. go.
распоя́сыва|ть(ся), ю(сь) *impf. of* **распоя́сать(ся)**
распра́в|а, ы *f.* **1.** (*hist.*) punishment. **2.** violence; reprisal; **крова́вая р.** massacre; **коро́ткая р.** short shrift; **у нас с ни́ми р. коротка́** we'll give them short shrift.
распра́в|ить, лю, ишь *pf.* (*of* **~ля́ть**) **1.** to straighten; to smooth out. **2.** to spread, stretch; **р. кры́лья** to spread one's wings (*also fig.*).
распра́в|иться[1], **ится** *pf.* (*of* **~ля́ться**) to get smoothed out.
распра́в|иться[2], **люсь, ишься** *pf.* (*of* **~ля́ться**) (**с**+*i.*) to deal (with), make short work (of); **р. без суда́** to take the law into one's own hands.
расправля́|ть(ся), ю(сь) *impf. of* **распра́вить(ся)**
распределе́ни|е, я *nt.* distribution; allocation, assignment; **р. нало́гов** assessment of taxes.
распредели́тел|ь, я *m.* **1.** distributor; retailer. **2.** (*elec.*) distributor; spreader.
распредели́тельн|ый *adj.* distributive, distributing; **р. щит** (*tech.*) switchboard; **р. вал** (*tech.*) cam shaft; **~ая коро́бка** (*elec.*) switch box, junction box.
распредел|и́ть, ю́, и́шь *pf.* (*of* **~я́ть**) to distribute; to allocate, assign.
распредел|я́ть, я́ю *impf. of* **~и́ть**
распрода|ва́ть, ю́, ёшь *impf. of* **~ть**
распрода́ж|а, и *f.* sale; clearance sale.
распрода́|ть, м, шь, ст, ди́м, ди́те, ду́т, *past* **распро́дал, ~ла́, распро́дало** *pf.* (*of* **~ва́ть**) to sell off; to sell out; **биле́ты распро́даны** all the tickets are sold.
распростер|е́ть, *fut. tense not used*, *past* **~, ~ла** *pf.* (*of* **распростира́ть**) to stretch out, extend.
распростер|е́ться, *fut. tense not used*, *past* **~ся, ~лась** *pf.* (*of* **распростира́ться**) **1.** to stretch o.s. out; to prostrate o.s. **2.** (*fig.*) to spread.
распростёр|тый *p.p.p. of* **~е́ть** *and adj.* **1.** outstretched; **встре́тить с ~тыми объя́тиями** to receive with open arms. **2.** prostrate, prone.
распростира́|ть(ся), ю(сь) *impf. of* **распростере́ть(ся)**
распро|сти́ться, щу́сь, сти́шься *pf.* (**с**+*i.*) to say goodbye (to); to bid farewell (to).
распростране́ни|е, я *nt.* spreading, diffusion; dissemination; **р. зара́зы** spreading of infection; **име́ть большо́е р.** to be widely practised.
распростран|ённый *p.p.p. of* **~и́ть** *and adj.* widespread; prevalent.
распростран|и́ть, ю, и́шь *pf.* (*of* **~я́ть**) **1.** to spread, diffuse; to disseminate; **р. слух** to spread a rumour; **р. но́вое уче́ние** to disseminate a new doctrine. **2.** to extend. **3.** to give off (*a smell*).
распростран|и́ться, ю́сь, и́шься *pf.* (*of* **~я́ться**) **1.** to spread; to extend; (*of a law, etc.*) to apply. **2.** (**о**+*p.*; *coll.*) to enlarge (on), dilate (on).
распростран|я́ть(ся), я́ю(сь) *impf. of* **~и́ть(ся)**
ра́спр|я, и, *g. pl.* **~ей** *f.* quarrel, feud.
распряга́|ть, ю *impf. of* **распря́чь**
распрям|и́ть, лю́, и́шь *pf.* (*of* **~ля́ть**) to straighten, unbend.
распрям|и́ться, лю́сь, и́шься *pf.* (*of* **~ля́ться**) to straighten (o.s.) up.
распрямля́|ть(ся), ю(сь) *impf. of* **распрями́ть(ся)**
распря́|чь, гу́, жёшь, гу́т, *past* **~г, ~гла́** *pf.* (*of* **~га́ть**) to unharness.
распуг|а́ть, а́ю *pf.* (*of* **~ивать**) to scare away, frighten away.
распуска́|ть(ся), ю(сь) *impf. of* **распусти́ть(ся)**
распу|сти́ть, щу́, ~стишь *pf.* (*of* **~ска́ть**) **1.** to dismiss; to disband; **р. парла́мент** to dissolve parliament. **2.** to let out; to relax; **р. во́лосы** to let one's hair down; **р. знамёна** to unfurl banners. **3.** (*fig.*) to allow to get out of hand; to spoil. **4.** to dissolve; to melt. **5.** (*coll.*) to spread (*rumours, etc.*).
распу|сти́ться, щу́сь, ~стишься *pf.* (*of* **~ска́ться**) **1.** (*bot.*) to open, come out. **2.** to come loose; **чуло́к у неё ~сти́лся** her stocking had come down. **3.** (*fig.*) to get out of hand, let o.s. go. **4.** to dissolve; to melt.
распу́т|ать, аю *pf.* (*of* **~ывать**) **1.** to untangle, disentangle; to unravel. **2.** to untie (*an animal*). **3.** (*fig.*) to disentangle, unravel; to puzzle out.
распу́т|аться, аюсь *pf.* (*of* **~ываться**) **1.** to get disentangled, come undone. **2.** (*fig.*, *coll.*) to get disentangled, be cleared up. **3.** (**с**+*i.*; *coll.*) to rid o.s. (of), shake off.
распу́тиц|а, ы *f.* time (*during spring and autumn*) of bad roads.
распу́тник, а *m.* profligate, libertine.
распу́тнича|ть, ю *impf.* to lead a dissolute life.
распу́т|ный (~ен, ~на) *adj.* dissolute, dissipated, debauched.
распу́тств|о, а *nt.* dissipation, debauchery, profligacy, libertinism.
распу́тыва|ть(ся), ю(сь) *impf. of* **распу́тать(ся)**
распу́ть|е, я *nt.* crossroads; **быть на р.** (*fig.*) to be at the crossroads.
распух|а́ть, а́ю *impf. of* **~нуть**
распу́х|нуть, ну, нешь, *past* **~, ~ла** *pf.* (*of* **~а́ть**) **1.** to swell up. **2.** (*fig.*, *coll.*) to swell, become inflated.
распуш|и́ть, у́, и́шь *pf. of* **пуши́ть**
распу́щенност|ь, и *f.* **1.** lack of discipline. **2.** dissoluteness, dissipation.
распу́|щенный *p.p.p. of* **~сти́ть** *and adj.* **1.** undisciplined; **р. ребёнок** spoiled child. **2.** dissolute.
распыли́тел|ь, я *m.* spray(er), atomizer.
распыл|и́ть, ю́, и́шь *pf.* (*of* **~я́ть**) **1.** to spray; to atomize; to pulverize. **2.** (*fig.*) to disperse, scatter.
распыл|я́ть, я́ю *impf. of* **~и́ть**
распя́ти|е, я *nt.* **1.** crucifixion. **2.** cross, crucifix.
расп|я́ть, ну́, нёшь *pf.* (*of* **~ина́ть**) to crucify.
расса́д|а, ы *no pl.*, *f.* seedlings.
расса|ди́ть, жу́, ~дишь *pf.* (*of* **~живать**) **1.** to seat, offer seats. **2.** to separate, seat separately. **3.** to transplant, plant out.
расса́дник, а *m.* **1.** seed-plot. **2.** (*fig.*) hotbed, breeding-ground.

рассáжива|ть, ю *impf. of* **рассадúть**
рассáжива|ться, юсь *impf. of* **рассéсться**[1]
рассве|стú, тёт, *past* **~лó** *pf.* (*of* **~тáть**) to dawn; **ужé ~лó** it was already light.
рассвéт, а *m.* dawn, daybreak.
рассветá|ть, ет *impf. of* **рассвестú; ~ет** day is breaking; it is getting light.
рассвирепé|ть, ю *pf.* (*of* **свирепéть**) to become savage; to turn nasty.
рассedá|ться, юсь *impf. of* **рассéсться**[2]
расседл|áть, áю *pf.* (*of* **~ывать**) to unsaddle.
рассéивани|е, я *nt.* dispersion; dispersal, scattering.
рассéива|ть(ся), ю(сь) *impf. of* **рассéять(ся)**
рассекá|ть, ю *impf. of* **рассéчь**
рассекрé|тить, чу, тишь *pf.* (*of* **~чивать**) to declassify.
рассекрéчива|ть, ю *impf. of* **рассекрéтить**
рассéлин|а, ы *f.* cleft, fissure.
рассел|úть, ю́, úшь *pf.* (*of* **~я́ть**) **1.** to settle (*in a new place*). **2.** to separate; to settle apart.
рассел|úться, ю́сь, úшься *pf.* (*of* **~я́ться**) **1.** to settle (*in a new place*). **2.** to separate, settle separately.
рассел|я́ть(ся), я́ю(сь) *impf. of* **~úть(ся)**
рассер|дúть, жý, ~дишь *pf.* to anger, make angry.
рассер|дúться, жýсь, ~дишься *pf.* (**на**+*a.*) to get, become angry (with).
рассéр|женный *p.p.p. of* **~дúть** *and adj.* angry.
рас|сéсться[1], **ся́дусь, ся́дешься,** *past* **~сéлся** *pf.* (*of* **~сáживаться**) to take one's seat.
рас|сéсться[2], **ся́дется,** *past* **~сéлся** *pf.* (*of* **~седáться**) to crack.
рассé|чь, кý, чёшь, кýт, *past* **~к, ~клá** *pf.* (*of* **~кáть**) **1.** to cut through; to cleave (*also fig.*). **2.** to gash; **я ~к себé пáлец** I have gashed my finger.
рассéяни|е, я *nt.* diffusion; dispersion.
рассéяннoст|ь, и *f.* absent-mindedness.
рассéя|нный *p.p.p. of* **~ть** *and adj.* **1.** diffused; **р. свет** (*phys.*) diffused light. **2.** scattered, dispersed; **~нное населéние** scattered population. **3.** absent-minded; **р. взгляд** vacant look.
рассé|ять, ю, ешь *pf.* (*of* **~ивать**) **1.** to scatter. **2.** (*fig.*) to place (about), dot (about). **3.** to disperse, scatter; (*fig.*) to dispel; **р. чьи-н. сомнéния** to dispel s.o.'s doubts.
рассé|яться, юсь, ешься *pf.* (*of* **~иваться**) **1.** to disperse, scatter; **толпá ~ялась** the crowd dispersed; **тумáн ~ялся** the fog cleared; **р. как дым** to vanish into thin air. **2.** to divert o.s., distract o.s.; **емý нáдо р.** he needs a break.
расскáз, а *m.* **1.** account, narrative. **2.** story, tale.
расска|зáть, жý, ~жешь *pf.* (*of* **~зывать**) to tell, narrate, recount.
расскáзчик, а *m.* story-teller, narrator.
расскáзыва|ть, ю *impf. of* **рассказáть**
расслáб|ить, лю, ишь *pf.* (*of* **~ля́ть**) to weaken, enfeeble; to enervate.
расслáб|ленный *p.p.p. of* **~ить** *and adj.* weak; limp.
расслабля́|ть, ю *impf. of* **расслáбить**
расслáива|ть, ю, ет *impf. of* **расслоúть**
расслéдовани|е, я *nt.* investigation; (*leg.*) inquiry; **произвестú р.** (+*g.*) to hold an inquiry (into).
расслéд|овать, ую *impf. and pf.* to investigate.
расслоéни|е, я *nt.* stratification (*also fig.*).
рассло|úть, ю́, úшь *pf.* (*of* **расслáивать**) to stratify (*also fig.*).
расслы́ш|ать, у, ишь *pf.* to catch; **я не ~ал вас** I didn't catch what you said.
рассмáтрива|ть, ю *impf.* **1.** *impf. of* **рассмотрéть. 2.** *impf. only* to regard (as), consider; **мы ~ем э́то как обмáн** we regard it as a fraud. **3.** *impf. only* to scrutinize, examine.
рассмеш|úть, ý, úшь *pf.* to make laugh.
рассме|я́ться, ю́сь, ёшься *pf.* to burst out laughing.
рассмотрéни|е, я *nt.* examination; consideration; **быть на ~и** to be under consideration.
рассмотр|éть, ю́, ~ишь *pf.* (*of* **рассмáтривать**) **1.** to discern, make out. **2.** to examine, consider; **р. заявлéние** to consider an application.
расс|овáть, ую́, уёшь *pf.* (*of* **~óвывать**) (*coll.*) to shove, stuff; **р. свои́ вéщи по чемодáнам** to stuff one's things into suitcases.
рассóвыва|ть, ю *impf. of* **рассовáть**
рассóл, а *m.* **1.** brine. **2.** (*cul.*) pickle.
рассóльник, а *m.* (*cul.*) rassolnik (*meat or fish soup with pickled cucumbers*).
рассóр|ить, ю, ишь *pf.* to set at loggerheads.
рассóр|иться, юсь, ишься *pf.* (**с**+*i.*) to fall out (with).
рассортир|овáть, ýю *pf.* (*of* **~óвывать**) to sort out.
рассортирóвк|а, и *f.* sorting out.
рассортирóвыва|ть, ю *impf. of* **рассортировáть**
рассóх|нуться, нется, *past* **~ся, ~лась** *pf.* (*of* **рассыхáться**) to crack.
расспрáшива|ть, ю *impf. of* **расспросúть**
расспрóс, а *m.* question, questioning; **надоéсть ~ами** to pester with questions.
расспро|сúть, шý, ~сишь *pf.* (*of* **расспрáшивать**) to question; **р. когó-н. о дорóге** to ask s.o. the way.
рассредотóчени|е, я *nt.* (*mil.*) dispersion, dispersal.
рассредотóчива|ть, ю *impf. of* **рассредотóчить**
рассредотóч|ить, у, ишь *pf.* (*of* **~ивать**) (*mil.*) to disperse.
рассрóчива|ть, ю *impf. of* **рассрóчить**
рассрóч|ить, у, ишь *pf.* (*of* **~ивать**) to spread (*over a period*); **р. издáние энциклопéдии на дéсять лет** to spread the publication of an encyclopaedia over a period of ten years.
рассрóчк|а, и *f.*: **в ~у** in instalments; **купúть в ~у** to purchase by instalments, on hire-purchase.
расставáни|е, я *nt.* parting; **при ~и** on parting.
расста|вáться, ю́сь, ёшься *impf. of* **расстáться**
расстáв|ить, лю, ишь *pf.* (*of* **~ля́ть**) **1.** (*impf. also* **расстанáвливать**) to place, arrange; **р. часовы́х** to post sentries. **2.** to move apart; **р. нóги** to stand with one's legs apart. **3.** (*tailoring*) to let out.
расставля́|ть, ю *impf. of* **расстáвить**
расстанáвлива|ть, ю *impf. of* **расстáвить**
расстанóвк|а, и *f.* **1.** placing, placement; arrangement. **2.** pause; spacing; **говорúть с ~ой** to speak slowly and deliberately.
расстá|ться, нусь, нешься *pf.* (*of* **~вáться**) (**с**+*i.*) **1.** to part (with); to leave; **~немся друзья́ми** let us part friends. **2.** to give up; **р. с мы́слью** to put the thought out of one's head.
расстёгива|ть(ся), ю(сь) *impf. of* **расстегнýть(ся)**
расстег|нýть, нý, нёшь *pf.* (*of* **~ивать**) to undo, unfasten; to unbutton; to unhook, unclasp, unbuckle.
расстег|нýться, нýсь, нёшься *pf.* (*of* **~иваться**) **1.** to come undone. **2.** to unbutton one's coat; to undo one's buttons.
рассtел|úться), ю́(сь), ~ишь(ся) *pf.* = **разостлáть(ся)**
расстилá|ть, ю *impf. of* **разостлáть**
расстилá|ться, юсь *impf.* **1.** *impf. of* **разостлáться. 2.** *impf. only* to extend, unfold.
расстоя́ни|е, я *nt.* distance, space, interval; **на бли́зком ~и (от)** at a short distance (from), a short way away (from); **онú живýт на ~и двух миль от ближáйшего совéда** they live two miles from their nearest neighbour; **держáться на ~и** to keep one's distance.
расстрáива|ть(ся), ю(сь) *impf. of* **расстрóить(ся)**
расстрéл, а *m.* **1.** execution (*by firing squad*); **приговорúть к ~у** to sentence to be shot. **2.** shooting up.

расстре́лива|ть, ю *impf. of* **расстреля́ть**
расстрел|я́ть, я́ю *pf.* (*of* **∼ивать**) **1.** to shoot; to execute (*by firing squad*). **2.** to shoot up; to fire upon at close range. **3.** to use up (*in firing*).
расстри́г|а, и *m.* unfrocked priest, unfrocked monk.
расстрига́|ть, ю *impf. of* **расстри́чь**
расстри́|чь, гу́, жёшь, гу́т, *past* **∼г, ∼гла** *pf.* (*of* **∼га́ть**) (*eccl.*) to unfrock.
расстро́|енный *p.p.p. of* **∼ить** *and adj.* disordered, deranged; **р. вид** downcast appearance.
расстро́|ить, ю, ишь *pf.* (*of* **расстра́ивать**) **1.** to disorder, derange; to throw into disorder; to unsettle; to upset; **р. желу́док** to upset one's stomach; **р. за́мыслы** to thwart schemes; **р. своё здоро́вье** to impair one's health; **р. чьи-н. пла́ны** to upset s.o.'s plans; **р. сва́дьбу** to break off an engagement; **р. хозя́йство** to ruin the economy. **2.** to upset, put out. **3.** (*mus.*) to throw out of tune.
расстро́|иться, юсь, ишься *pf.* (*of* **расстра́иваться**) **1.** to be thrown into disorder, fall apart; (*fig.*) to fall through; **все на́ши пла́ны ∼ились** all our plans have fallen through. **2. (от)** to be upset (over, about). **3.** (*mus.*) to get out of tune.
расстро́йств|о, а *nt.* **1.** disorder; derangement; confusion; **р. желу́дка** stomach upset; **р. пищеваре́ния** indigestion; **р. ре́чи** speech defect; **внести́ р.** (**в**+*a.*), **привести́ в р.** to throw into confusion, disorganize. **2.** (*coll.*) upset; **привести́ в р.** to upset; **быть в ∼е** to be upset.
расступ|а́ться, а́ется *impf. of* **∼и́ться**
расступ|и́ться, ∼ится *pf.* (*of* **∼а́ться**) to part, make way; **толпа́ ∼и́лась** the crowd parted.
рассуди́тельност|ь, и *f.* reasonableness; good sense.
рассуди́тел|ьный (∼ен, ∼ьна) *adj.* reasonable; sober-minded; sensible.
рассу|ди́ть, жу́, ∼дишь *pf.* **1.** to judge (between), arbitrate (between); **р. спор** to settle a dispute. **2.** to think, consider; to decide; **мы ∼ди́ли, что пришло́ вре́мя верну́ться домо́й** we decided that the time had come to return home.
рассу́д|ок, ка *m.* **1.** reason; intellect; **го́лос ∼ка** the voice of reason; **в по́лном ∼ке** in full possession of one's faculties; **лиши́ться ∼ка** to go out of one's mind. **2.** common sense, good sense.
рассу́доч|ный (∼ен, ∼на) *adj.* rational.
рассужда́|ть, ю *impf.* **1.** to reason. **2.** (**о**+*p.*) to discuss, debate; to argue (about); to discourse (on); **р. на каку́ю-н. те́му** to discuss a topic.
рассужде́ни|е, я *nt.* **1.** reasoning. **2.** (*usu. pl.*) discussion, debate; argument; discourse; **без ∼й** without argument.
рассу́чива|ть, ю, ет *impf. of* **рассучи́ть**
рассуч|и́ть, у́, ∼ишь *pf.* (*of* **∼ивать**) to untwist; to undo; **р. рукава́** to roll one's sleeves down.
рассчи́т|анный *p.p.p. of* **∼а́ть** *and adj.* **1.** calculated, deliberate; **∼анная гру́бость** calculated rudeness. **2.** (**на**+*a.*) intended (for), meant (for), designed (for).
рассчит|а́ть, а́ю *pf.* (*of* **∼ывать**) **1.** to calculate, compute. **2.** to dismiss, sack.
рассчит|а́ться, а́юсь *pf.* (*of* **∼ываться**) (**с**+*i.*) to settle up (with).
рассчи́тыва|ть, ю *impf.* **1.** *impf. of* **рассчита́ть** *and* **расче́сть. 2.** *impf. only* (**на**+*a.*) to count (on, upon), reckon (on, upon); (+*inf.*) to expect (to), hope (to). **3.** *impf. only* (**на**+*a.*) to count (on, upon).
рассчи́тыва|ться, юсь *impf. of* **рассчита́ться** *and* **расче́сться**
рассыла́|ть, ю *impf. of* **разосла́ть**
рассы́лк|а, и *f.* distribution, delivery.
рассы́льн|ый *adj.*: **∼ая кни́га** delivery book; *as n.* **р., ∼ого** *m.* delivery man, errand-boy.
рассы́п|ать, лю, лешь *pf.* (*of* **∼а́ть**) to spill; to strew, scatter.
рассы́п|аться, люсь, лешься *pf.* (*of* **∼а́ться**) **1.** to spill, scatter. **2.** to spread out, deploy. **3.** to crumble; to fall to pieces, disintegrate (*also fig.*). **4.** (**в**+*p.*) to be profuse (in); **р. в похвала́х** (+*d.*) to lavish praise (upon).
рассып|а́ть(ся), а́ю(сь) *impf. of* **∼ать(ся)**
рассы́пчат|ый (∼, ∼а) *adj.* friable; (*cul.*) short, crumbly; **∼ое пече́нье** shortbread.
рассыха́|ться, юсь *impf. of* **рассо́хнуться**
раста́лкива|ть, ю *impf. of* **растолка́ть**
раста́плива|ть(ся), ю, ет(ся) *impf. of* **растопи́ть(ся)**
раста́птыва|ть, ю *impf. of* **растопта́ть**
растаск|а́ть, а́ю *pf.* (*of* **∼ивать**) **1.** to take away, remove (*little by little, bit by bit*). **2.** to pilfer, filch.
раста́скива|ть, ю *impf. of* **растаска́ть** *and* **растащи́ть**
растафа́ри *c.g. & adj. indecl.* Rastafarian; Rasta.
раста́чива|ть, ю *impf. of* **расточи́ть**[2]
растащ|и́ть, у́, ∼ишь *pf.* (*of* **раста́скивать**) **1.** to part, separate, drag asunder. **2.** = **растаска́ть**
раста́|ять, ю, ешь *pf. of* **та́ять**
раство́р[1], **а** *m.* span; spread; **р. ци́ркуля** spread of a pair of compasses.
раство́р[2], **а** *m.* **1.** (*chem.*) solution. **2.** (*tech.*) mortar; **строи́тельный р.** grout.
растворе́ни|е, я *nt.* solution, dissolution.
раствори́мост|ь, и *f.* (*chem.*) solubility
раствори́м|ый (∼, ∼а) *adj.* (*chem.*) soluble; **р. ко́фе** instant coffee.
раствори́тел|ь, я *m.* (*chem.*) solvent.
раствор|и́ть[1], **ю́, ∼ишь** *pf.* (*of* **∼я́ть**) to open.
раствор|и́ть[2], **ю́, и́шь** *pf.* (*of* **∼я́ть**) to dissolve.
раствор|и́ться[1], **∼ится** *pf.* (*of* **∼я́ться**) to open.
раствор|и́ться[2], **и́тся** *pf.* (*of* **∼я́ться**) to dissolve.
раствор|я́ть(ся), я́ю(сь) *impf. of* **∼и́ть(ся)**
растека́|ться, юсь *impf. of* **расте́чься**
расте́ни|е, я *nt.* plant; **одноле́тнее р.** annual; **многоле́тнее р.** perennial; **ползу́чее р.** creeper.
растениево́дств|о, а *nt.* plant-growing.
растере́ть, разотру́, разотрёшь, *past* **растёр, растёрла** *pf.* (*of* **растира́ть**) **1.** to grind; **р. в порошо́к** to grind to powder. **2.** (**по**+*d.*) to rub (over), spread (over). **3.** to rub, massage.
растерз|а́ть, а́ю *pf.* (*of* **∼ывать**) to tear to pieces.
расте́рзыва|ть, ю *impf. of* **растерза́ть**
расте́рива|ть(ся), ю(сь) *impf. of* **растеря́ть(ся)**
расте́рянност|ь, и *f.* confusion, bewilderment.
расте́р|янный *p.p.p. of* **∼я́ть** *and adj.* confused, bewildered.
растер|я́ть, я́ю *pf.* (*of* **∼ивать**) to lose (bit by bit).
растер|я́ться, я́юсь *pf.* (*of* **∼иваться**) **1.** to get lost. **2.** to lose one's head.
расте́|чься, чётся, ку́тся, *past* **∼кся, ∼кла́сь** *pf.* (*of* **∼ка́ться**) **1.** to spill; to run. **2.** (*fig.*) to spread; **по её лицу́ ∼кла́сь улы́бка** a smile spread over her face.
раст|и́, у́, ёшь, *past* **рос, росла́** *impf.* **1.** (*biol., bot.*) to grow; (*of children*) to grow up; **он рос на Украи́не** he grew up in (the) Ukraine. **2.** (*fig.*) to grow, increase. **3.** (*fig.*) to advance, develop.
растира́ни|е, я *nt.* **1.** grinding. **2.** (*med.*) massage.
растира́|ть, ю *impf. of* **растере́ть**
расти́тельност|ь, и *f.* **1.** vegetation; verdure. **2.** hair (*on face or body*).
расти́тельн|ый *adj.* vegetable; **∼ое ма́сло** vegetable oil; **жить ∼ой жи́знью** (*fig., iron.*) to vegetate.
ра|сти́ть, щу́, сти́шь *impf.*. **1.** to raise, bring up; to train; **р. дете́й** to raise children. **2.** to grow, cultivate; **р. бо́роду** to grow a beard.
растлева́|ть, ю *impf. of* **растли́ть**
растле́ни|е, я *nt.* **1.** seduction (*of minors*). **2.** (*fig.*)

corruption; decay, decadence.
растлéнный *adj.* corrupt; decadent.
растлúтел|ь, я *m.*: **р. малолéтних детéй** child molester.
растл|úть, ю́, úшь *pf.* (*of* **~евáть**) **1.** to seduce (*minors*). **2.** (*fig.*) to corrupt.
растолкá|ть, ю *pf.* (*of* **растáлкивать**) **1.** to push asunder, apart. **2.** to shake (*in order to awaken*).
растолк|овáть, у́ю *pf.* (*of* **~óвывать**) to explain.
растолкóвыва|ть, ю *impf. of* **растолковáть**
растол|óчь, ку́, чёшь, ку́т, *past* **~óк, ~олкá** *pf. of* **толóчь**
растолстé|ть, ю *pf.* to grow stout, put on weight.
растоп|úть¹, лю́, ∠ишь *pf.* (*of* **растáпливать**) to light, kindle.
растоп|úть², лю́, ∠ишь *pf.* (*of* **растáпливать**) to melt; to (cause to) thaw.
растоп|úться¹, ∠ится *pf.* (*of* **растáпливаться**) to begin to burn.
растоп|úться², ∠ится *pf.* (*of* **растáпливаться**) to melt.
растóпк|а, и *f.* **1.** lighting, kindling. **2.** (*collect.*) kindling (wood).
растоп|тáть, чу́, ∠чешь *pf.* (*of* **растáптывать**) to trample, crush.
растопы́рива|ть, ю *impf. of* **растопы́рить**
растопы́р|ить, ю, ишь *pf.* (*of* **~ивать**) to spread wide, open wide.
расторг|áть, áю *impf. of* **∠нуть**
растóрг|нуть, ну, нешь, *past* **~, ~ла** *pf.* (*of* **~áть**) to annul, abrogate; **р. брак** to dissolve a marriage.
расторжéни|е, я *nt.* annulment, abrogation, dissolution.
растормош|úть, у́, úшь *pf.* (*coll.*) **1.** to tug (*in order to awaken*). **2.** (*fig.*) to stir up, spur to activity.
расторóп|ный (~ен, ~на) *adj.* (*coll.*) quick, prompt, smart; efficient.
расточ|áть, áю *pf.* (*of* **~úть¹**) **1.** to waste, squander, dissipate. **2.** (*fig.*) to lavish, shower; **р. похвалы́** (*+d.*) to lavish praise (on, upon).
расточúтел|ь, я *m.* squanderer, spendthrift.
расточúтел|ьный (~ен, ~ьна) *adj.* extravagant, wasteful.
расточ|úть¹, у́, úшь *pf.* (*of* **~áть**)
расточ|úть², у́, ∠ишь *pf.* (*of* **растáчивать**) (*tech.*) to bore (out).
растрав|úть, лю́, ∠ишь *pf.* (*of* **~ля́ть**) to irritate; **р. рáну** (*fig.*) to rub salt in a wound.
растравля́|ть, ю *impf. of* **растравúть**
растранжúр|ить, ю, ишь *pf. of* **транжúрить**
растрáт|а, ы *f.* **1.** waste, squandering. **2.** embezzlement.
растрá|тить, чу, тишь *pf.* (*of* **~чивать**) **1.** to waste, squander, dissipate; **р. своё врéмя** to fritter away one's time. **2.** to embezzle.
растрáтчик, а *m.* embezzler.
растрáчива|ть, ю *impf. of* **растрáтить**
растревóж|ить, у, ишь *pf.* (*coll.*) to alarm, agitate; **р. муравéйник** to stir up an ant-hill.
растрёп|а, ы *c.g.* (*coll.*) sloven, scruff.
растрёп|анный *p.p.p. of* **~áть** *and adj.* dishevelled; tattered.
растреп|áть, лю́, ∠лешь *pf.* **1.** to mess up; to tousle. **2.** to tatter, tear (*a book, etc.*).
растреп|áться, ∠лется *pf.* **1.** to get dishevelled. **2.** to get tattered, get torn.
растрéск|аться, ается *pf.* (*of* **~иваться**) to crack; (*of skin*) to chap.
растрéскива|ться, ется *impf. of* **растрéскаться**
растрóга|ть, ю *pf.* to move, touch; **р. когó-н. до слёз** to move s.o. to tears.
растрóга|ться, юсь *pf.* to be (deeply) moved, touched.
растру́б, а *m.* bell, bell-mouth; socket (*of pipe*); **с ~ом** bell-shaped, bell-mouthed.
растряс|тú, у́, ёшь, *past* **∠, ~лá** *pf.* **1.** to strew (*hay, etc.*). **2.** (*coll.*) to shake (*in order to awaken*). **3.** (*impers.*) to jolt about. **4.** (*coll.*) to squander.
растя́гива|ть(ся), ю(сь) *impf. of* **растяну́ть(ся)**
растяжéни|е, я *nt.* (*med.*) strain, sprain.
растяжúмост|ь, и *f.* tensility, tensile strength; extensibility; expansibility.
растяжúм|ый (~, ~а) *adj.* tensile; extensible; expansible; **~ое поня́тие** loose concept.
растя́жк|а, и *f.* stretching, extension.
растя́н|утый *p.p.p. of* **~у́ть** *and adj.* **1.** long-winded, prolix. **2.** stretched; **р. фронт** (*mil.*) extended front.
растя|ну́ть, ну́, ∠нешь *pf.* (*of* **∠гивать**) **1.** to stretch (out). **2.** (*med.*) to strain, sprain; **р. себé му́скул** to pull a muscle; **р. себé свя́зку** to strain a ligament. **3.** to stretch too far; (*fig.*) to prolong, drag out; **р. словá** to drawl.
растя|ну́ться, ну́сь, ∠нешься *pf.* (*of* **∠гиваться**) **1.** to stretch (out), lengthen out. **2.** to stretch too far; (*fig.*) to be prolonged, drag out. **3.** to stretch o.s. out, sprawl.
растя́п|а, ы *c.g.* (*coll.*) bungler.
расфас|овáть, у́ю *pf.* (*of* **~óвывать**) to pack up, parcel up.
расфасóвк|а, и *f.* packing, parcelling.
расфасóвыва|ть, ю *impf. of* **расфасовáть**
расформир|овáть, у́ю *pf.* (*of* **~óвывать**) to break up; (*mil.*) to disband.
расформирóвыва|ть, ю *impf. of* **расформировáть**
расфранчённый *adj.* (*coll.*) dressed up to the nines; overdressed.
расхáжива|ть, ю *impf.* to walk, pace; **р. по кóмнате** to pace up and down a room.
расхвáлива|ть, ю *impf. of* **расхвалúть**
расхвал|úть, ю́, ∠ишь *pf.* (*of* **∠ивать**) to lavish, shower praise (on, upon).
расхвáрыва|ться, юсь *impf. of* **расхворáться**
расхвáста|ться, юсь *pf.* (**о**+*p.*; *coll.*) to boast extravagantly (of, about); to shoot a line (about).
расхват|áть, áю *pf.* (*of* **∠ывать**) to snatch, seize (*with the object of purchasing, etc.*).
расхвáтыва|ть, ю *impf. of* **расхватáть**
расхворá|ться, юсь *pf.* (*of* **расхвáрываться**) to fall ill.
расхитúтел|ь, я *m.* embezzler.
расхú|тить, щу, тишь *pf.* (*of* **~щáть**) to embezzle, misappropriate.
расхищá|ть, ю *impf. of* **расхúтить**
расхищéни|е, я *nt.* embezzlement, misappropriation.
расхлеб|áть, áю *pf.* (*of* **∠ывать**) to disentangle.
расхлёбыва|ть, ю *impf. of* **расхлебáть; заварúл кáшу, тепéрь сам и ~й** (*coll.*) you got yourself into this mess, now get yourself out of it.
расхля́банност|ь, и *f.* **1.** looseness; instability. **2.** (*fig.*) slackness; laxity, lack of discipline.
расхля́банн|ый *adj.* (*coll.*) **1.** loose, unstable. **2.** (*fig.*) lax, undisciplined.
расхóд, а *m.* **1.** expense; (*pl.*) expenses, outlay, cost; **накладны́е ~ы** overheads; **дéньги на кармáнные ~ы** pocket-money. **2.** consumption; **р. горю́чего** fuel consumption. **3.** (*book-keeping*) expenditure, outlay; **прихóд и р.** income and expenditure; **списáть в р.** to write off; (*fig., coll.*) to liquidate. **4.: вы́вести в р.** (*coll.*) to shoot.
расхо|дúться, жу́сь, ∠дишься *impf. of* **разойтúсь**
расхóд|ный *adj. of* **~**; **~ная кнúга** expenses book.
расхóдовани|е, я *nt.* expense, expenditure.
расхóд|овать, ую *impf.* (*of* **из~**) **1.** to spend, expend. **2.** to use up, consume.
расхóд|оваться, уюсь *impf.* (*of* **из~**) **1.** (*coll.*) to spend; to lay out money. **2.** *pass. of* **~овать**

расхожде́ни|е, я *nt.* divergence; **р. во мне́ниях** difference of opinion.
расхола́жива|ть, ю *impf. of* **расхолоди́ть**
расхоло|ди́ть, жу́, ди́шь *pf.* (*of* **расхола́живать**) to damp the ardour (of).
расхо|те́ть, чу́, ∠чешь, ти́м, ти́те, тя́т *pf.* (+*inf.*; *coll.*) to cease to want.
расхо|те́ться, ∠чется *pf.* (*impers.*+*d.*; *coll.*) to cease to want; **мне ~те́лось есть** I no longer want to eat.
расхохо|та́ться, чу́сь, ∠чешься *pf.* to burst out laughing; to roar with laughter.
расхрабр|и́ться, ю́сь, и́шься *pf.* (*coll.*) to screw up one's courage, pluck up courage.
расцара́п|ать, аю *pf.* (*of* **~ывать**) to scratch (all over).
расцара́пыва|ть, ю *impf. of* **расцара́пать**
расцве|сти́, ту́, тёшь, *past* **∸л, ~ла́** *pf.* (*of* **~та́ть**) to bloom; to blossom (*also fig.*); (*fig.*) to flourish; **его́ лицо́ ~ло́ улы́бкой** his face was wreathed in smiles.
расцве́т, а *m.* bloom, blossoming; (*fig.*) flourishing; flowering, heyday; **в ~е сил** at the peak of one's powers, in one's prime.
расцвета́|ть, ю *impf. of* **расцвести́**
расцве|ти́ть, чу́, ти́шь *pf.* (*of* **∠чивать**) **1.** to paint in bright colours. **2.** to deck, adorn.
расцве́тк|а, и *f.* colours; colour scheme.
расцве́чива|ть, ю *impf. of* **расцвети́ть**
расцел|ова́ть, у́ю *pf.* to smother with kisses.
расцел|ова́ться, у́юсь *pf.* to exchange kisses.
расце́нива|ть, ю *impf. of* **расцени́ть**
расцен|и́ть, ю́, ∠ишь *pf.* (*of* **∠ивать**) **1.** to estimate, assess, value. **2.** (*fig.*) to rate, assess; to regard, consider; **как вы ~или его́ игру́?** what did you think of his acting?
расце́нк|а, и *f.* **1.** valuation. **2.** price. **3.** (wage-)rate.
расцеп|и́ть, лю́, ∠ишь *pf.* (*of* **~ля́ть**) to uncouple, unhook; to disengage, release.
расцеп|и́ться, ∠ится *pf.* (*of* **~ля́ться**) to come uncoupled, come unhooked.
расцепля́|ть(ся), ю, ет(ся) *impf. of* **расцепи́ть(ся)**
расче|са́ть, шу́, ∠шешь *pf.* (*of* **∸сывать**) **1.** to comb; to card. **2.** to scratch.
расче|са́ться, шу́сь, ∠шешься *pf.* (*of* **∸сываться**) (*coll.*) **1.** to comb one's hair. **2.** to scratch o.s.
расчёск|а, и *f.* comb.
расче́сть, разочту́, разочтёшь, *past* **расчёл, разочла́** *pf.* (*of* **рассчи́тывать**) **1.** to calculate, compute. **2.** to dismiss, sack.
расче́сться, разочту́сь, разочтёшься, *past* **расчёлся, разочла́сь** *pf.* (*of* **рассчи́тывать(ся)** (**с**+*i.*) to settle accounts (with).
расчёсыва|ть(ся), ю(сь) *impf. of* **расчеса́ть(ся)**
расчёт[1]**, а** *m.* **1.** calculation (*also tech.*); computation; estimate, reckoning; **из ~а** (+*g.*) on the basis (of), at a rate (of); **приня́ть в р.** to take into account, consideration; **по мои́м ~ам** by my reckoning; **э́то не входи́ло в мои́ ~ы** I had not reckoned with that; **ошиби́ться в свои́х ~ах** to miscalculate. **2.** (*coll.*) gain, advantage; **нет ~а** (+*inf.*) it is not worth while, there is no point. **3.** (**с**+*i.*) settling (with); **нали́чный р.** cash payment; **быть в ~е** (**с**+*i.*) to be quits (with), be even (with). **4.** dismissal, discharge; **дать р.** (+*d.*) to dismiss, sack; **взять р.** to hand in one's notice.
расчёт[2]**, а** *m.* (*mil.*) crew; **ору́дийный р.** gun crew.
расчётливост|ь, и *f.* thrift.
расчётлив|ый (~, ~а) *adj.* thrifty; careful.
расчётн|ый *adj.* **1.** calculation, computation. **2.** pay, accounts; **~ая кни́жка** pay-book; **р. отде́л** accounts department. **3.** (*tech.*) rated, designed; **~ая мо́щность** rated capacity; **~ая ско́рость** rated speed.
расчи́|стить, щу, стишь *pf.* (*of* **~ща́ть**) to clear.
расчи́стк|а, и *f.* clearing.
расчиха́|ться, юсь *pf.* to sneeze repeatedly.
расчища́|ть, ю, ет *impf. of* **расчи́стить**
расчлене́ни|е, я *nt.* dismemberment; partition.
расчлен|и́ть, ю́, и́шь *pf.* (*of* **~я́ть**) to dismember; to partition; to break up, divide.
расчлен|я́ть, я́ю *impf. of* **~и́ть**
расчу́вств|оваться, уюсь *pf.* (*coll.*) to be deeply moved.
расша́рк|аться, аюсь *pf.* (*of* **~иваться**) (*obs.*) to bow, scraping one's feet; (*fig.*) to bow and scrape.
расша́ркива|ться, юсь *impf. of* **расша́ркаться**
расша́т|анный *p.p.p. of* **~а́ть** *and adj.* shaky; rickety; tottering; **~анные не́рвы** shattered nerves.
расшат|а́ть, а́ю *pf.* (*of* **∠ывать**) **1.** to shake loose; to make rickety. **2.** (*fig.*) to shatter; to impair; **э́тот уда́р ~а́л её здоро́вье** the blow shattered her health; **р. дисципли́ну** to impair discipline.
расшат|а́ться, а́юсь *pf.* (*of* **∠ываться**) **1.** to come loose; to become rickety. **2.** (*fig.*) to go to pieces, crack up.
расша́тыва|ть(ся), ю(сь) *impf. of* **расшата́ть(ся)**
расшвы́рива|ть, ю *impf. of* **расшвыря́ть**
расшвыр|я́ть, я́ю *pf.* (*of* **∠ивать**) to throw around.
расшеве́лива|ть, ю *impf. of* **расшевели́ть**
расшевел|и́ть, ю́, и́шь *pf.* (*of* **∠ивать**) to stir, shake; (*fig.*) to stir, rouse.
расшиб|а́ть(ся), а́ю(сь) *impf. of* **расшиби́ть(ся)**
расшиб|и́ть, у́, ёшь, *past* **∠, ∠ла** *pf.* (*of* **~а́ть**) (*coll.*) **1.** to hurt; to knock, stub; **р. па́лец ноги́ об ка́мень** to stub one's toe on a rock. **2.** to break up, smash to pieces.
расшиб|и́ться, у́сь, ёшься, *past* **∠ся, ∠лась** *pf.* (*of* **~а́ться**) (*coll.*) to hurt o.s., knock o.s.
расшива́|ть, ю *impf. of* **расши́ть**
расшире́ни|е, я *nt.* **1.** broadening, widening. **2.** expansion. **3.** (*med.*) dilation; **р. вен** varicose veins.
расши́р|енный *p.p.p. of* **~ить** *and adj.* broadened, expanded; enlarged; dilated; **~енная програ́мма** expanded programme; **~енные зрачки́** dilated pupils; **с ~енными глаза́ми** wide-eyed.
расши́р|ить, ю, ишь *pf.* (*of* **~я́ть**) to broaden, widen; to enlarge; to expand; to extend; **р. чей-н. кругозо́р** to broaden s.o.'s outlook, mind; **р. сфе́ру влия́ния** to extend a sphere of influence.
расши́р|иться, юсь, ишься *pf.* (*of* **~я́ться**) **1.** to broaden, widen; to extend. **2.** (*phys.*) to expand, dilate.
расшир|я́ть(ся), я́ю(сь) *impf. of* **∠ить(ся)**
расши́ть[1]**, разошью́, разошьёшь** *pf.* (*of* **расшива́ть**) to embroider.
расши́ть[2]**, разошью́, разошьёшь** *pf.* (*of* **расшива́ть**) to undo, unpick.
расшифр|ова́ть, у́ю *pf.* (*of* **~о́вывать**) to decipher, decode; (*fig.*) to interpret.
расшифро́вк|а, и *f.* deciphering, decoding.
расшифро́выва|ть, ю *impf. of* **расшифрова́ть**
расшнур|ова́ть, у́ю *pf.* (*of* **~о́вывать**) to unlace.
расшнуро́выва|ть, ю *impf. of* **расшнурова́ть**
расшум|е́ться, лю́сь, и́шься *pf.* (*coll.*) to get noisy, kick up a din.
расще́др|иться, юсь, ишься *pf.* (*coll., also iron.*) to have a fit of generosity.
расще́лин|а, ы *f.* cleft, crevice.
расщеп|и́ть, лю́, и́шь *pf.* (*of* **~ля́ть**) to split, splinter.
расщеп|и́ться, и́тся *pf.* (*of* **~ля́ться**) to split, splinter.
расщепле́ни|е, я *nt.* **1.** splitting, splintering. **2.** (*phys.*) splitting, fission; **р. ядра́** nuclear fission.
расщепля́|ть(ся), ю, ет(ся) *impf. of* **расщепи́ть(ся)**
ратификацио́нн|ый *adj.*: **~ые гра́моты** (*dipl.*) instruments of ratification.
ратифика́ци|я, и *f.* (*dipl.*) ratification.

ратифици́р|овать, ую *impf. and pf.* (*dipl.*) to ratify.
ра́т|овать, ую *impf.* (**за**+*a.*) to fight (for), stand up (for); (**про́тив**) to inveigh (against).
ра́туш|а, и *f.* **1.** town hall. **2.** (*hist.*) town council.
рат|ь, и *f.* (*arch. or poet.*) **1.** host, army. **2.** war; battle; **идти́ на р.** to go into battle.
ра́унд, а *m.* (*sport*) round.
ра́ут, а *m.* (*obs.*) rout; reception.
рафина́д, а *m.* lump sugar.
рафина́д|ный *adj. of* ~; **р. заво́д** sugar refinery.
рафини́р|овать, ую *impf. and pf.* to refine.
раха́т-луку́м, а *m.* Turkish delight.
рахи́т, а *m.* (*med.*) rickets.
рацио́н, а *m.* ration.
рационализа́тор|ский *adj. of* ~; **~ское предложе́ние** proposal for improving production methods.
рационализа́ци|я, и *f.* rationalization, improvement.
рационализи́р|овать, ую *impf. and pf.* to rationalize, streamline.
рационали́зм, а *m.* (*phil.*) rationalism.
рационали́ст, а *m.* rationalist.
рационалисти́ческий *adj.* rationalistic.
рациона́льно *adv.* rationally; efficiently; **р. испо́льзовать** to make efficient use (of).
рациона́л|ьный (~ен, ~ьна) *adj.* **1.** rational; efficient; **~ьная дие́та** balanced diet; **~ьное пита́ние** sound nutrition. **2.** (*math.*) rational.
ра́ци|я, и *f.* walkie-talkie.
ра́чий *adj. of* **рак; ра́чьи глаза́** goggle eyes.
рачи́тел|ьный (~ен, ~ьна) *adj.* (*obs.*) zealous; assiduous.
ра́шпил|ь, я *m.* (*tech.*) rasp, rasp file; grater.
рван|у́ть, у́, ёшь *pf.* **1.** to jerk; to tug (at); **р. кого́-н. за рука́в** to tug s.o. by the sleeve. **2.** to start with a jerk; **вдруг ~у́л ве́тер** suddenly a wind got up.
рван|у́ться, у́сь, ёшься *pf.* to rush, dash, dart.
рва́н|ый *adj.* torn; lacerated; **~ая ра́на** (*med.*) laceration.
рван|ь, и *no pl., f.* **1.** rags. **2.** (*coll.*) scoundrel, scamp; (*collect.*) riff-raff.
рвать[1], **рву, рвёшь,** *past* **рвал, рвала́, рва́ло** *impf.* **1.** to tear; to rip; **р. в клочки́** to tear to piecesr; **р. и мета́ть** to rant and rave. **2.** to pull out, tear out; **р. зу́бы** to pull out teeth; **р. из рук у кого́-н.** to snatch out of s.o.'s handst. **3.** to pick, pluck. **4.** to blow up. **5.** (*fig.*) to break off, sever; **р. отноше́ния с кем-н.** to break off relations with s.o.
рвать[2], **рвёт,** *past* **рва́ло́** *impf.* (*of* **вы́рвать**[2]) (*impers.; coll.*) to vomit, throw up, be sick.
рва́|ться[1], **рвётся,** *past* **~лся, ~ла́сь, ~ло́сь** *impf.* **1.** to break; to tear. **2.** to burst, explode.
рва́|ться[2], **рвусь, рвёшься,** *past* **~лся, ~ла́сь, ~ло́сь** *impf.* to strain (to, at); to be bursting (to); **р. в бой** to be bursting to go into action; **р. в дра́ку** to be spoiling for a fight; **р. на свобо́ду** to be dying to be free; **р. с при́вязи** to strain at the leash.
рвач, а́ *m.* (*coll.*) self-seeker, grabber.
рва́ческий *adj.* (*coll.*) self-seeking, grabbing.
рва́честв|о, а *nt.* (*coll.*) self-seeking, grabbing.
рве́ни|е, я *nt.* zeal, fervour, ardour.
рво́т|а, ы *f.* vomiting, retching.
рво́тн|ый *adj.* emetic; **~ое сре́дство** (*also as n.* **~ое, ~ого** *nt.*) emetic.
рде|ть, ю *impf.* (*of sth. red*) to glow.
реабилита́ци|я, и *f.* rehabilitation.
реабилити́р|овать, ую *impf. and pf.* to rehabilitate.
реаге́нт, а *m.* (*chem.*) reagent.
реаги́р|овать, ую *impf.* (**на**+*a.*) **1.** to react (to). **2.** (*pf.* **от~**) to react(to), (*fig.*) respond (to).
реакти́в, а *m.* (*chem.*) reagent.
реакти́вн|ый *adj.* **1.** (*chem., phys.*) reactive. **2.** (*tech., aeron.*) jet(-propelled); **р. дви́гатель** jet engine.
реа́ктор, а *m.* (*phys., tech.*) reactor; **р.-размножи́тель, р. с расши́ренным воспроизво́дством я́дерного горю́чего** breeder reactor.
реакционе́р, а *m.* (*pol.*) reactionary.
реакцио́н|ный (~ен, ~на) *adj.* (*pol.*) reactionary.
реа́кци|я, и *f.* (*chem., phys., pol.; fig.*) reaction; (*pol., collect.*) reactionaries.
реализа́ци|я, и *f.* realization (= (*i*) *implementation*, (*ii*) *sale*).
реали́зм, а *m.* realism.
реализ|ова́ть, у́ю *impf. and pf.* to realize (= (*i*) *to implement*, (*ii*) *to sell*); **р. це́нные бума́ги** to realize securities.
реали́ст, а *m.* realist.
реалисти́ческий *adj.* **1.** (*art, liter., etc.*) realist. **2.** realistic.
реа́ли|я, и *f.* realia.
реа́льност|ь, и *f.* **1.** reality. **2.** practicability.
реа́л|ьный (~ен, ~ьна) *adj.* **1.** real. **2.** practicable, workable. **3.** realistic; practical; **вести́ ~ьную поли́тику** to pursue a realistic policy; **~ьная за́работная пла́та** real wages.
ребён|ок, ка (*as pl.* **ребя́та, ребя́т** *and* **де́ти, дете́й**) *m.* child, infant; **грудно́й р.** baby.
ребо́рд|а, ы *f.* flange.
ребри́ст|ый (~, ~а) *adj.* **1.** having prominent ribs. **2.** (*tech.*) ribbed; costate; finned.
ребр|о́, а́, *pl.* **~а, рёбер, ~ам** *nt.* **1.** (*anat., tech.*) rib; (*tech.*) fin; **пересчита́ть кому́-н. ~а** (*coll.*) to give s.o. a drubbing. **2.** edge; **поста́вить ~о́м** to place on its side; **поста́вить вопро́с ~о́м** to put a question point-blank.
ре́бус, а *m.* rebus.
ребя́та, ребя́т (*coll.*) **1.** (*sg.* **ребёнок** *m.*) children. **2.** (*of adults*) boys, lads.
ребяти́ш|ки, ек, кам *no sg.* (*coll.*) children, kids.
ребя́ческий *adj.* **1.** of a child, childish. **2.** (*fig.*) childish, infantile.
ребя́честв|о, а *nt.* childishness.
ребя́чий *adj.* (*coll.*) childish.
ребя́ч|иться, усь, ишься *impf.* (*coll.*) to behave childishly.
рёв, а *m.* **1.** roar; bellow, howl; **р. ве́тра** the howling of the wind. **2.** (*coll.*) howl (*of a child, etc.*).
рев... *comb. form, abbr. of* **революцио́нный**
рева́нш, а *m.* revenge; (*sport*) return match.
реванши́зм, а *m.* (*pol.*) revanchism.
реванши́ст, а *m.* (*pol.*) revanchist.
ревен|ный *adj. of* **~ь**
реве́н|ь, я́ *m.* rhubarb.
ревера́нс, а *m.* (*obs.*) curts(e)y; **сде́лать р.** to curts(e)y.
ревербера́ци|я, и *f.* (*tech.*) reverberation.
рев|е́ть, у́, ёшь *impf.* **1.** to roar; to bellow, howl. **2.** (*coll.*) to howl; **ревмя́ р.** to set up a fearful howl.
ревизиони́зм, а *m.* (*pol.*) revisionism.
ревизиони́ст, а *m.* (*pol.*) revisionist.
ревизио́нн|ый *adj.*: **~ая коми́ссия** inspection commission; auditing commission.
реви́зи|я, и *f.* **1.** inspection; audit. **2.** revision.
ревиз|ова́ть, у́ю *impf. and pf.* **1.** (*pf. also* **об~**) to inspect. **2.** to revise.
ревизо́р, а *m.* inspector.
ревмати́зм, а *m.* rheumatism; rheumatics.
ревма́тик, а *m.* rheumatic.
ревмати́ческий *adj.* rheumatic; **р. артри́т** rheumatoid arthritis.
рев|мя́ *see* **~е́ть**
ревни́в|ец, ца *m.* jealous person.
ревни́в|ый (~, ~а) *adj.* jealous.
ревни́тел|ь, я *m.* (+*g.*; *obs.*) ardent supporter (of).
ревн|ова́ть, у́ю *impf.* to be jealous; **она́ ~ова́ла му́жа к его́ рабо́те** she was jealous of her husband's work.

ре́вност|ный (~ен, ~на) *adj.* zealous, fervent.
ре́вност|ь, и *f.* **1.** jealousy. **2.** (*obs.*) zeal, fervour.
револьве́р, а *m.* revolver.
револьве́р|ный *adj.* **1.** *adj. of* **~. 2.** (*tech.*): **р. стано́к** capstan lathe, turret lathe.
революционе́р, а *m.* revolutionary.
революционизи́р|овать, ую *impf. and pf.* to revolutionize.
революцио́н|ный (~ен, ~на) *adj.* revolutionary.
револю́ци|я, и *f.* (*pol. and fig.*) revolution.
реву́н, а́ *m.* (*zool.*; *coll.*) howler.
ревю́ *nt. indecl.* revue.
рега́ли|и, й *pl.* (*sg.* **~я, ~и** *f.*) regalia.
ре́гби *nt. indecl.* Rugby (football), rugger.
рег|би́йный *adj. of* **~би**
ре́гги *nt. indecl.* = **рэ́ггей**
регенерати́вный *adj.* (*tech.*) regenerative.
регенера́ци|я, и *f.* (*tech.*) regeneration.
ре́гент, а *m.* **1.** regent. **2.** (*mus.*) precentor.
ре́гентств|о, а *nt.* regency.
регио́н, а *m.* region, area.
региона́льный *adj.* regional.
реги́стр, а *m.* register.
регистра́тор, а *m.* registrar.
регистрату́р|а, ы *f.* registry.
регистра́ци|я, и *f.* registration.
регистри́р|овать, ую *impf. and pf.* (*pf. also* **за~**) to register, record.
регистри́р|оваться, уюсь *impf. and pf.* (*pf. also* **за~**) **1.** to register (o.s.). **2.** to register one's marriage. **3.** *pass. of* **~овать**
регла́мент, а *m.* **1.** regulations; standing orders. **2.** (*at a meeting*) time-limit.
регламента́ци|я, и *f.* regulation.
регламенти́р|овать, ую *impf. and pf.* to regulate.
регла́н, а *m.* raglan (*coat*).
регресси́в|ный (~ен, ~на) *adj.* regressive.
регресси́р|овать, ую *impf.* to regress.
регули́ровани|е, я *nt.* **1.** regulation, control. **2.** adjustment.
регули́р|овать, ую *impf.* **1.** (*pf.* **у~**) to regulate; to control. **2.** (*pf.* **от~**) to adjust; to tune.
регулиро́вщик, а *m.* traffic-controller.
регуля́рност|ь, и *f.* regularity.
регуля́р|ный (~ен, ~на) *adj.* regular; **~ные войска́** regular troops, regulars.
регуля́тор, а *m.* (*tech.*) regulator; governor; (*pl.*) controls (*on TV*, *etc.*).
ред. *abbr. of* **1. реда́ктор** Ed., Editor. **2. реда́кция** Editorial Office.
ред... *comb. form*, *abbr. of* **редакцио́нный**
редакти́ровани|е, я *nt.* editing; **р. те́кста** word-processing.
редакти́р|овать, ую *impf.* **1.** (*pf.* **от~**) to edit. **2.** (*pf.* **с~**) to word.
реда́ктор, а *m.* **1.** editor; **гла́вный р.** editor-in-chief. **2.: р. те́кстов, те́кстовый р.** word-processor (*software*).
реда́кторский *adj.* editorial.
реда́кторств|о, а *nt.* editorship.
редакцио́нн|ый *adj.* editorial, editing; **~ая коми́ссия** drafting committee.
реда́кци|я, и *f.* **1.** editorial staff. **2.** editorial office. **3.** editing; **под ~ей** (*+g.*) edited (by). **4.** wording.
реде́|ть, ю *impf.* (*of* **по~**) to thin, thin out; **~ющие во́лосы** thinning hair.
реди́с, а *no pl.*, *m.* radish(es).
реди́ск|а, и *f.* radish.
ре́д|кий (~ок, ~ка́, ~ко) *adj.* **1.** thin, sparse; **~кие во́лосы** thin hair; **~кие зу́бы** widely spaced teeth; **~кая ткань** flimsy fabric. **2.** rare; uncommon.
ре́дко *adv.* **1.** sparsely; far apart. **2.** rarely, seldom.
редколле́ги|я, и *f.* editorial board.
ре́дкост|ный (~ен, ~на) *adj.* rare; uncommon.
ре́дкост|ь, и *f.* **1.** thinness, sparseness. **2.** rarity; **на р.** uncommonly, exceptionally. **3.** rarity, curiosity.
реду́кци|я, и *f.* reduction.
реду́т, а *m.* (*mil.*, *hist.*) redoubt.
ре́дьк|а, и *f.* radish.
редюи́т, а *m.* (*mil.*) reduit.
рее́стр, а *m.* list, roll, register.
ре́|же *comp. of* **~дкий** *and* **~дко**
режи́м, а *m.* **1.** (*pol.*) régime. **2.** routine; procedure; (*med.*) regimen; (*tech.*) mode of operation; **шко́льный р.** school routine; **р. пита́ния** diet; **р. безопа́сности** safety measures. **3.** conditions; (*tech.*) operating conditions.
режиссёр, а *m.* (*theatr.*) producer; (*cin.*) director.
режиссёр|ский *adj. of* **~**
режисси́р|овать, ую *impf.* (*theatr.*) to produce, stage; (*cin.*) to direct.
режиссу́р|а, ы *f.* (*theatr.*) **1.** producing; profession of producer. **2.** production. **3.** (*collect.*) producers.
ре́жущ|ий *pres. part. act. of* **ре́зать** *and adj.* cutting; sharp; **р. уда́р** slash.
реза́к, а́ *m.* **1.** chopping-knife, chopper; pole-axe. **2.** slaughterman.
ре́зан|ый *adj.* **1.** cut; **р. хлеб** cut loaf. **2.** (*sport*) slice, sliced; **р. уда́р** slice.
ре́|зать, жу, жешь *impf.* **1.** *impf. only* to cut; to slice. **2.** *impf. only* (*med.*) to operate, open. **3.** *impf. only* to cut (= *to have the power of cutting*); **э́ти но́жницы бо́льше не ~жут** these scissors do not cut any longer. **4.** (*pf.* **за~**) to kill; to slaughter; to knife. **5.** *impf. only* (**по**+*d.*) to carve (on), engrave (on). **6.** *impf. only* to cut (into); **реме́нь ~зал его́ плечо́** the strap was cutting into his shoulder; **р. глаза́** to irritate the eyes; **р. слух** to grate on one's ears. **7.** (*coll.*) to speak bluntly; **р. пра́вду в глаза́** to speak the truth boldly. **8.** (*pf.* **с~**) (*sport*) to slice, chop.
ре́|заться, жусь, зешься *impf.* **1.** (*pf.* **про~**) (*of teeth*) to come through; **у него́ уже́ ~жутся зу́бы** he is already teething. **2.** *impf. only* to play furiously.
резв|и́ться, лю́сь, и́шься *impf.* to gambol, romp.
ре́звост|ь, и *f.* **1.** playfulness, friskiness. **2.** (*sport*; *of a horse*) speed.
ре́зв|ый (~, ~а́, ~о) *adj.* **1.** playful, frisky. **2.** (*sport*; *of a horse*) fast.
резед|а́, ы́ *f.* (*bot.*) mignonette.
резе́кци|я, и *f.* (*med.*) resection.
резе́рв, а *m.* (*mil.*, *etc.*) reserve(s); **име́ть в ~е** to have in reserve; **перевести́ в р.** (*mil.*) to transfer to the reserve.
резерва́ци|я, и *f.* reservation.
резерви́р|овать, ую *impf. and pf.* to reserve.
резерви́ст, а *m.* (*mil.*) reservist.
резе́рвный *adj.* (*mil. and fin.*) reserve; (*comput.*) back-up; **~ая ко́пия** back-up copy.
резервуа́р, а *m.* reservoir, vessel, tank.
рез|е́ц, ца́ *m.* **1.** (*tech.*) cutter; cutting tool; chisel. **2.** (*tooth*) incisor.
резиде́нт, а *m.* (*dipl.*, *etc.*) resident (*esp. of member of Intelligence Service operating in foreign country*).
резиде́нци|я, и *f.* residence.
рези́н|а, ы *f.* rubber.
рези́нк|а, и *f.* **1.** rubber, eraser. **2.** (piece of) elastic. **3.** rubber band. **4.** chewing-gum.
рези́нов|ый *adj.* **1.** rubber. **2.** elastic.
ре́зк|а, и *f.* cutting.
ре́з|кий (~ок, ~ка́, ~ко) *adj.* sharp; harsh; abrupt; **р. го́лос** shrill voice; **р. за́пах** strong smell; **~кое измене́ние** abrupt change; **~кие мане́ры** abrupt manners; **р. свет** strong, harsh light; **~кие слова́** sharp words; **~кое увеличе́ние** dramatic increase.
ре́зкост|ь, и *f.* **1.** sharpness; harshness; abruptness. **2.** sharp words, harsh words.

резн|óй *adj.* carved, fretted; **~áя рабóта** (*archit.*) carving, fretwork.
резн|я́, и́ *f.* slaughter, butchery, carnage.
резолю́ци|я, и *f.* **1.** resolution. **2.** instructions.
резóн, а *m.* (*coll.*) reason.
резонáнс, а *m.* **1.** (*phys.*) resonance. **2.** (*fig.*) echo, response; **дать, имéть р.** to have repercussions.
резонёр, а *m.* moralizer.
резони́р|овать, ую *impf.* to resound.
резóн|ный (~ен, ~на) *adj.* reasonable.
результáт, а *m.* result; outcome; **дать ~ы** to yield results; **в ~е** (+*g.*) as a result (of).
результати́вный *adj.* successful.
рéз|че *comp. of* **~кий** *and* **~ко**
рéзчик, а *m.* engraver, carver.
рез|ь, и *f.* colic; gripe.
резьб|á, ы́ *f.* **1.** carving, fretwork. **2.** (*tech.*) thread.
резюмé *nt. indecl.* summary, résumé.
резюми́р|овать, ую *impf. and pf.* to summarize, recapitulate.
рейд[1], **а** *m.* (*naut.*) road(s), roadstead.
рейд[2], **а** *m.* **1.** (*mil.*) raid. **2.** 'swoop'; special (*journalistic*) assignment.
рéйк|а, и *f.* **1.** lath. **2.: зубчáтая р.** (*tech.*) rack. **3.** (*surveyor's*) rod, pole.
рейс, а *m.* trip, run; voyage, passage; flight; **нóмер ~а** flight number; **пéрвый р.** maiden voyage.
рейсши́н|а, ы *f.* T-square.
рéйтинг, а *m.* rating (*in opinion poll*).
рейтýз|ы, ~ *no sg.* **1.** (riding-)breeches. **2.** tights.
рейх, а *m.* Reich; **трéтий р.** Third Reich.
рекá, рéкý, реки́, *pl.* **рéки, рек, рéкáм, рéкáми, рéкáх** *f.* river; **ли́ться,** *etc.*, **рекóй** (*fig.*) to pour, flood.
рéквием, а *m.* (*eccl. and mus.*) requiem.
реквизи́р|овать, ую *impf. and pf.* to requisition, commandeer.
реквизи́т, а *m.* (*theatr.*) properties, props.
реквизи́ци|я, и *f.* requisition, commandeering.
реклáм|а, ы *f.* **1.** advertising, publicity; **крикли́вая р.** hype. **2.** advertisement; commercial.
рекламáци|я, и *f.* claim for replacement (*of defective goods, etc.*).
реклами́р|овать, ую *impf. and pf.* to advertise, publicize; to boost, push; **крикли́во р.** to hype.
реклáмный *adj.* publicity.
рекламодáтел|ь, я *m.* advertiser.
рекогносци́р|овать, ую *impf. and pf.* (*mil.*) to reconnoitre.
рекогносцирóвк|а, и *f.* (*mil.*) reconnaissance; reconnoitring.
рекогносцирóвочный *adj.* reconnaissance.
рекомендáтельн|ый *adj.*: **р. óтзыв** testimonial; **~ое письмó** letter of recommendation.
рекомендáци|я, и *f.* recommendation.
рекоменд|овáть, ýю *impf. and pf.* **1.** (*pf. also* **по~** *and* **от~**) to recommend; to speak well for. **2.** (*pf. also* **по~**) (+*inf.*) to recommend, advise; **я вам ~ýю посовéтоваться с дóктором** I recommend you to see a doctor.
рекоменд|овáться, ýюсь *impf. and pf.* **1.** (*pf. also* **от~**) to introduce o.s. **2.** *pass. of* **~овáть; не ~ýется** it is not recommended; it is not advisable.
реконструи́р|овать, ую *impf. and pf.* to reconstruct.
реконстрýкци|я, и *f.* reconstruction.
рекóрд, а *m.* record; **поби́ть р.** to break a record.
рекорди́ст, а *m.* (*agric.*) champion.
рекóрдный *adj.* record, record-breaking.
рекордсмéн, а *m.* record-holder; record-breaker.
рекордсмéн|ка, ки *f. of* **~**
рéкрут, а *m.* (*hist.*) recruit.
рéктор, а *m.* rector, vice-chancellor, principal.
релé *nt. indecl.* (*tech.*) relay.
религиóз|ный *adj.* **1.** religious; **р. обря́д** religious ceremony. **2. (~ен, ~на)** religious; pious.
рели́ги|я, и *f.* religion.
рели́кви|я, и *f.* relic.
рели́кт, а *m.* relic; survival.
рели́кт|овый *adj. of* **~**; surviving.
рельéф, а *m.* (*art and geol.*) relief.
рельéфно *adv.* in relief; **р.-тóчечный шрифт** Braille.
рельéф|ный (~ен, ~на) *adj.* relief, raised; **~ная рабóта** embossed work; **~ная кáрта** relief map.
рельс, а, *g. pl.* **~ов** *m.* rail; **постáвить на ~ы** (*fig.*) to launch.
рéльс|овый *adj. of* **~**; **р. путь** railway, track.
ремáрк|а, и *f.* (*theatr.*) stage direction.
ремённ|ый *adj.* belt; **~ая передáча** (*tech.*) belt-drive.
рем|éнь, ня́ *m.* strap; belt; **привязнóй р.** seat-belt.
ремéсленник, а *m.* artisan, craftsman.
ремéсленн|ый *adj.* **1.** handicraft; **~ое учи́лище** vocational school. **2.** (*fig., pej.*) mechanical, stereotyped.
ремес|лó, лá, *pl.* **~ла, ~ел** *nt.* handicraft; trade.
ремеш|óк, кá *m.* small strap; wristlet.
ремóнт, а *m.* repair(s); maintenance; **капитáльный р.** overhaul, refit, major repairs; **космети́ческий р.** face-lift; **в ~е** under repair.
ремонти́р|овать, ую *impf. and pf.* (*pf. also* **от~**) to repair; to refit, recondition, overhaul.
ремóнт|ный *adj. of* **~**; **~ная мастерскáя** repair shop.
ренегáт, а *m.* renegade.
ренегáтств|о, а *nt.* desertion; apostasy.
ренклóд, а *m.* greengage.
ренóнс, а *m.* (*cards*) revoke.
рéнт|а, ы *f.* **1.** rent; **земéльная р.** ground-rent. **2.** income (*from investments, etc.*); **ежегóдная р.** annuity.
рентáбел|ьный (~ен, ~ьна) *adj.* paying, profitable.
рентгéн, а *m.* X-rays.
рентгенизи́р|овать, ую *impf. and pf.* to X-ray.
рентгéнов *adj.*: **~ы лучи́** X-rays.
рентгéновск|ий *adj.* X-ray; **~ие лучи́** X-rays.
рентгенográмм|а, ы *f.* X-ray (photograph).
рентгенóлог, а *m.* radiologist.
рентгенолóги|я, и *f.* radiology.
рентгенотерапи́|я, и *f.* X-ray treatment.
Реомю́р, а *m.* Réaumur; **10° по ~у** 10° Réaumur.
реорганизáци|я, и *f.* reorganization.
реорганиз|овáть, ýю *impf. and pf.* to reorganize.
реостáт, а *m.* (*elec.*) rheostat.
рéп|а, ы *f.* turnip.
репар|аци́онный *adj. of* **~áция**
репарáци|я, и *f.* reparation.
репатриáнт, а *m.* repatriate.
репатриáци|я, и *f.* repatriation.
репатрии́р|овать, ую *impf. and pf.* to repatriate.
репéйник, а *m.* (*bot.*) burdock.
репéр, а *m.* (*surveying*) bench-mark, datum mark.
репертуáр, а *m.* (*theatr. and fig.*) repertoire.
репети́р|овать, ую *impf.* **1.** (*pf.* **про~** *and* **с~**) (*theatr.*) to rehearse. **2.** *impf. only* to coach.
репети́тор, а *m.* tutor, coach.
репетициóнный *adj.* rehearsal.
репети́ци|я, и *f.* rehearsal; **генерáльная р.** dress rehearsal.
рéплик|а, и *f.* **1.** rejoinder, retort; heckling comment. **2.** (*theatr.*) cue.
реполóв, а *m.* (*zool.*) linnet.
репортáж, а *m.* report; reporting.
репортёр, а *m.* reporter.
репресси́в|ный (~ен, ~на) *adj.* repressive.
репресси́р|овать, ую *impf. and pf.* to subject to repression.
репрéсси|я, и *f.* punitive measure.
репродýктор, а *m.* loud-speaker.
репродýкци|я, и *f.* reproduction (*of a picture, etc.*).

репута́ци|я, и *f.* reputation.
ре́пчатый *adj.* turnip-shaped; **р. лук** onion.
ресни́ц|а, ы *f.* eyelash.
респекта́бельност|ь, и *f.* respectability.
респекта́бел|ьный (~ен, ~ьна) *adj.* respectable.
респира́тор, а *m.* respirator.
респу́блик|а, и *f.* republic.
республика́н|ец, ца *m.* republican.
республика́нский *adj.* **1.** republican. **2.** of (situated in, *etc.*) a constituent republic of the former USSR.
рессо́р|а, ы *f.* spring (*of vehicle*).
рессо́рный *adj.* spring; sprung.
реставра́тор, а *m.* restorer.
реставра́ци|я, и *f.* restoration.
реставри́р|овать, ую *impf. and pf.* to restore.
** innoрестора́н, а** *m.* restaurant.
ресу́рс, а *m.* resource; **де́нежные ~ы** financial resources; **после́дний р.** the last resort.
рети́вост|ь, и *f.* zeal, ardour.
рети́в|ый (~, ~а) *adj.* (*coll.*) zealous, ardent.
рети́н|а, ы *f.* (*anat.*) retina.
ретир|ова́ться, у́юсь *impf. and pf.* to retire, withdraw.
рето́рт|а, ы *f.* (*chem.*) retort.
ретрогра́д, а *m.* reactionary.
ретрогра́д|ный (~ен, ~на) *adj.* reactionary.
ретроспекти́в|ный (~ен, ~на) *adj.* retrospective; **р. взгляд** backward glance.
ретушёр, а *m.* retoucher.
ретуши́р|овать, ую *impf. and pf.* (*pf. also* **от~**) to retouch.
ре́туш|ь, и *f.* retouching.
рефера́т, а *m.* **1.** synopsis, abstract. **2.** paper, essay.
рефере́ндум, а *m.* referendum.
рефере́нт, а *m.* **1.** reader of a paper; seminar leader, colloquium leader. **2.** assessor (*of thesis, book, etc.*).
рефери́р|овать, ую *impf. and pf.* to abstract, make a synopsis of.
рефле́кс, а *m.* reflex.
рефлекти́в|ный (~ен, ~на) *adj.* (*physiol.*) reflex.
рефле́ктор, а *m.* reflector.
рефлекто́рный *adj.* (*physiol., astron.*) reflex.
рефо́рм|а, ы *f.* reform.
реформа́тор, а *m.* reformer.
реформа́торский *adj.* reformative, reformatory.
реформа́|тский *adj. of* **Р~ция; ~тская це́рковь** Reformed Church.
Реформа́ци|я, и *f.* (*hist.*) Reformation.
реформи́р|овать, ую *impf. and pf.* to reform.
реформи́ст, а *m.* (*pol.*) reformist.
рефра́ктор, а *m.* (*phys., astron.*) refractor.
рефра́кци|я, и *f.* (*phys., astron.*) refraction.
рефре́н, а *m.* (*liter.*) refrain.
рефрижера́тор, а *m.* refrigerated lorry; refrigerated ship.
рехн|у́ться, у́сь, ёшься *pf.* (*coll.*) to go mad, go off one's head.
рецензе́нт, а *m.* reviewer.
рецензи́р|овать, ую *impf.* (*of* **про~**) to review.
реце́нзи|я, и *f.* review; (*theatr.*) notice; **р. на кни́гу, р. о кни́ге** book review.
реце́пт, а *m.* **1.** (*med.*) prescription. **2.** (*cul.*) recipe.
рециди́в, а *m.* **1.** (*med., etc.*) recurrence; relapse. **2.** (*leg.*) repeated commission (*of offence*).
рецидиви́зм, а *m.* (*leg.*) recidivism.
рецидиви́ст, а *m.* (*leg.*) recidivist.
рециркули́р|овать, ую *impf. and pf.* to recycle.
рециркуля́ци|я, и *f.* recycling.
речево́й *adj.* speech; vocal; **р. аппара́т** vocal organs.
рече́ни|е, я *nt.* set phrase; saying; (*ling.*) locution.
речи́ст|ый (~, ~а) voluble, garrulous.
речитати́в, а *m.* (*mus.*) recitative.
ре́чк|а, и *f.* small river; rivulet.
речн|о́й *adj.* river; fluvial; **~ы́е пути́ сообще́ния** inland waterways.
реч|ь, и *f.* **1.** speech; **дар ~и** gift of speech. **2.** enunciation, speech; **горта́нная р.** guttural speech; **отчётливая р.** distinct enunciation. **3.** language; **делова́я р.** business language. **4.** discourse; **о чём идёт р.?** what are you talking about?; **р. идёт о том, где сле́дует назна́чить ме́сто встре́чи** it is a question of where to fix the meeting-place; **об э́том не мо́жет быть и ~и** that is out of the question; **завести́ р.** (о+*p.*) to lead, turn the conversation (towards). **5.** speech; address; **вступи́тельная р.** opening address; **засто́льная р.** after-dinner speech; **торже́ственная р.** oration; **вы́ступить с ~ью** to make a speech. **6.** (*gram.*) speech; **пряма́я р.** direct speech; **ча́сти ~и** parts of speech.
реш|а́ть(ся), а́ю(сь) *impf. of* **~и́ть(ся)**
реша́|ющий *pres. part. act. of* **~ть** *and adj.* decisive, deciding; key, conclusive; **р. го́лос** casting vote.
реше́ни|е, я *nt.* **1.** decision; **приня́ть р.** to take a decision. **2.** decree, judg(e)ment; decision, verdict; **вы́нести р.** to deliver a judg(e)ment; to pass a resolution; **отмени́ть р.** to revoke a decision; (*leg.*) to quash a sentence. **3.** solution; answer (*to a problem*).
решётк|а, и *f.* **1.** grating; grille, railing; lattice; trellis; fender, fireguard; **за ~ой** (*fig., coll.*) behind bars; **посади́ть за ~у** to put behind bars. **2.** (fire-)grate.
решет|о́, а́, *pl.* **~а** *nt.* sieve.
решётчат|ый (*and* **реше́тчатый**) *adj.* lattice, latticed; trellised.
реши́мост|ь, и *f.* resolution, resoluteness.
реши́тельно *adv.* **1.** resolutely. **2.** decidedly, definitely; **р. отказа́ться** to refuse flatly; **я р. про́тив э́того прое́кта** I am firmly opposed to this scheme. **3.** absolutely; **э́то мне р. всё равно́** it makes absolutely no difference to me.
реши́тельност|ь, и *f.* resolution, determination.
реши́тел|ьный (~ен, ~ьна) *adj.* **1.** resolute, determined; firm; **~ьные ме́ры** strong measures; **р. тон** firm tone. **2.** definite; **р. отве́т** definite reply. **3.** decisive; crucial; **р. моме́нт** crucial point. **4.** (*coll.*) absolute, blatant; **р. дура́к** absolute fool.
реш|и́ть, у́, и́шь *pf.* (*of* **~а́ть**) **1.** (+*inf. or* +*a.*) to decide, determine; **р. чью-н. у́часть** to decide s.o.'s fate. **2.** to solve; to settle; **р. зада́чу** to solve a problem; to accomplish a task.
реш|и́ться, у́сь, и́шься *pf.* (*of* **~а́ться**) (**на**+*a. or* +*inf.*) to make up one's mind (to), decide (to), resolve (to); to bring o.s. (to).
ре́шк|а, и *f.* (*coll.*) tail (*of coin*); **орёл и́ли р.?** heads or tails?
ре́|ять, ю, ешь *impf.* **1.** to soar, hover. **2.** to flutter.
ржа́ве|ть, ет *impf.* (*of* **за~**) to rust.
ржа́вчин|а, ы *f.* **1.** rust. **2.** (*bot.*) mildew.
ржа́вый *adj.* rusty.
ржа́ни|е, я *nt.* neighing.
ржа́нк|а, и *f.* (*zool.*) plover.
ржано́й *adj.* rye.
рж|ать, у, ёшь *impf.* to neigh.
ри́г|а, и *f.* threshing barn.
ри́з|а, ы *f.* (*eccl.*) chasuble.
ри́зниц|а, ы *f.* (*eccl.*) vestry, sacristy.
рикоше́т, а *m.* ricochet, rebound; **~ом** on the rebound (*also fig.*).
рикошети́р|овать, ую *impf.* to ricochet.
ри́кш|а, и *f.* rickshaw.
Рим, а *m.* Rome.
ри́млян|ин, ина, *pl.* **~е, ~** *m.* Roman.
ри́мский *adj.* Roman; **па́па р.** the Pope.
ринг, а *m.* (*sport*) ring.
ри́н|уться, усь, ешься *pf.* to dash, dart.
рис, а *m.* rice; paddy.
рис. (*abbr. of* **рису́нок**) fig., figure.

риск, а *m.* risk; **на свой (страх и) р.** at one's own risk; **пойти́ на р.** to run a risk, take a chance.
рискн|у́ть, у́, ёшь *pf.* (*+inf.*) to take the risk (of), venture (to).
риско́ван|ный (~, ~на) *adj.* **1.** risky. **2.** risqué.
риск|ова́ть, у́ю *impf.* **1.** to run risks, take chances. **2.** (*+i.*) to risk; (*+inf.*) to risk, run the risk (of); **р. голово́й** to risk one's neck; **р. опозда́ть на по́езд** to risk missing the train.
рисова́льный *adj.* drawing.
рисова́льщик, а *m.* graphic artist.
рисова́ни|е, я *nt.* drawing.
рис|ова́ть, у́ю *impf.* (*of* **на~**) **1.** to draw; **р. акваре́лью** to paint in water-colours; **р. с нату́ры** to draw, paint from life. **2.** (*fig.*) to depict, portray.
рис|ова́ться, у́юсь *impf.* **1.** to be silhouetted; to appear. **2.** (*pej.*) to show off. **3.** *pass. of* **~ова́ть**
рисо́вк|а, и *f.* (*pej.*) showing off.
ри́сов|ый *adj.* rice; **~ая ка́ша** rice pudding.
рису́н|ок, ка *m.* drawing; illustration; (*in scientific work, article, etc.*) figure; pattern, design.
ритм, а *m.* rhythm.
ри́тмик|а, и *f.* **1.** (*liter.*) rhythm system. **2.** eurhythmics.
ритми́ческий *adj.* rhythmic(al).
ритми́чност|ь, и *f.* rhythm.
ритми́ч|ный (~ен, ~на) *adj.* rhythmic(al); **~ная рабо́та** smooth functioning.
рито́рик|а, и *f.* rhetoric.
ритори́ческий *adj.* rhetorical.
ритуа́л, а *m.* ritual; ceremonial.
ритуа́льный *adj.* ritual.
риф, а *m.* reef; **кора́лловый р.** coral reef.
рифлёный *adj.* (*tech.*) fluted, corrugated.
ри́фм|а, ы *f.* rhyme.
рифм|ова́ть, у́ю *impf.* (*of* **с~**) **1.** to rhyme. **2.** to select in order to make rhyme.
рифм|ова́ться, у́юсь *impf.* to rhyme.
рифмоплёт, а *m.* (*pej.*) rhymer, rhymester.
р-н (*abbr. of* **райо́н**) rayon, raion.
ро́ббер, а *m.* (*cards*) rubber.
робе́|ть, ю *impf.* (*of* **о~**) to be timid; to quail.
ро́б|кий (~ок, ~ка́, ~ко) *adj.* timid, shy.
ро́бост|ь, и *f.* timidity, shyness.
ро́бот, а *m.* robot.
робо(то)те́хник|а, и *f.* robotics.
ро́бче *comp. of* **ро́бкий**
ров, рва, о рве, во рву *m.* ditch; **крепостно́й р.** moat.
рове́сник, а *m.* person of the same age; **мы с ним ~и** we are the same age.
ро́вно *adv.* **1.** regularly, evenly. **2.** exactly; (*of time*) sharp; **р. пять рубле́й** five roubles exactly; **р. в час** at one o'clock sharp. **3.** (*coll.*) absolutely; **р. ничего́** absolutely nothing. **4.** (*coll.*) exactly like, just like.
ро́вност|ь, и *f.* regularity, evenness.
ро́в|ный (~ен, ~на́, ~но) *adj.* **1.** flat, even, level. **2.** regular, even; equable; **р. пульс** regular pulse; **р. хара́ктер** even temper. **3.** exact, even; equal; **для ~ного счёта** to make it even; **~ным счётом ничего́** (*coll.*) precisely nothing.
ро́вня́, ро́вни́ *c.g.* equal, match; **он ей не р.** he is no match for her.
ровня́|ть, ю *impf.* (*of* **с~**) to even, level; **р. с землёй** to raze to the ground.
рог, а, *pl.* **~а́, ~о́в** *m.* **1.** horn; antler; **брать быка́ за ~а́** (*coll.*) to take the bull by the horns; **наста́вить ~а́** (*+d.*; *coll.*) to cuckold; **согну́ть в бара́ний р.** (*coll.*) to make knuckle under; **сломи́ть ~а́** (*+d.*; *coll.*) to bring to one's knees. **2.** bugle, horn.
рога́ст|ый (~, ~а) *adj.* (*coll.*) large-horned.
рога́тк|а, и *f.* **1.** turnpike. **2.** (*boy's*) catapult.
рога́т|ый (~, ~а) *adj.* horned; **кру́пный р. скот** cattle; **ме́лкий р. скот** sheep and goats.
рога́ч, а́ *m.* **1.** stag. **2.** stag-beetle.
рогови́ц|а, ы *f.* (*anat.*) cornea.
рогов|о́й *adj.* horn; horny; **~ы́е очки́** horn-rimmed spectacles; **~а́я оболо́чка гла́за** (*anat.*) cornea; **~а́я му́зыка** music for horn.
рого́ж|а, и *f.* bast mat, matting.
рого́з, а *m.* (*bot.*) reed mace.
рогоно́с|ец, ца *m.* (*coll., joc.*) cuckold.
род, а, о ~́е, в ~у́, *pl.* **~ы́, ~о́в** *m.* **1.** family, kin, clan; **челове́ческий р.** the human race; **без ~́у, без пле́мени** without kith or kin. **2.** birth, origin, stock; generation; **он ~́ом из Ирла́ндии** he is a native of Ireland; **из ~́а в р.** from generation to generation; **ему́ на ~у́ напи́сано** (*+inf.*) he was preordained (to); **ей де́сять лет о́т ~у** she is ten years of age. **3.** (*biol.*) genus. **4.** sort, kind; **литерату́рный р.** literary genre; **р. войск** arm of the service; **вся́кого ~́а** of all kinds, all kind of; **тако́го ~́а** of such a kind, such; **в э́том ~́е** of this sort; **что-то в э́том ~́е** sth. of the kind; sth. to that effect; **в не́котором ~́е** in a way; to some extent; **в своём ~́е** in one's own way; **своего́ ~́а** a kind of; **он своего́ ~́а ге́ний** he is a genius in his own way. **5.** (*gram.*) gender.
роддо́м, а *m.* (*abbr. of* **роди́льный дом**) maternity home.
родео *nt. indecl.* rodeo.
роди́льниц|а, ы *f.* woman recently confined.
роди́льн|ый *adj.*: **р. дом** maternity home; **~ое отделе́ние** delivery room.
роди́м|ый *adj.* **1.** own; native. **2.:** **~ое пятно́** birthmark.
ро́дин|а, ы *f.* native land; home, homeland; **верну́ться на ~у** to return home; **тоска́ по ~е** homesickness, nostalgia.
ро́динк|а, и *f.* birth-mark.
роди́тел|и, ей *no sg.* parents.
роди́тел|ь, я *m.* (*obs.*) father.
роди́тельниц|а, ы *f.* (*obs.*) mother.
роди́тельный *adj.* (*gram.*) genitive.
роди́тельский *adj.* parental, parents'.
ро|ди́ть, жу́, ди́шь, *past* **~ди́л, ~дила́, ~ди́ло** *impf. and pf.* **1.** (*impf. also* **рожа́ть**) to bear, give birth (to); **в чём мать ~дила́** (*joc.*) in one's birthday suit. **2.** (*impf. also* **рожда́ть**) (*fig.*) to give birth, rise (to).
ро|ди́ться, жу́сь, ди́шься, *past* **~ди́лся́, ~ди́ла́сь, ~ди́ло́сь** *impf. and pf.* **1.** (*impf. also* **рожда́ться**) to be born; **р. преподава́телем** to be a born teacher. **2.** (*impf. also* **рожда́ться**) (*fig.*) to arise, come into being. **3.** to spring up, thrive; **кукуру́за у нас ~дила́сь хорошо́** we had a good maize-crop.
родни́к, а́ *m.* spring.
роднико́в|ый *adj. of* **родни́к; ~ая вода́** spring water.
родн|и́ть, ю́, и́шь *impf.* to make related, link.
родн|и́ться, ю́сь, и́шься *impf.* (*of* **по~**) (**с**+*i.*) to become related (with).
роднич|о́к, ка́ *m.* (*anat.*) fontanel(le).
родн|о́й *adj.* **1.** own (*by blood relationship in direct line*); **р. брат** brother (*opp. cousin, etc.*); *as n.* **~ы́е, ~ы́х** relatives. **2.** native; home; **~а́я страна́, ~а́я земля́** native land; **р. го́род** home town; **р. язы́к** mother tongue. **3.** (*as form of address*) (my) dear.
родн|я́, и́ *f.* **1.** (*collect.*) relatives, kinsfolk. **2.** relative.
родови́тост|ь, и *f.* noble birth, high birth.
родови́т|ый (~, ~а) *adj.* of noble birth, high-born.
родов|о́й[1] *adj.* **1.** (*ethnol.*) clan. **2.** ancestral; **~о́е име́ние, ~о́е иму́щество** patrimony. **3.** (*biol.*) generic. **4.** (*gram.*) gender.
родов|о́й[2] *adj.* birth, labour; **~ы́е схва́тки** contractions.
рододе́ндрон, а *m.* (*bot.*) rhododendron.

родонача́льник, а *m.* ancestor, forefather; (*fig.*) father.
родосло́вн|ая, ой *f.* genealogy, pedigree.
родосло́вн|ый *adj.* genealogical; **~ое де́рево** family tree.
ро́дственник, а *m.* relative; relation; **ближа́йший р.** next of kin.
ро́дствен|ный (~, ~на) *adj.* **1.** kindred, related; **~ные свя́зи** kinship ties. **2.** kindred, related; **~ные наро́ды** related peoples; **~ные языки́** cognate languages. **3.** familiar, intimate.
родств|о́, а́ *nt.* **1.** relationship, kinship (*also fig.*); **кро́вное р.** blood tie, consanguinity; **быть в ~е́** (**с**+*i.*) to be related (to). **2.** (*collect., coll.*) relatives.
ро́д|ы, ов *no sg.* birth; childbirth; **в ~ах** in labour; **стимуля́ция ~ов** induction (of labour).
ро́ж|а, и *f.* (*coll.*) mug, puss (= *ugly face*).
рожа́|ть, ю *impf. of* **роди́ть**
рожда́емост|ь, и *f.* birth-rate.
рожда́|ть(ся), ю(сь) *impf. of* **роди́ть(ся)**
рожде́ни|е, я *nt.* birth; **день ~я** birthday.
рождённый *p.p.p. of* **роди́ть**; (+*inf.*) born (to), destined (to).
рожде́ственск|ий *adj.* Christmas; **р. дед** Father Christmas; **~ая ёлка** Christmas-tree.
Рождеств|о́, а́ *nt.* Christmas; the Nativity; **на Р.** at Christmas(-time).
роже́ниц|а, ы *f.* woman in childbirth.
рож|о́к, ка́ *m.* **1.** small horn. **2.** (*mus.*) horn, clarion; bugle. **3. (слухово́й)** ear-trumpet. **4.** feeding-bottle. **5. (га́зовый)** (gas-)burner, (gas-)jet. **6.** shoe-horn.
рож|о́н, на́ *m.*: **лезть, идти́ на р.** (*coll.*) to kick against the pricks.
рожь, ржи *f.* rye.
ро́з|а, ы *f.* **1.** rose. **2.** rose-bush.
роза́ри|й, я *m.* rosarium, rose-garden.
ро́звальн|и, ей *no sg.* rozvalni (*low, wide sledge*).
ро́з|га, ги, *g. pl.* **~ог** *f.* birch (rod); **наказа́ть ~гой** to birch.
ро́зговень|е, я *nt.* (*eccl.*) first meal after fast.
розе́тк|а, и *f.* **1.** rosette. **2.** (*elec.*) socket; wall-plug. **3.** jam-dish.
розмари́н, а *m.* (*bot.*) rosemary.
ро́зниц|а, ы *f.* retail; **торгова́ть в ~у** to engage in retail trade.
ро́зничный *adj.* retail; **р. торго́вец** retailer.
ро́зно *adv.* (*coll.*) apart, separately.
розн|ь, и *f.* **1.** difference; **челове́к челове́ку р.** there are no two people alike; there are people and people. **2.** disagreement, dissension.
розове́|ть, ю *impf.* (*of* **по~**) to turn pink.
розовощёкий *adj.* rosy-cheeked.
ро́зов|ый (~, ~а) *adj.* **1.** *adj. of* **ро́за; ~ое де́рево** rosewood; **р. куст** rose-bush. **2.** pink, rose-coloured. **3.** (*fig.*) rosy; **смотре́ть сквозь ~ые очки́** to view through rose-coloured spectacles.
ро́зыгрыш, а *m.* **1.** drawing (*of a lottery, etc.*). **2.** (*sport*) playing off (*of a cup-tie, etc.*). **3.** (*sport*) draw, drawn game. **4.** practical joke.
ро́зыск, а *m.* **1.** search. **2.** (*leg.*) inquiry; **Уголо́вный р.** Criminal Investigation Department.
ро|и́ться, и́тся *impf.* (*of bees, etc.*) to swarm.
рой, ро́я, *pl.* **рои́** *m.* swarm (*of bees, etc.*).
рок[1], а *m.* fate.
рок[2], а *m.* rock (*var. of popular music*).
рок- *comb. form* rock.
рокир|ова́ть(ся), у́ю(сь) *impf. and pf.* (*chess*) to castle.
рокиро́вк|а, и *f.* (*chess*) castling.
рок-му́зык|а, и *f.* rock music.
рок-н-ро́лл, а *m.* rock 'n' roll.
роков|о́й *adj.* **1.** fateful; fated; **~а́я краса́вица** femme fatale. **2.** fatal.
рококо́ *nt. indecl.* rococo.
ро́кот, а *m.* roar, rumble.
роко|та́ть, чу́, ~́чешь *impf.* to roar, rumble.
ро́лик, а *m.* **1.** roller, castor. **2.** *pl.* roller skates. **3.: рекла́мный р.** (*cin.*) trailer.
ро́лик|овый *adj. of* **~**; **р. подши́пник** roller bearing.
роликодро́м, а *m.* roller-skating rink.
рол|ь, и, *pl.* **~́и, ~е́й** *f.* (*theatr.*) role (*also fig.*); part; **в ~́и** (+*g.*) in the role (of); **игра́ть р.** (+*g.*) to take the part (of), play; (*fig.*) to matter, count; **э́то не игра́ет ~́и** it is of no importance, it does not count.
ром, а *m.* rum.
рома́н, а *m.* **1.** novel. **2.** (*coll.*) love affair; romance.
романи́ст[1], а *m.* novelist.
романи́ст[2], а *m.* Romance philologist.
рома́нс, а *m.* (*mus.*) romance.
рома́нск|ий *adj.* Romance; **р. стиль** (*archit.*) Romanesque.
романти́зм, а *m.* romanticism.
рома́нтик, а *m.* romantic; romanticist.
рома́нтик|а, и *f.* romance; **р. медици́нских иссле́дований** the romance of medical research.
романти́ческий *adj.* romantic.
романти́ч|ный (~ен, ~на) *adj.* = **~еский**
рома́шк|а, и *f.* (*bot. and pharm.*) camomile.
ромб, а *m.* (*math.*) rhomb(us); (*mil.*) diamond formation.
ромби́ческий *adj.* (*math.*) rhombic.
ро́мовый *adj. of* **ром**
ромште́кс, а *m.* rump steak.
ро́ндо *nt. indecl.* (*mus.*) rondo.
роня́|ть, ю *impf.* (*of* **урони́ть**) **1.** to drop, let fall; **р. слёзы** to shed tears; **р. сло́во** to utter a word. **2.** *impf. only* to shed; **р. ли́стья** to shed its leaves; **р. опере́ние** to moult. **3.** (*fig.*) to injure, discredit; **р. себя́ в обще́ственном мне́нии** to drop in public estimation.
ро́пот, а *m.* murmur, grumble.
роп|та́ть, щу́, ~́щешь *impf.* to murmur, grumble.
рос, ла́ *see* **расти́**
рос|а́, ы́, *pl.* **~́ы** *f.* dew.
роси́нк|а, и *f.* dewdrop.
роси́ст|ый (~, ~а) *adj.* dewy.
роско́шеств|овать, ую *impf.* to luxuriate, live in luxury.
роско́ш|ный (~ен, ~на) *adj.* **1.** luxurious, sumptuous. **2.** (*coll.*) luxuriant, splendid.
ро́скош|ь, и *f.* **1.** luxury. **2.** luxuriance; splendour.
ро́слый *adj.* tall, strapping.
ро́сный *adj.*: **р. ла́дан** benzoin, benjamin.
росома́х|а, и *f.* (*zool.*) wolverene, glutton.
ро́спис|ь, и *f.* **1.** list, inventory. **2.** painting; **р. стен** wall-painting(s), mural(s).
ро́спуск, а *m.* dismissal; dissolution.
росси́йский *adj.* Russian.
Росси́|я, и *f.* Russia.
россия́н|ин, а, *pl.* **~е, ~** *m.* Russian.
россия́н|ка, ки *f. of* **~ин**
ро́ссказн|и, ей *no sg.* (*coll.*) old wives' tale, cock-and-bull story.
ро́ссып|ь, и *f.* **1.** scattering; **грузи́ть зерно́ ~ью** to load grain loose. **2.** (*pl.*; *min.*) deposit.
рост, а *m.* **1.** growth (*also fig.*); (*fig.*) increase, rise. **2.** height, stature; **~́ом** in height; **высо́кого ~́а** tall; **во весь р.** full length; (*fig.*) in all its magnitude; **встать во весь р.** to stand upright, stand up straight.
ро́стбиф, а *m.* roast beef.
ростовщи́к, а́ *m.* usurer, money-lender.
ростовщи́ческий *adj.* usurious.
ростовщи́честв|о, а *nt.* usury, money-lending.
рост|о́к, ка́ *m.* sprout, shoot; **пусти́ть ~ки́** to sprout.
ро́счерк, а *m.* flourish; **одни́м ~ом пера́** with a

stroke of the pen.
росянк|а, и *f.* (*bot.*) sundew.
рот, рта, о рте́, во рту́ *m.* mouth; **не брать в р.** (+*g.*) not to touch; **она́ мя́са в р. не брала́** she would never touch meat; **зажа́ть, за́ткнуть р. кому́-н.** to shut s.o. up; **смотре́ть в р. кому́-н.** to hang on s.o.'s every word.
ро́т|а, ы *f.* (*mil.*) company.
рота́тор, а *m.* duplicator, duplicating machine.
ротацио́нн|ый *adj.*: **~ая маши́на** (*typ.*) rotary press.
ротве́йлер, а *m.* Rottweiler.
ро́т|ный *adj. of* **~а**; *as n.* **р., ~ного** *m.* company commander.
ротозе́|й, я *m.* (*coll.*) scatter-brain, gaper.
ротозе́йств|о, а *nt.* (*coll.*) scatter-brainedness.
рото́нд|а, ы *f.* (*archit.*) rotunda.
ро́тор, а *m.* (*tech.*) rotor.
ро́щ|а, и *f.* small wood, grove.
роялист, а *m.* royalist.
роялистский *adj.* royalist.
роя́л|ь, я *m.* piano; grand piano; **у ~я** at the piano.
РСФСР *f. indecl.* (*hist.*) (*abbr. of* ***Росси́йская Сове́тская Федерати́вная Социалисти́ческая Респу́блика***) RSFSR (*Russian Soviet Federal Socialist Republic*).
рту́тный *adj.* mercury.
рту́т|ь, и *f.* mercury.
руба́н|ок, ка *m.* (*tech.*) plane.
руба́х|а, и *f.* shirt.
руба́шк|а, и *f.* **1.** shirt; **ночна́я р.** night-shirt; night-gown; **роди́ться в ~е** to be born with a silver spoon in one's mouth; **своя́ р. бли́же к те́лу** (*prov.*) charity begins at home. **2.** back (*of playing cards*).
рубе́ж, а́ *m.* **1.** boundary, border(line); **за ~о́м** abroad. **2.** (*mil.*) line; **р. ата́ки** assault position.
руб|е́ц[1], **ца́** *m.* **1.** scar; weal. **2.** hem, seam.
руб|е́ц[2], **ца́** *m.* **1.** (*zool.*) paunch (*ruminant's first stomach*). **2.** (*cul.*) tripe.
руби́н, а *m.* ruby.
руби́новый *adj.* ruby; ruby(-coloured).
руб|и́ть, лю́, ~ишь *impf.* **1.** to fell (*trees*). **2.** to hew, chop, hack. **3.** (*cul.*) to mince, chop up. **4.** to put up, erect (*of logs*).
руб|и́ться, лю́сь, ~ишься *impf.* to fight (with cold steel).
ру́бищ|е, а *no pl., nt.* rags, tatters.
ру́бк|а[1], **и** *f.* **1.** felling. **2.** hewing, chopping, hacking. **3.** mincing, chopping up.
ру́бк|а[2], **и** *f.* (*naut.*) deck house; **боева́я р.** conning tower; **рулева́я р.** wheel-house.
рублёвк|а, и *f.* (*coll.*) one-rouble note.
рубл|ёвый *adj.* **1.** *adj. of* **~ь. 2.** one rouble (*in price*).
ру́блен|ый *adj.* **1.** minced, chopped; **~ые котле́ты** rissoles. **2.**: **~ая изба́** log cabin.
рубл|ь, я́ *m.* rouble.
ру́брик|а, и *f.* **1.** rubric, heading. **2.** column (*of figures*).
рубц|ева́ться, у́ется *impf.* (*of* **за~**) to form a scar.
ру́бчатый *adj.* ribbed.
ру́бчик, а *m.* **1.** *dim. of* **рубе́ц**[1]. **2.** rib (*on material*).
ру́ган|ь, и *f.* bad language, swearing.
руга́тельн|ый *adj.* abusive; **~ые слова́** bad language, swear-words.
руга́тельств|о, а *nt.* swear-word.
руга́|ть, ю *impf.* (*of* **вы́~** *and* **из~**) to curse, swear (at).
руга́|ться, юсь *impf.* **1.** to curse, swear; **р. как изво́зчик** to swear like a trooper. **2.** to swear at one another.
руд|а́, ы́, *pl.* **~ы** *f.* ore; **желе́зная р.** iron-ore.
рудиме́нт, а *m.* rudiment.
рудимента́рный *adj.* rudimentary.
рудни́к, а́ *m.* mine, pit.
руднико́вый *adj. of* **рудни́к**
рудни́|чный *adj. of* **~к; р. газ** fire-damp; **~чная сто́йка** pit prop; **~чная ла́мпа** miner's lamp.
ру́д|ный *adj. of* **~а́; ~ная жи́ла** vein.
рудоко́п, а *m.* miner.
руже́йник, а *m.* gunsmith.
руже́йн|ый *adj. of* **ружьё; р. вы́стрел** rifle-shot; **р. ма́стер** armourer, gunsmith.
руж|ьё, ья́, *pl.* **~ья, ~ей, ~ьям** *nt.* (hand-)gun, rifle; **дробово́е р.** shot-gun; **быть под ~ьём** to be under arms; **призва́ть под р.** to call to arms, call to the colours.
руи́н|а, ы *f.* ruin (*usu. pl.*).
рук|а́, и́, *a.* **~у,** *pl.* **~и, ~, ~а́м** *f.*

I. 1. hand; arm; **пожа́ть ~у** (+*d.*) to shake hands (with); **~и вверх!** hands up!; **~а́ми не тро́гать!** please, do not touch!; **вести́ за́ ~у** to lead by the hand; **взя́ться за́ ~у** to join hands, link arms; **из ~ в ~и** from hand to hand; **взять на́ ~и** to take in one's arms; **держа́ть на ~а́х** to hold in one's arms; **р. о́б ~у** hand in hand; **написа́ть от ~и́** to write out by hand; **взять кого́-н. по́д ~у** to take s.o.'s arm; **идти́ с кем-н. по́д ~у** to walk arm in arm with s.o. **2.** hand, handwriting; signature; **приложи́ть ~у** to affix one's signature. **3.** side, hand; **на ле́вой ~е́** on the left; **по пра́вую ~у** at the right hand. **4.** *pl.* hands (*fig.* = *power*, *possession*); **взять в свои́ ~и** to take into one's own hands; **взять (себя́) в ~и** to take (o.s.) in hand; **держа́ть в свои́х ~а́х** to have in one's clutches; **попа́сться в ~и кому́-н.** to fall into s.o.'s hands; **прибра́ть к ~а́м** to appropriate; **ско́лько у вас на ~а́х иностра́нной валю́ты?** how much foreign currency have you on you?; **свобо́да ~** a free hand; **в со́бственные ~и** (*on cover of letter*, *etc.*) 'personal'. **5.** (*fig.*) hand; **проси́ть ~и́ у кого́-н.** to ask s.o.'s hand in marriage. **6.** (*fig.*) hand; source, authority; **из пе́рвых ~** at first hand; **узна́ть из ве́рных ~** to have on good authority.

II. (*fig.*) hand; **переда́ть де́ло в чьи-н. ~и** to put a matter in s.o.'s hands; **сон в ~у** the dream has come true; **из ~ вон (пло́хо)** (*coll.*) quite useless; **вы́дать на́ ~и** to hand out; **име́ть на ~а́х** to have on one's hands; **умере́ть на чьих-н. ~а́х** to die in s.o.'s arms; **ма́стер на все ~и** Jack of all trades; **э́то бу́дет им на́ ~у** that will serve their purpose; it will be playing into their hands; **на́ ~у нечи́ст** (*coll.*) dishonest, underhand; **на ско́рую ~у** off-hand; **дать кому́-н. по ~а́м** (*coll.*) to give a rap over the knuckles; **по ~а́м!** it's a deal!; done!; **говори́ть кому́-н. по́д ~у** to distract s.o. by talking; **под ~о́й** at hand, to hand; **под пья́ную ~у** under the influence (of drink); **с ~ доло́й** off one's hands; **сбыть с ~** to get off one's hands; **э́то тебе́ не сойдёт с ~** (*coll.*) you won't get away with it; **греть ~и (на+*p.*)** to make a good thing (out of); **дать во́лю ~а́м** (*coll.*) to bring one's fists into play; **э́то де́ло чужи́х ~** this is s.o. else's doing; **как ~о́й сня́ло** it has vanished as if by magic; **махну́ть ~о́й (на+*a.*)** to give up as lost; **наби́ть ~у** to get one's hand in; **наложи́ть на себя́ ~и** to lay hands on o.s.; **приложи́ть ~у (к)** to put one's hand (to), take a hand (in); **развяза́ть ~и** (+*d.*) to give a free hand; **р. у него́ не дро́гнет** (+*inf.*) he will not scruple (to); **~и у меня́ не дохо́дят до э́того** I've no time to do it; **~и прочь!** hands off!; **~о́й пода́ть** a stone's throw away; **умы́ть ~и (в+*p.*)** to wash one s hands (of); **у меня́ ~и че́шутся** (+*inf.*) my fingers are itching (to); I itch (to).
рука́в, а́, *pl.* **~а́** *m.* **1.** sleeve; **спустя́ ~а́** (*coll.*) in a slipshod manner. **2.** branch (*of river*). **3.** (*tech.*) hose.
рукави́ц|а, ы *f.* mitten; gauntlet; **держа́ть в ежо́вых ~ах** to rule with a rod of iron.
руководи́тел|ь, я *m.* **1.** leader; manager; **кла́ссный**

р. (*in school*) form monitor. **2.** instructor; guide; **нау́чный руководи́тель** supervisor of studies.
руково|ди́ть, жу́, ди́шь *impf.* (+*i.*) to lead; to guide; to direct, manage.
руково|ди́ться, жу́сь, ди́шься *impf.* (+*i.*) to follow; to be guided (by).
руково́дств|о, а *nt.* **1.** leadership; guidance; direction. **2.** guide; **р. к де́йствию** guide to action. **3.** handbook, guide, manual; **р. по эксплуата́ции** instructions for use. **4.** (*collect.*) (the) leadership, leaders; governing body.
руково́дств|оваться, уюсь *impf.* (+*i.*) to follow; to be guided (by).
руковод|я́щий *pres. part. act. of* **~и́ть** *and adj.* leading; guiding; senior; **~я́щая статья́** editorial, leader; **р. комите́т** steering committee.
рукоде́ли|е, я *nt.* needlework.
рукоде́льниц|а, ы *f.* needlewoman, needleworker.
рукомо́йник, а *m.* wash-stand, wash-hand-stand.
рукопа́шный *adj.* hand-to-hand.
рукопи́сный *adj.* manuscript.
ру́копис|ь, и *f.* manuscript
рукоплеска́ни|е, я *nt.* applause.
рукопле|ска́ть, щу́, ~́щешь *impf.* (+*d.*) to applaud.
рукопожа́ти|е, я *nt.* handshake.
рукоя́тк|а, и *f.* **1.** handle; hilt; haft, helve; shaft; **по ~у** up to the hilt. **2.** crank, crank handle.
рула́д|а, ы *f.* (*mus.*) roulade.
рулев|о́й *adj. of* **руль; ~о́е колесо́** steering wheel; **~а́я коло́нка** steering column; *as n.* **р., ~о́го** *m.* **1.** helmsman. **2.** (*sport*) cox(swain).
руле́т, а *m.* (*cul.*) **1.** roll; **мясно́й р.** meat loaf. **2.** boned gammon.
руле́тк|а, и *f.* **1.** tape-measure. **2.** roulette.
рул|и́ть, ю́, и́шь *impf.* (*aeron.*) to taxi.
руло́н, а *m.* roll.
рул|ь, я́ *m.* rudder; helm (*also fig.*); (steering-)wheel; handle-bars; **стать за р.** to take the helm; **стоя́ть на ~е́** (*fig.*) to be at the helm.
румы́н, а *m.* Romanian.
Румы́ни|я, и *f.* Romania, Rumania.
румы́н|ка, ки *f. of* **~**
румы́нский *adj.* Romanian.
румя́н|а, ~ *no sg.* rouge; blusher.
румя́н|ец, ца *m.* (high) colour; flush; blush.
румя́н|ить, ю, ишь *impf.* **1.** (*pf.* **за~**) to redden (*also fig.*); to cause to glow. **2.** (*pf.* **на~**) to rouge.
румя́н|иться, юсь, ишься *impf.* **1.** (*pf.* **за~**) to redden; to glow; to flush. **2.** (*pf.* **на~**) to use rouge.
румя́н|ый (~, ~а) *adj.* rosy, ruddy.
ру́н|а, ы *m.* rune.
руни́ческий *adj.* runic.
рун|о́, а́, *pl.* **~́а** *nt.* fleece; **золото́е р.** (*myth.*) the Golden Fleece.
ру́пи|я, и *f.* rupee.
ру́пор, а *m.* megaphone; loud hailer; (*fig.*) mouthpiece.
руса́к[1], а́ *m.* (grey) hare.
руса́к[2], а́ *m.* (*coll.*) Russian.
руса́лк|а, и *f.* mermaid.
руси́зм, а *m.* (*ling.*) Russianism, Russ(ic)ism.
руси́ст, а *m.* Russianist.
руси́стик|а, и *f.* Russian philology.
русифика́ци|я, и *f.* Russification.
русифици́р|овать, ую *impf. and pf.* to Russify.
ру́сл|о, а, *g. pl.* **~** *nt.* **1.** (river-)bed, channel; **измени́ть р. реки́** to change the course of a river. **2.** (*fig.*) course, direction; **мои́ дела́ пошли́ по но́вому ~у** my affairs have taken a new turn.
ру́сск|ая, ой *f.* **1.** *f. of* **~ий** *as n.* **2.** russkaya (*Russ. folk-dance*).
ру́сск|ий *adj.* Russian (*also as n.* **р., ~ого** *m.*).
ру́с|ый (~, ~а) *adj.* light-brown.
Рус|ь, и́ *f.* (*hist.*) Rus, Russia.
руте́ни|й, я *m.* (*chem.*) ruthenium.
рути́н|а, ы *f.* (*pej.*) routine; rut.
рутинёр, а *m.* slave to routine, person in a rut.
рутинёр|ский *adj. of* **~; ~́ские взгля́ды** rigid views.
рути́н|ный *adj. of* **~а**
ру́хлядь, и *f.* (*collect.*; *coll.*) junk, lumber.
ру́хн|уть, у, ешь *pf.* to crash down, tumble down, collapse; (*fig.*) to crash, fall through.
руча́тельств|о, а *nt.* guarantee; **с ~ом** guaranteed.
руча́|ться, юсь *impf.* (*of* **поручи́ться**) (**за**+*a.*) to warrant, guarantee; to answer (for), vouch (for); **р. голово́й** (**за**+*a.*) to stake one's life (on).
руче|ёк, йка́ *m. dim. of* **руче́й**
руч|е́й, ья́ *m.* brook, stream; **~ьи́ слёз** floods of tears.
ру́чк|а, и *f.* **1.** *dim. of* **рука́. 2.** handle; arm (*of chair*); **р. две́ри** door-handle, door-knob; **дойти́ до ~и** (*fig., coll.*) to reach the end of one's tether. **3.** penholder; pen; **автомати́ческая р.** fountain-pen.
ручн|о́й *adj.* **1.** hand; manual; **~а́я грана́та** hand grenade; **~а́я кладь** hand luggage; **р. труд** manual labour; **~ы́е часы́** wrist watch. **2.** tame; pet.
ру́ш|ить, у, ишь *impf.* to pull down.
ру́ш|иться, усь, ишься *impf. and pf.* to fall in, collapse; (*fig.*) to fall through.
ры́б|а, ы *f.* fish; (*pl., astron.*) Pisces; **ни р., ни мя́со** neither fish, flesh nor fowl.
рыба́к, а́ *m.* fisherman.
рыба́лк|а, и *f.* (*coll.*) fishing; fishing trip; **идти́ на ~у** to go fishing.
рыба́|цкий *adj. of* **~к; р. посёлок** fishing village.
рыба́|чий *adj. of* **~к; ~чья ло́дка** fishing-boat.
рыба́ч|ить, у, ишь *impf.* to fish.
рыбёшк|а, и *f.* (*coll.*) small fry.
ры́бий *adj.* fish; **р. жир** cod-liver oil; **р. клей** isinglass.
ры́бн|ый *adj.* fish; **~ые консе́рвы** tinned fish; **~ая ло́вля** fishing; **р. магази́н** fishmonger's.
рыбово́дческ|ий *adj.*: **~ая фе́рма** fish farm.
рыбозаво́д, а *m.* fish-factory; **плаву́чий р.** fish-factory ship.
рыбоконсе́рвный *adj.*: **р. заво́д** fish cannery.
рыболо́в, а *m.* fisherman; angler.
рыболо́вн|ый *adj.* fishing; **~ые принадле́жности, ~ая снасть** fishing tackle; **р. райо́н** fishing-ground, fishery.
рыболо́вств|о, а *nt.* fishing (*as branch of economy*).
рыботорго́в|ец, ца *m.* fishmonger.
рыботорго́вк|а, и *f.* fishwife.
рыв|о́к, ка́ *m.* **1.** jerk. **2.** (*sport*) burst, spurt.
рыг|а́ть, а́ю *impf.* (*of* **~ну́ть**) to belch.
рыг|ну́ть, ну́, нёшь *pf. of* **~а́ть**
рыда́|ть, ю *impf.* to sob.
рыжеволо́с|ый (~, ~а) *adj.* red-haired.
рыже́|ть, ю *impf.* (*of* **по~**) to turn reddish.
ры́ж|ий (~, ~а́, ~е) *adj.* **1.** red. **2.** red-haired, ginger; (*of a horse*) chestnut. **3.** *as n.* **р., ~его** *m.* circus clown.
ры́жик, а *m.* saffron milk-cap (*mushroom*).
рыка́|ть, ю *impf.* to roar.
ры́л|о, а *nt.* **1.** snout. **2.** (*coll.*) mug, puss.
ры́л|ьце, ьца, *g. pl.* **~ец** *nt.* **1.** *dim. of* **~о; у него́ р. в пуху́** he has been at the jam-pot. **2.** (*bot.*) stigma.
ры́нд|а, ы *f.* ship's bell.
ры́н|ок, ка *m.* **1.** market(-place). **2.** (*econ.*) market.
ры́ночник, а *m.* free-marketeer.
ры́но|чный *adj. of* **~к; р. день** market-day.
рыса́к, а́ *m.* trotter.
ры́с|ий *adj.* lynx; piercing; **~ьи глаза́** (*fig.*) lynx eyes.
рыси́ст|ый *adj.*: **~ая ло́шадь** trotter.
рыс|и́ть, и́шь *impf.* to trot.
ры́|скать, щу, щешь *impf.* **1.** to rove, roam. **2.** (**по**+*d.*) to scour, ransack; **р. по ска́лам** to scour

the cliffs; **р. по кармáнам** to ransack one's pockets.
рысц|á, ы́ *f.* jog-trot; **éхать ~óй** to go at a jog-trot.
рыс|ь[1], **и, о ~́и, на ~и́** *f.* trot; **на ~я́х** at a trot.
рыс|ь[2], **и** *f.* lynx.
ры́сью *adv.* at a trot.
ры́твин|а, ы *f.* rut, groove.
рыть, ро́ю, ро́ешь *impf.* to dig; to burrow; to root up; **р. око́пы** to dig trenches.
рыть|ё, я́ *nt.* digging.
ры́ться, ро́юсь, ро́ешься *impf.* (**в**+*p.*) to dig (in); (*fig.*) to rummage (in), ransack, burrow (in).
рыхле́|ть, ю *impf.* (*of* **по~**) to become friable.
рыхл|и́ть, ю́, и́шь *impf.* to loosen; to make friable.
ры́хл|ый (~, ~á, ~o) *adj.* **1.** friable; mellow (*of soil*); loose; porous. **2.** (*fig.*) podgy.
ры́цар|ский *adj.* **1.** *adj. of* **~ь; р. поеди́нок** joust; **р. ромáн** tale of chivalry. **2.** (*fig.*) chivalrous.
ры́царств|о, а *nt.* **1.** (*collect.*; *hist.*) knights. **2.** knighthood. **3.** (*fig.*) chivalry.
ры́цар|ь, я *m.* knight.
рычáг, á *m.* lever.
рычáни|е, я *nt.* growl, snarl.
рыч|áть, ý, и́шь *impf.* to growl, snarl.
рья́ност|ь, и *f.* zeal.
рья́н|ый (~, ~а) *adj.* zealous.
рэ́ггей *m. indecl.* reggae.
рэ́кет, а *m.* racket.
рэкети́р, а *m.* racketeer.
рюкзáк, á *m.* rucksack, knapsack; backpack.
рюкзáчник, а *m.* backpacker.
рю́мк|а, и *f.* (*small*) glass.
рю́мочк|а, и *f. dim. of* **рю́мка**
рябйн|а[1], **ы** *f.* **1.** rowan-tree, mountain ash. **2.** rowanberry, ashberry.
ряби́н|а[2], **ы** *f.* (*coll.*) pockmark.
ряб|и́ть, и́т *impf.* **1.** to ripple. **2.** (*impers.*): **у меня́ ~и́т в глазáх** I am dazzled.
ряб|óй (~, ~á, ~́о) *adj.* **1.** pock-marked. **2.** speckled.
ря́бчик, а *m.* (*zool.*) hazel-grouse, hazel-hen.
ряб|ь, и *f.* **1.** ripple(s). **2.** dazzle.
ря́вк|ать, аю *impf.* (*of* **~нуть**) (**на**+*a.*; *coll.*) to bellow (at), roar (at).
ря́вк|нуть, ну, нешь *pf. of* **~ать**
ряд, а, в ~́е *and* **в ~ý**, *pl.* **~ы́, ~óв** *m.* **1.** row; line; **пéрвый р., послéдний р.** (*theatr.*) front row, back row; **р. за ~́ом** row upon row; **из ~́а вон выходя́щий** outstanding, exceptional; **стоя́ть в одно́м ~ý** (**с**+*i.*) to rank (with), be on a par (with). **2.** (*mil.*) file, rank; **в ~áх áрмии** in the ranks of the army; **в пéрвых ~áх** in the first ranks; (*fig.*) in the forefront. **3.** series (*also math.*); number; **в цéлом ~́е слу́чаев** in a number of cases.
ря|ди́ться, жýсь, ~́дишься *impf.* **1.** (*coll.*) to dress up. **2.** (+*i.*) to dress up (as), disguise o.s. (as).
рядов|óй *adj.* **1.** ordinary, common. **2.** (*mil.*): **р. состáв** rank and file; men, other ranks; *as n.* **р., ~óго** *m.* private (soldier).
ря́дом *adv.* **1.** alongside, side by side; (**с**+*i.*) next to. **2.** nearby, close by, next door; **э́то совсéм р.** it is a stone's throw away; **он жил р. с бо́йней** he lived next door to the slaughterhouse.
ря́с|а, ы *f.* cassock.
ря́ск|а, и *f.* (*bot.*) duckweed.
ря́шк|а, и *f.* (*coll.*) mug (= *face*).

С (*abbr. of* **сéвер**) N, North.
с *prep.*

I. +*g.* **1.** from; off; **с ю́го-востóка** from the South-East; **с Вóлги** from the Volga; **с Кавкáза** from the Caucasus; **с головы́ до ног** from head to foot; **с пéрвого взгля́да** at first sight; **перевóд с рýсского** translation from Russian; **вернýться с рабóты** to return from work; **убрáть посýду со столá** the clear the things from the table; **устáть с дорóги** to be tired after a journey; **снять с когó-н. фотогрáфию** to take s.o.'s photograph; **взять примéр с когó-н.** to follow s.o.'s example; **довóльно с тебя́!** that's enough from you! **скóлько с меня́?** how much do I owe? **2.** for, from, with; **с рáдости** for joy; **со стыдá** with shame. **3.** on, from; **с лéвой стороны́ от желéзной дорóги** on the left-hand side of the railway; **с однóй, с другóй стороны́** on the one, on the other hand; **с какóй тóчки зрéния?** from what point of view? **4.** with (= *on the basis of*); **с вáшего соглáсия** with your consent. **5.** by, with (= *by means of*); **взять с бóю** to take by storm; **писáть с большóй бýквы** to write with a capital letter. **6.** (*of time*) from, since; as from; **с девяти́ (часóв) до пяти́** from nine (o'clock) till five; **с дéтства** from childhood; **с утрá** since morning; **мы с ней не ви́делись с января́** I have not seen her since January; **они́ бýдут в Москвé с двадцáтого числá** they will be in Moscow from the twentieth; **с 1850 по 1900** from 1850 to 1900.

II. +*a.* **1.: я бýду там с год** I shall be there about a year; **мы прошли́ с ми́лю** we walked about a mile. **2.** the size of; **с дом** the size of a house; **нáша дóчка рóстом с вáшу** our daughter is about the same height as yours; **мáльчик с пáльчик** Tom Thumb.

III. +*i.* **1.** with; and; **с удовóльствием** with pleasure; **мы с вáми** you and I; **он с сестрóй** he and his sister. **2.** (*indicates possession*) **хлеб с мáслом** bread and butter; **человéк со стрáнностями** queer, peculiar person. **3.** by, on (= *by means of*); **получи́ть с пéрвой пóчтой** to receive by first post; **я приéхал с экспрéссом** I came on the express. **4.** with (= *with the passage of*); **с годáми** with the years; **с кáждым днём** every day. **5.** with (*or not translated*) (= *in regard to, as regards*); **как обстои́т у вас с рабóтой?** how is the work going? **что с вáми?** what's up? **как у вас с деньгáми?** how are you off for money?
с. *abbr. of* **селó** village.
с... (*also* **со...** *and* **съ...**) *vbl. pref. indicating* **1.** *unification, movement from various sides to a point*, *as* **свари́ть** to weld. **2.** *movement or action made in a downward direction*, *as* **спусти́ться** to descend. **3.** *removal of sth. from somewhere*, *as* **сорвáть** to tear off.
саáм, а *m.* Lapp, Laplander.
саáм|ка, ки *f. of* **~**
саáмский *adj.* Lappish.
сáбельный *adj.* sabre.
сáб|ля, ли, *g.pl.* **~ель** *f.* sabre.
саботáж, а *m.* sabotage.

саботáжник, а *m.* saboteur
саботáжнича|ть, ю *impf.* (*coll.*) to engage in sabotage.
саботи́р|овать, ую *impf. and pf.* to sabotage.
сáван, а *m.* shroud; **снéжный с.** blanket of snow.
савáнн|а, ы *f.* (*geog.*) savannah.
саврáсый *adj.* (*of horses*) light brown with black mane and tail.
сáг|а, и *f.* saga.
сагити́р|овать, ую *pf. of* **агити́ровать**
сáго *nt. indecl.* (*bot.*) sago.
сáго|вый *adj. of* ~; **~вая кáша** sago pudding.
сад, а, о ~е, в ~ý, *pl.* **~ы́** *m.* garden; **фруктóвый с.** orchard; **зоологи́ческий с.** zoo; **дéтский с.** kindergarten.
сади́зм, а *m.* sadism.
сади́ст, а *m.* sadist.
сади́стский *adj.* sadistic.
са|ди́ть, жý, ~дишь *impf.* (*of* **по~**) to plant.
са|ди́ться, жýсь, ди́шься *impf.* (*of* **сесть**); **~ди́(те)сь!** (*polite request*) take a seat!
сáдн|ить, ит *impf.* (*impers.*; *coll.*) to smart, burn.
садóвник, а *m.* gardener.
садовóд, а *m.* gardener; horticulturist.
садовóдств|о, а *nt.* gardening; horticulture.
садовóдческий *adj.* horticultural.
сад|óвый *adj.* **1.** *adj. of* ~. **2.** garden, cultivated.
сад|óк, кá *m.* place for keeping live creatures; **крóличий с.** rabbit-hutch; **ры́бный с.** fish-pond.
садо-мазохи́зм, а *m.* sado-masochism.
сáж|а, и *f.* soot, lamp-black.
сажá|ть, ю *impf.* (*of* **посади́ть**) **1.** to plant. **2.** to seat; to set, put; to offer a seat; **с. в клéтку** to cage; **с. в тюрьмý** to put into prison, imprison, jail; **с. под арéст** to put under arrest.
сáжен|ец, ца *m.* seedling; sapling.
сáжéн|ь, и, *pl.* **~и, сáжен** *and* **сажéнéй** *f.* sazhen (*old Russ. measure of length, equivalent to 2.13 metres*); **морскáя с.** Russian fathom (*1.83 metres*).
сазáн, а *m.* (wild) carp.
сайг|á, и *f.* (*zool.*) saiga.
сáйк|а, и *f.* (*bread*) roll.
саквоя́ж, а *m.* travelling-bag.
сакé *nt. indecl.* sake.
сакраментáл|ьный (~ен, ~ьна) *adj.* sacramental; sacred.
сакс, а *m.* (*hist.*) Saxon.
саксóнский *adj.* Saxon.
саксофóн, а *m.* saxophone.
салáз|ки, ок *no sg.* hand sled, toboggan.
саламáндр|а, ы *f.* salamander.
салáт, а *m.* **1.** lettuce. **2.** salad.
салáтник, а *m.* salad-dish, salad-bowl.
салáтниц|а, ы *f.* = **салáтник**
салáт|ный *adj. of* ~; **~ного цвéта** light green.
сáл|ить, ю, ишь *impf.* to grease.
сáл|ки, ок *pl.* (*children's game*) tag.
сáл|о, а *nt.* **1.** fat, lard; suet. **2.** tallow. **3.** thin ice.
салóн, а *m.* **1.** salon; showroom; **дáмский с.** beauty parlour. **2.** saloon.
салóн-вагóн, а *m.* saloon car.
салóн|ный *adj. of* ~; **~ные бесéды** small talk.
салфéтк|а, и *f.* serviette, (table-)napkin; doily.
сáльдо *nt. indecl.* (*book-keeping*) balance.
сáльност|ь, и *f.* obscenity, bawdiness.
сáльн|ый *adj.* **1.** tallow; **~ая свечá** tallow candle. **2.** (*anat.*) sebaceous; **~ая железá** sebaceous gland. **3.** greasy. **4.** obscene, bawdy.
сáльто-мортáле *nt. indecl.* somersault.
салю́т, а *m.* (*mil.*, *naut.*) salute.
салют|овáть, ýю *impf. and pf.* (*pf. also* **от~**) (*+d.*) to salute.
сам, самогó *m.*; **самá, самóй,** *a.* **самоё** (*and* **самý**) *f.*; **~ó, самогó** *nt.*; *pl.* **сáми, сами́х** *refl. pron.* myself, yourself, himself, *etc.*; **с. по себé** in itself, per se; by o.s.; **с. собóй** of itself, of its own accord; **он с. не свой** he is not himself; **с. себé хозя́ин** one's own master; **онá — самá добротá** she is kindness itself.
самáн, а *m.* adobe.
самáн|ный *adj. of* ~
самаритя́н|ин, ина, *pl.* **~е,** ~ *m.* (*bibl.*, *hist.*) Samaritan.
сáмбо *nt. indecl.* (*abbr. of* ***самооборóна без орýжия***) unarmed combat.
сам|éц, цá *m.* male (*of species*).
самиздáт, а *m.* (*coll.*) samizdat.
сáмк|а, и *f.* female (*of species*).
само... *comb. form* self-, auto-.
самоанáлиз, а *m.* self-examination, introspection.
самобы́тност|ь, и *f.* originality.
самобы́т|ный (~ен, на) *adj.* original.
самовáр, а *m.* samovar.
самовлáсти|е, я *nt.* absolute power, despotism.
самовлáст|ный (~ен, ~на) *adj.* **1.** absolute. **2.** (*fig.*) despotic, autocratic.
самовлюблённост|ь, и *f.* narcissism, vanity.
самовлюблённый *adj.* narcissistic, vain.
самовнушéни|е, я *nt.* auto-suggestion.
самовозгорáни|е, я *nt.* spontaneous combustion.
самовóли|е, я *nt.* licence.
самовóл|ьный (~ен, ~ьна) *adj.* **1.** wilful, self-willed. **2.** unauthorized; **~ьная отлýчка** (*mil.*) absence without leave.
самовоспламенéни|е, я *nt.* spontaneous combustion.
самогóн, а *m.* home-made vodka, hooch.
самодви́жущийся *adj.* self-propelled.
самодéйствующий *adj.* self-acting, automatic.
самодéлк|а, и *f.* (*coll.*) home-made article.
самодéл|ьный (~ен, ~ьна) *adj.* home-made.
самодержáви|е, я *nt.* autocracy.
самодержáв|ный (~ен, ~на) *adj.* autocratic.
самодéрж|ец, ца *m.* autocrat.
самодéятельност|ь, и *f.* **1.** (individual) initiative. **2.** amateur production (*theatricals, music, etc.*); **вéчер ~и** amateurs' night.
самодéятельный *adj.* **1.** amateur. **2.** (*econ.*) self-employed.
самодисципли́н|а, ы *f.* self-discipline.
самодовлéющий *adj.* self-sufficient.
самодовóл|ьный (~ен, ~ьна) *adj.* self-satisfied, smug, complacent.
самодовóльств|о, а *nt.* self-satisfaction, smugness, complacency.
самодýр, а *m.* petty tyrant.
самодýрств|о, а *nt.* petty tyranny.
самозабвéни|е, я *nt.* selflessness.
самозарождéни|е, я *nt.* (*biol.*) spontaneous generation.
самозащи́т|а, ы *f.* self-defence.
самозвáн|ец, ца *m.* impostor, pretender.
самозвáнный *adj.* false, self-styled.
самокáт, а *m.* (*child's*) scooter.
самокри́тик|а, и *f.* self-criticism.
самокрити́ч|ный (~ен, ~на) *adj.* self-critical.
самолёт, а *m.* aeroplane, aircraft.
самолёт|ный *adj of* ~
самоли́чно *adv.* (*coll.*) oneself; on one's own; personally.
самолюби́в|ый (~, ~а) *adj.* proud, haughty.
самолю́би|е, я, *nt.* pride, self-esteem.
самомнéни|е, я *nt.* conceit, self-importance.
самонаблюдéни|е, я *nt.* (*psych.*) introspection.
самонадéянност|ь, и *f.* (*pej.*) conceit, arrogance.
самонадéян|ный (~, ~на) *adj.* (*pej.*) conceited, arrogant.

самоназва́ни|е, я *nt.* own name; **ро́мэни — с. цыга́н** 'Romany' is the gypsies' own name for themselves.
самооблада́ни|е, я *nt.* self-control, self-possession, composure.
самообма́н, а *m.* self-deception.
самооборо́н|а, ы *f.* self-defence.
самообразова́ни|е, я *nt.* self-education.
самообслу́живани|е, я *nt.* self-service.
самоопределе́ни|е, я *nt.* self-determination.
самоотверже́ни|е, я *nt.* = **самоотве́рженность**
самоотве́рженност|ь, и *f.* selflessness.
самоотве́ржен|ный (~, ~на) *adj.* selfless.
самоотво́д, а *m.* withdrawal (*of candidature*), refusal to accept (*nomination for an office, etc.*).
самоотрече́ни|е, я *nt.* self-denial, (self-)abnegation.
самоочеви́дный *adj.* self-evident.
самопи́с|ец, ца *m.*: **бортово́й с.** (*aeron.*) flight recorder.
самопоже́ртвовани|е, я *nt.* self-sacrifice.
самопо́мощ|ь, и *f.* self-help.
самопроизво́льност|ь, и *f.* spontaneity
самопроизво́л|ьный (~ен, ~ьна) *adj.* spontaneous.
самопу́ск, а *m.* (*tech.*) self-starter.
саморо́д|ок *m.* (*min.*) nugget; (*fig.*) natural (talent); **композѝтор-с.** born composer, natural composer.
самоса́д, а *m.* home-grown tobacco.
самосва́л, а *m.* tip-up (lorry), dump truck.
самосожже́ни|е, я *nt.* self-immolation.
самосозна́ни|е, я *nt.* (self-)consciousness.
самосохране́ни|е, я *nt.* self-preservation.
самостоя́тельно *adv.* independently; on one's own.
самостоя́тельност|ь, и *f.* independence.
самостоя́тел|ьный (~ен, ~ьна) *adj.* independent.
самостре́л[1]**, а** *m.* (*hist.*) cross-bow.
самостре́л[2]**, а** *m.* person with self-inflicted wound.
самосу́д, а *m.* mob law
самотёк, а *m.* drift (*also fig.*); **пусти́ть де́ло на с.** to let things slide.
самотёком *adv.* **1.** (*tech.*) by gravity. **2.** haphazard; of its own accord; **идти́ с.** to drift.
самоуби́йственный *adj.* suicidal (*also fig.*).
самоуби́йств|о, а *nt.* suicide; **поко́нчить жизнь ~ом** to commit suicide.
самоуби́йц|а, ы *c.g.* suicide (*agent*).
самоуваже́ни|е, я *nt.* self-esteem.
самоуве́ренност|ь, и *f.* self-confidence, self-assurance.
самоуве́рен|ный (~, ~на) *adj.* self-confident, self-assured.
самоуправле́ни|е, я *nt.* self-government; **ме́стное с.** local government.
самоуправля́ющийся *adj.* self-governing.
самоупра́вно *adv.* arbitrarily; **поступа́ть с.** to take the law into one's own hands.
самоупра́вный *adj.* arbitrary.
самоупра́вств|о, а *nt.* arbitrariness.
самоучи́тел|ь, я *m.* self-instructor, manual for self-tuition.
самоу́чк|а, и *c.g.* self-taught person.
самохва́льств|о, а *nt.* self-advertisement.
самохо́дк|а, и *f.* self-propelled gun.
самохо́дный *adj.* self-propelled.
самоцве́т, а *m.* semi-precious stone.
самоцве́т|ный *adj.*: **с. ка́мень** = **~**
самоце́л|ь, и *f.* end in itself.
самочи́нный *adj.* arbitrary, unauthorized.
самочу́встви|е, я *nt.* general state; **как ва́ше с.?** how are you feeling?
самура́|й, я *m.* samurai.
самши́т, а *m.* box(-tree).
са́м|ый *pron.* **1.** (*in conjunction with nn., esp. denoting points of time or place, and with* **тот** *and* **э́тот**) the very, right; **в ~ое вре́мя** at the right time; **с ~ого нача́ла** right from the start; **с ~ого утра́** ever since the morning, since first thing; **в ~ом углу́** right in the corner; **до ~ого ве́рха** to the very top, right to the top; **до ~ого Владивосто́ка** all the way to Vladivostok; **в с. раз** (*coll.*) just right; **в~ом де́ле** indeed; **в ~ом де́ле?** indeed?; really?; **на ~ом де́ле** actually, in (actual) fact; **тот с. челове́к, кото́рый...** the very man who...; **на э́том ~ом ме́сте** on this very spot. **2.: тот же с. (кото́рый, что); тако́й же с. (как)** the same (as); **э́тот же с.** the same. **3.** *forms superl. of adjs.; also expr. superl. in conjunction with certain nn. denoting degree of quantity or quality*; **с. глу́пый** the stupidest, the most stupid; **~ые пустяки́** the merest trifles.
сан, а *m.* rank; office; **высо́кий с.** high office; **духо́вный с.** holy orders; **быть посвящённым в духо́вный с.** to be ordained.
сан... *comb. form, abbr. of* **санита́рный**
санато́ри|й, я *m.* sanatorium.
сангвини́ческий *adj.* sanguine.
санда́л, а *m.* sandal-wood tree.
санда́ли|я, и *f.* sandal.
санда́ловый *adj.* sandal-wood.
са́н|и, е́й *no sg.* sledge, sleigh; **е́хать в, на ~я́х** to drive in a sledge.
санита́р, а *m.* hospital orderly; (*mil.*) medical orderly.
санитари́|я, и *f.* sanitation.
санита́рн|ый *adj.* **1.** medical; hospital; **~ая полева́я су́мка** (*mil.*) first-aid kit; **с. самолёт** ambulance plane; **~ое су́дно** hospital ship; **~ая часть** (*mil.*) medical unit. **2.** sanitary; **с. врач** sanitary inspector; **с. день** cleaning day; **~ые пра́вила** sanitary regulations.
са́н|ки, ок *no sg.* **1.** = **~и. 2.** toboggan.
Санкт-Петербу́рг, а *m.* St. Petersburg.
санкт-петербу́ргский *adj.* St. Petersburg.
санкт-петербурж|а́нка, а́нки *f. of* **~ец**
санкт-петербу́рж|ец, ца *m.* St. Petersburger.
санкциони́р|овать, ую *impf. and pf.* to sanction.
са́нкци|я, и *f.* **1.** sanction, approval. **2.** *pl.* (*pol., econ.*) sanctions.
са́н|ный *adj. of* **~и; с. путь** sleigh-road.
санови́т|ый (~, ~а) *adj.* **1.** high-ranking. **2.** (*fig.*) imposing.
сано́вник, а *m.* dignitary, high official.
сано́вный *adj.* high-ranking.
санскри́т, а *m.* Sanscrit.
санскрито́лог, а *m.* Sanscrit scholar.
санскри́тский *adj.* Sanscrit.
санте́хник|а, и *f.* sanitary engineering.
санте́хник, а *m.* sanitary engineer.
сантигра́мм, а *m.* centigram.
санти́м, а *m.* centime.
сантиме́нт|ы, ов *no sg.* (*coll.*) sentimentality.
сантиме́тр, а *m.* **1.** centimetre. **2.** tape-measure.
сану́з|ел, ла́ *m.* sanitary unit.
сап, а *m.* (*med.*) glanders.
са́п|а, ы *f.* (*mil.*) sap; **ти́хой ~ой** on the sly, on the quiet.
сапёр, а *m.* (*mil.*) sapper.
сапёр|ный *adj. of* **~; ~ные рабо́ты** field engineering.
сапо́г, а́, *g.pl.* **сапо́г** *m.* (high-)boot.
сапо́жник, а *m.* shoemaker, cobbler.
сапо́жн|ый *adj.* boot, shoe; **~ая ва́кса, с. крем** blacking, shoe-polish.
сапфи́р, а *m.* sapphire.
Сара́ев|о, а *nt.* Sarajevo.
сара́|й, я *m.* shed; (*fig.*; *of uncomfortable room or dwelling*) barn; **каре́тный с.** coach-house; **сенно́й с.** hay-loft; **с. для дров** wood-shed.
саранч|а́, и *no pl., f.* locust(s).
сарафа́н, а *m.* sarafan (*Russ. peasant women's dress, without sleeves and buttoning in front*); tunic dress.
сарде́льк|а, и *f.* saveloy.

сарди́н|а, ы *f.* sardine, pilchard.
сардони́ческий *adj.* sardonic.
са́рж|а, и *f.* (*text.*) serge.
сарка́зм, а *m.* sarcasm.
саркасти́ческий *adj.* sarcastic.
саркофа́г, а *m.* sarcophagus.
сары́ч, а́ *m.* (*zool.*) buzzard.
сатан|а́, ы́ *m.* Satan.
сатани́нский *adj.* Satanic.
сателли́т, а *m.* (*astron.*; *fig.*) satellite.
сати́н, а *m.* (*text.*) sateen.
сатине́т, а *m.* (*text.*) satinet(te).
сатини́р|овать, ую *impf. and pf.* to satin.
сати́н|овый *adj. of* ~
сати́р, а *m.* (*myth.*) satyr.
сати́р|а, ы *f.* satire.
сати́рик, а *m.* satirist.
сатири́ческий *adj.* satirical.
сатра́п, а *m.* satrap.
сатра́пи|я, и *f.* satrapy.
са́ун|а, ы *f.* sauna.
сафа́ри *nt. indecl.* safari; **«с.» зоопа́рк** safari park.
сафья́н, а *m.* morocco (leather).
сафья́новый *adj.* morocco(-leather).
са́хар, а (у) *m.* sugar.
Саха́р|а, ы *f.* the Sahara.
сахари́н, а *m.* saccharin(e).
са́харист|ый (~, ~а) *adj.* sugary; saccharine.
са́харниц|а, ы *f.* sugar-basin.
са́хар|ный *adj. of* ~; (*fig.*) sugary; **~ная боле́знь** (*med.*) diabetes; **~ная глазу́рь** icing; **~ная голова́** sugar-loaf; **с. заво́д** sugar-refinery; **с. песо́к** granulated sugar; **~ная пу́дра** icing sugar; **~ная свёкла** sugar-beet; **с. тростни́к** sugar-cane.
сахаро́з|а, ы *f.* (*chem.*) sucrose.
сачк|ова́ть, у́ю *impf.* (*coll.*) to skive, loaf.
сач|о́к[1], **ка́** *m.* net; **с. для ры́бы** landing-net; **с. для ба́бочек** butterfly-net.
сач|о́к[2], **ка́** *m.* (*coll.*) skiver, loafer.
сба́в|ить, лю, ишь *pf.* (*of* **~ля́ть**) **(с+*g.*)** to take off (from), deduct (from); **с. с цены́** to reduce the price; **с. в ве́се** to lose weight; **с. газ** (*tech.*) to throttle back.
сбавля́|ть, ю *impf. of* **сба́вить**
сбаланси́р|овать, ую *pf. of* **баланси́ровать**
сбе́га|ть, ю *pf.* **(за+*i.*;** *coll.*) to run (for), run and fetch.
сбега́|ть(ся), ю(сь) *impf. of* **сбежа́ть(ся)**
сбе|жа́ть, гу́, жи́шь гу́т *pf.* (*of* **~га́ть**) **1. (с+*g.*)** to run down (from); **с. с ле́стницы** to run downstairs. **2.** to run away. **3. (с+*g.*;** *fig.*) to disappear, vanish.
сбе|жа́ться, жи́тся, гу́тся *pf.* (*of* **~га́ться**) to come running.
сбер... *comb. form, abbr. of* **сберега́тельный**
сберега́тельн|ый *adj.*: **~ая ка́сса** savings bank; **~ая кни́жка** savings book.
сберега́|ть, ю *impf. of* **сбере́чь**
сбереже́ни|е, я *nt.* **1.** economy. **2.** (*pl.*) savings.
сбере́|чь, гу́, жёшь, гу́т, *past* **~̈г, ~гла́** *pf.* (*of* **~га́ть**) **1.** to save, preserve; to protect. **2.** to save, save up, put aside.
сберка́сс|а, ы *f.* savings bank.
сберкни́жк|а, и *f.* savings book.
сбива́лк|а, и *f.* (*cul.*) (egg-)whisk.
сбива́|ть, ю *impf. of* **сбить**
сбива́|ться, юсь *impf.* **1.** *impf. of* **сби́ться. 2.** *impf. only* **(на+*a.*)** to resemble; to remind one (of).
сби́вчив|ый (~, ~а) *adj.* inconsistent, contradictory.
сби́т|ый *p.p.p. of* **~ь** *and adj.*: **~ые сли́вки** whipped cream.
сбить, собью́, собьёшь *pf.* (*of* **сбива́ть**) **1.** to bring down, knock down; to knock off, dislodge; **с. самолёт** to shoot down an aircraft; **с. проти́вника с пози́ций** to dislodge the enemy from his positions; **с. це́ну** to beat down the price; **с. спесь с кого́-н.** to bring s.o. down a peg. **2.** to put out; to distract; to deflect; **с. с та́кта** to throw out of time; **с. кого́-н. с то́лку** to confuse s.o.; **с. с пути́ и́стинного** (*fig.*) to lead s.o. astray. **3.** to wear down. **4.** to knock together. **5.** (*impf. also* **бить**) to churn; to whip, whisk.
сби́ться, собью́сь, собьёшься *pf.* (*of* **сбива́ться**) **1.** to be dislodged; to slip; **с. с ног** (*coll.*) to be run off one's feet. **2.** to be deflected; to go wrong; **с. в вычисле́ниях** to be out in one's calculations; **с. с доро́ги, с. с пути́** to lose one's way; to go astray (*also fig.*); **с. со счёта** to lose count; **с. с та́кта** to get out of time. **3.** to become worn down; to become blunt. **4.: с. в ку́чу, с. толпо́й** to bunch, huddle.
сближа́|ть(ся), ю(сь) *impf. of* **сбли́зить(ся)**
сближе́ние, я *nt.* **1.** rapprochement. **2.** (*mil.*) approach, closing in. **3.** intimacy.
сбли́|зить, жу, зишь *pf.* (*of* **~жа́ть**) to bring together, draw together.
сбли́|зиться, жусь, зишься *pf.* (*of* **~жа́ться**) **1.** to draw together, converge. **2. (с+*i.*)** to become close friends (with). **3.** (*mil.*) to approach, close in.
сбо|й, я *m.* failure, shortcoming.
сбо́ку *adv.* from one side; on one side; **вид с.** side-view; **смотре́ть на кого́-н. с.** to look sideways at s.o.
сбор, а *m.* **1.** collection; **с. нало́гов** tax collection. **2.** dues; duty; takings, returns; **ге́рбовый с.** stamp-duty; **порто́вый с.** harbour dues; **тамо́женный с.** customs duty; **по́лный с.** (*theatr.*) full house; **де́лать хоро́шие ~̈ы** (*theatr.*) to play to packed houses. **3.** assembly, gathering. **4.** (*mil.*) muster. **5.** (*mil.*) (periodical) training; **уче́бный с.** refresher course. **6.** (*pl.*) preparations.
сбо́рищ|е, а *nt.* gathering, mob.
сбо́рк|а, и *f.* **1.** (*tech.*) assembly, erection. **2.** (*in dress, etc.*) gather.
сбо́рник, а *m.* collection; anthology.
сбо́рн|ый *adj.* **1.** that can be taken to pieces, detachable; **с. дом** prefabricated house. **2.** mixed, combined; **~ая кома́нда** (*sport*) combined team. **3.** (*mil.*) assembly; **с. пункт** assembly point.
сбо́рочный *adj.* (*tech.*) assembly; **с. конве́йер** assembly belt; **с. цех** assembly shop.
сбо́рщик, а *m.* **1.** collector; **с. нало́гов** tax-collector. **2.** (*tech.*) assembler, fitter.
сбра́сыва|ть, ю *impf. of* **сбро́сить**
сбрива́|ть, ю *impf. of* **сбрить**
сбрить, сбре́ю, сбре́ешь *pf.* (*of* **сбрива́ть**) to shave off.
сброд, а *no pl., m.* (*collect.*) riff-raff, rabble.
сбро́|сить, шу, сишь *pf.* (*of* **сбра́сывать**) **1.** to throw down; to drop; **с. бо́мбы** to drop bombs. **2.** to throw off (*also fig.*); to cast off, shed; **с. с себя́ одея́ло** to throw off a blanket; **с. и́го** to throw off the yoke. **3.** (*cards*) to discard.
сбру́|я, и *f.* (*collect.*) harness.
сбыва́|ть(ся), ю(сь) *impf. of* **сбы́ть(ся)**
сбыт, а *no pl., m.* (*econ., comm.*) sale; **ры́нок ~̈а** (seller's) market; **хоро́ший с.** good sales.
сбытово́й *adj.* (*econ., comm.*) selling, marketing.
сбы́тчик, а *m.*: **с. нарко́тиков** drug trafficker.
сбыть[1], **сбу́ду, сбу́дешь,** *past* **сбыл, сбыла́, сбы́ло** *pf.* (*of* **сбыва́ть**) **1.** to sell, market. **2.** (*coll.*) to get rid (of); (*comm.*) to dump; **с. с рук** to get off one's hands.
сбыть[2], **сбу́дет,** *past* **сбыл, сбыла́, сбы́ло** *pf.* (*of* **сбыва́ть**) (*of level of water*) to fall.
сбы́ться, сбу́дется, *past* **сбы́лся, сбыла́сь** *pf.* (*of* **сбыва́ться**) to come true, be realized.
св. (*abbr. of* **свято́й**) St, Saint.
сва́дебный *adj.* wedding; nuptial; **с. пода́рок** wedding present.

сва́д|ьба, ьбы, *g. pl.* **~еб** *f.* wedding; **справля́ть ~ьбу** to celebrate a wedding.
сва́йн|ый *adj.* pile; **~ые постро́йки** pile-dwellings.
сва́лива|ть(ся), ю(сь) *impf. of* **свали́ть(ся)**
свал|и́ть[1]**, ю́, ~́ишь** *pf.* (*of* **вали́ть**[1] *and* **~́ивать**) **1.** to throw down, bring down; to overthrow; to lay low. **2.** to heap up, pile up; **с. вину́ (на**+*a.*) to lump the blame (on).
свал|и́ть[2]**, ~и́т** *pf.* (*coll.*) to sink, drop, fall, abate.
свал|и́ться, ю́сь, ~́ишся *pf.* (*of* **вали́ться** *and* **~́иваться**) to fall (down), collapse; **с. как снег на́ го́лову** to come like a bolt from the blue.
сва́лк|а, и *f.* **1.** dump; scrap heap. **2.** (*coll.*) scuffle, fight; **о́бщая с.** free-for-all, mêlée.
сваля́|ть, ю *pf. of* **валя́ть 3., 4.**
сва́рива|ть, ю *impf. of* **свари́ть**
свар|и́ть, ю, ~́ишь *pf.* **1.** *pf. of* **вари́ть. 2.** (*impf.* **~́ивать**) (*tech.*) to weld.
свар|и́ться, ю́сь, ~́ишься *pf. of* **вари́ться**
сва́рк|а, и *f.* (*tech.*) welding.
сварли́в|ый (~, ~а) *adj.* quarrelsome; shrewish.
сварно́й *adj.* (*tech.*) welded; **с. шов** welded joint.
сва́рочн|ый *adj.* (*tech.*) welding; **~ая горе́лка** welding torch, burner; **~ое желе́зо** wrought iron.
сва́рщик, а *m.* welder.
сва́стик|а, и *f.* swastika.
сват, а *m.* **1.** matchmaker. **2.** son-in-law's father; daughter-in-law's father.
сва́та|ть, ю *impf.* (*of* **по~**) **1.** (*pf. also* **со~**) (+*a. and d.*) to propose as husband; (*also* +*a.* **за**+*a.*) to propose as wife; to (try to) marry off (to); to (try to) arrange a match (between); **ему́, за него́ ~ют каку́ю-то неме́цкую ба́рышню** they are trying to arrange a match for him with a German girl. **2.** to ask in marriage.
сва́та|ться, юсь *impf.* (*of* **по~**) (**к; за**+*a.*) to court; to ask, seek in marriage.
сва́ть|я, и *f.* son-in-law's mother; daughter-in-law's mother.
сва́х|а, и *f.* matchmaker.
сва́|я, и *f.* pile.
све́дени|е, я *nt.* **1.** piece of information; (*pl.*) information, intelligence. **2.** knowledge; attention, consideration, notice; **дойти́ до чьего́-н. ~я** to come to s.o.'s attention; **довести́ до чьего́-н. ~я** to bring to s.o.'s attention, inform s.o.; **приня́ть к ~ю** to take into consideration. **3.** (*pl.*) knowledge; **у него́ бо́льшие ~я по исто́рии Росси́и** he is very knowledgeable about the history of Russia.
сведе́ни|е, я *nt.* **1.** reduction; **с. счётов** settling of accounts. **2.** (*med.*) contraction, cramp.
све́дущ|ий (~, ~а) *adj.* (**в**+*p.*) knowledgeable (about); (well-)versed (in).
свеж|ева́ть, у́ю *impf.* (*of* **о~**) to skin, dress.
све́жест|ь, и *f.* freshness; coolness; **не пе́рвой ~и** (*coll.*) past its (*fig., joc.*; one's) best.
свеже́|ть, ю *impf.* (*of* **по~**) **1.** to become cooler; (*of the wind*) to freshen (up), blow up. **2.** to freshen up, acquire a glow of health.
све́ж|ий (~, ~а́, ~о́, ~́и) *adj.* fresh; **~ее бельё** clean underclothes; **с. ве́тер** fresh breeze; **на ~ем во́здухе** in the fresh air; **~ие но́вости** recent news; **со ~ими си́лами** with renewed strength; **с. цвет лица́** fresh complexion; **~о́ в па́мяти** fresh in one's memory; (*impers., as pred.*): **~о́** it is fresh, it is blowing up.
свез|ти́, у́, ёшь, *past* **~̈, ~ла́** *pf.* (*of* **свози́ть**[1]) **1.** to take, convey; **его́ ~ли́ в больни́цу** he has been taken to hospital. **2.** to take down. **3.** to take away, clear away.
свёкл|а, ы *f.* beet, beetroot; **са́харная с.** sugar-beet.
свеклови́ц|а, ы *f.* sugar-beet.
свеклови́|чный *adj. of* **~ца; с. са́хар** beet-sugar.
свеклоса́харный *adj.* sugar-beet; beet-sugar.
свеко́льник, а *m.* **1.** beetroot soup. **2.** beet tops.
свеко́льный *adj. of* **свёкла**
свёк|ор, ра *m.* father-in-law (*husband's father*).
свекро́в|ь, и *f.* mother-in-law (*husband's mother*).
сверг|а́ть, а́ю *impf. of* **~́нуть**
све́рг|нуть, ну, нешь, *past* **~, ~ла** *pf.* (*of* **~а́ть**) to overthrow; to depose; **с. с престо́ла** to dethrone.
сверже́ни|е, я *nt.* overthrow.
све́р|ить, ю, ишь *pf.* (*of* **~я́ть**) (+*a.* **с**+*i.*) to collate (with); to check (against); **с. корректу́ру с ру́кописью** to check proofs against a manuscript.
све́р|иться, юсь, ишься *pf.* (*of* **~я́ться**) (**с**+*i.*) to check (with).
све́рк|а, и *f.* collation.
сверка́ни|е, я *nt.* sparkling, twinkling; glitter; glare.
сверка́|ть, ю *impf.* to sparkle, twinkle; to glitter; to gleam.
сверкн|у́ть, у́, ёшь *pf.* to flash (*also fig.*).
сверли́льный *adj.* (*tech.*) boring, drilling.
сверл|и́ть, ю, и́шь *impf.* **1.** (*tech.*) to bore, drill; **с. зуб** to drill a tooth. **2.** to bore through. **3.** (*fig.*; *of mental or physical pain*) to nag (at), gnaw (at); **его́ ~и́ла мысль об уби́том** the image of the murdered man nagged at him; **у меня́ ~и́т в у́хе** I have a nagging earache.
сверл|о́, а́, *pl.* **~̈а** *nt.* (*tech.*) drill.
сверл|я́щий *pres. part. act. of* **~ить** *and adj.*; **~я́щая боль** nagging, gnawing pain.
сверн|у́ть, у́, ёшь *pf.* (*of* **свёртывать** *and* **свора́чивать**) **1.** to roll (up); **с. папиро́су** to roll a cigarette; **с. паруса́** to furl sails; **с. ше́ю кому́-н.** to wring s.o.'s neck. **2.** (*fig.*) to curtail, cut back. **3.** to turn; **с нале́во** to turn to the left; **с. с доро́ги** to turn off the road.
сверн|у́ться, у́сь, ёшься *pf.* (*of* **свёртываться** *and* **свора́чиваться**) **1.** to roll up, curl up; **с. клубко́м** to roll up into a ball. **2.** to curdle, coagulate, turn. **3.** (*fig.*) to contract. **4.** *pass. of* **~уть**
свержста́|ть, ю *pf. of* **верста́ть**[1]
све́рстник, а *m.* contemporary; peer; **мы с ним ~и** he and I are the same age.
свёрт|ок, ка *m.* package, parcel, bundle.
свёртывани|е, я *nt.* **1.** rolling (up). **2.** curdling; coagulation. **3.** (*fig.*) reduction, curtailment.
свёртыва|ть(ся), ю(сь) *impf. of* **сверну́ть(ся)**
сверх *prep.*+*g.* **1.** over, above, on top of. **2.** (*fig.*) above, beyond; over and above; in excess of; **с. пла́на** in excess of the plan; **с. сил** beyond one's strength; **с. (вся́кого) ожида́ния** beyond (all) expectations; **с. всего́** on top of everything else; **с. того́** moreover, besides.
сверх... *comb. form* super-, supra-, extra-, over-, preter-.
сверхдержа́в|а, ы *f.* superpower.
сверхзвуково́й *adj.* (*phys., aeron.*) supersonic.
сверхмагистра́л|ь, и *f.*: **информацио́нная с.** information superhighway.
сверхпри́был|ь, и *f.* excess profit.
сверхпроводи́мост|ь, и *f.* (*elec.*) superconductivity.
сверхсро́чн|ый *adj.* (*mil.*): **~ая слу́жба** additional service (*voluntarily undertaken after completion of statutory period*).
све́рху *adv.* **1.** from above (*also fig.*); from the top; **с. до́низу** from top to bottom. **2.** on the surface.
сверхуро́чн|ый *adj.* overtime; **~ая рабо́та** overtime; *as n.* **~ые, ~ых** (*payment for*) overtime.
сверхчелове́к, а *m.* superman.
сверхчелове́ческий *adj.* superhuman.
сверхчувстви́тельный *adj.* supersensitive.
сверхшта́тный *adj.* supernumerary.
сверхъесте́ственный *adj.* supernatural, preternatural.

сверч|о́к, ка́ *m.* (*zool.*) cricket.
сверша́|ть(ся), ю(сь) *impf.* = **соверша́ть(ся)**
сверш|и́ть(ся), у́(сь), и́шь (ся) *pf.* = **соверши́ть(ся)**
свер|я́ть(ся), я́ю(сь) *impf. of* **~и́ть(ся)**
све́|сить, шу, сишь *pf.* (*of* **~шивать**) **1.** to let down, lower; **сиде́ть, ~сив но́ги** to sit with one's legs dangling. **2.** to weigh.
све́|ситься, шусь, сишься *pf.* (*of* **~шиваться**) to lean over; to hang over, overhang; **с. че́рез пери́ла** to lean over the banisters.
све|сти́, ду́, дёшь, *past* **~л, ~ла́** *pf.* (*of* **своди́ть**[1]) **1.** to take; **с. дете́й в шко́лу** to take the children to school; **с. в моги́лу** to be the death (of). **2.** (**с**+*g.*) to take down (from, off); **с. с ума́** to drive mad. **3.** to take away; to lead off; **с. разгово́р на другу́ю те́му** to lead the conversation onto a different subject. **4.** to remove; **с. пятно́** to remove a stain. **5.** to bring together; to put together; to unite; **с. ста́рых друзе́й** to bring old friends together; **судьба́ ~ла́ их** fate threw them together; **с. да́нные в табли́цу** to tabulate data; **с. концы́ с конца́ми** to make (both) ends meet. **6.: с. дру́жбу** (**с**+*i.*), **с. знако́мство** (**с**+*i.*) to make friends (with). **7.** (**к, на**+*a.*) to reduce (to), bring (to); **с. на нет** to negate; to nullify. **8.** to trace, transfer. **9.** to cramp, convulse; **у меня́ ~ло́ но́гу** I have cramp in my foot.
све|сти́сь, дётся, *past* **~лся, ~ла́сь** *pf.* (*of* **своди́ться**) **1.** (**к, на**+*a.*) to come (to), reduce (to); **с. на нет** to come to naught. **2.** (*of a transfer*) to come off.
свет[1], **а** *m.* **1.** light (*also fig.*); **лу́нный с.** moonlight; **заже́чь с.** to turn the light on; **в ~е** (+*g.*) in the light (of); **предста́вить в невы́годном ~е** to represent in an unfavourable light; **на ~у́** in the light; **при ~е** (+*g.*) by the light (of). **2.** daybreak; **чем с.** first thing (in the morning); **чуть с.** at first light; **ни с., ни заря́** before dawn; (*iron.*) at the crack of dawn.
све́т[2], **а** *m.* **1.** world (*also fig.*); **ста́рый, но́вый с.** the Old, the New World; **тот с.** the next world; **коне́ц ~а** doomsday, the end of the world; **произвести́ на с.** to bring into the world; **(по)яви́ться на с.** to come into the world; **вы́пустить в с.** to bring out (= *to publish*); **ни за что на ~е** not for (anything in) the world. **2.** society; **вы́сший с.** high society; **мо́дный с.** the smart set.
света́|ть, ет *impf.*; (*impers.*): **~ет** it is dawning, it is getting light, day is breaking.
свети́л|о, а *nt.* luminary (*also fig.*); **небе́сные ~а** heavenly bodies.
свети́льник, а *m.* lamp.
све|ти́ть, чу́, ~тишь *impf.* **1.** to shine. **2.** (+*d.*) to give light; to shine a light (for); **он ~ти́л нам в тунне́ле** he lit us through the tunnel.
све|ти́ться, чу́сь, ~ти́шься *impf.* to shine, gleam; **в окне́ ~тится огонёк** there is a light in the window.
светле́|ть, у *impf.* (*of* **по~**) to brighten (*also fig.*); (*of weather*) to clear up, brighten up.
све́тло... *comb. form* light-.
све́тлост|ь, и *f.* **1.** brightness (*also fig.*); lightness. **2.: его́,** *etc.*, **с.** (*title of dukes and archbishops*) his, *etc.*, Grace.
све́т|лый (~ел, ~ла́, ~ло) *adj.* **1.** light; bright; **~лые во́лосы** light hair; **с. день** bright day; **на дворе́ ~ло́** it is daylight. **2.** (*fig.*) bright, radiant, joyous; pure, unclouded; **~лое бу́дущее** radiant future; **~лой па́мяти** of blessed memory. **3.** (*fig.*) lucid, clear; **~лые мину́ты** lucid intervals. **4.** (*eccl.*) Easter; **~лая неде́ля** Easter week.
светля́к, а *m.* glow-worm; fire-fly.
светов|о́й *adj. of* **свет**[1]; **~а́я волна́** light wave; **~а́я рекла́ма** illuminated signs; **с. эффе́кт** (*theatr.*) lighting effect.
светодио́д, а *m.* light-emitting diode, LED.
светомаскиро́вк|а, и *f.* black-out.
светонепроница́емый *adj.* light-proof.
светопреставле́ни|е, я *nt.* the end of the world, doomsday.
светофо́р, а *m.* traffic lights.
све́точ, а *m.* **1.** (*obs.*) torch, lamp. **2.** (*fig.*) leading light, luminary; torch-bearer.
светочувстви́тел|ьный (~ен, ~ьна) *adj.* photosensitive.
све́тск|ий *adj.* **1.** society, fashionable; **~ая жизнь** high life; **с. челове́к** man about town. **2.** (*obs.*) genteel, refined; **~ие мане́ры** genteel manners. **3.** temporal, lay, secular; worldly.
свет|я́щийся *pres. part. of* **~и́ться** *and adj.* luminous, luminescent, fluorescent, phosphorescent.
свеч|а́, и, *i.* **~о́й,** *pl.* **~и, ~е́й, ~а́м** *f.* **1.** candle; taper; **жечь ~у́ с двух концо́в** to burn the candle at both ends. **2.: запа́льная с.** sparking-plug. **3.** lamp candle-power; **ла́мпочка в пятьдеся́т ~е́й** lamp of fifty candle-power.
свече́ни|е, я *nt.* luminescence, fluorescence; phosphorescence.
све́чк|а, и *f.* **1.** candle. **2.** (*med.*) suppository.
свеч|но́й *adj. of* **~а́; с. ога́рок** candle-end.
све́ша|ть, ю *pf.* to weigh.
све́шива|ть(ся), ю(сь) *impf. of* **све́сить(ся)**
свива́льник, а *m.* swaddling-clothes.
свива́|ть, ю *impf.* **1.** *impf. of* **свить. 2.** *impf. only* to swaddle.
свида́ни|е, я *nt.* meeting; appointment; reunion; rendezvous; date; **до ~я!** good-bye!; **до ско́рого ~я!** see you soon!
свиде́тел|ь, я *m.* witness; bystander; **с. обвине́ния** witness for the prosecution; **с. Иего́вы** Jehovah's Witness.
свиде́тельств|о, а *nt.* **1.** evidence; testimony. **2.** certificate; **с. о рожде́нии/бра́ке** birth, marriage certificate.
свиде́тельств|овать, ую *impf.* **1.** (**о**+*p.*, +*a. or* +**что**) (*leg.*) to give evidence (concerning); to testify (to) (*also fig.*); (*fig.*) to attest to, be evidence (of); **письмо́ э́то ~ует о его́ беста́ктности** this letter is evidence of his tactlessness. **2.** (*pf.* **за~**) to witness; to attest, certify; **с. ко́пию** to certify a copy; **с. по́дпись** to witness a signature. **3.** (*pf.* **о~**) to examine, inspect; **с. больно́го** to examine a patient.
свина́рник, а *m.* pigsty.
свин|е́ц, ца́ *m.* lead.
свини́н|а, ы *f.* pork.
сви́нк|а[1], **ки** *f. dim. of* **~ья́; морска́я с.** guinea-pig.
сви́нк|а[2], **и** *f.* (*med.*) mumps.
свиново́д, а *m.* pig-breeder.
свиново́дств|о, а *nt.* pig-breeding.
свиново́д|ческий *adj. of* **~ство**
свин|о́й *adj. of* **~ья́; ~а́я ко́жа** pigskin; **~а́я котле́та** pork chop; **~о́е са́ло** lard.
свинома́тк|а, и *f.* sow.
свинопа́с, а *m.* swineherd.
свинофе́рм|а, ы *f.* pig-farm, piggery.
сви́нский *adj.* (*coll.*) swinish.
сви́нств|о, а *nt.* (*coll.*) swinishness; swinish trick.
свин|ти́ть, чу́, ти́шь *pf.* (*of* **~чивать**) **1.** to screw together. **2.** to unscrew.
свинцо́в|ый *adj.* lead; leaden; **~ые бели́ла** white lead; **с. блеск** (*min.*) galena; **~ая дробь** lead shot; **~ое отравле́ние** lead-poisoning; **с. су́рик** red lead.
сви́нчива|ть, ю *impf. of* **свинти́ть**
свин|ья́, ьи́, *pl.* **~ьи, ~е́й** *f.* **1.** pig, swine; hog; sow; **морска́я с.** porpoise. **2.** (*fig.*) swine; **подложи́ть ~ью́** (+*d.*; *coll.*) to play a dirty trick (on).
свире́л|ь, и *f.* (reed-)pipe.
свирепе́|ть, ю *impf.* to grow fierce, grow savage.

свире́пост|ь, и *f.* ferocity, savageness; truculence.
свире́пств|овать, ую *impf.* to rage.
свире́п|ый *adj.* fierce, ferocious, savage; truculent.
свиристе́л|ь, я *m.* (*zool.*) waxwing.
свис|а́ть, а́ю *impf.* (*of* **~нуть**) to hang down, droop.
сви́с|нуть, ну, нешь *pf. of* **~а́ть**
свист, а *m.* whistle; whistling; hiss, hissing.
сви|ста́ть, щу́, ~щешь *impf.* to whistle; **с. в свисто́к** to blow a whistle; **с. всех наве́рх** (*naut.*) to pipe all hands on deck.
сви|сте́ть, щу́, сти́шь *impf.* to whistle; to hiss; **ищи́ ~щи́** (*coll.*) you can whistle for it.
сви́стн|уть, у, ешь *pf.* **1.** to give a whistle. **2.** (*coll.*) to pinch, swipe.
свист|о́к, ка́ *m.* whistle.
свистопля́ск|а, и *f.* (*coll.*) pandemonium, bedlam.
свисту́льк|а, и *f.* penny whistle, tin whistle.
свисту́н, а́ *m.* whistler.
сви́т|а, ы *f.* suite, retinue.
сви́тер, а *m.* sweater.
сви́т|ок, ка *m.* roll; scroll.
свить, совью́, совьёшь, *past* **свил, свила́, сви́ло** *pf.* (*of* **вить** *and* **свива́ть**) to twist, wind.
сви́ться, совью́сь, совьёшься, *past* **сви́лся, свила́сь** *pf.* (*of* **ви́ться**) to roll up, curl up, coil.
свихн|у́ть, у́, ёшь *pf.* to dislocate, sprain.
свихн|у́ться, у́сь, ёшься *pf.* (*coll.*) **1.** to go off one's head. **2.** to go astray, go off the rails.
свищ, а́ *m.* **1.** (*in wood*) knot hole. **2.** (*med.*) fistula.
свия́з|ь, и *f.* (*zool.*) wigeon.
свобо́д|а, ы *f.* freedom, liberty; **с. во́ли** free will; **с. сло́ва** freedom of speech; **с. торго́вли** free trade; **вы́пустить на ~у** to set free; **предоста́вить по́лную ~у де́йствий** (+*d.*) to give a free hand, give carte blanche; **на ~е** (*i*) at leisure, (*ii*) at large.
свобо́дно *adv.* **1.** freely; easily, with ease; fluently; **она́ с. говори́т на пяти́ языка́х** she speaks five languages fluently. **2.** (*of clothing*) loose, loosely.
свобо́д|ный (~ен, ~на) *adj.* **1.** free (= *at liberty*). **2.** free (= *unhampered, unrestrained*); easy; **с. до́ступ** easy access; **с. уда́р** (*sport*) free kick; **с. от недоста́тков** free from defects. **3.** free (= *disengaged*); vacant; spare; **~ное вре́мя** free time; spare time; **~ное ме́сто** vacant place, vacant seat; **здесь ~но?** is this seat taken? **4.** free-and-easy, relaxed. **5.** (*of clothing*) loose, loose-fitting.
свободолюби́в|ый (~, ~а) *adj.* freedom-loving.
свободолю́би|е, я *nt.* love of freedom.
свободомы́сли|е, я *nt.* free-thinking.
свободомы́слящ|ий *adj.* free-thinking; *as n.* **с., ~его** *m.* free-thinker.
свод[1], **а** *m.* code; **с. зако́нов** code of laws.
свод[2], **а** *m.* arch, vault; **небе́сный с.** the firmament.
сво|ди́ть[1], **жу́, ~дишь** *impf. of* **свести́**
сво|ди́ть[2], **жу́, ~дишь** *pf.* to take (*and bring back*); **вчера́ мы ~ди́ли дете́й в кино́** we took the children to the cinema yesterday.
сво|ди́ться, жу́сь, ~дишься *impf. of* **свести́сь**
сво́дк|а, и *f.* summary; report; **с. пого́ды** weather forecast, weather report.
сво́дник, а *m.* pimp.
сво́днича|ть, ю *impf.* to pander.
сво́дничеств|о, а *nt.* procuring, pimping.
сво́дн|ый *adj.* **1.** composite, combined; consolidated; **с. отря́д** (*mil.*) combined force; **~ая табли́ца** summary table, index. **2.** step-; **с. брат** step-brother.
сво́дчатый *adj.* arched, vaulted.
своевла́ст|ный (~ен, ~на) *adj.* despotic.
своево́ли|е, я *nt.* self-will, wilfulness.
своево́л|ьный (~ен, ~ьна) *adj.* self-willed, wilful.
своевре́менно *adv.* in good time; opportunely.
своевре́мен|ный (~ен, ~на) *adj.* timely, opportune.
своекоры́сти|е, я *nt.* self-interest.
своекоры́ст|ный (~ен, ~на) *adj.* self-seeking.
своенра́ви|е, я *nt.* wilfulness.
своенра́в|ный (~ен, ~на) *adj.* wilful.
своеобра́зи|е, я *nt.* originality; peculiarity.
своеобра́з|ный (~ен, ~на) *adj.* original; peculiar, distinctive.
сво|зи́ть[1], **жу́, ~зишь** *impf. of* **свезти́**
сво|зи́ть[2], **жу́, ~зишь** *pf.* to take (*and bring back*); **мы ~зи́ли дете́й в цирк** we took the children to the circus.
свой *possessive adj.* one's (my, your, his, *etc.*, *in accordance with subject of sentence or clause*), one's own; **у них с. дом** they have a house of their own; **своё варе́нье** home-made jam; **свои́ войска́** friendly troops; **кри́кнуть не свои́м го́лосом** to give a frenzied scream; **в своё вре́мя** (*i*) at one time, in my, his, etc., time, (*ii*) in due time, in due course; **в своём ро́де** in one's own way; **он не в своём уме́** he is off his head; **на свои́х на двои́х** on Shanks' pony; **она́ сама́ не своя́** she is not herself; **он у нас с. челове́к** he's one of us; *as n.* **свои́** one's (own) people; **своё** one's own; **доби́ться своего́** to get one's own way; **получи́ть своё** to get one's own back.
сво́йственник, а *m.* relative by marriage; in-law; **он мне с.** he is related to me by marriage.
сво́йствен|ный (~ *and* ~ен, ~на) *adj.* (+*d.*) characteristic (of).
сво́йств|о, а *nt.* property, attribute, characteristic.
свойств|о́, а *nt.* relationship by marriage; **быть в ~е́ с кем-н.** to be related to s.o. by marriage.
свола́кива|ть, ю *impf. of* **своло́чь**
сво́лоч|ь, и, *g. pl.* **~е́й** *f.* (*coll.*) **1.** (*as term of abuse*) scum, swine. **2.** (*collect.*) riff-raff, rabble.
своло́|чь, ку́, чёшь, ку́т, *past* **~к, ~кла́** *pf.* (*of* **свола́кивать**) (*coll.*) **1.** to drag off. **2.** (*fig.*) to knock off.
сво́р|а, ы *f.* **1.** leash. **2.** (*collect.*) pack (*of hounds*); (*fig.*) gang.
свора́чива|ть, ю *impf. of* **сверну́ть** *and* **свороти́ть**
свор|ова́ть, у́ю *pf. of* **ворова́ть**
своро|ти́ть, чу́, ~тишь *pf.* (*of* **свора́чивать**) (*coll.*) **1.** to dislodge, displace, shift. **2.** to turn, swing (*also trans.*); **с. с доро́ги** to turn off the road; **с. с ума́** to go off one's head. **3.** to twist, dislocate; to break.
своя́к, а́ *m.* brother-in-law (*husband of wife's sister*).
своя́чениц|а, ы *f.* sister-in-law (*wife's sister*).
СВЧ-печ|ь, и *f.* (*abbr. of* **сверхвысокочасто́тная печь**) microwave (oven).
свык|а́ться, а́юсь *impf. of* **~нуться**
сви́к|нуться, нусь, нешься, *past* **~ся, ~лась** *pf.* (*of* **~а́ться**) (**с**+*i.*) to get used (to).
свысока́ *adv.* (*pej.*) condescendingly; **обраща́ться с кем-н. с.** to talk down to, patronize s.o.
свы́ше 1. *adv.* from above; (*relig.*) from on high. **2.** *prep.*+*g.* over, more than; beyond; **с. ты́сячи самолётов уча́ствовало в налёте** over a thousand planes took part in the raid; **э́то с. мои́х сил** it is beyond me.
свя́з|анный *p.p.p. of* **~а́ть** *and adj.* constrained; **~анная речь** halting speech.
свя|за́ть, жу́, ~жешь *pf.* (*of* **вяза́ть** *and* **~зывать**) **1.** to tie; to bind (*also fig.*); **с. по рука́м и нога́м** to bind hand and foot (*also fig.*); **с. свою́ судьбу́** (**с**+*i.*) to throw in one's lot (with). **2.** (*fig.*) to connect, link; **быть (те́сно) ~занным, ~зано** (**с**+*i.*) to be (closely) connected (with), be bound up (with), be tied up (with). **3. (быть) ~зано** (**с**+*i.*; *fig.*) to involve, entail; **э́то предприя́тие бу́дет ~зано с огро́мными расхо́дами** this undertaking will involve huge expense. **4.** to link, associate.
свя|за́ться, жу́сь, ~жешься *pf.* (*of* **~зываться**) (**с**+*i.*) **1.** to contact, get in touch (with). **2.** (*coll., pej.*) to get involved (with).

связи́ст, а *m.* (*mil.*) signaller.
свя́зк|а, и *f.* **1.** sheaf; bunch. **2.** (*anat.*) cord; ligament; **голосовы́е ~и** vocal cords. **3.** (*gram.*) copula.
связн|о́й *adj.* (*mil.*) liaison, communication; **с. самолёт** liaison aircraft; **~а́я соба́ка** messenger dog; *as n.* **с., ~о́го** *m.* messenger, runner.
свя́зный *adj.* coherent.
связу́ющий *adj.* connecting, linking.
свя́зыва|ть, ю *impf. of* **связа́ть**
свя́зыва|ться, юсь *impf.* **1.** *impf. of* **связа́ться. 2.** *impf. only* (**с**+*i.*) to have to do (with); **не ~йся с ни́ми** don't have anything to do with them.
связ|ь, и, о ≁и, в ≁и́ *f.* **1.** connection; **в ~и́ с э́тим** in this connection. **2.** link, tie, bond; **дру́жеские ≁и** ties of friendship; **потеря́ть с.** (**с**+*i.*) to lose touch (with). **3.** (*sexual*) liaison, relationship. **4.** (*pl.*) connections, contacts. **5.** communication; (*mil.*) intercommunication; signals; liaison. **6.** (*sg. only*) (postal and tele-) communications; **Министе́рство ≁и** Ministry of Communications; **рабо́тник ~и** post office worker. **7.** (*tech.*) tie, stay, brace, strut; (*elec.*) coupling.
святе́йшеств|о, а *nt.*: **его́ с.** (*title of Patriarchs and of the Pope*) His Holiness.
святе́йший *adj.* most holy (*pertaining to the Patriarchs and synod of the Orthodox Church, also to the Pope*); **с. патриа́рх** His Holiness the Patriarch.
святи́лищ|е, а *nt.* sanctuary.
свя|ти́ть, чу́, ти́шь *impf.* (*of* **о~**) to consecrate; to bless, sanctify.
свя́т|ки, ок *no sg.* Yuletide.
свя́то *adv.* piously; religiously; **с. бере́чь** to treasure; **с. чтить** to hold sacred.
свят|о́й (~, ~а́, ≁о) *adj.* **1.** holy; sacred (*also fig.*); **~а́я вода́** holy water; **с. долг** sacred duty; **~а́я (неде́ля)** Holy Week; **~а́я ~ы́х** holy of holies. **2.** saintly. **3.** (*fig.*) pious. **4.** *preceding name, or as n.* **с., ~о́го** *m.*, **~а́я, ~о́й** *f.* saint.
свя́тост|ь, и *f.* holiness; sanctity.
святота́тственный *adj.* sacrilegious.
святота́тств|о, а *nt.* sacrilege.
святота́тств|овать, ую *impf.* to commit sacrilege.
свя́т|очный *adj. of* **~ки; с. расска́з** Christmas tale.
свято́ш|а, и *c.g.* sanctimonious person.
свя́тц|ы, ев *no sg.* (church) calendar.
святы́н|я, и *f.* **1.** (*eccl.*) object of worship; sacred place. **2.** (*fig.*) sacred object.
свяще́нник, а *m.* priest (*of Orthodox Church*); clergyman.
свяще́ннический *adj.* priestly; sacerdotal.
свяще́н|ный (~ен, ~на) *adj.* holy; sacred (*also fig.*); **~ное писа́ние** Holy Writ.
свяще́нств|о, а *nt.* priesthood (*also collect.*).
сгиб, а *m.* **1.** bend. **2.** (*anat.*) flexion.
сгиба́|ть(ся), ю(сь) *impf. of* **согну́ть(ся)**
сги́н|уть, у, ешь *pf.* (*coll.*) to disappear, vanish.
сгла́|дить, жу, дишь *pf.* (*of* **~живать) 1.** to smooth out. **2.** (*fig.*) to smooth over, soften.
сгла́жива|ть, ю *impf. of* **сгла́дить**
сгла́|зить, жу, зишь *pf.* to put the evil eye (on, upon); (*fig., coll.*) to jinx; **что́бы не с.!** touch wood!
сглуп|и́ть, лю́, и́шь *pf. of* **глупи́ть**
сгнива́|ть, ю *impf. of* **сгнить**
сгни|ть, ю́, ёшь *pf.* (*of* **гнить** *and* **~ва́ть**) to rot, decay.
сгно|и́ть, ю́, и́шь *pf. of* **гнои́ть**
сгова́рива|ться, юсь *impf. of* **сговори́ться**
сго́вор, а *m.* **1.** (*obs.*) betrothal. **2.** (*usu. pej.*) agreement, deal.
сговор|и́ться, ю́сь, и́шься *pf.* (*of* **сгова́риваться**) (**с**+*i.*) **1.** to arrange (with); **мы ~и́лись встре́титься с ни́ми при вхо́де в парк** we arranged to meet them at the entrance to the park. **2.** to come to an arrangement (with), reach an understanding (with).
сгово́рчив|ый (~, ~а) *adj.* compliant, tractable.
сгоня́|ть, ю *impf. of* **согна́ть**
сгора́ни|е, я *nt.* combustion; **дви́гатель вну́треннего ~я** internal-combustion engine.
сгор|а́ть, а́ю *impf.* **1.** *impf. of* **~е́ть. 2.** (**от**; *fig.*) to be dying (of); **с. от сты́да, любопы́тства** to be dying of shame, curiosity.
сго́рб|ить(ся), лю(сь), ишь(ся) *pf. of* **го́рбить(ся)**
сго́рб|ленный *p.p.p. of* **~ить** *and adj.* crooked, bent; hunchbacked.
сгор|е́ть, ю́, и́шь *pf.* (*of* **~а́ть**) **1.** to burn down; to be burnt out, down; **наш дом ~е́л** our house was burnt down. **2.** (*of fuel*) to be consumed, be used up. **3.** (*fig., coll.*) to burn o.s. out.
сгоряча́ *adv.* in the heat of the moment; in a fit of temper.
сгреба́|ть, ю *impf. of* **сгрести́**
сгре|сти́, бу́, бёшь, *past* **≁̈б, ~бла́** *pf.* (*of* **~ба́ть**) **1.** to rake up, rake together. **2.** (**с**+*g.*) to shovel (off, from); **с. снег с кры́ши** to shovel snow off the roof.
сгруд|и́ться, и́тся *pf.* (*coll.*) to crowd, mill, bunch.
сгружа́|ть, ю *impf. of* **сгрузи́ть**
сгру|зи́ть, жу́, ≁зишь *pf.* (*of* **~жа́ть**) to unload.
сгруппир|ова́ть(ся), у́ю(сь) *pf. of* **группирова́ть(ся)**
сгрыза́|ть, ю *impf. of* **сгрызть**
сгрыз|ть, у́, ёшь, *past* **~, ≁ла** *pf.* (*of* **~а́ть**) to chew (up).
сгуб|и́ть, лю́, ≁ишь *pf.* (*coll.*) to ruin.
сгу|сти́ть, щу́, сти́шь *pf.* (*of* **~ща́ть**) to thicken; to condense; **с. кра́ски** (*fig.*) to lay it on thick.
сгу|сти́ться, сти́тся *pf.* (*of* **~ща́ться**) to thicken; to condense; to clot.
сгу́ст|ок, ка *m.* clot; **с. кро́ви** clot of blood.
сгуща́|ть(ся), ю, ет(ся) *impf. of* **сгусти́ть(ся)**
сгуще́ни|е, я *nt.* thickening, condensation; clotting.
сгу|щённый *p.p.p. of* **~сти́ть** *and adj.*; **~щённое молоко́** condensed milk, evaporated milk.
сда́брива|ть, ю *impf. of* **сдо́брить**
сда|ва́ть, ю́, ёшь *impf. of* **сдать; с. экза́мен** to take, sit an examination.
сда|ва́ться[1]**, ю́сь, ёшься** *impf. of* **≁ться**[1]
сда|ва́ться[2]**, ётся** *impf.* (*impers., coll.*) it seems; **мне ~ётся** it seems to me; I think.
сдав|и́ть, лю́, ≁ишь *pf.* (*of* **≁ливать**) to squeeze.
сда́влива|ть, ю *impf. of* **сдави́ть**
сда́точн|ый *adj.* delivery; **с. пункт** delivery point.
сдать[1]**, сдам, сдашь, сдаст, сдади́м, сдади́те, сдаду́т,** *past* **сдал, сдала́, сда́ло** *pf.* (*of* **сдава́ть**) **1.** to hand over, pass; **с. бага́ж на хране́ние** to deposit one's luggage. **2.** to let, let out, hire out; **с. в аре́нду** to lease. **3.** to give change; **с. пятьдеся́т копе́ек** to give fifty kopecks change. **4.** to surrender, give up. **5.** to pass (*an examination*); **он сдал то́лько латы́нь** he only passed in Latin. **6.** to deal (*cards*).
сдать[2]**, сдам, сдашь, сдаст, сдади́м, сдади́те, сдаду́т** *pf.* (*of* **сдава́ть**) **1.** to give out; **мото́р сдал** the engine gave out. **2.** to be weakened.
сда́|ться, мся, шься, стся, ди́мся, ди́тесь, ду́тся, *past* **~лся** *pf.* (*of* **~ва́ться**[1]) to surrender, give up; (*chess*) to resign.
сда́ч|а, и *f.* **1.** handing over. **2.** letting out, hiring out; **с. в аре́нду** leasing. **3.** surrender. **4.** change; **три рубля́ ~и** three roubles change; **дать ~и** (+*d.*; *fig., coll.*) to give as good as one got. **5.** (*cards*) deal; **ва́ша с.** it is your deal.
сдва́ива|ть, ю *impf. of* **сдвои́ть**
сдвиг, а *m.* **1.** displacement; (*geol.*) fault. **2.** (*fig.*) change (for the better), improvement.
сдвига́|ть(ся), ю(сь) *impf. of* **сдви́нуть(ся)**
сдви́|нуть, ну, нешь *pf.* (*of* **~га́ть**) **1.** to shift, move,

displace; **с. с ме́ста** (*fig.*) to get moving, set in motion. **2.** to move together, bring together.
сдви́|нуться, нусь, нешься *pf.* (*of* **~га́ться**) **1.** to move, budge; **с. с ме́ста** (*fig.*) to progress; **де́ло не ~нулось с ме́ста** no headway has been made. **2.** to come together.
сдво|и́ть, ю, и́шь *pf.* (*of* **сдва́ивать**) to double.
сде́ла|ть(ся), ю(сь) *pf. of* **де́лать(ся)**
сде́лк|а, и *f.* transaction, deal, bargain; **войти́ в ~у** (**с**+*i.*) to strike a bargain (with).
сде́льн|ый *adj.* by the piece; **~ая рабо́та** piecework.
сде́льщик, а *m.* pieceworker.
сде́льщин|а, ы *f.* piecework.
сдёргива|ть, ю *impf. of* **сдёрнуть**
сде́ржанно *adv.* with restraint, with reserve.
сде́ржанност|ь, и *f.* restraint, reserve.
сде́ржан|ный *p.p.p. of* **сдержа́ть** *and* (**~, ~на**) *adj.* restrained; reserved.
сдерж|а́ть[1]**, у́, ~ишь** *pf.* (*of* **~ивать**) **1.** to hold (back); to hold in check, contain. **2.** (*fig.*) to keep back, restrain; **с. слёзы** to suppress tears.
сдерж|а́ть[2]**, у́, ~ишь** *pf.* (*of* **~ивать**) to keep (*a promise, etc.*); **с. сло́во** to keep one's word.
сдерж|а́ться, у́сь, ~ишься *pf.* (*of* **~иваться**) to restrain o.s., contain o.s.; to check o.s.
сде́ржива|ть(ся), ю(сь) *impf. of* **сдержа́ть(ся)**
сдёр|нуть, ну, нешь *pf.* (*of* **~гивать**) to pull off.
сдира́|ть, ю *impf. of* **содра́ть**
сдо́б|а, ы *f.* **1.** (*cul.*) shortening. **2.** (fancy) cake, bun (*also collect*).
сдо́бн|ый *adj.* (*cul.*) rich; **~ая бу́лка** bun.
сдо́бр|ить, ю, ишь *pf.* (*of* **сда́бривать**) (+*i.*) to flavour (with), spice (with).
сдоброва́ть *only in phr.* **ему́** *etc.*, **не с.** (*coll.*) it will be a bad look out for him, *etc.*
сдо́хн|уть, у, ешь *pf.* (*of* **сдыха́ть**) (*of cattle, also coll. of people*) to die.
сдре́йф|ить, лю, ишь *pf. of* **дре́йфить**
сдруж|и́ть, у́, и́шь *pf.* to bring together, unite in friendship.
сдруж|и́ться, у́сь, и́шься *pf.* (**с**+*i.*) to become friends (with).
сдува́|ть, ю *impf. of* **сдуть**
сду́ру *adv.* (*coll.*) stupidly.
сду|ть, ~ю, ~ешь *pf.* (*of* **~ва́ть**) to blow away, blow off.
сдыха́|ть, ю *impf. of* **сдо́хнуть**
сё, сего́ *pron.* this (*arch. exc. in certain set phrr.*; *see* **тот**).
сеа́нс, а *m.* **1.** performance, showing. **2.** sitting.
себе́[1] *see* **себя́**
себе́[2] *particle* (*coll.*) **а они́ с. молча́ли** and they just kept their mouths shut; **он о́чень с. на уме́** he is very crafty; **ничего́ с.** not bad; **так с.** so-so.
себесто́имост|ь, и *f.* (*econ.*) cost (*of manufacture*); cost price; **прода́ть по ~и** to sell at cost price.
себя́, себе́, собо́й (собо́ю), о себе́ *refl. pron.* oneself; myself, yourself, himself, *etc.*; **собо́ю** in appearance; **хоро́ш собо́ю** nice-looking; **прийти́ в с. (от)** to come to one's senses; to get over; **не в себе́** not o.s.; **от с.** (*i*) away from o.s., outwards, (*ii*) for o.s., on one's own behalf; **рабо́та не по себе́** work that is beyond one; **ка́к-то не по себе́** not quite o.s.; **чита́ть про с.** to read to o.s.; **у с.** at home.
себялю́б|ец, ца *m.* egoist.
себялюби́в|ый (~, ~а) *adj.* egoistical, selfish.
себялю́би|е, я *nt.* self-love, egoism.
сев, а *m.* sowing.
се́вер, а *m.* north.
се́верн|ый *adj.* north, northern; northerly; **с. оле́нь** reindeer.
Се́верн|ый Ледови́т|ый океа́н, ~ого ~ого ~а *m.* the Arctic Ocean.
Се́верн|ый Поля́рн|ый круг, ~ого ~ого ~а *m.* the Arctic Circle.
се́веро-восто́к, а *m.* north-east.
се́веро-восто́чный *adj.* north-east, north-eastern.
се́веро-за́пад, а *m.* north-west.
се́веро-за́падный *adj.* north-west, north-western.
северя́н|ин, ина, *pl.* **~е, ~** *m.* northerner.
севооборо́т, а *m.* crop rotation.
севрю́г|а, и *f.* (*variety of*) sturgeon.
сегме́нт, а *m.* segment.
сего́дня *adv.* today; **с. ве́чером** this evening, tonight; **не с.-за́втра** any day now.
сего́дня|шний *adj. of* **~**; **с. день** today; **~шняя газе́та** today's paper.
седа́лищ|е, а *nt.* (*anat.*) seat, buttocks.
седа́лищн|ый *adj.* (*anat.*) sciatic; **воспале́ние ~ого не́рва** (*med.*) sciatica.
седе́льник, а *m.* saddler.
седе́льн|ый *adj. of* **седло́**
седе́|ть, ю *impf.* (*of* **по~**) to turn grey.
седи́л|ь, я *m.* cedilla.
седин|а́, ы́, *pl.* **~ы, ~** *f.* grey hair(s).
седла́|ть, ю *impf.* (*of* **о~**) to saddle.
сед|ло́, ла́, *pl.* **~ла, ~ел** *nt.* saddle.
седлови́н|а, ы *f.* **1.** arch, saddle (*of back of animal*). **2.** (*geog.*) col, saddle.
седовла́с|ый (~, ~а) *adj.* grey-haired.
седоволо́с|ый (~, ~а) *adj.* = **седовла́сый**
сед|о́й (~, ~а́, ~о) *adj.* (*of hair*) grey, gray; hoary; grey-haired; white-haired.
седо́к, а *m.* **1.** fare (*passenger*). **2.** rider, horseman.
седьм|о́й *adj.* seventh; **одна́ ~а́я** one seventh.
сеза́м, а *m.* (*bot.*) sesame.
сезо́н, а *m.* season.
сезо́нн|ый *adj.* season; seasonal; **с. биле́т** season ticket; **~ые рабо́ты** seasonal work.
сей *m.*, **сия́** *f.*, **сие́** *nt.*, *pl.* **сии́** *pron.* this; **сию́ мину́ту** this minute; at once, this instant; **сего́ го́да** of this year; **сего́ ме́сяца** (*abbr.* **с. м.**) of this month; **ва́ше письмо́ от 16-го с. м.** your letter of the 16th inst.; **до сих пор** until now, hitherto; **на с. раз** this time; **под сим ка́мнем поко́ится** here lies; **при сём прилага́ется** (there is) enclosed herewith.
сейсми́ческий *adj.* seismic.
сейсмо́граф, а *m.* seismograph.
сейсмо́лог, а *m.* seismologist.
сейсмологи́ческий *adj.* seismological.
сейсмоло́ги|я, и *f.* seismology.
сейсмо́метр, а *m.* seismometer.
сейсмоопа́с|ный (~ен, ~на) *adj.* earthquake-prone.
сейсмосто́йкий *adj.* earthquake-proof.
сейф, а *m.* safe.
сейча́с *adv.* **1.** (right) now, at present, at the moment; **они́ с. в Аме́рике** they are in America at present. **2.** just, just now; **она́ с. вы́шла** she has just gone out. **3.** presently, soon; **с. же** at once, immediately; **с.!** in a minute! **4.** (*coll.*) straight away, immediately.
сек. (*abbr. of* **секу́нда**) sec., second(s).
се́канс, а *m.* (*math.*) secant.
секве́стр, а *m.* (*leg.*) sequestration.
секвестр|ова́ть, у́ю *impf. and pf.* (*leg.*) to sequestrate.
секи́р|а, ы *f.* pole-axe; hatchet, axe.
секре́т, а *m.* secret; **по ~у** confidentially, in confidence; **под больши́м ~ом** in strict confidence; **с. полишине́ля** open secret.
секретариа́т, а *m.* secretariat.
секрета́рский *adj.* secretarial; secretary's.
секрета́рств|овать, ую *impf.* to act as secretary.
секрета́р|ша, ши *f.* (*coll.*) *f. of* **~ь 1.**
секрета́р|ь, я́ *m.* **1.** (*administrative assistant*) secretary; **ли́чный с.** private secretary; **2.** (*official*) **гене-**

ра́льный с. secretary-general; **непреме́нный с.** permanent secretary.
секре́тнича|ть, ю *impf.* (*coll.*) **1.** to be secretive; to keep things secret. **2.** to talk confidentially.
секре́тно *adv.* secretly, in secret; (*on documents, etc.*) 'secret'; 'confidential'; **соверше́нно с.** 'top secret'.
секре́тност|ь, и *f.* secrecy.
секре́т|ный (~ен, ~на) *adj.* secret; confidential; **с. замо́к** combination lock; **с. сотру́дник** secret agent, undercover agent.
секре́ци|я, и *f.* (*physiol.*) secretion.
секс, а *m.* sex; **с. вне бра́ка** extramarital sex.
сексапи́льност|ь, и *f.* sex appeal.
сексапи́л|ьный (~ен, ~ьна) *adj.* sexy.
се́кст|а, ы *f.* (*mus.*) sixth.
секста́нт, а *m.* sextant.
сексте́т, а *m.* (*mus.*) sextet.
сексуа́льност|ь, и *f.* sexuality.
сексуа́л|ьный (~ен, ~ьна) *adj.* sexual.
се́кт|а, ы *f.* sect.
секта́нт, а *m.* sectarian; member of a sect.
секта́нтский *adj.* sectarian.
секта́нтств|о, а *nt.* sectarianism.
се́ктор, а *m.* **1.** (*math., mil.*) sector; **с. Га́за** the Gaza Strip. **2.** section, department. **3.** (*econ.*) sector.
секуляриза́ци|я, и *f.* secularization.
секуляриз|ова́ть, у́ю *impf. and pf.* to secularize.
секу́нд|а, ы *f.* (*of time*) second; **сию́ ~у!** just a moment!
секунда́нт, а *m.* (*in a duel or in boxing*) second.
секу́нд|ный *adj. of* **~а; ~ная стре́лка** second hand.
секундоме́р, а *m.* stop-watch.
секу́щ|ая, ей *f.* (*math.*) secant.
секци|о́нный *adj.* sectional; modular.
се́кци|я, и *f.* **1.** section. **2.** unit (*of furniture*).
селёдк|а, и *f.* herring.
селёд|очный *adj. of* **~ка**
селезёнк|а, и *f.* (*physiol.*) spleen.
се́лез|ень, ня *m.* drake.
селе́ктор, а *m.* intercom.
селекци|я, и *f.* (*agric.*) selection, breeding.
селе́ни|е, я *nt.* settlement.
селени́т, а *m.* (*min.*) selenite.
seли́тр|а, ы *f.* (*chem.*) saltpetre, nitre; **кали́йная с.** potassium nitrate.
сели́тр|яный *adj. of* **~а; ~яная кислота́** nitric acid.
сел|и́ть, ю́ и́шь *impf.* (*of* **по~**) to settle.
сел|и́ться, ю́сь, и́шься *impf.* (*of* **по~**) to settle.
сел|о́, а́, *pl.* **~́а** *nt.* village; **на ~е́** (*collect.*) in the country; **ни к ~у́, не к го́роду** (*coll.*) for no reason at all; neither here nor there.
сель... *comb. form, abbr. of* **се́льский**
сельдере́|й, я *m.* celery.
сельд|ь, и, *pl.* **~и, ~е́й** *f.* herring; **как ~и в бо́чке** (*coll.*) like sardines.
се́льск|ий *adj.* **1.** country, rural; **~ое хозя́йство** agriculture. **2.** village.
сельскохозя́йственный *adj.* agricultural, farming.
се́льтерск|ий *adj.*: **~ая вода́** seltzer water.
сема́нтик|а, и *f.* semantics.
семанти́ческий *adj.* semantic.
семафо́р, а *m.* semaphore.
сёмг|а, и *f.* salmon.
семе́йн|ый *adj.* **1.** family; domestic; **о́тпуск по ~ым обстоя́тельствам** (*mil.*) compassionate leave. **2.** having a family; **с. челове́к** family man.
семе́йственност|ь, и *f.* **1.** attachment to family life. **2.** (*pej.*) nepotism.
семе́йственн|ый *adj.* **1.** attached to family life. **2.** (*fig., pej.*) nepotistic; **~ые отноше́ния** nepotism.
семе́йств|о, а *nt.* family.
семена́ *see* **се́мя**
семен|и́ть, ю́, и́шь *impf.* to mince (*of gait*).
семенни́к, а́ *m.* **1.** (*biol.*) testicle. **2.** (*bot.*) pericarp.
семенн|о́й *adj.* **1.** seed; **с. карто́фель** seed potato. **2.** (*biol.*) seminal; **~а́я нить** spermatozoon.
семёрк|а, и *f.* **1.** seven; number seven (*bus, tram, etc.*). **2.: с. треф** *etc.* (*cards*) the seven of clubs, *etc.* **3.** group of seven persons.
се́мер|о, ы́х *num.* (*collect.*) seven.
семе́стр, а *m.* term, semester.
се́меч|ко, ка, *pl.* **~ки, ~ек** *nt.* **1.** *dim. of* **се́мя. 2.** (*pl.*) sunflower seeds.
семивёрстн|ый *adj.*: **~ые сапоги́** seven-league boots.
семидесятиле́ти|е, я *nt.* **1.** seventy years. **2.** seventieth anniversary; seventieth birthday.
семидесятиле́тний *adj.* **1.** seventy-year. **2.** seventy-year-old.
семидеся́тый *adj.* seventieth.
семикра́тный *adj.* sevenfold, septuple.
семиле́ти|е, я *nt.* **1.** seven years; seven-year period. **2.** seventh anniversary.
семиле́тний *adj.* **1.** seven-year. **2.** seven-year-old.
семина́р, а *m.* seminar.
семинари́ст, а *m.* seminarist.
семина́ри|я, и *f.* seminary; **духо́вная с.** theological college.
семина́р|ский *adj. of* **~** *and* **~ия**
семисо́тый *adj.* seven-hundredth.
семи́т, а *m.* Semite.
семити́ческий *adj.* Semitic.
семи́т|ский = ~и́ческий
семиуго́льник *m.* (*math.*) heptagon.
семиуго́льный *adj.* heptagonal.
семичасово́й *adj.* **1.** seven-hour. **2.** seven o'clock.
семна́дцатый *adj.* seventeenth.
семна́дцат|ь, и *f., num.* seventeen.
сем|ь, и́, *i.* **~ью́** *num.* seven.
се́мьдесят, семи́десяти, семью́десятью *num.* seventy.
семьсо́т, семисо́т, семиста́м, семьюста́ми, о семиста́х *num.* seven hundred.
се́мью *adv.* seven times.
сем|ья́, ьи́, *pl.* **~ьи ~е́й, ~ьям** *f.* family.
семьяни́н, а, *pl.* **~ы** *m.* family man.
се́м|я, ени, *pl.* **~ена́, ~я́н, ~ена́м** *nt.* **1.** (*bot. and fig.*) seed; **пойти́ в ~ена́** to go to seed; **~ена́ раздо́ра** seeds of discord. **2.** semen, sperm.
семядо́л|я, и, *g. pl.* **~ей** *f.* (*bot.*) seed-lobe, cotyledon.
семяизлия́ни|е, я *nt.* (*physiol.*) ejaculation.
семяпо́чк|а, и *f.* (*bot.*) seed-bud.
сена́т, а *m.* senate.
сена́тор, а *m.* senator.
сена́торский *adj.* senatorial.
сена́т|ский *adj. of* **~**
сенберна́р, а *m.* St. Bernard (*dog*).
се́н|и, е́й *no sg.* (entrance-)hall, vestibule.
сенни́к, а́ *m.* hay-mattress.
сенн|о́й *adj.* hay; **~а́я лихора́дка** hay fever.
се́н|о, а *nt.* hay.
сенова́л, а *m.* hay-loft.
сеноко́с, а *m.* **1.** haymaking. **2.** haymaking (*time*). **3.** hayfield
сенокоси́лк|а, и *f.* (hay-)mowing machine.
сеноубо́рк|а, и *f.* hay harvesting, haymaking.
сенсацио́н|ный (~ен, ~на) *adj.* sensational.
сенса́ци|я, и *f.* sensation.
сенсо́рный *adj.* (*physiol.*) sensory.
сентенцио́зный *adj.* sententious.
сенте́нци|я, и *f.* maxim.
сентимента́льност|ь, и *f.* sentimentality.
сентимента́л|ьный (~ен, ~ьна) *adj.* sentimental.
сентя́бр|ь, я́ *m.* September.
сентя́бр|ьский *adj. of* **~**
сен|ь, и, о ~и, в ~и́ *f.* (*obs. or poet.*) canopy; **под**

∠ью (+*g.*) under the protection (of).
сепарати́вный *adj.* (*pol.*) separatist.
сепарати́зм, а *m.* (*pol.*) separatism.
сепарати́ст, а *m.* (*pol.*) separatist.
сепара́тный *adj.* (*pol.*) separate.
сепара́тор, а *m.* (*agric.*) separator.
се́пи|я, и *f.* **1.** sepia. **2.** sepia drawing; sepia photograph.
се́псис, а *m.* (*med.*) sepsis, septicaemia.
септи́ческий *adj.* (*med.*) septic.
се́р|а, ы *f.* **1.** (*chem.*) sulphur. **2.** ear-wax.
сера́л|ь, я *m.* seraglio.
серб, а *m.* Serb.
Се́рби|я, и *f.* Serbia.
се́рб|ка, ки *f. of* **~**
сербохорва́тский *adj.* = **сербскохорва́тский**
се́рбский *adj.* Serb, Serbian.
сербскохорва́тский *adj.* Serbo-Croat(ian); **с. язы́к** Serbo-Croat(ian).
серва́нт, а *m.* sideboard; dumb-waiter.
серви́з, а *m.* service, set; **столо́вый с.** dinner service.
сервир|ова́ть, у́ю *impf. and pf.* **1.: с. стол** to lay a table. **2.** to serve; **с. за́втрак** to serve breakfast.
сервиро́вк|а, и *f.* **1.** laying. **2.** (*collect.*) table appointments (*crockery and table linen*).
се́рвис, а *m.* (consumer) service.
серде́чник[1], **а** *m.* (*tech.*) core.
серде́чник[2], **а** *m.* (*coll.*) **1.** heart specialist. **2.** sufferer from heart disease.
серде́чност|ь, и *f.* cordiality; warmth.
серде́ч|ный (~ен, ~на) *adj.* **1.** of the heart (*also fig.*); (*anat.*) cardiac; **~ная боле́знь** heart disease; **с. припа́док** heart attack. **2.** cordial, hearty, heartfelt, sincere; **~ная благода́рность** heartfelt gratitude. **3.** warm, warm-hearted.
серди́тый *adj.* (**на**+*a.*) angry (with, at, about); irate.
сер|ди́ть, жу́, ∠дишь *impf.* (*of* **рас~**) to anger, make angry.
сер|ди́ться, жу́сь, ∠дишься *impf.* (*of* **рас~**) (**на**+*a.*) to be angry (with, at, about).
сердобо́ли|е, я *nt.* soft-heartedness.
сердобо́л|ьный (~ен, ~ьна) *adj.* (*coll.*) soft-hearted.
се́рд|це, ца, *pl.* **~ца́, ~е́ц** *nt.* heart; **в ~ца́х** in a fit of temper; **с глаз доло́й, из ~ца вон** (*prov.*) out of sight, out of mind; **приня́ть (бли́зко) к ~цу** to take to heart; **от всего́ ~ца** from the bottom of one's heart; **по́ ∠цу** (*coll.*) to one's liking; after one's own heart; **с. боли́т** (+*inf.*) it pains one, one's heart bleeds; **у него́ не лежи́т с. (к)** he has no inclination (to, for).
сердцебие́ни|е, я *nt.* palpitation; (*med.*) tachycardia.
сердцеви́д|ный (~ен, ~на) *adj.* heart-shaped.
сердцеви́н|а, ы *f.* core, pith, heart (*also fig.*).
сердцее́д, а *m.* (*coll.*) lady-killer.
серебри́ст|ый (~, ~а) *adj.* silvery.
серебр|и́ть, ю́, и́шь *impf.* (*of* **по~**) to silver, silver-plate.
серебр|и́ться, и́тся *impf.* **1.** to become silvery. **2.** *pass. of* **~и́ть**
серебр|о́, а́ *nt.* **1.** silver. **2.** (*collect.*) silver; **столо́вое с.** silver, plate; **сда́ча ~о́м** change in silver.
сере́бряник, а *m.* silversmith.
сере́бряный *adj.* silver.
среди́н|а, ы *f.* middle, midst; **золота́я с.** the golden mean.
середи́нный *adj.* middle, mean.
серёдк|а, и *f.* (*coll.*) middle, centre.
середня́к, а́ *m.* **1.** peasant of average means. **2.** (*fig., coll.*) middling person, undistinguished person.
серёжк|а *f.* **1.** ear-ring. **2.** (*bot.*) catkin.
серена́д|а, ы *f.* serenade.
сере́|ть, ю *impf.* (*pf.* **по~**) to turn grey, go grey.
сержа́нт, а *m.* sergeant.
сери́йный *adj.* (*tech., econ.*) serial.
се́ри|я, и *f.* series; set; (*of film*) part; **кинофи́льм в не́скольких ~ях** film in several parts.
сермя́г|а, и *f.* sermyaga (*coarse, undyed cloth or caftan of this material*).
се́рн|а, ы *f.* (*zool.*) chamois.
серни́ст|ый *adj.* (*chem.*) sulphureous; sulphide (of); **с. аммо́ний** ammonium sulphide.
сернокисл|ый *adj.* (*chem.*) sulphate (of); **~ая соль** sulphate.
се́рн|ый *adj.* sulphuric; **~ая кислота́** sulphuric acid.
сероводоро́д, а *m.* (*chem.*) hydrogen sulphide.
серп, а́ *m.* sickle; **с. луны́** crescent moon.
серпанти́н, а *m.* **1.** streamer. **2.** hairpin-bend road (*in mountainous terrain*).
серпови́дный *adj.* crescent(-shaped).
сертифика́т, а *m.* certificate.
се́рум, а *m.* (*med.*) serum.
се́рфинг, а *m.* surfing.
сёрфинг = се́рфинг
серфинги́ст, а *m.* surfer.
серча́|ть, ю *impf.* (*of* **о~**) (*coll.*) to be angry.
се́р|ый (~, ~а́, ~о) *adj.* **1.** grey. **2.** (*fig.*) grey, dull; drab. **3.** (*fig.*) dull, dim (= *uneducated*).
серьг|а́, и́, *pl.* **∠и, серёг, ~а́м** *f.* ear-ring.
серьёзно *adv.* seriously; earnestly; in earnest; **с.?** seriously?; really?
серьёзност|ь, и *f.* seriousness; earnestness.
серьёз|ный (~ен, ~на, ~но) *adj.* serious; earnest.
се́сси|я, и *f.* session.
сестр|а́, ы́, *pl.* **∸ы, сестёр, ∸ам** *f.* **1.** sister; **двою́родная с.** (first) cousin. **2.: медици́нская с.** nurse.
сестрёнк|а, и *f.* little sister.
се́стрин *adj.* sister's.
сестри́ц|а, ы *f. affectionate dim. of* **сестра́**
сесть[1], **ся́ду, ся́дешь,** *past* **сел, се́ла** *pf.* (*of* **сади́ться**) **1.** to sit down; **с. за стол** to sit down at the table; **с. обе́дать** to sit down to dinner; **с. в ва́нну** to get into the bath; **с. рабо́тать** to get down to work. **2.** (**в, на**+*a.*) to board, take; **с. на по́езд** to board a train; **с. на ло́шадь** to mount a horse. **3.** to alight, settle, perch; (*of an aircraft*) to land. **4.** (*of the heavenly bodies*) to set. **5.: с. в тюрьму́** to go to prison, jail.
сесть[2], **ся́дет,** *past* **сел** *pf.* (*of* **сади́ться**) to shrink.
сет, а *m.* (*sport*) set.
се́тк|а, и *f.* **1.** net, netting; (luggage) rack. **2.** (*coll.*) string-bag. **3.** (*geog.*) grid; (*collect.*) co-ordinates. **4.** (*radio*) grid. **5.** scale (*of charges, etc.*).
се́т|овать, ую *impf.* (*of* **по~**) **1.** (**на**+*a.*) to complain (of). **2.** (**о**+*p.*) to lament, mourn.
се́ттер, а *m.* setter (*dog*).
сетча́тк|а, и *f.* (*anat.*) retina.
се́тчат|ый *adj.* netted, network; reticular; **~ая ма́йка** string vest; **~ая оболо́чка гла́за** (*anat.*) retina.
сет|ь, и, о ∠и, в ∠и *and* **~и́,** *pl.* **∠и, ~е́й** *f.* **1.** net (*also fig.*); **расста́вить ∠и кому́-н.** to set a trap for s.o. **2.** network; system; **лока́льная с.** (*comput.*) local area network, LAN.
сече́ни|е, я *nt.* section; **ке́сарево с.** Caesarean (section); **попере́чное с.** cross section.
се́чк|а, и *f.* **1.** chopper, vegetable-cutting knife. **2.** chopped straw, chaff.
сечь, секу́, сечёшь, секу́т, *past* **сек, секла́** *impf.* **1.** (*impf. only*) to cut to pieces. **2.** (*pf.* **вы́~,** *past* **сек, се́кла**) to beat, flog.
се́|чься, чётся, ку́тся, *past* **~кся, ~клась** *impf.* (*of* **по~**) (*of hairs*) to split; (*of fabric*) to cut.
се́ялк|а, и *f.* (*agric.*) sowing-machine, seed drill.
се́ян|ец, ца *m.* seedling.
се́ятел|ь, я *m.* sower (*also fig., rhet.*); disseminator.
се́|ять, ю, ешь *impf.* (*of* **по~**) to sow (*also fig.*).
сжа́л|иться, юсь, ишься *pf.* (**над**) to take pity (on).

сжа́ти|е, я *nt.* **1.** pressing, pressure; grasp, grip. **2.** compression; **ка́мера ~я** compression chamber.
сжа́тост|ь, и *f.* **1.** compression. **2.** conciseness.
сжа́т|ый *p.p.p. of* **~ь**[1] *and* **~ь**[2] *and adj.* **1.** compressed (*air, gas*). **2.** (*fig.*) condensed, concise.
сжать[1], **сожму́, сожмёшь** *pf.* (*of* **сжима́ть**) to squeeze; to compress (*also fig.*); to grip; **с. гу́бы** to purse one's lips; **с. зу́бы** to grit one's teeth; **с. кулаки́** to clench one's fists; **с. в объя́тиях** to hug.
сжать[2], **сожну́, сожнёшь** *pf. of* **жать**[2]
сжа́|ться, сожму́сь, сожмёшься *pf.* (*of* **сжима́ться**) **1.** to tighten, clench. **2.** to shrink, contract; **её душа́ ~лась** her heart sank.
сжечь, сожгу́, сожжёшь, сожгу́т, *past* **сжёг, сожгла́** *pf.* (*of* **жечь** *and* **сжига́ть**) to burn (up, down); to cremate; **с. свой корабли́** (*fig.*) to burn one's boats.
сжива́|ть(ся), ю(сь) *impf. of* **сжи́ть(ся)**
сжига́|ть, ю *impf. of* **сжечь**
сжи|ди́ть, жу́, ди́шь *pf.* (*of* **~жа́ть**) to liquefy.
сжижа́|ть, ю *impf. of* **сжиди́ть**
сжиже́ни|е, я *nt.* (*chem.*) liquefaction.
сжи́женный *adj.* (*chem.*) liquefied.
сжима́|ть(ся), ю(сь) *impf. of* **сжа́ть**[1]**(ся)**
сжи|ть, ву́, вёшь, *past* **~л, ~ла́, ́~ло** *pf.* (*of* **~ва́ть**) (*coll.*) to force out; **с. со́ свету** to be the death (of).
сжи́|ться, ву́сь, вёшься, *past* **~лся,~ла́сь** *pf.* (*of* **~ва́ться**) (**с**+*i.*) to get used (to).
сжу́льнича|ть, ю *pf. of* **жу́льничать**
сза́ди *adv. and prep.*+*g.* **1.** *adv.* from behind; behind; from the end; from the rear; **вид с.** rear view. **2.** *prep.*+*g.* behind.
сзыва́|ть, ю *impf. of* **созва́ть**
сиа́мский *adj.* Siamese.
сибари́т, а *m.* sybarite.
сибари́тский *adj.* sybaritic.
сиби́рск|ий *adj.* Siberian; **~ая ко́шка** Persian cat; **~ая я́зва** (*med.*) anthrax.
Сиби́р|ь, и *f.* Siberia.
сибиря́к, а́ *m.* Siberian.
сибиря́|чка, чки *f. of* **~к**
си́вк|а, и *f.* dark grey (horse).
сиву́х|а, и *f.* raw vodka.
сиву́ч, а *m.* (*zool.*) Steller's sea lion.
си́в|ый (~, ~а́, ́~о) *adj.* **1.** (*of horses*) grey. **2.** (*of hair*) grey, greying.
сиг, а́ *m.* whitefish.
сиган|у́ть, у́, ёшь *pf.* (*coll.*) to leap.
сига́р|а, ы *f.* cigar.
сигаре́т|а, ы *f.* cigarette.
сигаре́т|ный *adj. of* **~а**
сига́р|ный *adj. of* **~а**
сигна́л, а *m.* signal; **пожа́рный с.** fire-alarm.
сигнализа́тор, а *m.* (*tech.*) signalling device.
сигнализа́ци|я, и *f.* signalling.
сигнализи́р|овать, ую *impf. and pf.* **1.** (*pf. also* **про~**) to signal. **2.** (+*a. or* **о**+*p.*; *fig.*) to warn (of).
сигна́л|ьный *adj. of* **~**; **~ьная бу́дка** signal-box.
сигна́льщик, а *m.* signaller, signal-man.
сигнату́р|а, ы *f.* (*pharm.*) label.
СИД *m.* (*indecl.*) (*abbr. of* **светоизлуча́ющий дио́д**) LED (*light-emitting diode*).
сиде́лк|а, и *f.* (sick-)nurse.
сиде́ни|е, я *nt.* sitting.
си́д|ень, ня *m.* (*coll.*) stay-at-home; **сиде́ть ~нем** to be a stay-at-home.
сиде́нь|е, я *nt.* seat.
си|де́ть, жу́, ди́шь *impf.* **1.** to sit; **с., поджа́в но́ги** to sit cross-legged; **с. верхо́м** to be on horseback; **с. на ко́рточках** to squat. **2.** to be; **с. (в тюрьме́)** to be in prison; **с. под аре́стом** to be under arrest; **с. без де́ла** to have nothing to do; **с. за кни́гой** to be (engaged in) reading. **3.** (**на**+*p.*; *of clothing*) to fit.
сид|е́ться, и́тся *impf.* (*impers.*+*d.*): **ему́, *etc.*, не ~и́тся до́ма** he, *etc.*, can't bear staying at home; **ей не ~и́тся на ме́сте** she can't keep still.
сидр, а *m.* cider.
сидя́ч|ий *adj.* **1.** sitting; **в ~ей по́зе** in a sitting posture. **2.** (*fig.*) sedentary.
сие́ *see* **сей**
сие́н|а, ы *f.* sienna.
си́з|ый (~, ~а́, ́~о) *adj.* blue-grey, dove-coloured.
сикомо́р, а *m.* (*bot.*) sycamore.
сикх, а *m.* Sikh.
си́кхский *adj.* Sikh.
си́л|а, ы *f.* **1.** strength, force; **в ~у** (+*g.*) on the strength (of), by virtue (of); **быть в ~ах** (+*inf.*) to be able(to), have the strength (to); **изо всех ~, что есть ~ы** with all one's might; **от ~ы** (*coll.*) at most; **сверх ~, свы́ше~, не по ~ам** beyond one's power(s); outside one's competence; **че́рез ~у** beyond one's powers; **~ой** by force; **свои́ми ~ами** unaided; **~ою** (+*g. or* **в**+*a.*) to the strength (of); **с. во́ли** will-power; **с. привы́чки** force of habit; **в ~у привы́чки** by force of habit. **2.** (*phys., tech.*) force, power; **лошади́ная с.** horse-power; **с. тя́жести, с. притяже́ния** force of gravity. **3.** (*leg. and fig.*) force; **име́ющий ~у** valid; **в ~е** in force, valid; **войти́, вступи́ть в ~у** to come into force; take effect. **4.** (*pl.*; *mil.*) forces; **вооружённые ~ы** armed forces.
сила́ч, а́ *m.* strong man.
силика́т, а *m.* (*min.*) silicate.
си́л|иться, юсь, ишься *impf.* to try, make efforts.
silко́м
силко́м *adv.* (*coll.*) by (main) force.
силлоги́зм, а *m.* (*phil.*) syllogism.
силов|о́й *adj.* **1.** power; **с. про́вод** (*elec.*) power-line; **~а́я ста́нция** power-station. **2.** of force, using force; **~а́я поли́тика** policy of force.
сил|о́к, ка́ *m.* snare.
силоме́р, а *m.* dynamometer.
си́лос, а *m.* (*agric.*) **1.** silo. **2.** silage.
силуэ́т, а *m.* silhouette.
си́льно *adv.* **1.** strongly; violently. **2.** very much, greatly; badly; **с. нужда́ться в чём-н** to want sth. badly.
сильноде́йствующий *adj.* potent, powerful; drastic.
си́л|ьный (~ен *and* **~ён, ~ьна́, ~ьно, ́~ьны́)** *adj.* strong; powerful; **~ьное жела́ние** intense desire; **с. моро́з** hard frost; **он не ~ён в языка́х** he is not good at languages.
сильф, а *m.* (*myth.*) sylph.
сильфи́д|а, ы *f.* (*myth. and fig.*) sylph.
симбио́з, а *m.* (*biol.*) symbiosis.
си́мвол, а *m.* symbol; emblem.
символизи́р|овать, ую *impf.* to symbolize.
символи́зм, а *m.* symbolism.
симво́лик|а, и *f.* symbolism.
символи́ческий *adj.* symbolic(al).
символи́ч|ный (~ен, ~на) *adj.* = **~еский**
симметри́ческий *adj.* symmetrical.
симметри́ч|ный (~ен, ~на) *adj.* = **~еский**
симметри́|я, и *f.* symmetry.
симпатизи́р|овать, ую *impf.* (+*d.*) be in sympathy (with), sympathize (with); to be fond (of).
симпати́ческ|ий *adj.* (*physiol., etc.*) sympathetic; **~ая не́рвная систе́ма** sympathetic nervous system; **~ие черни́ла** invisible ink.
симпати́ч|ный (~ен, ~на) *adj.* likeable, nice.
симпа́ти|я, и *f.* (**к**) liking, fondness (for).
симпто́м, а *m.* symptom.
симптомати́ческий *adj.* symptomatic.
симптомати́ч|ный (~ен, ~на) *adj.* = **~еский**
симули́р|овать, ую *impf. and pf.* to simulate, feign.
симуля́нт, а *m.* simulator; malingerer.
симуля́ци|я, и *f.* simulation.

симфони́ческий *adj.* symphonic; **с. орке́стр** symphony orchestra.
симфо́ни|я, и *f.* symphony.
синаго́г|а, и *f.* synagogue.
синдро́м, а *m.* syndrome.
синев|а́, ы́ *f.* blue colour; **с. небе́с** the blue of the sky; **с. под глаза́ми** dark patches under the eyes.
синева́т|ый (~, ~а) *adj.* bluish.
синегла́з|ый (~, ~а) *adj.* blue-eyed.
синеку́р|а, ы *f.* sinecure.
сине́л|ь, и *f.* chenille.
сине́|ть, ю *impf.* **1.** (*pf.* **по~**) to turn blue, become blue. **2.** (*impf. only*) to show blue.
син|ий (~ь, ~я́, ~е) *adj.* (dark) blue.
сини́льн|ый *adj.*: **~ая кислота́** (*chem.*) prussic acid.
син|и́ть, ю́, и́шь *impf.* (*of* **по~**) **1.** to paint blue. **2.** to blue.
сини́ц|а, ы *f.* tit, titmouse, tomtit.
синко́п|а, ы *f.* (*mus. and ling.*) syncope.
сино́д, а *m.* synod.
синода́льный *adj.* synodal.
сино́лог, а *m.* sinologist.
синоло́ги|я, и *f.* sinology.
сино́ним, а *m.* synonym.
синоними́ческий *adj.* synonymous.
синоними́ч|ный (~ен, ~на) *adj.* = **синоними́ческий**
сино́птик, а *m.* weather forecaster.
сино́птик|а, и *f.* weather forecasting.
синопти́ческ|ий *adj.* synoptical; **~ая ка́рта** weather-map.
си́нтаксис, а *m.* syntax.
синтакси́ческий *adj.* syntactical.
си́нтез, а *m.* synthesis.
синтеза́тор, а *m.* synthesizer.
синтези́р|овать, ую *impf. and pf.* to synthesize.
синтети́ческий *adj.* synthetic.
си́нус[1], **а** *m.* (*math.*) sine.
си́нус[2], **а** *m.* (*anat.*) sinus.
синхрониза́ци|я, и *f.* synchronization.
синхронизи́р|овать, ую *impf. and pf.* to synchronize.
синхрони́ст, а *m.* simultaneous interpreter.
синхрони́ческий *adj.* synchronic.
синхро́нный *adj.* synchronous; simultaneous.
син|ь, и *f.* blue colour.
синьг|а́, и́ *f.* (*zool.*) common scoter.
си́ньк|а, и *f.* **1.** blue, blueing. **2.** blueprint.
синя́к, а́ *m.* bruise; **с. под гла́зом** black eye; **~и́ под глаза́ми** dark patches under the eyes; **изби́ть до ~о́в** to beat black and blue.
сиони́зм, а *m.* Zionism.
сиони́ст, а *m.* Zionist.
сиони́стский *adj.* Zionist.
сип|е́ть, лю́, и́шь *impf.* **1.** to speak in a hoarse voice. **2.** (*impers.*) to be hoarse; **у него́ в го́рле ~и́т** he is hoarse.
си́плый *adj.* hoarse, husky.
си́пн|уть, у, ешь *impf.* (*coll.*) to become hoarse.
сипу́х|а, и *f.* (*zool.*) barn owl.
сире́н|а, ы *f.* siren.
сире́невый *adj.* lilac; lilac-coloured.
сире́н|ь, и *f.* lilac.
сири́|ец, йца *m.* Syrian.
сири́|йка, йки *f. of* **~ец**
сири́йский *adj.* Syrian.
Си́ри|я, и *f.* Syria.
сиро́кко *m. indecl.* sirocco.
сиро́п, а *m.* syrup.
сирот|а́, ы́, *pl.* **~ы** *c.g.* orphan.
сироте́|ть, ю *impf.* to be orphaned.
сиротли́в|ый (~, ~а) *adj.* lonely; (*fig.*) lost, stray.
сиро́т|ский *adj. of* **~а́**; **с. дом** orphanage.
сиро́тств|о, а *nt.* orphanhood.
систе́м|а, ы *f.* **1.** system. **2.** type.
систематиза́ци|я, и *f.* systematization.
систематизи́р|овать, ую *impf. and pf.* to systematize, order.
системати́ческий *adj.* systematic; methodical.
системати́ч|ный (~ен, ~на) *adj.* = **системати́ческий**
си́стол|а, ы *f.* (*med.*) systole.
си́с|ька, ьки, *g. pl.* **~ек** *f.* (*coll.*) nipple; tit.
си́т|ец, ца *m.* cotton (print); calico (print); chintz.
си́теч|ко, ка, *pl.* **~ки, ~ек** *nt. dim. of* **си́то; ча́йное с.** tea-strainer.
си́тник[1], **а** *m.* loaf made of sifted flour.
си́тник[2], **а** *m.* (*bot.*) rush.
си́т|о, а *nt.* sieve.
ситуа́ци|я, и *f.* situation.
си́т|цевый *adj. of* **~ец**
си́филис, а *m.* (*med.*) syphilis.
сифили́тик, а *m.* syphilitic.
сифилити́ческий *adj.* syphilitic.
сифо́н, а *m.* siphon.
сиюмину́т|ный (~ен, ~на) *adj.* present, current.
сия́ни|е, я *nt.* radiance; **се́верное с.** northern lights, Aurora Borealis.
сия́|ть, ю *impf.* to shine, beam; to be radiant.
скабрёзност|ь, и *f.* scabrousness; indecency; (*pl.*) foul language; **говори́ть ~и** to talk filth.
скабрёз|ный (~ен, ~на) *adj.* scabrous; indecent.
сказ, а *m.* (*Russ. liter.*) skaz (= *first-person narrative*).
сказа́ни|е, я *nt.* story, tale, legend.
ска|за́ть, жу́, ~́жешь *pf. of* **говори́ть; ~жи́(те)!** (*coll., iron.*) I say!; **как с.** how shall I put it?; **лу́чше с., верне́е с., точне́е с.** or rather; **не́чего с.!** well, I never!; **~́зано — сде́лано** (*coll.*) no sooner said than done.
ска|за́ться[1], **жу́сь, ~́жешься** *pf.* (*of* **~́зываться**) (*coll.*) (*+i.*) to report o.s.; **с. больны́м** to report sick.
ска|за́ться[2], **жу́сь, ~́жешься** *pf.* (*of* **~́зываться**) **1.** (**на**+*p.*) to tell (on), take its toll (on); **бомбёжка ~за́лась на её не́рвах** the bombing told on her nerves. **2.** (**в**+*p.*) to be manifest (in); be seen (in).
сказа́тел|ь, я *m.* folk-tale narrator, story-teller.
ска́зк|а, и *f.* **1.** tale, story; **волше́бная с.** fairy-tale. **2.** (*coll.*) (tall) story, fairy-tale (*fig.*).
ска́зочник, а *m.* story-teller.
ска́зочн|ый *adj.* fairytale; fabulous, fantastic; **~ая страна́** fairyland; **~ое бога́тство** fabulous wealth.
сказу́ем|ое, ого *nt.* (*gram.*) predicate.
ска́зыва|ться, юсь *impf. of* **сказа́ться**
скак *m. only found in p. sg.*: **на всём ~у́** at full tilt.
скака́лк|а, и *f.* skipping-rope.
ска|ка́ть, чу́, ~́чешь *impf.* **1.** to skip, jump; **с. на одно́й ноге́** to hop. **2.** to gallop.
скаков|о́й *adj.* race, racing; **~а́я доро́жка** racecourse; **~а́я ло́шадь** racehorse.
скаку́н, а́ *m.* racehorse.
скал|а́, ы́, *pl.* **~́ы** *f.* rock face, crag; **(отве́сная) с.** cliff; **подво́дная с.** reef.
скаламбу́р|ить, ю, ишь *pf. of* **каламбу́рить**
скали́ст|ый (~, ~а) *adj.* rocky; **С~ые го́ры** (*geog.*) the Rocky Mountains; the Rockies.
ска́л|ить, ю, ишь *impf.* (*of* **о~**); **с. зу́бы** to bare one's teeth; (*impf. only*) (*fig. pej.*) to grin, laugh.
ска́лк|а, и *f.* (*cul.*) rolling-pin.
скалола́з, а *m.* rock-climber.
ска́лыва|ть, ю *impf. of* **сколо́ть**
скалькир|овать, ую *pf. of* **калькирова́ть**
скалькули́р|овать, ую *pf. of* **калькули́ровать**
ска́льпел|ь, я *m.* scalpel.
скальпи́р|овать, ую *impf. and pf.* (*pf. also* **о~**) to scalp.
скаме́ечк|а, и *f.* small bench; **с. для ног** footstool.
скаме́йк|а, и *f.* bench.

скам|ья́, ьи́, *pl.* **~ьи, ~е́й** *f.* bench; **с. подсуди́мых** (*leg.*) the dock; **на шко́льной ~ье́** during one's schooldays; **со шко́льной ~ьи́** straight from school.
сканда́л, а *m.* **1.** scandal. **2.** brawl; row.
скандализи́р|овать, ую *impf. and pf.* to scandalize.
скандали́ст, а *m.* brawler; trouble-maker; rowdy.
сканда́л|ить, ю, ишь *impf.* **1.** (*pf.* **на~**) (*coll.*) to brawl; to start a row. **2.** (*pf.* **о~**) to scandalize.
сканда́л|иться, юсь, ишься *impf.* (*of* **о~**) to disgrace o.s.
сканда́л|ьный (~ен, ~ьна) *adj.* **1.** scandalous. **2.** (*coll.*) rowdy. **3.** quarrelsome, trouble-making.
скандина́в, а *m.* Scandinavian.
Скандина́ви|я, и *f.* Scandinavia.
скандина́в|ка, ки *f. of* **~**
скандина́вский *adj.* Scandinavian.
сканди́р|овать, ую *impf. and pf.* to declaim, recite (*stressing individual syllables of words*); to chant.
ска́нер, а *m.* (*comput., med.*) scanner.
ска́плива|ть(ся), ю(сь) *impf. of* **скопи́ть(ся)**
скарабе́|й, я *m.* scarab.
скарб, а *m.* (*coll.*) goods and chattels; **со всем ~ом** bag and baggage.
ска́ред|ный (~ен, ~на) *adj.* (*coll.*) stingy, miserly.
скарлати́н|а, ы *f.* (*med.*) scarlet fever.
скарлати́н|ный *adj. of* **~а**
ска́рмлива|ть, ю *impf. of* **скорми́ть**
скат[1]**, а** *m.* slope, incline; pitch.
скат[2]**, а** *m.* (*tech.*) wheelbase.
скат[3]**, а** *m.* (*zool.*) ray, skate.
скат|а́ть, а́ю *pf.* (*of* **~ывать**) to roll (up).
ска́терт|ь, и, *pl.* **~и, ~е́й** *f.* table-cloth; **~ью доро́га!** (*coll.*) good riddance!
ска|ти́ть, чу́, ~тишь *pf.* (*of* **~тывать**) to roll down.
ска|ти́ться, чу́сь, ~тшься *pf.* (*of* **~тываться**) to roll down; (*fig., pej.*) to slip, slide.
ска́тыва|ть, ю *impf. of* **ската́ть** *and* **скати́ть**
ска́тыва|ться, юсь *impf. of* **скати́ться**
ска́ут, а *m.* (boy) scout.
скафа́ндр, а *m.* protective suit.
ска́чк|а, и *f.* **1.** gallop, galloping. **2.** (*pl.*) horse-race; race meeting, the races.
скачкообра́з|ный (~ен, ~на) *adj.* spasmodic; uneven.
скач|о́к, ка́ *m.* **1.** jump, leap, bound; **~ка́ми** by leaps. **2.** (*fig.*) a great advance, leap forward.
ска́шива|ть, ю *impf. of* **скоси́ть**
ска́щива|ть, ю *impf. of* **скости́ть**
СКВ *f. indecl.* (*abbr. of* ***свобо́дно конверти́руемая валю́та***) hard currency, freely convertible currency.
сква́жин|а, ы *f.* slit, chink; **бурова́я с.** (*tech.*) bore-hole; **замо́чная с.** key-hole.
сквалы́г|а, и *c.g.* (*coll.*) miser, skinflint.
сквер, а *m.* public garden.
скве́рно *adv.* badly; **с. чу́вствовать себя́** to feel poorly; **с. поступи́ть с кем-н.** to treat s.o. badly.
скверносло́в, а *m.* foul-mouthed person.
скверносло́ви|е, я *nt.* foul language.
скверносло́в|ить, лю, ишь *impf.* to use foul language.
скве́р|ный (~ен, ~на́, ~но) *adj.* nasty, foul; bad; **~ная пого́да** foul weather; (*impers.*): **мне ~но** I feel awful.
сквита́|ться, юсь *pf.* (**с**+*i.*; *coll.*) to be quits (with), be even (with).
сквоз|и́ть, и́т *impf.* **1.** (*impers.*): **~и́т** there is a draught. **2.** to show through, be seen through (*also fig.*); **синева́ небе́с ~и́ла меж ветвя́ми** the blue of the sky could be seen through the branches; **в его́ слова́х ~и́ла жа́лость к себе́** there was a hint of self-pity in his words.
сквозн|о́й *adj.* **1.** through; **с. ве́тер** draught; **~о́е движе́ние** through traffic; **с. по́езд** through train. **2.** transparent; sheer.
сквозня́к, а́ *m.* draught.
сквозь *prep.*+*a.* through.
сквор|е́ц, ца́ *m.* starling.
скворе́чник, а *m.* nest(ing) box (*for starlings*).
скворе́ч|ня, ни, *g. pl.* **~ен** *f.* = **~ник**
сквош, а *m.* (*sport*) squash.
скейтбо́рд, а *m.* skateboard.
скейтбо́рдинг, а *m.* skateboarding.
скеле́т, а *m.* skeleton.
ске́птик, а *m.* sceptic.
скептици́зм, а *m.* scepticism.
скепти́ческий *adj.* sceptical.
скепти́ч|ный (~ен, ~на) *adj.* = **скепти́ческий**
ске́рцо *nt. indecl.* (*mus.*) scherzo.
ске́тинг-ринг, а *m.* roller-skating rink.
скетч, а *m.* (*theatr.*) sketch.
ски́дк|а, и *f.* **1.** reduction, discount. **2.** (**на**+*a.*; *fig.*) allowance(s) (for); **сде́лать ~у на во́зраст** to make allowances for age.
ски́дыва|ть, ю *impf. of* **ски́нуть**
ски́|нуть, ну, нешь *pf.* (*of* **~дывать**) **1.** (*coll.*) to throw off, down. **2.** (*coll.*) to knock off (*from price*).
ски́петр, а *m.* sceptre.
скипида́р, а *m.* turpentine.
скипида́р|ный *adj. of* **~**
скирд, а́, *pl.* **~ы** *m.* stack, rick.
скирд|а́, ы́, *pl.* **~ы, ~, ~а́м** *f.* = **~**
скис|а́ть, а́ю *impf. of* **~нуть**
ски́с|нуть, ну, нешь, *past* **~, ~ла** *pf.* (*of* **~а́ть**) to go sour, turn sour.
скита́л|ец, ьца *m.* wanderer.
скита́ни|е, я *nt.* wandering.
скита́|ться, юсь *impf.* to wander.
скиф[1]**, а** *m.* (*hist.*) Scythian.
скиф[2]**, а** *m.* skiff.
ски́фский *adj.* (*hist.*) Scythian.
склад[1]**, а** *m.* **1.** storehouse; (*mil.*) depot; **тамо́женный с.** bonded warehouse; **това́рный с.** warehouse. **2.** store; **с. боеприпа́сов** (*mil.*) ammunition dump.
склад[2]**, а** *m.* **1.** stamp, mould; **с. ума́** mentality. **2.** (*coll.*): **ни ~у, ни ла́ду** neither rhyme nor reason.
склад[3]**, а,** *pl.* **~ы** *m.* syllable; **чита́ть по ~а́м** to read out one syllable at a time, spell out.
склади́р|овать, ую *impf. and pf.* to store.
скла́дк|а, и *f.* **1.** fold; pleat, tuck; crease; **ю́бка в ~у** pleated skirt. **2.** wrinkle.
скла́дно *adv.* smoothly, coherently.
складн|о́й *adj.* folding, collapsible; **~а́я крова́ть** camp bed; **с. нож** pocket knife.
скла́д|ный (~ен, ~на́, ~но) *adj.* **1.** (*coll.*) well-built; well-proportioned **2.** (*coll.*) well-made; well-executed.
скла́дочн|ый *adj.* storage, warehousing; **~ое ме́сто** store-room, lumber-room.
склад|ско́й *adj.* = **~очный**
скла́дчин|а, ы *f.* pooling (of resources); **устро́ить ~у** to club together; **купи́ть автомоби́ль в ~у** to club together to buy a car.
скла́дыва|ть(ся), ю(сь) *impf. of* **сложи́ть(ся)**
скле́ива|ть(ся), ю(сь), ет(ся) *impf. of* **скле́ить(ся)**
скле́|ить, ю, ишь *pf.* (*of* **~ивать**) to stick together; to glue together, paste together.
скле́|иться, ится *pf.* (*of* **~иваться**) to stick together (*intrans.*).
скле́йк|а, и *f.* glueing together, pasting together.
склеп, а *m.* burial vault, crypt.
склеп|а́ть, а́ю *pf.* (*of* **~ывать**) to rivet.
склёпыва|ть, ю *impf. of* **склепа́ть**
склеро́з, а *m.* (*med.*) sclerosis; **рассе́янный с.** multiple sclerosis.
склероти́ческий *adj.* (*med.*) sclerotic.
скли́|кать, чу, чешь *pf. of* **~ка́ть**
склик|а́ть, а́ю *impf.* (*of* **~ать**) (*coll.*) to call together.

склóк|а, и *f.* squabble; row.
склон, а *m.* slope; **на ∠е лет** in one's declining years.
склонéни|е, я *nt.* **1.** (*math.*) inclination; (*astron.*) declination. **2.** (*gram.*) declension.
склон|и́ть, ю́, ∠ишь *pf.* (*of* **~я́ть**[1]) **1.** to incline, bend, bow; **с. гóлову (пéред)** (*fig.*) to bow one's head (to, before). **2.** (*fig.*) to talk over; to win over.
склон|и́ться, ю́сь, ∠ишься *pf.* (*of* **~я́ться**[1]) **1.** to bend, bow. **2.** (**к**; *fig.*) to give in (to), yield (to).
склóнност|ь, и *f.* (**к**) inclination (to, for); disposition (to); susceptibility (to); bent (for); penchant (for).
склóн|ный (~ен, ~нá, ~но) *adj.* (**к**) inclined (to), susceptible (to), given (to), prone (to).
склоня́|емый *pres. part. pass. of* **~ть**[2] *and adj.* (*gram.*) declinable.
склон|я́ть[1], **я́ю** *impf. of* **~и́ть**
склон|я́ть[2], **я́ю** *impf.* (*of* **про~**) (*gram.*) to decline.
склон|я́ться[1], **я́юсь** *impf. of* **~и́ться**
склон|я́ться[2], **я́ется** *impf.* (*gram.*) to be declined.
склóч|ный (~ен, ~на) *adj.* (*coll.*) quarrelsome, argumentative.
скля́нк|а, и *f.* **1.** phial; bottle. **2.** (*naut.*) bell (= *one half-hour*); **шесть скля́нок** six bells.
скоб|á, ы́, *pl.* **∠ы, ~áм** *f.* cramp(-iron), clamp; staple; catch, fastening; (*naut.*) shackle.
скóбк|а, и *f.* **1.** *dim. of* **скобá**. **2.** (*mark of punctuation, also math.*) bracket; *pl. also* parentheses.
скобл|и́ть, ю́, ∠и́шь *impf.* to scrape, plane.
скобян|óй *adj.*: **с. товáр, ~ы́е издéлия** hardware.
скóв|анный 1. *p.p.p. of* **~áть**; **с. льдáми** ice-bound. **2.** *adj.* constrained.
сковá|ть, скую́, скуёшь *pf.* (*of* **скóвывать**) **1.** to forge, hammer out. **2.** to forge together. **3.** to chain; to fetter (*also fig.*). **4.** (*mil.*; *fig.*) to pin down. **5.** (*of frost or ice*) to lock; **морóз ~л рéку** the river was frozen over.
сковород|á, ы́, *pl.* **скóвороды, сковорóд, ~áм** *f.* frying-pan.
сковорóдк|а, и *f.* (*coll.*) frying-pan.
скóвыва|ть, ю *impf. of* **сковáть**
сколáчива|ть, ю *impf. of* **сколоти́ть**
скóл|ок, ка *m.* **1.** chip. **2.** (*fig.*) copy.
сколо|ти́ть, чý, ∠тишь *pf.* (*of* **сколáчивать**) **1.** to knock together, knock up. **2.** (*fig., coll.*) to get together; to scrape up.
скол|óть[1], **ю́, ∠ешь** *pf.* (*of* **скáлывать**) to split off, chop off.
скол|óть[2], **ю́, ∠ешь** *pf.* (*of* **скáлывать**) to pin together.
сколь *adv.* how.
скольжéни|е, я *nt.* sliding, slipping.
сколь|зи́ть, жý, зи́шь *impf.* to slide, slip; to glide; **с. глазáми (по+*d.*)** to cast one's eye (over).
скóльз|кий (~ок, ~кá, ~ко) *adj.* slippery (*also fig.*); tricky; delicate, sensitive.
скользн|ýть, ý, ёшь *pf.* to slide, slip; **с. в дверь** to slip through the door.
скольз|я́щий *pres. part. act. of* **~и́ть** *and adj.* sliding; **~я́щая шкалá** sliding scale; **с. ýзел** slip-knot.
скóлько *interrog. and rel. adv.* **1.** how much; how many; **с. стóит?** how much does it cost?; **с. вам лет?** how old are you?; **с. врéмени?** what time is it? **2.** = **наскóлько**
скóлько-нибудь *adv.* any; **éсть у вас при себé с.-н. дéнег?** have you any money on you?
скомáнд|овать, ую *pf. of* **комáндовать**
скомбини́р|овать, ую *pf. of* **комбини́ровать**
скóмка|ть, ю *pf. of* **кóмкать**
скоморóх, а *m.* **1.** (*hist.*) skomorokh (*wandering minstrel-cum-clown*). **2.** (*fig.*) buffoon, clown.
скоморóшеств|о, а *nt.* buffoonery.
скомпили́р|овать, ую *pf. of* **компили́ровать**
скомпон|овáть, ýю *pf. of* **компоновáть**
скомпромети́р|овать, ую *pf. of* **компромети́ровать**
сконструи́р|овать, ую *pf. of* **конструи́ровать**
сконфý|женный *p.p.p. of* **~зить** *and adj.* confused, abashed, disconcerted.
сконфý|зить(ся), жу(сь), зишь(ся) *pf. of* **конфýзить(ся)**
сконцентри́р|овать, ую *pf. of* **концентри́ровать**
скончá|ться, юсь *pf.* to pass away (= *to die*).
скоп|á, ы́ *f.* (*zool.*) osprey.
скоп|éц, цá *m.* eunuch.
скопидóм, а *m.* (*coll.*) hoarder, miser.
скопидóмств|о, а *nt.* (*coll.*) hoarding; miserliness.
скопи́р|овать, ую *pf. of* **копи́ровать**
скоп|и́ть[1], **лю́, ∠ишь** *pf.* (*of* **скáпливать**) (+*a. or g.*) to save (up); to amass, pile up.
скоп|и́ть[2], **лю́, и́шь** *impf.* to castrate.
скоп|и́ться, ∠ится *pf.* (*of* **скáпливаться**) **1.** to accumulate, pile up. **2.** (*of people*) to gather, congregate.
скóпищ|е, а *nt.* (*pej.*) crowd, throng.
скоплéни|е, я *nt.* **1.** accumulation. **2.** crowd; concentration.
скóпом *adv.* (*coll.*) in a crowd, in a group, en masse.
скорб|éть, лю́, и́шь *impf.* (**о**+*p.*) to grieve (for, over), mourn (for, over), lament.
скóрб|ный (~ен, ~на) *adj.* sorrowful, mournful.
скорб|ь, и, *pl.* **∠и, ~éй** *f.* sorrow, grief.
скор|éе (*and* ~éй) 1. *comp. of* **~ый** *and* **∠о**; **как мóжно с.** as soon as possible. **2.** *adv.* rather, sooner; **с. всегó** most likely, most probably.
скорлуп|á, ы́, *pl.* **∠ы** *f.* shell; **замкнýться в свою́ ~ý** to withdraw into one's shell.
скорм|и́ть, лю́, ∠ишь *pf.* (*of* **скáрмливать**) (+*d.*) to feed (to).
скорня́жн|ый *adj.*: **с. товáр** furs.
скорня́к, á *m.* furrier.
скóро *adv.* **1.** quickly, fast. **2.** soon.
скорóб|иться, люсь, ишься *pf. of* **корóбиться**
скороговóрк|а, и *f.* **1.** patter. **2.** tongue-twister.
скорóм|ный (~ен, ~на) *adj.* (*of food*) not to be consumed during fast; **~ные дни** meat days; **~ное мáсло** animal (*opp. vegetable*) fat.
скоропали́тел|ьный (~ен, ~ьна) *adj.* (*coll.*) hasty, rash.
скорописный *adj.* cursive.
скóропис|ь, и *f.* cursive (hand).
скороподъёмност|ь, и *f.* (*aeron.*) rate of climb.
скоропóртящийся *adj.* perishable.
скоропости́жн|ый *adj.*: **~ая смерть** sudden death.
скороспéл|ый (~, ~а) *adj.* **1.** early; fast-ripening. **2.** (*fig., coll.*) premature; hasty.
скоростни́к, á *m.* high-speed worker.
скоростнóй *adj.* high-speed; **с. автóбус** express bus.
скорострéльный *adj.* rapid-firing.
скóрост|ь, и, *pl.* **~и, ~éй** *f.* **1.** speed; velocity; rate; **дозвóленная с. (езды́)** speed-limit; **со ~ью тридцатú миль в час** at thirty miles per hour. **2.** **корóбка ~éй** (*tech.*) gear-box; **перейти́ на другýю с.** to change gear.
скоросшивáтел|ь, я *m.* loose-leaf binder.
скоротá|ть, ю *pf. of* **коротáть**
скоротéч|ный (~ен, ~на) *adj.* transient, short-lived.
скорохóд, а *m.* **1.** (*obs.*) footman. **2.** fast runner; **конькобéжец-с.** high-speed skater.
скорпиóн, а *m.* scorpion; **С.** Scorpio (*sign of zodiac*).
скорч|и́ть, у, ишь *pf. of* **кóрчить**
скóр|ый (~, ~á, ~о) *adj.* **1.** quick, fast; rapid; **с. пóезд** fast train; **~ая пóмощь** ambulance (service); **на ~ую рýку** off-hand, in rough-and-ready fashion. **2.** near, forthcoming, impending; **в ~ом бýдущем** in the near future; **в ~ом врéмени** shortly, before

long; **до ~ого (свида́ния)!** see you soon!
скос, а *m.* slant, splay, chamfer, taper; **у́гол ~а** angle of taper.
ско|си́ть[1], шу́, ~сишь *pf.* (*of* **коси́ть[1]** *and* **ска́шивать**) to mow.
ско|си́ть[2], шу́, си́шь *pf.* (*of* **коси́ть[2]** *and* **ска́шивать**) to squint.
ско|сти́ть, щу́, сти́шь *pf.* (*of* **ска́щивать**) (*coll.*) to take off, knock off; **с. три рубля́ с цены́** to knock three roubles off the price.
скот, а́ *m.* **1.** (*collect.*) cattle; livestock. **2.** (*fig., coll.*) swine, beast.
скоти́н|а, ы *f.* **1.** (*collect.*) cattle; livestock. **2.** (*also m.*) (*fig., coll.*) swine, beast.
ско́тник, а *m.* herdsman; cowman.
ско́т|ный *adj. of* **~**; **с. двор** cattle-yard.
скотобо́|йня, йни, *g. pl.* **~ен** *f.* slaughter-house.
скотово́д, а *m.* cattle-breeder.
скотово́дств|о, а *nt.* cattle-breeding, cattle-raising.
скотово́дческий *adj.* cattle-breeding.
скотоло́жств|о, а *nt.* bestiality.
скотопригóнный *adj.*: **с. двор** stock-yard.
ско́тский *adj.* brutal, brutish, bestial.
скотств|о́, а́ *nt.* brutality, brutishness, bestiality.
скотч, а *m.* (*coll.*) adhesive tape; sellotape (*propr.*).
скра́дыва|ть, ю *impf.* to conceal.
скра́|сить, шу, сишь *pf.* (*of* **~шивать**) (*fig.*) to relieve; **он мно́го чита́л, что́бы с. своё одино́чество** he read a lot to relieve his loneliness.
скра́шива|ть, ю *impf. of* **скра́сить**
скребни́ц|а, ы *f.* curry-comb.
скреб|о́к, ка́ *m.* scraper.
скре́жет, а *m.* gnashing (*of teeth*).
скреже|та́ть, щу́, ~щешь *impf.* **(зуба́ми)** to gnash one's teeth.
скре́п|а, ы *f.* **1.** (*tech.*) tie, clamp, brace. **2.** countersignature.
скреп|и́ть, лю́, и́шь *pf.* (*of* **~ля́ть**) **1.** to fasten (together); to pin (together), to clamp, brace; **~я́ се́рдце** reluctantly, grudgingly. **2.** to countersign.
скре́пк|а, и *f.* paper-clip.
скрепля́|ть, ю *impf. of* **скрепи́ть**
скре|сти́, бу́, бёшь, *past* **~б, ~бла́** *impf.* **1.** to scrape; to scratch, claw. **2.** (*impers.; fig., coll.*) to nag; **у неё ~бло́ на се́рдце** she felt a nagging anxiety.
скре|сти́сь, бу́сь, бёшься, *past* **~бся, ~бла́сь** *impf.* to scratch, make a scratching noise.
скре|сти́ть, щу́, сти́шь *pf.* (*of* **~щивать**) **1.** to cross; **с. мечи́, с. шпа́ги (с+*i.*)** to cross swords (with) (*also fig.*). **2.** (*biol.*) to cross, interbreed.
скрест|и́ться, и́тся *pf.* (*of* **скре́щиваться**) **1.** to cross; (*fig.*) to clash. **2.** (*biol.*) to cross, interbreed.
скреще́ни|е, я *nt.* crossing; intersection.
скре́щивани|е, я *nt.* **1.** crossing. **2.** (*biol.*) crossing, interbreeding.
скре́щива|ть(ся), ю, ет(ся) *impf. of* **скрести́ть(ся)**
скрив|и́ть(ся), лю́(сь), и́шь(ся) *pf. of* **криви́ть(ся)**
скрижа́л|ь, и *f.* tablet, table (*with sacred text inscribed upon it*); **~и** (*fig., arch.*) annals.
скрип, а *m.* squeak, creak; crunch.
скрипа́ч, а́ *m.* violinist; fiddler.
скрип|е́ть, лю́, и́шь *impf.* to squeak, creak; to crunch.
скрипи́чный *adj.* violin; **с. ма́стер** violin-maker; **с. ключ** treble clef, G clef; **с. конце́рт** violin concerto.
скри́пк|а, и *f.* violin; fiddle.
скрипу́чий *adj.* (*coll.*) squeaky; croaky.
скро|и́ть, ю́, и́шь *pf. of* **кро́ить**
скро́мник, а *m.* modest person.
скро́мнича|ть, ю *impf.* to be overmodest.
скро́мност|ь, и *f.* modesty.
скро́м|ный (~ен, ~на́, ~но) *adj.* modest; **по моему́ ~ному мне́нию** in my humble opinion.
скрупулёз|ный (~ен, ~на) *adj.* scrupulous.
скру|ти́ть, чу́, ~тишь *pf.* (*of* **крути́ть** *and* **~чивать**) **1.** to twist; to roll. **2.** to bind, tie up.
скру́чива|ть, ю *impf. of* **скрути́ть**
скрыва́|ть, ю *impf. of* **скрыть**
скрыва́|ться, юсь *impf.* **1.** *impf. of* **скры́ться. 2.** *impf. only* to be in hiding; to lie low.
скры́тнича|ть, ю *impf.* (*coll.*) to be secretive.
скры́т|ный (~ен, ~на) *adj.* secretive.
скры́т|ый *p.p.p. of* **~ь** *and adj.* secret, concealed; **с. смысл** hidden meaning; **~ая теплота́** (*phys.*) latent heat.
скр|ыть, о́ю, о́ешь *pf.* (*of* **~ыва́ть**) **(от)** to hide (from), conceal (from).
скр|ы́ться, о́юсь, о́ешься *pf.* (*of* **~ыва́ться**) **(от) 1.** to hide (o.s.) (from); to go into hiding. **2.** to steal away (from), escape. **3.** to disappear, vanish.
скрюч|иться, усь, ишься *pf.* to bend (*intrans.*); to hunch o.s. up.
скря́г|а, и *c.g.* miser, skinflint.
скря́жнича|ть, ю *impf.* (*coll.*) to be a miser.
скуде́|ть, ю *impf.* (*of* **о~**) to run short; (+*i.*) to be short (of).
ску́д|ный (~ен, ~на́, ~но) *adj.* **1.** scanty; meagre; scant; **~ные сре́дства** slender means **2.** (+*i.*) poor (in), short (of).
ску́дост|ь, и *f.* scarcity; poverty.
ску́к|а, и *f.* boredom; **кака́я с.!** what a bore!
скул|а́, ы́, *pl.* **~ы** *f.* cheek-bone.
скула́ст|ый (~, ~а) *adj.* with prominent cheek-bones.
скул|и́ть, ю́, и́шь *impf.* to whine, whimper (*also fig.*).
ску́льптор, а *m.* sculptor.
скульпту́р|а, ы *f.* sculpture.
скульпту́рный *adj.* sculptural; (*fig.*) statuesque.
ску́мбри|я, и *f.* mackerel.
скунс, а *m.* skunk.
скуп|а́ть, а́ю *impf. of* **~и́ть**
скуперда́|й, я *m.* (*coll.*) miser, skinflint.
скуп|е́ц, ца́ *m.* miser, skinflint.
скуп|и́ть, лю́, ~ишь *pf.* (*of* **~а́ть**) to buy up.
скуп|и́ться, лю́сь, и́шься *impf.* (*of* **по~**) (+*inf. or* **на**+*a.*) to stint, grudge, skimp; to be sparing (of); **с. на де́ньги** to be close-fisted; **не с. на похвалы́** not to stint one's praise.
ску́пк|а, и *f.* buying up.
ску́по *adv.* sparingly.
скуп|о́й (~, ~а́, ~о) *adj.* **1.** stingy, miserly; **с. на слова́** sparing of words. **2.** (*fig.*) inadequate; **с. свет** inadequate illumination.
ску́пост|ь, и *f.* stinginess, miserliness.
ску́пщик, а *m.* buyer.
скуфе́йк|а, и *f. dim. of* **скуфья́**
скуфь|я́, и́ *f.* (*clerical*) skull-cap.
скуча́|ть, ю *impf.* **1.** to be bored. **2. (по+*d. or p.*)** to miss, yearn (for).
ску́ченност|ь, и *f.* density, congestion; **с. населе́ния** overcrowding.
ску́ченный *adj.* dense, congested.
ску́чива|ться, юсь *impf. of* **ску́читься**
ску́ч|иться, усь, ишься *pf.* (*of* **~иваться**) to cluster; to crowd together.
ску́ч|ный (~ен, ~на́, ~но) *adj.* **1.** boring, tedious, dull. **2.** bored; *as pred.* **мне,** *etc.*, **~но** I, *etc.*, am bored.
ску́ша|ть, ю *pf. of* **ку́шать**
слабе́|ть, ю *impf.* (*of* **о~**) to weaken, grow weak(er), (*of wind, etc.*) to slacken, drop.
слабин|а́, ы́ *no pl., f.* **1.** (*in a rope, etc.*) slack. **2.** (*coll.*) weak spot, weak point.
слаби́тельн|ый *adj.* (*med.*) laxative, purgative; *as n.* **~ое, ~ого** *nt.* laxative.
сла́б|ить, ит *impf.* (*of* **про~**) **1.** (*impers.*): **его́ ~ит** he has diarrhoea. **2.** to purge, act as a laxative.
слабоалкого́льный *adj.* low-alcohol.
слабово́ли|е, я *nt.* weak will.

слабово́л|ьный (~ен, ~ьна) *adj.* weak-willed.
слабора́звитый *adj.* (*econ.*) under-developed.
слабоси́ли|е, я *nt.* weakness, feebleness.
слабоси́л|ьный (~ен, ~ьна) *adj.* **1.** weak, feeble. **2.** (*tech.*) low-powered.
сла́бост|ь, и *f.* **1.** weakness, feebleness; debility. **2.** **(к)** weakness (for).
слабоу́ми|е, я *nt.* feeble-mindedness; **ста́рческое с.** senile dementia.
слабоу́м|ный (~ен, ~на) *adj.* feeble-minded.
сла́б|ый (~, ~а́, ~о) *adj.* weak; feeble; slack, loose; (*fig.*) poor; **~ое ме́сто** weak point; **~ая наде́жда** faint hope, slender hope; **~ое оправда́ние** lame excuse; **с. пол** the weaker sex.
сла́в|а, ы *f.* **1.** glory; fame; **во ~у** (*+g.*) to the glory (of); **на ~у** (*coll.*) wonderfully well, excellently; (*as int.*, *+d.*) hurrah (for)!; **с. Бо́гу** thank God. **2.** name, reputation; **до́брая с.** good name; **дурна́я с.** infamy.
слави́ст, а *m.* Slavist, Slavicist.
слави́стик|а, и *f.* Slavistics; Slavonic *or* Slavic studies.
сла́в|ить, лю, ишь *impf.* to glorify, sing the praises (of).
сла́в|иться, люсь, ишься *impf.* (*+i.*) to be renowned (for); to have a reputation (for).
сла́вк|а, и *f.* (*zool.*) warbler.
сла́в|ный (~ен, ~на́, ~но) *adj.* **1.** glorious; famous, renowned. **2.** (*coll.*) nice, splendid; **с. ма́лый** good chap, nice chap.
славосло́ви|е, я *nt.* glorification, eulogy.
славосло́в|ить, лю, ишь *impf.* to eulogize, extol.
славян|и́н, и́на, *pl.* **~́е, ~́** *m.* Slav.
славянофи́л, а *m.* Slavophil(e).
славянофи́л|ьский *adj. of* **~** *and* **~ьство**
славянофи́льств|о, а *nt.* Slavophilism.
славя́нский *adj.* Slavonic; Slavic; Slav.
слага́ем|ое, ого *nt.* **1.** (*math.*) item. **2.** (*fig.*) component.
слага́|ть(ся), ю(сь) *impf. of* **сложи́ть(ся)**
слад, а(у) *m.*, *now only in phr.* **с ним,** *etc.*, **~́у нет** (*coll.*) he, *etc.*, is unmanageable, is out of hand.
сла́|дить, жу, дишь *pf.* (*of* **~живать**) **1.** (*coll.*) to arrange. **2.** **(с+***i.***)** to cope (with), handle.
сла́д|кий (~ок, ~ка́, ~ко) *adj.* **1.** sweet (*also fig.*); **~кое мя́со** (*cul.*) sweetbread; *as n.* **~кое, ~кого** *nt.* sweet (course), dessert. **2.** (*fig., pej.*) sugary, honeyed.
сладкое́жк|а, и *c.g.* (*coll.*) (person with) sweet tooth.
сладкоречи́в|ый (~, ~а) *adj.* smooth-tongued.
сла́дост|ный (~ен, ~на) *adj.* sweet, delightful.
сладостра́сти|е, я *nt.* voluptuousness.
сладостра́стник, а *m.* voluptuary.
сладостра́ст|ный (~ен, ~на) *adj.* voluptuous.
сла́дост|ь, и *f.* **1.** sweetness. **2.** (*pl.*) sweets, sweetmeats.
сла́женност|ь, и *f.* co-ordination, harmony, order.
сла́|женный *p.p.p. of* **~дить** *and adj.* (well-)coordinated, harmonious, orderly.
сла́жива|ть, ю *impf. of* **сла́дить**
сла́|зить, жу, зишь *pf.* (*coll.*) to go; **с. в подва́л за дрова́ми** to go down to the cellar for logs.
слайд, а *m.* slide, transparency.
сла́лом, а *m.* (*sport*) slalom.
сла́н|ец, ца *m.* (*min.*) shale, schist; slate; **нефтено́сный с.** oil shale.
сла́нцев|ый *adj.* slate; shale; **~ое ма́сло** shale oil.
сла|сти́ть, щу́, сти́шь *impf.* (*of* **по~**) to sweeten.
сластолю́б|ец, ца *m.* voluptuary.
сластолюби́в|ый (~, ~а) *adj.* voluptuous.
сластолю́би|е, я *nt.* voluptuousness.
сласт|ь, и, *pl.* **~́и, ~е́й** *f.* **1.** (*pl.*) sweets, sweetmeats. **2.** (*fig.*) fun, pleasure; **что за с. гуля́ть одному́?** what fun is there in going out alone?
слать, шлю, шлёшь *impf.* to send.
слаща́в|ый (~, ~а) *adj.* (*liter. and fig.*) sugary, sickly-sweet.
сла́ще *comp. of* **сла́дкий**
сле́ва *adv.* **(от)** on the left (of), to the left (of); **с. напра́во** from left to right.
слегка́ *adv.* lightly, gently; slightly; **с. суту́литься** to stoop slightly; **с. гла́дить** to stroke gently.
след, а(у), *pl.* **~ы́, ~о́в** *m.* **1.** track; trail, footprint, footstep; **верну́ться по свои́м ~а́м** to retrace one's steps; **замести́ свои́ ~ы́** to cover up one's tracks; **идти́ по чьим-н. ~а́м** (*fig.*) to follow in s.o.'s footsteps. **2.** (*fig.*) trace, sign, vestige; **~́а нет его́** there is no trace of it; **~ы́ о́спы** pockmarks.
сле|ди́ть[1], жу́, ди́шь *impf.* **(за+***i.***)** **1.** to watch; to track; to shadow. **2.** (*fig.*) to follow; to keep up (with). **3.** to look after; to keep an eye (on); **с. за детьми́** to look after children; **с. за поря́дком** to keep order; **с. за тем, что́бы** to see to it that.
сле|ди́ть[2], жу́, ди́шь *impf.* (*of* **на~**) **(на+***p.***)** to mark; to leave traces (on), leave footprints (on).
сле́довани|е, я *nt.* movement; **по́езд да́льнего ~я** long-distance train; **во вре́мя ~я по́езда** while the train is moving; **на всём пути́ ~я** throughout the entire journey.
сле́довател|ь, я *m.* investigator.
сле́довательно *conj.* consequently, therefore.
сле́д|овать[1], ую *impf.* (*of* **по~**) **1.** **(за+***i.***)** to follow; **с. за кем-н. по пята́м** to follow hard on s.o.'s heels. **2.** (*+d.*) to follow; **с. отцу́** to follow in one's father's footsteps. **3.** (*+d.*) to follow; to comply (with). **4.** (*impf. only*) **(до, в+***a.***)** to be bound (for); **э́тот по́езд ~ует в Варша́ву** this train is (bound) for Warsaw. **5.** (*impf. only*) to follow; to result; **из э́того ~ует, что мы оши́блись** it follows from this that we were mistaken.
сле́д|овать[2], ует *impf.* (*impers.*) **1.** (*+d. and inf.*) ought, should; **вам ~ует обрати́ться к ре́ктору** you should approach the rector; **не ~ует забыва́ть** it should not be forgotten; **куда́ ~ует** to the proper quarter; **как и ~овало ожида́ть** as was to be expected; **как ~ует** properly, well and truly. **2.** (*+d.* **с+***g.*) to be owed, be owing; **ско́лько вам ~ует с меня́?** how much do I owe you?; **с вас ~ует де́сять рубле́й** you have ten roubles to pay.
сле́дом *adv.* **(за+***i.***)** immediately (after, behind); **идти́ с. за кем-н.** to follow s.o. close(ly).
следопы́т, а *m.* pathfinder, tracker.
сле́дств|енный *adj. of* **~ие**; investigatory; **~енная коми́ссия** committee of inquiry.
сле́дстви|е[1], я *nt.* consequence, result; **причи́на и с.** cause and effect.
сле́дстви|е[2], я *nt.* (*leg.*) investigation; **суде́бное с.** inquest.
сле́дуем|ый *adj.* (*+d.*) due (to); **отда́ть ка́ждому ~ое** to give each his due.
сле́д|ующий *pres. part. act. of* **~овать** *and adj.* following, next; **на с. день** next day; **на ~ующей неде́ле** next week.
слеж|а́ться, и́ться *pf.* (*of* **~́иваться**) to become caked; to deteriorate in storage.
слёжива|ться, ется *impf. of* **слежа́ться**
сле́жк|а, и *f.* surveillance; shadowing; **установи́ть ~у за кем-н.** to have s.o. shadowed.
слез|а́, ы́, *pl.* **~̈ы, ~̈, ~а́м** *f.* tear; **довести́ до ~̈** to reduce to tears; **э́то до ~̈ оби́дно** it is enough to make one weep.
слеза́|ть, ю *impf. of* **слезть**
слез|и́ться, и́тся *impf.* to water; **её глаза́ ~и́лись** her eyes were watering.
слезли́в|ый (~, ~а) *adj.* **1.** given to crying. **2.** tearful.
слёзн|ый *adj.* **1.** (*anat.*) lachrymal; **с. прото́к** tear duct. **2.** (*fig.*) plaintive.

слезоточи́в|ый (~, ~а) *adj.* **1.: ~ые глаза́** running eyes. **2.** lachrymatory; **с. газ** tear-gas.
слез|ть, у, ешь, *past* **~, ~ла** *pf.* (*of* **~а́ть**) **(с+g.) 1.** to climb down (from), get down (from); to dismount (from). **2.** to alight (from), get off; **с. с трамва́я** to get off a tram. **3.** (*of paint or skin*) to come off, peel.
сленг, а *m.* slang.
слеп|е́нь, ня́ *m.* gadfly, horse-fly.
слеп|е́ц, ца́ *m.* blind man.
слеп|и́ть[1], лю́, и́шь *impf.* to blind; to dazzle.
слеп|и́ть[2], лю́, ~ишь *pf. of* **лепи́ть**
слеп|и́ть[3], лю́, ~ишь *pf.* (*of* **~ля́ть**) **1.** to stick together. **2.** to make by sticking together.
слеп|и́ться, ~иться *pf.* (*of* **~ля́ться**) to stick together.
слепля́|ть(ся), ю(сь) *impf. of* **слепи́ть[3](ся)**
сле́п|нуть, ну, нешь, *past* **~, ~ла** *and* **~нул, ~нула** *impf.* to go blind.
сле́по *adv.* blindly.
слеп|о́й (~, ~а́, ~о) *adj.* blind (*also fig.*); **с. на оди́н глаз** blind in one eye; **с. ме́тод маши́нописи** touch-typing; *as n.* **с., ~о́го** *m.* blind person; (*pl.*, *collect.*) the blind.
сле́п|ок, ка *m.* mould, copy.
слепот|а́, ы *f.* blindness (*also fig.*).
слепы́ш, а́ *m.* mole-rat.
слеса́рн|ый *adj.* metal-work(ing); **~ое де́ло** metal work.
сле́сар|ь, я, *pl.* **~и, ~ей** *and* **~я́, ~е́й** *m.* metal worker; locksmith.
слёт, а *m.* **1.** flight (*of birds*). **2.** gathering, meeting; rally.
слета́|ть[1], ю *pf.* **1.** to fly (*there and back*). **2.** (*fig.*, *coll.*) to fly, dash, nip.
слет|а́ть[2], а́ю *impf. of* **~е́ть**
слет|а́ться, а́юсь *impf. of* **~е́ться**
сле|те́ть, чу́, ти́шь *pf.* (*of* **~та́ть[2]**) **(с+g.) 1.** to fly down (from). **2.** (*coll.*) to fall down, fall off; **с. с ло́шади** to fall from a horse. **3.** to fly away.
слет|е́ться, и́ться *pf.* (*of* **~а́ться**) to fly together; (*of birds*) to congregate.
слечь, сля́гу, сля́жешь, *past* **слёг, слегла́** *pf.* to take to one's bed.
сли́в|а, ы *f.* **1.** plum. **2.** plum-tree.
слива́|ть(ся), ю(сь) *impf. of* **сли́ть(ся)**
сли́в|ки, ок *no sg.* cream (*also fig.*); **с. о́бщества** the cream of society.
сли́в|овый *adj. of* **~а; с. джем** plum jam.
сли́вочник, а *m.* cream-jug.
сли́вочн|ый *adj.* cream; creamy; **~ое ма́сло** butter; **~ое моро́женое** ice-cream.
сливя́нк|а, и *f.* plum brandy.
сли|за́ть, жу́, ~жешь *pf.* (*of* **~зывать**) to lick off.
сли́зист|ый (~, ~а) *adj.* mucous; slimy; **~ая оболо́чка** (*anat.*) mucous membrane.
слизня́к, а́ *m.* slug.
сли́зыва|ть, ю *impf. of* **слиза́ть**
слиз|ь, и *f.* mucus; mucilage; slime.
слиня́|ть, ет *pf.* (*coll.*) to fade.
слип|а́ться, а́ется *impf. of* **~нуться**
сли́п|нуться, нется, *past* **~ся, ~лась** *pf.* (*of* **~а́ться**) to stick together.
сли́тно *adv.* **1.** together. **2.** (*of spelling*) as one word.
сли́тн|ый *adj.* joint, united, continuous; **~ое написа́ние слов** omission of hyphen from words.
сли́т|ок, ка *m.* ingot, bar; **зо́лото в ~ках** gold bullion.
слить, солью́, сольёшь, *past* **слил, слила́, сли́ло** *pf.* (*of* **слива́ть**) **1.** to pour out, pour off. **2.** to pour together; (*fig.*) to merge, amalgamate.
сли́ться, солью́сь, сольёшься, *past* **сли́лся, слила́сь** *pf.* (*of* **слива́ться**) **1.** to flow together. **2.** (*fig.*) to blend, mingle; to merge, amalgamate.
слич|а́ть, а́ю *impf. of* **~и́ть**
слич|и́ть, у́, и́шь *pf.* (*of* **~а́ть**) **(с+i.)** to collate (with), check (with, against).
сли́шком *adv.* too; too much.
слия́ни|е, я *nt.* **1.** confluence. **2.** (*fig.*) blending, merging, amalgamation; merger.
слобод|а́, ы́, *pl.* **сло́боды, слобо́д, ~а́м** *f.* (*hist.*) sloboda (*settlement exempted from normal State obligations*).
слова́к, а *m.* Slovak.
Слова́ки|я, и *f.* Slovakia.
слова́рный *adj.* **1.** lexical; **с. запа́с** vocabulary. **2.** lexicographic(al), dictionary.
слова́р|ь, я́ *m.* **1.** dictionary; glossary, vocabulary (*to particular text*); **энциклопеди́ческий с.** encyclopedia; **с. географи́ческих назва́ний** gazetteer. **2.** (*collect.*) vocabulary; lexis.
слова́цкий *adj.* Slovak, Slovakian.
слова́|чка, чки *f. of* **~к**
слове́н|ец, ца *m.* Slovene.
Слове́ни|я, и *f.* Slovenia.
слове́н|ка, ки *f. of* **~ец**
слове́нский *adj.* Slovene, Slovenian.
слове́сник, а *m.* **1.** philologist. **2.** language and literature teacher.
слове́сный *adj.* verbal; oral.
слове́ч|ко, ка, *pl.* **~ки, ~ек** *nt.*, (*coll.*) *dim. of* **сло́во; замо́лвить с. за кого́-н.** to put in a word for s.o.
сло́вник, а *m.* glossary; word-list (*for inclusion in a dictionary*).
сло́вно *conj.* **1.** as if. **2.** like, as.
сло́в|о, а, *pl.* **~а́** *nt.* **1.** word; **заи́мствованное с.** loanword; **други́ми ~а́ми** in other words; **одни́м ~ом** in a word; **с. в с.** word for word; **с. за́ с.** little by little; **к ~у (пришло́сь, сказа́ть)** by the way; **на ~а́х** (*i*) by word of mouth, (*ii*) in word; **ве́рить на́ с. кому́-н. в чём-н.** to take s.o.'s word for sth.; **челове́к ~а** a man of his word; **игра́ ~** play on words; **~ нет** (*coll.*) it goes without saying. **2.** speech, speaking; **дар ~а** talent for speaking; **свобо́да ~а** freedom of speech. **3.** speech, address; **заключи́тельное с.** concluding remarks; **надгро́бное с.** funeral oration; **дать, предоста́вить с.** (*+d.*) to give the floor, to ask, call upon to speak. **4.** (*liter.*; *hist.*) lay, tale.
сло́вом *adv.* in a word, in short.
словообразова́ни|е, я *nt.* (*ling.*) word-formation.
словообразова́тельный *adj.* word-forming.
словоохо́тливост|ь, и *f.* talkativeness, loquacity.
словоохо́тлив|ый (~, ~а) *adj.* talkative, loquacious.
словосочета́ни|е, я *nt.* combination of words; **усто́йчивое с.** set expression.
словц|о́, а́ *nt.* (*coll.*) word; **для кра́сного ~а́** for effect.
слог[1], а, *pl.* **~и, ~о́в** *m.* syllable
слог[2], а *m.* style.
слогово́й *adj.* syllabic.
слоён|ый *adj.*: **~ое те́сто** puff-pastry.
сложе́ни|е, я *nt.* **1.** adding; composition; (*math.*) addition. **2.** build, physique.
сложён|ный (~, ~а́) *adj.* formed, built; **хорошо́ с.** well-built.
сложи́|вшийся *p.p. of* **~ться; вполне́ с.** fully developed, fully formed.
слож|и́ть[1], у́, ~ишь *pf.* **1.** (*impf.* **скла́дывать**) to put (together), lay (together); to pile, heap, stack; **с. свои́ ве́щи в сунду́к** to pack one's things in a trunk. **2.** (*impf.* **скла́дывать**) to add (up). **3.** (*impf.* **скла́дывать**) to fold (up); **с. вдвое́** to fold in two; **с. ру́ки** to give up the struggle; **~а́ ру́ки** with arms folded; (*fig.*) idle. **4.** (*impf.* **слага́ть**) to compose; **с. пе́сню** to compose a song.
слож|и́ть[2], у́, ~ишь *pf.* **1.** (*impf.* **скла́дывать**) to

take off, put down, set down; **с. груз** to set down a load. **2.** (*impf.* **слага́ть**) (**с**+*g.*; *fig.*) to lay down; to relieve (of); **с. го́лову** (*rhet.*) to lay down one's life; **с. ору́жие** to lay down one's arms; **с. с себя́ обя́занности** to relinquish responsibility.

слож|и́ться[1], **у́сь, ~ишься** *pf.* (*of* **скла́дываться**) (**с**+*i.*) to club together (with); to pool one's resources.

слож|и́ться[2], **у́сь, ~ишься** *pf.* (*of* **скла́дываться**) to form, turn out; to take shape; to arise.

сложноподчинённ|ый *adj.*: **~ое предложе́ние** (*gram.*) complex sentence.

сложносокращённ|ый *adj.* compounded of abbreviations; **~ое сло́во** acronym.

сложносочинённ|ый *adj.*: **~ое предложе́ние** (*gram.*) compound sentence.

сло́жност|ь, и *f.* complication; complexity; **в о́бщей ~и** (all) in all.

сло́ж|ный (~ен, ~на́, ~но) *adj.* **1.** compound; complex, multiple; **~ное предложе́ние** (*gram.*) compound *or* complex sentence; **~ные проце́нты** compound interest; **~ное сло́во** compound word; **~ное число́** complex number. **2.** complicated, complex, intricate; sophisticated.

слоист|ый (~, ~а) *adj.* stratified; lamellar; flaky, foliated; **~ые облака́** strati.

сло|й, я, *pl.* **~и́** *m.* layer; stratum (*also fig.*); coat; **все ~и́ населе́ния** all sections of the population.

сло́йк|а, и *f.* puff-pastry.

слом, а *m.* demolition, breaking up; **пойти́ на с.** to be scrapped.

слома́|ть(ся), ю(сь) *pf. of* **лома́ть(ся)**

слом|и́ть, лю́, ~ишь *pf.* to break, smash (*fig.*) to overcome; **~я́ го́лову** (*coll.*) like mad, at breakneck speed.

слом|и́ться, лю́сь, ~ишься *pf.* to break.

слон, а́ *m.* **1.** elephant; **де́лать из му́хи ~а́** to make mountains out of mole-hills. **2.** (*chess*) bishop.

слон|ёнок, ёнка, *pl.* **~я́та, ~я́т** *m.* elephant calf.

слони́х|а, и *f.* she-elephant, cow-elephant.

слоно́вост|ь, и *f.* (*med.*) elephantiasis.

слоно́в|ый *adj. of* **слон**; elephantine; **~ая боле́знь** = **~ость; ~ая кость** ivory.

слоня́|ться, юсь *impf.* (*coll.*) to loiter, mooch about.

слуг|а́, и́, *pl.* **~и, ~** *m.* **1.** servant. **2.** manservant.

служа́нк|а, и *f.* (house)maid.

слу́жащ|ий, его *m.* employee; white-collar worker, office worker.

слу́жб|а, ы *f.* **1.** service; work; employment; **быть на ~е у кого́-н.** to work for s.o.; **по дела́м ~ы** on official business. **2.** (special) service; **с. движе́ния** (*rail.*) traffic management; **с. пути́** (*rail.*) track maintenance; **~ы ты́ла** (*mil.*) supply services.

служе́бн|ый *adj.* **1.** *adj. of* **слу́жба**; office; official; work; **~ое вре́мя** office hours; **~ое де́ло** official business; **~ая пое́здка** business trip; **в ~ом поря́дке** in the line of duty; **с. путь** official channels; **с. стаж** seniority; **~ая характери́стика** service record. **2.** auxiliary; secondary; **~ое сло́во** (*gram.*) connective word.

служе́ни|е, я *nt.* service, serving.

служи́тел|ь, я *m.* **1.** (*obs.*) servant. **2.** attendant; **с. ку́льта** priest, minister.

служ|и́ть, у́, ~ишь *impf.* (*of* **по~**) **1.** (+*d.*) to serve, devote o.s. (to). **2.** (+*i.*) to serve (as); to work (as), be employed (as), be; **с. в а́рмии** to serve in the Army; **с. доказа́тельством** (+*g.*) to serve as evidence (of). **3.** *impf. only* (+*i. or* **для**) to serve (for), do (for), be used (for); **гости́ная ~ит нам и спа́льней** our sitting-room serves also for a bedroom. **4.** to be in use, do duty, serve. **5.** (*eccl.*) to celebrate; to conduct, officiate (at); **с. обе́дню** to celebrate mass. **6.** *impf. only* (*of a dog*) to beg.

лука́в|ить, лю, ишь *pf. of* **лука́вить**

слуп|и́ть, лю́, ~ишь *pf. of* **лупи́ть**

слух, а *m.* **1.** hearing, ear; **абсолю́тный с.** absolute pitch; **игра́ть по ~у** to play by ear; **она́ вся обрати́лась в с.** she was all ears. **2.** rumour; hearsay; **есть с., что** it is rumoured that; **ни ~у ни ду́ху** (**о**+*p.*) (*coll.*) not a word has been heard (of).

слухов|о́й *adj.* acoustic, auditory, aural; **с. аппара́т** hearing aid; **~о́е окно́** dormer(-window); **с. рожо́к, ~а́я тру́бка** ear-trumpet.

слу́ча|й, я *m.* **1.** case; **во вся́ком ~е** in any case, anyhow, anyway; **ни в ко́ем ~е** in no circumstances; **в лу́чшем, ху́дшем ~е** at best, at worst; **в проти́вном ~е** otherwise; **в тако́м ~е** in that case; **в ~е чего́** (*coll.*) if anything crops up; **на вся́кий с.** to be on the safe side, just in case; **на кра́йний с.** in case of special emergency; **по ~ю** (+*g.*) by reason (of), on account (of), on the occasion (of). **2.** event, incident, occurrence; **несча́стный с.** accident. **3.** opportunity, occasion, chance; **упусти́ть удо́бный с.** to miss an opportunity; **при ~е** when an opportunity offers; **от ~я к ~ю** occasionally.

случа́йно *adv.* **1.** by chance, by accident, accidentally; **я с. подслу́шал их разгово́р** I happened to overhear their conversation. **2.** by any chance; **вы, с., не ви́дели моего́ зо́нтика?** have you by any chance seen my umbrella?

случа́йност|ь, и *f.* chance; **по счастли́вой ~и** by a lucky chance, by sheer luck.

случа́|йный (~ен, ~йна) *adj.* **1.** accidental, fortuitous; **~йная встре́ча** chance meeting. **2.** chance, casual, incidental; **с. за́работок** casual earnings.

случ|а́ть, а́ю *impf. of* **~и́ть**

случ|а́ться, а́ется *impf. of* **~и́ться**

случ|и́ть, у́, и́шь *pf.* (*of* **~а́ть**) (**с**+*i.*) (*of animals*) to couple (with), pair (with), mate (with).

случ|и́ться[1], **и́тся** *pf.* (*of* **~а́ться**) (*of animals*) to couple, pair, mate.

случ|и́ться[2], **и́тся** *pf.* (*of* **~а́ться**) **1.** to happen, come about; **что бы ни ~и́лось** whatever happens, come what may. **2.** (*impers.*; +*d. and inf.*) to happen; **мне ~и́лось попа́сть в Москву́** I happened to land up in Moscow. **3.** (*coll.*) to turn up, show up; **~и́лось у меня́ как раз пять рубле́й** I happened to have just five roubles on me.

слу́чк|а, и *f.* coupling, pairing, mating.

слу́шани|е, я *nt.* **1.** audition; hearing; **с. ле́кции** attendance at a lecture. **2.** (*leg.*) hearing.

слу́шател|ь, я *m.* **1.** listener; (*pl.*; *collect.*) audience. **2.** student.

слу́ша|ть, ю *impf.* (*of* **по~**) **1.** to listen (to), hear; **с. ле́кцию** to attend a lecture; **~й(те)!** (*coll.*) listen!, look here!; **~ю!** at your service!; very good!; (*on telephone*) hello! **2.** to attend lectures (on). **3.** to listen (to), obey. **4.** (*leg.*) to hear.

слу́ша|ться, юсь *impf.* (*of* **по~**) ((*obs.*)+*g.*) **1.** to listen (to), obey; **~юсь!** (*mil.*) yes, sir! (*indicating readiness to carry out order*). **2.** *pass. of* **~ть**

слы|ть, ву́, вёшь, *past* **~л, ~ла́, ~ло** *impf.* (*of* **про~**) (+*i. or* **за**+*a.*) to have a reputation (for), be said (to); to pass (for).

слыха́ть *no pres., impf.* **1.** to hear; **что у вас с.?** (*coll.*) tell us what you have been up to!; **ничего́ не с.** nothing can be heard. **2.** *as adv.* (*coll.*) apparently, it seems; **ты, с., пи́шешь но́вый рома́н** we hear you are writing a new novel.

слы́ш|ать, у, ишь *impf.* (*of* **у~**) **1.** to hear; **~ишь, ~ите** (*coll.*) do you hear? (*emph. command or direction*). **2.** (*impf. only*) to have the sense of hearing; **не с.** to be hard of hearing. **3.** to feel, sense.

слы́ш|аться, ится *impf.* (*of* **по~**) to be heard; to be audible.

слы́шимост|ь, и *f.* audibility.

слы́шно[1] *adv*. audibly.

слы́шно[2] *as pred*., *impers*. **1.** one can hear; **бы́ло с., как она́ рыда́ла** one could hear her sobbing. **2.** (*coll*.); **что с.?** what news?, any news?; **о них ничего́ не с.** nothing has been heard of them.

слы́ш|ный (∼ен, ∼на́, ∼но) *adj*. audible.

слюд|а́, ы́ *f*. mica.

слюдяно́й *adj*. mica.

слюн|а́, ы́ *f*. saliva.

слю́н|и, е́й *no sg*. (*coll*.) slobber, spittle; **пусти́ть с.** to slobber, drivel; **распусти́ть с.** (*coll*.) to dither.

слюн|и́ть, ю́, и́шь *impf*. **1.** (*pf*. **по∼**) to wet with saliva. **2.** (*pf*. **за∼**) to slobber over.

слю́н|ки, ок *no sg*., *dim*. *of* **∼и; от э́того с. теку́т** it makes one's mouth water.

слюноотделе́ни|е, я *nt*. salivation.

слюнтя́|й, я *m*. (*coll*.) ditherer.

слюня́в|ить, лю, ишь *impf*. (*coll*.) to slobber over.

слюня́вчик, а *m*. (*baby's*) bib.

слюня́вый *adj*. (*coll*.) dribbling, drivelling.

сля́котный *adj*. slushy.

сля́кот|ь, и *f*. slush.

см (*abbr*. *of* **сантиме́тр**) cm, centimetre(s).

см. (*abbr*. *of* **смотри́**) see, *vide*.

сма́|зать, жу, жешь *pf*. (*of* **∼зывать**) **1.** to oil, lubricate; to grease. **2.** (*fig*., *coll*.) to grease the palm (of), grease the wheels (of). **3.** to smudge; to rub off. **4.** (*fig*., *coll*.) to slur (over).

сма́|заться, жусь, жешься *pf*. (*of* **∼зываться**) **1.** to grease o.s. **2.** (*of paint*, *etc*.) to become smudged; to come off.

сма́зк|а, и *f*. **1.** lubrication. **2.** oil; lubricant; grease.

смазли́в|ый (∼, ∼а) *adj*. (*coll*.) pretty.

сма́зочн|ый *adj*. *of* **смазка; ∼ая коро́бка** oil can; **∼ое ма́сло** lubricating oil; **с. материа́л** lubricant.

сма́зчик, а *m*. greaser.

сма́зывани|е, я *nt*. **1.** oiling, lubrication; greasing. **2.** (*fig*.) slurring over.

сма́зыва|ть(ся), ю(сь) *impf*. *of* **сма́зать(ся)**

смак, а *m*. (*coll*.) relish, savour (*also fig*.); **со ∼́ом** with relish, with gusto.

смак|ова́ть, у́ю *impf*. (*coll*.) to savour; to eat, drink with relish; to relish (*also fig*.).

сма́нива|ть, ю *impf*. *of* **смани́ть**

сман|и́ть, ю́, ∼́ишь *pf*. (*of* **∼́ивать**) to entice, lure.

смастер|и́ть, ю́, и́шь *pf*. *of* **мастери́ть**

сма́тыва|ть, ю *impf*. *of* **смота́ть**

сма́тыва|ться, юсь *impf*. *of* **смота́ться**

сма́хива|ть[1]**, ю** *impf*. *of* **смахну́ть**

сма́хива|ть[2]**, ю** *impf*. (**на**+*a*.; *coll*.) to look like, resemble.

смах|ну́ть, ну́, нёшь *pf*. (*of* **∼́ивать**[1]) to brush (away, off), flick (away, off); **с. пыль** (**с**+*g*.) to dust.

сма́чива|ть, ю *impf*. *of* **смочи́ть**

сма́ч|ный (∼ен, ∼на́, ∼но) *adj*. (*coll*.) **1.** savoury, tasty. **2.** (*fig*., *pej*.) fruity; **∼ная ру́гань** colourful language.

смеж|а́ть, а́ю *impf*. *of* **∼и́ть**

смеж|и́ть, у́, и́шь *pf*. (*of* **∼а́ть**) (*obs. or poet*.); **с. глаза́** to close one's eyes.

сме́жник, а *m*. factory producing parts for use by another.

сме́жност|ь, и *f*. contiguity.

сме́ж|ный (∼ен, ∼на) *adj*. adjacent, contiguous, adjoining; **∼ные ко́мнаты** interconnecting rooms; **∼ные поня́тия** closely-related concepts.

смека́лист|ый (∼, ∼а) *adj*. (*coll*.) sharp, quick-witted.

смека́лк|а, и *f*. (*coll*.) native wit; nous; sharpness.

смек|а́ть, а́ю *impf*. (*of* **∼ну́ть**) (*coll*.) to see the point (of), grasp.

смек|ну́ть, ну́, нёшь *pf*. *of* **∼а́ть**

смеле́|ть, ю *impf*. (*of* **о∼**) to grow bold(er).

сме́ло *adv*. **1.** boldly; **я могу́ с. сказа́ть** I can safely say; **с.!** don't be afraid!, have a try! **2.** easily, with ease.

сме́лост|ь, и *f*. boldness, audacity; **взять на себя́ с.** (+*inf*.) to take the liberty (of), make bold (to).

сме́л|ый (∼, ∼а́, ∼о) *adj*. bold, audacious, daring.

смельча́к, а́ *m*. (*coll*.) bold spirit; dare-devil.

сме́н|а, ы *f*. **1.** changing; replacement; **с. карау́ла** changing of the guard; **идти́ на ∼у** (+*d*.) to come to take the place (of), come to relieve. **2.** (*collect*.) replacements; successors; (*mil*.) relief; **гото́вить себе́ ∼у** to prepare successors (*to take one's place*). **3.** shift; **у́тренняя, дневна́я, вече́рняя с.** morning, day, night shift. **4.** change (*of linen*, *etc*.).

смен|и́ть, ю́, ∼́ишь *pf*. (*of* **∼я́ть**[1]) **1.** to change; to replace; (*mil*.) to relieve; **с. гнев на ми́лость** to temper justice with mercy. **2.** to replace, relieve, succeed (s.o.).

смен|и́ться, ю́сь, ∼́ишься *pf*. (*of* **∼я́ться**) **1.** to hand over; (*mil*.) to be relieved; **с. с дежу́рства** to go off duty. **2.** (+*i*.) to give way (to); turn to.

сме́нн|ый *adj*. **1.** shift; **∼ая рабо́та** shift work. **2.** (*tech*.) removeable; **∼ое колесо́** spare wheel.

сменя́|емый *pres. part. pass. of* **∼ть**[1] *and adj*. removable, interchangeable.

смен|я́ть[1]**, я́ю** *impf*. *of* **∼и́ть**

смен|я́ть[2]**, я́ю** *pf*. (**на**+*a*.; *coll*.) to exchange (for).

смен|я́ться, я́юсь *impf*. *of* **смени́ться**

смер|де́ть, жу́, ди́шь *impf*. (*obs*.) to stink.

смерз|а́ться, а́ется *impf*. *of* **∼̋нуться**

смёрз|нуться, нется, *past* **∼ся, ∼лась** *pf*. (*of* **∼а́ться**) to freeze together.

сме́р|ить, ю, ишь *pf*. (*coll*.) to measure; **с. взгля́дом** to look (s.o.) up and down, measure at a glance.

смерк|а́ться, а́ется *impf*. (*of* **∼́нуться**) to get dark; **∼а́лось** it was getting dark.

сме́рк|нуться, нется *pf*. *of* **∼а́ться**

смерте́льно *adv*. **1.** mortally. **2.** (*coll*.) extremely, terribly; **с. уста́ть** to be dead tired, be dead-beat.

смерте́л|ьный (∼ен, ∼ьна) *adj*. **1.** mortal; deadly; **с. уда́р** mortal blow. **2.** (*coll*.) extreme, terrible.

сме́ртник, а *m*. prisoner sentenced to death.

сме́ртност|ь, и *f*. mortality, death-rate.

сме́рт|ный (∼ен, ∼на) *adj*. **1.** mortal; *as n*. **с., ∼ного** *m*. mortal; **просто́й с.** ordinary mortal. **2.** death; **с. бой** fight to the death; **∼ная казнь** capital punishment, death penalty; **с. пригово́р** death sentence; **с. час** last hour(s). **3.** (*fig*.) deadly, extreme.

смертоно́с|ный (∼ен, ∼на) *adj*. mortal, fatal, lethal; **с. уда́р** mortal blow.

смерт|ь, и, *pl*. **∼́и, ∼е́й** *f*. **1.** death, decease; **умере́ть голо́дной ∼́ью** to starve to death; **умере́ть свое́й ∼́ью** to die a natural death; **до́ ∼и** (*fig*., *coll*.) to death; **я уста́л до́ смерти** I'm dead tired; **боро́ться не на жизнь, а на с.** to fight to the death; **быть при́ ∼и** to be dying. **2.: с. как** *as adv*. (*coll*.) awfully, terribly; **ему́,** *etc*., **с. как хо́чется** (+*inf*.) he, *etc*., is dying (for).

смерч, а *m*. **1.** waterspout. **2.** sand-storm, tornado.

сме|си́ть, шу́, ∼́сишь *pf*. *of* **меси́ть**

сме|сти́, ту́, тёшь, *past* **∼̋л, ∼ла́** *pf*. (*of* **∼та́ть**[2]) **1.** to sweep off, sweep away; **с. с лица́ земли́** to wipe off the face of the earth. **2.** to sweep into, together.

сме|сти́ть, щу́, сти́шь *pf*. (*of* **∼ща́ть**) **1.** to displace, remove, move. **2.** (*fig*.) to remove, dismiss (*from one's post*).

сме|сти́ться, щу́сь, сти́шься *pf*. (*of* **∼ща́ться**) to change position, become displaced.

смес|ь, и *f*. mixture; blend, medley.

сме́т|а, ы *f*. (*fin*.) estimate.

смета́н|а, ы *f*. sour(ed) (cultured) cream.

смет|а́ть[1]**, а́ю** *pf*. (*of* **мета́ть** *and* **∼̋ывать**) to tack (together).

сметá|ть², **ю** *pf. of* **смести́**
смётк|а, и *f.* (*coll.*) quick-wittedness; gumption.
смéтлив|ый (~, ~а) *adj.* quick-witted.
смéт|ный *adj. of* **~а; ~ные ассигнóвки** budget allowances.
смётыва|ть, ю *impf. of* **сметáть**¹
сме|ть, ю *impf.* (*of* **по~**) to dare; to make bold; **не ~й(те)!** don't you dare!
смех, а (у) *m.* laughter; laugh; **разрази́ться ~ом** to burst out laughing; **без ~у** joking apart, in earnest; **в с., нá с., ~а рáди** for a joke, for fun, in jest; **нам не до ~у** we are in no mood for laughter.
смехотвóр|ный (~ен, ~на) *adj.* laughable, ludicrous, ridiculous.
смéш|анный *p.p.p. of* **~áть** *and adj.* mixed; combined; **~анное акционéрное óбщество** joint-stock company; **телефóн ~анного пóльзования** party-line; **~анная порóда** crossbreed.
смеш|áть, áю *pf.* (*of* **мешáть**² *and* **~ивать**) **1.** (**с**+*i.*) to mix (with), blend (with). **2.** to lump together. **3.** to confuse, mix up.
смеш|áться, áюсь *pf.* (*of* **~иваться**) **1.** to mix, blend in; to mingle; **с. с толпóй** to mingle in the crowd. **2.** to become confused, get mixed up.
смешéни|е, я *nt.* **1.** mixture, blending. **2.** confusion, mixing up; **с. поня́тий** confusion of ideas.
смéшива|ть(ся), ю(сь) *impf. of* **смешáть(ся)**
смеш|и́ть, ý, и́шь *impf.* to make laugh.
смешли́в|ый (~, ~а) *adj.* easily amused.
смеш|нóй (~óн, ~нá) *adj.* **1.** funny, droll; *as pred.* **~нó** it is funny, it makes one laugh; **вам ~нó?** do you find it funny? **2.** absurd ridiculous, ludicrous; **до ~нóго** to the point of absurdity.
смеш|óк, кá *m.* (*coll.*) chuckle; giggle.
смещá|ть(ся), ю(сь) *impf. of* **смести́ть(ся)**
смещéни|е, я *nt.* **1.** displacement, removal. **2.** (*geol.*) slip, upheaval, dislocation.
сме|я́ться, ю́сь, ёшься *impf.* **1.** to laugh; **с. шýтке** to laugh at a joke. **2.** (**над**) to laugh (at), mock (at), make fun (of). **3.** to joke, say in jest.
сми́л|оваться, уюсь *pf.* to have mercy, take pity.
смирéни|е, я *nt.* humbleness, humility, meekness.
смирéнност|ь, и *f.* humility.
смирéн|ный (~, ~на) *adj.* humble, meek.
смири́тельн|ый *adj.* **~ая рубáшка** straitjacket.
смир|и́ть, ю́, и́шь *pf.* (*of* **~я́ть**) to restrain, subdue.
смир|и́ться, ю́сь, и́шься *pf.* (*of* **~я́ться**) to submit; to resign o.s.
сми́рно *adv.* quietly; **с.!** (*mil. word of command*) attention!
сми́р|ный (~ен, ~нá, ~но) *adj.* quiet; submissive.
смир|я́ть(ся), я́ю(сь) *impf. of* **~и́ть(ся)**
см. на об. (*abbr. of* ***смотри́ на оборóте***) PTO (= *please turn over*), see over.
смог, а *m.* smog.
смоделúр|овать, ую *pf. of* **моделúровать**
смóкв|а, ы *f.* fig.
смóкинг, а *m.* dinner-jacket.
смокóвниц|а *f.* fig-tree.
смол|á, ы́, *pl.* **~ы** *f.* resin; pitch, tar.
смолёный *adj.* resined; tarred, pitched.
смоли́ст|ый (~, ~а) *adj.* resinous.
смол|и́ть, ю́, и́шь *impf.* (*of* **вы~** *and* **о~**) to resin; to tar, pitch.
смолк|áть, áю *impf. of* **~нуть**
смóлк|нуть, ну, нешь, *past* **~, ~ла** *pf.* (*of* **~áть**) to fall silent; (*of sound*) to cease.
смóлоду *adv.* from, in one's youth.
смоло|ти́ть, чý, ~тишь *pf. of* **молоти́ть**
смолóть, смелю́, смéлешь *pf. of* **молóть**
смолч|áть, ý, и́шь *pf.* to hold one's tongue.
смоль *only in phr.* **чёрный как с.** jet-black.
смол|янóй *adj. of* **~á; ~янáя бóчка** tar barrel; **с. кáмень** pitchstone; **~янóе мáсло** resin oil; **с. состáв** resinous compound.
смонти́р|овать, ую *pf. of* **монти́ровать**
сморкá|ть, ю *impf.* (*of* **вы́~**): **с. нос** to blow one's nose.
сморкá|ться, юсь *impf.* (*of* **вы́~**) to blow one's nose.
смородин|а, ы *no pl., f.* **1.** currant; currant bush. **2.** (*collect.*) currants; **крáсная, чёрная с.** redcurrants, blackcurrants.
сморóдин|ный *adj. of* **~а**
сморч|óк, кá *m.* morel (*mushroom*).
смóрщ|енный *p.p.p. of* **~ить** *and adj.* wrinkled.
смóрщ|ить(ся), у(сь), ишь(ся) *pf. of* **мóрщить(ся)**
смотá|ть, ю *pf.* (*of* **смáтывать**) to wind, reel; (*coll.*): **с. ýдочки** to take to one's heels, make off.
смотá|ться, юсь *pf.* (*of* **смáтываться**) (*coll.*) to take to one's heels, make off.
смотр, а *m.* **1.** (**на ~ý,** *pl.* **~ы́**) review, inspection; **произвести́ с.** (+*d.*) to review, inspect. **2.** (**на ~е,** *pl.* **~ы**) public showing.
смотр|éть, ю́, ~ишь *impf.* (*of* **по~**) **1.** (**на**+*a.*, **в**+*a.*) to look (at); **с. в окнó** to look out of the window; **с. в глазá, в лицó** (+*d.*) to look in the face; **с. сквозь пáльцы** (**на**+*a.*; *coll.*) to make light (of), wink (at). **2.** to see; to watch; **с. телеви́дение** to watch television. **3.** to examine; to review, inspect. **4.** (**за**+*i.*) to look (after); to be in charge (of); **с. за поря́дком** to keep order. **5.** (**на**+*a.*; *coll.*) to follow the example (of). **6.** *impf. only* (**в**+*a.*, **на**+*a.*) to look (on to, over); **óкна ~ят в сад** the windows look on to the garden. **7.** *impf. only* (+*i.*; *coll.*) to look (like); **он ~ит простакóм** he looks a simple fellow. **8.: ~и́(те)!** mind!, take care!; **~и́те, чтóбы нáшим гостя́м бы́ло удóбно** see that our guests are comfortable. **9.: ~я́ (где, как,** *etc.*) it depends (where, how, *etc.*); **~я́ (по**+*d.*) depending (on), in accordance (with).
смотр|éться, ю́сь, ~ишься *impf.* (*of* **по~**) **1.** to look at o.s.; **с. в зéркало** to look at o.s. in the mirror. **2.** *pass. of* **~éть**
смотри́тел|ь, я *m.* supervisor; keeper, custodian.
смотров|óй *adj.* **1.** (*mil.*) review. **2.: ~óе окнó** inspection window; **~áя щель** vision slit (*in tank*).
смоч|и́ть, ý, ~ишь *pf.* (*of* **смáчивать**) to damp, wet, moisten.
смо|чь, гý, ~жешь, *past* **~г, ~глá** *pf. of* **мочь**¹
смошéннича|ть, ю *pf. of* **мошéнничать**
смрад, а *m.* stink, stench.
смрáд|ный (~ен, ~на) *adj.* stinking.
смýгл|ый (~, ~á, ~о) *adj.* dark-complexioned.
смýт|а, ы *f.* (*obs.*) disturbance, sedition.
сму|ти́ть, щý, ти́шь *pf.* (*of* **~щáть**) **1.** to embarrass, confuse. **2.** to disturb, trouble.
сму|ти́ться, щýсь, ти́шься *pf.* (*of* **~щáться**) to be embarrassed, be confused.
смýт|ный (~ен, ~нá, ~но) *adj.* **1.** vague; confused, dim. **2.** disturbed, troubled; **~ное врéмя** (*hist.*) Time of Troubles (*1605–13*).
смутья́н, а *m.* (*coll.*) trouble-maker.
смущá|ть(ся), ю(сь) *impf. of* **смути́ть(ся)**
смущéни|е, я *nt.* embarrassment, confusion.
сму|щённый *p.p.p. of* **~ти́ть** *and adj.* embarrassed, confused.
смывá|ть(ся), ю(сь) *impf. of* **смы́ть(ся)**
смыкá|ть(ся), ю(сь) *impf. of* **сомкнýть(ся)**
смысл, а *m.* **1.** sense, meaning; **прямóй, перенóсный с.** literal, metaphorical sense; **в ~е** (+*g.*) as regards. **2.** sense, point; **имéть с.** to make sense; **нет никакóго ~а** (+*inf.*) there is no sense (in), there is no point (in). **3.** (good) sense; **здрáвый с.** common sense.
смы́сл|ить, ю, ишь *impf.* (**в**+*p.*; *coll.*) to understand.
смыслов|óй *adj. of* **смысл; ~ы́е оттéнки** shades of meaning.

смыть, смо́ю, смо́ешь *pf.* (*of* **смыва́ть**) **1.** to wash off; (*fig.*) to clear, wipe away; (*mil.*) to wipe out. **2.** to wash away.
смы́ться, смо́юсь, смо́ешься *pf.* (*of* **смыва́ться**) **1.** to wash off, come off. **2.** (*fig.*, *coll.*) to slip away.
смы́чк|а, и *f.* union; linking.
смыч|ко́вый *adj. of* **~о́к**
смыч|о́к, ка́ *m.* (*mus.*) bow.
смышлён|ый (~, ~а) *adj.* (*coll.*) clever, bright.
смягч|а́ть(ся), а́ю(сь) *impf. of* **~и́ть(ся)**
смягча́|ющий *pres. part. act. of* **~ть; ~ющие вину́ обстоя́тельства** extenuating circumstances.
смягче́ни|е, я *nt.* **1.** softening. **2.** mitigation.
смягч|и́ть, у́, и́шь *pf.* (*of* **~а́ть**) **1.** (*impf. also* **мягчи́ть**) to soften. **2.** to ease, alleviate; to assuage; **с. боль** to alleviate pain; **с. наказа́ние** to mitigate a punishment; **с. напряже́ние** to ease tension.
смягч|и́ться, у́сь, и́шься *pf.* (*of* **~а́ться**) **1.** to soften, become soft. **2.** to relent, relax; to grow mild; to ease (off). **3.** *pass. of* **~и́ть**
смяте́ни|е, я *nt.* confusion, disarray; commotion.
смяте́н|ный (~, ~а) *adj.* (*obs.*) troubled, perturbed.
смять, сомну́, сомнёшь *pf.* (*of* **мять**) **1.** to crumple; **с. пла́тье** to crush a dress. **2.** (*mil.*) to crush.
смя́ться, сомнётся *pf.* (*of* **мя́ться**[1]) to get creased; to get crumpled.
снаб|ди́ть, жу́, ди́шь *pf.* (*of* **~жа́ть**) (*+i.*) to supply (with), furnish (with), provide (with).
снабжа́|ть, ю *impf. of* **снабди́ть**
снабже́ни|е, я *nt.* supply, supplying, provision.
сна́доб|ье, ья, *g. pl.* **~ий** *nt.* (*coll.*) drug.
сна́йпер, а *m.* sniper; sharp-shooter.
снару́жи *adv.* on the outside; from (the) outside.
снаря́д, а *m.* **1.** projectile, missile; shell; **управля́емый с.** guided missile. **2.** contrivance, machine; **гимнасти́ческие ~ы** gymnastic apparatus.
снаря|ди́ть, жу́, ди́шь *pf.* (*of* **~жа́ть**) to equip, fit out.
снаря|ди́ться, жу́сь, ди́шься *pf.* (*of* **~жа́ться**) to equip o.s., get ready.
снаря́дн|ый *adj.* **1.** shell; ammunition. **2.: ~ая гимна́стика** (*sport*) apparatus work.
снаряжа́|ть(ся), ю(сь) *impf. of* **снаряди́ть(ся)**
снаряже́ни|е, я *nt.* equipment, outfit; **ко́нское с.** harness.
снаст|ь, и, *pl.* **~и, ~е́й** *f.* **1.** (*collect.*) tackle, gear. **2.** (*usu. pl.*) rigging.
снача́ла *adv.* **1.** at first, in the beginning. **2.** all over again.
сна́шива|ть, ю *impf. of* **сноси́ть**
СНГ *nt. indecl.* (*abbr. of* ***Содру́жество незави́симых госуда́рств***) CIS (*Commonwealth of Independent States*).
снег, а, *pl.* **~а́** *m.* snow; **мо́крый с.** sleet; **как с. на́ го́лову** like a bolt from the blue.
снеги́р|ь, я́ *m.* bullfinch.
снегов|о́й *adj.* snow.
снегоочисти́тел|ь, я *m.* snow-plough.
снегопа́д, а *m.* snow-fall.
снегосту́пы, ов *pl.* (*sport*) snow-shoes.
снегоубо́рочн|ый *adj.* snow-removal; **~ая маши́на** snow-plough.
снегохо́д, а *m.* snowmobile.
Снегу́рочк|а, и *f.* (*folklore*) Snow Maiden.
снеда́|ть, ю *impf.* to consume, gnaw.
снед|ь, и *f.* (*obs. or dial.*) food.
снежи́нк|а, и *f.* snow-flake.
сне́жн|ый *adj.* snow; snowy; **~ая ба́ба** snow man; **с. зано́с, с. сугро́б** snow-drift.
снеж|о́к, ка́ *m.* **1.** light snow. **2.** snowball; **игра́ть в ~ки́** to throw snowballs, have a snowball fight.
снес|ти́[1]**, у́, ёшь,** *past* **~, ~ла́** *pf.* (*of* **сноси́ть**) **1.** to take. **2.** to fetch down, bring down. **3.** (*usu. impers.*) to carry away; to blow off; **урага́ном ~ло́ кры́шу** a hurricane took the roof off. **4.** to demolish, take down, pull down. **5.** to cut off, chop off.
снес|ти́[2]**, у́, ёшь** *pf.* (*of* **сноси́ть**) to bring together, pile up.
снес|ти́[3]**, у́, ёшь** *pf.* (*of* **сноси́ть**) to bear, endure, suffer, stand, put up (with).
снес|ти́[4]**, у́, ёшь** *pf.* (*of* **нести́**[2]) to lay (eggs).
снес|ти́сь[1]**, у́сь, ёшься,** *past* **~ся, ~ла́сь** *pf.* (*of* **сноси́ться**) (**с**+*i.*) to communicate (with).
снес|ти́сь[2]**, ётся** *pf. of* **нести́сь**[2]
снижа́|ть(ся), ю(сь) *impf. of* **сни́зить(ся)**
сниже́ни|е, я *nt.* **1.** lowering, reduction; **с. зарпла́ты** wage cut. **2.** (*aeron.*) descent.
сни́|зить, жу, зишь *pf.* (*of* **~жа́ть**) **1.** to bring down, lower. **2.** (*fig.*) lower, reduce; **с. себесто́имость** to cut production costs; **с. по до́лжности** to reduce, demote.
сни́|зиться, жусь, зишься *pf.* (*of* **~жа́ться**) **1.** to descend, come down. **2.** (*fig.*) to fall, sink, come down; **це́ны ~зились** prices have come down.
снизо|йти́, йду́, йдёшь, *past* **~шёл, ~шла́** *pf.* (*of* **снисходи́ть**) (**к**) to condescend (to); **с. к чьей-н. про́сьбе** to deign to grant s.o.'s request.
сни́зу *adv.* from below (*pol.*; *also fig.*); from the bottom; **с. до́верху** from top to bottom.
сни́к|нуть, ну, нешь *pf. of* **ни́кнуть**
снима́|ть(ся), ю(сь) *impf. of* **снять(ся)**
сни́м|ок, ка *m.* photograph, photo, print.
сни|ска́ть, щу́, ~щешь *pf.* (*of* **сни́скивать**) (*obs.*) to gain, get, win.
сни́скива|ть, ю *impf. of* **сниска́ть**
снисходи́тельност|ь, и *f.* **1.** condescension **2.** tolerance, leniency.
снисходи́тел|ьный (~ен, ~ьна) *adj.* **1.** condescending. **2.** tolerant, lenient.
снисхо|ди́ть, жу́, ~дишь *impf. of* **снизойти́**
снисхожде́ни|е, я *nt.* indulgence, leniency.
сни́|ться, снюсь, сни́шься *impf.* (*of* **при~**) (*+d.*) to dream; **ей ~лось, что** she dreamed that; **мне ~лся лев** I dreamed about a lion.
сноб, а *m.* snob.
сноби́зм, а *m.* snobbery.
сно́ва *adv.* again, anew, afresh.
снова́ть[1]**, сную́, снуёшь** *impf.* to scurry about.
снова́ть[2]**, сную́, снуёшь** *impf.* (*text.*) to warp.
сновиде́ни|е, я *nt.* dream.
сногсшиба́тел|ьный (~ен, ~ьна) *adj.* (*coll.*, *joc.*) stunning.
сноп, а́ *m.* sheaf; **с. луче́й** shaft of light.
сноровист|ый (~, ~а) *adj.* (*coll.*) smart, clever.
сноро́вк|а, и *f.* skill, knack.
снос[1]**, а** *m.* **1.** demolition, pulling down; **дом назна́чен на с.** the house is to be pulled down. **2.** drift.
снос[2]**, а (у)** *m.* wear; **тако́й мате́рии ~у нет** this material won't wear out; **не знать ~у** to wear well.
снос[3]**: быть на ~ях** (*coll.*; *of a pregnant woman*) to be near her time.
сно|си́ть[1]**, щу́, ~сишь** *pf.* (*of* **сна́шивать**) to wear out.
сно|си́ть[2]**, шу́, ~сишь** *pf.* (*coll.*) to take (*and bring back*).
сно|си́ть[3]**, шу́, ~сишь** *impf. of* **снести́**[1,2,3]
сно|си́ться, шу́сь, ~сишься *impf. of* **снести́сь**[1]
сно́ск|а, и *f.* footnote.
сно́сно *adv.* (*coll.*) tolerably, so-so.
сно́с|ный (~ен, ~на) *adj.* (*coll.*) tolerable; fair.
снотво́р|ный (~ен, ~на) *adj.* soporific (*also fig.*); **~ное сре́дство** soporific, sleeping draught, tablet.
снох|а́, и́, *pl.* **~и** *f.* (father's) daughter-in-law.
сноше́ни|е, я *nt.* (*usu. pl.*) intercourse; relations, dealings; **име́ть ~я** (**с**+*i.*) to have dealings (with); to have (sexual) intercourse (with).

сну|ю, ёшь *see* **сновáть**

снЯти|е, я *nt.* **1.** taking down; **с. урожáя** gathering in the harvest. **2.** removal; **с. запрéта** lifting of a ban; **с. с рабóты** dismissal. **3.** taking, making; **с. кóпии** copying.

снят|óй *adj.*: **~óе молокó** skimmed milk.

сня|ть, снимý, снúмешь, *past* **~л, ~лá, ~ло** *pf.* (*of* **снимáть**) **1.** to take off; to take down; **с. урожáй** to gather in the harvest; **с. осáду** to raise a siege; **с. с себЯ** to divest o.s. (of); **с. с себЯ ответственность** to decline responsibility. **2.** (*fig.*) to remove; to withdraw, cancel; **с. запрéт** to lift a ban; **с. с рабóты** to discharge, sack; **с. с фрóнта** to withdraw from the front. **3.** (*mil.*) to pick off. **4.** to take, make; to photograph, make a photograph (of); **с. кóпию** (**с**+*g.*) to copy, make a copy (of); **с. мéрку с когó-н.** to take s.o.'s measurements; **с. показáние** to take (down) evidence; **с. фильм** to shoot a film. **5.** to take, rent (*a house, etc.*); **с. в арéнду** to take on lease. **6.** (*cards*) to cut.

снЯ|ться, снимýсь, снúмешься, *past* **~лся, ~лáсь** *pf.* (*of* **снимáться**) **1.** to come off. **2.** to move off; **с. с Якоря** to weigh anchor. **3.** to have one's photograph taken.

со *prep.* = **с**

со... *vbl. pref.* = **с...**

соáвтор, а *m.* co-author.

соáвторств|о, а *nt.* co-authorship.

собáк|а, и *f.* dog; **дворóвая с.** watchdog; **морскáя с.** dogfish; **с.-поводЫрь** guide-dog; **служéбная с.** guard dog; **устáть как с.** to be dog-tired; **вот где с. зарЫта!** so that's what it's all about!; **~у съесть** (**на**+*p.*; *coll.*) to know inside out.

собаковóд, а *m.* dog-breeder.

собá|чий *adj. of* **~ка**; canine; **~чья жизнь** dog's life; **с. хóлод** intense cold.

собáчк|а[1]**, и** *f.* little dog, doggie.

собáчк|а[2]**, и** *f.* **1.** trigger. **2.** (*tech.*) catch, trip; pawl (*of ratchet*).

собáчник, а *m.* (*coll.*) dog-lover.

собезьЯннича|ть, ю *pf. of* **обезьЯнничать**

СОБЕС, а *or* **собéс, а** *m.* (*abbr. of* **(отдéл) социáльного обеспéчения**) **1.** social security. **2.** social security department (*of local authority*).

собесéдник, а *m.* interlocutor; **он — забáвный с.** he is amusing company.

собесéдовани|е, я *nt.* conversation, discussion.

собирáтел|ь, я *m.* collector.

собирáтельный *adj.* (*gram.*) collective.

собирáтельств|о, а *nt.* collecting.

собирá|ть, ю *impf. of* **собрáть**

собирá|ться, юсь *impf.* **1.** (*impf. of* **собрáться**). **2.** (+*inf.*) to intend (to), be about (to); **я ~лся позвонúть вам** I was going to ring you up.

соблаговол|úть, ю́, úшь *pf.* (+*inf.*; *obs.*) to deign (to), condescend (to).

соблáзн, а *m.* temptation.

соблазнúтел|ь, я *m.* **1.** tempter. **2.** seducer.

соблазнúтельниц|а, ы *f.* temptress.

соблазнúтел|ьный (~ен, ~ьна) *adj.* **1.** tempting; alluring; seductive. **2.** suggestive, corrupting.

соблазн|úть, ю́, úшь *pf.* (*of* **~Ять**) **1.** to tempt. **2.** to seduce, entice.

соблазн|Ять, Яю *impf. of* **~úть**

соблюдá|ть, ю *impf. of* **соблюстú**

соблюдéни|е, я *nt.* observance; maintenance; **с. порЯдка** maintenance of order.

соблю|стú, дý, дёшь, *past* **~л, ~лá** *pf.* (*of* **~дáть**) to keep (to); to observe; **с. закóн** to observe a law.

собóй *see* **себЯ**

соболéзновани|е, я *nt.* sympathy, condolence.

соболéзн|овать, ую *impf.* (+*d.*) to sympathize (with), commiserate (with).

собóл|ий, ья, ье *adj. of* **сóболь; с. мех** sable.

собо|лúный *adj.* sable.

сóбол|ь, я, *pl.* **~Я́, ~éй** *and* **~и, ~ей** *m.* **1.** sable. **2.** (*pl.* **~Я́, ~éй**) sable (fur).

собóр, а *m.* **1.** (*hist.*) council, synod, assembly; **вселéнский с.** ecumenical council; **зéмский с.** Assembly of the Land (*in Muscovite Russia*). **2.** cathedral.

собóр|ный *adj. of* **~**

собóровани|е, я *nt.* (*eccl.*) extreme unction.

собóр|овать, ую *impf. and pf.* (*eccl.*) to administer extreme unction (to), anoint.

собóю = **собóй,** *see* **себЯ**

собрáни|е, я *nt.* **1.** meeting; **óбщее с.** general meeting; **с. правлéния** board meeting. **2.** assembly; **учредúтельное с.** constituent assembly. **3.** collection; **с. закóнов** code (of laws); **с. сочинéний** collected works.

сóбр|анный *p.p.p. of* **~áть** *and adj.*; **с. человéк** precise, accurate, self-disciplined person.

собрáт, а, *pl.* **~ья, ~ьев** *m.* colleague; **с. по орýжию** brother-in-arms.

собр|áть, соберý, соберёшь, *past* **~áл, ~лá, ~áло** *pf.* (*of* **собирáть**) **1.** to gather, collect, pick; **с. цветЫ** to pick flowers. **2.** to assemble, muster; to convene; **с. послéдние сúлы** to make a last effort. **3.** (*tech.*) to assemble, mount. **4.** to obtain, poll (*votes*). **5.** to prepare, make ready, equip; **с. когó-н. в дорóгу** to equip s.o. for a journey; **с. на стол** to lay the table. **6.** (*dressmaking*) to gather, take in.

собр|áться, соберýсь, соберёшься, *past* **~áлся, ~алáсь, ~áлóсь** *pf.* (*of* **собирáться**) **1.** to gather, assemble, muster. **2.** (**в**+*a.*) to prepare (for), make ready (for); **с. в гóсти** to get ready to go away (*to visit s.o.*). **3.** (+*inf.*) to intend (to), be about (to), be going (to). **4.** (**с**+*i.*, *fig.*) to collect; **с. с дýхом** (*i*) to get one's breath, (*ii*) to pluck up one's courage; **с. с мЫслями** to collect one's thoughts; **с. с сúлами** to summon up one's strength, brace o.s.

сóбственник, а *m.* owner, proprietor.

сóбственнический *adj.* possessive, proprietary.

сóбственно 1. *adv.* strictly; **с. говорЯ** strictly speaking, as a matter of fact. **2.** *particle* proper; **егó не интересýет с. медицúна** he is not interested in medicine proper.

собственнорýчно *adv.* with one's own hand.

собственнорýчн|ый *adj.* done, made, written with one's own hand(s); **~ая пóдпись** autograph.

сóбственност|ь, и *f.* **1.** property. **2.** possession, ownership; **приобрестú в с.** to become the owner (of).

сóбственн|ый *adj.* **1.** (one's) own; proper; **~ыми глазáми** with one's own eyes; **~ой персóной** in person; **úмя ~ое** (*gram.*) proper name. **2.** true, proper; **в ~ом смЫсле** in the true sense. **3.** (*tech.*) natural; internal; **~ая скóрость** actual speed.

собутЫльник, а *m.* (*coll.*) drinking companion.

событи|е, я *nt.* event; **текýщие ~я** current affairs.

сов... *comb. form, abbr. of* **совéтский**

сов|á, Ы, *pl.* **~ы** *f.* owl.

совáть, сую́, суёшь *impf.* (*of* **сýнуть**) to shove, thrust, poke; **с. рýки в кармáны** to stick one's hands in one's pockets; **с. нос** (**в**+*a.*) (*coll.*) to poke one's nose (into), pry (into).

совáться, сýюсь, суёшься *impf.* (*of* **сýнуться**) (*coll.*) **1.** to push, strain. **2.** (**в**+*a.*; *fig.*) to butt (in), poke one's nose (into).

соверш|áть(ся), áю, áет(ся) *impf. of* **~úть(ся)**

совершéни|е, я *nt.* accomplishment, fulfilment; perpetration.

совершéнно *adv.* **1.** perfectly. **2.** absolutely, utterly, completely, totally; **с. вéрно!** quite right!; perfectly true!; quite so!

совершеннолéти|е, я *nt.* majority; **достúгнуть ~я** to come of age, attain one's majority.

совершеннолéтний *adj.* of age.
совершéн|ный[1] **(~ен, ~на)** *adj.* **1.** perfect. **2.** (*coll.*) absolute, utter, complete, total, perfect.
совершéнный[2] *adj.* (*gram.*) perfective.
совершéнств|о, а *nt.* perfection; **в ~е** perfectly, to perfection.
совершéнств|овать, ую *impf.* (*of* **у~**) to perfect; to develop, improve.
совершéнств|оваться, уюсь *impf.* (*of* **у~**) (**в**+*p.*) to perfect o.s. (in); to improve.
соверш|и́ть, ý, и́шь *pf.* (*of* **~áть**) **1.** to accomplish, carry out; to perform; to commit; **с. оши́бку** to make a mistake. **2.** to complete, conclude; **с. сдéлку** to complete a transaction, make a deal.
сóве|стить, щу, стишь *impf.* to shame, put to shame.
сóве|ститься, щусь, стишься *impf.* (*of* **по~**) (+*g. or inf.*; *obs.*) to be ashamed (of).
сóвестлив|ый (~, ~а) *adj.* conscientious.
сóвестно *as pred.* (+*d. and inf.*) to be ashamed; **емý бы́ло с.** he was ashamed; **как вам не с.!** you ought to be ashamed of yourself!
сóвест|ь, и *f.* conscience; **чи́стая, нечи́стая с.** clear, guilty conscience; **со споко́йной ~ью** with a clear conscience; **по ~и (говоря́)** to be honest; **свобо́да ~и** freedom of worship.
совéт[1]**, а** *m.* advice, counsel; (*leg.*) opinion.
совéт[2]**, а** *m.* **1.** Soviet, soviet. **2.** council; **С. Безопáсности** Security Council. **3.** council, conference.
совéтник, а *m.* **1.** adviser. **2.** (*title of office*) councillor.
совéт|овать, ую *impf.* (*of* **по~**) (+*d.*) to advise.
совéт|оваться, уюсь *impf.* (*of* **по~**) (**с**+*i.*) to consult, ask advice (of), seek advice (from).
совéтск|ий *adj.* **1.** Soviet, of the Soviet Union; **~ая влáсть** Soviet rule *or* power; **с. нарóд** the Soviet people. **2.** soviet (= *of local soviets*).
Совéтск|ий Сою́з, ~ого ~а *m.* the Soviet Union.
совéтчик, а *m.* adviser, counsellor.
совещáни|е *nt.* conference, meeting; **с. на верхáх** summit conference.
совещáтельный *adj.* consultative, deliberative.
совещá|ться, юсь *impf.* **1.** (**о**+*p.*) to deliberate (on, about), consult (on, about). **2.** (**с**+*i.*) to confer (with).
сов|и́ный *adj. of* **~á**; owlish.
совкóвый *adj.* (*sl.*, *pej.*) Soviet.
совладá|ть, ю *pf.* (**с**+*i.*; *coll.*) to control; **с. с собóй** to control o.s.
совладéл|ец, ьца *m.* joint owner, joint proprietor.
совладéни|е, я *nt.* joint ownership.
совмести́мост|ь, и *f.* compatibility.
совмести́м|ый (~, ~а) *adj.* compatible.
совмести́тел|ь, я *m.* person holding more than one office, combining jobs; pluralist.
совмести́тельств|о, а *nt.* holding of more than one office; pluralism; **рабóтать по ~у** to hold more than one office, combine jobs.
совмести́тельств|овать, ую *impf.* to hold more than one office, combine jobs.
совме|сти́ть, щý, сти́шь *pf.* (*of* **~щáть**[2]) to combine.
совме|сти́ться, сти́тся *pf.* (*of* **~щáться**) **1.** to coincide. **2.** to be combined, combine.
совмéстно *adv.* in common, jointly.
совмéстн|ый *adj.* joint, combined; **~ые дéйствия** concerted action; **~ое обучéние** co-education; **~ое предприя́тие** joint venture; **~ая рабóта** team-work.
совмещá|ть[1]**, ю** *impf.* to hold more than one office, combine jobs.
совмещá|ть[2]**(ся), ю(сь)** *impf. of* **совмести́ть(ся)**
совнархóз, а *m.* (*abbr. of* **совéт нарóдного хозя́йства**) (*hist.*) Economic Council (*central or regional economic management board in USSR*).
сов|óк, кá *m.* shovel, scoop; **садóвый с.** trowel; **с. для мýсора** dustpan.
совокуп|и́ться, лю́сь, и́шься *pf.* (*of* **~ля́ться**) (**с**+*i.*) to copulate (with).
совокуплéни|е, я *nt.* copulation.
совокупля́|ть(ся), ю(сь) *impf. of* **совокупи́ть(ся)**
совокýпно *adv.* in common, jointly.
совокýпност|ь, и *f.* aggregate, sum total; totality; **в ~и** in the aggregate; **по ~и** (+*g.*) on the basis (of).
совокýпн|ый *adj.* joint, combined, aggregate; **~ые уси́лия** combined efforts.
совпадá|ть, ю *impf. of* **совпáсть**
совпадéни|е, я *nt.* coincidence.
совпá|сть, дý, дёшь, *past* **~л** *pf.* (*of* **~дáть**) **1.** (**с**+*i.*) to coincide (with); **части́чно с.** to overlap. **2.** to agree, concur, tally.
соврати́тел|ь, я *m.* perverter, seducer.
совра|ти́ть, щý, ти́шь *pf.* (*of* **~щáть**) to pervert, seduce; **с. с пути́ и́стинного** to lead astray.
совра|ти́ться, щусь, ти́шься *pf.* (*of* **~щáться**) to go astray.
совр|áть, ý, ёшь, *past* **~áл, ~алá, ~áло** *pf. of* **врать**
совращá|ть(ся), ю(сь) *impf. of* **соврати́ть(ся)**
совращéни|е, я *nt.* perverting, seducing, seduction.
совремéнник, а *m.* contemporary.
совремéнност|ь, и *f.* **1.** contemporaneity. **2.** the present (time).
совремéн|ный (~ен, ~на) *adj.* **1.** (+*d.*) contemporaneous (with), of the time (of). **2.** contemporary, present-day; modern; up-to-date; state-of-the-art.
совсéм *adv.* quite, entirely, completely; **с. не** not at all, not in the least; **с. не то** nothing of the kind.
совхóз, а *m.* sovkhoz, State farm.
совхóз|ный *adj. of* **~**
соглáси|е, я *nt.* **1.** consent; assent; **с вáшего ~я** with your consent. **2.** agreement; **в ~и** (**с**+*i.*) in accordance (with). **3.** accord; harmony.
согласи́тельн|ый *adj.* conciliatory; **~ая коми́ссия** conciliation commission.
согла|си́ть, шý, си́шь *pf.* (*of* **~шáть**) to reconcile.
согла|си́ться, шýсь, си́шься *pf.* (*of* **~шáться**) **1.** (**на**+*a. or* +*inf.*) to consent (to), agree (to). **2.** (**с**+*i.*) to agree (with), concur (with).
соглáсно *adv.* **1.** in accord, in harmony; **петь с.** to sing in harmony. **2.** *as prep.* (+*d. or* **с**+*i.*) in accordance (with); according (to); **с. договóру** in accordance with the treaty, under the treaty.
соглáсност|ь, и *f.* harmony, harmoniousness.
соглáс|ный[1] **(~ен, ~на)** *adj.* **1.** (**на**+*a.*) agreeable (to). **2.** (**с**+*i.*) in agreement (with); **быть ~ным** to agree (with); **~ен, ~на, ~ны?** do you agree? **3.** harmonious, concordant.
соглáс|ный[2] *adj.* (*gram.*) consonant(al); *as n.* **с., ~ого** *m.* consonant.
согласовáни|е, я *nt.* **1.** coordination; agreement. **2.** (*gram.*) agreement; **с. времён** sequence of tenses.
согласóванност|ь, и *f.* coordination; **с. во врéмени** synchronization.
согласóв|анный *p.p.p. of* **~áть** *and adj.* coordinated; **~анные дéйствия** concerted action.
соглас|овáть, ýю *pf.* (*of* **~óвывать**) (**с**+*i.*) **1.** to coordinate (with). **2. с. что-н. с кем-н.** to come to an agreement with s.o. about sth. **3.** (*gram.*) to make agree (with).
соглас|овáться, ýется *impf. and pf.* (**с**+*i.*) **1.** to accord (with), to conform (to). **2.** (*gram.*) to agree (with).
согласóвыва|ть, ю *impf. of* **согласовáть**
соглашáтел|ь, я *m.* (*pol.*; *pej.*) compromiser; appeaser.
соглашáтель|ский *adj. of* **~**; **~ская поли́тика** policy of compromise, appeasement policy.
соглашáтельств|о, а *nt.* (*pol.*; *pej.*) compromise, appeasement.

соглаша́|ть(ся), ю(сь) *impf. of* **согласи́ть(ся)**

соглаше́ни|е, я *nt.* **1.** agreement, understanding. **2.** agreement, covenant; **заключи́ть с.** to conclude an agreement.

соглядата́|й, я *m.* spy.

согна́|ть[1], **сгоню́, сго́нишь,** *past* **~л, ~ла́, ~ло** *pf.* (*of* **сгоня́ть**) to drive away.

согна́|ть[2], **сгоню́, сго́нишь,** *past* **~л, ~ла́, ~ло** *pf.* (*of* **сгоня́ть**) to drive together, round up.

согн|у́ть, у́, ёшь *pf.* (*of* **гнуть** *and* **сгиба́ть**) to bend, curve, crook.

согн|у́ться, у́сь, ёшься *pf.* (*of* **гну́ться** *and* **сгиба́ться**) to bend, bow (down); to stoop.

согражданин, а, *pl.* **сogра́ждане, сogра́ждан** fellow-citizen.

согрева́|ть(ся), ю(сь) *impf. of* **согре́ть(ся)**

согре́|ть, ю *pf.* (*of* **~ва́ть**) to warm, heat.

согре́|ться, юсь *pf.* (*of* **~ва́ться**) to get warm; to warm o.s.

согреше́ни|е, я *nt.* sin, trespass.

согреш|и́ть, у́, и́шь *pf.* (*of* **греши́ть**) (**про́тив**) to sin (against), trespass (against).

со́д|а, ы *f.* soda, sodium carbonate; **питьева́я с.** baking soda.

соде́йстви|е, я *nt.* assistance, help.

соде́йств|овать, ую *impf. and pf.* (*pf. also* **по~**) (*+d.*) to assist; to further, promote; to contribute (to).

содержа́ни|е, я *nt.* **1.** maintenance, upkeep; allowance; (*animal*) housing; **де́нежное с.** financial support; **с. под аре́стом** custody. **2.** pay; **окла́д ~я** rate of pay. **3.** content; **с больши́м ~ем** (*+g.*) rich (in). **4.** matter, substance; content. **5.** content(s); plot (*of a novel, etc.*). **6.** table of contents.

содержа́нк|а, и *f.* (*obs.*) kept woman.

содержа́тел|ь, я *m.* (*obs.*) landlord (*of an inn, etc.*).

содержа́тел|ьный (~ен, ~ьна) *adj.* rich in content; **~ьное письмо́** interesting letter.

содерж|а́ть, у́, ´~ишь *impf.* **1.** to keep, support; **с. семью́** to keep a family. **2.** to keep, have (*a business, enterprise, etc.*). **3.** (**в**+*p.*) to keep (*in a given state*); **с. в испра́вности** to keep going, in working order; **с. в поря́дке** to keep in order; **с. под аре́стом** to keep under arrest. **4.** to contain.

содерж|а́ться, у́сь, ´~ишься *impf.* **1.** to be kept, be maintained. **2.** to be kept, be; **с. под аре́стом** to be under arrest. **3.** (**в**+*p.*) to be contained (by).

содержи́м|ое, ого *nt.* contents.

соде́|ять, ю, ешь *pf.* (*obs. or rhet.*) to commit, carry out.

соде́|яться, ется *pf.* (*obs. or joc.*) to happen.

со́дов|ый *adj.* soda; **~ая вода́** soda (water).

содо́м, а *m.* (*coll.*) uproar, row; **подня́ть с.** to raise hell.

содра́|ть, сдеру́, сдерёшь, *past* **~л, ~ла́, ~ло** *pf.* (*of* **сдира́ть**) **1.** to tear off, strip off; **с. ко́жу** (**с**+*g.*) to skin, flay. **2.** *pf. only* (*fig., coll.*) to fleece.

содрога́ни|е, я *nt.* shudder.

содрог|а́ться, а́юсь *impf. of* **~ну́ться**

содрог|ну́ться, ну́сь, нёшься *pf.* (*of* **~а́ться**) to shudder, shake, quake.

содру́жеств|о, а *nt.* **1.** concord; **рабо́тать в те́сном ~е** (**с**+*i.*) to work in close co-operation (with). **2.** commonwealth; **Брита́нское с. на́ций** the British Commonwealth.

со́евый *adj.* soya; **с. тво́ро́г** tofu.

соедине́ни|е, я *nt.* **1.** joining, combination. **2.** (*tech.*) joint. **3.** (*chem.*) compound. **4.** (*mil.*) formation.

Соединённ|ое Короле́вств|о, ~ого ~а *nt.* the United Kingdom.

Соединённ|ые Шта́т|ы (Аме́рики), ~ых ~ов (А.) *no sg.* the United States (of America).

соедин|ённый *p.p.p. of* **~и́ть** *and adj.* united, joint.

соедини́тельн|ый *adj.* connecting; **~ое звено́** connecting link; **~ая коро́бка** (*elec.*) junction box; **с. сою́з** (*gram.*) copulative conjunction; **~ая ткань** (*biol.*) connective tissue; **~ая тя́га** coupling rod.

соедин|и́ть, ю́, и́шь *pf.* (*of* **~я́ть**) **1.** to join, unite. **2.** to connect, link; **с. по телефо́ну** to put through. **3.** (*chem.*) to combine.

соедин|и́ться, ю́сь, и́шься *pf.* (*of* **~я́ться**) **1.** to join, unite. **2.** (*chem.*) to combine. **3.** *pass. of* **~и́ть**

соедин|я́ть(ся), я́ю(сь) *impf. of* **~и́ть(ся)**

сожале́ни|е, я *nt.* **1.** (**о**+*p.*) regret (for); **к ~ю** unfortunately. **2.** (**к**) pity (for).

сожале́|ть, ю *impf.* (**о**+*p. or* **+что**) to regret, deplore.

сожже́ни|е, я *nt.* burning; cremation; **с. на костре́** burning at the stake.

сожи́тел|ь, я *m.* **1.** room-mate. **2.** lover.

сожи́тельниц|а, ы *f.* **1.** room-mate. **2.** mistress.

сожи́тельств|о, а *nt.* living together, cohabitation.

сожи́тельств|овать, ую *impf.* (**с**+*i.*) to live (with); to live together, cohabit.

сожр|а́ть, у́, ёшь, *past* **~а́л, ~ала́, ~а́ло** *pf. of* **жрать**

созва́нива|ться, юсь *impf. of* **созвони́ться**

созва́|ть, созову́, созовёшь, *past* **~л, ~ла́, ~ло** *pf.* **1.** (*impf.* **сзыва́ть**) to gather; to invite. **2.** (*impf.* **созыва́ть**) to call (together), summon; to convene; **с. ми́тинг** to call a meeting.

созве́зди|е, я *nt.* constellation.

созвон|и́ться, ю́сь, и́шься *pf.* (*of* **созва́ниваться**) **1.** (**с**+*i.*; *coll.*) to speak on the telephone (to). **2.** (**о**+*p.*; *coll.*) to arrange (sth.) on the phone.

созву́чи|е, я *nt.* **1.** (*mus.*) accord, consonance. **2.** (*liter.*) assonance.

созву́ч|ный (~ен, ~на) *adj.* **1.** harmonious. **2.** (*+d.*) consonant (with), in keeping (with).

созда|ва́ть(ся), ю́, ёт(ся) *impf. of* **´~ть(ся)**

созда́ни|е, я *nt.* **1.** creation, making. **2.** creation, work. **3.** creature.

созда́тел|ь, я *m.* **1.** creator; founder. **2.** the Creator.

созда́|ть, м, шь, ст, ди́м, ди́те, ду́т, *past* **со́зда́л, ~ла́, со́зда́ло** *pf.* (*of* **~ва́ть**) to create; to found; to establish; **с. впечатле́ние** to give the impression.

созда́|ться, стся, ду́тся, *past* **~лся, ~ла́сь** *pf.* (*of* **~ва́ться**) to be created; to arise; **у нас ~ло́сь впечатле́ние, что** we gained the impression that.

созерца́ни|е, я *nt.* contemplation.

созерца́тел|ьный (~ен, ~ьна) *adj.* contemplative.

созерца́|ть, ю *impf.* to contemplate.

созида́ни|е, я *nt.* creation.

созида́тел|ь, я *m.* creator.

созида́тел|ьный (~ен, ~ьна) *adj.* creative, constructive.

созида́|ть, ю *impf.* (*no pf.*) to build up.

созна|ва́ть, ю́, ёшь *impf.* **1.** *impf. of* **´~ть. 2.** to be conscious (of), realize; **я́сно с.** to be alive (to).

созна|ва́ться, ю́сь, ёшься *impf. of* **´~ться**

созна́ни|е, я *nt.* **1.** consciousness; **прийти́ в с.** to regain, recover consciousness. **2.** recognition, acknowledgement; **с. до́лга** sense of duty. **3.** confession.

созна́тельност|ь, и *f.* **1.** awareness; acumen; **полити́ческая с.** political awareness. **2.** deliberateness.

созна́тел|ьный (~ен, ~ьна) *adj.* **1.** conscious. **2.** intelligent. **3.** deliberate.

созна́|ть, ю *pf.* (*of* **~ва́ть**) to recognize, acknowledge; **с. свою́ оши́бку** to recognize one's mistake.

созна́|ться, юсь *pf.* (*of* **~ва́ться**) (**в**+*p.*) to confess (to); (*leg.*) to plead guilty.

созорнича́|ть, ю *pf. of* **озорнича́ть**

созрева́|ть, ю *impf. of* **созре́ть**

созре́|ть, ю *pf.* (*of* **~ва́ть**) to ripen, mature.

созы́в, а *m.* calling, summoning; convocation.

созыва́|ть, ю *impf. of* **созва́ть**

соизво́л|ить, ю, ишь *pf.* (*of* **~я́ть**) (*+inf.*; *obs.*) to

deign (to), be pleased (to).
соизвол|я́ть, я́ю *impf. of* **~и́ть**
соизмери́м|ый (~, ~а) *adj.* commensurable.
соиска́ни|е, я *nt.* (+*g.*) competition (for).
соиска́тел|ь, я *m.* (+*g.*) competitor (for).
со́йк|а, и, *g. pl.* **со́ек** *f.* (*zool.*) jay.
со|йти́[1], **йду́, йдёшь,** *past* **~шёл, ~шла́** *pf.* (*of* **сходи́ть**) **1.** to go down, come down; to descend, get off, alight; **с. с ле́стницы** to go downstairs; **с. с ло́шади** to dismount; **с. на не́т** to come to naught. **2.** to leave; **с. с доро́ги** to get out of the way, step aside; **с. с ре́льсов** to come off the rails; **снег ~шёл** the snow has melted; **с. с ума́** to go mad, go off one's head. **3.** (*of paint, skin, etc.*) to come off.
со|йти́[2], **йду́, йдёшь** *pf.* (*of* **сходи́ть**) **1.** (**за**+*a.*) to pass (for), be taken (for). **2.** (*coll.*) to pass, go off; **~шло́ благополу́чно** it went off all right; **э́то ~шло́ ему́ с рук** he got away with it.
со|йти́сь, йду́сь, йдёшься, *past* **~шёлся, ~шла́сь** *pf.* (*of* **сходи́ться**) **1.** to meet; to come together, gather. **2.** (**с**+*i.*) to meet, become friends (with); to become (*sexually*) intimate (with). **3.** (+*i.*, **в**+*p. or* **на**+*p.*) to agree (about); **с. в цене́** to agree about a price; **они́ не ~шли́сь хара́ктерами** they could not get on. **4.** (*fig.*) to agree, tally.
сок, а (у), о ~е, в *and* **на ~у́** *m.* juice; (*coll.*) **в (по́лном) ~у́** in the prime of life.
соквартира́нт, а *m.* flat-sharer, lodgings-sharer.
соковыжима́лк|а, и *f.* juicer.
со́кол, а *m.* falcon (*also fig., rhet.*; *of air aces*); **гол как соко́л** (*coll.*) as poor as a church mouse.
соколи́н|ый *adj. of* **со́кол**[1]; **~ая охо́та** falconry.
соко́льник, а *m.* (*hist.*) falconer.
сокра|ти́ть, щу́, ти́шь *pf.* (*of* **~ща́ть**) **1.** to shorten; to curtail; to abbreviate; to abridge. **2.** to reduce, cut down; **с. шта́ты** to cut down the staff. **3.** to dismiss, discharge, lay off. **4.** (*math.*) to cancel.
сокра|ти́ться, ти́тся *pf.* (*of* **~ща́ться**) **1.** grow shorter. **2.** to decrease, decline. **3.** (*coll.*) to cut down (*on expenses*). **4.** (**на**+*a.*; *math.*) to be cancelled (by). **5.** (*physiol.*) to contract.
сокраща́|ть(ся), ю(сь) *impf. of* **сократи́ть(ся)**
сокраще́ни|е, я *nt.* **1.** shortening. **2.** abridgement; **с ~ями** abridged. **3.** abbreviation. **4.** reduction, cutting down; **с. вооруже́ний** (*mil.*) arms build-down; **с. шта́тов** staff reduction. **5.** (*math.*) cancellation. **6.** (*physiol.*) contraction.
сокращённо *adv.* briefly; in abbreviated form.
сокра|щённый *p.p.p. of* **~ти́ть** *and adj.* brief; **~щённое сло́во** abbreviation, contraction.
сокрове́н|ный (~, ~на) *adj.* secret, concealed; **~ные мы́сли** innermost thoughts.
сокро́вищ|е, а *nt.* treasure; **ни за каки́е ~а** not for the world.
сокро́вищниц|а, ы *f.* treasure-house, storehouse.
сокруш|а́ть, а́ю *impf. of* **~и́ть**
сокруша́|ться, юсь *impf.* (**о**+*p.*) to grieve (for, over); to be distressed (about).
сокруше́ни|е, я *nt.* **1.** smashing, shattering. **2.** (*obs.*) grief, distress.
сокруш|ённый *p.p.p. of* **~и́ть** *and adj.* grief-stricken.
сокруши́тел|ьный (~ен, ~ьна) *adj.* shattering; **нанести́ с. уда́р** (+*d.*) to deal a crippling blow.
сокруш|и́ть, у́, и́шь *pf.* (*of* **~а́ть**) **1.** to shatter, smash. **2.** (*fig.*) to shatter; to distress.
сокры́ти|е, я *nt.* concealment; **с. кра́деного** receiving of stolen goods.
со|лга́ть, лгу́, лжёшь, лгу́т, *past* **~лга́л, ~лгала́, ~лга́ло** *pf. of* **лгать**
солда́т, а, *g. pl.* **~** *m.* soldier.
солда́тик, а *m.* **1.** *dim. of* **солда́т. 2.** toy soldier.
солда́тк|а, и *f.* soldier's wife.
солда́т|ский *adj. of* **~**
солда́тчин|а, ы *f.* **1.** (*hist.*) levy. **2.** military service.
солевaréни|е, я *nt.* salt production.
солева́р|енный (*and* **~ный**) *adj. of* **~е́ние; с. заво́д** salt-works.
солева́р|ня, ни, *g. pl.* **~ен** *f.* salt-works.
соле́ни|е, я *nt.* salting; pickling.
солено́ид, а *m.* (*elec.*) solenoid.
солён|ый *adj.* **1.** salt. **2.** (**со́лон, солона́, со́лоно**) salty; **у меня́ во рту́ со́лоно** I have a salty taste in my mouth. **3.** salted; pickled; **с. огуре́ц** pickled cucumber; *as n.* **~ое, ~ого** *nt.* pickles. **4.** (*fig., coll.*) salty, spicy; **с. анекдо́т** spicy story. **5.** (*short forms only*) (*fig.*) hot; **ему́ со́лоно пришло́сь** he got it hot; **верну́ться не со́лоно хлеба́вши** to come home empty-handed.
соле́нь|е, я *nt.* salted food(s); pickles.
солеци́зм, а *m.* solecism.
солидаризи́р|оваться, уюсь *impf. and pf.* (**с**+*i.*) to express one's solidarity (with), make common cause (with), identify o.s. (with).
солида́рност|ь, и *f.* solidarity; **из ~и** (**с**+*i.*) in sympathy (with); **ста́чка ~и** sympathetic strike.
солида́р|ный *adj.* (**~ен, ~на**) (**с**+*i.*) at one (with), in sympathy (with).
соли́д|ный (~ен, ~на) *adj.* **1.** solid, strong, sound. **2.** (*fig.*) solid, sound; reliable, respectable; **с. челове́к** a solid man. **3.** (*coll.*) respectable, sizable; **~ная су́мма** tidy sum. **4.** middle-aged; **челове́к ~ных лет** a middle-aged man.
соли́ст, а *m.* soloist.
солите́р, а *m.* (*min.*) solitaire (diamond).
солитёр, а *m.* tapeworm.
сол|и́ть, ю́, ~и́шь *impf.* (*of* **по~**) **1.** to salt. **2.** to pickle; **с. мя́со** to corn meat.
со́лк|а, и *f.* salting; pickling.
со́лнечн|ый *adj.* **1.** sun; solar; **~ая пане́ль** solar panel; **~ые пя́тна** (*astron.*) sun-spots; **с. свет** sunlight, sunshine; **~ая систе́ма** solar system; **~ое сплете́ние** (*anat.*) solar plexus; **с. уда́р** (*med.*) sunstroke; **~ые часы́** sun-dial. **2.** sunny.
со́лнц|е, а *nt.* sun; **го́рное с.** artificial sunlight, sunlamp; **на с.** in the sun; **гре́ться на с.** to sun o.s.
солнцепёк, а *m.*: **на ~е** right in the sun, in the full blaze of the sun.
солнцестоя́ни|е, я *nt.* solstice.
со́ло 1. *adv.* **2.** *n.*; *nt. indecl.* solo.
солов|е́й, ья́ *m.* nightingale.
солов|ьи́ный *adj. of* **~е́й**
со́лод, а *m.* malt.
соло|ди́ть, жу́, ди́шь *impf.* (*of* **на~**) to malt.
соло́дк|а, и *f.* liquorice.
солодко́вый *adj. of* **соло́дка; с. ко́рень** (*pharm.*) liquorice.
солодо́венный *adj.*: **с. заво́д** malt-house.
соло́м|а, ы *f.* straw; thatch; **крыть ~ой** to thatch.
соло́менн|ый *adj.* **1.** straw; **~ая вдова́** grass widow; **~ая кры́ша** thatch, thatched roof. **2.** straw-coloured.
соло́минк|а, и *f.* straw; **хвата́ться за ~у** to catch, clutch at a straw.
соло́мк|а, и *f.* **1.** *dim. of* **соло́ма. 2.** (drinking) straw. **3.** (*cul.*) long, thin biscuits; bread sticks.
солони́н|а, ы *f.* salted beef, corned beef.
соло́нк|а, и *f.* salt-cellar.
со́лоно *see* **солёный**
солонча́к, а́ *m* **1.** saline soil. **2.** salt-marsh.
сол|ь[1], **и,** *pl.* **~и, ~е́й** *f.* **1.** salt; **го́рькая с.** Epsom salts. **2.** (*fig.*) salt, spice; point; **с. земли́** the salt of the earth; **вот в чём вся с.** that's the whole point.
соль[2] *nt. indecl.* (*mus.*) so(h), sol; G.
со́л|ьный 1. *adj. of* **~о; с. но́мер** solo; **~ьная па́ртия** solo part. **2.** *adj. of* **~ь**[2]; **с. ключ** treble clef.
сольфе́джио *nt. indecl.* (*mus.*) solfeggio, sol-fa.
соля́нк|а, ~и *f.* solyanka (*a sharp-tasting Russ. soup*

of vegetables and meat or fish).
солян|óй *adj.* salt, saline; **с. раствóр** saline solution, brine.
солáри|й, я *m.* solarium.
сом, á *m.* sheat-fish.
соматúческий *adj.* somatic.
сóмкн|утый *p.p.p. of* **~уть** *and adj.*; **с. строй** (*mil.*) close order.
сомкн|ýть, ý, ёшь *pf.* (*of* **смыкáть**) to close; **с. глазá** to close one's eyes; **с. рядь́і** (*mil.*) to close ranks.
сомкн|ýться, ётся *pf.* (*of* **смыкáться**) to close (up).
сомнáмбул|а, ы *c.g.* sleep-walker, somnambulist.
сомнамбулúзм, а *m.* sleep-walking, somnambulism.
сомневá|ться, юсь *impf.* **1.** (**в**+*p.*) to doubt; to question. **2.** to worry; **вы мóжете не с.** you need not worry.
сомнéни|е, я *nt.* doubt; uncertainty; **без (всякого) ~я, вне ~я** without (any) doubt, beyond doubt.
сомнúтел|ьный (~ен, ~ьна) *adj.* **1.** doubtful, questionable; **~ьно** it is doubtful, it is open to question. **2.** dubious; equivocal; **~ьные делá** shady dealings.
сомнóжител|ь, я *m.* (*math.*) factor.
сон, сна *m.* **1.** sleep; **во сне, сквозь с.** in one's sleep; **со сна** half awake; **у менá сна ни в однóм глазý** (*coll.*) I am not in the least sleepy. **2.** dream; **вúдеть во сне** to dream, have a dream (about).
сонáт|а, ы *f.* (*mus.*) sonata.
сонéт, а *m.* sonnet.
сонлúвост|ь, и *f.* sleepiness, drowsiness.
сонлúв|ый (~, ~а) *adj.* sleepy, drowsy.
сонм, а *m.* (*arch. or joc.*) assembly, throng.
сóнн|ый *adj.* **1.** sleepy, drowsy (*also fig.*); **~ая артéрия** (*anat.*) carotid artery; **~ая болéзнь** (*med.*) sleeping sickness; **~ое цáрство** the land of Nod. **2.** sleeping, soporific; **~ые кáпли** sleeping-draught.
сонóрный *adj.* (*ling.*) sonorous; sonant.
сóн|я, и *f. and c.g.* **1.** *f.* dormouse. **2.** *c.g.* (*coll.*) sleepyhead.
соображá|ть, ю *impf.* **1.** *impf. of* **сообразúть. 2.** *impf. only* **хорошó с.** to be quick on the uptake.
соображéни|е, я *nt.* **1.** consideration, thought; **принять в с.** to take into consideration. **2.** understanding, grasp. **3.** consideration, reason; idea; **по финáнсовым ~ям** for financial reasons.
сообразúтельност|ь, и *f.* quickness, quick-wittedness.
сообразúтел|ьный (~ен, ~ьна) *adj.* quick-witted, quick, sharp, bright.
соöбра|зúть, жý, зúшь *pf.* (*of* **~жáть**) **1.** to consider, ponder; to weigh (the pros and cons of). **2.** to understand, grasp. **3.** (*coll.*) to think up, arrange.
сообрáзно *adv.* (**с**+*i.*) in conformity (with).
сообрáзност|ь, и *f.* conformity.
сообрáз|ный (~ен, ~на) *adj.* (**с**+*i.*) in conformity (with); **э́то ни с чем не ~но** it makes no sense at all.
сообраз|овáть, ýю *impf. and pf.* (**с**+*i.*) to conform (to), make conformable (to), adapt (to).
сообраз|овáться, ýюсь *impf. and pf.* (**с**+*i.*) to conform (to), adapt o.s. (to).
сообщá *adv.* together, jointly.
сообщ|áть, áю *impf. of* **~úть**
сообщ|áться, áюсь *impf.* **1.** *impf. of* **~úться. 2.** *impf. only* (**с**+*i.*) to communicate (with), be in communication (with).
сообщéни|е, я *nt.* **1.** communication, report; **срóчное** *or* **э́кстренное с.** news flash; **по послéдним ~ям** according to latest reports. **2.** communication; **прямóе с.** through connection; **путú ~я** communications (*rail, road, canal, etc.*).
сообществ|о, а *nt.* association; community; **в ~е** (**с**+*i.*) in association (with), together (with).
сообщ|úть, ý, úшь *pf.* (*of* **~áть**) **1.** (+*a. or* **о**+*p.*) to communicate, report, inform, announce; **с. послéдние извéстия** to communicate the latest news. **2.** to impart; **с. материáлу огнеупóрность** to make a material fireproof.
сообщ|úться, úтся *pf.* (*of* **~áться**) to be communicated, communicate itself.
соóбщник, а *m.* accomplice; partner (*in crime*); (*leg.*) accessory.
соóбщничеств|о, а *nt.* complicity.
сооору|дúть, жý, дúшь *pf.* (*of* **~жáть**) to build, erect.
сооружéни|е, я *nt.* **1.** building, erection. **2.** building, structure; **воéнные ~я** military installations; **оборонúтельные ~я** (*mil.*) defences.
соотвéтственно *adv.* **1.** accordingly. **2.** (+*d.*) according (to), in accordance (with), in conformity (with).
соотвéтствен|ный (~, ~на) *adj.* (+*d.*) corresponding (to).
соотвéтстви|е, я *nt.* accordance, conformity; **в ~и** (**с**+*i.*) in accordance (with); **привестú в с.** (**с**+*i.*) to bring into line (with).
соотвéтств|овать, ую *impf.* (+*d.*) to correspond (to, with), conform (to); **с. действúтельности** to correspond to the facts; **с. трéбованиям** to meet the requirements; **с. цéли** to answer the purpose.
соотвéтств|ующий *pres. part. act. of* **~овать** *and adj.* **1.** (+*d.*) corresponding (to). **2.** proper, appropriate, suitable; **~ующим óбразом** accordingly.
соотéчественник, а *m.* compatriot, fellow-countryman.
соотнес|тú, ý, ёшь, *past* **~̈, ~лá** *pf.* (*of* **соотносúть**) to correlate.
соотносúтел|ьный (~ен, ~ьна) *adj.* correlative.
соотно|сúть, шý, ~сишь *impf. of* **соотнестú**
соотно|сúться, ~сится *impf.* to correspond.
соотношéни|е, я *nt.* correlation, ratio; **с. сил** correlation of forces, alignment of forces.
сопéрник, а *m.* rival.
сопéрнича|ть, ю *impf.* to be rivals; (**с**+*i.*) to compete (with), vie (with).
сопéрничеств|о, а *nt.* rivalry.
соп|éть, лю́, úшь *impf.* to breathe heavily and noisily through the nose.
сóпк|а, и *f.* **1.** knoll, hill, mound. **2.** (*in Far East*) volcano.
соплúв|ый (~, ~а) *adj.* (*coll.*) snotty.
соп|лó, á, *pl.* **~ла, ~ел** *nt.* (*tech.*) nozzle.
сопл|я́, ú, *pl.* **~и, ~éй** *f.* (nose-)drip; (*pl.*) snot.
сопля́к, á *m.* (*coll., pej.*) **1.** sniveller. **2.** spineless creature.
сопоставúм|ый (~, ~а) *adj.* comparable.
сопостáв|ить, лю, ишь *pf.* (*of* **~ля́ть**) (**с**+*i.*) to compare (with), confront (with).
сопоставлéни|е, я *nt.* comparison, confrontation.
сопоставля́|ть, ю *impf. of* **сопостáвить**
сопрáно *indecl.* (*mus.*) **1.** *nt.* soprano (*voice*). **2.** *f.* soprano (*singer*).
сопредéл|ьный (~ен, ~ьна) *adj.* contiguous; (*fig.*) kindred, related.
сопрé|ть, ю *pf. of* **преть**
соприкасá|ться, юсь *impf.* (*of* **соприкоснýться**) (**с**+*i.*) **1.** to adjoin, be contiguous (to). **2.** (*fig.*) to come into contact (with).
соприкосновéни|е, я *nt.* contiguity; (*mil. and fig.*) contact; **имéть с.** (**с**+*i.*) to come into contact (with).
соприкосн|ýться, ýсь, ёшься *pf. of* **соприкасáться**
сопроводúтел|ь, я *m.* escort.
сопроводúтел|ьный *adj.* accompanying; **~ое письмó** covering letter.
сопрово|дúть, жý, дúшь *pf. of* **~ждáть**
сопровождá|ть, ю *impf.* (*of* **сопроводúть**) to accompany; to escort; to convoy.

сопровожде́ни|е, я *nt.* accompaniment; escort, convoy; **в ~и** (+*g.*) accompanied (by); escorted (by); **звуково́е с.** soundtrack.
сопротивле́ни|е, я *nt.* resistance, opposition; (*phys.*, *tech.*) strength; (*elec.*) resistance, impedance; **оказа́ть с.** to put up resistance; **идти́ по ли́нии наиме́ньшего ~я** to take the line of least resistance.
сопротивля́емост|ь, и *f.* capacity to resist.
сопротивля́|ться, юсь *impf.* (+*d.*) to resist, oppose.
сопряжён|ный (~, ~а́) *adj.* **1.** (**с**+*i.*) linked (with), attended (by), entailing; **ваш прое́кт ~ с больши́м ри́ском** your scheme entails great risk.
сопу́тств|овать, ую *impf.* (+*d.*) to accompany; **~ующие обстоя́тельства** attendant circumstances, concomitants.
сор, а *m.* litter, dust; **не выноси́ть ~а из избы́** not to wash one's dirty linen in public.
соразме́р|ить, ю, ишь *pf.* (*of* **~я́ть**) (**с**+*i.*) to make commensurate (with), balance.
соразме́рност|ь, и *f.* proportionality.
соразме́р|ный (~ен, ~на) *adj.* proportionate, commensurate; balanced.
соразмер|я́ть, я́ю *impf. of* **~ить**
сора́тник, а *m.* comrade-in-arms.
сорван|е́ц, ца́ *m.* (*coll.*; *of a child*) a terror; (*of a girl*) tomboy.
сорв|а́ть, у́, ёшь, *past* **~а́л, ~ала́, ~а́ло** *pf.* (*of* **срыва́ть**) **1.** to tear off, tear away; to pick, pluck; **с. ве́тку** to break off a branch. **2.** (*coll.*) to get, extract. **3.** (**на**+*p.*) to vent (upon); **с. гнев на ком-н.** to vent one's anger upon s.o. **4.** to smash, wreck, ruin; **с. вра́жеские пла́ны** to foil, frustrate the enemy's plans; **с. рабо́ту** to upset work; **с. банк** (*cards*) to break the bank.
сорв|а́ться, у́сь, ёшься, *past* **~а́лся, ~ала́сь, ~а́ло́сь** *pf.* (*of* **срыва́ться**) **1.** to break away, break loose; **с. с пе́тель** to come off its hinges; **с. с ме́ста** (*coll.*) to dart off; **с. с языка́** to escape one's lips. **2.** to fall, come down. **3.** (*coll.*) to fall through.
сорвиголов|а́, ы́, *pl.* **сорвиго́ловы, сорвиголо́в, сорвиголова́м** *c.g.* (*coll.*) daredevil; desperado.
сорганиз|ова́ть, у́ю *pf. of* **организова́ть**
со́рго *nt. indecl.* (*bot.*) sorghum.
соревнова́ни|е, я *nt.* **1.** (*sport*) competition, contest; event; **кома́ндное с.** team event; **отбо́рочные ~я** elimination contests; **с. на пе́рвенство ми́ра** world championship. **2.** competition, emulation.
соревн|ова́ться, у́юсь *impf.* (**с**+*i.*) to compete (with, against), contend (with).
соревн|у́ющийся *pres. part. of* **~ова́ться**; *as n.* **с., ~у́ющегося** *m.* competitor, contender.
соригина́льнича|ть, ю *pf. of* **оригина́льничать**
сори́нк|а, и *f.* mote; speck of dust.
сор|и́ть, ю́, и́шь *impf.* (*of* **на~**) (+*a. or i.*) to litter; to throw about (*also fig.*); **с. деньга́ми** to throw one's money about.
со́рн|ый *adj.* **1.** *adj. of* **сор. 2. ~ая трава́** weed; (*collect.*) weeds.
сорня́к, а́ *m.* weed.
соро́дич, а *m.* **1.** relative. **2.** fellow-countryman.
со́рок *all other cases* **а́**, *num. forty.*
соро́к|а, и *f.* magpie.
сорокале́ти|е, я *nt.* **1.** forty years. **2.** fortieth anniversary, fortieth birthday.
сорокале́тний *adj.* **1.** forty-year. **2.** forty-year-old.
сороков|о́й *adj.* fortieth; **~ы́е го́ды** the forties.
сороконо́жк|а, и *f.* centipede.
соро́чк|а, и *f.* **1.** shirt; blouse; camisole; **ночна́я с.** night-shirt, night-dress. **2.** reverse (*of playing-card*). **3.**: **роди́ться в ~е** to be born with a silver spoon in one's mouth.
сорт, а, *pl.* **~а́** *m.* **1.** grade, quality; brand; **вы́сший с.** best quality; **пе́рвого ~а** high-grade; first-rate. **2.** sort, kind, variety.
сортир|ова́ть, у́ю *impf.* to sort, assort, grade.
сортиро́вк|а, и *f.* sorting, grading, sizing.
сортиро́вочн|ая, ой *f.* marshalling yard.
сортиро́вочный *adj.* sorting.
сортиро́вщик, а *m.* sorter.
сортов|о́й *adj.* high-grade, of high quality.
соса́ни|е, я *nt.* sucking, suction.
соса́тельный *adj.* sucking.
сос|а́ть, у́, ёшь *impf.* to suck.
сосва́та|ть, ю *pf. of* **сва́тать**
сосе́д, а, *pl.* **~и, ~ей** *m.* neighbour; **с. по кварти́ре** flatmate; **с. по купе́** (*rail.*) fellow passenger.
сосе́дн|ий *adj.* neighbouring; adjacent, next.
сосе́д|ский *adj. of* **~**; **~ские де́ти** the neighbours' children, the children next door.
сосе́дств|о, а *nt.* neighbourhood, vicinity; **по ~у** (+*g.*) in the neighbourhood (of), in the vicinity (of).
соси́ск|а, и *f.* sausage; frankfurter.
со́ск|а, и *f.* (*baby's*) dummy.
соска́блива|ть, ю *impf. of* **соскобли́ть**
соска́кива|ть, ю *impf. of* **соскочи́ть**
соска́льзыва|ть, ю *impf. of* **соскользну́ть**
соскобл|и́ть, ю́, ~и́шь *pf.* (*of* **соска́бливать**) to scrape off.
соскользн|у́ть, у́, ёшь *pf.* (*of* **соска́льзывать**) to slip off, slide off; to slide down.
соскоч|и́ть, у́, ~ишь *pf.* (*of* **соска́кивать**) **1.** to jump off; to jump down; **с. с крова́ти** to jump out of bed. **2.** to come off; **с. с пе́тель** to come off its hinges.
соску́ч|иться, усь, ишься *pf.* **1.** to become bored. **2.** (**по**+*p.*, *preceding sg. nn.*; **по**+*d.*, *preceding pl. nn.*) to miss; **с. по дере́вне** to miss the country; **с. по друзья́м** to miss one's friends.
сослага́тельный *adj.* (*gram.*) subjunctive.
со|сла́ть, шлю́, шлёшь *pf.* (*of* **ссыла́ть**) to exile, banish, deport.
со|сла́ться[1], шлю́сь, шлёшься *pf.* (*of* **ссыла́ться**) (**на**+*a.*) **1.** to refer (to), allude (to), cite, quote. **2.** to plead; **с. на недомога́ние** to plead indisposition.
со|сла́ться[2], шлю́сь, шлёшься *pf.* (*of* **ссыла́ться**) *pass. of* **~сла́ть**
со́слепа *adv.* (*coll.*) due to poor sight.
со́слеп|у *adv.* = **~а**
сосло́ви|е, я *nt.* estate; **дворя́нское с.** the nobility; **духо́вное с.** the clergy; **купе́ческое с.** the merchants.
сосло́в|ный *adj. of* **~и; с. предрассу́док** class prejudice.
сослужи́в|ец, ца *m.* colleague, fellow-employee.
сослуж|и́ть, у́, ~ишь *pf.*: **с. кому́-н. слу́жбу** to do s.o. a good turn, stand s.o. in good stead.
сосн|а́, ы́, *pl.* **~ы, со́сен** *f.* pine(-tree).
сосно́в|ый *adj.* pine; pinewood; deal; **с. бор** pine forest; **~ая ме́бель** deal furniture.
сосн|у́ть, у́, ёшь *pf.* (*coll.*) to have, take a nap.
сосня́к, а́ *m.* pine forest.
сос|о́к, ка́ *m.* nipple, teat.
сосредото́чени|е, я *nt.* (*mil.*, *etc.*) concentration.
сосредото́ченност|ь, и *f.* (degree of) concentration.
сосредото́ч|енный *p.p.p. of* **~ить** *and adj.* concentrated; (*tech.*) lumped, centred; **с. взгляд** fixed stare; **~енное внима́ние** rapt attention.
сосредото́чива|ть(ся), ю(сь) *impf. of* **сосредото́чить(ся)**
сосредото́ч|ить, у, ишь *pf.* (*of* **~ивать**) to concentrate; to focus; **с. внима́ние (на**+*p.*) to concentrate one's attention (on, upon).
сосредото́ч|иться, усь, ишься *pf.* (*of* **~иваться**) **1.** (**на**+*p.*) to concentrate (on, upon). **2.** *pass. of* **~ить**
соста́в, а *m.* **1.** composition, make-up; **социа́льный**

с. social structure; **хими́ческий с.** (*i*) chemical composition, (*ii*) chemical compound; **входи́ть в с.** (+*g.*) to form part (of); **с. преступле́ния** (*leg.*) corpus delicti. **2.** staff; membership, composition, strength; **ли́чный с.** personnel; **с. (актёров)** cast; **офице́рский с.** the officers; **в по́лном ~е** with its full complement; in, at full strength; **в ~е** (+*g.*) numbering, consisting (of); **делега́ция в ~е тридцати́ челове́к** a delegation of thirty (persons); **входи́ть в с.** (+*g.*) to be(come) a member (of). **3.** train; **подвижно́й с.** rolling-stock.

состави́тел|ь, я *m.* compiler, author.

соста́в|ить[1]**, лю, ишь** *pf.* (*of* **~ля́ть**) **1.** to put together, make up; **с. посу́ду** to stack crockery. **2.** to compose, draw up; to compile; to form, construct; **с. мне́ние** to form an opinion; **с. предложе́ние** to construct a sentence; **с. прое́кт** to draw up a draft. **3.** to be, constitute, make. **4.** to form, amount to, total; **с. в сре́днем** to average. **5.: с. себе́** to make (for o.s.); **с. себе́ и́мя** to make a name for o.s.

соста́в|иться, ится *pf.* (*of* **~ля́ться**) to form, be formed, come into being.

составля́|ть(ся), ю(сь) *impf. of* **соста́вить(ся)**

составн|о́й *adj.* **1.** compound, composite; **~а́я кни́жная по́лка** sectional book-shelf. **2.** component; **~а́я часть** component, constituent.

соста́р|ить(ся), ю(сь) *pf. of* **ста́рить(ся)**

состоя́ни|е, я *nt.* **1.** state, condition; position; **в хоро́шем ~и** in good condition; **быть в ~и** (+*inf.*) to be able (to), be in a position (to). **2.** fortune; **нажи́ть с.** to make a fortune.

состоя́тельност|ь[1]**, и** *f.* **1.** solvency. **2.** wealth.

состоя́тельност|ь[2]**, и** *f.* strength (*of an argument, etc.*).

состоя́тел|ьный[1] **(~ен, ~ьна)** *adj.* **1.** solvent. **2.** well-off, well-to-do.

состоя́тел|ьный[2] **(~ен, ~ьна)** *adj.* well-grounded.

состо|я́ть, ю́, и́шь *impf.* **1. (из)** to consist (of), comprise, be made up (of); **кварти́ра ~и́т из трёх ко́мнат** the flat consists of three rooms. **2.** (**в**+*p.*) to consist (in), lie (in), be; **ра́зница ~и́т в том, что** the difference is that. **3.** to be; **с. чле́ном о́бщества** to be a member of a society; **с. под судо́м** to be awaiting trial; **с. при посо́льстве** to be attached to the embassy.

состо|я́ться, и́тся *pf.* to take place; **визи́т не ~я́лся** the visit did not take place.

сострада́ни|е, я *nt.* compassion, sympathy.

сострада́тел|ьный (~ен, ~ьна) *adj.* compassionate, sympathetic.

сострига́|ть, ю *impf. of* **состри́чь**

состр|и́ть, ю́, и́шь *pf. of* **остри́ть**

состри́|чь, гу́, жёшь, гу́т, *past* **~г, ~гла** *pf.* (*of* **~га́ть**) to shear, clip off.

состро́|ить, ю, ишь *pf. of* **стро́ить 3.; с. грима́су, с. ро́жу** (*coll.*) to make a face.

состря́па|ть, ю *pf. of* **стря́пать**

состык|ова́ть(ся), у́ю(сь) *pf. of* **стыкова́ть(ся)**

состяза́ни|е, я *nt.* competition, contest; match; **с. в пла́вании** swimming contest; **с. в остроу́мии** battle of wits.

состяза́|ться, юсь *impf.* (**с**+*i.*) to compete (with).

сосу́д, а *m.* vessel; **кровено́сные ~ы** blood vessels.

сосу́дистый *adj.* (*anat., biol.*) vascular.

сосу́льк|а, и *f.* icicle.

сосуществова́ни|е, я *nt.* coexistence.

сосуществ|ова́ть, у́ю *impf.* to coexist.

сосчита́|ть, ю *pf. of* **счита́ть**

сосчита́|ться, юсь *pf.* (**с**+*i.*) to settle accounts (with), get even (with) (*also fig.*).

сотворе́ни|е, я *nt.* creation, making; **с. ми́ра** the creation of the world.

сотвор|и́ть, ю́, и́шь *pf. of* **твори́ть**

со́тенный *adj.* (*coll.*) worth a hundred roubles.

сотк|а́ть, у́, ёшь, *past* **~а́л, ~ала́, ~а́ло** *pf. of* **ткать**

со́т|ня, ни, *g. pl.* **~ен** *f.* **1.** a hundred (*esp. a hundred roubles*). **2.** (*hist.*) sotnya, company (*mil. unit, originally of a hundred men*).

сотова́рищ, а *m.* associate, partner.

со́т|овый *adj.* **1.** *adj. of* **~ы; с. мёд** comb-honey. **2.** (*tech.; fig.*) honeycomb.

сотру́дник, а *m.* **1.** collaborator. **2.** employee, official; **нау́чный с.** research fellow, research assistant (*of a learned body or scientific institution*); **с. посо́льства** embassy official. **3.** contributor (*to a newspaper, journal, etc.*).

сотру́днича|ть, ю *impf.* **1.** (**с**+*i.*) to collaborate (with). **2.** (**в**+*p.*) to contribute (to); **с. в газе́те** to contribute to a newspaper; to work on a newspaper.

сотру́дничеств|о, а *nt.* collaboration, co-operation.

сотряс|а́ть(ся), а́ю(сь) *impf. of* **~ти́(сь)**

сотрясе́ни|е, я *nt.* shaking; **с. мо́зга** (*med.*) concussion.

сотряс|ти́, у́, ёшь, *past* **∠, ~ла́** *pf.* (*of* **~а́ть**) to shake.

сотряс|ти́сь, у́сь, ёшься, *past* **∠ся, ла́сь** *pf.* (*of* **~а́ться**) to shake, tremble.

со́т|ы, ов *no sg.* honeycombs; **мёд в ~ах** honey in combs.

со́т|ый *adj.* hundredth; **с. год** the year one hundred; *as n.* **~ая, ~ой** *f.* (a) hundredth.

со́ул, а *m.*: **(му́зыка) с.** soul music.

со́ус, а *m.* sauce; gravy; dressing.

со́усник, а *m.* sauce-boat, gravy-boat.

соуча́сти|е, я *nt.* participation; complicity.

соуча́стник, а *m.* accomplice; **с. преступле́ния, с. в преступле́нии** (*leg.*) accessory to a crime.

соучени́к, а́ *m.* schoolmate, schoolfellow.

соф|а́, ы́, *pl.* **∠ы** *f.* sofa.

софи́зм, а *m.* sophism, sophistry.

софи́ст, а *m.* sophist.

софи́стик|а, и *f.* sophistry.

софисти́ческий *adj.* sophistic(al).

сох|а́, и́, *pl.* **∠и** *f.* (*wooden*) plough.

со́х|нуть, ну, нешь, *past* **~, ~ла** *impf.* **1.** to dry, get dry; to become parched. **2.** to wither; (*fig.*) to pine.

сохране́ни|е, я *nt.* **1.** preservation; conservation; care, custody; **отда́ть кому́-н. на с.** to give into s.o.'s charge. **2.** retention.

сохран|и́ть, ю́, и́шь *pf.* (*of* **~я́ть**) **1.** to preserve, keep; to keep safe; **с. ве́рность** (+*d.*) to remain faithful, loyal (to); **с. на па́мять** to keep as a souvenir. **2.** to keep, retain, reserve; **с. за собо́й пра́во** to reserve the right.

сохран|и́ться, ю́сь, и́шься *pf.* (*of* **~я́ться**) **1.** to remain (intact); to last out; **он хорошо́ ~и́лся** he is well preserved. **2.** *pass. of* **~и́ть**

сохра́нно *adv.* safely, intact.

сохра́нност|ь, и *f.* **1.** safety, undamaged state; **в ~и** safe; intact. **2.** safe keeping.

сохра́н|ный (~ен, ~на) *adj.* safe; undamaged.

сохраня́емост|ь, и *f.* shelf-life.

сохран|я́ть(ся), я́ю(сь) *impf. of* **~и́ть(ся)**

соц... *comb. form, abbr. of* **1. социа́льный. 2. социалисти́ческий**

соцве́ти|е, я *nt.* (*bot.*) inflorescence.

социа́л-демокра́т, а *m.* social democrat.

социа́л-демократи́ческий *adj.* social democratic.

социа́л-демокра́ти|я, и *f.* social democracy.

социализа́ци|я, и *f.* socialization.

социализи́р|овать, ую *impf. and pf.* to socialize.

социали́зм, а *m.* socialism.

социали́ст, а *m.* socialist.

социалисти́ческий *adj.* socialist.

социа́льно-бытово́й *adj.* social, welfare.

социа́льн|ый *adj.* social; **~ое обеспе́чение** social security; **~ое положе́ние** social status.

социóлог, а *m.* sociologist.
социологи́ческий *adj.* sociological.
социолóги|я, и *f.* sociology.
соцреали́зм, а *m.* socialist realism.
сочéльник, а *m.* (*eccl.*) **рождéственский с.** Christmas Eve; **крещéнский с.** Twelfth-night.
сочетáни|е, я *nt.* combination.
сочетá|ть, ю *impf. and pf.* (**с**+*i.*) to combine (with).
сочетá|ться, юсь *impf. and pf.* **1.** to combine. **2.** (**с**+*i.*) to harmonize (with), go (with); to match.
сочинéни|е, я *nt.* **1.** composing. **2.** (*literary*) work. **3.** (*school*) composition, essay.
сочини́тел|ь, я *m.* **1.** (*obs.*) writer, author. **2.** (*coll.*) story-teller, fabricator.
сочин|и́ть, ю́, и́шь *pf.* (*of* **~я́ть**) **1.** to compose (*liter. or mus. work*); to write. **2.** to make up, fabricate.
сочин|я́ть, я́ю *impf.* **~и́ть**
соч|и́ть, ý, и́шь *impf.* to ooze (out), exude.
соч|и́ться, и́тся *impf.* to ooze (out), trickle; **с. крóвью** to bleed.
сóчност|ь, и *f.* juiciness, succulence.
сóч|ный (~ен, ~нá, ~но) *adj.* **1.** juicy (*also fig.*); succulent. **2.** (*fig.*) rich; lush; **~ная расти́тельность** lush vegetation.
сочýвствен|ный (~, ~на) *adj.* sympathetic.
сочýвстви|е, я *nt.* sympathy.
сочýвств|овать, ую *impf.* (+*d.*) to sympathize (with), feel (for).
сочýвств|ующий *pres. part. act. of* **~овать** *and adj.* sympathetic; *as n.* **с., ~ующего** *m.* sympathizer.
сóшк|а, и *f.*: **мéлкая с.** (*coll.*) small fry.
сошни́к, á *m.* ploughshare.
сощýрива|ть(ся), ю(сь) *impf. of* **сощýрить(ся)**
сощýр|ить, ю, ишь *pf.* (*of* **щýрить** *and* **~ивать**); **с. глазá** to screw up one's eyes.
сощýр|иться, юсь, ишься *pf.* (*of* **щýриться** *and* **~иваться**) to screw up one's eyes.
союз[1], а *m.* **1.** alliance, union. **2.** union; league; **профессионáльный с.** trade union.
союз[2], а *m.* (*gram.*) conjunction.
сою́зник, а *m.* ally.
сою́знический *adj.* ally's.
сою́зн|ый *adj.* allied; **~ые держáвы** allied powers; (*hist.*) the Allies.
сó|я, и *f.* soya bean.
спагéтти *nt. and pl. indecl.* spaghetti.
спад, а *m.* **1.** (*econ.*) slump, recession. **2.** abatement.
спадá|ть, ю *impf. of* **спасть**
спазм, а *m.* spasm.
спáзм|а, ы *f.* = **~**
спáива|ть[1], ю *impf. of* **споить**
спáива|ть[2], ю *impf. of* **спая́ть**
спáйк|а, и *f.* **1.** soldering; soldered joint. **2.** (*fig.*) cohesion; union.
спал|и́ть, ю́, и́шь *pf. of* **пали́ть[1]**
спáльн|ый *adj.* sleeping; **с. вагóн** sleeping-car; **~ое мéсто** berth, bunk; **с. мешóк** sleeping-bag.
спáл|ьня, ьни, *g. pl.* **~ен** *f.* bedroom; **с.-гости́ная** bed-sitting room.
спань|ё, я́ *nt.* sleep(ing).
спáр|енный *p.p.p. of* **~ить** *and adj.* paired, coupled; **~енная ездá** (*rail.*) double-manning.
спáрж|а, и *f.* asparagus.
спáрива|ть(ся), ю(сь) *impf. of* **спáрить(ся)**
спáр|ить, ю, ишь *pf.* (*of* **~ивать**) **1.** to couple, pair, mate (*animals*). **2.** to pair off (*to work together*).
спáр|иться, юсь, ишься *pf.* (*of* **~иваться**) **1.** (*of animals*) to couple, pair, mate. **2.** to pair off (*to work together*).
спартакиáд|а, ы *f.* sports and/or athletics meeting.
спартáн|ец, ца *m.* Spartan.
спартáн|ка, ки *f. of* **~ец**
спартáнский *adj.* Spartan.
спáрхива|ть, ю *impf. of* **спорхнýть**
спáрыва|ть, ю *impf. of* **спорóть**
Спас, а *m.* (*relig.*) the Saviour.
спасáни|е, я *nt.* rescuing, life-saving.
спасáтел|ь, я *m.* **1.** (*at sea*) lifeguard; rescuer; (*pl.*) rescue party *or* team. **2.** lifeboat.
спасáтельн|ый *adj.* rescue, life-saving; **с. круг, с. пóяс** lifebelt; **~ая лóдка** lifeboat.
спасá|ть(ся), ю(сь) *impf. of* **спасти́(сь)**
спасéни|е, я *nt.* **1.** rescuing, saving. **2.** rescue, escape; salvation.
спаси́бо *particle* thanks; thank you; **с. и на том** we must be thankful for small mercies; *as n.* thanks; **большóе вам с.** thank you very much; **сдéлать что-н. за (однó) с.** (*coll.*) to do sth. for love.
спаси́тел|ь, я *m.* **1.** rescuer, saviour. **2.** (*relig.*) the Saviour.
спаси́тел|ьный (~ен, ~ьна) *adj.* saving; salutary; **с. вы́ход, ~ьное срéдство** means of escape.
спас|овáть, ýю *pf. of* **пасовáть[1]**
спас|ти́, ý, ёшь, *past* **~, ~лá** *pf.* (*of* **~áть**) to save; to rescue; **с. положéние** to save the situation.
спас|ти́сь, ýсь, ёшься, *past* **~ся, ~лáсь** *pf.* (*of* **~áться**) **1.** to save o.s., escape. **2.** (*relig.*) to be saved, save one's soul.
спа|сть, дý, дёшь, *past* **~л** *pf.* (*of* **~дáть**) **1.** (**с**+*i.*) to fall down (from); **с. с тéла** (*coll.*) to lose weight. **2.** to abate; (*of water*) to fall.
спа|ть, сплю, спишь, *past* **~л, ~лá, ~ло** *impf.* to sleep, be asleep; **с. мёртвым сном** to be fast asleep; **лечь с.** to go to bed; **порá с.** it is bedtime.
спá|ться, спи́тся, *past* **~лóсь** *impf.* (*impers.*, +*d.*): **мне не спи́тся** (*i*) I cannot (get to) sleep, (*ii*) I am not sleepy; **ей плóхо ~лóсь** she did not sleep well.
спáянност|ь, и *f.* cohesion, unity.
спа|я́ть, я́ю *pf.* (*of* **~ивать[2]**) **1.** to solder together, weld. **2.** (*fig.*) to weld together.
СПБ, СПб (*abbr. of* **Санкт-Петербýрг**) St. Petersburg.
спевá|ться, юсь *impf. of* **спéться**
спéвк|а, и *f.* (choir) practice, rehearsal.
спектáкл|ь, я *m.* (*theatr.*) performance; show.
спектр, а *m.* (*phys.*) spectrum.
спектрáльный *adj.* (*phys.*) spectral, spectrum.
спектроскóп, а *m.* (*phys.*) spectroscope.
спекули́р|овать, ую *impf.* **1.** (+*i. or* **на**+*p.*) to speculate (in); to profiteer (in). **2.** (**на**+*p.*; *fig.*) to gamble (on), reckon (on); to profit (by).
спекуля́нт, а *m.* speculator, profiteer.
спекуляти́вн|ый *adj.* speculative.
спекуля́ци|я, и *f.* **1.** (+*i.*, **с**+*i.*, or **на**+*p.*) speculation (in); profiteering. **2.** (**на**+*p.*; *fig.*) gamble (on).
спеленá|ть, ю *pf. of* **пеленáть**
спелеóлог, а *m.* **1.** speleologist. **2.** (**спортсмéн-**)**с.** caver, potholer.
спéл|ый (~, ~á, ~о) *adj.* ripe.
спервá *adv.* (*coll.*) at first; first.
спéреди *adv. and prep.*+*g.* in front (of); at the front, from the front.
спер|éть, сопрý, сопрёшь, *past* **~, ~ла** *pf.* (*of* **перéть 5.**) (*coll.*) to filch, pinch.
спéрм|а, ы *f.* sperm.
сперматозóид, а *m.* (*biol.*) spermatozoon.
спёр|тый *adj.* close, stuffy.
спеси́в|ый (~, ~а) *adj.* arrogant, conceited, haughty.
спес|ь, и *f.* arrogance, conceit, haughtiness; **сбить с. с когó-н.** to take s.o. down a peg.
спе|ть[1], ет *impf.* to ripen.
спеть[2], спою́, споёшь *pf. of* **петь**
спéться, спою́сь, споёшься *pf.* **1.** (*impf.* **спевáться**) (*of a choir*) to practise, rehearse. **2.** *pf. only* (*coll.*) to get on, agree, see eye to eye.
спех, а (у) *m.* (*coll.*) hurry; **что за с.?** what's the hurry?; **мне не к ~у** I'm in no hurry.

спец... *comb. form, abbr. of* **специа́льный**
специализа́ци|я, и *f.* specialization.
специализи́рова|нный *adj.* specialized.
специализи́р|оваться, уюсь *impf. and pf.* (**в**+*p. or* **по**+*d.*) to specialize (in).
специали́ст, а *m.* (**в**+*p. or* **по**+*d.*) specialist (in), expert (in).
специа́льно *adv.* specially, especially.
специа́льност|ь, и *f.* **1.** speciality, special interest. **2.** profession; trade.
специа́л|ьный *adj.* **1.** special, especial; **со ~ьной це́лью** with the express purpose. **2. (~ен, ~ьна)** specialist; **с. те́рмин** technical term.
специ́фик|а, и *f.* specific character.
спецификаци|я, и *f.* specification.
специфици́р|овать, ую *impf. and pf.* to specify.
специфи́ческий *adj.* specific.
спе́ци|я, и *f.* spice.
спецку́рс, а *m.* special course.
спецна́з *m.* (*coll.*) (*abbr. of* **подразделе́ние специа́льного назначе́ния**) special unit; riot police.
спецна́з|овец, овца *m.* (*coll.*) member of ~
спецоде́жд|а, ы *f.* working clothes, overalls.
спе́шива|ть(ся), ю(сь) *impf. of* **спе́шить(ся)**
спе́ш|ить, у, ишь *pf.* (*of* **~ивать**) to dismount.
спеш|и́ть, у́, и́шь *impf.* (*of* **по~**) **1.** to hurry, be in a hurry; to make haste; (**с**+*i.*) to hurry up (with); **с. домо́й** to be in a hurry to get home; **де́лать не ~а́** to do in leisurely style, take one's time over. **2.** (*of a timepiece*) to be fast.
спе́ш|иться, усь, ишься *pf.* (*of* **~иваться**) to dismount.
спе́шк|а, и *f.* hurry, haste, rush.
спе́шност|ь, и *f.* hurry, haste.
спе́ш|ный (~ен, ~на) *adj.* urgent, pressing; **с. зака́з** rush order; **~ная по́чта** express delivery.
спива́|ться, юсь *impf. of* **спи́ться**
СПИД, а *m.* (*abbr. of* **синдро́м приобретённого иммýнного дефици́та**) (*med.*) AIDS (*acquired immune deficiency syndrome*).
спидве́|й, я *m.* speedway (racing).
спидо́метр, а *m.* speedometer.
спики́р|овать, ую *pf. of* **пики́ровать**
спи́лива|ть, ю *impf. of* **спили́ть**
спил|и́ть, ю́, ⁓ишь *pf.* (*of* **⁓ивать**) to saw down; to saw off.
спин|а́, ы́, *a.* **⁓у,** *pl.* **⁓ы** *f.* back; **за ~о́й у кого́-н.** (*fig.*) behind s.o.'s back; **гнуть ⁓у (пе́ред)** to cringe (to), kowtow (to); **нож в ⁓у** (*fig.*) stab in the back.
спи́нк|а, и *f.* **1.** *dim. of* **спина́. 2.** back (*of article of furniture or clothing*).
спинно́й *adj.* spinal; **с. мозг** spinal cord; **с. хребе́т** spinal column.
спира́л|ь, и *f.* spiral.
спира́льный *adj.* spiral, helical.
спири́т, а *m.* spiritualist.
спирити́зм, а *m.* spiritualism.
спирити́ческий *adj.* spiritualistic.
спиритуали́зм, а *m.* (*phil.*) spiritualism.
спиритуали́ст, а *m.* (*phil.*) spiritualist.
спирт, а *m.* alcohol, spirit(s); **безво́дный с.** absolute alcohol; **древе́сный с.** wood alcohol.
спиртн|о́й *adj.* alcoholic; **~ы́е напи́тки** alcoholic drinks, spirits; *as n.* **~о́е, ~о́го** *nt.* = **~ы́е напи́тки**
спирто́вк|а, и *f.* spirit-lamp.
спиртов|о́й *adj.* alcoholic, spirit.
спи|са́ть, шу́, ⁓шешь *pf.* (*of* **⁓сывать**) **1.** (**с**+*i.*) to copy from. **2.** (**у**) to copy (off). **3.** (*fin.*) to write off.
спи|са́ться, шу́сь, ⁓шешься *pf.* (*of* **⁓сываться**) (**с**+*i.*) **1.** to arrange by letter. **2.** to exchange letters.
спи́с|ок, ка *m.* **1.** list; roll; **именно́й с.** nominal roll; **с. избира́телей** electoral roll; **с. опеча́ток** errata; **с. уби́тых и ра́неных** casualty list; **с. ли́чного соста́ва** (*mil.*) muster-roll. **2.** record; **послужно́й с.** service record.
спи́сыва|ть(ся), ю(сь) *impf. of* **списа́ть(ся)**
спито́й *adj.* (*coll.*; *of hot beverages*) weak.
спи́|ться, сопью́сь, сопьёшься, *past* **⁓лся́, ~ла́сь, ⁓ло́сь** *pf.* (*of* **~ва́ться**) to become a drunkard, take to drink.
спи́хива|ть, ю *impf. of* **спихну́ть**
спих|ну́ть, ну́, нёшь *pf.* (*of* **⁓ивать**) to push aside, shove aside; to push down.
спи́ц|а, ы *f.* **1.** knitting needle. **2.** spoke.
спич, а *m.* speech, address.
спи́чечниц|а, ы *f.* **1.** match-box. **2.** match-box stand.
спи́ч|ечный *adj. of* **~ка; ~ечная коро́бка** match-box.
спи́чк|а, и *f.* match.
сплав[1]**, а** *m.* (*tech.*) alloy; fusion.
сплав[2]**, а** *m.* (timber) floating.
спла́в|ить[1]**, лю, ишь** *pf.* (*of* **~ля́ть**) (*tech.*) to alloy, melt, fuse.
спла́в|ить[2]**, лю, ишь** *pf.* (*of* **~ля́ть**) **1.** to float (*timber*); to raft. **2.** (*coll.*) to send packing.
спла́в|иться, ится *pf.* (*of* **~ля́ться**) to fuse together, coalesce.
сплавля́|ть(ся), ю, ет(ся) *impf. of* **спла́вить(ся)**
сплани́р|овать, ую *pf. of* **плани́ровать**[2]
спла́чива|ть(ся), ю(сь) *impf. of* **сплоти́ть(ся)**
сплёвыва|ть, ю *impf. of* **сплю́нуть**
сплe|сти́, ту́, тёшь, *past* **⁓̈л, ~ла́** *pf.* (*of* **плести́** *and* **~та́ть**) to weave, plait, interlace.
сплета́|ть, ю *impf. of* **сплести́**
сплете́ни|е, я *nt.* **1.** interlacing; **с. лжи** tissue of lies; **с. обстоя́тельств** combination of circumstances. **2.** (*anat.*) plexus.
спле́тник, а *m.* gossip.
спле́тниц|а, ы *f. of* **спле́тник**
спле́тнича|ть, ю *impf.* (*of* **на~**) to gossip.
спле́т|ня, ни, *g. pl.* **~ен** *f.* gossip; piece of scandal.
сплеча́ *adv.* **1.** straight from the shoulder (*also fig.*). **2.** (*fig., coll.*) on the spur of the moment.
спло|ти́ть, чу́, ти́шь *pf.* (*of* **спла́чивать**) **1.** to join. **2.** (*fig.*) to unite, rally; **с. ряды́** to close the ranks.
спло|ти́ться, чу́сь, ти́шься *pf.* (*of* **спла́чиваться**) to unite, rally; to close the ranks.
сплох|ова́ть, у́ю *pf.* (*coll.*) to make a blunder.
сплочённост|ь, и *f.* cohesion, unity.
спло|чённый *p.p.p. of* **~ти́ть** *and adj.* **1.** unbroken. **2.** united, firm; **~чённые ряды́** serried ranks.
сплоша́|ть, ю *pf. of* **плоша́ть**
сплошн|о́й *adj.* **1.** unbroken, continuous; **с. лес** dense forest; **~а́я ма́сса** solid mass. **2.** all-round, complete. **3.** (*fig., coll.*) sheer, complete and utter; **с. восто́рг** sheer joy; **~а́я чепуха́** utter rubbish.
сплошь *adv.* **1.** all over; without a break; **с. и** (*or* **да**) **ря́дом** (*coll.*) nearly always; pretty often. **2.** (*coll.*) completely, utterly; without exception.
сплут|ова́ть, у́ю *pf. of* **плутова́ть**
сплы́ва|ть(ся), ет(ся) *impf. of* **сплы́ть(ся)**
сплы|ть, вёт, *past* **~л, ~ла́, ⁓ло** *pf.* (*of* **~ва́ть**) (*coll.*) **1.** to be carried away (*by a current of water, by a flood*); **бы́ло да ⁓ло** it was a short-lived joy; it's all over. **2.** to overflow, run over.
сплы́|ться, вётся, *past* **~лся, ~ла́сь** *pf.* (*of* **~ва́ться**) (*coll.*) to run (together), merge, blend.
сплю́н|уть, у, ешь *pf.* (*of* **сплёвывать**) **1.** to spit. **2.** (*coll.*) to spit out.
сплю́щива|ть(ся), ю(сь) *impf. of* **сплю́щить(ся)**
сплю́щ|ить, у, ишь *pf.* (*of* **плю́щить** *and* **~ивать**) to flatten, laminate.
сплю́щ|иться, ится *pf.* (*of* **~иваться**) to become flat.
спля|са́ть, шу́, ⁓шешь *pf.* to dance.
сподви́жник, а *m.* (*rhet.*) associate; comrade-inarms.

сподру́ч|ный[1] **(~ен, ~на)** *adj.* (*coll.*) easy; convenient, handy.
спозара́нку *adv.* (*coll.*) very early (in the morning).
спо|и́ть, ю́, и́шь *pf.* (*of* **спа́ивать**[1]) **1.** to give to drink. **2.** to make a drunkard (of).
споко́|йный (~ен, ~йна) *adj.* **1.** quiet; calm, tranquil; **с. о́браз жи́зни** quiet life; **~йная со́весть** clear conscience; **~йная улы́бка** serene smile; **бу́дьте ~йны!** don't worry!, rest assured!; **~йной но́чи!** good night! **2.** quiet, composed. **3.** comfortable.
споко́йстви|е, я *nt.* **1.** quiet, tranquillity; calm. **2.** order; **наруше́ние обще́ственного ~я** breach of the peace. **3.** composure; **с. ду́ха** peace of mind.
спола́скива|ть, ю *impf. of* **сполосну́ть**
сполз|а́ть, а́ю *impf. of* **~ти́**
сполз|ти́, у́, ёшь, *past* **~, ~ла́** *pf.* (*of* **~а́ть**) **(с+***g.***)** to climb down (from).
сполна́ *adv.* completely, in full.
сполосн|у́ть, у́, ёшь *pf.* (*of* **спола́скивать**) to rinse (out).
споло́х|и, ов *no sg.* (*dial.*) **1.** northern lights. **2.** lightning.
спо́нсор, а *m.* sponsor, backer.
спонта́нност|ь, и *f.* spontaneity.
спонта́нный *adj.* spontaneous.
спор, а *m.* **1.** argument; controversy; debate; **~́у нет** undoubtedly; there's no denying. **2.** (*leg.*) dispute.
спо́р|а, ы *f.* (*biol.*) spore.
споради́ческий *adj.* sporadic.
спора́нги|й, я *m.* (*biol.*) sporangium, spore-case.
спо́р|ить, ю, ишь *impf.* (*of* **по~**) **(о+***p.***) 1.** to argue (about); to dispute (about), debate; **о вку́сах не ~ят** tastes differ. **2.** to dispute; **с. о насле́дстве** to dispute a legacy. **3.** to bet (on), have a bet (on).
спор|и́ться, и́тся *impf.* (*coll.*) to succeed, go well; **у него́ всё ~и́тся** he never puts a foot wrong.
спо́р|ный (~ен, ~на) *adj.* debatable, questionable; disputed; **с. вопро́с** moot point, vexed question.
спор|о́ть, ю́, ~́ешь *pf.* (*of* **спа́рывать**) to unstitch, take off (*by cutting stitches*).
спорт, а *m.* sport; **ко́нный с.** equestrianism.
спорти́вн|ый *adj.* sports, sporting; casual (*of clothing*); **с. зал** gymnasium; **~ая площа́дка** sports ground, playing-field.
спортсме́н, а *m.* sportsman.
спортсме́нк|а, и *f.* sportswoman.
спортсме́нский *adj.* sportsmanlike.
спорхн|у́ть, у́, ёшь *pf.* (*of* **спа́рхивать**) to flutter off; to flutter away.
спо́рщик, а *m.* debater, wrangler.
спо́р|ый (~, ~а́, ~о) *adj.* (*coll.*) successful, profitable; **~ая рабо́та** good work.
спо́соб, а *m.* way, method; means; **таки́м ~ом** in this way; **сле́дующим ~ом** as follows.
спосо́бност|ь, и *f.* **1.** (*usu. pl.*; **к**) ability (for), aptitude (for); **челове́к с больши́ми ~ями** person of great abilities; **с. к языка́м** linguistic ability. **2.** capacity; **покупа́тельная с.** purchasing power.
спосо́б|ный (~ен, ~на) *adj.* **1.** able, talented, clever; **с. к матема́тике** good at mathematics. **2.** **(на+** *a. or +inf.*) capable (of), able (to); **они́ ~ны на всё** they are capable of anything.
спосо́бств|овать, ую *impf.* (*of* **по~**) (*+d.*) **1.** to assist. **2.** to be conducive (to), further, promote.
споткн|у́ться, у́сь, ёшься *pf.* (*of* **спотыка́ться**) **1.** **(о+***a.***)** to stumble (against, over). **2.** **(на+***p. or* **о+***a.*; *fig., coll.*) to get stuck (on).
спотыка́|ться, юсь *impf. of* **споткну́ться**
спохва|ти́ться, чу́сь, ~́тишься *pf.* (*of* **~́тываться**) (*coll.*) to remember suddenly, think suddenly.
спра́ва *adv.* **(от)** to the right (of).
справедли́вост|ь, и *f.* **1.** justice; fairness; **по ~и (говоря́)** in (all) fairness, by rights. **2.** correctness.
справедли́в|ый (~, ~а) *adj.* **1.** just; fair; **с. судья́** impartial judge. **2.** justified, correct.
спра́в|ить[1]**, лю, ишь** *pf.* (*of* **~ля́ть**) (*coll.*) to celebrate; **с. сва́дьбу** to celebrate one's wedding.
спра́в|иться[1]**, люсь, ишься** *pf.* (*of* **~ля́ться**) **(с+***i.***)** **1.** to cope (with), manage; **с. с зада́чей** to cope with a task, be equal to a task. **2.** to deal (with), get the better (of); **я с ним ~люсь!** I'll deal with him!
спра́в|иться[2]**, люсь, ишься** *pf.* (*of* **~ля́ться**) **(о+***p.***)** to ask (about), inquire (about); **с. в словаре́** to consult a dictionary.
спра́вк|а, и *f.* **1.** information; **навести́ ~у (о+***p.***)** to inquire (about). **2.** certificate; **с. с ме́ста рабо́ты** reference.
справля́|ть(ся), ю(сь) *impf. of* **спра́вить(ся)**
спра́вочник, а *m.* reference book, handbook, guide; **телефо́нный с.** telephone directory.
спра́вочн|ый *adj.* inquiry, information; **~ое бюро́, с. стол** inquiries office, information bureau.
спра́шива|ть, ю *impf. of* **спроси́ть**
спра́шива|ться, юсь *impf.* **1.** *impf. of* **спроси́ться. 2.** *impf. only* **~ется** the question is, arises.
спресс|ова́ть, у́ю *pf. of* **прессова́ть**
спринт, а *m.* (*sport*) sprint.
спри́нтер, а *m.* (*sport*) sprinter.
спринц|ева́ть, у́ю *impf.* to syringe.
спринцо́вк|а, и *f.* **1.** syringing. **2.** syringe.
спрова́|дить, жу, дишь *pf.* (*of* **~живать**) (*coll.*) to show out, show the door, send on one's way.
спрова́жива|ть, ю *impf. of* **спрова́дить**
спровоци́р|овать, ую *pf. of* **провоци́ровать**
спроекти́р|овать, ую *pf. of* **проекти́ровать**[1]
спрос, а *m.* **1.** (*econ.*) demand; **(на+***a.***)** demand (for), run (on); **с. и предложе́ние** supply and demand; **по́льзоваться больши́м ~́ом** to be much in demand. **2.:** **без ~́а (~́у)** (*coll.*) without permission.
спро|си́ть, шу́, ~́сишь *pf.* (*of* **спра́шивать**) **1.** **(о+***p.***)** to ask (about), inquire (about). **2.** (*+a. or g.*) to ask (for); to ask to see; **с. рези́нку** to ask for a rubber; **с. сове́та** to ask (for) advice; **~си́те хозя́йку** ask to see the landlady. **3.** **(с+***g.***)** to make answer (for), make responsible (for).
спро|си́ться, шу́сь, ~́сишься *pf.* (*of* **спра́шиваться**) **1.** (*+g. or* **у**) to ask permission (of). **2.** (*impers.*): **~́сится с него́,** *etc.*, he, *etc.*, will be answerable.
спросо́нок *adv.* (*coll.*) being only half-awake.
спроста́ *adv.* (*coll.*) without reflection.
спрут, а *m.* octopus.
спры́гива|ть, ю *impf. of* **спры́гнуть**
спры́г|нуть, ну, нешь *pf.* (*of* **~ивать**) **(с+***g.***)** to jump off (from); to jump down (from).
спры́скива|ть, ю *impf. of* **спры́снуть**
спры́с|нуть, ну, нешь *pf.* (*of* **~кивать**) **1.** to sprinkle. **2.** (*coll.*) to celebrate, drink (to).
спряга́|ть, ю *impf.* (*of* **про~**) (*gram.*) to conjugate.
спряга́|ться, ется *impf.* (*gram.*) to conjugate, be conjugated.
спряже́ни|е, я *m.* (*gram.*) conjugation.
спря|сть, ду́, дёшь, *past* **~л, ~ла́, ~́ло** *pf. of* **прясть**
спря́|тать(ся), чу(сь), чешь(ся) *pf. of* **пря́тать(ся)**
спу́гива|ть, ю *impf. of* **спугну́ть**
спуг|ну́ть, ну́, нёшь *pf.* (*of* **~́ивать**) to frighten off, scare off.
спуд, а *m.* (*arch.*) bushel; *now only used in phrr.* (*i*) **под ~́ом** under a bushel; **держа́ть под ~́ом** (*fig.*) to hide under a bushel; (*ii*) **из-под ~́а** from hiding.
спуск, а *m.* **1.** lowering; **с. корабля́** launch(ing). **2.** descent, descending. **3.** release; draining. **4.** slope, descent. **5.** (*coll.*) quarter; **не дава́ть ~́у (***+d.***)** to give no quarter, not to let off.
спуска́|ть, ю *impf. of* **спусти́ть; не с. глаз (с+***g.***)** not to let out of one's sight.

спуска́|ться, юсь *impf. of* **спусти́ться**
спускн|о́й *adj.* drain; **с. кран** drain-cock; **~а́я труба́** drain-pipe.
спусков|о́й *adj.* trigger; **с. крючо́к** trigger; **с. механи́зм** trigger mechanism.
спу|сти́ть, щу́, ~стишь *pf.* (*of* **~ска́ть**) **1.** to let down, lower; **с. кора́бль (на во́ду)** to launch a ship; **с. флаг** to lower a flag; **~стя́ рукава́** (*coll.*) in a slipshod fashion, carelessly; **с. с ле́стницы** (*fig., coll.*) to kick downstairs. **2.** to let loose, release; **с. куро́к** to pull, release the trigger; **с. затво́р** (*phot.*) to release the shutter; **с. пе́тлю** to drop a stitch. **3.** to let out, drain; **с. во́ду в убо́рной** to flush a lavatory. **4.** to send down, send out. **5.** (*of objects inflated with air*) to go down. **6.** (*coll.*) to pardon, let off, let go. **7.** (*coll.*) to lose, throw away, squander.
спу|сти́ться, щу́сь, ~стишься *pf.* (*of* **~ска́ться**) **1.** to descend; to come down, go down; to go downstream; (*of darkness*) to fall; **с. с ле́стницы** to come downstairs. **2.** *pass. of* **~сти́ть**
спустя́ *prep.+a.* after; later; **с. год** a year later.
спу́та|ть(ся), ю(сь) *pf. of* **пу́тать(ся)**
спу́тник, а *m.* **1.** (travelling) companion. **2.** concomitant. **3.** (*astron.*) satellite; **иску́сственный с. земли́** artificial earth satellite, sputnik.
спья́на *adv.* in a state of drunkenness.
спья́н|у *adv.* = **~а**
спя́|тить, чу, тишь *pf.*: **с. с ума́** (*coll.*) to go barmy, go off one's rocker.
спя́чк|а, и *f.* **1.** (*of animals*) hibernation. **2.** (*coll.*) sleepiness, lethargy.
ср. (*abbr. of* **сравни́**) cf., compare.
сраба́тыва|ться, юсь *impf. of* **срабо́таться**
срабо́танност|ь[1], **и** *f.* harmony in work.
срабо́танност|ь[2], **и** *f.* wear.
срабо́танный *adj.* worn (out).
срабо́та|ть, ю *pf.* (*coll.*) **1.** to make. **2.** (*+i.*) to work, operate.
срабо́та|ться[1], **юсь** *pf.* to work well together.
срабо́та|ться[2], **ется** *pf.* to wear out.
сравне́ни|е, я *nt.* **1.** comparison; **по ~ю (с+*i.*)** by comparison (with), as compared (with); **не идёт в с. (с+*i.*)** it cannot be compared (with). **2.** (*liter.*) simile.
сра́внива|ть, ю *impf. of* **сравни́ть** *and* **сравня́ть**
сравни́тельно *adv.* **1.** **(с+*i.*)** by comparison (with). **2.** comparatively.
сравни́тел|ьный *adj.* comparative; **~ая сте́пень** (*gram.*) comparative (degree).
сравн|и́ть, ю́, и́шь *pf.* (*of* **~ивать**) **(с+*i.*)** to compare (to, with).
сравн|и́ться, ю́сь, и́шься *pf.* **(с+*i.*)** to compare (with), come up (to), touch.
сравн|я́ть, я́ю *pf.* (*of* **равня́ть** *and* **~ивать**) to make even; **с. счёт** (*sport*) to equalize, bring the score level.
сравня́|ться, юсь *pf. of* **равня́ться**
сража́|ть, ю *impf. of* **срази́ть**
сража́|ться, юсь *impf.* (*of* **срази́ться**) **(с+*i.*)** to fight; to join battle (with).
сраже́ни|е, я *nt.* battle, engagement.
сра|зи́ть, жу́, зи́шь *pf.* (*of* **~жа́ть**) **1.** (*obs.*) to slay, strike down. **2.** (*fig.*) to overwhelm, crush.
сра|зи́ться, жу́сь, зи́шься *pf. of* **~жа́ться**
сра́зу *adv.* **1.** at once. **2.** straight away, right away.
срам, а *m.* shame; **како́й с.!** for shame!
срам|и́ть, лю́, и́шь *impf.* (*of* **о~**) to shame, put to shame.
срам|и́ться, лю́сь, и́шься *impf.* (*of* **о~**) to cover o.s. with shame.
срамни́к, а́ *m.* (*coll.*) shameless person.
срамн|о́й *adj.* (*coll.*) shameless.
сраста́ни|е, я *nt.* (*of bones*) knitting.
сраст|а́ться, а́ется *impf. of* **~и́сь**
сраст|и́сь, ётся, *past* **сро́сся, сросла́сь** *pf.* (*of* **~а́ться**) (*physiol.*) to grow together; (*of bones*) to knit.
сра|сти́ть, щу́, сти́шь *pf.* (*of* **~щивать**) **1.** to join, joint. **2.** to splice.
ср|ать, у, ёшь *impf.* (*of* **насра́ть**) (*vulg.*) to shit.
сраще́ни|е, я *nt.* union.
сра́щивани|е, я *nt.* **1.** joining; splicing. **2.** (*fig.*) fusion, merging.
сра́щива|ть, ю *impf. of* **срасти́ть**
сре́бреник, а *m.* silver coin, piece of silver.
сред|а́[1], **ы,** *a.* **~у́,** *pl.* **~ы** *f.* **1.** environment, surroundings; milieu; (*biol.*) habitat; **в на́шей ~е́** in our midst, among us. **2.** (*phys.*) medium.
сред|а́[2], **ы́,** *a.* **~у,** *pl.* **~ы, ~а́м** *f.* Wednesday.
средакти́р|овать, ую *pf. of* **редакти́ровать**
среди́ *prep.+g.* **1.** among, amongst; amidst. **2.** in the middle (of); **с. бе́ла дня** in broad daylight.
Средизе́мн|ое мо́р|е, ~ого ~я *nt.* the Mediterranean (Sea).
средиземномо́рский *adj.* Mediterranean.
среди́н|а, ы *f.* (*obs.*) middle.
среди́нн|ый *adj.* middle.
сре́дне *adv.* (*coll.*) middling, so-so.
среднеазиа́тский *adj.* Central Asian (*in context of former USSR*).
среднеангли́йский *adj.*: **с. язы́к** Middle English.
средневеко́вый *adj.* medieval.
средневеко́вь|е, я *nt.* the Middle Ages.
сре́дн|ий *adj.* **1.** middle; medium; **~ие века́** the Middle Ages; **~их лет** middle-aged; **~его ро́ста** of medium height. **2.** mean, average; **с. за́работок** average earnings; **~яя оши́бка** standard deviation; *as n.* **~ее, ~его** *nt.* mean, average; **в ~ем** on average; **вы́ше ~его** above average. **3.** (*coll.*) middling, average. **4.** (*in education*) secondary; **~яя шко́ла** secondary school. **5.: с. род** (*gram.*) neuter (gender).
средото́чи|е, я *nt.* focus, centre point.
сре́дств|о, а *nt.* **1.** means; facilities; **~а сообще́ния** means of communication. **2.** **(от)** remedy (for); **с. от ка́шля** cough medicine; **с. от насеко́мых** insect repellent; **с. от поте́ния** antiperspirant. **3.** (*pl.*) resources; credits. **4.** (*pl.*) means; **челове́к со ~ами** man of means; **жить не по ~ам** to live beyond one's means.
средь *prep.+g.* = **среди́**
срез, а *m.* **1.** cut; microscopic section. **2.** (*tech.*) shear, shearing. **3.** (*sport*) slice, slicing.
сре́|зать, жу, жешь *pf.* **1.** (*impf.* **~за́ть**) to cut off; **с. у́гол** (*fig.*) to take a short cut; **с. на экза́мене** (*school sl.*) to fail an exam. **2.** (*impf.* **ре́зать**) (*sport*) to slice, cut, chop.
среза́|ть, ю *impf. of* **сре́зать**
сре́|заться, жусь, жешься *pf.* (*of* **~за́ться**) (*school sl.*) to fail.
среза́|ться, юсь *impf. of* **сре́заться**
срепети́р|овать, ую *pf. of* **репети́ровать**
срис|ова́ть, у́ю *pf.* (*of* **~о́вывать**) to copy.
срисо́выва|ть, ю *impf. of* **срисова́ть**
сровня́|ть, ю *pf. of* **ровня́ть**
сродни́ *adv.* akin; **быть с.** (*+d.*) to be related (to).
сродн|и́ть, ю́, и́шь *pf.* **(с+*i.*)** to link (with).
сродн|и́ться, ю́сь, и́шься *pf.* **(с+*i.*)** to become closely linked (with); to get used (to).
сро́д|ный (~ен, ~на) *adj.* (*+d. or* **с+*i.***) related (to).
сродств|о́, а́ *nt.* relationship, affinity.
сро́ду *adv.* (*coll.*) in one's life.
срок, а (у) *m.* **1.** time, period; term; **в кратча́йший с.** in the shortest possible time; **с. вое́нной слу́жбы** call-up period; **с. де́йствия** period of validity; **с. полномо́чий** term of office; **с. рабо́ты** life (*of machine, etc.*); **продли́ть с. ви́зы** to extend a visa;

∼ом до трёх ме́сяцев within three months; **да́й(те) с.** (*coll.*) wait a minute!, give us time! **2.** date, term; **кра́йний с.** closing date; **с. аре́нды** term of lease; **с. платежа́** date of payment; **с. хране́ния** shelf life; **пропусти́ть с. платежа́** to fail to pay by the date fixed; **в ука́занный с.** by the date fixed; **в с., к ∼у** in time, to time.

сро́чно *adv.* urgently; quickly.

сро́чност|ь, и *f.* urgency; hurry.

сро́ч|ный (∼ен, ∼на́, ∼но) *adj.* **1.** urgent, pressing; **с. зака́з** rush order. **2.** at a fixed date; for a fixed period; **∼ная слу́жба** (*mil.*) service for a fixed period. **3.** periodic, routine.

сруб, а *m.* **1.** felling; **на с.** for timber. **2.** frame(work), shell (*of an izba, well, etc.*). **3.** (*hist.*) framework.

сруб|а́ть, а́ю *impf. of* **∼и́ть**

сруб|и́ть, лю́, ∼ишь *pf.* (*of* **∼а́ть**) **1.** to fell, cut down. **2.** to build (*of logs*).

срыв, а *m.* disruption; frustration; **с. перегово́ров** break-down of talks; **с. рабо́ты** stoppage.

срыва́|ть[1], **ю** *impf. of* **сорва́ть**

срыва́|ть[2], **ю** *impf. of* **срыть**

срыва́|ться, юсь *impf. of* **сорва́ться**

срыть, сро́ю, сро́ешь *pf.* (*of* **срыва́ть**[2]) to raze, level to the ground.

сря́ду *adv.* (*coll.*) running; **два ра́за с.** twice running.

сса́дин|а, ы *f.* scratch, abrasion.

сса|ди́ть[1], **жу́, ∼дишь** *pf.* (*of* **∼живать**) (*coll.*) to scratch.

сса|ди́ть[2], **жу́, ∼дишь** *pf.* (*of* **∼живать**) **1.** to help down, help to alight. **2.** to put off, make get off (*from public transport*).

сса́жива|ть, ю *impf. of* **ссади́ть**

ссо́р|а, ы *f.* **1.** quarrel; falling-out; **они́ в ∼е друг с дру́гом** they have fallen out. **2.** slanging-match.

ссо́р|ить, ю, ишь *impf.* (*of* **по∼**) to cause to quarrel, cause to fall out.

ссо́р|иться, юсь, ишься *impf.* (*of* **по∼**) (**с**+*i.*) to quarrel (with), fall out (with).

ссо́х|нуться, нется, *past* **∼ся, ∼лась** *pf.* (*of* **ссыха́ться**) **1.** to shrink, shrivel, warp. **2.** to harden out, dry out.

СССР *m. indecl.* (*hist.*) (*abbr. of* ***Сою́з Сове́тских Социалисти́ческих Респу́блик***) USSR (*Union of Soviet Socialist Republics*).

ссу́д|а, ы *f.* loan, grant.

ссу|ди́ть, жу́, ∼дишь *pf.* (*of* **∼жа́ть**) (+*a. and i. or* +*d. and a.*) to lend, loan.

ссужа́|ть, ю *impf. of* **ссуди́ть**

ссуту́л|ить(ся), ю(сь), ишь(ся) *pf. of* **суту́лить(ся)**

ссуч|и́ть, у́, ∼ишь *pf. of* **сучи́ть**

ссыла́|ть(ся), ю(сь) *impf. of* **сосла́ть(ся)**

ссы́лк|а[1], **и** *f.* exile, banishment; deportation.

ссы́лк|а[2], **и** *f.* reference.

ссы́л|очный *adj. of* **∼ка**[2]; **∼очное примеча́ние** reference note.

ссы́льн|ый, ого *m.* exile.

ссып|а́ть, а́ю *impf. of* **∼ать**

ссы́п|ать, лю, лешь *pf.* (*of* **∼а́ть**) to pour.

ссыха́|ться, ется *impf. of* **ссо́хнуться**

ст. *abbr. of* **1. статья́** Art., Article (*of law, etc.*). **2. столе́тие** C, century.

стабилиза́тор, а *m.* (*tech.*) stabilizer; (*aeron.*) tail-plane.

стабилиза́ци|я, и *f.* stabilization.

стабилизи́р|овать, ую *impf. and pf.* to stabilize.

стабилизи́р|оваться, уюсь *impf. and pf.* to become stable.

стаби́льност|ь, и *f.* stability.

стаби́л|ьный (∼ен, ∼ьна) *adj.* stable, firm; **с. уче́бник** standard text-book.

ста́в|ень, ня, *g. pl.* **∼ней** *m.* shutter (*on window*).

ста́в|ить, лю, ишь *impf.* (*of* **по∼**) **1.** to put, place, set; to stand; **с. цветы́ в ва́зу** to put flowers in a vase; **с. буты́лки в ряд** to stand bottles in a row; **с. диа́гноз** to diagnose; **с. реко́рд** to set up, create a record; **с. то́чку** to put a full stop; **с. часы́** to set a clock; **с. самова́р** to put a samovar on; **с. в вину́ что-н. кому́-н.** to accuse s.o. of sth.; **с. в тупи́к** to nonplus; **с. за пра́вило** to make it a rule; **с. кого́-н. на ме́сто** to put s.o. in his place. **2.** to put up, erect; to install; **с. па́мятник** to erect a monument. **3.** (*coll.*) to put in, install. **4.** to apply, put on; **с. кому́-н. термо́метр** to take s.o.'s temperature. **5.** to put, present; to put on, stage; **с. резолю́цию** to put a resolution. **6.** (**на**+*a.*) to place, stake (*money on*); **с. на ло́шадь** to back a horse.

ста́вк|а[1], **и** *f.* **1.** rate. **2.** stake; **де́лать ∼у (на**+*a.*) (*fig.*) to count (on).

ста́вк|а[2], **и** *f.* (*mil.*) headquarters; **с. главнокома́ндующего** General Headquarters.

ста́вленник, а *m.* protégé.

ста́вн|я, и *f.* = **ста́вень**

стадио́н, а *m.* stadium.

ста́ди|я, и *f.* stage.

ста́дный *adj.* gregarious; **с. инсти́нкт** herd instinct.

ста́д|о, а, *pl.* **∼а́** *nt.* herd; flock.

стаж, а *m.* **1.** length of service; record. **2.** (**испыта́тельный**) **с.** probation; **проходи́ть с.** to work on probation.

стажёр, а *m.* probationer.

стажи́р|овать, ую *impf.* to work on probation.

ста́ива|ть, ю *impf. of* **стоя́ть**

ста́йер, а *m.* (*sport*) long-distance runner.

стака́н, а *m.* glass, tumbler, beaker.

стакка́то (*mus.*) **1.** *adv.* **2.** *n.*; *nt. indecl.* staccato.

сталагми́т, а *m.* stalagmite.

сталакти́т, а *m.* stalactite.

сталева́р, а *m.* steelworker.

сталелите́йный *adj.*: **с. заво́д** steel mill, steel works.

сталелите́йщик, а *m.* steelworker.

сталепрока́тный *adj.*: **с. заво́д** steel-rolling mill.

ста́линск|ий *adj.* Stalin's, of Stalin.

ста́лкива|ть(ся), ю(сь) *impf. of* **столкну́ть(ся)**

ста́ло быть *conj.* (*coll.*) consequently, therefore.

стал|ь, и *f.* steel; **нержаве́ющая с.** stainless steel.

стальн|о́й *adj.* steel; **∼о́го цве́та** steel-blue; **∼а́я во́ля** iron will; **∼ы́е не́рвы** nerves of steel.

стаме́ск|а, и *f.* (*tech.*) chisel.

стан[1], **а** *m.* figure, torso.

стан[2], **а** *m.* camp (*also fig.*); **в ∼е врага́** in the enemy's camp.

стан[3], **а** *m.* (*tech.*) mill.

станда́рт, а *m.* standard.

стандартиза́ци|я, и *f.* standardization.

стандартиз|ова́ть, у́ю *impf. and pf.* to standardize.

станда́рт|ный (∼ен, ∼на) *adj.* standard.

стани́н|а, ы *f.* (*tech.*) mounting, bed (plate).

станио́л|ь, я *m.* tin foil.

стани́ц|а[1], **ы** *f.* stanitsa (*large Cossack village*).

стани́ц|а[2], **ы** *f.* (*obs.*) flock.

станко́в|ый *adj. of* **стано́к; с. пулемёт** (*mil.*) heavy machine-gun.

станкострое́ни|е, я *nt.* machine-tool construction.

станов|и́ться, лю́сь, ∼ишься *impf. of* **стать**

становле́ни|е, я *nt.* (*phil.*) coming into being; **в проце́ссе ∼я** in the making.

станово́й *adj.* main, chief; **с. хребе́т** (*fig.*) backbone.

стан|о́к, ка́ *m.* **1.** (*tech.*) machine-tool, machine; bench; **печа́тный с.** printing-press; **тка́цкий с.** loom; **тока́рный с.** lathe; **рабо́чий от ∼ка́** bench worker. **2.** (*mil.*) mount, mounting.

стано́чник, а *m.* machine operator, machine minder.

станс, а *m.* (*liter.*) stanza.

станцио́нный *adj. of* **ста́нция; с. зал** waiting-room;

с. смотри́тель (*obs.*) postmaster.
ста́нци|я, и *f.* station; **гидроэлектри́ческая с.** hydro-electric power station; **телефо́нная с.** telephone exchange.
ста́пел|ь, я *m.* (*naut.*) building slip(s), stocks; **на ~е, на ~ях** on the stocks.
ста́птыва|ть(ся), ю(сь) *impf. of* **стопта́ть(ся)**
стара́ни|е, я *nt.* effort; diligence; **приложи́ть все ~я** to do one's utmost, do one's best.
стара́тел|ь, я *m.* gold prospector, gold-digger.
стара́тельност|ь, и *f.* application, diligence.
стара́тел|ьный (~ен, ~ьна) *adj.* assiduous, diligent, painstaking.
стара́|ться, юсь *impf.* (*of* **по~**) to try, endeavour, seek; **с. изо всех сил** to do one's utmost.
старе́йшин|а, ы *m.* (*hist.*, *ethnol.*) elder.
старе́|ть, ю *impf.* (*of* **по~**) to grow old, age.
ста́р|ец, ца *m.* **1.** elder, (venerable) old man. **2.** elderly monk. **3.** spiritual adviser.
стари́к, а́ *m.* old man.
старин|а́[1], **ы́** *f.* **1.** antiquity, olden times; **в ~у́** in olden times, in days of old. **2.** (*collect.*) antiques.
старин|а́[2], **ы́** *m.* (*coll.*) old fellow, old chap.
стари́нк|а *f.* (*coll.*) old fashion, old custom(s); **по ~е** in the old fashion, in the old way.
стари́нный *adj.* **1.** ancient, old; antique. **2.** old, of long standing; **с. друг** old friend.
ста́р|ить, ю, ишь *impf.* (*of* **со~**) to age; to make look old(er).
ста́р|иться, юсь, ишься *impf.* (*of* **со~**) to age; to grow old, age.
старич|о́к, ка́ *m.* little old man.
старове́р, а *m.* (*relig.*) Old Believer.
староде́вний *adj.* ancient.
староде́вност|ь, и *f.* antiquity.
старожи́л, а *m.* old inhabitant, old resident.
старозаве́т|ный (~ен, ~на) *adj.* **1.** (*of persons*) old-fashioned, conservative. **2.** (*pej.*) old, antiquated.
старомо́д|ный (~ен, ~на) *adj.* old-fashioned; out-of-date.
старообра́з|ный (~ен, на) *adj.* old-looking.
старообря́д|ец, ца *m.* (*relig.*) Old Believer.
старосве́тский *adj.* old-world; old-fashioned.
старославя́нский *adj.* (*ling.*) Old Church Slavonic.
ста́рост|а, ы *m.* (*elected*) head; **се́льский с.** (*hist.*) village headman, elder; **церко́вный с.** churchwarden; **с. кла́сса** (*in school*) form prefect, monitor.
ста́рост|ь, и *f.* old age; **на ~и лет** in one's old age.
старт, а *m.* **1.** (*sport*) start; **на с.!** on your marks! **2.** (*aeron.*) take-off point.
ста́ртер, а *m.* (*tech.*) starter.
стартёр, а *m.* (*sport*) starter.
старт|ова́ть, у́ю *impf. and pf.* **1.** (*sport*) to start. **2.** (*aeron.*) to take off.
ста́ртовый *adj.* starting.
стару́х|а, и *f.* old woman, old lady.
стару́шк|а, и *f.* (little) old lady, old woman.
ста́рческ|ий *adj.* **1.** of old age. **2.** senile; **~ое слабоу́мие** senile dementia.
ста́рше *comp. of* **ста́рый; она́ с. меня́ на три го́да** she is three years older than me.
старшекла́ссник, а *m.* senior (pupil).
старшеку́рсник, а *m.* senior student.
ста́рш|ий *adj.* **1.** elder; *as n.* **~ие, ~их** (one's) elders. **2.** oldest, eldest. **3.** senior, superior; chief, head; **с. врач** head physician; **~ая медсестра́** sister; *as n.* **с., ~его** *m.* chief; (*mil.*) man in charge. **4.** senior, upper, higher; **с. класс** (*school*) higher form.
старшин|а́, ы́ *m.* **1.** (*mil.*) sergeant-major; (*naut.*) petty officer. **2.** leader, senior representative (*of social group, professional organization, etc.*); **с. прися́жных заседа́телей** foreman of the jury.
старшинств|о́, а́ *nt.* seniority.
ста́р|ый (~, ~а́, ~́о) *adj.* old; **по ~ой па́мяти** for old times' sake; from force of habit; *as n.* **~ые, ~ых** the old, old people; **~ое, ~ого** *nt.* the old, the past.
старь|ё, я́ *nt.* (*collect.*; *coll.*) old things, old clothes.
старьёвщик, а *m.* old-clothes dealer; junk dealer.
ста́скива|ть, ю *impf. of* **стащи́ть**
стас|ова́ть, у́ю *pf. of* **тасова́ть**
ста́тик|а, и *f.* statics.
стати́ст, а *m.* (*theatr.*) super, extra, mute.
стати́стик, а *m.* statistician.
стати́стик|а, и *f.* statistics.
статисти́ческий *adj.* statistical.
стати́ческий *adj.* static.
ста́т|ный (~ен, ~на) *adj.* stately.
статс-секрета́р|ь, я́ *m.* Secretary of State.
ста́тус-кво́ *m. indecl.* status quo.
стату́т, а *m.* statute.
статуэ́тк|а, и *f.* statuette, figurine.
ста́ту|я, и *f.* statue.
стать[1]**, ста́ну, ста́нешь** *pf.* (*of* **станови́ться**) **1.** to stand; **с. на коле́ни** to kneel; **с. в о́чередь** to queue (up); **с. в по́зу** to strike an attitude; **с. на чью-н. сто́рону** to take s.o.'s side, stand up for s.o. **2.** to take up position; **с. ла́герем** to camp, encamp; **с. в карау́л** to mount guard; **с. на я́корь** to anchor. **3.** to stop, come to a halt; **река́ ста́ла** the river has frozen over; **за чем де́ло ста́ло?** (*coll.*) what's holding things up? **4.** (**в**+*a.*; *coll.*) to cost; **во что бы то ни ста́ло** at any price, at all costs.
стать[2]**, ста́ну, ста́нешь** *pf.* (*of* **станови́ться**) **1.** (+*inf.*) to begin (to), start; **она́ ста́ла говори́ть во сне** she began talking in her sleep. **2.** (+*i.*) to become, get, grow; **он стал машини́стом** he became an engine-driver; **ста́ло темно́** it got dark; **ей ста́ло лу́чше** she was better; she had got better. **3.** (**с**+*i.*) to become (of); **что с ни́ми ста́ло?** what has become of them? **4.: не с.** (*impers.*+*g.*) to cease to be; **её отца́ давно́ не ста́ло** her father passed away long ago.
стат|ь[3]**, и,** *pl.* **~́и, ~е́й** *f.* **1.** figure, build. **2.** character, type; **быть под с.** (+*d.*) to be (well) matched (with).
стат|ь[4]**, и** *f.* (*coll.*, *obs.*) need, necessity; **с како́й ~́и?** (*coll.*) why?, what for?
ста́|ться, нется *pf.* (*coll.*) to happen, become; **что с на́ми ~нется?** what will become of us?; **вполне́ мо́жет с.** it is quite possible.
стат|ья́, ьи́, *g. pl.* **~е́й** *f.* **1.** article; **передова́я с.** editorial. **2.** clause; item; (dictionary) entry; **с. догово́ра** clause of a treaty; **расхо́дная с.** debit item. **3.** (*coll.*) matter, job. **4.** (*naut.*) class, rating; **матро́с пе́рвой ~ьи́** able seaman.
стациона́р, а *m.* permanent establishment; **(лечéбный) с.** hospital.
стациона́рн|ый *adj.* **1.** stationary; **с. объе́кт** (*mil.*) stationary target. **2.** permanent, fixed. **3.: с. больно́й** in-patient; **~ое лече́ние** hospitalization.
ста́чечник, а *m.* striker.
ста́ч|ечный *adj. of* **~ка**
ста́чива|ть, ю *impf. of* **сточи́ть**
ста́чк|а, и *f.* strike.
стащ|и́ть, у́, ~́ишь *pf.* (*of* **ста́скивать**) **1.** to drag off; to drag down. **2.** (*coll.*) to pinch, swipe.
ста́|я, и *f.* (*of birds*) flock; (*of fish*) school, shoal; (*of dogs or wolves*) pack.
ста́|ять, ет *pf.* (*of* **~ивать**) to melt.
ствол, а́ *m.* **1.** (*of tree*) trunk. **2.** (*of firearm*) barrel.
створ, а *m.* = **~ка**
ство́рк|а, и *f.* leaf, fold; door, gate, shutter (*one of a pair*).
створо́ж|иться, ится *pf.* to curdle.
ство́рчатый *adj.* folding; valved.

стеари́н, а *m.* stearin.
сте́б|ель, ля, *pl.* **~ли, ~ле́й** *m.* stem, stalk.
стёганк|а, и *f.* (*coll.*) quilted jacket.
стёган|ый *adj.* quilted; **~ое одея́ло** quilt.
стега́|ть[1]**, ю** *impf.* (*of* **от~** *and* **стегну́ть**) to whip, lash.
стега́|ть[2]**, ю** *impf.* (*of* **вы́~**) to quilt.
стег|ну́ть, ну́, нёшь *pf. of* **~а́ть**[1]
стеж|о́к, ка́ *m.* stitch.
стез|я́, и́, *g. pl.* **~е́й** *f.* (*rhet.*) path, way.
стека́|ть(ся), ю(сь) *impf. of* **сте́чь(ся)**
стеклене́|ть, ет *impf.* (*of* **о~**) to become glassy.
стек|ло́, ла́, *pl.* **⁓ла, ⁓ол** *nt.* glass; *pl.* lenses (*for spectacles*); **око́нное с.** window-pane; **пере́днее с.** wind-screen.
стеклова́т|а, ы *f.* fibreglass.
стекловолокн|о́, а́ *nt.* fibreglass.
стеклоду́в, а *m.* glass-blower.
стекля́нн|ый *adj.* **1.** glass; **~ая бума́га** glass-paper; **~ые изде́лия** glassware. **2.** (*fig.*) glassy.
стекля́рус, а *m.* (*collect.*) bugles (*tubular glass beads*).
стеко́льный *adj.* glass; vitreous; **с. заво́д** glass-works, glass-factory.
стеко́льщик, а *m.* glazier.
стел|и́ть(ся), ю́(сь), ⁓ешь(ся) *impf.* = **стлать(ся)**
стелла́ж, а́ *m.* **1.** shelves. **2.** rack, stand.
сте́льк|а, и *f.* insole, sock; **пьян как с.** (*coll.*) drunk as a lord.
стемне́|ть, ю *pf. of* **темне́ть**
стен|а́, ы́, *a.* **⁓у,** *pl.* **⁓ы, ~а́м** *f.* wall (*also fig.*); **жить с. в ⁓у** (**с**+*i.*) to live right on top (of); **в ~а́х** (+*g.*) within the precincts (of).
стена́|ть, ю *impf.* (*obs.*) to groan, moan.
стенгазе́т|а, ы *f.* (*abbr. of* **стенна́я газе́та**) wall newspaper.
стенд, а *m.* stand (*at exhibition, etc.*).
сте́ндер, а *m.* stand-pipe.
сте́нк|а, и *f.* **1.** wall; **гимнасти́ческая с.** wall-bars. **2.** (*anat., etc.*) side, wall. **3.** (*furniture*) wall unit.
стенн|о́й *adj.* wall; mural.
стеноби́тный *adj.*: **с. тара́н** battering-ram.
стеногра́мм|а, ы *f.* shorthand report.
стено́граф, а *m.* stenographer.
стенографи́р|овать, ую *impf. and pf.* to take down in shorthand.
стенографи́ст, а *m.* = **стено́граф**
стенографи́ст|ка, ки *f. of* **~**
стенографи́ческий *adj.* stenographic, shorthand.
стеногра́фи|я, и *f.* stenography, shorthand.
сте́нопис|ь, и *f.* mural (painting).
сте́ньг|а, и *f.* (*naut.*) topmast.
степе́н|ный (~ен, ~на) *adj.* staid, steady.
сте́пен|ь, и, *g. pl.* **~е́й** *f.* **1.** degree, extent; **в вы́сшей ~и** in the highest degree; **до не́которой ~и** to some extent, to a certain extent. **2.** (*math.*) power; **возвести́ в тре́тью с.** to raise to the third power. **3. (учёная) с.** (*academic*) degree.
степ|но́й *adj. of* **~ь**
степ|ь, и, о ⁓и, в ~и́, *pl.* **⁓и, ~е́й** *f.* steppe.
сте́рв|а, ы *f.* (*vulg.*; *as term of abuse*) bastard, shit.
стервя́тник, а *m.* carrion-crow.
стерео... *comb. form* stereo-.
стереоме́три|я, и *f.* solid geometry.
стереоско́п, а *m.* stereoscope.
стереоскопи́ческий *adj.* stereoscopic.
стереоти́п, а *m.* stereotype.
стереоти́пн|ый *adj.* **1.** stereotype. **2.** (*fig.*) stereotyped; **~ая фра́за** stock phrase.
стереофони́ческий *adj.* stereophonic.
стер|е́ть, сотру́, сотрёшь, *past* **⁓, ⁓ла** *pf.* (*of* **стира́ть**[1]) **1.** to rub out; to wipe off; **с. с лица́ земли́** to wipe off the face of the earth. **2.** to rub sore.
стер|е́ться, сотрётся, *past* **⁓ся, ⁓лась** *pf.* (*of* **стира́ться**[1]) **1.** to rub off; (*fig.*) to fade; **с. в па́мяти** to sink into oblivion. **2.** to become worn down.
стере́|чь, гу́, жёшь, гу́т, *past* **⁓г, ~гла́** *impf.* **1.** to guard, watch (over). **2.** to watch (for).
сте́рж|ень, ня *m.* **1.** (*tech.*) pivot; shank, rod. **2.** (*fig.*) core.
стержнево́й *adj.*: **с. вопро́с** key question.
стерилиза́тор, а *m.* sterilizer.
стерилиза́ци|я, и *f.* sterilization.
стерилиз|ова́ть, у́ю *impf. and pf.* to sterilize.
стери́льност|ь, и *f.* sterility.
стери́л|ьный (~ен, ~ьна) *adj.* sterile; germ-free.
сте́рлинг, а *m.* (*fin.*) sterling; **фунт ~ов** pound sterling.
сте́рлинг|овый *adj. of* **~**; **~овая зо́на** sterling area.
сте́рляд|ь, и *f.* (*zool.*) sterlet.
стерн|ь, и *f.* **1.** harvest-field. **2.** (*collect.*) stubble.
стерн|я́, и́ *f.* = **~ь**
стеро́ид, а *m.* steroid.
стерп|е́ть, лю́, ⁓ишь *pf.* to bear, suffer, endure.
стерп|е́ться, ⁓ишься *pf.* (**с**+*i.*; *coll.*) to get used (to), accept.
стёр|тый *p.p.p. of* **~е́ть** *and adj.* worn, effaced.
стесне́ни|е, я *nt.* constraint; **без вся́ких ~й** quite uninhibitedly.
стесн|ённый *p.p.p. of* **~и́ть** *and adj.* **~ённые обстоя́тельства** straitened circumstances.
стесни́тельност|ь, и *f.* **1.** shyness; inhibition(s). **2.** difficulty, inconvenience.
стесни́тел|ьный (~ен, ~ьна) *adj.* **1.** shy; inhibited. **2.** difficult, inconvenient.
стесн|и́ть, ю́, и́шь *pf.* (*of* **~я́ть**) to constrain; to hamper; to inhibit.
стесн|и́ться, ю́сь, и́шься *pf.* (*of* **тесни́ться**) to crowd together.
стесн|я́ть, я́ю *impf. of* **~и́ть**
стесня́|ться, юсь *impf.* (*of* **по~**) (+*inf.*) to feel too shy (to), be ashamed (to); (+*g.*) to feel shy (before, of); **не ~йтесь!** don't be shy!
стетоско́п, а *m.* (*med.*) stethoscope.
стече́ни|е, я *nt.* confluence; **с. обстоя́тельств** coincidence.
сте|чь, чёт, ку́т, *past* **⁓к, ~кла́** *pf.* (*of* **~ка́ть**) to flow down.
сте́|чься, чётся, ку́тся, *past* **⁓кся, ~кла́сь** *pf.* (*of* **~ка́ться**) to flow together; to gather, throng.
сти́бр|ить, ю, ишь *pf. of* **ти́брить**
стил|ево́й *adj. of* **~ь**
стиле́т, а *m.* stiletto.
стилиза́ци|я, и *f.* stylization.
стилиз|ова́ть, у́ю *impf. and pf.* to stylize.
стили́ст, а *m.* stylist.
стили́стик|а, и *f.* (*study of*) style, stylistics.
стилисти́ческий *adj.* stylistic.
стил|ь, я *m.* style.
сти́л|ьный (~ен, ~ьна) *adj.* stylish; **~ьная ме́бель** period furniture.
стиля́г|а, и *c.g.* stilyaga (*young person given to uncritical display of extravagant fashion*).
сти́мул, а *m.* stimulus, incentive.
стимули́р|овать, ую *impf. and pf.* to stimulate.
стипе́нди|я, и *f.* grant, scholarship.
стира́льн|ый *adj.* washing; **~ая маши́на** washing machine.
стира́|ть[1]**, ю** *impf. of* **стере́ть**
стира́|ть[2]**, ю** *impf.* (*of* **вы́~**) to wash, launder.
стира́|ться[1]**, юсь** *impf. of* **стере́ться**
стира́|ться[2]**, ется** *impf.* to wash; **хорошо́ с.** to wash well.
сти́рк|а, и *f.* washing, laundering; **отда́ть в ~у** to send to the wash, send to the laundry.
сти́скива|ть, ю *impf. of* **сти́снуть**
сти́с|нуть, ну, нешь *pf.* (*of* **~кивать**) to squeeze;

с. зу́бы to clench one's teeth.
стих, а́ *m.* **1.** verse; line (*of poetry*); **бе́лый с.** blank verse; **разме́р ~а́** metre. **2.** (*pl.*) verses; poetry.
стиха́р|ь, я́ *m.* (*eccl.*) surplice.
стих|а́ть, а́ю *impf. of* **~нуть**
стихи́йност|ь, и *f.* spontaneity.
стихи́|йный (~ен, ~йна) *adj.* **1.** elemental; **~йное бе́дствие** natural calamity. **2.** (*fig.*) spontaneous.
стихи́|я, и *f.* element; **быть в свое́й ~и** to be in one's element.
сти́х|нуть, ну, нешь, *past* **~, ~ла** *pf.* (*of* **~а́ть**) to abate, subside; to die down; to calm down.
стихоплёт, а *m.* (*coll.*) rhymester, versifier.
стихосложе́ни|е, я *nt.* versification.
стихотворе́ни|е, я *nt.* poem.
стихотво́рн|ый *adj.* in verse form.
стихотво́рчеств|о, а *nt.* poetry-writing.
стиш|о́к, ка́ *m.* (*coll.*) verse, rhyme.
стлать, стелю́, сте́лешь *impf.* (*of* **по~**) to spread; **с. посте́ль** to make a bed.
стла́ться, сте́лется *impf.* to spread; **с. по земле́** (*of mists, smoke, etc.*) to creep; to hang about.
сто, ста, *pl.* **ста, сот, стам, ста́ми, стах** *num.* hundred.
стог, а, *pl.* **~а́** *m.* (*agric.*) stack, rick.
сто́ик, а *m.* (*phil. and fig.*) stoic.
сто́имост|ь, и *f.* **1.** cost; **с. перево́зки** carriage. **2.** (*econ.*) value; **приба́вочная с.** surplus value.
сто́|ить, ю, ишь *impf.* **1.** to cost (*also fig.*); **ско́лько ~ит э́то пла́тье?** how much is this dress?; **до́рого с.** to cost dear. **2.** (*+g.*) to be worth; to deserve; (*impers.*): **~ит** it is worth while; **не ~ит того́** (*coll.*) it is not worth while; **не ~ит (благода́рности)** don't mention it. **3.: ~ит то́лько** (*impers.+inf.*) one has only (to).
стоици́зм, а *m.* (*phil. and fig.*) stoicism.
стои́ческий *adj.* (*phil.*) stoic; (*fig.*) stoical.
сто́йк|а, и *f.* **1.** (*sport*) stand, stance; **с. на рука́х** hand-stand. **2.** (*tech.*) support, prop; stanchion, upright; (*aeron*) strut. **3.** bar, counter.
сто́|йкий (~ек, ~йка́, ~йко) *adj.* **1.** firm, stable; (*chem.*) stable. **2.** (*fig.*) stable; steadfast, staunch.
сто́йкост|ь, и *f.* **1.** firmness, stability. **2.** (*fig.*) steadfastness, staunchness.
сто́йл|о, а *nt.* stall.
стойм́я *adv.* upright.
сток, а *m.* **1.** flow; drainage. **2.** drain, gutter; sewer.
Стокго́льм, а *m.* Stockholm.
сто́кер, а *m.* (*tech.*) (mechanical) stoker.
стокра́т *adv.* (*obs.*) a hundred times.
стокра́тный *adj.* hundredfold.
сто́л, а *m.* **1.** table; **пи́сьменный с.** desk; **сесть за с.** to sit down to table; **за ~о́м** at table. **2.** board; cooking, cuisine; diet; **с. и кварти́ра** board and lodging. **3.** department; office; **с. ли́чного соста́ва** personnel department; **с. нахо́док** lost property office.
столб, а́ *m.* post, pole, pillar, column; **телегра́фный с.** telegraph pole; **пыль ~о́м** a cloud of dust.
столбене́|ть, ю *impf.* (*of* **о~**) (*coll.*) to be rooted to the ground.
столб|е́ц, ца́ m. column (*in dictionary, newspaper, etc.*).
сто́лбик, а *m.* **1.** *dim. of* **столб. 2.** (*bot.*) style.
столбня́к, а́ *m.* **1.** (*med.*) tetanus. **2.** (*coll.*) stupor.
столбов|о́й *adj. of* **столб**; (*fig., coll.*) main, chief; **~а́я доро́га** high road, highway (*also fig.*).
столе́ти|е, я *nt.* **1.** century. **2.** centenary.
столе́тн|ий *adj.* **1.** of a hundred years' duration; **~яя война́** the Hundred Years' War. **2.** a hundred years old; **~яя годовщи́на** centenary.
сто́л|ик, а *m. dim. of* **~**; **ни́зкий с.** coffee table.
столи́ц|а, ы *f.* capital; metropolis.
столи́|чный *adj. of* **~ца; с. го́род** capital (city).
столкнове́ни|е, я *nt.* collision; (*mil. and fig.*) clash; **вооружённое с.** armed conflict, hostilities.
столкн|у́ть, у́, ёшь *pf.* (*of* **ста́лкивать**) **1.** to push off, push away. **2.** to cause to collide; to knock together. **3.** (*coll.*) to bring together.
столкн|у́ться, у́сь, ёшься *pf.* (*of* **ста́лкиваться**) **1.** (**с**+*i.*) to collide (with); (*fig.*) to clash (with), conflict (with). **2.** (**с**+*i.*; *fig., coll.*) to run (into), bump (into).
столк|ова́ться, у́юсь *pf.* (*of* **~о́вываться**) (**с**+*i.*; *coll.*) to come to an agreement (with).
столко́выва|ться, юсь *impf. of* **столкова́ться**
стол|ова́ться, у́юсь *impf.* to have meals.
столо́в|ая, ой *f.* dining-room; mess; canteen.
столо́в|ый *adj.* **1.** table; **~ая ло́жка** table-spoon; **с. прибо́р** cover; **~ое серебро́** (*collect.*) silver, plate. **2.** feeding, catering; **~ые де́ньги** dinner money. **3.: ~ые го́ры** (*geog.*) mesa, tableland.
стол|о́чь, ку́, чёшь, ку́т, *past* **~о́к, ~кла́** *pf.* (*of* **толо́чь**) to pound, grind.
столп, а́ *m.* (*arch. or fig.*) pillar, column; **~ы́ о́бщества** pillars of society.
столп|и́ться, и́тся *pf.* to crowd.
столпотворе́ни|е, я *nt.*: **вавило́нское с.** babel.
столь *adv.* so; **э́то не с. ва́жно** it is of no particular importance.
сто́лько *adv.* so much; so many; **ещё с. же** as much again, as many again; **не с. ... ско́лько** not so much ... as; **сто́лько-то** so much, some.
столя́р, а́ *m.* joiner.
столя́рнича|ть, ю *impf.* to be a joiner.
столя́рн|ый *adj.* joiner's; **~ое де́ло** joinery.
стоматоло́ги|я, и *f.* stomatology.
стон, а *m.* moan, groan.
стон|а́ть, у́, ~ешь *and* **~а́ю, ~а́ешь** *impf.* to moan, groan (*also fig.*).
стоп *int.* stop!; **сигна́л с.** stop signal.
стоп|а́[1], ы́ *f.* **1.** (*pl.* **~ы́**) foot (*also fig.*); **идти́ по чьим-н. ~а́м** to follow in s.o.'s footsteps. **2.** (*pl.* **~ы**) (*liter.*) foot.
стоп|а́[2], ы́, *pl.* **~ы** *f.* **1.** ream. **2.** pile, heap.
сто́пк|а[1], и *f.* pile, heap.
сто́пк|а[2], и *f.* small drinking vessel.
сто́пор, а *m.* (*tech.*) stop, catch, locking device.
сто́пор|ить, ю, ишь *impf.* (*tech.*) to stop, lock; (*fig., coll.*) to bring to a standstill.
сто́пор|иться, ится *impf.* (*coll.*) to come to a standstill.
сто́пор|ный *adj. of* **~**; **с. кран** stopcock; **с. механи́зм** stop gear, locking device.
стопроце́нтный *adj.* hundred per cent.
стоп-сигна́л, а *m.* brake-light (*on car*).
стоп|та́ть, чу́, ~чешь *pf.* (*of* **ста́птывать**) **1.** to wear down (*footwear*). **2.** (*coll.*) to trample.
стоп|та́ться, ~чется *pf.* (*of* **ста́птываться**) to wear down, be worn down (*of footwear*).
сторг|ова́ть(ся), у́ю(сь) *pf. of* **торгова́ть(ся)**
стори́цею *adv.* (*obs.*) a hundredfold; **возда́ть с.** (*+d.*) to return a hundredfold, repay with interest.
сто́рож, а, *pl.* **~а́, ~е́й** *m.* watchman, guard.
сторожев|о́й *adj.* watch; **~а́я бу́дка** sentry-box; **~а́я вы́шка** watch-tower; **с. кора́бль** escort vessel; **с. пёс** watch-dog; **с. пост** sentry post.
сторож|и́ть, у́, и́шь *impf.* to guard, watch.
сторо́жк|а, и *f.* lodge.
сторон|а́, ы́, *a.* **сто́рону,** *pl.* **сто́роны, сторо́н, ~а́м** *f.* **1.** side; hand (*also fig.*); feature, aspect; **в сто́рону** (*theatr.*) aside; **шу́тки в сто́рону** (*coll.*) joking aside; **в ~е́** aside; **держа́ться в ~е́** to keep aloof; **на ~е́** (*coll.*) elsewhere, not on the spot; **продава́ть на́ сторону** sell on the black market; **по ту сто́рону** (*+g.*) on the other side (of); **с пра́вой, с ле́вой ~ы́** on the right, left side; **с мое́й ~ы́** for my part; **э́то о́чень любе́зно с ва́шей ~ы́** it is very kind of you;

со ~ы́ (+*g.*) (*indicating line of descent*) on the side of; **с одно́й ~ы́..., с друго́й ~ы́** on the one hand ..., on the other hand; **узна́ть ~о́й** to find out indirectly. **2.** side, party; **вы на чьей ~е́?** whose side are you on?; **взять чью-н. сто́рону** to take s.o.'s part, side with s.o. **3.** land, place; parts; **на чужо́й ~е́** in foreign parts.

сторон|и́ться, ю́сь, ~́ишься *impf.* (*of* **по~**) **1.** to stand aside, make way. **2.** (+*g.*) to shun, avoid.

сторо́нний *adj.* **1.** strange, foreign; **с. наблюда́тель** detached observer. **2.** indirect.

сторо́нник, а *m.* supporter, advocate; **с. ми́ра** peace campaigner.

стоск|ова́ться, у́юсь *pf.* (**по**+*p.*, **о**+*p.*) to pine (for), yearn (for).

сточ|и́ть, у́, ~́ишь *pf.* (*of* **ста́чивать**) to grind off.

сто́чн|ый *adj.* sewage, drainage; **~ые во́ды** sewage.

стошн|и́ть, и́т *pf.* (*impers.*) to be sick, vomit; **меня́ ~и́ло** I was sick.

сто́я *adv.* upright.

стоя́к, а́ *m.* **1.** post, upright. **2.** chimney.

стоя́ни|е, я *nt.* standing.

стоя́нк|а, и *f.* **1.** stop; parking; **«с. запрещена́!»** 'no parking!' **2.** stopping place; parking space; moorage; **автомоби́льная с.** car park; **с. такси́** taxi-rank.

сто|я́ть, ю́, и́шь *impf.* **1.** to stand; **с. в о́череди** to stand in a queue; **с. на коле́нях** to kneel; **с. на четвере́ньках** to be on all fours. **2.** to be, be situated, lie; **село́ ~и́т на возвы́шенности** the village is situated on rising ground; **стака́ны ~я́т в шкафу́** the glasses are in the cupboard; **с. во главе́** (+*g.*) to be at the head (of), head; **с. на я́коре** to be at anchor; **с. у вла́сти** to be in power; **с. у руля́** to be at the helm. **3.** (*of weather conditions, etc.*) to be; to continue; **~и́т моро́з** there is a frost; **~я́ла хоро́шая пого́да** the weather continued fine. **4.** to stay, put up; (*mil.*) to be stationed; **с. ла́герем** to be encamped. **5.** (**за**+*a.*) to stand up (for); (**на**+*p.*) to stand (on), insist (on); **с. на чьей-н. то́чке зре́ния** to share s.o.'s point of view. **6.** to stop; to come to a halt; **мои́ часы́ ~я́т** my watch has stopped; **рабо́та ~и́т** work has come to a standstill; **~й(те)!** stop!; halt!

стоя́ч|ий *adj.* **1.** standing; upright; **~ая ла́мпа** standard lamp; **~ая труба́** stand-pipe. **2.** stagnant.

сто́|ящий *pres. part. act. of* **~ить** *and adj.* deserving; worth-while.

стр. *abbr. of* **1. страни́ца** p., page. **2. страни́цы** pp., pages.

страв|и́ть, лю́, ~́ишь *pf.* (*of* **~́ливать** *and* **~ля́ть**) to set on (*to fight*); **с. одного́ с други́м** to play off one against another.

стра́влива|ть, ю *impf. of* **страви́ть**

стравля́|ть, ю *impf.* = **стра́вливать**

страд|а́, ы́, *pl.* **~́ы** *f.* hard work at harvest-time; period of hard work; (*fig.*) toil, drudgery.

страда́л|ец, ьца *m.* sufferer.

страда́льческ|ий *adj.* full of suffering.

страда́ни|е, я *nt.* suffering.

страда́тельный *adj.* (*gram.*) passive.

страда́|ть, ю *impf.* **1.** *impf. only* (+*i.*) to suffer (from); to be subject (to); **с. бессо́нницей** to suffer from insomnia. **2.** *impf. only* (**от**) to suffer (from); **с. от зубно́й бо́ли** to have (a) toothache; **с. от любви́** to be in love. **3.** *impf. only* **с. за кого́-н.** to feel for s.o. **4.** *impf. only* (**по**+ *d. or p.*; *coll.*) to miss; to long (for). **5.** (*pf.* **по~**) to suffer; **с. за ве́ру** to suffer for one's faith; **с. по свое́й вине́** to suffer through one's own fault. **6.** *impf. only* (*coll.*) to be weak, be poor; **у неё па́мять ~ет** she has a poor memory.

стра́д|ный *adj. of* **~а́; ~ная пора́** busy period.

страж, а *m.* **1.** (*obs., now only rhet.*) guard, custodian. **2.: с. ми́ра** peacekeeper.

стра́ж|а, и *f.* guard, watch; **быть, стоя́ть на ~е** (+*g.*) to guard; **под ~ей** under arrest, in custody; **взять, заключи́ть под ~у** to take into custody.

стран|а́, ы́, *pl.* **~́ы** *f.* **1.** country; land. **2.: с. све́та** cardinal point (*of compass*).

страни́ц|а, ы *f.* page (*also fig., rhet.*).

стра́нник, а *m.* wanderer (*esp.* religious pilgrim).

стра́нниц|а, ы *f. of* **стра́нник**

стра́нно *adv.* **1.** strangely, in a strange way. **2.** *as pred.* it is strange, funny, odd, queer.

стра́нност|ь, и *f.* **1.** strangeness. **2.** oddity, eccentricity; **за ним води́лись ~и** he was an odd person.

стра́н|ный (~ен, ~на́, ~но) *adj.* strange; funny, odd, queer.

странове́дени|е, я *nt.* regional studies.

стра́нстви|е, я *nt.* (*obs.*) wandering, travelling.

стра́нствовани|е, я *nt.* wandering, travelling.

стра́нств|овать, ую *impf.* to wander, travel.

стра́нств|ующий *pres. part. act. of* **~овать** *and adj.*; **с. актёр** strolling player; **с. ры́царь** knight-errant.

Страсбу́рг, а *m.* Strasbourg.

страстн|о́й *adj.* of Holy Week; **~а́я неде́ля** Holy Week; **~а́я пя́тница** Good Friday; **С. четве́рг** Maundy Thursday.

стра́стност|ь, и *f.* passion.

стра́ст|ный (~ен, ~на́, ~но) *adj.* passionate; impassioned; ardent.

страст|ь[1]**, и,** *g. pl.* **~е́й** *f.* **1.** (**к**) passion (for); **до ~́и** (*coll.*) passionately; **люби́ть до ~́и** to be passionately fond (of); **со ~́ью** with fervour. **2.: ~́и Христо́вы** (*relig.*) the Passion. **3.** (*coll.*) horror; **расска́зывать (про) вся́кие ~́и** to recount all manner of horrors.

страсть[2] *adv.* (*coll.*) **1.** (**как, како́й**) awfully, frightfully; **мне с. как хо́чется ви́деть э́тот фильм** I want awfully to see this film. **2.** an awful lot, a terrific number.

стратаге́м|а, ы *f.* stratagem.

страте́г, а *m.* strategist.

стратеги́ческий *adj.* strategic.

страте́ги|я, и *f.* strategy.

стратифика́ци|я, и *f.* stratification.

стратосфе́р|а, ы *f.* stratosphere.

стратосфе́рный *adj.* stratospheric.

стра́ус, а *m.* ostrich.

стра́ус|овый *adj. of* **~; ~овое перо́** ostrich feather.

страх[1]**, а** *m.* **1.** fear; terror; **с. Бо́жий** the fear of God; **с. пе́ред неизве́стностью** fear of the unknown; **под ~́ом сме́рти** on pain of death; **~́а ра́ди** for fear, from fear. **2.** (*pl.*) terrors. **3.** risk, responsibility; **на свой с.** at one's own risk.

страх[2] *adv.* (*coll.*) (**как**) terribly; **им с. хо́чется побыва́ть во Фра́нции** they want terribly to go to France.

страх... *comb. form, abbr. of* **страхово́й**

страхка́сс|а, ы *f.* insurance office.

страхова́ни|е, я *nt.* insurance; **с. жи́зни** life insurance; **с. от огня́** fire insurance.

страх|ова́ть, у́ю *impf.* (*pf.* **за~**) (**от**) to insure (against); **с. себя́** (**от** *fig.*) to insure (against), safeguard o.s. (against).

страх|ова́ться, у́юсь *impf.* (*of* **за~**) (**от**) to insure o.s. (against) (*also fig.*).

страхо́вк|а, и *f.* insurance.

страхово́й *adj.* insurance; **с. по́лис** insurance policy.

страхо́вщик, а *m.* insurer.

страши́лищ|е, а *nt.* fright (*object inspiring fear*).

страш|и́ть, у́, и́шь *impf.* to frighten, scare.

страш|и́ться, у́сь, и́шься *impf.* (+*g.*) to be afraid (of), fear.

стра́шно *adv.* **1.** terribly, awfully. **2.** *as pred.* it is terrible; it is terrifying; **нам бы́ло с.** we were terrified.

стра́ш|ный (~ен, ~на́, ~но) *adj.* terrible, awful,

dreadful, frightful; **с. сон** bad dream; **с. шум** (*coll.*) awful din; **С. суд** the Day of Judgement.

страща́|ть, ю *impf.* (*of* **по~**) (*coll.*) to frighten.

стре́ж|ень, ня *m.* channel, main stream (*of river*).

стрека́ч, а́ *m. now only in phr.* **(за)да́ть ~а́** (*coll.*) to take to one's heels, run for it.

стрекоз|а́, ы́, *pl.* **~ы** *f.* dragon-fly.

стре́кот, а *m.* chirr (*of grasshoppers*); (*fig.*) rattle, chatter (*of machine-gun fire, etc.*).

стрекота́ни|е, я *nt.* chirring; (*fig.*) rattle, chatter.

стреко|та́ть, чу́, ~чешь *impf.* to chirr (*of grasshoppers*); (*fig.*) to rattle (*of machine-guns, etc.*).

стрел|а́, ы́, *pl.* **~ы** *f.* **1.** arrow (*also fig.*); (*fig.*) shaft, dart; **пусти́ть ~у́** to shoot an arrow. **2.** (*bot.*) shaft. **3.** (*tech.*) arm (*of crane*), boom, jib. **4.: с. мо́ста** cantilever.

стрел|е́ц, ьца́ *m.* **1.** (*hist.*) strelets (*member of military corps in Muscovite Russia in the 16th and 17th centuries*). **2. С.** (*astron.*) Sagittarius (*constellation*).

стре́лк|а, и *f.* **1.** pointer, indicator; hand (*of clock or watch*); needle (*of compass, etc.*). **2.** arrow (*on diagram, etc.*). **3.** (*rail.*) point(s), switch; **перевести́ ~у** to change the points. **4.** (*geog.*) spit.

стрелко́в|ый *adj.* **1.** rifle, shooting; **~ое мастерство́** marksmanship; **~ое ору́жие** small arms; **с. спорт** shooting; **с. тир** rifle range. **2.** (*mil.*) rifle, infantry; **~ые войска́** infantry.

стреловид|ный (~ен, ~на) *adj.* arrow-shaped; **~ное крыло́** (*aeron.*) swept-back wing.

стрел|о́к, ка́ *m.* **1.** shot; **иску́сный с., отли́чный с.** good shot. **2.** (*mil.*) rifleman; (*aeron.*) gunner.

стрелокры́лый *adj.*: **с. самолёт** swing-wing aircraft.

стре́лочник, а *m.* (*rail.*) pointsman, switchman.

стрельб|а́, ы́, *pl.* **~ы** *f.* shooting, firing; **руже́йная с.** small arms fire; **уче́бная с.** practice shoot.

стре́льбищ|е, а *nt.* shooting range, target range.

стрельн|у́ть, у́, ёшь *pf.* (*coll.*) **1.** to fire a shot. **2.** (*impers.*): **у меня́ ~у́ло в у́хе** I had a stab of pain in my ear. **3.** to rush away.

стре́льчат|ый *adj.* **1.** (*archit.*) lancet. **2.** arched, pointed; **~ые бро́ви** arched eyebrows.

стре́лян|ый *adj.* (*coll.*) **1.** shot. **2.** that has been under fire; **с. воробе́й** old hand. **3.** used, fired, spent.

стреля́|ть, ю *impf.* **1.** (**в**+*a.*, **по**+*d.*) to shoot (at), fire (at); **хорошо́ с.** to be a good shot; **с. из револьве́ра** to fire a revolver; **с. в цель** to shoot at a target; **с. по самолёту** to fire at an aeroplane. **2.** to shoot (= *to hunt, kill by shooting*). **3.: с. глаза́ми** (*coll.*) to dart glances (at); to make eyes (at). **4.** (*sl.*) to cadge. **5.** (*impers.*) to have a shooting pain. **6.** to produce a sharp sound; **стреля́ть кнуто́м** crack a whip.

стреля́|ться, юсь *impf.* **1.** (*coll.*) to shoot o.s. **2.** to fight a duel (with firearms). **3.** *pass. of* **~ть 2.**

стремгла́в *adv.* headlong.

стреми́тел|ьный (~ен, ~ьна) *adj.* swift, headlong; impetuous.

стрем|и́ться, лю́сь, и́шься *impf.* **1.** (*obs.*) to rush. **2. (к)** to strive (for), seek, aspire (to); (+*inf.*) to try (to); **с. к соверше́нству** to strive for perfection.

стремле́ни|е, я *nt.* **(к)** striving (for), aspiration (to).

стремни́н|а, ы *f.* rapids (*in a river*).

стре́м|я, *g.*, *d. and p.* **~ени,** *i.* **~енем,** *pl.* **~ена́, ~я́н, ~ена́м** *nt.* stirrup.

стремя́нк|а, и *f.* step-ladder, steps.

стрено́ж|ить, у, ишь *pf. of* **трено́жить**

стрептоко́кк, а *m.* (*biol., med.*) streptococcus.

стрептомици́н, а *m.* (*med.*) streptomycin.

стресс, а *m.* (*psych.*) stress.

стрех|а́, и́, *pl.* **~и** *f.* eaves.

стригу́щий *pres. part. act. of* **стричь; с. лиша́й** (*med.*) ring-worm.

стриж, а́ *m.* (*zool.*) martin, swift.

стри́женый *adj.* **1.** short-haired, close-cropped. **2.** (*of hair*) short; (*of sheep*) sheared; (*of tree*) clipped.

стри́жк|а, и *f.* **1.** hair-cutting; shearing; clipping. **2.** cut, hair-style, hair-do.

стрипти́з, а *m.* striptease.

стрихни́н, а *m.* (*med.*) strychnine.

стри|чь, гу́, жёшь, гу́т, *past* **~г, ~гла** *impf.* (*of* **о~**) **1.** to cut, clip, (*hair or nails*). **2.: с. кого́-н.** to cut s.o.'s hair; **с. ове́ц** to shear sheep; **с. пу́деля** to clip a poodle.

стри́|чься, гу́сь, жёшься, гу́тся, *past* **~гся, ~глась** *impf.* (*of* **о~**) **1.** to cut one's hair; to have one's hair cut. **2.** to wear one's hair short. **3.** *pass. of* **~чь**

стробоско́п, а *m.* (*phys.*) stroboscope.

строга́льный *adj.* (*tech.*): **с. стано́к** planing machine.

строга́льщик, а *m.* plane operator, planer.

строга́|ть, ю *impf.* (*of* **вы́~**) (*tech.*) to plane, shave.

стро́г|ий (~, ~а́, ~о) *adj.* strict; severe; **~ие ме́ры** strong measures; **под ~им секре́том** in strict confidence.

стро́го *adv.* strictly; severely; **с. говоря́** strictly speaking; **«с. воспреща́ется»** 'strictly forbidden'.

стро́гост|ь, и *f.* strictness; severity.

строево́й[1] *adj.* building; **с. лес** timber.

строев|о́й[2] *adj.* (*mil.*) **1.** combatant, line; **с. офице́р** officer serving in line. **2.** drill; **~а́я подгото́вка** drill.

строе́ни|е, я *nt.* **1.** building, structure. **2.** (*fig.*) structure, composition; (*biol.*) texture.

строжа́йший *superl. of* **стро́гий**

стро́же *comp. of* **стро́гий** *and* **стро́го**

строи́тел|ь, я *m.* builder (*also fig.*).

строи́тельн|ый *adj.* building, construction; **~ое иску́сство** civil engineering; architecture; **~ая площа́дка** building site; **с. раство́р** lime mortar.

строи́тельств|о, а *nt.* **1.** building, construction (*also fig.*). **2.** building site, construction project. **3.** (*fig.*) organization, structuring.

стро́|ить, ю, ишь *impf.* **1.** (*pf.* **по~**) to build, construct; **с. но́вую жизнь** to make a new life. **2.** (*pf.* **по~**) (*maths., etc.*) to construct; to formulate; **с. многоуго́льник** to construct a polygon; **с. у́гол** to plot an angle; **с. фра́зу** to construct a sentence. **3.** (*pf.* **со~**) (*in phrr. denoting facial expressions, etc.*) to make; **с. гла́зки** to make eyes; **с. грима́сы** to make, pull faces. **4.** (**на**+*p.*) to base (on). **5.** (*impf. only*): **с. пла́ны** to make plans, plan. **6.** (*pf.* **по~**) (*mil.*) to draw up, form (up).

стро́|иться, юсь, ишься *impf.* (*of* **по~**) **1.** to build (*a house, etc.*) for o.s. **2.** (*mil.*) to draw up, form up; **стро́йся!** (*mil.*) fall in! **3.** *pass. of* **~ить**

стро|й, я, о ~е, в ~ю́, *pl.* **~и, ~ев** *m.* **1.** system, order, régime; **обще́ственный с.** social system. **2.** (*ling.*) system, structure. **3.** (*mus.*) pitch. **4.** (*pl.* **~и́, ~ёв**) (*mil., naut., aeron.*) formation; **со́мкнутый с.** close order; **с. фро́нта** (*naut.*) line abreast; **в ко́нном ~ю́** mounted; **в пе́шем ~ю́** dismounted. **5.** (*mil.*) unit in formation; **пе́ред ~ем** in front of the ranks. **6.** (*mil. and fig.*) service, commission; **ввести́ в с.** to put into commission; **вы́вести из ~я** to disable; to put out of action; **вступи́ть в с.** to come into operation; **вы́йти из ~я** to be disabled; to become unserviceable.

строй... *comb. form, abbr. of* **строи́тельный**

стро́йк|а, и *f.* **1.** building, construction. **2.** building-site.

стро́|йный (~ен, ~йна́, ~йно) *adj.* **1.** (*of the human figure*) well-proportioned; (*of a woman*) shapely, having a good figure. **2.** (*mus., etc.*) harmonious; well-balanced; orderly.

строк|а́, и́, *pl.* **~и, ~, ~а́м** *f.* line; **с. в ~у́** line by line; **нача́ть с но́вой ~и́** to begin a new paragraph; **чита́ть ме́жду ~** to read between the lines.

стро́нци|й, я *m.* (*chem.*) strontium.

стропи́л|о, а *nt.* rafter, beam.
строптѝвост|ь, и *f.* obstinacy.
строптѝв|ый (~, ~а) *adj.* obstinate; shrewish.
строф|á, ы́, *pl.* **~ы, ~, ~áм** *f.* (*liter.*) stanza.
строч|и́ть, у́, ~и́шь *impf.* (*of* **на~**[1]) **1.** to stitch. **2.** (*coll.*) to scribble, dash off. **3.** (*coll.*) to bang away (*with automatic weapons*).
стро́чк|а[1], **и** *f.* stitch.
стро́чк|а[2], **и** *f.* = **строкá**
строчн|о́й *adj.*: **~áя бу́ква** small letter, lower-case letter; **писáть с ~о́й бу́квы** to write a small letter.
струг, а *m.* (*tech.*) plane.
стру́жк|а, и *f.* shaving, filing.
стру|и́ться, и́тся *impf.* to stream, flow.
стру́йно-черни́льный *adj.*: **с. при́нтер** inkjet printer.
структу́р|а, ы *f.* structure.
структу́рный *adj.* structural; structured.
струн|á, ы́, *pl.* **~ы** *f.* string (*of mus. instrument, tennis racket, etc.*); **слáбая с.** weak point.
стру́н|ка, ки *f. dim. of* **~á; вы́тянуться в ~ку, стать в ~ку** to stand at attention; **ходи́ть по ~ке (у, пéред)** to be at the beck and call (of).
стру́нный *adj.* (*mus.*): **с. инструмéнт** stringed instrument; **с. оркéстр** string orchestra.
струп, а, *pl.* **~ья, ~ьев** *m.* scab.
стру́|сить, шу, сишь *pf. of* **тру́сить**
стручко́вый *adj.* leguminous; **с. пéрец** capsicum; **с. горо́шек** peas in the pod.
струч|о́к, кá *m.* pod.
стру|я́, и́, *pl.* **~и** *f.* **1.** jet, spurt, stream; current (*of air*); **бить ~ёй** to spurt. **2.** (*fig.*) spirit; impetus.
стря́па|ть, ю *impf.* (*of* **со~**) (*coll.*) to cook; (*fig.*) to cook up, concoct.
стряпн|я́, и́ *f.* (*coll.*) cooking; (*fig., pej.*) concoction.
стряс|áть, áю *impf. of* **~ти́**
стряс|ти́, у́, ёшь, *past* **~, ~лá** *pf.* (*of* **~áть**) to shake off, shake down.
стряс|ти́сь, ётся, *past* **~ся, ~лáсь** *pf.* (**над, с**+*i.*; *coll.*) to befall; **бедá ~лáсь с нáми** a disaster befell us.
стря́хива|ть, ю *impf. of* **стряхну́ть**
стрях|ну́ть, ну́, нёшь *pf.* (*of* **~ивать**) to shake off.
ст. ст. (*abbr. of* **стáрый стиль**) OS, Old Style (*of calendar*).
студéнт, а *m.* student, undergraduate; **с.-мéдик** medical student; **с.-юри́ст** law student.
студéнт|ка, ки *f. of* **~**
студéнческ|ий *adj. of* **студéнт**; **~ое общежи́тие** student hostel, hall of residence.
студéнчеств|о, а *nt.* **1.** (*collect.*) students. **2.** student days.
студён|ый (~, ~а) *adj.* (*coll.*) very cold, freezing.
сту́д|ень, ня *m.* aspic; (meat- *or* fish-)jelly.
студи́йн|ый *adj. of* **сту́дия**
сту|ди́ть, жу́, ~дишь *impf.* (*of* **о~**) to cool.
сту́ди|я, и *f.* **1.** (*artist's or broadcasting*) studio, workshop. **2.** (*art, drama, music, etc.*) school.
сту́ж|а, и *f.* severe cold, hard frost.
стук, а *m.* knock; tap; thump; **с. в дверь** knock at the door; **с. колёс** rumble of wheels.
сту́к|ать(ся), аю(сь) *impf. of* **~нуть(ся)**
стукáч, á *m.* (*sl.*) stool-pigeon (= *informer*).
сту́к|нуть, ну, нешь *pf.* (*of* **~ать**) **1.** to knock; to bang; to tap; **с. в дверь** to knock, to bang at (on) the door; **с. кулако́м по́ столу** to bang one's fist on the table. **2.** to hit, strike. **3.** *pf. only* (*impers.*+*d.*; *coll.*): **ему́ пятьдеся́т ско́ро ~нет** he will soon be fifty.
сту́к|нуться, нусь, нешься *pf.* (*of* **~аться**) (**о, обо**+*a.*) to knock o.s. (against), bump o.s. (against).
стукотн|я́, и́ *f.* (*coll.*) knocking, banging, tapping.
стул, а, *pl.* **~ья, ~ьев** *m.* **1.** chair; **сидéть мéжду двух ~ьев** to fall between two stools. **2.** (*med.*) stool.
стульчáк, á *m.* (lavatory) seat.
сту́льчик, а *m.* stool.
сту́п|а, ы *f.* mortar.
ступ|áть, áю *impf. of* **~и́ть; ~áй(те) сюдá!** come here!; **~áй(те)!** be off!, clear out!
ступéнчатый *adj.* stepped, graduated, graded.
ступ|éнь, éни *f.* **1.** (*g. pl.* **~éней**) step (*of stairs*); rung. **2.** (*g. pl.* **~енéй**) stage, grade, level.
ступéнь|ка, ки *f.* = **~ 1.**
ступ|и́ть, лю́, ~ишь *pf.* (*of* **~áть**) to step, take a step; to tread; **тяжело́ с.** to tread heavily.
ступи́ц|а, ы *f.* hub (*of a wheel.*).
ступн|я́, и́, *pl.* **~и́, ~éй** *f.* **1.** foot. **2.** sole (*of foot*).
стуч|áть, у́, и́шь *impf.* **1.** (*pf.* **по~**) to knock; to bang; to rap; (*of teeth*) to chatter. **2.** *impf.* (*3rd pers. only*) to hammer, thump, pound; **сéрдце у неё ~áло** her heart was pounding.
стуч|áться, у́сь, и́шься *impf.* (*of* **по~**) (**в**+*a.*) to knock (at); **с. в дверь** to knock at the door.
стуш|евáться, у́юсь *pf.* (*of* **~ёвываться**) **1.** (*art*) to shade off. **2.** (*coll.*) to retire into the background; to efface o.s. **3.** to be covered with confusion.
стушёвыва|ться, юсь *impf. of* **стушевáться**
стыд, á *m.* shame; **к нáшему ~у́** to our shame.
сты|ди́ть, жу́, ди́шь *impf.* (*of* **при~**) to shame, put to shame.
сты|ди́ться, жу́сь, ди́шься *impf.* (*of* **по~**) (+*g.*) to be ashamed (of).
стыдли́в|ый (~, ~а) *adj.* bashful.
сты́дно *as pred.* it is a shame; **ему́,** *etc.*, **с.** he, *etc.*, is ashamed; **как тебé не с.!** you ought to be ashamed of yourself!
сты́дный *adj.* shameful.
стык, а *m.* **1.** (*tech.*) joint, junction. **2.** (*fig.*) junction, meeting-point; **с. доро́г** road junction; **на ~е двух веко́в** at the turn of the century.
стык|овáть, у́ю *impf.* (*of* **со~**) (*tech.*) to join.
стык|овáться, у́юсь *impf.* (*of* **со~**) (*tech.*) to join (*intrans.*); (*of space vehicles*) to dock.
стыко́вк|а, и *f.* (*of space vehicles*) docking.
сты́н|уть, у, ешь, *past* **стыл, сты́ла** *impf.* **1.** to cool, get cool. **2.** to become frozen over. **3.** (*fig.*): **кровь ~ет в жи́лах** one's blood runs cold.
стыть = сты́нуть
сты́чк|а, и *f.* **1.** skirmish, clash. **2.** (*coll.*) squabble.
стюардéсс|а, ы *f.* stewardess; air hostess.
стяг, а *m.* (*rhet.*) banner.
стя́гива|ть(ся), ю(сь) *impf. of* **стяну́ть(ся)**
стяжáтел|ь, я *m.* money-grubber.
стяжáтел|ьный (~ен, ~ьна) *adj.* greedy, grasping.
стяжá|ть, ю *impf. and pf.* **1.** to gain, win. **2.** (*impf. only*) to seek, court; **с. слáву** to court fame.
стя|ну́ть[1], **ну́, ~нешь** *pf.* (*of* **~гивать**) **1.** to tighten; to pull together; **с. на себé по́яс** to tighten one's belt. **2.** (*mil.*) to gather, assemble (*trans.*). **3.** (*impers., coll.*) to have cramp; **но́гу у меня́ ~ну́ло** I have cramp in my legs.
стя|ну́ть[2], **ну́, ~нешь** *pf.* (*of* **~гивать**) **1.** to pull off. **2.** (*coll.*) to pinch, steal.
стя|ну́ться, ну́сь, ~нешься *pf.* (*of* **~гиваться**) **1.** to tighten (*intrans.*). **2.** (*mil.*) to gather, assemble.
суахи́ли *m. indecl.* Swahili.
субарéнд|а, ы *f.* sub-lease.
суббо́т|а, ы *f.* Saturday.
суббо́т|ний *adj. of* **~а**
суббо́тник, а *m.* subbotnik (*in former USSR, voluntary unpaid work on days off, originally esp. on Saturdays*).
сублимáт, а *m.* (*chem.*) sublimate.
сублимáци|я, и *f.* (*chem.*) sublimation.
сублими́р|овать, ую *impf. and pf.* (*chem.*) to sublimate.
субординáци|я, и *f.* (system of) seniority.

субсиди́р|овать, ую *impf. and pf.* to subsidize.
субси́ди|я, и *f.* subsidy, grant(-in-aid).
субста́нци|я, и *f.* (*phil.*) substance.
субстра́т, а *m.* substratum.
субти́льност|ь, и *f.* delicateness; frailty.
субти́л|ьный (~ен, ~ьна) *adj.* (*coll.*) delicate; frail.
субти́тр, а *m.* subtitle (*in film*).
субтро́пик|и, ов *no sg.* subtropics.
субтропи́ческий *adj.* subtropical.
субъе́кт, а *m.* **1.** (*phil.*, *gram.*) subject; (*phil.*) the self, the ego. **2.** (*med.*, *leg.*) subject. **3.** (*coll.*) fellow, character, type.
субъективи́зм, а *m.* **1.** (*phil.*) subjectivism. **2.** subjectivity.
субъекти́вност|ь, и *f.* subjectivity.
субъекти́в|ный (~ен, ~на) *adj.* subjective.
сувени́р, а *m.* souvenir.
сувере́н, а *m.* (*pol.*, *leg.*) sovereign.
суверените́т, а *m.* (*pol.*, *leg.*) sovereignty.
сувере́нный *adj.* (*pol.*, *leg.*) sovereign.
сугли́нистый *adj.* loamy.
сугли́н|ок, ка *m.* loam, loamy soil.
сугро́б, а *m.* snow-drift.
сугу́бо *adv.* especially, particularly.
сугу́б|ый (~, ~а) *adj.* **1.** (*obs.*) double. **2.** especial, particular.
суд, а́ *m.* **1.** court, law-court; **зал ~а́** court-room; **заседа́ние ~а́** sitting of the court; **на ~е́** in court. **2.** (*fig.*) court; trial, legal proceedings; **вы́звать в с.** to summons, subpoena; **отда́ть под с., преда́ть ~у́** to prosecute; **быть под ~о́м** to be on trial; **на тебя́ и ~а́ нет** no one can blame you. **3.** (*collect.*) the judges; the bench. **4.** judgement, verdict.
суда́к, а́ *m.* pike-perch (*fish*).
Суда́н, а *m.* (the) Sudan.
суда́рын|я, и *f.* (*obs.*; *mode of address*) madam.
су́дар|ь, я *m.* (*obs.*; *mode of address*) sir.
суда́ч|ить, у, ишь *impf.* (*coll.*) to gossip.
суде́бн|ый *adj.* judicial; legal; forensic; **~ые изде́ржки** costs; **с. исполни́тель** officer of the court; **~ая оши́бка** miscarriage of justice; **~ое реше́ние** court decision, court order; **с. сле́дователь** investigator; coroner; **~ое сле́дствие** investigation in court, inquest.
суде́йский *adj.* **1.** judge's. **2.** (*sport*) referee's, umpire's; **с. свисто́к** referee's whistle.
суди́мост|ь, и *f.* (*leg.*) conviction(s); **снять с кого́-н. с.** to expunge s.o.'s previous convictions.
су|ди́ть, жу́, ∠дишь *impf.* **1.** to judge; to form an opinion; **наско́лько мы могли́ с.** as far as we could judge; **~ди́те са́ми** judge for yourself; **∠дя (по+*d.*)** judging (by); **∠дя по всему́** to all appearances. **2.** (*leg.*) to try. **3.** to judge, pass judgement (upon); **не ~ди́те их стро́го** don't be hard on them. **4.** (*sport*) to referee, umpire. **5.** (*also pf.*) to predestine; **но Бог ~ди́л ино́е** but God decreed a different fate.
су|ди́ться, жу́сь, ∠дишься *impf.* (**с**+*i.*) to sue.
су́д|но[1], **на,** *pl.* **~а́, ~о́в** *nt.* vessel, craft; **с. на возду́шной поду́шке** hovercraft; **с. на подво́дных кры́льях** hydrofoil.
су́д|но[2], **на,** *pl.* **~на, ~ен** *nt.* chamber-pot; **подкладно́е с.** bed-pan.
су́дный *adj.* (*obs.*) **1.** court; judicial. **2.: С. день** (*relig.*) Day of Judgement.
судове́рф|ь, и *f.* shipyard.
судовладе́л|ец, ьца *m.* shipowner.
судоводи́тел|ь, я *m.* navigator.
судовожде́ни|е, я *nt.* navigation.
судов|о́й *adj.* ship's; marine.
суд|о́к, ка́ *m.* **1.** gravy-boat. **2.** cruet(-stand). **3.** (*usu. pl.*) set of dishes with covers (*for carrying food*).
судомо́йк|а, и *f.* scullery maid, washer-up.
судопроизво́дств|о, а *nt.* legal proceedings.
су́дорог|а, и *f.* cramp, convulsion, spasm.
су́дорож|ный (~ен, ~на) *adj.* convulsive, spasmodic (*also fig.*).
судострое́ни|е, я *nt.* shipbuilding.
судострои́тел|ь, я *m.* shipbuilder, shipwright.
судострои́тельный *adj.* shipbuilding.
судоустро́йств|о, а *nt.* judicial system.
судохо́д|ный (~ен, ~на) *adj.* **1.** navigable; **с. кана́л** ship canal. **2.: ~ная компа́ния** shipping company.
судохо́дств|о, а *nt.* navigation, shipping.
суд|ьба́, ьбы́, *pl.* **∠ьбы, ∠еб, ∠ьбам** *f.* fate, fortune, destiny; **благодари́ть ~ьбу́** to thank one's lucky stars; **искуша́ть ~ьбу́** to tempt fate; **каки́ми ~ьба́ми?** (*coll.*) fancy meeting you here!; how did you get here?; **не с. нам** (+*inf.*) we are not fated (to).
суд|ья́, ьи́, *pl.* **∠ьи, ~е́й, ∠ьям** *m.* **1.** judge; **трете́йский с.** arbitrator. **2.** (*sport*) referee, umpire; **с. на ли́нии** linesman.
су́д|я *see* **~и́ть**
суеве́ри|е, я *nt.* superstition.
суеве́р|ный (~ен, ~на) *adj.* superstitious.
сует|а́, ы́ *f.* **1.** vanity; **с. суе́т** vanity of vanities. **2.** bustle, fuss.
сує|ти́ться, чу́сь, ти́шься *impf.* to bustle, fuss.
суетли́в|ый (~, ~а) *adj.* fussy, bustling.
су́ет|ный (~ен, ~на) *adj.* vain, empty.
сужде́ни|е, я *nt.* opinion; judgement (*in logic*).
суждён|ный (~, ~а́) *p.p.p. of* **суди́ть; нам бы́ло ~о́ встре́титься** we were fated to meet.
су́жива|ть(ся), ю, ет(ся) *impf. of* **су́зить(ся)**
су́|зить, жу, зишь *pf.* (*of* **~живать**) to narrow (*trans.*).
су́|зиться, зится *pf.* (*of* **~живаться**) to narrow (*intrans*), get narrow; to taper.
сук, а́, о ~е́, на ~у́, *pl.* **~и́, ~о́в** *and* **су́чья, су́чьев** *m.* **1.** bough. **2.** knot (*in wood*).
су́к|а, и *f.* bitch (*also as term of abuse*).
су́к|ин *adj. of* **~а; с. сын** (*as term of abuse*) son of a bitch.
сук|но́, на́, *pl.* **∠на, ∠он** *nt.* (heavy, coarse) cloth; **положи́ть под с.** (*fig.*) to shelve.
сукнова́льн|ый *adj.* fulling; **~ая гли́на** fuller's earth.
суко́нк|а, и *f.* piece of cloth, rag.
суко́нн|ый *adj.* **1.** cloth; **~ая фа́брика** cloth mill. **2.** (*fig.*) rough, clumsy, crude; **с. язы́к** rough tongue.
сул|и́ть, ю́, и́шь *impf.* (*of* **по~**) to promise; **э́то не ~и́т ничего́ хоро́шего** this does not bode well.
султа́н[1], **а** *m.* sultan.
султа́н[2], **а** *m.* plume (*on headdress*, *etc.*).
султана́т, а *m.* sultanate.
сульфа́т, а *m.* (*chem.*) sulphate.
сульфи́д, а *m.* (*chem.*) sulphide.
сум|а́, ы́ *f.* bag, pouch; **ходи́ть с ~о́й** to beg, go a-begging.
сумасбро́д, а *m.* madcap.
сумасбро́д|ка, ки *f. of* **~**
сумасбро́|дить, жу, дишь *impf.* (*coll.*) to behave wildly, extravagantly.
сумасбро́д|ный (~ен, ~на) *adj.* wild, extravagant.
сумасбро́дств|о, а *nt.* wild, extravagant behaviour.
сумасше́дш|ий *adj.* **1.** mad; *as n.* **с., ~его** *m.* madman, lunatic; **~ая, ~ей** *f.* madwoman. **2.: с. дом** (*coll.*) lunatic asylum, madhouse. **3.** (*fig.*) mad, lunatic.
сумасше́стви|е, я *nt.* madness, lunacy.
сумато́х|а, и *f.* confusion, chaos, turmoil.
сумато́шлив|ый (~, ~а) *adj.* (*coll.*) given to fussing.
сумато́ш|ный (~ен, ~на) *adj.* = **~ливый**
сумбу́р, а *m.* confusion, chaos.
сумбу́р|ный (~ен, ~на) *adj.* confused, chaotic.
су́мереч|ный (~ен, ~на) *adj.* twilight, dusk.
су́мер|ки, ек *no sg.* twilight, dusk.
суме́|ть, ю *pf.* (*of* **уме́ть**) (+*inf.*) to be able (to), manage (to).

су́мк|а, и *f.* **1.** bag, handbag; **поясна́я с.** waist *or* hip-pouch; bum-bag. **2.** (*biol.*) pouch.
су́мм|а, ы *f.* sum; **о́бщая с.** sum total; **в ~е** all in all.
сумма́р|ный (~ен, ~на) *adj.* **1.** total. **2.** summary.
сумми́р|овать, ую *impf.* **1.** to sum up. **2.** to summarize.
сумня́ся, сумня́шеся *see* **ничто́же**
су́мрак, а *m.* dusk, twilight.
су́мрач|ный (~ен, ~на) *adj.* gloomy (*also fig.*).
су́мчат|ый *adj.* (*zool.*) marsupial.
сумя́тиц|а, ы *f.* confusion, chaos.
сунду́к, а́ *m.* trunk, box, chest.
су́н|уть(ся), у(сь), ешь(ся) *pf. of* **сова́ть(ся)**
суп, а, *pl.* **~ы́** *m.* soup.
супероблóжк|а, и *f.* dust-cover, jacket (*of book*).
су́пес|ь, и *f.* sandy soil, sandy loam.
су́п|ить, лю, ишь *impf.* (*of* **на~**): **с. бро́ви** to knit one's brows, frown.
супов|о́й *adj. of* **суп; ~а́я ло́жка** soup ladle; **~а́я ми́ска** soup tureen.
супру́г, а *m.* **1.** husband, spouse. **2.** (*pl.*) husband and wife, married couple.
супру́г|а, и *f.* wife, spouse.
супру́жеский *adj.* conjugal, matrimonial.
супру́жеств|о, а *nt.* matrimony, wedlock.
сургу́ч, а́ *m.* sealing-wax.
сургу́ч|ный *adj. of* **~**
сурди́нк|а, и *f.* (*mus.*) mute; **под ~у** on the quiet.
суре́пиц|а, ы *f.* (*bot.*) **1.** cole-seed, rape. **2.** charlock.
суре́п|ный *adj. of* **~ица; ~ное ма́сло** rape-oil.
су́рик, а *m.* (*chem.*) red lead.
суро́вост|ь, и *f.* severity, sternness.
суро́в|ый (~, ~а) *adj.* **1.** severe, stern; rigorous; bleak. **2.** (*text.*) unbleached, brown.
сур|о́к, ка́ *m.* marmot; **спать как с.** to sleep like a log.
суррога́т, а *m.* substitute.
суррога́тный *adj.* substitute, ersatz.
сурьм|а́, ы́ *f.* (*chem.*) antimony.
суса́льн|ый *adj.* **1.** tinsel; **~ое зо́лото** gold leaf. **2.** (*fig., coll.*) sugary.
су́слик, а *m.* (*zool.*) gopher.
су́сл|о, а *nt.* **1.: виногра́дное с.** must; **пивно́е с.** wort. **2.** grape-juice.
суспензо́ри|й, я *m.* (*sport*) jock-strap.
суста́в, а *m.* (*anat.*) joint.
суставно́й *adj. of* **суста́в**
сутенёр, а *m.* pimp.
су́т|ки, ок *no sg.* twenty-four hours; twenty-four-hour period; **це́лые с.** for days and nights.
су́толок|а, и *f.* commotion, hubbub.
су́точн|ый *adj.* twenty-four-hour; daily; round-the-clock; *as n.* **~ые, ~ых** per diem.
суту́л|ить, ю, ишь *impf.* (*of* **с~**) to stoop.
суту́лост|ь, и *f.*: **с. фигу́ры** round shoulders, stoop.
суту́л|ый (~, ~а) *adj.* round-shouldered, stooping.
сут|ь[1], **и** *f.* essence; **с. де́ла** the heart, crux of the matter; **по ~и де́ла** as a matter of fact.
сут|ь[2] (*arch.*) *3rd pers. pl. pres. of* **быть; э́то не с. ва́жно** (*coll.*) this is not so important.
суфле́ *nt. indecl.* (*cul.*) soufflé.
суфлёр, а *m.* (*theatr.*) prompter.
суфлёр|ский *adj. of* **~; ~ская бу́дка** prompt-box.
суфли́р|овать, ую *impf.* (*+d.*) (*theatr.*) to prompt.
суфражи́стк|а, и *f.* suffragette.
су́ффикс, а *m.* (*gram.*) suffix.
суха́р|ь, я́ *m.* **1.** rusk. **2.** (*fig., coll.*) dried-up person.
сух|а́я, о́й *f.* (*sport*) whitewash (*game in which loser fails to score a single point*).
су́хо *adv.* **1.** drily; coldly; **нас при́няли с.** we were received coldly. **2.** *as pred.* it is dry; **на у́лице с.** it is dry out of doors.
сухове́|й, я *m.* hot dry wind.
сухожи́ли|е, я *nt.* (*anat.*) tendon, sinew.
сух|о́й (~, ~а́, ~о) *adj.* **1.** dry; dried-up; arid; **~и́м путём** by land, overland; **вы́йти ~и́м из воды́** to come out unscathed. **2.** (*of foodstuffs, etc.*) dry, dried; **~о́е молоко́** dried milk. **3.** (*of part of body*) dried-up, withered (*also fig.*; *of persons*). **4.** dry (= *unconnected with, opp. to liquid*); **с. док** dry-dock; **с. зако́н** (*hist.*) 'dry law' (*e.g. in USA*). **5.** (*fig.*) dry (= *dull, boring*). **6.** (*fig.*) chilly, cold; **с. приём** chilly reception.
сухомя́тк|а, и *f.* (*coll.*) dry food (*without any beverage*).
сухопа́р|ый (~, ~а) *adj.* (*coll.*) lean, skinny.
сухопу́тн|ый *adj.* land (*opp. marine, air*); **~ые си́лы** (*mil.*) ground forces.
сухосто́|й, я *m.* (*collect.*) dead standing trees.
су́хост|ь, и *f.* **1.** dryness; aridity. **2.** (*fig.*) chilliness, coldness.
сухот|а́, ы́ *f.* **1.** dryness; **у меня́ в го́рле с.** my throat is parched. **2.** dry spell (*of weather*).
сухофру́кт|ы, ов *no sg.* dried fruits.
сухоща́в|ый (~, ~а) *adj.* lean, skinny.
сучёный *adj.* twisted.
суч|и́ть, у́, ~ишь *impf.* (*of* **с~**) **1.** to twist, spin. **2.** (*cul.*) to roll out (*dough*).
сучкова́т|ый (~, ~а) *adj.* knotty; gnarled.
суч|о́к, ка́ *m.* **1.** twig. **2.** knot (*in wood*); **без ~ка́, без задо́ринки** (*coll.*) without a hitch.
су́ш|а, и *f.* (dry) land (*opp. sea*).
су́ше *comp. of* **сухо́й** *and* **су́хо**
суше́ни|е, я *nt.* drying.
сушёный *adj.* dried.
суши́лк|а, и *f.* **1.** drying apparatus, dryer; **напо́льная с.** airer; clothes horse. **2.** drying-room.
суши́льный *adj.* (*tech.*) drying.
суши́л|ьня, ьни, *g. pl.* **~ен** *f.* drying-room.
суш|и́ть, у́, ~ишь *impf.* to dry (out, up).
суш|и́ться, у́сь, ~ишься *impf.* to dry, get dry.
су́шк|а, и *f.* **1.** drying. **2.** (*cul.*) dry (*ring-shaped*) cracker.
суш|ь, и *f.* **1.** dry spell. **2.** dry place. **3.** dry object.
суще́ствен|ный (~, ~на) *adj.* essential; material; important; **~ное замеча́ние** remark of material significance; **игра́ть ~ную роль** to play a vital part.
существи́тельн|ое *adj., only in phr.* **и́мя с.** *or as n.* **с., ~ого** *nt.* noun, substantive.
существ|о́, а́ *nt.* **1.** essence; **по ~у́** in essence, essentially; **говори́ть по ~у́** to speak to the point; **не по ~у́** beside the point. **2.** being, creature; **люби́мое с.** loved one.
существова́ни|е, я *nt.* existence.
существ|ова́ть, у́ю *impf.* to exist.
су́щ|ий *adj.* **1.** (*obs.*) existing. **2.** (*coll.*) real; absolute, utter, downright; **с. ад** absolute hell.
су́щност|ь, и *f.* essence; **в ~и** in essence, at bottom; **в ~и говоря́** really and truly.
сфабрик|ова́ть, у́ю *pf. of* **фабрикова́ть**
сфа́гнум, а *m.* (*bot.*) sphagnum, bog-moss.
сфальши́в|ить, лю, ишь *pf. of* **фальши́вить**
сфантази́р|овать, ую *pf. of* **фантази́ровать**
сфе́р|а, ы *f.* **1.** sphere; realm; **с. влия́ния** (*pol.*) sphere of influence; **вы́сшие ~ы** influential circles. **2.** (*mil.*) zone, area; **с. огня́** zone of fire.
сфери́ческий *adj.* spherical.
сферо́ид, а *m.* (*math.*) spheroid.
сфероида́льный *adj.* (*math.*) spheroidal.
сфинкс, а *m.* sphinx.
сформир|ова́ть(ся), у́ю(сь) *pf. of* **формирова́ть(ся)**
сформ|ова́ть, у́ю *pf. of* **формова́ть**
сформули́р|овать, ую *pf. of* **формули́ровать**
сфотографи́р|овать(ся), ую(сь) *pf. of* **фотографи́ровать(ся)**

схва|ти́ть, чу́, ∠тишь *pf.* **1.** *pf. of* **хвата́ть**[1]. **2.** (*impf.* **∠тывать**) (*coll.*) to catch (*a cold, etc.*). **3.** (*impf.* **∠тывать**) (*coll.*) to grasp, comprehend.
схва|ти́ться, чу́сь, ∠тишься *pf.* **1.** *pf. of* **хвата́ться. 2.** (*impf.* **∠тываться**) (**с**+*i.*) to grapple (with), come to grips (with) (*also fig.*).
схва́тк|а, и *f.* **1.** skirmish, fight. **2.** (*coll.*) squabble.
схва́т|ки, ок *no sg.* contractions (*of muscles*); fit, spasm; **родовы́е с.** labour, birth pangs.
схва́тыва|ть(ся), у(сь) *impf. of* **схвати́ть(ся)**
схе́м|а, ы *f.* **1.** diagram, chart. **2.** sketch, outline, plan; **с. рома́на** plan of a novel. **3.** (*elec.*) circuit.
схемати́ческий *adj.* **1.** diagrammatic, schematic. **2.** sketchy, over-simplified.
схемати́ч|ный (~ен, ~на) *adj.* sketchy, over-simplified.
схи́зм|а, ы *f.* (*eccl.*) schism.
схитр|и́ть, ю́, и́шь *pf. of* **хитри́ть**
схлы́н|уть, у, ешь *pf.* **1.** (*of waves*) to break and flow back. **2.** (*of a crowd*) to break up; to dwindle. **3.** (*of emotions*) to subside.
сход[1]**, а** *m.* **1.** coming off, alighting. **2.** descent.
сход[2]**, а** *m.* (*obs.*) gathering, assembly.
схо|ди́ть[1]**, жу́, ∠дишь** *impf. of* **сойти́**
схо|ди́ть[2]**, жу́, ∠дишь** *pf.* to go (*and come back*); (**за**+*i.*) to go to fetch; **с. посмотре́ть** to go to see; **~ди́ за до́ктором!** go and fetch a doctor!
схо|ди́ться, жу́сь, ∠дишься *impf. of* **сойти́сь**
схо́дк|а, и *f.* (*obs.*) gathering, assembly.
схо́дн|и, ей *pl.* (*sg.* **~я, ~и** *f.*) gangway, gang-plank.
схо́д|ный (~ен, ~на́, ~но) *adj.* **1.** similar. **2.** (*coll.*) reasonable, fair (*of prices, etc.*).
схо́дств|о, а *nt.* likeness, similarity, resemblance.
схо́жест|ь, и *f.* likeness, similarity.
схо́ж|ий (~, ~а) *adj.* like, similar.
схорон|и́ть(ся), ю́(сь), ∠ишь(ся) *pf. of* **хорони́ть(ся)**
сца́па|ть, ю *pf.* (*coll.*) to catch hold (of).
сцара́п|ать, аю *pf.* (*of* **~ывать**) to scratch off.
сцара́пыва|ть, ю *impf. of* **сцара́пать**
сц|ать, у, ишь, *3d pers. pl.* **ат, ут** *impf.* (*of* **посца́ть**) (*vulg.*) to piss.
сце|ди́ть, жу́, ∠дишь *pf.* (*of* **∠живать**) to pour off, strain off. decant.
сце́жива|ть, ю *impf. of* **сцеди́ть**
сце́н|а, ы *f.* **1.** (*theatr.*) stage; **ста́вить на ~е** to stage; **сойти́ со ~ы** to go off the scene, make one's exit (*also fig.*). **2.** (*theatr., liter.*) scene. **3.** (*coll.*) scene; **устра́ивать ~ы** to make scenes.
сцена́ри|й, я *m.* **1.** scenario. **2.** film script.
сценари́ст, а *m.* scenario writer; script writer.
сцени́ческ|ий *adj.* stage; **~ая рема́рка** stage direction; **с. шёпот** stage whisper.
сцени́ч|ный (~ен, ~на) *adj.* suitable for the theatre, effective on the stage.
сцено́граф, а *m.* (*theatr.*) set designer.
сцеп|и́ть, лю́, ∠ишь *pf.* (*of* **~ля́ть**) to couple.
сцеп|и́ться, лю́сь, ∠ишься *pf.* (*of* **~ля́ться**) **1.** to be coupled. **2.** (**с**+*i.*; *coll.*) to grapple (with).
сцепле́ни|е, я *nt.* **1.** coupling. **2.** (*tech.*) clutch; **выключе́ние ~я** clutch release. **3.** (*fig.*) accumulation; **с. обстоя́тельств** chain of events.
сцепля́|ть(ся), ю(сь) *impf. of* **сцепи́ть(ся)**
сцепн|о́й *adj.* (*tech.*) coupling.
счастли́в|ец, ца *m.* lucky man.
счастли́виц|а, ы *f.* lucky woman.
счастли́вчик, а *m.* (*coll.*) = **счастли́вец**
сча́стливо *adv.* happily; with luck; **с. отде́латься (от)** to have a lucky escape (from); **счастли́во (остава́ться)!** good luck!
счастли́в|ый (сча́стли́в, ~а) *adj.* **1.** happy. **2.** lucky, fortunate. **3.** successful; **~ого пути́!** bon voyage!
сча́сть|е, я *nt.* **1.** happiness. **2.** luck, good fortune; **к ~ю, на с., по ~ю** luckily, fortunately; **на на́ше с.** luckily for us.
сче́сть(ся), сочту́(сь), сочтёшь(ся), *past* **счёл(ся), сочла́(сь)** *impf. of* **счита́ть(ся)**[1]
счёт, а (у), *pl.* **~ы** *and* **~а́** *m.* **1.** *sg. only* counting, calculation, reckoning; **вести́ с.** (+*d.*) to keep count (of); **потеря́ть с.** (+*d.*) to lose count (of); **он не в с.** he does not count; **в два ~а** in a jiffy; **без ~у, ~у нет** countless. **2.** *sg. only* (*sport*) score. **3.** (*pl.* **~а́**) bill, account; **пода́ть с.** to present a bill. **4.** (*pl.* **~а́**) (*book-keeping*) account; **откры́ть с.** to open an account; **за с.** (+*g.*) at the expense (of); **на с.** on account; **на с.** (+*g.*) to the account (of). **5.** (*fig.*) account, expense; **в с.** (+*g.*) on the strength (of); **в коне́чном ~е** in the end; **за с.** (+*g.*) at the expense (of); owing (to); **на свой с.** on one's own account; **на чужо́й с.** at others' expense; **на э́тот с.** (*i*) on this score, (*ii*) in this respect; **быть на хоро́шем ~у́** to be in good (repute); to stand well; **име́ть на своём ~у́** to have to one's credit. **6. ~ы** (*no sg.*; *fig.*) accounts, score(s); **свести́ ~ы (с**+*i.*) to settle a score (with), get even (with). **7.** *see* **~ы**
счётн|ый *adj.* **1.** counting, calculating; **~ая лине́йка** slide-rule; **~ая маши́на** calculator, calculating machine. **2.** accounts, accounting; **с. рабо́тник** accounts clerk; **~ая часть** accounts department.
счетово́д, а *m.* accountant; accounts clerk.
счетово́дн|ый *adj.* accounting.
счетово́дств|о, а *nt.* accounting.
счётчик[1]**, а** *m.* teller; counter (*pers.*).
счётчик[2]**, а** *m.* meter; counter (*instrument*); **га́зовый с.** gas meter; **с. километра́жа** milometer.
счёт|ы[1]**, ов** *no sg.* abacus, counting frame.
счёт|ы[2] *see* **~ 6.**
счисле́ни|е, я *nt.* **1.** counting; **систе́ма ~я** (*math.*) scale of notation. **2.: с. пути́** (*naut.*) dead reckoning.
счи́|стить, щу, стишь *pf.* (*of* **~ща́ть**) to clear away.
счи́|ститься, стится *pf.* (*of* **~ща́ться**) (*of dirt, etc.*) to come off.
счи́тан|ный (~, ~а) *p.p.p. of* **счита́ть; остаю́тся ~ные дни (до)** one can count the days (until).
счита́|ть[1]**, ю** *impf.* (*of* **счесть**) **1.** (*pf. also* **со~**) to count; **с. до ста** to count up to a hundred; **не ~я** not counting. **2.** (+*i. or* **за**+*a.*) to count, consider, think; to regard (as); **с. ну́жным, с. за ну́жное** to consider it necessary; **с. за сча́стье** to count it one's good fortune. **3. (что)** to consider (that), hold (that).
счита́|ться[1]**, юсь** *impf.* (*of* **сче́сться**) (**с**+*i.*) to settle accounts (with) (*also fig.*).
счита́|ться[2]**, юсь** *impf.* (*no pf.*) **1.** (+*i.*) to be considered; to be regarded (as). **2.** (**с**+*i.*) to consider, take into consideration, to take into account, reckon (with).
счища́|ть(ся), ю(сь) *impf. of* **счи́стить(ся)**
США *no sg., indecl.* (*abbr. of* ***Соединённые Шта́ты Аме́рики***) USA (*United States of America*).
сшиб|а́ть(ся), а́ю(сь) *impf. of* **~и́ть(ся)**
сшиб|и́ть, у́, ёшь, *past* **~, ∠ла** *pf.* (*of* **~а́ть**) (*coll.*) to knock off; **с. с ног** to knock down, knock over.
сшиб|и́ться, у́сь, ёшься, *past* **∠ся, ∠лась** *pf.* (*of* **~а́ться**) (*coll.*) **1.** to collide; to come to blows. **2.** *pass. of* **~и́ть**
сшива́|ть, ю *impf. of* **сшить**
сшить, сошью́, сошьёшь *pf.* **1.** *pf. of* **шить. 2.** (*impf.* **сшива́ть**) to sew together; (*med.*) to suture.
съ... *vbl. pref.* = **с...**
съеда́|ть, ю *impf.* to eat (up).
съеде́ни|е, я *nt., only in phr.* **отда́ть на с.** (+*d.*) to put at the mercy (of).
съедо́б|ный (~ен, ~на) *adj.* edible.
съёжива|ться, юсь *impf. of* **съёжиться**
съёж|иться, усь, ишься *pf.* (*of* **ёжиться** *and* **~иваться**) to huddle up; to shrivel, shrink.

съезд, а *m.* congress; convention.
съе́з|дить, жу, дишь *pf.* to go, drive (*and come back*).
съезжа́|ть(ся), ю(сь) *impf. of* **съе́хать(ся)**
съел *see* **съесть**
съёмк|а, и *f.* **1.** removal. **2.** survey, surveying. **3.** (*phot.*) exposure; shooting.
съёмный *adj.* detachable, removable.
съём|очный *adj. of* **~ка; ~очная гру́ппа** film-crew; **~очная площа́дка** film-set.
съёмщик, а *m.* **1.** tenant, lessee. **2.** surveyor.
съестн|о́й *adj.* food; **~ы́е припа́сы** food supplies, provisions; *as n.* **~о́е, ~о́го** *nt.* = **~ы́е припа́сы**
съе|сть, м, шь, ст, ди́м, ди́те, дя́т, *past* **~л, ~ла** *pf. of* **есть**[1]; **с. соба́ку (на+***p.*; *coll.*) to have at one's finger-tips, know inside out.
съе́|хать, ду, дешь *pf.* (*of* **~зжа́ть**) **1.** to go down, come down. **2.: с. на́ берег** (*naut.*) to go ashore. **3.** to move (*house*). **4.** (*fig., coll.*) to come down, slip.
съе́|хаться, дусь, дешься *pf.* (*of* **~зжа́ться**) **1.** to meet. **2.** to gather, assemble.
съехи́днича|ть, ю *pf. of* **ехи́дничать**
съязв|и́ть, лю́, и́шь *pf. of* **язви́ть**
сы́вороткa|а, и *f.* **1.** whey. **2.** (*biol., med.*) serum.
сы́гранност|ь, и *f.* team-work.
сыгра́|ть, ю *pf. of* **игра́ть; с. шу́тку (с+***i.*) to play a practical joke (on).
сыгра́|ться, юсь *pf.* to achieve team-work; to play well together.
сы́змала *adv.* (*coll.*) since childhood.
сы́знова *adv.* (*coll.*) anew, afresh; all over again.
сымпровизи́р|овать, ую *pf. of* **импровизи́ровать**
сын, а, *pl.* **~овья́, ~ове́й** *m.* son.
сыни́шк|а, и *m.* (*coll.*) *dim. of* **сын**
сыно́вний *adj.* filial.
сын|о́к, ка́' *m. dim. of* **~**; (*as mode of address*) sonny.
сы́п|ать, лю, лешь *impf.* **1.** to pour. **2.** (+*a. or i.*; *fig., coll.*) to pour forth; spout; **с. жа́лобами** to pour forth complaints; **с. деньга́ми** to squander money.
сы́п|аться, лется *impf.* **1.** to fall; to pour out; to scatter; **мука́ ~алась из мешка́** flour poured out of the bag. **2.** (*of sounds, etc.*; *coll.*) to pour forth (*intrans.*), rain down; **уда́ры ~ались гра́дом** blows were raining down. **3.** (*of plaster, etc.*) to flake off.
сыпно́й *adj.*: **с. тиф** (*med.*) typhus.
сыпу́ч|ий (~, ~а) *adj.* friable, free-flowing; **с. песо́к** quicksand; **ме́ры ~их тел** dry measures.
сып|ь, и *f.* (*med.*) rash, eruption.
сыр, а, *pl.* **~ы́** *m.* cheese.
сыр-бо́р *now only in phr.* **вот отку́да с. загоре́лся** (*coll.*) that was the spark that set the forest on fire.
сыре́|ть, ю *impf.* (*of* **от~**) to become damp.
сыр|е́ц, ца́ *m.* product in raw state; **кирпи́ч-с.** adobe; **шёлк-с.** raw silk.
сы́рник, а *m.* curd fritter.
сы́р|ный *adj. of* **~**; **~ная неде́ля** Shrovetide.
сы́ро *as predicate* it is damp.
сыроваре́ни|е, я *nt.* cheese-making.
сыроe̋жк|а, и *f.* russula (*mushroom*).
сыр|о́й (~, ~а́, ~о) *adj.* **1.** damp. **2.** raw, uncooked; **~а́я вода́** unboiled water. **3.** green, unripe. **4.** raw; unfinished; **~ы́е материа́лы** raw materials.
сыромя́тн|ый *adj.*: **~ая ко́жа** rawhide.
сы́ромят|ь, и *f.* rawhide.
сы́рост|ь, и *f.* dampness, humidity.
сырь|ё, я́ *no pl., nt.* raw material(s).
сыск, а *m.* (*obs.*) investigation (*of criminals*).
сы|ска́ть, щу́, ~щешь *pf.* (*coll.*) to find.
сы|ска́ться, щу́сь, ~щешься *pf.* (*coll.*) to be found.
сыск|но́й *adj. of* **~**; **~на́я поли́ция** (*obs.*) criminal investigation department.
сы́тно *adv.* well; **с. пое́сть** to have a good meal.
сы́т|ный (~ен, ~на́, ~но) *adj.* (*of a meal*) substantial, filling.
сы́тост|ь, и *f.* satiety, repletion.
сы́т|ый (~, ~а́, ~о) *adj.* satisfied, full; **я ~ по го́рло** I have eaten my fill, I am full up.
сычу́жин|а, ы *f.* rennet.
сы́щик, а *m.* detective.
сы́щиц|а, ы *f. of* **сы́щик**
СЭВ, а *m.* (*abbr. of* ***Сове́т Экономи́ческой Взаимопо́мощи***) COMECON (*Council for Mutual Economic Assistance*).
сэконо́м|ить, лю, ишь *pf. of* **эконо́мить**
сэр, а *m.* sir.
сюда́ *adv.* here, hither.
сюже́т, а *m.* subject; topic.
сюже́т|ный *adj. of* **~**
сюзере́н, а *m.* (*hist.*) suzerain.
сюзере́н|ный *adj. of* **~**
сюи́т|а, ы *f.* (*mus.*) suite.
сюрпри́з, а *m.* surprise.
сюрреали́зм, а *m.* surrealism.
сюрреали́ст, а *m.* surrealist.
сюрту́к, а́ *m.* frock-coat.
сюсю́ка|ть, ю *impf.* to lisp.
сяк *adv.* (*coll.*): **и так и с., see так**
сям *adv.*: **и там и с., ни там ни с.,** *see* **там**

Т

т (*abbr. of* **то́нна**) t., ton(s), tonne(s).
т. *abbr. of* **1. това́рищ** Comrade. **2. том** vol., volume.
таба́к, а́ (у́) *m.* tobacco; **ню́хательный т.** snuff; **де́ло — т.!** (*coll.*) things are in a bad way.
табаке́рк|а, и *f.* snuff-box.
табаково́д, а *m.* tobacco-grower.
табаково́дств|о, а *nt.* tobacco-growing.
табаково́д|ческий *adj. of* **~ство**
таба́чный *adj.* tobacco; **т. кисе́т** tobacco-pouch.
та́бел|ь, я *m.* **1.** table; **т. о ра́нгах** (*hist.*) Table of Ranks. **2.** time-board (*in factory, etc.*).
та́бель|ный *adj. of* **~**; **~ная доска́** time-board; **~ные часы́** time-clock.
та́бельщик, а *m.* timekeeper.
табле́тк|а, и *f.* tablet, pill; **т. аспири́на** an aspirin.
табли́ц|а, ы *f.* table; plate (*with illustrations or diagrams*); **т. умноже́ния** multiplication table; **т. Менделе́ева** (*chem.*) periodic table; **электро́нная т.** (*comput.*) spreadsheet; **т. вы́игрышей** prize-list; **т. (ро́зыгрыша) пе́рвенства** (*sport*) (score-)table; **внести́ в ~у** to tabulate.
табли́чный *adj.* **1.** tabular. **2.** standard.
табло́ *indec., nt.* indicator board; scoreboard.
табльдо́т, а *m.* table d'hôte.
та́бор, а *m.* **1.** camp. **2.** Gypsy encampment.
табу́ *nt. indecl.* taboo.
табу́н, а́ *m.* herd (*usu. of horses, reindeer etc.*).
табу́нщик, а *m.* herdsman.
табуре́т, а *m.* = **~ка**
табуре́т|ка, ки *f.* stool.
таве́рн|а, ы *f.* tavern, inn.
та́волг|а, и *f.* (*bot.*) meadow-sweet.
таво́т, а *m.* (*tech.*) axle grease, lubricating grease.
таврёный *adj.* branded.
тавр|и́ть, ю́, и́шь *impf.* (*of* **за~**) to brand.
тавр|о́, а́, *pl.* **~а, ~, ~а́м** *nt.* brand (*on cattle, etc.*).

тавтологи́ческий *adj.* tautological.
тавтоло́ги|я, и *f.* tautology.
тага́н, а́ *m.* trivet.
таджи́к, а *m.* Tadzhik.
Таджикиста́н, а *m.* Tadzhikistan.
таджи́кский *adj.* Tadzhik.
таджи́|чка, чки *f. of* **~к**
таёжник, а *m.* taiga dweller.
таёжный *adj. of* **тайга́**
таз[1], **а, в ~у́,** *pl.* **~ы́** *m.* basin; wash-basin.
таз[2], **а, в ~е** *and* **в ~у́,** *pl.* **~ы́** *m.* (*anat.*) pelvis.
тазобе́дренный *adj.* (*anat.*) hip; **т. суста́в** hip joint.
та́зовый *adj.* (*anat.*) pelvic.
таи́нственност|ь, и *f.* mystery.
таи́нствен|ный (~, ~на) *adj.* **1.** mysterious. **2.** secret. **3.** secretive; **т. вид** secretive look.
та́инств|о, а *nt.* **1.** (*relig.*) sacrament. **2.** (*obs.*) mystery, secret.
та|и́ть, ю́, и́шь *impf.* to hide, conceal (*emotion, etc.*); to harbour; **т. в себе́** to be fraught (with); **т. зло́бу (про́тив)** to harbour a grudge (against).
та|и́ться, ю́сь, и́шься *impf.* **1.** (*coll.*) to be (in) hiding, lurk. **2.** (*fig.*) to lurk, be lurking. **3.** (*coll.*) to hold back (= *to decline to reveal*).
Тайва́н|ь, я *m.* Taiwan.
тайва́ньский *adj.* Taiwanese.
тайг|а́, и́ *f.* (*geog.*) taiga.
тайко́м *adv.* in secret, surreptitiously; on the quiet, behind s.o.'s back.
тайм, а *m.* (*sport*) half, period (*of game*).
тайм-ше́р, а *m.* time-share.
та́йн|а, ы *f.* **1.** mystery. **2.** secret; **держа́ть в ~е** to keep secret; **храни́ть ~у** to keep a secret.
тайни́к, а́ *m.* hiding-place; cache; **в ~а́х души́** in the innermost recesses of the heart.
та́йнопис|ь, и *f.* cryptographic writing.
та́йный *adj.* secret; clandestine; **т. аге́нт** undercover agent; **т. коммуни́ст** crypto-Communist; **т. сове́т** (*hist.*) Privy Council.
та́йский *adj.* Thai.
тайфу́н, а *m.* typhoon.
так 1. *adv.* so; in this way, like this; in such a way; **т. мно́го** so many; **мы сде́лали т.** this is what we did; **т. же** in the same way; **т. и быть** (*coll.*) all right, right you are; **т. и есть** (*coll.*) so it is; **т. ему́** *etc.*, **и на́до** serves him, *etc.*, right; **т. и́ли ина́че** (*i*) whatever happens, (*ii*) one way or another; **т. называ́емый** so-called; **т. себе́** so-so, not too good; **т. сказа́ть** so to speak; **и т.** even so; as it is; **и т. да́лее** and so on; **и т. и сяк** this way and that; **когда́ т.** (*coll.*) if so; **(не) т. ли?** isn't it so? **2.** *adv.* as it should be; **не т.** amiss, wrong; **т. ли я говорю́?** am I right?; **что́-то бы́ло не совсе́м т.** sth. was not quite right. **3.** *adv.* just like that (= *without further action or consequences*); **т. ему́ э́то не пройдёт** he won't get away with it like that. **4.** *adv.*: **т. (то́лько), про́сто т.** for no special reason; for the sake of it. **5.**: **т. и** (*as emph. particle*) simply, just; **её глаза́ т. и сверка́ли гне́вом** her eyes were simply blazing with anger. **6.** *conj.* then (*or not translated*); **е́хать, т. е́хать** if we are going, let's go; **не сего́дня, т. за́втра** if not today, then tomorrow. **7.** *conj.* so; **т. вы зна́ете друг дру́га?** so you know one another? **8.**: **т. как** *conj.* as, since. **9.** *affirmative or emph. particle* yes; **т. то́чно** (*in mil. parlance*) yes.
такела́ж, а *m.* (*naut.*) rigging.
та́кже *adv.* also, too, as well; (*after neg.*) or, nor.
-таки *particle* (*coll.*) however, though; **всё-т.** nevertheless; **опя́ть-т.** again.
тако́в *m.*, **~а́** *f.*, **~о́** *nt.*, *pl.* **~ы́,** *pron.* such; **все они́ ~ы́** they are all the same; **и был т.** (*coll.*) and that was the last we saw of him.
таков|о́й *adj.* **1.** (*obs.*) such; **е́сли ~ы́е име́ются** if any. **2.**: **как т.** as such.
так|о́й *pron.* **1.** such; so; **т. же** the same; **он т. до́брый!** he is such a kind man; **~о́е пальто́ мне ну́жно** I need a coat like that; **~и́м о́бразом** thus, in this way; **в ~о́м слу́чае** in that case; **до ~о́й сте́пени** to such an extent. **2.**: **кто он т.?** who is he?; **что э́то ~о́е?** what is this?; **что ~о́е** what's that?; what did you say?; **куда́ ~о́е он пошёл?** (*coll.*) wherever has he gone?
тако́й-то *pron.* so-and-so; such-and-such.
та́кс|а[1], **ы** *f.* statutory price; tariff.
та́кс|а[2], **ы** *f.* dachshund.
такси́ *nt. indecl.* taxi.
такси́р|овать, ую *impf. and pf.* to fix the price (of).
такси́ст, а *m.* taxi-driver.
таксо́метр, а *m.* (taxi)meter; 'clock'.
таксомото́р, а *m.* taxi.
таксомото́р|ный *adj. of* **~;** **т. парк** fleet of taxis.
таксофо́н, а *m.* automatic telephone.
так-ся́к *adv. as pred.* (*coll.*) it is tolerable, it is passable.
такт[1], **а** *m.* (*mus., etc.*) time; measure; bar; **отбива́ть т.** to beat time; **в т.** in time.
такт[2], **а** *m.* tact.
та́к-таки *particle* (*coll.*) after all; really.
та́ктик, а *m.* tactician.
та́ктик|а, и *f.* tactics.
такти́ческий *adj.* tactical.
такти́чност|ь, и *f.* tact.
такти́ч|ный (~ен, ~на) *adj.* tactful.
тала́нт, а *m.* **1.** talent, gift(s). **2.** gifted person.
тала́нтливост|ь, и *f.* talent, gifts.
тала́нтлив|ый (~, ~а) *adj.* talented, gifted.
талидоми́д, а *m.* (*pharm.*) thalidomide.
талисма́н, а *m.* talisman, charm, mascot.
та́ли|я, и *f.* waist; **пла́тье в ~ю** dress fitting at the waist.
талму́д, а *m.* (*relig.*) Talmud.
талмуди́ст, а *m.* Talmudist; (*fig.*) doctrinaire.
талмуди́стский *adj.* Talmudistic; (*fig.*) doctrinaire.
талмуди́ческий = **талмуди́стский**
тало́н, а *m.* coupon; stub (*of cheques, etc.*); **т. на обе́д** luncheon voucher; **поса́дочный т.** boarding pass.
та́л|ый *adj.* thawed, melted.
тальк, а *m.* talc; talcum powder.
та́льк|овый *adj. of* **~.**
там *adv.* there; **т. же** in the same place; (*in footnotes, etc.*) ibidem; **и т. и сям** here, there and everywhere.
тамад|а́, ы́ *m.* master of ceremonies, toast-master.
та́мбур[1], **а** *m.* **1.** lobby. **2.** platform (*of rail. carriage*).
та́мбур[2], **а** *m.* chain-stitch.
тамбури́н, а *m.* tambourine.
та́мбур|ный *adj. of* **~**[2]; **т. шов** chain-stitch.
тамо́женник, а *m.* customs official.
тамо́женн|ый *adj.* customs; **~ые по́шлины** customs (*duties*).
тамо́жн|я, и *f.* custom-house.
та́мошн|ий *adj.* (*coll.*) of that place; local.
тампо́н, а *m.* (*med.*) tampon, plug; **гигиени́ческий т.** sanitary towel *or* pad.
тамта́м, а *m.* tom-tom.
та́нгенс, а *m.* (*math.*) tangent.
тангенциа́льный *adj.* (*math.*) tangential.
та́нго *nt. indecl.* tango.
та́н|ец, ца *m.* **1.** dance; dancing. **2.** (*pl.*) a dance, dancing; **пойти́ на ~цы** to go to a dance, go dancing.
тани́н, а *m.* tannin.
танк[1], **а** *m.* (*mil.*) tank.
танк[2], **а** *m.* container (*for transportation of liquids*).
та́нкер, а *m.* (*naut.*) tanker.
танке́тк|а[1], **и** *f.* small tank.
танке́тк|а[2], **и** *f.* (*coll.*) (*ladies'*) wedge-heeled shoe.

танки́ст, а *m.* member of tank crew.
та́нковый *adj.* tank, armoured.
тантье́м|а, ы *f.* bonus.
танцева́льный *adj.* dancing; **т. ве́чер** a dance.
танц|ева́ть, у́ю *impf.* to dance.
танцо́вщик, а *m.* (ballet) dancer.
танцо́вщиц|а, ы *f. of* **танцо́вщик**
танцо́р, а *m.* dancer.
танцо́рк|а, и *f. of* **танцо́р**
тапёр, а *m.* ballroom pianist.
тапио́к|а, и *f.* tapioca.
тапи́р, а *m.* tapir.
та́почк|а, и *f.* (*coll.*) slipper; **спорти́вная т.** sports shoe, plimsoll.
та́р|а, ы *f.* **1.** packing, packaging. **2.** (*comm.*) tare.
тараба́н|ить, ю, ишь *impf.* (*coll.*) to clatter.
тараба́рщин|а, ы *f.* (*coll.*) double Dutch, gibberish.
тарака́н, а *m.* cockroach.
тара́н, а *m.* **1.** (*hist.*) battering ram. **2.** (*mil.*) ram.
тара́н|ить, ю, ишь *impf.* (*of* **про~**) to ram.
таранта́с, а *m.* tarantass (*springless carriage*).
тара́нтул, а *m.* tarantula.
тара́н|ь, и *f.* sea-roach.
тарара́м, а *m.* (*coll.*) row, racket, hullabaloo.
тарата́йк|а, и *f.* cabriolet, gig.
тарато́р|а, ы *c.g.* (*coll.*) chatterbox, gabbler.
тарато́р|ить, ю, ишь *impf.* (*coll.*) to jabber, natter.
тарах|те́ть, чу́, ти́шь *impf.* (*coll.*) to rattle, rumble.
тара́щ|ить, у, ишь *impf.* **т. глаза́ (на**+*a.*) to goggle (at).
таре́лк|а, и *f.* **1.** plate; **глубо́кая т.** soup-plate; **быть не в свое́й ~е** to be not quite o.s. **2.** (*tech.*) plate, disc. **3.** (*pl.*) cymbals.
таре́л|очный *adj. of* **~ка**; **~очная ми́на** (*mil.*) flat anti-tank mine.
таре́льчат|ый *adj.* (*tech.*) plate, disc; **т. то́рмоз** disc brake.
тари́ф, а *m.* tariff, rate.
тари́ф|ный *adj. of* **~**
та́ры-ба́ры *pl. indecl.* (*coll.*) tittle-tattle.
таска́|ть, ю *impf.* (*indet. of* **тащи́ть**) **1.** *see* **тащи́ть. 2.** (*pf.* **от~**) (*coll.*) to pull (*as punishment*); **т. кого́-н. за́ волосы** to pull s.o.'s hair. **2.** (*coll.*) to wear.
таска́|ться, юсь *impf.* (*indet. of* **тащи́ться**) **1.** *see* **тащи́ться. 2.** (*coll., pej.*) to roam about; to hang about.
тас|ова́ть, у́ю *impf.* (*of* **с~**) to shuffle (*cards in a pack*).
тасо́вк|а, и *f.* shuffle, shuffling (*of playing cards*).
тата́р|ин, ина, *pl.* **~ы, ~** *m.* Ta(r)tar.
тата́р|ка, ки *f. of* **~ин**
тата́рский *adj.* Ta(r)tar.
тату́ир|овать, ую *impf. and pf.* to tattoo.
тату́ир|оваться, уюсь *impf. and pf.* to tattoo o.s.; to have o.s. tattooed.
татуиро́вк|а, и *f.* tattooing.
тафт|а́, ы́ *f.* taffeta.
тахо́метр, а *m.* tachometer.
тахт|а́, ы́ *f.* ottoman.
тача́нк|а, и *f.* cart (*used in Ukraine and Caucasus*).
тача́|ть, ю *impf.* (*of* **вы́~**) to stitch.
та́чк|а, и *f.* wheelbarrow.
тащ|и́ть, у́, ~́ишь *impf.* (*det. of* **таска́ть**) **1.** to pull; to drag, lug; to carry. **2.** (*coll.*) to take; (*fig.*) to drag off; **т. кого́-н. в кино́** to drag s.o. off to the cinema. **3.** to pull out. **4.** (*coll.*) to pinch, swipe.
тащ|и́ться, у́сь, ~́ишься *impf.* (*det. of* **таска́ться**) **1.** to drag o.s. along. **2.** to drag, trail.
та́яни|е, я *nt.* thaw, thawing.
та́|ять, ю, ешь *impf.* (*of* **рас~**) **1.** to melt; to thaw; **~ет** it is thawing. **2.** (*fig.*) to melt away, dwindle, wane; **его́ си́лы ~яли** his strength was ebbing. **3.** (**от**; *fig.*) to melt (with), languish (with). **4.** (*impf. only*) to waste away.
твар|ь, и *f.* creature; (*collect.*) creatures; all creation (*also pej.*).
тверде́|ть, ю *impf.* to harden, become hard.
твер|ди́ть, жу́, ди́шь *impf.* **1.** (+*a. or* **о**+*p.*) to repeat, say over and over again. **2.** to memorize, learn by rote.
твёрдо *adv.* hard; firmly, firm.
твердока́менный *adj.* (*rhet.*) steadfast, staunch.
твердоло́б|ый (~, ~а) *adj.* **1.** thick-skulled. **2.** (*pol.*) diehard.
твёрдост|ь, и *f.* hardness; (*fig.*) firmness.
твёрд|ый (~, ~а́, ~о) *adj.* **1.** hard. **2.** firm; solid; **~ое те́ло** (*phys., chem.*) solid. **3.** (*fig.*) firm; stable; steadfast; **~ое зада́ние** specified task; **~ые зна́ния** sound knowledge; **т. срок** fixed time-limit. **4.** (*ling.*) hard; **т. знак** hard sign (*name of Russian letter* **'ъ'**).
тверды́н|я, и *f.* (*obs.*) stronghold (*also fig.*).
твид, а *m.* tweed.
тви́д|овый *adj. of* **~**
тво|й, его́ *m.*, **~я́, ~е́й** *f.*, **~ё, ~его́** *nt.*, *pl.* **~и́, ~и́х** *possessive pron.* your, yours; *as n.* **~и́, ~и́х** your people.
творе́ни|е, я *nt.* **1.** creation; work. **2.** creature, being.
твор|е́ц, ца́ *m.* creator.
твори́тельный *adj.*: **т. паде́ж** (*gram.*) instrumental case.
твор|и́ть, ю́, и́шь *impf.* (*of* **со~**) **1.** to create. **2.** to do; to make; **т. добро́** to do good; **т. чудеса́** to work wonders.
твор|и́ться[1], и́тся *impf.* (*coll.*) to happen, go on; **что тут ~и́тся?** what is going on here?
твор|и́ться[2], и́тся *impf., pass. of* **~и́ть[2]**
творо́г, а́ *and* **тво́рог, а** *m.* curds, cottage cheese; **со́евый т.** tofu.
творо́жник, а *m.* curd pancake.
творо́жн|ый *adj.* curd; **т. сыро́к** cottage cheese.
тво́рческ|ий *adj.* creative; **~ая си́ла** creative power.
тво́рчеств|о, а *nt.* **1.** creation; creative work. **2.** (*collect.*) works (*of an author*).
т. е. (*abbr. of* **то есть**) i.e., that is, viz.
теа́тр, а *m.* **1.** theatre; **т. вое́нных де́йствий** (*mil.*) theatre of operations. **2.** (*fig.*) the stage. **3.** (*collect.*) (the) plays; **т. Шекспи́ра** the plays of Shakespeare.
театра́л, а *m.* theatre-goer, playgoer.
театра́л|ьный (~ен, ~ьна) *adj.* **1.** theatre; theatrical; **т. зал** auditorium; **~ьная ка́сса** box-office; **~ьная шко́ла** drama school. **2.** (*fig.*) theatrical, stagy.
тевто́н, а *m.* Teuton.
тевто́нский *adj.* Teutonic.
теза́урус, а *m.* thesaurus.
те́зис, а *m.* thesis, proposition; **вы́двинуть т.** to advance a thesis.
тёзк|а, и *c.g.* namesake.
теи́зм, а *m.* theism.
теи́ст, а *m.* theist.
теисти́ческий *adj.* theistic.
текст, а *m.* **1.** text. **2.** words, libretto.
тексти́л|ь, я *no pl., m.* (*collect.*) textiles.
тексти́льный *adj.* textile.
тексти́льщик, а *m.* textile worker.
тексту́ал|ьный (~ен, ~ьна) *adj.* **1.** verbatim, word-for-word. **2.** (*philol.*) textual.
текто́ник|а, и *f.* (*geol.*) tectonics.
теку́чест|ь, и *f.* **1.** (*phys.*) fluidity. **2.** fluctuation; **т. рабо́чей си́лы** fluctuation of manpower.
теку́ч|ий (~, ~а) *adj.* **1.** (*phys.*) fluid. **2.** fluctuating, unstable.
теку́щ|ий *pres. part. act. of* **течь** *and adj.* **1.** current; of the present moment; **в ~ем году́** in the current year; **~ие собы́тия** current events, current affairs. **2.** routine, ordinary; **т. ремо́нт** routine repairs.

тел. (*abbr. of* **телефо́н**) tel., telephone.
теле... *comb. form* tele-.
телеавтома́т, а *m.* video games machine.
телеви́дени|е, я *nt.* television, TV; **за́мкнутое т.** closed-circuit TV.
телевизио́нный *adj.* television.
телеви́зор, а *m.* television set.
теле́г|а, и *f.* cart, wagon.
телегра́мм|а, ы *f.* telegram.
телегра́ф, а *m.* **1.** telegraph. **2.** telegraph office.
телеграфи́р|овать, ую *impf. and pf.* to telegraph, wire.
телеграфи́ст, а *m.* telegraphist.
телеграфи́|я, и *f.* telegraphy.
телегра́фн|ый *adj.* telegraph; telegraphic; **~ая ле́нта** ticker-tape; **т. стиль** telegraphese.
теле́жк|а, и *f.* **1.** small cart, hand-cart. **2.** bogie, trolley.
тележурна́л, а *m.* current affairs programme (*on TV*).
телезри́тел|ь, я *m.* (television) viewer.
телекоммуника́ци|и, й *no sg.* telecommunications.
те́лекс, а *m.* telex.
телемарафо́н, а *m.*: **(благотвори́тельный) т.** telethon.
телемо́ст, а *m.* satellite (TV) link-up.
тел|ёнок, ёнка, *pl.* **~я́та, ~я́т** *m.* calf.
телеобъекти́в, а *m.* (*phot.*) telephoto lens.
телеологи́ческий *adj.* teleological.
телеоло́ги|я, и *f.* teleology.
телепати́ческий *adj.* telepathic.
телепа́ти|я, и *f.* telepathy.
телепереда́ч|а, и *f.* television transmission.
телеско́п, а *m.* telescope.
телескопи́ческий *adj.* telescopic.
теле́сн|ый *adj.* **1.** bodily; corporal; physical; **~ое наказа́ние** corporal punishment; **~ого цве́та** flesh-coloured. **2.** corporeal.
телесту́ди|я, и *f.* television studio.
телесуфлёр, а *m.* teleprompter, Autocue (*propr.*).
телеуправле́ни|е, я *nt.* remote control.
телефа́кс, а *m.* (tele)fax (machine).
телефо́н, а *m.* **1.** telephone; **позвони́ть по ~у** (*+d.*) to telephone, phone, ring up; **т.-автома́т** public telephone, public call-box; **т.-отве́тчик** answerphone. **2.** (*coll.*) telephone number.
телефони́р|овать, ую *impf. and pf.* to telephone.
телефони́ст, а *m.* telephone operator, telephonist.
телефони́ст|ка, ки *f. of* **~**
телефо́н|ный *adj. of* **~**
тел|е́ц, ьца́ *m.* **1.** (*obs.*) calf. **2. Т.** (*astron.*) Taurus.
телеце́нтр, а *m.* television centre.
те́лик, а *m.* (*coll.*) (the) telly, the (goggle-)box.
тел|и́ться, ́~ится *impf.* (*of* **о~**) to calve.
тёлк|а, и *f.* **1.** heifer.
те́л|о, а, *pl.* **~а́, ~, ~а́м** *nt.* body; **держа́ть в чёрном ~е** to ill-treat, maltreat.
телогре́йк|а, и *f.* padded jacket (*usu. sleeveless*).
телодвиже́ни|е, я *nt.* movement, motion.
телосложе́ни|е, я *nt.* build, frame.
телохрани́тел|ь, я *m.* bodyguard.
теля́тин|а, ы *f.* veal.
теля́ч|ий *adj.* **1.** *adj. of* **телёнок; ~ья ко́жа** calf(skin). **2.** (*cul.*) veal. **3.: т. восто́рг** (*coll.*) foolish raptures.
тем 1. *i. sg. m. and nt., d. pl. of* **тот. 2.** *conj.* (so much) the; **чем вы́ше, т. лу́чше** the taller, the better; **т. лу́чше** so much the better; **т. бо́лее, что** especially as; **т. не ме́нее** none the less, nevertheless.
те́м|а, ы *f.* **1.** subject, topic, theme; **перейти́ к друго́й ~е** to change the subject. **2.** (*mus.*) theme; **т. с вариа́циями** theme and variations.
тема́тик|а, и *f.* (*collect.*) subject-matter.
темати́ческий *adj.* **1.** *adj. of* **тема́тика; т. план** plan of subjects. **2.** (*mus.*) thematic.
тембр, а *m.* timbre.
те́мен|ь, и *f.* (*coll.*) darkness.
Те́мз|а, ы *f.* the Thames (*river*).
те́ми *i. pl. of* **тот**
темне́|ть, ю *impf.* **1.** (*pf.* **по~**) to grow *or* become dark; to darken. **2.** (*pf.* **с~**): **~ет** (*impers.*) it is getting dark. **3.** (*impf. only*) to show up darkly; loom.
темн|и́ть, ю́, и́шь *impf.* to darken; to make darker.
темни́ц|а, ы *f.* (*obs.*) dungeon.
темно́ *as pred.* it is dark; **у меня́ в глаза́х ста́ло т.** everything went dark before my eyes.
темно... *comb. form* dark-.
темноко́жий *adj.* dark-skinned, swarthy.
темноси́ний *adj.* dark blue; navy blue.
темнот|а́, ы́ *f.* dark, darkness; **в ~е́** in the dark.
тём|ный (~ен, ~на́, ~но́) *adj.* **1.** dark; **~ное пятно́** (*fig.*) dark stain, blemish. **2.** obscure, vague. **3.** sombre. **4.** shady, suspicious; **~ное де́ло** shady business. **5.** ignorant.
темп, а *m.* **1.** (*mus.*) tempo. **2.** (*fig.*) tempo; rate, speed, pace; **уско́рить т.** to accelerate.
те́мпер|а, ы *f.* **1.** distemper (*paint*). **2.** tempera.
темпера́мент, а *m.* temperament; **челове́к с ~ом** energetic person, spirited person.
темпера́мент|ный (~ен, ~на) *adj.* energetic; spirited, vigorous.
температу́р|а, ы *f.* temperature; **т. кипе́ния** boiling-point; **т. замерза́ния** freezing-point; **ме́рить кому́-н. ~у** to take s.o.'s temperature.
температу́р|ить, ю, ишь *impf.* (*coll.*) to have a temperature.
температу́р|ный *adj. of* **~а**
тем|ь, и *f.* (*coll.*) dark, darkness.
те́м|я, ени *no pl., nt.* (*anat.*) crown, top of the head.
тенденцио́з|ный (~ен, ~на) *adj.* (*pej.*) tendentious, biased.
тенде́нци|я, и *f.* **1. (к)** tendency (to, towards). **2.** (*pej.*) bias; **с ~ей** tendentious, biased.
те́ндер, а *m.* **1.** (*rail.*) tender. **2.** (*naut.*) cutter.
тенев|о́й *adj.* shady (*also fig.*); **~а́я сторона́** shady side; (*fig.*) bad side, seamy side.
тенёт|а, ~ *no sg.* snare.
тени́ст|ый (~, ~а) *adj.* shady.
те́ннис, а *m.* tennis.
теннеси́ст, а *m.* tennis-player.
те́нниск|а, и *f.* (*coll.*) tennis shirt, short-sleeved shirt.
те́ннисн|ый *adj.* tennis; **т. корт, ~ая площа́дка** tennis-court.
те́нор, а, *pl.* **~а́, ~о́в** *m.* (*mus.*) tenor.
теноро́вый *adj. of* **те́нор**
тент, а *m.* awning.
тен|ь, и, в ~и́, *pl.* **́~и, ~е́й** *f.* **1.** shade; **сиде́ть в ~и́** to sit in the shade; **держа́ться в ~и́** (*fig.*) to keep in the background. **2.** shadow; **дава́ть т.** to cast a shadow; **от него́ оста́лась одна́ т.** he is but a shadow of his former self. **3.** shadow, ghost; **бле́ден, как т.** pale as a ghost. **4.** (*fig.*) shadow, particle; **нет ни ́~и сомне́ния** there is not a shadow of doubt. **5.** suspicion; **бро́сить т. на кого́-н.** to cast suspicion on s.o.
теократи́ческий *adj.* theocratic.
теокра́ти|я, и *f.* theocracy.
теологи́ческий *adj.* theological.
теоло́ги|я, и *f.* theology.
теоре́м|а, ы *f.* theorem.
теоретизи́р|овать, ую *impf.* to theorize.
теоре́тик, а *m.* theorist.
теорети́ческий *adj.* theoretical.
тео́ри|я, и *f.* theory.
теософи́ческий *adj.* theosophical.
теосо́фи|я, и *f.* theosophy.
тепе́решн|ий *adj.* (*coll.*) present; **~ие лю́ди** people

(of) today; **в ~ее врéмя** nowadays.
тепéрь *adv.* now; nowadays, today.
теплé|ть, ет *impf.* (*of* **по~**) to get warm.
тéпл|иться, ится *impf.* to flicker, glimmer (*also fig.*); **~ится надéжда** there is still a glimmer of hope.
теплúц|а, ы *f.* greenhouse, hothouse, conservatory.
теплú|чный *adj. of* **~ца**
теплó[1] *adv.* **1.** warmly. **2.** *as pred.* it is warm.
тепл|ó[2], **á** *nt.* heat; warmth; **дéсять грáдусов ~á** ten degrees (*Celsius*) above zero.
тепловóз, а *m.* diesel locomotive.
тепловóзный *adj.* diesel.
теплов|óй *adj.* heat; thermal; **~áя единúца** thermal unit; **т. удáр** heat stroke.
теплоёмкост|ь, и *f.* (*phys.*) thermal capacity; **удéльная т.** specific heat.
теплокрóвный *adj.* (*zool.*) warm-blooded.
тепломéр, а *m.* (*phys.*) calorimeter.
теплопровóд, а *m.* hot-water system.
теплопровóдный *adj.* heat-conducting.
теплостóйкий *adj.* heat-proof, heat-resistant.
теплот|á, ы́ *f.* **1.** (*phys.*) heat. **2.** warmth (*also fig.*); **душéвная т.** warm-heartedness.
теплотéхник, а *m.* heating engineer.
теплохóд, а *m.* motor ship.
теплоцентрáл|ь, и *f.* heating plant.
теплýшк|а, и *f.* (*coll.*) heated goods van (*for transportation of human beings*).
тёп|лый (~ел, ~лá, ~лó, ~лы) *adj.* **1.** warm; **~лая одéжда** warm clothing; **~лое местéчко** (*coll.*) cushy job. **2.** warmed, heated. **3.** (*fig.*) warm, cordial; affectionate; **т. приём** warm welcome. **4.** heartfelt.
теплы́н|ь, и *f.* (*coll.*) warm weather.
терапéвт, а *m.* therapeutist.
терапевтúческий *adj.* therapeutic.
терапú|я, и *f.* therapy; **интенсúвная т.** intensive care.
тереб|úть, лю́, úшь *impf.* **1.** to pull (at), pick (at). **2.:** **т. лён** to pull flax. **3.** (*fig., coll.*) to pester, bother.
тéрем, а, *pl.* **~á** *m.* (*hist.*) (tower-)chamber; tower.
терéть, тру, трёшь, *past* **тёр, тёрла** *impf.* **1.** to rub. **2.** to grate, grind. **3.** to rub, chafe.
терéться, трусь, трёшься, *past* **тёрся, тёрлась** *impf.* **1.** to rub o.s.; (**о, обо**+*a.*) to rub (against). **2.** (**óколо**; *fig., coll.*) to hang (about, round).
терзá|ть, ю *impf.* **1.** to tear to pieces; to pull about. **2.** to torment, torture.
терзá|ться, юсь *impf.* (+*i.*) to suffer; to be a prey (to).
тёрк|а, и *f.* (*cul.*) grater.
тéрмин, а *m.* term.
терминологúческий *adj.* terminological.
терминолóги|я, и *f.* terminology.
термúт, а *m.* (*zool.*) termite.
термúческ|ий *adj.* (*phys., tech.*) thermal.
термодинáмик|а, и *f.* thermodynamics.
термодинамúческий *adj.* thermodynamic.
термóметр, а *m.* thermometer; **постáвить т. комý-н.** to take s.o.'s temperature.
термопáр|а, ы *f.* (*phys.*) thermocouple.
тéрмос, а *m.* thermos (flask).
термостáт, а *m.* thermostat.
термоя́дерный *adj.* thermonuclear.
тёрн, а *m.* (*bot.*) **1.** blackthorn. **2.** sloe(s).
тéрни|е, я *nt.* (*obs.*) **1.** prickly plant. **2.** prickle, thorn.
тернóвник, а *m.* (*bot.*) blackthorn.
тернóв|ый *adj.* **1.** *adj. of* **тёрн** *and* **~ник. 2.** thorny, prickly; **т. венéц** crown of thorns.
тернослúв, а *m.* damson.
терпелúвост|ь, и *f.* patience.
терпелúв|ый (~, ~а) *adj.* patient.
терпéни|е, я *nt.* patience; **вы́вести из ~я** to exasperate; **вы́йти из ~я** to lose patience.
терп|éть, лю́, ∠ишь *impf.* **1.** (*pf.* **по~**) to suffer, undergo; **т. поражéние** to suffer a defeat. **2.** to bear, endure, stand. **3.** to have patience. **4.** to tolerate, suffer, put up (with); **не (мочь) т.** to be unable to bear, endure, stand; **т. не могý** I can't stand it; **врéмя ∠ит** there is plenty of time; **врéмя не ∠ит** there is no time to be lost.
терп|éться, ∠ится *impf.* (*impers.*): **емý,** *etc.*, **не ∠ится** (+*inf.*) he, *etc.*, is impatient (to).
терпúмост|ь, и *f.* tolerance; indulgence.
терпúм|ый (~, ~а) *adj.* **1.** tolerant; indulgent. **2.** tolerable, bearable.
тéрп|кий (~ок, ~кá) *adj.* astringent; tart, sharp.
тéрпкост|ь, и *f.* astringency; tartness, sharpness.
терракóт|а, ы *f.* terracotta.
терракóт|овый *adj. of* **~а**
террáс|а, ы *f.* terrace.
территориáльн|ый *adj.* territorial.
территóри|я, и *f.* territory, confines; area.
террóр, а *m.* terror.
терроризúр|овать, ую *impf. and pf.* to terrorize.
террорúзм, а *m.* terrorism.
террорúст, а *m.* terrorist.
террористúческий *adj.* terrorist.
тёрт|ый *adj.* **1.** ground; grated. **2.** (*fig., coll.*) hardened, experienced; **т. калáч** old stager, old hand.
тéрци|я, и *f.* (*mus.*) mediant; third.
терьéр, а *m.* terrier (*dog.*).
теря́|ть, ю *impf.* (*of* **по~**) to lose; **т. надéжду** to lose hope; **не т. головы́** to keep one's head; **т. сúлу** to become invalid; **т. врéмя на что-н.** to waste time on sth.; **т. в вéсе** to lose weight; **т. в чьём-н. мнéнии** to sink in s.o.'s estimation; **не т. из вúду** to keep in sight; (*fig.*) to remember, bear in mind; **нам нéчего т.** we have nothing to lose.
теря́|ться, юсь *impf.* (*of* **по~**) **1.** to get lost; to disappear. **2.** to fail, decline, weaken; **пáмять у негó ~ется** his memory is failing. **3.** to pass unnoticed; to fail to attract notice. **4.** to become flustered; **~юсь, умá не приложý** I am at my wits' end. **5.:** **т. в предположéниях** to be lost in conjecture.
тёс, а (у) *m.* (*collect.*) boards, planks.
тесáк, á *m.* cutlass.
те|сáть, шý, ∠шешь *impf.* to cut, hew.
тесёмк|а, и *f.* tape, ribbon, braid.
тесёмчатый *adj.* tape-like; **т. глист** tape-worm.
тесúн|а, ы *f.* board, plank.
тес|лó, лá, *pl.* **∸ла, ∸ел** *nt.* adze.
теснúн|а, ы *f.* gorge, ravine.
тесн|úть, ю́, úшь *impf.* **1.** (*pf.* **по~**) to press, crowd. **2.** to squeeze, constrict; (*of clothing*) to be too tight; **мне грудь ~úт** I have a tightness in my chest.
тесн|úться, ю́сь, úшься *impf.* **1.** (*pf.* **по~**) to press through, push a way through. **2.** (*pf.* **с~**) to crowd, cluster (*also fig.*; *of thoughts, etc.*).
тéсно *adv.* **1.** closely (*also fig.*); tightly; narrowly; **быть т. свя́зано (с**+*i.*) to be closely linked (with). **2.** *as pred.* it is crowded; it is (too) tight; **в трамвáе бы́ло óчень т.** the tram was very crowded; **мне т. под мы́шками** it feels tight in the arm-pits.
теснот|á, ы́ *f.* **1.** crowded state; tightness; closeness. **2.** crush, squash; **жить в ~é** to live cooped up; **в ~é, да не в обúде** the more the merrier.
тéс|ный (~ен, ~нá, ~но) *adj.* **1.** crowded, cramped; **мир ~ен!** it's a small world. **2.** narrow; **т. прохóд** narrow passage. **3.** (too) tight. **4.** close, compact; **~ные ряды́** close ranks. **5.** (*fig.*) close, tight; **~ная дрýжба** close friendship.
тесóвый *adj.* board, plank.
тéст|о, а *nt.* dough; pastry; **т. для блинóв** batter.
тест|ь, я *m.* father-in-law (*wife's father*).
тесьм|á, ы́ *f.* tape, ribbon, braid.
тётеньк|а, и *f.* (*affectionate form of* **тётя**, *also used by children to address an unknown woman*) aunty.

те́терев, а, *pl.* **~а́, ~о́в** *m.* (*zool.*) black grouse.
тетёрк|а, и *f.* grey-hen (*fem. of black grouse*).
тете́р|я, и *f.* **1.** (*dial.*) = **те́терев. 2.** (*coll., joc.*): **лени́вая т.** lazybones; **со́нная т.** sleepyhead.
тетив|а́, ы *f.* bowstring.
тётк|а, и *f.* **1.** aunt. **2.** (*as term of address to any elderly woman; coll.*) ma, lady.
тетра́д|ка, ки *f.* = **~ь**
тетра́д|ь, и *f.* **1.** exercise book; **т. для рисова́ния** drawing-book; sketch-book. **2.: т. пи́счей бума́ги** packet of notepaper.
тёт|я, и, *g. pl.* **~ей** *f.* **1.** aunt. **2.** (*used by children to any unknown woman*) lady. **3.** (*joc.*) woman.
те́фтел|и, ей *no sg.* (*cul.*) meat-balls.
тех *g., a., p. pl. of* **тот**
тех... *comb. form, abbr. of* **техни́ческий**
те́хник, а *m.* **1.** technician; **зубно́й т.** dental mechanic. **2.** technically qualified person.
те́хник|а, и *f.* **1.** engineering; technology. **2.** technique, art; **э́то — де́ло ~и** it is a matter of technique; **овладе́ть ~ой** to master the art. **3.** (*collect.*) technical devices; **т. безопа́сности** safety devices.
те́хникум, а *m.* technical college, training college.
техни́чески *adv.* technically.
техни́ческ|ий *adj.* **1.** technical; engineering; **~ие нау́ки** engineering sciences; **т. персона́л** technical staff; **т. реда́ктор**, *see* **техре́д**; **~ие усло́вия** specifications. **2.** (*mil*) maintenance; **~ое обслу́живание** maintenance. **3.: ~ие культу́ры** (*agric.*) industrial crops. **4.** assistant; **т. сотру́дник** junior member of staff.
техно́лог, а *m.* technologist.
технологи́ческий *adj.* technological.
техноло́ги|я, и *f.* technology; **высокосло́жная т.** high technology.
техосмо́тр, а *m.* (*abbr. of* **техни́ческий осмо́тр**) check-up (*of motor vehicle*); **листо́к ~а** ≃ MOT (*Ministry of Transport*) certificate (*of roadworthiness*).
техре́д, а *m.* (*abbr. of* **техни́ческий реда́ктор**) technical editor, copy editor.
тече́ни|е, я *nt.* **1.** flow. **2.** (*fig.*) course; **с ~ем вре́мени** in the course of time, in time. **3.** current, stream (*also fig.*); **по ~ю, про́тив ~я** with the current. against the current (*also fig.*). **4.** (*fig.*) trend, tendency. **5.: в т.** (*+g.*) during, in the course (of).
те́чк|а, и *f.* heat (*in animals*).
теч|ь[1], **и** *f.* leak; **дать т.** to spring a leak.
течь[2], **теку́, течёшь, теку́т**, *past* **тёк, текла́** *impf.* **1.** to flow (*also fig.*); to stream; (*fig.; of time*) to pass; **у него́ из носу течёт** his nose is running; **у меня́ слю́нки текли́** my mouth was watering. **2.** to leak, be leaky.
те́ш|ить, у, ишь *impf.* (*of* **по~**) **1.** to amuse, entertain. **2.** to gratify, please.
те́ш|иться, усь, ишься *impf.* (*of* **по~**) **1.** (*+i*) to amuse o.s. (with), play (with). **2. (над)** to make fun (of).
тёщ|а, и *f.* mother-in-law (*wife's mother*).
тиа́р|а, ы *f.* tiara.
тибе́тский *adj.* Tibetan.
ти́бр|ить, ю, ишь *impf.* (*of* **с~**) (*coll.*) to pinch.
ти́г|ель, ля *m.* (*tech.*) crucible.
тигр, а *m.* tiger.
тигр|ёнок, ёнка, *pl.* **~я́та, ~я́т** *m.* tiger cub.
тигри́ц|а, ы *f.* tigress.
тигро́в|ый *adj. of* **тигр; ~ая шку́ра** tiger-skin.
тик[1], **а** *m.* (*med.*) tic.
тик[2], **а** *m.* tick, ticking (*material*).
тик[3], **а** *m.* (*bot.*) teak.
ти́кань|е, я *nt.* tick, ticking (*of a clock*).
ти́ка|ть, ю *impf.* (*coll.*) to tick.
ти́ковый[1] *adj. of* **тик**[2]
ти́ков|ый[2] *adj. of* **тик**[3]
ти́льд|а, ы *f.* (*typ.*) tilde, swung dash.
тимиа́н = **тимья́н**
тимья́н, а *m.* (*bot.*) thyme.
ти́н|а, ы *no pl., f.* slime, mud; mire (*also fig.*).
ти́нистый *adj.* slimy, muddy.
тинкту́р|а, ы *f.* tincture.
тип, а *m.* **1.** type; model. **2.** (*coll.*) fellow, character; **стра́нный т.** odd character.
типа́ж, а́ *m.* (*liter., art*) type; prototype.
типизи́р|овать, ую *impf. and pf.* to typify.
типи́ческий *adj.* **1.** typical (= *constituting a type*). **2.** model, standard.
типи́чност|ь, и *f.* typicalness, typical nature.
типи́ч|ный (~ен, ~на) *adj.* typical (= *characteristic*).
типов|о́й *adj.* model; standard.
типо́граф, а *m.* printer.
типогра́фи|я, и *f.* printing-house, press.
типогра́фск|ий *adj.* typographical; **~ое иску́сство** typography.
тир[1], **а** *m.* shooting-range; shooting gallery.
тира́д|а, ы *f.* tirade; sally.
тира́ж, а́ *m.* **1.** drawing (*of loan or lottery*); **вы́йти в т.** to be drawn; (*fig.*) to retire from the scene. **2.** circulation; edition; print run.
тира́н, а *m.* tyrant.
тира́н|ить, ю, ишь *impf.* to tyrannize, torment.
тирани́ческий *adj.* tyrannical.
тирани́|я, и *f.* (*hist. and fig.*) tyranny.
тира́нств|о, а *nt.* tyranny.
тира́нств|овать, ую *impf.* **(над)** to tyrannize (over).
тире́ *nt. indecl.* dash.
тис, а *m.* yew(-tree).
ти́ска|ть, ю *impf.* (*of* **ти́снуть**) to press, squeeze.
тиск|и́, о́в *no sg.* (*tech.*) vice; **зажа́ть в т.** to grip in a vice; **в ~а́х** (*+g.*) in the grip (of).
тисне́ни|е, я *nt.* **1.** stamping. **2.** imprint; design.
тиснёный *adj.* stamped, printed; **т. шрифт** raised (Braille) type.
ти́с|нуть, ну, нешь *pf. of* **~кать**
ти́с|овый *adj. of* **~**
тита́н[1], **а** *m.* (*myth. and fig.*) titan.
тита́н[2], **а** *m.* (*chem.*) titanium.
тита́н[3], **а** *m.* boiler.
титани́ческий *adj.* titanic.
тита́н|овый *adj. of* **~**[2]; titanic.
титр, а *m.* (*cin.*) caption, credit.
титрова́ни|е, я *nt.* (*chem.*) titration.
титр|ова́ть, у́ю *impf. and pf.* (*chem.*) to titrate.
ти́тул, а *m.* **1.** title. **2.** title-page.
титуло́в|анный *p.p.p. of* **~а́ть** *and adj.* titled.
титул|ова́ть, у́ю *impf. and pf.* to style, call by one's title.
ти́тул|ьный *adj. of* **~; т. лист** title-page.
тиф, а *m.* typhus; **брюшно́й т.** typhoid; **сыпно́й т.** typhus.
тифо́зн|ый *adj.* typhus; typhoid.
ти́х|ий (~, ~а́, ~о) *adj.* **1.** quiet; (*of sounds*) low, soft, gentle, faint; **т. го́лос** low voice. **2.** silent; still. **3.** (*fig.*) quiet, calm; gentle; still; **т. нрав** gentle disposition; **~ая пого́да** calm weather. **4.** slow, slow-moving; **т. ход** slow speed, slow pace.
Ти́х|ий океа́н, ~ого ~а *m.* the Pacific (Ocean).
ти́хо[1] *adv.* **1.** quietly; softly, gently. **2.** silently. **3.** (*fig.*) quietly, calmly; still; **сиде́ть т.** to sit still; **т.** gently!, careful! **4.** slowly; **дела́ иду́т т.** things are slack.
ти́хо[2] *as pred.* **1.** it is quiet, there is not a sound; **ста́ло т.** it became quiet. **2.** (*fig.*) it is quiet; it is calm; **на душе́ у меня́ ста́ло т.** my mind is at rest. **3.** (*comm.*) it is slack; **с хло́пком т.** cotton is slack.
тихомо́лком *adv.* (*coll.*) quietly, without a sound.
тихо́нько *adv.* (*coll.*) quietly; softly, gently.
тихо́н|я, и, *g. pl.* **~ей** *c.g.* demure person.

тихоокеа́нский *adj.* Pacific.
тихохо́д, а *m.* (*zool.*) sloth.
тихохо́д|ный (~ен, ~на) *adj.* slow.
ти́ше 1. *comp. of* **ти́хий** *and* **ти́хо. 2. т.!** (*i*) (be) quiet!, silence! (*ii*) gently!; careful!
тишин|а́, ы́ *f.* quiet, silence; stillness; **нару́шить ~у́** to break the silence; **соблюда́ть ~у́** to keep quiet.
тиш|ь, и, в ~и́ *f.* quiet, silence; stillness; **т. да гладь** peace and quiet.
т. к. (*abbr. of* **так как**) as, since.
тка́ный *adj.* woven.
ткан|ь, и *f.* **1.** fabric, cloth; **льняны́е ~и** linen(s); **шёлковые ~и** silks. **2.** (*anat.*) tissue.
тканьё, я́ *nt.* **1.** weaving. **2.** woven fabrics, cloth.
ткать, тку, ткёшь, *past* **ткал, ткала́, тка́ло** *impf.* (*of* **со~**) to weave; **т. паути́ну** to spin a web.
тка́цк|ий *adj.* weaver's, weaving; **~ое де́ло** weaving; **т. стано́к** loom; **т. челно́к** shuttle.
ткач, а́ *m.* weaver.
ткачи́х|а, и *f. of* **ткач**
ткн|у́ть(ся), у́(сь), ёшь(ся) *pf. of* **ты́кать(ся)**
тле́ни|е, я *nt.* **1.** decay, decomposition. **2.** smouldering.
тле́н|ный (~ен, ~на) *adj.* (*obs.*) liable to decay.
тлетво́р|ный (~ен, ~на) *adj.* **1.** putrid. **2.** (*fig.*) pernicious, noxious.
тле́|ть, ет *impf.* **1.** to rot, decay, decompose. **2.** to smoulder (*also fig.*).
тле́|ться, ется *impf.* to smoulder.
тл|я, и, *g. pl.* **~ей** *f.* plant-louse, aphis.
тмин, а *m.* **1.** caraway. **2.** (*collect.*) caraway-seeds.
тми́н|ный *adj. of* **~**
то[1] *pron.* (*nom. and a. sg. nt. of* **тот**) that; **то, что...** the fact that ...; **то, что́** that which; **то был, была́, бы́ло** that was; **то бы́ли** those were; **то́ есть** that is (to say); **а то,** *see* **а; (да) и то** and that, at that.
то[2] *conj.* **1.** (*in apodosis of conditional sentence*) then (*or not translated*); **е́сли вас там не бу́дет, то и я не пойду́** if you won't be there, (then) I shan't go either. **2.: то..., то** now ..., now. **3.: не то..., не то** either ... or; whether ... or; half ..., half; **не то по глу́пости, не то по зло́бе** either through stupidity or through malice. **4.: не то, что́бы..., но** it is not, it was not that ... (but). **5.: то и де́ло, то и знай** (*coll.*) time and again; perpetually.
-то[1] *emph. particle* (*in coll. Russ. oft. merely adds familiar tone*) just, precisely, exactly (*or not translated*); **в то́м-то и де́ло** that's just it; **чего́ же ва́м-то боя́ться?** what have *you* to be afraid of?
-то[2] *particle forming indef. prons and advs.* (**кто́-то, како́й-то, когда́-то,** *etc.*).
т. о. (*abbr. of* **таки́м о́бразом**) thus, in this way.
тобо́й, тобо́ю *i. of* **ты**
тов. (*abbr. of* **това́рищ**) Comrade.
това́р, а *m.* goods; article; commodity; **~ы широ́кого потребле́ния** consumer goods.
това́рищ, а *m.* **1.** comrade; friend; colleague; **т. по ору́жию** comrade-in-arms; **т. по рабо́те** colleague; workmate; **т. по шко́ле** school-friend. **2.** (*as style and as term of address in former USSR*) Comrade. **3.** person; **вот т. из Министе́рства** here is the man from the ministry.
това́рищеск|ий *adj.* **1.** comradely; friendly; **с ~им приве́том** (*epistolary formula*) with fraternal greetings. **2.** (*sport*) friendly, unofficial; **~ое состяза́ние, ~ая встре́ча** friendly (match).
това́риществ|о, а *nt.* **1.** comradeship, fellowship; **чу́вство ~а** feeling of solidarity. **2.** company; association, society.
това́рност|ь, и *f.* (*econ.*) marketability.
това́рн|ый *adj.* **1.** goods; **т. знак** trade mark; **т. склад** warehouse. **2.** (*rail.*) goods, freight; **т. ваго́н** goods truck; **т. соста́в** goods train. **3.** (*econ.*) commodity; **~ая проду́кция** commodity output. **4.** (*econ.*) marketable; **~ое зерно́** marketable grain.
товарове́д, а *m.* commodity researcher.
товарове́дени|е, я *nt.* commodity research.
товарообме́н, а *m.* (*econ.*) barter.
товарооборо́т, а *m.* commodity circulation.
то́г|а, и *f.* (*hist.*) toga.
тогда́ 1. *adv.* then (= (*i*) at that time, (*ii*) in that case). **2.: когда́..., т.** (*conj.*) when; **когда́ решу́сь, т. тебе́ напишу́** I will write to you when I have decided. **3.: т. как** (*conj.*) whereas, while.
тогда́шний *adj.* (*coll.*) of that time; the then.
того́ *g. sg. m. and nt. of* **тот**
тожде́ственност|ь, и *f.* identity.
тожде́ствен|ный (~, ~на) *adj.* identical, one and the same.
то́ждеств|о, а *nt.* identity.
то́же *adv.* also, as well, too.
ток[1]**, а** *m.* current; **т. высо́кого напряже́ния** (*elec.*) high-tension current; **переме́нный т.** alternating current; **постоя́нный т.** direct current.
ток[2]**, а, о ~е, на ~у́,** *pl.* **~а́, ~о́в** *m.* (*birds'*) mating-place.
ток[3]**, а, о ~е́, на ~у́,** *pl.* **~а́** *and* **~и, ~о́в** *m.* threshing-floor.
ток[4]**, а** *m.* toque.
тока́рн|ый *adj.* (*tech.*) turning; **т. стано́к** lathe; **т. цех** turning shop.
то́кар|ь, я, *pl.* **~и** *and* **~я́** *m.* turner, lathe operator.
ток|ова́ть, у́ет *impf.* (*of birds*) to utter the mating-call.
токоприёмник, а *m.* (*elec.*) current collector, trolley (*of elec. locomotive, trolleybus, etc.*).
токсикологи́ческий *adj.* toxicological.
токсиколо́ги|я, и *f.* toxicology.
токси́н, а *m.* (*med.*) toxin.
токси́ческий *adj.* toxic.
тол, а *m.* (*chem.*) TNT.
толи́к|а, и *f.* (*coll.*): **ма́лая т., не́которая т.** a little, a small quantity; a few.
толк[1]**, а (у)** *m.* **1.** sense; understanding; **бе́з ~у** senselessly; **с ~ом** sensibly, intelligently; **сбить с ~у** to confuse; **взять в т.** (*coll.*) to understand, grasp, get; **от него́ ~у не добьёшься** you'll get no sense out of him. **2.** (*coll.*) use, profit; **из э́того не вы́йдет ~у** nothing will come of it; **понима́ть, знать т.** (**в**+*p.*) to know what one is talking about (in).
толка́тел|ь, я *m.*: **т. ядра́** (*sport*) shot-putter.
толк|а́ть, а́ю *impf.* (*of* **~ну́ть**) **1.** to push, shove; to jog; **т. ло́ктем** to nudge. **2.** (*sport*) **т. шта́нгу** to weight-lift; **т. ядро́** to put the shot. **3.** (**на**+*a.*) to push (into), incite (to).
толк|а́ться, а́юсь *impf.* **1.** (*impf. only*) to push (one another). **2.** (*pf.* **~ну́ться**): **т. в дверь** to knock on the door. **3.** (*pf.* **~ну́ться**) (**к**) to try to see, try to get access (to). **4.** (*impf. only*) (*coll.*) to knock about.
толка́ч, а́ *m.* **1.** (*coll.*) pusher, go-getter, fixer (*in industrial enterprises*).
то́лк|и, ов *pl.* talk; rumours, gossip; **иду́т т. о том, что** it is said that, it is rumoured that.
толк|ну́ть, ну́, нёшь *pf. of* **~а́ть**
толк|ну́ться, ну́сь, нёшься *pf. of* **~а́ться 2., 3.**
толкова́ни|е, я *nt.* **1.** interpretation. **2.** (*pl.*) commentary.
толкова́тел|ь, я *m.* interpreter, commentator.
толк|ова́ть, у́ю *impf.* **1.** to interpret; **ло́жно т. чьи-н. слова́** to misconstrue s.o.'s words. **2.** (*+d.*; *coll.*) to explain (to). **3.** (*coll.*) to talk; to say.
толко́в|ый (~, ~а) *adj.* **1.** intelligent, sensible. **2.** intelligible, clear. **3.** (*full form only*) **т. слова́рь** explanatory dictionary.
то́лком *adv.* (*coll.*) **1.** plainly, clearly; **поговори́ть т.** to talk straight. **2.** seriously, in all seriousness.

толкотн|я́, и́ *f.* (*coll.*) crush, scrum, squash.
тол|ку́, ку́т *see* **~о́чь**
толку́чий *adj.*: **т. ры́нок** (*coll.*) flea market.
толку́ч|ка, ки *f.* (*coll.*) **1.** crush, scrum, squash. **2.** = **~ий ры́нок**
толокн|о́, а́ *nt.* oat flour.
тол|о́чь, ку́, чёшь, ку́т, *past* **~о́к, ~кла́** *impf.* (*of* **рас~** *and* **с~**) to pound, crush; **т. во́ду в сту́пе** to beat the air, mill the wind.
тол|о́чься, ку́сь, чёшься, ку́тся, *past* **~о́кся, ~кла́сь** *impf.* (*coll.*) to knock about; to gad about; (*fig.*) to swarm.
толп|а́, ы́, *pl.* **~ы** *f.* crowd; throng; multitude.
толп|и́ться, и́тся *impf.* to crowd; to throng.
толсте́|ть, ю *impf.* (*of* **по~**) to grow fat; to put on weight.
толст|и́ть, и́т *impf.* (*coll.*) to make (look) fat; **хлеб о́чень ~и́т** bread is very fattening.
толсто́вк|а, и *f.* tolstovka (*long belted blouse*).
толстогу́б|ый (~, ~а) *adj.* thick-lipped.
толстоко́ж|ий (~, ~а) *adj.* **1.** thick-skinned (*also fig.*). **2.** (*zool.*): **~ее живо́тное** pachyderm.
толстосу́м, а *f.* (*obs.*, *coll.*) money-bags.
толсту́х|а, и *f.* (*coll.*) fat woman; fat girl.
толсту́шк|а, и *f. affectionate form of* **толсту́ха**
то́лст|ый (~, ~а́, ~о) *adj.* **1.** fat; stout; **т. нос** big nose. **2.** thick; heavy; **т. про́вод** heavy-gauge wire; **~ая кишка́** (*anat.*) large intestine.
толстя́к, а́ *m.* fat man; fat boy.
толуо́л, а *m.* (*chem.*) toluene.
толчёный *adj.* pounded, crushed; ground.
тол|чёт *see* **~о́чь**
толче|я́, и́ *f.* (*coll.*) crush, scrum, squash.
толч|о́к, ка́ *m.* **1.** push, shove; (*sport*) put. **2.** jolt, bump; (earthquake) shock, tremor. **3.** (*fig.*) push, shove; stimulus; **дать т. к эконо́мике** to kick-start the economy.
то́лщ|а, и *f.* **1.** thickness; **т. сне́га** depth of snow. **2.**: **в ~е наро́да** in the (thick of the) people.
то́лще *comp. of* **то́лстый**
толщин|а́, ы́ *f.* **1.** fatness, corpulence. **2.** thickness.
тол|ь, я *m.* (tarred) roofing paper.
то́лько 1. *adv.* only; solely; alone; just; **не т...., но и** not only ..., but also; **поду́май(те) т.!** just think!; **т. и всего́, да и т.** (*coll.*) that's all; **т. что не** (*coll.*) the only thing lacking (is, was); **не т. что** (*coll.*) not to mention, let alone; **т. за после́дние пять лет...** in the last five years alone .... **2.**: **т. что** (*adv. and conj.*) just, only just; **он т. что позвони́л** he has just rung up. **3.** *conj.* (**+как, лишь**) as soon as; one has only to ...; **т. ска́жешь, я уйду́** you have only to say (the word) and I will go. **4.** *conj.* only, but; **с удово́льствием, т. не сего́дня** with pleasure, only not today. **5.**: **т. бы** (*+inf.*) (*particle*) if only; **т. бы получи́ть о нём ве́сточку** if only we could hear news of him. **6.** *particle intensifying interrog. prons. and advs.*: **заче́м т.?** why on earth?; **где т. они́ не быва́ли?** where have they *not* been?
том, а, *pl.* **~а́, ~о́в** *m.* volume.
томага́вк, а *m.* tomahawk.
тома́т, а *m.* **1.** tomato. **2.** tomato purée.
тома́тный *adj.* tomato; **т. сок** tomato juice.
то́мик, а *m. dim. of* **том**
томи́тел|ьный (~ен, ~на) *adj.* tedious, wearing; tiresome; agonizing; **т. зной** trying heat; **~ьное ожида́ние** agonizing suspense; tedious wait.
том|и́ть, лю́, и́шь *impf.* (*of* **ис~**) **1.** to tire, wear; to torment; to wear down; **т. в тюрьме́** to leave to languish in prison; **меня́ ~и́т жа́жда** I am parched. **2.** (*cul.*) to stew; to braise.
том|и́ться, лю́сь, и́шься *impf.* **1.** to pine; to languish; **т. жа́ждой** to be parched with thirst; **т. в тюрьме́** to languish in captivity. **2.** *pass. of* **~и́ть**

томле́ни|е, я *nt.* languor.
то́мност|ь, и *f.* languor.
то́м|ный (~ен, ~на́) *adj.* languid, languorous.
тон, а, *pl.* **~ы** *and* **~а́** *m.* **1.** (*pl.* **~ы**) (*mus. and fig.*) tone; **~ом вы́ше** a tone higher; **хоро́ший, дурно́й т.** good, bad form; **зада́ть т.** to set the tone; **перемени́ть т.** to change one's tone; **попа́сть в т.** to hit the right note. **2.** (*pl.* **~а́**) (colour) tone, tint.
тона́льност|ь, и *f.* (*mus.*) key.
то́ненький *adj.* thin; slender, slim.
тонзу́р|а, ы *f.* tonsure.
тонизи́р|овать, ую *impf. and pf.* (*physiol.*) to tone up.
то́ник, а *m.* tonic (water).
тони́ческий[1] *adj.* (*mus.*, *liter.*) tonic.
тони́ческий[2] *adj.* (*physiol.*, *med*) tonic.
то́н|кий (~ок, ~ка́, ~ко) *adj.* **1.** thin; slim; **т. ло́мтик** thin slice; **~кая кишка́** (*anat.*) small intestine. **2.** fine; delicate; refined; **~кое бельё** fine linen; **т. за́пах** delicate perfume; **~кие черты́ лица́** refined features. **3.**: **т. го́лос** thin voice. **4.** (*fig.*) subtle, delicate; fine; **т. кри́тик** shrewd critic; **т. намёк** gentle hint; **~кое разли́чие** subtle, fine, nice distinction. **5.** (*of the senses*) keen. **6.**: **т. сон** light sleep.
то́нко *adv.* **1.** thinly. **2.** subtly, delicately, nicely.
тонкоко́ж|ий (~, ~а) *adj.* thin-skinned.
то́нкост|ь, и *f.* **1.** thinness; slimness. **2.** fineness. **3.** subtlety. **4.** nice point, subtle point; **до ~ей** to a nicety; **вдава́ться в ~и** to split hairs.
то́нн|а, ы *f.* (*metric*) ton, tonne.
тонна́ж, а *m.* tonnage.
тонне́ль = тунне́ль
то́нус, а *m.* (*physiol.*, *med.*) tone.
тон|у́ть, у́, ~ешь *impf.* **1.** (*pf.* **по~**) to sink, go down. **2.** (*pf.* **у~**) to drown. **3.** (*pf.* **у~**) (**в+***p.*) to sink (in); to be lost (in); to be hidden (in, by); **т. в поду́шках** to sink in the pillows; **т. в дела́х** to be up to one's eyes in work.
то́ньше *comp. of* **то́нкий** *and* **то́нко**
топа́з, а *m.* (*min.*) topaz.
топа́з|овый *adj. of* **~**
то́п|ать, аю *impf.* (*pf.* **~нуть**) to stamp; **т. нога́ми** to stamp one's feet.
топ|и́ть[1]**, лю́, ~ишь** *impf.* **1.** to stoke (*a boiler, a stove, etc.*). **2.** to heat.
топ|и́ть[2]**, лю́, ~ишь** *impf.* **1.** to melt (down), render. **2.**: **т. молоко́** to bake milk.
топ|и́ть[3]**, лю́, ~ишь** *impf.* **1.** (*pf.* **по~**) to sink. **2.** (*pf.* **у~**) to drown; (*fig.*, *coll.*) to wreck, ruin.
топ|и́ться[1]**, ~ится** *impf.* (*of a stove, etc.*) to burn, be alight.
топ|и́ться[2]**, ~ится** *impf.* **1.** to melt. **2.** *pass of* **~и́ть**[2]
топ|и́ться[3]**, лю́сь, ~ишься** *impf.* (*of* **у~**) to drown o.s.
то́пк|а[1]**, и** *f.* **1.** stoking. **2.** heating. **3.** furnace.
то́пк|а[2]**, и** *f.* melting (down).
то́п|кий (~ок, ~ка́, ~ко) *adj.* boggy, marshy.
топлён|ый *adj.* melted; **~ое молоко́** baked milk.
то́плив|ный *adj. of* **~о**; **~ная нефть** fuel oil.
то́плив|о, а *nt.* fuel; **жи́дкое т.** fuel oil; **твёрдое т.** solid fuel.
то́п|нуть, ну, нешь *pf. of* **~ать**
топо́граф, а *m.* topographer.
топографи́ческий *adj.* topographical.
топогра́фи|я, и *f.* topography.
то́пол|евый *adj. of* **~ь**
то́пол|ь, я, *pl.* **~и** *and* **~я́** *m.* poplar.
топони́ми|я, и *f.* toponymy.
топо́р, а́ *m.* axe.
топо́рик, а *m.* hatchet.
топори́щ|е, а *nt.* axe-handle.
топо́р|ный (~ен, ~на) *adj.* clumsy, crude; uncouth.
топо́рщ|ить, ит *impf.* (*coll.*) to bristle.

топо́рщ|иться, ится *impf.* (*coll.*) **1.** to bristle (*intrans.*). **2.** to puff up.
то́пот, а *m.* tramp; **ко́нский т.** clatter of horses' hoofs.
топо|та́ть, чу́, ~чешь *impf.* (*coll.*) to stamp; (*of horses*) to clatter.
то́почн|ый *adj.* furnace; **~ая коро́бка** fire-box; **~ое простра́нство** combustion chamber.
то́псел|ь, я *m.* (*naut.*) topsail.
топ|та́ть, чу́, ~чешь *impf.* **1.** to trample (down). **2.** to make dirty (*with one's feet*). **3.** to trample out (*grapes, etc.*); **т. гли́ну** to knead clay.
топ|та́ться, чу́сь, ~чешься *impf.* to stamp; **т. на ме́сте** to mark time (*also fig.*).
топча́к, а́ *m.* treadmill.
топ|ь, и *f.* bog, marsh, swamp.
то́р|а, ы *f.* (*relig.*) Torah, Pentateuch.
то́рб|а, ы *f.* bag; **носи́ться (с+***i.***) как с пи́саной ~ой** (*coll.*) to make a great song and dance (about).
торг[1]**, а, о ~е, на ~у́,** *pl.* **~и́** *m.* **1.** trading; bargaining, haggling. **2.** (*obs.*) market. **3.** (*pl.*) auction; **прода́ть с ~о́в** to sell by auction. **4.** (*pl.*) tender.
торг[2]**, а** *m.* (*abbr. of* ***торго́вая организа́ция***) trading organization.
торг... *comb. form, abbr. of* **торго́вый**
...торг *comb. form, abbr. of* **1. торг**[2]**. 2. торго́вля**
торг|ова́ть, у́ю *impf.* **1.** (*impf. only*) (+*i.*) to trade (in), deal (in), sell. **2.** (*impf. only*) (*of a shop or business*) to be open.
торг|ова́ться, у́юсь *impf.* (*pf.* **с~**) (**с**+*i.*) to bargain (with), haggle (with).
торго́в|ец, ца *m.* merchant; dealer; tradesman; **т. нарко́тиками** drug trafficker *or* pusher.
торго́вк|а, и *f.* stall-holder; woman street-trader.
торго́вл|я, и *f.* trade, commerce; **посы́лочная т.** mail-order.
торго́во-посы́лочн|ый *adj.*: **~ая фи́рма** mail-order firm.
торго́в|ый *adj.* trade, commercial; **т. дом** firm; **~ая пала́та** chamber of commerce; **т. представи́тель** trade representative; **~ое су́дно** merchant ship.
торгпре́д, а *m.* (*abbr. of* ***торго́вый представи́тель***) trade representative.
торгпре́дств|о, а *nt.* (*abbr. of* ***торго́вое представи́тельство***) trade delegation.
торгфло́т, а *m.* merchant navy.
тореадо́р, а *m.* toreador.
тор|е́ц, ца́ *m.* **1.** butt-end, face (*of beam, plank*). **2.** wooden paving-block.
торже́ственност|ь, и *f.* solemnity.
торже́ствен|ный (~, ~на) *adj.* **1.** ceremonial; festive; gala; **т. день** red-letter day; **~ная оде́жда** ceremonial attire. **2.** solemn; **~ная кля́тва** solemn vow.
торжеств|о́, а́ *nt.* **1.** celebration; (*pl.*) festivities. **2.** triumph (= *victory*). **3.** triumph, exultation; **сказа́ть с ~о́м** to say triumphantly.
торжеств|ова́ть, у́ю *impf.* **1.** to celebrate; **т. побе́ду** to celebrate a victory; (*fig.*) to be victorious. **2. (над)** to triumph (over); to exult (over).
торжеству́ющий *adj.* triumphant, exultant.
то́ри *m. indecl.* (*pol.*) Tory.
торма́шк|и: вверх т., вверх ~ами (*coll.*) head over heels, upside down, topsy-turvy.
торможе́ни|е, я *nt.* **1.** (*tech.*) braking. **2.** (*psych.*) inhibition.
то́рмоз, а *m.* **1.** (*pl.* **~а́**) brake. **2.** (*pl.* **~ы**) (*fig.*) brake; drag, hindrance, obstacle.
тормо|зи́ть, жу́, зи́шь *impf.* (*of* **за~**) **1.** (*tech.*) to brake, apply the brake (to). **2.** (*fig.*) to hamper, impede, be a drag (on). **3.** (*psych.*) to inhibit.
тормозн|о́й *adj.* (*tech.*) brake, braking; **т. башма́к** brake-shoe; **~а́я ракéта** retro-rocket.
тормош|и́ть, у́, и́шь *impf.* (*coll.*) **1.** to pull about. **2.** (*fig.*) to pester, plague.
то́рн|ый *adj.* smooth, even; **пойти́ по ~ой доро́ге** (*fig.*) to stick to the beaten track.
торова́т|ый (~, ~а) *adj.* (*coll.*) liberal, generous.
тороп|и́ть, лю́, ~ишь *impf.* (*of* **по~**) **1.** to hurry, hasten; to press. **2.** to precipitate.
тороп|и́ться, лю́сь, ~ишься *impf.* (*of* **по~**) to hurry, be in a hurry, hasten.
торопли́во *adv.* hurriedly, hastily; in a hurry.
торопли́вост|ь, и *f.* hurry, haste.
торопли́в|ый (~, ~а) *adj.* hurried, hasty.
торо́с, а *m.* ice-hummock.
торпе́д|а, ы *f.* torpedo.
торпеди́р|овать, ую *impf. and pf.* to torpedo.
торпе́д|ный *adj. of* **~а; т. аппара́т** torpedo-tube; **т. ка́тер** motor torpedo boat (*abbr.* MTB).
торс, а *m.* trunk; torso.
торт, а *m.* cake.
торф, а *m.* peat.
торфодобы́ч|а, и *f.* peat-extraction, peat-cutting.
торфяни́ст|ый (~, ~а) *adj.* peaty.
торфян|о́й *adj.* peat; **~о́е боло́то** peatbog.
торч|а́ть, у́, и́шь *impf.* **1.** to stick up, stick out; to stand on end. **2.** (*coll.*) to hang about; **т. пе́ред чьи́ми-н. глаза́ми** to be under s.o.'s feet.
торчко́м *adv.* (*coll.*) on end, sticking up.
торше́р, а *m.* standard lamp.
тоск|а́, и́ *f.* **1.** melancholy; anguish; **у неё т. на се́рдце** she is sick at heart; **т. любви́** pangs of love. **2.** ennui, boredom; **сплошна́я т.** a frightful bore. **3.** (**по**+*d. or p.*) longing (for); yearning (for), nostalgia (for); **т. по ро́дине** home-sickness.
тоскли́в|ый (~, ~а) *adj.* **1.** melancholy; depressed. **2.** dull, dreary; **~ая пого́да** depressing weather.
тоск|ова́ть, у́ю *impf.* **1.** to be melancholy, be depressed. **2.** (**по**+*d. or p.*) to long (for), yearn (for), pine (for), miss.
тост[1] **, а** *m.* toast; **провозгласи́ть, предложи́ть, т.** (**за**+*a.*) to toast, drink (to); to propose a toast (to).
тост[2]**, а** *m.* piece of toast; **т. с сы́ром** Welsh rarebit.
то́стер, а *m.* toaster.
тот *m.*, **та** *f.*, **то** *nt.*, *pl.* **те**, *pron.* **1.** (*opp.* **э́тот**) that; (*pl.*) those; **мне бо́льше нра́вится та карти́на** I like that picture better; **в тот раз** on that occasion; **в то вре́мя** then, at that time; **в том слу́чае** in that case. **2.** (*opp.* **э́тот**) the former; (*replacing 3rd pers. sg. pron.*) he; she; it. **3.** (*opp.* **э́тот**) the other; the opposite; **на той стороне́** on the other side; **по ту сто́рону** (+*g.*) beyond, on the other side (of). **4.** (*opp.* **сей** *in certain set phrr.*) that, the other; **то да сё** one thing and another; **ни то ни сё** neither one thing nor another; **поговори́ть о том, о сём** to talk about this and that. **5.** (*opp.* **друго́й, ино́й**) the one; **и тот и друго́й** both; **ни тот ни друго́й** neither; **не тот, так друго́й** if not one, then the other. **6.: тот..., (кото́рый)** the ... (which); **тот, (кто)** the one (who), the person (who); **тот фильм кото́рый вы ви́дели вчера́** the film (which) you saw yesterday; **тот факт, что** the fact that (*see also* **то**[1]). **7.: тот (же), тот (же) са́мый** the same; **одно́ и то же** one and the same thing; **в то же са́мое вре́мя** at the same time; **он тепе́рь не тот** he is not the man he was. **8.** the right; **не тот** the wrong; **э́то тот но́мер?** is this the (right) room?. **9.** +*preps. forms the following conjs.*: **для того́, что́бы** in order that, in order to; **до того́, что** (*i*) until, (*ii*) to such an extent that; **ме́жду тем, как** whereas; **несмотря́ на то, что** in spite of the fact that; **пе́ред тем, как** before; **по́сле того́, как** after; **по ме́ре того́, как** in proportion as; **с тем, что́бы** (*i*) in order to, (*ii*) on condition that, provided that. **10.** *forms part of var. adv. phrr. and particles* (*see also* **то**[1]): **вме́сте с тем** at the same time; **к тому́ же** moreover; **кро́ме того́** besides; **ме́жду тем, тем вре́менем** meanwhile; **со всем тем**

notwithstanding all this; **тем са́мым** hereby; **тому́ наза́д** ago; **и тому́ подо́бное (и т. п.)** and so forth; **и без того́** as it is.

тоталитари́зм, а *m.* (*pol.*) totalitarianism.

тоталита́рный *adj.* (*pol.*) totalitarian.

тота́льный *adj.* total.

тоте́м, а *m.* totem.

тотеми́зм, а *m.* totemism.

то́-то *particle* (*coll.*) **1.** *emph. point of utterance*: **(вот) то́-то, (вот) то́-то и оно́, (вот) то́-то и есть** that's just it; precisely, exactly. **2.** *in exclamations, expr. emotion or emotional judgement*: **то́-то прекра́сно!** there, isn't that lovely! **3.** *expr. reproach, or recalls warning or threat conveyed in previous utterance*: **ну, то́-то же!** well, what did I tell you!

то́тчас *adv.* at once; immediately.

точёный *adj.* **1.** sharpened. **2.** (*tech.*) turned. **3.** (*fig.*; *of bodily features*) finely-moulded, chiselled.

точи́лк|а, и *f.* (*coll.*) steel, knife-sharpener; pencil-sharpener.

точи́л|о, а *nt.* whetstone, grindstone.

точи́льный *adj.* grinding, sharpening; **т. ка́мень** whetstone, grindstone; **т. реме́нь** strop.

точи́льщик, а *m.* grinder.

точ|и́ть[1], **у́, ~́ишь** *impf.* **1.** (*pf* **на~**) to sharpen; to grind; to hone; **т. зу́бы на кого́-н.** to have a grudge against s.o. **2.** (*impf. only*) to turn (*on a lathe*).

точ|и́ть[2], **у́, ~́ишь** *impf.* to eat away, gnaw away; to corrode; (*fig.*) to gnaw (at), prey (upon).

точ|и́ться, ~́ится *impf.*, *pass. of* **~и́ть**[1,2]

то́чк|а[1], **и** *f.* **1.** spot, dot; **бе́лое пла́тье в ро́зовых ~ах** white dress with pink spots; **ста́вить ~и на „и"** to dot one's 'i's' (and cross one's 't's'). **2.** (*gram*) full stop; **т. с запято́й** semicolon; **поста́вить ~у** to place a full stop; (*fig.*) to finish, come to the end. **3.** (*mus.*) dot. **4.** (*math.*, *phys.*, *tech.*) point; **т. опо́ры** fulcrum, point of support; **мёртвая т.** dead point, dead centre; (*fig.*) standstill; **дойти́ до мёртвой ~и** to come to a standstill, to a full stop. **5.** (*mil.*) point; **т. попада́ния** point of impact; **т. прице́ливания** point of aim. **6.: т. замерза́ния, кипе́ния, плавле́ния** freezing, boiling, melting point. **7.** (*fig.*) point; **т. зре́ния** point of view; **т. соприкоснове́ния** point of contact; **горя́чая т.** trouble spot; **т. в ~у** (*coll.*) exactly; to the letter; **попа́сть в (са́мую) ~у** (*coll.*) to hit the nail on the head; **до ~и** (*coll.*) to the limit, to the extreme point; **дойти́ до ~и** (*coll.*) to come to the end of one's tether.

то́чк|а[2], **и** *f.* **1.** sharpening; grinding. **2.** (*tech.*) turning (*on a lathe*).

то́чно[1] *adv.* **1.** exactly, precisely; punctually; **приходи́те, пожа́луйста, т. в час** please, come at one o'clock sharp. **2.: т. так** just so, exactly, precisely; **т. тако́й (же)** just the same. **3.** indeed.

то́чно[2] *particle* (*coll.*) yes; true; **так т.** (*in mil. parlance*) yes, sir!

то́чно[3] *conj.* as though, as if; like; **он там стоя́л т. окамене́лый** he stood there as if turned to stone.

то́чност|ь, и *f.* exactness; precision; accuracy; punctuality; **в ~и** exactly; accurately; to the letter; **вы́числить с ~ью до...** to calculate to within ...; **с ~ью часово́го механи́зма** like clockwork.

то́ч|ный (~ен, ~на́, ~но) *adj.* exact, precise; accurate; punctual; **~ная бомбардиро́вка** precision bombing; **~ные нау́ки** exact sciences; **т. прибо́р** precision instrument; **т. челове́к** punctual person.

то́чь-в-то́чь *adv.* (*coll.*) exactly; word for word; **он — т.-в-т. оте́ц** he is the spit and image of his father.

тошн|и́ть, и́т *impf.* (*impers.*): **меня́**, *etc.*, **~и́т** I, *etc.*, feel sick; **меня́ от э́того ~и́т** (*fig.*) it makes me sick, it sickens me.

то́шно *as pred.* (*coll.*) **1. мне,** *etc.*, **т.** I, *etc.*, feel sick; (*fig.*) I, *etc.*, feel wretched, awful. **2.** (*+inf.*) it is sickening, it makes one sick, it is nauseating.

тошнот|а́, ы *f.* sickness, nausea (*also fig.*); **испы́тывать ~у́** to feel sick; **у́тренняя т.** morning sickness.

тошнотво́р|ный (~ен, ~на) *adj.* sickening, nauseating (*also fig.*).

то́ш|ный (~ен, ~на́, ~но) *adj.* (*coll.*) **1.** tiresome, tedious. **2.** sickening, nauseating.

тоща́|ть, ю *impf.* (*of* **о~**) (*coll.*) to become thin.

то́щ|ий (~, ~а́, ~е) *adj.* **1.** gaunt, emaciated; skinny. **2.** empty; **на т. желу́док** on an empty stomach. **3.** poor (= *with low content of some substance*); **~ее мя́со** lean meat; **~ая по́чва** poor soil.

тпру *int.* (*to horses*) wo!; whoa!

трав|а́, ы́, *pl.* **~́ы** *f.* grass; herb; **лека́рственные ~́ы** medicinal herbs; **морска́я т.** sea-weed; **со́рная т.** weed; **хоть т. не расти́** (*coll.*) (everything else) can go to hell.

трави́нк|а, и *f.* blade of grass.

трав|и́ть[1], **лю́, ~́ишь** *impf.* **1.** (*pf.* **вы́~**) to exterminate. **2.** (*coll.*) to poison. **3.** (*pf.* **вы́~**) to etch. **4.** (*pf.* **по~**) (*of cattle, etc.*) to trample down. **5.** (*pf.* **за~**) to hunt; (*fig.*) to persecute, torment.

трав|и́ть[2], **лю́, ~́ишь** *impf.* (*naut.*) to pay out (*rope*).

трав|и́ться[1], **лю́сь, ~́ишься** *impf.* (*coll.*) to poison o.s.

трав|и́ться[2], **лю́сь, ~́ишься** *impf.*, *pass. of* **~и́ть**[1,2]

тра́в|ка, ки *f. dim of* **~а́**

травле́ни|е, я *nt.* **1.** extermination. **2.** etching.

тра́вленый[1] *adj.* etched.

тра́вленый[2] *adj.* hunted.

тра́вл|я, и *f.* hunting; (*fig.*) persecution, tormenting.

тра́вм|а, ы *f.* (*med.*) trauma, injury.

травмати́зм, а *m.* (*med.*) traumatism; (*collect.*) injuries; **произво́дственный т.** industrial injuries.

травмати́ческий *adj.* (*med.*, *psych.*) traumatic.

травматологи́ческий *adj.*: **т. пункт** casualty (department).

травми́р|овать, ую *impf. and pf.* to traumatize.

травокоси́лк|а, и *f.* lawn mower.

траволече́ни|е, я *n.* herbal medicine.

травоя́дный *adj.* herbivorous.

травяни́ст|ый (~, ~а) *adj.* **1.** grass; herbaceous. **2.** grassy. **3.** (*coll.*) tasteless, insipid.

травян|о́й *adj.* **1.** grass; herbaceous. **2.** grassy; **т. цвет** grass-green. **3.: ~а́я насто́йка** herb-tea.

траге́ди|я, и *f.* tragedy.

траги́зм, а *m.* tragic element.

тра́гик, а *m.* **1.** tragic actor. **2.** tragedian.

трагикоме́ди|я, и *f.* tragicomedy.

трагикоми́ческий *adj.* tragicomic.

траги́ческ|ий *adj.* tragic; **т. актёр** tragic actor.

траги́чност|ь, и *f.* tragedy, tragic nature.

траги́ч|ный (~ен, ~на) *adj.* tragic (= *sad, terrible*; *not in theatr. sense*).

традицио́н|ный (~ен, ~на) *adj.* traditional.

тради́ци|я, и *f.* tradition.

траекто́ри|я, и *f.* trajectory.

тракт, а *m.* **1.** high road, highway; **желу́дочно-кише́чный т.** (*anat.*) alimentary canal. **2.** route.

тракта́т, а *m.* **1.** treatise. **2.** treaty.

тракти́р, а *m.* (*obs.*) inn, eating-house.

тракти́р|ный *adj. of* **~**

тракти́рщик, а *m.* (*obs.*) innkeeper.

тракт|ова́ть, у́ю *impf.* **1.** (**о**+*p.*) to treat (of), discuss. **2.** to interpret (*a part in a play, etc.*).

тракт|ова́ться, у́ется *impf.* to be treated, be discussed.

тракто́вк|а, и *f.* treatment; interpretation.

тра́ктор, а *m.* tractor; **т. на гу́сеничном ходу́, гу́сеничный т.** caterpillar tractor.

трактори́ст, а *m.* tractor driver.

тра́ктор|ный *adj. of* **~**; **т. парк** fleet of tractors; **на ~ной тя́ге** tractor-drawn.

трал, а *m.* **1.** trawl. **2.** (*mil.*) mine-sweep.
трáл|ить, ю, ишь *impf.* **1.** to trawl. **2.** (*mil.*) to sweep.
трáльщик, а *m.* **1.** trawler. **2.** (*mil.*) mine-sweeper.
трамб|овáть, ýю *impf.* to ram.
трамвá|й, я *m.* tram(-car); **речнóй т.** river bus.
трамвáй|ный *adj. of* **~**; **~ные рéльсы** tram-lines.
трамвáйщик, а *m.* tram worker.
трампли́н, а *m.* (*sport and fig.*) spring-board; jumping-off place, ski-jump.
транжи́р, а *m.* (*coll.*) spendthrift.
транжи́р|а, ы *c.g.* = **~**
транжи́р|ить, ю, ишь *impf.* (*of* **рас~**) (*coll.*) to blow, squander.
транзи́т, а *m.* transit.
транзи́т|ный *adj. of* **~**; **~ная ви́за** transit visa.
транквилизáтор, а *m.* tranquillizer.
транс, а *m.* trance.
транс... *pref.* trans-.
трансагéнтств|о, а *nt.* (*abbr. of* ***трáнспортное агéнтство***) removal company.
трансатланти́ческий *adj.* transatlantic.
транскриби́р|овать, ую *impf. and pf.* to transcribe.
транскри́пци|я, и *f.* transcription.
трансли́р|овать, ую *impf. and pf.* to broadcast, transmit (*by radio*); to relay.
транслитерáци|я, и *f.* transliteration.
трансля́ци|я, и *f.* broadcast, transmission.
трансмисс|иóнный *adj. of* **~и́я**
трансми́сси|я, и *f.* (*tech.*) transmission.
транснационáльный *adj.* multinational.
транспарáнт, а *m.* **1.** black-lined paper (*placed under unruled writing-paper*). **2.** transparency; banner.
трансплантáци|я, и *f.* (*med.*) transplantation.
транспони́р|овать, ую *impf. and pf.* (*mus.*) to transpose.
транспони́ровк|а, и *f.* (*mus.*) transposition.
трáнспорт, а *m.* **1.** transport. **2.** transportation. **3.** consignment. **4.** (*mil.*) train, transport. **5.** (*naut.*) transport, supply ship; troopship.
транспóрт, а *m.* (*book-keeping*) carrying forward.
транспортáбел|ьный (~ен, ~ьна) *adj.* transportable, mobile.
транспортёр, а *m.* **1.** (*tech.*) conveyor. **2.** (*mil.*) carrier.
транспорти́р, а *m.* protractor.
транспорти́ровать[1], **ую** *impf. and pf.* to transport.
транспорти́р|овать[2], **ую** *impf. and pf.* (*book-keeping*) to carry forward.
транспорти́ровк|а, и *f.* transport, transportation.
трáнспортник, а *m.* transport worker.
трáнспорт|ный *adj. of* **~**
транссексуали́ст, а *m.* transsexual.
транссиби́рск|ий *adj.* Trans-Siberian; **~ая магистрáль** the Trans-Siberian Railway.
трансформáтор[1], **а** *m.* (*elec.*) transformer.
трансформáтор[2], **а** *m.* **1.** quick-change actor. **2.** conjuror, illusionist.
трансформáци|я, и *f.* transformation.
трансформи́р|овать, ую *impf. and pf.* to transform.
трансцендентáльный *adj.* (*phil.*) transcendental.
трансцендéнт|ный (~ен, ~на) *adj.* (*phil., math.*) transcendental.
траншé|йный *adj. of* **~я**
траншé|я, и *f.* (*mil.*) trench.
трап, а *m.* (*naut.*) ladder; (*aeron.*) gangway.
трáпéз|а, ы *f.* **1.** dining-table (*esp. in a monastery*). **2.** meal. **3.** refectory.
трáпез|ный *adj. of* **~а**; *as n.* **~ная, ~ной** *f.* refectory.
трапéци|я, и *f.* **1.** (*math.*) trapezium. **2.** trapeze.
трáсс|а, ы *f.* **1.** line, course; direction; **воздýшная т.** airway. **2.** route.
трассáнт, а *m.* (*fin.*) drawer.
трасси́р|овать, ую *impf. and pf.* to mark out, trace.
трасси́р|ующий *pres. part. act. of* **~овать** *and adj.* (*mil.*) tracer; **~ующая пýля** tracer bullet.
трáт|а, ы *f.* expenditure; **пустáя т. врéмени** waste of time.
трá|тить, чу, тишь *impf.* (*of* **ис~** *and* **по~**) to spend, expend, use up; to waste.
трá|титься, чусь, тишься *impf.* (*of* **ис~** *and* **по~**) (**на**+*a.*; *coll.*) to spend one's money (on), spend up (on).
трáулер, а *m.* trawler.
трáур, а *m.* mourning.
трáурн|ый *adj.* **1.** mourning; funeral; **т. марш** funeral march; **~ое шéствие** funeral procession. **2.** mournful, sorrowful; funereal.
трафарéт, а *m.* **1.** stencil; **раскрáсить, расписáть по ~у** to stencil. **2.** engraved inscription. **3.** (*fig.*) conventional, stereotyped pattern; cliché.
трафарéт|ный *adj.* **1.** stencilled; **т. рисýнок** stencil drawing. **2. (~ен, ~на)** (*fig.*) conventional, stereotyped; hackneyed.
трах *int.* bang!
трáх|ать, аю *impf. of* **~нуть**
трáх|аться, аюсь *impf. of* **~нуться**
трахéйный *adj.* (*anat.*) tracheal.
трахеотоми́|я, и *f.* (*med.*) tracheotomy.
трахé|я, и *f.* (*anat.*) trachea, windpipe.
трáх|нуть, ну, нешь pf. (*of* **~ать**) (*coll.*) **1.** to bang, crash; **т. из ружья́** to loose off with a gun. **2.** (*vulg.*) to screw, hump.
трáх|нуться, нусь, нешься *pf.* (*of* **~аться**) (*vulg.*) to screw, hump.
трахóм|а, ы *f.* (*med.*) trachoma.
трéбовани|е, я *nt.* **1.** demand, request; **по ~ю** on demand, by request; **по ~ю** (+*g.*) at the request (of); **по ~ю судá** by order of the court. **2.** demand, claim; **согласи́ться на чьи-н. ~я** to agree to s.o.'s demands. **3.** requirement, condition; **отвечáть ~ям** to meet requirements. **4.** (*pl.*) aspirations; needs. **5.** requisition, order; **т. на тóпливо** fuel requisition.
трéбовател|ьный (~ен, ~ьна) *adj.* demanding, exacting; particular.
трéб|овать, ую *impf.* (*of* **по~**) **1.** (+*g. or* **+чтóбы**) to demand, request, require; **т. извинéния у когó-н.** to demand an apology from s.o. **2.** (*impf. only*) (+*g.* **от**) to expect (from), ask (of). **3.** (*pf.* **по~**) (+*g.*) to require, need, call (for); **т. немéдленного решéния** to require an immediate decision. **4.** to send for, call, summon.
трéб|оваться, уется *impf.* (*of* **по~**) **1.** to be needed, be required; **на э́то ~уется мнóго врéмени** it takes a lot of time; **что и ~овалось доказáть** (*math.*) Q.E.D. (*abbr. of* quod erat demonstrandum). **2.** *pass. of* **~овать**
требух|á, и́ *no pl., f.* **1.** entrails; (*cul.*) offal, tripe. **2.** (*fig., coll.*) tripe, rubbish.
тревóг|а, и *f.* **1.** alarm, anxiety. **2.** alarm, alert; **воздýшная т.** air-raid warning, alert; **пожáрная т.** fire-alarm; **бить ~у** to sound the alarm (*also fig.*).
тревóж|ить, у, ишь *impf.* **1.** (*of* **вс~**) to alarm; worry, trouble. **2.** (*pf.* **по~**) to disturb, interrupt. **3.** to annoy, bait; **не т.** to leave alone.
тревóж|иться, усь, ишься *impf.* **1.** to worry, be alarmed, be uneasy. **2.** (*pf.* **по~**) to trouble o.s., put o.s. out; **не ~ьтесь!** don't bother (yourself)!
тревóж|ный (~ен, ~на) *adj.* **1.** anxious, uneasy, troubled. **2.** alarming, disturbing; **~ные слýхи** alarming reports. **3.** alarm; **т. звонóк** alarm (bell).
треволнéни|е, я *nt.* (*now coll., joc.*) agitation, disquiet.
трéзвенник, а *m.* teetotaller, abstainer.
трéзвеннически|ий *adj.* temperance; **~ое движéние** temperance movement.

трезвé|ть, ю *impf.* (*of* **о~**) to sober (up), become sober.
трезвóн, а *m.* **1.** peal (of bells). **2.** (*coll., joc.*) talk, gossip. **3.** (*coll., pej.*) row, shindy.
трезвóн|ить, ю, ишь *impf.* **1.** to ring (a peal). **2.** (**о**+*p.*; *coll.*) to noise abroad; to proclaim.
трéзвост|ь, и *f.* **1.** soberness, sobriety (*also fig.*). **2.** abstinence; temperance.
трезвýчи|е, я *nt.* (*mus.*) triad.
трéзв|ый (~, ~á, ~о) *adj.* **1.** sober (*also fig.*). **2.** teetotal, abstinent.
трезýб|ец, ца *m.* trident.
трек, а *m.* (*sport*) track.
трел|ь, и *f.* (*mus.*) trill; warble.
трелья́ж, а *m.* **1.** trellis. **2.** three-leaved mirror.
трéмоло *nt. indecl.* (*mus.*) tremolo.
тренажёр, а *m.* training apparatus; **гребнóй т.** rowing machine; **лётный т.** flight simulator.
трéнер, а *m.* (*sport*) trainer, coach.
трéнзел|ь, я, *pl.* **~и** *and* **~я́** *m.* snaffle.
трéни|е, я *nt.* **1.** friction, rubbing. **2.** (*pl., fig.*) friction.
тренир|овáть, ýю *impf.* (*of* **на~**) to train, coach.
тренир|овáться, ýюсь *impf.* (*of* **на~**) to train o.s., coach o.s.; to be in training.
тренирóвк|а, и *f.* training, coaching.
тренирóвочный *adj.* training; practice.
тренóг|а, и *f.* tripod.
тренóгий *adj.* three-legged.
тренóж|ить, у, ишь *impf.* (*of* **с~**) to hobble.
тренóжник, а *m.* tripod.
трéнька|ть, ю *impf.* (*coll.*) to strum.
трепáк, á *m.* trepak (*Russ. folk-dance*).
трепáл|о, а *nt.* (*tech.*) swingle, scutcher.
трёпаный *adj.* **1.** torn, tattered. **2.** dishevelled.
треп|áть, лю́, ~́лешь *impf.* **1.** (*pf.* **по~**) to pull about; (*of the wind*) to blow about; to dishevel, tousle; **т. когó-н. за вóлосы** to pull s.o.'s hair; **т. языкóм** (*coll.*) to prattle, blather; **т. чьи-н. нéрвы** to get on s.o.'s nerves; **егó ~́лет лихорáдка** he is feverish. **2.** (*pf.* **по~**) (*coll.*) to tear; to wear out.
треп|áться, лю́сь, ~́лешься *impf.* **1.** (*pf.* **по~**) to tear, fray; to wear out. **2.** (*impf. only*) to flutter, blow about.
трéпет, а *m.* trembling, quivering (*from fear, etc. or from pleasurable sensation*); **быть в ~е** to be a-tremble, be in a dither.
трепе|тáть, щý, ~́щешь *impf.* **1.** to tremble, quiver; to flicker; to palpitate. **2.** (*fig.*) to tremble; to thrill, palpitate; **т. от востóрга** to thrill with joy.
трéпетный *adj.* **1.** trembling; flickering; palpitating. **2.** anxious. **3.** timid.
трёпк|а, и *f.* **1.** (*coll.*) dressing-down, scolding. **2.: т. нéрвов** nervous strain.
трепыхá|ться, юсь *impf.* (*coll.*) to flutter, quiver.
треск, а *m.* **1.** crack; crackle, crackling; **т. ломáющихся сýчьев** snapping of twigs; **т. мотóра** popping of an engine; **с ~́ом провали́ться** (*fig., coll.*) to flop. **2.** (*fig., coll.*) noise, fuss.
треск|á, и́ *f.* cod.
трéска|ться[1], ется *impf.* (*of* **по~**) to crack; to chap.
трéска|ться[2], юсь *impf. of* **трéснуться**
треск|óвый *adj. of* **~á; т. жир** cod-liver oil.
трескотн|я́, и́ *f.* (*coll.*) **1.** crackle, crackling; chirring (*of grasshoppers*). **2.** (*fig.*) chatter.
трескýч|ий (~, ~а) *adj.* **1.** (*pej.*) highfalutin(g), high-flown. **2.: т. морóз** hard frost, ringing frost.
трéсн|уть, у, ешь *pf.* **1.** to snap, crackle, pop. **2.** to crack; to chap; (*fig., coll.*) to crash, flop. **3.** (+*i.* **по**+*d.* *or* +*a.* **по**+*d.*; *coll.*) to bring down with a crash (on); to hit, bang; **т. кулакóм по столý** to bang one's fist on the table.
трéс|нуться, нусь, нешься *pf.* (*of* **~каться**[2]) (+*i.* **о**+*a.*; *coll.*) to bang (against); **т. головóй о двéрцу шкáфа** to bang one's head against the door of a cupboard.
трест, а *m.* (*econ.*) trust.
третéйский *adj.* arbitration; **т. суд** arbitration tribunal; **т. судья́** arbitrator.
трéт|ий, ья, ье *adj.* **1.** third; **т. нóмер** number three; **полови́на ~ьего** half past two; **~ьего дня** the day before yesterday; **~ье лицó** (*gram.*) third person; **~ья сторонá** third party. **2.** *as n.* **~ье, ~ьего** *nt.* sweet, dessert.
трети́р|овать, ую *impf.* to slight.
трети́чный *adj.* (*geol., chem., etc.*) tertiary, ternary.
трет|ь, и, *pl.* **~́и, ~éй** *f.* third.
третьесóртный *adj.* third-rate.
третьестепéнный *adj.* **1.** insignificant. **2.** third-rate.
треугóлк|а, и *f.* cocked hat.
треугóльник, а *m.* triangle.
треугóльный *adj.* three-cornered, triangular.
трефнóй *adj.* (*of food*) tref, non-kosher.
трéфовый *adj.* (*cards*) of clubs.
трéф|ы, ~ *pl.* (*sg.* **~а, ~ы** *f.*) (*cards*) clubs; **дáма ~** queen of clubs.
трёх... *comb. form* three-, tri-.
трёхвалéнтный *adj.* (*chem.*) trivalent.
трёхвёрст|ка, ки *f.* = **~ная кáрта**
трёхгоди́чный *adj.* three-year.
трёхгодовáлый *adj.* three-year-old.
трёхгрáнный *adj.* three-edged; (*math.*) trihedral.
трёхднéвн|ый *adj.* three-day.
трёхколёсный *adj.* three-wheeled; **т. велосипéд** tricycle.
трёхлéти|е, я *nt.* **1.** period of three years. **2.** third anniversary.
трёхлéтний *adj.* **1.** three-year. **2.** three-year-old.
трёхмéрный *adj.* three-dimensional.
трёхмéстный *adj.* three-seater.
трёхмéсячный *adj.* **1.** three-month; quarterly. **2.** three-month-old.
трёхнедéльный *adj.* **1.** three-week. **2.** three-week-old.
трёхслóжный *adj.* trisyllabic.
трёхслóйный *adj.* three-layered; three-ply.
трёхсотлéти|е, я *nt.* **1.** three hundred years. **2.** tercentenary.
трёхсотлéтний *adj.* **1.** of three hundred years. **2.** tercentennial.
трёхсóтый *adj.* three-hundredth.
трёхсторóнний *adj.* **1.** three-sided; (*math.*) trilateral. **2.** tripartite.
трёхцвéтный *adj.* three-coloured; tricolour(ed).
трёхчасовóй *adj.* **1.** three-hour. **2.** three o'clock.
трёхчлéн, а *m.* (*math.*) trinomial.
трёхчлéн|ный *adj. of* **~**
трёхэтáжный *adj.* three-storeyed.
трещ|áть, ý, и́шь *impf.* **1.** to crack; (*fig.*) to crack up; **у меня́ головá ~и́т** I have a splitting headache. **2.** to crackle; (*of furniture*) to creak; (*of grasshoppers*) to chirr; **~áт морóзы** there is a ringing frost. **3.** (*coll.*) to jabber, chatter.
трéщин|а, ы *f.* crack, split (*also fig.*); fissure; chap (*of skin*); **дать ~у** to crack, split.
трещóтк|а, и *f. and c.g.* **1.** *f.* rattle. **2.** *c.g.* (*fig., coll.*) chatterbox.
три, трёх, трём, тремя́, о трёх *num.* three.
триáд|а, ы *f.* triad.
триангуля́ци|я, и *f.* (*math., geod.*) triangulation.
триáсовый *adj.* (*geol.*) Triassic.
трибýн, а *m.* (*hist. or rhet.*) tribune.
трибýн|а, ы *f.* **1.** platform, rostrum. **2.** stand (*at sports stadiums*).
трибунáл, а *m.* tribunal.
тривиáльност|ь, и *f.* triviality, banality.
тривиáл|ьный (~ен, ~ьна) *adj.* trivial, banal; trite.

тригонометри́ческий *adj.* trigonometric(al).
тригономе́три|я, и *f.* trigonometry.
три́девять: за т. земе́ль (*in legends and fig., coll.*) at the other end of the world.
тридцатиле́ти|е, я *nt.* **1.** thirty years. **2.** thirtieth anniversary.
тридцатиле́тний *adj.* **1.** thirty-year. **2.** thirty-year-old.
тридца́т|ый *adj.* thirtieth; **~ые го́ды** the thirties.
три́дцат|ь, и́, *i.* **ью́** *num.* thirty.
три́жды *adv.* three times, thrice.
тризм, а *m.* (*med.*) lockjaw, trismus.
трико́ *nt. indecl.* **1.** tricot (*woollen fabric*). **2.** tights; leotard, body stocking.
трикота́ж, а *m.* **1.** jersey. **2.** (*collect.*) knitwear.
трикота́жн|ый *adj.* jersey; knitted; **~ые изде́лия** knitwear; **~ая фа́брика** knitted goods factory.
триктра́к, а *m.* backgammon.
трили́стник, а *m.* (*bot.*) trefoil.
три́ллер, а *m.* thriller (*book, film etc.*).
триллио́н, а *m.* trillion.
трило́ги|я, и *f.* trilogy.
триме́стр, а *m.* term (*at educational establishment*).
трина́дцатый *adj.* thirteenth.
трина́дцат|ь, и *num.* thirteen.
три́о *nt. indecl.* (*mus.*) trio.
трио́д, а *m.* (*radio*) triode.
трио́л|ь, и *f.* (*mus.*) triplet.
три́плекс, а *m.* triplex (*safety glass*).
три́ппер, а *m.* (*med.*) gonorrhoea.
трипси́н, а *m.* (*biol.*) trypsin.
три́ста, трёхсо́т, трёмста́м, тремяста́ми, трёхста́х *num.* three hundred.
трито́н, а *m.* (*zool.*) triton; newt.
триумвира́т, а *m.* triumvirate.
триу́мф, а *m.* triumph.
триумфа́льный *adj.* triumphal.
тро́гател|ьный (~ен, ~ьна) *adj.* touching; moving.
тро́га|ть[1]**, ю** *impf.* (*of* **тро́нуть**) **1.** to touch. **2.** to disturb; **не ~й его́!** don't disturb him! **3.** to touch, move, affect; **т. до слёз** to move to tears.
тро́га|ть[2]**, ю** *impf.* (*of* **тро́нуть**) (*coll.*) to start; **ну ~й!** go ahead!; get going!
тро́га|ться[1]**, юсь** *impf.* (*of* **тро́нуться**[1]) *pass. of* **~ть**[1]; to be touched, moved, be affected.
тро́га|ться[2]**, юсь** *impf. of* **тро́нуться**[2]
троглоди́т, а *m.* troglodyte (*also fig. of a person*).
тро́е, трои́х *num.* (*preceding m. nn. denoting living beings and pluralia tantum*) three; **т. су́ток** seventy-two hours.
троекра́тный *adj.* thrice-repeated.
Тро́иц|а, ы *f.* **1.** (*theol.*) Trinity. **2.** (*eccl.*) Trinity; Whitsun(day). **3.** (*coll.*) trio.
Тро́ицын *adj.*: **Т. день** Trinity; Whitsun(day).
тро́йк|а, и *f.* **1.** three. **2.** (*school mark*) three (*out of five*). **3.** (*cards*) the three (*of a suit*). **4.** troika. **5.** (*coll.*) three-piece suit. **6.** No. 3 bus, tram, *etc.*
тройн|о́й *adj.* triple, threefold, treble; **т. кана́т** three-ply rope; **в ~о́м разме́ре** threefold, treble.
тро́йн|я, и *f.* triplets.
тро́йственн|ый *adj.* triple; tripartite.
тролле́йбус, а *m.* trolleybus.
тролле́йбус|ный *adj. of* **~**
тромб, а *m.* (*med.*) clot of blood.
тромбо́з, а *m.* (*med.*) thrombosis.
тромбо́н, а *m.* trombone.
тромбони́ст, а *m.* trombonist.
трон, а *m.* throne.
тро́н|ный *adj. of* **~**; **т. зал** throne-room.
тро́|нуть, ну, нешь *pf. of* **~гать**
тро́|нуться[1]**, нусь, нешься** *pf.* **1.** *pf. of* **~гаться**[1]. **2.** (*pf. only*) (*fig., coll.*) to be touched (= *to lose one's mind*).
тро́|нуться[2]**, нусь, нешься** *pf.* (*of* **~гаться**[2]) to start, set out; **т. с ме́ста** to make a move, get going; **по́езд ~нулся** the train started; **лёд ~нулся** the ice has begun to break (*also fig.*).
троп|а́, ы́, *pl.* **~́ы, ~, ~́ам** *f.* path.
тро́пик, а *m.* (*geog.*) **1.** tropic; **т. Ра́ка** tropic of Cancer; **т. Козеро́га** tropic of Capricorn. **2.** (*pl.*) the tropics.
тропи́нк|а, и *f.* path.
тропи́ческ|ий *adj.* tropical; **~ая лихора́дка** jungle fever; **т. по́яс** torrid zone.
тропосфе́р|а, ы *f.* (*meteor.*) troposphere.
трос, а *m.* rope, cable, hawser.
трости́нк|а, и *f.* thin reed.
тростни́к, а́ *m.* reed; rush; **са́харный т.** sugar-cane.
тростнико́вый *adj.* reed; **т. са́хар** cane-sugar.
тро́сточк|а, и *f.* = **трость**
трост|ь, и, *pl.* **~́и, ~е́й** *f.* cane, walking-stick.
троти́л, а *m.* (*chem., mil.*) trinitrotoluene (*abbr.* TNT).
тротуа́р, а *m.* pavement.
трофе́|й, я *m.* trophy (*also fig.*); (*pl.*) spoils of war, booty; captured material.
трофе́йный *adj.* (*mil.*) captured.
трохеи́ческий *adj.* (*liter.*) trochaic.
трохе́|й, я *m.* (*liter.*) trochee.
троцки́ст, а *m.* Trotskyite, Trotskyist.
троюро́дн|ый *adj.*: **т. брат, ~ая сестра́** second cousin.
троя́кий *adj.* threefold, triple.
троя́нский *adj.*: **т. конь** Trojan horse.
труб|а́, ы́, *pl.* **~́ы** *f.* **1.** pipe; tube. **2.** chimney-flue; funnel, smoke-stack. **3.** (*mus.*) trumpet; **игра́ть на ~е́** to play the trumpet. **4.** (*anat.*) tube; duct. **5.** *as symbol of failure or ruin*: **вы́лететь в ~у́** (*coll.*) to go bust, go smash; **пусти́ть в ~у́** to blow, squander.
трубаду́р, а *m.* troubadour.
труба́ч, а́ *m.* trumpeter; trumpet-player.
труб|и́ть, лю́, и́шь *impf.* **1.** (**в**+*a.*; *mus.*) to blow. **2.** (*of trumpets, etc.*) to sound; to blare. **3.** to sound (*by blast of trumpet, etc.*); **т. сбор** (*mil.*) to sound assembly. **4.** (**о**+*p.*; *coll.*) to trumpet, proclaim.
тру́бк|а, и *f.* **1.** tube; pipe; **сверну́ть ~ой** to roll up. **2.** (tobacco-)pipe; **наби́ть ~у** to fill a pipe. **3.** (*mil., etc.*) fuse. **4.** (*telephone*) receiver.
трубкозу́б, а *m.* (*zool.*) aardvark.
тру́бный *adj.* trumpet; **т. сигна́л** trumpet-call.
трубопрово́д, а *m.* pipe-line; piping, tubing.
трубочи́ст, а *m.* chimney-sweep.
тру́бочный *adj. of* **тру́бка; т. таба́к** pipe tobacco.
тру́бчатый *adj.* tubular.
труд, а́ *m.* **1.** labour, work. **2.** difficulty, trouble; **взять на себя́ т., дать себе́ т.** (*+inf.*) to take the trouble (to); **не сто́ит ~а́** it is not worth the trouble; **с ~о́м** with difficulty, hardly. **3.** (scholarly) work; (*pl., in titles of scholarly periodicals, etc.*) transactions.
тру|ди́ться, жу́сь, ~́дишься *impf.* to toil, labour, work; **не ~ди́тесь!** (please) don't trouble.
тру́дно *as pred.* it is hard, it is difficult; **т. сказа́ть** it is hard to say; **т. мне суди́ть** it is hard for me to tell.
тру́дност|ь, и *f.* difficulty; obstacle.
тру́д|ный (~ен, ~на́, ~но) *adj.* **1.** difficult, hard. **2.** difficult, awkward. **3.** (*coll., of illness*) serious, grave; **т. больно́й** patient seriously ill.
трудов|о́й *adj.* **1.** labour, work; **т. день** day's work; **т. коллекти́в** work force. **2.** working; living on one's own earnings; **т. наро́д** working people. **3.** earned.
трудод|е́нь, ня́ *m.* (*hist.*) work-day (*unit of payment on collective farms*).
трудоём|кий (~ок, ~ка) *adj.* labour-intensive.
трудолюби́в|ый (~, ~а) *adj.* hard-working, industrious.
трудолю́би|е, я *nt.* industriousness.
трудосберега́ющий *adj.* labour-saving.

трудоспосо́бност|ь, и *f.* ability to work.
трудоспосо́б|ный (~ен, ~на) *adj.* able-bodied; capable of working.
трудотерапи́|я, и *f.* occupational therapy.
трудоустро́йств|о, а *nt.* placing in a job; resettlement (*of demobilized servicemen in civilian occupations*).
труд|я́щийся *adj.* working; *as n.* **~я́щиеся, ~я́щихся** the working people, the workers.
тру́женик, а *m.* toiler.
трун|и́ть, ю́, и́шь *impf.* (**над**; *coll.*) to make fun (of), mock.
труп, а *m.* dead body, corpse; carcass.
тру́п|ный *adj. of* ~; **т. за́пах** putrid smell; **~ное разложе́ние** putrefaction; **т. яд** ptomaine.
тру́пп|а, ы *f.* troupe, company.
трус, а *m.* coward.
тру́сик|и, ов *no sg.* **1.** shorts. **2.** swimming trunks. **3.** (under)pants.
тру́|сить, шу, сишь *impf.* (*of* **с~**) **1.** to be a coward; to funk; to have cold feet. **2.** (**пе́ред** *or* +*a.*) to be afraid (of), be frightened (of).
тру|си́ть, шу́, си́шь *impf.* to trot, jog.
труси́х|а, и *f. of* **трус**[1]
трусли́в|ый (~, ~а) *adj.* cowardly.
тру́сост|ь, и *f.* cowardice.
трусц|а́, ы́ *f.* (*coll.*) jog-trot; **бег ~о́й** (*sport*) jogging.
трус|ы́, о́в *no sg.* = **~́ики**
трут, а *m.* tinder.
тру́т|ень, ня *m.* drone (*also fig.*).
трух|а́, и́ *f.* dust (*of rotted wood*); hay-dust; (*fig.*) trash.
трухля́в|ый (~, ~а) *adj.* mouldering; rotten.
трущо́б|а, ы *f.* **1.** overgrown place (*in forest, etc.*). **2.** (*fig.*) out-of-the-way place. **3.** slum.
трын-трава́ *as pred.* (+*d.*; *coll.*) it makes no odds; it's all the same.
трюк, а *m.* **1.** feat, stunt; **рекла́мный т.** advertising gimmick. **2.** (*fig., pej.*) trick.
трюка́ч, а́ *m.* **1.** crafty, wily person. **2.** stuntman.
трю́к|овый *adj. of* ~ **1.**; **т. но́мер** turn.
трюм, а *m.* (*naut.*) hold.
трю́м|ный *adj. of* ~; **~ая вода́** bilge-water.
трюмо́ *nt. indecl.* cheval-glass, pier-glass.
трю́фел|ь, я, *pl.* **~и, ~е́й** *m.* truffle.
тряпи́чник, а *m.* (*obs.*) rag-and-bone man *or* merchant.
тряпи́чный *adj.* rag.
тря́пк|а, и *f.* **1.** rag; duster. **2.** (*pl., coll.*) finery, glad rags. **3.** (*coll., pej.*) milksop, spineless creature.
тряпь|ё, я́ *nt.* (*collect.*) rags.
тряси́н|а, ы *f.* quagmire.
тря́ск|а, и *f.* shaking, jolting.
тря́с|кий (~ок, ~ка) *adj.* **1.** shaky, jolty. **2.** bumpy.
трясогу́зк|а, и *f.* (*zool.*) wagtail.
тряс|ти́, у́, ёшь, *past* **~, ~ла́** *impf.* **1.** to shake. **2.** to shake out. **3.** to cause to shake, cause to shiver (*usu. impers.*); **его́ ~ла́ лихора́дка** he was in the grip of a fever; **её ~ло́ от стра́ха** she was trembling with fear. **4.** (+*i.*) to swing; to shake; **т. гри́вой** (*of an animal*) to toss its mane. **5.** (*coll.*) to jolt.
тряс|ти́сь, у́сь, ёшься, *past* **~́ся, ~ла́сь** *impf.* **1.** to shake; to tremble; **т. от хо́лода** to shiver with cold. **2.** (*coll.*) to bump along; to be jolted. **3.** (**над**; *coll.*) to watch (over) (= *to fear to lose*); **они́ ~у́тся над ка́ждой копе́йкой** they watch every penny.
тряхн|у́ть, у́, ёшь *pf.* **1.** to shake. **2.**: **т. мо́лодостью** (*coll.*) to hark back to (the days of) one's youth. **3.** (+*i.*; *coll.*) to make free (with).
тсс *int.* ssh!; (s)hush!
тт. *abbr. of* **1.** ***това́рищи*** Comrades. **2.** ***тома́*** vols; volumes.
туале́т, а *m.* **1.** dress; toilet. **2.** toilet, dressing. **3.** dressing-table. **4.** lavatory, toilet; **обще́ственный т.** public convenience.
туале́т|ный *adj. of* ~; **~ная бума́га** toilet-paper; **т. сто́лик** dressing-table.
ту́б|а, ы *f.* (*mus.*) tuba.
туберкулёз, а *m.* tuberculosis; **т. лёгких** pulmonary tuberculosis, consumption.
туберкулёз|ный *adj. of* ~; **т. больно́й** tubercular (patient); *as n.* **т., ~ного** *m.* = **т. больно́й**
тубеpо́з|а, ы *f.* (*bot.*) tuberose.
ту́го *adv.* **1.** tight(ly), taut; **т. наби́ть чемода́н** to pack a suitcase tight. **2.** with difficulty; **т. продвига́ться вперёд** to make slow progress. **3.** *as pred.* **т. приходи́ться** (+*d.*; *coll.*) to have difficulties; **с деньга́ми у нас т.** we are in a tight spot financially.
тугоду́м, а *m.* (*coll.*) slow-witted person.
туг|о́й (~, ~а́, ~́о) *adj.* **1.** tight; taut. **2.** tightly-filled; **т. кошелёк** tightly-stuffed purse. **3.**: **т. на́ ухо** hard of hearing. **4.** (*fig., coll.*) tight, close (*with money*); **т. на распла́ту** close-fisted. **5.** (*fig., coll.*) difficult; **дела́ у них ~и́е** they are in a (tight) spot.
туда́ *adv.* there; that way; to the right place; **т. и обра́тно** there and back; **биле́т т. и обра́тно** return ticket; **не т.!** not that way!; **ни т. ни сюда́** neither one way nor the other; **вы не т. попа́ли** (*on telephone*) you have got the wrong number; **т. ему́ и доро́га** (*coll.*) it serves him right.
туда́-сюда́ *adv.* (*coll.*) **1.** hither and thither. **2.** *as pred.* it will do, it will pass muster.
ту́же *comp. of* **туго́й** *and* **ту́го**
туж|и́ть, у́, ~́ишь *impf.* (**о, по**+*p.*; *coll.*) to grieve (for).
ту́ж|иться, усь, ишься *impf.* (*coll.*) to make an effort.
тужу́рк|а, и *f.* (*man's*) double-breasted jacket.
туз, а́ *m.* **1.** (*cards*) ace; **пойти́ с ~а́** to lead an ace. **2.** (*coll.*) bigwig; big shot.
тузе́м|ец, ца *m.* native.
тузе́м|ка, ки *f. of* **~ец**
тузе́мный *adj.* native, indigenous.
ту|зи́ть, жу́, зи́шь *impf.* (*of* **от~**) (*coll.*) to punch; to pummel.
ту́к|ать, аю *impf.* (*of* **~нуть**) (*coll.*) to bash, bonk.
ту́к|нуть, ну, нешь *pf. of* **~ать**
ту́к|нуться, нусь, нешься *pf.* (**о**+*a.*; *coll.*) to bang o.s. (against, on).
ту́ловищ|е, а *nt.* trunk; torso.
тулу́п, а *m.* sheepskin coat.
тул|ья́, ьи́, *g. pl.* **~е́й** *f.* crown (*of headgear*).
тума́к, а́ *m.* (*coll.*) cuff, punch.
тума́н, а *m.* fog; mist, haze.
тума́н|ить, ит *impf.* to dim, cloud, obscure (*also fig.*).
тума́н|иться, ится *impf.* **1.** to grow misty; to become enveloped in mist. **2.** (*fig., coll.*) to be in a fog.
тума́нно *as pred.* it is foggy, it is misty.
тума́нност|ь, и *f.* **1.** fog, mist. **2.** (*astron.*) nebula. **3.** haziness, obscurity.
тума́н|ный (~ен, ~на) *adj.* **1.** foggy; misty; **~ная полоса́** fog patch. **2.** (*fig.*) hazy, obscure, vague.
ту́мб|а, ы *f.* **1.** curbstone; post; **прича́льная т.** (*naut.*) bollard. **2.** pedestal.
ту́мбочк|а, и *f.* **1.** bedside table. **2.** *dim. of* **ту́мба**
ту́ндр|а, ы *f.* (*geog.*) tundra.
ту́ндр|овый *adj. of* **~а**
тун|е́ц, ца́ *m.* tunny(-fish).
тунея́д|ец, ца *m.* parasite, sponger.
тунея́дств|о, а *nt.* parasitism, sponging.
туни́к|а, и *f.* tunic.
тунне́л|ь, я *m.* tunnel; subway.
тупе́|ть, ю *impf.* (*of* **о~**) to become blunt; to grow dull.
ту́пик, а *m.* (*zool.*) puffin.
тупи́к, а́ *m.* **1.** blind alley, cul-de-sac. **2.** (*rail.*) siding. **3.** (*fig.*) impasse, deadlock; **зайти́ в т.** to reach a deadlock. **4.**: **поста́вить в т.** to stump, nonplus; **стать в т.** to be stumped, be at a loss.

туп|и́ть, лю́, ⌣ишь *impf.* to blunt.
туп|и́ться, ⌣ится *impf.* to become blunt.
тупи́ц|а, ы *c.g.* (*coll.*) dolt, blockhead, dimwit.
тупоголо́в|ый (~, ~а) *adj.* (*coll.*) dim-witted.
туп|о́й (~, ~а́, ⌣о) *adj.* **1.** blunt. **2.: т. у́гол** (*math.*) obtuse angle. **3.** (*fig.*) dull (*pain, sensation, etc.*). **4.** (*fig.*) vacant, stupid; **~а́я улы́бка** vacant smile. **5.** (*fig.*) dull, obtuse; **т. ум** dull wits.
ту́пост|ь, и *f.* **1.** bluntness. **2.** (*fig.*) dullness, slowness.
тупоу́ми|е, я *nt.* dullness, obtuseness.
тупоу́м|ный (~ен, ~на) *adj.* dull, obtuse.
тур¹, а *m.* **1.** turn (*in a dance*). **2.** (*at sports and games; also fig.*) round.
тур², а *m.* (*zool.*) **1.** aurochs. **2.** Caucasian wild goat.
тур|а́, ы́ *f.* (*chess*) castle, rook.
турба́з|а, ы *f.* tourist centre.
турби́н|а, ы *f.* (*tech.*) turbine.
турби́нный *adj.* turbine.
турбовинтово́й *adj.* (*tech., aeron.*) turbo-prop.
турбореакти́вный *adj.* (*tech., aeron.*) turbo-jet.
туре́цк|ий *adj.* Turkish; **т. бараба́н** bass drum; **~ие бобы́** haricot beans; **т. горо́х** chick pea.
тури́зм, а *m.* tourism; outdoor pursuits; **во́дный т.** boating; **го́рный т.** mountaineering.
тури́ст, а *m.* tourist; hiker.
туристи́ческ|ий *adj.* tourist; **т. похо́д** walking tour.
тури́стск|ий *adj.* tourist; **~ая ба́за** tourist centre.
туркме́н, а, *g. pl.* **т.** *m.* Turkmen.
Туркмениста́н, а *m.* Turkmenistan.
туркме́н|ка, ки *f. of* **~**
туркме́нский *adj.* Turkmen.
ту́рман, а *m.* tumbler-pigeon.
турне́ *nt. indecl.* tour (*esp. of artistes or sportsmen*).
турне́пс, а *m.* swede.
турни́к, а́ *m.* (*sport*) horizontal bar.
турнике́т, а *m.* **1.** turnstile. **2.** (*med.*) tourniquet.
турни́р, а *m.* tournament (*at chess, etc., also hist.*)
ту́р|ок, ка, *g. pl.* **т.** *m.* Turk.
Ту́рци|я, и *f.* Turkey.
турча́нк|а, и *f. of* **ту́рок**
ту́скл|ый (~, ~а́, ~о) *adj.* **1.** dim, dull; matt; tarnished. **2.** wan; lacklustre. **3.** (*fig.*) dim, dull; colourless; **т. го́лос** flat voice.
тускне́|ть, ет *impf.* (*of* **по~**) **1.** to grow dim; to tarnish; to lose its lustre. **2.** (**пе́ред;** *fig.*) to pale (before).
тусо́вк|а, и *f.* (*coll.*) get-together, do.
тут *adv.* **1.** here; **кто т.?** who's there?; **и всё т.** (*coll.*) and that's it; **т. как т.** (*coll.*) there he is, there they are. **2.** now; **т. же** there and then.
ту́товник, а *m.* **1.** mulberry (tree). **2.** mulberry grove.
ту́тов|ый *adj.* mulberry; **~ое де́рево** mulberry (tree); **т. шелкопря́д** silkworm.
туф, а *m.* (*geol., min.*) tufa.
ту́фл|я, и *f.* shoe; slipper.
ту́хл|ый (~, ~а́, ~о) *adj.* rotten, bad; **~ое мя́со** tainted meat.
тухля́тин|а, ы *f.* (*coll.*) bad food; tainted meat.
ту́х|нуть¹, нет, *past* **~, ~ла** *impf.* (*of* **по~**) (*of source of light or heat*) to go out.
ту́х|нуть², нет, *past* **~, ~ла** *impf.* to go bad, become rotten.
ту́ч|а, и *f.* **1.** (rain) cloud; storm cloud (*also fig.*). **2.** *as symbol of sombre appearance or gloomy mood*: **смотре́ть ~ей** to look black, scowl.
туч|ево́й *adj. of* **⌣а**
ту́чк|а, и *f. dim. of* **ту́ча**
тучне́|ть, ю *impf.* (*of* **по~**) **1.** to grow fat. **2.** (*of soil*) to become fertile.
ту́чност|ь, и *f.* **1.** stoutness, obesity, corpulence. **2.** (*of soil*) richness, fertility.
ту́ч|ный (~ен, ~на́, ~но) *adj.* **1.** fat, stout, obese. **2.** (*of soil*) rich, fertile. **3.** (*of grass*) succulent.
туш, а *m.* (*mus.*) flourish.
ту́ш|а, и *f.* carcass.
туше́ *nt. indecl.* **1.** (*mus.*) touch. **2.** (*fencing*) touché.
туш|ева́ть, у́ю *impf.* (*of* **за~**) to shade.
тушёвк|а, и *f.* shading.
тушёный *adj.* (*cul.*) braised, stewed.
туш|и́ть¹, у́, ⌣ишь *impf.* (*of* **по~**) **1.** to extinguish, put out. **2.** (*fig.*) to suppress, stifle.
туш|и́ть², у́, ⌣ишь *impf.* (*cul.*) to braise, stew.
туш|ь, и *f.* Indian ink; **т. (для ресни́ц)** mascara.
тща́тельност|ь, и *f.* thoroughness; care.
тща́тел|ьный (~ен, ~ьна) *adj.* thorough, careful; painstaking.
тщеду́ши|е, я *nt.* feebleness, frailty.
тщеду́ш|ный (~ен, ~на) *adj.* feeble, frail, weak.
тщесла́ви|е, я *nt.* vanity.
тщесла́в|ный (~ен, ~на) *adj.* vain.
тще́тно *adv.* vainly, in vain.
тще́тност|ь, и *f.* futility.
тще́т|ный (~ен, ~на) *adj.* vain, futile; unavailing.
тщ|и́ться, усь, и́шься *impf.* (*+inf.; obs.*) to try (to), endeavour (to).
ты, тебя́, тебе́, тобо́й (*and* **тобо́ю**), **о тебе́** *2nd pers. sg. pers. pron.* you; **быть „на ты“ (с+***i*), **говори́ть „ты“** (*+d*) to be on familiar terms (with).
ты́|кать¹, чу, чешь *impf.* (*of* **ткнуть**) **1.** (*+i.* **в**+*a.* *or +a.* **в**+*a.*) to stick (into) (*also fig.*); to poke (into); to jab (into); **т. була́вкой во что-н.** to stick a pin into sth.; **т. па́лкой** to prod with a stick; **т. (свой) нос** (**в**+*a.*; *fig., pej.*) to stick, poke one's nose (into). **2.: т. па́льцем** (**на**+*a.*; *coll.*) to point (at), poke one's finger (at).
ты́ка|ть², ю *impf.* (*coll.*) to address as **„ты“**; be on familiar terms (with).
ты́|каться, чусь, чешься *impf.* (*of* **ткну́ться**) (*coll.*) **1.** (**в**+*a.*) to knock (against, into). **2.** to rush about, fuss about.
ты́кв|а, ы *f.* pumpkin, gourd.
ты́кв|енный *adj. of* **~а**
тыл, а, о ⌣е, в ~у́, *pl.* **~ы́** *m.* **1.** back, rear. **2.** (*mil.*) rear; home front; **напа́сть с ⌣а** to attack in the rear. **3.** (*pl.; mil.*) rear services.
тылов|о́й *adj.* (*mil.*) rear; **т. го́спиталь** base hospital.
ты́льн|ый *adj.* **1.** back, rear; **~ая пове́рхность руки́** back of the hand. **2.** (*mil.*) rear.
тын, а *m.* paling; palisade.
ты́сяч|а, и, *i.* **~ей** *and* **~ью** *num. and n., f.* thousand; **в ~у раз** a thousand times (*also fig.*).
тысячеле́ти|е, я *nt.* **1.** a thousand years; millennium. **2.** thousandth anniversary.
тысячеле́тний *adj.* thousand-year; millennial.
ты́сячн|ый *adj.* **1.** thousandth; *as n.* **~ая ~ой** *f.* thousandth. **2.** of many thousands.
тычи́нк|а, и *f.* (*bot.*) stamen.
тыч|о́к, ка́ *m.* **1.** sharp object sticking up. **2.** hit, prod, jab.
тьм|а¹, ы *no pl., f.* darkness (*also fig. = ignorance*).
тьм|а², ы, *g. pl.* **тем** *f.* (*coll.*) host, swarm, multitude.
тьфу *int.* (*coll.*) pah!; **т. про́пасть!** confound it!
тюбете́йк|а, и tyubeteyka (*embroidered skull-cap worn in Central Asia*).
тю́бик, а *m.* tube (*of toothpaste, etc.*).
тюк, а́ *m.* bale, package.
тю́к|ать, аю *impf.* (*of* **~нуть**) (*coll.*) to chop, hack.
тю́к|нуть, ну, нешь *pf. of* **~ать**
тю́левый *adj.* (*text.*) tulle.
тюле́невый *adj.* sealskin.
тюле́н|ий *adj. of* **~ь.**
тюле́н|ь, я *m.* (*zool.*) seal.
тюл|ь, я *m.* (*text.*) tulle.
тюльпа́н, а *m.* tulip.
тюльпа́н|ный *adj. of* **~; ~ное де́рево** tulip-tree.
тюрба́н, а *m.* turban.

тюр|е́мный *adj. of* **~ьма́; ~е́мное заключе́ние** imprisonment; **т. смотри́тель** prison governor.
тю́ркский *adj.* (*ethnol.*, *ling.*) Turkic.
тюр|ьма́, ьмы́, *pl.* **~́ьмы, ~́ем** *f.* **1.** prison; jail; **заключи́ть в ~ьму́** to imprison, jail; **сиде́ть в ~ьме́** to be in prison. **2.** imprisonment.
тюфя́к, а́ *m.* mattress (*filled with straw, hay, etc.*).
тя́вк|ать, аю *impf.* (*of* **~нуть**) to yap, yelp.
тя́вк|нуть, ну, нешь *pf. of* **~ать**
тяг, у *m.*: **дать ~́у** (*coll.*) to take to one's heels.
тя́г|а, и *f.* **1.** traction; locomotion; **на ко́нной ~е** horse-drawn. **2.** (*aeron.*) thrust. **3.** (*in boiler chimney, etc.*) draught. **4.** (**к, на**+*a.*; *fig.*) pull (towards), attraction (towards), thirst (for), craving (for); inclination (to, for); **т. к зна́нию** thirst for knowledge.
тяга́|ться, юсь *impf.* (*of* **по~**) (**с**+*i.*) (*coll.*) to contend (with), vie (with), compete (with).
тяга́ч, а́ *m.* tractor (*for pulling train of trailers*).
тя́гл|о[1], **а** *nt.* (*collect.*) draught animals.
тя́гл|о[2], **а,** *g. pl.* **тя́гол** *nt.* (*hist.*) **1.** tax, impost. **2.** household (*as unit for tax assessment*).
тя́гловый[1] *adj.* = **тя́глый**
тя́гловый[2] *adj.* (*hist.*) taxed, liable to tax.
тя́глый *adj.* draught (*of cattle*).
тя́гов|ый *adj.* traction, tractive; **т. кана́т** hauling rope; **т. сте́ржень** drawbar; **~ая си́ла** tractive force.
тягоме́р, а *m.* (*tech.*) draught gauge; suction gauge; blast meter.
тя́гост|ный (~ен, ~на) *adj.* **1.** burdensome, onerous. **2.** painful, distressing.
тя́гост|ь, и *f.* **1.** weight, burden; **быть кому́-н. в т.** to be a burden to s.o. **2.** fatigue.
тягот|а́, ы́, *pl.* **тя́готы** *f.* weight, burden.
тяготе́ни|е, я *nt.* **1.** (*phys.*) gravity; **зако́н (всеми́рного) ~я** law of gravity. **2.** (**к**) attraction (towards), taste (for); inclination (to, for).
тяготе́|ть, ю *impf.* **1.** (**к**) (*phys.*) to gravitate (towards). **2.** (**к**) (*fig.*) to gravitate (towards), be drawn (by, towards). **3.** (**над**) to hang (over), threaten.
тяго|ти́ть, щу́, ти́шь *impf.* to burden, be a burden (on, to); to lie heavy (on).
тяго|ти́ться, щу́сь, ти́шься *impf.* to be weighed down, oppressed.
тягу́чест|ь, и *f.* **1.** malleability. **2.** viscosity.
тягу́ч|ий (~, ~а) *adj.* **1.** malleable, ductile. **2.** viscous. **3.** (*fig.*) slow, unhurried.
тягча́йш|ий *superl. of* **тя́жкий; ~ее преступле́ние** very serious crime.
тя́жб|а, ы *f.* **1.** (*obs.*) lawsuit; litigation. **2.** (*fig.*, *coll.*) competition, rivalry.
тяжеле́|ть, ю *impf.* **1.** to become heavier; to put on weight. **2.** to become heavy with sleep (*of eyes*).
тяжело́[1] *adv.* **1.** heavily. **2.** seriously, gravely. **т. бо́лен** seriously ill. **3.** with difficulty.
тяжело́[2] *as pred.* **1.** it is hard; it is painful, it is distressing. **2. ему́,** *etc.*, **т.** he, *etc.*, feels miserable, wretched.
тяжелоатле́т, а *m.* weight-lifter; athlete competing in weight-lifting and/or wrestling.
тяжелове́с, а *m.* (*sport*) heavyweight.
тяжелове́с|ный (~ен, ~на) *adj.* **1.** heavily-loaded; **т. соста́в** heavy goods train. **2.** (*fig.*, *pej.*) heavy, ponderous; heavy-handed.
тяжёл|ый (~, ~а́) *adj.* **1.** heavy; **т. чемода́н** heavy suitcase; **~ая атле́тика** (*sport*) weight-lifting and/or wrestling; **~ое дыха́ние** heavy breathing; **~ая промы́шленность** heavy industry; **т. шаг** heavy step, tread. **2.** *expr. idea of excessive, disagreeable heaviness*: **т. во́здух** close air; **т. за́пах** oppressive, strong smell; **~ая пи́ща** heavy, indigestible food. **3.** hard, difficult; **~ая зада́ча** hard task. **4.** slow; **т. ум** slow brain, wits. **5.** heavy, severe; **~ые поте́ри** heavy casualties; **~ое наказа́ние** severe punishment; **т. уда́р** severe blow. **6.** (*of illness, etc.*) serious, grave; **~ое ране́ние** serious injury. **7.** heavy, hard, painful; **~ое чу́вство** heavy heart; misgivings; **~ые времена́** hard times; **~ая обя́занность** painful duty. **8.** (*of liter. style, etc.*) heavy, ponderous.
тя́жест|ь, и *f.* **1.** (*phys.*) gravity; **центр ~и** centre of gravity (*also fig.*). **2.** weight, heavy object; **подня́тие ~ей** (*sport*) weight-lifting. **3.** weight, heaviness; **вся т. чего́-н.** (*fig.*) the whole weight, the brunt of sth. **4.** difficulty. **5.** heaviness, severity.
тя́ж|кий (~ек, ~ка́, ~ко) *adj.* **1.** (*fig.*) heavy, hard. **2.** severe; grave; **~кая боле́знь** dangerous illness; **т. уда́р** severe blow. **3.: пусти́ться во все ~кие** (*coll.*) to plunge into dissipation.
тян|у́ть, у́, ~́ешь *impf.* **1.** to pull, draw; to haul; to drag; **т. на букси́ре** to tow; **т. кого́-н. за рука́в** to tug at s.o.'s sleeve. **2.** (*tech.*) to draw (*wire*). **3.** to lay; to put up (*wire, cable, etc.*); **т. телефо́нную ли́нию** to lay a telephone cable. **4.: т. жре́бий** to draw lots. **5.** (*fig.*) to draw, attract; **меня́,** *etc.* **~́ет** I long; **его́ ~́ет домо́й** he wants to go home; **меня́ ~́ет ко сну** I feel sleepy. **6.** to drawl, drag out; **т. слова́** to drawl; **т. но́ту** to sustain a note. **7.** to drag out, protract, delay; **т. с отве́том** to delay one's answer. **8.** to weigh (*intrans.*). **9.** to draw up; to take in; **т. в себя́ во́здух** to inhale deeply; **т. че́рез соло́минку** to suck through a straw. **10. (из, с)** to extract (from); to extort (from); **т. все си́лы из кого́-н.** to exhaust all the strength from s.o. **11.** (*of a chimney, etc.*) to draw; **пе́чь пло́хо ~́ет** the stove is not drawing well. **12.** *impers.*, *+i.*; *of a stream of air, of a smell*: **~́ет хо́лодом из-под две́ри** there is a draught coming from beneath the door; **от поле́й ~у́ло за́пахом се́на** a smell of hay was wafted from the fields.
тян|у́ться, у́сь, ~́ешься *impf.* **1.** (*of rubber, etc.*) to stretch. **2.** (*pf.* **по~**) to stretch out, stretch o.s. **3.** (*of landscape features, etc.*) to stretch, extend; **по ту сто́рону на со́тни киломе́тров ~́ется тайга́** on that side for hundreds of kilometres stretches the taiga. **4.** (*of time*) to drag on; to hang heavy. **5.** (*coll.*) to last out, hold out; **запа́сы ещё ~́нутся** supplies are still holding out. **6. (к)** to reach (for), reach out (for); **т. к сла́ве** to strive after fame. **7.** (**за**+*i.*; *fig.*, *coll.*) to try to keep up (with). **8.** (*of clouds, smoke, etc.*) to drift.
тяну́чк|а, и *f.* toffee, caramel.
тя́нущ|ий *adj.*: **~ая боль** nagging, persistent pain.
тя́пк|а, и *f.* chopper.

у *prep.+g.* **1.** by; at; **у окна́** by the window; **у воро́т** at the gate; **у мо́ря** by the sea; **у вла́сти** in power. **2.** at; with (*oft.* = *French* 'chez'); **у нас** (*i*) at our place, (*ii*) in our country; **у себя́** at one's (own) place, at home; **я был у парикма́хера** I was at the hairdresser's; **она́ учи́лась у знамени́того испа́нского скрипача́** she was taught by a celebrated Spanish violinist. **3.** *expr. relationship of possession, of part to whole, etc.*: **зуб у меня́ боли́т** my tooth aches; **ши́на у пере́днего колеса́ ло́пнула** there is a puncture in (the tyre of) the front wheel. **4.** (*indi-*

cating source, place of origin, etc., of sth. obtained) from, of; **я за́нял де́сять рубле́й у сосе́да** I borrowed ten roubles from a neighbour; **спроси́те у него́ о́ттиск** ask him to let you have an offprint. **5.: у меня́**, *etc.*, I, *etc.*, have; **у них великоле́пный дог** they have a magnificent Great Dane; **есть у вас радиоприёмник?** have you a radio?; **у меня́ к вам ма́ленькая про́сьба** I have a small favour to ask of you.

у... *vbl. pref. indicating* **1.** *movement away from a place, as* **улете́ть** to fly away. **2.** *insertion in sth., as* **умести́ть** to put in. **3.** *covering of sth. all over, as* **усе́ять** to strew. **4.** *reduction, curtailment, etc., as* **уба́вить** to reduce. **5.** *achievement of aim sought, as* **уговори́ть** to persuade; *with adj. roots forms vv. expr. comp. degree, as* **уско́рить** to accelerate.

уба́в|ить, лю, ишь *pf.* (*of* **~ля́ть**) **1.** (+*a. or g.*) to reduce, diminish; **у. ход** to reduce speed; **у. рука́в** to shorten a sleeve. **2.: у. в ве́се** to lose weight.

уба́в|иться, ится *pf.* (*of* **~ля́ться**) to diminish, decrease; **дни ~ились** the days are shorter.

убавля́|ть(ся), ю(сь) *impf. of* **уба́вить(ся)**

убаю́к|ать, аю *pf.* (*of* **~ивать**) to lull (*also fig.*).

убаю́кива|ть, ю *impf. of* **убаю́кать**

убега́|ть, ю *impf. of* **убежа́ть**

убеди́тельност|ь, и *f.* persuasiveness, cogency.

убеди́тел|ьный (~ен, ~ьна) *adj.* **1.** convincing, persuasive; **быть ~ьным** to carry conviction. **2.** pressing; earnest; **~ьная про́сьба** pressing request.

убе|ди́ть, *1st pers. sg. not used,* **ди́шь** *pf.* (*of* **~жда́ть**) **1.** (**в**+*p.*) to convince (of). **2.** (+*inf.*) to persuade (to), prevail on (to).

убе|ди́ться, *1st pers. sg. not used,* **ди́шься** *pf.* (*of* **~жда́ться**) **1.** (**в**+*p.*) to make certain (of), satisfy o.s. (of). **2.** *pass. of* **~жда́ть**

убе|жа́ть, гу́, жи́шь, гу́т *pf.* (*of* **~га́ть**) **1.** to run away, run off. **2.** to escape. **3.** (*coll.*) to boil over.

убежда́|ть(ся), ю(сь) *impf. of* **убеди́ть(ся)**

убежде́ни|е, я *nt.* **1.** persuasion; **путём ~я** by means of persuasion. **2.** conviction, belief.

убеждённо *adv.* with conviction.

убеждённост|ь, и *f.* conviction.

убеждён|ный *p.p.p. of* **убеди́ть** *and adj.* **1.** (**~, ~а́**) (**в**+*p.*) convinced (of), persuaded (of); **я в э́том соверше́нно ~** I am absolutely convinced of this. **2.** convinced, confirmed; staunch; **у. пацифи́ст** convinced pacifist; **у. сторо́нник** staunch supporter.

убе́жищ|е, а *nt.* **1.** refuge, asylum; **пра́во ~а** a right of asylum. **2.** (air-raid, *etc.*) shelter; (*mil.*) dug-out.

уберега́|ть(ся), ю(сь) *impf. of* **убере́чь(ся)**

убере́|чь, гу́, жёшь, гу́т, *past* **~г, ~гла́** *pf.* (*of* **~га́ть**) (**от**) to protect (against), guard (against), keep safe (from), preserve (from).

убере́|чься, гу́сь, жёшься, гу́тся, *past* **~гся, ~гла́сь** *pf.* (*of* **~га́ться**) (**от**) to protect o.s. (against), guard (*intrans.*) (against).

убива́|ть, ю *impf. of* **уби́ть**

убива́|ться, юсь *impf.* **1.** (*impf. only*) (**о**+*p.*; *coll.*) to grieve (over). **2.** *impf. of* **уби́ться**

уби́йствен|ный (~, ~на) *adj.* **1.** (*obs.*) death-dealing; **~ная стрела́** deadly arrow. **2.** (*fig., coll.*) killing, murderous; **у. взгляд** murderous look.

уби́йств|о, а *nt.* murder; assassination.

уби́йц|а, ы *c.g.* murderer; assassin; killer.

убира́|ть(ся), ю(сь) *impf. of* **убра́ть(ся)**; **~йся!** clear off!, beat it!, hop it!

уби́т|ый (~, ~а) 1. *p.p.p. of* **~ь; неприя́тель потеря́л две ты́сячи ~ыми** the enemy lost two thousand killed; *as n.* **у., ~ого** *m.* dead man; **спать как у.** to sleep like a log; **ходи́ть, как у.** to be dazed (with grief, *etc.*). **2.** *adj.* (*fig.*) crushed, broken.

уб|и́ть, ью́, ьёшь *pf.* (*of* **~ива́ть**) **1.** to kill; to murder; to assassinate; **хоть ~е́й** (*coll.*) for the life of me. **2.** (*fig.*) to kill, finish; to smash; **её отка́з ~и́л его́** her refusal finished him; **у. чьи-н. наде́жды** to smash s.o.'s hopes. **3.** (*coll.*) to expend; to waste; **у. вре́мя** to kill time.

уб|и́ться, ью́сь, ьёшься *pf.* (*of* **~ива́ться**) **1.** (*coll.*) to hurt o.s., bruise o.s. **2.** *pass. of* **~и́ть**

ублаж|а́ть, а́ю *impf. of* **~и́ть**

ублаж|и́ть, у́, и́шь *pf.* (*of* **~а́ть**) (*coll.*) to indulge; to gratify.

ублю́д|ок, ка *m.* mongrel (*also fig.*).

убо́г|ий (~, ~а) *adj.* **1.** poverty-stricken (*also fig.*); wretched, squalid; **~ое жили́ще** wretched habitation; *as n.* **у., ~ого** *m.* pauper. **2.** (*obs.*) crippled.

убо́гост|ь, и *f.* poverty (*also fig.*); wretchedness, squalor.

убо́жеств|о, а *nt.* **1.** (*obs.*) physical disability; infirmity. **2.** (*fig.*) poverty; mediocrity; **у. иде́й** poverty of ideas.

убо́|й, я *m.* slaughter (*of livestock*); **корми́ть на у.** to fatten (*livestock*); (*fig.*) to feed up, stuff with food.

убо́йн|ый *adj.* **1.: у. скот** livestock for slaughter. **2.** (*mil.*) killing, destructive, lethal; **~ая мо́щность** destructive power.

убо́р, а *m.* **1.** (*obs.*) dress, attire. **2.: головно́й у.** headgear, headdress.

убо́рист|ый (~, ~а) *adj.* close (*of handwriting, etc.*)

убо́рк|а, и *f.* **1.** harvesting; picking. **2.** clearing up, tidying up.

убо́рн|ая, ой *f.* **1.** (*theatr.*) dressing-room. **2.** lavatory; public convenience.

убо́рочн|ый *adj.* harvest(ing); **~ая маши́на** harvester.

убо́рщик, а *m.* cleaner.

убо́рщиц|а, ы *f.* cleaner (*in offices, etc.*); char-(woman), charlady.

убра́нств|о, а *nt.* furnishings; (*poet.*) attire.

убра́|ть, уберу́, уберёшь, *past* **~л, ~ла́, ~ло** *pf.* (*of* **убира́ть**) **1.** to remove, take away; **у. с доро́ги** to put out of the way (*also fig.*); **у. со стола́** to clear the table. **2.** (*fig., coll.*) to kick out; to sack. **3.** to put away; to store. **4.** to harvest, gather in. **5.** to clear up, tidy up; **у. ко́мнату** to do a room; **у. посте́ль** to make the bed. **6.** to decorate, adorn.

убра́|ться, уберу́сь, уберёшься, *past* **~лся, ~ла́сь, ~ло́сь** *pf.* (*of* **убира́ться**) **1.** (*coll.*) to clear up, tidy up, clean up. **2.** (*coll.*) to clear off, beat it.

убыва́|ть, ю *impf. of* **убы́ть**

у́был|ь, и *f.* **1.** diminution, decrease; subsidence (*of water*); **идти́ на у.** to decrease; to subside, recede. **2.** (*mil.*) losses, casualties.

убы́стр|ить, ю́, и́шь *pf.* (*of* **~я́ть**) to speed up.

убыстр|я́ть, я́ю *impf. of* **~и́ть**

убы́т|ок, ка *m.* **1.** loss; **терпе́ть, нести́ ~ки** to incur losses; **в у., с ~ком** at a loss. **2.** (*pl.*) damages; **взыска́ть ~ки** to claim damages.

убы́точ|ный (~ен, ~на) *adj.* unprofitable; **~ная торго́вля** trading at a loss.

убы́ть, убу́ду, убу́дешь, *past* **у́был, убыла́, у́было** *pf.* (*of* **убыва́ть**) **1.** to decrease, diminish; (*of water*) to subside, go down; (*of the moon*) to wane (*also fig.*). **2.** to go away, leave; **у. в командиро́вку** to go away on business; **у. по боле́зни** to go sick.

уважа́|емый *pres. part. pass. of* **~ть** *and adj.* respected; (*in opening formal letter*) dear.

уважа́|ть, ю *impf.* to respect, esteem.

уваже́ни|е, я *nt.* respect, esteem; **внуша́ть у.** to command respect; **из ~я (к)** out of respect (for); **с уваже́нием** (*in letters*) yours sincerely.

уважи́тельност|ь, и *f.* **1.** validity. **2.** respectfulness.

уважи́тел|ьный (~ен, ~ьна) *adj.* **1.** valid; **~ьная причи́на** valid cause. **2.** respectful, deferential.

ува́ж|ить, у, ишь *pf.* **1.** to comply (with). **2.** (*coll.*) to humour.

у́вал|ень, ьня *m.* (*coll.*) bumpkin, clodhopper.
ува́рива|ться, ется *impf. of* **навари́ться**
увар|и́ться, ~и́тся *pf.* (*of* **~иваться**) (*coll.*) **1.** to be thoroughly cooked. **2.** to boil away.
уве́дом|ить, лю, ишь *pf.* (*of* **~ля́ть**) to inform, notify.
уведомле́ни|е, я *nt.* information, notification.
уведомля́|ть, ю *impf. of* **уве́домить**
увез|ти́, у́, ёшь, *past* **~́, ~ла́** *pf.* (*of* **увози́ть**) **1.** to take (away); to take with one. **2.** to abduct, kidnap.
увекове́чива|ть, ю *impf. of* **увекове́чить**
увекове́ч|ить, у, ишь *pf.* (*of* **~ивать**) **1.** to immortalize. **2.** to perpetuate.
увеличе́ни|е, я *nt.* **1.** increase. **2.** magnification; (*phot.*) enlargement.
увели́чива|ть(ся), ю(сь) *impf. of* **увели́чить(ся)**
увеличи́тельн|ый *adj.* magnifying; **~ое стекло́** magnifying glass; **у. аппара́т** (*phot.*) enlarger.
увели́ч|ить, у, ишь *pf.* (*of* **~ивать**) **1.** to increase. **2.** to magnify; (*phot.*) to enlarge.
увели́ч|иться, ится *pf.* (*of* **~иваться**) to increase, grow, rise.
увенч|а́ть, а́ю *pf.* (*of* **венча́ть 1., 2.** *and* **~́ивать**) to crown.
увенч|а́ться, а́ется *pf.* (*of* **~́иваться**) (*+i.*; *fig., rhet.*) to be crowned (with); **у. успе́хом** to be crowned with success.
уве́нчива|ть(ся), ю(сь) *impf. of* **увенча́ть(ся)**
увере́ни|е, я *nt.* assurance.
уве́ренност|ь, и *f.* **1.** confidence; **у. в себе́** self-confidence. **2.** confidence, certainty; **мо́жно с ~ью сказа́ть** it is safe to say.
уве́рен|ный (~, ~на) *adj.* **1.** confident, sure; **~ная рука́** sure hand. **2.** *as pred.* **(~, ~а)** confident, sure, certain; **бу́дь(те) ~(ы)!** you may be sure.
уве́р|ить, ю, ишь *pf.* (*of* **~я́ть**) to assure.
уве́р|иться, юсь, ишься *pf.* (*of* **~я́ться**) to assure o.s., satisfy o.s.
увер|ну́ться, ну́сь, нёшься *pf.* (*of* **~́тываться**) (**от**) to dodge; to evade (*also fig.*).
уве́р|овать, ую *pf.* (**в**+*a.*) to come to believe (in).
увёртк|а, и *f.* dodge, evasion; subterfuge.
увёртлив|ый (~, ~а) *adj.* evasive, shifty.
увёртыва|ться, юсь *impf. of* **уверну́ться**
увертю́р|а, ы *f.* (*mus.*) overture.
увер|я́ть(ся), я́ю(сь) *impf. of* **~́ить(ся)**
увеселе́ни|е, я *nt.* entertainment, amusement.
увесели́тельн|ый *adj.* pleasure, entertainment, amusement; **~ая пое́здка** pleasure-trip, jaunt.
увесел|и́ть, ю́, и́шь *pf.* (*of* **~я́ть**) to entertain, amuse.
увесел|я́ть, я́ю *impf. of* **~и́ть**
уве́сист|ый (~, ~а) *adj.* (*coll.*) weighty; heavy.
уве|сти́, ду́, дёшь, *past* **~́л, ~ла́** *pf.* (*of* **уводи́ть**) **1.** to take (away). **2.** (*coll.*) to carry off, lift, walk off with (= *to steal*).
уве́ч|ить, у, ишь *impf.* to maim, mutilate, cripple.
уве́чь|е, я *nt.* maiming, mutilation.
уве́ш|ать, аю *pf.* (*of* **~ивать**) to cover (*with objects suspended*); **у. сте́ну карти́нами** to cover a wall with pictures.
уве́шива|ть, ю *impf. of* **уве́шать**
увеща́ни|е, я *nt.* exhortation, admonition.
увеща́|ть, ю *impf.* (*obs.*) = **увещева́ть**
увещева́|ть, ю *impf.* to exhort, admonish.
увива́|ть, ю *impf. of* **уви́ть**
увива́|ться, юсь *impf.* (**за**+*i.*; *coll., pej.*) to hang round.
увида́|ть, ю *pf.* (*of* **вида́ть**) (*coll.*) to see.
увида́|ться, юсь *pf.* (*coll.*) to see one another.
уви́|деть, жу, дишь *pf.* **1.** *pf. of* **ви́деть. 2.** to catch sight of.
уви́|деться, жусь, дишься *pf. of* **ви́деться**
уви́лива|ть, ю *impf.* (**от**) **1.** *impf. of* **увильну́ть. 2.** (*impf. only*) to try to get out (of).
увильн|у́ть, у́, ёшь *pf.* (*of* **уви́ливать**) (**от**; *coll.*) **1.** to dodge. **2.** (*fig.*) to evade; get out (of).
ув|и́ть, ью́, ьёшь, *past* **~и́л, ~ила́, ~и́ло** *pf.* (*of* **~ива́ть**) to twine all over, entwine.
увлажни́тел|ь, я *m.*: **у. во́здуха** humidifier.
увлажн|и́ть, ю́, и́шь *pf.* (*of* **~я́ть**) to moisten, dampen, wet.
увлажн|я́ть, я́ю *impf. of* **~и́ть**
увлажня́ющий *adj.*: **у. крем** moisturizer.
увлека́тел|ьный (~ен, ~ьна) *adj.* fascinating; absorbing.
увлека́|ть(ся), ю(сь) *impf. of* **увле́чь(ся)**
увлече́ни|е, я *nt.* **1.** animation. **2.** (*+i.*) passion (for); enthusiasm (for); crush (on). **3.** (object of) passion; **планери́зм — его́ у.** he is mad about gliding.
увле́|чь, ку́, чёшь, ку́т, *past* **~́к, ~кла́** *pf.* (*of* **~ка́ть**) **1.** to carry along. **2.** (*fig.*) to carry away, distract. **3.** to captivate, fascinate. **4.** to entice.
увле́|чься, ку́сь, чёшься, ку́тся, *past* **~́кся, ~кла́сь** *pf.* (*of* **~ка́ться**) (*+i.*) **1.** to be carried away (by); to become keen (on), become mad (about); **ора́тор ~́кся** the speaker got carried away. **2.** to become enamoured (of), fall (for).
уво́д, а *m.* **1.** taking away; **у. войск** withdrawal of troops. **2.** (*coll.*) carrying off; lifting (= *stealing*).
уво|ди́ть, жу́, ~́дишь *impf. of* **увести́**
уво́з, а *m.* (*coll.*) abduction; carrying off, lifting.
уво|зи́ть, жу́, ~́зишь *pf. of* **увезти́**
увола́кива|ть, ю *impf. of* **уволо́чь**
уво́л|ить, ю, ишь *pf.* (*of* **~ьня́ть**) **1.** to discharge, dismiss; to sack, fire; **у. в отста́вку** to retire, pension off. **2.** (*pf. only*) (**от**; *obs.*) to spare; **~ьте нас от подро́бного расска́за** spare us the details.
уво́л|иться, юсь, ишься *pf.* (*of* **~ьня́ться**) **1.** to retire; (*mil.*) to get one's discharge; **у. в отста́вку** to retire, go into retirement. **2.** *pass. of* **~ить**
увол|о́чь, оку́, очёшь, оку́т, *past* **~о́к, ~окла́** *pf.* (*of* **~а́кивать**) (*coll.*) **1.** to drag away. **2.** to carry off, make off with.
увольне́ни|е, я *nt.* discharge, dismissal.
увольни́тельн|ый *adj.* discharge, dismissal; **у. биле́т, ~ая запи́ска** (*mil.*) leave-pass.
увольня́|ть(ся), ю(сь) *impf. of* **уво́лить(ся)**
увы́ *int.* alas!
увяда́|ть, ю *impf. of* **увя́нуть**
увя|за́ть[1], жу́, ~́жешь *pf.* (*of* **~́зывать**) **1.** to tie up; to pack up. **2.** to co-ordinate.
увяз|а́ть[2], а́ю *impf. of* **~́нуть**
увя|за́ться, жу́сь, ~́жешься *pf.* (*of* **~́зываться**) (*coll.*) **1.** to pack. **2. (за кем-н.)** to dog (s.o.'s footsteps).
увя́зк|а, и *f.* **1.** tying up. **2.** co-ordination.
увя́з|нуть, ну, нешь, *past* **~, ~ла** *pf.* (*of* **~а́ть[2]**) (**в**+*p.*) to get stuck (in); to get bogged down (in).
увя́зыва|ть, ю *impf. of* **увяза́ть[1]**
увя́зыва|ться, юсь *impf. of* **увяза́ться**
увя́|нуть, ну, нешь *pf.* (*of* **~да́ть**) to fade, wither.
угад|а́ть, а́ю *pf.* (*of* **~́ывать**) to guess (right), divine.
уга́дыва|ть, ю *impf. of* **угада́ть**
уга́р, а *m.* **1.** carbon monoxide fumes. **2.** carbon monoxide poisoning. **3.** (*fig.*) ecstasy, intoxication; **в ~е** (*+g.*) carried away (by).
уга́рный *adj.* full of (monoxide) fumes; (*tech.*): **у. газ** coal-gas, carbon monoxide.
угас|а́ть, а́ет *impf.* **1.** *impf. of* **~́нуть. 2.** (*impf. only*) to die down (*of a fire and fig.*); to fade; wane.
уга́с|нуть, нет *pf.* (*of* **~а́ть**) to go out.
углево́д, а *m.* (*chem.*) carbohydrate.
углеводоро́д, а *m.* (*chem.*) hydrocarbon.
угледобы́ч|а, и *f.* coal extraction.
углекислот|а́, ы́ *f.* (*chem.*) carbonic acid, carbon dioxide.

углеки́слый *adj.* (*chem.*) carbonate (of); **у. газ** carbon dioxide; **у. аммо́ний** ammonium carbonate.
углеко́п, а *m.* (*obs.*) coal-miner, collier.
углеро́д, а *m.* (*chem.*) carbon.
углеро́дист|ый *adj.* (*chem.*) carbon; carbide (of).
углова́т|ый (~, ~а) *adj.* **1.** angular. **2.** (*fig.*) awkward.
углов|о́й *adj.* **1.** (*math., phys., tech.*) angle; angular; **~а́я ско́рость** angular velocity. **2.** angle; corner; **у. дом** corner house; *as n.* **у., ~о́го** *m.* (*sport*) corner; **пода́ть у.** to take a corner.
углуб|и́ть, лю́, и́шь *pf.* (*of* **~ля́ть**) **1.** to deepen, make deeper. **2.** (*fig.*) to extend; **у. свои́ зна́ния** to extend one's knowledge.
углуб|и́ться, лю́сь, и́шься *pf.* (*of* **~ля́ться**) **1.** to deepen, become deeper. **2.** (**в**+*a.*) to go deep (into); to delve deeply (into) (*also fig.*). **3.** (**в**+*a.*; *fig.*) to become absorbed (in); **у. в кни́гу.** to become absorbed in a book; **у. в себя́** to become introspective.
углубле́ни|е, я *nt.* **1.** deepening. **2.** (*fig.*) extending; intensification. **3.** (*geog.*) hollow, depression, dip.
углубля́|ть(ся), ю(сь) *impf. of* **углуби́ть(ся)**
угля|де́ть, жу́, ди́шь *pf.* (*coll.*) **1.** to espy, spot. **2.** (**за**+*i.*) to look after.
угна́|ть, угоню́, уго́нишь, *past* **~л, ~ла́, ~ло** *pf.* (*of* **угоня́ть**) **1.** to drive away. **2.** (*coll.*) to steal, lift.
угна́|ться, угоню́сь, уго́нишься, *past* **~лся, ~ла́сь, ~ло́сь** *pf.* (**за**+*i.*) to keep pace (with); to keep up (with) (*also fig., coll.*).
угнезд|и́ться, и́шься *pf.* (*coll.*) to nestle.
угнета́тел|ь, я *m.* oppressor.
угнета́тельский *adj.* oppressive.
угнета́|ть, ю *impf.* **1.** to oppress. **2.** to depress.
угнете́ни|е, я *nt.* **1.** oppression. **2.** depression; **быть в ~и** to be depressed.
угнетённ|ый *adj.* **1.** oppressed. **2.** depressed; **быть в ~ом состоя́нии** to be depressed.
угова́рива|ть, ю *impf.* **1.** *impf. of* **уговори́ть. 2.** (*impf. only*) to try to persuade, urge.
угова́рива|ться, юсь *impf. of* **уговори́ться**
угово́р, а *m.* **1.** persuasion. **2.** agreement, compact; **с ~ом...** on condition ....
уговор|и́ть, ю́, и́шь *pf.* (*of* **угова́ривать**) (+*inf.*) to persuade (to); to talk (into).
уговор|и́ться, ю́сь, и́шься *pf.* (*of* **угова́риваться**) (+*inf.*) to arrange (to), agree (to).
уго́д|а, ы *f.*: **в ~у** (+*d.*) to please.
уго|ди́ть[1]**, жу́, ди́шь** *pf.* (*of* **~жда́ть**) (+*d. or* **на**+*a.*) to please, oblige.
уго|ди́ть[2]**, жу́, ди́шь** *pf.* (*coll.*) **1.** (**в**+*a.*) to fall (into), get (into); to bang (against); **у. в тюрьму́** to land up in prison. **2.** (+*d.* **в**+*a.*) to hit (in, on).
уго́длив|ый (~, ~а) *adj.* obsequious.
уго́дник, а *m.* **1.** (*coll.*) person anxious to please. **2.** saint.
уго́днича|ть, ю *impf.* (**пе́ред**; *coll.*) to fawn (on).
уго́дничеств|о, а *nt.* subservience, servility.
уго́дно 1. *as pred.* (+*d.*) **что вам у.?** what would you like?, what can I do for you?; **как вам у.** as you wish; please yourself; **ско́лько душе́ у.** to one's heart's content. **2.** *forms indef. prons. and advs.*: **кто у.** anyone (you like); **что у.** anything (you like); **ско́лько у.** as much as you like; any amount.
уго́д|ный (~ен, ~на) *adj.* pleasing, welcome.
уго́д|ье, ья, *g. pl.* **~ий** *nt.* object or area of economic significance; **лесны́е ~ья** forests; **полевы́е ~ья** arable land; **ры́бные ~ья** fishing-ground.
угожда́|ть, ю *impf. of* **угоди́ть**[1]
у́г|ол, ла́, об ~ле́, в ~лу́ *m.* **1.** (**в ~ле́**) (*math., phys.*) angle; (*fig.*) point of view; **под прямы́м ~ло́м** at right angles. **2.** corner; **в ~лу́** in the corner; **на ~лу́** at the corner; **за ~ло́м** round the corner; **поста́вить в у.** to put in the corner, make stand in the corner. **3.** part of a room. **4.** place; **име́ть свой у.** to have a place of one's own; **глухо́й у., медве́жий у.** remote part, godforsaken spot.
угол|ёк, ька́ *m.* small piece of coal.
уголо́вник, а *m.* criminal.
уголо́вн|ый *adj.* criminal; **у. ко́декс** criminal code; **~ое пра́во** criminal law.
угол|о́к, ка́ *m. dim. of* **у́гол**; corner; **кра́сный у.** recreation and reading room.
у́голь, угля́ *m.* **1.** (*pl.* **у́гли, у́гле́й**) coal; **ка́менный у.** coal; **древе́сный у.** charcoal. **2.** (*pl.* **у́гли, угле́й** *and* **~я, ~ев**) a coal; piece of coal; **сиде́ть как на ~ях** to be on thorns. **3.** (*art*) charcoal.
уго́льник, а *m.* set square.
у́гольн|ый *adj.* **1.** coal; **у. бассе́йн** coal-field; **у. райо́н** coal-mining area. **2.** carbon. **3.** (*chem.*) carbonic; **~ая кислота́** carbonic acid.
у́гольщик, а *m.* **1.** coal-miner. **2.** charcoal-burner.
угомон|и́ть, ю, и́шь *pf.* (*coll.*) to calm.
угомон|и́ться, ю́сь, и́шься *pf.* (*coll.*) to calm down.
уго́н, а *m.* **1.** driving away. **2.** (*coll.*) lifting, stealing; hijacking; **у. маши́ны** car theft.
уго́нщик, а *m.* thief; hijacker; **у. маши́ны** car thief; **у.-лиха́ч** joyrider.
угоня́|ть, ю *impf. of* **угна́ть**
угора́зд|ить, ит *pf.* (+*inf.*, *usu. impers.*; *coll.*) to urge, make; **как э́то его́ ~ило жени́ться на ней?** what on earth made him marry her?
угор|а́ть, а́ю *impf. of* **~е́ть**
угоре́лый *adj.*: **как у.** like a madman.
угор|е́ть, ю́, и́шь *pf.* (*of* **~а́ть**) **1.** to be poisoned by fumes, get carbon monoxide poisoning. **2.** (*coll.*) to be mad; **что ты, ~е́л?** are you out of your mind?
у́г|орь[1]**, ря́** *m.* eel; **живо́й как у.** as lively as a cricket.
у́г|орь[2]**, ря́** *m.* blackhead.
уго|сти́ть, щу́, сти́шь *pf.* (*of* **~ща́ть**) (+*i.*) to entertain (to), treat (to); **у. кого́-н. обе́дом** to have s.o. to dinner.
угото́в|ить, лю, ишь *pf.* (*obs.*) to prepare.
угоща́|ть, ю *impf. of* **угости́ть**
угоще́ни|е, я *nt.* **1.** (+*i.*) entertaining (to, with), treating (to). **2.** refreshments; fare.
угрева́т|ый (~, ~а) *adj.* covered with blackheads; pimply.
угрожа́|ть, ю *impf.* to threaten.
угрожа́|ющий *adj.* threatening, menacing; **~ющая катастро́фа** impending disaster.
угро́з|а, ы *f.* threat, menace; **под ~ой** (+*g.*) under threat (of); **поста́вить под ~у** to threaten, endanger.
угрызе́ни|е, я *nt.* pangs; **~я со́вести** remorse; **чу́вствовать ~я со́вести** to feel pangs of conscience.
угрю́м|ый (~, ~а) *adj.* sullen, morose, gloomy.
уда́в, а *m.* (*zool.*) boa, boa constrictor.
уда|ва́ться, ётся *impf. of* **~́ться**
удав|и́ть, лю́, ~́ишь *pf.* to strangle.
удавле́ни|е, я *nt.* strangling, strangulation.
удале́ни|е, я *nt.* **1.** removal; **у. зу́ба** extraction of a tooth. **2.** sending away; **у. с по́ля** (*sport*) sending off the field. **3.** moving off.
удалённост|ь, и *f.* remoteness, distance.
удал|ённый *p.p.p. of* **~и́ть** *and adj.* remote.
удал|е́ц, ьца́ *m.* daring person.
удал|и́ть, ю́, и́шь *pf.* (*of* **~я́ть**) **1.** to remove; **у. зуб** to extract a tooth. **2.** to remove, send away; **у. с рабо́ты** to dismiss, sack; **у. с по́ля** (*sport*) to send off (the field). **3.** to move away.
удал|и́ться, ю́сь, и́шься *pf.* (*of* **~я́ться**) **1.** to move off, move away. **2.** to leave, withdraw, retire; **у. на поко́й** to retire to a quiet life.
удал|о́й (уда́л, ~а́, уда́ло) *adj.* daring, bold.
у́дал|ь, и *f.* daring, boldness.
удальств|о́, а́ *nt.* (*coll.*) = **у́даль**
удал|я́ть(ся), я́ю(сь) *impf. of* **~и́ть(ся)**
уда́р, а *m.* **1.** blow; stroke; **одни́м ~ом** at one stroke;

нанести́ у. to strike a blow; **у. в спи́ну** (*fig.*) stab in the back; **у. гро́ма** thunder-clap. **2.** stroke (*sound*). **3.** (*mil.*) blow; attack; thrust; **у. с во́здуха** air strike; **под ~ом** exposed (to attack). **4.: быть в ~е** (*coll.*) to be in good form. **5.** (*med.*) stroke, seizure; **со́лнечный у.** sun-stroke.

ударе́ни|е, я *nt.* **1.** (*ling.*) stress, accent; (*fig.*) stress, emphasis; **сде́лать у.** (**на**+*p. or* **на**+*a.*) to stress, emphasize. **2.** stress(-mark).

уда́ренный *adj.* (*ling.*) stressed, accented.

уда́р|ить, ю, ишь *pf.* (*of* **~я́ть** *and, in some senses, of* **бить**) **1.** (+*a.* **по**+*d. or* **в**+*a.*) to strike; to hit; **у. кого́-н. по лицу́** to slap s.o.'s face; **у. кулако́м по́ столу** to bang on the table with one's fist. **2.** (**в**+*a. or* +*a.*) to strike; to sound; to beat; **у. в бараба́н** to beat a drum; **у. трево́гу** to sound the alarm; **часы́ ~или по́лночь** the clock struck midnight. **3.: у. в го́лову** (*of blood*) to rush to one's head; (*of wine, etc.*) to go to one's head. **4.** (**на**+*a. or* **по**+*d.*) (*mil.*) to attack. **5.** (**по**+*d.*) to strike (at); to combat; **у. по кумовству́** to combat nepotism. **6.: у. по рука́м** to strike a bargain.

уда́р|иться, юсь, ишься *pf.* (*of* **~я́ться**) **1.** (**о**+*a. or* **в**+*a.*) to strike (against), hit; **у. о подво́дный ка́мень** to strike a reef. **2.** (**в**+*a. or* +*inf.*) to break (into); **у. в слёзы** to burst into tears. **3.: у. в кра́йность** to go to an extreme.

уда́рник[1], **а** *m.* shock-worker, udarnik.

уда́рник[2], **а** *m.* (*in fire-arm*) striker, firing pin; (*in detonator*) plunger.

уда́рн|ый *adj.* **1.** (*tech. and mil.*) percussion; **у. ка́псюль** percussion cap; **~ая си́ла** striking power, force of impact. **2.** (*mus.*) percussion. **3.** (*mil.*) striking, shock; **~ая гру́ппа** striking force; **~ые ча́сти** shock troops. **4.** shock(-working); **~ая рабо́та** shock work. **5.** urgent; **~ое зада́ние** urgent task, rush job.

удар|я́ть(ся), я́ю(сь) *impf. of* **≈ить(ся)**

уда́|ться, стся, ду́тся, *past* **~лся, ~ла́сь** *pf.* (*of* **~ва́ться**) **1.** to succeed, be successful, work (well); **опера́ция ~ла́сь** the operation was a success. **2.** (*impers.*+*d. and inf.*) to succeed, manage; **мне не ~ло́сь прису́тствовать на их сва́дьбе** I did not manage to attend their wedding.

уда́ч|а, и *f.* success; good luck, good fortune; **жела́ть ~и** to wish good luck.

уда́члив|ый (~, ~а) *adj.* successful, lucky.

уда́чник, а *m.* (*coll.*) lucky person.

уда́ч|ный (~ен, ~на) *adj.* **1.** successful. **2.** felicitous, apt, good; **у. перево́д** felicitous translation.

удва́ива|ть, ю *impf. of* **удво́ить**

удвое́ни|е, я *nt.* doubling, redoubling.

удво́|ить, ю, ишь *pf.* (*of* **удва́ивать**) to double, redouble; **у. свои́ уси́лия** to redouble one's efforts.

уде́л, а *m.* lot, destiny; **доста́ться в у. кому́-н.** to fall to one's lot.

удел|и́ть, ю́, и́шь *pf.* (*of* **~я́ть**) to give, spare, devote; **у. вре́мя чему́-н.** to spare the time for sth.

уде́льн|ый *adj.* (*phys.*) specific; **у. вес** specific gravity; (*fig.*) proportion, share.

удел|я́ть, я́ю *impf. of* **~и́ть**

у́держ, у *m.*: **без ~у** (*coll.*) uncontrollably, without restraint; **пла́кать без ~у** to weep uncontrollably; **~у нет ему́, на него́** (*coll.*) there's no holding him; **~у не знать** (*coll.*) to know no bounds.

удержа́ни|е, я *nt.* **1.** keeping, retention. **2.** deduction; **у. из зарпла́ты** money stopped from wages.

удерж|а́ть, у́, ≈ишь *pf.* (*of* **≈ивать**) **1.** to hold, hold on to. **2.** to keep, retain; **у. в па́мяти** to retain in one's memory. **3.** to hold back, restrain; **у. лошаде́й** to hold horses back. **4.** to keep down, suppress; **у. слёзы** to stifle one's tears. **5.** to deduct, keep back; **у. из зарпла́ты** to stop from wages.

удерж|а́ться, у́сь, ≈ишься *pf.* (*of* **≈иваться**) **1.** to hold one's ground, hold out; to stand firm; **у. на нога́х** to remain on one's feet. **2.** (**от**) to keep (from); **у. от собла́зна** to resist a temptation; **мы не могли́ у. от сме́ха** we couldn't help laughing.

уде́ржива|ть(ся), ю(сь) *impf. of* **удержа́ть(ся)**

удесятер|и́ть, ю́, и́шь *pf.* (*of* **~я́ть**) to increase tenfold.

удесятер|и́ться, и́тся *pf.* (*of* **~я́ться**) to increase (*intrans.*) tenfold.

удесятер|я́ть(ся), я́ю, я́ет(ся) *impf. of* **~и́ть(ся)**

удешев|и́ть, лю́, и́шь *pf.* (*of* **~ля́ть**) to reduce the price (of).

удешев|и́ться, и́тся *pf.* (*of* **~ля́ться**) to become cheaper.

удешевля́|ть(ся), ю, ет(ся) *impf. of* **удешеви́ть(ся)**

удиви́тельно *adv.* **1.** astonishingly, surprisingly. **2.** wonderfully, marvellously. **3.** very, extremely.

удиви́тел|ьный (~ен, ~ьна) *adj.* **1.** astonishing, surprising, amazing; **~ьно** (*as pred.*) it is astonishing, it is surprising, it is amazing; **не ~ьно, что** no wonder that. **2.** wonderful, marvellous.

удив|и́ть, лю́, и́шь *pf.* (*of* **~ля́ть**) to astonish, surprise, amaze.

удив|и́ться, лю́сь, и́шься *pf.* (*of* **~ля́ться**) (+*d.*) to be astonished (at), be surprised (at); to marvel (at).

удивле́ни|е, я *nt.* astonishment, surprise, amazement; **к моему́ вели́кому ~ю** to my great surprise; **на у.** (*as pred.*; *coll.*) excellent(ly), splendid(ly); **приём вы́шел на у.** the reception went off splendidly.

удивля́|ть(ся), ю(сь) *impf. of* **удиви́ть(ся)**

удил|а́, уди́л, ~а́м *no sg.* bit; **закуси́ть у.** to take the bit between one's teeth (*also fig.*).

уди́лищ|е, а *nt.* fishing-rod.

уди́льщик, а *m.* angler.

удира́|ть, ю *impf. of* **удра́ть**

уди́ть, ужу́, у́дишь *impf.*: **у. ры́бу** to fish, angle.

уди́ться, у́дится *impf.* (*of fish*) to bite.

удлине́ни|е, я *nt.* lengthening; **у. сро́ка** extension (of time).

удлин|и́ть, ю́, и́шь *pf.* (*of* **~я́ть**) to lengthen; to extend, prolong.

удлин|и́ться, и́тся *pf.* (*of* **~я́ться**) to become longer; to be extended, be prolonged.

удлин|я́ть(ся), я́ю(сь) *impf. of* **~и́ть(ся)**

удо́бно[1] *adv.* **1.** comfortably. **2.** conveniently.

удо́бно[2] *as pred.* **1.** (+*d.*) to be comfortable; **нам здесь вполне́ у.** we are very comfortable here. **2.** (+*d.*) it is convenient (for), it suits; **у. ли вам сра́зу же прие́хать?** is it convenient for you to come at once? **3.** it is proper, it is in order; **у. ли зада́ть тако́й вопро́с?** is it proper to ask such a question?

удо́б|ный (~ен, ~на) *adj.* **1.** comfortable; cosy. **2.** convenient, opportune; **по́льзоваться ~ным слу́чаем** to take an opportunity. **3.** proper, in order.

удобовари́м|ый (~, ~а) *adj.* digestible.

удобре́ни|е, я *nt.* **1.** fertilization. **2.** fertilizer.

удо́бр|ить, ю, ишь *pf.* (*of* **~я́ть**) to fertilize.

удобр|я́ть, я́ю *impf. of* **≈ить**

удо́бств|о, а *nt.* **1.** comfort. **2.** convenience; **кварти́ра со все́ми ~ами** flat with all conveniences.

удовлетворе́ни|е, я *nt.* satisfaction; **тре́бовать ~я у кого́-н.** to demand satisfaction from s.o.

удовлетворённост|ь, и *f.* satisfaction, contentment.

удовлетворённый *adj.* satisfied, contented.

удовлетвори́тельно 1. *adv.* satisfactorily. **2.** *n.*; *nt. indecl.* 'satisfactory', 'fair' (*as school mark*).

удовлетвори́тельный (~ен, ~ьна) *adj.* satisfactory.

удовлетвор|и́ть, ю́, и́шь *pf.* (*of* **~я́ть**) **1.** to satisfy; to comply (with); **у. запро́сы** to satisfy requirements; **у. про́сьбу** to comply with a request. **2.** (+*d.*) to answer, meet; **у. тре́бованиям** to answer requirements. **3.** (+*i.*) to supply (with), furnish (with).

удовлетвор|и́ться, ю́сь, и́шься *pf.* (*of* **~я́ться**) **1.** (+*i.*) to content o.s. (with), be satisfied (with). **2.** *pass. of* **~и́ть**

удовлетвор|я́ть(ся), я́ю(сь) *impf. of* **~и́ть(ся)**

удово́льстви|е, я *nt.* **1.** (*sg. only*) pleasure; **доста́вить у.** (+*d.*) to give pleasure. **2.** amusement.

удово́льств|оваться, уюсь *pf. of* **дово́льствоваться**

удо́|й, я *m.* **1.** yield of milk. **2.** milking.

удо́й|ный *adj.* **1.** *adj. of* **~**. **2.** yielding much milk.

удорожа́ни|е, я *nt.* rise in price(s).

удорож|а́ть, а́ю *impf. of* **~и́ть**

удорож|и́ть, у́, и́шь *pf.* (*of* **~а́ть**) to raise the price (of).

удоста́ива|ть(ся), ю(сь) *impf. of* **удосто́ить(ся)**

удостовере́ни|е, я *nt.* **1.** certification, attestation; **в у.** (+*g.*) in witness (of). **2.** certificate; **у. ли́чности** identity card, ID; **у. пра́ва вожде́ния автомоби́ля** driving licence; **у. о сме́рти** death certificate.

удостове́р|ить, ю, ишь *pf.* (*of* **~я́ть**) to certify, attest, witness; **у. по́дпись** to witness a signature.

удостове́р|иться, юсь, ишься *pf.* (*of* **~я́ться**) (**в**+*p.*) to make sure (of), to assure o.s. (of).

удостовер|я́ть(ся), я́ю(сь) *impf. of* **~́ить(ся)**

удосто́|ить, ю, ишь *pf.* (*of* **удоста́ивать**) **1.** (+*a. and g.*) to award (to), confer (on); **у. кого́-н. Но́белевской пре́мии** to award s.o. a Nobel prize. **2.** (+*i.*; *usu. iron.*) to favour (with).

удосто́|иться, юсь, ишься *pf.* (*of* **удоста́иваться**) (+*g.*) **1.** to receive, be awarded (*an honour*, *a prize*, *etc.*). **2.** (*usu. iron.*) to be favoured (with).

удосу́жива|ться, юсь *impf. of* **удосу́житься**

удосу́ж|иться, усь, ишься *pf.* (*of* **~иваться**) (+*inf.*; *coll.*) to find time (to), to manage.

удочер|и́ть, ю́, и́шь *pf.* (*of* **~я́ть**) to adopt (*a girl*).

удочер|я́ть, я́ю *impf. of* **~и́ть**

у́дочк|а, и *f.* (fishing-)rod (*also in fig., coll. phrr.*); **заки́нуть ~у** to put a line out (= *to try to discover sth.*); **пойма́ть на ~у** to catch out; **попа́сться на ~у** to swallow the bait.

удра́|ть, удеру́, удерёшь, *past* **~л, ~ла́, ~ло** *pf.* (*of* **удира́ть**) (*coll.*) to make off; to do a bunk.

удруж|и́ть, у́, и́шь *pf.* (+*d.*; *coll.*) to do a good turn.

удруч|а́ть, а́ю *impf. of* **~и́ть**

удручённост|ь, и *f.* depression, despondency.

удруч|и́ть, у́, и́шь *pf.* (*of* **~а́ть**) to depress, dispirit.

удуш|а́ть, а́ю *impf. of* **~и́ть**

удуше́ни|е, я *nt.* suffocation; asphyxiation.

удуш|и́ть, у́, ~́ишь *pf.* (*of* **~а́ть**) to smother, stifle, suffocate; to asphyxiate.

уду́шлив|ый (~, ~а) *adj.* stifling, suffocating; **~ая жара́** stifling heat; **у. газ** asphyxiating gas.

уду́шь|е, я *nt.* suffocation.

уедине́ни|е, я *nt.* solitude; seclusion.

уединённост|ь, и *f.* solitariness, seclusion.

уединён|ный (~, ~на) *adj.* solitary, secluded.

уедин|и́ть, ю́, и́шь *pf.* (*of* **~я́ть**) to seclude, set apart.

уедин|и́ться, ю́сь, и́шься *pf.* (*of* **~я́ться**) (**от**) to retire (from), withdraw (from); to go off (by o.s.).

уедин|я́ть(ся), я́ю(сь) *impf. of* **~и́ть(ся)**

уе́зд, а *m.* (*hist.*) uyezd (*administrative unit*).

уе́зд|ный *adj. of* **~**; **у. го́род** chief town of uyezd.

уе́ть, уебу́, уебёшь, *past* **уёб, уебли́** *pf.* (*of* **еба́ть**) (*vulg.*) to fuck.

уе́хать, уе́ду, уе́дешь, *imper.* **уезжа́й(те)** *pf.* (*of* **уезжа́ть**) to go away, leave, depart.

уж[1]**, а́** *m.* grass-snake.

уж[2] **1.** *adv.* = **уже́**. **2.** *emph. particle* (*coll.*) to be sure, indeed, certainly; **уж он узна́ет** he is sure to find out. **3.** *particle emph. certain prons. and advs.* very; **э́то не так уж сло́жно** it's not so very complicated.

ужа́л|ить, ю, ишь *pf. of* **жа́лить**

у́жас, а *m.* **1.** horror, terror; **к моему́ ~у** to my horror. **2.** (*usu. pl.*) horrors; **~ы оса́ды** the horrors of a siege. **3.** *as pred.* (*coll.*) it is awful. **4.: у. (как)** *as adv.* (*coll.*) awfully; **у. как гро́мко** awfully loud.

ужас|а́ть(ся), а́ю(сь) *impf. of* **~ну́ть(ся)**

ужа́сно[1] *adv.* **1.** horribly, terribly; **у. себя́ чу́вствовать** to feel awful. **2.** (*coll.*) awfully, terribly.

ужа́сно[2] *as pred.* (*coll.*) it is awful, it is terrible.

ужас|ну́ть, ну́, нёшь *pf.* (*of* **~а́ть**) to horrify, terrify.

ужас|ну́ться, ну́сь, нёшься *pf.* (*of* **~а́ться**) to be horrified, be terrified.

ужа́с|ный (~ен, ~на) *adj.* awful, terrible, ghastly, frightful; **у. вид** awful sight; **у. на́сморк** awful cold.

у́же *comp. of* **у́зкий** *and* **у́зко**

уже́ 1. *adv.* already; now; by now; **у. не** no longer; **они́ у. при́были** they are here already; **она́ у. не ребёнок** she is no longer a child. **2.** *emph. particle* = **уж; э́то у. друго́е де́ло** that's quite a different matter.

уже́ни|е, я *nt.* fishing, angling.

ужива́|ться, юсь *impf. of* **ужи́ться**

ужи́вчив|ый (~, ~а) *adj.* easy to get on with.

ужи́мк|а, и *f.* grimace.

у́жин, а *m.* supper.

у́жина|ть, ю *impf.* (*of* **по~**) to have supper.

ужи́|ться, ву́сь, вёшься, *past* **~лся, ~ла́сь** *pf.* (*of* **~ва́ться**) (**с**+*i.*) to get on (with); **мы с ней так и не ~ли́сь** she and I simply couldn't get on.

узаконе́ни|е, я *nt.* **1.** legalization. **2.** statute.

узако́нива|ть, ю *impf. of* **узако́нить**

узако́н|ить, ю, ишь *pf.* (*of* **~ивать**) to legalize, legitimize.

узбе́к, а *m.* Uzbek.

Узбекиста́н, а *m.* Uzbekistan.

узбе́кский *adj.* Uzbek.

узбе́|чка, чки *f. of* **~к**

узд|а́, ы́, *pl.* **~́ы** *f.* bridle (*also fig.*); **держа́ть в ~** to keep in check, restrain.

узде́чк|а, и *f.* bridle.

у́з|ел, ла́ *m.* **1.** knot (*also naut. measurement of speed*); **завяза́ть у.** to tie a knot. **2.** junction; centre; **у. доро́г** road junction; **промы́шленный у.** industrial centre. **3.: не́рвный у.** (*anat.*) ganglion. **4.** (*bot.*) node. **5.** (*tech.*) group, assembly. **6.** bundle, pack.

узел|о́к, ка́ *m.* **1.** small knot. **2.** (*bot.*) nodule. **3.** small bundle.

у́з|кий (~ок, ~ка́, ~ко) *adj.* **1.** narrow; **~кое ме́сто** (*fig.*) bottleneck. **2.** tight. **3.** (*fig.*) narrow, limited. **4.** (*fig.*) narrow, narrow-minded.

узкоколе́йный *adj.* narrow-gauge.

узколо́б|ый (~, ~а) *adj.* narrow-minded.

узлова́т|ый (~, ~а) *adj.* knotty; gnarled.

узлов|о́й *adj.* **1.** junction; **~а́я ста́нция** (*rail.*) junction. **2.** main, key; **у. вопро́с** central question.

узна|ва́ть, ю́, ёшь *impf. of* **~́ть**

узна́|ть, ю *pf.* (*of* **~ва́ть**) **1.** to recognize. **2.** to get to know; become familiar with. **3.** to learn, find out.

у́зник, а *m.* (*obs. or rhet.*) prisoner.

узо́р, а *m.* pattern, design.

узо́р|ный *adj.* **1.** *adj. of* **~**. **2.** decorated with a pattern, design.

узо́рчат|ый (~, ~а) *adj.* decorated with a pattern, design.

у́зост|ь, и *f.* narrowness (*also fig.*); tightness.

узр|е́ть, ю́, ~́ишь *pf.* **1.** *pf. of* **зреть**[2]. **2.** (*fig.*) to see; to take (as).

узурпа́тор, а *m.* usurper.

узурпа́ци|я, и *f.* usurpation.

узурпи́р|овать, ую *impf. and pf.* to usurp.

у́з|ы, ~ *no sg.* (*fig.*) bonds, ties.

уй|ду́, дёшь *see* **~ти́**

у́йм|а, ы *no pl., f.* (*coll.*) lots (of), masses (of).

уйм|у́, ёшь *see* **уня́ть**
уй|ти́, ду́, дёшь, *past* **ушёл, ушла́** *pf.* (*of* **уходи́ть**) **1.** to go away, leave; **у. из ко́мнаты** to leave the room. **2. (от, из)** to escape (from), get away (from); to evade. **3. (от, из, с)** to retire (from), give up; **у. от поли́тики** to retire from politics; **у. от жи́зни** to retire from life; **у. из жи́зни** to pass away (= *to die*); **у. со сце́ны** to quit the stage. **4. (в**+*a.*) to sink (into); (*fig.*) to bury o.s. (in); **у. в себя́** to retire into one's shell. **5.** to be used up, be spent. **6.** (*of time, youth, etc.*) to pass away, slip away. **7.** (*coll.*) to boil over.
ука́з, а *m.* **1.** decree; edict, ukase. **2.** *as pred.* (+*neg.*) (it is) not an order, not obligatory; **ты мне не у.** I'm not obliged to do as *you* say.
указа́ни|е, я *nt.* **1.** indication, pointing out. **2.** instruction, direction; **дать ~я** to give instructions.
ука́з|анный *p.p.p. of* **~а́ть** *and adj.* fixed, appointed; **на ~анном ме́сте** at the place appointed.
указа́тел|ь, я *m.* **1.** indicator; marker; (*comput.*) cursor; **у. направле́ния** road sign. **2.** index. **3.** guide, directory.
указа́тельн|ый *adj.* **1.** indicating; **у. па́лец** index finger; **у. столб** road sign. **2.: ~ое местоиме́ние** (*gram.*) demonstrative pronoun.
ука|за́ть, жу́, ∠жешь *pf.* (*of* **∠зывать**) **1.** to show, indicate. **2. (на**+*a.*) to point (at, to); (*fig.*) to point out; **у. на оши́бку** to point out a mistake. **3.** to explain; to give directions.
ука́зк|а, и *f.* **1.** pointer. **2.** (*coll., pej.*) orders; **по чужо́й ~е** at s.o. else's bidding.
ука́зчик, а *m.* (*coll.*) person who gives orders.
ука́зыва|ть, ю *impf. of* **указа́ть**
ука́лыва|ть, ю *impf. of* **уколо́ть**
укат|а́ть, а́ю *pf.* (*of* **∠ывать**[1]) to roll (out); **у. доро́гу** to roll, make smooth a road.
ука|ти́ть, чу́, ∠тишь *pf.* (*of* **∠тывать**[2]) **1.** to roll away. **2.** (*coll.*) to drive off.
ука|ти́ться, чу́сь, ∠тишься *pf.* (*of* **∠тываться**[2]) to roll away (*intrans.*).
ука́тыва|ть[1]**, ю** *impf. of* **украта́ть**
ука́тыва|ть(ся)[2]**, ю(сь)** *impf. of* **укати́ть(ся)**
укач|а́ть, а́ю *pf.* (*of* **∠ивать**) **1.** to rock to sleep. **2.** (*of motion of sea or of means of transport*) to make sick; (*impers.*): **меня́ ~а́ло на парохо́де** I was sea(sick) on the boat.
ука́чива|ть, ю *impf. of* **укача́ть**
укла́д, а *m.* structure; **у. жи́зни** style of life; **обще́ственно-экономи́ческий у.** social and economic structure.
укла́дк|а, и *f.* **1.** packing; stacking, piling. **2.** laying (*of rails, sleepers, pipes, etc.*).
укла́дчик, а *m.* **1.** packer. **2.** layer (*of rails etc.*).
укла́дыва|ть, ю *impf. of* **уложи́ть**
укла́дыва|ться[1]**, юсь,** *impf. of* **уложи́ться**
укла́дыва|ться[2]**, юсь,** *impf. of* **уле́чься**
укло́н, а *m.* **1.** slope; inclination; gradient. **2.** (*fig.*) bias, tendency. **3.** (*pol.*) deviation.
уклоне́ни|е, я *nt.* deviation; **у. от те́мы** digression; **у. от вое́нной слу́жбы** evasion of military service.
уклон|и́ться, ю́сь, ∠ишься *pf.* (*of* **~я́ться**) **1. (от)** to avoid; to evade; **у. от уда́ра** to dodge a blow; **у. от прямо́го отве́та** to avoid giving a direct answer. **2.** to turn off, turn aside.
укло́нчив|ый (~, ~а) *adj.* evasive.
уклон|я́ться, я́юсь *impf. of* **~и́ться**
уклю́чин|а, ы *f.* rowlock.
уко́л, а *m.* **1.** prick; jab. **2.** injection, 'jab'.
укол|о́ть, ю́, ∠ешь *pf.* (*of* **ука́лывать**) **1.** to prick. **2.** (*fig.*) to sting, wound.
укомплектова́ни|е, я *nt.* bringing up to strength.
укомплект|ова́ть, у́ю *pf.* (*of* **комплектова́ть**) **1.** to complete; to bring up to (full) strength; to man. **2.** (+*i.*) to equip (with), furnish (with).
уко́р, а *m.* reproach.
укора́чива|ть, ю *impf. of* **укороти́ть**
укорене́ни|е, я *nt.* **1.** implanting. **2.** taking root.
укорен|и́ть, ю́, и́шь *pf.* (*of* **~я́ть**) to implant, inculcate.
укорен|и́ться, ю́сь, и́шься *pf.* (*of* **~я́ться**) to take, strike root (*also fig.*).
укорен|я́ть(ся), я́ю(сь) *impf. of* **~и́ть(ся)**
укори́зн|а, ы *f.* reproach.
укори́зненный *adj.* reproachful.
укор|и́ть, ю́, и́шь *pf.* (*of* **~я́ть**) (+*a.* **в**+*p.*) to reproach (with).
укоро|ти́ть, чу́, ти́шь *pf.* (*of* **укора́чивать**) to shorten.
укор|я́ть, я́ю *impf. of* **~и́ть**
уко́с, а *m.* hay-harvest, hay crop.
укра́дкой *adv.* stealthily, furtively, by stealth.
Украи́н|а, ы *f.* (the) Ukraine.
украи́н|ец, ца *m.* Ukrainian.
украи́н|ка, ки *f. of* **~ец**
украи́нский *adj.* Ukrainian.
укра́|сить, шу, сишь *pf.* (*of* **~ша́ть**) to adorn, decorate, ornament (*also fig.*).
укра́|ситься, шусь, сишься *pf.* (*of* **~ша́ться**) **1.** *pass. of* **~сить. 2.** to adorn o.s.
укра́|сть, ду́, дёшь, *past* **~л** *pf.* (*of* **красть**) to steal.
украша́|ть(ся), ю(сь) *impf. of* **укра́сить(ся)**
украше́ни|е, я *nt.* **1.** adorning, decoration. **2.** adornment, decoration, ornament.
укреп|и́ть, лю́, и́шь *pf.* (*of* **~ля́ть**) **1.** to strengthen; to reinforce. **2.** (*mil.*) to fortify. **3.** (*fig.*) to strengthen; **у. дисципли́ну** to tighten up discipline.
укреп|и́ться, лю́сь, и́шься *pf.* (*of* **~ля́ться**) **1.** to become stronger. **2.** (*mil.*) to fortify one's position. **3.** (*fig.*) to become firmly established.
укрепле́ни|е, я *nt.* **1.** strengthening, reinforcing. **2.** (*mil.*) fortification.
укрепля́|ть(ся), ю(сь) *impf. of* **укрепи́ть(ся)**
укро́м|ный (~ен, ~на) *adj.* secluded; sheltered.
укро́п, а *m.* (*bot.*) dill.
укроти́тел|ь, я *m.* (animal-)tamer.
укро|ти́ть, щу́, ти́шь *pf.* (*of* **~ща́ть**) **1.** to tame. **2.** to curb, subdue, check.
укро|ти́ться, щу́сь, ти́шься *pf.* (*of* **~ща́ться**) **1.** to become tame. **2.** to calm down, die down.
укроща́|ть(ся), ю(сь) *impf. of* **укроти́ть(ся)**
укрупне́ни|е, я *nt.* enlargement; amalgamation.
укрупн|и́ть, ю́, и́шь *pf.* (*of* **~я́ть**) to enlarge, extend; to amalgamate.
укрупн|я́ть, я́ю *impf. of* **~и́ть**
укрыва́тел|ь, я *m.* (*leg.*) harbourer; **у. кра́деного** receiver (of stolen goods).
укрыва́тельств|о, а *nt.* (*leg.*) concealment, harbouring; **у. кра́деного** receiving (of stolen goods).
укрыва́|ть(ся), ю(сь) *impf. of* **укры́ть(ся)**
укры́ти|е, я *nt.* (*mil., etc.*) cover, concealment; shelter; **у. от огня́** cover (from fire).
укр|ы́ть, о́ю, о́ешь *pf.* (*of* **~ыва́ть**) **1.** to cover (up). **2.** to conceal, harbour; to give shelter; **у. от дождя́** to give shelter from the rain.
укр|ы́ться, о́юсь, о́ешься *pf.* (*of* **~ыва́ться**) **1.** to cover o.s. (up). **2.** to take cover; to seek shelter. **3.** to escape notice; **от меня́ не ~ы́лось** it has not escaped my notice.
у́ксус, а (у) *m.* vinegar.
уксуснoки́сл|ый *adj.* (*chem.*) acetate (of); **~ая соль** acetate.
у́ксусн|ый *adj.* **1.** *adj. of* **у́ксус. 2.** acetic; **~ая кислота́** acetic acid.
уку́порива|ть, ю *impf. of* **уку́порить**
уку́пор|ить, ю, ишь *pf.* (*of* **~ивать**) **1.** to cork (up). **2.** (*coll.*) to pack (up), crate.
уку́с, а *m.* bite; sting.

уку|си́ть, шу́, ~сишь *pf.* to bite; to sting.
уку́т|ать, аю *pf.* (*of* **~ывать**) (**в**+*a.*) to wrap up (in).
уку́т|аться, аюсь *pf.* (*of* **~ываться**) to wrap o.s. up.
уку́тыва|ть(ся), ю(сь) *impf. of* **уку́тать(ся)**
ул. (*abbr. of* **у́лица**) St., Street; Rd., Road.
ула́влива|ть, ю *impf. of* **улови́ть**
ула́|дить, жу, дишь *pf.* (*of* **~живать**) **1.** to settle, arrange. **2.** (*obs.*) to reconcile.
ула́жива|ть, ю *impf. of* **ула́дить**
ула́мыва|ть, ю *impf. of* **улома́ть**
у́л|ей, ья *m.* (bee)hive.
улепет|ну́ть, ну́, нёшь *pf. of* **~ывать**
улепётыва|ть, ю *impf.* (*of* **улепетну́ть**) (*coll.*) to make off, bolt; **~й!** hop it!
улет|а́ть, а́ю *impf. of* **~е́ть**
уле|те́ть, чу́, ти́шь *pf.* (*of* **~та́ть**) **1.** to fly (away). **2.** (*fig.*) to fly; **вре́мя ~те́ло** the time had flown by.
улету́чива|ться, юсь *impf. of* **улету́читься**
улету́ч|иться, усь, ишься *pf.* (*of* **~иваться**) **1.** to evaporate. **2.** (*coll.*) to vanish, disappear.
ул|е́чься, я́гусь, я́жешься, я́гутся, *past* **~ёгся, ~егла́сь** *pf.* **1.** (*impf.* **укла́дываться**[2]) to lie down. **2.** (*impf.* **укла́дываться**[2]) to find room (*lying down*). **3.** (*of dust, etc.*) to settle. **4.** (*fig.*) to subside; to calm down; **ве́тер ~ёгся** the wind dropped.
улизн|у́ть, у́, ёшь *pf.* (*coll.*) to slip away, steal away.
ули́к|а, и *f.* (piece of) evidence.
ули́тк|а, и *f.* (*zool.*) snail.
у́лиц|а, ы *f.* street; **на ~е** (*i*) in the street, (*ii*) out (of doors), outside; **с ~ы** from out of doors.
улич|а́ть, а́ю *impf. of* **~и́ть**
улич|и́ть, у́, и́шь *pf.* (*of* **~а́ть**) (**в**+*p.*) to establish the guilt (of).
у́личн|ый *adj.* street.
уло́в, а *m.* catch (*of fish*).
улови́мый *adj.* perceptible; audible.
улов|и́ть, лю́, ~ишь *pf.* (*of* **ула́вливать**) **1.** (*tech.*) to catch, pick up (*a sound wave, etc.*). **2.** to detect, perceive. **3.** (*coll.*) to seize (*an opportunity, etc.*).
уло́вк|а, и *f.* trick, ruse, subterfuge.
уложе́ни|е, я *nt.* (*leg.*) code (*esp. hist.*).
улож|и́ть, у́, ~ишь *pf.* (*of* **укла́дывать**) **1.** to lay; **у. в посте́ль** to put to bed. **2.** to pack; to stow; to pile, stack. **3.** (+*i.*) to cover (with), lay (with). **4.** to lay (*rails, sleepers, etc.*).
улож|и́ться, у́сь, ~ишься *pf.* (*of* **укла́дываться**[1]) **1.** to pack (up). **2.** (**в**+*a.*) to go (in), fit (in). **3.** (**в**+*a.*; *coll.*) to keep (within), confine o.s. (to); **у. в полчаса́** to confine o.s. to half an hour. **4.:** **у. в голове́, в созна́нии** to sink in, go in.
улома́|ть, ю *pf.* (*of* **ула́мывать**) (*coll.*) to talk round; (+*inf.*) to talk into, prevail upon (to).
у́лочк|а, и *f. dim. of* **у́лица**
улуч|а́ть, а́ю *impf. of* **~и́ть**
улуч|и́ть, у́, и́шь *pf.* (*of* **~а́ть**) (*coll.*) to find, seize, catch; **у. удо́бный слу́чай** to seize an opportunity.
улучш|а́ть(ся), а́ю(сь) *impf. of* **~ить(ся)**
улучше́ни|е, я *nt.* improvement, amelioration.
улу́чш|ить, у, ишь *pf.* (*of* **~а́ть**) to improve; to make better; to better.
улу́чш|иться, усь, ишься *pf.* (*of* **~а́ться**) to improve; to get better.
улыб|а́ться, а́юсь *impf.* (*of* **~ну́ться**) **1.** to smile. **2.** (+*d.*; *fig.*) to smile (upon). **3.** (*impf. only*) (+*d.*; *coll.*) to please; appeal to.
улы́бк|а, и *f.* smile.
улыб|ну́ться, ну́сь, нёшься *pf.* **~а́ться**
улы́бчив|ый (~, ~а) *adj.* (*coll.*) smiling; happy.
ультима́тум, а *m.* ultimatum.
ультра... *comb. form* ultra-
ультразвуково́й *adj.* (*phys.*, *aeron.*) supersonic.
ультракоро́тк|ий *adj.* (*radio*) ultra-short; **~ие во́лны** VHF (*abbr. of* very high frequency) waveband.
ультрамари́н, а *m.* ultramarine.
ультрафиоле́товый *adj.* ultra-violet.
улюлю́ка|ть, ю *impf.* (*hunting*) to halloo.
ум, а́ *m.* mind, intellect; wits; **склад ~а́** mentality; **~а́ не приложу́** (*coll.*) it's beyond me; I give up; **быть без ~а́ (от)** to be mad, crazy (about); (**счи-та́ть**, *etc.*) **в ~е́** (to count, *etc.*) in one's head; **в уме́ ли ты?** (*coll.*) are you in your right mind?; **взя́ться за ум** (*coll.*) to come to one's senses; **прийти́ на ум** (+*d.*) (*coll.*) to occur to one; **быть на ~е́** (*coll.*) to be on one's mind; **свести́ с ~а́** (*coll.*) to drive mad; (*fig.*) to make wild (*with delight, admiration*); **сойти́ с ~а́** to go mad; **с ~о́м** (*coll.*) intelligently; **с ума́ сойти́!** (*coll.*) incredible!
умале́ни|е, я *nt.* belittling, disparagement.
умал|и́ть, ю, и́шь *pf.* (*of* **~я́ть**) to belittle, disparage.
умалишённ|ый *adj.* mad, lunatic; *as n.* **у., ~ого** *m.*; **~ая, ~ой** *f.* madman; lunatic; madwoman; **дом ~ых** lunatic asylum.
ума́лчива|ть, ю *impf. of* **умолча́ть**
умал|я́ть, я́ю *impf. of* **~и́ть**
ума́слива|ть, ю *impf. of* **ума́слить**
ума́сл|ить, ю, ишь *pf.* (*of* **~ивать**) (*coll.*) to butter up.
ума́|ять, ю *pf.* (*coll.*) to tire out.
у́мбр|а, ы *f.* umber.
уме́л|ец, ьца *m.* skilled craftsman.
уме́л|ый *adj.* able, skilful.
уме́ни|е, я *nt.* ability, skill; know-how.
уменьш|а́ть(ся), а́ю(сь) *impf. of* **~и́ть(ся)**
уменьше́ни|е, я *nt.* reduction, diminution, decrease; **у. ско́рости** deceleration.
уменьши́тельн|ый *adj.* **1.** (*gram.*) diminutive. **2.:** **~ое и́мя** pet name (*as* Kolya *for* Nikolai).
уме́ньш|ить, ~у́, ~и́шь *pf.* (*of* **~а́ть**) to reduce, diminish, decrease, lessen; **у. ход** to reduce speed.
уме́ньш|иться, ~у́сь, ~и́шься *pf.* (*of* **~а́ться**) **1.** to diminish, decrease; to abate. **2.** *pass. of* **~ить**
уме́ренност|ь, и *f.* moderation; temperance.
уме́р|енный *adj.* **1.** (**~ен, ~енна**) moderate (*pol.*; *also fig.*); **у. аппети́т** moderate appetite. **2.** (*geog.*, *meteor.*) temperate; moderate.
умер|е́ть, умру́, умрёшь, *past* **у́мер, ~ла́, у́мерло** *pf.* (*of* **умира́ть**) to die; **у. есте́ственной сме́ртью** to die a natural death.
уме́р|ить, ю, ишь *pf.* (*of* **~я́ть**) to moderate, to restrain.
умер|тви́ть, щвлю́, тви́шь *pf.* (*of* **~щвля́ть**) to kill, destroy (*also fig.*); to mortify.
умерщвле́ни|е, я *nt.* killing; mortification.
умерщвля́|ть, ю *impf. of* **умертви́ть**
умер|я́ть, я́ю *impf. of* **~ить**
уме|сти́ть, щу́, сти́шь *pf.* (*of* **~ща́ть**) to get in, fit in; **она́ не могла́ у. все поку́пки в су́мку** she could not get all her purchases into her bag.
уме|сти́ться, щу́сь, сти́шься *pf.* (*of* **~ща́ться**) to go in, fit in, find room.
уме́стно[1] *adv.* appropriately; opportunely.
уме́стно[2] *as pred.* it is appropriate, it is in order; **у. бы́ло бы сде́лать намёк** it would not be out of place to drop a hint.
уме́ст|ный (~ен, ~на) *adj.* appropriate; pertinent; opportune, timely; **ва́ше предложе́ние вполне́ ~но** your suggestion is quite in order.
уме́|ть, ю *impf.* (*of* **с~**) (+*inf.*) to be able (to), know how (to).
умеща́|ть(ся), ю(сь) *impf. of* **умести́ть(ся)**
умиле́ни|е, я *nt.* emotion; tenderness; **прийти́ в у.** to be moved; **лить слёзы ~я** to weep with emotion.
умили́тел|ьный (~ен, ~ьна) *adj.* moving, touching, affecting.
умил|и́ть, ю́, и́шь *pf.* (*of* **~я́ть**) to move, touch.

умил|и́ться, ю́сь, и́шься *pf.* (*of* **~я́ться**) to be moved, be touched.
умил|я́ть(ся), я́ю(сь) *impf. of* **~и́ть(ся)**
умира́ни|е, я *nt.* dying.
умира́|ть, ю *impf. of* **умере́ть**
умиротворе́ни|е, я *nt.* pacification; appeasement.
умиротвор|и́ть, ю́, и́шь *pf.* (*of* **~я́ть**) to pacify; to appease.
умиротвор|я́ть, я́ю *impf. of* **~и́ть**
умла́ут, а *m.* (*ling.*) umlaut.
умн|е́е *comp. of* **~ый** *and* **~о**
умне́|ть, ю *impf.* (*of* **по~**) to grow wiser.
у́мник, а *m.* **1.** good boy; (*coll.*) clever person. **2.** (*iron.*) know-all, smart alec.
у́мниц|а, ы *f. and c.g.* (*coll.*) **1.** *f.* good girl. **2.** *c.g.* clever person.
у́мно[1] *adv.* cleverly, wisely; sensibly.
у́мно[2] *as pred.* it is wise; it is sensible.
умнож|а́ть(ся), а́ю(сь) *impf. of* **~́ить(ся)**
умноже́ни|е, я *nt.* **1.** increase, rise. **2.** (*math.*) multiplication.
умно́ж|ить, у, ишь *pf.* (*of* **мно́жить** *and* **~а́ть**) **1.** to increase, augment. **2.** (*math.*) to multiply.
умно́ж|иться, усь, ишься *pf.* (*of* **мно́житься** *and* **~а́ться**) **1.** to increase, multiply (*intrans.*). **2.** *pass. of* **~ить**
у́м|ный (~ён, ~на́, ~но) *adj.* clever, wise, intelligent; sensible.
умозаключ|а́ть, а́ю *impf. of* **~и́ть**
умозаключе́ни|е, я *nt.* deduction; conclusion.
умозаключ|и́ть, у́, и́шь *pf.* (*of* **~а́ть**) to deduce; to conclude.
умозре́ни|е, я *nt.* (*phil.*) speculation.
умозри́тел|ьный (~ен, ~ьна) *adj.* (*phil.*) speculative.
умоисступле́ни|е, я *nt.* delirium.
умол|и́ть, ю́, и́шь *pf.* (*of* **~я́ть**) to prevail upon.
у́молк: без ~у (*to talk, etc.*) unceasingly, incessantly.
умолк|а́ть, а́ю *impf. of* **~́нуть**
умо́лк|нуть, ну, нешь, *past* **~, ~ла** *pf.* (*of* **~а́ть**) to fall silent; (*of noises*) to cease, stop.
умолча́ни|е, я *nt.* passing over in silence, failure to mention, suppression.
умолча́|ть, ю *pf.* (*of* **ума́лчивать**) (**о**+*p.*) to pass over in silence, fail to mention, suppress, hush up.
умол|я́ть, я́ю *impf.* **1.** *impf. of* **~и́ть. 2.** to entreat, implore.
умоля́ющий *adj.* imploring, pleading, suppliant.
умонастрое́ни|е, я *nt.* mood; mentality.
умопомеша́тельств|о, а *nt.* derangement of mind.
умопомраче́ни|е, я *nt.* (*obs.*) derangement of mind; fit of insanity.
умопомрачи́тел|ьный (~ен, ~ьна) *adj.* (*coll.*) stupendous, tremendous, terrific.
умо́р|а, ы *f. as pred.* (*coll.*) it's hilarious; it's a scream.
умори́тел|ьный (~ен, ~ьна) *adj.* (*coll.*) hilarious.
умор|и́ть, ю́, и́шь *pf.* (*of* **мори́ть**[1]) (*coll.*) **1.** to kill; (*fig.*) to be the death (of); **у. кого́-н. со́ смеху** to make s.o. die of laughing. **2.** to tire out, exhaust.
у́мственн|о *adv. of* **~ый; у. отста́лый** mentally retarded.
у́мственн|ый *adj.* mental, intellectual; **у. бага́ж** mental equipment, store of knowledge.
умудр|и́ть, ю́, и́шь *pf.* (*of* **~я́ть**) to teach, make wiser.
умудр|и́ться, ю́сь, и́шься *pf.* (*of* **~я́ться**) (*coll.*) to contrive, manage.
умудр|я́ть(ся), я́ю(сь) *impf. of* **~и́ть(ся)**
умч|а́ть, у́, и́шь *pf.* to whirl, hurtle away.
умч|а́ться, у́сь, и́шься *pf.* **1.** to whirl, hurtle away (*intrans.*). **2.** (*fig.*) to fly away.
умыва́льник, а *m.* wash-(hand-)stand; wash-basin.
умыва́льный *adj.* wash, washing.
умыва́|ть(ся), ю(сь) *impf. of* **умы́ть(ся)**
у́мыс|ел, ла *m.* design, intention; **со злым ~лом** with malicious intent.
ум|ы́ть, о́ю, о́ешь *pf.* (*of* **~ыва́ть**) to wash.
ум|ы́ться, о́юсь, о́ешься *pf.* (*of* **~ыва́ться**) to wash (o.s.).
умы́шленно *adv.* purposely, intentionally.
умы́шленный *adj.* intentional, deliberate, premeditated.
умягч|а́ть, а́ю *impf. of* **~и́ть**
умягч|и́ть, у́, и́шь *pf.* (*of* **~а́ть**) to soften; to mollify.
унаво́|зить, жу, зишь *pf.* (*of* **наво́зить**) to manure.
унасле́д|овать, ую *pf. of* **насле́довать 1.**
унес|ти́, у́, ёшь, *past* **~̈, ~ла́** *pf.* (*of* **уноси́ть**) **1.** to take away. **2.** (*coll.*) to carry off, make off with. **3.** to carry away, remove; (*impers.*): **ло́дку ~ло́ тече́нием** the boat was carried away by the current. **4.** (*fig.*) to carry (*in thought*).
унес|ти́сь, у́сь, ёшься, *past* **~̈ся, ~ла́сь** *pf.* (*of* **уноси́ться**) **1.** to whirl away (*intrans.*). **2.** (*fig.*) to fly away, fly by; **го́ды ~ли́сь** the years flew by. **3.** (*fig.*) to travel (*in thought*).
униа́т, а *m.* (*relig.*) member of Uniat(e) Church.
униа́тский *adj.* (*relig.*) Uniat(e).
универма́г, а *m.* (*abbr. of* ***универса́льный магази́н***) department store.
универса́л|ьный (~ен, ~ьна) *adj.* **1.** universal; all-round; **~ьное сре́дство** panacea; **у. магази́н** department store. **2.** many-sided; versatile. **3.** (*tech.*) multi-purpose, all-purpose; **~ьное пита́ние** (*elec.*) mains-or-battery power supply.
универса́м, а *m.* (*abbr. of* ***универса́льный магази́н самообслу́живания***) supermarket.
университе́т, а *m.* university; **поступи́ть в у.** to enter, go up to university; **око́нчить у.** to graduate (from a university).
университе́т|ский *adj. of* **~**
унижа́|ть(ся), ю(сь) *impf. of* **уни́зить(ся)**
униже́ни|е, я *nt.* humiliation, degradation, abasement.
уни́жен|ный *adj.* (**~, ~на**) humble.
уни|за́ть, жу́, ~́жешь *pf.* (*of* **~́зывать**) (+*i.*) to cover (with), stud (with).
унизи́тел|ьный (~ен, ~ьна) *adj.* humiliating, degrading.
уни́|зить, жу, зишь *pf.* (*of* **~жа́ть**) to humble, humiliate; to lower, degrade.
уни́|зиться, жусь, зишься *pf.* (*of* **~жа́ться**) to debase o.s.; **у. до шантажа́** to stoop to blackmail.
уни́зыва|ть, ю *impf. of* **униза́ть**
уника́л|ьный (~ен, ~ьна) *adj.* unique.
у́никум, а *m.* unique object (*of its kind*).
унима́|ть(ся), ю(сь) *impf. of* **уня́ть(ся)**
унисо́н, а *m.* (*mus. and phys.*) unison; **в у.** in unison; (*fig.*) in unison, in concert.
унита́з, а *m.* lavatory pan.
унифика́ци|я, и *f.* unification; standardization.
унифици́р|овать, ую *impf. and pf.* to standardize.
уничижи́тел|ьный (~ен, ~ьна) *adj.* **1.** (*obs.*) disparaging. **2.** (*gram.*) pejorative.
уничтож|а́ть, а́ю *impf. of* **~́ить**
уничтожа́|ющий *adj.* destructive; **у. взгляд** murderous look; **~ющее замеча́ние** scathing comment.
уничтоже́ни|е, я *nt.* **1.** destruction, annihilation. **2.** abolition, elimination.
уничто́ж|ить, у, ишь *pf.* (*of* **~а́ть**) **1.** to destroy, annihilate; to wipe out; to obliterate; **у. си́лы проти́вника** to wipe out the enemy's forces. **2.** to abolish; to do away with; **у. крепостно́е пра́во** to abolish serfdom.
у́ни|я, и *f.* (*hist., eccl.*) union.
уно|си́ть(ся), шу́(сь), ~́сишь(ся) *impf. of* **унести́(сь)**

у́нтер-офице́р, а *m.* non-commissioned officer (*abbr.* NCO).

у́нци|я, и *f.* ounce (*measure*).

уныва́|ть, ю *impf.* to be depressed, be dejected.

уны́л|ый (~, ~а) *adj.* **1.** (*of persons*) dejected, despondent, downcast. **2.** (*of thoughts, looks, etc.*) melancholy, doleful, cheerless.

уны́ни|е, я *nt.* dejection, despondency; **впасть в у.** to become depressed; **навести́ у.** to depress.

уня́|ть, уйму́, уймёшь, *past* **~л, ~ла́, ~ло** *pf.* (*of* **унима́ть**) **1.** to calm, soothe, pacify. **2.** (*coll.*) to stop, check. **3.** to suppress (*feelings*).

уня́|ться, уйму́сь, уймёшься, *past* **~лся, ~ла́сь** *pf.* (*of* **унима́ться**) **1.** to calm down. **2.** (*coll.*) to stop, abate, die down.

упа́д: до ~у to the point of exhaustion, till one drops.

упа́д|ок, ка *m.* **1.** decline (*of pol. system, culture, etc.*); **в. состоя́нии ~ка** on the decline. **2.** decline, decay, collapse (*of physical or spiritual faculties*); **у. ду́ха** depression; **у. сил** breakdown.

упа́дочнический *adj.* decadent.

упа́дочничеств|о, а *n.* decadence.

упа́доч|ный (~ен, ~на) *adj.* **1.** decadent. **2.** depressive; **~ное настрое́ние** depression.

упак|ова́ть, у́ю *pf.* (*of* **пакова́ть** *and* **~о́вывать**) to pack (up), wrap (up), bale.

упако́вк|а, и *f.* **1.** packing (*action*), wrapping. **2.** packing (*material*), package.

упако́вочн|ый *adj.* packing.

упако́вшик, а *m.* packer.

упако́выва|ть, ю *impf. of* **упакова́ть**

упас|ти́, у́, ёшь, *past* **~́, ~ла́** *pf.* (*coll.*) to save, preserve; **~и́ Бог, Бо́же ~и́** (*i*) (*expr. warning not to do sth.*) God preserve you!; heaven help you!, (*ii*) (*expr. vigorous denial*) God forbid!

упа́|сть, ду́, дёшь, *past* **~л** *pf.* (*of* **па́дать 1.**) to fall.

упека́|ть, ю *impf. of* **упе́чь**

упер|е́ть, упру́, упрёшь, *past* **~̈, ~̈ла** *pf.* (*of* **упира́ть**) (*a.* **в**+*a.*) to rest (against), prop (against), lean (against); **у. ле́стницу в сте́ну** to rest a ladder against the wall; **у. глаза́ в кого́-н.** (*coll.*) to fasten one's gaze upon s.o.

упер|е́ться, упру́сь, упрёшься, *past* **~̈ся, ~̈лась** *pf.* (*of* **упира́ться**) **1.** (+*i.* **в**+*a.*) to rest (against), prop (against), lean (against); **у. ло́ктем в стол** to rest one's elbow on the table; **у. нога́ми в зе́млю** to dig one's heels in the ground. **2.** (**в**+*a.*; *coll.*) to come up (against), bump (into) (*an obstacle*). **3.** (*coll.*) (*fig.*) to dig one's heels in.

упе́|чь, ку́, чёшь, ку́т, *past* **~̈к, ~кла́** *pf.* (*of* **~ка́ть**) **1.** to bake thoroughly. **2.** (*coll.*) to drag off (*against one's will*); **у. под суд** to drag into court.

упива́|ться, юсь *impf. of* **упи́ться**

упира́|ть, ю *impf.* **1.** *impf. of* **упере́ть. 2.** (*impf. only*) (**на**+*a.*; *coll.*) to stress, insist (on).

упира́|ться, юсь *impf.* **1.** *impf. of* **упере́ться. 2.** (*impf. only*) (**в**+*a.*; *coll.*) to come up (against), be held up (by), be stuck (on account of).

упи|са́ть, шу́, ~́шешь *pf.* (*of* **~́сывать**) (*coll.*) to get through, consume (= *to eat up*).

упи́сыва|ть, ю *impf. of* **уписа́ть**

упи́тан|ный *adj.* **(~, ~на)** well-fed; fattened; plump.

упи́|ться, упью́сь, упьёшься, *past* **~лся, ~ла́сь** *pf.* (*of* **~ва́ться**) (+*i.*) **1.** (*coll.*) to get drunk (on). **2.** (*fig.*) to revel (in), be intoxicated (by).

упла́т|а, ы *f.* payment, paying; **в ~у** on account, in payment; **подлежа́щий ~е** payable.

упла|ти́ть, чу́, ~́тишь *pf.* (*of* **~́чивать**) to pay; **у. по счёту** to pay a bill, settle an account.

упле|сти́, ту́, тёшь, *past* **~̈л, ~ла́** *pf.* (*of* **~та́ть**) (*coll.*) to tuck in (to).

уплета́|ть, ю *impf. of* **уплести́**

уплотне́ни|е, я *nt.* **1.** compression; packing (in); **у. рабо́чего дня** tightening up time-schedules to increase amount of work done. **2.** (*med.*) hardening (*of skin*).

уплотн|и́ть, ю́, и́шь *pf.* (*of* **~я́ть**) to consolidate, compress; to pack (in); **у. рабо́чий день** to plan the working day to increase amount of work done.

уплотн|и́ться, ю́сь, и́шься *pf.* (*of* **~я́ться**) **1.** (*med.*) to harden. **2.** (+*i.*) to take in, give up part of one's accommodation (to). **3.** to condense, thicken.

уплотн|я́ть(ся), я́ю(сь) *impf. of* **~и́ть(ся)**

уплыва́|ть, ю *impf. of* **уплы́ть**

уплы́|ть, ву́, вёшь, *past* **~л, ~ла́, ~ло** *pf.* (*of* **~ва́ть**) **1.** to swim away; to sail, steam away. **2.** (*fig., coll.*) to pass, elapse; **нема́ло вре́мени ~ло** much water has flowed beneath the bridges.

упова́ни|е, я *nt.* (*obs.*) hope.

упова́|ть, ю *impf.* (**на**+*a.*) to put one's trust (in); (+*inf.*) to hope to.

уподо́б|ить, лю, ишь *pf.* (*of* **~ля́ть**) to liken.

уподо́б|иться, люсь, ишься *pf.* (*of* **~ля́ться**) (+*d.*) to become like.

уподобля́|ть(ся), ю(сь) *impf. of* **уподо́бить(ся)**

упое́ни|е, я *nt.* ecstasy, rapture, thrill.

упоённый *adj.* (+*i.*) intoxicated (with), thrilled (by), in raptures (about, over).

упои́тел|ьный (~ен, ~ьна) *adj.* intoxicating, ravishing.

упокое́ни|е, я *nt.* rest, repose; **ме́сто ~я** resting-place (= *grave*).

уполз|а́ть, а́ю *impf. of* **~ти́**

уполз|ти́, у́, ёшь, *past* **~́, ~ла́** *pf.* (*of* **~а́ть**) to creep, crawl away.

уполномо́ченн|ый, ого *m.* plenipotentiary, representative, person authorized.

уполномо́чива|ть, ю *impf. of* **уполномо́чить**

уполномо́чи|е, я *nt.* authorization; **подписа́ть докуме́нт по ~ю кого́-н.** to sign a document on s.o.'s authority.

уполномо́ч|ить, у, ишь *pf.* (*of* **~ивать**) to authorize, empower.

упомина́ни|е, я *nt.* mentioning; (**о**+*p.*) mention (of).

упомина́|ть, ю *impf. of* **упомяну́ть**

упо́мн|ить, ю, ишь *pf.* (*coll.*) to remember.

упомян|у́ть, у́, ~́ешь *pf.* (*of* **упомина́ть**) (+*a. or* **о**+*p.*) to mention, refer (to).

упо́р, а *m.* **1.** rest, prop, support; (*tech.*) stay, brace. **2.: в у.** (*mil.*) point-blank (*also fig.*); **сказа́ть кому́-н. в у.** to tell s.o. point-blank, flat(ly). **3.: сде́лать у.** (**на**+*a. or p.*) to lay special stress (on).

упо́р|ный (~ен, ~на) *adj.* **1.** stubborn, obstinate; persistent; sustained; **у. челове́к** stubborn person; **у. ка́шель** persistent cough; **~ная оборо́на** sustained defence. **2.** (*tech.*) supporting; **у. като́к** bogie wheel. **3.** (*tech.*) stop; **у. рыча́г** stop lever.

упо́рств|о, а *nt.* stubbornness, obstinacy; persistence.

упо́рств|овать, ую *impf.* to be stubborn, unyielding; (**в**+*p.*) to persist (in).

упорхн|у́ть, у́, ёшь *pf.* to fly, flit away.

упоря́дочива|ть, ю *impf. of* **упоря́дочить**

упоря́доч|ить, у, ишь *pf.* (*of* **~ивать**) to regulate, put in (good) order, set to rights.

употреби́тел|ьный (~ен, ~ьна) *adj.* (widely-)used; common, generally accepted, usual.

употреб|и́ть, лю́, и́шь *pf.* (*of* **~ля́ть**) to use; to make use (of); to take (*drink, medicine, etc.*); **у. все уси́лия** to make every effort.

употребле́ни|е, я *nt.* use; application; **спо́соб ~я** directions for use (*of medicine, etc.*); **для вну́треннего ~я** to be taken internally; **вы́йти из ~я** to go out of use, fall into disuse.

употребля́|ть, ю *impf. of* **употреби́ть**

упра́в|а, ы *f.* **1.** (*coll.*) justice, satisfaction; **иска́ть ~ы** to seek justice; **найти́ на кого́-н. ~у** to obtain satisfaction from s.o. **2.** (*hist.*) office, board.

управи́тел|ь, я *m.* (*obs.*) manager, bailiff, steward.

упра́в|иться, люсь, ишься *pf.* (*of* **~ля́ться**) (**с**+*i.*; *coll.*) **1.** to cope (with), manage. **2.** to deal (with) (= *to get the better of*).

управле́ни|е, я *nt.* **1.** management, administration; direction. **2.** (*tech.*) control; driving; steering; **у. по ра́дио** radio control; **теря́ть у.** to get out of control. **3.** government; **о́рганы ме́стного ~я** local government organs. **4.** (*governmental organ*) administration, authority, board. **5.** (*tech.*) controls; steering; **щит ~я** control panel. **6.** (*gram.*) government.

управле́н|ческий *adj. of* **~ие 3., 4.**; **у. аппара́т** government apparatus.

управля́емый *adj.* guided; **у. снаря́д** guided missile.

управля́|ть, ю *impf.* (+*i.*) **1.** to manage, administer, direct, run; to govern; to be in charge (of). **2.** (*tech.*) to control, operate (*a machine*); to drive (*a car, etc.*); to steer; **у. су́дном** (*naut.*) to navigate a vessel. **3.** (*gram.*) to govern.

управл|я́ющий *pres. part. act. of* **~я́ть** *and adj.* control, controlling; **у. вал** (*tech.*) camshaft; *as n.* **у., ~я́ющего** *m.* manager; **у. по́ртом** harbour master.

упражне́ни|е, я *nt.* exercise.

упражня́|ть, ю *impf.* to exercise, train; **у. му́скулы** to exercise one's muscles.

упражня́|ться, юсь *impf.* (**в**+*p.*, **на**+*p.*, **с**+*i.*) to practise, train (at).

упраздне́ни|е, я *nt.* abolition.

упраздн|и́ть, ю́, и́шь *pf.* (*of* **~я́ть**) to abolish.

упраздн|я́ть, я́ю *impf. of* **~и́ть**

упра́шива|ть, ю *impf. of* **упроси́ть**

упрева́|ть, ю *impf. of* **упре́ть**

упре|ди́ть, жу́, ди́шь *pf.* (*of* **~жда́ть**) (*obs.*) **1.** to warn. **2.** to forestall, anticipate.

упрежда́|ть, ю *impf. of* **упреди́ть**

упрежда́ющий *adj.* (*mil.*) pre-emptive; **у. уда́р** pre-emptive strike.

упрёк, а *m.* reproach, reproof; **ста́вить кому́-н. что-н. в у.** to hold sth. against s.o.

упрек|а́ть, а́ю *impf.* (*of* **~ну́ть**) to reproach, reprove; (**в**+*p.*) to accuse (of), charge (with).

упрек|ну́ть, ну́, нёшь *pf. of* **~а́ть**

упре́|ть, ю *pf.* (*of* **~ва́ть**) (*coll.*) to be well stewed.

упро|си́ть, шу́, ~́сишь *pf.* (*of* **упра́шивать**) **1.** to beg, entreat. **2.** (*pf. only*) to prevail upon.

упро|сти́ть, щу́, сти́шь *pf.* (*of* **~ща́ть**) **1.** to simplify; (**до**) to reduce (to). **2.** (*pej.*) to oversimplify.

упро|сти́ться, сти́тся *pf.* (*of* **~ща́ться**) to become simpler, be simplified.

упро́чени|е, я *nt.* strengthening, consolidation.

упро́чива|ть(ся), ю(сь) *impf. of* **упро́чить(ся)**

упро́ч|ить, у, ишь *pf.* (*of* **~ивать**) to strengthen, consolidate.

упро́ч|иться, усь, ишься *pf.* (*of* **~иваться**) **1.** to be strengthened, consolidated; **на́ше положе́ние ~илось** our position is firmly established. **2.** to establish o.s. (firmly), settle o.s. **3.** (**за**+*i.*) to be ensured; to become firmly attached (to); **про́звище ~илось за ней** the nickname stuck to her.

упроща́|ть(ся), ю(сь) *impf. of* **упрости́ть(ся)**

упроще́ни|е, я *nt.* simplification.

упрощённый *adj.* **1.** simplified. **2.** oversimplified.

упроще́нческий *adj.* (*pej.*) oversimplified.

упроще́нчеств|о, а *nt.* (*pej.*) oversimplification.

упру́г|ий (~, ~а) *adj.* elastic, resilient; **~ая похо́дка** springy gait.

упру́гост|ь, и *f.* elasticity, resilience.

упря́жк|а, и *f.* **1.** team, relay (*of horses, dogs, etc.*). **2.** harness, gear.

упряжн|о́й *adj.* draught; **~а́я ло́шадь** draught-horse, carriage-horse; **~а́я тя́га** draw-bar.

у́пряж|ь, и *f.* harness, gear.

упря́м|ец, ца *m.* (*coll.*) obstinate person.

упря́м|иться, люсь, ишься *impf.* to be obstinate; (**в**+*p.*) to persist (in).

упря́мств|о, а *nt.* obstinacy, stubbornness.

упря́м|ый (~, ~а) *adj.* **1.** obstinate, stubborn. **2.** persistent.

упря́|тать, чу, чешь *pf.* (*of* **~тывать**) **1.** to hide, conceal. **2.** (*fig., coll.*) to put away, banish.

упря́тыва|ть, ю *impf. of* **упря́тать**

упуска́|ть, ю *impf. of* **упусти́ть**

упу|сти́ть, щу́, ~́стишь *pf.* (*of* **~ска́ть**) **1.** to let go, let slip, let fall. **2.** (*fig.*) to let go, let slip; to miss; to lose; **у. возмо́жность** to miss an opportunity; **у. и́з виду** to overlook, fail to take account (of).

упуще́ни|е, я *nt.* **1.** omission. **2.** (careless) slip; negligence; **у. по слу́жбе** dereliction of duty.

упы́р|ь, я́ *m.* (*coll.*) vampire; ghoul; bloodsucker.

ура́ *int.* hurrah!; hurray! (*exclamation* (*i*) *expr. exultation or approbation*, (*ii*) *of troops going in to attack*); **на у.** (*i*) (*mil.*) by storm, (*ii*) (*iron.*) by luck (= *without due preparation*).

уравне́ни|е, я *nt.* **1.** equalization. **2.** (*math.*) equation; **у. пе́рвой сте́пени** simple equation.

ура́внива|ть[1], ю *impf. of* **уравня́ть**

ура́внива|ть[2], ю *impf. of* **уровня́ть**

уравни́тельн|ый *adj.* equalizing, levelling.

уравнове́|сить, шу, сишь *pf.* (*of* **~шивать**) **1.** to balance. **2.** (*fig.*) to counterbalance; to neutralize.

уравнове́шенност|ь, и *f.* (*fig.*) steadiness, composure.

уравнове́шенный *adj.* balanced, steady, composed.

уравнове́шива|ть, ю *impf. of* **уравнове́сить**

уравня́|ть, ю *pf.* (*of* **ура́внивать**[1]) to equalize, make equal, make level.

урага́н, а *m.* hurricane; (*fig.*) storm.

уразумева́|ть, ю *impf. of* **уразуме́ть**

уразуме́|ть, ю *pf.* (*of* **~ва́ть**) to comprehend.

Ура́л, а *m.* the Urals.

ура́льский *adj.* (*geog.*) Ural(s).

ура́н, а *m.* **1. У.** (*astron.*) Uranus. **2.** (*chem.*) uranium.

ура́новый *adj.* uranium.

урв|а́ть, у́, ёшь, *past* **~а́л, ~ала́, ~а́ло** *pf.* (*of* **урыва́ть**) (*coll.*) to snatch (*also fig.*), grab; **у. мину́ту-две для бесе́ды** to snatch a minute or two for a chat.

урду́ *m. indecl.* Urdu (*language*).

урегули́ровани|е, я *nt.* regulation; settlement.

урегули́р|овать, ую *pf.* (*of* **регули́ровать**) to regulate; to settle; **у. спо́рную пробле́му** to settle a dispute.

уре́|зать, жу, жешь *pf.* (*of* **~за́ть** *and* **~зывать**) **1.** (*coll.*) to cut off; to shorten. **2.** to cut down, reduce; to axe; **у. шта́ты** to cut down the staff.

урез|а́ть, а́ю *impf. of* **~́ать**

урезо́нива|ть, ю *impf. of* **урезо́нить**

урезо́н|ить, ю, ишь *pf.* (*of* **~ивать**) (*coll.*) to make to see reason, bring to reason.

уре́зыва|ть ю *impf.* = **уреза́ть**

уре́тр|а, ы *f.* (*anat.*) urethra.

у́рн|а, ы *f.* **1.** urn. **2.: избира́тельная у.** ballot-box. **3.** refuse bin.

у́ров|ень, ня *m.* **1.** level; standard; **у. мо́ря** sea level; **в у.** (**с**+*i.*) (*i*) level (with); flush (with), (*ii*) (*fig.*) abreast (of), in pace (with); **на ~не земли́** at ground level; **быть на ~не** to satisfy requirements. **2.** (*tech.*) level, gauge.

уровня́|ть, ю *pf.* (*of* **ура́внивать**[2]) to level, make even.

уро́д, а *m.* **1.** freak, monster. **2.** ugly person.

уро́дин|а, ы *c.g.* (*coll.*) = **уро́д**

уро|ди́ть, жу́, ди́шь *pf.* (*coll.*) to bear, bring forth.

уро|ди́ться, жу́сь, ди́шься *pf.* **1.** (*of crops, etc.*) to ripen; (*of a human being*) to be born. **2.** (**в**+*a.*; *coll.*) to take after.

уро́дливост|ь, и *f.* **1.** deformity. **2.** ugliness.
уро́длив|ый (~, ~а) *adj.* **1.** deformed, misshapen. **2.** ugly. **3.** (*fig.*) bad; abnormal; faulty; distorted.
уро́д|овать, ую *impf.* (*of* **из~**) **1.** to deform, disfigure, mutilate. **2.** to make ugly. **3.** (*fig.*) to distort.
уро́д|ский *adj.* (*coll.*) **1.** *adj. of* **~**. **2.** distorted.
уро́дств|о, а *nt.* **1.** deformity; disfigurement. **2.** ugliness. **3.** (*fig.*) abnormality.
урожа́|й, я *m.* harvest; crop; **собра́ть у.** to gather in the harvest.
урожа́йност|ь, и *f.* productivity (*of crops*), yield.
урожа́|йный (~ен, ~йна) *adj.* **1.** *adj. of* **~й. 2.** producing high yield, productive; **у. год** good year (*for a crop*).
урождённ|ый *adj.*: **~ая** (*before maiden name*) née.
уроже́н|ец, ца *m.* (+*g.*) native (of).
уроже́н|ка, ки *f. of* **~ец**
уро́к, а *m.* **1.** lesson (*also fig.*); **брать ~и** (+*g.*) to have lessons (in); **дава́ть ~и** (+*g.*) to give lessons (in); **дать кому́-н. у.** (*fig.*) to teach s.o. a lesson. **2.** homework; **зада́ть у.** to set homework.
уро́лог, а *m.* (*med.*) urologist.
урологи́ческий *adj.* (*med.*) urological.
уроло́ги|я, и *f.* (*med.*) urology.
уро́н, а *no pl., m.* losses, casualties; **нанести́ у.** to inflict casualties.
урон|и́ть, ю́, ~́ишь *pf. of* **роня́ть**
уро́чищ|е, а *nt.* (*geog.*) natural boundary.
уро́чн|ый *adj.* **1.** (*obs.*) fixed, agreed; **~ая цена́** fixed price. **2.** usual, established.
урча́ни|е, я *nt.* rumbling.
урч|а́ть, у́, и́шь *impf.* to rumble.
урыва́|ть, ю *impf. of* **урва́ть**
уры́вками *adv.* (*coll.*) in snatches, by fits and starts.
урю́к, а (у) *no pl., m.* (*collect.*) dried apricots.
ус, а *m.* **1.** (*see also* **~ы́**) moustache hair; **и в ус не дуть** (*coll.*) not to give a damn. **2.** whisker (*of an animal*). **3.** antenna, feeler (*of an insect*). **4.** (*bot.*) tendril. **5.: кито́вый ус** whalebone, baleen.
уса|ди́ть, жу́, ~́дишь *pf.* (*of* **~́живать**) **1.** to seat, help sit down; **у. в тюрьму́** (*coll.*) to throw into jail. **2.** (**за**+*a. or* +*inf.*) to set (to, at); **у. кого́-н. за роя́ль** to set s.o. to (play at) the piano. **3.** (+*i.*) to plant (with).
уса́дк|а, и *f.* shrinking; shrinkage; contraction.
уса́дьб|а, ы, *g. pl.* **~** *and* **уса́деб** *f.* **1.** (*hist.*) country estate; country seat. **2.** farmstead.
уса́жива|ть, ю *impf. of* **усади́ть**
уса́жива|ться, юсь *impf. of* **усе́сться**
уса́т|ый (~, ~а) *adj.* **1.** with a (big) moustache. **2.** (*of animals*) whiskered.
уса́ч, а́ *m.* **1.** (*coll.*) man with a (big) moustache. **2.** barbel (*fish*).
усва́ива|ть, ю *impf. of* **усво́ить**
усвое́ни|е, я *nt.* mastering; assimilation.
усво́|ить, ю, ишь *pf.* (*of* **усва́ивать**) **1.** to adopt, acquire (*a habit, etc.*); to imitate; **у. чужо́й вы́говор** to pick up s.o. else's accent. **2.** to master (= *to learn*); to assimilate. **3.** to assimilate (*food, medicine, etc.*).
усе́ива|ть, ю *impf. of* **усе́ять**
усека́|ть, ю *impf. of* **усе́чь**
усе́рди|е, я *nt.* zeal; diligence.
усе́рд|ный (~ен, ~на) *adj.* zealous, diligent, painstaking.
усе́рдств|овать, ую *impf.* to be zealous; to take pains.
усе́|сться, ускя́дусь, уся́дешься, *past* **~лся, ~лась** *pf.* (*of* **уса́живаться**) **1.** to take a seat; to settle (down). **2.** (**за**+*a. or* +*inf.*) to settle down (to); **у. за ка́рты** to settle down to (a game of) cards.
усе́|чь, ку́, чёшь, ку́т, *past* **~́к, ~кла́** *pf.* (*of* **~ка́ть**) to cut off, truncate.
усе́|ять, ю, ешь *pf.* (*of* **~ивать**) (+*i.*) **1.** to sow (with). **2.** to cover (with), dot (with), stud (with), strew (with); **лицо́, ~янное весну́шками** face covered with freckles.
уси|де́ть, жу́, ди́шь *pf.* **1.** to keep one's place, remain sitting. **2.** (*coll.*) to keep a job.
уси́дчивост|ь, и *f.* assiduity.
уси́дчив|ый (~, ~а) *adj.* assiduous; painstaking.
у́сик, а *m.* **1.** (*pl.*) small moustache. **2.** (*bot.*) tendril; runner (*of strawberry, etc.*). **3.** (*zool.*) antenna, feeler.
усиле́ни|е, я *nt.* **1.** strengthening; reinforcement. **2.** intensification; (*radio*) amplification.
уси́ленн|ый *adj.* **1.** intensified, increased; **~ая рабо́та** high pressure of work. **2.** earnest, urgent, importunate; **~ые про́сьбы** earnest entreaties.
уси́лива|ть, ю *impf. of* **уси́лить**
уси́лива|ться, юсь *impf.* **1.** *impf. of* **уси́литься. 2.** (+*inf.*; *obs.*) to try (to), make an effort (to).
уси́ли|е, я *nt.* effort; exertion; **приложи́ть все ~я** to make every effort.
усили́тел|ь, я *m.* **1.** (*tech.*) booster. **2.** (*radio*) amplifier.
уси́л|ить, ю, ишь *pf.* (*of* **~ивать**) **1.** to strengthen, reinforce. **2.** to intensify, increase, heighten; (*radio*) to amplify.
уси́л|иться, ится *pf.* (*of* **~иваться**) to become stronger; to intensify, increase (*intrans.*); (*of sound*) to swell, grow louder.
уска|ка́ть, чу́, ~́чешь *pf.* **1.** to bound away; (*coll.*) to skip off. **2.** to gallop off.
ускольз|а́ть, а́ю *impf. of* **~ну́ть**
ускольз|ну́ть, ну́, нёшь *pf.* (*of* **~а́ть**) **1.** to slip off. **2.** (*coll., of a pers.*) to slip off, steal away. **3.** (*fig.*) to disappear; to escape; **у. от внима́ния** to escape one's notice. **4.** (**от**; *coll.*) to evade, avoid; **у. от прямо́го отве́та** to avoid giving a direct answer.
ускоре́ни|е, я *nt.* acceleration; speeding up.
уско́ренн|ый *adj.* accelerated; rapid; crash; **~ая програ́мма** crash programme.
ускори́тел|ь, я *m.* (*tech.*) accelerator.
уско́р|ить, ю, ишь *pf.* (*of* **~я́ть**) **1.** to quicken; to speed up, accelerate; **у. шаг** to quicken one's pace. **2.** to hasten; to precipitate.
уско́р|иться, ится *pf.* (*of* **~я́ться**) **1.** to quicken; to accelerate. **2.** *pass of* **~ить**
ускор|я́ть, я́ю *impf. of* **~́ить**
ускор|я́ться, я́ется *impf. of* **~́иться**
усла́вливаться = усло́вливаться
усла́д|а, ы *f.* (*obs.*) joy, delight; enjoyment.
усла|ди́ть, жу́, ди́шь *pf.* (*of* **~жда́ть**) (*obs. or poet.*) **1.** to delight, charm. **2.** to soften, mitigate.
усла|ди́ться, жу́сь, ди́шься *pf.* (*of* **~жда́ться**) (+*i.*; *obs. or poet.*) to delight (in).
услажда́|ть(ся), ю(сь) *impf. of* **услади́ть(ся)**
усла́ть, ушлю́, ушлёшь *pf.* (*of* **усыла́ть**) to send away, dispatch.
усле|ди́ть, жу́, ди́шь *pf.* (**за**+*i.*) **1.** to keep an eye (on), mind. **2.** to follow.
усло́ви|е, я *nt.* **1.** condition; term; stipulation; **поста́вить ~ем** to make it a condition, stipulate; **при ~и, что** on condition that, provided that. **2.** (*obs.*) agreement; **заключи́ть у.** to conclude an agreement. **3.** (*pl.*) conditions; **~я пого́ды** weather conditions; **при про́чих ра́вных ~ях** other things being equal.
усло́в|иться, люсь, ишься *pf.* (*of* **~ливаться**) to agree; to arrange, make arrangements; **мы ~ились о ме́сте свида́ния** we agreed on a meeting-place.
усло́вленный *adj.* agreed, fixed, stipulated; **в у. час** at the hour agreed.
усло́влива|ться, юсь *impf. of* **усло́виться**
усло́вност|ь, и *f.* convention, conventionality.
усло́в|ный *adj.* **1.** conventional; agreed, prearranged; **у. знак** conventional sign. **2. (~ен, ~на)** conditional; **у. пригово́р** (*leg.*) suspended sentence. **3. (~ен, ~на)** relative. **4.** (*gram.*) conditional. **5.: у.**

рефле́кс (*physiol.*) conditioned reflex.
усложне́ни|е, я *nt.* complication.
усложн|и́ть, ю́, и́шь *pf.* (*of* **~я́ть**) to complicate.
усложн|и́ться, и́тся *pf.* (*of* **~я́ться**) to become complicated.
усложн|я́ть, я́ю *impf. of* **~и́ть**
усложн|я́ться, я́ется *impf. of* **~и́ться**
услу́г|а, и *f.* **1.** service; good turn; **до́брые ~и** (*dipl.*) good offices; **предложи́ть свои́ ~и** to offer one's services; **к ва́шим ~ам** at your service. **2.** (*pl.*) service(s); **ко́мната со всеми ~ами** room with service; **коммуна́льные ~и** public utilities.
услу́жива|ть, ю *impf.* (*obs.*) **1.** *impf. of* **услужи́ть. 2.** to serve, act as a servant.
услуж|и́ть, у́, ~ишь *pf.* (*of* **~ивать**) (+*d.*) to do a service, good turn.
услу́жлив|ый (~, ~а) *adj.* obliging.
услыха́ть = услы́шать
услы́ш|ать, у, ишь *pf.* (*of* **слы́шать**) **1.** to hear. **2.** (*coll.*) to perceive, sense; (*of animals*) to scent.
усма́трива|ть, ю *impf. of* **усмотре́ть**
усмех|а́ться, а́юсь *impf. of* **~ну́ться**
усмех|ну́ться, ну́сь, нёшься *pf.* (*of* **~а́ться**) to smile; to grin.
усме́шк|а, и *f.* smile, grin.
усмире́ни|е, я *nt.* suppression; pacification.
усмир|и́ть, ю́, и́шь *pf.* (*of* **~я́ть**) **1.** to pacify; to quieten. **2.** to suppress, put down (*a mutiny, etc.*).
усмир|я́ть, я́ю *impf. of* **~и́ть**
усмотре́ни|е, я *nt.* discretion, judgement; **поступи́ть по своему́ ~ю** to use one's own discretion.
усмотр|е́ть, ю́, ~ишь *pf.* (*of* **усма́тривать**) **1.** (**за**+*i.*) to keep an eye (on). **2.** (*coll.*) to perceive, observe. **3.** (**в**+*p.*) to see (in); to regard (as), interpret (as); **у. угро́зу в заявле́нии** to interpret the statement as a threat.
усн|у́ть, у́, ёшь *pf.* to go to sleep, fall asleep.
усоверше́нствовани|е, я *nt.* **1.** improvement, refinement. **2.**: **ку́рсы ~я** advanced training course(s).
усоверше́нств|овать(ся), ую(сь) *pf. of* **соверше́нствовать(ся)**
усо́ве|стить, щу, стишь *pf.* (*of* **~щивать**) to appeal to the conscience (of); to make ashamed.
усо́ве|ститься, щусь, стишься *pf.* (*of* **~щиваться**) to be sorry, be conscience-stricken.
усо́вещива|ть(ся), ю(сь) *impf. of* **усо́вестить(ся)**
усомн|и́ться, ю́сь, и́шься *pf.* (**в**+*p.*) to doubt.
усо́пш|ий *adj.* (*obs.*) deceased; *as n.* **у., ~его** *m.*, **~ая, ~ей** *f.* the deceased.
усо́х|нуть, ну, нешь, *past* **~, ~ла** *pf.* (*of* **усыха́ть**) to dry up, dry out.
успева́емост|ь, и *f.* progress (*in studies*).
успева́|ть, ю *impf.* **1.** *impf. of* **успе́ть. 2.** (*impf. only*) (**в**+*p. or* **по**+*d.*) to make progress (in), get on well (in, at) (*of studies*).
успе́ется *impers., pf.* (*coll.*) there's plenty of time.
успе́ни|е, я *nt.* (*eccl.*) **1.** death, passing. **2. У.** (Feast of) the Dormition, Assumption (of the Virgin).
успе́н|ский *adj. of* **~ие 2.**
успе́|ть, ю *pf.* (*of* **~ва́ть**) **1.** to have time; to manage; **у. на заседа́ние** to be in time for the meeting; **у. к по́езду** to manage to catch the train. **2.** (**в**+*p.*) to succeed (in), be successful (in).
успе́х, а *m.* **1.** success; **име́ть большо́й у.** to be a great success; **по́льзоваться ~ом** to be a success; **с тем же ~ом** equally well, with the same result. **2.** (*pl.*) success, progress; **как ва́ши ~и?** how are you getting on? **де́лать ~и** (**в**+*p.*) to make progress (in).
успе́шност|ь, и *f.* success; progress.
успе́ш|ный (~ен, ~на) *adj.* successful.
успока́ива|ть(ся), ю(сь) *impf. of* **успоко́ить(ся)**
успока́ивающ|ий *adj.* sedative; **~ее сре́дство** sedative.
успокое́ни|е, я *nt.* **1.** calming, quieting, soothing. **2.** calm; peace, tranquillity.
успокои́тел|ьный (~ен, ~ьна) *adj.* calming, soothing; reassuring; *as n.* **~ьное, ~ьного** *nt.* sedative.
успоко́|ить, ю, ишь *pf.* (*of* **успока́ивать**) **1.** to calm, quiet, soothe; to reassure, set one's mind at rest. **2.** to assuage, deaden (*pain, etc.*); **у. чьи-н. подозре́ния** to still s.o.'s suspicions. **3.** (*coll.*) to reduce to order; **у. дете́й** to make children be quiet.
успоко́|иться, юсь, ишься *pf.* (*of* **успока́иваться**) **1.** to calm down. **2.** (**на дости́гнутом**) to rest content (with what has been achieved). **3.** (*of pain, etc.*) to abate; (*of the sea*) to become still. **4.** *pass. of* **~ить**
уст|а́, ~, ~а́м *no sg.* (*obs. or poet.*) mouth, lips; **из ~ в у.** by word of mouth; **узна́ть из пе́рвых ~** to learn at first hand; **э́то у всех на ~а́х** everyone's talking about it; **твои́ми бы ~а́ми мёд пить** if only you were right.
уста́в, а *m.* regulations, rules, statutes; (*mil.*) service regulations; (*monastic*) rule; **у. университе́та** university statutes; **У. ООН** UN Charter.
уста|ва́ть, ю́, ёшь *impf. of* **~ть; не ~ва́я** (*as adv.*) incessantly, uninterruptedly.
уста́в|ить, лю, ишь *pf.* (*of* **~ля́ть**) (*coll.*) **1.** to set, arrange; **у. ме́бель в ко́мнате** to arrange furniture about the room. **2.** (+*i.*) to cover (with), fill (with), pile (with); **у. стол буты́лками** to cover a table with bottles. **3.** (**глаза́**, *etc.* **на**+*a.*) to direct, fix (one's gaze, *etc.*, upon).
уста́в|иться, люсь, ишься *pf.* (*of* **~ля́ться**) (*coll.*) **1.** to find room, go in. **2.** (**на**+*a.*) to fix one's gaze (upon), stare (at).
уставля́|ть(ся), ю(сь) *impf. of* **уста́вить(ся)**
уста́вный *adj.* regulation, statutory, prescribed.
уста́лост|ь, и *f.* fatigue, tiredness.
уста́лый *adj.* tired, weary.
у́стал|ь, и *f.* (*obs. or coll.*) = **~ость; без ~и** tirelessly, unceasingly.
устана́влива|ть(ся), ю(сь) *impf. of* **установи́ть(ся)**
установ|и́ть, лю́, ~ишь *pf.* (*of* **устана́вливать**) **1.** to place, set up; (*tech.*) to install. **2.** (**на**+*a.*; **по**+*d.*) to adjust, set (to; by); **у. часы́ по ра́дио** to set one's watch by the radio. **3.** to establish, institute; **у. связь** (**с**+*i.*; *mil.*) to establish communication (with). **4.** to fix; **у. сро́ки о́тдыха** to fix holidays. **5.** to secure, obtain; **у. тишину́** to secure quiet. **6.** to establish; to ascertain; **у. причи́ну ава́рии** to establish the cause of a crash.
установ|и́ться, лю́сь, ~ишься *pf.* (*of* **устана́вливаться**) **1.** to be established; to set in; **~и́лся обы́чай** it has become a custom; **пого́да ~и́лась** the weather has become settled. **2.** (*of character, etc.*) to be formed, be fixed.
устано́вк|а, и *f.* **1.** placing, setting up, arrangement; (*tech.*) installation. **2.** adjustment, setting. **3.** (*tech.*) plant, unit, installation. **4.** aim, purpose; **име́ть ~у** (**на**+*a.*) to aim (at). **5.** directions, directive.
установле́ни|е, я *nt.* establishment.
устано́вленн|ый *adj.* established, fixed, prescribed, regulation; **в ~ом поря́дке** in prescribed manner.
устано́в|очный *adj.* **1.** (*tech.*) *adj. of* **~ка 1., 2.; у. винт** adjusting screw. **2.** *adj. of* **~ка 5.; у. вопро́с** fundamental question.
устарева́|ть, ю *impf. of* **устаре́ть**
устаре́вший *adj.* obsolete.
устаре́лый *adj.* obsolete; antiquated, out of date.
устаре́|ть, ю *pf.* (*of* **~ва́ть**) to become obsolete; to become antiquated, out of date.
уста́|ть, ну, нешь *pf.* (*of* **~ва́ть**) to become tired; **я ~л** I am tired.
устерега́|ть, ю *impf. of* **устере́чь**
устере́|чь, гу́, жёшь, гу́т, *past* **~г, ~гла́** *pf.* (*of* **~га́ть**) (**от**; *coll.*) to guard (against).

устила́|ть, ю *impf. of* **устла́ть**
устла́ть, устелю́, усте́лешь *pf.* (*of* **устила́ть**) (*+i.*) to cover (with); to pave (with).
у́стно *adv.* orally, by word of mouth.
у́стн|ый *adj.* oral, verbal; **~ая речь** spoken language.
усто́|й[1], я *m.* **1.** (*tech.*) abutment, pier (*of bridge*). **2.** foundation, support. **3.** (*pl.*; *fig.*) foundations, bases.
усто́|й[2], я *m.* (*coll.*) thickened layer on surface of liquid; **у. молока́** cream.
усто́йчивост|ь, и *f.* stability, steadiness, firmness.
усто́йчив|ый (~, ~а) *adj.* stable, steady, firm (*also fig.*); **~ая валю́та** stable currency; **~ая пого́да** settled weather.
усто|я́ть, ю́, и́шь *pf.* **1.** to keep one's balance, remain standing. **2.** (*fig.*) to stand one's ground. **3.** to resist; **у. пе́ред собла́зном** to resist a temptation.
усто|я́ться, и́тся *pf.* **1.** (*esp. of liquids*) to settle. **2.** (*coll.*) to become fixed, become permanent.
устра́ива|ть(ся), ю(сь) *impf. of* **устро́ить(ся)**
устране́ни|е, я *nt.* removal, elimination.
устран|и́ть, ю́, и́шь *pf.* (*of* **~я́ть**) **1.** to remove, eliminate. **2.** to remove (*from office*), dismiss.
устран|и́ться, ю́сь, и́шься *pf.* (*of* **~я́ться**) **1.** to resign, retire, withdraw. **2.** *pass. of* **~и́ть**
устран|я́ть(ся), я́ю(сь) *impf. of* **~и́ть(ся)**
устраш|а́ть(ся), а́ю(сь) *impf. of* **~и́ть(ся)**
устраш|и́ть, у́, и́шь *pf.* (*of* **~а́ть**) to frighten, scare.
устраш|и́ться, у́сь, и́шься *pf.* (*of* **~а́ться**) to be afraid, take fright, be scared.
устрем|и́ть, лю́, и́шь *pf.* (*of* **~ля́ть**) (**на**+*a.*) **1.** (*obs.*) to throw (*troops, etc.*) (against). **2.** to direct (to, at); **у. глаза́ на что-н.** to fasten one's gaze upon sth.
устрем|и́ться, лю́сь, и́шься *pf.* (*of* **~ля́ться**) **1.** (**на**+*a.*) to rush (upon, at). **2.** (**на**+*a.*; **к**) to be directed (at, towards), be fixed (upon); (*of a pers.*) to concentrate (on).
устремле́ни|е, я *nt.* **1.** rush. **2.** striving, aspiration.
устремля́|ть(ся), ю(сь) *impf. of* **устреми́ть(ся)**
у́стриц|а, ы *f.* oyster.
у́стри|чный *adj. of* **~ца**
устро́йтел|ь, я *m.* organizer.
устро́|ить, ю, ишь *pf.* (*of* **устра́ивать**) **1.** to make, construct. **2.** to arrange, organize; **у. конце́рт** to arrange a concert. **3.** (*fig., coll.*) to make, create; **у. сканда́л** to make a scene. **4.** to settle, order, put in (good) order. **у. свои́ дела́** to put one's affairs in order. **5.** to place; to get; **у. кого́-н. на рабо́ту** to fix s.o. up with work. **у. кому́-н. ко́мнату** (*coll.*) to get s.o. a room. **6.** (*impers.*; *coll.*) to suit, be convenient (to, for).
устро́|иться, юсь, ишься *pf.* (*of* **устра́иваться**) **1.** to work out (well). **2.** to manage, make arrangements. **3.** to settle down. **4.** to get fixed up (*in a job*); **он ~ился на желе́зную доро́гу кочега́ром** he has got a job on the railway as a fireman.
устро́йств|о, а *nt.* **1.** arrangement, organization. **2.** layout; (*tech.*) working principle(s). **3.** apparatus, device; **запомина́ющее у.** (*comput.*) storage (device), memory. **4.** structure, system; **обще́ственное у.** social structure.
усту́п, а *m.* shelf, ledge (*of wall or cliff*); terrace; **располо́женный ~ами** terraced.
уступ|а́ть, а́ю *impf. of* **~и́ть**
уступи́тельный *adj.* (*gram.*) concessive.
уступ|и́ть, лю́, ~ишь *pf.* (*of* **~а́ть**) **1.** (*+d.*) to let have, give up (to); to cede (to); **у. кому́-н. ме́сто** to give up one's place to s.o.; **у. доро́гу** (*+d.*) to make way (for). **2.** (*+d.*) to yield (to), give in (to). **3.** (*+d.*) to be inferior (to). **4.** (*coll.*) to let have (= *to sell*). **5.** (*coll.*) to take off, knock off (= *to reduce the price by*).
усту́пк|а, и *f.* **1.** concession; **сде́лать ~и** to make concessions, compromise. **2.** reduction (*of price*).
усту́пчив|ый (~, ~а) pliant, pliable; compliant.
усты|ди́ть, жу́, ди́шь *pf.* to shame, put to shame.
усты|ди́ться, жу́сь, ди́шься *pf.* (*+g.*) to be ashamed (of); to feel embarrassed (for).
у́сть|е, я, *g. pl.* **~ев** *nt.* **1.** mouth, estuary (*of a river*). **2.** mouth, orifice (*of furnace, pipe, etc.*)
усугу́б|ить, ~лю, ~ишь *pf.* (*of* **~ля́ть**) to increase; to intensify; to aggravate.
усугубля́|ть, ю *impf. of* **усугу́бить**
ус|ы́, о́в *pl.* (*sg.* **ус, а** *m.*) moustache (*see also* **ус**); **мы,** *etc.* **са́ми с ~а́ми** (*coll.*) we, *etc.*, weren't born yesterday.
усыла́|ть, ю *impf. of* **усла́ть**
усынов|и́ть, лю́, и́шь *pf.* (*of* **~ля́ть**) to adopt.
усыновле́ни|е, я *nt.* adoption.
усыновля́|ть, ю *impf. of* **усынови́ть**
усыпа́льниц|а, ы *f.* burial-vault.
усы́п|ать, лю, лешь *pf.* (*of* **~а́ть**) (*+i.*) to strew (with), scatter (with); (*fig.*) to cover (with).
усып|а́ть, а́ю *impf. of* **~ать**
усыпи́тел|ьный (~ен, ~ьна) *adj.* soporific (*also fig.*); **~ьное сре́дство** sleeping-draught.
усып|и́ть, лю́, и́шь *pf.* (*of* **~ля́ть**) **1.** to put to sleep (*by means of narcotics, etc.*); to lull to sleep. **2.** (*fig.*) to lull; **у. боль** to deaden pain. **3.** to put (*an animal*) to sleep.
усыпля́|ть, ю *impf. of* **усыпи́ть**
усыха́|ть, ю *impf. of* **усо́хнуть**
ута́ива|ть, ю *impf. of* **утаи́ть**
ута|и́ть, ю́, и́шь *pf.* (*of* **~ивать**) **1.** to conceal; to keep to o.s., keep secret. **2.** to appropriate.
ута́йк|а, и *f.* (*coll.*) concealment; **без ~и** frankly, openly.
ута́птыва|ть, ю *impf. of* **утопта́ть**
ута́скива|ть, ю *impf. of* **утащи́ть**
утащ|и́ть, у́, ~ишь *pf.* (*of* **ута́скивать**) **1.** to drag away, off (*also fig.*); **у. кого́-н. в кино́** (*coll.*) to drag s.o. off to the cinema. **2.** (*coll.*) to walk off with (= *to steal*).
у́твар|ь, и *no pl., f.* (*collect.*) utensils, equipment.
утверди́тел|ьный (~ен, ~ьна) *adj.* affirmative.
утвер|ди́ть, жу́, ди́шь *pf.* (*of* **~жда́ть**) **1.** to establish (*securely, firmly*); **у. диктату́ру** to establish a dictatorship. **2.** (**в**+*p.*) to confirm (in) (*intention, opinion, etc.*) **3.** to approve; to confirm; **у. пове́стку дня** to approve an agenda; **у. кого́-н. в до́лжности** to confirm s.o.'s tenure of an office.
утвер|ди́ться, жу́сь, ди́шься *pf.* (*of* **~жда́ться**) **1.** to gain a foothold (*also fig.*); to become firmly established. **2.** (**в**+*p.*) to be confirmed in (*one's resolve, etc.*); **у. в мы́сли** to become firmly convinced.
утвержда́|ть, ю *impf.* **1.** *impf. of* **утверди́ть. 2.** (*impf. only*) to assert, maintain, claim.
утвержда́|ться, юсь *impf. of* **утверди́ться**
утвержде́ни|е, я *nt.* **1.** assertion, claim, allegation. **2.** approval; confirmation; (*leg.*) probate. **3.** establishment.
утека́|ть, ю *impf. of* **уте́чь**
ут|ёнок, ёнка, *pl.* **~я́та, ~я́т** *m.* duckling.
утепл|и́ть, ю́, и́шь *pf.* (*of* **~я́ть**) to warm, heat.
утепл|я́ть, я́ю *impf. of* **~и́ть**
утер|е́ть, утру́, утрёшь, *past* **~, ~ла** *pf.* (*of* **утира́ть**) to wipe (off); to wipe dry; **у. пот со лба** to wipe the sweat off one's brow.
утерп|е́ть, лю́, ~ишь *pf.* to restrain o.s.
уте́р|я, и *f.* loss.
утеря́|ть, ю *pf.* to lose, mislay.
утёс, а *m.* cliff, crag.
утёсист|ый (~, ~а) *adj.* steep, precipitous.
утёх|а, и *f.* (*coll.*) **1.** pleasure; delight; **для ~и** for fun. **2.** comfort, consolation.
уте́чк|а, и *f.* leak, leakage (*also fig.*); loss, wastage; **у. га́за** gas escape; **«у. умо́в»** brain drain.

уте́|чь, ку́, чёшь, ку́т, *past* **∸к, ~кла́** *pf.* (*of* **~ка́ть**) **1.** to leak; (*of gas, etc.*) to escape; **мно́го воды́ ~кло́** (*fig.*) much water has flowed (*under the bridges*). **2.** (*of time*) to pass, go by.
утеш|а́ть(ся), а́ю(сь) *impf. of* **∸ить(ся)**
утеше́ни|е, я *nt.* comfort, consolation.
утеши́тел|ь, я *m.* comforter.
утеши́тел|ьный (~ен, ~ьна) *adj.* comforting, consoling.
уте́ш|ить, у, ишь *pf.* (*of* **~а́ть**) to comfort, console.
уте́ш|иться, усь, ишься *pf.* (*of* **~а́ться**) **1.** to console o.s. **2.** (+*i.*) to take comfort (in).
утилизацио́нный *adj.*: **у. цех** salvage department.
утилиза́ци|я, и *f.* **1.** utilization. **2.** salvaging.
утилизи́р|овать, ую *impf. and pf.* to utilize.
утилитари́зм, а *m.* utilitarianism.
утилита́рный *adj.* utilitarian.
ути́л|ь, я *no pl., m.* (*collect.*) salvage, scrap.
ути́ль|ный *adj. of* **~**; **~ное желе́зо** scrap iron.
утильсырь|ё, я́ *no pl., nt.* (*collect.*) = **ути́ль**
ути́ный *adj. of* **у́тка 1.**
утира́|ть(ся), ю(сь) *impf. of* **утере́ть(ся)**
утих|а́ть, а́ю *impf. of* **∸нуть**
ути́х|нуть, ну, нешь, *past* **~, ~ла** *pf.* (*of* **~а́ть**) **1.** to become quiet, still; (*of sounds*) to die away. **2.** to abate, subside; (*of wind*) to drop. **3.** to become calm.
утихоми́рива|ть(ся), ю(сь) *impf. of* **утихоми́рить(ся)**
утихоми́р|ить, ю, ишь *pf.* (*of* **~ивать**) (*coll.*) to calm down; to pacify, placate.
утихоми́р|иться, юсь, ишься *pf.* (*of* **~иваться**) (*coll.*) to calm down; to abate.
у́тк|а, и *f.* **1.** duck. **2.** canard, false report; **пусти́ть ~у** to start a canard. **3.** bedpan.
уткн|у́ть, у́, ёшь *pf.* (*coll.*) to bury; to fix; **у. нос в кни́гу** to bury o.s. in a book.
уткн|у́ться, у́сь, ёшься *pf.* (**в**+*a.*; *coll.*) **1.** to bury o.s. (in), one's head (in). **2.** to bump (into); **ло́дка ~у́лась в бе́рег** the boat bumped into the bank.
утконо́с, а *m.* (*zool.*) duck-billed platypus.
утле́гар|ь, я *m.* (*naut.*) jib-boom.
у́тлый *adj.* **1.** frail; unseaworthy. **2.** poor, wretched.
ут|о́к, ка́ *m.* (*text.*) woof, weft.
утол|и́ть, ю́, и́шь *pf.* (*of* **~я́ть**) **1.** to quench, slake (*thirst*); to satisfy (*hunger*). **2.** to relieve, alleviate.
утол|сти́ть, щу́, сти́шь *pf.* (*of* **~ща́ть**) to thicken.
утолща́|ть, ю *impf. of* **утолсти́ть**
утолще́ни|е, я *nt.* **1.** thickening. **2.** bulge.
утол|я́ть, я́ю *impf. of* **~и́ть**
утоми́тел|ьный (~ен, ~ьна) *adj.* **1.** tiring, fatiguing. **2.** tiresome; tedious.
утом|и́ть, лю́, и́шь *pf.* (*of* **~ля́ть**) to tire, weary, fatigue.
утом|и́ться, лю́сь, и́шься *pf.* (*of* **~ля́ться**) to get tired.
утомле́ни|е, я *nt.* tiredness, weariness, fatigue.
утомлённый *adj.* tired, weary, fatigued.
утомля́|ть(ся), ю(сь) *impf. of* **утоми́ть(ся)**
утон|у́ть, у́, ∸ешь *pf.* (*of* **тону́ть** *and* **утопа́ть**) **1.** to drown, sink. **2.** (**в**+*p.*; *fig.*) to be lost (in).
утонч|а́ть, а́ю *impf. of* **~и́ть**
утончённост|ь, и *f.* refinement.
утончённый *adj.* refined; exquisite, subtle.
утонч|и́ть, у́, и́шь *pf.* (*of* **~а́ть**) **1.** to make thinner; to taper. **2.** (*fig.*) to refine, make refined.
утопа́|ть, ю *impf.* **1.** *impf. of* **утону́ть. 2.** (*impf. only*) (**в**+*p.*; *fig.*) to roll (in), wallow (in).
утопи́зм, а *m.* Utopianism.
утоп|и́ть, лю́, ∸ишь *pf.* (*of* **топи́ть**) **1.** to drown. **2.** (*fig., coll.*) to ruin. **3.** to bury, embed.
утоп|и́ться, лю́сь, ∸ишься *pf.* (*of* **топи́ться**) to drown o.s.
утопи́ческий *adj.* Utopian.
уто́пи|я, и *f.* Utopia.
уто́пленник, а *m.* drowned man.
утоп|та́ть, чу́, ∸чешь *pf.* (*of* **ута́птывать**) to trample down, pound.
у́точк|а, и *f. dim. of* **у́тка; ходи́ть ~ой** to waddle.
уточне́ни|е, я *nt.* more precise definition; clarification.
уточн|и́ть, ю́, и́шь *pf.* (*of* **~я́ть**) to make more precise, define more precisely.
уточн|я́ть, я́ю *impf. of* **~и́ть**
утра́ива|ть, ю *impf. of* **утро́ить**
утрамб|ова́ть, у́ю *pf.* (*of* **~о́вывать**) to ram, tamp (*road material, etc.*).
утрамбо́выва|ть, ю *impf. of* **утрамбова́ть**
утра́т|а, ы *f.* loss; **у. трудоспосо́бности** disablement.
утра́|тить, чу, тишь *pf.* (*of* **~чивать**) to lose.
утра́чива|ть, ю *impf. of* **утра́тить**
у́тренн|ий *adj.* morning, early.
у́тренник, а *m.* **1.** morning frost. **2.** morning performance, matinée.
у́трен|я, и *f.* (*eccl.*) matins.
утри́р|овать, ую *impf. and pf.* to exaggerate.
утриро́вк|а, и *f.* exaggeration.
у́тр|о, а (до ~а́, с ~а́), *d.* **у (к ~у́),** *pl.* **~а, ~, ~ам (по ~а́м)** *nt.* morning; **в семь часо́в ~а́** at 7 a.m.; **с ~а́** early in the morning; **с ~а́ до ве́чера** from morn till night; **до́брое у.!** good morning!
утро́б|а, ы *f.* **1.** womb. **2.** (*coll.*) belly.
утро́бный *adj.* **1.** uterine, foetal; **у. плод** foetus. **2.** internal; (*of sounds*) deep; **у. смех** belly-laugh.
утро́|ить, ю, ишь *pf.* (*of* **утра́ивать**) to treble.
у́тром *adv.* in the morning; **сего́дня у.** this morning.
утру|ди́ть, жу́, ди́шь *pf.* (*of* **~жда́ть**) to trouble, to tire.
утру|ди́ться, жу́сь, ди́шься *pf.* (*of* **~жда́ться**) (*coll.*) to trouble o.s., take trouble.
утружда́|ть(ся), ю(сь) *impf. of* **утруди́ть(ся)**
утряс|а́ть, а́ю *impf. of* **~ти́**
утряс|ти́, у́, ёшь *pf.* (*of* **~а́ть**) (*coll.*) **1.** to shake down. **2.** to shake up. **3.** to settle; **у. вопро́с** to have a matter out.
утучн|и́ть, ю́, и́шь *pf.* (*of* **~я́ть**) to fatten.
утучн|я́ть, я́ю *impf. of* **~и́ть**
утуш|а́ть, а́ю *impf. of* **~и́ть**
утю́г, а́ *m.* (*flat*) iron.
утю́ж|ить, у, ишь *impf.* (*of* **вы~**) to iron, press.
утю́жк|а, и *f.* ironing, pressing.
утя́гива|ть, ю *impf. of* **утяну́ть**
утяжел|и́ть, ю́, и́шь *pf.* (*of* **~я́ть**) to make heavier, increase the weight (of).
утяжел|я́ть, я́ю *impf. of* **~и́ть**
утян|у́ть, у́, ∸ешь *pf.* (*of* **утя́гивать**) to drag away, off.
утя́тин|а, ы *f.* (*cul.*) duck.
уф *int.* (*expr.* (i) *relief,* (ii) *fatigue, physical discomfort, etc.*) ooh!; gosh!; phew!; **уф, жа́рко!** phew, it's hot!
ух *int.* (*expr. various strong feelings*) ooh!; gosh!
ух|а́, и́ *f.* ukha (*fish-soup*).
уха́б, а *m.* pot-hole, pit (*in road*).
уха́бист|ый (~, ~а) *adj.* full of pot-holes; bumpy.
ухажёр, а *m.* (*coll.*) ladies' man; admirer.
уха́жива|ть, ю *impf.* (**за**+*i.*) **1.** to nurse, tend; to look after. **2.** to court (*a woman*); to pay court (to). **3.** to make up (to).
у́хар|ь, я *m.* (*coll.*) 'lad', smart fellow; dashing fellow.
у́ха|ть, ю *impf. of* **у́хнуть**
ухва|ти́ть, чу́, ∸тишь *pf.* to grasp.
ухва|ти́ться, чу́сь, ∸тишься *pf.* (**за**+*a.*) **1.** to grasp, lay hold (of). **2.** (*coll.*) to set (to, about); **у. за но́вую рабо́ту** to get stuck in to a new job. **3.** (*fig., coll.*) to seize; to jump (at); **у. за предложе́ние** to jump at an offer.
ухва́тк|а, и *f.* (*coll.*) **1.** grip. **2.** (*fig.*) grasp; (a) skill; trick. **3.** manner.

ухитр|и́ться, ю́сь, и́шься *pf.* (*of* **~я́ться**) (*+inf.*; *coll.*) to manage (to), contrive (to).
ухитр|я́ться, я́юсь *impf. of* **~и́ться**
ухищре́ни|е, я *nt.* contrivance, device, trick, dodge.
ухищря́|ться, юсь *impf.* to contrive; to resort to contrivance.
ухло́п|ать, аю *pf.* (*of* **~ывать**) (*coll.*) **1.** to kill. **2.** to squander.
ухло́пыва|ть, ю *impf. of* **ухло́пать**
ухмы́лк|а, и *f.* (*coll.*) smirk, grin.
ухмыльн|у́ться, у́сь, ёшься *pf.* (*of* **ухмыля́ться**) (*coll.*) to smirk, grin.
ухмыл|я́ться, я́юсь *impf. of* **~ьну́ться**
у́хн|уть, у, ешь *pf.* (*of* **у́хать**) (*coll.*) **1.** to cry out (*from surprise, pain, etc.*); (*of owls*) to hoot. **2.** to crash, bang; **вдруг ~ул гром** there was a sudden crash of thunder. **3.** to slip, fall. **4.** (*fig.*) to come to grief. **5.** to lose, squander.
у́х|о, а, *pl.* **у́ши, уше́й** *nt.* **1.** ear; **и ~ом не вести́** not to listen (= *to pay no heed*); **кра́ем ~а слу́шать** to listen with half an ear; **у. в у.** (**с**+*i.*) level (with), alongside; **дать кому́-н. в у.** (*coll.*) to box s.o.'s ear; **во все у́ши слу́шать** to be all ears; **пропусти́ть ми́мо уше́й** (*coll.*) to turn a deaf ear (to), pay no heed (to); **говори́ть кому́-н. на́ у.** to have a word in s.o.'s ear, have a private word with s.o.; **по́ уши** up to one's eyes (*in work, etc.*), head over heels (*in love, etc.*). **2.** ear-flap (*of cap, etc.*) **3.** (*tech.*) ear, lug.
уховёртк|а, и *f.* (*zool.*) earwig.
ухо́д[1]**, а** *m.* leaving, departure; withdrawal.
ухо́д[2]**, а** *m.* (**за**+*i.*) nursing, tending; care (of); maintenance.
ухо|ди́ть[1]**, жу́, ~́дишь** *impf. of* **уйти́**
ухудш|а́ть(ся), а́ю, а́ет(ся) *impf. of* **~́ить(ся)**
ухудше́ни|е, я *nt.* worsening, deterioration.
уху́дш|ить, у, ишь *pf.* (*of* **~а́ть**) to make worse.
уху́дш|иться, ится *pf.* (*of* **~а́ться**) to become worse, worsen, deteriorate (*intrans.*).
уцеле́|ть, ю *pf.* to remain intact, escape destruction; to remain alive, survive.
уце́нива|ть, ю *impf. of* **уцени́ть**
уцен|и́ть, ю́, ~́ишь *pf.* (*of* **~́ивать**) to reduce the price (of).
уцеп|и́ть, лю́, ~́ишь *pf.* (*coll.*) to catch hold (of).
уцеп|и́ться, лю́сь, ~́ишься *pf.* (**за**+*a.*) **1.** to catch hold (of), grasp, seize. **2.** (*fig., coll.*) to jump (at).
уча́ств|овать, ую *impf.* **1.** (**в**+*p.*) to take part (in), participate (in). **2.** (**в**+*p.*) to have a share (in), have shares (in); **у. в акционе́рном о́бществе** to have shares in a (joint-stock) company.
уча́сти|е, я *nt.* **1.** taking part, participation; **при ~и, с ~ем** (*+g.*) with the participation (of), with assistance (of), featuring; **принима́ть у.** (**в**+*p.*) to take part (in), participate (in). **2.** share, sharing. **3.** sympathy, concern; **принима́ть у. в ком-н.** to display concern for s.o.
уча|сти́ть, щу́, сти́шь *pf.* (*of* **~ща́ть**) to make more frequent.
участ|и́ться, и́тся *pf.* (*of* **учаща́ться**) to become more frequent; (*of pulse*) to quicken.
участко́в|ый *adj. of* **уча́сток; у. уполномо́ченный** divisional inspector (*of police*); *as n.* **у., ~ого** *m.* = **у. уполномо́ченный.**
уча́стлив|ый (~, ~а) *adj.* sympathetic.
уча́стник, а *m.* (*+g.*) participant (in), member (of); **у. состяза́ния** competitor.
уча́ст|ок, ка *m.* **1.** (*of land*) plot, strip. **2.** part, section; length (*of road, etc.*). **3.** (*mil.*) sector; area, zone. **4.** district (*as administrative unit*); **избира́тельный у.** (*i*) electoral district, ward, (*ii*) polling station. **5.** (*fig.*) field, sphere (*of activity*). **6.** (*hist.*) (*i*) police division, district; (*ii*) police-station.
у́част|ь, и *f.* lot, fate.
учаща́|ть(ся), ю, ет(ся) *impf. of* **участи́ть(ся)**
уча́щ|ийся, ~егося *m.* student; pupil.
учёб|а, ы *f.* **1.** studies; learning; **за ~ой** at one's studies. **2.** drill, training.
уче́бник, а *m.* text-book; manual, primer.
уче́бно... *comb. form, abbr. of* **уче́бный**
уче́бн|ый *adj.* **1.** educational; school; **у. год** academic year, school year; **~ое заведе́ние** educational institution; **у. план** curriculum; **заве́дующий ~ой ча́стью** director of studies. **2.** (*mil.*) training, practice; **у. патро́н** dummy cartridge (*used in training*); **~ое по́ле** training ground; **~ая стрельба́** firing practice.
уче́ни|е, я *nt.* **1.** learning; studies; apprenticeship. **2.** teaching, instruction. **3.** (*mil.*) exercise; (*pl.*) training. **4.** teaching, doctrine.
учени́к, а́ *m.* **1.** pupil; **у.-лётчик** student pilot. **2.** apprentice. **3.** disciple, follower.
учени́ц|а, ы *f. of* **учени́к**
учени́|ческий *adj.* **1.** *adj. of* **~к. 2.** crude, immature.
учени́честв|о, а *nt.* **1.** period spent as a pupil, student. **2.** apprenticeship.
учёност|ь, и *f.* learning, erudition.
учён|ый (~, ~а) *adj.* **1.** learned, erudite. **2.** scholarly; academic; **~ая сте́пень** (university) degree. **3.** *in titles of certain academic posts and institutions in former USSR*: **у. секрета́рь** academic secretary; **у. сове́т** academic council. **4.** (*of animals*) trained. **5.** *as n.* **у., ~ого** *m.* scholar; scientist; academic.
уч|е́сть, учту́, учтёшь, *past* **~ёл, ~ла́** *pf.* (*of* **~и́тывать**) **1.** to take into account, consideration. **2.** to take stock (of). **3.** (*fin.*) to discount.
учёт, а *m.* **1.** stock-taking; inventory; calculation; **вести́ у.** (*+g.*) to take stock (of). **2.** taking into account; **без ~а** (*+g.*) disregarding. **3.** registration; **взять на у.** to register; **встать, стать на у.** to be registered. **4.** (*fin.*) discount, discounting.
учетвер|и́ть, ю́, и́шь *pf.* (*of* **~я́ть**) to quadruple.
учетвер|я́ть, я́ю *impf. of* **~и́ть**
учётн|ый *adj.* **1.** registration; **~ая ка́рточка** registration form; **~ое отделе́ние** records section. **2.** (*fin.*) discount; **~ая ста́вка ба́нковского проце́нта** bank rate.
учи́лищ|е, а *nt.* school, college (*institution providing specialist instruction at secondary level*); **реме́сленное у.** trade school.
учин|и́ть, ю́, и́шь *pf.* (*of* **~я́ть**) to make, commit; **у. сканда́л** (*coll.*) to make a scene.
учин|я́ть, я́ю *impf. of* **~и́ть**
учи́тел|ь, я *m.* **1.** (*pl.* **~я́**) teacher. **2.** (*pl.* **~и**) (*fig.*) teacher, master (= *authority*).
учи́тельниц|а, ы *f. of* **учи́тель**
учи́тель|ский *adj. of* **~**; *as n.* **~ская, ~ской** *f.* teachers' common room, staff (common) room.
учи́тыва|ть, ю *impf. of* **уче́сть**
уч|и́ть, у́, ~́ишь *impf.* **1.** (*pf.* **вы́~, на~** *and* **об~**) (*+a. and d. or +inf.*) to teach; **у. кого́-н. неме́цкому языку́** to teach s.o. German; **у. игра́ть на скри́пке** to teach to play the violin. **2. (что)** (*of a theory, etc.*) to teach (that), say (that). **3.** (*pf.* **вы́~**) (*+a.*) to learn; to memorize.
уч|и́ться, у́сь, ~́ишься *impf.* **1.** (*pf.* **вы́~, на~** *and* **об~**) (*+d. or +inf.*) to learn, study. **2.** to be a student; **у. в шко́ле** to go to, be at school. **3.** (**на кого́-н.**; *coll.*) to study (to be, to become), learn (to be); **он ~́ится на перево́дчика** he is studying to be an interpreter.
учреди́тел|ь, я *m.* founder.
учреди́тельн|ый *adj.* constituent; **~ое собра́ние** (*pol.*) constituent assembly.
учре|ди́ть, жу́, ди́шь *pf.* (*of* **~жда́ть**) to found, establish, set up; to institute.
учрежда́|ть, ю *impf. of* **учреди́ть**

учреждéни|е, я *nt.* **1.** founding, establishment (*action*), setting up. **2.** establishment, institution.
учти́вост|ь, и *f.* civility, courtesy.
учти́в|ый (~, ~а) *adj.* civil, courteous.
учу́|ять, ю, ешь *pf.* (*coll.*) to smell; (*fig.*) to sense.
уша́нк|а, и *f.* (*coll.*) cap with ear-flaps.
уша́ст|ый (~, ~а) *adj.* (*coll.*) big-eared.
уша́т, а *m.* tub (*carried on a pole inserted through handles*).
у́ши *see* **у́хо**
уши́б, а *m.* injury; knock; bruise.
ушиб|а́ть(ся), а́ю(сь) *impf. of* **~и́ть(ся)**
ушиб|и́ть, у́, ёшь, *past* **~, ~ла** *pf.* (*of* **~а́ть**) to hurt, injure (*by knocking*); to bruise.
ушиб|и́ться, у́сь, ёшься, *past* **~ся, ~лась** *pf.* (*of* **~а́ться**) to hurt o.s., give o.s. a knock; to bruise o.s.
ушива́|ть, ю *impf. of* **уши́ть**
уш|и́ть, ью́, ьёшь *pf.* (*of* **~ива́ть**) (*dressmaking*) to take in.
у́шк|о, а, *pl.* **~и, у́шек** *nt. dim. of* **у́хо; у него́ ~и на маку́шке** he is on the qui-vive.
ушк|о́, а́, *pl.* **~и́, ~о́в** *nt.* **1.** (*tech.*) eye, lug. **2.** tab, tag (*of boot*). **3.** eye (*of needle*). **4.** (*pl.*) (*cul.*) noodles.
ушн|о́й *adj.* ear, aural; **~а́я боль** ear-ache; **у. врач** ear-specialist; **~а́я ра́ковина** (*anat.*) auricle.
ущéл|ье, ья, *g. pl.* **~ий** *nt.* ravine, gorge, canyon.
ущем|и́ть, лю́, и́шь *pf.* (*of* **~ля́ть**) **1.** to pinch, jam; **у. себé па́лец двéрью** to pinch one's finger in the door. **2.** (*fig.*) to limit; to encroach (upon). **3.** (*fig.*) to wound, hurt; **у. чьё-н. самолю́бие** to hurt s.o.'s pride.
ущемлéни|е, я *nt.* **1.** pinching, jamming. **2.** (*fig.*) limitation. **3.** (*fig.*) wounding, hurting.
ущемля́|ть, ю *impf. of* **ущеми́ть**
ущéрб, а *m.* **1.** detriment; damage, injury; **без ~а (для)** without prejudice (to); **в у.** (*+d.*) to the detriment (of). **2.: на ~е** (*of the moon*) on the wane; (*fig.*) on the decline.
ущéрбный *adj.* (*of the moon*) waning; (*fig.*) on the decline.
ущипн|у́ть, у́, ёшь *pf.* to pinch, tweak.
Уэ́льс, а *m.* Wales.
уэ́льс|ец, ца *m.* Welshman.
уэ́льский *adj.* Welsh.
ую́т, а *m.* comfort, cosiness.
ую́т|ный (~ен, ~на) *adj.* comfortable, cosy.
уязви́м|ый (~, ~а) *adj.* vulnerable (*also fig.*); **~ое мéсто** (*fig.*) weak spot, sensitive spot.
уязв|и́ть, лю́, и́шь *pf.* (*of* **~ля́ть**) to wound, hurt.
уязвля́|ть, ю *impf. of* **уязви́ть**
уясн|и́ть, ю́, и́шь *pf.* (*of* **~я́ть**) **1. (себé)** to understand, make out. **2.** (*obs.*) to explain.
уясн|я́ть, я́ю *impf. of* **~и́ть**

Ф

фа *nt. indecl.* (*mus.*) fa(h); F.
фа́брик|а, и *f.* factory, mill.
фабрика́нт, а *m.* factory-owner, mill-owner; manufacturer.
фабрика́т, а *m.* finished product.
фабрика́ци|я, и *f.* fabrication (*also fig.*).
фабрик|ова́ть, у́ю *impf.* **1.** (*obs.*) to manufacture, make. **2.** (*pf.* **с~**) (*fig., coll.*) to fabricate, forge.
фабри́чн|ый *adj.* **1.** factory; manufacturing; **ф. го́род** manufacturing town; **~ая ма́рка** trade mark; **~ое произво́дство** manufacturing; *as n.* **ф., ~ого** *m.*, **~ая, ~ой** *f.* factory worker. **2.** factory-made.
фа́бул|а, ы *f.* (*liter.*) plot, story.
фавн, а *m.* (*myth.*) faun.
фаво́р, а *m.*: **быть в ~е (у)** to be in favour (with); **быть не в ~е у кого́-н.** to be in s.o.'s bad books.
фавори́т, а *m.* favourite (*also sport*).
фаворити́зм, а *m.* favouritism.
фаго́т, а *m.* (*mus.*) bassoon.
фаготи́ст, а *m.* bassoon-player.
фагоци́т, а *m.* (*biol.*) phagocyte.
фа́з|а, ы *f.* phase; stage.
фаза́н, а *m.* pheasant.
фаза́н|ий *adj. of* **~**
фа́зис, а *m.* phase.
файл, а *m.* (*comput.*) file.
файл-сéрвер, а *m.* (*comput.*) file server.
фа́кел, а *m.* torch, flare.
фа́кел|ьный *adj. of* **~; ~ьное шéствие** torch-light procession.
фа́кельщик, а *m.* **1.** torch-bearer. **2.** (*fig., pej.*) incendiary, fire-bug.
faки́р, а *m.* fakir.
фа́кс, а *m.* fax; **посла́ть по ~у** to fax.
факси́миле *indecl.* **1.** *adj.* **2.** *n.*; *nt.* facsimile.
факс|ими́льный *adj. of* **~; ф. аппара́т** fax (machine).
факт, а *m.* **1.** fact; **соверши́вшийся ф.** fait accompli; **факт, что** (*coll.*) it is a fact that; **ф. остаётся ~ом** the fact remains.
факти́чески *adv.* in fact, actually; practically, virtually, to all intents and purposes.
факти́ческ|ий *adj.* actual; factual; de-facto.
фа́ктор, а *m.* factor.
факто́ри|я, и *f.* trading station.
факту́р|а, ы *f.* **1.** (*arts and liter.*) style; manner of execution; texture. **2.** (*comm.*) invoice, bill.
факультати́в|ный (~ен, ~на) *adj.* optional.
факультéт, а *m.* faculty, department.
фал, а *m.* (*naut.*) halyard.
фала́нг|а, и *f.* (*hist.*; *fig.*) phalanx.
фа́лд|а, ы *f.* tail, skirt (*of coat*).
фалли́ческий *adj.* phallic.
фалло́пиев *adj.*: **~а труба́** (*med.*) Fallopian tube.
фа́ллос, а *m.* phallus.
фальсифика́тор *m.* falsifier; forger.
фальсифика́ци|я, и *f.* **1.** falsification; forging. **2.** adulteration. **3.** forgery, fake, counterfeit.
фальсифици́р|овать, ую *impf. and pf.* **1.** to falsify; to forge. **2.** to adulterate.
фальцéт, а *m.* (*mus.*) falsetto.
фальши́в|ить, лю, ишь *impf.* **1.** to be a hypocrite; to act insincerely. **2.** (*pf.* **с~**) (*mus.*) to sing, play out of tune.
фальши́вк|а, и *f.* (*coll.*) forged document.
фальшивомонéтчик, а *m.* counterfeiter.
фальши́в|ый (~, ~а) *adj.* **1.** false; forged; fake; imitation; **ф. докумéнт** forged document; **~ые зу́бы** false teeth; **ф. жéмчуг** imitation pearl. **2.** false; insincere; **ф. комплимéнт** insincere compliment. **3.** (*mus.*) false (= *out of tune*).
фальш|ь, и *f.* **1.** deception, trickery. **2.** falseness; hypocrisy, insincerity. **3.** (*mus.*) singing, playing out of tune.
фами́ли|я, и *f.* surname, last name.
фами́льный *adj.* family.
фамилья́рнича|ть, ю *impf.* (*coll.*) to be (over-)familiar; to take liberties.
фамилья́рност|ь, и *f.* (over-)familiarity.
фамилья́р|ный (~ен, ~на) *adj.* (over-)familiar; unceremonious.

фанабе́ри|я, и *f.* (*coll.*) arrogance, bumptiousness.
фанати́зм, а *m.* fanaticism.
фана́тик, а *m.* fanatic.
фанати́ческий *adj.* fanatical.
фанати́ч|ный (~ен, ~на) *adj.* fanatic(al).
фане́р|а, ы *f.* **1.** veneer. **2.** plywood.
фане́р|ный *adj. of* **~а**
фант, а *m.* forfeit; **игра́ть в ~ы** to play forfeits.
фантазёр, а *m.* dreamer, visionary.
фантази́р|овать, ую *impf.* **1.** (*impf. only*) to dream, indulge in fantasies. **2.** (*pf.* **с~**) to make up, dream up. **3.** (*impf. only*) to improvise (*on piano, etc.*).
фанта́зи|я, и *f.* **1.** fantasy; imagination; **бога́тая ф.** fertile imagination. **2.** fantasy, fancy; **предава́ться ~ям** to indulge in fantasies. **3.** fabrication. **4.** (*coll.*) fancy, whim. **5.** (*mus.*) fantasia.
фантасмаго́ри|я, и *f.* phantasmagoria.
фанта́ст, а *m.* **1.** dreamer, visionary. **2.** writer, artist treating the fantastic.
фанта́стик|а, и *f.* **1.** the fantastic; (*collect.*; *liter.*) fantastic tales. **2.** fantasy (*opp. reality*); **нау́чная ф.** science fiction; sci-fi.
фантасти́ческий *adj.* **1.** fantastical. **2.** fantastic; fabulous; imaginary.
фантасти́ч|ный (~ен, ~на) *adj.* = **~еский**
фанто́м, а *m.* phantom.
фанфа́р|а, ы *f.* (*mus.*) **1.** bugle. **2.** fanfare.
фанфаро́н, а *m.* (*coll.*) braggart.
фа́р|а, ы *f.* headlight; **поса́дочные ~ы** landing lights.
фарао́н, а *m.* **1.** (*hist.*) Pharaoh. **2.** faro (*card-game*).
фарва́тер, а *m.* (*naut.*) fairway, channel.
Фаренге́йт, а *m.* Fahrenheit; **80° по ~у** 80° Fahrenheit.
фарисе́|й, я *m.* Pharisee (*also fig.*).
фарисе́йский *adj.* pharisaical (*also fig.*).
фармако́лог, а *m.* pharmacologist.
фармакологи́ческий *adj.* pharmacological.
фармаколо́ги|я, и *f.* pharmacology.
фармакопе́|я, и *f.* pharmacopoeia.
фармаце́вт, а *m.* pharmaceutical chemist.
фармаце́втик|а, и *f.* pharmaceutics.
фармацевти́ческий *adj.* pharmaceutical.
фармаци́|я, и *f.* pharmacy.
фарс, а *m.* (*theatr.*) farce (*also fig.*).
фа́ртук, а *m.* apron.
фарфо́р, а *m.* **1.** porcelain, china. **2.** (*collect.*) china.
фарфо́р|овый *adj. of* **~**; **~овая гли́на** china clay, kaolin; **~овая посу́да** china(-ware).
фарцо́вщик, а *m.* (*sl.*) black marketeer.
фарш, а *m.* (*cul.*) force-meat; sausage-meat; stuffing.
фарширо́в|анный *p.p.p. of* **~а́ть** *and adj.* (*cul.*) stuffed.
фаршир|ова́ть, у́ю *impf.* (*of* **за~**) (*cul.*) to stuff.
фас, а *m.* front, façade; **в ф.** en face; full face.
фаса́д, а *m.* façade, front.
фасе́т, а *m.* facet.
фас|ова́ть, у́ю *impf.* (*comm.*) to prepack.
фасо́вк|а, и *f.* (*comm.*) prepacking.
фасо́вочный *adj.* (*comm.*) (pre)packing, packaging.
фасо́л|евый *adj. of* **~ь**
фасо́л|ь, и *f.* haricot bean, French bean; **туре́цкая ф.** runner beans.
фасо́н, а *m.* **1.** cut; fashion, style. **2.** (*coll.*) manner, style.
фасо́нист|ый (~, ~а) *adj.* (*coll.*) fashionable, stylish.
фасо́нный *adj.* (*tech.*) fashioned, shaped.
фат, а *m.* fop.
фат|а́, ы́ *f.* (*bridal*) veil.
фатали́зм, а *m.* fatalism.
фатали́ст, а *m.* fatalist.
фаталисти́ческий *adj.* **1.** fatalistic. **2.** fatal.
фата́л|ьный (~ен, ~ьна) *adj.* **1.** fatal, fated. **2.** of resignation; **ф. вид** resigned appearance.
фатова́т|ый (~, ~а) *adj.* foppish.
фа́ун|а, ы *f.* fauna.
фаши́зм, а *m.* Fascism.
фаши́ст, а *m.* Fascist.
фаши́стский *adj.* Fascist.
фаэто́н, а *m.* phaeton.
фая́нс, а *m.* faience, glazed earthenware.
фая́нс|овый *adj. of* **~**
ФБР *nt. indecl.* (*abbr. of* **Федера́льное бюро́ рассле́дований**) FBI (*Federal Bureau of Investigation*).
февра́л|ь, я́ *m.* February.
февра́ль|ский *adj. of* **~**
федерали́зм, а *m.* federalism.
федерали́ст, а *m.* federalist.
федера́льный *adj.* federal.
федерати́вный *adj.* federative; federal.
федера́ци|я, и *f.* federation.
феери́ческий *adj.* **1.** (*theatr.*) (based on a) fairytale. **2.** fairy-like; magical.
фее́ри|я, и *f.* **1.** play, ballet, *etc.*, based on a fairy-tale. **2.** magical sight.
фейерве́рк, а *m.* firework(s).
фельдма́ршал, а *m.* field-marshal.
фе́льдшер, а, *pl.* **~а́** *m.* medical assistant.
фельето́н, а *m.* satirical article.
фельетони́ст, а *m.* writer of satirical articles.
фельето́нный *adj.* satirical; humorous.
фемини́зм, а *m.* feminism.
фемини́ст, а *m.* feminist.
фемини́ст|ка, ки *f. of* **~**
фемини́стский *adj.* feminist.
фен, а *m.* hair-drier.
фе́никс, а *m.* (*mythol.*) phoenix.
фено́л, а *m.* (*chem.*) phenol.
фено́мен, а *m.* phenomenon; marvel.
феномена́л|ьный (~ен, ~ьна) *adj.* phenomenal.
фе́нхел|ь, я *m.* (*bot.*) fennel.
фео́д, а *m.* (*hist.*) fief.
феода́л, а *m.* (*hist.*) feudal lord.
феодали́зм, а *m.* feudalism.
феода́льный *adj.* feudal.
фе́рз|евый *adj. of* **~ь**
ферз|ь, я́, *pl.* **~и́, ~е́й** *m.* (*chess*) queen.
фе́рм|а¹, ы *f.* farm.
фе́рм|а², ы *f.* (*tech.*) girder.
ферме́нт, а *m.* (*biol.*, *chem.*) ferment.
ферменти́р|овать, ую *impf.* to ferment.
фе́рмер, а *m.* farmer.
фе́рмер|ский *adj. of* **~**; **ф. дом** farm-house.
фе́рмерств|о, а *nt.* **1.** farming. **2.** (*collect.*) farmers.
фе́ск|а, и *f.* fez.
фестива́л|ь, я *m.* festival.
фесто́н, а *m.* (*dressmaking*) scallops.
фети́ш, а *m.* fetish.
фетишизи́р|овать, ую *impf.* to make a fetish (of).
фетиши́зм, а *m.* fetishism.
фетиши́ст, а *m.* fetishist.
фетр, а *m.* felt.
фе́тр|овый *adj. of* **~**
фехтова́льный *adj.* fencing.
фехтова́льщик, а *m.* fencer; **ф. шпа́гой** épéeist.
фехтова́ни|е, я *nt.* fencing.
фехт|ова́ть, у́ю, *impf.* to fence.
фешене́бел|ьный (~ен, ~ьна) *adj.* fashionable.
фе́|я, и *f.* fairy.
фи *int.* fie!; pah!
фиа́лк|а, и *f.* violet.
фиа́ско *nt. indecl.* fiasco; failure; **потерпе́ть ф.** to be a flop.
фи́бр|а, ы *f.* fibre (*also fig.*); **все́ми ~ами души́** in every fibre (of one's being).
фибро́зный *adj.* fibrous.
фи́г|а, и *f.* **1.** fig (tree). **2.** (*coll.*) = **ку́киш**

фигля́р, а *m.* **1.** (*obs.*) (circus) acrobat; clown. **2.** poseur; (*pej.*) actor.
фи́г|овый *adj. of* **~а; ~овое де́рево** fig tree; **ф. листо́к** fig-leaf (*also fig.*).
фигу́р|а, ы *f.* **1.** figure. **2.** (*cards*) picture-card. **3.** piece, chess-man (*excluding pawns*).
фигура́л|ьный (~ен, ~ьна) *adj.* figurative, metaphorical.
фигури́р|овать, ую *impf.* to figure, appear.
фигури́ст, а *m.* figure skater.
фигури́ст|ка, ки *f. of* ~
фигу́р|ка, ки *f.* **1.** *dim. of* **~а. 2.** figurine, statuette.
фигу́рн|ый *adj.* **1.** figured; ornamented. **2.: ~ое ката́ние на конька́х** figure skating.
фи́зик, а *m.* physicist.
фи́зик|а, и *f.* physics.
физио́лог, а *m.* physiologist.
физиологи́ческий *adj.* physiological.
физиоло́ги|я, и *f.* physiology.
физионо́ми|я, и *f.* face; physiognomy (*also joc.*).
физиотерапе́вт, а *m.* physiotherapist.
физиотерапи́|я, и *f.* physiotherapy.
физи́ческ|ий *adj.* **1.** physical; **~ая культу́ра** physical training; **ф. труд** manual labour. **2.** *adj. of* **фи́зика; ф. кабине́т** physics laboratory.
физкульту́р|а, ы *f.* physical training; physical education; **уро́к ~ы** PE class.
физкульту́рник, а *m.* athlete, sportsman.
физкульту́рни|ца, цы *f. of* **~к**
физкульту́рн|ый *adj.* gymnastic; athletic; **ф. зал** gymnasium.
фикса́ж, а *m.* (*phot.*) fixing solution, fixer.
фикси́р|овать, ую *impf. and pf.* (*pf. also* **за~**) **1.** to record (*in writing, etc.*). **2.** to fix; **ф. день свида́ния** to fix a date to meet.
фикти́в|ный (~ен, ~на) *adj.* fictitious.
фи́кус, а *m.* rubber plant.
фи́кци|я, и *f.* fiction.
филантро́п, а *m.* philanthropist.
филантропи́ческий *adj.* philanthropic.
филантро́пи|я, и *f.* philanthropy.
филармо́ни|я, и *f.* philharmonic society.
филатели́ст, а *m.* philatelist, stamp collector.
филатели́|я, и *f.* philately.
филе́ *nt. indecl.* (*cul.*) **1.** sirloin. **2.** fillet (*of meat or fish*).
филёнк|а, и *f.* panel, slat.
филёр, а *m.* detective, sleuth.
филиа́л, а *m.* branch.
филиа́л|ьный *adj. of* **~; ~ьное отделе́ние** branch (office).
филигра́нный *adj.* **1.** filigree. **2.** (*fig.*) meticulous.
филигра́н|ь, и *f.* filigree.
фи́лин, а *m.* eagle owl.
фили́ппик|а, и *f.* philippic.
филиппи́нский *adj.* Philippine; Filipino.
фило́лог, а *m.* philologist.
филологи́ческий *adj.* philological; **ф. факульте́т** faculty of philology.
филоло́ги|я, и *f.* philology.
фило́н, а *m.* (*coll.*) idler, loafer.
фило́н|ить, ю, ишь *impf.* (*coll.*) to idle, loaf.
фило́соф, а *m.* philosopher.
филосо́фи|я, и *f.* philosophy.
филосо́фский *adj.* philosophic(al).
филосо́фств|овать, ую *impf.* to philosophize.
филфа́к, а *m.* (*abbr. of* **филологи́ческий факульте́т**) faculty of philology.
филфа́ков|ец, ца *m.* (*coll.*) philology student.
фильм, а *m.* (*cin.*) film; **приключе́нческий ф.** thriller.
фильмоте́к|а, и *f.* film library.
фильтр, а *m.* filter.
фильтра́ци|я, и *f.* filtration.
фильтрова́льный *adj.*: **ф. насо́с** filter pump.
фильтр|ова́ть, у́ю *impf.* (*of* **про~**) **1.** to filter. **2.** (*fig., coll.*) screen.
фимиа́м, а *m.* incense; **кури́ть ф.** (*+d.*) to praise to the skies, sing the praises (of).
фина́л, а *m.* **1.** finale. **2.** (*sport*) final.
финали́ст, а *m.* finalist.
фина́льный *adj.* final; **ф. матч** (*sport*) final.
финанси́р|овать, ую *impf. and pf.* to finance.
финанси́ст, а *m.* financier.
фина́нсовый *adj.* financial; **ф. год** fiscal year; **ф. отде́л** finance department.
фина́нс|ы, ов *no sg.* **1.** finance(s). **2.** (*coll.*) money.
фи́ник, а *m.* date (*fruit*).
финики́йский *adj.* Phoenician.
фи́ник|овый *adj. of* **~; ~овая па́льма** date-palm.
фини́фт|ь, и *f.* enamel.
фи́ниш, а *m.* (*sport*) finish; finishing post, line.
финиши́р|овать, ую *impf. and pf.* (*sport*) to finish.
фи́ниш|ный *adj. of* **~; ~ная ле́нточка** finishing tape.
фи́нк|а[1]**, и** *f. of* **финн**
фи́нк|а[2]**, и** *f.* (*coll.*) knife.
Финля́нди|я, и *f.* Finland.
финля́ндский *adj.* Finnish.
финн, а *m.* Finn.
фи́нно-уго́рский *adj.* (*ling.*) Finno-Ugric.
фи́нский *adj.* Finnish; **ф. зали́в** Gulf of Finland.
финт, а *m.* (*sport*) feint.
фин|ти́ть, чу́, ти́шь *impf.* (*coll.*) to be crafty, resort to ruses.
финтифлю́шк|а, и *f.* (*coll.*) **1.** bauble, bagatelle. **2.** flibbertigibbet.
фиоле́товый *adj.* violet.
фио́рд, а *m.* (*geog.*) fiord, fjord.
фи́рм|а, ы *f.* (*econ.*) firm.
фи́рм|енный *adj. of* **~а; ~енная этике́тка** proprietary label; **ф. бланк** letterhead.
фисгармо́ни|я, и *f.* (*mus.*) harmonium.
фиска́л, а *m.* (*coll.*) sneak, tale-bearer.
фиска́л|ить, ю, ишь *impf.* (*coll.*) to (be a) sneak.
фиста́шк|а, и *f.* pistachio(-tree).
фиста́шков|ый *adj.* **1.** pistachio; **~ая смола́** mastic. **2.** pistachio-green.
фи́стул|а́[1]**, ы-ы́** *f.* (*med.*) fistula.
фистул|а́[2]**, ы́** *f.* **1.** (*mus.*) pipe, flute. **2.** falsetto.
фити́л|ь, я́ *m.* wick; fuse.
фи́шк|а, и *f.* **1.** counter, chip. **2.** (*sl.*) face.
флаг, а *m.* flag; **под ~ом** (*+g.*) (*i*) flying the flag (of), (*ii*) (*fig.*) under the guise (of).
фла́гман, а *m.* (*naut.*) **1.** flag-officer. **2.** flag-ship.
фла́гман|ский *adj. of* **~; ф. кора́бль = ~ 2.**
флагшто́к, а *m.* flagstaff.
фла́жный *adj.* flag.
флаж|о́к, ка́ *m.* (*small*) flag; signal flag.
флако́н, а *m.* (scent-)bottle, flask.
флама́нд|ец, ца *m.* Fleming.
флама́нд|ка, ки *f. of* **~ец**
флама́ндский *adj.* Flemish.
флами́нго *m. indecl.* flamingo.
фланг, а *m.* (*mil.*) flank; wing.
флангo̍вый *adj.* (*mil.*) flank; flanking.
флане́левый *adj.* flannel.
флане́л|ь, и *f.* flannel.
флáн|ец, ца *m.* (*tech.*) flange.
флани́р|овать, ую *impf.* (*coll.*) to idle; to mooch.
фланки́р|овать, ую *impf. and pf.* (*mil.*) to flank.
флеби́т, а *m.* (*med.*) phlebitis.
фле́гм|а, ы *f.* **1.** (*fig.*) phlegm. **2.** (*coll.*) phlegmatic person.
флегма́тик, а *m.* phlegmatic person.
флегмати́ч|ный (~ен, ~на) *adj.* phlegmatic.
фле́йт|а, ы *f.* flute.

флейти́ст, а *m.* flautist.
фле́кси|я, и *f.* (*ling.*) inflection.
флекти́вный *adj.* (*ling.*) inflected.
флёр, а *m.* crêpe.
фли́гел|ь, я, *pl.* **~я́, ~е́й** *m.* **1.** wing (*of building*). **2.** outhouse, outbuilding.
флирт, а *m.* flirtation.
флирт|ова́ть, у́ю *impf.* (**с**+*i.*) to flirt (with).
флома́стер, а *m.* felt-tip pen, felt-tip; marker (pen).
фло́р|а, ы *f.* flora.
флот, а *m.* **1.** fleet; **вое́нно-морско́й ф.** navy. **2.: возду́шный ф.** air force.
флоти́ли|я, и *f.* flotilla.
фло́тск|ий *adj.* naval.
флуоресце́нци|я, и *f.* fluorescence.
флуоресци́р|овать, ует *impf.* (*phys.*) to fluoresce; **~ующий** fluorescent.
флюга́рк|а, и *f.* **1.** (*naut.*) pennant; distinguishing plate (*of boat*). **2.** weather-vane.
флю́гер, а, *pl.* **~а́** *m.* weather-vane.
флюс[1]**, а,** *pl.* **~ы** *m.* gumboil.
флюс[2]**, а,** *pl.* **~ы́** *m.* (*tech.*) flux.
фля́г|а, и *f.* **1.** flask; (*mil.*) water bottle. **2.** churn.
фля́жк|а, и *f. dim. of* **фля́га**
фо́би|я, и *m.* phobia.
фойе́ *nt. indecl.* foyer, lobby.
фок, а *m.* (*naut.*) **1.** foresail. **2.** foremast.
фок-ма́чт|а, ы (*naut.*) foremast.
фокстерье́р, а *m.* fox-terrier.
фокстро́т, а *m.* foxtrot.
фо́кус[1]**, а** *m.* focus.
фо́кус[2]**, а** *m.* (conjuring) trick; **пока́зывать ~ы** to perform conjuring tricks.
фокуси́р|овать, ую *impf.* to focus.
фо́кусник, а *m.* conjurer.
фо́кусничa|ть, ю *impf.* (*coll.*) to play tricks.
фо́кусный *adj.* focal.
фолиа́нт, а *m.* folio.
фолли́кул, а *m.* (*anat.*) follicle.
фо́льг|а, и *f.* foil.
фолькло́р, а *m.* folklore.
фольклори́ст, а *m.* folklorist.
фон, а *m.* background (*also fig.*).
фона́рик, а *m.* small lamp; torch, flash-light.
фона́рщик, а *m.* (*obs.*) lamplighter.
фона́р|ь, я́ *m.* **1.** lantern; lamp; light. **2.** (*archit.*) light; skylight. **3.** (*coll.*) black eye.
фонд, а *m.* **1.** (*fin.*) fund; stock, reserves; **валю́тный ф.** currency reserves; **земе́льный ф.** available land; **золото́й ф.** gold reserves; **о́бщий ф.** pool. **2.** (*pl.*) (*fin.*) stocks. **3.** fund, foundation. **4.** archive.
фо́нд|овый *adj. of* **~; ~овая би́ржа** stock exchange.
фоне́м|а, ы *f.* (*ling.*) phoneme.
фоне́тик|а, и *f.* phonetics.
фонети́ст, а *m.* phonetician.
фонети́ческий *adj.* phonetic.
фонogра́мм|а, ы *m.* recording.
фоно́граф, а *m.* phonograph.
фоноло́ги|я, и *f.* phonemics.
фоноте́к|а, и *f.* sound recording library.
фонта́н, а *m.* fountain; (*fig.*) stream; **нефтяно́й ф.** oil gusher; **бить ~ом** to gush forth.
фонтани́р|овать, ует *impf.* to gush forth.
фо́р|а, ы *f.*: **дать ~у** (+*d.*) to give a start (*in a game*).
фо́рвард, а *m.* (*sport.*) forward.
форе́йтор, а *m.* postilion.
форе́л|ь, и *f.* trout.
фо́рзац, а *m.* fly-leaf.
фо́рм|а, ы *f.* **1.** form. **2.** shape; (*pl.*) contours (*of human body*). **3.** (*tech.*) mould, cast; **отли́ть в ~у** to mould, cast. **4.** uniform. **5.: быть в ~е** (*coll.*) to be in (good) form.
формали́зм, а *m.* formalism.
формали́ст, а *m.* formalist.
формали́стик|а, и *f.* formalities.
формальдеги́д, а *m.* (*chem.*) formaldehyde.
форма́льност|ь, и *f.* formality.
форма́л|ьный (~ен, ~ьна) *adj.* formal.
форма́т, а *m.* size, format.
форма́ци|я, и *f.* **1.** structure. **2.** mentality. **3.** (*geol.*) formation.
фо́рменный *adj.* **1.** uniform. **2.** (*obs.*) formal. **3.** (*coll.*) proper, regular, positive.
формирова́ни|е, я *nt.* **1.** forming; organizing. **2.** (*mil.*) unit, formation.
формир|ова́ть, у́ю *impf.* (*of* **с~**) to form; to organize; **ф. хара́ктер** to form character; **ф. батальо́н** to raise a battalion; **ф. по́езд** to make up a train.
формир|ова́ться, у́юсь *impf.* (*of* **с~**) **1.** to form, develop (*intrans.*). **2.** *pass. of* **~ова́ть**
форм|ова́ть, у́ю *impf.* (*of* **с~**) to form, shape; to model; (*tech.*) to mould, cast.
фо́рмул|а, ы *f.* formula; formulation.
формули́р|овать, ую *impf. and pf.* (*pf. also* **с~**) to formulate.
формулиро́вк|а, и *f.* **1.** formulation. **2.** formula.
формуля́р, а *m.* **1.** (*obs.*) record of service. **2.** (*tech.*) logbook. **3.** library card.
форпо́ст, а *m.* (*mil.*) advanced post; outpost (*also fig.*).
форс, а (у) *m.* (*coll.*) swank; **для ~а** for show; **сбить кому́-н. ф.** to take s.o. down a peg.
форси́ров|анный *p.p.p. of* **~ать** *and adj.* forced; accelerated; **ф. марш** forced march.
форси́р|овать, ую *impf. and pf.* **1.** to force; to speed up. **2.** (*mil.*) to force (*a crossing of*).
фор|си́ть, шу́, си́шь *impf.* (*coll.*) to show off.
форсу́нк|а, и *f.* (*tech.*) sprayer; fuel injector.
форт, а, о ~е, в ~у́, *pl.* **~ы́** *m.* (*mil.*) fort.
фо́ртел|ь, я *m.* (*coll.*) trick, stunt.
фортепья́нный *adj.* piano; **ф. конце́рт** piano concerto.
фортепья́но *nt. indecl.* piano.
фортификацио́нный *adj.* fortification.
фортифика́ци|я, и *f.* fortification.
фо́рточк|а, и *f.* fortochka (*small hinged pane for ventilation in window of Russ. houses*).
фо́рум, а *m.* forum.
форшла́г, а *m.* (*mus.*) grace-note.
форште́в|ень, ня *m.* (*naut.*) stem.
фосге́н, а *m.* (*chem.*) phosgene.
фосфа́т, а *m.* (*chem.*) phosphate.
фо́сфор, а *m.* (*chem.*) phosphorus.
фосфоресце́нци|я, и *f.* phosphorescence.
фосфоресци́р|овать, ую *impf.* to phosphoresce; **~ующий** phosphorescent; luminous.
фо́сфорный *adj.* (*chem.*) phosphorous, phosphoric.
фо́то *nt. indecl.* (*coll.*) photo.
фотоальбо́м, а *m.* photograph album.
фотоаппара́т, а *m.* camera.
фотогени́ч|ный (~ен, ~на) *adj.* photogenic.
фото́граф, а *m.* photographer.
фотографи́р|овать, ую *impf.* (*of* **с~**) to photograph.
фотографи́р|оваться, уюсь *impf.* (*of* **с~**) to be photographed, have one's photo taken.
фотографи́ческ|ий *adj.* photographic.
фотогра́фи|я, и *f.* **1.** photography. **2.** photograph. **3.** photographer's studio.
фотока́рточк|а, и *f.* photograph; snapshot.
фотокомпозицио́нный *adj.*: **ф. портре́т** photofit.
фотокопирова́льный *adj.*: **ф. аппара́т** photocopier.
фотоко́пи|я, и *f.* photocopy.
фотолюби́тел|ь, я *m.* amateur photographer.
фото́н, а *m.* (*phys.*) photon.
фотонабо́р, а *m.* photo typesetting.

фотонабо́рный *adj.*: **ф. аппара́т** phototypesetter; photo-typesetting machine.
фотоохо́т|а, ы *f.* wildlife photography.
фотоохо́тник, а *m.* wildlife photographer.
фоторепортёр, а *m.* press photographer.
фотоси́нтез, а *m.* (*bot.*) photosynthesis.
фототе́к|а, и *f.* photograph library.
фотоэлеме́нт, а *m.* (*elec.*) photoelectric cell.
фо́фан, а *m.* (*coll.*) dim-wit.
фрагме́нт, а *m.* fragment; detail; **ф. фи́льма** film clip.
фрагмента́р|ный (~ен, ~на) *adj.* fragmentary.
фра́з|а, ы *f.* **1.** sentence. **2.** phrase.
фразеологи́зм, а *m.* (*ling.*) idiom, idiomatic expression.
фразеологи́ческий *adj.* phraseological; **ф. оборо́т** idiom.
фразеоло́ги|я, и *f.* **1.** phraseology. **2.** rhetoric.
фразёр, а *m.* phrase-monger.
фрак, а *m.* tail-coat, tails.
фракцио́нност|ь, и *f.* (*pol.*) factionalism.
фракцио́нный *adj.* (*pol.*) factional.
фра́кци|я, и *f.* (*pol.*) faction.
фраму́г|а, и *f.* transom.
франк[1]**, а** *m.* (*hist.*) Frank.
франк[2]**, а** *m.* franc.
франки́р|овать, ую *impf. and pf.* to prepay the postage (on).
франкмасо́н, а *m.* freemason.
франкоязы́чный *adj.* francophone.
фра́нкский *adj.* (*hist.*) Frankish.
франт, а *m.* dandy.
фран|ти́ть, чу́, ти́шь *impf.* (*coll.*) to dress foppishly.
франти́х|а, и *f. of* **франт**
франтова́т|ый (~, ~а) *adj.* (*coll.*) dandified.
франтовско́й *adj.* = **франтова́тый**
франтовств|о́, а́ *nt.* dandyism, foppishness.
Фра́нци|я, и *f.* France.
францу́женк|а, и *f.* Frenchwoman.
францу́з, а *m.* Frenchman.
францу́зский *adj.* French.
фрахт, а *m.* freight.
фрахт|ова́ть, у́ю *impf.* (*of* **за~**) to charter.
фра́чн|ый *adj. of* **фрак**
ФРГ *f. indecl.* (*abbr. of* **Федерати́вная Респу́блика Герма́нии**) FRG (*Federal Republic of Germany*).
фрега́т, а *m.* **1.** (*naut.*) frigate. **2.** frigate-bird.
фрез|а́, ы́ *f.* (*tech.*) milling cutter.
фре́зерный *adj.* (*tech.*) milling; **ф. стано́к** milling machine.
фрезер|ова́ть, у́ю *impf. and pf.* (*tech.*) to mill, cut.
фре́йлин|а, ы *f.* (*hist.*) lady-in-waiting.
френо́лог, а *m.* phrenologist.
френоло́ги|я, и *f.* phrenology.
френч, а *m.* service jacket.
фре́ск|а, и *f.* fresco.
фриво́л|ьный (~ен, ~ьна) *adj.* frivolous.
фриз, а *m.* (*archit.*) frieze.
фрикаде́льк|а, и *f.* meat-ball, fish-ball.
фрикасе́ *nt. indecl.* (*cul.*) fricassee.
фрикати́вный *adj.* (*ling.*) fricative.
фритю́р, а *m.* (*cul.*) deep-fat.
фритю́рниц|а, ы *f.* deep-fat fryer.
фриц, а *m.* (*sl.*) Jerry (= *German soldier*).
фри́ц|евский *adj. of* **~**
фронт, а, *pl.* **~́ы, ~о́в** *m.* (*mil.*, *meteor.*; *fig.*) front; **стать во ф.** to stand to attention.
фронта́льный *adj.* frontal.
фронтиспи́с, а *m.* (*archit.*, *typ.*) frontispiece.
фронтови́к, а́ *m.* front-line soldier.
фронтов|о́й *adj.* (*mil.*) front(-line); **~ы́е пи́сьма** letters from the front.
фронто́н, а *m.* (*archit.*) pediment.
фрукт, а *m.* **1.** piece of fruit. **2.** (*pl.*) fruit.
фрукто́вый *adj.* fruit; **ф. сад** orchard.
фтор, а *m.* (*chem.*) fluorine.
фторирова́ни|е, я *nt.* (*med.*) fluoridation.
фто́ристый *adj.* fluorine; fluoride (of).
фу *int.* **1.** (*expr. contempt, revulsion, etc.*) ugh! **2.** (*expr. fatigue, etc.*) oh!; ooh!
фу́г|а, и *f.* (*mus.*) fugue.
фуга́с, а *m.* (*mil.*) landmine.
фуга́ск|а, и *f.* (*coll.*) **1.** landmine. **2.** high-explosive bomb.
фуга́с|ный *adj.* **1.** *adj. of* **~**. **2.** high-explosive.
фуже́р, а *m.* tall wineglass.
фу́к|ать, аю *impf. of* **~нуть**
фу́к|нуть, ну, нешь *pf.* (*of* **~ать**) (*coll.*) **1.** to blow; to blow out. **2.** to snort.
фу́кси|я, и *f.* fuchsia.
фунда́мент, а *m.* foundation, base (*also fig.*).
фундамента́л|ьный (~ен, ~ьна) *adj.* **1.** solid, sound; (*fig.*) thorough(-going). **2.** main, basic; **~ьная библиоте́ка** main library.
фуникулёр, а *m.* funicular (railway).
функциона́льный *adj.* functional.
фунциони́р|овать, ую *impf.* to function.
фу́нкци|я, и *f.* function.
фунт[1]**, а** *m.* **1.** (*obs.*) pound (*Russ. measure of weight, equivalent to 409.5 grams*). **2.** pound (*imperial measure of weight, equivalent to 453.6 grams*).
фунт[2]**, а** *m.* (*fin.*): **ф. (сте́рлингов)** pound (sterling).
фу́нтик, а *m.* (*cone-shaped*) paper bag.
фу́ра, ы *f.* (baggage-)wagon.
фура́ж, а́ *m.* forage, fodder.
фура́жк|а, и *f.* peak-cap; (*mil.*) service cap.
фура́ж|ный *adj. of* **~**; **~ное зерно́** feed grain.
фурго́н, а *m.* **1.** van; estate car. **2.** caravan.
фу́ри|я, и *f.* **1.** (*myth.*) Fury. **2.** (*fig.*) shrew, virago.
фуро́р, а *m.* furore.
фуру́нкул, а *m.* (*med.*) furuncle; boil.
фут, а *m.* foot (*measure of length*).
футбо́л, а *m.* football, soccer.
футболи́ст, а *m.* football-player, footballer.
футбо́лк|а, и *f.* (*coll.*) sweatshirt.
футбо́л|ьный *adj. of* **~**; **ф. мяч** football.
футля́р, а *m.* case; **ф. для очко́в** spectacle-case.
фу́товый *adj.* one-foot.
футури́зм, а *m.* futurism.
футури́ст, а *m.* futurist.
футуристи́ческий *adj.* futuristic.
фуфа́йк|а, и *f.* jersey.
фьорд = **фио́рд**
фы́рк|ать, аю *impf.* (*of* **~нуть**) **1.** to snort (*also fig.*). **2.** (*coll.*) to chuckle. **3.** (*coll.*) to grouse.
фы́рк|нуть, ну, нешь *pf. of* **~ать**
фюзеля́ж, а *m.* (*aeron.*) fuselage.

ха́живать *pres. tense not used, impf.* (*coll.*) *freq. of* **ходи́ть**
ха́ки *indecl.* **1.** *adj.* **2.** *n.*; *nt.* khaki.
хала́т, а *m.* **1.** dressing-gown. **2.** overall; **до́кторский х.** doctor's smock. **3.** (*oriental*) robe.
хала́тност|ь, и *f.* negligence.
хала́т|ный *adj.* **1.** *adj. of* **~**. **2. (~ен, ~на)** negligent.

халв|а́, ы́ *f.* (*cul.*) halva.
хали́ф, а *m.* (*hist.*) caliph.
халифа́т, а *m.* (*hist.*) caliphate.
халту́р|а, ы *f.* (*coll.*) **1.** hack-work; rubbish. **2.** extra work; money made on the side.
халту́р|ный *adj. of* **~а**
халту́рщик, а *m.* (*coll.*) **1.** hack. **2.** person making money on the side; moonlighter.
халу́п|а, ы *f.* peasant hut, shack.
халцедо́н, а *m.* (*min.*) chalcedony.
хам, а *m.* (*coll.*) boor, lout.
хамелео́н, а *m.* chameleon (*also fig.*).
хам|и́ть, лю́, и́шь *impf.* (*+d.*) to be rude (to).
ха́мский *adj.* (*coll.*) boorish, loutish.
ха́мств|о, а *nt.* (*coll.*) boorishness, loutishness.
хан, а *m.* khan.
хандр|а́, ы́ *f.* depression.
хандр|и́ть, ю́, и́шь *impf.* to be depressed.
ханж|а́, и́, *g. pl.* **~е́й** *c.g.* sanctimonious person; hypocrite.
ха́нжеск|ий (*and* **~о́й)** *adj.* sanctimonious; hypocritical.
ханжеств|о́, а́ *nt.* sanctimoniousness; hypocrisy.
ханж|и́ть, у́, и́шь *impf.* (*coll.*) to display sanctimoniousness; to play the hypocrite.
ха́нств|о, а *nt.* khanate.
хао́с, а *m.* chaos.
хаоти́ческий *adj.* chaotic.
хаоти́чност|ь, и *f.* chaotic character; state of chaos.
хаоти́ч|ный (~ен, ~на) *adj.* = **~еский**
ха́п|ать, аю *impf. of* **~нуть**
ха́п|нуть, ну, нешь *pf.* (*of* **~ать**) (*coll.*) **1.** to seize, grab. **2.** (*fig.*) to pinch, nab.
хапу́г|а, и *c.g.* (*coll.*) thief.
хара́ктер, а *m.* **1.** character, personality, nature, disposition (*of a human being*); **они́ не сошли́сь ~ами** they could not get on (together); **э́то не в его́ ~е** it's not like him. **2.** (strong) character; **челове́к с ~ом** strong-willed person. **3.** character, type; **х. рабо́ты** type of work.
характериз|ова́ть, у́ю *impf. and pf.* **1.** to describe. **2.** to be characteristic (of).
характериз|ова́ться, у́юсь *impf.* (*+i.*) to be characterized (by).
характери́стик|а, и *f.* **1.** description. **2.** (character) reference.
хара́ктерный *adj.* (*coll.*) strong-willed; temperamental.
характе́р|ный (~ен, ~на) *adj.* **1.** characteristic; typical; **э́то для него́ ~но** it is typical of him. **2.** distinctive. **3.** (*theatr.*) character; **х. актёр** character actor.
хариджа́н, а *m.* Harijan, untouchable.
ха́рк|ать, аю *impf.* (*of* **~нуть**) (*coll.*) to spit, expectorate; **х. кро́вью** to spit blood.
ха́рк|нуть, ну, нешь *pf. of* **~ать**
ха́рти|я, и *f.* charter.
харче́вн|я, и *f.* (*obs.*) eating-house.
харч|и́, е́й *pl.* (*sg.* **~,** **~а** *m.*) (*coll.*) grub.
харчо́ *nt. indecl.* kharcho (*Caucasian mutton soup*).
ха́р|я, и *f.* (*sl.*) mug (*= face*).
хаси́дский *adj.* (*relig.*) Hasidic.
ха́т|а, ы *f.* peasant hut; **моя́ х. с кра́ю** it's no concern of mine; that's your, their, *etc.*, funeral.
ха́|ять, ю, ешь *impf.* (*of* **о~**) (*coll.*) to run down, knock (*fig.*).
хвал|а́, ы́ *f.* praise.
хвале́б|ный (~ен, ~на) *adj.* laudatory, eulogistic.
хвалёный *adj.* (*iron.*) much-vaunted, celebrated.
хвал|и́ть, ю́, ~ишь *impf.* (*of* **по~**) to praise.
хвал|и́ться, ю́сь, ~ишься *impf.* (*of* **по~**) (*+i.*) to boast (of), brag (about).
хва́ста|ться, юсь *impf.* (*of* **по~**) (*+i.*) to boast (of).
хвастли́в|ый (~, ~а) *adj.* boastful.
хвастовств|о́, а́ *nt.* boasting, bragging.
хвасту́н, а́ *m.* (*coll.*) boaster, braggart.
хват, а *m.* (*coll.*) dashing blade.
хват|а́ть¹, а́ю *impf.* (*of* **~и́ть¹** *and* **схвати́ть**) **1.** to snatch, seize, catch hold (of); to grab, grasp. **2.** (*impf. only*) (*coll.*) to bite (*of fish*). **3.** (*impf. only*) (*coll.*) to pick up (*= to detain*).
хват|а́ть², а́ет *impf.* (*of* **~и́ть²**) *impers.* **1.** (*+g.*) to suffice, be sufficient, enough; to last out; **у меня́,** *etc.*, **не ~а́ет** I, *etc.*, am short (of); **у нас не ~а́ет де́нег** we haven't enough money. **2.** (*+g.* **на**+*a.*) to be capable (of); **его́ не ~а́ет на тако́й посту́пок** he is not capable of such an act.
хват|а́ться, а́юсь *impf.* (*of* **~и́ться** *and* **схвати́ться**) (**за**+*a.*) **1.** to snatch (at), catch (at), pluck (at); **х. за соло́минку** to grasp at a straw. **2.** to take up.
хва|ти́ть¹, чу́, ~тишь *pf.* (*coll.*) **1.** *pf. of* **~та́ть¹**. **2.** to drink up, knock back; **х. ли́шнего** to have one too many. **3.** to suffer, endure. **4.** to stick one's neck out; to blurt out; **х. че́рез край** to go too far. **5.** to strike; to hit; **его́ ~ти́л уда́р** he has had a stroke; (*impers.*): **моро́зом ~ти́ло посе́в** the frost hit the crops. **6.** to strike up, start up; **х. плясову́ю** to strike up a tune for dancing.
хват|и́ть², ~ит *pf.* (*of* **~а́ть²**); **~ит!** that will do!; that's enough!; **с меня́ ~ит!** I've had enough!; **~ит тебе́ хны́кать!** that's enough of your whining!
хва|ти́ться, чу́сь, ~тишься *pf.* **1.** *pf. of* **~та́ться.** **2.** (*+g.*; *coll.*) to miss, notice the absence (of).
хва́тк|а, и *f.* **1.** grasp, grip. **2.** skill.
хва́т|кий (~ок, ~ка́, ~ко) *adj.* (*coll.*) **1.** strong (*of hands, grip, etc.*); tenacious. **2.** skilful, crafty.
хво́йн|ый *adj.* **1.** *adj. of* **хво́я.** **2.** coniferous; *as n.* **~ые, ~ых** (*bot.*) conifers.
хвора́|ть, ю *impf.* (*coll.*) to be ill, sick.
хво́рост, а (у) *m.* (*collect.*) **1.** brushwood. **2.** (*cul.*) (pastry) straws.
хворости́н|а, ы *f.* stick, switch.
хво́р|ый (~, ~а́, ~о) *adj.* (*coll.*) ill, sick.
хвор|ь, и *f.* (*coll.*) illness, ailment.
хвост, а́ *m.* **1.** tail (*also fig.*); **маха́ть ~о́м** to wag one's tail; **показа́ть х.** (*coll.*) to show a clean pair of heels. **2.** (*fig.*) tail, rear, tail-end; **х. по́езда** rear of train; **быть, плести́сь в ~е́** to lag behind. **3.** (*coll.*) train (*of dress*). **4.** (*coll.*) queue, line; **х. за хле́бом** bread queue.
хвоста́т|ый (~, ~а) *adj.* **1.** having a tail; caudate. **2.** having a large tail.
хво́стик, а *m. dim. of* **хвост; с ~ом** and a little more; **сто с ~ом** a hundred odd.
хвостов|о́й *adj. of* **хвост; ~а́я ве́на** (*anat.*) caudal vein; **х. ого́нь** (*aeron.*) tail light; **~о́е опере́ние** (*aeron.*) tail unit.
хвощ, а́ *m.* (*bot.*) needle-tail, mare's tail.
хво́|я, и *f.* **1.** needle(s) (*of conifer*). **2.** (*collect.*) branches (*of conifer*).
Хе́льсинки *m. indecl.* Helsinki.
хе́льсинкский *adj.* Helsinki.
хе́рес, а (у) *m.* sherry.
херуви́м, а *m.* cherub.
херуви́м|ский *adj.* **1.** *adj. of* **~.** **2.** (*coll.*) cherubic.
хе́ттский *adj.* (*hist. and ling.*) Hittite.
хиба́р|а, ы *f.* (*coll.*) shack, hovel.
хиба́р|ка, ки *f. dim. of* **~а**
хи́жин|а, ы *f.* shack, hut.
хиле́|ть, ю *impf.* (*of* **за~**) (*coll.*) to become weak, sickly.
хи́л|ый (~, ~а́, ~о) *adj.* weak, sickly; puny; decrepit.
химе́р|а, ы *f.* **1.** chimera. **2.** (*archit.*) gargoyle.
химери́ческий *adj.* chimerical.
хи́мик, а *m.* chemist.
химика́л|ии, ий *no sg.* chemicals.

химика́т|ы, ов *pl.* (*sg.* **~**, **~а** *m.*) = **химика́лии**
химиотерапи́|я, и *f.* chemotherapy.
хими́ческ|ий *adj.* **1.** chemical; **х. каранда́ш** indelible pencil; **~ие препара́ты** chemicals; **~ая чи́стка** dry-cleaning. **2.** chemistry; **х. кабине́т** chemistry laboratory. **3.** (*mil.*): **~ая бо́мба** gas bomb; **~ое подразделе́ние** chemical warfare unit.
хи́ми|я, и *f.* chemistry.
химчи́стк|а, и *f.* **1.** dry-cleaning. **2.** dry-cleaner's.
хи́нди *m. indecl.* Hindi (*language*).
хини́н, а *m.* quinine.
хи́нн|ый *adj.*: **~ое де́рево** cinchona (*tree*).
хире́|ть, ю *impf.* (*of* **за~**) to grow sickly; (*of plants*) to wither; (*fig.*) to decay.
хирома́нт, а *m.* palmist.
хирома́нти|я, и *f.* palmistry.
хиропра́ктик, а *m.* chiropractor.
хиру́рг, а *m.* surgeon.
хирурги́ческ|ий *adj.* surgical; **~ие но́жницы** forceps; **~ая сестра́** theatre nurse.
хирурги́|я, и *f.* surgery.
хитре́ц, а́ *m.* cunning person; (*coll.*) slyboots.
хитрец|а́, ы́ *f.* (*coll.*) cunning, guile.
хитри́нк|а, и *f.* = **хитреца́**
хитр|и́ть, ю́, и́шь *impf.* (*of* **с~**) to use cunning, guile; to dissemble.
хитросплете́ни|е, я *nt.* **1.** cunning trick, stratagem. **2.** (*pl.*) fanciful construction; hair-splitting.
хи́трост|ь, и *f.* **1.** cunning, guile. **2.** ruse, stratagem. **3.** (*coll.*) ingenuity, subtlety.
хитроу́ми|е, я *nt.* cunning; resourcefulness.
хитроу́м|ный (~ен, ~на) *adj.* **1.** cunning; resourceful. **2.** intricate, complicated.
хи́т|рый (~ёр, ~ра́, ~ро) *adj.* **1.** cunning, sly, crafty, wily. **2.** (*coll.*) skilful, resourceful. **3.** (*coll.*) intricate, subtle; complicated.
хихи́к|ать, аю *impf.* (*of* **~нуть**) to giggle; to snigger.
хихи́к|нуть, ну, нешь *pf. of* **~ать**
хище́ни|е, я *nt.* theft; embezzlement, misappropriation.
хи́щник, а *m.* **1.** beast, bird of prey. **2.** (*fig.*) plunderer; predator.
хи́щнический *adj.* **1.** *adj. of* **хи́щник. 2.** predatory, rapacious. **3.** destructive.
хи́щничеств|о, а *nt.* **1.** preying. **2.** predatoriness; rapaciousness.
хи́щ|ный (~ен, ~на) *adj.* **1.** predatory; **~ные пти́цы** birds of prey. **2.** rapacious.
хладнокро́ви|е, я *nt.* composure, sang-froid.
хладнокро́в|ный (~ен, ~на) *adj.* cool, composed.
хлам, а *m.* (*collect.*) rubbish, trash.
хлеб, а, *pl.* **∠ы** *and* **~а́** *m.* **1.** (*sg. only*) bread (*also fig.*). **2.** (*pl.* **∠ы**) loaf. **3.** (*pl.* **~а́**) bread-grain; (*pl.*) corn; cereals.
хлеба́|ть, ю *impf.* to gulp (down).
хле́б|ец, ца *m.* small loaf.
хле́бниц|а, ы *f.* bread-plate; bread-basket.
хлебн|у́ть, у́, ёшь *pf.* (*coll.*) **1.** to drink down. **2.** (+*g.*) to go through, endure, experience.
хле́бн|ый *adj.* **1.** *adj. of* **хлеб 1.; ~ые дро́жжи** baker's yeast. **2.** *adj. of* **хлеб 3.; х. амба́р** granary; **~ые зла́ки** bread-grains, cereals; **х. спирт** grain alcohol. **3.** rich (*in grain*), fertile; grain-producing. **4.** (*coll.*) lucrative, profitable.
хлебопёк, а *m.* baker.
хлеборо́б, а *m.* farmer.
хлебосо́л, а *m.* hospitable person.
хлебосо́л|ьный (~ен, ~ьна) *adj.* hospitable.
хлебосо́льств|о, а *nt.* hospitality.
хле́б-со́ль, хле́ба-со́ли bread and salt (*symbol of hospitality*); hospitality.
хлев, а, в ∠е *or* **в ~у́,** *pl.* **~а́** *m.* cowshed, byre; (*fig., coll.*) pig-sty.
хле|ста́ть, щу́, ∠щешь *impf.* (*of* **~сну́ть**) **1.** (+*a. or* **по**+*d.*) to lash; to whip. **2.** (*of rain, etc.*) to lash (down), beat (down), pour; to stream, gush.
хлёст|кий (~ок, ~ка́, ~ко) *adj.* **1.** biting. **2.** (*fig.*) biting, scathing; trenchant. **3.** (*of sounds, etc.*) sharp.
хлест|ну́ть, ну́, нёшь *pf. of* **~а́ть**
хлёст|че *comp. of* **~кий**
хли́п|кий (~ок, ~ка́, ~ко) *adj.* (*coll.*) **1.** rickety, shaky. **2.** (*fig.*) weak, fragile. **3.** watery, slushy.
хлоп *int.* bang! (*as pred.*; *stands for pres. and past tenses of* **∠ать, ∠нуть** *and* **∠аться**).
хло́па|ть, ю *impf.* (*of* **хло́пнуть**) **1.** (+*i. or* **по**+d.) to bang; to slap; **х. кого́-н. по спине́** to slap s.o. on the back; **х. глаза́ми/уша́ми** (*i*) to look blank, (*ii*) to be at a loss what to say. **2. (в ладо́ши)** (+*d.*) to clap, applaud. **3.** (*coll.*) to shoot. **4.** (*coll.*) to knock back (= *to drink*).
хло́па|ться, юсь *impf.* (*of* **хло́пнуться**) (*coll.*) to flop down.
хло́п|ец, ца *m.* (*coll.*) lad.
хлопково́д, а *m.* cotton-grower.
хлопково́дств|о, а *nt.* cotton-growing.
хлопково́дческий *adj.* cotton-growing.
хло́пков|ый *adj.* cotton; **~ое ма́сло** cotton-seed oil.
хло́п|нуть(ся), ну(сь), нешь(ся) *pf. of* **~ать(ся)**
хло́п|ок, ка *m.* cotton; **х.-сыре́ц** raw cotton.
хлоп|о́к, ка́ *m.* **1.** clap. **2.** bang.
хлопо|та́ть, чу́, ∠чешь *impf.* (*of* **по~**) **1.** (*impf. only*) to busy o.s.; to bustle about. **2.** (**о**+*p. or* +**что́бы**) to make efforts; to take trouble, go to pains; to petition (for); **х., что́бы привести́ кого́-н. в чу́вство** to endeavour to bring s.o. round. **3.** (**за**+*a. or* **о**+*p.*) to plead (for), make efforts on behalf (of).
хлопотли́в|ый (~, ~а) *adj.* **1.** onerous; exacting. **2.** busy, bustling, restless.
хло́пот|ный (~ен, ~на) *adj.* (*coll.*) onerous; exacting.
хлопотн|я́, и́ *f.* (*coll.*) efforts, labour, toil.
хлопоту́н, а́ *m.* (*coll.*) busy, restless person.
хло́пот|ы, хлопо́т, ~ам *no sg.* **1.** trouble. **2.** (**о**+*p.*) efforts (on behalf of, for); pains.
хлопу́шк|а, и *f.* **1.** fly-swatter. **2.** (Christmas) cracker. **3.** (*cin.*) clapperboard.
хлопча́тк|а, и *f.* (*coll.*) cotton (*fabric*).
хлопча́тник, а *m.* cotton-plant.
хлопчатобума́жный *adj.* cotton.
хло́пь|я, ев *no sg.* flakes (*of snow, etc., or as component of name of certain cereal foods*); **кукуру́зные х.** corn flakes.
хлор, а *m.* (*chem.*) chlorine.
хлори́р|овать, ую *impf. and pf.* to chlorinate.
хло́ристый *adj.* (*chem.*) chlorine; chloride (of); **х. водоро́д** hydrogen chloride.
хло́рк|а, и *f.* (*coll.*) bleaching powder.
хло́р|ный *adj. of* **~**
хлорофи́лл, а *m.* (*bot.*) chlorophyll.
хлорофо́рм, а *m.* chloroform.
хлы́н|уть, у, ешь *pf.* **1.** (*of blood, rain, etc.*) to gush, pour. **2.** (*fig.*) to pour, rush, surge; **на пло́щадь ~ула толпа́ наро́ду** a crowd poured into the square.
хлыст[1]**, а́** *m.* whip, switch; **х. и пря́ник** (*fig., coll.*) stick and carrot.
хлыст[2]**, а́** *m.* Khlyst (*member of Russ. religious sect*).
хлыщ, а́ *m.* (*coll.*) fop.
хлю́па|ть, ю *impf.* (*coll.*) **1.** to squelch. **2.** to flounder (*through mud, etc.*). **3.** to snivel; **х. но́сом** to sniff.
хлю́п|кий (~ок, ~ка́, ~ко) *adj.* (*coll.*) **1.** soggy. **2.** rickety. **3.** (*fig.*) frail, feeble.
хляб|ь, и *f.* **1.** (*poet.*) abyss; **∠и небе́сные разве́рзлись** (*joc.*) the heavens opened. **2.** (*coll.*) mud, muddy ground.
хля́стик, а *m.* half-belt (*at the back of a coat*).
хмел|ёк, ька́ *m. dim. of* **~ь; под ~ько́м** tipsy, tight.

хмеле́|ть, ю *impf.* (*of* **за~** *and* **о ~**) to become tipsy, get tight.
хмел|ь, я *m.* **1.** (*bot.*) hop(s); hop-plant. **2. (о ~́е, во ~ю́)** drunkenness, tipsiness; **под ~́ем, во ~ю́,** tipsy, tight.
хмел|ьно́й (~ён, ~ьна́) *adj.* **1.** drunken, tipsy. **2.** intoxicating; *as n.* **~ьно́е, ~ьно́го** *nt.* intoxicating liquor, alcohol.
хму́р|ить, ю, ишь *impf.* (*of* **на~**): **х. лицо́** to frown; **х. бро́ви** to knit one's brows.
хму́р|иться, юсь, ишься *impf.* (*of* **на~**) **1.** to frown. **2.** to be overcast.
хму́рост|ь, и *f.* **1.** gloom. **2.** cloudiness.
хму́р|ый (~, ~а́, ~о) *adj.* **1.** gloomy, sullen. **2.** overcast, cloudy; **х. день** dull day.
хн|а, ы *f.* henna.
хны́ка|ть, ю (*and* **хны́ч|у, ешь**) *impf.* (*coll.*) to whimper, snivel; (*fig.*) to whine.
хо́бби *nt. indecl.* hobby.
хо́бот, а *m.* (*zool.*) trunk, proboscis.
ход, а (у), о ~́е, в (на) ~́е *and* **~у́** *m.* **1. (в ~́е, на ~у́)** motion, movement, travel, going; speed, pace; **три часа́ ~́у** three hours' walk; **за́дний х.** reversing; **ма́лый х., ти́хий х.** slow speed; **по́лный х.** full speed; **по́лный х.!** full speed ahead!; **по́лным ~́ом** (*fig.*) in full swing; **дать х.** (+*d.*) to set in motion, set going; **дать ~́у** (*i*) (*coll.*) to increase pace, go faster, (*ii*) (*coll.*) to take to one's heels; **не дать ~́у кому́-н.** not to give s.o. a chance; **идти́ свои́м ~́ом** (*i*) to travel under one's own steam, (*ii*) to take its course; **пойти́ в х.** to come to be widely used; **пусти́ть в х.** to start, set in motion, set going (*also fig.*), put into service; **быть в ~у́** to be in demand, be in vogue; **на ~у́** (*i*) in transit, on the move, without halting, (*ii*) in motion, in operation; **на по́лном ~у́** at full speed; **с ~́у** (*coll.*) straight off. **2.** (*eccl.*) procession. **3. (в, на ~́е)** (*fig.*) course, progress; **х. мы́слей** train of thought; **х. собы́тий** course of events. **4. (в ~́е, на ~́е** *and* **~у́)** (*tech.*) work, operation, running; **на холосто́м ~у́** idling. **5. (в, на ~́е;** *pl.* **~́ы, ~о́в)** (*tech.*) stroke (*of piston*). **6. (на ~́е;** *pl.* **~́ы)** (*chess, draughts*) move; (*cards*) lead. **7. (в ~́е;** *pl.* **~́ы)** (*fig.*) move, gambit; **ло́вкий х.** shrewd move. **8. (в ~́е** *and* **~у́;** *pl.* **~ы́)** entrance (*to building*); **знать все ~ы́ и вы́ходы** to know all the ins and outs. **9. (в, на ~́е** *and* **~у́;** *pl.* **~́ы, ~о́в)** passage(way). **10. (в, на ~у́;** *pl.* **~ы́** *and* **~а́, ~о́в)** (*tech.*) wheel-base; runners (*of sledge*); **гу́сеничный х.** caterpillar tracks.
хода́та|й, я *m.* intercessor, mediator.
хода́тайств|о, а *nt.* **1.** petitioning; entreaty, pleading. **2.** petition; application.
хода́тайств|овать, ую *impf.* (*of* **по~**) **1. (о**+*p. or* **за**+*a.*) to petition (for); to apply (for). **2. (за**+*a.*) to intercede (on behalf of), plead (for).
хо́дик|и, ов *no sg.* (*coll.*) grandfather clock.
хо|ди́ть, жу́, ~́дишь *impf.* **1.** to (be able to) walk. **2.** (*indet. of* **идти́**) to go (*on foot*); **х. в кино́** to go to the cinema; **х. в ата́ку** to go into the attack; **х. на паруса́х** to go sailing. **3.** (*of trains, etc.*) to run. **4.** to pass, go round; **х. из рук в ру́ки, по рука́м** to pass from hand to hand; **недо́брые ве́сти ~́дят** bad news is going round. **5.** (*cards*) to lead, play; (*chess, etc.*) to move; **х. ферзём** to move one's queen. **6.** (*indet. only*) **(за**+*i.*) to look after, care for, tend. **7. (в**+*p.*) to wear.
хо́д|кий (~ок, ~ка́, ~ко) *adj.* (*coll.*) **1.** fast, fleet. **2.** fast-selling; popular; **х. това́р** popular line; **~кое выраже́ние** popular phrase.
ходов|о́й *adj.* **1.** (*tech.*) running, working; **~о́е вре́мя** working time; **~ы́е испыта́ния** running tests; **х. механи́зм** running gear. **2.** in (good) working order. **3.** (*coll.*) popular; current; **х. анекдо́т** popular story.
ходо́к, а́ *m.* **1.** walker. **2.: быть ~о́м (куда́-н.)** (*coll.*) to make regular visits (to). **3.** envoy. **4. (на**+*a.*, **по**+*d.*) (*coll.*) person clever (at).
ходу́л|и, ей *pl.* (*sg.* **~я, ~и** *f.*) stilts.
ходу́л|ьный (~ен, ~ьна) *adj.* stilted; pompous.
ходу́н, а́ *m. now only in phr.* **~о́м ходи́ть** (*coll.*) to shake, rock; (*fig.*) to rush about.
ходьб|а́, ы́ *f.* walking; walk; **це́рковь нахо́дится в пяти́ мину́тах ~ы́ отсю́да** the church is five minutes' walk from here.
ходя́ч|ий *adj.* **1.** walking; able to walk. **2.** (*fig., coll., iron.*) the personification (of); **~ая доброде́тель** virtue personified. **3.** popular; current; **~ее выраже́ние** current phrase.
хожде́ни|е, я *nt.* **1.** walking; going; **х. по му́кам** (*fig.*) purgatory. **2.: име́ть х.** to be in circulation.
хозрасчёт, а *m.* (*econ.*) operation on a self-supporting basis; self-financing.
хозрасчёт|ный *adj. of* **~**
хозя́|ин, ина, *pl.* **~ева, ~ев** *m.* **1.** owner, proprietor. **2.** master; boss. **3.** landlord. **4.** host; **~ева по́ля** (*sport*) the home team. **5.: хоро́ший, плохо́й х.** good, bad manager. **6.** (*biol.*) host.
хозя́йк|а, и, *g. pl.* **хозя́ек** *f.* **1.** owner, proprietress. **2.** mistress. **3.** landlady.
хозя́йнича|ть, ю *impf.* **1.** to manage. **2.** to keep house. **3.** (*fig., pej.*) to lord it; to throw one's weight around.
хозя́йский *adj.* **1.** *adj. of* **хозя́ин. 2.** solicitous, careful. **3.** (*pej.*) proprietary; imperious.
хозя́йственник, а *m.* economic planner.
хозя́йствен|ный (~, ~на) *adj.* **1.** economic. **2.** household; home management. **3.** economical, thrifty.
хозя́йств|о, а *nt.* **1.** economy; **се́льское х.** agriculture; **дома́шнее х.** housekeeping; **вести́ х.** to manage. **2.** equipment. **3.** (*agric.*) farm, holding. **4.** housekeeping.
хозя́йств|овать, ую *impf.* to manage.
хозя́йчик, а *m.* (*coll.*) small proprietor.
хокке́ист, а *m.* hockey-player.
хокке́|й, я *m.* hockey; **х. с ша́йбой** ice hockey; **ко́нный х.** polo.
хокке́й|ный *adj. of* **~**; **~ная клю́шка** hockey-stick.
хо́леный *adj.* well-groomed, carefully tended; sleek.
холе́р|а, ы *f.* (*med.*) cholera.
холе́рик, а *m.* **1.** choleric person. **2.** (*coll.*) cholera victim.
холери́ческий *adj.* choleric.
холе́р|ный *adj. of* **~а**; **х. вибрио́н** cholera bacillus.
хо́л|ить, ю, ишь *impf.* to tend, care for.
хо́лк|а, и *f.* withers.
холл, а *m.* hall, vestibule, foyer.
холм, а́ *m.* hill.
холми́ст|ый (~, ~а) *adj.* hilly.
хо́лод, а (у), *pl.* **~а́, ~о́в** *m.* **1.** cold; coldness (*also fig.*); **ди́кий х.** bitter cold. **2.** (*pl.*) cold weather.
холода́|ть, ю *impf.* (*pf.* **по~**; *impers.*) to become cold, turn cold.
холоде́|ть, ю *impf.* (*of* **по~**) to grow cold; (*impers.*) to turn cold.
холод|е́ц, ца́ *m.* (*coll.*) meat *or* fish in jelly.
холоди́льник, а *m.* refrigerator; **двухсекцио́нный х.** fridge-freezer.
холоди́льн|ый *adj.* refrigeration; **~ая устано́вка** cold storage plant.
холо|ди́ть, жу́, ди́шь *impf.* **1.** (*pf.* **на~**) (*coll.*) to cool. **2.** to cause a cold sensation (*also impers.*)
хо́лодно[1] *adv.* (*fig.*) coldly.
хо́лодно[2] *as pred.* it is cold; **мне,** *etc.*, **х.** I, *etc.*, am cold.
холоднова́т|ый (~, ~а) *adj.* rather cold, chilly.
холоднокро́вный *adj.* (*zool.*) cold-blooded.
хо́лодност|ь, и *f.* coldness.

холо́д|ный (хо́лоден, ~на́, хо́лодно) *adj.* **1.** cold; **х. ве́тер** cold wind; **х. отве́т** cold reply; **х. по́яс** (*geog.*) frigid zone; **~ная война́** cold war; **~ное ору́жие** side-arms, cold steel. **2.** light, thin (*of clothing, etc.*).
холод|о́к, ка́ *m.* **1.** coolness, chill (*also fig.*). **2.** cool breeze. **3.** cool place. **4.** cool of the day.
холо́п, а *m.* **1.** (*hist.*) villein, bond slave. **2.** serf. **3.** (*fig., pej.*) lackey.
холо́п|ский *adj.* **1.** *adj. of* **~. 2.** servile.
холо́пств|о, а *nt.* **1.** (*hist.*) villeinage, bond slavery. **2.** servility.
холо́пств|овать, ую *impf.* to display servility.
холо|сти́ть, щу́, сти́шь *impf.* to castrate, geld.
холост|о́й (хо́лост, ~а́) *adj.* **1.** unmarried, single; bachelor. **2.** (*tech.*) idle, free-running; **на ~о́м ходу́** idling. **3.** (*mil.*) blank; **х. патро́н** blank cartridge.
холостя́к, а́ *m.* bachelor.
холостя́|цкий *adj. of* **~к**
холоще́ни|е, я *nt.* castration, gelding.
холощёный *adj.* castrated, gelded.
холст, а́ *m.* **1.** canvas; sackcloth. **2.** (*art*) canvas.
холсти́н|а, ы *f.* **1.** = **холст. 2.** piece of canvas.
холсти́нк|а, и *f.* (*text.*) gingham.
холу́|й, я́ *m.* lackey.
холщо́вый *adj. of* **холст 1.**
хо́л|я, и *f.* (*coll.*) care, attention; **жить в ~е** to be well cared for.
хому́т, а́ *m.* (*horse's*) collar.
хомя́к, а́ *m.* hamster.
хонинг|ова́ть, у́ю *impf.* (*tech.*) to hone.
хор, а, *pl.* **~ы́** (*and* **∸ы**) *m.* **1.** choir. **2.** (*mus. and fig.*) chorus; **∸ом** all together.
хора́л, а *m.* chorale.
хорва́т, а *m.* Croat.
Хорва́ти|я, и *f.* Croatia.
хорва́т|ка, ки *f. of* **~**
хорва́тский *adj.* Croatian, Croat.
хо́рд|а, ы *f.* (*math.*) chord.
хорейческий *adj.* (*liter.*) trochaic.
хоре́|й, я *m.* (*liter.*) trochee.
хор|ёк, ька́ *m.* polecat, ferret.
хореографи́ческий *adj.* choreographic.
хореогра́фи|я, и *f.* choreography.
хоре́|я, и *f.* (*med.*) chorea.
хори́ст, а *m.* chorister.
хорме́йстер, а *m.* choirmaster.
хорово́д, а *m.* round dance.
хорово́й *adj.* choral.
хорон|и́ть, ю́, ∸ишь *impf.* (*of* **по~**) (*pf. also* **за~** *and* **с~**) to bury (*also fig.*); to inter.
хорохо́р|иться, юсь, ишься *impf.* (*coll.*) to swagger; to boast.
хоро́шенький *adj.* pretty, nice (*also iron.*).
хороше́нько *adv.* (*coll.*) properly, thoroughly, well and truly.
хороше́|ть, ю *impf.* (*of* **по~**) to grow prettier.
хоро́ш|ий (~, ~а́, ~о́) *adj.* **1.** good. **2.** nice (*oft. iron.*) **3.** (*short forms*) pretty, good-looking.
хорошо́[1] **1.** *adv.* well; nicely. **2.** *particle, expr. agreement, acceptance* all right!; very well! **3.** *n.*; *nt. indecl.* good (*mark*).
хорошо́[2] *as predicate* it is good; it is nice; **х., что вы успе́ли прие́хать** it is good that you managed to come; **им х. — ведь у них своя́ маши́на** it is all right for them, they have a car of their own.
хо́р|ы, ~ *and* **∸ов** (*musicians'*) gallery.
хор|ь, я́ *m.* polecat.
хор|ько́вый *adj. of* **~ёк**
хо́спис, а *m.* hospice.
хоте́ни|е, я *nt.* desire, wish.
хоте́|ть, хочу́, хо́чешь, хо́чет, хоти́м, хоти́те, хотя́т *impf.* (*of* **за~**) (*+g., inf. or* **что́бы**) to want, desire; **я ~л бы** I should like; **х. пить** to be thirsty; **х. сказа́ть** to mean.
хоте́|ться, хо́чется *impf.* (*of* **за~**) (*impers.+d.*) to want; to feel like; **мне хо́чется** I want; **мне ~лось бы** I should like.
хоть *conj. and particle* **1.** *conj.* although. **2.** *conj.* even if (*esp. in set phrr.*); **у него́ де́нег х. отбавля́й** he has more than enough money; **х. убе́й, не скажу́** I couldn't tell you to save my life; **х. бы и так** (*coll.*) even so. **3.** *particle* (*also* **х. бы**) at least, if only; **ты бы посмотре́л х. на мину́точку** you should take a look, if only for a minute. **4.** *particle* (*coll.*) for example, even; **вот, х. его́ семиле́тняя сестрёнка, ведь, догада́лась** why, even his little seven-year-old sister had guessed it. **5.: х. бы** if only. **6.** *+rel. pron. forms indef. pron.*: **х. кто** anyone; **х. где** anywhere, everywhere; **х. куда́** (*as pred.*; *coll.*) first-rate, terrific. **7.: х. бы что** (*+d.*; *coll.*) it does not bother.
хотя́ *conj.* **1.** although, though. **2.: х. бы** even if. **3.** *as particle* **х. бы** if only.
хохла́т|ый (~, ~а) *adj.* crested, tufted.
хо́хл|иться, юсь, ишься *impf. of* **на~**
хо́хм|а, ы *f.* joke, quip, gag.
хох|о́л, ла́ *m.* **1.** crest; topknot. **2.** (*joc.*) Ukrainian.
хо́хот, а *m.* guffaw, loud laugh.
хохо|та́ть, чу́, ∸чешь *impf.* to guffaw, laugh loudly.
хохоту́н, а́ *m.* (*coll.*) joker.
храбре́ц, а́ *m.* brave person.
храбр|и́ться, ю́сь, и́шься *impf.* (*coll.*) to try to appear brave.
хра́брост|ь, и *f.* bravery, valour.
хра́бр|ый (~, ~а́, ~о) *adj.* brave, valiant.
храм, а *m.* temple.
хране́ни|е, я *nt.* safekeeping, custody; storage; **ка́мера ~я** left luggage office; **сдать на х.** to deposit for safekeeping.
храни́лищ|е, а *nt.* storehouse, depository; vault.
храни́тел|ь, я *m.* **1.** keeper, custodian. **2.** curator.
хран|и́ть, ю́, и́шь *impf.* to keep; to preserve, maintain; to store **х. молча́ние** to keep silence; **х. в та́йне** to keep secret.
храп, а *m.* snore; snoring.
храп|е́ть, лю́, и́шь *impf.* **1.** to snore. **2.** (*of an animal*) to snort.
храпови́к, а́ *m.* (*tech.*) ratchet.
храпов|о́й *adj. of* **~и́к**
хреб|е́т, та́ *m.* **1.** (*anat.*) spine, spinal column; (*fig., coll.*) back. **2.** (mountain) range; ridge.
хреб|то́вый *adj. of* **~е́т**
хрен, а(у), *m.* horseradish; **говя́дина под ∸ом** roast beef with horseradish sauce; **х. ре́дьки не сла́ще** (*fig.*) it's six of one to half a dozen of the other; **ста́рый х.** (*fig., coll.*) old fogey; **х. с** (*+i.*) to hell (with).
хрен|о́вый *adj. of* **~**; (*sl.*) rotten, lousy.
хрестома́ти|я, и *f.* reader.
хризанте́м|а, ы *f.* chrysanthemum.
хрип, а *m.* wheeze, wheezing sound.
хрип|е́ть, лю́, и́шь *impf.* to wheeze.
хри́пл|ый (~, ~а́, ~о) *adj.* hoarse; wheezy.
хри́п|нуть, ну, нешь, *past* **~, ~ла** *impf.* (*of* **о~**) to become hoarse, lose one's voice.
хрипот|а́, ы́ *f.* hoarseness.
христи|ани́н, ани́на, *pl.* **~а́не, ~а́н** *m.* Christian.
христиа́н|ка, ки *f. of* **~и́н**
христиа́нский *adj.* Christian.
христиа́нств|о, а *nt.* Christianity.
Христо́с, Христа́ *m.* Christ.
хром[1]**, а** *m.* (*chem.*) chromium; chrome.
хром[2]**, а** *m.* box-calf.
хромати́ческий *adj.* chromatic.
хрома́|ть, ю *impf.* **1.** to limp, be lame; **х. на о́бе ноги́** (*fig., coll.*) to be in a poor way. **2.** (*fig., coll.*) to be weak; **арифме́тика у тебя́ ~ет** your arithmetic is very shaky.

хромé|ть, ю *impf.* (*of* **о~**) to go lame.
хроми́р|овать, ую *impf. and pf.* to chromium-plate.
хрóм|истый *adj. of* **~**[1]
хрóмовый[1] *adj.* (*chem.*) chromium, chromic.
хрóм|овый[2] *adj. of* **~**[2]
хром|óй (~, ~á, ~́о) *adj.* lame; **х. на лéвую нóгу** lame in the left leg; *as n.* **х., ~óго** *m.*; **~áя, ~óй** *f.* lame man, woman.
хромонóг|ий (~, ~а) *adj.* lame.
хромосóм|а, ы *f.* (*biol.*) chromosome.
хромот|á, ы́ *f.* lameness.
хрóник, а *m.* (*coll.*) chronic invalid.
хрóник|а, и *f.* **1.** chronicle. **2.** news items. **3.** (*cin.*) newsreel.
хроникáльный *adj. of* **хрóника 2., 3.**; **х. фильм** = **хрóника 3.**
хрони́ческ|ий *adj.* chronic.
хронологи́ческий *adj.* chronological.
хронолóги|я, и *f.* chronology.
хронóметр, а *m.* chronometer.
хронометрáж, а *m.* time study, time-keeping.
хрономнетражи́ст, а *m.* time study specialist, time-keeper.
хрýп|кий (~ок, ~кá, ~ко) *adj.* **1.** fragile, brittle. **2.** (*fig.*) fragile, frail; delicate.
хрýпкост|ь, и *f.* **1.** fragility, brittleness. **2.** (*fig.*) fragility, frailness.
хруст, а *m.* crunch; crackle.
хрустáлик, а *m.* (*anat.*) crystalline lens.
хрустáл|ь, я́ *m.* cut glass, crystal.
хрустáльный *adj.* **1.** cut glass, crystal. **2.** (*fig.*) crystal-clear.
хру|стéть, щý, сти́шь *impf.* (*of* **~́стнуть**) to crunch (*of snow, etc.*); to crackle.
хрýст|нуть, ну, нешь *pf. of* **~éть**
хруст|я́щий *pres. part. of* **~éть** *and adj.* **х. картóфель** potato crisps.
хрущ, á *m.* cockchafer, may bug.
хрю́кань|е, я *nt.* grunting (*of a pig*).
хрю́к|ать, аю *impf.* (*of* **~нуть**) to grunt.
хрю́к|нуть, ну, нешь *pf.* (*of* **~ать**) to give a grunt.
хряк, á *m.* hog.
хрящ, á *m.* (*anat.*) cartilage, gristle.
хрящевáт|ый (~, ~а) *adj.* cartilaginous, gristly.
хрящ|евóй *adj. of* **~**
худé|ть, ю *impf.* (*of* **по~**) to grow thin, lose wight.
хýд|о[1], **а** *nt.* harm, ill, evil; **нет ~а без добрá** every cloud has a silver lining.
хýдо[2] *adv.* ill, badly.
хýдо[3] *as pred.* (*impers.+d.*) **емý,** *etc.*, **х.** (*i*) he, *etc.*, feels poorly, unwell, (*ii*) he, *etc.*, is in a bad way; he, *etc.*, is having a bad time.
худоб|á, ы́ *f.* thinness, leanness.
худóжественност|ь, и *f.* artistry, artistic merit.
худóжествен|ный (~, ~на) *adj.* **1.** of art, of the arts; **~ная литератýра** fiction; **х. фильм** feature film; **~ная шкóла** art school. **2.** artistic.
худóжеств|о, а *nt.* **1.** art; *pl.* (*obs.*) the arts; **Акадéмия ~** Academy of Arts. **2..** (*coll.*) trick, escapade.
худóжник, а *m.* artist.
худ|óй[1] **(~, ~á, ~́о)** *adj.* thin, lean.
худ|óй[2] **(~, ~á, ~́о)** *adj.* bad; **на х. конéц** if the worst comes to the worst.
худ|óй[3] **(~, ~á, ~́о)** *adj.* (*coll.*) full of holes; worn; tumbledown.
худощáв|ый (~, ~а) *adj.* thin, lean.
хýд|ший *superl. of* **~óй**[2] *and* **плохóй**; (the) worst.
хуёвин|а, ы *f.* (*euph.*) = **хуйня́**
ху|ёвый *adj. of* **~й**; (*vulg.*) shitty, crap(py) (= *awful*).
хý|же *comp. of* **~дóй**[2] *and* **~до**[2], **плохóй** *and* **плóхо**; worse.
хуй, хýя *m.*(*vulg.*) prick, cock (= *penis*); **ни хуя́** (*vulg.*) fuck all.
хуйн|я́, и́ *f.* (*vulg.*) bollocks (= *utter nonsense*).
хул|á, ы́ *f.* (verbal) abuse.
хулигáн, а *m.* hooligan, hoodlum.
хулигáн|ить, ю, ишь *impf.* to act like a hooligan.
хулигáн|ский *adj. of* **~**
хулигáнств|о, а *nt.* hooliganism.
хули́тел|ьный (~ен, ~ьна) *adj.* abusive.
хул|и́ть, ю́, и́шь *impf.* to abuse, criticize.
хýнт|а, ы *f.* (*pol.*) junta.
хунти́ст, а *m.* (*pol.*) member of a junta.
хурм|á, ы́ *f.* (*bot.*) persimmon.
хýтор, а, *pl.* **~á** *m.* **1.** farm; farmstead. **2.** village.
хуторск|óй *adj. of* **хýтор**
хутор|я́н|ин, ина, *pl.* **~е, ~** *m.* **1.** farmer. **2.** villager.

Ц

ц. (*abbr. of* **цéнтнер**) q., quintal(s).
цáп|ать, аю *impf.* (*of* **~нуть**) to snatch, grab.
цáп|ля, ли, *g. pl.* **~ель** *f.* heron.
цаpáп|ать, аю *impf.* **1.** (*pf.* **о~** *and* **~нуть**) to scratch. **2.** (*coll.*) to scribble.
царáпа|ться, юсь *impf.* to scratch (*intrans.*); to scratch one another.
царáпин|а, ы *f.* scratch; abrasion.
царáп|нуть, ну, нешь *pf. of* **~ать**
царéвич, а *m.* tsarevich.
царéв|на, ны, *g. pl.* **~ен** *f.* tsarevna.
цареуби́йств|о, а *nt.* regicide.
цари́зм, а *m.* tsarism.
цари́стский *adj.* tsarist.
цар|и́ть, ю́, и́шь *impf.* **1.** (*obs.*) to reign. **2.** (*fig.*) to reign, prevail; **~и́ла тишинá** silence reigned.
цари́ц|а, ы *f.* **1.** tsarina. **2.** (*fig.*) queen.
цáрск|ий *adj.* **1.** tsar's, of the tsar; royal. **2.** tsarist. **3.** (*fig.*) regal; **~ая рóскошь** regal splendour.
цáрствен|ный (~, ~на) *adj.* regal.
цáрств|о, а *nt.* **1.** kingdom, realm. **2.** reign. **3.** (*fig.*) realm, domain; **живóтное ц.** animal kingdom.
цáрствовани|е, я *nt.* reign; **в ц.** (*+g.*) during the reign (of).
цáрств|овать, ую *impf.* to reign (*also fig.*).
цар|ь, я́ *m.* **1.** tsar; **он без ~я́ в головé** (*coll.*) he's off his head. **2.** (*fig.*) king, ruler.
цве|сти́, тý, тёшь, *past* **~̈л, ~лá, ~лó** *impf.* **1.** to flower, bloom, blossom (*also fig.*); **ц. здорóвьем** to be radiant with health. **2.** (*fig.*) to prosper, flourish.
цвет[1], **а,** *pl.* **~á** *m.* colour; **ц. лицá** complexion.
цвет[2], **а** *m.* **1.** (*pl.* **~ы́**) (*coll.*) flower. **2.** (*fig.*) flower, cream, pick (*best part*). **3.** blossom-time; (*fig.*) prime; **в цветý** in blossom; **дать ц.** to blossom, flower; **во ~́е сил** in one's prime. **4.** blossom.
цветéни|е, я *nt.* (*bot.*) flowering, blossoming.
цвети́ст|ый (~, ~а) *adj.* **1.** multi-coloured, variegated. **2.** (*fig.*) flowery, florid.
цветкóв|ый *adj.*: **~ые растéния** (*bot.*) flowering plants.
цветни́к, á *m.* flower-bed.
цветн|óй *adj.* **1.** coloured; colour; **~óе стеклó** stained glass; **~áя капýста** cauliflower. **2.** (*tech.*) non-ferrous.
цветовóдств|о, а *nt.* floriculture.
цветов|óй *adj. of* **цвет**[1]; **~áя гáмма** colour spectrum; **~áя слепотá** colour-blindness.

цвет|о́к, ка́, *pl.* **~ы́, ~о́в** *m.* flower; (*pl. also* **~ки́, ~ко́в**) flower.
цветоло́ж|е, а *nt.* (*bot.*) receptacle.
цветоно́жк|а, и *f.* (*bot.*) peduncle.
цвето́ч|ек, ка *m. dim. of* **цвето́к**
цвето́чник, а *m.* florist; flower-seller.
цвето́чниц|а, ы *f.* flower-girl.
цвето́чн|ый *adj. of* **цвето́к; ~ая клу́мба** flower-bed; **ц. магази́н** flower-shop, florist's.
цвету́щий *pres. part. act. of* **цвести́** *and adj.* **1.** flowering, blossoming, blooming (*also fig.*). **2.** (*fig.*) prosperous, flourishing.
цеди́лк|а, и *f.* (*coll.*) strainer, filter.
цеди́льн|ый *adj.* filter, filtering; **~ая бума́га** filter paper; **~ая поду́шка** filter pad.
це|ди́ть, жу́, ⁓дишь *impf.* **1.** to strain, filter. **2.** to decant (*liquids*). **3.** (*coll.*) to say (*through clenched teeth*).
це́др|а, ы *f.* (dried) lemon *or* orange peel.
це́зи|й, я *m.* (*chem.*) caesium.
цезу́р|а, ы *f.* (*liter.*) caesura.
Цейло́н, а *m.* Ceylon.
цейло́н|ец, ца *m.* Ceylonese.
цейло́н|ка, ки *f. of* **~ец**
цейло́нский *adj.* Ceylonese; Ceylon.
цейтно́т, а *m.* time-trouble (*at chess*).
целе́бност|ь, и *f.* curative, healing properties.
целе́б|ный (~ен, ~на) *adj.* curative, healing, medicinal.
цел|ево́й *adj.* **1.** *adj. of* **~ь. 2.** for a specified purpose.
целенапра́влен|ный (~, ~на) *adj.* purposeful, single-minded.
целесообра́зност|ь, и *f.* expediency.
целесообра́з|ный (~ен, ~на) *adj.* expedient.
целеустремлён|ный (~, ~а́) *adj.* purposeful.
целико́м *adv.* **1.** whole; **проглоти́ть ц.** to swallow whole. **2.** wholly, entirely; **ц. и по́лностью** utterly and completely.
целин|а́, ы́ *f.* virgin lands, virgin soil.
цели́н|ный *adj. of* **~а́; ~ные зе́мли** virgin lands.
цели́тел|ьный (~ен, ~ьна) *adj.* curative, healing, medicinal.
це́л|ить, ю, ишь *impf.* (*of* **на~**) to take aim; (**в**+*a.*) to aim (at).
це́л|иться, юсь, ишься *impf.* (*of* **на~**) = **~ить**
целлофа́н, а *m.* cellophane.
целлуло́ид, а *m.* celluloid.
целлюло́з|а, ы *f.* cellulose.
цел|ова́ть, у́ю *impf.* (*of* **по~**) to kiss.
цел|ова́ться, у́юсь *impf.* (*of* **по~**) to kiss (one another); to exchange kisses.
це́л|ое, ого *nt.* **1.** whole. **2.** (*math.*) integer.
целому́дрен|ный (~, ~на) *adj.* chaste.
целому́дри|е, я *nt.* chastity.
це́лостност|ь, и *f.* integrity.
це́лост|ный (~ен, ~на) *adj.* integral; complete.
це́лост|ь, и *f.* **1.** safety; **в ~и и сохра́нности** intact; safe and sound. **2.** unity.
це́л|ый *adj.* **1.** whole, entire; **~ое число́** whole number, integer; **в ~ом** as a whole; **по ~ым неде́лям** for weeks on end. **2. (~, ~а́, ~о)** safe, intact; **~ и невреди́м** safe and sound.
цел|ь, и *f.* **1.** target; **попа́сть в ц.** to hit the target; **бить ми́мо ⁓и** to miss the target. **2.** aim, object, goal, end, purpose; **с ⁓ью** (+*inf.*) with the object (of), in order (to); **отвеча́ть ⁓и** to answer the purpose; **пресле́довать ц.** to pursue a goal.
це́л|ьный *adj.* **1.** of one piece, solid. **2. (~ен, ~ьна́, ~ьно)** entire, integral; single. **3.** whole, undiluted.
це́льност|ь, и *f.* wholeness, entirety, integrity.
Це́льси|й, я *m.* Celsius, centigrade; **10° по ~ю** 10° Celsius.

цеме́нт, а *m.* cement.
цементи́р|овать, ую *impf. and pf.* **1.** (*tech.*) to cement; to case-harden. **2.** (*fig.*) to cement.
цеме́нт|ный *adj. of* **~**
цен|а́, ы́, *a.* **⁓у**, *pl.* **⁓ы** *f.* **1.** price, cost; **~о́ю** (+*g.*) at the cost (of); **любо́й ~о́й** at any price; **э́тому ~ы́ нет** it is invaluable; **э́то в ~е́** it is very costly. **2.** worth, value; **знать ⁓у** (+*d.*) to know the worth (of).
ценз, а *m.* qualification, reqirement.
це́нз|овый *adj. of* **~**
це́нзор, а *m.* censor.
цензу́р|а, ы *f.* censorship.
цензу́р|ный *adj.* **1.** *adj. of* **~а. 2. (~ен, ~на)** decent, printable.
цени́тел|ь, я *m.* judge, connoisseur, expert.
цен|и́ть, ю́, ⁓ишь *impf.* **1.** (*coll.*) to fix a price for; (*fig.*) to assess, evaluate. **2.** to value, appreciate; **высоко́ ц.** to rate highly.
це́нник, а *m.* price-list.
це́нност|ь, и *f.* **1.** price, value. **2.** (*fig.*) value, importance. **3.** (*pl.*) valuables; values.
це́н|ный (~ен, ~на) *adj.* **1.** containing valuables; representing a stated value; **~ная бандеро́ль** registered postal packet; **~ные бума́ги** (*fin.*) securities. **2.** valuable.
цент, а *m.* cent (*unit of currency*).
це́нтнер, а *m.* quintal (= *100 kilograms*).
центр, а *m.* centre; **ц. тя́жести** centre of gravity.
централиза́ци|я, и *f.* centralization.
централиз|ова́ть, у́ю *impf. and pf.* to centralize.
центра́льн|ый *adj.* central; **~ые газе́ты** national newspapers; **ц. нападА́ющий** (*sport*) centre forward.
центри́ст, а *m.* (*pol.*) centrist.
центри́ст|ский *adj. of* **~**
центрифу́г|а, и *f.* **1.** (*tech.*) centrifuge. **2.** spin drier.
центробе́жный *adj.* centrifugal.
центрово́й *adj.* (*tech.*) central, centre.
центростреми́тельный *adj.* centripetal.
цеп, а́ *m.* (*agric.*) flail.
цепене́|ть, ю *impf.* (*of* **о~**) to freeze, be rooted to the spot (*from cold or from strong emotion*).
це́п|кий (~ок, ~ка́, ~ко) *adj.* **1.** tenacious, strong (*also fig.*); prehensile. **2.** (*of soil, mud, etc.*) sticky, tacky, loamy. **3.** (*coll.*) persistent, dogged.
це́пкост|ь, и *f.* **1.** tenacity, strength. **2.** (*coll.*) persistence, doggedness.
цепля́|ться, юсь *impf.* **1.** (**за**+*a.*) to clutch (at), try to grasp. **2.** (**за**+*a.*; *coll.*) to cling (to); to stick (to).
цеп|но́й *adj. of* **~ь; ~на́я соба́ка** watchdog, house-dog; **~но́е колесо́** sprocket wheel; **~на́я реа́кция** (*chem., phys.*; *fig.*) chain reaction.
цепо́чк|а, и *f.* **1.** (small) chain. **2.** file, series; **идти́ ~ой** to walk in file.
цеп|ь, и, о ⁓и, на ~и́, *pl.* **⁓и, ~е́й** *f.* **1.** chain; (*pl.*) chains (= *fetters*; *also fig.*); **посади́ть на ц.** to chain (up). **2.** range (*of mountains*). **3.** (*fig.*) series, succession; **ц. катастро́ф** succession of disasters. **5.** (*elec.*) circuit.
церемониа́л, а *m.* ceremonial, ritual.
церемониа́л|ьный *adj.* **1.** *adj. of* **~. 2.** solemn, ceremonial; **ц. марш** (*mil.*) march-past.
церемо́н|иться, юсь *impf.* (*of* **по~**) **1.** to stand upon ceremony. **2.** (**с кем-н.**) to be too soft (on).
церемо́ни|я, и *f.* ceremony; **без дальне́йших ~й** without further ado.
церемо́н|ный (~ен, ~на) *adj.* ceremonious.
церко́вник, а *m.* churchman, clergyman.
церковнославя́нский *adj.* (*ling.*) Church Slavonic.
церко́вный *adj.* church; **ц. ста́роста** churchwarden; **ц. сто́рож** sexton.
це́рк|овь, ви, *i.* **~овью**, *pl.* **~ви, ~ве́й, ~ва́м** *f.* church.

цесаре́вич, а *m.* cesarevitch, crown prince.
цеса́рк|а, и *f.* guinea-fowl.
цех, а, в ∸е *and* (*coll.*) **в ~у́,** *pl.* **~и** *and* (*coll.*) **~а́** *m.* **1.** shop, section (*in factory*). **2.** (*hist.*) guild.
цех|ово́й *adj. of* ~
цеце́ *f. indecl.* tsetse (fly).
циа́н, а *m.* (*chem.*) cyanogen.
циа́нистый *adj.* (*chem.*) cyanogen; cyanide (of); **ц. ка́лий** potassium cyanide.
циа́нов|ый *adj.* (*chem.*) cyanic.
циано́з, а *m.* (*med.*) cyanosis.
цивилиза́ци|я, и *f.* civilization.
цивилизо́в|анный *p.p.p. of* **~а́ть** *and adj.* civilized.
цивилиз|ова́ть, у́ю *impf. and pf.* to civilize.
цигéйк|а, и *f.* beaver lamb.
цигéйковый *adj.* beaver-lamb.
цика́д|а, ы *f.* cicada.
цикл, а *m.* cycle; series.
цикламéн, а *m.* cyclamen.
цикли́ческий *adj.* cyclical.
цикли́ч|ный (~ен, ~на) *adj.* = **~еский**
цикло́н, а *m.* (*meteor.*) cyclone.
циклони́ческий *adj.* (*meteor.*) cyclonic.
циклотро́н, а *m.* (*phys.*) cyclotron.
цико́ри|й, я *m.* chicory.
цико́р|ный *adj. of* **~ий**
цику́т|а, ы *f.* (*bot.*) water hemlock.
цили́ндр, а *m.* **1.** cylinder. **2.** top hat.
цилиндри́ческий *adj.* cylindrical.
цимбали́ст, а *m.* cymbalist.
цимба́л|ы, ~ *no sg.* (*mus.*) cymbals.
цинг|а́, и́ *f.* (*med.*) scurvy.
цини́зм, а *m.* cynicism.
ци́ник, а *m.* cynic.
цини́ческий *adj.* cynical.
цини́ч|ный (~ен, ~на) *adj.* cynical.
цинк, а *m.* (*chem.*) zinc.
ци́нковый *adj.* zinc.
цино́вк|а, и *f.* mat.
цирк, а *m.* circus.
цирка́ч, а́ *m.* (*coll.*) circus artiste.
цирк|ово́й *adj. of* ~
цирко́н, а *m.* (*min.*) zircon.
цирко́ни|й, я *m.* (*chem.*) zirconium.
циркули́р|овать, ую *impf.* to circulate.
ци́ркул|ь, я *m.* (pair of) compasses; dividers.
циркуля́р, а *m.* (*official*) instruction.
циркуля́ци|я, и *f.* circulation.
цирро́з, а *m.* (*med.*) cirrhosis.
цирю́льник, а *m.* (*obs.*) barber.
цирю́л|ьня, ьни, *g. pl.* **~ен** *f.* (*obs.*) barber's shop.
цистéрн|а, ы *f.* cistern, tank; tanker.
цитадéл|ь, и *f.* citadel; (*fig.*) bulwark, stronghold.
цита́т|а, ы *f.* quotation.
цити́р|овать, ую *impf.* (*of* **про~**) to quote.
цитоло́ги|я, и *f.* (*biol.*) cytology.
ци́тр|а, ы *f.* (*mus.*) zither.
ци́трус, а *m.* citrus.
цитрусово́дств|о, а *nt.* citrus-growing.
ци́трус|овый *adj. of* ~; *as n.* **~овые, ~овых** citrus plants.
цифербла́т, а *m.* dial; face.
ци́фр|а, ы *f.* **1.** figure; number, numeral. **2.** (*pl.*) figures (= *statistical data*).
цифров|о́й *adj.* **1.** numerical. **2.** digital; **~а́я за́пись** digital recording.
ци́церо *nt. indecl.* (*typ.*) pica.
ЦК *m. indecl.* (*abbr. of* **Центра́льный Комитéт**) Central Committee.
цо́к|ать[1], аю *impf.* (*of* **~нуть**) to clatter.
цо́к|ать[2], аю *impf.* to pronounce **ч** as **ц** (*as in some North Russ. dialects*).
цо́к|нуть, ну *pf. of* **~ать[1]**
цо́кол|ь, я *m.* (*archit.*) socle, plinth, pedestal.
цо́коль|ный *adj. of* ~; **ц. эта́ж** ground floor.
цо́кот, а *m.* clatter.
ЦРУ *nt. indecl.* (*abbr. of* **Центра́льное разве́дывательное управлéние**) CIA (*Central Intelligence Agency*).
цуг, а *m.* team (*of horses harnessed tandem or in pairs*).
цу́гом *adv.* (in) tandem.
цука́т, а *m.* candied fruit; candied peel.
цыга́н, а, *pl.* **~е,** ~ *m.* Gypsy.
цыга́н|ка, ки *f. of* ~
цыга́нский *adj.* Gypsy.
цы́п|ки, ок *pl.* (*coll.*) red spots (*on hands, etc.*).
цыпл|ёнок, ёнка, *pl.* **~я́та, ~я́т** *m.* chick(en).
цы́почк|и: на ц., на ~ах on tiptoe.
цыц *int.* (*coll.*) (s)hush!
цэрэу́шник, а *m.* (*coll.*) CIA (*Central Intelligence Agency*) agent.
Цю́рих, а *m.* Zurich.

Ч

ч. (*abbr. of* **час**) hour; o'clock.
чаба́н, а́ *m.* shepherd.
ча́б|ер, ра *and* **чаб|ёр, ра́** *m.* (*bot., cul.*) savory.
чабре́ц, а́ *m.* (*bot., cul.*) thyme.
ча́вк|ать, аю *impf.* (*of* **~нуть) 1.** to champ; to munch. **2.** to tramp; to squelch.
ча́вк|нуть, ну, нешь *pf. of* **~ать**
чад, а (у), о ∸е, в~у́ *m.* **1.** fumes. **2.** (*fig.*) intoxication.
ча|ди́ть, жу́, ди́шь *impf.* (*of* **на~**) to smoke, emit fumes.
ча́д|ный (~ен, ~на, ~но) *adj.* **1.** smoky, smoke-laden; **~но** (*as pred.*) it is smoky, full of smoke. **2.** (*fig.*) doped, drugged, stupefied; stupefying.
ча́д|о, а *nt.* **1.** (*joc.*) child, offspring, progeny. **2.** (*fig.*) child, product, creature; **ч. двадца́того ве́ка** product of the twentieth century.
чадр|а́, ы́ *f.* chador (*veil worn by Moslem women*).
чаёвник, а *m.* (*coll.*) tea-drinker.
чаёвнича|ть, ю *impf.* (*coll.*) to drink tea, have tea.
чаево́д, а *m.* tea-grower.
чаево́дств|о, а *nt.* tea-growing.
чаево́д|ческий *adj. of* **~ство**
чаев|ы́е, ы́х *no sg.* tip, gratuity.
чаепи́ти|е, я *nt.* tea-drinking.
ча́инк|а, и *f.* tea-leaf.
ча|й, я (ю), *pl.* **~и́, ~ёв** *m.* **1.** tea. **2.** tea(-drinking); **за ∸ем, за ча́шкой ∸я** over (a cup of) tea. **3.: дать** (+*d.*) **на ч.** to tip.
ча́йк|а, и, *g. pl.* **ча́ек** *f.* (sea-)gull.
ча́йн|ая, ой *f.* tea-room, tea-shop.
ча́йник, а *m.* teapot; kettle.
ча́йниц|а, ы *f.* tea-caddy.
ча́йн|ый *adj.* tea; **ч. куст** tea-plant; **~ая ло́жка** teaspoon; **~ая ча́шка** teacup.
чайхан|а́, ы́ *f.* chaikhana (*tea-drinking establishment in Central Asia*).
ча́л|ить, ю, ишь *impf.* (*naut.*) to tie up, moor.
ча́лк|а, и *f.* (*naut.*) tie-rope, mooring rope.
чалм|а́, ы́ *f.* turban.
ча́лый *adj.* roan.

чан, а, в ∼е *or* **в ∼у́,** *pl.* **∼ы́** *m.* vat, tub, tank.
ча́р|а, ы *f.* (*folk poet.*) cup, goblet.
ча́р|ка, ки *f.* = **∼а**
чар|ова́ть, у́ю *impf.* to charm, captivate, enchant.
чаро́де́|й, я *m.* sorcerer, magician (*also fig.*).
чаро́де́йств|о, а *nt.* sorcery.
ча́ртерный *adj.*: **ч. рейс** (*aeron.*) charter flight.
ча́р|ы, ∼ *no sg.* magic, charms (*also fig.*)
час, а, о ∼е, в ∼у́ *and* **в ∼е,** *pl.***∼ы́** *m.* **1.** hour (*also fig.*); **че́тверть ∼а́** a quarter of an hour; **ч. о́т ∼у** with every passing hour; **с ∼у на ч.** (*i*) hourly, with every passing hour, (*ii*) any moment; **че́рез ч.** (*i*) in an hour, (*ii*) at hourly intervals; **в до́брый ч.!** good luck! **2.** (*in time measurement*: *g. sg.* **∼а́** *after numerals 2, 3, 4*) o'clock; **час** one o'clock; **два ∼а́** two o'clock; **во второ́м ∼у́** between one and two (o'clock); **кото́рый ч.?** what is the time? **3.** (*usu. pl.*) hours, time, period; **ч. пик, ∼ы́ пик** rush hour; **∼ы́ заня́тий** working hours; **«золоты́е ∼ы́»** prime (*television viewing*) time. **4. ∼ы́** (*mil.*) guard-duty; **стоя́ть на ∼а́х** to stand guard.
часа́ми *adv.* for hours.
часо́в|ня, ни, *g. pl.* **∼ен** *f.* chapel.
часов|о́й[1]**, о́го** *m.* sentry, sentinel, guard.
часов|о́й[2] *adj.* (*of* **час**) **1.** of one hour's duration; **ч. переры́в** one hour's interval. **2.** (measured) by the hour; **∼а́я опла́та** payment by the hour; **ч. по́яс** time zone. **3.** one o'clock; **ч. по́езд** one o'clock train.
часов|о́й[3] *adj. of* **часы́; ч. магази́н** watchmaker's; **∼ы́х дел ма́стер** watchmaker; **ч. механи́зм** clockwork; **∼а́я стре́лка** clock hand, hour hand; **по ∼о́й стре́лке** clockwise.
часовщи́к, а́ *m.* watchmaker.
часте́нько *adv.* (*coll.*) quite often, fairly often.
ча|сти́ть, щу́, сти́шь *impf.* (*coll.*) **1.** to do sth. *or* speak rapidly, hurriedly. **2. (к)** to visit frequently, see much (of).
части́ц|а, ы *f.* **1.** small part. **2.** (*phys.*) particle. **3.** (*gram.*) particle.
части́чно *adv.* partly, partially.
части́ч|ный (∼ен, ∼на) *adj.* partial.
ча́стник, а *m.* (*coll.*) private trader.
ча́стн|ое, ого *nt.* (*math.*) quotient.
ча́стност|ь, и *f.* detail; **в ∼и** in particular.
ча́стн|ый *adj.* **1.** private, personal; **∼ым о́бразом** privately. **2.** (*econ.*) private; **∼ая со́бственность** private property. **3.** particular, individual; *as n.* **∼ое, ∼ого** *nt.* the particular.
ча́сто *adv.* often, frequently.
частоко́л, а *m.* fence, paling; palisade.
частот|а́, ы́, *pl.* **∼ы** *f.* frequency.
часто́т|ный *adj.* (*tech.*) *of* **∼а́**
часту́шк|а, и *f.* chastushka (*two-line or four-line rhymed poem or ditty*).
ча́ст|ый (∼, ∼а́, ∼о) *adj.* **1.** frequent. **2.** close (together); dense, thick; **ч. гре́бень** fine-tooth comb; **∼ые дере́вни** villages close together; **ч. дождь** steady rain; **∼ое си́то** fine sieve. **3.** quick, rapid; **ч. ого́нь** (*mil.*) rapid fire.
част|ь, и, *pl.* **∼и, ∼е́й** *f.* **1.** part; portion; **∼и ре́чи** (*gram.*) parts of speech; **разобра́ть на ∼и** to take to pieces, dismantle; **бо́льшей ∼ью, по бо́льшей ∼и** for the most part, mostly; **рвать кого́-н. на ∼и** to give s.o. no peace. **2.** section, department. **3.** sphere, field; **э́то не по мое́й ∼и** this is not my province; **по ∼и** (+*g.*) in connection (with). **4.** (*mil.*) unit.
ча́стью *adv.* partly, in part.
час|ы́[1]**, о́в** *no sg.* clock, watch.
часы́[2] *see* **час 4.**
ча́хл|ый (∼, ∼а) *adj.* **1.** (*of vegetation*) stunted; poor. **2.** sickly.
ча́х|нуть, ну, нешь, *past* **∼, ∼ла** *impf.* (*of* **за∼**) **1.** (*of vegetation*) to wither away. **2.** to become weak, (go into a) decline; (*fig.*) to tire o.s. out.
чахо́тк|а, и *f.* (*coll.*) consumption.
чахо́точный *adj.* (*coll.*) consumptive.
ча-ча-ча́ *nt. indecl.* the cha-cha (*dance*).
ча́ш|а, и *f.* cup, bowl (*also fig.*); (*eccl.*) chalice; **ч. весо́в** scale, pan; **ч. на́шего терпе́ния перепо́лнилась** our patience was exhausted.
чашели́стик, а *m.* (*bot.*) sepal.
ча́шечк|а, и *f.* **1.** *dim. of* **ча́шка. 2.** (*bot.*) calyx.
ча́шк|а, и *f.* **1.** cup; bowl, pan. **2.: ч. весо́в** pan (*of scales*). **3. (коле́нная)** knee-cap.
ча́щ|а, и *f.* thicket.
ча́ще *comp. of* **ча́стый** *and* **ча́сто** more often, more frequently; **ч. всего́** most often, mostly.
ча́яни|е, я *nt.* expectation; aspiration; **па́че ∼я, сверх ∼я** unexpectedly, contrary to expectation.
ча́|ять, ю, ешь *impf.* (*coll.*) (+*g. or inf.*) to hope (for), expect; **души́ не ч. в**+*p.* to dote upon.
чва́н|иться, юсь, ишься *impf.* to boast.
чванли́в|ый (∼, ∼а) *adj.* arrogant, conceited.
чва́нный *adj.* conceited, arrogant.
чва́нств|о, а *nt.* conceit, arrogance.
чебуре́к, а *m.* cheburek (*kind of meat pasty*).
чего́[1] *interrog. adv.* (*coll.*) why? what for?
чего́[2] *g. of* **что**
чей, чья, чьё *interrog. and rel. pron.* whose.
че́й-либо *pron.* anyone's.
че́й-нибудь *pron.* anyone's.
че́й-то *pron.* someone's.
чек, а *m.* **1.** cheque; **вы́писать ч.** to draw a cheque. **2.** (*in shops, etc.*) bill, chit (*indicating amount to be paid*); receipt (*for payment, to be presented at counter when claiming purchase*).
чек|а́[1]**, и́** *f.* pin, linchpin, cotter-pin.
Чек|а́[2] *f. indecl. or* (*coll.*) *g.* **∼и́** *f.* (*coll.*) (*hist.*) Cheka (*abbr. of* **Чрезвыча́йная коми́ссия по борьбе́ с контрреволю́цией и сабота́жем** *the Soviet state security organ, 1918–1922*).
чека́н, а *m.* stamp, die.
чека́н|ить, ю, ишь *impf.* **1.** (*pf.* **вы́∼, от∼**) to mint, coin; to engrave, emboss. **2.** (*pf.* **от∼**) to do, make with precision; **ч. слова́** to enunciate one's words clearly.
чека́нк|а, и *f.* **1.** coining, minting; engraving, embossing. **2.** stamp, engraving, relief work.
чека́нн|ый *adj.* **1.** engraving, embossing; **∼ая рабо́та = чека́нка 2.. 2.** engraved, embossed. **3.** (*fig.*) precise, expressive, sharp.
чеки́ст, а *m.* (state) security officer; (*hist.*) Chekist, Cheka agent (*see also* **Чека́**[2]).
че́к|овый *adj. of* **∼; ∼овая кни́жка** cheque book.
челе́ст|а, ы *f.* (*mus.*) glockenspiel.
чёлк|а, и *f.* fringe; forelock.
чёлн, а́, *pl.* **∼ы́,** *or* **∼ы** *m.* dug-out (canoe).
челно́к, а́ *m.* **1.** = **чёлн. 2.** shuttle.
челно́|чный *adj. of* **∼к 2.; ч. полёт** (*aeron.*) shuttle flight; **∼чная диплома́тия** shuttle diplomacy.
чел|о́, а́ *nt.* forehead, brow; **бить ∼о́м кому́-н.** (*hist. or iron.*) (*i*) to bow to s.o. (*in greeting*), (*ii*) to petition s.o., (*iii*) to offer s.o. humble thanks.
челове́к, а, *pl.* **лю́ди** (*g. pl., etc.,* **челове́к, ∼ам, ∼ами, о ∼ах** *only in comb. with nums.*) *m.* man, person, human being.
челове́ко-де́нь, ч.-дня́ *m.* (*econ.*) man-day.
человеконенави́стник, а *m.* misanthrope.
человеконенави́стнический *adj.* misanthropic.
человеконенави́стничеств|о, а *nt.* misanthropy
человекообра́з|ный (∼ен, ∼на) *adj.* anthropomorphous; (*zool.*) anthropoid.
человекоподо́б|ный (∼ен, ∼на) *adj.* humanoid.
челове́ко-час, а *m.* (*econ.*) man-hour.
челове́ч|ек, ка *m.* little man.

человéческий *adj.* **1.** human. **2.** humane.
человéчеств|о, а *nt.* humanity, mankind.
человéчност|ь, и *f.* humaneness, humanity.
человéч|ный (~ен, ~на) *adj.* humane.
челюстнóй *adj.* jaw; (*anat.*) maxillary
чéлюст|ь, и *f.* **1.** jaw, jaw-bone; (*anat.*) maxilla. **2.** dental plate, set of false teeth.
чéляд|ь, и *f.* (*collect.*; *hist.*) servants, retainers.
чем *conj.* **1.** than. **2.** (*+comp.*) **ч...., тем...** the more ..., the more ...; **ч. скорéе, тем лýчше** the sooner, the better. **3.** (*+inf.*) rather than, instead of; **чем писáть, ты бы лýчше позвонúл** you'd do better to ring up rather than write.
чемодáн, а *m.* suitcase.
чемпиóн, а *m.* champion.
чемпионáт, а *m.* championship.
чемпиóн|ка, ки *f. of* ~
чемпиóнств|о, а *nt.* champion's title.
чепé *nt. indecl.* (*abbr. of* ***чрезвычáйное происшéствие***) incident, emergency.
чеп|éц, цá *m.* (*woman's*) cap.
чепух|á, ú *f.* (*coll.*) **1.** nonsense, rubbish. **2.** a trifle, trifling matter; trivialities.
чéпчик, а *m.* **1.** = **чепéц. 2.** (*child's*) bonnet.
червеобрáзный *adj.* vermiform, vermicular.
чéрв|и[1], **éй** *and* **~ы, ~** *pl.* (*sg.*~**а, ~ы** *f.*) hearts (*card suit*); **корóль ~éй** king of hearts.
чéрв|и[2] *pl. of* **~ь**
червúве|ть, ет *impf.* (*of* **о~**) to become worm-eaten.
червúв|ый (~, ~а) *adj.* worm-eaten.
червóн|ец, ца *m.* (*hist.*) chervonets (*gold coin of 3, 5, or 10 roubles' denomination*; *or 10 rouble banknote in circulation 1922–47*).
черв|óнный *adj. of* **∸и**[1]; **ч. туз** ace of hearts.
червотóчин|а, ы *f.* **1.** worm-hole. **2.** (*fig.*) rottenness.
черв|ь, я́, *pl.* **∸и, ~éй** *m.* **1.** worm; maggot. **2.** (*fig.*): **егó тóчит ч. сомнéния** he is nagged by doubts.
червя́к, á *m.* **1.** = **червь. 2.** (*tech.*) worm.
червя́чн|ый *adj. of* **червя́к 2.**; **~ое колесó, ~ая шестерня́** worm wheel.
червяч|óк, кá *m. dim. of* **червя́к 1.**; **заморúть ~кá** (*coll.*) to have a bite to eat.
чердáк, á *m.* attic, loft.
чердá|чный *adj. of* **~к**
черёд, á, о ~é, в ~ý *m.* turn; **идтú своúм ~óм** to take its course.
черед|á, ы́ *f.* **1.** (*obs.*) = **черёд 1.**. **2.** sequence. **3.** file (*of people*).
чередовáни|е, я *nt.* alternation, interchange, rotation; **ч. глáсных** (*ling.*) vowel interchange.
черед|овáть, ýю *impf.* (**с**+*i.*) to alternate (with).
черед|овáться, ýюсь *impf.* to alternate; to take turns.
чéрез *prep.+a.* **1.** (*of place*) across; over; through. **2.** via. **3.** through; **ч. перевóдчика** through an interpreter. **4.** (*of time*) in; **ч. полчасá** in half an hour's time; **я вернýсь ч. год** I shall be back in a year's time. **5.** (*of space*) after; (further) on **ч. три киломéтра** three kilometres (further) on. **6.** (*i*) *indicates repetition at stated unit of time or space*: **принимáть ч. час по столóвой лóжке** to take one tablespoonful every hour; **ч. кáждые три странúцы** every three pages, (*ii*) *indicates repetition alternating at stated unit of time or space*: **дежýрить ч. день** to be on duty every other day, on alternate days; **печáтать ч. строкý** to double-space.
черёмух|а, и *f.* bird cherry (*Padus*).
черен|óк, кá *m.* **1.** handle, haft. **2.** (*hort.*) graft, cutting.
чéреп, а, *pl.* **~á** *m.* skull, cranium.
черепáх|а, и *f.* **1.** tortoise; turtle. **2.** tortoise-shell.
черепáховый *adj.* tortoise, turtle; tortoise-shell.
черепá|ший *adj.* **1.** *adj. of* **~ха 1.**. **2.** (*fig.*) snail-like.
черепúц|а, ы *f.* tile.
черепúчный *adj.* tile; tiled.
черепн|óй *adj. of* **чéреп**; **~áя корóбка** cranium.
череп|óк, кá *m.* fragment of pottery.
чересседéльник, а *m.* back-band.
чересчýр *adv.* too; too much.
черéшн|евый *adj. of* **~я**
черéшн|я, и *f.* cherry(-tree).
черкá|ть, ю (*and* **чёрка|ть, ю)** *impf.* (*coll.*) to cross out, cross through.
черкéс, а *m.* Circassian.
черкéсский *adj.* Circassian.
черкéшенк|а, и *f. of* **черкéс**
черкн|ýть, ý, ёшь *pf.* (*coll.*) **1.** to make, leave a line on. **2.** to dash off, scribble.
чернé|ть, ю *impf.* **1.** (*pf.* **по~**) to turn black. **2.** to show up black.
черúк|а, и *f.* bilberry (bush).
чернúл|а, ~ *no sg.* ink.
чернúльниц|а, ы *f.* ink-pot, ink-well.
чернúл|ьный *adj. of* **~а**; **ч. карандáш** indelible pencil.
черн|úть, ю́, úшь *impf.* **1.** (*pf.* **за~** *and* **на~**) to blacken, paint black. **2.** (*pf.* **о~**) (*fig.*) to blacken, slander.
чернú|чный *adj. of* **~ка**
чёрно-бéлый *adj.* black-and-white.
чернобýрк|а, и *f.* (*coll.*) silver fox (fur).
черновúк, á *m.* rough copy, draft.
чернов|óй *adj.* **1.** rough, draft; preparatory. **2.**: **~áя рабóта** (*coll.*) rough work.
чернозём, а *m.* (*agric.*, *geol.*) chernozem, black earth.
чернокóж|ий (~, ~а) *adj.* black; *as n.* **ч., ~его** *m.* negro, black (man).
черномáз|ый (~, ~а) *adj.* (*coll.*) swarthy.
чернорабóч|ий, его *m.* unskilled labourer.
черносли́в, а (у) *m.* (*collect.*) prunes.
чернот|á, ы́ *f.* blackness (*also fig.*); darkness.
чёр|ный (~ен, ~нá, ~нó) *adj.* **1.** black; **ч. ры́нок** black market; **(отложúть на) ч. день** (to put by for) a rainy day; **~ное дéрево** ebony; **~ное зóлото** 'black gold' (= *oil*); **~ным по бéлому** in black and white; *as n.* **ч., ~ного** *m.* negro, black (man). **2.** back; **ч. ход** back entrance, back door. **3.** (*of work*) heavy; unskilled. **4.** (*tech.*) ferrous. **6.** (*fig.*) gloomy, sombre.
черн|ь, и *f.* mob, common people.
черпáк, á *m.* scoop; bucket; grab.
черпáлк|а, и *f.* scoop; ladle.
чéрп|ать, аю *impf.* (*of* **~нýть) 1.** to draw (up); to scoop; to ladle. **2.** (*fig.*) to extract, derive, draw.
черп|нýть, нý, нёшь *pf. of* **∸ать**
черствé|ть, ю *impf.* **1.** (*pf.* **за~**) to become stale. **2.** (*pf.* **о~**) to grow hardened, become hard (*fig.*).
чёрств|ый (~, ~á, ~о) *adj.* **1.** stale. **2.** (*fig.*) hard, callous.
чёрт, а, *pl.* **чéрти, ~éй** *m.* devil; **ч. (егó) возьмú!** damn it!; **ч. егó знáет!** God knows!; **до ~а** hellishly; **на кой ч.?** why the hell?; **~а с два** like hell!; **у ~а на рогáх, на кулúчках** at the back of beyond.
черт|á, ы́ *f.* **1.** line; **провестú ~ý** to draw a line. **2.** boundary. **3.** trait, characteristic; **~ы́ лицá** features; **в óбщих ~áх** in general outline.
чертёж, á *m.* draught, drawing, sketch.
чертёжник, а *m.* draughtsman.
чертёжн|ый *adj.* drawing; **~ая доскá** drawing board.
чертён|ок, ка, *pl.* **~я́та, ~я́т** *m.* (*coll.*) imp.
чер|тúть, чý, ∸тишь *impf.* (*of* **на~**) to draw; to draw up.
чёртов *adj.* **1.** devil's; **~а дю́жина** baker's dozen. **2.** (*coll.*) devilish, hellish.
чертóвский *adj.* (*coll.*) devilish, damnable.

чертовщи́н|а, ы *f.* **1.** (*collect.*) devils, demons. **2.** (*fig.*, *coll.*) devilry; idiocy.
черто́г, а *m.* (*obs.*) hall, mansion.
чертополо́х, а *m.* thistle.
чёрточк|а, и *f.* **1.** *dim. of* **черта́ 1. 2.** hyphen.
чертых|а́ться, а́юсь *impf.* (*of* **~ну́ться**) (*coll.*) to swear.
чертых|ну́ться, ну́сь, нёшься *pf. of* **~а́ться**
черче́ни|е, я *nt.* drawing; sketching.
чеса́лк|а, и *f.* (*text.*) comb, combing machine.
чеса́льный *adj.* (*text.*) combing, carding.
че|са́ть, шу́, ~́шешь *impf.* (*of* **по~**) **1.** to scratch; **ч. заты́лок, в заты́лке** to scratch one's head (*also fig.*); **ч. язы́к** to wag one's tongue. **2.** (*coll.*) to comb (*hair*). **3.** (*text.*) to comb, card.
че|са́ться, шу́сь, ~́шешься *impf.* (*of* **по~**) **1.** to scratch o.s. **2.** (*impf. only*) to itch; **ру́ки у него́** *etc.* **~́шутся** (*+inf.*) he is, *etc.*, itching to .... **3.** (*coll.*) to comb one's hair.
чесно́к, а́ (у́) *m.* garlic.
чесно́|чный *adj. of* **~к**
чесо́тк|а, и *f.* **1.** (*med.*) scabies; rash; mange. **2.** itch.
че́ствовани|е, я *nt.* **(кого́-н.)** celebration (in honour of s.o.).
че́ств|овать, ую *impf.* to celebrate (*an occasion*, *etc.*); to honour, pay tribute to (*s.o.*).
че|сти́ть, щу́, сти́шь *impf.* (*coll.*) to abuse.
че́стност|ь, и *f.* honesty.
че́ст|ный (~ен, ~на́, ~но) *adj.* honest; upright; **~ное сло́во!** upon my honour!
честолю́б|ец, ца *m.* ambitious person.
честолюби́в|ый (~, ~а) *adj.* ambitious.
честолю́би|е, я *nt.* ambition.
чест|ь, и *f.* honour; **в ч.** (*+g.*) in honour (of); **отда́ть ч.** (*+d.*) (*i*) to salute, (*ii*) (*joc.*) to do honour (to); **проси́ть ~́ью** to urge; **пора́ и ч. знать** (*coll.*) it is time we were going; **ч. ~́ью** (*coll.*) fittingly, properly.
чёт, а *m.* even number.
чет|а́, ы́ *f.* pair, couple; **счастли́вая ч.** (the) happy couple; **не ч. кому́-н.** no match for s.o.
четве́рг, а́ *m.* Thursday.
четвере́ньк|и (*coll.*): **на ч., на ~ах** on all fours, on one's hands and knees.
четвёрк|а, и *f.* (*coll.*) **1.** number '4'; No. 4 (*bus*, *tram*, *etc.*). **2.** 'four' (*as school mark — out of five*, *hence* = 'good'). **3.** four (*at cards*; *team of horses*; *rowing boat*, *etc.*).
четверно́й *adj.* fourfold, quadruple.
четверн|я́, и́ *f.* **1.** team of four horses. **2.** quadruplets.
че́твер|о, ы́х *num.* four; **нас бы́ло ч.** there were four of us.
четвероно́г|ий *adj.* four-legged; *as n.* **~ое, ~ого** *nt.* quadruped.
четверости́ши|е, я *nt.* (*liter.*) quatrain.
четвертно́й *adj.* quarter.
четверт|ова́ть, у́ю *impf. and pf.* to quarter (*as means of execution*; *hist.*)
четвёртый *adj.* fourth.
че́тверт|ь, и, *g. pl.* **~е́й** *f.* **1.** quarter (of an hour); **без ~и час** a quarter to one; **ч. деся́того** a quarter past nine. **2.** (*mus.*) fourth. **3.** term.
четвертьфина́л, а *m.* (*sport*) quarter-final.
чёт|ки, ок *no sg.* (*eccl.*) rosary.
чёт|кий (~ок, ~ка́, ~ко) *adj.* **1.** precise; clear-cut; **~кое движе́ние** precise movement. **2.** clear, well-defined; (*of handwriting*) legible; (*of sound*) plain, distinct; (*of speech*) articulate.
чёткост|ь, и *f.* **1.** precision. **2.** clarity, definition; legibility; distinctness.
чётный *adj.* even (*of numbers*).
четы́р|е, ёх, ём, ьмя́, о ~ёх *num.* four.
четы́режды *adv.* four times.
четы́р|еста, ёхсо́т, ёмста́м, ьмяста́ми, о ~ёхста́х *num.* four hundred.
четырёх... *comb. form* four-, quadri-, tetra-.
четырёхгоди́чный *adj.* four-year.
четырёхголо́сный *adj.* (*mus.*) four-part.
четырёхгра́нник, а *m.* (*math.*) tetrahedron.
четырёхгра́нный *adj.* (*math.*) tetrahedral.
четырёхкра́тный *adj.* fourfold.
четырёхле́ти|е, я *nt.* **1.** four-year period. **2.** fourth anniversary.
четырёхле́тний *adj.* **1.** four years', of four years' duration. **2.** four-year-old.
четырёхме́стный *adj.* four-seater.
четырёхме́сячный *adj.* **1.** four-month, four months', of four months' duration. **2.** four-month-old.
четырёхсотле́ти|е, я *nt.* **1.** four hundred years. **2.** quatercentenary
четырёхсотле́тний *adj.* **1.** four hundred years', of four hundred years' duration **2.** quatercentenary.
четырёхсо́тый *adj.* fourhundredth.
черырёхсто́пный *adj.* (*liter.*) tetrameter.
четырёхсторо́нний *adj.* **1.** quadrilateral. **2.** (*pol.*, *etc.*) quadripartite.
четырёхта́ктный *adj.* **1.** (*tech.*) four-stroke. **2.** (*mus.*) four-beat.
четырёхуго́льник, *adj.* quadrangle.
четырёхуго́льный *adj.* quadrangular.
четы́рнадцатый *adj.* fourteenth.
четы́рнадцат|ь, и *num.* fourteen.
чех, а *m.* Czech.
чехард|а́, ы́ *f.* leap-frog.
Че́хи|я, и *f.* Czech Republic.
чех|о́л, ла́ *m.* cover, case.
чечеви́ц|а, ы *f.* lentil.
чечеви́|чный *adj. of* **~ца; прода́ть за ~чную похлёбку** to sell for a mess of pottage.
чече́н|ец, ца *m.* Chechen.
чечётк|а, и *f.* chechotka (*kind of tap-dance*).
че́шк|а, и *f. of* **чех**
че́шский *adj.* Czech.
чешу́йчатый *adj.* scaly.
чешу|я́, и́ *no pl.*, *f.* (*zool.*) scales.
чи́бис, а *m.* (*zool.*) lapwing.
чиж, а́ *m.* (*zool.*) siskin.
чи́жик, а *m.* = **чиж**
Чи́ли *nt. indecl.* Chile.
чили́|ец, йца *m.* Chilean.
чили́|йка, йки *f. of* **~ец**
чили́йск|ий *adj.* Chilean.
чин, а, *pl.* **~ы́** *m.* **1.** rank; **быть в ~а́х** to hold, be of high rank. **2.** official. **3.** rite, ceremony; **ч. ~́ом** properly, fittingly; **без ~о́в** without ceremony.
чина́р, а *m.* plane (tree).
чина́р|а, ы *f.* = **~**
чин|и́ть¹, ю́, ~́ишь *impf.* (*of* **по~**) to repair, mend.
чин|и́ть², ю́, ~́ишь *impf.* (*of* **о~**) to sharpen.
чин|и́ть³, ю́, и́шь *impf.* to carry out, execute; to cause; **ч. препя́тствия** (*+d.*) to impede; **ч. распра́ву** to carry out reprisals.
чи́нност|ь, и *f.* decorum, propriety, orderliness.
чи́н|ный (~ен, ~на́, ~но) *adj.* decorous, proper, orderly; well-ordered.
чино́вник, а *m.* **1.** (*hist.*) official, functionary. **2.** (*pej.*) bureaucrat.
чино́вни|ческий *adj.* **1.** *adj. of* **~к. 2.** (*pej.*) bureaucratic.
чино́вничеств|о, а *nt.* **1.** (*collect.*) officials, officialdom. **2.** (*pej.*) red tape.
чино́вничий *adj.* = **~еский**
чину́ш|а, и *m.* (*pej.*) bureaucrat.
чи́пс|ы, ов *no sg.* (potato) crisps.
чи́р|ей, ья *m.* (*coll.*) boil.

чири́ка|ть, ю *impf.* to chirp, twitter.
чири́кн|уть, у, ешь *pf.* to give a chirp.
чи́рк|ать, аю *impf.* (*of* **~нуть**) (**о**+*a.* **по**+*d.*) to strike sharply (against, on); **ч. спи́чкой** to strike a match.
чи́рк|нуть, ну, нешь *pf. of* **~ать**
чир|о́к, ка́ *m.* (*zool.*) teal.
чи́сленност|ь, и *f.* numbers; (*mil.*) strength.
чи́сленный *adj.* numerical.
числи́тел|ь, я *m.* (*math.*) numerator.
числи́тельн|ое, ого *nt.* (*gram.*) numeral.
числи́тельн|ый *adj.*: **и́мя ~ое** (*gram.*) numeral.
чи́сл|ить, ю, ишь *impf.* to count, reckon.
чи́сл|иться, юсь, ишься *impf.* **1.** to be; **в на́шей дере́вне ~ится три́ста жи́телей** there are three hundred inhabitants in our village; **ч. в отпуску́** to be (recorded as being) on leave. **2.** (+*i.*) to be officially, be on paper; **он ещё ~ился заве́дующим отде́лом, а все обя́занности исполня́ли его́ замести́тели** he was still officially head of the department, but all the duties were being performed by his deputies. **3.** (**за**+*i.*) to be attributed (to), have; **за ним ~ится мно́го недоста́тков** he has many failings.
чис|ло́, ла́, *pl.* **~ла, ~ел** *nt.* **1.** number; **~ло́м** in number; **в ~ле́** (+*g.*) among; **в том ~ле́** including. **2.** date, day (*of month*); **како́е сего́дня ч.?** what is the date today?; **како́го ~ла́ вы уезжа́ете?** what is the date of your departure?; **без ~ла́** undated; **поме́тить (за́дним) ~ло́м** to date (antedate). **3.** (*gram.*) number; **еди́нственное, мно́жественное ч.** singular, plural.
числово́й *adj.* numerical.
чисти́лищ|е, а *nt.* (*relig.*) purgatory.
чи́стильщик, а *m.* cleaner; **ч. сапо́г** bootblack.
чи́|стить, щу, стишь *impf.* **1.** (*pf.* **по~, вы́~**) to clean; **(щёткой)** to brush; to scour; **ч. посу́ду** to wash dishes, wash up; **ч. трубу́** to sweep a chimney. **2.** (*pf.* **по~, вы́~**) to clear; to dredge. **3.** (*pf.* **о~**) to peel. **4.** (*pf.* **по~**) (*pol.*) to purge.
чи́|ститься, щусь, стишься *impf.* **1.** (*pf.* **по~, вы́~**) to clean o.s. (up). **2.** *pass. of* **~стить**
чи́стк|а, и *f.* **1.** cleaning; **отда́ть в ~у** to have cleaned. **2.** (*pol.*) purge; **этни́ческая ч.** ethnic cleansing.
чи́сто[1] *as pred.* it is clean.
чи́ст|о[2] *adv.* **1.** *adv. of* **~ый; ч.-на́чисто** spotlessly clean. **2.** purely, merely; completely. **3.** *as conj.* (*coll.*) just like, just as if.
чистови́к, а́ *m.* (*coll.*) fair copy.
чистово́й *adj.* fair, clean; **ч. экземпля́р** fair copy.
чистога́н, а *m.* (*coll.*) cash, ready money.
чистокро́вный *adj.* thoroughbred.
чистописа́ни|е, я *nt.* calligraphy.
чистопло́т|ный (~ен, ~на) *adj.* **1.** clean; neat, tidy. **2.** (*fig.*) clean, decent, upright.
чистопоро́д|ный (~ен, ~на) *adj.* thoroughbred.
чистопро́бный *adj.* pure (*of gold or silver*).
чистосерде́ч|ие, ия *nt.* = **~ность**
чистосерде́чност|ь, и *f.* frankness, sincerity.
чистосерде́ч|ный (~ен, ~на) *adj.* frank, sincere.
чистот|а́, ы́ *f.* **1.** cleanliness. **2.** purity.
чи́ст|ый (~, ~а́, ~о) *adj.* **1.** clean; (*of speech, voice, etc.*) pure; **экологи́чески ч.** eco-friendly. **2.** (*fig.*) pure, unsullied; **с ~ой со́вестью** with a clear conscience. **3.** pure; undiluted, neat; **~ое зо́лото, ~ая шерсть** pure gold, wool; **~ой воды́** (*min.*) of the first water; (*fig.*) pure, first-class; **вы́вести на ~ую во́ду** to expose, unmask. **4.** clear; open; **~ое не́бо** clear sky; **на ~ом во́здухе** in the open air; **ч. лист** blank sheet. **5.** (*fin., etc.*) net, clear; **~ая при́быль** clear profit. **6.** (*coll.*) pure, utter; sheer; **ч. вздор** utter nonsense; **~ая случа́йность** pure chance.
чита́льн|ый *adj.*: **ч. зал** = **~я**
чита́л|ьня, ьни, *g. pl.* **~ен** *f.* reading-room.
чита́тел|ь, я *m.* reader.
чита́тель|ский *adj. of* **~**
чита́|ть, ю *impf.* (*of* **про~, проче́сть**) **1.** to read; **ч. с губ** to lip-read. **2.: ч. ле́кцию** to give a lecture; **ч. стихи́** to recite poetry; **ч. кому́-н. наставле́ния, нравоуче́ния** to lecture s.o.
чита́|ться, ется *impf.* **1.** *pass. of* **~ть. 2.** to be legible. **3.** (*fig.*) to be visible. **4.** (*impers.*): **мне,** *etc.*, **не ~ется** I, *etc.*, don't feel like reading.
чи́тк|а, и *f.* reading; read through.
чих, а *m.* (*coll.*) sneeze.
чиха́нь|е, я *nt.* sneezing.
чих|а́ть, а́ю *impf.* (*of* **~ну́ть**) to sneeze.
чих|ну́ть, ну́, нёшь *pf. of* **~а́ть**
чи́ще *comp. of* **чи́стый, чи́сто**
член, а *m.* **1.** member; Fellow; **ч.-корреспонде́нт** corresponding member (*of an Academy*); Associate (*of learned body*); **ч. Короле́вского о́бщества** Fellow of the Royal Society; FRS. **2.** (*math.*) term; (*gram.*) part (*of sentence*). **3.** limb, member. **4.** (*gram.*) article.
член|и́ть, ю́, и́шь *impf.* (*of* **рас~**) to divide into parts, articulate.
членовреди́тельств|о, а *nt.* maiming, mutilation; self-mutilation.
членоразде́л|ьный (~ен, ~ьна) *adj.* articulate.
чле́н|ский *adj. of* **~; ~ские взно́сы** membership dues.
чле́нств|о, а *nt.* membership.
чмо́к|ать, аю *impf.* (*of* **~нуть**) **1.** to smack one's lips. **2.** (*coll.*) to give a smacking kiss. **3.** to squelch.
чмо́к|нуть, ну, нешь *pf. of* **~ать**
чо́кань|е, я *nt.* clinking of glasses.
чо́к|аться, аюсь *impf.* (*of* **~нуться**) to clink glasses (*when drinking toasts*).
чо́кнутый *adj.* odd, rum.
чо́к|нуться, нусь, нешься *pf. of* **~аться**
чо́порност|ь, и *f.* primness; standoffishness.
чо́пор|ный (~ен, ~на) *adj.* prim; standoffish.
чо́хом *adv.* (*coll.*) wholesale.
ЧП = **чепе́**
чрева́т|ый (~, ~а) *adj.* (+*i.*) fraught (with).
чре́в|о, а *nt.* (*rhet., fig.*) belly; womb.
чревовеща́ни|е, я *nt.* ventriloquy.
чревовеща́тел|ь, я *m.* ventriloquist.
чрезвыча́йно *adv.* extremely, extraordinarily.
чрезвыча́|йный (~ен, ~йна) *adj.* **1.** extraordinary. **2.** emergency; **~йные ме́ры** emergency measures; **~йное положе́ние** state of emergency; **ч. и полномо́чный посо́л** ambassador extraordinary and plenipotentiary.
чрезме́рно *adv.* excessively, to excess.
чрезме́р|ный (~ен, ~на) *adj.* excessive, inordinate.
чте́ни|е, я *nt.* **1.** reading; **ч. ле́кций** lecturing; **ч. с губ** lip-reading. **2.** reading-matter.
чтец, а́ *m.* reader; (*professional*) reciter.
чти́в|о, а *nt.* (*coll., pej.*) reading-matter.
чтить, чту, чтишь, чтят (*and* **чтут**) *impf.* to honour.
чти́ц|а, ы *f. of* **чтец**
что[1], **чего́, чему́, о чём** *interrog. pron.* **1.** what?; **что с тобо́й?** what's the matter (with you)?; **что де́лать, что поде́лаешь?** it can't be helped; **для чего́?** why?, what ... for?; **к чему́?** why?; **что ты (вы)!** (*expr. surprise, fear, etc.*) you don't mean to say so!; **что ему́** *etc.* **до...?** what does it matter to him, *etc.*? **2.** how?; **что сего́дня На́дя?** how is Nadya today? **3.** why?; **что вы не пьёте?** why aren't you drinking? **4.** (*coll.*) how much?; **что сто́ит?** how much does it cost?
что[2] (*sometimes printed* **что́**) *rel. pron.* which, that; (*coll.*) who; **я зна́ю, что вы име́ете в виду́** I know what you mean; **па́рень, что стоя́л ря́дом со мной** the fellow (who was) standing next to me; **он всё**

молча́л, что для него́ не характе́рно he said nothing the whole time, which is unlike him.
что[3] (*coll.*) = **что́-нибудь; е́сли что случи́тся** if anything happens.
что[4] as far as; **что есть мо́чи** with all one's might; **что до, что каса́ется** (+*g.*) as for, as far as ... is concerned.
что[5] *conj.* that; **то, что...** the fact that ....
чтоб = **что́бы**
что́бы *conj.* **1.** (*expr. purpose*) in order to, in order that; **ч.... не** lest. **2.** (*after neg.*) (that); **я никогда́ не вида́л, ч. он яви́лся пья́ным на рабо́ту** I have never seen him turn up drunk for work; **сомнева́юсь, ч. вам э́то понра́вилось** I doubt whether you will like it. **3.** (*as particle*) *expr. wish*: **ч. я тебя́ бо́льше не ви́дел!** may I never see your face again!
что ж (*coll.*) *expr. admission, acceptance of argument*: yes; all right; right you are.
что за (*coll.*) **1.** (*interrog.*) what?; what sort of ... ?; **что э́то за пти́ца?** what sort of bird is that? **2.** (*int.*): **что за день!** what a (marvellous) day!; **что за ерунда́!** what (utter) nonsense!
что ли (*coll.*) *expr. uncertainty or hesitation*: **пора́ нам идти́, что ли?** perhaps we should be going?; **позвони́ть тебе́, что ли?** do you want me to ring you, then?
что́-либо, чего́-либо *indef. pron.* anything.
что ни *indef. pron.*: **что ни день** every day, not a day passes but ... ; **что ни говори́** say what you like; **во что бы то ни ста́ло** at whatever cost.
что́-нибудь, чего́-нибудь *indef. pron.* anything
что́-то[1], **чего́-то** *indef. pron.* sth.
что́-то[2] *adv.* (*coll.*) **1.** somewhat, slightly; **на слу́шателей его́ выступле́ние произвело́ что́-то не о́чень прия́тное впечатле́ние** his speech made a somewhat disagreeable impression on the audience. **2.** somehow, for some reason; **что́-то мне не хо́чется идти́** I don't feel like going for some reason.
чуб, а, *pl.* **~ы́** *m.* forelock.
чуба́рый *adj.* (*of a horse's coat*) dappled.
чува́ш, а (*and* **а́**), *pl.* **~и, ~ей** (*and* **~и́, ~е́й**) *m.* Chuvash.
чува́ш|ка, ки *f. of* **~**
чува́шский *adj.* Chuvash.
чуви́х|а, и *f.* (*sl.*) bird (= *girl*).
чу́вственност|ь, и *f.* sensuality.
чу́вствен|ный *adj.* **1.** (**~, ~на**) sensual. **2.** (*phil.*) perceptible, sensible; **~ное восприя́тие** perception.
чувстви́тельност|ь, и *f.* **1.** sensitivity; (*of photog. film*) speed. **2.** perceptibility, sensibility. **3.** sentimentality. **4.** tenderness; (deep) feeling.
чувстви́тел|ьный (**~ен, ~ьна**) *adj.* **1.** sensitive. **2.** perceptible, sensible. **3.** sentimental. **4.** tender; (*of feelings*) deep.
чу́вств|о, а *nt.* **1.** (*physiol.*) sense **ч. вку́са** sense of taste; **обма́н ~** delusion. **2.** (*sg. or pl.*) senses (= *consciousness*); **без ~** unconscious; **лиши́ться ~, упа́сть без ~** to faint, lose consciousness; **привести́ в ч.** to bring round; **прийти́ в ч.** to come to, regain consciousness. **3.** feeling; sense; **ч. ло́ктя** feeling of comradeship; **ч. ю́мора** sense of humour.
чу́вств|овать, ую *impf.* (*of* **по~**) **1.** to feel, sense; **ч. себя́** to feel (*intrans.*); **ч. го́лод** to feel hungry; **дава́ть себя́ ч.** to make itself felt; **как вы себя́ ~уете?** how do you feel? **2.** to appreciate, have a feeling (for) (*music, etc.*).
чу́вств|оваться, уется *impf.* **1.** to be perceptible; to make itself felt. **2.** *pass. of* **~овать**
чугу́н, а́ *m.* **1.** cast iron. **2.** cast-iron pot, vessel.
чугу́нный *adj.* cast-iron (*also fig.*).
чугунолите́йный *adj.*: **ч. заво́д** iron foundry.
чуда́к, а́ *m.* eccentric, crank.
чуда́ческий *adj.* eccentric.
чуда́честв|о, а *nt.* eccentricity, crankiness.
чуда́чк|а, и *f. of* **чуда́к**
чуде́с|ный (**~ен, ~на**) *adj.* **1.** miraculous. **2.** marvellous, wonderful.
чуд|и́ть, *1st pers. not used*, **и́шь** *impf.* (*coll.*) to behave eccentrically, oddly.
чу́д|иться, ится *impf.* (*of* **по~** *and* **при~**) (*coll.*) to seem.
чуд|но́й (**~ён, ~на́, ~но́**) *adj.* strange, odd; **~но́** (*as pred.*) it is strange, it is odd.
чу́д|ный (**~ен, ~на**) *adj.* marvellous, wonderful, lovely; **~но** *as pred.* it is marvellous, wonderful, lovely.
чу́д|о, а, *pl.* **~еса́, ~е́с** *nt.* **1.** miracle. **2.** wonder, marvel; **~еса́ те́хники** wonders of technology; **ч. как** *as adv.* marvellously; **ч., что...** *as pred.* it is a marvel that ....
чудо́вищ|е, а *nt.* monster; **лохне́сское ч.** Loch Ness monster.
чудо́вищ|ный (**~ен, ~на**) *adj.* monstrous (*also fig., pej.*).
чудоде́йствен|ный (**~, ~на**) *adj.* miracle-working; miraculous; **~ное лека́рство** wonder drug.
чу́дом *adv.* miraculously; **ч. спасти́сь** to be saved by a miracle.
чудотво́р|ец, ца *m.* miracle-worker.
чудотво́рный *adj.* miracle-working; (*fig.*) marvellous.
чужа́к, а́ *m.* (*coll.*) stranger; (*pej.*) alien, interloper.
чужби́н|а, ы *f.* foreign land, country.
чужда́|ться, юсь *impf.* (+*g.*) to shun, avoid; to stand aloof (from).
чу́жд|ый (**~, ~а́, ~о**) *adj.* **1.** (+*d.*) alien (to); extraneous. **2.** (+*g.*) free (from), devoid (of); **он ~ зло́бы** he is devoid of malice.
чужезе́м|ец, ца *m.* (*obs.*) foreigner.
чужезе́мный *adj.* (*obs.*) foreign.
чужеро́д|ный (**~ен, ~на**) *adj.* alien, foreign.
чужестра́н|ец, ца *m.* (*obs.*) = **чужезе́мец**
чужестра́нный *adj.* (*obs.*) = **чужезе́мный**
чуж|о́й *adj.* **1.** s.o. else's, another's, others'; **на ч. счёт** at s.o. else's expense; **с ~и́х слов** at second-hand; *as n.* **~о́е, ~о́го** *nt.* s.o. else's belongings. **2.** strange, alien; foreign; **~и́е края́** = **~би́на**; *as n.* **ч., ~о́го** *m.* stranger.
чуко́тский *adj.* Chukchi.
чу́кч|а, и *m.* Chukchi (man).
чук|ча́нка, ча́нки *f. of* **~ча**
чула́н, а *m.* **1.** store-room, lumber-room. **2.** larder.
чул|о́к, ка́, *g. pl.* **ч.** *m.* stocking.
чуло́чно-носо́чн|ый *adj.* **~ые изде́лия** hosiery.
чуло́чный *adj. of* **чуло́к**
чум|а́, ы *f.* plague.
чума́з|ый (**~, ~а**) *adj.* (*coll.*) grubby, dirty.
чум|но́й *adj. of* **~а́**; plague-stricken.
чур *int.* (*coll.*) keep away!; mind out!; **ч. меня́** (*in children's games, etc.*) keep away from me!
чура́|ться, юсь *impf.* (+*g.*; *coll.*) to shun, avoid, steer clear (of).
чурба́н, а *m.* block, log.
чу́рк|а, и *f.* block, lump.
чу́т|кий (**~ок, ~ка́, ~ко**) *adj.* **1.** (*of senses of hearing and smell*) keen, sharp, quick; **ч. нюх** keen sense of smell; **~кая соба́ка** keen-nosed dog; **ч. сон** light sleep. **2.** (*fig.*) sensitive; sympathetic; tactful.
чу́ткост|ь, и *f.* **1.** keenness, sharpness, quickness. **2.** sensitivity; sympathetic attitude; tactfulness.
чу́точк|а, и *f.*: **ни ~и** (*coll.*) not in the least.
чу́точку *adv.* (*coll.*) a little, a wee bit.
чу́т|че *comp. of* **~кий**
чуть (*coll.*) **1.** *adv.* hardly, scarcely; just; **ч. (бы́ло) не, ч. ли не** almost, nearly. **2.** *adv.* (just) a little, very slightly. **3.** *conj.* as soon as; **ч. свет** at daybreak, at first light; **ч. что** at the slightest provocation.

чуть|ё, я́ *nt.* **1.** (*of animals*) scent. **2.** (*fig.*) flair, feeling (for).
чуть-чу́ть *adv.* (*coll.*) a tiny bit; **ч.-ч. не = чуть не.**
чу́чел|о, а *nt.* **1.** stuffed animal. **2.** scarecrow (*also fig.*).
чу́шк|а, и *f.* **1.** (*coll.*) piglet. **2.** (*tech.*) pig, ingot, bar.
чуш|ь, и *f.* (*coll.*) nonsense, rubbish.
чу́|ять, ю, ешь *impf.* to scent, smell; (*fig.*) to sense, feel.

ша́баш, а *m.* (*relig.*) sabbath; **ш. ведьм** witches' sabbath; (*fig.*) orgy.
шаба́ш *as pred.* that's enough!; that'll do!
шаба́ш|ить, у, ишь *impf.* (*coll.*) (*trans. and intrans.*) to stop (work); to knock off.
шаба́шник, а *m.* (*coll., pej.*) moonlighter.
шаба́шнича|ть, ю *impf.* (*coll., pej.*) to moonlight.
ша́бер, а *m.* (*tech.*) scraper.
шабло́н, а *m.* **1.** (*tech.*) template, pattern; mould, form; stencil. **2.** (*fig., pej.*) cliché; routine.
шабло́н|ный *adj.* **1.** *adj. of* **~. 2.** (**~ен, ~на**) trite, banal; stereotyped; routine.
ша́вк|а, и *f.* (*coll.*) (small) dog.
шаг, а (у) (*after numerals 2, 3, 4* **~а́**) **о ~е, в (на) ~у́,** *pl.* **~и́, ~о́в** *m.* step (*also fig.*); pace; stride; **ни ~у да́льше!** stay where you are!; **идти́ бы́стрыми ~а́ми** make rapid strides; **~у ступи́ть нельзя́ (не даю́т)** one can't do anything; **заме́длить ш.** to slow down; **приба́вить ~у** to quicken one's pace; **в двух ~а́х, в не́скольких ~а́х** a stone's throw away; **у́зки в ~у́** (*of cut of trousers*) tight in the seat; **на ка́ждом ~у́** everywhere, at every turn, continually.
шаг|а́ть, а́ю *impf.* (*of* **~ну́ть**) **1.** to step; to walk, stride. **2.** (*coll.*) to go, come.
шаги́стик|а, и *f.* (*pej.*) square-bashing (*as part of mil. training*).
шаг|ну́ть, ну́, нёшь *pf.* (*of* **~а́ть**) to take a step; (*fig.*) to make progress; **ш. нельзя́ (не даю́т)** one can't do anything.
ша́гом *adv.* at a walk, at a walking pace; slowly; **ш. марш!** (*mil.*) quick march!
шагоме́р, а *m.* pedometer.
шаж|о́к, ка́ *m., dim. of* **шаг**
ша́йб|а, ы *f.* **1.** (*tech.*) washer. **2.** (*sport*) puck; **хокке́й с ~ой** ice hockey.
ша́йк|а[1]**, и,** *g. pl.* **ша́ек** *f.* tub.
ша́йк|а[2]**, и,** *g. pl.* **ша́ек** *f.* gang, band.
шака́л, а *m.* jackal.
шала́нд|а, ы *f.* scow, lighter.
шала́ш, а́ *m.* hut, cabin (*made of branches and straw, etc.*).
шале́|ть, ю *impf.* (*of* **о~**) (*coll.*) to go crazy.
шал|и́ть, ю́, и́шь *impf.* to be naughty; to play up, play tricks.
шаловли́в|ый (~, ~а) *adj.* naughty; mischievous; flirtatious.
шалопа́|й, я *m.* (*coll.*) idler, skiver.
ша́лост|ь, и *f.* prank; (*pl.*) mischief.
шалу́н, а́ *m.* naughty child.
шалу́н|ья, ьи *f. of* **~**
шалфе́|й, я *m.* (*bot.*) sage.
ша́лый *adj.* (*coll.*) mad, crazy.
шал|ь, и *f.* shawl.
шальн|о́й *adj.* mad, crazy; **~ы́е де́ньги** easy money; **~а́я пу́ля** stray bullet.
шама́н, а *m.* (*relig.*) shaman.
шама́нств|о, а *nt.* (*relig.*) shamanism.
ша́мка|ть, ю *impf.* to mumble.
шампа́нск|ое, ого *nt.* champagne.
шампиньо́н, а *m.* (field) mushroom.
шампу́н|ь, я *m.* shampoo.
шанкр, а *m.* (*med.*) chancre.
шанс, а *m.* chance; **име́ть мно́го ~ов, бо́льшие ~ы (на**+*a.*) to have a good chance (of).
шансоне́тк|а, и *f.* **1.** (music-hall) song. **2.** singer (*in music-hall or café chantant*).
шансонье́ *m. indecl.* balladeer; singer-songwriter.
шанта́ж, а́ *m.* blackmail.
шантажи́р|овать, ую *impf.* to blackmail.
шантажи́ст, а *m.* blackmailer.
ша́пк|а, и *f.* **1.** cap; **дать по ~е** (+*d.*; *coll.*) (*i*) to hit, strike, (*ii*) to sack, fire (= *dismiss*); **получи́ть по ~е** (*coll.*) (*i*) to receive a blow, (*ii*) to be sacked, fired. **2.** banner headline(s).
ша́почк|а, и *f. dim. of* **ша́пка**
ша́почн|ый *adj. of* **ша́пка; ~ое знако́мство** nodding acquaintance; **прийти́ к ~ому разбо́ру** (*fig., coll.*) to miss the bus.
шар, а (*after numerals 2, 3, 4* **~а́**), *pl.* **~ы́** *m.* **1.** (*math.*) sphere; **земно́й ш.** the Earth, globe. **2.** spherical object, ball; **возду́шный ш.** balloon; **хоть ~о́м покати́** completely empty.
шара́х|ать, аю *impf.* (*of* **~нуть**) (*coll.*) to strike; to hit, shoot.
шара́х|аться, аюсь *impf.* (*of* **~нуться**) (*coll.*) **1.** to shy (*of a horse*); to start (up); to rush, dash. **2.** (**о**+*a.*) to hit, strike.
шара́х|нуть(ся), ну(сь), нешь(ся) *pf. of* **~ать(ся)**
шарж, а *m.* caricature, cartoon.
шаржи́р|овать, ую *impf.* to caricature.
ша́рик, а *m. dim. of* **шар; (кровяно́й) ш.** (blood) corpuscle.
ша́рик|овый *adj. of* **~; ~овая ру́чка** ball-point pen; **ш. подши́пник** (*tech.*) ball-bearing.
шарикоподши́пник, а *m.* (*tech.*) ball-bearing.
ша́р|ить, ю, ишь *impf.* (**в**+*p.* **по**+*d.*) to grope about, feel, fumble (in, through); to sweep (*in order to locate a target*).
ша́рканье, я *nt.* shuffling (*of the feet or footwear*).
ша́рк|ать, аю *impf.* (*of* **~нуть**) **1.** (+*i.*) to shuffle. **2.** (**ного́й**; *obs.*) to click one's heels.
ша́рк|нуть, ну, нешь *pf. of* **~ать**
шарлата́н, а *m.* charlatan; quack.
шарлата́н|ский *adj. of* **~**
шарлата́нств|о, а *nt.* charlatanism.
шарма́нк|а, и *f.* barrel-organ, street organ.
шарма́нщик, а *m.* organ-grinder.
шарни́р, а *m.* (*tech.*) hinge, joint; **на ~ах** hinged.
шарова́р|ы, ~ *no sg.* baggy trousers.
шарови́д|ный (~ен, ~на) *adj.* spherical; globose.
шар|ово́й *adj. of* **~**; globular; **ш. кла́пан** ball-cock; **ш. шарни́р** ball and socket joint.
шарообра́з|ный (~ен, ~на) *adj.* spherical.
шарф, а *m.* scarf.
шасси́ *nt. indecl.* **1.** chassis. **2.** (*aeron.*) undercarriage.
шата́ни|е, я *nt.* **1.** swaying, reeling. **2.** roaming, wandering. **3.** (*fig.*) vacillation; instability.
шата́|ть, ю *impf.* to rock, shake, cause to reel.
шата́|ться, юсь *impf.* **1.** (*intrans.*) to rock, sway, reel. **2.** to be, come loose; to be unsteady. **3.** (*coll.*) to roam; to loaf, lounge about.
шате́н, а *m.* person with auburn, brown hair.
шате́н|ка, ки *f. of* **~**
шат|ёр, ра́ *m.* tent, marquee.
ша́т|кий (~ок, ~ка) *adj.* **1.** unsteady; shaky; loose.

2. (*fig.*) unstable, insecure, shaky; unreliable; vacillating.

шату́н, а́ *m.* (*tech.*) connecting rod.

ша́фер, а, *pl.* **~а́** *m.* best man (*at wedding*).

шафра́н, а *m.* (*bot.*) saffron.

шафра́н|ный *adj. of* **~**

шах[1]**, а** *m.* Shah.

шах[2]**, а** *m.* (*chess*) check.

шахмати́ст, а *m.* chess-player.

ша́хматн|ый *adj.* **1.** chess; **~ая доска́** chess-board; **~ая па́ртия** game of chess. **2.** check(ed); chequered; **~ая ска́терть** check table-cloth; **ш. флажо́к** chequered flag.

ша́хмат|ы, ~ *no sg.* **1.** chess. **2.** chessmen.

ша́хт|а, ы *f.* **1.** mine, pit. **2.** (*tech.*) shaft.

шахтёр, а *m.* miner.

шахтёр|ский *adj. of* **~**

ша́хт|ный *adj. of* **~а; ш. ствол** pit-shaft.

ша́хт|овый *adj. of* **~а**

ша́шечниц|а, ы *f.* draught-board, chess-board.

ша́шк|а[1]**, и** *f.* **1.** draught, draughtsman (*piece in game of draughts*). **2.** (*pl.*) draughts (*game*).

ша́шк|а[2]**, и** *f.* sabre, cavalry sword.

шашлы́к, а́ *m.* (*cul.*) shashlik, kebab.

ша́шн|и, ей *no sg.* (*coll., pej.*) **1.** tricks. **2.** amorous intrigues; affair; **завести́ ш. с** (*+i.*) to take up with.

шва *g. sg. of* **шов**

шва́бр|а, ы *f.* mop, swab.

швал|ь, и *f.* (*coll.*) **1.** (*collect.*) rubbish, junk. **2.** good-for-nothing.

шварто́в, а *m.* (*naut.*) hawser, mooring line.

шварт|ова́ть, у́ю *impf.* (*of* **при~**) (*naut.*) to moor.

шварт|ова́ться, у́юсь *impf.* (*of* **при~**) (*naut.*) to moor, make fast.

швед, а *m.* Swede.

шве́д|ка, ки *f. of* **~**

шве́дский *adj.* Swedish.

шве́йник, а *m.* clothing industry worker.

шве́йн|ый *adj.* sewing; **~ая маши́на** sewing-machine; **~ая фа́брика** garment factory.

швейца́р, а *m.* porter, commissionaire.

швейца́р|ец, ца *m.* Swiss.

Швейца́ри|я, и *f.* Switzerland.

швейца́р|ка, ки *f. of* **~ец**

швейца́рский *adj.* Swiss.

швец, а́ *m.* (*obs.*) tailor; **и ш., и жнец, и в ду́ду игре́ц** (*fig.*) jack of all trades.

Шве́ци|я, и *f.* Sweden.

шве|я́, и́ *f.* seamstress.

шво́р|ень, ня *m.* = **шкво́рень**

швыр|ну́ть, ну́, нёшь *pf. of* **~я́ть**

швыр|о́к, ка́ *m.* **1.** throw. **2.** (*collect.*) logs, firewood. **3.** (*moving*) practice target.

швыр|я́ть, я́ю *impf.* (*of* **~ну́ть**) (*+a. or i.; coll.*) to throw, fling, chuck, hurl; **ш. де́ньги (деньга́ми)** to fling one's money about.

швыря́|ться, юсь *impf.* (*coll.*) (*+i.*) **1.** to throw, fling, hurl (at one another). **2.** to make light (of), trifle (with).

шевел|и́ть, ю́, и́шь *impf.* (*of* **~ьну́ть** *and* **по~**) **1.** to turn over. **2.** (*+i.*) to move, stir, budge; **ш. мозга́ми** (*coll., joc.*) to use one's loaf.

шевел|и́ться, ю́сь, и́шься *impf.* (*of* **~ьну́ться** *and* **по~**) **1.** to move, stir. **2.** (*fig.*) to stir (*of hopes, fears, etc.*). **3. ~и́сь; ~и́тесь!** (*coll.*) get a move on!; get cracking!

шевел|ьну́ть, ьну́, ьнёшь *pf.* (*of* **~и́ть**); **па́льцем не ш.** not to lift a finger.

шевел|ьну́ться, ьну́сь, ьнёшься *pf. of* **~и́ться**

шевелю́р|а, ы *f.* (head of) hair.

шевио́т, а *m.* (*text.*) cheviot (*cloth*).

шевио́т|овый *adj. of* **~**

шевро́ *nt. indecl.* kid (*leather*).

шевро́|вый *adj. of* **~**

шевро́н, а *m.* (*mil.*) long-service stripe.

шеде́вр, а *m.* masterpiece.

шезло́нг, а *m.* deck-chair; lounger.

ше́йк|а, и, *g. pl.* **ше́ек** *f.* **1.** *dim. of* **ше́я. 2.** neck; (*tech.*) pin, journal; **ш. ги́льзы** cartridge neck; **ш. ре́льса** web (*of rail*). **3.** (*anat.*) cervix.

ше́йный *adj. of* **ше́я**; (*anat.*) jugular, cervical.

шейх, а *m.* sheikh.

шёл *see* **идти́**

ше́лест, а *m.* rustle, rustling.

шелест|е́ть *1st pers. not used,* **и́шь** *impf.* to rustle.

шёлк, а (у), о ~е, на (в) ~у́, *pl.* **~а́** *m.* silk; **ш.-сыре́ц** raw silk; **в долгу́ как в ~у́** up to one's eyes in debt.

шелкови́нк|а, и *f.* silk thread.

шелкови́ст|ый (~, ~а) *adj.* silky.

шелкови́ц|а, ы *f.* mulberry (tree).

шелкови́|чный *adj. of* **~ца; ш. червь** silk-worm.

шелково́д, а *m.* silkworm breeder.

шелково́дств|о, а *nt.* sericulture.

шелково́д|ческий *adj. of* **~ство**

шёлковый *adj.* **1.** silk. **2.** (*fig., coll.*) meek, docile.

шелкопря́д, а *m.* silkworm.

шелохн|у́ть, у́, ёшь *pf.* to stir, agitate.

шелохн|у́ться, у́сь, ёшься *pf.* to stir, move.

шелуди́в|ый (~, ~а) *adj.* (*coll.*) mangy.

шелух|а́, и́ *f.* skin (*of vegetables or fruit*); peel; pod.

шелуш|и́ть, у́, и́шь *impf.* to peel; to shell.

шелуш|и́ться, и́тся *impf.* to peel (off).

ше́льм|а, ы *c.g.* (*coll.*) rascal, scoundrel.

шельм|ова́ть, у́ю *impf.* (*of* **о~**) (*coll.*) to blacken (*fig.*); to defame.

шельф, а *m.* (*geog.*) shelf.

шемя́кин *adj., only in phr.* **ш. суд** unfair trial.

шепеля́в|ить, лю, ишь *impf.* to lisp.

шепеля́в|ый (~, ~а) *adj.* lisping.

шеп|ну́ть, ну́, нёшь *pf. of* **~та́ть**

шёпот, а *m.* whisper (*also fig.*).

шёпотом *adv.* in a whisper.

шептал|а́, ы́ *f.* (*collect.*) dried apricots *or* peaches.

шеп|та́ть, чу́, ~́чешь *impf.* (*of* **~ну́ть**) to whisper.

шеп|та́ться, чу́сь, ~́чешься *impf.* to whisper, converse in whispers.

шепту́н, а́ *m.* (*coll.*) **1.** whisperer. **2.** (*fig.*) tell-tale, informer.

щербе́т, а *m.* sherbet.

шере́нг|а, и *f.* rank (= *row*); file, column.

шери́ф, а *m.* sheriff.

шероховá́тост|ь, и *f.* roughness; unevenness.

шерохова́т|ый (~, ~а) *adj.* rough; uneven; rugged.

шерсти́нк|а, и *f.* strand of wool.

шерсти́ст|ый (~, ~а) *adj.* woolly, fleecy.

шерст|и́ть, и́т *impf.* to irritate, tickle (*of garment*).

шерст|ь, и, *pl.* **~́и, ~е́й** *f.* **1.** hair (*of animals*); **гла́дить кого́-н. про́тив ~́и** (*fig.*) to rub s.o. up the wrong way. **2.** wool.

шерстян|о́й *adj.* wool, woollen.

шерша́ве|ть, ет *impf.* to become rough.

шерша́в|ый (~, ~а) *adj.* rough.

ше́рш|ень, ня *m.* hornet.

шест, а́ *m.* pole; staff.

ше́стви|е, я *nt.* procession.

ше́ств|овать, ую *impf.* to walk (*as in procession*).

шестерёнк|а, и *f. dim. of* **шестерня́**

шестёрк|а, и *f.* **1.** figure '6'; six, group of six. **2.** (*cards*) six. **3.** team of six horses. **4.** six-oar (boat).

шестер|ня́, ни́, *g. pl.* **~ён** *f.* (*tech.*) gear (wheel), cogwheel, pinion.

ше́стер|о, ы́х *collect. num.* six.

шести... *comb. form* six-.

шестидесятиле́ти|е, я *nt.* **1.** sixty years, sixty-year period. **2.** sixtieth anniversary.

шестидесятиле́тний *adj.* **1.** of sixty years, sixty-year. **2.** sixty-year-old.
шестидеся́тник, а *m.* (*hist.*) 'man of the sixties'.
шестидеся́тый *adj.* sixtieth.
шестисо́тый *adj.* six-hundredth.
шестиуго́льник, а *m.* (*math.*) hexagon.
шестиуго́льный *adj.* hexagonal.
шестна́дцатый *adj.* sixteenth.
шестна́дцат|ь, и *num.* sixteen.
шестови́к, а́ *m.* (*sport*) pole-vaulter.
шест|о́й *adj.* sixth; **одна́ ~а́я** one sixth.
шест|о́к, ка́ *m.* **1.** hearth (*in Russ. stove*). **2.** roost.
шест|ь, и́, ью́ *num.* six.
шестьдеся́т, шести́десяти, шестью́десятью, о шести́десяти *num.* sixty.
шест|ьсо́т, ~исо́т, ~иста́м, ~ьюста́ми, о ~иста́х *num.* six hundred.
ше́стью *adv.* six times.
шеф, а *m.* **1.** (*coll.*) boss, chief. **2.** patron, sponsor.
шеф-по́вар, а, *pl.* **~а́, ~о́в** *m.* chef.
ше́ф|ский *adj. of* **~ство**
ше́фств|о, а *nt.* patronage, sponsorship; **взять ш. (над)** to take under one's patronage.
ше́фств|овать, ую *impf.* **(над)** to act as patron, sponsor (to).
ше́|я, и *f.* neck; **броса́ться на ~ю кому́-н.** to throw one's arms around s.o.'s neck; **прогна́ть, вы́толкать кого́-н. в ~ю** (*coll.*) to throw s.o. out on his ear; **сиде́ть на ~е у кого́-н.** (*coll.*) to live off s.o.
ши́б|кий (~ок, ~ка́, ~ко) *adj.* (*coll.*) fast, quick.
ши́бк|о *adv.* (*coll.*) **1.** *adv. of* **~ий. 2.** hard; much, very; **ш. испуга́ться** to be scared stiff.
ши́б|че *comp. of* **~кий** *and* **~ко**
ши́ворот, а *m.* (*coll.*): **за ш.** by the scruff of the neck; **ш.-навы́ворот** (*adv.*) topsy-turvy, upside down.
шизофре́ник, а *m.* (*med.*) schizophrenic.
шизофрени́|я, и *f.* (*med.*) schizophrenia.
шии́т, а *m.* Shiite; **мусульма́нин-ш.** Shiite Muslim.
шии́тский *adj.* Shiite.
шик, а (у) *m.* stylishness; style.
шика́рно *as pred.* it is splendid, magnificent.
шика́р|ный (~ен, ~на) *adj.* **1.** chic, smart, stylish. **2.** (*coll.*) splendid, magnificent.
ши́к|ать, аю *impf.* (*of* **~нуть**) (*coll.*) **1.** **(на+*a.*)** to hush. **2.** (+*d.*) to hiss (at), boo, catcall.
ши́к|нуть, ну, нешь *pf. of* **~ать**
ши́л|о, а, *pl.* **~ья, ~ьев** *nt.* awl.
шилохво́ст|ь, и *f.* (*zool.*) pintail.
шимпанзе́ *m. indecl.* chimpanzee.
ши́н|а, ы *f.* **1.** tyre. **2.** (*med.*) splint.
шине́л|ь, и *f.* (*mil.*) greatcoat.
шинка́р|ь, я́ *m.* (*obs.*) tavern-keeper, publican.
шинк|ова́ть, у́ю *impf.* (*cul.*) to shred, chop.
ши́н|ный *adj. of* **~а; ш. заво́д** tyre factory.
шин|о́к, ка́ *m.* (*obs.*) tavern.
шинши́лл|а, ы *f.* chinchilla.
шип[1]**, а́** *m.* **1.** (*bot.*) thorn. **2.** spike; crampon. **3.** (*tech.*) tenon; **ш. и гнездо́** mortise and tenon.
шип[2]**, а** *m.* (*coll.*) hissing (sound).
шипе́ни|е, я *nt.* hissing; sizzling; sputtering.
шип|е́ть, лю́, и́шь *impf.* to hiss; to sizzle; to fizz; to sputter.
шипо́вник, а *m.* (*bot.*) dogrose.
шипу́чий *adj.* (*of drinks*) sparkling; fizzy.
шипу́чк|а, и *f.* (*coll.*) fizzy drink.
шип|я́щий *pres. part. act. of* **~е́ть** *and adj.* (*ling.*) sibilant.
ши́р|е *comp. of* **~о́кий** *and* **~о́ко́**
ширин|а́, ы́ *f.* width, breadth; gauge (*of rail. track*).
шири́нк|а, и *f.* (*coll.*) fly (*of trousers*).
ши́р|ить, ю, ишь *impf.* to extend, expand.
ши́р|иться, ится *impf.* to spread, expand (*intrans.*).
ши́рм|а, ы *f.* screen (*also fig.*).
широ́к|ий (~, ~а́, ~о́, *pl.* **~и́)** *adj.* **1.** wide, broad (*also fig.*). **2.** (*fig.*) big, extensive, general; **~ие пла́ны** big plans; **~ие ма́ссы** the general public; **ш. чита́тель** the average reader; **това́ры ~ого потребле́ния** (*econ.*) consumer goods; **жить на ~ую но́гу** to live in grand style.
широко́ *adv.* **1.** wide, widely, broadly (*also fig.*); **ш. толкова́ть** to interpret loosely. **2.** extensively, on a large scale.
широко... *comb. form* wide-, broad-.
широковеща́ни|е, я *nt.* (*radio*) broadcasting.
широковеща́тельный *adj.* **1.** broadcasting. **2.** (*pej.*) loud, loud-mouthed.
ширококоле́йный *adj.* (*rail.*) broad-gauge.
широкопле́ч|ий (~, ~а) *adj.* broad-shouldered.
широкопо́лый *adj.* wide-brimmed (*of hats*).
широт|а́, ы́, *pl.* **~ы, ~** *f.* **1.** width, breadth; **ш. взгля́дов** broad-mindedness. **2.** (*geog.*) latitude.
широ́тный *adj.* (*geog.*) latitudinal, of latitude.
ширпотре́б, а *m.* (*econ.*; *coll.*) consumption; (*collect.*) consumer goods.
шир|ь, и *f.* (*wide*) expanse; **во всю ш.** to full width; (*fig.*) to the full extent.
ши́т|ый *p.p.p. of* **~ь** *and adj.* embroidered.
шить, шью, шьёшь *impf.* (*of* **с~**) **1.** to sew. **2.** make (*by sewing*); **ш. себе́ что-н.** to have sth. made. **3.** (*impf. only*) to embroider.
шить|ё, я́ *nt.* **1.** sewing, needlework; **лоску́тное ш.** patchwork. **2.** embroidery.
ши́фер, а *m.* slate.
ши́фер|ный *adj. of* **~; ~ное ма́сло** shale oil.
шифо́н, а *m.* (*text.*) chiffon.
шифонье́рк|а, и *f.* chest of drawers.
шифр, а *m.* **1.** cipher; code. **2.** pressmark.
шифрова́льщик, а *m.* cypher clerk.
шифро́в|анный *p.p.p. of* **~а́ть** *and adj.* (in) cypher.
шифр|ова́ть, у́ю *impf.* (*of* **за~**) to encipher, encode.
шифро́вк|а, и *f.* **1.** enciphering. **2.** (*coll.*) coded message.
шиш, а́ *m.* (*coll.*) **1.** (*vulg.*) fig; **показа́ть ш.** to pull a long nose. **2.** nothing; **ни ~а́** damn all.
ши́шк|а, и *f.* **1.** (*bot.*) cone. **2.** bump; lump. **3.** (*coll., joc.*) big shot, big wheel.
шишкова́т|ый (~, ~а) *adj.* knobbly; bumpy.
шишкови́д|ный (~ен, ~на) *adj.* cone-shaped.
шишконо́сный *adj.* (*bot.*) coniferous.
шкал|а́, ы́, *pl.* **~ы** *f.* scale; dial.
шка́нц|ы, ев *no sg.* (*naut.*) quarterdeck.
шкату́лк|а, и *f.* box, casket, case.
шкаф, а, о ~е, в ~у́, *pl.* **~ы́** *m.* cupboard, wardrobe; dresser; **кни́жный ш.** bookcase (*with doors*); **несгора́емый ш.** safe.
шка́фчик, а *m.* closet, locker.
шквал, а *nt.* squall.
шква́листый *adj.* squally.
шква́р|ки, ок *pl.* (*sg.* **~ка, ~ки** *f.*) (*cul.*) crackling.
шкво́р|ень, ня *m.* (*tech.*) kingpin, kingbolt.
шкив, а, *pl.* **~ы́** *m.* (*tech.*) pulley.
шки́пер, а, *pl.* **~ы** *and* **~а́** *m.* (*naut.*) skipper, master.
шко́л|а, ы *f.* **1.** school; **ходи́ть в ~у** to go to school; **око́нчить ~у** to leave school; **ш.-интерна́т** boarding school; **вы́сшая ш.** university, college. **2.** schooling, training.
шко́л|ить, ю, ишь *impf.* (*of* **вы~**) (*coll.*) to train, discipline.
шко́льник, а *m.* schoolboy.
шко́льниц|а, ы *f.* schoolgirl.
шко́льнический *adj.* schoolboy(ish).
шко́льничеств|о, а *nt.* schoolboyish behaviour, schoolboy tricks.
шко́льн|ый *adj.* school; **ш. во́зраст** school age; **со ~ой скамьи́** since one's schooldays.

шку́р|а, ы *f.* skin (*also fig.*), hide, pelt; **быть в чьей-н. ~е** to be in s.o.'s shoes; **драть ~у (с кого́-н.)** to fleece s.o.; **дрожа́ть за свою́ ~у** to be concerned for one's own skin; **чу́вствовать что-н. на свое́й ~е** to know what sth. feels like.
шку́рк|а, и *f.* **1.** skin. **2.** emery paper, sandpaper.
шку́рник, а *m.* (*coll., pej.*) person concerned only with self-advantage.
шку́рный *adj.* (*pej.*) selfish, self-seeking.
шла *see* **идти́**
шлагба́ум, а *m.* barrier (*of swing-beam type, at road or rail crossing*).
шлак, а *m.* slag; clinker.
шланг, а *m.* hose.
шлейф, а *m.* train (*of dress*).
шлем[1], а *m.* helmet; **вя́заный ш.** balaclava; **защи́тный ш.** (*on building site, etc.*) hard hat.
шлем[2], а *m.* (*cards*) slam; **большо́й ш.** grand slam.
шлёпан|цы, цев *pl.* (*sg.* **~ец, ~ца** *m.*) bedroom slippers.
шлёп|ать, аю *impf.* (*of* **~нуть**) **1.** to smack, spank. **2.** (*coll.*) to shuffle; to tramp.
шлёп|аться, аюсь *impf.* (*of* **~нуться**) (*coll.*) to fall with a plop, thud.
шлёп|нуть(ся), ну(сь), нешь(ся) *pf. of* **~ать(ся)**
шлеп|о́к, ка́ *m.* smack, slap.
шли[1] *see* **идти́**
шли[2] *see* **слать**
шлифова́льный *adj.* (*tech.*) polishing, burnishing; grinding; **ш. материа́л** abrasive(s).
шлиф|ова́ть, у́ю *impf.* (*of* **от~**) **1.** (*tech.*) to polish, burnish; to grind. **2.** (*fig.*) to polish, perfect.
шлифо́вк|а, и *f.* (*tech.*) **1.** polishing, burnishing; grinding. **2.** polish (*result of action*).
шло *see* **идти́**
шлюз, а *m.* lock, sluice, floodgate.
шлю́пк|а, и *f.* launch; **спаса́тельная ш.** lifeboat.
шлю́х|а, и *f.* (*vulg.*) streetwalker, tart.
шля́гер, а *m.* (*coll.*) hit (song).
шля́п|а, ы *f. and c.g.* **1.** *f.* hat; **де́ло в ~е** (*coll.*) it's in the bag. **2.** *c.g.* (*coll., pej.*) duffer.
шля́пк|а, и *f.* **1.** (*woman's*) hat. **2.** head (*of nail, etc.*); cap (*of mushroom*).
шля́пник, а *m.* milliner, hatter.
шля́п|ный *adj. of* **~а**
шля́|ться, юсь *impf.* (*coll.*) to loaf about.
шмел|ь, я́ *m.* bumble-bee.
шмо́т|ки, ок *no sg.* (*coll.*) clothes.
шмыг|ать, аю *impf.* (*of* **~ну́ть**) (*coll.*) **1.** (*+i.*) to rub, brush; **ш. но́сом** to sniff. **2.** to rush up and down.
шмыг|ну́ть, ну́, нёшь *pf.* (*coll.*) **1.** *inst. pf. of* **~ать. 2.** to dart, nip, sneak.
шмя́к|ать, аю *impf.* (*of* **~нуть**) (*coll.*) to drop with a thud.
шмя́к|нуть, ну, нешь *pf. of* **~ать**
шнит(т)-лу́к, а *m.* chive.
шни́цел|ь, я *m.* (*cul.*) schnitzel.
шнур, а́ *m.* **1.** cord; lace. **2.** (*electr.*) flex, cable.
шнур|ова́ть, у́ю *impf.* (*pf.* **за~**) to lace up.
шнур|ова́ться, у́юсь *impf.* (*of* **за~**) **1.** to lace o.s. up. **2.** *pass. of* **~ова́ть**
шнуро́вк|а, и *f.* lacing, tying.
шнур|о́к, ка́ *m.* lace.
шныр|ну́ть, ну́, нёшь *pf. of* **~я́ть**
шныр|я́ть, я́ю *impf.* (*of* **~ну́ть**) (*coll.*) to dart about.
шов, шва *m.* **1.** seam; **без шва** seamless; **треща́ть по всем швам** (*fig.*) to burst at the seams, fall to pieces. **2.** stitch (*in embroidery*). **3.** (*med.*) stitch, suture; **наложи́ть швы** to put in stitches. **4.** (*tech.*) joint, junction.
шовини́зм, а *m.* chauvinism.
шовини́ст, а *m.* chauvinist.
шовинисти́ческий *adj.* chauvinistic.
шок, а *m.* (*med.*) shock.
шоки́р|овать, ую *impf.* to shock.
шо́ков|ый *adj.*: **~ая терапи́я** shock therapy.
шокола́д, а *m.* chocolate.
шокола́дк|а, и *f.* (*coll.*) bar of chocolate; a chocolate (sweet).
шокола́д|ный *adj. of* **~**
шо́мпол, а, *pl.* **~а́** *m.* (*mil.*) **1.** cleaning rod. **2.** (*obs.*) ramrod.
шо́рник, а *m.* saddler, harness-maker.
шо́рн|ый *adj.* harness; **~ая мастерска́я = ~я**
шо́рн|я, и *f.* saddler's shop, harness-maker's.
шо́рох, а *m.* rustle.
шо́рт|ы, ~ *no sg.* shorts.
шо́р|ы, ~ *no sg.* blinkers (*also fig.*).
шоссе́ *nt. indecl.* highway; surfaced road.
шоссе́|йный *adj. of* **~; ~йная доро́га = ~**
шосси́р|овать, ую *impf. and pf.* to surface (*a road*).
шотла́нд|ец, ца *m.* Scotsman, Scot.
Шотла́нди|я, и *f.* Scotland; **Но́вая Ш.** Nova Scotia.
шотла́нд|ка[1], ки *f. of* **~ец**
шотла́нд|ка[2], ки *f.* (*text.*) tartan, plaid.
шотла́ндский *adj.* Scottish, Scots.
шофёр, а *m.* driver (*of a motor vehicle*), chauffeur.
шофёр|ский *adj. of* **~**
шпа́г|а, и *f.* sword; (*sport*) épée; **обнажи́ть ~у** to draw one's sword; **скрести́ть ~и** to cross swords (*also fig.*).
шпага́т, а *m.* **1.** string, cord; (*agric.*) binder twine. **2.** (*gymnastics*) the splits.
шпакл|ева́ть, ю́ю, ю́ешь *impf.* (*of* **за~**) to fill, putty, stop (*holes*); (*naut.*) to caulk.
шпаклёвк|а, и *f.* **1.** filling, stoppng up. **2.** putty.
шпа́л|а, ы *f.* (*rail.*) sleeper.
шпале́р|а, ы *f.* **1.** trellis, lattice-work. **2.** hedge, line of trees (*lining road*). **3.** (*mil.*) line (*of soldiers along ceremonial route*); **стоя́ть ~ами** to line the route.
шпан|а́, ы́ *f.* (*coll.*) hooligan; (*also collect.*) rabble.
шпанго́ут, а *m.* (*tech.*) frame (*of aircraft*); ribs (*of ship*).
шпа́н|ка, ки *f.* **1.** black cherry. **2.** = **~ская му́шка**
шпа́нск|ий *adj.*: **~ая му́шка** (*zool., med.*) Spanish fly.
шпарга́лк|а, и *f.* (*coll.*) crib (*in school*).
шпа́р|ить, ю, ишь *impf.* (*of* **о~**) (*coll.*) to scald, pour boiling water on.
шпат, а *m.* (*min.*) spar; **полево́й ш.** feldspar.
шпа́тел|ь, я *m.* **1.** (*tech., art*) palette-knife. **2.** (*med.*) spatula.
шпа́ци|я, и *f.* (*typ.*) space.
шпен|ёк, ька́ *m.* pin, peg, prong.
шпиг|ова́ть, у́ю *impf.* (*of* **на~**) **1.** (*cul.*) to lard. **2.** (*coll.*): **ш. кого́-н.** to put it into s.o.'s head.
шпик, а́ *m.* (*coll.*) secret agent; detective.
шпил|ь, я *m.* **1.** spire, steeple. **2.** (*naut.*) capstan.
шпи́льк|а, и *f.* **1.** hairpin; hat-pin. **2.** (*tech.*) peg, dowel; tack, brad. **3.** (*fig.*) caustic remark; **подпусти́ть ~и (кому́-н.)** to get at, have a dig at (s.o.).
шпина́т, а *m.* spinach.
шпингале́т, а *m.* catch, latch (*of door or window*).
шпио́н, а *m.* spy.
шпиона́ж, а *m.* espionage.
шпио́н|ить, ю, ишь *impf.* (**за**+*i.*) to spy (on).
шпио́н|ский *adj. of* **~**
шпиц, а *m.* Pomeranian (*dog*).
шпон, а *m.* (*typ.*) lead.
шпо́нк|а, и *f.* (*tech.*) bushing key, dowel.
шпо́р|а, ы *f.* spur; **дать ~ы** (*+d.*) to spur on.
шприц, а *m.* (*med.*) syringe.
шпро́т|ы, ~ *pl.* (*sg.* **~а, ~ы** *f. and* **~, ~а** *m.*) sprats.
шпу́льк|а, и *f.* spool, bobbin.
шпыня́|ть, ю *impf.* (*coll.*) to needle, nag.
шрам, а *m.* scar.

шрапне́л|ь, и *f.* shrapnel.
Шри-Ла́нк|а, и *f.* Sri Lanka.
шрифт, а, *pl.* **~ы́** *m.* **1.** type, type face. **2.** script.
штаб, а, *pl.* **~ы́** *m.* (*mil.*) staff; headquarters.
шта́бел|ь, я, *pl.* **~я́, ~е́й** *m.* stack, pile.
штаб-кварти́р|а, ы *f.* (*mil.*) headquarters.
штаб|но́й *adj. of* **~**
штаке́тник, а *m.* fence, fencing.
штамп, а *m.* **1.** (*tech.*) die, punch. **2.** stamp, impress; letter-head. **3.** (*fig., pej.*) cliché, stock phrase.
штампова́льный *adj.* (*tech.*) punching, stamping.
штампо́в|анный *p.p.p. of* **~а́ть** *and adj.* **1.** (*tech.*) punched, stamped, pressed. **2.** (*fig.*) trite; stock.
штамп|ова́ть, у́ю *impf.* **1.** (*tech.*) to punch, press. **2.** to stamp, die. **3.** (*fig.*) to carry out mechanically.
штампо́вк|а, и *f.* **1.** (*tech.*) punching, pressing. **2.** (die-)stamping.
штампо́вщик, а *m.* puncher; stamp operator.
шта́нг|а, и *f.* **1.** (*tech.*) bar, rod, beam. **2.** (*sport*) weight. **3.** (*sport*) post (*of goal*).
штанги́ст, а *m.* (*sport*) weight-lifter.
штанда́рт, а *m.* (*obs.*) standard.
штани́н|а, ы *f.* (*coll.*) trouser-leg.
штани́ш|ки, ек *no sg., dim. of* **штаны́**
штан|ы́, о́в *no sg.* trousers, breeches.
штат[1], а *m.* state (*administrative unit*); **Соединённые ~ы Аме́рики** United States of America.
штат[2], а *m.* (*sg. or pl.*) staff, establishment; **сокраще́ние ~ов** reduction of staff; **зачи́слить в ш.** to take on the staff, establish.
штати́в, а *m.* tripod, base, support, stand.
шта́т|ный *adj. of* **~**[2]; **~ная до́лжность** established post; **ш. рабо́тник** permanent member of staff.
шта́тск|ий *adj.* civilian; **~ое (пла́тье)** civilian clothes, civvies, mufti; *as n.* **ш., ~ого** *m.* civilian.
ште́в|ень, ня *m.* (*naut.*) stern-post.
штемпел|ева́ть, ю́ю, ю́ешь *impf.* (*of* **за~**) to stamp; to frank, postmark.
ште́мпел|ь, я, *pl.* **~я́** *m.* stamp; **почто́вый ш.** postmark.
ште́мпель|ный *adj. of* **~**
ште́псел|ь, я, *pl.* **~я́** *m.* (*electr.*) plug, socket.
ште́псель|ный *adj. of* **~**; **~ная ви́лка** plug; **~ная розе́тка** socket.
штибле́т|ы, ~ *pl.* (*sg.* **~а, ~ы** *f.*) (*lace-up*) boots, shoes.
штил|ево́й *adj. of* **~ь**
штил|ь, я *m.* (*naut.*) calm.
штифт, а́ *m.* (*tech.*) (joint-)pin, dowel, sprig.
шток, а *m.* (*tech.*) (coupling) rod; **ш. по́ршня** piston rod.
штокро́з|а, ы *f.* (*bot.*) hollyhock.
што́пальный *adj.* darning.
што́па|ть, ю *impf.* (*of* **за~**) to darn.
што́пк|а, и *f.* **1.** darning. **2.** darning thread, wool. **3.** (*coll.*) darn (*darned place*).
што́пор, а *m.* **1.** corkscrew. **2.** (*aeron.*) spin.
што́р|а, ы *f.* blind.
шторм, а *m.* (*naut.*) strong gale (*wind force 9*).
шторм|ова́ть, у́ет *impf.* (*naut.*) to ride out a storm.
шторм|ово́й *adj. of* **~**; **ве́тер ~ово́й си́лы** gale-force wind; **ш. костю́м** weatherproof clothing.
штоф[1], а *m.* shtof (*old Russ. unit of liquid measure, equivalent to 1.23 litres, or bottle of this measure*).
штоф[2], а *m.* (*text.*) damask, brocade.
што́ф|ный[1] *adj. of* **~**[1]; **~ная ла́вка** drinking-shop.
што́ф|ный[2] *adj. of* **~**[2]
штраф, а *m.* fine; **наложи́ть ш.** to impose a fine.
штраф|но́й *adj.* **1.** *adj. of* **~**. **2.** penal, penalty; **ш. батальо́н** (*mil.*) penal battalion; **~на́я площа́дка** (*sport*) penalty area; **ш. уда́р** (*sport*) penalty kick.
штраф|ова́ть, у́ю *impf.* (*of* **о~**) to fine.
штрейкбре́хер, а *m.* strike-breaker, blackleg.
штрих, а́ *m.* **1.** stroke (*in drawing*). **2.** (*fig.*) feature, trait.
штрих|ова́ть, у́ю *impf.* (*of* **за~**) to shade, hatch.
штрих|ово́й *adj. of* **~**; **ш. рису́нок** line drawing.
штуди́р|овать, ую *impf.* (*of* **про~**) to study.
шту́к|а, и *f.* **1.** item, one of a kind (*oft. not translated*); **по рублю́ ш.** one rouble each; **пять ~ яиц** five eggs; **я возьму́ шесть ~** I'll have six (*of item in question*). **2.** (*coll.*) thing; **вот так ш.!** well I'll be damned! **3.** (*coll.*) trick; **сыгра́ть ~у** to play a trick.
штука́р|ь, я́ *m.* (*coll.*) joker; rogue.
штукату́р, а *m.* plasterer.
штукату́р|ить, ю, ишь *impf.* (*of* **о~** *and* **от~**) to plaster.
штукату́рк|а, и *f.* **1.** plastering. **2.** plaster. **3.** stucco.
штукату́р|ный *adj. of* **~ка**
штурва́л, а *m.* steering-wheel; controls; **стоя́ть за ~ом** to be at the wheel, helm, controls.
штурва́л|ьный *adj. of* **~**; *as n.* **ш., ~ьного** *m.* helmsman, pilot.
штурм, а *m.* (*mil.*) storm, assault.
шту́рман, а, *pl.* **~ы** *and* **~а́** *m.* navigator.
штурм|ова́ть, у́ю *impf.* to storm, assault.
штурмови́к, а́ *m.* low-flying attack aircraft.
штурмо́вк|а, и *f.* low-flying air attack.
штурм|ово́й *adj. of* **~** *and* **~о́вка; ~ова́я авиа́ция** ground support aircraft; **~ова́я ло́дка** assault craft.
шту́чн|ый *adj.* (by the) piece; **ш. това́р** goods sold by the piece (*and not by weight*).
штык, а́ *m.* bayonet; **встре́тить, приня́ть в ~и́** (*fig.*) to give a hostile reception (to), oppose adamantly.
штык|ово́й *adj. of* **~**; **ш. уда́р** bayonet thrust.
штыр|ь, я́ *m.* (*tech.*) pin, dowel.
шу́б|а, ы *f.* fur coat.
шуг|а́, и́ *f.* sludge ice.
шу́лер, а, *pl.* **~а́** *m.* card-sharper, cheat.
шу́лер|ский *adj. of* **~**
шу́лерств|о, а *nt.* card-sharping, sharp practice.
шум, а (у) *m.* **1.** noise. **2.** din, racket; **подня́ть ш.** to kick up a racket. **3.** (*fig.*) sensation, stir. **4.** (*med.*) murmur; **ш. се́рдца** cardiac murmur.
шум|е́ть, лю́, и́шь *impf.* **1.** to make a noise. **2.** (*coll.*) to row, wrangle. **3.** (*coll.*) to make a stir, fuss.
шуми́х|а, и *f.* (*coll.*) sensation, stir.
шумли́в|ый (~, ~а) *adj.* noisy.
шу́м|ный (~ен, ~на́, ~но) *adj.* **1.** noisy; loud. **2.** sensational.
шумови́к, а́ *m.* (*theatr.*) sound effects man.
шумо́вк|а, и *f.* (*cul.*) perforated spoon, straining ladle.
шум|ово́й *adj. of* **~**; **~овы́е эффе́кты** sound effects.
шум|о́к, ка́ *m.* (*coll.*) noise; **под ш.** on the quiet.
шу́р|ин, ина, *pl.* **~ья́, ~ьёв** *m.* brother-in-law (*wife's brother*).
шуру́п, а *m.* (*tech.*) screw.
шурш|а́ть, у́, и́шь *impf.* to rustle (*also +i., trans.*).
шу́ст|рый (~ёр, ~ра́, ~ро) *adj.* (*coll.*) smart, bright.
шут, а́ *m.* **1.** (*hist.*) fool, jester. **2.** fool, buffoon, clown; **разыгра́ть ~а́** to play the fool.
шу|ти́ть, чу́, ~тишь *impf.* (*of* **по~**) **1.** to joke, jest; **я же не ~чу́** but I'm not joking. **2.** (**с**+*i.*) to play (with), trifle (with); **ш. с огнём** to play with fire. **3.** **(над)** to laugh (at), make fun (of).
шути́х|а, и *f.* **1.** *f. of* **шут. 2.** firecracker, rocket.
шу́тк|а, и *f.* **1.** joke, jest; **не ш.** it's no joke; **с ней ~и пло́хи** she is not to be trifled with; **~и в сто́рону, ~и прочь** let's get down to business; **без шу́ток** joking apart; **сказа́ть в ~у** to say as a joke; **не на ~у** in earnest. **2.** trick; **сыгра́ть ~у (с**+*i.*) to play a trick (on).
шутли́в|ый (~, ~а) *adj.* **1.** humorous. **2.** joking, light-hearted.
шутни́к, а́ *m.* joker, wag.

шут|овско́й *adj.* *of* **шут; ш. колпа́к** fool's cap; **~овски́е вы́ходки** clowning, buffoonery.
шутовств|о́, а́ *nt.* buffoonery.
шу́точ|ный (~ен, ~на) *adj.* comic; joking; **де́ло не ~ное** it's no joke, no laughing matter.
шут|я́ *pres. ger. of* **~и́ть** *and adv.* **1.** easily, lightly. **2.** for fun, in jest; **не ш.** in earnest.
шушу́ка|ться, юсь *impf.* (*coll.*) to whisper; (*fig.*) to gossip.
шхе́р|ы, ~ *no sg.* (*geog.*) skerries.
шху́н|а, ы *f.* schooner.
ш-ш *int.* ssh!; (s)hush!

щаве́л|евый *adj.* **1.** *adj. of* **~ь. 2.** (*chem.*) oxalic; **~евая кислота́** oxalic acid.
щаве́л|ь, я́ *m.* (*bot.*) sorrel.
щаве́льник, а *m.* (*coll.*) sorrel soup.
ща|ди́ть, жу́, ди́шь *impf.* (*of* **по~**) to spare; to have mercy (on); **щ. чьи-н. чу́вства** to spare s.o.'s feelings; **не щ. враго́в** to give one's enemies no quarter.
щебёнк|а, и *f.* = **ще́бень**
ще́б|ень, ня *m.* **1.** crushed stone, ballast. **2.** (*geol.*) detritus.
ще́бет, а *m.* twitter, chirp.
щебета́ни|е, я *nt.* twittering, chirping.
щебе|та́ть, чу́, ~́чешь *impf.* to twitter, chirp.
щег|о́л, ла́ *m.* goldfinch.
щеголева́т|ый (~, ~а) *adj.* foppish, dandified.
щёгол|ь, я *m.* fop, dandy.
щегол|ьну́ть, ьну́, ьнёшь *pf. of* **~я́ть 2.**
щегольско́й *adj.* foppish, dandified.
щегольств|о́, а́ *nt.* foppishness, dandyism.
щегол|я́ть, я́ю *impf.* **1.** to dress ultra-fashionably; to strut around. **2.** (*pf.* **~ьну́ть**) (*+i.*; *coll.*) to show off, parade, flaunt.
ще́дрост|ь, и *f.* generosity.
ще́др|ый (~, ~а́, ~о) *adj.* **1.** generous. **2.** lavish, liberal; **щ. на похвалы́** lavish in praises.
щек|а́, и́, *a.* **~́у,** *pl.* **~́и, ~, ~а́м** *f.* cheek; **уда́рить кого́-н. по ~е́** to slap s.o.'s face; **упи́сывать, уплета́ть за о́бе ~и́** (*coll.*) to eat ravenously, guzzle.
щеко́лд|а, ы *f.* latch; catch.
щеко|та́ть, чу́, ~́чешь *impf.* (*of* **по~**) **1.** to tickle (*also fig.*). **2.** (*impers.*): **у меня́ в го́рле,** *etc.*, **~́чет** I have a tickle in my throat, *etc.*
щеко́тк|а, и *f.* tickling; **боя́ться ~и** to be ticklish.
щекотли́в|ый (~, ~а) *adj.* ticklish, delicate; **~ая те́ма** delicate topic.
щеко́тно *as pred.* (*impers.*; *+i.*) it tickles.
щели́нный *adj.* (*ling.*) fricative.
щели́ст|ый (~, ~а) *adj.* (*coll.*) full of chinks.
щёлк|а, и *f.* chink.
щёлкань|е, я *nt.* **1.** flicking. **2.** clicking, snapping, cracking, popping. **3.** trilling (*of some birds*).
щёлк|ать, аю *impf.* (*of* **~нуть**) **1.** to flick. **2.** (*+i.*) to click, snap, crack, pop; **щ. затво́ром** to click the shutter (*of a camera*); **щ. па́льцами** to snap one's fingers; **щ. кнуто́м** to crack a whip. **3.** (*impf. only*) to crack (*nuts*). **4.** (*impf. only*) to trill (*of some birds*).
щёлк|нуть, ну, нешь *pf. of* **~ать**
щелкопёр, а *m.* (*obs.*, *pej.*) scribbler, hack.
щёлок, а *m.* alkaline solution, lye.
щелочно́й *adj.* (*chem.*) alkaline.
щёлочност|ь, и *f.* (*chem.*) alkalinity.
щёлоч|ь, и, *pl.* **~и, ~е́й** *f.* (*chem.*) alkali.
щелч|о́к, ка́ *m.* **1.** flick (of the fingers). **2.** (*fig.*, *coll.*) insult, slight.
щел|ь, и, *pl.* **~́и, ~е́й** *f.* **1.** crack; chink; slit; slot. **2.** (*mil.*) slit trench. **3.: голосова́я щ.** (*anat.*) glottis.
щем|и́ть, и́т *impf.* **1.** (*coll.*) to press, pinch. **2.** to oppress, grieve (*also impers*).
щем|я́щий *pres. part. act. of* **~и́ть** *and adj.* **1.** aching, nagging; **~я́щая боль** ache. **2.** (*fig.*) painful, oppressive.
щен|и́ться, и́тся *impf.* (*of* **о~**) to whelp, cub.
щен|о́к, ка́, *pl.* **~ки́, ~ко́в** *and* **~я́та, ~я́т** *m.* puppy, pup (*also fig.*); whelp, cub.
щеп|а́, ы́, *pl.* **~́ы, ~, ~а́м** *f.* (*wood*) splinter, chip; (*collect.*) kindling.
щеп|а́ть, лю́, ~́лешь *impf.* to chip, chop (*wood*).
щепети́л|ьный (~ен, ~ьна) *adj.* punctilious; finicky, (over-)scrupulous.
ще́пк|а, и *f.* = **щепа́; худо́й как щ.** thin as a rake.
щепо́т|ка, ки *f.* = **ще́по́ть**
ще́по́т|ь, и *f.* pinch (*of salt, snuff, etc.*).
щерба́т|ый (~, ~а) *adj.* **1.** dented; chipped. **2.** (*coll.*) pock-marked. **3.** (*coll.*) gap-toothed.
щерби́н|а, ы *f.* **1.** indentation; gap. **2.** pockmark.
щети́н|а, ы *f.* bristle; (*coll.*) stubble (*of beard*).
щети́нист|ый (~, ~а) *adj.* bristly.
щети́н|иться, ится *impf.* (*of* **о~**) to bristle (*also fig.*).
щётк|а, и *f.* **1.** brush; **зубна́я щ.** toothbrush; **щ. для воло́с** hairbrush. **2.** fetlock.
щёт|очный *adj. of* **~ка**
щёчный *adj. of* **щека́**
щи, щей, щам, ща́ми, о щах *no sg.* shchi (*cabbage soup*); **попа́сть как кур во́ щи** to get into hot water.
щи́колотк|а, и *f.* ankle.
щип|а́ть, лю́, ~́лешь *impf.* **1.** (*pf.* **~ну́ть**) to pinch, nip, tweak. **2.** (*impf. only*) to sting, bite (*of frost, etc.*); to burn (*of hot liquids, etc.*). **3.** (*impf. only*) to nibble, munch, browse (on). **4.** (*pf.* **об~** *and* **о~**) to pluck.
щип|а́ться, лю́сь, ~́лешься *impf.* (*coll.*) **1.** to pinch (each other). **2.** *pass. of* **~а́ть**
щипко́в|ый *adj.*: **~ые музыка́льные инструме́нты** (*mus.*) stringed instruments played by plucking.
щипко́м *adv.* (*mus.*) pizzicato.
щип|ну́ть, ну́, нёшь *pf. of* **~а́ть 1.**
щип|о́к, ка́ *m.* pinch, nip, tweak.
щипц|ы́, о́в *no sg.* tongs, pincers, pliers; forceps; **щ. для зави́вки воло́с** curling-irons; **щ. для са́хара** sugar-tongs.
щи́пчик|и, ов *no sg.* tweezers.
щит, а́ *m.* **1.** shield; **живо́й щ.** human shield; **подня́ть на щ.** to extol, eulogize; **верну́ться на ~е́** to suffer defeat; **верну́ться со ~о́м** to be triumphant, victorious. **2.** (*tech.*) shield, screen. **3.** sluice-gate. **4.** (*zool.*) (tortoise-)shell. **5.** (display) board. **6.** (*tech.*) panel; **распредели́тельный щ.** switchboard.
щитови́дный *adj.* (*anat.*) thyroid.
щит|о́к, ка́ *m.* **1.** *dim. of* **~ 2.–6.**; dashboard (*of motor vehicle*). **2.** (*zool.*) thorax. **3.** (*sport*) shin-pad.
щу́к|а, и *f.* pike (*fish*).
щуп, а *m.* (*tech.*) **1.** probe, sounding borer. **2.** (*mil.*) probing rod (*in mine detection*). **3.** (*coll.*) dipstick.
щу́пальц|е, а, *g. pl.* **щу́палец** *nt.* (*zool.*) tentacle; antenna.
щу́па|ть, ю *impf.* (*of* **по~**) to feel (for), touch; **щ. глаза́ми** to scan; **щ. пульс** (*med.*) to feel the pulse.
щу́пл|ый (~, ~а́, ~о) *adj.* weak, puny, frail.
щу́р|ить, ю, ишь *impf.* (*of* **со~**); **щ. глаза́ = ~иться**
щу́р|иться, юсь, ишься *impf.* (*of* **со~**) **1.** to screw

up one's eyes; to squint. **2.** (*of the eyes*) to narrow.
щу́рк|а, и *f.* (*zool.*) bee-eater.
щу́|чий *adj. of* **~ка; как по ~чьему веле́нью** as if of its own volition; as if by magic.

Э

эбе́новый *adj.* ebony.
эвакуацио́нный *adj. of* **эвакуа́ция; э. пункт** evacuation centre; **э. райо́н** evacuation area.
эвакуа́ци|я, и *f.* evacuation.
эвакуи́ров|анный *p.p.p. of* **~ать**; *as n.* **э., ~анного** *m.*, **~анная, ~анной** *f.* evacuee.
эвакуи́р|овать, ую *impf. and pf.* to evacuate (*trans.*).
эвакуи́р|оваться, уюсь *impf. and pf.* **1.** to evacuate (*intrans.*). **2.** *pass. of* **~овать**
эвкали́пт, а *m.* (*bot.*) eucalyptus.
эвкали́пт|овый *adj. of* **~; ~овое ма́сло** eucalyptus oil.
ЭВМ *f. indecl.* (*abbr. of* ***электро́нно-вычисли́тельная маши́на***) computer; **больша́я Э.** mainframe computer; **персона́льная Э.** personal computer.
эволюциони́р|овать, ую *impf. and pf.* to evolve.
эволюциони́ст, а *m.* evolutionist.
эволюцио́нн|ый *adj.* evolutionary; **~ое уче́ние** (*biol.*) doctrine of evolution.
эволю́ци|я, и *f.* evolution.
эвфеми́зм, а *m.* euphemism.
эвфемисти́ческий *adj.* euphemistic.
эвфони́ческий *adj.* euphonious.
эвфони́|я, и *f.* euphony.
эги́д|а, ы *f.* aegis; **под ~ой** (+*g.*) under the aegis (of).
эгои́зм, а *m.* egoism, selfishness.
эгои́ст, а *m.* egoist.
эгоисти́ческий *adj.* egoistic, selfish.
эгоисти́ч|ный (~ен, ~на) *adj.* = **~еский**
эготи́зм, а *m.* egotism.
эдельве́йс, а *m.* (*bot.*) edelweiss.
эди́пов *adj.*: **э. ко́мплекс** (*psych.*) Oedipus complex.
эй *int.* heigh!; hi!
эйтана́зи|я, и *f.* euthanasia.
эйфори́|я, и *f.* euphoria.
эк (*and* **э́ко, э́ка)** *particle* (*coll.*) *expr. surprise*, *indignation, etc.*, my goodness!
эква́тор, а *m.* equator.
экваториа́льный *adj.* equatorial.
эквивале́нт, а *m.* equivalent.
эквивале́нт|ный (~ен, ~на) *adj.* equivalent.
эквилибри́ст, а *m.* tightrope-walker.
эквилибри́стик|а, и *f.* tightrope-walking (*also fig.*).
экз. (*abbr. of* **экземпля́р**) copy.
экзальта́ци|я, и *f.* exaltation; excitement.
экзальтиро́ван|ный (~, ~на) *adj.* in a state of exaltation, excited.
экза́мен, а *m.* examination; **держа́ть, сдава́ть э.** to take, sit an examination; **вы́держать, сдать э.** to pass an examination; **провали́ться на ~е** to fail an examination; **э. на вожде́ние** driving test.
экзамена́тор, а *m.* examiner.
экзамен|ацио́нный *adj. of* **экза́мен; э. биле́т** examination question(-paper); **~ацио́нная се́ссия** examination period, exams.
экзамен|ова́ть, у́ю *impf.* (*of* **про~**) to examine.
экзамен|ова́ться, у́юсь *impf.* (*of* **про~**) **1.** to go in for an examination. **2.** *pass. of* **~ова́ть**
экзамен|у́ющийся *pres. part. of* **~ова́ться**; *as n.* **э., ~у́ющегося** *m.* examinee.
экзе́м|а, ы *f.* (*med.*) eczema.
экземпля́р, а *m.* **1.** copy; **в двух, трёх ~ах** in duplicate, in triplicate; **переписа́ть в двух ~ах** to make two copies; **резе́рвный э.** (*comput.*) backup (copy). **2.** specimen, example.
экзистенциали́зм, а *m.* existentialism.
экзистенциали́ст, а *m.* existentialist.
экзо́тик|а, и *f.* exotica, exotic objects.
экзоти́ческий *adj.* exotic.
экиво́к|и, ов *pl.* (*sg.* **~, ~а** *m.*) **1.** double entendre. **2.** quibbling, evasion, hedging; **говори́ть без ~ов** to call a spade a spade. **3.** subtleties, intricacies.
э́кий *pron.* (*coll.*) what (a).
экипа́ж[1], а *m.* carriage.
экипа́ж[2], а *m.* crew (*of ship*, *aircraft*, *tank*); ship's company.
экипир|ова́ть, у́ю *impf. and pf.* to equip.
экипиро́вк|а, и *f.* **1.** equipping. **2.** equipment.
эклекти́зм, а *m.* eclecticism.
экле́ктик, а *m.* eclectic.
эклекти́ч|ный (~ен, ~на) *adj.* eclectic.
экли́птик|а, и *f.* (*astron.*) ecliptic.
эко... *comb. form* eco-.
экологи́ческий *adj.* ecological.
эколо́ги|я, и *f.* ecology.
эконо́м, а *m.* (*obs.*) **1.** steward, housekeeper. **2.** economist.
экономáйзер, а *m.* (*tech.*) economiser, waste gas heater.
экономи́зм, а *m.* (*hist.*, *pol.*) economism.
эконо́мик|а, и *f.* **1.** economics. **2.** economy (*of a country*, *etc.*).
экономи́ст, а *m.* economist.
эконо́м|ить, лю, ишь *impf.* (*of* **с~**) **1.** to use sparingly, husband; to save. **2.** (**на**+*p.*) to economise (on), save (on).
экономи́ческ|ий *adj.* economic; **э. райо́н** economic region; **э. журна́л** economics journal; **~ая ско́рость** cruising speed.
экономи́ч|ный (~ен, ~на) *adj.* economical.
эконо́ми|я, и *f.* **1.** economy, saving; **режи́м ~и** economy effort; **соблюда́ть ~ю** to economize. **2.: полити́ческая э.** political economy.
эконо́мк|а, и *f.* housekeeper.
эконо́мнича|ть, ю *impf.* (*coll.*) to be (excessively) economical.
эконо́м|ный (~ен, ~на) *adj.* economical; careful, thrifty.
экосисте́м|а, ы *f.* ecosystem.
экра́н, а *m.* **1.** (*cinema*) screen. **2.** (*fig.*) screen (= *cinema industry*, *cinema art*). **3.** (*phys.*, *tech.*) screen, shield, shade.
экраниза́ци|я, и *f.* (*cinema.*) filming, screening; film version (*of novel*, *etc.*).
экранизи́р|овать, ую *impf. and pf.* (*cinema*) to film, screen.
экрани́р|овать, ую *impf. and pf.* (*tech.*) to screen, shield.
экра́нн|ый *adj.* (*comput.*) on-screen; **~ая гра́фика** on-screen graphics.
экс-... *pref.* ex-.
экскава́тор, а *m.* (*tech.*) excavator, earth-moving machine.
экскава́торщик, а *m.* excavator operator.
экскреме́нт|ы, ов *no sg.* excrement.
э́кскурс, а *m.* digression.
экскурса́нт, а *m.* tourist; participant in (conducted) tour *or* excursion.

экскурс|ио́нный *adj. of* ∼**ия**
экску́рси|я, и *f.* **1.** excursion, (conducted) tour, trip. **2.** tourist group, excursion party.
экскурсово́д, а *m.* guide.
экслі́брис, а *m.* book-plate.
экспанси́в|ный (∼ен, ∼на) *adj.* effusive.
экспансиони́зм, а *m.* (*pol.*) expansionism.
экспа́нси|я, и *f.* (*pol.*) expansion.
экспедицио́нный *adj.* **1.** dispatch, forwarding. **2.** expeditionary.
экспеди́ци|я, и *f.* **1.** dispatch, forwarding. **2.** dispatch office. **3.** expedition.
экспериме́нт, а *m.* experiment.
эксперимента́льный *adj.* experimental.
экспериментá́тор, а *m.* experimenter.
эксперименти́р|овать, ую *impf.* (**над, с**+*i.*) to experiment (on, with).
экспе́рт, а *m.* expert.
эксперти́з|а, ы *f.* (*leg., med.*) **1.** (*expert*) examination, expert opinion; **э. на СПИД** AIDS test; **произвести́ ∼у** to make an examination. **2.** commission of experts.
экспе́рт|ный *adj. of* ∼; **∼ная коми́ссия** commission of experts.
эксплуата́тор, а *m.* exploiter.
эксплуатац|ио́нный *adj. of* ∼**ия 2.**; **∼ио́нные ка́чества** operating characteristics; **∼ио́нные расхо́ды** running costs; **∼ио́нные усло́вия** working conditions.
эксплуата́ци|я, и *f.* **1.** (*pol.*; *pej.*) exploitation. **2.** exploitation (*econ.*); utilization; operation; **сдать в ∼ю** to commission, put into operation.
эксплуати́р|овать, ую *impf.* **1.** (*pol.*; *pej.*) to exploit. **2.** to exploit (*econ.*); to operate, run.
экспози́ци|я, и *f.* **1.** layout (*of an exhibition, etc.*). **2.** (*phot.*) exposure.
экспона́т, а *m.* exhibit.
экспоне́нт, а *m.* **1.** exhibitor. **2.** (*math.*) exponent.
экспони́р|овать, ую *impf. and pf.* **1.** to exhibit. **2.** (*phot.*) to expose.
экспоно́метр, а *m.* (*phot.*) exposure meter.
э́кспорт, а *m.* export.
экспортёр, а *m.* exporter.
экспорти́р|овать, ую *impf. and pf.* to export.
э́кспорт|ный *adj. of* ∼
экспре́сс, а *m.* express (*train, motor coach, etc.*).
экспресси́в|ный (∼ен, ∼на) *adj.* expressive.
экспрессиони́зм, а *m.* (*art*) expressionism.
экспре́сси|я, и *f.* expression.
экспре́сс|ный *adj. of* ∼
экспро́мт, а *m.* impromptu, improvisation, extemporisation.
экспро́мтом *adv.* **1.** impromptu; **петь, игра́ть,** *etc.*, **э.** to extemporize, improvise. **2.** without warning.
экспроприа́тор, а *m.* expropriator.
экспроприа́ци|я, и *f.* expropriation.
экспроприи́р|овать, ую *impf. and pf.* to expropriate, dispossess.
экста́з, а *m.* ecstasy.
экстенси́в|ный (∼ен, ∼на) *adj.* extensive.
экстéрн, а *m.* external student; **око́нчить университе́т ∼ом** to take an external degree.
экстерна́т, а *m.* external studies.
экстерриториа́л|ьный (∼ен, ∼ьна) *adj.* extraterritorial, exterritorial.
экстравага́нт|ный (∼ен, ∼на) *adj.* eccentric, bizarre, preposterous.
экстраги́р|овать, ую *impf. and pf.* (*chem., med.*) to extract.
экстради́ци|я, и *f.* (*leg.*) extradition.
экстра́кт, а *m.* **1.** (*cul.*) extract. **2.** résumé, précis.
экстра́кци|я, и *f.* (*chem., med.*) extraction.
экстраордина́р|ный (∼ен, ∼на) *adj.* extraordinary.
экстрасе́нс, а *m.* psychic.
э́кстрен|ный (∼, ∼на) *adj.* **1.** urgent; emergency; **э. вы́зов** urgent summons; **в ∼ном слу́чае** in case of emergency. **2.** extra, special; **∼ное заседа́ние** extraordinary session.
эксце́нтрик[1]**, а** *m.* **1.** clown. **2.** (*obs.*) eccentric (*pers.*).
эксце́нтрик[2] *m.* (*tech.*) cam.
эксцентри́ческий *adj.* (*tech.*) eccentric, off-centre.
эксцентри́чност|ь, и *f.* eccentricity.
эксцентри́ч|ный (∼ен, ∼на) *adj.* eccentric.
эксце́сс, а *m.* excess.
экумени́ческий *adj.* ecumenical.
экю́ *m. and nt. indecl.* écu.
эласти́ч|ный (∼ен, ∼на) *adj.* **1.** elastic (*also fig.*); **∼ные брю́ки** stretch pants. **2.** (*fig.*) springy, resilient.
элева́тор, а *m.* **1.** (*agric.*) elevator. **2.** (*tech.*) hoist.
элега́нтност|ь, и *f.* elegance.
элега́нт|ный (∼ен, ∼на) *adj.* elegant, smart.
элеги́ческий *adj.* (*liter., mus.*) elegiac.
элеги́ч|ный (∼ен, ∼на) *adj.* melancholy.
эле́ги|я, и *f.* (*liter., mus.*) elegy.
электриз|ова́ть, у́ю *impf.* **1.** (*phys., med.*) to electrify, subject to electric charge(s). **2.** (*fig.*) to electrify.
эле́ктрик, а *m.* electrician.
электри́к *adj. indecl.* electric blue.
электрифика́ци|я, и *f.* electrification.
электрифици́р|овать, ую *impf. and pf.* (*tech.*) to electrify.
электри́ческий *adj.* electric(al).
электри́честв|о, а *nt.* **1.** electricity. **2.** electric light; **заже́чь э.** to turn on the light.
электри́чк|а, и *f.* (*coll.*) (suburban) electric train.
электро... *comb. form* electro-, electric.
электробытов|о́й *adj.* electrical; **∼ы́е прибо́ры** (electrical) household appliances.
электрово́з, а *m.* electric locomotive.
электро́д, а *m.* (*phys.*) electrode.
электродви́гател|ь, я *m.* electric motor.
электродина́мик|а, и *f.* electrodynamics.
электроёмкост|ь, и *f.* (*phys.*) capacity.
электрока́р, а *m.* electric trolley, float.
электрокардиостимуля́тор, а *m.* (*med.*) pacemaker (*device*).
электрола́мп|а, ы *f.* electric light bulb.
электролече́ни|е, я *nt.* (*med.*) electrical treatment.
электро́лиз, а *m.* (*phys.*) electrolysis.
электромагни́т, а *m.* electromagnet.
электромагни́тный *adj.* electromagnetic.
электромеха́ник|а, и *f.* electromechanics.
электромонтёр, а *m.* electrician.
электро́н, а *m.* (*phys.*) electron.
электро́ник|а, и *f.* electronics.
электро́нно... *comb. form* electronic-.
электро́н|ный *adj.* **1.** *adj. of* ∼; **∼ная ла́мпа** electron tube; **э. микроско́п** electron microscope. **2.** electronic; **∼ная вычисли́тельная маши́на** electronic computer.
электропереда́ч|а, и *f.* electricity transmission.
электропли́тк|а, и *f.* (electric) hotplate.
электропо́езд, а *m.* electric train.
электрополоте́нц|е, а *nt.* hand-drier.
электроприбо́р, а *m.* electrical appliance.
электропро́вод, а *m.* electricity cable.
электропрово́дк|а, и *f.* electric wiring.
электросилово́й *adj.* electric power.
электроста́нци|я, и *f.* electric power station.
электроте́хник, а *m.* electrical engineer.
электроте́хник|а, и *f.* electrical engineering.
электротех|ни́ческий *adj. of* ∼**ника**
электроцентра́л|ь, и *f.* electric power plant.
электроча́йник, а *m.* electric kettle.

электроэне́рги|я, и *f.* electric power.
элеме́нт, а *m.* **1.** element; **э. изображе́ния** (*comput.*) pixel. **2.** (*coll.*) type, character; **подозри́тельный э.** suspicious type. **3.** (*electr.*) cell, battery; **сухо́й э.** dry cell; **рабо́тать от ~ов** to be battery-operated.
элемента́р|ный (~ен, ~на) *adj.* elementary.
элеро́н, а *m.* (*aeron.*) aileron.
эли́т|а, ы *f.* **1.** (*collect.*; *agric.*) best specimens. **2.** élite.
эли́т|ный *adj. of* **~а**
э́ллин, а *m.* ancient Greek, Hellene.
э́ллинг, а *m.* **1.** (*naut.*) slipway. **2.** (*aeron.*) shed, hangar (*for airships or balloons*).
э́ллин|ка, ки *f. of* **~**
э́ллинский *adj.* ancient Greek, Hellenic.
э́ллипс, а *m.* (*math.*, *liter.*) ellipse.
э́ллипс|ис, а *m.* = **~**
эллипти́ческий *adj.* elliptic(al).
эл|ь, я *m.* ale.
эльф, а *m.* elf.
эма́левый *adj.* enamel.
эмалиро́в|анный *p.p.p. of* **~а́ть** *and adj.* enamelled; **~анная посу́да** enamel ware.
эмалир|ова́ть, у́ю *impf.* to enamel.
эмалиро́вк|а, и *f.* **1.** enamelling. **2.** enamel.
эма́л|ь, и *f.* enamel.
эмана́ци|я, и *f.* emanation.
эмансипа́ци|я, и *f.* emancipation; **боре́ц за ~ю же́нщин** women's liberationist; women's libber.
эмансипи́р|овать, ую *impf. and pf.* to emancipate.
эмба́рго *nt. indecl.* (*econ.*) embargo; **наложи́ть э.** (**на**+*a.*) to embargo, place an embargo (on).
эмбле́м|а, ы *f.* **1.** emblem. **2.** (*mil.*) insignia.
эмболи́|я, и *f.* (*med.*) embolism.
эмбриоло́ги|я, и *f.* embryology.
эмбрио́н, а *m.* (*biol.*) embryo.
эмигра́нт, а *m.* emigré, emigrant.
эмигра́нт|ский *adj. of* **~**
эмигра|цио́нный *adj. of* **~́ция**
эмигра́ци|я, и *f.* **1.** emigration. **2.** (*collect.*) emigration, emigrés.
эмигри́р|овать, ую *impf. and pf.* to emigrate.
эмисса́р, а *m.* emissary.
эми́сси|я, и *f.* (*fin.*, *phys.*) emission.
эмоциона́л|ьный (~ен, ~ьна) *adj.* emotional.
эмо́ци|я, и *f.* emotion.
эмпири́зм, а *m.* empiricism.
эмпи́рик, а *m.* empiricist.
эмпири́ческий *adj.* empirical.
эмпири́ч|ный (~ен, ~на) *adj.* = **~еский**
э́му *m. indecl.* emu.
эму́льси|я, и *f.* emulsion.
эндокри́нн|ый *adj.* (*physiol.*) endocrine; **~ые же́лезы** endocrine glands, ductless glands.
эндокриноло́ги|я, и *f.* endocrinology.
э́ндшпил|ь, я *m.* (*chess*) end-game.
энерге́тик, а *m.* power engineering specialist.
энерге́тик|а, и *f.* power engineering.
энергет|и́ческий *adj. of* **~́ика**
энерги́ч|ный (~ен, ~на) *adj.* energetic, vigorous, forceful.
эне́рги|я, и *f.* **1.** (*phys.*) energy; power; **затра́та ~и** energy consumption; **растра́та ~и** energy loss; **э. ве́тра** wind power. **2.** (*fig.*) energy; vigour, effort.
энерго... *comb. form* power-.
энергоёмкий *adj.* power-consuming.
энергосберега́ющий *adj.* energy-saving.
энергосисте́м|а, ы *f.* power (supply) system.
э́нн|ый *adj.* (*expr. indefinite quantity, size, duration of time, etc.*): **в ~ой сте́пени** to the *n*th degree; **~ое коли́чество вре́мени** any number of hours.
э́нск|ий *adj.* (*used to designate sth. that cannot be identified for reasons of security*) ... 'X'; a certain ... (that shall remain nameless); **э. заво́д** factory 'X'.
энтомо́лог, а *m.* entomologist.
энтомологи́ческий *adj.* entomological.
энтомоло́ги|я, и *f.* entomology.
энтузиа́зм, а *m.* enthusiasm.
энтузиа́ст, а *m.* (+*g.*) enthusiast (about, for), devotee (of); **э. футбо́ла** football enthusiast.
энцефали́т, а *m.* (*med.*) encephalitis.
энцефалопати́|я, и *f.* (*med.*): **бы́чья губкови́дная э.** bovine spongiform encephalopathy (*abbr.* BSE).
энци́клик|а, и *f.* (*eccl.*) encyclical.
энциклопеди́ческий *adj.* encyclopaedic; **э. слова́рь** encyclopaedia; **э. ум** encyclopaedic brain.
энциклопе́ди|я, и *f.* encyclopaedia; **ходя́чая э.** (*joc.*) walking encyclopaedia.
эоли́т, а *m.* (*archaeol.*) eolithic period.
эпати́р|овать, ую *impf. and pf.* to shock.
эпиго́н, а *m.* (*pej.*) imitator, unoriginal follower.
эпигра́мм|а, ы *f.* epigram.
эпи́граф, а *m.* epigraph.
эпиде́ми|я, и *f.* epidemic.
эпиде́рмис, а *m.* (*biol.*) epidermis.
эпизо́д, а *m.* episode.
эпизоди́ческий *adj.* episodic; occasional, sporadic.
э́пик, а *m.* epic poet.
э́пик|а, и *f.* epic poetry.
эпикуре́|ец, йца *m.* epicurean.
эпикуре́йский *adj.* epicurean.
эпиле́пси|я, и *f.* (*med.*) epilepsy.
эпиле́птик, а *m.* epileptic (*pers.*).
эпилепти́ческий *adj.* epileptic.
эпило́г, а *m.* epilogue.
эпистоля́рный *adj.* epistolary.
эпита́фи|я, и *f.* epitaph.
эпи́тет, а *m.* epithet.
эпице́нтр, а *m.* (*geol.*) epicentre.
эпи́ческий *adj.* epic.
эполе́т|ы, ~ *pl.* (*sg.* **~а, ~ы** *f.*) epaulettes.
эпопе́|я, и *f.* (*liter. or fig.*) epic.
эпо́х|а, и *f.* epoch, age, era.
эпоха́льный *adj.* epoch-making.
э́р|а, ы *f.* era; **до на́шей ~ы** BC (*before Christ*); **на́шей ~ы** AD (*Anno Domini*).
эрг, а *m.* erg (*unit of work*).
эре́кци|я, и *f.* (*physiol.*) erection.
эрза́ц, а *m.* ersatz.
эроге́нн|ый *adj.* erogenous; **~ые зо́ны** erogenous zones.
эро́зи|я, и *f.* erosion.
эроти́зм, а *m.* eroticism.
эро́тик|а, и *f.* sensuality.
эроти́ческий *adj.* erotic, sensual.
эроти́ч|ный (~ен, ~на) *adj.* = **~еский**
эруди́рован|ный (~, ~на) *adj.* erudite.
эруди́т, а *m.* **1.** polymath. **2.** **«э.»** 'Polymath' (*Scrabble* (*propr.*)*-like board game*).
эруди́ци|я, и *f.* erudition.
эрцге́рцог, а *m.* archduke.
эрцгерцоги́н|я, и *f.* archduchess.
эрцге́рцогств|о, а *nt.* archduchy, archdukedom.
эсе́р, а *m.* (*hist.*) S.R. (*member of Socialist Revolutionary Party*).
эсе́ровский *adj.* (*hist.*) S.R. (*Socialist Revolutionary*).
эска́др|а, ы *f.* (*naut.*) squadron.
эска́др|енный *adj. of* **~а**; **э. бронено́сец** (*obs.*) battleship; **э. миноно́сец** destroyer.
эскадри́л|ьный *adj. of* **~ья**
эскадри́л|ья, ьи, *g. pl.* **~ий** *f.* (*aeron.*) squadron.
эскадро́н, а *m.* (*mil.*) (*cavalry*) squadron, troop.
эскадро́н|ный *adj. of* **~**
эскала́тор, а *m.* escalator.
эскала́ци|я, и *f.* (*mil.*) escalation.

эскало́п, а *m.* (*cul.*) escalope.
эска́рп, а *m.* (*mil.*) scarp, escarpment.
эски́з, а *m.* sketch, study; draft, outline.
эски́з|ный *adj. of* ~; **э. чертёж** draft, outline sketch.
эскимо́ *nt. indecl.* choc(olate) ice.
эскимо́с, а *m.* Eskimo, Inuit.
эскимо́с|ка, ки *f. of* ~
эскимо́сский *adj.* Eskimo, Inuit.
эско́рт, а *m.* (*mil.*) escort.
эскорти́р|овать, ую *impf. and pf.* (*mil.*) to escort.
эсми́н|ец, ца *m.* (*abbr. of* **эска́дренный миноно́сец**) (*naut.*) destroyer.
эссе́ *nt. indecl.* essay.
эссе́нци|я, и *f.* essence.
эстака́д|а, ы *f.* **1.** viaduct, platform (*carrying elevated rail.*); gantry. **2.** flyover. **3.** (*naut.*) pier. **4.** (*naut.*) boom (*of harbour*).
эстака́д|ный *adj. of* ~**а**; ~**ная желе́зная доро́га** elevated railway; **э. кран** gantry crane.
эста́мп, а *m.* (*art*) print, engraving, plate.
эстафе́т|а, ы *f.* **1.** (*sport*) relay race. **2.** baton (*in relay race*); **приня́ть у кого́-н.** ~**у** (*fig.*) to carry on s.o.'s work, maintain s.o.'s tradition.
эсте́т, а *m.* aesthete.
эстети́зм, а *m.* aestheticism.
эсте́тик|а, *f.* **1.** aesthetics. **2.** design; **промы́шленная э.** industrial design.
эстети́ческий *adj.* aesthetic.
эсте́т|ский *adj. of* ~
эсто́н|ец, ца *m.* Estonian.
Эсто́ни|я, и *f.* Estonia.
эсто́н|ка, ки *f. of* ~**ец**
эсто́нский *adj.* Estonian.
эстраго́н, а *m.* (*bot.*) tarragon.
эстра́д|а, ы *f.* **1.** stage, platform; **вы́йти на** ~**у** to come on stage. **2.** variety (*art*); **арти́ст** ~**ы** variety performer, artiste.
эстра́д|ный *adj. of* ~**а**; **э. конце́рт** variety show; ~**ная му́зыка** popular music.
эсэнго́вский *adj.* (*coll.*) CIS (*Commonwealth of Independent States*).
эсэ́сов|ец, ца *m.* (*hist.*) SS (*Schutz-Staffel*) man.
эсэ́совский *adj.* (*hist.*) SS (*Schutz-Staffel*).
эта́ж, а́ *m.* storey, floor; **пе́рвый, второ́й,** *etc.*, **э.** ground floor, first floor, *etc.*
этаже́рк|а, и *f.* bookcase, shelves.
э́так *adv.* (*coll.*) **1.** so, thus; **мо́жно э́то сде́лать и так и э.** you can do it like this or like that. **2.** about, approximately.
э́такий *pron.* (*coll.*) such (a), what (a).
этало́н, а *m.* standard (*of weights and measures*).
эта́н, а *m.* (*chem.*) ethane.
эта́п, а *m.* **1.** stage, phase. **2.** (*sport*) lap. **3.** halting-place, stage (*for troops*; *formerly*, *for groups of deported convicts in transit*); **отпра́вить по** ~**у,** ~**ом** to transport, deport (*under guard*).
эта́пник, а *m.* (*hist.*) convict in transit.
эта́п|ный *adj. of* ~; ~**ное собы́тие** (*fig.*) landmark, turning-point; **отпра́вить** ~**ным поря́дком** (*hist.*) to transport, deport (*under guard*).
э́тик|а, и *f.* ethics.
этике́т, а *m.* etiquette.
этике́тк|а, и *f.* label.
эти́л, а *m.* (*chem.*) ethyl.
этиле́н, а *m.* (*chem.*) ethylene.
эти́л|овый *adj. of* ~; **э. спирт** ethyl alcohol.
этимо́лог, а *m.* etymologist.
этимологи́ческий *adj.* etymological.
этимоло́ги|я, и *f.* etymology.
эти́ческий *adj. of* **э́тика**
эти́ч|ный (~**ен,** ~**на)** *adj.* ethical.
этни́ческий *adj.* ethnic.
этно́граф, а *m.* ethnographer, social anthropologist.
этнографи́ческий *adj.* ethnographic(al).
этногра́фи|я, и *f.* ethnography.
э́то[1] *see* **э́тот**
э́то[2] *emph. particle* (*coll.*); **куда́ э. он де́лся?** wherever has he got to?; **что э. ты не гото́в?** why on earth aren't you ready?; **э. вы спра́шивали?** was it *you* who was asking?
э́то[3] *pron.* (*as n.*) this (is), that (is); **э. наш дом** this is our house; **э. вам помо́жет** this will help you; **э. ве́рно** that is true; **не в э́том де́ло** that's not the point; **об э́том я вам пото́м расскажу́** I will tell you about it later; **э. я ви́жу** so I can see.
э́тот, э́та, э́то, *pl.* **э́ти** *pron.* this (these); *as n.* (*i*) this one, (*ii*) the latter.
этру́ск, а *m.* Etruscan.
этру́сский *adj.* Etruscan.
этю́д, а *m.* **1.** (*art, liter.*) study, sketch. **2.** (*mus.*) étude. **3.** (*mus.*) exercise; (*chess*) problem.
эфеме́р|ный (~**ен,** ~**на)** *adj.* ephemeral.
эфе́с, а *m.* hilt, handle (*of sword, sabre, etc.*).
эфио́п, а *m.* Ethiopian.
Эфио́пи|я, и *f.* Ethiopia.
эфио́п|ка, ки *f. of* ~
эфио́пский *adj.* Ethiopian.
эфи́р, а *m.* **1.** ether; (*fig.*) air; **вре́мя в** ~**е** air time; **передава́ть в э.** to put on the air, broadcast. **2.** (*chem.*) ether; **просто́й э.** ether; **сло́жный э.** ester.
эфи́р|ный (~**ен,** ~**на)** *adj.* **1.** ethereal. **2.** (*chem.*) ether, ester; ~**ное ма́сло** essential oil, volatile oil.
эффе́кт, а *m.* **1.** effect, impact; **произвести́ э.** (**на**+*a.*) to have an effect (on), make an impression (on); **парнико́вый** *or* **тепли́чный э.** greenhouse effect. **2.** (*econ.*) result, consequences. **3.** (*pl.*) (*theatr.*) effects; **шумовы́е** ~**ы** sound effects.
эффекти́в|ный (~**ен,** ~**на)** *adj.* effective, efficacious.
эффе́кт|ный (~**ен,** ~**на)** *adj.* **1.** effective (= *making an impact*), striking; eye-catching; snazzy. **2.** done for effect.
эх *int. expr. regret, reproval, amazement, etc.*; eh!; oh!
э́х|о, а *nt.* echo.
эхоло́т, а *m.* (*naut.*) sonic depth finder, echo sounder.
эшафо́т, а *m.* scaffold; **взойти́ на э.** to mount the scaffold.
эшело́н, а *m.* **1.** (*mil.*) échelon. **2.** special train.

Ю

Ю (*abbr. of* **юг**) S, South.
юа́н|ь, я *m.* yuan (*Chinese currency unit*).
ЮАР *f. indecl.* (*abbr. of* **Ю́жно-Африка́нская Респу́блика**) Republic of South Africa.
юа́ров|ец, ца *m.* South African.
юа́ровский *adj.* South African.
юбиле́|й, я *m.* **1.** anniversary; jubilee. **2.** anniversary celebrations.
юбиле́й|ный *adj. of* ~
юбиля́р, а *m.* person (*or* institution) whose anniversary is celebrated.
ю́бк|а, и *f.* skirt; **ю.-брю́ки** split skirt, culottes; **держа́ться за чью-н.** ~**у** to cling to s.o.'s apron-strings.
ю́бочк|а, и *f.* short skirt.
ю́бочник, а *m.* (*coll.*) womanizer.

юб|очный *adj. of* **~ка**
ювели́р, а *m.* jeweller.
ювели́р|ный *adj.* **1.** *adj. of* **~**; **~ные изде́лия** gold and silver ware, jewellery; **ю. магази́н** jeweller's. **2.** (*fig.*) fine, intricate.
юг, а *m.* south; the South (*of Russia, etc.*); **на ю́ге** in the south; **к ю́гу от** to the south of.
ю́го-восто́к, а *m.* south-east.
ю́го-восто́чный *adj.* south-east(ern).
ю́го-за́пад, а *m.* south-west.
ю́го-за́падный *adj.* south-west(ern).
югосла́в, а *m.* Yugoslav.
Югосла́ви|я, и *f.* Yugoslavia.
югосла́в|ка, ки *f. of* **~**
югосла́вский *adj.* Yugoslav.
юдофо́б, а *m.* anti-Semite.
юдофо́бств|о, а *nt.* anti-Semitism.
южа́н|ин, ина, *pl.* **~е, ~** *m.* southerner.
южн|ée, *comp. of* **~ый; ю. Ло́ндона** to the south of London.
Ю́жно-Африка́нск|ая Респу́блик|а, ~ой ~и *f.* Republic of South Africa.
ю́жный *adj.* south, southern; **Ю. по́люс** South Pole; **Ю. поля́рный круг** antarctic circle; **ю. темпера́мент** (*fig.*) southern temperament.
Ю́жн|ый океа́н, ~ого ~а *m.* the Antarctic Ocean.
ю́зом, *adv.* skidding, in a skid.
ю́кк|а, и *f.* (*bot.*) yucca.
юл|á, ы *f.* **1.** top (*child's toy*). **2.** (*coll.*) fidget. **3.** (*zool.*) woodlark.
юл|и́ть, ю́, и́шь *impf.* (*coll.*) **1.** to fuss, fidget. **2.** **(пе́ред)** to play up (to).
ю́мор, а *m.* humour; **чу́вство ~а** a sense of humour.
юморе́ск|а, и *f.* (*mus., liter.*) humoresque.
юмори́ст, а *m.* humorist.
юмористи́ческий *adj.* humorous, comic, funny.
ю́нг|а, и *m.* cabin boy; sea cadet.
юн|е́ц, ца́ *m.* (*coll.*) youth.
ю́нкер, а *m.* (*hist.*) **1.** (*pl.* **~а́, ~о́в**) cadet. **2.** (*pl.* **~ы, ~ов**) Junker (*Prussian landowner*).
ю́нкер|ский *adj. of* **~**
ю́ност|ь, и *f.* youth (*age*).
ю́нош|а, и *m.* youth (*pers.*).
ю́ношеский *adj.* youthful.
ю́ношеств|о, а *nt.* **1.** youth (*age*). **2.** (*collect.*) youth, young people.
ю́н|ый (~, ~á, ~о) *adj.* **1.** young; **теа́тр ~ого зри́теля** young people's theatre. **2.** youthful.
юпи́тер, а *m.* floodlight.
юр, а *m. only in phr.* **на ~у́** (*i*) in a high , exposed place, (*ii*) (*fig.*) in the limelight, in the forefront.
ю́р|а, ы *f.* (*geol.*) Jurassic period.
юриди́ческ|ий *adj.* legal, juridical; **~ая консульта́ция** legal advice office; **~ое лицо́** juridical person; **~ие нау́ки** jurisprudence, law; **ю. факульте́т** faculty of law.
юрисди́кци|я, и *f.* jurisdiction.
юриско́нсульт, а *m.* legal adviser.
юриспруде́нци|я, и *f.* jurisprudence, law (*as academic discipline*).
юри́ст, а *m.* legal expert, lawyer.
ю́р|кий (~ок, ~ка́, ~ко) *adj.* **1.** quick-moving, agile. **2.** (*fig., coll.*) clever, sharp, smart.
юркн|у́ть, у́, ёшь *pf.* to scamper away, dart away.
юро́див|ый *adj.* **1.** crazy, simple, touched. **2.** *as n.* **ю., ~ого** *m.* 'God's fool' (*idiot believed to possess divine gift of prophecy*).
юро́дств|о, а *nt.* **1.** craziness, idiocy. **2.** idiotic action.
юро́дств|овать, ую *impf.* to behave like an idiot.
ю́рский *adj.* (*geol.*) Jurassic.
ю́рт|а, ы *f.* yurt, yurta (*nomad's tent in Central Asia*).
Ю́рьев *adj.*: **Ю. день** St George's Day; **вот тебе́ и Ю. день!** here's a fine how d'ye do!
юсти́ци|я, и *f.* justice.
ют, а *m.* (*naut.*) quarter-deck.
ю|ти́ться, чу́сь, ти́шься *impf.* to huddle (together); to take shelter.
ю́фт|евый *adj. of* **~ь**
юфт|ь, и *f.* yuft, Russia leather.

Я

я, меня́, мне, мной (мно́ю), обо мне 1. *pers. pron.* I (me); **я не я** (*coll.*) it's nothing to do with me; **(я) не я бу́ду, е́сли не добью́сь от него́ извине́ния** I'll damn well see that I get an apology from him. **2.** *n.*; *nt. indecl.* the self, the ego; **второ́е я** alter ego.
я́бед|а, ы *f. and c.g.* **1.** *f.* (*obs.*) information, slander. **2.** *c.g.* = **~ник**
я́бедник, а *m.* (*coll.*) informer, sneak.
я́беднича|ть, ю *impf.* (*of* **на~**) (**на**+*a.*; *coll.*) to inform (on), tell tales (about).
я́блок|о, а, *pl.* **~и, ~** *nt.* apple; **глазно́е я.** eyeball; **в ~ах** (*of a horse's coat*) dappled; **я. раздо́ра** bone of contention; **~у не́где упа́сть** there isn't room to swing a cat.
я́блон|евый *adj. of* **~я**
я́блон|ный = **~евый**
я́блон|я, и *f.* apple-tree.
я́блочк|о, а *dim. of* **я́блоко**
я́бло|чный *adj. of* **~ко**
яв|и́ть, лю́, ~ишь *pf.* (*of* **~ля́ть**) to show, display; **я. (собо́й) приме́р** (+*g.*) to give an example (of), display.
яв|и́ться, лю́сь, ~ишься *pf.* (*of* **~ля́ться**) **1.** to appear, present o.s.; to report; **я. в суд** to appear before the court; **я. на слу́жбу** to report for duty; **я. с пови́нной** to give o.s. up. **2.** to turn up, arrive, show up. **3.** to arise, occur; **у меня́ ~и́лась блестя́щая мысль** I had a brilliant idea; **~и́лся удо́бный слу́чай** a suitable opportunity presented itself.
я́вк|а, и *f.* **1.** appearance, attendance; **я. в суд** appearance in court. **2.** secret rendezvous.
явле́ни|е, я *nt.* **1.** phenomenon; occurrence, happening; **стихи́йное я.** natural calamity. **2.** (*theatr.*) scene.
явля́|ть, ю *impf. of* **яви́ть**
явля́|ться, юсь *impf.* **1.** *impf. of* **яви́ться. 2.** (*impf. only*) (+*i.*) to be; to serve (as); **э́то ~ется кощу́нством** this is blasphemy.
я́вно[1] *adv.* manifestly, patently; obviously.
я́вно[2] *as pred.* it is manifest; it is obvious.
я́в|ный (~ен, ~на) *adj.* **1.** manifest; overt, explicit. **2.** obvious.
я́вор, а *m.* sycamore (*tree*).
я́вор|овый *adj. of* **~**
я́вочн|ый *adj.* **1.** *adj. of* **я́вка 2.**; **~ая кварти́ра** secret rendezvous. **2.** (*mil.*) reporting, recruiting; **я. пункт** reporting point (*for conscripts*); **я. уча́сток** recruiting office. **3.:** **~ым поря́дком** on the spur of the moment, without prior arrangement.
я́вствен|ный (~, ~на) *adj.* clear, distinct.
я́вств|овать, ует *impf.* to appear; to be clear, apparent, obvious; to follow (*logically*).

яв|ь, и *f.* reality.
ягдта́ш, а *m.* game-bag.
я́гел|ь, я *m.* (*bot.*) Iceland moss, reindeer moss.
ягн|ёнок, ёнка, *pl.* **~я́та, ~я́т** *m.* lamb.
ягн|и́ться, и́тся *impf.* (*of* **о~**) to lamb.
ягня́тник, а *m.* (*zool.*) lammergeyer.
я́год|а, ы *f.* berry; (*collect.*) soft fruit (*strawberries, blackcurrants, etc.*); **ви́нная я.** dried fig; **пойти́ по ~ы** to go berry-picking; **одного́ по́ля я.** soul-mate; kindred spirit.
я́годиц|а, ы *f.* buttock.
я́годи|чный *adj. of* **~ца**
я́годник, а *m.* **1.** berry plantation. **2.** berry bush. **3.** (*coll.*) berry-picker.
я́год|ный *adj. of* **~а**
ягуа́р, а *m.* jaguar.
яд, а (у) *m.* poison; venom (*also fig.*).
я́дерн|ый *adj.* **1.** (*phys.*) nuclear; **~ое расщепле́ние** nuclear fission; **я. реа́ктор** nuclear reactor; **~ая фи́зика** nuclear physics. **2.** *adj. of* **ядро́**
я́дерщик, а *m.* (*coll.*) nuclear scientist.
ядови́т|ый (~, ~а) *adj.* **1.** poisonous; toxic; **~ая змея́** poisonous snake. **2.** (*fig.*) venomous, malicious.
ядохимика́т, а *m.* (*agric.*) (chemical) pesticide.
ядрён|ый (~, ~а) *adj.* (*coll.*) **1.** having a large kernel (*of nuts*); juicy (*of fruit*); hearty (*of cabbages*). **2.** (*fig.*) healthy, vigorous. **3.** (*fig.*) fresh, bracing.
ядр|о́, а́, *pl.* **́~а, я́дер, ́~ам** *nt.* **1.** kernel; core. **2.** (*phys.*) nucleus. **3.** (*mil., etc.*) main body (*of a unit, group*). **4.** (*hist., mil.*) ball, shot. **5.** (*sport*) shot; **толка́ние ~а́** putting the shot.
я́зв|а, ы *f.* **1.** ulcer, sore; **я. желу́дка** stomach ulcer; **морова́я я.** plague; **сиби́рская я.** malignant anthrax. **2.** (*fig.*) plague, curse. **3.** (*fig., coll.*) malicious person; (*as term of abuse*) scum.
я́звенн|ый *adj.* ulcerous; **~ая боле́знь** stomach ulcer.
язви́тел|ьный (~ен, ~ьна) *adj.* caustic, biting, sarcastic.
язв|и́ть, лю́, и́шь *impf.* (*of* **съ~**) **1.** (*obs.*) to wound; to sting. **2.** to say sarcastically; to mock; **я. на чей-н. счёт** to be sarcastic at s.o.'s expense.
язы́к[1]**, а́,** *pl.* **~и́** *m.* **1.** tongue; **у него́ я. без косте́й** he is too fond of talking; **держа́ть я. за зуба́ми, придержа́ть я.** to hold one's tongue; **прикуси́ть я.** (*coll.*) to shut up; **я. у него́ хорошо́ подве́шен** (*coll.*) he has a glib tongue; **распусти́ть я.** (*coll.*) to talk too glibly; **сорвало́сь с ~а́** (*fig.*) it slipped out; **лиши́ться ~а́** (*fig.*) to lose one's tongue; **я. у меня́ не поверну́лся э́то сказа́ть** (*coll.*) I could not bring myself to say it; **чеса́ть, болта́ть ~о́м** (*coll.*) to natter, blather; **я. у меня́ чеса́лся** (*coll.*) I was itching to speak. **2.** (*cul.*) tongue; **копчёный я.** smoked tongue. **3.** clapper (*of a bell*). **4.** (*mil.; coll.*) prisoner who will talk (*will provide information when interrogated*). **5.: морско́й я.** (*zool.*) sole.
язы́к[2]**, а́,** *pl.* **~и́,** *m.* language (*also fig.*); **владе́ть мно́гими ~а́ми** to know many languages; **говори́ть на ло́маном ру́сском ~е́** to talk in broken Russian; **найти́ о́бщий я.** (*fig.*) to find a common language.
языка́ст|ый (~, ~а) *adj.* (*coll.*) sharp-tongued.
языкове́д, а *m.* linguist, specialist on linguistics.
языкове́дени|е, я *nt.* linguistics.
языково́й *adj.* linguistic.
языко́вый *adj.* **1.** (*anat.*) tongue. **2.** (*cul.*) tongue.
языкозна́ни|е, я *nt.* linguistics, science of language.
язы́ческий *adj.* heathen, pagan.
язы́честв|о, а *nt.* heathenism, paganism.
языч|ко́вый *adj. of* **~о́к; я. инструме́нт** (*mus.*) reed instrument.
язы́чник, а *m.* heathen, pagan.
язы́|чный *adj. of* **~к**[1] **1.**
языч|о́к, ка́ *m.* **1.** (*anat.*) uvula. **2.** (*mus.*) reed. **3.** (*tech.*) catch. lug. **4.** *dim. of* **язы́к**
яз|ь, я́ *m.* ide (*fish of carp family*).
я́ичк|о, а *pl.* **~и** *nt.* **1.** (*anat.*) testicle. **2.** *dim. of* **яйцо́**
я́ичник, а *m.* (*anat.*) ovary.
я́ичниц|а, ы *f.* (*cul.*) fried eggs (*also* **я.-глазу́нья**); **я.-болту́нья** scrambled eggs.
яи́чн|ый *adj. of* **яйцо́; я. бело́к** white of eggs; **я. желто́к** yolk of egg; **я. порошо́к** dried egg(s); **~ая скорлупа́** egg-shell.
яйцеви́д|ный (~ен, ~на) *adj.* egg-shaped, oval.
яйцево́д, а *m.* (*anat.*) oviduct.
яйцекле́тк|а, и *f.* (*biol.*) ovule.
яйцеро́дный *adj.* (*zool.*) oviparous.
яйц|о́, а́, *pl.* **́~а, яи́ц, ́~ам** *nt.* **1.** egg; (*biol.*) ovum; **нести́ ́~а** to lay eggs; **я. всмя́тку** lightly-boiled egg; **я. вкруту́ю** hard-boiled egg; **я. в мешо́чек** medium-boiled egg. **2.** (*pl. coll.*) balls, nuts (= *testicles*).
як, а *m.* yak.
якоби́н|ец, ца *m.* (*hist., pol.*) Jacobin.
якоби́н|ский *adj. of* **~ец**
я́кобы 1. *conj.* (*expr. doubt about validity of another's statement*) that; **говоря́т, я. он у́мер** they say (= *they claim*) that he has died. **2.** *conj.* as if, as though; **он вообрази́л, я. его́ произвели́ в генера́лы** he imagined he had been made a general. **3.** *particle* supposedly, allegedly; **мы посмотре́ли э́ту я. стра́шную карти́ну** we have seen this supposedly dreadful film.
я́кор|ный *adj. of* **~ь; ~ная лебёдка** capstan; **~ное ме́сто, ~ная стоя́нка** anchorage.
я́кор|ь, я, *pl.* **~я́, ~е́й** *m.* **1.** (*naut.*) anchor; **я. спасе́ния** (*fig.*) last hope; **стать на я.** to anchor; **бро́сить я.** to cast, drop anchor; **стоя́ть на ~е** to ride at anchor; **сня́ться с ~я** to weigh anchor. **2.** (*electr.*) armature; rotor.
яку́т, а *m.*Yakut.
яку́т|ка, ки *f. of* **~**
яку́тский *adj.* Yakut.
якша́|ться, юсь *impf.* (**с**+*i.*; *coll.*) to consort (with), hobnob (with).
ял, а *m.* whaler, pinnace; yawl.
я́лик, а *m.* skiff, dinghy; yawl.
я́ловый *adj.* barren, dry (*of cows*).
Я́лт|а, ы *f.* Yalta.
я́м|а, ы *f.* **1.** pit, hole; **возду́шная я.** air pocket; **выгребна́я я.** cesspit; **у́гольная я.** coal bunker. **2.** (*geog.; coll.*) depression, hollow. **3.** (*obs.*) prison.
яма́|ец, йца *m.* Jamaican.
Яма́йк|а, и *f.* Jamaica.
яма́йский *adj.* Jamaican; **я. ром** Jamaica rum.
ямб, а *m.* (*liter.*) iambus, iambic verse.
ямби́ческий *adj.* iambic.
я́мк|а, и *f. dim. of* **я́ма; я. на щека́х** dimple.
ямщи́к, а́ *m.* coachman.
янва́р|ский *adj. of* **~ь**
янва́р|ь, я́ *m.* January.
я́нки *m.*Yankee.
янта́рн|ый *adj.* **1.** amber. **2.** amber-coloured.
янта́р|ь, я́ *m.* amber.
япо́н|ец, ца *m.* Japanese.
Япо́ни|я, и *f.* Japan.
япо́н|ка, ки *f. of* **~ец**
япо́нский *adj.* Japanese; **я. лак** Japan lacquer, japan.
яр[1]**, а, о ́~е, на ~у́** *m.* **1.** steep bank (*of river, lake, etc.*); slope (*of ravine*). **2.** ravine.
ярд, а *m.* yard (*measure*).
яре́мн|ый *adj. of* **ярмо́; ~ая ве́на** (*anat.*) jugular vein.
я́р|кий (~ок, ~ка́, ~ко) *adj.* **1.** bright (*of light, colours, etc.*). **2.** (*fig.*) colourful, striking; vivid, graphic; **~кая карти́на** graphic picture; **я. приме́р** striking example. **3.** (*fig.*) brilliant, outstanding; **~кая речь**

brilliant speech; **я. тала́нт** outstanding gifts.
я́ркост|ь, и *f.* **1.** brightness. **2.** (*fig.*) brilliance.
ярлы́к, а́ *m.* **1.** label, tag. **2.** (*fig.*) label; **приклеи́ть я. кому́-н.** to pin a label on s.o.
я́рмарк|а, и *f.* (trade) fair.
я́рмар|очный *adj. of* **~ка**
ярм|о́, а́, *pl.* **~́а** *nt.* yoke (*also fig.*); **сбро́сить с себя́ я.** (*fig.*) to cast off the yoke.
яров|о́й *adj.* (*agric.*) spring; **~а́я пшени́ца** spring wheat; *as n.* **~о́е, ~о́го** *nt.* spring crop.
я́рост|ный (~ен, ~на) *adj.* furious, fierce, savage.
я́рост|ь, и *f.* fury, rage.
я́рус, а *m.* **1.** (*theatr.*) circle. **2.** tier.
я́рус|ный *adj.* **1.** *adj. of* **~. 2.** tiered; stepped; graduated.
ярча́йший *superl. of* **я́ркий**
я́р|че *comp. of* **~кий**
я́р|ый (~, ~а) *adj.* **1.** furious; violent. **2.** vehement, fervent.
я́рь-медя́нка, я́ри-медя́нки *f.* (*chem.*) verdigris.
я́с|ельный *adj. of* **~ли**
я́сен|евый *adj. of* **~ь**
я́сен|ь, я *m.* ash-tree.
я́сл|и, ей *no sg.* **1.** manger, crib (*for cattle*). **2.** crèche, day nursery.
ясне́|ть, ет *impf.* to become clear(er).
я́сн|о[1] *adv. of* **~ый**
я́сно[2] *as pred.* **1.** (*of weather*) it is fine. **2.** (*fig.*) it is clear. **3.** (*as affirmative particle*) yes, of course.
яснови́дени|е, я *nt.* clairvoyance.
ясновид|ец, ца *m.* clairvoyant.
ясновидящий *adj.* (*also as n.*) clairvoyant.
я́сност|ь, и *f.* clearness, clarity; lucidity; **внести́ я. во что-н.** to clarify sth.
я́с|ный (~ен, ~на́, ~но) *adj.* **1.** clear; bright; (*of weather*) fine; **~ное не́бо** clear sky; **гром средь ~ного не́ба** a bolt from the blue. **2.** distinct. **3.** (*fig.*) clear, plain; **сде́лать ~ным** to make it clear; **~ное де́ло** of course. **5.** lucid; **я. ум** precise mind.
я́ств|а, ~ *pl.* (*sg.* **~о, ~а** *nt.*) viands, victuals.
я́стреб, а, *pl.* **~а́** *and* **~ы** *m.* hawk.
ястреби́н|ый *adj. of* **я́стреб; ~ая охо́та** falconry; **с ~ым взгля́дом** hawk-eyed; **я. нос** hawk nose.
ястреб|о́к, ка́ *m.* **1.** *dim. of* **я́стреб. 2.** (*coll.*) fighter (*plane*).
ятага́н, а *m.* scimitar.
ятроге́нный *adj.* iatrogenic.
ят|ь, я *m.* yat´ (*name of old Russ. letter* **'ѣ'**, *replaced by* **'е'** *in 1918*); **на я.** (*coll.*) first-class; splendid(ly).
я́хонт, а *m.* **(кра́сный)** ruby; **(си́ний)** sapphire.
я́хонт|овый *adj. of* **~**
я́хт|а, ы *f.* yacht.
яхт-клу́б, а *m.* yacht club.
яхтсме́н, а *m.* yachtsman.
яче́ист|ый (~, ~а) *adj.* cellular, porous.
яче́йк|а, и, *g. pl.* **яче́ек** *f.* **1.** (*biol.*, *pol.*) cell. **2.** (*mil.*) foxhole; slit trench.
ячме́н|ный *adj. of* **~ь**[1]; **~ное зерно́** barley-corn; **я. отва́р** barley-water; **я. са́хар** barley-sugar.
ячме́н|ь[1]**, я́** *m.* barley.
ячме́н|ь[2]**, я́** *m.* sty (*in the eye*).
я́чнев|ый *adj.*: **~ая крупа́** fine-ground barley.
я́шм|а, ы *f.* (*min.*) jasper.
я́шм|овый *adj. of* **~а**
я́щериц|а, ы *f.* lizard.
я́щик, а *m.* **1.** box, chest; cabinet; (*coll.*, *joc.*) the box (= *television*); **му́сорный я.** dustbin; **почто́вый я.** letter-box; pillar-box; **откла́дывать в до́лгий я.** (*fig.*) to shelve, put off. **2.** drawer.
я́щур, а *m.* foot-and-mouth disease.
я́щур|ный *adj.* **1.** *adj. of* **~. 2.** infected with foot-and-mouth disease.

Thematic Wordfinder/ Темати́ческий спра́вочник слов

This section of thematically organized vocabulary lists is designed as an aid to self-expression, and is a valuable reference for writing papers, essays, speeches, business reports, or articles. The subject areas covered have been chosen for their topicality and relevance to the needs of today's student. The lists are intended not only to provide the concrete vocabulary you require, but also to help with construction and usage, allowing you to express your opinion and structure your views clearly and idiomatically.

Этот тематический словарь предназначен для того, чтобы помогать читателю выражать свою мысль. Его можно использовать при написании диссертаций, сочинений, речей, деловых докладов или статей. Темы, включённые в этот раздел, выбраны из-за их актуальности и необходимости для сегодняшего студента. Эти списки рассчитаны не только на то, чтобы помогать вам с синтаксисом и словоупотреблением, причём вы сможете свободно выражать своё мнение и излагать свои взгляды, употребляя подходящую лексику.

Contents

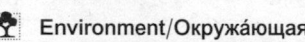

Expression of one's Point of View / Выраже́ние свое́й то́чки зре́ния

Agreeing	**Согла́сие**
as... has underlined	как подчеркну́л(а)...
I admit that ...	призна́юсь, что...
I agree, share your opinion	я согла́сен (согла́сна)
I am pleased to accept	я соглаша́юсь с удово́льствием
I quite agree with you	я вполне́ согла́сен (согла́сна) с ва́ми
I share your concern about...	я разделя́ю ва́ше беспоко́йство о...
I share your reluctance to...	я разделя́ю ва́ше нежела́ние...
I think that is an excellent idea	я ду́маю, что э́то отли́чная иде́я
it seems to me to be completely justified to...	мне ка́жется совсе́м есте́ственно...
it's a good idea	э́то хоро́шая мысль
that's correct, true	э́то пра́вильно, ве́рно
we agree on the need to...	мы согласи́лись, что ну́жно...
X states, quite rightly, that...	Х справедли́во утвержда́ет, что...
you're right	вы пра́вы

continued...

continued...

Disagreeing / Несогла́сие

Disagreeing	Несогла́сие
do you accept that...?	вы признаёте, что...?
don't you admit that...?	ра́зве вы не признаёте, что...?
don't you think that...?	не ду́маете ли вы, что...?
frankly, honestly	че́стно (говоря́)
I cannot believe that...	я не могу́ пове́рить, что...
I didn't expect that of you	я э́того от вас не ожида́л(а)
I don't agree at all	я совсе́м не согла́сен (согла́сна)
I don't agree with you	я не согла́сен (согла́сна) с ва́ми
I don't quite agree	я не вполне́ согла́сен (согла́сна)
I must admit	на́до призна́ться
I must contradict you	я вы́нужден (вы́нуждена) возрази́ть вам
I think it is totally inappropriate to...	по-мо́ему, соверше́нно неуме́стно...
I think we must moderate our judgement	мо-мо́ему, нам на́до смягчи́ть оце́нку
I very much regret that...	я о́чень сожале́ю, что....
I'm afraid I can't agree	я бою́сь, что не могу́ согласи́ться
I'm afraid I must refuse	бою́сь, что мне на́до отказа́ться
I'm surprised at you!	вы меня́ удивля́ете!
it is a pity that...	жаль, что...
it is difficult to believe that...	тру́дно пове́рить, что...
it is unthinkable that...	недопусти́мо, что...
on the contrary, it seems to me that...	напро́тив, мне ка́жется, что...
really?	серьёзно? пра́вда? неуже́ли?
surely not!	неуже́ли!
we have diametrically opposed opinions on...	у нас диаметра́льно противополо́жные мне́ния о...
we have different opinions about that	у нас ра́зные мне́ния об э́том
what are you saying?...doing?	да что́ вы?
what are you talking about?	о чём вы говори́те?
what do you mean?	что вы хоти́те сказа́ть?, что вы име́ете в виду́?
you are in a minority	вы в меньшинстве́
you're wrong	вы непра́вы
you've got it all wrong	вы всё перепу́тали

Giving your Opinion / Выража́я своё мне́ние

Giving your Opinion	Выража́я своё мне́ние
forgive me, but I can't agree with you	извини́те меня́, но я не могу́ согласи́ться с ва́ми
from your point of view	с ва́шей то́чки зре́ния
I (dis)approve of...	я (не) одобря́ю...
I am afraid that...	бою́сь, что...
I am certain that...	я уве́рен (уве́рена), что...
I am convinced that...	я убеждён (убеждена́), что...
I can't help thinking that...	не могу́ не ду́мать, что...
I consider that...	счита́ю, что...
I don't deny, that...	я не отрица́ю, что...
I doubt whether...	я сомнева́юсь, что́бы...
I get the impression that...	у меня́ сложи́лось впечатле́ние, что...
I greatly admire	я глубоко́ уважа́ю
I hate	я ненави́жу
I must say that...	на́до сказа́ть, что...
I must stress that...	я до́лжен (должна́) подчеркну́ть, что...
I prefer	я предпочита́ю, бо́льше люблю́
I see no advantage in...	не ви́жу никако́й по́льзы...
I should be very surprised if...	я был(а́) бы о́чень удивлён (удивлена́), е́сли бы...
I suggest, maintain that...	я полага́ю, утвержда́ю, что...
I suppose that...	я полага́ю, что...
I think it's important to say...	по-мо́ему, ва́жно сказа́ть...
I think that...	я ду́маю, что...

continued...

in my opinion	по-мо́ему (мне́нию), на мой взгляд
it is difficult for me to give my opinion about...	мне тру́дно вы́разить своё мне́ние о...
it is undeniable that...	неоспори́мо, что...
it must be difficult to...	должно́ быть тру́дно...
it seems to me that...	мне ка́жется, что...
it's obvious that...	очеви́дно, что...
point of view	то́чка зре́ния
that's just the point	в то́м-то и де́ло
the fact is that...	де́ло в том, что...
to have a high / low opinion of...	быть высо́кого / невысо́кого мне́ния о...

Structuring your Views / Организа́ция то́чки зре́ния

admittedly,	призна́ться,
although	хотя́
...and finally	...и в заключе́ние
at any rate	во вся́ком слу́чае
be that as it may	пусть бу́дет, как бу́дет
consequently	сле́довательно
finally,	наконе́ц,
hence, therefore	поэ́тому
however,	одна́ко,
I must admit that...	на́до призна́ться, что...
I wish to start with...	я хочу́ нача́ть с (чего́)
in addition	вдоба́вок, к тому́ же
in alphabetical order	в алфави́тном поря́дке
in conclusion,	в заключе́ние,
in fact	на са́мом де́ле
in order of importance	по сте́пени ва́жности
in other words	ины́ми, други́ми слова́ми
in short	коро́че говоря́
in spite of	несмотря́ на
in the first place	во-пе́рвых
in the second place	во-вторы́х
indeed, really	в са́мом де́ле, действи́тельно
it may be a good thing for adults, but...	мо́жет быть, э́то хорошо́ для взро́слых, но...
moreover	к тому́ же, вдоба́вок
nevertheless	тем не ме́нее, одна́ко
not only..., but also...	не то́лько..., но и...
on the contrary	наоборо́т
on the face of it...	на пе́рвый взгляд
on the one hand...on the other hand	с одно́й стороны́... с друго́й стороны́
or else, otherwise...	а то, ина́че
some people maintain..., but others say...	одни́ утвержда́ют..., а други́е говоря́т...
that is less important than...	э́то ме́нее ва́жно, чем...
that is why...	вот почему́, поэ́тому
the most important thing	са́мое ва́жное
the sequence of events	ход собы́тий
to begin with,	пре́жде всего́,
to sum up	сло́вом...
to summarize	подвести́ ито́г

Environment/ Окружа́ющая среда́

The Protection of the Environment/ Охра́на окружа́ющей среды́

biodegradable	подве́рженный биологи́ческому разложе́нию
car with a low fuel consumption	маши́на, потребля́ющая ма́логорю́чего
catalytic converter	каталити́ческий нейтрализа́тор
CFC-free spray	аэрозо́ль (м.) без хлори́рованных флоруглеро́дов, фрео́на
closed to traffic	закры́т(а) для движе́ния тра́нспорта
container	сосу́д
ecological	экологи́ческий
environmentalist	сторо́нник защи́ты окружа́ющей среды́, эко́лог
environmentally friendly	не принося́щий вреда́ окружа́ющей среде́
glass, paper recycling	перерабо́тка стекла́, бума́ги
Green Party	па́ртия зелёных
hydro-electric power station	гидроэлектроста́нция
non-pollutant product	проду́кт, не загрязня́ющий окружа́ющую сре́ду
organic product	органи́ческий проду́кт
ozone-friendly	не поврежда́ющий озо́новый слой
polar ice-cap	поля́рный ледниќовый покро́в
private cars	ли́чные маши́ны
protection of nature	охра́на, защи́та приро́ды
public transport	обще́ственный тра́нспорт
rainforest	тропи́ческий лес
recyclable	перераба́тываемый
recycling centre	центр перерабо́тки
reforestation	восстановле́ние лесны́х масси́вов
refuse collection	убо́рка (дома́шнего) му́сора
sense of responsibility among the public	чу́вство отве́тственности среди́ й обще́ственности
to campaign for	вести́ кампа́нию за (что)
to establish standards of air quality	устана́вливать/установи́ть но́рмы ка́чества во́здуха
to fight pollution	боро́ться с загрязне́нием
to fine polluting companies	штрафова́ть/о- загрязня́ющие компа́нии
to fit a vehicle (with)	снабжа́ть/снабди́ть маши́ну (чем)
to limit waste production	ограни́чивать/ограни́чить коли́чество му́сора, отхо́дов
to pedestrianize	запреща́ть/запрети́ть автомоби́льное движе́ние в (чём)
to protect	защища́ть/защити́ть, охраня́ть/охрани́ть
to protect endangered species	защища́ть/защити́ть вымира́ющие ви́ды
to raise the alarm	поднима́ть/подня́ть трево́гу
to realize the risk	осознава́ть/осозна́ть риск
to reduce waste	уменьша́ть/уме́ньшить растра́ту материа́лов
to replant a forest (with trees)	сно́ва сажа́ть/посади́ть (дере́вья) в лес
to restock a forest (with animals)	сно́ва заполня́ть/запо́лнить лес (живо́тными)
to salvage, to reclaim recyclable waste	собира́ть/собра́ть ути́ль
to save energy	эконо́мить/с- эне́ргию
unleaded petrol	неэтили́рованный бензи́н
waste processing	перерабо́тка отхо́дов
wildlife sanctuary	запове́дник

The Deterioration of the Environment/ Ухудше́ние окружа́ющей среды́

acid rain	кисло́тные дожди́
barrel	бо́чка
carbon dioxide	углеки́слый газ
CFC (chloroflourocarbon)	хлори́рованные флороуглеро́ды, фрео́н
climate	кли́мат
climatic change	измене́ние кли́мата
deforestation	обезле́сение
desertification	опусты́нивание
destruction of the flora and fauna	уничтоже́ние фло́ры и фа́уны
drought	за́суха
ecological disaster	экологи́ческое бе́дствие, экологи́ческая катастро́фа
factory	фа́брика, заво́д
famine	го́лод
garbage dump	му́сорная сва́лка
global warming	глоба́льное потепле́ние
greenhouse effect	тепли́чный, па́рниковый эффе́кт
• to increase the greenhouse effect	• увели́чить тепли́чный эффе́кт
• to reduce the greenhouse effect	• уме́ньшить тепли́чный эффе́кт
heatwave	волна́ си́льной жары́
lack of rain (see also 'drought')	недоста́ток дожде́й
oil slick	нефтяна́я плёнка на воде́
oil tanker	та́нкер
oil-well	нефтяна́я сква́жина
oilfield	месторожде́ние не́фти
open-cast mining	откры́тые го́рные рабо́ты
ozone layer	озо́новый слой
pollutant	загрязня́ющее вещество́
pollution	загрязне́ние
• air pollution	• загрязне́ние во́здуха
• atmospheric pollution	• атмосфе́рное загрязне́ние
• urban pollution	• городско́е загрязне́ние
• water pollution	• загрязне́ние воды́
power station	электроста́нция
• nuclear power station	• а́томная электроста́нция
• thermal power station	• теплова́я электроста́нция
seepage	проса́чивание
shrinkage of the permafrost	уса́дка ве́чной мерзлоты́
spray, aerosol	аэрозо́ль (м.)
temperature	температу́ра
to dump toxic	сбра́сывать/сбро́сить токси́ч-

waste (into)	ные отхо́ды
o exhaust natural resources	истоща́ть/истощи́ть есте́ственные ресу́рсы
to upset nature's balance	наруша́ть/нару́шить приро́дный бала́нс
oxic cloud	о́блако токси́чных веще́ств
waste	отхо́ды/отбро́сы/му́сор
• industrial waste	• промы́шленные отхо́ды
• radioactive waste	• радиоакти́вные отхо́ды
• toxic waste	• токси́чные отхо́ды

Natural Disasters/Стихи́йные бе́дствия, катастро́фы

active	де́йствующий
ash	зола́/пе́пел
avalanche	лави́на/обва́л (сне́жный обва́л)
bed (of river)	ру́сло (реки́)
crater	кра́тер
cyclone	цикло́н
disaster	бе́дствие, катастро́фа
downstream	вниз по тече́нию
earth tremor	подзе́мный толчо́к
earthquake	землетрясе́ние
emergency shelter	убе́жище
epicentre	эпице́нтр
flood	наводне́ние
forest fire	лесно́й пожа́р
gale	бу́ря
hurricane	урага́н
landslide	обва́л/о́ползень (м.)
lava	ла́ва
magma	ма́гма
monsoon	муссо́н, муссо́нные дожди́
natural phenomena	приро́дное явле́ние
rainy season	сезо́н дожде́й
Richter scale	шкала́ Ри́хтера
river in spate	разли́в
rockfall (blocking the road)	зава́л (на доро́ге)
storm at sea	шторм
thaw	о́ттепель (ж.)
thunderstorm	гроза́
tidal wave	прили́вная волна́
to evacuate an area	эвакуи́ровать райо́н
to overflow	разлива́ться/разли́ться
to overflow its banks	выходи́ть/вы́йти из берего́в
to rumble	громыха́ть, греме́ть
to tame nature	укроща́ть/укроти́ть приро́ду
tornado	торна́до
typhoon	тайфу́н
upstream	вверх по тече́нию
vagaries of nature	капри́зы приро́ды
volcanic eruption	изверже́ние вулка́на
volcano	вулка́н
• active volcano	• де́йствующий вулка́н
• extinct volcano	• поту́хший вулка́н
whirlpool	водоворо́т
whirlwind	вихрь (м.)

Society/Общество

Politics/Поли́тика

abstention (from voting)	воздержа́ние (от голосова́ния)
ballot box	у́рна для голосова́ния
candidate	кандида́т
constituency	избира́тельный о́круг
deputy	депута́т, член парла́мента
economic policy	экономи́ческая поли́тика
election campaign	предвы́борная, избира́тельная кампа́ния
election(s)	вы́боры (мн.)
electoral roll	спи́сок избира́телей
electorate, voters	избира́тели
executive power	исполни́тельная власть
extremist	экстреми́ст
foreign policy	вне́шняя поли́тика
general election	всео́бщие вы́боры (мн.)
government	прави́тельство
left-wing	ле́вый
legislative power	законода́тельная власть
majority (of votes)	большинство́ (голосо́в)
minister	мини́стр
ministry	министе́рство
moderate	челове́к, приде́рживающийся уме́ренных взгля́дов, центри́ст
opinion poll	опро́с обще́ственного мне́ния
opposition	оппози́ция
parliament	парла́мент
policy	поли́тика
political cant	полити́ческий жарго́н
political party	полити́ческая па́ртия
political scandal	полити́ческий сканда́л
politician	поли́тик
polling station	избира́тельный уча́сток
popularity rating	ре́йтинг популя́рности
president	президе́нт
presidential election	президе́нтские вы́боры (мн.)
prime minister	премье́р-мини́стр
public opinion	обще́ственное мне́ние
referendum (on)	рефере́ндум (по чему́)
republic	респу́блика
right to vote	пра́во го́лоса, избира́тельное пра́во
right-wing	пра́вый
Russian National Assembly	Госду́ма
second round, run-off	второ́й тур
senate	сена́т
speech	речь (ж.)
the Left	ле́вые, ле́вые па́ртии
the Right	пра́вые, пра́вые па́ртии
to abstain (from voting)	воздержа́ться (от голосова́ния)
to appoint	назнача́ть/назна́чить
to belong to a party	быть чле́ном па́ртии
to call upon (s.o.) to vote	призыва́ть/призва́ть (кого́) проголосова́ть

to campaign	вести́ кампа́нию
to cast a vote	отдава́ть/отда́ть го́лос
to elect (s.o.)	избира́ть/избра́ть
to form a government	формирова́ть/сформирова́ть прави́тельство
to give one's opinion on	выража́ть/вы́разить своё мне́ние о (чём)
to make a speech	произноси́ть/произнести́ речь выступа́ть/вы́ступить с ре́чью
to stand for election	выставля́ть/вы́ставить свою́ кандидату́ру на вы́борах
to vote	голосова́ть/про-
voting paper	избира́тельный бюллете́нь
when the votes are counted	когда́ подсчи́таны голоса́

Emigration and Immigration/Эмигра́ция и иммигра́ция

asylum-seeker	челове́к, про́сящий убе́жища
border	грани́ца
brain drain	уте́чка мозго́в
business visa	делова́я ви́за
country of origin	ро́дина
country of refuge	страна́, где про́сят убе́жища
culture shock	культу́рный шок
customs	тамо́жня
emigrant	эмигра́нт(ка)
exodus	ма́ссовый отъе́зд
expatriate	экспатриа́нт(ка)
foreign resident	иностра́нец, прожива́ющий в стране́
host country	страна́, принима́ющая (иммигра́нтов)
illegal	незако́нный, нелега́льный
illegal immigrant	нелега́льный иммигра́нт
immigrant	иммигра́нт(ка)
immigration	иммигра́ция
integration	интегра́ция
intolerance	нетерпи́мость (ж.)
law	зако́н
law on immigration	иммиграцио́нный зако́н
law on nationality	зако́н о гражда́нстве
naturalization	натурализа́ция
naturalize	натурализова́ть
permit	разреше́ние, про́пуск
political asylum	полити́ческое убе́жище
political refugee	полити́ческий бе́женец
quota	кво́та, но́рма
resident's permit	вид, разреше́ние на жи́тельство
student visa	студе́нческая ви́за
temporary visa	вре́менная ви́за
to acquire American nationality	получа́ть/получи́ть америка́нское гражда́нство
to close the borders	закрыва́ть/закры́ть грани́цу
to deport	депорти́ровать
to go through customs	проходи́ть/пройти́ тамо́женный досмо́тр
to renew a visa	продлева́ть/продли́ть, возобновля́ть/возобнови́ть ви́зу
to turn back (tr.)	верну́ть
to turn (s.o.) back at the border	отка́зывать/отказа́ть кому́-либо во въе́зде в страну́
to uproot	выселя́ть/вы́селить, переселя́ть/пересели́ть
tourist visa	туристи́ческая ви́за
visa	ви́за
wave of immigration	волна́ иммигра́ции
work permit	разреше́ние на рабо́ту

Social Issues and Youth Concerns/ Обще́ственные вопро́сы и пробле́мы молодёжи

abortion	або́рт
Aids	СПИД
anti-racist movement	движе́ние про́тив раси́зма (анти-раси́стское)
anti-semitism	антисемити́зм
benefit (grant)	посо́бие
block of flats	жило́й, многокварти́рный дом
contraception	контраце́пция
contraceptive, condom	противозача́точное сре́дство, презервати́в
discrimination against young people/women/ disabled people/ old people, etc.	дискримина́ция молодёжи/ же́нщин/инвали́дов/ста́рых, и т.д.
drug	нарко́тик
drug addict	нарком́ан(ка)
environment	среда́
equality	ра́венство, равнопра́вие
ethnic group	этни́ческая гру́ппа
family environment	семе́йная среда́
fight against Aids	борьба́ со СПИДом
fight against racism	борьба́ с раси́змом
gang	ша́йка, ба́нда
generation gap	пробле́ма отцо́в и дете́й, разобще́ние поколе́ний
group of young people	гру́ппа молоды́х люде́й
homeless person	бездо́мный челове́к, бомж
hooligan	хулига́н
housing estate	жило́й кварта́л, жило́й масси́в, микрорайо́н
illiteracy	безгра́мотность (ж.)
minority	меньшинство́
overdose	передозиро́вка, чрезме́рная до́за
prejudice	предубежде́ние, предрассу́док
privileged/ underprivileged background	привилегиро́ванное/непривилегиро́ванное происхожде́ние
(racial) segregation	(ра́совая) сегрега́ция
racism	раси́зм
sexism	пренебрежи́тельное отноше́ние к же́нщинам
single parent family	семья́ с ма́терью- или отцо́м-одино́чкой
slum	трущо́ба
social worker	рабо́тник(-ница) социа́льной сфе́ры, соцрабо́тник
solvent abuse	токсикома́ния
solvent abuser	токсикома́н(ка)
suburb	при́город, предме́стье

suicide attempt	попы́тка самоуби́йства
to attack (s.o.)	напада́ть/напа́сть на (кого́)
to be the victim of racism	быть же́ртвой раси́зма
to drop out of society	устраня́ться/устрани́ться от о́бщества
to go to university	поступа́ть/поступи́ть в университе́т
to leave school at 16	ока́нчивать/око́нчить шко́лу в 16 лет
to mug (s.o.)	обкра́дывать/обокра́сть (кого́) (на у́лице)
to rebel (against society)	отвора́чиваться/отверну́ться (от о́бщества)
to rebel (i.e. to rise up against…)	восстава́ть/восста́ть, бунтова́ть
to take drugs	принима́ть/приня́ть нарко́тики
tramp	бродя́га, бомж
unemployment	безрабо́тица
unqualified, unskilled	неквалифици́рованный
vandalism	ванда́лизм
xenophobia	ксенофо́бия

Business and Industry/ Комме́рция и промы́шленность

Employment and Unemployment/ Рабо́та и безрабо́тица

enefits package	компле́кт, набо́рка посо́бий
ontract	контра́кт, догово́р
ismissal	увольне́ние
mployee	слу́жащий, рабо́тник
mployer	хозя́ин, работода́тель (м.)
mployment agency	аге́нство по на́йму
ll-time job	рабо́та, занима́ющая всё рабо́чее вре́мя
uaranteed minimum wage	гаранти́рованная минима́льная за́работная пла́та
igher education	вы́сшее образова́ние
ı office/ working hours	в рабо́чее вре́мя
b	рабо́та, ме́сто
b interview	собесе́дование
b security	гара́нтия рабо́ты
b-seeker	челове́к, и́щущий рабо́ту
bour	труд
y-offs	сокраще́ние ка́дров
ng-term unemployed	безрабо́тный в тече́ние до́лгого вре́мени
ertime	сверхуро́чная рабо́та
ırt-time job	рабо́та на полста́вки
dundancy	безрабо́тица
lary, wage	окла́д, зарпла́та
lf-employed person	рабо́тающий не по на́йму
ːk pay	опла́та по (больни́чному) бюллете́ню
ke-home pay	чи́стый за́работок
the workers are underpaid	рабо́чим ма́ло пла́тят
thirty-five hour week	35-часова́я рабо́чая неде́ля
to change jobs	сменя́ть/смени́ть ме́сто рабо́ты
to create job opportunities	создава́ть/созда́ть рабо́чие места́
to give notice	предупрежда́ть/предупреди́ть
to have a good salary	получа́ть хоро́шую зарпла́ту
to have a job	име́ть рабо́ту
to help create new jobs	помога́ть/помо́чь в созда́нии но́вых мест
to hire	нанима́ть/наня́ть
to interview (s.o.)	проводи́ть/провести́ собесе́дование с (кем)
to look for a job	иска́ть рабо́ту
to lose one's job/ be made redundant	быть уво́ленным
to put in an application	подава́ть/пода́ть заявле́ние
to receive a salary/ benefits	получа́ть зарпла́ту, посо́бие
to resign (from a job)	увольня́ться/уво́литься с рабо́ты
to sign on at the unemployment office	регистри́роваться/за- в ка́честве безрабо́тного
to temp	рабо́тать вре́менно
to work	рабо́тать
• to work part-time/ full-time	• рабо́тать на непо́лной ста́вке/ по́лный рабо́чий день
• to work shifts	• рабо́тать посме́нно
• to work without declaring one's earnings	• рабо́тать, не деклари́руя дохо́ды
training course	курс подгото́вки, обуче́ния
unemployed people no longer eligible for benefit	безрабо́тные, кото́рым уже́ не поло́жено платёжное посо́бие
unemployed person	безрабо́тный
unemployment	безрабо́тица
unemployment benefit	посо́бие по безрабо́тице
unemployment is on the increase	безрабо́тица растёт/ увели́чивается
wage earner	наёмный рабо́чий
work conditions	усло́вия труда́
working population	рабо́чие, рабо́чее населе́ние

Trade and Commerce/Торго́вля и комме́рция

according to safety standards	согла́сно но́рмам безопа́сности
at the lower end of the market	ни́зшего со́рта
at the top end of the market	пе́рвого, вы́сшего со́рта
balance of trade	торго́вый бала́нс
car fair	автомоби́льная я́рмарка
car manufacturer	производи́тель (м.) автомоби́лей
chain of stores	сеть (ж.) магази́нов
chamber of commerce	торго́вая пала́та
clearance sale	распрода́жа

cost effective	рента́бельный
cost price	себесто́имость (ж.)
customer services	отде́л по рабо́те с клие́нтами
deficit	дефици́т
delivery	доста́вка
department store	универма́г
exhibition	вы́ставка
fair	я́рмарка
finished goods	гото́вые изде́лия
foreign trade	вне́шняя торго́вля
free trade	свобо́дная торго́вля
inclusive of tax	включа́я нало́г
income tax	подохо́дный нало́г
large supermarket (hypermarket)	кру́пный универса́м
mail-order selling	прода́жа по почто́вым зака́зам
make-up/clothing/ etc. line	сорт космети́ческих това́ров, оде́жды, и т.д.
manufacturer	изготови́тель (м.), производи́тель (м.)
manufacturing fault	дефе́кт при изготовле́нии, брак
mass-produced product	проду́кт ма́ссового произво́дства
mass-production	ма́ссовое произво́дство
oddment	оста́ток, обре́зок
opening hours	часы́ рабо́ты
order	зака́з
out of stock	не име́ющийся в нали́чии, в прода́же
product	проду́кт
profit	при́быль (ж.)
purchasing power	покупа́тельная спосо́бность
quality control	прове́рка за ка́чеством
raw material	сырьё
sales representative	коммивояжёр, торго́вый аге́нт
shop	магази́н
shop assistant	продаве́ц (продавщи́ца)
shopkeeper	владе́лец (владе́лица) магази́на
shopping centre	торго́вый центр
shopping precinct	торго́вый пасса́ж
sole distributor	еди́нственный распредели́тель
stock	запа́с, инвента́рь (м.)
stock shortage	дефици́т в запа́се това́ров
supermarket	универса́м, суперма́ркет
supplier	поставщи́к
supply and demand	спрос и предложе́ние
to be well-stocked	име́ть (вполне́) доста́точный запа́с
to buy a shop	покупа́ть/купи́ть магази́н
to buy out a business	выкупа́ть/вы́купить компа́нию
to compete with (s.o.)	конкури́ровать, сопе́рничать с (кем)
to develop a product	разраба́тывать/разрабо́тать проду́кт
to distribute a product	распределя́ть/распредели́ть проду́кт
to do the stock-taking	инвентаризова́ть
to dress a window	оформля́ть/офо́рмить витри́ну
to export	экспорти́ровать, вывози́ть/вы́везти
to go bankrupt	обанкро́титься
to import	импорти́ровать, ввози́ть/ввезти́
to launch a product on the market	выпуска́ть/вы́пустить проду́кт в прода́жу
to make out an invoice	выпи́сывать/вы́писать счёт, факту́ру
to open a shop	открыва́ть/откры́ть магази́н
to place an order	зака́зывать/заказа́ть
to reach trade agreements	заключа́ть/заключи́ть догово́ры о торго́вле
to rent a shop	нанима́ть/наня́ть магази́н
to retail	продава́ть/прода́ть в ро́зницу
• to sell at a loss	• продава́ть/прода́ть с убы́тком
• to sell at a profit	• продава́ть/прода́ть вы́годно
• to sell retail	• продава́ть/прода́ть в ро́зницу
• to sell wholesale	• продава́ть/прода́ть о́птом
to test a product	подверга́ть/подве́ргнуть проду́кт испыта́нию
trading partner	партнёр, компаньо́н
value for money	вы́годная поку́пка
VAT	нало́г на доба́вленную сто́имость
warehouse	(това́рный) склад
wholesaler	оптови́к

Marketing and Publicity/Ма́ркетинг и реклами́рование

advertisement	рекла́ма
advertising	реклами́рование
advertising agency	рекла́мное аге́нтство
advertising campaign	рекла́мная кампа́ния
advertising space	ме́сто для рекла́мы
brand, make	сорт, ма́рка
brand name	фи́рменное назва́ние
buoyant market	оживлённая торго́вля
commercial	комме́рческий
competition	сопе́рничество, конкуре́нция
consumer survey	опро́с потреби́телей
discount	ски́дка
discount voucher	льго́тный тало́н
market share	до́ля прода́ж на ры́нке
market trends	направле́ние на ры́нке
marketing department	отде́л ма́ркетинга
poster	афи́ша, плака́т
public relations, PR	свя́зи с обще́ственностью
radio advert	рекла́ма на ра́дио
rapidly growing market	бы́стро расту́щий (расширя́ющийся) ры́нок
reply card	ка́рточка для отве́та (на опро́с)
sales and marketing person	слу́жащий отде́ла сбы́та и ма́ркетинга
sales department	отде́л сбы́та
sales executive	ме́неджер по сбы́ту
sales strategy	страте́гия сбы́та

slogan	ло́зунг, деви́з, рекла́мная фо́рмула
special offer	специа́льное предложе́ние
survey	опро́с, иссле́дование обще́ственного мне́ния
telephone sales	прода́жа по телефо́ну
to advertise	реклами́ровать
to break into a market	пробива́ться/проби́ться на ры́нок
to dominate a market	преоблада́ть на ры́нке
to find a gap in the market	находи́ть/найти́ ни́шу на ры́нке
to market a product	выпуска́ть/вы́пустить това́р на ры́нок
to promote a product	реклами́ровать проду́кт
to secure the loyalty of a customer to a brand	обеспе́чивать/обеспе́чить приве́рженность покупа́теля к ма́рке
to sponsor an event	финанси́ровать собы́тие
TV advert	рекла́ма по ТВ

Communication/ Коммуника́ция

Telephone/Телефо́н

answering machine	автоотве́тчик
can I take a message for him?	что ему́ переда́ть?
car phone	автотелефо́н
cardphone	телефо́н, рабо́тающий по ка́рточке
cordless telephone	радиотелефо́н
could I speak to...?	позови́те, пожа́луйста, ... к телефо́ну
dialling code of a region/country	код
emergency telephone number	но́мер для экстрема́льной ситуа́ции
extension number	доба́вочный (но́мер)
freefone number	но́мер, на кото́рый мо́жно позвони́ть беспла́тно
hello	алло́!, слу́шаю
hold the line	не ве́шайте тру́бку
I get few/a lot of calls	мне мно́го/ма́ло звонко́в
I'm putting you through	я вас соединя́ю
mobile phone	моби́льный телефо́н
operator	телефони́ст(ка)
phonebook, directory	телефо́нная кни́га, телефо́нный спра́вочник
phonecard	телефо́нная ка́рточка
price of the call	цена́ звонка́
public phone	телефо́н-автома́т
receiver, handset	телефо́нная тру́бка
speaking	говори́т...
telephone	телефо́н
telephone cord	телефо́нный шнур
the number is engaged	но́мер за́нят
the person you are calling	абоне́нт, кото́рому вы звони́те
there is no answer	не отвеча́ют, нет отве́та
to answer the phone	подходи́ть/подойти́ к телефо́ну
to be ex-directory	не име́ть своего́ но́мера в телефо́нной кни́ге
to dial a number	набира́ть/набра́ть но́мер
to hang up	ве́шать/пове́сить тру́бку
to hear the phone ring	слы́шать/у- телефо́нный звоно́к
to leave a message after the tone	оставля́ть/оста́вить сообще́ние по́сле сигна́ла
to let the phone ring 10 times	подожда́ть 10 звонко́в
to phone s.o. and reverse the charges	звони́ть/по- за счёт абоне́нта
to pick up the receiver	снима́ть/снять тру́бку
to ring directory enquiries	звони́ть/по- в телефо́нную спра́вочную
to wait for the dialling tone	подожда́ть сигна́ла
yellow pages	золоты́е страни́цы
you have dialled the wrong number	вы не туда́ попа́ли

Media and Arts/Сре́дства ма́ссовой информа́ции, и иску́сство

Television/Телеви́дение

advert	рекла́ма
aerial	анте́нна
announcer	ди́ктор
broadcasting satellite	спу́тник ра́дио и телеви́дения
cable TV	ка́бельное телеви́дение
camcorder	камко́рдер
cathode ray tube	като́дная тру́бка
channel	кана́л
children's programme	де́тская переда́ча
commentator	коммента́тор, обозрева́тель (м.)
commercial	рекла́мная переда́ча
decoder	деко́дер
documentary	документа́льный (фильм)
entertainment programme	развлека́тельная переда́ча
episode	эпизо́д
fast forward	ускоре́нно вперёд
freeze-frame	па́уза
high definition television	ТВ с чётким изображе́нием
interference	поме́хи
live broadcast	прямо́й эфи́р
main aerial	гла́вная анте́нна
news	после́дние изве́стия, но́вости

peak viewing time	лу́чшие часы́ для пока́за переда́ч
play	пье́са
portable television	портати́вный телеви́зор
presenter	обозрева́тель (м.)
private channel	ча́стный кана́л
programme	переда́ча
remote control	дистанцио́нное управле́ние
report	докла́д, сообще́ние
rewind	перема́тывать/перемота́ть
satellite dish	спу́тниковая анте́нна
screen	экра́н
serial, soap	сериа́л
state-owned channel	госуда́рственный кана́л
subscription TV channel	пла́тный кана́л
televised debate	теледеба́ты
television (the medium)	телеви́дение
television (set)	телеви́зор
to be on TV	появля́ться/появи́ться по телеви́дению
to flick through the channels	просма́тривать/просмотре́ть что идёт по кана́лам
to pay for the TV licence	плати́ть/за- за лице́нзию ТВ
to subscribe to cable TV	плати́ть/за- за приём ка́бельного ТВ
to watch television	смотре́ть телеви́зор
TV game show	телевизио́нное шо́у
TV movie	телевизио́нный фильм
TV programme	телевизио́нная переда́ча
TV series	многосери́йная переда́ча по телеви́дению
video cassette	видеокассе́та
video recorder, VCR	видеомагнитофо́н
videoclip	отры́вок из видеофи́льма, видеокли́п
voice-over	го́лос за ка́дром, зака́дровый го́лос
weather forecast	прогно́з пого́ды

Journalism/Журнали́стика

burning issue	актуа́льный вопро́с
cartoon	карикату́ра
chief editor	гла́вный реда́ктор
classified advertisements	объявле́ния
column, section	коло́нка
critic	кри́тик
daily (paper)	ежедне́вная газе́та
debate	диску́ссия, пре́ния, деба́ты
editorial	передова́я статья́
editorial offices	реда́кция
editorial staff	редакцио́нная колле́гия
freedom of the press	свобо́да печа́ти
gutter press	бульва́рная, жёлтая пре́сса
he was in the headlines	о нём крича́ли в газе́тах
headline	заголо́вок
investigation (into)	рассле́дование (чего́)
job advertisements	объявле́ния о рабо́те
journalist	журнали́ст(ка)
letters to the editor	пи́сьма в реда́кцию
mass circulation daily	ма́ссовая ежедне́вная газе́та
monthly magazine	ежеме́сячный журна́л
news	изве́стия, но́вости
news agency	информацио́нное аге́нтство
news flash	экстре́нное сообще́ние
news in brief	но́вости вкра́тце
news magazine	информацио́нный журна́л
news reader	ди́ктор
newspaper	газе́та
our correspondent in New York	наш корреспонде́нт в Нью-Йо́рке
photographer	фото́граф
photoreporter	фотокорреспонде́нт
press conference	пресс-конфере́нция
press pass	журнали́стский про́пуск
press release	сообще́ние для печа́ти
reporter	репортёр
review of the papers	обзо́р печа́ти
special correspondent	специа́льный корреспонде́нт
special edition	специа́льный вы́пуск
sub-editor, copy editor	помо́щник реда́ктора, техре́д (техни́ческий реда́ктор)
to cover an event	освеща́ть/освети́ть собы́тие
to found a newspaper	осно́вывать/основа́ть газе́ту
to grant an interview	соглаша́ться/согласи́ться на интервью́
to listen to the radio news	слу́шать после́дние изве́стия по ра́дио
to write an article	писа́ть/на- статью́
topical issue	актуа́льный вопро́с
TV news	телено́вости
weekly magazine	еженеде́льник
with a circulation of 10,000	с тиражо́м де́сять ты́сяч экземпля́ров
women's sport magazine	журна́л о же́нском спо́рте

Cinema, Theatre, and Music/Кино́, теа́тр и му́зыка

actor, actress	актёр, актри́са
adventure film	приключе́нческий фильм
avant-garde theatre	авангарди́стский теа́тр
backstage	за кули́сами
band	орке́стр
blockbuster	высокобюдже́тный фильм
brass band	духово́й орке́стр
(censor's) certificate	рекоменда́ция для просмо́тра фи́льма
choir	хор
cinema, movie theatre	кино́, кинотеа́тр
cinema complex	киноце́нтр
cinema enthusiast	киноведа́, кинома́н
circle	бельэта́ж, балко́н
classical music concert	конце́рт класси́ческой му́зыки

close-up	кру́пный план
comedy	коме́дия
composer	компози́тор
concert hall	конце́ртный зал
conductor	дирижёр
credits	ти́тры
detective film	детекти́в
director, film director	режиссёр, кинорежиссёр
drama	дра́ма
dress rehearsal, final rehearsal	генера́льная репети́ция
dubbed	дубли́рованный
extra, bit player	стати́ст(ка)
farce	фарс
film	фильм
• film club	• киноклу́б
• film star	• кинозвезда́
• film studio	• киносту́дия, киноателье́
intermission, interval	антра́кт
jazz band	джаз-банд
lead role,	гла́вная роль
light comedy	лёгкая коме́дия
musical	музыка́льная коме́дия, опере́тта
musician	музыка́нт
on the set (of a film)	на съёмочной площа́дке
open-air theatre	зелёный теа́тр, теа́тр под откры́тым не́бом
orchestra, band	орке́стр
original version	по́длинник
piano concerto	фортепья́нный конце́рт
preview	предвари́тельный просмо́тр
production (film, play)	постано́вка
rock concert	конце́рт рок-му́зыки
scene	сце́на
sci-fi film	научно-фантасти́ческий фильм
screenplay	киносцена́рий
screenwriter	кинодрамату́рг
scriptwriter	сценари́ст
shooting (of a film)	киносъёмка
singer	певе́ц (певи́ца)
sound effects	шумовы́е эффе́кты
soundtrack	звуково́е сопровожде́ние
special effects	специа́льные эффе́кты, спецэффе́кты
spectacular	эффе́ктное зре́лище
stage	сце́на, эстра́да
• stage door	• служе́бный, актёрский вход
• stage fright	• страх пе́ред пу́бликой
supporting actor	актёр на вторы́х роля́х
the film was released	фильм был вы́пущен (на экра́ны)
the tickets are sold out	все биле́ты распро́даны
theatre	теа́тр
to act in a play	игра́ть/сыгра́ть роль в пье́се
to adapt a novel for the cinema	адапти́ровать рома́н для постано́вки в кино́
to conduct an orchestra	дирижи́ровать орке́стром
to edit (e.g. film)	монти́ровать/с-
to go on the stage	станови́ться/стать актёром (актри́сой) в теа́тре
to go on tour	гастроли́ровать
to manage a theatre	заве́довать теа́тром
to play (a piece of) music	игра́ть/сыгра́ть му́зыку (музыка́льную пье́су)
to produce a film	выпуска́ть/вы́пустить фильм
to produce a play	режисси́ровать
to reserve tickets	зака́зывать/заказа́ть биле́ты
to stage a play	ста́вить/по- пье́су
to star in…	игра́ть/сыгра́ть гла́вную роль в (чём)
tragedy	траге́дия
trailer	вы́держки из реклами́руемого фи́льма
variety show	эстра́дное представле́ние
with subtitles	с субти́трами
with X as…	роль…исполня́ет X

женский род	**ж**	feminine
мужской род	**м**	masculine
множественное число	**мн**	plural

Guide to exploring the Internet/ Инструкции по использованию Internet

Getting started

Netscape Navigator version 3.0 or later is the only browser that will work with Cyrillic text. At least 16 megabytes of memory will be needed. If you have more memory, use version 4 out of preference. It can be downloaded from: **http://home.netscape.com**

You will also need a utility for expanding and decoding archived software (zipped, binhexed, etc.). StuffIt™ Expander is available free from Aladdin Systems at: **http://www.aladdinsys.com/expander**

At this site, select the appropriate Expander for your operating system, then click on GO. For a Windows environment, choose the self-extracting version. Once the expander has downloaded, install it on your hard disk/desktop. To do this in Windows, double-click on the downloaded file. If you are using a Mac, double-click on the StuffIt™ installer and follow the instructions given in the dialog box until a message confirms that the expander has been successfully installed.

Fonts

Cyrillic fonts for Internet use can be obtained free from: **http://www.brama.com/compute**

Downloading decoding utilities and fonts from the Internet is quite a long process (allow a couple of hours), but once installed on your computer, you won't have to do it again. You will need to set up the preferences and encoding options (steps 5–7) before each session.

Not all Russian sites use the same encoding system, so it is a good idea to download all the most commonly used fonts (*see below for details*). At the Brama homepage, follow the links to the software for your operating system and then follow the relevant instructions below.

If you are a Macintosh user:

1 Download the fonts, **ERBukinist Macintosh.hqx**, **ERKurierMacintosh.hqx**, **ERBukinistkoi8.hqx**, **ERKurierkoi8.hqx**, **ERBukinist1251.hqx** and **ERKurier1251.hqx** on to your desktop.
2 If the archives have not been automatically expanded, drop them on to your copy of StuffIt™ expander.
3 Place these expanded files (font suitcases) into your Fonts folder in your System folder.
4 Return to Netscape Navigator.
5 If using Version 3 go to the **Options** menu, select **General preferences**, then **Fonts**. If using Version 4 go to the **Edit** menu, select **Preferences**, followed by **Appearances**, then **Fonts**.
6 Now select the proportional font (**Bukinist**), and the corresponding fixed width font (**Kurier/Courier**).
7 Click OK to return to the browser. Go to the site of your choice. The Russian text will probably appear as rows of Latin characters with diacritical marks or as a nonsensical series of Cyrillic characters. Go to **View** and **Encoding**. Select **Cyrillic**.

Mac users can also download default fonts (**Прямой проп** and **АРСКурьер**) for Cyrillic from the archive **Fonts-1.hqx** obtainable from Apple's ftp site at: **ftp://ftp.apple.com/devworld/System_Software_Archive/Russian_7.01/**

If you are a PC user:

1 Download the fonts **bkkoi8.zip (Bukinist)**, **cokoi8.zip (courier)**, **bk1251.zip** and **co1251.zip** by double-clicking on the files and saving them on to your hard disk. If you have a problem at this stage, the **readme.txt file**, will give you useful information.
2 If the zipped archives have not automatically expanded, use an appropriate utility (e.g. StuffIt™ Expander (*see above*) or PKUnzip). You can either open the expander, drag and drop the zipped files on to it or just double-click on the zipped files.
3 Once the files are expanded, install the fonts using the **fonts** option in your Control Panel.
4 Return to Netscape Navigator.
5 If using Version 3 go to the **Options** menu, select **General preferences**, then **Fonts**. If using Version 4 go to the **Edit** menu, select **Preferences**, followed by **Appearances**, then **Fonts**.
6 For the Encoding select **Cyrillic** or **Cyrillic KOI8** and then select the proportional font (**Bukinist**), and the fixed width font (**Kurier/Courier**).
7 Click OK to return to the browser. Go to the site of your choice. The Russian text will probably appear as rows of Latin characters with diacritical marks or as a nonsensical series of Cyrillic characters. Go to the **Options** or **View** menu again and to **Document encoding**. Select **Cyrillic**.

If the characters are still not showing correctly, it could mean that the site you are visiting uses a different type of encoding. You may need to switch (for example, if you have selected KOI8, change to 1251). Alternatively, you can try clicking on the appropriate KOI(8), Win (1251) or Mac Cyrillic button. These buttons usually appear in a row at the top or bottom of most Russian websites. (*See right*)

For further information on encoding see:
http://www.siber.com/sib/russify *or*
http://koi.www.online.ru/ehelp/index.html#russ/

Вы видите русские буквы

бШ БХДХРЕ ПСЯЯЙХЕ АСЙВШ

„К е Б ЮЦАА Ц К

ГК рьтьБу ЮЦААзьу яЦзрК

„Ш БХДХРЕ ПСЯЯЙХЕ АСЙВШ

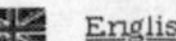
English

Search engines

These are essentially websites containing searchable databases of Uniform Resource Locators (URLs), indexed by topic and content. To perform a Net search open the location of a search engine, type a key word or phrase into the text box and click the Search button. A list of websites containing the chosen word or phrase will be returned in the form of clickable links. As these can run into thousands, it is best to make maximum use of the online help available. This can narrow down the scope of the search considerably. Special attention to the search engine's syntax is also recommended if you want to avoid excessively long lists of partially relevant URLs.

Search engine	Address
AltaVista	http://www.altavista.digital.com
Excite	http://www.excite. com
HotBot	http://www.hotbot.com
Infoseek	http://www.infoseek.com
Lycos	http://www.uk.lycos.de
LookSmart	http://www.looksmart.com
Webcrawler	http://www.webcrawler.com
Yahoo!	http://www.yahoo.com http://www.yahoo.co.uk

Different search engines sometimes have unique features. Lycos, for example, enables you to restrict your search to pictures or sounds. However, the World Wide Web is such a rapidly changing area that it is difficult for search engines to keep their indices up to date and it is not an uncommon experience to click a link which turns out to have moved or to be otherwise unobtainable.

Net searches in Russian

To perform a Net search in Russian you will need to obtain a Cyrillic keyboard driver such as ParaWin (Windows) or rScript (Macintosh) in addition to the fonts previously mentioned. These will enable you to type the desired word or by clicking on the letters to form it in a utility window, copy it and paste it into the search engine's text box. **KOI8** encoding is the one most likely to produce the desired result, followed by **Win 1251** as the next most likely. Yahoo! is the engine that consistently returns the greatest number of responses to a search word in Russian.

Email directories

These work on a similar principle to search engines, but enable you to locate email addresses in many different countries. Since all email addresses are written in Latin script, no special procedures are required to locate one in Russia.

Directory	Address
Four11 Email directory	http://www.four11.com
The Ultimate Email Directory	http://www.theultimates.com/email

A typical email interface

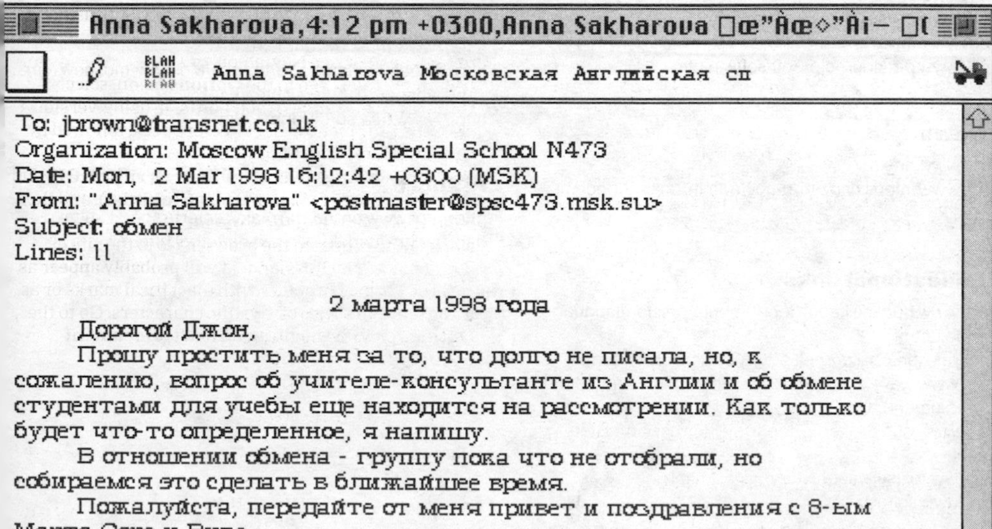
Anna Sakharova,4:12 pm +0300,Anna Sakharova □œ"Àœ◇"Ài– □(

Anna Sakharova Московская Английская сп

To: jbrown@transnet.co.uk
Organization: Moscow English Special School N473
Date: Mon, 2 Mar 1998 16:12:42 +0300 (MSK)
From: "Anna Sakharova" <postmaster@spsc473.msk.su>
Subject: обмен
Lines: 11

2 марта 1998 года

Дорогой Джон,

Прошу простить меня за то, что долго не писала, но, к сожалению, вопрос об учителе-консультанте из Англии и об обмене студентами для учебы еще находится на рассмотрении. Как только будет что-то определенное, я напишу.

В отношении обмена - группу пока что не отобрали, но собираемся это сделать в ближайшее время.

Пожалуйста, передайте от меня привет и поздравления с 8-ым Марта Сэре и Вике.

Анна

Email in Russian

The 8-bit nature of Cyrillic characters in most methods of encoding makes them impossible to send in the body of an email message without becoming corrupted by the transfer protocol. Instead you have to save your message as a plain text file and send it as an attachment protected in transmission by a system of encoding such as UUEncode or BinHex. Depending on the mail package and the mail server, it may end up being received in the body of an email text message. Similarly, a message that started out in one form of Cyrillic encoding may be changed in transit to another. It is a common practice to convert all Cyrillic text in transit to KOI8, as the most universally accepted Internet standard. On receiving such a message, if your mail package does not allow you to select the text and put it into a KOI8 font, copy and paste it into a word processor and change the font there. Email in Russian works most reliably where an established link exists between correspondents and it is known which forms of encoding can be handled at either end.

Russian-language websites

▶ Software and technical issues relating to use of Cyrillic

http://www.brama.com/compute
http://www.camtours.demon.co.uk/context.html
http://www.gy.com/www/ww1/ww2/smar13.htm
http://www.yacc.yakutia.su/FAQ/faq3.html
http://www.siber.com/sib/russify/ms-windows/netscape.html
http://sunsite.oit.unc.edu/sergei/Software/Software.html
http://www.gy.com/www/cat1/cy_cat.htm
http://www.relcom.ru/Russification/
http://www.apple.ru/

▶ Miscellaneous

http://www.funet.fi/pub/culture/russian/html_pages/links.html
http://www.mark-itt.ru/cgi-bin/www-list.pl/sortgroup
http://www.dux.ru/project.html
http://www.online.ru
http://www.peterlink.ru
http://www.piter-press.ru/yp
http://www.cross.ru
http://www.ifmo.ru/
http://www.pitt.edu/~cjp/Soft/softwin.html

▶ News

http://www.nns.ru
http://www.inforis.nnov.su/n-nov/admin/doklad/become.html.k

▶ Educational links

http://www.bucknell.edu/departments/russian/language/index.html
http://russian.dmll.cornell.edu/russian.web/material
http://www.wavefront.com/%7Eswithee/dictionary/menus/mainmenu.html
http://www.bucknell.edu/departments/russian/history.html
http://www.russia.net/history/history.html
http://uwh.lib.msu.su

▶ Cultural links

http://www.mkniga.ru
http://www.friends-partners.org/friends/opt-tables-mac-english-
http://alice.ibpm.serpukhov.su/friends/opt-tables-mac-english-

▶ Newspapers and journals

http://www.simplex.ru/lit.html
http://www.ropnet.ru/ogonyok
http://www.spb.ru/chaspik/current
http://www.relis.ru/MEDIA/mediacom.html
http://www.petropressa.ru

▶ Literature

http://koi.www.online.ru/sp/eel/russian
http://www.enjoy.ru:80/lit/lichno.html

▶ Tourism and travel

http://www.machaon.ru/most-tour/tour18.html
http://www.moscow-guide.ru
http://mech.math.msu.su/church/Moscow/moscow.html
w.transport.ru/9/tr_air.htm#E11E5
http://www.tula.su/cit/dom1.html

▶ Sport

http://koi.www.online.ru/rmain/rentert/rsports.xhtml
http://www.quark.lu.se/~oxana/futbol.html

Англоязычные Website*

Поисковые системы

Поисковые системы являются необходимыми инструментами Internet и служат указателями Website. Их легко использовать и они позволяют пользователю найти Website, относящиеся к определенным предметам, что было бы почти невозможно без них, имея в виду широту сети. Нужно только набрать ключевое слово и поисковая система список Website, которые относятся к теме. Они позволяют поиск по ключевым словам на любом языке, и многие поисковые системы позволяют ограничить поиск отдельной страной или языком, таким образом увеличивая число удачных результатов поиска по выбранной теме.

Поисковая система	Адрес
AltaVista	http://www.altavista.digital.com
Excite	http://www.excite. com
HotBot	http://www.hotbot.com
Infoseek	http://www.infoseek.com
Lycos	http://www.uk.lycos.de
LookSmart	http://www.looksmart.com
Webcrawler	http://www.webcrawler.com
Yahoo!	http://www.yahoo.com
	http://www.yahoo.co.uk

Указатели адресов электронной почты*

Они работают, как поисковые системы, но занимаются поиском личных адресов электронной почты во всем мире.

Directory	Адрес
Four11 Email Directory	http://www.four11.com
The Ultimate Email Directory	http://www.theultimates.com/email

▶ Информационные Website

Site	Адрес
BBC	http://www.bbc.co.uk
CNN Interactive	http://www.cnn.com
The Economist	http://www.economist.co.uk
New York Times	http://www.nytimes.com
Reuters	http://www.reuters.com
Time Magazine	http://www.time.com
The Times (London)	http://www.the-times.co.uk

Эта иллюстрация показывает типичный интерфейс Internet

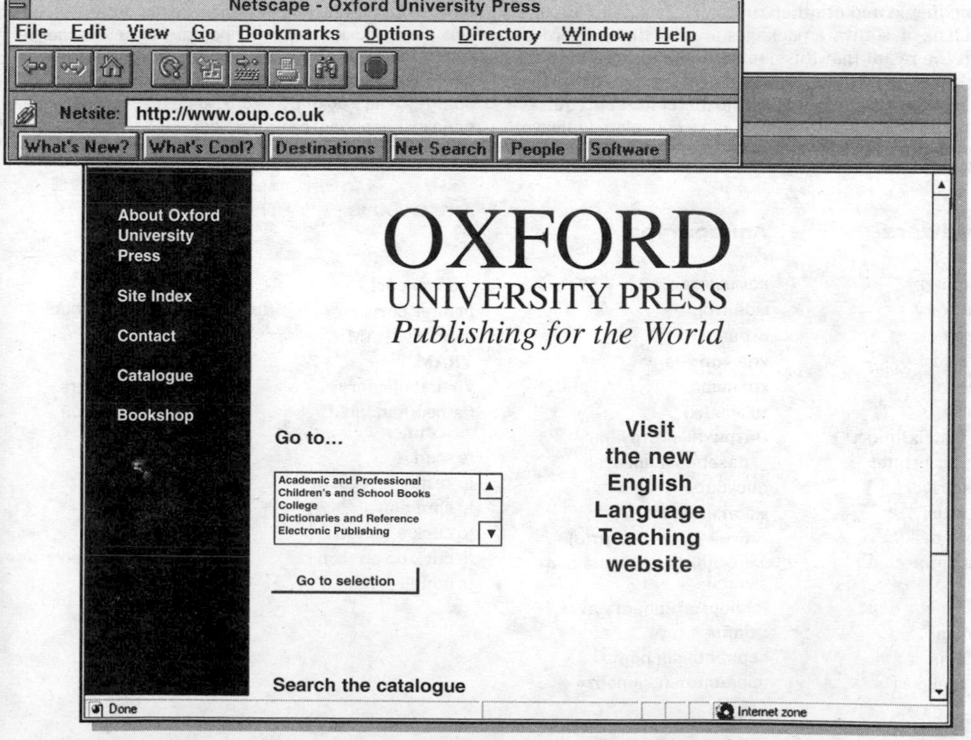

▶ Адреса образовательных Website

Site	Адрес
The Discovery Channel	http://www.discovery.com
National Geographic	http://www.nationalgeographic.com
English Server	http://english-server.hss.cmu.edu
Oxford University Press	http://www.oup.co.uk
Travlang	http://www.travlang.com
Yahooligans!	http://www.yahooligans.com

▶ Адреса Website по искусству и культуре

Site	Адрес
All Music Guide	http://www.allmusic.com
Internet Movie Database	http://www.imdb.com
Museum of Modern Art	http://www.moma.org

Russian Computer Speak/ Русский компьютерный жаргон

The Russian language is evolving rapidly. A massive influx of Western ways and goods has brought in its wake a vast number of foreign borrowings, mostly from English. In few areas has this been more marked than in that of computer terminology. English words now regularly appear in Latin script in the middle of a Russian sentence, in some cases with Russian grammatical terminations added. This makes it hard to determine with any degree of certainty which words have been fully assimilated and which are still regarded as 'exotic' Anglicisms. The terms 'Internet' and 'Web', for example, are sometimes seen in Latin characters and sometimes in Cyrillic. Sometimes they are treated as indeclinable and at other times are declined. Russian versions of software packages are not that numerous with the result that Russians are quite accustomed to working with Anglo-American versions. Many terms are never translated and have no direct Russian equivalent. The following, though, may be considered to have genuine Russian counterparts.

Русский язык быстро развивается. Большой наплыв западных новшеств и товаров принес огромное количество иностранных заимствований, преимущественно из английского языка. В особенности это относится к компьютерной терминологии. Сейчас можно встретить английские слова, написанные латинскими буквами в середине русского предложения, иногда к ним добавляются русские грамматические окончания. Поэтому трудно точно сказать, какие слова полностью ассимилировались и какие еще считаются 'экзотическими' англицизмами. Даже термины Internet и Web, к примеру, можно встретить написанными или латинским или русским шрифтом. В некоторых случаях они считаются несклоняемыми, а в других их склоняют. Так как русских версий программного обеспечения мало, русские пользователи привыкли к работе с англоязычными версиями. Многие термины не переводятся и не имеют русского эквивалента. Следующие, однако, переводятся на русский.

Hardware	Аппарату́ра
computer	компью́тер
monitor	монито́р
screen	экра́н
keyboard	клавиату́ра
key	кла́виша
mouse	мышь (ж)
dot matrix/inkjet/laser printer	ма́тричный/стру́йный/ла́зерный при́нтер
disk drive	дисково́д
hard disk	жёсткий диск
floppy disk	ги́бкий диск, диске́т(а)
write protected	защищён, защищена́ ... от за́писи
to format a disk	(с)формати́ровать диск
modem	моде́м
serial port	сериа́льный порт
parallel port	паралле́льный порт
modem port	моде́мный порт
printer port	порт печа́ти
memory (RAM)	па́мять (ж)
VRAM	видеопа́мять (ж)
virtual memory	виртуа́льная па́мять
flatbed/handheld scanner	планше́тный/ручно́й ска́нер
to scan	скани́ровать
to restart/reboot	перезагрузи́ть
to shut down	усыпи́ть
to click a button	нажа́ть на кно́пку
to click on an icon	щёлкнуть на карти́нку
to double-click	два́жды щёлкнуть

Software	**Програ́ммное обеспече́ние**
operating system	операцио́нная систе́ма
to install	установи́ть
installation	устано́вка
to reinstall	переустанови́ть
application	приложе́ние
control panel	пульт
utility	ути́лита
driver	дра́йвер
word processor	текстово́й реда́ктор
spreadsheet	табли́ца
database	ба́за да́нных
desktop publisher	насто́льная изда́тельская систе́ма
graphics	гра́фика
graphics package	графи́ческая програ́мма
multimedia	мультиме́диа
mail package	почто́вая програ́мма
browser	бро́узер
virus	ви́рус
window	окно́
desktop	стол
folder	па́пка
alias	псевдони́м
(default) font	шрифт (по умолча́нию)
template	шабло́н
toolbar	пане́ль (ж) инструме́нтов
status bar	строка́ ста́туса
scroll bar	лине́йка прокру́тки
menu bar	лине́йка меню́
pull-down/pop-up menu	выпада́ющее/всплыва́ющее меню́
File	Файл
Open	Откры́ть
Close	Закры́ть
Save	Сохрани́ть
Print	Распеча́тать
Import	И́мпорт
Export	Э́кспорт
Exit	Вы́ход
Quit	Заверши́ть
Edit	Реда́ктор
Cut	Вы́резать
Copy	Скопи́ровать
Paste	Помести́ть, Вста́вить
Delete/Erase	Стере́ть
Select all	Вы́брать всё
View	Просмо́тр
Options	Пара́метры
dialog	диало́г
Cancel	Отмени́ть
Confirm	Подтверди́ть
highlighted	вы́деленный
data	да́нные
saved	сохранён, сохранена́ ...
corrupted	повреждён, повреждена́... испо́рчен, испо́рчена
text file	те́кстовый файл

Getting connected	**Подключе́ние к се́ти**
to connect to	подключи́ться к
network	сеть (ж)
file sharing	о́бщий до́ступ
terminal	термина́л
(file) server	(фа́йловый) се́рвер
log in	вы́ход из систе́мы
log out	вход в систе́му
to enter a password	набра́ть паро́ль (м)
the Web	веб, паути́на
website	ве́бсайт
bookmark	закла́дка
home page	дома́шняя страни́ца, страни́чка
hypertext	гиперте́кст
link	ссы́лка
cache	кеш, бу́фер
online (adj.)	онла́йновый
news group	гру́ппа новосте́й
search	по́иск
search engine	по́исковая систе́ма
request	запро́с
to upload	вы́грузить
to download	загрузи́ть
file transfer	переда́ча фа́йлов
transfer rate	ско́рость (ж) обме́на да́нными
archive	архи́в
to archive	архиви́ровать
to encode	закоди́ровать
encoder	кодиро́вщик
encoding	кодиро́вка
to decode	раскоди́ровать
compression	компре́ссия
decompression	декомпре́ссия
video-conference	видео-конфере́нция

Email	**Электро́нная по́чта**
mailbox	почто́вый я́щик
mail server	почто́вый се́рвер
email address	электро́нный а́дрес
address book	записна́я кни́жка, спра́вочник
sender	отправи́тель (м)
recipient	получа́тель (м)
new message	но́вое сообще́ние
attachment	приложе́ние

*The website addresses were accurate at the time of going to press. Oxford University Press cannot be held responsible for any subsequent changes.

***Ко времени выхода в печать даны правильные адреса Website. Oxford University Press не несет ответственности за возможные изменения.**

A [eɪ] *letter*: **from ~ to Z** от нача́ла до конца́; **~ road** магистра́льная доро́га; **A1** *adj.* (*coll.*) первокла́ссный.

A [eɪ] *n.* **1.** (*mus.*) ля (*nt. indecl.*). **2.** (*acad. mark*) «отли́чно», «пятёрка»; **he got an ~ in physics** он получи́л «отли́чно» *or* «пятёрку» по фи́зике.

a [ə, eɪ], **an** [æn, ən] *indef. art.* **1.** *not usu. translated*: **it's an elephant** э́то слон. **2.** (*~ certain*): **~ Mr. Smith rang** звони́л не́кий господи́н Смит; **in ~ sense** в како́м-то смы́сле; **an old friend of mine** оди́н мой ста́рый знако́мый. **3.** (*distributive*, *in each*) в+*a.*; **twice ~ week** два ра́за в неде́лю; **10 miles an hour** де́сять миль в час; (*for each*) за+*a.*; **50p ~ pound** 50 пе́нсов за фунт; (*to each*): **he gave out £5 ~ person** он вы́дал ка́ждому по пять фу́нтов; (*from each*) с+*g.*; **they charged £1 ~ head** они́ взя́ли по фу́нту с челове́ка.

AA (*abbr. of* ***Automobile Association***) Ассоциа́ция автомобили́стов.

aback [ə'bæk] *adv.*: **I was taken ~ by his audacity** я растеря́лся от его́ на́глости.

abacus ['æbəkəs] *n.* счё|ты (*pl.*, *g.* -ов).

abandon [ə'bænd(ə)n] *n.* несде́ржанность, самозабве́ние; **with ~** не сде́рживаясь; самозабве́нно.

v.t. **1.** (*forsake*, *desert*) пок|ида́ть, -и́нуть; **~ ship!** поки́нуть кора́бль! **2.** (*renounce*) отка́з|ываться, -а́ться от+*g.*; **they had ~ed all hope** они́ потеря́ли вся́кую наде́жду. **3.** (*discontinue*) прекра|ща́ть, -ти́ть. **4.** (*surrender*): **the town was ~ed to the enemy** го́род был оста́влен врагу́.

abandoned [ə'bænd(ə)nd] *adj.* оста́вленный, забро́шенный.

abandonment [ə'bændənmənt] *n.* **1.** (*forsaking*) оставле́ние. **2.** (*being forsaken*) забро́шенность. **3.** (*renunciation*) отка́з (*от чего*). **4.** (*termination*) прекраще́ние.

abase [ə'beɪs] *v.t.* ун|ижа́ть, -и́зить.

abasement [ə'beɪsmənt] *n.* униже́ние.

abash [ə'bæʃ] *v.t.* сму|ща́ть, -ти́ть.

abate [ə'beɪt] *v.i.* (*diminish*) ум|еньша́ться, -е́ньшиться; (*weaken*) ослаб|ева́ть, -е́ть; (*of storm*, *epidemic etc.*) ут|иха́ть, -и́хнуть.

abatement [ə'beɪtmənt] *n.* (*reduction*) уменьше́ние; (*weakening*) ослабле́ние; (*lowering*) сниже́ние; **noise ~** сниже́ние у́ровня шу́ма; (*of storm etc.*) затиха́ние.

abattoir ['æbə,twɑ:(r)] *n.* скотобо́йня.

abbess ['æbɪs] *n.* аббати́са.

abbey ['æbɪ] *n.* абба́тство.

abbot ['æbət] *n.* абба́т.

abbreviate [ə'bri:vɪ,eɪt] *v.t.* сокра|ща́ть, -ти́ть.

abbreviation [ə,bri:vɪ'eɪʃ(ə)n] *n.* сокраще́ние.

ABC [,eɪbi:'si:] *n.* (*alphabet*) а́збука, алфави́т; **it's as easy as ~** э́то (про́сто) как два́жды два — четы́ре; (*reading primer*) буква́рь (*m.*); а́збука; (*fig.*, *rudiments*) а́збука; осно́вы (*f. pl.*).

abdicate ['æbdɪ,keɪt] *v.t.* отка́з|ываться, -а́ться от+*g.*; **~ the throne** (*also* ~ *v.i.*) отр|ека́ться, -е́чься от престо́ла.

abdication [,æbdɪ'keɪʃ(ə)n] *n.* отка́з (*от чего*); отрече́ние (от престо́ла).

abdomen ['æbdəmən] *n.* живо́т.

abdominal [æb'dɒmɪn(ə)l] *adj.* брюшно́й; **~ pain** боль в животе́.

abduct [əb'dʌkt] *v.t.* пох|ища́ть, -и́тить; (наси́льно) ув|ози́ть, -езти́.

abduction [əb'dʌkʃ(ə)n] *n.* похище́ние; уво́з.

abductor [əb'dʌktə(r)] *n.* похити́тель (*m.*).

aberrant [ə'berənt] *adj.* анорма́льный.

aberration [,æbə'reɪʃ(ə)n] *n.* **1.** (*error of judgement or conduct*) заблужде́ние; **mental ~** помраче́ние созна́ния. **2.** (*deviation*) отклоне́ние от но́рмы.

abet [ə'bet] *v.t.* подстрека́ть (*impf.*) к+*d.*; **he was ~ted by X** его́ посо́бником был X.

abettor [ə'betə(r)] *n.* посо́бник.

abeyance [ə'beɪəns] *n.* **1.** (*suspension*) вре́менная отме́на. **2. in ~: the matter is in ~** де́ло вре́менно прекращено́.

abhor [əb'hɔ:(r)] *v.t.* пита́ть (*impf.*) (*or* испы́т|ывать, -а́ть) отвраще́ние к+*d.*; **nature ~s a vacuum** приро́да не те́рпит пустоты́.

abhorrence [əb'hɒrəns] *n.* отвраще́ние.

abhorrent [əb'hɒrənt] *adj.* отврати́тельный.

abidance [ə'baɪdəns] *n.*: **~ by the rules** соблюде́ние пра́вил.

abide [ə'baɪd] *v.t.* терпе́ть (*impf.*); выноси́ть (*impf.*).

v.i. **1.** (*remain*) пребыва́ть (*impf.*). **2.**: **~ by** (*comply with*) приде́рживаться (*impf.*) +*g.*; **~ by the law** соблюда́ть (*impf.*) зако́н.

abiding [ə'baɪdɪŋ] *adj.* постоя́нный, неизме́нный.

ability [ə'bɪlɪtɪ] *n.* **1.** (*capacity in general*) спосо́бность; **to the best of one's ~** по ме́ре спосо́бностей; **he shows an ~ for music** он проявля́ет музыка́льные спосо́бности; (*knowing how*) уме́ние; (*mental competence*) спосо́бность; **a man of ~** спосо́бный челове́к. **2.** (*pl.*, *gifts*) спосо́бности (*f. pl.*); **natural ~** врождённые спосо́бности.

abject ['æbdʒekt] *adj.* (*humble*) уни́женный; (*despicable*) презре́нный; (*pitiful*, *wretched*) жа́лкий; **in ~ poverty** в кра́йней нищете́.

ablaze [ə'bleɪz] *pred. adj.*: **the buildings were ~** зда́ния бы́ли охва́чены огнём.

adv.: **set a house ~** подж|ига́ть, -е́чь дом.

able ['eɪb(ə)l] *adj.* **1.**: **be ~ to** мочь, с-; быть в состоя́нии; (*have the strength or power to*): **he was not ~ to walk any farther** он был не в си́лах идти́ да́льше; (*know how to*) уме́ть (*impf.*): **he is ~ to swim** он уме́ет пла́вать. **2.** (*skilful*) уме́лый; (*capable*) спосо́бный.

cpd. **~-bodied** *adj.* здоро́вый, кре́пкий; (*mil.*) го́дный к вое́нной слу́жбе.

ablution [ə'blu:ʃ(ə)n] *n.* (*usu. pl.*, *act of washing o.s.*) умыва́ние; **perform one's ~s** мы́ться, вы́-; ум|ыва́ться, -ы́ться.

abnormal [æb'nɔːm(ə)l] *adj.* ненорма́льный; (*deviating from type*) анома́льный.

abnormality [ˌæbnɔː'mælɪtɪ] *n.* ненорма́льность; анома́лия.

aboard [ə'bɔːd] *adv.* **1.** (*on a ship*) на корабле́; (*ship or aircraft*) на борту́. **2.** (*on to a ship etc.*) на кора́бль; на́ борт; **all ~!** поса́дка зака́нчивается!; (*rail.*) по ваго́нам!; **go ~** сади́ться, сесть на су́дно *и т.п.*; **take ~** взять (*pf.*) на́ борт.

prep.: **~ ship** на борт(у́) корабля́.

abode [ə'bəʊd] *n.* жили́ще; **of no fixed ~** без постоя́нного местожи́тельства.

abolish [ə'bɒlɪʃ] *v.t.* уничт|ожа́ть, -о́жить; (*laws, taxes etc.*) отмен|я́ть, -и́ть; (*customs etc.*) упраздн|я́ть, -и́ть.

abolition [ˌæbə'lɪʃ(ə)n] *n.* уничтоже́ние; отме́на; упраздне́ние.

abominable [ə'bɒmɪnəb(ə)l] *adj.* отврати́тельный.

abominate [ə'bɒmɪˌneɪt] *v.t.* пита́ть (*impf.*) отвраще́ние к+*d*.

abomination [əˌbɒmɪ'neɪʃ(ə)n] *n.* (*detestation*) отвраще́ние; (*detestable thg.*): **this building is an ~** э́то зда́ние про́сто у́жас.

aboriginal [ˌæbə'rɪdʒɪn(ə)l] *adj.* тузе́мный, коренно́й; (*primitive*) первобы́тный.

aborigine [ˌæbə'rɪdʒɪnɪ] *n.* тузе́м|ец (*fem.* -ка); абориге́н.

abort [ə'bɔːt] *v.t.* **1.** (*terminate pregnancy of*) де́лать, с- або́рт +*d*. **2.** (*fig., terminate or cancel prematurely*) приостан|а́вливать, -ови́ть.

abortion [ə'bɔːʃ(ə)n] *n.* **1.** (*miscarriage*) або́рт, вы́кидыш; **she had an ~** (*by surgery*) она́ сде́лала або́рт. **2.** (*cancellation*) прекраще́ние.

abortionist [ə'bɔːʃənɪst] *n.* подпо́льный акуше́р.

abortive [ə'bɔːtɪv] *adj.* (*fig.*) мертворождённый; неуда́вшийся.

abound [ə'baʊnd] *v.i.* **1.** (*exist in large numbers or quantities*) быть в изоби́лии. **2.: ~ in** (*be rich in*) изоби́ловать (*impf.*) +*i*.; **the country ~s in oil** страна́ бога́та не́фтью.

about [ə'baʊt] *adv.* **1.** (*here and there*): **don't leave your clothes ~** не оставля́йте свое́й оде́жды, где попа́ло. **2.** (*in the vicinity*; *in circulation*) вокру́г, круго́м; **is he anywhere ~?** нет его́ где́-нибудь побли́зости?; **up and ~** на нога́х. **3.** (*to face the other way*): **~ turn!** (*mil.*) круго́м!; (*alternately*) **turn and turn ~** по о́череди. **4.** (*almost*) почти́; **that's ~ right** приме́рно так; **it's ~ time we went** пора́ бы нам идти́; **and ~ time too!** давно́ пора́! **5.** (*approximately*) о́коло+*g*.; приблизи́тельно; **~ 3 o'clock** о́коло трёх часо́в; **he is ~ your height** он приблизи́тельно ва́шего ро́ста; **it costs ~ £100** э́то сто́ит фу́нтов сто; **in ~ half an hour** че́рез каки́е-нибудь полчаса́. **6. ~ to** (*ready to, just going to*): **I was ~ to say** я собира́лся сказа́ть; **the train is ~ to leave** по́езд сейча́с тро́нется. **7.** *For phrasal vv. with ~, see relevant v. entries.*

prep. **1.** (*around*; *near*) вокру́г+*g*.; **somewhere ~ here** где́-то здесь; **I have no money ~ me** у меня́ нет при себе́ де́нег. **2.** (*at or to var. places, in*) по +*d*.; **walk ~ the streets** ходи́ть (*indet.*) по у́лицам. **3.** (*fig., in*) в+*p*.; **there was no vanity ~ him** в нём не́ было тщесла́вия. **4.** (*concerning*) о+*p*.; насчёт+*g*.; по по́воду+*g*.; относи́тельно+*g*.; **what are you talking ~?** о чём вы говори́те?; **how ~ a game of cards?** не сыгра́ть ли нам в ка́рты?; **what is it all ~?** в чём де́ло?; **he has called ~ the rent** он зашёл насчёт квартпла́ты; **much ado ~ nothing** мно́го шу́ма из ничего́; **there is no doubt ~ it** в э́том нет сомне́ния. **5.** (*engaged in*): **be ~ one's business** занима́ться (*impf.*) свои́ми дела́ми.

cpds. **~-face, ~-turn** *nn.* (*lit.*) поворо́т круго́м; (*fig.*) ре́зкое измене́ние.

above [ə'bʌv] *n.*: **the ~** вышеупомя́нутое; вышеизло́женное.

adj. (**~-*mentioned***) вышеупомя́нутый; (*foregoing*) предыду́щий.

adv. **1.** (*overhead*; *upstairs*) наверху́; **we live in the flat ~** мы живём в кварти́ре этажо́м вы́ше; (*expr. motion*) наве́рх; **from ~** све́рху. **2.** (*higher up*) вы́ше. **3.** (*in text, speech etc.*) вы́ше; ра́ньше.

prep. **1.** (*over*; *higher than*) над+*i*.; вы́ше+*g*.; **his voice was heard ~ the noise** его́ го́лос доноси́лся сквозь шум. **2.** (*more than*) свы́ше+*g*. **3.** (*fig.*): **~ me in rank** вы́ше меня́ чи́ном; **~ all praise** вы́ше вся́ких похва́л; **~ suspicion** вне подозре́ния; **he is living ~ his means** он живёт не по сре́дствам; **~ all** пре́жде/бо́льше всего́; са́мое гла́вное; **over and ~** вдоба́вок к+*d*.; **this is ~ my head** э́то вы́ше моего́ понима́ния.

cpds. **~-board** *adj.* (*honourable*) че́стный; (*open, frank*) откры́тый; **~-mentioned** *adj.* вышеупомя́нутый.

abracadabra [ˌæbrəkə'dæbrə] *n.* абракада́бра.

abrade [ə'breɪd] *v.t.* сдира́ть, содра́ть.

abrasion [ə'breɪʒ(ə)n] *n.* сса́дина.

abrasive [ə'breɪsɪv] *n.* абрази́вный материа́л.

adj. сдира́ющий, обдира́ющий; (*fig.*) колю́чий; **an ~ personality** ре́зкий хара́ктер.

abreast [ə'brest] *adv.* в ряд; **three ~** по́ трое в ряд; (*fig.*): **~ of events** в ку́рсе собы́тий.

abridge [ə'brɪdʒ] *v.t.* **1.** (*shorten*) сокра|ща́ть, -ти́ть. **2.** (*curtail*) ограни́чи|вать, -ть.

abridgement [ə'brɪdʒmənt] *n.* сокраще́ние; ограниче́ние.

abroad [ə'brɔːd] *adv.* за грани́цей/рубежо́м; (*motion*) за грани́цу; **from ~** из-за грани́цы; (*fig., in circulation*): **there are rumours ~** хо́дят слу́хи.

abrogate ['æbrəˌgeɪt] *v.t.* отмен|я́ть, -и́ть.

abrogation [ˌæbrə'geɪʃ(ə)n] *n.* отме́на.

abrupt [ə'brʌpt] *adj.* **1.** (*disconnected*) отры́вистый. **2.** (*brusque*) ре́зкий. **3.** (*sudden*) внеза́пный. **4.** (*steep, precipitous*) крутой, обры́вистый.

abruptness [ə'brʌptnɪs] *n.* отры́вистость; ре́зкость; внеза́пность; крутизна́.

abscess ['æbsɪs] *n.* абсце́сс.

abscond [əb'skɒnd] *v.i.* скр|ыва́ться, -ы́ться.

abseil ['æbseɪl, -ziːl] *n.* спуск на верёвке.

v.i. спус|ка́ться, -ти́ться на верёвке.

absence ['æbs(ə)ns] *n.* отсу́тствие; **in his ~** в его́ отсу́тствие; **leave of ~** о́тпуск.

absent[1] ['æbs(ə)nt] *adj.* отсу́тствующий; **~ without leave** в самово́льной отлу́чке; **be ~** отсу́тствовать (*impf.*); **he was ~ from school** его́ не́ было в шко́ле.

cpds. **~-minded** *adj.* рассе́янный; **~-mindedness** *n.* рассе́янность.

absent[2] [əb'sent] *v.t.*: **~ o.s.** отлуч|а́ться, -и́ться (от+*g*.).

absentee [ˌæbsən'tiː] *n.* отсу́тствующий; **there were six ~s** отсу́тствовало шесть челове́к.

absenteeism [ˌæbsən'tiːɪz(ə)m] *n.* абсентеи́зм; прогу́л.

absinth(e) ['æbsɪnθ] *n.* (*liqueur*) полы́нная во́дка, абсе́нт.

absolute ['æbsəˌluːt, -ˌljuːt] *adj.* (*perfect*): **~ beauty** соверше́нная красота́; **~ monarchy** абсолю́тная мона́рхия; (*consummate*): **an ~ ruffian** зако́нченный негодя́й; (*indubitable*): **~ proof** несомне́нное доказа́тельство.

absolutely ['æbsəˌluːtlɪ, -ˌljuːtlɪ] *adv.* **1.** (*completely*) вполне́, абсолю́тно; соверше́нно; (*unquestionably*) безусло́вно. **2. ~!** (*expr. agreement*) безусло́вно/коне́чно!

absolution [ˌæbsə'luːʃ(ə)n, -'ljuːʃ(ə)n] *n.* (*forgiveness*) проще́ние; (*eccl.*) отпуще́ние грехо́в.

absolutism ['æbsəluːˌtɪz(ə)m, -ljuːˌtɪz(ə)m] *n.* абсолюти́зм.

absolutist ['æbsə,lu:tɪst, -,lju:tɪst] *n.* абсолютист.
adj. абсолютистский.
absolve [əb'zɒlv] *v.t.* (*of blame*) призн|авáть, -áть невинóвным; (*of sins*) отпус|кáть, -тúть грехú +*d.*; (*of obligation*) освобо|ждáть, -дúть.
absorb [əb'sɔ:b, -'zɔ:b] *v.t.* **1.** (*soak up*) вс|áсывать, -осáть. **2.** (*fig.*): ~ **knowledge** впúт|ывать, -áть знáния. **3.** (*engross*) погло|щáть, -тúть; **he was ~ed in reading** он был погружён в чтéние. **4.** (*of shock, vibration etc.*) амортизúровать (*impf., pf.*).
absorbent [əb'sɔ:bənt, -'zɔ:bənt] *adj.* всáсывающий, поглощáющий; ~ **cotton** (*US*) (гигроскопúческая) вáта.
absorbing [əb'sɔ:bɪŋ, -'zɔ:bɪŋ] *adj.* (*engrossing*) захвáтывающий.
absorption [əb'sɔ:pʃ(ə)n, -'zɔ:pʃ(ə)n] *n.* **1.** (*soaking up*) всáсывание; впúтывание. **2.** (*engrossment*): **his ~ in his studies** егó погружённость в занятия.
abstain [əb'steɪn] *v.i.* воздéрж|иваться, -áться; **the Opposition ~ed (from voting)** оппозúция воздержáлся (от голосовáния).
abstainer [əb'steɪnə(r)] *n.* воздержáвшийся.
abstemious [æb'sti:mɪəs] *adj.* воздéржанный.
abstemiousness [æb'sti:mɪəsnɪs] *n.* воздéржанность.
abstention [əb'stenʃ(ə)n] *n.* воздержáние (*от чего*): **the resolution was passed with three ~s** резолюция былá принятá при трёх воздержáвшихся.
abstinence ['æbstɪnəns] *n.* воздержáние (*от чего*).
abstract[1] ['æbstrækt] *n.* (*summary*) резюмé (*indecl.*); (*of dissertation*) реферáт; **in the ~** в абстрáкции; отвлечённо.
adj. отвлечённый; абстрáктный; ~ **art** абстрáктное искýсство.
abstract[2] [əb'strækt] *v.t.* **1.** (*summarize*) резюмúровать (*impf., pf.*). **2.** (*consider ~ly*) абстрагúровать (*impf., pf.*).
abstraction [əb'strækʃ(ə)n] *n.* **1.** (*process of thought or idea*) отвлечéние; абстрáкция. **2.** (*absence of mind*) рассéянность.
abstruse [əb'stru:s] *adj.* замысловáтый, мудрёный.
absurd [əb'sɜ:d] *adj.* нелéпый, абсýрдный; **don't be ~!** какóй вздор!; **she looks ~ in that hat** в э́той шля́пе у неё нелéпый вид; **he was ~ly generous** он был до абсýрда щедр.
absurdity [əb'sɜ:dɪtɪ] *n.* нелéпость, абсýрдность; **reduce to ~** дов|одúть, -естú до абсýрда.
abundance [ə'bʌnd(ə)ns] *n.* (*plenty*) изобúлие; **there was food in ~** еды́ бы́ло вдóволь; **live in ~** жить в достáтке; (*superfluity*) избы́ток.
abundant [ə'bʌnd(ə)nt] *adj.* (из)обúльный (*чем*); **be ~** изобúловать (*impf.*); **~ly clear** предéльно я́сно.
abuse[1] [ə'bju:s] *n.* **1.** (*misuse*; *corrupt practice*) злоупотреблéние; **~ of confidence** злоупотреблéние довéрием. **2.** (*reviling*) рýгань, брань.
abuse[2] [ə'bju:z] *v.t.* **1.** (*misuse*) злоупотреб|ля́ть, -úть +*i.* **2.** (*revile*) ругáть (*impf.*); оскорб|ля́ть, -úть.
abusive [ə'bju:sɪv] *adj.* (*insulting*) оскорбúтельный; (*using curses*) брáнный, ругáтельный.
abut [ə'bʌt] *v.i.*: ~ **on** прилегáть (*impf.*) к+*d.*; примыкáть (*impf.*) к+*d.*
abutment [ə'bʌtmənt] *n.* **1.** (*junction*) стык. **2.** (*part of structure*) пятá; контрфóрс.
abysmal [ə'bɪzm(ə)l] *adj.* безграничный; ужасáющий.
abyss [ə'bɪs] *n.* бéздна, прóпасть.
AC (*abbr. of* **alternating current**) перемéнный ток.
acacia [ə'keɪʃə] *n.* акáция.
academia [,ækə'di:mɪə] *n.* академúческий мир.
academic [,ækə'demɪk] *n.* учёный.
adj. академúческий; ~ **year** учéбный год; (*unpractical*) кабинéтный.
academician [ə,kædə'mɪʃ(ə)n] *n.* академик.
academy [ə'kædəmɪ] *n.* акадéмия; учúлище; **military ~** воéнное учúлище.
accede [æk'si:d] *v.i.* **1.** (*agree, assent*) согла|шáться, -сúться (с+*i.*). **2.**: ~ **to** (*grant*): ~ **to a request** удовлетвор|я́ть, -úть прóсьбу; (*assume*) вступ|áть, -úть в+*a.*; ~ **to the throne** взойтú (*pf.*) на престóл.
accelerate [ək'selə,reɪt] *v.t. & i.* уск|оря́ть(ся), -óрить(ся); (*motoring*) да|вáть, -ть газ.
acceleration [ək,selə'reɪʃ(ə)n] *n.* ускорéние.
accelerator [ək'selə,reɪtə(r)] *n.* (*of car*) акселерáтор; (*phys., etc.*) ускорúтель (*m.*).
accent[1] ['æks(ə)nt, -sent] *n.* **1.** (*orthographical sign*; *emphasis*) ударéние; акцéнт. **2.** (*mode of speech*) акцéнт.
accent[2] [æk'sent] *v.t.* **1.** (*emphasize*) дéлать, с- ударéние/акцéнт на+*p.*; акцентúровать (*impf.*). **2.** (*put written ~s on*) стáвить, по- ударéние на+*a.*
accentuate [æk'sentjʊ,eɪt] *v.t.* акцентúровать (*impf.*); подч|ёркивать, -еркнýть.
accept [ək'sept] *v.t.* **1.** (*agree to receive*) прин|имáть, -я́ть. **2.** (*recognize, admit*) призн|авáть, -áть; **I ~ that it may take time** не спóрю, что для э́того потрéбуется врéмя; **it is an ~ed fact** э́то общепризнанный факт.
acceptability [ək,septə'bɪlɪtɪ] *n.* приéмлемость.
acceptable [ək'septəb(ə)l] *adj.* приéмлемый.
acceptance [ək'sept(ə)ns] *n.* (*willing receipt*) приня́тие; (*approval*) одобрéние.
access ['ækses] *n.* (*possibility of reaching, using, etc.*) дóступ; (*means of approach*; *way in*) подхóд; ~ **road** подъезднóй путь.
accessibility [ək,sesɪ'bɪlɪtɪ] *n.* достýпность; удóбство подхóда.
accessible [ək'sesɪb(ə)l] *adj.* достýпный.
accession [ək'seʃ(ə)n] *n.* **1.** (*attaining*) вступлéние; ~ **to power** прихóд к влáсти; ~ **to the throne** вступлéние на престóл. **2.** (*of book into library etc.*) поступлéние.
accessory [ək'sesərɪ] *n.* **1.** соучáстник; ~ **to a crime** соучáстник преступлéния. **2.** *pl.* (*equipment*) принадлéжности (*f. pl.*); (*clothing*) аксессуáры (*m. pl.*).
adj. вспомогáтельный; дополнúтельный.
accident ['æksɪd(ə)nt] *n.* **1.** (*chance*) слýчай, случáйность; **by (sheer) ~** (чúсто) случáйно. **2.** (*unintentional action*): **I'm sorry, it was an ~** простúте, я нечáянно. **3.** (*mishap*) несчáстный слýчай; **road ~** автомобúльная катастрóфа; **his car met with an ~** егó автомобúль попáл в авáрию.
cpd. **~-prone** *adj.* невезýчий.
accidental [,æksɪ'dent(ə)l] *adj.* случáйный.
acclaim [ə'kleɪm] *n.* (*welcome*) привéтствие; (*applause*) овáция.
v.t. (*welcome*) привéтствовать (*impf.*); (*applaud*) бýрно аплодúровать (*impf.*) +*d.*
acclamation [,æklə'meɪʃ(ə)n] *n.* шýмное одобрéние; **his books won ~** егó кнúги вы́звали шýмное одобрéние.
acclimatization [ə,klaɪmətaɪ'zeɪʃ(ə)n] *n.* акклиматизáция.
acclimatize [ə'klaɪmə,taɪz] *v.t. & i.* акклиматизúровать(ся) (*impf., pf.*).
accolade ['ækə,leɪd, -'leɪd] *n.* похвалá; наградá.
accommodat|e [ə'kɒmə,deɪt] *v.t.* **1.** (*house*) разме|щáть, -стúть; (*single person*) поме|щáть, -стúть. **2.** (*hold, seat*) вме|щáть, -стúть; **a hall ~ing 500** зал на 500 человéк. **3.** (*oblige*) окáз|ывать, -áть услýгу +*d.* **4.** (*adapt*) приспос|обля́ть, -óбить; примен|я́ть, -úть; **she ~ed herself to circumstances** онá применúлась/приспосóбилась к обстоя́тельствам.
accommodating [ə'kɒmə,deɪtɪŋ] *adj.* сговóрчивый, услýжливый.
accommodation [ə,kɒmə'deɪʃ(ə)n] *n.* **1.** (*lodgings*) жильё; **hotel ~ is scarce** гостúничных мест не хватáет. **2.** (*adaptation*) приспособлéние. **3.** (*settlement*) соглашéние. **4.** (*convenience*) удóбство.

accompaniment [ə'kʌmpənɪmənt] *n.* **1.** (*accompanying*) сопровожде́ние. **2.** (*mus.*) аккомпанеме́нт.

accompanist [ə'kʌmpənɪst] *n.* (*mus.*) аккомпаниа́тор.

accompan|y [ə'kʌmpənɪ] *v.t.* **1.** (*lit.*, *go or be with*; *fig.*, *occur with*) сопровожда́ть (*impf.*); **~ied by friends** в сопровожде́нии друзе́й; (*escort*): **may I ~y you home?** разреши́те проводи́ть вас домо́й? **2.** (*fig.*, *supplement*) сопрово|жда́ть, -ди́ть (*что чем*); **your offer must be ~ied by a letter** ва́ше предложе́ние необходи́мо сопроводи́ть письмо́м. **3.** (*mus.*) аккомпани́ровать (*impf.*) +*d.*

accomplice [ə'kʌmplɪs, -'kɒm-] *n.* соуча́стник, соо́бщник.

accomplish [ə'kʌmplɪʃ, ə'kɒm-] *v.t.* (*complete*) заверш|а́ть, -и́ть; (*fulfil*, *perform*) выполня́ть, вы́полнить; соверш|а́ть, -и́ть.

accomplished [ə'kʌmplɪʃd, ə'kɒm-] *adj.* **1.** (*completed*) совершённый; **an ~ fact** соверши́вшийся факт. **2.** (*skilled*) соверше́нный, зако́нченный. **3.** (*egregious*): **an ~ liar** зако́нченный лгун.

accomplishment [ə'kʌmplɪʃmənt, ə'kɒm-] *n.* заверше́ние; выполне́ние; (*achievement*) достиже́ние; **a man of many ~s** разносторо́нний челове́к.

accord [ə'kɔːd] *n.* **1.** (*agreement*) согла́сие, соглаше́ние; **with one ~** единоду́шно; **be in ~ with** быть согла́сным с+*i.*; согласо́вываться (*impf.*) с+*i.* **2.** (*volition*): **of one's own ~** по со́бственному почи́ну; сам по себе́.

v.t. предост|авля́ть, -а́вить (*что кому*); **he was ~ed a hero's welcome** его́ встре́тили как геро́я.

v.i.: **~ with** быть в согла́сии с+*i.*; согласо́в|ываться, -а́ться с+*i.*

accordance [ə'kɔːd(ə)ns] *n.* соотве́тствие; **in ~ with** в соотве́тствии с+*i.*, согла́сно+*d.*

according [ə'kɔːdɪŋ] *adv.*: **~ to** (*in keeping or conformity with*) согла́сно+*d.*; **~ to the laws** согла́сно зако́нам; (*in a manner or degree consistent with*; *corresponding to*) в соотве́тствии с+*i.*, по+*d.*; (*depending on*): **~ to circumstances** в зави́симости от обстоя́тельств; (*on the authority or information of*) по+*d.*, согла́сно +*d.*; по мне́нию/слова́м/сообще́нию +*g.*

accordingly [ə'kɔːdɪŋlɪ] *adv.* **1.** (*as circumstances suggest*) соотве́тственно. **2.** (*therefore*) поэ́тому; таки́м о́бразом.

accordion [ə'kɔːdɪən] *n.* аккордео́н.

accordionist [ə'kɔːdɪənɪst] *n.* аккордеони́ст.

accost [ə'kɒst] *v.t.* прист|ава́ть, -а́ть к+*d.*

account [ə'kaʊnt] *n.* **1.** (*comm.*) счёт (*pl.* -а́); **current ~** теку́щий счёт; **joint ~** о́бщий счёт; **keep ~s** вести́ (*det.*) счета́; **can you give me a little on ~?** мо́жете ли вы мне дать небольшо́й зада́ток?; (*fig.*): **settle ~s with s.o.** (*take revenge*) свести́ (*pf.*) счёты с кем-н. **2.** (*description*) описа́ние; расска́з. **3.** (*purpose*; *benefit*) по́льза; вы́года; **turn sth. to (good) ~** извл|ека́ть, -е́чь по́льзу из чего́-н. **4.** (*statement*, *report*) отчёт; **by his own ~** по его́ со́бственным слова́м; **by all ~s** су́дя по всему́; **call to ~** приз|ыва́ть, -ва́ть (*кого*) к отве́ту; **give a good ~ of o.s.** хорошо́ показа́ть (*pf.*) себя́. **5.** (*consideration*) расчёт, значе́ние; **take into ~** уч|и́тывать, -е́сть; прин|има́ть, -я́ть в расчёт. **6.** (*reason*, *cause*): **on ~ of** (*for the sake of*) ра́ди+*g.*; (*because of*) из-за+*g.*; (*in consequence of*) по причи́не +*g.*; (*as a result of*) всле́дствие+*g.*; **on no ~** ни в ко́ем слу́чае.

v.i. **~ for:** (*lit.*, *fig.*, *give a reckoning of*) отчи́т|ываться, -а́ться в+*p.*; да|ва́ть, -ть отчёт в+*p.*; (*fig.*, *answer for*) отв|еча́ть, -е́тить за+*a.*; (*explain*) объясн|я́ть, -и́ть; **there's no ~ing for tastes** о вку́сах не спо́рят; (*be reason for*) явля́ться (*impf.*) причи́ной +*g.*; (*comprise*) сост|авля́ть, -а́вить.

accountability [ə,kaʊntə'bɪlɪtɪ] *n.* отве́тственность; (*for money*) подотчётность.

accountable [ə'kaʊntəb(ə)l] *adj.* отве́тственный; **he is ~ to me** он отчи́тывается пе́редо мной; **he is not ~ for his actions** он не отвеча́ет за свои́ посту́пки.

accountancy [ə'kaʊntənsɪ] *n.* счетово́дство, бухгалте́рия.

accountant [ə'kaʊnt(ə)nt] *n.* счетово́д, бухга́лтер.

accounting [ə'kaʊntɪŋ] *n.* (*profession*) бухга́лтерское де́ло.

accoutrements [ə'kuːtrəmənt, -təmənt] *n.* ли́чное снаряже́ние.

accredit [ə'kredɪt] *v.t.* аккредитова́ть (*impf.*, *pf.*).

accreditation [ə,kredɪ'teɪʃ(ə)n] *n.* аккредитова́ние.

accredited [ə'kredɪtɪd] *adj.* (*officially recognized*) аккредито́ванный; (*generally accepted*) общепри́нятый.

accretion [ə'kriːʃ(ə)n] *n.* прираще́ние, приро́ст.

accrue [ə'kruː] *v.i.* **1.** (*accumulate*) нараст|а́ть, -и́; **~d interest** наро́сшие проце́нты (*m. pl.*). **2.**: **~ to** (*fall to the lot of*) дост|ава́ться, -а́ться +*d.*

accumulate [ə'kjuːmjʊ,leɪt] *v.t.* нак|а́пливать, -опи́ть; **~d experience** нако́пленный о́пыт; **he ~d a fine library** он собра́л хоро́шую библиоте́ку.

v.i. накоп|ля́ться, -и́ться; скоп|ля́ться, -и́ться.

accumulation [ə,kjuːmjʊ'leɪʃ(ə)n] *n.* (*amassing*) накопле́ние; (*gathering together*) собра́ние.

accumulator [ə'kjuːmjʊ,leɪtə(r)] *n.* (*elec.*) аккумуля́тор.

accuracy ['ækjʊrəsɪ] *n.* то́чность; (*of aim or shot*) ме́ткость.

accurate ['ækjʊrət] *adj.* (*of persons*, *statements*, *instruments etc.*) то́чный; (*of aim or shot*) ме́ткий.

accursed [ə'kɜːsɪd, ə'kɜːst] *adj.* прокля́тый.

accusation [,ækjuː'zeɪʃ(ə)n] *n.* обвине́ние; **bring an ~ against** выдвига́ть, вы́двинуть обвине́ние про́тив+*g.*

accusative [ə'kjuːzətɪv] *adj.* вини́тельный; **~ case** вини́тельный паде́ж.

accusatory [ə'kjuːzətərɪ] *adj.* обвини́тельный.

accuse [ə'kjuːz] *v.t.* обвин|я́ть, -и́ть; **he was ~d of stealing** его́ обвини́ли в кра́же.

accused [ə'kjuːzd] *n.*: **the ~** обвиня́емый.

accuser [ə'kjuːzə(r)] *n.* обвини́тель (*m.*).

accusing [ə'kjuːzɪŋ] *adj.* укори́зненный, обвиня́ющий.

accustom [ə'kʌstəm] *v.t.* приуч|а́ть, -и́ть (**to**: к+*d.*); **~ o.s., become ~ed** прив|ыка́ть, -ы́кнуть (**to**: к+*d.*).

accustomed [ə'kʌstəmd] *adj.* (*usual*) обы́чный, привы́чный.

ace [eɪs] *n.* **1.** (*single pip on dice*, *cards*, *dominoes*) очко́. **2.** (*card*) туз. **3.** (*pilot*, *etc.*) ас. **4.**: **within an ~ of** на волосо́к от+*g.*

adj. (*coll.*) первокла́ссный.

acerbic [ə'sɜːbɪk] *adj.* (*astringent*) те́рпкий; (*of speech*, *manner etc.*) ре́зкий.

acerbity [ə'sɜːbɪtɪ] *n.* те́рпкость; ре́зкость.

acetate ['æsɪ,teɪt] *n.* ацета́т; уксуснокислая соль.

acetic [ə'siːtɪk] *adj.* у́ксусный.

acetone ['æsɪ,təʊn] *n.* ацето́н.

acetylene [ə'setɪ,liːn] *n.* ацетиле́н.

adj. ацетиле́новый.

ach|e [eɪk] *n.* боль.

v.i. боле́ть (*impf.*); ныть (*impf.*); **my head ~es** у меня́ боли́т голова́; **my bones ~e** у меня́ но́ют ко́сти; **my heart ~es for him** у меня́ душа́ боли́т за него́; **I ~e to see him** я жа́жду уви́деть его́.

achievable [ə'tʃiːvəb(ə)l] *adj.* достижи́мый.

achieve [ə'tʃiːv] *v.t.* дост|ига́ть, -и́чь +*g.*; доби́ться (*pf.*) +*g.*

achievement [ə'tʃiːvmənt] *n.* (*attainment*) достиже́ние; (*success*) успе́х, завоева́ние.

Achilles [ə'kɪliːz] *n.*: **~' heel** ахилле́сова пята́.

acid ['æsɪd] *n.* кислота́; **~ rain** кисло́тные дожди́; **~ test** (*fig.*) про́бный ка́мень.

adj. (*lit. and fig.*) ки́слый.
acidity [ə'sɪdɪtɪ] *n.* кисло́тность.
acknowledge [ək'nɒlɪdʒ] *v.t.* **1.** (*recognize; admit*) призн|ава́ть, -а́ть; **he refused to ~ defeat** он отказа́лся призна́ть пораже́ние. **2.** (*confirm receipt of*): **~ a letter** подтвер|жда́ть, -ди́ть получе́ние письма́; **~ a greeting** отве́тить (*pf.*) на приве́тствие.
acknowledg(e)ment [ək'nɒlɪdʒmənt] *n.* **1.** (*recognition, admission*) призна́ние. **2.** (*confirmation*) подтвержде́ние. **3.** (*reward*): **this is in ~ of your kindness** э́то в благода́рность за ва́шу доброту́.
acme ['ækmɪ] *n.* верх, верши́на.
acne ['æknɪ] *n.* угри́ (*m.pl.*).
acorn ['eɪkɔːn] *n.* жёлудь (*m.*).
acoustic [ə'kuːstɪk] *adj.* акусти́ческий.
acoustics [ə'kuːstɪks] *n.* аку́стика.
acquaint [ə'kweɪnt] *v.t.* знако́мить, по-; **I ~ed him with the facts** я ознако́мил его́ с фа́ктами; **be ~ed with s.o.** быть знако́мым с кем-н.
acquaintance [ə'kweɪnt(ə)ns] *n.* знако́мство; **make the ~ of** познако́миться (*pf.*) с+*i.*; **strike up an ~** зав|оди́ть, -ести́ знако́мство; (*pers.*) знако́мый; **an ~ of mine** оди́н мой знако́мый.
acquiesce [ˌækwɪ'es] *v.i.* (*agree tacitly*) согла|ша́ться, -си́ться.
acquiescence [ˌækwɪ'esəns] *n.* согла́сие.
acquiescent [ˌækwɪ'esənt] *adj.* усту́пчивый.
acquire [ə'kwaɪə(r)] *v.t.* приобре|та́ть, -сти́; **~ a habit** усв|а́ивать, -о́ить привы́чку; **asparagus is an ~d taste** к спа́рже на́до привы́кнуть.
acquisition [ˌækwɪ'zɪʃ(ə)n] *n.* приобрете́ние; поступле́ние; **the ~ of language** овладе́ние языко́м; **the library's new ~s** но́вые библиоте́чные поступле́ния.
acquisitive [ə'kwɪzɪtɪv] *adj.* стяжа́тельский.
acquisitiveness [ə'kwɪzɪtɪvnɪs] *n.* стяжа́тельство.
acquit [ə'kwɪt] *v.t.* **1.** (*declare not guilty*) опра́вд|ывать, -а́ть. **2.**: **~ o.s. well** хорошо́ прояви́ть (*pf.*) себя́.
acquittal [ə'kwɪt(ə)l] *n.* оправда́ние.
acre ['eɪkə(r)] *n.* акр.
acreage ['eɪkərɪdʒ] *n.* пло́щадь земли́ в а́крах.
acrid ['ækrɪd] *adj.* е́дкий (*lit., fig.*).
acrimonious [ˌækrɪ'məʊnɪəs] *adj.* язви́тельный, е́дкий.
acrimon|iousness [ˌækrɪ'məʊnɪəsnɪs], **-y** ['ækrɪmənɪ] *n.* язви́тельность, е́дкость.
acrobat ['ækrəˌbæt] *n.* акроба́т.
acrobatic [ˌækrə'bætɪk] *adj.* акробати́ческий.
acrobatics [ˌækrə'bætɪks] *n.* акроба́тика.
acronym ['ækrənɪm] *n.* аббревиату́ра.
acropolis [ə'krɒpəlɪs] *n.* акро́поль (*m.*).
across [ə'krɒs] *adv.* **1.** (*crosswise*) попёрек; (*in crosswords*) по горизонта́ли. **2.** (*on the other side*) на той стороне́; (*to the other side*) на ту сто́рону. **3.** (*in width*): **the river here is more than six miles ~** ширина́ реки́ здесь бо́льше шести́ миль.
prep. **1.** (*from one side of to the other*) че́рез+*a.*, *sometimes omitted with vv. compounded with* пере...; **he went ~ the street** он перешёл у́лицу; **they were talking ~ the table** они́ говори́ли че́рез стол. **2.** (*over the surface of*) по+*d.*; **he drew a line ~ the page** он провёл черту́ на страни́це; **he hit me ~ the face** он уда́рил меня́ по лицу́; **~ the board** (*fig.*) для всех; во всех слу́чаях. **3.** (*athwart*) попёрек+*g.* **4.** (*on the other side of*) на той стороне́ +*g.*, по ту сто́рону +*g.*; **he lives ~ (the street) from the park** он живёт напро́тив па́рка.
cpd. **~-the-board** *adj.* всео́бщий, поголо́вный; **an ~ agreement** всеобъе́млющее соглаше́ние.
acrostic [ə'krɒstɪk] *n.* акрости́х.
acrylic [ə'krɪlɪk] *n.* акри́л.
adj. акри́ловый.
act [ækt] *n.* **1.** (*action*) посту́пок; (*feat*) по́двиг; **~ of God** стихи́йное бе́дствие; **catch in the ~** пойма́ть (*pf.*) с поли́чным. **2.** (*document*) акт; **~ of sale** акт о прода́же. **3.** (*law*) акт, зако́н, постановле́ние; **~ of Parliament** парла́ментский акт. **4.** (*of drama*) де́йствие; **a 3-~ play** пье́са в трёх де́йствиях. **5.** (*performance*) но́мер; **circus ~** цирково́й но́мер; (*fig., coll.*): **put on an ~** притвор|я́ться, -и́ться.
v.t. игра́ть (*impf.*); **~ a part** (*lit., fig.*) игра́ть роль; **~ the fool** валя́ть (*impf.*) дурака́; **~ a play** игра́ть, разыгра́ть (*or* да|ва́ть, -ть) пье́су.
v.i. **1.** (*behave*) поступ|а́ть, -и́ть; вести́ (*det.*) себя́; (*take action, intervene*) прин|има́ть, -я́ть ме́ры; **~ on advice** сле́довать, по- сове́ту; **~ (up)on an order** де́йствовать (*impf.*) по прика́зу; **it is time to ~** пора́ де́йствовать. **2.** (*serve, function*) де́йствовать (*impf.*): **~ for s.o.** де́йствовать от и́мени кого́-л.; **~ against s.o.** выступа́ть, вы́ступить про́тив кого́-н.; **he is ~ing as interpreter** он слу́жит перево́дчиком. **3.** (*have or take effect*) де́йствовать, по- (**on:** на+*a*). **4.** (*theatr.*) игра́ть; **he wants to ~** он хо́чет игра́ть на сце́не.
with advs. **~ out** *v.t.* разы́гр|ывать, -а́ть; **~ up** *v.i.* (*coll., misbehave*) шали́ть (*impf.*), поша́ливать (*impf.*); (*give trouble*) **my car has been ~ing up** моя́ маши́на поша́ливает.
acting ['æktɪŋ] *n.* (*theatr.*) игра́; (*as skill*) актёрское мастерство́.
adj. (*doing duty temporarily*): **~ manager** исполня́ющий обя́занности (*abbr.* и.о.) заве́дующего.
action ['ækʃ(ə)n] *n.* **1.** (*acting; activity; effect*) де́йствие; **in ~** в де́йствии; **come into ~** вступ|а́ть, -и́ть в де́йствие; **bring into ~** вв|оди́ть, -ести́ в де́йствие; **put out of ~** выводи́ть, вы́вести из стро́я; **out of ~** него́дный к употребле́нию; **take ~** прин|има́ть, -я́ть ме́ры; **what we need is some ~** ну́жно де́йствовать. **2.** (*deed*) де́ло; **~s speak louder than words** дела́ говоря́т са́ми за себя́. **3.** (*functioning*): **the ~ of the heart** де́ятельность се́рдца; (*of a gun, piano etc.*) де́йствие. **4.** (*physical movement*) движе́ние. **5.** (*theatr.*): **the ~ takes place in London** де́йствие происхо́дит в Ло́ндоне. **7.** (*leg.*) иск, де́ло; **~ for damages** иск об убы́тках; **bring an ~ against** предъяв|ля́ть, -и́ть иск к+*d.* **8.** (*mil.*) бой; **killed in ~** уби́тый в бою́; **go into ~** вступ|а́ть, -и́ть в бой.
activate ['æktɪˌveɪt] *v.t.* прив|оди́ть, -ести́ в де́йствие.
active ['æktɪv] *adj.* **1.** (*lively; energetic; displaying activity*) де́ятельный, акти́вный; **take an ~ interest in** прояв|ля́ть, -и́ть живо́й интере́с к+*d.*; **an ~ brain** живо́й/де́ятельный ум; **an ~ volcano** де́йствующий вулка́н. **2.** (*gram.*) действи́тельный. **3.** (*phys., chem.*) акти́вный. **4.** (*mil.*): **on ~ service** на действи́тельной слу́жбе; **~ division** боева́я диви́зия.
activist ['æktɪvɪst] *n.* активи́ст (*fem.* -ка).
activit|y [æk'tɪvɪtɪ] *n.* **1.** (*being active; exertion of energy*) акти́вность. **2.** (*usu. pl., pursuit, sphere of action; doings*) де́ятельность.
actor ['æktə(r)] *n.* актёр.
actress ['æktrɪs] *n.* актри́са.
actual ['æktʃʊəl, 'æktjʊəl] *adj.* (*real*) действи́тельный; факти́ческий; (*genuine*) по́длинный; **in ~ fact** в действи́тельности.
actuality [ˌæktʃʊ'ælɪtɪ, ˌæktjʊ-] *n.* действи́тельность; **in ~** в действи́тельности.
actually ['æktʃʊəlɪ] *adv.* (*really; in fact*) действи́тельно; в су́щности; (*in expansion or correction of former statement*) в/на са́мом де́ле; (*in sense 'to tell the truth'*) вообще́-то (говоря́); со́бственно (говоря́).
actuate ['æktʃʊˌeɪt] *v.t.* прив|оди́ть, -ести в де́йствие.
acuity [ə'kjuːɪtɪ] *n.* (*lit., fig.*) острота́.
acumen ['ækjʊmən] *n.* (*judgement*) сообрази́тельность; (*penetration*) проница́тельность.
acupuncture ['ækjuːˌpʌŋktʃə(r)] *n.* акупункту́ра, иглоука́лывание.

acupuncturist ['ækju:ˌpʌŋktʃərɪst] *n.* иглотерапе́вт.

acute [ə'kju:t] *adj.* (*in var. senses*) о́стрый; ~ **shortage** о́страя нехва́тка; ~ **sense of smell** то́нкое обоня́ние.

AD (*abbr. of* **Anno Domini**) н.э., (на́шей э́ры).

ad [æd] (*coll.*) = **advertisement**

adage ['ædɪdʒ] *n.* погово́рка.

adagio [ə'dɑ:ʒɪəʊ] *n., adj. & adv.* ада́жио (*indecl.*).

Adam ['ædəm] *n.* Ада́м; ~**'s apple** ада́мово я́блоко, кады́к.

adamant ['ædəmənt] *adj.* (*fig.*) непрекло́нный.

adapt [ə'dæpt] *v.t.* **1.** приспос|обля́ть, -о́бить. **2.** (*modify*) адапти́ровать (*impf., pf.*); ~ **for the stage** инсцени́ровать (*impf., pf.*).

adaptability [əˌdæptə'bɪlɪtɪ] *n.* приспособля́емость.

adaptable [ə'dæptəb(ə)l] *adj.* легко́ приспоса́бливающийся.

adaptation [ˌædæp'teɪʃ(ə)n] *n.* приспособле́ние; (*of book etc.*) адапта́ция, инсцениро́вка.

adapt|er, -or [ə'dæptə(r)] *n.* **1.** (*of book etc.*) а́втор адапта́ции. **2.** (*tech.*) ада́птер.

add [æd] *v.t.* **1.** (*make an addition of*) приб|авля́ть, -а́вить; ~ **sugar to tea** положи́ть (*pf.*) са́хар в чай; ~ **salt to** подс|а́ливать, -оли́ть; ~ **fuel to the fire/flames** подл|ива́ть, -и́ть ма́сла в ого́нь; (*build on*) пристр|а́ивать, -о́ить; **a garage was** ~**ed to the house** к до́му пристро́или гара́ж. **2.** (*say in addition*) доб|авля́ть, -а́вить; **I have nothing to** ~ мне не́чего доба́вить; **what can I** ~**?** что я могу́ ещё сказа́ть? **3.** (*math.*) скла́дывать, сложи́ть.

v.i. **1.** ~ **to** (*increase, enlarge*) увели́чи|вать, -ть; уси́ли|вать, -ть; (*knowledge etc.*) углуб|ля́ть, -и́ть; **this will** ~ **to the expense** э́то увели́чит расхо́ды; ~ **to a house** пристр|а́ивать, -о́ить к до́му. **2.** (*perform addition*) *see* ~ **up** *v.i.*; **3.** ~ **to** (*total*) *see* ~ **up** *v.i.*

with advs. ~ **in** *v.t.* включ|а́ть, -и́ть; ~ **on** *v.t.* приб|авля́ть, -а́вить; (*build on*): **the porch was** ~**ed on later** крыльцо́ пристро́или по́зже; ~ **together** *v.t.* скла́дывать, сложи́ть; ~ **up** *v.t.* (*find sum of*) подсч|и́тывать, -ита́ть; подыто́жи|вать, -ть; *v.i.* (*perform addition*): **you can't** ~ **up!** вы не уме́ете счита́ть!; (*total*): **it** ~**s up to 50** э́то составля́ет в су́мме 50; (*coll.*): **it** ~**s up to this, that ...** э́то сво́дится к тому́, что...; **it doesn't** ~ **up** (*make sense*) концы́ не схо́дятся.

addendum [ə'dendəm] *n.* приложе́ние; дополне́ние.

adder ['ædə(r)] *n.* (*snake*) гадю́ка; (*US*) уж.

addict[1] ['ædɪkt] *n.* (**drug** ~) наркома́н; **theatre** ~ завзя́тый театра́л.

addict[2] [ə'dɪkt] *v.t.*: **be, become** ~**ed to** пристрасти́ться (*pf.*) к+*d.*

addiction [ə'dɪkʃ(ə)n] *n.* пристра́стие (*к чему*); **drug** ~ наркома́ния.

addictive [ə'dɪktɪv] *adj.* выраба́тывающий привыка́ние.

addition [ə'dɪʃ(ə)n] *n.* **1.** (*adding; supplement*) прибавле́ние; добавле́ние; **an** ~ **to the family** прибавле́ние семе́йства; **in** ~ **to** в дополне́ние к+*d.*; **in** ~ (*as well*) вдоба́вок; (*moreover*) к тому́ же. **2.** (*math.*) сложе́ние.

additional [ə'dɪʃən(ə)l] *adj.* доба́вочный, дополни́тельный.

additive ['ædɪtɪv] *n.* доба́вка, добавле́ние.

addle ['æd(ə)l] *adj.*: **an** ~ **(d) egg** ту́хлое яйцо́.

v.i. (*of an egg*) ту́хнуть, про-.

cpds. ~**-brained** *adj.* пу́таный.

address [ə'dres] *n.* **1.** (*of letter etc.; place of residence*) а́дрес; ~ **book** записна́я кни́жка; а́дресная кни́га. **2.** (*discourse*) речь; **deliver an** ~ выступа́ть, вы́ступить с ре́чью. **3.** (*pl., courtship*) уха́живание; **pay one's** ~**es to** уха́живать (*impf.*) за+*i.* **4.: form of** ~ фо́рма обраще́ния.

v.t. **1.** (*a letter*) адресова́ть (*impf., pf.*). **2.** (*speak to*) обра|ща́ться, -ти́ться к+*d.*; **he** ~**ed the meeting** он обрати́лся с ре́чью к собра́вшимся. **3.** (*direct*): ~ **one's remarks to** адресова́ть свои́ замеча́ния +*d.*

addressee [ˌædre'si:] *n.* адреса́т.

adduce [ə'dju:s] *v.t.* прив|оди́ть, -ести́.

adenoids ['ædɪˌnɔɪdz] *n.* адено́иды (*m. pl.*); **he had his** ~ **out** ему́ удали́ли адено́иды.

adept ['ædept, ə'dept] *adj.* уме́лый; све́дущий (**at, in:** в+*p.*); **he is** ~ **at finding excuses** он ма́стер находи́ть оправда́ния.

adequacy ['ædɪkwəsɪ] *n.* доста́точность.

adequate ['ædɪkwət] *adj.* доста́точный.

adhere [əd'hɪə(r)] *v.i.* (*lit.*) прил|ипа́ть, -и́пнуть (к+*d.*); (*fig.*): ~ **to a programme** (твёрдо) сле́довать (*impf.*) програ́мме.

adherence [əd'hɪərəns] *n.* приве́рженность.

adherent [əd'hɪərənt] *n.* приве́рженец.

adhesion [əd'hi:ʒ(ə)n] *n.* прилипа́ние; скле́ивание.

adhesive [əd'hi:sɪv] *n.* клей; кле́йкое вещество́.

adj. ли́пкий; (*sticky*) кле́йкий; ~ **tape** кле́йкая ле́нта.

ad hoc [æd 'hɒk] *adv.* для да́нного слу́чая; (*attr.*): ~ **committee** вре́менный комите́т.

adieu [ə'dju:] *n.* проща́ние; **make one's** ~**s** про|ща́ться, -сти́ться.

int. проща́й(те).

ad infinitum [æd ˌɪnfɪ'naɪtəm] *adv.* до бесконе́чности.

adipose ['ædɪˌpəʊz] *adj.* жи́рный.

adjacent [ə'dʒeɪs(ə)nt] *adj.* (*geom.*): ~ **angles** сме́жные углы́; (*neighbouring*) сосе́дний; сме́жный; ~ **to** примыка́ющий к+*d.*; **our house is** ~ **to the school** наш дом примыка́ет к шко́ле.

adjectival [ˌædʒɪk'taɪv(ə)l] *adj.* адъекти́вный.

adjective ['ædʒɪktɪv] *n.* (и́мя) прилага́тельное.

adjoin [ə'dʒɔɪn] *v.t.* примыка́ть (*impf.*) к+*d.*; прилега́ть (*impf.*) к+*d.*

v.i. примыка́ть (*impf.*), прилега́ть (*impf.*); **the two houses** ~ э́ти два до́ма примыка́ют друг к дру́гу; **in the** ~**ing house** в сосе́днем до́ме.

adjourn [ə'dʒɜ:n] *v.t.* (*postpone*) от|кла́дывать, -ложи́ть; (*break off*): **they** ~**ed the meeting till 2 o'clock** они́ объяви́ли переры́в в заседа́нии до двух часо́в.

v.i. **1.** (*suspend proceedings*) закр|ыва́ть, -ы́ть заседа́ние; (*disperse*) ра|сходи́ться, -зойти́сь; **Parliament has** ~**ed for the summer** парла́мент распу́щен на ле́то. **2.** (*coll., move*): **shall we** ~ **to the dining-room?** перейдём в столо́вую?

adjournment [ə'dʒɜ:nmənt] *n.* (*postponement*) отсро́чка; (*dispersal*) ро́спуск; (*break in proceedings*) переры́в.

adjudge [ə'dʒʌdʒ] *v.t.*: ~ **s.o. guilty** призн|ава́ть, -а́ть кого́-н. вино́вным.

adjudicate [ə'dʒu:dɪˌkeɪt] *v.t.* (*decide upon*) выноси́ть, вы́нести реше́ние по+*d.*

adjudication [əˌdʒu:dɪ'keɪʃ(ə)n] *n.* суде́бное/арбитра́жное реше́ние.

adjudicator [ə'dʒu:dɪˌkeɪtə(r)] *n.* арби́тр.

adjunct ['ædʒʌŋkt] *n.* (*appendage*) приложе́ние; (*addition*) дополне́ние.

adjure [ə'dʒʊə(r)] *v.t.* заклина́ть (*impf.*); умоля́ть (*impf.*).

adjust [ə'dʒʌst] *v.t.* **1.** (*arrange; put right or straight*) регули́ровать, от-; прив|оди́ть, -ести́ в поря́док; попр|авля́ть, -а́вить; (*of mechanism*) регули́ровать, от-; нала́|живать, -дить. **2.** (*fit, adapt*) приг|оня́ть, -на́ть; под|гоня́ть, -огна́ть; ~ **to** приспос|обля́ться, -о́биться к+*d.*; **well-**~**ed** (*of pers.*) уравнове́шенный.

adjustable [ə'dʒʌstəb(ə)l] *adj.* регули́руемый; подвижно́й; ~ **spanner** разводно́й (га́ечный) ключ.

adjustment [ə'dʒʌstmənt] *n.* (*regulation*) регул|и́рование, -иро́вка; (*correction*) исправле́ние, попра́вка; (*fitting*) пригонка; (*adaptation*) приспособле́ние.

adjutant ['ædʒʊt(ə)nt] *n.* адъюта́нт; ≃ нача́льник штаба ча́сти.

ad-lib [æd 'lɪb] (*coll.*) *n.* экспро́мт.

v.i. говори́ть (*impf.*) экспро́мтом.

administer [əd'mɪnɪstə(r)] *v.t.* **1.** (*manage, govern*) управля́ть (*impf.*) +*i.*; заве́довать (*impf.*) +*i.* **2.**: ~ **a blow** нанести́ (*pf.*) уда́р (*кому*); ~ **medicine** да|ва́ть, -ть лека́рство; ~ **an oath to s.o.** прив|о-ди́ть, -ести́ кого́-н. к прися́ге; **the priest ~ed the sacrament of marriage** свяще́нник соверши́л обря́д венча́ния.

administration [əd,mɪnɪ'streɪʃ(ə)n] *n.* **1.** (*management*) управле́ние, организа́ция. **2.** (*of public affairs*) администра́ция; **the A~** прави́тельство; **during the Kennedy ~** при администра́ции Ке́ннеди. **3.**: ~ **of justice** отправле́ние правосу́дия. **4.**: ~ **of an oath** приведе́ние к прися́ге.

administrative [əd'mɪnɪstrətɪv] *adj.* администрати́вный.

administrator [əd'mɪnɪ,streɪtə(r)] *n.* администра́тор.

admirable ['ædmərəb(ə)l] *adj.* замеча́тельный, прекра́сный.

admiral ['ædmər(ə)l] *n.* адмира́л.

admiralty ['ædmərəltɪ] *n.* адмиралте́йство.

admiration [,ædmɪ'reɪʃ(ə)n] *n.* восхище́ние; **fill with** ~ прив|оди́ть, -ести́ в восхище́ние; **lost in** ~ вне себя́ от восто́рга.

admir|e [əd'maɪə(r)] *v.t.* (*view with pleasure*) любова́ться (*impf.*) +*i.* (*or* на+*a.*); (*be delighted with*) восхи|ща́ться, -ти́ться +*i.*; восторга́ться (*impf.*) +*i.*; **~ing glances** восхищённые взгля́ды.

admirer [əd'maɪərə(r)] *n.* покло́нник.

admissible [əd'mɪsɪb(ə)l] *adj.* прие́млемый; допусти́мый.

admission [əd'mɪʃ(ə)n] *n.* **1.** (*permitted entry or access*) вход; до́ступ; **'no ~'** «вход воспреща́ется»; «нет вхо́да»; ~ **charge** входна́я пла́та. **2.** (*acknowledgement*) призна́ние.

admit [əd'mɪt] *v.t. & i.* **1.** (*allow, accept*) допус|ка́ть, -ти́ть; **you must ~ he is right** вы должны́ призна́ть, что он прав. **2.** (*let in*) впус|ка́ть, -ти́ть; прин|има́ть, -я́ть; **this ticket ~s one (person)** э́то биле́т на одно́ лицо́; **children are not ~ted** де́тям вход воспрещён. **3.** (*confess*) призн|ава́ть, -а́ть; **I don't mind ~ting** гото́в призна́ть(ся).

admittance [əd'mɪt(ə)ns] *n.* (*entry*) вход; **'no ~!'** «вход запрещён!»; (*access*) до́ступ.

admittedly [əd'mɪtɪdlɪ] *adv.* пра́вда; призна́ться.

admixture [æd'mɪkstʃə(r)] *n.* при́месь.

admonish [əd'mɒnɪʃ] *v.t.* **1.** (*reprove*) де́лать, с-внуше́ние/замеча́ние +*d.* **2.** (*exhort*) увещева́ть (*impf.*); наст|авля́ть, -а́вить.

admoni|shment [əd'mɒnɪʃmənt], **-tion** [,ædmə'nɪʃ(ə)n] *n.* (*reproof*) внуше́ние; (*exhortation*) увещева́ние, наставле́ние.

ad nauseam [æd 'nɔːzɪ,æm] *adv.* до тошноты́.

ado [ə'duː] *n.* (*fuss*) сует́а; **without further ~** без дальне́йших церемо́ний; **much ~ about nothing** мно́го шу́ма из ничего́.

adobe [ə'dəʊbɪ] *n.* кирпи́ч-сыре́ц; **an ~ hut** глинобитная хи́жина.

adolescence [,ædə'lesəns] *n.* о́трочество.

adolescent [,ædə'les(ə)nt] *n.* подро́сток.

adj. подро́стко́вый, о́троческий.

adopt [ə'dɒpt] *v.t.* **1.** (*a son*) усынов|ля́ть, -и́ть; (*a daughter*) удочер|я́ть, -и́ть; **~ed child** приёмный ребёнок, приёмыш. **2.** (*acquire*) усв|а́ивать, -о́ить. **3.** (*accept*) прин|има́ть, -я́ть; **the resolution was ~ed** резолю́ция была́ принята́; (*take over*) перен|има́ть, -я́ть; (*take up*) зан|има́ть, -я́ть; **he ~ed a condescending attitude** он стал держа́ться снисходи́тельно. **4.** (*ling., borrow*) заи́мствовать (*impf., pf.*). **5.** (*choose*) выбира́ть, вы́брать; **he was ~ed as candidate** его́ кандидату́ру при́няли.

adoption [ə'dɒpʃ(ə)n] *n.* **1.** усыновле́ние; удочере́ние. **2.** усвое́ние. **3.** приня́тие. **4.** заи́мствование. **5.** вы́бор; **country of ~** второ́е оте́чество.

adoptive [ə'dɒptɪv] *adj.* приёмный; ~ **parent** усынови́тель (*fem.* -ница).

adorable [ə'dɔːrəb(ə)l] *adj.* преле́стный, восхити́тельный.

adoration [,ædə'reɪʃ(ə)n] *n.* обожа́ние.

ador|e [ə'dɔː(r)] *v.t.* (*worship*) обожа́ть ; поклоня́ться (*impf.*) +*d.*

adorn [ə'dɔːn] *v.t.* (*lit., fig.*) укр|аша́ть, -а́сить.

adornment [ə'dɔːnmənt] *n.* украше́ние.

adrenal [ə'driːn(ə)l] *adj.* надпо́чечный; ~ **glands** надпо́чечные же́лезы (*f. pl.*).

adrenalin [ə'drenəlɪn] *n.* адренали́н.

adrift [ə'drɪft] *pred. adj. & adv.* (*of a boat or its crew*): **go ~** дрейфова́ть (*impf.*); **cut ~** (*v.t.*) пус|ка́ть, -ти́ть.

adroit [ə'drɔɪt] *adj.* (*dexterous*) ло́вкий; (*skilful*) иску́сный; (*resourceful*) нахо́дчивый.

adroitness [ə'drɔɪtnɪs] *n.* ло́вкость; иску́сность; нахо́дчивость.

adulation [,ædjʊ'leɪʃ(ə)n] *n.* низкопокло́нство, лесть.

adult [ə'dʌlt, 'ædʌlt] *n. & adj.* взро́слый; ~ **education** обуче́ние взро́слых.

adulterate [ə'dʌltə,reɪt] *v.t.* (*debase*) по́ртить, ис-; (*dilute*) разб|авля́ть, -а́вить.

adulteration [ə,dʌltə'reɪʃ(ə)n] *n.* по́рча; разбавле́ние.

adulterer [ə'dʌltərə(r)] *n.* неве́рный супру́г.

adulteress [ə'dʌltərɪs] *n.* неве́рная супру́га.

adulterous [ə'dʌltərəs] *adj.* неве́рный.

adultery [ə'dʌltərɪ] *n.* адюльте́р, прелюбодея́ние; **to commit ~** соверш|а́ть, -и́ть прелюбодея́ние.

adulthood ['ædʌlthʊd, ə'dʌlthʊd] *n.* зре́лость; возмужа́лость.

adumbrate ['ædʌm,breɪt] *v.t.* **1.** (*sketch out*) набр|а́сывать, -оса́ть. **2.** (*foreshadow*) предвеща́ть (*impf.*).

advance [əd'vɑːns] *n.* **1.** (*forward move*) продвиже́ние; (*mil.: also*) наступле́ние; (*pl., overtures to a person*): **make ~s to** заи́грывать (*impf.*) с+*i.* **2.** (*progress*) прогре́сс; (*in rank, social position etc.*) продвиже́ние; **~s of science** прогре́сс нау́ки; **~s of civilization** достиже́ния (*nt. pl.*) цивилиза́ции; **the country has made great ~s** страна́ доби́лась больши́х успе́хов. **3.** (*loan*) ссу́да; (*payment beforehand*) ава́нс; **an ~ on salary** ава́нс под зарпла́ту. **4.**: **in ~** (*in front*) вперёд; (*beforehand*) зара́нее; **in ~ of** впереди́+*g.*; **he expects to be paid in ~** он ожида́ет, что ему́ запла́тят вперёд. **5.** (*attr.*): ~ **copy** (*of book*) сигна́льный экземпля́р; ~ **copy of a speech** предвари́тельный текст ре́чи; ~ **guard** аванга́рд; **I had ~ knowledge of this** я зара́нее знал об э́том; ~ **payment** ава́нсовый платёж.

v.t. **1.** (*move forward*) продв|ига́ть, -и́нуть. **2.** (*fig., put forward*): ~ **an opinion** вы́сказать (*pf.*) мне́ние; ~ **a proposal** выдвига́ть, вы́двинуть предложе́ние. **3.** (*fig., further*): ~ **s.o.'s interests** соде́йствовать (*impf.*) чьим-н. интере́сам; послужи́ть (*pf.*) на по́льзу кому́-н. **4.** (*of payment*) плати́ть, за- ава́нсом; (*lend*) ссу|жа́ть, -ди́ть. **5.** (*bring forward; make earlier*): ~ **the date of** перенести́ (*pf.*) на бо́лее ра́нний срок.

v.i. **1.** (*move forward*) продв|ига́ться, -и́нуться; ~ **on** наступа́ть (*impf.*) на+*a.* **2.** (*progress*) разв|ива́ться, -и́ться; де́лать, с- успе́хи.

advanced [əd'vɑːnsd] *adj.* **1.** (*far on*): ~ **age, years** преклóнный во́зраст; **he is very ~ for his years** он о́чень ра́звит для свои́х лет. **2.** (*opp. elementary*): **an ~ course** курс для продви́нутого эта́па (обуче́ния). **3.** (*progressive*) передово́й.

advancement [əd'vɑːnsmənt] *n.* продвиже́ние.

advantage [əd'vɑːntɪdʒ] *n.* **1.** (*superiority*) преиму́щество, досто́инство; **gain, win an ~ over**

брать, взять верх над+*i*. **2.** (*profit, benefit*) вы́года, по́льза; **it is to your ~ to sell** вам бу́дет вы́годно прода́ть; **gain ~ from** извл|ека́ть, -е́чь вы́году из+*g*.; **turn sth. to ~** обра|ща́ть, -ти́ть что-н. себе́ на по́льзу; **take ~ of sth.** воспо́льзоваться (*pf.*) чем-н.; **use to ~** вы́годно испо́льзовать (*pf.*). **3.** (*tennis*): **~ in/out** «бо́льше»/«ме́ньше».

advantageous [ˌædvənˈteɪdʒəs] *adj.* (*favourable*) благоприя́тный; (*profitable*) вы́годный.

advent [ˈædvent] *n.* **1.** (*arrival*) прибы́тие. **2.** (*appearance; occurrence*) появле́ние. **3.** (**A~**: *eccl.*) рожде́ственский пост.

adventure [ədˈventʃə(r)] *n.* (*exciting incident or episode*) приключе́ние; (*risky or irresponsible activity*) авантю́ра; **~ story** приключе́нческий рома́н.

adventurer [ədˈventʃərə(r)] *n.* (*seeker of adventure*) иска́тель (*m.*) приключе́ний; (*speculator*) авантюри́ст.

adventurism [ədˈventʃəˌrɪz(ə)m] *n.* авантюри́зм.

adventurist [ədˈventʃərɪst] *n.* авантюри́ст.

adventurous [ədˈventʃərəs] *adj.* **1.** (*of pers.*) сме́лый; (*enterprising*) предприи́мчивый. **2.** (*of actions*) риско́ванный, авантю́рный.

adverb [ˈædvɜːb] *n.* наре́чие.

adverbial [ədˈvɜːbɪəl] *adj.* наре́чный.

adversary [ˈædvəsərɪ] *n.* проти́вник.

adverse [ˈædvɜːs] *adj.* (*unfavourable*) неблагоприя́тный; (*harmful*) вре́дный; **~ winds** проти́вные ве́тры (*m.pl.*).

adversity [ədˈvɜːsɪtɪ] *n.* бе́дствия (*nt. pl.*), несча́стья (*nt. pl.*); **show courage in ~** прояви́ть (*pf.*) му́жество в беде́.

advertise [ˈædvəˌtaɪz] *v.t.* & *i.* (*boost, publicize*) реклами́ровать (*impf., pf.*); (*in newspaper*) да|ва́ть, -ть объявле́ние (о+*p*.).

advertisement [ədˈvɜːtɪsmənt, -tɪzmənt] *n.* рекла́ма; объявле́ние.

advertiser [ˈædvəˌtaɪzə(r)] *n.* рекламода́тель (*m.*).

advertising [ˈædvəˌtaɪzɪŋ] *n.* реклами́рование.

advice [ədˈvaɪs] *n.* **1.** сове́т; **give s.o. a piece, word of ~** посове́товать кому́-н.; **seek s.o.'s ~** сове́товаться, по- с кем-н.; **take, follow s.o.'s ~** сле́довать, по- чьему́-н. сове́ту. **2.** (*information*) сообще́ние. **3.** (*comm.*: *notification*) извеще́ние.

advisability [ədˌvaɪzəˈbɪlɪtɪ] *n.* целесообра́зность.

advisable [ədˈvaɪzəb(ə)l] *adj.* целесообра́зный.

advise [ədˈvaɪz] *v.t.* **1.** (*counsel*) сове́товать, по- +*d*.; **what do you ~ (me to do)?** что вы мне сове́туете де́лать?; **you would be well ~d to go** вам сто́ило бы пойти́; (*give professional advice to*) консульти́ровать (*impf.*). **2.** (*comm.*: *notify*) изве|ща́ть, -сти́ть (*кого о чём*).

advisedly [ədˈvaɪzɪdlɪ] *adv.* наме́ренно.

advis|er, -or [ədˈvaɪzə(r)] *n.* сове́тник; (*professional*) консульта́нт.

advisory [ədˈvaɪzərɪ] *adj.* совеща́тельный, консультати́вный; **in an ~ capacity** в ка́честве сове́тника.

advocacy [ˈædvəkəsɪ] *n.* защи́та, отста́ивание.

advocate[1] [ˈædvəkət] *n.* **1.** (*defender*) защи́тник; (*supporter*) сторо́нник. **2.** (*lawyer*) адвока́т.

advocate[2] [ˈædvəˌkeɪt] *v.t.* (*speak in favour of*) выступа́ть, вы́ступить за+*a*.; (*advise, recommend*) сове́товать, по-.

adze [ædʒ] *n.* тесло́.

aegis [ˈiːdʒɪs] *n.*: **under the ~ of** под эги́дой +*g*.

aeon [ˈiːɒn] *n.* (*geol.*) э́ра; (*fig.*) (це́лая) ве́чность.

aerate [ˈeəreɪt] *v.t.* прове́три|вать, -ть.

aeration [ˌeəˈreɪʃ(ə)n] *n.* прове́тривание; (*of the soil*) аэра́ция.

aerial [ˈeərɪəl] *n.* анте́нна.

adj. **1.** (*lit., fig.*) возду́шный; **~ photography** аэрофотосъёмка.

aerobics [eəˈrəʊbɪks] *n.* аэро́бика.

aerodrome [ˈeərəˌdrəʊm] *n.* аэродро́м.

aerodynamic [ˌeərəʊdaɪˈnæmɪk] *adj.* аэродинами́ческий.

aerodynamics [ˌeərəʊdaɪˈnæmɪks] *n.* аэродина́мика.

aeronaut [ˌeərəʊˈnɔːt] *n.* аэрона́вт; воздухопла́ватель (*m.*).

aeronautic(al) [ˌeərəʊˈnɔːtɪk(ə)l] *adj.* аэронавигацио́нный, авиацио́нный.

aeronautics [ˌeərəʊˈnɔːtɪks] *n.* аэрона́втика.

aeroplane [ˈeərəˌpleɪn] *n.* самолёт.

aerosol [ˈeərəˌsɒl] *n.* аэрозо́ль (*m.*).

aerospace [ˈeərəʊˌspeɪs] *n.* возду́шно-косми́ческое простра́нство.

adj. авиацио́нно-косми́ческий.

aesthete [ˈiːsθiːt] *n.* эсте́т.

aesthetic [iːsˈθetɪk] *adj.* эстети́ческий.

aesthetics [iːsˈθetɪks] *n.* эсте́тика.

afar [əˈfɑː(r)] *adv.* (*also* **~ off**) вдалеке́; **from ~** и́здали, издалека́.

affability [ˌæfəˈbɪlɪtɪ] *n.* приве́тливость; любе́зность.

affable [ˈæfəb(ə)l] *adj.* приве́тливый; любе́зный.

affair [əˈfeə(r)] *n.* **1.** (*business, matter*) де́ло; **~s of state** госуда́рственные дела́; **Ministry of Foreign A~s** министе́рство иностра́нных дел. **2.** (*also* **love ~**) любо́вная связь; рома́н.

affect[1] [əˈfekt] *v.t.* **1.** (*act on*) де́йствовать, по- на+*a*.; влия́ть, по- на+*a*. **2.** (*concern*) каса́ться, косну́ться +*g*.; **everyone is ~ed by the rise in prices** повыше́ние цен затра́гивает всех. **3.** (*touch emotionally*) тро́|гать, -нуть. **4.** (*of disease*): **the lung is ~ed** лёгкое пораже́но; **several hundred cattle were ~ed** пострада́ло не́сколько сот голо́в скота́.

affect[2] [əˈfekt] *v.t.* (*pretend*) притвор|я́ться, -и́ться; прики́|дываться, -нуться.

affectation [ˌæfekˈteɪʃ(ə)n] *n.* **1.** (*pretence*) притво́рство. **2.** (*unnatural behaviour*) аффекта́ция. **3.** (*of language or style*) иску́сственность.

affected [əˈfektɪd] *adj.* (*pretended*) притво́рный; (*not natural*) аффекти́рованный.

affection [əˈfekʃ(ə)n] *n.* привя́занность (**for:** к+*d*).

affectionate [əˈfekʃənət] *adj.* не́жный.

affidavit [ˌæfɪˈdeɪvɪt] *n.* пи́сьменное показа́ние; **make, swear an ~** да|ва́ть, -ть показа́ние под прися́гой.

affiliate [əˈfɪlɪˌeɪt] *v.t.* **1.** (*join, attach*) присоедин|я́ть, -и́ть (**to:** к+*d*.). **2.** (*adopt as member*) прин|има́ть, -я́ть в чле́ны.

v.i. присоедин|я́ться, -и́ться (**with:** к+*d*.).

affiliation [əˌfɪlɪˈeɪʃ(ə)n] *n.* **1.** присоедине́ние. **2.** приня́тие в чле́ны.

affinity [əˈfɪnɪtɪ] *n.* **1.** (*resemblance*) схо́дство; (*relationship*) родство́; (*connection*) связь. **2.** (*liking, attraction*) влече́ние, скло́нность.

affirm [əˈfɜːm] *v.t.* (*assert*) утвер|жда́ть, -ди́ть; (*leg.*: *make an ~ation*) торже́ственно заяв|ля́ть, -и́ть (вме́сто прися́ги).

affirmation [ˌæfəˈmeɪʃ(ə)n] *n.* утвержде́ние; (*leg.*) торже́ственное заявле́ние.

affirmative [əˈfɜːmətɪv] *n.*: **he answered in the ~** он отве́тил утверди́тельно.

adj. утверди́тельный.

affix [əˈfɪks] *v.t.* прикреп|ля́ть, -и́ть (*что к чему*); **~ one's signature** ста́вить, по- по́дпись; **~ a seal/stamp** при|кла́дывать, -ложи́ть печа́ть/ште́мпель (*m.*); **~ a postage stamp** прикле́и|вать, -ть ма́рку.

afflict [əˈflɪkt] *v.t.*: **be ~ed with** страда́ть (*impf.*) +*i*.; **he is ~ed with rheumatism** он страда́ет ревмати́змом.

affliction [əˈflɪkʃ(ə)n] *n.* (*grief*) го́ре; (*misfortune*) несча́стье; бе́дствие; (*illness*) боле́знь.

affluence [ˈæflʊəns] *n.* (*wealth*) бога́тство; (*plenty*) изоби́лие.

affluent [ˈæflʊənt] *adj.* (*wealthy*) бога́тый; (*abounding*) изоби́льный.

afford [əˈfɔːd] *v.t.* **1.** (*with* **can**, *expr. possibility*): **I can't**

~ all these books я не в состоя́нии купи́ть все э́ти кни́ги; **they can ~ a new car** они́ мо́гут позво́лить себе́ но́вую маши́ну; **I can't ~ it** э́то мне не по карма́ну; **I can't ~ the time** мне не́когда. **2.** (*yield*; *supply*; *give*) предост|авля́ть, -а́вить; да|ва́ть, -ть; **it will ~ me an opportunity to speak to her** э́то даст мне возмо́жность поговори́ть с ней; **it ~s me great pleasure** э́то доставля́ет мне большо́е удово́льствие; **the hill ~ed a fine view** с холма́ открыва́лся прекра́сный вид.

affront [ə'frʌnt] *n.* оскорбле́ние.

v.t. оскорб|ля́ть, -и́ть.

Afghan ['æfgæn] *n.* афга́н|ец (*fem.* -ка); (~ *hound*) афга́нская борза́я.

adj. афга́нский.

Afghanistan [æf'gænɪˌstɑːn, -stæn] *n.* Афганиста́н.

afield [ə'fiːld] *adv.*: **far ~** вдалеке́, вдали́.

afire [ə'faɪə(r)] *pred. adj. & adv.*: **the house was ~** дом был охва́чен огнём; **set sth. ~** подж|ига́ть, -е́чь что-н.

aflame [ə'fleɪm] *pred. adj. & adv.*: **his clothes were ~** его́ оде́жда загоре́лась; (*fig.*): **the woods were ~ with colour** леса́ горе́ли ра́зными кра́сками.

afloat [ə'fləʊt] *pred. adj. & adv.* **1.** (*floating on water*) на воде́; (*in sailing order*) на плаву́; **get a ship ~** (*after grounding*) сн|има́ть, -ять кора́бль с ме́ли. **2.** (*at sea*) в мо́ре; **life ~** жизнь на воде́/мо́ре. **3.** **keep ~** (*fig., solvent*) *v.t.*: **they kept the newspaper ~** они́ подде́рживали существова́ние газе́ты; *v.i.* быть свобо́дным от долго́в.

afoot [ə'fʊt] *pred. adj. & adv.* (*in progress or preparation*): **there is a plan ~** гото́вится план; **there is sth. ~** что́-то затева́ется.

afore- [ə'fɔː(r)] *comb. form*: **~mentioned** *adj.* вышеупомя́нутый; **~said** *adj.* вышеска́занный; **malice ~thought** злой у́мысел.

afraid [ə'freɪd] *pred. adj.* испу́ганный; **I'm ~** мне стра́шно; **don't be ~** не бо́йтесь!; **I'm ~ he will die** бою́сь, что он умрёт; **I'm ~ he is out** к сожале́нию, его́ нет; **be ~ of** боя́ться (*impf.*) +*g.*

afresh [ə'freʃ] *adv.* снова.

Africa ['æfrɪkə] *n.* А́фрика.

African ['æfrɪkən] *n.* африка́н|ец (*fem.* -ка).

adj. африка́нский.

Afrikaans [ˌæfrɪ'kɑːns] *n.* (язы́к) африка́анс.

Afrikaner [ˌæfrɪ'kɑːnə(r)] *n.* африка́нер.

aft [ɑːft] *adv.* (*naut.*) на корме́; **fore and ~** от но́са к корме́.

after ['ɑːftə(r)] *adv.* **1.** (*subsequently*; *then*) пото́м, зате́м; **soon ~** вско́ре по́сле э́того. **2.** (*later*) поздне́е, по́зже; **3 days ~** спустя́ три дня; **3.** (*in consequence*) впосле́дствии.

prep. **1.** (*in expressions of time*) по́сле+*g.*; за+*i.*; че́рез+*a.*; спустя́+*a.*; **~ dinner** по́сле обе́да; **~ you!** за ва́ми!; **~ that** пото́м, зате́м; **the day ~ tomorrow** послеза́втра; **I am tired ~ my journey** я уста́л с доро́ги; **the week ~ next** неде́ля по́сле сле́дующей; (*in adv. sense*) че́рез две неде́ли; **they met ~ 10 years** они́ встре́тились че́рез де́сять лет; **~ midday** за́ полдень, по́сле полу́дня; **~ midnight** за́ полночь, по́сле полу́ночи; **it's ~ 6 (o'clock)** уже́ седьмо́й час; (*in sequence*) **day ~ day** день за днём; **one ~ another** оди́н за други́м; (*in spite of*) несмотря́ на+*a.*; **~ all my care** в отве́т на все мои́ забо́ты; **~ all** (*in the end*) в коне́чном счёте; в конце́ концо́в; (*nevertheless*) всё-таки. **2.** (*in expressions of place*) за+*i* .; **shut the door ~ you** закро́йте за собо́й дверь; **run ~ s.o.** бежа́ть за кем-н.; **we shouted ~ him** мы крича́ли ему́ вслед. **3.** (*in search of*; *trying to get*): **the police are ~ him** его́ разы́скивает поли́ция; **what is he ~?** на что он ме́тит?; что он замышля́ет? **4.** (*in accordance with*) по+*d.*, согла́сно+*d.*; **a man ~ my own heart** челове́к мне по ду́ше; **~ a fashion** как-нибу́дь; **he paints ~ a fashion** он в своём ро́де худо́жник; **named ~** на́званный по+*d.* (*or* в честь +*g.*); **he takes ~ his father** он похо́ж на отца́.

conj. по́сле того́, как.

cpds. **~birth** *n.* после́д; **~-dinner** *adj.* послеобе́денный; **~-effect** *n.* после́дствие; **~glow** *n.* вече́рняя заря́; **~life** *n.* загро́бная жизнь; **~math** *n.* ота́ва; (*fig.*) после́дствия (*nt. pl.*); **~noon** *n.* послеполу́денное вре́мя; **in the ~noon** днём; по́сле обе́да; пополу́дни; во второ́й полови́не дня; **at 3 in the ~noon** в три часа́ дня; **good ~noon!** (*in greeting*) до́брый день!; **~taste** *n.* при́вкус; **~thought** *n.* запозда́лая мысль.

afterwards ['ɑːftəwədz] *adv.* (*then*) пото́м; (*subsequently*) впосле́дствии; (*later*) по́зже.

again [ə'geɪn, ə'gen] *adv.* **1.** (*expr. repetition*) опя́ть; (*afresh, anew*) сно́ва, вновь; (*once more*) ещё раз; (*with certain vv.*) *by use of pref.* пере...; **read ~** перечи́т|ывать, -а́ть; **open ~** вновь откр|ыва́ть, -ы́ть; **time and ~** то и де́ло; **now and ~** вре́мя от вре́мени; **once ~** ещё раз. **2.** (*with neg.*: *any more*) бо́льше; **never ~** никогда́ бо́льше; **don't do it ~!** бо́льше э́того не де́лайте! **3.** (*in addition*): **as far ~** вдво́е да́льше; **as much ~** ещё сто́лько же. **4.** (*expr. return to original state or position*): **back ~** обра́тно; **you'll soon be well ~** вы ско́ро попра́витесь. **5.** (*moreover*; *besides*) кро́ме того́; (*on the other hand*) с друго́й стороны́.

against [ə'geɪnst, ə'genst] *prep.* **1.** (*in opposition to*) про́тив+*g.*; **I have nothing ~ it** я ничего́ не име́ю про́тив э́того; **I acted ~ my will** я де́йствовал не по свое́й во́ле; **swim ~ the current** (*lit., fig.*) плыть (*impf.*) про́тив тече́ния; **act ~ the law** поступ|а́ть, -и́ть противозако́нно; **~ the rules** не по пра́вилам; **fight, struggle ~** боро́ться (*impf., pf.*) про́тив+*g.* (*or* с+*i.*); **the battle ~ drunkenness** борьба с пья́нством; **speak ~** (*oppose*) выступа́ть, вы́ступить про́тив+*g.* **2.** (*in spite of*) вопреки́+*d.*; **~ reason** вопреки́ рассу́дку; **~ my better judgement** вопреки́ го́лосу рассу́дка. **3.** (*to the disfavour of*): **her age is ~ her** во́зраст её подво́дит. **4.** (*to oppose or combat*) на+*a.*; **march ~ the enemy** наступа́ть (*impf.*) на врага́. **5.** (*to withstand*) от+*g.*; **a shelter ~ the storm** убе́жище от бу́ри; **defend o.s. ~ the enemy** защища́ться (*impf.*) от врага́. **6.** (*in readiness for, anticipation of*): **~ a rainy day** на чёрный день; **they bought provisions ~ the winter** они́ купи́ли прови́зии на́ зиму. **7.** (*compared with*): **3 deaths this year ~ 20 last year** три сме́рти в э́том году́ про́тив двадцати́ в про́шлом. **8.** (*in contrast with*): **it shows up ~ a dark background** э́то выделя́ется на тёмном фо́не. **9.** (*in collision with*) о+*a.*; **knock ~ sth.** уда́риться (*pf.*) о что-н.; **he banged his head ~ a stone** он уда́рился голово́й о ка́мень. **10.** (*into contact with*) к+*d.*; **he moved the chair ~ the wall** он придви́нул стул к стене́. **11.** (*facing*): **over ~ the church** напро́тив це́ркви; **we are up ~ strong competition** у нас си́льная конкуре́нция.

agape [ə'geɪp] *pred. adj. & adv.* рази́нув рот.

agate ['ægət] *n.* ага́т; (*attr.*) ага́товый.

agave [ə'geɪvɪ] *n.* столе́тник, ага́ва.

age [eɪdʒ] *n.* **1.** (*time of life*) во́зраст; **what ~ is he?** како́го он во́зраста?; (*expecting exact answer*) ско́лько ему́ лет?; **he is 40 years of ~** ему́ со́рок лет; **he and I are the same ~** мы с ним рове́сники; **when I was your ~** когда́ я был в ва́шем во́зрасте; **a man (of) your ~** челове́к ва́шего во́зраста; **she doesn't look her ~** она́ вы́глядит моло́же свои́х лет; **at an early ~** в де́тском/ра́ннем во́зрасте; **over ~** ста́рше поло́женного во́зраста; **~ of consent** бра́чный во́зраст. **2.** (*majority*): **be of ~** быть совершенноле́тним; **come of ~** дост|ига́ть, -и́чь совершеннолéтия; **he is under ~** он несовершеннолéтний. **3.** (*old ~*) стáрость; **he lived to a ripe (old) ~** он дóжил до преклóнных лет. **4.** (*period*) períод; (*century*) век; **Ice A~** ледникóвый períод; **Stone A~** кáменный век; **the Middle A~s** срéдние векá; (*coll., often pl., long time*): **the bus left ~s ago** автóбус ушёл давны́м-давнó; **we have not seen each other for ~s** мы не видáлись цéлую вéчность.

v.t. стáрить, со-; (*of wine*) выдéрживать, вы́держать.

v.i. (*of pers.*) старéть, по-; (*of thg.*) старéть.

cpds. **~-group** *n.* возрастнáя грýппа; **~-limit** *n.* предéльный вóзраст; **~-old** *adj.* вековóй.

aged[1] [eɪdʒd] *adj.* (*of the age of*): **~ six** шести́ лет.

aged[2] ['eɪdʒɪd] *adj.* (*very old*) престарéлый.

adj. **the ~** пожилы́е лю́ди, престарéлые.

ag(e)ing ['eɪdʒɪŋ] *n.* старéние.

adj. старéющий.

ageism ['eɪdʒɪz(ə)m] *n.* дискриминáция по вóзрасту.

ageist ['eɪdʒɪst] *n.* сторóнник дискриминáции по вóзрасту.

adj. дискримини́рующий по вóзрасту.

ageless ['eɪdʒlɪs] *adj.* (*always young*) нестарéющий; (*eternal*) вéчный.

agency ['eɪdʒənsɪ] *n.* **1.** (*action*) дéйствие; (*instrumentality*) посрéдство; **by the ~ of** посрéдством+*g.*; чéрез+*a.* **2.** (*comm.*) агéнтство; **employment ~** агéнтство по наймý; **travel ~** бюрó (*indecl.*) путешéствий. **3.** (*organization*): **government ~** прави́тельственное учреждéние.

agenda [ə'dʒendə] *n.* повéстка дня.

agent ['eɪdʒ(ə)nt] *n.* **1.** (*person acting for others*) агéнт; (*representative*) представи́тель (*m.*).

agent provocateur [ˌɑ:ʒɑ̃ prəˌvɒkə'tɜ:(r)] *n.* провокáтор.

aggrandize [ə'grændaɪz] *v.t.* увели́чи|вать, -ть; расш|ирять, -и́рить.

aggrandizement [ə'grændɪzmənt] *n.* увеличéние; расширéние.

aggravat|e ['ægrəˌveɪt] *v.t.* **1.** (*make worse*) ух|удшáть, -ýдшить; (*of pain*) обостр|я́ть, -и́ть. **2.** (*coll., exasperate*) раздраж|áть, -и́ть.

aggravation [ˌægrə'veɪʃ(ə)n] *n.* **1.** ухудшéние; обострéние. **2.** раздражéние.

aggregate[1] ['ægrɪgət] *n.* совокýпность; **in the ~** в совокýпности.

adj. óбщий.

aggregate[2] ['ægrɪˌgeɪt] *v.t.* **1.** (*collect into a mass*) соб|ирáть, -рáть в цéлое. **2.** (*amount to*) сост|авля́ть, -áвить; состоя́ть (*impf.*) (в óбщей слóжности) из+*g.*

v.i. (*collect or come together*) соб|ирáться, -рáться.

aggression [ə'greʃ(ə)n] *n.* агрéссия.

aggressive [ə'gresɪv] *adj.* агресси́вный; (*assertive*) напóристый.

aggressiveness [ə'gresɪvnɪs] *n.* агресси́вность.

aggressor [ə'gresə(r)] *n.* агрéссор.

aggrieve [ə'gri:v] *v.t.* огор|чáть, -чи́ть; **feel (o.s.) ~d** быть огорчённым; огорч|áться, -и́ться.

aghast [ə'gɑ:st] *pred. adj.* (*terrified*) в ýжасе (*от чего*).

agile ['ædʒaɪl] *adj.* провóрный; **an ~ mind** живóй ум.

agility [ə'dʒɪlɪtɪ] *n.* провóрство.

agitate ['ædʒɪˌteɪt] *v.t.* **1.** (*excite*) волновáть, вз-; **be ~d about sth.** волновáться (*impf.*) из-за чегó-н.; **in an ~d voice** взволнóванным гóлосом. **2.** (*shake*) трясти́ (*impf.*); (*liquids*) взб|áлтывать, -олтáть.

v.i. агити́ровать (*impf.*) (*for, against*: за+*a.*, прóтив+*g.*).

agitation [ˌædʒɪ'teɪʃ(ə)n] *n.* **1.** (*disturbance*) волнéние; **in a state of ~** взволнóванный. **2.** (*pol.*) агитáция.

agitator ['ædʒɪˌteɪtə(r)] *n.* агитáтор.

aglow [ə'gləʊ] *pred. adj.* (*lit.*): **be ~** пылáть (*impf.*); (*fig.*) **his face was ~** он раскраснéлся.

agnostic [æg'nɒstɪk] *n.* агнóстик.

adj. агности́ческий.

agnosticism [æg'nɒstɪˌsɪz(ə)m] *n.* агностици́зм.

ago [ə'gəʊ] *adv.* томý назáд; **long ~** давнó; **not long ~** недáвно.

agog [ə'gɒg] *pred. adj.*: **she was ~ with excitement** онá былá вне себя́ от волнéния.

adv.: **he listened ~** он слýшал, затаи́в дыхáние.

agonize ['ægəˌnaɪz] *v.i.* мýчиться (*impf.*); **he ~ed over his speech** он мýчился над своéй рéчью.

agony ['ægənɪ] *n.* (*torment*) мучéние; (*suffering*) страдáние; (*pains of death*) агóния; **I was in ~** я óчень страдáл.

agrarian [ə'greərɪən] *adj.* агрáрный.

agree [ə'gri:] *v.t.* **1.** (*reach agreement on*) соглacóв|ывать, -áть (*что с кем*). **2.** (*accept as correct*) утвер|ждáть, -ди́ть; прин|имáть, -я́ть.

v.i. **1.** (*concur; be of like opinion*): **I quite ~ with you** я совершéнно с вáми соглáсен. **2.** (*reach agreement; make common decision*): **we ~d to go together** мы договори́лись éхать вмéсте; **~ on a price** договори́ться о ценé. **3.** (*consent*) согла|шáться, -си́ться (*на что*). **4.** (*accept*): **I ~ that it was wrong** соглáсен, что э́то бы́ло непрáвильно; **~ with** (*accept as correct or right*): **I don't ~ with his policy** я не соглáсен с егó полити́кой. **5.**: **~ with** (*suit*) под|ходи́ть, -ойти́ +*d.*; **oysters don't ~ with me** от ýстриц мне бывáет плóхо. **6.** (*tally*): **his story ~s with mine** егó расскáз схóдится с мои́м.

agreeable [ə'gri:əb(ə)l] *adj.* **1.** (*pleasant*) прия́тный. **2.** (*acceptable*): **if that is ~ to you** éсли вас э́то устрáивает. **3.** (*prepared to agree*): **be ~ to sth.** согла|шáться, -си́ться на что-н.

agreement [ə'gri:mənt] *n.* **1.** (*consent*) соглáсие; **by mutual ~** по взаи́мному соглáсию. **2.** (*treaty*) соглашéние, договóр; **come to an ~** при|ходи́ть, -йти́ к соглашéнию; **enter into an ~ with** заключ|áть, -и́ть соглашéние/договóр с+*i.* **3.** (*gram.*) согласовáние.

agricultural [ˌægrɪ'kʌltʃər(ə)l] *adj.* сельскохозя́йственный.

agricultur(al)ist [ˌægrɪ'kʌltʃər(əl)ɪst] *n.* земледе́лец.

agriculture ['ægrɪˌkʌltʃə(r)] *n.* сéльское хозя́йство.

agronomist [ə'grɒnəmɪst] *n.* агронóм.

agronomy [ə'grɒnəmɪ] *n.* агронóмия.

aground [ə'graʊnd] *pred. adj. & adv.*: **the ship was ~** корáбль сидéл на мели́; **run ~** (*v.i.*) сесть (*pf.*) на мель.

ah [ɑ:] *int.* ах!; а!

aha [ɑ:'hɑ:, ə'hɑ:] *int.* агá!

ahead [ə'hed] *adv.* впереди́; (*expr. motion*) вперёд; **he was ten yards ~ of us** он был на дéсять я́рдов впереди́ нас; **be, get ~ of** опере|жáть, -ди́ть; **move ~** продви́нуться (*pf.*) вперёд; **go ~!** ну давáйте!; **~ of time** досрóчно; **look ~** (*fig.*) смотрéть (*impf.*) вперёд.

ahem [ə'həm, ə'hem] *int.* гм!

ahoy [ə'hɔɪ] *int.*: **ship ~!** на кораблé/сýдне!

aid [eɪd] *n.* **1.** (*help, assistance*) пóмощь; (*support*) поддéржка; **first ~** пéрвая пóмощь; **~ agency** организáция по оказáнию пóмощи; **~ worker** рабóтн|ик (*fem.* -ица) организáции по оказáнию пóмощи; **with the ~ of** при пóмощи +*g.*; **call on s.o.'s ~** приб|егáть, -éгнуть к чьей-н. пóмощи; **go to s.o.'s ~** при|ходи́ть, -йти́ комý-н. на пóмощь; **mutual ~** взаимопóмощь; **in ~ of** в пóмощь +*d.* **2.** (*appliance*) посóбие; **visual ~s** нагля́дные посóбия.

v.t. (*help*) пом|огáть, -óчь +*d.*; (*promote*) спосóбствовать (*impf.*) +*d.*; **~ing and abetting** посóбничество и подстрекáтельство.

aide [eɪd] *n.* помóщни|к (*fem.* -ца).

cpds. **~-de-camp** *n.* адъютáнт; **~-memoire** *n.* пáмятная запи́ска.

AIDS [eɪdz] *n.* (*abbr. of* **acquired immune deficiency syndrome**) СПИД, (синдро́м приобретённого иммýнного дефици́та).
aiguillette [ˌeɪgwɪ'let] *n.* аксельба́нт.
ail [eɪl] *v.i.*: **he is always ~ing** он постоя́нно хвора́ет.
aileron ['eɪləˌrɒn] *n.* элеро́н.
ailment ['eɪlmənt] *n.* боле́знь; нездоро́вье.
aim [eɪm] *n.* **1.** (*purpose*) цель; **with the ~ of** с це́лью +*g.*; **fall short of one's ~s** не дост|ига́ть, -и́чь свое́й це́ли. **2.** (*of a gun, etc.*) прице́л; **take ~ at** прице́л|иваться, -иться в+*a.*; **miss one's ~** не попа́сть (*pf.*) в цель.
v.t. нав|оди́ть, -ести́; **~ a rifle at** напр|авля́ть, -а́вить винто́вку на+*a.*; **~ a stone at** це́литься (*impf.*) ка́мнем в+*a.*; **~ a blow at** зама́х|иваться, -ну́ться на+*a.*
v.i. це́лить (*impf.*); **~ at** (*with rifle*) прице́л|иваться, -иться в+*a.*; (*fig.*): **~ at** (*aspire to*) стреми́ться (*impf.*) к+*d.*; **~ high** ме́тить (*impf.*) высоко́; **what are you ~ing at?** что вы име́ете в виду́; **~ for** напр|авля́ться, -а́виться в/на+*a.*
aimless ['eɪmlɪs] *adj.* бесце́льный.
air [eə(r)] *n.* **1.** (*lit.*) во́здух; **stale ~** спёртый во́здух; **get some fresh ~** подыша́ть (*pf.*) све́жим во́здухом; **in the open ~** на откры́том во́здухе; **let some ~ into a room** прове́три|вать, -ть ко́мнату; **let the ~ out of** (*balloon, tyre*) выпуска́ть, вы́пустить воздух из+*g.*; **take to the ~** взлет|а́ть, -е́ть; **into the ~** вверх; **travel by ~** лета́ть (*impf.*) (самолётом); **a change of ~** переме́на обстано́вки; **~ current** возду́шное тече́ние; **~ pollution** загрязне́ние во́здуха. **2.** (*in fig. phrr.*): **a plan is in the ~** гото́вится план; **the question was left in the ~** вопро́с пови́с в во́здухе; **clear the ~** разря|жа́ть, -ди́ть атмосфе́ру; **hot ~** (*coll.*) хвастовство́, пустозво́нство; **he vanished into thin ~** его́ и след просты́л; **live on ~** пита́ться (*impf.*) во́здухом; **castles in the ~** возду́шные за́мки; **he was walking on ~** он ног под собо́й не чу́ял; **with his, her head in the ~** задра́в нос. **3.** (*appearance, manner*) вид; **with a triumphant ~** с торжеству́ющим ви́дом; **~s and graces** мане́рность; **put on** (*or* **give o.s.**) **~s** задава́ться (*impf.*). **4.** (*mus., song*) пе́сня; (*tune*) моти́в. **5.** (*radio*): **the programme is on the ~** програ́мма в эфи́ре; **go on the ~** выходи́ть, вы́йти в эфи́р; (*of pers.*) выступа́ть, вы́ступить по ра́дио; **go off the ~** (*of station*) зак|а́нчивать, -о́нчить радиопереда́чу. **6.** (*attr., pert. to aviation*) возду́шный; авиацио́нный, авиа...; (*mil.*) вое́нно-возду́шный; **~ force** вое́нно-возду́шные си́лы; **~ defence** противовозду́шная оборо́на; **~ base** авиаба́за; **~ crash** авиакатастро́фа; **~ display** возду́шный пара́д; **~ hostess** бортпроводни́ца; **~ show** авиасало́н; **~ terminal** (городско́й) аэровокза́л; **~ waves** *n.* радиово́лны.
v.t. (*ventilate*) прове́три|вать, -ть; (*dry*) суши́ть, вы-.
v.i.: **she hung the clothes out to ~** она́ разве́сила ве́щи для просу́шки.
cpds. **~-bed** *n.* надувно́й матра́ц; **~borne** *ad.* (*landed by ~*) возду́шно-деса́нтный; **~-conditioned** *adj.* с кондициони́рованным во́здухом; **~-conditioner** *n.* кондиционе́р (во́здуха); **~-conditioning** *n.* кондициони́рование во́здуха; **~-cooled** *adj.* охлажда́емый во́здухом; **~craft** *n.* самолёт, (*collect.*) самолёты, авиа́ция; **~craft-carrier** *n.* авиано́сец; **~crew** *n.* лётный соста́в; **~field** *n.* аэродро́м; **~gun** *n.* духово́е ружьё; **~-letter** *n.* авиаписьмо́; **~lift** *n.* возду́шная перево́зка; *v.t.* перев|ози́ть, -езти́ (*or* перебр|а́сывать, -о́сить) по во́здуху; **~line** *n.* авиали́ния; **~-liner** *n.* возду́шный ла́йнер; **~mail** *n.* авиапо́чта; **~man** *n.* лётчик; **~-pocket** *n.* (*aeron.*) возду́шная я́ма; **~port** *n.* аэропо́рт; **~-raid** *n.* возду́шный налёт; **~-raid warning** возду́шная трево́га; **~-raid shelter** бомбоубе́жище; **~-rifle** *n.* пневмати́ческая винто́вка; **~ship** *n.* дирижа́бль (*m.*); **~sick** *adj.*: **I was ~ sick** меня́ укача́ло в самолёте; **~sickness** *n.* возду́шная боле́знь; **~space** *n.* возду́шное простра́нство; **~speed** *n.* возду́шная ско́рость; **~strip** *n.* взлётно-поса́дочная полоса́; **~tight** *adj.* гермети́ческий; **~-traffic controller** авиадиспе́тчер; **~way** *n.* (*route*) возду́шная тра́сса; **~worthy** *adj.* го́дный к полёту.
airer ['eərə(r)] *n.* суши́лка.
airily ['eərɪlɪ] *adv.* за́просто; с лёгкостью.
airing ['eərɪŋ] *n.* прове́тривание; **~ cupboard** суши́льный шкаф.
airless ['eəlɪs] *adj.* (*stuffy*) ду́шный; (*still*) безве́тренный.
airy ['eərɪ] *adj.* **1.** (*well-ventilated*) просто́рный, прове́триваемый. **2.** (*light in movement etc.*) возду́шный. **3.** (*superficial; light-hearted*) ве́треный, беспе́чный.
aisle [aɪl] *n.* боково́й неф; (*in theatre etc.*) прохо́д.
ajar [ə'dʒɑː(r)] *pred. adj.* приоткры́тый.
akimbo [ə'kɪmbəʊ] *adj.* подбоче́нясь; **stand with arms ~** подбоче́ниться (*pf.*).
akin [ə'kɪn] *pred. adj. & adv.* (*related*) ро́дственный; **~ to** сродни́ +*d*; (*similar*) сро́дный, похо́жий.
alabaster ['æləˌbɑːstə(r), -ˌbæstə(r)] *n.* алеба́стр; (*attr.*) алеба́стровый.
à la carte [ˌɑː lɑː 'kɑːt] *adv.* порцио́нно, на зака́з.
alacrity [ə'lækrɪtɪ] *n.* (*liveliness*) жи́вость; (*zeal*) рве́ние.
alarm [ə'lɑːm] *n.* **1.** (*warning; warning signal*) трево́га; **false ~** ло́жная трево́га; **give, raise, sound the ~** подн|има́ть, -я́ть трево́гу; **fire ~** пожа́рная трево́га. **2.** (*~-clock*) буди́льник; **I set the ~ for 6** я поста́вил буди́льник на 6 часо́в. **3.** (*fright*): **he ran away in ~** он убежа́л в смяте́нии; испуга́ться +*g.*
v.t. трево́жить; **~ing news** трево́жные но́вости (*f. pl.*); **there's nothing to be ~ed about** ничего́ стра́шного.
alarming [ə'lɑːmɪŋ] *adj.* трево́жный.
alarmist [ə'lɑːmɪst] *n.* паникёр (*fem.* -ша).
alas [ə'læs, ə'lɑːs] *int.* увы́!
Alaska [ə'læskə] *n.* Аля́ска; **in ~** на Аля́ске.
Albania [æl'beɪnɪə] *n.* Алба́ния.
albatross ['ælbəˌtrɒs] *n.* альбатро́с.
albeit [ɔːl'biːɪt] *conj.* хотя́ и.
albinism ['ælbɪˌnɪz(ə)m] *n.* альбини́зм.
albino [æl'biːnəʊ] *n.* альбино́с (*fem.* -ка).
album ['ælbəm] *n.* альбо́м.
albumen ['ælbjʊmɪn] *n.* (*white of egg*) я́ичный бело́к; (*chem.*) альбуми́н.
alchemist ['ælkəmɪst] *n.* алхи́мик.
alchemy ['ælkəmɪ] *n.* алхи́мия.
alcohol ['ælkəˌhɒl] *n.* (*chem.*) алкого́ль (*m.*); (*spirit*) спирт.
alcoholic [ˌælkə'hɒlɪk] *n.* алкого́лик.
adj. алкого́льный; **~ beverages** спиртно́е; спиртны́е напи́тки (*m. pl.*).
alcoholism ['ælkəhɒˌlɪz(ə)m] *n.* алкоголи́зм.
alcove ['ælkəʊv] *n.* алько́в, ни́ша.
alder ['ɔːldə(r)] *n.* ольха́ (чёрная).
ale [eɪl] *n.* эль (*m.*); (*beer*) пи́во.
cpd. **~-house** *n.* пивна́я.
alert [ə'lɜːt] *n.* **1.** (*alarm*) трево́га; **give the ~** подня́ть (*pf.*) трево́гу. **2.**: **on the ~** наготове; **keep s.o. on the ~** держа́ть (*impf.*) кого́-н. в постоя́нной гото́вности.
adj. (*vigilant*) насторо́женный; (*lively*) живо́й.
v.t. прив|оди́ть, -ести́ в состоя́ние гото́вности; **~ s.o. to a danger** предупреди́ть (*pf.*) кого́-н. об опа́сности.
alertness [ə'lɜːtnɪs] *n.* насторо́женность; жи́вость.
A level ['eɪ levəl] *n.* (*Br.*) экза́мен по програ́мме

сре́дней шко́лы на повы́шенном у́ровне.

alfalfa [æl'fælfə] *n.* люце́рна.

alfresco [æl'freskəʊ] *adv.* на откры́том во́здухе.

algae ['ældʒi:, 'ælgi:] *n. pl.* морска́я во́доросль.

algebra ['ældʒɪbrə] *n.* а́лгебра.

algebraic [ˌældʒɪ'breɪɪk] *adj.* алгебраи́ческий.

Algeria [æl'dʒɪərɪə] *n.* Алжи́р.

algorithm ['ælgəˌrɪð(ə)m] *n.* алгори́тм.

alias ['eɪlɪəs] *n.* кли́чка, про́звище; **his ~ was ...** он называ́л себя́....

adv. ина́че называ́емый; он же.

alibi ['ælɪˌbaɪ] *n.* **1.** (*plea or proof of being elsewhere*) а́либи (*nt. indecl.*); **establish an ~** устан|а́вливать, -ови́ть а́либи; **produce an ~** предст|авля́ть, -а́вить а́либи. **2.** (*coll., excuse*) отгово́рка.

alien ['eɪlɪən] *n.* чужестра́н|ец (*fem.* -ка), иностра́н|ец (*fem.* -ка).

adj. **1.** (*foreign*) иностра́нный; (*extra-terrestrial*) внеземно́й. **2.: ~ to** чу́ждый *+d.*

alienate ['eɪlɪəˌneɪt] *v.t.* **1.** (*estrange, antagonize*) отдал|я́ть, -и́ть; отвра|ща́ть, -ти́ть. **2.** (*leg.*) отчужда́ть (*impf.*).

alienation [ˌeɪlɪə'neɪʃ(ə)n] *n.* отчужде́ние.

alight[1] [ə'laɪt] *pred. adj. & adv.* **1.** (*on fire*) в огне́; **set ~** заж|ига́ть, -е́чь; **is your cigarette ~?** у вас сигаре́та гори́т? **2.** (*illuminated*) освещённый.

alight[2] [ə'laɪt] *v.i.* **1.** (*dismount from horse or vehicle*) сходи́ть, сойти́ (с+*g.*). **2.** (*come to earth: of birds etc.*) сади́ться, сесть; (*of aircraft*) приземл|я́ться, -и́ться.

align [ə'laɪn] *v.t.* выра́внивать, вы́ровнять; **~ o.s. with s.o.** стать (*pf.*) на чью-н. сто́рону.

alignment [ə'laɪnmənt] *n.* выра́внивание; **out of ~** неро́вно, не в ряд; (*arrangement*) расстано́вка.

alike [ə'laɪk] *pred. adj.* (*similar*) похо́жий, подо́бный; **they are very much ~** они́ о́чень похо́жи друг на дру́га; (*as one*) одина́ковый.

adv. подо́бно, одина́ково; **treat everyone ~** обраща́ться (*impf.*) одина́ково со все́ми; **winter and summer ~** как зимо́й, так и ле́том.

alimentary [ˌælɪ'mentərɪ] *adj.* (*of food*): **~ products** пищевы́е проду́кты; (*digestive*): **~ canal** пищевари́тельный тракт.

alimony ['ælɪmənɪ] *n.* (*leg.*) алиме́нт|ы (*pl., g.* -ов).

alive [ə'laɪv] *pred. adj. & adv.* **1.** (*living*) живо́й; в живы́х; **buried ~** за́живо похоро́ненный; **~ and kicking** жив-здоро́в (*coll.*); **more dead than ~** е́ле живо́й. **2.** (*alert*): **be ~ to the danger** сознава́ть (*impf.*) опа́сность; быть начеку́. **3.** (*elec.*) под напряже́нием. **4.** (*infested*): **the bed was ~ with fleas** крова́ть кише́ла бло́хами.

alkali ['ælkəˌlaɪ] *n.* щёлочь; (*attr.*) щелочно́й.

alkaline ['ælkəˌlaɪn] *adj.* щелочно́й.

alkaloid ['ælkəˌlɔɪd] *n.* алкало́ид.

all [ɔ:l] *n.*: **he lost his ~** он потеря́л всё, что име́л; **he staked his ~** он поста́вил на ка́рту всё.

pron. (*everybody*) все; (*everything*) всё; **~ of us** мы все; **the score is 2 ~** счёт 2:2; **~ and sundry** ка́ждый и вся́кий; **~ but** (*almost*) почти́, едва́ не, чуть не; **he ~ but died** он чуть бы́ло не у́мер; **~ in the day's work** де́ло привы́чное; **~ in good time** всё в своё вре́мя; **~ in ~** (*in general*) в о́бщем и це́лом; **it's ~ one to me** мне всё равно́; **~ together now!** а тепе́рь все вме́сте!; **that's ~ very well, but ...** всё это прекра́сно, но...; *see also* **well**[2]; **above ~** пре́жде всего́; **after ~** в конце́ концо́в; в коне́чном счёте; **he came after ~** он всё же пришёл; **any card at ~** люба́я ка́рта; **not at ~** совсе́м/во́все/соверше́нно не; нисколько, ничу́ть; **'Thank you.' — 'Not at ~!'** «Спаси́бо.» — «Не́ за что!»; **he has no money at ~** у него́ совсе́м нет де́нег; **you have eaten nothing at ~** вы ничего́ не е́ли; **for good and ~**; **once and for ~** раз навсегда́; **in ~**; **~ told** в це́лом; всего́.

adj. весь; (*every*) вся́кий; **~ his life** всю свою́ жизнь; **~ day long** весь день; **~ the time** всё вре́мя; **at ~ times** в любо́е вре́мя; всегда́; **at ~ costs** любо́й цено́й; во что бы то ни ста́ло; **beyond ~ doubt** без/вне вся́кого сомне́ния; **by ~ accounts** су́дя по всему́; **for ~ that** всё-таки; **for ~ time** навсегда́; **on ~ fours** на четвере́ньках; **... and ~ that** и так да́лее; и про́чее; **it's not as hard as ~ that** э́то не так уж тру́дно.

adv. (*quite*) совсе́м, соверше́нно; целико́м; **~ along the road** всю доро́гу; на всём пути́; **I knew it ~ along** я всегда́ э́то знал; **~ around** повсю́ду, круго́м; **~ at once** соверше́нно внеза́пно; и вдруг; **she did it ~ by herself** она́ сде́лала э́то сама́; **I am ~ ears** я весь слух; **~ in** включа́я всё; **~ over the room** по всей ко́мнате; **~ the world over** по всему́ ми́ру; **it's ~ over now** тепе́рь всё ко́нчено; с э́тим поко́нчено; **~ over again** (всё) сно́ва; **~ the rage** после́дний крик мо́ды; **~ right** (*satisfactory*) ла́дно; идёт; хорошо́; (*safe*): **we got back ~ right** мы верну́лись благополу́чно; (*in good order*) в поря́дке; (*in replies*) хорошо́; (*implying threat*): **~ right, you wait!** ну хорошо́ же, погоди́те!; **~ the better** тем лу́чше; **~ the same** (*however*) всё-таки; **if it's ~ the same to you** е́сли вам всё равно́; **~ too soon** сли́шком ско́ро; **you're ~ wrong** вы соверше́нно не пра́вы.

cpds. **~-American** чи́сто америка́нский; **~-clear** *n.* отбо́й (трево́ги); **sound the ~-clear** дать (*pf.*) отбо́й; **~-embracing** *adj.* всеобъе́млющий; **~-out** *adj.*: **an ~-out effort** максима́льное уси́лие; **~-party** *adj.* общепарти́йный; **~-powerful** *adj.* всеси́льный; **~-purpose** *adj.* универса́льный; **~-round** *adj.*: **an ~-round view** всесторо́нний подхо́д; **~-round sportsman** разносторо́нний спортсме́н; **~-Russian** *adj.* всеросси́йский; **~spice** *n.* души́стый/ямайский пе́рец; **~-star** *adj.*: **with an ~-star cast** с уча́стием звёзд; **~-time** *adj.*: **at an ~-time low** на небыва́ло ни́зком у́ровне; **~-time record** непревзойдённый реко́рд; **~-weather** *adj.* всепого́дный.

Allah ['ælə] *n.* Алла́х.

allay [ə'leɪ] *v.t.* успок|а́ивать, -о́ить; смягч|а́ть, -и́ть; **~ suspicions** усып|ля́ть, -и́ть подозре́ния.

allegation [ˌælɪ'geɪʃ(ə)n] *n.* заявле́ние, утвержде́ние.

allege [ə'ledʒ] *v.t.* утвержда́ть (*impf.*); **he ~d ill health** он сосла́лся на нездоро́вье; **he is ~d to have died** его́ счита́ют уме́ршим; **an ~d murderer** подозрева́емый в уби́йстве.

allegedly [ə'ledʒɪdlɪ] *adv.* бу́дто бы, я́кобы.

allegiance [ə'li:dʒ(ə)ns] *n.* (*loyalty*) ве́рность; (*devotion*) пре́данность.

allegorical [ˌælɪ'gɒrɪk(ə)l] *adj.* аллегори́ческий.

allegory ['ælɪgərɪ] *n.* аллего́рия.

allegretto [ˌælɪ'gretəʊ] *n., adj. & adv.* аллегре́тто (*indecl.*).

allegro [ə'leɪgrəʊ] *n., adj. & adv.* алле́гро (*indecl.*).

alleluia [ˌælɪ'lu:jə] *n. & int.* аллилу́йя.

allergen ['ælədʒ(ə)n] *n.* аллерге́н.

allergic [ə'lɜ:dʒɪk] *adj.* аллерги́ческий; **I'm ~ to strawberries** у меня́ аллерги́я к клубни́ке.

allergy ['ælədʒɪ] *n.* аллерги́я.

alleviate [ə'li:vɪˌeɪt] *v.t.* (*relieve, lighten*) облегч|а́ть, -и́ть; (*mitigate, soften*) смягч|а́ть, -и́ть.

alleviation [əˌli:vɪ'eɪʃ(ə)n] *n.* облегче́ние; смягче́ние.

alley ['ælɪ] *n.* переу́лок; **blind ~** тупи́к; **that's right up my ~** (*coll.*) э́то как раз по мое́й ча́сти.

alliance [ə'laɪəns] *n.* сою́з.

allied ['ælaɪd] *adj.* (*joined by alliance*) сою́зный; (*related*) ро́дственный; **~ sciences** сме́жные нау́ки.

alligator ['ælɪˌgeɪtə(r)] *n.* аллига́тор.

alliteration [əˌlɪtə'reɪʃ(ə)n] *n.* аллитера́ция.

allocate ['æləˌkeɪt] *v.t.* (*fin.: allot, earmark*) выделя́ть, вы́делить; ассигнова́ть (*impf., pf.*).

allocation [ˌælə'keɪʃ(ə)n] *n.* выделе́ние; ассигнова́ние.
allot [ə'lɒt] *v.t.* (*distribute*) распредел|я́ть, -и́ть; (*assign*) назн|ача́ть, -а́чить; ~ **a task** да|ва́ть, -ть зада́ние.
allotment [ə'lɒtmənt] *n.* **1.** (*in vbl. senses*) распределе́ние; назначе́ние. **2.** (*plot of land*) (земе́льный) уча́сток.
allow [ə'laʊ] *v.t.* **1.** (*permit*) позв|оля́ть, -о́лить; разреш|а́ть, -и́ть; ~ **me!** разреши́те!; **as far as circumstances** ~ наско́лько позволя́ют обстоя́тельства; **I will not** ~ **you to be deceived** я не допущу́, что́бы вас обману́ли; ~ **no discussion** запре|ща́ть, -ти́ть вся́кое обсужде́ние; **smoking is not** ~**ed** кури́ть воспреща́ется; **no dogs** ~**ed** вход с соба́ками воспрещён. **2.** (*grant, provide*) да|ва́ть, -ть; предост|авля́ть, -а́вить; допус|ка́ть, -ти́ть; **I** ~**ed him a free hand** я предоста́вил ему́ свобо́ду де́йствий; ~ **discount** предост|авля́ть, -а́вить ски́дку. **3.** (*admit*) допус|ка́ть, -ти́ть; (*recognize*) призн|ава́ть, -а́ть; **his claim was allowed** его́ тре́бование бы́ло при́нято.
v.i. **1.** ~ **for** (*take into account*) уч|и́тывать, -е́сть; **not** ~**ing for expenses** не принима́я в расчёт изде́ржек; ~ **£50 for emergencies** выделя́ть, вы́делить 50 фу́нтов на чрезвыча́йный слу́чай; ~ **for his being ill** приня́ть (*pf.*) во внима́ние то, что он бо́лен. **2.** ~ **of: his tone** ~**ed of no reply** его́ тон не допуска́л возраже́ний.
allowance [ə'laʊəns] *n.* **1.** (*amount provided*): **monthly** ~ ме́сячное содержа́ние; **family** ~ посо́бие на семью́; **make s.o. an** ~ назна́чить (*pf.*) содержа́ние кому́-н.; (*mil.*) дово́льствие. **2.** (*discount*) ски́дка; ~ **for cash** ски́дка за платёж нали́чными. **3.** (*concession*): **we will make an** ~ **in your case** мы сде́лаем для вас исключе́ние; **make** ~**(s) for** прин|има́ть, -я́ть во внима́ние.
alloy ['ælɔɪ, ə'lɔɪ] *n.* сплав.
v.t. спл|авля́ть, -а́вить.
allud|e [ə'lu:d, ə'lju:d] *v.i.*: ~ **to** ссыла́ться, сосла́ться на+*a.*; упом|ина́ть, -яну́ть; (*mean*): **what are you** ~**ing to?** на что вы намека́ете?
allure [ə'ljʊə(r)] *n.* привлека́тельность, пре́лесть.
v.t. (*entice, attract*) зама́н|ивать, -и́ть; (*charm*) завл|ека́ть, -е́чь; очаро́в|ывать, -а́ть.
allurement [ə'ljʊəmənt] *n.* (*enticement*) привлече́ние; (*charm*) привлека́тельность, пре́лесть.
alluring [ə'ljʊərɪŋ] *adj.* зама́нчивый; очарова́тельный.
allusion [ə'lu:ʒ(ə)n, ə'lju:-] *n.* намёк; ссы́лка.
alluvial [ə'lu:vɪəl] *adj.* аллювиа́льный.
alluvium [ə'lu:vɪəm] *n.* аллю́вий.
ally[1] ['ælaɪ] *n.* сою́зник.
all|y[2] [ə'laɪ] *v.t.* (*connect*) соедин|я́ть, -и́ть; ~**ied to** (*of things*) соединённый с+*i.*; **to be** ~**ied to, with** (*of nations*) быть в сою́зе с+*i.*; ~**y o.s. with** вступ|а́ть, -и́ть в сою́з с+*i.*
almanac ['ɔ:lməˌnæk, 'ɒl-] *n.* альмана́х.
almighty [ɔ:l'maɪtɪ] *n.* **the A**~ Всевы́шний.
adj. всемогу́щий; (*coll., great*): **an** ~ **blow** мо́щный уда́р.
almond ['ɑ:mənd] *n.* минда́ль (*m.*).
adj. минда́льный.
almost ['ɔ:lməʊst] *adv.* почти́; (*with vv.*) почти́, чуть не, едва́ не.
alms [ɑ:mz] *n.* ми́лостыня; **give** ~ подава́ть ми́лостыню.
cpds. ~**-box** *n.* я́щик для же́ртвований; ~**house** *n.* богаде́льня.
aloe ['æləʊ] *n.* ало́э (*nt. indecl.*); **(bitter)** ~**s** ало́э.
aloft [ə'lɒft] *adv.* наверху́; (*of motion*) наве́рх; (*naut.*) на ма́рсе; (*aeron.*) в во́здухе.
alone [ə'ləʊn] *adj.* **1.** (*by o.s., itself*) оди́н; еди́нственный; **he came** ~ он пришёл оди́н; **not by bread** ~ не хле́бом еди́ным. **2.** (*... and no other(s)*): **in the month of June** ~ то́лько в ию́не ме́сяце; **she and I are** ~ **(together)** мы с ней вдвоём/одни́; (*pred.*: *the only one(s)*): **he was** ~ **opposing the suggestion** он оди́н был про́тив предложе́ния; **we are not** ~ **in thinking so** не то́лько мы так ду́маем. **3.: let, leave** ~**: his parents left him** ~ **all day** роди́тели оста́вили его́ на це́лый день одного́; **I should leave the dog** ~ я бы оста́вил соба́ку в поко́е; **let** ~ (*coll.*) не говоря́ уже́ о+*p*.
along [ə'lɒŋ] *adv.* **1.** (*on; forward*): **move** ~ продв|ига́ться, -и́нуться; **move** ~**, please!** проходи́те/продвига́йтесь, пожа́луйста!; **come** ~**!** пошли́!; **a few doors** ~ **from the station** в не́скольких шага́х от вокза́ла; **get** ~ **with** уж|ива́ться, -и́ться с+*i.*. **2.** (*denoting accompaniment*): **come** ~ **with me** пойдёмте/иди́те со мной; **he brought a book** ~ он принёс с собо́й кни́гу. **3.** (*over there*; *over here*): **he went** ~ **to the exhibition** он пошёл на вы́ставку; **he'll be** ~ **in 10 minutes** он бу́дет че́рез де́сять мину́т. **4.: all** ~ (*the whole time*) всё вре́мя; **I said so all** ~ я э́то всегда́ говори́л.
prep. вдоль+*g.*; по+*d.*; вдоль по; **she was walking** ~ **the river** она́ шла вдоль реки́; **they sailed** ~ **the river** они́ плы́ли по реке́.
alongside [əlɒŋ'saɪd] *adv.* ря́дом, сбо́ку.
prep. (*also* ~ **of**) ря́дом с+*i.*; бок о́ бок +*i.*; у+*g.*; ~ **the quay** у при́стани; **come** ~ **a ship/wharf** прист|ава́ть, -а́ть к кораблю́/ве́рфи; (*compared with*) в сравне́нии с+*i.*
aloof [ə'lu:f] *adj.* сде́ржанный, сухова́тый.
adv.: **keep, hold** ~ держа́ться (*impf.*) в стороне́ (*or* особняко́м).
aloofness [ə'lu:fnɪs] *n.* сде́ржанность, отчуждённость.
aloud [ə'laʊd] *adv.* вслух.
alp [ælp] *n.*: **the A**~**s** А́льп|ы (*pl., g.* —).
alpaca [æl'pækə] *n.* альпака́ (*c.g. indecl.*).
alpha ['ælfə] *n.* а́льфа; ~ **particle** а́льфа-части́ца.
alphabet ['ælfəˌbet] *n.* а́збука, алфави́т.
alphabetical [ˌælfə'betɪk(ə)l] *adj.* а́збучный, алфави́тный; **in** ~ **order** в алфави́тном поря́дке.
alpine ['ælpaɪn] *adj.* альпи́йский.
already [ɔ:l'redɪ] *adv.* уже́.
Alsatian [æl'seɪʃ(ə)n] *n.* неме́цкая овча́рка.
also ['ɔ:lsəʊ] *adv.* то́же; та́кже; (*moreover*) к тому́ же; **not only ... but** ~ **...** не то́лько... но и...
altar ['ɔ:ltə(r), 'ɒl-] *n.* престо́л; (*in fig. uses*) алта́рь (*m.*); **high** ~ гла́вный престо́л; **lead to the** ~ вести́ (*det.*) под вене́ц; (*pagan*) алта́рь, же́ртвенник.
cpd. ~**-screen** *n.* (*in Russian church*) иконоста́с.
alter ['ɔ:ltə(r), 'ɒl-] *v.t. & i.* меня́ть(ся) (*impf.*); измен|я́ть(ся), -и́ть(ся); ~ **for the worse** измени́ться к ху́дшему; (*re-make*) переде́л|ывать, -ать; **the dress needs** ~**ing** э́то пла́тье на́до переде́лать.
alteration [ˌɔ:ltə'reɪʃ(ə)n, 'ɒl-] *n.* (*change*) измене́ние; (*replacement*) переме́на; (*re-making e.g. of clothes*) переде́лка; (*re-building*) перестро́йка.
altercation [ˌɔ:ltə'keɪʃ(ə)n, ˌɒl-] *n.* ссо́ра, перебра́нка.
alter ego [ˌæltər 'i:gəʊ, 'egəʊ] *n.* «а́льтер э́го» (*indecl.*), второ́е «я».
alternate[1] [ɔ:l'tɜ:nət, ɒl-] *n.* (*US*) замести́тель (*m.*).
alternate[2] [ɔ:l'tɜ:nət, ɒl-] *adj.* **1.** (*changing*) переме́нный; (*taking turns*) чередую́щийся; **on** ~ **Saturdays** че́рез суббо́ту; ~**ly** попереме́нно. **2.** (*held in reserve*) запасно́й.
alternat|e[3] ['ɔ:ltəˌneɪt, 'ɒl-] *v.t. & i.* чередова́ть(ся) (*impf.*); перемежа́ть(ся) (*impf.*); ~**ing current** переме́нный ток.
alternation [ˌɔ:ltə'neɪʃ(ə)n, ˌɒl-] *n.* чередова́ние; **the** ~ **of day and night** сме́на дня и но́чи.
alternative [ɔ:l'tɜ:nətɪv, ɒl-] *n.* альтернати́ва; **there is no** ~ друго́го вы́бора нет.
adj. альтернати́вный; **an** ~ **proposal** встре́чное

предложе́ние; (*held in reserve*) запасно́й.

alternatively [ɔ:l'tɜ:nətɪvlɪ, ɒl-] *adv.*: **a £50 fine, ~ one month's imprisonment** штраф 50 фу́нтов и́ли оди́н ме́сяц тюре́много заключе́ния.

alternator ['ɔ:ltəˌneɪtə(r), 'ɒl-] *n.* (*elec.*) генера́тор переме́нного то́ка.

although [ɔ:l'ðəʊ] *conj.* хотя́; (*despite the fact that*) несмотря́ на то, что; **~ ill, he came** несмотря́ на боле́знь, он пришёл.

altimeter ['æltɪˌmi:tə(r)] *n.* альтиме́тр; высотоме́р.

altitude ['æltɪˌtju:d] *n.* высота́; **at an ~ of 10,000 metres** на высоте́ 10 000 ме́тров.

alto ['æltəʊ] *n.* альт; (*attr.*) альто́вый.

altogether [ˌɔ:ltə'geðə(r)] *adv.* **1.** (*entirely*) вполне́; соверше́нно; **it is ~ out of the question** э́то соверше́нно исключено́; (*completely*) совсе́м. **2.** (*in all, in general*; *as a whole*) в це́лом, в о́бщем, вообще́; всего́; **how much is that ~?** ско́лько всего́?

altruism ['æltru:ˌɪz(ə)m] *n.* альтруи́зм.

altruist ['æltru:ɪst] *n.* альтруи́ст.

altruistic [ˌæltru:'ɪstɪk] *adj.* альтруисти́ческий.

alum ['æləm] *n.* квасц|ы́ (*pl.*, *g.* -о́в).

alumin|ium (*US* **-um**) [ˌæljʊ'mɪnɪəm; ə'lu:mɪnəm] *n.* алюми́ний.

alumna [ə'lʌmnə] *n.* (бы́вшая) учени́ца; (*of a university*) (бы́вшая) студе́нтка.

alumnus [ə'lʌmnəs] *n.* (бы́вший) учени́к; (*of a university*) (бы́вший) студе́нт.

always ['ɔ:lweɪz] *adv.* всегда́; (*constantly*) постоя́нно, всё вре́мя; **~ the same old thing** всё одно́ и то же.

a.m. (*abbr. of* ***ante meridiem***) утра́; у́тром; **6 ~** шесть часо́в утра́.

amalgam [ə'mælgəm] *n.* амальга́ма.

amalgamate [ə'mælgəˌmeɪt] *v.t. & i.* (*of metals*) амальгами́ровать(ся) (*impf.*, *pf.*); (*fig.*, *unite*) объедин|я́ть(ся), -и́ть(ся).

amalgamation [əˌmælgə'meɪʃ(ə)n] *n.* амальгами́рование; объедине́ние; (*merging*) слия́ние.

amass [ə'mæs] *v.t.* накоп|ля́ть, -и́ть.

amateur ['æmətə(r)] *n.* люби́тель (*m.*); (*pej.*) дилета́нт; (*attr.*) люби́тельский; **~ theatricals** театра́льная самоде́ятельность.

amateurish ['æmətərɪʃ] *adj.* дилета́нтский.

amaz|e [ə'meɪz] *v.t.* изум|ля́ть, -и́ть; **be ~ed at** изум|ля́ться, -и́ться +*d.*; **~ing** изуми́тельный.

amazement [ə'meɪzmənt] *n.* изумле́ние; **he looked at me in ~** он посмотре́л на меня́ с изумле́нием; **to everyone's ~** ко всео́бщему изумле́нию.

Amazon ['æməz(ə)n] *n.* (*myth.*, *fig.*) амазо́нка.

ambassador [æm'bæsədə(r)] *n.* посо́л; (*representative*) представи́тель (*m.*).

ambassadorial [ˌæmbæsə'dɔ:rɪəl] *adj.* посо́льский.

amber ['æmbə(r)] *n.* **1.** (*resin*) янта́рь (*m.*). **2.** (*colour*) янта́рный цвет, цвет янтаря́.

ambergris ['æmbəgrɪs, -ˌgri:s] *n.* се́рая а́мбра.

ambidext(e)rous [ˌæmbɪ'dekstrəs] *adj.* одина́ково владе́ющий обе́ими рука́ми.

ambience ['æmbɪəns] *n.* среда́; атмосфе́ра.

ambiguity [ˌæmbɪ'gju:ɪtɪ] *n.* двусмы́сленность.

ambiguous [æm'bɪgjʊəs] *adj.* двусмы́сленный.

ambition [æm'bɪʃ(ə)n] *n.* (*desire for distinction*) честолю́бие, амби́ция; (*aspiration*) стремле́ние; **her great ~ is to be a dancer** её заве́тная мечта́ — стать танцо́вщицей.

ambitious [æm'bɪʃəs] *adj.* честолюби́вый; амбицио́зный; **he is too ~** он сли́шком мно́гого хо́чет; **an ~ attempt** сме́лая попы́тка; **an ~ plan** грандио́зный план.

ambivalence [æm'bɪvələns] *n.* дво́йственность.

ambivalent [æm'bɪvələnt] *adj.* дво́йственный.

amble ['æmb(ə)l] *n.* (*horse's pace*) и́ноходь; (*easy gait*) лёгкая похо́дка.

v.i. (*of horse*) идти́ (*det.*) и́ноходью; (*of pers.*) идти́ (*det.*) лёгкой похо́дкой.

ambrosia [æm'brəʊzɪə, -ʒjə] *n.* амбро́зия.

ambulance ['æmbjʊləns] *n.* маши́на ско́рой по́мощи; **~ station** медици́нский пункт; **call an ~!** вы́зовите ско́рую по́мощь!

ambush ['æmbʊʃ] *n.* заса́да; **lie in ~** сиде́ть (*impf.*) в заса́де; **run into an ~** поп|ада́ть, -а́сть в заса́ду.

v.t. нап|ада́ть, -а́сть на (*кого*) из заса́ды.

ameliorate [ə'mi:lɪəˌreɪt] *v.t. & i.* ул|учша́ть(ся), -у́чшить(ся).

amelioration [əˌmi:lɪə'reɪʃ(ə)n] *n.* улучше́ние.

amen [ɑ:'men, eɪ-] *int.* ами́нь.

amenable [ə'mi:nəb(ə)l] *adj.* (*tractable*) пода́тливый, послу́шный; (*responsive*) поддаю́щийся (*чему*); **~ to reason** досту́пный го́лосу ра́зума.

amend [ə'mend] *v.t.* **1.** (*correct*) испр|авля́ть, -а́вить; (*improve*) ул|учша́ть, -у́чшить. **2.** (*make changes to*) вн|оси́ть, -ести́ попра́вки/добавле́ния в+*a.*

amendment [ə'mendmənt] *n.* **1.** (*reform*) исправле́ние. **2.** (*of document etc.*) попра́вка, добавле́ние.

amends [ə'mendz] *n.* возмеще́ние; исправле́ние; **make ~ to s.o.** компенси́ровать (*impf.*, *pf.*) кому́-н. (*за что*).

amenit|y [ə'mi:nɪtɪ, ə'menɪtɪ] *n.* (*usu. pl.*, *comforts, pleasures*) удо́бства, удово́льствия (*both nt. pl.*).

America [ə'merɪkə] *n.* Аме́рика.

American [ə'merɪkən] *n.* америка́н|ец (*fem.* -ка).

adj. америка́нский; **~ English** америка́нский вариа́нт англи́йского языка́.

amethyst ['æmɪθɪst] *n.* амети́ст; (*attr.*) амети́стовый.

amiability [ˌeɪmɪə'bɪlɪtɪ] *n.* доброду́шие; приве́тливость.

amiable ['eɪmɪəb(ə)l] *adj.* доброду́шный; приве́тливый.

amicability [ˌæmɪkə'bɪlɪtɪ] *n.* дружелю́бие.

amicable ['æmɪkəb(ə)l] *adj.* дружелю́бный; **they reached an ~ arrangement** они пришли́ к дру́жескому соглаше́нию.

amid(st) [ə'mɪdst] *prep.* среди́+*g.*

cpd. **~ships** *adv.* по середи́не корабля́.

amino acid [əˌmi:nəʊ 'æsɪd] *n.* аминокислота́.

amiss [ə'mɪs] *pred. adj.* непра́вильный; **something is ~** что́-то нела́дно; **what's ~?** в чём де́ло?

adv. **1.** (*wrongly*) непра́вильно; **take ~** (*misinterpret*) толкова́ть (*impf.*) превра́тно; (*take offence at*) об|ижа́ться, -и́деться на+*a.* **2.** (*out of place*) некста́ти.

amity ['æmɪtɪ] *n.* дру́жба; дру́жеские отноше́ния.

ammonia [ə'məʊnɪə] *n.* (*gas*) аммиа́к; (*attr.*) аммиа́чный; (*solution*; *spirit of ~*); нашаты́рный спирт.

ammonium [ə'məʊnɪəm] *n.* аммо́ний; **~ chloride** хло́ристый аммо́ний; **~ nitrate** аммони́йная сели́тра.

ammunition [ˌæmjʊ'nɪʃ(ə)n] *n.* боевы́е припа́сы, боеприпа́сы (*m. pl.*); **~ belt** патро́нная ле́нта, патронта́ш; **~ dump** склад боеприпа́сов.

amnesia [æm'ni:zɪə] *n.* амнези́я.

amnesty ['æmnɪstɪ] *n.* амни́стия.

v.t. амнисти́ровать (*impf.*, *pf.*); да|ва́ть, -ть амни́стию +*d.*

amniocentesis [ˌæmnɪəʊsen'ti:sɪs] *n.* про́ба амнioти́ческой жи́дкости.

amoeba [ə'mi:bə] *n.* амёба.

amok [ə'mɒk] *adv.*: **run ~** бу́йствовать (*impf.*); беси́ться (*impf.*).

among(st) [ə'mʌŋst] *prep.* **1.** (*between*) ме́жду+*i.*; **conversation ~ friends** разгово́р ме́жду друзья́ми. **2.** (*in the midst of*) среди́+*g.*; ме́жду+*g.*; **~ the trees** среди́ дере́вьев; **~ those present** в числе́ прису́тствующих; (*shared by*): **there was a legend ~ the Greeks** у гре́ков существова́ла леге́нда. **3.** (*expr. one of a number*) из+*g.*; **only one ~ his friends** то́лько оди́н из его́ друзе́й; **he was numbered ~ the dead** его́ счита́ли поги́бшим.

amoral [eɪ'mɒr(ə)l] *adj.* амора́льный.

amorous [ˈæmərəs] *adj.* (*inclined to love*) влюбчивый; (*in love*) влюблённый; (*pert. to love*) любо́вный.

amorousness [ˈæmərəsnɪs] *n.* влю́бчивость; влюблённость.

amorphous [əˈmɔːfəs] *adj.* (*shapeless*) бесфо́рменный; (*chem. etc.*) амо́рфный.

amortization [əˌmɔːtaɪˈzeɪʃ(ə)n] *n.* погаше́ние до́лга в рассро́чку.

amortize [əˈmɔːtaɪz] *v.t.* пога|ша́ть, -си́ть в рассро́чку.

amount [əˈmaʊnt] *n.* **1.** (*sum*) су́мма; **to the ~ of** на су́мму в+*a.* **2.** (*quantity*) коли́чество.

v.i.: **~ to** (*add up to*) сост|авля́ть, -а́вить +*g.*; дост|ига́ть, -и́чь +*g.*; **an invoice ~ing to £100** счёт на су́мму в сто фу́нтов; (*be equivalent to*) быть ра́вным/равноси́льным +*d.*; **it ~s to the same thing** э́то сво́дится всё к тому́ же; **~ to very little, not ~ to much** быть незначи́тельным; **he will never ~ to much** из него́ никогда́ ничего́ пу́тного не вы́йдет; (*signify*): **what does it ~ to?** к чему́ э́то сво́дится?

amp [æmp] *n.* (*abbr. of* **ampere**) А, (ампе́р).

ampere [ˈæmpeə(r)] *n.* ампе́р.

ampersand [ˈæmpəˌsænd] *n.* знак «&».

amphibian [æmˈfɪbɪən] *n.* **1.** (*animal*) земново́дное; амфи́бия. **2.** (*mil.*) (*aircraft*) самолёт-амфи́бия; (*tank*) танк-амфи́бия; (*car*) пла́вающий автомоби́ль.

amphibi|ous [æmˈfɪbɪəs], **-an** [æmˈfɪbɪən] *adj.* земново́дный; (*mil.*) пла́вающий; -амфи́бия (*as suff.*); **~ assault** морско́й деса́нт.

amphitheatre [ˈæmfɪˌθɪətə(r)] *n.* амфитеа́тр.

amphora [ˈæmfərə] *n.* а́мфора.

ample [ˈæmp(ə)l] *adj.* (*sufficient*) доста́точный; **we have ~ time** у нас доста́точно вре́мени; (*spacious*) просто́рный; широ́кий; (*extensive*) простра́нный; (*abundant*) оби́льный.

amplification [ˌæmplɪfɪˈkeɪʃ(ə)n] *n.* (*expansion, extension*) расшире́ние; (*enlargement*) увеличе́ние; (*of sound, radio signal etc.*) усиле́ние.

amplifier [ˈæmplɪˌfaɪə(r)] *n.* усили́тель (*m.*).

amplify [ˈæmplɪˌfaɪ] *v.t.* (*expand, extend*) расш|иря́ть, -и́рить; (*enlarge*) увеличи|вать, -ть; (*of sound, radio signal etc.*) усили|вать, -ть.

amplitude [ˈæmplɪˌtjuːd] *n.* (*width*) широта́, разма́х; (*phys., elec.*) амплиту́да.

amply [ˈæmplɪ] *adv.* (*sufficiently*) доста́точно; (*fully*) вполне́; оби́льно.

ampoule [ˈæmpuːl] *n.* а́мпула.

amputate [ˈæmpjʊˌteɪt] *v.t.* ампути́ровать (*impf., pf.*); отн|има́ть, -я́ть.

amputation [ˌæmpjʊˈteɪʃ(ə)n] *n.* ампута́ция.

amulet [ˈæmjʊlɪt] *n.* амуле́т.

amuse [əˈmjuːz] *v.t.* (*entertain, divert*) развл|ека́ть, -е́чь; забавля́ть (*impf.*); (*make laugh*) смеши́ть (*impf.*).

amusement [əˈmjuːzmənt] *n.* **1.** (*diversion*) развлече́ние, заба́ва; **~ arcade, park** аттракцио́ны (*m. pl.*), павильо́н, парк аттракцио́нов. **2.** (*tendency to laughter*): **to everyone's ~ the clown fell over** ко всео́бщему удово́льствию, кло́ун упа́л.

anachronism [əˈnækrəˌnɪz(ə)m] *n.* анахрони́зм.

anachronistic [əˌnækrəˈnɪstɪk] *adj.* анахрони́ческий.

anaconda [ˌænəˈkɒndə] *n.* анако́нда.

anaemia [əˈniːmɪə] *n.* малокро́вие, анеми́я.

anaemic [əˈniːmɪk] *adj.* малокро́вный, анеми́чный.

anaesthesia [ˌænɪsˈθiːzɪə] *n.* анестези́я; обезбо́ливание.

anaesthetic [ˌænɪsˈθetɪk] *n.* анестези́рующее сре́дство; анесте́тик; **general/local ~** о́бщий/ме́стный нарко́з.

adj. анестези́рующий; обезбо́ливающий.

anaesthetist [əˈniːsθətɪst] *n.* анестезио́лог.

anaesthetize [əˈniːsθəˌtaɪz] *v.t.* анестези́ровать (*impf., pf.*).

anagram [ˈænəˌgræm] *n.* анагра́мма.

anal [ˈeɪn(ə)l] *adj.* заднепрохо́дный, ана́льный.

analgesic [ˌænælˈdʒiːsɪk, -zɪk] *adj.* болеутоля́ющий.

analogous [əˈnæləgəs] *adj.* аналоги́чный.

analogue [ˈænəˌlɒg] *n.* ана́лог.

analogy [əˈnælədʒɪ] *n.* анало́гия; схо́дство; **by ~ with** по анало́гии с+*i.*

analyse [ˈænəˌlaɪz] *v.t.* анализи́ровать (*impf., pf.*); (*psych.*) подв|ерга́ть, -е́ргнуть психоана́лизу.

analysis [əˈnælɪsɪs] *n.* ана́лиз; (*gram.*) разбо́р; **in the last ~** в коне́чном счёте; (*psycho ~*) психоана́лиз.

analyst [ˈænəlɪst] *n.* психоанали́тик.

analytic(al) [ˌænəˈlɪtɪk(ə)l] *adj.* аналити́ческий.

anapaest [ˈænəˌpiːst] *n.* ана́пест.

anarchic(al) [əˈnɑːkɪk(ə)l] *adj.* анархи́ческий.

anarchism [ˈænəˌkɪz(ə)m] *n.* анархи́зм.

anarchist [ˈænəkɪst] *n.* анархи́ст (*fem.* -ка).

adj. анархи́стский.

anarchy [ˈænəkɪ] *n.* ана́рхия.

anathema [əˈnæθəmə] *n.* ана́фема.

anathematize [əˈnæθəməˌtaɪz] *v.t.* пред|ава́ть, -а́ть ана́феме.

anatomical [ˌænəˈtɒmɪk(ə)l] *adj.* анатоми́ческий.

anatomist [əˈnætəmɪst] *n.* ана́том.

anatomize [əˈnætəˌmaɪz] *v.t.* анатоми́ровать (*impf., pf.*).

anatomy [əˈnætəmɪ] *n.* **1.** (*science*) анато́мия. **2.** (*dissection*) анатоми́рование. **3.** (*body*) те́ло.

ancestor [ˈænsestə(r)] *n.* пре́док.

ancestral [ænˈsestr(ə)l] *adj.* родово́й.

ancestry [ˈænsestrɪ] *n.* происхожде́ние.

anchor [ˈæŋkə(r)] *n.* я́корь (*m.*); **lie, ride at ~** стоя́ть на я́коре; **weigh ~** сн|има́ться, -я́ться с я́коря.

v.t. ста́вить, по- на я́корь.

v.i. (*of vessel*) ста|нови́ться, -ть на я́корь; (*of crew*: *cast ~*) бр|оса́ть, -о́сить я́корь.

anchorage [ˈæŋkərɪdʒ] *n.* я́корная стоя́нка.

anchorman [ˈæŋkəmən] *n.* (*TV, radio*) веду́щий.

anchovy [ˈæntʃəvɪ, ænˈtʃəʊvɪ] *n.* анчо́ус.

ancient [ˈeɪnʃ(ə)nt] *n.* **the ~s** дре́вние наро́ды (*m. pl.*): (*writers*) анти́чные писа́тели (*m. pl.*).

adj. дре́вний; анти́чный; (*very old*) стари́нный; веково́й; **~ history** дре́вняя исто́рия; **~ monument** па́мятник старины́; **an ~ castle** стари́нный за́мок.

ancillary [ænˈsɪlərɪ] *adj.* (*auxiliary*) вспомога́тельный; (*subordinate*) подчинённый.

and [ænd, ənd] *conj.* **1.** (*connecting words or clauses*) и; (*in addition*) и, да; (*with certain closely linked pairs, esp. of persons*) с+*i.*; **bread ~ butter** хлеб с ма́слом; **you ~ I** мы с ва́ми; (*with nums. denoting addition*) и; плюс; **2 ~ 2 are 4** два и два — четы́ре; (*to form cpd. num.*) *omitted*: **260** две́сти шестьдеся́т; (*with following fraction*) с+*i.*; 41/2 четы́ре с полови́ной. **2.** (*intensive*): **he ran ~ ran** он всё бежа́л и бежа́л; **better ~ better** всё лу́чше (и лу́чше); **they talked for hours ~ hours** они́ разгова́ривали часа́ми. **3.** (*in order to*) *omitted before inf.*: **try ~ find out** постара́йтесь узна́ть; **wait ~ see!** погоди́те — ещё уви́дите! **4.** (*in contrast*) а; **I shall go, ~ you stay here** я пойду́, а вы остава́йтесь здесь.

andante [ænˈdæntɪ] *n., adj. and adv.* анда́нте (*indecl.*).

Andes [ˈændiːz] *n.* А́нды (*pl., g.* —).

anecdotal [ˌænɪkˈdəʊt(ə)l] *adj.* анекдоти́ческий.

anecdote [ˈænɪkˌdəʊt] *n.* исто́рия; (*joke*) анекдо́т.

anemone [əˈnemənɪ] *n.* анемо́н; (*windflower, wood-~*) ве́треница; **sea ~** морско́й анемо́н; акти́ния.

anew [əˈnjuː] *adj.* (*again*) сно́ва; (*in a different way*) за́ново.

angel [ˈeɪndʒ(ə)l] *n.* (*lit., fig.*) а́нгел; **guardian ~** а́нгел-храни́тель; **good/bad ~** до́брый/злой ге́ний.

angelic [ænˈdʒelɪk] *adj.* а́нгельский.

angelica [ænˈdʒelɪkə] *n.* дя́гиль (*m.*).

anger [ˈæŋgə(r)] *n.* гнев; **I said it in ~** я сказа́л э́то сгоряча́.

v.t. серди́ть, рас-; разгне́вать (*pf.*).

angina [æn'dʒaɪnə] *n.* анги́на; ~ **(pectoris)** стенокарди́я, грудна́я жа́ба.

angle[1] ['æŋg(ə)l] *n.* у́гол; **acute** ~ о́стрый у́гол; **obtuse** ~ тупо́й у́гол; **right** ~ прямо́й у́гол; **at right ~s** под прямы́м угло́м; (*fig.*, *viewpoint*) то́чка зре́ния, подхо́д; **one must consider all ~s of a question** на́до уче́сть все аспе́кты вопро́са; **we examined the matter from every** ~ мы всесторо́нне рассмотре́ли вопро́с.

v.t. ста́вить, по- под угло́м; **he ~d the lamp to shine on his book** он поста́вил ла́мпу так, что́бы свет па́дал на кни́гу; (*fig.*): **the news was ~d** но́вости бы́ли подо́браны/по́даны тенденцио́зно.

angl|e[2] ['æŋg(ə)l] *v.i.* (*fish*) уди́ть (*impf.*) ры́бу; **~e for trout** лови́ть форе́ль; (*fig.*): **~e for compliments** напра́шиваться (*impf.*) на комплиме́нты.

angler ['æŋglə(r)] *n.* рыболо́в.

Anglican ['æŋglɪkən] *n.* англика́нец.

adj. англика́нский.

Anglicanism ['æŋglɪkənɪz(ə)m] *n.* англика́нство.

Anglicism ['æŋglɪˌsɪz(ə)m] *n.* англици́зм.

Anglicize ['æŋglɪˌsaɪz] *v.t.* англизи́ровать (*impf.*, *pf.*).

angling ['æŋglɪŋ] *n.* (спорти́вное) рыболо́вство.

Anglophile ['æŋgləʊˌfaɪl] *n.* англофи́л.

Anglo-Saxon [ˌæŋgləʊ'sæks(ə)n] *n.* англоса́кс; чистокро́вный англича́нин.

adj. англосаксо́нский, древнеангли́йский.

angora [æŋ'gɔːrə] *n.* (*cloth*) анго́рская шерсть.

angry ['æŋgrɪ] *adj.* серди́тый, разгне́ванный; **be ~ with** серди́ться/гне́ваться (*both impf.*) на+*a.* **(over, about sth.:** за что-н.); **get ~ with** рассерди́ться (*pf.*) на+*a.*; **make** ~ серди́ть, рас-; (*annoyed*): **he is ~ about the delay** он раздражён опозда́нием.

anguish ['æŋgwɪʃ] *n.* муче́ние; му́ка; страда́ние; (*pain*) боль; **a look of ~, an ~ed look** му́ченический/страда́льческий взгляд.

angular ['æŋgjʊlə(r)] *adj.* **1.** (*forming or pert. to an angle*) углово́й; ~ **velocity** углова́я ско́рость. **2.** (*having angles*) углова́тый; **an ~ face** лицо́ с ре́зкими черта́ми. **3.** (*of pers.*, *thin*, *bony*) худо́й, костля́вый; (*fig.*, *awkward*) углова́тый.

aniline ['ænɪˌliːn, -lɪn, -ˌlaɪn] *n.* анили́н.

adj. анили́новый.

animal ['ænɪm(ə)l] *n.* живо́тное; **domestic ~s** дома́шние живо́тные; **wild** ~ зверь (*m.*), ди́кое живо́тное.

adj. живо́тный; **the ~ kingdom** живо́тное ца́рство; ~ **husbandry** животново́дство.

animate[1] ['ænɪmət] *adj.* (*living*) живо́й; **an ~ noun** одушевлённое и́мя существи́тельное; (*lively*) оживлённый.

animate[2] ['ænɪˌmeɪt] *v.t.* (*enliven*) ожив|ля́ть, -и́ть; (*give life to*) вдохну́ть (*pf.*) жизнь в+*a.*; (*inspire*, *actuate*) вдохнов|ля́ть, -и́ть; (во)одушев|ля́ть, -и́ть; **become ~d** ожив|ля́ться, -и́ться; **~d cartoon** мультипликацио́нный фильм.

animation [ˌænɪ'meɪʃ(ə)n] *n.* (*liveliness*) оживле́ние; (*enthusiasm*) воодушевле́ние.

animism ['ænɪˌmɪz(ə)m] *n.* аними́зм.

animist ['ænɪmɪst] *n.* аними́ст.

animosity [ˌænɪ'mɒsɪtɪ] *n.* (*hostility*) вражде́бность; **feel ~ against** пита́ть (*impf.*) вражду́ к+*d.*

aniseed ['ænɪˌsiːd] *n.* ани́с; ани́совое се́мя.

anisette [ˌænɪ'zet] *n.* ани́совый ликёр.

ankle ['æŋk(ə)l] *n.* лоды́жка, щи́колотка.

cpds. **~-boot** *n.* боти́нок; **~-length** *adj.*: **~-length dress** пла́тье по щи́колотку; **~-socks** носки́ (*m. pl.*).

annals ['æn(ə)lz] *n.* анна́л|ы (*pl.*, *g.* -ов); ле́топись.

anneal [ə'niːl] *v.t.* отж|ига́ть, -е́чь; (*fig.*) закал|я́ть, -и́ть.

annex(e)[1] ['æneks] *n.* (*to document*) приложе́ние; (*to a building*) пристро́йка, фли́гель (*m.*); (*separate building*) отде́льный ко́рпус.

annex[2] [æ'neks, ə'n-] *v.t.* присоедин|я́ть, -и́ть; (*territory etc.*) аннекси́ровать (*impf.*, *pf.*).

annexation [ˌænek'seɪʃ(ə)n, ˌən-] *n.* присоедине́ние; анне́ксия, аннекси́рование.

annihilate [ə'naɪəˌleɪt, ə'naɪl-] *v.t.* (*destroy*) уничт|ожа́ть, -о́жить; (*extirpate*) истреб|ля́ть, -и́ть.

annihilation [əˌnaɪə'leɪʃ(ə)n, əˌnaɪl-] *n.* уничтоже́ние; истребле́ние.

anniversary [ˌænɪ'vɜːsərɪ] *n.* годовщи́на; **on his fifth wedding** ~ в пя́тую годовщи́ну его́ сва́дьбы.

adj.: ~ **edition** юбиле́йное изда́ние.

Anno Domini [ˌænəʊ 'dɒmɪˌnaɪ] *adv.* на́шей э́ры (*abbr.* н.э.); **400 AD** 400 г. на́шей э́ры.

annotate ['ænəʊˌteɪt, 'ænəˌteɪt] *v.t.* снаб|жа́ть, -ди́ть примеча́ниями (*impf.*, *pf.*).

annotation [ˌænəʊ'teɪʃ(ə)n, ˌænə'teɪʃ(ə)n] *n.* примеча́ние; аннота́ция.

announce [ə'naʊns] *v.t.* (*state*; *declare*) объяв|ля́ть, -и́ть (*что or о чём*); заяв|ля́ть, -и́ть (*что or о чём or relative clause*); (*notify*, *tell*) да|ва́ть, -ть знать (*о чём кому*); **he ~d the results of his researches** он сообщи́л о результа́тах свои́х иссле́дований; **the footman ~d the guests as they arrived** лаке́й докла́дывал о прибы́тии госте́й.

announcement [ə'naʊnsmənt] *n.* объявле́ние, заявле́ние; (*written notification*) извеще́ние; (*on radio etc.*) сообще́ние; **the ~ of his death was made at 4 o'clock** о его́ сме́рти сообщи́ли в 4 часа́.

announcer [ə'naʊnsə(r)] *n.* (*on radio etc.*) ди́ктор; (*of stage entertainment*) конферансье́ (*m. indecl.*).

annoy [ə'nɔɪ] *v.t.* (*vex*) доса|жда́ть, -ди́ть +*d.*; (*irritate*) раздража́ть (*impf.*); де́йствовать (*impf.*) на не́рвы +*d.*; **I was ~ed with him** я был на него́ серди́т.

annoyance [ə'nɔɪəns] *n.* раздраже́ние; (*cause of* ~) доса́да, неприя́тность.

annoying [ə'nɔɪɪŋ] *adj.* доса́дный; **how ~!** кака́я доса́да!

annual ['ænjʊəl] *n.* **1.** (*publication*) ежего́дник. **2.** (*plant*) однолє́тнее расте́ние, одноле́тник.

adj. **1.** (*happening once a year*): ~ **meeting** ежего́дное собра́ние. **2.** (*pert. to whole year*): ~ **income** годово́й дохо́д; ~ **report** годово́й отчёт. **3.** (*bot.*, *lasting for one year*) одноле́тний.

annually ['ænjʊəlɪ] *adv.* ежего́дно.

annuity [ə'njuːɪtɪ] *n.* ежего́дная ре́нта.

annul [ə'nʌl] *v.t.* отмен|я́ть, -и́ть (*impf.*, *pf.*); **the marriage was ~led** брак был при́знан недействи́тельным.

annulment [ə'nʌlmənt] *n.* отме́на, аннули́рование.

Annunciation [əˌnʌnsɪ'eɪʃ(ə)n] *n.* (*relig.*) Благове́щение.

anode ['ænəʊd] *n.* ано́д; (*attr.*) ано́дный.

anoint [ə'nɔɪnt] *v.t.* пома́з|ывать, -ать.

anomalous [ə'nɒmələs] *adj.* анома́льный.

anomaly [ə'nɒməlɪ] *n.* анома́лия.

anon [ə'nɒn] *adv.* ско́ро, вско́ре; **see you ~!** пока́!

anonymity [ˌænə'nɪmɪtɪ] *n.* анони́мность.

anonymous [ə'nɒnɪməs] *adj.* анони́мный.

anorak ['ænəˌræk] *n.* анора́к, ку́ртка с капюшо́ном.

anorexia [ˌænə'reksɪə] *n.* отсу́тствие аппети́та; ~ **nervosa** не́рвная анорекси́я.

anorexic [ænə'reksɪk] *n.* больн|о́й (*fem.* -а́я) анорекси́ей.

adj. страда́ющий анорекси́ей.

another [ə'nʌðə(r)] *pron.* & *adj.* **1.** (*additional*) ещё; ~ **cup of tea?** ещё ча́шку ча́ю?; **will you have ~ (drink)?** хоти́те ещё вы́пить?; **have ~ go!** попыта́йтесь ещё раз!; **in ~ 10 years** ещё че́рез де́сять лет; **and ~ thing** и вот ещё что; **not ~ word!** ни сло́ва бо́льше!; **without ~ word** не говоря́ ни сло́ва. **2.** (*similar*): **such ~ as I** подо́бный мне; ~ **Tolstoy** второ́й Толсто́й. **3.** (*different*) друго́й; ~ **time** в друго́й раз; **that's ~ matter altogether** э́то совсе́м друго́е де́ло; **one way or ~** так и́ли ина́че. **4.: one ~** (*refl.*) *see* **one**

answer ['ɑːnsə(r)] *n.* **1.** (*reply*) отве́т; **what was his ~?** что он отве́тил?; **in ~ to your letter** в отве́т на ва́ше письмо́; (*retort*) возраже́ние; (*defence*): **he has a complete ~ to the charges** он мо́жет отвести́ все обвине́ния. **2.** (*solution*) отве́т; реше́ние; **there is no simple ~ to the problem** пробле́му реши́ть нелегко́.

v.t. **1.** (*reply to*) отв|еча́ть, -е́тить (*кому, на что*); **the question was not ~ed** вопро́с оста́лся без отве́та; **~ the door** откр|ыва́ть, -ы́ть дверь; **~ the door-bell (*or* a knock at the door)** откр|ыва́ть, -ы́ть (дверь) на звоно́к (*or* на стук); **~ the telephone** под|ходи́ть, -ойти́ к телефо́ну; отвеча́ть (*impf.*) на телефо́нные звонки́. **2.** (*fulfil*): **~ requirements** отвеча́ть (*impf.*) тре́бованиям; **~ the purpose** соотве́тствовать (*impf.*) це́ли. **3.** (*correspond to*): **he ~s the description exactly** он то́чно соотве́тствует описа́нию. **4.** (*refute*): **~ a charge** опров|ерга́ть, -е́ргнуть обвине́ние. **5.** (*solve*) реш|а́ть, -и́ть.

v.i. **1.** (*reply*) отв|еча́ть, -е́тить. **2.** (*respond; react*): **the dog ~s to the name of Rex** соба́ка отзыва́ется на кли́чку Рекс. **3. ~ for** (*vouch, accept responsibility for*) руча́ться, поручи́ться за+*a.*; (*suffer, bear responsibility for*): **you will ~ for your words** вы отве́тите за э́ти слова́. **4.** (*give an account*): **I ~ to no one** я никому́ не обя́зан отчётом. **5. ~ back** дерзи́ть, на-.

cpd. **~phone** ['ɑːnsəˌfəʊn] *n.* автоотве́тчик.

answerable ['ɑːnsərəb(ə)l] *adj.* отве́тственный (*перед кем за что*); **you are ~ to me for your conduct** вы несёте передо мной отве́тственность за свой посту́пки.

ant [ænt] *n.* мураве́й; (*attr.*) муравьи́ный.

cpds. **~-eater** *n.* муравье́д; **~-hill, ~-heap** *nn.* мураве́йник.

antacid [ænt'æsɪd] *n.* сре́дство, нейтрализу́ющее кислоту́.

antagonism [æn'tægəˌnɪz(ə)m] *n.* антагони́зм.

antagonist [æn'tægənɪst] *n.* антагони́ст; (*adversary*) проти́вник.

antagonistic [ænˌtægə'nɪstɪk] *adj.* антагонисти́ческий.

antagonize [æn'tægəˌnaɪz] *v.t.* раздража́ть (*impf.*); нерви́ровать (*impf.*).

Antarctic [ænt'ɑːktɪk] *n.*: **the A~** Анта́рктика.

adj. антаркти́ческий; **A~ Circle** Ю́жный поля́рный круг; **A~ Ocean** Ю́жный океа́н.

Antarctica [ænt'ɑːktɪkə] *n.* Антаркти́да.

ante ['æntɪ] *n.* (*stake*) ста́вка; **raise the ~** пов|ыша́ть, -ы́сить ста́вку.

antecedent [ˌæntɪ'siːd(ə)nt] *n.* **1.** (*preceding thg. or circumstance*) предше́ствующее, предыду́щее. **2.** (*pl., the past*) про́шлое; (*past life*) про́шлая жизнь.

adj. предше́ствующий, предыду́щий.

antechamber ['æntɪˌtʃeɪmbə(r)] *n.* пере́дняя, вестибю́ль (*m.*).

antedate [ˌæntɪ'deɪt] *v.t.* **1.** (*put earlier date on*) пом|еча́ть, -е́тить за́дним число́м. **2.** (*precede*) предше́ствовать (*impf.*) +*d.*

antediluvian [ˌæntɪdɪ'luːvɪən, -'ljuːvɪən] *adj.* (*lit., fig.*) допото́пный.

antelope ['æntɪˌləʊp] *n.* антило́па.

antenatal [ˌæntɪ'neɪt(ə)l] *adj.* утро́бный; дородово́й.

antenna [æn'tenə] *n.* (*radio*) анте́нна; (*of insect*) щу́пальце, у́сик.

anterior [æn'tɪərɪə(r)] *adj.* (*of place*) пере́дний; (*of time*) предше́ствующий.

ante-room ['æntɪˌruːm, -ˌrʊm] *n.* пере́дняя, прихо́жая.

anthem ['ænθəm] *n.* гимн; **national ~** госуда́рственный гимн.

anther ['ænθə(r)] *n.* пы́льник.

anthology [æn'θɒlədʒɪ] *n.* антоло́гия.

anthracite ['ænθrəˌsaɪt] *n.* антраци́т.

anthrax ['ænθræks] *n.* сиби́рская я́зва.

anthropoid ['ænθrəˌpɔɪd] *n.* антропо́ид.

adj. человекообра́зный, антропо́идный.

anthropological [ˌænθrəpə'lɒdʒɪk(ə)l] *adj.* антропологи́ческий.

anthropologist [ˌænθrə'pɒlədʒɪst] *n.* (*biological*) антропо́лог; **social ~** этно́граф.

anthropology [ˌænθrə'pɒlədʒɪ] *n.* (*biological*) антрополо́гия; **social ~** этногра́фия.

anthropomorphic [ˌænθrəpə'mɔːfɪk] *adj.* антропоморфи́ческий.

anthropomorphism [ˌænθrəpə'mɔːfɪz(ə)m] *n.* антропоморфи́зм.

anti- ['æntɪ] *pref.* анти..., противо...

anti-aircraft [ˌæntɪ'eəkrɑːft] *adj.* зени́тный; **~ defence** противовозду́шая оборо́на (*abbr.* ПВО).

antibiotic [ˌæntɪbaɪ'ɒtɪk] *n.* антибио́тик.

adj. антибиоти́ческий.

antibody ['æntɪˌbɒdɪ] *n.* антите́ло.

Antichrist ['æntɪˌkraɪst] *n.* анти́христ.

anticipate [æn'tɪsɪˌpeɪt] *v.t.* **1.** (*do, use in advance*) де́лать, с- ра́ньше сро́ка; испо́льзовать (*impf., pf.*) ра́ньше вре́мени. **2.** (*precede*) опере|жа́ть, -ди́ть. **3.** (*foresee*) предви́деть (*impf.*); предчу́вствовать (*impf.*); (*expect*) ожида́ть (*impf.*). **4.** (*forestall*) предвосх|ища́ть, -и́тить; предупре|жда́ть, -ди́ть.

anticipation [ænˌtɪsɪ'peɪʃ(ə)n] *n.* **1.** (*looking forward to*) ожида́ние; **in ~ of your early reply** в ожида́нии ва́шего ско́рого отве́та. **2.** (*foreseeing*) предви́дение, предвосхище́ние.

anticlimax [ˌæntɪ'klaɪmæks] *n.* (ре́зкий) спад (интере́са *и т.п.*); разочарова́ние.

anticlockwise [ˌæntɪ'klɒkwaɪz] *adj. & adv.* про́тив часово́й стре́лки.

anti-Communist [ˌæntɪ'kɒmjʊnɪst] *n.* проти́вник коммуни́зма.

adj. антикоммунисти́ческий.

antics ['æntɪks] *n. pl.* (*physical*) кривля́нье, ужи́мки (*f. pl.*); (*behaviour*) проде́лки (*f. pl.*).

anticyclone [ˌæntɪ'saɪkləʊn] *n.* антицикло́н.

antidepressant [ˌæntɪdɪ'pres(ə)nt] *n.* антидепресса́нт.

antidote ['æntɪˌdəʊt] *n.* противоя́дие.

antifreeze ['æntɪˌfriːz] *n.* антифри́з.

anti-missile [ˌæntɪ'mɪsaɪl] *adj.* противораке́тный.

antimony ['æntɪmənɪ] *n.* сурьма́; (*attr.*) сурьмя́ный.

antipathetic [ˌæntɪpə'θetɪk] *adj.* антипати́чный.

antipathy [æn'tɪpəθɪ] *n.* антипа́тия; **have, feel an ~ to, against, for** пита́ть (*impf.*) антипа́тию к+*d.*

anti-personnel [ˌæntɪˌpɜːsə'nel] *adj.* противопехо́тный; **~ (*fragmentation*) bomb** оско́лочная бо́мба.

antiperspirant [ˌæntɪ'pɜːspɪrənt] *n.* антиперспира́нт, сре́дство от поте́ния.

antipodes [æn'tɪpəˌdiːz] *n.* антипо́ды (*m. pl.*).

antiquarian [ˌæntɪ'kweərɪən] *n.* антиква́р, антиква́рий.

adj. антиква́рный.

antiquary ['æntɪkwərɪ] *n.* антиква́р, антиква́рий.

antiquated ['æntɪˌkweɪtɪd] *adj.* (*obsolete*) устаре́лый; (*old-fashioned*) старомо́дный.

antique [æn'tiːk] *n.* антиква́рная вещь; **~ shop** антиква́рный магази́н.

adj. (*ancient*) дре́вний, стари́нный; (*pert. to ancient, esp. classical times*) анти́чный.

antiquit|y [æn'tɪkwɪtɪ] *n.* (*great age; olden times*) дре́вность; (*classical times*) анти́чность; (*pl., ancient objects*) рели́квии (*f. pl.*).

antirrhinum [ˌæntɪ'raɪnəm] *n.* льви́ный зев.

anti-Semite [ˌæntɪ'siːmaɪt] *n.* антисеми́т (*fem.* -ка).

anti-Semitic [ˌæntɪsɪ'mɪtɪk] *adj.* антисеми́тский.

anti-Semitism [ˌæntɪ'semɪˌtɪz(ə)m] *n.* антисемити́зм.

antisepsis [ˌæntɪ'sepsɪs] *n.* антисе́птика.

antiseptic [ˌæntɪ'septɪk] *n.* антисе́птик.

adj. антисепти́ческий.

anti-social [ˌæntɪˈsəʊʃ(ə)l] *adj.* антиобще́ственный.
anti-Soviet [ˌæntɪˈsəʊvɪət] *adj.* антисове́тский.
anti-submarine [ˌæntɪsʌbməˈriːn] *adj.* противоло́дочный.
anti-tank [ˌæntɪˈtæŋk] *adj.* противота́нковый.
antithesis [ænˈtɪθɪsɪs] *n.* (*contrast of opposite ideas*) антите́за; (*contrast*) контра́ст; (*opposite*) противополо́жность.
antithetic(al) [ˌæntɪˈθetɪk(ə)l] *adj.* антитети́ческий.
antitoxin [ˌæntɪˈtɒksɪn] *n.* антитокси́н.
antler [ˈæntlə(r)] *n.* оле́ний рог.
antonym [ˈæntənɪm] *n.* анто́ним.
anus [ˈeɪnəs] *n.* за́дний прохо́д, а́нус.
anvil [ˈænvɪl] *n.* накова́льня.
anxiety [æŋˈzaɪətɪ] *n.* **1.** (*uneasiness*) беспоко́йство; (*alarm*) трево́га; **be full of ~** волнова́ться (*impf.*); **feel ~ for, over** беспоко́иться (*impf.*) о+*p.* **2.** (*desire*; *keenness*) жела́ние/стремле́ние +*inf.* **3.** (*pl.*, *cares*, *worries*) забо́ты (*f. pl.*).
anxious [ˈæŋkʃəs] *adj.* **1.** (*worried*, *uneasy*) озабо́ченный; **be ~ about, for, over** беспоко́иться (*impf.*) о+*p.* **2.** (*causing anxiety*) трево́жный, беспоко́йный. **3.** (*keen*, *desirous*): **I am ~ to see him** мне о́чень хо́чется его́ ви́деть.
any [ˈenɪ] *pron.* **1.** (*in interrog. or conditional sentences*) кто́-нибудь; что́-нибудь; **if ~ of them should see him** е́сли его́ кто́-нибудь из них уви́дит. **2.** (*in neg. sentences*) никто́; ничто́; ни оди́н; **I don't like ~ of these actors** мне не нра́вится ни оди́н из э́тих арти́стов; **he never spoke to ~ of our friends** он не говори́л ни с кем из на́ших друзе́й; **I looked for the books but couldn't find ~** я иска́л кни́ги, но не нашёл ни одно́й. **3.** (*in affirmative sentences*) любо́й; **take ~ of these books** возьми́те любу́ю/любы́е из э́тих книг.

adj. **1.** (*in interrog. or conditional sentences*) *untranslated*: **have you ~ children?** у вас есть де́ти?; **were there ~ Russians there?** бы́ли там ру́сские?; **is there ~ news?** есть каки́е-нибудь но́вости?; (*no matter what*) любо́й, како́й уго́дно. **2.** (*in neg. sentences*): **we haven't ~ milk** у нас нет молока́; (*not ~ at all*, *not a single*) никако́й, ни оди́н; **there wasn't ~ hope** никако́й наде́жды не́ было; (*with* **hardly**, *vv. of prevention etc.*): **there is hardly ~ doubt** нет почти́ никако́го сомне́ния; **without ~ doubt** без вся́кого сомне́ния; **they stopped us from scoring ~ goals** они́ не да́ли нам заби́ть ни одного́ гола́. **3.** (*no matter which*) любо́й; **at ~ time** в любо́е вре́мя; **at ~ hour of the day** в любо́е вре́мя дня; (*every*) вся́кий; **in ~ case** во вся́ком слу́чае; **~ student knows this** э́то зна́ет ка́ждый/любо́й студе́нт; **~ amount** *see* **amount**

adv. **1.** (*in interrog. or conditional sentences*) *untranslated or* ско́лько-нибудь; **do you want ~ more tea?** хоти́те ещё ча́ю?; **will he be ~ better for it?** ра́зве от э́того ему́ бу́дет лу́чше?. **2.** (*in neg. sentences*) *untranslated or* ниско́лько; ничу́ть; отню́дь; **I can't go ~ farther** я не могу́ идти́ да́льше; **I am not ~ better** мне ничу́ть не лу́чше; **he did not get ~ nearer** он ниско́лько не прибли́зился. **3.** (*US*, *at all*): **it didn't snow ~ yesterday** вчера́ сне́га во́все не́ было; **that didn't help us ~** э́то нам ниско́лько не помогло́.
anybody [ˈenɪˌbɒdɪ], **anyone** [ˈenɪˌwʌn] *n.* & *pron.* **1.** (*in interrog. or conditional sentences*) кто́-нибудь; кто́-либо; кто; **did you meet ~?** вы кого́-нибудь встре́тили?; **is this ~'s seat?** э́то ме́сто за́нято?; **is ~ hurt?** никто́ не ра́нен? **2.** (*in neg. sentences*) никто́; **I didn't speak to ~** я ни с кем не говори́л. **3.** (*~ at all*; *no matter who*) вся́кий, ка́ждый; любо́й; **~ will tell you** вся́кий вам ска́жет; **~ but you** кто уго́дно, то́лько не вы; **~ else** кто́-нибудь друго́й/ещё; **he speaks better than ~** он говори́т лу́чше всех; **there was hardly ~ there** там почти́ никого́ не́ было; **he loved her more than ~** он люби́л её бо́льше всех.
anyhow [ˈenɪˌhaʊ] *adv.* **1.** (*in one manner or another*) так и́ли и́наче; ка́к-нибудь. **2.** (*haphazardly*; *carelessly*) ко́е-как; ка́к-нибудь; **the work was done ~** рабо́та была́ сде́лана ко́е-как. **3.** (*anyway*, *in any case*) во вся́ком слу́чае; **I shall go ~** я всё равно́ пойду́.
anyone [ˈenɪˌwʌn] = **anybody**
anything [ˈenɪθɪŋ] *n.* & *pron.* **1.** (*in interrog. or conditional sen tences*) что́-нибудь; что́-либо; что; **is there ~ I can get for you?** вам что́-нибудь ну́жно? я принесу́; **can I do ~ to help?** чем я могу́ помо́чь?; **have you ~ to say?** у вас (*or* вам) есть что сказа́ть?; **better, if ~** вро́де бы лу́чше. **2.** (*in neg. sentences*) ничто́; **I haven't ~ to say to that** мне не́чего сказа́ть на э́то. **3.** (*everything*) всё; **I'd give ~ to see him again** я о́тдал бы всё, что́бы уви́деть его́ опя́ть; **we were left without ~** мы оста́лись без ничего́/всего́; **more, better than ~** бо́льше всего́. **4.** (*~ at all*, *~ you please*) всё что уго́дно; **it's as simple as ~** э́то про́ще просто́го. **5.** (*whatever*): **I will do ~ you suggest** я сде́лаю всё, что вы ска́жете. **6.: ~ but: he is ~ but a genius** он совсе́м не ге́ний; **it is ~ but** (*far from*) **clear** э́то далеко́ не я́сно.
anyway [ˈenɪˌweɪ] = **anyhow 3.**
anywhere [ˈenɪˌweə(r)] *adv.* **1.** (*in interrog. and conditional sentences*) где́-нибудь; где́-либо; (*of motion*) куда́-нибудь; куда́-либо; **is there a chemist's ~?** здесь есть апте́ка?; **have you ~ to stay?** у вас есть где останови́ться? **2.** (*in neg. sentences*) нигде́; (*of motion*) никуда́. **3.** (*in any place at all*; *everywhere*) где уго́дно; везде́; (по)всю́ду; **it is miles from ~** э́то у чёрта на кули́чках; **it isn't ~ near finished** э́то ещё далеко́ не зако́нчено.
aorta [eɪˈɔːtə] *n.* ао́рта.
apace [əˈpeɪs] *adv.* по́лным хо́дом.
apart [əˈpɑːt] *adv.* **1.** (*on*, *to one side*) в стороне́; в сто́рону; **his height set him ~** он выделя́лся свои́м ро́стом; **joking ~** шу́тки в сто́рону; **~ from** (*with the exception of*) за исключе́нием +*g.*, кро́ме+*g.*; (*other than*; *besides*) кро́ме/поми́мо +*g.* **2.** (*separate*; *into parts*) отде́льно; на ча́сти; **the dish came ~ in her hands** таре́лка слома́лась у неё в рука́х; **the baby pulled its rattle ~** ребёнок разлома́л погрему́шку на ча́сти; **they took the machine ~** они́ разобра́ли маши́ну на ча́сти; **I could not tell them ~** я не мог их различи́ть/отличи́ть; **with one's feet wide ~** расста́вив но́ги. **3.** (*distant*): **the houses are a mile ~** дома́ нахо́дятся в ми́ле друг от дру́га.
apartheid [əˈpɑːteɪt] *n.* апартейд.
apartment [əˈpɑːtmənt] *n.* **1.** (*room*) ко́мната. **2.: the royal ~s** короле́вские апартаме́нты (*m. pl.*). **3.** (*US*) кварти́ра; **~ house** многокварти́рный дом.
apathetic [ˌæpəˈθetɪk] *adj.* апати́чный.
apathy [ˈæpəθɪ] *n.* апа́тия.
APC (*abbr. of* **armoured personnel carrier**) БТР, бронетранспортёр.
ape [eɪp] *n.* (*lit.*, *fig.*) обезья́на; **play the ~** обезья́нничать (*impf.*).

v.t. **1.** (*imitate*) подража́ть (*impf.*) +*d.* **2.** (*mock*) передра́зн|ивать, -и́ть.

cpd. **~-like** *adj.* обезьяноподо́бный.
aperitif [əˌperɪˈtiːf, əˈpe-] *n.* аперити́в.
aperture [ˈæpəˌtjʊə(r)] *n.* отве́рстие; (*opt.*) аперту́ра.
apex [ˈeɪpeks] *n.* (*lit.*, *fig.*) верши́на, верх.
aphasia [əˈfeɪzɪə] *n.* афа́зия.
aphid [ˈeɪfɪd], **aphis** [ˈeɪfɪs] *nn.* тля.
aphorism [ˈæfəˌrɪz(ə)m] *n.* афори́зм.
aphrodisiac [ˌæfrəˈdɪzɪˌæk] *n.* сре́дство, уси́ливающее полово́е влече́ние.

apiary [ˈeɪpɪərɪ] *n.* пчéльник, пáсека.

apiece [əˈpiːs] *adv.* **1.** (*of thg.*): **I sell books for a dollar ~** я продаю́ кни́ги по до́ллару (за ка́ждую). **2.** (*of pers.*): **we had £10 ~** у нас бы́ло по де́сять фу́нтов на челове́ка; **he gave them 5 roubles ~** он дал им по пять рубле́й (ка́ждому); **they scored two goals ~** ка́ждый из них заби́л по два го́ла.

aplomb [əˈplɒm] *n.* апло́мб.

apocalypse [əˈpɒkəlɪps] *n.* апока́липсис.

apocalyptic [əˌpɒkəˈlɪptɪk] *adj.* апокалипти́ческий.

Apocrypha [əˈpɒkrɪfə] *n.* апо́крифы (*m. pl.*).

apocryphal [əˈpɒkrɪf(ə)l] *adj.* **1.** (*bibl.*) апокрифи́ческий. **2.** (*of doubtful authenticity*) недостове́рный.

apogee [ˈæpəˌdʒiː] *n.* (*lit.*, *fig.*) апоге́й.

apolitical [ˌeːpəˈlɪtɪk(ə)l] *adj.* аполити́чный.

Apollo [əˈpɒləʊ] *n.* Аполло́н.

apologetic [əˌpɒləˈdʒetɪk] *adj.* извиня́ющийся; **he was very ~** он о́чень извиня́лся; **an ~ smile** винова́тая улы́бка.

apologetics [əˌpɒləˈdʒetɪks] *n.* апологе́тика.

apologia [ˌæpəˈləʊdʒɪə] *n.* аполо́гия.

apologist [əˈpɒlədʒɪst] *n.* апологе́т.

apologize [əˈpɒləˌdʒaɪz] *v.i.* извин|я́ться, -и́ться (*перед кем за что*).

apolog|y [əˈpɒlədʒɪ] *n.* извине́ние; **make, offer an ~y to s.o. for sth.** прин|оси́ть, -ести́ извине́ние кому́-н. за что-н.; **please accept my ~ies** приму́те мои́ извине́ния; **they sent their ~ies** они́ переда́ли свои́ извине́ния.

apoplectic [ˌæpəˈplektɪk] *adj.*: **an ~ fit** апоплекси́ческий уда́р.

apoplexy [ˈæpəˌpleksɪ] *n.* апопле́ксия.

apostasy [əˈpɒstəsɪ] *n.* (*abandonment or loss of faith, principles etc.*) отсту́пничество, апоста́зия; (*desertion of cause or party*) ренега́тство.

apostate [əˈpɒsteɪt] *n.* отсту́пник; ренега́т.

adj. отсту́пнический.

a posteriori [ˌeɪ pɒˌsterɪˈɔːraɪ] *adj.* апостерио́рный.

adv. апостерио́ри.

apostle [əˈpɒs(ə)l] *n.* апо́стол.

apostolic [ˌæpəˈstɒlɪk] *adj.*: **~ succession** апо́стольское насле́дование; **A~ See** па́пский престо́л.

apostrophe [əˈpɒstrəfɪ] *n.* (*gram.*) апостро́ф.

apothecary [əˈpɒθəkərɪ] *n.* (*arch.*) апте́карь (*m.*).

apothegm [ˈæpəˌθem, ˈæpəfˌθem] = **apo(ph)thegm**

apotheosis [əˌpɒθɪˈəʊsɪs] *n.* (*lit.*, *fig.*) апофео́з.

appal [əˈpɔːl] *v.t.* ужас|а́ть, -ну́ть; **we were ~led at the sight** мы ужасну́лись (*or* пришли́ в у́жас) при ви́де э́того.

appalling [əˈpɔːlɪŋ] *adj.* ужа́сный, жу́ткий.

apparatus [ˌæpəˈreɪtəs, ˈæp-] *n.* **1.** (*instrument*; *appliance*) прибо́р, инструме́нт. **2.** (*in laboratory*) аппарату́ра; обору́дование. **3.** (*gymnastic*) снаря́ды (*m. pl.*). **4.** (*set of institutions*) аппара́т; **~ of government** прави́тельственный аппара́т.

apparel [əˈpær(ə)l] *n.* одея́ние, наря́д, облаче́ние.

apparent [əˈpærənt] *adj.* **1.** (*visible*) ви́димый. **2.** (*plain*, *obvious*) очеви́дный; я́вный; **heir ~** зако́нный/прямо́й насле́дник; **be, become ~** обнару́жи|ваться, -ться.

apparently [əˈpærəntlɪ] *adv.* **1.** (*clearly*) очеви́дно, я́вно. **2.** (*seemingly*) по-ви́димому; (как) бу́дто; **~ he's the local doctor** он как бу́дто зде́шний врач.

apparition [ˌæpəˈrɪʃ(ə)n] *n.* **1.** (*manifestation, esp. of ghost*) (по)явле́ние. **2.** (*ghost*) привиде́ние, виде́ние, при́зрак.

appeal [əˈpiːl] *n.* **1.** (*earnest request, plea*) обраще́ние (с про́сьбой); (*official*) воззва́ние; (*call*) призы́в; **an ~ to public opinion** обраще́ние к обще́ственному мне́нию; **an ~ for sympathy** про́сьба отнести́сь сочу́вственно; **an ~ for silence** призы́в к тишине́. **2.** (*reference to higher authority*) апелля́ция, обжа́лование; **court of ~** апелляцио́нный суд; **an ~ to the referee** обраще́ние к судье́. **3.** (*attraction*) привлека́тельность.

v.i. **1.** (*make earnest request*) обра|ща́ться, -ти́ться с про́сьбой; **she ~ed to him for mercy** она́ моли́ла его́ о милосе́рдии. **2.** (*leg.*) апелли́ровать (*impf.*, *pf.*); под|ава́ть, -а́ть апелля́цию; обжа́ловать (*pf.*) пригово́р. **3.**: **~ to** (*attract*) привлека́ть (*impf.*); нра́виться (*impf.*) +*d.*

appealing [əˈpiːlɪŋ] *adj.* (*imploring*) умоля́ющий; (*attractive*) привлека́тельный.

appear [əˈpɪə(r)] *v.i.* **1.** (*become visible*) пока́з|ываться, -а́ться; появ|ля́ться, -и́ться; (*of qualities etc.*) проявл|я́ться, -и́ться. **2.** (*present o.s.*) выступа́ть, вы́ступить; **~ in court** предст|ава́ть, -а́ть пе́ред судо́м; (*of actor*) игра́ть (*impf.*) на сце́не; снима́ться (*impf.*) в кино́; (*make an entrance on stage*) выходи́ть, вы́йти на сце́ну; (*of book*) выходи́ть, вы́йти (в свет). **3.** (*seem*) каза́ться, по-; (*follow as inference*) сле́довать (*impf.*); (*be manifest*) я́вствовать (*impf.*); **it ~s strange to me** мне э́то ка́жется стра́нным; **he ~s to have left** он, ка́жется, уе́хал. **4.** (*turn out*) ока́з|ываться, -а́ться; **if it ~s that this is so** е́сли ока́жется, что э́то так.

appearance [əˈpɪərəns] *n.* **1.** (*act of appearing*) появле́ние; (*in public*) выступле́ние; **make (*or* put in) an ~** пока́з|ываться, -а́ться; появ|ля́ться, -и́ться; **make one's first ~** дебюти́ровать (*impf.*, *pf.*). **2.** (*phenomenon*) явле́ние. **3.** (*look*, *aspect*) вид; о́блик; нару́жность; вне́шность; **~s are deceptive** нару́жность обма́нчива; **judge by ~(s)** суди́ть (*impf.*) по вне́шнему ви́ду; **in ~** на вид; по ви́ду; **to, by all ~s** по всем при́знакам; су́дя по всему́. **4.** (*semblance*) вид, ви́димость; **keep up ~s** соблюда́ть (*impf.*) прили́чия (*nt. pl.*); **for ~'s sake** для ви́димости; напока́з.

appease [əˈpiːz] *v.t.* (*pol.*, *buy off*) умиротвор|я́ть, -и́ть; (*appetites*, *passions*, *demands*) утол|я́ть, -и́ть.

appeasement [əˈpiːzmənt] *n.* **1.** умиротворе́ние. **2.** (*of hunger, desire etc.*) утоле́ние.

appeaser [əˈpiːzə(r)] *n.* умиротвори́тель (*m.*); успоко́итель (*m.*).

appellant [əˈpelənt] *n.* апелля́нт.

appellate [əˈpelət] *adj.* апелляцио́нный.

appellati|on [ˌæpəˈleɪʃ(ə)n] *n.* назва́ние.

append [əˈpend] *v.t.* **1.** (*join*) присоедин|я́ть, -и́ть; (*fasten*) прикреп|ля́ть, -и́ть. **2.** (*add, in writing etc.*) прил|ага́ть, -ожи́ть; приб|авля́ть, -а́вить; **they wish to ~ a clause to the treaty** они́ хотя́т доба́вить статью́ к догово́ру.

appendage [əˈpendɪdʒ] *n.* прида́ток.

appendectomy [ˌæpenˈdektəmɪ] *n.* опера́ция аппендици́та.

appendicitis [əˌpendɪˈsaɪtɪs] *n.* аппендици́т.

appendix [əˈpendɪks] *n.* **1.** (*anat.*) аппе́ндикс. **2.** (*of a book, document etc.*) приложе́ние.

apperception [ˌæpəˈsepʃ(ə)n] *n.* апперце́пция; самосозна́ние.

appertain [ˌæpəˈteɪn] *v.i.* (*belong*) принадлежа́ть (*impf.*); (*relate*) относи́ться (*impf.*); (*be appropriate*) соотве́тствовать (*impf.*).

appetite [ˈæpɪˌtaɪt] *n.* **1.** (*for food*) аппети́т; **I have lost my ~** у меня́ пропа́л аппети́т. **2.** (*natural desire*) потре́бность; **sexual ~** полово́е влече́ние; (*thirst*) жа́жда; **~ for revenge** жа́жда ме́сти; (*inclination*) скло́нность (к+*d.*).

appetizer [ˈæpɪˌtaɪzə(r)] *n.* (*aperitif*) аперити́в; (*hors d'oeuvre*) заку́ска.

appetizing [ˈæpɪˌtaɪzɪŋ] *adj.* аппети́тный; (*attractive*) привлека́тельный.

applaud [əˈplɔːd] *v.t.* (*also v.i.*, *clap*) аплоди́ровать (*impf.*) +*d.*; (*approve*) од|обря́ть, -о́брить.

applause [əˈplɔːz] *n.* аплодисме́нты (*m. pl.*); рукоплеска́ния (*nt. pl.*).

apple ['æp(ə)l] *n.* я́блоко; ~ **of discord** я́блоко раздо́ра.

cpds. ~**-blossom** *n.* я́блоневый цвет; ~**-juice** *n.* я́блочный сок; ~**-orchard** *n.* я́блоневый сад; ~**-pie** *n.* я́блочный пиро́г; ~**-sauce** *n.* я́блочное пюре́ (*indecl.*); ~**-tree** *n.* я́блоня.

appliance [ə'plaɪəns] *n.* **1.** (*act of applying*) примене́ние. **2.** (*instrument*) прибо́р, приспособле́ние; **dental** ~ проте́з; **domestic** ~ бытово́й прибо́р; **electric** ~ эле́ктроприбо́р.

applicable ['æplɪkəb(ə)l, ə'plɪkəb(ə)l] *adj.* примени́мый; (*appropriate*) подходя́щий; **the rule is not** ~ **to this case** пра́вило неримени́мо к э́тому слу́чаю.

applicant ['æplɪkənt] *n.* кандида́т; претенде́нт (*for a situation*: на до́лжность).

application [,æplɪ'keɪʃ(ə)n] *n.* **1.** (*applying; putting on to a surface*) прикла́дывание; наложе́ние; ~ **of paint** наложе́ние кра́ски. **2.** (*employment*) примене́ние; приложе́ние. **3.** (*diligence*) прилежа́ние. **4.** (*request*) заявле́ние; проше́ние; ~ **form** бланк, фо́рма; ~ **for payment** тре́бование упла́ты; **prices are sent on** ~ расце́нки высыла́ются по тре́бованию; **make** (*or* **put in**) **an** ~ под|ава́ть, -а́ть заявле́ние.

applied [ə'plaɪd] *adj.*: ~ **sciences** прикладны́е нау́ки.

appliqué [æ'pli:keɪ] *n.* апплика́ция.

appl|y [ə'plaɪ] *v.t.* **1.** (*lay, put on*) при|кла́дывать, -ложи́ть; ~**y the liniment twice a day** сма́зывать (*impf.*) два́жды в день. **2.** (*bring into action*) прил|ага́ть, -ожи́ть; ~**y the brakes** тормози́ть, за-. **3.** (*make use of*) примен|я́ть, -и́ть; **he** ~**ied his knowledge well** он хорошо́ примени́л свои́ зна́ния. **4.**: ~**y o.s. to** зан|има́ться, -я́ться +*i.*

v.i.: ~**y to** (*concern; relate to*) относи́ться (*impf.*) к+*d.*; (*approach, request*) обра|ща́ться, -ти́ться к+*d.*; **I** ~**ied to him for permission** я обрати́лся к нему́ за разреше́нием; **have you** ~**ied for a pass?** вы заказа́ли про́пуск?

appoint [ə'pɔɪnt] *v.t.* **1.** (*fix*) назн|ача́ть, -а́чить; определ|я́ть, -и́ть; **at the** ~**ed time** в назна́ченное вре́мя. **2.** (*nominate*) назн|ача́ть, -а́чить; **he was** ~**ed ambassador** он был назна́чен посло́м; **they** ~**ed him to the post** они́ назна́чили его́ на э́ту до́лжность. **3.** (*equip*): **well** ~**ed** хорошо́ обору́дованный.

appointment [ə'pɔɪntmənt] *n.* **1.** (*act of appointing*) назначе́ние; **by** ~ **to Her Majesty the Queen** поставщи́к Её Вели́чества. **2.** (*office*) до́лжность; **permanent** ~ шта́тная до́лжность; **hold an** ~ занима́ть (*impf.*) до́лжность. **3.** (*arrangement to meet*): **I have an** ~ **with my dentist for 4 o'clock** я запи́сан на приём к зубно́му врачу́ в четы́ре часа́; **she was late for the** ~ она́ опозда́ла на свида́ние; **make an** ~ **to meet s.o.** назна́чить (*pf.*) встре́чу с кем-н. **4.** (*pl., fittings*) обстано́вка; обору́дование.

apportion [ə'pɔ:ʃ(ə)n] *v.t.* распредел|я́ть, -и́ть.

apportionment [ə'pɔ:ʃənmənt] *n.* распределе́ние.

apposite ['æpəzɪt] *adj.* (*suitable*) подходя́щий; (*to the point*) уме́стный; уда́чный.

apposition [,æpə'zɪʃ(ə)n] *n.* **1.** (*placing side by side*) прикла́дывание. **2.** (*gram.*) приложе́ние.

appraisal [ə'preɪz(ə)l] *n.* оце́нка.

appraise [ə'preɪz] *v.t.* оце́н|ивать, -и́ть.

appraiser [ə'preɪzə(r)] *n.* оце́нщик.

appreciable [ə'pri:ʃəb(ə)l] *adj.* (*perceptible*) заме́тный; (*considerable*) значи́тельный.

appreciate [ə'pri:ʃɪ,eɪt, -sɪ,eɪt] *v.t.* **1.** (*value*) оц|е́нивать, -ени́ть; (высоко́) цени́ть (*impf.*); **we** ~ **your help** мы це́ним ва́шу по́мощь. **2.** (*understand*) пон|има́ть, -я́ть; (*take into account*) прин|има́ть, -я́ть во внима́ние. **3.** (*enjoy*): **he doesn't** ~ **French cooking** он не признаёт францу́зскую ку́хню; (*through understanding*): **he has learnt to** ~ **music** он научи́лся понима́ть и цени́ть му́зыку.

v.i. (*rise in value*) пов|ыша́ться, -ы́ситься; **furniture has** ~**d in value** це́ны на ме́бель повы́сились.

appreciation [ə,pri:ʃɪ'eɪʃ(ə)n, ə,pri:s-] *n.* **1.** (*estimation, judgement*) оце́нка. **2.** (*critique*) реце́нзия. **3.** (*understanding*) понима́ние, призна́ние досто́инств. **4.** (*rise in value*) повыше́ние в цене́. **5.** (*gratitude*) призна́тельность; **in** ~ **of your kindness** в знак призна́тельности за ва́шу любе́зность.

appreciative [ə'pri:ʃətɪv] *adj.* **1.** (*perceptive of merit*): **an** ~ **audience** понима́ющая аудито́рия. **2.** (*grateful*) благода́рный, призна́тельный (за+*a*).

apprehend [,æprɪ'hend] *v.t.* **1.** (*understand*) пон|има́ть, -я́ть. **2.** (*arrest*) аресто́в|ывать, -а́ть; заде́рж|ивать, -а́ть.

apprehension [,æprɪ'henʃ(ə)n] *n.* **1.** понима́ние. **2.** опасе́ние. **3.** аре́ст, задержа́ние.

apprehensive [,æprɪ'hensɪv] *adj.* встрево́женный, по́лный трево́ги; предчу́вствующий; **I am** ~ **for you** я опаса́юсь за вас.

apprentice [ə'prentɪs] *n.* учени́к, подмасте́рье (*m.*).

v.t. отд|ава́ть, -а́ть в уче́ние ремеслу́.

apprenticeship [ə'prentɪsʃɪp] *n.* учени́чество; (*period*) срок уче́ния; **serve one's** ~ про|ходи́ть, -йти́ обуче́ние.

apprise [ə'praɪz] *v.t.* изве|ща́ть, -сти́ть.

approach [ə'prəʊtʃ] *n.* **1.** (*drawing near; advance*) приближе́ние; наступле́ние; **at our** ~ при на́шем приближе́нии; как/когда́ мы подошли́. **2.** (*fig.*) подхо́д; **his** ~ **to the subject** его́ подхо́д к предме́ту. **3.** (*way, passage*) подхо́д; **the** ~ **to the river** подхо́д к реке́. **4.** (*access*) по́дступ; **the** ~**es to the town** по́дступы к го́роду; **easy of** ~ (*lit., fig.*) (легко)досту́пный. **5.** (*fig., overture*) предложе́ние; **they made unofficial** ~**es** они́ де́лали неофициа́льные ава́нсы.

v.t. **1.** (*come near to*) прибл|ижа́ться, -и́зиться к+*d.*; (*come up to — on foot*) под|ходи́ть, -ойти́ к+*d.*; (*come up to — by riding*) подъ|езжа́ть, -е́хать к+*d.*; (*fig.*): **he** ~**ed the subject in a light-hearted way** он подошёл к вопро́су несерьёзно; **he is difficult to** ~ к нему́ тру́дно подступи́ться. **2.** (*make overtures to*) обра|ща́ться, -ти́ться к+*d.*. **3.** (*approximate to*) прибл|ижа́ться, -и́зиться к+*d.*

v.i. прибл|ижа́ться, -и́зиться; под|ходи́ть, -ойти́; подъ|езжа́ть, -е́хать.

approachable [ə'prəʊtʃəb(ə)l] *adj.* досту́пный.

approaching [ə'prəʊtʃɪŋ] *adj.* приближа́ющийся; **the** ~ **storm** надвига́ющаяся бу́ря.

approbation [,æprə'beɪʃ(ə)n] *n.* (*approval*) одобре́ние; (*sanction*) апроба́ция.

appropriate[1] [ə'prəʊprɪət] *adj.* соотве́тствующий; **remarks** ~ **to the occasion** соотве́тствующие слу́чаю замеча́ния; (*suitable*) подходя́щий; (*to the point*) уме́стный.

appropriate[2] [ə'prəʊprɪ,eɪt] *v.t.* **1.** (*devote to special purpose*) предназн|ача́ть, -а́чить; (*funds*) ассигнова́ть (*impf., pf.*). **2.** (*take possession of*) присв|а́ивать, -о́ить.

appropriation [ə,prəʊprɪ'eɪʃ(ə)n] *n.* **1.** назначе́ние; ассигнова́ние. **2.** присвое́ние.

approval [ə'pru:v(ə)l] *n.* одобре́ние; (*confirmation*) утвержде́ние; (*consent*) согла́сие; **meet with** ~ получ|а́ть, -и́ть одобре́ние; **on** ~ на про́бу.

approv|e [ə'pru:v] *v.t.* од|обря́ть, -о́брить; (*confirm*) утвер|жда́ть, -ди́ть; **the report was** ~**ed** отчёт был утверждён.

v.i. ~**e of** од|обря́ть, -о́брить; **an** ~**ing glance** одобри́тельный взгляд.

approximate[1] [ə'prɒksɪmət] *adj.* приблизи́тельный.

approximate[2] [ə'prɒksɪ,meɪt] *v.t.* **1.** (*bring near*) прибл|ижа́ть, -и́зить (*что к чему*). **2.** (*come near to*) прибл|ижа́ться, -и́зиться к+*d.*

v.i.: ~ **to** прибл|ижа́ться, -и́зиться к+*d*.

approximation [əˌprɒksɪ'meɪʃ(ə)n] *n.* приближе́ние; **this is an ~ to the truth** э́то бли́зко к и́стине.

appurtenance [ə'pɜ:tɪnəns] *n.* (*accessory*) принадле́жность; (*appendage*) прида́ток.

apricot ['eɪprɪˌkɒt] *n.* (*fruit or tree*) абрико́с; ~ **jam** абрико́совый джем.

April ['eɪprɪl, 'eɪpr(ə)l] *n.* апре́ль (*m.*); ~ **fool** первоапре́льский дурачо́к; ~ **Fool!** с пе́рвым апре́ля! ~ **fool's day** пе́рвое апре́ля.
adj. апре́льский; ~ **shower** внеза́пный дождь.

a priori [ˌeɪ praɪ'ɔ:raɪ] *adj.* априо́рный.
adv. априо́ри.

apron ['eɪprən] *n.* пере́дник; фа́ртук.
cpd. ~**-strings** *n.*: **he is tied to his mother's ~-strings** он ма́менькин сыно́к.

apropos ['æprəˌpəʊ, -'pəʊ] *adj. & adv.* (*appropriate*) уме́стн|ый, -о́; (*by the way*) кста́ти, ме́жду про́чим; ~ **of** по по́воду +*g*.

apse [æps] *n.* апси́да.

apt [æpt] *adj.* **1.** (*suitable*) подходя́щий; (*apposite*) уме́стный, уда́чный. **2.** (*intelligent*) спосо́бный. **3.**: ~ **to** скло́нный к+*d*.; **he is ~ to fall asleep** он всё вре́мя засыпа́ет.

aptitude ['æptɪˌtju:d] *n.* (*capacity*) спосо́бность; ~ **for work** работоспосо́бность; ~ **test** прове́рка спосо́бностей; (*propensity*): ~ **for** скло́нность к+*d*.

aqualung ['ækwəˌlʌŋ] *n.* аквала́нг.

aquamarine [ˌækwəmə'ri:n] *n.* (*min.*) аквамари́н; (*colour*) зеленова́то-голубо́й цвет.
adj. аквамари́новый; зеленова́то-голубо́й.

aquarium [ə'kweərɪəm] *n.* аква́риум.

Aquarius [ə'kweərɪəs] *n.* Водоле́й.

aquatic [ə'kwætɪk] *adj.* (*of plant or animal*) водяно́й; (*of bird*) водопла́вающий; (*of sport*) во́дный.

aquatint ['ækwətɪnt] *n.* аквати́нта.

aqueduct ['ækwɪˌdʌkt] *n.* акведу́к.

aquiline ['ækwɪˌlaɪn] *adj.* орли́ный.

Arab ['ærəb] *n.* ара́б (*fem.* -ка).
adj. ара́бский.

arabesque [ˌærə'besk] *n.* арабе́ск(а).

Arabia [ə'reɪbɪə] *n.* Ара́вия.

Arabian [ə'reɪbɪən] *adj.* арави́йский; **the ~ Nights** Ты́сяча и одна́ ночь.

Arabic ['ærəbɪk] *n.* ара́бский язы́к; **in ~** по-ара́бски.
adj. ара́бский; **a~ numerals** ара́бские ци́фры.

arable ['ærəb(ə)l] *n.* па́хотная земля́.
adj. па́хотный; ~ **farming** земледе́лие.

Aramaic [ˌærə'meɪɪk] *n.* араме́йский язы́к.
adj. араме́йский.

arbiter ['ɑ:bɪtə(r)] *n.* **1.** (*judge*) арби́тр; ~ **of fashion** законода́тель (*m.*) мод. **2.** (*third party*) трете́йский судья́; посре́дник..

arbitrariness ['ɑ:bɪtrərɪnɪs] *n.* произво́л; произво́льность.

arbitrary ['ɑ:bɪtrərɪ] *adj.* (*random, capricious*) произво́льный; (*dictatorial*) деспоти́ческий.

arbitrate ['ɑ:bɪˌtreɪt] *v.t.* (*decide*) реш|а́ть, -и́ть трете́йским судо́м; (*refer to arbitration*) перед|ава́ть, -а́ть в арбитра́ж.
v.i. (*act as arbiter*) быть арби́тром; быть трете́йским судьёй.

arbitration [ˌɑ:bɪ'treɪʃ(ə)n] *n.* арбитра́ж; трете́йский суд; **refer, submit to ~** перед|ава́ть, -а́ть в арбитра́ж.

arbitrator ['ɑ:bɪˌtreɪtə(r)] *n.* трете́йский судья́; арби́тр.

arboretum [ˌɑ:bə'ri:təm] *n.* древе́сный пито́мник.

arbour ['ɑ:bə(r)] *n.* бесе́дка.

arc [ɑ:k] *n.* дуга́.
cpds. ~**-lamp** *n.* дугова́я ла́мпа; ~**-light** *n.* дугово́й свет.

arcade [ɑ:'keɪd] *n.* (*covered passage*) арка́да; (*with shops*) пасса́ж.

arcane [ɑ:'keɪn] *adj.* скры́тый, та́йный.

arch[1] [ɑ:tʃ] *n.* (~*way*) а́рка; (~*ed roof*; *vault*) свод; ~ **of the foot** свод стопы́; **he suffers from fallen ~es** у него́ плоскосто́пие.
v.t. прид|ава́ть, -а́ть фо́рму а́рки +*d*.; **the cat ~ed its back** ко́шка вы́гнула спи́ну; **she ~d her eyebrows** она́ подняла́/вски́нула бро́ви.
v.i. (*form an ~*) выгиба́ться, вы́гнуться.
cpd. ~**way** *n.* сво́дчатый прохо́д.

arch[2] [ɑ:tʃ] *adj.* лука́вый, игри́вый.

arch-[3] [ɑ:tʃ] *comb. form* архи...; гла́вный.

archaeological [ˌɑ:kɪə'lɒdʒɪk(ə)l] *adj.* археологи́ческий.

archaeologist [ˌɑ:kɪ'ɒlədʒɪst] *n.* архео́лог.

archaeology [ˌɑ:kɪ'ɒlədʒɪ] *n.* археоло́гия.

archaic [ɑ:'keɪɪk] *adj.* архаи́чный; устаре́вший.

archaism ['ɑ:keɪˌɪz(ə)m] *n.* архаи́зм.

archangel ['ɑ:kˌeɪndʒ(ə)l] *n.* арха́нгел.

archbishop [ɑ:tʃ'bɪʃəp] *n.* архиепи́скоп.

archdeacon [ɑ:tʃ'di:kən] *n.* архидья́кон.

archduchess [ɑ:tʃ'dʌtʃɪs] *n.* эрцгерцоги́ня.

archduchy [ɑ:tʃ'dʌtʃɪ] *n.* эрцге́рцогство.

archduke [ɑ:tʃ'dju:k] *n.* эрцге́рцог.

arched [ɑ:tʃd] *adj.* **1.** (*furnished with, consisting of, arches*) сво́дчатый, а́рочный. **2.** (*bent, curved*) изо́гнутый.

arch-enemy [ɑ:tʃ'enəmɪ] *n.* закля́тый враг.

archer ['ɑ:tʃə(r)] *n.* лу́чни|к (*fem.* -ца); стрело́к из лу́ка.

archery ['ɑ:tʃərɪ] *n.* стрельба́ из лу́ка; ~ **range** лукодро́м.

archetypal [ˌɑ:kɪ'taɪp(ə)l] *adj.* (*typical*) типи́чный.

archetype ['ɑ:kɪˌtaɪp] *n.* прототи́п.

archimandrite [ˌɑ:kɪ'mændraɪt] *n.* архимандри́т.

Archimedean [ˌɑ:kɪ'mi:dɪən] *adj.*: ~ **principle** зако́н Архиме́да.

archipelago [ˌɑ:kɪ'peləˌgəʊ] *n.* архипела́г.

architect ['ɑ:kɪˌtekt] *n.* архите́ктор; **naval ~** корабе́льный инжене́р; (*fig.*) а́втор, творе́ц.

architectural [ˌɑ:kɪ'tektʃər(ə)l] *adj.* архитекту́рный; строи́тельный.

architecture ['ɑ:kɪˌtektʃə(r)] *n.* (*science*) архитекту́ра, зо́дчество; (*fig., structure, construction*) построе́ние, структу́ра.

archival [ɑ:'kaɪv(ə)l] *adj.* архи́вный.

archive ['ɑ:kaɪv] *n.* (*also pl.*) архи́в.

archivist ['ɑ:kɪvɪst] *n.* архива́риус.

arctic ['ɑ:ktɪk] *n.*: **the A~** А́рктика.
adj. аркти́ческий; **A~ Circle** Се́верный поля́рный круг; **A~ Ocean** Се́верный Ледови́тый океа́н.

ardent ['ɑ:d(ə)nt] *adj.* (*fervent*) горя́чий, пы́лкий; (*passionate*) стра́стный; (*zealous*) ре́вностный.

ardour ['ɑ:də(r)] *n.* жар, пы́лкость, пыл, рве́ние.

arduous ['ɑ:dju:əs] *adj.* (*difficult*) тру́дный; тя́жкий; **an ~ ascent** тру́дный подъём; **an ~ road** тяжёлая доро́га.

area ['eərɪə] *n.* **1.** (*measurement*) пло́щадь; **what is the ~ of this triangle?** какова́ пло́щадь э́того треуго́льника?; **a room 12 square metres in ~** ко́мната пло́щадью в 12 $м^2$. **2.** (*defined or designated space*): **the ~ under cultivation** посевна́я пло́щадь; **landing ~** поса́дочная площа́дка; **training ~** полиго́н; **vast ~s of forest** огро́мные лесны́е простра́нства; (*portion*) уча́сток. **3.** (*region, tract, zone*) райо́н, край, зо́на; **residential ~** жило́й райо́н; **wheat-growing ~** пло́щадь под пшени́цей; **sterling ~** сте́рлинговая зо́на; ~ (*regional*) **studies** странове́дение. **4.** (*scope, range*) разма́х; (*sphere*) о́бласть, сфе́ра; **broad ~s of agreement** соглаше́ние по широ́кому кру́гу вопро́сов.

arena [ə'ri:nə] *n.* (*lit., fig.*) аре́на.

Argentina [ˌɑ:dʒən'ti:nə] *n.* (*also* **the Argentine**) Аргенти́на.

argon [ˈɑːgɒn] *n.* арго́н.

argot [ˈɑːgəʊ] *n.* арго́ (*indecl.*), жарго́н.

arguable [ˈɑːgjʊəb(ə)l] *adj.* **1.** (*open to argument*) спо́рный. **2.** (*demonstrable by argument*) доказу́емый; **it is ~ that ...** есть основа́ния полага́ть, что...; мо́жно утвержда́ть, что...

argue [ˈɑːgjuː] *v.t.* **1.** (*discuss, debate*) обсу|жда́ть, -ди́ть; **let's not ~ the point** дава́йте об э́том не спо́рить. **2.** (*contend*) дока́зывать (*impf.*); **it was ~d that ...** утвержда́лось, что... **3.** (*speak in support of*) дока́зывать (*impf.*), отста́ивать (*impf.*); убежда́ть (*impf.*) (*кого в чём*).

v.i. **1.** (*debate; disagree; quarrel*) спо́рить (*impf.*); препира́ться (*impf.*); (*object*) возража́ть (*impf.*); **get dressed and don't ~!** одева́йся — и никаки́х разгово́ров!; **they ~d over who should drive** они́ спо́рили, кому́ вести́. **2.** (*give reasons*) выступа́ть, вы́ступить (**against:** про́тив+*g.*; *for, in favour of*: в по́льзу +*g.*); прив|оди́ть, -ести́ до́воды.

with advs.: **~ away: one cannot ~ away the fact that ...** невозмо́жно затушева́ть тот факт, что...; **~ out: let's ~ the matter out** дава́йте обсу́дим вопро́с доскона́льно.

argument [ˈɑːgjʊmənt] *n.* **1.** (*reason*) аргуме́нт; до́вод; **advance ~s for** прив|оди́ть, -ести́ до́воды в по́льзу +*g.*. **2.** (*process of reasoning*) аргумента́ция; **the ~ ran as follows** аргумента́ция была́ такова́. **3.** (*discussion, debate*) спор; **a heated ~ took place** разгоре́лся жа́ркий спор; **who won the ~?** кто победи́л в спо́ре?; **a matter of ~** спо́рный вопро́с; **have an ~ over, about** спо́рить (*impf.*) о+*p*.

argumentation [ˌɑːgjʊmenˈteɪʃ(ə)n] *n.* (*reasoning*) аргумента́ция; (*debate*) спор.

argumentative [ˌɑːgjʊˈmentətɪv] *adj.* любя́щий спо́рить; спо́рный.

aria [ˈɑːrɪə] *n.* а́рия.

arid [ˈærɪd] *adj.* (*of soil etc.*) сухо́й, пересо́хший; (*of climate; lit., fig.*) (*dry*) сухо́й; (*barren*) беспло́дный.

aridity [əˈrɪdɪtɪ] *n.* (*lit.*) засу́шливость; (*lit., fig.*) су́хость; беспло́дность.

Aries [ˈeəriːz] *n.* Ове́н.

aright [əˈraɪt] *adv.* пра́вильно.

arise [əˈraɪz] *v.i.* **1.** (*lit., get up; stand up*) вст|ава́ть, -а́ть; (*lit., fig., rise*) восст|ава́ть, -а́ть; (*from the dead*) воскр|еса́ть, -е́снуть. **2.** (*fig., come into being*) возн|ика́ть, -и́кнуть; **if the need should ~** е́сли возни́кнет необходи́мость; **the question arose** встал вопро́с; **a shout arose from the crowd** из толпы́ разда́лся крик; (*appear*) появ|ля́ться, -и́ться.

aristocracy [ˌærɪˈstɒkrəsɪ] *n.* аристокра́тия.

aristocrat [ˈærɪstəˌkræt] *n.* аристокра́т.

aristocratic [ˌærɪstəˈkrætɪk] *adj.* аристократи́ческий.

arithmetic [əˈrɪθmətɪk] *n.* арифме́тика.

arithmetical [əˌrɪθˈmetɪk(ə)l] *adj.* арифмети́ческий.

ark [ɑːk] *n.* ковче́г; **Noah's ~** Но́ев ковче́г; **A~ of the Covenant** ковче́г заве́та.

arm[1] [ɑːm] *n.* **1.** (*of pers.*) рука́; **with a book under his ~** с кни́гой под мы́шкой; **she had a basket on her ~** на руке́ у неё висе́ла корзи́на; **he offered her his ~** он предложи́л ей ру́ку; **within ~'s reach** под руко́й; **he broke his ~** он слома́л себе́ ру́ку; **he kept me at ~'s length** он меня́ бли́зко не подпуска́л; **~ in ~** по́д руку; **twist s.o.'s ~** (*fig., coerce*) брать кого́-н. (*impf.*) за го́рло; **with open ~s** (*lit., fig.*) с распростёртыми объя́тиями; **fold one's ~s** сложи́ть (*pf.*) ру́ки; **take s.o.'s in one's ~s** заключ|а́ть, -и́ть кого́-н. в объя́тия; **he gathered the books (up) in his ~s** он собра́л кни́ги в оха́пку. **2.** (*of object*): **~ of a garment** рука́в; **~ of a chair** ру́чка кре́сла. **3.** (*fig., reach*): **the (long) ~ of the law** (кара́ющая) рука́ зако́на.

cpds. **~band** *n.* нарука́вная повя́зка; **~chair** *n.* кре́сло; **~pit** *n.* подмы́шка; **under one's ~pit** под мы́шкой; **~-rest** *n.* подлоко́тник.

arm[2] [ɑːm] *n.* **1.** (*mil., force*): **air ~** вое́нно-возду́шные си́лы (*f. pl.*). **2.** (*pl., weapons*) ору́жие; **small ~s** стрелко́вое ору́жие; **~s race** го́нка вооруже́ний; **under ~s** под ружьём; **take up ~s** бра́ться, взя́ться за ору́жие; **bear ~s** носи́ть (*impf.*) ору́жие; **lay down one's ~s** (*lit., fig.*) сложи́ть (*pf.*) ору́жие; **by force of ~s** си́лой ору́жия; **they were up in ~s** (*fig.*) они́ взбунтова́лись. **3.** (*her.*) **(coat of) ~s** герб.

v.t. воору|жа́ть, -жи́ть; (*equip*) снаб|жа́ть, -ди́ть; **~ o.s.** (*lit., fig.*) вооруж|а́ться, -и́ться; **~ed forces** вооружённые си́лы.

v.i. вооруж|а́ться, -и́ться.

armada [ɑːˈmɑːdə] *n.* арма́да.

armadillo [ˌɑːməˈdɪləʊ] *n.* армади́лл; броненосе́ц.

armament [ˈɑːməmənt] *n.* **1.** (*also pl., weapons; military equipment*) вооруже́ние; **~ factory** вое́нный заво́д. **2.** (*armed forces*) вооружённые си́лы (*f. pl.*).

armature [ˈɑːməˌtjʊə(r)] *n.* (*elec.*) я́корь (*m.*), броня́ (ка́беля).

Armenia [ɑːˈmiːnɪə] *n.* Арме́ния.

armful [ˈɑːmfʊl] *n.* оха́пка.

armistice [ˈɑːmɪstɪs] *n.* переми́рие.

armour [ˈɑːmə(r)] *n.* (*for body*) доспе́хи (*m. pl.*); **he wore (a suit of) ~** он был в доспе́хах; (*of plant or animal*) па́нцирь (*m.*); (*of vehicle, ship etc.*) броня́; (*coll., armoured vehicles*) бронета́нковые си́лы (*f. pl.*).

v.t. брони́ровать (*impf., pf.*).

cpds. **~-bearer** *n.* оруженосе́ц; **~-clad, ~-plated** *adjs.* брони́рованный; **~-plate** *n.* бронева́я плита́.

armoured [ˈɑːmərd] *adj.* брони́рованный, бронено́сный; **~ car** бронеавтомоби́ль (*m.*), броневи́к; **~ column** бронета́нковая коло́нна; **~ concrete** железобето́н; **~ cruiser** броненосный кре́йсер; **~ glass** арми́рованное стекло́; **~ train** бронепо́езд.

armoury [ˈɑːmərɪ] *n.* арсена́л.

army [ˈɑːmɪ] *n.* а́рмия; **he served in the regular ~** он служи́л в регуля́рных частя́х; **join the ~** вступ|а́ть, -и́ть в а́рмию; **~ command** кома́ндование а́рмии; **Salvation A~** А́рмия спасе́ния; (*fig., large number*) а́рмия; мно́жество; (*attr.*) арме́йский; **~ chaplain** арме́йский свяще́нник; **~ corps** арме́йский ко́рпус; **~ general** генера́л а́рмии.

arnica [ˈɑːnɪkə] *n.* а́рника.

aroma [əˈrəʊmə] *n.* арома́т.

aromatic [ˌærəˈmætɪk] *adj.* арома́тный; благово́нный.

around [əˈraʊnd] (*see also* **round**) *adv.* вокру́г; круго́м; **all ~** повсю́ду; **from all ~** отовсю́ду; **for miles ~** на ми́ли вокру́г; **they were standing ~** они́ стоя́ли побли́зости; **he's been ~** (*coll.*) он вида́л ви́ды; он челове́к быва́лый; **he travels ~** он мно́го путеше́ствует.

prep. **1.** (*encircling*) вокру́г+*g.*; круго́м+*g.*; **the path goes ~ the garden** доро́жка огибает сад; **his arm was ~ her waist** он обнима́л её за та́лию. **2.** (*over*): **he walked ~ the town** он броди́л по го́роду; **he looked ~ the house** он осмотре́л дом. **3.** (*in the vicinity of*) о́коло+*g.* **4.** (*in var. parts of*): **the child played ~ the house** ребёнок игра́л по всему́ до́му; **he stayed ~ the house** он не выходи́л и́з дому. **5.** (*approximately*) о́коло+*g.*; приблизи́тельно.

arousal [əˈraʊz(ə)l] *n.* пробужде́ние.

arouse [əˈraʊz] *v.t.* (*awaken from sleep*) буди́ть, раз-; (*fig.*) возбу|жда́ть, -ди́ть; **his interest was ~d** у него́ пробуди́лся интере́с; **my suspicions were ~d** у меня́ возни́кли подозре́ния.

arpeggio [ɑːˈpedʒɪəʊ] *n.* арпе́джио (*indecl.*).

arraign [əˈreɪn] *v.t.* (*bring to trial*) привл|ека́ть, -е́чь к суду́; (*accuse*) обвин|я́ть, -и́ть.

arraignment [əˈreɪnmənt] *n.* привлече́ние к суду́; обвине́ние.

arrang|e [ə'reɪndʒ] *v.t.* **1.** (*put in order*) прив|оди́ть, -ести́ в поря́док; устр|а́ивать, -о́ить; **she was ~ing flowers** она расставля́ла цветы́; **I must ~e my hair** мне на́до сде́лать причёску. **2.** (*put in a certain order*; *group*) распол|ага́ть, -ожи́ть; расст|авля́ть, -а́вить; **~ed in alphabetical order** располо́женный в алфави́тном поря́дке; **he ~ed books on the shelves** он расста́вил кни́ги по по́лкам. **3.** (*settle*) ула́|живать, -дить. **4.** (*organize*) устр|а́ивать, -о́ить; организо́в|ывать, -а́ть; (*prepare*; *plan in advance*) подгот|а́вливать, -о́вить; нала́|живать, -дить. **5.** (*mus.*) аранжи́ровать (*impf.*, *pf.*).

v.i. догов|а́риваться, -ори́ться; усл|а́вливаться, -о́виться; **I ~ed with my friend to go to the theatre** мы с дру́гом договори́лись пойти́ в теа́тр.

arrangement [ə'reɪndʒmənt] *n.* **1.** (*setting in order*) приведе́ние в поря́док. **2.** (*specific order*) расположе́ние. **3.** (*planning*, *preparation*) подгото́вка; (*pl.*) приготовле́ния (*nt. pl.*); **make ~s for** организо́в|ывать, -а́ть; устр|а́ивать, -о́ить; **he made the ~s for the concert** он устро́ил/организова́л э́тот конце́рт. **4.** (*agreement*, *understanding*) соглаше́ние; **they came to an ~** они́ пришли́ к соглаше́нию/договорённости. **5.** (*mus.*) аранжиро́вка.

arrant ['ærənt] *adj.* (*liter.*) отъя́вленный; су́щий; **~ nonsense** су́щий вздор; **an ~ fool** кру́глый дура́к.

array [ə'reɪ] *n.* **1.** (*order*): **in battle ~** в боево́м поря́дке. **2.** (*display*) собра́ние, колле́кция. **3.** (*dress*, *apparel*) наря́д, одея́ние.

v.t. **1.** (*place in order or line*) выстра́ивать, вы́строить; **the troops were ~ed for battle** войска́ бы́ли вы́строены в боево́м поря́дке. **2.** (*set out*, *display*) выставля́ть, вы́ставить. **3.** (*adorn*) укр|аша́ть, -а́сить; (*deck out*, *dress*) од|ева́ть, -е́ть; **~ o.s.** наряди́ться (*pf.*).

arrears [ə'rɪəz] *n.* задо́лженность; просро́чка; **~ of rent** задо́лженность по квартпла́те; **fall into ~** (*of pers.*) просро́чи|вать, -ть платёж.

arrest [ə'rest] *n.* **1.** (*seizure*; *leg. apprehension*) аре́ст; **place under ~** сажа́ть, посади́ть под аре́ст; **be under ~** сиде́ть (*impf.*) под аре́стом; **you are under ~!** вы аресто́ваны; **he was put under ~** его́ арестова́ли; **the police made several ~s** поли́ция произвела́ не́сколько аре́стов. **2.** (*stoppage*): **cardiac ~** (*med.*) остано́вка се́рдца.

v.t. **1.** (*apprehend*) аресто́в|ывать, -а́ть; (*fig.*, *seize*): **~ s.o.'s attention** прико́в|ывать, -а́ть чьё-н. внима́ние. **2.** (*check*) заде́рж|ивать, -а́ть; **~ed development** заме́дленное разви́тие; (*stop*) приостан|а́вливать, -ови́ть.

arresting [ə'restɪŋ] *adj.* захва́тывающий; прико́вывающий внима́ние.

arrival [ə'raɪv(ə)l] *n.* **1.** (*act or moment of arriving*) прибы́тие; **'to await ~'** «оста́вить до прибы́тия адреса́та»; (*of pers. etc. on foot*; *of vehicles*) прихо́д; (*of pers. by vehicle*) прие́зд; (*by air*) прилёт. **2.** (*pers. or thg.*): **new ~** вновь прибы́вший; (*baby*) новорождённый.

arrive [ə'raɪv] *v.i.* **1.** (*reach destination*) приб|ыва́ть, -ы́ть; (*of persons on foot*; *of vehicles*; *also fig.*) при|ходи́ть, -йти́; (*by land transport*) при|езжа́ть, -е́хать; (*by air*) прилет|а́ть, -е́ть. **2.**: **~ at a decision** прийти́ (*pf.*) к реше́нию. **3.** (*of time*) насту|па́ть, -и́ть.

arrogance ['ærəgəns] *n.* высокоме́рие, надме́нность.

arrogant ['ærəgənt] *adj.* высокоме́рный, надме́нный.

arrogate ['ærə,geɪt] *v.t.* (*claim*) присв|а́ивать, -о́ить себе́.

arrow ['ærəʊ] *n.* стрела́; (*as symbol or indicator*) стре́лка.

cpds. **~-head** *n.* наконе́чник стрелы́; **~root** *n.* арроу́т; **~-shaped** *adj.* стрелови́дный.

arse [ɑːs] (*US* **ass**) *n.* жо́па (*vulg.*), за́дница.

arsenal ['ɑːsən(ə)l] *n.* (*lit.*, *fig.*) арсена́л.

arsenic ['ɑːsənɪk] *n.* мышья́к.

adj. мышьяко́вый.

arson ['ɑːs(ə)n] *n.* поджо́г.

arsonist ['ɑːsənɪst] *n.* поджига́тель (*m.*).

art [ɑːt] *n.* **1.** (*skill*, *craft*) иску́сство; **a work of ~** произведе́ние иску́сства; **mechanical, useful ~s** ремёсла (*nt. pl.*). **2.** (*esp. pl.*) (*device*, *trick*) уло́вки (*f. pl.*); **there's an ~ to making an omelette** пригото́вить омле́т — то́же иску́сство. **3.** (*decorative*) иску́сство; **fine ~s** изя́щные/изобрази́тельные иску́сства; **applied ~s** прикладны́е иску́сства; **~ school** худо́жественное учи́лище; **~ gallery** худо́жественная галере́я; **~ critic** искусствове́д. **4.** (*pl.*, *humanities*) гуманита́рные нау́ки (*f. pl.*); **Bachelor of Arts** бакала́вр гуманита́рных нау́к. **5.** (*attr.*, *artistic*) худо́жественный; (*artificial*) иску́сственный.

artefact, artifact ['ɑːtɪ,fækt] *n.* худо́жественное изде́лие; поде́лка.

artel [ɑː'tel] *n.* арте́ль.

arterial [ɑː'tɪərɪəl] *adj.* **1.** (*anat.*) артериа́льный. **2.**: **~ road** магистра́льная доро́га; магистра́ль.

arteriosclerosis [ɑː,tɪərɪəʊsklɪə'rəʊsɪs] *n.* артериосклеро́з.

artery ['ɑːtərɪ] *n.* (*anat.*) арте́рия; (*road*) магистра́ль.

artesian [ɑː'tiːzɪən, -ʒ(ə)n] *adj.* артезиа́нский.

artful ['ɑːtfʊl] *adj.* хи́трый.

arthritic [ɑː'θrɪtɪk] *n.* больн|о́й (*fem.* -а́я) артри́том.

adj. артри́тный; **an ~ old woman** стару́ха, страда́ющая артри́том.

arthritis [ɑː'θraɪtɪs] *n.* артри́т.

artichoke ['ɑːtɪ,tʃəʊk] *n.* артишо́к; **Jerusalem ~** земляна́я гру́ша.

article ['ɑːtɪk(ə)l] *n.* **1.** (*item*) предме́т; изде́лие; **~ of clothing** предме́т оде́жды; **~ of food** пищево́й проду́кт; (*of trade*) **consumer ~s** потреби́тельские това́ры (*m. pl.*). **2.** (*clause etc. of document*) статья́; пара́граф; **~ of faith** догма́т ве́ры. **3.** (*piece of writing*) статья́; **leading ~** передова́я статья́. **4.** (*gram.*): **(in)definite ~** (не)определённый арти́кль.

articulate[1] [ɑː'tɪkjʊlət] *adj.* (*of speech*) членоразде́льный; (*of thoughts*) отчётливый; (*of pers.*) чётко выража́ющий свои́ мы́сли.

articulate[2] [ɑː'tɪkjʊ,leɪt] *v.t.* **1.** (*speech*) отчётливо произн|оси́ть, -ести́. **2.** (*connect by joints*): **~d lorry** автопо́езд.

v.i.: **he ~s well** у него́ хоро́шая артикуля́ция.

articulation [ɑː,tɪkjʊ'leɪʃ(ə)n] *n.* артикуля́ция.

artifice ['ɑːtɪfɪs] *n.* (*device*, *contrivance*) изобрете́ние; (*cunning*) хи́трость.

artificial [,ɑːtɪ'fɪʃ(ə)l] *adj.* (*not natural*) иску́сственный; **~ respiration** иску́сственное дыха́ние; (*feigned*) притво́рный.

artificiality [,ɑːtɪfɪʃɪ'ælɪtɪ] *n.* иску́сственность.

artillery [ɑː'tɪlərɪ] *n.* артилле́рия; (*attr.*) артиллери́йский.

cpd. **~man** *n.* артиллери́ст.

artisan [,ɑːtɪ'zæn, 'ɑː-] *n.* ремесленник.

artist ['ɑːtɪst] *n.* **1.** (*practiser of art*) худо́жник. **2.** (*skilled performer*) арти́ст.

artiste [ɑː'tiːst] *n.* (эстра́дный) арти́ст; (*fem.*) (эстра́дная) арти́стка.

artistic [ɑː'tɪstɪk] *adj.* худо́жественный; артисти́ческий.

artistry ['ɑːtɪstrɪ] *n.* артисти́чность, мастерство́.

artless ['ɑːtlɪs] *adj.* (*unskilled*) неиску́сный; (*ingenuous*) простоду́шный; (*natural*) безыску́сственный.

artlessness ['ɑːtlɪsnɪs] *n.* неиску́сность; простоду́шие; безыску́сственность.

Aryan ['eərɪən] *n.* ари́|ец (*fem.* -ка).

adj. ари́йский.

as [æz, əz] *pron.*: **such men ~ knew him** те, кото́рые зна́ли его́; **such ~ need our help** те, кто нужда́ется в на́шей по́мощи.

adv. & conj. **1.** (*expr. comparison or conformity*) как; ~ **I was saying** как я говори́л; ~ **follows** сле́дующим о́бразом; **the same** ~ ... то же са́мое, что...; ~ **heavy** ~ **lead** тяжёлый, как свине́ц; **he is** ~ **clever** ~ **she** он так же умён, как она́; **he is** ~ **kind** ~ **he is rich** он и добр и бога́т; **I am** ~ **tall** ~ **he** я одного́ с ним ро́ста; ~ **quickly** ~ **possible** как мо́жно скоре́е; **just** ~ так же, как; ~ **usual** как всегда́; ~ **things are, you cannot go** положе́ние дел таково́, что вы не мо́жете идти́; **he is tall,** ~ **are his brothers** как и его́ бра́тья, он высо́кого ро́ста; ~ **it were** так сказа́ть; как бы; **he arranged matters so** ~ **to suit everyone** он устро́ил всё так, что́бы все бы́ли дово́льны; ~ **a man sows, so shall he reap** что посе́ешь, то и пожнёшь; **he was not so foolish** ~ **to say ...** он был не так глуп, что́бы сказа́ть...; **so** ~ **to** (*expr. purpose*) что́бы; (*expr. manner*) так, что́бы; **that's** ~ **may be** ну, поло́жим; мо́жет быть и так. **2.** (*expr. capacity or category*) как; **I regard him** ~ **a fool** я счита́ю его́ дурако́м; **his appointment** ~ **colonel** присвое́ние ему́ зва́ния полко́вника; ~ **your guardian, I ...** как ваш опеку́н, я...; **he appeared** ~ **Hamlet** он вы́ступил в ро́ли Га́млета; ~ **a rule** как пра́вило; **I said it** ~ **a joke** я сказа́л э́то в шу́тку; **I recognized him** ~ **the new tenant** я узна́л в нём но́вого жильца́. **3.** (*concessive*): **young** (*US* ~ **young**) ~ **I am** хоть я и мо́лод; **much** ~ **I should like to** хотя́ мне и о́чень хоте́лось бы; **try** ~ **he would** как он ни стара́лся. **4.** (*temporal*) когда́; в то вре́мя как; **(just)** ~ **I reached the door** когда́ (*or* как то́лько) я подошёл к две́ри. **5.** (*causative*) е́сли; раз; ~ **you are ready, let us begin** поско́льку вы уже́ гото́вы, дава́йте начнём. **6.** (*in proportion* ~) по ме́ре того́, как. **7.** (*var.*): ~ **far** ~ **I know** наско́лько мне изве́стно; **he walked** ~ **far** ~ **the station** он дошёл до ста́нции; ~ **far back** ~ **1920** ещё/уже́ в 1920 году́; ~ **for you** что каса́ется вас; ~ **from January** начина́я с пе́рвого января́; **he was** ~ **good** ~ **his word** он сдержа́л своё сло́во; **be so good** ~ **to tell me** бу́дьте добры́, скажи́те мне; ~ **if** бу́дто (бы); как бу́дто (бы); **he made** ~ **if to go** он дви́нулся бы́ло уходи́ть; **I will stay** ~ **long** ~ **you want me** я пробу́ду сто́лько, ско́лько вы захоти́те; **keep it** ~ **long** ~ **you like** держи́те э́то, ско́лько вам уго́дно; ~ **much** ~ ... сто́лько, ско́лько...; **I thought** ~ **much!** так я и ду́мал!; ~ **of this moment** в да́нный моме́нт; ~ **often** ~ (*whenever*) **he comes** вся́кий раз, когда́ он прихо́дит; ~ **regards** что каса́ется +*g.*; относи́тельно+*g.*; ~ **soon** ~ как то́лько; **I would just** ~ **soon go** я предпочёл бы пойти́; **the drawings** ~ **such** рису́нки как таковы́е; ~ **though** бу́дто (бы); как бу́дто (бы); ~ **to** (*regarding*) что каса́ется +*g.*; **he said nothing** ~ **to when he would come** он ничего́ не сказа́л насчёт того́, когда́ он придёт; ~ **well** (*in addition*) та́кже, то́же; **he came** ~ **well** ~ **John** и он и Джон пришли́; **it is just** ~ **well you came** хорошо́, что вы пришли́; ~ **yet** ещё; до сих пор.

a.s.a.p. (*abbr. of* **as soon as possible**) как мо́жно скоре́е.

asbestos [æz'bestɒs, æs-] *n.* асбе́ст; (*attr.*) асбе́стовый.

ascend [ə'send] *v.t.* подн|има́ться, -я́ться по+*d.* (*or* на+*a.*); ~ **the throne** взойти́ (*pf.*) на престо́л.

v.i. подн|има́ться, -я́ться; восходи́ть (*impf.*).

ascendancy [ə'send(ə)nsɪ] *n.* госпо́дство; **gain, obtain** ~ **over** брать, взять власть над+*i.*

ascendant [ə'send(ə)nt] *adj.* (*rising*) восходя́щий; (*predominant*) госпо́дствующий.

ascension [ə'senʃ(ə)n] *n.* (*act of ascending*) восхожде́ние; (*relig.*) **the A~** Вознесе́ние.

ascent [ə'sent] *n.* **1.** (*rise in ground; slope*) подъём. **2.** (*act of climbing or rising*) восхожде́ние, подъём; ~ **of a mountain** восхожде́ние на́ гору; **they made the** ~ **in 5 hours** они́ подняли́сь за пять часо́в.

ascertain [ˌæsə'teɪn] *v.t.* устан|а́вливать, -ови́ть; выясня́ть, вы́яснить.

ascetic [ə'setɪk] *n.* аске́т.

adj. аскети́ческий.

asceticism [ə'setɪˌsɪz(ə)m] *n.* аскети́зм.

ascorbic [ə'skɔ:bɪk] *adj.* аскорби́новый.

ascribe [ə'skraɪb] *v.t.* припи́с|ывать, -а́ть.

asepsis [eɪ'sepsɪs, ə-] *n.* асе́птика.

aseptic [eɪ'septɪk] *adj.* асепти́ческий.

asexual [eɪ'seksjʊəl, æ-] *adj.* беспо́лый.

ash[1] [æʃ] *n.* (*bot.*) я́сень (*m.*); **mountain** ~ ряби́на.

ash[2] [æʃ] *n.* **1.** (*also pl.*) зола́; пе́пел; **this coal makes a lot of** ~ от э́того у́гля мно́го золы́; **cigarette** ~ пе́пел; **they burnt the town to** ~**es** они́ сожгли́ го́род дотла́; **A~ Wednesday** пе́рвый день Вели́кого поста́. **2.** (*pl., human remains*) прах; (*fig.*) **his hopes turned to** ~**es** его́ наде́жды ру́хнули.

cpds. ~**-blond** *n.* пе́пельная блонди́нка; ~**-box,** ~**-pan** *nn.* зо́льник; я́щик для золы́; ~**-can** *n.* (*US*) му́сорный я́щик; ~**-grey** *adj.* пе́пельно-се́рый; ~**tray** *n.* пе́пельница.

ashamed [ə'ʃeɪmd] *adj.* пристыжённый; **I am, feel** ~ мне сты́дно; **be** ~ **of** стыди́ться (*impf.*) +*g.*; **be, feel** ~ **for s.o.** стыди́ться за кого́-н.; **you ought to be** ~ **of yourself** как вам не сты́дно!

ashen ['æʃ(ə)n] *adj.* (*ash-coloured*) пе́пельного цве́та; (*pale*) ме́ртвенно-бле́дный.

ashore [ə'ʃɔ:(r)] *adv.* (*position*) на берегу́; (*motion*) на бе́рег; **go** ~ сойти́ на бе́рег; **put** ~ выса́живать, вы́садить на бе́рег.

Asia ['eɪʃə, -ʒə] *n.* А́зия; ~ **Minor** Ма́лая А́зия.

Asia|n ['eɪʃ(ə)n, -ʒ(ə)n], **-tic** [ˌeɪʃɪ'ætɪk, ˌeɪz-] *nn.* азиа́т (*fem.* -ка).

adjs. азиа́тский.

aside [ə'saɪd] *n.* ре́плика в сто́рону.

adv. (*place*) в стороне́; (*motion*) в сто́рону; (*in reserve*) отде́льно, в резе́рве; **joking** ~ кро́ме шу́ток; ~ **from** (*US*) за исключе́нием +*g.*; кро́ме+*g.*; **take s.o.** ~ отв|оди́ть, -ести́ кого́-н. в сто́рону; **set, put** ~ от|кла́дывать, -ложи́ть.

asinine ['æsɪˌnaɪn] *adj.* глу́пый; дура́цкий.

ask [ɑ:sk] *v.t.* **1.** (*enquire*) спр|а́шивать, -оси́ть (*что у кого or кого о чём*); **he was** ~**ed his name** у него́ спроси́ли фами́лию; **he** ~**ed me the time** он спроси́л меня́, кото́рый час; ~ **him the way!** спроси́те его́, как пройти́!; **one might** ~ спра́шивается; **I** ~ **you!** скажи́те пожа́луйста! **2.** (*pose*): ~ **a question** зад|ава́ть, -а́ть вопро́с. **3.** (*request permission*): **he** ~**ed to leave the room** он попроси́л разреше́ния вы́йти из ко́мнаты; **he went off without** ~**ing** он ушёл не спрося́сь. **4.** (*request*) проси́ть, по- (*что у кого or кого о чём*); **I** ~**ed him to do it** я попроси́л его́ сде́лать э́то; (*require*) тре́бовать, по- +*g.*; **the society** ~**s obedience of its members** о́бщество тре́бует от свои́х чле́нов подчине́ния; **if it's not too much to** ~ е́сли э́то вас не затрудни́т; *see also* **asking. 5.** (*charge*) проси́ть, за-; **he** ~**ed a high price** он запроси́л высо́кую це́ну; **what is he** ~**ing for his car?** ско́лько он про́сит за свою́ маши́ну?; ~**ing price** запра́шиваемая цена́. **6.** (*invite*) звать, по-; пригла|ша́ть, -си́ть; **why don't you** ~ **him in?** почему́ вы не пригласи́те его́ войти́?; ~ **a girl out** пригла|ша́ть, -си́ть де́вушку на свида́ние; **we have been** ~**ed out to dinner** нас позва́ли на у́жин.

v.i. **1.** (*make enquiries*): **she** ~**ed after your health** она́ осве́домилась/справля́лась о ва́шем здоро́вье; (~ *to see*): **I** ~**ed for Mr. Smith** я спроси́л г-на Сми́та. **2.** (*make a request*) проси́ть, по-; ~ **for help** проси́ть (*impf.*) о по́мощи; ~ **for trouble** (*coll.*) напра́шиваться на неприя́тности.

askance [ə'skæns, -'skɑ:ns] *adv.* ко́со, и́скоса; **he looked at me** ~ он посмотре́л на меня́ и́скоса.

askew [ə'skju:] *adv.* кри́во, ко́со.

asking ['ɑ:skɪŋ] *n.*: **it is yours for the ~** сто́ит то́лько попроси́ть; **food was there for the ~** еды́ там бы́ло ско́лько уго́дно.

aslant [ə'slɑ:nt] *adv.* на́искось, ко́со.

asleep [ə'sli:p] *pred. adj.* спя́щий; **he was sound, fast ~** он спал кре́пким сном; **fall ~** зас|ыпа́ть, -ну́ть; **my leg is ~** я отсиде́л но́гу; (*fig., mentally*) со́нный.

asp [æsp] *n.* а́спид.

asparagus [ə'spærəgəs] *n.* спа́ржа; **~ tips** спа́ржевые голо́вки.

aspect ['æspekt] *n.* **1.** (*look, appearance; expression*) вид, выраже́ние. **2.** (*fig., facet; mode of presentation*) аспе́кт, сторона́; (*point of view*) то́чка зре́ния; **have you considered the question in all its ~s?** вы рассмотре́ли вопро́с со всех то́чек зре́ния? **3.** (*outlook*) вид; **my house has a north ~** мой дом смо́трит на се́вер. **4.** (*gram.*) вид.

aspen ['æspən] *n.* оси́на; (*attr.*) оси́новый.

aspersion [ə'spɜ:ʃ(ə)n] *n.* (*slur*) клевета́; **cast ~s** клевета́ть (*impf.*) на+*a.*

asphalt ['æsfælt] *n.* асфа́льт; (*attr.*) асфа́льтовый.

v.t. асфальти́ровать (*impf., pf.*).

asphyxia [æs'fɪksɪə] *n.* уду́шье; асфи́ксия.

asphyxiate [æs'fɪksɪ,eɪt] *v.t.* вызыва́ть, вы́звать уду́шье у+*g.*; (*suffocate*) души́ть, за-; **be ~d** задыха́ться.

asphyxiation [æs,fɪksɪ'eɪʃ(ə)n] *n.* уду́шье, удуше́ние.

aspic ['æspɪk] *n.* заливно́е; **veal in ~** заливна́я теля́тина.

aspirant ['æspɪrənt, ə'spaɪərənt] *n.* претенде́нт.

aspirate ['æspə,reɪt] *v.t.* произн|оси́ть, -ести́ с приды-ха́нием.

aspiration [,æspɪ'reɪʃ(ə)n] *n.* **1.** (*desire*) стремле́ние; **his ~s to fame** его́ стремле́ние к сла́ве. **2.** (*phon.*) придыха́ние.

aspirator ['æspɪ,reɪtə(r)] *n.* аспира́тор.

aspir|e [ə'spaɪə(r)] *v.i.* стреми́ться (*impf.*); **he ~es to be a leader** он наде́ется стать ли́дером.

aspirin ['æsprɪn] *n.* аспири́н; (*tablet*) табле́тка аспири́на.

ass[1] [æs] (*donkey, lit., fig.*) осёл; **~'s** *or* **~es'** (*as adj.*) осли́ный; **he made an ~ of himself** он сваля́л дурака́; **he was made an ~ of** он оста́лся в дурака́х.

ass[2] [æs] (*US vulg.*) = **arse**

assail [ə'seɪl] *v.t.* (*lit., fig.*) нап|ада́ть, -а́сть на+*a.*; **I was ~ed by doubts** меня́ одолева́ли сомне́ния; **~ with criticism** обру́шиться (*pf.*) с кри́тикой на+*a.*

assailant [ə'seɪlənt] *n.* напада́ющая/атаку́ющая сторона́.

assassin [ə'sæsɪn] *n.* уби́йца (*c.g.*).

assassinate [ə'sæsɪ,neɪt] *v.t.* уб|ива́ть, -и́ть (по полити́ческим моти́вам).

assassination [ə,sæsɪ'neɪʃ(ə)n] *n.* (преда́тельское) уби́йство; (*fig.*) **character ~** подры́в репута́ции.

assault [ə'sɔ:lt, ə'sɒlt] *n.* (*in general*) нападе́ние; (*mil.*) ата́ка, штурм, при́ступ; **carry, take by ~** брать (*impf.*) шту́рмом/при́ступом; **mount an ~** предприн|има́ть, -я́ть ата́ку; **~ troops** штурмовы́е ча́сти; **~ craft** деса́нтный ка́тер; штурмова́я ло́дка; (*leg.*): **~ and battery** оскорбле́ние де́йствием; **indecent ~** изнаси́лование.

v.t. нап|ада́ть, -а́сть на+*a.*; (*mil.*) атакова́ть (*impf., pf.*); (*sexually*) наси́ловать, из-.

assay [ə'seɪ, 'æseɪ] *n.* (*test*) испыта́ние; (*analysis*) ана́лиз.

v.t. (*test*) испы́т|ывать, -а́ть; (*analyze*) анализи́ровать (*impf., pl.*).

assemblage [ə'semblɪdʒ] *n.* **1.** (*bringing or coming together*) собира́ние, сбор. **2.** (*collection*) собра́ние, скопле́ние.

assemble [ə'semb(ə)l] *v.t.* (*gather together*) соб|ира́ть, -ра́ть; (*call together*) соз|ыва́ть, -ва́ть; (*tech., fit together*) монти́ровать, с-.

v.i. соб|ира́ться, -ра́ться.

assembly [ə'semblɪ] *n.* **1.** (*company of persons*) собра́ние; (*school*) **~ hall** а́ктовый зал; **unlawful ~** незако́нное сбо́рище. **3.** (*pol.*) собра́ние; ассамбле́я. **4.** (*mil.*) сбор; **~ area** райо́н сбо́ра. **5.** (*of machine parts*) сбо́рка; **~ line** сбо́рочный конве́йер; **~ shop** сбо́рочный цех; **~ worker** сбо́рщик.

assent [ə'sent] *n.* согла́сие; **the Royal ~** короле́вская са́нкция.

v.i. согла|ша́ться, -си́ться (*с чем or на что*).

assert [ə'sɜ:t] *v.t.* **1.** (*declare; affirm*) утвер|жда́ть, -ди́ть; заяв|ля́ть, -и́ть. **2.** (*stand up for*) отст|а́ивать, -оя́ть; защи|ща́ть, -ти́ть; **~ one's rights** отст|а́ивать, -оя́ть свои́ права́.

assertion [ə'sɜ:ʃ(ə)n] *n.* **1.** (*statement*) утвержде́ние. **2.** (*defence*) отста́ивание.

assertive [ə'sɜ:tɪv] *adj.* утверди́тельный; (*dogmatic*) догмати́ческий; (*insistent*) насто́йчивый.

assess [ə'ses] *v.t.* **1.** (*estimate value of; appraise; also fig.*) оце́н|ивать, -и́ть. **2.** (*determine amount of*) определ|я́ть, -и́ть су́мму/разме́р +*g.*; **damages were ~ed at £10,000** убы́тки оцени́ли в 10 000 фу́нтов.

assessment [ə'sesmənt] *n.* (*valuation*) оце́нка; (*for taxation*) обложе́ние; (*sum to be levied*) су́мма обложе́ния.

assessor [ə'sesə(r)] *n.* **1.** (*of taxes, property etc.*) нало́говый чино́вник. **2.** (*leg., adviser*) экспе́рт(-консульта́нт).

asset ['æset] *n.* **1.** (*advantage; useful quality*) це́нность; **knowledge of French is an ~ in this job** зна́ние францу́зского языка́ осо́бенно ва́жно для э́той рабо́ты. **2.** (*pl., fin.: possessions with money value*) акти́в; **current ~s** оборо́тные сре́дства; **fixed ~s** основны́е сре́дства; **personal ~s** дви́жимое иму́щество.

assiduity [,æsɪ'dju:ɪtɪ] *n.* прилежа́ние; усе́рдие.

assiduous [ə'sɪdjʊəs] *adj.* приле́жный; усе́рдный.

assign [ə'saɪn] *v.t.* **1.** (*leg., transfer*) перед|ава́ть, -а́ть. **2.** (*appoint; allot*) переуступ|а́ть, -и́ть; **the task was ~ed to me** на меня́ была́ возло́жена зада́ча; **have you had any homework ~ed to you?** тебе́ за́дали уро́ки на́ дом? **3.** (*ascribe*) припи́с|ывать, -а́ть; **they could ~ no cause to the fire** они́ не могли́ установи́ть причи́ну пожа́ра.

assignation [,æsɪg'neɪʃ(ə)n] *n.* **1.** (*appointment*) назначе́ние. **2.** (*illicit meeting*) та́йное свида́ние. **3.** (*leg., transfer*) переда́ча, переусту́пка.

assignment [ə'saɪnmənt] *n.* **1.** (*allotment*) распределе́ние; (пред)назначе́ние. **2.** (*task, duty*) поруче́ние; зада́ние; рабо́та; (*involving journey*) командиро́вка; (*schoolwork*) зада́ние. **3.** (*fin., transfer*) переда́ча, переусту́пка.

assimilate [ə'sɪmɪ,leɪt] *v.t.* (*absorb by digestion etc., and fig.*) ассимили́ровать (*impf., pf.*); усв|а́ивать, -о́ить; **the immigrants were quickly ~d** иммигра́нты бы́стро ассимили́ровались; **new ideas take time to ~** но́вые иде́и привива́ются не сра́зу.

v.i. ассимили́роваться (*impf., pf.*).

assimilation [ə,sɪmɪ'leɪʃ(ə)n] *n.* (*physiol., ling.*) ассимиля́ция; (*of knowledge etc.*) усвое́ние.

assist [ə'sɪst] *v.t.* (*help*) пом|ога́ть, -о́чь +*d.*; (*cooperate with*) соде́йствовать (*impf., pf.*) +*d.*; **she was ~ed to her feet by a passer-by** прохо́жий помо́г ей подня́ться на́ ноги.

assistance [ə'sɪstəns] *n.* по́мощь; соде́йствие; **he rendered valuable ~** он оказа́л це́нную по́мощь; **can you come to my ~?** вы мо́жете мне помо́чь?; **may I be of ~?** могу́ я че́м-нибудь помо́чь?

assistant [ə'sɪst(ə)nt] *n.* помо́щник; ассисте́нт; **~ manager** помо́щник заве́дующего; **~ professor** ≃ доце́нт; (*in shop*) продав|е́ц (*fem.* -щи́ца).

assize [ə'saɪz] *n.* (*usu. pl.*) суде́бное заседа́ние; выездна́я се́ссия суда прися́жных.

associate[1] [əˈsəʊʃɪət, -sɪət] *n.* **1.** (*colleague*) колле́га (*c.g.*), това́рищ, партнёр; (*in business*) компаньо́н; **his ~s in crime** его́ соо́бщники в преступле́нии. **2.** (*commerce*) член о́бщества.

adj. (*closely connected*) свя́занный; (*united*) объединённый; **~ member** непо́лный член; член-корреспонде́нт; **~ editor** помо́щник реда́ктора.

associate[2] [əˈsəʊʃɪˌeɪt, -sɪˌeɪt] *v.t.* соедин|я́ть, -и́ть; свя́з|ывать, -а́ть; (*esp. psych.*) ассоции́ровать (*impf.*, *pf.*); **~ o.s. with** присоедин|я́ться, -и́ться к+*d.*

v.i. води́ться (*impf.*), обща́ться (*impf.*).

association [əˌsəʊsɪˈeɪʃ(ə)n] *n.* **1.** (*uniting; joining*) объедине́ние; соедине́ние. **2.** (*consorting*) обще́ние. **3.** (*connection; bond*) связь. **4.** (*group*) ассоциа́ция, о́бщество; (*union*) сою́з.

assonance [ˈæsənəns] *n.* ассона́нс; непо́лная ри́фма.

assorted [əˈsɔːtɪd] *adj.* (*sorted, classified*) сортиро́ванный; (*selected*) подо́бранный; **~ chocolates** шокола́дный набо́р; (шокола́дное) ассорти́ (*indecl.*); (*varied*) разнообра́зный.

assortment [əˈsɔːtmənt] *n.* ассортиме́нт; набо́р; **an ~ of books** вы́бор книг.

assuage [əˈsweɪdʒ] *v.t.* (*soothe*) успок|а́ивать, -о́ить; (*alleviate*) смягч|а́ть, -и́ть; (*appetite etc.*) утол|я́ть, -и́ть.

assum|e [əˈsjuːm] *v.t.* **1.** (*take on*) прин|има́ть, -я́ть; **he ~ed command** он при́нял кома́ндование; **I ~e full responsibility** я принима́ю на себя́ по́лную отве́тственность; **~e control of** брать, взять на себя́ управле́ние/руково́дство +*i.* **2.** (*feign*) напус|ка́ть, -ти́ть на себя́; **he went under an ~ed name** он был изве́стен под вы́мышленным и́менем; **she ~ed an air of indifference** она́ напусти́ла на себя́ равноду́шный вид. **3.** (*suppose*) предпол|ага́ть, -ожи́ть; допус|ка́ть, -ти́ть; **let us ~e that ...** допу́стим, что…

assumption [əˈsʌmpʃ(ə)n] *n.* **1.** (*taking on*) приня́тие (на себя́); **his ~ of power** его́ прихо́д к вла́сти. **2.** (*pretence*): **~ of indifference** притво́рное равноду́шие. **3.** (*supposition*) предположе́ние; допуще́ние; **on the ~ that ...** исходя́ из того́, что…; е́сли допусти́ть, что… **4.** (*eccl.*): **the A~** Успе́ние.

assurance [əˈʃʊərəns] *n.* **1.** (*act of assuring; promise; guarantee*) завере́ние, увере́ние; **have I your ~ of this?** вы мо́жете за э́то поручи́ться?. **2.** (*confidence*) уве́ренность (в себе́). **3.** (*insurance*) страхова́ние; **life ~ company** о́бщество по страхова́нию жи́зни.

assure [əˈʃʊə(r)] *v.t.* **1.** (*ensure*) обеспе́чи|вать, -ть; **~ o.s. of sth.** обеспе́чить (*pf.*) себе́ что-н.; **he is ~d of a steady income** ему́ обеспе́чен постоя́нный дохо́д. **2.** (*assert confidently*) ув|еря́ть, -е́рить; зав|еря́ть, -е́рить; **you may rest ~d that ...** мо́жете быть уве́рены, что…

assuredly [əˈʃʊərɪdlɪ] *adv.* несомне́нно.

aster [ˈæstə(r)] *n.* а́стра.

asterisk [ˈæstərɪsk] *n.* звёздочка.

astern [əˈstɜːn] *adv.* за кормо́й; на корме́; (*of motion*) наза́д; **full speed ~** по́лный ход наза́д.

asteroid [ˈæstəˌrɔɪd] *n.* астеро́ид.

asthma [ˈæsmə] *n.* а́стма.

asthmatic [æsˈmætɪk] *n.* астма́тик.

adj. (*pertaining to asthma*) астмати́ческий; (*suffering from asthma*) страда́ющий а́стмой.

astigmatic [ˌæstɪgˈmætɪk] *adj.* астигмати́ческий.

astigmatism [əˈstɪgməˌtɪz(ə)m] *n.* астигмати́зм.

astir [əˈstɜː(r)] *pred. adj.* (*out of bed*) на нога́х; (*agog*) взбудора́женный.

astonish [əˈstɒnɪʃ] *v.t.* удив|ля́ть, -и́ть; изум|ля́ть, -и́ть; **be ~ed at** удив|ля́ться, -и́ться +*d.*; изум|ля́ться, -и́ться +*d.*; **his success was ~ing** он име́л порази́тельный успе́х.

astonishment [əˈstɒnɪʃmənt] *n.* удивле́ние, изумле́ние; **to my ~** к моему́ изумле́нию.

astound [əˈstaʊnd] *v.t.* изум|ля́ть, -и́ть; пора|жа́ть, -зи́ть; **he had an ~ing memory** у него́ была́ порази́тельная па́мять.

astrakhan [ˌæstrəˈkæn] *n.* (*lambskin*) кара́куль (*m.*); (*attr.*) кара́кулевый.

astral [ˈæstr(ə)l] *adj.* звёздный; астра́льный; **~ body** астра́льное те́ло.

astray [əˈstreɪ] *pred. adj. & adv.*: **go ~** (*lit., miss one's way*) заблуди́ться (*pf.*); (*fig.*) сб|ива́ться, -и́ться с пути́; **lead ~** (*fig.*) сб|ива́ть, -ить с пути́.

astride [əˈstraɪd] *adv.* (*on animal*) верхо́м; (*with legs apart*) расста́вив но́ги.

prep.: **~ his father's knee** на коле́нях у отца́.

astringency [əˈstrɪndʒ(ə)nsɪ] *n.* вя́жущее сво́йство; (*fig.*) суро́вость.

astringent [əˈstrɪndʒ(ə)nt] *n.* вя́жущее сре́дство.

adj. вя́жущий; (*fig.*) суро́вый.

astrolabe [ˈæstrəˌleɪb] *n.* астроля́бия.

astrologer [əˈstrɒlədʒə(r)] *n.* астро́лог, звездочёт.

astrological [ˌæstrəˈlɒdʒɪk(ə)l] *adj.* астрологи́ческий.

astrology [əˈstrɒlədʒɪ] *n.* астроло́гия.

astronaut [ˈæstrəˌnɔːt] *n.* космона́вт.

astronomer [əˈstrɒnəmə(r)] *n.* астроно́м.

astronomical [ˌæstrəˈnɒmɪk(ə)l] *adj.* (*lit., fig.*) астрономи́ческий.

astronomy [əˈstrɒnəmɪ] *n.* астроно́мия.

astrophysicist [ˌæstrəʊˈfɪzɪsɪst] *n.* астрофи́зик.

astrophysics [ˌæstrəʊˈfɪzɪks] *n.* астрофи́зика.

astute [əˈstjuːt] *adj.* **1.** (*shrewd*) проница́тельный. **2.** (*crafty*) хи́трый; ло́вкий.

astuteness [əˈstjuːtnɪs] *n.* **1.** проница́тельность. **2.** хи́трость; ло́вкость.

asunder [əˈsʌndə(r)] *adv.* на куски́, на ча́сти; **tear ~** (*lit.*) разорва́ть (*pf.*) на ча́сти; (*fig., of persons*) разлуч|а́ть, -и́ть.

asylum [əˈsaɪləm] *n.* **1.** (*sanctuary*) прию́т; (*place of refuge*) убе́жище. **2.** (*mental home*) сумасше́дший дом.

asymmetrical [ˌeɪsɪˈmetrɪk(ə)l, ˌæsɪˈmetrɪk(ə)l] *adj.* асимметри́ческий.

asymmetry [eɪˈsɪmɪtrɪ, æˈsɪmɪtrɪ] *n.* асимме́трия.

at [æt, *unstressed* ət] *prep.* **1.** (*denoting place*) в/на+*p.*; (*near, by*) у+*g.*, при+*p.*; **~ the university** в университе́те; **~ № 10** в до́ме (но́мер) де́сять; **~ home** до́ма; **~ sea** (*lit.*) в мо́ре; **~ the battle** в би́тве; **~ church** в це́ркви; **~ school** в шко́ле; **~ the station** на вокза́ле/ста́нции; **~ the corner** на углу́; **~ the fork in the road** у разви́лки доро́ги; **~ the concert** на конце́рте; **~ that distance** на э́том расстоя́нии; **~ hand** под руко́й; **~ the piano** у роя́ля; за роя́лем; **~ the helm** у руля́; **~ my aunt's** у мое́й тётки; **~ table** за столо́м; **~ his feet** у его́ ног; **~ the gates** у воро́т; **~ Court** при дворе́; **a translator ~ the UN** перево́дчик при ООН. **2.** (*denoting motion or direction; lit., fig.*): **he tapped ~ the window** он постуча́л в окно́; **he sat down ~ the table** он сел за стол; **she fell ~ his feet** она́ упа́ла к его́ нога́м; **he arrived ~ the station** он при́был на ста́нцию; **he went in ~ this door** он вошёл в/че́рез э́ту дверь; **he came out ~ this door** он вы́шел из э́той две́ри; **throw a stone ~** бро́сить (*pf.*) ка́мень/ка́мнем в+*a.* **3.** (*denoting time or order*): **~ night** но́чью; **~ present** в настоя́щее вре́мя; **~ 2 o'clock** в два часа́; **~ half-past 2** в полови́не тре́тьего; **~ any moment** в любо́й моме́нт; **~ (the age of) 15** (в во́зрасте) пятна́дцати лет; **~ his death** в моме́нт его́ сме́рти; **~ the first attempt** с пе́рвой попы́тки; **~ intervals** с переры́вами; **~ his signal** по его́ сигна́лу; **~ Easter** на Па́сху; **~ dawn** на рассве́те; **~ twilight** в су́мерках; **~ midday** в по́лдень; **~ that time** в э́то вре́мя; **~ what hour?** в кото́ром часу́?; **~ the beginning** в нача́ле; **~ first** снача́ла. **4.** (*of activity, state, manner, rate etc.*): **~ work** на рабо́те; **good ~ languages**

способный к языкам; ~ **war** в состоянии войны; ~ **peace** в мире; ~ **a gallop** галопом; ~ **one blow** одним ударом; ~ **a sitting** в один присест; ~ **60 m.p.h.** со скоростью шестьдесят миль в час; ~ **full speed** на полной скорости; ~ **my expense** за мой счёт; **estimate** ~ оценивать (*impf.*) в+*a.*; ~ **best** в лучшем случае; ~ **least** по крайней мере; ~ **most** самое большее; ~ **your own risk** на ваш/свой страх и риск; ~ **all** вообще; (*with neg.*) совсем; ~ **your service** к вашим услугам; ~ **my request** по моей просьбе; ~ **his dictation** под его диктовку; ~ **that** (*moreover*) к тому же; ~ **first sight** с первого взгляда; ~ **a reduced price** по сниженной цене; ~ **a high remuneration** за большое вознаграждение; ~ **your discretion** по вашему усмотрению. **5.** (*of cause*): **be impatient** ~ **the delay** волноваться (*impf.*) из-за задержки; **delighted** ~ в восторге от+*g.*

atavism ['ætə,vɪz(ə)m] *n.* атавизм.

atavistic [,ætə'vɪstɪk] *adj.* атавистический.

ataxia [ə'tæksɪə] *n.* атаксия.

atheism ['eɪθɪ,ɪz(ə)m] *n.* атеизм, безбожие.

atheist ['eɪθɪɪst] *n.* атеист, безбожник.

atheistic [,eɪθɪ'ɪstɪk] *adj.* атеистический.

athlete ['æθli:t] *n.* спортсмен (*fem.* -ка); атлет.

athletic [æθ'letɪk] *adj.* атлетический.

athletics [æθ'letɪks] *n.* атлетика.

athwart [ə'θwɔ:t] *adv.* косо, поперёк.

prep. поперёк+*g.*; через+*a.*

Atlantic [ət'læntɪk] *n.* Атлантический океан; **North ~ Treaty Organization (NATO)** Североатлантический союз (НАТО).

adj. атлантический.

atlas ['ætləs] *n.* атлас.

atmosphere ['ætməs,fɪə(r)] *n.* (*lit., fig.*) атмосфера; (*fig.*) колорит, обстановка.

atmospheric [,ætməs'ferɪk] *adj.* атмосферный.

atoll ['ætɒl] *n.* атолл.

atom ['ætəm] *n.* атом; **split the** ~ расщеп|лять, -ить атом; ~ **bomb** атомная бомба.

atomic [ə'tɒmɪk] *adj.* атомный; ~ **bomb** атомная бомба.

cpd. **~-powered** *adj.* с атомными двигателями.

atomize [,ætə'maɪz] *v.t.* распыл|ять, -ить.

atomizer ['ætə,maɪzə(r)] *n.* атомизатор; (*spray*) пульверизатор, распылитель (*m.*).

atonal [eɪ'təʊn(ə)l, ə-] *adj.* атональный.

atonality [eɪ,təʊ'nælɪtɪ, ə-] *n.* атональность.

atone [ə'təʊn] *v.i.*: ~ **for** искуп|ать, -ить.

atonement [ə'təʊnmənt] *n.* искупление.

atop [ə'tɒp] *adv. & prep.* на вершине (+*g.*); наверху.

atrocious [ə'trəʊʃəs] *adj.* зверский; (*very bad*) ужасный.

atrocit|y [ə'trɒsɪtɪ] *n.* зверство; **many ~ies were committed** было совершено много зверств.

atroph|y ['ætrəfɪ] *n.* атрофия.

v.t. & i. атрофировать(ся) (*impf., pf.*).

atropine ['ætrə,pi:n, -pɪn] *n.* атропин.

attach [ə'tætʃ] *v.t.* **1.** (*fasten*) прикреп|лять, -ить; (*by tying*) привяз|ывать, -ать; (*by sticking*) прикле|ивать, -ить; ~ **a seal** приложить (*pf.*) печать; **the ~ed document** прилагаемый документ. **2.** (*fig., of pers.*) присоедин|ять, -ить; (*appoint*) назн|ачать, -ачить. **3.:** ~ **o.s. to** присоедин|яться, -иться к+*d.* **4.** (*assign*) прид|авать, -ать; (*ascribe*) припис|ывать, -ать; ~ **blame to** возл|агать, -ожить вину на+*a.* **5.** (*of affection*): **she is very ~ed to her brother** она очень привязана к своему брату. **I am ~ed to this necklace** это ожерелье мне очень дорого.

v.i. ~ **to** (*inhere in*): **the responsibility that ~es to this position** ответственность, связанная с этой должностью.

attaché [ə'tæʃeɪ] *n.* атташе (*m. indecl.*); ~ **case** портфель (*m.*).

attachment [ə'tætʃmənt] *n.* **1.** (*part attached to a larger unit*) прикрепление, привязывание. **2.** (*affection*) привязанность; **form an ~ for** привязаться (*pf.*) к+*d.*; (*devotion*) преданность.

attack [ə'tæk] *n.* **1.** нападение; (*mil.*) атака, наступление, нападение, приступ; **make an ~ on** атаковать (*impf., pf.*); **we went into the ~** мы пошли в атаку; **our troops were under ~** наши войска были атакованы. **2.** (*fig., criticism*) напад|ки (*pl., g.* -ок). **3.** (*of illness*) приступ; припадок; **he had a heart ~** с ним случился сердечный приступ.

v.t. **1.** (*lit., fig.*) нап|адать, -асть на+*a*; атаковать (*impf., pf.*); обруши|ваться, -ться на+*a.*; **he was ~ed in the press** его атаковали в печати. **2.** (*of illness*) пора|жать, -зить. **3.** (*harm*) повре|ждать, -дить +*d.*; (*of chemical action*) разъ|едать, -есть. **4.** (*a task etc.*) набр|асываться, -оситься на+*a.*

v.i.: **the enemy ~ed** враг бросился/пошёл в атаку.

attacker [ə'tækə(r)] *n.* нападающий; (*mil.*) атакующий.

attain [ə'teɪn] *v.t.* (*also* ~ **to**) (*reach; gain; accomplish*) дост|игать, -игнуть (*or* -ичь) +*g.*; доб|иваться, -иться +*g.*; **our ends were ~ed** мы добились своего.

attainable [ə'teɪnəb(ə)l] *adj.* достижимый.

attainment [ə'teɪnmənt] *n.* (*attaining*) достижение; (*acquisition*) приобретение; (*accomplishment*): **linguistic ~s** лингвистические познания.

attempt [ə'tempt] *n.* **1.** (*endeavour*) попытка; опыт; **they made no ~ to escape** они не пытались убежать; **at the first ~** с первой попытки. **2.** (*assault*) покушение; **an ~ was made on his life** покушались на его жизнь.

v.t. **1.** (*try; try to do*) пытаться, по-; **~ed theft** попытка воровства; **he was charged with ~ed murder** его обвинили в покушении на жизнь.

attend [ə'tend] *v.t.* **1.** (*be present at*) присутствовать (*impf.*) на+*p.*; **the concert was well ~ed** на концерте было много публики; ~ **school** посещать (*impf.*) школу. **2.** (*serve professionally*) ухаживать (*impf.*) за+*i.*; **three nurses ~ed him** три медсестры ухаживали за ним; **he was ~ed by Dr. Smith** его лечил доктор Смит.

v.i. **1.** (*be present*) присутствовать (*impf.*). **2.** (*direct one's mind*) удел|ять, -ить внимание +*d.*; обра|щать, -тить внимание на+*a.*; (*listen carefully*): ~ **to what I am saying** слушайте меня внимательно. **3.:** ~ **to** (*take care of, look after*) следить (*impf.*) за+*i.*; заботиться, по- о+*p.*; **she ~ed to the children** она присматривала за детьми; ~ **to one's duties** исполнять (*impf.*) свои обязанности; ~ **to one's correspondence** заниматься (*impf.*) своей перепиской; **are you being ~ed to?** (*in shop*) вас (уже) обслуживают?; **I have things to ~ to** у меня есть дела. **4.:** ~ **upon** (*serve*) прислуживать (*impf.*), обслуживать (*impf.*); **he ~ed upon the queen** он сопровождал королеву.

attendance [ə'tend(ə)ns] *n.* **1.** (*presence*) присутствие; (*number of visits or of those present*) посещаемость; **there was a high, large ~ at church today** сегодня в церкви было много народу; (*body of persons present*) аудитория; публика. **2.** (*looking after s.o.*) уход; **the doctor is in ~ from 3 to 5** врач принимает с трёх до пяти (часов). **3.** (*service to, accompaniment of s.o.*) обслуживание.

attendant [ə'tend(ə)nt] *n.* служитель (m.); (*one who waits upon or accompanies another*) обслуживающее/сопровождающее лицо; **medical ~** врач.

adj. (*accompanying*) сопровождающий; (*present*) присутствующий; обслуживающий.

attender [ə'tendə(r)] *n.*: **he is a regular ~ at church** он регулярно ходит в церковь.

attention [ə'tenʃ(ə)n] *n.* **1.** (*heed*) внима́ние; **pay, give ~ to** обра|ща́ть, -ти́ть внима́ние на+*a.*; **pay, devote much/little ~ to** удел|я́ть, -и́ть мно́го/ма́ло внима́ния +*d.*; **pay ~!** бу́дьте внима́тельны!; **direct, draw ~ to** привл|ека́ть, -е́чь внима́ние к+*d.*; **(for the) ~ (of)** (*on letters etc.*) на рассмотре́ние +*g.* **2.** (*mil. command*) сми́рно!; (*posture*) **stand to ~** стоя́ть (*impf.*) сми́рно; **he came to ~** он при́нял сто́йку сми́рно (*or* строеву́ю сто́йку). **3.** (*care*) ухо́д; **he was given immediate medical ~** ему́ была́ ока́зана неме́дленная медици́нская по́мощь. **4.** (*politeness*; *courtesy*) забо́тливость; внима́ние, внима́тельность.

attentive [ə'tentɪv] *adj.* **1.** внима́тельный; **~ to detail** внима́тельный к ча́стностям. **2.** (*solicitous*) забо́тливый.

attentiveness [ə'tentɪvnɪs] *n.* внима́тельность; забо́тливость.

attenuat|e [ə'tenjʊˌeɪt] *v.t.* (*fig., reduce gravity of*) смягч|а́ть, -и́ть; **~ing circumstances** смягча́ющие обстоя́тельства.

attest [ə'test] *v.t.* (*certify*) удостов|еря́ть, -е́рить; (*bear witness to*) свиде́тельствовать, за-; (*confirm*) подтвер|жда́ть, -ди́ть.

v.i. **~ to** свиде́тельствовать (*impf.*) о+*p.*

attestation [ˌæte'steɪʃ(ə)n] *n.* засвиде́тельствование, удостовере́ние, подтвержде́ние.

attic[1] ['ætɪk] *n.* манса́рда, черда́к.

attire [ə'taɪə(r)] *n.* наря́д, одея́ние; **in night ~** в ночно́м облаче́нии.

v.t. (*dress*) наря|жа́ть, -ди́ть; од|ева́ть, -е́ть; **she was ~d in white** она́ была́ вся в бе́лом.

attitude ['ætɪˌtju:d] *n.* **1.** (*pose*) по́за; **strike an ~** прин|има́ть, -я́ть по́зу. **2.** (*fig., disposition*) отноше́ние; **~ of mind** склад ума́; **what is your ~ to this book?** как вы отно́ситесь к э́той кни́ге?

attn. [ə'tenʃ(ə)n] *n.* (*abbr. of* **for the attention of**) вним., (внима́нию) (+*g.*).

attorney [ə'tɜ:nɪ] *n.* уполномо́ченный, дове́ренный; адвока́т; **by ~** по дове́ренности; **power of ~** дове́ренность.

attract [ə'trækt] *v.t.* **1.** (*of physical forces*) притя́|гивать, -ну́ть; (*fig.*) привл|ека́ть, -е́чь (к себе́). **2.** (*captivate*) плен|я́ть, -и́ть; **he found himself ~ed to her** он почу́вствовал, что увлечён е́ю; **I am not ~ed by the idea** меня́ э́та иде́я не привлека́ет.

attraction [ə'trækʃ(ə)n] *n.* **1.** (*phys.*) притяже́ние, тяготе́ние. **2.** (*charm, allure*) прима́нка, привлека́тельность; **the ~s of a big city** собла́зны большо́го го́рода. **3.** (*in theatre etc.*) аттракцио́н.

attractive [ə'træktɪv] *adj.* **1.** (*phys.*): **~ force** си́ла притяже́ния. **2.** (*fig.*) притяга́тельный; привлека́тельный; **an ~ dress** ми́лое/симпати́чное пла́тье.

attractiveness [ə'træktɪvnɪs] *n.* привлека́тельность.

attributable [ə'trɪbjʊtəb(ə)l] *adj.* припи́сываемый; **his illness is ~ to drink** его́ боле́знь объясня́ется пья́нством.

attribute[1] ['ætrɪˌbju:t] *n.* **1.** (*quality*) сво́йство; (*characteristic*) характе́рная черта́. **2.** (*accompanying feature, emblem*) атрибу́т. **3.** (*gram.*) атрибу́т; определе́ние.

attribute[2] [ə'trɪbju:t] *v.t.*: **~ sth to** припи́с|ывать, -а́ть что-н. +*d.*; отн|оси́ть, -ести́ что-н. к+*d.*

attribution [ˌætrɪ'bju:ʃ(ə)n] *n.* (*ascription*) припи́сывание, отнесе́ние.

attributive [ə'trɪbjʊtɪv] *adj.* атрибути́вный; определи́тельный.

attrition [ə'trɪʃ(ə)n] *n.* тре́ние; истира́ние; (*fig.*) истоще́ние; измо́р; **war of ~** война́ на истоще́ние.

attune [ə'tju:n] *v.t.* (*lit., fig.*) настр|а́ивать, -о́ить.

atypical [eɪ'tɪpɪk(ə)l] *adj.* атипи́ческий.

aubergine ['əʊbəˌʒi:n] *n.* баклажа́н.

auburn ['ɔ:bən] *adj.* тёмно-ры́жий.

auction ['ɔ:kʃ(ə)n] *n.* аукцио́н; **put up for ~** выставля́ть, вы́ставить на аукцио́не; продава́ть (*impf.*) с молотка́; **the house is for sale by ~** дом продаётся с аукцио́на.

v.t. (*also* **~ off**) прод|ава́ть, -а́ть с аукцио́на.

auctioneer [ˌɔ:kʃə'nɪə(r)] *n.* аукциони́ст.

audacious [ɔ:'deɪʃəs] *adj.* (*bold*) сме́лый; (*daring*) отва́жный; (*impudent*) де́рзкий.

audacity [ɔ:'dæsɪtɪ] *n.* отва́га, сме́лость; де́рзость.

audibility [ˌɔ:dɪ'bɪlɪtɪ] *n.* слы́шимость; вня́тность.

audible ['ɔ:dɪb(ə)l] *adj.* слы́шимый, слы́шный; (*distinct*) вня́тный.

audience ['ɔ:dɪəns] *n.* **1.** (*listeners*) аудито́рия; слу́шатели (*m. pl.*); (*spectators*) зри́тели (*m. pl.*); пу́блика. **2.** (*hearing*; *interview*) аудие́нция.

audiotape ['ɔ:dɪəʊˌteɪp] *n.* плёнка звукоза́писи.

audiotypist [ˌɔ:dɪəʊ'taɪpɪst] *n.* фономашини́стка.

audio-visual [ˌɔ:dɪəʊ'vɪʒjʊəl] *adj.* а́удио-визуа́льный.

audit ['ɔ:dɪt] *n.* прове́рка, реви́зия.

v.t. пров|еря́ть, -е́рить отчётность +*g.*; ревизова́ть (*impf., pf.*).

audition [ɔ:'dɪʃ(ə)n] *n.* (*listening*) слу́шание; (*trial hearing*) про́ба.

v.t. прослу́ш|ивать, -ать.

auditor ['ɔ:dɪtə(r)] *n.* бухга́лтер-ревизо́р; фина́нсовый инспе́ктор.

auditorium [ˌɔ:dɪ'tɔ:rɪəm] *n.* (*where audience sits*) зри́тельный зал; (*public building*) аудито́рия, зал.

auditory ['ɔ:dɪtərɪ] *adj.* слухово́й.

au fait [əʊ 'feɪ] *pred. adj.* в ку́рсе; осведомлённый; **can you put me ~ with the situation?** могли́ бы вы ввести́ меня́ в курс де́ла?

auger ['ɔ:gə(r)] *n.* сверло́; (*woodworking tool*) бура́в.

augment [ɔ:g'ment] *v.t.* увели́чи|вать, -ть; приб|авля́ть, -а́вить +*g.*

v.i. увели́чи|ваться, -ться; уси́ли|ваться, -ться.

augmentation [ˌɔ:gmen'teɪʃ(ə)n] *n.* увеличе́ние; прираще́ние.

augur ['ɔ:gə(r)] *n.* (*hist.*) авгу́р; (*soothsayer*) прорица́тель (*m.*).

v.t. (*portend*) предвеща́ть (*impf.*); (*of pers.*: *predict*) предска́з|ывать, -а́ть.

v.i. (*of things*) служи́ть (*impf.*) предзнаменова́нием; (*of pers.*) предви́деть (*impf.*).

augury ['ɔ:gjərɪ] *n.* (*divination*) предсказа́ние; (*omen*; *sign*) предзнаменова́ние.

August[1] ['ɔ:gəst] *n.* а́вгуст; (*attr.*) а́вгустовский.

august[2] [ɔ:'gʌst] *adj.* вели́чественный.

auk [ɔ:k] *n.* гага́рка.

aunt [ɑ:nt] *n.* тётя, тётка.

aunt|ie, -y ['ɑ:ntɪ] *n.* тётушка, тётенька.

au pair [əʊ 'peə(r)] *n.* ≃ ня́ня-иностра́нка; помо́щница по хозя́йству из иностра́нок.

aura ['ɔ:rə] *n.* арома́т; (*atmosphere*) атмосфе́ра.

aureole ['ɔ:rɪˌəʊl] *n.* (*halo*) орео́л; (*crown*) ве́нчик.

auricle ['ɔ:rɪk(ə)l] *n.* (*of ear*) нару́жное у́хо; (*of heart*) предсе́рдие.

aurochs ['ɔ:rɒks, 'aʊrɒks] *n.* зубр.

aurora [ɔ:'rɔ:rə] *n.* **1** (*poet., dawn*) авро́ра, у́тренняя заря́. **2.** (*atmospheric phenomenon*): **~ borealis/australis** се́верное/ю́жное сия́ние.

auscultation [ˌɔ:skəl'teɪʃ(ə)n] *n.* выслу́шивание, аускульта́ция.

auspices ['ɔ:spɪsɪz] *n.* **1.** (*omens*) предзнаменова́ния (*nt. pl.*); **under favourable ~** при благоприя́тных усло́виях. **2.** (*patronage*) покрови́тельство; эги́да.

auspicious [ɔ:'spɪʃəs] *adj.* (*favourable*) благоприя́тный; **on this ~ day** в э́тот знамена́тельный день.

austere [ɒ'stɪə(r), ɔ:'stɪə(r)] *adj.* (*lit., fig.*) стро́гий, суро́вый.

austerity [ɒ'sterɪtɪ, ɔ:'sterɪtɪ] *n.* стро́гость, суро́вость; (*economy*) стро́гая эконо́мия.

Australia [ɒ'streɪlɪə] *n.* Австра́лия.

Australian [ɒ'streɪlɪən] *n.* австрали́|ец (*fem.* -йка).
adj. австрали́йский.
Austria ['ɒstrɪə] *n.* А́встрия.
Austrian ['ɒstrɪən] *n.* австри́|ец (*fem.* -йка).
adj. австри́йский.
authentic [ɔː'θentɪk] *adj.* (*genuine*) по́длинный.
authenticate [ɔː'θentɪˌkeɪt] *v.t.* удостов|еря́ть, -е́рить по́длинность +*g.*
authenticity [ˌɔːθen'tɪsɪtɪ] *n.* по́длинность.
author ['ɔːθə(r)] *n.* (*of specific work*) а́втор; (*writer in general*) писа́тель (*m.*).
authoritarian [ɔːˌθɒrɪ'teərɪən] *adj.* авторита́рный, деспоти́ческий.
authoritative [ɔː'θɒrɪtətɪv] *adj.* авторите́тный.
authority [ɔː'θɒrɪtɪ] *n.* **1.** (*power*; *right*) власть; (*legal*) полномо́чие; ~ **to sign** пра́во по́дписи; **who is in ~ here?** кто здесь гла́вный/нача́льник?; **on one's own ~** на свою́ отве́тственность; **I did it on his ~** я э́то сде́лал по его́ поруче́нию; **who gave you ~ over me?** кто вам дал пра́во мне прика́зывать? **2.** (*usu. pl.*: *public bodies*) вла́сти (*f. pl.*); о́рганы (*m. pl.*) вла́сти; **he is always getting into trouble with ~** у него́ всё вре́мя неприя́тности с властя́ми. **3.** (*influence*, *weight*) авторите́т; **carry, have ~** по́льзоваться (*impf.*) авторите́том; **he speaks with ~** он говори́т авторите́тно. **4.** (*source*) достове́рный исто́чник; **I have it on good ~** я э́то зна́ю из достове́рного исто́чника; **what is your ~ for saying so?** на основа́нии чего́ вы э́то говори́те? **5.** (*expert*): **he is an ~ on Greek** он кру́пный специали́ст по гре́ческому языку́.
authorization [ˌɔːθəraɪ'zeɪʃ(ə)n] *n.* (*authorizing*) уполномо́чивание; (*sanction*) разреше́ние.
authorize ['ɔːθəˌraɪz] *v.t.* **1.** (*give authority to*) уполномо́чи|вать, -ть. **2.** (*permit*; *sanction*) разреш|а́ть, -и́ть; дозв|оля́ть, -о́лить; **~d expenditure** утверждённые расхо́ды.
authorship ['ɔːθəʃɪp] *n.* а́вторство.
autism ['ɔːtɪz(ə)m] *n.* аути́зм.
autistic [ɔː'tɪstɪk] *adj.* аутисти́ческий.
autobahn ['ɔːtəʊˌbɑːn] *n.* автостра́да.
autobiographer [ˌɔːtəʊbaɪ'ɒgrəfə(r)] *n.* автобио́граф.
autobiographical [ˌɔːtəʊbaɪə'græfɪk(ə)l] *adj.* автобиографи́ческий, автобиографи́чный.
autobiography [ˌɔːtəʊbaɪ'ɒgrəfɪ] *n.* автобиогра́фия.
autocracy [ɔː'tɒkrəsɪ] *n.* самодержа́вие, автокра́тия.
autocrat ['ɔːtəˌkræt] *n.* самоде́ржец.
autocratic [ˌɔːtə'krætɪk] *adj.* самодержа́вный; (*dictatorial*) деспоти́ческий.
autocross ['ɔːtəʊˌkrɒs] *n.* автокро́сс.
autocue ['ɔːtəʊˌkjuː] *n.* (*propr.*) телесуфлёр; автосуфлёр.
autogiro [ˌɔːtəʊ'dʒaɪərəʊ] *n.* автожи́р.
autograph ['ɔːtəˌgrɑːf] *n.* авто́граф.
v.t. надпи́с|ывать, -а́ть; **~ed copy** экземпля́р с авто́графом.
automat ['ɔːtəˌmæt] *n.* автома́т; (*cafeteria*) заку́сочная-автома́т.
automated ['ɔːtəˌmeɪtɪd] *adj.* автоматизи́рованный.
automatic [ˌɔːtə'mætɪk] *n.* (*firearm*) автомати́ческое ору́жие.
adj. автомати́ческий; ~ **pilot** автопило́т; ~ **pistol** самозаря́дный пистоле́т; ~ **machine** автома́т.
automation [ˌɔːtə'meɪʃ(ə)n] *n.* автоматиза́ция.
automaton [ɔː'tɒmət(ə)n] *n.* автома́т.
automobile ['ɔːtəməˌbiːl] *n.* автомоби́ль (*m.*); (*attr.*) автомоби́льный.
autonomous [ɔː'tɒnəməs] *adj.* автоно́мный.
autonomy [ɔː'tɒnəmɪ] *n.* автоно́мия.
autopsy ['ɔːtɒpsɪ, ɔː'tɒpsɪ] *n.* вскры́тие тру́па.
auto-suggestion [ˌɔːtəʊsə'dʒestʃ(ə)n] *n.* самовнуше́ние.
autumn ['ɔːtəm] *n.* о́сень; **in ~** о́сенью; (*attr.*) осе́нний; ~ **crocus** лугово́й шафра́н.
autumnal [ɔː'tʌmn(ə)l] *adj.* осе́нний.
auxiliary [ɔːg'zɪljərɪ] *n.* (*assistant*) помо́щник; (*gram.*, ~ **verb**) вспомога́тельный глаго́л; (*mil.*) солда́т вспомога́тельных войск; (*pl.*) вспомога́тельные войска́.
adj. (*helpful*; *supporting*) вспомога́тельный; (*additional*) доба́вочный; (*in reserve*) запасно́й.
avail [ə'veɪl] *n.* (*use*) по́льза; (*profit*) вы́года; **his entreaties were of no ~** его́ мольбы́ бы́ли безуспе́шны.
v.t. **1.** (*benefit*) быть поле́зным/вы́годным +*d.*; **our efforts ~ed us nothing** на́ши уси́лия ни к чему́ не привели́. **2.**: **~o.s. of** воспо́льзоваться (*pf.*) +*i.*
availability [əˌveɪlə'bɪlɪtɪ] *n.* (*presence*) нали́чие; (*accessibility*) досту́пность.
available [ə'veɪləb(ə)l] *adj.* **1.** (*present*, *to hand*) нали́чный; (*pred.*) в нали́чии, в распоряже́нии; **if there is money ~** е́сли есть де́ньги (в нали́чии); **make ~** предост|авля́ть, -а́вить. **2.** (*accessible*) досту́пный.
avalanche ['ævəˌlɑːnʃ] *n.* (*lit.*, *fig.*) лави́на.
avant-garde [ˌævɑ̃'gɑːd] *n.* авангарди́сты; (*attr.*) авангарди́стский.
avarice ['ævərɪs] *n.* ску́пость, ска́редность.
avaricious [ˌævə'rɪʃəs] *adj.* скупо́й, ска́редный.
Av(e). ['ævəˌnjuː] *n.* (*abbr. of* **Avenue**) пр., (проспе́кт); авеню́.
avenge [ə'vendʒ] *v.t.* мстить, ото- за+*a.*
avenger [ə'vendʒə(r)] *n.* мсти́тель (*m.*).
avenue ['ævəˌnjuː] *n.* **1.** (*tree-lined road*) алле́я; (*wide street*) проспе́кт. **2.** (*fig.*, *approach*, *way*) путь (*m.*); ~ **to fame** путь к сла́ве; **explore every ~** испо́льзовать (*impf.*, *pf.*) все пути́/кана́лы.
aver [ə'vɜː(r)] *v.t.* утвер|жда́ть, -ди́ть.
average ['ævərɪdʒ] *n.* (*mean*) сре́днее число́; **strike an ~** выводи́ть, вы́вести сре́днее число́; (*norm*) сре́днее; **above/below ~** вы́ше/ни́же сре́днего; **on an, the ~** в сре́днем.
adj. сре́дний; **the ~ age of the class is 12** сре́дний во́зраст кла́сса — двена́дцать лет; **the ~ man** сре́дний челове́к.
v.t. & i. **1.** (*find the ~ of*) выводи́ть, вы́вести сре́днее число́ +*g.*; **his salary, when ~d, was £200 a month** его́ сре́дняя зарпла́та соста́вила 200 фу́нтов в ме́сяц. **2.** (*amount to on ~*): **my expenses ~ £10 a day** мои́ расхо́ды составля́ют в сре́днем де́сять фу́нтов в день; **it ~s out in the end** к концу́ э́то всё ура́внивается.
averse [ə'vɜːs] *pred. adj.*: ~ **to** нерасполо́женный к+*d.*; **I am not ~ to a good dinner** я не прочь хорошо́ пообе́дать.
aversion [ə'vɜːʃ(ə)n] *n.* (*dislike*) отвраще́ние, антипа́тия; **have an ~ to** пита́ть (*impf.*) отвраще́ние к+*d.*
avert [ə'vɜːt] *v.t.* **1.** (*turn aside*): ~ **one's glance, eyes** отв|оди́ть, -ести́ взгляд; ~ **one's thoughts** отвл|ека́ть, -е́чь мы́сли. **2.** (*ward off*) предотвра|ща́ть. -ти́ть; **the danger has been ~ed** опа́сность предотврати́ли.
aviary ['eɪvɪərɪ] *n.* пти́чник.
aviation [ˌeɪvɪ'eɪʃ(ə)n] *n.* авиа́ция; (*attr.*) авиацио́нный; ~ **spirit** авиабензи́н.
aviator ['eɪvɪˌeɪtə(r)] *n.* авиа́тор.
avid ['ævɪd] *adj.* жа́дный, а́лчный; **he was ~ to hear the results** он жа́ждал узна́ть результа́ты.
avidity [ə'vɪdɪtɪ] *n.* жа́дность, а́лчность.
avionics [ˌeɪvɪ'ɒnɪks] *n.* авиацио́нная электро́ника.
avocado [ˌævə'kɑːdəʊ] *n.* (~ *pear*) авока́до (*indecl.*).
avocation [ˌævə'keɪʃ(ə)n] *n.* побо́чное заня́тие.
avoid [ə'vɔɪd] *v.t.* **1.** объе́хать (*pf.*); (*escape*, *evade*) избе|га́ть, -жа́ть +*g.*; (*shun*) сторони́ться (*impf.*) +*g.*; (*refrain from*) уклон|я́ться, -и́ться от+*g.*
avoidance [ə'vɔɪd(ə)ns] *n.* **1.** избежа́ние; уклоне́ние;

~ of strong drink воздержа́ние от употребле́ния спиртно́го. **2.** (*leg.*) аннули́рование.
avow [ə'vaʊ] *v.t.* призн|ава́ть, -а́ть; **he is an ~ed racist** он открове́нный раси́ст; **it was his ~ed intent to emigrate** он откры́то выража́л наме́рение эмигри́ровать; **~edly** по со́бственному призна́нию.
avowal [ə'vaʊ(ə)l] *n.* призна́ние.
avuncular [ə'vʌŋkjʊlə(r)] *adj.* дя́дин; **~ manner** оте́ческое обраще́ние.
await [ə'weɪt] *v.t.* ожида́ть (*impf.*) +*g.*; **~ing your reply** в ожида́нии ва́шего отве́та.
awake [ə'weɪk] *pred. adj.*: **1. are you ~ or asleep?** вы спи́те и́ли нет?; **is he ~ yet?** он просну́лся?; **he lay ~ thinking** он лежа́л без сна и ду́мал; **she stayed ~ till her husband came home** она́ не засыпа́ла, пока́ муж не верну́лся домо́й; **the baby was wide ~** у ребёнка сна не́ было ни в одно́м глазу́. **2.** (*fig.*, *vigilant*, *alert*) бди́тельный; начеку́; **he is not ~ to his opportunity** он упуска́ет слу́чай; **we must be ~ to the possibility of defeat** пораже́ние возмо́жно, и мы не должны́ закрыва́ть на э́то глаза́.
v.t. **1.** (*rouse from sleep*) буди́ть, раз-; **I was awoken by the song of birds** меня́ разбуди́ло пе́ние птиц.
v.i. **1.** (*wake from sleep*) прос|ыпа́ться, -ну́ться. **2.**: **~ to** (*fig.*, *realize*) осозн|ава́ть, -а́ть.
awaken [ə'weɪkən] *v.t.* **1.** (*lit.*) = **awake** *v.t.*
awakening [ə'weɪkənɪŋ] *n.* пробужде́ние; **a rude ~** (*fig.*) го́рькое разочарова́ние.
award [ə'wɔːd] *n.* награ́да, приз.
v.t. прису|жда́ть, -ди́ть (*что кому*); **he was ~ed a medal** его награди́ли меда́лью.
aware [ə'weə(r)] *pred. adj.*: **be ~ of** сознава́ть (*impf.*); (*realise*) знать (*impf.*); **I am well ~ of the dangers** я вполне́ представля́ю себе́ все опа́сности; **he became ~ of someone following him** он почу́вствовал, что за ним следя́т; **I was not ~ of that** я э́того не знал; **you are probably ~ that ...** вам, вероя́тно, изве́стно, что...
awareness [ə'weərnɪs] *n.* созна́ние.
awash [ə'wɒʃ] *pred. adj.* омы́тый водо́й.
away [ə'weɪ] *adv.* **1.** (*at a distance*): **the shops are ten minutes' walk ~** магази́ны нахо́дятся в десяти́ мину́тах ходьбы́ отсю́да; **the sea is only 5 miles ~ from our villa** мо́ре всего́ в пяти́ ми́лях от на́шей ви́ллы; **her mother lived half an hour ~ by bus** её мать жила́ в получа́се езды́ на авто́бусе. **2.** (*not present or near*): **he is ~** он в отъе́зде; **he was ~ on leave** он был в о́тпуске; **how long have you been ~?** ско́лько же (вре́мени) вас не́ было?; **we shall be ~ in July** в ию́ле нас не бу́дет. **3.** (*fig.*, *of time or degree*): **far and ~ the best** наилу́чший. **4.** (*expr. continuance*): **he works ~** он знай себе́ рабо́тает; **he was talking ~ to himself** он всё вре́мя сам с собо́й разгова́ривал; **all the time the clock was ticking ~** всё э́то вре́мя часы́ ти́кали не перестава́я. **5.**: **right, straight ~** сейча́с; неме́дленно. **6.**: **~ with him!** доло́й его́! чтоб его́ здесь не́ было!; **~ with you!** убира́йтесь.
awe [ɔː] *n.* благогове́йный страх; свяще́нный тре́пет; **he stands in ~ of his teacher** он испы́тывает благогове́йный страх пе́ред учи́телем.
v.t. внуш|а́ть, -и́ть (*кому*) благогове́йный страх/тре́пет.
cpds. **~-inspiring** *adj.* внуша́ющий благогове́йный стра́х; **~-struck** *adj.* прони́кнутый свяще́нным тре́петом.
awesome ['ɔːsəm] *adj.* внуша́ющий страх.
awful ['ɔːfʊl] *adj.* **1.** (*terrible*; *also coll.*: *very bad*, *great etc.*) ужа́сный, стра́шный; **it's an ~ shame** ужа́сно доса́дно; **he has an ~ lot of money** у него́ у́йма де́нег. **2.** (*inspiring awe*) внуша́ющий страх.
awfully ['ɔːfəlɪ, -flɪ] *adv.* ужа́сно; **~ nice** стра́шно ми́лый; **thanks ~** огро́мное вам спаси́бо; **I'm ~ sorry** прости́те, ра́ди Бо́га.
awhile [ə'waɪl] *adv.* на не́которое вре́мя; **I shan't be ready to leave yet ~** я не смогу́ пое́хать сра́зу.
awkward ['ɔːkwəd] *adj.* **1.** (*clumsy*) неуклю́жий, нело́вкий. **2.** (*inconvenient*, *uncomfortable*) неудо́бный. **3.** (*difficult*): **an ~ problem** ка́верзная пробле́ма; **an ~ turning** тру́дный поворо́т. **4.** (*embarrassing*): **an ~ silence** нело́вкое молча́ние. **5.** (*of pers.*, *hard to manage*) тру́дный; **he's being ~ (about it)** он чини́т препя́тствия.
awkwardness ['ɔːkwədnɪs] *n.* неуклю́жесть, нело́вкость; неудо́бство.
awl [ɔːl] *n.* ши́ло.
awning ['ɔːnɪŋ] *n.* наве́с; тент.
awry [ə'raɪ] *pred. adj.* криво́й; (*distorted*) искажённый.
adv. ко́со; (*on*, *to one side*) на́бок; (*fig.*): **things went ~** дела́ пошли́ скве́рно.
axe (*US* **ax**) [æks] *n.* **1.** (*tool*) топо́р; **I have no ~ to grind** (*fig.*) у меня́ нет коры́стных побужде́ний. **2.** (*coll.*: *reduction of expenditure*) уре́зывание.
v.t. (*fig.*) (*terminate*) отмен|я́ть, -и́ть; **the government intends to ~ public expenditure** прави́тельство наме́рено уре́зать расхо́ды на обще́ственные ну́жды; **many workers have been ~d** уво́лено мно́го рабо́чих.
axial ['æksɪəl] *adj.* осево́й.
axiom ['æksɪəm] *n.* аксио́ма.
axiomatic [,æksɪə'mætɪk] *adj.* аксиомати́чный.
axis ['æksɪs] *n.* ось.
axle ['æks(ə)l] *n.* ось.
ayatollah [,aɪə'tɒlə] *n.* аятолла́ (*m.*).
ay(e) [aɪ] *n.* (*affirmative vote*) го́лос «за»; **the ~s have it** большинство́ за.
int. да; есть; **~, ~, Sir!** есть!
azalea [ə'zeɪlɪə] *n.* аза́лия.
Azerbaijan [,æzəbaɪ'dʒɑːn] *n.* Азербайджа́н.
azimuth ['æzɪməθ] *n.* а́зимут.
Aztec ['æztek] *n.* ацте́к.
adj. ацте́кский.
azure ['æʒə(r), -zjə(r), 'eɪ-] *n.* лазу́рь.
adj. лазу́рный, голубо́й.

B

B [biː] *n.* **1.** (*mus.*) си (*nt. indecl.*). **2.** (*acad. mark*) 4, четвёрка.
BA (*abbr. of* ***Bachelor of Arts***) бакала́вр гуманита́рных нау́к; **he has a ~ in Russian** он име́ет сте́пень бакала́вра по ру́сскому языку́.
baa [bɑː] *v.i.* бле́ять (*impf.*).
babble ['bæb(ə)l] *n.* (*imperfect speech*) ле́пет; (*idle talk*) болтовня́; (*of water etc.*) журча́ние.
v.t. & i. болта́ть (*impf.*); лепета́ть (*impf.*).
babbler ['bæbl(ə)r] *n.* болту́н (*fem.* -нья).
babe [beɪb] *n.* (*lit.*, *fig.*) младе́нец.
babel ['beɪb(ə)l] *n.* **1.: the tower of B~** вавило́нская ба́шня. **2.** (*fig.*) вавило́нское столпотворе́ние.
baboon [bə'buːn] *n.* бабуи́н, павиа́н.
baby ['beɪbɪ] *n.* **1.** младе́нец; **the ~ of the family** мла́дший в семье́; **empty out the baby with the bathwater** (*fig.*) вме́сте с водо́й вы́плеснуть (*pf.*) и ребёнка; **they left me holding the ~** (*fig.*) мне пришло́сь за них отдува́ться. **2.** (*of animals etc.*) детёныш. **3.** (*coll.*, *sweetheart*) де́тка. **4.** (*attr.*): **~**

elephant слонёнок; ~ **grand (piano)** кабине́тный роя́ль.

v.t. обраща́ться (*impf.*) (*с кем*) как с младе́нцем.

cpds. **~-carriage** *n.* де́тская коля́ска; **~-sit** *v.i.* присма́тривать (*impf.*) за детьми́ в отсу́тствие роди́телей; **~-sitter** *n.* приходя́щая ня́ня; **~-sitting** *n.* присмо́тр за детьми́; **~-talk** *n.* де́тский язы́к, де́тский ле́пет.

babyish ['beɪbɪɪʃ] *adj.* ребя́ческий.

baccalaureate [ˌbækə'lɔːrɪət] *n.* бакала́врство.

baccarat ['bækəˌrɑː] *n.* баккара́ (*nt. indecl.*).

bachelor ['bætʃələ(r)] *n.* **1.** холостя́к. **2.** (*acad.*) бакала́вр.

bachelorhood ['bætʃələ(r)hʊd] *n.* холостя́цкая жизнь.

bacillus [bə'sɪləs] *n.* баци́лла.

back [bæk] *n.* **1.** (*part of body*) спина́; ~ **to** ~ спино́й к спине́; **break one's** ~ перелома́ть (*pf.*) спинно́й хребе́т; **he fell on his** ~ он упа́л на́ спину; **turn one's** ~ **on** (*lit.*) отв|ора́чиваться, -ерну́ться от+*g.*; (*fig.*) пок|ида́ть, -и́нуть; **as soon as my** ~ **was turned** не успе́л я отверну́ться. **2.** (*fig. uses*): **behind my** ~ за мое́й спино́й; **on one's** ~ (*as burden*) на ше́е; **put s.o.'s** ~ **up** рассерди́ть (*pf.*) кого́-н.; **break the** ~ **of a task** одоле́ть (*pf.*) трудне́йшую часть зада́ния; **see the** ~ **of** (*get rid of*) отде́латься (*pf.*) от+*g.*; **with one's** ~ **against the wall** припёртый к сте́нке; **put one's** ~ **into sth.** вложи́ть (*pf.*) все си́лы во что-н. **3.** (*of chair, dress*) спи́нка. **4.** (*other side, rear*): ~ **of an envelope** обра́тная сторона́ конве́рта; ~ **of one's head** заты́лок; ~ **of one's hand** ты́льная сторона́ руки́; **know sth. like the** ~ **of one's hand** знать (*impf.*) что-н. как свои́ пять па́льцев; ~ (*spine*) **of a book** корешо́к кни́ги; **at the** ~ **of the house** в за́дней ча́сти до́ма; (*behind it*) позади́ до́ма; **at the** ~ **of one's mind** подсозна́тельно; в глубине́ души́; **at the** ~ **of beyond** на краю́ све́та. **5.** (*sport*): **full** ~ защи́тник, бек. **6.** (*attr.*; *see also cpds. as separate headwords*): ~ **door** чёрный ход; ~ **seat** за́днее сиде́нье; ~ **street** глуха́я у́лица.

adv. **1.** (*to or at the rear*) наза́д, сза́ди; ~ **and forth** взад и вперёд; **hold the crowd** ~ сде́рживать (*impf.*) толпу́; **sit** ~ **in one's chair** отки́нуться (*pf.*) на спи́нку сту́ла; **(in)** ~ **of** (*US*) позади́+*g.*; ~ **from the road** в стороне́ от доро́ги. **2.** (*returning to former position etc.*) обра́тно; **he is** ~ **again** он сно́ва здесь; **we shall be** ~ **before dark** мы вернёмся за́светло; **take** ~ **a statement** отказа́ться (*pf.*) от своего́ заявле́ния; **pay s.o.** ~ отпла́|чивать, -ти́ть кому́-н.; **hit** ~ уд|аря́ть, -а́рить в отве́т; **get one's own** ~ отплати́ть (*pf.*) (*кому*). **3.** (*ago*) тому́ наза́д; ~ **in 1930** ещё в 1930 году́.

v.t. **1.** (*move backwards*) дви́|гать, -нуть наза́д (*or* в обра́тном направле́нии). **2.** (*support*; *also* ~ **up**) подде́рж|ивать, -а́ть; ~ (*bet on*) **a horse** ста́вить, по- на ло́шадь. **3.** (*line*) покр|ыва́ть, -ы́ть. **4.** (*form* ~ *of*) примыка́ть (*impf.*) сза́ди; быть фо́ном (*чего*).

v.i. **1.** (*move backwards*) пя́титься, по-; (*of motor car*) идти́ (*det.*) за́дним хо́дом. **2.** ~ **down (from)** отсту́п|аться, -и́ться (*от чего*); ~ **out (of)** уклон|я́ться, и́ться (*от чего*).

backache ['bækeɪk] *n.* боль в спине́.

backbencher ['bæk'bentʃə(r)] *n.* заднескаме́ечник, рядово́й член парла́мента.

backbite ['bækbaɪt] *v.t. & i.* злосло́вить (*impf.*) (*о ком*).

backbiter ['bækˌbaɪtə(r)] *n.* зло́бный спле́тник.

backbiting ['bækˌbaɪtɪŋ] *n.* злосло́вие.

backbone ['bækbəʊn] *n.* **1.** спинно́й хребе́т, позвоно́чник. **2.** (*basis*) осно́ва; (*support*) опо́ра; (*strength of character*) твёрдость хара́ктера.

back-date [bæk'deɪt] *v.t.* пом|еча́ть, -е́тить за́дним число́м.

backdrop ['bækdrɒp] *n.*: **against the** ~ **of crisis** на фо́не кри́зиса.

backer ['bækə(r)] *n.* ока́зывающий подде́ржку; субсиди́рующий.

backfire ['bækfaɪə(r)] *n.* (*of a car*) обра́тная вспы́шка.

v.t. да|ва́ть, -ть обра́тную вспы́шку; (*fig.*) прив|оди́ть, -ести́ к обра́тным результа́там.

backgammon ['bækˌgæmən, bæk'gæmən] *n.* трикта́к.

background ['bækgraʊnd] *n.* **1.** за́дний план, фон; **on a dark** ~ на тёмном фо́не; **keep in the** ~ (*fig.*) держа́ть(ся) (*impf.*) в тени́. **2.** (*of pers.*) ≃ происхожде́ние; образова́ние; о́пыт. **3.** (*to a situation*) предысто́рия. **4.**: ~ **music** музыка́льное сопровожде́ние.

backhand ['bækhænd] *n.* (*sport*: ~ *stroke*) уда́р сле́ва.

backhanded [bæk'hændɪd] *adj.* (*fig.*) сомни́тельный, двусмы́сленный.

backhander ['bækˌhændə(r)] (*bribe*) *n.* взя́тка.

backing ['bækɪŋ] *n.* **1.** (*assistance*) подде́ржка; (*subsidy*) субсиди́рование. **2.** (*of cloth*) подкла́дка; (*covering*) покры́тие.

backlash ['bæklæʃ] *n.* (*fig.*) реа́кция.

backlog ['bæklɒg] *n.* за́лежи (*f. pl.*) накопи́вшейся рабо́ты.

backpack ['bækpæk] *n.* рюкза́к.

backside [bæk'saɪd, 'bæk-] *n.* (*coll., buttocks*) зад, за́дница.

backstage ['bæksteɪdʒ] *adj.* (*also fig.*) закули́сный.

adv. за кули́сами.

backstreet ['bækstriːt] *adj.* (*illicit*) подпо́льный.

backstroke ['bækstrəʊk] *n.* пла́вание на спине́.

back-track ['bæktræk] *v.i.* идти́ (*det.*) за́дним хо́дом; пя́титься, по-; (*fig.*) идти́ (*det.*) на попя́тный/попя́тную.

back-up ['bækʌp] (*comput.*) резе́рвная ко́пия.

adj. запасно́й; (*comput.*) резе́рвный.

backward ['bækwəd] *adj.* **1.** (*towards the back*) обра́тный; **a** ~ **glance** взгля́д наза́д. **2.** (*lagging*) отста́лый; (*retarded*) слабора́звитый, недора́звитый.

adv.: *see next entry.*

backward(s) ['bækwədz] *adv.* (*in backward direction*) наза́д; (*in opposite direction*) в обра́тном направле́нии; (*in reverse order*) в обра́тном поря́дке; **sit** ~ **on a horse** сиде́ть (*impf.*) на ло́шади за́дом наперёд; **walk** ~ пя́титься, по-; ~ **and forwards** взад и вперёд; туда́ и обра́тно; **know sth.** ~ знать (*impf.*) что-н. от ко́рки до ко́рки; **lean over** ~ (*fig.*) из ко́жи вон лезть (*pf.*).

backwardness ['bækwədnɪs] *n.* отста́лость.

backwater ['bækˌwɔːtə(r)] *n.* за́водь; (*fig.*) ти́хая за́водь.

backwoods ['bækwʊdz] *n.* (лесна́я) глушь.

bacon ['beɪkən] *n.* бе́ко́н; ~ **and eggs** яи́чница с беко́ном; (*fig.*): **save one's** ~ спа|са́ть, -сти́ свою шку́ру.

bacterial [bæk'tɪərɪəl] *adj.* бактери́йный.

bacteriological [ˌbæktɪə'lɒdʒɪk(ə)l] *adj.* бактериологи́ческий.

bacteriology [ˌbæktɪərɪ'ɒlədʒɪ] *n.* бактериоло́гия.

bacterium [bæk'tɪərɪəm] *n.* бакте́рия.

bad [bæd] *n.* (*evil*) дурно́е, плохо́е; ху́до.

adj. **1.** плохо́й, дурно́й, скве́рный; **not** ~! непло́хо!; **things went from** ~ **to worse** дела́ шли всё ху́же и ху́же; **too** ~! о́чень жаль!; **it is too** ~ **of him** э́то о́чень некраси́во с его́ стороны́; **a** ~ **light** (*to read in*) сла́бый свет. **2.** (*morally bad*) плохо́й, дурно́й; **a** ~ **name** дурна́я репута́ция. **3.** (*spoilt*) испо́рченный; **go** ~ по́ртиться, ис-. **4.** (*severe*) си́льный; **I caught a** ~ **cold** я си́льно простуди́лся; **a** ~ **wound** тяжёлая ра́на. **5.** (*harmful*) вре́дный; **smoking is** ~ **for one** куре́ние вре́дно для здоро́вья. **6.** (*of health*) больно́й; **I feel** ~ я чу́вствую себя́ пло́хо. **7.** (*var.*): **a** ~ **mistake** гру́бая оши́бка; **a** ~ **debt** безнадёжный долг; ~ **language** ру́гань.

cpds. **~-mannered** *adj.* невоспи́танный; **~-tempered** *adj.* раздражи́тельный.
badge [bædʒ] *n.* значо́к; (*fig.*) си́мвол.
badger ['bædʒə(r)] *n.* барсу́к.
v.t. (*coll.*) трави́ть (*impf.*); **~ s.o. for sth.** пристава́ть (*impf.*) к кому́-н. с про́сьбой о чём-н.
badly ['bædlɪ] *adv.* **1.** (*not well*) пло́хо. **2.** (*very much*) о́чень; си́льно; (*urgently*) сро́чно. **3.: ~ off** в нужде́.
badminton ['bædmɪnt(ə)n] *n.* бадминто́н.
baffle ['bæf(ə)l] *v.t.* (*perplex*) сби|ва́ть, -ть с то́лку; **the police are ~d** поли́ция не зна́ет, что де́лать.
baffling ['bæf(ə)lɪŋ] *adj.* сбива́ющий с то́лку; ста́вящий в тупи́к; зага́дочный.
bag [bæg] *n.* **1.** су́мка; (*small ~, hand ~*) су́мочка; **shopping ~** хозя́йственная су́мка. **2.** (*large ~, sack*) мешо́к. **3.** (*luggage*) чемода́н; **pack one's ~s** упакова́ться (*pf.*); **~ and baggage** со все́ми пожи́тками. **4.** (*game shot by sportsman*) добы́ча. **5.: by diplomatic ~** дипломати́ческой по́чтой. **6.** (*pl., coll., trousers*) штан|ы́ (*pl., g.* -о́в). **7.** (*pl., coll., plenty*): **~s of room** полно́ ме́ста; **~ of money** мешки́ (*m. pl.*) де́нег. **8.** (*var.*): **in the ~** (*coll., assured*) ≃ уже́ в карма́не; **~s under the eyes** мешки́ под глаза́ми; **a ~ of bones** (*fig.*) ко́жа да ко́сти; **old ~** (*sl., pej., woman*) ста́рая хрычо́вка.
v.t. **1.** (*put in bag*) класть, положи́ть в мешо́к. **2.** (*shoot down*): **~ game** бить (*impf.*) дичь. **3.: ~s I first place!** чур я пе́рвый! (*coll.*).
v.i.: **his trousers ~ at the knees** его́ брю́ки пузы́рятся на коле́нях.
cpds. **~pipe(s)** *n.* волы́нка; **~piper** *n.* волы́нщик.
baggage ['bægɪdʒ] *n.* **1.** бага́ж. **2.** (*mil.*) вози́мое иму́щество. **3.** (*attr.*) бага́жный; (*mil.*) вещево́й; **~ room** ка́мера хране́ния; **~ train** вещево́й обо́з.
baggy ['bægɪ] *adj.* мешкова́тый.
bah [bɑ:] *int.* ба!
bail[1] [beɪl] *n.* **1.** (*pledge*) зало́г; поручи́тельство; **release on ~** отпус|ка́ть, -ти́ть на пору́ки. **2.: stand, go ~ for s.o.** поручи́ться (*pf.*) за кого́-н.
v.t.: **~ s.o. out** брать, взять кого́-н. на пору́ки.
bail[2], **bale** [beɪl] *v.t.* (*also* **~ out**) вычё́рпывать, вы́черпать (*воду из лодки*).
v.i.: **~ out** (*aeron.*) выбра́сываться, вы́броситься с парашю́том.
bailiff ['beɪlɪf] *n.* суде́бный при́став; бе́йлиф.
bait [beɪt] *n.* прима́нка; (*fishing*) наса́дка, нажи́вка; **rise to the ~** (*lit., fig.*) попа́сться (*pf.*) на у́дочку.
v.t. **1.** (*attach ~ to*) наса́|живать, -ди́ть нажи́вку на+*a.* **2.** (*entice*) прима́н|ивать, -и́ть. **3.** (*tease*) пресле́довать (*impf.*), изводи́ть (*impf.*).
baize [beɪz] *n.* ба́йка; **green ~** зелё́ное сукно́.
bake [beɪk] *v.t.* печь, с-; (*of bricks*) обж|ига́ть, -е́чь.
v.i. пе́чься; **we were baking in the sun** мы жа́рились на со́лнце; **baking-powder** пека́рный порошо́к.
bakelite ['beɪkə,laɪt] *n.* бакели́т.
baker ['beɪkə(r)] *n.* пе́карь (*m.*); (*in charge of ~'s shop*) бу́лочник; **~'s dozen** чё́ртова дю́жина.
bakery ['beɪkərɪ] *n.* пека́рня; (*shop*) бу́лочная.
Balaclava [,bælə'klɑ:və] *n.*: **~ helmet** вя́заный шлем.
balalaika [,bælə'laɪkə] *n.* балала́йка.
balance ['bæləns] *n.* **1.** (*machine*) вес|ы́ (*pl., g.* -о́в); **spring ~** пружи́нные весы́. **2.** (*equilibrium*) равнове́сие; **lose one's ~** (*fig.*) теря́ть, по- душе́вное равнове́сие; **hang in the ~** висе́ть (*impf.*) на волоске́. **3.** (*counterbalance*) противове́с. **4.** (*bookkeeping*) бала́нс; са́льдо (*indecl.*); **~ of account**; **~ in hand** са́льдо в ба́нке; оста́ток счё́та в ба́нке; **adverse ~** пасси́вный бала́нс; **~ sheet** бухга́лтерский бала́нс; **~ of payments** платё́жный бала́нс; **~ of trade** торго́вый бала́нс; **on ~** в ито́ге, в коне́чном счё́те.
v.t. **1.** (*lit.*): **he ~d a pole on his chin** он баланси́ровал шест на подборо́дке. **2.** (*make equal*) уравнове́|шивать, -сить. **3.** (*weigh one thg. against another*) взве́|шивать, -сить; сопо|ставля́ть, -а́вить (*что с чем*). **4.** (*comm.*) баланси́ровать, с/за-; **~ the books** забаланси́ровать (*pf.*) бухга́лтерские кни́ги.
v.i. (*of accounts*) сходи́ться (*impf.*); (*be in equilibrium*) баланси́ровать (*impf.*).
cpd. **~-wheel** *n.* ма́ятник.
balanced ['bælənsd] *adj.* (*of pers.*) уравнове́шенный; **~ judgement** проду́манное сужде́ние; **~ diet** сбаланси́рованная дие́та.
balcony ['bælkənɪ] *n.* балко́н.
bald [bɔ:ld] *adj.* **1.** лы́сый, плеши́вый; **as ~ as a coot** (*coll.*) го́лый, как коле́но; **~ patch** лы́сина, плешь.
cpd. **~-headed** *adj.* лы́сый, плеши́вый.
balderdash ['bɔ:ldə,dæʃ] *n.* галиматья́.
balding ['bɔ:ldɪŋ] *adj.* лысе́ющий.
baldness ['bɔ:ldnɪs] *n.* плеши́вость.
bale [beɪl] *n.* ки́па.
v.t. упако́в|ывать, -а́ть в ки́пы; тюкова́ть (*impf.*).
baleful ['beɪlfʊl] *adj.* злове́щий.
balk, baulk [bɔ:lk] *v.t.* (*hinder*) меша́ть, по- (*кому, чему, в чём*); (*frustrate*) расстр|а́ивать, -о́ить.
v.i. **1.** (*of horses*) арта́читься, за- (*при чём*). **2.: ~ at food** отка́з|ываться, -а́ться от пи́щи; **he ~ed at the expense** таки́е расхо́ды его́ испуга́ли.
Balkan ['bɔ:lkən] *n.*: **the ~s** Балка́н|ы (*pl., g.* —); Балка́нский полуо́стров.
adj. балка́нский.
balky ['bɔ:lkɪ] *adj.* стропти́вый.
ball[1] [bɔ:l] *n.* (*dance*) бал; **open the ~** откр|ыва́ть, -ы́ть бал; **give a ~** устр|а́ивать, -о́ить бал; **fancy-dress ~** маскара́д.
cpds. **~-dress** *n.* ба́льное пла́тье; **~room** *n.* танцева́льный зал.
ball[2] [bɔ:l] *n.* **1.** (*sphere*) шар; **billiard ~** билья́рдный шар. **2.** (*in outdoor games*) мяч; **play ~** игра́ть (*impf.*) в мяч. **3.** (*of wool*) клубо́к. **4.** (*bullet*) пу́ля; (*for cannon*) ядро́; **load with ~** заряди́ть (*pf.*) боевы́ми патро́нами. **5.** (*of thumb, foot*) поду́шечка. **6.** (*pl., sl.: testicles*) я́йца (*nt. pl.*) (*vulg.*); (*nonsense*) чепуха́. **7.** (*tech.*): **~ and socket** шарово́й шарни́р. **8.** (*var. fig. uses*): **on the ~** сметли́вый, (*coll.*) расторо́пный; **have, keep one's eye on the ~** (*pursue objective single-mindedly*) идти́ (*det.*) пря́мо к це́ли; быть целеустремлё́нным; **keep the ~ rolling** (*in conversation*) подде́рж|ивать, -а́ть разгово́р; **set the ~ rolling** (*start sth.*) пус|ка́ть, -ти́ть что-н. в ход.
cpds. **~-bearing** *n.* шарикоподши́пник; **~-point** (*pen*) *n.* ша́риковая ру́чка, ша́рик.
ballad ['bæləd] *n.* балла́да, наро́дная пе́сня, шансо́н.
ballade [bæ'lɑ:d] *n.* балла́да.
balladeer [,bælə'dɪə(r)] *n.* шансонье́ (*m. indecl.*).
ballast ['bæləst] *n.* балла́ст.
v.t. грузи́ть, на- балла́стом.
ballerina [,bælə'ri:nə] *n.* балери́на.
ballet ['bæleɪ] *n.* бале́т.
cpds. **~-dancer** *n.* арти́ст (*fem.* -ка) бале́та; **~-master** *n.* балетме́йстер.
ballistic [bə'lɪstɪk] *adj.* баллисти́ческий; **~ missile** баллисти́ческий снаря́д.
ballistics [bə'lɪstɪks] *n.* балли́стика.
balloon [bə'lu:n] *n.* возду́шный шар; (*in comic strip, etc.*) ова́л; **barrage ~** аэроста́т загражде́ния.
v.i. (*fly in ~*) лета́ть (*indet.*) на возду́шном ша́ре.
balloonist [bə'lu:nɪst] *n.* воздухопла́ватель (*m.*), аэрона́вт.
ballot ['bælət] *n.* (*~-paper*) избира́тельный бюллете́нь; (*vote*) баллотиро́вка; **put a question to the ~, take a ~** ста́вить, по- вопро́с на голосова́ние;

(*number of votes*) коли́чество по́данных голосо́в.
cpd. **~-box** *n.* избира́тельная у́рна; я́щик для бюллете́ней.
ballyhoo [ˌbælɪ'huː] *n.* (*coll.*) шуми́ха.
balm [bɑːm] *n.* (*fragrance*; *also fig.*) бальза́м; (*ointment*) бальза́м, болеутоля́ющее сре́дство.
balmy ['bɑːmɪ] *adj.* **1.** (*fragrant*) арома́тный. **2.** (*soft*) мя́гкий; (*of wind*) не́жный.
baloney [bə'ləʊnɪ] *n.* (*sl.*) ерунда́.
balsa ['bɒlsə, 'bɔːl-] *n.* ба́льза.
balsam ['bɒlsəm, 'bɔːl-] *n.* бальза́м.
Baltic ['bɔːltɪk, 'bɒl-] *n.*: **the ~** Балти́йское мо́ре.
adj. балти́йский; прибалти́йский; **~ states** прибалти́йские госуда́рства, Приба́лтика.
baluster ['bæləstə(r)] *n.* баля́сина.
balustrade [ˌbælə'streɪd] *n.* балюстра́да.
bamboo [bæm'buː] *n.* бамбу́к; (*attr.*) бамбу́ковый.
ban [bæn] *n.* запреще́ние, запре́т.
v.t. запре|ща́ть, -ти́ть.
banal [bə'nɑːl] *adj.* бана́льный.
banality [bə'nælɪtɪ] *n.* бана́льность; (*remark*) бана́льное замеча́ние.
banana [bə'nɑːnə] *n.* бана́н.
band[1] [bænd] *n.* **1.** (*braid*) тесьма́; (*for decoration*) ле́нта; **rubber ~** рези́нка. **2.** (*strip*) полоса́. **3.** (*radio*): **frequency ~** полоса́ часто́т.
cpds. **~box** *n.* карто́нка для шляп; **~-saw** *n.* ле́нточная пила́.
band[2] [bænd] *n.* (*company*) гру́ппа; (*detachment*) отря́д; (*gang*) ба́нда, ша́йка; (*mus.*) орке́стр; **jazz ~** джаз-ба́нд, джаз-орке́стр.
v.t. & i. **~ together** соб|ира́ть(ся), -ра́ть(ся).
cpds. **~master** *n.* капельме́йстер; **~sman** *n.* оркестра́нт; **~stand** *n.* эстра́да для орке́стра.
bandage ['bændɪdʒ] *n.* бинт; (*blindfold*) повя́зка.
v.t. бинтова́ть, за-; перевя́з|ывать, -а́ть.
bandan(n)a [bæn'dænə] *n.* цветно́й плато́к.
bandit ['bændɪt] *n.* разбо́йник, банди́т.
banditry ['bændɪtrɪ] *n.* бандити́зм.
bandy[1] ['bændɪ] *adj.* криво́й.
cpd. **~-legged** *adj.* кривоно́гий.
band|y[2] ['bændɪ] *v.t.*: **have one's name ~ied about** быть предме́том то́лков; **~y words** перебра́сываться (*impf.*) слова́ми.
bane [beɪn] *n.* прокля́тие; **it is the ~ of my life** э́то отравля́ет мне жизнь.
baneful ['beɪnfʊl] *adj.* па́губный, губи́тельный.
bang[1] [bæŋ] *n.* (*of hair*) чёлка.
bang[2] [bæŋ] *n.* **1.** (*blow*) уда́р. **2.** (*crash*) гро́хот; стук. **3.** (*sound of a gun*) вы́стрел; (*of explosion*) взрыв.
v.t. (*strike*, *thump*) уд|аря́ть, -а́рить; (*at the door etc.*) ст|уча́ть, -у́кнуть +*a.*; **~ a drum** уда́рить (*pf.*) в бараба́н; **~ one's fist on the table** сту́кнуть (*pf.*) кулако́м по столу́; **~ the door** хло́пнуть (*pf.*) две́рью; **~ the lid down** захло́пнуть (*pf.*) кры́шку.
v.i. (*of door, window etc.*; *also* **~ to**) захло́пнуться (*pf.*); **the door is ~ing** дверь хло́пает; (*of pers.*): **~ at the door** стуча́ть/колоти́ть (*impf.*) в дверь.
adv. **1.**: **go ~** (*of gun*) ба́хнуть (*pf.*). **2.** (*just, exactly*) пря́мо; как раз; **~ on** (*coll.*) в аккура́т.
int. бац!; бах!
banger ['bæŋə(r)] *n.* (*coll.*) (*sausage*) соси́ска; (*car*) драндуле́т.
bangle ['bæŋg(ə)l] *n.* брасле́т.
banish ['bænɪʃ] *v.t.* (*exile*) высыла́ть, вы́слать; (*dismiss*) прог|оня́ть, -на́ть; изг|оня́ть, -на́ть; (*from one's mind*) от|гоня́ть, -огна́ть.
banishment ['bænɪʃmənt] *n.* вы́сылка, ссы́лка; изгна́ние.
banisters ['bænɪstəz] *n.* пери́л|а (*pl.*, *g.*—).
banjo ['bændʒəʊ] *n.* ба́нджо (*indecl.*).
bank[1] [bæŋk] *n.* **1.** (*of river*) бе́рег. **2.** (*under-water shelf*) ба́нка. **3.**: **~ of clouds** гряда́ облако́в; **~ of fog** полоса́ тума́на; (*of snow*) зано́с, сугро́б; (*sand-~*) о́тмель; **~s of earth** земляны́е валы́. **4.** (*embankment*) на́сыпь.
v.t. (*aeron.*) крени́ть, на-.
v.i. **1.** (*also* **~ up,** *of snow etc.*) образо́в|ывать, -а́ть зано́сы. **2.** (*aeron.*) накрен|я́ться, -и́ться.
bank[2] [bæŋk] *n.* (*tier of oars*) ряд вёсел; (*row of keys*) ряд клавиату́ры.
bank[3] [bæŋk] *n.* **1.** (*fin.*) банк; **~ account** счёт в ба́нке; **B~ of England** Англи́йский банк; **~ rate** учётная ста́вка; **clearing ~** кли́ринговый банк; **savings ~** сберега́тельная ка́сса; **~ of issue** эмиссио́нный банк. **2.** (*at cards etc.*) банк; **break the ~** сорва́ть (*pf.*) банк. **3.** (*attr.*) ба́нковый, ба́нковский; **~ book** ба́нковская кни́жка; **~ card** ба́нковская креди́тная ка́рта; **~ clerk** ба́нковский слу́жащий; **~ holiday** ≃ пра́здничный день.
v.t. (*put into ~*) класть, положи́ть в банк.
v.i. (*keep money in ~*) держа́ть (*impf.*) де́ньги в ба́нке; (*at cards*) мета́ть (*impf.*) банк; **~ on** (*fig.*, *rely on*) пол|ага́ться, -ожи́ться на+*a.*; де́лать, с-ста́вку на+*a.*
cpd. **~-note** *n.* креди́тный биле́т; банкно́т.
banker ['bæŋkə(r)] *n.* банки́р; (*at cards*) банкомёт.
banking ['bæŋkɪŋ] *n.* (*aeron.*) крен; (*fin.*) ба́нковое де́ло.
bankrupt ['bæŋkrʌpt] *n.* банкро́т, несостоя́тельный должни́к.
adj. (*also fig.*) обанкро́тившийся; **go ~** обанкро́титься (*pf.*).
v.t. де́лать, с- несостоя́тельным; дов|оди́ть, -ести́ до банкро́тства.
bankruptcy ['bæŋkˌrʌptsɪ] *n.* банкро́тство, несостоя́тельность; **file a declaration of ~** официа́льно объяв|ля́ть, -и́ть себя́ несостоя́тельным.
banner ['bænə(r)] *n.* (*lit.*, *fig.*) зна́мя (*nt. pl.*); (*flag*) флаг; (*with slogan*) плака́т; **~ headlines** кру́пные заголо́вки.
banns [bænz] *n.* оглаше́ние (предстоя́щего бра́ка); **ask, call, read the ~** огла|ша́ть, -си́ть имена́ жениха́ и неве́сты.
banquet ['bæŋkwɪt] *n.* пир; (*formal*) банке́т.
v.i. пирова́ть (*impf.*).
bantam ['bæntəm] *n.* (*fowl*) бента́мка.
cpd. **~-weight** *n.* боксёр легча́йшего ве́са.
banter ['bæntə(r)] *n.* подшу́чивание, подтру́нивание.
banyan ['bænɪən, -jən] *n.* баньа́н.
baobab ['beɪəʊˌbæb] *n.* баоба́б.
baptism ['bæptɪz(ə)m] *n.* креще́ние; **~ of fire** боево́е креще́ние.
baptismal [bæp'tɪzm(ə)l] *adj.* крести́льный.
Baptist ['bæptɪst] *n.* **1.**: **St John the B~** Иоа́нн Крести́тель (*m.*). **2.** (*member of sect*) бапти́ст.
baptist(e)ry ['bæptɪstərɪ] *n.* баптисте́рий.
baptize [bæp'taɪz] *v.t.* крести́ть, о́-; нар|ека́ть, -е́чь; **he was ~d Peter** он был наречён Петро́м.
bar[1] [bɑː(r)] *n.* **1.** (*strip*, *flat piece*) полоса́; (*ingot*) сли́ток; (*lever*) ва́га; **parallel ~s** паралле́льные бру́сья (*m. pl.*); **horizontal ~** перекла́дина; (*rod, pole*) шта́нга; (*of chocolate*) пли́тка; (*of soap*) кусо́к. **2.** (*bolt*) затво́р, засо́в. **3.** (*obstacle*) прегра́да; препя́тствие; **colour ~** цветно́й барье́р; **~ to marriage** препя́тствие к вступле́нию в брак. **4.** (*usu. pl.*) решётка; **behind ~s** за решёткой. **5.** (*naut.*) бар, о́тмель. **6.** (*mus.*) та́ктовая черта́, такт.
v.t. (*bolt, lock*) зап|ира́ть, -ере́ть на засо́в; (*obstruct*) прегра|жда́ть, -ди́ть; (*close*) закр|ыва́ть, -ы́ть; загор|а́живать, -оди́ть; (*exclude*) исключ|а́ть, -и́ть; (*prohibit*) запре|ща́ть, -ти́ть; **~ o.s. in** зап|ира́ться, -ере́ться; **~ s.o. out** не впус|ка́ть, -ти́ть кого́-н.; **soldiers ~red the way** солда́ты загороди́ли доро́гу.
cpd. **~-code** *n.* бар-ко́д.

bar[2] [bɑː(r)] *n.* (*legal profession*) адвокату́ра; **read for the ~** гото́виться (*impf.*) к адвокату́ре; **he was called to the ~** он получи́л пра́во адвока́тской пра́ктики; **prisoner at the ~** обвиня́емый (на скамье́ подсуди́мых).

bar[3] [bɑː(r)] *n.* (*room*) бар, буфе́т; (*counter*) прила́вок; **snack ~** заку́сочная.

cpds. **~maid** *n.* буфе́тчица, официа́нтка в пивно́й; **~man, ~-tender** *nn.* буфе́тчик, ба́рмен.

bar[4] [bɑː(r)] *n.* (*unit of pressure*) бар.

bar[5] [bɑː(r)] *prep.* (*coll., excluding*) исключа́я, не счита́я; **~ none** без исключе́ния; **it's all over ~ the shouting** (*fig.*) ко́нчен бал.

barb [bɑːb] *n.* **1.** (*fish's feeler*) у́сик. **2.** (*sting, spike*) колю́чка. **3.** (*of arrow, fish-hook etc.*) зубе́ц. **4.** (*cutting remark*) ко́лкость.

barbarian [bɑːˈbeərɪən] *n.* ва́рвар.

adj. ва́рварский.

barbaric [bɑːˈbærɪk] *adj.* ва́рварский.

barbarism [ˈbɑːbəˌrɪz(ə)m] *n.* ва́рварство; (*ling.*) варвари́зм.

barbarity [bɑːˈbærɪtɪ] *n.* ва́рварство.

barbarous [ˈbɑːbərəs] *adj.* ва́рварский; (*cruel*) бесчелове́чный.

barbecue [ˈbɑːbɪˌkjuː] *n.* (*party*) пи́кник, где подаю́т мя́со, зажа́ренное на ве́ртеле.

v.t. жа́рить, за- на ве́ртеле.

barbed [bɑːbd] *adj.* **1.** колю́чий; име́ющий колю́чки/шипы́; **~ wire** колю́чая про́волока. **2.: a ~ remark** ко́лкое замеча́ние.

barber [ˈbɑːbə(r)] *n.* парикма́хер; **~'s shop** парикма́херская.

barberry [ˈbɑːbərɪ] *n.* барбари́с.

barbiturate [bɑːˈbɪtjʊrət, -ˌreɪt] *n.* барбитура́т.

bard [bɑːd] *n.* бард, менестре́ль (*m.*), певе́ц.

bare [beə(r)] *adj.* **1.** (*naked, not covered*) го́лый, наго́й; обнажённый; **with one's ~ hands** го́лыми рука́ми; **~ feet** бо́сые но́ги; **in one's ~ skin** голышо́м, нагишо́м; **~ shoulders** обнажённые пле́чи; **with ~ head** с непокры́той голово́й; **lay ~** (*fig.*) вскры|ва́ть, -ть; раскр|ыва́ть, -ы́ть. **2.** (*threadbare*) поно́шенный. **3.** (*empty*) пусто́й; **the room was ~ of furniture** в ко́мнате не́ было ме́бели. **4.** (*unadorned*) просто́й, неприкра́шенный. **5.** (*slight*) мале́йший; **a ~ majority** о́чень незначи́тельное большинство́; **~ necessities of life** насу́щные потре́бности жи́зни. **6.** (*elec.*) го́лый, неизоли́рованный.

v.t. обнаж|а́ть, -и́ть; огол|я́ть, -и́ть; **~ one's head** обнаж|а́ть, -и́ть го́лову; **~ one's teeth** ска́лить, о- зу́бы.

cpds. **~back** *adv.* без седла́; **~faced** *adj.* (*fig.*) на́глый, бессты́дный; **~foot** *adj.* босо́й; *adv.* босико́м; **~footed** *adj.* босо́й, босоно́гий; **~headed** *adj.* простоволо́сый, с непокры́той голово́й.

barely [ˈbeəlɪ] *adv.* (*simply*) то́лько, про́сто; (*scarcely*) едва́; **I have ~ enough money** мне едва́ хва́тит де́нег.

bargain [ˈbɑːgɪn] *n.* **1.** (*deal*) сде́лка, соглаше́ние; **good/bad ~** вы́годная/невы́годная сде́лка; **make, strike, drive a ~** заключ|а́ть, -и́ть сде́лку; **it's a ~!** по рука́м!; **into the ~** в прида́чу. **2.** (*thg. cheaply acquired*) вы́годная поку́пка; **~ price** распрода́жная цена́.

v.i. торгова́ться, с-; (*agree*) догов|а́риваться, -ори́ться; **~ for** (*expect*) ожида́ть (*impf.*); **it was more than I ~ed for** на э́то я не рассчи́тывал.

bargainer [ˈbɑːgɪnə(r)] *n.*: **he is a hard ~** он упо́рно торгу́ется.

bargaining [ˈbɑːgɪnɪŋ] *n.*: **pay ~** перегово́ры о зарпла́те.

barge [bɑːdʒ] *n.* ба́ржа.

v.i. (*coll.*): **~ about** носи́ться (*impf.*), мета́ться (*impf.*); **~ into, against** налет|а́ть, -е́ть на+*a.*; **~ in** (*intrude*) вва́л|иваться, -и́ться.

bargee [bɑːˈdʒiː] *n.* ба́рочник.

baritone [ˈbærɪˌtəʊn] *n.* (*voice, singer*) барито́н.

adj. баритона́льный.

barium [ˈbeərɪəm] *n.* ба́рий.

bark[1] [bɑːk] *n.* (*of tree etc.*) кора́.

bark[2] [bɑːk] *n.* (*vessel*) барк.

bark[3] [bɑːk] *n.* (*of dog*) лай; **his ~ is worse than his bite** ≃ он гро́зен лишь на слова́х.

v.t.: **~ out** (*e.g. an order*) ря́вк|ать, -нуть.

v.t. (*of dog etc.*) ла́ять (*impf.*) (**at:** на+*a.*); **~ up the wrong tree** (*fig.*) обра|ща́ться, -ти́ться не по а́дресу.

barley [ˈbɑːlɪ] *n.* ячме́нь (*m.*); **pearl ~** перло́вая ка́ша.

cpds. **~-sugar** *n.* леденцы́ (*m. pl.*); **~-water** *n.* ячме́нный отва́р.

bar mitzvah [bɑː ˈmɪtzvə] *n.* бар-ми́цва.

barmy [ˈbɑːmɪ] *adj.* (*coll., silly*) чо́кнутый, тро́нутый; **go ~** тро́нуться (*pf.*); спя́тить (*pf.*) (с ума́).

barn [bɑːn] *n.* амба́р, сара́й; (*threshing-floor*) гумно́; (*fig., comfortless building*) сара́й.

cpds. **~-owl** *n.* сипу́ха; **~stormer** *n.* (*coll.*) бродя́чий актёр.

barnacle [ˈbɑːnək(ə)l] *n.* **1.** морска́я у́точка. **2.: ~ goose** белощёкая каза́рка.

barometer [bəˈrɒmɪtə(r)] *n.* баро́метр.

barometric [ˌbærəʊˈmetrɪk] *adj.* барометри́ческий.

baron [ˈbærən] *n.* баро́н; (*industrial leader*) магна́т.

baroness [ˈbærənɪs] *n.* барone´сса.

baronet [ˈbærənɪt] *n.* барone´т.

baronial [bəˈrəʊnɪəl] *adj.* баро́нский; (*fig.*) ба́рский.

barony [ˈbærənɪ] *n.* баро́нство.

baroque [bəˈrɒk] *n.* баро́кко (*indecl.*).

adj. баро́чный.

barrack[1] [ˈbærək] *n.* (*usu. pl.*) каза́рма; **confinement to ~s** каза́рменный аре́ст.

v.t. (*lodge in ~s*) разме|ща́ть, -сти́ть в каза́рмах.

barrack[2] [ˈbærək] *v.i.* (*coll.*) (*jeer at*) гро́мко высме́ивать (*impf.*).

barracuda [ˌbærəˈkuːdə] *n.* баррaку́да.

barrage [ˈbærɑːʒ] *n.* **1.** (*in watercourse*) запру́да; (*dam*) плоти́на. **2.** (*mil.*) загражде́ние; (*gunfire*) огнево́й вал; (*fig.*): **a ~ of questions** град/шквал вопро́сов.

barrel [ˈbær(ə)l] *n.* **1.** бо́чка. **2.** (*of firearm*) ствол, (*muzzle*) ду́ло; (*of fountain pen*) резервуа́р.

cpd. **~-organ** *n.* шарма́нка.

barren [ˈbærən] *adj.* (*of woman*) беспло́дная; (*of plants, trees etc.*) беспло́дный, неплодоно́сный; **~ land** неплодоро́дная земля́.

barrenness [ˈbærənnɪs] *n.* (*of woman*) беспло́дие; (*of trees, plants*) неплодоно́сность; (*of land*) неплодоро́дность; (*fig.*) беспло́дность.

barricade [ˌbærɪˈkeɪd] *n.* баррика́да.

v.t. баррикади́ровать, за-.

barrier [ˈbærɪə(r)] *n.* барье́р; **sound ~** звуково́й барье́р; (*dividing-line*) прегра́да; (*obstacle*) поме́ха.

v.t.: **~ in** загра|жда́ть, -ди́ть; огра|жда́ть, -ди́ть; **~ off** прегра|жда́ть, -ди́ть.

barring [ˈbɑːrɪŋ] *prep.* за исключе́нием +*g.*

barrister [ˈbærɪstə(r)] *n.* адвока́т.

barrow[1] [ˈbærəʊ] *n.* (*archaeol.*) курга́н.

barrow[2] [ˈbærəʊ] *n.* (*hand-~*) ручна́я теле́жка; (*wheel~*) та́чка.

barter [ˈbɑːtə(r)] *n.* менова́я торго́вля, товарообме́н.

v.t. обме́н|ивать, -я́ть (*что на что*).

v.i. обме́н|иваться, -я́ться +*i.*

basal [ˈbeɪs(ə)l] *adj.* основно́й, лежа́щий в осно́ве.

basalt [ˈbæsɔːlt] *n.* база́льт; (*attr.*) база́льтовый.

base[1] [beɪs] *n.* **1.** (*of wall, column etc.*) фунда́мент, пьедеста́л, основа́ние, ба́зис. **2.** (*fig., basis; also math.*) основа́ние. **3.** (*chem.*) основа́ние. **4.** (*gram.*)

осно́ва. **5.** (*mil. etc.*) ба́за; ~ **hospital** ба́зовый го́спиталь; ~ **of operations** операцио́нная ба́за, плацда́рм. **6.: get to first** ~ (*fig.*) доби́ться (*pf.*) пе́рвого успе́ха.

v.t. осно́в|ывать, -а́ть; ~ **one's hopes on** возл|ага́ть, -ожи́ть наде́жды на+*a*; ~ **o.s. on** полага́ться (*impf.*) на+*a*..

cpds. ~**ball** *n.* бейсбо́л; ~**line** *n.* исхо́дная ли́ния.

base² [beɪs] *adj.* ни́зкий, ни́зменный, по́длый; ~ **metal** неблагоро́дный мета́лл.

baseless ['beɪslɪs] *adj.* необосно́ванный.

basement ['beɪsmənt] *n.* подва́л; (*attr.*) подва́льный.

baseness ['beɪsnɪs] *n.* ни́зость, ни́зменность.

bash [bæʃ] (*coll.*) *n.* (*attempt*) попы́тка; **have a** ~ попыта́ться, попро́бовать.

v.t. тра́хнуть (*pf.*); ~ **s.o.'s head against a wall** тра́хнуть (*pf.*) кого́-н. башко́й об сте́ну (*coll.*); **give s.o. a** ~ **on the head** тра́хнуть (*pf.*) кого́-н. по башке́ (*coll.*).

bashful ['bæʃfʊl] *adj.* засте́нчивый.

bashfulness ['bæʃfʊlnɪs] *n.* засте́нчивость.

basic ['beɪsɪk] *adj.* основно́й.

basically ['beɪsɪkəlɪ] *adv.* в основно́м.

basil ['bæz(ə)l] *n.* базили́к.

basilica [bə'zɪlɪkə] *n.* базили́ка.

basin ['beɪs(ə)n] *n.* **1.** таз, ми́ска. **2.** (*of fountain*) ча́ша. **3.** (*of dock, river*) бассе́йн.

basis ['beɪsɪs] *n.* осно́ва, ба́зис; ~ **of negotiations** осно́ва для перегово́ров; **on the** ~ **of** на осно́ве +*g.*; **on this** ~ на э́том основа́нии.

bask [bɑ:sk] *v.i.* гре́ться (*impf.*) (**in the sun:** на со́лнце); (*fig.*): ~ **in glory** купа́ться (*impf.*) в луча́х сла́вы.

basket ['bɑ:skɪt] *n.* корзи́на, корзи́нка; **clothes, laundry** ~ корзи́на для гря́зного белья́; **shopping** ~ корзи́на/корзи́нка для поку́пок.

cpds. ~**-ball** *n.* баскетбо́л; ~**-chair** *n.* плетёное кре́сло.

basket|ry ['bɑ:skɪtrɪ] *n.* плете́ние; (*product*) плетёные изде́лия (*nt. pl.*).

bas-relief [ˌbɑ: rɪ'li:f] *n.* барелье́ф.

bass¹ [bæs] *n.* (*zool.*) ка́менный о́кунь.

bass² [beɪs] *n.* (*mus.*) бас.

adj. басо́вый; **he has a** ~ **voice** у него́ бас; ~ **drum** туре́цкий бараба́н; ~ **viol** контраба́совая вио́ла.

basset ['bæsɪt] *n.* (~**-hound**) ба́с(с)ет.

bassoon [bə'su:n] *n.* фаго́т.

bassoonist [bə'su:nɪst] *n.* фаготи́ст.

bast [bæst] *n.* луб, лы́ко, моча́ло; (*strip of* ~) лубо́к; (*attr.*) лубяно́й, лы́ковый; ~ **shoe** ла́поть(*m.*).

bastard ['bɑ:stəd, 'bæ-] *n.* **1.** (*child*) внебра́чный ребёнок. **2.** (*hybrid*) по́месь. **3.** (*as term of abuse etc.*) мерза́вец.

baste¹ [beɪst] *v.t.* (*stitch*) смёт|ывать, -а́ть; сши|ва́ть, -ть на живу́ю ни́тку.

baste² [beɪst] *v.t.* (*cul.*) пол|ива́ть, -и́ть (*жаркое*).

bastion ['bæstɪən] *n.* бастио́н; (*fig.*) опло́т.

bat¹ [bæt] *n.* (*zool.*) летучая мышь; **blind as a** ~ соверше́нно слепо́й; **like a** ~ **out of hell** о́чень бы́стро, внеза́пно.

bat² [bæt] *n.* (*at games*) бита́, лапта́; (*fig.*): **off one's own** ~ по со́бственному почи́ну; самостоя́тельно; **right off the** ~ с ме́ста в карье́р.

v.t. бить (*impf.*) (*or* уд|аря́ть, -а́рить) бито́й/лапто́й.

bat³ [bæt] *v.t.*: **he did not** ~ **an eyelid** он и гла́зом не моргну́л.

bat⁴ [bæt] (*coll.*) *v.i.*: ~ **along** нести́сь (*impf.*), мча́ться (*impf.*).

batch [bætʃ] *n.* **1.** (*of bread*) вы́печка. **2.** (*of pottery etc.*) па́ртия. **3.** (*consignment, collection*) ку́чка, па́чка; гру́ппа; ~ **of letters** па́чка пи́сем.

bated ['beɪtɪd] *adj.*: **with** ~**d breath** затаи́в дыха́ние.

bath [bɑ:θ] *n.* ва́нна; (*steam* ~) ба́ня; **take, have a** ~ прин|има́ть, -я́ть ва́нну; купа́ться, вы́-/ис-; **run me a** ~! напусти́те мне ва́нну!; **swimming** ~**(s)** пла́вательный бассе́йн.

v.t. & i. купа́ть(ся), вы́/ис-.

cpds. ~**-attendant** *n.* ба́нщик; ~**-house** *n.* купа́льня, ба́ня; ~**-mat** *n.* ко́врик для ва́нной; ~**robe** *n.* купа́льный хала́т; ~**room** *n.* ва́нная (ко́мната); ~**-towel** *n.* купа́льное полоте́нце; ~**-tub** *n.* ва́нна.

bathe [beɪð] *n.* купа́ние; **go for a** ~ искупа́ться (*pf.*).

v.t. **1.** (*one's face etc.*) мыть, по-; обм|ыва́ть, -ы́ть; ~ **one's eyes, a wound** пром|ыва́ть, -ы́ть глаза́/ра́ну. **2.: he was** ~**d in sweat** он облива́лся по́том; **a face** ~**d in tears** лицо́, за́литое слеза́ми. **3.** (*of light, warmth*) зал|ива́ть, -и́ть.

v.i. купа́ться, вы́-/ис-.

bather ['beɪðə(r)] *n.* купа́льщи|к (*fem.* -ца).

bathing ['beɪðɪŋ] *n.* купа́ние.

cpds. ~**-cabin** *n.* каби́на для переодева́ния; ~**-cap** *n.* купа́льная ша́почка; ~**-costume,** ~**-suit** *nn.* купа́льный костю́м; ~**-trunks** *n.* пла́в|ки (*pl., g.* -ок).

batiste [bæ'ti:st] *n.* бати́ст; (*attr.*) бати́стовый.

baton ['bæt(ə)n] *n.* **1.** (*staff of office*) жезл. **2.** (*mus.*) дирижёрская па́лочка. **3.** (*sport*) эстафе́тная па́лочка. **4.** (*policeman's*) дуби́нка.

batsman ['bætsmən] *n.* игро́к с би́той; отбива́ющий мяч.

battalion [bə'tælɪən] *n.* батальо́н; **labour** ~ строи́тельный батальо́н.

batten ['bæt(ə)n] *n.* ре́йка, пла́нка.

v.t.: ~ **down** (*naut.*) задра́и|вать, -ть.

batter¹ ['bætə(r)] *n.* (*cul.*) взби́тое те́сто.

batter² ['bætə(r)] *n.* (*US*) = **batsman**

batter³ ['bætə(r)] *v.t. & i.* **1.** (*beat*) колоти́ть, по-; дуба́сить, от-; ~ **a wall down** разру́шить (*pf.*) сте́ну; ~**ing-ram** тара́н. **2.** (*knock about*): **a** ~**ed old car/hat** потрёпанная ста́рая маши́на/шля́па.

battery ['bætərɪ] *n.* **1.** (*beating*): **assault and** ~ (*leg.*) побо́|и (*pl., g.* -ев); оскорбле́ние де́йствием. **2.** (*group of guns*) батаре́я; (*artillery unit*) дивизио́н. **3.** (*elec.*) батаре́я; (*in torch*) батаре́йка. **4.:** ~ **farming** выра́щивание живо́тных в (клёточных) батаре́ях; ~ **hens** бро́йлерные ку́ры.

cpd. ~**-operated** *adj.* на батаре́ях; с батаре́йным пита́нием; ~**-farmed** *adj.* вы́ращенный в батаре́е.

battle ['bæt(ə)l] *n.* би́тва, сраже́ние, бой; (*struggle*) борьба́; **drawn** ~ безрезульта́тный бой; **join** ~ вступи́ть (*pf.*) в бой; **give** ~ дать (*pf.*) бой; **do** ~ сража́ться (*impf.*); **order of** ~ боево́й поря́док; ~ **of Britain** би́тва за А́нглию; ~ **of Waterloo** сраже́ние при Ватерло́о; ~ **of Stalingrad** би́тва под Сталингра́дом; ~ **casualties** поте́ри в бою́; **the** ~ **is ours** побе́да за на́ми; **the** ~ **of life** би́тва жи́зни; **fight a losing** ~ вести́ (*det.*) безнадёжную борьбу́; **fight s.o.'s** ~**s for him** лезть (*det.*) в дра́ку за кого́-н.; **fight one's own** ~**s** постоя́ть (*pf.*) за себя́; **half the** ~ (*fig.*) зало́г успе́ха, полде́ла.

v.i. боро́ться (*impf.*); сража́ться (*impf.*).

cpds. ~**-axe** *n.* (*fig., termagant*) бой-ба́ба; ~**-dress** *n.* похо́дная фо́рма; ~**field,** ~**-ground** *n.* по́ле сраже́ния/бо́я; ~**ship** *n.* лине́йный кора́бль, линко́р.

battlement ['bæt(ə)lmənt] *n.* зубча́тая стена́.

batty ['bætɪ] *adj.* чо́кнутый, тро́нутый (*coll.*).

bauble ['bɔ:b(ə)l] *n.* (*trifle*) безделу́шка.

bauxite ['bɔ:ksaɪt] *n.* бокси́т.

bawdy ['bɔ:dɪ] *adj.* непристо́йный, похабный.

bawl [bɔ:l] *v.t. & i.* ора́ть (*impf.*); выкри́кивать, вы́крикнуть; ~ **at s.o.** ора́ть на кого́-н.; ~ **s.o. out** (*coll.*) наора́ть (*pf.*) на кого́-н.

bay[1] [beɪ] *n.* (*bot.*) лавр; (*attr.*) лавро́вый.
cpd. **~-tree** *n.* лавр, ла́вровое де́рево.

bay[2] [beɪ] *n.* (*geog.*) зали́в, бу́хта.

bay[3] [beɪ] *n.* **1.** (*of wall*) пролёт, пане́ль. **2.** (*window recess*) ни́ша. **3.**: **sick ~** (*naut.*) судово́й лазаре́т.

bay[4] [beɪ] *n.* **1.** (*bark*) лай. **2.** (*fig. uses*): **keep s.o. at ~** держа́ть (*impf.*) кого́-н. на расстоя́нии; **keep the enemy at ~** сде́рживать (*impf.*) неприя́теля; **bring to ~** загна́ть (*pf.*), затрави́ть (*pf.*).
v.t. & *i.* ла́ять (*impf.*); **~ (at) the moon** выть на луну́.

bay[5] [beɪ] *n.* (*horse*) гнеда́я (ло́шадь).
adj. гнедо́й.

bayonet ['beɪə,net] *n.* штык.
v.t. коло́ть, за- штыко́м.

bazaar [bə'zɑ:(r)] *n.* база́р.

bazooka [bə'zu:kə] *n.* противота́нковый гранатомёт.

BBC (*abbr. of* ***British Broadcasting Corporation***) Би-Би-Си́ (*nt. indecl.*); **~ English** нормати́вный англи́йский язы́к.

BC (*abbr. of* ***before Christ***) до н.э., (до на́шей э́ры).

be [bi:, bɪ] *v.i.* **1.** быть (*impf.*); (*exist*) существова́ть (*impf.*); (*as copula in the present tense, usu. omitted or expr. by dash*): **the world is round** земля́ кру́глая; **that is a dog** э́то соба́ка. **2.** (*more emphatic uses*): **an order is an order** прика́з есть прика́з; **there is a God** Бог есть; **we should love people as they are** ну́жно люби́ть люде́й таки́ми, каки́е они́ есть; **there are books on all subjects** име́ются кни́ги по всем те́мам. **3.** (*expr. frequency*) быва́ть (*impf.*); **he is in London every Tuesday** он быва́ет в Ло́ндоне по вто́рникам; **there is no smoke without fire** нет ды́ма без огня́. **4.** (*more formally, with complement*) явля́ться (*impf.*) +*i.*; представля́ть (*impf.*) собо́й; (*of membership etc.*) состоя́ть (*impf.*) +*i.* **5.** (*expr. present continuous*): **she is crying** она́ пла́чет. **6.** (*of place, time, cost etc.*): **it is a mile away** э́то в ми́ле отсю́да; **where is the office?** где́ нахо́дится бюро́?; **he is 21 today** ему́ сего́дня исполня́ется два́дцать оди́н год; **it is 25 pence a yard** э́то сто́ит два́дцать пять пе́нсов в ярд; (*of pers. or obj. in a certain position*) стоя́ть, лежа́ть, сиде́ть (*acc. to sense*; *all impf.*); **the books are on the floor** кни́ги лежа́т на полу́; **the books are on the shelf** кни́ги стоя́т на по́лке; **the ship is at anchor** кора́бль стои́т на я́коре; **Paris is on the Seine** Пари́ж стои́т на Се́не; **he is in hospital** он лежи́т в больни́це; **he is in prison** он (сиди́т) в тюрьме́; **I was at home all day** я сиде́л до́ма весь день; (*of continuing states*): **the weather was settled** пого́да стоя́ла хоро́шая; **prices are high** це́ны сохраня́ются высо́кие. **7.** (*become*): **what are you going to ~ when you grow up?** кем ты ста́нешь/бу́дешь, когда́ вы́растешь? **8.** (*behave, act a part*): **you are ~ing silly** вы ведёте себя́ глу́по; **am I ~ing a bore?** я вам надое́л?. **9.** (*take place, happen*): **there is a party next door** в сосе́днем до́ме идёт вечери́нка; **the meeting is** (*will be*) **on Friday** заседа́ние состои́тся в пя́тницу. **10.** (*exist, live*): **he is no more** его́ бо́льше нет; **the government that was** тогда́шнее прави́тельство. **11.** (*remain*): **let him ~!** оста́вьте его́!; **don't ~ too long!** не заде́рживайтесь! **12.** (*expr. motion*): **he is off to London** он уезжа́ет в Ло́ндон; **the dog was after him** за ним гнала́сь соба́ка; **has the postman been?** по́чта уже́ была́? **13.** (*expr. pass.*): **the house is ~ing built** дом стро́ится; **I am told** мне сказа́ли. **14.** (*uses of pres. part. and gerund*): **~ing a doctor, he knew what to do** бу́дучи врачо́м, он знал, что де́лать; **for the time ~ing** пока́ что, на вре́мя; **he is far from ~ing an expert** он далеко́ не специали́ст. **15.** (*with* **at**): **what are you at?** что вы хоти́те?; что вы де́лаете? **16.** (*with* **for**): **I am for tariff reform** я за тари́фную рефо́рму. **17.** (*with* **to**): **I am to inform you** я до́лжен сообщи́ть вам; **he is to ~ married today** он сего́дня же́нится; **you are not to do that** вам нельзя́ (*or* не сле́дует) э́то де́лать; **how was I to know?** как же я мог знать?; **the book is not to ~ found** э́той кни́ги нигде́ не найти́; **when am I to ~ there?** когда́ мне на́до быть там?; **it is to ~ hoped that ...** на́до наде́яться, что...; **it is not to ~** э́тому не суждено́ соверши́ться; **his wife to ~** его́ бу́дущая жена́. **18.** (*var.*): **so ~ it!** так и быть; **how are you?** как пожива́ете?; **~ that as it may** как бы то ни́ было; **what is that to me?** что мне до э́того?; **as you were!** (*mil.*) отста́вить!
cpd. **~-all** *n.* (*also* **~-all and end-all**) суть; коне́ц и нача́ло всего́.
See also **being**

beach [bi:tʃ] *n.* пляж.
v.t. (*run ashore*) посади́ть (*pf.*) на мель; (*haul up*) выта́скивать, вы́тащить на бе́рег.
cpds. **~-head** *n.* (*mil.*) примо́рский плацда́рм; **~-wear** *n.* пля́жная оде́жда.

beacon ['bi:kən] *n.* (*signal light, fire*) сигна́льный ого́нь; (*lighthouse*) мая́к; (*buoy*) ба́кен; (*at crossing*) знак пешехо́дного перехо́да.

bead [bi:d] *n.* **1.** бу́син(к)а, би́серина; **glass ~s** би́сер; **pearl ~s** жемчу́жины (*f. pl.*); **string of ~s** бу́сы (*pl. g.* —). **2.** (*drop of liquid*) ка́пля.

beady ['bi:dɪ] *adj.*: **~ eyes** глаза́-бу́синки; **a ~ look** испыту́ющий взгля́д.

beagle ['bi:g(ə)l] *n.* бигль (*m.*).

beak [bi:k] *n.* клюв.

beaker ['bi:k(ə)r] *n.* (*for drinking*) ку́бок, ча́ша; (*in laboratory*) мензу́рка.

beam[1] [bi:m] *n.* **1.** (*of timber etc.*) брус, ба́лка, перекла́дина. **2.** (*naut.*) бимс; **broad in the ~** (*lit.*) с широ́кими би́мсами; (*fig., coll.*) толстоза́дый.

beam[2] [bi:m] *n.* **1.** (*ray*) луч; (*of particles etc.*) пучо́к луче́й; (*as radio signal*) радиосигна́л. **2.** (*smile*) сия́ющая улы́бка.
v.t. напр|авля́ть, -а́вить (сигна́л).
v.i. (*shine*) свети́ть (*impf.*), сия́ть (*impf.*); (*smile broadly*) сия́ть улы́бкой; **she ~ed with delight** она́ сия́ла от ра́дости.

beaming ['bi:mɪŋ] *adj.* сия́ющий.

bean [bi:n] *n.* **1.** боб; **broad ~s** бобы́ (*m. pl.*); **French ~s** фасо́ль; **string ~s** зелёная фасо́ль. **2.** (*coll., coin*) грош; **I haven't a ~** у меня́ нет ни гроша́. **3.** (*coll. uses*): **spill the ~s** проболта́ться (*pf.*); **full of ~s** по́лный задо́ра.
cpds. **~-feast** *n.* пиру́шка, пир горо́й; **~-pod** *n.* бобо́вый стручо́к.

bear[1] [beə(r)] *n.* **1.** (*zool., also fig.*) медве́дь (*m.*); **she-~** медве́дица; **~ cub** медвежо́нок; **Teddy ~** ми́шка. **2.** (*astron.*) **Great/Little B~** Больша́я/Ма́лая Медве́дица.
cpds. **~-garden** *n.* (*fig.*) (шу́мное) сбо́рище, база́р; **~-skin** *n.* (*lit.*) медве́жья шку́ра; (*headgear*) мехово́й ки́вер.

bear[2] [beə(r)] *v.t.* **1.** (*carry*) носи́ть (*indet.*), нести́, по- (*det.*); **~ arms** носи́ть ору́жие; **~ one's head high** высоко́ нести́/держа́ть (*impf.*) го́лову; **~ in mind** име́ть (*impf.*) в виду́. **2.**: **~ o.s.** (*behave*) держа́ться (*impf.*). **3.** (*show, have*): **the document ~s your signature** на докуме́нте есть ва́ша по́дпись; **a monument ~ing an inscription** па́мятник с на́дписью; **~ a resemblance to** име́ть (*impf.*) схо́дство с+*i.*; **~ the marks of ill-treatment** нести́ (*det.*) на себе́ следы́ дурно́го обраще́ния. **4.** (*harbour*): **~ ill-will** пита́ть (*impf.*) дурны́е чу́вства. **5.** (*provide*): **~ false witness** лжесвиде́тельствовать (*impf.*). **6.** (*sustain, support*): **the ice will ~ his weight** лёд вы́держит его́; **~ responsibility** нести́ (*det.*) отве́тственность. **7.** (*endure, tolerate*) терпе́ть, с-; выноси́ть, вы́нести; **I cannot ~ him** я его́ не выношу́.

8. (*be fit for, capable of*): **the joke ~s repeating** этот анекдот можно повторить ещё раз; **~ comparison** выдерживать (*impf.*) сравнение. **9.** (*give birth to*): **she bore him a son** она родила ему сына; **be born** родиться (*impf., pf.*); **a man born in 1919** человек 1919 года рождения. **10.** (*yield*): **trees/efforts ~ fruit** деревья/усилия приносят плоды; **the bonds ~ 5% interest** облигации приносят пять процентов дохода.

v.i. **1.** (*of direction*): **the road ~s to the right** дорога идёт вправо; **the guns ~ on the trench** орудия направлены на окоп. **2.** (*exert pressure, affect*): **he bore heavily on a stick** он тяжело опирался на палку; **bring one's energy to ~ on** направить (*pf.*) энергию на+*a.*; **this ~s on our problem** это относится к нашей проблеме; **~ with** терпеть (*impf.*), переносить (*impf.*).

with advs.: **~ away** *v.t.* ун|осить, -ести; **he was borne away (by his feelings)** он был увлечён; **~ out** *v.t.* (*confirm*) подтвер|ждать, -дить; подкреп|лять, -ить; **~ up** *v.i.* (*endure*) держаться (*impf.*).

bearable [ˈbeərəb(ə)l] *adj.* терпимый, сносный.

beard [bɪəd] *n.* **1.** борода; **grow a ~** растить, отбороду; **he had three days' ~** у него была трёхдневная щетина. **2.** (*of animal*) бородка.

bearded [ˈbɪədɪd] *adj.* бородатый.

beardless [ˈbɪədlɪs] *adj.* безбородый; (*youthful*) безусый.

bearer [ˈbeərə(r)] *n.* несущий, носящий; **~ of good news** добрый вестник; (*of letter*) податель (*m.*); (*of a cheque*) предъявитель (*m.*).

bearing [ˈbeərɪŋ] *n.* **1.** (*carrying*) ношение. **2.** (*behaviour*) поведение; (*deportment*) манера держаться. **3.** (*relevance*) отношение (к+*d.*). **4.** (*direction*) пеленг; **take a compass ~** определ|ять, -ить магнитный азимут; **find, get, take one's ~s** ориентироваться (*impf., pf.*); **lose one's ~s** потерять (*pf.*) ориентировку. **5.** (*tech.*) опора; **roller ~** роликовый подшипник. **6.** (*pl., her.*) девиз.

beast [bi:st] *n.* **1.** (*animal*) животное; (*wild animal*) зверь (*m.*); (*pl., cattle*) рогатый скот; **~ of burden** вьючное животное; **~ of prey** хищный зверь. **2.** (*savage person*) зверь; (*nasty person*) скот, скотина (*c.g.*).

beastly [ˈbi:stlɪ] *adj.* (*like a beast*) звериный; (*unpleasant*) отвратительный; **~ weather** ужасная погода.

beat¹ [bi:t] *n.* **1.** (*of drum*) бой; (*of heart*) биение; (*rhythm*) ритм; (*mus.*) такт; (*of baton*) отбивание такта. **2.** (*policeman's*) район обхода; **be on the ~** совершать (*impf.*) обход.

v.t. **1.** (*strike*) бить, по-; уд|арять, -арить; колотить, по-; **~ s.o. black and blue** исколотить (*pf.*) кого-н.; **~ one's breast** бить (*impf.*) себя в грудь; **~ a carpet** выбивать, выбить ковёр; **~ a drum** бить (*impf.*) в барабан; **~ eggs** взби|вать, -ть яйца; **~ one's head against a wall** (*lit., fig.*) биться (*impf.*) головой о стенку; **~ a retreat** (*lit., fig.*) бить (*impf.*) отбой; **he ~ the table with his fists** он колотил кулаками по столу; **~ time** отбивать (*impf.*) такт; **the bird ~s its wings** птица бьёт крыльями; **~ it!** (*sl.*) катись!; **~ one's brains out over sth.** ломать (*impf.*) голову над чем-н.; **~ a stick into the ground** вбить (*pf.*) палку в землю. **2.** (*defeat, surpass*) поб|ивать, -ить; побе|ждать, -дить; одерж|ивать, -ать победу над+*i.*; **he ~ me at chess** он обыграл меня в шахматы; **he always ~s me at golf** он всегда выигрывает, когда мы играем в гольф; **these armies have never been ~en** эти армии не знали поражения; **he ~ the record** он побил рекорд; **can you ~ it?** (*coll.*) как вам это нравится?; **I'll ~ you to the top of the hill** я быстрее вас доберусь до вершины холма.

v.i.: **his heart is ~ing** его сердце бьётся; **he heard drums ~ing** он слышал барабанный бой; **the rain ~ against the windows** дождь стучал в окна; **~ about the bush** (*fig.*) ходить (*indet.*) вокруг да около; **~ at, on a door** колотить (*impf.*) в дверь.

with advs.: **~ back** *v.t.* отб|ивать, -ить; **~ down** *v.t.*: **the rain ~ down the corn** дождь побил хлеба; **he ~ down the price** он сбил цену; *v.i.*: **the sun ~ down on us** солнце нещадно палило нас; **~ in** *v.t.*: **~ a door in** выломать (*pf.*) дверь; **~ off** *v.t.*: **~ off an attack** отб|ивать, -ить атаку; **~ out** *v.t.*: **~ out a fire** зат|аптывать, -оптать огонь; **~ out a path** проб|ивать, -ить тропинку; **~ out a rhythm** отбивать (*impf.*) ритм; **~ s.o.'s brains out** вышибать, вышибить мозги кому-н.; **~ up** *v.t.*: **~ up eggs/cream** взби|вать, -ть яйца/сливки; **~ s.o. up** изб|ивать, -ить кого-н.

See also **beaten**

beat² [bi:t] *adj.* (*coll., tired*): **dead ~** смертельно усталый.

beaten [ˈbi:t(ə)n] *adj.* битый, побитый, избитый; (*conquered*) разбитый; **off the ~ track** не по проторённой дорожке.

beatific [ˌbi:əˈtɪfɪk] *adj.* **1.** (*making blessed*) благословенный. **2.**: **a ~ smile** блаженная улыбка.

beatification [bi:ˌætɪfɪˈkeɪʃ(ə)n] *n.* беатификация, причисление к лику блаженных.

beatify [bi:ˈætɪˌfaɪ] *v.t.* (*eccl.*) ≃ канонизировать (*impf. pf.*).

beating [ˈbi:tɪŋ] *n.* **1.** (*of heart*) биение. **2.** (*thrashing*) битьё, порка; **give s.o. a good ~** отлупить (*pf.*) кого-н. **3.** (*defeat*) разгром, поражение.

beatitude [bi:ˈætɪˌtju:d] *n.* блаженство.

beat(nik) [ˈbi:tnɪk] *n.* (*sl.*) битник.

beau [bəʊ] *n.* (*admirer*) ухажёр, поклонник.

beautician [bju:ˈtɪʃ(ə)n] *n.* косметолог, косметичка.

beautiful [ˈbju:tɪˌfʊl] *adj.* красивый; (*excellent*) прекрасный; **~ly warm** необыкновенно тепло.

beautify [ˈbju:tɪˌfaɪ] *v.t.* укр|ашать, -асить.

beauty [ˈbju:tɪ] *n.* **1.** (*quality*) красота; **~ is skin-deep** красота недолговечна; **~ sleep** сон до полуночи; **~ spot** живописная местность; (*on face*) мушка. **2.** (*woman*) красавица. **3.** (*excellence, fine specimen*): **that's the ~ of it** в этом-то вся прелесть; **his car is a ~** у него прекрасная машина.

beaver [ˈbi:və(r)] *n.* **1.** (*zool.*) бобр. **2.** (*fur*) бобёр; (*hat*) бобровая шапка.

v.i. (*coll., toil*) вкалывать (*impf.*).

becalm [bɪˈkɑ:m] *v.t.*: **be ~ed** (*naut.*) штилевать (*impf.*); заштил|евать, -еть; **a ~ed ship** заштилевший корабль.

because [bɪˈkɒz] *conj.* потому что; (*since*) так как; **all the more ~** тем более, что; **~ of** из-за+*g.*, (*thanks to*) благодаря+*d.*

beck [bek] *n.*: **be at s.o.'s ~ and call** быть у кого-н на побегушках.

beckon [ˈbekən] *v.t. & i.* манить, по-; заз|ывать, -вать; **I ~ed (to) him to approach** я поманил его к себе.

becloud [bɪˈklaʊd] *v.t.* завол|акивать, -очь; (*of the mind*) затумани|вать, -ть.

become [bɪˈkʌm] *v.t.* (*befit*) годиться, подобать; **it doesn't ~ you to complain** вам не к лицу жаловаться; (*look well on*) идти (*det.*); **the dress ~s you** это платье вам идёт; *see also* **becoming**

v.i. (*come to be*) ста|новиться, -ть +*i.*; *often expr. by v. in* …еть; **~ pale** побледнеть; **~ rich** разбогатеть; **~ smaller** уменьшиться (*all pf.*); **what became of him?** что с ним сталось?; **he became a waiter** он поступил в официанты; **the weather became worse** погода испортилась.

becoming [bɪˈkʌmɪŋ] *adj.* (*proper*) подобающий; (*of dress etc.*) (идущий) к лицу; **she wore a ~ hat** шляпка ей очень шла.

bed [bed] *n.* **1.** (*esp. bedstead*) крова́ть; (*esp. bedding*) посте́ль; (*in hospital*) ко́йка; (*dog's etc. bedding*) подсти́лка; **go to ~** ложи́ться, лечь спать; **put to ~** укла́дывать, уложи́ть спать; **send to ~** отпр|авля́ть, -а́вить спать; **get into ~** ложи́ться, лечь в посте́ль/крова́ть; **get out of ~** вста|ва́ть, -ть с посте́ли/крова́ти; **get out of ~ on the wrong side** (*fig.*) встать (*pf.*) с ле́вой ноги́; **make a ~** (*arrange for sleep*) стлать, по- (*or* стели́ть, по-) посте́ль; (*tidy after sleep*) заст|ила́ть, -ла́ть (*or* уб|ира́ть, -ра́ть) посте́ль; **take to one's ~** слечь (*pf.*); **out of ~** (*up, recovered*) на нога́х. **2.** (*base, bottom*): (*of concrete etc.*) основа́ние, фунда́мент; (*of rock, clay etc.*) пласт, слой; (*of a road*) полотно́; (*of the sea*) морско́е дно; (*of a river*) речно́е ру́сло. **3.** (*place of cultivation*): **~ of flowers** клу́мба; **~ of nettles** за́росль крапи́вы; **~ of potatoes** карто́фельная гря́дка.

v.t. (*of flowers*; *also* **~ out**) сажа́ть, посади́ть; выса́живать, вы́садить.

v.i. **~ down** распол|ага́ться, -ожи́ться на ночлёг.

cpds. **~bug** *n.* клоп; **~clothes** *n.* посте́ль; посте́льные принадле́жности (*f. pl.*); **~-cover** *n.* покрыва́ло; **~fellow** *n.* сожи́тель (*fem.* -ница); **~-linen** *n.* посте́льное бельё; **~-pan** *n.* подкладно́е су́дно; **~ridden** *adj.* прико́ванный к посте́ли; **~room** *n.* спа́льня; **~side** *n.*: **watch at s.o.'s ~side** сиде́ть (*impf.*) у посте́ли больно́го; **a good ~side manner** уме́лый подхо́д к больно́му, враче́бный такт; **~ side table** ту́мбочка; **~-sit(ting-room)** *n.* однoко́мнатная кварти́ра; **~spread** *n.* покрыва́ло; **~stead** *n.* крова́ть; **~time** *n.* вре́мя ложи́ться/идти́ спать; **my ~time is at 11** я ложу́сь спать в оди́ннадцать часо́в.

bedding ['bedɪŋ] *n.* посте́ль; посте́льные принадле́жности (*f. pl.*).

bedeck [bɪ'dek] *v.t.* укр|аша́ть, -а́сить.

bedevil [bɪ'dev(ə)l] *v.t.* (*confuse*) спу́т|ывать, -ать; вн|оси́ть, -ести́ неразбери́ху в+*a*.

bedlam ['bedləm] *n.* (*fig.*) бедла́м.

Bed(o)uin ['bedʊɪn] *n.* бедуи́н (*fem.* -ка).

adj. бедуи́нский.

bedraggled [bɪ'dræg(ə)ld] *adj.* забры́зганный.

bee [bi:] *n.* **1.** пчела́; **have a ~ in one's bonnet** быть поме́шанным (*на чём*). **2.** (*gathering*) совме́стная рабо́та.

cpds. **~hive** *n.* у́лей; **~-keeper** *n.* пчелово́д; **~-keeping** *n.* пчелово́дство; **~-line** *n.* пряма́я; **make a ~-line for** стрело́й помча́ться (*pf.*) к+*d.*; **~swax** *n.* пчели́ный воск.

beech [bi:tʃ] *n.* бук.

cpd. **~mast** *n.* бу́ковый оре́шек.

beef[1] [bi:f] *n.* (*meat*) говя́дина; (*fig., energy*) си́ла, эне́ргия.

v.t.: **~ up** (*coll., strengthen, increase*) укреп|ля́ть, -и́ть.

cpds. **~burger** ру́бленый бифште́кс; **~steak** *n.* бифште́кс.

beef[2] [bi:f] *v.i.* (*sl., complain*) стона́ть (*impf.*).

beefy ['bi:fɪ] *adj.* (*like beef*) мяси́стый; (*muscular*) му́скули́стый.

beep [bi:p] *n.* гудо́к.

v.i. гуде́ть, про-.

beer [bɪə(r)] *n.* пи́во.

beet [bi:t] *n.* свёкла; (*sugar ~*) са́харная свёкла, свеклови́ца.

cpd. **~root** *n.* свёкла, бура́к; **he blushed as red as a ~root** он покрасне́л как рак.

beetle[1] ['bi:t(ə)l] *n.* жук.

beetle[2] ['bi:t(ə)l] *adj.*: **~-browed** *adj.* с нави́сшими бровя́ми.

befall [bɪ'fɔ:l] *v.t. & i.* (*liter.*) приключ|а́ться, -и́ться (с+*i.*); пост|ига́ть, -и́гнуть (*кого/что*); **what has ~en him?** что с ним ста́ло?

befit [bɪ'fɪt] *v.t.* под|ходи́ть, -ойти́ +*d*.

before [bɪ'fɔ:(r)] *adv.* **1.** (*sooner, previously*) ра́ньше; **six weeks ~** шестью неде́лями ра́ньше; **18 years ~** 18 лет наза́д. **2.** (*of place*) впереди́.

prep. **1.** (*of time*) пе́ред+*i.*; **~ leaving** пе́ред отъе́здом; (*earlier than*) до+*g.*; **~ the war** до войны́; **since ~ the war** с довое́нного вре́мени; **long ~ that** задо́лго до э́того; **~ now** пре́жде; **the week ~ last** позапро́шлая неде́ля; **don't come ~ I call you** не приходи́те, пока́ я вас не позову́. **2.** (*rather than*) скоре́е чем; **he would die ~ lying** он скоре́е умрёт, чем солжёт. **3.** (*of place*) пе́ред+*i.*; впереди́+*g.*; **your whole life is ~ you** у вас вся жизнь впереди́; **~ the court** пе́ред судо́м; **~ witnesses** при свиде́телях; **~ my eyes** на мои́х глаза́х. **4.** (*fig., ahead of*): **he is ~ me in class** он впереди́ меня́ в кла́ссе. **5.** (*naut.*): **~ the wind** по ве́тру.

conj. (*earlier than*) ра́ньше чем; (*immediately ~*) пре́жде/пе́ред тем, как; (*at a previous time*)до того́ как; **do it ~ you forget** сде́лайте э́то, пока́ не забы́ли; **it will be years ~ we meet** пройду́т го́ды, пока́ мы встре́тимся; **just ~ you arrived** пе́ред са́мым ва́шим прихо́дом.

cpds. **~hand** *adv.* зара́нее; **~-tax** *adj.* начи́сленный до упла́ты нало́гов.

befoul [bɪ'faʊl] *v.t.* па́чкать, за-.

befriend [bɪ'frend] *v.t.* дружи́ться, по- с+*i.*

befuddle [bɪ'fʌd(ə)l] *v.t.* одурма́ни|вать, -ть.

beg [beg] *v.t.* проси́ть, по-; умол|я́ть (*impf.*); **~ money of s.o.** проси́ть (*impf.*) у кого́-н. де́нег; **~ s.o. to do sth.** умоля́ть (*impf.*) кого́-н. сде́лать что-н.; **~ a favour of s.o.** проси́ть, по- кого́-н. о любе́зности; **they ~ged to come with us** они́ умоля́ли нас взять их с собо́й.

v.i. **1.** (*ask for charity*) проси́ть подая́ния, ни́щенствовать, (*coll.*) побира́ться (*all impf.*); **~ from door to door** побира́ться по двора́м; **~ging letter** проси́тельное письмо́. **2.**: **~ for sth.** выпра́шивать, вы́просить что-н.; **I ~ of you not to go** я умоля́ю вас не ходи́ть. **3.**: **the cakes are going ~ging** пирожки́ зря пропада́ют.

beget [bɪ'get] *v.t.* (*lit., fig.*) поро|жда́ть, -ди́ть.

beggar ['begə(r)] *n.* **1.** ни́щий; **~ woman** ни́щенка. **2.** (*fellow*) па́рень (*m.*), ма́лый; **poor ~** бедня́га (*m.*), бе́дный ма́лый; **little ~s** малыши́ (*m. pl.*).

v.t.: **it ~s description** э́то не поддаётся описа́нию.

beggarly ['begəlɪ] *adj.* ни́щенский, жа́лкий.

beggary ['begərɪ] *n.* нищета́, ни́щенство.

begin [bɪ'gɪn] *v.t.* нач|ина́ть, -а́ть; **he began English** он на́чал изуча́ть англи́йский язы́к; **he began the meeting** он откры́л собра́ние; **I began to think she would not come** я поду́мал бы́ло, что она́ не придёт; (*often translated by* за-): **~ to sing** запе́ть (*pf.*); **he began to cry** он запла́кал.

v.i. нач|ина́ть(ся), -а́ть(ся); **he began at the beginning** он на́чал с са́мого нача́ла; **the meeting began** собра́ние начало́сь; **before winter ~s** до нача́ла зимы́; до того́ как начнётся зима́; **he began as a reporter** он на́чал свою́ карье́ру с рабо́ты репортёра; **to ~ with** во-пе́рвых.

beginner [bɪ'gɪnə(r)] *n.* начина́ющий.

beginning [bɪ'gɪnɪŋ] *n.* нача́ло; (*source*) исто́чник; **at the ~ of April** в нача́ле (*or* в пе́рвых чи́слах) апре́ля; **make a ~** нача́ть (*pf.*).

begonia [bɪ'gəʊnjə] *n.* бего́ния.

begrudge [bɪ'grʌdʒ] *v.t.* зави́довать, по- (*кому чему*); **I ~ the time** мне жаль вре́мени; **they ~d him his food** они́ укоря́ли/попрека́ли его́ куско́м хле́ба.

beguile [bɪ'gaɪl] *v.t.* **1.** (*charm*) очаро́в|ывать, -а́ть. **2.** (*delude*) завл|ека́ть, -е́чь; **they ~d him into giving them his money** они́ (обма́ном) вы́удили у него́ де́ньги.

behalf [bɪ'hɑ:f] *n.*: **on/in my ~** от моего́ и́мени; ра́ди меня́; в мои́х интере́сах, в мою́ по́льзу; **he is going on our ~** он идёт за нас; **plead on s.o.'s ~** выступа́ть (*impf.*) в защи́ту кого́-н.

behave [bɪ'heɪv] *v.i.* вести́ (*det.*) себя́, держа́ться (*impf.*); **~ well, ~ o.s.** вести́ себя́ хорошо́; **~ badly** пло́хо поступ|а́ть, -и́ть; **~ (well *etc.*) towards s.o.** (хорошо́) относи́ться (*impf.*) к кому́-н.

behaviour [bɪ'heɪvjə(r)] *n.* поведе́ние; отноше́ние (*к кому*), обраще́ние (*с кем*); **be on one's best ~** вести́ (*det.*) себя́ безупре́чно.

behavioural [bɪ'heɪvjər(ə)l] *adj.* поведе́нческий.

behaviourism [bɪ'heɪvjə,rɪz(ə)m] *n.* бихевиори́зм.

behead [bɪ'hed] *v.t.* обезгла́в|ливать, -ить.

behemoth [bɪ'hi:mɒθ] *n.* чу́дище; (*bibl.*) бегемо́т.

behest [bɪ'hest] *n.* (*liter.*) повеле́ние.

behind [bɪ'haɪnd] *n.* (*coll.*) зад, за́дница.

adv. сза́ди, позади́; **a long way ~** далеко́ позади́; **from ~** сза́ди; **he is ~ in his studies** он отста́л в учёбе; **he is ~ with his payments** он запа́здывает с упла́той.

prep. (*expr. place*) за+*i.*; (*expr. motion*) за+*a.*; (*more emphatic*) сза́ди, позади́+*g.*; (*after*) по́сле+*g.*; **from ~** из-за+*g.*; **he walked ~ me** он шёл сле́дом за мной; **what is ~ it all?** что стои́т за всем э́тим?; **he has the army ~ him** его́ подде́рживает а́рмия; **he put the idea ~ him** он бро́сил э́ту мысль; **the country is ~ its neighbours** страна́ отста́ла от свои́х сосе́дей.

cpd. **~hand** *adj.* & *adv.*: **he is ~hand in his work** он запусти́л рабо́ту; **I am ~hand with the rent** я задолжа́л за кварти́ру.

behold [bɪ'həʊld] *v.t.* узре́ть (*pf.*); **lo and ~!** и вдруг; о чу́до!

beholden [bɪ'həʊld(ə)n] *pred. adj.* обя́зан, призна́телен.

behove [bɪ'həʊv] (*US* **behoove**) [bɪ'hu:v] *v.t.* (*liter.*): **it ~s you to work** вам надлежи́т рабо́тать; **it ill ~s him to complain** ему́ не к лицу́ жа́ловаться.

beige [beɪʒ] *adj.* беж (*indecl.*), бе́жевый.

being ['bi:ɪŋ] *n.* **1.** (*existence*) бытие́, существова́ние; **come into ~** возн|ика́ть, -и́кнуть; **call, bring into ~** вы́звать (*pf.*) к жи́зни. **2.** (*creature, person*) существо́; **human ~** челове́к.

belabour [bɪ'leɪbə(r)] *v.t.* (*thrash*) взду́ть (*pf.*); изб|ива́ть, -и́ть; (*over-emphasize*): **~ the obvious** дока́зывать (*impf.*) очеви́дное.

Belarus [belə'rʌs] *n.* Белару́сь.

belated [bɪ'leɪtɪd] *adj.* запозда́лый.

belch [beltʃ] *n.* отры́жка; **give a ~** рыгну́ть (*pf.*); (*of smoke etc.*) столб.

v.t. (*smoke etc.*; *also* **~ forth, out**) выбра́сывать, вы́бросить; (*oaths etc.*) изрыг|а́ть, -ну́ть.

beleaguer [bɪ'li:gə(r)] *v.t.* оса|жда́ть, -ди́ть.

belfry ['belfrɪ] *n.* колоко́льня.

Belgian ['beldʒ(ə)n] *n.* бельги́|ец (*fem.* -йка).

adj. бельги́йский.

Belgium ['beldʒəm] *n.* Бе́льгия.

belie [bɪ'laɪ] *v.t.* противоре́чить (*impf.*) +*d.*

belief [bɪ'li:f] *n.* **1.** (*trust*) ве́ра (в+*a.*); дове́рие (к+*d.*). **2.** (*acceptance as true*; *thg. believed*) ве́ра, ве́рование; **entertain the ~ that** пита́ть (*impf.*) уве́ренность в том, что; **to the best of my ~** по моему́ убежде́нию; **he has a strong ~ in education** он глубоко́ убеждён в необходи́мости образова́ния; **beyond ~** невероя́тно.

believable [bɪ'li:vəb(ə)l] *adj.* правдоподо́бный.

believe [bɪ'li:v] *v.t.* ве́рить, по- (*кому, во что*); ду́мать (*impf.*); **I ~ so** ду́маю, что э́то так; мне так ка́жется; **~ one's eyes** ве́рить, по- свои́м глаза́м; **~ it or not; would you ~ it?** хоти́те ве́рьте, хоти́те — нет; **~ me** мо́жете мне пове́рить; **make ~** де́лать вид, притворя́ться (*impf.*).

v.i. ве́рить (*impf.*); (*esp. relig.*) ве́ровать (*impf.*); **~ in God** ве́рить (*impf.*) в Бо́га; **~ in s.o.** ве́рить (*impf.*) в кого́-н.; име́ть (*impf.*) дове́рие к кому́-н.; **I ~ in taking exercise** я ве́рю в по́льзу заря́дки.

believer [bɪ'li:və(r)] *n.* **1.** (*relig.*) ве́рующий. **2.** (*advocate*) сторо́нник +*g.*

belittle [bɪ'lɪt(ə)l] *v.t.* преум|еньша́ть, -е́ньшить; ума-л|я́ть, -и́ть.

bell [bel] *n.* **1.** ко́локол; (*smaller*) колоко́льчик; (*of door, telephone, bicycle etc.*) звоно́к; **ring the ~** звони́ть (*impf.*) в звоно́к/ко́локол; **that rings a ~** (*fig., coll.*) да, я что́-то припомина́ю; **answer the ~** откры́ть (*pf.*) дверь; **clear as a ~** чи́стый как звон колоко́льчика; **sound as a ~** в полне́йшем поря́дке. **2.** (*naut.*) ры́нда; **ring the ~s** бить (*impf.*) скля́нки. **3.** (*of flower*) ча́шечка.

cpds. **~-bottomed** *adj.*: **~-bottomed trousers** брю́ки-клёш; **~boy** *n.* коридо́рный; **~-jar** *n.* стекля́нный колпа́к; **~-push** *n.* кно́пка звонка́; **~ringer** *n.* звона́рь (*m.*).

belladonna [,belə'dɒnə] *n.* (*plant, drug*) беллadóнна.

belle [bel] *n.* краса́вица; **the ~ of the ball** цари́ца ба́ла.

belligerency [bɪ'lɪdʒərənsɪ] *n.* состоя́ние войны́; (*aggressiveness*) вои́нственность, агресси́вность.

belligerent [bɪ'lɪdʒərənt] *n.* вою́ющая сторона́.

adj. (*waging war*) вою́ющий; (*aggressive*) вои́нственный, задири́стый.

bellow ['beləʊ] *n.* мыча́ние.

v.t. (*also* **~ forth, out**) ора́ть (*impf.*).

v.i. **1.** (*of animal*) мыча́ть, про-; реве́ть (*impf.*). **2.** (*shout*) ора́ть (*impf.*); (*roar with pain*) реве́ть (*impf.*); (*of thunder, cannon etc.*) греме́ть (*impf.*).

bellows ['beləʊz] *n.* мехи́ (*m. pl.*).

belly ['belɪ] *n.* живо́т, (*coll.*) брю́хо; **pot ~** то́лстое брю́хо; пу́зо.

cpds. **~-ache** *n.* бо́ль в животе́; *v.i.* (*sl.*) хны́кать, ныть (*all impf.*); **~-band** *n.* подпру́га; **~-flop** *n.* (*coll.*) уда́р живото́м (*при прыжке в воду*).

bellyful ['belɪfʊl] *n.*: **he has had his ~ of it** он сыт по го́рло э́тим.

belong [bɪ'lɒŋ] *v.i.* **1.: ~ to** (*be the property of*) принадле́жать (*impf.*) +*d.*; (*be a member of*) состоя́ть (*impf.*) в+*p.*; (*befit, appertain*): **it ~s to me to decide** мне реша́ть; **that ~s to my duties** э́то вхо́дит в мои́ обя́занности. **2.** (*of place*): **these books ~ here** э́ти кни́ги стоя́т здесь; э́ти кни́ги отсю́да; **I ~ here** (*was born here*) я ро́дом отсю́да; (*live here*) я отсю́да; (*am rightly placed here*) я здесь на ме́сте; **this ~s under 'Science'** э́то отно́сится к разде́лу «Нау́ка».

belongings [bɪ'lɒŋɪŋz] *n.* ве́щи (*f. pl.*) пожи́тк|и (*pl., g.* -ов).

Belorussian [,beləʊ'rʌʃ(ə)n] *n.* белору́с (*fem.* -ка).

adj. белору́сский.

beloved [bɪ'lʌvɪd, *pred. also* -lʌvd] *n.* возлю́бленн|ый (*fem.* -ая).

adj. возлю́бленный, люби́мый.

below [bɪ'ləʊ] *adv.* (*of place*) внизу́; (*of motion*) вниз; (*in text etc.*) ни́же; **from ~** сни́зу; **go ~** (*naut.*) спусти́ться (*pf.*) вниз.

prep. (*of place*) под+*i.*; (*of motion*) под+*a.*; (*lower, downstream*) ни́же +*g.*; **~ 60** моло́же шести́десяти; **~ £10** деше́вле/ме́ньше десяти́ фу́нтов; **he is ~ average height** он ни́же сре́днего ро́ста.

belt [belt] *n.* **1.** (*of leather*) реме́нь (*m.*); (*of linen etc.*) по́яс (*pl.* -а́); **seat ~** реме́нь безопа́сности. **2.** (*zone*) по́яс, полоса́; **cotton ~** хло́пковый по́яс. **3.** (*tech.*) (приводно́й) реме́нь.

v.t. **1.** (*fasten*): **~ on a sword** опоя́с|ываться, -аться мечо́м. **2.** (*coll., thrash*) поро́ть, вы́-. **3.: ~ out a song** горла́нить (*impf.*) пе́сню.

beluga [bə'lu:gə] *n.* белу́га.

bemoan [bɪ'məʊn] *v.t.* опла́к|ивать, -ать.

bemuse [bɪ'mju:z] *v.t.* ошелом|ля́ть, -и́ть.

bench [bentʃ] *n.* **1.** (*seat*) скамья́, ла́вка. **2.** (*work-table*) верста́к, стано́к. **3.** (*judges*) су́дьи (*m. pl.*).
cpd. **~-mark** *n.* репе́р.

bend [bend] *n.* **1.** (*curve*) изги́б; (*in river*) излу́чина; **~ of the arm** локтево́й сгиб руки́; **round the ~** (*coll.*) свихну́вшийся. **2.: the ~s** (*disease*) кессо́нная боле́знь.
v.t. **1.** (*twist, incline*): **~ a branch** гнуть, при-ве́тку; **~ an iron bar** из|гиба́ть, -огну́ть желе́зный брус; **a bent pin** со́гнутая була́вка; **the axle is bent** ось погну́лась; **on ~ed knee** преклони́в коле́на; **knees ~!** коле́ни согну́ть!; **~ s.o. to one's will** подчин|я́ть, -и́ть кого́-н. свое́й во́ле. **2.** (*direct*): **~ one's steps homewards** напра́вить (*pf.*) стопы́ к до́му; **all eyes were bent on him** все взо́ры бы́ли напра́влены на него́.
v.i.: **the river ~s here** река́ здесь изгиба́ется; **the trees bent in the wind** дере́вья гну́лись на ветру́; **~ at the knees** сгиба́ться, согну́ться в коле́нях; **~ over one's desk** сгиба́ться, согну́ться над столо́м; **~ before s.o.'s will** склон|я́ться, -и́ться пе́ред чьей-н. во́лей; **~ forward** наклон|я́ться, -и́ться (вперёд); **~ over backwards** (*fig.*) ≃ из ко́жи вон лезть.
with advs.: **~ back** *v.t.* (*e.g. a finger*) оття́|гивать, -ну́ть наза́д; **~ down** *v.t.* наг|иба́ть, -ну́ть; сгиба́ть, согну́ть; *v.i.* (*also* **~ over**) наг|иба́ться, -ну́ться; перег|иба́ться, -ну́ться.

beneath [bɪ'ni:θ] *adv.* внизу́.
prep. (*of place*) под+*i.*; (*of motion*) под+*a.*; (*lower than*) ни́же+*g.*; **~ criticism** ни́же вся́кой кри́тики; **it is ~ you to complain** жа́ловаться — недосто́йно вас; **it is ~ contempt** э́то не заслу́живает ничего́, кро́ме презре́ния.

benediction [ˌbenɪ'dɪkʃ(ə)n] *n.* благослове́ние.

benefactor ['benɪˌfæktə(r)] *n.* (*one who confers benefit*) благоде́тель (*m.*); (*donor*) благотвори́тель (*m.*).

benefactress ['benɪˌfæktrɪs] *n.* благоде́тельница; благотвори́тельница.

beneficence [bɪ'nefɪsəns] *n.* благодея́ние; благо-твори́тельность.

beneficent [bɪ'nefɪs(ə)nt] *adj.* благотвори́тельный.

beneficial [ˌbenɪ'fɪʃ(ə)l] *adj.* благотво́рный, поле́з-ный, вы́годный; **mutually ~** взаимовы́годный.

beneficiary [ˌbenɪ'fɪʃərɪ] *n.* (*leg.*) бенефициа́рий.

benefit ['benɪfɪt] *n.* **1.** (*advantage*) по́льза, вы́года, преиму́щество; **for the ~ of the poor** в по́льзу бе́д-ных; **for the ~ of mankind** на бла́го челове́чества; **give s.o. the ~ of one's advice** помо́чь (*pf.*) кому́-н. сове́том; **I gave him the ~ of the doubt** я ему́ пове́рил (на э́тот раз); **reap the ~ of** пожина́ть (*impf.*) плоды́ +*g.*; **she wore a new dress for his ~** она́ наде́ла но́вое пла́тье ра́ди него́. **2.** (*favour*) благодея́ние; **confer ~s on** ока́зывать (*impf.*) бла-годея́ния +*d.* **3.** (*grant*) посо́бие; **maternity ~** посо́-бие по бере́менности и ро́дам. **4.: ~ concert** благо-твори́тельный конце́рт.
v.t. прин|оси́ть, -ести́ по́льзу +*d.*
v.i. извл|ека́ть, -е́чь по́льзу (из+*g.*).

benevolence [bɪ'nevələns] *n.* благожела́тельность, доброжела́тельность.

benevolent [bɪ'nevələnt] *adj.* благожела́тельный, доброжела́тельный.

benign [bɪ'naɪn] *adj.* (*of pers.*) добросерде́чный; (*of climate*) благотво́рный; (*med.*) доброка́чественный.

bent [bent] *n.* (*inclination*) скло́нность; (*aptitude*) накло́нность.
adj. (*coll., corrupt*) нече́стный, извращённый.
also p.p. of **bend,** *q.v.*

benz|ene ['benzi:n], **-ol** ['benzɒl] *nn.* бензо́л.

benzine ['benzi:n] *n.* бензи́н.

benzol ['benzɒl] = **benzene**

bequeath [bɪ'kwi:ð] *v.t.* завеща́ть (*impf., pf.*); (*fig.*) оста́вить (*pf.*).

bequest [bɪ'kwest] *n.* (*object*) вещь, оста́вленная в насле́дство; (*as part of museum collection*) фонд, посме́ртный дар; (*act*) завеща́тельный отка́з иму́-щества; **make a ~ of** завеща́ть (*impf., pf.*).

berate [bɪ'reɪt] *v.t.* брани́ть (*impf.*).

bereave [bɪ'ri:v] *v.t.*: **a ~d husband** неда́вно овдо-ве́вший муж; **an accident bereft him of his children** несча́стный слу́чай о́тнял у него́ дете́й; **bereft of hope** лишённый наде́жды.

bereavement [bɪ'ri:vmənt] *n.* тяжёлая утра́та.

beret ['bereɪ] *n.* бере́т.

beriberi [ˌberɪ'berɪ] *n.* бе́ри-бе́ри (*f. indecl.*).

Bermuda [bə'mju:də] *n.*: **~ shorts** шо́рты-берму́ды.

berry ['berɪ] *n.* я́года; (*coffee bean*) зерно́; (*of caviar*) икри́нка.

berserk [bə'sɜ:k, -'zɜ:k] *n.*: **go ~** разъяри́ться (*pf.*), обезу́меть (*pf.*).

berth [bɜ:θ] *n.* **1.** (*place at wharf*) при́стань, прича́л. **2.: give s.o. a wide ~** (*fig.*) обходи́ть (*impf.*) кого́-н. стороно́й (*or* за версту́). **3.** (*sleeping-place on ship*) ко́йка; (*on train*) спа́льное ме́сто.
v.t. (*moor*) ста́вить (*impf.*) к прича́лу.
v.i. (*of ship*) прича́ли|вать, -ть.

beryl ['berɪl] *n.* бери́лл; (*attr.*) бери́лловый.

beryllium [bə'rɪlɪəm] *n.* бери́ллий.

beseech [bɪ'si:tʃ] *v.t.* умол|я́ть, -и́ть; моли́ть (*impf.*).

beset [bɪ'set] *v.t.* окруж|а́ть, -и́ть; оса|жда́ть, -ди́ть.

beside [bɪ'saɪd] *prep.* **1.** (*alongside*) ря́дом с+*i.*; (*near*) о́коло+*g.*, у+*g.* **2.** (*compared with*) по сравне́нию с+*i.*; пе́ред+*i.*; **set ~** поста́вить (*pf.*) ря́дом с+*i.* **3.** (*wide of*) ми́мо+*g.*; **that is ~ the point** э́то к де́лу не отно́сится. **4.: ~ o.s.** вне себя́. **5.** (*as well as*) кро́ме+*g.*

besides [bɪ'saɪdz] *adv.* сверх того́; кро́ме того́.
prep. кро́ме+*g.*

besiege [bɪ'si:dʒ] *v.t.* (*lit., fig.*) оса|жда́ть, -ди́ть.

besmirch [bɪ'smɜ:tʃ] *v.t.* па́чкать, вы́-; (*fig.*) запа́ч-кать, опоро́чить (*both pf.*).

besom ['bi:z(ə)m] *n.* метла́, ве́ник.

besotted [bɪ'sɒtɪd] *adj.* одурма́ненный.

bespatter [bɪ'spætə(r)] *v.t.* забры́зг|ивать, -ать.

bespeak [bɪ'spi:k] *v.t.* (*order*) зака́з|ывать, -а́ть; (*reveal*) свиде́тельствовать, говори́ть (*both impf.*) о.

bespoke [bɪ'spəʊk] *adj.* сде́ланный на зака́з; **~ tailor** портно́й, рабо́тающий на зака́з.

besprinkle [bɪ'sprɪŋk(ə)l] *v.t.* (*with liquid*) обры́з-г|ивать, -ать; (*with powder etc.*) обс|ыпа́ть, -ы́пать.

best [best] *n.* (**~** *performance*) лу́чший результа́т; *see also adj.*
adj. лу́чший; **the ~ way to the station** са́мый лу́чший путь к ста́нции; **we are the ~ of friends** мы бли́зкие друзья́; **at ~** в лу́чшем слу́чае; **I did it for the ~** я де́лал э́то с лу́чшими наме́рениями; **get the ~ of it** взять (*pf.*) верх; **do one's ~** сде́лать (*pf.*) всё возмо́жное; **I know what is ~ for him** я лу́чше зна́ю, что ему́ ну́жно; **to the ~ of one's ability** в ме́ру свои́х сил/спосо́бностей; **to the ~ of my knowledge** наско́лько мне изве́стно; **in the ~ of health** в до́бром здра́вии; **all the ~!** всего́ наилу́чшего!; **hope for the ~** наде́яться (*impf.*) на лу́чшее; **turn out for the ~** оберну́ться (*pf.*) к лу́чшему; **may the ~ man win** пусть победи́т сильне́йший; **have the ~ of the bargain** оказа́ться (*pf.*) в вы́игрыше; **~ pupil** пе́рвый учени́к; **~ quality** вы́сший сорт; (*greater*): **the ~ part of a week** бо́льшая часть неде́ли; **I waited for the ~ part of an hour** я ждал почти́ це́лый час; **~ man** (*at wedding*) ша́фер.
adv. лу́чше всего́; **he works ~** (*better than others*) он рабо́тает лу́чше всех; **you know ~** вам лу́чше знать; **I had ~ tell him** мне бы сле́довало сказа́ть ему́; **do as you think ~** де́лайте, как вам ка́жется лу́чше; **which town did you like ~?** како́й го́род

вам бо́льше всего́ понра́вился?; **I liked her ~ (of all)** она́ мне понра́вилась бо́льше всех; **it is ~ forgotten** лу́чше всего́ забы́ть об э́том.

v.t. брать, взять верх над+*i.*

cpds. **~-dressed** *adj.* са́мый элега́нтный; **~-looking** *adj.* са́мый краси́вый; **~-seller** *n.* (*book*) бестсе́ллер.

bestial [ˈbestɪəl] *adj.* звери́ный; (*brutish*) зве́рский.

bestiality [ˌbestɪˈælɪtɪ] *n.* зве́рство.

bestir [bɪˈstɜː(r)] *v.t.*: **~ o.s.** встряхну́ться (*pf.*).

bestow [bɪˈstəʊ] *v.t.* (*confer*): **~ gifts on s.o.** ода́р|ивать, -и́ть кого́-н.; **he ~ed a fortune on his nephew** он переда́л племя́ннику це́лое состоя́ние; **~ a title on s.o.** присв|а́ивать, -о́ить кому́-н. ти́тул; **~ honours** возд|ава́ть, -а́ть по́чести.

bestowal [bɪˈstəʊəl] *n.* **1.** (*donation*) дар. **2.:** **~ of a title** присвое́ние ти́тула; **~ of honours** воздая́ние по́честей.

bestrew [bɪˈstruː] *v.t.* ус|ыпа́ть, -ы́пать.

bet [bet] *n.* пари́ (*nt. indecl.*), ста́вка; **make, lay a ~** держа́ть (*impf.*) пари́; **accept a ~** идти́ (*det.*) на пари́; **your best ~ is to go there** вам лу́чше всего́ пойти́ туда́.

v.t. & i. держа́ть (*impf.*) пари́; **he ~ £5 on a horse** он поста́вил 5 фу́нтов на ло́шадь; **he ~ me £10 I wouldn't do it** он поспо́рил со мной на 10 фу́нтов, что я не сде́лаю э́того; **I ~ he doesn't turn up** держу́ пари́, что он не придёт; **you ~ (your life)!** (*coll.*) ещё вы!; ещё как!

beta [ˈbiːtə] *n.*: **~ blocker** (*pharm.*) бе́та-блока́тор; **~ particle** бе́та-части́ца; **~ rays** бе́та-лучи́.

betake [bɪˈteɪk] *v.t.*: **~ o.s. to** (*a place*) отпр|авля́ться, -а́виться к+*d.*

betel [ˈbiːt(ə)l] *n.* бе́тель (*m.*).

cpd. **~-nut** *n.* аре́ковое се́мя.

betide [bɪˈtaɪd] (*arch.*) *v.t.*: **woe ~ you** го́ре вам!

betoken [bɪˈtəʊkən] *v.t.* (*indicate*) ука́з|ывать, -а́ть на+*a.*; (*signify*) означа́ть (*impf.*).

betray [bɪˈtreɪ] *v.t.* **1.** (*abandon treacherously*) измен|я́ть, -и́ть +*d.*; пред|ава́ть, -а́ть. **2.** (*seduce*) обма́н|ывать, -у́ть. **3.:** **~ s.o.'s hopes** обману́ть (*pf.*) чьи-н. наде́жды; **~ s.o.'s trust** обману́ть чьё-н. дове́рие. **4.** (*disclose, evince*) выдава́ть, вы́дать; **~ surprise** выража́ть, вы́разить удивле́ние.

betrayal [bɪˈtreɪəl] *n.* (*treachery*) преда́тельство, изме́на; (*disclosure*) вы́дача; (*seduction, disappointment*) обма́н.

betrayer [bɪˈtreɪə(r)] *n.* преда́тель (*m.*); изме́нник.

betroth [bɪˈtrəʊð] *v.t.* (*liter.*) обруч|а́ть, -и́ть; помо́лвить (*pf.*).

betrothal [bɪˈtrəʊðəl] *n.* обруче́ние, помо́лвка.

better [ˈbetə(r)] *adj.* лу́чший, лу́чше; **~ still** ещё лу́чше; **all the ~** тем лу́чше; **I hoped for ~ things** я наде́ялся на лу́чшее; **it is ~ that you go** вам бы лу́чше уйти́; **get ~** ул|учша́ться, -у́чшиться; (*in health*) попр|авля́ться, -а́виться; **things are getting ~** дела́ иду́т лу́чше; **get the ~ of s.o.** взять (*pf.*) верх над кем-н.; превзойти́ (*pf.*) кого́-н.; **he got the ~ of his anger** он преодоле́л свой гнев; **a change for the ~** переме́на к лу́чшему; **for ~, for worse** на го́ре и ра́дость; **you will be the ~ for a holiday** о́тдых пойдёт вам на по́льзу; **he is no ~ than a fool** он по́просту дура́к; **appeal to s.o.'s ~ feelings** взыва́ть (*impf.*) к чьим-н. лу́чшим чу́вствам; **the ~ part of a day** бо́льшая часть дня; **one's ~s** вышестоя́щие ли́ца.

adv. лу́чше; (*more*) бо́льше; **~ and ~** всё лу́чше и лу́чше; **the more the ~** чем бо́льше, тем лу́чше; **you had ~ stay here** вам бы лу́чше оста́ться здесь; **I thought ~ of it** я разду́мал/переду́мал; **~ off** бо́лее состоя́тельный.

v.t. **1.** (*improve*) ул|учша́ть, -у́чшить; **he ~ed himself** он продви́нулся. **2.** (*improve on*) превзойти́ (pf.).

betterment [ˈbetəmənt] *n.* улучше́ние.

betting [ˈbetɪŋ] *n.*: **what's the ~ he marries her?** на ско́лько спо́рим, что он на ней же́нится?

adj.: **he is not a ~ man** он челове́к не аза́ртный.

between [bɪˈtwiːn] *adv.*: **I attended the two lectures and had lunch in ~** я посети́л две ле́кции и пообе́дал в переры́ве.

prep. ме́жду+*g. or i.*; **~ you and me** ме́жду на́ми; **(in) ~ times** вре́мя от вре́мени; **~ two and three months** от двух до трёх ме́сяцев; **choose ~ the two** выбира́ть, вы́брать одно́ из двух; **~ now and then** к тому́ вре́мени; **they scored 150 ~ them** они́ набра́ли сто пятьдеся́т очко́в вме́сте; **we have only a pound ~ us** у нас на двои́х всего́ оди́н фунт.

betwixt [bɪˈtwɪkst] *adv.*: **~ and between** ни то ни сё.

bevel [ˈbev(ə)l] *n.* (*tool*) ма́лка; (*surface*) скос; **~ edge** фаце́т.

v.t. ск|а́шивать, -оси́ть.

beverage [ˈbevərɪdʒ] *n.* напи́ток.

bevy [ˈbevɪ] *n.* ста́я, ста́до; (*fig.*) ста́йка.

bewail [bɪˈweɪl] *v.t.* опла́к|ивать, -ать.

beware [bɪˈweə(r)] *v.t. & i.* остер|ега́ться, -е́чься (*impf.*) +*g.*; **~ lest you fall** осторо́жно, а то упадёте; **'~ of the dog'** «осторо́жно, зла́я соба́ка».

bewilder [bɪˈwɪldə(r)] *v.t.* сби|ва́ть, -ть с то́лку; прив|оди́ть, -ести́ в замеша́тельство; **~ed** смущённый, озада́ченный.

bewilderment [bɪˈwɪldəmənt] *n.* замеша́тельство, озада́ченность.

bewitch [bɪˈwɪtʃ] *v.t.* (*put spell on*) околдо́в|ывать, -а́ть; (*delight*) очаро́в|ывать, -а́ть.

bewitching [bɪˈwɪtʃɪŋ] *adj.* чару́ющий.

beyond [bɪˈjɒnd] *n.*: **he lives at the back of ~** он живёт на краю́ све́та.

adv. вдали́; вдаль.

prep. (*of place*) за+*i.*; (*of motion*) за+*a.*; (*later than*) по́сле+*g.*; **~ doubt** вне сомне́ния; **~ dispute** бесспо́рно; **~ my comprehension** вы́ше моего́ понима́ния; **~ my powers** не в мои́х си́лах; **~ belief** невероя́тно; **~ expression** невырази́мо; **~ my expectations** сверх мои́х ожида́ний; **succeed ~ one's hopes** да́же не ожида́ть (*impf.*) тако́го успе́ха; **this is ~ a joke** здесь уже́ не до шу́ток; **live ~ one's income** жить (*impf.*) не по сре́дствам; **~ measure** сверх ме́ры, чрезме́рно; **~ hope** безнадёжно; **~ cure** неизлечи́мый; **go ~ one's duty** сде́лать (*pf.*) бо́льше, чем обя́зан.

biannual [baɪˈænjʊəl] *adj.* выходя́щий два́жды в год; полугодово́й.

bias [ˈbaɪəs] *n.* **1.** предрассу́док, предвзя́тое отноше́ние (*к чему*); (*favourable prejudice*) пристра́стие (к+*d.*); (*adverse*) предубежде́ние (про́тив+*g.*). **2.** (*of material*): **cut on the ~** кро́ить, с- по косо́й ли́нии.

v.t. (*influence*) склон|я́ть, -и́ть; (*prejudice*) предубе|жда́ть, -ди́ть; **~ s.o. against an idea** настр|а́ивать, -о́ить кого́-н. про́тив како́й-н. иде́и; **a ~(s)ed opinion** предвзя́тое мне́ние.

bib [bɪb] *n.* нагру́дник.

Bible [ˈbaɪb(ə)l] *n.* Би́блия; (*fig.*) би́блия.

biblical [ˈbɪblɪk(ə)l] *adj.* библе́йский.

bibliographer [ˌbɪblɪˈɒgrəfə(r)] *n.* библио́граф.

bibliographic(al) [ˌbɪblɪəˈgræfɪk(ə)l] *adj.* библиографи́ческий.

bibliography [ˌbɪblɪˈɒgrəfɪ] *n.* библиогра́фия.

bibliophile [ˈbɪblɪəʊˌfaɪl] *n.* библиофи́л.

bicameral [baɪˈkæmər(ə)l] *adj.* двухпала́тный.

bicarbonate [baɪˈkɑːbənɪt] *n.*: **~ of soda** двууглеки́слый на́трий, питьева́я со́да.

bicentenary [ˌbaɪsenˈtiːnərɪ] *n.* двухсотле́тие.

adj. двухсотле́тний.

bicentennial [ˌbaɪsenˈtenɪəl] *n.* двухсотле́тие.

biceps [ˈbaɪseps] *n.* би́цепс.

bicker [ˈbɪkə(r)] *v.t.* (*squabble*) перебра́ниваться (*impf.*).

bicycle ['baɪsɪk(ə)l] *n.* велосипéд.
v.i. éздить (*indet.*), éхать, по- (*det.*) на велосипéде.

bicyclist ['baɪsɪklɪst] *n.* велосипедúст.

bid [bɪd] *n.* **1.** (*at auction*) заявка; предложéние цены́. **2.** (*tender*) заявка. **3.** (*claim, demand*) заявка (на+*a.*); претéнзия. **4.** (*attempt*) стáвка; попытка. **5.** (*at cards*) заявка.
v.t. & i. **1.** (*at auction*) предл|агáть, -ожи́ть цéну (*за что*); **~ against s.o.** наб|авля́ть, -áвить цéну прóтив когó-н. **2.** (*at cards*) объяв|ля́ть, -и́ть. **3.** (*tender*): **~ for a contract** дéлать, с- заявку на контрáкт. **4.** (*liter., order*): **~ him come in!** вели́те емý войти́!; **do as you are ~(den)!** дéлай как скáзано! **5.** (*liter., say*): **~ s.o. farewell** про|щáться, -сти́ться с кем-н.; **~ s.o. welcome** привéтствовать (*impf.*) когó-н.; **~ s.o. goodnight** пожелáть (*pf.*) покóйной нóчи комý-н.

bidder ['bɪdə(r)] *n.* покупщи́к; **the highest ~** предложи́вший наивы́сшую цéну.

bidding ['bɪdɪŋ] *n.* **1.** (*at auction*) предложéние цены́. **2.** (*command*): **do s.o.'s ~** исп|олня́ть, -óлнить чьи-н. приказáния. **3.** (*at cards*) объявлéние.

bide [baɪd] *v.t.*: **~ one's time** ждать (*impf.*) благоприя́тного слýчая.

bidet ['bi:deɪ] *n.* бидé (*indecl.*).

biennial [baɪ'enɪəl] *n.* (*bot.*) двулéтник.
adj. двухлéтний.

bier [bɪə(r)] *n.* катафáлк.

bifocal [baɪ'fəʊk(ə)l] *adj.* двухфóкусный, бифокáльный; **~ spectacles** (*also* **~s**) бифокáльные очки́.

bifurcate ['baɪfə,keɪt] *v.t. & i.* разветв|ля́ть(ся), -и́ть(ся); (*of road, river: also*) раздв|áиваться, -óиться; **a ~d tail** раздвоённый хвост.

bifurcation [,baɪfə'keɪʃ(ə)n] *n.* раздвоéние.

big [bɪg] *adj.* (*in size*) большóй, крýпный; (*great*) крýпный, вели́кий; (*extensive*) обши́рный; (*intense*) си́льный; (*tall*) высóкий; (*adult*) взрóслый; (*magnanimous*) великодýшный; (*important*) вáжный; **a ~ man** (*in stature*) крýпный мужчи́на; (*in importance*) крýпная фигýра; **a ~ voice** си́льный гóлос; **a ~ landowner** крýпный землевладéлец; **these boots are too ~ for me** э́ти сапоги́ мне велики́; **~ (*capital*) letters** прописны́е бýквы; **a ~ fire** си́льный пожáр; **~ and small** от мáла до вели́ка; **as ~ as** величинóй в+*a.*; **my ~ brother** мой стáрший брат; **in a ~ way** с ширóким размáхом; **a ~ name** (*celebrity*) знамени́тость.
cpds. **~-headed** *adj.* (*conceited*) зазнáвшийся; **~-hearted** *adj.* великодýшный; **~wig** *n.* ши́шка (*coll.*).

bigamist ['bɪgəmɪst] *n.* двоежéнец, (*fem.*) двумýжница.

bigamous ['bɪgəməs] *adj.* бигами́ческий, двубрáчный; имéющий/имéющая двух жён/мужéй.

bigamy ['bɪgəmɪ] *n.* бигáмия; (*of man*) двоежёнство; (*of woman*) двоемýжие.

bigot ['bɪgət] *n.* фанáтик.

bigoted ['bɪgətɪd] *adj.* фанати́ческий.

bigotry ['bɪgətrɪ] *n.* фанати́зм.

bike [baɪk] *n.* **1.** (*coll.*) = **bicycle. 2.** (*motorcycle*) мотоци́кл.
v.i. éздить (*indet.*) на мотоци́кле.

biker ['baɪkə(r)] *n.* мотоцикли́ст (*fem.* -ка).

bikeway ['baɪkweɪ] *n.* велосипéдная дорóжка.

bikini [bɪ'ki:nɪ] *n.* бики́ни (*nt. indecl.*).

bilateral [baɪ'lætər(ə)l] *adj.* двусторóнний.

bilberry ['bɪlbərɪ] *n.* черни́ка (*collect.*); я́года черни́ки.

bile [baɪl] *n.* жёлчь; (*fig.*) жёлчность.
cpd. **~-duct** *n.* жёлчный протóк.

bilingual [baɪ'lɪŋgw(ə)l] *adj.* двуязы́чный.

bilingualism [baɪ'lɪŋgw(ə)lɪz(ə)m] *n.* двуязы́чие.

bilious ['bɪljəs] *adj.* **1.** жёлчный; **a ~ headache** мигрéнь. **2.** (*fig.*) жёлчный, раздражи́тельный.

bilk [bɪlk] *v.t.*: **~ s.o. of sth.** надýть (*pf.*) (*coll.*) когó-н. на что-н.

bill[1] [bɪl] *n.* (*beak*) клюв.
v.i.: **~ and coo** ворковáть (*impf.*).

bill[2] [bɪl] *n.* **1.** (*parl.*) законопроéкт, билль (*m.*). **2.** (*certificate*): **clean ~ of health** каранти́нное свидéтельство. **3.** (*comm.*) счёт (*pl.* -á); **pay a ~, foot the ~** заплати́ть (*pf.*) по счёту; оплá|чивать, -ти́ть счёт; **run up a ~** набрáть (*pf.*) мнóго в долг. **4.** (*advertisement*): **~ of fare** меню́ (*nt. indecl.*); **theatre ~** театрáльная афи́ша; **stick no ~s** (*as notice*) наклéивать объявлéния воспрещáется; **fill the ~** (*satisfy requirements*) отвечáть (*impf.*) всем трéбованиям. **5.** (*US, banknote*) банкнóта; **dollar ~** дóлларовый билéт.
v.t. **1.** (*announce*) объяв|ля́ть, -и́ть; **get top ~ing** быть помещённым в афи́ше на пéрвом мéсте. **2.** (*charge*): **~ me for the goods** пришли́те мне счёт за товáры.
cpds. **~board** *n.* доскá объявлéний; **~fold** *n.* (*US*) бумáжник; **~-poster** *n.* расклéйщик афи́ш.

billet ['bɪlɪt] *n.* помещéние для постóя; **be in ~s** быть на постóе.
v.t. (*assign to ~*) расквартирóв|ывать, -áть; назн|ачáть, -áчить (*or* стáвить, по-) на постóй (**on s.o.:** к комý-н.).

billiard|s ['bɪljədz] *n.* бильярд.
cpds. **~-ball** *n.* бильярдный шар; **~-cue** *n.* кий; **~-table** *n.* бильярд.

billion ['bɪljən] *n.* (*million millions*) биллиóн; (*thousand millions*) миллиáрд.

billionaire [,bɪljə'neə(r)] *n.* миллиардéр.

billow ['bɪləʊ] *n.* вал.
v.i. вздымáться (*impf.*); волновáться (*impf.*).

billy ['bɪlɪ] *n.* (*also* **~can**) жестянóй (похóдный) котелóк.

billy-goat ['bɪlɪ,gəʊt] *n.* козёл.

bimetallic [,baɪmɪ'tælɪk] *adj.* биметалли́ческий.

bimetallism [baɪ'metə,lɪz(ə)m] *n.* биметалли́зм.

bimonthly [baɪ'mʌnθlɪ] *adj.* (*two-monthly*) выходя́щий (*u m.n.*) раз в два мéсяца.
adv. раз в два мéсяца.

bin [bɪn] *n.* (*for coal*) бýнкер; (*for corn*) закрóм, ларь (*m.*); (*for ashes, dust*) мýсорное ведрó.

binary ['baɪnərɪ] *adj.* (*math.*) двои́чный.

bind [baɪnd] *v.t.* **1.** (*tie, fasten*) свя́з|ывать, -áть; **~ on one's skis** привя́з|ывать, -áть лы́жи; **~ up one's hair** подвя́з|ывать, -áть вóлосы; **~ up a wound** перевя́з|ывать, -áть рáну; **~ together** свя́з|ывать, -áть. **2.** (*secure*): **~ the edge of a carpet** закреп|ля́ть, -и́ть край коврá. **3.** (*books etc.*) перепле|тáть, -сти́. **4.** (*oblige, exact promise*) обя́з|ывать, -áть; **~ s.o. to secrecy** обя́з|ывать, -áть когó-н. храни́ть тáйну; **I am bound to say** я дóлжен сказáть; **I'll be bound** увéрен; **~ o.s.** обязáться (*pf.*); **~ over** (*leg.*) обя́з|ывать, -áть. *See also* **binding, bound**[3]
cpd. **~weed** *n.* вьюнóк.

binder ['baɪndə(r)] *n.* **1.** (*book ~*) переплётчик. **2.** (*cover for magazines etc.*) пáпка.

binding ['baɪndɪŋ] *n.* (*of book*) переплёт; (*braid etc.*) обши́вка.
adj. обя́зывающий; имéющий обязáтельную си́лу.

binge [bɪndʒ] *n.* (*sl.*) кутёж; пья́нка; **go on the ~** закути́ть, запи́ть (*both pf.*).

bingo ['bɪŋgəʊ] *n.* лотó (*indecl.*).

binoculars [bɪ'nɒkjʊləz] *n.* бинóкль (*m.*).

binomial [baɪ'nəʊmɪəl] *adj.* двучлéнный, биномиáльный; **the ~ theorem** бинóм Нью́тона.

biochemical [,baɪəʊ'kemɪk(ə)l] *adj.* биохими́ческий.

biochemist [,baɪəʊ'kemɪst] *n.* биохи́мик.

biochemistry [,baɪəʊ'kemɪstrɪ] *n.* биохи́мия.

biodegradable [,baɪəʊdɪ'greɪdəb(ə)l] *adj.* подвéрженный биологи́ческому разложéнию.

biodiversity [ˌbaɪəʊdaɪ'vɜːsɪtɪ] *n.* биологи́ческое разнообра́зие.
bioengineering [ˌbaɪəʊˌendʒɪ'nɪərɪŋ] *n.* биоинжене́рия.
biographer [baɪ'ɒgrəfə(r)] *n.* био́граф.
biographic(al) [ˌbaɪə'græfɪk(ə)l] *adj.* биографи́ческий.
biography [baɪ'ɒgrəfɪ] *n.* биогра́фия.
biological [ˌbaɪə'lɒdʒɪk(ə)l] *adj.* биологи́ческий; ~ **warfare** бактериологи́ческая война́.
biologist [baɪ'ɒlədʒɪst] *n.* био́лог.
biology [baɪ'ɒlədʒɪ] *n.* биоло́гия.
biophysics [ˌbaɪəʊ'fɪzɪks] *n.* биофи́зика.
biopsy ['baɪɒpsɪ] *n.* биопси́я.
bioresources ['baɪɒrɪˌsɔːsɪs] *n.* биоресу́рс|ы, (*pl.*, *g.* -ов).
biotechnology [ˌbaɪəʊtek'nɒlədʒɪ] *n.* биотехноло́гия.
bipartisan [ˌbaɪpɑːtɪ'zæn, baɪ'pɑːtɪz(ə)n] *adj.* двухпарти́йный.
bipartite [baɪ'pɑːtaɪt] *adj.* двусторо́нний.
biped ['baɪped] *n.* двуно́гое.
biplane ['baɪpleɪn] *n.* бипла́н.
birch [bɜːtʃ] *n.* **1.** (*tree*) берёза; (*attr.*) берёзовый. **2.** (*rod*) ро́зга.
v.t. сечь, вы́-.
bird [bɜːd] *n.* **1.** пти́ца; ~ **of prey** хи́щная пти́ца; **game** ~ дичь; ~ **of paradise** ра́йская пти́ца; ~**'s eye view** вид с (высоты́) пти́чьего полёта; **a** ~ **in the hand is worth two in the bush** лу́чше сини́ца в ру́ки, чем жура́вль в не́бе; ~**s of a feather flock together** рыба́к рыбака́ ви́дит издалека́; **kill two** ~**s with one stone** уби́ть (*pf.*) двух за́йцев одни́м уда́ром; **the early** ~ **catches the worm** кто ра́но встаёт, тому́ Бог подаёт; **an early** ~ ра́нняя пта́шка; **night** ~ (*fig.*) ночно́й гуля́ка. **2.** (*sl.*, *girl*) де́вка.
cpds. ~**-brain** *n.* (*fig.*) кури́ные мо́зги (*m. pl.*); ~**-cage** *n.* кле́тка для птиц; ~**-call** *n.* пти́чий крик; ~**-fancier** *n.* люби́тель (*m.*) птиц; ~**-lime** *n.* пти́чий клей; ~**-seed** *n.* пти́чий корм; ~**'s nest** *n.* пти́чье гнездо́; ~**-table** *n.* корму́шка для птиц; ~**-watcher** *n.* орнито́лог-люби́тель (*m.*).
Biro ['baɪərəʊ] *n.* (*propr.*) ша́риковая ру́чка, ша́рик.
birth [bɜːθ] *n.* **1.** рожде́ние; **he weighed 7lbs. at** ~ он ве́сил 7 фу́нтов при рожде́нии; **give** ~ **to** роди́ть (*impf.*, *pf.*), рожа́ть (*impf.*); (*fig.*) произвести́ (*pf.*) на свет; **premature** ~ преждевре́менные ро́ды (*pl.*, *g.* -ов); **since** ~ с рожде́ния; о́т роду; **still** ~ рожде́ние мёртвого ребёнка; **there are more** ~**s than deaths** рожда́емость превыша́ет сме́ртность; ~ **certificate** свиде́тельство о рожде́нии; ~ **control** (*contraception*) противозача́точные ме́ры (*f. pl.*). **2.** (*descent*): **of noble** ~ благоро́дного происхожде́ния; **an Englishman by** ~ англича́нин по происхожде́нию. **3.** (*fig.*): ~ **of an idea** зарожде́ние мы́сли; **new** ~ второ́е рожде́ние.
cpds. ~**day** *n.* день рожде́ния; рожде́ние; ~**day present** пода́рок ко дню рожде́ния; ~**day cake** ≃ имени́нный пиро́г; **in one's** ~**day suit** (*joc.*) в чём мать родила́; ~**mark** *n.* роди́мое пятно́; ~**place** *n.* ме́сто рожде́ния; ро́дина; ~**rate** *n.* рожда́емость; ~**right** *n.* пра́во первоporо́дства.
biscuit ['bɪskɪt] *n.* пече́нье; **ship's** ~ гале́та; **take the** ~ (*coll.*) превосходи́ть (*impf.*) всё.
bisect [baɪ'sekt] *v.t.* дели́ть, раз- попола́м.
bisexual [baɪ'seksjʊəl] *adj.* (*having organs of both sexes*) двупо́лый, гермафроди́тный; (*attracted by both sexes*) бисексуа́льный.
bishop ['bɪʃəp] *n.* (*eccl.*) епи́скоп; (*chess*) слон.
bishopric ['bɪʃəprɪk] *n.* (*office*) епи́скопство; (*diocese*) епа́рхия.
bismuth ['bɪzməθ] *n.* ви́смут.
bison ['baɪs(ə)n] *n.* бизо́н.
bistro ['biːstrəʊ] *n.* бистро́ (*indecl.*).
bit[1] [bɪt] *n.* **1.** кусо́к, кусо́чек; **a** ~ **of paper** листо́к бума́ги; **come to** ~**s** развали́ться (*pf.*) на куски́. **2.** (*abstr. uses*): **a** ~ **of news** но́вость; **a** ~ **of advice** сове́т; **I am a** ~ **late** я немно́го опозда́л; **not a** ~ **of it!** ниско́лько!; ничу́ть!; **wait a** ~! подожди́те чуть-чуть!; **a good** ~ **older** значи́тельно ста́рше; ~ **by** ~ ма́ло-пома́лу; **not a** ~ **of use** никако́й по́льзы; **every** ~ **as good** так же хоро́ш; ниско́лько не ху́же; **a** ~ **of a coward** трусова́тый; **a nasty** ~ **of work** (*pers.*) проти́вная осо́ба; **do one's** ~ внести́ (*pf.*) свою́ ле́пту; **it will take a** ~ **of doing** э́то бу́дет нелегко́ сде́лать; ~ **part** (*theatr.*) ма́ленькая роль; ~ **player** (*theatr.*) актёр на эпизоди́ческих роля́х.
bit[2] [bɪt] *n.* (*comput.*) бит.
cpd. ~**-mapped** *adj.* (*comput.*) би́товый.
bit[3] [bɪt] *n.* **1.** (*of drill*) коро́нка; сверло́, бур; (*of plane*) ле́звие. **2.** (*of bridle*) уд|ила́ (*pl.*, *g.* -и́л); мундшту́к; **take the** ~ **between one's teeth** (*fig.*) закуси́ть (*pf.*) удила́.
bitch [bɪtʃ] *n.* **1.** (*of dog*) су́ка. **2.** (*coll.*, *spiteful woman*) сте́рва; (*promiscuous woman*) су́ка.
v.i. (*sl.*) стона́ть, ныть (*both impf.*).
bitchiness ['bɪtʃɪnɪs] *n.* (*coll.*) стерво́зность.
bitchy ['bɪtʃɪ] *adj.* (*coll.*) стерво́зный.
bite [baɪt] *n.* **1.** (*act of biting*) куса́ние; **eat sth. at one** ~ съе́сть (*pf.*) что-н. зара́з. **2.** (*mouthful*): **I haven't had a** ~ **to eat** у меня́ куска́ во рту́ не́ было; **have a** ~ **of food** перекуси́ть (*pf.*), закуси́ть (*pf.*). **3.** (*wound caused by biting*) уку́с; **snake** ~ змеи́ный уку́с. **4.** (*of fish*) клёв; **I have been fishing all day and haven't had a** ~ весь день сижу́, а ры́ба не клюёт. **5.** (*sharpness*, *pungency*): **there is a** ~ **in the air** моро́з пощи́пывает.
v.t. **1.** куса́ть, укуси́ть; **he bit the apple** он откуси́л я́блоко; **the dog bit him in the leg** соба́ка укуси́ла его́ за́ ногу; **a piece was bitten from the apple** я́блоко бы́ло надку́сано; **he was bitten by midges** его́ искуса́ли комары́. **2.** (*fig.*): ~ **off more than one can chew** ≃ де́ло не по плечу́; ~ **s.o.'s head off** откуси́ть (*pf.*) кому́-н. го́лову; **he was bitten by this craze** он зарази́лся э́тим увлече́нием; ~ **the dust** быть пове́рженным; **once bitten, twice shy** пу́ганая воро́на куста́ бои́тся.
v.i.: **does your dog** ~? ва́ша соба́ка куса́ется?; **the fish won't** ~ ры́ба не клюёт; ~ **into sth.** вгр|ыза́ться, -ы́зться во что-н.; **acid** ~**s into metal** кислота́ разъеда́ет мета́лл.
biting ['baɪtɪŋ] *adj.* куса́ющий; (*of cold*) ре́зкий; (*of wind*) ре́зкий; (*of satire*) е́дкий, язви́тельный.
bitter ['bɪtə(r)] *adj.* (*lit.*, *fig.*) го́рький; **a** ~ **wind** ре́зкий ве́тер; ~ **conflict** о́стрый конфли́кт; ~ **enemy** зле́йший/закля́тый враг; **to the** ~ **end** до са́мого конца́.
adv.: ~ **cold** ужа́сно хо́лодно.
cpd. ~**-sweet** *adj.* горькова́то-сла́дкий.
bittern ['bɪt(ə)n] *n.* выпь.
bitumen ['bɪtjʊmɪn] *n.* биту́м; асфа́льт.
bituminous [bɪ'tjuːmɪnəs] *adj.* биту́мный, асфа́льтовый.
bivalve ['baɪvælv] *n.* двуство́рчатый моллю́ск.
bivouac ['bɪvʊˌæk] *n.* бива́к.
v.i. распол|ага́ться, -ожи́ться бивако́м.
bi-weekly [baɪ'wiːklɪ] *adj.* (*fortnightly*) двухнеде́льный; выходя́щий (*и т.п.*) ра́з в две неде́ли.
adv. раз в две неде́ли.
bizarre [bɪ'zɑː(r)] *adj.* чудно́й, дико́винный.
blab [blæb] *v.t.* (*also* ~ **out**) выба́лтывать, вы́болтать; разб|а́лтывать, -олта́ть.
v.i. болта́ть (*impf.*)
blabber ['blæbə(r)] *n.* болту́н; пустоме́ля (*c.g.*).
black [blæk] *n.* **1.** (*colour*) чернота́, чёрное; **dress in** ~ одева́ться (*impf.*) в чёрное; **wear** ~ **for s.o.** носи́ть (*indet.*) тра́ур по кому́-н.; **be in the** ~ вести́ де́ло с при́былью. **2.** (*negro*) чёрный, чернoко́жий; негр, (*fem.*) -итя́нка. **3.** (*fig.*): **two** ~**s don't make a white** злом зла не попра́вишь; **swear** ~ **is white**

называ́ть (*impf.*) чёрное бе́лым.

adj. **1.** (*colour*) чёрный; **as ~ as ink** (*etc.*) чёрный как смоль; **a ~ eye** подби́тый глаз. **2.** (*fig.*): **a ~ deed** чёрное де́ло; **he is not so ~ as he is painted** он не так плох, как его́ изобража́ют; **a ~ heart** чёрная душа́; **~ despair** безысхо́дное отча́яние. **3.** (*negro*) чёрный; **~ man** чёрный, чернoко́жий; **B~ Power** «Власть чёрным». **4.** (*var.*): **~ and tan** чёрно-ры́жий; **~ and white** чёрно-бе́лый; **in ~ and white** (*in writing*) чёрным по бе́лому; **he beat him ~ and blue** он изби́л его́ до полусме́рти; **~ art** чёрная ма́гия; **~ bread** чёрный/ржано́й хлеб; **~ coffee** чёрный ко́фе; **~ earth** чернозём; **~ hole** (*astron.*) чёрная дыра́; **~ ice** гололе́дица; **it is a ~ mark against him** э́то его́ поро́чит; **~ market** чёрный ры́нок; **B~ Sea** Чёрное мо́ре.

v.t. **1.** (*paint black*) кра́сить (*impf.*) в чёрное; (*boots etc.*) ва́ксить, на-; **~ one's face** кра́сить, вы́-лицо́ чёрным. **2.** (*boycott*) бойкоти́ровать (*impf.*, *pf.*). **3.: ~ out** (*light*) затемн|я́ть, -и́ть.

v.i.: **~ out** (*lose consciousness*) теря́ть, по- созна́ние.

cpds. **~ball** *v.t.* забаллоти́ровать (*pf.*); **~-beetle** *n.* чёрный тарака́н; **~berry** *n.* ежеви́ка (*collect*); я́года ежеви́ки; **~bird** *n.* чёрный дрозд; **~board** *n.* кла́ссная доска́; ; **~currant** *n.* чёрная сморо́дина; **~guard** *n.* негодя́й; **~head** *n.* у́горь (*m.*); **~jack** *n.* (*US*, *bludgeon*) дуби́нка; **~leg** *n.* штрейкбре́хер; **~-list** *v.t.* вн|оси́ть, -ести́ в чёрный спи́сок; **~mail** *n.* шанта́ж; *v.t.* шантажи́ровать (*impf.*); **~mailer** *n.* шантажи́ст; **~-marketeer** *n.* спекуля́нт; **~out** *n.* (*in wartime*) затемне́ние; (*electricity failure*) вре́менное отсу́тствие электри́ческого освеще́ния; (*loss of consciousness or awareness*) поте́ря созна́ния; *v.t.* затемн|я́ть, -и́ть; **~smith** *n.* кузне́ц; **~thorn** *n.* (*plant*) тёрн.

blacken ['blækən] *v.t.* **1.** (*paint black*) кра́сить, по- в чёрное; (*boots etc.*) ва́ксить, на. **2.** (*soil, dirty*) грязни́ть, за-. **3.** (*reputation*) черни́ть, о-.

v.i. черне́ть, по-.

blacking ['blækıŋ] *n.* (*for boots etc.*) ва́кса.

blackish ['blækıʃ] *adj.* темнова́тый.

blackness ['blæknıs] *n.* чернота́; (*darkness*) темнота́.

bladder ['blædə(r)] *n.* (*anat.*, *bot.*) пузы́рь (*m.*); (*in seaweed*) пузырёк.

blade [bleıd] *n.* **1.** (*of knife etc.*) ле́звие. **2.** (*of oar etc.*) ло́пасть, лопа́тка; (*of fan*) крыло́. **3.** (*of grass etc.*) были́нка, стебелёк. **4.** (*fig.*, *sword*) клино́к.

blame [bleım] *n.* (*censure*) порица́ние; осужде́ние; (*fault*) вина́; **his conduct was free from ~** его́ поведе́ние бы́ло безупре́чным; **the ~ is mine** я винова́т; **lay, put the ~ on s.o.** возложи́ть (*pf.*) вину́ на кого́-н.; **bear, take the ~** приня́ть (*pf.*) на себя́ вину́/отве́тственность; **where does the ~ lie?** кто винова́т?

v.t. порица́ть (*impf.*); вини́ть (*impf.*); осу|жда́ть, -ди́ть (*кого за что*); **he was ~d for the mistake** вину́ за оши́бку возложи́ли на него́; **he cannot be ~d for it** он не винова́т в э́том; **I am in no way to ~** мне не́ в чем упрекну́ть себя́; **he is entirely to ~** э́то по́лностью его́ вина́; **~ sth. on s.o.** взва́л|ивать, -ить вину́ за что-н. на кого́-н.

cpd. **~worthy** *adj.* предосуди́тельный.

blameless ['bleımlıs] *adj.* безупре́чный; неви́нный.

blanch [blɑ:ntʃ] *v.t.* бели́ть, вы́-; **~ed almonds** бланширо́ванный минда́ль.

v.i. (*go pale*) беле́ть, по-.

blancmange [blə'mɒndʒ] *n.* бланманже́ (*indecl.*).

bland [blænd] *adj.* мя́гкий.

blandishment ['blændıʃmənt] *n.* (*usu. pl.*) обха́живание, лесть.

blank [blæŋk] *n.* **1.** (*empty space*) про́пуск; (*fig.*) **his death leaves a ~** по́сле его́ сме́рти жизнь опусте́ла; **my mind is a ~ on this subject** у меня́ э́то вы́летело из головы́. **2.** (*in lottery*): **draw a ~** вы́тянуть (*pf.*) пусто́й биле́т; (*fig.*) иска́ть (*impf.*) беспло́дно/напра́сно. **3.** (*US*, *form*) бланк.

adj. **1.** (*empty*): **a ~ sheet of paper** пусто́й лист бума́ги; **a ~ cheque** незапо́лненный чек; **a ~ space** про́пуск; пусто́е ме́сто; **~ cartridge** холосто́й патро́н. **2.** (*bare, plain*): **a ~ wall** глуха́я стена́; **we are up against a ~ wall** (*fig.*) мы упёрлись в глуху́ю сте́ну; **a ~ key** болва́нка ключа́; **~ verse** бе́лый стих. **3.** (*fig.*): **my memory is ~** ничего́ не по́мню; **look ~** (*of pers.*) вы́глядеть (*impf.*) растеря́нным; **the future looks ~** бу́дущее ничего́ не сули́т.

blanket ['blæŋkıt] *n.* одея́ло; **~ of fog** пелена́ тума́на; **~ of smoke** пелена́ ды́ма; **the hills lay under a ~ of snow** холмы́ бы́ли покры́ты сло́ем сне́га (*or* бы́ли под снегов́ым покрыва́лом); **~ instructions** о́бщие указа́ния.

v.t. (*cover*) оку́т|ывать, -ать.

blankly ['blæŋklı] *adv.* (*without expression*) бессмы́сленно, ту́по.

blare [bleə(r)] *n.* рёв.

v.t.: **~ out** труби́ть, про-.

v.i. труби́ть, про-; реве́ть (*impf.*).

blarney ['blɑ:nı] *n.* загова́ривание зубо́в.

v.t. & i. загов|а́ривать, -ори́ть зу́бы (*кому*).

blasé ['blɑ:zeı] *adj.* пресы́щенный (жи́знью).

blaspheme [blæs'fi:m] *v.t.* (*revile*) поноси́ть (*impf.*), хули́ть (*impf.*).

v.i. богоху́льствовать (*impf.*), богоху́льничать (*impf.*).

blasphemer [blæs'fi:mə(r)] *n.* богоху́льник.

blasphemous ['blæsfiməs] *adj.* богоху́льный.

blasphemy ['blæsfəmı] *n.* богоху́льство.

blast [blɑ:st] *n.* **1.: ~ of wind** поры́в ве́тра; **~ of hot air** волна́ горя́чего во́здуха. **2.** (*from explosion*) взрыв. **3.: at full ~** (*fig.*) в по́лном разга́ре; по́лным хо́дом. **4.** (*of an instrument*): **~ on a whistle** свисто́к.

v.t. **1.** (*explode rocks etc.*) вз|рыва́ть, -орва́ть. **2.** (*curse*): **~ it!** прокля́тие!; пропади́ всё про́падом; **~ you!** чтоб тебя́ разорва́ло!; чтоб ты ло́пнул!

v.i.: **~ off** (*rocketry*) взлет|а́ть, -е́ть; стартова́ть (*impf.*, *pf.*).

cpds. **~-furnace** *n.* до́мна, до́менная печь; **~-off** *n.* взлёт; моме́нт ста́рта.

blasted ['blɑ:stıd] *adj.* (*cursed*) прокля́тый.

blasting ['blɑ:stıŋ] *n.* (*of rocks etc.*) подрывны́е рабо́ты (*f. pl.*).

blatant ['bleıt(ə)nt] *adj.* крикли́вый; бессты́дный; (*flagrant*) я́вный.

blaz|e[1] [bleız] *n.* **1.** (*of fire*) пла́мя (*nt.*); **burst into a ~e** запыла́ть (*pf.*). **2.** (*of colour, light*) я́ркость; **the garden was a ~e of colour** сад пыла́л я́ркими кра́сками. **3.** (*conflagration*) пожа́р. **4.** (*fig.*): **~e of publicity** шу́мная рекла́ма. **5.** (*expletive*): **go to ~es!** иди́/убира́йся к чёрту!; **what the ~es do you want?** како́го чёрта вам на́до?; **run like ~es** нести́сь, по- (*det.*) сломя́ го́лову.

v.i.: **a fire was ~ing in the hearth** в ками́не пыла́л ого́нь; **the building was ~ing** зда́ние полыха́ло; **he was ~ing with anger** он пыла́л гне́вом.

with advs.: **~e away** *v.i.* (*with rifle etc.*) вести́ (*det.*) ого́нь; (*work vigorously*) рабо́тать (*impf.*) вовсю́.

blaze[2] [bleız] *v.t.*: **~ a trail** про|кла́дывать, -ложи́ть путь.

blazer ['bleızə(r)] *n.* ≃ ку́ртка, пиджа́к, бле́йзер.

blazing ['bleızıŋ] *adj.* **1.** (*of fire*) пыла́ющий. **2.** (*of light*) сверка́ющий, сия́ющий. **3.: he was in a ~ fury** он пыла́л я́ростью. **5.** (*coll.*, *expletive*): **what's the ~ hurry?** како́го чёрта торопи́ться?; что за спе́шка, чёрт побери́?

bleach [bli:tʃ] *n.* отбе́ливающее вещество́.

v.t. бели́ть (*impf.*); отбе́л|ивать, -и́ть; **~ing powder** бели́льная и́звесть; (*of hair*) обесцве́|чивать, -тить; **the sun ~ed the curtains** занаве́ски вы́горели на со́лнце.

v.i. беле́ть (*impf.*).

bleak [bli:k] *adj.* уны́лый, безра́достный; (*gloomy*) мра́чный.

bleary-eyed [blɪə(r)] *adj.* с затума́ненными/му́тными глаза́ми.

bleat [bli:t] *n.* бле́яние, мыча́ние.

v.t. & i. мыча́ть (*impf.*), бле́ять (*impf.*).

bleed [bli:d] *v.t.* пус|ка́ть, -ти́ть кровь +*d.*; **~ s.o.** (*for money*) об|ира́ть, -обра́ть кого́-н.; **~ s.o. white** (*fig.*) обескро́в|ливать -ить кого́-н.

v.i. (*of pers.*) ист|ека́ть, -е́чь кро́вью; (*of wound*) кровоточи́ть (*impf.*); **his nose is ~ing** у него́ кровь идёт но́сом; **he bled to death** он у́мер от поте́ри кро́ви; **my heart ~s for him** у меня́ се́рдце кро́вью облива́ется при мы́сли о нём.

bleeding ['bli:dɪŋ] *n.* кровотече́ние (*from the nose*: из носу).

adj. кровото́чащий; истека́ющий кро́вью.

blemish ['blemɪʃ] *n.* (*defect*) недоста́ток, изъя́н; (*stain*) пятно́.

v.t. пятна́ть, за.

blend [blend] *n.* смесь; (*of colours*) сочета́ние.

v.t. сме́ш|ивать, -а́ть; (*colours, ideas*) сочета́ть (*impf.*); **the two rivers ~ their waters** э́ти две реки́ слива́ются.

v.i. сме́ш|иваться, -а́ться; (*of colours, ideas*) сочета́ться (*impf.*); гармони́ровать (*impf.*); (*of sounds, waters*) слива́ться, -и́ться.

blender ['blendə(r)] *n.* (*cul.*) смеси́тель (*m.*), ми́ксер.

bless [bles] *v.t.* **1.** (*relig.*) благослов|ля́ть, -и́ть; **~ me!, ~ my soul!** Го́споди, поми́луй!; **(God) ~ you!** дай вам Бог здоро́вья; (*after sneeze*) бу́дьте здоро́вы!; **~ o.s.** (*cross o.s.*) перекрести́ться (*pf.*). **2.** (*prosper, favour*): **he was ~ed with good health** Бог награди́л его́ здоро́вьем.

blessed ['blesɪd, blest] *adj.* **1.** (*holy*) благослове́нный; **of ~ memory** блаже́нной па́мяти. **2.** (*happy*) блаже́нный, благослове́нный.

blessing ['blesɪŋ] *n.* **1.** благослове́ние; **give, pronounce a ~ upon** благослов|ля́ть, -и́ть; **ask, say a ~** (*at meal*) произн|оси́ть, -ести́ засто́льную моли́тву; **with official ~** с благослове́ния нача́льства. **2.: the ~s of civilization** блага́ цивилиза́ции; **what a ~ that he came!** како́е сча́стье, что он пришёл!

blight [blaɪt] *n.* **1.** (*disease*) головня́; ржа. **2.: it cast a ~ on her youth** э́то омрачи́ло её ю́ность.

v.t. **1.** пора|жа́ть, -зи́ть ржой. **2.: ~ s.o.'s hopes** разр|уша́ть, -у́шить чьи-н. наде́жды; (*career, plans*) погуби́ть (*pf.*).

blighted ['blaɪtəd] *adj.* (*of plants*) поги́бший; поражённый ржой; (*of plans etc.*) погу́бленный.

blind [blaɪnd] *n.* (*screen*) што́ра, ста́вень (*m.*); **Venetian ~** жалюзи́ (*nt. indecl.*); **shop ~** (*over pavement*) марки́за, тент.

adj. **1.** слепо́й; **the ~** (*as n.*) слепы́е, слепцы́ (*m. pl.*); **as ~ as a bat** слепа́я ку́рица; **~ in one eye** слепо́й на оди́н глаз; криво́й; **go ~, be struck ~** осле́пнуть (*pf.*); **~ spot** слепо́е пятно́; (*fig.*) пробе́л; **~ man's buff** жму́р|ки (*pl., g.* -ок); **turn a ~ eye to sth.** закр|ыва́ть, -ы́ть глаза́ на что-н. **2.** (*concealed*): **a ~ corner** непросма́тривающийся поворо́т; **a ~ date** (*coll.*) свида́ние с незнако́мым/незнако́мой. **3.** (*closed up*): **a ~ alley** (*lit., fig.*) тупи́к. **4.: he didn't take a ~ bit of notice** (*coll.*) он э́то абсолю́тно проигнори́ровал.

adv.: **fly ~** лета́ть (*indet.*) по прибо́рам; **~ drunk** мертве́цки пья́ный.

v.t. ослеп|ля́ть, -и́ть (*also fig.*); (*temporarily*) слепи́ть (*impf.*); **he was ~ed, went ~ in the left eye** он осле́п на ле́вый глаз.

cpd. **~fold** *adj.* с завя́занными глаза́ми; *adv.* (*recklessly*) вслепу́ю; *v.t.* завя́з|ывать, -а́ть глаза́ +*d.*

blindly ['blaɪndlɪ] *adv.* (*gropingly*) о́щупью; (*recklessly*) сле́по.

blindness ['blaɪndnɪs] *n.* слепота́; (*fig.*) ослепле́ние.

blink [blɪŋk] *n.* (*of eye*) морга́ние, мига́ние; (*of light*) мерца́ние; про́блеск.

v.t. & i. (*of pers.*) миг|а́ть, -ну́ть; морг|а́ть, -ну́ть; (*of light*) мерца́ть (*impf.*); **~ at** (*fig., ignore*) закр|ыва́ть, -ы́ть глаза́ на+*a.*

blinkers ['blɪŋkəz] *n.* шо́р|ы (*pl., g.* —) (*also fig.*); нагла́зники (*m. pl.*).

bliss [blɪs] *n.* блаже́нство.

blissful ['blɪsfʊl] *adj.* блаже́нный.

blister ['blɪstə(r)] *n.* (*on skin*) волды́рь (*m.*); (*on paint*) пузы́рь (*m.*).

v.t. вызыва́ть, вы́звать волдыри́/пузыри́ на+*p.*

v.i. покр|ыва́ться, -ы́ться волдыря́ми/пузыря́ми.

blithe ['blaɪð] *adj.* жизнера́достный, беспе́чный.

blitz [blɪts] *n.* бомбёжка.

v.t. разбомби́ть (*pf.*).

blitzkrieg ['blɪtskri:g] *n.* молниено́сная война́.

blizzard ['blɪzəd] *n.* бура́н, вью́га.

bloated ['bləʊtɪd] *adj.* (*swollen*) разду́тый, разду́вшийся.

blob [blɒb] *n.* ка́пля; ша́рик.

bloc [blɒk] *n.* блок.

block [blɒk] *n.* **1.** (*of wood*) чурба́н, коло́да; (*of stone, marble*) глы́ба; **~ of soap** брусо́к мы́ла; **children's ~s** ку́бики (*m. pl.*). **2.** (*for execution*) пла́ха. **3.** (*of houses*) кварта́л; (*of shares, tickets etc.*) па́чка; **~ of flats** многокварти́рный дом. **4.** (*for hats*) болва́нка, болва́н. **5.** (*for lifting*: *also* **~ and tackle**) блок, лебёдка. **6.: writing ~** блокно́т. **7.** (*obstruction*): **~ in a pipe** заку́порка трубы́; **traffic ~** про́бка; (*fig.*): **mental ~** у́мственное торможе́ние. **8.** (*stolid person*) бревно́. **9.: ~ voting** представи́тельное голосова́ние; **in ~** целико́м; в це́лом.

v.t. **1.** (*obstruct physically*): **roads ~ed by snow** доро́ги, занесённые сне́гом; **~ (up) an entrance** загор|а́живать, -оди́ть вход; **mud ~ed the pipe** грязь заби́ла трубу́; **the sink is ~ed** ра́ковина засори́лась; **~ s.o.'s way** прегра|жда́ть, -ди́ть кому́-н. путь. **2.** (*fig.*): **~ the enemy's plan** срыва́ть, сорва́ть пла́ны неприя́теля. **3.: ~ in, out** (*sketch*) набр|а́сывать, -оса́ть.

cpds. **~head** *n.* болва́н, тупи́ца (*c.g.*); **~house** *n.* блокга́уз.

blockade [blɒ'keɪd] *n.* блока́да; **raise a ~** снять (*pf.*) блока́ду.

v.t. блоки́ровать (*impf., pf.*).

bloke [bləʊk] *n.* (*coll.*) тип; па́рень (*m.*).

blond(e) [blɒnd] *n.* блонди́н (*fem.* -ка).

adj. белоку́рый, све́тлый.

blood [blʌd] *n.* **1.** кровь; **the ~ rushed to his head** кровь бро́силась/уда́рила ему́ в го́лову; **hands covered with ~** ру́ки в крови́; **sweat ~** рабо́тать (*impf.*) до крова́вого по́та; **taste ~** вку|ша́ть, -си́ть кро́ви. **2.** (*attr.*): **~ bank** до́норский пункт; **~ clot** сгу́сток кро́ви; **~ donor** до́нор; **~ orange** королёк; **~ plasma** пла́зма; **~ sports** охо́та; **~ test** ана́лиз кро́ви; (*for paternity*) иссле́дование кро́ви; **~ transfusion** перелива́ние кро́ви; *see also cpds.* **3.** (*var. fig. uses*): **it made my ~ boil** э́то меня́ взбеси́ло; **his ~ ran cold** кровь сты́ла/ледене́ла у него́ в жи́лах; **in cold ~** хладнокро́вно; **we need new ~** нам нужны́ но́вые си́лы; **there is bad ~ between them** они́ вражду́ют. **4.** (*lineage, kinship*): **blue ~** голуба́я кровь; **~ is thicker than water** кровь не води́ца.

cpds. **~-and-thunder** *adj.* (*story etc.*) по́лный у́жасов; **~-bath** *n.* крова́вая ба́ня; **~curdling** *adj.* леденя́щий кровь; **~-heat** *n.* температу́ра человéческого тéла; **~hound** *n.* ищéйка; **~-letting** *n.* (*med.*) кровопускáние; (*bloodshed*) кровопролúтие; **~-poisoning** *n.* заражéние крóви; **~-pressure** *n.* кровянóе давлéние; **~shed** *n.* кровопролúтие; **~shot** *adj.* нáлитый крóвью; **~stain** *n.* кровáвое пятнó; **~stained** *adj.* запáчканный крóвью; **~stained hands** рýки в кровú; **~stone** *n.* гелиотрóп, кровáвик; **~stream** *n.* ток крóви; **~sucker** *n.* (*insect*) пиявка; (*fig.*) кровопúйца (*c.g.*); **~thirsty** *adj.* кровожáдный; **~-vessel** *n.* кровенóсный сосýд.

bloodless [ˈblʌdlɪs] *adj.* бескрóвный.

bloody [ˈblʌdɪ] *adj.* **1.** кровáвый; (*smeared with blood*) окровáвленный; **give s.o. a ~ nose** разбúть (*pf.*) комý-н. нос в кровь. **2.** (*expletive*): **a ~ liar** отчáянный лгун; **stop that ~ row!** прекратúте э́тот чёртов скандáл!; **not a ~ thing** ни чертá/хренá; **no ~ fear!; not ~ likely!** чёрта с два!; фиг-то!

adv. (*sl.*): **~ awful** чертóвский; сквéрный.

v.t. окровáвить (*pf.*).

cpds. **~-minded** *adj.* (*coll.*, *obstructive*) зловрéдный; **~-mindedness** *n.* зловрéдность.

bloom [blu:m] *n.* **1.** (*flower*) цвет; цветы́ (*m. pl.*); (*single flower*) цветóк; **in ~** в цветý; **burst into ~** расцве|тáть, -стú. **2.** (*prime*) расцвéт; **in the ~ of youth** в расцвéте ю́ности. **3.** (*on cheeks*) румя́нец. **4.** (*down*) пушóк.

v.i. цвестú (*impf.*); (*come into ~*) расцве|тáть, -стú; **finish ~ing** отцве|тáть, -стú.

bloomer [ˈblu:mə(r)] *n.* **1.** (*coll.*, *mistake*) прóмах; (*in speech*) оговóрка; **make a ~** дéлать, с- прóмах; огов|áриваться, -орúться. **2.** (*pl.*) (*undergarment*) панталóн|ы (*pl.*, *g.* —).

blooming [ˈblu:mɪŋ] *adj.* (*flowering*, *flourishing*) цветýщий; (*expletive*): **a ~ fool** набúтый дурáк.

blossom [ˈblɒsəm] *n.* цвет, цветéние; **in ~** в цветý; **come into ~** расцве|тáть, -стú.

v.i. цвестú (*impf.*); **finish ~ing** отцве|тáть, -стú; (*fig.*): **he ~ed into a statesman** он вы́рос в госудáрственного дéятеля.

blot [blɒt] *n.* (*on paper*) кля́кса; (*blemish*) пятнó; **it is a ~ on the landscape** э́то пóртит вид/пейзáж.

v.t. & i. **1.** (*smudge*) пáчкать, за-; стáвить, по- кля́ксу. **2.** (*dry*) промок|áть, -нýть; **~ting-pad** бювáр; **~ting-paper** промокáтельная бумáга. **3.** (*sully*) пятнáть, за-; **~ one's copybook** (*fig.*) пятнáть, за- свою́ репутáцию; **without a ~ on one's character** с незапя́тнанной репутáцией.

with adv.: **~ out** *v.t.* (*from one's memory*) изглá|живать, -дить (or ст|ирáть, -ерéть) из пáмяти; (*a view*) закр|ывáть, -ы́ть; заслон|я́ть, -úть.

blotch [blɒtʃ] *n.* пятнó; (*of ink*) кля́кса.

blotter [ˈblɒtə(r)] *n.* бювáр.

blouse [blaʊz] *n.* (*workman's*) блýза; (*woman's*) кóфточка, блýзка.

blow[1] [bləʊ] *n.* (*of air*, *wind*) дуновéние, поры́в; **give your nose a good ~!** вы́сморкайся хорошéнько (*or* как слéдует).

v.t. **1.** дуть, дýнуть; **~ a horn** дуть, дýнуть в рог; трубúть (*impf.*); **~ a whistle** свистéть, за- в свистóк; дать (*pf.*) свистóк; **~ one's nose** сморк|áться, -нýться; **~ the dust off a book** сду|вáть, -ть пыль с кнúги; **~ s.o. a kiss** пос|ылáть, -лáть комý-н. воздýшный поцелýй; **~ bubbles** пускáть (*impf.*) пузырú; **~ one's own trumpet** (*fig.*) хвалúться, похваля́ться (*both impf.*). **2.** (*of wind*): **the ship was ~n off course** корáбль снеслó с кýрса; **the wind blew the papers out of my hand** вéтер вы́рвал бумáги у меня́ из рук; **he was ~n ashore** егó вы́несло на бéрег; **we were ~n out to sea** нас унеслó в мóре. **3.** (*with bellows*): **he blew the fire** он раздýл огóнь. **4.** (*elec.*): **~ a fuse** переж|игáть, -éчь прóбку. **5.: ~ £25 on a dinner** прсá|живать, -дúть (*coll.*) 25 фýнтов на обéд. **6.** (*coll.*, *curse*): **I'm ~ed if I know** ей-Бóгу, не знáю; **well, I'm ~ed!** так тáк!; вóт-те рáз!

v.i. **1.** (*of wind or pers*) дуть, по-, дýнуть; **it is ~ing hard** сúльно дýет; óчень вéтрено; **~ hot and cold** (*fig.*) поминýтно меня́ть (*impf.*) мнéние. **2.** (*of thg.*): **the door blew open** дверь распахнýлась; **dust blew into the room** пыль налетéла в кóмнату; **the whistle blew** раздáлся свистóк; гудóк загудéл; **the fuse blew** прóбка перегорéла.

with advs.: **~ about** *v.t.*: **the wind blew her hair about** вéтер развевáл её вóлосы; *v.i.*: **the leaves blew about** носúлись лúстья; **~ away** *v.t. & i.* ун|осúть(ся), -естú(сь); **~ down** *v.t.* валúть, по-; **he was blown down from the roof** егó снеслó с кры́ши; *v.i.*: **the tree blew down** бýря повалúла дéрево; **~ in** *v.t.*: **the gale blew the windows in** ураráном разбúло óкна; *v.i.*: **the wind blows in through the door** вéтер дýет в дверь; **~ off** *v.t.*: **the wind blew his hat off** вéтер сорвáл с негó шля́пу; *v.i.*: **his hat blew off** у негó слетéла шля́па; **~ out** *v.t.*: **he blew the candle out** он задýл свечý; **~ one's brains out** пустúть (*pf.*) себé пýлю в лоб; **the bomb blew out the doors** от взры́ва бóмбы вы́летели двéри; *v.i.*: **the candle blew out** свечá погáсла; **~ over** *v.t.*: **he was blown over by the wind** егó свалúло с ног вéтром; *v.i.*: **the storm blew over** бýря утúхла; **~ up** *v.t.*: **~ up a bridge** взрывáть, взорвáть мост; **~ up a tyre** над|увáть, -ýть шúну; **~ up a photograph** увелúчи|вать, -ть фотогрáфию; **the boss blew him up** (*coll.*) начáльник сдéлал емý разнóс; *v.i.*: **the mine blew up** мúна взорвáлась.

cpds. **~-fly** *n.* мяснáя мýха; **~-lamp** *n.* паяльная лáмпа; **~-out** *n.* (*of tyre*) разры́в; **~-out** (*oil*) фонтáн (нéфти); (*coll.*, *feast*) кутёж, пирýшка; **~pipe** *n.* (*tool*) пая́льная трýбка; **~-torch** *n.* пая́льная лáмпа.

blow[2] [bləʊ] *n.* (*lit.*, *fig.*: *stroke*) удáр; **deliver, deal, strike a ~** нан|осúть, -естú удáр; **at a ~** однúм удáром; **they came to ~s** онú подрáлись; **without striking a ~** без дрáки; **her death was a ~ to us** её смерть былá удáром для нас; **it was a ~ to our hopes** э́то разбúло нáши надéжды.

blowy [ˈbləʊɪ] *adj.* вéтреный.

blubber [ˈblʌbə(r)] *n.* (*whale-fat*) вóрвань.

bludgeon [ˈblʌdʒ(ə)n] *n.* дубúнка.

v.t. бить (*impf.*) дубúнкой.

blue [blu:] *n.* **1.** (*colour*) синевá, голубизнá; **navy ~** тёмно-сúний цвет. **2.** (*sky*): **out of the ~** (*fig.*) ни с тогó ни с сегó; **he arrived out of the ~** он нагря́нул неожúданно; **like a bolt from the ~** (*fig.*) как гром средú я́сного нéба. **3.** (*sea*) (сúнее) мóре. **4.: the ~s** (*coll.*) тоскá, уны́ние, хандрá; **have the ~s** хандрúть (*impf.*). **5.: ~s** (*mus.*) блюз.

adj. **1.** (*colour*) (*dark*) сúний; (*light*) голубóй; **her hands were ~ with cold** её рýки посинéли от хóлода; **his arms are ~ (with bruises)** у негó все рýки в синякáх; **he shouted till he was ~ in the face** он кричáл до изнеможéния; **once in a ~ moon** раз в сто лет; **scream ~ murder** кричáть (*impf.*) во всю глóтку; **~ blood** голубáя кровь. **2.** (*coll.*, *sad*): **feel ~** хандрúть (*impf.*); **look ~** (*of pers.*) вы́глядеть (*impf.*) уны́лым.

v.t. (*of laundry*) синúть (*impf.*); подсúн|ивать, -úть.

cpds. **~bell** *n.* колокóльчик; **~bottle** *n.* мяснáя мýха; **~-eyed** *adj.* синеглáзый, голубоглáзый; ; **~-grey** *adj.* сúзый; **~print** *n.* (*phot.*) светокóпия, сúнька; (*fig.*) намётка.

bluff[1] [blʌf] *n.* (*headland*) утёс.

adj. (*of cliffs etc.*) обры́вистый, отвéсный; (*of pers.*) грубовáто-добродýшный; прямодýшный.

bluff[2] [blʌf] *n.* блеф; **call s.o.'s ~** застáвить когó-н. раскры́ть кáрты.

v.t. & i. блефова́ть (*impf.*); втира́ть (*impf.*) очки́ +*d.*; пуска́ть (*impf.*) пыль в глаза́ +*d.*

bluish ['blu:ɪʃ] *adj.* синева́тый; голубова́тый.

blunder ['blʌndə(r)] *n.* оши́бка, оплóшность.

v.i. блужда́ть (*impf.*); (*grope*) óщупью пробира́ться/дви́гаться (*impf.*); ~ **into a table** наткну́ться/натолкну́ться (*pf.*) на стол; ~ **through one's work** де́лать (*impf.*) рабо́ту ко́е-как.

blunderbuss ['blʌndə,bʌs] *n.* мушкето́н.

blunt [blʌnt] *adj.* (*not sharp*) тупо́й; **a ~ pencil** неотто́ченный каранда́ш; (*plain-spoken*) прямо́й.

v.t. тупи́ть (*impf.*); **~ a needle** притуп|ля́ть, -и́ть иглу́; **~ a knife/scissors** затуп|ля́ть, -и́ть нож/но́жницы; (*feelings etc.*) притуп|ля́ть, -и́ть.

bluntness ['blʌntnɪs] *n.* (*lit.*) ту́пость; (*frankness*) прямота́.

blur [blɜ:(r)] *n.* (*confused effect*) ды́мка; **she saw him through a ~ of tears** она́ ви́дела его́ сквозь ды́мку слёз.

v.t. (*make indistinct*) сма́з|ывать, -ать; (*fig.*) зату-ма́ни|вать, -ть; затемн|я́ть, -и́ть.

blurb [blɜ:b] *n.* (*coll.*) (изда́тельская) аннота́ция.

blurry ['blɜ:rɪ] *adj.* затума́ненный.

blurt [blɜ:t] *v.t.*: **~ out** выпа́ливать, вы́палить.

blush [blʌʃ] *n.* **1.** кра́ска; **spare s.o.'s ~es** пощади́ть (*pf.*) чью-н. стыдли́вость; **a ~ rose to her cheeks** кра́ска залила́ её щёки. **2.** (*glow*) румя́нец.

v.i. красне́ть, по-; зарде́ться (*pf.*).

blushing ['blʌʃɪŋ] *adj.* (*modest*) засте́нчивый, стыдли́вый; **a ~ bride** стыдли́вая неве́ста.

bluster ['blʌstə(r)] *n.* (*of storm*) рёв; (*of pers.*) гро́мкие слова́, угро́зы (*f. pl.*).

v.i. (*of storm*) реве́ть (*impf.*); (*of pers.*) расшуме́ться (*pf.*), разбушева́ться (*pf.*).

BO (*abbr. of* ***body odour***) дурно́й за́пах (те́ла).

boa ['bəʊə] *n.* (*zool.*) боа́ (*m. indecl.*); **~ constrictor** уда́в; (*wrap*) боа́ (*nt. indecl.*).

boar [bɔ:(r)] *n.* каба́н.

board [bɔ:d] *n.* **1.** (*piece of wood*) доска́ (*also for chess etc.*); **~ game** насто́льная игра́. **2.** (*pl., theatr.*) подмо́стк|и (*pl., g.* -ов); **go on the ~s** пойти́ (*pf.*) на сце́ну. **3.** (*pl., cover of book*) переплёт; **cloth ~s** коленко́ровый переплёт. **4.** (*food*) стол; **~ and lodging; bed and ~** кварти́ра и стол; **full ~** по́лный пансио́н. **5.** (*table*): **above ~** (*fig.*) в откры́тую, че́стно; **sweep the ~** (*at cards*) заб|ира́ть, -ра́ть все ста́вки. **6.** (*council*) правле́ние; **~ of enquiry** коми́ссия по рассле́дованию; **~ of directors** правле́ние дирекbuilt торо́в. **7.** (*naut. etc.*): **on ~** на борту́; **come, go on ~ a ship/aircraft** сади́ться, сесть на кора́бль/самолёт.

v.t. **1.** (*cover with ~s; also ~* **up**) обш|ива́ть, -и́ть (*or* покр|ыва́ть, -ы́ть) до́сками. **2.:** **~ a ship** (*go on ~*) сади́ться, сесть на кора́бль; (*attack*) брать, взять кора́бль на абorда́ж.

v.i. (*reside*) жить (*impf.*) на по́лном пансио́не; (*at school*) быть пансионе́ром.

cpds. **~-room** *n.* помеще́ние правле́ния директоро́в; **~walk** *n.* доща́тый насти́л.

boarder ['bɔ:də(r)] *n.* пансионе́р (*also at school*) (*fem.* -ка); жиле́ц; **take in ~s** брать (*impf.*) жильцо́в.

boarding ['bɔ:dɪŋ] *n.* **1.** (*boards*) обши́вка до́сками. **2.** (*naut.*) аборда́ж; (*aeron.*) поса́дка.

cpds. **~-card** *n.* поса́дочный биле́т; **~-house** *n.* пансио́н; **~-school** *n.* шко́ла-интерна́т.

boast [bəʊst] *n.* хвастовство́; **their ~ is that ...** они́ похваля́ются тем, что...; (*pers. or thg. ~ed of*) го́рдость, предме́т го́рдости.

v.t. & i. **1.** (*~ of*) хва́стать(ся), по- +*i.*; хвали́ться (*or* похваля́ться), по- +*i.*; **it is nothing to ~ of** похва́статься не́чем. **2.** (*possess*) горди́ться (*impf.*) +*i.*

boaster ['bəʊstə(r)] *n.* хвасту́н (*fem.* -ья).

boastful ['bəʊstfʊl] *adj.* хвастли́вый.

boat [bəʊt] *n.* (*small, rowing ~*) ло́дка, шлю́пка; (*vessel*) су́дно; (*large ~*) кора́бль (*m.*), парохо́д; **in the same ~** (*fig.*) в одина́ковом положе́нии; **burn one's ~s** (*fig.*) сжечь (*pf.*) (свой) корабли́; **miss the ~** (*fig.*) прозева́ть (*pf.*) слу́чай.

v.i. (*go ~ing*) ката́ться (*indet.*) на ло́дке.

cpds. **~-hook** *n.* баго́р; **~house** *n.* э́ллинг; **~man** *n.* ло́дочник; **~swain** *n.* бо́цман.

boater ['bəʊtə(r)] *n.* соло́менная шля́па.

bob[1] [bɒb] *n.* **1.** (*weight*) подве́сок; (*on fishing-line*) поплаво́к. **2.** (*hair-style*) коро́ткая стри́жка.

v.t. (*of hair*) ко́ротко стричь (*impf.*).

cpd. **~tail** *n.* (*tail*) обре́занный хвост; ку́цый хвост.

bob[2] [bɒb] *n.* (*jerk, e.g. of the head*) киво́к; (*curtsey*) приседа́ние, рэвера́нс.

v.i. **1.** (*move up and down*) подпры́г|ивать, -нуть; **~ up** выска́кивать, вы́скочить. **2.** (*curtsey*) прис|еда́ть, -е́сть; **she ~bed him a curtsey** она́ присе́ла в рэвера́нсе пе́ред ним.

bob[3] [bɒb] *n.* (*coll., shilling*) ши́ллинг.

bob[4] [bɒb] *n.*: **~'s your uncle** (*coll.*) всё в поря́дке.

bobbin ['bɒbɪn] *n.* (*reel, spool*) кату́шка, шпу́лька.

bobble ['bɒb(ə)l] *n.* помпо́н(чик).

bobby ['bɒbɪ] *n.* (*coll.*) полисме́н.

bob-sled ['bɒbsled], **bob-sleigh** ['bɒbsleɪ] *nn.* бо́бслей.

bode [bəʊd] *v.t. & i.*: **~ ill/well** предвеща́ть (*impf.*) недо́брое/хоро́шее; **it ~s no good** э́то не предвеща́ет ничего́ хоро́шего.

bodice ['bɒdɪs] *n.* корса́ж, лиф.

bodily ['bɒdɪlɪ] *adj.* теле́сный, физи́ческий; **~ harm** физи́ческое поврежде́ние.

adv.: **he was carried ~ to the doors** его́ на рука́х вы́несли к дверя́м; **the house was moved ~** дом был передви́нут целико́м.

body ['bɒdɪ] *n.* **1.** (*of pers. or animal*) те́ло; (*build*) телосложе́ние; **strong in ~** физи́чески си́льный; **keep ~ and soul together** своди́ть (*impf.*) концы́ с конца́ми; **he is ours ~ and soul** он пре́дан нам душо́й и те́лом. **2.** (*trunk*) ту́ловище, торс. **3.** (*dead person*) мёртвое те́ло; уби́т|ый (*fem.* -ая); **~ bag** похоро́нный мешо́к; **~ count** поте́ри уби́тыми. **4.** (*main portion*): **the ~ of a hall/building** гла́вная часть за́ла/зда́ния; (*of ship*) ко́рпус; (*of car*) ку́зов; (*of aircraft*) фюзеля́ж; **the ~ of his supporters** все его́ сторо́нники; (*of letter, book*) основна́я часть. **5.** (*quantity, aggregate*) ма́сса, гру́ппа; **~ of evidence** совоку́пность доказа́тельств. **6.** (*group, institution, system*): **governing ~** о́рган управле́ния; **legislative ~** законода́тельный о́рган; **learned ~** учёное о́бщество; **public ~** обще́ственная организа́ция; **in a ~** в по́лном соста́ве; **main ~** (*mil.*) гла́вные си́лы (*f. pl.*); **~ of cavalry** отря́д кавале́рии. **7.** (*object*) те́ло; **the heavenly bodies** небе́сные тела́. **9.** (*strength, consistency*) консисте́нция, вя́зкость.

cpds. **~-blow** *n.* (*lit.*) уда́р в ко́рпус; (*fig.*) сокруши́тельный уда́р; **~-builder** *n.* (*pers.*) культури́ст; (*apparatus*) экспанде́р; **~-building** *n.* культури́зм; **~guard** *n.* телохрани́тель (*m.*); **~-snatcher** *n.* похити́тель (*m.*) тру́пов; **~-stocking** *n.* трико́ (*indecl.*); **~warmer** *n.* телогре́йка; **~work** *n.* (*of vehicle*) ку́зов.

Boer ['bəʊə(r), bʊə(r)] *n.* бур.

adj. бу́рский; **~ War** а́нгло-бу́рская война́.

bog [bɒg] *n.* боло́то, тряси́на.

v.t.: **get ~ged down** (*fig.*) увя́знуть, завя́знуть (*both pf.*).

bogeyman ['bəʊgɪ,mæn] = **bogyman**

boggle ['bɒg(ə)l] *v.i.* отша́т|ываться, -ну́ться; отпря́нуть (*pf.*); **the mind ~s** уму́ непостижи́мо.

boggy ['bɒgɪ] *adj.* боло́тистый.

bogus ['bəʊgəs] *adj.* фикти́вный, притво́рный.

bog|yman, -eyman ['bəʊgɪˌmæn] *n.* бу́ка, пу́гало.
Bohemian [bəʊ'hi:mɪən] *adj.* (*fig.*) боге́мный.
boil[1] [bɔɪl] *n.* (*tumour*) нары́в, чи́рей.
boil[2] [bɔɪl] *v.t.* (*state of* ~*ing*) кипе́ние; **come to the** ~ вскипе́ть (*pf.*), закипе́ть (*pf.*); **bring to the** ~ довести́ (*pf.*) до кипе́ния; **be on the** ~ кипе́ть (*impf.*); **go off the** ~ переста́ть (*pf.*) кипе́ть.
v.t.: ~ **water** кипяти́ть, вс- во́ду; ~ **fish/an egg** вари́ть, с- ры́бу/яйцо́.
v.i.: **the water is** ~**ing** вода́ кипи́т; **the egg has** ~**ed** яйцо́ свари́лось; **the kettle has** ~**ed dry** ча́йник совсе́м вы́кипел.
with advs.: ~**away** *v.i.*: **the kettle was** ~**ing away** ча́йник кипе́л вовсю́; ~ **down** *v.t.* (*lit.*) выпа́ривать; вы́парить; (*abridge*) сж|има́ть, -ать; *v.i.*: **it** ~**s down to this, that ...** э́то сво́дится к тому́, что...; ~ **over** *v.i.* (*lit.*) убе|га́ть, -жа́ть че́рез край; **the milk** ~**ed over** молоко́ убежа́ло; (*fig., with rage*) вскипе́ть (*pf.*); **he was** ~**ing over** всё в нём кипе́ло; ~ **up** *v.t.* вскипяти́ть (*pf.*); *v.i.* вскип|а́ть, -е́ть.
boiler ['bɔɪlə(r)] *n.* кипяти́льный котёл, бо́йлер; (*of steam engine*) парово́й котёл; (*for domestic heating*) котёл отопле́ния; бо́йлер; (*for laundry*) бак.
cpds. ~**-house** *n.* коте́льная; ~**-maker** *n.* коте́льщик; ~**-suit** *n.* комбинезо́н.
boiling ['bɔɪlɪŋ] *n.* кипе́ние, кипяче́ние, ва́рка.
adj. (*also of waves etc.*) кипя́щий; ~ **water** кипято́к; ~ **hot** горя́чий, как кипято́к; **a** ~ **hot day** зно́йный день.
cpd. ~**-point** *n.* то́чка кипе́ния.
boisterous ['bɔɪstərəs] *adj.* бу́йный, шумли́вый.
bold [bəʊld] *n.* (*typ.*) жи́рный шрифт.
adj. **1.** сме́лый, отва́жный; **grow** ~ осмеле́ть (*pf.*); **make so** ~ **as to** осме́ли|ваться, -ться; **make** ~ **with sth.** во́льно обраща́ться (*impf.*) с чем-н.; (*impudent*) наха́льный; **as** ~ **as brass** бессты́жий. **2.** (*prominent*): ~ **features** ре́зкие черты́ лица́. **3.** (*clear*) чёткий.
cpds. ~**-face** *n.* (*typ.*) жи́рный шрифт; ~**-faced** *adj.* (*impudent*) на́глый, бессты́жий; (*of type*) жи́рный.
boldness ['bəʊldnɪs] *n.* сме́лость, отва́жность; (*impudence*) на́глость.
Bolivia [bəl'ɪvɪə] *n.* Боли́вия.
boll [bəʊl] *n.* семенна́я коро́бочка.
cpd. ~**-weevil** *n.* долгоно́сик.
bollard ['bɒlɑ:d] *n.* (*on ship or quay*) пал; (*on traffic island*) ту́мба.
Bolshevi|k ['bɒlʃəvɪk], **-st** ['bɒlʃəvɪst] *nn.* большеви́|к (*fem.* -чка).
adj. большеви́стский.
Bolshevism ['bɒlʃəˌvɪz(ə)m] *n.* большеви́зм.
bolster ['bəʊlstə(r)] *n.* ва́лик; (*fig.*) опо́ра.
v.t. (*prop; also fig.*) подп|ира́ть, -ере́ть.
bolt[1] [bəʊlt] *n.* **1.** (*on door etc.*) засо́в, задви́жка. **2.** (*screw*) болт. **3.** (*thunderbolt*) уда́р гро́ма. **5.** (*measure of cloth*) руло́н.
adv.: ~ **upright** пря́мо; вы́тянувшись.
v.t.: ~ **the door** зап|ира́ть, -ере́ть дверь на засо́в/задви́жку.
v.i.: **the door** ~**s on the inside** дверь запира́ется изнутри́.
bolt[2] [bəʊlt] *n.* (*escape*): **make a** ~ **for it** удра́ть (*pf.*); дать (*pf.*) стрекача́.
v.t. (*gulp down*) глота́ть, проглоти́ть.
v.i. (*of horse*) понести́ (*pf.*); (*of pers.*) помча́ться (*pf.*), удра́ть (*pf.*).
cpd. ~**-hole** *n.* заго́н; (*fig.*) прибе́жище.
bomb [bɒm] *n.* бо́мба; (*mortar* ~) ми́на; (*shell*) снаря́д; **incendiary** ~ зажига́тельная бо́мба; **drop a** ~ сбро́сить (*pf.*) бо́мбу; ~ **disposal** обезвре́живание неразорва́вшихся бомб; (*fig.*) **to cost a** ~ сто́ить бе́шеных де́нег.
v.t. & i. бомби́ть, раз-.
with advs.: ~ **out** *v.t.* (*a building*) разбомби́ть (*pf.*).
cpds. ~**-bay** *n.* бо́мбовый отсе́к; ~**-proof** *adj.* бомбосто́йкий; ~**shell** *n.* артиллери́йский снаря́д; **the news came as a** ~**shell to them** весть их как гро́мом порази́ла; ~**-shelter** *n.* бомбоубе́жище; ~**-site** *n.* разбомблённый уча́сток.
bombard [bɒm'bɑ:d] *v.t.* **1.** бомби́ть, раз-; бомбардирова́ть (*impf.*); обстре́л|ивать, -ять. **2.** (*fig.*): ~ **s.o. with abuse** ос|ыпа́ть, -ы́пать кого́-н. оскорбле́ниями; ~ **s.o. with questions** бомбардирова́ть (*impf.*) кого́-н. вопро́сами.
bombardier [ˌbɒmbə'dɪə(r)] *n.* бомбарди́р.
bombardment [bɒm'bɑ:dmənt] *n.* бомбардиро́вка, бомбёжка; (*with shells*) артиллери́йский обстре́л.
bombast ['bɒmbæst] *n.* высокопа́рность, напы́щенность.
bombastic [bɒm'bæstɪk] *adj.* высокопа́рный, напы́щенный.
bomber ['bɒmə(r)] *n.* (*aircraft*) бомбардиро́вщик; (*pers.*) бомбомета́тель (*m.*).
bombing ['bɒmɪŋ] *n.* бомбомета́ние, бомбардиро́вка; **precision** ~ прице́льное бомбомета́ние.
bona fide [ˌbəʊnə 'faɪdɪ] *adj.* добросо́вестный, че́стный.
adv. че́стно; без обма́на.
bona fides [ˌbəʊnə 'faɪdi:z] *n.* че́стное наме́рение; че́стность.
bond [bɒnd] *n.* **1.** (*link*) связь; **love of music was a** ~ **between us** нас свя́зывала любо́вь к му́зыке. **2.** (*shackle*): **in** ~**s** в око́вах; в заключе́нии. **3.** (*obligation*) гара́нтия; **his word is as good as his** ~ на его́ сло́во мо́жно положи́ться. **4.** (*fin.*) облига́ция.
v.t. (*comm.*): ~**ed warehouse** приписно́й тамо́женный склад.
cpds. ~**holder** *n.* держа́тель (*m.*) облига́ций; ~**sman** *n.* крепостно́й; (*guarantor*) поручи́тель (*m.*); ~**swoman** *n.* крепостна́я.
bondage ['bɒndɪdʒ] *n.* нево́ля; закрепоще́ние.
bone [bəʊn] *n.* **1.** кость; **drenched to the** ~ промо́кший до косте́й; **he is all skin and** ~ он ко́жа да ко́сти; **I feel in my** ~**s that ...** чу́ет моё се́рдце, что...; **near the** ~ (*coll.*) риско́ванный; **the bare** ~**s** (*of a subject*) элемента́рные поня́тия/зна́ния; **make no** ~**s about sth.** не церемо́ниться (*impf.*) с чем-н.; **he made no** ~**s about telling me ...** он не постесня́лся сказа́ть мне...; ~ **of contention** я́блоко раздо́ра; **I have a** ~ **to pick with you** у меня́ к вам прете́нзия. **2.** (*substance*) кость; **buttons made of** ~ костяны́е пу́говицы; ~ **china** твёрдый англи́йский фарфо́р.
v.t.: ~ **fish/meat** отдел|я́ть, -и́ть ры́бу/мя́со от косте́й.
v.i.: ~ **up on** (*coll.*) зубри́ть, вы́-.
cpds. ~**-dry** *adj.* соверше́нно сухо́й; ~**head** *n.* (*sl.*) ду́рень (*m.*), балда́ (*c.g.*); ~**headed** *adj.* (*sl.*) тупоголо́вый; ~**-idle** *adj.* ужа́сно лени́вый; ~**meal** *n.* костяна́я мука́.
boneless [bəʊnlɪs] *adj.* беско́стный.
boner ['bəʊnə(r)] *n.* (*sl.*) про́мах, оплóшность.
bonfire ['bɒnˌfaɪə(r)] *n.* костёр.
bonkers ['bɒŋkəz] *adj.* (*coll.*): **he's** ~ он чо́кнутый; он с приве́том.
bonnet ['bɒnɪt] *n.* **1.** (*woman's hat*) ка́пор; чепе́ц, че́пчик. **2.** (*of car*) капо́т.
bonny ['bɒnɪ] *adj.* (*comely*) хоро́шенький; (*healthy*): **a** ~ **baby** кре́пкий ребёнок.
bonus ['bəʊnəs] *n.* пре́мия, премиа́льные (*pl.*).
bony ['bəʊnɪ] *adj.* **1.** (*of, like bone*) костяно́й. **2.** (*of pers.*) костяно́й, кости́стый; ~ **fingers** костля́вые па́льцы.
boo [bu:] *n.* ши́канье.
v.t. осви́ст|ывать, -а́ть.
v.i. улюлю́кать (*impf.*).

int. **1.** (*expr. disapproval*) шш!; у-у! **2.** (*used to startle*) у-у!

boob [bu:b] *n.* **1.** (*coll., simpleton*) простофи́ля (*c.g.*), дурале́й. **2.** (*coll., mistake*) прома́шка. **3.** (*pl., breasts*) буфера́ (*m. pl.*) (*sl.*).

v.i. (*coll.*) оплоша́ть (*pf.*); дать (*pf.*) прома́шку.

booby ['bu:bɪ] *n.* дурачо́к, дурале́й.

cpd. **~-trap** *n.* (*mil.*) ми́на-лову́шка; *v.t.* устан|а́вливать, -ови́ть ми́ны-лову́шки в/на+*p*.

book [bʊk] *n.* **1.** кни́га; (*small*) кни́жка; **go by the ~** сле́довать (*impf.*) предписа́нию/пра́вилам. **2.** (*set*): **~ of tickets** па́чка биле́тов; **~ of matches/stamps** кни́жечка спи́чек/ма́рок. **3.** (*account*): **he is on the firm's ~s** (*an employee*) он в шта́те э́той фи́рмы; **keep the ~s** вести́ (*det.*) бухга́лтерские/счётные кни́ги; **in s.o.'s good/bad ~s** на хоро́шем/плохо́м счету́ у кого́-н.; **bring s.o. to ~** призва́ть (*pf.*) кого́-н. к отве́ту; **that suits my ~** э́то меня́ устра́ивает.

v.t. (*reserve, engage*) зака́з|ывать, -а́ть; зан|има́ть, -я́ть; **~ one's passage** купи́ть (*pf.*) биле́т на парохо́д; **I am ~ed (up) on Wednesday** я (по́лностью) за́нят в сре́ду; **~ s.o. in at a hotel** брони́ровать, за- для кого́-н. но́мер в гости́нице.

v.i.: **he ~ed in/out last night** он въе́хал/вы́ехал вчера́ ве́чером.

cpds. **~binder** *n.* переплётчик; **~binding** *n.* переплётное де́ло; **~case** *n.* кни́жный шкаф; (*open-fronted*) кни́жные по́лки (*f. pl.*); **~-ends** *n.* подста́вки (*f. pl.*) для книг; **~-jacket** *n.* суперобло́жка; **~keeper** *n.* бухга́лтер, счетово́д; **~keeping** *n.* бухгалте́рия, счетово́дство; **~-lover** *n.* кни́жник, книголю́б; **~maker** *n.* букме́кер; **~mark(er)** *n.* (кни́жная) закла́дка; **~plate** *n.* экслибрис; **~-post** *n.* бандеро́ль; **by ~-post** бандеро́лью; **~seller** *n.* торго́вец кни́гами; **second-hand ~seller** букини́ст; **~shelf** *n.* кни́жная по́лка; **~shop, ~store** *nn.* кни́жный магази́н; **~stall** *n.* кни́жный кио́ск; **~worm** *n.* (*lit., fig.*) кни́жный червь.

booking ['bʊkɪŋ] *n.* зака́з; **advance ~** предвари́тельный зака́з.

cpds. **~-clerk** *n.* касси́р; **~-office** *n.* биле́тная ка́сса.

bookish ['bʊkɪʃ] *adj.* (*literary, studious*) кни́жный; (*pedantic*) педанти́чный.

bookishness ['bʊkɪʃnɪs] *n.* кни́жность; педанти́чность.

booklet ['bʊklɪt] *n.* брошю́ра, букле́т.

boom[1] [bu:m] *n.* (*of gun, thunder, waves*) гул, ро́кот; (*of voice*) гул; **supersonic ~** сверхзвуково́й хлопо́к.

v.t. & i. (*of gun*) бу́хать (*impf.*), грохота́ть (*impf*); (*of thunder*) глу́хо грохота́ть (*impf.*); (*of waves*) рокота́ть (*impf.*); **the clock ~ed out the hour** часы́ гу́лко про́били час.

int. бум!

boom[2] [bu:m] *n.* (*comm.*) бум, оживле́ние; **~ town** бы́стро расту́щий го́род.

v.i.: **business is ~ing** де́ло процвета́ет.

boomerang ['bu:mə,ræŋ] *n.* бумера́нг.

v.i. (*fig.*): **his plan ~ed** его́ зате́я обрати́лась про́тив него́.

boon [bu:n] *n.* (*favour*) дар, благоде́яние; (*advantage*) бла́го.

boor ['bʊə(r)] *n.* (*peasant*) мужи́к, дереве́нщина (*c.g.*); (*coarse person*) хам, мужи́к.

boorish ['bʊərɪʃ] *adj.* ха́мский, мужи́цкий.

boorishness ['bʊərɪʃnɪs] *n.* ха́мство, мужикова́тость.

boost [bu:st] *n.* **1.** (*advertisement*) реклами́рование, рекла́ма. **2.**: **give a ~ to the economy** стимули́ровать (*impf., pf.*) эконо́мику.

v.t. (*advertise*) реклами́ровать (*impf., pf.*); (*increase*) пов|ыша́ть, -ы́сить; **~ s.o.'s reputation** создава́ть (*impf.*) кому́-н. репута́цию.

booster ['bu:stə(r)] *n.* **1.** (*elec.*) побуди́тель (*m.*), усили́тель (*m.*). **2.**: **~ rocket** раке́тный ускори́тель; **~ injection** (*med.*) повто́рная приви́вка.

boot[1] [bu:t] *n.* **1.** (*footwear*) боти́нок, башма́к; (*knee-length*) сапо́г; **riding ~** (высо́кий) сапо́г; **football ~s** бу́тсы (*f. pl.*); **he is too big for his ~s** он зазна́лся; **the ~ is now on the other foot** тепе́рь уж всё наоборо́т; **put the ~ in** прибе́гнуть (*pf.*) к жёстким ме́рам; **you bet your ~s!** (*coll.*) бу́дьте уве́рены! **2.** (*dismissal*): **give s.o. the ~** вы́турить (*pf.*) (*coll.*) кого́-н. (с рабо́ты); **get the ~** вы́лететь (*pf.*) (*coll.*) (с рабо́ты). **3.** (*of a car*) бага́жник.

v.t.: **~ s.o. out of his job** вы́турить (*pf.*) (*coll.*) кого́-н. (с рабо́ты).

cpds. **~black** *n.* чи́стильщик сапо́г; **~lace** *n.* шнуро́к для боти́нок; **~leg** *n.* (*fig.*): **~leg whisky** контраба́ндное ви́ски; **~legger** *n.* самого́нщик; **~licker** *n.* (*coll.*) лизоблю́д, подхали́м; **~maker** *n.* сапо́жник; **~-polish** *n.* ва́кса.

boot[2] [bu:t] *n.*: **to ~** в прида́чу.

bootee [bu:'ti:] *n.* (*woman's*) да́мский боти́нок; (*child's*) пине́тка; вя́заный башмачо́к.

booth [bu:ð, bu:θ] *n.* бу́дка; (*stall in market*) пала́тка; (*tent at fair*) балага́н; (*polling-~*) каби́на для голосова́ния.

booty ['bu:tɪ] *n.* добы́ча.

booze [bu:z] *n.* вы́пивка; попо́йка; **go on the ~** запи́ть (*pf.*); **be on the ~** пья́нствовать (*impf.*).

v.i. пья́нствовать (*impf.*), выпива́ть (*impf.*).

cpd. **~-up** *n.* попо́йка .

boozer ['bu:zə(r)] *n.* (*pers.*) выпиво́ха (*c.g.*); (*pub*) забега́ловка.

borax ['bɔ:ræks] *n.* бура́; (*attr.*) бо́рный.

border ['bɔ:də(r)] *n.* **1.** (*side, edging*): **~ of a lake** бе́рег о́зера; (*of a sheet of paper*) кайма́; (*of a handkerchief*) каёмка; **a ~ of tulips** бордю́р из тюльпа́нов; **herbaceous ~** бордю́р из многоле́тних цвето́в. **2.** (*frontier*) грани́ца; (*fig.*) грань.

v.t.: **the garden is ~ed by a stream** сад ограни́чен ручьём; вокру́г са́да протека́ет руче́й.

v.i.: **these countries ~ on one another** э́ти стра́ны грани́чат друг с дру́гом; **he is ~ing on sixty** ему́ под шестьдеся́т; **this ~s on fanaticism** э́то грани́чит с фанати́змом.

cpd. **~line** *n.* грани́ца; (*fig.*) грань; (*demarcation line*) демаркацио́нная ли́ния; **a ~line case** промежу́точный слу́чай.

bore[1] [bɔ:(r)] *n.* (*of tube, pipe*) расто́ченное отве́рстие; (*calibre*) кали́бр, кана́л ствола́.

v.t. сверли́ть, про-; бури́ть, про-.

v.i. бури́ть (*impf.*); **~ for oil** бури́ть (*impf.*) в по́исках не́фти.

cpd. **~-hole** *n.* бурова́я сква́жина.

bore[2] [bɔ:(r)] *n.* (*pers.*) ску́чный челове́к; зану́да (*c.g.*); (*thg.*) (что-н.) надое́дливое.

v.t. надо|еда́ть, -е́сть +*d*.

bored ['bɔ:d] *adj.* скуча́ющий; **I am ~** мне ску́чно; **in a ~ voice** ску́чным/скуча́ющим го́лосом; **I am ~ with him** он мне надое́л.

boredom ['bɔ:dəm] *n.* ску́ка, тоска́.

boric ['bɔ:rɪk] *adj.* бо́рный.

boring ['bɔ:rɪŋ] *adj.* (*tedious*) ску́чный, надое́дливый.

born [bɔ:n] *adj.* **1.**: **a ~ poet/fool** прирождённый поэ́т/дура́к. **2.**: **be ~** роди́ться (*pf.*); **he was ~ with a silver spoon in his mouth** он роди́лся в соро́чке; **I wasn't ~ yesterday** я не вчера́ роди́лся. **3.**: **in all my ~ days** за всю мою́ жизнь.

Borneo ['bɔ:nɪ,əʊ] *n.* Борне́о (*indecl.*).

boron ['bɔ:rɒn] *n.* бор.

borough ['bʌrə] *n.* (*town*) го́род; (*section of town*) райо́н; **parliamentary ~** го́род, предста́вленный в парла́менте.

borrow ['bɒrəʊ] *v.t. & i.* **1.** (*take for a time*) брать, взять на вре́мя; заи́мствовать, по-; зан|има́ть, -я́ть (*also math.*); (*money*) брать, взять взаймы́; **he is always ~ing** он постоя́нно берёт взаймы́ (*or* в долг); ~ **an idea from s.o.** заимствовать (*impf.*, *pf.*) у кого́-н. иде́ю. **2.** (*ling.*) заи́мствовать (*impf.*).

borrowing ['bɒrəʊɪŋ] *n.* **1.** ода́лживание; ~ **is a bad habit** брать взаймы́ — плоха́я привы́чка. **2.** (*ling.*) заи́мствование.

bor(t)sch [bɔːʃ] *n.* борщ.

borzoi ['bɔːzɔɪ] *n.* ру́сская борза́я.

Bosnia and Herzegovina ['bɒznɪə ˌhɜːtsɪgə'viːnə] *n.* Бо́сния и Герцегови́на.

bosom ['bʊz(ə)m] *n.* **1.** (*breast*) грудь. **2.** (*fig.*) се́рдце, душа́; ~ **friend** закады́чный друг; **in one's (own)** ~ в глубине́ души́; **in the** ~ **of one's family** в ло́не семьи́.

boss[1] [bɒs] *n.* (*protuberance*) ши́шка; (*archit.*) орна́мент в места́х пересече́ний ба́лок.

boss[2] [bɒs] *n.* (*master*) босс, хозя́ин.

v.t.: ~ **s.o. about** кома́ндовать (*impf.*) кем-н.

bossy ['bɒsɪ] *adj.* (*overbearing*) команди́рский.

botanical [bə'tænɪk(ə)l] *adj.* ботани́ческий.

botanist ['bɒtənɪst] *n.* бота́ник.

botany ['bɒtənɪ] *n.* бота́ника.

botch [bɒtʃ] *v.t.* (*bungle*) зава́л|ивать, -и́ть; (*patch roughly*) зала́т|ывать, -а́ть.

both [bəʊθ] *pron. & adj.* о́ба (*m.*, *nt.*), о́бе (*f.*); и тот и друго́й; ~ **sledges** о́бе па́ры сане́й; ~ **of us** мы о́ба; **of** ~ **sexes** обо́его по́ла; **you cannot have it** ~ **ways** выбира́йте одно́ из двух.

adv.: ~ **... and ...** и... и...; **he is** ~ **tired and hungry** он и уста́л и к тому́ же го́лоден; **I am fond of music,** ~ **ancient and modern** я люблю́ му́зыку, как ста́рую, так и совреме́нную.

bother ['bɒðə(r)] *n.* беспоко́йство; хло́п|оты (*pl.*, *g.* -о́т); **I had no** ~ **finding the book** я нашёл кни́гу без труда́.

v.t. (*disturb*) беспоко́ить, по-; (*importune*) надоеда́ть (*impf.*) +*d.*; ~ **(it)!** чёрт возьми́!; **he is always** ~**ing me to lend him money** он ве́чно приста́ёт ко мне с про́сьбой одолжи́ть ему́ де́нег; **I can't be** ~**ed** мне лень.

v.i. беспоко́иться, по-.

bothersome ['bɒðəsəm] *adj.* доса́дный, надое́дливый.

bottle ['bɒt(ə)l] *n.* **1.** буты́лка; (*for infants*) рожо́к; **over a** ~ **of wine** за буты́лкой вина́; **bring up a child on the** ~ вска́рмливать (*impf.*) ребёнка иску́сственно; **hot-water** ~ гре́лка. **2.** (*fig.*): **he is fond of the** ~ он прикла́дывается к буты́лке; **keep s.o. from the** ~ удéрж|ивать, -а́ть кого́-н. от пья́нства.

v.t. (*put in* ~*s*) разл|ива́ть, -и́ть по буты́лкам; ~**d in Moscow** моско́вского разли́ва; ~ **fruit** консерви́ровать (*impf.*, *pf.*) фру́кты; ~ **up** (*conceal*) скры́|ва́ть, -ть; (*restrain*) сдéрж|ивать, -а́ть; ~ **up one's feelings** скры|ва́ть, -ть свои́ чу́вства.

cpds. ~**-fed** *adj.* иску́сственно вско́рмленный; ~**neck** *n.* (*fig.*) зато́р; про́бка; у́зкое ме́сто; ~**-top** *n.* колпачо́к на буты́лку.

bottled ['bɒt(ə)ld] *adj.*: ~ **beer** буты́лочное пи́во.

bottom ['bɒtəm] *n.* **1.** (*lowest part*) дно; (*of mountain*) подно́жие; (*of page*) низ, коне́ц; (*of stairs*) низ, основа́ние; ~ **shelf** ни́жняя по́лка; (*of coat*) подо́л; ~ **up(wards)** вверх дном; ~**s up!** пей до дна!; **at the** ~ **of the class** отстаю́щий в кла́ссе. **2.** (*further end*): **at the** ~ **of the bed** в нога́х крова́ти; ~ **(end) of the table** ни́жний коне́ц стола́; ~ **of the garden** за́дняя часть са́да; ~ **of the street** коне́ц у́лицы. **3.** (*of sea*) дно; **send to the** ~ пус|ка́ть, -ти́ть на дно. **4.** (*anat.*) зад; за́дняя часть; за́днее ме́сто. **5.** (*of ship*) дни́ще. **6.** (*fig.*): **from the** ~ **of my heart** из глубины́ души́; от всего́ се́рдца; **get to the** ~ **of sth.** доб|ира́ться, -ра́ться до су́ти чего́-н.; **he was at the** ~ **of it** за э́тим стоя́л он; **prices touched** ~ це́ны дости́гли са́мого ни́зкого у́ровня; **he came** ~ **in algebra** он был после́дним по а́лгебре.

bottomless ['bɒtəmlɪs] *adj.* бездо́нный; ~ **pit** бездо́нная я́ма; (*hell*) ад, преиспо́дняя; (*immeasurable*) безграни́чный, беспреде́льный.

boudoir ['buːdwɑː(r)] *n.* будуа́р.

bough [baʊ] *n.* сук.

bouillon [buː'jɔ̃, 'buːjɒn] *n.* бульо́н.

boulder ['bəʊldə(r)] *n.* валу́н.

boulevard ['buːləˌvɑːd, 'buːlvɑː(r)] *n.* бульва́р.

bounce [baʊns] *n.* (*of ball*) подпры́гивание, отско́к.

v.t. (*eject*) выки́дывать, вы́кинуть; ~ **a ball** бить (*impf.*) мячо́м об пол (о зе́млю, об сте́нку *и т.п.*).

v.i. (*of ball etc.*) отск|а́кивать, -очи́ть; подпры́г|ивать, -нуть; (*coll.*, *of cheque*) верну́ться (*pf.*); (*of pers.*): ~ **into a room** влете́ть (*pf.*) в ко́мнату; ~ **out of a room** вы́скочить (*pf.*) из ко́мнаты; ~ **back** (*fig.*) бы́стро опра́виться.

bouncer ['baʊnsə(r)] *n.* вышиба́ла (*m.*).

bouncing ['baʊnsɪŋ] *adj.* **1.** (*of ball*) пры́гающий, подпры́гивающий. **2.** (*healthy*) здоро́вый; (*lusty*) здорове́нный.

bouncy ['baʊnsɪ] *adj.* (*lit.*, *resilient*) упру́гий; (*in manner*) ре́звый, живо́й.

bound[1] [baʊnd] *n.* (*usu. pl.*, *limit*) грани́ца, преде́л; **set** ~**s to sth.** ста́вить, по- преде́л чему́-н.; ограни́чи|вать, -ть что-н.; **know no** ~**s** не знать (*impf.*) грани́ц; **beyond the** ~**s of reason** за преде́лами разу́много; **within the** ~**s of possibility** в преде́лах возмо́жного; **the town is out of** ~**s to troops** вход в го́род солда́там воспрещён.

v.t. (*limit*) ограни́чи|вать, -ть.

bound[2] [baʊnd] *n.* (*jump*) прыжо́к; скачо́к; **by leaps and** ~**s** гало́пом; не по дням, а по часа́м; **at a** ~ одни́м прыжко́м; (*bounce*) отско́к.

v.i. пры́г|ать, -нуть; скак|а́ть, -ну́ть; ~ **over a ditch** переск|а́кивать, -очи́ть че́рез кана́ву; **he** ~**ed off to fetch the book** он подпры́гнул, что́бы доста́ть кни́гу.

bound[3] [baʊnd] *adj.* **1.** (*connected*) свя́занный; **this is** ~ **up with politics** э́то свя́зано с поли́тикой. **2.** (*absorbed*): **he is** ~ **up in his work** он поглощён рабо́той. **3.** (*certain*): **he is** ~ **to win** он непреме́нно вы́играет; **I'll be** ~ я уве́рен. **4.** (*obliged*): **you are not** ~ **to go** вам не обяза́тельно идти́. **5.** (*of book*) переплетённый; в переплёте. **6.** (*en route*): **the ship is** ~ **for New York** парохо́д направля́ется в Нью-Йо́рк; **homeward** ~ направля́ющийся на ро́дину.

boundary ['baʊndərɪ, -drɪ] *n.* (*of a field etc.*) грани́ца, рубе́ж; (*fig.*) преде́л; (*attr.*) пограни́чный.

boundless ['baʊndlɪs] *adj.* безграни́чный, беспреде́льный.

bounteous ['baʊntɪəs] *adj.* (*generous*) ще́дрый; (*plentiful*) оби́льный.

bountiful ['baʊntɪˌfʊl] *adj.* ще́дрый; оби́льный.

bounty ['baʊntɪ] *n.* **1.** (*generosity*) ще́дрость. **2.** (*mil.*, *naut.*) поощри́тельная пре́мия.

bouquet [buː'keɪ, bəʊ-] *n.* (*of flowers, wine*) буке́т.

bourgeois ['bʊəʒwɑː] *n.* буржуа́ (*m. indecl.*).

adj. буржуа́зный.

bourgeoisie [ˌbʊəʒwɑː'ziː] *n.* буржуази́я.

bout [baʊt] *n.* **1.** (*at games*) бой, встре́ча, схва́тка; **fencing** ~ бой в фехтова́нии; **wrestling** ~ схва́тка в борьбе́; **have a** ~ **with** схва́т|ываться, -и́ться с+*i.* **2.** (*of illness*) при́ступ. **3.** (*drinking-*~) запо́й.

boutique [buː'tiːk] *n.* (небольшо́й) мо́дный магази́н.

bovine ['bəʊvaɪn] *adj.* (*zool.*) быча́чий, бы́чий.

bow[1] [bəʊ] *n.* **1.** (*weapon*) лук; **draw a** ~ натя́|гивать, -ну́ть тетиву́ лу́ка. **2.** (*rainbow*) ра́дуга. **3.** (*of violin etc.*) смычо́к. **4.** (*knot*) бант; **tie a** ~ завя́з|ывать, -а́ть бант; **tie sth. in a** ~ завя́з|ывать, -а́ть что-н. ба́нтиком.

cpds. ~**-legged** *adj.* кривоно́гий; ~**-line** *n.* (*rope*) були́нь (*m.*); ~**man** *n.* (*archer*) лу́чник; ~**string** *n.* тетива́; ~**-tie** *n.* (га́лстук-)ба́бочка; ~**-window** *n.* э́ркер.

bow[2] [baʊ] *n.* (*salutation*) покло́н; **make a deep/low ~** ни́зко кла́няться, поклони́ться.

v.t.: **~ the knee** преклон|я́ть, -и́ть коле́на; **~ one's head** склон|я́ть, -и́ть го́лову; **the wind ~ed the trees** ве́тер гнул/клони́л дере́вья; **~ed down by grief** сло́мленный го́рем.

v.i. **1.** (*salute*) кла́няться, поклони́ться; **~ and scrape** расша́ркиваться (*перед кем-н.*); **~ down** (*worship*) преклон|я́ться, -и́ться (пе́ред+*i.*); **~ out** (= *retire*): **~ out of politics** распрости́ться (*pf.*) с поли́тикой. **2.** (*defer*) склон|я́ться, -и́ться (**to, before:** перед+*i.*); **~ to fate** смир|я́ться, -и́ться с судьбо́й.

bow[3] [baʊ] *n.* (*naut.*) нос; **cross s.o.'s ~s** (*fig.*) пере|бе|га́ть, -жа́ть кому́-н. доро́гу.

bowel ['baʊəl] *n.* **1.** кишка́; **have a ~ movement** име́ть (*impf.*) стул; испражня́ться; **are your ~s regular?** регуля́рно ли де́йствует у вас кише́чник? **2.: ~s of the earth** не́дра (*pl., g.* —) земли́.

bower ['baʊə(r)] *n.* (*arbour*) бесе́дка.

bowl[1] [bəʊl] *n.* **1.** (*vessel*) ча́ша, ва́за, ми́ска; **crystal ~** хруста́льная ва́за; **wooden ~** деревя́нная ми́ска. **2.** (*of pipe*) ча́шечка; (*of spoon*) углубле́ние.

bowl[2] [bəʊl] *n.* (*ball*) ке́гельный шар; **play ~s** игра́ть (*impf.*) в ке́гли/шары́.

v.t. (*roll*) ката́ть (*indet.*), кати́ть, по-; **~ over** (*lit.*) сшиб|а́ть, -и́ть; (*fig.*); **he was ~ed over by the news** он был ошеломлён э́тим изве́стием.

v.i. **1.: ~ along** бы́стро кати́ться. **2.** (*play bowls*) игра́ть (*impf.*) в ке́гли/шары́; **~ing-alley** кегельба́н; **~ing-green** лужа́йка для игры́ в шары́.

bowler[1] ['bəʊlə(r)] *n.* (*at games*) подаю́щий/броса́ющий мяч.

bowler[2] ['bəʊlə(r)] *n.* (**~** *hat*) котело́к.

bowsprit ['bəʊsprɪt] *n.* бушпри́т.

box[1] [bɒks] *n.* (*bot.*) (*also* **~wood**) самши́т.

box[2] [bɒks] *n.* **1.** (*receptacle*) коро́бка, я́щик; **letter-~** почто́вый я́щик; **P.O.** (*abbr. of* ***post office***) **box** почто́вый я́щик; **~ number** но́мер почто́вого я́щика; **cardboard ~** карто́нка. **2.: Christmas ~** рожде́ственский пода́рок. **3.** (*theatr.*) ло́жа. **4.** (*television*) я́щик, те́лик. **5.** (*for horse*) сто́йло; **loose ~** широ́кое сто́йло. **6.** (*witness-~*) ме́сто для свиде́телей; **be in the ~** свиде́тельствовать (*impf.*); **put s.o. in the ~** вы́звать (*pf.*) кого́-н. в ка́честве свиде́теля.

v.t. **1.** класть, положи́ть в коро́бку/я́щик. **2. ~ in, up** (*confine*) сти́с|кивать, -нуть; вти́с|кивать, -нуть; **~ed in** сти́снутый, зажа́тый.

cpds. **~-camera** *n.* я́щичный фотоаппара́т; **~-car** *n.* (*rail*) това́рный ваго́н; **~-kite** *n.* коро́бчатый возду́шный змей; **~-office** *n.* (театра́льная) ка́сса; **~room** *n.* кладова́я; **~-seat** *n.* (*theatr.*) ме́сто в ло́же.

box[3] [bɒks] *n.*: **~ on the ear** оплеу́ха.

v.t.: **~ s.o.'s ears** да|ва́ть, -ть кому́-н. оплеу́ху (*or* по́ уху).

v.i. (*sport*) бокси́ровать (*impf.*).

boxer ['bɒksə(r)] *n.* (*sportsman; dog*) боксёр.

boxing ['bɒksɪŋ] *n.* (*sport*) бокс.

cpd. **~-glove** *n.* боксёрская перча́тка.

Boxing Day ['bɒksɪŋ] *n.* второ́й день Рождества́, день рожде́ственских пода́рков.

boy [bɔɪ] *n.* **1.** (*child*) ма́льчик; **I knew him as** (*when I was*) **a ~** я знал его́, когда́ я был ребёнком; (*when he was*) я знал его́ ма́льчиком; **~ scout** бойска́ут. **2.** (*son*) сын. **3.: old ~** старина́ (*m.*), стари́к; **~s!** ребя́та! (*m. pl.*); **oh ~!** (*coll.*) здо́рово!; вот э́то да́!

cpd. **~-friend** *n.* ≃ (*её*) па́рень (*m.*), молодо́й челове́к.

boyar ['bɔɪə] *n.* боя́рин; (*attr.*) боя́рский.

boycott ['bɔɪkɒt] *n.* бойко́т.

v.t. бойкоти́ровать (*impf., pf.*).

boyhood ['bɔɪhʊd] *n.* о́трочество.

boyish ['bɔɪɪʃ] *adj.* мальчи́шеский.

bra [brɑː] *n.* ли́фчик, бюстга́льтер.

brace [breɪs] *n.* **1.** (*support*) подпо́рка, распо́рка; (*clasp*) скре́па; (*stay*) оття́жка; (*tie*) связь; (*in building*) связь, подко́с, скоба́. **2.** (*strap*) сво́ра; **~s** (*to wear*) по́дтяж|ки (*pl., g.* -ек). **3.** (*pair*) па́ра. **4.: ~ and bit** коловоро́т. **5.** (*dentistry etc.*) (ортодонти́ческие) ско́бы (*pl., g.* —).

v.t. **1.** (*make fast*) скреп|ля́ть, -и́ть; подкреп|ля́ть, -и́ть; (*support*) подп|ира́ть, -ере́ть; **he ~d himself against the wall** он опёрся о сте́ну. **2.** (*of nerves*) укреп|ля́ть, -и́ть; **~ s.o. (up)** подбод|ря́ть, -и́ть кого́-н.; **he ~d himself to do it** он собра́лся с ду́хом сде́лать э́то.

bracelet ['breɪslɪt] *n.* брасле́т.

bracing ['breɪsɪŋ] *adj.* бодря́щий, укрепля́ющий.

bracken ['brækən] *n.* орля́к; (*collect.*) па́поротник.

bracket ['brækɪt] *n.* **1.** (*support*) кронште́йн. **2.** (*typ.*) ско́бка; **square/round ~** квадра́тная/кру́глая ско́бка; **open/close ~s** откры́ть/закры́ть (*pf.*) ско́бки. **4.** (*fig.*): **the higher income ~s** гру́ппа населе́ния с бо́лее высо́кими дохо́дами.

v.t. **1.** (*enclose in ~s*) заключ|а́ть, -и́ть в ско́бки. **2.** (*link with a ~*) соедин|я́ть, -и́ть ско́бкой; (*fig.*): **do not ~ me with him** не ста́вьте меня́ с ним на одну́ до́ску.

cpd. **~-lamp** *n.* ла́мпа на кронште́йне.

brackish ['brækɪʃ] *adj.* солонова́тый.

bradawl ['brædɔːl] *n.* ши́ло.

brag [bræg] *n.* хвастовство́.

v.i. хва́стать(ся), по- (*чем*).

braggart ['brægət] *n.* хвасту́н.

bragging ['brægɪŋ] *n.* хвастовство́.

Brahmin ['brɑːmɪn] *n.* брами́н, брахма́н.

Brahminism ['brɑːmɪnɪz(ə)m] *n.* брахмани́зм.

braid [breɪd] *n.* (*of hair*) коса́; (*band, ribbon*) тесьма́; (*cord-like fabric*) галу́н; **gold ~** золото́й галу́н.

v.t. (*interweave*) плести́, с-; (*arrange in braids*) запле|та́ть, -сти́; (*edge with braid*) обш|ива́ть, -и́ть тесьмо́й.

Braille [breɪl] *n.* шрифт Бра́йля; **read ~** чита́ть (*impf.*) по Бра́йлю.

brain [breɪn] *n.* **1.** (*anat.*) мозг; (*pl., cul.*) мозги́. **2.** (*intellect*): **overtax one's ~** перенапряга́ть (*impf.*) свои́ мозги́; **rack one's ~s** лома́ть (*impf.*) го́лову (над+*i.*); **use one's ~s** шевели́ть (*impf.*) мозга́ми; **he has that tune on the ~** э́тот моти́в нейдёт у него́ из головы́; **he's the ~s of the family** он са́мый башкови́тый/мозгови́тый в семье́; **a great ~** (*pers.*) све́тлая голова́.

cpds. **~-child** *n.* де́тище/плод ра́зума/воображе́ния; **~ drain** *n.* «уте́чка мозго́в»; **~storm** *n.* припа́док безу́мия; **~-wash** *v.t.* пром|ыва́ть, -ы́ть мозги́ +*d.*; **~wave** *n.*: **he had a ~wave** ему́ пришла́ счастли́вая мысль; **~-work** *n.* у́мственная де́ятельность/рабо́та; **~-worker** *n.* рабо́тник у́мственного труда́.

brainless ['breɪnlɪs] *adj.* безмо́зглый, пустоголо́вый.

brainy ['breɪnɪ] *adj.* (*coll.*) башкови́тый, мозгови́тый.

braise [breɪz] *v.t.* туши́ть (*impf.*).

brake [breɪk] *n.* (*on vehicle*) то́рмоз (*pl.* -á); **put on the ~** затормози́ть (*pf.*).

v.t. & i. тормози́ть, за-.

cpds. **~-drum** *n.* тормозно́й бараба́н; **~-light** *n.* фона́рь (*m.*) сигна́ла торможе́ния (*or* стоп-сигна́ла); **~-shoe** *n.* тормозно́й башма́к.

bramble ['bræmb(ə)l] *n.* ежеви́ка.

bran [bræn] *n.* о́труб|и (*pl., g.* -ей).

branch [brɑːntʃ] *n.* (*of tree*) ветвь; ве́тка; (*of river*) рука́в; (*of road*) ответвле́ние; (*of family, genus*) ли́ния, ветвь; (*of railway line*) ве́тка; (*comm.*)

филиа́л, отделе́ние; ~ **office** филиа́льное отделе́ние, филиа́л; (*of knowledge, subject, industry*) о́трасль.

v.i. (*of plants*): ~ **forth, out** разветв|ля́ться, -и́ться; (*of organization*): ~ **out** разветв|ля́ться, -и́ться; (*of pers.*): ~ **out in a new direction** расш|иря́ть, -и́рить де́ятельность в но́вом направле́нии; (*of road or rail., also* ~ **off**) разветв|ля́ться, -и́ться; (*of river*) раздел|я́ться, -и́ться на рукава́.

brand [brænd] *n.* **1.** (*piece of burning wood*) головня́, голове́шка. **2.** (*mark of* ~*ing, also fig.*) клеймо́, тавро́, печа́ть. **3.** (*trade-mark*) фабри́чная ма́рка; фабри́чное клеймо́. **4.** (*species of goods*) сорт, ма́рка; ~ **name** фи́рменное назва́ние.

v.t. **1.** (*cattle etc.*) таври́ть, за-; клейми́ть, за-; ~**ing-iron** клеймо́. **2.** (*fig., imprint*): ~ **sth. on s.o.'s memory** запечатле́ть (*pf.*) что-н. в чьей-н. па́мяти. **3.** (*comm.*): ~**ed goods** това́ры с фабри́чным клеймо́м.

cpd. ~**-new** *adj.* соверше́нно но́вый, с иго́лочки.

brandish ['brændɪʃ] *v.t.* разма́хивать (*impf.*) +*i.*

brandy ['brændɪ] *n.* коньяк.

brash [bræʃ] *adj.* нагловáтый, де́рзкий.

brass [brɑːs] *n.* **1.** (*metal*) лату́нь, жёлтая медь; ~ **plate** ме́дная доще́чка (на две́ри); **the top** ~ (*sl.*) вы́сшее нача́льство; **get down to** ~ **tacks** дойти́ (*pf.*) до су́ти де́ла; **it is not worth a** ~ **farthing** э́то ло́маного гроша́ не сто́ит. **2.** (*also* ~**-ware**) лату́нные/ме́дные изде́лия. **3.** (*mus.*): **the** ~**es** духовы́е инструме́нты (*m. pl.*); ~ **band** духово́й орке́стр. **4.** (*sl., money*) деньга́ (*coll.*).

brassière ['bræzɪə(r), -sɪˌeə(r)] *n.* ли́фчик, бюстга́льтер.

brassy ['brɑːsɪ] *adj.* (*of colour*) ме́дный; (*of sound*) металли́ческий.

brat [bræt] *n.* щено́к, (*coll.*) сопля́к.

bravado [brə'vɑːdəʊ] *n.* брава́да.

brave [breɪv] *adj.* (*courageous*) хра́брый, сме́лый; (*bold*) де́рзкий; (*fearless, intrepid*) бесстра́шный, му́жественный.

v.t. (*danger etc.*) бр|оса́ть, -о́сить вы́зов +*d.*; ~ **the storm** боро́ться (*impf.*) с бу́рей.

bravery ['breɪvərɪ] *n.* (*courage*) хра́брость, сме́лость.

bravo [brɑː'vəʊ] *int.* бра́во!

bravura [brə'vʊərə, -'vjʊərə] *n.* (*mus.*) браву́рность; (*attr.*) браву́рный.

brawl [brɔːl] *n.* сканда́л.

v.i. сканда́лить (*impf.*).

brawn [brɔːn] *n.* (*meat*) зельц; (*fig.*) му́скулы (*m. pl.*).

brawny ['brɔːnɪ] *adj.* му́скули́стый.

bray [breɪ] *n.* (*of ass, trumpet etc.*) рёв.

v.i. реве́ть (*impf.*).

braze [breɪz] *v.t.* (*solder*) пая́ть (*impf.*) твёрдым припо́ем.

brazen ['breɪz(ə)n] *adj.* ме́дный, бро́нзовый; (*fig., shameless*) на́глый, бессты́дный.

brazier ['breɪzɪə(r), -ʒə(r)] *n.* (*worker*) ме́дник; (*pan*) жаро́вня.

Brazil [brə'zɪl] *n.* Брази́лия; ~ **nut** америка́нский оре́х.

breach [briːtʃ] *n.* **1.** (*violation, interruption*) наруше́ние; ~ **of duty** невыполне́ние обяза́тельств; ~ **of trust** злоупотребле́ние дове́рием; ~ **of good manners** наруше́ние пра́вил поведе́ния. **2.** (*gap*) проло́м, брешь; **step into the** ~ (*fig.*) прийти́ (*pf.*) на по́мощь.

v.t. прор|ыва́ть, -ва́ть.

bread [bred] *n.* хлеб; **brown** ~ се́рый хлеб; **loaf of** ~ бато́н, буха́нка; ~ **and butter** (*fig.*) хлеб с ма́слом; **daily** ~ (*lit., fig.*) хлеб насу́щный; **be on** ~ **and water** сиде́ть (*impf.*) на хле́бе и воде́; **he knows which side his** ~ **is buttered on** он зна́ет свою́ вы́году; **half a loaf is better than no** ~ на безры́бье и рак ры́ба.

cpds. ~**-bin** *n.* хле́бница; ~**-crumb** *n.* кро́шка; (*pl., cul.*) толчёные сухари́ (*m. pl.*); ~**line** *n.*: **on the** ~**line** в тяжёлом материа́льном положе́нии; ~**winner** *n.* корми́лец.

breadth [bredθ] *n.* **1.** (*width*) ширина́; **he missed by a hair's** ~ он был на волосо́к от це́ли. **2.** (*fig.*): ~ **of mind** широта́ ума́.

break[1] [breɪk] *n.* **1.** (*broken place, gap*) тре́щина, разры́в. **2.**: ~ **of day** рассве́т. **3.** (*interval*) переры́в, па́уза; (*rest*) переды́шка. **4.** (*change*) переме́на; **the trip made a pleasant** ~ пое́здка внесла́ прия́тное разнообра́зие; (*in voice at puberty*) ло́мка. **5.** (*coll., opportunity*): **give him a** ~! да́йте ему́ то́лько возмо́жность!; (*piece of luck*) уда́ча. **6.** (*escape*): **prison** ~ побе́г из тюрьмы́.

v.t. (*see also* **broken**) **1.** (*fracture, divide, destroy*) лома́ть, с-; **he broke his leg** он слома́л но́гу; **she broke the plate in two** таре́лка у неё слома́лась попола́м; ~ **sth. in pieces** разл|а́мывать, -ома́ть что-н. на куски́; ~ **a piece off sth.** отл|а́мывать, -ома́ть (*or* -оми́ть) кусо́к от чего́-н.; ~ **the ice** (*lit., fig.*) лома́ть, с- лёд; ~ **the skin** прор|ыва́ть, -ва́ть ко́жу; ~ **s.o.'s head (open)** прол|а́мывать, -оми́ть кому́-н. че́реп; ~ **s.o.'s nose** разби́ть (*pf.*) кому́-н. нос. **2.** (*fig.*): ~ **new ground** про|кла́дывать, -ложи́ть но́вые пути́; ~ **cover** выходи́ть, вы́йти из укры́тия; ~ **camp** сн|има́ться, -я́ться с ла́геря; ~ **a record** поби́ть (*pf.*) реко́рд; ~ (*defeat*) **a strike** срыва́ть, сорва́ть забасто́вку; ~ **wind** (*fart*) по́ртить, ис- во́здух; ~ (*into*) **a five-pound note** разме́н|ивать, -я́ть пятифунто́вую бума́жку; ~ **s.o.'s heart** разб|ива́ть, -и́ть кому́-н. се́рдце; ~ **a spell** разр|уша́ть, -у́шить ча́ры; ~ **the back of a task** одол|ева́ть, -е́ть трудне́йшую часть зада́ния; **he was broken by the failure of his business** его́ сломи́ла неуда́ча в де́ле. **3.** (*tame*): ~ **a horse to harness** приуч|а́ть, -и́ть ло́шадь к у́пряжи. **4.** (*disaccustom*): ~ **s.o. of a habit** отуч|а́ть, -и́ть кого́-н. от привы́чки. **5.** (*convey*): ~ **the news** сообщи́ть (*pf.*) (неприя́тные) но́вости. **6.** (*weaken*): ~ **a blow** смягч|а́ть, -и́ть уда́р; ~ **a fall** осл|абля́ть, -а́бить си́лу паде́ния. **7.** (*violate, e.g. the law, a promise*) нар|уша́ть, -у́шить; ~ **a secret** разгл|аша́ть, -аси́ть та́йну; ~ **a cypher** расшифро́в|ывать, -а́ть (*pf.*) код. **8.** (*interrupt, put an end to*): ~ **silence** нар|уша́ть, -у́шить молча́ние; ~ **one's journey** прер|ыва́ть, -ва́ть путеше́ствие; ~ **a fast** прекра|ща́ть, -ти́ть пост; ~ **a circuit** (*elec.*) прер|ыва́ть, -ва́ть ток. **9.** (*destroy uniformity or completeness of*): ~ **a set of books** разро́зни|ва́ть, -ть компле́кт книг; ~ **ranks** выходи́ть, вы́йти из стро́я; ~ (*refuse to join*) **a strike** быть штре́йкбре́хером.

v.i. **1.** (*fracture, divide, disperse*) лома́ться, с-; об|рыва́ться, -орва́ться; (*of glass, china*) би́ться (*or* разбива́ться), раз-; (*of rope etc.*) ло́паться, ло́пнуть; (*of ice*) треща́ть, тре́снуть; ~ **in two** лома́ться, с- попола́м; ~ **in pieces** разл|а́мываться, -ома́ться на куски́; **the door broke open** дверь поддала́сь; **the waves** ~ **on the beach** во́лны бью́тся о бе́рег; **the clouds broke** ту́чи рассе́ялись. **2.** (*fig.*): **his heart broke** он был (соверше́нно) уби́т; **their spirit broke** они́ па́ли ду́хом; ~**ing-point** преде́л. **3.** (*burst, dawn*): **the blister/bubble broke** волды́рь/пузы́рь ло́пнул; **day broke** рассвело́; **the storm broke** разрази́лась гроза́; **the news broke at 5 o'clock** об э́том ста́ло изве́стно в 5 часо́в. **4.** (*change*): **his voice broke** (*puberty*) у него́ слома́лся го́лос; (*emotion*) его́ го́лос дро́гнул; **the weather broke** пого́да испо́ртилась. **5.** (*var.*): ~ **even** ост|ава́ться, -а́ться при свои́х; **we broke for lunch** мы сде́лали переры́в на обе́д.

with preps.: **burglars broke into the house** граби́тели ворвали́сь в дом; **the house was broken into** в до́ме произошёл грабёж со взло́мом; ~ **into song** запе́ть (*pf.*); ~ **into a trot** пусти́ться (*pf.*) ры́сью; ~ **into laughter** рассмея́ться (*pf.*); ~ **into a £5 note** разме́н|ивать, -я́ть пятифунто́вую бума́жку; ~ **into the publishing world** проб|ива́ться, -и́ться в изда́тельский мир; **cattle broke through the fence** скот прорва́лся че́рез забо́р; **the sun broke through the cloud** со́лнце проби́лось сквозь ту́чи; **he broke with her** он порва́л с ней; ~ **with old habits** поко́нчить (*pf.*) со ста́рыми привы́чками.

with advs.: ~ **away** *v.i.*: ~ **away from one's gaolers** вы́рваться (*pf.*) из рук тюре́мщиков; ~ **away from old habits** отка́з|ываться, -а́ться от ста́рых привы́чек; ~ **away from a group** отк|а́лываться, -оло́ться от гру́ппы; ~ **down** *v.t.*: ~ **down a door** выла́мывать, вы́ломать дверь; ~ **down resistance** сломи́ть (*pf.*) сопротивле́ние; *v.i.*: **the bridge broke down** мост ру́хнул; **negotiations broke down** перегово́ры сорва́лись; **the car broke down** маши́на слома́лась; **he broke down** он не вы́держал; ~ **forth** *v.i.* вырыва́ться, вы́рваться вперёд; ~ **in** *v.t.*: ~ **in a door** вл|а́мываться, -оми́ться в дверь; ~ **in a horse** выезжа́ть, вы́ездить ло́шадь; *v.i.*: ~ **in on a conversation** вме́ш|иваться, -а́ться в разгово́р; ~ **off** *v.t.*: ~ **off a twig** отл|а́мывать, -оми́ть ве́точку; ~ **off relations** пор|ыва́ть, -ва́ть отноше́ния (с+*i.*); ~ **off an engagement** раст|орга́ть, -о́ргнуть помо́лвку; *v.i.*: **the nib broke off** ко́нчик пера́ отломи́лся; **he broke off** (*speaking*) он замолча́л; ~ **open** *v.t.*: ~ **open a chest** взл|а́мывать, -ома́ть сунду́к; ~ **out** *v.t.*: ~ **out a flag** развёр|тывать, -ну́ть зна́мя; *v.i.*: **the prisoner broke out** заключённый сбежа́л; **fire broke out** вспы́хнул пожа́р; **war broke out** разрази́лась/вспы́хнула война́; ~ **up** *v.t.*: ~ **up furniture** переломáть (*pf.*) ме́бель; ~ **up a meeting** прекра|ща́ть, -ти́ть собра́ние; ~ **it up!** (*coll.*, *desist*) конча́йте; ~ **up a family** (*separate*) разб|ива́ть, -и́ть семью́; (*cause to quarrel*) вн|оси́ть, -ести́ разла́д в семью́; *v.i.* **school** ~**s up tomorrow** уча́щихся за́втра распуска́ют на кани́кулы; **the crowd broke up** толпа́ разошла́сь.

cpds. ~**away** *n.* (*secession*) отко́л, отделе́ние; **a** ~**away faction** отколо́вшаяся фра́кция; ~**down** *n.* (*mechanical*) поло́мка; ~**down van** авари́йный грузови́к; маши́на техни́ческой по́мощи; (*of health*) упа́док сил; **nervous** ~**down** не́рвное расстро́йство; (*of negotiations etc.*) срыв; (*analysis*) подразделе́ние; ~**-in** *n.* (*raid*) взлом; ~**neck** *adj.*: ~**neck speed** головокружи́тельная ско́рость; ~**-out** *n.* (*escape*) побе́г; ~**through** *n.* (*mil.*) проры́в; (*fig.*, *e.g. in science*) скачо́к, перело́м; ~**-up** *n.* разва́л, распа́д; (*of school, assembly*) ро́спуск; (*of friendship*) разры́в; ~**water** *n.* волноло́м.

breakable ['breɪkəb(ə)l] *adj.* ло́мкий.

breakage ['breɪkɪdʒ] *n.* (*break*) поло́мка; (*pl.*, *broken articles*) бой, поло́мка.

breaker ['breɪkə(r)] *n.* (*wave*) вал, буру́н.

breakfast ['brekfəst] *n.* за́втрак; **have** ~ за́втракать, по-.

v.i. за́втракать, по-.

bream [bri:m] *n.* лещ.

breast [brest] *n.* **1.** грудь; **give a child the** ~ да|ва́ть, -ть ребёнку грудь; **child at the** ~ грудно́й ребёнок. **2.** (*fig.*) грудь, душа́; **make a clean** ~ **of sth.** чистосерде́чно созн|ава́ться, -а́ться в чём-н. **3.** (*cul.*): ~ **of lamb** бара́нья груди́нка.

cpds. ~**bone** *n.* грудна́я кость, груди́на; ~**-feeding** *n.* кормле́ние гру́дью; ~**-pocket** *n.* ве́рхний карма́н; ~**-stroke** *n.* брасс; **do the** ~**-stroke** пла́вать (*indet.*), плыть (*det.*) бра́ссом.

breath [breθ] *n.* дыха́ние; (*single* ~) вздох; **draw** ~ дыша́ть (*impf.*); **lose one's** ~ зад|ыха́ться, -охну́ться; **take** ~ перев|оди́ть, -ести́ дух; отд|ыха́ть, -охну́ть; **take a deep** ~ сде́лать (*pf.*) глубо́кий вздох; **out of** ~ задыха́ясь; **recover one's** ~ отдыша́ться (*pf.*); **bad** ~ дурно́й за́пах изо рта; **waste one's** ~ говори́ть (*impf.*) на ве́тер; **hold one's** ~ зата́|ивать, -и́ть дыха́ние; **take s.o.'s** ~ **away** захва́т|ывать, -и́ть дух у кого́-н.; **with bated** ~ затаи́в дыха́ние; **under one's** ~ о́чень ти́хо; **in the same** ~ еди́ным/одни́м ду́хом; **there is not a** ~ **of air** не́чем дыша́ть; **get a** ~ **of air** подыша́ть (*pf.*) све́жим во́здухом.

cpd. ~**-taking** *adj.* захва́тывающий.

breathalyse ['breθəlaɪz] *v.t.* прове́рить (*pf.*) на алкого́ль.

Breathalyser ['breθə,laɪzə(r)] *n.* (*propr.*) алкоме́тр, алкого́льно-респирато́рная тру́бка.

breathe [bri:ð] *v.t.* **1.**: ~ **fresh air** дыша́ть (*impf.*) све́жим во́здухом; ~ **one's last** испусти́ть (*pf.*) дух (*or* после́дний вздох). **2.**: ~ **new life into** вд|ыха́ть, -охну́ть но́вую жизнь в+*a*. **3.** (*utter softly*): **he** ~**d these words** он произнёс э́ти слова́ полушёпотом; ~ **a sigh** изд|ава́ть, -а́ть вздох; **don't** ~ **a word!** ни сло́ва бо́льше!; не пророни́те ни сло́ва!

v.i. дыша́ть (*impf.*); (*fig.*): ~ **again, freely** вздохну́ть (*pf.*) с облегче́нием (*or* свобо́дно); **give me a chance to** ~ да́йте мне вздохну́ть.

breather ['bri:ðə(r)] *n.* переды́шка.

breathing ['bri:ðɪŋ] *n.* дыха́ние; **his** ~ **is heavy** он тяжело́ ды́шит.

cpd. ~**-space** *n.* переды́шка.

breathless ['breθlɪs] *adj.* **1.** (*panting*) задыха́ющийся, запыха́вшийся.

breech [bri:tʃ] *n.* **1.** (*pl.*, *knee-*~**es**) пантало́н|ы (*pl.*, *g.* —); (*riding-*~**es**) бри́дж|и (*pl.*, *g.* -ей). **2.** (*of a gun*) казённая часть.

breed [bri:d] *n.* поро́да.

v.t. **1.** (*engender, cause*) поро|жда́ть, -ди́ть. **2.** (*animals*) раз|води́ть, -вести́.

v.i. размножа́ться (*impf.*), плоди́ться (*impf.*).

breeder ['bri:də(r)] *n.* **1.** (*animal*) производи́тель (*m.*). **2.** (*stock-*~) животново́д, скотово́д; **he is a** ~ **of horses** он разво́дит лошаде́й. **3.**: ~ **reactor** (*phys.*) реа́ктор-размножи́тель (*m.*).

breeding ['bri:dɪŋ] *n.* **1.** (*by animals*) размноже́ние; ~ **season** пери́од размноже́ния; ~ **stock** племенно́й скот. **2.** (*by stock-breeders*) разведе́ние. **3.** (*training, education*) воспита́ние, образова́ние. **4.** (*manners etc.*) воспи́танность.

cpd. ~**-ground** *n.* (*fig.*) расса́дник, оча́г.

breeze [bri:z] *n.* ветеро́к; бриз.

v.i.: ~ **in/out** (*coll.*) влете́ть/вы́лететь (*pf.*).

breezy ['bri:zɪ] *adj.* (*of weather*) све́жий; (*of locality*) обдува́емый ветра́ми; (*fig.*, *of pers.*) живо́й, беззабо́тный.

brethren ['breðrɪn] *n.* собра́тья (*m. pl.*); бра́тия (*f. sg.*).

brevity ['brevɪtɪ] *n.* кра́ткость.

brew [bru:] *n.* (*amount brewed*: *of beer*) ва́рка; (*of tea*) зава́рка; (*beverage*) сва́ренный напи́ток.

v.t. (*beer*) вари́ть, с-; (*tea*) зава́р|ивать, -и́ть.

v.i. **1.** (*of tea etc.*) зава́р|иваться, -и́ться. **2.**: **a storm is** ~**ing** (*lit.*) собира́ется гроза́; (*fig.*) гроза́ надвига́ется; **there's trouble** ~**ing** быть беде́.

brewer ['bru:ə(r)] *n.* пивова́р.

brewery ['bru:ərɪ] *n.* пивова́ренный заво́д.

briar ['braɪə(r)] = **brier**[1,2]

bribe [braɪb] *n.* взя́тка, по́дкуп.

v.t. да|ва́ть, -ть взя́тку +*d.*; подкуп|а́ть, -и́ть.

bribery ['braɪbərɪ] *n.* взя́точничество.

bric-à-brac ['brɪkə,bræk] *n.* старьё; безделу́шки (*f. pl.*).

brick [brɪk] *n.* **1.** кирпи́ч; ~**s** (*collect.*) кирпи́ч; (*attr.*) кирпи́чный; **drop a** ~ ля́пнуть (*pf.*) (*coll.*); **drop sth. like a hot** ~ бежа́ть (*det.*) от чего́-н. как от чумы́. **2.** (*toy*): ~**s** ку́бики (*m. pl.*).

v.t.: ~ **up** за|кла́дывать, -ложи́ть кирпича́ми.

cpds. **~layer** *n.* ка́менщик; **~-red** *adj.* кирпи́чно-кра́сный; **~work** *n.* кирпи́чная кла́дка.

bridal ['braɪd(ə)l] *adj.* сва́дебный.

bride [braɪd] *n.* неве́ста.

cpds. **~groom** *n.* жени́х; **~smaid** *n.* подру́жка неве́сты.

bridge[1] [brɪdʒ] *n.* **1.** мост; **suspension ~** вися́чий мост; **throw a ~ over a river** навести́/перебро́сить (*pf.*) мост через ре́ку; **we'll cross that ~ when we come to it** не́чего зара́нее волнова́ться. **2.** (*naut.*) капита́нский мо́стик. **3.** (*of nose*) перено́сица. **4.** (*of violin*) кобы́лка.

v.t.: **~ a river** нав|оди́ть, -ести́ мост че́рез ре́ку; (*join by bridging*) соедин|я́ть, -и́ть мосто́м; (*fig.*): **~ a gap** зап|олня́ть, -о́лнить пробе́л.

cpd. **~head** *n.* плацда́рм (*also fig.*); предмо́стное укрепле́ние.

bridge[2] [brɪdʒ] *n.* (*game*) бридж.

bridle ['braɪd(ə)l] *n.* узда́, узде́чка.

v.t. (*of horse, also* **~ in**) взну́зд|ывать, -а́ть; (*fig.*) обу́зд|ывать, -а́ть.

v.i. (*fig.*) зад|ира́ть, -ра́ть нос.

cpds. **~-path** *n.* верхова́я тропа́; **~-rein** *n.* по́вод.

brief [bri:f] *n.* **1.** (*lawyer's*) изложе́ние де́ла; **hold a ~ for s.o.** вести́ (*det.*) чьё-н. де́ло в суде́. **2.** (*mil. etc., instructions*) инстру́кция. **3.** (*pl., coll., underpants*) трус|ы́ (*pl., g.* -о́в).

adj. (*of duration*) коро́ткий, недо́лгий; (*concise*) кра́ткий, сжа́тый; **in ~** вкра́тце.

v.t. **1.: ~ a lawyer** поруч|а́ть, -и́ть адвока́ту веде́ние де́ла. **2.** (*mil. etc.*) инструкти́ровать (*impf., pf.*).

cpd. **~-case** *n.* портфе́ль (*m.*).

briefing ['bri:fɪŋ] *n.* (*also* **~ meeting**) инструкта́ж; (*press*) бри́финг.

briefly ['bri:flɪ] *adv.* кра́тко, сжа́то.

brier, briar[1] ['braɪə(r)] *n.* (*prickly bush*; *also* **sweet ~**) шипо́вник.

cpd. **~-rose** *n.* шипо́вник.

brier, briar[2] ['braɪə(r)] *n.* (*heather*) ве́реск, э́рика; **(~ pipe)** тру́бка из ко́рня э́рики.

Brig.[1] [ˌbrɪgə'dɪə(r)] *n.* (*abbr. of* **Brigadier**) брига́дный генера́л.

brig[2] [brɪg] *n.* бриг.

brigade [brɪ'geɪd] *n.* брига́да; **fire ~** пожа́рная кома́нда.

brigadier [ˌbrɪgə'dɪə(r)] *n.* (*also* **~-general**) брига́дный генера́л.

brigand ['brɪgənd] *n.* разбо́йник.

brigandage ['brɪgəndɪdʒ] *n.* разбо́й.

bright [braɪt] *adj.* **1.** (*clear, shining*) я́ркий, све́тлый; **a ~ day** я́сный день; **~ red** я́рко-кра́сный; **the sun shines ~** со́лнце све́тит я́рко; **a ~ room** све́тлая ко́мната. **2.** (*cheerful*): **~ faces** весёлые ли́ца; **look on the ~ side** смотре́ть (*impf.*) на ве́щи оптимисти́чески. **3.** (*clever*): **a ~ girl** толко́вая де́вочка; **a ~ idea** блестя́щая мысль.

brighten ['braɪt(ə)n] *v.t.* (*also* **~ up**): (*polish*) полирова́ть, от-; (*enliven*) ожив|ля́ть, -и́ть; подб|а́дривать (*or* -одря́ть), -одри́ть.

v.i. (*also* **~ up**): **the weather ~ed** пого́да проясни́лась; **his face ~ed** его́ лицо́ просветле́ло; **things are ~ing up** дела́ улучша́ются.

brightness ['braɪtnɪs] *n.* (*lustre*) я́ркость; (*cheer*) весёлость.

brilliance ['brɪlɪəns] *n.* (*brightness*) я́ркость; (*magnificence*) великоле́пие, блеск; (*intelligence*) блеск (ума́); блестя́щие спосо́бности (*f. pl.*).

brilliant ['brɪlɪənt] *n.* (*diamond*) бриллиа́нт.

adj. (*lit., fig.*) сверка́ющий, блестя́щий.

brim [brɪm] *n.* край; **fill a glass to the ~** нап|олня́ть, -о́лнить стака́н до краёв; (*of hat*) поля́ (*nt. pl.*).

v.i. (*of vessel*) нап|олня́ться, -о́лниться до краёв.

cpd. **~-full** *adj.* по́лный до краёв.

brimstone ['brɪmstəʊn] *n.* саморо́дная се́ра.

brine [braɪn] *n.* рассо́л.

bring [brɪŋ] *v.t.* **1.** (*cause to come, deliver*): (*a thg.*) прин|оси́ть, -ести́; (*a pers.*) прив|оди́ть, -ести́; (*thg. or pers., by vehicle*) прив|ози́ть, -езти́; **~ s.o. into the world** произвести́ (*pf.*) кого́-н. на свет; **it brought tears to my eyes** э́то вы́звало у меня́ слёзы; **spring ~s warm weather** с весно́й прихо́дит тепло́; **~ into action, effect, play** прив|оди́ть, -ести́ в де́йствие; **~ to light** выявля́ть, вы́явить; **~ to pass** осуществ|ля́ть, -и́ть; **~ to mind** прив|оди́ть, -ести́ на ум; нап|омина́ть, -о́мнить; **~ to an end** зак|а́нчивать, -о́нчить; заверш|а́ть, -и́ть; **~ pressure to bear on** ока́з|ывать, -а́ть давле́ние на+*a.*; **~ s.o. to his senses** (*lit.*) прив|оди́ть, -ести́ кого́-н. в созна́ние; (*fig.*) образу́м|ливать, -ить кого́-н.; **~ a misfortune upon o.s.** навл|ека́ть, -е́чь на себя́ беду́. **2.** (*yield*): **this ~s me (in) £5000 a year** э́то прино́сит мне 5000 фу́нтов в год; **the harvest will not ~ much** урожа́й не бу́дет больши́м. **3.** (*induce*): **I could not ~ him to agree** я не мог убеди́ть его́ дать согла́сие; **I cannot ~ myself to do it** я не могу́ заста́вить себя́ сде́лать э́то. **4.** (*leg.*): **~ an action against s.o.** возбу|жда́ть, -ди́ть де́ло про́тив кого́-н.; **~ a charge** выдвига́ть, вы́двинуть обвине́ние.

with advs.: **~ about** *v.t.* (*cause*) вызыва́ть, вы́звать; произв|оди́ть, -ести́; **~ back** *v.t.* прин|оси́ть, -ести́ (*or* прив|оди́ть, -ести́) наза́д; **they brought back the news that ...** они́ верну́лись с но́востью, бу́дто...; **it ~s back the past** э́то напомина́ет бы́лое; **~ s.o. back to health** возвраща́ть, верну́ть кому́-н. здоро́вье; **~ down** *v.t.* (*an aircraft*) сби|ва́ть, -ть; (*a bird*) подстре́л|ивать, -и́ть; **~ prices down** сн|ижа́ть, -и́зить це́ны; **~ forth** *v.t.* (*give birth to*) произв|оди́ть, -ести́; **his speech brought forth protests** его́ речь вы́звала проте́сты; **~ forward** *v.t.*: **~ a chair forward** выдвига́ть, вы́двинуть стул; **~ forward a proposal** выдвига́ть, вы́двинуть предложе́ние; (*advance date of*) перен|оси́ть, -ести́ на бо́лее ра́нний срок; (*bookkeeping*) де́лать, с- перено́с счёта на сле́дующую страни́цу; **~ in** *v.t.* вн|оси́ть, -ести́; вв|оди́ть, -ести́; **~ off** *v.t.*: **~ off a manoeuvre** успе́шно заверш|а́ть, -и́ть опера́цию; **~ on** *v.t.*: **this brought on a bad cold** э́то вы́звало си́льный на́сморк; **~ out** *v.t.* выноси́ть, вы́нести; выводи́ть, вы́вести; (*publish*) выпуска́ть, вы́пустить; **the sun ~s out the roses** ро́зы распуска́ются под со́лнечными луча́ми; **~ over** *v.t.* (*convert, convince*) переубе|жда́ть, -ди́ть; **~ round** *v.t.* (*deliver*) прив|ози́ть, -езти́; дост|авля́ть, -а́вить; (*restore to consciousness*) прив|оди́ть, -ести в себя́; (*persuade*) убе|жда́ть, -ди́ть; **he brought the conversation round to politics** он перевёл разгово́р на поли́тику; **~ through** *v.t.*: **the doctors brought him through** доктора́ вы́тянули его́; **~ to** *v.t.* (*restore to consciousness*) прив|оди́ть, -ести́ в созна́ние/себя́; **~ together** *v.t.* (*assemble*) соб|ира́ть, -ра́ть; св|оди́ть, -ести́ вме́сте; (*reconcile*) примир|я́ть, -и́ть; **~ under** *v.t.* (*subdue*) подчин|я́ть, -и́ть; **~ up** *v.t.* (*carry up*) прин|оси́ть, -ести́ наве́рх; (*educate*) воспи́т|ывать, -а́ть; **I was brought up to believe that ...** мне с де́тства внуша́ли, что...; (*vomit*): **he brought up his dinner** его́ вы́рвало по́сле обе́да; **~ up a subject** подн|има́ть, -я́ть (*pf.*) вопро́с; **~ up the rear** замыка́ть (*impf.*) коло́нну/ше́ствие.

brink [brɪŋk] *n.* край (*also fig.*); **on the ~ of despair** на гра́ни отча́яния; **he was on the ~ of tears** он едва́ сде́рживал слёзы.

briny ['braɪnɪ] *adj.* солёный.

briquette [brɪ'ket] *n.* брике́т.

brisk [brɪsk] *adj.* (*of movement*) ско́рый; (*of air, wind*) све́жий; **~ demand** большо́й спрос; **~ trade** оживлённая торго́вля.

brisket ['brɪskɪt] *n.* груди́нка.

bristle ['brɪs(ə)l] *n.* щети́на.

v.i. (*of hair*) стоя́ть (*impf.*) ды́бом; вста́ть (*pf.*) ды́бом; (*of animal, also fig., of pers.*) ощети́ни|ваться, -ться; **the cat ~d** шерсть у ко́шки подняла́сь ды́бом.

bristly ['brɪslɪ] *adj.* щети́нистый.

Britain ['brɪt(ə)n] *n.* А́нглия, Брита́ния; (*also* **Great ~**) Великобрита́ния.

Briticism ['brɪtɪˌsɪz(ə)m] *n.* англици́зм.

British ['brɪtɪʃ] *n.*: **the ~** англича́не, брита́нцы (*both m. pl.*).

adj. брита́нский (*also of ancient Britons*); великобрита́нский, англи́йский; **~ Isles** Брита́нские острова́.

Briton ['brɪt(ə)n] *n.* брита́н|ец (*fem.* -ка); англича́н|ин (*fem.* -ка).

brittle ['brɪt(ə)l] *adj.* ло́мкий, хру́пкий.

broach [brəʊtʃ] *v.t.* (*discussion*) откр|ыва́ть, -ы́ть; **~ a subject** подн|има́ть, -я́ть вопро́с.

broad [brɔːd] *adj.* **1.** (*wide*) широ́кий; **the river is 50 feet ~** ширина́ реки́ 50 фу́тов. **2.** (*extensive*): **~ lands** обши́рные зе́мли. **3.: in ~ daylight** средь бе́ла дня. **4.** (*decided*): **a ~ hint** то́лстый намёк; **a ~ accent** си́льный акце́нт. **5.** (*approximate*): **a ~ definition** о́бщее определе́ние; **in ~ outline** в о́бщих черта́х.

cpds. **~cast** *n.* радиопереда́ча, радиовеща́ние, трансля́ция; (*attr.*) радиовеща́тельный; *v.t.* (*agric.*) се́ять, по- вразбро́с; (*radio*) перед|ава́ть, -а́ть по ра́дио; (*spread, of news etc.*) распростран|я́ть, -и́ть; *v.i.* вести́ (*det.*) радиопереда́чу; **~caster** *n.* радиожурнали́ст; **~casting** *n.* радиовеща́ние, трансля́ция; **~cloth** *n.* то́нкое чёрное сукно́; **~-gauge** *adj.* ширококоле́йный; **~-minded** *adj.* широ́ких взгля́дов; **~side** *n.* **fire a ~side** дать (*pf.*) бортово́й залп; (*fig., vbl. onslaught*) обру́шиться (*pf.*) с ре́зкими напа́дками; **~sword** *n.* пала́ш; **~tail** *n.* каракульча́.

broaden ['brɔːd(ə)n] *v.t. & i.* (*lit., fig.*) расш|иря́ть(ся), -и́рить(ся).

broadly ['brɔːdlɪ] *adv.* (*in the main*) в основно́м; **~ speaking** вообще́ говоря́.

brocade [brə'keɪd, brəʊ-] *n.* парча́.

v.t.: **a ~d gown** парчо́вый наря́д.

broccoli ['brɒkəlɪ] *n.* бро́кколи (*nt. indecl.*); капу́ста спа́ржевая.

brochure ['brəʊʃə(r), brəʊ'ʃjʊə(r)] *n.* брошю́ра.

broil [brɔɪl] *v.t.* (*cul.*) жа́рить, за- на ве́ртеле (*or* на откры́том огне́).

v.i. (*cul.*) жа́риться, за- *etc. as above*.

broke [brəʊk] *adj.* (*coll.*) разори́вшийся, безде́нежный; **stony ~** без гроша́.

broken ['brəʊkən] *adj.* **1.: a ~ leg** сло́манная нога́; **~ English** ло́маный англи́йский язы́к. **2.** (**~-*down***): **a ~ marriage** расстро́енный брак; **a ~ home** разби́тая семья́. **3.** (*crushed*): **a ~ man** сло́мленный челове́к; **~ spirits** пода́вленное настрое́ние. **4.** (*rough*): **~ ground** пересечённая ме́стность. **5.** (*interrupted*): **~ sleep** пре́рванный сон. **6.** (**~ in,** *of a horse*) вы́езженный, объе́зженный.

cpds. **~-down** *adj.* (*of pers.*) надло́мленный; (*of machine*) сло́манный; **~-hearted** *adj.* с разби́тым се́рдцем.

broker ['brəʊkə(r)] *n.* (*of shares etc.*) ма́клер; (*of distrained goods*) комиссионе́р; (*go-between*) посре́дник; **marriage ~** сват.

brokerage ['brəʊkərɪdʒ] *n.* (*business*) ма́клерство; (*commission*) комиссио́нное вознагражде́ние.

bromide ['brəʊmaɪd] *n.* (*chem.*) броми́д; (*fig., coll.*) бана́льность.

bromine ['brəʊmiːn] *n.* бром.

bronch|i ['brɒŋkaɪ], **-ia** ['brɒŋkɪə] *nn.* (*anat.*) бро́нхи (*m. pl.*).

bronchial ['brɒŋkɪəl] *adj.* бронхиа́льный.

bronchitis [brɒŋ'kaɪtɪs] *n.* бронхи́т.

brontosaurus [ˌbrɒntə'sɔːrəs] *n.* бронтоза́вр.

bronze [brɒnz] *n.* бро́нза; (*article*) бро́нза, изде́лие из бро́нзы; (*attr.*) бро́нзовый.

v.t. бронзи́ровать (*impf., pf.*); (*tan*) покр|ыва́ть, -ы́ть зага́ром; **~d cheeks** загоре́лые щёки.

brooch [brəʊtʃ] *n.* брошь.

brood [bruːd] *n.* вы́водок.

v.i. **1.** (*of bird*) сиде́ть (*impf.*) на я́йцах. **2.: ~ over one's plans** вына́шивать (*impf.*) пла́ны; **~ over an insult** копи́ть (*impf.*) в себе́ оби́ду.

cpds. **~-hen** *n.* насе́дка; **~-mare** *n.* племенна́я кобы́ла.

brook[1] [brʊk] *n.* (*stream*) руче́й.

brook[2] [brʊk] *v.t.* (*liter.*): **this ~s no delay** э́то не те́рпит отлага́тельства.

broom [bruːm] *n.* **1.** (*bot.*) раки́тник. **2.** (*implement*) метла́; (*besom*) ве́ник; **a new ~ sweeps clean** но́вая метла́ чи́сто метёт.

cpd. **~stick** *n.* метлови́ще; (*witch's*) помело́.

Bros. ['brʌðəz] *n.* (*abbr. of* **Brother(s)**) Бра́тья (*в названии фирмы*).

broth [brɒθ] *n.* мясно́й бульо́н; **Scotch ~** перло́вый суп.

brothel ['brɒθ(ə)l] *n.* публи́чный дом, дом терпи́мости.

brother ['brʌðə(r)] *n.* **1.** (*also relig.*) брат; **own, full ~** родно́й брат; **half ~** сво́дный брат; **the Ivanov ~s** бра́тья Ивано́вы. **2.** (*fig.*): **~ in arms** собра́т по ору́жию.

cpd. **~-in-law** *n.* (*sister's husband*) зять (*m.*); (*wife's ~*) шу́рин; (*husband's ~*) де́верь (*m.*); (*wife's sister's husband*) своя́к.

brotherhood ['brʌðəˌhʊd] *n.* (*kinship*) бра́тство; (*comradeship*) бра́тские отноше́ния; (*association, community*) содру́жество.

brotherly ['brʌðəlɪ] *adj.* бра́тский.

brow [braʊ] *n.* (*eye ~*) бровь; **knit one's ~s** хму́рить, на- бро́ви; (*forehead*) лоб, чело́; (*of hill*) гре́бень (*m.*); **over the ~ of the hill** за гре́бнем холма́.

cpd. **~beat** *v.t.* наг|оня́ть, -на́ть страх на+*a.*; запу́г|ивать, -а́ть.

brown [braʊn] *n.* (*colour*) кори́чневый цвет.

adj. **1.** кори́чневый; (*grey-~*) бу́рый; **light-~** све́тло-кори́чневый; **~ eyes** ка́рие глаза́; **~ hair** кашта́новые во́лосы; **~ bear** бу́рый медве́дь; **~ bread** се́рый хлеб; **~ sugar** кори́чневый са́хар; **~ paper** обёрточная бума́га. **2.** (*toasted*) поджа́ренный, подрумя́ненный. **3.** (*tanned*) загоре́лый; **as ~ as a berry** чёрный, как га́лка; **he returned from his holidays quite ~** он верну́лся из о́тпуска тёмным от зага́ра. **4.** (*dark-skinned*) сму́глый.

v.t. (*roast, toast*) поджа́ри|вать, -ть.

cpds. **~-eyed** *adj.* с ка́рими глаза́ми; **~-haired** *adj.* с тёмно-ру́сыми волоса́ми.

brownie ['braʊnɪ] *n.* (*goblin*) домово́й.

browse [braʊz] *v.i.* щипа́ть (*impf.*) траву́; пасти́сь (*impf.*); (*fig.*): **~ through a book** просм|а́тривать, -отре́ть кни́гу.

bruise [bruːz] *n.* синя́к, кровоподтёк; (*of fruit*) помя́тость.

v.t. подст|авля́ть, -а́вить синя́к +*d.*; (*fruit*) помя́ть, поби́ть (*both pf.*); **I ~d my shoulder** я ушиб плечо́; **this apple is ~d** э́то я́блоко поби́то.

v.i. ушиб|а́ться, -и́ться.

brunette [bruː'net] *n.* брюне́тка.

adj. тёмный, темноволо́сый.

brunt [brʌnt] *n.* гла́вный уда́р; **bear the ~ of the work** вы́нести (*pf.*) всю тя́жесть рабо́ты.

brush [brʌʃ] *n.* **1.** (*brushwood*) куста́рник, хво́рост. **2.** (*for sweeping*) щётка; (*painter's*) кисть. **3.** (*skirmish, tiff*) сты́чка. **4.** (*brushing*) чи́стка; **give sth. a good ~** хорошо́ почи́стить (*pf.*) что-н.

v.t. (*clean*) чи́стить, по-; ~ **mud off a coat** счи́стить (*pf.*) грязь с пальто́; (*touch slightly*): **the twigs ~ed my cheek** ве́тки легко́ косну́лись мое́й щеки́.

v.i.: ~ **against sth.** слегка́ каса́ться, косну́ться чего́-н.; ~ **past s.o.** прон|оси́ться, -ести́сь ми́мо кого́-н.

with advs.: ~ **aside** *v.t.*: ~ **aside difficulties** отме|та́ть, -сти́ тру́дности; ~ **away** *v.t.*: ~ **away a fly** смахну́ть (*pf.*) му́ху; ~ **off** *v.i.*: **the mud will ~ off** грязь счи́стится; ~ **out** *v.t.*: ~ **out a room** подме|та́ть, -сти́ ко́мнату; ~ **out one's hair** причеса́ть (*pf.*) щёткой во́лосы; ~ **up** *v.t.*: ~ **up one's French** восстан|а́вливать, -ови́ть свои́ зна́ния во францу́зском языке́; *v.i.*: ~ **up on a subject** освеж|а́ть, -и́ть зна́ния по како́му-н. предме́ту.

cpds. **~-down** *n.*: **give s.o. a ~-down** почи́стить (*pf.*) кого́-н.; **~-off** *n.*: **give s.o. the ~-off** (*coll.*) отряхну́ть (*pf.*) кого́-н.; **~-up** *n.*: **have a wash and ~-up** привести́ (*pf.*) себя́ в поря́док; **~wood** *n.* хво́рост; **~work** *n.* живопи́сная мане́ра.

brusque [brʊsk, bru:sk, brʌsk] *adj.* ре́зкий.

brusqueness ['brʊsknɪs, bru:sknɪs, brʌsknɪs] *n.* ре́зкость.

Brussels ['brʌs(ə)lz] *n.*: ~ **sprouts** брюссе́льская капу́ста.

brutal ['bru:t(ə)l] *adj.* (*rough*) гру́бый; (*cruel*) жесто́кий.

brutality [bru:'tælɪtɪ] *n.* гру́бость; жесто́кость; (*cruel act*) зве́рство.

brute [bru:t] *n.* (*animal*) живо́тное, зверь (*m.*); (*pers.*) скоти́на (*c.g.*).

adj.: ~ **strength, force** физи́ческая си́ла.

B.Sc. (*abbr. of* ***Bachelor of Science***) бакала́вр (есте́ственных) нау́к.

BST (*abbr. of* ***British Summer Time***) Брита́нское ле́тнее вре́мя.

bubble ['bʌb(ə)l] *n.* **1.** пузы́рь (*m.*); (*of air, gas in liquid*) пузырёк; **blow ~s** пус|ка́ть, -ти́ть пузыри́; **prick a, the ~** (*lit.*) проткну́ть (*pf.*) пузы́рь. **2.** (*gurgle*) бу́льканье.

v.i. (*of water*) пузыри́ться (*impf.*), кипе́ть (*impf.*); (*of a fountain*) кипе́ть (*impf.*); ~ **up** бить (*impf.*) ключо́м; бу́лькать (*impf.*); ~ **(over) with laughter** залива́ться (*impf.*) сме́хом.

bubbly ['bʌblɪ] *adj.* (*of wine*) шипу́чий, пе́нящийся.

bubonic [bju:'bɒnɪk] *adj.* бубо́нный; ~ **plague** бубо́нная чума́.

buccaneer [,bʌkə'nɪə(r)] *n.* пира́т.

buck[1] [bʌk] *n.* **1.** (*male deer*) оле́нь (*m.*). **2.** (*male animal*) саме́ц; ~ **rabbit** саме́ц кро́лика. **3.** (*coll., dollar*) до́ллар; **big ~s** ку́ча де́нег. **4.: pass the ~** (*coll.*) снять (*pf.*) с себя́ отве́тственность.

cpds. **~shot** *n.* кру́пная дробь; **~skin** *n.* оле́нья (*or* лоси́ная) ко́жа; **~thorn** *n.* круши́на; **~-tooth** *n.* выступа́ющий зуб.

buck[2] [bʌk] *v.t.* **1.: the horse ~ed him off** ло́шадь сбро́сила его́. **2.: ~ s.o. up** (*cheer*) подбодри́ть (*pf.*) кого́-н.; ~ **things up** (*hasten*) подтолкну́ть (*pf.*) де́ло.

v.i. **1.** (*of horse*) вста|ва́ть, -ть на дыбы́. **2.: ~ against fate** проти́виться (*impf.*) судьбе́. **3. ~ up** (*coll.*) (*cheer up*) подбодри́ться, оживи́ться (*all pf.*); (*get a move on*) пошеве́ливаться (*impf.*).

bucket ['bʌkɪt] *n.* **1.** ведро́; **the rain came down in ~s** дождь лил как из ведра́; **kick the ~** сыгра́ть (*pf.*) в я́щик (*sl.*). **2.** (*of dredger*) черпа́к, ковш.

v.i.: (*rain*) **it's ~ing down** льёт, как из ведра́.

buckle ['bʌk(ə)l] *n.* пря́жка.

v.t. **1.** (*fasten*) застёг|ивать, -ну́ть; ~ **on one's sword** пристёг|ивать, -ну́ть меч. **2.** (*crumple*) из|гиба́ть, -огну́ть; сгиба́ть, согну́ть.

v.i. **1.** (*fasten*) застёг|иваться, -ну́ться. **2.: ~ down to a task, ~ to** прин|има́ться, -я́ться за де́ло. **3.** (*also* ~ **up**, *of metal etc.*) сгиба́ться, согну́ться; (*of wheel*) погну́ться (*pf.*).

buckram ['bʌkrəm] *n.* клеёнка; (*attr.*) клеёнчатый.

buckwheat ['bʌkwi:t] *n.* гречи́ха; (*attr.*) гречи́шный, (*cooked*) гре́чневый.

bucolic [bju:'kɒlɪk] *adj.* буколи́ческий.

bud [bʌd] *n.* по́чка; (*flower not fully opened*) буто́н; **the trees are in ~** на дере́вьях появи́лись по́чки; **nip sth. in the ~** уничт|ожа́ть, -о́жить что-н. в заро́дыше.

v.i. (*of plant*) покр|ыва́ться, -ы́ться по́чками; (*fig.*) распус|ка́ться, -ти́ться; расцве|та́ть, -сти́.

Buddha ['bʊdə] *n.* Бу́дда (*m.*).

Buddhism ['bʊdɪz(ə)m] *n.* будди́зм.

Buddhist ['bʊdɪst] *n.* будди́ст.

adj. будди́йский.

buddy ['bʌdɪ] *n.* (*US coll.*) дружи́ще (*m.*), прия́тель (*m.*), брато́к.

budge [bʌdʒ] *v.t.*: **I cannot ~ this rock** я не могу́ сдви́нуть э́тот ка́мень.

v.i.: **he never ~d the whole time** за всё вре́мя он не пошевельну́лся; **the bookcase won't ~ an inch** кни́жный шкаф невозмо́жно с ме́ста сдви́нуть.

budgerigar ['bʌdʒərɪ,gɑ:(r)] *n.* волни́стый попуга́йчик.

budget ['bʌdʒɪt] *n.* бюдже́т.

v.t. & i.: ~ **(funds) for a project** ассигнова́ть (*impf., pf.*) определённую су́мму на прое́кт.

budgetary ['bʌdʒɪtərɪ] *adj.* бюдже́тный.

buff [bʌf] *n.* (*ox-hide*) бы́чья ко́жа; (*buffalo-hide*) бу́йволовая ко́жа; (*coll., human skin*): **in the ~** нагишо́м; (*colour*) тёмно-жёлтый цвет.

adj. тёмно-жёлтый.

v.t. (*metal*) полирова́ть, от- ко́жей.

buffalo ['bʌfə,ləʊ] *n.* бу́йвол, бизо́н.

buffer ['bʌfə(r)] *n.* бу́фер; (*fig.*): ~ **state** бу́ферное госуда́рство.

buffet[1] [bʌfɪt] *v.t.* уд|аря́ть, -а́рить в+*a.*; **they were ~ed by waves** их швыря́ло по волна́м; **they were ~ed by the crowd** их затолка́ла толпа́.

buffet[2] ['bʊfeɪ, 'bʌfeɪ] *n.* (*sideboard*) буфе́т, серва́нт; (*refreshment bar*) буфе́т; (*supper, reception*) а-ля фурше́т.

buffoon [bə'fu:n] *n.* шут, фигля́р.

buffoonery [bə'fu:nərɪ] *n.* шутовство́, фигля́рство.

bug [bʌg] *n.* (*bedbug*) клоп; (*any small insect*) бука́шка, жучо́к; (*coll., germ*) зара́за; (*concealed microphone*) подслу́шка; (*craze*) пове́трие; **he's got the travelling ~** он поме́шан на путеше́ствиях.

v.t.: **the room was ~ged** (*coll.*) в ко́мнате бы́ли устано́влены подслу́шивающие устро́йства; **the conversation was ~ged** разгово́р подслу́шивали.

bugaboo ['bʌgə,bu:] *n.* бу́ка, пу́гало.

bugbear ['bʌgbeə(r)] *n.* (*bogy*) бу́ка, пу́гало; (*object of aversion*) жу́пел.

bugger ['bʌgə(r)] *n.* (*sodomite*) содоми́т; (*vulg., as term of abuse*) тип; **poor ~** несча́стный.

v.t. **1.** (*commit sodomy with*) занима́ться (*impf.*) содоми́ей с+*i.* **2.** (*vulg. uses*): ~ **s.o. about** трави́ть, за- кого́-н.; ~ **sth. up** исковéркать/запоро́ть (*pf., sl.*) что-н.; **I'm ~ed if I know** чёрта с два, е́сли я зна́ю; ~ **all** ни шиша́; ни хрена́; ~ **(it)!** чёрт возьми́! ~ **them!** да хрен с ни́ми!

v.i.: ~ **off!** (*vulg.*) прова́ливай!; убира́йся!

buggery ['bʌgərɪ] *n.* содоми́я.

buggy ['bʌgɪ] *n.* (*horse-drawn*) кабриоле́т; (*beach, dune etc.*) ба́гги.

bugle[1] ['bju:g(ə)l] *n.* горн.

cpd. **~-call** *n.* сигна́л го́рна.

bugle[2] ['bju:g(ə)l] *n.* (*bead*) стекля́рус.

bugler ['bju:glə(r)] *n.* горни́ст.

build [bɪld] *n.* (*structure*) констру́кция; фо́рма; (*of human body*) телосложе́ние; **a man of powerful ~**

челове́к могу́чего сложе́ния.

v.t. **1.** стро́ить, по-; выстра́ивать, вы́строить; **~ a nest** вить, с- гнездо́; **~ a fire** (*in the open*) разв|о-ди́ть, -ести́ костёр. **2.: a well-built man** хорошо́ сложённый челове́к. **3.** (*fig.*): **~ a new world** созд|ава́ть, -а́ть но́вый мир; **he is not built that way** он сде́лан из друго́го те́ста. **4.** (*base*): **~ one's hopes on sth.** стро́ить, по- наде́жды на чём-н.

v.i.: **I shan't ~ if I can find a suitable house** я не бу́ду стро́иться, если найду́ подходя́щий дом.

with advs.: **~ in** *v.t.*: (*surround*): **~ in a garden with a wall** обн|оси́ть, -ести́ сад стено́й; (*insert into structure*) вмонти́ровать (*pf.*); *see also* **built-in; ~ on** *v.t.*: **~ a wing on to a house** пристр|а́ивать, -о́ить крыло́ к до́му; **~ up** *v.t.*: **~ s.o. up** (*in health*) укреп|ля́ть, -и́ть кому́-н. здоро́вье; (*in prestige*) созд|ава́ть, -а́ть и́мя кому́-н.; **~ up a theory** стро́ить, по- тео́рию; **~ up a business** созд|ава́ть, -а́ть де́ло; *v.i.*: **work has built up over the past year** накопи́лось мно́го рабо́ты за после́дний год; **our forces are ~ing up** на́ши си́лы расту́т (*see also* **built-up**).

cpds. **~-up** *n.* (*accumulation*) скопле́ние; рост, разви́тие; (*coll.*, *boosting*) популяриза́ция, созда́ние и́мени; **arms ~-up** нара́щивание вооруже́ний.

builder ['bɪldə(r)] *n.* строи́тель (*m.*); (*housing contractor*) подря́дчик.

building ['bɪldɪŋ] *n.* **1.** (*structure*) зда́ние, постро́йка, строе́ние; (*large edifice*) сооруже́ние; (*premises*) помеще́ние. **2.** (*activity*) (по)стро́йка; (*esp. large-scale*) строи́тельство; **~ of socialism** построе́ние социали́зма; **~ of houses** жили́щное строи́тельство; **~ materials** строи́тельные материа́лы; **~ land** земля́ под постро́йку; **~ society** жили́щно-строи́тельное о́бщество.

built-in [bɪlt] *adj.*: **a ~ cupboard** встро́енный/стенно́й шкаф.

built-up [bɪlt] *adj.*: **~ area** застро́енный райо́н.

bulb [bʌlb] *n.* (*bot.*, *anat.*) лу́ковица; (*of lamp*) ла́мпочка.

bulbous ['bʌlbəs] *adj.* лу́ковичный.

Bulgaria [bʌl'geərɪə] *n.* Болга́рия.

bulg|e [bʌldʒ] *n.* вы́пуклость.

v.i. (*swell*) выпя́чиваться, вы́пятиться; (*of bag etc.*) над|ува́ться, -у́ться; разд|ува́ться, -у́ться; **his pockets were ~ing with apples** его́ карма́ны оттопы́ривались от я́блок.

bulimia [bju:'lɪmɪə] *n.* булими́я, ненорма́льно повы́шенное чу́вство го́лода.

bulk [bʌlk] *n.* **1.** (*size*, *mass*, *volume*) величина́, ма́сса, объём. **2.** (*in large quantities*): **~ purchase** поку́пка гурто́м; ма́ссовая заку́пка; **~ buying** о́птовые заку́пки. **3.** (*greater part*) основна́я ма́сса/часть.

cpd. **~head** *n.* перебо́рка, перегоро́дка.

bulky ['bʌlkɪ] *adj.* (*large*) объёмистый; (*unwieldy*) громо́здкий.

bull[1] [bʊl] *n.* бык; (*elephant*, *whale etc.*) саме́ц; (*fig.*): **~ in a china shop** слон в посу́дной ла́вке; **take the ~ by the horns** взять (*pf.*) быка́ за рога́; **go at sth. like a ~ at a gate** лезть/пере́ть (*impf.*) напроло́м.

cpds. **~dog** *n.* бульдо́г; **~doze** *v.t.* (*clear with ~dozer*) расч|ища́ть, -и́стить бульдо́зером; **~dozer** *n.* бульдо́зер; **~fight, ~fighting** *nn.* бой быко́в; **~fighter** *n.* тореадо́р; **~finch** *n.* снеги́рь (*m.*); **~frog** *n.* лягу́шка-бык; **~-ring** *n.* аре́на для бо́я быко́в; **~'s-eye** *n.* (*of target*) я́блоко; **hit the ~'s-eye** (*fig.*) поп|ада́ть, -а́сть в цель.

bull[2] [bʊl] *n.* (*edict*) бу́лла.

bullet ['bʊlɪt] *n.* пу́ля.

cpds. **~-hole** *n.* пулево́е отве́рстие; **~-proof** *adj.* пуленепробива́емый; **~proof vest** бронежиле́т.

bulletin ['bʊlɪtɪn] *n.* (*periodical*; *official statement*) бюллете́нь (*m.*); (*news report*) бюллете́нь (*m.*), вы́пуск, сообще́ние.

bullion ['bʊlɪən] *n.*: **gold ~** зо́лото в сли́тках.

bullock ['bʊlək] *n.* вол.

bullshit ['bʊlʃɪt] *n.* (*vulg.*) брехня́, бредя́тина.

bully ['bʊlɪ] *n.* громи́ла (*m.*), зади́ра (*m.*).

v.t. запу́г|ивать, -а́ть; **~ s.o. into doing sth.** запу́гиванием заст|авля́ть, -а́вить кого́-н. сде́лать что-н.

bulrush ['bʊlrʌʃ] *n.* камы́ш.

bulwark ['bʊlwək] *n.* (*rampart*) бастио́н, бо́льверк; (*fig.*): **~ of freedom** опло́т свобо́ды.

bum [bʌm] *n.* (*coll.*) **1.** (*buttocks*) зад, за́дница. **2.** (*loafer*) ло́дырь (*m.*); (*US*, *vagrant*) бродя́га (*m.*).

adj. дрянно́й.

v.t. (*sl.*, *cadge*, *scrounge*) кля́нчить, вы́-.

v.i.: **~ around** шата́ться (*impf.*).

bumble-bee ['bʌmb(ə)l,bi:] *n.* шмель (*m.*).

bum|f, -ph ['bʌmf] *n.* (*papers*) бума́жки (*f. pl.*).

bump [bʌmp] *n.* **1.** (*thump*) глухо́й уда́р; **he landed with a ~ on the floor** он шлёпнулся/гро́хнулся на́ пол; (*collision*) толчо́к; **2.** (*swelling*, *protuberance*) ши́шка. **3.** (*in a road*) уха́б, буго́р.

adv.: **he went ~ into the door** он так и вре́зался в дверь.

v.t. уд|аря́ть, -а́рить; ушиб|а́ть, -и́ть; **the car ~ed the one in front** маши́на сту́кнулась о другу́ю, стоя́вшую/ше́дшую впереди́; **I ~ed the table and spilt the ink** я толкну́л стол и проли́л черни́ла; **~ off** (*kill*) пусти́ть (*pf.*) в расхо́д (*sl.*).

v.i.: **~ against a tree** уда́риться (*pf.*) о де́рево; наскочи́ть/наткну́ться (*pf.*) на дерево; **~ along** (*in cart etc.*) трясти́сь (*impf.*); **his car ~ed into ours** его́ маши́на вре́залась в на́шу; **I ~ed into him in London** я наткну́лся на него́ в Ло́ндоне.

bumper ['bʌmpə(r)] *n.* **1.** (*of car*) бу́фер. **2.: ~ crop** небыва́лый/неви́данный урожа́й.

bumph ['bʌmf] = **bumf**

bumpkin ['bʌmpkɪn] *n.* мужла́н.

bumpy ['bʌmpɪ] *adj.* (*of road*) уха́бистый, тря́ский; **we had a ~ journey** нас трясло́ всю доро́гу.

bun [bʌn] *n.* **1.** (*cul.*) бу́лочка, плю́шка. **2.** (*of hair*) пучо́к.

bunch [bʌntʃ] *n.* **1.** (*of flowers*) буке́т; (*of grapes*) кисть, гроздь; (*of bananas*) гроздь; **~ of keys** свя́зка ключе́й. **2.** (*coll.*, *group*) компа́ния, гру́ппа.

bundle ['bʌnd(ə)l] *n.* **1.** (*of clothes etc.*) у́зел; (*of sticks*) вяза́нка; (*of hay*) оха́пка. **2.** (*packet*) паке́т. **3.: she is a ~ of nerves** она́ комо́к не́рвов.

v.t. **1. ~ up** свя́з|ывать, -а́ть в у́зел/вяза́нку. **2.** (*shove*) запи́х|ивать, -а́ть; **~ s.o. into a room** втолкну́ть (*pf.*) кого́-н. в ко́мнату; **~ off** спрова́|живать, -дить.

bung [bʌŋ] *n.* заты́чка, вту́лка.

v.t. **1.** (*cask etc.*) зат|ыка́ть, -кну́ть; закупо́ри|вать, -ть; **the sink is ~ed up** ра́ковина засори́лась; **my nose is ~ed up** у меня́ зало́жен нос.

bungalow ['bʌŋgə,ləʊ] *n.* бу́нгало (*indecl.*); одноэта́жная да́ча.

bungle ['bʌŋg(ə)l] *v.t.* по́ртить, на-; пу́тать, с-.

bunion ['bʌnjən] *n.* о́пухоль/ши́шка на ноге́.

bunk[1] [bʌŋk] *n.* (*sleeping-berth*) ко́йка; **~ bed** двухъя́русная крова́ть.

bunk[2] [bʌŋk] *n.* (*sl.*, *nonsense*) чепуха́, чушь.

bunker ['bʌŋkə(r)] *n.* (*ship's*) бу́нкер; (*underground shelter*) блинда́ж; (*golf*) я́ма.

bunkum ['bʌŋkəm] *n.* (*coll.*) чушь, пустосло́вие.

bunny ['bʌnɪ] *n.* (*coll.*) кро́лик, за́йчик.

Bunsen burner ['bʌns(ə)n] *n.* бу́нзеновская горе́лка.

bunting[1] ['bʌntɪŋ] *n.* (*zool.*) овся́нка; **snow ~** пу́ночка.

bunting[2] ['bʌntɪŋ] *n.* (*cloth*) фла́жная мате́рия; (*naut.*) флагду́к; (*fig.*, *flags*) фла́ги (*m. pl.*).

buoy [bɔɪ] *n.* буй, ба́кен; **mooring-~** швартóвная бо́чка; (*life-~*) спаса́тельный буй/круг.

v.t. (*mark with ~*) отм|еча́ть, -е́тить буя́ми ; **~**

up (*fig.*) поддéрж|ивать, -áть.
buoyancy ['bɔɪənsɪ] *n.* плавýчесть; (*fig.*) жизнерáдостность; оживлéние.
buoyant ['bɔɪənt] *adj.* плавýчий; (*of pers.*) жизнерáдостный; (*of hopes, market*) оживлённый.
bur, burr [bɜ:(r)] *n.* репéй, репéйник.
burden ['bɜ:d(ə)n] *n.* **1.** (*load*) нóша, груз; (*fig.*) брéмя (*nt.*); **beast of ~** вьючное живóтное; **~ of proof** брéмя докáзывания; **become a ~ on s.o.** стать (*pf.*) в тягость комý-н.
v.t. (*load*) нагру|жáть, -зи́ть; (*fig.*) обремен|я́ть, -и́ть; **~ s.o. with expenses** взвáл|ивать, -и́ть на когó-н. расхóды.
burdensome ['bɜ:d(ə)nsəm] *adj.* обремени́тельный, тя́гостный.
burdock ['bɜ:dɒk] *n.* лопýх.
bureau ['bjʊərəʊ, -'rəʊ] *n.* (*desk*) бюрó (*indecl.*); (*chest*) комóд; (*office*) бюрó; **information ~** спрáвочное бюрó; **employment ~** бюрó по нáйму; **marriage ~** брáчное бюрó; **~ de change** размéнная контóра.
bureaucracy [bjʊə'rɒkrəsɪ] *n.* бюрокрáтия.
bureaucrat ['bjʊərə,kræt, -rəʊ,kræt] *n.* бюрокрáт.
bureaucratic [bjʊərə'krætɪk, -rəʊ'krætɪk] *adj.* бюрократи́ческий.
burgeon ['bɜ:dʒ(ə)n] *v.i.* да|вáть, -ть пóчки; распус|кáться, -ти́ться.
burger ['bɜ:gə(r)] *n.* котлéта; **~ bar** гáмбургерная, котлéтная.
burgher ['bɜ:gə(r)] *n.* бю́ргер, горожáнин.
burglar ['bɜ:glə(r)] *n.* грабúтель (*m.*), взлóмщик.
burglary ['bɜ:glərɪ] *n.* грабёж; крáжа со взлóмом.
burgle ['bɜ:g(ə)l] (*also* **burglarize**) *v.t.*: грáбить, о-.
v.i. соверш|áть, -и́ть крáжу со взлóмом.
burgomaster ['bɜ:gə,mɑ:stə(r)] *n.* бургоми́стр.
burial ['berɪəl] *n.* (*interment*) погребéние, захоронéние; (*funeral*) пóхор|оны (*pl., g.* -он); **~ service** заупокóйная слýжба.
cpds. **~-ground** *n.* клáдбище, погóст; **~-mound** *n.* кургáн; **~-place** *n.* мéсто погребéния.
burlap ['bɜ:læp] *n.* дерю́га.
burlesque [bɜ:'lesk] *n.* (*parody*) бурлéск.
adj. бурлéскный.
burly ['bɜ:lɪ] *adj.* здоровéнный, дю́жий.
Burma ['bɜ:mə] *n.* Би́рма.
burn [bɜ:n] *n.* (*injury*) ожóг.
v.t. **1.** (*sting*) жечь, с-; (*destroy by fire*) сж|игáть, -ечь; **~ o.s.** обж|игáться, -éчься; **~ one's fingers** (*lit.*) обжéчь (*pf.*) себé пáльцы; (*fig.*) обжéчься (*pf.*) (*на чём*); **~ a hole in sth.** прожéчь (*pf.*) дырý в чём-н.; **the meat is ~t** мя́со сгорéло/подгорéло; **a ~t taste/smell** вкус/зáпах горéлого; **the ship ~s oil** корáбль рабóтает на нéфти; **acid ~s the carpet** кислотá прожигáет ковёр; **pepper ~s one's mouth** от пéрца жжёт во ртý; **~ paint off a wall** сжечь (*pf.*) крáску со стены́. **2.** (*bricks, charcoal etc.*) обж|игáть, -éчь. **3.** (*tan*) опал|я́ть, -и́ть; обж|игáть, -éчь. **4.** (*fig.*): **~ one's boats** сжéчь (*pf.*) свои́ корабли́; **he has money to ~** у негó дéнег кýры не клюю́т; **money ~s a hole in his pocket** дéньги у негó не дéржатся.
v.i. **1.** горéть (*impf.*) (*also fig.*): **the house is ~ing** дом гори́т; в дóме пожáр; **the lamp is ~ing low** лáмпа догорáет; **acid ~s into metal** кислотá разъедáет метáлл; **he ~t with fever** он был в жарý; он горéл в лихорáдке; **he ~t with shame** он сгорáл от стыдá; **he ~t with passion** он пылáл стрáстью; **he ~t with anger** он кипéл от злóсти.
with advs.: **~ down** *v.t.* сж|игáть, -ечь; *v.i.*: **the house ~t down** дом сгорéл дотлá; **~ out** *v.t.*: **the fire ~t itself out** пожáр/костёр догорéл и заглóх; **~ o.s. out** (*fig.*) сгорéть (*pf.*); **~ out a fuse** (*elec.*) пережéчь (*pf.*) прóбку; *v.i.*: **the fire ~t out** огóнь потýх; костёр заглóх; **~ up** *v.i.*: **make the fire ~ up** разж|игáть, -éчь пéчку/ками́н.
burner ['bɜ:nə(r)] *n.* (*of stove etc.*) горéлка; **to put on the back burner** отодви́нуть (*pf.*) на зáдний план.
burning ['bɜ:nɪŋ] *n.* горéние; обжигáние, óбжиг.
adj. (*of fever*) сжигáющий; (*of shame*) жгýчий.
burnish ['bɜ:nɪʃ] *v.t.* полировáть, от-.
burp [bɜ:p] (*coll.*) *n.* отры́жка, рыгáнье.
v.t.: **~ a baby** да|вáть, -ть ребёнку отрыгнýть.
v.i. рыг|áть, -нýть.
burr[1] [bɜ:(r)] *n.* (*in speech*) картáвость; **speak with a ~** картáвить (*impf.*).
burr[2] [bɜ:(r)] *n.* (*on metal*) заусéнец, грат.
burrow ['bʌrəʊ] *n.* норá.
v.t.: **~ a hole** рыть, вы- нóру.
v.i. (*of rabbit/mole*) рыть, вы- нóру/ходы́; **~ among archives** ры́ться (*impf.*) в архи́вах.
bursar ['bɜ:sə] *n.* (*treasurer*) казначéй.
bursary ['bɜ:sərɪ] *n.* (*office*) канцеля́рия казначéя; (*grant*) стипéндия.
burst [bɜ:st] *n.* взрыв; разры́в; **the ~ of a shell** разры́в снаря́да; **a ~ of energy** вспы́шка/взрыв энéргии; **work in sudden ~s** рабóтать (*impf.*) рывкáми; **~ of applause** взрыв аплодисмéнтов; **~ of anger** вспы́шка гнéва; **~ of tears** внезáпный потóк слёз; **~ of machine-gun fire** пулемётная óчередь.
v.t. (*e.g. a shell. tyre, balloon, blood-vessel*) раз|рывáть, -орвáть; **the river ~ its banks** рекá вы́шла из берегóв; **~ one's sides with laughing** надорвáть (*pf.*) живóт от смéха; **~ a door open** распахнýть (*pf.*) дверь.
v.i.: **the shell ~** снаря́д разорвáлся; **the bubble ~** пузы́рь лóпнул; **the dam ~** плоти́ну прорвáло; **full to ~ing** пóлный до откáза; **he is ~ing with health** он пы́шет здорóвьем; **~ with laughter** расхохотáться (*pf.*); **he was ~ing with pride** егó распирáло от гóрдости; **I was ~ing to tell her** мне не терпéлось сказáть ей; **the door ~ open** дверь распахнýлась.
with preps.: **~ into bloom** распусти́ться (*pf.*), расцвести́ (*pf.*): **~ into song** запéть (*pf.*); **~ into tears** разрыдáться (*pf.*); **~ into a room** ворвáться (*pf.*) в кóмнату; **~ into flame** вспы́хнуть (*pf.*); **oil ~ out of the ground** из земли́ заби́ла нефть; **the sun ~ through the clouds** сóлнце прорвáлось сквозь тýчи; **shouts ~ upon our ears** внезáпно нас оглуши́ли кри́ки; **the news ~ upon the world** э́та нóвость потряслá мир.
with advs.: **~ in** *v.i.* **he ~ in upon us** он ворвáлся к нам; **~ out** *v.i.* (*exclaim*) вы́палить (*pf.*); **~ out laughing** расхохотáться (*pf.*).
bur|y ['berɪ] *v.t.* **1.** (*inter*) хорони́ть, по-; погре|бáть, -сти́; **he is dead and ~ied** егó нет в живы́х. **2.** (*hide in earth*) зар|ывáть, -ы́ть; зак|áпывать, -опáть. **3.** (*remove from view*): **~y one's face in one's hands** закры́ть (*pf.*) лицó рукáми; **~y o.s. in one's books** зары́ться (*pf.*) в кни́ги; **~y o.s. in the country** похорони́ть (*pf.*) себя́ в дерéвне.
bus [bʌs] *n.* автóбус.
v.i. (*also* **~ it**) éхать (*det.*) автóбусом.
cpds. **~-conductor** *n.* кондýктор автóбуса; **~-conductress** *n.* жéнщина-кондýктор; **~-driver** *n.* води́тель (*m.*) автóбуса; **~-shelter** *n.* автопавильóн; **~-stop** *n.* автóбусная останóвка.
bush [bʊʃ] *n.* (*shrub*) куст; (*thicket*) кустáрник; (*wild land*) некультиви́рованная земля́.
bushel ['bʊʃ(ə)l] *n.* бýшель (*m.*).
bushing ['bʊʃɪŋ] *n.* втýлка, вклáдыш.
bushy ['bʊʃɪ] *adj.* (*covered with bush*) покры́тый кустáрником; (*of beard etc.*) густóй.
busily ['bɪzɪlɪ] *adv.* делови́то; энерги́чно.
business ['bɪznɪs] *n.* **1.** (*task, affair*) дéло; **he made it his ~ to find out ...** он счёл свои́м дóлгом узнáть...;

what is your ~ here? что вам здесь на́до?; **it is none of your ~** э́то не ва́ше де́ло; э́то вас не каса́ется; **mind your own ~** не вме́шивайтесь не в своё де́ло; **it is his ~ to keep a record** его́ обя́занность — вести́ за́писи; **you have no ~ to say that** не вам э́то говори́ть; **funny, monkey ~** нечи́стое де́ло; **I am sick of the whole ~** мне вся э́та исто́рия надое́ла; **'any other ~'** (*on agenda*) «Ра́зное». **2.** (*trouble*): **what a ~ it is!** кака́я возня́/исто́рия!; **make a great ~ of sth.** преувели́чивать (*impf.*) значе́ние чего́-н. **3.** (*serious purpose, work*): **he means ~** он име́ет серьёзные наме́рения; **get down to ~** бра́ться, взя́ться за де́ло. **4.** (*comm. etc.*): **man of ~** (*agent*) аге́нт; пове́ренный; **~ of the day, meeting** пове́стка дня; **~ hours; hours of ~** (*of an office*) часы́ приёма/заня́тий/рабо́ты; **~ year** хозя́йственный год; **~ card** визи́тная ка́рточка; **~ before pleasure** де́лу вре́мя, поте́хе час; **big ~** большо́й би́знес; **~ as usual** фи́рма рабо́тает как обы́чно; **set up in ~** нач|ина́ть, -а́ть торго́вое де́ло; **go into ~** заня́ться (*pf.*) комме́рцией; **~ is ~** де́ло есть де́ло; **on ~** по де́лу; **put s.o. out of ~** разор|я́ть, -и́ть кого́-н.; **do ~ with s.o.** вести́ (*det.*) дела́ с кем-н.; **lose ~** теря́ть, по- клие́нтов; **talk ~** говори́ть (*impf.*) по де́лу/существу́; **~ is slow/brisk** дела́ иду́т вя́ло/хорошо́; **~ deal, piece of ~** сде́лка. **5.** (*establishment*) фи́рма, предприя́тие; (*office*) конто́ра.

cpds. **~-like** *adj.* делово́й, практи́чный; **~man** *n.* коммерса́нт, бизнесме́н, деле́ц.

bust[1] [bʌst] *n.* (*sculpture*; *bosom*) бюст; (*upper part of body*) грудь.

bust[2] [bʌst] (*coll.*) *v.t.* раскол|а́чивать, -оти́ть; **~ up** разб|ива́ть, -и́ть.

v.i. (*also* **go ~**) раскол|а́чиваться, -оти́ться; **~ up** разб|ива́ться, -и́ться; **the business went ~** де́ло ло́пнуло.

bustard [ˈbʌstəd] *n.* дрофа́.

bustle [ˈbʌs(ə)l] *n.* (*activity*) сумато́ха, суета́.

v.i. (*also* **~ about**) суети́ться, тормоши́ться (*both impf.*).

bustling [ˈbʌslɪŋ] *adj.* суетли́вый, суетя́щийся; **a ~ city** оживлённый го́род.

busy [ˈbɪzɪ] *adj.* **1.** (*occupied*) за́нятый; **I had a ~ day** я был за́нят весь день; **he was ~ packing** он был за́нят упако́вкой; **keep s.o. ~** зан|има́ть (*impf.*) кого́-н. (*чем-н.*); **get ~ on sth.** заня́ться (*pf.*) чем-н. **2.** (*unresting*) занято́й. **3.: a ~ street** шу́мная/оживлённая у́лица. **4.** (*meddlesome*) суетли́вый.

v.t.: **~ o.s.** зан|има́ться, -я́ться.

cpd. **~body** *n.* доку́чливый/назо́йливый челове́к.

but [bʌt] *n.*: **(~ me) no ~s** никаки́х «но»; без вся́ких «но».

adv. (*liter.*): (*only*) всего́ (лишь); **we can ~ try** попы́тка — не пы́тка.

prep. & conj. (*except*): **no one ~ me** никто́, кроме меня́; **she is anything ~ beautiful** она́ далеко́ не краса́вица; **he all ~ failed** он то́лько что не провали́лся; **nothing remains ~ to thank her** остаётся то́лько поблагодари́ть её; **he had no choice ~ to go there** ему́ не остава́лось ничего́ друго́го, кроме как пойти́ туда́; **next door ~ one** че́рез одну́ дверь; **the last ~ one** предпосле́дний; **~ for me he would have stayed** е́сли бы не я, он бы оста́лся; **he cannot ~ agree** ему́ остаётся то́лько согласи́ться; **I do not doubt ~ that he is honest** я не сомнева́юсь в его́ че́стности; **I cannot help ~ think ...** я не могу́ не ду́мать, что...

conj. (*adversative*) но; (*less emphatic*) а; **~ yet, then, again** но всё же; но опя́ть-таки.

butane [ˈbjuːteɪn, bjuːˈteɪn] *n.* бута́н.

butcher [ˈbʊtʃə(r)] *n.* **1.** (*tradesman*) мясни́к; **~'s (shop)** мясна́я ла́вка, мясно́й магази́н. **2.** (*murderer*) пала́ч.

v.t. (*cattle*) забива́ть (*impf.*); (*people*) истреб|ля́ть, -и́ть; выреза́ть, вы́резать.

butchery [ˈbʊtʃərɪ] *n.* (*massacre*) резня́.

butler [ˈbʌtlə(r)] *n.* дворе́цкий.

butt[1] [bʌt] (*fig., target*): **a ~ for ridicule** мише́нь для насме́шек.

butt[2] [bʌt] *n.* (*of rifle*) прикла́д; (*of tree*) ко́мель (*m.*); (*of cigarette*) оку́рок.

butt[3] [bʌt] *n.* (*blow with the head*) уда́р голово́й.

v.t. бода́ть, за-.

v.i.: **~ in** (*interrupt*) встр|ева́ть, -ять; вмеш|иваться, -а́ться.

butter [ˈbʌtə(r)] *n.* ма́сло; **melted ~** топлёное ма́сло; **fry sth. in ~** жа́рить, под- что-н. на ма́сле.

v.t. нама́з|ывать, -ать ма́слом; (*a dish*) сма́з|ывать, -ать ма́слом; **~ up** (*fig.*) льсти́ть, по- +*d.*; ума́сл|ивать, -ить.

cpds. **~-bean** *n.* боб (кароли́нский); **~cup** *n.* лю́тик; **~-dish** *n.* маслёнка; **~milk** *n.* па́хта, па́хтанье.

butterfly [ˈbʌtəˌflaɪ] *n.* **1.** ба́бочка; **I have butterflies in my stomach** у меня́ се́рдце ёкает. **2.** (*fig., flighty person*) мотылёк. **3.: ~ stroke** (*swimming*) баттерфля́й.

buttocks [ˈbʌtəks] *n.* я́годицы (*f. pl.*).

button [ˈbʌt(ə)n] *n.* **1.** пу́говица. **2.** (*knob*) кно́пка; **press a ~** наж|има́ть, -а́ть кно́пку.

v.t. (*also* **~ up**) застёг|ивать, -ну́ть.

v.i. застёг|иваться, -ну́ться; **the dress ~s up the back** пла́тье застёгивается на спине́.

cpd. **~hole** *n.* петля́, петли́ца; (*flower*) бутонье́рка; *v.t.* (*fig.*) заде́рж|ивать, -а́ть разгово́ром.

buttress [ˈbʌtrɪs] *n.* (*archit.*) контрфо́рс; (*fig.*) опо́ра, подде́ржка; **flying ~** аркбута́н.

v.t. (*archit.*) подп|ира́ть, -е́ть контрфо́рсом; (*fig.*) укреп|ля́ть, -и́ть; служи́ть (*impf.*) опо́рой +*d.*

buxom [ˈbʌksəm] *adj.* (*of woman*) полногру́дая.

buy [baɪ] *n.*: **a good ~** вы́годная поку́пка.

v.t. **1.** покупа́ть, купи́ть; **money cannot ~ happiness** сча́стья не ку́пишь; **~ s.o. a drink** ста́вить, по- кому́-н. вы́пивку. **2.** (*bribe*) подкуп|а́ть, -и́ть.

with advs.: **~ in** *v.t.* (*stock up*) закуп|а́ть, -и́ть; **~ off** *v.t.* откуп|а́ться, -и́ться (*от кого*); **~ out** *v.t.*: **~ o.s. out of the army** откупи́ться (*pf.*) от вое́нной слу́жбы; **~ up** *v.t.* скуп|а́ть, -и́ть.

cpd. **~-out** *n.* (*comm.*) вы́куп.

buyer [ˈbaɪə(r)] *n.* **1.** покупа́тель (*m.*). **2.** (*firm's agent*) заку́пщи|к (*fem.* -ца).

buzz [bʌz] *n.* **1.** (*of bee etc.*) жужжа́ние; (*of talk*) гул, жужжа́ние. **2.: give s.o. a ~** (*ring*) звя́кнуть (*pf.*) кому́-н. (*coll.*).

v.i. **1.** (*of insect, projectile*) жужжа́ть (*impf.*); (*of place, people*) гуде́ть (*impf.*); **my ears were ~ing** у меня́ гуде́ло в уша́х. **2.: ~ off!** (*sl.*) убира́йся!; прова́ливай!

cpd. **~-word** *n.* мо́дное слове́чко.

buzzard [ˈbʌzəd] *n.* сары́ч; каню́к.

buzzer [ˈbʌzə(r)] *n.* (*elec.*) зу́ммер.

by [baɪ] *adv.* (*near*) побли́зости; (*alongside*) ря́дом; (*past*) ми́мо; **the days went ~** дни шли за дня́ми; **~ and large** в це́лом.

prep. **1.** (*near, close to*): **sit ~ the fire(side)** сиде́ть (*impf.*) уками́на; **I was going ~ the house** я шёл ми́мо до́ма; **she sat ~ the sick man** она́ сиде́ла у посте́ли больно́го; **~ o.s.** (*alone*) (соверше́нно) оди́н/одна́; (*unaided*) сам/сама́, самостоя́тельно; **he played billiards ~ himself** он игра́л в билья́рд сам с собо́й; **~ and ~** вско́ре; сейча́с; **side ~ side** ря́дом; **pass ~ s.o.** про|ходи́ть, -йти́ ми́мо кого́-н.; **a path ~ the river** доро́жка у/вдоль реки́; **~ the way** кста́ти. **2.** (*along, via*): **~ land and sea** по су́ше и по мо́рю; **~ the nearest road** ближа́йшей доро́гой; **we travelled ~ (way of) Paris** мы е́хали че́рез Пари́ж; **~ water** по воде́. **3.** (*during*): **~ day/**

night днём/но́чью; ~ **daylight** при дневно́м све́те. **4.** (*of time-limit*): ~ **Thursday** к четвергу́; ~ **then** к тому́ вре́мени; ~ **now** тепе́рь; **he should know** ~ **now** пора́ бы уж ему́ зна́ть. **5.** (*manner, means or agency*) *often expr. by i. case*; (~ *means of*) при по́мощи +*g.*; **divide** ~ **two** дели́ть, раз- на́ два; **lead** ~ **the hand** вести́ (*det.*) за́ руку; ~ **the name of George** по и́мени Гео́ргий; **have children** ~ **s.o.** име́ть (*impf.*) дете́й от кого́-н.; **a Frenchman** ~ **blood** францу́з по происхожде́нию; **pull up** ~ **the roots** выта́скивать, вы́тащить с ко́рнем; **a book** ~ **Tolstoy** кни́га Толсто́го; **know** ~ **experience** знать (*impf.*) по о́пыту; ~ **my watch** по мои́м часа́м; ~ **rail** по желе́зной доро́ге; ~ **taxi** на/в такси́; **work** ~ **electric light** рабо́тать при электри́ческом све́те; ~ **law** по зако́ну; ~ **radio** по ра́дио; ~ **no means** ни в ко́ем слу́чае; **hang** ~ **a thread** висе́ть (*impf.*) на волоске́; ~ **post** по́чтой, по по́чте; ~ **telephone** по телефо́ну; ~ **nature/profession** по приро́де/профе́ссии; **cautious** ~ **nature** осторо́жный от приро́ды; **a letter written** ~ **hand** письмо́, напи́санное от руки́; ~ **means of** при по́мощи +*g.*; **I knew** ~ **his eyes that he was afraid** я по́нял по его́ глаза́м, что он бои́тся; **he led her** ~ **the hand** он вёл её за́ руку; **what is meant** ~ **this word?** что означа́ет э́то сло́во? **6.** (*of rate or measurement*): **pay** ~ **the day** плати́ть (*impf.*) подённо; ~ **degrees** постепе́нно; **little** ~ **little** ма́ло-пома́лу; ~ **what amount do expenses exceed income?** на каку́ю су́мму расхо́ды превыша́ют дохо́ды?; **better** ~ **far** намно́го лу́чше; **tomatoes are sold** ~ **weight** помидо́ры продаю́тся на вес; ~ **the dozen** дю́жинами; **one** ~ **one** оди́н за други́м; **day** ~ **day** день за днём; **a room 13 feet** ~ **12** ко́мната трина́дцать фу́тов на двена́дцать. **7.**: ~ **God!** кляну́сь Бо́гом!

bye [baɪ] *n.*: **draw a** ~ (*sport*) быть свобо́дным от игры́.

bye-bye ['baɪbaɪ, bə'baɪ] *int.* (*good-bye*) пока́!; всего́ хоро́шего!

by-election ['baɪɪ,lekʃ(ə)n] *n.* дополни́тельные вы́боры (*m. pl.*).

bygone ['baɪgɒn] *n.* (*usu. pl.*): **let** ~**s be** ~**s** что бы́ло, то прошло́.

adj. проше́дший, мину́вший; **in** ~ **days** в давно́ мину́вшие времена́.

by-law, bye-law ['baɪlɔː] *n.* распоряже́ние, постановле́ние (ме́стной вла́сти).

by-pass ['baɪpɑːs] *n.* объе́зд, обхо́д; обхо́дный путь.

v.t. об|ходи́ть, -ойти́ (*also fig.*).

by-product ['baɪ,prɒdʌkt] *n.* побо́чный проду́кт.

by-road ['baɪrəʊd] *n.* бокова́я доро́га.

bystander ['baɪ,stændə(r)] *n.* зри́тель (*m.*); прохо́жий.

byte [baɪt] *n.* (*comput.*) байт.

Byzantine [bɪ'zæntaɪn, baɪ-, 'bɪzən,tiːn, 'bɪzən,taɪn] *adj.* (*lit., fig.*) византи́йский.

C

C[1] [siː] *n.* **1.** (*mus.*) до (*indecl.*). **2.** (*acad. mark*) 3, тро́йка; **she got a** ~ **in maths** она получи́ла тро́йку по матема́тике.

C[2] (*abbr. of* **Celsius** ['selsɪəs] *or* **centigrade** ['sentɪ,greɪd]) (шкала́) Це́льсия; **20°C** 20°Ц (по Це́льсию).

c. *abbr. of* **1. century** ['sentʃərɪ, -tjʊrɪ] в., (век); ст., (столе́тие). **2. circa** ['sɜːkə] ок., (о́коло). **3. cent(s)** [sent(s)] цент.

cab [kæb] *n.* **1.** такси́ (*nt. indecl.*); **go by** ~ е́хать (*det.*) на такси́. **2.** (*of lorry etc.*) каби́на (води́теля).

cpds. ~**-driver** *n.* шофёр такси́; ~**-rank,** ~**-stand** *nn.* стоя́нка такси́.

cabal [kə'bæl] *n.* полити́ческая кли́ка.

cabaret ['kæbə,reɪ] *n.* (*place*) кабаре́ (*indecl.*); (*entertainment*) кабаре́, эстра́дное представле́ние.

cabbage ['kæbɪdʒ] *n.* капу́ста; ~ **butterfly** капу́стница.

cabin ['kæbɪn] *n.* каби́на; (*dwelling*) хи́жина; (*in ship etc.*) каю́та; ~ **class** каю́тный класс; (*of aeroplane*) каби́на; ~ **boy** каю́т-ю́нга (*m.*).

cabinet ['kæbɪnɪt] *n.* **1.** (*piece of furniture*) го́рка, шкаф; **filing** ~ картоте́чный шкаф; **medicine** ~ апте́чка. **2.** (*of radio set etc.*) ко́рпус. **3.** (*pol.*) кабине́т; ~ **minister** член кабине́та.

cpd. ~**-maker** *n.* краснодере́вец.

cable ['keɪb(ə)l] *n.* **1.** (*rope*) кана́т, трос. **2.** (*wire*) ка́бель (*m.*); ~ **car** ваго́н подвесно́й доро́ги; фуникулёр; ~ **TV** ка́бельное телеви́дение. **3.** (*telegram*) телегра́мма.

v.t. & i. телеграфи́ровать (*impf., pf.*).

cablegram ['keɪb(ə)l,græm] *n.* каблогра́мма, телегра́мма.

cabriolet [,kæbrɪəʊ'leɪ] *n.* кабриоле́т.

cacao [kə'kɑːəʊ, -'keɪəʊ] *n.* кака́о (*indecl.*).

cache [kæʃ] *n.* тайни́к, та́йный склад.

cackle ['kæk(ə)l] *n.* куда́хтанье; (*fig., chatter*) трескотня́, болтовня́; **cut the** ~! дово́льно треща́ть!; (*laugh*) хихи́канье.

v.t. & i. куда́хтать (*impf.*); хихи́к|ать, -нуть.

cacophonous [kə'kɒfənəs] *adj.* какофони́ческий.

cacophony [kə'kɒfənɪ] *n.* какофо́ния.

cactus ['kæktəs] *n.* ка́ктус.

cad [kæd] *n.* хам.

cadaver [kə'deɪvə(r), -'dɑːvə(r)] *n.* труп.

cadaverous [kə'dævərəs] *adj.* ме́ртвенно-бле́дный.

caddish ['kædɪʃ] *adj.* ни́зкий, ха́мский.

caddy ['kædɪ] *n.* ча́йница.

cadence ['keɪd(ə)ns] *n.* каде́нция; (*rhythm*) ритм.

cadenza [kə'denzə] *n.* каде́нция.

cadet [kə'det] *n.* (*mil.*) каде́т, курса́нт; ~ **corps** каде́тский ко́рпус.

cadge [kædʒ] *v.t. & i.* выкля́нчивать, вы́клянчить; (*coll.*) стрел|я́ть, -ьну́ть (*что у кого*).

cadmium ['kædmɪəm] *n.* ка́дмий.

cadre ['kɑːdə(r), 'kɑːdrə] *n.* (*mil. etc.*) ка́дровый соста́в; (*pl., key personnel*) ка́дры (*m. pl.*).

caecum ['siːkəm] *n.* слепа́я кишка́.

Caesarean [sɪ'zeərɪən] *adj.*: ~ **birth, section** ке́сарево сече́ние.

caesium ['siːzɪəm] *n.* це́зий.

café ['kæfeɪ, 'kæfɪ] *n.* кафе́ (*indecl.*).

cafeteria [,kæfɪ'tɪərɪə] *n.* кафете́рий.

caffeine ['kæfiːn] *n.* кофеи́н.

c|aftan, k- ['kæftæn] *n.* кафта́н.

cage [keɪdʒ] *n.* (*for animals etc.*) кле́тка; (*of lift etc.*) каби́на.

v.t. сажа́ть, посади́ть в кле́тку; **a** ~**d lion** лев в кле́тке.

cag(e)y ['keɪdʒɪ] *adj.* (*coll.*) скры́тный.

cagoule [kə'guːl] *n.* кагу́ль (*m.*), водонепроница́емая ку́ртка.

cahoots [kə'huːts] *n.* (*sl.*): **in** ~ **with s.o.** в сго́воре с кем-н.

caisson ['keɪs(ə)n, kə'suːn] *n.* (*ammunition chest*) заря́дный я́щик; (*underwater chamber*) кессо́н.

cajole [kə'dʒəʊl] *v.t.* обха́живать (*impf.*); уле|ща́ть, -сти́ть.

cajolery [kə'dʒəʊlərɪ] *n.* лесть; обха́живание.

cake [keɪk] *n.* **1.** (*food*) кекс, торт; (*fancy* ~) пиро́жное. **2.** (*flat piece*) брусо́к, пли́тка; ~ **of soap** кусо́к мы́ла. **3.** (*fig.*): **a piece of** ~ (*coll.*) пустяко́вое де́ло;

they sell like hot ~s э́то раскупа́ется нарасхва́т.

v.t.: **his shoes were ~d with mud** его́ боти́нки бы́ли обле́плены гря́зью.

v.i. сп|ека́ться, -е́чься.

calamitous [kə'læmɪtəs] *adj.* бе́дственный.

calamity [kə'læmɪtɪ] *n.* бе́дствие.

calcify ['kælsɪ,faɪ] *v.t. & i.* обызвеств|ля́ть(ся), -и́ть(ся).

calcium ['kælsɪəm] *n.* ка́льций; **~ chloride** хло́ристый ка́льций.

calculat|e ['kælkjʊ,leɪt] *v.t.* **1.** (*compute*) вычисля́ть, вы́числить; рассчи́т|ывать, -а́ть; высчи́тывать, вы́считать; **a ~ing machine** счётная маши́на. **2.** (*estimate*) рассчи́т|ывать, -а́ть; калькули́ровать, с-. **3.** (*plan*): **a ~ed insult** наме́ренное оскорбле́ние; **a ~ risk** обду́манный риск. **4.** (*past part.*: *fit*, *likely*): **that is ~ed to offend him** весьма́ возмо́жно, что э́то его́ оби́дит.

v.i. (*rely*) рассчи́тывать (*impf.*) (на+*a.*).

calculating ['kælkjʊ,leɪtɪŋ] *adj.* (*of pers.*) расчётливый, себе́ на уме́.

calculation [,kælkjʊ'leɪʃ(ə)n] *n.* **1.** (*mathematical*) вычисле́ние. **2.** (*planning*, *forecast*) расчёт; **my ~s were at fault** мои́ расчёты оказа́лись оши́бочными. **3.** (*estimate*) калькуля́ция.

calculator ['kælkjʊ,leɪtə(r)] *n.* **1.** (*pers.*) вычисли́тель (*m.*), калькуля́тор. **2.** (*machine*) счётная маши́на; арифмо́метр.

calculus ['kælkjʊləs] *n.* исчисле́ние.

calendar ['kælɪndə(r)] *n.* календа́рь (*m.*); **~ month** календа́рный ме́сяц.

calender ['kælɪndə(r)] *n.* кала́ндр.

calf[1] [kɑːf] *n.* **1.** (*of cattle*) телёнок; **a cow in ~** сте́льная коро́ва; (*of seal*, *whale etc.*) детёныш. **2.** (*leather*) теля́чья ко́жа; опо́ек.

cpd. **~skin** *n.* опо́ек; теля́чья ко́жа.

calf[2] [kɑːf] *n.* (*of leg*) икра́.

calibrate ['kælɪ,breɪt] *v.t.* калиброва́ть (*impf.*), градуи́ровать (*impf.*, *pf.*).

calibration [,kælɪ'breɪʃ(ə)n] *n.* калибро́вка.

calibre ['kælɪbə(r)] *n.* (*lit.*, *fig.*) кали́бр.

calico ['kælɪ,kəʊ] *n.* коленко́р, митка́ль (*m.*).

caliph ['keɪlɪf, 'kæl-] *n.* кали́ф, хали́ф.

caliphate ['keɪlɪ,feɪt] *n.* халифа́т.

call [kɔːl] *n.* **1.** (*cry*, *shout*) зов, о́клик; **I heard a ~ for help** я услы́шал крик о по́мощи; **they came at my ~** они́ пришли́ на мой зов. **2.** (*of bird*) крик; (*of bugle*) зов, сигна́л. **3.** (*message*): **telephone ~** вы́зов по телефо́ну; телефо́нный звоно́к; **he took the ~ in his study** он подошёл к телефо́ну в своём кабине́те. **4.** (*visit*): **pay a ~** нан|оси́ть, -ести́ визи́т; **port of ~** порт захо́да. **5.** (*invitation*, *summons*, *demand*) зов, клич, призы́в; **the ~ of the sea** зов мо́ря; **the doctor is on ~** врач на вы́зове; **he answered his country's ~** он откли́кнулся на призы́в свое́й ро́дины; **I have many ~s on my time** у меня́ почти́ нет свобо́дного вре́мени. **6.** (*need*): **there is no ~ for him to worry** ему́ не́чего волнова́ться. **7.** (*at cards*) объявле́ние игры́.

v.t. **1.** (*name*, *designate*): наз|ыва́ть, -ва́ть; **he is ~ed John** его́ зову́т Джон; **he ~s himself a colonel** он называ́ет себя́ полко́вником; **~ s.o. names** об|зыва́ть, -озва́ть кого́-н.; **we have nothing we can ~ our own** у нас нет ничего́, что мы могли́ бы счита́ть свои́м; **I ~ that a shame** я счита́ю э́то посты́дным; **let's ~ it £5** сойдёмся на пяти́ фу́нтах; **~ a halt** объяв|ля́ть, -и́ть переры́в/остано́вку; **~ a strike** приз|ыва́ть, -ва́ть к забасто́вке. **2.** (*summon*, *arouse attention of*): **~ a doctor/taxi!** вы́зовите врача́/такси́!; **duty ~s** долг вели́т; **~ me at 6** разбуди́те меня́ в 6 часо́в; **(this is) London ~ing** говори́т Ло́ндон; *for US sense 'telephone' see* **~ up. 3.** (*announce*): **~ a meeting** соз|ыва́ть, -ва́ть собра́ние. **4.** (*var. idioms*): **~ in question** ста́вить, по- под сомне́ние; **~ to mind** вызыва́ть, вы́звать в па́мяти; **~ into being** вызыва́ть, вы́звать к жи́зни; **~ attention to** обра|ща́ть, -ти́ть (*чьё-н.*) внима́ние на+*a.*; **~ to witness** приз|ыва́ть, -ва́ть в свиде́тели; **~ to order** приз|ыва́ть, -ва́ть к поря́дку.

v.i. **1.** (*cry*, *shout*) звать, по-; окл|ика́ть, -и́кнуть; **I heard someone ~** я слы́шал, как кто́-то позва́л; **I ~ed to him** я окли́кнул его́. **2.** (*pay a visit*) за|ходи́ть, -йти́; **I ~ed on him** я зашёл к нему́; **the ship ~ed at Naples** парохо́д зашёл в Неа́поль; **the train ~s at every station** по́езд остана́вливается на ка́ждой ста́нции. **3. ~ for** (*pick up*): **I ~ed for him at 6** я зашёл за ним в 6 часо́в; **to be ~ed for** до востре́бования; (*demand*): **the situation ~s for courage** обстоя́тельства тре́буют му́жества. **4. ~ on, upon** (*require*): **I ~ on you to keep your promise** я призыва́ю вас сдержа́ть своё обеща́ние; (*appeal to*): **I ~ed on him for help** я призва́л его́ на по́мощь; (*invite*) предл|ага́ть, -ожи́ть (*что кому*); **I ~ on Mr. Grey to speak** я предоставля́ю сло́во г-ну Гре́ю; **I feel ~ed on to reply** я чу́вствую, что до́лжен отве́тить.

with advs.: **~ away** *v.t.* от|зыва́ть, -озва́ть; **~ back** *v.t. & i.* (*answer*) откл|ика́ться, -и́кнуться (на+*a.*); (*on telephone*) позвони́ть (*pf.*) сно́ва (+*d.*); перезвони́ть (*pf.*); **~ down** *v.t.*: **~ down curses on s.o.'s head** приз|ыва́ть, -ва́ть прокля́тия на чью-н. го́лову; **~ forth** *v.t.* (*lit.*, *fig.*) вызыва́ть, вы́звать; **~ in** *v.t.* (*books*) тре́бовать, за- наза́д; (*a specialist*) вызыва́ть, вы́звать; **~ off** *v.t.* (*e.g. a dog*) от|зыва́ть, -озва́ть; (*cancel*) отмен|я́ть, -и́ть; **~ out** *v.t.* (*announce*) выклика́ть, вы́кликнуть; (*summon away*) от|зыва́ть, -озва́ть; (*workers*, *on strike*) приз|ыва́ть, -ва́ть (к+*d.*); (*to a duel*) вызыва́ть, вы́звать; *v.i.* выклика́ть, вы́кликнуть; выкри́кивать, вы́крикнуть; **~ over** *v.t.* **I ~ ed him over** (*i.e. to come over*) я подозва́л его́; **~ up** *v.t.* (*telephone*) звони́ть, по- (*кому*) по телефо́ну; (*evoke*) вызыва́ть, вы́звать; (*for mil. service*) приз|ыва́ть, -ва́ть.

cpds. **~-box** *n.* телефо́нная бу́дка; **~-sign** *n.* (*radio*) позывно́й (сигна́л); **~up** *n.* (*mil.*) призы́в.

caller ['kɔːlə(r)] *n.* (*visitor*) посети́тель (*fem.* -ница); (*telephone*) позвони́вший (по телефо́ну).

calligrapher [kə'lɪgrəfə(r)] *n.* каллигра́ф.

calligraphic [,kælɪ'græfɪk] *adj.* каллиграфи́ческий.

calligraphy [kə'lɪgrəfɪ] *n.* каллигра́фия.

calling ['kɔːlɪŋ] *n.* (*summoning*) созы́в; (*profession*, *occupation*) призва́ние, заня́тие.

callipers ['kælɪpəz] *n.* кронци́ркуль.

callisthenics [,kælɪs'θenɪks] *n.* ритми́ческая гимна́стика; пласти́ческая гимна́стика.

callous ['kæləs] *n.* = **callus**

adj. (*of skin*) огрубе́лый, мозо́листый; (*fig.*) чёрствый.

callousness ['kæləsnɪs] *n.* чёрствость.

callow ['kæləʊ] *adj.* (*unfledged*; *also fig.*) неопери́вшийся.

callus ['kæləs] *n.* ко́стная мозо́ль.

calm [kɑːm] *n.* споко́йствие, тишина́; **a dead ~** мёртвая тишина́; (*at sea*) штиль (*m.*), безве́трие.

adj. споко́йный.

v.t. & i. успок|а́ивать(ся), -о́ить(ся).

calmness ['kɑːmnɪs] *n.* споко́йствие, тишина́, поко́й

caloric ['kælərɪk] *adj.* теплово́й, терми́ческий.

calorie ['kælərɪ] *n.* кало́рия.

calorific [,kælə'rɪfɪk] *adj.* теплово́й, теплотво́рный; калори́йный; **~ value** калори́йность.

calorimeter [,kælə'rɪmɪtə(r)] *n.* калори́метр.

calque [kælk] *n.* (*ling.*) ка́лька.

calumniate [kə'lʌmnɪ,eɪt] *v.t.* клевета́ть, о-.

calumniator [kə'lʌmnɪ,eɪtə(r)] *n.* клеветни́к.

calumnious [kə'lʌmnɪəs] *adj.* клеветни́ческий.

calumny ['kæləmnɪ] *n.* клевета́.

calve [kɑːv] *v.i.* тели́ться, о-.
calyx ['keɪlɪks, 'kæl-] *n.* ча́шечка.
cam [kæm] *n.* кулачо́к, копи́р, па́лец.
cpd. **~shaft** кулачко́вый вал.
camaraderie [ˌkæmə'rɑːdərɪ] *n.* това́рищеские отноше́ния.
Cambodia [kæm'bəʊdɪə] *n.* Камбо́джа.
cambric ['kæmbrɪk] *n.* бати́ст.
camcorder ['kæmˌkɔːdə(r)] *n.* камко́рдер.
camel ['kæm(ə)l] *n.* верблю́д; **Arabian ~** дромаде́р.
cpd. **~-hair** *adj.*: **~-hair coat** пальто́ из верблю́жьей ше́рсти.
camel(l)ia [kə'miːlɪə] *n.* каме́лия.
cameo ['kæmɪˌəʊ] *n.* каме́я (*fig.*) скетч, эссе́ (*indecl.*), винье́тка; **~ role** эпизоди́ческая роль.
camera ['kæmrə, -ərə] *n.* **1.** (*phot.*) фотоаппара́т. **2. in ~** при закры́тых дверя́х.
cpd. **~man** (*photographer*) фото́граф, фоторепортёр; (*cin.*) (кино)опера́тор.
camomile ['kæməˌmaɪl] *n.* рома́шка.
camouflage ['kæməˌflɑːʒ] *n.* камуфля́ж; (*also fig.*) маскиро́вка.
v.t. (*lit., fig.*) маскирова́ть, за-.
camp[1] [kæmp] *n.* ла́герь (*m.*; *pl. in mil. etc. sense* лагеря́, *in pol. sense* ла́гери); бива́к; **pitch ~** расположи́ться ла́герем; **break, strike ~** сн|има́ться, -я́ться с ла́геря.
v.i. распол|ага́ться, -ожи́ться ла́герем; **go ~ing** отпр|авля́ться, -а́виться в (туристи́ческий) похо́д; жить в пала́тках; **~ out** спать (*impf.*) на откры́том во́здухе; **~ing site** ке́мпинг, турба́за.
cpds. **~-bed** *n.* похо́дная крова́ть; **~-fire** *n.* бива́чный костёр.
camp[2] [kæmp] *adj.* (*coll.*) аффекти́рованный, мане́рный.
campaign [kæm'peɪn] *n.* похо́д; (*lit., fig.*) камп́ания.
v.i. уча́ствовать (*impf.*) в похо́де; (*fig.*) вести́ (*det.*) кампа́нию.
campaigner [kæm'peɪnə(r)] *n.* уча́стник кампа́нии; боре́ц; **old ~** ста́рый вои́ка; **peace ~** боре́ц за мир.
campanula [kæm'pænjʊlə] *n.* колоко́льчик.
camper ['kæmpə(r)] *n.* (*pers.*) ночу́ющий на откры́том во́здухе; тури́ст, живу́щий в пала́тке; (*vehicle*) жило́й/тури́стский автоприце́п.
camphor ['kæmfə(r)] *n.* камфара́.
Campuchea [ˌkæmpʊ'tʃɪə] *n.* Кампучи́я.
campus ['kæmpəs] *n.* университе́тский городо́к; (*attr.*) университе́тский, студе́нческий.
can[1] [kæn] *n.* **1.** (*for liquids*) бидо́н; **milk-~** моло́чный бидо́н. **2.** (*for food etc.*) (консе́рвная) ба́нка.
v.t. консерви́ровать (*impf., pf.*); **~ned food** консе́рв|ы (*pl., g.* -ов); **~ned vegetables** овощны́е консе́рвы; **~ned music** му́зыка в за́писи.
cpd. **~-opener** *n.* консе́рвный ключ/нож.
can[2] [kæn] *v.i.* (*expr. ability or permission*) мочь (*impf.*); (*expr. capability*) уме́ть (*impf.*); **I ~ speak French** я уме́ю говори́ть по-францу́зски; **I ~ see him** я ви́жу его́; **I could have laughed for joy** я гото́в был смея́ться от ра́дости; **I ~not but feel that ...** я не могу́ не чу́вствовать, что...; **~ it be true?** неуже́ли э́то пра́вда?; **as soon as you ~** как то́лько смо́жете; как мо́жно скоре́е; **we ~ but try** мо́жно всё-таки попыта́ться.
Canada ['kænədə] *n.* Кана́да.
Canadian [kə'neɪdɪən] *n.* (*pers.*) кана́д|ец (*fem.* -ка).
adj. кана́дский.
canal [kə'næl] *n.* **1.** (*channel through land*) кана́л; **~ boat** су́дно для кана́лов. **2.** (*anat.*) кана́л, прохо́д; **alimentary ~** пищевари́тельный тракт.
canard [kə'nɑːd, 'kænɑːd] *n.* ло́жный слух, (газе́тная) у́тка.
canary [kə'neərɪ] *n.* канаре́йка.
cpds. **~-yellow** *n.* канаре́ечный цвет.
cancan ['kænkæn] *n.* канка́н.
cancel ['kæns(ə)l] *n.* (*cancelling*) отме́на; (*on postage stamps*) погаше́ние.
v.t. **1.** (*cross out*) вычёркивать, вы́черкнуть. **2.** (*countermand*) отмен|я́ть, -и́ть; аннули́ровать (*impf., pf.*). **3.** (*nullify*) св|оди́ть, -ести́ на нет.
v.i.: **these items ~ out** э́ти пу́нкты сво́дят друг дру́га на нет.
cancellation [ˌkænsə'leɪʃ(ə)n] *n.* отме́на, аннули́рование; погаше́ние; вычёркивание.
cancer ['kænsə(r)] *n.* **1.** (*astron.*) Рак; **Tropic of C~** тро́пик Ра́ка. **2.** (*med.*) рак. **3.** (*fig.*) я́зва.
cancerous ['kænsərəs] *adj.* (*med.*) ра́ковый; (*fig.*) разъеда́ющий.
candelabr|a [ˌkændɪ'lɑːbrə] *n.* канделя́бр.
candid ['kændɪd] *adj.* (*frank*) чистосерде́чный, открове́нный; (*unbiased*) беспристра́стный.
candidacy ['kændɪdəsɪ] *n.* кандидату́ра.
candidate ['kændɪdət, -ˌdeɪt] *n.* кандида́т.
candidature ['kændɪdətjə(r)] *n.* кандидату́ра.
candle ['kænd(ə)l] *n.* свеча́; **the game is not worth the ~** игра́ не сто́ит свеч; **burn the ~ at both ends** прожига́ть (*impf.*) жизнь.
cpds. **~-light** *n.* свет свечи́/свече́й; свечно́е освеще́ние; **~-power** *n.* (*elec.*) си́ла све́та в свеча́х; **~stick** *n.* подсве́чник.
candour ['kændə(r)] *n.* открове́нность, чистосерде́чие; беспристра́стность.
candy ['kændɪ] *n.* леденцы́ (*m. pl.*) караме́ль; (*US*) конфе́та, сла́сти (*f. pl.*).
v.t.: **candied fruit(s)** заса́харенные фру́кты.
candyfloss ['kændɪˌflɒs] *n.* са́харная ва́та.
cane [keɪn] *n.* **1.** (*bot.*) камы́ш, тростни́к; **~ chair** плетёное кре́сло. **2.** (*walking-stick*) трость, па́лка. **3.** (*for punishment*) па́лка; **the boy got the ~** ма́льчика отлупи́ли.
v.t. **1.: ~ a chair** плести́, с- кре́сло из камыша́. **2.: ~ a pupil** нака́з|ывать, -а́ть ученика́ па́лкой.
cpd. **~-sugar** *n.* тростнико́вый са́хар.
canine ['keɪnaɪn, 'kæn-] *adj.* соба́чий; **~ tooth** клык.
caning ['keɪnɪŋ] *n.* (*punishment*) наказа́ние па́лкой.
canister ['kænɪstə(r)] *n.* ба́нка, коро́бка.
cpd. **~-shot** *n.* карте́чь.
canker ['kæŋkə(r)] *n.* (*med.*) (я́зненный) стомати́т, моло́чница; (*agr.*) рак расте́ний; некро́з плодо́вых дере́вьев.
cannabis ['kænəbɪs] *n.* гаши́ш.
cannery ['kænərɪ] *n.* консе́рвный заво́д.
cannibal ['kænɪb(ə)l] *n.* канниба́л, людое́д.
adj. канниба́льский, людое́дский.
cannibalism ['kænɪbəˌlɪz(ə)m] *n.* каннибали́зм, людое́дство.
cannibalistic [ˌkænɪbə'lɪstɪk] *adj.* канниба́льский, людое́дский.
cannibalize ['kænɪbəˌlaɪz] *v.t.* (*mil. etc.*): **~ a machine** сн|има́ть, -ять го́дные дета́ли с неиспра́вной маши́ны.
canniness ['kænɪnɪs] *n.* хи́трость, осторо́жность.
canning ['kænɪŋ] *n.* консерви́рование.
cpd. **~-factory** *n.* консе́рвный заво́д.
cannon ['kænən] *n.* **1.** (*gun*) пу́шка, ору́дие. **2.** (*artillery*) артилле́рия. **3.** (*at billiards*: *also US* **carom**) карамбо́ль (*m.*).
v.i. (*collide*) ст|а́лкиваться, -олкну́ться; (*at billiards*) сде́лать (*pf.*) карамбо́ль.
cpds. **~-ball** *n.* пу́шечное ядро́; **~-fodder** *n.* пу́шечное мя́со; .
cannonade [ˌkænə'neɪd] *n.* канона́да, ору́ди́йный ого́нь.
canny ['kænɪ] *adj.* (*shrewd, cautious*) хи́трый, осторо́жный; смека́листый, себе́ на уме́.
canoe [kə'nuː] *n.* кано́э (*nt. indecl.*), челно́к, чёлн, байда́рка.

v.i. плыть (*det.*) в челноке́ (*or* на байда́рке).
canoeist [kə'nu:ɪst] *n.* каноúст, байда́рочник.
canon ['kænən] *n.* **1.** (*church decree*) кано́н; ~ **law** канони́ческое пра́во. **2.** (*criterion*) пра́вило. **3.** (*body of writings*) кано́н. **4.** (*list of saints*) свя́тц|ы (*pl.*, *g.* -ев). **5.** (*priest*) кано́ник. **6.** (*mus.*) кано́н.
canonical [kə'nɒnɪk(ə)l] *adj.* канони́ческий.
canonize ['kænə,naɪz] *v.t.* (*recognise as a saint*) канонизи́ровать (*impf.*, *pf.*).
canopy ['kænəpɪ] *n.* **1.** (*covering over bed etc.*) балдахи́н, по́лог. **2.** (*of parachute*) ку́пол. **3.** (*fig.*) по́лог, покро́в.
cant [kænt] *n.* (*insincere talk*) ха́нжество; (*jargon*): **thieves'** ~ воровско́й жарго́н, блатна́я му́зыка.
cantaloup(e) ['kæntə,lu:p] *n.* канталу́па; (му́скусная) ды́ня.
cantankerous [kæn'tæŋkərəs] *adj.* сварли́вый.
cantata [kæn'tɑ:tə] *n.* канта́та.
canteen [kæn'ti:n] *n.* **1.** (*shop*) войскова́я ла́вка, вое́нный магази́н. **2.** (*eating-place*) столо́вая. **3.** (*water-container*) фля́га. **4.** (*case of cutlery*) (похо́дный) я́щик со столо́выми принадле́жностями.
canter ['kæntə(r)] *n.* лёгкий гало́п.
v.i. е́хать (*impf.*) лёгким гало́пом.
cantilever ['kæntɪ,li:və(r)] *n.* консо́ль, кронште́йн; ~ **bridge** консо́льный мост.
canto ['kæntəʊ] *n.* песнь.
canton ['kæntɒn] *n.* канто́н.
cantonal ['kæntən(ə)l, kæn'tɒn(ə)l] *adj.* кантона́льный.
cantor ['kæntɔ:(r)] *n.* ка́нтор.
canvas ['kænvəs] *n.* **1.** (*cloth*) холст; паруси́на, брезе́нт; **under** ~ (*in camp*) в пала́тках; (*with sails spread*) под паруса́ми. **2.** (*for painting*) холст. **3.** (*fig., picture*) полотно́, холст. **4.** (*attr.*) холщо́вый; брезе́нтовый, паруси́новый; **a** ~ **bag** холщо́вый мешо́к.
canvass ['kænvəs] *n.* (*for votes*) предвы́борная агита́ция.
v.t. & *i.*: ~ **a constituency** вести́ (*det.*) предвы́борную агита́цию в избира́тельном о́круге; ~ **opinions** соб|ира́ть, -ра́ть мне́ния.
canvasser ['kænvəsə(r)] *n.* агита́тор.
canyon ['kænjən] *n.* каньо́н; глубо́кое уще́лье.
cap [kæp] *n.* **1.** (*worker's*) ке́пка; (*of uniform, incl. school*) фура́жка; (*without peak*) ша́пка; **dunce's** ~ дура́цкий колпа́к; **fool's** ~ шутовско́й колпа́к; (*lady's, servant's or nurse's*) чепе́ц; (*baby's*) че́пчик. **2.** (*of mountain*) верху́шка, верши́на. **3.** (*e.g. of pen or bottle*) кры́шка; **percussion** ~ писто́н, ка́псюль (*m.*). **4.** (*contraceptive*) колпачо́к.
v.t. **1.** (*put a* ~ *on, cover*) над|ева́ть, -е́ть ша́пку на+*a.* **2.** (*excel*) прев|осходи́ть, -зойти́; (*a joke etc.*) перещеголя́ть (*pf.*); **to** ~ **our misfortunes** в доверше́ние на́ших злоключе́ний. **3.** (*sport*) прин|има́ть, -я́ть в соста́в кома́нды.
capability [,keɪpə'bɪlɪtɪ] *n.* спосо́бность, возмо́жность.
capable ['keɪpəb(ə)l] *adj.* **1.** (*gifted*) спосо́бный. **2.** (~ *of*) спосо́бный на+*a.* **3.** (*susceptible*) поддаю́щийся; **the situation is** ~ **of improvement** положе́ние мо́жно испра́вить.
capacious [kə'peɪʃəs] *adj.* просто́рный.
capacity [kə'pæsɪtɪ] *n.* **1.** (*ability to hold*) вмести́мость; **measure of** ~ ме́ра объёма; **the hall's seating** ~ **is 500** вмести́мость за́ла — пятьсо́т мест; **the room was filled to** ~ ко́мната была́ запо́лнена до отка́за; **play to** ~ (*theatr.*) де́лать (*impf.*) по́лные сбо́ры. **2.** (*of engine*) (наибо́льшая) мо́щность, нагру́зка; (*of ship*) вмести́мость; **to work at, to** ~ рабо́тать (*impf.*) в по́лную си́лу. **3.** (*position, character*): **in my** ~ **as critic** как кри́тик; в ро́ли/ка́честве кри́тика; **I have come in the** ~ **of a friend** я пришёл как друг; **legal** ~ правоспосо́бность. **5.** (*elec.*) электри́ческая ёмкость.
cape[1] [keɪp] *n.* (*garment*) наки́дка с капюшо́ном.
cape[2] [keɪp] (*geog.*) мыс; **the C**~ **(of Good Hope)** мыс До́брой Наде́жды.
caper[1] ['keɪpə(r)] *n.* (*pl.*, *cul.*) ка́персы (*m. pl.*).
caper[2] ['keɪpə(r)] *n.* (*leap*) прыжо́к.
v.i. (*also* **cut** ~**s**) скака́ть (*impf.*).
capillary [kə'pɪlərɪ] *adj.* капилля́рный.
capital ['kæpɪt(ə)l] *n.* **1.** (*principal city*) столи́ца; (*attr.*) столи́чный. **2.** (*upper-case letter*) прописна́я/загла́вная бу́ква; **block** ~**s** прописны́е печа́тные бу́квы. **3.** (*wealth*) капита́л; **circulating** ~ оборо́тный капита́л; **fixed** ~ основно́й капита́л; **loan** ~ ссу́дный капита́л; ~ **and interest** основна́я су́мма и наро́сшие проце́нты. **4.** (*fig., advantage*) вы́игрыш, капита́л; **he made** ~ **out of our mistakes** он ло́вко воспо́льзовался на́шими оши́бками. **5.** (*employers*) капита́л; ~ **and labour** труд и капита́л.
adj. **1.** (*major*) гла́вный, основно́й. **2.** (*excellent*) капита́льный, превосхо́дный. **3.** (*involving death penalty*): **a** ~ **offence** преступле́ние, кара́емое сме́ртью; ~ **punishment** сме́ртная казнь. **4.** (*econ.*): ~ **goods** сре́дства произво́дства; ~ **expenditure** капита́льные затра́ты; ~ **assets** основны́е сре́дства; ~ **gains tax** нало́г на дохо́ды от приро́ста капита́ла. **5.** (*upper-case*) прописна́я/загла́вная бу́ква.
capitalism ['kæpɪtə,lɪz(ə)m] *n.* капитали́зм.
capitalist ['kæpɪtəlɪst] *n.* капитали́ст.
capitalistic [,kæpɪtə'lɪstɪk] *adj.* капиталисти́ческий.
capitalization [,kæpɪtəlaɪ'zeɪʃ(ə)n] *n.* **1.** (*writing with capital letter*) письмо́ прописны́ми бу́квами. **2.** (*econ.*) капитализа́ция.
capitalize ['kæpɪtə,laɪz] *v.t.* & *i.* **1.** (*write with capital letter*) писа́ть, на- прописны́ми бу́квами. **2.** (*econ.*) капитализи́ровать (*impf.*, *pf.*). **3.** (*fig.*) наж|ива́ться, -и́ться; ~ **on s.o.'s misfortune** извл|ека́ть, -е́чь вы́году из чьего́-н. несча́стья.
capitation [,kæpɪ'teɪʃ(ə)n] *n.* исчисле́ние с головы́.
capitulate [kə'pɪtjʊ,leɪt] *v.t.* капитули́ровать (*impf.*, *pf.*).
capitulation [kə,pɪtjʊ'leɪʃ(ə)n] *n.* (*surrender*) капитуля́ция.
capon ['keɪpən] *n.* каплу́н.
caprice [kə'pri:s] *n.* при́хоть, капри́з, причу́да.
capricious [kə'prɪʃəs] *adj.* прихотли́вый, капри́зный.
Capricorn ['kæprɪ,kɔ:n] *n.* Козеро́г; **Tropic of** ~ тро́пик Козеро́га.
capsicum ['kæpsɪkəm] *n.* стручко́вый пе́рец.
capsize [kæp'saɪz] *v.t.* & *i.* опроки́|дывать(ся), -нуть(ся).
capstan ['kæpst(ə)n] *n.* кабеста́н.
capsule ['kæpsju:l] *n.* **1.** (*bot.*) семенна́я коро́бочка. **2.** (*med.*) ка́псула. **3.** (*metal cap*) кры́шка, колпачо́к. **4.** (*for space travel*) ка́псула, отсе́к. **5.** (*fig.*): ~ **biography** кра́ткая биогра́фия.
Capt. ['kæptɪn] *n.* (*abbr. of* **Captain**) кап., (капита́н).
captain ['kæptɪn] *n.* **1.** (*leader*) руководи́тель (*m.*); ~ **of industry** промы́шленный магна́т; (*head of team*) капита́н кома́нды. **2.** (*army rank*) капита́н. **3.** (*naval rank*) капита́н пе́рвого ра́нга; команди́р корабля́.
v.i. руководи́ть (*impf.*); вести́ (*det.*); быть капита́ном +*g.*
captaincy ['kæptɪnsɪ] *n.* зва́ние/до́лжность капита́на.
caption ['kæpʃ(ə)n] *n.* (*title, words accompanying picture*) по́дпись к карти́нке; (*film subtitle*) титр.
captious ['kæpʃəs] *adj.* придирчивый.
captivate ['kæptɪ,veɪt] *v.t.* плен|я́ть, -и́ть; очаро́в|ывать, -а́ть.
captivating ['kæptɪ,veɪtɪŋ] *adj.* плени́тельный, чару́ющий.
captive ['kæptɪv] *n.* пле́нник, пле́нный; **take** ~ брать, взять в плен; **hold** ~ держа́ть (*impf.*) в плену́.

adj. плéнный; ~ **audience** слу́шатели (*m. pl.*) поневóле.

captivity [kæp'tɪvɪtɪ] *n.* плен, пленéние.

captor ['kæptə(r), -tɔː(r)] *n.* захвати́вший в плéн; взя́вший приз.

capture ['kæptʃə(r)] *n.* (*action*) поймка, захвáт; (*thg.* ~*d*) добы́ча.

v.t. брать, взять в плен; захвáт|ывать, -и́ть; ~ **s.o.'s attention** прикóв|ывать, -áть чьё-н. внимáние.

Capuchin ['kæpjuːtʃɪn] *n.* (*friar*; *monkey*) капуци́н.

capybara [ˌkæpɪ'bɑːrə] *n.* водосви́нка.

car [kɑː(r)] *n.* **1.** (*motor vehicle*) (легковóй) автомоби́ль, маши́на; ~ **boot sale** продáжа (пря́мо) из багáжника; ~ **pool** автобáза предприя́тия (*or* учреждéния). **2.** (*rail vehicle*) вагóн; **dining-**~ вагóн-ресторáн; **sleeping-**~ спáльный вагóн.

cpds. ~**-driver** *n.* шофёр; ~**-ferry** *n.* автопарóм; ~**-hire** *n.* прокáт автомоби́ля; ~**-park** *n.* пáркинг, автостоя́нка; ~**phone** *n.* автотелефóн; ~**-port** *n.* навéс для автомоби́ля; ~**-race** *n.* автогóнка; ~**-sick** *adj.*: **he was** ~**-sick** егó укачáло в маши́не.

caracul, karakul ['kærəˌkʊl] *n.* карáкуль (*m.*).

carafe [kə'ræf, -rɑːf] *n.* графи́н.

caramel ['kærəˌmel] *n.* (*burnt sugar*) карамéль; (*sweetmeat*) карамéль, карамéлька.

carapace ['kærəˌpeɪs] *n.* щитóк (*черепахи и т.п.*).

carat ['kærət] (*also US* **karat**) *n.* карáт.

caravan ['kærəˌvæn] *n.* каравáн; (*Gypsy's*) фургóн, кры́тая телéга; (*trailer*) дом-автоприцéп.

v.i.: **go** ~**ing** путешéствовать в дóме-автоприцéпе.

caravel ['kærəˌvel] *n.* каравéлла.

caraway ['kærəˌweɪ] *n.* тмин; ~ **seed** тми́нное сéмя.

carbide ['kɑːbaɪd] *n.* карби́д; **calcium** ~ карби́д кáльция.

carbine ['kɑːbaɪn] *n.* караби́н.

carbohydrate [ˌkɑːbə'haɪdreɪt] *n.* углевóд.

carbolic [kɑː'bɒlɪk] *adj.* карбóловый.

carbon ['kɑːbən] *n.* **1.** (*element*) углерóд; ~ **monoxide** угáрный газ; ~ **dioxide** углеки́слый газ; ~ **dating** дати́рование по (радио)углерóду. **2.** (*elec.*) у́голь (*m.*); у́гольный электрóд. **3.** (~*-paper*) копировáльная бумáга, копи́рка; ~ **copy** (*lit.*) кóпия под копи́рку; (*fig.*) (тóчная) кóпия.

carbonic [kɑː'bɒnɪk] *adj.* у́гольный, углерóдный, углерóдистый; ~ **acid** углекислотá.

carbonize ['kɑːbəˌnaɪz] *v.t.* **1.** (*convert into carbon*) карбонизи́ровать (*impf.*, *pf.*). **2.** (*apply carbon black to*) покр|ывáть, -ы́ть углём. **3.** (*char*) обугли|вать, -ть; коксовáть (*impf.*).

carborundum [ˌkɑːbə'rʌndəm] *n.* карбору́нд.

carbuncle ['kɑːbʌŋk(ə)l] *n.* (*jewel*; *med.*) карбу́нкул.

carburettor [ˌkɑːbjʊ'retə(r), ˌkɑːbə-] *n.* карбюрáтор.

carcas|e ['kɑːkəs], **-s** ['kɑːkəs] *n.* **1.** (*of animal*) ту́ша; ~ **meat** парнóе мя́со. **2.** (*of building, ship etc.*) каркáс, остóв, кóрпус.

carcinogen [kɑː'sɪnədʒ(ə)n] *n.* канцерогéнное веществó.

carcinogenic [ˌkɑːsɪnə'dʒenɪk] *adj.* канцерогéнный.

card[1] [kɑːd] *n.* **1.** (*piece of pasteboard*) кáрточка; (*postcard*) откры́тка; **calling-, visiting-**~ визи́тная кáрточка; **Party** ~ парти́йный билéт; **Christmas** ~ рождéственская откры́тка; **birthday** ~ поздрави́тельная кáрточка/откры́тка ко дню рождéния; **identity** ~ удостоверéние ли́чности. **2.** (*playing-*~) игрáльная кáрта; **play** ~**s** игрáть, сыгрáть в кáрты; **play a** ~ пойти́ (*pf.*) с (какóй-н.) кáрты; **house of** ~**s** (*lit.*, *fig.*) кáрточный дóмик. **3.** (*in libraries etc.*) каталóжная кáрточка; ~**s** (*documents of employment*) учётная кáрточка; **give s.o. his** ~**s** (*dismiss him*) увóлить (*pf.*) когó-н. **4.** (*fig.*): **he put his** ~**s on the table** он раскры́л свои́ кáрты; **I have a** ~ **up my sleeve** у меня́ есть в запáсе кóзырь; **he plays his** ~**s well** он умéло испóльзует обстоя́тельства; **it is on the** ~**s that we shall go** возмóжно, что мы пойдём.

cpds. ~**-carrying** *adj.* зарегистри́рованный, состоя́щий в организáции; ~**-index** *n.* картотéка; *v.t.* (*enter on* ~*s*) зан|оси́ть, -ести́ на кáрточки; каталогизи́ровать (*impf.*, *pf.*); ~**-player** *n.* игрóк в кáрты; ~**-playing** *n.* игрá в кáрты; ~**-sharp(er)** *n.* шу́лер; ~**-table** *n.* лóмберный стол.

card[2] [kɑːd] *v.t.* чесáть, по-; прочёс|ывать, -áть; ~**ing-machine** кардочесáльная маши́на.

cardam|om, -um ['kɑːdəməm] *n.* кардамóн.

cardboard ['kɑːdbɔːd] *n.* картóн; ~ **box** картóнная корóбка.

cardiac ['kɑːdɪˌæk] *adj.* сердéчный; ~ **murmur** шум сéрдца.

cardigan ['kɑːdɪgən] *n.* шерстянáя кóфта; кардигáн; (*man's*) вя́заная ку́ртка.

cardinal ['kɑːdɪn(ə)l] *n.* (*eccl.*, *zool.*) кардинáл.

adj. (*principal*) кардинáльный; ~ **number** коли́чественное числи́тельное; ~ **point** странá свéта; **a matter of** ~ **importance** дéло чрезвычáйной вáжности.

cardiogram ['kɑːdɪəʊˌgræm] *n.* кардиогрáмма.

cardiology [ˌkɑːdɪ'ɒlədʒɪ] *n.* кардиолóгия.

care [keə(r)] *n.* **1.** (*serious attention*, *caution*) осторóжность; **he works with** ~ он старáтельно рабóтает; **'handle with** ~**!'** «осторóжно!»; **handle this with** ~ обращáйтесь с э́тим осторóжно; **take** ~ **you don't fall** смотри́те, не упади́те; **have a** ~**!** береги́тесь! **2.** (*charge*, *responsibility*) забóта, попечéние; **he is under the doctor's** ~ он нахóдится под наблюдéнием врачá; **the child is in my** ~ ребёнок на моём попечéнии; **take a child into** ~ взять (*pf.*) ребёнка в систéму госудáрственного призрéния; **Mr. Smith,** ~ **of Mr. Jones** г-ну Джóнсу для передáчи г-ну Сми́ту; **that will take** ~ **of** (*meet*) **our needs** э́то обеспéчит нас необходи́мым. **3.** (*anxiety*): **free from** ~ свобóдный от забóт; не знáющий забóт.

v.i. **1.** (*feel concern or anxiety*): **I don't** ~ **what they say** мне всё равнó, что они́ скáжут; **he doesn't** ~ **a bit** емý наплевáть (*coll.*); **who** ~**s?** не всё ли равнó?; **I couldn't** ~ **less** (*coll.*) мне-то что?; мне наплевáть; **that's all he** ~**s about** он бóльше ничéм не интересу́ется. **2.** (*feel inclination*): **would you** ~ **for a walk?** не хоти́те ли пойти́ погуля́ть?; **I don't** ~ **for asparagus** я не люблю́ спáржу; **I knew she** ~**d for him** я знал, что он ей нрáвится; **you might** ~ **to look at this letter** вам, мóжет быть, бу́дет интерéсно взгляну́ть на э́то письмó. **3.** (*look after*): **he is well** ~**d for** за ним хорóший ухóд.

cpds. ~**free** *adj.* беззабóтный; ~**taker** *n.* стóрож, смотри́тель (*m.*) здáния; ~**taker government** врéменное прави́тельство; ~**worn** *adj.* изму́ченный забóтами.

careen [kə'riːn] *v.t.* кренговáть (*impf.*), килевáть (*impf.*).

v.i. (*heel over*) крени́ться (*impf.*); (*US*, *career*) нести́сь, по- (*det.*).

career [kə'rɪə(r)] *n.* **1.** (*life story*) жи́зненный путь. **2.** (*profession*) карьéра, профéссия; ~ **diplomat(ist)** профессионáльный дипломáт; ~**s teacher** (*at school*) консультáнт по профессионáльной ориентáции.

v.i. нести́сь, по- (*det.*); мчáться (*impf.*).

careerist [kə'rɪərɪst] *n.* карьери́ст.

careful ['keəfʊl] *adj.* **1.** (*attentive*) осторóжный; забóтливый, внимáтельный; **be** ~ **not to fall** бу́дьте осторóжны, не упади́те; **he is** ~ **with his money** он не трáтит дéнег зря. **2.** (*of work etc.*) тщáтельный, аккурáтный.

carefulness ['keəfʊlnɪs] *n.* осторóжность; забóтливость, внимáтельность; тщáтельность.

careless ['keəlɪs] *adj.* (*thoughtless*) неосторо́жный, неосмотри́тельный; **a ~ driver** неосторо́жный води́тель; **a ~ mistake** оши́бка по невнима́тельности; (*negligent*) небре́жный; (*carefree, unconcerned*) беззабо́тный, беспе́чный.

carelessness ['keəlɪsnɪs] *n.* небре́жность, неосторо́жность; (*negligence*) неосмотри́тельность.

carer ['keərə(r)] *n.* челове́к, уха́живающий за больны́м/ста́рым.

caress [kə'res] *n.* ла́ска.

v.t. ласка́ть (*impf.*).

caressing [kə'resɪŋ] *adj.* ласка́ющий, ла́сковый.

cargo ['kɑːgəʊ] *n.* груз; **~ ship, boat** торго́вое/грузово́е су́дно.

Caribbean [ˌkærɪ'biːən, kə'rɪbɪən] *adj.* кар(а)и́бский; (*as n.*) **the ~ (sea)** Кар(а)и́бское мо́ре; (*region*) стра́ны (*fem. pl.*) бассе́йна Кар(а)и́бского мо́ря.

caribou ['kærɪˌbuː] *n.* кари́бу (*m. indecl.*), кана́дский оле́нь.

caricature ['kærɪkətjʊə(r)] *n.* карикату́ра.

v.t. изобра|жа́ть, -зи́ть в карикату́рном ви́де.

caricaturist ['kærɪkəˌtjʊərɪst] *n.* карикатури́ст.

caries ['keəriːz, -rɪˌiːz] *n.* костое́да, ка́риез.

carillon [kə'rɪljən, 'kærɪljən] *n.* подбо́р колоколо́в; перезво́н.

caring ['keərɪŋ] *adj.* забо́тливый.

carious ['keərɪəs] *adj.* карио́зный.

carmine ['kɑːmaɪn] *n.* карми́н.

adj. карми́нный.

carnage ['kɑːnɪdʒ] *n.* бо́йня.

carnal ['kɑːn(ə)l] *adj.* (*sensual*) пло́тский, теле́сный; (*sexual*) полово́й.

carnation [kɑː'neɪʃ(ə)n] *n.* гвозди́ка.

carnival ['kɑːnɪv(ə)l] *n.* карнава́л.

carnivore ['kɑːnɪˌvɔː(r)] *n.* плотоя́дное/хи́щное живо́тное.

carnivorous [kɑː'nɪvərəs] *adj.* плотоя́дный.

carol ['kær(ə)l] *n.* (*song*) пе́сня; (*Xmas song*) рожде́ственский гимн.

carom ['kærəm] = **cannon** *n.* **3.** *& v.i.*

carotid [kə'rɒtɪd] *adj.*: **~ artery** со́нная арте́рия.

carousal [kə'raʊzəl] *n.* попо́йка, гуля́нка.

carouse [kə'raʊz] *v.i.* бра́жничать (*impf.*).

carousel [ˌkærə'sel, -'zel] *n.* (*roundabout*) карусе́ль.

carouser [kə'raʊzə(r)] *n.* гуля́ка (*c.g.*), кути́ла (*m.*).

carp[1] [kɑːp] *n.* (*zool.*) карп.

carp[2] [kɑːp] *v.i.* придира́ться (*impf.*) (**at:** к+*d.*); **~ing criticism** приди́рчивая кри́тика.

carpenter ['kɑːpɪntə(r)] *n.* пло́тник.

carpentry ['kɑːpɪntrɪ] *n.* пло́тничество, пло́тничье де́ло.

carpet ['kɑːpɪt] *n.* ковёр; **~ bombing** бомбомета́ние по пло́щади; **~ slippers** тёплые та́почки.

v.t. покр|ыва́ть, -ы́ть ковро́м; уст|ила́ть, -ла́ть ковра́ми; (*reprimand*) да|ва́ть, -ть нагоня́й/взбу́чку +*d.*; вызыва́ть, вы́звать на ковёр (*coll.*).

cpds. **~-bag** *n.* саквоя́ж; **~-sweeper** *n.* щётка для ковра́.

carriage ['kærɪdʒ] *n.* **1.** (*road vehicle*) экипа́ж, каре́та, коля́ска. **2.** (*rail car*) пассажи́рский ваго́н. **3.** (*transport of goods*) перево́зка, доста́вка. **4.** (*manner of standing or walking*) оса́нка; мане́ра держа́ться. **5.** (*gun-~*) лафе́т. **6.** (*of typewriter etc.*) каре́тка.

carrier ['kærɪə(r)] *n.* **1.** (*transport agent*) транспортёр. **2.** (*receptacle or support for luggage etc.*) бага́жник; **~ bag** су́мка для поку́пок. **3.** (*of disease*) бациллоноси́тель (*m.*), вирусоноси́тель (*m.*). **4.** (*aircraft-~*) авиано́сец. **5.:** **~ pigeon** почто́вый го́лубь.

carrion ['kærɪən] *n.* па́даль, мертвечи́на; **~ crow** воро́на чёрная.

carrot ['kærət] *n.* морко́вка; (*pl., collect.*) морко́вь.

carroty ['kærətɪ] *adj.* рыжева́тый, рыжеволо́сый.

carry ['kærɪ] *v.t.* **1.** (*bear, transport*) носи́ть, нести́; (*of or by vehicle*) вози́ть (*indet.*), везти́ (*det.*); пере|вози́ть, -везти́; **this bicycle has carried me 500 miles** на э́том велосипе́де я прое́хал 500 миль; **pipes ~ water** вода́ идёт по тру́бам; **wires ~ sound** звук передаётся по провода́м; **pillars ~ an arch** коло́нны подде́рживают а́рку; **he carries himself well** он хорошо́ де́ржится; **the police carried him off to prison** поли́ция увезла́ его́ в тюрьму́. **2.** (*have on or about one*): **I always ~ an umbrella (money) with me** у меня́ всегда́ с собо́й зо́нтик (всегда́ де́ньги при себе́); **the police ~ arms** поли́ция вооружена́; **~ figures in one's head** держа́ть (*impf.*) ци́фры в голове́; **this crime carries a heavy penalty** э́то преступле́ние влечёт за собо́й тяжёлое наказа́ние. **3.** (*fig.*): **~ into effect** осуществ|ля́ть, -и́ть; **the argument carries conviction** э́тот аргуме́нт убеди́телен; **~ the day** одéрж|ивать, -а́ть побе́ду; **the bill was carried** законопрое́кт был при́нят. **4.** (*include*): **the book carries many tables** кни́га соде́ржит мно́го табли́ц; **the newspaper carried this report** газе́та помести́ла э́то сообще́ние. **5.** (*fin., comm.*): **the loan carries interest** заём прино́сит проце́нты/дохо́д; **the shop carries hardware** э́тот магази́н торгу́ет скобяны́ми това́рами. **6.** (*math.*): **put down 6 and ~ 1** записа́ть (*pf.*) 6 и держа́ть (*impf.*) в уме́ оди́н; **'~ 1'** «оди́н в уме́».

v.i.: **the shot carried 200 yards** снаря́д пролете́л 200 я́рдов; **his voice carries well** у него́ зву́чный го́лос.

with advs.: **~ away** *v.t.* (*lit.*) ун|оси́ть, -ести́; **the masts were carried away by the storm** бу́рей унесло́ ма́чты; (*fig.*): **he was carried away by his feelings** он оказа́лся во вла́сти чувств; **~ back** *v.t.* (*lit.*) прин|оси́ть, -ести́ обра́тно; (*fig.*): **the incident carried me back to my schooldays** э́тот слу́чай перенёс меня́ обра́тно в мои́ шко́льные го́ды; **~ forward, over** *vv.t.* (*transfer*) перен|оси́ть, -ести́; **~ off** *v.t.* (*remove*) ун|оси́ть, -ести́; **death carried off several of them** не́которых из них унесла́ смерть; **he carried the situation off well** он хорошо́ вы́шел из положе́ния; **~ on** *v.t.* (*conduct, perform*): **~ on a conversation/business** вести́ (*det.*) разгово́р/де́ло; *v.i.* (*continue*) прод|олжа́ть, -о́лжить; **~ on with your work** продолжа́йте рабо́ту; (*talk, behave excitedly*) волнова́ться (*impf.*); проявля́ть (*impf.*) несде́ржанность; **don't ~ on so!** не распаля́йтесь так!; **~ out** *v.t.* (*lit.*) выноси́ть, вы́нести; (*execute*) выполня́ть, вы́полнить; **~ through** *v.t.* (*bring out of difficulties*) выводи́ть, вы́вести из затрудне́ний.

cpd. **~-cot** *n.* переносна́я де́тская крова́тка.

cart [kɑːt] *n.* двуко́лка, теле́жка; **put the ~ before the horse** (*fig.*) ста́вить (*impf.*) теле́гу пе́ред ло́шадью.

v.t. (*carry in ~*) вози́ть (*indet.*) в теле́жке; **~ away** ув|ози́ть, -езти́; (*coll., carry*) тащи́ть (*impf.*).

cpds. **~-horse** *n.* ломова́я ло́шадь; **~-road, ~-track** *nn.* просёлочная доро́га; **~wheel** *n.* колесо́ теле́ги; **turn ~wheels** кувырк|а́ться, -ну́ться колесо́м.

cartel [kɑː'tel] *n.* (*comm.*) карте́ль (*m.*).

carter ['kɑːtə(r)] *n.* во́зчик.

cartilage ['kɑːtɪlɪdʒ] *n.* хрящ.

cartilaginous [ˌkɑːtɪ'lædʒɪnəs] *adj.* хрящево́й.

cartographer [kɑː'tɒgrəfə(r)] *n.* карто́граф.

cartography [kɑː'tɒgrəfɪ] *n.* картогра́фия.

carton ['kɑːt(ə)n] *n.* (*container*) карто́нка; блок.

cartoon [kɑː'tuːn] *n.* (*in newspaper*) карикату́ра; (*film*) мультипликация, мультфи́льм.

cartoonist [kɑː'tuːnɪst] *n.* карикатури́ст; (*film*) мультиплика́тор.

cartridge ['kɑːtrɪdʒ] *n.* патро́н, заря́д; **blank ~** холосто́й патро́н.

cpds. **~-belt** *n.* патронта́ш; патро́нная ле́нта; **~-**

case *n.* патро́нная ги́льза; **~-paper** *n.* пло́тная бума́га (*для рисования и т.п.*).

carv|e [kɑːv] *v.t.* (*cut*) ре́зать (*impf.*); выреза́ть, вы́резать; (*shape by cutting*): **~e a statue out of wood** выреза́ть, вы́резать ста́тую из де́рева; **~e meat** ре́зать, на- мя́со; **~ing-fork/knife** ви́лка/нож для нареза́ния мя́са.

with adv.: **~e up** *v.t.* (*fig.*, *of wealth etc.*) раздел|я́ть, -и́ть.

carver [ˈkɑːvə(r)] *n.* ре́зчик.

carving [ˈkɑːvɪŋ] *n.* (*object*) резна́я рабо́та, резьба́.

caryatid [ˌkærɪˈætɪd] *n.* кариати́да.

cascade [kæsˈkeɪd] *n.* каска́д; водопа́д.

v.i. па́дать/ниспада́ть (*both impf.*) каска́дом.

case[1] [keɪs] *n.* **1.** (*instance*, *circumstances*) слу́чай, обстоя́тельство, де́ло; **it is (not) the ~ that ...** де́ло обстои́т (не) так, что...; **such being the ~** поско́льку э́то так; **that alters the ~** э́то меня́ет де́ло; **a ~ in point** приме́р; **a hard ~** (*difficult point to decide*) тру́дный вопро́с; (*hardened criminal*) закорене́лый престу́пник; **in that ~** в тако́м/э́том слу́чае; **in any ~** во вся́ком слу́чае; **as the ~ may be** как полу́чится; в зави́симости от обстоя́тельств; **in ~ of fire** (*if fire breaks out*) в слу́чае пожа́ра; **in the ~ of Mr. Smith** что каса́ется г-на Сми́та. **2.** (*med.*) слу́чай; больно́й, ра́неный; **there were five ~s of influenza** бы́ло пять слу́чаев гри́ппа; **the worst ~s were taken to hospital** наибо́лее тяжело́ ра́неных отвезли́ в больни́цу; **stretcher ~** носи́лочный больно́й (*or* ра́неный); **mental ~** душевнобольно́й. **3.** (*hypothesis*): **put the ~ that ...** предполо́жим, что...; **take an umbrella in ~ it rains** возьми́те зо́нтик на слу́чай дождя́; **just in ~** на вся́кий слу́чай. **4.** (*leg.*) суде́бное де́ло; **try a ~** раз|бира́ть, -обра́ть де́ло в суде́. **5.** (*sum of arguments*): **he makes out a good ~ for the change** его́ до́воды в защи́ту измене́ния убеди́тельны. **6.** (*gram.*) паде́ж.

case[2] [keɪs] *n.* **1.** (*container*) я́щик, ларе́ц, коро́бка; (*for spectacles etc.*) футля́р; **glass ~** витри́на. **2.** (*typ.*) набо́рная ка́сса; **lower ~** стро́чные бу́квы (*f. pl.*).

casein [ˈkeɪsɪɪn, ˈkeɪsiːn] *n.* казе́ин.

casemate [ˈkeɪsmeɪt] *n.* эска́рповая галере́я; казема́т.

casement [ˈkeɪsmənt] *n.* (*frame*) ство́рный око́нный переплёт; (*window*) окно́.

cash [kæʃ] *n.* (*ready money*; *also hard ~*) нали́чные (де́н|ьги, *pl.*, *g.* -ег); **on a ~ basis** за нали́чные; за нали́чный расчёт; **~ on delivery** нало́женным платежо́м; **petty ~** ме́лкие су́ммы (*f. pl.*); ка́сса для ме́лких расхо́дов; **~ dispenser** де́нежный автома́т; **~ register** ка́сса.

v.t.: **~ a cheque** получ|а́ть, -и́ть де́ньги по че́ку.

v.i.: **~ in on** (*fig.*) воспо́льзоваться (*pf.*) +*i.*

cashcard [ˈkæʃkɑːd] *n.* ка́рточка для де́нежного автома́та.

cashew [ˈkæʃuː, kæˈʃuː] *n.* оре́х ке́шью (*indecl.*).

cashier[1] [kæˈʃɪə(r)] *n.* касси́р.

cashier[2] [kæˈʃɪə(r)] *v.t.* ув|ольня́ть, -о́лить со слу́жбы.

cashmere [ˈkæʃmɪə(r)] *n.* кашеми́р; (*attr.*) кашеми́ровый.

casino [kəˈsiːnəʊ] *n.* казино́ (*indecl.*).

cask [kɑːsk] *n.* бо́чка, бочо́нок.

casket [ˈkɑːskɪt] *n.* шкату́лка; (*US*, *coffin*) гроб.

Caspian [ˈkæspɪən] *n.* (**the ~ Sea**) Каспи́йское мо́ре.

cassava [kəˈsɑːvə] *n.* манио́ка.

casserole [ˈkæsəˌrəʊl] *n.* кастрю́лечка; блю́до, пригото́вленное в кастрю́лечке.

cassette [kæˈset, kə-] *n.* кассе́та; **~ recorder** кассе́тный магнитофо́н.

cassock [ˈkæsək] *n.* ря́са, сута́на.

cast [kɑːst] *n.* **1.** (*act of throwing*) броса́ние, мета́ние, бросо́к. **2.** (*mould*) фо́рма для отли́вки; (*moulded object*): **plaster ~** ги́псовый сле́пок. **3.** (*theatr.*) соста́в актёров; спи́сок исполни́телей. **4.: ~ of mind** склад ума́.

v.t. **1.** (*throw*) бр|оса́ть, -о́сить; кида́ть, ки́нуть. **2.** (*fig.*): **~ a vote** проголосова́ть (*pf.*); **~ lots** броса́ть/кида́ть (*both impf.*) жре́бий; **~ doubt on** подв|ерга́ть, -е́ргнуть сомне́нию; **~ an eye over** бро́сить (*pf.*) взгля́д на+*a.*; **~ in one's lot with** свя́з|ывать, -а́ть свою́ судьбу́ с+*i.*; **~ a spell (up)on** околдо́в|ывать, -а́ть; **~ing vote** реша́ющий го́лос. **3.** (*pour*, *form in a mould*) отл|ива́ть, -и́ть; **~ iron** чугу́н. **4.** (*theatr.*): **~ a play** распредел|я́ть, -и́ть ро́ли в пье́се; **he was ~ for the part of Hamlet** ему́ была́ пору́чена роль Га́млета.

with advs.: **~ about** *v.i.*: **~ about for** разы́скивать, оты́скивать (*both impf.*); **~ away** *v.t.* (*reject*) отбр|а́сывать, -о́сить; **~ down** *v.t.* (*depress*) угнета́ть (*impf.*); подав|ля́ть, -и́ть; **~ off** *v.t.* (*abandon*) сбр|а́сывать, -о́сить; *v.i.* (*naut.*) отва́л|ивать, -и́ть.

cpds. **~away** *n.* & *adj.* потерпе́вший кораблекруше́ние; **~-iron** *adj.* чугу́нный; (*fig.*) стально́й, желе́зный; несгиба́емый; **~-off** *n.* & *adj.*: **~-off clothing** обно́ск|и (*pl.*, *g.* -ов), старьё.

castanets [ˌkæstəˈnets] *n.* кастанье́ты (*f. pl.*).

caste [kɑːst] *n.* ка́ста.

castigate [ˈkæstɪˌgeɪt] *v.t.* нака́з|ывать, -а́ть; бичева́ть (*impf.*).

castigation [ˌkæstɪˈgeɪʃ(ə)n] *n.* наказа́ние; бичева́ние.

casting [ˈkɑːstɪŋ] *n.* **1.** (*tech.*): (*process*) литьё, отли́вка; (*product*) отли́вка. **2.** (*theatr.*) распределе́ние роле́й.

castle [ˈkɑːs(ə)l] *n.* за́мок; **~s in Spain** возду́шные за́мки; (*at chess*) ладья́, тура́.

v.i. (*at chess*) рокирова́ться (*impf.*, *pf.*).

cast|or,[1] [ˈkɑːstə(r)] *n.* **1.** (*wheel on furniture*) ро́лик. **2.: ~ sugar** са́харный песо́к.

castor[2] [ˈkɑːstə(r)] *n.*: **~ oil** касто́ровое ма́сло.

castrate [kæˈstreɪt] *v.t.* кастри́ровать (*impf.*, *pf.*).

castration [kæˈstreɪʃ(ə)n] *n.* кастра́ция.

casual [ˈkæʒʊəl, -zjʊəl] *adj.* **1.** (*chance*, *occasional*) случа́йный; **a ~ meeting** случа́йная встре́ча; **~ labourer** рабо́чий, живу́щий на случа́йные за́работки. **2.** (*careless*) небре́жный, беспе́чный; **clothes for ~ wear** проста́я/бу́дничная оде́жда.

casualness [ˈkæʒʊəlnɪs, -zjʊəlnɪs] *n.* случа́йность; небре́жность, беспе́чность.

casualty [ˈkæʒʊəltɪ, ˈkæzjʊ-] *n.* **1.** (*accident*) несча́стный слу́чай. **2.** (*pers.*) пострада́вший от несча́стного слу́чая; (*mil.*) ра́неный, уби́тый; **~ list** спи́сок уби́тых и ра́неных; **~ ward** пала́та ско́рой по́мощи.

casuist [ˈkæzjuːɪst, ˈkæʒʊɪst] *n.* казуи́ст.

casuistic(al) [kæzjuːˈɪstɪk(ə)l, kæʒʊˈɪstɪk(ə)l] *adj.* казуисти́ческий.

casuistry [ˈkæzjʊɪstrɪ] *n.* казуи́стика.

cat [kæt] *n.* **1.** ко́шка; **tom ~** кот; **wild ~** ди́кая ко́шка. **2.: ~ o'nine tails** ко́шка. **3.** (*idioms and provs.*): **let the ~ out of the bag** проб|а́лтываться, -олта́ться; выба́лтывать, вы́болтать секре́т; **there's not room to swing a ~** поверну́ться не́где; **a ~ may look at a king** за просмо́тр де́нег не беру́т; **like a ~ on hot bricks** как на иго́лках; **when the ~'s away the mice will play** без кота́ мыша́м раздо́лье; **~'s pyjamas, whiskers** (*sl.*) что на́до; пе́рвый сорт.

cpds. **~call** *n.* осви́стывание; **~'s-eye** *n.* (*reflector*) катафо́т; **~walk** *n.* рабо́чие мостки́ (*pl.*, *g.* -о́в); (*in fashion-house*) помо́ст.

cataclysm [ˈkætəˌklɪz(ə)m] *n.* катакли́зм.

cataclysmic [ˌkætəˈklɪzmɪk] *adj.* катастрофи́ческий.

catacomb [ˈkætəˌkuːm, -ˌkəʊm] *n.* катако́мба.

catafalque [ˈkætəˌfælk] *n.* катафа́лк.

catalepsy [ˈkætəˌlepsɪ] *n.* катале́псия.

cataleptic [ˌkætəˈleptɪk] *adj.* каталепти́ческий.

catalogue ['kætə,lɒg] (*US* **catalog**) *n.* катало́г.
v.t. каталогизи́ровать (*impf., pf.*).
cataloguer ['kætə,lɒgə(r)] *n.* каталогиза́тор.
catalysis [kə'tælɪsɪs] *n.* ката́лиз.
catalyst ['kætəlɪst] *n.* катализа́тор.
catalytic [,kætə'lɪtɪk] *adj.* каталити́ческий; ~ **converter** каталити́ческий нейтрализа́тор.
catamaran [,kætəmə'ræn] *n.* катамара́н.
catapult ['kætə,pʌlt] *n.* (*toy*) рога́тка; (*hist., aeron.*) катапу́льта.
v.t. выбра́сывать, вы́бросить катапу́льтой; катапульти́ровать (*impf., pf.*).
cataract ['kætə,rækt] *n.* (*waterfall*) водопа́д; (*med.*) катара́кта.
catarrh [kə'tɑ:(r)] *n.* ката́р.
catastrophe [kə'tæstrəfɪ] *n.* катастро́фа; **natural** ~ стихи́йное бе́дствие.
catastrophic [,kætə'strɒfɪk] *adj.* катастрофи́ческий.
catch [kætʃ] *n.* **1.** (*act of catching*) пои́мка, захва́т; **play** ~ игра́ть (*impf.*) в са́лки. **2.** (*amount caught*) уло́в, добы́ча. **3.** (*trap*) уло́вка, лову́шка; **there must be a** ~ **in it** здесь, должно́ быть, кро́ется подво́х; **a** ~ **question** ка́верзный вопро́с. **4.** (*device for fastening etc.*) защёлка, шпингале́т.
v.t. & i. **1.** (*seize*) лови́ть, пойма́ть; хвата́ть, схвати́ть; **he caught the ball** он пойма́л мяч; ~ **a fish** пойма́ть (*pf.*) ры́бу; **she caught hold of him** она́ схвати́ла его́; ~ **at** хвата́ться, схвати́ться за+*a.* **2.** (*of entanglement, fastening etc.*): **her dress caught on a nail; the nail caught her dress** она́ зацепи́лась пла́тьем за гвоздь; **I caught my finger in the door** я прищеми́л себе́ па́лец две́рью; **he caught his foot** у него́ застря́ла нога́. **3.** (*intercept, detect*): **I caught him stealing** я заста́л его́, когда́ он крал; **I caught him as he was leaving the house** я заста́л/захвати́л его́ как раз, когда́ он выходи́л и́з дому; **I was caught by the rain** меня́ захвати́ло дождём; **we were caught in the storm** нас засти́гла бу́ря. **4.** (*be in time for*): ~ **a train** поспе́ть (*pf.*) к по́езду; **he caught the post** он успе́л отпра́вить письмо́ с э́той по́чтой. **5.** (*fig.*) пойма́ть, улови́ть, схвати́ть (*all pf.*); ~ **s.o.'s words** расслы́шать (*pf.*) чьи-н. слова́; **I didn't** ~ **what you said** я прослу́шал, что вы сказа́ли; ~ **s.o.'s meaning** улови́ть (*pf.*) чью-н. мысль; ~ **one's breath** затаи́ть (*pf.*) дыха́ние; ~ **s.o.'s eye** привле́чь (*pf.*) чьё-н. внима́ние; ~ **fire, alight** загоре́ться (*pf.*); ~ **a glimpse of** уви́деть (*pf.*) ме́льком; ~ **hold of** схвати́ть, улови́ть (*both pf.*). **6.** (*be hit by*): **he caught it on the forehead** он получи́л уда́р в лоб (*or* по лбу); (*of punishment*): **you'll** ~ **it!** тебе́ доста́нется/попадёт. **7.** (*be infected by; lit., fig.*) схвати́ть, получи́ть (*both pf.*); **he caught a fever** он схвати́л лихора́дку; ~ **cold** простуди́ться (*pf.*); **he was caught with the general enthusiasm** его́ захвати́л/увлёк о́бщий энтузиа́зм.
with advs.: ~ **on** *v.i.*: **the fashion did not** ~ **on** э́та мо́да не приви́лась; ~ **out** *v.t.*: **he was caught out in a mistake** его́ пойма́ли на оши́бке; ~ **up** *v.t. & i.* (*pick up quickly*) подхва́т|ывать, -и́ть; **he caught up with the others** он догна́л остальны́х; **I must** ~ **up on my work** я запусти́л рабо́ту — тепе́рь на́до нагоня́ть; **this paper got caught up with the others** э́та бума́га затеря́лась среди́ остальны́х; **the police caught up with him** поли́ция насти́гла его́.
cpds. ~**-phrase** *n.*, ~**word** *n.* мо́дное слове́чко.
catching ['kætʃɪŋ] *adj.* (*of disease*) зара́зный, зарази́тельный, прили́пчивый.
catchment ['kætʃmənt] *n.*: ~ **area, basin** бассе́йн реки́; водосбо́рная пло́щадь; микрорайо́н, обслу́живаемый шко́лой *и т.п.*
catchy ['kætʃɪ] *adj.* привлека́тельный; (*of tune etc.*) легко́ запомина́ющийся, прили́пчивый.
catechism ['kætɪ,kɪz(ə)m] *n.* катехи́зис.
categorical [,kætɪ'gɒrɪk(ə)l] *adj.* категори́ческий.
categorize ['kætɪgə,raɪz] *v.t.* распредел|я́ть, -и́ть по катего́риям.
category ['kætɪgərɪ] *n.* катего́рия.
cater ['keɪtə(r)] *v.i.*: ~ **for** пост|авля́ть, -а́вить прови́зию для+*g.*; (*fig.*) удовлетвор|я́ть, -и́ть (*кого* or *чьи-н. вкусы*); уго|жда́ть, -ди́ть (*кому*); **the** ~**ing trade** рестора́нное де́ло.
caterer ['keɪtərə(r)] *n.* поставщи́к прови́зии.
caterpillar ['kætə,pɪlə(r)] *n.* (*zool., tech.*) гу́сеница; (*attr.*) гу́сеничный.
catgut ['kætgʌt] *n.* кетгу́т, кише́чная струна́.
catharsis [kə'θɑ:sɪs] *n.* (*med.*) очище́ние желу́дка; (*fig.*) ка́тарсис.
cathartic [kə'θɑ:tɪk] *adj.* (*med.*) слаби́тельный; (*fig.*) очища́ющий.
cathedral [kə'θi:dr(ə)l] *n.* (кафедра́льный) собо́р.
catheter ['kæθɪtə(r)] *n.* кате́тер.
cathode ['kæθəʊd] *n.* като́д; ~ **rays** като́дные лучи́.
catholic ['kæθəlɪk, 'kæθlɪk] *n.* като́л|ик (*fem.* -и́чка).
adj. (*relig.*) католи́ческий; **Roman** ~ ри́мско-католи́ческий; (*liberal*): **a man of** ~ **tastes** челове́к широ́ких вку́сов.
Catholicism [kə'θɒlɪ,sɪz(ə)m] *n.* католици́зм, католи́чество.
catkin ['kætkɪn] *n.* серёжка.
cattle ['kæt(ə)l] *n.* (*livestock*) скот, скоти́на; (*bovines*) кру́пный рога́тый скот; (*fig., pej.*) скот, скоти́на.
cpds. ~**-dealer** *n.* скотопромы́шленник; ~**-truck** *n.* ваго́н для перево́зки скота́.
catty ['kætɪ] *adj.* ехи́дный.
Caucasian [kɔ:'keɪʒ(ə)n, -'keɪzɪən] *n.* (*of Caucasus*) кавка́з|ец (*fem.* -ка); (*of white race*) челове́к бе́лой ра́сы.
adj. кавка́зский.
Caucasus ['kɔ:kəsəs] *n.* Кавка́з.
cauldron ['kɔ:ldrən] *n.* котёл.
cauliflower ['kɒlɪ,flaʊə(r)] *n.* цветна́я капу́ста.
ca(u)lk [kɔ:k] *v.t.* конопа́тить, за-.
causal ['kɔ:z(ə)l] *adj.* казуа́льный, причи́нный.
causality [kɔ:'zælɪtɪ] *n.* казуа́льность, причи́нность.
cause [kɔ:z] *n.* **1.** (*that which* ~*s*) причи́на, по́вод. **2.** (*need*) причи́на, основа́ние. **3.** (*purpose, objective*): **the workers'** ~ де́ло трудя́щихся; **he pleaded his** ~ он защища́л своё де́ло; **a lost** ~ прои́гранное де́ло.
v.t. вызыва́ть, вы́звать; ~ **a disturbance** произв|оди́ть, -ести́ беспоря́дки; ~ **s.o. trouble** причин|я́ть, и́ть кому́-н. беспоко́йство; **what** ~**d the accident?** от чего́ произошёл несча́стный слу́чай?; **he** ~**d them to be put to death** он повеле́л уби́ть их.
cause célèbre [,kɔ:z se'lebr] *n.* гро́мкий/сканда́льный проце́сс.
causeway ['kɔ:zweɪ] *n.* да́мба; гать; мощёная доро́га.
caustic ['kɔ:stɪk] *adj.* каусти́ческий; ~ **soda** е́дкий натр; (*fig.*) е́дкий, ко́лкий, язви́тельный.
cauter|ization [,kɔ:təraɪ'zeɪʃ(ə)n] *n.* прижига́ние.
cauterize ['kɔ:tə,raɪz] *v.t.* приж|ига́ть, -е́чь.
caution ['kɔ:ʃ(ə)n] *n.* **1.** (*prudence*) осторо́жность; **with** ~ осторо́жно. **2.** (*warning*) предостереже́ние, предосторо́жность; '~!' «Внима́ние!»; «Осторо́жно!»; **he was let off with a** ~ его́ отпусти́ли с предостереже́нием.
v.t. предостер|ега́ть, -е́чь.
cautionary ['kɔ:ʃənərɪ] *adj.* предостерега́ющий.
cautious ['kɔ:ʃəs] *adj.* осторо́жный, осмотри́тельный.
cavalcade [,kævəl'keɪd] *n.* кавалька́да.
cavalier [,kævə'lɪə(r)] *n.* (*gallant; royalist*) кавале́р.
adj. бесцеремо́нный, надме́нный.
cavalry ['kævəlrɪ] *n.* кавале́рия, ко́нница; **two hundred** ~ две́сти ко́нников.
cpd. ~**man** *n.* кавалери́ст.
cave[1] [keɪv] *n.* пеще́ра.

cpds. **~-man** *n.* (*lit.*, *fig.*) пещéрный человéк, троглодúт; **~-painting** *n.* пещéрная живопись.

cave[2] [keɪv] *v.i.*: **~ in** (*lit.*) провáл|иваться, -úться; продáв|ливаться, -úться; (*fig.*) сд|авáться, -áться.

caveat ['kævɪˌæt] *n.* предостережéние.

cavern ['kæv(ə)n] *n.* грот, пещéра.

cavernous ['kæv(ə)nəs] *adj.* пещéристый.

caviar(e) ['kævɪˌɑː(r), ˌkævɪ'ɑː(r)] *n.* икрá.

cavil ['kævɪl] *n.* придúрка.

v.i.: **~ at** прид|ирáться, -рáться к+*d.*

cavity ['kævɪtɪ] *n.* пóлость, впáдина; (*in tooth*) дуплó.

cavort [kə'vɔːt] *v.i.* скакáть (*impf.*).

caw ['kɔː] *n.* кáрканье.

v.t. & *i.* кáрк|ать -нуть.

cayenne [keɪ'en] *n.*: **~ pepper** кайéнский пéрец.

CD (*abbr. of* ***compact disk***) компáкт-дúск; **~-player** проúгрыватель (*m.*) компáкт-дúсков.

CD-ROM (*abbr. of* ***compact disk — read-only memory***) компáкт-дúск ПЗУ.

cease [siːs] *n.*: **without ~** непрестáнно, не переставáя.

v.t. прекра|щáть, -тúть; перест|авáть, -áть; **~ talking** прекратúть (*pf.*) разговóр; замолчáть (*pf.*); **~ fire** прекратúть (*pf.*) огóнь.

v.i. прекра|щáться, -тúться.

cpd. **~-fire** *n.* прекращéние огня́.

ceaseless ['siːslɪs] *adj.* непрестáнный, непреры́вный.

cedar ['siːdə(r)] *n.* кедр; (*attr.*) кедрóвый.

cede [siːd] *v.t.* сда|вáть, -áть; уступ|áть, -úть.

cedilla [sɪ'dɪlə] *n.* седúль (*m.*).

ceiling ['siːlɪŋ] *n.* (*lit.*, *fig.*) потолóк; (*fig.*) максимáльный ýровень; **hit the ~** (*fig.*, *fly into a rage*) рассвирепéть (*pf.*); нá стену лезть (*impf.*).

celandine ['selənˌdaɪn] *n.* чистотéл.

celebrate ['selɪˌbreɪt] *v.t.* & *i.* **1.** (*mark an occasion*) прáздновать, от-. **2.** (*praise*) просл|авля́ть, -áвить. **3.** (*relig.*) отпр|авля́ть, -áвить (церкóвную слýжбу).

celebrated ['selɪˌbreɪtɪd] *adj.* прослáвленный, знаменúтый.

celebration [selɪ'breɪʃ(ə)n] *n.* прáзднование, торжествá (*nt. pl.*); **this calls for a ~** э́то слéдует отпрáздновать/отмéтить.

celebrity [sɪ'lebrɪtɪ] *n.* (*fame*) знаменúтость, извéстность; (*pers.*) знаменúтость.

celerity [sɪ'lerɪtɪ] *n.* быстротá.

celery ['selərɪ] *n.* сельдерéй.

celestial [sɪ'lestɪəl] *adj.* (*astron.*, *fig.*) небéсный.

celibacy ['selɪbəsɪ] *n.* целибáт, безбрáчие.

celibate ['selɪbət] *n.* & *adj.* холостя́к, холостóй; дáвший обéт безбрáчия.

cell [sel] *n.* **1.** (*in prison*) кáмера. **2.** (*in monastery*) кéлья. **3.** (*of honeycomb*) ячея́, ячéйка. **4.** (*elec.*) элемéнт. **5.** (*biol.*) клéтка. **6.** (*pol.*) ячéйка.

cpd. **~-mate** *n.* сокáмерник.

cellar ['selə(r)] *n.* пóгреб, подвáл.

cellist ['tʃelɪst] *n.* виолончелúст.

cello ['tʃeləʊ] *n.* виолончéль.

cellophane ['seləˌfeɪn] *n.* целлофáн; (*attr.*) целлофáновый.

cellular ['seljʊlə(r)] *adj.* клéточный, ячéистый.

celluloid ['seljʊˌlɔɪd] *n.* целлулóид; (*attr.*) целлулóидный.

cellulose ['seljʊˌləʊz, -ˌləʊs] *n.* (*chem.*) целлюлóза; клетчáтка.

C|elt (*also* **K-**) [kelt, selt] *n.* кельт.

C|eltic (*also* **K-**) ['keltɪk, 'seltɪk] *adj.* кéльтский.

cement [sɪ'ment] *n.* цемéнт; (*attr.*) цемéнтный.

v.t. цементúровать (*impf.*, *pf.*); (*fig.*): **~ relations** упрóч|ивать, -ить отношéния; укреп|ля́ть, -úть свя́зи.

cpd. **~-mixer** *n.* мешáлка для цемéнтного раствóра.

cemetery ['semɪtərɪ] *n.* клáдбище.

cenotaph ['senəˌtɑːf] *n.* кенотáф.

censer ['sensə(r)] *n.* кадúло, курúльница.

censor ['sensə(r)] *n.* цéнзор.

v.t. цензуровáть (*impf.*); подв|ергáть, -éргнуть цензýре.

censorship ['sensərʃɪp] *n.* цензýра.

censure ['sensjə(r)] *n.* осуждéние, порицáние; **pass a vote of ~** вы́нести (*pf.*) вóтум недовéрия.

v.t. осу|ждáть, -дúть; порицáть (*impf.*).

census ['sensəs] *n.* пéрепись (населéния); **take a ~** произв|одúть, -естú пéрепись (населéния).

cent [sent] *n.* **1.** (*coin*) цент. **2.**: **per ~** процéнт, на сóтню.

centaur ['sentɔː(r)] *n.* кентáвр.

centenarian [ˌsentɪ'neərɪən] *n.* человéк, достúгший столéтнего вóзраста.

adj. столéтний.

centen|ary [sen'tiːnərɪ], **-nial** [sen'tenɪəl] *n.* столéтие.

adj. столéтний.

centigrade ['sentɪˌgreɪd] *adj.*: **~ thermometer** термóметр Цéльсия; **20° ~** 20 грáдусов по Цéльсию.

centigram(me) ['sentɪˌgræm] *n.* сантигрáмм.

centime ['sɑ̃tiːm] *n.* сантúм.

centimetre ['sentɪˌmiːtə(r)] *n.* сантимéтр.

centipede ['sentɪˌpiːd] *n.* многонóжка.

central ['sentr(ə)l] *adj.* **1.** (*pert. to a centre*) центрáльный; **~ Asia** Срéдняя Áзия; **the house is very ~** дом нахóдится в сáмом цéнтре гóрода. **2.** (*principal*) центрáльный, глáвный.

centralization [ˌsentrəlaɪ'zeɪʃ(ə)n] *n.* централизáция.

centralize ['sentrəˌlaɪz] *v.t.* централизовáть (*impf.*, *pf.*).

centre ['sentə(r)] *n.* **1.** (*middle point or section*) центр; (*of a chocolate*) начúнка; **~ of gravity** центр тя́жести; **dead ~** мёртвая тóчка. **2.** (*fig.*, *key-point*): **~ of attraction** центр внимáния; **shopping ~** торгóвый центр. **3.** (*pol.*) центр. **4.** (*attr.*) центрáльный.

v.t. **1.** (*fix in central position*) поме|щáть, -стúть в цéнтре. **2.** (*fig.*) сосредотóчи|вать, -ть; концентрúровать, с-.

v.i. сосредотóчи|ваться, -ться; концентрúроваться, с-.

cpds. **~-forward** *n.* (*sport*) цéнтр нападéния, центрфóрвард; **~piece** *n.* (*fig.*) украшéние (*коллекции*); **~-right** *adj.* (*pol.*) правоцентрúстский.

centrifugal [ˌsentrɪ'fjuːg(ə)l, sen'trɪfjʊg(ə)l] *adj.* центробéжный.

centrifuge ['sentrɪˌfjuːdʒ] *n.* центрифýга.

centripetal [sen'trɪpɪt(ə)l] *adj.* центростремúтельный.

centrist ['sentrɪst] *n.* центрúст.

century ['sentʃərɪ, -tjʊrɪ] *n.* столéтие, век.

ceramic [sɪ'ræmɪk, kɪ-] *adj.* керамúческий.

ceramics [sɪ'ræmɪks, kɪ-] *n.* керáмика.

cereal ['sɪərɪəl] *n.* хлéбный злак; (*breakfast*) **~** корнфлéкс, геркулéс *и т.п.*

adj. хлéбный, зерновóй.

cerebellum [ˌserɪ'beləm] *n.* мозжечóк.

cerebral ['serɪbr(ə)l] *adj.* мозговóй, церебрáльный; **~ haemorrhage** кровоизлия́ние в мозг.

cerebrum ['serɪbrəm] *n.* головнóй мозг.

ceremonial [ˌserɪ'məʊnɪəl] *n.* (*relig. rites*) церемониáл, обря́д, ритуáл.

adj. церемониáльный, обря́довый.

ceremonious [ˌserɪ'məʊnɪəs] *adj.* церемóнный.

ceremony ['serɪmənɪ] *n.* (*rite*) обря́д, церемóния; **wedding ~** обря́д венчáния; (*formal behaviour*) церемóнность; **stand (up)on ~** церемóниться (*impf.*); наст|áивать, -оя́ть на соблюдéнии формáльностей; **without ~** без церемóний.

cerise [sə'riːz, -'riːs] *adj.* свéтло-крáсный.

certain ['sɜːt(ə)n, -tɪn] *adj.* **1.** (*undoubted*) несомнéнный; **I cannot say for ~** я не могý сказáть наверняка́; **make ~ of** (*ascertain*) удостов|ера́ться, -е́риться в чём-н.; (*ensure possession of*) обеспе́чи|вать, -ть; **he is ~ to succeed** он наверняка́/несомне́нно преуспе́ет. **2.** (*confident*) уве́ренный. **3.** (*definite but unspecified*) изве́стный, не́который; оди́н; **a ~ person** не́кто, не́кое лицо́; **in a ~ town** в одно́м го́роде; **a ~ Mr. Jones** не́кий г. Джо́унс; **a ~ type of people** лю́ди изве́стного ро́да; **under ~ conditions** при изве́стных усло́виях; **a ~** (*some*) **pleasure** не́которое удово́льствие.

certainly ['sɜːtənlɪ, -tɪnlɪ] *adv.* (*without doubt*) несомне́нно, наверняка́, наве́рно; (*expr. obedience or consent*) коне́чно, безусло́вно; **~ not** ни в ко́ем слу́чае.

certainty ['sɜːtəntɪ, -tɪntɪ] *n.* **1.** (*being certainly true*) несомне́нность. **2.** (*certain fact*) несомне́нный факт; **for a ~** наверняка́. **3.** (*confidence*) уве́ренность. **4.** (*accuracy*): **I cannot say with ~** не могу́ определённо сказа́ть.

certificate [sə'tɪfɪkət] *n.* удостовере́ние, свиде́тельство, сертифика́т; **birth ~** свиде́тельство о рожде́нии, ме́трика.

certification [ˌsɜːtɪfɪ'keɪʃ(ə)n] *n.* удостовере́ние.

certify ['sɜːtɪˌfaɪ] *v.t.* удостов|еря́ть, -е́рить; зав|еря́ть, -е́рить; **this is to ~ that ...** настоя́щим удостоверя́ется, что....

certitude ['sɜːtɪˌtjuːd] *n.* уве́ренность; несомне́нность.

ceruse ['sɪəruːs, sɪ'ruːs] *n.* бели́л|а (*pl., g.* —).

cervical [sɜː'vaɪk(ə)l, 'sɜːvɪk(ə)l] *adj.* ше́йный; **~ smear** мазо́к ше́йки ма́тки.

cervix ['sɜːvɪks] *n.* ше́я; (*of womb*) ше́йка (ма́тки).

Cesarean [sɪ'zeərɪən] (*US*) = **Caesarean**

cessation [se'seɪʃ(ə)n] *n.* прекраще́ние, остано́вка; **~ of hostilities** прекраще́ние вое́нных де́йствий.

cession ['seʃ(ə)n] *n.* усту́пка, переда́ча.

cess|pit ['sespɪt], **-pool** ['sespuːl] *nn.* выгребна́я/помо́йная я́ма; (*fig.*) помо́йная я́ма, клоа́ка.

CFCs (*abbr. of* **chloro-fluorocarbons**) хлори́рованные фторуглеро́ды.

chafe [tʃeɪf] *v.t.* (*rub*) тере́ть (*impf.*); (*make sore*) нат|ира́ть, -ере́ть.

v.i. нат|ира́ться, -ере́ться; **her skin ~s easily** у неё ко́жа легко́ воспаля́ется; **he ~d at the delay** отсро́чка раздража́ла его́.

chaff [tʃɑːf] *n.* (*husks*) мяки́на.

chaffinch ['tʃæfɪntʃ] *n.* зя́блик.

chagrin ['ʃægrɪn, ʃə'griːn] *n.* огорче́ние, доса́да.

v.t. огорч|а́ть, -и́ть.

chain [tʃeɪn] *n.* цепь; цепо́чка; **mountain ~** го́рная цепь; (*pl., fetters*) це́пи (*f. pl.*), око́в|ы (*pl., g.* —); (*fig.*): **~ of events** цепь собы́тий; **~ reaction** цепна́я реа́кция.

v.t. прико́в|ывать, -а́ть це́пью; **the dog is ~ed up** соба́ка поса́жена на цепь.

cpds. **~-mail** *n.* кольчу́га; **~-gang** *n.* гру́ппа каторжа́н, ско́ванных о́бщей це́пью; **~-smoker** *n.* зая́длый кури́льщик; **~-stitch** *n.* та́мбурная стро́чка; **~-store** *n.* однoти́пный фи́рменный магази́н.

chair [tʃeə(r)] *n.* **1.** стул. **2.** (*~manship*) председа́тельство; **Mr. X took/left the ~** г-н X за́нял/поки́нул председа́тельское ме́сто. **3.** (*~man*) председа́тель (*m.*); **Madam C~man!** госпожа́ председа́тель! **4.** (*professorship*) ка́федра; **he holds the ~ of physics** он заве́дует ка́федрой фи́зики.

v.t. (*preside over*) председа́тельствовать (*impf.*) на+*p*.

cpds. **~-lift** подвесно́й подъёмник; **~man, ~-person** *nn.* = **chair 3.**

chaise longue [ʃeɪz 'lɒŋ] *n.* шезло́нг.

chalcedony [kæl'sedənɪ] *n.* халцедо́н.

chalet ['ʃæleɪ] *n.* шале́ (*indecl.*).

chalice ['tʃælɪs] *n.* (*goblet*) ку́бок, ча́ша; (*eccl.*) поти́р.

chalk [tʃɔːk] *n.* **1.** (*material*) мел; (*attr.*) мелово́й. **2.** (*fig.*): **not by a long ~** отню́дь нет; далеко́ не.

v.t. (*write or mark with ~*) писа́ть, на- ме́лом; (*whiten with ~*) бели́ть, по-; **~ up** (*register*) отм|еча́ть, -е́тить.

chalky ['tʃɔːkɪ] *adj.* (*like chalk*) мелово́й; (*containing chalk*) известко́вый.

challenge ['tʃælɪndʒ] *n.* (*to a race etc.*) вы́зов; **~ cup** переходя́щий ку́бок; (*sentry's*) о́клик.

v.t. вызыва́ть, вы́звать; (*dispute*) оспа́ривать (*impf.*); **~ s.o. to a race/duel** вызыва́ть, вы́звать кого́-н. на состяза́ние/дуэ́ль.

challenger ['tʃælɪndʒə(r)] *n.* претенде́нт.

challenging ['tʃælɪndʒɪŋ] *adv.* (*of opportunity etc.*) тру́дный, но интере́сный.

chamber ['tʃeɪmbə(r)] *n.* **1.** (*room*) ко́мната; (*pl., apartment*) кварти́ра; (*office*) адвока́тская конто́ра; ка́мера, кабине́т судьи́; **~ of horrors** зал у́жасов; **bridal ~** спа́льня новобра́чных; **~ music** ка́мерная му́зыка. **2.** (*hall, e.g. of parliament*) зал, за́ла. **3.** (*official body*) пала́та; **~ of deputies** пала́та депута́тов. **4.** (*of revolver*) патро́нник.

cpd. **~maid** *n.* го́рничная.

chamberlain ['tʃeɪmbəlɪn] *n.* мажордо́м, камерге́р.

chameleon [kə'miːlɪən] *n.* (*lit., fig.*) хамелео́н.

chammy ['ʃæmɪ] (*US*) = **shammy**

chamois ['ʃæmwɑː, *sense* **2.** 'ʃæmɪ] *n.* **1.** (*zool.*) се́рна. **2.** (*~-leather*) за́мша.

champ[1] [tʃæmp] *n.* (*chewing action or noise*) ча́вканье.

v.t. & i. (*chew noisily*) ча́вкать (*impf.*); (*bite on*): **~ the bit** грызть (*impf.*) удила́.

champ[2] [tʃæmp] (*coll.*) = **champion 2.**

champagne [ʃæm'peɪn] *n.* шампа́нское.

champion ['tʃæmpɪən] *n.* **1.** (*defender*) побо́рни|к, защи́тни|к (*fem.* -ца); боре́ц. **2.** (*prize-winning pers. or thg.*) чемпио́н (*fem., coll.* -ка); **a ~ chess-player** чемпио́н по ша́хматам.

championship ['tʃæmpɪənʃɪp] *n.* (*advocacy*) защи́та; (*sport*) чемпио́нство, чемпиона́т, пе́рвенство.

chance [tʃɑːns] *n.* **1.** (*casual occurrence*) слу́чай, случа́йность; **by ~** случа́йно; **he left it to ~** он оста́вил э́то на во́лю слу́чая. **2.** (*possibility, likelihood, opportunity*) шанс, возмо́жность; **the ~s are that he will come** все ша́нсы за то, что он придёт; **I had no ~ of winning** у меня́ не́ было никаки́х ша́нсов на успе́х; **the ~ of a lifetime** раз в жи́зни предста́вившийся слу́чай; **a fat ~ he has!** куда́ уж ему́ (*coll.*); **a ~ companion** случа́йный попу́тчик.

v.t.: **let's ~ it** рискнём!

v.i. (*happen*) случ|а́ться, -и́ться; **I ~d to see him** мне довело́сь уви́деть его́.

chancellery ['tʃɑːnsələrɪ] *n.* канцеля́рия.

chancellor ['tʃɑːnsələ(r)] *n.* ка́нцлер; **C~ of the Exchequer** ка́нцлер казначе́йства, мини́стр фина́нсов; (*of university*) ре́ктор, ка́нцлер.

chancre ['ʃæŋkə(r)] *n.* твёрдый шанкр.

chancy ['tʃɑːnsɪ] *adj.* (*coll.*) риско́ванный.

chandelier [ˌʃændɪ'lɪə(r)] *n.* канделя́бр, лю́стра.

chandler ['tʃɑːndlə(r)] *n.* москате́льщик.

change [tʃeɪndʒ] *n.* **1.** (*alteration*) измене́ние; (*substitution*) переме́на; **~ of air, scene** переме́на обстано́вки; **~ of life** (*med.*) климакте́рий; **for a ~** для разнообра́зия; **~ of heart** измене́ние наме́рений; **a ~ for the better** переме́на к лу́чшему. **2.** (*spare set*) сме́на; **he took a ~ of linen with him** он взял с собо́й сме́ну белья́. **3.** (*money*) ме́лкие де́н|ьги (*pl., g.* -ег); ме́лочь; (*returned as balance*) сда́ча; **have you ~ for a pound?** мо́жете ли вы разменя́ть фунт?. **4.** (*of trains etc.*) переса́дка.

v.t. **1.** (*alter, replace*) меня́ть, по-; **she ~d her address** она́ перее́хала на друго́е ме́сто; **~ (one's) clothes** переод|ева́ться, -е́ться; смен|я́ть, -и́ть оде́жду; **~ one's shoes** переоб|ува́ться, -у́ться; ~

one's mind разду́м|ывать, -ать; переду́м|ывать, -ать; **~ hands** (*of a property*) пере|ходи́ть, -йти́ из рук в ру́ки; **~ sides** пере|ходи́ть, -йти́ на другу́ю сто́рону; **~ trains** перес|а́живаться, -е́сть на друго́й по́езд; **~ gear** меня́ть (*impf.*) ско́рость; переключи́ть (*pf.*) переда́чу; **~ the subject** смени́ть/перемени́ть (*pf.*) те́му разгово́ра. **2.** (*re-clothe etc.*): **~ a child** переод|ева́ть, -е́ть ребёнка; (*of baby*) перепелена́ть (*pf.*); **~ a bed** меня́ть (*impf.*) посте́льное бельё. **3.** (*money*): **~ a pound note** разменя́ть (*pf.*) фу́нтовую бума́жку; **~ francs into pounds** обменя́ть (*pf.*) фра́нки на фу́нты сте́рлингов. **4.** (*exchange*): **~ a book** обменя́ть (*pf.*) кни́гу; **~ places with s.o.** (*lit.*) поменя́ться (*pf.*) места́ми с кем-н.; **~ing of the guard** сме́на карау́ла.

v.i.: **he has ~d a lot** он си́льно измени́лся; **caterpillars ~ into butterflies** гу́сеницы превраща́ются в ба́бочек; **we ~d to central heating** мы перешли́ на центра́льное отопле́ние; **the weather ~d to rain** пого́да перемени́лась и пошёл дождь; **the wind ~d** ве́тер перемени́лся; (*rail.*) перес|а́живаться, -е́сть; **all ~!** коне́чная остано́вка!; переса́дка, по́езд да́льше не пойдёт!

with advs.: **~ down** *v.i.* (*motoring*) перейти́ (*pf.*) на бо́лее ни́зкую ско́рость; **~ over** *v.i.*: **the railways ~d over to electricity** желе́зные доро́ги перешли́ на электри́чество/электроэне́ргию; **~ up** *v.i.* (*motoring*) перейти́ (*pf.*) на бо́лее высо́кую ско́рость.

cpd. **~-over** *n.*: **~-over to electricity** перехо́д на электроэне́ргию; (*of leader etc.*) сме́на.

changeability [ˌtʃeɪndʒəˈbɪlɪtɪ] *n.* переме́нчивость; изме́нчивость.

changeable [ˈtʃeɪndʒəb(ə)l] *adj.*: **~ weather** изме́нчивая пого́да; (*of pers.*) изме́нчивый, непостоя́нный.

changing-room [ˈtʃeɪndʒɪŋˌruːm] *n.* раздева́лка; приме́рочная.

channel [ˈtʃæn(ə)l] *n.* **1.** (*strait*) проли́в, кана́л; **the English C~** Ла-Ма́нш; **the C~ Islands** Норма́ндские острова́; **C~ tunnel** тонне́ль под Ла-Ма́ншем. **2.** (*bed of a stream*) ру́сло. **3.** (*deeper part of a waterway*) фарва́тер. **4.** (*fig.*): **through the usual ~s** обы́чным путём; **~ of information** исто́чник информа́ции. **5.** (*television*) кана́л.

v.t. (*make a ~ in*) пров|оди́ть, -ести́ кана́л в+*p.*; (*cause to flow*): **the river ~led its way through the rocks** река́ проложи́ла себе́ путь че́рез ска́лы; (*fig.*): **we ~led the information to him** мы переда́ли ему́ э́ти све́дения; **his energies are ~led into sport** вся его́ эне́ргия ухо́дит на спорт.

chant [tʃɑːnt] *n.* песнь; (*eccl.*) пе́ние.

v.t. восп|ева́ть, -е́ть.

v.i. петь (*impf.*).

chaos [ˈkeɪɒs] *n.* хао́с.

chaotic [keɪˈɒtɪk] *adj.* хаоти́ческий, хаоти́чный.

chap[1] [tʃæp] *v.t.* произв|оди́ть, -ести́ тре́щину в+*p.*; **~ped hands** потре́скавшиеся ру́ки.

chap[2] [tʃæp] *n.* (*coll.*, *fellow*) па́рень (*m.*), ма́лый; **a good ~** сла́вный ма́лый; **old ~** старина́ (*m.*).

chapel [ˈtʃæp(ə)l] *n.* **1.** (*small church*) часо́вня, моле́льня; (*Catholic*) капе́лла. **2.** (*part of church*) приде́л с алтарём.

chaperon(e) [ˈʃæpəˌrəʊn] *n.* компаньо́нка.

v.t. сопрово|жда́ть, -ди́ть.

chaplain [ˈtʃæplɪn] *n.* капелла́н, свяще́нник.

chapter [ˈtʃæptə(r)] *n.* **1.** (*of book*) глава́; **~ and verse** (*fig.*) то́чная ссы́лка. **2.** (*of clergy*) собра́ние кано́ников (*or* чле́нов мона́шеского о́рдена).

cpd. **~-house** *n.* дом капи́тула.

char[1] [tʃɑː(r)] *v.t.* обу́гли|вать, -ть.

v.i. обу́гли|ваться, -ться.

char[2] [tʃɑː(r)] *n.* (*coll.*) = **~woman**

v.t. (*coll.*, *perform housework*) уб|ира́ть, -ра́ть помеще́ние подённо.

cpds. **~lady, ~woman** *nn.* приходя́щая рабо́тница; (подённая) убо́рщица.

character [ˈkærɪktə(r)] *n.* **1.** (*nature*) сво́йство, ка́чество; **a book of that ~** кни́га тако́го ро́да. **2.** (*personal qualities*) хара́ктер; **a man of ~** челове́к с си́льным хара́ктером; **he lacks ~** он бесхара́ктерный челове́к; **an interesting ~** интере́сный челове́к. **3.** (*eccentric or distinctive person*): **she is quite a ~** она́ оригина́льная ли́чность; **a weird ~** стра́нный субъе́кт; **a ~ actor** характе́рный актёр. **4.** (*fictional*) геро́й, тип, о́браз, персона́ж; **in the ~ of Hamlet** в о́бразе Га́млета. **5.** (*reputation*) репута́ция; **~ assassination** подры́в репута́ции. **6.** (*letter, graphic symbol*) бу́ква, ли́тера; **Chinese ~s** кита́йские иеро́глифы (*m. pl.*); **Runic ~s** руни́ческое письмо́.

characteristic [ˌkærɪktəˈrɪstɪk] *n.* характе́рная черта́, сво́йство, осо́бенность; (*math.*) характери́стика.

adj. характе́рный, типи́чный; **it is ~ of him** э́то характе́рно для него́.

characterization [ˌkærɪktəraɪˈzeɪʃ(ə)n] *n.* **1.** характери́стика.

characterize [ˈkærɪktəˌraɪz] *v.t.* **1.** (*describe*) характеризова́ть (*impf.*, *pf.*). **2.** (*distinguish*) отлич|а́ть, -и́ть; **he is ~d by honesty** он отлича́ется свое́й че́стностью.

charade [ʃəˈrɑːd] *n.* шара́да.

charcoal [ˈtʃɑːkəʊl] *n.* древе́сный у́голь; **a ~ drawing** рису́нок углём.

charge [tʃɑːdʒ] *n.* **1.** (*load*) нагру́зка, груз. **2.** (*for gun etc.*) заря́д. **3.** (*elec.*) заря́д, заряжа́ние; **the battery is being ~d** батаре́я заряжа́ется. **4.** (*expense*) цена́, расхо́ды (*m. pl.*); **what is the ~?** ско́лько э́то сто́ит?; **his ~s are reasonable** у него́ це́ны вполне́ уме́ренные; **a ~ account** счёт в магази́не; **at his own ~** на его́/свой со́бственный счёт; **free of ~** беспла́тно. **5.** (*duty, care*): **the child is in my ~** э́тот ребёнок на моём попече́нии; **I am in ~ here** я здесь заве́дую; **take ~ of a business** взять (*pf.*) на себя́ руково́дство де́лом. **6.** (*person entrusted*): **the nurse took her ~s for a walk** ня́ня повела́ свои́х пито́мцев на прогу́лку. **7.** (*accusation*) обвине́ние; **bring a ~ against s.o.** выдвига́ть, вы́двинуть обвине́ние про́тив кого́-н.; **he pleaded guilty to the ~ of speeding** он призна́л себя́ вино́вным в превыше́нии ско́рости. **8.** (*attack*) нападе́ние, ата́ка; **return to the ~** (*fig.*) возобнови́ть (*pf.*) ата́ку.

v.t. **1.** (*load, fill*) нагру|жа́ть, -зи́ть; **~ your glasses!** напо́лните свои́ стака́ны!; (*elec.*) заря|жа́ть, -ди́ть. **2.** (*make responsible*): **he was ~d with an important mission** ему́ бы́ло пору́чено ва́жное зада́ние. **3.** (*instruct*): **I ~ you to obey him** я тре́бую, что́бы вы повинова́лись ему́. **4.** (*accuse*) обвин|я́ть, -и́ть; **he is ~d with murder** его́ обвиня́ют в уби́йстве. **5.** (*debit*): **~ the goods to me** запиши́те това́ры на мой счёт; **the debt was ~d to his estate** за его́ име́нием чи́слился долг; **tax is ~d on the proceeds of the sale** дохо́ды с прода́жи подлежа́т обложе́нию нало́гом. **6.** (*ask price*): **he ~d £5 for the book** он запроси́л 5 фу́нтов за э́ту кни́гу. **7.** (*also v.i.*; *attack*): **the troops ~d the enemy** войска́ атакова́ли неприя́теля; **he ~d at me** он набро́сился на меня́.

cpds. **~-nurse** *n.* ста́ршая медсестра́ отделе́ния; **~-sheet** *n.* полице́йский протоко́л.

chargeable [ˈtʃɑːdʒəb(ə)l] *adj.* **1. ~** (*to be debited*) **to** относи́мый за счёт +*g.* **2.** (*liable to be accused*): **he is ~ with theft** он мо́жет быть обвинён в кра́же.

chargé d'affaires [ˌʃɑːʒeɪ dæˈfeə(r)] *n.* пове́ренный в дела́х.

charger [ˈtʃɑːdʒə(r)] *n.* (*horse*) строева́я ло́шадь; боево́й конь.

chariot [ˈtʃærɪət] *n.* колесни́ца.

charioteer [ˌtʃærɪə'tɪə(r)] *n.* возни́ца (*m.*).
charisma [kə'rɪzmə] *n.* хари́зма, обая́ние.
charismatic [ˌkærɪz'mætɪk] *adj.* харизмати́ческий.
charitable ['tʃærɪtəb(ə)l] *adj.* (*in judgement etc.*) ми́лостивый, снисходи́тельный; (*in almsgiving*) благотвори́тельный.
charity ['tʃærɪtɪ] *n.* **1.** (*kindness*) любо́вь к бли́жнему; ~ **begins at home** своя́ руба́шка бли́же к те́лу; **he lives on** ~ он живёт ми́лостыней. **2.** (*indulgence*) милосе́рдие; снисхожде́ние. **3.** (*almsgiving*) благотвори́тельность; ми́лостыня; **give, dispense** ~ под|ава́ть, -а́ть ми́лостыню. **4.** (*institution*) благотвори́тельное учрежде́ние.
charlatan ['ʃɑ:lət(ə)n] *n.* шарлата́н.
charlatanism ['ʃɑ:lətənˌɪz(ə)m] *n.* шарлата́нство.
charm [tʃɑ:m] *n.* **1.** (*attraction*) обая́ние, очарова́ние, очарова́тельность; **her ~s** её пре́лести (*f. pl.*). **2.** (*spell*) ча́ры (*pl., g.* —); **under a** ~ заколдо́ванный; очаро́ванный; **it worked like a** ~ э́то оказа́ло маги́ческое де́йствие. **3.** (*talisman*) амуле́т.
v.t. **1.** (*attract, delight*) очаро́в|ывать, -а́ть. **2.** (*use magic on*) чарова́ть (*impf.*); зачаро́в|ывать, -а́ть; **he bears a ~ed life** он как бы неуязви́м.
charmer ['tʃɑ:mə(r)] *n.* **1.** (*beauty*) чаровни́ца, чароде́йка. **2.** (*charming person*) обая́тельный/очарова́тельный челове́к.
charming ['tʃɑ:mɪŋ] *adj.* очарова́тельный, обая́тельный, чару́ющий.
chart [tʃɑ:t] *n.* (*nautical map*) морска́я ка́рта; (*record*) табли́ца, гра́фик; **weather** ~ синопти́ческая ка́рта.
v.t. черти́ть, на- ка́рту +*g.*; нан|оси́ть, -ести́ на ка́рту; ~ **an ocean** начерти́ть (*pf.*) ка́рту океа́на; ~ **s.o.'s progress** сде́лать (*pf.*) диагра́мму чьего́-н. продвиже́ния; ~ **a course of action** наме́тить (*pf.*) план де́йствий.
charter ['tʃɑ:tə(r)] *n.* **1.** (*grant of rights*) ха́ртия, гра́мота. **2.** (*of society*): **C~ of the United Nations** Уста́в ООН; ~ **member** член-основа́тель (*m.*) организа́ции. **3.** (*hire*) фрахто́вка, наём; ~ **flight** зафрахто́ванный полёт.
v.t. **1.** (*grant diploma etc. to*) дарова́ть (*impf., pf.*) ха́ртию/привиле́гию +*d.*; **~ed accountant** бухга́лтер-экспе́рт, ауди́тор. **2.** (*provide on hire*) сд|ава́ть, -ать внаём по ча́ртеру. **3.** (*procure on hire*) фрахтова́ть, за-.
chary ['tʃeərɪ] *adj.* осторо́жный, сде́ржанный.
chase [tʃeɪs] *n.* **1.** (*act of chasing*) пого́ня; **give ~ to** погна́ться (*pf.*) за+*i.*; **in ~ of** в пого́не за+*i.*; **wild goose** ~ напра́сная пого́ня. **2.**: **the** ~ (*hunting*) охо́та.
v.t. гоня́ться (*indet.*), гна́ться (*det.*) за+*i.*
v.i.: ~ **after** гна́ться, по- за+*i.*; охо́титься (*impf.*) за+*i.*; ~ **off** помча́ться (*pf.*).
chasm ['kæz(ə)m] *n.* бе́здна, про́пасть (*also fig.*).
chassis ['ʃæsɪ] *n.* шасси́ (*nt. indecl.*).
chaste [tʃeɪst] *adj.* целому́дренный.
chasten ['tʃeɪs(ə)n] *v.t.* (*punish, subdue*) смир|я́ть, -и́ть; **the rebuke had a ~ing effect** упрёк поде́йствовал отрезвля́юще.
chastise [tʃæs'taɪz] *v.t.* нака́з|ывать, -а́ть; кара́ть, по-.
chastisement [tʃæs'taɪzmənt] *n.* наказа́ние.
chastity ['tʃæstɪtɪ] *n.* целому́дрие.
chasuble ['tʃæzjʊb(ə)l] *n.* ри́за.
chat [tʃæt] *n.* болтовня́, бесе́да; ~ **show** бесе́да/интервью́ (*nt. indecl.*) со знамени́тостью.
v.t.: ~ **s.o. up** (*coll.*) заи́грывать (*impf.*) с кем-н.
v.i. болта́ть, по-; бесе́довать, по-.
château ['ʃætəʊ] *n.* за́мок.
chattel ['tʃæt(ə)l] *n.* дви́жимое иму́щество; **goods and ~s** всё иму́щество.
chatter ['tʃætə(r)] *n.* **1.** (*talk*) болтовня́, трескотня́. **2.** (*of birds*) щебета́ние.
v.i. **1.** болта́ть, тарато́рить (*both impf.*). **2.** щебета́ть, треща́ть (*both impf.*). **3.**: **his teeth are ~ing** у него́ стуча́т зу́бы.
cpd. **~box** *n.* болту́н (*fem.* -ья); тарато́рка, трещо́тка (*both c.g.*).
chatty ['tʃætɪ] *adj.* болтли́вый, говорли́вый.
chauffeur ['ʃəʊfə(r), -'fɜ:(r)] *n.* (наёмный) шофёр.
chauvinism ['ʃəʊvɪˌnɪz(ə)m] *n.* шовини́зм.
chauvinist ['ʃəʊvɪnɪst] *n.* шовини́ст (*fem.* -ка); **male** ~ сторо́нник дискримина́ции же́нщин.
chauvinistic [ʃəʊvɪ'nɪstɪk] *adj.* шовинисти́ческий.
cheap [tʃi:p] *adj.* **1.** (*low in price*) дешёвый; **I bought it** ~ я дёшево э́то купи́л; **on the** ~ по дешёвке; **he got off** ~ он дёшево отде́лался. **2.** (*facile, tawdry, petty, vulgar*): ~ **flattery** дешёвая лесть; **a** ~ **remark** по́шлое замеча́ние.
cheapen ['tʃi:pən] *v.t.* (*make cheap*) удешев|ля́ть, -и́ть; де́лать, с- деше́вле; ~ **o.s.** (*fig.*) роня́ть (*impf.*) себя́.
cheat [tʃi:t] *n.* обма́нщик, плут, жу́лик.
v.t. & i. обма́н|ывать, -у́ть; плутова́ть, на-/с-; ~ **s.o. out of sth.** обма́ном лиши́ть кого́-н. чего́-н.; ~ **at cards** жу́льничать, с- в ка́ртах; плутова́ть, на-/с- в ка́ртах.
check[1] [tʃek] *n.* **1.** (*restraint*) заде́ржка; **wind acts as a ~ upon speed** ве́тер замедля́ет ско́рость; **they held the enemy in** ~ они́ сде́рживали проти́вника. **3.** (*verification*) контро́ль (*m.*); прове́рка; **keep a ~ on his expenses** держа́ть под контро́лем его́ расхо́ды. **4.** (*for hat, luggage etc.*) номеро́к; квита́нция. **5.** (*at chess*) шах. **6.** (*US, at cards etc.*) фи́шка, ма́рка. **7.** (*US*) = **cheque. 8.** (*US*) = **bill. 9.** (*US, tick*) га́лочка.
v.t. **1.** (*restrain*) сде́рж|ивать, -а́ть; **he ~ed himself from speaking** он сдержа́лся и промолча́л; **the car ~ed its speed** автомоби́ль заме́длил ско́рость. **2.** (*stop*) остан|а́вливать, -ови́ть; заде́рж|ивать, -а́ть. **3.** (*rebuke*) проб|ира́ть, -ра́ть. **4.** (*verify*) пров|еря́ть, -е́рить. **5.** (*deposit, of luggage etc.*) сд|ава́ть, -ать под квита́нцию. **6.** (*at chess*) объяв|ля́ть, -и́ть шах +*d.*; шахова́ть (*impf.*). **7.** (*US, tick*) отм|еча́ть, -е́тить га́лочкой.
v.i. **1.** (*pause*) остан|а́вливаться, -ови́ться. **2.** ~ **on** = ~ **up. 3.**: ~ (*accord*) **with** совп|ада́ть, -а́сть с+*i.*
with advs.: ~ **in** *v.i.* (*at hotel*) регистри́роваться, за-; ~ **out** *v.i.* (*from hotel*) выпи́сываться, вы́писаться; ~ **up** *v.i.*: ~ **up on sth.** пров|еря́ть, -е́рить что-н.
cpds. **~-list** *n.* контро́льный спи́сок, пе́речень (*m.*); **~out** *n.* ка́сса; **~-point, ~-post** *nn.* контро́льный пункт; **~room** *n.* гардеро́б; **~-up** *n.* прове́рка; (техни́ческий/медици́нский) осмо́тр.
int. **~!** (*US, coll.*) то́чно!; (*at chess*) шах!
check[2] [tʃek] *n.* (*pattern*) кле́тка; (*attr., also* **~ed**) клётчатый.
checkers ['tʃekəz] *n.* ша́ш|ки (*pl., g.* -ек).
checkmate ['tʃekmeɪt] *n.* шах и мат; (*fig.*) мат.
v.t. де́лать, с- мат +*d.*
cheek [tʃi:k] *n.* **1.** (*part of face*) щека́; **turn the other** ~ подст|авля́ть, -а́вить другу́ю щёку. **2.** (*impudence*) на́глость; **he had the ~ to say ...** у него́ хвати́ло на́глости сказа́ть...
cpd. **~-bone** *n.* скула́.
cheeky ['tʃi:kɪ] *adj.* наха́льный.
cheep [tʃi:p] *n.* писк. *v.t. & i.* пища́ть, пи́скнуть.
cheer ['tʃɪə(r)] *n.* **1.** (*comfort*): **words of** ~ ободря́ющие слова́; **be of good ~!** не унывайте! **2.** (*shout*): **a round of ~s** кругово́е ура́; **three ~s for our visitors!** троекра́тное ура́ на́шим гостя́м!; **~s!** (*as toast*) (за) ва́ше здоро́вье!
v.t. **1.** (*comfort, encourage*) подбодр|я́ть, -и́ть; ободр|я́ть, -и́ть; **~ing news** прия́тная но́вость. **2.** (*acclaim*) приве́тствовать (*impf.*).
v.i. подбодр|я́ться, -и́ться; ободр|я́ться, -и́ться; (*utter ~s*) изд|ава́ть, -а́ть восто́рженные кри́ки.
with adv.: ~ **up** *v.t. & i.* ободр|я́ть(ся), -и́ть(ся);

v.i. повеселе́ть (*pf.*); ~ **up!** не унывайте!
cpd. ~**-leader** *n.* заводи́ла (*c.g.*).
cheerful ['tʃɪəfʊl] *adj.* весёлый, ра́достный; **a ~ room** весёлая/све́тлая ко́мната.
cheer|fulness ['tʃɪəfʊlnɪs] *n.* весёлость, ра́достность.
cheerio [,tʃɪrɪ'əʊ] *int.* (*coll.*) всего́ хоро́шего!; всего́!
cheerless ['tʃɪəlɪs] *adj.* уны́лый.
cheery ['tʃɪərɪ] *adj.* весёлый, ра́достный.
cheese [tʃi:z] *n.* сыр; **ripe ~** вы́держанный сыр.
cpds. ~**burger** *n.* чизбу́ргер; ~**cake** *n.* ватру́шка.
cheesy ['tʃi:zɪ] *adj.* сы́рный.
cheetah ['tʃi:tə] *n.* гепа́рд.
chef [ʃef] *n.* шеф-по́вар.
chemical ['kemɪk(ə)l] *n.* хими́ческий проду́кт; (*pl.*) химика́ли|и (*pl.*, *g.* -й); химика́ты (*m. pl.*).
adj. хими́ческий; ~ **warfare** хими́ческая война́.
chemise [ʃə'mi:z] *n.* же́нская соро́чка/руба́шка.
chemist ['kemɪst] *n.* **1.** (*scientist*) хи́мик. **2.** (*pharmacist*) апте́карь (*m.*); ~**'s shop** апте́ка.
chemistry ['kemɪstrɪ] *n.* хи́мия.
chemotherapy [,ki:mə'θerəpɪ] *n.* химиотерапи́я.
chenille [ʃə'ni:l] *n.* (*yarn*) сине́ль; (*fabric*) шени́ль.
che|que [tʃek] (*US* **-ck**) *n.* чек; **he made the ~ out to me** он вы́писал чек на моё и́мя; **blank ~** незапо́лненный чек; **traveller's ~** тури́стский чек.
cpd. ~**-book** *n.* че́ковая кни́жка.
chequer ['tʃekə(r)] *v.t.* (*mark in ~s*) графи́ть, раз- в клётку; ~**ed flag** ша́хматный флажо́к; ~**ed career** (*fig.*) бу́рная жизнь.
cherish ['tʃerɪʃ] *v.t.* **1.** (*love, care for*) не́жно люби́ть (*impf.*); леле́ять (*impf.*). **2.** (*of hopes etc.*) леле́ять (*impf.*); дорожи́ть (*impf.*) *+i.*
cherry ['tʃerɪ] *n.* (*fruit*) ви́шня; чере́шня; (*tree*) ви́шня; ~ **orchard** вишнёвый сад.
cpds. ~**-blossom** *n.* вишнёвый цвет; ~**-pie** *n.* (*cul.*) пиро́г с ви́шнями.
cherub ['tʃerəb] *n.* (*relig.*, *art*) херуви́м.
cherubic [tʃɪ'ru:bɪk] *adj.* херуви́мский.
chess [tʃes] *n.* ша́хмат|ы (*pl.*, *g.* —).
cpds. ~**-board** *n.* ша́хматная доска́; ~**-man** *n.* ша́хматная фигу́ра; ~**-player** *n.* шахмати́ст (*fem.* -ка).
chest [tʃest] *n.* **1.** (*furniture*) сунду́к; ~ **of drawers** комо́д; **medicine ~** апте́чка. **2.** (*anat.*) грудна́я клётка; грудь; **get sth. off one's ~** облегчи́ть (*pf.*) ду́шу; ~ **cold** просту́да.
chestnut ['tʃesnʌt] *n.* **1.** (*tree, fruit*) кашта́н. **2.** (*stale anecdote*) анекдо́т с бородо́й. **3.** (*horse*) гнеда́я ло́шадь. **4.** (*attr.*, *of colour*) кашта́новый.
chesty ['tʃestɪ] *adj.* (*of cold*) грудно́й.
chevron ['ʃevrən] *n.* шевро́н.
chew [tʃu:] *v.t. & i.* жева́ть (*impf.*); ~ **the cud** жева́ть жва́чку; ~ **over** (*fig.*) пережёвывать (*impf.*); ~**ing-gum** жева́тельная рези́нка.
chewy ['tʃu:ɪ] *adj.* (*coll.*) тягу́чий.
chic [ʃi:k] *n.* элега́нтность, шик.
adj. элега́нтный, шика́рный.
chicane(ry) [ʃɪ'keɪnərɪ] *n.* крючкотво́рство.
chick [tʃɪk] *n.* птене́ц; цыплёнок; (*sl.*, *girl*) цы́почка.
cpds. ~**pea** *n.* (*bot.*) туре́цкий горо́х; ~**weed** *n.* (*bot.*) алзи́на.
chicken ['tʃɪkɪn] *n.* цыплёнок; (*as food*) куря́тина, цыплёнок, ку́рица; (*fig.*, *coward*) трус.
cpds. ~**-feed** *n.* (*fig.*) пустяки́ (*m. pl.*); ~**-hearted,** ~**-livered** *adjs.* трусли́вый, малоду́шный; ~**-pox** *n.* ветряна́я о́спа; ~**-run** *n.* заго́н для кур.
chicory ['tʃɪkərɪ] *n.* цико́рий (полево́й).
chide [tʃaɪd] *v.t.* попрек|а́ть, -ну́ть; брани́ть, вы-.
chief [tʃi:f] *n.* **1.** (*leader, ruler*) вождь (*m.*), глава́ (*m.*); ~ **of state** глава́ госуда́рства. **2.** (*boss, senior official*) шеф, нача́льник; **C~ of Staff** нача́льник шта́ба.
adj. **1.** (*most important*) гла́вный, основно́й, важне́йший. **2.** (*senior*) гла́вный, ста́рший; **C~ Justice** верхо́вный судья́; председа́тель (*m.*) верхо́вного суда́; ~ **constable** нача́льник поли́ции.
chiefly ['tʃi:flɪ] *adv.* гла́вным о́бразом; в пе́рвую о́чередь.
chieftain ['tʃi:ft(ə)n] *n.* вождь (*m.*).
chiffon ['ʃɪfɒn] *n.* шифо́н.
chiffonier [,ʃɪfə'nɪə(r)] *n.* шифонье́рка.
chignon ['ʃi:njɔ̃] *n.* шиньо́н.
chilblain ['tʃɪlbleɪn] *n.* обморо́женное ме́сто.
child [tʃaɪld] *n.* ребёнок; ~**'s play** (*fig.*) де́тские игру́шки; **with ~** бере́менная, в положе́нии; ~ **molester** растли́тель *m.* малоле́тних дете́й; ~ **labour** де́тский труд; ~ **welfare** охра́на младе́нчества.
cpds. ~**-bearing** *n.* деторожде́ние; **of ~-bearing age** деторо́дного во́зраста; ~**birth** *nn.* ро́ды (*pl.*, *g.* -ов); **she died in ~birth** она́ умерла́ от ро́дов; ~**-minder** *n.* приходя́щая ня́ня; ~**-minding** *n.* присмо́тр за детьми́.
childhood ['tʃaɪldhʊd] *n.* де́тство.
childish ['tʃaɪldɪʃ] *adj.* де́тский, ребя́ческий.
childishness ['tʃaɪldɪʃnɪs] *n.* ребя́чество.
childless ['tʃaɪldlɪs] *adj.* безде́тный.
childlike ['tʃaɪldlaɪk] *adj.* де́тский, младе́нческий.
Chile ['tʃɪlɪ] *n.* Чи́ли (*nt. indecl.*).
chill [tʃɪl] *n.* **1.** (*physical*) хо́лод; **there is a ~ in the air** прохла́дно; холода́ет; **take the ~ off wine** подогре́ть (*pf.*) вино́. **2.** (*fig.*) хо́лод; расхола́живание. **3.** (*med.*) просту́да; **catch a ~** просту|жа́ться, -ди́ться.
adj. холо́дный; расхола́живающий.
v.t. охлажда́ть, -ди́ть; осту|жа́ть, -ди́ть.
chil(l)i ['tʃɪlɪ] *n.* кра́сный стручко́вый пе́рец.
chilliness ['tʃɪlɪnɪs] *n.* (*lit.*) хо́лод; (*fig.*) хо́лодность, су́хость; зя́бкость.
chilly ['tʃɪlɪ] *adj.* холо́дный; (*fig.*) холо́дный, сухо́й.
chime [tʃaɪm] *n.* перезво́н.
v.t.: **the clock ~d midnight** часы́ про́били по́лночь; **the clock ~s the quarters** часы́ отбива́ют ка́ждую че́тверть часа.
v.i. трезво́нить (*impf.*).
chimera [kaɪ'mɪərə, kɪ-] *n.* химе́ра.
chimerical [tʃɪ'merɪk(ə)l] *adj.* химери́ческий.
chimney ['tʃɪmnɪ] *n.* труба́, дымохо́д.
cpds. ~**-pot** *n.* колпа́к дымово́й трубы́; ~**-sweep** *n.* трубочи́ст.
chimpanzee [,tʃɪmpən'zi:] *n.* шимпанзе́ (*m. indecl.*).
chin [tʃɪn] *n.* подборо́док; **(keep your) ~ up!** (*fig.*) не унывай(те)!
China[1] ['tʃaɪnə] *n.* Кита́й; ~ **ink** (кита́йская) тушь.
cpds. ~**man** *n.* кита́ец; ~**town** *n.* кита́йский кварта́л.
china[2] ['tʃaɪnə] *n.* фарфо́р.
cpds. ~**-closet,** ~**-cupboard** *nn.* буфе́т, серва́нт; ~**ware** *n.* фарфо́р, фарфо́ровые изде́лия.
chinchilla [tʃɪn'tʃɪlə] *n.* шинши́лла.
Chinese [tʃaɪ'ni:z] *n.* (*pers.*) кит|а́ец (*fem.* -ая́нка); (*language*) кита́йский язы́к.
adj. кита́йский; ~ **lantern** лампио́н.
chink[1] [tʃɪŋk] *n.* (*crevice*) щель.
chink[2] [tʃɪŋk] *n.* (*sound*) звя́канье.
v.i. звя́к|ать, -нуть.
chintz [tʃɪnts] *n.* си́тец; (*attr.*) си́тцевый.
chip [tʃɪp] *n.* **1.** (*of wood*) щепа́, ще́пка; стру́жка; (*of stone*) обло́мок; (*of china*) оско́лок. **2.** (*fig.*): **he is a ~ off the old block** он вы́литый оте́ц; **he has a ~ on his shoulder** он боле́зненно оби́дчив. **3.: the cup has a ~** на ча́шке щерби́на. **4.** (*food*): **fish and ~s** жа́реная ры́ба с чи́псами. **5.** (*at games*) фи́шка, ма́рка; **bargaining ~** (*fig.*) ко́зырь (*m.*) (в запа́се); **he's in the ~s** (*sl.*, *well-off*) он при деньга́х. **6.** (*in microelectronics*) чип.
v.t. струга́ть, вы́стругать; отк|а́лывать, -оло́ть; отб|ива́ть, -и́ть; **the plates have ~ped edges** у таре́лок отби́тые/щерба́тые края́; ~ **potatoes** то́нко

нарез|а́ть, -е́зать карто́фель.

v.i. **1.** отк|а́лываться, -оло́ться; отб|ива́ться, -и́ться. **2.** ~ **in** (*coll.*) вме́ш|иваться, -а́ться; влез|а́ть, -ть (в разгово́р).

cpd. ~**board** *n.* фиброли́т; (*attr.*) фиброли́товый.

chipmunk ['tʃɪpmʌŋk] *n.* бурунду́к.

chipper ['tʃɪpə(r)] *adj.* (*coll.*) бо́дрый.

chiropodist [kɪ'rɒpədɪst] *n.* мозо́льный опера́тор, (*fem.*) педикю́рша.

chiropody [kɪ'rɒpədɪ] *n.* педикю́р.

chirp [tʃɜːp] *n.* чири́канье, щебета́ние.

v.t. & i. чири́кать (*impf.*); щебета́ть (*impf.*).

chisel ['tʃɪz(ə)l] *n.* (*sculptor's*) резе́ц; (*carpenter's*) долото́, стаме́ска, зуби́ло.

v.t. **1.** вая́ть, из-; высека́ть, вы́сечь; **finely ~led features** точёные черты́ лица́. **2.** (*sl., cheat*) над|у-ва́ть, -у́ть.

chit [tʃɪt] *n.* (*note*) запи́ска.

chit-chat ['tʃɪttʃæt] *n.* болтовня́, пересу́д|ы (*pl., g.* -ов).

chivalrous ['ʃɪvəlrəs] *adj.* ры́царский.

chivalry ['ʃɪvəlrɪ] *n.* ры́царство; ры́царское поведе́ние.

chive [tʃaɪv] *n.* лук-ре́занец.

chloric ['klɔːrɪk] *adj.*: ~ **acid** хлорнова́тая кислота́.

chloride ['klɔːraɪd] *n.* хлори́д; ~ **of lime** хло́рная и́звесть; **sodium** ~ хло́ристый на́трий.

chlorinate ['klɔːrɪ,neɪt] *v.t.* (*impf., pf.*) хлори́ровать.

chlorination [,klɔːrɪ'neɪʃ(ə)n] *n.* хлори́рование.

chlorine ['klɔːriːn] *n.* хлор.

chloroform ['klɒrə,fɔːm, 'klɔːrə-] *n.* хлорофо́рм.

v.t. хлороформи́ровать (*impf., pf.*).

chlorophyll ['klɒrəfɪl] *n.* хлорофи́лл.

choc-ice [tʃɒk] *n.* моро́женое в шокола́де.

chock [tʃɒk] *n.* клин; подпо́рка; тормозна́я коло́дка.

v.t. подп|ира́ть, -ере́ть; под|кла́дывать, -ложи́ть клин под+*a.*; ~ **up** (*fig.*) загромозди́ть (*pf.*).

cpds. ~**-a-block** *adj.* загромождённый; ~**-full** *adj.* битко́м наби́тый.

chocolate ['tʃɒkələt, 'tʃɒklət] *n.* **1.** шокола́д (*also drink*); (*~-coated sweet*) шокола́дная конфе́та; ~ **biscuit** шокола́дное пече́нье. **2.** (*attr., colour*) шокола́дный.

choice [tʃɔɪs] *n.* **1.** (*act or power of choosing*) вы́бор, отбо́р; **I have no ~ but to ...** у меня́ нет друго́го вы́бора, кро́ме как (+*inf.*); **the girl of his ~** его́ избра́нница; **for ~** предпочти́тельно; **take your ~!** выбира́йте! **2.** (*thg. chosen*) вы́бор; **this is my ~** я выбира́ю э́то; вот мой вы́бор. **3.** (*variety*) вы́бор; **the shop has a large ~ of hats** в магази́не широ́кий ассортиме́нт головны́х убо́ров.

adj. отбо́рный.

choir ['kwaɪə(r)] *n.* (*singers*) хор; (*part of church*) кли́рос.

cpds. ~**boy** *n.* пе́вчий; ~**master** *n.* хорме́йстер.

choke [tʃəʊk] *n.* (*in car*) дро́ссель (*m.*).

v.t. **1.** (*throttle*) души́ть, за-; ~ **the life out of s.o.** вы́шибить (*pf.*) дух из кого́-н.; **anger ~d him** его́ удуши́л гнев. **2.** (*block*) заку́пор|ивать, -ить; засо-р|я́ть, -и́ть; **the drain is ~d** сток засори́лся; **the garden is ~d with weeds** сорняки́ заглуши́ли сад. **3.**: **he ~d back his anger** он сдержа́л свой гнев; **he ~d off enquiries** он отде́лался от расспро́сов.

v.i. зад|ыха́ться, -охну́ться; **he ~d on a plum-stone** он подави́лся сли́вовой ко́сточкой; **he spoke with a choking voice** он говори́л прерыва́ющимся го́лосом.

cholera ['kɒlərə] *n.* холе́ра.

choleric ['kɒlərɪk] *adj.* холери́ческий.

choose [tʃuːz] *v.t.* выбира́ть, вы́брать; изб|ира́ть, -ра́ть; **there are five to ~ from** мо́жно выбира́ть из пяти́; **there is little to ~ between them** оди́н друго́го сто́ит; **I cannot ~ but obey** я вы́нужден повинова́ться; **he was chosen king** его́ вы́брали/избра́ли королём; **I chose to remain** я предпочёл оста́ться.

v.i. **pick and ~** (*fig.*) быть разбо́рчивым.

choos(e)y ['tʃuːzɪ] *adj.* разбо́рчивый.

chop[1] [tʃɒp] *n.* **1.** (*cut*) ру́бящий уда́р. **2.** (*of meat*) отбивна́я котле́та.

v.t. руби́ть (*impf.*); (*cut*) нар|еза́ть, -е́зать; кроши́ть (*impf.*); ~ **up** нар|еза́ть, -е́зать; ~ **a branch off a tree** сруби́ть (*pf.*) ве́тку с де́рева; ~ **a way through the bushes** проруб|а́ть, -и́ть доро́гу че́рез кусты́; ~ **a tree down** сруби́ть (*pf.*) де́рево.

chop[2] [tʃɒp] *v.i.* (*change*; *also* ~ **about**) меня́ться (*impf.*); ~ **and change** постоя́нно меня́ть свои́ взгля́ды.

chopper ['tʃɒpə(r)] *n.* (*implement*) нож, коса́рь (*m.*); (*sl., helicopter*) вертолёт.

choppy ['tʃɒpɪ] *adj.* (*of sea*) неспоко́йный; (*of wind, changeable*) поры́вистый.

chopstick ['tʃɒpstɪk] *n.* па́лочка для еды́.

chop-suey [tʃɒp'suːɪ] *n.* кита́йское рагу́ (*indecl*).

choral ['kɔːr(ə)l] *adj.* хорово́й.

chorale [kɔː'rɑːl] *n.* хора́л.

chord [kɔːd] *n.* **1.** (*string of harp etc.*) струна́; **strike a ~** (*fig., remind of sth.*) вы́звать (*pf.*) о́тклик. **2.** (*anat.*): **vocal ~s** голосовы́е свя́зки (*f. pl.*); **spinal ~** спинно́й мозг. **3.** (*combination of notes*) акко́рд.

chore [tʃɔː(r)] *n.* (*odd job*) случа́йная рабо́та; (*heavy task*) бре́мя (*nt.*); **household ~s** дома́шняя рабо́та.

choreographer [,kɒrɪ'ɒgrəfə(r)] *n.* хорео́граф.

choreographic [,kɒrɪə'græfɪk] *adj.* хореографи́ческий.

choreography [,kɒrɪ'ɒgrəfɪ] *n.* хореогра́фия.

chorister ['kɒrɪstə(r)] *n.* хори́ст, пе́вчий.

chortle ['tʃɔːt(ə)l] *v.i.* фы́ркать (*impf.*); дави́ться (*impf.*) от сме́ха.

chorus ['kɔːrəs] *n.* **1.** (*singers*; *also in anc. drama*) хор; **in ~** (*lit., fig.*) хо́ром; ~ **of approval** хвале́бный хор. **2.** (*refrain*) припе́в, рефре́н.

v.t. & i. петь, с- (*or* произн|оси́ть, -ести́) хо́ром.

cpd. ~**-girl** *n.* хори́стка.

Christ [kraɪst] *n.* **1.** Христо́с; **the ~ child** младе́нец Ису́с; **before ~** до на́шей э́ры (*abbr.* до н.э.). **2.** *as int.* Бо́же (мой)!; Го́споди!

christen ['krɪs(ə)n] *v.t.* крести́ть (*impf., pf.*); **he was ~ed John** ему́ при креще́нии да́ли и́мя Джон; его́ нарекли́ Джо́ном.

Christendom ['krɪsəndəm] *n.* христиа́нский мир.

christening ['krɪs(ə)nɪŋ] *n.* крести́н|ы (*pl., g.* —); креще́ние.

Christian ['krɪstɪən, 'krɪstʃ(ə)n] *n.* христи|ани́н (*fem.* -а́нка).

adj. христиа́нский; ~ **name** и́мя (*nt.*).

Christianity [,krɪstɪ'ænɪtɪ] *n.* христиа́нство.

Christmas ['krɪsməs] *n.* Рождество́; ~ **box, present** рожде́ственский пода́рок; ~ **day** пе́рвый день Рождества́; ~ **eve** соче́льник; **Father ~** дед-моро́з; **at ~** на Рождество́; ~ **tree** рожде́ственская ёлка.

cpds. ~**-time,** ~**-tide** *nn.* свя́т|ки (*pl., g.* -ок).

chromatic [krə'mætɪk] *adj.* **1.** (*pert. to colour*) цветно́й. **2.** (*mus.*) хромати́ческий.

chrome [krəʊm] *n.* **1.** (*chem.*) хром. **2.** (*pigment, also ~ yellow*) хром; жёлтый цвет.

chromium ['krəʊmɪəm] *n.* хром.

cpds. ~**-plated** *adj.* хроми́рованный; ~**-plating** *n.* хроми́рование, хромиро́вка.

chromosome ['krəʊmə,səʊm] *n.* хромосо́ма.

chronic ['krɒnɪk] *adj.* **1.** (*med.*) хрони́ческий. **2.** (*fig., incessant*) ве́чный, постоя́нный. **3.** (*coll., very bad*) ужа́сный.

chronicle ['krɒnɪk(ə)l] *n.* хро́ника, ле́топись.

v.t. вести́ (*det.*) хро́нику +*g.*; (*hist.*) зан|оси́ть, -ести́ в ле́топись.

chronicler ['krɒnɪklə(r)] *n.* летопи́сец, исто́рик.

chronological [,krɒnə'lɒdʒɪk(ə)l] *adj.* хронологи́ческий.

chronology [krəˈnɒlədʒɪ] *n.* хроноло́гия.
chronometer [krəˈnɒmɪtə(r)] *n.* хроно́метр.
chrysalis [ˈkrɪsəlɪs] *n.* ку́колка.
chrysanthemum [krɪˈsænθəməm] *n.* хризанте́ма.
chub [tʃʌb] *n.* голáвль (*m.*).
chubby [ˈtʃʌbɪ] *adj.* то́лстенький, пу́хленький.
chuck [tʃʌk] *v.t.* **1.: ~ s.o. under the chin** потрепа́ть (*pf.*) кого́-н. по подборо́дку. **2.** (*coll.*, *throw*) швы|ря́ть, -ну́ть. **3.** (*coll.*, *give up*) бр|оса́ть, -о́сить; **~ it!** бро́сьте!
with advs.: (*coll.*): **~ away** *v.t.* (*lit.*) выбра́сывать, вы́бросить; (*fig.*): **~ away a chance** упусти́ть (*pf.*) слу́чай; **~ out** *v.t.* (*thg. or pers.*) вы́кинуть (*pf.*); вы́швырнуть (*pf.*); **~ up** *v.t.* (*give up*) бр|оса́ть, -о́сить.
chuckle [ˈtʃʌk(ə)l] *n.* сда́вленный смешо́к, смех.
v.i. фы́ркать (*impf.*) от сме́ха, посме́иваться (*impf.*).
chug [tʃʌg] *v.i.*: **the boat ~ged past** ло́дка пропыхте́ла ми́мо.
chum [tʃʌm] *n.* прия́тель (*m.*), дружо́к.
v.i.: **~ up with s.o.** сдружи́ться (*pf.*) с кем-н.
chummy [ˈtʃʌmɪ] *adj.* дружелю́бный, общи́тельный.
chump [tʃʌmp] *n.* (*log*; *blockhead*) чурба́н; (*head*) башка́; **he is off his ~** он рехну́лся/спя́тил (*coll.*).
chunk [tʃʌŋk] *n.* то́лстый кусо́к/ломо́ть (*m.*).
chunky [ˈtʃʌŋkɪ] *adj.* корена́стый, пло́тный.
church [tʃɜːtʃ] *n.* **1.** (*institution*) це́рковь; (*building*) це́рковь (*esp. Orthodox*), храм; **C~ Slavonic** церковнославя́нский (язы́к). **2.** (*holy orders*): **he entered the ~** он при́нял духо́вный сан.
cpds. **~goer** *n.*: **he is a regular ~goer** он регуля́рно хо́дит в це́рковь; **~going** *n.* посеще́ние це́ркви; **~warden** *n.* кти́тор, церко́вный ста́роста; **~yard** *n.* пого́ст, кла́дбище при це́ркви.
churl [tʃɜːl] *n.* хам, мужи́к.
churlish [ˈtʃɜːlɪʃ] *adj.* ха́мский, гру́бый.
churn [tʃɜːn] *n.* (*tub*) маслобо́йка; (*can*) бидо́н.
v.t.: **~ butter** сби|ва́ть, -ть ма́сло; (*fig.*): **he ~s out novels** он печёт рома́ны (как блины́); **the propeller ~ed up the waves** винт взвихри́л во́лны.
chute [ʃuːt] *n.* (*slide*, *slope*) жёлоб, спуск; (*for amusement*) гора́, го́рка; (*for rubbish*) мусоропрово́д.
chutney [ˈtʃʌtnɪ] *n.* ча́тни (*nt. indecl.*).
CIA (*abbr. of* ***Central Intelligence Agency***) ЦРУ, (Центра́льное разве́дывательное управле́ние).
cicada [sɪˈkɑːdə, -ˈkeɪdə] *n.* цика́да.
CID (*abbr. of* ***Criminal Investigation Department***) отде́л/департа́мент уголо́вного ро́зыска.
cider [ˈsaɪdə(r)] *n.* сидр.
cpd. **~-press** *n.* я́блочный пресс.
cigar [sɪˈgɑː(r)] *n.* сига́ра.
cpds. **~-case** *n.* сига́рочница; **~-holder** *n.* мундшту́к.
cigarette [ˌsɪgəˈret] *n.* сигаре́та; (*of Russ. type*) папиро́са.
cpds. **~-case** *n.* портсига́р; **~-end, ~-stub** *nn.* оку́рок; **~-holder** *n.* мундшту́к; **~-lighter** *n.* зажига́лка; **~-paper** *n.* папиро́сная бума́га.
C.-in-C. (*abbr. of* ***Commander-in-Chief***) главко́м, (главнокома́ндующий).
cinch [sɪntʃ] *n.* (*sl.*) де́ло ве́рное.
cinder [ˈsɪndə(r)] *n.*: (*pl.*) шлак, зола́, пе́пел; **burn sth. to a ~** сжечь (*pf.*) что-н. дотла́; **~ path, track** (бегова́я) га́ревая доро́жка.
Cinderella [ˌsɪndəˈrelə] *n.* Зо́лушка.
cine-camera [ˈsɪnɪ-] *n.* киноаппара́т.
cine-film [ˈsɪnɪ-] *n.* киноплёнка.
cinema [ˈsɪnɪˌmɑː, -mə] *n.* (*art*) кино́ (*indecl.*), кинематогра́фия; (*place*) кино́ (*indecl.*), кинотеа́тр.
cinematography [ˌsɪnɪməˈtɒgrəfɪ] *n.* кинематогра́фия.
cine-projector [ˈsɪnɪ] *n.* кинопроекцио́нный аппара́т.
cinnabar [ˈsɪnəˌbɑː(r)] *n.* (*min.*, *chem.*) ки́новарь.
cinnamon [ˈsɪnəmən] *n.* кори́ца; (*colour*) све́тло-кори́чневый цвет.
cipher [ˈsaɪfə(r)] *n.* **1.** (*figure 0*) нуль, ноль (*both m.*). **2.** (*secret writing*) шифр, код; **message in ~, ~ message** (за)шифро́ванное сообще́ние; **~ officer** шифрова́льщик; **~ room** шифрова́льная.
v.t. шифрова́ть, за-.
circa [ˈsɜːkə] *prep.* приблизи́тельно; о́коло+*g.*
circle [ˈsɜːk(ə)l] *n.* **1.** (*math.*, *fig.*) круг, окру́жность; **a ~ of trees** кольцо́ дере́вьев; **they stood in a ~** они́ ста́ли в кру́г; они́ стоя́ли кольцо́м; **Arctic/Antarctic ~** Се́верный/Ю́жный поля́рный круг; **vicious ~** поро́чный круг; **go round in a ~** (*fig.*, *e.g. argument*) возвраща́ться (*impf.*) к исхо́дной то́чке; **run round in ~s** (*fig.*) верте́ться (*impf.*), как бе́лка в колесе́. **2.** (*theatr.*): **dress ~** бельэта́ж; **upper ~** балко́н. **3.** (*of seasons etc.*) цикл; по́лный оборо́т; **come full ~** описа́ть (*pf.*) по́лный круг; заверши́ть (*pf.*) цикл.
v.t.: **the earth ~s the sun** земля́ враща́ется вокру́г со́лнца; **he ~d the misspelt words** он обвёл кружка́ми непра́вильно напи́санные слова́.
v.i.: **the hawk ~d** я́стреб кружи́лся (*or* опи́сывал круги́); **the news ~d round** но́вость распространи́лась повсю́ду.
circuit [ˈsɜːkɪt] *n.* **1.** (*distance*, *journey round*): **the ~ of the walls is 3 miles** окру́жность стен 3 ми́ли; **he made a ~ of the camp** он обошёл ла́герь; (*detour*) окружно́й путь, объе́зд. **2.** (*itinerary*) маршру́т. **3.** (*elec.*) цепь; схе́ма; **integrated ~** интегра́льная схе́ма; **short ~** коро́ткое замыка́ние; **~ breaker** автомати́ческий выключа́тель; **closed-~ television** ка́бельное телеви́дение (по за́мкнутому кана́лу).
v.t. & i. об|ходи́ть, -ойти́ (вокру́г+*g.*).
circuitous [sɜːˈkjuːɪtəs] *adj.* кру́жный, око́льный.
circular [ˈsɜːkjʊlə(r)] *n.* (*letter etc.*) циркуля́р; (*commercial*) проспе́кт.
adj. кругово́й; (*round in shape*) кру́глый, кругообра́зный; **~ saw** кру́глая/циркуля́рная пила́; **~ road** (*round a town*) окружна́я доро́га; **~ letter** циркуля́рное письмо́.
circulate [ˈsɜːkjʊˌleɪt] *v.t.* (*put about*, *e.g. rumour*) распростран|я́ть, -и́ть; перед|ава́ть, -а́ть; (*pass round*, *e.g. port*) передава́ть (*impf.*) по кру́гу.
v.i. циркули́ровать (*impf.*, *pf.*); **she ~d among the guests** она́ переходи́ла от одного́ го́стя к друго́му.
circulation [ˌsɜːkjʊˈleɪʃ(ə)n] *n.* **1.** (*of blood*) кровообраще́ние; (*of air*) циркуля́ция. **2.** (*of banknotes etc.*) обраще́ние. **3. Smith is back in ~** Смит сно́ва появи́лся на горизо́нте. **4.** (*of newspaper etc.*) тира́ж; **this paper has a ~ of 5,000** у э́той газе́ты тира́ж 5 000.
circumcise [ˈsɜːkəmˌsaɪz] *v.t.* соверш|а́ть, -и́ть обреза́ние +*d.*
circumcision [ˌsɜːkəmˈsɪʒ(ə)n] *n.* обреза́ние.
circumference [sɜːˈkʌmfərəns] *n.* окру́жность.
circumflex [ˈsɜːkəmˌfleks] *n.* (*~ accent*) циркумфле́кс, знак облегчённого ударе́ния.
circumlocution [ˌsɜːkəmləˈkjuːʃ(ə)n] *n.* многосло́вие, околи́чности (*f. pl.*).
circumnavigate [ˌsɜːkəmˈnævɪˌgeɪt] *v.t.* пла́вать (*indet.*) вокру́г+*g.*; **Drake ~d the globe** Дрейк соверши́л кругосве́тное путеше́ствие.
circumscribe [ˈsɜːkəmˌskraɪb] *v.t.* (*draw line round*) опи́с|ывать, -а́ть; (*fig.*, *restrict*) ста́вить, по- преде́л +*d.*; ограни́чи|вать, -ть.
circumscription [ˌsɜːkəmˈskrɪpʃ(ə)n] *n.* ограниче́ние, преде́л.
circumspect [ˈsɜːkəmˌspekt] *adj.* осмотри́тельный.
circumspection [ˌsɜːkəmˈspekʃ(ə)n] *n.* осмотри́тельность.
circumstance [ˈsɜːkəmst(ə)ns] *n.* **1.** (*fact*, *detail*) обстоя́тельство, усло́вие; **in, under the ~s** в да́нных

усло́виях/обстоя́тельствах; **in, under no ~s** ни при каки́х усло́виях/обстоя́тельствах; **extenuating ~s** смягча́ющие обстоя́тельства. **2.** (*condition of life*) материа́льное положе́ние; **in easy ~s** в хоро́шем материа́льном положе́нии.

circumstantial [ˌsɜːkəmˈstænʃ(ə)l] *adj.*: **~ evidence** ко́свенные ули́ки (*f. pl.*).

circumvent [ˌsɜːkəmˈvent] *v.t.* об|ходи́ть, -ойти́; (*outwit, cheat*) перехитри́ть (*pf.*).

circus [ˈsɜːkəs] *n.* **1.** (*also hist.*) цирк. **2.** (intersection of *streets*) (кру́глая) пло́щадь.

cirrhosis [sɪˈrəʊsɪs] *n.* цирро́з.

CIS (*abbr. of* **Commonwealth of Independent States**) СНГ, (Содру́жество незави́симых госуда́рств).

cistern [ˈsɪst(ə)n] *n.* цисте́рна, бак.

citadel [ˈsɪtəd(ə)l, -ˌdel] *n.* (*lit., fig.*) цитаде́ль.

citation [saɪˈteɪʃ(ə)n] *n.* **1.** (*quotation*) цита́ция, цити́рование. **2.** (*for bravery*) упомина́ние в прика́зе.

cite [saɪt] *v.t.* **1.** (*quote*) цити́ровать, про-. **2.** (*for bravery*) отм|еча́ть, -е́тить в прика́зе.

citizen [ˈsɪtɪz(ə)n] *n.* гражд|ани́н (*fem.* -а́нка); (*of city*) жи́тель (*fem.* -ница); **private ~** ча́стное лицо́.

citizenship [ˈsɪtɪzənʃɪp] *n.* (*nationality*) гражда́нство.

citric [ˈsɪtrɪk] *adj.* лимо́нный.

citrus [ˈsɪtrəs] *n.* ци́трус; **~ fruit** ци́трусовые (*m. pl.*).

city [ˈsɪtɪ] *n.* го́род; (*of London*) Си́ти (*nt. indecl.*); **~ centre** центр го́рода; **~ council** городско́й сове́т; **~ hall** ра́туша.

civet [ˈsɪvɪt] *n.* (*also* **~-cat**) виве́рра.

civic [ˈsɪvɪk] *adj.* гражда́нский; **~ activity** обще́ственная де́ятельность.

civil [ˈsɪv(ə)l, -ɪl] *adj.* **1.** (*pert. to a community*): **~ war** гражда́нская война́; **~ rights** гражда́нские права́; **~ servant** госуда́рственный слу́жащий, чино́вник; **~ service** госуда́рственная слу́жба; **~ law** гражда́нское пра́во; **~ engineer** инжене́р-строи́тель (*m.*). **2.** (*civilian*) гражда́нский, шта́тский; **~ defence** гражда́нская оборо́на. **3.** (*polite*) ве́жливый, любе́зный.

civilian [sɪˈvɪlɪən] *n. & adj.* шта́тский; **~ population** ми́рные жи́тели; **what did you do in ~ life?** чем вы занима́лись до а́рмии?

civility [sɪˈvɪlɪtɪ] *n.* ве́жливость, любе́зность; (*pl.*) любе́зности (*f. pl.*).

civilization [ˌsɪvɪlaɪˈzeɪʃ(ə)n] *n.* цивилиза́ция.

civilize [ˈsɪvɪˌlaɪz] *v.t.* цивилизова́ть (*impf., pf.*).

clack [klæk] *n.* (*sharp sound*) треск, щёлканье; (*talk*) трескотня́.

v.i. (*lit., fig.*) треща́ть, щёлкать (*both impf.*); **tongues were ~ing** языки́ болта́ли.

claim [kleɪm] *n.* **1.** (*assertion of right*) притяза́ние; **lay ~ to sth.** предъяви́ть (*pf.*) прете́нзии на что-н.; претендова́ть (*impf.*) на что-н. **2.** (*assertion*) утвержде́ние, заявле́ние. **3.** (*demand*) тре́бование.

v.t. **1.** (*demand*) тре́бовать (*impf.*) +*g.*; **where do I ~ my baggage?** где здесь выдаю́т бага́ж? **2.** (*assert as fact*) утвер|жда́ть, -ди́ть; **he ~s to own the land** он заявля́ет, что э́та земля́ принадлежи́т ему́. **3.** (*of things*) тре́бовать, по- +*g.*; **this matter ~s attention** э́тот вопро́с заслу́живает внима́ния.

claimant [ˈkleɪmənt] *n.* претенде́нт (*на что*).

clairvoyance [kleəˈvɔɪəns] *n.* ясновиде́ние.

clairvoyant [kleəˈvɔɪənt] *n.* ясновид|ец (*fem.* -ица).

clam [klæm] *n.* (*shellfish*) двуство́рчатый морско́й моллю́ск; **he shut up like a ~** (*fig.*) он храни́л упо́рное молча́ние.

clamber [ˈklæmbə(r)] *v.i.* кара́бкаться, вс- (*на что*).

clammy [ˈklæmɪ] *adj.* холо́дный и ли́пкий.

clamorous [ˈklæmərəs] *adj.* шу́мный, шумли́вый.

clamour [ˈklæmə(r)] *n.* шум, кри́ки (*m. pl.*).

v.i. шуме́ть (*impf.*), крича́ть (*impf.*).

clamp [klæmp] *n.* (*implement*) зажи́м, скоба́.

v.t. заж|има́ть, -а́ть; скреп|ля́ть, -и́ть.

v.i.: **~ down on** (*fig., suppress*) зажа́ть (*pf.*); прижа́ть (*pf.*).

cpd. **~down** *n.* стро́гий запре́т, стро́гие ме́ры (*против чего*).

clan [klæn] *n.* клан, род.

clandestine [klænˈdestɪn] *adj.* та́йный, подпо́льный.

clang [ˈklæŋ] *n.* лязг, звон.

v.t. & i. ля́зг|ать, -нуть; звене́ть (*impf.*).

clanger [ˈklæŋə(r)] *n.*: **he dropped a ~** (*sl.*) он сде́лал ля́псус; он дал ма́ху (*coll.*).

clank [klæŋk] *n.* звон, лязг, бряца́ние.

v.t. & i. ля́зг|ать, -нуть; бряца́ть (*impf.*).

clannish [ˈklænɪʃ] *adj.* держа́щийся своего́ кла́на (*or* свое́й гру́ппы).

clap [klæp] *n.* (*of thunder*) уда́р; (*of applause*) хлопо́к, хло́панье; **let's give him a ~!** похло́паем ему́!; (*slap*) хлопо́к; **a ~ on the back** хлопо́к по спине́.

v.t. **1.** (*strike, slap*) хло́п|ать, -нуть; **he ~ped me on the back** он хло́пнул меня́ по спине́; **~ one's hands** хло́п|ать, -нуть в ладо́ши. **2.** (*put*): **~ s.o. in prison** упе́чь (*pf.*) кого́-н. в тюрьму́; **~ handcuffs on s.o.** наде́ть (*pf.*) нару́чники на кого́-н. **3.** (*applaud*) аплоди́ровать (*impf.*) +*d.*

v.i. хло́пать (*impf.*); аплоди́ровать (*impf.*).

clapper [ˈklæpə(r)] *n.* (*of bell*) язы́к; *pl.* **go like the ~s** мча́ться как угоре́лый.

claque [klæk, klɑːk] *n.* кла́ка.

claret [ˈklærət] *n.* кларе́т; бордо́ (*indecl.*).

cpd. **~-coloured** *adj.* цве́та бордо́; бордо́вый.

clarification [ˌklærɪfɪˈkeɪʃ(ə)n] *n.* проясне́ние, разъясне́ние; (*of liquid*) очище́ние.

clarify [ˈklærɪˌfaɪ] *v.t.* вн|оси́ть, -ести́ я́сность в+*a.*; разъясн|я́ть, -и́ть; **~ one's mind about sth.** уясни́ть (*pf.*) себе́ что-н.

clarinet [ˌklærɪˈnet] *n.* кларне́т.

clarinettist [ˌklærɪˈnetɪst] *n.* кларнети́ст (*fem.* -ка).

clarion [ˈklærɪən] *n.* рог, рожо́к; **~ call** (*fig.*) призы́вный звук; боево́й клич.

clarity [ˈklærɪtɪ] *n.* я́сность.

clash [klæʃ] *n.* **1.** (*sound*) гул, лязг, звон. **2.** (*conflict*): **I had a ~ with him** у меня́ бы́ло с ним столкнове́ние; **~ of views** расхожде́ние во взгля́дах; **~ of colours** дисгармо́ния цвето́в; (*of dates*) совпаде́ние по вре́мени.

v.t.: **he ~ed the cymbals** он уда́рил в цимба́лы.

v.i. **1.** (*sound*): **the cymbals ~ed** зазвене́ли цимба́лы. **2.** (*conflict*): **the armies ~ed** а́рмии столкну́лись; **my interests ~ with his** у нас с ним ста́лкиваются интере́сы; **the two concerts ~** о́ба конце́рта совпада́ют по вре́мени; **the colours ~** э́ти цвета́ не гармони́руют друг с дру́гом.

clasp [klɑːsp] *n.* **1.** (*fastener*) пря́жка, застёжка. **2.** (*grip, handshake*) пожа́тие, сжа́тие, объя́тие.

v.t.: **~ a bracelet round one's wrist** застёг|ивать, -ну́ть на руке́ брасле́т; **~ one's hands** сплести́ (*pf.*) па́льцы рук; **~ s.o. by the hand** сж|има́ть, -ать кому́-н. ру́ку.

v.i.: **the necklace won't ~** ожере́лье не застёгивается.

class [klɑːs] *n.* **1.** (*group, category*) класс, разря́д; (*railway etc.*): **he went first ~** он е́хал пе́рвым кла́ссом; (*fig.*): **he is not in the same ~ as X** ему́ о́чень далеко́ до X; (*biol.*) класс. **2.** (*social*) класс; **middle ~** буржуази́я; **upper ~(es)** аристокра́тия. **3.** (*scholastic*) класс; **he is top of the ~** он пе́рвый учени́к в кла́ссе; (*period of instruction*): **a mathematics ~** уро́к матема́тики; **Mr. X is taking the ~** г-н X ведёт заня́тия; **he attended ~es in French** он посеща́л заня́тия по францу́зскому языку́; (*US*): **the ~ of 1955** вы́пуск 1955 го́да. **4.** (*mil.*): **the ~ of 1960** набо́р 1960 го́да. **5.** (*distinction*) класс, шик.

v.t. классифици́ровать (*impf., pf.*).

cpds. **~-conscious** *adj.* кла́ссово-созна́тельный;

~fellow, ~mate *nn.* одноклáссни|к (*fem.* -ца); **~room** *n.* клáссная кóмната, класс.

classic ['klæsɪk] *n.* **1.** (*writer etc.*) клáссик. **2.** (*book etc.*) классúческое произведéние. **3.** (*ancient writer*) клáссик, антúчный áвтор; **the ~s** клáссика, классúческая литератýра. **4.** (*pl.*, *studies*): **he studied ~s** он изучáл классúческую филолóгию.

adj. классúческий.

classical ['klæsɪk(ə)l] *adj.* классúческий; **~ scholar** клáссик.

classicism ['klæsɪˌsɪz(ə)m] *n.* классицúзм; (*classical scholarship*) изучéние классúческой филолóгии.

classicist ['klæsɪˌsɪst] *n.* классицúст.

classification [ˌklæsɪfɪ'keɪʃ(ə)n] *n.* классификáция.

classif|y ['klæsɪˌfaɪ] *v.t.* классифицúровать (*impf.*, *pf.*); **~ied** (*secret*) засекрéченный.

classless ['klɑːslɪs] *adj.* бесклáссовый.

classy ['klɑːsɪ] *adj.* клáссный (*coll.*).

clatter ['klætə(r)] *n.* **1.** (*of metal*) грóхот; (*of hoofs*, *plates*, *cutlery etc.*) стук, звон, звя́канье. **2.** (*chatter*, *noise*) трескотня́.

v.t. стучáть, гремéть, звя́кать (*all impf.*).

v.i. гремéть; грохотáть (*both impf.*).

clause [klɔːz] *n.* **1.** (*gram.*) предложéние. **2.** (*provision*) клáузула, оговóрка; **escape ~** пункт, предусмáтривающий откáз от взя́того обязáтельства.

claustrophobia [ˌklɔːstrə'fəʊbɪə] *n.* боя́знь зáмкнутого прострáнства; клаустрофóбия.

claustrophobic [ˌklɔːstrə'fəʊbɪk] *adj.* клаустрофобúчный.

clavichord ['klævɪˌkɔːd] *n.* клавикóрд|ы (*pl.*, *g.* -ов).

clavicle ['klævɪk(ə)l] *n.* ключúца.

claw [klɔː] *n.* (*of animal*, *bird*) кóготь (*m.*); (*of crustacean*) клешня́; (*of machinery*) кулáк, лáпа, клéщ|и (*pl.*, *g.* -ей).

v.t. & i. царáпать(ся); рвать когтя́ми (*both impf.*); **the cat ~ed at the door** кóшка царáпалась в дверь.

cpd. **~-hammer** *n.* молотóк с гвоздодёром.

clay [kleɪ] *n.* глúна; **~ pigeon** тарéлочка для стрельбы́ (*в тире*); **~ pipe** глúняная трýбка.

clayey ['kleɪɪ] *adj.* глúнистый.

clean [kliːn] *n.* чúстка, убóрка; **he gave the table a good ~** он хорошéнько вы́тер стол.

adj. **1.** (*not dirty*) чúстый; **wash sth. ~** дóчиста вы́мыть (*pf.*) что-н.; **keep a room ~** содержáть (*impf.*) кóмнату в чистотé. **2.** (*fresh*): **a ~ sheet of paper** чúстый лист бумáги; **a ~ copy** (*of draft*) чистовúк, беловúк. **3.** (*pure*, *unblemished*) чúстый, незапя́тнанный. **4.** (*neat*, *smooth*): **the ship has ~ lines** у корабля́ плáвные обвóды; **a ~ cut** рóвный разрéз. **5.** (*fig.*): **my hands are ~** я невинóвен; **he showed a ~ pair of heels** у негó пя́тки засверкáли; **come ~** (*coll.*, *confess or vouchsafe the truth*) сознáться (*pf.*).

adv.: **I ~ forgot** я нáчисто забы́л; **the bullet went ~ through his shoulder** пýля прошлá у негó (навы́лет) сквозь плечó.

v.t. чúстить (*impf.*; *for forms of pf. see examples*); **~ one's nails** почúстить (*pf.*) нóгти; **~ a suit** чúстить, вы́-/по- костю́м; **~ streets** уб|ирáть, -рáть ýлицы; **~ a car** мыть, вы́- машúну; **~ a window** прот|ирáть, -ерéть окнó; **~ a rifle** проч|ищáть, -úстить ружьё; **he had his suit ~ed** он отдáл костю́м в чúстку.

v.i. чúститься (*impf.*); **the sink ~s easily** рáковина хорошó мóется; **~ing day** (*in hostels, shops etc.*) санитáрный день.

with advs.: **~ out** *v.t.*: **~ out a room** убрáть (*pf.*) кóмнату; **he was ~ed out** (*fig.*) он остáлся без копéйки; **~ up** *v.t.*: **~ o.s. up** почúститься (*pf.*); **~ up a city** (*fig.*) почúстить (*pf.*) гóрод; *v.i.*: **they ~ed up after the picnic** онú всё убрáли за собóй пóсле пикникá.

cpds. **~-cut** *adj.* рéзко очéрченный; **~-cut features** прáвильные черты́ лицá; **~-out** *n.* чúстка, убóрка; **~-shaven** *adj.* брúтый; **~-up** *n.* (*lit.*) чúстка; (*fig.*) чúстка, очúстка; приведéние в поря́док.

cleaner ['kliːnə(r)] *n.* (*pers.*) убóрщи|к (*fem.* -ца); чúстильщик (*fem.* -ца); **he sent the suit to the ~'s** он отдáл костю́м в чúстку; (*tool*, *machine*, *substance*) очистúтель (*m.*).

cleanliness ['klenlɪnɪs] *n.* чистотá.

cleanly ['kliːnlɪ] *adj.* чистоплóтный, опря́тный.

cleanness ['kliːnnɪs] *n.* чистотá.

cleans|e [klenz] *v.t.* оч|ищáть, -úстить; **~ing cream** очищáющий крем; **~ing department** санитáрное управлéние; **ethnic ~ing** этнúческая чúстка.

cleanser ['klenzə(r)] *n.* срéдство для очúстки кóжи.

clear [klɪə(r)] *adj.* **1.** (*easy to see*) я́сный, отчётливый; (*evident*) я́вный, очевúдный. **2.** (*bright*, *unclouded*) я́ркий, я́сный; **a ~ sky** я́сное нéбо; **on a ~ day** в погóжий день. **3.** (*transparent*) прозрáчный. **4.** (*of sound*) чúстый, отчётливый. **5.** (*intelligible*, *certain*): **make sth. ~ to s.o.** объясн|я́ть, -úть что-н. комý-н.; **make o.s. ~** объясн|я́ться, -úться; **I am not ~ what he wants** мне нея́сно, чегó он хóчет; **crystal ~** я́сно как день; **~ as mud** (*coll.*) совершéнно нея́сно. **6.** (*safe*, *free*, *unencumbered*) свобóдный; **the 'all ~'** отбóй (*воздушной тревоги*); **~ of debt** свобóдный от долгóв; **~ of suspicion** вне подозрéний; **my conscience is ~** моя́ сóвесть чистá; **~ profit** чúстая прúбыль; **three ~ days** цéлых три дня; **keep a ~ head** сохраня́ть (*impf.*) я́сный ум.

adv.: **he spoke loud and ~** он говорúл грóмко и я́сно; **keep ~ of** держáться (*impf.*) в сторонé от+*g.*; остерегáться (*impf.*) +*g.*; избегáть (*impf.*) +*g.*

v.t. **1.** (*make ~*, *empty*) оч|ищáть, -úстить; **~ land** расч|ищáть, -úстить зéмлю; **he ~ed his desk** он убрáл свой стол; **she ~ed the table** онá убралá со столá; **our talk ~ed the air** наш разговóр разрядúл атмосфéру; **~ o.s. (of a charge)** оправдáться (*pf.*); опровéргнуть (*pf.*) обвинéние; **~ s.o.'s mind of doubt** рассé|ивать, -ять чьи-н. сомнéния; **to ~ one's conscience** для очúстки сóвести; **he ~ed his throat** он откáшлялся; **~ sth. out of the way** уб|ирáть, -рáть что-н. с дорóги; отодв|игáть, -úнуть что-н.; **he ~ed the children out of the garden** он вы́гнал детéй из сáда. **2.** (*jump over*, *get past*): **the horse ~ed the hedge** лóшадь взялá барьéр; **the car ~ed the gate** автомобúль прошёл в ворóта. **3.** (*make profit of*): **we ~ed £50** мы получúли 50 фýнтов прúбыли. **4.**: **~ an account** оплá|чивать, -тúть счёт.

v.i.: *cf.* **~ up; his brow ~ed** егó лицó прояснúлось.

with advs.: **~ away** *v.t.* уб|ирáть, -рáть; *v.i.* (*disperse*) рассé|иваться, -яться; **~ off** *v.t.*: **~ off a debt** погасúть (*pf.*) долг; *v.i.* (*coll.*, *go away*) убрáться (*pf.*); **~ out** *v.t.*: **she ~ed out the cupboard** онá очúстила шкаф; *v.i.* (*coll.*, *go away*) убрáться (*pf.*); **~ up** *v.t.* (*tidy*, *remove*) убрáть (*pf.*); **~ up a mystery** распýтать (*pf.*) тáйну; *v.i.*: **the weather ~ed up** погóда прояснúлась; **please ~ up after you** бýдьте добры́, уберúте за собóй.

cpds. **~-cut** *adj.* чёткий; **~-headed** *adj.* толкóвый, ýмный; **~-sighted** *adj.* проницáтельный, дальновúдный; **~way** *n.* скоростнáя автострáда.

clearance ['klɪərəns] *n.* **1.** (*removal of obstruction etc.*) очúстка, расчúстка; **~ sale** распродáжа. **2.** (*free space*) зазóр; промежýток. **3.** (*customs*) очúстка от тамóженных пóшлин. **4.**: **security ~** дóпуск к секрéтной рабóте; **medical ~** свидéтельство о гóдности по здорóвью.

clearing ['klɪərɪŋ] *n.* **1.** (*glade*) прóсека, поля́на. **2.** (*fin.*) клúринг; **~ agreement** клúринговое соглашéние; **~ house** расчётная палáта.

clearly [ˈklɪəlɪ] *adv.* (*distinctly*) я́сно; (*evidently*) очеви́дно, коне́чно; **it is too dark to see ~** сли́шком темно́, что́бы разгляде́ть.

cleat [kliːt] *n.* (*on sole or heel of shoe*) ско́бка, гвоздь (*m.*).

cleavage [ˈkliːvɪdʒ] *n.* **1.** (*splitting*) расщепле́ние, раска́лывание. **2.** (*fig., discord*) расхожде́ние, раско́л. **3.** (*of bosom*) ложби́нка бю́ста.

cleave [kliːv] *v.t.* **1.** (*split*) раск|а́лывать, -оло́ть; расс|ека́ть, -е́чь. **2.: cleft palate** (*med.*) во́лчья пасть.

cleaver [ˈkliːvə(r)] *n.* нож мясника́.

clef [klef] *n.* ключ; **treble ~** скрипи́чный ключ; **bass ~** басо́вый ключ.

cleft[1] [kleft] *n.* тре́щина, рассе́лина.

cleft[2] [kleft] *adj.* = **cleave 2.**

clematis [ˈklemətɪs, kləˈmeɪtɪs] *n.* ломоно́с.

clemency [ˈklemənsɪ] *n.* (*of pers.*) милосе́рдие; **the defence lawyer appealed for ~** защи́тник призва́л к снисхожде́нию; (*of weather*) мя́гкость.

clench [klentʃ] *v.t.*: **~ one's teeth** сти́с|кивать, -нуть зу́бы; **~ one's fist** сж|има́ть, -ать кулаки́.

clergy [ˈklɜːdʒɪ] *n.* духове́нство.

cpd. **~man** *n.* духо́вное лицо́; (*Protestant*) па́стор.

cleric [ˈklerɪk] *n.* церко́вник, духо́вное лицо́.

clerical [ˈklerɪk(ə)l] *adj.* **1.** (*of clergy*) клерика́льный; **~ collar** па́сторский воротни́к. **2.** (*of clerks*) канцеля́рский, конто́рский.

clerk [klɑːk] *n.* **1.** (*person in charge of correspondence*) секрета́рь (*m.*); **bank ~** ба́нковский слу́жащий. **2.** (*official*) слу́жащий, чино́вник; **town ~** секрета́рь (*m.*) городско́го сове́та; (*of court*) регистра́тор. **3.** (*US, shop assistant*) продаве́ц, прика́зчик; (*hotel receptionist*) (дежу́рный) администра́тор.

clever [ˈklevə(r)] *adj.* у́мный, сообрази́тельный; (*skilful*) ло́вкий; **he is ~ at arithmetic** он спосо́бен к арифме́тике; **he is ~ with his fingers** у него́ уме́лые ру́ки.

cleverness [ˈklevənɪs] *n.* сметли́вость; (*skill*) ло́вкость, уме́ние.

cliché [ˈkliːʃeɪ] *n.* (*fig.*) клише́ (*indecl.*), штамп.

click [klɪk] *n.* щёлканье, щёлк, щелчо́к.

v.t. щёлк|ать, -нуть +*i.*; прищёлк|ивать, -нуть +*i.*.

v.i. щёлк|ать, -нуть; **the door ~ed shut** дверь защёлкнулась.

client [ˈklaɪənt] *n.* **1.** клие́нт. **2.** (*customer*) клие́нт, зака́зчик.

clientele [ˌkliːɒnˈtel] *n.* клиенту́ра.

cliff [klɪf] *n.* утёс, скала́.

climate [ˈklaɪmɪt] *n.* кли́мат; (*fig.*) атмосфе́ра; **~ of opinion** состоя́ние обще́ственного мне́ния.

climatic [ˌklaɪˈmætɪk] *adj.* климати́ческий.

climax [ˈklaɪmæks] *n.* кульмина́ция; (*orgasm*) орга́зм.

v.t. (*top off, crown*) довести́ (*pf.*) до кульмина́ции.

v.i. (*culminate*) кульмини́ровать (*impf., pf.*); дойти́ (*pf.*) до кульмина́ции.

climb [klaɪm] *n.* подъём, восхожде́ние.

v.t. вл|еза́ть, -езть на+*a.*

v.i. ла́зить (*indet.*), лезть (*det.*); подн|има́ться, -я́ться; **~ up a tree** влезть (*pf.*) на де́рево; **~ over a wall** переле́зть (*pf.*) че́рез сте́ну; **~ down a ladder** слезть (*pf.*) с ле́стницы; **~ on to a table** зал|еза́ть, -е́зть на стол; **the aircraft ~ed slowly** самолёт ме́дленно поднима́лся; **~ down** (*lit.*) слез|а́ть, -ть; (*fig.*) отступ|а́ть, -и́ть.

cpd. **~-down** *n.* (*fig.*) отступле́ние, усту́пка.

climber [ˈklaɪmə(r)] *n.* (*pers.*) альпини́ст (*fem.* -ка); (*plant*) вью́щееся расте́ние.

climbing [ˈklaɪmɪŋ] *n.* (*mountaineering*) альпини́зм.

clinch [klɪntʃ] *v.t.* (*make fast*) заклёп|ывать, -а́ть; (*fig.*): **~ an argument** заверши́ть (*pf.*) спор; **~ a bargain** закрепи́ть (*pf.*) сде́лку.

cling [klɪŋ] *v.i.* (*adhere*) цепля́ться (*impf.*) (за+*a.*); льну́ть (*impf.*) (к+*d.*); (*fig.*): **he clung to his possessions** он цепля́лся за своё иму́щество; **they clung together** они́ держа́лись вме́сте; **the child clung to its mother** ребёнок льну́л к ма́тери; **a ~ing dress** облега́ющее пла́тье; **a ~ing person** привя́зчивый челове́к.

clinic [ˈklɪnɪk] *n.* кли́ника.

clinical [ˈklɪnɪk(ə)l] *adj.* **1.** клини́ческий; **~ record** исто́рия боле́зни. **2.** (*fig.*) бесстра́стный.

clink[1] [klɪŋk] *n.* звон.

v.t. звене́ть (*impf.*) +*i.*; **~ glasses with s.o.** чо́к|аться, -нуться с кем-н.

v.i. звене́ть (*impf.*); чо́к|аться, -нуться.

clink[2] [klɪŋk] *n.* (*prison*) куту́зка.

clip[1] [klɪp] *n.* **1.** (*slide-on ~*) скре́пка; (*grip-~*) зажи́м, зажи́мка. **2.** (*ornament*) клипс. **3.** (*of cartridges*) обо́йма.

v.t. заж|има́ть, -а́ть; скреп|ля́ть, -и́ть; **~ a paper to a board** прикреп|ля́ть, -и́ть бума́гу к доске́.

cpd. **~board** *n.* доска́ с зажи́мом для бума́ги; **~-on** *adj.* пристёгивающийся, прикрепля́ющийся.

clip[2] [klɪp] *n.* **1.** (*shearing*) стри́жка. **2.** (*coll., blow*): **a ~ on the jaw** уда́р по скуле́. **3.** (*coll., speed*): **at a fast ~** бы́стрым хо́дом. **4.** (*cin.*) отры́вок из фи́льма.

v.t. **1.** (*cut*): **~ a hedge** подстр|ига́ть, -и́чь живу́ю и́згородь; **~ s.o.'s wings** (*fig.*) подре́зать (*pf.*) кому́-н. кры́лышки; **~ an article out of a newspaper** выреза́ть, вы́резать статью́ из газе́ты; **~ tickets** пробива́ть (*impf.*) (*or* компости́ровать) биле́ты. **2.** (*hit*): **~ s.o. on the jaw** съе́здить (*pf.*) кому́-н. по физионо́мии (*coll.*).

clipper [ˈklɪpə(r)] *n.* **1.** (*pl., for hair*) маши́нка для стри́жки воло́с; (*pl., for nails*) куса́ч|ки (*pl., g.* -ек). **2.** (*naut.*) кли́пер.

clipping [ˈklɪpɪŋ] *n.* (*from newspaper*) вы́резка.

clique [kliːk] *n.* кли́ка.

clitoris [ˈklɪtərɪs, ˈklaɪ-] *n.* кли́тор, похотни́к.

cloak [kləʊk] *n.* (*garment*) плащ, ма́нтия; (*covering*): **a ~ of snow** сне́жный покро́в; **under the ~ of darkness** под покро́вом темноты́; (*fig., pretext*) ма́ска.

v.t. (*fig.*) прикр|ыва́ть, -ы́ть; скр|ыва́ть, -ы́ть.

cpd. **~room** *n.* (*for clothes*) гардеро́б, раздева́льня; (*for luggage*) ка́мера хране́ния; (*lavatory*) убо́рная.

cloche [klɒʃ, kləʊʃ] *n.* (*for plants*) стекля́нный колпа́к.

clock [klɒk] *n.* час|ы́ (*pl., g.* -о́в); **he works round the ~** он рабо́тает кру́глые су́тки; **put the ~ forward** поста́вить (*pf.*) часы́ вперёд; **put the ~ back** (*lit.*) отвести́ (*pf.*) часы́ наза́д.

v.t. (*time*) хронометри́ровать (*impf., pf.*); (*register*): **she ~ed 11 seconds in this race** она́ показа́ла вре́мя 11 секу́нд в э́том забе́ге.

v.i.: **~ in, on** отм|еча́ться, -е́титься по прихо́де на рабо́ту; **~ out, off** отм|еча́ться, -е́титься при ухо́де с рабо́ты.

cpds. **~-face** *n.* цифербла́т; **~-maker** *n.* часовщи́к; **~work** *n.* часово́й механи́зм; **~work toy** заводна́я игру́шка; **the ceremony went like ~work** церемо́ния шла без сучка́, без задо́ринки.

clockwise [ˈklɒkwaɪz] *adj. & adv.* (дви́жущийся) по часово́й стре́лке.

clod [klɒd] *n.* ком, глы́ба.

cpd. **~-hopper** *n.* болва́н, дереве́нщина (*c.g.*).

clog[1] [klɒg] *n.* (*shoe*) башма́к на деревя́нной подо́шве.

clog[2] [klɒg] *v.t.* (*lit., fig.*) засор|я́ть, -и́ть; **the sink is ~ged** ра́ковина засори́лась.

cloister [ˈklɔɪstə(r)] *n.* монасты́рь (*m.*); (*covered walk*) арка́да.

v.t. (*fig.*): **he led a ~ed life** он вёл уединённую жизнь.

clone [kləʊn] *n.* клон.

v.t. размн|ожа́ть, -о́жить вегетати́вным путём; клони́ровать (*impf., pf.*).

clop [klɒp] *n.* (*of hoofs*) цо́канье, цо́кот.

close[1] [kləʊs] *n.* (*enclosure, precinct*) двор.

adj. **1.** (*near*) бли́зкий; **he fired at ~ range** он стреля́л с бли́зкого расстоя́ния; **~ combat** бли́жний бой; **~ contact** те́сное обще́ние; **~ competition** о́страя конкуре́нция; **~ resemblance** большо́е схо́дство. **2.** (*intimate*) бли́зкий; **a ~ friend** бли́зкий друг; **his sister was very ~ to him** они́ с сестро́й бы́ли о́чень близки́. **3.** (*serried, compact*): **~ texture** пло́тная ткань; **~ column** (*mil.*) со́мкнутая коло́нна. **4.** (*strict, attentive*): **keep a ~ watch on s.o.** тща́тельно следи́ть (*impf.*) за кем-н.; **~ examination** тща́тельное обсле́дование; **~ attention** при́стальное внима́ние; **~ confinement** стро́гая изоля́ция; **a ~ translation** то́чный перево́д. **5.** (*restricted*) закры́тый; **~ season** вре́мя, когда́ охо́та запрещена́. **6.** (*of games etc.*): **a ~ contest** упо́рная борьба́, состяза́ние с почти́ ра́вными ша́нсами. **7.** (*stingy*) скупо́й, прижи́мистый. **8.** (*reticent, secret*) скры́тный; **he is ~ about his affairs** он де́ржит свои́ дела́ в секре́те. **9.** (*stuffy*): (*of air*) ду́шный, спёртый; (*of weather*) ду́шный, тяжёлый.

adv.: **he lives ~ to, by the church** он живёт побли́зости от це́ркви; **keep ~ to me** не отходи́те от меня́; **follow ~ behind s.o.** сле́довать(*impf.*) непосре́дственно за кем-н.; **stand ~ against the wall** стоя́ть (*impf.*) вплотну́ю к стене́; **cut one's hair ~** ко́ротко подстри́чься (*pf.*); **come ~r together** (*fig.*) сбли́зиться (*pf.*); подойти́ (*pf.*) вплотну́ю друг к дру́гу; **sail ~ to the wind** (*lit.*) идти́ (*det.*) кру́то к ве́тру; (*fig.*) ходи́ть (*indet.*) по острию́ (ножа́).

cpds. **~-cropped** *adj.* ко́ротко остри́женный; **~-fisted** *adj.* прижи́мистый, скупо́й; **~-fitting** *adj.* облега́ющий; **~-set** *adj.* бли́зко поста́вленный; **~-up** *n.* (*cin.*) кру́пный план.

close[2] [kləʊz] *n.* (*end*) коне́ц; **at ~ of day** в конце́ дня; **~ of play** коне́ц игры́; **bring to a ~** довести́ (*pf.*) до конца́; **the day reached its ~** день ко́нчился; **the meeting drew to a ~** собра́ние подошло́ к концу́.

v.t. **1.** (*shut*) закр|ыва́ть, -ы́ть; **~ a gap** зап|олня́ть, -о́лнить пробе́л; **~ one's hand** сжать (*pf.*) ру́ку в кула́к; **~ one's lips** сомкну́ть (*pf.*) гу́бы; **~d shop** предприя́тие, нанима́ющее то́лько чле́нов профсою́за; **'road ~d'** «прое́зд закры́т»; **the museum is ~d** музе́й не рабо́тает. **2.** (*end, complete, settle*): **~ a meeting** закр|ыва́ть, -ы́ть собра́ние; **~ a deal** заключи́ть (*pf.*) сде́лку; **the closing scene of the play** заключи́тельная сце́на пье́сы; **the closing date is December 1** после́дний срок — пе́рвое декабря́. **3.: ~ the ranks** сомкну́ть (*pf.*) ряды́.

v.i. **1.** (*shut*) закр|ыва́ться, -ы́ться; **the door ~d** дверь закры́лась; **closing day** выходно́й день. **2.** (*cease*): **the performance ~d last night** вчера́ пье́са шла в после́дний раз; **he ~d with this remark** он зако́нчил э́тим замеча́нием. **3.** (*come closer*) сбл|ижа́ться, -и́зиться; прибл|ижа́ться, -и́зиться; **the soldiers ~d up** солда́ты сомкну́ли ряды́.

with advs.: **~ down** *v.t.* закр|ыва́ть, -ы́ть; *v.i.* (*e.g. of a factory*) закр|ыва́ться, -ы́ться; (*broadcasting*) зак|а́нчивать, -о́нчить переда́чу; **~ in** *v.i.*: **the days are closing in** дни стано́вятся коро́че; **the darkness ~d in on us** нас оку́тала темнота́; **the enemy ~d in upon us** неприя́тель подступи́л вплотну́ю; **~ up** *v.t. & i.* закр|ыва́ть(ся), -ы́ть(ся).

closely ['kləʊslɪ] *adv.*: **it ~ resembles pork** э́то о́чень напомина́ет свини́ну; (*attentively*) внима́тельно; **watch ~** при́стально следи́ть (*impf.*) за+*i.*; **~ connected** те́сно свя́занный; **we worked ~ together** мы рабо́тали в те́сном сотру́дничестве; **they questioned him ~** его́ подро́бно расспра́шивали.

closeness ['kləʊsnɪs] *n.* (*proximity, resemblance; intimacy*) бли́зость; (*of texture etc.*) пло́тность; (*attentiveness*) при́стальность; (*reticence*) скры́тность; (*parsimony*) прижи́мистость, ску́пость; (*of air etc.*) духота́, спёртость.

closet ['klɒzɪt] *n.* (*cupboard*) шкаф; **china ~** буфе́т.

v.t. зап|ира́ть, -ере́ть; **he was ~ed with his solicitor** он совеща́лся со свои́м адвока́том наедине́.

closure ['kləʊʒə(r)] *n.* закры́тие.

clot [klɒt] *n.* (*of blood etc.*) сгу́сток, комо́к; (*sl., stupid person*) болва́н, тупи́ца (*c.g.*).

v.i. свёр|тываться, -ну́ться; сгу|ща́ться, -сти́ться; **~ted cream** густы́е топлёные сли́вки.

cloth [klɒθ] *n.* **1.** (*material*) ткань, мате́рия; **bound in ~** в матерча́том переплёте. **2.** (*piece of ~*) тря́пка; (*table ~*) ска́терть. **3.** (*fig., clerical status*) духо́вный сан. **4. a ~ cap** (матерча́тая) ке́пка.

clothe [kləʊð] *v.t.* од|ева́ть, -еть; **~ o.s.** (*acquire clothing*) приоде́ться (*pf.*).

clothes [kləʊðz] *n.* пла́тье, оде́жда; **evening ~** вече́рнее пла́тье; (*bed ~*) посте́льное бельё; **in plain ~** (*out of uniform*) в шта́тском (пла́тье).

cpds. **~-basket** *n.* корзи́на для белья́; **~-brush** *n.* платяна́я щётка; **~-horse** *n.* напо́льная суши́лка; **~-line** *n.* верёвка для белья́; **~-peg** *n.* зажи́мка для белья́.

clothier ['kləʊðɪə(r)] *n.* торго́вец мужско́й оде́ждой.

clothing ['kləʊðɪŋ] *n.* оде́жда.

cloud [klaʊd] *n.* **1.** (*in the sky*) о́блако; ту́ча; **every ~ has a silver lining** нет ху́да без добра́; **~ cuckoo land** мир фанта́зий. **2.** (*of smoke*) клубы́ (*m. pl.*); (*of dust*) о́блако. **3.** (*of unhappiness etc.*): **this cast a ~ over our meeting** э́то омрачи́ло на́шу встре́чу; **under a ~** (*fig.*) в неми́лости.

v.t. покр|ыва́ть, -ы́ть облака́ми; (*fig.*) омрач|а́ть, -и́ть; **eyes ~ed with tears** глаза́, затума́ненные слеза́ми.

v.i. омрач|а́ться, -и́ться; покр|ыва́ться, -ы́ться облака́ми/ту́чами; нахму́ри|ваться, -ться; **the sky ~ed over** не́бо затяну́ло облака́ми/ту́чами.

cpds. **~berry** *n.* моро́шка; **~burst** *n.* ли́вень (*m.*).

cloudiness ['klaʊdɪnɪs] *n.* о́блачность; (*fig.*) тума́нность, нея́сность.

cloudless ['klaʊdlɪs] *adj.* безо́блачный.

cloudy ['klaʊdɪ] *adj.* о́блачный; (*of liquid etc.*) му́тный; (*fig., of ideas*) тума́нный.

clout [klaʊt] *n.* (*coll., blow*) затре́щина; (*coll., influence*) влия́ние.

v.t. (*coll., hit*) тре́снуть (*pf.*).

clove[1] [kləʊv] *n.* (*section of bulb*) зубо́к; **a ~ of garlic** зубо́к чеснока́.

clove[2] [kləʊv] *n.* (*aromatic*) гвозди́ка.

clover ['kləʊvə(r)] *n.* кле́вер; **we are in ~** у нас не жизнь, а ма́сленица; мы живём припева́ючи.

clown [klaʊn] *n.* кло́ун.

v.i. стро́ить (*impf.*) из себя́ шута́.

clowning ['klaʊnɪŋ] *n.* шутовство́, пая́сничание.

clownish ['klaʊnɪʃ] *adj.* кло́унский, шутовско́й.

cloy [klɔɪ] *v.t.* прес|ыща́ть, -ы́тить.

club[1] [klʌb] *n.* (*weapon*) дуби́нка; (*at golf*) клю́шка; (*pl., at cards*) тре́фы (*f. pl.*).

v.t. бить (*impf.*) дуби́нкой.

cpds. **~-foot** *n.* изуро́дованная ступня́; **~-footed** *adj.* с изуро́дованной ступнёй; косола́пый.

club[2] [klʌb] *n.* (*society, building*) клуб.

v.i. скла́дываться, сложи́ться; устр|а́ивать, -о́ить скла́дчину; **they ~bed together to pay the fine** они́ сложи́лись и уплати́ли штраф.

cpd. **~-house** *n.* клуб, помеще́ние клу́ба.

cluck [klʌk] *n.* куда́хтанье, клохта́нье.

v.i. куда́хтать, клохта́ть (*both impf.*).

clue (*US* **clew**) [klu:] *n.* ключ, нить; **the police found a ~** поли́ция нашла́ ули́ку; **the ~ to this mystery** ключ к разга́дке э́той та́йны; **I haven't a ~** (*coll.*) поня́тия не име́ю.

clueless ['klu:lɪs] *adj.* (*coll.*) бестолко́вый; не в ку́рсе.
clump[1] [klʌmp] *n.* (*cluster*) гру́ппа, ку́па.
v.t. соб|ира́ть, -ра́ть в ку́чу; **they are ~ed together** они́ сва́лены в ку́чу.
clump[2] [klʌmp] *n.* (*heavy tread*) то́пот.
v.i. (*tread heavily*) то́пать (*impf.*).
clumsiness ['klʌmzɪnɪs] *n.* неуклю́жесть.
clumsy ['klʌmzɪ] *adj.* неуклю́жий, нело́вкий.
cluster ['klʌstə(r)] *n.* (*of grapes*) гроздь, кисть; (*of flowers*) кисть; (*of bees*) рой; (*of trees*) ку́па.
v.i. расти́ (*impf.*) пучка́ми; собира́ться (*impf.*) гру́ппами; **the children ~ed round the teacher** де́ти столпи́лись вокру́г учи́теля.
clutch[1] [klʌtʃ] *n.* **1.** (*act of ~ing*) сжа́тие, захва́т, схва́тывание. **2.** (*pl., grasp*) ла́пы (*f. pl.*), ко́гти (*m. pl.*); **they fell into his ~es** (*fig.*) они́ попа́ли к нему́ в ла́пы. **3.** (*of car*) сцепле́ние; **let in the ~** отпусти́ть сцепле́ние.
v.t. & i. хвата́ться, (с)хвати́ться (за+*a.*); сж|има́ть, -ать.
clutch[2] [klʌtʃ] *n.* (*of eggs*) я́йца (*nt. pl.*) под насе́дкой; (*brood*) вы́водок.
clutter ['klʌtə(r)] *n.* (*confused mess*) сумато́ха, суета́; (*untidiness*) хао́с, беспоря́док.
v.t. (*also* **~ up**) загромо|жда́ть, -зди́ть.
cm. ['sentɪ,mi:tə(r)(z)] *n.* (*abbr. of* **centimetre(s)**) см., (сантиме́тр).
CND (*abbr. of* ***Campaign for Nuclear Disarmament***) Кампа́ния за я́дерное разоруже́ние.
CO (*abbr. of* ***Commanding Officer***) команди́р.
Co. [kəʊ] *n.* (*abbr. of* **company**) К°, (компа́ния).
coach[1] [kəʊtʃ] *n.* **1.** (*horse-drawn*) каре́та, экипа́ж. **2.** (*railway*) пассажи́рский ваго́н. **3.** (*motor-bus*) (тури́стский междугоро́дный) авто́бус.
cpds. **~-house** *n.* каре́тный сара́й; **~man** *n.* ку́чер; **~-party** *n.* экскурса́нты (*m. pl.*); **~-tour** *n.* экску́рсия.
coach[2] [kəʊtʃ] *n.* (*tutor*) репети́тор; (*trainer*) тре́нер.
v.t. репети́ровать (*impf.*); (*train*) тренирова́ть, на-; (*prepare for questioning, e.g. a witness*) ната́скивать (*impf.*).
coagulant [kəʊ'ægjʊlənt] *n.* коагуля́нт.
coagulate [kəʊ'ægjʊ,leɪt] *v.t.* сгу|ща́ть, -сти́ть; коагули́ровать (*impf., pf.*); свёрт|ывать. -ну́ть.
v.i. коагули́роваться (*impf., pf.*); свёр|тываться, -ну́ться.
coagulation [,kəʊægjʊ'leɪʃ(ə)n] *n.* коагуля́ция, свёртывание.
coal [kəʊl] *n.* (*mineral*) ка́менный у́голь; **~s** у́гли (*m. pl.*); **a live ~** горя́щий уголёк; (*fig.*): **carry ~s to Newcastle** е́хать (*det.*) в Ту́лу со свои́м самова́ром; **haul s.o. over the ~s** да|ва́ть, -ть нагоня́й кому́-н.
cpds. **~-black** *adj.* (*e.g. hair*) чёрный как смоль; **~-cellar** *n.* подва́л для хране́ния у́гля́; **~-face** *n.* забо́й; грудь забо́я; **~-field** *n.* каменноу́го́льный бассе́йн; **~-gas** *n.* каменноу́го́льный/свети́льный газ; **~-mine, ~-pit** *nn.* у́гольная ша́хта; **~-miner** *n.* шахтёр; **~-scuttle** *n.* ведёрко для у́гля́; **~-seam** *n.* у́гольный пласт; **~-tar** *n.* каменноу́го́льная смола́; дёготь (*m.*).
coalesce [,kəʊə'les] *v.i.* соедин|я́ться, -и́ться; объедин|я́ться, -и́ться.
coalescence [,kəʊə'lesəns] *n.* соедине́ние, объедине́ние.
coalition [,kəʊə'lɪʃ(ə)n] *n.* (*pol.*) коали́ция; (*attr.*) коалицио́нный.
coarse [kɔ:s] *adj.* (*of material*) гру́бый; (*of sand, sugar*) кру́пный; **~ manners** гру́бые/вульга́рные мане́ры.
coarsen ['kɔ:s(ə)n] *v.t.* де́лать, с- гру́бым.
v.i. грубе́ть, о-.
coarseness ['kɔ:snɪs] *n.* (*lit.*) гру́бость; (*fig.*) гру́бость, вульга́рность.
coast [kəʊst] *n.* (*sea-~*) морско́й бе́рег; побере́жье; **the ~ is clear** (*fig.*) путь свобо́ден.
v.i. (*bicycle downhill*) кати́ться (*impf.*) на велосипе́де с горы́.
cpds. **~guard** *n.* (*collect.*) берегова́я стра́жа; **~line** *n.* берегова́я ли́ния.
coastal ['kəʊstəl] *adj.* берегово́й, прибре́жный; **~ command** берегова́я охра́на; **~ waters** прибре́жные во́ды (*f. pl.*).
coaster ['kəʊstə(r)] *n.* подно́с, подста́вка.
coat [kəʊt] *n.* **1.** (*overcoat*) пальто́ (*indecl.*); (*man's jacket*) пиджа́к; (*woman's jacket*) жаке́т; **~ of arms** герб. **2.** (*of animal*) шерсть, мех. **3.** (*of paint etc.*) слой; **this wall needs a ~ of paint** э́ту сте́ну на́до покра́сить.
v.t. покр|ыва́ть, -ы́ть; облиц|о́вывать, -ева́ть; **the pill is ~ed with sugar** пилю́ля в са́харной оболо́чке; **he ~ed the wall with whitewash** он побели́л сте́ну; **his tongue is ~ed** у него́ обло́жен язы́к.
cpds. **~-hanger** *n.* ве́шалка; **~-tails** *n.* фа́лды (*f. pl.*) фра́ка.
coating ['kəʊtɪŋ] *n.* (*layer*) слой.
co-author [,kəʊ'ɔ:θə(r)] *n.* соа́втор.
v.t. писа́ть, на- в соа́вторстве.
coax [kəʊks] *v.t.* угов|а́ривать, -ори́ть; зад|а́бривать, -о́брить; **he ~ed the child to take its medicine** он уговори́л ребёнка приня́ть лека́рство.
coaxial [kəʊ'æksɪəl] *adj.* (*tech.*): **~ cable** коаксиа́льный ка́бель.
cob [kɒb] *n.* **1.** (*swan*) ле́бедь-саме́ц. **2.** (*nut*) оре́х. **3.** (*of maize*) поча́ток; **corn on the ~** поча́ток кукуру́зы.
cobalt ['kəʊbɔ:lt, -bɒlt] *n.* (*chem.*) ко́бальт; (*pigment*) ко́бальтовая синь.
cobble ['kɒb(ə)l] *n.* (*also* **~-stone**) булы́жник.
v.t. (*pave*) мости́ть, за-/вы- булы́жником.
cobbler ['kɒblə(r)] *n.* (*shoemaker*) сапо́жник.
COBOL ['kəʊbɒl] *n.* (*comput.*) КОБОЛ.
cobra ['kəʊbrə, 'kɒbrə] *n.* очко́вая змея́.
cobweb ['kɒbweb] *n.* паути́на; нить паути́ны.
coca ['kəʊkə] *n.* ко́ка
Coca-Cola [,kəʊkə'kəʊlə] *n.* (*propr.*) ко́ка-ко́ла.
cocaine [kə'keɪn, kəʊ-] *n.* кокаи́н.
coccyx ['kɒksɪks] *n.* ко́пчик.
cochineal ['kɒtʃɪ,ni:l, -'ni:l] *n.* кошени́ль.
cock[1] [kɒk] *n.* **1.** (*male domestic fowl*) пету́х. **2.** (*male bird*) пету́х, саме́ц.
v.t. **~ up** (*sl.*) пу́тать, на-; портá́чить, на-.
cpds. **~-a-doodle-doo** *n.* кукареку́ (*nt. indecl.*); **~-and-bull** *adj.*: **~-and-bull story** вздор, небыли́ца (в ли́цах); **~chafer** *n.* ма́йский жук, хрущ; **~-crow** *n.* рассве́т; **before ~-crow** до петухо́в; **~-fighting** *n.* петуши́ные бои́ (*m. pl.*); **~pit** *n.* (*aeron.*) каби́на; **~roach** *n.* тарака́н; **~scomb** *n.* (*crest of ~*) петуши́ный гре́бень; **~sure** *adj.* самоуве́ренный; **~tail** *n.* (*drink*) кокте́йль (*m.*); **~tail party** кокте́йль (*m.*); **~-up** *n.* (*sl., muddle*) неразбери́ха, пу́таница; **make a ~-up of sth.** пу́тать, на-; порта́чить, на-.
cock[2] [kɒk] *n.* **1.** (*tap*) кран. **2.** (*lever in gun*) куро́к. **3.** (*vulg., penis*) хуй.
cock[3] [kɒk] *v.t.* **1.** (*stick up etc.*): **~ one's hat** заломи́ть (*pf.*) ша́пку набекре́нь; **he ~ed an eye at me** он подмигну́л мне; **~ one's nose** (*or* **a snook**) **at s.o.** показа́ть (*pf.*) нос кому́-н.; **~ed hat** треуго́лка. **2.** (*of gun*) взв|оди́ть, -ести́ курок +*g.*
cpd. **~-eyed** *adj.* (*squinting*) косогла́зый, косо́й; (*askew*) косо́й; (*absurd*) дура́цкий.
cockade [kɒ'keɪd] *n.* кока́рда.
cock-a-hoop [,kɒkə'hu:p] *adj.* хвастли́вый и самодово́льный.
cockatoo [,kɒkə'tu:] *n.* какаду́ (*m. indecl.*).

cockerel ['kɒkər(ə)l] *n.* петушóк.
cockiness ['kɒkɪnɪs] *n.* бóйкость, нахáльство.
cockle[1] ['kɒk(ə)l] *n.* (*plant*) кýколь (*m.*), плевéл.
cockle[2] ['kɒk(ə)l] *n.* **1.** (*shellfish*) сердцеви́дка. **2.: it warms the ~s of one's heart** э́то согревáет дýшу.
cockney ['kɒknɪ] *n.* & *adj.* кóкни (*c.g. indecl.*); **~ accent** акцéнт кóкни.
cocky ['kɒkɪ] *adj.* нахáльный; разбитнóй.
coco ['kəʊkəʊ] *n.* **(~ palm)** кокóсовая пáльма.
cpd. **~nut** *n.* кокóс, кокóсовый орéх; **~nut fibre** кокóсовое волокнó; **~nut matting** цинóвка из кокóсового волокнá.
cocoa ['kəʊkəʊ] *n.* (*powder or drink*) какáо (*indecl.*); (*attr.*) какáовый; **~ bean** боб какáо.
cocoon [kə'ku:n] *n.* кóкон.
COD *abbr. of* **1.** ***cash on delivery*** уплáта при достáвке. **2.** ***Concise Oxford Dictionary*** Крáткий оксфóрдский словáрь (англи́йского языкá).
cod [kɒd] *n.* **(~fish)** трескá.
cpd. **~-liver oil** *n.* ры́бий жир.
coddle ['kɒd(ə)l] *v.t.* нéжить (*or* изнéживать), из-.
code [kəʊd] *n.* (*of laws*) кóдекс; свод закóнов; **building ~** положéние о застрóйке; (*of conduct*) кóдекс; нóрмы (*f. pl.*); (*set of symbols, cipher*) код; **Morse ~** код/áзбука Мóрзе.
v.t. (*encode*) коди́ровать (*impf., pf.*); шифровáть, за- по кóду.
codeine ['kəʊdi:n] *n.* кодеи́н.
codicil ['kəʊdɪsɪl, 'kɒd-] *n.* дополни́тельное распоряжéние к завещáнию.
codification [ˌkəʊdɪfɪ'keɪʃ(ə)n] *n.* кодификáция.
codify ['kəʊdɪˌfaɪ, 'kɒd-] *v.t.* кодифици́ровать (*impf., pf*).
co-education [ˌkəʊedju:'keɪʃ(ə)n] *n.* совмéстное обучéние.
co-educational [ˌkəʊedju:'keɪʃ(ə)nəl] *adj.* совмéстного обучéния.
coefficient [ˌkəʊɪ'fɪʃ(ə)nt] *n.* коэффициéнт.
coerce [kəʊ'ɜ:s] *v.t.* прину|ждáть, -ди́ть; **~ into silence** застáвить (*pf.*) молчáть.
coercion [kəʊ'ɜ:ʃ(ə)n] *n.* принуждéние; **he paid under ~** он заплати́л под давлéнием.
coercive [kəʊ'ɜ:sɪv] *adj.* принуди́тельный.
coexist [ˌkəʊɪg'zɪst] *v.i.* сосуществовáть (*impf*).
coexistence [ˌkəʊɪg'zɪstəns] *n.* сосуществовáние.
C. of E. (*abbr. of* ***Church of England***) Англикáнская цéрковь.
coffee ['kɒfɪ] *n.* кóфе (*m. indecl.*); **black ~** чёрный кóфе; **white ~** кофе с молокóм; **ground ~** мóлотый кóфе; **instant ~** растворúмый кóфе.
cpds. **~-bar** *n.* буфéт; **~-bean** *n.* кофéйный боб; (*pl.*) кóфе в зёрнах; **~-break** *n.* переры́в на кóфе; **~-cup** *n.* кофéйная чáшка; **~-grinder, ~-mill** *nn.* кофéйница, кофéйная мéльница; **~-house** *n.* кафé (*indecl.*); **~-maker** кофевáрка; **~-pot** *n.* кофéйник; **~-table** *n.* ни́зенький стóлик.
coffer ['kɒfə(r)] *n.* (*chest*) сундýк; (*pl., fig., funds*) казнá.
coffin ['kɒfɪn] *n.* гроб.
cog [kɒg] *n.* зуб (*pl.* -ья); зубéц; вы́ступ.
cpd. **~-wheel** *n.* зýбчатое колесó.
cogency ['kəʊdʒənsɪ] *n.* убеди́тельность.
cogent ['kəʊdʒ(ə)nt] *adj.* убеди́тельный.
cogitate ['kɒdʒɪˌteɪt] *v.i.* размышля́ть (*impf.*) (*o чём or над чем*).
cogitation [ˌkɒdʒɪ'teɪʃ(ə)n] *n.* размышлéние, обдýмывание.
cognac ['kɒnjæk] *n.* конья́к.
cognate ['kɒgneɪt] *adj.* рóдственный.
cognition [kɒg'nɪʃ(ə)n] *n.* познáние; знáние.
cognitive ['kɒgnɪtɪv] *adj.* познавáтельный.
cognizance ['kɒgnɪz(ə)ns, 'kɒn-] *n.* знáние, узнавáние; **take ~ of** приня́ть (*pf.*) во внимáние.
cognizant ['kɒgnɪz(ə)nt, 'kɒn-] *adj.* знáющий, осведомлённый.
cohabit [kəʊ'hæbɪt] *v.t.* сожи́тельствовать (*impf.*).
cohabitation [ˌkəʊhæbɪ'teɪʃ(ə)n] *n.* (внебрáчное) сожи́тельство.
cohere [kəʊ'hɪə(r)] *v.t.* (*stick, together*) сцеп|ля́ться, -и́ться; быть соединённым; (*fig., be consistent*) быть свя́зным.
coherence [kəʊ'hɪərəns] *n.* свя́зность, послéдовательность.
coherent [kəʊ'hɪərənt] *adj.* свя́зный, послéдовательный.
cohesion [kəʊ'hi:ʒ(ə)n] *n.* сцеплéние; сплочённость.
cohesive [kəʊ'hi:sɪv] *adj.* спосóбный к сцеплéнию; (*united*) сплочённый.
coil [kɔɪl] *n.* **1.** (*of rope, snake etc.*) витóк; кольцó. **2.** (*elec.*) катýшка.
v.t. & i. (*also* **~ up**) свёр|тывать(ся), -нýть(ся) кольцóм (*or* в кольцó).
coin [kɔɪn] *n.* монéта; **spin, toss a ~** подки́|дывать, -нуть монéтку.
v.t. чекáнить (*impf.*) (*монеты*); **~ a phrase** созд|авáть, -áть выражéние.
cpds. **~-box** *n.* монéтник (*автомата*); телефóн-автомáт; **~-operated** *adj.* монéтный.
coinage ['kɔɪnɪdʒ] *n.* **1.** (*monetary system*) монéтная систéма; **decimal ~** десяти́чная дéнежная систéма. **2.** (*inventing*) создáние (слов). **3.** (*coined word*) неологи́зм.
coincide [ˌkəʊɪn'saɪd] *v.i.* (*also math.*) совп|адáть, -áсть.
coincidence [kəʊ'ɪnsɪd(ə)ns] *n.* **1.** (*fact of coinciding*) совпадéние. **2.** (*curious chance*) совпадéние, стечéние обстоя́тельств.
coincidental [kəʊˌɪnsɪ'dent(ə)l] *adj.* случáйный.
coit|ion [kəʊ'ɪʃ(ə)n], **-us** ['kəʊɪtəs] *nn.* совокуплéние, кóитус.
Coke[1] [kəʊk] *n.* (*propr.*) «Кóка-кóла», «Кок».
coke[2] [kəʊk] *n.* кокс; **~ oven** кóксовая/коксовáльная печь.
v.t. коксовáть (*impf.*); **coking coal** коксýющийся ýголь.
Col. ['kɜ:n(ə)l] *n.* (*abbr. of* **Colonel**) полк., (полкóвник).
colander ['kʌləndə(r)] *n.* дуршлáг.
cold [kəʊld] *n.* **1.** хóлод; **he was left out in the ~** (*fig.*) егó поки́нули. **2.** (*illness*) простýда; **catch (a) ~** просту|жáться, -ди́ться; схвати́ть (*pf.*) нáсморк; **~ in the head** нáсморк; **~ in the chest** простýда.
adj. **1.** (*at low temperature*) холóдный; **I am, feel ~** мне хóлодно. **2.** (*fig.*): **throw ~ water on s.o.'s plan** окати́ть ушáтом холóдной воды́ когó-н.; **in ~ blood** хладнокрóвно; **~ steel** холóдное орýжие; **get ~ feet** (*fig., coll.*) струсить (*pf.*). **3.** (*unemotional, unfeeling*): **a ~ person** холóдный человéк; **~ facts** гóлые фáкты; **~ comfort** слáбое утешéние; **the idea leaves me ~** э́та мысль не волнýет меня́. **4.** (*of scent*) осты́вший.
cpds. **~-blooded** *adj.* (*of animal*) холоднокрóвный; (*fig.*) бесчýвственный, безжáлостный; **~-hearted** *adj.* бессердéчный; **~-shoulder** *v.t.* окáз|ывать, -áть комý-н. холóдный приём.
coldness ['kəʊldnɪs] *n.* (*of temperature*) хóлод; (*of character etc.*) хóлодность.
coleslaw ['kəʊlslɔ:] *n.* капýстный салáт.
colic ['kɒlɪk] *n.* кóлик|и (*pl., g.* —).
colitis [kə'laɪtɪs] *n.* коли́т.
collaborate [kə'læbəˌreɪt] *v.i.* сотрýдничать (*impf.*).
collaboration [kəˌlæbə'reɪʃ(ə)n] *n.* сотрýдничество.
collaborator [kə'læbəˌreɪtə(r)] *n.* сотрýдник; (*hist.*) коллаборациони́ст.
collage ['kɒlɑ:ʒ, kə'lɑ:ʒ] *n.* коллáж.
collapse [kə'læps] *n.* (*of a building etc.*) обвáл, падéние, обрушéние; (*of hopes etc.*) крушéние; (*of

resistance etc.) разва́л, крах; (*med.*) колла́пс, изнеможе́ние; **nervous ~** не́рвное истоще́ние.

v.t. (*e.g. a telescope*) скла́дывать, сложи́ть.

v.i. (*of a building etc.*) обва́л|иваться, -и́ться; ру́хнуть (*pf.*); (*of pers.*) свали́ться (*pf.*); **the house ~d** дом ру́хнул/обвали́лся; **this table ~s** (*folds up*) э́тот стол скла́дывается; **the plan ~d** план ру́хнул.

collapsible [kə'læpsɪb(ə)l] *adj.* складно́й, разбо́рный.

collar ['kɒlə(r)] *n.* **1.** (*part of a garment*) воротни́к; (*detachable*) воротничо́к; **hot under the ~** (*fig., excited, vexed*) рассе́рженный, рассвирипе́вший. **2.** (*of dog*) оше́йник; (*of horse*) хому́т.

v.t. (*seize*) схва́т|ывать, -и́ть за во́рот/ши́ворот.

cpd. **~-bone** *n.* (*anat.*) ключи́ца.

collateral [kə'lætər(ə)l] *adj.* побо́чный, дополни́тельный; **~ security** дополни́тельное обеспе́чение.

colleague ['kɒli:g] *n.* колле́га (*c.g.*); сослужи́в|ец (*fem.* -ица).

collect [kə'lekt] *v.t.* **1.** (*gather together*) соб|ира́ть, -ра́ть; **~ed works** (по́лное) собра́ние сочине́ний. **2.** (*of debts, taxes*) соб|ира́ть, -ра́ть; получ|а́ть, -и́ть. **3.** (*of stamps etc.*) коллекциони́ровать (*impf.*). **4.** (*fetch*) заб|ира́ть, -ра́ть; за|ходи́ть, -йти́ за +*i.*; **he ~ed the children from school** он забра́л дете́й из шко́лы. **5.** (*keep in hand*): **~ o.s.** брать, взять себя́ в ру́ки; **~ one's thoughts** собра́ться (*pf.*) с мы́слями.

v.i. соб|ира́ться, -ра́ться; **a crowd ~ed** собрала́сь толпа́; **dust ~s** пыль ска́пливается.

collected [kə'lektɪd] *adj.* (*calm*) со́бранный; споко́йный.

collection [kə'lekʃ(ə)n] *n.* (*of valuables etc.*) колле́кция; (*accumulation*) скопле́ние; (*church etc.*) сбор, собира́ние; (*of mail*) вы́емка.

collective [kə'lektɪv] *n.* (*co-operative unit*) коллекти́в.

adj. коллекти́вный; **~ farm** колхо́з; **~ farmer** колхо́зни|к (*fem.* -ца); (*gram.*): **~ noun** собира́тельное существи́тельное.

collectivism [kə'lektɪ,vɪz(ə)m] *n.* коллективи́зм.

collectivization [kə,lektɪvaɪ'zeɪʃ(ə)n] *n.* коллективиза́ция.

collectivize [kə'lektɪ,vaɪz] *v.t.* коллективизи́ровать (*impf., pf.*).

collector [kə'lektə(r)] *n.* (*of stamps etc.*) коллекционе́р; (*of taxes, debts*) сбо́рщик; (*of tickets*) контролёр.

college ['kɒlɪdʒ] *n.* **1.** (*school*) колле́дж. **2.** (*university*) университе́т; институ́т; вуз; **a ~ education** университе́тское образова́ние. **3.** (*within university*) университе́тский колле́дж. **4.** (*body of colleagues*) колле́гия.

collegiate [kə'li:dʒət] *adj.* **1.** (*of college*) университе́тский. **2.** (*of collegium*) коллегиа́льный. **3.** (*of students*) студе́нческий.

collegium [kə'li:dʒɪəm] *n.* колле́гия.

collide [kə'laɪd] *v.i.* ст|а́лкиваться, -олкну́ться.

collie ['kɒlɪ] *n.* ко́лли (*m. indecl.*), шотла́ндская овча́рка.

colliery ['kɒlɪərɪ] *n.* каменноуго́льная ша́хта.

collision [kə'lɪʒ(ə)n] *n.* столкнове́ние; **come into ~ with** столкну́ться (*pf.*) с+*i.*; **~ course** пу́ть, на кото́ром неизбе́жно столкнове́ние.

collodion [kə'ləʊdɪən] *n.* колло́дий.

colloquial [kə'ləʊkwɪəl] *adj.* разгово́рный.

colloquialism [kə'ləʊkwɪə,lɪz(ə)m] *n.* разгово́рное выраже́ние/сло́во.

collusion [kə'lu:ʒ(ə)n, -'lju:ʒ(ə)n] *n.* сго́вор; **act in ~** де́йствовать (*impf.*) по сго́вору.

Colombia [kə'lɒmbɪə] *n.* Колу́мбия.

colon[1] ['kəʊlən, -lɒn] *n.* (*anat.*) ободо́чная кишка́.

colon[2] ['kəʊlən, -lɒn] *n.* (*gram.*) двоето́чие.

colonel ['kɜ:n(ə)l] *n.* полко́вник.

cpds. **~-general** *n.* генера́л-полко́вник; **~-in-chief** *n.* шеф полка́.

colonial [kə'ləʊnɪəl] *n.* жи́тель (*fem.* -ница) коло́нии.

adj. колониа́льный.

colonialism [kə'ləʊnɪə,lɪz(ə)m] *n.* колониали́зм.

colonialist [kə'ləʊnɪəlɪst] *n.* колониали́ст.

colonist ['kɒlənɪst] *n.* колони́ст (*fem.* -ка); (*settler*) поселе́нец.

colonization ['kɒlə,naɪ'zeɪʃ(ə)n] *n.* колониза́ция.

colonize ['kɒlə,naɪz] *v.t.* колонизи́ровать (*impf., pf.*); (*settle in*) засел|я́ть, -и́ть.

colonizer ['kɒlə,naɪzə(r)] *n.* колониза́тор.

colonnade [,kɒlə'neɪd] *n.* колонна́да.

colony ['kɒlənɪ] *n.* коло́ния.

coloration [,kʌlə'reɪʃ(ə)n] *n.* (*putting on colour*) окра́шивание; (*varied colour*) окра́ска, раскра́ска.

colossal [kə'lɒs(ə)l] *adj.* колосса́льный, грома́дный.

colossus [kə'lɒsəs] *n.* коло́сс.

colour ['kʌlə(r)] *n.* **1.** (*lit.*) цвет; (*of horses*) масть; **primary ~s** основны́е цвета́; **secondary ~s** составны́е цвета́; **complementary ~s** дополни́тельные цвета́; **change ~** (*lit.*) меня́ть (*impf.*) цвет; **the film is in ~** э́то цветно́й фильм; **what ~ are his eyes?** како́го цве́та у него́ глаза́?; **~ code** цветово́й код; **~ scheme** подбо́р цвето́в; **~ television** цветно́е телеви́дение; (*pl., of team*) фо́рма; **what are their ~s?** в како́й фо́рме они́ игра́ют? **2.** (*of face*) цвет лица́; румя́нец; **she has very little ~** у неё бле́дное лицо́; **off ~** (*out of sorts*) не в фо́рме. **3.** (*pl., paints*) кра́ски; **water ~s** акваре́ль; **oil ~s** ма́сляные кра́ски; **paint sth. in bright ~s** (*fig.*) рисова́ть, на- что-н. я́ркими кра́сками; **see sth. in its true ~s** (*fig.*) ви́деть (*impf.*) что-н. в и́стинном све́те. **4.** (*semblance, probability*): **this fact lent ~ to his tale** э́тот факт прида́л не́которое правдоподо́бие его́ расска́зу; **he gave a false ~ to the news** он предста́вил но́вость в ло́жном све́те. **5.** (*liveliness*): **local ~** ме́стный колори́т. **6.** (*pl., flag; also fig.*): **he spent 5 years with the ~s** он прослужи́л 5 лет в а́рмии; **pass an examination with flying ~s** сдать (*pf.*) экза́мен с бле́ском; **show one's true ~s** предста́ть (*pf.*) в и́стинном све́те.

v.t. **1.** (*paint, endow with ~*) кра́сить (*impf.*); окра́|шивать, -сить. **2.** (*embellish*) приукра́|шивать, -сить. **3.** (*imbue*): **his action was ~ed by vengefulness** его́ посту́пок был отча́сти продикто́ван мсти́тельностью. *See also* **coloured**

v.i. **1.** (*take on ~*): **the leaves ~ in autumn** о́сенью ли́стья меня́ют свой цвет. **2.** (*blush*) красне́ть, по-.

cpds. **~-bar** *n.* цветно́й барье́р; **~-blind** *adj.* страда́ющий дальтони́змом; **~-blind person** не различа́ющий цвето́в, дальто́ник; **~-blindness** *n.* неспосо́бность различа́ть цвета́, дальтони́зм; **~-fast** *adj.* цветосто́йкий; **~-printing** *n.* хромоти́пия, многокра́сочная печа́ть.

coloured ['kʌləd] *adj.* цветно́й; (*of race*): **~ people** цветны́е (*pl.*).

colourful ['kʌlə,fʊl] *adj.* кра́сочный, я́ркий; **a ~ personality** я́ркая/колори́тная ли́чность.

colouring ['kʌlərɪŋ] *n.* окра́ска; (*complexion*) цвет лица́; **~ book** (*for children*) альбо́м для раскра́шивания.

adj. кра́сящий; **~ matter** кра́сящее вещество́.

colourless ['kʌləlɪs] *adj.* (*lit., fig.*) бесцве́тный.

colt [kəʊlt] *n.* жеребёнок.

column ['kɒləm] *n.* **1.** (*pillar*) коло́нна. **2.** (*vertical object or mass*) столб; **~ of smoke** столб ды́ма; **spinal ~** позвоно́чный столб; **mercury ~** рту́тный сто́лбик. **3.** (*in book etc.*) столбе́ц. **4.** (*regular feature in newspaper*): **weekly ~** еженеде́льная коло́нка. **5.** (*of figures*) столбе́ц, коло́нка. **6.** (*mil. etc.*) коло́нна; **close ~** со́мкнутая коло́нна; **fifth ~** (*fig.*) пя́тая коло́нна.

columnist ['kɒləmɪst] *n.* обозрева́тель (*fem.* -ница).

coma ['kəʊmə] *n.* кóма.

comatose ['kəʊmə,təʊz] *adj.* коматóзный; **he is ~** он в кóме.

comb [kəʊm] *n.* **1.** (*for ~ing hair*) расчёска, гребёнка, гребешóк; (*as adornment*) грéбень (*m.*). **2.** (*of bird*) гребешóк, грéбень (*m.*).

v.t. **1.** (*hair etc.*) чесáть (*impf.*); расчёс|ывать, -áть; причёс|ывать, -áть; (*wool, flax etc.*) чесáть (*impf.*). **2.** (*fig., search*) причёс|ывать, -áть.

combat ['kɒmbæt, 'kʌm-] *n.* бой; **single ~** единобóрство, поеди́нок; (*mil.*): **~ fatigue** боевáя психи́ческая трáвма; **~ zone** зóна боевы́х дéйствий.

v.t. борóться (*impf.*) с+*i.* (*or* прóтив+*g.*).

v.i. борóться; сражáться (*both impf.*).

combatant ['kɒmbət(ə)nt, 'kʌm-] *n.* боéц; вою́ющая сторонá.

adj. бóрющийся; сражáющийся.

combative ['kɒmbɪnətɪv, 'kʌm-] *adj.* боевóй, задиристый.

combination [,kɒmbɪ'neɪʃ(ə)n] *n.* **1.** (*combining*) сочетáние, комбинáция; **in ~ with** в сочетáнии с+*i.* **2.** (*of a safe*) кóдовая комбинáция; **~ lock** секрéтный замóк.

combine[1] ['kɒmbaɪn] *n.* **1.** (*group of concerns*) комбинáт, синдикáт. **2.** (**~ harvester**) комбáйн.

combine[2] [kəm'baɪn] *v.t.* сочетáть (*impf.*); объедин|я́ть, -и́ть; комбини́ровать, с-; **~ forces** соедин|я́ть, -и́ть си́лы; **he ~s business with pleasure** он сочетáет приятное с полéзным; **~d operations** (*mil.*) общевойсковáя оперáция.

combustible [kəm'bʌstɪb(ə)l] *adj.* горю́чий.

combustion [kəm'bʌstʃ(ə)n] *n.* воспламенéние; сгорáние; **spontaneous ~** самовоспламенéние; **internal ~ engine** двигатель внýтреннего сгорáния.

come [kʌm] *v.i.* **1.** (*move near, arrive*) при|ходи́ть, -йти́; приб|ывáть, -ы́ть; при|езжáть, -éхать; **~ and see us!** приходи́те/заходи́те к нам!; **he came running** он прибежáл; **he has ~ a hundred miles** он приéхал за сто миль; **he came near to falling** он чуть не упáл; **~ along!** пойдёмте!; **~ into the house!** заходи́те/зайди́те в дом! **2.** (*of inanimate things; lit., fig.*): **the dress ~s to her knees** плáтье дохóдит ей до колéн; **the sunshine came streaming into the room** лучи́ сóлнца лили́сь в кóмнату; **a parcel has ~** полýчена посы́лка; **the feeling ~s and goes** э́то чýвство то появля́ется, то исчезáет; **these shirts ~ in three sizes** э́ти рубáшки бывáют трёх размéров; **it came as a shock to me** э́то бы́ло для меня́ удáром; **it came into my head** э́то пришлó мне в гóлову; **the water came to the boil** водá закипéла; **the solution came to me** я (вдруг) нашёл решéние; **what are we coming to?** до чегó мы дóжили?; **she takes things as they ~** онá спокóйно относи́тся ко всемý, что бы ни случи́лось. **3.** (*fig. uses with 'to': see also relevant nn.*): **~ to a decision** прийти́ (*pf.*) к решéнию; **~ to blows** дойти́ (*pf.*) до рукопáшной; **~ to terms** прийти́ (*pf.*) к соглашéнию; **~ to light** обнарýжиться (*pf.*); **~ to one's senses** образýмиться (*pf.*). **4.** (*fig. uses with 'into': see also relevant nn.*): **he has ~ into a fortune** он получи́л большóе наслéдство; **he came into his own** он доби́лся признáния/своегó; **they came into sight** они́ появи́лись; **the party came into power** пáртия пришлá к влáсти. **5.** (*occur, happen*) случáться, бывáть (*both impf.*); **Christmas ~s once a year** Рождествó бывáет раз в годý; **who ~s next?** кто слéдующий; **no harm will ~ to you** с вáми ничегó не случи́тся; **he had it coming to him** емý слéдовало э́того ожидáть; **how ~ he was late?** как э́то получи́лось, что он опоздáл?; **how did you ~ to meet him?** как случи́лось, что вы с ним встрéтились?; **no good will ~ of it** ничегó хорóшего из э́того не вы́йдет; **in years to ~** в послéдующие гóды; **~ what may** будь что бýдет; **how ~?** (*US, sl.*) э́то почемý же?; как так? **6.** (*amount, result*): **the bill ~s to £5** счёт составля́ет 5 фýнтов; **it ~s to this, that ...** дéло свóдится к томý, что...; **it ~s to the same thing** получáется то же сáмое; **if it ~s to that** éсли уж на то пошлó; **his plans came to nothing** из егó плáнов ничегó не вы́шло. **7.** (*become, prove to be*): **his dreams came true** егó мечты́ осуществи́лись/сбыли́сь; **it ~s naturally to him** емý э́то легкó даётся; **it all came right in the end** всё кóнчилось благополýчно; **~ clean** (*sl., confess*) вы́ложить (*pf.*) всё. **8.** (*fig., find o.s. in a position*): **I have ~ to see that he is right** я убеди́лся, что он прав. **9.** (*of pers., originate*) прои|сходи́ть, -зойти́; **he ~s from Scotland** он урожéнец Шотлáндии. **10.** (*coll. uses*): **it will be 5 years ago ~ Christmas that ...** на Рождествó бýдет пять лет с тех пор, как...; **~ off it** (*desist*)! кончáй!; перестáнь! **11.** (*imper., fig.*): **~, ~!** (*expostulatory*) ну! ну!; ну, что вы!

with preps. (*see also* **3.** *and* **4.** *above*): **~ across** (*traverse*) пере|ходи́ть, -йти́ чéрез+*a.*; (*encounter*) нат|áлкиваться, -олкнýться на+*a.*; **~ after** (*follow*) слéдовать (*impf.*) за+*i.*; **~ at** (*reach*): **the truth is hard to ~ at** до прáвды трýдно добрáться; (*attack*): **the dog came at me** собáка набрóсилась на меня́; **~ before** (*appear before*): **he came before the court** он предстáл пéред судóм; **~ by** (*obtain*) дост|авáть, -áть; **~ for** (*attack*): **he came for us with a stick** он набрóсился на нас с пáлкой; **~ from: wine ~s from grapes** винó получáется из виногрáда; **~ into: he came into a large estate** емý достáлось большóе имéние; **~ off** (*lit.*): **~ off the grass!** сойди́те с травы́; (*become detached from*): **a button came off my coat** от моегó пальтó оторвалáсь пýговица; (*fall off*): **she came off her bicycle** онá упáла с велосипéда; **~ out of** (*lit.*): **he came out of the house** он вы́шел и́з дому; **~ over** (*fig.*): **what came over you?** что на вас нашлó?; **~ round: he came round the corner** он повернýл зá угол; **~ through: he came through both wars** он прошёл óбе войны́; **~ under: what heading does this ~ under?** к какóй рýбрике э́то относи́тся; **he came under her influence** он попáл под её влия́ние; **~ upon** (*find*) напáсть (*pf.*) на+*a.*

with advs.: **~ about** *v.i.* (*happen*) прои|сходи́ть, -зойти́; **~ again** *v.i.*: **~ again?** (*coll., what did you say?*) нý-ка повтори́!; скажи́ снóва!; **~ apart** *v.i.* (*unfastened*) ра|сходи́ться, -зойти́сь; развáл|иваться, -и́ться на чáсти; **~ away** *v.i.* (*become detached*) отл|áмываться, -оми́ться (*om+g.*); **~ back** *v.i.* (*return*) возвра|щáться, -ти́ться; вернýться (*pf.*); **his name came back to me** я вспóмнил егó и́мя; **~ by** *v.i.* (*pass by*) миновáть (*impf., pf.*); про|ходи́ть, -йти́ ми́мо; **~ down** *v.i.*: **he came down off the ladder** он сошёл с лéстницы; **her hair ~s down to her waist** у неё вóлосы дохóдят до пóяса; (*of prices*) пáдать, упáсть; (*fig.*): **he has ~ down in the world** он опусти́лся; **the story has ~ down to us** до нас дошлá э́та истóрия; **he came down with influenza** он слёг с гри́ппом; **~ forward** *v.i.* (*offer one's services*) предл|агáть, -ожи́ть свои́ услýги; **~ in** *v.i.* (*lit.*) входи́ть, войти́; **~ in!** (*to s.o. knocking*) войди́те!; **the tide came in** наступи́л прили́в; **short skirts came in** корóткие ю́бки вошли́ в мóду; **the Conservatives came in** консервáторы победи́ли на вы́борах; **information came in** поступи́ли свéдения; **where do I ~ in?** какóе э́то имéет ко мне отношéние?; **it came in handy** э́то пригоди́лось; **~ off** *v.i.* (*become detached*) отвáл|иваться, -и́ться; (*happen, succeed*): **the marriage came off** брак состоя́лся; **the experiment came off** óпыт удáлся; **he came off best** он вы́шел победи́телем; (**~** *off duty*): **he ~s off at 10** он ухóдит со слýжбы в 10; **~**

on *v.i.* (*follow*) следовать (*impf.*); **he came on later** он появился позднее; ~ **on!** (*impatient*) ну!; ~ **on! I'll race you** давайте побежим наперегонки!; (*progress*) делать (*impf.*) успехи; **the garden is coming on well** всё в саду хорошо растёт; (*start, set in*): **it came on to rain** начался дождь; **I have a cold coming on** у меня начинается простуда; (*of actor; appear*) появ|ляться, -иться; (*of play; be performed*): **the play ~s on next week** пьеса будет представлена на следующей неделе; ~ **out** *v.i.* (*lit.*) выходить, выйти; **the sun came out** солнце появилось; **the flowers came out** цветы распустились; (*become known, appear*): **the news came out** новость стала известной; **the paper ~s out on Thursday** эта газета выходит по четвергам; **he came out well in the photograph** он хорошо вышел на фотографии; (*disappear*): **the stains came out** пятна сошли; **the colour came out** (*faded*) краска выцвела; (*of results*): **the sum came out** задача получилась; **he came out first in the exam** он был лучшим на этом экзамене; (*declare o.s.*): **he came out against the plan** он выступил против плана; **the total came out at 700** общий итог оказался равным 700; (*go on strike*) выходить, выйти на забастовку; **he came out with the truth** он рассказал всю правду; **she came out in a rash** она покрылась сыпью; ~ **over** *v.i.*: **they came over to England** они приехали в Англию; **he came over to our side** он перешёл на нашу сторону; **he came over dizzy** (*coll.*) у него закружилась голова; ~ **round** *v.i.* (*make trip*): ~ **round and see us!** заходите к нам!; (*recur*): **Christmas will soon ~ round** скоро (наступит) Рождество; (*yield*): **she'll ~ round** она согласится; (*recover consciousness*) прийти (*pf.*) в себя; ~ **through** *v.i.* (*survive experience*) пережить (*pf.*); (*teleph.*): **the call came through at 3 o'clock** разговор состоялся в 3 часа; ~ **to** *v.i.* (*recover one's senses*) прийти (*pf.*) в себя; очнуться (*pf.*); ~ **up** *v.i.*: **the sun came up** солнце взошло; **he came up to me** он подошёл ко мне; **the water came up to my waist** вода доходила мне до пояса; **the question came up** встал вопрос; **the book came up to my expectations** книга оправдала мои ожидания; **he came up against a difficulty** он натолкнулся на трудности; **he came up with a suggestion** он внёс предложение.

cpds. **~back** *n.* (*return*) возвращение; **~-down** *n.* унижение; **~-hither** *adj.* (*coll.*): **a ~-hither look** завлекающий взгляд; **~-uppance** *n.* (*coll.*): **he got his ~-uppance** он получил по заслугам.

comedian [kə'mi:dıən] *n.* комик.

comedienne [kə,mi:dı'en] *n.* комическая актриса.

comedy ['kɒmıdı] *n.* комедия.

comely ['kʌmlı] *adj.* миловидный.

comet ['kɒmıt] *n.* комета.

comfort ['kʌmfət] *n.* **1.** (*physical ease*) комфорт; удобства (*nt. pl.*). **2.** (*relief of suffering*) утешение, отрада; **cold ~** слабое утешение. **3.** (*thg. that brings ~*) утешение, успокоение.

v.t. утешать, -ешить; успок|аивать, -оить.

comfortabl|e ['kʌmftəb(ə)l, -fətəb(ə)l] *adj.* удобный, комфортабельный; **I am ~e here** мне здесь удобно; **the car holds six people ~y** эта машина свободно вмещает шесть человек; **he makes a ~e living** он прилично зарабатывает; **he is ~y off** он живёт в достатке.

comforter ['kʌmfətə(r)] *n.* **1.** (*pers.*) утешитель. **2.** (*teat*) соска, пустышка.

comforting ['kʌmfətıŋ] *adj.* утешительный, успокоительный.

comic ['kɒmık] *n.* **1.** (*coll., comedian*) комик, юморист. **2.** (*pl., ~ papers*) комиксы (*m. pl.*).

adj. комический, юмористический; **~ book** книжка комиксов; **~ strip** комикс.

comical ['kɒmık(ə)l] *adj.* комичный, смешной.

coming ['kʌmıŋ] *n.* приезд, приход; **the Second C~** второе пришествие (Христа).

adj. будущий, наступающий; **the ~ week** будущая неделя.

comma ['kɒmə] *n.* запятая; **inverted ~s** кавыч|ки (*pl., g.* -ек).

command [kə'mɑ:nd] *n.* **1.** (*order*) команда; **at the word of ~** по команде. **2.** (*authority*) командование; **he is in ~ of the army** он командует армией. **3.** (*control*) контроль (*m.*); **~ of the air** господство в воздухе; **~ of one's emotions** владение своими чувствами. **4.** (*knowledge, ability to use*): **she has a good ~ of French** она хорошо владеет французским языком. **5.** (*mil.*) командование; **High C~** верховное командование; (*attr.*) командный; **~ post** командный пункт.

v.t. & i. **1.** (*give orders to*) приказ|ывать, -ать +*d.* **2.** (*have authority over*) командовать (*impf.*) +*i.* **3.** (*be able to use or enjoy*) располагать (*impf.*) +*i.*; **he ~s respect** он внушает к себе уважение. **4.** (*of things*): **this article ~s a high price** этот товар продаётся по высокой цене; **the window ~s a fine view** из окна открывается прекрасный вид.

commandant [,kɒmən'dænt, 'kɒm-] *n.* комендант.

commandeer [,kɒmən'dıə(r)] *v.t.* реквизировать (*impf., pf.*).

commander [kə'mɑ:ndə(r)] *n.* командир, командующий; **C~-in-Chief** главнокомандующий; (*naval rank*) капитан третьего ранга.

commanding [kə'mɑ:ndıŋ] *adj.* (*in command*) командующий; **~ officer** командир; **a ~ tone** повелительный тон; **~ heights** командные высоты.

commandment [kə'mɑ:ndmənt] *n.*: **the Ten C~s** десять заповедей.

commando [kə'mɑ:ndəʊ] *n.* (*force*) десантно-диверсионный отряд; (*pers.*) солдат десантно-диверсионного отряда.

commemorate [kə'memə,reıt] *v.t.* (*celebrate memory of*) отм|ечать, -етить память +*g.*; ознаменовать (*pf.*); (*be in memory of*): **this monument ~s the victory** этот памятник воздвигнут в честь победы.

commemoration [kə,memə'reıʃ(ə)n] *n.* ознаменование памяти (*кого/чего*).

commemorative [kə'memərətıv] *adj.* памятный, мемориальный.

commence [kə'mens] *v.t. & i.* нач|инать(ся), -ать(ся).

commencement [kə'mensmənt] *n.* начало; (*acad.*) торжественное вручение дипломов.

commend [kə'mend] *v.t.* **1.** (*praise*) хвалить, по-. **2.** (*recommend*) рекомендовать (*impf., pf.*).

commendable [kə'mendəb(ə)l] *adj.* похвальный.

commendation [,kɒmen'deıʃ(ə)n] *n.* похвала, рекомендация.

commensura|ble [kə'menʃərəb(ə)l, -sjərəb(ə)l], **-te** [kə'menʃərət, -sjərət] *adjs.* соизмеримый.

comment ['kɒment] *n.* замечание, комментарий; отзыв, отклик.

v.t. & i. комментировать (*impf., pf.*); делать, с- замечания.

commentary ['kɒməntərı] *n.* комментарий.

commentator ['kɒmən,teıtə(r)] *n.* (*textual*) комментатор; (*radio etc.*) комментатор, обозреватель (*m.*).

commerce ['kɒmɜ:s] *n.* коммерция, торговля.

commercial [kə'mɜ:ʃ(ə)l] *n.* (*coll., TV advertisement*) рекламная передача.

adj. коммерческий, торговый; **~ traveller** коммивояжёр; **~ vehicle** грузовая машина.

commercialism [kə'mɜ:ʃ(ə),lız(ə)m] *n.* стремление к прибыли.

commercialize [kə'mɜ:ʃə,laız] *n.* ставить, по- на коммерческую ногу; вн|осить, -ести коммерческий дух в+*a.*

commiserate [kəˈmɪzəˌreɪt] *v.i.* (*feel sympathy*) сочу́вствовать (*impf.*) (*кому*); (*express sympathy*) выража́ть, вы́разить соболе́знование (*кому*).

commiseration [kəˌmɪzəˈreɪʃ(ə)n] *n.* сочу́вствие, соболе́знование.

commissar [ˈkɒmɪˌsɑ:(r)] *n.* комисса́р.

commissariat [ˌkɒmɪˈseərɪət, -ˈsærɪˌæt] *n.* **1.** (*office of commissar*) комиссариа́т. **2.** (*mil.*) интенда́нтство.

commissary [ˈkɒmɪsərɪ, kəˈmɪs-] *n.* (*US, mil. store*) вое́нный магази́н.

commission [kəˈmɪʃ(ə)n] *n.* **1.** (*authorization*) полномо́чие. **2.** (*errand*) поруче́ние. **3.** (*action*) соверше́ние. **4.** (*reward*) комиссио́нн|ые (*pl.*, *g.* -ых); **he sells goods on ~** он продаёт това́ры за комиссио́нное вознагражде́ние. **5.** (*officer's*) пате́нт на офице́рский чин. **6.** (*official body*) комиссариа́т; **high ~** верхо́вный комиссариа́т. **7.: in ~** (*fit for action*) в испра́вности; **out of ~** (*out of working order*) в неиспра́вности.

v.t. поруч|а́ть, -и́ть (*что кому*); **he ~ed me to buy this** он поручи́л мне купи́ть э́то; **he ~ed a portrait from the artist** он заказа́л худо́жнику портре́т; **the ship was ~ed** кора́бль был введён в строй; **a ~ed officer** офице́р; **he was ~ed from the ranks** он был произведён в офице́ры из рядовы́х.

commissionaire [kəˌmɪʃəˈneə(r)] *n.* швейца́р.

commissioner [kəˈmɪʃənə(r)] *n.* комисса́р; **high ~** верхо́вный комисса́р.

commit [kəˈmɪt] *v.t.* **1.** (*perform*) соверш|а́ть, -и́ть. **2.** (*entrust, consign*): **~ s.o. for trial** пред|ава́ть, -а́ть кого́-н. суду́; **~ to paper** изл|ага́ть, -ожи́ть на бума́ге; **~ to memory** зау́ч|ивать, -и́ть. **3.** (*engage*): **he ~ted himself to helping her** он взя́лся помо́чь ей; **he would not ~ himself** он уклони́лся от чёткого отве́та. **4.: ~ troops to battle** вв|оди́ть, -ести́ войска́ в бой. **5.: a ~ted writer** иде́йный писа́тель.

commitment [kəˈmɪtmənt] *n.* (*obligation*) обяза́тельство; **~ to a cause** пре́данность де́лу.

committal [kəˈmɪt(ə)l] *n.*: **~ for trial** преда́ние суду́.

committee[1] [kəˈmɪtɪ] *n.* (*body of persons*) комите́т, коми́ссия.

commode [kəˈməʊd] *n.* (*chest of drawers*) комо́д; (*for chamber-pot*) стульча́к для ночно́го горшка́.

commodious [kəˈməʊdɪəs] *adj.* просто́рный.

commodity [kəˈmɒdɪtɪ] *n.* това́р, предме́т потребле́ния; (*attr.*) това́рный.

commodore [ˈkɒməˌdɔ:(r)] *n.* (*in navy or merchant marine*) коммодо́р, капита́н пе́рвого ра́нга; (*of yacht club*) командо́р.

common [ˈkɒmən] *n.* **1.** (*land*) пусты́рь (*m.*), вы́гон. **2.** (*sth. usual or shared*): **they have some tastes in ~** у них есть о́бщие вку́сы.

adj. **1.** (*belonging to more than one, general*) о́бщий; **it is ~ ground between us that ...** мы согла́сны в том, что...; **it is ~ knowledge that ...** общеизве́стно, что... **2.** (*belonging to the public or a specific group*): **~ law** о́бщее/обы́чное/некодифици́рованное пра́во. **3.** (*ordinary, usual*) обы́чный, обыкнове́нный; **the ~ people** (просто́й) наро́д; **~ sense** здра́вый смысл; **~ or garden** (*coll.*) обыкнове́нный. **4.** (*vulgar*) вульга́рный, по́шлый. **5.** (*gram.*): **~ gender** о́бщий род.

cpds. **~-law** *adj.*: **~-law marriage** незарегистри́рованный брак; **~-law wife** сожи́тельница; **~place** *n.* бана́льность; *adj.* бана́льный; **~-room** *n.* (*senior*) учи́тельская, профе́ссорская; (*junior*) студе́нческая ко́мната о́тдыха; **~-sense** *adj.* здра́вый, разу́мный.

commoner [ˈkɒmənə(r)] *n.* недворяни́н, челове́к незна́тного происхожде́ния.

commonly [ˈkɒmənlɪ] *adv.* (*usually*) обы́чно, обыкнове́нно.

commons [ˈkɒmənz] *n.* (*common people*) простонаро́дье; **(House of) C~** пала́та о́бщин.

commonwealth [ˈkɒmənˌwelθ] *n.*: **the British C~** брита́нское Содру́жество (на́ций); **C~ of Independent States** Содру́жество незави́симых госуда́рств.

commotion [kəˈməʊʃ(ə)n] *n.* волне́ние, возня́.

communal [ˈkɒmjʊn(ə)l] *adj.* обще́ственный, коммуна́льный.

commune[1] [ˈkɒmju:n] *n.* (*administrative unit*) общи́на, комму́на; (*Russ. hist., peasant ~*) мир.

commune[2] [ˈkɒmju:n] *v.i.* обща́ться (*impf.*) (с+*i.*); быть в те́сном обще́нии (с+*i.*); **~ with nature** обща́ться с приро́дой.

communicable [kəˈmju:nɪkəb(ə)l] *adj.* передаю́щийся; **a ~ disease** зара́зная боле́знь.

communicate [kəˈmju:nɪˌkeɪt] *v.t.* сообщ|а́ть, -и́ть; (*a disease, also*) перед|ава́ть, -а́ть.

v.i. свя́з|ываться, -а́ться; сообщ|а́ть, -и́ть (*кому о чём*); **~ with s.o.** сн|оси́ться, -ести́сь с кем-н.

communication [kəˌmju:nɪˈkeɪʃ(ə)n] *n.* **1.** (*act of communicating*) обще́ние; связь, сообще́ние, коммуника́ция; **get into ~ with s.o.** установи́ть (*pf.*) связь с кем-н.; **lack of ~** (*understanding*) отсу́тствие взаимопонима́ния. **2.** (*message*) сообще́ние. **3.** (*means of ~*) сре́дства свя́зи/сообще́ния; (*pl.*: *roads, railways etc.*) пути́ (*m. pl.*) сообще́ния. **4.** (*mil.*): **lines of ~** коммуника́ции.

communicative [kəˈmju:nɪkətɪv] *adj.* общи́тельный, разгово́рчивый.

communion [kəˈmju:nɪən] *n.* **1.** (*intercourse*) обще́ние; **~ with nature** обще́ние с приро́дой. **2.** (*sacrament*) прича́стие.

communiqué [kəˈmju:nɪˌkeɪ] *n.* (*indecl.*) коммюнике́.

communism [ˈkɒmjʊˌnɪz(ə)m] *n.* коммуни́зм.

communist [ˈkɒmjʊnɪst] *n.* коммуни́ст (*fem.* -ка).

adj. коммунисти́ческий.

community [kəˈmju:nɪtɪ] *n.* **1.** (*commonness; joint ownership*): **~ of interest** о́бщность интере́сов. **2.** (*society*) о́бщество. **3.** (*pol., social etc. group*) общи́на, гру́ппа населе́ния.

commutation [ˌkɒmju:ˈteɪʃ(ə)n] *n.* (*leg., of sentence*) смягче́ние (пригово́ра).

commute [kəˈmju:t] *v.t.* (*leg.*) смягч|а́ть, -и́ть (*приговор*).

v.i. (*travel to and fro*) соверша́ть (*impf.*) регуля́рные пое́здки из при́города в го́род.

commuter [kəˈmju:tə(r)] *n.* (*traveller*) регуля́рный пассажи́р (*человек, живущий за городом, который регулярно ездит в город на работу*).

compact[1] [ˈkɒmpækt] *n.* (*pact*) соглаше́ние, догово́р.

compact[2] [ˈkɒmpækt] *n.* (*cosmetic case*) пу́дреница.

compact[3] [kəmˈpækt] *adj.* (*closely packed*) компа́ктный; (*tense, concise*) сжа́тый, компа́ктный; **~ disk** компа́кт-ди́ск; **~ disk player** прои́грыватель компа́кт-ди́сков.

v.t. (*press together*) сж|има́ть, -ать; стис|кивать, -нуть; уплотн|я́ть, -и́ть.

companion [kəmˈpænjən] *n.* **1.** (*person who accompanies*): **my ~ on the journey** мой попу́тчик; **he is an excellent ~** с ним мо́жно отли́чно провести́ вре́мя. **2.** (*object matching another*) па́ра; (*attr.*) па́рный; **~ volume** сопроводи́тельный том. **3.** (*woman paid to keep another company*) компаньо́нка. **4.** (*handbook*) спра́вочник.

companionable [kəmˈpænjənəb(ə)l] *adj.* общи́тельный, (*coll.*) компане́йский.

companionship [kəmˈpænjənʃɪp] *n.* дру́жеское обще́ние; дру́жеские отноше́ния.

company [ˈkʌmpənɪ] *n.* **1.** (*companionship*): **I was glad of his ~** я был рад его́ о́бществу; **keep s.o. ~** сост|авля́ть, -а́вить кому́-н. компа́нию; **part ~** расста́ться (*pf.*); **we parted ~** на́ши пути́ разошли́сь; **in ~ with** совме́стно с+*i.*; **he is good ~** с ним не соску́чишься. **2.** (*associates, guests*): **we have ~ this**

evening у нас сего́дня бу́дут го́сти; **two's ~ (but three is none)** где дво́е, там тре́тий ли́шний. **3.** (*commercial firm*) това́рищество, компа́ния; **Jones and Company** Джо́унз и компа́ния; **~ car** служе́бная маши́на. **4.** (*theatr.*) тру́ппа. **5.** (*naut.*) кома́нда, экипа́ж. **6.** (*mil.*) ро́та.

comparable ['kɒmpərəb(ə)l] *adj.* сравни́мый.

comparative [kəm'pærətɪv] *adj.* **1.** (*proceeding by comparison*) сравни́тельный. **2.** (*relative*) относи́тельный; **he is a ~ newcomer** он сравни́тельно неда́вно при́был сюда́. **3.** (*gram.*) сравни́тельный.

compare [kəm'peə(r)] *n.* (*liter.*): **beyond ~** вне сравне́ния.

v.t. **1.** (*assess degree of similarity*) сра́вн|ивать, -и́ть; слич|а́ть, -и́ть; **~ notes with s.o.** обме́н|иваться, -я́ться впечатле́ниями с кем-н. **2.** (*assert similarity of*) сра́вн|ивать, -и́ть; **he is not to be ~d with his father** ему́ далеко́ до отца́.

v.i. сра́вн|иваться, -и́ться; **he ~s favourably with his predecessor** он вы́годно отлича́ется от своего́ предше́ственника; **he cannot ~ with her** его́ нельзя́ и сравни́ть с ней.

comparison [kəm'pærɪs(ə)n] *n.* сравне́ние; **make a ~** пров|оди́ть, -ести́ сравне́ние; **there is no ~ between them** их нельзя́ сра́внивать; **in, by ~ with** по сравне́нию с+*i.*

compartment [kəm'pɑːtmənt] *n.* (*railway*) купе́ (*indecl.*); (*of ship*) отсе́к.

compass ['kʌmpəs] *n.* **1.** (*mariner's*) ко́мпас; (*surveying ~*) буссо́ль; **points of the ~** стра́ны све́та. **2.** (*geom.*, *also* **pair of ~es**) ци́ркуль (*m.*).

compassion [kəm'pæʃ(ə)n] *n.* сострада́ние.

compassionate [kəm'pæʃənət] *adj.* сострада́тельный.

compatibility [kəm,pætə'bɪlɪtɪ] *n.* совмести́мость.

compatible [kəm'pætəb(ə)l] *adj.* совмести́мый.

compatriot [kəm'pætrɪət] *n.* сооте́чественник.

compel [kəm'pel] *v.t.* заст|авля́ть, -а́вить; прин|ужда́ть, -уди́ть.

compelling [kəm'pelɪŋ] *adj.* непреодоли́мый, неотрази́мый; (*fascinating*) захва́тывающий.

compendium [kəm'pendɪəm] *n.* компе́ндиум, конспе́кт.

compensate ['kɒmpen,seɪt] *v.t. & i.* компенси́ровать (*impf., pf.*) (*кому что*).

compensation [,kɒmpen'seɪʃ(ə)n] *n.* компенса́ция (*also psych.*); **pay ~** вы́платить (*pf.*) компенса́цию; **in ~ for the loss** в компенса́цию за понесённые убы́тки.

compensatory [-'pensətərɪ, -'seɪtərɪ] *adj.* компенси́рующий (*also psych.*); компенсацио́нный.

compère ['kɒmpeə(r)] *n.* конферансье́ (*m. indecl.*).

v.t. & i. конфери́ровать (*impf., pf.*).

compete [kəm'piːt] *v.i.* (*vie*) конкури́ровать (*impf.*); сопе́рничать (*impf.*); **~ with, against s.o. for sth.** конкури́ровать (*impf.*) с кем-н. из-за чего́-н.; (*in sport*) состяза́ться (*impf.*).

competenc|e ['kɒmpɪt(ə)ns] *n.* (*ability, authority*) уме́ние, компете́нтность.

competent ['kɒmpɪt(ə)nt] *adj.* компете́нтный.

competition [,kɒmpə'tɪʃ(ə)n] *n.* **1.** (*rivalry*) сопе́рничество, конкуре́нция; **they are in ~ with us** они́ конкури́руют с на́ми. **2.** (*contest*) состяза́ние, соревнова́ние. **3.** (*examination*) ко́нкурсный экза́мен.

competitive [kəm'petɪtɪv] *adj.* (*competing*) конкури́рующий; **~ examination** ко́нкурсный экза́мен; **~ prices** конкурентоспосо́бные це́ны.

competitor [kəm'petɪtə(r)] *n.* конкуре́нт.

compilation [,kɒmpɪ'leɪʃ(ə)n] *n.* (*act*) собира́ние, компили́рование; (*result*) собра́ние, компиля́ция.

compile [kəm'paɪl] *v.t.* соб|ира́ть, -ра́ть; сост|авля́ть, -а́вить; компили́ровать (*impf., pf.*).

compiler [kəm'paɪlə(r)] *n.* состави́тель (*m.*); компиля́тор.

complacency [kəm'pleɪsənsɪ] *n.* самодово́льство.

complacent [kəm'pleɪs(ə)nt] *adj.* самодово́льный.

complain [kəm'pleɪn] *v.i.* **1.** (*express dissatisfaction*) жа́ловаться (*impf.*). **2.** (*to an authority*) под|ава́ть, -а́ть жа́лобу (на+*a.*); жа́ловаться, по- (на+*a.*). **3.**: **he ~s of frequent headaches** он жа́луется на ча́стые головны́е бо́ли.

complaint [kəm'pleɪnt] *n.* жа́лоба; причи́на недово́льства; (*ailment*) неду́г, боле́знь.

complaisant [kəm'pleɪz(ə)nt] *adj.* обходи́тельный, услу́жливый.

complement ['kɒmplɪmənt] *n.* **1.** (*that which completes*) дополне́ние. **2.** по́лный компле́кт. **3.** (*gram.*) дополне́ние.

v.t. доп|олня́ть, -о́лнить.

complementary [,kɒmplɪ'mentərɪ] *adj.* дополни́тельный.

complete [kəm'pliːt] *adj.* **1.** (*whole*) по́лный; **~ edition** по́лное изда́ние. **2.** (*finished*) зако́нченный, завершённый. **3.** (*thorough*) соверше́нный; **he is a ~ stranger to me** он мне соверше́нно не знако́м; **a ~ surprise** по́лная неожи́данность.

v.t. зак|а́нчивать, -о́нчить; заверш|а́ть, -и́ть; (*fill in*) зап|олня́ть, -о́лнить.

completely [kəm'pliːtlɪ] *adv.* соверше́нно, по́лностью.

completeness [kəm'pliːtnɪs] *n.* полнота́; зако́нченность.

completion [kəm'pliːʃ(ə)n] *n.* заверше́ние, оконча́ние; (*of a form*) заполне́ние.

complex ['kɒmpleks] *n.* (*abstr. or physical whole, also psych.*) ко́мплекс.

adj. сло́жный, ко́мплексный; (*gram.*): **~ sentence** сложноподчинённое предложе́ние.

complexion [kəm'plekʃ(ə)n] *n.* **1.** (*of face*) цвет лица́. **2.** (*character, aspect*) вид, аспе́кт; **that puts a different ~ on the matter** э́то представля́ет де́ло в ино́м све́те.

complexity [kəm'pleksɪtɪ] *n.* сло́жность.

compliance [kəm'plaɪəns] *n.* усту́пчивость, пода́тливость; **in ~ with his orders** согла́сно его́ прика́зам.

compliant [kəm'plaɪənt] *adj.* усту́пчивый, пода́тливый.

complicate ['kɒmplɪ,keɪt] *v.t.* осложн|я́ть, -и́ть; усложн|я́ть, -и́ть.

complicated ['kɒmplɪ,keɪtɪd] *adj.* сло́жный.

complication [,kɒmplɪ'keɪʃ(ə)n] *n.* (*complexity*) сло́жность; (*complicating circumstance*) осложне́ние; (*med.*): **~s set in** после́довали осложне́ния.

complicity [kəm'plɪsɪtɪ] *n.* соуча́стие.

compliment ['kɒmplɪmənt] *n.* **1.** (*praise*) комплиме́нт; похвала́. **2.** (*greeting*) приве́т, поздравле́ние; **~s of the season** нового́дние (*и т.п.*) поздравле́ния.

v.t. говори́ть (*impf.*) комплиме́нты +*d.* (*по поводу чего*); хвали́ть, по- (за+*a.*).

complimentary [,kɒmplɪ'mentərɪ] *adj.* **1.** (*laudatory*) похва́льный, ле́стный. **2. ~ copy** (*of book*) беспла́тный экземпля́р; **~ ticket** контрама́рка, пригласи́тельный биле́т.

comply [kəm'plaɪ] *v.i.*: **~ with** уступ|а́ть, -и́ть (+*d.*); слу́шаться, по- (+*g.*); подчин|я́ться, -и́ться (+*d.*).

component [kəm'pəʊnənt] *n.* компоне́нт; составна́я часть; дета́ль.

adj. составно́й, составля́ющий.

comport [kəm'pɔːt] *v.t. & i.*: **~ o.s.** держа́ться (*impf.*); вести́ (*det.*) себя́.

comportment [kəm'pɔːtmənt] *n.* мане́ра держа́ться; поведе́ние.

compose [kəm'pəʊz] *v.t. & i.* **1.** (*make up, constitute*) сост|авля́ть, -а́вить; **the party was ~d of teachers** гру́ппа состоя́ла из учителе́й. **2.** (*liter., mus.*) сочин|я́ть, -и́ть; **~ a picture** сост|авля́ть, -а́вить компози́цию карти́ны. **3.** (*control, assuage*): **~ o.s.**

успок|аиваться, -оиться; **a ~d manner** сдéржанная манéра. **4.** (*typ.*) наб|ирáть, -рáть.
composedly [kəm'pəʊzɪdlɪ] *adv.* сдéржанно, спокóйно.
composer [kəm'pəʊzə(r)] *n.* (*mus.*) композитор.
composite ['kɒmpəzɪt, -,zaɪt] *n.* составнóй предмéт.
adj. составнóй.
composition [,kɒmpə'zɪʃ(ə)n] *n.* **1.** (*act or art of composing*) сочинéние, составлéние. **2.** (*liter. or mus. work*) произведéние, сочинéние. **3.** (*school exercise*) сочинéние. **4.** (*arrangement*) компози́ция. **5.** (*make-up*) сострáв; **~ of the soil** состáв пóчвы. **6.** (*typ.*) набóр.
compositor [kəm'pɒzɪtə(r)] *n.* набóрщик.
compos mentis [,kɒmpɒs 'mentɪs] *adj.* в здрáвом умé.
compost ['kɒmpɒst] *n.* компóст.
composure [kəm'pəʊʒə(r)] *n.* спокóйствие.
compote ['kɒmpəʊt, -pɒt] *n.* компóт.
compound[1] ['kɒmpaʊnd] *n.* (*enclosure*) огорóженное мéсто.
compound[2] ['kɒmpaʊnd] *n.* (*mixture*) смесь; (*gram.*) слóжное слóво; (*chem.*) соединéние.
adj. составнóй, слóжный; **~ interest** слóжные процéнты; **~ fracture** осложнённый перелóм.
compound[3] [kəm'paʊnd] *v.t.* **1.** (*mix, combine*) смéш|ивать, -áть; соедин|я́ть, -и́ть. **2.** (*aggravate*) отягчáть (*impf.*).
comprehend [,kɒmprɪ'hend] *v.t.* (*understand*) пон|имáть, -я́ть; пост|игáть, -и́гнуть; (*include*) включ|áть, -и́ть; охвáт|ывать, -и́ть.
comprehensible [,kɒmprɪ'hensɪb(ə)l] *adj.* поня́тный, постижи́мый.
comprehension [,kɒmprɪ'henʃ(ə)n] *n.* (*understanding*) понимáние, постижéние; (*inclusion, scope*) охвáт, включéние.
comprehensive [,kɒmprɪ'hensɪv] *adj.* (*pert. to understanding*) поня́тливый, схвáтывающий, (*of wide scope*) всеобъéмлющий; **~ school** еди́ная срéдняя шкóла.
compress[1] ['kɒmpres] *n.* (*to relieve inflammation*) компрéсс; (*to ~ artery etc.*) давя́щая повя́зка.
compress[2] [kəm'pres] *v.t.* (*physically*) сж|имáть, -ать; **~ed air** сжáтый вóздух; (*make more concise*) сокра|щáть, -ти́ть.
compression [kəm'preʃ(ə)n] *n.* (*lit.*) сжáтие; (*fig.*) сжáтие, сокращéние; (*tech.*) компрéссия.
compressor [kəm'presə(r)] *n.* компрéссор.
comprise [kəm'praɪz] *v.t.* включ|áть, -и́ть в себя́; состоя́ть (*impf.*) из+*g.*
compromise ['kɒmprə,maɪz] *n.* компроми́сс.
v.t. (*expose to discredit*) компромети́ровать; (*endanger*) стáвить, по- под угрóзу.
v.i. пойти́ (*pf.*) на компроми́сс; (*reach ~*) при|ходи́ть, -йти́ к компроми́ссу.
comptroller [kən'trəʊlə(r)] = **controller**
compulsion [kəm'pʌlʃ(ə)n] *n.* принуждéние; **on, under ~** по принуждéнию.
compulsive [kəm'pʌlsɪv] *adj.* принуди́тельный.
compulsory [kəm'pʌlsərɪ] *adj.* обязáтельный, принуди́тельный; **~ military service** вóинская пови́нность.
compunction [kəm'pʌŋkʃ(ə)n] *n.* угрызéния (*nt. pl.*) сóвести; раскáяние.
computation [,kɒmpjuː'teɪʃ(ə)n] *n.* вычислéние.
compute [kəm'pjuːt] *v.t. & i.* вычисля́ть, вы́числить.
computer [kəm'pjuːtə(r)] *n.* (*pers.*) счётчик; (*machine*) электрóнно-вычисли́тельная маши́на (*abbr.* ЭВМ); компью́тер; **~ programming** программи́рование; **~ programmer** программи́ст; **~ science** вычисли́тельная тéхника.
cpds. **~-aided design** *n.* автоматизи́рованное проекти́рование; **~-aided learning** *n.* маши́нное обучéние; **~-assisted** *adj.* автоматизи́рованный.
computerate [kəm'pjuːtərət] *adj.* владéющий основны́ми компью́терными нáвыками.
comrade ['kɒmreɪd, -rɪd] *n.* товáрищ; **~-in-arms** сорáтник.
comradeship ['kɒmreɪdʃɪp, -rɪdʃɪp] *n.* товáрищество.
con[1] [kɒn] *see* **pro**[1]
con[2] [kɒn] *v.t.* (*sl., dupe*) над|увáть, -ýть; **~ man** мошéнник, жýлик.
concave ['kɒnkeɪv] *adj.* вóгнутый.
concavity [kɒn'kævɪtɪ] *n.* вóгнутость.
conceal [kən'siːl] *v.t.* скр|ывáть, -ы́ть; (*keep secret*) утá|ивать, -и́ть.
concealment [kən'siːlmənt] *n.* сокры́тие, утáивание.
concede [kən'siːd] *v.t.* уступ|áть, -и́ть; **the candidate ~d the election** кандидáт признáл себя́ побеждённым на вы́борах.
conceit [kən'siːt] *n.* (*vanity*) самомнéние, самонадéянность, зазнáйство.
conceited [kən'siːtɪd] *adj.* самонадéянный, зазнáвшийся.
conceivabl|e [kən'siːvəb(ə)l] *adj.* мы́слимый, постижи́мый; **he may ~y be right** не исключенó, что он прав.
conceive [kən'siːv] *v.t.* **1.** (*form in the mind, imagine*) задýм|ывать, -ать. **2.** (*formulate*) выражáть, вы́разить. **3.** (*become pregnant with*) зачáть (*pf.*).
v.i. зачáть, забеременеть (*both pf.*).
concentrate ['kɒnsən,treɪt] *n.* (*of product*) концентрáт.
v.t. **1.** (*bring together, focus*) сосредотóчи|вать, -ть; концентри́ровать, с-. **2.** (*increase strength of*) концентри́ровать, с-; **~d food** концентрáты (*m. pl.*).
v.i. сосредотóчи|ваться, -ться; концентри́роваться, с-.
concentration [,kɒnsən'treɪʃ(ə)n] *n.* **1.** (*chem.*) концентрáция, крéпость. **2.** (*of troops etc.*) сосредотóчение, концентрáция; **~ camp** концентраціóнный лáгерь. **3.** (*of attention etc.*) сосредотóченность.
concentric [kən'sentrɪk] *adj.* концентри́ческий.
concept ['kɒnsept] *n.* поня́тие.
conception [kən'sepʃ(ə)n] *n.* **1.** (*notion*) концéпция, поня́тие. **2.** (*physiol.*) зачáтие.
concern [kən'sɜːn] *n.* **1.** (*affair*) отношéние; **it is no ~ of mine** э́то меня́ не касáется. **2.** (*business*) концéрн, предприя́тие; **a going ~** дéйствующее предприя́тие. **3.** (*share*) учáстие, интерéс; **he has a ~ in the enterprise** он учáствует в э́том предприя́тии. **4.** (*importance*) вáжность; значи́тельность. **5.** (*anxiety*) беспокóйство.
v.t. **1.** (*have to do with*) касáться (*impf.*) +*g.*; **~ed** (*involved*) заинтересóванный; **I am not ~ed** э́то меня́ не касáется; **as far as that is ~ed** что касáется э́того. **2.** (*cause anxiety to*) беспокóить (*impf.*): **~ed** (*anxious*) озабóченный, обеспокóенный; **I am ~ed about the future** меня́ беспокóит бýдущее.
concerning [kən'sɜːnɪŋ] *prep.* относи́тельно+*g.*; касáтельно+*g.*
concert ['kɒnsət] *n.* концéрт.
cpds. **~-goer** *n.* посети́тель (*m.*) концéртов; **~-hall** *n.* концéртный зал.
concerted [kən'sɜːtɪd] *adj.* согласóванный; **take ~ action** дéйствовать (*impf.*) согласóванно; **~ attack** одноврéменная атáка.
concertina [,kɒnsə'tiːnə] *n.* концерти́но, гармóника.
concerto [kən'tʃeətəʊ, -'tʃɜːtəʊ] *n.* концéрт.
concession [kən'seʃ(ə)n] *n.* **1.** (*yielding; thg. yielded*) устýпка. **2.** (*mining etc.*) концéссия.
concessionaire [kən,seʃə'neə(r)] *n.* концессионéр.
conciliate [kən'sɪlɪ,eɪt] *v.t.* примир|я́ть, -и́ть.
conciliation [kən,sɪlɪ'eɪʃ(ə)n] *n.* примирéние.
conciliator [kən'sɪlɪ,eɪtə(r)] *n.* миротвóрец, посрéдник.
conciliatory [kən'sɪlɪətərɪ] *adj.* примири́тельный.
concise [kən'saɪs] *adj.* крáткий, сжáтый.

concis|eness [kən'saɪsnɪs], **-ion** [kən'sɪʒ(ə)n] *nn.* крáткость, сжáтость.

conclave ['kɒnkleɪv] *n.* конклáв; (*fig.*) тáйное совещáние.

conclud|e [kən'klu:d] *v.t.* **1.** (*terminate*) зак|áнчивать, -óнчить; заверш|áть, -и́ть; **~ing** заключи́тельный; (*session etc.*) закр|ывáть, -ы́ть. **2.** (*agreement etc.*) заключ|áть, -и́ть. **3.** (*infer*) дéлать, с- вы́вод, что...; при|ходи́ть, -йти́ к вы́воду, что...

v.i. (*end*) зак|áнчиваться, -óнчиться; **he ~ed by saying** в заключéние он сказáл.

conclusion [kən'klu:ʒ(ə)n] *n.* **1.** (*end*) окончáние, заключéние; **bring to a ~** дов|оди́ть, -ести́ до концá; **in ~** в заключéние. **2.** (*of agreement etc.*) заключéние. **3.** (*inference*) вы́вод, заключéние; **he jumps to ~s** он дéлает поспéшные вы́воды.

conclusive [kən'klu:sɪv] *adj.* решáющий, окончáтельный.

concoct [kən'kɒkt] *v.t.* (*of drink etc.*) стря́пать, со-; (*of story etc.*) стря́пать, со-; сочин|я́ть, -и́ть.

concoction [kən'kɒkʃ(ə)n] *n.* (*drink etc.*) смéшивание, смесь; (*invention of story*) сочинéние; (*story invented*) вы́думка.

concomitant [kən'kɒmɪt(ə)nt] *adj.* сопу́тствующий.

concord ['kɒnkɔ:d, 'kɒŋ-] *n.* соглáсие, соглашéние.

concordat [kən'kɔ:dæt] *n.* конкордáт.

concourse ['kɒnkɔ:s, 'kɒŋ-] *n.* (*of railway station*) вестибю́ль (*m.*) вокзáла.

concrete[1] ['kɒnkri:t, 'kɒŋ-] *n.* (*building material*) бетóн; **reinforced ~** железобетóн.

v.t. бетони́ровать (*impf.*).

cpd. **~-mixer** *n.* бетономешáлка.

concrete[2] ['kɒnkri:t, 'kɒŋ-] *adj.* конкрéтный.

concubine ['kɒŋkjʊ,baɪn] *n.* нало́жница.

concur [kən'kɜ:(r)] *v.i.* **1.** (*of circumstance etc.*) совп|адáть, -áсть; сходи́ться, сойти́сь. **2.** (*agree, consent*) согла|шáться, -си́ться (c+*i.*).

concurrence [kən'kʌr(ə)ns] *n.* (*of things*) совпадéние; (*agreement, consent*) соглáсие.

concurrent [kən'kʌrənt] *adj.* совпадáющий; **~ly** одноврéмéнно.

concussion [kən'kʌʃ(ə)n] *n.* (*med.*) сотрясéние мóзга.

condemn [kən'dem] *v.t.* осу|ждáть, -ди́ть; приго-в|áривать, -ори́ть; (*blame*) порицáть (*impf.*); **~ed cell** кáмера смéртника; (*declare forfeit*) конфисковáть (*impf., pf*); (*declare unfit for use*) призн|авáть, -áть непригóдным; **the building was ~ed** здáние бы́ло при́знано непригóдным для жилья́.

condemnation [,kɒndem'neɪʃ(ə)n] *n.* осуждéние.

condemnatory [,kɒndem'neɪtərɪ] *adj.* осуждáющий.

condensation [,kɒnden'seɪʃ(ə)n] *n.* (*phys.*) конденсáция; (*liquefaction*) сжижéние; (*abridgement*) сокращéние.

condense [kən'dens] *v.t.* **1.** (*phys.*) конденси́ровать (*impf., pf.*); сжи|жáть, -ди́ть; **~d milk** сгущённое молокó. **2.** (*fig.*): **a ~d account of events** сжáтый отчёт о собы́тиях.

condenser [kən'densə(r)] *n.* конденсáтор.

condescend [,kɒndɪ'send] *v.i.* сни|сходи́ть, -зойти́.

condescending [,kɒndɪ'sendɪŋ] *adj.* снисходи́тельный.

condescension [,kɒndɪ'senʃ(ə)n] *n.* снисхождéние, снисходи́тельность.

condiment ['kɒndɪmənt] *n.* припрáва.

condition [kən'dɪʃ(ə)n] *n.* **1.** (*state*) состоя́ние, положéние. **2.** (*fitness*): **the athlete is out of ~** спортсмéн не в фóрме. **3.** (*pl., circumstances*) услóвия; обстоя́тельства (*both nt. pl.*). **4.** (*requisite, stipulation*) услóвие; **on ~ that ...** при услóвии, что...; **on no ~** ни при каки́х услóвиях.

v.t. **1.** (*determine, govern*) обуслóв|ливать, -ить; **~ed reflex** услóвный рефлéкс. **2.** (*of athletes*) тренировáть, на-. **3.** (*indoctrinate*) приуч|áть, -и́ть; **he was ~ed to obey unquestioningly** егó приучи́ли беспрекословно подчиня́ться.

conditional [kən'dɪʃən(ə)l] *adj.* услóвный, обуслóвленный; **my agreement is ~ on his coming** я соглáсен при услóвии, что он придёт; (*gram.*): **the ~ (mood)** услóвное наклонéние.

condole [kən'dəʊl] *v.i.* соболéзновать (*impf.*) (+*d.*); выражáть, вы́разить соболéзнование.

condolence [kən'dəʊləns] *n.* (*also pl.*) соболéзнование.

condom ['kɒndɒm] *n.* презервати́в, кондóм.

condominium [,kɒndə'mɪnɪəm] *n.* кондоми́ниум.

condone [kən'dəʊn] *v.t.* про|щáть, -сти́ть.

condor ['kɒndɔ:(r)] *n.* кóндор.

conducive [kən'dju:sɪv] *adj.* спосóбствующий; **health is ~ to happiness** здорóвье — помóщник счáстью.

conduct[1] ['kɒndʌkt] *n.* **1.** (*behaviour*) поведéние. **2.** (*manner of ~ing*) ведéние. **3.**: **safe ~** гарáнтия неприкосновéнности, охрáнная грáмота.

conduct[2] [kən'dʌkt] *v.t.* **1.** (*lead, guide*) води́ть (*indet*), вести́ (*det.*); руководи́ть (*impf.*) +*i.*; **a ~ed tour** экску́рсия с ги́дом. **2.** (*manage*) вести́ (*det.*); **~ an experiment** стáвить, по- óпыт; **~ o.s.** вести́ себя́, держáться (*impf.*). **3.** (*mus., also v.i.*) дирижи́ровать (*impf.*) (+*i.*). **4.** (*phys.*) проводи́ть (*impf.*).

conductivity [,kɒndʌk'tɪvɪtɪ] *n.* (*tech.*) (удéльная) проводи́мость; электропровóдность.

conductor [kən'dʌktə(r)] *n.* **1.** (*leader*) руководи́тель (*m.*). **2.** (*mus.*) дирижёр. **3.** (*of bus or tram*) кондýктор. **4.** (*phys.*) проводни́к.

conductress [kən'dʌktrɪs] *n.* (*on bus*) жéнщина-кондýктор.

conduit ['kɒndɪt, -djʊɪt] *n.* трубопровóд; водопровóдная трубá; (*elec.*) изоляциóнная тру́бка.

cone [kəʊn] *n.* **1.** (*geom.*) кóнус. **2.** (*bot.*) ши́шка. **3.** (*for ice-cream*) вáфельный стакáнчик.

cpd. **~-shaped** *adj.* конусообрáзный.

coney ['kəʊnɪ] = **cony**

confection [kən'fekʃ(ə)n] *n.* слáст|и (*pl., g.* -éй), конфéт|ы (*pl., g.* —).

confectioner [kən'fekʃənə(r)] *n.* конди́тер.

confectionery [kən'fekʃənərɪ] *n.* (*wares*) конди́терские издéлия; (*shop*) конди́терская.

Confederacy [kən'fedərəsɪ] *n.* (*hist.*) Конфедерáция.

confederate [kən'fedərət] *n.* сóобщник, сою́зник; (*conjurer's*) посóбник.

adj. сою́зный; (*US hist.*) конфедерати́вный.

confederation [kən,fedə'reɪʃ(ə)n] *n.* сою́з; федерáция.

confer[1] [kən'fɜ:(r)] *v.t.* присв|áивать, -óить; прису|ждáть, -ди́ть; даровáть (*impf.*); (*all что кому*); **~ a degree** (*acad.*) прису|ждáть, -ди́ть учёную стéпень; **~ a title** присв|áивать, -óить ти́тул; **~ a favour** оказáть (*pf.*) услýгу.

confer[2] [kən'fɜ:(r)] *v.i.* (*consult*) совещáться; совéтоваться (*both impf.*) (c+*i.*).

conference ['kɒnfərəns] *n.* конферéнция, совещáние; **he is in ~** он на совещáнии.

cpd. **~-table** *n.* стол переговóров.

confess [kən'fes] *v.t. & i.* **1.** призн|авáть, -áть; призн|авáться, -áться (*or* созн|авáться, -áться) (в чём); **I ~ I haven't read it** признаю́сь, я э́того не читáл; **he ~ed to the crime** он признáлся в преступлéнии. **2.** (*eccl.*) (*hear confession of*) исповéд|овать, -ать; (*~ one's sins*) исповéд|оваться, -аться.

confession [kən'feʃ(ə)n] *n.* **1.** (*avowal*) признáние, сознáние. **2.** (*profession of faith*) исповéдание. **3.** (*to a priest*) и́споведь.

confessional [kən'feʃən(ə)l] *n.* исповедáльня.

confessor [kən'fesə(r)] *n.* (*priest*) исповéдник, духовни́к; **Edward the C~** Эдуáрд Исповéдник.

confetti [kən'fetɪ] *n.* конфетти́ (*nt. indecl.*).

confidant, -e [,kɒnfɪ'dænt, 'kɒn-] *nn.* напéрсни|к (*fem.* -ца); довéренное лицó.

confide [kən'faɪd] *v.t.* **1.** (*entrust*) поруч|áть, -и́ть;

вв|еря́ть, -е́рить. **2.** (*impart*) сообщ|а́ть, -и́ть; пов|еря́ть, -е́рить; вв|еря́ть, -е́рить; **he ~d his secret to me** он дове́рил мне свою́ та́йну.

v.i. **~ in** дели́ться, по- (*своими планами и т.п.*) +*i*.

confidence ['kɒnfɪd(ə)ns] *n.* **1.** (*confiding of secrets*) дове́рие; **I tell you this in ~** я говорю́ вам э́то конфиденциа́льно (*or* по секре́ту); **take s.o. into one's ~** дов|еря́ть, -е́рить кому́-н. свои́ та́йны. **2.** (*secret*) та́йна. **3.** (*trust*): **I have ~ in him** я уве́рен в нём; я ве́рю в него́; **he enjoys her ~** он по́льзуется её дове́рием. **4.** (*certainty, assurance*) уве́ренность; самоуве́ренность; **he spoke with ~** он говори́л с уве́ренностью. **5.: ~ trick** моше́нничество.

confident ['kɒnfɪd(ə)nt] *adj.* уве́ренный, самоуве́ренный; **I am ~ of success** я уве́рен в успе́хе.

confidential [,kɒnfɪ'denʃ(ə)l] *adj.* конфиденциа́льный, секре́тный; **a ~ tone** довери́тельный тон.

configuration [kən,fɪgjʊ'reɪʃ(ə)n, -gə'reɪʃ(ə)n] *n.* конфигура́ция.

confine[1] ['kɒnfaɪn] *n.* (*usu. pl.*) грани́цы (*f. pl.*), преде́лы (*m. pl.*).

confine[2] [kən'faɪn] *v.t.* ограни́чи|вать, -ть; заклю-ч|а́ть, -и́ть; **~ yourself to the subject** приде́рживайтесь те́мы.

confinement [kən'faɪnmənt] *n.* **1.** (*restriction*) ограниче́ние. **2.** (*imprisonment*) заключе́ние; **solitary ~** одино́чное заключе́ние. **3.** (*childbirth*) ро́д|ы (*pl., g.* -ов).

confirm [kən'fɜ:m] *v.t.* **1.** (*strengthen, e.g. power*) подтвер|жда́ть, -ди́ть; подкреп|ля́ть, -и́ть. **2.** (*establish as certain*) утвер|жда́ть, -ди́ть; подтвер|жда́ть, -ди́ть; **his appointment was ~ed** его́ назначе́ние бы́ло утверждено́. **3.** (*of pers.*): **I was ~ed in this belief by the fact that ...** меня́ укрепи́л в э́том убежде́нии тот фа́кт, что...; **a ~ed bachelor** убеждённый холостя́к. **4.** (*relig.*) конфирмова́ть (*impf., pf.*).

confirmation [,kɒnfə'meɪʃ(ə)n] *n.* **1.** (*of report etc.*) подтвержде́ние, утвержде́ние. **2.** (*relig.*) конфирма́ция.

confiscate ['kɒnfɪ,skeɪt] *v.t.* конфискова́ть (*impf. pf.*).

confiscation [,kɒnfɪ'skeɪʃ(ə)n] *n.* конфиска́ция.

conflagration [,kɒnflə'greɪʃ(ə)n] *n.* большо́й пожа́р.

conflict[1] ['kɒnflɪkt] *n.* конфли́кт, противоре́чие.

conflict[2] [kən'flɪkt] *v.t.* быть в конфли́кте (с+*i.*); противоре́чить (*impf.*) (+*d.*).

confluence ['kɒnflʊəns] *n.* слия́ние.

conform [kən'fɔ:m] *v.t.* приспос|а́бливать, -о́бить; сообразо́в|ывать, -а́ть.

v.i. приспос|а́бливаться, -о́биться (к+*d.*); сообразо́в|ываться, -а́ться (с+*i.*).

conformism [kən'fɔ:mɪz(ə)m] *n.* конформи́зм.

comformist [kən'fɔ:mɪst] *n.* конформи́ст.

conformity [kən'fɔ:mɪtɪ] *n.* соотве́тствие.

confound [kən'faʊnd] *v.t.* **1.** (*amaze*) пора|жа́ть, -зи́ть; потряс|а́ть, -ти́. **2.** (*confuse*) сме́ш|ивать, -а́ть; спу́т|ывать, -ать. **3.** (*as expletive*): **~ it!** чёрт возьми́!

confront [kən'frʌnt] *v.t.* **1.** (*bring face to face*) ста́вить, по- лицо́м к лицу́ (с+*i.*). **2.** (*face*) смотре́ть (*impf.*) в лицо́ +*d.*; встр|еча́ть, -е́тить; **many difficulties ~ed us** мы столкну́лись со мно́гими тру́дностями.

confrontation [,kɒnfrʌn'teɪʃ(ə)n] *n.* конфронта́ция.

confuse [kən'fju:z] *v.t.* **1.** (*throw into confusion*) сму|ща́ть, -ти́ть; прив|оди́ть, -ести́ в замеша́тельство; **the situation is ~d** положе́ние запу́танное. **2.** (*mistake*) спу́т|ывать, -ать; сме́ш|ивать, -а́ть.

confusion [kən'fju:ʒ(ə)n] *n.* смуще́ние, замеша́тельство; (*mix-up*) пу́таница, беспоря́док.

congeal [kən'dʒi:l] *v.t.* замор|а́живать, -о́зить; сгу|ща́ть, -сти́ть.

v.i. свёр|тываться, -ну́ться; сгу|ща́ться, -сти́ться; заст|ыва́ть, -ы́ть.

congenial [kən'dʒi:nɪəl] *adj.* бли́зкий по ду́ху; **a ~ companion** прия́тный спу́тник; **a ~ climate** благоприя́тный кли́мат; **~ employment** рабо́та по душе́.

congeniality [kən,dʒi:nɪ'ælɪtɪ] *n.* конгениа́льность; духо́вная бли́зость.

congenital [kən'dʒenɪt(ə)l] *adj.*: **~ defect** врождённый дефе́кт.

congested [kən'dʒestɪd] *adj.* перенаселённый; перегру́женный; (*of street*) запру́женный; (*med.*) перепо́лненный кро́вью, засто́йный.

congestion [kən'dʒestʃ(ə)n] *n.* перенаселённость; перегру́женность; (*med.*) гиперемия, засто́й.

conglomerate[1] [kən'glɒmərət] *n.* конгломера́т.

adj. конгломера́тный.

conglomerate[2] [kən'glɒmə,reɪt] *v.t. & i.* соб|ира́ть(ся), -ра́ть(ся); ск|а́пливать(ся), -опи́ться.

conglomeration [kən,glɒmə'reɪʃ(ə)n] *n.* конгломера́т.

Congo ['kɒŋgəʊ] *n.* (река́, Респу́блика) Ко́нго (*indecl.*).

congratulate [kən'grætjʊ,leɪt] *v.t.* поздр|авля́ть, -а́вить (*кого с чем*).

congratulation [kən,grætjʊ'leɪʃ(ə)n] *n.* поздравле́ние; **~s!** поздравля́ю!

congratulatory [kən'grætjʊlətərɪ] *adj.* поздрави́тельный.

congregate ['kɒŋgrɪ,geɪt] *v.t.* соб|ира́ть, -ра́ть.

v.i. соб|ира́ться, -ра́ться; сходи́ться, сойти́сь.

congregation [,kɒŋgrɪ'geɪʃ(ə)n] *n.* (*assembly*) собра́ние; (*in church*) прихожа́не (*m. pl.*), па́ства.

congress ['kɒŋgres] *n.* **1.** (*organized meeting*) конгре́сс, съе́зд. **2.** (*pol., hist.*) конгре́сс; **C~ of Vienna** Ве́нский конгре́сс.

cpds. **~man** *n.* конгрессме́н; **~woman** *n.* же́нщина-член конгре́сса.

congruence ['kɒŋgrʊəns] *n.* согласо́ванность, соотве́тствие.

congruent ['kɒŋgrʊənt] *adj.* соотве́тствующий, подходя́щий; (*geom.*) конгрує́нтный.

conical ['kɒnɪk(ə)l] *adj.* кони́ческий, ко́нусный.

conifer ['kɒnɪfə(r), 'kəʊn-] *n.* хво́йное де́рево.

coniferous [kə'nɪfərəs] *adj.* хво́йный, шишконо́сный.

conjectural [kən'dʒektʃər(ə)l] *adj.* предположи́тельный.

conjecture [kən'dʒektʃə(r)] *n.* предположе́ние, дога́дка.

v.t. & i. предпол|ага́ть, -ожи́ть; гада́ть (*impf.*).

conjugal ['kɒndʒʊg(ə)l] *adj.* супру́жеский, бра́чный; **~ rights** супру́жеские права́.

conjugate ['kɒndʒʊ,geɪt] *v.t.* спряга́ть, про-.

conjugation [,kɒndʒʊ'geɪʃ(ə)n] *n.* спряже́ние.

conjunction [kən'dʒʌŋkʃ(ə)n] *n.* **1.** (*union*) соедине́ние, связь; **in ~ with** совме́стно с+*i.*; **~ of circumstances** стече́ние обстоя́тельств. **2.** (*gram.*) сою́з.

conjunctivitis [kən,dʒʌŋktɪ'vaɪtɪs] *n.* коньюктиви́т.

conjur|e ['kʌndʒə(r)] *v.t. & i.* **1.** (*evoke by magic spell*) вызыва́ть, вы́звать. **2.** (*fig.*): **~e up** вызыва́ть, вы́звать в воображе́нии. **3.** (*perform tricks*) пока́з|ывать, -а́ть фо́кусы; **he ~ed a rabbit out of a hat** он извлёк из шля́пы за́йца; **~ing trick** фо́кус.

conjur|er, or ['kʌndʒərə(r)] *n.* фо́кусник, заклина́тель (*m.*).

conk [kɒŋk] *v.i.* (*usu.* **~ out**) (*break down*) загло́хнуть (*pf.*); (*die*) загну́ться (*pf.*) (*sl.*).

connect [kə'nekt] *v.t.* (*join*) соедин|я́ть, -и́ть; свя́з|ывать, -а́ть; **the towns are ~ed by railway** э́ти города́ соединены́ желе́зной доро́гой; **what firm are you ~ed with?** с како́й фи́рмой вы свя́заны?; **he is well ~ed** у него́ хоро́шие свя́зи; (*associate*) свя́з|ывать, -а́ть; ассоции́ровать (*impf., pf.*); **I ~ him with music** его́ и́мя ассоции́руется у меня́ с му́зыкой.

v.i. соедин|я́ться, -и́ться; свя́з|ываться, -а́ться; **the train ~s with the one from London** э́тот по́езд согласо́ван по расписа́нию с ло́ндонским по́ездом.

connecting-rod [kə'nektɪŋ] *n.* шату́н, тя́га.

conne|ction, -xion [kəˈnekʃ(ə)n] *n.* **1.** (*joining up, installation*) соединéние, связь. **2.** (*fig., link*) связь; **in this ~** в э́той связи́. **3.** (*of transport*) согласо́ванность расписа́ния; **the train runs in ~ with the ferry** расписа́ние поездо́в и паро́мов согласо́вано; **I missed my ~** я не успе́л сде́лать переса́дку. **4.** (*association*) связь; **he formed a ~ with her** он вступи́л с ней в связь. **5.** (*teleph.*): **the ~ was bad** телефо́н пло́хо рабо́тал. **6.** (*tech.*): **a loose ~ in the engine** сла́бый конта́кт в электросисте́ме дви́гателя.

connective [kəˈnektɪv] *adj.* соедини́тельный, связу́ющий.

connexion [kəˈnekʃ(ə)n] = **connection**

conning-tower [ˈkɒnɪŋ] *n.* (*naut.*) боева́я ру́бка.

connivance [kəˈnaɪv(ə)ns] *n.* потво́рство, попусти́тельство.

connive [kəˈnaɪv] *v.i.*: **~ at** потво́рствовать (*impf.*) +*d.*; попусти́тельствовать (*impf.*) +*d.*

connoisseur [ˌkɒnəˈsɜː(r)] *n.* знато́к, цени́тель (*m.*).

connotation [ˌkɒnəˈteɪʃ(ə)n] *n.* побо́чное значе́ние; ассоциа́ция.

connote [kəˈnəʊt] *v.t.* означа́ть (*impf.*).

connubial [kəˈnjuːbɪəl] *adj.* супру́жеский, бра́чный.

conquer [ˈkɒŋkə(r)] *v.t.* & *i.* (*overcome; obtain by conquest*) завоёв|ывать, -а́ть; покор|я́ть, -и́ть; **~ one's feelings** совлада́ть (*pf.*) со свои́ми чу́вствами.

conqueror [ˈkɒŋkərə(r)] *n.* завоева́тель (*m.*); **William the C~** (*hist.*) Вильге́льм Завоева́тель.

conquest [ˈkɒŋkwest] *n.* завоева́ние, побе́да.

consanguineous [ˌkɒnsæŋˈgwɪnɪəs] *adj.* единокро́вный, ро́дственный.

consanguinity [ˌkɒnsæŋˈgwɪnɪtɪ] *n.* родство́.

conscience [ˈkɒnʃ(ə)ns] *n.* со́весть; **clear ~** чи́стая со́весть; **guilty ~** нечи́стая со́весть; **have you no ~?** как то́лько у вас со́вести хвата́ет?; **in all ~** по со́вести говоря́.

conscientious [ˌkɒnʃɪˈenʃəs] *adj.* созна́тельный, добросо́вестный, со́вестливый; **~ objector** отка́зывающийся от вое́нной слу́жбы по убежде́нию.

conscientiousness [ˌkɒnʃɪˈenʃəsnɪs] *n.* добросо́вестность.

conscious [ˈkɒnʃəs] *adj.* **1.** (*physically aware*) сознающий, ощуща́ющий; **he was ~ to the last** он был в созна́нии до после́дней мину́ты; **~ of pain** чу́вствующий боль; **I was ~ of what I was doing** я де́йствовал созна́тельно. **2.** (*mentally aware*) сознающий, понима́ющий; **I was ~ of having offended him** я сознава́л, что оскорби́л его́. **3.** (*realized*) сознающий, созна́тельный; **a ~ effort** созна́тельное уси́лие. **4.** (*as suff.*): **class-~** кла́ссово созна́тельный; **security-~** бди́тельный.

consciousness [ˈkɒnʃəsnɪs] *n.* **1.** (*physical*) созна́ние; **he lost ~** он потеря́л созна́ние; **she regained ~** она́ пришла́ в себя́/созна́ние. **2.** (*mental*) созна́тельность.

conscript[1] [ˈkɒnskrɪpt] *n.* новобра́нец, призывни́к.

adj. при́званный на вое́нную слу́жбу; **~ soldiers** солда́ты-призывники́.

conscript[2] [kənˈskrɪpt] *v.t.* приз|ыва́ть, -ва́ть на вое́нную слу́жбу.

conscription [kənˈskrɪpʃ(ə)n] *n.* во́инская пови́нность; (*call-up*) призы́в на вое́нную слу́жбу.

consecrate [ˈkɒnsɪˌkreɪt] *v.t.* освя|ща́ть, -ти́ть; посвя|ща́ть, -ти́ть.

consecration [ˌkɒnsɪˈkreɪʃ(ə)n] *n.* освяще́ние, посвяще́ние.

consecutive [kənˈsekjʊtɪv] *adj.* после́довательный; **(on) five ~ days** пять дней подря́д.

consensus [kənˈsensəs] *n.* согла́сие, единоду́шие.

consent [kənˈsent] *n.* согла́сие; **with one ~** единоду́шно, с о́бщего согла́сия; **age of ~** бра́чный во́зраст.

v.i. согла|ша́ться, -си́ться; да|ва́ть, -ть согла́сие.

consequence [ˈkɒnsɪkwəns] *n.* **1.** (*result*) сле́дствие, после́дствие; **in ~ of** всле́дствие+*g.*; в результа́те +*g.* **2.** (*importance*) ва́жность, значе́ние; **it is of no ~** э́то не име́ет значе́ния.

consequent [ˈkɒnsɪkwənt] *adj.* вытека́ющий (*из чего*).

consequently [ˈkɒnsɪˌkwentlɪ] *adv.* сле́довательно.

conservancy [kənˈsɜːvənsɪ] *n.* (*preservation*) охра́на (приро́ды).

conservation [ˌkɒnsəˈveɪʃ(ə)n] *n.* сохране́ние, охра́на; **~ area** запове́дник; **energy ~** сохране́ние эне́ргии.

conservationist [ˌkɒnsəˈveɪʃənɪst] *n.* боре́ц за охра́ну приро́ды.

conservatism [kənˈsɜːvətɪz(ə)m] *n.* консервати́зм.

conservative [kənˈsɜːvətɪv] *n.* консерва́тор.

adj. консервати́вный; **a ~ estimate** скро́мный/уме́ренный подсчёт.

conservatoire [kənˈsɜːvəˌtwɑː(r)] *n.* консервато́рия.

conservatory [kənˈsɜːvətərɪ] *n.* **1.** (*greenhouse*) оранжере́я. **2.** (*US, mus.*) консервато́рия.

conserve [kənˈsɜːv] *v.t.* консерви́ровать, за-; сохран|я́ть, -и́ть; сбер|ега́ть, -е́чь; **~ one's strength** бере́чь (*impf.*) свои́ си́лы.

consider [kənˈsɪdə(r)] *v.t.* & *i.* рассм|а́тривать, -отре́ть; счита́ть (*impf.*); **we are ~ing going to Canada** мы поду́мываем о пое́здке в Кана́ду; **~ yourself under arrest** счита́йте, что вы аресто́ваны; **he is ~ed clever** его́ счита́ют у́мным; (*make allowance for*) счита́ться (*impf.*) с+*i.*; прин|има́ть, -я́ть во внима́ние; **we must ~ his feelings** мы должны́ счита́ться с его́ чу́вствами; **all things ~ed** приня́в всё во внима́ние.

considerable [kənˈsɪdərəb(ə)l] *adj.* значи́тельный.

considerate [kənˈsɪdərət] *adj.* внима́тельный, забо́тливый.

consideration [kənˌsɪdəˈreɪʃ(ə)n] *n.* **1.** (*reflection*) рассмотре́ние; **take into ~** прин|има́ть, -я́ть во внима́ние; **the matter is under ~** де́ло рассма́тривается. **2.** (*making allowance*): **in ~ of his youth** принима́я во внима́ние его́ мо́лодость; **he showed ~ for my feelings** он счита́лся с мои́ми чу́вствами. **3.** (*reason, factor*) соображе́ние; **money is no ~** де́ньги не име́ют значе́ния; **on no ~** ни под каки́м ви́дом. **4.** (*requital*) вознагражде́ние.

considering [kənˈsɪdərɪŋ] *adv.* & *prep.* учи́тывая; принима́я во внима́ние.

consign [kənˈsaɪn] *v.t.* (*forward*) пересы|ла́ть, -ла́ть; пос|ыла́ть, -ла́ть; (*condemn*) обр|ека́ть, -е́чь; (*entrust*) поруч|а́ть, -и́ть; вруч|а́ть, -и́ть.

consignment [kənˈsaɪnmənt] *n.* (*act of consigning*) отпра́вка; (*goods*) па́ртия това́ра.

consist [kənˈsɪst] *v.i.*: **~ of** состоя́ть (*impf.*) из+*g.*; заключа́ться (*impf.*) в+*p.*; **~ in: his task ~s in defining work norms** его́ рабо́та состои́т в определе́нии норм вы́работки.

consistency [kənˈsɪstənsɪ] *n.* **1.** (*of mixture etc.*) консисте́нция. **2.** (*adherence to logic or principle*) после́довательность.

consistent [kənˈsɪst(ə)nt] *adj.* после́довательный; **this fact is ~ with his having written the book** э́тот факт не противоре́чит тому́, что он явля́ется а́втором э́той кни́ги.

consolation [ˌkɒnsəˈleɪʃ(ə)n] *n.* утеше́ние, отра́да; **it is a ~ that he is here** утеши́тельно знать, что он здесь; **~ prize** утеши́тельный приз.

console[1] [ˈkɒnsəʊl] *n.* **1.** (*bracket*) консо́ль, кронште́йн. **2.** (*panel*) пульт управле́ния. **3.** (*cabinet*) ко́рпус, шка́фчик (*радиоприёмника и т.п.*).

console[2] [kənˈsəʊl] *v.t.* ут|еша́ть, -е́шить.

consolidate [kənˈsɒlɪˌdeɪt] *v.t.* укреп|ля́ть, -и́ть; консолиди́ровать (*impf., pf.*).

v.i. укреп|ля́ться, -и́ться; консолиди́роваться (*impf., pf.*).

consolidation [kənˌsɒlɪˈdeɪʃ(ə)n] *n.* консолида́ция;

укреплéние.
consommé [kən'sɒmeɪ] *n.* бульóн.
consonance ['kɒnsənəns] *n.* (*agreement*) соглáсие; (*mus.*) консонáнс.
consonant ['kɒnsənənt] *n.* (*phon.*) соглáсный (звук), консонáнт.
adj. (*in accord*) соглáсный, созвýчный.
consort[1] ['kɒnsɔːt] *n.* консóрт, супрýг (*fem.* -а); **Prince C~** принц-консóрт.
consort[2] [kən'sɔːt] *v.t.* **1.** (*associate*) общáться (*impf.*). **2.** (*harmonize*) согласóв|ываться, -áться.
consortium [kən'sɔːtɪəm] *n.* консóрциум.
conspicuous [kən'spɪkjʊəs] *adj.* замéтный; бросáющийся в глазá; **he was ~ by his absence** егó отсýтствие бросáлось в глазá.
conspiracy [kən'spɪrəsɪ] *n.* зáговор; конспирáция.
conspirator [kən'spɪrətə(r)] *n.* заговóрщик; конспирáтор.
conspiratorial [kən,spɪrə'tɔːrɪəl] *adj.* заговóрщический, конспирáторский.
conspire [kən'spaɪə(r)] *v.t. & i.* устр|áивать, -óить зáговор; сгов|áриваться, -ори́ться; **events ~d against him** собы́тия склáдывались прóтив негó.
constable ['kʌnstəb(ə)l] *n.* полицéйский; **Chief C~** начáльник поли́ции.
constabulary [kən'stæbjʊlərɪ] *n.* поли́ция.
adj. полицéйский.
constancy ['kɒnstənsɪ] *n.* постоя́нство; неизмéнность.
constant ['kɒnst(ə)nt] *n.* (*math., phys.*) констáнта.
adj. постоя́нный; (*faithful*) неизмéнный.
constantly ['kɒnst(ə)ntlɪ] *adj.* постоя́нно.
constellation [,kɒnstə'leɪʃ(ə)n] *n.* созвéздие.
consternation [,kɒnstə'neɪʃ(ə)n] *n.* смятéние, ýжас.
constipate ['kɒnstɪ,peɪt] *v.t.* (*med.*) вызывáть, вы́звать запóр у+*g.*; **he is ~d** у негó запóр.
constipation [,kɒnstɪ'peɪʃ(ə)n] *n.* запóр.
constituency [kən'stɪtjʊənsɪ] *n.* избирáтельный óкруг.
constituent [kən'stɪtjʊənt] *n.* (*elector*) избирáтель (*fem.* -ница); (*element*) составнáя часть.
adj. составля́ющий часть цéлого; (*pol.*) избирáющий; **~ assembly** учреди́тельное собрáние.
constitute ['kɒnstɪ,tjuːt] *v.t.* (*make up*) сост|авля́ть, -áвить; (*set up*) учре|ждáть, -ди́ть; устан|áвливать, -ови́ть.
constitution [,kɒnstɪ'tjuːʃ(ə)n] *n.* **1.** (*make-up*) строéние, структýра; **the ~ of one's mind** склад умá. **2.** (*of body*) (тéло)сложéние. **3.** (*pol.*) конститýция.
constitutional [,kɒnstɪ'tjuːʃən(ə)l] *n.* (*walk*) моциóн, прогýлка.
adj. (*of body*) органи́ческий, конституционáльный; (*pol.*) конституциóнный.
constrain [kən'streɪn] *v.t.* прин|уждáть, -ýдить; заст|авля́ть, -áвить; вынуждáть, вы́нудить.
constraint [kən'streɪnt] *n.* (*compulsion*) принуждéние, давлéние; (*repression of feelings*) скóванность.
constrict [kən'strɪkt] *v.t.* сж|имáть, -ать; сужáть, сýзить; **a ~ed outlook** ограни́ченный кругозóр.
constriction [kən'strɪkʃ(ə)n] *n.* сжáтие, сужéние; **I feel a ~ in the chest** я чýвствую стеснéние в груди́.
construct [kən'strʌkt] *v.t.* конструи́ровать (*impf., pf.*); (*also gram., geom.*) стрóить, по-.
construction [kən'strʌkʃ(ə)n] *n.* **1.** (*building, structure*) построéние, строи́тельство, стрóйка; **the road is under ~** дорóга стрóится; **a car of solid ~** маши́на прóчной констрýкции. **2.** (*interpretation*) истолковáние; **he put a wrong ~ on my words** он неправи́льно истолковáл мои́ словá. **3.** (*gram.*) констрýкция.
constructive [kən'strʌktɪv] *adj.* (*pert. to construction; helpful*) конструкти́вный.
constructor [kən'strʌktə(r)] *n.* строи́тель (*m.*).
construe [kən'struː] *v.t.* истолкóв|ывать, -áть.
consul ['kɒns(ə)l] *n.* кóнсул.
consular ['kɒnsjʊlə(r)] *adj.* кóнсульский.
consulate ['kɒnsjʊlət] *n.* (*also hist.*) кóнсульство.
consult [kən'sʌlt] *v.t.* (*refer to*): **~ a book** спр|авля́ться, -áвиться в кни́ге; **~ one's watch** посмотрéть (*pf.*) на часы́; **~ a lawyer** совéтоваться, по- с юри́стом.
v.i. совéтоваться, по- (с+*i.*); **~ with s.o.** консульти́роваться (*impf., pf.*) с кем-н.; совещáться (*impf.*) с кем-н.; **~ing physician** (врач-)консультáнт; **~ing hours** приёмные часы́; **~ing room** кабинéт (врачá).
consultant [kən'sʌlt(ə)nt] *n.* консультáнт.
consultation [,kɒnsəl'teɪʃ(ə)n] *n.* консультáция; **he acted in ~ with me** он дéйствовал, совéтуясь со мной.
consultative [,kən'səltətɪv] *adj.* консультати́вный, совещáтельный.
consume [kən'sjuːm] *v.t.* **1.** (*eat or drink*) съ|едáть, -есть; погло|щáть, -ти́ть. **2.** (*use up*) потреб|ля́ть, -и́ть. **3.** (*destroy*) истреб|ля́ть, -и́ть; **the fire ~d the huts** пожáр уничтóжил лачýги. **4.: he was ~d with envy** егó снедáла зáвисть.
consumer [kən'sjuːmə(r)] *n.* потреби́тель (*m.*); **~ goods** потреби́тельские товáры.
consumerism [kən'sjuːmə,rɪz(ə)m] *n.* потреби́тельство.
consummate[1] [kən'sʌmɪt, 'kɒnsəmɪt] *adj.* совершéнный, закóнченный; **a ~ artist** блестя́щий худóжник.
consummate[2] ['kɒnsə,meɪt] *v.t.* (*e.g. happiness*) заверш|áть, -и́ть; (*marriage*) осуществ|ля́ть, -и́ть (*брачные отношения*).
consummation [,kɒnsə'meɪʃ(ə)n] *n.* (*completion, achievement*) заверш́ение; (*of marriage*) осуществлéние.
consumption [kən'sʌmpʃ(ə)n] *n.* **1.** (*eating etc.*) потреблéние, поглощéние; **the ~ of beer has gone up** потреблéние пи́ва поднялóсь. **2.** (*using up*) потреблéние. **3.** (*med.*) чахóтка, туберкулёз.
consumptive [kən'sʌmptɪv] *n. & adj.* (*med.*) чахóточный, туберкулёзный (больнóй).
contact ['kɒntækt] *n.* **1.** (*lit., fig.*) контáкт, соприкосновéние; **bring, come into ~ with** установи́ть (*pf.*) контáкт с+*i.*; войти́ (*pf.*) в контáкт с+*i.*; **keep in ~ with** поддéрживать (*impf.*) связь с+*i.*; **our troops are in ~ with the enemy** нáши войскá вошли́ в соприкосновéние с проти́вником; **make/break ~** (*elec.*) включи́ть/вы́ключить (*both pf.*) ток; **~ lenses** контáктные ли́нзы. **2.** (*of pers.*): **he made useful ~s** он завязáл полéзные знакóмства/свя́зи; **~ man** агéнт.
v.t. (*coll.*) связáться (*pf.*) с+*i.*
contagion [kən'teɪdʒ(ə)n] *n.* зарáза.
contagious [kən'teɪdʒəs] *adj.* зарáзный, инфекциóнный; **laughter is ~** смех заразúтелен.
contain [kən'teɪn] *v.t.* **1.** (*hold within itself*) содержáть (*impf.*) в себé; **the newspaper ~s interesting reports** в газéте есть/имéются интерéсные сообщéния. **2.** (*comprise*) содержáть (*impf.*); состоя́ть (*impf.*) из+*g.*; **a gallon ~s eight pints** в галлóне вóсемь пинт. **3.** (*be capable of holding*) вмещáть (*impf.*); **how much does this bottle ~?** скóлько вмещáет э́та буты́лка? **4.** (*control*) сдéрж|ивать, -áть; **~ yourself!** возьми́те себя́ в рýки! **5.** (*hold in check*) сдéрж|ивать, -áть; **our forces ~ed the enemy** нáши войскá сдéрживали проти́вника.
container [kən'teɪnə(r)] *n.* **1.** (*receptacle*) сосýд. **2.** контéйнер, тáра; **~ ship** контéйнерное сýдно.
containment [kən'teɪnmənt] *n.* (*of enemy forces etc.*) сдéрживание.
contaminate [kən'tæmɪ,neɪt] *v.t.* зара|жáть, -зи́ть; загрязн|я́ть, -и́ть.
contamination [kən,tæmɪ'neɪʃ(ə)n] *v.t.* заражéние, загрязнéние.
contemplate ['kɒntəm,pleɪt] *v.t.* **1.** (*gaze at*) созер-

ца́ть (*impf.*); при́стально рассма́тривать (*impf.*). **2.** (*view mentally*) рассма́тривать (*impf.*); созерца́ть (*impf*). **3.** (*envisage, plan*) обду́м|ывать, -ать; зам|ышля́ть, -ы́слить.

contemplation [ˌkɒntəmˈpleɪʃ(ə)n] *n.* созерца́ние, размышле́ние, обду́мывание.

contemplative [kənˈtemplətɪv] *adj.* созерца́тельный.

contemporaneous [kənˌtempəˈreɪnɪəs] *adj.* совреме́нный, одновре́ме́нный.

contemporary [kənˈtempərərɪ] *n.* совреме́нни|к, све́рстни|к (*fem.* -ца).

adj. совреме́нный; ~ **history** нове́йшая исто́рия.

contempt [kənˈtempt] *n.* презре́ние; **have ~ for** презира́ть (*impf.*); **in ~ of rules** невзира́я на пра́вила; **~ of court** оскорбле́ние суда́.

contemptible [kənˈtemptɪb(ə)l] *adj.* презре́нный.

contemptuous [kənˈtemptjʊəs] *adj.* презри́тельный.

contend [kənˈtend] *v.t.* утвержда́ть (*impf.*).

v.i. (*fight*) боро́ться (*impf.*) (**with:** с+*i.*; *for:* за+*a.*); (*compete*) состяза́ться (*impf.*); **~ for a prize** боро́ться (*impf.*) за приз; оспа́ривать (*impf.*) приз.

contender [kənˈtendə(r)] *n.* сопе́рник, претенде́нт.

content[1] [ˈkɒntent] *n.* (*lit., fig.*) содержа́ние; **the sugar ~ of beet** содержа́ние са́хара в свёкле; (*pl.*) содержи́мое; **(table of) ~s** оглавле́ние.

content[2] [kənˈtent] *n.*: **to one's heart's ~** в своё удово́льствие, вво́лю, всласть.

adj. дово́льный.

v.t. удовлетвор|я́ть, -и́ть; **~ o.s.** дово́льствоваться; **a ~ed look** дово́льный вид.

contention [kənˈtenʃ(ə)n] *n.* (*strife*) спор, раздо́р; (*assertion*) утвержде́ние.

contentious [kənˈtenʃəs] *adj.* вздо́рный, зади́ристый.

contentment [kənˈtentmənt] *n.* удовлетворённость, дово́льство.

contest [ˈkɒntest; *v. only* kənˈtest] *n.* ко́нкурс, состяза́ние; **beauty ~** ко́нкурс красоты́.

v.t. & i. **1.** (*dispute*) осп|а́ривать, -о́рить. **2.** (*contend for*) отст|а́ивать, -оя́ть; боро́ться (*impf.*) за+*a.*; **he ~ed the election** он боро́лся на вы́борах.

contestable [kənˈtestəb(ə)l] *adj.* спо́рный.

contestant [kənˈtest(ə)nt] *n.* уча́стник состяза́ния.

context [ˈkɒntekst] *n.* (*textual*) конте́кст; (*connection*) связь; **in the ~ of today's America** в усло́виях совреме́нной Аме́рики.

contiguity [ˌkɒntɪˈgjuːɪtɪ] *n.* сме́жность, соприкоснове́ние.

contiguous [kənˈtɪgjʊəs] *adj.* сме́жный, соприкаса́ющийся, прилега́ющий.

continence [ˈkɒntɪnəns] *n.* воздержа́ние.

continent [ˈkɒntɪnənt] *n.* контине́нт, матери́к; **the C~** (*Europe*) (континента́льная) Евро́па.

continental [ˌkɒntɪˈnent(ə)l] *adj.* континента́льный; **~ shelf** материко́вая о́тмель.

contingency [kənˈtɪndʒənsɪ] *n.* **1.** (*uncertainty*) случа́йность, слу́чай. **2.** (*possible event*) возмо́жное обстоя́тельство; **~ plan** вариа́нт пла́на.

contingent [kənˈtɪndʒ(ə)nt] *n.* (*mil.*) континге́нт.

adj. случа́йный; возмо́жный.

continual [kənˈtɪnjʊəl] *adj.* постоя́нный, беспреры́вный, беспреста́нный.

continuation [kənˌtɪnjʊˈeɪʃ(ə)n] *n.* продолже́ние.

continue [kənˈtɪnjuː] *v.t.* прод|олжа́ть, -о́лжить; **'to be ~d'** (*of story etc.*) продолже́ние сле́дует.

v.i. прод|олжа́ться, -о́лжиться; **the wet weather ~s** сыра́я пого́да де́ржится.

continuer [kənˈtɪnjuːə(r)] *n.* продолжа́тель (*m.*).

continuity [ˌkɒntɪˈnjuːɪtɪ] *n.* непреры́вность, беспреры́вность; **~ girl** (*cin.*) монта́жница.

continuous [kənˈtɪnjʊəs] *adj.* непреры́вный, беспреры́вный; (*gram.*) дли́тельный.

contort [kənˈtɔːt] *v.t.* иска|жа́ть, -зи́ть; искрив|ля́ть, -и́ть.

contortion [kənˈtɔːʃ(ə)n] *n.* искаже́ние; искривле́ние.

contortionist [kənˈtɔːʃənɪst] *n.* челове́к-змея́.

contraband [ˈkɒntrəˌbænd] *n.* контраба́нда; **~ goods** контраба́ндные това́ры.

contraception [ˌkɒntrəˈsepʃ(ə)n] *n.* предупрежде́ние бере́менности; примене́ние противозача́точных средств.

contraceptive [ˌkɒntrəˈseptɪv] *n.* противозача́точное сре́дство.

adj. противозача́точный.

contract[1] [ˈkɒntrækt] *n.* (*agreement*) контра́кт, догово́р; **breach of ~** наруше́ние догово́ра/контра́кта; **~ price** догово́рная цена́.

contract[2] [kənˈtrækt] *v.t.* (*conclude*) заключ|а́ть, -и́ть (*договор/контракт*); **~ a marriage** вступи́ть в брак; (*incur*): **~ an illness** заболе́ть (*pf.*).

v.i. (*agree*) прин|има́ть, -я́ть на себя́ обяза́тельство; **he ~ed to build a bridge** он подряди́лся вы́строить мост; **~ing parties** (*dipl.*) догова́ривающиеся сто́роны (*f. pl.*); **~ out** отказа́ться (*pf.*) от уча́стия в (*чём*).

contract[3] [kənˈtrækt] *v.t.* (*shorten*) сокра|ща́ть, -ти́ть; (*tighten*) сж|има́ть, -ать.

v.i. (*shorten*) сокра|ща́ться, -ти́ться; **metal ~s** мета́лл сжима́ется; (*tighten*) сж|има́ться, -а́ться.

contraction [kənˈtrækʃ(ə)n] *n.* **1.** (*shortening*) сокраще́ние, суже́ние. **2.** (*of metal*) сжа́тие; (*of muscle etc.*) сокраще́ние. **3.** (*of marriage*) заключе́ние; (*of illness*) заболева́ние (*чем*).

contractor [kənˈtræktə(r)] *n.* подря́дчик.

contractual [kənˈtræktjʊəl] *adj.* догово́рный.

contradict [ˌkɒntrəˈdɪkt] *v.t.* противоре́чить (*impf.*) +*d.*; (*rumours etc.*) опров|ерга́ть, -е́ргнуть.

contradiction [ˌkɒntrəˈdɪkʃ(ə)n] *n.* противоре́чие, опроверже́ние; **~ in terms** логи́ческая несообра́зность.

contradictory [ˌkɒntrəˈdɪktərɪ] *adj.* противоречи́вый.

contradistinction [ˌkɒntrədɪˈstɪŋkʃ(ə)n] *n.* противопоставле́ние, противополо́жность; **in ~ to** в отли́чие от+*g.*

contralto [kənˈtræltəʊ] *n.* (*voice, singer*) контра́льто (*nt. & f., indecl.*).

contraption [kənˈtræpʃ(ə)n] *n.* (*coll.*) приспособле́ние.

contrapuntal [ˌkɒntrəˈpʌnt(ə)l] *adj.* (*mus.*) контрапункти́ческий.

contrariness [ˈkɒntrərɪnɪs] *n.* (*coll., perversity*) своево́лие, своенра́вность, своенра́вие.

contrary[1] [ˈkɒntrərɪ] *n.* противополо́жность; противополо́жное, обра́тное; **on, quite the ~** (как раз) наоборо́т; **to the ~** в обра́тном смы́сле; **unless I hear to the ~** е́сли я не услы́шу чего́-нибудь ино́го; **there is no evidence to the ~** нет доказа́тельств проти́вного.

adj. противополо́жный, проти́вный, обра́тный; **~ information** противополо́жные сообще́ния.

adv.: **he acted ~ to the rules** он поступи́л про́тив пра́вил; **~ to my expectations** вопреки́ мои́м ожида́ниям.

contrary[2] [kənˈtreərɪ] *adj.* (*coll.*) своево́льный, своенра́вный.

contrast [ˈkɒntrɑːst] *n.* контра́ст; противополо́жность; **in ~ to** в противополо́жность +*d.*; **by ~ with** по сравне́нию с+*i.*

v.t. противопост|авля́ть, -а́вить; сопост|авля́ть, -а́вить.

v.i. контрасти́ровать (*impf., pf.*).

contravene [ˌkɒntrəˈviːn] *v.t.* противоре́чить (*impf.*) +*d.*; **he ~d the law** он нару́шил зако́н.

contravention [ˌkɒntrəˈvenʃ(ə)n] *n.* наруше́ние; **in ~ of** в наруше́ние +*g.*

contretemps [ˈkɔːntrəˌtɑ̃] *n.* неприя́тность.

contribute [kənˈtrɪbjuːt] *v.t.* (*money etc.*) же́ртвовать, по-; **he ~d £5** он внёс 5 фу́нтов; **he ~d new infor-**

mation он сообщи́л но́вые све́дения.

v.i. соде́йствовать (*impf.*) +*d.*; спосо́бствовать (*impf.*) +*d.*; **he ~s to our magazine** он пи́шет для на́шего журна́ла.

contribution [ˌkɒntrɪ'bju:ʃ(ə)n] *n.*: **a ~ of £5** поже́ртвование/взнос в пять фу́нтов; **his ~ to our success** его́ вклад в наш успе́х.

contributor [kən'trɪbjʊtə(r)] *n.* (*writer*) (постоя́нный) сотру́дник; (*of funds*) же́ртвователь (*m.*).

contributory [kən'trɪbjʊtərɪ] *adj.* соде́йствующий, спосо́бствующий; **a ~ pension scheme** пенсио́нная систе́ма, осно́ванная на отчисле́ниях из за́работка рабо́тающих.

contrite ['kɒntraɪt, kən'traɪt] *adj.* сокруша́ющийся, ка́ющийся.

contrition [kən'trɪʃ(ə)n] *n.* раска́яние, пока́яние.

contrivance [kən'traɪv(ə)ns] *n.* (*device*) приспособле́ние, изобрете́ние.

contrive [kən'traɪv] *v.t.* (*devise*) заду́м|ывать, -ать; изобре|та́ть, -сти; (*succeed*) наловчи́ться (*pf.*); **he ~d to offend everybody** он ухитри́лся всех оби́деть; **~d** (*artificial*) иску́сственный.

control [kən'trəʊl] *n.* **1.** (*power to direct etc.*) управле́ние, регули́рование; **he lost ~ of the car** он потеря́л управле́ние автомоби́лем; **he is in ~ of the situation** он хозя́ин положе́ния; **the situation is under ~** наведён поря́док; **the children are out of ~** де́ти не слу́шаются; **remote ~** дистанцио́нное управле́ние. **2.** (*means of regulating*) контро́ль (*m.*); **government ~s** госуда́рственный контро́ль; **birth ~** регули́рование рожда́емости. **3.** (*pl., of a machine etc.*) рычаги́ (*m. pl.*) управле́ния; **volume ~** регуля́тор гро́мкости/усиле́ния. **4.: ~ experiment** контро́льный о́пыт; **~ panel** пульт управле́ния; **~ room** пункт управле́ния; **~ tower** (*aeron.*) контро́льно-диспе́тчерский пункт.

v.t. **1.** (*master, regulate*) регули́ровать (*impf., pf.*); держа́ть (*impf.*) в повинове́нии; **~ children** держа́ть (*impf.*) дете́й в послуша́нии; **~ one's temper** владе́ть (*impf.*) собо́й; **~ prices** регули́ровать це́ны. **2.** (*verify*) контроли́ровать (*impf., pf.*).

controller [kən'trəʊlə(r)] *nn.* контролёр, инспе́ктор.

controversial [ˌkɒntrə'vɜ:ʃ(ə)l] *adj.* спо́рный, полеми́ческий.

controversy ['kɒntrəˌvɜ:sɪ] *n.* поле́мика, спор.

contuse [kən'tju:z] *v.t.* контузи́ть (*pf.*).

contusion [kən'tju:ʃ(ə)n, -ʒ(ə)n] *n.* конту́зия, ушиб.

conundrum [kə'nʌndrəm] *n.* зага́дка, головоло́мка.

conurbation [ˌkɒnɜ:'beɪʃ(ə)n] *n.* конурба́ция.

convalesce [ˌkɒnvə'les] *v.i.* выздора́вливать (*impf.*).

convalescence [ˌkɒnvə'lesəns] *n.* выздоровле́ние.

convalescent [ˌkɒnvə'les(ə)nt] *n.* выздора́вливающий.

adj. (*of patient*) выздора́вливающий, поправля́ющийся; **~ home** санато́рий для выздора́вливающих.

convection [kən'vekʃ(ə)n] *n.* конве́кция.

convector [kən'vektə(r)] *n.* конве́ктор.

convene [kən'vi:n] *v.t.* (*people*) соб|ира́ть, -ра́ть; (*meeting*) соз|ыва́ть, -ва́ть.

v.i. соб|ира́ться, -ра́ться.

convener [kən'vi:nə(r)] *n.* организа́тор/инициа́тор собра́ния.

convenience [kən'vi:nɪəns] *n.* **1.** удо́бство; **marriage of ~** брак по расчёту; **at your ~** когда́ вам бу́дет удо́бно; **~ foods** пищевы́е полуфабрика́ты. **2.** (*appliance*) удо́бства (*nt. pl.*); **all modern ~s** все удо́бства. **3.: public ~** обще́ственная убо́рная.

convenient [kən'vi:nɪənt] *adj.* удо́бный, подходя́щий; **if it is ~ for you** е́сли вам удо́бно.

convent ['kɒnv(ə)nt, -vent] *n.* (же́нский) монасты́рь.

convention [kən'venʃ(ə)n] *n.* **1.** (*congress*) съезд; **C~** (*Fr. hist.*) конве́нт. **2.** (*treaty*) конве́нция. **3.** (*custom*) обы́чай, усло́вность.

conventional [kən'venʃən(ə)l] *adj.* обы́чный, традицио́нный; **a ~ greeting** (обще)при́нятое приве́тствие; **~ sign** усло́вный знак; **~ armaments** вооруже́ние обы́чного ти́па.

conventionality [kənˌvenʃə'nælɪtɪ] *n.* усло́вность.

converge [kən'vɜ:dʒ] *v.i.* сходи́ться, сойти́сь; (*math.*) стреми́ться (*impf.*) к преде́лу; **the armies ~d on the city** а́рмии прибли́зились к го́роду.

convergence [kən'vɜ:dʒəns] *n.* сходи́мость, конверге́нция.

conversant [kən'vɜ:s(ə)nt] *adj.* знако́мый (с+*i.*), осведомлённый (в+*p.*).

conversation [ˌkɒnvə'seɪʃ(ə)n] *n.* разгово́р, бесе́да; **~s** (*e.g. dipl.*) перегово́ры (*pl., g.* -ов); **make ~** вести́/подде́рживать (*impf.*) пусто́й разгово́р.

conversational [ˌkɒnvə'seɪʃən(ə)l] *adj.* (*pert. to conversation*) разгово́рный; (*talkative*) разгово́рчивый.

converse[1] ['kɒnvɜ:s] *n.* (*logic, math.*) обра́тное положе́ние; обра́тная теоре́ма.

converse[2] [kən'vɜ:s] *v.i.* (*talk*) бесе́довать (*impf.*), разгова́ривать (*impf.*).

conversely ['kɒnvɜ:slɪ, kən'vɜ:slɪ] *adv.* наоборо́т.

conversion [kən'vɜ:ʃ(ə)n] *n.* **1.** (*transformation*) превраще́ние, перехо́д; **~ of cream into butter** сбива́ние сли́вок в ма́сло. **2.** (*relig. etc.*) обраще́ние (в+*a.*); **there were many ~s to Islam** мно́гие перешли́ в исла́м. **3.** (*math.*) преобразова́ние, перево́д; **~ of pounds into dollars** перево́д фу́нтов в до́ллары. **4.** (*fin., of stocks etc.*) конве́рсия.

convert[1] ['kɒnvɜ:t] *n.* (ново)обращённый; **he is a ~ to Buddhism** он перешёл в будди́зм.

convert[2] [kən'vɜ:t] *v.t.* **1.** (*change*) превра|ща́ть, -ти́ть; **the house was ~ed into flats** дом был разби́т на кварти́ры. **2.** (*relig. etc.*) обра|ща́ть, -ти́ть. **3.** (*math.*) пере|води́ть, -вести́; **~ pounds into francs** перевести́ (*pf.*) фу́нты сте́рлингов во фра́нки.

v.i.: **he ~ed to Buddhism** он обрати́лся в будди́зм; он при́нял будди́йскую ве́ру.

convertibility [kənˌvɜ:tɪ'bɪlɪtɪ] *n.* (*fin.*) обрати́мость.

convertible [kən'vɜ:tɪb(ə)l] *n.* (*car*) автомоби́ль (*m.*) с откидны́м/открыва́ющимся ве́рхом.

adj. обрати́мый, конверти́руемый; **~ currency** конверти́руемая валю́та.

convex ['kɒnveks] *adj.* вы́пуклый, вы́гнутый.

convey [kən'veɪ] *v.t.* **1.** (*carry, transmit*) перев|ози́ть, -езти́; перепр|авля́ть, -а́вить. **2.** (*impart*) перед|ава́ть, -а́ть; **the words ~ nothing to me** э́ти слова́ мне ничего́ не говоря́т; **~ my greetings to him** переда́йте ему́ приве́т от меня́. **3.** (*leg.*) перед|ава́ть, -а́ть (*имущество, права*).

conveyance [kən'veɪəns] *n.* (*transmission*) перево́зка, переда́ча; (*vehicle*) тра́нспортное сре́дство.

conveyancing [kən'veɪənsɪŋ] *n.* (*leg.*) составле́ние нотариа́льных а́ктов о переда́че иму́щества.

conveyer [kən'veɪə(r)] *n.* конве́йер, транспортёр; **~ belt** конве́йерная ле́нта; ле́нточный транспортёр.

convict[1] ['kɒnvɪkt] *n.* осуждённый, ка́торжник.

convict[2] [kən'vɪkt] *v.t.* осу|жда́ть, -ди́ть (*в чём*).

conviction [kən'vɪkʃ(ə)n] *n.* **1.** (*leg.*) осужде́ние; призна́ние кого́-н. вино́вным. **2.** (*settled opinion*) убежде́ние, убеждённость. **3.** (*persuasive force*) убежде́ние; **these arguments carry ~** э́ти аргуме́нты убеди́тельны; **he spoke without ~** он говори́л неуве́ренно.

convince [kən'vɪns] *v.t.* убе|жда́ть, -ди́ть.

convincing [kən'vɪnsɪŋ] *adj.* убеди́тельный.

convivial [kən'vɪvɪəl] *adj.* (*of pers.*) компане́йский, весёлый; (*of evening etc.*) весёлый.

conviviality [kənˌvɪvɪ'ælɪtɪ] *n.* весёлость, весе́лье.

convocation [ˌkɒnvə'keɪʃ(ə)n] *n.* созы́в, собра́ние.

convoke [kən'vəʊk] *v.t.* соз|ыва́ть, -ва́ть.

convoluted ['kɒnvəˌlu:tɪd] *adj.* зави́тый, изо́гнутый;

(*fig.*) запу́танный.
convolvulus [kən'vɒlvjʊləs] *n.* вьюно́к.
convoy ['kɒnvɔɪ] *n.* конво́й; тра́нспортная коло́нна с конво́ем.
convulse [kən'vʌls] *v.t.* сотряс|а́ть, -ти́; потряс|а́ть, -ти́; **he was ~d with laughter** он ко́рчился от сме́ха.
convulsion [kən'vʌlʃ(ə)n] *n.* сотрясе́ние; (*fig.*) потрясе́ние; (*pl., med.*) конву́льсия, су́дорога.
convulsive [kən'vʌlsɪv] *adj.* конвульси́вный, су́дорожный.
cony ['kəʊnɪ] *n.* (*fur*) кро́лик; кро́личий мех.
coo [ku:] *n.* воркова́нье.
v.t. & i. воркова́ть (*impf.*).
cooee ['ku:i:] *int.* ау́!
cook [kʊk] *n.* (*male*) по́вар; (*fem.*) куха́рка.
v.t. вари́ть, с-; стря́пать, со-; гото́вить, с-/при-; **~ one's own meals** гото́вить самому́; **~ up a story** (*coll.*) состря́пать (*pf.*) исто́рию.
v.i. вари́ться, с-; гото́виться, при-; **these apples ~ well** э́ти я́блоки хорошо́ пеку́тся; **what's ~ing?** (*coll.*) что тут затева́ется?
cpd. **~-house** *n.* похо́дная ку́хня; (*on ship*) ка́мбуз.
cooker ['kʊkə(r)] *n.* плита́; печь.
cookery ['kʊkərɪ] *n.* кулина́рия, стряпня́.
cpd. **~-book** (*also* **cook-book**) *n.* пова́ренная кни́га.
cookie ['kʊkɪ] *n.* (*US, small cake*) пече́нье.
cooking ['kʊkɪŋ] *n.* (*cuisine*) ку́хня.
adj. столо́вый, ку́хонный; **~ apple** я́блоко для ва́рки.
cool [ku:l] *n.* **1.** прохла́да; **in the ~ of the evening** в вече́рней прохла́де. **2.: lose one's ~** (*coll.*) вы́йти (*pf.*) из себя́, потеря́ть (*pf.*) самооблада́ние.
adj. **1.** (*lit.*) прохла́дный, све́жий. **2.** (*unexcited*) хладнокро́вный, невозмути́мый. **3.** (*impudent*) на́глый, беззасте́нчивый. **4.** (*unenthusiastic*) прохла́дный, холо́дный.
v.t. охла|жда́ть, -ди́ть; осту|жа́ть, -ди́ть; освеж|а́ть, -и́ть; **rain ~ed the air** по́сле дождя́ ста́ло прохла́дно.
v.i. охла|жда́ться, -ди́ться; освеж|а́ться, -и́ться; ост|ыва́ть, -ы́ть; **his anger ~ed** его́ гнев осты́л; **~ down, off** ост|ыва́ть, -ы́ть.
cpds. **~-headed** *adj.* уравнове́шенный, споко́йный; **~-headedness** *n.* уравнове́шенность, споко́йствие.
coolie ['ku:lɪ] *n.* ку́ли (*m. indecl.*).
coolness ['ku:lnɪs] *n.* прохла́да, хо́лод; (*of manner*) холодо́к, хо́лодность; (*estrangement*) охлажде́ние; (*impudence*) беззасте́нчивость.
coop [ku:p] *n.* куря́тник.
v.t. сажа́ть, посади́ть в кле́тку; **~ up, in** (*fig.*) держа́ть (*impf.*) взаперти́.
co-op ['kəʊɒp] *n.* (*coll.*) кооперати́вный магази́н.
cooper ['ku:pə(r)] *n.* бонда́рь (*m.*), боча́р.
co-operate [kəʊ'ɒpə,reɪt] *v.i.* сотру́дничать (*impf.*).
co-operation [kəʊ,ɒpə'reɪʃ(ə)n] *n.* сотру́дничество.
co-operative [kəʊ'ɒpərətɪv] *n.* кооперати́в.
adj. кооперати́вный; (*helpful*) гото́вый к сотру́дничеству.
co-ordinate [kəʊ'ɔ:dɪnət; *v. only* kəʊ'ɔ:dɪ,neɪt] *n.* (*math.*) координа́та.
adj. координи́рованный; ра́вный по значе́нию.
v.t. координи́ровать (*impf., pf.*).
co-ordination [kəʊ,ɔ:dɪ'neɪʃ(ə)n] *n.* координа́ция.
coot [ku:t] *n.* лысу́ха.
cop [kɒp] *n.* (*sl., policeman*) полице́йский.
copartner [kəʊ'pɑ:tnə(r)] *n.* компаньо́н, уча́стник в при́былях.
copartnership [kəʊ'pɑ:tnəʃɪp] *n.* това́рищество, уча́стие в при́былях.
cope [kəʊp] *v.i.* спр|авля́ться, -а́виться (с+*i.*).
copeck (*also* **kope(c)k**) ['kəʊpek, 'kɒpek] *n.* копе́йка.
Copenhagen [,kəʊpən'heɪgən] *n.* Копенга́ген.
copier ['kɒpɪə(r)] *n.* (*pers.*) перепи́счик; (*machine*) мно́жительный аппара́т.
co-pilot ['kəʊ,paɪlət] *n.* второ́й пило́т.
copious ['kəʊpɪəs] *adj.* оби́льный.
copper[1] ['kɒpə(r)] *n.* медь; **~ wire** ме́дная про́волока; (**~** *coin*) ме́дная моне́та.
cpds. **~-bottomed** *adj.* обши́тый ме́дью; (*fig., coll.*) надёжный, ве́рный; **~head** *n.* щитомо́рдник; **~plate** *n.* ме́дная гравирова́льная доска́; **~plate handwriting** каллиграфи́ческий по́черк; **~-smith** *n.* ме́дник.
copper[2] ['kɒpə(r)] *n.* (*sl., policeman*) полице́йский.
coppice ['kɒpɪs], **copse** [kɒps] *nn.* подле́сок, ро́щица.
copra ['kɒprə] *n.* ко́пра.
copse [kɒps] = **coppice**
copulate ['kɒpjʊ,leɪt] *v.i.* совокуп|ля́ться, -и́ться.
copulation [,kɒpjʊ'leɪʃ(ə)n] *n.* совокупле́ние.
copy ['kɒpɪ] *n.* **1.** (*imitation, version*) ко́пия, ру́копись; **fair, clean ~** чистова́я ру́копись; **rough ~** чернови́к. **2.** (*of book etc.*) экземпля́р. **3.** (*for printer*) текст, материа́л; **advertising ~** текст рекла́много объявле́ния.
v.t. & i. перепи́с|ывать, -а́ть; копи́ровать, с-; (*imitate*) подража́ть (*impf.*) +*d.*; **he copied in the examination** он спи́сывал на экза́мене.
cpds. **~-book** *n.* тетра́дь; **~-cat** *n.* (*coll.*) подража́тель (*fem.* -ница); **~-editor** *n.* техни́ческий реда́ктор; **~right** *n.* а́вторское пра́во; *adj.* охраня́емый а́вторским пра́вом; *v.t.* обеспе́чи|вать, -ть а́вторское пра́во на+*a.*; **~-typist** машини́стка-перепи́счица.
copyist ['kɒpɪɪst] *n.* перепи́счик, копиро́вщик.
coquetry ['kɒkɪtrɪ, 'kəʊk-] *n.* коке́тство.
coquette [kɒ'ket, kə'ket] *n.* коке́тка.
coquettish [kɒ'ketɪʃ, kə'ketɪʃ] *adj.* коке́тливый.
cor [kɔ:(r)] *int.* (*vulg. or joc.*) Го́споди!; Бо́же мой!
coral ['kɒr(ə)l] *n.* кора́лл; (*attr., also fig.*) кора́лловый.
cord [kɔ:d] *n.* (*rope, string*) верёвка, бечёвка; (*flex*) шнур; **spinal ~** спинно́й мозг; **vocal ~s** голосовы́е свя́зки (*f. pl.*).
v.t. свя́з|ывать, -а́ть верёвкой; **~ed** (*ribbed*) в ру́бчик; ру́бчатый.
cordial ['kɔ:dɪəl] *n.* подслащённый напи́ток.
adj. (*friendly*) серде́чный, раду́шный.
cordiality [,kɔ:dɪ'ælɪtɪ] *n.* серде́чность, раду́шие.
cordite ['kɔ:daɪt] *n.* корди́т.
cordless ['kɔ:dlɪs] *adj.* беспроводно́й, бесшнурово́й.
cordon ['kɔ:d(ə)n] *n.* (*of police etc.*) кордо́н.
v.t. (*also* **~ off**) оцеп|ля́ть, -и́ть.
corduroy ['kɔ:də,rɔɪ, -djʊ,rɔɪ] *n.* вельве́т; ру́бчатый плис; (*pl.*, **~** *trousers*) вельве́товые брю́к|и (*pl., g.* —).
core [kɔ:(r)] *n.* **1.** (*of fruit*) сердцеви́на; (*fig.*) центр, ядро́, суть; **rotten at the ~** гнило́й изнутри́; **English to the ~** англича́нин до мо́зга косте́й; **~ of a problem** суть пробле́мы; **hard ~** (*attr.*) закорене́лый, отча́янный. **2.** (*elec.*) жи́ла ка́беля; (*of nuclear reactor*) акти́вная зо́на.
v.t. выреза́ть, вы́резать сердцеви́ну +*g.*
co-religionist [,kəʊrɪ'lɪdʒənɪst] *n.* единове́р|ец (*fem.* -ка).
co-respondent [,kəʊrɪ'spɒnd(ə)nt] *n.* (*leg.*) соотве́тчик (в бракоразво́дном проце́ссе).
corgi ['kɔ:gɪ] *n.* ко́рги (*m. indecl.*).
coriander [,kɒrɪ'ændə(r)] *n.* (*bot., also* **~ seed**) кориа́ндр; (*cul.*) fresh (leaves) кинза́.
cork [kɔ:k] *n.* (*material, stopper*) про́бка; (*attr.*) про́бковый; (*float*) поплаво́к.
v.t. (*stop up*) зат|ыка́ть, -кну́ть про́бкой; **~ up one's feelings** сде́рживать (*impf.*) свои́ чу́вства.
cpd. **~screw** *n.* што́пор; *v.i.* дви́гаться (*impf.*)

по спира́ли.

corker ['kɔːkə(r)] *n.* (*sl., excellent or astonishing thg. or pers.*) (не́что) шика́рное/потряса́ющее; блеск.

corking ['kɔːkɪŋ] *adj.* (*sl., excellent*) шика́рный.

cormorant ['kɔːmərənt] *n.* большо́й баклан.

corn[1] [kɔːn] *n.* **1.** (*grain, seed*) зерно́. **2.** (*cereals in general*) зерновы́е (*pl.*), хлеб; ~ **exchange** хле́бная би́ржа. **3.** (*wheat*) пшени́ца; **a field of** ~ пшени́чное по́ле. **4.** (*US, maize*) кукуру́за.

cpds. **~-cob** *n.* сте́ржень (*m.*) кукуру́зного поча́тка; **~crake** *n.* коросте́ль (*m.*); **~flakes** *n.* корнфле́кс; **~flour** *n.* кукуру́зная мука́; **~flower** *n.* василёк.

corn[2] [kɔːn] *n.* (*on foot*) мозо́ль.

corn[3] [kɔːn] *v.t.*: **~ed beef** солони́на.

cornea ['kɔːnɪə] *n.* рогови́ца; рогова́я оболо́чка.

cornelian [kɔː'niːlɪən] *n.* сердоли́к.

corner ['kɔːnə(r)] *n.* **1.** (*place where lines etc. meet*) у́гол; **at, on the** ~ на углу́; **round the** ~ (*lit.*) за угло́м; (*fig., near*) ря́дом, побли́зости; **cut a** ~ (*of car*) сре́зать (*pf.*) поворо́т; **he was driven into a** ~ (*fig.*) он был за́гнан в у́гол; **in a tight** ~ в затрудне́нии; **turn the** ~ (*of illness*) благополу́чно перенести́ (*pf.*) кри́зис (боле́зни); **he looked out of the** ~ **of his eye** он следи́л уголко́м гла́за. **2.** (*hidden place etc.*) уголо́к. **3.** (*region*) край; **all the** ~**s of the earth** все уголки́ земли́. **4.** (*football*) углово́й уда́р, ко́рнер.

v.t. заг|оня́ть, -на́ть в у́гол; **the fugitive was ~ed** беглеца́ загна́ли в у́гол; **he ~ed the market** он завладе́л ры́нком, скупи́в весь това́р.

v.i. (*of car*) брать, взять углы́.

cpd. **~-stone** *n.* (*fig.*) краеуго́льный ка́мень.

cornet ['kɔːnɪt] *n.* **1.** (*mus. instrument*) корне́т. **2.** (*for ice-cream*) ва́фельный рожо́к.

cornice ['kɔːnɪs] *n.* карни́з.

cornucopia [ˌkɔːnjʊ'kəʊpɪə] *n.* рог изоби́лия.

corny ['kɔːnɪ] *adj.* (*coll., hackneyed*) пло́ский, изби́тый.

corolla [kə'rɒlə] *n.* ве́нчик.

corollary [kə'rɒlərɪ] *n.* сле́дствие, вы́вод.

corona [kə'rəʊnə] *n.* коро́на, вене́ц.

coronary ['kɒrənərɪ] *n.* коронаротромбо́з.

adj. (*anat.*) корона́рный, вене́чный; ~ **artery** вене́чная арте́рия; ~ **(thrombosis)** тромбо́з вене́чных арте́рий.

coronation [ˌkɒrə'neɪʃ(ə)n] *n.* корона́ция.

coroner ['kɒrənə(r)] *n.* сле́дователь (*m.*), веду́щий дела́ о наси́льственной или скоропости́жной сме́рти.

coronet ['kɒrənɪt, -ˌnet] *n.* (*small crown*) коро́на, диаде́ма; (*garland*) вено́к, вене́ц.

Corp. [ˌkɔːpə'reɪʃ(ə)n] *n.* (*abbr. of* **Corporation**) корпора́ция.

corporal[1] ['kɔːpr(ə)l] *n.* (*officer*) капра́л.

corporal[2] ['kɔːpr(ə)l] *adj.* теле́сный; ~ **punishment** теле́сное наказа́ние.

corporate ['kɔːpərət] *adj.* **1.** (*collective*) о́бщий, коллекти́вный. **2.** (*of, forming a corporation*) корпорати́вный. **3.:** ~ **state** корпорати́вное госуда́рство.

corporation [ˌkɔːpə'reɪʃ(ə)n] *n.* (*public body*) корпора́ция; (*US, company*) акционе́рное о́бщество; (*coll., paunch*) пу́зо, брю́хо.

corporeal [kɔː'pɔːrɪəl] *adj.* теле́сный.

corps [kɔː(r)] *n.* (*mil., dipl.*) ко́рпус; ~ ***de ballet*** кордебале́т.

corpse [kɔːps] *n.* труп.

corpulence ['kɔːpjʊləns] *n.* полнота́, ту́чность, доро́дность.

corpulent ['kɔːpjʊlənt] *adj.* по́лный, ту́чный, доро́дный.

corpus ['kɔːpəs] *n.* (*body of writings etc.*) свод, ко́декс; ~ **delicti** соста́в преступле́ния.

corpuscle ['kɔːpʌs(ə)l] *n.* корпу́скула, те́льце, части́ца.

corral [kɒ'rɑːl] *n.* (*enclosure*) заго́н.

v.t. (*drive together*) заг|оня́ть, -на́ть в заго́н.

correct [kə'rekt] *adj.* **1.** (*right, true*) пра́вильный, ве́рный, то́чный. **2.** (*of behaviour*) корре́ктный.

v.t. **1.** (*make right*) испр|авля́ть, -а́вить; попр|авля́ть, -а́вить; **I ~ed my watch by the time signal** я вы́верил свои́ часы́ по сигна́лу вре́мени. **2.** (*admonish, punish*) нака́з|ывать, -а́ть; де́лать, с- замеча́ние +*d*.

correction [kə'rekʃ(ə)n] *n.* **1.** (*act of correcting*) исправле́ние, поправле́ние, пра́вка; **these figures are subject to** ~ э́ти ци́фры подлежа́т исправле́нию. **2.** (*thg. substituted for what is wrong*) попра́вка, исправле́ние. **3.** (*punishment*) наказа́ние; **house of** ~ исправи́тельный дом.

corrective [kə'rektɪv] *adj.* исправи́тельный.

correctness [kə'rektnɪs] *n.* пра́вильность, ве́рность; (*of behaviour*) корре́ктность.

correlate ['kɒrəˌleɪt, 'kɒrɪ-] *v.t.* прив|оди́ть, -ести́ в соотноше́ние.

correlation [ˌkɒrə'leɪʃ(ə)n, ˌkɒrɪ-] *n.* соотноше́ние.

correlative [kɒ'relətɪv, kə-] *adj.* соотноси́тельный.

correspond [ˌkɒrɪ'spɒnd] *v.i.* **1.** (*match, harmonize*) соотве́тствовать (*impf.*) (+*d.*). **2.** (*exchange letters*) перепи́сываться (*impf.*) (с+*i.*).

correspondence [ˌkɒrɪ'spɒnd(ə)ns] *n.* **1.** (*analogy, agreement*) соотве́тствие. **2.** (*letter-writing*) корреспонде́нция, перепи́ска; **I am in** ~ **with him** я с ним перепи́сываюсь; ~ **column** ру́брика пи́сем (в газе́те); ~ **course** курс зао́чного обуче́ния.

correspondent [ˌkɒrɪ'spɒnd(ə)nt] *n.* (*writer of letters; reporter*) корреспонде́нт.

corresponding [ˌkɒrɪ'spɒndɪŋ] *adj.* **1.** (*matching*) соотве́тствующий. **2.:** ~ **member** (*of a society*) член-корреспонде́нт.

corridor ['kɒrɪˌdɔː(r)] *n.* коридо́р.

corroborate [kə'rɒbəˌreɪt] *v.t.* подтвер|жда́ть, -ди́ть.

corroboration [kəˌrɒbə'reɪʃ(ə)n] *n.* подтвержде́ние; **in** ~ в подтвержде́ние (*чего*).

corroborat|ive [kə'rɒbərətɪv] *adj.* подтвержда́ющий.

corrode [kə'rəʊd] *v.t.* разъ|еда́ть, -е́сть.

v.i. ржаве́ть, за-.

corrosion [kə'rəʊʒ(ə)n] *n.* корро́зия, ржа́вчина.

corrosive [kə'rəʊsɪv] *adj.* коррози́йный, разъеда́ющий, е́дкий.

corrugate ['kɒrʊˌgeɪt] *v.t.* гофрирова́ть (*impf., pf.*); **~d iron** волни́стое/рифлёное желе́зо.

corrupt [kə'rʌpt] *adj.* **1.** (*depraved*) развращённый. **2.** (*venal*) прода́жный; ~ **practices** корру́пция, подку́пность и прода́жность.

v.t. **1.** (*deprave*) развра|ща́ть, -ти́ть; разл|ага́ть, -ожи́ть. **2.** (*bribe*) подкуп|а́ть, -и́ть.

corruption [kə'rʌpʃ(ə)n] *n.* **1.** (*depravity*) разложе́ние; развраще́ние. **3.** (*bribery*) корру́пция. **4.** (*deformation*) по́рча, искаже́ние; **this word is a** ~ **of that** э́то сло́во — испо́рченный вариа́нт того́ сло́ва.

corsage [kɔː'sɑːʒ] *n.* (*bodice*) корса́ж; (*US, flower adornment*) цвето́к, прико́лотый к корса́жу.

corset ['kɔːsɪt] *n.* корсе́т.

cortège [kɔː'teɪʒ] *n.* корте́ж.

cortex ['kɔːteks] *n.* (*bark*) кора́; (*anat.*) кора́ больши́х полуша́рий головно́го мо́зга.

cortisone ['kɔːtɪˌzəʊn] *n.* кортизо́н.

corundum [kə'rʌndəm] *n.* кору́нд.

coruscat|e ['kɒrəˌskeɪt] *v.i.* (*lit., fig.*) сверк|а́ть, -ну́ть.

cosecant [kəʊ'siːkənt] *n.* (*math.*) косе́канс.

cosh [kɒʃ] *n.* дуби́нка.

cosine ['kəʊsaɪn] *n.* ко́синус.

cosiness ['kəʊzɪnɪs] *n.* ую́т.

cosmetic [kɒz'metɪk] *n.* косме́тика.

adj. космети́ческий.

cosmic ['kɒzmɪk] *adj.* косми́ческий.

cosmologist [kɒz'mɒlədʒɪst] *n.* космо́лог.

cosmology [kɒz'mɒlədʒɪ] *n.* космоло́гия.
cosmonaut ['kɒzmə,nɔ:t] *n.* космона́вт.
cosmopolitan [,kɒzmə'pɒlɪt(ə)n] *n.* космополи́т.
adj. космополити́ческий.
cosmopolitanism [kɒzmə'pɒlɪtən,ɪz(ə)m] *n.* космополити́зм.
cosmos ['kɒzmɒs] *n.* ко́смос.
Cossack ['kɒsæk] *n.* каза́|к (*fem.* -чка); (*attr.*) каза́цкий, каза́чий; ~ **hat** папа́ха.
cosset ['kɒsɪt] *v.t.* балова́ть (*impf.*); не́жить (*impf.*).
cost [kɒst] *n.* **1.** (*monetary*) цена́, сто́имость; ~ **price** себесто́имость; **he sold it at** ~ он про́дал э́то по себесто́имости; ~ **accounting** хозрасчёт; ~ **of living** прожи́точный ми́нимум; ~ **of production** изде́ржки (*f. pl.*) произво́дства. **2.** (*expense, loss*) цена́; **at all** ~**s** любо́й цено́й; **at the** ~ **of his life** цено́й жи́зни; **count the** ~ (*fig.*) взве́сить (*pf.*) возмо́жные после́дствия. **3.** (*pl., leg.*) суде́бные изде́ржки (*f. pl.*).
v.t. & i. **1.** (*involve expense*) сто́ить (*impf.*); об|ходи́ться, -ойти́сь (*кому во что*); **this** ~ **me £5** э́то сто́ило мне 5 фу́нтов; э́то обошло́сь мне в 5 фу́нтов; **it will** ~ **you dear** э́то вам до́рого обойдётся. **2.** (*assess* ~ *of*) оце́н|ивать, -и́ть изде́ржки (*предприятия и т.п.*).
cpds. ~**-effective** *adj.* рента́бельный.
co-star ['kəʊstɑ:(r)] *n.* партнёр (*fem.* -ша) (в друго́й гла́вной ро́ли).
costing ['kɒstɪŋ] *n.* калькуля́ция изде́ржек произво́дства (*чего*).
costly ['kɒstlɪ] *adj.* дорого́й, дорогосто́ящий.
costume ['kɒstju:m] *n.* костю́м; (*attr.*): ~ **ball** костюми́рованный бал; ~ **jewellery** ювели́рные украше́ния к пла́тью.
cosy (*US* **cozy**) ['kəʊzɪ] *adj.* ую́тный.
cot [kɒt] *n.* (*small bed*) де́тская крова́тка; (*cradle*) лю́лька, колыбе́ль; ~ **death** внеза́пная сме́рть (ребёнка грудно́го во́зраста).
cotangent [kəʊ'tændʒ(ə)nt] *n.* кота́нгенс.
co-tenancy [kəʊ'tenənsɪ] *n.* сoаре́нда.
co-tenant [kəʊ'tenənt] *n.* соаренда́тор.
coterie ['kəʊtərɪ] *n.* кружо́к.
cotill(i)on [kə'tɪljən] *n.* котильо́н.
cottage ['kɒtɪdʒ] *n.* котте́дж; за́городный дом, до́мик, да́ча; ~ **cheese** (прессо́ванный) творо́г; ~ **industry** надо́мное произво́дство; куста́рная промы́шленность; ~ **pie** карто́фельная запека́нка с мя́сом.
cotton[1] ['kɒt(ə)n] *n.* **1.** (*plant*) хло́пок, хлопча́тник. **2.** (*fabric*) (хлопча́то)бума́жная ткань; ~ **print** си́тец. **3.** (*thread*) ни́тки (*f. pl.*); (*piece of thread*) ни́тка. **4.** (*attr.*) хло́пковый, хлопча́тый, хлопчатобума́жный. **5.** (*US*) = ~**-wool**
cpds. ~**-gin** *n.* хлопкоочисти́тельная маши́на; ~**-mill** *n.* хлопкопряди́льная фа́брика; ~**-picker** *n.* хлопкоро́б; ~**-seed** *n.* хло́пковое се́мя; ~**-wool** *n.* ва́та.
cotton[2] ['kɒt(ə)n] *v.i.* (*coll.*): ~ **on to** поня́ть (*pf.*), (*coll.*) усе́чь (*pf.*).
cotyledon [,kɒtɪ'li:d(ə)n] *n.* семядо́ля.
couch [kaʊtʃ] *n.* (*sofa*) куше́тка, дива́н; (*bed*) крова́ть.
v.t.: (*express*): **he** ~**ed his reply in friendly terms** он облёк свой отве́т в дру́жескую фо́рму.
couchette [ku:'ʃet] *n.* спа́льное ме́сто.
cougar ['ku:gə(r)] *n.* пу́ма, кугуа́р.
cough [kɒf] *n.* ка́шель (*m.*); **he has a bad** ~ у него́ си́льный ка́шель.
v.t. & i. ка́шлять (*impf.*); ~ **up** (*lit.*) отка́шл|ивать, -яну́ть; (*fig., coll.*) вы́кла́дывать, вы́ложить.
cpds. ~**-drop** *n.* пасти́лка/табле́тка от ка́шля; ~**-medicine,** ~**-mixture** *nn.* миксту́ра от ка́шля.
could [kʊd] *v. aux.*, *see* **can**[2]
council ['kaʊns(ə)l] *n.* сове́т; **town** ~ городско́й сове́т; муниципалите́т; **Church** ~ церко́вный собо́р; ~ **tax** муниципа́льный нало́г.
cpd. ~**-house** *n.* (*dwelling*) муниципа́льный дом; жило́й дом, принадлежа́щий муниципа́льному сове́ту.
councillor ['kaʊnsələ(r)] *n.* член сове́та.
counsel ['kaʊns(ə)l] *n.* **1.** (*advice, consultation*) сове́т, совеща́ние; **take** ~ **with s.o.** совеща́ться (*impf.*) с кем-н.; **keep one's (own)** ~ пома́лкивать (*impf.*). **2.** (*barrister(s)*) адвока́т; ~ **for the defence** защи́тник; ~ **for the plaintiff** адвока́т истца́.
counsellor ['kaʊnsələ(r)] *n.* сове́тник.
count[1] [kaʊnt] *n.* (*nobleman*) граф.
count[2] [kaʊnt] *n.* **1.** (*reckoning*) счёт, подсчёт; **keep** ~ счита́ть (*impf.*); вести́ (*det.*) счёт; **lose** ~ потеря́ть (*pf.*) счёт. **2.** (*total*) ито́г; **the** ~ **was 200** ито́г равня́лся 200 (двумста́м). **3.** (*leg.*) пункт обвини́тельного заключе́ния; **he was found guilty on all** ~**s** его́ призна́ли вино́вным по всем пу́нктам обвини́тельного заключе́ния. **4.** (*boxing*): **he took** (*or* **went down for) the** ~ он был нокаути́рован.
v.t. (*number, reckon*) счита́ть, со-; подсчи́т|ывать, -а́ть; пересчи́т|ывать, -а́ть; **he** ~**ed (up) the men** он пересчита́л солда́т; ~ **your change!** прове́рьте сда́чу!; ~ **ten!** сосчита́йте до десяти́!; **50 people, not** ~**ing the children** 50 челове́к, не счита́я дете́й; **I** ~ **him among my friends** я счита́ю его́ мои́м дру́гом; ~ **me in/out!** включи́те/исключи́те меня́; **I shall** ~ **it an honour to serve you** я почту́ за че́сть служи́ть вам; **do not** ~ **that against him** не ста́вьте ему́ э́того в вину́; **the boxer was** ~**ed out** боксёр был объя́влен нокаути́рованным.
v.i. **1.** (*reckon, number*) счита́ть (*impf.*); ~ **up to 10!** счита́йте до десяти́!; ~ **down from 10 to 0!** счита́йте в обра́тном поря́дке от десяти́ до нуля́!; ~**ing-house** бухгалте́рия. **2.** (*be reckoned*) счита́ться (*impf.*); **that doesn't** ~ э́то не в счёт (*or* не счита́ется); ~ **for much** име́ть большо́е значе́ние; ~ **for little** не име́ть (*impf.*) большо́го значе́ния; ~ **for nothing** не име́ть никако́го значе́ния. **3.** (*rely*) рассчи́тывать (*impf.*) (на+*a.*); **I** ~ **(up)on you to help** я рассчи́тываю на ва́шу по́мощь.
cpd. ~**-down** *n.* обра́тный отсчёт вре́мени.
countenance ['kaʊntɪnəns] *n.* **1.** (*face*) лицо́, о́блик; выраже́ние лица́. **2.** (*composure*) споко́йствие. **3.** (*sanction*) подде́ржка.
v.t. подде́рж|ивать, -а́ть.
counter[1] ['kaʊntɪnəns] *n.* **1.** (*at games*) фи́шка, ма́рка. **2.** (*in shop*) прила́вок; **under the** ~ (*fig.*) из-под полы́/прила́вка. **3.** (*device for counting*) счётчик; **Geiger** ~ счётчик Ге́йгера.
counter[2] ['kaʊntɪnəns] *adj. & adv.* (*contrary*) противополо́жный; напро́тив; **this runs** ~ **to my wishes** э́то идёт вразре́з с мои́ми жела́ниями.
v.t. & i. (*oppose, parry*) противоде́йствовать (*impf.*) +*d.*
counteract [,kaʊntə'rækt] *v.t.* противоде́йствовать (*impf.*) +*d.*
counteraction [,kaʊntər'ækʃ(ə)n] *n.* противоде́йствие.
counter-attack ['kaʊntərə,tæk] *n.* контрата́ка.
v.t. & i. контратакова́ть (*impf., pf.*).
counter-attraction ['kaʊntərə,trækʃ(ə)n] *n.* зама́нчивая альтернати́ва.
counterbalance ['kaʊntə,bæləns] *n.* противове́с.
v.t. уравнове́|шивать, -сить.
counterblow ['kaʊntər,bləʊ] *n.* контруда́р; встре́чный уда́р.
countercharge ['kaʊntə,tʃɑ:dʒ] *n.* встре́чное обвине́ние.
v.t. предъяв|ля́ть, -и́ть встре́чное обвине́ние +*p.*
counter-claim ['kaʊntə,kleɪm] *n.* встре́чный иск; контробвине́ние.

v.t. предъяв|ля́ть, -и́ть встре́чный иск (*кому*) на+*a*.
counter-clockwise [ˌkaʊntəˈklɒkwaɪz] *adj.* & *adv.* (дви́жущийся) про́тив часово́й стре́лки.
counter-espionage [ˌkaʊntərˈespɪəˌnɑːʒ, -ɪdʒ] *n.* контрразве́дка.
counterfeit [ˈkaʊntəfɪt, -ˌfiːt] *n.* подде́лка, подло́г.
adj. подде́льный, подло́жный.
v.t. & *i.* подде́л|ывать, -ать.
counterfeiter [ˈkaʊntəfɪtə(r), -ˌfiːtə(r)] *n.* фальшивомоне́тчик.
counterfoil [ˈkaʊntəˌfɔɪl] *n.* корешо́к (че́ка *и т.п.*).
counter-intelligence [ˌkaʊntərɪnˈtelɪdʒ(ə)ns] *n.* контрразве́дка.
countermand [ˌkaʊntəˈmɑːnd] *v.t.* отмен|я́ть, -и́ть.
counter-measure [ˈkaʊntəˌmeʒə(r)] *n.* контрме́ра.
counter-offensive [ˈkaʊntərəˌfensɪv] *n.* контрнаступле́ние.
counterpane [ˈkaʊntəˌpeɪn] *n.* покрыва́ло.
counterpart [ˈkaʊntəˌpɑːt] *n.* па́ра (*к чему*), дополне́ние; (*pers.*) двойни́к, колле́га (*c.g.*).
counterpoint [ˈkaʊntəˌpɔɪnt] *n.* контрапу́нкт.
counterpoise [ˈkaʊntəˌpɔɪz] *n.* противове́с.
counter-productive [ˌkaʊntəprəˈdʌktɪv] *adj.* приводя́щий к обра́тным результа́там; нецелесообра́зный.
counter-proposal [ˈkaʊntəprəˌpəʊz(ə)l] *n.* встре́чное предложе́ние; контрпредложе́ние.
counter-revolution [ˌkaʊntəˌrevəˈluːʃ(ə)n] *n.* контрреволю́ция.
counter-revolutionary [ˌkaʊntəˌrevəˈluːʃənərɪ] *n.* контрреволюционе́р.
adj. контрреволюцио́нный.
countersign [ˈkaʊntəˌsaɪn] *n.* (*watchword*) паро́ль (*m.*), о́тзыв.
v.t. (*add signature to*) скреп|ля́ть, -и́ть по́дписью.
countersignature [ˈkaʊntəˌsɪgnətʃə(r)] *n.* втора́я по́дпись.
counterstroke [ˈkaʊntəˌstrəʊk] *n.* контруда́р.
counterweight [ˈkaʊntəˌweɪt] *n.* противове́с.
countess [ˈkaʊntɪs] *n.* графи́ня.
countless [ˈkaʊntlɪs] *adj.* бесчи́сленный, несчётный, неисчисли́мый.
country [ˈkʌntrɪ] *n.* **1.** (*geog.*, *pol.*) страна́; **~ of birth** ро́дина. **2.** (*motherland*) ро́дина, оте́чество. **3.** (*opp. town*) дере́вня; **in the ~** за́ городом; (*~side*) приро́да, се́льская ме́стность; **~ life** дереве́нская жизнь; **~ gentleman** землевладе́лец, поме́щик; **~ house, seat** поме́стье; **~ club** за́городный клуб. **4.** (*terrain*) ме́стность; **difficult ~** труднопроходи́мая ме́стность. **5.** (*fig.*, *domain*) о́бласть, сфе́ра; **the subject is unknown ~ to me** э́то неизве́стная для меня́ о́бласть.
cpds. **~folk** *n.* се́льские жи́тели (*m. pl.*); **~man** *n.* дереве́нский/се́льский жи́тель (*m.*); (*fellow-~man*) сооте́чественник, земля́к; **~side** *n.* се́льская ме́стность; ландша́фт; **~woman** *n.* дереве́нская/се́льская жи́тельница; (*fellow-~woman*) сооте́чественница, земля́чка.
county [ˈkaʊntɪ] *n.* гра́фство; **~ town** гла́вный го́род гра́фства.
coup [kuː] *n.* уда́чный ход; *see also* **~ d'état**
cpds. **~ de grâce** *n.* заверша́ющий уда́р; **~ d'état** *n.* госуда́рственный переворо́т.
couple [ˈkʌp(ə)l] *n.* (*objects or people*) па́ра; **married ~** супру́жеская па́ра; **engaged ~** жени́х и неве́ста.
v.t. **1.** (*rail*) сцеп|ля́ть, -и́ть. **2.** (*associate, assemble*) соедин|я́ть, -и́ть; свя́з|ывать, -а́ть.
coupling [ˈkʌplɪŋ] *n.* (*rail.*) сцепле́ние, сце́пка; (*tech.*) связь, му́фта.
coupon [ˈkuːpɒn] *n.* купо́н, тало́н.
courage [ˈkʌrɪdʒ] *n.* хра́брость, му́жество; **take, pluck up ~** мужа́ться (*impf.*); соб|ира́ться, -ра́ться с ду́хом; **lose ~** пасть (*pf.*) ду́хом; **take one's ~ in both hands** мобилизова́ть (*impf.*, *pf.*) всё своё му́жество.
courageous [kəˈreɪdʒəs] *adj.* хра́брый, му́жественный.
courgette [kʊəˈʒet] *n.* кабачо́к.
courier [ˈkʊrɪə(r)] *n.* (*messenger*) курье́р, на́рочный; (*travel guide*) экскурсово́д.
course [kɔːs] *n.* **1.** (*movement, process*) ход, тече́ние; **~ of events** ход собы́тий; **in ~ of time** с тече́нием вре́мени; **in the ordinary ~** (*of events*) при норма́льном разви́тии собы́тий; **in due ~** в своё вре́мя; **of ~** коне́чно; **as a matter of ~** обы́чным поря́дком; **he takes my help as a matter of ~** он принима́ет мою́ по́мощь как не́что само́ собо́й разуме́ющееся; **the disease must run its ~** боле́знь должна́ пройти́ все ста́дии. **2.** (*direction*) курс, направле́ние; (*of a river*) тече́ние; (*naut.*) курс; **our ~ lies due north** мы де́ржим курс (*or* направле́ние) на се́вер; **we are on ~** мы идём по ку́рсу; **we are off ~** мы сби́лись с ку́рса. **3.** (*line of conduct*): **this is the only ~ open to us** э́то — еди́нственная ли́ния поведе́ния, досту́пная нам. **4.** (*race-~*) скаково́й круг, доро́жка; **stay the ~** (*fig.*) держа́ться (*impf.*) до конца́. **5.** (*series*) курс; **a ~ of lectures** курс ле́кций; **a ~ of treatment** курс лече́ния. **6.** (*cul.*) блю́до; **main ~** второ́е блю́до; **sweet ~** сла́дкое, десе́рт.
v.i. (*run about*) бе́гать (*indet.*); (*of water*) бежа́ть (*det.*); (*of blood*) течь (*impf.*).
court [kɔːt] *n.* **1.** (*yard*) двор. **2.** (*space for playing games*) площа́дка для игр; (*tennis*) корт; **hard ~** бетони́рованный корт; **grass ~** земляно́й корт. **3.** (*sovereign's etc.*) двор; **hold ~** (*maintain a ~*) содержа́ть (*impf.*) двор. **4.** (*leg.*) суд; **~ of law, justice** суд; **~ of inquiry** сле́дственная коми́ссия; **they settled (the case) out of ~** они́ пришли́ к (полюбо́вному) соглаше́нию; **he was brought to ~** (*for trial*) он предста́л пе́ред судо́м. **5.: pay ~ to s.o.** уха́живать (*impf.*) за кем-н.
v.t. **1.** (*a woman*) уха́живать (*impf.*) за+*i.* **2.** (*seek*): **she ~ed his approval** она́ добива́лась его́ одобре́ния. **3.** (*risk*): **he is ~ing disaster** он игра́ет с огнём.
cpds. **~-house** *n.* зда́ние суда́; **~-martial** *n.* вое́нный суд; *v.t.* суди́ть (*impf.*) вое́нным судо́м; **~-room** *n.* зал суда́; **~yard** *n.* двор.
courteous [ˈkɜːtɪəs] *adj.* ве́жливый, учти́вый.
courtesan [ˌkɔːtɪˈzæn, ˈkɔːt-] *n.* куртиза́нка.
courtesy [ˈkɜːtɪsɪ] *n.* (*politeness*) ве́жливость, учти́вость; (*polite act*) любе́зность.
courtier [ˈkɔːtɪə(r)] *n.* придво́рный.
courtly [ˈkɔːtlɪ] *adj.* обходи́тельный.
courtship [ˈkɔːtʃɪp] *n.* уха́живание.
cousin [ˈkʌz(ə)n] *n.* (*also* **first ~**) (*male*) кузе́н; двою́родный брат; (*fem.*) кузи́на; двою́родная сестра́; **second ~** трою́родный брат (*fem.* трою́родная сестра́); **our American ~s** на́ши америка́нские ро́дственники.
couturier [kuːˈtjʊərɪˌeɪ] *n.* моделье́р.
cove [kəʊv] *n.* (*bay*) бу́хточка.
coven [ˈkʌv(ə)n] *n.* шаба́ш ведьм.
covenant [ˈkʌvənənt] *n.* соглаше́ние, догово́р; **C~ of the League of Nations** уста́в Ли́ги На́ций; (*relig.*) заве́т.
v.t. & *i.* заключ|а́ть, -и́ть соглаше́ние; догов|а́риваться, -ори́ться (*с кем о чём*).
cover [ˈkʌvə(r)] *n.* **1.** (*lid*) кры́шка, покры́шка. **2.** (*loose ~ing of chair etc.*) чехо́л; (*pl.*, *bedclothes*) посте́ль. **3.** (*of book etc.*) переплёт, обло́жка; **I read the book from ~ to ~** я прочёл кни́гу от ко́рки до ко́рки; (*dust-~*) суперобло́жка. **4.** (*wrapper, envelope*) обёртка, конве́рт; **under separate ~** в отде́льном конве́рте. **5.** (*shelter, protection*) укры́тие, прикры́тие; **take ~** укр|ыва́ться, -ы́ться; **under ~ of darkness** под покро́вом темноты́. **6.** (*pretence, pretext*) личи́на, ма́ска, ши́рма; **under ~ of**

friendship под личи́ной дру́жбы. **7.** (*mil.*, *protective force*) прикры́тие; **fighter ~** прикры́тие истреби́телями.

v.t. **1.** (*overspread etc.*; *also* **~ up, ~ over**) покр|ыва́ть, -ы́ть; закр|ыва́ть, -ы́ть; прикр|ыва́ть, -ы́ть; накр|ыва́ть, -ы́ть; **~ a chair** об|ива́ть, -и́ть стул; **cats are ~ed with hair** ко́шки покры́ты ше́рстью; **she ~ed her face in, with her hands** она́ закры́ла лицо́ рука́ми; **the roads are ~ed with snow** доро́ги занесены́ сне́гом; **trees ~ed with blossom** дере́вья в цвету́; **well ~ed** (*with clothes*) тепло́ оде́тый; (*with flesh*) в те́ле; **~ed** (*indoor*) **court** (*for tennis*) закры́тый корт; **~ed way** кры́тая галере́я. **2.** (*fig.*) покр|ыва́ть, -ы́ть; скр|ыва́ть, -ыть; **he ~ed himself with glory** он покры́л себя́ сла́вой. **3.** (*protect*) закр|ыва́ть, -ы́ть; прикр|ыва́ть, -ы́ть; **are you ~ed against theft?** вы застрахо́ваны от кра́жи? **4.** (*aim weapon at*) це́литься (*impf.*) в+*a.*; **he ~ed him** (*with his revolver*) он це́лился в него́ (из револьве́ра); **our guns ~ed the road** на́ши ору́дия прикрыва́ли доро́гу (от неприя́теля). **5.** (*travel*) покр|ыва́ть, -ы́ть; **we ~ed 5 miles by nightfall** мы прошли́ расстоя́ние в 5 миль до наступле́ния темноты́. **6.** (*meet*, *satisfy*) покр|ыва́ть, -ы́ть; **£10 will ~ my needs** 10 фу́нтов хва́тит на мои́ ну́жды; **we only just ~ed expenses** мы едва́ покры́ли свои́ расхо́ды. **7.** (*embrace*, *deal with*): **the lectures ~ a wide field** ле́кции охва́тывают широ́кий круг вопро́сов; **the reporter ~ed the conference** корреспонде́нт дава́л репорта́жи о хо́де конфере́нции; **this salesman ~s Essex** э́тот торго́вый аге́нт обслу́живает Э́ссекс. **8.** (*of correspondence*): **~ing letter** сопроводи́тельное письмо́.

cpd. **~-up** *n.* (*pretext*) предло́г, ши́рма.

coverage ['kʌvərɪdʒ] *n.* **1.** (*extent or amount dealt with*) охва́т; **news ~** освеще́ние в печа́ти (*or* по ра́дио). **2.** (*fin.*) покры́тие; гаранти́йный фонд. **3.** (*insurance*) страхова́ние.

coverlet ['kʌvəlɪt] *n.* покрыва́ло.

covert ['kʌvət] *adj.* скры́тый.

covet ['kʌvɪt] *v.t.* вожделе́ть (*impf.*) к+*d.*; жа́ждать (*impf.*) +*g.*; (*coll.*) за́риться (*impf.*) на+*a.*

covetous ['kʌvɪtəs] *adj.* жа́дный.

cow[1] [kaʊ] *n.* **1.** (*bovine*) коро́ва; **till the ~s come home** (*coll.*) до второ́го прише́ствия; (*of other mammals*) са́мка, коро́ва; *expr. by suff.*, *e.g.* **~ elephant** слони́ха. **2.** (*pej.*, *woman*) коро́ва.

cpds. **~boy** *n.* ковбо́й; **~hide** *n.* (*leather*) воло́вья ко́жа; **~pox** *n.* коро́вья о́спа; **~-shed** *n.* хлев, коро́вник.

cow[2] [kaʊ] *v.t.* запу́г|ивать, -а́ть.

coward ['kaʊəd] *n.* трус (*fem.* -и́ха).

cowardice ['kaʊədɪs] *n.* тру́сость.

cowardly ['kaʊədlɪ] *adj.* трусли́вый.

cower ['kaʊə(r)] *v.i.* съёжи|ваться, -ться.

cowl [kaʊl] *n.* (*hood*) капюшо́н; (*chimney-~*) зонт над домово́й трубо́й.

cowling ['kaʊlɪŋ] *n.* (*tech.*) капо́т дви́гателя.

cowslip ['kaʊslɪp] *n.* первоцве́т.

cox [kɒks] *n.* рулево́й.

v.t.: **~ a boat** управля́ть (*impf.*) рулём ло́дки; сиде́ть (*impf.*) на руле́.

coy [kɔɪ] *adj.* (*bashful*) стыдли́вый; (*affectedly*) жема́нный; (*secretive*) скры́тный.

coyote [kɔɪ'əʊtɪ, 'kɔɪəʊt] *n.* койо́т.

cozy ['kəʊzɪ] = **cosy**

Cpl. ['kɔːpər(ə)l] *n.* (*abbr. of* **Corporal**) капра́л.

CPSU (*abbr. of* ***Communist Party of the Soviet Union***) КПСС, (Коммунисти́ческая па́ртия Сове́тского Сою́за).

CPU (*abbr. of* ***central processing unit***) (*comput.*) ЦП, (центра́льный проце́ссор).

crab[1] [kræb] *n.* краб; (*astron.*): **the C~** Рак; (*fig.*, *crossgrained person*) брюзга́ (*c.g.*).

v.i. (*grumble*) брюзжа́ть (*impf.*).

crab[2] [kræb] *n.* (*also* **~-apple**) ди́кое я́блоко.

crabby ['kræbɪ] *adj.* брюзгли́вый.

crack [kræk] *n.* **1.** (*in a cup, ice etc.*) тре́щина; (*in the ground*) рассе́лина; (*in wall, floor etc.*) щель. **2.** (*sudden noise*) треск, щёлканье; (*of thunder*) треск, уда́р. **3.**: **at ~ of dawn** с (пе́рвой) заре́й. **4.** (*blow*) затре́щина; **he got a ~ on the head** он получи́л затре́щину. **5.** (*coll.*, *facetious remark*) остро́та. **6.** (*coll.*, *attempt*) попы́тка; **have a ~ at sth.** попыта́ть (*pf.*) свои́ си́лы в чём-н. **7.**: **a ~ regiment** отбо́рный полк; **a ~ shot** первокла́ссный стрело́к. **8.** (*drug*) крэк.

v.t. **1.** (*make a ~ in*, *break open*) проб|ива́ть, -и́ть щель в (чём); взл|а́мывать, -ома́ть; **he fell and ~ed his skull** он упа́л и пролома́л себе́ го́лову; **~ a nut** расколо́ть (*pf.*) оре́х; **~ a code** разгада́ть (*pf.*) шифр; **~ a safe** взлома́ть (*pf.*) сейф. **2.**: **~ a whip** щёлк|ать, -нуть бичо́м; **~ a joke** отпусти́ть (*pf.*) шу́тку.

v.i. **1.** (*get broken or fissured*) да|ва́ть, -ть тре́щину; тре́снуть (*pf.*); **the glass ~ed** стекло́ тре́снуло. **2.** (*of sound*) щёлк|ать, -нуть; **a rifle ~ed (out)** разда́лся винто́вочный вы́стрел. **3.**: **the boy's voice ~ed** у ма́льчика слома́лся го́лос.

with advs.: **~ down** *v.i.* **~ down on** прин|има́ть, -я́ть круты́е ме́ры про́тив+*g.*; **~ up** *v.t.* (*praise*) захва́л|ивать, -и́ть; **the book is not all it's ~ed up to be** э́та кни́га не та́к хороша́, как её распи́сывают; *v.i.*: **the plane ~ed up on landing** самолёт разби́лся при поса́дке; (*of pers.*: *suffer collapse*) надломи́ться (*pf.*).

cpds. **~-pot** *adj.* поме́шанный; **~-down** *n.* расправа; **~-up** *n.* (*breakdown*) упа́док сил.

cracker ['krækə(r)] *n.* **1.** (*firework*) хлопу́шка, шути́ха. **2.** (*biscuit*) кре́кер. **3.** (*pl.*, *nut-~s*) щипц|ы́ (*pl.*, *g.* -о́в) для оре́хов.

crackerjack ['krækəˌdʒæk] *adj.* (*coll.*) первокла́ссный; вы́сшего кла́сса.

crackers ['krækəz] *adj.* (*sl.*, *mad*) рехну́вшийся.

cracking ['krækɪŋ] *adj.* & *adv.*: **at a ~ pace** стреми́тельно; бо́дрым ша́гом; **we had a ~ good time** мы здо́рово провели́ вре́мя; **get ~!** пошеве́ливайся!; за рабо́ту!

crackle ['kræk(ə)l] *n.* треск, потре́скивание.

v.i. (*of sound*) потре́скивать (*impf.*).

crackling ['kræklɪŋ] *n.* **1.** (*sound*) треск, хруст. **2.** (*cul.*) шква́рки (*f. pl.*).

cradle ['kreɪd(ə)l] *n.* колыбе́ль; лю́лька; **from ~ to grave** всю жизнь.

v.t.: **~ a child in one's arms** держа́ть (*impf.*) ребёнка на рука́х.

cpd. **~-song** *n.* колыбе́льная (пе́сня).

craft [krɑːft] *n.* **1.** (*guile*) хи́трость, хитроу́мие. **2.** (*skill*) ло́вкость, уме́ние. **3.** (*occupation*) ремесло́; **arts and ~s** иску́сства и ремёсла (*nt. pl.*) **4.** (*boat*) су́дно.

cpds. **~sman** *n.* реме́сленник, ма́стер; **~smanship** *n.* мастерство́.

crafty ['krɑːftɪ] *adj.* хи́трый.

crag [kræg] *n.* скала́, утёс.

craggy ['krægɪ] *adj.* скали́стый.

cram [kræm] *v.t.* **1.** (*insert forcefully*) запи́х|ивать, -а́ть/-ну́ть; впи́х|ивать, -ну́ть; **the shelves are ~med with books** по́лки ло́мятся от книг. **2.** (*v.t.* & *i.*) (*teach*, *study intensively*) репети́ровать (*impf.*); зубри́ть (*impf.*); **~ pupils** репети́ровать/ната́скивать (*impf.*) ученико́в.

cpd. **~-full** *adj.* по́лный до отка́за; битко́м наби́тый.

crammer ['kræmə(r)] *n.* (*tutor*) репети́тор.

cramp [kræmp] *n.* (*of muscles*) су́дорога; **the swim-**

mer was seized with ~ пловца́ схвати́ла су́дорога.

v.t. (*hamper*) стесн|я́ть, -и́ть; **we are ~ed for room** у нас здесь поверну́ться не́где; **~ s.o.'s style** (*fig.*) не дава́ть (*impf.*) кому́-н. разверну́ться.

crampon ['kræmpən] *n.* (*pl., hooked levers*) грузовы́е клё́щ|и (*pl., g.* -е́й); схва́ты (m. pl.); (*plate with spikes*) подо́шва с шипа́ми; (*pl.*) ко́шки (*f. pl.*).

cranberry ['krænbərɪ] *n.* клю́ква (*collect.*); я́года клю́квы.

crane [kreɪn] *n.* (*bird*) жура́вль (*m.*); (*machine*) (грузо)подъё́мный кран.

v.t.: **~ one's neck** вытя́гивать, вы́тянуть ше́ю.

cpd. **~-fly** *n.* долгоно́жка.

cranial ['kreɪnɪəl] *adj.* черепно́й.

cranium ['kreɪnɪəm] *n.* че́реп.

crank[1] [kræŋk] *n.* (*handle*) кривоши́п; коле́нчатый рыча́г; рукоя́тка; заводна́я ру́чка.

v.t.: **~ up a car** зав|оди́ть, -ести́ мото́р вручну́ю; **~ a film camera** крути́ть (*impf.*) киноаппара́т.

cpds. **~case** *n.* (*tech.*) ка́ртер (дви́гателя); **~shaft** *n.* (*tech.*) коле́нчатый вал.

crank[2] [kræŋk] *n.* (*pers.*) чуда́|к (*fem.* -чка).

cranky ['kræŋkɪ] *adj.* (*eccentric*) с причу́дами; (*peevish*) раздражи́тельный.

cranny ['krænɪ] *n.* тре́щина.

crap[1] [kræp] (*vulg.*) *n.* (*shit*) говно́; (*nonsense*) вздо́р, чепуха́.

v.i. (*shit*) срать (*impf.*).

crap[2] [kræp] *n.* (*pl., game; also* **~-shooting**) игра́ в ко́сти; **shoot ~s** броса́ть (*impf.*) ко́сти.

cpd. **~shooter** *n.* игро́к в ко́сти.

crash [kræʃ] *n.* **1.** (*noise*) гро́хот, гром. **2.** (*fall, smash*) ава́рия, круше́ние; **he was killed in a car ~** он поги́б в автомоби́льной катастро́фе; (*fig., disaster*) катастро́фа, крах. **3.: a ~** (*intensive*) **programme** ускоренная програ́мма.

v.t. разб|ива́ть, -и́ть; гро́хнуть (*pf.*); **he ~ed his fist down on the table** он гро́хнул кулако́м по́ столу; **~** (*gate-~*) **a party** ворва́ться (*pf.*) на ве́чер без приглаше́ния.

v.i.: **the plane ~ed** самолё́т разби́лся; **the cars ~ed together** автомоби́ли столкну́лись; **he ~ed into the room** он вломи́лся в ко́мнату.

cpds. **~-helmet** *n.* шлем автого́нщика/мотоцикли́ста; мотошле́м; **~-landing** *n.* авари́йная поса́дка.

crass [kræs] *adj.* гру́бый; тупо́й; **~ stupidity** непроходи́мая ту́пость.

crate [kreɪt] *n.* я́щик, конте́йнер.

v.t. паковать, у- в я́щик(и).

crater ['kreɪtə(r)] *n.* кра́тер; (*bomb-~*) воро́нка.

cravat [krə'væt] *n.* широ́кий га́лстук; ше́йный плато́к.

crave [kreɪv] *v.t. & i.* **1.** (*beg for*) умоля́ть (*impf.*) (*кого о чём*). **2.** (*desire*) жа́ждать (*impf.*) +*g.*; **he ~d for a drink** ему́ до́ смерти хоте́лось вы́пить.

craven ['kreɪv(ə)n] *adj.* трусли́вый, малоду́шный.

craving ['kreɪvɪŋ] *n.* стра́стное жела́ние.

craw [krɔ:] *n.* зоб

crawfish ['krɔ:fɪʃ] = **crayfish**

crawl [krɔ:l] *n.* **1.** (*~ing motion*) по́лзание; **traffic was reduced to a ~** тра́нспорт тащи́лся е́ле-е́ле. **2.** (*swimming stroke*) кроль (*m.*).

v.i. **1.** (*e.g. of reptile*) по́лзать (*indet.*), ползти́ (*det.*); **he ~ed on his hands and knees** он полз на четвере́ньках. **2.** (*go very slowly*) ползти́ (*det.*). **3.** (*kowtow*) по́лзать (*indet.*) (*перед кем*); пресмыка́ться (*impf.*) (*перед кем*). **4.: the ground is ~ing with ants** земля́ кишмя́ киши́т муравья́ми.

crawler ['krɔ:lə(r)] *n.* **1.** (*obsequious person*) низкопокло́нник, подхали́м. **2.** (*pl., baby's garment*) ползунк|и́ (*pl., g.* -о́в).

cray|fish ['kreɪfɪʃ], **craw-** ['krɔ:fɪʃ] *nn.* речно́й рак.

crayon ['kreɪən, -ɒn] *n.* цветно́й каранда́ш.

v.t. & i. рисова́ть (*impf.*) цветны́м карандашо́м.

craze [kreɪz] *n.* ма́ния; пова́льная мо́да.

v.t. св|оди́ть, -ести́ с ума́.

craziness ['kreɪzɪnɪs] *n.* (*madness*) безу́мие, сумасше́ствие.

crazy ['kreɪzɪ] *adj.* безу́мный, сумасше́дший; **~ about sth.** поме́шанный на чё́м-н.; **he is ~ about her** он схо́дит по ней с ума́.

creak [kri:k] *n.* скрип.

v.i. скрипе́ть (*impf.*).

cream [kri:m] *n.* **1.** (*top part of milk*) сли́в|ки (*pl., g.* -ок); **whipped ~** взби́тые сли́вки; **~ cheese** сли́вочный сыро́к. **2.** (*dish or sweet*) крем; **~ cake** торт с кре́мом; кре́мовое пиро́жное; **chocolate ~s** шокола́дные конфе́ты (*f. pl.*); **salad ~** майоне́з; **~ of celery (soup)** суп-пюре́ из сельдере́я. **3.** (*polish, cosmetic etc.*) крем, мазь; **face ~** крем для лица́; **cold ~** кольдкре́м. **4.** (*of other liquid*) пе́на; **~ of tartar** ви́нный ка́мень. **5.** (*best part*): **the ~ of society** сли́вки о́бщества. **6.** (*attr., ~-coloured*) кре́мового цве́та.

cpds. **~-coloured** *adj.* кре́мового цве́та; кре́мовый; **~-jug** *n.* сли́вочник.

creamer ['kri:mə(r)] *n.* (*milk, cream substitute*) освети́тель (*m.*).

creamery ['kri:mərɪ] *n.* (*place of sale*) моло́чная; (*factory*) маслобо́йня.

creaminess ['kri:mɪnɪs] *n.* жи́рность (молока́).

creamy ['kri:mɪ] *adj.* сли́вочный, кре́мовый.

crease [kri:s] *n.* скла́дка, морщи́на; (*in trousers*) скла́дка.

v.t. (*wrinkle*) мять с-.

v.i. (*form ~s*) мя́ться с-.

cpd. **~-resisting** *adj.* немну́щийся.

create [kri:'eɪt] *v.t.* созд|ава́ть, -а́ть; твори́ть, со-; произв|оди́ть, -ести́; **God ~d the world** Бог сотвори́л мир; **Dickens ~d many characters** Ди́ккенс со́здал мно́го о́бразов; **it ~d a bad impression** э́то произвело́ дурно́е впечатле́ние.

creation [kri:'eɪʃ(ə)n] *n.* **1.** (*act, process*) созда́ние, созида́ние; **~ of the world** сотворе́ние ми́ра. **2.** (*the universe*) мирозда́ние. **3.** (*product of imagination*) творе́ние, произведе́ние.

creative [kri:'eɪtɪv] *adj.* тво́рческий.

creativeness [kri:'eɪtɪvnɪs] *n.* тво́рческий дар.

creator [kri:'eɪtə(r)] *n.* созда́тель (*m.*), творе́ц.

creature ['kri:tʃə(r)] *n.* **1.** (*living being*) созда́ние, существо́; **poor ~** бедня́жка (*c.g.*); **a good ~** хоро́ший челове́к. **2.: ~ comforts** земны́е блага́.

crèche [kreʃ, kreɪʃ] *n.* (де́тские) я́сл|и (*pl., g.* -ей).

credence ['kri:d(ə)ns] *n.* ве́ра, дове́рие; **give ~ to** пове́рить (*pf.*) +*d.*

credential [krɪ'denʃ(ə)l] *n.* (*usu. pl.*) **1.** (*testimonial*) удостовере́ние; манда́т; **~s committee** манда́тная коми́ссия. **2.** (*ambassador's*) вери́тельная гра́мота.

credibility [ˌkredɪ'bɪlɪtɪ] *n.* (*of pers.*) спосо́бность вы́звать дове́рие; (*of thg.*) правдоподо́бие, достове́рность; (*plausibility*) убеди́тельность.

credible ['kredɪb(ə)l] *adj.* (*of pers.*) заслу́живающий дове́рия; (*of thg.*) правдоподо́бный, вероя́тный.

credit ['kredɪt] *n.* **1.** (*belief, trust, confidence*) ве́ра, дове́рие; **give ~ to, place ~ in** (*a report etc.*) пове́рить (*pf.*) +*d.*; доверя́ть (*impf.*) +*d.*; **this lends ~ to the story** э́то де́лает расска́з правдоподо́бным. **2.** (*honour, reputation*): **a man of the highest ~** челове́к с прекра́сной репута́цией; **the work does you ~** э́та рабо́та де́лает вам честь; **this is to his ~** э́то говори́т в его́ по́льзу; **give ~ where ~ is due** возда́ть (*pf.*) до́лжное кому́ сле́дует; **~ titles** (*cin., also ~s*) вступи́тельные ти́тры (*m. pl.*). **3.** (*book-keeping*) кре́дит; (*fin.*) креди́т; **buy on ~** покупа́ть (*pf.*) в креди́т; **~ balance** кре́дитовый бала́нс, са́льдо (*indecl.*); ~ **card** креди́тная ка́рточка; **letter of** ~ аккредити́в; **this shop gives no** ~ э́тот магази́н не продаёт това́ры в креди́т; **his** ~ **is good for £50** он име́ет креди́т на 50 фу́нтов; **place the sum to my credit** внеси́те э́ту су́мму на мой счёт.

v.t. **1.** (*believe sth.*) ве́рить, по- +*d.*; доверя́ть (*impf.*) +*d.* **2.: I ~ed him with more sense** я счита́л его́ бо́лее благоразу́мным. **3.** (*fin.*): **I ~ed him with £10** я внёс 10 фу́нтов на его́ счёт.

cpds. **~-worthiness** *n.* кредитоспосо́бность; **~-worthy** *adj.* заслу́живающий креди́та, кредитоспосо́бный.

creditable ['kredɪtəb(ə)l] *adj.* (*praiseworthy*) де́лающий честь (+*d.*); (*believable*) правдоподо́бный, вероя́тный.

creditor ['kredɪtə(r)] *n.* кредито́р.

credo ['kreɪdəʊ, 'kriː-] *n.* кре́до (*indecl.*).

credulity [krɪ'djuːlɪtɪ] *n.* легкове́рие, дове́рчивость.

credulous ['kredjʊləs] *adj.* легкове́рный, дове́рчивый.

creed [kriːd] *n.* вероуче́ние; (*fig.*) убежде́ния (*nt. pl.*), кре́до (*indecl.*).

creek [kriːk] *n.* (*inlet*) зали́в, бу́хта; (*small river*) ре́чка.

creep [kriːp] *n.* **1.** (*act of ~ing*) по́лзание. **2.: it gives me the ~s** (*coll.*) от э́того у меня́ моро́з по ко́же. **3.** (*sl., obnoxious person*) несно́сный/отврати́тельный тип.

v.i. **1.** (*crawl, move stealthily*) по́лзать (*indet.*), ползти́ (*det.*); кра́сться (*impf.*). **2.** (*fig.*): **old age ~s upon me** ста́рость подкра́дывается ко мне. **3.** (*of plants*) стла́ться (*impf.*); ви́ться (*impf.*).

creeper ['kriːpə(r)] *n.* (*plant*) ползу́чее/вью́щееся расте́ние.

creepy ['kriːpɪ] *adj.* **1.** (*producing horror*) броса́ющий в дрожь; (*coll., obnoxious*) отврати́тельный, несно́сный. **2.** (*of flesh*) в мура́шках.

cpd. **~-crawly** *n.* бука́шка.

cremate [krɪ'meɪt] *v.t.* креми́ровать (*impf., pf.*) .

cremation [krɪ'meɪʃ(ə)n] *n.* крема́ция.

crematorium [ˌkremə'tɔːrɪəm] *n.* кремато́рий.

crenellate ['krenəˌleɪt] *v.t.*: **~d walls** зу́бчатые сте́ны.

Creole ['kriːəʊl] *n.* (*of European descent*) крео́л (*fem.* -ка); (*of part-Negro descent, also*) мула́т (*fem.* -ка).

adj. крео́льский.

creosote ['kriːəˌsəʊt] *n.* креозо́т.

crêpe [kreɪp] *n.* креп; ~ **paper** гофриро́ванная бума́га; ~ **soles** каучу́ковые подо́швы; ~ **de Chine** крепдеши́н.

crescendo [krɪ'ʃendəʊ] *n.* креще́ндо (*indecl.*).

crescent ['krez(ə)nt, 'kres-] *n.* **1.** (*moon*) лу́нный серп. **2.** (*symbol of Islam*) полуме́сяц. **3.** (*street, row of houses*) ряд домо́в, располо́женных полукру́гом.

cpd. **~-shaped** *adj.* серпови́дный.

cress [kres] *n.* кресс(-сала́т).

crest [krest] *n.* **1.** (*tuft of feathers*) гре́бень (*m.*), хохоло́к. **2.** (*helmet*) шлем; (*top of helmet*) гре́бень (*m.*) шле́ма. **3.** (*her. device*) герб. **4.** (*of wave*) гре́бень (*m.*).

cpd. **~fallen** *adj.* упа́вший ду́хом; удручённый.

cretin ['kretɪn] *n.* (*lit., fig.*) крети́н.

cretinous ['kretɪnəs] *adj.* слабоу́мный (*also fig.*).

cretonne [kre'tɒn, 'kre-] *n.* крето́н.

crevasse [krə'væs] *n.* рассе́лина в леднике́.

crevice ['krevɪs] *n.* щель, расще́лина.

crew [kruː] *n.* **1.** (*of vessel*) кома́нда, экипа́ж; (*of aircraft*) экипа́ж; (*of train*) брига́да; (*aeron.*): **ground** ~назе́мный обслу́живающий персона́л. **2.** (*team*) брига́да; (*lot, gang*) ба́нда. **3.:** ~ **cut** стри́жка ёжиком.

v.t. обслу́живать (*impf.*) (*корабль*).

crib [krɪb] *n.* **1.** (*cot*) де́тская крова́тка с се́ткой. **2.** (*manger*) я́с|ли (*pl., g.* -ей), корму́шка. **3.** (*for cheating*) шпарга́лка (*coll.*).

v.t. (*of schoolboy*) шпарга́лить (*impf.*) (*sl.*).

cpd. **crib death** (*US*) = **cot death**

cricket[1] ['krɪkɪt] *n.* (*insect*) сверчо́к.

cricket[2] ['krɪkɪt] *n.* (*game*) кри́кет; **it isn't** ~ (*fig.*) э́то нече́стно; э́то не по пра́вилам.

cricketer ['krɪkɪtə(r)] *n.* игро́к в кри́кет.

crier ['kraɪə(r)] *n.* (*official*) глаша́тай.

crime [kraɪm] *n.* **1.** (*act*) преступле́ние. **2.** (*~s in general*) престу́пность; ~ **fiction** детекти́вный рома́н.

Crimea [kraɪ'mɪə] *n.* Крым; **native of** ~ крымча́|к (*fem.* -чка).

Crimean [kraɪ'mɪən] *adj.* кры́мский.

criminal ['krɪmɪn(ə)l] *n.* престу́пни|к (*fem.* -ца).

adj. **1.** (*guilty*) престу́пный. **2.** (*pert. to crime*) уголо́вный, кримина́льный; ~ **action** (*prosecution*) уголо́вное де́ло; ~ **court** суд по уголо́вным дела́м; ~ **law** уголо́вное пра́во.

criminologist [ˌkrɪmɪ'nɒlədʒɪst] *n.* кримино́лог.

criminology [ˌkrɪmɪ'nɒlədʒɪ] *n.* криминоло́гия.

crimp [krɪmp] *v.t.* гофрирова́ть (*impf., pf.*); **~ing-iron** щипцы́ для зави́вки воло́с.

crimson ['krɪmz(ə)n] *n.* мали́новый цвет; тёмно-кра́сный цвет.

adj. мали́новый; тёмно-кра́сный.

cringe [krɪndʒ] *v.i.* (*shrink*) съёжи|ваться, -ться (*от чего*); (*behave servilely*) раболе́пствовать (*impf.*).

crinkle ['krɪŋk(ə)l] *n.* морщи́на.

v.t. & i. мо́рщить(ся), на-/с-.

crinkly ['krɪŋklɪ] *adj.* смо́рщенный.

crinoline ['krɪnəlɪn] *n.* кринoли́н.

crippl|e ['krɪp(ə)l] *n.* кале́ка (*c.g.*).

v.t. кале́чить, ис-; уро́довать, из-; (*fig.*); **the ship was ~ed by the storm** бу́ря покале́чила кора́бль; **strikes are ~ing industry** забасто́вки расша́тывают промы́шленность; **~ing expenses** разори́тельные расхо́ды.

crisis ['kraɪsɪs] *n.* кри́зис, перело́м.

crisp [krɪsp] *n.* (*potato* ~) жа́реная карто́фельная стру́жка; (*pl.*) хрустя́щий карто́фель.

adj. (*of substance*) хрустя́щий; **a** ~ **biscuit** рассы́пчатое пече́нье; **a** ~ **lettuce** све́жий сала́т; (*of style, orders etc.*) чека́нный, отчётливый; (*of air*) бодря́щий, све́жий.

cpd. **~bread** *n.* сухари́ (*m. pl.*); хрустя́щие хле́бцы (*m. pl.*).

criss-cross ['krɪskrɒs] *n.* перекре́щивание.

adj. перекре́щивающийся, перекрёстный.

adv. крест-на́крест; (*fig.*) вкривь и вкось.

v.t. расчёр|чивать, -ти́ть крест-на́крест.

criterion [kraɪ'tɪərɪən] *n.* крите́рий.

critic ['krɪtɪk] *n.* кри́тик.

critical ['krɪtɪk(ə)l] *adj.* **1.** (*decisive; judicious*) крити́ческий; **the patient's condition is** ~ больно́й в крити́ческом состоя́нии. **2.** (*fault-finding*) крити́ческий, крити́чный.

criticism ['krɪtɪˌsɪz(ə)m] *n.* кри́тика; **textual** ~ крити́ческий разбо́р те́кста; **I have only one** ~ **to make** у меня́ то́лько одно́ замеча́ние.

criticize ['krɪtɪˌsaɪz] *v.t.* подв|ерга́ть, -е́ргнуть крити́ческому разбо́ру; (*adversely*) критикова́ть (*impf*).

critique [krɪ'tiːk] *n.* кри́тика; (*review*) реце́нзия, крити́ческая статья́.

croak [krəʊk] *n.* ква́канье.

v.t. & i. ква́кать (*impf.*).

Croat ['krəʊæt] *n.* хорва́т (*fem.* -ка).

Croatia [krəʊ'eɪʃə] *n.* Хорва́тия.

Croatian [krəʊ'eɪʃ(ə)n] *adj.* хорва́тский.

crochet ['krəʊʃeɪ, -ʃɪ] *n.* вя́зка крючко́м.

v.t. & i. вяза́ть крючко́м.

cpd. **~-hook** *n.* вяза́льный крючо́к.

crock [krɒk] *n.* (*pot*) гли́няный кувши́н/горшо́к.

crockery ['krɒkərɪ] *n.* гли́няная/фая́нсовая посу́да.
crocodile ['krɒkə,daɪl] *n.* крокоди́л.
crocus ['krəʊkəs] *n.* кро́кус.
croft [krɒft] *n.* ху́тор.
crofter ['krɒftə(r)] *n.* хутоpя́нин.
croissant ['krwʌsɑ̃] *n.* рога́лик.
crone [krəʊn] *n.* сго́рбленная стару́ха.
crony ['krəʊnɪ] *n.* дружо́к, закады́чный друг.
cronyism ['krəʊnɪ,ɪz(ə)m] *n.* панибра́тство.
crook [krʊk] *n.* **1.** (*shepherd's*) по́сох. **2.** (*bend*) поворо́т, изги́б. **3.** (*coll., criminal*) моше́нник, жу́лик.
crooked ['krʊkɪd] *adj.* **1.** (*bent*) со́гнутый, изо́гнутый; (*with age*) сго́рбленный. **2.: you have got your hat on ~** у вас шля́па ко́со/кри́во наде́та. **3.** (*coll., dishonest*) бесче́стный, моше́ннический.
croon [kru:n] *v.t. & i.* напева́ть (*impf.*) вполго́лоса.
crop [krɒp] *n.* **1.** (*craw*) зоб. **2.** (*of whip*) кнутови́ще; (*hunting-~*) охо́тничий хлы́ст. **3.** (*produce*) урожа́й, жа́тва; **potato ~** урожа́й карто́феля; (*pl.*) посе́вы (*m. pl.*), (*grain*) хлеба́ (*m. pl.*). **4.** (*fig.*): **a ~ of questions** ку́ча вопро́сов.
v.t. **1.** (*bite off*) щипа́ть (*impf.*); объ|еда́ть, -е́сть; **the sheep ~ped the grass short** о́вцы ощипа́ли траву́. **2.** (*cut short*): (*hair, hedge*) подстр|ига́ть, -и́чь. **3.** (*sow, plant*) зас|ева́ть, -е́ять.
v.i. **1.** (*yield a ~*) да|ва́ть, -ть урожа́й; **the beans ~ped well** бобы́ да́ли хоро́ший урожа́й. **2. ~ up, out** (*of rock etc.*) обнаж|а́ться, -и́ться. **3.** (*fig.*): **difficulties ~ped up** появи́лись/возни́кли тру́дности.
cpd. **~-dusting** *n.* опы́ливание посе́вов.
cropper ['krɒpə(r)] *n.*: **he came a ~** (*coll.*) (*lit.*) он шлёпнулся; (*fig.*) он провали́лся.
croquet ['krəʊkeɪ, -kɪ] *n.* кроке́т.
cro|sier, -zier ['krəʊzɪə(r), -ʒə(r)] *n.* епи́скопский по́сох.
cross [krɒs] *n.* **1.** крест; **he made a ~ on the document** он поста́вил кре́стик на докуме́нте. **2.** (*of crucifixion*) крест; **he made the sign of the ~** он перекрести́лся; он осени́л себя́ кресто́м (*or* кре́стным зна́мением). **3.** (*fig.*): **take up one's ~** нести́ (*pf.*) свой крест; **he is a ~ I have to bear** он крест, кото́рый мне суждено́ нести́. **4.: cut on the ~** (*diagonally*) разре́занный на́искось (*or* по диагона́ли). **5.** (*mixing of breeds*) по́месь, гибри́д; **a mule is a ~ between a horse and an ass** мул — по́месь ло́шади с осло́м.
adj. (*see also cpds.*) **1.** (*transverse*) попере́чный, перекрёстный; **~ ventilation** сквозна́я вентиля́ция; **~ wind** (*sidewind*) боково́й/косо́й ве́тер. **2.** (*angry*) серди́тый; злой (на+*a.*); раздражённый.
v.t. **1.** (*go across, traverse; also* **~ over**): **~ a road** пере|ходи́ть, -йти́ че́рез доро́гу; **~ the Channel** перепл|ыва́ть, -ы́ть Ла-Манш; **~ s.o.'s path** перебежа́ть (*pf.*) кому́-н. доро́гу; (*fig.*) повстреча́ться (*impf.*) с кем-н.; **the idea never ~ed my mind** э́та мысль никогда́ не приходи́ла мне в го́лову; **the ship ~ed our bows** кора́бль пересёк наш путь. **2.** (*draw lines across*): **~ a cheque** перечёрк|ивать, -ну́ть чек. **3.** (*place across*) скре́|щивать, -сти́ть; **~ one's legs** скрести́ть (*pf.*) но́ги; **~ swords with s.o.** (*fig.*) скрести́ть (*pf.*) мечи́/шпа́ги с кем-н.; **keep one's fingers ~ed** (*fig., expr. hope*) ≃ как бы не сгла́зить; **the wires are ~ed** (*lit.*) провода́ запу́тались; **~ wires** (*fig.*) запу́т|ывать, -ать де́ло. **4.: ~ o.s.** перекрести́ться (*pf.*); **~ my heart!** вот те крест! **5.** (*travel in opposite direction to*): **we ~ed each other on the way** мы размину́лись в пути́; **my letter ~ed your telegram** моё письмо́ размину́лось с ва́шей телегра́ммой. **6.** (*thwart*): **he was ~ed in love** он потерпе́л неуда́чу в любви́; **do not ~ me** не станови́тесь на моём пути́; не перебега́йте мне доро́гу. **7.** (*breed*) скре́|щивать, -сти́ть.
v.i. **1.** (*go across*): **he ~ed to where I was sitting** он перешёл к тому́ ме́сту, где я сиде́л; **he ~ed from Dover to Calais** он перепра́вился из Ду́вра в Кале́. **2.: our letters ~ed** на́ши пи́сьма размину́лись.
with advs.: **~ off, out** *vv.t.* вычёркивать, вы́черкнуть.
cpds. **~bar** *n.* попере́чина, тра́верса, ри́гель (*m.*); **~-bench** *n.* (*parl.*) скамья́ для незави́симых депута́тов; **~-bencher** *n.* (*parl.*) незави́симый депута́т; **~bill** *n.* клёст; **~bow** *n.* самостре́л; **~-bred** *adj.* скрещённый, гибри́дный; **~-breed** *n.* по́месь, гибри́д; *v.t. & i.* скре́|щивать(ся), -сти́ть(ся); **~-channel** *adj.*: **~-channel steamer** парохо́д, пересека́ющий Ла-Ма́нш; **~-country** *adj.*: **a ~-country race** кросс; **~-country runner** кроссме́н; **~-country vehicle** вездехо́д; **~-current** *n.* пересека́ющий пото́к; **~-cut** *adj.*: **~-cut saw** попере́чная пила́; **~-examination** *n.* перекрёстный допро́с; **~-examine** *v.t.* подв|ерга́ть, -е́ргнуть перекрёстному допро́су; (*fig.*) допр|а́шивать, -оси́ть; **~-eyed** *adj.* косогла́зый, косо́й; **~-fertilization** *n.* перекрёстное опыле́ние; **~-fire** *n.* (*mil.*) перекрёстный ого́нь; **~-legged** *adj.* (сидя́щий) положи́в но́гу на́ ногу; **~-patch** *n.* (*coll.*) брюзга́ (*c.g.*), злю́ка (*c.g.*); **~piece** *n.* попере́чина, крестови́на; **~-pollination** *n.* перекрёстное опыле́ние; **~-purposes** *n.* недоразуме́ние; **~-question** *v.t.* допр|а́шивать, -оси́ть; **~-reference** *n.* перекрёстная ссы́лка; **~road** *n.* перекрёсток; **at the ~ roads** (*fig.*) на распу́тье; **~-section** *n.* попере́чное сече́ние; попере́чный разре́з; **~-stitch** *n.* вы́шивка кре́стиком; **~word** *n.* кроссво́рд.
crossing ['krɒsɪŋ] *n.* **1.** (*going across*) перехо́д; перее́зд. **2.** (*of sea*) перепра́ва, перехо́д. **3.** (*of road and/or rail*) перекрёсток; перехо́д; перее́зд; **level ~** пересече́ние желе́зной доро́ги с шоссе́ (на одно́м у́ровне); **pedestrian ~** пешехо́дный перехо́д.
cross|wise ['krɒswaɪz], **-ways** ['krɒsweɪz] *adj.* крестообра́зный.
adv. крест-на́крест.
crotch [krɒtʃ] *n.* (*anat.; also* **crutch**) проме́жность; **the trousers are tight in the ~** брю́ки жмут в шагу́.
crotchet ['krɒtʃɪt] *n.* (*mus.*) четвертна́я но́та.
crotchety ['krɒtʃɪtɪ] *adj.* (*peevish*) раздражи́тельный, брюзгли́вый.
crouch [kraʊtʃ] *v.i.* сгиба́ться, согну́ться.
croup [kru:p] *n.* круп.
croupier ['kru:pɪə(r), -ɪ,eɪ] *n.* крупье́ (*m. indecl.*).
croûton ['kru:tɒn] *n.* (*cul.*) грено́к.
crow[1] [krəʊ] *n.* воро́на; **carrion ~** чёрная воро́на; **as the ~ flies** по прямо́й; **~'s nest** (*naut.*) «воро́нье гнездо́».
cpd. **~bar** *n.* лом.
crow[2] [krəʊ] *n.* (*of cock*) кукаре́канье.
v.t. (*of cock*) кукаре́кать (*impf.*); **~ over s.o.** восторжествова́ть (*pf.*) над кем-н.
crowd [kraʊd] *n.* **1.** (*throng*) толпа́; **follow (*or* go with) the ~** (*fig.*) плыть (*impf.*) по тече́нию. **2.** (*clique, social set*) компа́ния, о́бщество.
v.t. **1.** (*overfill*) зап|олня́ть, -о́лнить; переп|олня́ть, -о́лнить; **the buses are ~ed** авто́бусы перепо́лнены; **~ed street** у́лица, запру́женная наро́дом; **the room was ~ed with furniture** ко́мната была́ загромождена́ ме́белью; **a life ~ed with incident** жизнь, бога́тая происше́ствиями. **2.: patients are ~ed out of the hospitals** больни́цы перегру́жены; больны́м бо́льше нет ме́ста; **his article was ~ed out of the magazine** его́ статья́ была́ вы́теснена из журна́ла други́м материа́лом.
v.i. (*assemble in a ~*) толпи́ться, с-; наб|ива́ться, -и́ться битко́м; **they ~ed round the teacher** они́ столпи́лись вокру́г учи́теля; **they ~ed into the room** они́ хлы́нули в ко́мнату.

crown [kraʊn] *n.* **1.** коро́на, вене́ц. **2.** (*fig.*, *sovereignty or sovereign*) коро́на, престо́л; **he succeeded to the ~** он унасле́довал коро́ну; **this land belongs to the C~** э́та земля́ принадлежи́т коро́не; **witness for the C~** свиде́тель обвине́ния. **3.** (*wreath*) вене́ц, вено́к. **4.** (*coin*) кро́на. **5.** (*of head*) маку́шка, те́мя (*nt.*); (*of hat*) тулья́; (*of tree*) кро́на, верху́шка. **6.** (*dental work*) коро́нка. **7.** (*fig.*, *culmination or reward*) вене́ц, заверше́ние, верши́на; **the ~ of one's achievements** верши́на достиже́ний. **8.** (*attr.*): **~ jewels** короле́вские/ца́рские рега́лии (*f. pl.*); **~ prince** насле́дный принц; **~ princess** насле́дная принце́сса.

v.t. **1.: he was ~ed king** его́ короновáли (на ца́рство). **2.: the hill is ~ed with a wood** верши́на холма́ покры́та ле́сом. **3.** (*fig.*, *reward*): **his efforts were ~ed with success** его́ уси́лия увенча́лись успе́хом. **4.** (*put finishing touch to*) заверш|а́ть, -и́ть; **to ~ it all, a storm broke out** в доверше́ние всего́ разрази́лась бу́ря. **5.** (*hit on the head*) тре́снуть (*pf.*) по башке́ (*coll.*). **6.** (*at draughts*) пров|оди́ть, -ести́ в да́мки. **7.: ~ a tooth** ста́вить, по- коро́нку на зуб.

crozier ['krəʊzɪə(r), -ʒə(r)] = **crosier**

crucial ['kruːʃ(ə)l] *adj.* (*decisive*) реша́ющий.

crucible ['kruːsɪb(ə)l] *n.* ти́гель (*m.*); (*fig.*) горни́ло.

crucifix ['kruːsɪfɪks] *n.* распя́тие; (*cross*) крест.

crucifixion [ˌkruːsɪ'fɪkʃ(ə)n] *n.* распя́тие (на кресте́).

cruciform ['kruːsɪˌfɔːm] *adj.* крестообра́зный.

crucify ['kruːsɪˌfaɪ] *v.t.* расп|ина́ть, -я́ть.

crude [kruːd] *adj.* **1.** (*of materials*): **~ oil** сыра́я нефть; **~ sugar** неочи́щенный са́хар. **2.** (*graceless*) гру́бый, неотёсанный. **3.** (*awkward*, *ill-made*): **~ paintings** аляпова́тые карти́ны; **a ~ log cabin** гру́бо сколо́ченная деревя́нная хи́жина. **4.** (*unripe*, *undigested*): **~ schemes** неразрабо́танные пла́ны; **~ facts** го́лые фа́кты.

crud|eness ['kruːdnɪs], **-ity** ['kruːdɪtɪ] *nn.* гру́бость, неотёсанность.

cruel ['kruːəl] *adj.* жесто́кий.

cruelty ['kruːəltɪ] *n.* жесто́кость; **~ to animals** жесто́кое обраще́ние с живо́тными.

cruet ['kruːɪt] *n.* графи́нчик, сосу́д.

cpd. **~-stand** *n.* судо́к.

cruis|e [kruːz] *n.* (*of ship*) пла́вание; (*of aircraft*) полёт; (*pleasure voyage*) морско́е путеше́ствие, круи́з; **~ missile** крыла́тая раке́та.

v.i. крейси́ровать (*impf.*); соверша́ть (*impf.*) ре́йсы; **~ing speed** (*of aircraft*) кре́йсерская ско́рость; (*of car*) эксплуатацио́нная ско́рость.

cruiser ['kruːzə(r)] *n.* (*warship*) кре́йсер; **cabin ~** прогу́лочный ка́тер с каю́той.

crumb [krʌm] *n.* **1.** (*small piece*) кро́шка; (*fig.*): **~s of information** обры́вки (*m. pl.*) све́дений; **~ of comfort** сла́бое утеше́ние. **2. ~s!** (*coll.*) ну и ну!

crumble ['krʌmb(ə)l] *n.* (*cul.*) слоёный фрукто́вый пу́динг.

v.t. (*bread etc.*) кроши́ть, рас-.

v.i. кроши́ться (*impf.*); (*of a wall*) обру́ши|ваться, -ться; (*fig.*, *of empires*, *hopes etc.*) ру́шиться (*impf.*, *pf.*).

crumbly ['krʌmblɪ] *adj.* кроша́щийся; (*of bread*) рассыпча́тый.

crummy ['krʌmɪ] *adj.* (*inferior*) дрянно́й, жа́лкий.

crumpet ['krʌmpɪt] *n.* ≃ сдо́бная лепёшка.

crumple ['krʌmp(ə)l] *v.t.* мять с-; **~ one's clothes** смять (*pf.*) свою́ оде́жду; **~ up a sheet of paper** ско́мкать (*pf.*) лист бума́ги.

v.i. мя́ться (*or* смина́ться), с-; **these sheets ~** э́ти про́стыни мну́тся; **the wings of the aircraft ~d up** кры́лья самолёта помя́лись.

crunch [krʌntʃ] *n.* (*noise*) хруст; (*crucial moment*) реша́ющий моме́нт.

v.t. & i. грызть (*impf.*) с хру́стом; хрусте́ть (*impf.*).

crusade [kruː'seɪd] *n.* (*lit.*, *fig.*) кресто́вый похо́д.

v.i. (*fig.*) идти́ (*det.*) в похо́д (*против чего or за что*).

crusader [kruː'seɪdə(r)] *n.* крестоно́сец; (*fig.*) боре́ц.

crush [krʌʃ] *n.* **1.** (*crowd*) толчея́, толкотня́, да́вка. **2.** (*infatuation*): **she has a ~ on him** она́ от него́ без ума́. **3.** (*fruit drink*) вы́жатый фрукто́вый сок.

v.t. **1.** (*press*, *squash*) разда́в|ливать, -и́ть; **some people were ~ed to death** кое-кого́ задави́ло. **2.** (*crumple*) мять, из-/с-; **her dresses were badly ~ed** её пла́тья си́льно помя́лись. **3.** (*defeat*, *overcome*) сокруш|а́ть, -и́ть; **he ~ed his enemies** он разгроми́л свои́х враго́в; **our hopes were ~ed** на́ши наде́жды ру́хнули; **a ~ing defeat** по́лное пораже́ние, разгро́м.

v.i. мя́ться, из-/с-; изм|ина́ться, -я́ться; прот|а́лкиваться, -олка́ться; проти́с|киваться, -нуться; **they ~ed into the front seats** они́ проти́снулись/протолка́лись на места́ пе́рвого ря́да.

with advs.: **~ out** *v.t.* (*extinguish*): **~ out a cigarette** погаси́ть (*pf.*) сигаре́ту; **~ up** *v.t.* (*make into powder*) толо́чь, рас-/ис-.

crust [krʌst] *n.* (*of bread*) ко́рка; (*of pastry*) ко́рочка; **the earth's ~** земна́я кора́.

crustacean [krʌ'steɪʃ(ə)n] *n.* ракообра́зное.

crusty ['krʌstɪ] *adj.* (*lit.*) покры́тый ко́ркой; с ко́рочкой; (*fig.*) ре́зкий, жёлчный.

crutch [krʌtʃ] *n.* **1.** (*support*) косты́ль (*m.*); (*fig.*) опо́ра. **2.** = **crotch**

crux [krʌks] *n.* (*essential point*) суть; коренно́й вопро́с.

cry [kraɪ] *n.* **1.** (*weeping*) плач; **she had a good ~** она́ вспла́сть попла́кала. **2.** (*shout*) крик. **3.** (*of animal*) крик; **in full ~** (*of hounds*) в бе́шеной пого́не. **4.** (*watch-word*) клич, ло́зунг. **5.** (*entreaty*, *demand*) мольба́; **there was a ~ for reform** подняли́сь голоса́, тре́бующие рефо́рмы. **6.** (*outcry*, *clamour*) крик, вопль (*m.*); **they raised the ~ of discrimination** они́ по́дняли крик/во́пли о дискримина́ции.

v.t. **1.** (*weep*) пла́кать (*impf.*); **~ one's eyes out** вы́плакать (*pf.*) (все) глаза́; **she cried herself to sleep** она́ усну́ла в слеза́х. **2.** (*shout*, *exclaim*) крича́ть (*impf.*); вскри́к|ивать, -нуть; **"Enough!" he cried** «Дово́льно!» — закрича́л он.

v.i. **1.** (*weep*) пла́кать (*impf.*); **~ over sth.** опла́кивать (*impf.*) что-н.. **2.** (*shout*, *exclaim*, *plead*) крича́ть (*impf.*); вскри́к|ивать, -нуть; **he cried with pain** он вскри́кнул от бо́ли; **they cried for mercy** они́ умоля́ли о милосе́рдии.

with advs.: **~ off** *v.t. & i.* (*an engagement*) отмен|я́ть, -и́ть (свида́ние); **~ out** *v.i.* (*in pain or distress*) вскри́к|ивать, -нуть.

cpd. **~-baby** *n.* пла́кса (*c.g.*).

crying ['kraɪɪŋ] *n.* (*weeping*) плач.

adj.: **a ~ shame** безобра́зие; **~ need** о́страя нужда́.

cryogenics [ˌkraɪəʊ'dʒenɪks] *n.* криоге́ника.

crypt [krɪpt] *n.* кри́пта, склеп.

cryptic ['krɪptɪk] *adj.* та́инственный, зага́дочный.

crypto-Communist [ˌkrɪptəʊ-'kɒmjʊnɪst] *n.* та́йный коммуни́ст.

cryptogram ['krɪptəˌgræm] *n.* криптогра́мма.

cryptographer [krɪp'tɒgrəfə(r)] *n.* шифрова́льщик

cryptographic [ˌkrɪptə'græfɪk] *adj.* криптографи́ческий, шифрова́льный.

cryptography [krɪp'tɒgrəfɪ] *n.* криптогра́фия.

crystal ['krɪst(ə)l] *n.* **1.** (*substance*) го́рный хруста́ль; **~ ornaments** хруста́льные украше́ния. **2.** (*glassware*) хруста́ль (*m.*); **~ ball** маги́ческий криста́лл. **3.** (*aggregation of molecules*) криста́лл. **4.** (*fig.*): **the ~ waters of the lake** прозра́чные во́ды о́зера. **5.** (*US*, *watch-glass*) стекло́ ручны́х часо́в.

cpds. **~-clear** *adj.* (*fig.*) я́сный как бо́жий день; **~-gazing** *n.* гада́ние.

crystalline ['krɪstə,laɪn] *adj.* хрустáльный; (*fig., also*) кристáльный.

crystallization [,krɪstəlaɪ'zeɪʃ(ə)n] *n.* (*lit.*) кристаллизáция.

crystallize ['krɪstə,laɪz] *v.t.* **1.** (*form into crystals*) кристаллизовáть (*impf., pf.*); за- (*pf.*). **2.** (*clarify*) вопло|щáть, -тúть в определённую фóрму. **3.:** **~d fruit** засáхаренные фрýкты.

v.i. **1.** (*form into crystals*) кристаллизовáться (*impf., pf.*); вы- (*pf.*). **2.:** **his plans ~d** егó плáны стáли определёнными.

crystallography [,krɪstə'lɒgrəfɪ] *n.* кристаллогрáфия.

cub [kʌb] *n.* детёныш; (*bear*) медвежóнок; (*lion*) львёнок; (*tiger*) тигрёнок.

Cuba [,kju:bə] *n.* Кýба; **in ~** на Кýбе.

Cuban ['kju:bən] *n.* кубúн|ец (*fem.* -ка).

adj. кубúнский.

cubby-hole ['kʌbɪ-] *n.* (*small room*) кóмнатка, камóрка.

cube [kju:b] *n.* **1.** (*math.: of a number*) куб; **~ root** кубúческий кóрень. **2.** (*solid*) кýбик; **~ sugar** пилёный сáхар; **sugar ~** кусóк пилёного сáхара.

v.t. **1.** (*calculate ~ of*) возв|одúть, -естú (*число*) в куб; **4 ~d** 4 в кýбе. **2.** (*cut into ~s*) нар|езáть, -éзать кýбиками.

cubic ['kju:bɪk] *adj.* кубúческий.

cubicle ['kju:bɪk(ə)l] *n.* кабúна.

cubism ['kju:bɪz(ə)m] *n.* кубúзм.

cubit ['kju:bɪt] *n.* лóкоть (*m.*) (*мера длины*).

cuckold ['kʌkəʊld] *n.* рогонóсец.

v.t. наст|авлять, -áвить рогá +*d*.

cuckoo ['kʊku:] *n.* кукýшка; **~ clock** часы́ (*m. pl.*) с кукýшкой.

adj. (*coll., crazy*) чóкнутый, трóнутый.

v.i. (*utter ~'s cry*) кковáть (*impf.*).

cucumber ['kju:kʌmbə(r)] *n.* огурéц; **~ salad** салáт из огурцóв; **cool as a ~** хладнокрóвный, невозмутúмый.

cud [kʌd] *n.* жвáчка; **chew the ~** (*lit., fig.*) жевáть (*impf.*) жвáчку.

cuddle ['kʌd(ə)l] *v.t. & i.* обн|имáть(ся).

v.i.: **~ up (to s.o.)** приж|имáться, -áться (к комý-н.).

cuddl|esome ['kʌd(ə)lsəm], **-y** ['kʌdlɪ] *adjs.* располагáющий к лáске; мúлый, прия́тный; **~ toy** мягконабивнáя игрýшка.

cudgel ['kʌdʒ(ə)l] *n.* дубúнка, пáлка; **take up the ~s for s.o.** (*fig.*) вы́ступить (*pf.*) в защúту когó-н.

v.t. бить (*impf.*) дубúнкой/пáлкой.

cue[1] [kju:] *n.* (*theatr.*) рéплика; (*fig., hint*) намёк; **take one's ~ from** взять (*pf.*) примéр с (*кого*).

cue[2] [kju:] *n.* (*billiards*) кий.

cuff[1] [kʌf] *n.* **1.** (*part of sleeve*) манжéта; **off the ~** (*fig.*) экспрóмтом. **2.** (*US, trouser turnup*) отворóт.

cpd. **~-links** *n.* зáпонки (*f. pl.*).

cuff[2] [kʌf] *n.* (*blow*) шлепóк.

v.t. шлёп|ать, -нуть.

cuirass [kwɪ'ræs] *n.* (*armour*) кирáса.

cuisine [kwɪ'zi:n] *n.* кýхня.

cul-de-sac ['kʌldə,sæk, 'kʊl-] *n.* (*also fig.*) тупúк.

culinary ['kʌlɪnərɪ] *adj.* кулинáрный.

cull [kʌl] *n.* (*of seals*) отбóр, бракóвка.

v.t. **1.** (*select*) от|бирáть, -обрáть; (*flowers etc.*) соб|ирáть, -рáть. **2.** (*slaughter*) бить (*impf.*).

culminate ['kʌlmɪ,neɪt] *v.i.* дост|игáть, -úгнуть вы́сшей тóчки (*or* апогéя).

culmination [,kʌlmɪ'neɪʃ(ə)n] *n.* кульминáция; кульминациóнный пункт.

culottes [kju:'lɒts] *n. pl.* ю́бка-брю́ки.

culpability [,kʌlpə'bɪlɪtɪ] *n.* винóвность.

culpable ['kʌlpəb(ə)l] *adj.* винóвный.

culprit ['kʌlprɪt] *n.* винóвник.

cult [kʌlt] *n.* культ.

cultivate ['kʌltɪ,veɪt] *v.t.* **1.** (*land*) возделы|вать, -ать; (*crops*) культивúровать (*impf.*); **~d area** посевнáя плóщадь. **2.:** **~ one's mind** развивáть (*impf.*) ум; **~ one's style** совершéнствовать (*impf.*) свой стиль; **a ~d person** культýрный человéк. **3.:** **~ s.o.('s acquaintance)** поддéрживать (*impf.*) знакóмство с кем-н.

cultivation [,kʌltɪ'veɪʃ(ə)n] *n.* **1.** (*agric.*) (*of soil*) обрабóтка, культивáция, возделывание; (*of plants*) культивúрование, разведéние. **2.** (*culture*) культýра. **3.** (*of acquaintance*) поддéрживание (знакóмства).

cultivator ['kʌltɪ,veɪtə(r)] *n.* (*pers.*) землéдéлец; (*implement*) культиватóр.

cultural ['kʌltʃər(ə)l] *adj.* культýрный; **~ agreement** договóр о культýрном обмéне.

culture ['kʌltʃə(r)] *n.* **1.** (*tillage*) возделывание, культивáция. **2.** (*rearing, production*) разведéние, возделывание. **3.** (*colony of bacteria*) культýра, штáмм. **4.** (*civilization, way of life*) культýра, быт; **a man of ~** интеллигéнтный человéк.

v.t.: **~d pearls** культивúрованный жéмчуг.

cultured ['kʌltʃəd] *adj.* (*of pers.*) культýрный.

cumbersome ['kʌmbəsəm] *adj.* громóздкий.

cummerbund ['kʌmə,bʌnd] *n.* ширóкий пóяс (под смóкинг).

cum(m)in ['kʌmɪn] *n.* тмин.

cumulative ['kju:mjʊlətɪv] *adj.* кумулятúвный, накóпленный; **~ evidence** (*leg.*) совокýпность улúк.

cumulus ['kju:mjʊləs] *n.* (*cloud*) кучевы́е облакá.

cuneiform ['kju:nɪ,fɔ:m] *n.* (*~ writing*) клúнопись.

cunning ['kʌnɪŋ] *n.* (*craftiness*) хúтрость; (*skill*) лóвкость.

adj. (*crafty*) хúтрый.

cunt [kʌnt] *n.* пиздá (*vulg.*).

cup [kʌp] *n.* **1.** (*for tea etc.*) чáшка, (*liter.*) чáша; **that is my ~ of tea** (*fig.*) э́то в моём вкýсе. **2.** (*as prize*) кýбок; **~ final** финáл рóзыгрыша кýбка.

v.t.: **~ one's hand** держáть (*impf.*) рýку гóрстью; **~ one's hands round a glass** обхватúть (*pf.*) стакáн обéими рукáми; **~ one's chin in one's hands** подп|ирáть, -ерéть подборóдок ладóнями.

cpds. **~-cake** *n.* крýглый кекс; **~-tie** *n.* футбóльный матч на кýбок.

cupboard ['kʌbəd] *n.* шкаф, буфéт.

Cupid ['kju:pɪd] *n.* Купидóн.

cupidity [kju:'pɪdɪtɪ] *n.* áлчность, жáдность.

cupola ['kju:pələ] *n.* кýпол.

cur [kɜ:(r)] *n.* дворня́жка.

curable ['kjʊərəb(ə)l] *adj.* излечúмый.

curate ['kjʊərət] *n.* викáрий, млáдший прихóдский свящéнник.

curative ['kjʊərətɪv] *adj.* целéбный, целúтельный.

curator [kjʊə'reɪtə(r)] *n.* (*of museum etc.*) хранúтель (*m.*).

curb [kɜ:b] *n.* **1.** уздá. **2.** = **kerb**

v.t. **1.** (*of horse*) над|евáть, -éть уздý на+*a*. **2.** (*fig.*) обýзд|ывать, -áть.

curd [kɜ:d] *n.* твóрóг.

curdle ['kɜ:d(ə)l] *v.t.* створ|áживать, -ожúть; **~ the blood** (*fig.*) леденúть (*impf.*) кровь.

v.i. свёр|тываться, -нýться; створ|áживаться, -óжиться; (*fig.*): **one's blood ~s** кровь леденéет; кровь сты́нет в жúлах.

cure ['kjʊə(r)] *n.* **1.** (*remedy*) лекáрство, срéдство; **past ~** неизлечúмый. **2.** (*treatment*) лечéние.

v.t. **1.** (*make healthy*) вылéчивать, вы́лечить; **he was ~d of asthma** он вы́лечился от áстмы. **2.** (*remedy*): (*disease*) вылéчивать, вы́лечить; излéч|ивать, -úть; (*poverty*) уничт|ожáть, -óжить; (*drunkenness*) изж|ивáть, -úть. **3.** (*meat*) солúть, по-; вя́лить, про-; (*hides*) обраб|áтывать, -óтать.

v.i.: **the disease ~d of itself** болéзнь прошлá самá по себé.

cpd. **~-all** *n.* панацéя.

curfew ['kɜːfjuː] *n.* комендáнтский час; **impose a ~** устан|áвливать, -ови́ть комендáнтский час; **lift a ~** отмен|я́ть, -и́ть комендáнтский час.

curio ['kjʊərɪəʊ] *n.* антиквáрная вещь, рéдкость.

curiosity [ˌkjʊərɪ'ɒsɪtɪ] *n.* **1.** (*inquisitiveness*) любопы́тство, любознáтельность. **2.** (*unusual object*) дикóвин(к)а; рéдкость.

curious ['kjʊərɪəs] *adj.* **1.** (*interested*): **I am ~ to know what he said** я хочý знáть, что он сказáл. **2.** (*inquisitive*) любопы́тный, любознáтельный. **3.** (*odd*) стрáнный, дикóвинный; **~ly enough** как ни стрáнно.

curium ['kjʊərɪəm] *n.* кю́рий.

curl [kɜːl] *n.* (*of hair*) лóкон, завитóк; (*pl.*, **~y** *hair*) кудря́вые вóлосы (*m. pl.*); (*of string*) завитóк, спирáль; (*of smoke*) кольцó; (*of lip*) презри́тельная усмéшка/улы́бка.

v.t.: **~ a string around one's finger** закрути́ть (*pf.*) шнурóк вокрýг пáльца; **~ one's hair** зав|ивáть, -и́ть вóлосы; **~ing-tongs** щипцы́ (*m. pl.*) для зави́вки; **~ one's lip** презри́тельно скриви́ть (*pf.*) гýбы.

v.i.: **her hair ~s naturally** у неё кудря́вые от прирóды вóлосы; **the smoke ~ed upwards** клу́бы ды́ма поднимáлись вверх; **the dog ~ed up by the fire** собáка свернýлась клубкóм уками́на.

curlers ['kɜːləz] *n.* бигуди́ (*nt. pl.*, *indecl.*).

curlew ['kɜːljuː] *n.* кроншнéп.

curlicue ['kɜːlɪˌkjuː] *n.* завитýшка.

curly ['kɜːlɪ] *adj.* кудря́вый, курчáвый, вью́щийся.

cpd. **~-headed** *adj.* кудря́вый.

currant ['kʌrənt] *n.* **1.** (*fruit*, *bush*) сморóдина. **2.** (*in cake etc.*) изю́м, кори́нка; **~ bun** бýлочка с изю́мом.

currency ['kʌrənsɪ] *n.* **1.** (*acceptance*, *validity*): **the rumour gained ~** э́тот слух прони́к всю́ду; **give ~ to a rumour** распространи́ть (*pf.*) слух (*о чём*); **during the ~ of the contract** в течéние срóка дéйствия договóра. **2.** (*money*) валю́та; дéн|ьги (*pl.*, *g.* -ег); **paper ~** бумáжные дéньги; **gold ~** золотáя валю́та; **hard ~** конверти́руемая валю́та; **soft ~** неконверти́руемая валю́та; **the mark is German ~** мáрка — дéнежная едини́ца Гермáнии.

current ['kʌrənt] *n.* **1.** (*of air*, *water*) струя́, потóк. **2.** (*elec.*) ток; **alternating ~** перемéнный ток; **direct ~** постоя́нный ток. **3.** (*course*, *tendency*) течéние, ход.

adj. **1.** (*in general use*, *e.g. words*, *opinions*) ходя́чий, распространённый. **2.** (*of present time*) текýщий; **~ events** текýщие собы́тия; **at ~ prices** по существýющим цéнам. **3.**: **~ account** (*comm.*) текýщий счёт.

currently ['kʌrəntlɪ] *adv.* **1.** (*generally*, *commonly*) обы́чно. **2.** (*at present*) ны́не, в настоя́щее врéмя.

curriculum [kə'rɪkjʊləm] *n.* курс обучéния; учéбный план; **~ vitae** (крáткая) биогрáфия.

curry[1] ['kʌrɪ] *n.* (*cul.*) кэ́рри (*nt. indecl.*).

v.t.: **curried lamb** барáнина, припрáвленная кэ́рри.

cpd. **~-powder** *n.* порошóк кэ́рри.

curry[2] ['kʌrɪ] *v.t.*: **~ favour with s.o.** подли́з|ываться, -áться к комý-н.

curse [kɜːs] *n.* **1.** (*execration*) проклятие; **he is under a ~** над ним тяготéет проклятие. **2.** (*bane*) проклятие, бич; **the ~ of drink** бич пья́нства. **3.** (*oath*) богохýльство, ругáтельство.

v.t. **1.** (*pronounce ~ on*) прокл|инáть, -я́сть. **2.** (*abuse*, *scold*) ругáть (*impf.*); проклинáть (*impf.*).

v.i. (*swear*, *utter ~s*) ругáться (*impf.*); **~ at s.o.** осыпáть (*pf.*) когó-н. проклятиями.

cursed ['kɜːsɪd, kɜːst] *adj.* прокля́тый.

cursive ['kɜːsɪv] *adj.* скорописный.

cursor ['kɜːsə(r)] *n.* стрéлка, указáтель (*m.*), движóк.

cursory ['kɜːsərɪ] *adj.* бéглый, повéрхностный.

curt [kɜːt] *adj.* отры́вистый, рéзкий.

curtail [kɜː'teɪl] *v.t.* (*shorten*) сокра|щáть, -ти́ть; **~ an allowance** урéзать (*impf.*) посóбие.

curtailment [kɜː'teɪlmənt] *n.* сокращéние, урéзывание.

curtain ['kɜːt(ə)n] *n.* **1.** (*of window*, *door*) занавéска, штóра; **draw the ~s** (*close*) задёрнуть (*pf.*) занавéски; (*open*) отдёрнуть (*pf.*) занавéски. **2.** (*fig.*) завéса; **draw a ~ over sth.** покры́ть (*pf.*) что-н. завéсой тáйны; **lift the ~ of secrecy** приподня́ть (*pf.*) завéсу тáйны; **Iron C~** желéзный зáнавес. **3.** (*theatr.*) зáнавес; **ring up the ~** подня́ть (*pf.*) зáнавес; дать (*pf.*) звонóк к подня́тию зáнавеса; **ring down the ~** опусти́ть (*pf.*) зáнавес; **~ call** вы́зов.

v.t. занавé|шивать, -сить; **~ off** отгор|áживать, -оди́ть занавéской.

curts(e)y ['kɜːtsɪ] *n.* реверáнс, приседáние.

v.i. прис|едáть, -éсть; дéлать, с- реверáнс.

curvature ['kɜːvətʃə(r)] *n.* кривизнá, изги́б, кривáя; **~ of the spine** искривлéние позвонóчника.

curve [kɜːv] *n.* (*line*) кривáя; (*pl.*, *of female body*) изги́бы (*m. pl.*); (*bend in road*) изги́б.

v.i. из|гибáться, -огнýться; **the road ~s** дорóга извивáется; **the river ~s round the town** рекá огибáет гóрод.

curvilinear [ˌkɜːvɪ'lɪnɪə(r)] *adj.* криволинéйный.

cushion ['kʊʃ(ə)n] *n.* (дивáнная) подýшка; (*billiards*) борт.

v.t.: **~ed** (*padded*) **seats** мя́гкие сидéнья; **~ a blow** смягч|áть, -и́ть удáр.

cushy ['kʊʃɪ] *adj.* (*coll.*): **~ job** тёпленькое местéчко.

custard ['kʌstəd] *n.* слáдкий крем/сóус из яи́ц и молокá.

custodian [kʌ'stəʊdɪən] *n.* (*guardian*) опекýн; (*of property etc.*) администрáтор; (*of museum etc.*) храни́тель (*m.*); (*caretaker*) стóрож.

custody ['kʌstədɪ] *n.* **1.** (*guardianship*) опéка, попечéние. **2.** (*keeping*): **in safe ~** на (со)хранéнии. **3.** (*arrest*): **take into ~** брать, взять под стрáжу; арестóв|ывать, -áть.

custom ['kʌstəm] *n.* **1.** (*habit*, *accepted behaviour*) обы́чай. **2.** (*business patronage*, *clientele*) клиентýра, покупáтели (*m. pl.*). **3.** (*pl.*, *import duties*) тамóженные пóшлины (*f. pl.*); **~s officer** тамóженник; **we got through the ~s** мы прошли́ тамóженный досмóтр.

cpds. **~-house** *n.* тамóжня; **~-made** *adj.* сдéланный на закáз.

customary ['kʌstəmərɪ] *adj.* обы́чный, привы́чный; **it is ~ to tip** при́нято давáть на чай.

customer ['kʌstəmə(r)] *n.* (*purchaser*) покупáтель (*m.*); (*giving order*) закáзчик; (*of bank etc.*) клиéнт; (*of restaurant*) посети́тель (*m.*); (*coll.*, *fellow*) субъéкт, тип; **ugly ~** жýткий субъéкт.

cut [kʌt] *n.* **1.** (*act of ~ting*) рéзка, рéзание; **~ and thrust** схвáтка; (*result of stroke*) порéз, разрéз; **he has ~s on his face from shaving** у негó на лицé порéзы от бритья́; **he got a nasty ~** он си́льно порéзался. **2.** (*reduction*) снижéние, понижéние; **~ in salary** снижéние жáлованья; **power ~** прекращéние подáчи электроэнéргии. **3.** (*omission*): **there were ~s in the film** в фи́льме бы́ли сдéланы купю́ры (*f. pl.*). **4.** (*piece or quantity ~*): **a ~ off the joint** ломóть (*m.*) жáреного мя́са; **cold ~s** мяснóй ассорти́мéнт. **5.** (*of clothes*) покрóй. **6.**: **short ~** кратчáйший путь; **take a short ~** пойти́ (*pf.*) напрями́к. **7.**: **he is a ~ above you** он нá голову вы́ше вас. **8.** (*coll.*, *rake-off*) дóля, часть; **his ~ was 20%** егó дóля составля́ла 20%.

v.t. **1.** (*divide*, *separate*, *wound*, *extract by ~ting*) рéзать (*impf.*); разр|езáть, -éзать; отр|езáть, -éзать; **the knife ~ his finger** нож порéзал емý пáлец; **he ~ himself on the tin** он порéзался о консéрвную бáнку; **the wheat has been ~** пшени́ца сжáта; **~ wood** руби́ть (*impf.*) лес; колóть (*impf.*) дровá; **~**

(*p.p.*) **flowers** срезанные цветы; ~ **coal** (*in a mine*) вырубать, вырубить уголь; ~ **sth. in two** разр|езать, -езать что-н. пополам; ~ **to pieces** (*lit.*) разрезать (*pf.*) на куски; (*fig.*, *defeat utterly*) изничтожить (*pf.*); ~ **short** (*an article*) сокра|щать, -тить; (*s.o.'s life*) оборвать (*pf.*); ~ **open** (*e.g. an orange*) разр|езать, -езать; (*cin.*) ~! (*stop shooting*) стоп! **2.** (*make by* ~*ting*): ~ **me a piece of cake** отрежьте мне кусок торта; ~ **steps in the ice** прорубать, -ить ступеньки во льду; ~ **an inscription** высекать, высечь надпись (на камне); ~ **a key** вырезать, вырезать ключ; ~ **a jewel** гранить (*impf.*) драгоценный камень; ~ **glass** гранёное стекло; хрусталь (*m.*). **3.** (*trim*) подстр|игать, -ичь; ~ **one's nails** подстр|игать, -ичь ногти; **have one's hair** ~ стричься, по-; ~ **s.o.'s hair** стричь, о- кого-н. **4.** (*ignore*, *neglect*): **she** ~ **me (dead)** она не пожелала меня узнать; ~ **a lecture** пропус|кать, -тить лекцию. **5.** (*intersect*) пересекать (*impf.*). **6.** (*reduce*) сн|ижать, -изить; сокра|щать, -тить; **fares were** ~ плата за проезд была снижена; **the play was** ~ пьесу сократили. **7.** (*of clothes*) кроить, с-. **8.**: **the baby** ~ **a tooth** у ребёнка прорезался зуб. **9.** (*at cards*): ~ **the pack** сн|имать, -ять колоду. **10.** (*fig.*): **he was** ~ **to the heart** это его задело за живое; ~ (*break*) **one's connection with s.o.** пор|ывать, -вать отношения с кем-н.; **that** ~**s no ice with me** (*coll.*) это на меня не действует.

v.i. **1.** (*make incision*) резать (*impf.*); **this knife doesn't** ~ этот нож не режет. **2.** (*in pass. sense*) резаться (*impf.*); **sandstone** ~**s easily** песчаник легко режется. **3.** (*fig.*): **he** ~ **into the conversation** он вмешался в разговор; **it** ~ **into** (*took up*) **his time** это отняло у него время. **4.** (*aim a blow*; *thrust*): **he** ~ **at me with a stick** он замахнулся на меня палкой; **it** ~**s across our plans** это срывает наши планы. **5.** (*cards*): **we** ~ **for partners** снятием карт мы определили партнёров. **6.** (*run, take short* ~): **the boy** ~ **away** мальчик удрал/умчался; **we** ~ **across the fields** мы прошли кратчайшим путём через поля.

with advs.: ~ **away** *v.t.* (*e.g. dead wood from a tree*) ср|езать, -езать; ~ **back** *v.t.* (*prune*) подр|езать, -езать; (*fig, reduce, limit*) сокра|щать, -тить; ~ **down** *v.t.* (*e.g. a tree*) рубить, с-; (*an opponent*) сра|жать, -зить; ~ **down expenses** сокра|щать, -тить расходы; ~ **in** *v.t.*: ~ **s.o. in** (*give them a share*) выделять, выделить кому-н. долю; *v.i.* (*interrupt a speaker*) вмеш|иваться, -аться; (*of a driver*) перерезать (*pf.*) дорогу кому-н.; ~ **off** *v.t.*: **he** ~ **off a yard from the roll (of cloth)** он отрезал ярд материи от куска; **I was** ~ **off while talking** меня прервали во время разговора; **they** ~ **off our electricity** у нас отключили электричество; **the army was** ~ **off from its base** армия была отрезана от базы; ~ **off supplies** прекра|щать, -тить подвоз припасов; **he** ~ **himself off from the world** он отгородился от мира; **he** ~ **his son off** он лишил своего сына наследства; **he was** ~ **off in his prime** он погиб в расцвете лет; ~ **(off) a corner** ср|езать, -езать угол; ~ **out** *v.t.*: **he** ~ **out a picture from the paper** он вырезал картинку из газеты; **she** ~ **out a dress** она скроила платье; **he is not** ~ **out for the work** он не создан для этой работы; **he has his work** ~ **out** ему предстоит нелёгкая задача; (*eliminate*): ~ **out the details** (*in talking*) отбр|асывать, -осить подробности; ~ **out smoking** бросить (*pf.*) курить; **the engine** ~ **out** (*failed*) мотор сдал; ~ **up** *v.t.*: **he** ~ **up his meat** он нарезал мясо; **he was** ~ **up by the news** (*coll.*) его подкосило это известие; *v.i.*: **the cloth** ~ **up into three suits** из этого материала вышло три костюма; **he** ~ **up rough** (*coll.*) он рассвирепел.

cpds. ~**away** *adj.*: ~**away view of an engine** разрез машины; ~**back** *n.* (*reduction*) подрезка; ~**-off** *n.*: ~**-off date** (*terminal date of a narrative etc.*) последняя дата; ~**-out** *n.* (*figure*) вырезанная фигура; (*elec.*) автоматический выключатель; ~**-price** *adj.* продаваемый по сниженной цене; ~**throat** *n.* головорез; ~**throat razor** опасная бритва; ~**throat competition** ожесточённая конкуренция.

cute [kju:t] *adj.* (*shrewd*) находчивый; (*appealing*) симпатичный.

cuticle ['kju:tɪk(ə)l] *n.* кутикула.

cutlass ['kʌtləs] *n.* абордажная сабля.

cutlery ['kʌtlərɪ] *n.* ножевые изделия.

cutlet ['kʌtlɪt] *n.* отбивная котлета.

cutter ['kʌtə(r)] *n.* (*tailor*) закройщик; (*boat*) катер.

cutting ['kʌtɪŋ] *n.* **1.** (*road, rail etc.*) выемка. **2.** (*press* ~) вырезка. **3.** (*of plant*) отросток. **4.** (*cin.*) монтаж.

adj.: **a** ~ **wind** резкий ветер; **a** ~ **retort** язвительный ответ.

cuttle-fish ['kʌt(ə)lfɪʃ] *n.* каракатица, сепия.

c.v. (*abbr. of* ***curriculum vitae***) (краткая) автобиография.

cwt ['hʌndrəd,weɪt] *n.* (*abbr. of* **hundredweight**) (*Imperial — approx. 50.8 kilograms*) английский центнер; (*US — approx. 45.4 kilograms*) американский центнер.

cyanide ['saɪə,naɪd] *n.* цианид.

cyanogen [saɪ'ænədʒ(ə)n] *n.* циан.

cyanosis [,saɪə'nəʊsɪs] *n.* цианоз, синюха.

cybernetic [,saɪbə'netɪk] *adj.* кибернетический.

cybernetics [,saɪbə'netɪks] *n.* кибернетика.

cyberspace ['saɪbə,speɪs] *n.* киберпространство.

cyclamen ['sɪkləmən] *n.* цикламен.

cycle ['saɪk(ə)l] *n.* **1.** (*series, rotation*) цикл, круг; **the** ~ **of the seasons** времена (*nt. pl.*) года. **2.** (*bicycle*) велосипед. **3.** (*elec.*) период переменного тока.

v.i. **1.** (*revolve*) делать (*impf.*) обороты. **2.** ездить (*indet.*) на велосипеде.

cpd. ~**-track** *n.* велосипедная дорожка; (*for race*) велотрек.

cyclic(al) ['saɪklɪk(ə)l, 'sɪk-] *adj.* циклический.

cyclist ['saɪklɪst] *n.* велосипедист.

cyclone ['saɪkləʊn] *n.* циклон.

cyclonic [,saɪ'klɒnɪk] *adj.* циклонический.

cyclotron ['saɪklə,trɒn] *n.* циклотрон.

cygnet ['sɪgnɪt] *n.* молодой лебедь.

cylinder ['sɪlɪndə(r)] *n.* **1.** (*geom. & eng.*) цилиндр; ~ **head** крышка цилиндра; **fire on all** ~**s** (*lit., fig.*) работать (*impf.*) в полную мощность. **2.** (*typ.*) цилиндр, валик.

cylindrical [,sɪ'lɪndrɪk(ə)l] *adj.* цилиндрический.

cymbal ['sɪmb(ə)l] *n.* тарелка.

cynic ['sɪnɪk] *n.* циник.

cynical ['sɪnɪk(ə)l] *adj.* циничный.

cynicism ['sɪnɪ,sɪz(ə)m] *n.* цинизм.

cypress ['saɪprəs] *n.* кипарис; (*attr.*) кипарисовый.

Cyprus ['sɑɪprəs] *n.* Кипр; **in** ~ на Кипре.

Cyrillic [sɪ'rɪlɪk] *adj.*: ~ **alphabet** кириллица.

cyst [sɪst] *n.* киста.

cystic fibrosis [,sɪstɪk faɪ'brəʊsɪs] *n.* кистозный фиброз.

cystitis [sɪ'staɪtɪs] *n.* цистит.

cytology [saɪ'tɒlədʒɪ] *n.* цитология.

czar [zɑ:(r)] *etc. see* **tsar** *etc.*

Czech [tʃek] *n.* чех (*fem.* чешка); (*language*) чешский язык.

adj. чешский; ~ **Republic** Чехия.

Czechoslovakia [,tʃekəslə'vækɪə] *n.* Чехословакия.

D

D [di:] *n.* **1.** (*mus.*) ре (*indecl.*). **2.** (*acad. mark*) 2, двóйка; **he got a ~ in English** он получи́л двóйку по англи́йскому языку́.

dab[1] [dæb] *n.* (*small quantity*) мазóк.
v.t. & i. при|клáдывать, -ложи́ть; **she ~bed (at) her eyes with a handkerchief** онá приклáдывала к глазáм платóк; **he ~bed paint on the picture** он нанёс крáски на холст/полотнó.

dab[2] [dæb] *n.*: **~ hand** спец, дóка (*c.g.*) (*coll.*).

dabble ['dæb(ə)l] *v.i.*: **~ at** (*fig.*) игрáть (*impf.*) в+*a.*; баловáться (*impf.*) +*i.*; **he ~s in politics** он игрáет в поли́тику.

dabbler ['dæblə(r)] *n.* дилетáнт.

dacha ['dætʃə] *n.* дáча.

dachshund ['dækshʊnd] *n.* тáкса.

dacron ['deɪkrɒn, 'dæk-] *n.* (*propr.*) дакрóн.

dactyl ['dæktɪl] *n.* дáктиль (*m.*).

dactylic [dæk'tɪlɪk] *adj.* дактили́ческий.

dad [dæd], **-dy** ['dædɪ] *nn.* (*coll.*) пáпа (*m.*).

daddy ['dædɪ] = **dad**
cpd. **~-long-legs** *n.* долгонóжка; паýк-сенокóсец.

daffodil ['dæfədɪl] *n.* нарци́сс жёлтый.

daft [dɑ:ft] *adj.* трóнутый, дурнóй (*coll.*).

dagger ['dægə(r)] *n.* **1.** (*weapon*) кинжáл; **they are at ~s drawn** они́ на ножáх; **she looked ~s at him** онá пронзи́ла егó взгля́дом. **2.** (*typ.*) ≃ крéстик.

dahlia ['deɪlɪə] *n.* георги́н.

daily ['deɪlɪ] *n.* **1.** (*newspaper*) ежеднéвная газéта. **2.** (*charwoman*) приходя́щая домрабóтница.
adj. ежеднéвный; **one's ~ bread** хлеб насýщный.
adv. ежеднéвно, кáждый день.

dainty ['deɪntɪ] *adj.* **1.** (*refined, delicate*) утончённый, изя́щный. **2.** (*fastidious*) привередливый.

dairy ['deərɪ] *n.* **1.** (*room or building*) маслодéльня. **2.** (*shop*) молóчная; (*attr.*) молóчный.
cpds. **~maid** доя́рка; **~man** доя́р.

dais ['deɪɪs] *n.* помóст.

daisy ['deɪzɪ] *n.* маргари́тка; **fresh as a ~** пы́шущий здорóвьем.

dale [deɪl] *n.* доли́на, дол.

dally ['dælɪ] *v.i.* **1.** (*play, toy*) баловáться (*impf.*) (*чем*). **2.** (*waste time*) трáтить (*impf.*) врéмя пóпусту.

Dalmatian [dæl'meɪʃ(ə)n] *n.* (*dog*) далмáтский дог.

dam[1] [dæm] *n.* **1.** (*barrier*) дáмба, плоти́на, запрýда. **2.** (*reservoir*) водохрани́лище.
v.t. запрý|живать, -ди́ть; **~ up a valley** перекр|ывáть, -ы́ть доли́ну.

dam[2] [dæm] *n.* (*zool.*) мáтка.

damag|e ['dæmɪdʒ] *n.* **1.** (*harm, injury*) вред, повреждéние; ущéрб; **do ~e to sth.** нан|оси́ть, -ести́ ущéрб/вред чемý-н. **2.** (*coll., cost*): **what's the ~e?** скóлько с нас причитáется? **3.** (*pl., leg.*) убы́тк|и (*pl., g.* -ов); **sue s.o. for ~es** возбу|ждáть, -ди́ть дéло прóтив когó-н. за убы́тки.
v.t. (*physically or morally*) повре|ждáть, -ди́ть +*d.*

damask ['dæməsk] *n.* **1.** (*material*) дамáст, штоф; **~ silk** дамáст, камкá; **~ table-cloth** камчáтная скáтерть. **2.**: **~ rose** дамáсская рóза.

dame [deɪm] *n.* **1.** (*arch. or joc., lady*) госпожá, дáма. **2.** (*fem. equiv. of knight*) дейм, кавалéрственная дáма. **3.** (*US, woman*) бабёнка (*coll.*).

damn [dæm] *n.*: **I don't care a ~** мне наплевáть.
v.t. **1.** (*doom to hell*) осу|ждáть, -ди́ть на вéчные мýки. **2.** (*condemn*): **the critics ~ed the play** крити́ки забраковáли пьéсу. **3.** (*as expletive*): **~ (it all)!** чёрт возьми́!; **I'm ~ed if I know** ей-Бóгу, не знáю; **well, I'm ~ed!** чёрт бы меня́ побрáл!; **~ your impudence!** чёрт бы побрáл твоё нахáльство!; **~ all** (*coll., nothing*) ни чертá; **I'm ~ed if I'll go** провали́ться мне на э́том мéсте, éсли я пойдý. *see also* **damned**

damnable ['dæmnəb(ə)l] *adj.* прокля́тый.

damnation [dæm'neɪʃ(ə)n] *n.* **1.** (*condemnation to hell*) прокля́тие; осуждéние на вéчные мýки. **2.** (*adverse judgment*) осуждéние. **3.** **~!** прокля́тие!

damned [dæmd] *n., adj. & adv.* **1.**: **the ~** осуждённые на вéчные мýки; прóклятые. **2.**: **a ~ fool** наби́тый дурáк; **it's a ~ nuisance** э́то чертóвски досáдно.

damning ['dæmɪŋ] *adj.* губи́тельный; **~ evidence** изобличáющие ули́ки.

damp [dæmp] *n.* **1.** (*moisture*) влáжность, сы́рость. **2.** (**~** *atmosphere*) сы́рость, влáжность.
adj. влáжный, сырóй; **~ course** гидроизоля́ция.
v.t. (*also* **dampen**) (*lit.*) см|áчивать, -очи́ть; увлажн|я́ть, -и́ть; **~ down a fire** туши́ть, по- огóнь.
cpd. **~-proof** *adj.* влагонепроницáемый; *v.t.* предохран|я́ть, -и́ть от влáги.

damper ['dæmpə(r)] *n.* **1.** (*plate in stove etc.*) заслóнка; (*shock absorber*) амортизáтор; (*silencer*) глуши́тель (*m.*). **2.** (*fig.*): **the news put a ~ on the stock market** нóвости привели́ к понижéнию конъюнктýры на би́рже. **3.** (*in piano*) дéмпфер.

dampness ['dæmpnɪs] *n.* сы́рость.

damsel ['dæmz(ə)l] *n.* (*arch.*) деви́ца.

damson ['dæmz(ə)n] *n.* (*fruit*) терносли́в; (*tree*) тёрн.

dance [dɑ:ns] *n.* **1.** тáнец; **we joined the ~** мы присоедини́лись к танцýющим. **2.** (*party*) танцевáльный вéчер; тáнцы (*m. pl.*); **give a ~** устр|áивать, -óить тáнцы. **3.** (*fig.*): **lead s.o. a (fine, pretty)** води́ть (*indet.*) когó-н. зá нос.
v.t. **1.** танцевáть, с-. **2.**: **~ a baby on one's knee** качáть (*impf.*) ребёнка на колéнях. **3.** (*fig.*): **~ attendance on s.o.** ходи́ть (*indet.*) пéред кем-н. на зáдних лáпках.
v.i. танцевáть, с-; плясáть, с-; **he ~d for joy** он плясáл от рáдости; **the leaves ~d in the wind** ли́стья кружи́лись на ветрý; **the boat ~d on the waves** лóдка качáлась на вóлнáх.
cpds. **~-band** *n.* оркéстр (на тáнцах); **~-hall** *n.* танцевáльный зал.

dancer ['dɑ:nsə(r)] *n.* танцóр (*fem.* -ка); (*professional*) танцóвщи|к (*fem.* -ца).

dancing ['dɑ:nsɪŋ] *n.* тáнцы (*m. pl.*).
cpds. **~-master** *n.* учи́тель (*m.*) тáнцев; **~-partner** *n.* партнёр; **~-shoes** *n.* танцевáльные тýфли (*f. pl.*).

dandelion ['dændɪ,laɪən] *n.* одувáнчик.

dander ['dændə(r)] *n.* (*US coll.*): **get s.o.'s ~ up** вы́вести (*pf.*) когó-н. из себя́.

dandle ['dænd(ə)l] *v.t.* качáть (*impf.*).

dandruff ['dændrʌf] *n.* пéрхоть.

dandy ['dændɪ] *n.* дéнди (*m. indecl.*), щёголь (*m.*), франт.
adj. (*US coll.*) превосхóдный.

Dane [deɪn] *n.* датчáн|ин (*fem.* -ка); **Great ~** дог.

danger ['deɪndʒə(r)] *n.* **1.** (*risk of injury*) опáсность; **'~!'** «осторóжно!»; **in ~** в опáсности; **out of ~** вне опáсности; **he is in ~ of falling** он рискýет упáсть; **~ money** плáта за опáсную рабóту; **~ zone** опáсная зóна. **2.** (*pers. or thg. presenting risk*) опáсность, угрóза.

dangerous ['deɪndʒərəs] *adj.* опáсный, рискóванный; **the dog looks ~** у собáки грóзный вид.

dangle ['dæŋg(ə)l] *v.t.* качáть (*impf.*); покáчивать (*impf.*).
v.i. **1.** (*lit.*) качáться (*impf.*); болтáться (*impf.*).

Danish ['deɪnɪʃ] *n.* (*language*) да́тский язы́к.
adj. да́тский.
dank [dæŋk] сыро́й, промо́зглый.
dapper ['dæpə(r)] *adj.* щеголева́тый.
dapple ['dæp(ə)l] *adj.* (*also* **~d**) пёстрый, пятни́стый.
cpd. **~-grey** *n. & adj.* (*horse*) се́рый в я́блоках (конь).
dare [deə(r)] *n.* (*challenge*) вы́зов; **take a ~** приня́ть (*pf.*) вы́зов.
v.t. (*challenge*) бр|оса́ть, -о́сить вы́зов +*d.*; **I ~ you to jump over the wall!** а ну, перепры́гни че́рез э́ту сте́ну!
v.i. **1.** (*have courage*) осме́ли|ваться, -ться; сметь, по-. **2.** (*have impudence*) сметь, по-; **how ~ you say that!** как вы сме́ете говори́ть тако́е! **3.: I ~ say (that) ...** на́до ду́мать (*or* полага́ю), что...
cpd. **~-devil** *adj.* отча́янный, бесшаба́шный.
daring ['deərɪŋ] *n.* отва́га.
adj. отва́жный, де́рзкий.
dark [dɑːk] *n.* темнота́, тьма; **before/after ~** до/по́сле наступле́ния темноты́; (*ignorance*) неве́жество, неве́дение; **I am in the ~ as to his plans** его́ пла́ны мне неве́домы; (*dark colour*) тень.
adj. **1.** (*lacking light*) тёмный; **pitch ~** темны́м-темно́; **~ glasses** (*spectacles*) тёмные/со́лнечные очки́; **~ room** (*phot.*) ка́мера-обску́ра. **2.** (*of colour*) тёмный. **3.** (*of complexion*) сму́глый. **4.** (*fig.*) тёмный; **a ~ horse** тёмная лоша́дка; **keep the news ~** держа́ть (*impf.*) но́вости в секре́те; **the future is ~** бу́дущее неизве́стно; **the D~ Ages** ра́ннее средневеко́вье.
darken ['dɑːkən] *v.t.* затемн|я́ть, -и́ть.
v.i. темне́ть, по-; ста|нови́ться, -ть тёмным.
darkness ['dɑːknɪs] *n.* темнота́; **the Prince of D~** принц тьмы.
darling ['dɑːlɪŋ] *n.* дорого́й, ми́лый, родно́й, люби́мый; **she's a ~** она́ пре́лесть; (*favourite*) люби́мец.
adj. (*beloved*) люби́мый, дорого́й; (*delightful*) очарова́тельный.
darn[1] [dɑːn] *n.* што́пка.
v.t. & i. (*mend*) што́пать, за-; *see also* **darning**
darn[2] [dɑːn] *n.* (*coll.*): **I don't give a ~** мне наплева́ть.
v.t. (*as expletive*) проклина́ть (*impf.*); **~ (it)!** про́пасть!; чёрт возьми́!
darning ['dɑːnɪŋ] *n.* **1.** (*action*) што́панье, што́пка. **2.** (*things to be darned*) ве́щи (*f. pl.*) для што́пки.
cpds. **~-needle** *n.* што́пальная игла́; **~-wool** *n.* шерстяна́я ни́тка.
dart[1] [dɑːt] *n.* стрела́, дро́тик.
cpd. **~board** *n.* мише́нь для стрел.
dart[2] [dɑːt] *n.* (*run*) бросо́к, рыво́к; **he made a ~ for the door** он рвану́лся/бро́сился к две́ри.
v.t. мета́ть (*impf.*); **she ~ed an angry look at him** она́ метну́ла на него́ зло́бный взгляд.
v.i. устреми́ться; помча́ться; бро́ситься (*all pf.*); **she ~ed into the shop** она́ стрело́й влете́ла в магази́н.
dart[3] [dɑːt] *n.* (*dressmaking*) вы́тачка, шов.
dash [dæʃ] *n.* **1.** (*sudden rush, race*) рыво́к, бросо́к; **let's make a ~ for it** побежи́м-ка туда́; **the 100 yards ~** забе́г на 100 я́рдов. **2.** (*impact*) уда́р, взмах; **the ~ of cold water revived him** струя́ холо́дной воды́ привела́ его́ в чу́вство. **3.** (*admixture*): **a ~ of pepper in the soup** щепо́тка пе́рца в су́пе. **4.** (*written stroke; also in Morse*) тире́ (*indecl.*).
v.t. **1.** (*throw violently*) швыр|я́ть, -ну́ть; **the ship was ~ed against the cliff** су́дно швырну́ло о скалу́; **he ~ed the book down** он отшвырну́л кни́гу. **2.** (*perform rapidly*): **he ~ed off a sketch** он наброса́л эски́з. **3.** (*fig., disappoint*) разб|ива́ть, -и́ть; **his hopes were ~ed** его́ наде́жды ру́хнули. **4.** (*as expletive*): **~ it (all)!** к чёрту!; чёрт побери́!
v.i. **1.** (*move violently*) бро́ситься (*pf.*); ри́нуться (*pf.*); **the waves ~ed over the rocks** во́лны разбива́лись о ска́лы. **2.** (*run*) мча́ться (*impf.*); нести́сь (*det.*); **she ~ed into the shop** она́ ворвала́сь в магази́н.
dashboard ['dæʃbɔːd] *n.* прибо́рная доска́.
dashing ['dæʃɪŋ] *adj.* лихо́й, стреми́тельный.
dastard ['dæstəd] *n.* трус, подле́ц.
dastardly ['dæstədlɪ] *adj.* трусли́вый, по́длый.
data ['deɪtə] = **datum**
database ['deɪtəˌbeɪs] *n.* ба́за да́нных.
date[1] [deɪt] *n.* (**~-palm**) фи́никовая па́льма; (*fruit*) фи́ник.
date[2] [deɪt] *n.* **1.** (*indication of time*) да́та, число́; **what's the ~ today?** како́е сего́дня число́?; **the ~ of the letter is 6 October** письмо́ дати́ровано шесты́м окрября́. **2.** (*period*) пери́од; **at an early ~** (*soon*) в ближа́йшем бу́дущем; **by the earliest possible ~** в наикратча́йший срок; **out of ~** устаре́лый; **go out of ~** выходи́ть, вы́йти из мо́ды; **up to ~** нове́йший, совреме́нный; **bring s.o. up to ~** вв|оди́ть, -ести́ кого́-н. в курс де́ла; **bring a catalogue up to ~** обнов|ля́ть, -и́ть катало́г. **3.** (*coll., appointment*) свида́ние.
v.t. **1.** (*indicate ~ on*) дати́ровать (*impf., pf.*); **he ~d the letter 24 May** он дати́ровал письмо́ 24-ым ма́я; *see also* **dated. 2.** (*estimate ~ of*): **can you ~ these coins?** к како́му пери́оду, по-ва́шему, отно́сятся э́ти моне́ты? **3.** (*coll., make appointment with*) назн|ача́ть, -а́чить свида́ние +*d. or* с+*i.*
v.i. **1.** (*originate*): **this church ~s from the 14th century** э́та це́рковь отно́сится к 14-му ве́ку. **2.** (*become obsolete, show signs of age*) старе́ть (*impf.*); устар|ева́ть, -е́ть; **the play ~s terribly** э́та пье́са ужа́сно устаре́ла.
cpds. **~-line** *n.* (*meridian*) демаркацио́нная ли́ния (су́точного) вре́мени; **~-stamp** *n.* ште́мпель-календа́рь (*m.*).
dated ['deɪtɪd] *adj.* (*out of date*) устаре́вший, устаре́лый.
dative ['deɪtɪv] *n. & adj.* да́тельный (паде́ж).
datum ['deɪtəm, 'dɑːtəm] *n.* **1.** (*thg. known or granted*) исхо́дный факт. **2.** (*assumption, premise*) исхо́дная то́чка. **3.** (*pl.*, **data**) да́нные (*nt. pl.*); материа́л; **personal ~** биографи́ческие да́нные; **~ bank** банк да́нных; **~ processing** обрабо́тка информа́ции.
daub [dɔːb] *v.t. & i.* **1.** (*smear*) обма́з|ывать, -ать; ма́зать, на-; **~ paint on a wall; ~ a wall with paint** ма́зать сте́ну кра́ской. **2.** (*paint badly*) па́чкать; ма́зать (*both impf.*).
daughter ['dɔːtə(r)] *n.* дочь.
cpd. **~-in-law** *n.* неве́стка, сноха́.
daunt [dɔːnt] *v.t.* устраш|а́ть, -и́ть; обескура́жи|вать, -ть; **nothing ~ ed, he asked for more** нима́ло не смуща́ясь, он попроси́л доба́вки.
dauntless ['dɔːntlɪs] *adj.* бесстра́шный, неустраши́мый.
dauphin ['dɔːfɪn, 'dəʊfæ̃] *n.* дофи́н.
dawdle ['dɔːd(ə)l] *v.t.*: **~ away one's time** зря тра́тить (*impf.*) вре́мя.
v.i. безде́льничать (*impf.*), ло́дырничать (*impf.*).
dawdler ['dɔːd(ə)lə(r)] *n.* ло́дырь (*m.*), безде́льник.
dawn [dɔːn] *n.* **1.** (*daybreak*) рассве́т, заря́; **at ~** на рассве́те; на заре́. **2.** (*fig.*): **the ~ of civilization** заря́ цивилиза́ции.
v.i. **1.** (*of daybreak*) света́ть (*impf.*); рассве|та́ть, -сти́; **the day is ~ing** света́ет. **2.** (*fig.*): **it ~ ed on me that ...** меня́ осени́ло, что...; **the truth ~ed upon him** ему́ всё ста́ло я́сно.
day [deɪ] *n.* **1.** (*time of daylight*) день (*m.*); (*attr.*) дневно́й; **by ~** днём; **twice a ~** два ра́за в день; **time of ~** вре́мя дня; **pass the time of ~ with s.o.** обменя́ться (*pf.*) приве́тствиями с кем-н.; **break of ~** рассве́т; **late in the ~** (*fig.*) сли́шком по́здно. **2.**

(*24 hours*) сýт|ки (*pl.*, *g.* ок); **a ~ and a half** пóлтора сýток. **3.** (*as point of time*): **what ~ (of the week) is it?** какóй сегóдня день (недéли)?; **one ~** (*past*) однáжды; (*future*) когдá-нибудь; **the other ~** на днях; **every other ~** чéрез день; **one of these (fine) ~s** в оди́н прекрáсный день; **this isn't my ~** (*coll.*) мне сегóдня чтó-то не везёт; **~ of judgement** день стрáшного судá; **she's thirty if she's a ~** ей никáк не мéньше тридцати́ лет; **live from ~ to ~** жить (*impf.*) со дня нá день; **~ in, ~ out; ~ after ~** изо дня в день; **(on) the ~ before** наканýне (*чего*); **to this ~** до сегóдняшнего дня; **she named the ~** онá назнáчила день свáдьбы; **I took a ~ off** я взял выходнóй; **we had a ~ out** мы провели́ день вне дóма. **4.** (*as work period*): **he works a 5-hour ~** у негó пятичасовóй рабóчий день; **he is paid by the ~** емý плáтят подённо; **let's call it a ~** (*coll.*) на сегóдня хвáтит; **it's all in the ~'s work** э́то в порядке вещéй. **5.** (*festival*) прáздничный день; **May D~** день Пéрвого мáя. **6.** (*period*) порá, врéмя (*nt.*); **the present ~** сегóдня; **these ~s** (*nowadays*) тепéрь, сейчáс; в нáши дни; **in those ~s** в те дни; в то врéмя; **in ~s of old** в бы́лые дни; **in ~s to come** в бýдущем; **in this ~ and age** в нáше врéмя; **his ~s are numbered** егó дни́ сочтены́; **end one's ~s** скончáться (*pf.*); **the great men of the ~** ви́дные лю́ди эпóхи; **he has had his ~** он отслужи́л своё; **save for a rainy ~** от|клáдывать, -ложи́ть на чёрный день. **7.** (*denoting contest*): **win, carry the ~** одéрж|ивать, -áть побéду; **his arrival saved the ~** егó приéзд спас положéние.

cpds. **~-bed** *n.* кушéтка; **~-boarder** *n.* полупансионéр; **~-break** *n.* рассвéт; **~-dream** *n.* грёза, мечтá; *v.i.* мечтáть (*impf.*); грéзить (*impf.*) (наявý); **~light** *n.* (*period*): **in broad ~light** средь бéла дня; (*dawn*) дневнóй свет; рассвéт; (*fig.*): **let in some ~light on the subject** проли́ть (*pf.*) свет на предмéт; **I begin to see ~light** мне ужé ви́ден просвéт; (*fig.*): **beat the ~lights out of s.o.** вы́бить (*pf.*) дýшу из когó-н.; **~-nursery** *n.* (*crèche*) дéтские ясл|и (*pl.*, *g.* -ей); **~-care: ~-care facilities** детсáд; ясл|и (*pl.*, *g.* -ей); дéтск|ие учреждéн|ия (*pl.*, *g.* -их -ий); **~time** *n.* день (*m.*); **in the ~time** днём; *adj.* дневнóй; **~-to-~** *adj.* повседнéвный.

daze [deɪz] *n.*: **he was in a ~** он был как в дурмáне.

v.t. порa|жáть, -зи́ть; ошарáши|вать, -ть.

dazzle ['dæz(ə)l] *v.t.* **1.** (*lit.*) ослеп|лять, -и́ть. **2.** (*fig.*) порa|жáть, -зи́ть; ослеп|лять, -и́ть; **she was ~d by his wealth** онá былá ослепленá егó богáтством.

DC (*abbr. of* **direct current**) постоя́нный ток.

deacon ['di:kən] *n.* дья́кон.

deaconess [ˌdi:kə'nes, 'di:kənɪs] *n.* диакони́са.

dead [ded] *n.*: **at ~ of night** глубóкой нóчью.

adj. **1.** (*no longer living*) мёртвый, умéрший; (*in accident etc.*) поги́бший, уби́тый; (*of animal*) дóхлый; **~ body** труп, мёртвое тéло; **~ flowers** увя́дшие цветы́; **he is ~** он ýмер/уби́т; **~ and gone** (*fig.*) давнó прошéдший; **more ~ than alive** полумёртвый; **~ wood** (*lit.*) сухостóй; (*fig.*) баллáст; (*as n.*: **the ~**) умéршие, покóйные. **2.** (*inanimate, sterile*) неодушевлённый; неплодорóдный; **~ matter** неживáя матéрия. **3.** (*numb, insensitive*) онемéлый, омертвéлый; **my foot has gone ~** у меня́ ногá онемéла; **~ with hunger** умирáющий с гóлоду; **~ with fatigue** смертéльно устáлый; **he is ~ to the world** (*drunk*) он мертвéцки пьян; (*asleep*) он спит мёртвым сном. **4.** (*inert, motionless*) спокóйный, неподви́жный; **~ end** (*lit.*, *fig.*) тупи́к; **a ~ end job** бесперспекти́вная рабóта. **5.** (*used, spent, uncharged*): **~ match** испóльзованная спи́чка; **the telephone went ~** телефóн умóлк; **the furnace is ~** тóпка погáсла; **the law is a ~ letter** э́тот закóн утрáтил си́лу; **~ volcano** потýхший вулкáн. **6.** (*dull, of sound or colour*) глухóй, тýсклый. **7.** (*obsolete, no longer valid*): **~ language** мёртвый язы́к. **8.** (*abrupt, exact, complete*) внезáпный; пóлный; совершéнный; **in ~ earnest** совершéнно серьёзно; **come to a ~ stop** останови́ться (*pf.*) как вкóпанному; **~ level** совершéнно рóвная мéстность; **he's the ~ spit of his father** (*coll.*) он вы́литый отéц; **~ calm** мёртвый штиль; **~ loss** (*fig.*, *failure*) пóлный провáл; **he's a ~ loss** он неудáчник; **a ~ faint** глубóкий óбморок; **a ~ certainty** пóлная увéренность; **he's a ~ shot** он мéткий стрелóк; **~ centre** (*mech.*) мёртвая тóчка.

adv.: **he stopped ~** он останови́лся как вкóпанный; **~ on time** тóчно вóвремя; **~ drunk** мертвéцки пья́ный; **~ straight** совершéнно пря́мо; **~ tired** смертéльно устáлый; **~ against** реши́тельно прóтив; **he is ~ set on going to London** он реши́л во что бы то ни стáло поéхать в Лóндон; **~ slow** óчень мéдленно; **~ certain** совершéнно увéренный.

cpds. **~-beat** *n.* (*coll.*, *loafer*) бездéльник; парази́т; *adj.* (*coll.*, *worn out*) смертéльно устáлый; **~line** *n.* предéл; **~lock** *n.* мёртвая тóчка; тупи́к; **break a ~lock** вы́йти (*pf.*) из тупикá; *v.t.*: **the negotiations are ~locked** переговóры зашли́ в тупи́к; **~pan** *adj.* (*coll.*) с невырази́тельным лицóм; **~-reckoning** *n.* навигациóнное счислéние.

deaden ['ded(ə)n] *v.t.* заглуш|áть, -и́ть; **the drug ~s pain** лекáрство притупляет боль; **the walls ~ sound** стéны заглушáют шум.

deadly ['dedlɪ] *adj.* смертéльный; смертонóсный; **~ sin** смéртный грех; (*intense*) ужáсный.

deaf [def] *adj.* **1.** глухóй; **~ in one ear** глухóй на однó ýхо; **~ and dumb** глухонемóй; **~ and dumb language** язык глухонемы́х; **~ mute** глухонемóй; (*as n.*: **the ~**) глухи́е. **2.** (*fig.*): **turn a ~ ear to** не слýшать (*impf.*); не обращáть (*impf.*) внимáния на+*a.*; **~ to all entreaty** глух ко всем мольбáм.

cpd. **~-aid** *n.* слуховóй аппарáт.

deafen ['def(ə)n] *v.t.* оглуш|áть, -и́ть.

deafening ['defənɪŋ] *adj.* оглуши́тельный.

deafness ['defnɪs] *n.* глухотá.

deal [di:l] *n.* **1.** (*amount*) коли́чество; **a great, good ~ (of)** мнóго +*g.*; **she's a good ~ better today** ей сегóдня горáздо лýчше; **he didn't succeed, not by a good ~** он далекó не преуспéл (*в чём*). **2.** (*business agreement*) сдéлка; **it's a ~!** договори́лись!; по рукáм!; **give s.o. a raw/square ~** (*coll.*) несправедли́во/чéстно обойти́сь (*pf.*) с кем-н. **3.** (*at cards*) сдáча; **it' s my ~** моя́ óчередь сдавáть.

v.t. **1.** (*cards*) сда|вáть, -ть. **2.** (*apportion*) разд|авáть, -áть; распредéл|ять, -и́ть; **the money was ~t out fairly** дéньги бы́ли разделены́ чéстно. **3.** (*inflict*): **~ s.o. a blow** нан|оси́ть, -ести́ комý-н. удáр.

v.i. **1.** (*do business*) торговáть (*impf.*); **he is a difficult man to ~ with** с ним трýдно имéть дéло; **he ~s in furs** он торгýет мехáми. **2.** (*treat, manage*) обращáться (с+*i.*); поступáть (с+*i.*) (*all impf.*); **what is the best way of ~ing with young criminals?** как лýчше всегó поступáть с молоды́ми престýпниками?; **he ~t with the problem skilfully** он умéло подошёл к э́тому вопрóсу. **3.** (*treat of*) занимáться (*impf.*) +*i.*; **the book ~s with African affairs** э́та кни́га рассмáтривает африкáнские проблéмы. **4.** (*conduct o.s.*) обходи́ться (*impf.*); поступáть (*impf.*); **he ~s justly with all** он поступáет со всéми справедли́во.

dealer ['di:lə(r)] *n.* **1.** (*at cards*) сдаю́щий кáрты. **2.** торгóвец.

dealing ['di:lɪŋ] *n.* **1.** (*action*) распределéние; **plain ~** прямотá. **2.** (*trade*): **~ in real estate** торгóвля недвижи́мостью. **3.** (*pl.*, *association*) торгóвые делá; сдéлки (*f. pl.*); **have ~s with s.o.** вести́ (*det.*) делá с кем-н.

dean [diːn] *n.* (*eccl.*) дека́н, настоя́тель (*m.*); (*acad.*) дека́н.

dear [dɪə(r)] *n.* ми́лый, возлю́бленный, дорого́й; **he's a (perfect) ~** он о́чень мил; **be a ~ and do this for me** бу́дьте так добры́, сде́лайте э́то для меня́.

adj. **1.** (*beloved*) люби́мый, дорого́й. **2.** (*lovable*) сла́вный, ми́лый. **3.** (*as polite address*): **my ~ fellow** дорого́й (мой); (*in formal letters*) уважа́емый. **4.** (*precious*) дорого́й; **for ~ life** (*fig.*) отча́янно, изо всех сил. **5.** (*heartfelt*): **his ~est wish** его́ сокрове́нное жела́ние; **6.** (*costly*) дорого́й.

int.: **oh ~!; ~ me!** о, Го́споди!; ой-ой-ой!

dearly ['dɪəlɪ] *adv.* (*fondly*) не́жно; (*at a high price*) до́рого.

dearth [dɜːθ] *n.* нехва́тка, недоста́ток.

death [deθ] *n.* **1.**(*act or fact of dying*) смерть; **die the ~** (*liter.*) поги́бнуть (*pf.*); **meet one's ~** найти́ (*pf.*) свою́ смерть; **natural ~** есте́ственная смерть; **violent ~** наси́льственная смерть; **~ certificate** свиде́тельство о сме́рти; **~ duties** нало́г на насле́дство; **~ penalty** сме́ртная казнь; **be burnt to ~** сгоре́ть (*pf.*) за́живо; **drink o.s. to ~** умере́ть (*pf.*) от пья́нства; **work o.s. to ~** рабо́тать (*impf.*) на изно́с; **bleed to ~** истéчь (*pf.*) кро́вью; **at ~'s door** на поро́ге сме́рти; **catch one's ~ (of cold)** просту-ди́ться (*pf.*) на́смерть; **put to ~** казни́ть (*pf.*); уби́ть (*pf.*); **sentence to ~** приговори́ть (*pf.*) к сме́рти; **he held on like grim ~** он держа́лся изо всех сил; **he looks like ~** (*coll.*) ≃ кра́ше в гроб кладу́т. **2.** (*instance of dying*) коне́ц, ги́бель; **there were many ~s in the accident** в ава́рии поги́бло мно́го люде́й. **3.** (*destruction*): **the ~ of his hopes** круше́ние его́ наде́жд. **4.** (*utmost limit*): **he was bored to ~** ему́ бы́ло до́ смерти ску́чно; **tired to ~** смерте́льно уста́лый; **I'm sick to ~ of it** мне э́то до́ смерти надое́ло. **5.** (*cause of death*): **this work will be the ~ of me** э́та рабо́та сведёт меня́ в моги́лу.

cpds. **~-bed** *n.* сме́ртное ло́же; **~-blow** *n.* смерте́льный уда́р; **~-mask** *n.* посме́ртная ма́ска; **~-rate** *n.* сме́ртность; **~-rattle** *n.* предсме́ртный хрип; **~-warrant** *n.* распоряже́ние о приведе́нии в исполне́ние сме́ртного пригово́ра; **~-watch** *adj.*: **~-watch beetle** жук-моги́льщик.

deathly ['deθlɪ] *adj.* & *adv.* смерте́льный; **~ pale** смерте́льно бле́дный.

débâcle [deɪ'bɑːk(ə)l] *n.* катастро́фа.

debar [dɪ'bɑː(r)] *v.t.* препя́тствовать, вос- *+d.*; не допус|ка́ть, -ти́ть *+g.*; **~ s.o. from voting** лиш|а́ть, -и́ть кого́-н. пра́ва го́лоса.

debark [diː'bɑːk, dɪ-] *v.t.* & *i.* = **disembark**

debarkation [ˌdiːbɑː'keɪʃ(ə)n] *n.* = **disembarkation**

debase [dɪ'beɪs] *v.t.* **1.** (*lower morally*) ун|ижа́ть, -и́зить. **2.** (*depreciate, e.g. coinage*) пон|ижа́ть, -и́зить ка́чество/це́нность *+g.*

debatable [dɪ'beɪtəb(ə)l] *adj.* спо́рный, оспа́риваемый.

debat|e [dɪ'beɪt] *n.* диску́ссия; пре́ния (*nt. pl.*); деба́т|ы (*pl., g.* -ов); **the question under ~e** обсужда́емый вопро́с; **beyond ~e** бесспо́рный.

v.t. & *i.* **1.** (*discuss*) обсу|жда́ть, -ди́ть; дебати́ровать (*impf.*); дискути́ровать (*impf., pf.*); спо́рить (*impf.*) о+*p.*; **~ing society** дискуссио́нный клуб. **2.** (*ponder*) обду́м|ывать, -ать; взве́|шивать, -сить; **I was ~ing whether to go out or not** я размышля́л, сто́ит выходи́ть и́ли нет.

debauch [dɪ'bɔːtʃ] *v.t.* **1.** (*pervert morally*) развра|ща́ть, -ти́ть. **2.** (*seduce*) совра|ща́ть, -ти́ть.

debauchery [dɪ'bɔːtʃərɪ] *n.* развра́т, распу́щенность.

debenture [dɪ'bentʃə(r)] *n.* долгово́е обяза́тельство; облига́ция акционе́рного о́бщества.

debilitate [dɪ'bɪlɪˌteɪt] *v.t.* осл|абля́ть, -а́бить; рассл|абля́ть, -а́бить.

debility [dɪ'bɪlɪtɪ] *n.* сла́бость, бесси́лие.

debit ['debɪt] *n.* де́бет.

v.t. дебетова́ть (*impf., pf.*).

debonair [ˌdebə'neə(r)] *adj.* (*suave, urbane*) обходи́тельный, учти́вый.

debrief [diː'briːf] *v.t.* расспр|а́шивать, -оси́ть; **~ s.o.** заслу́ш|ивать, -ать чей-н. отчёт.

debriefing [diː'briːfɪŋ] *n.* расспро́с, опро́с.

debris ['debriː, 'deɪ-] *n.* оско́лки (*m. pl.*); обло́мки (*m. pl.*).

debt [det] *n.* **1.** (*of money*) долг; **get, run into ~** влез|а́ть, -ть в долги́; **bad ~** безнадёжный долг; **~ of honour** долг че́сти. **2.** (*obligation*): **I owe him a ~ of gratitude** я пе́ред ним в долгу́; **I am greatly in your ~** я вам чрезвыча́йно обя́зан.

debtor ['detə(r)] *n.* должни́к; **~'s prison** долгова́я тюрьма́.

debunk [diː'bʌŋk] *v.t.* (*coll.*) разве́нч|ивать, -а́ть.

debut ['deɪbjuː, -buː] *n.* дебю́т.

debutante ['debjuːˌtɑːnt, 'deɪb-] *n.* дебюта́нтка.

decade ['dekeɪd] *n.* десятиле́тие.

decadence ['dekəd(ə)ns] *n.* упа́док, декаде́нтство.

decadent ['dekəd(ə)nt] *n.* декаде́нт.

adj. упа́днический, декаде́нтский.

decaffeinated [diː'kæfɪˌneɪtɪd] *adj.* без кофеи́на; **~ coffee** бескофеи́новый ко́фе.

decagon ['dekəgən] *n.* десятиуго́льник.

decahedron [ˌdekə'hiːdrən] *n.* десятигра́нник.

decamp [dɪ'kæmp] *v.i.* (*leave camp*) сн|има́ться, -я́ться с ла́геря; (*abscond*) сбе|га́ть, -жа́ть; уд|ира́ть, -ра́ть.

decant [dɪ'kænt] *v.t.* (*pour wine*) сце́|живать, -ди́ть; перел|ива́ть, -и́ть из буты́лки в графи́н.

decanter [dɪ'kæntə(r)] *n.* графи́н.

decapitate [dɪ'kæpɪˌteɪt] *v.t.* обезгла́в|ливать, -ить.

decapitation [dɪˌkæpɪ'teɪʃ(ə)n] *n.* обезгла́вливание.

decathlete [dɪ'kæθliːt] *n.* десятибо́рец.

decathlon [dɪ'kæθlən] *n.* десятибо́рье.

decay [dɪ'keɪ] *n.* **1.** (*physical*) гние́ние, разложе́ние; **tooth ~** разруше́ние зубо́в; **the house is in ~** дом разруша́ется. **2.** (*decayed part*) гниль. **3.** (*moral*) упа́док, разложе́ние.

v.i. гнить, с-; разл|ага́ться, -ожи́ться; **~ing vegetables** гнию́щие о́вощи.

deceased [dɪ'siːst] *adj.* поко́йный, сконча́вшийся, уме́рший; (*as n.*: **the ~**) поко́йник, отоше́дший.

deceit [dɪ'siːt] *n.* обма́н, лжи́вость.

deceitful [dɪ'siːtfʊl] *adj.* обма́нчивый, лжи́вый.

deceive [dɪ'siːv] *v.t.* & *i.* обма́н|ывать, -у́ть; **~ o.s.** обма́н|ываться, -у́ться; **I have been ~d in him** я в нём обману́лся; **we were ~d into believing that ...** нас обма́ном заста́вили пове́рить, что...

decelerate [diː'seləˌreɪt] *v.t.* & *i.* зам|едля́ть, -е́длить (ход).

deceleration [diːˌselə'reɪʃ(ə)n] *n.* замедле́ние; торможе́ние.

December [dɪ'sembə(r)] *n.* дека́брь (*m.*); (*attr.*) дека́брьский.

Decembrist [dɪ'sembrɪst] *n.* декабри́ст.

adj. декабри́стский.

decenc|y ['diːsənsɪ] *n.* (*seemliness*) прили́чие, благопристо́йность; **offence against ~y** наруше́ние прили́чий; **observe the ~ies** соблюда́ть (*impf.*) прили́чия.

decent ['diːs(ə)nt] *adj.* **1.** (*not obscene*) прили́чный; благопристо́йный. **2.** (*proper, adequate*) прили́чный, подходя́щий; **~ living conditions** прили́чные жили́щные усло́вия. **3.** (*coll., kind, well-conducted*) поря́дочный; **he was very ~ to me** он вёл себя́ поря́дочно по отноше́нию ко мне.

decentralization [diːˌsentrəlaɪ'zeɪʃ(ə)n] *n.* децентрализа́ция.

decentralize [diː'sentrəˌlaɪz] *v.t.* децентрализова́ть (*impf., pf.*).

deception [dɪ'sepʃ(ə)n] *n.* обма́н; **practise a ~ on** обма́н|ывать, -у́ть.

deceptive [dɪ'septɪv] *adj.* обма́нчивый.
decibel ['desɪ,bel] *n.* децибе́л.
decide [dɪ'saɪd] *v.t.* реш|а́ть, -и́ть; прин|има́ть, -я́ть реше́ние +*p.*; ~ **a dispute** разреш|а́ть, -и́ть спор; **what ~d you to give up your job?** почему́ вы реши́ли бро́сить рабо́ту?
v.i. реш|а́ться, -и́ться; прин|има́ть, -я́ть реше́ние; ~ **between alternatives** сде́лать (*pf.*) вы́бор; ~ **on going** реши́ть (*pf.*) пое́хать; ~ **against going** реши́ть (*pf.*) не е́хать; **she ~d on the green hat** она́ вы́брала зелёную шля́пу; **they ~d on the youngest candidate** они́ останови́ли свой вы́бор на са́мом молодо́м кандида́те.
decided [dɪ'saɪdɪd] *adj.* (*clear-cut*) определённый; **a ~ difference** бесспо́рное разли́чие.
decidedly [dɪ'saɪdɪdlɪ] *adv.* реши́тельно, я́вно.
deciduous [dɪ'sɪdjʊəs] *adj.* ли́ственный, листопа́дный.
decigram(me) ['desɪ,græm] *n.* децигра́мм.
decilitre ['desɪ,li:tə(r)] *n.* децили́тр.
decimal ['desɪm(ə)l] *n.* десяти́чная дробь.
adj. десяти́чный; ~ **point** запята́я, отделя́ющая це́лое от дро́би; ~ **coinage** десяти́чная моне́тная систе́ма.
decimate ['desɪ,meɪt] *v.t.* (*devastate*) опустош|а́ть, -и́ть.
decimetre ['desɪ,mi:tə(r)] *n.* децимéтр.
decipher [dɪ'saɪfə(r)] *v.t.* **1.** (*lit.*) расшифро́в|ывать, -а́ть. **2.** (*fig., make out*) раз|бира́ть, -обра́ть.
decipherment [dɪ'saɪfəmənt] *n.* расшифро́вка, дешифро́вка.
decision [dɪ'sɪʒ(ə)n] *n.* реше́ние; **make, take, come to a ~** приня́ть (*pf.*) реше́ние.
decisive [dɪ'saɪsɪv] *adj.* (*conclusive*) реша́ющий; ~ **answer** оконча́тельный отве́т; (*resolute*) реши́тельный.
decisiveness [dɪ'saɪsɪvnɪs] *n.* реши́тельность.
deck[1] [dek] *n.* **1.** (*of ship*) па́луба; ~ **house** ру́бка; **go up on ~** подня́ться (*pf.*) на па́лубу; **below ~(s)** под па́лубой; **clear the ~s** (*for action*) (*nav.*) пригото́виться (*pf.*) к бо́ю; (*fig.*) пригото́виться (*pf.*) к де́йствиям; **all hands on ~!** все наве́рх!; авра́л! **2.** (*of bus*): **top ~** ве́рхний эта́ж. **3.** (*US, of cards*) коло́да.
cpds. **~-chair** *n.* шезло́нг; **~-hand** *n.* матро́с.
deck[2] [dek] *v.t.* (*adorn; also* ~ **out**) укр|аша́ть, -а́сить.
declaim [dɪ'kleɪm] *v.t. & i.* деклами́ровать (*impf.*).
declamation [,deklə'meɪʃ(ə)n] *n.* (*act*) деклами́рование; (*art*) деклама́ция.
declamatory [dɪ'klæmətərɪ] *n.* декламацио́нный; ора́торский.
declaration [,deklə'reɪʃ(ə)n] *n.* **1.** (*proclamation*) заявле́ние, деклара́ция; ~ **of independence** деклара́ция незави́симости; ~ **of war** объявле́ние войны́. **2.** (*affirmation*): ~ **of one's income** нало́говая деклара́ция; ~ **of love** призна́ние в любви́.
declarative [,de'klærətɪv] *adj.* деклarати́вный.
declare [dɪ'kleə(r)] *v.t. & i.* **1.** (*proclaim, make known*) объяв|ля́ть, -и́ть; ~ **one's love** объясн|я́ться, -и́ться в любви́. **2.** (*say solemnly*) заяв|ля́ть, -и́ть; провозгла|ша́ть, -си́ть; **he ~d that he was innocent** он заяви́л о свое́й невино́вности. **3.** (*pronounce*) объяв|ля́ть, -и́ть; **I ~ the meeting open** объявля́ю собра́ние откры́тым; ~ **o.s.** (*avow intentions*) де́лать, с- призна́ние; ~ **for/against s.o.** выска́зываться, вы́сказаться за/про́тив кого́-н. **4.** (*at customs*) деклари́ровать (*impf., pf.*); **have you anything to ~?** предъяви́те ве́щи, подлежа́щие обложе́нию по́шлиной.
declassify [di:'klæsɪ,faɪ] *v.t.* рассекре́|чивать, -тить (*документы*).
declension [dɪ'klenʃ(ə)n] *n.* (*gram.*) склоне́ние.
declinable [dɪ'klaɪnəb(ə)l] *adj.* (*gram.*) склоня́емый.
declination [,deklɪ'neɪʃ(ə)n] *n.* (*astron.*) магни́тное склоне́ние; отклоне́ние.
decline [dɪ'klaɪn] *n.* **1.** (*fall*) паде́ние; ~ **in prices** сниже́ние/пониже́ние цен. **2.** (*decay*) упа́док, зака́т. **3.** (*in health*) ухудше́ние; **fall into a ~** слабе́ть (*impf.*).
v.t. **1.** (*refuse*) отклон|я́ть, -и́ть; **he ~d the invitation** он отклони́л приглаше́ние. **2.** (*gram.*) склоня́ть, про-.
v. i. **1.** (*sink, draw to a close*) клони́ться (*impf.*) (к+*d.*); **his strength ~d** его́ си́ла пошла́ на у́быль; **prices ~** це́ны па́дают; **his declining years** его́ прекло́нные го́ды. **2.** (*refuse*) отка́з|ываться, -а́ться.
decoction [dɪ'kɒkʃ(ə)n] *n.* (*boiling down*) выва́ривание; (*liquor*) отва́р.
decode [di:'kəʊd] *v.t.* расшифро́в|ывать, -а́ть.
décolletage [,deɪkɒl'tɑ:ʒ] *n.* декольте́ (*indecl.*), вы́рез.
décolleté [deɪ'kɒlteɪ] *adj.* декольтиро́ванный.
decolonization [,di:kɒlənaɪ'zeɪʃ(ə)n] *n.* деколониза́ция.
decompose [,di:kəm'pəʊz] *v.t.* разл|ага́ть, -ожи́ть.
v.i. (*decay*) разл|ага́ться, -ожи́ться.
decomposition [,di:kɒmpə'zɪʃ(ə)n] *n.* разложе́ние.
decompression [,di:kəm'preʃ(ə)n] *n.* декомпре́ссия.
decompressor [,di:kəm'presə(r)] *n.* декомпре́ссор.
decontaminate [,di:kən'tæmɪ,neɪt] *v.t.* обеззара́|живать, -зить; дегази́ровать (*impf., pf.*).
decontamination [,di:kəntæmɪ'neɪʃ(ə)n] *n.* обеззара́живание, дегаза́ция.
decontrol [,di:kən'trəʊl] *v.t.* освобо|жда́ть, -ди́ть от контро́ля.
decor ['deɪkɔ:(r), 'de-] *n.* декора́ции (*f. pl.*); убра́нство.
decorate ['dekə,reɪt] *v.t.* **1.** (*adorn*) укр|аша́ть, -а́сить; декори́ровать (*impf., pf.*). **2.** (*paint, furnish etc.*) отде́л|ывать, -ать. **3.** (*confer medal upon*) награ|жда́ть, -ди́ть.
decoration [,dekə'reɪʃ(ə)n] *n.* **1.** (*adornment*) украше́ние. **2.** (*furnishing etc. of house*) отде́лка; обстано́вка. **3.** (*order, medal*) о́рден, знак отли́чия.
decorative ['dekərətɪv] *adj.* декорати́вный.
decorator ['dekə,reɪtə(r)] *n.* **1.** (*manual worker*) маля́р, обо́йщик. **2.**: **interior ~** худо́жник по интерье́ру.
decorous ['dekərəs] *adj.* прили́чный, присто́йный.
decorum [dɪ'kɔ:rəm] *n.* вне́шнее прили́чие; этике́т, деко́рум.
decoy ['di:kɔɪ, dɪ'kɔɪ] *n.* прима́нка; ~ **duck** мано́к для ди́ких у́ток.
v.t. зама́н|ивать, -и́ть; прима́н|ивать, -и́ть.
decrease ['di:kri:s] *n.* уменьше́ние; **crime is on the ~** престу́пность идёт на у́быль.
v.t. ум|еньша́ть, -е́ньшить.
v.i. ум|еньша́ться, -е́ньшиться; уб|ыва́ть, -ы́ть.
decreasingly [,di:'kri:sɪŋlɪ] *adv.* всё ме́ньше и ме́ньше.
decree [dɪ'kri:] *n.* **1.** (*pol.*) ука́з, декре́т, постановле́ние. **2.** (*leg.*) реше́ние.
v.t. & i. изд|ава́ть, -а́ть декре́т; декрети́ровать (*impf., pf.*); **fate ~d otherwise** судьба́ реши́ла ина́че.
decrepit [dɪ'krepɪt] *adj.* дря́хлый.
decrepitude [dɪ'krepɪtju:d] *n.* дря́хлость.
decry [dɪ'kraɪ] *v.t.* хули́ть (*impf.*).
dedicate ['dedɪ,keɪt] *v.t.* (*devote; also book etc.*) посвя|ща́ть, -ти́ть; (*assign, set apart*) предназн|ача́ть, -а́чить.
dedicated ['dedɪ,keɪtɪd] *adj.* самозабве́нный, беззаве́тный.
dedication [,dedɪ'keɪʃ(ə)n] *n.* (*devotion*) пре́данность, самоотве́рженность; (*inscription*) посвяще́ние.
deduce [dɪ'dju:s] *v.t.* (*infer*) выводи́ть, вы́вести; заключ|а́ть, -и́ть.
deduct [dɪ'dʌkt] *v.t.* вычита́ть, вы́честь; уде́рж|ивать, -а́ть.
deduction [dɪ'dʌkʃ(ə)n] *n.* (*subtraction*) вы́чет, удержа́ние; (*inference*) вы́вод, заключе́ние.

deed [di:d] *n.* **1.** (*sth. done*) де́йствие, посту́пок. **2.** (*feat*) по́двиг. **3.** (*actual fact*) де́ло, дея́ние; **in word and ~** сло́вом и де́лом. **4.** (*leg.*) акт, докуме́нт.
deem [di:m] *v.t.* (*hold, consider*) полага́ть, счита́ть (*both impf.*).
deep [di:p] *adj.* **1.** глубо́кий; **a ~ shelf** широ́кая по́лка; **in ~ water** (*trouble*) в беде́. **2.** (*with measurement*): **a hole 6 feet ~** отве́рстие глубино́й в 6 фу́тов; **ankle ~ in mud** по щи́колотку в грязи́. **3.** (*submerged, lit., fig.*): **a village ~ in the valley** дере́вня, располо́женная в глубине́ доли́ны; **~ in thought** заду́мавшийся; **~ in a book** уше́дший с голово́й в кни́гу; **~ in debt** увя́зший в долга́х; **~ in love** по́ уши влюблённый. **4.** (*extreme, profound*) глубо́кий; **~ sorrow** глубо́кая печа́ль; **in ~ mourning** в глубо́ком тра́уре; **take a ~ breath** де́лать, с- глубо́кий вдох; **heave a ~ sigh** глубоко́ взд|ыха́ть, -охну́ть. **5.** (*of colour*) тёмный, густо́й; **~ red** тёмно-кра́сный; **a ~ sun-tan** си́льный зага́р. **6.** (*low-pitched*) ни́зкий.
adv. глубоко́; **drink ~** кре́пко/си́льно выпива́ть (*impf.*); **~ into the night** до глубо́кой но́чи; **still waters run ~** в ти́хом о́муте че́рти во́дятся.
cpds. **~-freeze** *n.* морози́льник; *v.t.* глубоко́ замор|а́живать, -о́зить; **~-frozen** *adj.* моро́женный; **~-fry** *v.t.* жа́рить, за- во фритю́ре; **~-rooted** *adj.*: **~-rooted belief** глубоко́ укорени́вшееся мне́ние; **~-sea** *adj.*: **~-sea fishing** глубоково́дный лов; **~-seated** *adj.*: **~-seated emotion** затаённое чу́вство.
deepen ['di:pən] *v.t. & i.* **1.** (*make, become deeper*) углуб|ля́ть(ся), -и́ть(ся). **2.** (*intensify*) уси́ли|вать(ся), -ть(ся).
deeply ['di:plɪ] *adv.* глубо́ко́; **he is ~ in debt** он по́ уши в долга́х; **he feels ~ about it** э́то его́ глубоко́ волну́ет.
deer [dɪə(r)] *n.* оле́нь (*m.*).
cpds. **~-forest, ~-park** *nn.* оле́ний запове́дник; **~skin** *n.* лоси́на, за́мша; (*attr.*) лоси́ный, за́мшевый; **~stalker** *n.* (*cap*) охо́тничий шлем.
de-escalate [di:'eskə,leɪt] *v.t.* прекра|ща́ть, -ти́ть эскала́цию.
de-escalation [di:eskə'leɪʃ(ə)n] *n.* деэскала́ция.
deface [dɪ'feɪs] *v.t.* (*spoil appearance of*) иска|жа́ть, -зи́ть; по́ртить, ис-; уро́довать, из-.
de facto [di: 'fæktəʊ, deɪ] *adj.* факти́ческий.
adv. де-фа́кто; на де́ле.
defamation [,defə'meɪʃ(ə)n, ,di:f-] *n.* клевета́, диффама́ция; **~ of character** диффама́ция ли́чности.
defamatory [dɪ'fæmətərɪ] *adj.* клеветни́ческий.
defame [dɪ'feɪm] *v.t.* клевета́ть, о-; поро́чить, о-.
default [dɪ'fɔ:lt, -'fɒlt] *n.* **1.** (*want, absence*) отсу́тствие, недоста́ток; **in ~ of** за отсу́тствием +*g.* **2.** (*neglect, failure to act or appear*): **he won the match by ~** он вы́играл матч из-за нея́вки проти́вника. **3.** (*failure to pay*) неупла́та.
v.i. **1.** (*fail to perform a duty*) не выполня́ть (*impf*) обяза́тельства. **2.** (*fail to appear in court*) не яв|ля́ться, -и́ться в суд. **3.** (*fail to meet debts*) прекра|ща́ть, -ти́ть платежи́; **~ on a debt** не выпла́чивать (*impf.*) долг.
defeat [dɪ'fi:t] *n.* пораже́ние.
v.t. нан|оси́ть, -ести́ пораже́ние +*d.*; разб|ива́ть, -и́ть; одержа́ть (*pf.*) побе́ду над+*i.*; **our hopes were ~ed** на́ши наде́жды ру́хнули; **they were ~ed** они́ потерпе́ли пораже́ние.
defeatism [dɪ'fi:tɪz(ə)m] *n.* пораже́нчество.
defeatist [dɪ'fi:tɪst] *n.* пораже́нец; (*fig.*) пессими́ст.
adj. пораже́нческий, пессимисти́ческий.
defecate ['defɪ,keɪt] *v.i.* испражн|я́ться, -и́ться.
defecation [,defɪ'keɪʃ(ə)n] *n.* испражне́ние.
defect[1] [dɪ'fekt, ,di:fekt] *n.* недоста́ток, изъя́н; дефе́кт; поро́к (*also leg.*).
defect[2] [di:'fekt] *v.i.* перебе|га́ть, -жа́ть.
defection [dɪ'fekʃ(ə)n] *n.* дезерти́рство; **there were several ~s from the party** не́сколько челове́к вы́шло из па́ртии.
defective [dɪ'fektɪv] *n.* дефекти́вный; **mental ~s** у́мственно отста́лые.
adj. несоверше́нный; дефе́ктный; **~ memory** плоха́я па́мять; **~ translation** нето́чный перево́д.
defector [dɪ'fektə(r)] *n.* перебе́жчик, невозвраще́нец.
defence (*US* **defense**) [dɪ'fens] *n.* **1.** оборо́на, защи́та; **in ~ of** в защи́ту +*g.*; **he died in ~ of his country** он поги́б, защища́я ро́дину; **~ industry** оборо́нная промы́шленность. **2.** (*means or system of defending*) укрепле́ния (*nt. pl.*); оборони́тельные сооруже́ния; **his ~s are down** он беззащи́тен. **3.** (*leg.*) защи́та; **counsel for the ~** защи́тник.
defenceless [dɪ'fenslɪs] *adj.* беззащи́тный.
defend [dɪ'fend] *v.t.* **1.** оборон|я́ть, -и́ть; защи|ща́ть, -ти́ть; **~ o.s.** защи|ща́ться, -ти́ться. **2.** (*leg.*) защи|ща́ть, -ти́ть; выступа́ть, вы́ступить защи́тником +*g.*
defendant [dɪ'fend(ə)nt] *n.* отве́тчик, подсуди́мый, обвиня́емый.
defender [dɪ'fendə(r)] *n.* защи́тник.
defense [dɪ'fens] = **defence**
defensive [dɪ'fensɪv] *n.* оборо́на; **on the ~** в оборо́не.
adj. оборони́тельный.
defer [dɪ'fɜ:(r)] *v.t.* (*postpone*) отсро́чи|вать, -ть; **~ one's departure** от|кла́дывать, -ложи́ть отъе́зд; **~red payment** отсро́чка платежа́.
deference ['defərəns] *n.* уваже́ние, почти́тельность; **show ~ to s.o.** относи́ться (*impf.*) почти́тельно к кому́-н.; **with all (due) ~ to** при всём уваже́нии к+*d.*
deferential [,defə'renʃ(ə)l] *adj.* почти́тельный.
deferment [dɪ'fɜ:mənt] *n.* откла́дывание, отсро́чка.
defiance [dɪ'faɪəns] *n.* вы́зов; **bid ~ to** пренебр|ега́ть, -е́чь +*i*; **in ~ of orders** вопреки́ распоряже́ниям.
defiant [dɪ'faɪənt] *adj.* вызыва́ющий.
deficiency [dɪ'fɪʃənsɪ] *n.* **1.** (*lack*) нехва́тка, отсу́тствие. **2.** (*pl., shortcomings*) недоста́тки (*m. pl.*).
deficient [dɪ'fɪʃ(ə)nt] *adj.* недоста́точный, непо́лный; **mentally ~** слабоу́мный.
deficit ['defɪsɪt] *n.* дефици́т; **meet a ~** покр|ыва́ть, -ы́ть дефици́т.
defile [dɪ'faɪl] *v.t.* загрязн|я́ть, -и́ть; осквер|ня́ть, -и́ть.
defilement [dɪ'faɪlmənt] *n.* загрязне́ние, оскверне́ние.
define [dɪ'faɪn] *v.t.* **1.** (*state meaning of*) определ|я́ть, -и́ть; толкова́ть (*impf.*); да|ва́ть, -ть определе́ние +*d.* **2.** (*state clearly*): **I ~d his duties** я очерти́л/установи́л круг его́ обя́занностей; **he ~d his position** он определи́л/вы́сказал своё отноше́ние. **3.** (*delimit*): **his powers are ~d by law** его́ полномо́чия устана́вливаются зако́ном; **the frontier is not clearly ~ d** нет определённой/чёткой грани́цы. **4.** (*show clearly*): **a well ~d image** чётко оче́рченный о́браз.
definite ['defɪnɪt] *adj.* **1.** (*specific*) определённый. **2.** (*clear, exact*) то́чный, чёткий.
definitely ['defɪnɪtlɪ] *adv.* определённо, то́чно, чётко; **he is ~ coming** он непреме́нно придёт.
definition [,defɪ'nɪʃ(ə)n] *n.* (*clearness of outline*) я́сность, чёткость; (*statement of meaning*) определе́ние.
definitive [dɪ'fɪnɪtɪv] *adj.* оконча́тельный.
deflate [dɪ'fleɪt] *v.t.* **1.** выка́чивать, вы́качать во́здух/газ из+*g.*; **~ a tyre** вы́пустить (*pf.*) во́здух из ши́ны. **2.** (*fig.*): **~ s.o.'s conceit** сбить (*pf.*) с кого́-н. спесь.
deflation [dɪ'fleɪʃ(ə)n] *n.* (*fin.*) дефля́ция.
deflect [dɪ'flekt] *v.t. & i.* отклон|я́ть(ся), -и́ть(ся).
deflection [dɪ'flekʃ(ə)n] *n.* отклоне́ние.
deforest [di:'fɒrɪst] *v.t.* обезле́сить (*pf.*).
deforestation [di:,fɒrɪ'steɪʃ(ə)n] *n.* обезле́сение.
deform [dɪ'fɔ:m] *v.t.* уро́довать, из-; иска|жа́ть, -зи́ть;

he has a ~ed foot у него́ деформи́рована стопа́.
deformation [ˌdiːfɔːˈmeɪʃ(ə)n] *n.* уро́дование, деформа́ция.
deformity [dɪˈfɔːmɪtɪ] *n.* уро́дливость, уро́дство.
defraud [dɪˈfrɔːd] *v.t.* обма́н|ывать, -у́ть.
defray [dɪˈfreɪ] *v.t.* опла́|чивать, -ти́ть; **~ expenses** возме|ща́ть, -сти́ть расхо́ды.
defrost [diːˈfrɒst] *v.t.* отта́|ивать, -ять; размор|а́живать, -о́зить; **~ a refrigerator** раст|а́пливать, -опи́ть лёд в холоди́льнике.
defroster [diːˈfrɒstə(r)] *n.* антиобледени́тель (*m.*).
deft [deft] *adj.* ло́вкий, иску́сный.
defunct [dɪˈfʌŋkt] *adj.* уме́рший, поко́йный; **a ~ newspaper** бо́лее не существу́ющая газе́та.
defuse [diːˈfjuːz] *v.t.* сн|има́ть, -ять взрыва́тель *+g.*; (*fig.*) разряди́ть (*pf.*).
defy [dɪˈfaɪ] *v.t.* **1.** (*challenge*) вызыва́ть, вы́звать; бр|оса́ть, -о́сить вы́зов *+d.*; **I ~ you to prove it** руча́юсь, что вы э́того не дока́жете. **2.** (*disobey*) пренебр|ега́ть, -е́чь *+i.* **3.** (*fig.*): **the problem defies solution** пробле́му реши́ть невозмо́жно.
degeneracy [dɪˈdʒenərəsɪ] *n.* дегенерати́вность.
degenerate [dɪˈdʒenərət; *v.* dɪˈdʒenəˌreɪt] *n.* дегенера́т.
adj. вы́родившийся, дегенерати́вный.
v.i. вырожда́ться, вы́родиться; дегенери́ровать (*impf., pf.*).
degeneration [dɪˌdʒenəˈreɪʃ(ə)n] *n.* вырожде́ние, дегенера́ция.
degradation [ˌdegrəˈdeɪʃ(ə)n] *n.* **1.** (*in rank*) пониже́ние. **2.** (*moral*) упа́док, деграда́ция.
degrade [dɪˈgreɪd] *v.t.* (*reduce in rank*) пон|ижа́ть, -и́зить. **2.** (*lower morally*) прин|ижа́ть, -и́зить; ун|ижа́ть, -и́зить.
v.i. деград́ировать (*impf., pf.*).
degrading [dɪˈgreɪdɪŋ] *adj.* унизи́тельный.
degree [dɪˈgriː] *n.* **1.** (*unit of measurement*) гра́дус. **2.** (*step, stage*) ступе́нь, сте́пень; у́ровень (*m.*); **their work shows varying ~s of skill** их рабо́та пока́зывает разли́чную сте́пень мастерства́; **by ~s** постепе́нно; **to the last ~** до после́дней сте́пени; **not in the slightest ~** ничу́ть, ниско́лько, ни в како́й сте́пени; **in some ~** в не́которой сте́пени. **3.** (*social position*) положе́ние; **of high ~** высокопоста́вленный. **4.** (*acad.*) дипло́м; (*higher ~*) сте́пень; **take one's ~** получи́ть (*pf.*) сте́пень. **5.** (*gram.*) сте́пень; **~s of comparison** сте́пени сравне́ния.
dehydrate [diːˈhaɪdreɪt, ˌdiːhaɪˈdreɪt] *v.t.* обезво́|живать, -дить.
dehydration [ˌdiːhaɪˈdreɪʃ(ə)n] *n.* обезво́живание.
de-ice [diːˈaɪs] *v.t.* устран|я́ть, -и́ть обледене́ние *+g.*
de-icer [diːˈaɪsə(r)] *n.* антиобледени́тель (*m.*).
deification [ˌdiːɪfɪˈkeɪʃ(ə)n, ˌdeɪɪfɪˈkeɪʃ(ə)n] *n.* обожествле́ние, обоготворе́ние.
deify [ˈdiːɪˌfaɪ, ˈdeɪɪ-] *v.t.* обожеств|ля́ть, -и́ть; обоготвор|я́ть, -и́ть.
deign [deɪn] *v.t.* сни|сходи́ть, -зойти́; соизво́лить (*pf.*); **he did not ~ to answer us** он не удосто́ил нас отве́том.
deism [ˈdiːɪz(ə)m, ˈdeɪ-] *n.* деи́зм.
deist [ˈdiːɪst, ˈdeɪɪst] *n.* деи́ст.
deity [ˈdiːɪtɪ, ˈdeɪɪ-] *n.* (*divine nature*) боже́ственность; (*god*) божество́.
dejected [dɪˈdʒektɪd] *adj.* удручённый, пода́вленный.
dejection [dɪˈdʒekʃ(ə)n] *n.* уны́ние.
de jure [diː ˈdʒʊərɪ, deɪ ˈjʊəreɪ] *adj.* юриди́ческий.
adv. де-ю́ре; юриди́чески.
delay [dɪˈleɪ] *n.* заде́ржка, отсро́чка, промедле́ние; **without ~** неме́дленно; **after several ~s** по́сле не́скольких отсро́чек.
v.t. от|кла́дывать, -ложи́ть; заде́рж|ивать, -а́ть; ме́длить (*impf.*); **I was ~ed by traffic** я задержа́лся из-за про́бок; **~ed action mine** ми́на заме́дленного де́йствия.
v.i. заде́рж|иваться, -а́ться.
delectable [dɪˈlektəb(ə)l] *adj.* преле́стный.
delectation [ˌdiːlekˈteɪʃ(ə)n] *n.* наслажде́ние, удово́льствие, услажде́ние.
delegate [ˈdelɪgət] *n.* делега́т, представи́тель (*m.*).
v.t. **~ s.o.** делеги́ровать (*impf., pf.*) кого́-н.; посла́ть (*pf.*) кого́-н. делега́том; **~ authority** перед|ава́ть, -а́ть полномо́чие; **~ a task** поруч|а́ть, -и́ть рабо́ту (*кому*).
delegation [ˌdelɪˈgeɪʃ(ə)n] *n.* **1.** (*of task, authority*) поруче́ние, переда́ча. **2.** (*body of delegates*) делега́ция, депута́ция.
delete [dɪˈliːt] *v.t.* вычёркивать, вы́черкнуть.
deleterious [ˌdelɪˈtɪərɪəs] *adj.* вре́дный.
deletion [dɪˈliːʃ(ə)n] *n.* вычёркивание.
deliberate[1] [dɪˈlɪbərət] *adj.* (*intentional*) преднаме́ренный, умы́шленный, нарочи́тый; (*slow, prudent*) осторо́жный, осмотри́тельный.
deliberate[2] [dɪˈlɪbəˌreɪt] *v.i.* совеща́ться (*impf.*); **~ on, over, about a matter** обсу|жда́ть, -ди́ть вопро́с.
deliberation [dɪˌlɪbəˈreɪʃ(ə)n] *n.* (*pondering*) обду́мывание; (*slowness*) нетороплив́ость.
deliberative [dɪˈlɪbərətɪv] *adj.* совеща́тельный.
delicacy [ˈdelɪkəsɪ] *n.* (*exquisiteness, subtlety*) утончённость, то́нкость; (*proneness to injury*) хру́пкость, делика́тность; (*critical nature*) щекотли́вость; (*sensitivity*) чувстви́тельность; (*tact*) делика́тность, щепети́льность; (*choice food*) деликате́с, ла́комство.
delicate [ˈdelɪkət] *adj.* **1.** (*fine, exquisite*) изя́щный, то́нкий; **~ complexion** не́жная ко́жа. **2.** (*subtle, dainty*) то́нкий, утончённый; **~ flavour** то́нкий арома́т. **3.** (*easily injured*) хру́пкий, сла́бый; **a ~ child** боле́зненный ребёнок. **4.** (*critical, ticklish*) щекотли́вый, затрудни́тельный; **a ~ operation** то́нкая опера́ция. **5.** (*sensitive*) то́нкий, о́стрый; **~ instruments** чувстви́тельные прибо́ры. **6.** (*tactful, considerate*) делика́тный, такти́чный. **7.** (*careful of propriety*) щепети́льный, осторо́жный.
delicatessen [ˌdelɪkəˈtes(ə)n] *n.* (*food*) деликате́сы (*m. pl.*); (*shop*) гастрономи́ческий магази́н, гастроно́м.
delicious [dɪˈlɪʃəs] *adj.* о́чень вку́сный.
delight [dɪˈlaɪt] *n.* **1.** (*pleasure*) удово́льствие, наслажде́ние; **take ~ in sth.** на|ходи́ть, -йти́ удово́льствие в чём-н. **2.** (*source of pleasure*): **music is her ~** му́зыка для неё — исто́чник наслажде́ния.
v.t. дост|авля́ть, -а́вить наслажде́ние *+d.*; **I am ~ed to accept the invitation** я о́чень рад приня́ть приглаше́ние.
v.i. насла|жда́ться, -ди́ться.
delightful [dɪˈlaɪtfʊl] *adj.* восхити́тельный, очарова́тельный.
delimit [dɪˈlɪmɪt] *v.t.* определ|я́ть, -и́ть грани́цы *+g.*; размежёв|ывать, -а́ть.
delimitation [dɪˌlɪmɪˈteɪʃ(ə)n] *n.* размежева́ние; определе́ние.
delineate [dɪˈlɪnɪˌeɪt] *v.t.* (*e.g. a frontier*) оче́р|чивать, -ти́ть; (*e.g. character*) изобра|жа́ть, -зи́ть.
delineation [dɪˌlɪnɪˈeɪʃ(ə)n] *n.* оче́рчивание, изображе́ние.
delinquency [dɪˈlɪŋkwənsɪ] *n.* престу́пность; **juvenile ~** престу́пность несовершенноле́тних.
delinquent [dɪˈlɪŋkwənt] *adj.* правонаруши́тель (*fem.* -ница); **juvenile ~** малоле́тний престу́пник.
adj. вино́вный.
delirious [dɪˈlɪrɪəs] *adj.* (*raving*) в бреду́.
delirium [dɪˈlɪrɪəm] *n.* бред.
deliver [dɪˈlɪvə(r)] *v.t.* **1.** (*rescue, set free*) освобо|жда́ть, -ди́ть; изб|авля́ть, -а́вить; **God ~ us!** изба́ви Бог! **2.** (*of birth*): **he ~ed her** он при́нял ро́ды у неё; **the child was ~ed by forceps** при ро́дах пришло́сь наложи́ть щипцы́. **3.** (*give, present*): **~**

judgment выноси́ть, вы́нести реше́ние; ~ **a speech** произн|оси́ть, -ести́ речь. **4.** (*hand over*) сда|ва́ть, -ть; перед|ава́ть, -а́ть. **5.** (*aim, launch*) нан|оси́ть, -ести́; ~ **a blow** нанести́ (*pf.*) уда́р. **6.** (*send out, convey*) пост|авля́ть, -а́вить; вруч|а́ть, -и́ть; пере-д|ава́ть, -а́ть; **the shop ~s daily** магази́н доставля́ет това́ры на́ дом ежедне́вно; **the postman ~s letters** почтальо́н разно́сит пи́сьма.

deliverance [dɪ'lɪvərəns] *n.* избавле́ние.

deliverer [dɪ'lɪvərə(r)] *n.* (*saviour, rescuer*) избави́тель (*m.*), спаси́тель (*m.*).

delivery [dɪ'lɪvərɪ] *n.* **1.** (*childbirth*) ро́ды (*pl., g.* -ов); ~ **room** роди́льная пала́та. **2.** (*distribution of goods or letters*) доста́вка; **charges payable on** ~ опла́та при доста́вке; ~ **the letter came by the first** ~ письмо́ пришло́ с пе́рвой по́чтой; ~ **note** накладна́я; ~ **man** доста́вщик; ~ **van** фурго́н для доста́вки поку́пок на́ дом. **3.** (*of speech etc.*) произнесе́ние (ре́чи); ди́кция; **his ~ was poor** он говори́л о́чень невня́тно.

dell [del] *n.* леси́стая доли́на; лощи́на.

delphinium [del'fɪnɪəm] *n.* дельфи́ниум.

delta ['deltə] *n.* де́льта.

deltoid ['deltɔɪd] *adj.* дельтови́дный, треуго́льный.

delude [dɪ'lu:d, -'lju:d] *v.t.* вв|оди́ть, -ести́ в заблужде́ние; **he ~d himself into believing that ...** он уве́рил себя́ в то́м, что...

deluge ['delju:dʒ] *n.* **1.** (*lit.*) пото́п. **2.** (*fig.*) пото́к, град; **a ~ of protest** пото́к проте́стов.

v.t. затоп|ля́ть, -и́ть; **he was ~d with questions** его́ засы́пали гра́дом вопро́сов.

delusion [dɪ'lu:ʒ(ə)n, -'lju:ʒ(ə)n] *n.* заблужде́ние; **be under a ~** заблужда́ться (*impf.*); **~s of grandeur** ма́ния вели́чия.

de luxe [də 'lʌks, 'lʊks] *adj.* роско́шный; **a ~ cabin** каю́та-лю́кс.

delve [delv] *v.i.* копа́ть (*impf.*); ~ **in archives** ры́ться (*impf.*) в архи́вах.

demagnetize [di:'mægnɪ,taɪz] *v.t.* размагни́|чивать, -тить.

demagogic [,demə'gɒgɪk] *adj.* демагоги́ческий.

demagogue ['demə,gɒg] *n.* демаго́г.

demagogy ['demə,gɒgɪ] *n.* демаго́гия.

demand [dɪ'mɑ:nd] *n.* **1.** (*claim*) тре́бование. **2.** (*desire to obtain*) потре́бность, спро́с; **there is no ~ for this article** на э́тот това́р нет спро́са.

v.t. тре́бовать, по- +*g.*.

demarcate ['di:mɑ:,keɪt] *v.t.* разграни́чи|вать, -ть.

demarcation [,di:mɑ:'keɪʃ(ə)n] *n.* демарка́ция.

démarche [deɪ'mɑ:ʃ] *n.* дема́рш.

demean [dɪ'mi:n] *v.t.* (*abase*) ун|ижа́ть, -и́зить; ~ **o.s.** роня́ть (*impf.*) своё досто́инство.

demeanour [dɪ'mi:nə(r)] *n.* поведе́ние; мане́ра вести́ себя́.

demented [dɪ'mentɪd] *adj.* сумасше́дший.

dementia [dɪ'menʃə] *n.* слабоу́мие.

demerit [di:'merɪt] *n.* недоста́ток; дурна́я черта́.

demigod ['demɪ,gɒd] *n.* полубо́г.

demilitarization [di:,mɪlɪtəraɪ'zeɪʃ(ə)n] *n.* демилитариза́ция.

demilitarize [di:'mɪlɪtə,raɪz] *v.t.* демилитаризи́ровать (*impf., pf.*).

demise [dɪ'maɪz] *n.* кончи́на.

demist [di:'mɪst] *v.t.* предохран|я́ть, -и́ть от запотева́ния; обогр|ева́ть, -е́ть (*стекло*).

demister [di:'mɪstə(r)] *n.* деми́стер; обогрева́тель (*m.*) стекла́.

demi-tasse ['demɪ,tæs, dəmɪ'tæs] *n.* (*US*) ча́шечка чёрного ко́фе.

demo ['deməʊ] (*coll.*) = **demonstration**

demob [di:'mɒb] (*coll.*) = **demobilize**

demobilization [di:,məʊbɪlaɪ'zeɪʃ(ə)n] *n.* демобилиза́ция.

demobilize [di:'məʊbɪ,laɪz] *v.t.* демобилизова́ть (*pf.*).

democracy [dɪ'mɒkrəsɪ] *n.* демокра́тия; **Britain is a ~** А́нглия — демократи́ческое госуда́рство.

democrat ['demə,kræt] *n.* демокра́т.

democratic [,demə'krætɪk] *adj.* демократи́ческий.

democratize [dɪ'mɒkrə,taɪz] *v.t.* демократизи́ровать (*impf., pf.*).

demographer [dɪ'mɒgrəfə(r)] *n.* демо́граф.

demographic [,demə'græfɪk] *adj.* демографи́ческий.

demography [dɪ'mɒgrəfɪ] *n.* демогра́фия.

demolish [dɪ'mɒlɪʃ] *v.t.* (*e.g. house*) сн|оси́ть, -ести́; разр|уша́ть, -у́шить; (*e.g. theory*) разб|ива́ть, -и́ть.

demolition [,demə'lɪʃ(ə)n] *n.* **1.** (*lit.*) разруше́ние, снос. **2.** (*of argument etc.*) опроверже́ние.

demon ['di:mən] *n.* **1.** (*devil*) де́мон, дья́вол, бес. **2.** (*fierce or energetic person*): **he's a ~ for work** он рабо́тает как чёрт.

demoniac(al) [,di:mə'naɪək(ə)l] *adj.* демони́ческий.

demonstrable ['demɒnstrəb(ə)l, dɪ'mɒnstrəb(ə)l] *adj.* доказу́емый.

demonstrate ['demən,streɪt] *v.t.* **1.** (*prove*) дока́з|ывать, -а́ть; ~ **one's sympathies** прояв|ля́ть, -и́ть свои́ симпа́тии. **2.** (*show in operation*) демонстри́ровать, про-.

v.i. устр|а́ивать, -о́ить демонстра́цию; уча́ствовать (*impf.*) в демонстра́ции.

demonstration [,demən'streɪʃ(ə)n] *n.* (*proof*) доказа́тельство; (*exhibition*): ~ **of affection** проявле́ние чу́вства; ~ **of a machine** демонстри́рование маши́ны; (*public manifestation*) демонстра́ция.

demonstrative [dɪ'mɒnstrətɪv] *adj.* **1.** (*of proof*) нагля́дный, убеди́тельный. **2.** (*showing feelings*) экспанси́вный, несде́ржанный. **3.** (*gram.*) указа́тельный.

demonstrator ['demən,streɪtə(r)] *n.* **1.** (*one who displays*) демонстра́тор. **2.** (*pol.*) демонстра́нт.

demoralization [dɪ,mɒrəlaɪ'zeɪʃ(ə)n] *n.* деморализа́ция; (*corruption*) разложе́ние.

demoralize [dɪ'mɒrə,laɪz] *v.t.* деморализова́ть (*impf., pf.*); (*corrupt*) разл|ага́ть, -ожи́ть.

demote [dɪ'məʊt, di:-] *v.t.* пон|ижа́ть, -и́зить в до́лжности.

demotion [dɪ'məʊʃ(ə)n] *n.* пониже́ние в до́лжности.

demur [dɪ'mɜ:(r)] *v.i.* возра|жа́ть, -зи́ть (~ **at, to:** про́тив+*g.*).

demure [dɪ'mjʊə(r)] *adj.* скро́мный, серьёзный.

den [den] *n.* **1.** (*animal's lair*) берло́га, ло́говище, ло́гово. **2.** (*of thieves*) прито́н. **3.** (*study*) рабо́чий кабине́т.

denature [di:'neɪtʃə(r)] *v.t.* денатури́ровать (*impf., pf.*); **~d alcohol** денатура́т.

denial [dɪ'naɪəl] *n.* **1.** (*denying*) отрица́ние, опроверже́ние; **a flat ~** категори́ческое опроверже́ние/отрица́ние. **2.** (*refusal*) отка́з; **I'll take no ~** я не приму́ отка́за; ~ **of justice** отка́з в правосу́дии. **3.** (*disavowal*) отрече́ние (от+*g.*).

denier ['denjə(r)] *n.* (*unit of fineness*) денье́ (*indecl.*).

denigrate ['denɪ,greɪt] *v.t.* (*defame*) черни́ть, о-; клевета́ть, о-; поро́чить, о-.

denigration [,denɪ'greɪʃ(ə)n] *n.* клевета́, опоро́чение.

denigrator ['denɪ,greɪtə(r)] *n.* клеветни́к.

denim ['denɪm] *n.* джинсо́вая ткань.

adj. джинсо́вый.

denizen ['denɪz(ə)n] *n.* (*inhabitant*) жи́тель (*m.*), обита́тель (*m.*); **~s of the deep** обита́тели глуби́н.

Denmark ['denmɑ:k] *n.* Да́ния.

denomination [dɪ,nɒmɪ'neɪʃ(ə)n] *n.* **1.** (*name, nomenclature*) наименова́ние. **2.** (*relig.*) вероиспове́дание. **3.**: **money of small ~s** купю́ры (*f. pl.*) ма́лого досто́инства.

denominator [dɪ'nɒmɪ,neɪtə(r)] *n.* (*math.*) знамена́тель (*m.*); **reduce to a common ~** прив|оди́ть, -ести́ к о́бщему знамена́телю.

denotation [ˌdiːnəˈteɪʃ(ə)n] *n.* обозначе́ние.
denote [dɪˈnəʊt] *v.t.* обозн|ача́ть, -а́чить.
dénouement [deɪˈnuːmɑ̃] *n.* развя́зка.
denounce [dɪˈnaʊns] *v.t.* **1.** (*inveigh against*) осу|жда́ть, -ди́ть. **2.** (*inform against*) дон|оси́ть, -ести́ на+*a.*
dense [dens] *adj.* **1.** (*of liquids, vapour*) пло́тный, густо́й. **2.** (*of objects*) густо́й. **3.** (*stupid*) тупо́й.
density [ˈdensɪtɪ] *n.* пло́тность, густота́; ~ **of population** пло́тность населе́ния; населённость.
dent [dent] *n.* вмя́тина, вы́боина.
v.t. ост|авля́ть, -а́вить вмя́тину в/на+*p.*; вдав|ливать, -и́ть; **the car got ~ed in the collision** при столкнове́нии маши́на получи́ла вмя́тину.
v.i. гну́ться, про-; **this metal ~s easily** э́тот мета́лл легко́ гнётся.
dental [ˈdent(ə)l] *adj.* (*of teeth*) зубно́й; ~ **plaque** зубно́й налёт; (*of dentistry*) зубовраче́бный.
dentifrice [ˈdentɪfrɪs] *n.* зубно́й порошо́к; зубна́я па́ста.
dentist [ˈdentɪst] *n.* зубно́й врач, стомато́лог.
dentistry [ˈdentɪstrɪ] *n.* профе́ссия зубно́го врача́.
denture [ˈdentʃə(r)] *n.* зубно́й проте́з.
denude [dɪˈnjuːd] *v.t.* огол|я́ть, -и́ть; обнаж|а́ть, -и́ть.
denunciation [dɪˌnʌnsɪˈeɪʃ(ə)n] *n.* осужде́ние; доно́с.
denunciatory [dɪˈnʌnsɪətərɪ, -ˈnʌnʃɪətərɪ] *adj.* осужда́ющий.
den|y [dɪˈnaɪ] *v.t.* **1.** (*contest truth of*) отрица́ть (*impf.*). **2.** (*repudiate*) отр|ека́ться, -е́чься от+*g.* **3.** (*refuse*) отка́з|ывать, -а́ть (*кому в чём*); **he was ~ied admittance** его́ не впусти́ли; **~y o.s. sth.** отка́з|ывать, -а́ть себе́ в чём-н.
deodorant [diːˈəʊdərənt] *n.* дезодора́тор.
deodorize [diːˈəʊdəˌraɪz] *v.t.* дезодори́ровать (*impf., pf.*).
depart [dɪˈpɑːt] *v.t.*: ~ **this life** пок|ида́ть, -и́нуть э́тот мир.
v.i. **1.** (*go away*) отпр|авля́ться, -а́виться; отб|ыва́ть, -ы́ть. **2.:** ~ **from** (*custom, plan etc.*) отсту|п|а́ть, -и́ть от+*g.*
departed [dɪˈpɑːtɪd] *n.*: **the (dear)** ~ поко́йный, отоше́дший.
adj. (*bygone*) бы́лой, мину́вший.
department [dɪˈpɑːtmənt] *n.* **1.** отде́л; ~ **store** универма́г. **2.** (*of government*) департа́мент, ве́домство. **3.** (*of univ.*) ка́федра.
departmental [ˌdiːpɑːtˈment(ə)l] *adj.* ве́домственный.
departure [dɪˈpɑːtʃə(r)] *n.* **1.** (*going away*) отъе́зд, отправле́ние; **take one's** ~ уходи́ть, уйти́; уезжа́ть, уе́хать. **2.** (*deviation, change*) отклоне́ние.
depend [dɪˈpend] *v.i.* **1.** (*be conditional*) зави́сеть (*impf.*) (от+*g.*); **that ~s; it all ~s** как сказа́ть; посмо́трим; смотря́ (*где, когда, что и т.п.*). **2.** (*rely*) пол|ага́ться, -ожи́ться (на+*a.*); рассчи́тывать (*impf.*) (на+*a.*).
dependable [dɪˈpendəb(ə)l] *adj.* надёжный.
dependant [dɪˈpend(ə)nt] *n.* иждиве́н|ец (*fem.* -ка).
dependence [dɪˈpend(ə)ns] *n.* зави́симость (от+*g.*); (*reliance*) дове́рие (к+*d.*).
dependency [dɪˈpendənsɪ] *n.* (*pol.*) коло́ния.
dependent [dɪˈpend(ə)nt] *adj.* **1.** (*conditional*) зави́симый. **2.** (*financial*) зави́симый, находя́щийся на иждиве́нии. **3.** (*gram.*) подчинённый.
depersonalize [diːˈpɜːsənəˌlaɪz] *v.t.* обезли́чи|вать, -ть.
depict [dɪˈpɪkt] *v.t.* изобра|жа́ть, -зи́ть.
depiction [dɪˈpɪkʃ(ə)n] *n.* описа́ние, изображе́ние.
depilatory [dɪˈpɪlətərɪ] *n.* сре́дство для удале́ния воло́с.
deplete [dɪˈpliːt] *v.t.* истощ|а́ть, -и́ть; исче́рп|ывать, -а́ть; **~d strength** (*physical*) уга́сшие си́лы.
depletion [dɪˈpliːʃ(ə)n] *n.* истоще́ние, исче́рпывание.
deplorable [dɪˈplɔːrəb(ə)l] *adj.* плаче́вный, приско́рбный.
deplore [dɪˈplɔː(r)] *v.t.* сожале́ть (*impf.*) о+*p.*; счита́ть (*impf.*) возмути́тельным.
deploy [dɪˈplɔɪ] *v.t.* развёр|тывать, -ну́ть.
deployment [dɪˈplɔɪmənt] *n.* развёртывание; размеще́ние.
depopulate [diːˈpɒpjʊˌleɪt] *v.t.* обезлю́дить (*pf.*).
deport [dɪˈpɔːt] *v.t.* **1.:** ~ **o.s.** вести́ (*det.*) себя́. **2.** (*remove, banish*) высыла́ть, вы́слать.
deportation [ˌdiːpɔːˈteɪʃ(ə)n] *n.* вы́сылка, депорта́ция.
deportment [dɪˈpɔːtmənt] *n.* мане́ра держа́ться; оса́нка.
depose [dɪˈpəʊz] *v.t.* (*monarch etc.*) св|ерга́ть, -е́ргнуть (с престо́ла); низл|ага́ть, -ожи́ть.
deposit [dɪˈpɒzɪt] *n.* **1.** (*sum in bank*) вклад. **2.** (*act of placing*) депози́т; ~ **account** депози́тный счёт. **3.** (*advance payment*) зада́ток; (*layer*) отложе́ние. **4.** (*of ore etc.*) за́лежь, ро́ссыпь.
v.t. класть, положи́ть; (*place in bank*) депони́ровать (*impf., pf.*).
deposition [ˌdiːpəˈzɪʃ(ə)n, ˌdep-] *n.* (*dethronement*) сверже́ние; (*evidence*) показа́ние под прися́гой.
depositor [dɪˈpɒzɪtə(r)] *n.* (*fin.*) депози́тор, депоне́нт, вкла́дчик.
depository [dɪˈpɒzɪtərɪ] *n.* храни́лище.
depot [ˈdepəʊ] *n.* (*place of storage*) склад; (*for motor transport*) автоба́за.
deprave [dɪˈpreɪv] *v.t.* развра|ща́ть, -ти́ть.
depravity [dɪˈprævɪtɪ] *n.* развра́т, развращённость.
deprecate [ˈdeprɪˌkeɪt] *v.t.* осу|жда́ть, -ди́ть; выска́зываться, вы́сказаться про́тив+*g.*
depreciate [dɪˈpriːʃɪˌeɪt, -sɪˌeɪt] *v.t.* обесце́ни|ва́ть, -ть; (*disparage*) умал|я́ть, -и́ть.
v.i. обесце́ни|ваться, -ться.
depreciation [dɪˌpriːʃɪˈeɪʃ(ə)n, -sɪˈeɪʃ(ə)n] *n.* обесце́нение.
depredation [ˌdeprɪˈdeɪʃ(ə)n] *n.* грабёж.
depress [dɪˈpres] *v.t.* **1.** (*push down*) наж|има́ть, -а́ть на+*a.* **2.** (*fig.*) угнета́ть (*impf.*); **~ed area** райо́н, пострада́вший от экономи́ческой депре́ссии. **3.** (*make sad*) удруч|а́ть, -и́ть; угнета́ть (*impf.*); подав|ля́ть, -и́ть.
depressing [dɪˈpresɪŋ] *adj.* удруча́ющий; тру́дный.
depression [dɪˈpreʃ(ə)n] *n.* **1.** (*hollow, sunken place*) впа́дина, углубле́ние. **2.** (*slump*) депре́ссия, засто́й. **3.** (*low spirits*) депре́ссия, тоска́.
deprivation [ˌdeprɪˈveɪʃ(ə)n, ˌdiːpraɪ-] *n.* лише́ние.
deprive [dɪˈpraɪv] *v.t.* лиш|а́ть, -и́ть (*кого чего*); **~d** (*underprivileged*) обездо́ленный.
depth [depθ] *n.* **1.** (*deepness*) глубина́; **6 feet in ~** глубино́й в шесть фу́тов; **at a ~ of 6 feet** на глубине́ шести́ фу́тов; **be out of one's ~** не достава́ть (*impf.*) нога́ми дна; (*fig.*): **I am out of my ~ in this job** э́та рабо́та мне не по плечу́; **in ~** (*fig., thoroughly*) глубоко́. **2.** (*profundity*) глубина́. **3.** (*extremity*): **~ of despair** по́лное отча́яние; **~ of winter** разга́р зимы́; **in the ~(s) of the country** в глуши́.
cpd. **~-charge** *n.* глуби́нная бо́мба.
deputation [ˌdepjʊˈteɪʃ(ə)n] *n.* депута́ция.
deputize [ˈdepjʊˌtaɪz] *v.i.*: ~ **for s.o.** заме|ща́ть (*impf.*) кого́-н.
deputy [ˈdepjʊtɪ] *n.* **1.** (*substitute*) замести́тель (*m.*); ~ **chairman** замести́тель (*m.*) председа́теля. **2.** (*member of parliament*) депута́т.
derail [dɪˈreɪl, diː-] *v.t.* св|оди́ть, -ести́ с ре́льсов; **the train was ~ ed** по́езд сошёл с ре́льсов; **the partisans ~ed the train** партиза́ны пусти́ли по́езд под отко́с.
derailment [dɪˈreɪlmənt, diː-] *n.* сход с ре́льсов.
derange [dɪˈreɪndʒ] *v.t.* св|оди́ть, -ести́ с ума́.
derangement [dɪˈreɪndʒmənt] *n.* (у́мственное) расстро́йство.
derelict [ˈderəlɪkt, ˈderɪ-] *adj.* (*abandoned*) забро́шенный, запу́щенный.
dereliction [ˌderɪˈlɪkʃ(ə)n] *n.* забро́шенность, запу́щенность; ~ **of duty** наруше́ние до́лга.

deride [dɪˈraɪd] *v.t.* высме́ивать, вы́смеять; осме́|ивать, -я́ть.
derision [dɪˈrɪʒ(ə)n] *n.* осмея́ние, высме́ивание.
derisive [dɪˈraɪsɪv] *adj.* (*scornful*) насме́шливый; (*absurd*) смехотво́рный.
derisory [dɪˈraɪsərɪ] *adj.* (*ludicrous*) неле́пый, смешно́й, ничто́жный.
derivation [ˌderɪˈveɪʃ(ə)n] *n.* происхожде́ние.
derivative [dəˈrɪvətɪv, dɪ-] *adj.* произво́дный.
derive [dɪˈraɪv] *v.t.* **1.** (*obtain*) извл|ека́ть, -е́чь; **~ pleasure from** получ|а́ть, -и́ть удово́льствие от+*g.* **2.** (*trace*) выводи́ть, вы́вести; возв|оди́ть, -ести́. **3.** (*originate*) происходи́ть (*impf.*); **words ~d from Latin** слова́ лати́нского происхожде́ния.
dermatologist [ˌdɜːməˈtɒlədʒɪst] *n.* дермато́лог.
dermatology [ˌdɜːməˈtɒlədʒɪ] *n.* дерматоло́гия.
derogatory [dɪˈrɒgətərɪ] *adj.* пренебрежи́тельный; **~ to s.o.'s dignity** унижа́ющий чьё-н. досто́инство.
derrick [ˈderɪk] *n.* **1.** (*crane*) де́ррик(-кран). **2.** (*over oil-well*) бурова́я вы́шка.
dervish [ˈdɜːvɪʃ] *n.* де́рвиш.
desalinate [diːˈsælɪˌneɪt] *v.t.* опресн|я́ть, -и́ть.
desalination [diːˌsælɪˈneɪʃ(ə)n] *n.* опресне́ние (воды́).
descant [ˈdeskænt] *n.* (*mus.*) ди́скант.
descend [dɪˈsend] *v.t.* сходи́ть, сойти́ с+*g.*; **~ a hill** спус|ка́ться, -ти́ться с холма́; **he ~ed the stairs** он спусти́лся/сошёл по ле́стнице.
v.i. **1.** (*go down*) спус|ка́ться, -ти́ться; сходи́ть, сойти́; **in ~ing order (of importance)** в нисходя́щем поря́дке. **2.** (*originate*) происходи́ть (*impf.*); **he is ~ed from a ducal family** он происхо́дит из ге́рцогской семьи́. **3.** (*make an attack*) набр|а́сываться, -о́ситься. **4.** (*lower o.s. morally*) опус|ка́ться, -ти́ться.
descendant [dɪˈsend(ə)nt] *n.* пото́мок.
descent [dɪˈsent] *n.* **1.** (*downward slope*) скат, склон. **2.** (*act of descending*) спуск, сниже́ние. **3.** (*ancestry*) происхожде́ние.
describe [dɪˈskraɪb] *v.t.* опи́с|ывать, -а́ть (*also geom.*); охарактеризова́ть (*pf.*); **~ s.o. as a scoundrel** изобрази́ть/назва́ть (*both pf.*) кого́-н. подлецо́м; **he ~s himself as a doctor** он называ́ет себя́ врачо́м.
description [dɪˈskrɪpʃ(ə)n] *n.* **1.** (*act of describing*) описа́ние; **answer a ~** соотве́тствовать (*impf.*) описа́нию; **beyond ~** неопису́емый. **2.** (*kind*) род, сорт.
descriptive [dɪˈskrɪptɪv] *adj.* описа́тельный.
descry [dɪˈskraɪ] *v.t.* зам|еча́ть, -е́тить; различ|а́ть, -и́ть.
desecrate [ˈdesɪˌkreɪt] *v.t.* оскверн|я́ть, -и́ть.
desecration [ˌdesɪˈkreɪʃ(ə)n] *n.* оскверне́ние.
desegregate [diːˈsegrɪˌgeɪt] *v.t. & i.* десегреги́ровать (*impf., pf.*)
desegregation [ˌdiːsegrɪˈgeɪʃ(ə)n] *n.* десегрега́ция.
desert[1] [dɪˈzɜːt] *n.* (*merit*) заслу́га; **get one's ~s** получ|а́ть, -и́ть по заслу́гам.
desert[2] [ˈdezət] *n.* (*waste land*) пусты́ня.
adj. пусты́нный; **~ island** необита́емый о́стров.
desert[3] [dɪˈzɜːt] *v.t.* **1.** (*go away from*) ост|авля́ть, -а́вить; пок|ида́ть, -и́нуть; **the streets were ~ed** у́лицы бы́ли пусты́нны. **2.** (*abandon*) пок|ида́ть, -и́нуть; **he ~ed his wife** он бро́сил свою́ жену́.
v.i. дезерти́ровать (*impf., pf.*).
deserter [dɪˈzɜːtə(r)] *n.* дезерти́р.
desertion [dɪˈzɜːʃ(ə)n] *n.* дезерти́рство.
deserve [dɪˈzɜːv] *v.t. & i.* заслу́ж|ивать, -и́ть; **he ~s to be well treated** он заслу́живает хоро́шего отноше́ния.
deserved [dɪˈzɜːvd] *adj.* заслу́женный.
deserving [dɪˈzɜːvɪŋ] *adj.* похва́льный, досто́йный.
desiderat|um [dɪˌzɪdəˈrɑːtəm, dɪˌsɪd-] *n.* жела́емое; **~a** (*pl.*) пожела́ния (*nt. pl.*).
design [dɪˈzaɪn] *n.* **1.** (*drawing, plan*) план; (*industrial*) диза́йн; **~ for a dress** эски́з пла́тья. **2.** (*art of drawing*) рисова́ние; **school of ~** худо́жественное учи́лище. **3.** (*tech.: layout, system*) констру́кция, прое́кт; **~ of a car** констру́кция автомоби́ля; **~ of a building** прое́кт зда́ния. **4.** (*pattern*) узо́р, рису́нок. **5.** (*purpose*) у́мысел; **by ~** с у́мыслом; **he has ~s on my job** он име́ет ви́ды на мою́ рабо́ту.
v.t. **1.** (*make designs for*) сост|авля́ть, -а́вить план +*g.*; проекти́ровать, с-; (*e.g. a book*) оф|ормля́ть, -о́рмить; **~ a garden** плани́ровать, рас- сад. **2.** (*intend*) зам|ышля́ть, -ы́слить; предназн|ача́ть, -а́чить.
v.i.: **he ~s for a dressmaker** он де́лает эски́зы для портни́хи.
designate[1] [ˈdezɪgnət] *adj.* назна́ченный.
designate[2] [ˈdezɪgˌneɪt] *v.t.* обозн|ача́ть, -а́чить; назн|ача́ть, -а́чить.
designation [ˌdezɪgˈneɪʃ(ə)n] *n.* (*appointment*) назначе́ние; (*title*) зва́ние.
designedly [dɪˈzaɪnɪdlɪ] *adv.* умы́шленно.
designer [dɪˈzaɪnə(r)] *n.* (*of dresses, decorations*) моделье́р; (*tech.*) констру́ктор; (*industrial*) диза́йнер.
designing [dɪˈzaɪnɪŋ] *adj.* (*scheming*) интригу́ющий.
desirability [dɪˌzaɪərəˈbɪlɪtɪ] *n.* жела́тельность.
desirable [dɪˈzaɪərəb(ə)l] *adj.* жела́тельный.
desire [dɪˈzaɪə(r)] *n.* **1.** (*wish, longing*) жела́ние. **2.** (*lust*) вожделе́ние. **3.** (*request*) про́сьба, пожела́ние. **4.** (*thg. desired*) предме́т жела́ния; **he got all his ~s** все его́ жела́ния сбыли́сь.
v.t. **1.** (*wish*) жела́ть, по-; **it leaves much to be ~ed** э́то оставля́ет жела́ть мно́го лу́чшего. **2.** (*request*) проси́ть, по-.
desirous [dɪˈzaɪərəs] *adj.* жела́ющий.
desist [dɪˈzɪst] *v.i.* отка́з|ываться, -а́ться (от+*g.*).
desk [desk] *n.* пи́сьменный стол; конто́рка; **(school ~)** па́рта; (*information centre*) пункт; (*attr.*) насто́льный; **~ work** канцеля́рская рабо́та.
desktop [ˈdesktɒp] *adj.* насто́льный; **~ publishing** насто́льная полигра́фия.
desolate[1] [ˈdesələt] *adj.* (*ruined, neglected*) забро́шенный, запу́щенный; (*wretched, lonely*) забро́шенный, поки́нутый.
desolate[2] [ˈdesəˌleɪt] *v.t.* (*lay waste*) разор|я́ть, -и́ть; опустош|а́ть, -и́ть; (*make sad*) прив|оди́ть, -ести́ в отча́яние.
desolation [ˌdesəˈleɪʃ(ə)n] *n.* (*waste*) забро́шенность, опустоше́ние; (*sorrow*) забро́шенность, скорбь.
despair [dɪˈspeə(r)] *n.* отча́яние.
v.i. отча́|иваться, -яться.
despatch [dɪˈspætʃ] = **dispatch**
desperado [ˌdespəˈrɑːdəʊ] *n.* головоре́з.
desperate [ˈdespərət] *adj.* **1.** (*wretched, hopeless*) отча́янный, беспросве́тный. **2.** (*in extreme need*): **he is ~ for money** он отча́янно нужда́ется в деньга́х; **a ~ remedy** кра́йнее сре́дство. **3.**: **a ~ criminal** закорене́лый престу́пник.
desperation [ˌdespəˈreɪʃ(ə)n] *n.* отча́яние.
despicable [ˈdespɪkəb(ə)l, dɪˈspɪk-] *adj.* презре́нный.
despise [dɪˈspaɪz] *v.t.* презира́ть (*impf.*); пренебр|ега́ть, -е́чь +*i.*.
despite [dɪˈspaɪt] *prep.* несмотря́ на+*a.*
despoil [dɪˈspɔɪl] *v.t.* гра́бить, о-; разор|я́ть, -и́ть.
despondency [dɪˈspɒndənsɪ] *n.* уны́ние.
despondent [dɪˈspɒnd(ə)nt] *adj.* уны́лый; пода́вленный.
despot [ˈdespɒt] *n.* де́спот.
despotic [ˌdeˈspɒtɪk] *adj.* деспоти́ческий.
despotism [ˈdespəˌtɪz(ə)m] *n.* деспоти́зм.
dessert [dɪˈzɜːt] *n.* (*sweet course*) десе́рт, сла́дкое, тре́тье.
cpd. **~-spoon** *n.* десе́ртная ло́жка.
destabilize [diːˈsteɪbɪˌlaɪz] *v.t.* дестабилизи́ровать (*impf., pf.*).
destination [ˌdestɪˈneɪʃ(ə)n] *n.* ме́сто назначе́ния.
destine [ˈdestɪn] *v.t.* предназн|ача́ть, -а́чить; **his parents ~d him for the army** роди́тели про́чили его́ в

а́рмию; **he was ~ed to become Prime Minister** ему́ суждено́ бы́ло стать премье́р-мини́стром.

destiny ['destɪnɪ] *n.* судьба́.

destitute ['destɪ,tju:t] *adj.* (*in penury*) нужда́ющийся, обездо́ленный; (*devoid*) лишённый (*чего*).

destitution [,destɪ'tju:ʃ(ə)n] *n.* (*poverty*) нищета́; (*deprivation*) лише́ние.

destroy [dɪ'strɔɪ] *v.t.* разр|уша́ть, -у́шить; разб|ива́ть, -и́ть; уничт|ожа́ть, -о́жить; **his hopes were ~ed** его́ наде́жды ру́хнули.

destroyer [dɪ'strɔɪə(r)] *n.* **1.** (*one who destroys*) разруши́тель (*m.*). **2.** (*nav.*) эсми́нец; эска́дренный миноно́сец.

destruction [dɪ'strʌkʃ(ə)n] *n.* уничтоже́ние, разруше́ние.

destructive [dɪ'strʌktɪv] *adj.* разруши́тельный; **~ criticism** уничтожа́ющая кри́тика; **he is a ~ child** э́тот ребёнок всё лома́ет.

desultory ['dezəltərɪ] *adj.* отры́вочный.

detach [dɪ'tætʃ] *v.t.* отдел|я́ть, -и́ть; разъедин|я́ть, -и́ть; **a ~ed house** особня́к.

detached [dɪ'tætʃd] *adj.* беспристра́стный; **a ~ attitude** равноду́шный подхо́д.

detachment [dɪ'tætʃmənt] *n.* (*separation*) отделе́ние; (*indifference*) равноду́шие; (*body of troops etc.*) отря́д.

detail[1] ['di:teɪl] *n.* **1.** подро́бность, дета́ль; **go into ~(s)** вдава́ться (*impf.*) в подро́бности; **in ~** подро́бно. **2.** (*mil., detachment*) наря́д.

detail[2] ['di:teɪl] *v.t.* **1.** (*give particulars of*) входи́ть, вдава́ться (*both impf.*) в подро́бности +*g.* **2.** (*appoint*) откомандиро́в|ывать, -а́ть.

detain [dɪ'teɪn] *v.t.* заде́рж|ивать, -а́ть; **he was ~ed at the office** его́ задержа́ли на рабо́те; **he was ~ed by the police** он был заде́ржан поли́цией.

detect [dɪ'tekt] *v.t.* (*track down*) высле́живать, вы́следить; (*perceive*) обнару́жи|вать, -ть.

detectable [dɪ'tektəb(ə)l] *adj.* заме́тный.

detection [dɪ'tekʃ(ə)n] *n.* (*of crime*) рассле́дование, раскры́тие; **he escaped ~** он избежа́л разоблаче́ния; (*perception*) обнаруже́ние.

detective [dɪ'tektɪv] *n.* сы́щик, детекти́в; **~ novel** детекти́в.

detector [dɪ'tektə(r)] *n.* (*radio*) дете́ктор.

détente [deɪ'tɑ̃t] *n.* (*pol.*) разря́дка.

detention [dɪ'tenʃ(ə)n] *n.* (*at school*) оставле́ние по́сле уро́ков; (*arrest, confinement*) заключе́ние, задержа́ние.

deter [dɪ'tɜ:(r)] *v.t.* уде́рж|ивать, -а́ть.

detergent [dɪ'tɜ:dʒ(ə)nt] *n.* мо́ющее сре́дство; стира́льный порошо́к.

deteriorate [dɪ'tɪərɪə,reɪt] *v.t. & i.* ух|удша́ть(ся), -у́дшить(ся).

deterioration [dɪ,tɪərɪə'reɪʃ(ə)n] *n.* ухудше́ние.

determinant [dɪ'tɜ:mɪnənt] *n.* реша́ющий фа́ктор.
adj. реша́ющий.

determinate [dɪ'tɜ:mɪnət] *adj.* определённый, устано́вленный.

determination [dɪ,tɜ:mɪ'neɪʃ(ə)n] *n.* **1.** (*deciding upon*) реше́ние. **2.** (*calculating*) установле́ние. **3.** (*resoluteness*) реши́мость, реши́тельность.

determine [dɪ'tɜ:mɪn] *v.t.* **1.** (*be deciding factor*) определ|я́ть, -и́ть; **this ~d him to accept** э́то убеди́ло его́ согласи́ться. **2.** (*take decision*) реш|а́ть, -и́ть; **he is ~d to go** он твёрдо реши́л е́хать; **~ the date of a meeting** установи́ть (*pf.*) да́ту собра́ния. **3.** (*ascertain*) устан|а́вливать, -ови́ть.

determined [dɪ'tɜ:mɪnd] *adj.* (*resolute*) реши́тельный.

determinism [dɪ'tɜ:mɪ,nɪz(ə)m] *n.* детермини́зм.

deterrence [dɪ'terəns] *n.* устраше́ние, отпу́гивание.

deterrent [dɪ'terənt] *n.* сре́дство сде́рживания; **nuclear ~** я́дерный арсена́л (сде́рживания).

detest [dɪ'test] *v.t.* ненави́деть (*impf.*).

detestable [dɪ'testəb(ə)l] *adj.* отврати́тельный.

detestation [,di:te'steɪʃ(ə)n] *n.* не́нависть, отвраще́ние.

dethrone [di:'θrəʊn] *v.t.* св|ерга́ть, -е́ргнуть с престо́ла.

detonate ['detə,neɪt] *v.t.* детони́ровать (*impf., pf.*).
v.i. вз|рыва́ться, -орва́ться.

detonation [,detə'neɪʃ(ə)n] *n.* детона́ция.

detonator ['detə,neɪtə(r)] *n.* (*part of bomb or shell*) детона́тор.

detour ['di:tʊə(r)] *n.* объе́зд; око́льный путь; **make a ~** де́лать, с- крюк.

detract [dɪ'trækt] *v.i.*: **~ from** умал|я́ть, -и́ть.

detraction [dɪ'trækʃ(ə)n] *n.* (*disparagement*) умале́ние; (*slander*) клевета́.

detractor [dɪ'træktə(r)] *n.* клеветни́к.

detriment ['detrɪmənt] *n.* уще́рб; **he works long hours to the ~ of his health** он мно́го рабо́тает в уще́рб своему́ здоро́вью.

detrimental [,detrɪ'ment(ə)l] *adj.* вре́дный.

deuce[1] [dju:s] *n.* (*cards or dice*) дво́йка; (*tennis*) ра́вный счёт.

deuce[2] [dju:s] *n.* (*euph., devil*) чёрт, дья́вол; **~ take it!** чёрт подери́!; **where the ~ did I put it?** куда́ к чёрту я э́то дел?

deuterium [dju:'tɪərɪəm] *n.* дейте́рий.

Deuteronomy [,dju:tə'rɒnəmɪ] *n.* Второзако́ние.

devaluation [di:,vælju:'eɪʃ(ə)n] *n.* обесце́нение; (*fin.*) девальва́ция.

devalue [di:'vælju:] *v.t.* обесце́ни|вать, -ть; (*fin.*) девальви́ровать (*impf., pf.*).
v.i. пров|оди́ть, -ести́ девальва́цию (*чего*).

devastate ['devə,steɪt] *v.t.* опустош|а́ть, -и́ть; разор|я́ть, -и́ть; **a ~ing remark** уничтожа́ющее замеча́ние.

devastation [,devə'steɪʃ(ə)n] *n.* опустоше́ние.

develop [dɪ'veləp] *v.t.* **1.** (*cause to unfold*) разв|ива́ть, -и́ть; обраб|а́тывать, -о́тать. **2.** (*phot.*) прояв|ля́ть, -и́ть. **3.** (*contract*): **he ~ed a cough** у него́ появи́лся ка́шель. **4.** (*open up for residence etc.*) разв|ива́ть, -и́ть; (*resources*) осв|а́ивать, -о́ить; разраб|а́тывать, -о́тать.
v.i. **1.** (*unfold*) разв|ива́ться, -и́ться; разв|ёртываться, -ерну́ться; превра|ща́ться, -ти́ться; **London ~ed into a great city** Ло́ндон разро́сся в большо́й го́род. **2.** (*come to light*) выясня́ться, вы́ясниться.

developer [dɪ'veləpə(r)] *n.*: **1.: he was a late ~** он по́здно разви́лся. **2.** (*phot., substance*) прояви́тель (*m.*). **3.** (*builder*) застро́йщик.

development [dɪ'veləpmənt] *n.* **1.** (*unfolding*) разви́тие, рост. **2.** (*event*) собы́тие, обстоя́тельство. **3.** (*of land etc.*) разви́тие (райо́на); (*building*) застро́йка.

deviant ['di:vɪənt] *adj.* отклоня́ющийся от но́рмы

deviate ['di:vɪ,eɪt] *v.i.* отклон|я́ться, -и́ться (от+*g.*).

deviation [,di:vɪ'eɪʃ(ə)n] *n.* отклоне́ние, отхо́д.

device [dɪ'vaɪs] *n.* **1.** (*plan, scheme*) план, схе́ма; (*method*) приём; **he was left to his own ~s** он был предоста́влен самому́ себе́. **2.** (*instrument, contrivance*) приспособле́ние, прибо́р.

devil ['dev(ə)l] *n.* **1.** чёрт, дья́вол; **between the ~ and the deep (blue) sea** ме́жду двух огне́й; **go to the ~!** иди́ к чёрту!; **~ take it!** чёрт побери́!; **talk of the ~!** лёгок на поми́не; **he has the ~'s own luck** ему чёрто́вски везёт. **2.** (*wretched person*): **poor ~!** бедня́га! **3.** (*as expletive*): **what the ~ do you mean?** что вы э́тим хоти́те сказа́ть, чёрт возьми́?; **he ran like the ~** он бежа́л как чёрт; **a ~ of a fellow** отча́янный па́рень; **there'll be the devil to pay** рассчита́ться за э́то бу́дет нелегко́.
cpd. **~-may-care** *adj.* бесшаба́шный, разуда́лый.

devilish ['devəlɪʃ] *adj.* дья́вольский.
adv. (*coll.*) черто́вски.

devilment ['devəlmənt] *n.* прока́зы (*f. pl.*), чертовщи́на.

devious ['di:vıəs] *adj.* (*lit.*) окóльный; (*fig.*) лукáвый, неискренний.
devise [dı'vaız] *v.t.* (*think out*) придýм|ывать, -ать; изобре|тáть, -сти́.
devoid [dı'vɔıd] *adj.* лишённый; **~ of shame** бесстыдный; **~ of fear** бесстрáшный.
devolution [,di:və'lu:ʃ(ə)n, -'lju:ʃ(ə)n] *n.* (*delegation*) передáча влáсти.
devolve [dı'vɒlv] *v.t.* (*delegate*) перед|авáть, -áть.
v.i. пере|ходи́ть, -йти́; **the work ~d on me** рабóта свалилась на меня́.
devote [dı'vəʊt] *v.t.* посвя|щáть, -ти́ть; **she is ~d to her children** онá прéдана свои́м дéтям; онá всю себя́ отдаёт дéтям; **a ~d friend** прéданный друг.
devotee [,devə'ti:] *n.* привéрженец.
devotion [dı'vəʊʃ(ə)n] *n.* **1.** (*being devoted*) прéданность. **2.** (*love*) прéданность, привя́занность. **3.** (*pl., prayers*) моли́твы (*f. pl.*).
devour [dı'vaʊə(r)] *v.t.* **1.** (*eat greedily*) пож|ирáть, -рáть. **2.** (*fig.*) погло|щáть, -ти́ть; **she ~ed his story** онá жáдно слýшала егó расскáз; **he ~ed the book** он проглоти́л кни́гу.
devout [dı'vaʊt] *adj.* (*religious*) благочести́вый; (*devoted*) прéданный.
dew [dju:] *n.* росá.
cpds. **~berry** *n.* ежеви́ка (*collect.*); я́года ежеви́ки; **~drop** *n.* роси́нка.
dewlap ['dju:læp] *n.* подгрýдок.
dewy ['dju:ı] *adj.* роси́стый.
cpd. **~-eyed** *adj.* (*fig.*) с неви́нным взгля́дом; простодýшный.
dexterity [dek'sterıtı] *n.* лóвкость, провóрство.
dext(e)rous ['dekstrəs] *adj.* лóвкий, провóрный.
diabetes [,daıə'bi:ti:z] *n.* диабéт; сáхарная болéзнь.
diabetic [,daıə'betık] *n.* диабéтик.
adj. диабети́ческий.
diabolic(al) [,daıə'bɒlık(l)] *adj.* дья́вольский.
diacritic [,daıə'krıtık] *n. & adj.* диакрити́ческий (знак).
diadem ['daıə,dem] *n.* (*crown*) диадéма; (*wreath*) венóк, венéц.
diaeresis [daı'ıərəsıs] *n.* диерéза.
diagnose ['daıəg,nəʊz] *v.t.* стáвить, по- диáгноз *+g*; диагности́ровать (*impf., pf.*); **he ~d (the illness as) cancer** он установи́л, что у больнóго рак.
diagnosis [,daıəg'nəʊsıs] *n.* диáгноз; **make a ~** стáвить, по- диáгноз.
diagnostic [,daıəg'nɒstık] *adj.* диагности́ческий.
diagnostician [,daıəgnɒ'stıʃ(ə)n] *n.* диагнóст.
diagnostics [,daıəg'nɒstıks] *n.* диагнóстика.
diagonal [daı'ægən(ə)l] *n.* диагонáль.
adj. диагонáльный; **~ly** по диагонáли.
diagram ['daıə,græm] *n.* диагрáмма, схéма.
diagrammatic [,daıəgrə'mætık] *adj.* схемати́ческий.
dial ['daı(ə)l] *n.* **1.** (*of clock*) цифербла́т. **2.** (*of radio etc.*) шкалá. **3.** (*of telephone*) диск.
v.t. & i.: **~ a number** наб|ирáть, -рáть нóмер.
dialect ['daıə,lekt] *n.* диалéкт, нарéчие, гóвор.
dialectal [,daıə'lekt(ə)l] *adj.* диалéктный.
dialectic(s) [,daıə'lektıks] *n.* диалéктика.
adj. (*also* **-al**) диалекти́ческий.
dialogue ['daıə,lɒg] *n.* диалóг, разговóр.
diameter [daı'æmıtə(r)] *n.* диáметр; **two feet in ~** два фýта диáметром.
diametric(al) [,daıə'metrık(ə)l] *adj.* диаметрáльный.
diamond ['daıəmənd] *n.* **1.** (*precious stone*) алмáз. **2.** (*geom.*) ромб. **3.** (*at cards*) бýб|ны (*pl., g.* -ён); **the queen of ~s** бубнóвая дáма. **4.** (*attr.*) алмáзный; бриллиáнтовый; **~ mine** алмáзная копь; **~ ring** бриллиáнтовое кольцó.
diaper ['daıəpə(r)] *n.* (*baby's napkin*) пелёнка.
diaphanous [daı'æfənəs] *adj.* прозрáчный, просвéчивающий.
diaphragm ['daıə,fræm] *n.* **1.** (*anat.*) диафрáгма. **2.** (*of camera lens*) перегорóдка. 3. (*of telephone receiver*) мембрáна.
diarrhoea [,daıə'rıə] *n.* понóс; расстрóйство желýдка; **he got over his ~** егó закрепи́ло.
diary ['daıərı] *n.* (*journal*) дневни́к; (*engagement book*) календáрь (*m.*).
diaspora [daı'æspərə] *n.* диáспора, рассéяние.
diatonic [,daıə'tɒnık] *adj.* диатони́ческий.
diatribe ['daıə,traıb] *n.* диатри́ба.
dice [daıs] *n.* (*see also* **die**) (*cube*) игрáльные кóсти (*f. pl.*); (*game of ~*) игрá в кóсти.
v.t. & i. **1.** (*play at ~*) игрáть (*impf.*) в кóсти. **2.** (*cul.*) нар|езáть, -éзать кýбиками.
dicey ['daısı] *adj.* (*sl.*) рискóванный.
dichotomy [daı'kɒtəmı] *n.* дихотоми́я, раздвóенность.
dickens ['dıkınz] *n.* (*coll.*) чёрт; **what the ~ are you up to?** что вы замышля́ете, чёрт возьми́?
dicky[1] ['dıkı] *n.* (*shirt-front*) мани́шка.
dicky[2] ['dıkı] *adj.* (*coll.*) слáбый; (*unstable*) шáткий, нетвёрдый.
Dictaphone ['dıktə,fəʊn] *n.* (*propr.*) диктофóн.
dictate[1] ['dıkteıt] *n.* велéние.
dictate[2] [dık'teıt] *v.t. & i.* (*recite, specify, command*) диктовáть, про-; **I won't be ~d to** я не позвóлю стáвить мне услóвия.
dictation [dık'teıʃ(ə)n] *n.* **1.** (*to secretary, class etc.*) диктáнт, диктóвка; **take ~** писáть (*impf.*) под диктóвку. **2.** (*orders*) предписáние; **I did it at his ~** я сдéлал э́то по егó прикáзу.
dictator [dık'teıtə(r)] *n.* диктáтор.
dictatorial [,dıktə'tɔ:rıəl] *adj.* диктáторский.
dictatorship [dık'teıtəʃıp] *n.* диктатýра.
diction ['dıkʃ(ə)n] *n.* ди́кция.
dictionary ['dıkʃənrı, -nərı] *n.* словáрь (*m.*); **a walking ~** ходя́чая энциклопéдия.
dictum ['dıktəm] *n.* изречéние, афори́зм.
didactic [daı'dæktık, dı-] *adj.* поучи́тельный, дидакти́ческий.
didacticism [daı'dæktı,sız(ə)m, dı-] *n.* дидакти́зм.
die[1] [daı] *n.* (*cf.* **dice**) игрáльная кость; **the ~ is cast** жрéбий брóшен; **straight as a ~** (*fig.*) прямóй, чéстный.
die[2] [daı] *n.* (*engraving stamp*) штамп.
die[3] [daı] *v.i.* **1.** (*of pers.*) ум|ирáть, -eréть; скончáться (*pf.*); ги́бнуть, по-; (*of animals*) сд|ыхáть, -óхнуть; (*of plants*) ув|ядáть, -я́нуть; вя́нуть, за-; **he ~d a beggar** он ýмер ни́щим; **never say ~!** никогдá не отчáивайся!; **old habits ~ hard** стáрые привы́чки живýчи; **he ~d by violence** он ýмер наси́льственной смéртью. **2.** (*fig.*): **I'm dying to see him** я ужáсно хочý егó ви́деть; **we ~d of laughing** мы умирáли сó смеху. **3.** (*of things*): **his anger ~d** егó гнев ути́х; **the wind ~d** вéтер зати́х; **the engine ~d** мотóр заглóх.
with advs.: **~ away** (*of sound*) зам|ирáть, -ерéть; (*of feeling etc.*) ум|ирáть. -ерéть; **~ down** (*of fire*) уг|асáть, -áснуть; (*of noise*) ут|ихáть, -и́хнуть; (*of feeling*) ум|ирáть. -ерéть; **~ off** умирáть (*impf.*) оди́н за други́м; **~ out** вымирáть, вы́мереть; **the dinosaur ~d out** динозáвры вы́мерли; **the belief ~d out** э́то повéрье óтмерло.
cpds. **~hard** *n.* догмáтик; *adj.* твердолóбый.
diesel ['di:z(ə)l] *n.* (**~ engine, motor**) ди́зель (*m.*); **~ locomotive** тепловóз; **~ oil** ди́зельное тóпливо.
diet ['daıət] *n.* **1.** (*customary food*) пи́ща, стол. **2.** (*medical régime*) диéта; **he is on a ~** он на диéте; **put s.o. on a ~** посади́ть (*pf.*) когó-н. на диéту.
v.t. & i. соблюдáть (*impf.*) диéту; быть (*impf.*) на диéте.
diet|ary ['daıətrı], **-etic** [,daıə'tetık] *adjs.* диети́ческий.
dietetics [,daıə'tetıks] *n.* диетéтика.
dietitian [,daıə'tıʃ(ə)n] *n.* диетврáч.

differ ['dɪfə(r)] *v.i.* **1.** (*be different*) отличáться (*impf.*); различáться (*impf.*); **we ~ in our tastes** нáши вкýсы различны; **tastes ~** (*prov.*) о вкýсах не спóрят; **they ~ in size** они различáются размéром. **2.** (*disagree*) ра|сходи́ться, -зойти́сь во мнéниях; **I ~ed with him** я с ним не согласи́лся; **I beg to ~** я позвóлю себé не согласи́ться.

difference ['dɪfrəns] *n.* **1.** (*state of being unlike*) отли́чие, рáзница; **that makes all the ~** в э́том вся рáзница; **it makes no ~ whether you go or not** совершéнно безразли́чно, идёте вы и́ли нет. **2.** (*extent of inequality*) рáзница; (*math.*) рáзность; **I will pay the ~** я доплачý рáзницу. **3.** (*dispute*) разноглáсие, спор.

different ['dɪfrənt] *adj.* **1.** (*unlike*) рáзный, различный; **that is quite ~** э́то совсéм другóе дéло; **she wears a ~ hat each day** онá кáждый день надевáет нóвую шля́пу; **of ~ kinds** рáзного рóда; **he became a ~ person** он стал други́м человéком; **~ from** непохóжий на+*a.*; отли́чный от+*g.*; **everyone gave him a ~ answer** все отвечáли емý по-рáзному. **2.** (*unusual*) необы́чный. **3.** (*various*) различный, рáзный; **we talked of ~ things** мы говори́ли о рáзных вещáх; **at ~ times** в рáзное врéмя.

differential [ˌdɪfə'renʃ(ə)l] *n.* **1.** (*difference in wage-rates*) дифференци́рованная оплáта трудá. **2.** (*of a car etc.; also* **~ gear**) дифференциáл.

adj. дифференциáльный.

differentiate [ˌdɪfə'renʃɪˌeɪt] *v.t.* **1.** (*constitute difference*) отлич|áть, и́ть. **2.** (*perceive difference*) различ|áть, -и́ть. **3.** (*make, point out difference*) дéлать, с- различие.

v.i. (*become different*) различ|áться, -и́ться; отлич|áться, -и́ться.

differentiation [ˌdɪfərenʃɪ'eɪʃ(ə)n] *n.* **1.** (*change*) видоизменéние. **2.** (*act of distinguishing*) различéние. **3.** (*discrimination*) дифференциáция.

differently ['dɪfrəntlɪ] *adv.* по-другóму; инáче.

difficult ['dɪfɪkəlt] *adj.* трýдный (*also of pers.*); **a ~ child** трудновоспитýемый ребёнок; **he is ~ to please** емý трýдно угоди́ть; **~ of access** недостýпный.

difficult|y ['dɪfɪkəltɪ] *n.* трýдность, затруднéние; **I have ~y in understanding him** я с трудóм егó понимáю; **we ran into ~ies** мы столкнýлись с трýдностями; **he is in financial ~ies** он испы́тывает материáльные затруднéния.

diffidence ['dɪfɪdəns] *n.* застéнчивость; стесни́тельность.

diffident ['dɪfɪd(ə)nt] *adj.* застéнчивый, стесни́тельный.

diffuse[1] [dɪ'fju:s] *adj.* (*of light etc.*) рассéянный.

diffuse[2] [dɪ'fju:z] *v.t.* (*light etc.*) рассé|ивать, -ять; **~d lighting** рассéянный свет; (*learning etc.*) распростран|я́ть, -и́ть.

v.i. рассé|иваться, -яться; распростран|я́ться, -и́ться.

diffusion [dɪ'fju:ʒ(ə)n] *n.* (*phys.*) диффýзия, рассéивание; распространéние.

dig [dɪg] *n.* **1.** (*thrust, poke*) толчóк; **~ in the ribs** толчóк в бок. **2.** (*fig.*) шпи́лька; **that remark was a ~ at me** э́то замечáние — кáмешек в мой огорóд. **3.** (*archaeol. site, expedition*) раскóпки (*f. pl.*); **we went on a ~** мы вы́ехали на раскóпки. **4.** (*pl., coll., lodgings*) кварти́ра, «берлóга».

v.t. & i. **1.** (*excavate ground*) коп|áть, -нýть; рыть, вы́-; **they are ~ging potatoes** они́ копáют картóшку; **he dug a hole** он вы́рыл я́му; **~ging for gold** они́ и́щут зóлото. **2.** (*fig.*) отк|áпывать, -опáть; **he dug into the archives** он зары́лся в архи́вы. **3.** (*thrust*) толк|áть, -нýть; **he dug me in the ribs** он толкнýл меня́ в бок; **he dug his fork into the pie** он вонзи́л ви́лку в пирóг.

with advs.: **~ in** *v.t.* зак|áпывать, -опáть; **the soldiers dug (themselves) in** солдáты окопáлись; **~ out** *v.t.* выкáпывать, вы́копать; **victims of the accident were dug out** жéртвы катастрóфы бы́ли откры́ты; **~ up** *v.t.* отк|áпывать, -опáть; **they dug up the land** они́ вскопáли зéмлю; **they dug up an ancient statue** они́ вы́рыли дрéвнюю стáтую; **where did you ~ him up?** (*fig.*) где вы егó откопáли?

digest[1] ['daɪdʒest] *n.* компéндиум, резюмé (*indecl.*).

digest[2] [daɪ'dʒest, dɪ-] *v.t.* (*food*) перевáр|ивать, -и́ть; (*information etc.*) усв|áивать, -óить.

v.i. перевáр|иваться, -и́ться.

digestible [daɪ'dʒestɪb(ə)l, dɪ-] *adj.* удобовари́мый.

digestion [daɪ'dʒestʃ(ə)n] *n.* пищеварéние.

digestive [dɪ'dʒestɪv, daɪ-] *adj.* пищевари́тельный.

digger ['dɪgə(r)] *n.* копáтель (*m.*); землекóп.

digging ['dɪgɪŋ] *n.* (*action*) рытьё, копáние.

digit ['dɪdʒɪt] *n.* (*finger or toe*) пáлец; (*numeral*) ци́фра.

digital ['dɪdʒɪt(ə)l] *adj.* цифровóй; **~ clock** цифровы́е/электрóнные часы́ (*pl., g.* -óв).

digitalis [ˌdɪdʒɪ'teɪlɪs] *n.* дигитáлис, наперстя́нка.

dignified ['dɪgnɪˌfaɪd] *adj.* пóлный достóинства; величáвый.

dignify ['dɪgnɪˌfaɪ] *v.t.* облагор|áживать, -óдить; величáть (*impf.*).

dignitary ['dɪgnɪtərɪ] *n.* санóвник; высокопостáвленное лицó.

dignity ['dɪgnɪtɪ] *n.* **1.** (*worth*) достóинство; **it is beneath my ~ to reply** отвечáть на э́то — ни́же моегó достóинства. **2.** (*dignified behaviour*): **keep one's ~** сохран|я́ть, -и́ть своё достóинство.

digress [daɪ'gres] *v.i.* отвл|екáться, -éчься; отклон|я́ться, -и́ться.

digression [daɪ'greʃ(ə)n] *n.* отклонéние, отступлéние.

dike, dyke [daɪk] *n.* (*ditch*) ров, канáва; (*embankment*) дáмба.

diktat ['dɪktæt] *n.* дикт́ат.

dilapidated [dɪ'læpɪˌdeɪtɪd] *adj.* вéтхий, полуразрýшенный.

dilate [daɪ'leɪt] *v.t.* расш|иря́ть, -и́рить.

v.i. расш|иря́ться, -и́риться; распростран|я́ться, -и́ться; **his eyes ~d** егó глазá расши́рились.

dilat|ion [daɪ'leɪʃ(ə)n] *n.* расширéние.

dilatory ['dɪlətərɪ] *adj.* замедля́ющий, медли́тельный.

dilemma [daɪ'lemə, dɪ-] *n.* дилéмма; **he is on the horns of a ~** он стои́т пéред дилéммой.

dilettante [ˌdɪlɪ'tæntɪ] *n.* дилетáнт.

adj. дилетáнтский.

dilettantism [ˌdɪlɪ'tæntɪz(ə)m] *n.* дилетáнтство.

diligence ['dɪlɪdʒ(ə)ns] *n.* (*zeal*) прилежáние, усéрдие, старáтельность.

diligent ['dɪlɪdʒ(ə)nt] *adj.* прилéжный, усéрдный, старáтельный.

dill [dɪl] *n.* укрóп; **~ pickle** маринóванный огурéц.

dilly-dally [ˌdɪlɪ'dælɪ] *v.i.* (*coll.*) мéшкать (*impf.*); колебáться (*impf.*).

dilute ['daɪlju:t] *adj.* разбáвленный; разведённый.

v.t. разв|оди́ть, -ести́; разб|авля́ть, -áвить.

dilution [daɪ'lju:ʃ(ə)n] *n.* разведéние, разбавлéние.

dim [dɪm] *adj.* (*of light etc.*) тýсклый; (*of memory etc.*) смýтный; (*of eyes*) слáбый, затумáненный; (*coll., stupid*) тупóй; **I take a ~ view of it** (*coll.*) я смотрю́ на э́то неодобри́тельно.

v.t. затумáни|вать, -ть; **~ one's headlights** перейти́ (*pf.*) на «мáлый» свет.

v.i. затумáни|ваться, -ться; тускнéть, по-.

cpds. (*coll.*): **~wit** *n.* тупи́ца (*c.g.*); **~-witted** *adj.* тупоýмный.

dime [daɪm] *n.* десятицéнтовик.

dimension [daɪ'menʃ(ə)n, dɪ-] *n.* **1.** (*extent*) размéр; (*capacity*) объём. **2.** (*direction of measurement*) измерéние; **the fourth ~** четвёртое измерéние.

diminish [dɪ'mɪnɪʃ] *v.t.* ум|еньшáть, -éньшить; **~ed**

responsibility (*leg.*) ограни́ченная уголо́вная отве́тственность; **law of ~ing returns** зако́н сокраща́ющихся дохо́дов.

v.i. ум|еньша́ться, -е́ньшиться.

diminuendo [dɪˌmɪnjʊ'endəʊ] *n. & adv.* диминуэ́ндо (*indecl.*).

diminution [ˌdɪmɪ'nju:ʃ(ə)n] *n.* уменьше́ние.

diminutive [dɪ'mɪnjʊtɪv] *n.* (*gram.*) уменьши́тельное сло́во.

adj. (*small*) миниатю́рный.

dimness ['dɪmnɪs] *n.* (*of light*) ту́склость; (*of wit*) ту́пость.

dimple ['dɪmp(ə)l] *n.* я́мочка.

din [dɪn] *n.* гро́хот, галдёж.

v.t. вд|а́лбливать, -олби́ть; **he ~ned it into me that I must obey** он вда́лбливал мне в го́лову, что я до́лжен подчини́ться.

din|e [daɪn] *v.i.* обе́дать, по- (**on, off:** *чем*); у́жинать, по-; **~ing-car** ваго́н-рестора́н; **~ing-hall** обе́денный зал, столо́вая; **~ing-room** столо́вая; **~ing-table** обе́денный стол.

diner ['daɪnə(r)] *n.* (*pers.*) обе́дающий, у́жинающий; (*dining-car*) ваго́н-рестора́н.

ding-dong ['dɪŋdɒŋ] *adj.*: **a ~ battle** би́тва с переме́нным успе́хом.

dinghy ['dɪŋɪ, 'dɪŋgɪ] *n.* я́лик; (*inflatable*) надувна́я ло́дка.

dingy ['dɪndʒɪ] *adj.* гря́зный, тёмный, мра́чный.

dinner ['dɪnə(r)] *n.* обе́д; (*evening meal*) у́жин; **at ~** за у́жином; **ask s.o. to ~** пригла|ша́ть, -си́ть кого́-н. на у́жин; **have ~** у́жинать, по-; **what's for ~?** что на у́жин?

cpds. **~-jacket** *n.* смо́кинг; **~-party** *n.* зва́ный обе́д; **~-plate** *n.* ме́лкая таре́лка; **~-service, ~-set** *nn.* обе́денный серви́з; **~-time** *n.* обе́денное вре́мя; вре́мя у́жина.

dinosaur ['daɪnəˌsɔ:(r)] *n.* диноза́вр.

dint [dɪnt] *n.*: **by ~ of** посре́дством+*g.*; при по́мощи +*g.*

diocese ['daɪəsɪs] *n.* епа́рхия.

diode ['daɪəʊd] *n.* дио́д.

dioxide [daɪ'ɒksaɪd] *n.* двуо́кись.

dip [dɪp] *n.* **1.** (*immersion*) погруже́ние; **lucky ~** лотере́йный бараба́н. **2.** (*bathe*): **have, take a ~** пойти́ (*pf.*) вы́купаться/попла́вать. **3.** (*slope*) спуск, укло́н. **4.** (*cul.*) со́ус.

v.t. **1.** (*immerse*) окун|а́ть, -у́ть; мак|а́ть, -ну́ть; погру|жа́ть, -зи́ть; **~ one's pen into ink** обмак|ивать, -ну́ть перо́ в черни́ла; **~ one's hand into a bag** запусти́ть (*pf.*) ру́ку в су́мку. **2.** (*lower briefly*) приспус|ка́ть, -ти́ть; **~ headlights** переключ|а́ть, -и́ть фа́ры на бли́жний свет.

v.i. **1.** (*go below surface*) окун|а́ться, -у́ться; погру|жа́ться, -зи́ться; **the sun ~ped below the horizon** со́лнце скры́лось за горизо́нтом. **2.** (*fig.*): **~ into one's purse** раскошели|ваться, -ться. **3.** (*slope away*): **the land ~s to the south** уча́сток име́ет накло́н к ю́гу. **4.** (*scan, peer*) загля́|дывать, -ну́ть; **I ~ped into the book** я загляну́л в э́ту кни́гу. **5.** (*fall slightly or temporarily*) пон|ижа́ться, -и́зиться; **the road ~s here** здесь доро́га идёт под укло́н.

cpd. **~-stick** *n.* уровнеме́р, (*coll.*) щуп.

diphtheria [dɪp'θɪərɪə] *n.* дифтери́я, дифтери́т.

diphthong ['dɪfθɒŋ] *n.* дифто́нг.

diploma [dɪ'pləʊmə] *n.* дипло́м (по+*d.*).

diplomacy [dɪp'ləʊməsɪ] *n.* диплома́тия; (*tact*) диплома́ти́чность.

diplomat ['dɪpləˌmæt], **-ist** [dɪ'pləʊmətɪst] *nn.* (*lit., fig.*) диплома́т.

diplomatic [ˌdɪplə'mætɪk] *adj.* (*lit., fig.*) дипломати́ческий; **~ service** дипломати́ческая слу́жба.

dipper ['dɪpə(r)] *n.* **1.** (*ladle*) ковш, черпа́к; **the Big/Little D~** (*astron.*) Больша́я/Ма́лая Медве́дица. **2.** (*bird*) оля́пка. **3.** (*switchback*) америка́нские го́ры (*f. pl.*).

dire ['daɪə(r)] *adj.* ужа́сный; **he is in ~ need of help** он кра́йне нужда́ется в по́мощи.

direct [daɪ'rekt, dɪ-] *adj.* (*straight*; *without intermediary*) прямо́й; (*straightforward*) прямо́й, непосре́дственный; **he has a ~ way of speaking** он говори́т всё пря́мо в лицо́; **the ~ opposite** по́лная противополо́жность; **~ current** постоя́нный ток.

adv. пря́мо.

v.t. **1.** (*indicate the way*): **can you ~ me to the station?** не ска́жете ли вы, как пройти́ на вокза́л? **2.** (*address*) адресова́ть (*impf., pf.*); напр|авля́ть, -а́вить. **3.** (*manage, control*) руководи́ть (*impf.*) +*i.*; **he ~ed the orchestra** он дирижи́ровал орке́стром; **he ~ed the play** он поста́вил пье́су; **the policeman ~s traffic** полице́йский регули́рует движе́ние. **4.** (*command*) предпи́с|ывать, -а́ть; да|ва́ть, -ть указа́ние.

direction [daɪ'rekʃ(ə)n, dɪ-] *n.* **1.** (*course, point of compass*) направле́ние; **he went in the ~ of London** он напра́вился к Ло́ндону; **they dispersed in all ~s** они́ разошли́сь по всем направле́ниям; **he has a good sense of ~** он хорошо́ ориенти́руется. **2.** (*pl., instructions*) указа́ния (*nt. pl.*); **I followed the ~s on the label** я сле́довал указа́ниям на ярлыке́. **3.** (*command, control*) руково́дство. **4.** (*theatr.*): **~ of a play** режиссу́ра пье́сы; **stage ~** а́вторская рема́рка.

cpd. **~-finder** *n.* радиопеленга́тор.

directional [daɪ'rekʃən(ə)l, dɪ-] *adj.*: **~ radio** радиопеленга́ция; **~ transmitter** радиопеленга́торная ста́нция.

directive [daɪ'rektɪv, dɪ-] *n.* директи́ва, указа́ние.

directly [daɪ'rektlɪ, dɪ-] *adv.* **1.** (*in var. senses of direct*) пря́мо. **2.** (*soon*): **I'll be there ~** я вскоре/сейча́с там бу́ду. **3.** (*at once*) неме́дленно, то́тчас.

conj. как то́лько.

directness [daɪ'rektnɪs, dɪ-] *n.* прямота́, открове́нность.

director [daɪ'rektə(r), dɪ-] *n.* **1.** (*one who directs*) руководи́тель (*m.*). **2.** (*of company etc.*) дире́ктор; **managing ~** управля́ющий. **3.** (*theatr.*) режиссёр.

directorate [daɪ'rektərət, dɪ-] *n.* (*group of directors*) директора́т; (*admin. body*) управле́ние.

directorial [ˌdaɪrek'tɔ:rɪəl, ˌdɪ-] *adj.* дире́кторский.

directory [daɪ'rektərɪ, dɪ-] *n.* спра́вочник, указа́тель (*m.*); **~ enquiries** спра́вочная; **telephone ~** телефо́нная кни́га.

dirge [dɜ:dʒ] *n.* погреба́льное пе́ние.

dirigible ['dɪrɪdʒɪb(ə)l, dɪ'rɪdʒ-] *n.* дирижа́бль (*m.*).

dirt [dɜ:t] *n.* **1.** (*unclean matter*) грязь; **this dress shows the ~** э́то пла́тье ма́ркое. **2.** (*loose earth or soil*) грунт, земля́; **a ~ road** грунтова́я доро́га.

cpd. **~-cheap** *adv.* деше́вле па́реной ре́пы; малоце́нный; **I bought the radio ~-cheap** я купи́л ра́дио по дешёвке.

dirtiness ['dɜ:tɪnɪs] *n.* грязь, га́дость.

dirty [dɜ:tɪ] *adj.* **1.** (*not clean*) гря́зный. **2.** (*rough, stormy*) бу́рный. **3.** (*obscene*) похá́бный, па́костный; **~ story** похá́бный анекдо́т. **4.** (*nasty*) гря́зный, га́дкий; **he played a ~ trick on me** он подложи́л мне свинью́; **he gave me a ~ look** он серди́то посмотре́л на меня́.

v.t. & i. грязни́ть(ся), за-; па́чкать(ся), за-.

disability [ˌdɪsə'bɪlɪtɪ] *n.* (*inability to work*) нетрудоспосо́бность; (*physical defect*) инвали́дность.

disable [dɪs'eɪb(ə)l] *v.t.* (*physically*) кале́чить, ис-; **~d soldier** инвали́д войны́.

disabuse [ˌdɪsə'bju:z] *v.t.* выводи́ть, вы́вести из заблужде́ния.

disadvantage [ˌdɪsəd'vɑ:ntɪdʒ] *n.* невы́года; невы́годное положе́ние; **be at a ~** ока́з|ываться, -а́ться в невы́годном положе́нии; **put s.o. at a ~** поста́вить (*pf.*) кого́-н. в невы́годное положе́ние.

v.t. де́йствовать (*impf.*) в уще́рб +*d.*
disadvantageous [dɪs,ædvən'teɪdʒəs] *adj.* невы́годный.
disaffected [,dɪsə'fektɪd] *adj.* недово́льный, неблагонаме́ренный.
disagree [,dɪsə'gri:] *v.i.* **1.** (*differ, not correspond*) не соотве́тствовать (*impf.*) (+*d.*). **2.** (*in opinion*) не согла|ша́ться, -си́ться; **I ~ with you** я с ва́ми не согла́сен; **the witnesses ~** свиде́тели расхо́дятся в показа́ниях. **3.** (*have adverse effect*): **oysters ~ with me** я пло́хо переношу́ у́стриц.
disagreeable [,dɪsə'gri:əb(ə)l] *adj.* (*unpleasant*) непри-я́тный; (*of pers.*) неприве́тливый.
disagreement [,dɪsə'gri:mənt] *n.* разногла́сие, несогла́сие.
disallow [,dɪsə'laʊ] *v.t.* (*reject*) отклон|я́ть, -и́ть.
disappear [,dɪsə'pɪə(r)] *v.i.* исч|еза́ть, -е́знуть; проп|ада́ть, -а́сть.
disappearance [,dɪsə'pɪərəns] *n.* исчезнове́ние.
disappoint [,dɪsə'pɔɪnt] *v.t.* разочаро́в|ывать, -а́ть; **he was ~ed at this** он был э́тим разочаро́ван; **I am ~ed in you** я в вас разочарова́лся.
disappointing [,dɪsə'pɔɪntɪŋ] *adj.* разочаро́вывающий.
disappointment [,dɪsə'pɔɪntmənt] *n.* разочарова́ние; **to my ~** к моему́ огорче́нию.
disapproval [,dɪsə'pru:vəl] *n.* неодобре́ние.
disapprove [,dɪsə'pru:v] *v.t. & i.* не од|обря́ть, -о́брить.
disapproving [,dɪsə'pru:vɪŋ] *adj.* неодобри́тельный.
disarm [dɪs'ɑ:m] *v.t.* разоруж|а́ть, -и́ть; (*fig.*) обезору́жи|вать, -ть.
v.i. разоруж|а́ться, -и́ться.
disarmament [dɪs'ɑ:məmənt] *n.* разоруже́ние.
disarrange [,dɪsə'reɪndʒ] *v.t.* прив|оди́ть, -ести́ в беспоря́док.
disarray [,dɪsə'reɪ] *n.* смяте́ние, расстро́йство.
disassemble [,dɪsə'semb(ə)l] *v.t.* раз|бира́ть, -обра́ть.
disassembly [,dɪsə'semblɪ] *n.* разбо́рка.
disassociate [,dɪsə'səʊʃɪ,eɪt, -sɪ,eɪt] = **dissociate**
disaster [dɪ'zɑ:stə(r)] *n.* бе́дствие; **he is courting ~** он накли́кает беду́.
disastrous [dɪ'zɑ:strəs] *adj.* ги́бельный, бе́дственный.
disavow [,dɪsə'vaʊ] *v.t.* дезавуи́ровать (*impf., pf.*); отрица́ть (*impf.*).
disavowal [,dɪsə'vaʊəl] *n.* дезавуи́рование; отрица́ние.
disband [dɪs'bænd] *v.t.* распус|ка́ть, -ти́ть; расформиро́в|ывать, -а́ть.
v.i. разбе|га́ться, -жа́ться; рассе́|иваться, -яться.
disbar [dɪs'bɑ:(r)] *v.t.* лиш|а́ть, -и́ть зва́ния адвока́та.
disbelief [,dɪsbɪ'li:f] *n.* неве́рие.
disbelieve [,dɪsbɪ'li:v] *v.t.* не ве́рить (*impf.*) +*d.* (*or* в+*a.*).
disburse [dɪs'bɜ:s] *v.t.* выпла́чивать, вы́платить.
disbursement [dɪs'bɜ:smənt] *n.* (*act of paying*) опла́та; (*sum paid*) вы́плаченная су́мма.
disc, disk [dɪsk] *n.* **1.** (*round object*) диск; **identification ~** ли́чный знак. **2.** (*gramophone record*) пласти́нка. **3.** (*med.*): **slipped ~** смеще́ние межпозвоно́чного ди́ска. **4.** (*comput.*): **floppy ~** ги́бкий диск; **~ drive** дисково́д, накопи́тель на ди́сках.
cpd. **~-jockey** диск-жоке́й.
discard ['dɪskɑ:d] *v.t.* выбра́сывать, вы́бросить; **~ winter clothing** сбр|а́сывать, -о́сить зи́мнюю оде́жду; **~ old beliefs** отбр|а́сывать, -о́сить ста́рые убежде́ния.
discern [dɪ'sɜ:n] *v.t.* разгля́д|ывать, -е́ть; рассм|а́тривать, -отре́ть; различ|а́ть, -и́ть.
discernible [dɪ,sɜ:n'ɪb(ə)l] *adj.* различи́мый.
discerning [dɪ'sɜ:nɪŋ] *adj.* проница́тельный.
discernment [dɪ'sɜ:nmənt] *n.* проница́тельность.
discharge ['dɪstʃɑ:dʒ, dɪs'tʃɑ:dʒ] *n.* **1.** (*unloading*) разгру́зка. **2.** (*emission of fluid etc.*) выделе́ния (*pl.*); (*elec.*) разря́д. **3.** (*performance, e.g. of duty*) исполне́ние; (*of a debt*) упла́та. **4.** (*release, dismissal*) увольне́ние, освобожде́ние; (*from the army*) демобилиза́ция, увольне́ние. **5.** (*firing of a gun*) вы́стрел, залп.
v.t. **1.** (*unload*) разгру|жа́ть, -зи́ть. **2.** (*emit liquid, current etc.*) спус|ка́ть, -ти́ть; разря|жа́ть, -ди́ть; **the clouds ~ electricity** облака́ разряжа́ются электри́чеством. **3.** (*fire, let fly*) стреля́ть (*impf.*); выстре́ливать, вы́стрелить. **4.** (*release, dismiss*): (*from the army*) демобилизова́ть (*impf., pf.*); (*from hospital*) выпи́сывать, вы́писать; (*from service*) увольня́ть, -о́лить.
disciple [dɪ'saɪp(ə)l] *n.* учени́|к (*fem.* -ца).
disciplinarian [,dɪsɪplɪ'neərɪən] *n.* сторо́нник дисципли́ны.
disciplinary ['dɪsɪplɪnərɪ, -'plɪnərɪ] *adj.* дисциплина́рный.
discipline ['dɪsɪplɪn] *n.* (*good order; branch of studies*) дисципли́на.
v.t. дисциплини́ровать (*impf., pf.*).
disclaim [dɪs'kleɪm] *v.t.* отр|ека́ться, -е́чься от+*g.*; отка́з|ываться, -а́ться от+*g.*
disclaimer [dɪs'kleɪmə(r)] *n.* отрече́ние, отка́з.
disclose [dɪs'kləʊz] *v.t.* раскр|ыва́ть, -ы́ть; разоблач|а́ть, -и́ть; обнару́жи|вать, -ть.
disclosure [dɪs'kləʊʒə(r)] *n.* раскры́тие, разоблаче́ние, обнаруже́ние.
disco ['dɪskəʊ] *n.* (*coll.*) = **discotheque**
discoloration [dɪs,kʌlə'reɪʃ(ə)n] *n.* обесцве́чивание.
discolour [dɪs'kʌlə(r)] *v.t. & i.* обесцве́|чивать(ся), -тить(ся).
discomfit [dɪs'kʌmfɪt] *v.t.* (*disconcert*) сму|ща́ть, -ти́ть; прив|оди́ть, -ести́ в замеша́тельство.
discomfiture [dɪs'kʌmfɪtjə(r)] *n.* смуще́ние, замеша́тельство.
discomfort [dɪs'kʌmfət] *n.* неудо́бство.
discommode [,dɪskə'məʊd] *v.t.* причин|я́ть, -и́ть неудо́бство +*d.*
disconcert [,dɪskən'sɜ:t] *v.t.* (*agitate*) волнова́ть, вз-; (*disturb*) расстр|а́ивать, -о́ить.
disconnect [,dɪskə'nekt] *v.t.* разъедин|я́ть, -и́ть; (*gas etc.*) отключ|а́ть, -и́ть; **we were ~ed** (*telephone*) нас разъедини́ли.
disconnected [,dɪskə'nektɪd] *adj.* **1.** (*tech.*) разъединённый, вы́ключенный. **2.** (*ideas etc.*) обры́вочный, бессвя́зный.
disconsolate [dɪs'kɒnsələt] *adj.* неуте́шный.
discontent [,dɪskən'tent] *n.* недово́льство.
discontinue [,dɪskən'tɪnju:] *v.t.* прекра|ща́ть, -ти́ть.
discord ['dɪskɔ:d] *n.* (*disagreement*) разногла́сие; (*disharmony*) разла́д, раздо́р; (*mus.*) диссона́нс.
discordant [dɪ'skɔ:d(ə)nt] *adj.* несогла́сный; (*inharmonious*) диссони́рующий; нестро́йный.
discothèque ['dɪskə,tek] *n.* дискоте́ка.
discount ['dɪskaʊnt] *n.* (*rebate*) ски́дка.
v.t. (*bill of exchange etc.*) дисконти́ровать (*impf., pf.*); (*fig., treat sceptically*) отн|оси́ться, -ести́сь с недове́рием к+*d.*; **I ~ed his story** я не о́чень пове́рил его́ расска́зу.
discourage [dɪ'skʌrɪdʒ] *v.t.* (*deprive of courage*) обескура́жи|вать, -ть; лиш|а́ть, -и́ть му́жества; (*dissuade*) отгов|а́ривать, -ори́ть.
discouragement [dɪ'skʌrɪdʒmənt] *n.* обескура́живание; (*dissuasion*) отгова́ривание.
discourse[1] ['dɪskɔ:s, -'skɔ:s] *n.* речь, рассужде́ние.
discourse[2] [dɪ'skɔ:s] *v.i.* рассужда́ть (*impf.*).
discourteous [dɪs'kɜ:tɪəs] *adj.* неве́жливый.
discourtesy [dɪs'kɜ:təsɪ] *n.* неве́жливость.
discover [dɪ'skʌvə(r)] *v.t.* (*find*) на|ходи́ть, -йти́; откр|ыва́ть, -ы́ть; обнару́жи|вать, -ть; раскр|ыва́ть, -ы́ть; (*find out*) узн|ава́ть, -а́ть.
discoverer [dɪ'skʌvərə(r)] *n.* иссле́дователь (*m.*) (но́вых земе́ль); (перво)открыва́тель (*m.*); **she was the ~ of radium** она́ откры́ла ра́дий.

discovery [dɪ'skʌvərɪ] *n.* откры́тие.
discredit [dɪs'kredɪt] *n.* (*loss of repute*) дискредита́ция; **bring s.o. into ~** (*or* **bring ~ upon s.o.**) компромети́ровать, с- кого́-н.; **he is a ~ to the school** он позо́рит шко́лу.
v.t. дискредити́ровать (*impf.*, *pf.*).
discreet [dɪ'skri:t] *adj.* осмотри́тельный; (*tactful*) такти́чный; **a ~ silence** благоразу́мное молча́ние.
discrepancy [dɪs'krepənsɪ] *n.* расхожде́ние, разногла́сие.
discretion [dɪ'skreʃ(ə)n] *n.* **1.** (*prudence, good judgment*) осмотри́тельность, благоразу́мие; **~ is the better part of valour** благоразу́мие — гла́вное досто́инство хра́брости. **2.** (*freedom to judge*) усмотре́ние; **I leave this to your ~** я оставля́ю э́то на ва́ше усмотре́ние; **at ~** по усмотре́нию; **I gave him wide ~** я дал ему́ широ́кие полномо́чия.
discretionary [dɪ'skreʃənərɪ] *adj.* дискрецио́нный.
discriminate [dɪ'skrɪmɪˌneɪt] *v.t.* (*distinguish*) отлич|а́ть, -и́ть; различ|а́ть, -и́ть.
v.i.: **~ against** дискримини́ровать (*impf.*, *pf.*).
discriminating [dɪ'skrɪmɪˌneɪtɪŋ] *adj.* разбо́рчивый; **~ taste** то́нкий вкус.
discrimination [dɪˌskrɪmɪ'neɪʃ(ə)n] *n.* (*judgment, taste*) разбо́рчивость; (*bias*) дискримина́ция (**against s.o.** кого́-н.).
discriminatory [dɪ'skrɪmɪnətərɪ] *adj.* пристра́стный, дифференциа́льный.
discursive [dɪ'skɜ:sɪv] *adj.* разбро́санный.
discus ['dɪskəs] *n.* диск.
discuss [dɪ'skʌs] *v.t.* обсу|жда́ть, -ди́ть.
discussion [dɪ'skʌʃ(ə)n] *n.* обсужде́ние, диску́ссия; **the question is under ~** вопро́с обсужда́ется.
disdain [dɪs'deɪn] *n.* презре́ние.
v.t. през|ира́ть, -ре́ть; пренебр|ега́ть, -е́чь +*i.*
disdainful [dɪs'deɪnfʊl] *adj.* презри́тельный.
disease [dɪ'zi:z] *n.* боле́знь.
diseased [dɪ'zi:zd] *adj.* (*lit.*, *fig.*) больно́й.
disembark [ˌdɪsɪm'bɑ:k] *v.t.* & *i.* выса́живать(ся), вы́садить(ся); выгружа́ть(ся), вы́грузить(ся).
disembarkation [ˌdɪsɪmbɑ:'keɪʃ(ə)n] *n.* вы́садка, вы́грузка.
disembowel [ˌdɪsɪm'baʊəl] *v.t.* потроши́ть, вы́-.
disenchant [ˌdɪsɪn'tʃɑ:nt] *v.t.* разочаро́в|ывать, -а́ть.
disenchantment [ˌdɪsɪn'tʃɑ:ntmənt] *n.* разочарова́ние.
disengage [ˌdɪsɪn'geɪdʒ] *v.t.* высвобожда́ть, вы́свободить; освобо|жда́ть, -ди́ть.
v.i. высвобожда́ться, вы́свободиться; освобо|жда́ться, -ди́ться; (*mil.*) от|рыва́ться, -орва́ться от проти́вника; выходи́ть, вы́йти из бо́я.
disengagement [ˌdɪsɪn'geɪdʒmənt] *n.* (*disentangling*) освобожде́ние, высвобожде́ние; (*pol.*, *mil.*) вы́ход из бо́я; взаи́мный вы́вод вооружённых сил.
disentangle [ˌdɪsɪn'tæŋg(ə)l] *v.t.* & *i.* распу́т|ывать(ся), -ать(ся); выпу́тывать(ся), вы́путать(ся).
disestablish [ˌdɪsɪ'stæblɪʃ] *v.t.* (*eccl.*) отдел|я́ть, -и́ть (*церковь*) от госуда́рства.
disfavour [dɪs'feɪvə(r)] *n.* неми́лость, опа́ла.
disfigure [dɪs'fɪgə(r)] *v.t.* уро́довать, из-; обезобра́|живать, -зить.
disfigurement [dɪs'fɪgərmənt] *n.* уро́дство.
disfranchise [dɪs'fræntʃaɪz] *v.t.* лиш|а́ть, -и́ть избира́тельного пра́ва.
disgorge [dɪs'gɔ:dʒ] *v.t.* изв|ерга́ть, -е́ргнуть.
disgrace [dɪs'greɪs] *n.* (*loss of respect*) бесче́стье, позо́р; **bring ~ upon, bring into ~** навл|ека́ть, -е́чь позо́р на+*a.* **2.** (*disfavour*) неми́лость, опа́ла; **he is in ~** он в неми́лости.
v.t. позо́рить, о-; (*dismiss with ignominy*) разжа́ловать (*pf.*); (*bring shame upon*): **he ~d the family name** он покры́л позо́ром свою́ семью́.
disgraceful [dɪs'greɪsfʊl] *adj.* позо́рный, недосто́йный.
disgruntled [dɪs'grʌnt(ə)ld] *adj.* недово́льный; в дурно́м настрое́нии.
disguise [dɪs'gaɪz] *n.* **1.** (*clothing*) маскиро́вка; **in the ~ of a beggar** переоде́тый ни́щим. **2.** (*concealment*) маскиро́вка, личи́на.
v.t. маскирова́ть, за-; переод|ева́ть, -е́ть; **he ~d his voice** он измени́л го́лос; (*fig.*): **he ~d his feelings** он скрыл свои́ чу́вства; **there is no disguising the fact that ...** для вся́кого очеви́дно, что...
disgust [dɪs'gʌst] *n.* отвраще́ние.
v.t. внуш|а́ть, -и́ть отвраще́ние +*d.*
disgusting [dɪs'gʌstɪŋ] *adj.* отврати́тельный.
dish [dɪʃ] *n.* **1.** (*vessel*) посу́да, блю́до; **wash, do the ~es** мыть, вы́- посу́ду. **2.** (*contents*) блю́до.
v.t. (*serve*; *also* **~ up**) под|ава́ть, -а́ть к столу́; **~ out** (*food*) ра|скла́дывать, -зложи́ть (*еду*) по таре́лкам; выкла́дывать, вы́ложить (*еду*) на блю́до.
cpds. **~-cloth, ~-towel** *nn.* ку́хонное/посу́дное полоте́нце; **~-washer** *n.* (*fem.*) судомо́йка; (*machine*) посудомо́ечная маши́на; **~-water** *n.* помо́|и (*pl.*, *g.* -ев).
disharmony [dɪs'hɑ:mənɪ] *n.* дисгармо́ния, разла́д, разногла́сие.
dishearten [dɪs'hɑ:t(ə)n] *v.t.* прив|оди́ть, -ести́ в уны́ние; **I was ~ed** я упа́л ду́хом.
dishevelled [dɪ'ʃev(ə)ld] *adj.* взъеро́шенный, всклоко́ченный, растрёпанный.
dishonest [dɪs'ɒnɪst] *adj.* нече́стный.
dishonesty [dɪs'ɒnɪstɪ] *n.* нече́стность.
dishonour [dɪs'ɒnə(r)] *n.* бесче́стье, позо́р.
v.t. бесче́стить, о-; позо́рить, о-; **~ one's promise** не сдержа́ть (*pf.*) обеща́ния; (*comm.*): **~ a bill** отка́з|ывать, -а́ть в акце́пте ве́кселя.
dishonourable [dɪs'ɒnərəb(ə)l] *adj.* бесче́стный.
disillusion [ˌdɪsɪ'lu:ʒ(ə)n, -'lju:ʒ(ə)n] *v.t.* разочаро́в|ывать, -а́ть; разр|уша́ть, -у́шить иллю́зии +*g.*
disillusionment [ˌdɪsɪ'lu:ʒənmənt, -'lju:ʒənmənt] *n.* разочарова́ние; утра́та иллю́зий.
disincentive [ˌdɪsɪn'sentɪv] *n.* сде́рживающее обстоя́тельство.
disinclination [ˌdɪsɪnklɪ'neɪʃ(ə)n] *n.* нежела́ние, неохо́та.
disincline [ˌdɪsɪn'klaɪn] *v.t.* отб|ива́ть, -и́ть чью-н. охо́ту к+*d.*; **he was ~d to help me** ему́ не хоте́лось мне помо́чь.
disinfect [ˌdɪsɪn'fekt] *v.t.* дезинфици́ровать (*impf.*, *pf.*); обеззара́|живать, -зить.
disinfectant [ˌdɪsɪn'fekt(ə)nt] *n.* дезинфици́рующее сре́дство.
disinfection [ˌdɪsɪn'fekʃ(ə)n] *n.* дезинфе́кция.
disinformation [ˌdɪsɪnfə'meɪʃ(ə)n] *n.* дезинформа́ция.
disingenuous [ˌdɪsɪn'dʒenjʊəs] *adj.* неи́скренний.
disinherit [ˌdɪsɪn'herɪt] *v.t.* лиш|а́ть, -и́ть насле́дства.
disinheritance [ˌdɪsɪn'herɪtəns] *n.* лише́ние насле́дства.
disintegrate [dɪs'ɪntɪˌgreɪt] *v.i.* расп|ада́ться, -а́сться.
disintegration [dɪsˌɪntɪ'greɪʃ(ə)n] *n.* распа́д.
disinter [ˌdɪsɪn'tɜ:(r)] *v.t.* эксгуми́ровать (*impf.*, *pf.*).
disinterest [dɪs'ɪntrɪst] *n.* **1.** (*lack of bias*) беспристра́стие. **2.** (*lack of self-interest*) бескоры́стие. 3. (*lack of concern*) безуча́стность.
disinterested [dɪs'ɪntrɪstɪd] *adj.* **1.** (*unprejudiced*) беспристра́стный. **2.** (*not self-seeking*) бескоры́стный.
disjointed [dɪs'dʒɔɪntɪd] *adj.* (*fig.*) бессвя́зный, несвя́зный.
disk [dɪsk] = **disc**
diskette [dɪ'sket] *n.* (*comput.*) диске́т.
dislikable [dɪs'laɪkəb(ə)l] *adj.* неприя́тный, антипати́чный.
dislike [dɪs'laɪk] *n.* нелюбо́вь, нерасположе́ние, антипа́тия; **I took a ~ to him** я невзлюби́л его́.
v.t. не люби́ть (*impf.*) +*g.*; **I ~ having to go** мне

неохо́та идти́; **he made himself ~d** он вы́звал к себе́ неприя́знь.

dislocate [ˈdɪslə,keɪt] *v.t.* вы́вихнуть (*pf.*).

dislocation [,dɪsləˈkeɪʃ(ə)n] *n.* вы́вих; наруше́ние.

dislodge [dɪsˈlɒdʒ] *v.t.* сме|ща́ть, -сти́ть; (*evict*) выбива́ть, вы́бить; вытесня́ть, вы́теснить.

disloyal [dɪsˈlɔɪəl] *adj.* нелоя́льный.

disloyalty [dɪsˈlɔɪəltɪ] *n.* нелоя́льность.

dismal [ˈdɪzm(ə)l] *adj.* мра́чный, уны́лый.

dismantle [dɪsˈmænt(ə)l] *v.t.* (*strip of defences etc.*) демонти́ровать (*impf., pf.*); (*take to pieces*) раз|бира́ть, -обра́ть.

dismay [dɪsˈmeɪ] *n.* смяте́ние, потрясе́ние.

v.t. прив|оди́ть, -ести́ в смяте́ние; потрясти́ (*pf.*).

dismember [dɪsˈmembə(r)] *v.t.* расчлен|я́ть, -и́ть.

dismemberment [dɪsˈmembəmənt] *n.* расчлене́ние.

dismiss [dɪsˈmɪs] *v.t.* **1.** (*send away*) распус|ка́ть, -ти́ть; отпус|ка́ть, -ти́ть. **2.** (*discharge from service*) ув|ольня́ть, -о́лить; прог|оня́ть, -на́ть. **3.** (*put out of consideration, reject*): **he ~ed it from his mind** он вы́бросил э́то из головы́; **I ~ed the idea** я оста́вил э́ту мысль. **4.** (*leg.*): (*a case*) прекра|ща́ть, -ти́ть; (*an appeal*) отклон|я́ть, -и́ть.

dismissal [dɪsˈmɪsəl] *n.* ро́спуск; (*from service*) увольне́ние.

dismissive [dɪsˈmɪsɪv] *adj.* (*contemptuous*) презри́тельный.

dismount [dɪsˈmaʊnt] *v.i.* (*from horse*) спе́ши|ваться, -ться; (*from vehicle etc.*) сходи́ть, сойти́.

disobedience [,dɪsəˈbiːdɪəns] *n.* неповинове́ние, непослуша́ние.

disobedient [,dɪsəˈbiːdɪənt] *adj.* непослу́шный.

disobey [,dɪsəˈbeɪ] *v.t.* не слу́шаться, по- +*g.*; не повинова́ться (*impf., pf.*) +*d.*

disorder [dɪsˈɔːdə(r)] *n.* (*untidiness*) беспоря́док; (*confusion*) расстро́йство; (*riot*) беспоря́дки (*m. pl.*); (*med.*) расстро́йство; **mental ~** психи́ческое наруше́ние.

v.t. расстр|а́ивать, -о́ить; прив|оди́ть, -ести́ в беспоря́док.

disorderly [dɪsˈɔːdəlɪ] *adj.* (*untidy*) беспоря́дочный; (*unruly*) бу́йный; **~ conduct** хулига́нство.

disorganization [dɪs,ɔːgənaɪˈzeɪʃ(ə)n] *n.* дезорганиза́ция.

disorganize [dɪsˈɔːgə,naɪz] *v.t.* дезорганизова́ть (*impf., pf.*).

disorient(ate) [dɪsˈɔːrɪən,teɪt] *v.t.* дезориенти́ровать (*impf., pf.*).

disorientation [dɪs,ɔːrɪənˈteɪʃ(ə)n] *n.* дезориента́ция.

disown [dɪsˈəʊn] *v.t.* отка́з|ываться, -а́ться от+*g.*; отр|ека́ться, -е́чься от+*g.*

disparage [dɪˈspærɪdʒ] *v.t.* (*belittle*) преум|еньша́ть, -е́ньшить; говори́ть (*impf.*) с пренебреже́нием о+*p.*

disparagement [dɪˈspærɪdʒmənt] *n.* преуменьше́ние.

disparaging [dɪˈspærɪdʒɪŋ] *adj.* пренебрежи́тельный.

disparate [ˈdɪspərət] *adj.* разнообра́зный, несоотве́тственный.

disparity [dɪˈspærɪtɪ] *n.* расхожде́ние, несоотве́тствие.

dispassionate [dɪˈspæʃənət] *adj.* бесстра́стный.

dispatch, despatch [dɪˈspætʃ] *n.* **1.** (*sending off*) отпра́вка. **2.** (*message*) депе́ша, донесе́ние. **3.** (*promptitude*) быстрота́.

v.t. **1.** (*send off*) отпр|авля́ть, -а́вить. **2.** (*deal with, e.g. business*) спр|авля́ться, -а́виться с+*i.* **3.** (*kill*) поко́нчить (*pf.*) с+*i.*

cpd. **~-rider** *n.* мотоцикли́ст свя́зи.

dispel [dɪˈspel] *v.t.* рассе́|ивать, -ять.

dispensable [dɪˈspensəb(ə)l] *adj.* необяза́тельный.

dispensary [dɪˈspensərɪ] *n.* апте́ка; (*clinic*) амбулато́рия.

dispensation [,dɪspenˈseɪʃ(ə)n] *n.* **1.** (*dealing out*) разда́ча. **2.** (*exemption*) освобожде́ние.

dispens|e [dɪˈspens] *v.t.* **1.** (*deal out*) разд|ава́ть, -а́ть. **2.** (*of prescription*) пригот|овля́ть, -о́вить; **~ing chemist** апте́карь (*m.*), фармаце́вт.

v.i. **~ with** (*do without*) об|ходи́ться, -ойти́сь без+*g.*

dispenser [dɪˈspensə(r)] *n.* (*container*) (торго́вый) автома́т.

dispersal [dɪˈspɜːsəl] *n.* рассе́ивание; разго́н.

disperse [dɪˈspɜːs] *v.t.* рассе́|ивать, -ять; раз|гоня́ть, -огна́ть; **the troops were ~d over a wide front** войска́ бы́ли рассредото́чены по широ́кому фро́нту.

v.i. рассе́|иваться, -яться; ра|сходи́ться, -зойти́сь.

dispirit [dɪˈspɪrɪt] *v.t.* удруч|а́ть, -и́ть; прив|оди́ть, -ести́ в уны́ние.

displace [dɪsˈpleɪs] *v.t.* **1.** (*put in wrong place*) сме|ща́ть, -сти́ть; **~d persons** перемещённые ли́ца. **2.** (*replace*) заме|ща́ть, -сти́ть; вытесня́ть, вы́теснить.

displacement [dɪsˈpleɪsmənt] *n.* (*ousting*) смеще́ние, вытесне́ние; (*replacement*) замеще́ние; (*of ship*) водоизмеще́ние.

display [dɪˈspleɪ] *n.* **1.** (*manifestation*) пока́з, проявле́ние. **2.** (*ostentation*) хвастовство́. **3.** (*of goods etc.*) вы́ставка. **4.** (*of computer*) диспле́й.

v.t. прояв|ля́ть, -и́ть; обнару́жи|вать, -ть; (*goods etc.*) выставля́ть, вы́ставить (на пока́з); **he ~s his ignorance** он выка́зывает своё неве́жество.

displease [dɪsˈpliːz] *v.t.* не нра́виться (*impf.*) +*d.*; вызыва́ть, вы́звать недово́льство +*g.*; **I am ~d with you** я недово́лен ва́ми.

displeasing [dɪsˈpliːzɪŋ] *adj.* неприя́тный.

displeasure [dɪsˈpleʒə(r)] *n.* недово́льство, неудово́льствие; **incur s.o.'s ~** навл|ека́ть, -е́чь на себя́ чьё-н. недово́льство.

disposable [dɪˈspəʊzəb(ə)l] *adj.* однора́зового по́льзования; выбра́сываемый.

disposal [dɪˈspəʊz(ə)l] *n.* **1.** (*getting rid of*) удале́ние, убо́рка; **the ~ of rubbish** удале́ние му́сора; **bomb ~** обезвре́живание бомб. **2.** (*arrangement*) размеще́ние. **3.** (*management, control*) распоряже́ние; **the money is at your ~** де́ньги в ва́шем распоряже́нии.

dispose [dɪˈspəʊz] *v.t.* **1.** (*arrange*) распол|ага́ть, -ожи́ть. **2.** (*determine*) распол|ага́ть, -ожи́ть. **3.** (*incline*) склон|я́ть, -и́ть; **I am not ~d to help him** я не скло́нен ему́ помога́ть; **he is well ~d towards me** он ко мне хорошо́ отно́сится.

v.i. (*with prep.* **of**) **1.** (*get rid of*) отде́л|ываться, -аться от+*g.*; изб|авля́ться, -а́виться от+*g.* **2.** (*deal with*): **he ~d of his work/dinner** он упра́вился с рабо́той/обе́дом. **3.** (*account for, overcome*) разде́латься (*pf.*) с+*i.*; **that argument is soon ~d of** э́тот аргуме́нт легко́ опрове́ргнуть.

disposition [,dɪspəˈzɪʃ(ə)n] *n.* **1.** (*arrangement*) расположе́ние. **2.** (*character*) нрав, хара́ктер; **he has a cheerful ~** у него́ весёлый нрав. **3.** (*inclination*) скло́нность; **there was a general ~ to leave early** большинство́ бы́ло скло́нно уйти́ ра́но.

dispossess [,dɪspəˈzes] *v.t.* лиш|а́ть, -и́ть (*кого чего*); от|бира́ть, -обра́ть (*что у кого*).

disproportion [,dɪsprəˈpɔːʃ(ə)n] *n.* диспропо́рция.

disproportionate [,dɪsprəˈpɔːʃənət] *adj.* непропорциона́льный, чрезме́рный.

disprove [dɪsˈpruːv] *v.t.* опров|ерга́ть, -е́ргнуть.

disputable [dɪˈspjuːtəb(ə)l, ˈdɪspjʊ-] *adj.* спо́рный, недока́занный.

disputation [,dɪspjuːˈteɪʃ(ə)n] *n.* ди́спут, спор.

disputatious [,dɪspjuːˈteɪʃ(ə)s] *adj.* лю́бящий спо́рить.

dispute [dɪˈspjuːt, ˈdɪspjuːt] *n.* **1.** (*debate, argument*) ди́спут; **the ownership of the house is in ~** пра́во со́бственности на э́тот дом оспа́ривается; **beyond ~** бесспо́рно, вне вся́ких сомне́ний. **2.** (*quarrel*) ссо́ра, разногла́сие.

v.t. **1.** (*call in question, oppose*) осп|а́ривать, -о́рить; **the will was ~d** завеща́ние бы́ло опротесто́вано.

v.i. (*argue*) спо́рить, по-.

disqualification [dɪsˌkwɒlɪfɪˈkeɪʃ(ə)n] *n.* дисквалифика́ция; **age is no ~** во́зраст — не поме́ха.

disqualify [dɪsˈkwɒlɪˌfaɪ] *v.t.* дисквалифици́ровать (*impf., pf.*).

disquiet [dɪsˈkwaɪət] *n.* беспоко́йство.
v.t. беспоко́ить, о-.

disquieting [dɪsˈkwaɪətɪŋ] *adj.* трево́жный, беспоко́йный.

disquietude [dɪsˈkwaɪəˌtjuːd] *n.* беспоко́йство.

disquisition [ˌdɪskwɪˈzɪʃ(ə)n] *n.* тракта́т.

disregard [ˌdɪsrɪˈgɑːd] *n.* пренебреже́ние +*i.*; **he showed ~ for his teachers** он проявля́л неуваже́ние к учителя́м.
v.t. пренебр|ега́ть, -е́чь +*i.*

disrepair [ˌdɪsrɪˈpeə(r)] *n.* неспра́вность; **the house is in ~** дом в запу́щенном состоя́нии; **fall into ~** при|ходи́ть, -йти́ в упа́док.

disreputable [dɪsˈrepjʊtəb(ə)l] *adj.* позо́рный, непр́ли́чный; по́льзующийся дурно́й сла́вой.

disrepute [ˌdɪsrɪˈpjuːt] *n.* дурна́я сла́ва; **fall into ~** приобре|та́ть, -сти́ дурну́ю сла́ву.

disrespect [ˌdɪsrɪˈspekt] *n.* неуваже́ние (к+*d.*); непочте́ние; непочти́тельность.

disrespectful [ˌdɪsrɪˈspektfʊl] *adj.* непочти́тельный.

disrobe [dɪsˈrəʊb] *v.t.* & *i.* (*undress*) разд|ева́ть(ся), -е́ть(ся); (*take off robes*) разоблач|а́ть(ся), -и́ть(ся).

disrupt [dɪsˈrʌpt] *v.t.* под|рыва́ть, -орва́ть; срыва́ть, сорва́ть.

disruption [dɪsˈrʌpʃ(ə)n] *n.* подры́в, срыв.

disruptive [dɪsˈrʌptɪv] *adj.* разруши́тельный, подрывно́й.

dissatisfaction [ˌdɪsætɪsˈfækʃ(ə)n] *n.* неудовлетворённость, недово́льство, неудово́льствие.

dissatisf|y [dɪˈsætɪsˌfaɪ] *v.t.* не удовлетвор|я́ть, -и́ть; **he is ~ied with his job** он недово́лен свое́й рабо́той.

dissect [dɪˈsekt] *v.t.* вскр|ыва́ть, -ы́ть; (*fig.*) раз|бира́ть, -обра́ть.

dissection [dɪˈsekʃ(ə)n] *n.* вскры́тие; разбо́р.

dissemble [dɪˈsemb(ə)l] *v.t.* скры|ва́ть, -ть; **he ~s his emotions** он скрыва́ет свои́ чу́вства; **~ a fact** ум|а́лчивать, -олча́ть о фа́кте.
v.i. притвор|я́ться, -и́ться; лицеме́рить (*impf.*).

disseminate [dɪˈsemɪˌneɪt] *v.t.* распростран|я́ть, -и́ть.

dissemination [dɪˌsemɪˈneɪʃ(ə)n] *n.* распростране́ние.

dissension [dɪˈsenʃ(ə)n] *n.* разла́д, раздо́р.

dissent [dɪˈsent] *n.* несогла́сие; (*eccl.*) раско́л.

dissenter [dɪˈsentə(r)] *n.* диссиде́нт; (*rebel*) бунта́рь (*m.*); (*eccl.*) раско́льник.

dissertation [ˌdɪsəˈteɪʃ(ə)n] *n.* диссерта́ция.

disservice [dɪsˈsɜːvɪs] *n.* плоха́я услу́га, уще́рб; **he did me a ~** он оказа́л мне плоху́ю услу́гу; он повреди́л мне.

dissidence [ˈdɪsɪd(ə)ns] *n.* инакомы́слие.

dissident [ˈdɪsɪd(ə)nt] *n.* диссиде́нт, инакомы́слящий.
adj. несогла́сный, диссиде́нтский.

dissimilar [dɪˈsɪmɪlə(r)] *adj.* несхо́дный.

dissimilarity [ˌdɪsɪmɪˈlærɪtɪ] *n.* несхо́дство.

dissipate [ˈdɪsɪˌpeɪt] *v.t.* (*lit., fig.*) рассе́|ивать, -ять; (*squander*) растра́|чивать, -тить; пром|а́тывать, -ота́ть.

dissipated [ˈdɪsɪˌpeɪtɪd] *adj.* беспу́тный, разгу́льный.

dissipation [ˌdɪsɪˈpeɪʃ(ə)n] *n.* беспу́тство, разгу́л.

dis|sociate [dɪˈsəʊʃɪˌeɪt, -sɪˌeɪt], **-associate** [ˌdɪsəˈsəʊʃɪˌeɪt, -sɪˌeɪt] *v.t.* (*disunite*) разобщ|а́ть, -и́ть; **I ~ myself from what has been said** я отмежёвываюсь от того́, что бы́ло ска́зано; (*think of as separate*) диссоции́ровать (*impf., pf.*).

dissolute [ˈdɪsəˌluːt, -ˌljuːt] *adj.* распу́щенный, беспу́тный, распу́тный.

dissoluteness [ˈdɪsəˌluːtnɪs, -ˌljuːtnɪs] *n.* распу́щенность, беспу́тство, распу́тство.

dissolution [ˌdɪsəˈluːʃ(ə)n, -ˈljuːʃ(ə)n] *n.* (*phys.*) растворе́ние; (*of marriage etc.*) расторже́ние; (*of parliament*) ро́спуск.

dissolve [dɪˈzɒlv] *v.t.* **1.** (*phys.*) раствор|я́ть, -и́ть. **2.: the queen ~d parliament** короле́ва распусти́ла парла́мент. **3.** (*marriage*) раст|орга́ть, -о́ргнуть; **the marriage was ~d** брак был расто́ргнут.
v.i. (*phys.*) раствор|я́ться, -и́ться; **she ~d into tears** она́ залила́сь слеза́ми.

dissonance [ˈdɪsənəns] *n.* диссона́нс; неблагозву́чие.

dissonant [ˈdɪsənənt] *adj.* нестро́йный.

dissuade [dɪˈsweɪd] *v.t.* отгов|а́ривать, -ори́ть (*кого от чего*); отсове́товать (*pf.*) (*что кому́*).

distaff [ˈdɪstɑːf] *n.* пря́лка; **on the ~ side** по же́нской ли́нии.

distance [ˈdɪst(ə)ns] *n.* **1.** (*measure of space*) диста́нция, расстоя́ние; **it is some ~ to the school** до шко́лы дово́льно далеко́; **no ~ at all** совсе́м недалеко́; **he lives within walking ~ of the office** от его́ до́ма до рабо́ты мо́жно дойти́ пешко́м; **at what ~?** на како́м расстоя́нии?; **in the ~** вдалеке́; **from a ~** и́здали, издалека́; **middle ~** сре́дний план. **2.** (*fig.*): **keep one's ~** держа́ться (*impf.*) в стороне́ (от+*g.*); **keep s.o. at a ~** держа́ть (*impf.*) кого́-н. на расстоя́нии.

distant [ˈdɪst(ə)nt] *adj.* **1.** (*in space*) далёкий, да́льний, отдалённый; **we had a ~ view of the mountains** вдали́ мы ви́дели го́ры. **2.** (*in time*) далёкий. **3.** (*fig., remote*): **a ~ cousin** да́льний ро́дственник; **a ~ likeness** отдалённое схо́дство. **4.** (*reserved*) сде́ржанный, холо́дный.

distaste [dɪsˈteɪst] *n.* отвраще́ние (к+*d.*).

distasteful [dɪsˈteɪstfʊl] *adj.* проти́вный, неприя́тный.

distemper[1] [dɪˈstempə(r)] *n.* (*disease of dogs*) соба́чья чума́.

distemper[2] [dɪˈstempə(r)] *n.* (*method of painting*) те́мпера; (*type of paint*) клеева́я кра́ска.
v.t. кра́сить, по- клеево́й кра́ской.

distend [dɪˈstend] *v.t.* & *i.* над|ува́ть(ся), -у́ть(ся); раз|дува́ть(ся), -у́ть(ся).

distil [dɪˈstɪl] *v.t.* дистилли́ровать (*impf., pf.*); (*e.g. salt water*) опресн|я́ть, -и́ть; **~ whisky** гнать (*det.*) ви́ски.

distillation [ˌdɪstɪˈleɪʃ(ə)n] *n.* дистилля́ция, перего́нка; винокуре́ние.

distiller [dɪˈstɪlə(r)] *n.* дистилля́тор.

distillery [dɪˈstɪlərɪ] *n.* виноку́ренный заво́д.

distinct [dɪˈstɪŋkt] *adj.* **1.** (*clear, perceptible*) вня́тный, отчётливый; **a ~ improvement** заме́тное улучше́ние. **2.** (*different*) отли́чный (от+*g.*).

distinction [dɪˈstɪŋkʃ(ə)n] *n.* **1.** (*difference*) отли́чие. **2.** (*discrimination*) разли́чие. **3.** (*special or superior quality*) отличи́тельная осо́бенность; **a writer of ~** выдаю́щийся писа́тель; **his style lacks ~** его́ стиль не отлича́ется оригина́льностью. **4.** (*mark of honour*) отли́чие; **he received several ~s** он получи́л не́сколько зна́ков отли́чия.

distinctive [dɪˈstɪŋktɪv] *adj.* отличи́тельный, характе́рный, осо́бый.

distinctly [dɪˈstɪŋktlɪ] *adv.* отчётливо; (*perceptibly*) заме́тно; **~ better** значи́тельно лу́чше; **he spoke ~** он говори́л чётко; **I ~ heard** я я́сно слы́шал.

distinguish [dɪˈstɪŋgwɪʃ] *v.t.* 1. (*perceive*) разли́ч|а́ть, -и́ть. **2.** (*discern or point out difference*) различ|а́ть, -и́ть. **3.** (*characterize*) отлич|а́ть, -и́ть. **4.: ~** (*do credit to*) **o.s.** отлич|а́ться, -и́ться.

distinguishable [dɪˈstɪŋgwɪʃəb(ə)l] *adj.* (*visible*) различи́мый; (*different*) отличи́мый.

distinguished [dɪˈstɪŋgwɪʃt] *adj.* выдаю́щийся.

distort [dɪˈstɔːt] *v.t.* иска|жа́ть, -зи́ть; искрив|ля́ть, -и́ть; **~ facts** извра|ща́ть, -ти́ть фа́кты.

distortion [dɪˈstɔːʃ(ə)n] *n.* искаже́ние, извраще́ние.

distract [dɪˈstrækt] *v.t.* **1.** (*draw away; make inattentive*) отвл|ека́ть, -е́чь. **2.** (*derange mentally*) св|оди́ть,

-ести́ с ума́; **he drove her ~ed** он довёл её до безу́мия.

distraction [dɪ'strækʃ(ə)n] *n.* (*act of diverting*) отвлече́ние; (*cause of inattention*) поме́ха; (*amusement*) развлече́ние; (*frenzy, derangement*) безу́мие; **he loves her to ~** он безу́мно её лю́бит; **drive s.o. to ~** дов|оди́ть, -ести́ кого́-н. до безу́мия.

distraught [dɪ'strɔ:t] *adj.* обезу́мевший.

distress [dɪ'stres] *n.* **1.** (*physical suffering*) утомле́ние, изнеможе́ние; **the runner showed signs of ~** бегу́н заме́тно утоми́лся. **2.** (*mental suffering*) огорче́ние, го́ре. **3.** (*indigence*) бе́дность, нужда́. **4.** (*danger*) бе́дствие; **a ship in ~** су́дно, те́рпящее бе́дствие.

v.t. **1.** (*grieve*) огорч|а́ть, -и́ть. **2.** (*impoverish*) истощ|а́ть, -и́ть; **~ed area** райо́н бе́дствия.

distressing [dɪ'stresɪŋ] *adj.* огорчи́тельный.

distribute [dɪ'strɪbju:t, 'dɪ-] *v.t.* **1.** (*deal out*) распредел|я́ть, -и́ть; разд|ава́ть, -а́ть. **2.** (*spread*) ра|скла́дывать, -зложи́ть; **wealth is unfairly ~d** бога́тства распределя́ются несправедли́во.

distribution [ˌdɪstrɪ'bju:ʃ(ə)n] *n.* **1.** (*dealing out, spreading*) распределе́ние, разда́ча; **the ~ of population is uneven** населе́ние распределено́ неравноме́рно; **~ of prizes** разда́ча награ́д. **2.** (*marketing*) распределе́ние, распростране́ние.

distributive [dɪ'strɪbjʊtɪv] *adj.* распредели́тельный; **the ~ trades** ро́зничная торго́вля.

distributor [dɪ'strɪbjʊtə(r)] *n.* распредели́тель (*m.*); (*tech.*) распредели́тель (*m.*) зажига́ния.

district ['dɪstrɪkt] *n.* райо́н, о́круг; (*attr.*) райо́нный, окружно́й; (*US, constituency*) избира́тельный уча́сток; **D~ of Columbia** о́круг Колу́мбия; **~ attorney** окружно́й прокуро́р.

distrust [dɪs'trʌst] *n.* недове́рие.

v.t. не доверя́ть (*impf.*) +*d.*

distrustful [dɪs'trʌstfʊl] *adj.* недове́рчивый.

disturb [dɪ'stɜ:b] *v.t.* беспоко́ить, о-; меша́ть, по- +*d.*; **~ s.o.'s sleep** нар|уша́ть, -у́шить чей-н. сон; **do not ~ yourself** не беспоко́йтесь; **he was ~ed by the news** он был обеспоко́ен но́востью; **his mind was ~ed** у него́ помути́лся рассу́док; **do not ~ these papers** не тро́гайте э́ти бума́ги.

disturbance [dɪ'stɜ:bəns] *n.* (*act of troubling*) наруше́ние; (*cause of trouble*) трево́га; (*riot*) волне́ния (*nt. pl.*); беспоря́дки (*m. pl.*).

disturbing [dɪ'stɜ:bɪŋ] *adj.* трево́жный.

disuse [dɪs'ju:s] *n.*: **fall into ~** выходи́ть, вы́йти из употребле́ния.

disused [dɪs'ju:sd] *adj.*: **a ~ well** забро́шенный коло́дец.

disyllabic [ˌdɪsɪ'læbɪk, ˌdaɪ-] *adj.* двусло́жный.

ditch [dɪtʃ] *n.* кана́ва; ров.

v.t.: **~ a car** завезти́ маши́ну (*pf.*) в кана́ву; **~ one's plane** сажа́ть, посади́ть самолёт на́ воду; **~ s.o.** (*sl.*) бр|оса́ть, -о́сить кого́-н.

cpd. **~-water** *n.*: **dull as ~-water** смерте́льно ску́чный.

dither ['dɪðə(r)] *n.* (*coll.*) смяте́ние; **she was in a ~** она́ не́рвничала (*or* колеба́лась).

v.i. (*coll.*) колеба́ться, по-; быть в нереши́тельности; не́рвничать (*impf.*).

ditto ['dɪtəʊ] *n.* то же; сто́лько же.

ditty ['dɪtɪ] *n.* пе́сенка.

diuretic [ˌdaɪjʊ'retɪk] *n.* мочего́нное сре́дство.

adj. мочего́нный.

diurnal [daɪ'ɜ:n(ə)l] *adj.* дневно́й, ежедне́вный.

divan [dɪ'væn, daɪ-, 'daɪ-] *n.* тахта́, дива́н; **~ bed** дива́н-крова́ть.

dive [daɪv] *n.* **1.** (*act of diving*) нырóк, ныря́ние; **high ~** прыжо́к в во́ду с вы́шки; (*of submarine*) погруже́ние; (*of aircraft*) пики́рование; **the plane went into a ~** самолёт спики́ровал. **2.** (*underground bar etc.*) погребо́к. **3.** (*drinking or gambling den*) прито́н.

v.i. **1.** (*plunge into water*) ныр|я́ть, -ну́ть; (*in diving suit; also of submarine*) погру|жа́ться, -зи́ться. **2.** (*move sharply downwards*): **the animal ~d into its hole** зверёк юркну́л в но́ру. **3.** (*fig., immerse o.s.*) углуб|ля́ться, -и́ться. *See also* **diving**

cpds. **~-bomb** *v.t.* бомби́ть (*impf.*) с пики́рования; **~-bomber** *n.* пики́рующий бомбардиро́вщик.

diver ['daɪvə(r)] *n.* ныря́льщик; водола́з; (*for pearls*) иска́тель (*m.*) же́мчуга.

diverge [daɪ'vɜ:dʒ] *v.i.* ра|сходи́ться, -зойти́сь; откло|ня́ться, -и́ться.

divergence [daɪ'vɜ:dʒəns] *n.* расхожде́ние, отклоне́ние.

divergent [daɪ'vɜ:dʒ(ə)nt] *adj.* расходя́щийся, отклоня́ющийся.

diverse [daɪ'vɜ:s, 'daɪ-, dɪ-] *adj.* ра́зный, разнообра́зный.

diversification [daɪˌvɜ:sɪfɪ'keɪʃ(ə)n] *n.* расшире́ние ассортиме́нта.

diversify [daɪ'vɜ:sɪˌfaɪ] *v.t.* разнообра́зить (*impf.*).

diversion [daɪ'vɜ:ʃ(ə)n, dɪ-] *n.* **1.** (*turning aside*) отклоне́ние; **~ of a stream** отво́д ручья́; **traffic ~** объе́зд. **2.** (*mil.*) диве́рсия. **3.** (*amusement*) развлече́ние. **4.: create a ~** отвл|ека́ть, -е́чь внима́ние.

diversionary [daɪ'vɜ:ʃənərɪ, dɪ-] *adj.* диверсио́нный.

diversity [daɪ'vɜ:sɪtɪ, dɪ-] *n.* (*differentness*) разли́чие; (*variety*) разнообра́зие.

divert [daɪ'vɜ:t, dɪ-] *v.t.* (*deflect*) отклон|я́ть, -и́ть; отвл|ека́ть, -е́чь; (*entertain*) развл|ека́ть, -е́чь.

divest [daɪ'vest] *v.t.* (*fig.*) лиш|а́ть, -и́ть; **~ o.s. of functions** сложи́ть (*pf.*) с себя́ обя́занности.

divide [dɪ'vaɪd] *v.t.* **1.** (*share*) дели́ть, раз-; **they ~d the money equally** они́ раздели́ли де́ньги по́ровну. **2.** (*math.*) дели́ть, раз-; **~ 27 by 3** дели́ть, раз- 27 на́ 3. **3.** (*separate*) раздел|я́ть, -и́ть; **dividing-line** разграниче́ние. **4.** (*cause disagreement*) разъедин|я́ть, -и́ть; раздел|я́ть, -и́ть; **we are ~d on this question** мы расхо́димся в э́том вопро́се; **a ~-and-rule policy** поли́тика «разделя́й и вла́ствуй».

v.i. дели́ться, раз-; **the road ~s** доро́га разветвля́ется; **the House ~d** пала́та проголосова́ла; (*math.*): **18 ~s by 3** 18 де́лится на́ 3.

dividend ['dɪvɪˌdend] *n.* (*math.*) дели́мое; (*fin.*) дивиде́нд.

dividers [dɪ'vaɪdəz] *n.* (*compasses*) ци́ркуль (*m.*).

divination [ˌdɪvɪ'neɪʃ(ə)n] *n.* (*foretelling the future*) гада́ние, прорица́ние.

divin|e [dɪ'vaɪn] *adj.* боже́ственный; (*coll., superb*) боже́ственный; **~e right of kings** пра́во пома́занника бо́жьего; **~e service** богослуже́ние.

v.t. (*guess, intuit*) уга́д|ывать, -а́ть; **~ing-rod** прут для отыска́ния воды́.

diving ['daɪvɪŋ] *n.* ныря́ние.

cpds. **~-board** *n.* трампли́н, вы́шка (для прыжко́в в во́ду); **~-suit** *n.* скафа́ндр.

divinity [dɪ'vɪnɪtɪ] *n.* (*quality*) боже́ственность; (*divine being*) божество́; (*theology*) богосло́вие.

divisibility [dɪˌvɪzɪ'bɪlɪtɪ] *n.* дели́мость.

divisible [dɪ'vɪzɪb(ə)l] *adj.* (раз)дели́мый.

division [dɪ'vɪʒ(ə)n] *n.* **1.** (*math.*) деле́ние. **2.** (*dividing*) разделе́ние, разде́л; **~ of labour** разделе́ние труда́; **a fair ~ of the money** справедли́вое распределе́ние де́нег. **3.** (*separation*) разделе́ние; **class ~s** кла́ссовые разли́чия. **4.** (*mil.*) диви́зия. **5.** (*department*) отде́л. **6.** (*electoral district*) избира́тельный о́круг. **7.** (*parl. vote*) голосова́ние.

divisional [dɪ'vɪʒənəl] *adj.* (*mil.*) дивизио́нный; **~ headquarters** штаб диви́зии.

divisive [dɪ'vaɪsɪv] *adj.* разделя́ющий, вызыва́ющий разногла́сия.

divisor [dɪ'vaɪzə(r)] *n.* (*math.*) дели́тель (*m.*).

divorce [dɪ'vɔːs] *n.* развóд; ~ **court** суд по бракоразвóдным делáм; ~ **rate** разводи́мость, процéнт развóдов.

v.t. **1.** (*separate*) отдел|я́ть, -и́ть; ~ **a word from its context** вырывáть, вы́рвать слóво из контéкста. **2.** (*leg.*) разв|оди́ть, -ести́; **he ~d his wife** он развёлся с женóй; **she is ~d** онá разведенá.

v.i. разв|оди́ться, -ести́сь.

divorcee [ˌdɪvɔː'siː] *n.* разведённый муж, разведённая женá.

divulge [daɪ'vʌldʒ, dɪ-] *v.t.* разглa|шáть, -си́ть.

DIY (*abbr. of* ***do it yourself***): ~ **store** магази́н «умéлые рýки».

dizziness ['dɪzɪnɪs] *n.* головокружéние.

dizzy ['dɪzɪ] *adj.* (*feeling giddy*) испы́тывающий головокружéние; (*causing giddiness*) головокружи́тельный; **I feel** ~ у меня́ крýжится головá.

DJ (*abbr. of* ***disc jockey***) диск-жокéй.

DNA (*abbr. of* ***deoxyribonucleic acid***) ДНК, (дезоксирибонуклеи́новая кислотá).

do[1] [duː, də] *n.* (*coll.*) **1.** (*entertainment*) вечери́нка. **2.** (*share*): **fair do's!** всем пóровну! **3.** (*advice*): **~'s and don'ts** совéты (*m. pl.*).

v.t. & aux. **1.** (*as aux. or substitute for v. already used: not translated unless emph.*): **I ~ not smoke** я не курю́; **did you not see me?** рáзве вы меня́ не ви́дели?; **I ~ want to go** я óчень хочý пойти́; ~ **tell me** пожáлуйста, расскажи́те мне; **they promised to help, and they did** они́ обещáли помóчь и помогли́; **so ~ I** я тóже; **he went, but I did not** он пошёл, а я нет; **she plays better than she did** онá игрáет лýчше, чем прéжде; **he ~es not work, nor ~ I** ни он, ни я не рабóтаем. **2.** (*perform, carry out*): **what can I ~ for you?** чем могý служи́ть?; **what ~es he ~ (for a living)?** чем он занимáется?; кем он рабóтает?; **what ~es your father ~?** кто ваш отéц?; **the team did well** комáнда вы́ступила успéшно; **what's ~ne cannot be undone** сдéланного не ворóтишь; ~ **one's duty** выполня́ть, вы́полнить свой долг; **easier said than ~ne** легкó сказáть, но трýдно сдéлать; **well ~ne!** молодéц!; **it isn't ~ne!** э́то не при́нято! **3.** (*bestow, render*): **it ~es him credit** э́то дéлает емý честь; **he did me a service** он оказáл мне услýгу; **it won't ~ any good** э́то бесполéзно. **4.** (*effect, produce*): **that's ~ne it! now you've ~ne it!** (*iron.*) поздравля́ю! **5.** (*finish*): **I have ~ne with algebra** я покóнчил с áлгеброй. **6.** (*work at*): **he's ~ing algebra** он изучáет áлгебру. **7.** (*solve*): ~ **a sum** реш|áть, -и́ть арифмети́ческую задáчу. **8.** (*attend to*): **the barber did me first** парикмáхер обслужи́л меня́ пéрвым; **he ~es book reviews** он рецензи́рует кни́ги; **we did geography today** сегóдня мы проходи́ли геогрáфию. **9.** (*arrange, clean, tidy*): ~ **one's hair** прич|ёсываться, -есáться; ~ **a room** уб|ирáть, -рáть кóмнату; ~ **the dishes** мыть, вы́- посýду. **10.** (*cook*): **well ~ne** хорошó прожáренный; **the potatoes are ~ne** картóшка свари́лась/готóва. **11.** (*enact*): **he did Hamlet** он игрáл Гáмлета. **12.** (*undergo*): **he did 6 years for forgery** он отсидéл 6 лет за подлóг. **13.** (*cater for*): **they ~ you well at the Savoy** в «Савóе» хорóшее обслýживание. **14.** (*coll., swindle*) над|увáть, -ýть. **15.** (*achieve speed etc.*): **we did 70 miles in two hours** мы продéлали 70 миль за два часá; **he was ~ing 60 (miles an hour)** он éхал со скóростью 60 миль в час. **16.: ~ne!** (*agreed*) по рукáм! **17.: I can ~** (*sell*) **you this coat at £50** я уступлю́ вам э́то пальтó за 50 фýнтов.

v.i. **1.** (*act, behave*): ~ **as I tell you** слýшайся меня́; **you would ~ well to go there** вы хорошó сдéлаете, éсли пойдёте тудá; **we must ~ or die** мы должны́ держáться до концá. **2.** (*be satisfactory, fitting or advisable*): **the scraps will ~ for the dog** объéдки пригодя́тся для собáки; **this will never ~** э́то никудá не годи́тся; **that will ~!** (*is enough*) хвáтит!; довóльно!; **tomorrow will ~** мóжно и зáвтра. **3.** (*fare, succeed*): **how ~ you ~?** здрáвствуйте!; как поживáете?; **how did he ~ in his exams?** как он сдáл экзáмены?; **the patient is ~ing well** больнóй поправля́ется. **4.** (*happen*): **is anything ~ing at the club?** что происхóдит в клýбе?; **nothing ~ing!** (*refusal*) не вы́йдет!

with preps.: **what shall we ~ about lunch?** как насчёт обéда?; **nothing can be ~ne about it** с э́тим ничегó не подéлаешь; ~ **well by s.o.** хорошó обращáться (*impf.*) с кем-н.; (*defeat, destroy, damage*): **these shoes are ~ne for** э́тим тýфлям конéц; **if he finds out, I am ~ne for** éсли он об э́том узнáет — я пропáл; **we're ~ne for** нам кры́шка (*coll.*); **what will you ~ for food?** как вы устрóитесь с питáнием?; ~ **s.o. out of sth.** (*cheat, deprive of*) вымáнивать, вы́манить что-н. у когó-н.; **what have you ~ne to my watch?** что вы сдéлали с мои́ми часáми?; **what have you ~ne with the keys?** кудá вы дéли ключи́?; **I could ~ with a drink** я охóтно (*or* с удовóльствием) вы́пил бы; **that coat could ~ with a clean** не помешáло бы вы́чистить э́то пальтó; **we shall have to make ~ with margarine** нам придётся обойти́сь маргари́ном; **he ~esn't know what to ~ with himself** он не знáет, чем заня́ться; **it is nothing to ~ with you** э́то вас не касáется; **hard work had a lot to ~ with his success** упóрный труд сыгрáл большýю роль в егó успéхе; **we must ~ without luxuries** мы должны́ обойти́сь без рóскоши; **I can ~ without his silly jokes** мне надоéли егó дурáцкие шýтки.

with advs.: ~ **away** *v.i.*: ~ **away with** кончáть, покóнчить с+*i.*; ~ **away with o.s.** покóнчить (*pf.*) с собóй; ~ **in** *v.t.* (*sl., kill*) уб|ирáть, -рáть; (*coll., exhaust*): **I am ~ne in** я измóтан; ~ **out** *v.t.* (*clean, e.g. a room*) уб|ирáть, -рáть; (*clear, e.g. a cupboard*) вы́чистить (*pf.*); ~ **over (again)** *v.t.* передéл|ывать, -ать; ~ **up** *v.t.* (*repair, refurnish*): ~ **up a room** отдéл|ывать, -ать кóмнату; (*fasten*): ~ **up a parcel** завя́з|ывать, -áть пакéт; ~ **up a dress** застёг|ивать, -нýть плáтье.

cpds. **~-it-yourself** *adj.* самодéльный; **~-nothing** *n.* лóдырь (*m.*); *adj.* ленúвый; **~-or-die** *adj.* отчáянный.

do[2] [dəʊ] *n.* = **doh**

docile ['dəʊsaɪl] *adj.* послýшный, покóрный.

docility [dəʊ'sɪlɪtɪ] *n.* послушáние, покóрность.

dock[1] [dɒk] *n.* (*in court*) скамья́ подсуди́мых.

dock[2] [dɒk] *n.* **1.** (*naut.*) док; **dry ~** сухóй док. **2.** (*pl., port facilities*) верфь. **3.** (*wharf*) при́стань.

v.t. (*bring into ~*) стáвить, по- (*сýдно*) в док.

v.i. (*go into ~*) входи́ть, войти́ в док; (*of space vehicles*) стыковáться, со-.

cpd. **~yard** *n.* верфь.

dock[3] [dɒk] *v.t.* **1.** (*shorten tail of*) обруб|áть, -и́ть хвост +*g. or d.* **2.** (*fig., reduce*) урéз|ывать, -ать.

docker ['dɒkə(r)] *n.* дóкер; портóвый рабóчий.

docket ['dɒkɪt] *n.* **1.** (*summary*) аннотáция; (*list*) пéречень (*m.*). **2.** (*US, leg.*) реéстр судéбных дел.

docking ['dɒkɪŋ] *n.* (*of space vehicles*) стыкóвка.

doctor ['dɒktə(r)] *n.* **1.** (*acad.*) дóктор. **2.** (*of medicine*) врач, дóктор; **woman ~** жéнщина-врач.

v.t. (*falsify*) поддéл|ывать, -ать; фальсифици́ровать (*impf., pf.*).

doctoral ['dɒktər(ə)l] *adj.* дóкторский.

doctorate ['dɒktərət] *n.* стéпень дóктора.

doctrinaire [ˌdɒktrɪ'neə(r)] *n.* доктринёр.

adj. доктринёрский.

doctrine ['dɒktrɪn] *n.* доктри́на, учéние.

document ['dɒkjʊmənt] *n.* докумéнт.

v.t. документи́ровать (*impf., pf.*).

documentary [ˌdɒkjʊ'mentərɪ] *n. & adj.* документа́льный (фильм).
documentation [ˌdɒkjʊmen'teɪʃ(ə)n] *n.* документа́ция.
dodder ['dɒdə(r)] *v.i.* трясти́сь (*impf.*); **a ~ing old man** дря́хлый стари́к.
doddery ['dɒdərɪ] *adj.* трясу́щийся от ста́рости; дря́хлый.
dodge [dɒdʒ] *n.* увёртка.
v.t. увил|ивать, -ьну́ть от+*g.*; **~ a blow** уверну́ться от (*pf.*) уда́ра; **~ military service** уклоня́ться (*impf.*) от вое́нной пови́нности.
v.i. уклон|я́ться, -и́ться (от+*g.*); **he ~d behind a tree** он (бы́стро) укры́лся за де́ревом.
dodgy ['dɒdʒɪ] *adj.* (*coll.*) (*artful*) изворо́тливый; (*tricky, difficult*) ка́верзный; (*unsafe*) ненадёжный.
doe [dəʊ] *n.* са́мка (*оленя, зайца и т.п.*).
cpd. **~skin** *n.* оле́нья ко́жа; за́мша.
doff [dɒf] *v.t.* сн|има́ть, -ять.
dog [dɒg] *n.* **1.** соба́ка, пёс (*also fig., pej.*); (*attr.*) соба́чий, пёсий. **2.** (*male*) кобе́ль (*m.*); **~ fox** саме́ц лисы́. **3.** (*coll., fellow*): **lucky ~** счастли́вчик; **lazy ~** лентя́й; **sly ~** хитре́ц; **dirty ~** су́кин сын; **top ~** хозя́ин положе́ния. **4.** (*other fig. uses*): **go to the ~s** разори́ться (*pf.*), пойти́ (*pf.*) пра́хом; **a ~'s life** соба́чья жизнь; **let sleeping ~s lie** не тронь ли́ха, пока спит ти́хо; **not a ~'s chance** нет ни мале́йшего ша́нса; **take a hair of the ~** опохме́л|я́ться, -и́ться; **you can't teach an old ~ new tricks** ≃ нельзя́ переучи́ть кого́-н. на ста́рости лет; **~'s dinner** (*sl., mess, hotchpotch*) мешани́на; неразбери́ха; **hot ~** (*coll.*) бу́лка с горя́чей соси́ской.
v.t. ходи́ть (*indet.*) по пята́м за+*i.*; (*fig.*) пресле́довать (*impf.*).
cpds. **~-biscuit** *n.* гале́та для соба́к; **~-collar** *n.* оше́йник; (*coll., clergyman's*) кру́глый стоя́чий воротни́к; **~-ear** (*fig.*) *n.* за́гнутый уголо́к страни́цы; **~fight** *n.* (*aeron.*) возду́шный бой; **~fish** *n.* аку́ла; **~-food** *n.* корм для соба́к; **~house** *n.* (*US*) конура́; **in the ~house** (*coll.*) в неми́лости; **~-paddle** *v.i.* пла́вать (*indet.*) по-соба́чьи; **~-racing** *n.* соба́чьи бега́; **~rose** *n.* шипо́вник; **~sbody** *n.* иша́к, работя́га (*c.g.*); **~-show** *n.* вы́ставка соба́к; **~-tired** *adj.* уста́лый как соба́ка; **~wood** *n.* кизи́л.
doge [dəʊdʒ] *n.* дож.
dogged ['dɒgɪd] *adj.* упо́рный, насты́рный.
doggerel ['dɒgər(ə)l] *n.* ви́рш|и (*pl., g.* -ей).
doggone ['dɒgɒn] *adj.* (*US sl.*) чёртов.
doggy ['dɒgɪ] *n.* соба́чка.
dogma ['dɒgmə] *n.* до́гма; (*specific*) догма́т.
dogmatic [dɒg'mætɪk] *adj.* догмати́ческий.
dogmatism ['dɒgməˌtɪz(ə)m] *n.* догмати́зм.
dogmatist ['dɒgmətɪst] *n.* догма́тик.
doh, do [dəʊ] *n.* (*mus.*) до (*indecl.*).
doily, doyley ['dɔɪlɪ] *n.* кружевна́я салфе́точка.
doing ['du:ɪŋ] *n.*: **this was his ~** э́то де́ло его́ рук; **it will take some ~** э́то потре́бует труда́.
doldrums ['dɒldrəmz] *n.* (*geog.*) штилева́я полоса́; (*fig.*) уны́ние, хандра́; **be in the ~** быть в уны́нии, хандри́ть (*impf.*).
dole [dəʊl] *n.* подая́ние; посо́бие по безрабо́тице; **he is on the ~** он безрабо́тный, он получа́ет посо́бие.
v.t. **~ out** ску́по выдава́ть, вы́дать.
doleful ['dəʊlfʊl] *adj.* ско́рбный.
doll [dɒl] *n.* ку́кла; **~'s house** ку́кольный до́мик.
v.t. & i.: **~ (o.s) up** разоде́ться (*pf.*).
dollar ['dɒlə(r)] *n.* до́ллар; **~ diplomacy** диплома́тия до́ллара; **(one's) bottom ~** после́дний грош.
dollop ['dɒləp] *n.* соли́дная по́рция, окова́лок.
dolly ['dɒlɪ] *n.* **1.** = **doll. 2.** (*platform for camera*) опера́торская теле́жка.
dolomite ['dɒləˌmaɪt] доломи́т.
dolphin ['dɒlfɪn] *n.* дельфи́н.
dolt [dəʊlt] *n.* болва́н, тупи́ца.
doltish ['dəʊltɪʃ] *adj.* тупо́й, глупова́тый.
domain [də'meɪn] *n.* **1.** (*estate*) владе́ние, име́ние. **2.** (*realm*) сфе́ра. **3.** (*fig.*) о́бласть; **these matters are in his ~** э́ти дела́ вхо́дят в его́ компете́нцию.
dome [dəʊm] *n.* ку́пол.
domestic [də'mestɪk] *n.* (*servant*) слуга́ (*m.*); прислу́га, домрабо́тница.
adj. **1.** (*of the home or family*) дома́шний; **~ science** домово́дство; **~ troubles** семе́йные неприя́тности. **2.** (*home-loving*) семе́йственный. **3.** (*of animals*) дома́шний. **4.** (*not foreign*) оте́чественный, вну́тренний.
domesticate [də'mestɪˌkeɪt] *v.t.* (*tame*) прируч|а́ть, -и́ть; (*interest in household*) приуч|а́ть, -и́ть к веде́нию хозя́йства; **she is not ~d** она́ не домосе́дка.
domestication [dəˌmestɪ'keɪʃ(ə)n] *n.* прируче́ние; приуче́ние к веде́нию хозя́йства.
domesticity [ˌdɒmə'stɪsɪtɪ, ˌdəʊ-] *n.* дома́шняя жизнь.
domicile ['dɒmɪˌsaɪl, -sɪl] *n.* (*dwelling*) местожи́тельство.
v.t.: **~d in England** име́ющий постоя́нное местожи́тельство в А́нглии.
dominance ['dɒmɪnəns] *n.* госпо́дство.
dominant ['dɒmɪnənt] *adj.* домини́рующий; госпо́дствующий.
dominate ['dɒmɪˌneɪt] *v.t. & i.* **1.** (*prevail*) домини́ровать (*impf.*) (над+*i.*). **2.** (*influence*) ока́з|ывать, -а́ть давле́ние. **3.** (*of heights, buildings etc.*) домини́ровать (*impf.*) над+*i.*; возвыша́ться (*impf.*) над+*i.*
domination [ˌdɒmɪ'neɪʃ(ə)n] *n.* госпо́дство.
domineer [ˌdɒmɪ'nɪə(r)] *v.i.*: **~ over** помыка́ть (*impf.*) (*кем*); кома́ндовать (*impf.*) (*кем*).
domineering [ˌdɒmɪ'nɪərɪŋ] *adj.* вла́стный.
dominion [də'mɪnɪən] *n.* (*lordship*) влады́чество; (*realm*) владе́ние; (*pol. hist.*) доминио́н.
domino ['dɒmɪˌnəʊ] *n.* кость домино́; (*pl., also name of game*) домино́ (*indecl.*).
don[1] [dɒn] *n.* **1.** (*Spanish title*) дон; **D~ Juan** (*fig.*) донжуа́н. **2.** (*univ.*) преподава́тель (*m.*); профе́ссор.
don[2] [dɒn] *v.t.* над|ева́ть, -е́ть.
donate [dəʊ'neɪt] *v.t.* дари́ть, по-; же́ртвовать, по-.
donation [dəʊ'neɪʃ(ə)n] *n.* дар; поже́ртвование.
donkey ['dɒŋkɪ] *n.* осёл (*also fig.*); **for ~'s years** (*coll.*) с незапа́мятных времён.
cpd. **~-work** *n.* (*coll.*) чёрная рабо́та.
donor ['dəʊnə(r)] *n.* же́ртвователь (*m.*); (*of blood, transplant*) до́нор.
doodle ['du:d(ə)l] *n.* кара́кули (*f. pl.*).
v.t. & i. чи́ркать (*impf.*).
doom [du:m] *n.* (*ruin*) ги́бель.
v.t. обр|ека́ть, -е́чь на+*a.*
cpd. **~sday** *n.* день стра́шного суда́; **till ~sday** (*fig.*) до второ́го прише́ствия.
door [dɔ:(r)] *n.* **1.** (*of room etc.*) дверь; (*of car etc.*) две́рца; **sliding ~** задвижна́я дверь; **revolving ~** враща́ющаяся дверь; **front ~** пара́дная дверь; **back ~** за́дняя дверь; чёрный ход; **side ~** бокова́я дверь; **answer the ~** откр|ыва́ть, -ы́ть дверь; **he lives next ~** он живёт в сосе́днем до́ме; **the boy next ~** сосе́дский ма́льчик; **out of ~s** на све́жем/откры́том во́здухе; на дворе́/у́лице; **within ~s** до́ма; **show s.o. the ~** (*expel*) выставля́ть, вы́ставить кого́-н. за дверь; **behind closed ~s** (*in secret*) за закры́тыми дверя́ми. **2.** (*fig., expr. proximity*): **that is next ~ to slander** от э́того оди́н шаг до клеветы́; **lay a crime at s.o.'s ~** вали́ть, с- вину́ на кого́-н.; **he shall never darken my ~ again** ноги́ его́ бо́льше не бу́дет в моём до́ме. **3.** (*fig.*): **a ~ to success** путь к успе́ху; **close the ~ to, upon** отр|еза́ть, -е́зать путь к+*d.*; **force an open ~** ломи́ться (*impf.*) в откры́тую дверь.

cpds. **~-bell** *n.* (дверно́й) звоно́к; **~-handle** *n.* дверна́я ру́чка; **~-keeper, ~man** *nn.* привра́тник; швейца́р; **~knob** *n.* кру́глая дверна́я ру́чка; **~man** *n.* = **~keeper; ~mat** *n.* полови́к; **~post** *n.* дверно́й躺 кося́к; **~step** *n.* поро́г; **~way** *n.* дверно́й проём.

dope [dəʊp] *n.* **1.** (*drug*) дурма́н, нарко́тик; **~ fiend** наркома́н; **~ merchant** нелега́льно торгу́ющий нарко́тиками. **2.** (*sl., fool*) ду́рень (*m.*). **3.** (*sl., information*) све́дения (*nt. pl.*).

v.t. **1.** (*make unconscious*) дурма́нить, о-. **2.** (*stimulate with drug*) взб|а́дривать, -одри́ть нарко́тиками.

dopey ['dəʊpɪ] *adj.* (*bemused by drug or sleep*) одурма́ненный; (*sl., foolish*) чо́кнутый.

dormant ['dɔːmənt] *adj.* (*of animals*) в спя́чке; **~ volcano** неде́йствующий вулка́н.

dormer(-window) ['dɔːmə(r)] *n.* слухово́е окно́.

dormitory ['dɔːmɪtərɪ] *n.* дортуа́р.

dormouse ['dɔːmaʊs] *n.* со́ня.

dorsal ['dɔːs(ə)l] *adj.* спинно́й.

dosage ['dəʊsɪdʒ] *n.* (*dosing*) дозиро́вка; (*dose*) до́за.

dose [dəʊs] *n.* до́за; (*fig.*) по́рция.

v.t. лечи́ть (*impf.*) до́зами лека́рства.

dossier ['dɒsɪə(r), -ɪ,eɪ] *n.* досье́ (*indecl.*), де́ло.

dot [dɒt] *n.* то́чка; **on the ~** то́чно; **~s and dashes** а́збука Мо́рзе; **in the year ~** (*coll.*) о́чень давно́.

v.t. **1.** (*place ~ on*): **~ one's i's** (*lit., fig.*) ста́вить, по- то́чки над «i». **2.** (*mark, indicate with ~s*) отм|еча́ть, -е́тить то́чками; **~ted line** пункти́рная ли́ния; **sign on the ~ted line** (*fig.*) безогово́рочно согла|ша́ться, -си́ться. **3.** (*scatter*) усе́|ивать, -ять; **villages ~ted about** дере́вни, разбро́санные вокру́г; **sea ~ted with ships** мо́ре, усе́янное корабля́ми.

dotage ['dəʊtɪdʒ] *n.* ста́рческое слабоу́мие; **he is in his ~** он впал в де́тство.

dote [dəʊt] *v.i.*: **~ on** обожа́ть (*impf.*); сходи́ть (*impf.*) с ума́ по+*d.*

doting ['dəʊtɪŋ] *adj.* безу́мно лю́бящий.

dotty ['dɒtɪ] *adj.* (*silly*) придуркова́тый, чо́кнутый.

double ['dʌb(ə)l] *n.* **1.** (*twofold quantity or measure*): **ten is the ~ of five** де́сять вдво́е бо́льше пяти́. **2.** (*pers. or thg. resembling another*) двойни́к. **3.** (*running pace*) бе́глый шаг; **at the ~** бе́глым ша́гом. **4.** (*pl., tennis*) па́рная игра́; **mixed ~s** сме́шанные па́ры (*f. pl.*).

adj. (*in two parts; twice as much*) двойно́й; (*happening twice*) двукра́тный; **~ bed** дву(х)спа́льная крова́ть; **~ bend** (*on road*) зигза́г; **~ doors** двойны́е две́ри; **~ knock** двукра́тный стук; **~ room** ко́мната на двои́х; **~ saucepan** кастрю́ля с двойны́м дном; **'Anna' is spelt with a ~ 'n'** «А́нна» пи́шется с двумя́ (*or* че́рез два) н; **serve a ~ purpose** служи́ть, по- двум це́лям. **3.** (*ambiguous, deceitful*): **~ dealer** двуру́шник; **~ dealing** двуру́шничество; **~ meaning** двусмы́сленность; **~ standard** двойна́я ме́рка. **4.** (*mus.*): **~ bass** контраба́с.

adv. вдво́е; **bend ~** сгиба́ть(ся), согну́ть(ся) вдво́е; **pay ~** плати́ть (*impf.*) вдвойне́; **he sees ~** у него́ двои́тся в глаза́х; **it costs ~ what it used to** э́то сто́ит вдво́е доро́же, чем ра́ньше.

v.t. **1.** (*make twice as great*) удв|а́ивать, -о́ить. **2.** (*fold, clench*): **~ a shawl** скла́дывать, сложи́ть шаль вдво́е; **~ up one's legs** под|гиба́ть, -огну́ть но́ги. **3.** (*cause to bend in pain*) скрю́чи|вать, -ть; **the blow ~d him up** он согну́лся попола́м от уда́ра.

v.i. **1.** (*become twice as great*) удв|а́иваться, -о́иться. **2.** (*turn sharply*): **he ~d back on his tracks** он поверну́л обра́тно по своему́ сле́ду. **3.** (*bend*) ско́рчи|ваться, -ться; **he ~d up with the pain** он скрю́чился от бо́ли. **4.** (*share room etc.*): **you will have to ~ up** вам придётся помести́ться вдвоём в одно́й ко́мнате. **5.** (*combine roles*): **the porter ~s as waiter** носи́льщик рабо́тает официа́нтом по совмести́тельству.

cpds. **~-barrelled** *adj.* двуство́льный; **~-breasted** *adj.* двубо́ртный; **~-check** *v.t.* перепров|еря́ть, -е́рить; **~-cross** *v.t.* обма́н|ывать, -у́ть; **~-decker** *n.* (*bus*) двухэта́жный авто́бус; **~ Dutch** *n.* кита́йская гра́мота; **~-edged** *adj.* (*lit., fig.*) обоюдоо́стрый; **~-quick** *adv.* о́чень бы́стро; **~-talk** *n.* укло́нчивые ре́чи (*f. pl.*).

double entendre [,duːb(ə)l ɑːn'tɑːndrə] *n.* двусмы́сленность.

doubly ['dʌb(ə)lɪ] *adv.* вдвойне́.

doubt [daʊt] *n.* сомне́ние; **I have my ~s** у меня́ есть сомне́ние; **there is no (room for) ~ that ...** нет сомне́ния в том, что...; **the question is in ~** э́тот вопро́с ещё не я́сен; **without ~** вне сомне́ния; несомне́нно; **no ~** без сомне́ния; вероя́тно.

v.t. & i. сомнева́ться (*impf.*) (в+*p.*); **I ~ that he will come** я не ду́маю, что́бы он пришёл.

doubtful ['daʊtfʊl] *adj.* **1.** (*feeling doubt*) сомнева́ющийся; **I am ~ about going** я сомнева́юсь, идти́ и́ли нет. **2.** (*causing doubt*) сомни́тельный; **he is a ~ character** он сомни́тельная ли́чность; **~ weather** неопределённая пого́да.

doubtless ['daʊtlɪs] *adv.* несомне́нно.

dough [dəʊ] *n.* те́сто; (*sl., money*) моне́та.

cpd. **~nut** *n.* по́нчик.

doughty ['daʊtɪ] *adj.* до́блестный, бра́вый.

dour [dʊə(r)] *adj.* суро́вый, непрекло́нный.

douse [daʊs] *v.t.* (*drench*) зал|ива́ть, -и́ть; (*extinguish*) гаси́ть, по-.

dove [dʌv] *n.* го́лубь (*m.*); **my ~** голу́бчик.

cpds. **~-coloured** *adj.* си́зый; **~cote** *n.* голубя́тня; **~tail** *n.* (*tech.*) ла́сточкин хвост; *v.t.* соедин|я́ть, -и́ть ла́сточкиным хвосто́м; *v.i.* (*fig.*) увя́з|ываться, -а́ться.

dowager ['daʊədʒə(r)] *n.* вдова́; **~ empress** вдо́вствующая императри́ца; (*elderly lady*) матро́на.

dowdy ['daʊdɪ] *adj.* неря́шливо/ду́рно одева́ющийся.

dowel ['daʊəl] *n.* (*tech.*) дю́бель (*m.*), штифт.

down[1] [daʊn] *n.* (*open high land*) безле́сная возвы́шенность.

down[2] [daʊn] *n.* (*hair, fluff*) пух, пушо́к.

down[3] [daʊn] *n.* **1.** (*reverse, of fortune etc.*) невзго́да; **ups and ~s** взлёты (*m. pl.*) и паде́ния (*nt. pl.*). **2.** (*coll., dislike*): **have a ~ on s.o.** име́ть зуб про́тив кого́-н.

adj. напра́вленный вниз/книзу́; **~ draught** (*tech.*) ни́жняя тя́га; **~ grade** спуск, укло́н; упа́док; **~ payment** ава́нс.

adv. **1.** (*expr. direction/state*) вниз/внизу́; **he is not ~ yet** (*from bedroom*) он ещё не сошёл вниз; **the sun is ~** со́лнце се́ло; **the blinds are ~** што́ры спу́щены; **~ south** на ю́ге; **prices are ~** це́ны сни́зились; (*fig.*): **he is ~ with fever** он слёг с высо́кой температу́рой; **he is ~ and out** он разби́т и уничто́жен; **~ under** (*coll.*) в Австра́лии. **2.** (*expr. movement to lower level*): **climb ~** слез|а́ть, -ть; **come ~** спус|ка́ться, -ти́ться; **~!** (*to a dog*) лежа́ть!; **we have read ~ to here** мы дочита́ли до э́того ме́ста. **3.** (*expr. change of position*): **sit ~** сади́ться, сесть; **lie ~** ложи́ться, лечь; **fall ~** па́дать, упа́сть; **knock s.o. ~** сби|ва́ть, -ть; **he bent ~** он нагну́лся. **4.** (*movement to less important place*): **we went ~ to Brighton for the day** мы съе́здили на́ день в Бра́йтон. **5.** (*reduction*): **the wind died ~** ве́тер ути́х; **the quality of these goods has gone ~** ка́чество э́тих това́ров уху́дшилось; **the house burnt ~** дом сгоре́л дотла́. **6.** (*of writing*): **write sth. ~** запи́с|ывать, -а́ть что-н. **7.** (*to end of scale*): **everyone from the manager ~ to the office-boy** все — от дире́ктора до посы́льного. **8.** (*at once*): **pay cash ~** плати́ть, нали́чными. **9.** (*var.*): **~ with tyranny!** доло́й тирани́ю!; **get ~ to business** взя́ться (*pf.*) за де́ло; **up and ~** (*to and fro*) взад и вперёд; *for other phrasal* *vv. see relevant v. entry.*

v.t. (*coll., overcome*) оси́ли|вать, -ть; (*coll., swallow*) прогл|а́тывать, -оти́ть; (*drop*) бр|оса́ть, -о́сить; ~ **tools** (*leave off work*) прекра|ща́ть, -ти́ть рабо́ту; (*strike*) забастова́ть (*pf.*).

prep. **1.** (*expr. downward direction*): **we walked ~ the hill** мы шли́ с горы́ (*or* по́д гору); **tears ran ~ her face** слёзы текли́ у неё по лицу́. **2.** (*at, to a lower or further part of*): **we sailed ~ the Volga** мы плы́ли вниз по Во́лге; **he lives ~ the street** он живёт да́льше по э́той у́лице. **3.** (*along*): **he walked ~ the street** он шёл по у́лице. **4.** (*var.*): **~ (the) wind** (*expr. place*) под ве́тром; (*expr. motion*) по ве́тру; **~ the ages** (*since earliest times*) с да́вних времён; **~ stage** (*theatr.*) на авансце́не.

down-and-out [daʊnə'naʊt] *n.* бродя́га (*m.*); бездо́мный.

downcast ['daʊnkɑːst] *adj.* (*dejected*) удручённый; пода́вленный.

downfall ['daʊnfɔːl] *n.* паде́ние, ги́бель.

downgrade ['daʊngreɪd] *v.t.* пон|ижа́ть, -и́зить в чи́не.

downhearted [daʊn'hɑːtɪd] *adj.* пода́вленный, угнетённый.

downhill ['daʊnhɪl] *adj.* накло́нный.

adv. по́д гору; вниз.

download [daʊn'ləʊd] *v.t.* (*comput.*) загру|жа́ть, -зи́ть.

downpour ['daʊnpɔː(r)] *n.* ли́вень (*m.*).

downright ['daʊnraɪt] *adj.* (*straightforward, blunt*) прямо́й; (*absolute*) соверше́нный; я́вный.

adv. соверше́нно, я́вно.

Down's syndrome [daʊnz] *n.*боле́знь Да́уна.

downstairs ['daʊnsteəz] *adj.*: **~ rooms** ко́мнаты пе́рвого этажа́.

adv. (*expr. place*) внизу́; (*expr. motion*) вниз.

downstream ['daʊnstriːm] *adv.* вниз по тече́нию.

downtown ['daʊntaʊn] *adj.* (*US*) располо́женный в делово́й ча́сти го́рода.

downtrodden ['daʊn,trɒd(ə)n] *adj.* угнетённый.

downward ['daʊnwəd] *adj.* спуска́ющийся, опуска́ющийся.

downwards ['daʊnwədz] *adv.* вниз.

downy ['daʊnɪ] *adj.* пуши́стый.

dowry ['daʊərɪ] *n.* прида́ное.

doze [dəʊz] *n.* дремо́та.

v.i. дрема́ть (*impf.*); **~ off** задрема́ть (*pf.*).

dozen ['dʌz(ə)n] *n.* дю́жина; **by the ~** дю́жинами; **talk nineteen to the ~** говори́ть (*impf.*) без у́молку; **~s of times** ты́сячу раз.

dozy ['dəʊzɪ] *adj.* дремо́тный, сонли́вый.

Dr. ['dɒktə(r)] *n.* (*abbr. of* **Doctor**) д-р, (до́ктор).

drab [dræb] *adj.* се́рый.

drabness ['dræbnɪs] *n.* се́рость.

Draconian [drə'kəʊnɪən] *adj.* драко́новский.

draft [drɑːft] *n. see also* **draught. 1.** (*outline, rough copy*) набро́сок, чернови́к. **2.** (*order for payment*) чек. **3.** (*US, conscription*) призы́в; **~ evasion** уклоне́ние от вое́нной слу́жбы.

v.t. **1.** (*detach for duty*) откомандиро́в|ывать, -а́ть. **2.** (*conscript*) приз|ыва́ть, -ва́ть. **3.** (*prepare ~ of*) набр|а́сывать, -оса́ть чернови́к +*g.*

drag [dræg] *n.* **1.** (*also* **~-net**) бре́день (*m.*). **2.** (*hindrance*) то́рмоз, препя́тствие. **3.** (*pull on cigarette etc.*) затя́жка. **4.** (*coll.*) же́нское пла́тье (трансвести́та).

v.t. **1.** (*pull*) тяну́ть, волочи́ть, тащи́ть (*all impf.*); **he could hardly ~ his feet along** он е́ле волочи́л но́ги; **~ one's feet** (*fig.*) тяну́ть (*impf.*); ме́длить (*impf.*). **2.** (*search, dredge*) драги́ровать (*impf., pf.*); чи́стить, по- дно +*g.*

v.i. **1.** (*trail*) волочи́ться (*impf.*); тащи́ться (*impf.*). **2.** (*be slow or tedious*) тяну́ться (*impf.*) затя́|гиваться, -ну́ться.

with advs.: **~ down** *v.t.*: **he ~ged the luggage down** он стащи́л чемода́ны вниз; **~ on** *v.i.*: **the performance ~ged on till 11** представле́ние затяну́лось до оди́ннадцати часо́в; **~ out** *v.t.* (*protract*) растя́|гивать, -ну́ть.

dragon ['drægən] *n.* (*fabulous beast*) драко́н; (*formidable woman*) гро́зная осо́ба.

cpd. **~-fly** *n.* стрекоза́.

dragoon [drə'guːn] *n.* драгу́н.

drain [dreɪn] *n.* **1.** (*channel carrying off sewage etc.*) водосто́к; (*pl.*) канализа́ция; **throw money down the ~** (*fig.*) тра́тить (*impf.*) де́ньги впусту́ю; **go down the ~** (*fig.*) кати́ться, по- по накло́нной пло́скости. **2.** (*cause of exhaustion*) истоще́ние; **it is a ~ on my energy** э́то истоща́ет мою эне́ргию.

v.t. **1.** (*water etc.*) отв|оди́ть, -ести́. **2.** (*land etc.*) осуш|а́ть, -и́ть; дрени́ровать (*impf., pf.*); **~ing-board** суши́лка. **3.** (*deplete*) истощ|а́ть, -и́ть. **4.** (*drink contents of*) осуш|а́ть, -и́ть.

v.i. **1.** (*flow away*) ут|ека́ть, -ечь. **2.** (*lose moisture, become dry*) высыха́ть, вы́сохнуть; **the field ~s into the river** вода́ с по́ля стека́ет в ре́ку.

cpd. **~pipe** *n.* дрена́жная труба́.

drainage ['dreɪnɪdʒ] *n.* **1.** (*draining*) дрена́ж, осуше́ние. **2.** (*system of drains*) канализа́ция.

drake [dreɪk] *n.* се́лезень (*m.*).

drama ['drɑːmə] *n.* дра́ма.

dramatic [drə'mætɪk] *adj.* драмати́ческий, театра́льный; драмати́чный, порази́тельный.

dramatics [drə'mætɪks] *n.* **1.** (*staging plays*) драмати́ческое иску́сство; **amateur ~** самоде́ятельный спекта́кль. **2.** (*theatrical behaviour*) драмати́зм.

dramatist ['dræmətɪst] *n.* драмату́рг.

dramatization [,dræmətaɪ'zeɪʃ(ə)n] *n.* инсцениро́вка.

dramatize ['dræmə,taɪz] *v.t.* (*turn into a play*) инсцени́ровать (*impf., pf.*); (*exaggerate*) драматизи́ровать (*impf., pf.*).

drape [dreɪp] *n.* драпиро́вка; (*US, curtain*) занаве́ска.

v.t. драпирова́ть, за-.

drapery ['dreɪpərɪ] *n.* (*trade*) торго́вля тексти́лем; (*goods*) тексти́льные изде́лия; тка́ни (*f. pl.*); (*clothing arranged in folds*) драпиро́вка.

drastic ['dræstɪk, 'drɑː-] *adj.* реши́тельный, круто́й.

draught [drɑːft] *n. see also* **draft. 1.** (*current of air*) тя́га; сквозня́к; **there is a ~ in this room** в э́той ко́мнате сквози́т. **2.** (*of ships*) оса́дка. **3.** (*supply of liquor*): **~ beer** пи́во из бо́чки. **4.** (*amount drunk*) глото́к; **he drank the glassful in one ~** он за́лпом вы́пил це́лый стака́н. **5.** (*traction by animals*) тя́га. **6.** (*pl., game*) ша́шки (*f. pl.*).

cpds. **~-board** *n.* ша́шечная доска́; **~-horse** *n.* ломова́я ло́шадь.

draughtsman ['drɑːftsmən] *n.* **1.** (*one who makes drawings etc.*) чертёжник. **2.** (*in game of draughts*) ша́шка.

draughty ['drɑːftɪ] *adj.*: **this is a ~ room** в э́той ко́мнате постоя́нный сквозня́к.

draw [drɔː] *n.* (*in lottery*) ро́зыгрыш; (*attraction*) прима́нка; (**~n** *game*) ничья́.

v.t. **1.** (*pull, move*) тяну́ть (*or* натя́гивать), на-; таска́ть (*indet.*), тащи́ть, по- (*det.*); **~ one's hand across one's forehead** пров|оди́ть, -ести́ руко́й по лбу; **~ s.o. aside** отв|оди́ть, -ести́ кого́-н. в сто́рону; **~ the curtains** (*close*) задёр|гивать, -нуть занаве́ски; (*open*) отдёр|гивать, -нуть занаве́ски; **the train was ~n by two engines** по́езд шёл двойно́й тя́гой. **2.** (*extract*) вытя́скивать, вы́тащить; **he drew a handkerchief out of his pocket** он вы́тащил плато́к из карма́на; **~ a knife** вы́хватить (*pf.*) нож; **~ blood** ра́нить (*pf.*) кого́-н. до кро́ви; **~ the sword** обнаж|а́ть, -и́ть меч; **have a tooth ~n; ~ a tooth** вы́дернуть/вы́рвать (*both pf.*) зуб; **~ lots** тяну́ть (*impf.*) жре́бий; **~ a blank** (*fig.*) потерпе́ть (*pf.*) неуда́чу; **her story ~s tears** её расска́з вызыва́ет слёзы. **3.** (*obtain from a source*): **~ water from a well** чéрпать (*impf.*) вóду из колóдца; **~ one's salary (money from the bank)** получ|áть, -йть зарплáту (дéньги в бáнке); **~ inspiration from nature** чéрпать (*impf.*) вдохновéние в прирóде; **~ on one's savings** трáтить (*impf.*) из своих сбережéний; **~ on s.o.'s help** приб|егáть, -éгнуть к чьей-н. пóмощи. **4.** (*attract*) привл|екáть, -ечь; **the film drew large audiences** фильм привлёк мнóго зрителей; **I drew him into the conversation** я втянýл егó в разговóр; **she felt ~n towards him** её тянýло к немý. **5.** (*stretch*): **he drew the metal into a long wire** он протянýл метáлл в длинную прóволоку; **his face was ~n with pain** егó лицó осýнулось от бóли. **6.** (*trace, depict*) рисовáть, на-; чертить, на-; **~ a line** пров|одить, -ести линию. **7.** (*of mental operations*): **~ a distinction** пров|одить, -ести различие; **~ conclusions** при|ходить, -йти к вы́водам. **8.** (*of documents*): **~ (up) a contract** сост|авлять, -áвить договóр. **9.** (*of ship*): **she ~s 20 feet of water** сýдно имéет осáдку в 20 фýтов. **10.** (*of contest*): **the match was ~n** матч был сы́гран (*or* окóнчился) вничью.

v.i. **1.** (*admit air*) тянýть, по-; втя|гивать, -нýть; **this pipe ~s well** э́та трýбка хорошó тя́нет. **2.** (*move, come*) придв|игáться, -инуться; **he drew near** он придвинулся поближе; **they drew round the table** они собрались вокрýг столá; **the day drew to a close** день близился к концý. **3.** (*pull*): **~ at a cigarette** затя|гиваться, -нýться папирóсой. *See also* **drawing**

with advs.: **~ back** *v.t.*: **he drew back the curtain** он отдёрнул занавéску; **~ down** *v.t.* (*e.g. blinds*) спус|кáть, -тить; **~ in** *v.t.*: **he drew in the details** он изобразил детáли; *v.i.*: **the train drew in** пóезд подошёл к перрóну; (*shorten*): **the days are ~ing in** дни станóвятся корóче; **~ off** *v.t.* (*e.g. water*) чéрп|ать, -нýть; **~ on** *v.t.*: **~ on one's gloves** натя|гивать, -нýть перчáтки; *v.i.* (*advance*): **autumn ~s on** óсень приближáется; **~ out** *v.t.* (*extract*) вытя́гивать, вы́тянуть; (*prolong*) протя|гивать, -нýть; (*encourage to speak*): **~ s.o. out** вызывáть, вы́звать когó-н. на разговóр; *v.i.*: **the train drew out** пóезд вы́шел (со стáнции); **~ up** *v.t.*: **~ o.s. up** (*to one's full height*) выпрямля́ться, вы́прямиться; **~ one's chair up to the table** пододв|игáть, -инуть стул к столý; **~ up troops** выстрáивать, вы́строить войскá; (*plan, contract etc.*) сост|авлять, -áвить; оф|ормлять, -óрмить; *v.i.*: **the taxi drew up at the door** такси подъéхало к двéри.

cpds. **~back** *n.* (*disadvantage*) недостáток, помéха; **~bridge** *n.* подъёмный мост.

drawer ['drɔ:ə(r), *senses* **2.** *and* **3.** drɔ:(r)] *n.* **1.** (*fin.*) трассáнт; (*of cheque*) чекодáтель (*m.*). **2.** (*in table etc.*) (выдвижнóй) я́щик; **chest of ~s** комóд. **3.** (*pl., underpants*) кальсóн|ы (*pl., g.* —).

drawing ['drɔ:ɪŋ] *n.* **1.** (*technique*) рисовáние. **2.** (*picture*) рисýнок.

cpds. **~-board** *n.* чертёжная доскá; **~-pin** *n.* кнóпка; **~-room** *n.* гостиная.

drawl [drɔ:l] *n.* протя́жное произношéние.

v.t. & i. тянýть (*impf.*) (словá).

dray [dreɪ] *n.* ломовáя телéга.

cpds. **~-horse** *n.* ломовáя лóшадь; **~man** *n.* ломовóй извóзчик.

dread [dred] *n.* ýжас, страх.

adj. ужáсный, грóзный.

v.t. боя́ться (*impf.*) *+g.*; **I ~ to think what may happen** мне стрáшно подýмать, что мóжет случиться.

cpd. **~nought** *n.* дреднóут.

dreadful ['dredfʊl] *adj.* ужáсный.

dream [dri:m] *n.* **1.** (*appearance in sleep*) сон, сновидéние. **2.** (*fantasy*) мечтá, мечтáние. **3.** (*bemused state*): **he goes about in a ~** он хóдит как во сне. **4.** (*delightful object*) мечтá, скáзка; **~ house** домскáзка.

v.t. & i. **1.** (*in sleep*) видеть (*impf.*) сон; **I ~t that I was in the forest** мне снилось, что я в лесý; **I ~t of you** вы мне снились; я вас видел во сне. **2.** (*imagine*) фантазировать (*impf.*); **I never ~t of doing so** я и не помышля́л сдéлать э́то; **he ~t up a plan** (*coll.*) он сочинил план. **3.** (*spend time in reverie*) грéзить (*impf.*); мечтáть (*impf.*); **he ~t away his life** он провёл жизнь в мечтáх.

cpds. **~-land, ~-world** *nn.* цáрство грёз; **~-like** *adj.* скáзочный.

dreamer ['dri:mə(r)] *n.* мечтáтель (*m.*).

dreamy ['dri:mɪ] *adj.* мечтáтельный.

dreariness ['drɪərɪnɪs] *n.* сéрость.

dreary ['drɪərɪ] *adj.* (*gloomy*) тоскливый; (*dull*) сéрый.

dredge [dredʒ] *n.* (*net*) дрáга; (*machine*) дрáга, землечерпáлка.

v.i. & i. драгировать (*impf., pf.*); **~ a harbour** оч|ищáть, -истить порт; **~ up** вылáвливать, вы́ловить.

dredger ['dredʒə(r)] *n.* землечерпáлка, землесóс.

dreg [dreg] *n.* (*usu. pl.*) **1.** (*of liquor*) отстóй, осáдок. **2.** (*pl., fig.*) подóнки (*m. pl.*).

drench [drentʃ] *v.t.* пром|áчивать, -очить; **he was ~ed to the skin** он вы́мок до нитки; он промóк до костéй.

dress [dres] *n.* **1.** (*clothing, costume*) наря́д, туалéт, плáтье; **national ~** национáльный костю́м; **~ circle** бельетáж; **~ coat** фрак; **~ rehearsal** генерáльная репетиция; **~ shirt** фрáчная сорóчка. **2.** (*woman's garment*) плáтье.

v.t. **1.** (*clothe*) од|евáть, -éть; **the boy can ~ himself** мáльчик умéет сам одевáться; **she was ~ed in white** онá былá одéта в бéлое. **2.** (*prepare*) припр|авлять, -áвить; **~ leather** выдéлывать, вы́делать кóжу; **~ a salad** запр|авлять, -áвить салáт; **~ (clean) a chicken** потрошить, вы- кýрицу. **3.** (*of a wound*) перевя́з|ывать, -áть. **4.** (*adorn*) наря|жáть, -дить; **~ a shop window** оф|ормлять, -óрмить витрину. **5.** (*mil., align*) вырáвнивать, вы́ровнять.

v.i. **1.** (*put on one's clothes*) од|евáться, -éться; **~ up** (**~** *elaborately*) наря|жáться, -диться; разря|жáться, -диться; **they ~ed up as pirates** они нарядились пирáтами. **2.** (*put on evening ~*) перeод|евáться, -éться в вечéрнее плáтье. **3.** (*of troops*) вырáвниваться, вы́ровняться; **right ~!** равнéние напрáво!

cpds. **~maker** *n.* портниха; **~maker's** *n.* ательé (*indecl.*) (мод).

dresser[1] ['dresə(r)] *n.* (*chooser of clothes etc.*): **she is a good ~** онá умéет одевáться.

dresser[2] ['dresə(r)] *n.* (*sideboard*) кýхонный шкаф.

dressing ['dresɪŋ] *n.* **1.** (*art of dress*) одевáние. **2.** (*for wounds*) перевя́зочный материáл; перевя́зки (*f. pl.*). **3.** (*of salad etc.*) припрáва. **4.** (*manure*) удобрéние.

cpds. **~down** *n.* (*coll.*) головомóйка, трёпка; **~-gown** *n.* халáт; **~-room** *n.* (*theatr., etc.*) грим-убóрная; **~-table** *n.* туалéт, туалéтный стóлик.

dribble ['drɪb(ə)l] *n.* (*trickle*) стрýйка.

v.t.: **~ a ball** вести (*det.*) мяч.

v.i. (*of baby*) пускáть, распустить слю́ни.

drier ['draɪə(r)] *n.* (**hair-~**) сушилка; (**clothes-~**) сушильный автомáт.

drift [drɪft] *n.* **1.** (*heap of snow, leaves etc.*) нанóс, кýча. **2.** (*meaning*) смысл; **I get his ~** я понимáю, кудá он клóнит.

v.t.: **the wind ~ed the snow into high banks** вéтер намёл высóкие сугрóбы.

v.i. дрейфовáть (*impf.*); **the boat ~ed out to sea** лóдку унеслó в мóре; **they were friends but ~ed apart** они бы́ли друзья́ми, но их пути постепéнно разошлись.

cpd. **~wood** *n.* сплавно́й лес.

drifter ['drɪftə(r)] *n.* (*aimless pers.*) лету́н; перекати́-по́ле.

drill[1] [drɪl] *n.* (*instrument*) сверло́, бура́в.

v.t. сверли́ть, про-; бури́ть, про-; **~ a tooth** сверли́ть (*impf.*) зуб.

v.i. бури́ть (*impf.*); **~ for oil** бури́ть (*impf.*) нефтяну́ю сква́жину.

drill[2] [drɪl] *n.* **1.** (*military exercise*) строева́я подгото́вка. **2.** (*thorough practice*) трениро́вка. **3.** (*coll., procedure*) процеду́ра.

v.t. **1.** (*troops*) обуч|а́ть, -и́ть стро́ю; муштрова́ть, вы́-. **2.: ~ s.o. in grammar** ната́ск|ивать, -а́ть кого́-н. по грамма́тике.

v.i. упражня́ться (*impf.*); про|ходи́ть, -йти́ строево́е обуче́ние; **the troops were ~ing all morning** войска́ обуча́лись стро́ю всё у́тро.

cpd. **~-sergeant** *n.* сержа́нт-инстру́ктор по стро́ю.

drily, dryly ['draɪlɪ] *adv.* ирони́чно.

drink [drɪŋk] *n.* **1.** (*liquid*) питьё, напи́ток. **2.** (*quantity*) глото́к; **give me a ~ of water** да́йте мне воды́. **3.** (*alcoholic*) спиртно́й напи́ток; **take to ~** пристрасти́ться (*pf.*) к вину́; **drive s.o. to ~** дов|оди́ть, -ести́ кого́-н. до пья́нства.

v.t. **1.** (*consume liquid*) пить, вы́-; **~ down** выпива́ть, вы́пить за́лпом; **~ up** доп|ива́ть, -и́ть; **~ing-fountain** питьево́й фонта́нчик; **~ing-water** питьева́я вода́. **2.** (*of plants, soil etc.*) впи́т|ывать, -а́ть. **3.** (*absorb with the mind*) впи́т|ывать, -а́ть. **4.** (*of alcoholic liquor*) пить (*or* выпива́ть) вы́-; **~ s.o. under the table** перепи́ть (*pf.*) кого́-н.; **~ing-bout** попо́йка; **~ing-song** засто́льная пе́сня. **5.: ~ a toast** провозгласи́ть (*pf.*) тост; **~ s.o.'s health** пить (*impf.*) за чьё-н. здоро́вье; **I ~ to your success** я пью за ваш успе́х.

v.i. (*consume liquid*) пить (*impf.*); (*be a drunkard*) пить запо́ем, пья́нствовать (*impf.*); **do you ~?** вы пьёте?; **he ~s like a fish** он пьёт как сапо́жник.

cpd. **~-driving** *n.* вожде́ние в нетре́звом состоя́нии.

drinkable ['drɪŋkəb(ə)l] *adj.* (*capable of being drunk*) питьево́й, го́дный для питья́; (*palatable*) вку́сный.

drinker ['drɪŋkə(r)] *n.* (*one who drinks, esp. alcohol*) пью́щий; **he is an occasional ~** он иногда́ выпива́ет; (*drunkard*) пья́ница.

drip [drɪp] *n.* ка́панье; (*sl., weak or dull person*) зану́да (*c.g.*).

v.t.: **he was ~ping sweat** с него́ кати́лся пот.

v.i. ка́пать (*impf.*); па́дать (*impf.*) ка́плями; **~ping wet** насквозь промо́кший.

dripping ['drɪpɪŋ] *n.* (*cul.*) топлёный жир.

drive [draɪv] *n.* **1.** (*ride in vehicle*) езда́; **go for a ~** прокати́ться (*det.*), поката́ться (*indet.*) (*both pf.*) на маши́не; **the station is an hour's ~ away** до ста́нции час езды́. **2.** (*private road*) подъездна́я доро́га. **3.** (*hit, stroke, at tennis etc.*) драйв, си́льный уда́р. **4.** (*energy*) напо́ристость, си́ла. **5.** (*organized effort*) кампа́ния. **6.** (*tournament*) состяза́ние. **7.** (*driving gear*) переда́ча, приво́д; **left-hand ~** ле́вое рулево́е управле́ние.

v.t. **1.** (*force to move*) гоня́ть (*indet.*), гнать (*det.*); **~ away** прог|оня́ть, -на́ть; **~ in** заг|оня́ть, -на́ть; **~ out** выгоня́ть, вы́гнать; **~ cattle to market** гнать (*det.*) скот на ры́нок; **~ s.o. into a corner** (*fig.*) загна́ть (*pf.*) кого́-н. в у́гол. **2.** (*operate*) управля́ть (*impf.*) +*i.*; пра́вить (*impf.*) +*i.*; **~ a car** води́ть (*indet.*) маши́ну; **the machinery is ~n by steam** маши́на рабо́тает на пару́. **3.** (*convey*) отв|ози́ть, -езти́. **4.** (*impel, of objects*): **he drove a nail into the plank** он вбил гвоздь в до́ску; **he drove the ball into our court** (*tennis*) он посла́л мяч на на́шу полови́ну ко́рта; **~n snow** сугро́б; **~ home** (*nail etc.*) загоня́ть, загна́ть; вкол|а́чивать, -оти́ть; **~ sth. home to s.o.** довести́ (*pf.*) кого́-н. до созна́ния чего́-н.; **this drove the matter out of my head** э́то вы́шибло у меня́ всё из головы́. **5.** (*impel, fig.*): **~ s.o. mad** св|оди́ть, -ести́ кого́-н. с ума́; **hunger drove him to steal** го́лод заста́вил его́ ворова́ть. **6.** (*force to work hard*) гоня́ть, гна́ть; **he has been driving his staff too much** он соверше́нно загоня́л свои́х подчинённых. **7.** (*engineering*) про|кла́дывать, -ложи́ть; пров|оди́ть, -ести́; **~ a tunnel through a hill** проложи́ть (*pf.*) тунне́ль че́рез го́ру. **8.** (*effect, conclude*): **~ a bargain** заключ|а́ть, -и́ть сде́лку.

v.i. **1.** (*operate vehicle*) води́ть (*indet.*), вести́ (*det.*) маши́ну; **we drove up to the door** мы подъе́хали пря́мо к две́ри. **2.** (*be impelled*): **rain drove against the panes** дождь бил в око́нные стёкла; **driving rain** проливно́й дождь. **3.** (*be active*): **what is he driving at?** к чему́ он кло́нит?; куда́ он гнёт? **4.** (*of vehicle*): **the car ~s easily** э́ту маши́ну легко́ вести́.

drivel ['drɪv(ə)l] *n.* (*nonsense*) чушь.

v.t. & i. поро́ть (*impf.*) чушь; плести́ (*impf.*) вздор/чепуху́.

driver ['draɪvə(r)] *n.* (*of vehicle*) води́тель (*m.*), шофёр; (*of animals*) пого́нщик, гуртовщи́к.

driving ['draɪvɪŋ] *n.* езда́; вожде́ние автомоби́ля; **~ instructor** преподава́тель (*m.*) автошко́лы.

cpds. **~-belt** *n.* приводно́й реме́нь; **~-licence** *n.* води́тельские права́; **~-school** *n.* автошко́ла; **~-test** *n.* экза́мен на вожде́ние; **~-wheel** *n.* веду́щее колесо́.

drizzle ['drɪz(ə)l] *n.* и́зморось.

v.i. мороси́ть (*impf.*).

droll [drəʊl] *adj.* чудно́й, заба́вный.

dromedary ['drɒmɪdərɪ, 'drʌm-] *n.* дромаде́р.

drone [drəʊn] *n.* **1.** (*bee; also fig., idler*) тру́тень (*m.*). **2.** (*of engine*) гуде́ние; (*of voice*) жужжа́ние.

v.t. & i. (*hum*) жужжа́ть (*impf.*); гуде́ть (*impf.*); (*speak monotonously*) бубни́ть (*impf.*).

drool [dru:l] *v.i.* пус|ка́ть, -ти́ть слю́ни.

droop [dru:p] *v.i.* (*of flowers etc.*) склон|я́ться, -и́ться; (*fig.*): **his spirits ~ed** он пал ду́хом.

drop [drɒp] *n.* **1.** (*small quantity of liquid*) ка́пля; **~ by ~** ка́пля по ка́пле; (*fig.*): **a ~ in the ocean** ка́пля в мо́ре; **he had a ~ too much** он хвати́л ли́шнего. **2.** (*small round object*): **acid ~** ледене́ц. **3.** (*fall*) паде́ние; **~ in prices/temperature** паде́ние цен; пониже́ние температу́ры; **at the ~ of a hat** (*fig.*) сра́зу/то́тчас же; **there is a ~ of 30 feet behind this wall** за э́той стено́й обры́в в 30 фу́тов высоты́.

v.t. **1.** (*allow, cause to fall*) роня́ть, урони́ть; **~ anchor** бр|оса́ть, -о́сить я́корь; **~ a stitch** спус|ка́ть, -ти́ть петлю́; **~ a letter into the box** опус|ка́ть, -ти́ть письмо́ в я́щик; **~ supplies by parachute** сбр|а́сывать, -о́сить припа́сы на парашю́те. **2.** (*impel, force down*) сра|жа́ть, -зи́ть; **~ shells into a town** обстре́л|ивать, -я́ть го́род. **3.** (*lower*): **~ one's voice** пон|ижа́ть, -и́зить го́лос; **~ one's eyes** потупи́ть (*pf.*) глаза́. **4.** (*send, utter casually*): **~ s.o. a line** черкну́ть (*pf.*) кому́-н. па́ру строк; **~ a hint** oброни́ть (*pf.*) намёк. **5.** (*omit, cease*) опус|ка́ть, -ти́ть; пропус|ка́ть, -ти́ть; **~ it!** бро́сьте! **6.** (*allow to descend, disembark*) выса́живать, вы́садить; **please ~ me at the station** пожа́луйста, вы́садите меня́ у ста́нции. **7.** (*abandon*) бр|оса́ть, -о́сить; **let us ~ the subject** дава́йте оста́вим э́ту те́му; **you should ~ smoking** вы должны́ бро́сить кури́ть. **8.: ~ a goal** заб|ива́ть, -и́ть гол.

v.i. **1.** (*fall, descend*) па́дать, упа́сть; опус|ка́ться, -ти́ться; **~ into one's club** загля́|дывать, -ну́ть в клуб. **2.** (*become weaker or lower*) па́дать, упа́сть; пон|ижа́ться, -и́зиться; **the wind ~ped** ве́тер стих; **prices ~ped** це́ны упа́ли; **his voice ~ped** он понизил голос. **3.** (*expr. separation etc.*): ~ **behind the others** отст|ава́ть, -а́ть от остальны́х; **he ~ped from sight** он исче́з из по́ля зре́ния. **4.** (*sink, collapse*) па́дать, упа́сть; опус|ка́ться, -ти́ться; **he ~ped (on) to his knees** он упа́л/опусти́лся на коле́ни; **he ~ped dead** он внеза́пно у́мер; ~ **dead!** (*coll.*) подо́хни!; чтоб ты сдох! **5.** (*cease, be abandoned*): **we let the matter ~** мы бро́сили э́то.

with advs.: ~ **in** *v.i.* (*coll.*): **he ~ped in on me** он загляну́л ко мне; ~ **off** *v.i.* (*become fewer or less*) ум|еньша́ться, -е́ньшиться; **attendance ~ped off** посеща́емость упа́ла; (*coll., doze off*) засну́ть (*pf.*); ~ **out** *v.i.*: **five runners ~ped out** пять бегуно́в вы́были из состяза́ния; **he ~ped out of school** он бро́сил шко́лу.

cpd. **~-out** *n.* челове́к, поста́вивший себя́ вне о́бщества; (*from school*) недоу́чка (*c.g.*).

droplet ['drɒplət] *n.* ка́пелька.

dropper ['drɒpə(r)] *n.* пипе́тка; ка́пельница.

dropping ['drɒpɪŋ] *n.* (*pl.*) помёт.

dropsy ['drɒpsɪ] *n.* водя́нка.

droshky ['drɒʃkɪ] *n.* дро́ж|ки (*pl., g.* -ек).

dross [drɒs] *n.* шлак, дросс; (*fig.*) отбро́сы (*m. pl.*).

drought [draʊt] *n.* за́суха.

drove [drəʊv] *n.* (*herd*) ста́до, гурт; (*crowd*) толпа́.

drover ['drəʊvə(r)] *n.* гуртовщи́к.

drown [draʊn] *v.t.* **1.** (*kill by immersion*) топи́ть, у-; ~ **one's sorrows in drink** топи́ть, у- го́ре в вине́; ~ **o.s.** топи́ться, у-; **be ~ed** утону́ть (*pf.*). **2.** (*of sound*) приглуш|а́ть, -и́ть. **3.** (*bathe, immerse*) погру|жа́ть, -зи́ть; **like a ~ed rat** (*fig.*) мо́крый как мышь.

v.i. тону́ть, у-; утопа́ть (*impf.*); **death by ~ing** утопле́ние.

drowsiness ['draʊzɪnɪs] *n.* дремо́та, сонли́вость.

drowsy ['draʊzɪ] *adj.* (*feeling sleepy*) со́нный, дре́млющий.

drub [drʌb] *v.t.* колоти́ть, по-.

drubbing ['drʌbɪŋ] *n.* трёпка, взбу́чка; **give s.o. a ~** над|ава́ть, -а́ть кому́-н. колоту́шек.

drudgery ['drʌdʒərɪ] *n.* изнури́тельная рабо́та.

drug [drʌg] *n.* **1.** (*medicinal substance*) медикаме́нт, лека́рство. **2.** (*narcotic or stimulant*) нарко́тик; ~ **addict** наркома́н.

v.t. (*food etc.*) подме́ш|ивать, -а́ть яд/нарко́тики в (*еду*); (*pers.*) да|ва́ть, -ть нарко́тики +*d.*; одурма́ни|вать, -ть.

cpd. **~store** *n.* (*US*) ≃ апте́ка.

druggist ['drʌgɪst] *n.* апте́карь (*m.*).

drum [drʌm] *n.* **1.** (*instrument*) бараба́н; **bass ~** большо́й бараба́н. **2.** (*container for oil etc.*) желе́зная бо́чка.

v.t. бараба́нить (*impf.*); бить (*impf.*) в бараба́н; ~ **up support** соз|ыва́ть, -ва́ть на подмо́гу; ~ **sth. into s.o.'s head** вд|а́лбливать, -олби́ть что-н. кому́-н. в го́лову.

v.i. бараба́нить (*impf.*); бить (*impf.*) в бараба́н; ~ **with one's fingers on the table** бараба́нить (*impf.*) па́льцами по́ столу.

cpds. **~-beat** *n.* бараба́нный бой; **~stick** *n.* бараба́нная па́лочка; (*of fowl*) но́жка.

drummer ['drʌmə(r)] *n.* (*also* **~-boy**) бараба́нщик.

drunk [drʌŋk] *n.* пья́ный.

adj. пья́ный; ~ **driver** автоалкого́лик; **half ~** подвы́пивший; **dead ~** мертве́цки пья́ный.

drunkard ['drʌŋkəd] *n.* пья́ница (*c.g.*).

drunken ['drʌŋkən] *adj.* пья́ный.

drunkenness ['drʌŋkənnɪs] *n.* пья́нство.

dry [draɪ] *adj.* **1.** (*free from moisture or rain*) сухо́й; засо́хший; **wipe ~** вытира́ть, вы́тереть на́сухо. **2.** (*not supplying water etc.*) вы́сохший, сухо́й; **a ~ well** вы́сохший коло́дец. **3.**: ~ **run** (*trial*) про́бный забе́г. **4.** (*of wine*) сухо́й. **5.** (*of humour*) сухо́й, сухова́тый; (*of remark etc.*) ирони́ческий; *see also* **drily**. **6.**: ~ **shampoo** сухо́й шампу́нь. **7.**: **the country went dry** в стране́ ввели́ сухо́й зако́н.

v.t. суши́ть, вы́-; ~ **o.s.** вытира́ться, вы́тереться; ~ **one's tears** ут|ира́ть, -ере́ть слёзы; ~ **the dishes** вытира́ть, вы́тереть посу́ду; **dried fruit(s)** сушёные фру́кты; **dried egg** яи́чный порошо́к; **dried milk** сухо́е молоко́.

v.i. со́хнуть (*impf.*); суши́ться, вы́-; **our clothes have dried** на́ша оде́жда вы́сохла; **the well dried up** коло́дец вы́сох; **his imagination dried up** его́ фанта́зия исся́кла; ~ **up!** заткни́сь! (*coll.*); **hang sth. up to ~** ве́шать, пове́сить что-н. для просу́шки.

cpds. **~-clean** *v.t.* подв|ерга́ть, -е́ргнуть хими́ческой чи́стке; **~-cleaning** *n.* хими́ческая чи́стка, химчи́стка.

dryly ['draɪlɪ] = **drily**

dryness ['draɪnɪs] *n.* су́хость, сушь.

DSS (*abbr. of* ***Department of Social Security***) Министе́рство социа́льного обеспе́чения.

DTP (*abbr. of* ***desktop publishing***) насто́льная полигра́фия.

DT's [diː'tiːz] *n.* (*coll.*) бе́лая горя́чка.

dual ['djuːəl] *adj.* двойственный, двойно́й; ~ **ownership** совме́стное владе́ние; ~ **control** двойно́е управле́ние; ~ **nationality** двойно́е по́дданство.

cpd. **~-purpose** *adj.* двойно́го назначе́ния.

dualism ['djuːə,lɪz(ə)m] *n.* дуали́зм.

duality [,djuː'ælɪtɪ] *n.* дво́йственность.

dub [dʌb] *v.t.* **1.** (*a knight*) посвя|ща́ть, -ти́ть в ры́цари; (*fig., call*) проз|ыва́ть, -ва́ть; крести́ть, о-. **2.** (*coll., film*) дубли́ровать (*impf.*).

dubious ['djuːbɪəs] *adj.* (*feeling doubt*) сомнева́ющийся; (*inspiring mistrust; ambiguous*) сомни́тельный.

ducal ['djuːk(ə)l] *adj.* ге́рцогский.

ducat ['dʌkət] *n.* дука́т.

duchess ['dʌtʃɪs] *n.* герцоги́ня.

duchy ['dʌtʃɪ] *n.* ге́рцогство, кня́жество; **Grand D~ of Muscovy** Вели́кое кня́жество Моско́вское.

duck[1] [dʌk] *n.* **1.** (*water-bird*) у́тка; (*as food*) утя́тина; **like water off a ~'s back** как с гу́ся вода́; **dead ~** (*fig.*) ко́нченый челове́к; ги́блое де́ло; **lame ~** неуда́чник. **2.** (*zero score*) нулево́й счёт; **make a ~** сыгра́ть (*pf.*) с нулевы́м счётом.

cpds. **~-bill (platypus)** *n.* утконо́с; **~weed** *n.* ря́ска.

duck[2] [dʌk] *v.t.* погру|жа́ть, -зи́ть; окун|а́ть, -у́ть; ~ **one's head** бы́стро нагну́ть (*pf.*) го́лову; ~ **s.o.** окун|а́ть, -у́ть кого́-н.; (*evade*): ~ **a question** увёр|тываться, -ну́ться от отве́та.

v.i. окун|а́ться, -у́ться; ~ **to avoid a blow** накло-н|я́ться, -и́ться, что́бы избежа́ть уда́ра.

duckling ['dʌklɪŋ] *n.* утёнок; **ugly ~** га́дкий утёнок.

duct ['dʌkt] *n.* (*anat.*) кана́л, прото́к.

ductile ['dʌktaɪl] *adj.* (*tech.*) тягу́чий, ко́вкий.

ductless ['dʌktlɪs] *adj.*: ~ **gland** железа́ вну́тренней секре́ции.

dud [dʌd] *n.* (*coll.*) (*bomb*) неразорва́вшаяся бо́мба; (*shell*) неразорва́вшийся снаря́д; (*cheque etc.*) подде́лка; (*pers.*) пусто́е ме́сто.

adj. непригóдный, подде́льный.

due [djuː] *n.* **1.** (~ *credit*) до́лжное; **to give him his ~, he tried hard** на́до отда́ть ему́ до́лжное — он о́чень стара́лся. **2.** (*pl., charges*) сбо́ры (*m. pl.*), взно́сы (*m. pl.*); **membership ~s** чле́нские взно́сы.

adj. **1.** (*owing, payable*) причита́ющийся; **debts ~ to us** причита́ющиеся нам долги́; **when is the rent ~?** когда́ на́до плати́ть за кварти́ру?; **the bill falls ~ on October 1** срок платежа́ по ве́кселю наступа́ет пе́рвого октября́. **2.** (*proper*) до́лжный, **with ~ attention** с до́лжным внима́нием; **in ~ time** в своё вре́мя; **after ~ consideration** по́сле надлежа́щего рассмотре́ния; **in ~ course** в свою́ о́чередь. **3.** (*expected*): **he is ~ to speak twice** он должен вы́ступить два́жды; **the mail is ~ tomorrow** по́чта должна́ быть за́втра. **4.:** ~ **to** (*coll.*, *owing to*) благодаря́+*d.*; из-за+*g.*

adv. то́чно, пря́мо; **it lies ~ south** э́то лежи́т пря́мо на юг отсю́да.

duel ['dju:əl] *n.* дуэ́ль, поеди́нок.

v.i. дра́ться (*impf.*) на дуэ́ли.

duellist ['dju:əlɪst] *n.* дуэля́нт.

duet [dju:'et] *n.* дуэ́т.

duffle ['dʌf(ə)l] *n.* **1.** (*text.*): ~ **coat** коро́ткое пальто́ из шерстяно́й ба́йки с капюшо́ном. **2.:** ~ **bag** (*kit-bag*) вещево́й мешо́к.

dug-out ['dʌgaʊt] *n.* (*shelter*) блинда́ж; (*canoe*) челно́к.

duke [dju:k] *n.* ге́рцог; **grand** ~ вели́кий князь.

dukedom ['dju:kdəm] *n.* ге́рцогство; кня́жество.

dulcet ['dʌlsɪt] adj. сла́дкий; не́жный.

dulcimer ['dʌlsɪmə(r)] *n.* цимба́л|ы (*pl.*, *g.* —).

dull [dʌl] *adj.* **1.** (*not clear or bright*) ту́склый; **a ~ sound** глухо́й звук; ~ **weather** па́смурная пого́да. **2.** (*slow in understanding*) тупо́й. **3.** (*uninteresting*) ску́чный. **4.** (*not sharp*) тупо́й; **a ~ knife** тупо́й нож; **a ~ pain** тупа́я боль.

v.t. притуп|ля́ть, -и́ть.

cpd. **~-witted** *adj.* тупоу́мный.

dullard ['dʌləd] *n.* тупи́ца.

dullness ['dʌlnɪs] *n.* ту́пость.

duly ['dju:lɪ] *adv.* до́лжным о́бразом; в до́лжное вре́мя; своевре́менно.

dumb [dʌm] *adj.* **1.** (*unable to speak*) немо́й; ~ **animals** бесслове́сные живо́тные. **2.** (*temporarily silent*) онеме́вший, немо́й; **he was struck ~** он онеме́л. **3.** (*US coll.*, *stupid*) глу́пый.

cpd. **~-bell** *n.* ганте́ль.

dum(b)found [dʌm'faʊnd] *v.t.* ошара́ш|ивать, -ить.

dummy ['dʌmɪ] *n.* **1.** ку́кла; **tailor's ~** манеке́н; **baby's ~** со́ска. **2.** (*at cards*) «болва́н». **3.** (*stand-in*) подставно́е лицо́.

adj. (*imitation*) подставно́й; ~ **run** испыта́тельный рейс.

dump [dʌmp] *n.* **1.** (*heap of refuse*) му́сорная ку́ча. **2.** (*place for tipping refuse*) сва́лка. **3.** (*ammunition store*) вре́менный полево́й скла́д. **4.** (*seedy place*) дыра́ (*coll.*).

v.t. **1.** (*put in a ~*) выбра́сывать, вы́бросить на сва́лку. **2.** (*deposit carelessly*) сва́л|ивать, -и́ть.

dumpling ['dʌmplɪŋ] *n.* клёцка.

dumps [dʌmps] *n.* (*coll.*): **the ~** уны́ние.

dunce [dʌns] *n.* тупи́ца (*m.*).

dunderhead ['dʌndə,hed] *n.* болва́н.

dune [dju:n] *n.* дю́на.

dung [dʌŋ] *n.* наво́з.

dungarees [,dʌngə'ri:z] *n.* рабо́чий комбинезо́н.

dungeon ['dʌndʒ(ə)n] *n.* темни́ца.

dunk [dʌŋk] *v.t.* мак|а́ть, -ну́ть.

duo ['dju:əʊ] *n.* дуэ́т; па́ра.

duodenal [,dju:əʊ'di:nəl] *adj.* дуодена́льный.

duodenum [,dju:əʊ'di:nəm] *n.* двенадцатипе́рстная кишка́.

dupe [dju:p] *n.* же́ртва обма́на, простофи́ля (*c.g.*).

v.t. ост|авля́ть, -а́вить в дурака́х; над|ува́ть, -у́ть.

duplex ['dju:pleks] *adj.* двойно́й; ~ **house** двухкварти́рный дом; ~ **apartment** кварти́ра, располо́женная на двух этажа́х.

duplicate[1] ['dju:plɪkət] *n.* дублика́т; (то́чная) ко́пия; **in ~** в двух экземпля́рах.

adj. двойно́й; одина́ковый.

duplicate[2] ['dju:plɪ,keɪt] *v.t.* (*double*) удв|а́ивать, -о́ить; (*copy*) дубли́ровать (*impf.*); сн|има́ть, -я́ть ко́пию с+*g.*

duplication [,dju:plɪ'keɪʃ(ə)n] *n.* удвое́ние; сня́тие ко́пии.

duplicator ['dju:plɪ,keɪtə(r)] *n.* (*machine*) копирова́льный аппара́т.

duplicity [dju:'plɪsɪtɪ] *n.* двули́чность.

durability [,djʊərə'bɪlɪtɪ] *n.* про́чность.

durable ['djʊərəb(ə)l] *n.*: **consumer ~s** това́ры (*m. pl.*) дли́тельного по́льзования.

adj. про́чный.

duralumin [djʊə'ræljʊmɪn] *n.* дюралюми́ний.

duration [djʊə'reɪʃ(ə)n] *n.* продолжи́тельность, продолже́ние; **for the ~ of** на вре́мя +*g.*; **of short ~** непродолжи́тельный, недолгове́чный.

duress [djʊə'res, 'djʊə-] *n.* принужде́ние, нажи́м, давле́ние; **under ~** под нажи́мом/давле́нием.

during ['djʊərɪŋ] *prep.* (*throughout*) в тече́ние+*g.*; (*at some point in*) во вре́мя+*g.*

dusk [dʌsk] *n.* су́мер|ки (*pl.*, *g.* -ек).

dust [dʌst] *n.* **1.** (*powdered earth etc.*) пыль; **bite the ~** па́|дать, -сть сражённым; **shake the ~ off one's feet** отрясти́ (*pf.*) прах с ног свои́х. **2.** (*human remains*) прах.

v.t. **1.** (*remove ~ from*) ст|ира́ть, -ере́ть пыль с +*g.*; ~ **a room** уб|ира́ть, -ра́ть ко́мнату. **2.** (*sprinkle*) пос|ыпа́ть, -ы́пать; ~ **sugar on to a cake** пос|ыпа́ть, -ы́пать торт са́харной пу́дрой.

cpds. **~bin** *n.* му́сорный я́щик; **~-cart** *n.* фурго́н для сбо́ра му́сора, мусорово́з; **~-jacket** *n.* (*of book*) супероблo̓жка; **~man** *n.* му́сорщик; **~pan** *n.* сово́к для му́сора; **~-storm** *n.* пы́льная бу́ря.

duster ['dʌstə(r)] *n.* пы́льная тря́пка.

dusty ['dʌstɪ] *adj.* пы́льный.

Dutch [dʌtʃ] *n.* голла́ндский/нидерла́ндский язы́к; **double ~** кита́йская гра́мота.

cpds. **~man** *n.* голла́ндец; **that's Smith, or I'm a ~man** я не я бу́ду, е́сли э́то не Смит; **~woman** *n.* голла́ндка.

dutiful ['dju:tɪ,fʊl] *adj.* послу́шный, пре́данный.

duty ['dju:tɪ] *n.* **1.** (*moral obligation*) долг, обя́занность; **he has a strong sense of ~** у него́ си́льно ра́звито чу́вство до́лга; **a ~ call** официа́льный визи́т. **2.** (*official employment*) служе́бные обя́занности; дежу́рство; **on ~** на дежу́рстве; **come on ~** при|ходи́ть, -йти́ на дежу́рство; **off ~** свобо́дный; в свобо́дное/неслуже́бное вре́мя; **go off ~** уходи́ть, уйти́ с дежу́рства; **take up one's duties** присту́п|а́ть, -и́ть к исполне́нию свои́х обя́занностей; ~ **officer** дежу́рный (офице́р). **3.** (*fig.*, *of things*): **a box did ~ for a table** я́щик служи́л столо́м. **4.** (*fin.*) по́шлина, сбор; **customs ~** тамо́женная по́шлина.

cpds. **~-free** *adj.* беспо́шлинный.

duvet ['du:veɪ] *n.* пухо́вая пери́на.

dwarf [dwɔ:f] *n.* ка́рлик.

v.t. (*fig.*): **our efforts are ~ed by his** его́ уси́лия затмева́ют на́ши.

dwarfish ['dwɔ:fɪʃ] *adj.* ка́рликовый.

dwell [dwel] *v.i.* **1.** (*live*) жить (*impf.*); обита́ть (*impf.*). **2.** ~ **(up)on** (*expatiate on*) распространя́ться (*impf.*) о+*p.*; **it is unnecessary to ~ on the difficulties** не ну́жно остана́вливаться на тру́дностях.

dweller ['dwelə(r)] *n.* жи́тель, обита́тель (*fem.* -ница).

dwelling ['dwelɪŋ] *n.* жили́ще.

cpd. **~-place** *n.* местожи́тельство.

dwindle ['dwɪnd(ə)l] *v.i.* сокра|ща́ться, -ти́ться; ум|еньша́ться, -е́ньшиться.

dye [daɪ] *n.* кра́ска.

v.t. кра́сить, по-; окра́|шивать, -сить; ~ **a dress black** кра́сить, по- пла́тье в чёрный цвет; **~d-in-the-wool** (*fig.*) закорене́лый.

cpds. **~stuff** *n.* краси́тель (*m.*); **~-works** *n.* краси́льня.

dyer ['daɪə(r)] *n.* краси́льщик.

dying ['daɪɪŋ] *adj.* умира́ющий, предсме́ртный; **till one's ~ day** до конца́ дней свои́х.

dyke [daɪk] = **dike**

dynamic [daɪ'næmɪk] *n.* (*pl.*, *science*) дина́мика.

adj. (*pertaining to force*) динами́ческий; (*energetic*), динами́чный.
dynamism ['daɪnə,mɪz(ə)m] *n.* динами́зм.
dynamite ['daɪnə,maɪt] *n.* динами́т (*also fig.*).
v.t. вз|рыва́ть, -орва́ть динами́том.
dynamo ['daɪnə,məʊ] *n.* дина́мо (*indecl.*).
dynamometer [,daɪnə'mɒmɪtə(r)] *n.* динамо́метр.
dynastic [dɪ'næstɪk] *adj.* династи́ческий.
dynasty ['dɪnəstɪ] *n.* дина́стия.
dyne [daɪn] *n.* ди́на.
dysentery ['dɪsəntərɪ, -trɪ] *n.* дизентери́я.
dyslexia [dɪs'leksɪə] *n.* дисле́ксия.
dyslexic [dɪs'leksɪk] *adj.*: **he is ~** он дисле́ктик.
dyspepsia [dɪs'pepsɪə] *n.* диспепси́я.
dystrophy ['dɪstrəfɪ] *n.* дистрофи́я.

E

E [i:] *n.* **1.** (*mus.*) ми (*nt. indecl.*). **2.** (*acad. mark*) 1, едини́ца; **he got an ~ in physics** он получи́л едини́цу по фи́зике.
each [i:tʃ] *pron. & adj.* ка́ждый; **he gave ~ (one) of us a book** он ка́ждому из нас дал по кни́ге; **he sat with a child on ~ side of him** он сиде́л ме́жду двух дете́й; **the apples cost 5 pence ~** я́блоки сто́ят пять пе́нсов шту́ка; **~ other** друг дру́га; **~ and every one** все без исключе́ния; **2 ~** два/дво́е; **5 ~** по пяти́; **100 ~** по́ сто.
eager ['i:gə(r)] *adj.* стремя́щийся (к+*d.*); **he is ~ to go** он рвётся идти́.
eagerness ['i:gənɪs] *n.* рве́ние, стремле́ние.
eagle ['i:g(ə)l] *n.* орёл; **~ eye** зо́ркий взгляд; **~ owl** фили́н.
cpd. **~-eyed** *adj.* зо́ркий, проница́тельный.
eaglet ['i:glɪt] *n.* орлёнок.
ear[1] [ɪə(r)] *n.* **1.** (*anat.*) у́хо; (*dim. e.g. baby's*) у́шко. **2.**: **~ for music** музыка́льный слух; **she plays by ~** она́ игра́ет по слу́ху; **play it by ~** (*fig.*) пол|ага́ться, -ожи́ться на чутьё. **3.** (*var. idioms*): **I am all ~s** я весь обрати́лся в слух; **it went in at one ~ and out at the other** в одно́ у́хо вошло́, в друго́е вы́шло; **up to one's ~s in work/debt** по́ уши в рабо́те/долга́х; **prick up one's ~s** навостри́ть (*pf.*) у́ши; **I could not believe my ~s** я свои́м уша́м не пове́рил; **lend an ~ to** прислу́ш|иваться, -аться к+*d.*; **turn a deaf ~ to** пропусти́ть (*pf.*) ми́мо уше́й; **it came to my ~s that ...** до меня́ дошли́ слу́хи, что...; **he has his ~ to the ground** (*fig.*) он де́ржит у́хо востро́.
cpds. **~ache** *n.* боль в у́хе; **~drop** *n.* (*pl., medicinal*) ушны́е ка́пли (*f. pl.*); **~drum** *n.* бараба́нная перепо́нка; **~-flap** *n.* нау́шник ша́пки; **~mark** *v.t.* (*fig.*) предназн|ача́ть, -а́чить; **~phone** *n.* нау́шник; **~-piercing** *adj.* пронзи́тельный; **~ring** *n.* серьга́; **~shot** *n.*: **within ~shot** в преде́лах слы́шимости; **~-trumpet** *n.* слухово́й рожо́к; **~-wax** *n.* ушна́я се́ра.
ear[2] [ɪə(r)] *n.* (*bot.*) ко́лос.
earl [ɜ:l] *n.* граф.
earl|y ['ɜ:lɪ] *adj.* ра́нний; **he is an ~y riser** он ра́но встаёт; **in one's ~y days** в ю́ности/мо́лодости; **in the ~y part of this century** в нача́ле э́того столе́тия; **we are ~y** мы пришли́ ра́но; **on Tuesday at (the) ~iest** не ра́ньше вто́рника; **~y man** первобы́тный челове́к; **~ music** стари́нная му́зыка; **~ warning** (*radar*) да́льнее обнару́же́ние.
adv. ра́но; **come as ~y as possible** приходи́те как мо́жно ра́ньше; **~y on** в нача́ле; **~ier on** ра́ньше, ра́нее; **two hours ~ier** на два часа ра́ньше; **as ~y as March** уже́/ещё в ма́рте.
earn [ɜ:n] *v.t. & i.* зараб|а́тывать, -о́тать; (*deserve*) заслу́ж|ивать, -и́ть; **~ one's living** зараба́тывать (*impf.*) на жизнь; **~ed income** трудово́й дохо́д.
earnest ['ɜ:nɪst] *n.*: **in ~** серьёзно, всерьёз; **I am in ~** (*not joking*) я не шучу́; я говорю́ серьёзно.
adj. серьёзный.
earnings ['ɜ:nɪŋz] *n.* за́работок.
earth [ɜ:θ] *n.* **1.** (*planet, world*) земля́; **why on ~?** с како́й ста́ти?; заче́м то́лько?; **who on ~?** кто то́лько?; **like nothing on ~** ни на что не похо́жий; **down to ~** (*fig.*) практи́чный, тре́звый. **2.** (*dry land*) земля́. **3.** (*soil*) земля́, по́чва. **4.** (*animal's hole*) нора́; **run s.o. to ~** (*fig.*) высле́живать, вы́следить кого́-н. **5.** (*chem.*) по́чва, грунт. **6.** (*elec.*) земля́, заземле́ние.
v.t.: **~ an aerial** заземл|я́ть, -и́ть анте́нну.
cpds. **~quake** *n.* землетрясе́ние; **~works** *n.* земляны́е рабо́ты (*f. pl.*); **~worm** *n.* земляно́й червь.
earthen ['ɜ:θ(ə)n] *adj.* земляно́й.
cpd. **~ware** *n.* гонча́рные изде́лия; гли́няная посу́да.
earthly ['ɜ:θlɪ] *adj.* земно́й; **there is no ~ reason why ...** нет ни мале́йшей причи́ны, что́бы...
earthy ['ɜ:θɪ] *adj.* (*smell etc.*) земляно́й; (*fig.*) приземлённый, грубова́тый.
earwig ['ɪəwɪg] *n.* уховёртка.
ease [i:z] *n.* **1.** (*facility*) лёгкость. **2.** (*comfort*) поко́й, о́тдых; **take one's ~** отд|ыха́ть, -охну́ть; **a life of ~** лёгкая жизнь; **he was ill at ~** ему́ бы́ло не по себе́; **stand at ~** (*mil.*) стоя́ть (*impf.*) во́льно; **be, feel at ~** чу́вствовать (*impf.*) себя́ непринуждённо.
v.t. **1.** (*loosen*) отпус|ка́ть, -ти́ть; **~ a drawer** испра́вить (*pf.*) я́щик, что́бы он ле́гче выдвига́лся. **2.** (*relieve*) облегч|а́ть, -и́ть; **~ s.o.'s anxiety** успок|а́ивать, -о́ить кого́-н.
v.i. (*relax*) облегч|а́ться, -и́ться; слабе́ть, о-; **tension ~d (off)** напряже́ние осла́бло; **~ off on drinking** (*coll.*) пить (*impf.*) ме́ньше; **the pressure of work ~d (up)** напряжённость рабо́ты спа́ла.
easel ['i:z(ə)l] *n.* мольбе́рт.
easily ['i:zɪlɪ] *adv.* (*freely*) свобо́дно; (*without difficulty*) легко́, без труда́; **he is ~ the best** он безусло́вно са́мый лу́чший; **he may ~ be late** он вполне́ мо́жет опозда́ть.
east [i:st] *n. & adv.* восто́к; на восто́к; к восто́ку; **Far E~** Да́льний Восто́к; **Near E~** Бли́жний Восто́к; **Middle E~** Сре́дний/Бли́жний Восто́к; **the wind is in the ~** ве́тер ду́ет с восто́ка; **(to the) ~ of London** к восто́ку от Ло́ндона.
adj. восто́чный.
Easter ['i:stə(r)] *n.* Па́сха; (*attr.*) пасха́льный; **at ~** на Па́сху; **~ Day, Sunday** Све́тлое/Христо́во Воскресе́нье; Па́сха.
easterly ['i:stəlɪ] *adj.*: **the wind is ~** ве́тер ду́ет с восто́ка.
eastern ['i:st(ə)n] *adj.* восто́чный.
easternmost ['i:st(ə)n,məʊst] *adj.* са́мый восто́чный.
eastward ['i:stwəd] *adj.* дви́жущийся на восто́к.
adv. (*also* **~s**) на восто́к; в восто́чном направле́нии.
easy ['i:zɪ] *adj.* **1.** (*not difficult*) лёгкий; **the book is ~ to read** кни́га легко́ чита́ется; **~ money** легко́ на́житые де́ньги; **~ come, ~ go** как на́жито, так и про́жито; **easier said than done** легко́ сказа́ть; **as ~ as ABC** ле́гче лёгкого; про́ще просто́го. **2.** (*comfortable, unconstrained*) споко́йный, лёгкий; **he leads an ~ life** у него́ лёгкая жизнь; **~ chair** кре́сло; **in E~ Street** в дово́льстве/доста́тке; **on ~ terms** на лёгких усло́виях; **I am ~** (*coll., have no preference*) мне всё равно́.

adv.: ~ **does it!** ти́ше е́дешь — да́льше бу́дешь; ~! споко́йно!; **take it** ~! (*don't worry*) не волну́йтесь!; (*don't hurry*) не спеши́те!

cpds. ~**-going** *adj.* (*of pers.*) благоду́шный.

eat [i:t] *v.t. & i.* **1.** (*of pers.*) есть, съ-; (*politely, of others*) ку́шать, по-/с-; ~ **one's dinner** пообе́дать/поу́жинать (*pf.*); **he ~s well** он хоро́ший едо́к; у него́ хоро́ший аппети́т; (~*s good food*) он хорошо́ пита́ется; **good to** ~ (*edible*) съедо́бный; (*palatable*) вку́сный. **2.** (*of animal etc.*) есть, съ-; жрать, со-. **3.** (*of physical substances*) раз|ъеда́ть, -е́сть. **4.** (*idioms*): ~ **one s words** брать, взять свои́ слова́ наза́д; ~ **one's heart out** исстрада́ться (*pf.*); ~ **s.o. out of house and home** объ|еда́ть, -е́сть кого́-н.

with advs.: ~ **away** *v.t.* разъ|еда́ть, -е́сть; ~ **in** *v.i.* (*at home*) пита́ться (*impf.*) до́ма; ~ **out** *v.i.* есть (*impf.*) вне до́ма; ~ **up** *v.t.* до|еда́ть, -е́сть.

eatable ['i:təb(ə)l] *adj.* съедо́бный.

eater ['i:tə(r)] *n.* едо́к; **he is a big** ~ едо́к он о́чень хоро́ший.

eating ['i:tɪŋ] *adj.*: **are these** ~ **apples?** мо́жно э́ти я́блоки есть сыры́ми?

eau-de-Cologne [ˌəʊdəkə'ləʊn] *n.* одеколо́н.

eaves [i:vz] *n.* карни́з.

cpd. ~**drop** *v.i.* подслу́ш|ивать, -ать.

ebb [eb] *n.* (*of tide*) отли́в; ~ **and flow** отли́в и прили́в; (*fig.*) упа́док; **his strength is at a low** ~ его́ си́лы иссяка́ют.

v.i. (*of tide*) уб|ыва́ть, -ы́ть; (*fig.*) ослаб|ева́ть, -е́ть; **daylight is** ~**ing away** день угаса́ет; **his strength is** ~**ing** его́ си́лы слабе́ют.

cpd. ~**-tide** *n.* отли́в.

ebonite ['ebəˌnaɪt] *n.* эбони́т.

ebony ['ebənɪ] *n.* эбе́новое/чёрное де́рево.

ebullience [ɪ'bʌlɪəns] *n.* кипу́честь.

ebullient [ɪ'bʌlɪənt] *adj.* кипу́чий.

eccentric [ɪk'sentrɪk, ek-] *n.* чуда́к; оригина́л.

adj. **1.** (*of pers.*) эксцентри́чный. **2.** (*math., astron.*) эксцентри́ческий.

eccentricity [ˌɪksen'trɪsɪtɪ, ˌek-] *n.* (*of pers.*) чуда́чество, эксцентри́чность.

ecclesiastical [ɪˌkli:zɪ'æstɪk(ə)l] *adj.* духо́вный, церко́вный.

echelon ['eʃəˌlɒn, 'eɪʃəˌlɔ̃] *n.* **1.** (*mil. formation*) эшело́н. **2.** (*grade*) чин, ранг.

echo ['ekəʊ] *n.* э́хо.

v.t. вто́рить (*impf.*) +*d.*

v.i. отд|ава́ться, -а́ться э́хом.

éclair [eɪ'kleə(r), ɪ'kleə(r)] *n.* эклер.

eclectic [ɪ'klektɪk] *adj.* эклекти́ческий; эклекти́чный.

eclecticism [ɪ'klektɪˌsɪz(ə)m] *n.* эклекти́зм.

eclipse [ɪ'klɪps] *n.* затме́ние.

v.t. (*lit., fig.*) затм|ева́ть, -и́ть.

ecliptic [ɪ'klɪptɪk] *n.* экли́птика.

ecological [ˌi:kə'lɒdʒɪk(ə)l] *adj.* экологи́ческий.

ecology [ɪ'kɒlədʒɪ] *n.* эколо́гия.

economic [ˌi:kə'nɒmɪk, ˌek-] *adj.* **1.** экономи́ческий, хозя́йственный. **2.** (*paying*) рента́бельный.

economical [ˌi:kə'nɒmik(ə)l, ˌek-] *adj.* эконо́мный, бережли́вый, хозя́йственный.

economics [ˌi:kə'nɒmɪks, ˌek-] *n.* эконо́мика.

economist [ɪ'kɒnəmɪst] *n.* экономи́ст; (*thrifty person*) бережли́вый челове́к.

economize [ɪ'kɒnəˌmaɪz] *v.t. & i.* эконо́мить, с-.

econom|y [ɪ'kɒnəmɪ] *n.* **1.** (*thrift*) эконо́мия, хозя́йственность, бережли́вость; **false** ~**y** бессмы́сленная эконо́мия. **2.** (~*ic system*) эконо́мика, хозя́йство; **rural** ~**y** се́льское хозя́йство; **political** ~**y** полити́ческая эконо́мия.

ecstas|y ['ekstəsɪ] *n.* экста́з; **she went into** ~**ies over it** э́то привело́ её в экста́з.

ecstatic [ɪk'stætɪk] *adj.* (*joyful*) экстати́ческий, в экста́зе.

ectoplasm ['ektəʊˌplæz(ə)m] *n.* эктопла́зма.

Ecuador ['ekwəˌdɔ:(r)] *n.* Эквадо́р.

ecumenical [ˌi:kju:'menɪk(ə)l, 'ek-] *adj.* (*eccles.*) вселе́нский; ~ **council** вселе́нский собо́р.

eczema ['eksɪmə] *n.* экзе́ма.

eddy ['edɪ] *n.* водоворо́т.

edelweiss ['eɪd(ə)lˌvaɪs] *n.* эдельве́йс.

edge [edʒ] *n.* **1.** (*sharpened side*) остриё, ле́звие; **take the** ~ **off** (*lit.*) притуп|ля́ть, -и́ть; (*fig., e.g. appetite*) испо́ртить (*pf.*). **2.** (*fig.*): **be on** ~ быть в не́рвном состоя́нии; **set one's teeth on** ~ вызыва́ть, вы́звать ощуще́ние оско́мины. **3.** (*border*) грань; край. **4.**: **have the** ~ **on s.o.** (*coll.*) име́ть преиму́щество над кем-н.

v.t. & i. **1.** (*border*) окайм|ля́ть, -и́ть; ~ **a path with plants** обса́|живать, -ди́ть доро́жку цвета́ми. **2.** (*move obliquely*): ~ **one's way through a crowd** проб|ира́ться, -ра́ться че́рез толпу́; ~ **one's chair towards the fire** пододви́нуть (*pf.*) стул к ками́ну.

edge|ways ['edʒweɪz], **-wise** ['edʒwaɪz] *adv.* бо́ком; **I could not get a word in** ~ я не мог сло́ва вста́вить.

edging ['edʒɪŋ] *n.* (*border*) кайма́.

edgy ['edʒɪ] *adj.* (*irritable*) раздражи́тельный.

edible ['edɪb(ə)l] *adj.* съедо́бный.

edict ['i:dɪkt] *n.* ука́з.

edification [ˌedɪfɪ'keɪʃ(ə)n] *n.* назида́ние, поуче́ние.

edifice ['edɪfɪs] *n.* зда́ние; (*fig.*) структу́ра, систе́ма.

edify ['edɪˌfaɪ] *v.t.* наст|авля́ть, -а́вить; поуча́ть (*impf.*).

edifying ['edɪˌfaɪɪŋ] *adj.* назида́тельный, поучи́тельный.

edit ['edɪt] *v.t.* (*a text, newspaper*) редакти́ровать, от-; **the passage was** ~**ed out** э́тот отры́вок вы́черкнули; (*film etc.*) монти́ровать, с-.

edition [ɪ'dɪʃ(ə)n] *n.* изда́ние; (*e.g. of newspaper*) вы́пуск.

editor ['edɪtə(r)] *n.* реда́ктор; **sports** ~ реда́ктор спорти́вного отде́ла.

editorial [ˌedɪ'tɔ:rɪəl] *n.* передова́я статья́.

adj. редакцио́нный; реда́кторский; ~ **office** реда́кция; ~ **staff** редакцио́нная колле́гия.

educate ['edjʊˌkeɪt] *v.t.* да|ва́ть, -ть образова́ние +*d.*; воспи́т|ывать, -а́ть; **where were you** ~**d?** где вы получи́ли образова́ние?; **a well** ~**d man** образо́ванный челове́к.

education [ˌedjʊ'keɪʃ(ə)n] *n.* образова́ние; (*upbringing*) воспита́ние; **universal compulsory** ~ всео́бщее обяза́тельное обуче́ние; **higher** ~ вы́сшее образова́ние; **Ministry of E**~ Министе́рство просвеще́ния; **lack of** ~ необразо́ванность; **physical** ~ физкульту́ра.

educational [ˌedjʊ'keɪʃənəl] *adj.* (*pert. to education*) образова́тельный; (*instructive*) воспита́тельный, уче́бный; ~ **film** уче́бный фильм.

educator ['edjʊˌkeɪtə(r)] *n.* воспита́тель (*m.*), педаго́г.

EEC (*abbr. of* ***European Economic Community***) ЕЭС, (Европе́йское экономи́ческое соо́бщество).

eel [i:l] *n.* у́горь (*m.*).

eer|ie (*US* **-y**) ['ɪərɪ] *adj.* жу́ткий.

efface [ɪ'feɪs] *v.t.* ст|ира́ть, -ере́ть; (*fig.*) изгла́|живать, -дить.

effect [ɪ'fekt] *n.* **1.** (*result*) результа́т; **of no** ~ безрезульта́тный; **to no** ~ безрезульта́тно; **take** ~ (*e.g. medicine*) де́йствовать, по-; **give** ~ **to a decision** осуществ|ля́ть, -и́ть реше́ние; **in** ~ в су́щности, факти́чески. **2.** (*validity*) де́йствие; **come into** ~ вступ|а́ть, -и́ть в си́лу; **put, bring into** ~ вводи́ть (*impf.*) в де́йствие; **with** ~ **from today** начина́я с сего́дняшнего дня; **in** ~ (*operative*) де́йствующий, в си́ле. **3.** (*sensual etc. impression*) впечатле́ние, эффе́кт; **sound** ~**s** (*e.g. on radio*) шумовы́е эффе́кты; **he does it all for** ~ он де́лает всё напока́з. **4.** (*meaning*) содержа́ние, смысл; **he spoke to this** ~ смысл его́ слов был сле́дующий;

or words to that ~ или что-то в этом роде. **5.** (*pl., property*) пожитк|и (*pl., g.* -ов); имущество.

v.t.: ~ **one's purpose** осуществ|лять, -ить цель; ~ **a cure** излечить (*pf.*) больного.

effective [ɪ'fektɪv] *adj.* **1.** (*efficacious*) эффективный. **2.** (*striking*) эффектный. **3.** (*operative*) имеющий силу; действующий; **become** ~ входить, войти в силу; ~ **strength** (*of an army*) наличный состав. **4.** (*virtual*) действительный.

effectiveness [ɪ'fektɪvnɪs] *n.* (*efficacy*) эффективность, действенность.

effectual [ɪ'fektʃʊəl, -tjʊəl] *adj.* действенный.

effectuate [ɪ'fektjʊˌeɪt] *v.t.* прив|одить, -ести в исполнение.

effeminate [ɪ'femɪnət] *adj.* женоподобный.

effervesce [ˌefə'ves] *v.i.* пузыриться (*impf.*).

effervescence [ˌefə'vesəns] *n.* шипение; (*fig.*) весёлое оживление.

effervescent [ˌefə'vesənt] *adj.* пузырящийся, шипучий; (*fig.*) искрящийся.

effete [ɪ'fiːt] *adj.* слабый, упадочный; (*degenerate*) выродившийся.

efficacious [ˌefɪ'keɪʃəs] *adj.* эффективный, действенный.

efficacy ['efɪkəsɪ] *n.* эффективность, действенность.

efficiency [ɪ'fɪʃənsɪ] *n.* деловитость; эффективность, производительность.

efficient [ɪ'fɪʃ(ə)nt] *adj.* деловитый, исполнительный; эффективный, производительный.

effigy ['efɪdʒɪ] *n.* изображение; **burn s.o. in** ~ сжечь (*pf.*) чьё-н. изображение/чучело.

effluent ['eflʊənt] *n.* поток, вытекающий из озера/реки; (*of sewage etc.*) сток.

effort ['efət] *n.* усилие, попытка; (*pl.*) работа; **make an** ~ приложить (*pf.*) усилие; **spare no** ~ не щадить (*impf.*) усилий; (*coll., performance*): **a good** ~ удачная попытка.

effortless ['efətlɪs] *adj.* непринуждённый; не требующий усилий.

effrontery [ɪ'frʌntərɪ] *n.* наглость, нахальство.

effulgent [ɪ'fʌldʒ(ə)nt] *adj.* лучезарный.

effusion [ɪ'fjuːʒ(ə)n] *n.* излияние (*also fig.*).

effusive [ɪ'fjuːsɪv] *adj.* экспансивный; **he was** ~ **in his gratitude** он рассыпался в благодарностях.

e.g. (*abbr. of* ***exempli gratia***) напр., (например).

egalitarian [ɪˌgælɪ'teərɪən] *adj.* эгалитарный.

egg[1] [eg] *n.* яйцо; **lay** ~**s** нестись (*impf.*); нести, с-яйца; **boiled** ~ яйцо в мешочек; **soft-boiled** ~ яйцо всмятку; **hard-boiled** ~ крутое яйцо; **fried** ~ яичница-глазунья; **scrambled** ~**s** яичница-болтунья; **poached** ~ яйцо-пашот; **rotten** ~ тухлое яйцо; **put all one's** ~**s in one basket** ≃ поставить (*pf.*) всё на карту.

cpds. ~**-beater,** ~**-whisk** *nn.* весёлка, мутовка; ~**-cup** *n.* рюмка для яйца; ~**head** *n.* (*sl.*) интеллигентик; ~**-plant** *n.* баклажан; ~**-shaped** *adj.* яйцевидный; ~**-shell** *n.* скорлупа; ~**-whisk** *n.* = ~**-beater**

egg[2] [eg] *v.t.*: ~ **on** подстрек|ать, -нуть.

ego ['iːgəʊ] *n.* эго (*indecl.*); (*amour-propre*) самолюбие; (*selfishness*) эгоизм.

egocentric [ˌiːgəʊ'sentrɪk] *adj.* эгоцентрический.

egoism ['iːgəʊˌɪz(ə)m] *n.* эгоизм.

egoist ['iːgəʊɪst, 'eg-] *n.* эгоист (*fem.* -ка).

egoistic(al) [ˌiːgəʊ'ɪstɪk(ə)l, 'eg-] *adj.* эгоистический.

egotism ['iːgəˌtɪz(ə)m] *n.* эготизм.

egotist ['iːgəˌtɪst, 'eg-] *n.* эготист (*fem.* -ка).

egotistic(al) [ˌiːgə'tɪstɪk(ə)l, ˌeg-] *adj.* эгоцентрический.

egregious [ɪ'griːdʒəs] *adj.* вопиющий.

egress ['iːgres] *n.* выход.

egret ['iːgrɪt] *n.* белая цапля.

Egypt ['iːdʒɪpt] *n.* Египет.

Egyptian [ɪ'dʒɪpʃ(ə)n] *n.* египтян|ин (*fem.* -ка).

adj. египетский.

Egyptologist [ˌiːdʒɪp'tɒlədʒɪst] *n.* египтолог.

Egyptology [ˌiːdʒɪp'tɒlədʒɪ] *n.* египтология.

eh [eɪ] *int.* а?; да неужели?; как?

eider ['aɪdə(r)] *n.* (*also* ~ **duck**) гага.

cpd. ~**down** *n.* (*feathers*) гагачий пух; (*quilt*) пуховое одеяло.

eight [eɪt] *n.* (число/номер) восемь; (~ *people*) восьмеро, восемь человек; ~ **each** по восьми; (*figure of* ~) восьмёрка; (*with var. nn. expressed or understood*: *cf. examples under* **five**): **piece of** ~ мексиканский доллар; **he had one over the** ~ (*coll.*) он хватил лишнего.

adj. восемь *+g. pl.*; (*for people and pluralia tantum, also*) восьмеро *+g. pl.*

cpd. ~**fold** *adj.* восьмикратный; *adv.* в восемь раз (больше).

eighteen [eɪ'tiːn] *n.* восемнадцать; **in the 1820s** в двадцатые годы (*or* в двадцатых годах) XIX (девятнадцатого) века.

adj. восемнадцать *+g. pl.*

eighteenth [eɪ'tiːnθ] *n.* (*date*) восемнадцатое число.

adj. восемнадцатый.

eighth [eɪtθ] *n.* (*date*) восьмое (число); (*fraction*) одна восьмая; восьмая часть.

adj. восьмой.

eightieth ['eɪtɪɪθ] *adj.* восьмидесятый.

eight|y ['eɪtɪ] *n.* восемьдесят; **in the** ~**ies** (*decade*) в восьмидесятых годах; в восьмидесятые годы; **he is in his** ~**ies** ему за восемьдесят.

Eire ['eərə] *n.* Эйре (*indecl.*).

either ['aɪðə(r), 'iːðə(r)] *pron. & adj.* (*one or other*) любой, каждый; тот или другой; ~ **book will do** любая из этих книг годится; **I do not like** ~ **(one)** мне не нравится ни тот, ни другой; ~ **way you will lose** и так и этак вы проиграете; **on** ~ **side of the window** по обеим сторонам окна; ~ **of you may come** любой из вас может прийти; **has** ~ **of you seen him?** кто-нибудь из вас видел его?

adv. & conj. **I do not like Smith, or Jones** ~ я не люблю ни Смита, ни Джонса; **he did not go, and I did not** ~ ни он, ни я не пошли; (*intensive*): **it was not long ago** ~ это было не так уж давно; ~ **... or** или... или; либо... либо; то ли... то ли; не то... не то.

ejaculate [ɪ'dʒækjʊˌleɪt] *v.t.* (*utter suddenly*) воскл|ицать, -икнуть; (*emit*) изв|ергать, -ергнуть.

ejaculation [ɪˌdʒækjʊ'leɪʃ(ə)n] *n.* (*exclamation*) восклицание; (*sexual*) семяизвержение, эякуляция.

eject [ɪ'dʒekt] *v.t.* (*lit., fig.*) выбрасывать, выбросить; (*emit*) изв|ергать, -ергнуть.

v.i. (*aeron.*): **the pilot** ~**ed** лётчик катапультировался.

ejection [ɪ'dʒekʃ(ə)n] *n.* (*expulsion*) исключение; (*from house*) выселение; (*emission*) извержение.

ejector [ɪ'dʒektə(r)] *n.*: ~ **seat** (*aeron.*) катапультируемое сиденье.

eke [iːk] *v.t.*: ~ **out a livelihood** кое-как перебиваться (*impf.*).

elaborate[1] [ɪ'læbərət] *adj.* искусно сделанный; сложный; **an** ~ **pattern** замысловатый рисунок; **an** ~ **dinner** изысканный обед.

elaborate[2] [ɪ'læbəˌreɪt] *v.t.* разраб|атывать, -отать.

elaboration [ɪˌlæbə'reɪʃ(ə)n] *n.* разработка.

elapse [ɪ'læps] *v.i.* про|ходить, -йти; прот|екать, -ечь.

elastic [ɪ'læstɪk, ɪ'lɑːstɪk] *n.* резинка.

adj. (*lit.*) эластичный; упругий; ~ **band** резинка; (*fig.*) гибкий; ~ **rules** нестрогие правила.

elasticity [ɪlæs'tɪsɪtɪ] *n.* эластичность, упругость; (*fig.*) гибкость.

elate [ɪ'leɪt] *v.t.* прив|одить, -ести в восторг; **he was** ~**d at the news** новость окрылила его.

elation [ɪ'leɪʃ(ə)n] *n.* ликование, восторг.

elbow ['elbəʊ] *n.* локоть (*m.*); **at one's** ~ (*fig.*) под рукóй; **more power to his ~!** (*coll.*) дай Бог емý удáчи!; **rub ~s with** якшáться (*impf.*) с+*i*. (*coll.*).

v.t. пих|áть, -нýть; толкáть (*impf.*) локтями; **~ one's way** прот|áлкиваться, -олкнýться.

cpd. **~-room** *n.* простóр.

elder[1] ['eldə(r)] *n.* **1.** (*older person*) стáрец, стáрший; **he is my ~ by seven years** он стáрше меня на семь лет. **2.** (*official, senior member of tribe*) старéйшина (*m.*).

adj. стáрший; **which is the ~ of the two?** кто из них двух стáрше?

elder[2] ['eldə(r)] *n.* (*bot.*) бузинá.

cpd. **~berry** *n.* ягода бузины.

elderly ['eldəlɪ] *adj.* пожилóй.

eldest ['eldɪst] *adj.* сáмый стáрший.

elect [ɪ'lekt] *adj.* избранный; **president ~** избранный президéнт.

v.t. изб|ирáть, -рáть; выбирáть, выбрать; **they ~ed him king** они избрáли егó королём; **the president is ~ed** президéнт избирáется; **he ~ed to go** он предпочёл пойти.

election [ɪ'lekʃ(ə)n] *n.* **1.** (*pol.*) выборы (*m. pl.*); **general ~** всеóбщие выборы; **hold an ~** пров|одить, -ести выборы; **~ campaign** предвыборная/избирáтельная кампáния. **2.** (*choice*) избрáние.

elective [ɪ'lektɪv] *adj.* **1.** (*filled by election*) выборный; **an ~ office** выборная дóлжность. **2.** (*empowered to elect*): **an ~ assembly** избирáтельное собрáние. **3.** (*optional*) факультативный.

elector [ɪ'lektə(r)] *n.* избирáтель (*m.*).

electoral [ɪ'lektər(ə)l] *adj.* избирáтельный; **~ college** коллéгия выборщиков; **~ register** список избирáтелей.

electorate [ɪ'lektərət] *n.* избирáтели (*m. pl.*).

electric [ɪ'lektrɪk] *adj.* электрический; **~ blanket** одеяло-грéлка; **~ locomotive** электровóз.

electrical [ɪ'lektrɪk(ə)l] *adj.* электрический; **~ engineer** инженéр-элéктрик; **~ engineering** электротéхника.

electrician [,ɪlek'trɪʃ(ə)n] *n.* (электро)монтёр.

electricity [,ɪlek'trɪsɪtɪ, ,el-] *n.* электричество.

electrification [ɪ,lektrɪfɪ'keɪʃ(ə)n] *n.* электрификáция.

electrify [ɪ'lektrɪ,faɪ] *v.t.* **1.** (*charge with electricity; also fig.*) электризовáть, на-. **2.** (*e.g. a railway*) электрифицировать (*impf., pf.*).

electrocardiogram [ɪ,lektrəʊ'kɑːdɪə,græm] *n.* электрокардиогрáмма.

electrocute [ɪ'lektrə,kjuːt] *v.t.* (*execute*) казнить (*impf., pf.*) на электрическом стýле; **he was ~d** (*by accident*) егó убило тóком.

electrocution [ɪ,lektrə'kjuːʃ(ə)n] *n.* казнь на электрическом стýле.

electrode [ɪ'lektrəʊd] *n.* электрóд.

electrolysis [,ɪlek'trɒlɪsɪs, ,el-] *n.* электрóлиз.

electrolyte [ɪ'lektrə,laɪt] *n.* электролит.

electromagnet [ɪ,lektrəʊ'mægnɪt] *n.* электромагнит.

electromagnetic [ɪ,lektrəʊmæg'netɪk] *adj.* электромагнитный.

electron [ɪ'lektrɒn] *n.* электрóн.

electronic [,ɪlek'trɒnɪk, ,el-] *adj.* электрóнный; **~ tagging** электрóнная слéжка.

electronics [,ɪlek'trɒnɪks, ,el-] *n.* электрóника.

elegance ['elɪgəns] *n.* элегáнтность, изящество.

elegant ['elɪgənt] *adj.* элегáнтный, изящный.

elegiac [,elɪ'dʒaɪək] *adj.* элегический.

elegiacs [,elɪ'dʒaɪəks] *n.* элегические стихи (*m. pl.*).

elegy ['elɪdʒɪ] *n.* элéгия.

element ['elɪmənt] *n.* **1.** (*earth, air etc.*) стихия; **exposed to the ~s** брóшенный на произвóл стихий; (*fig.*): **in one's ~** в своéй стихии. **2.** (*chem.*) элемéнт. **3.** (*pl., rudiments*) начáла (*nt. pl.*). **4.** (*feature, constituent*) элемéнт; составнáя часть. **5.** (*trace*) след, дóля. **6.** (*elec.*) элемéнт.

elemental [,elɪ'ment(ə)l] *adj.* стихийный.

elementary [,elɪ'mentərɪ] *adj.* элементáрный; **~ school** начáльная шкóла.

elephant ['elɪfənt] *n.* слон; **~ calf** слонёнок; **~ cow** слониха.

elephantiasis [,elɪfən'taɪəsɪs] *n.* слонóвая болéзнь.

elevate ['elɪ,veɪt] *v.t.* (*lit.*) подн|имáть, -ять; (*fig.*) пов|ышáть, -ысить; **he was ~d to the peerage** егó возвели в звáние пэ́ра.

elevated ['elɪ,veɪtɪd] *adj.* (*lofty*) высóкий, возвышенный.

elevating ['elɪ,veɪtɪŋ] *adj.* облагорáживающий; подъёмный.

elevation [,elɪ'veɪʃ(ə)n] *n.* **1.** (*act of raising*) поднятие, возвышéние. **2.** (*height*) возвышéние, возвышенность. **3.** (*drawing*) вертикáльный разрéз; **front ~** фасáд; **side ~** боковóй фасáд.

elevator ['elɪ,veɪtə(r)] *n.* **1.** (*machine*) грузоподъёмник, элевáтор. **2.** (*US, lift*) лифт; **~ operator** лифтёр.

eleven [ɪ'lev(ə)n] *n.* одиннадцать; **chapter ~** одиннадцатая главá; **at ~ (o'clock)** в одиннадцать (часóв); **half past ~** половина двенáдцатого.

elevenses [ɪ'levənzɪz] *n.* (*coll.*) лёгкий зáвтрак óколо одиннадцати часóв утрá.

eleventh [ɪ'levənθ] *n.* (*date*) одиннадцатое (числó).

adj. одиннадцатый; **at the ~ hour** (*fig.*) в послéднюю минýту.

elf [elf] *n.* эльф.

elicit [ɪ'lɪsɪt, e'lɪsɪt] *v.t.* извл|екáть, -éчь; допыт|ываться, -áться; **~ a fact** выявлять, выявить факт; **~ a reply** добиться (*pf.*) отвéта.

eligibility [,elɪdʒɪ'bɪlɪtɪ] *n.* (*pol.*) прáво на избрáние.

eligible ['elɪdʒɪb(ə)l] *adj.* мóгущий быть избранным; **an ~ young man** подходящий жених.

eliminate [ɪ'lɪmɪ,neɪt] *v.t.* **1.** (*do away with*) устран|ять, -ить. **2.** (*rule out*) исключ|áть, -ить. **3.** (*physiol., chem.*) оч|ищáть, -истить. **4.** (*sport*): **he was ~d on the first round** он выбыл в пéрвом тýре.

elimination [ɪ,lɪmɪ'neɪʃ(ə)n] *n.* устранéние, исключéние, очищéние; (*sport*) отбóрочное соревновáние.

élite [eɪ'liːt, ɪ-] *n.* элита.

elixir [ɪ'lɪksɪə(r)] *n.* эликсир.

elk [elk] *n.* лось (*m.*).

ellipse [ɪ'lɪps] *n.* э́ллипс, овáл.

ellipsis [ɪ'lɪpsɪs] *n.* э́ллипсис.

ellipsoid [ɪ'lɪpsɔɪd] *n.* эллипсóид.

elliptical [ɪ'lɪptɪkəl] *adj.* (*math., gram.*) эллиптический.

elm [elm] *n.* вяз.

elocution [,elə'kjuːʃ(ə)n] *n.* орáторское искýсство; тéхника рéчи.

elongate ['iːlɒŋ,geɪt] *adj.* (*also* **~d**) удлинённый.

v.t. удлин|ять, -ить.

elope [ɪ'ləʊp] *v.i.* (тáйно) бежáть (*det.*) (с возлюбленным).

eloquence ['eləkwəns] *n.* красноречие.

eloquent ['eləkwənt] *adj.* красноречивый.

else [els] *adj. & adv.* другóй; **no-one ~** никтó другóй; бóльше никтó; **everyone ~** все остальные; **nowhere ~** ни в какóм другóм мéсте; **nowhere ~ but ...** нигдé, крóме...; **everywhere ~** вездé, тóлько не здéсь/там; **someone ~'s** не свой, чужóй; **what ~ could I say?** что ещё я мог сказáть?; **do you want anything ~** (*more*)? вы хотите ещё что-нибýдь?; **or ~** или же; инáче; а (не) то; **run, or ~ you'll be late** бегите, а то опоздáете.

cpd. **~where** *adv.* гдé-нибудь ещё (в другóм мéсте); кудá-нибудь ещё (в другóе мéсто).

elucidate [ɪ'luːsɪ,deɪt, ɪ'ljuːs-] *v.t.* разъясн|ять, -ить; прол|ивáть, -ить свет на+*a*.

elucidation [ɪ,luːsɪ'deɪʃ(ə)n, ɪ,ljuːs-] *n.* разъяснéние.

elude [ɪ'luːd, ɪ'ljuːd] *v.t.* изб|егáть, -éгнуть *g.*; ускольз|áть, -нýть от+*g*.

elusive [ɪ'lu:sɪv, ɪ'lju:sɪv] *adj.* неулови́мый; (*evasive*) укло́нчивый.
emaciate [ɪ'meɪsɪ,eɪt, ɪ'meɪʃɪ,eɪt] *v.t.* истощ|а́ть, -и́ть.
email ['i:meɪl] *n.* (*also* **e-mail**) электро́нная по́чта.
emanate ['emə,neɪt] *v.i.* излуча́ться (*impf.*); истека́ть (*impf.*).
emanation [,emə'neɪʃ(ə)n] *n.* истече́ние, излуче́ние.
emancipate [ɪ'mænsɪ,peɪt] *v.t.* эмансипи́ровать (*impf., pf.*); свобо|жда́ть, -ди́ть.
emancipation [ɪ,mænsɪ'peɪʃ(ə)n] *n.* эмансипа́ция, освобожде́ние.
emancipator [ɪ'mænsɪ,peɪtə(r)] *n.* эмансипа́тор, освободи́тель (*m.*).
emasculate [ɪ'mæskjʊ,leɪt] *v.t.* (*castrate*) кастри́ровать (*impf., pf.*); (*fig.*) выхола́щивать, вы́холостить.
emasculation [ɪ,mæskjʊ'leɪʃ(ə)n] *n.* кастра́ция; выхола́щивание.
embalm [ɪm'bɑ:m] *v.t.* бальзами́ровать, на-.
embankment [ɪm'bæŋkmənt] *n.* (*wall etc.*) на́сыпь; (*roadway*) на́бережная.
embargo [em'bɑ:gəʊ, ɪm-] *n.* эмба́рго (*indecl.*); **oil is under ~** торго́вля не́фтью запрещена́.
v.t. (*forbid trade in*) нал|ага́ть, -ожи́ть эмба́рго на+*a.*; (*seize*) конфискова́ть (*impf., pf.*).
embark [ɪm'bɑ:k] *v.t.* (*goods*) грузи́ть, на-; (*people*) грузи́ть, по-.
v.i. (*go on board*) сади́ться, сесть на кора́бль; (*fig.*) пус|ка́ться -ти́ться (в+*a.*); **~ on an undertaking** предприн|има́ть, -я́ть де́ло.
embarkation [,embɑ:'keɪʃ(ə)n] *n.* (*of goods*) погру́зка; (*of people*) поса́дка.
embarrass [ɪm'bærəs] *v.t.* (*cause confusion to*) сму|ща́ть, -ти́ть; прив|оди́ть, -ести́ в замеша́тельство.
embarrassing [ɪm'bærəsɪŋ] *adj.* вызыва́ющий смуще́ние; затрудни́тельный.
embarrassment [ɪm'bærəsmənt] *n.* смуще́ние, замеша́тельство.
embassy ['embəsɪ] *n.* посо́льство.
embed [ɪm'bed] *v.t.*: **stones ~ded in rock** ка́мни, вмуро́ванные в скалу́; **facts ~ded in one's memory** фа́кты, вре́завшиеся в па́мять.
embellish [ɪm'belɪʃ] *v.t.* укр|аша́ть, -а́сить; (*a tale etc.*) приукра́|шивать, -сить.
embellishment [ɪm'belɪʃmənt] *n.* приукра́шивание.
embers ['embəz] *n. pl.* (*coals etc.*) тле́ющие уголькú (*m. pl.*).
embezzle [ɪm'bez(ə)l] *v.t.* растра́|чивать, -тить.
embezzlement [ɪm'bezəlmənt] *n.* растра́та.
embezzler [ɪm'bezələ(r)] *n.* растра́тчик.
embitter [ɪm'bɪtə(r)] *v.t.* озл|obля́ть, -о́бить; ожесточ|а́ть, -и́ть.
emblem ['embləm] *n.* эмбле́ма.
emblematic [,emblə'mætɪk] *adj.* эмблемати́ческий.
embodiment [ɪm'bɒdɪmənt] *n.* воплоще́ние, олицетворе́ние.
embod|y [ɪm'bɒdɪ] *v.t.* вопло|ща́ть, -ти́ть; олицетвор|я́ть, -и́ть; (*contain*) содержа́ть (*impf.*).
embolism ['embə,lɪz(ə)m] *n.* эмболи́я.
emboss [ɪm'bɒs] *v.t.* выбива́ть, вы́бить; чека́нить, от-/вы́-; **~ed notepaper** тиснёная бума́га.
embrace [ɪm'breɪs] *n.* объя́тие.
v.t. **1.** (*clasp in one's arms*) обн|има́ть, -я́ть. **2.** (*an offer, theory etc.*) прин|има́ть, -я́ть. **3.** (*include, comprise*) включ|а́ть, -и́ть. **4.** (*take in with eye or mind*) охва́т|ывать, -и́ть.
v.i. обн|има́ться, -я́ться.
embrasure [ɪm'breɪʒə(r)] *n.* (*for gun*) амбразу́ра, бойни́ца; (*of door, window*) проём.
embroider [ɪm'brɔɪdə(r)] *v.t.* вышива́ть, вы́шить; (*a story etc.*) приукра́|шивать, -сить.
embroidery [ɪm'brɔɪdərɪ] *n.* вышива́ние, вы́шивка.
embroil [ɪm'brɔɪl] *v.t.* (*confuse*) запу́т|ывать, -ать; (*involve in quarrel*) ссо́рить, по- (*кого с кем*).
embryo ['embrɪəʊ] *n.* (*biol.*) эмбрио́н; (*fig.*) заро́дыш; **in ~** в заро́дыше.
embryology [,embrɪ'ɒlədʒɪ] *n.* эмбриоло́гия.
embryonic [,embrɪ'ɒnɪk] *adj.* эмбриона́льный; (*fig.*) недора́звитый; в заро́дыше.
emerald ['emər(ə)ld] *n.* изумру́д; *attr.* изумру́дный; **~ green** изумру́дно-зелёный.
emerge [ɪ'mɜ:dʒ] *v.i.* всплы|ва́ть, -ть; появ|ля́ться, -и́ться; **the moon ~d from behind clouds** луна́ вы́шла из-за облако́в; (*fig.*) возн|ика́ть, -и́кнуть.
emergence [ɪ'mɜ:dʒəns] *n.* появле́ние, возникнове́ние.
emergency [ɪ'mɜ:dʒənsɪ] *n.* кра́йняя необходи́мость; ава́рия; чрезвыча́йное положе́ние; (*attr.*) чрезвыча́йный, э́кстренный; (*for use in ~*) запасно́й, запа́сный, вре́менный; **~ landing** вы́нужденная поса́дка; **~ powers** чрезвыча́йные полномо́чия; **~ ration** неприкоснове́нный запа́с.
emeritus [ɪ'merɪtəs] *adj.*: **professor ~** заслу́женный профе́ссор в отста́вке.
emery ['emərɪ] *n.* нажда́к; **~ paper** нажда́чная бума́га.
emetic [ɪ'metɪk] *n.* рво́тное сре́дство.
adj. рво́тный; (*fig.*) тошнотво́рный.
emigrant ['emɪgrənt] *n.* эмигра́нт (*fem.* -ка).
emigrate ['emɪ,greɪt] *v.i.* эмигри́ровать (*impf., pf.*).
emigration [,emɪ'greɪʃ(ə)n] *n.* эмигра́ция.
émigré ['emɪ,greɪ] *n.* эмигра́нт (*fem.* -ка).
eminence ['emɪnəns] *n.* **1.** (*high ground*) высота́; возвыше́ние. **2.** (*celebrity*) знамени́тость.
eminent ['emɪnənt] *adj.* (*of pers.*) выдаю́щийся, знамени́тый; (*of qualities*) замеча́тельный, выдаю́щийся; **~ly suitable** на ре́дкость подходя́щий.
emir [e'mɪə(r)] *n.* (*ruler*) эми́р.
emirate ['emɪərət] *n.* эмира́т.
emissary ['emɪsərɪ] *n.* эмисса́р.
emission [ɪ'mɪʃ(ə)n] *n.* (*of light*) излуче́ние; (*of heat*) теплоотда́ча.
emit [ɪ'mɪt] *v.t.* (*e.g. smoke*) испус|ка́ть, -ти́ть; (*light, heat etc.*) излуч|а́ть, -и́ть.
emotion [ɪ'məʊʃ(ə)n] *n.* (*feeling*) эмо́ция; (*agitation*) волне́ние.
emotional [ɪ'məʊʃən(ə)l] *adj.* эмоциона́льный; **an ~ appeal** волну́ющий призы́в.
empathy ['empəθɪ] *n.* эмпа́тия.
emperor ['empərə(r)] *n.* импера́тор.
emphasis ['emfəsɪs] *n.* **1.** (*stress, prominence*) ударе́ние, вырази́тельность; **lay ~ on** подчёрк|ивать, -ну́ть. **2.** (*phon.*) ударе́ние, акце́нт.
emphasize ['emfə,saɪz] *v.t.* подчёрк|ивать, -ну́ть; де́лать, с- упо́р на+*a.*
emphatic [ɪm'fætɪk] *adj.* вырази́тельный; **he was ~ on this point** он придава́л осо́бое значе́ние э́тому; **that is my ~ opinion** э́то моё твёрдое убежде́ние.
emphysema [,emfɪ'si:mə] *n.* эмфизе́ма.
empire ['empaɪə(r)] *n.* импе́рия; **Russian E~** Росси́йская импе́рия.
empiric(al) [ɪm'pɪrɪk(ə)l] *adj.* эмпири́ческий.
empiricism [ɪm'pɪrɪ,sɪz(ə)m] *n.* эмпири́зм.
empiricist [ɪm'pɪrɪsɪst] *n.* эмпи́рик.
emplacement [ɪm'pleɪsmənt] *n.* **1.** (*location*) местоположе́ние. **2.** (*mil.*) ору́дийный око́п.
employ [ɪm'plɔɪ] *n.* заня́тие, слу́жба; **he is in my ~** он рабо́тает у меня́.
v.t. **1.** (*engage*) нан|има́ть, -я́ть; держа́ть (*impf.*) на слу́жбе; предост|авля́ть, -а́вить рабо́ту +*d.*; **~ o.s.** занима́ться (*impf.*) (*чем*); **be ~ed** (*for hire*) рабо́тать (*impf.*), служи́ть (*impf.*). **2.** (*use*) примен|я́ть, -и́ть; употреб|ля́ть, -и́ть.
employee [,emplɔɪ'i:, -'plɔɪi:] *n.* слу́жащий; **he is an ~ of this firm** он рабо́тает в э́той фи́рме.
employer [ɪm'plɔɪə(r)] *n.* работода́тель (*m.*).
employment [ɪm'plɔɪmənt] *n.* **1.** (*service for pay*) рабо́та, слу́жба; **in ~** на слу́жбе/рабо́те; **out of ~**

без рабо́ты; **full ~** по́лная за́нятость; **~ agency** аге́нтство по на́йму рабо́чей си́лы. **2.** (*occupation*) заня́тие. **3.** (*use*) примене́ние, испо́льзование.

emporium [em'pɔ:rɪəm] *n.* (*trading centre*) торго́вый центр; (*shop*) большо́й магази́н.

empower [ɪm'paʊə(r)] *v.t.* уполномо́чи|вать, -ть.

empress ['emprɪs] *n.* императри́ца; (*fig.*) цари́ца.

emptiness ['emptɪnɪs] *n.* (*lit., fig.*) пустота́.

empt|y ['emptɪ] *adj.* **1.** пусто́й; поро́жний; (*fig.*): **~y words** пусты́е слова́; **on an ~y stomach** на пусто́й желу́док; **I feel ~y** я го́лоден. **2.** (*pl.*, *~y bottles etc.*) поро́жняя та́ра; буты́лки из-под вина́ и т.п.

v.t. опор|а́жнивать, -ожни́ть; **~y one drawer into another** пере|кла́дывать, -ложи́ть ве́щи из одного́ я́щика в друго́й; **~y water out of a jug** вы́лить (*pf.*) во́ду из кувши́на.

v.i. опорожн|я́ться, -и́ться; **the Rhine ~ies into the North Sea** Рейн впада́ет в Се́верное мо́ре; **the streets ~ied** у́лицы опусте́ли.

cpds. **~y-handed** *adj.* с пусты́ми рука́ми; **~y-headed** *adj.* пустоголо́вый.

emu ['i:mju:] *n.* э́му (*m. indecl.*).

emulate ['emjʊ,leɪt] *v.t.* соревнова́ться (*impf.*) с+*i.*

emulsion [ɪ'mʌlʃ(ə)n] *n.* эму́льсия.

enable [ɪ'neɪb(ə)l] *v.t.* (*make able*) да|ва́ть, -ть возмо́жность +*d.*; (*authorize*) уполномо́чи|вать, -ть; (*make possible*) де́лать, с- возмо́жным.

enact [ɪ'nækt] *v.t.* (*ordain*) постанов|ля́ть, -и́ть; предпи́с|ывать, -а́ть; (*act*) игра́ть, сыгра́ть (*роль*); разы́гр|ывать, -а́ть.

enactment [ɪ'næktmənt] *n.* (*ordaining*) постановле́ние, предписа́ние; (*ordinance*) постановле́ние, ука́з; (*theatr.*) игра́.

enamel [ɪ'næm(ə)l] *n.* (*also of teeth*) эма́ль; **~ paint** эма́левые кра́ски; **~ware** эмалиро́ванная посу́да.

v.t. эмалирова́ть (*impf.*).

enamour [ɪ'næmə(r)] *v.t.*: **he was ~ed of her** он был е́ю очаро́ван.

encamp [ɪn'kæmp] *v.t.* & *i.* распол|ага́ть(ся), -ожи́ть(ся) ла́герем.

encampment [ɪn'kæmpmənt] *n.* расположе́ние ла́герем; (*camp*) ла́герь (*m.*).

encephalitis [en,kefə'laɪtɪs, en,sef-] *n.* энцефали́т.

enchant [ɪn'tʃɑ:nt] *v.t.* (*bewitch*) зачаро́в|ывать, -а́ть; заколдо́в|ывать, -а́ть; (*delight*) обвор|а́живать, -ожи́ть; восхи|ща́ть, -ти́ть.

enchanter [ɪn'tʃɑ:ntə(r)] *n.* (*wizard*) волше́бник, чаро́дей.

enchanting [ɪn'tʃɑ:ntɪŋ] *adj.* чару́ющий, обворожи́тельный.

enchantment [ɪn'tʃɑ:ntmənt] *n.* (*spell*) волшебство́; (*charm*) очарова́ние, обая́ние; (*delight*) восхище́ние.

enchantress [ɪn'tʃɑ:ntrɪs] *n.* (*witch, charmer*) волше́бница, чаро́дейка.

encipher [ɪn'saɪfə(r)] *v.t.* зашифро́в|ывать, -а́ть.

encircle [ɪn'sɜ:k(ə)l] *v.t.* окруж|а́ть, -и́ть.

encirclement [ɪn'sɜ:kəlmənt] *n.* окруже́ние.

enclave ['enkleɪv] *n.* анкла́в.

enclos|e [ɪn'kləʊz] *v.t.* **1.** (*surround, fence*) окруж|а́ть, -и́ть; **~e a garden with a wall** обн|оси́ть, -ести́ сад стено́й; **~e in parentheses** заключ|а́ть, -и́ть в ско́бки. **2.** (*in letter etc.*) при|кла́дывать, -ложи́ть; **I ~e herewith** при сём прилага́ю; **a letter ~ing an invoice** письмо́ с приложе́нием счёта.

enclosure [ɪn'kləʊʒə(r)] *n.* (*act of enclosing*) огора́живание; (*fence*) огражде́ние, огра́да; (*in letter*) приложе́ние.

encode [ɪn'kəʊd] *v.t.* коди́ровать (*impf., pf.*); шифрова́ть, за-.

encompass [ɪn'kʌmpəs] *v.t.* (*surround*) окруж|а́ть, -и́ть; (*contain, comprise*) заключ|а́ть, -и́ть; (*cope with, accomplish*) охва́т|ывать, -и́ть.

encore ['ɒŋkɔ:(r)] *n.* & *int.* бис; **he gave six ~s** он бисирова́л шесть раз.

encounter [ɪn'kaʊntə(r)] *n.* (*meeting*) встре́ча; (*contest, competition*) состяза́ние.

v.t. встр|еча́ться, -е́титься с+*i.*; ст|а́лкиваться, -олкну́ться с+*i.*

encourage [ɪn'kʌrɪdʒ] *v.t.* ободр|я́ть, -и́ть; поощр|я́ть, -и́ть; подде́рж|ивать, -а́ть; спосо́бствовать (*impf.*) +*d.*; **I ~d him to go** я угова́ривал его́ идти́.

encouragement [ɪn'kʌrɪdʒmənt] *n.* ободре́ние, поощре́ние, подде́ржка; **this acted as an ~ to him** э́то ободри́ло его́.

encouraging [ɪn'kʌrɪdʒɪŋ] *adj.* ободря́ющий, обнадёживающий.

encroach [ɪn'krəʊtʃ] *v.i.* поку|ша́ться, -си́ться (на+*a.*); вт|орга́ться, -о́ргнуться (в+*a.*); **~ on s.o.'s rights** посяг|а́ть, -ну́ть на чьи-н. права́.

encroachment [ɪn'krəʊtʃmənt] *n.* посяга́тельство; вторже́ние.

encrust [ɪn'krʌst] *v.t.* & *i.* покр|ыва́ть(ся), -ы́ть(ся).

encumber [ɪn'kʌmbə(r)] *v.t.* **1.** (*burden*) обремен|я́ть, -и́ть. **2.** (*cram*) загромо|жда́ть, -зди́ть.

encumbrance [ɪn'kʌmbrəns] *n.* обу́за, препя́тствие.

encyclical [en'sɪklɪk(ə)l] *n.* энци́клика.

encyclopedia [en,saɪklə'pi:dɪə, ɪn-] *n.* энциклопе́дия.

encyclopedic [en,saɪklə'pi:dɪk, ɪn-] *adj.* энциклопеди́ческий.

end [end] *n.* (*extremity*; *lit., fig.*) коне́ц; **the ~ house** кра́йний дом; **two hours on ~** (*in succession*) два часа́ подря́д; **he began at the wrong ~** он на́чал не с того́ конца́; **third from the ~** тре́тий с кра́ю; **is everything all right at your ~?** всё ли благополу́чно у вас?; **to the ~s of the earth** ≃ к чёрту на кули́чки; **at the ~ of the world** на краю́ све́та; **at the ~ of August** в конце́ а́вгуста. **2.** (*of elongated object*) коне́ц, край; **he stood the box on (its) ~** он поста́вил я́щик стоймя́; **he placed the tables ~ to ~** он соста́вил столы́ в длину́ оди́н к друго́му; **her hair stood on ~** у неё во́лосы вста́ли ды́бом. **3.** (*var. idioms*): **keep one's ~ up** ≃ не уда́рить (*pf.*) лицо́м в грязь; **I am at the ~ of my tether** я дошёл до то́чки/ру́чки; **this is the ~!** (*coll., last straw, limit*) да́льше е́хать не́куда!; **he got hold of the wrong ~ of the stick** он по́нял всё наоборо́т; **loose ~s** (*unfinished business*) запу́щенные дела́; **I am at a loose ~** я шата́юсь без де́ла; **make (both) ~s meet** своди́ть (*impf.*) концы́ с конца́ми. **4.** (*remnant, small part*): **candle ~** ога́рок; **cigarette ~** оку́рок. **5.** (*conclusion, termination*) оконча́ние; **in the ~** в конце́ концо́в; в коне́чном счёте; **the war is at an ~** войне́ коне́ц; **our stores are at an ~** на́ши запа́сы на исхо́де; **come to an ~** ок|а́нчиваться, -о́нчиться; **put an ~ to, make an ~ of** класть, положи́ть коне́ц +*d.*; **there s an ~ (of it)!** вот и всё!; **what will the ~ be?** чем э́то ко́нчится?; **till the ~ of time** наве́чно; **dead ~** тупи́к; **he came to a bad ~** он пло́хо ко́нчил; **the ~ of the matter was that ...** де́ло ко́нчилось те́м, что...; **they fought to the bitter ~** они́ сража́лись до после́дней ка́пли кро́ви; **~ product** коне́чный проду́кт; **he has no ~ of books** у него́ у́йма книг; **we had no ~ of a time** мы прекра́сно провели́ вре́мя. **6.** (*death*) коне́ц; **he is nearing his ~** он при́ сме́рти; **she came to an untimely ~** она́ безвре́менно сконча́лась. **7.** (*purpose*) цель; **gain, win, achieve one's ~** дост|ига́ть, -и́чь свое́й це́ли; **to this ~, with this ~ in view** с э́той це́лью; **any means to an ~** все сре́дства хороши́.

v.t. конча́ть, ко́нчить; **~ a quarrel** прекра|ща́ть, -ти́ть ссо́ру; **~ one's days** рассчита́ться с жи́знью.

v.i. конча́ться, ко́нчиться; **the story ~s happily** э́то расска́з со счастли́вым концо́м; **he will ~ by marrying her** он в конце́ концо́в на ней же́нится; **all's well that ~s well** всё хорошо́, что хорошо́ конча́ется.

with advs.: ~ **off** *v.t.*: **he ~ed off his speech with a quotation** он закóнчил свою́ речь цитáтой; ~ **up** *v.i.*: **he ~ed up in jail** он кóнчил за решёткой; **he ~ed up at the opera** в концé концóв он попáл-таки в óперу.

cpds. **~-game** *n.* (*at chess*) э́ндшпиль (*m.*); **~ways, ~wise** *advs.* зáдом наперёд; (*end to end*) в длину́ (оди́н к другóму); (*upright*) стоймя́.

endanger [ɪn'deɪndʒə(r)] *v.t.* подв|ергáть, -éргнуть опáсности; стáвить (*impf.*) под угрóзу; **~ed species** вымирáющий вид.

endear [ɪn'dɪə(r)] *v.t.*: ~ **o.s. to s.o.** внуш|áть, -и́ть комý-н. любóвь к себé; **this speech ~ed him to me** э́та речь расположи́ла меня́ к немý; **an ~ing smile** покоря́ющая/подкупáющая улы́бка.

endearment [ɪn'dɪəmənt] *n.* лáска; **term of ~** лáсковое обращéние.

endeavour [ɪn'devə(r)] *n.* старáние.

v.i. старáться, по-.

endemic [en'demɪk] *adj.* эндеми́ческий.

ending ['endɪŋ] *n.* окончáние (*also gram.*); **happy ~** счастли́вый конéц.

endive ['endaɪv, -dɪv] *n.* салáт энди́вий.

endless ['endlɪs] *adj.* бесконéчный, нескончáемый; **~ patience** беспредéльное терпéние.

endocrine ['endəʊˌkraɪn, -ˌkrɪn] *adj.* эндокри́нный; **~ glands** жéлезы вну́тренней секрéции.

endocrinology [ˌendəʊkrɪ'nɒlədʒɪ] *n.* эндокринолóгия.

endorse [ɪn'dɔːs] *v.t.* **1.** (*sign*) индосси́ровать (*impf., pf.*); ~ **a cheque** распи́с|ываться, -áться на чéке. **2.** (*support*) поддéрж|ивать, -áть; **I ~ your opinion** я поддéрживаю вáше мнéние; **he ~d Blank's pills** он реклами́ровал пилю́ли Блáнка.

endorsement [ɪn'dɔːsmənt] *n.* **1.** передáточная нáдпись; индоссамéнт. **2.** (*support, approval*) подтверждéние; одобрéние.

endow [ɪn'daʊ] *v.t.* одар|я́ть, -и́ть; надел|я́ть, -и́ть; ~ **a school** пожéртвовать (*pf.*) капитáл на содержáние шкóлы.

endowment [ɪn'daʊmənt] *n.* **1.** дар, пожéртвование, фонд. **2.** (*talent*) одарённость. **3.**: ~ **insurance** страховáние-вклад.

endurance [ɪn'djʊərəns] *n.* (*physical*) прóчность; **~ test** испытáние на прóчность; (*mental*) выносли́вость; **past, beyond ~** невыноси́мый.

endure [ɪn'djʊə(r)] *v.t.* выноси́ть, вы́нести; терпéть, вы-; выдéрживать, вы́держать; перен|оси́ть, -ести́; ~ **toothache** терпéть зубну́ю боль; **I cannot ~ him** я егó терпéть не могу́.

v.i. (*suffer*) терпéть (*impf.*); (*last*) прод|олжáться, -óлжиться; дли́ться, про-.

enduring [ɪn'djʊərɪŋ] *adj.* (*lasting*) дли́тельный, продолжи́тельный.

enema ['enɪmə] *n.* кли́зма.

enemy ['enəmɪ] *n.* **1.** враг; **make an ~ of s.o.** нaж|ивáть, -и́ть себé врагá в ком-н.; **he is his own worst ~** он сам себé злéйший враг. **2.** (*mil., in collect. sense*) враг, проти́вник, неприя́тель (*m.*); **20 of the ~ were killed** проти́вник потеря́л 20 человéк уби́тыми. **3.** (*attr.*) врáжеский, неприя́тельский.

energetic [ˌenə'dʒetɪk] *adj.* энерги́чный.

energize ['enəˌdʒaɪz] *v.t.* побуждáть (*impf.*) к дéйствию; (*tech.*) питáть (*impf.*) энéргией.

energ|y ['enədʒɪ] *n.* (*phys. or mental*) энéргия; **devote all one's ~ies to a task** приложи́ть (*pf.*) все си́лы к выполнéнию задáчи.

enervat|e ['enəˌveɪt] *v.t.* обесси́ли|вать, -ть; рассл|аблять, -áбить; **~ing** обесси́ливающий.

enfeeble [ɪn'fiːb(ə)l] *v.t.* осл|абля́ть, -áбить; рассл|аблять, -áбить.

enfold [ɪn'fəʊld] *v.t.* (*contain, envelop*) закýт|ывать, -ать; (*embrace*) обн|имáть, -я́ть.

enforce [ɪn'fɔːs] *v.t.* **1.** (*strengthen*) уси́ли|вать, -ть; ~ **an argument** подкреп|ля́ть, -и́ть аргумéнт. **2.**: ~ **obedience on s.o.** заст|авля́ть, -áвить когó-н. подчини́ться. **3.**: ~ **a judgment** (*leg.*) прив|оди́ть, -ести́ в исполнéние судéбное решéние; ~ **a law** следи́ть (*impf.*) за соблюдéнием закóна; ~ **payment** взыскáть (*pf.*) платёж.

enforcement [ɪn'fɔːsmənt] *n.* осуществлéние; **law ~** наблюдéние за соблюдéнием закóнов.

enfranchise [ɪn'fræntʃaɪz] *v.t.* предост|авля́ть, -áвить избирáтельные правá +*d*.

engage [ɪn'geɪdʒ] *v.t.* **1.** (*hire*) нан|имáть, -я́ть; ~ **s.o. as a guide** нан|имáть, -я́ть когó-н. ги́дом. **2.** (*occupy*) зан|имáть, -я́ть; **he is ~d in reading** он зáнят чтéнием; **he ~d me in conversation** он вовлёк меня́ в разговóр; **the line is ~d** (*teleph.*) нóмер зáнят; **the lavatory is ~d** убóрная занятá. **3.** (*attract*) привл|екáть, -éчь. **4.** (*pledge to marry*): **Tom and Mary are ~d** Том и Мэ́ри помóлвлены; **to whom is he ~d?** с кем он помóлвлен?; **they got ~d** они́ обручи́лись. **5.** (*attack*) вступ|áть, -и́ть в бой с+*i.*; **we ~d the enemy** мы откры́ли огóнь по врагý. **6.** (*tech.*) зацеп|ля́ть, -и́ть; включ|áть, -и́ть.

v.i. **1.** (*undertake, promise*) брáться, взя́ться; обещáть (*impf., pf.*). **2.** (*embark, busy o.s.*) зан|имáться, -я́ться чем-н.; **he ~d in this venture** он взя́лся за э́то предприя́тие. **3.** (*lock together*) зацеп|ля́ть, -и́ть.

engagement [ɪn'geɪdʒmənt] *n.* **1.** (*hiring*) наём. **2.** (*promise, debt*) обязáтельство; **he cannot meet his ~s** он не мóжет вы́полнить свои́х обязáтельств. **3.** (*to marry*) помóлвка; **she broke off the ~** онá растóргла помóлвку; **~ ring** обручáльное кольцó. **4.** (*appointment to meet etc.*) свидáние, встрéча; **~ book** календáрь (*m.*). **5.** (*mil.*) бой. **6.** (*of wheels etc.*) зацеплéние.

engaging [ɪn'geɪdʒɪŋ] *adj.* привлекáтельный; **an ~ smile** располагáющая улы́бка; **with ~ frankness** с подкупáющей и́скренностью.

engender [ɪn'dʒendə(r)] *v.t.* (*fig.*) поро|ждáть, -ди́ть.

engine ['endʒɪn] *n.* дви́гатель (*m.*); мотóр.

cpds. **~-driver** *n.* машини́ст; **~-room** *n.* маши́нное отделéние.

engineer [ˌendʒɪ'nɪə(r)] *n.* **1.** (*technician*) инженéр, мехáник; **civil ~** инженéр-строи́тель; **mechanical ~** инженéр-мехáник. **2.** (*man in charge of engines*) мехáник; (*US, engine-driver*) машини́ст. **3.** (*mil.*) сапёр.

v.t. (*tech.*) конструи́ровать, с-; (*fig.*) зат|евáть, -éять; осуществ|ля́ть, -и́ть.

engineering [ˌendʒɪ'nɪərɪŋ] *n.* машинострoéние; **civil ~** граждáнское строи́тельство; **chemical ~** хими́ческая технолóгия; **genetic ~** гéнная инженéрия.

England ['ɪŋglənd] *n.* Áнглия.

English ['ɪŋglɪʃ] *n.* **1.** (*language*) англи́йский язы́к; **he speaks ~** он говори́т по-англи́йски; **American ~** америкáнский вариáнт англи́йского языкá; **standard ~** нормати́вный/литератýрный англи́йский язы́к; **what is the ~ for 'стол'?** как по-англи́йски «стол»? **2.**: **the ~** (*people*) англичáне.

adj. англи́йский.

cpds. **~man** *n.* англичáнин; **~woman** *n.* англичáнка.

engrave [ɪn'greɪv] *v.t.* гравировáть, вы́-; **~d with an inscription** с вы́гравированной нáдписью.

engraver [ɪn'greɪvə(r)] *n.* гравёр.

engraving [ɪn'greɪvɪŋ] *n.* (*craft*) гравирóвка, гравировáние; (*product*) гравю́ра.

engross [ɪn'grəʊs] *v.t.* (*absorb*) погло|щáть, -ти́ть; **an ~ing conversation** захвáтывающий разговóр.

engulf [ɪn'gʌlf] *v.t.* погло|щáть, -ти́ть.

enhance [ɪn'hɑːns] *v.t.* уси́ли|вать, -ть; (*of price*) пов|ышáть, -ы́сить.

enigma [ɪ'nɪgmə] *n.* зага́дка.
enigmatic [ˌenɪg'mætɪk] *adj.* зага́дочный.
enjoin [ɪn'dʒɔɪn] *v.t.* **1.** (*order*) предпи́с|ывать, -а́ть; веле́ть (*impf.*, *pf.*); **~ silence upon s.o.** веле́ть кому́-н. молча́ть. **2.** (*leg.*, *prohibit*) запре|ща́ть, -ти́ть.
enjoy [ɪn'dʒɔɪ] *v.t.* **1.** (*get pleasure from*) насла|жда́ться, -ди́ться +*i.*; **~ one's food** есть (*impf.*) с удово́льствием; люби́ть (*impf.*) пое́сть; **I ~ed talking to him** мне доставля́ло удово́льствие говори́ть с ним; **how did you ~ the play?** как вам понра́вилась пье́са?; **we ~ed our holiday** мы хорошо́ провели́ о́тпуск; **~ o.s.** весели́ться (*impf.*); наслажда́ться (*impf.*); **we ~ed ourselves** нам бы́ло ве́село/прия́тно. **2.** (*possess*) располага́ть (*impf.*) +*i.*; облада́ть (*impf.*) +*i.*; **~ good health** облада́ть хоро́шим здоро́вьем.
enjoyable [ɪn'dʒɔɪəb(ə)l] *adj.* прия́тный.
enjoyment [ɪn'dʒɔɪmənt] *n.* **1.** (*pleasure*) наслажде́ние, удово́льствие; **~ of music** любо́вь к му́зыке. **2.** (*possession*) облада́ние +*i.*
enlarge [ɪn'lɑːdʒ] *v.t.* увели́чи|вать, -ть; **~ one's house** де́лать, с- пристро́йку к до́му.
v.i. расш|иря́ться, -и́риться; **he ~d on the point** он подро́бнее останови́лся на э́том.
enlargement [ɪn'lɑːdʒmənt] *n.* увеличе́ние; расшире́ние.
enlarger [ɪn'lɑːdʒə(r)] *n.* (*phot.*) увеличи́тель (*m.*).
enlighten [ɪn'laɪt(ə)n] *v.t.* просве|ща́ть, -ти́ть.
enlightening [ɪn'laɪt(ə)nɪŋ] *adj.* поучи́тельный.
enlightenment [ɪn'laɪtənmənt] *n.* просвеще́ние.
enlist [ɪn'lɪst] *v.t.* вербова́ть, за-; **~ a recruit** вербова́ть, за- новобра́нца; **~ed man** (*US*) рядово́й; **~ s.o.'s support** заруч|а́ться, -и́ться чьей-н. подде́ржкой.
v.i. поступ|а́ть, -и́ть на вое́нную слу́жбу.
enlistment [ɪn'lɪstmənt] *n.* вербо́вка; поступле́ние на вое́нную слу́жбу.
enliven [ɪn'laɪv(ə)n] *v.t.* ожив|ля́ть, -и́ть.
en masse [ɑ̃ 'mæs] *adv.* в ма́ссе.
enmity ['enmɪtɪ] *n.* вражда́.
ennoble [ɪ'nəʊb(ə)l] *v.t.* (*raise to peerage*) возв|оди́ть, -ести́ в дворя́нство; (*make nobler*) облагор|а́живать, -о́дить.
enormity [ɪ'nɔːmɪtɪ] *n.* (*grossness*) чудо́вищность.
enormous [ɪ'nɔːməs] *adj.* грома́дный, огро́мный; **~ly** чрезвыча́йно.
enough [ɪ'nʌf] *n.* дово́льно, доста́точно; **he has ~ and to spare** у него́ бо́лее чем доста́точно; **it is ~ to make one weep** э́того доста́точно, что́бы расплА́каться; **(that's) ~!** доста́точно!; дово́льно!; **~ said!** всё поня́тно; **there is ~ to go round** хва́тит на всех; **I have had ~ of your lies** надое́ла мне ва́ша ложь.
adj. доста́точный; **is there ~ wine for all of us?** хва́тит ли вина́ на всех?; **I have just ~ money** де́нег у меня́ в обре́з (на+*a.*).
adv. доста́точно; **are you warm ~?** вы не замёрзли?; вам тепло́?; **you know well ~** вы прекра́сно зна́ете; **I was foolish ~ to believe her** я был насто́лько глуп, что пове́рил ей; (*fairly*, *rather*) дово́льно; **she sings well ~** она́ непло́хо поёт; **curiously ~** как ни стра́нно; **sure ~, he came** он действи́тельно пришёл.
en passant [ˌɑ̃ pæ'sɑ̃] *adv.* (*by the way*) мимохо́дом; (*chess*) на прохо́де.
enquire (*see also* **inquire**) [ɪn'kwaɪə(r), ɪŋ-] *v.t.* спр|а́шивать, -оси́ть; запр|а́шивать, -оси́ть.
v.i. осв|едомля́ться, -е́домиться; **~ into a matter** рассле́довать (*pf.*) де́ло; **~ after s.o.** спр|а́шивать, -оси́ть о ком-н.; **I ~d after his wife** я спроси́л, как пожива́ет его́ жена́; **~ for s.o.** спр|а́шивать, -оси́ть кого́-н.; **~ for the furnishing department** (*in a shop*) спроси́ть (*pf.*), где нахо́дится ме́бельный отде́л.
enquiring [ɪn'kwaɪərɪŋ, ɪŋ-] *adj.*: **an ~ look** вопроси́тельный взгляд; **an ~ mind** пытли́вый ум.
enquir|y [ɪn'kwaɪərɪ, ɪŋ-] *n.* (*see also* **inquiry**) расспро́сы (*m. pl.*); рассле́дование; **make ~ies** нав|оди́ть, -ести́ спра́вки.
enrage [ɪn'reɪdʒ] *v.t.* беси́ть, вз-.
enrapture [ɪn'ræptʃə(r)] *v.t.* восхи|ща́ть, -ти́ть.
enrich [ɪn'rɪtʃ] *v.t.* обога|ща́ть, -ти́ть.
enrichment [ɪn'rɪtʃmənt] *n.* обогаще́ние.
enrol [ɪn'rəʊl] *v t. & i.* зач|исля́ть(ся), -и́слить(ся); запи́с|ывать(ся), -а́ться.
enrolment [ɪn'rəʊlmənt] *n.* зачисле́ние, приём.
en route [ɑ̃ 'ruːt] *adv.* по/в пути́.
ensconce [ɪn'skɒns] *v.t.*: **~ o.s.** устро́иться (*pf.*).
ensemble [ɒn'sɒmb(ə)l] *n.* (*dress*, *music*) анса́мбль (*m.*).
enshrine [ɪn'ʃraɪn] *v.t.* поме|ща́ть, -сти́ть в ра́ку.
enshroud [ɪn'ʃraʊd] *v.t.* оку́т|ывать, -ать.
ensign ['ensaɪn, -s(ə)n] *n.* **1.** (*flag*) (кормово́й) флаг. **2.** (*US nav.*) мла́дший лейтена́нт.
enslave [ɪn'sleɪv] *v.t.* порабо|ща́ть, -ти́ть.
enslavement [ɪn'sleɪvmənt] *n.* порабоще́ние.
ensnare [ɪn'sneə(r)] *v.t.* лови́ть, пойма́ть в лову́шку.
ensu|e [ɪn'sjuː] *v.i.* (*result*) сле́довать (*impf.*) из+*g.*; (*follow*) сле́довать (*impf.*) за+*i.*; **in ~ing years** в после́дующие го́ды.
en suite [ɑ̃ 'swiːt] *adj.* (*with bathroom*) с ва́нной.
ensure (*see also* **insure**) [ɪn'ʃʊə(r)] *v.t.* (*make safe*) гаранти́ровать (*impf.*); (*make certain*; *secure*) обеспе́чи|вать, -ть.
entail [ɪn'teɪl, en-] *v.t.* (*necessitate*) влечь (*impf.*) за собо́й; **the work ~s expense** э́та рабо́та свя́зана с расхо́дами.
entangle [ɪn'tæŋg(ə)l] *v.t.* (*lit.*) запу́т|ывать, -ать (*fig.*) **he ~d himself with women** он запу́тался в отноше́ниях с же́нщинами.
enter ['entə(r)] *v.t. & i.* **1.** (*go into*) входи́ть, войти́ в+*a.*; **~ hospital** ложи́ться, лечь в больни́цу; **~ school** поступ|а́ть, -и́ть в шко́лу; **~ the army** вступ|а́ть, -и́ть в а́рмию; **~ the Church** (*be ordained*) прин|има́ть, -я́ть сан свяще́нника; **France ~ed the war** Фра́нция вступи́ла в войну́; **the idea never ~ed my head** э́та мысль никогда́ не приходи́ла мне в го́лову. **2.** (*include in record*) запи́с|ывать, -а́ть; **~ one's name in a list** внести́ (*pf.*) своё и́мя в спи́сок; **~ (o.s.) for an examination** пода́ть (*pf.*) на уча́стие в экза́мене; **~ a protest** заяв|ля́ть, -и́ть проте́ст.
with prep.: **~ into conversation** вступ|а́ть, -и́ть в разгово́р; **~ into details** входи́ть (*impf.*) в подро́бности; **~ into s.o.'s feelings** пон|има́ть, -я́ть чьи-н. чу́вства; **the fact ~ed into our calculations** э́тот факт входи́л в на́ши расчёты.
enteritis [ˌentə'raɪtɪs] *n.* энтери́т.
enterprise ['entəˌpraɪz] *n.* **1.** (*undertaking*, *adventure*) предприя́тие. **2.** (*initiative*) предприи́мчивость. **3.** (*econ.*): **private ~** ча́стное предпринима́тельство.
enterprising ['entəˌpraɪzɪŋ] *adj.* предприи́мчивый.
entertain [ˌentə'teɪn] *v.t.* развл|ека́ть, -е́чь; прин|има́ть, -я́ть; **~ friends** уго|ща́ть, -сти́ть друзе́й; **he ~s a great deal** у него́ ча́сто быва́ют го́сти; (*amuse*) развл|ека́ть, -е́чь; **~ a proposal** разду́мывать (*impf.*) над предложе́нием; **~ ideas** носи́ться (*impf.*) с иде́ями; **~ doubts** пита́ть (*impf.*) сомне́ния.
entertainer [ˌentə'teɪnə(r)] *n.* арти́ст эстра́ды.
entertaining [ˌentə'teɪnɪŋ] *adj.* занима́тельный.
entertainment [ˌentə'teɪnmənt] *n.* **1.** (*social*) приём госте́й. **2.** (*amusement*) развлече́ние. **3.** (*spectacle*) представле́ние.
enthral [ɪn'θrɔːl] *v.t.* (*fascinate*) увл|ека́ть, -е́чь; **an ~ling play** захва́тывающая пье́са.
enthrone [ɪn'θrəʊn] *v.t.* (*a king*, *bishop*) возв|оди́ть, -ести́ на престо́л.
enthuse [ɪn'θjuːz, -'θuːz] *v.i.* (*coll.*) восторга́ться (*impf.*) (*чем*).

enthusiasm [ɪn'θju:zɪ,æz(ə)m, -'θu:zɪ,æz(ə)m] *n.* восто́рг, энтузиа́зм.
enthusiast [ɪn'θju:zɪ,æst, -'θu:zɪ,æst] *n.* энтузиа́ст.
enthusiastic [ɪn,θju:zɪ'æstɪk, -,θu:zɪ'æstɪk] *adj.* восто́рженный; по́лный энтузиа́зма.
entice [ɪn'taɪs] *v.t.* соблазн|я́ть, -и́ть; зама́н|ивать, -и́ть; перема́н|ивать, -и́ть.
enticement [ɪn'taɪsmənt] *n.* (*action*) зама́нивание; (*lure*) прима́нка.
entire [ɪn'taɪə(r)] *adj.* це́лый, по́лный, це́льный; **that is the ~ cost** по́лная сто́имость; **~ly** целико́м, соверше́нно; **he is ~ly wrong** он соверше́нно непра́в.
entirety [ɪn'taɪərətɪ] *n.* полнота́, це́льность; **in its ~** по́лностью; во всей полноте́.
entitle [ɪn'taɪt(ə)l] *v.t.* **1.** (*a book etc.*) озагла́в|ливать, -ить; **a book ~d 'Progress'** кни́га под загла́вием «Прогре́сс». **2.** (*bestow title on*) жа́ловать, по- ти́тул *+d.* **3.** (*authorize*) да|ва́ть, -ть пра́во на*+a.*; **you are ~d to two books a month** вам полага́ется две кни́ги в ме́сяц.
entity ['entɪtɪ] *n.* (*object, body*) существо́, органи́зм, организа́ция.
entomb [ɪn'tu:m] *v.t.* (*bury*) погре|ба́ть, -сти́.
entomological [,entəmə'lɒdʒɪk(ə)l] *adj.* энтомологи́ческий.
entomologist [,entə'mɒlədʒɪst] *n.* энтомо́лог.
entomology [,entə'mɒlədʒɪ] *n.* энтомоло́гия.
entourage [,ɒntʊə'rɑ:ʒ] *n.* окруже́ние.
entrails ['entreɪlz] *n.* вну́тренности (*f. pl.*).
entrance[1] ['entrəns] *n.* **1.** (*door, passage etc.*) вход; **front ~** пара́дный ход; **back ~** чёрный ход. **2.** (*entering*) вход, вступле́ние; **upon his ~** когда́ он вошёл; **~s and exits** (*theatr.*) вы́ходы и вхо́ды (*m. pl.*); **~ examination** вступи́тельный экза́мен; **~ hall** прихо́жая, вестибю́ль (*m.*).
entranc|e[2] [ɪn'trɑ:ns] *v.t.* восторга́ть (*impf.*); **an ~ing sight** восхити́тельный вид.
entrant ['entrənt] *n.* (*person entering school, profession etc.*) поступа́ющий, приступа́ющий; (*competitor*) уча́стник.
entrap [ɪn'træp] *v.t.* лови́ть, пойма́ть в лову́шку.
entreat [ɪn'tri:t] *v.t.* умол|я́ть, -и́ть; упр|а́шивать, -оси́ть.
entreaty [ɪn'tri:tɪ] *n.* мольба́.
entrée ['ɒntreɪ, 'ɑ̃treɪ] *n.* **1.** (*admittance*) до́ступ; **he has the ~ to the Minister** у него́ есть до́ступ к мини́стру. **2.** (*cul.*) блю́до, подава́емое пе́ред жарки́м; (*US, main dish*) гла́вное блю́до.
entrench [ɪn'trentʃ] *v.t.* окруж|а́ть, -и́ть око́пами; **~ o.s.** ок|а́пываться, -опа́ться; (*fig.*) **customs ~ed by tradition** обы́чаи, закреплённые тради́цией.
entrepreneur [,ɒntrəprə'nɜ:(r)] *n.* предпринима́тель (*m.*).
entrust [ɪn'trʌst] *v.t.* вв|еря́ть, -е́рить; возл|ага́ть, -ожи́ть; **I ~ed the task to him** (*or* **~ed him with the task**) я дал ему́ (*or* возложи́л на него́) поруче́ние.
entry ['entrɪ] *n.* **1.** (*going in*) вход; **the ~ of the US into the war** вступле́ние США в войну́; **the Romans' ~ into Britain** вторже́ние ри́млян в Брита́нию. **2.** (*access*) до́ступ. **3.** (*place of ~*) вход; **the south ~ of a church** ю́жный вход це́ркви. **4.** (*item*) за́пись; **dictionary ~** слова́рная статья́; **~ in a diary** за́пись в дневнике́; **bookkeeping by double ~** двойна́я бухгалте́рия. **5.** (*inscription; competitor*): **~ form** вступи́тельная анке́та; **there was a large ~ for the race** на ска́чках записа́лось мно́го уча́стников. **6.** (*immigration*) въезд; **~ permit** разреше́ние на въезд.
entwine [ɪn'twaɪn] *v.t.* (*interweave*) впле|та́ть, -сти́; (*wreathe*) обв|ива́ть, -и́ть.
enumerate [ɪ'nju:mə,reɪt] *v.t.* переч|исля́ть, -и́слить.
enumeration [ɪ,nju:mə'reɪʃ(ə)n] *n.* перечисле́ние; (*list*) пе́речень (*m.*).
enunciate [ɪ'nʌnsɪ,eɪt] *v.t.* (*set forth*) формули́ровать, с-; (*pronounce*) произн|оси́ть, -ести́.
enunciation [ɪ,nʌnsɪ'eɪʃ(ə)n] *n.* формулиро́вка, произноше́ние.
envelop [ɪn'veləp] *v.t.* обёр|тывать, ну́ть; оку́т|ывать, -ать; **hills ~ed in mist** холмы́, оку́танные тума́ном; **~ed in mystery** покры́тый та́йной; (*mil.*) окруж|а́ть, -и́ть; охва́т|ывать, -и́ть.
envelope ['envə,ləʊp, 'ɒn-] *n.* конве́рт.
envelopment [ɪn'veləpmənt] *n.* обёртывание; (*mil.*) окруже́ние, охва́т.
enviable ['envɪəb(ə)l] *adj.* зави́дный.
envious ['envɪəs] *adj.* зави́стливый.
environment [ɪn'vaɪərənmənt] *n.* окруже́ние, среда́; **the ~** окружа́ющая среда́.
cpd. **~-friendly** *adj.* природобезвре́дный.
environmental [ɪn,vaɪərən'ment(ə)l] *adj.*: **~ studies** изуче́ние окружа́ющей среды́.
environmentalist [ɪn,vaɪərən'mentəlɪst] *n.* сторо́нник защи́ты окружа́ющей среды́.
environs [ɪn'vaɪərənz, 'envɪrənz] *n.* окре́стности (*f. pl.*).
envisage [ɪn'vɪzɪdʒ] *v.t.* (*consider*) рассм|а́тривать, -отре́ть; (*visualize*) предви́деть (*impf.*); **I had not ~d seeing him so soon** я не предполага́л, что уви́жу его́ так ско́ро.
envision [ɪn'vɪʒ(ə)n] *v.t.* предст|авля́ть, -а́вить себе́.
envoy ['envɔɪ] *n.* (*messenger*) посла́нец; (*diplomat*) диплома́т; **~ extraordinary** чрезвыча́йный посла́нник.
envy ['envɪ] *n.* за́висть; **she was green with ~** она́ чуть не ло́пнула от за́висти.
v.t. зави́довать, по- *+d.*; **I ~ him** я ему́ зави́дую.
enzyme ['enzaɪm] *n.* энзи́м.
epaulette ['epələt, 'epɔ:,let, 'epəʊ,let, ,epə'let] *n.* эполе́т.
ephemeral [ɪ'femər(ə)l, ɪ'fi:m-] *adj.* однодне́вный, кратковре́менный; (*fig.*) эфеме́рный.
epic ['epɪk] *n.* эпи́ческая поэ́ма, эпопе́я.
adj. эпи́ческий; (*on a grand scale*) грандио́зный.
epicentre ['epɪ,sentə(r)] *n.* эпице́нтр.
epicure ['epɪ,kjʊə(r)] *n.* эпикуре́ец.
epicurean [,epɪkjʊə'ri:ən] *adj.* эпикуре́йский.
epidemic [,epɪ'demɪk] *n.* эпиде́мия.
adj. эпидеми́ческий.
epidemiology [,epɪdi:mɪ'ɒlədʒɪ] *n.* эпидемиоло́гия.
epidermis [,epɪ'dɜ:mɪs] *n.* эпиде́рмис.
epidural [,epɪ'djʊər(ə)l] *n.* эпидура́льная инъе́кция.
epiglottis [,epɪ'glɒtɪs] *n.* надгорта́нник.
epigram ['epɪ,græm] *n.* эпигра́мма.
epigrammatic [,epɪgrə'mætɪkəl] *adj.* эпиграммати́ческий.
epigraph ['epɪ,grɑ:f] *n.* эпи́граф.
epilepsy ['epɪ,lepsɪ] *n.* эпиле́псия.
epileptic [,epɪ'leptɪk] *n.* эпиле́птик.
adj. эпилепти́ческий.
epilogue ['epɪ,lɒg] *n.* эпило́г.
Epiphany [e'pɪfənɪ, ɪ'pɪf-] *n.* Богоявле́ние, Креще́ние.
episcopal [ɪ'pɪskəp(ə)l] *adj.* (*of bishop*) епи́скопский; (*of system*) епископа́льный.
Episcopalian [ɪ,pɪskə'peɪlɪən] *n.* (*Anglican*) член англика́нской це́ркви; (*pl.*) англика́нцы.
episode ['epɪ,səʊd] *n.* эпизо́д; (*occurrence*) слу́чай.
episodic [,epɪ'sɒdɪk] *adj.* (*composed of episodes*) состоя́щий из отде́льных эпизо́дов; (*incidental, occasional*) эпизоди́ческий.
epistemology [ɪ,pɪstɪ'mɒlədʒɪ] *n.* эпистемоло́гия.
epistle [ɪ'pɪs(ə)l] *n.* посла́ние.
epistolary [ɪ'pɪstələrɪ] *adj.* эпистоля́рный.
epitaph ['epɪ,tɑ:f] *n.* эпита́фия, надгро́бная на́дпись.
epithelium [,epɪ'θi:lɪəm] *n.* эпите́лий.
epithet ['epɪ,θet] *n.* эпи́тет.
epitome [ɪ'pɪtəmɪ] *n.* (*summary*) конспе́кт; (*personification*) эпито́м, воплоще́ние.
epitomize [ɪ'pɪtə,maɪz] *v.t.* (*summarize*) резюми́ровать (*impf., pf.*); (*personify*) вопло|ща́ть, -ти́ть.

epoch [ˈiːpɒk] *n.* эпо́ха.

cpd. **~-making** *adj.* эпоха́льный.

eponymous [ɪˈpɒnɪməs] *adj.* эпони́мный.

Epsom salts [ˈepsəm] *n.* англи́йская соль.

equable [ˈekwəb(ə)l] *adj.* (*of climate, temper*) ро́вный, уравнове́шенный.

equal [ˈiːkw(ə)l] *n.* (*pers. or thg.*) ро́вня; **he has no ~** ему́ нет ра́вного; **he was her ~ at tennis** он игра́л в те́ннис не ху́же её.

adj. **1.** (*same, equivalent*) ра́вный, одина́ковый; **~ in** (*or* **of ~**) **ability** одина́ковых спосо́бностей; **the totals are ~** ито́ги равны́; **other things being ~** при про́чих ра́вных усло́виях; **~ shares** ро́вные до́ли; **two boys of ~ height** два ма́льчика одного́ ро́ста; **he speaks French and German with ~ ease** он одина́ково свобо́дно говори́т по-францу́зски и по-неме́цки. **2.** (*capable, adequate*) спосо́бный; **he is ~ to the task** он вполне́ мо́жет спра́виться с э́той зада́чей. **3.** (*unbiased, evenly balanced, stable*) ро́вный, равнопра́вный, уравнове́шенный; **~ laws** ра́вные права́; **an ~ fight** ра́вный бой.

v.t. & i. **1.** (*math.*) равня́ться (*impf.*) (*чему*); **twice 2 ~s 4** два́жды два равня́ется четырём; **x = y** x ра́вен y; **the ~s sign** знак ра́венства. **2.:** **he ~s me in strength** он ра́вен мне по си́ле; **I know nothing to ~ it** я не зна́ю ничего́ подо́бного.

equality [ɪˈkwɒlɪtɪ] *n.* ра́венство, равнопра́вие.

equalization [ˌiːkwəlaɪˈzeɪʃ(ə)n] *n.* уравне́ние.

equalize [ˈiːkwəˌlaɪz] *v.t. & i.* ура́вн|ивать, -я́ть; **~ (the score)** равня́ть (*or* сра́внивать), с- счёт.

equally [ˈiːkwəlɪ] *adv.* **1.** (*to an equal extent*) одина́ково; **he is ~ to blame** он винова́т в той же сте́пени. **2.** (*also, likewise*) ра́вным о́бразом; **~ it can be said that ...** с таки́м же успе́хом мо́жно сказа́ть, что... **3.** (*evenly*): **he divided the money ~** он раздели́л де́ньги по́ровну.

equanimity [ˌekwəˈnɪmɪtɪ, ˌiːk-] *n.* душе́вное равнове́сие; споко́йствие; **with ~** споко́йно.

equate [ɪˈkweɪt] *v.t.* (*make equal*) ура́вн|ивать, -я́ть; (*consider or treat as equal*) отождеств|ля́ть, -и́ть; прира́вн|ивать, -я́ть.

v.i.: **~ with** (*be equal, correspond to*) быть ра́вным +*d*.

equation [ɪˈkweɪʒ(ə)n] *n.* **1.** (*making equal, balancing*) выра́внивание. **2.** (*math., chem.*) уравне́ние.

equator [ɪˈkweɪtə(r)] *n.* эква́тор.

equatorial [ˌekwəˈtɔːrɪəl, ˌiːk-] *adj.* экваториа́льный.

equestrian [ɪˈkwestrɪən] *adj.* ко́нный.

equestrianism [ɪˈkwestrɪəˌnɪz(ə)m] *n.* ко́нный спорт.

equidistant [ˌiːkwɪˈdɪst(ə)nt] *adj.* равноотстоя́щий; **these towns are ~ from London** э́ти города́ располо́жены на одина́ковом расстоя́нии от Ло́ндона.

equilateral [ˌiːkwɪˈlætər(ə)l] *adj.* равносторо́нний.

equilibrium [ˌiːkwɪˈlɪbrɪəm] *n.* (*lit., fig.*) равнове́сие.

equine [ˈiːkwaɪn, ˈek-] *adj.* лошади́ный, ко́нский.

equinox [ˈiːkwɪˌnɒks, ˈek-] *n.* равноде́нствие.

equip [ɪˈkwɪp] *v.t.* снаря|жа́ть, -ди́ть; (*a ship*) осна|ща́ть, -сти́ть; **~ o.s. with sth.** вооруж|а́ться, -и́ться чем-н.

equipment [ɪˈkwɪpmənt] *n.* снаряже́ние, экипиро́вка.

equitable [ˈekwɪtəb(ə)l] *adj.* справедли́вый.

equitation [ˌekwɪˈteɪʃ(ə)n] *n.* верхова́я езда́.

equity [ˈekwɪtɪ] *n.* **1.** (*fairness*) справедли́вость. **2.** (*pl., fin.*) обыкнове́нные а́кции (*f. pl.*).

equivalence [ɪˈkwɪvələns] *n.* эквивале́нтность.

equivalent [ɪˈkwɪvələnt] *n.* эквивале́нт.

adj. эквивале́нтный; **his words were ~ to an insult** его́ слова́ бы́ли равноси́льны оскорбле́нию.

equivocal [ɪˈkwɪvək(ə)l] *adj.* двусмы́сленный.

equivocate [ɪˈkwɪvəˌkeɪt] *v.i.* говори́ть (*impf.*) двусмы́сленно; увил|ивать, -ну́ть от прямо́го отве́та.

equivocation [ɪˌkwɪvəˈkeɪʃ(ə)n] *n.* укло́нчивость.

era [ˈɪərə] *n.* э́ра.

eradicate [ɪˈrædɪˌkeɪt] *v.t.* искорен|я́ть, -и́ть.

eradication [ɪˌrædɪˈkeɪʃ(ə)n] *n.* искорене́ние.

erase [ɪˈreɪz] *v.t.* ст|ира́ть, -ере́ть; **~ sth. from one's memory** вычёркивать, вы́черкнуть что-н. из па́мяти.

eraser [ɪˈreɪzə(r)] *n.* рези́нка.

erasure [ɪˈreɪʒə(r)] *n.* стира́ние, подчи́стка.

erect [ɪˈrekt] *adj.* прямо́й; **with head ~** с по́днятой голово́й; **stand ~** держа́ться пря́мо.

v.t. (*build, set up*) воздв|ига́ть, -и́гнуть; соору|жа́ть, -ди́ть; **~ a tent** ста́вить, по- пала́тку.

erection [ɪˈrekʃ(ə)n] *n.* (*setting up*) сооруже́ние; (*building*) зда́ние; (*physiol.*) эре́кция.

ergo [ˈɜːɡəʊ] *adv.* сле́довательно.

ergonomic [ˌɜːɡəˈnɒmɪk] *adj.* эргономи́ческий.

ergonomics [ˌɜːɡəˈnɒmɪks] *n.* эргоно́мика.

ermine [ˈɜːmɪn] *n.* (*animal, fur*) горноста́й.

erode [ɪˈrəʊd] *v.t.* разъ|еда́ть, -е́сть; (*fig.*) подт|а́чивать, -очи́ть.

erogenous [ɪˈrɒdʒɪnəs] *adj. adj.* эроге́нный.

erosion [ɪˈrəʊʒ(ə)n] *n.* разъеда́ние, эро́зия.

erotic [ɪˈrɒtɪk] *adj.* эроти́ческий.

eroticism [ɪˈrɒtɪˌsɪz(ə)m] *n.* эроти́чность.

err [ɜː(r)] *v.i.* ошиб|а́ться, -и́ться; заблужда́ться (*impf.*).

errand [ˈerənd] *n.* поруче́ние; **go on ~s for s.o.** исполня́ть (*impf.*) чьи-н. поруче́ния.

cpd. **~-boy** *n.* рассы́льный.

errant [ˈerənt] *adj.* **1.** (*mistaken*) заблужда́ющийся. **2.** (*stray, wandering*) стра́нствующий. **3.** (*misbehaving*) заблу́дший.

erratic [ɪˈrætɪk] *adj.* неусто́йчивый; (*of pers.*) беспоря́дочный; **~ally** нерегуля́рно.

errat|um [ɪˈrɑːtəm] *n.* опеча́тка; **~a** (*pl., list*) спи́сок опеча́ток.

erroneous [ɪˈrəʊnɪəs] *adj.* оши́бочный.

error [ˈerə(r)] *n.* **1.** (*mistake*) оши́бка, заблужде́ние; **make, commit an ~** соверш|а́ть, -и́ть оши́бку; **he is in ~** он заблужда́ется; **the letter was sent in ~** письмо́ бы́ло по́слано по оши́бке; **clerical ~** опи́ска; **printer's ~** опеча́тка; **~ of judgment** неве́рное сужде́ние; **he saw the ~ of his ways** он осозна́л свои́ оши́бки. **2.** (*transgression*) просту́пок; **the ~s of his youth** грехи́ (*m. pl.*) его́ мо́лодости.

ersatz [ˈɜːzæts, ˈeə-] *n.* эрза́ц, суррога́т; **~ coffee** эрза́ц-ко́фе (*m. indecl.*).

erstwhile [ˈɜːstwaɪl] *adj.* да́вний; **an ~ friend** да́вний/стари́нный друг.

erudite [ˈeruːˌdaɪt] *adj.* эруди́рованный, учёный.

erudition [ˌeruːˈdɪʃ(ə)n] *n.* эруди́ция.

erupt [ɪˈrʌpt] *v.i.* (*of volcano etc.*) изв|ерга́ться, -е́ргнуться; (*of teeth*) прор|еза́ться, -е́заться.

eruption [ɪˈrʌpʃ(ə)n] *n.* **1.** (*of volcano etc.*) изверже́ние. **2.** (*on face etc.*) сыпь. **3.** (*fig.*) взрыв.

escalate [ˈeskəˌleɪt] *v.t.* эскали́ровать (*impf., pf.*); обостр|я́ть, -и́ть.

v.i. разраста́ться (*impf.*).

escalation [ˌeskəˈleɪʃ(ə)n] *n.* эскала́ция.

escalator [ˈeskəˌleɪtə(r)] *n.* эскала́тор.

escapade [ˈeskəˌpeɪd, ˌeskəˈpeɪd] *n.* эскапа́да; вы́ходка.

escape [ɪˈskeɪp] *n.* **1.** (*becoming free*) побе́г, бе́гство; **make one's ~** убежа́ть (*pf.*); **~ hatch** авари́йный люк; **~ ladder** пожа́рная ле́стница. **2.** (*avoidance*) спасе́ние, избавле́ние; **he had a narrow ~ from shipwreck** он едва́ спа́сся при кораблекруше́нии; **that was a lucky ~** э́то бы́ло счастли́вым избавле́нием. **3.** (*of gas etc.*) уте́чка.

v.t. избе|га́ть, -жа́ть +*g.*; **he ~d death** он оста́лся в живы́х; **he ~d with a scratch** он отде́лался цара́пиной; **the words ~d his lips** слова́ сорвали́сь у него́ с языка́; **nothing ~s you!** вы всё замеча́ете!; **his name ~s me** не могу́ припо́мнить его́ фами́лии.

v.i. бежа́ть (*det.*); уходи́ть, уйти́; соверши́ть (*pf.*) побе́г; **the prisoner ~d** заключённый (с)бежа́л; **an**

~d prisoner беглый арестант; **gas is escaping** происходит утечка газа.
escapee [ɪskeɪ'pi:] *n.* беглец.
escapism [ɪ'skeɪpɪz(ə)m] *n.* бегство от действительности; эскапизм.
escapist [ɪ'skeɪpɪst] *n.* человек, уходящий от действительности; эскапист.
adj. уходящий от действительности; эскапистский.
escapologist [ˌeskə'pɒlədʒɪst] *n.* фокусник, выполняющий трюк самоосвобождения от цепей.
escarp(ment) [ɪ'skɑ:pmənt] *n.* (*geol.*) вертикальное обнажение породы.
eschew [ɪs'tʃu:] *v.t.* воздерж|иваться, -аться от+*g.*; сторониться (*impf.*) +*g.*
escort[1] ['eskɔ:t] *n.* (*mil.*, *nav.*) конвой, эскорт; **~ ship, vessel** сторожевой/эскортный корабль; **police ~** (*of criminal*) конвой; **her ~ to the ball** её кавалер на балу.
escort[2] [ɪ'skɔ:t] *v.t.* сопрово|ждать, -дить; (*mil.*, *nav.*) эскортировать (*impf.*, *pf.*); конвоировать(*impf.*); **I ~ed him to his seat** я провёл его на место.
Eskimo ['eskɪˌməʊ] *n.* эскимос (*fem.* -ка).
adj. эскимосский; **~ dog** лайка.
esophagus [i:'sɒfəgas] = **oesophagus**
esoteric [ˌi:səʊ'terɪk, ˌe-] *adj.* эзотерический.
espalier [ɪ'spælɪə(r)] *n.* шпалера.
especial [ɪ'speʃ(ə)l] *adj.* специальный; особенный.
Esperantist [ˌespə'ræntɪst] *n.* эсперантист (*fem.* -ка).
Esperanto [ˌespə'ræntəʊ] *n.* эсперанто (*m. indecl.*); **in ~** на языке эсперанто.
espionage ['espɪəˌnɑ:ʒ] *n.* шпионаж.
esplanade [ˌesplə'neɪd] *n.* (*promenade*) эспланада.
espouse [ɪ'spaʊz] *v.t.*: **~ a cause** (целиком) отд|аваться, -аться делу.
espy [ɪ'spaɪ] *v.t.* зам|ечать, -етить.
essay[1] ['eseɪ] *n.* (*attempt*) попытка, проба; (*literary composition*) очерк.
essay[2] [e'seɪ] *v.t.* пробовать, по-.
v.i. пытаться, по-.
essayist ['eseɪɪst] *n.* очеркист.
essence ['es(ə)ns] *n.* **1.** (*philos.*) сущность, существо; (*gist*) суть. **2.** (*extract*) эссенция.
essential [ɪ'senʃ(ə)l] *n.* (*~ feature*, *element*) сущность; **~s of mathematics** основы (*f. pl.*) математики.
adj. **1.** (*necessary*) необходимый; **it is ~ that I should know** очень важно, чтобы я знал. **2.** (*fundamental*) существенный; **~ly** по существу; в сущности. **3.:** **~ oils** эфирные масла.
establish [ɪ'stæblɪʃ] *v.t.* **1.** (*found*, *set up*) учре|ждать, -дить; устан|авливать, -овить; **~ o.s. in business** осно́в|ывать, -ать дело. **2.** (*settle*) устр|аивать, -оить; **we are ~ed in our new home** мы обжились на новом месте. **3.** (*prove*, *gain acceptance for*) утвер|ждать, -дить; **~ a claim** обосно́в|ывать, -ать претензию; **~ one's reputation** созд|авать, -ать себе репутацию; **an ~ed custom** укоренившийся обычай; **~ed church** государственная церковь.
establishment [ɪ'stæblɪʃmənt] *n.* **1.** (*setting up*) учреждение, установление. **2.** (*of a claim*, *fact etc.*) установление, обоснование. **3.** (*business concern*) заведение, дело. **4.** (*household*) дом. **5.** (*institution*) учреждение, заведение; **educational ~** учебное заведение. **6.** (*set of institutions or key persons*): **the ~** «истеблишмент».
estate [ɪ'steɪt] *n.* **1.** (*landed property*) поместье, имение; **~ agent** агент по продаже недвижимости; **~ car** автомобиль с кузовом «универсал»; **housing ~** жилой массив; **industrial ~** промышленный комплекс. **2.** (*property*) имущество; **real ~** недвижимость; **personal ~** движимость.
esteem [ɪ'sti:m] *n.* уважение; **we have great ~ for you** мы питаем к вам большое уважение; **he lowered himself in my ~** он упал в моих глазах.
v.t. уважать (*impf.*); **I ~ him highly** я его высоко ценю.
esthete ['i:sθi:t] *etc.*, *see* **aesthete** *etc.*
estimable ['estɪməb(ə)l] *adj.* достойный уважения.
estimate[1] ['estɪmət] *n.* **1.** (*assessment*) оценка. **2.** (*comm.*) смета; **the builder exceeded his ~** строитель превысил смету.
estimate[2] ['estɪˌmeɪt] *v.t.* оцен|ивать, -ить.
v.i. сост|авлять, -авить смету (*чего*).
estimation [ˌestɪ'meɪʃ(ə)n] *n.* (*judgment*) оценка, суждение.
Estonia [ɪ'stəʊnɪə] *n.* Эстония.
Estonian [ɪ'stəʊnɪən] *n.* эстон|ец (*fem.* -ка).
adj. эстонский.
estrange [ɪ'streɪndʒ] *v.t.* отдал|ять, -ить; **Mr X is ~d from his wife** г-н и г-жа X живут врозь.
estrangement [ɪ'streɪndʒmənt] *n.* отчуждение, разрыв.
estuary ['estjʊərɪ] *n.* эстуарий, устье.
et al [et 'æl] (*abbr. of* **et alii**) и другие.
etc. [et 'setərə, 'setrə] *adv.* (*abbr. of* **et cetera**) и т.д., и т.п., (и так далее; и тому подобное).
et cetera [et 'setərə, 'setrə] *adv.* & *n.* и так далее; и тому подобное.
etch [etʃ] *v.t.* & *i.* травить, вы-; гравировать, вы-; (*fig.*): **it is ~ed on my memory** это запечатлелось у меня в памяти.
etcher ['etʃə(r)] *n.* гравёр.
etching ['etʃɪŋ] *n.* (*craft*) гравировка; (*product*) офорт, гравюра.
eternal [ɪ'tɜ:n(ə)l] *adj.* вечный (*also fig.*).
eternity [ɪ'tɜ:nɪtɪ] *n.* вечность; **for all ~** на веки вечные.
ether ['i:θə(r)] *n.* (*phys.*, *chem.*) эфир.
ethereal [ɪ'θɪərɪəl] *adj.* эфирный, неземной.
ethic ['eθɪk] *n.* (*moral code*; *also* **~s**) этика; мораль.
adj. этический; этичный.
ethical ['eθɪk(ə)l] *adj.* (*pert. to ethics*) этический; (*conforming to a code*) этичный; **it is not ~ for doctors to advertise** врачам неэтично создавать себе рекламу.
Ethiopia [ˌi:θɪ'əʊpɪə] *n.* Эфиопия.
Ethiopian [ˌi:θɪ'əʊpɪən] *n.* эфиоп (*fem.* -ка).
adj. эфиопский.
ethnic ['eθnɪk(ə)l] *adj.* этнический; **~ group** (*within a state*) национальность; **~ cleansing** этническая чистка.
ethnographer [eθ'nɒgrəfə(r)] *n.* этнограф.
ethnographic(al) [ˌeθnə'græfɪk(ə)l] *adj.* этнографический.
ethnography [eθ'nɒgrəfɪ] *n.* этнография.
ethnological [ˌeθnə'lɒdʒɪk(ə)l] *adj.* этнологический.
ethnologist [eθ'nɒlədʒɪst] *n.* этнолог.
ethnology [eθ'nɒlədʒɪ] *n.* этнология.
ethos ['i:θɒs] *n.* дух.
ethyl ['i:θaɪl, 'eθɪl] *n.* этил.
etiquette ['etɪˌket, -'ket] *n.* этикет.
étude ['eɪtju:d, -'tju:d] *n.* (*mus.*) этюд.
etymological [ˌetɪmə'lɒdʒɪk(ə)l] *adj.* этимологический.
etymologist [ˌetɪ'mɒlədʒɪst] *n.* этимолог.
etymology [ˌetɪ'mɒlədʒɪ] *n.* этимология.
eucalyptus [ju:kə'lɪptəs] *n.* эвкалипт.
Eucharist ['ju:kərɪst] *n.* евхаристия.
Euclidean [ju:'klɪdɪən] *adj.* эвклидов.
eugenic [ju:'dʒenɪk] *adj.* евгенический.
eugenics [ju:'dʒenɪks] *n.* евгеника.
eulogize ['ju:ləˌdʒaɪz] *v.t.* восхвал|ять, -ить.
eulogy ['ju:lədʒɪ] *n.* панегирик; похвала.
eunuch ['ju:nək] *n.* евнух, кастрат.
euphemism ['ju:fɪˌmɪz(ə)m] *n.* эвфемизм.
euphemistic [ˌju:fɪ'mɪstɪk] *adj.* эвфемистический.
euphonious [ju:'fəʊnɪəs] *adj.* благозвучный.
euphony ['ju:fənɪ] *n.* благозвучность, благозвучие.

euphoria [juːˈfɔːrɪə] *adj.* эйфори́я.
euphoric [juːˈfɒrɪk] *adj.* в припо́днятом настрое́нии.
eureka [jʊəˈriːkə] *int.* э́врика!
Euro- [ˈjʊərəʊ] *comb. form* евро...; **~parliament** европарла́мент; **~-MP** депута́т европарла́мента.
Europe [ˈjʊərəp] *n.* Евро́па; **to go into ~** (*pol.*) войти́ (*pf.*) в Евро́пу.
European [jʊərəˈpɪən] *n.* европе́|ец (*fem.* -йка).
adj. европе́йский.
Europeanism [jʊərəˈpɪənɪz(ə)m] *n.* иде́я еди́ной Евро́пы.
Europeanist [jʊərəˈpɪənɪst] *n.* сторо́нник еди́ной Евро́пы.
Eustachian tube [juːˈsteɪʃ(ə)n] *n.* евста́хиева труба́.
euthanasia [juːθəˈneɪzɪə] *n.* умерщвле́ние из милосе́рдия; эйтана́зия.
evacuate [ɪˈvækjʊˌeɪt] *v.t.* **1.** (*pers. or place*) эвакуи́ровать (*impf., pf.*). **2.** (*physiol.*) оч|ища́ть, -и́стить.
evacuation [ɪˌvækjʊˈeɪʃ(ə)n] *n.* (*removal*) эвакуа́ция; (*physiol.*) очище́ние кише́чника, испражне́ние.
evade [ɪˈveɪd] *v.t.* избе|га́ть, -жа́ть +*g.*; избе́гнуть (*pf.*) +*g.*; уклон|я́ться, -и́ться от+*g.*; **~ paying one's debts** уклон|я́ться, -и́ться от упла́ты долго́в.
evaluate [ɪˈvæljʊˌeɪt] *v.t.* оце́н|ивать, -и́ть.
evaluation [ɪˌvæljʊˈeɪʃ(ə)n] *n.* оце́нка.
evanescent [ˌiːvəˈnes(ə)nt, ˌe-] *adj.* исчеза́ющий, мимолётный.
evangelical [ˌiːvænˈdʒelɪk(ə)l] *n.* протеста́нт.
adj. ева́нгельский; (*Protestant*) евангели́ческий.
evangelism [ɪˈvændʒəˌlɪz(ə)m] *n.* про́поведь Ева́нгелия; (*fig.*) пропове́дничество.
evangelist [ɪˈvændʒəlɪst] *n.* (*author of gospel*) евангели́ст; (*preacher*) пропове́дник Ева́нгелия.
evaporate [ɪˈvæpəˌreɪt] *v.t. & i.* испар|я́ть(ся), -и́ть(ся) (*also fig.*); **his anger ~d** его́ гнев рассе́ялся.
evaporation [ɪˌvæpəˈreɪʃ(ə)n] *n.* испаре́ние.
evasion [ɪˈveɪʒ(ə)n] *n.* (*avoidance*) уклоне́ние; (*prevarication*) увёртка.
evasive [ɪˈveɪsɪv] *adj.* (*of answer*) укло́нчивый; (*of pers.*) увёртливый.
eve [iːv] *n.* (*day or evening before*) кану́н (*also fig.*); **on the ~ of** накану́не +*g.*; **Christmas E~** (Рожде́ственский) соче́льник; **New Year's E~** нового́дняя ночь, кану́н Но́вого го́да.
even [ˈiːv(ə)n] *adj.* **1.** (*level, smooth*) ро́вный; **fill** (*glass, etc.*) **~ with the brim** напо́лнить (*pf.*) до краёв; **~ with the ground** вро́вень с землёй. **2.** (*uniform*) равноме́рный; **his work is not very ~** он рабо́тает дово́льно неро́вно; **at an ~ speed** с постоя́нной ско́ростью. **3.** (*equal*) ра́вный; **the score is ~** счёт ра́вный; **an ~ chance** ра́вные ша́нсы; **get ~ with s.o.** расквита́ться (*pf.*) с кем-н.; **now we are ~** тепе́рь мы кви́ты; **break ~** ост|ава́ться, -а́ться при свои́х. **4.** (*divisible by 2*) чётный. **5.** (*calm*) ро́вный, споко́йный; **~ temper** ро́вный хара́ктер. **6.** (*exact*) ро́вный; **an ~ dozen** ро́вно дю́жина.
adv. да́же; и; хотя́ бы; **he disputes ~ the facts** он оспа́ривает да́же фа́кты; **he won't ~ notice** он и не заме́тит; **~ if** е́сли да́же; **~ so** всё равно́; да́же в тако́м слу́чае; **not ~** да́же не; **does he ~ suspect the danger?** подозрева́ет ли он вообще́ об опа́сности?; **this applies ~ more to French** э́то ещё в бо́льшей сте́пени отно́сится к францу́зскому языку́; **~ as I spoke, I realised ...** уже́ когда́ я говори́л э́то, я по́нял...; **~ as a child he was ...** ещё/уже́ ребёнком он был...
v.t. (*make even or equal*) выра́внивать, вы́ровнять; **that ~s (up) the score** э́то ура́внивает счёт.
v.i. выра́вниваться, вы́ровняться.
cpds. **~-handed** *adj.* беспристра́стный; **~-tempered** *adj.* уравнове́шенный.
evening [ˈiːvnɪŋ] *n.* ве́чер; **in the ~** ве́чером; **(on) that ~** в тот ве́чер; **one ~** одна́жды ве́чером; **this ~** сего́дня ве́чером; (*attr.*) вече́рний; **~ service** (*relig.*) вече́рня; вече́рняя моли́тва; **~ dress** (*men's or women's*) вече́рний туале́т.
evenly [ˈiːvənlɪ] *adv.* ро́вно, равноме́рно; **spread the butter ~** нама́з|ывать, -ать ма́сло ро́вным сло́ем; **the odds are ~ balanced** ша́нсы — ра́вные.
evenness [ˈiːvənnɪs] *n.* (*uniformity*) равноме́рность; (*of temper, tone etc.*) ро́вность, уравнове́шенность; (*of odds, contest etc.*) ра́венство.
evensong [ˈiːv(ə)nˌsɒŋ] *n.* вече́рняя моли́тва.
event [ɪˈvent] *n.* **1.** (*occurrence*) собы́тие; **current ~s** теку́щие собы́тия; **in the natural course of ~s** при норма́льном разви́тии собы́тий. **2.** (*outcome*) исхо́д; **in the ~ he was unsuccessful** в коне́чном счёте он потерпе́л неуда́чу. **3.** (*hypothesis*) слу́чай; **in the ~ of his coming** в слу́чае его́ прихо́да; **in any ~** в любо́м слу́чае; **in either ~** так и́ли ина́че; **at all ~s** во вся́ком слу́чае. **4.** (*sports item*) забе́г, зае́зд; вид спо́рта.
eventful [ɪˈventfʊl] *adj.* насы́щенный собы́тиями.
eventual [ɪˈventjʊəl] *adj.* коне́чный, оконча́тельный; **~ success** успе́шный коне́ц.
eventuality [ɪˌventjʊˈælɪtɪ] *n.* возмо́жность, слу́чай; **prepared for any ~** гото́вый ко вся́ким случа́йностям.
eventually [ɪˈventjʊəlɪ] *adv.* в конце́ концо́в; в коне́чном счёте.
eventuate [ɪˈventjʊˌeɪt] *v.i.* (*turn out*) разреш|а́ться, -и́ться (*чем*); (*happen*) случ|а́ться, -и́ться.
ever [ˈevə(r)] *adv.* **1.** (*always*) всегда́; **for ~ (and a day** *or* **and ~)** навсегда́, наве́чно; **~ after, since** с тех пор; **~ since** (*conj.*) с тех пор, как...; **yours ~, ~ yours, as ~** (*in letters*) Ваш/Твой...; пре́данный Вам. **2.** (*at any time*): **do you ~ see him?** вы его́ когда́-нибудь ви́дите?; **nothing ~ happens** ничего́ не происхо́дит; **scarcely, hardly ~** почти́ никогда́; о́чень ре́дко; **as good as ~** не ху́же, чем ра́ньше; **better than ~** лу́чше, чем когда́-либо; **this is the best ~** тако́го ещё не быва́ло. **3.** (*intensive*): **why ~ did you do it?** заче́м же вы э́то сде́лали?; **how ~ did you manage it?** как то́лько вам э́то удало́сь?; **~ so rich** ужа́сно бога́тый; **thank you ~ so much** я вам чрезвыча́йно благода́рен.
cpds. **~green** *n.* (*bot.*) вечнозелёное расте́ние; *adj.* вечнозелёный; **~lasting** *adj.* ве́чный; **~more** *adv.*: **for ~more** навсегда́, наве́чно; **~-present** *adj.* постоя́нный.
every [ˈevrɪ] *adj.* ка́ждый, вся́кий; **I wish you ~ success** жела́ю вам вся́ческого/по́лного успе́ха; **~ ten minutes** ка́ждые де́сять мину́т; **~ other car** ка́ждый второ́й автомоби́ль; **(on) ~ other day** че́рез день; **~ one of them** все до одного́; **~ now and again; ~ so often; ~ once in a while** вре́мя от вре́мени; **this is ~ bit as good** э́то ничу́ть не уступа́ет; **~ bit as much** то́чно сто́лько же; **in ~ way** во всех отноше́ниях; **I expect him ~ minute** я жду его́ с мину́ты на мину́ту.
cpds. **~body, ~one** *pron.* ка́ждый; вся́кий; все (*pl.*); **~body knows that!** э́то ка́ждый зна́ет; **~body else** все остальны́е; **~body knows ~body else** все со все́ми знако́мы; **~day** *adj.* повседне́вный; обыкнове́нный; **~one** *pron.* = **~body; ~thing** *pron.* всё; **money is not ~thing** де́ньги — э́то ещё не всё; **~thing is not clear** не всё я́сно; **~where** *adv.* везде́, повсю́ду; **~where else** во всех други́х места́х.
evict [ɪˈvɪkt] *v.t.* выселя́ть, вы́селить.
eviction [ɪˈvɪkʃ(ə)n] *n.* выселе́ние.
evidence [ˈevɪd(ə)ns] *n.* **1.** (*clarity, visibility*) очеви́дность; **he was much in ~ at the party** он о́чень выделя́лся на вечери́нке. **2.** (*indication, confirmation*) доказа́тельство, свиде́тельство; **there is no ~ for this belief** нет основа́ний для э́того убежде́ния. **3.** (*leg.*) свиде́тельское показа́ние; да́нные

(*nt. pl.*); **give ~** да|ва́ть, -ть свиде́тельское показа́ние; **circumstantial ~** ко́свенные ули́ки (*f. pl.*); **cumulative ~** совоку́пность ули́к.

v.t. служи́ть, по- доказа́тельством (*чего*).

evident [ˈevɪd(ə)nt] *adj.* очеви́дный, я́сный; **~ly not** (*as reply*) разуме́ется, нет; ока́зывается, что нет.

evil [ˈiːv(ə)l, -ɪl] *n.* зло; **the ~s of civilization** поро́ки (*m. pl.*) цивилиза́ции.

adj. злой, дурно́й.

cpds. **~-doer** *n.* злоде́й; **~-doing** *n.* злодея́ние; **~-minded** *adj.* злонаме́ренный.

evince [ɪˈvɪns] *v.t.* прояв|ля́ть, -и́ть.

eviscerate [ɪˈvɪsəˌreɪt] *v.t.* потроши́ть, вы́-.

evocative [ɪˈvɒkətɪv] *adj.* навева́ющий воспомина́ния.

evoke [ɪˈvəʊk] *v.t.* вызыва́ть, вы́звать; пробу|жда́ть, -ди́ть.

evolution [ˌiːvəˈluːʃ(ə)n, -ˈljuːʃ(ə)n] *n.* эволю́ция; **theory of ~** эволюцио́нная тео́рия.

evolutionary [ˌiːvəˈluːʃənərɪ, -ˈljuːʃənərɪ] *adj.* эволюцио́нный.

evolve [ɪˈvɒlv] *v.t.* разв|ива́ть, -и́ть; **he ~d a plan** он разрабо́тал план.

v.i. разв|ива́ться, -и́ться; эволюциони́ровать (*impf., pf.*).

ewe [juː] *n.* овца́.

ex- [eks] *pref.* (*former*) экс-..., бы́вший; **~ husband/president** бы́вший муж/президе́нт.

exacerbate [ekˈsæsəˌbeɪt, ɪg-] *v.t.* (*pers.*) раздраж|а́ть, -и́ть; (*pain etc.*) обостр|я́ть, -и́ть.

exacerbation [ekˌsæsəˈbeɪʃ(ə)n, ɪg-] *n.* раздраже́ние, обостре́ние.

exact [ɪgˈzækt] *adj.* то́чный.

v.t. (*e.g. payment*) взыск|ивать, -а́ть; (*e.g. obedience*) тре́бовать, по- +*g*.

exacting [ɪgˈzæktɪŋ] *adj.* взыска́тельный, тре́бовательный.

exactly [ɪgˈzæktlɪ] *adv.* то́чно; (*of numbers, quantities*) ро́вно; **he measured it ~** он э́то то́чно изме́рил; **~ a kilogram** ро́вно килогра́мм; **(in) ~ (the same way) as** так то́чно как; **~ the same** то же са́мое; **~!** (*as reply*) и́менно!; **~ how much do you need?** ско́лько и́менно вам ну́жно?

exactness [ɪgˈzæktnɪs] *n.* то́чность.

exaggerate [ɪgˈzædʒəˌreɪt] *v.t.* преувели́чи|вать, -ть.

exaggeration [ɪgˌzædʒəˈreɪʃ(ə)n] *n.* преувеличе́ние.

exalt [ɪgˈzɔːlt] *v.t.* (*make higher in rank etc.*) пов|ыша́ть, -ы́сить; (*praise*) превозн|оси́ть, -ести́.

exaltation [ˌegzɔːlˈteɪʃ(ə)n] *n.* **1.** (*raising in rank etc.*) повыше́ние. **2.** (*worship*) возвели́чение. **3.** (*mental or emotional transport*) экзальта́ция.

exam [ɪgˈzæm] (*coll.*) = **examination 3.**

examination [ɪgˌzæmɪˈneɪʃ(ə)n] *n.* **1.** (*inspection*) осмо́тр; **customs ~** тамо́женный досмо́тр; **~ of passports** прове́рка паспорто́в. **2.** (*interrogation*) допро́с; **the prisoner is under ~** заключённого допра́шивают. **3.** (*acad. etc.*; *also* **exam**) экза́мен; **~ paper** (*written by examinee*) экзаменацио́нная рабо́та; (*questions set*) вопро́сы (*m. pl.*) (для экзаменацио́нной рабо́ты); **entrance ~** вступи́тельный экза́мен; **take an ~** сда|ва́ть, -ть экза́мен; **sit an ~** экзаменова́ться, про-; **pass an ~** сдать/вы́держать (*both pf.*) экза́мен; **fail (in) an ~** провали́ться (*pf.*) на экза́мене.

examine [ɪgˈzæmɪn] *v.t.* **1.** (*inspect*) осм|а́тривать, -отре́ть; **~ passports** пров|еря́ть, -е́рить паспорта́; **~ records** изуч|а́ть, -и́ть докуме́нты; **~ a patient** осм|а́тривать, -отре́ть больно́го; **~ one's conscience** спр|а́шивать, -оси́ть свою́ со́весть. **2.** (*interrogate*) допр|а́шивать, -оси́ть. **3.** (*acad.*) экзаменова́ть, про-.

examiner [ɪgˈzæmɪnə(r)] *n.* (*acad.*) экзамена́тор; (*of a prisoner, witness etc.*) сле́дователь (*m.*).

example [ɪgˈzɑːmp(ə)l] *n.* **1.** (*illustration, model*) приме́р; **for (*or* by way of) ~** наприме́р; **set an ~ to s.o.** подава́ть (*impf.*) кому́-н. приме́р. **2.** (*warning*) уро́к; **let this be an ~ to you** пусть э́то послу́жит вам уро́ком. **3.** (*specimen*) образе́ц.

exasperate [ɪgˈzɑːspəˌreɪt] *v.t.* изв|оди́ть, -ести́; раздраж|а́ть, -и́ть.

exasperating [ɪgˈzɑːspəˌreɪtɪŋ] *adj.* раздража́ющий.

exasperation [ɪgˌzɑːspəˈreɪʃ(ə)n] *n.* раздраже́ние.

excavate [ˈekskəˌveɪt] *v.t.* копа́ть (*impf.*); раск|а́пывать, -опа́ть.

excavation [ˌekskəˈveɪʃ(ə)n] *n.* раско́пки (*f. pl.*).

excavator [ˈekskəˌveɪtə(r)] *n.* экскава́тор.

exceed [ɪkˈsiːd] *v.t.* прев|ыша́ть, -ы́сить; **~ expectations** превзойти́ (*pf.*) ожида́ния.

exceedingly [ɪkˈsiːdɪŋlɪ] *adv.* чрезвыча́йно.

excel [ɪkˈsel] *v.t.* прев|осходи́ть, -зойти́.

v.i. выдава́ться (*impf.*); выделя́ться (*impf.*); **he ~s in sport** он превосхо́дный спортсме́н.

excellence [ˈeksələns] *n.* превосхо́дство; превосхо́дное ка́чество; **~ in French** соверше́нство во францу́зском языке́.

excellency [ˈeksələnsɪ] *n.*: **His E~** его́ превосходи́тельство.

excellent [ˈeksələnt] *adj.* отли́чный.

except [ɪkˈsept] *v.t.* исключ|а́ть, -и́ть; **present company ~ed** о прису́тствующих не говоря́т.

prep. (*also* **~ing**) исключа́я+*a.*; кро́ме+*g.*; за исключе́нием+*g.*; ра́зве то́лько; **the essay is good ~ for the spelling mistakes** сочине́ние хоро́шее, е́сли не счита́ть орфографи́ческих оши́бок; **I knew nothing ~ that he was away** я не знал ничего́, кро́ме того́, что его́ не́ было.

exception [ɪkˈsepʃ(ə)n] *n.* **1.** (*sth. excepted*) исключе́ние; **with the ~ of** за исключе́нием+*g.*; **an ~ to a rule** исключе́ние из пра́вила. **2.** (*objection*) оби́да; **take ~ to** об|ижа́ться, -и́деться на+*a*.

exceptional [ɪkˈsepʃən(ə)l] *adj.* исключи́тельный.

excerpt [ˈeksɜːpt] *n.* вы́держка, цита́та.

excess [ɪkˈses, ˈekses] *n.* **1.** (*exceeding*) изли́шек, избы́ток; **in ~ of £20** свы́ше двадцати́ фу́нтов; **expenditure in ~ of income** расхо́ды, превыша́ющие дохо́д. **2.** (*exceeding what is proper or normal*) эксце́сс, кра́йность; **drink to ~** злоупотребля́ть (*impf.*) алкого́лем; **~ postage** почто́вая допла́та; **~ luggage** изли́шек багажа́.

excessive [ɪkˈsesɪv] *adj.* изли́шний; (*extreme*) чрезме́рный.

exchange [ɪksˈtʃeɪndʒ] *n.* **1.** (*act of exchanging*) обме́н +*g./i.*; **in ~ for** в обме́н на+*a.*; **~ of prisoners** обме́н пле́нными; **~ is no robbery** ме́на — не грабёж. **2.** (*fin.*) разме́н, обме́н; **~ rate/control** валю́тный курс/контро́ль; **lose on the ~** потеря́ть (*pf.*) на обме́не де́нег. **3.** (*place of business*) би́ржа; **stock ~** фо́ндовая би́ржа. **4.** (*teleph.*) (центра́льная) телефо́нная ста́нция; (*in building*) коммута́тор.

v.t. меня́ть, об-/по- (*что на что*); (*reciprocally*) обме́ниваться (*impf.*) +*i.*; **we ~d places** мы поменя́лись места́ми; **we ~d opinions** мы обменя́лись мне́ниями; **he ~d one job for another** он перешёл с одно́й рабо́ты на другу́ю.

v.i.: **he ~d with me on the roster** мы с ним поменя́лись дежу́рствами; **a mark ~s for one Swiss franc** ма́рка обме́нивается на оди́н швейца́рский франк.

exchequer [ɪksˈtʃekə(r)] *n.* казначе́йство, казна́.

excise[1] [ˈeksaɪz] *n.* акци́з.

excise[2] [ˈeksaɪz] *v.t.* выреза́ть, вы́резать; отр|еза́ть, -е́зать.

excitable [ɪkˈsaɪtəb(ə)l] *adj.* легко́ возбуди́мый.

excite [ɪkˈsaɪt] *v.t.* **1.** (*cause, arouse, stimulate*) возбу|жда́ть, -ди́ть; вызыва́ть, вы́звать. **2.** (*thrill, agitate*) волнова́ть, вз-; **don't ~ yourself (*or* get ~d)** не волну́йтесь.

excitement [ɪkˈsaɪtmənt] *n.* возбужде́ние, волне́ние;

what is all the ~ about? что за шум?; в чём де́ло?
exciting [ɪk'saɪtɪŋ] *adj.* захва́тывающий, увлека́тельный; **how ~!** как интере́сно!
exclaim [ɪk'skleɪm] *v.t. & i.* воскл|ица́ть, -и́кнуть.
exclamation [,ekskləˈmeɪʃ(ə)n] *n.* восклица́ние; **~ mark** восклица́тельный знак.
exclamatory [ɪk'sklæmətərɪ] *adj.* восклица́тельный.
exclude [ɪk'sklu:d] *v.t.* исключ|а́ть, -и́ть.
exclusion [ɪk'sklu:ʒ(ə)n] *n.* исключе́ние.
exclusive [ɪk'sklu:sɪv] *adj.* **1.** (*sole*) исключи́тельный, еди́нственный. **2.: ~ of** (*not counting*) без+*g.*, не счита́я+*g.* **3.** (*reserved, restricted*) специа́льный, исключи́тельный; **an ~ interview** интервью́, да́нное то́лько одно́й газе́те; **an ~ club** клуб для и́збранных.
exclusiveness [ɪk'sklu:sɪvnɪs] *n.* исключи́тельность.
excommunicate [,ekskəˈmju:nɪ,keɪt] *v.t.* отлуч|а́ть, -и́ть от це́ркви.
excommunication [ekskə,mju:nɪ'keɪʃ(ə)n] *n.* отлуче́ние от це́ркви.
excoriate [eks'kɔ:rɪ,eɪt] *v.t.* разн|оси́ть, -ести́.
excoriation [eks,kɔ:rɪ'eɪʃ(ə)n] *n.* разно́с.
excrement ['ekskrɪmənt] *n.* экскреме́нты (*m. pl.*).
excrescence [ɪk'skres(ə)ns] *n.* наро́ст.
excrete [ɪk'skri:t] *v.t.* выделя́ть, вы́делить.
excretion [ɪk'skri:ʃ(ə)n] *n.* выделе́ние.
excretory [ɪk'skri:tərɪ] *adj.* экскрето́рный, выдели́тельный.
excruciating [ɪk'skru:ʃɪ,eɪtɪŋ] *adj.* мучи́тельный.
exculpate ['ekskʌl,peɪt] *v.t.* опра́вд|ывать, -а́ть.
excursion [ɪk'skɜ:ʃ(ə)n] *n.* (*trip*) экску́рсия; **make** (*or* **go on) an ~** идти́/пое́хать (*det.*) на экску́рсию.
excusable [ɪk'skju:zəb(ə)l] *adj.* прости́тельный, извини́тельный.
excuse[1] [ɪk'skju:s, ek-] *n.* извине́ние, оправда́ние, отгово́рка; **ignorance is no ~** незна́ние — не оправда́ние; **a poor ~** сла́бая отгово́рка; **please make my ~s to the hostess** пожа́луйста, переда́йте мои́ извине́ния хозя́йке.
excuse[2] [ɪk'skju:z] *v.t.* **1.** (*justify, palliate*) опра́вд|ывать, -а́ть; **~ o.s.** прин|оси́ть, -ести́ извине́ния. **2.** (*forgive*) извин|я́ть, -и́ть; про|ща́ть, -сти́ть; **~ me, what time is it?** прости́те, кото́рый час? **3.** (*dispense, release*): **I ~d him from attending** я позво́лил ему́ не прису́тствовать; **may I be ~d from coming?** могу́ я не приходи́ть?
execute ['eksɪ,kju:t] *v.t.* **1.** (*carry out*) выполня́ть, вы́полнить; исп|олня́ть, -о́лнить; **~ a will** исп|олня́ть, -о́лнить завеща́ние. **2.** (*put to death*) казни́ть (*impf., pf.*).
execution [,eksɪ'kju:ʃ(ə)n] *n.* **1.** (*carrying out*) исполне́ние, выполне́ние. **2.** (*capital punishment*) казнь; **there were five ~s last year** в про́шлом году́ казни́ли пятеры́х.
executioner [,eksɪ'kju:ʃənə(r)] *n.* пала́ч.
executive [ɪg'zekjʊtɪv] *n.* (руководя́щий) рабо́тник.
adj. **1.** (*executing laws etc.*) исполни́тельный. **2.** (*managing*) руководя́щий; **~ ability** администрати́вные спосо́бности.
executor [ɪg'zekjʊtə(r)] *n.* (*of a will*) душеприка́зчик.
exemplary [ɪg'zemplərɪ] *adj.* приме́рный, образцо́вый.
exemplify [ɪg'zemplɪ,faɪ] *v.t.* служи́ть, по- приме́ром +*g.*
exempt [ɪg'zempt] *adj.* освобождённый, свобо́дный (*от чего*).
v.t. освобожда́ть, -ди́ть.
exemption [ɪg'zempʃ(ə)n] *n.* освобожде́ние (*от чего*).
exercise ['eksə,saɪz] *n.* **1.** (*use, exertion*) проявле́ние (*чего*); выка́зывание (*чего*). **2.** (*physical activity*) заря́дка, упражне́ние; **you should take more ~** вам ну́жно де́лать бо́льше физи́ческих упражне́ний. **3.** (*mental or physical training*) упражне́ние, трениро́вка. **4.** (*trial operation*) уче́ние; **military ~s** строево́е уче́ние.
v.t. **1.** (*exert, use*) выка́зывать, вы́казать; прояв|ля́ть, -и́ть; **~ authority** примен|я́ть, -и́ть власть; **~ one's rights** осуществ|ля́ть, -и́ть свои́ права́. **2.** (*physically*) упражня́ть (*impf.*); **~ a dog** прогу́ливать (*impf.*) соба́ку. **3.** (*worry, perplex*) беспоко́ить (*impf.*), трево́жить (*impf.*); **the problem ~d our minds** пробле́ма заста́вила нас заду́маться.
v.i. упражня́ться (*impf.*).
cpd. **~-book** *n.* (учени́ческая) тетра́дь.
exert [ɪg'zɜ:t] *v.t.* осуществ|ля́ть, -и́ть; ока́з|ывать, -а́ть; **~ influence** ока́з|ывать, -а́ть влия́ние; **~ o.s.** постара́ться (*pf.*).
exertion [ɪg'zɜ:ʃ(ə)n] *n.* напряже́ние, уси́лие.
exhalation [,ekshə'leɪʃ(ə)n] *n.* выдыха́ние.
exhale [eks'heɪl, ɪgz-] *v.t.* выдыха́ть, вы́дохнуть.
exhaust [ɪg'zɔ:st] *n.* (*apparatus*) вы́хлоп, вы́пуск; (*expelled gas*) отрабо́танный газ; **~ pipe** выхлопна́я труба́.
v.t. **1.** (*consume, tire out*) истощ|а́ть, -и́ть; изнур|я́ть, -и́ть; **my patience is ~ed** моё терпе́ние исся́кло; **be ~ed** изнем|ога́ть, -о́чь; **I feel ~ed** я соверше́нно без сил. **2.** (*empty*) исче́рп|ывать, -ать; **~ land** истощ|а́ть, -и́ть зе́млю. **3.** (*explore thoroughly*) исче́рп|ывать, -ать.
exhausting [ɪg'zɔ:stɪŋ] *adj.* изнури́тельный, утоми́тельный.
exhaustion [ɪg'zɔ:stʃ(ə)n] *n.* изнуре́ние, истоще́ние; (*fatigue*) переутомле́ние, изнеможе́ние.
exhaustive [ɪg'zɔ:stɪv] *adj.* исче́рпывающий.
exhibit [ɪg'zɪbɪt] *n.* экспона́т.
v.t. **1.** (*e.g. painting*) экспони́ровать (*impf., pf.*); выставля́ть, вы́ставить. **2.** (*fig., display*) прояв|ля́ть, -и́ть.
exhibition [,eksɪ'bɪʃ(ə)n] *n.* (*public show*) вы́ставка; (*showing*) пока́з.
exhibitionism [,eksɪ'bɪʃə,nɪz(ə)m] *n.* (*showing off*) рисо́вка; хвастовство́.
exhibitionist [eksɪ'bɪʃənɪst] *n.* хвасту́н, (*coll.*) вообража́ла (*c.g.*).
exhibitor [ɪg'zɪbɪtə(r)] *n.* экспоне́нт.
exhilarat|e [ɪg'zɪlə,reɪt] *v.t.* весели́ть, раз-; ра́довать, об-; **he felt ~ed** он был в припо́днятом настрое́нии; **~ing news** ра́достное изве́стие.
exhilaration [ɪg,zɪlə'reɪʃ(ə)n] *n.* весе́лье; прия́тное возбужде́ние.
exhort [ɪg'zɔ:t] *v.t.* приз|ыва́ть, -ва́ть (*кого к чему*); увещева́ть (*impf.*).
exhortation [,egzɔ:'teɪʃ(ə)n, ,eks-] *n.* призы́в, увещева́ние.
exhumation [eks,hju:'meɪʃ(ə)n, ɪg,zju:'meɪʃ(ə)n] *n.* эксгума́ция.
exhume [eks'hju:m, ɪg'zju:m] *v.t.* эксгуми́ровать (*impf., pf.*); (*fig.*) раск|а́пывать, -опа́ть.
exigency ['eksɪdʒənsɪ, ɪg'zɪdʒ-] *n.* неотло́жность, кра́йность; кра́йняя необходи́мость.
exigent ['eksɪdʒ(ə)nt] *adj.* (*urgent*) неотло́жный, сро́чный; (*demanding*) тре́бовательный.
exile ['eksaɪl, 'egz-] *n.* **1.** (*banishment*) изгна́ние; ссы́лка; **send into ~** ссыла́ть, сосла́ть. **2.** (*pers.*) изгна́нник; ссы́льный.
v.t. изг|оня́ть, -на́ть; ссыла́ть, сосла́ть.
exist [ɪg'zɪst] *v.i.* **1.** (*be, live*) существова́ть (*impf.*), жить (*impf.*). **2.** (*be found*) име́ться, встреча́ться, находи́ться (*all impf.*).
existence [ɪg'zɪst(ə)ns] *n.* существова́ние; (*presence*) нали́чие; (*life*) жизнь; **in ~** существу́ющий, нали́чный, име́ющийся.
existent [ɪg'zɪst(ə)nt] *adj.* существу́ющий.
existential [,egzɪ'stenʃ(ə)l] *adj.* экзистенциа́льный.
existentialism [,egzɪ'stenʃə,lɪz(ə)m] *n.* экзистенциали́зм.
existentialist [,egzɪ'stenʃəlɪst] *n.* экзистенциали́ст.

exit ['eksɪt, 'egzɪt] *n.* вы́ход; **make one's ~** у|ходи́ть, -йти́.
v.i. у|ходи́ть, -йти́.
ex-libris [eks'li:brɪs] *n.* экслибрис.
exodus ['eksədəs] *n.* ма́ссовый отъе́зд/ухо́д; **E~** (*bibl.*) Исхо́д, Втора́я кни́га Моисе́ева.
exonerate [ɪg'zɒnə,reɪt] *v.t.* опра́вд|ывать, -а́ть.
exoneration [ɪg,zɒnə'reɪʃ(ə)n] *n.* оправда́ние.
exorbitant [ɪg'zɔ:bɪt(ə)nt] *adj.* непоме́рный.
exorcism ['eksɔ:,sɪz(ə)m] *n.* изгна́ние злых ду́хов.
exorcist ['eksɔ:sɪst] *n.* заклина́тель (*m.*).
exorcize ['eksɔ:,saɪz] *v.t.* изг|оня́ть, -на́ть злых ду́хов из+*g.*
exotic [ɪg'zɒtɪk] *adj.* экзоти́ческий.
expand [ɪk'spænd] *v.t.* (*lit.*, *fig.*) расш|иря́ть, -и́рить; **heat ~s metals** при нагрева́нии мета́ллы расширя́ются.
v.i. расш|иря́ться, -и́риться.
expanse [ɪk'spæns] *n.* широ́кое простра́нство; (*of sea, sky etc.*) просто́р; ширь.
expansion [ɪk'spænʃ(ə)n] *n.* расшире́ние; (*pol.*) экспа́нсия; (*increase*) подъём; **territorial ~** территориа́льные захва́ты (*m. pl.*).
expansionism [ɪk'spænʃ(ə),nɪz(ə)m] *n.* (*pol.*) экспансиони́зм.
expansive [ɪk'spænsɪv] *adj.* (*of pers.*) экспанси́вный.
expatiate [ɪk'speɪʃɪ,eɪt] *v.i.* распространя́ться (*impf.*) (*на какую-н. тему*).
expatriate[1] [eks'pætrɪət, -'peɪtrɪət] *n.* экспатриа́нт (*fem.* -ка); **an ~ American** америка́нец-экспатриа́нт.
expatriate[2] [eks'pætrɪ,eɪt, -'peɪtrɪ,eɪt] *v.t.* экспатрии́ровать (*impf.*, *pf.*).
expatriation [eks,pætrɪ'eɪʃ(ə)n, -,peɪtrɪ'eɪʃ(ə)n] *n.* экспатриа́ция.
expect [ɪk'spekt] *v.t.* **1.** (*of future or probable event*) ждать (*impf.*), ожида́ть (*impf.*) +*g.*; **I ~ to see him** я рассчи́тываю встре́титься с ним; **I ~ him to dinner** я жду его́ к обе́ду; **just as I ~ed** так я и ду́мал. **2.** (*require*) ожида́ть (*impf.*) +*g.*; рассчи́тывать (*impf.*) на+*a.*; тре́бовать (*impf.*) +*g.*. **3.** (*suppose*) полага́ть (*impf.*); предполага́ть (*impf.*); **I ~ you are hungry** я полага́ю, что вы голодны́. **4.: she is ~ing** (*coll.*, *pregnant*) она́ ожида́ет ребёнка.
expectancy [ɪk'spektənsɪ] *n.* ожида́ние; предвкуше́ние.
expectant [ɪk'spekt(ə)nt] *adj.* выжида́ющий; **an ~ mother** бу́дущая мать.
expectation [,ekspek'teɪʃ(ə)n] *n.* **1.** (*anticipation*) ожида́ние; **in ~ of** в ожида́нии +*g.*; **contrary to ~** вопреки́ ожида́ниям; **come up to ~s** оправда́ть (*pf.*) ожида́ния. **2.** (*prospect*) наде́жда; **~ of life** вероя́тная продолжи́тельность жи́зни.
expectorate [ek'spektə,reɪt] *v.t. & i.* отха́рк|ивать(ся), -нуть(ся).
expedienc|e [ɪk'spi:dɪəns], **-y** [ɪk'spi:dɪənsɪ] *nn.* целесообра́зность.
expedient [ɪk'spi:dɪənt] *adj.* целесообра́зный; (*advantageous*) вы́годный.
expedite ['ekspɪ,daɪt] *v.t.* уск|оря́ть, -о́рить.
expedition [,ekspɪ'dɪʃ(ə)n] *n.* экспеди́ция.
expeditionary [,ekspɪ'dɪʃənərɪ] *adj.* экспедицио́нный; **~ force** экспедицио́нные войска́.
expeditious [,ekspɪ'dɪʃəs] *adj.* бы́стрый, ско́рый.
expel [ɪk'spel] *v.t.* (*emit*) пос|ыла́ть, -ла́ть; (*compel to leave*) исключ|а́ть, -и́ть; выгоня́ть, вы́гнать; (*dislodge, e.g. troops*) изг|оня́ть, -на́ть.
expend [ɪk'spend] *v.t.* (*capital*) расхо́довать, из-; тра́тить, ис-; (*ammunition*) расхо́довать, из-; (*time, efforts*) тра́тить, ис-/по-.
expendable [ɪk'spendəb(ə)l] *adj.* ли́шний.
expenditure [ɪk'spendɪtʃə(r)] *n.* расхо́д, тра́та; **~ of energy** затра́та эне́ргии.
expense [ɪk'spens] *n.* **1.** (*monetary cost*) расхо́д; **at my ~** (*lit.*) за мой счёт; **at public ~** за казённый счёт; **go to ~** нести́ (*det.*) расхо́ды; **spare no ~** не жале́ть (*impf.*) расхо́дов; **~ account** счёт подотчётных сумм; **travelling ~s** доро́жные расхо́ды. **2.** (*detriment*): **a joke at my ~** шу́тка на мой счёт; **idealism at others' ~** идеали́зм за чужо́й счёт.
expensive [ɪk'spensɪv] *adj.* дорого́й.
experience [ɪk'spɪərɪəns] *n.* **1.** (*process of gaining knowledge etc.*) о́пыт; **we learn by ~** мы у́чимся на со́бственном о́пыте; **I know that from ~** я зна́ю э́то по о́пыту. **2.** (*event*) слу́чай.
v.t. испы́т|ывать, -а́ть; переж|ива́ть, -и́ть.
experienced [ɪk'spɪərɪənst] *adj.* о́пытный.
experiment [ɪk'sperɪmənt, -,ment] *n.* экспериме́нт, о́пыт.
v.i. эксперименти́ровать (*impf.*).
experimental [ɪk,sperɪ'ment(ə)l] *adj.* эксперимента́льный, про́бный; **at the ~ stage** на ста́дии экспериме́нта.
experimentation [ɪk,sperɪmen'teɪʃ(ə)n] *n.* эксперименти́рование.
expert ['ekspɜ:t] *n.* экспе́рт, знато́к, специали́ст (*по чему*).
adj. квалифици́рованный; **an ~ driver** о́пытный шофёр; **~ advice** сове́т специали́ста.
expertise [,ekspɜ:'ti:z] *n.* (*skill, knowledge*) компете́нтность.
expiate ['ekspɪ,eɪt] *v.t.* искуп|а́ть, -и́ть.
expiation [,ekspɪ'eɪʃ(ə)n] *n.* искупле́ние.
expiatory ['ekspɪətərɪ, 'ekspɪ,eɪtərɪ] *adj.* искупи́тельный.
expiration [,ekspɪ'reɪʃ(ə)n] *n.* (*breathing out*) вы́дох; (*expiry*) истече́ние (*срока*).
expire [ɪk'spaɪə(r)] *v.i.* **1.** (*breathe out*) выдыха́ть, вы́дохнуть. **2.** (*of period, truce, licence etc.*) ист|ека́ть, -е́чь. **3.** (*die*) уг|аса́ть, -а́снуть.
expiry [ɪk'spaɪərɪ] *n.* истече́ние (сро́ка).
explain [ɪk'spleɪn] *v.t.* объясн|я́ть, -и́ть; **~ o.s.** (*make o.s. clear*) разъясни́ть (*pf.*) свою́ то́чку зре́ния; (*account for one's conduct*) опра́вд|ываться, -а́ться; **~ sth. away** на|ходи́ть, -йти́ объясне́ние (*неудобному факту*).
explainable [ɪk'spleɪnəb(ə)l] *adj.* объясни́мый.
explanation [,eksplə'neɪʃ(ə)n] *n.* объясне́ние; **in (by way of) ~** в ка́честве объясне́ния.
explanatory [ɪk'splænətərɪ] *adj.* объясни́тельный.
expletive [ɪk'spli:tɪv] *n.* бра́нное выраже́ние.
explicable [ɪk'splɪkəb(ə)l, 'ek-] *adj.* объясни́мый.
explicit [ɪk'splɪsɪt] *adj.* я́сный, чёткий, то́чный.
explode [ɪk'spləʊd] *v.t.* вз|рыва́ть, -орва́ть; (*fig.*): **~ a theory** опров|ерга́ть, -е́ргнуть тео́рию.
v.i. вз|рыва́ться, -орва́ться; (*fig.*): **he ~d with rage/laughter** он разрази́лся гне́вом/сме́хом.
exploit[1] ['eksplɔɪt] *n.* по́двиг.
exploit[2] [ɪk'splɔɪt] *v.t.* (*use or develop economically*) разраб|а́тывать, -о́тать; эксплуати́ровать (*impf.*). **2.** (*an advantage etc.*) по́льзоваться, вос- +*i.* **3.** (*a person*) эксплуати́ровать (*impf.*).
exploitable [ɪk'splɔɪtəb(ə)l] *adj.* го́дный для разрабо́тки.
exploitation [,eksplɔɪ'teɪʃ(ə)n] *n.* разрабо́тка; эксплуата́ция (*also of pers.*).
exploiter [ɪk'splɔɪtə(r)] *n.* эксплуата́тор.
exploration [,eksplə'reɪʃ(ə)n] *n.* (*geog.*) иссле́дование; (*of possibilities etc.*) изуче́ние.
exploratory [ɪk'splɒrətərɪ] *adj.* иссле́довательский; **~ talks** предвари́тельные перегово́ры.
explore [ɪk'splɔ:(r)] *v.t.* **1.** (*geog.*) иссле́довать (*impf.*, *pf.*). **2.** (*possibilities etc.*) изуч|а́ть, -и́ть.
explorer [ɪk'splɔ:rə(r)] *n.* иссле́дователь (*m.*).
explosion [ɪk'spləʊʒ(ə)n] *n.* (*of bomb etc.*) взрыв; (*of rage etc.*) вспы́шка; (*fig.*): **population ~** демографи́ческий взрыв.

explosive [ɪk'spləʊsɪv] *n.* взры́вчатое вещество́.

adj. взры́вчатый, взрывно́й; ~ **bomb** фуга́сная бо́мба; ~ **bullet** разрывна́я пу́ля; (*fig.*) вспы́льчивый.

exponent [ɪk'spəʊnənt] *n.* **1.** (*advocate*) сторо́нник; представи́тель (*m.*). **2.** (*math.*) показа́тель (*m.*) сте́пени.

exponential [ˌekspə'nenʃ(ə)l] *adj.* (*math.*) экспоненциа́льный, показа́тельный.

export[1] ['ekspɔːt] *n.* э́кспорт, вы́воз; ~ **duty** э́кспортная по́шлина.

export[2] [ek'spɔːt, 'ek-] *v.t.* экспорти́ровать (*impf.*, *pf.*); вывози́ть, вы́везти.

exportation [ˌekspɔː'teɪʃ(ə)n] *n.* экспорти́рование.

exporter [ek'spɔːtə(r)] *n.* экспортёр.

expose [ɪk'spəʊz] *v.t.* **1.** (*physically*) выставля́ть, вы́ставить; ~ **one's body to sunlight** подст|авля́ть, -а́вить те́ло со́лнцу; ~**d to the weather** незащищённый от непого́ды; **an** ~**d position** (*mil.*) незащищённая пози́ция. **2.** (*fig.*, *subject*) подв|ерга́ть, -е́ргнуть; **he was** ~**d to insult** его́ сде́лали мише́нью для оскорбле́ний. **3.** (*display*) выставля́ть, вы́ставить. **4.** (*fig.*, *unfold*) раскр|ыва́ть, -ы́ть. **5.** (*unmask*) разоблач|а́ть, -и́ть. **6.** (*phot.*) экспони́ровать (*impf.*).

exposé [ek'spəʊzeɪ] *n.* (*exposition*) экспозе́ (*indecl.*).

exposition [ˌekspə'zɪʃ(ə)n] *n.* (*setting forth facts etc.*) изложе́ние; (*exhibition*) экспози́ция, вы́ставка.

expository [ɪk'spɒzɪtərɪ] *adj.* объясни́тельный.

expostulate [ɪk'spɒstjʊˌleɪt] *v.i.*: ~ **with s.o.** увещева́ть (*impf.*) кого́-н.

expostulation [ɪkˌspɒstjʊ'leɪʃ(ə)n] *n.* увещева́ние.

exposure [ɪk'spəʊʒə(r)] *n.* **1.** (*physical*): ~ **to light** выставле́ние на свет; **he died of** ~ он поги́б от хо́лода; **house with a southern** ~ дом о́кнами на юг. **2.** (*subjection*): ~ **to ridicule** выставле́ние на посме́шище. **3.** (*unmasking*) разоблаче́ние. **4.** (*phot.*) экспози́ция; ~ **meter** экспоно́метр.

expound [ɪk'spaʊnd] *v.t.* (*a theory*) изл|ага́ть, -ожи́ть; (*a text*) толкова́ть (*impf.*).

express[1] [ɪk'spres] *n.* (~ *train*) экспре́сс; курье́рский по́езд.

adj. сро́чный; ~ **mail** э́кстренная по́чта.

adv. сро́чно, спе́шно; с на́рочным; **the goods were sent** ~ (*urgently*) това́р был отпра́влен большо́й ско́ростью.

express[2] [ɪk'spres] *adj.* **1.** (*clear*) чёткий. **2.** (*exact*, *specific*) то́чный, осо́бенный; **for the** ~ **purpose of** со специа́льной це́лью +*g*.

v.t. **1.** (*press out*) выжима́ть, вы́жать. **2.** (*show in words etc.*) выража́ть, вы́разить; ~ **o.s.** выража́ться, вы́разиться; выска́зывать, вы́сказать.

expression [ɪk'spreʃ(ə)n] *n.* **1.** (*act of expressing*) выраже́ние; **beyond** ~ невырази́мый; **give** ~ **to** выража́ть, вы́разить; **find** ~ выража́ться, вы́разиться. **2.** (*word*, *term*) выраже́ние (*also math.*).

expressive [ɪk'spresɪv] *adj.* вырази́тельный.

expressiveness [ɪk'spresɪvnɪs] *n.* вырази́тельность.

expropriate [eks'prəʊprɪˌeɪt] *v.t.* экспроприи́ровать (*impf.*, *pf.*).

expropriation [eksˌprəʊprɪ'eɪʃ(ə)n] *n.* экспроприа́ция.

expulsion [ɪk'spʌlʃ(ə)n] *n.* изгна́ние; исключе́ние.

expunge [ɪk'spʌndʒ] *v.t.* вычёркивать, вы́черкнуть.

expurgate ['ekspəˌgeɪt] *v.t.*: ~ **a book** исключ|а́ть, -и́ть нежела́тельные места́ из кни́ги.

exquisite [ek'skwɪzɪt] *adj.* (*perfected*) утончённый; (*delicate*) то́нкий.

ex-serviceman [eks'sɜːvɪsmən] *n.* демобилизо́ванный; отставно́й вое́нный.

extant [ek'stænt, ɪk'st-, 'ekst(ə)nt] *adj.* сохрани́вшийся.

extempore [ɪk'stempərɪ] *adj.* импровизи́рованный.

adv. экспро́мтом.

extemporize [ɪk'stempəˌraɪz] *v.t.* & *i.* и|мпровизи́ровать, сы-; **he** ~**d a speech** он произнёс импровизи́рованную речь.

extend [ɪk'stend] *v.t.* **1.** (*stretch out*) протя́|гивать, -ну́ть; ~ **a rope between two posts** натя́|гивать, -ну́ть верёвку ме́жду двумя́ столба́ми. **2.** (*offer*, *accord*) ока́з|ывать, -а́ть; ~ **a welcome** выка́зывать, вы́казать раду́шие; раду́шно встр|еча́ть, -е́тить (*кого*). **3.** (*make longer*, *wider or larger*) удлин|я́ть, -и́ть; расш|иря́ть, -и́рить; ~ **one's premises** расш|иря́ть, -и́рить помеще́ние. **4.** (*prolong*) продл|ева́ть, -и́ть; **an** ~**ed** (*lengthy*) **visit** дли́тельный визи́т. **5.** (*fig.*, *enlarge*, *widen*) увели́чи|вать, -ть; расш|иря́ть, -и́рить; ~ **one's influence** распростран|я́ть, -и́ть своё влия́ние. **6.** (*exert*): ~ **o.s.** напр|яга́ться, -я́чься; **we are fully** ~**ed** мы на преде́ле (на́ших) сил.

v.i. простира́ться (*impf.*); **my leave** ~**s till Tuesday** мой о́тпуск продолжа́ется до вто́рника; **this rule** ~**s to first-year students** э́то пра́вило распространя́ется и на первоку́рсников.

extension [ɪk'stenʃ(ə)n] *n.* **1.** (*extent*) протяже́ние. **2.** (*stretching out*) вытя́гивание, удлине́ние. **3.** (*enlarging in space or time*) расшире́ние, увеличе́ние; ~ **ladder** раздвижна́я ле́стница; ~ **of leave** продле́ние о́тпуска; **an** ~ **course in physics** дополни́тельный курс фи́зики. **4.** (*additional part of building etc.*) пристро́йка (к+*d*.). **5.** (*teleph.*) доба́вочный (но́мер).

extensive [ɪk'stensɪv] *adj.* (*wide*, *far-reaching*) простра́нный; **an** ~ **park** обши́рный парк; ~ **knowledge** обши́рные зна́ния; ~ **plans** далеко́ иду́щие пла́ны.

extent [ɪk'stent] *n.* **1.** (*phys. size*, *length etc.*) протяже́ние. **2.** (*fig.*, *range*) разме́р; круг; диапазо́н; ~ **of s.o.'s knowledge** круг чьих-н. зна́ний; ~ **of damage** разме́р поврежде́ний. **3.** (*degree*) сте́пень; **to some** (*or* **a certain**) ~ до не́которой/изве́стной сте́пени; **to a large** ~ в значи́тельной ме́ре.

extenuat|e [ɪk'stenjʊˌeɪt] *v.t.* преум|еньша́ть, -е́ньшить; ~**ing circumstances** смягча́ющие обстоя́тельства.

exterior [ɪk'stɪərɪə(r)] *n.* (*of object*) вне́шняя сторона́; (*of pers.*) вне́шность; нару́жность.

adj. вне́шний.

exterminate [ɪk'stɜːmɪˌneɪt] *v.t.* (*disease*; *ideas*) искорен|я́ть, -и́ть; (*people*) уничт|ожа́ть, -о́жить; (*people*, *vermin*) истреб|ля́ть, -и́ть.

extermination [ɪkˌstɜːmɪ'neɪʃ(ə)n] *n.* искорене́ние; уничтоже́ние; истребле́ние.

external [ɪk'stɜːn(ə)l] *n.* вне́шность.

adj. вне́шний; ~ **affairs** иностра́нные дела́; **an** ~ **student** экстéрн, зао́чни|к (*fem.* -ца); **for** ~ **use only** то́лько для нару́жного употребле́ния.

extinct [ɪk'stɪŋkt] *adj.* (*of volcano*) поту́хший; (*of species*, *custom*) вы́мерший; (*of feelings etc.*) уга́сший.

extinction [ɪk'stɪŋkʃ(ə)n] *n.* угаса́ние; (*of a species etc.*) вымира́ние; (*of a disease*) ликвида́ция, искорене́ние.

extinguish [ɪk'stɪŋgwɪʃ] *v.t.* (*light*, *fire*) гаси́ть, по-; (*hopes etc.*) уб|ива́ть, -и́ть.

extinguisher [ɪk'stɪŋgwɪʃə(r)] *n.* огнетуши́тель (*m.*).

extirpate ['ekstəˌpeɪt] *v.t.* вырыва́ть, вы́рвать с ко́рнем; искорен|я́ть, -и́ть.

extirpation [ˌekstə'peɪʃ(ə)n] *n.* искорене́ние.

extol [ɪk'stəʊl, ɪk'stɒl] *v.t.* превозн|оси́ть, -ести́.

extort [ɪk'stɔːt] *v.t.* вымога́ть (*impf.*).

extortion [ɪk'stɔːʃ(ə)n] *n.* вымога́тельство.

extortionate [ɪk'stɔːʃənət] *adj.* вымога́тельский.

extortioner [ɪk'stɔːʃənə(r)] *n.* вымога́тель (*m.*).

extra ['ekstrə] *n.* **1.** (*additional item*) что-н. дополни́тельное; **music is an** ~ му́зыка преподаётся факультати́вно; **no** ~**s** без вся́ких припла́т; (*edition*) э́кстренный вы́пуск. **2.** (*minor performer*) стати́ст (*fem.* -ка).

adj. **1.** (*additional*) доба́вочный, дополни́тельный; **it costs £1, postage** ~ э́то сто́ит 1 фунт без пересы́лки; **I paid an ~ £5** я заплати́л ли́шних 5 фу́нтов; **£5 ~** 5 фу́нтов дополни́тельно. **2.** (*special*) осо́бый.

adv. сверх-, осо́бо; **~ strong** (*e.g. drink*) осо́бой кре́пости.

extract[1] ['ekstrækt] *n.* **1.** (*concentrated substance*) экстра́кт. **2.** (*from book etc.*) вы́держка.

extract[2] [ɪk'strækt] *v.t.* (*cork*) выта́скивать, вы́тащить; (*tooth*) удал|я́ть, -и́ть; (*bullet from wound*) извл|ека́ть, -е́чь; (*information, admission*) вырыва́ть, вы́рвать; (*money*) вымога́ть (*impf.*); (*pleasure from a situation*) извл|ека́ть, -е́чь; **~ passages** (*from a book*) де́лать, с- вы́держки; (*juices etc.*) выжима́ть, вы́жать.

extraction [ɪk'strækʃ(ə)n] *n.* (*extracting*) извлече́ние; (*of tooth*) удале́ние; (*descent, origin*) происхожде́ние.

extractor [ɪk'stræktə(r)] *n.* экстра́ктор; **~ fan** вентиля́тор.

extra-curricular [,ekstrəkə'rɪkjʊlə(r)] *adj.* проводи́мый сверх уче́бного пла́на; вне програ́ммы.

extradite ['ekstrə,daɪt] *v.t.* (*hand over*) выдава́ть, вы́дать (*обвиняемого преступника*).

extradition [,ekstrə'dɪʃ(ə)n] *n.* вы́дача (престу́пника).

extra-marital [,ekstrə'mærɪt(ə)l] *adj.*: **~ affair** внебра́чная связь.

extramural [,ekstrə'mjʊər(ə)l] *adj.* (*acad.*): **~ student** ≃ вече́рни|к (*fem.* -ца).

extraneous [ɪk'streɪnɪəs] *adj.* посторо́нний, чужо́й.

extraordinary [ɪk'strɔːdɪnərɪ, ,ekstrə'ɔːdɪnərɪ] *adj.* чрезвыча́йный, необыча́йный, выдаю́щийся.

extrapolate [ɪk'stræpə,leɪt] *v.t. & i.* (*math., fig.*) экстраполи́ровать (*impf., pf.*).

extrapolation [ɪk,stræpə'leɪʃ(ə)n] *n.* (*math.*) экстраполя́ция.

extrasensory [,ekstrə'sensərɪ] *adj.*: **~ perception** внечу́вственное восприя́тие.

extraterrestrial [,ekstrətɪ'restrɪəl] *adj.* внеземно́й.

extravagance [ɪk'strævəgəns] *n.* экстравага́нтность; расточи́тельность.

extravagant [ɪk'strævəgənt] *adj.* **1.** (*excessive*) изли́шний. **2.** (*fantastic*) экстравага́нтный, сумасбро́дный. **3.** (*over-spending*) расточи́тельный.

extreme [ɪk'striːm] *n.* **1.** (*high degree*) кра́йность. **2.** (*of conduct etc.*) кра́йность; **he went to the opposite ~** он впал в другу́ю кра́йность; **carry things to ~s** впада́ть (*impf.*) в кра́йность. **3.** (*pl., opposing qualities etc.*): **~s of behaviour** кра́йности поведе́ния; **~s of heat and cold** кра́йне высо́кие и ни́зкие температу́ры.

adj. **1.** (*furthest, utmost, last*) кра́йний, преде́льный; **the ~ edge of the city** са́мая окра́ина го́рода; **(the one) on the ~ right** кра́йний спра́ва; **~ old age** глубо́кая ста́рость; **the ~ penalty of the law** вы́сшая ме́ра наказа́ния. **2.** (*very great*) чрезвыча́йный. **3.** (*taking sth. to its highest pitch*) кра́йний, преде́льный; **an ~ fashion** (*in clothes*) экстравага́нтная мо́да.

extremely [ɪk'striːmlɪ] *adv.* кра́йне.

extremism [ɪk'striːmɪz(ə)m] *n.* экстреми́зм.

extremist [ɪk'striːmɪst] *n.* экстреми́ст.

adj. экстреми́стский.

extremit|y [ɪk'stremɪtɪ] *n.* **1.** (*end, extreme point*) край. **2.** (*pl., hands and feet*) коне́чности (*f. pl.*). **3.** (*extreme quality*) кра́йность. **4.** (*hardship*) кра́йность; **reduced to ~y** доведённый до кра́йности. **5.** (*pl., extreme measures*) кра́йние ме́ры (*f. pl.*).

extricate ['ekstrɪ,keɪt] *v.t.* высвобожда́ть, вы́свободить; **~ o.s. from a difficulty** вы́путаться (*pf.*) из затрудне́ния.

extrovert ['ekstrə,vɜːt] *n.* челове́к с откры́той нату́рой, экстрове́рт.

exuberance [ɪg'zjuːbərəns] *n.* (*profusion*) изоби́лие; (*of character*) экспанси́вность.

exuberant [ɪg'zjuːbərənt] *adj.* (*of foliage etc.*) бу́йный; (*of imagination etc.*) бога́тый, бу́йный; (*of spirits etc.*) экспанси́вный.

exude [ɪg'zjuːd] *v.i.* просту́п|а́ть, -и́ть; выделя́ть, вы́делить; **he ~d cheerfulness** он излуча́л весе́лье.

exult [ɪg'zʌlt] *v.i.* торжествова́ть (*impf.*); ликова́ть (*impf.*).

exultant [ɪg'zʌltənt] *adj.* торжеству́ющий, лику́ющий.

exultation [ɪg,zʌl'teɪʃ(ə)n] *n.* торжество́, ликова́ние.

eye [aɪ] *n.* **1.** (*organ of vision*) глаз; (*dim.*) глазо́к (*pl.* гла́зки); **glass ~** стекля́нный глаз; **have a cast in one's ~** быть косогла́зым; **I can see well out of this ~** я хорошо́ ви́жу э́тим гла́зом; **I have sth. in my ~** мне что́-то попа́ло в глаз; **blind in one ~** криво́й. **2.** (*var. idioms*): **give s.o. a black ~** подби́ть (*pf.*) глаз кому́-н.; **~s right!/left!** (*mil.*) равне́ние напра́во/нале́во!; **with the naked ~** невооружённым гла́зом; **in the twinkling of an ~** в мгнове́ние о́ка; **make ~s at s.o.** (*coll.*) стро́ить (*impf.*) гла́зки кому́-н.; **be all ~s** гляде́ть (*impf.*) во все глаза́; **set, lay ~s on** зам|еча́ть, -е́тить; **fix, one's ~s on** не спуска́ть (*impf.*) глаз с+*g.*; уста́виться (*pf.*) на+*a.*; **keep an ~ on** следи́ть (*impf.*) за+*i.*; **keep one's ~s open, peeled** (*coll.*) смотре́ть (*impf.*) в о́ба; **take one's ~s off s.o./sth.** отв|оди́ть, -ести́ глаза́ от кого́/чего́-н.; **an ~ for an ~** о́ко за о́ко; **pull the wool over s.o.'s ~s** вт|ира́ть, -ере́ть очки́ кому́-н.; **under, before s.o.'s very ~s** на глаза́х у кого́-н.; **he has an ~ for colour** он чу́вствует цвет; **he has an ~ for the ladies** он зна́ет толк в же́нщинах; **cry one's ~s out** вы́плакать (*pf.*) все глаза́; **dry one's ~** осуши́ть (*pf.*) слёзы; **I could not believe my ~s** я не мог пове́рить свои́м глаза́м; **he ran his ~ over the paper** он пробежа́л глаза́ми газе́ту; **feast one's ~s on** (*a sight*) наслажда́ться (*impf.*) (зре́лищем); **I caught her ~** я пойма́л её взгляд; **have ~s at the back of one's head** всё ви́деть/подмеча́ть (*impf.*); **have one's ~ on the ball** (*fig.*) быть начеку́; **see ~ to ~ with** сходи́ться (*impf.*) во взгля́дах с+*i.*; **up to the ~s in work** по́ уши в рабо́те; **I opened his ~s to the situation** я откры́л ему́ глаза́ на положе́ние веще́й; **he closed his ~s to the danger** он закрыва́л глаза́ на опа́сность; **turn a blind ~ to** смотре́ть (*impf.*) сквозь па́льцы на+*a.*; **in my ~s** (*judgment*) в мои́х глаза́х, на мой взгляд; **in the public ~** в це́нтре внима́ния; **he has an ~ to business** у него́ комме́рческий подхо́д к веща́м; **there is more in this than meets the ~** э́то не так про́сто, как ка́жется на пе́рвый взгляд. **3.** (*special senses*): **~ of a needle** иго́льное ушко́; **in the ~ of the storm** в эпице́нтре бу́ри; **private ~** (*sl., detective*) ча́стный сы́щик.

v.t. разгля́д|ывать, -е́ть; наблюда́ть (*impf.*); **he ~d me with suspicion** он разгля́дывал меня́ с подозре́нием.

cpds. **~ball** *n.* глазно́е я́блоко; **~-bath, ~-cup** *nn.* глазна́я ва́нночка; **~brow** *n.* бровь; **up to the ~brows** (*fig.*) по́ уши; **raise one's ~brows** (*fig.*) подня́ть (*pf.*) бро́ви от удивле́ния, неодобре́ния и т.п.; **~-catching** *adj.* эффе́ктный; **~glass** *n.* (*monocle*) моно́кль (*m.*); (*pl., spectacles*) очк|и́ (*pl., g.* -о́в); **~lash** *n.* ресни́ца; **~-level** *n.*: **at ~-level** на у́ровне глаз; **~lid** *n.* ве́ко; **without batting an ~lid** (*coll.*) гла́зом не моргну́в; **~-opener** *n.* (*coll., revelation*) открове́ние; **~-shadow** *n.* те́ни (*f. pl.*) для век; **~sight** *n.* зре́ние; **~-socket** *n.* глазни́ца, глазна́я впа́дина; **~sore** *n.* уро́дство; **~strain** *n.* напряже́ние зре́ния; **~-tooth** *n.* глазно́й зуб; **~wash** *n.* (*lotion*) примо́чка для глаз; (*fig., coll.*) очковтира́тельство; **~witness** *n.* очеви́дец.

eyeful ['aɪfʊl] *n.* (*coll.*) зре́лище.

eyelet ['aɪlɪt] *n.* ушко́; пете́лька.

F

F[1] [ef] *n.* (*mus., also* **fa, fah**) фа (*nt. indecl.*).

F[2] ['færən,haɪt] (*abbr. of* **Fahrenheit**) °Ф, (шкала́ термо́метра Фаренге́йта); **30°F** 30°Ф (гра́дусов по Фаренге́йту).

FA (*abbr. of* ***Football Association***) Футбо́льная ассоциа́ция; ~ **Cup** кубо́к Футбо́льной ассоциа́ции.

fa [fɑː] *n.* = **fah**

fable ['feɪb(ə)l] *n.* ба́сня.

fabled ['feɪbəld] *adj.* (*celebrated*) легенда́рный; (*fictitious*) легенда́рный, ска́зочный.

fabric ['fæbrɪk] *n.* (*text.*) ткань, мате́рия; (*of a building etc.*) констру́кция, структу́ра; (*fig.*) структу́ра.

fabricate ['fæbrɪ,keɪt] *v.t.* (*invent*) сочин|я́ть, -и́ть; (*falsify, forge*) фабрикова́ть, с-; подде́л|ывать, -ать.

fabrication [,fæbrɪ'keɪʃ(ə)n] *n.* (*story etc.*) вы́думка; **complete** ~ сплошна́я вы́думка; (*falsification*) фабрика́ция, подде́лка.

fabulist ['fæbjʊlɪst] *n.* баснопи́сец.

fabulous ['fæbjʊləs] *adj.* (*legendary*) легенда́рный; (*coll., marvellous*) роско́шный, басносло́вный.

facade [fə'sɑːd] *n.* (*archit.*) фаса́д.

face [feɪs] *n.* **1.** (*front part of head*) лицо́; **he fell on his** ~ он упа́л ничко́м; **he hit him in the** ~ он уда́рил его́ по лицу́; **look s.o. in the** ~ (*lit.*) посмотре́ть (*pf.*) кому́-н. в глаза́; **I came** ~ **to** ~ **with him** я столкну́лся с ним лицо́м к лицу́; **I brought them** ~ **to face** я свёл их друг с дру́гом; **I told him so to his** ~ я сказа́л ему́ э́то в лицо́; **I dare not show my** ~ **there** я не сме́ю глаз показа́ть там; **the sun was shining in our** ~**s** со́лнце свети́ло нам пря́мо в лицо́; **she laughed in my** ~ она́ рассмея́лась мне в лицо́; **he shut the door in my** ~ он захло́пнул дверь пе́ред мои́м но́сом; **it's written all over his** ~ э́то у него́ на лице́ напи́сано; **she had her** ~ **lifted** ей подтяну́ли ко́жу на лице́; **in the** ~ **of danger** пе́ред лицо́м опа́сности; **in the** ~ **of difficulties** несмотря́ на тру́дности; **ruin stares us in the** ~ нам грози́т разоре́ние. **2.** (*facial expression*) лицо́; выраже́ние лица́; **he made a** ~ он ско́рчил/состро́ил ро́жу; **he pulled a long** ~ у него́ вы́тянулось лицо́; **he kept a straight** ~ он храни́л невозмути́мый вид; **he put a bold** ~ **on the matter** он сде́лал хоро́шую ми́ну при плохо́й игре́; **his** ~ **fell** он измени́лся в лице́; у него́ вы́тянулось лицо́. **3.** (*composure, effrontery*): **he saved his** ~ он спас свою́ репута́цию; **he had the** ~ **to tell me ...** у него́ хвати́ло на́глости сказа́ть мне... **4.** (*outward show, aspect*) вне́шний вид; **on the** ~ **of it** (*apparently*) на пе́рвый взгляд. **5.** (*physical surface, facade*) лицо́; лицева́я сторона́; (*of clock*) цифербла́т; **they disappeared from the** ~ **of the earth** они́ исче́зли с лица́ земли́; **he laid the card** ~ **down** он положи́л ка́рту лицо́м вниз; **the miner worked at the coal** ~ шахтёр рабо́тал в у́гольном забо́е; ~ **value** (*of currency*) номина́льная сто́имость; **I took his words at** ~ **value** я при́нял его́ слова́ за чи́стую моне́ту.

v.t. **1.** (*physically*) стоя́ть (*impf.*) лицо́м к+*d.*; смотре́ть (*impf.*) на+*a.*; **a seat facing the engine** сиде́нье по хо́ду по́езда. **2.** (*confront*) смотре́ть (*impf.*) в лицо́ (*чему*); **we must** ~ **facts** на́до смотре́ть фа́ктам в лицо́; **let's** ~ **it!** (*coll.*) на́до гляде́ть пра́вде в глаза́!; **the problem that** ~**s us** зада́ча, стоя́щая пе́ред на́ми; **we are** ~**d with bankruptcy** мы стои́м пе́ред банкро́тством. **3.** (*mil., cause to turn*) пов|ора́чивать, -ерну́ть. **4.** (*cover*): **a wall** ~**d with stone** стена́, облицо́ванная ка́мнем; **a coat** ~**d with silk** пальто́, отде́ланное шёлком.

v.i.: **the house** ~**s on to a park** о́кна до́ма выхо́дят на парк; **their house** ~**s ours** их дом — напро́тив на́шего; **he** ~**d up to the difficulties** он не испуга́лся тру́дностей; (*mil.*) **about** ~**!** круго́м!

cpds. ~**-cloth** *n.* ли́чное полоте́нце; ~**-cream** *n.* крем для лица́; ~**-lift** *n.* опера́ция подня́тия ко́жи на лице́; (*fig.*) вне́шнее обновле́ние, космети́ческий ремо́нт; ~**-pack** *n.* космети́ческая ма́ска; ~**-powder** *n.* пу́дра; ~**-saving** *adj.* (*fig.*) для спасе́ния репута́ции/прести́жа.

faceless ['feɪslɪs] *adj.* безли́чный, безли́кий.

facet ['fæsɪt] *n.* грань, фаце́т; (*fig.*) аспе́кт.

facetious [fə'siːʃəs] *adj.* шутли́вый, шу́точный.

facia ['feɪʃɪə] *n.* (*over shop-front*) вы́веска; (*dashboard*) щито́к; прибо́рная доска́.

facial ['feɪʃ(ə)l] *n.* масса́ж лица́.

adj. лицево́й; ~ **expression** выраже́ние лица́.

facile ['fæsaɪl] *adj.* (*easy, fluent*) лёгкий, свобо́дный; (*superficial*) пове́рхностный.

facilitate [fə'sɪlɪ,teɪt] *v.t.* облегч|а́ть, -и́ть; спосо́бствовать (*impf.*) +*d.*; соде́йствовать (*impf.*) +*d.*

facilit|y [fə'sɪlɪtɪ] *n.* (*ease*) лёгкость; (*skill*) спосо́бность (*к чему*); (*aid, appliance, installation*) сооруже́ние; ~**ies for study** усло́вия (*nt. pl.*) для учёбы; **sports** ~**ies** спорти́вное обору́дование, помеще́ния (*nt. pl.*) для заня́тия спо́ртом.

facing ['feɪsɪŋ] *n.* (*of wall etc.*) облицо́вка; (*of coat etc.*) отде́лка.

facsimile [fæk'sɪmɪlɪ] *n.* факсимиле́ (*indecl.*).

fact [fækt] *n.* факт; **as a matter of** ~ факти́чески; на са́мом де́ле; **the** ~ **is that ...** де́ло в том, что...; **in (point of)** ~ (*actually*) факти́чески; на са́мом де́ле; (*intensifying*): **very much, in** ~ о́чень да́же; **I think so, in** ~ **I'm quite sure** я так ду́маю, бо́лее того́, я уве́рен в э́том; (*summing up*): **in** ~ **the whole thing is most unsatisfactory** в су́щности, всё э́то весьма́ неудовлетвори́тельно; **a story founded on** ~ расска́з, осно́ванный на действи́тельном происше́ствии.

cpd. ~**-finding** *adj.* занима́ющийся собира́нием фа́ктов; ~**-finding tour** ознакоми́тельная пое́здка.

faction ['fækʃ(ə)n] *n.* фра́кция, кли́ка.

factious ['fækʃəs] *adj.* фракцио́нный.

factor ['fæktə(r)] *n.* **1.** (*math.*) мно́житель (*m.*), фа́ктор. **2.** (*contributing cause*) фа́ктор; **this was a** ~ **in his success** э́то соде́йствовало его́ успе́ху.

factory ['fæktərɪ] *n.* фа́брика, заво́д; (*attr.*) фабри́чный, заводско́й.

factual ['fæktjʊəl] *adj.* факти́ческий.

facult|y ['fækəltɪ] *n.* **1.** (*power, aptitude*) спосо́бность; **in possession of one's** ~**ies** в здра́вом уме́. **2.** (*acad.*) факульте́т. **3.** (*US, body of teachers*) преподава́тельский соста́в.

fad [fæd] *n.* (*craze*) увлече́ние, пове́трие.

fade [feɪd] *v.t.* **1.** (*cause to lose colour*) обесцве́|чивать, -тить; **the sunlight** ~**d the curtains** занаве́ски вы́горели на со́лнце. **2.** (*cin., radio*): ~ **one scene into another** пла́вно перев|оди́ть, -ести́ одну́ сце́ну в другу́ю; ~ **out** постепе́нно ум|еньша́ть, -е́ньшить си́лу зву́ка; ~ **in** постепе́нно увели́чи|вать, -ть си́лу зву́ка.

v.i. **1.** (*lose colour*) обесцве́|чиваться, -титься; **the flowers** ~**d** цветы́ завя́ли/поблёкли; (*of sound*) зам|ира́ть, -ере́ть; (*of strength*) уг|аса́ть, -а́снуть. **2.** (*fig.*): **his hopes** ~**d** его́ наде́жды испари́лись; **she is fading away** (*dying*) она́ та́ет.

faeces ['fi:si:z] *n.* испражне́ния (*nt. pl.*).
fag[1] [fæg] *v.t.* (*tire*) утом|ля́ть, -и́ть; **I am ~ged out** я вконе́ц вы́мотался.
fag[2] [fæg] *n.* (*coll.*, *cigarette*) сигаре́та, папиро́ска.
cpd. **~-end** *n.* (*butt*) оку́рок; (*fig.*) оста́ток (*чего*).
faggot ['fægət] *n.* (*bundle of sticks*) вяза́нка, фаши́на.
fa(h) [fɑ:] *n.* (*mus.*) фа (*nt. indecl.*).
Fahrenheit ['færən,haɪt] *n.* (*abbr.* **F**) Фаренге́йт.
faience ['faɪɑ̃s] *n.* фая́нс.
fail [feɪl] *n.*: **without ~** обяза́тельно, непреме́нно.
v.t. **1.** (*reject in exam*) прова́л|ивать, -и́ть. **2.** (*disappoint*, *desert*) подв|оди́ть, -ести́; **words ~ me** я не нахожу́ слов; **his heart ~ ed him** у него́ не хвати́ло ду́ху.
v.i. **1.** (*fall short*, *decline*) ух|удша́ться, -у́дшиться; недостава́ть (*impf.*); **the crops ~ed** хлеб не уроди́лся; **the water supply ~ed** водоснабже́ние прекрати́лось; **his eyesight is ~ing** его́ зре́ние слабе́ет; **he is in ~ing health** его́ здоро́вье ухудша́ется. **2.** (*not succeed*): **he ~ed in the exam** он провали́лся на экза́мене; **his scheme ~ed** его́ план провали́лся; **he ~ed to convince her** ему́ не удало́сь убеди́ть её; **I ~ to see why ...** я не понима́ю, почему́... **3.** (*omit*) упус|ка́ть, -ти́ть; **he never ~s to write** он никогда́ не забыва́ет писа́ть; **he ~ed to let us know** он не дал нам знать. **4.** (*go bankrupt*): **the bank ~ed** банк ло́пнул.
failing ['feɪlɪŋ] *n.* (*defect*) недоста́ток, сла́бость.
prep. за неиме́нием+*g.*; **~ this** за неиме́нием э́того; е́сли э́того не случи́тся; **~ an answer** не получи́в отве́та.
failure ['feɪljə(r)] *n.* **1.** (*unsuccess*) неуда́ча, неуспе́х, прова́л; **the venture was a ~** зате́я провали́лась. **2.** (*pers.*) неуда́чник. **3.** (*of crops etc.*) неурожа́й. **4.** (*bankruptcy*) банкро́тство. **5.** (*non-functioning*) ава́рия; **heart ~** парали́ч се́рдца; **engine ~** отка́з дви́гателя.
faint [feɪnt] *n.* (*loss of consciousness*) о́бморок; **in a dead ~** в глубо́ком о́бмороке.
adj. **1.** (*weak*, *indistinct*) сла́бый, неотчётливый; **his strength grew ~** его́ си́лы угаса́ли; **he was ~ with hunger** он осла́б от го́лода; **I haven't the ~est idea** я не име́ю ни мале́йшего поня́тия. **2.** (*giddy*, *likely to swoon*) бли́зкий к о́бмороку; **I feel ~** мне ду́рно.
v.i. (*lose consciousness*) па́дать, упа́сть в о́бморок; (*grow weak*) слабе́ть (*impf.*); **he was ~ing with hunger** он слабе́л от го́лода; **~ fit** о́бморок.
cpds. **~-hearted** *adj.* малоду́шный; **~-heartedness** *n.* малоду́шие.
faintly ['feɪntlɪ] *adv.* (*feebly*) сла́бо; (*slightly*) сла́бо, слегка́.
faintness ['feɪntnɪs] *n.* сла́бость; (*giddiness*), дурнота́.
fair[1] [feə(r)] *n.* (*open-air market etc.*) я́рмарка; (*exhibition*) вы́ставка.
cpd. **~-ground** *n.* я́рмарочная пло́щадь.
fair[2] [feə(r)] *adj.* **1.** (*beautiful*) прекра́сный, краси́вый. **2.** (*specious*) показно́й; **~ words** краси́вые слова́. **3.** (*of weather*) я́сный; **the barometer is at set ~** баро́метр стои́т на «я́сно». **4.** (*abundant*, *favourable*): **a ~ wind** попу́тный ве́тер; **a ~ amount** (*a lot*) значи́тельное/изря́дное коли́чество. **5.** (*average*) сно́сный, посре́дственный; **he has a ~ chance of success** у него́ неплохи́е ша́нсы на успе́х; **she has a ~ amount of sense** у неё доста́точно здра́вого смы́сла; **'~'** (*as school mark*) посре́дственно; **~ to middling** так себе́; нева́жный. **6.** (*equitable*): **~ share** справедли́вая до́ля; **~ price** подходя́щая цена́; **~ play** че́стная игра́; справедли́вость; **by ~ means or foul** любы́ми сре́дствами; **it is ~ to say that ...** со всей справедли́востью мо́жно сказа́ть, что...; **~ and square** откры́тый, че́стный; **~ game** зако́нная добы́ча; **~ comment** беспристра́стная кри́тика. **7.** (*clean*, *unblemished*): **~ copy** чистови́к. **8.** (*of hair*) све́тлый, (*blond*) белоку́рый; **a ~ complexion** све́тлый цвет лица́.
adv.: **he fought ~** он боро́лся че́стно; **he bids ~ to succeed** у него́ есть ша́нсы на успе́х.
cpds. **~-dealing** *n.* че́стность, прямота́; *adj.* че́стный, прямо́й; **~-haired** *adj.* белоку́рый; **~-minded** *adj.* справедли́вый; **~-mindedness** *n.* справедли́вость.
fairly ['feəlɪ] *adv.* **1.** (*completely*, *positively*) факти́чески, буква́льно; **he ~ shook with indignation** он буква́льно дрожа́л от негодова́ния. **2.** (*moderately*) дово́льно, сно́сно, терпи́мо. **3.** (*justly*) че́стно, справедли́во.
fairness ['feənɪs] *n.* (*equity*) справедли́вость, че́стность; **in all ~** со всей справедли́востью.
fairy ['feərɪ] *n.* фе́я; **bad ~** зла́я фе́я; (*attr.*) волше́бный, ска́зочный; **~ lamps, lights** цветны́е фона́рики.
cpds. **~land** *n.* волше́бное ца́рство; ска́зочная страна́; **~-like** *adj.* подо́бный фе́е; **~-story, ~-tale** *nn.* ска́зка; (*fig.*) ска́зка, небыли́ца.
fait accompli [,feɪt ə'kɒmpli:, ə'kɔ̃pli:] *n.* соверши́вшийся факт.
faith [feɪθ] *n.* **1.** (*trust*) ве́ра, дове́рие; **put one's ~ in s.o.** дов|еря́ться, -е́риться кому́-н.; **I have no ~ in doctors** я не ве́рю доктора́м. **2.** (*relig. conviction*) ве́ра. **3.** (*relig. system*) вероиспове́дание, ве́ра. **4.** (*promise*, *warranty*) обеща́ние, руча́тельство; **keep/break ~ with s.o.** сдержа́ть/нару́шить (*pf.*) обеща́ние, да́нное кому́-н.; **breach of ~** наруше́ние обеща́ния. **5.** (*sincerity*) че́стность; **good ~** добросо́вестность; **in bad ~** с нече́стными наме́рениями; **in good ~** че́стно, добросо́вестно; с чи́стой со́вестью.
faithful ['feɪθfʊl] *adj.* то́чный, достове́рный; **a ~ translation** то́чный перево́д; (*as n.*) **the ~** (*believers*) правове́рные.
faithfully ['feɪθfʊlɪ] *adv.* то́чно, ве́рно; **yours ~** (*letter-ending*) с соверше́нным почте́нием; **deal ~ with** (*treat candidly*) добросо́вестно относи́ться к+*d.*
faithfulness ['feɪθfʊlnɪs] *n.* ве́рность.
faithless ['feɪθlɪs] *adj.* вероло́мный.
fake [feɪk] *n.* (*sham*) подде́лка, фальши́вка; (*attr.*) подде́льный, фальши́вый.
v.t. подде́л|ывать, -ать; **a ~d illness** притво́рная боле́знь.
faker ['feɪkə(r)] *n.* (*fabricator*) подде́лыватель (*m.*); (*fraudulent person*) обма́нщик.
fakery ['feɪkərɪ] *n.* подде́лка; притво́рство.
falcon ['fɔ:lkən, 'fɒlkən] *n.* со́кол.
falconry ['fɔ:lkənrɪ, 'fɒl-] *n.* соколи́ная охо́та.
fall [fɔ:l] *n.* **1.** (*physical drop*, *act of ~ing*) паде́ние; **he had a bad ~** он упа́л и си́льно ушибся; **a heavy ~ of rain** ли́вень (*m.*), проливно́й дождь; **~ of snow** снегопа́д. **2.** (*moral*) паде́ние; **~ from grace** нра́вственное паде́ние; **the ~ of man** (*relig.*) грехопаде́ние. **3.**: **the ~ of the Roman Empire** паде́ние Ри́мской импе́рии. **4.** (*diminution*) пониже́ние; **~ in prices** паде́ние цен. **5.** (*pl.*, *waterfall*) водопа́д; **Niagara F~s** Ниага́рский водопа́д. **6.** (*US*, *autumn*) о́сень.
v.i. **1.** па́дать, упа́сть; **he fell over a chair** он упа́л, споткну́вшись о стул; **he fell full length** он растяну́лся во весь рост; **he fell dead** он у́мер на ме́сте; **rain fell at last** наконе́ц вы́пал дождь; **many trees fell in the storm** бу́рей повали́ло мно́го дере́вьев; **leaves ~** ли́стья опада́ют; **the river ~s into the lake** река́ впада́ет в о́зеро; **the arrow fell short** стрела́ не долете́ла до це́ли; **he fell on his feet** (*fig.*) он счастли́во отде́лался; **the joke fell flat** шу́тка не име́ла успе́ха; **his work fell short of expectations** его́ рабо́та не оправда́ла ожида́ний; **he fell into the trap** он попа́л(ся) в лову́шку; **~ over o.s.** (*coll.*) (*from eagerness*) перестара́ться (*pf.*); лезть (*impf.*)

из ко́жи вон. **2.** (*drop, sink*) па́дать, па́сть (*or* упа́сть); **the river has ~en** вода́ в реке́ спа́ла; **prices fell** це́ны сни́зились/упа́ли; **the temperature fell** температу́ра упа́ла; **my spirits fell ~** я упа́л ду́хом; **his eyes fell** он опусти́л глаза́; **the wind fell** ве́тер стих. **3.** (*of defeat etc.*) па́|дать, -сть; **the city fell** го́род пал; **he fell in battle** он пал в бою́; **the ~en** (*in war*) па́вшие (*m. pl.*) в боя́х; **the government fell** прави́тельство па́ло. **4.** (*morally*): **he was tempted and fell** он подда́лся искуше́нию. **5.** (*hang down*) па́дать (*impf.*); **his beard fell to his chest** борода́ па́дала ему́ на грудь; **her hair fell over her shoulders** во́лосы па́дали ей на пле́чи. **6.** (*pass into a state*): **he fell silent** он замолча́л; **he fell ill** он заболе́л; **the rent fell due** подошёл срок плати́ть за кварти́ру; **he fell into disgrace** он впал в неми́лость; **the garden fell into neglect** сад пришёл в запусте́ние; **he fell in love with her** он влюби́лся в неё; **they fell into conversation** они́ разговори́лись. **7.** (*come, alight*): **darkness fell** наступи́ла темнота́; **I fell to wondering** я заду́мался; **his eye fell on a strange object** его́ взгляд упа́л на стра́нный предме́т; **suspicion fell on her** подозре́ние па́ло на неё; **it fell to his lot** ему́ вы́пало на до́лю; **it fell to me to welcome the speaker** мне на́до бы́ло приве́тствовать ора́тора; **Christmas Day ~s on a Tuesday** Рождество́ прихо́дится на вто́рник; **Easter ~s early this year** в э́том году́ ра́нняя Па́сха.

with preps. (*further examples*): **~ for** (*~ in love with*) увл|ека́ться, -е́чься +i.; влюб|ля́ться, -и́ться в+a.; (*be taken in by*): **he fell for her story** он пове́рил её слова́м; **~ over: he fell over a cliff** он сорва́лся со скалы́; **he fell over a bucket** он споткну́лся о ведро́ и упа́л; **~ to** (*begin*): **he fell to work** он приня́лся за рабо́ту; **~ upon** (*attack*) нап|ада́ть, -а́сть; набр|а́сываться, -о́ситься; **they fell upon the enemy** они́ напа́ли на врага́; **he fell upon his dinner** он набро́сился на еду́.

with advs.: **~ about (with laughter)** (*coll.*) лежа́ть (*impf.*) (от сме́ха); **the audience fell about** пу́блика лежа́ла; **~ apart** расп|ада́ться, -а́сться; **~ away: his supporters fell away** сторо́нники поки́нули его́; **~ back** (*retreat*) приб|ега́ть, -е́гнуть к чему́-н.; **~ back on sth.** приб|ега́ть, -е́гнуть к чему́-н.; **~ behind** (*e.g. in walking*) отст|ава́ть, -а́ть; (*with letters*) заде́рж|иваться, -а́ться с отве́том; (*with rent*) зап|а́здывать, -озда́ть с упла́той за кварти́ру; **~ down** (*lit.*) упасть (*pf.*); **he fell down on the task** (*coll.*) он не спра́вился с зада́нием; **~ in** впасть (*во что*); **the roof fell in** кры́ша ру́хнула/обвали́лась; **the soldiers fell in** солда́ты ста́ли в строй; **~ in!** (*mil.*) станови́сь!; **he fell in with my views** он согласи́лся со мной; **~ off** упа́сть (*с чего*); **attendance is ~ing off** посеща́емость па́дает; **the quality fell off** ка́чество сни́зилось; **~ing-off** (*deterioration*) паде́ние, упа́док; **~ out** выпада́ть, вы́пасть; **his hair fell out** у него́ вы́пали во́лосы; (*quarrel*) поссо́риться (*pf.*); **~ing-out** (*quarrel*) размо́лвка, ссо́ра; (*mil.*) выходи́ть, вы́йти из стро́я; разойти́сь (*pf.*); **~ out!** разойди́сь!; (*withdraw*): **six competitors fell out** ше́стеро вы́пали из соревнова́ний; **~ over** (*lit.*) упа́сть; **he fell over backwards to please** он лез из ко́жи вон, что́бы угоди́ть +*d.*; **~ through** прова́л|иваться, -и́ться; **~ to** (*start eating or fighting*) набр|а́сываться, -о́ситься (друг на дру́га)(на еду́).

cpd. **~-out** *n.* (*nuclear*) радиоакти́вные оса́дки (*m. pl.*); выпаде́ние радиоакти́вных оса́дков.

fallacious [fəˈleɪʃəs] *adj.* оши́бочный, ло́жный.

fallaciousness [fəˈleɪʃəsnɪs] *n.* оши́бочность, ло́жность.

fallacy [ˈfæləsɪ] *n.* (*false belief*) заблужде́ние; **popular ~** распространённое заблужде́ние; (*false reasoning*) оши́бочный вы́вод.

fallibility [ˌfælɪˈbɪlɪtɪ] *n.* погреши́мость; подве́рженность оши́бкам.

fallible [ˈfælɪb(ə)l] *adj.* подве́рженный оши́бкам.

Fallopian tube [fəˈləʊpɪən] *n.* Фалло́пиева труба́.

fallow [ˈfæləʊ] *adj.* вспа́ханный под пар; **~ land** пар; **lie ~** ост|ава́ться, -а́ться под па́ром.

fallow-deer [ˈfæləʊ] *n.* лань.

false [fɒls, fɔːls] *adj.* **1.** (*wrong, incorrect*) ло́жный, оши́бочный, фальши́вый; **a ~ note** фальши́вая но́та; **a ~ step** ло́жный шаг; **is this statement true or ~?** ве́рно э́то утвержде́ние и́ли нет?; **~ pride** ло́жная го́рдость; **~ start** фальста́рт (*races*); срыв в са́мом нача́ле; **~ alarm** ло́жная трево́га. **2.** (*deceitful, treacherous*) лжи́вый, вероло́мный; **bear ~ witness** лжесвиде́тельствовать (*impf.*); **he was ~ to her** он был ей неве́рен; **sail under ~ colours** (*fig.*) выступа́ть (*impf.*) под ма́ской/личи́ной; **~ pretences** обма́н, притво́рство; (*adv.*): **he played me ~** он пре́дал меня́. **3.** (*sham, apparent*) фальши́вый; **~ hair** накладны́е во́лосы; **~ teeth** иску́сственные зу́бы.

falsehood [ˈfɒlshʊd, ˈfɔːls-] *n.* ложь, непра́вда.

falseness [ˈfɒlsnɪs, ˈfɔːlsnɪs] *n.* (*wrongness*) ло́жность; (*insincerity*) нei̇скренность; (*treachery*) лжи́вость.

falsetto [fɒlˈsetəʊ, fɔːl-] *n.* фальце́т.

falsification [ˌfɒlsɪfɪˈkeɪʃ(ə)n, ˌfɔːls-] *n.* фальсифика́ция.

falsifier [ˈfɒlsɪˌfaɪə(r), ˈfɔːls-] *n.* фальсифика́тор.

falsif|y [ˈfɒlsɪˌfaɪ, ˈfɔːls-] *v.t.* (*e.g. accounts*) подде́л|ывать, -ать; фальсифици́ровать (*impf., pf.*).

falsity [ˈfɒlsɪtɪ, ˈfɔːlsɪtɪ] *n.* (*falsehood, inaccuracy*) ло́жность, оши́бочность.

falter [ˈfɒltə(r), ˈfɔːl-] *v.t. & i.* (*move, walk or act hesitatingly*) поша́тываться, спотыка́ться, колеба́ться (*all impf.*).

faltering [ˈfɒltərɪŋ, ˈfɔːl-] *adj.* запина́ющийся, прерыва́ющийся; **~ gait** неве́рная похо́дка; **a ~ voice** дрожа́щий го́лос; **he spoke ~ly** он говори́л с запи́нкой.

fame [feɪm] *n.* сла́ва; репута́ция.

v.t.: **he was ~d for valour** он просла́вился свое́й до́блестью.

familiar [fəˈmɪlɪə(r)] *adj.* **1.** (*common, usual*) обы́чный, привы́чный. **2.** (*of acquaintance*) знако́мый; **I am ~ with the subject** я знако́м с э́тим предме́том; **your face is ~** ва́ше лицо́ мне знако́мо. **3.** (*friendly*) дру́жеский. **4.** (*casual, impudent*) бесцеремо́нный, фамилья́рный.

familiarity [fəˌmɪlɪˈærɪtɪ] *n.* **1.** (*close acquaintance with pers. or thg.*) бли́зкое знако́мство (с+*i.*). **2.** (*of manner*) фамилья́рность.

familiarization [fəˌmɪlɪəraɪˈzeɪʃ(ə)n] *n.* ознакомле́ние (*с чем*).

familiarize [fəˈmɪlɪəˌraɪz] *v.t.* ознак|омля́ть, -о́мить (*кого с чем*); **~ o.s. with sth.** ознако́миться (*pf.*) с чем-н.

family [ˈfæmɪlɪ, ˈfæmlɪ] *n.* **1.** (*parents and children*) семья́. **2.** (*children*) де́т|и (*pl., g.* -е́й); **they have a large ~** у них мно́го дете́й. **3.** (*descendants of common ancestor*) семья́, род; **a man of good ~** челове́к из хоро́шей семьи́. **4.** (*of animals etc.*) семе́йство. **5.** (*attr.*) семе́йный; **~ allowance** семе́йное посо́бие; **a ~ man** семе́йный челове́к; **~ likeness** семе́йное схо́дство; **~ name** (*surname*) фами́лия; **~ tree** родосло́вное де́рево; **~ planning** контро́ль (*m.*) над рожда́емостью; **in the ~ way** в интере́сном положе́нии.

famine [ˈfæmɪn] *n.* го́лод.

famish [ˈfæmɪʃ] *v.t.*: **I'm ~ed** я си́льно проголода́лся; я умира́ю с го́лоду; **the child looks half ~ed** у ребёнка голо́дный вид.

famous [ˈfeɪməs] *adj.* знамени́тый; **the road is ~ for its views** э́та доро́га изве́стна тем, что о́чень живопи́сна.

fan[1] [fæn] *n.* ве́ер; (*ventilator*) вентиля́тор.

v.t.: **~ o.s.** обма́хиваться (*impf.*) ве́ером; **he ~ned**

the spark into a blaze он разжёг из и́скры пла́мя; **the breeze ~ned our faces** ветеро́к обвева́л нам лицо́.

v.i.: **~ out** (*e.g. roads*) расходи́ться (*impf.*) ве́ером; (*e.g. soldiers*) развёр|тываться, -ну́ться ве́ером.

cpd. **~-belt** *n.* реме́нь (*m.*) вентиля́тора.

fan[2] [fæn] *n.* (*coll., devotee*) боле́льщик, люби́тель (*m.*).

cpd. **~-mail** *n.* пи́сьма (*nt. pl.*) от покло́нников.

fanatic [fəˈnætɪk] *n.* фана́тик.

adj. (*also* **~al**) фанати́чный, фанати́ческий.

fanaticism [fəˈnætɪˌsɪz(ə)m] *n.* фанати́зм.

fanciful [ˈfænsɪˌfʊl] *adj.* капри́зный; причу́дливый.

fancy [ˈfænsɪ] *n.* **1.** (*imagination*) фанта́зия, воображе́ние. **2.** (*thg. imagined, supposition*) фанта́зия. **3.** (*liking*) скло́нность; **he took a ~ to her** он е́ю увлёкся; **it caught my ~** э́то мне понра́вилось; **a passing ~** мимолётное увлече́ние. **4.** (*as adj.*): **a ~ portrait** (*based on imagination*) вообража́емый портре́т; **~ cakes** фигу́рные пиро́жные; **~ dress** маскара́дный костю́м; **a ~ price** непоме́рная цена́; **~ goods** безделу́шки (*f. pl.*); **this dress is too ~ to wear to work** для рабо́ты ну́жно пла́тье поскромне́е.

v.t. **1.** (*imagine*) вообра|жа́ть, -зи́ть; **~ (that)!** вообрази́те!; поду́мать то́лько!; **~ his being here!** кто б мог поду́мать, что он здесь! **2.** (*suppose, feel*) полага́ть (*impf.*); счита́ть (*impf.*); **I ~ he will come** мне сдаётся, что он придёт. **3.** (*like, wish*) хоте́ть (*impf.*) +*g.*; жела́ть (*impf.*); **I don't ~ this place** мне не по душе́ (*or* не нра́вится) э́то ме́сто; **he fancies himself as a speaker** он вообража́ет себя́ ора́тором; **what do you ~ for dinner?** чего́ бы вам хоте́лось на у́жин?

cpd. **~-free** *adj.* свобо́дный от привя́занностей; невлюблённый.

fanfare [ˈfænfeə(r)] *n.* фанфа́ра.

fang [fæŋ] *n.* (*of wolf etc.*) клык; (*of snake*) ядови́тый зуб.

fantasize [ˈfæntəˌsaɪz] *v.i.* фантази́ровать (*impf.*).

fantastic [fænˈtæstɪk] *adj.* (*wild, strange, absurd*) фантасти́ческий; (*coll., marvellous*) потряса́ющий, изуми́тельный.

fantasy [ˈfæntəsɪ, -zɪ] *n.* фанта́зия.

far [fɑː(r)] *n.* (*of distance or amount*): **have you come from ~?** вы издалека́ прие́хали?; **this is better by ~** э́то намно́го лу́чше.

adj. да́льний, далёкий, отдалённый; **a ~ country** далёкая страна́; **the F~ East** Да́льний Восто́к; **at the ~ end of the street** на друго́м конце́ у́лицы.

adv. далеко́; **~ away, off** о́чень далеко́; **~ and near, wide** повсю́ду; **they came from ~ and wide** они́ съе́хались отовсю́ду; **~ into the night** далеко́ за́ полночь; **~ better** (на)мно́го/гора́здо лу́чше; **~ different** соверше́нно друго́й; **~ (and away) the best** намно́го лу́чше други́х; **it is ~ from true** э́то совсе́м не так; **~ from satisfactory** весьма́ неудовлетвори́тельный; **not ~ wrong** не так уж далеко́ от и́стины; **~ from it!** ничу́ть!; отню́дь нет!; **~ be it from me to condemn him** я далёк от того́, что́бы осужда́ть его́; **as ~ back as January** ещё/уже́ в январе́; **so ~** (*until now*) до сих пор; пока́ (что); **so ~, so good** пока́ всё хорошо́; **as, so ~ as** (*of distance*) до (*чего*); (*of extent*) наско́лько; поско́льку; **as ~ as I know** наско́лько мне изве́стно; **as ~ as I am concerned** что каса́ется меня́; **he went so ~ as to say ...** он да́же сказа́л...; **in so ~ as** (*to the extent that*) поско́льку, насто́лько; **how ~** (*of distance*) как далеко́; (*of extent*) наско́лько; **he will go ~** (*succeed*) он далеко́ пойдёт; **he has gone too ~ this time** на э́то раз он зашёл сли́шком далеко́; **few and ~ between** ре́дкие (*pl.*).

cpds. **~-away** *adj.* (*distant*) далёкий, отдалённый; (*absent*): **a ~-away look** отсу́тствующий взгляд; **F~ Eastern** *adj.* дальневосто́чный; **~-fetched** *adj.* с натя́жкой; притя́нутый за́ уши; **~-flung** *adj.* обши́рный; широко́ раски́нувшийся; **~-off** *adj.* отдалённый; **~-reaching** *adj.* име́ющий серьёзные после́дствия; **~-sighted** *adj.* (*prudent etc.*) дальнови́дный; (*long-sighted*) дальнозо́ркий.

farce [fɑːs] *n.* (*theatr., fig.*) фарс.

farcical [ˈfɑːsɪk(ə)l] *adj.* смехотво́рный, неле́пый.

fare[1] [feə(r)] *n.* **1.** (*cost of journey*) пла́та за прое́зд; **what is the ~?** ско́лько сто́ит прое́зд/биле́т? **2.** (*passenger*) пассажи́р.

v.i. (*progress, prosper*): **how did you ~ on the journey?** как вы съе́здили?

cpds. **~-paying** *adj.* платя́щий за прое́зд.

fare[2] [feə(r)] *n.* (*food*) стол; **bill of ~** меню́ (*nt. indecl.*).

farewell [feəˈwel] *n.* проща́ние; **~ dinner** проща́льный у́жин; **make one's ~s, bid ~ (to)** про|ща́ться, -сти́ться (с+*i.*).

int. проща́й(те)!

farm [fɑːm] *n.* фе́рма; (*in former USSR, collective ~*) колхо́з; **state ~** совхо́з; **dairy ~** моло́чная фе́рма; **~ worker** рабо́тни|к (*fem.* -ца) на фе́рме; сельскохозя́йственный рабо́чий.

v.t. & i. **1.** (*agric.*) занима́ться (*impf.*) се́льским хозя́йством; быть фе́рмером; **he ~s 200 hectares** он обраба́тывает 200 гекта́ров земли́. **2.**: **~ out** (*taxes*) отд|ава́ть, -а́ть на о́ткуп; **~ out work** отда́ть (*pf.*) часть рабо́ты.

cpds. **~-hand, ~-labourer** *nn.* рабо́тник на фе́рме; сельскохозя́йственный рабо́чий; **~house** *n.* фе́рмерский дом; **~yard** *n.* двор фе́рмы.

farmer [ˈfɑːmə(r)] *n.* фе́рмер.

arrow [ˈfærəʊ] *n.* опоро́с.

v.i. пороси́ться, о-.

fart [fɑːt] (*vulg.*) *n.* пердёж.

v.i. перде́ть, пёрнуть.

farther [ˈfɑːðə(r)] (*see also* **further**) *adj.* бо́лее отдалённый; дальне́йший.

adv. да́льше, да́лее.

farthest [ˈfɑːðɪst] (*see also* **furthest**) *adj.* са́мый да́льний.

adv. да́льше всего́.

farthing [ˈfɑːðɪŋ] *n.* (*hist.*) фа́ртинг; **I don t care a brass ~!** мне наплева́ть!

fascinate [ˈfæsɪˌneɪt] *v.t.* очаро́в|ывать, -а́ть.

fascinating [ˈfæsɪˌneɪtɪŋ] *adj.* очарова́тельный; (*story*) захва́тывающий.

fascination [ˌfæsɪˈneɪʃ(ə)n] *n.* очарова́ние, обая́ние, пре́лесть.

Fascism [ˈfæʃɪz(ə)m] *n.* фаши́зм.

Fascist [ˈfæʃɪst] *n.* фаши́ст (*fem.* -ка).

adj. фаши́стский.

fashion [ˈfæʃ(ə)n] *n.* **1.** (*way*) о́браз, мане́ра; **after a ~** (*indifferently*) до не́которой сте́пени; **after the ~ of** по образцу́ +*g.* **2.** (*prevailing style*) мо́да; **in ~** в мо́де; **out of ~** вы́шедший из мо́ды; **in the height of ~** после́дний крик мо́ды; **~ designer** моделье́р; **~ house** дом моде́лей; **~ magazine** журна́л мод; **~ parade** пока́з мод.

v.t. (*e.g. an object*) прид|ава́ть, -а́ть фо́рму +*d.*; (*e.g. s.o.'s taste*) формирова́ть, с-.

cpd. **~-plate** *n.* мо́дная карти́нка.

fashionable [ˈfæʃnəb(ə)l] *adj.* мо́дный.

fast[1] [fɑːst] *n.* пост.

v.i. пости́ться (*impf.*).

cpd. **~-day** *n.* по́стный день.

fast[2] [fɑːst] *adj.* (*firm, secure*) про́чный, кре́пкий; **the post is ~ in the ground** столб про́чно вбит в зе́млю; **he made the boat ~** он привяза́л ло́дку; **the door is ~** дверь пло́тно закры́та; **~ colours** сто́йкие цвета́.

adv. про́чно, кре́пко; **she was ~ asleep** она́ кре́пко спала́; **he stood ~** он стоя́л твёрдо; (*fig.*) он твёрдо стоя́л на своём; **the car stuck ~** маши́на застря́ла/завя́зла.

fast[3] [fɑːst] *adj.* **1.** (*rapid*) ско́рый, бы́стрый; **he is a ~ worker** он бы́стро рабо́тает; **my watch is ~** мои́ часы́ спеша́т; **pull a ~ one on s.o.** наду́ть (*pf.*) кого́-н. **2.** (*dissipated*) беспу́тный; **a ~ woman** же́нщина лёгкого поведе́ния.

fasten ['fɑːs(ə)n] *v.t.* (*doors, windows*) зап|ира́ть, -ере́ть; (*dress, glove*) застёг|ивать, -ну́ть; (*shoelaces*) завя́з|ывать, -а́ть; (*with rope etc.*) привя́з|ывать, -а́ть; (*make firmer*) прикреп|ля́ть, -и́ть; **he ~ed the sheets of paper together** он скрепи́л вме́сте листы́ бума́ги.

v.i. **1.** зап|ира́ться, -ере́ться; **the door won't ~** дверь не закрыва́ется/запира́ется; **the dress ~s down the back** пла́тье застёгивается на спине́. **2.: he ~ed upon the idea** он ухвати́лся за э́ту мысль.

fasten|er ['fɑːs(ə)nə(r)], **-ing** ['fɑːsnɪŋ] *nn.* запо́р, задви́жка; (*on dress*) застёжка.

fastidious [fæ'stɪdɪəs] *adj.* привере́дливый, щепети́льный; разбо́рчивый.

fat [fæt] *n.* жир; са́ло.

adj. **1.** (*of pers. etc.*) то́лстый, жи́рный, ту́чный; **get ~** растолсте́ть (*pf.*); **~ cheeks** пу́хлые щёки; **~ fingers** то́лстые па́льцы; (*of food*) жи́рный. **2.** (*rich, fertile*): **a ~ profit** больша́я при́быль; (*pej.*) жи́рный кусо́к. **3.** (*coll., iron.*): **a ~ lot you care!** о́чень тебя́ э́то беспоко́ит!; **that's a ~ lot of use** мно́го с э́того то́лку.

cpds. **~head** *n.* (*coll.*) болва́н, тупи́ца (*c.g.*) **~-headed** *adj.* тупоголо́вый.

fatal ['feɪt(ə)l] *adj.* **1.** (*causing death*) смерте́льный, ги́бельный, па́губный; **a ~ accident** несча́стный слу́чай со смерте́льным исхо́дом. **2.** (*fateful*) роково́й, фата́льный.

fatalism ['feɪtə,lɪz(ə)m] *n.* фатали́зм.

fatalist ['feɪtəlɪst] *n.* фатали́ст.

fatalistic [,feɪtə'lɪstɪk] *adj.* фаталисти́ческий.

fatality [fə'tælətɪ] *n.* (*natural calamity*) стихи́йное бе́дствие; (*fatal accident*) смерть от несча́стного слу́чая.

fate [feɪt] *n.* **1.** (*personified destiny*) судьба́, рок; **as sure as ~** несомне́нно. **2.** (*what is in store for one*) судьба́, у́часть, до́ля. **3.** (*death*) ги́бель, смерть; **he sent him to his ~** он посла́л его́ на ги́бель.

v.t. предопредел|я́ть, -и́ть; **he was ~d to die** ему́ суждено́ бы́ло поги́бнуть.

fateful ['feɪtfʊl] *adj.* роково́й.

father ['fɑːðə(r)] *n.* **1.** (*male parent, also fig.*) оте́ц, роди́тель (*m.*); **God the F~** Бог-Оте́ц; **our Heavenly F~** Оте́ц Небе́сный; **Our F~** (*prayer*) О́тче наш. **2.** (*pl., ancestors*) отцы́, де́ды (*m. pl.*). **3.** (*founder, leader*) оте́ц, родонача́льник; **city ~s** отцы́ го́рода. **4.** (*oldest member*) старе́йшина (*m.*). **5.** (*in personifications*): **F~ Christmas** дед-моро́з; **F~ Thames** ма́тушка Те́мза. **6.** (*priest*) оте́ц, ба́тюшка; (*as title*): **F~ Sergius** оте́ц Се́ргий.

v.t. **1.** (*beget*) поро|жда́ть, -ди́ть; быть (*impf.*)/стать (*pf.*) отцо́м +*g.* **2.** (*fig., originate*) поро|жда́ть, -ди́ть.

cpds. **~-figure** *n.* кто-н., заменя́ющий отца́; **~-in-law** *n.* (*husband's ~*) свёкор; (*wife's ~*) тесть (*m.*); **~land** *n.* оте́чество, отчи́зна, ро́дина.

fatherhood ['fɑːðəhʊd] *n.* отцо́вство.

fatherly ['fɑːðəlɪ] *adj.* оте́ческий.

fathom ['fæð(ə)m] *n.* морска́я саже́нь.

v.t. (*fig.*) пост|ига́ть, -и́гнуть; вн|ика́ть, -и́кнуть в+*a.*

fatigue [fə'tiːg] *n.* уста́лость (*also* **metal ~**); (*mil.*) хозя́йственная рабо́та; (*pl. dress*) наря́д на рабо́ту.

v.t. утом|ля́ть, -и́ть.

cpds. **~-dress** *n.* рабо́чая оде́жда; спецоде́жда; **~-duty** *n.* хозя́йственные рабо́ты (*f. pl.*).

fatness ['fætnɪs] *n.* полнота́.

fatten ['fæt(ə)n] *v.t.* (*animal*) отк|а́рмливать, -орми́ть на убо́й.

v.i. жире́ть (*impf.*); толсте́ть (*impf.*).

fattening ['fæt(ə)nɪŋ] *adj.* калори́йный.

fatty ['fætɪ] *n.* (*coll.*) толстя́к.

adj. жи́рный, жирово́й; **~ tissue** жирова́я ткань.

fatuous ['fætjʊəs] *adj.* самодово́льно-глу́пый; бессмы́сленный.

faucet ['fɔːsɪt] *n.* (*US, tap*) кран.

fault [fɒlt, fɔːlt] *n.* **1.** (*imperfection*) недоста́ток; **generous to a ~** чересчу́р ще́дрый; **find ~ with s.o.** на|ходи́ть, -йти́ недоста́тки у кого́-н.; **my memory was at ~** па́мять мне измени́ла. **2.** (*physical defect*) дефе́кт. **3.** (*error*) оши́бка. **4.** (*blame*) вина́; **it's (all) your ~** э́то ва́ша вина́; э́то всё из-за вас; **the ~ lies with him** он винова́т. **5.** (*at tennis etc.*) непра́вильная пода́ча; **double ~** двойна́я оши́бка. **6.** (*geol.*) разло́м, сдвиг.

v.t. на|ходи́ть, -йти́ недоста́тки в+*p.*; прид|ира́ться, -ра́ться к+*d.*

cpd. **~-finder** *n.* приди́ра (*c.g.*).

faultless ['fɒltlɪs, 'fɔːlt-] *adj.* (*without blame*) непогреши́мый; безоши́бочный; (*without blemish*): **~ precision** безупре́чная то́чность.

faulty ['fɒltɪ, 'fɔːltɪ] *adv.* оши́бочный; с изъя́ном; **a ~ memory** сла́бая па́мять; **a ~ connection** (*tech.*) повреждённое соедине́ние.

fauna ['fɔːnə] *n.* фа́уна.

favour ['feɪvə(r)] *n.* **1.** (*goodwill*) благоскло́нность; расположе́ние (к+*d.*); **win s.o.'s ~; find ~ in s.o.'s eyes** сниска́ть (*pf.*) чьё-н. расположе́ние; **look with ~ on** благоскло́нно/доброжела́тельно относи́ться (*impf.*) к+*d.*; **he is out of ~ with his superiors** он не в чести́ у нача́льства; **I am in ~ of the plan** я — за э́тот план. **2.** (*kindly act*) одолже́ние, любе́зность, услу́га; **he did me a ~** он оказа́л мне любе́зность; он сде́лал мне одолже́ние. **3.** (*advantage, credit*) по́льза; **this is in his ~** э́то говори́т в его́ по́льзу; **the exchange rate is in our ~** курс обме́на валю́ты вы́годен для нас. **4.** (*privilege*): **I don't ask for any ~s** я не прошу́ одолже́ний/привиле́гий.

v.t. **1.** (*approve, support*) благоприя́тствовать (*impf.*) +*d.*; подде́рж|ивать, -а́ть; **this ~s my theory** э́то подтвержда́ет мою́ тео́рию. **2.** (*choose*) предпоч|ита́ть, -е́сть; **she ~ed a pink dress** она́ вы́брала ро́зовое пла́тье. **3.** (*treat with partiality*) ока́з|ывать, -а́ть предпочте́ние +*d.*; быть пристра́стным к +*d.*. **4.** (*oblige, treat favourably*): **she ~ed us with a song** она́ оказа́ла нам любе́зность, испо́лнив пе́сню; **the ~ed few** немно́гие и́збранные. **5.** (*resemble*) походи́ть (*impf.*) на+*a.*; **the child ~s its father** ребёнок похо́ж на своего́ отца́.

favourable ['feɪvərəb(ə)l] *adj.* благоприя́тный, благоскло́нный; **a ~ report** положи́тельный отчёт.

favourite ['feɪvərɪt] *n.* (*preferred person*) люби́мец, фавори́т; (*preferred thg.*) люби́мая вещь; (*horse*) фавори́т.

adj. люби́мый, излю́бленный.

favouritism ['feɪvərɪ,tɪz(ə)m] *n.* фаворити́зм.

fawn[1] [fɔːn] *n.* молодо́й оле́нь.

adj. (*also* **~-coloured**) желтова́то-кори́чневый.

fawn[2] [fɔːn] *v.i.* (*of pers.*): **~ on s.o.** подли́з|ываться, -а́ться к кому́-н.; выслу́живаться (*impf.*) пе́ред кем-н.

fax [fæks] *n.* факс; **~ machine** факсими́льный аппара́т, телефа́кс.

v.t. перед|ава́ть, -а́ть по фа́ксу.

faze [feɪz] *v.t.* сму|ща́ть, -ти́ть; прив|оди́ть, -ести́ в недоуме́ние.

FBI (*abbr. of* ***Federal Bureau of Investigation***) ФБР, (Федера́льное бюро́ рассле́дований).

fear [fɪə(r)] *n.* **1.** (*terror, anxiety*) страх, опасе́ние; **in**

~ and trembling дрожа́ от стра́ха; **he was in ~ of his life** он боя́лся за свою́ жи́знь; **your ~s are groundless** ва́ши опасе́ния напра́сны. **2.** (*of precaution, likelihood*): **I was silent for ~ of offending him** я молча́л, боя́сь оби́деть его́; **there is no ~ of my losing the money** не бо́йтесь, я не потеря́ю де́ньги.

v.t. & i. боя́ться (*impf.*) +*g.*; опаса́ться (*impf.*) +*g.*; **he ~s death** он бои́тся сме́рти; **I ~ the worst** я опаса́юсь ху́дшего; **I ~ for his life** я опаса́юсь за его́ жизнь; **he will come, never ~!** не бо́йтесь, он придёт; (*expr. regret*): **I ~ you must stay** бою́сь, вам придётся оста́ться.

fearful ['fɪəfʊl] *adj.* (*terrible*) стра́шный, ужа́сный; (*coll., frightful*) ужа́сный, стра́шный; (*timorous*) ро́бкий, боязли́вый; **I was ~ of waking him** я боя́лся разбуди́ть его́.

fearless ['fɪəlɪs] *adj.* бесстра́шный, неустраши́мый.

fearsome ['fɪəsəm] *adj.* устраша́ющий, гро́зный.

feasibility [ˌfi:zɪ'bɪlɪtɪ] *n.* осуществи́мость.

feasible ['fi:zɪb(ə)l] *adj.* осуществи́мый, выполни́мый.

feast [fi:st] *n.* **1.** (*relig.*) (церко́вный) пра́здник. **2.** (*meal*) пир.

v.t. & i. пирова́ть (*impf.*); пра́здновать (*impf.*); **they ~ed away the night** они́ (про)пирова́ли всю ночь; **he ~ed his friends** он ще́дро угоща́л свои́х друзе́й; **he ~ed his eyes on the scene** он любова́лся э́тим зре́лищем.

cpd. **~-day** *n.* пра́здник, пра́здничный день.

feat [fi:t] *n.* по́двиг; **~ of engineering** выдаю́щееся достиже́ние инжене́рного иску́сства.

feather ['feðə(r)] *n.* перо́; **that is a ~ in his cap** он мо́жет э́тим горди́ться.

v.t. опер|я́ть, -и́ть; **our ~ed friends** на́ши перна́тые друзья́; **~ one's nest** (*fig.*) наби́ть (*pf.*) себе́ карма́н.

cpds. **~-bed** *n.* пери́на, пухови́к; **~-brained** *adj.* пустоголо́вый; **~weight** *n.* вес пера́; *adj.* в ве́се пера́; о́чень лёгкий.

feathery ['feðərɪ] *adj.* пухово́й; лёгкий.

feature ['fi:tʃə(r)] *n.* **1.** (*part of face*) черта́; **he has strong ~s** у него́ волево́е лицо́. **2.** (*geog.*) черта́/подро́бность релье́фа; **a ~ of the landscape** осо́бенность ландша́фта. **3.** (*aspect*) черта́, осо́бенность; **the main ~s of his programme** основны́е пу́нкты (*m. pl.*) его́ програ́ммы. **4.** (*object of special attention, main item*): **this journal makes a ~ of sport** э́тот журна́л широко́ освеща́ет спорти́вные собы́тия; **~ (article)** темати́ческая статья́; **~ (film)** худо́жественный фильм.

v.t. (*give prominence to*) поме|ща́ть, -сти́ть на ви́дном ме́сте; **the film ~s a new actress** в фи́льме гла́вную роль поручи́ли но́вой актри́се.

v.i. (*figure prominently*) быть характе́рной черто́й.

cpds. **~-length** *adj.* (*film*) полнометра́жный; **~-writer** *n.* очерки́ст.

febrile ['fi:braɪl] *adj.* (*lit., fig.*) лихора́дочный.

February ['februərɪ] *n.* февра́ль (*m.*); (*attr.*) февра́льский.

feces ['fi:si:z] = **faeces**

feckless ['feklɪs] *adj.* безала́берный.

fecklessness ['feklɪsnɪs] *n.* безала́берность.

fecund ['fi:kənd, 'fek-] *adj.* плодоро́дный, плодови́тый.

fecundity [fɪ'kʌndɪtɪ] *n.* плодоро́дие, плодови́тость.

federal ['fedər(ə)l] *adj.* федера́льный; (*in titles of states*) федерати́вный; **F~ Republic of Germany** Федерати́вная Респу́блика Герма́нии.

federalism ['fedərəˌlɪz(ə)m] *n.* федерали́зм.

federalist ['fedərəlɪst] *n.* федерали́ст.

federate[1] ['fedərət] *adj.* федерати́вный.

federate[2] ['fedəˌreɪt] *v.t. & i.* объедин|я́ть(ся), -и́ть(ся) на федерати́вных нача́лах.

federation [ˌfedə'reɪʃ(ə)n] *n.* федера́ция; (*of societies etc.*) объедине́ние.

fee [fi:] *n.* (*professional charge*) гонора́р; **school ~s** пла́та за обуче́ние; **club ~s** чле́нские взно́сы (*m. pl.*) в клуб; **(TV, radio) licence ~** абонеме́нтная пла́та.

feeble ['fi:b(ə)l] *adj.* хи́лый, сла́бый.

cpds. **~-minded** *adj.* слабоу́мный; **~-mindedness** *n.* слабоу́мие.

feed [fi:d] *n.* (*animal's*) корм; (*baby's*) еда́; (*coll.*): **we had a good ~** мы хорошо́ перекуси́ли.

v.t. **1.** (*give food to*) корми́ть, на-; пита́ть, на-; да|ва́ть, -ть корм +*d.*; **what do you ~ your dog on?** чем вы ко́рмите свою́ соба́ку?; **the hotel ~s you well** в гости́нице хорошо́ ко́рмят; **the child cannot ~ itself** ребёнок ещё не мо́жет есть сам; **~ing-bottle** (де́тский) рожо́к; (*fig.*): **I am fed up** (*coll.*) я сыт по го́рло; мне надое́ло. **2.** (*give as food*) ск|а́рмливать, -орми́ть; **we ~ oats to horses** мы ко́рмим лошаде́й овсо́м. **3.** (*fig.*): **the lake is fed by two rivers** вода́ в о́зеро поступа́ет из двух рек; **he fed information into the computer** он ввёл да́нные в компью́тер.

v.i. (*of animals*) корми́ться (*impf.*); (*graze*) пасти́сь (*impf.*); (*coll., of pers.*) пита́ться (*impf.*).

cpds. **~-back** *n.* (*elec.*) обра́тное пита́ние; (*fig.*) о́тклик, реа́кция; **~-back from readers** о́тклики чита́телей; **~-bag** *n.* (*horse's*) то́рба.

feel [fi:l] *n.* (*sensation*) ощуще́ние; (*contact*) осяза́ние; **cold to the ~** холо́дный на о́щупь; **have a ~ of this cloth** пощу́пайте э́ту мате́рию; **there will be frost tonight by the ~ of it** чу́вствуется, что но́чью бу́дет моро́з; **if you practise you'll soon get the ~ of it** е́сли вы бу́дете упражня́ться, то ско́ро осво́ите э́тот приём (*or* набьёте ру́ку); **he has a ~ for language** у него́ есть чу́вство языка́.

v.t. **1.** (*explore by touch*) щу́пать, по-; ощу́п|ывать, -ать; **~ the edge of a knife** потро́гать (*pf.*) ле́звие ножа́; **~ s.o.'s pulse** пощу́пать (*pf.*) кому́-н. пу́льс; **~ the weight of this box!** чу́вствуете, ско́лько ве́сит э́тот я́щик!; **~ whether there are any bones broken** пощу́пайте, не сло́маны ли ко́сти. **2.** (*grope*) пробира́ться (*impf.*) о́щупью; **they are ~ing their way towards an agreement** они́ нащу́пывают по́чву для соглаше́ния. **3.** (*be aware of*) чу́вствовать, по-; ощу|ща́ть, -ти́ть; **I can ~ a nail in my shoe** я чу́вствую, у меня́ в боти́нке гвоздь; **did you ~ the earthquake?** вы почу́вствовали землетрясе́ние? **4.** (*be affected by*) чу́вствовать, по-; ощу|ща́ть, -ти́ть; пережива́ть (*impf.*); **he felt the insult** он почу́вствовал оскорбле́ние; **he ~s the heat** жара́ на него́ пло́хо де́йствует; он пло́хо перено́сит жару́; **he felt the loss of his mother keenly** он о́стро пережива́л сме́рть ма́тери. **5.** (*be of opinion*): **I ~ you should go** по-мо́ему, вам сле́дует пойти́; **I ~ the plan to be unwise** я счита́ю, что э́тот план неблагоразу́мен.

v.i. **1.** (*experience sensation*): **I ~ cold** мне хо́лодно; **I ~ hungry** я го́лоден; **I ~ sure** я уве́рен; **I don't ~ quite myself** мне не по себе́; **I ~ bound to say ...** я до́лжен сказа́ть...; **I ~ bad about not inviting him** мне со́вестно, что я не пригласи́л его́; **I ~ strongly about this** у меня́ твёрдое мне́ние на э́то счёт; **I ~ like (going for) a walk** мне хо́чется прогуля́ться; **I don't ~ up to going** я не в состоя́нии идти́; **it ~s like rain** похо́же, что быть дождю́; **I ~ for you** я вам сочу́вствую. **2.** (*produce sensation*) да|ва́ть, -ть ощуще́ние (*чего*); **your hands ~ cold** у вас холо́дные ру́ки; **how does it ~ to be home?** каково́ оказа́ться до́ма? **3.** (*grope*): **he felt in his pocket for a coin** он поша́рил в карма́не, ища́ моне́ту; **he felt along the wall for the door** он пыта́лся нащу́пать дверь в стене́.

feeler ['fi:lə(r)] *n.* (*zool.*) ýсик; (*fig.*): **he put out ~s** он заки́нул ýдочку; он пусти́л про́бный шар.

feeling ['fi:lɪŋ] *n.* **1.** (*power of sensation*) ощуще́ние, чу́вство; **sense of ~** ощуще́ние; **he lost all ~ in his legs** у него́ онеме́ли но́ги. **2.** (*sense, sensation*) созна́ние, чу́вство. **3.** (*opinion*): **I have a ~ he won't come** у меня́ предчу́вствие, что он не придёт; **the general ~ is that ...** о́бщее мне́ние таково́, что... **4.** (*emotion*) чу́вство, страсть; **he spoke with ~** он говори́л с чу́вством; **I have mixed ~s** у меня́ э́то вызыва́ет сме́шанные чу́вства; **no hard ~s, I hope** наде́юсь, никако́й оби́ды; **~ ran high** стра́сти разгоре́лись. **5.** (*sensitivity*) чувстви́тельность; **you hurt his ~s** вы его́ оби́дели. **6.** (*sympathy*) сочу́вствие.

feign [feɪn] *v.t.* (*simulate*) притвор|я́ться, -и́ться +*i.*; **~ madness** симули́ровать безу́мие.

feint [feɪnt] *n.* (*pretence*) притво́рство; (*sham attack*) ло́жная ата́ка, финт.

v.i. нан|оси́ть, -ести́ отвлека́ющий уда́р.

fel(d)spar ['feldspɑ:(r)] *n.* полево́й шпат.

felicitate [fə'lɪsɪ,teɪt] *v.t.* поздр|авля́ть, -а́вить.

felicitation [fə,lɪsɪ'teɪʃ(ə)n] *n.* (*usu. pl.*) поздравле́ние.

felicitous [fə'lɪsɪtəs] *adj.* ме́ткий, уме́стный, уда́чный.

felicity [fə'lɪsɪtɪ] *n.* (*bliss*) блаже́нство; (*aptness*) уме́стность.

feline ['fi:laɪn] *adj.* коша́чий.

fell [fel] *v.t.* (*pers.*) сби|ва́ть, -ть с ног; (*tree*) руби́ть, с-; вали́ть, с-/по-.

fellow ['feləʊ] *n.* **1.** (*chap; also coll.* **feller**) (*man, boy*) па́рень (*m.*); **a good ~** сла́вный ма́лый; **my dear ~** дорого́й мой!; **old ~!** стари́на́ (*m.*), дружи́ще (*m.*); **a little ~** малы́ш; **poor ~** бедня́га (*m.*). **2.** (*comrade, companion*) това́рищ, собра́т; **~s in misfortune** това́рищи по несча́стью. **3.** (*equal, contemporary etc.*) ра́вный; све́рстник; това́рищ. **4.** (*acad. & professional*) колле́га; сотру́дник; (*of a college*) член сове́та колле́джа.

cpds. **~-citizen** *n.* согражд|ани́н (*fem.* -а́нка); **~-countryman** *n.* сооте́чественник; **~-countrywoman** *n.* сооте́чественница; **~-creature** *n.* бли́жний; **~-feeling** *n.* симпа́тия, сочу́вствие; **~-student** *n.* това́рищ по университе́ту; соку́рсник; **~-traveller** *n.* (*lit., fig.*) попу́тчик.

fellowship ['feləʊʃɪp] *n.* (*companionship*) това́рищество, бра́тство; (*association*) корпора́ция; колле́гия (*адвокатов и т.п.*); (*of a college*) зва́ние чле́на сове́та колле́джа.

felon ['felən] *n.* уголо́вный престу́пник.

felonious [fɪ'ləʊnɪəs] *adj.* престу́пный.

felony ['felənɪ] *n.* уголо́вное преступле́ние.

felt [felt] *n.* (*material*) во́йлок, фетр; **~ boots** ва́ленки (*m. pl.*); **~ hat** фе́тровая шля́па.

cpd. **~-tip** *n.*: **~-tip (pen)** флома́стер.

female ['fi:meɪl] *n.* (*woman or girl*) же́нщина; (*animal*) са́мка, ма́тка.

adj. же́нский; **~ child** де́вочка; **~ worker** рабо́тница.

feminine ['femɪnɪn] *adj.* же́нский; (*gram.*) же́нского ро́да.

femininity [,femɪ'nɪnɪtɪ] *n.* же́нственность.

feminism ['femɪ,nɪz(ə)m] *n.* фемини́зм.

feminist ['femɪnɪst] *n.* фемини́ст (*fem.* -ка).

adj. фемини́стский.

femur ['fi:mə(r)] *n.* бедро́.

fence[1] [fens] *n.* забо́р, и́згородь, огра́да; (*fig.*) **sit on the ~** держа́ться (*impf.*) нейтра́льной пози́ции.

v.t. (*also* **~ in, off, round**) огор|а́живать, -оди́ть.

fence[2] [fens] *v.i.* фехтова́ть.

fencer ['fensə(r)] *n.* фехтова́льщик.

fencing ['fensɪŋ] *n.* **1.** (*fences*) и́згородь, забо́р, огра́да; (*material*) до́ски (*f. pl.*) для забо́ра; материа́л для и́згороди. **2.** (*swordplay*) фехтова́ние.

fend [fend] *v.t.* отра|жа́ть, -зи́ть; пари́ровать (*impf., pf.*); **~ off a blow** отра|жа́ть, -зи́ть уда́р.

v.i.: **~ for o.s.** полага́ться (*impf.*) на себя́.

fender ['fendə(r)] *n.* **1.** (*in front of fire*) ≃ ками́нная решётка. **2.** (*of train*) предохрани́тельная решётка. **3.** (*US, of car*) крыло́.

fennel ['fen(ə)l] *n.* фе́нхель (*m.*).

feral ['fɪər(ə)l, 'fer(ə)l] *adj.* ди́кий, одича́вший.

ferment[1] ['fɜ:ment] *n.* заква́ска; ферме́нт; (*fig.*): **in a ~** в броже́нии.

ferment[2] [fə'ment] *v.t.* (*e.g. beer*) выха́живать, вы́ходить.

v.i. броди́ть (*impf.*).

fermentation [,fɜ:men'teɪʃ(ə)n] *n.* броже́ние (*also fig.*).

fern [fɜ:n] *n.* па́поротник.

ferocious [fə'rəʊʃəs] *adj.* свире́пый, лю́тый.

ferocity [fə'rɒsɪtɪ] *n.* свире́пость, лю́тость.

ferret ['ferɪt] *n.* (*zool.*) хорёк.

v.t.: **~ out** (*fig.*) выи́скивать, вы́искать; разню́х|ивать, -ать.

ferrety ['ferɪtɪ] *adj.* хорько́вый; **~ eyes** ры́сьи глаза́.

Ferris wheel ['ferɪs] *n.* чёртово колесо́; колесо́ обозре́ния.

ferroconcrete [,ferəʊ'kɒŋkri:t] *n.* железобето́н.

ferrous ['ferəs] *adj.* желе́зистый; **~ metals** чёрные мета́ллы.

ferry ['ferɪ] *n.* паро́м.

v.t. (*convey to and fro*) перев|ози́ть, -езти́ (*or* перепр|авля́ть, -а́вить) на паро́ме.

cpds. **~-boat** *n.* паро́м; **~man** *n.* паро́мщик, перево́зчик.

fertile ['fɜ:taɪl] *adj.* **1.** (*of soil*) плодоро́дный; (*of eggs*) оплодотворённый; (*of humans, animals*) плодови́тый. **2.** (*fig.*): **a ~ imagination** бога́тое воображе́ние.

fertility [,fɜ:'tɪlɪtɪ] *n.* плодоро́дие; плодови́тость.

fertilization [,fɜ:tɪlaɪ'zeɪʃ(ə)n] *n.* (*biol.*) оплодотворе́ние; (*of soil*) удобре́ние.

fertilize ['fɜ:tɪ,laɪz] *v.t.* (*biol.*) оплодотвор|я́ть, -и́ть; (*of soil*) уд|обря́ть, -о́брить.

fertilizer ['fɜ:tɪ,laɪzə(r)] *n.* удобре́ние.

ferule ['feru:l] *n.* феру́ла.

fervent ['fɜ:v(ə)nt] *adj.* (*fig.*) горя́чий, пы́лкий.

fervid ['fɜ:vɪd] *adj.* пы́лкий, пла́менный.

fervour ['fɜ:və(r)] *n.* жар, пыл.

fester ['festə(r)] *v.i.* гнои́ться, за-/на-; нагн|а́иваться, -ои́ться.

festival ['festɪv(ə)l] *n.* фестива́ль (*m.*); пра́здненство; **Church ~** церко́вный пра́здник.

festive ['festɪv] *adj.* пра́здничный.

festivit|y [fe'stɪvɪtɪ] *n.* пра́зднество, торжество́; **wedding ~ies** сва́дебные торжества́.

festoon [fe'stu:n] *n.* гирля́нда; (*archit.*) фесто́н.

v.t укр|аша́ть, -а́сить гирля́ндами/фесто́нами.

fet|al ['fi:t(ə)], **-us** ['fi:t(ə)s] = **foet|al, -us**

fetch [fetʃ] *v.t.* **1.** (*go and get*) прин|оси́ть, -ести́; прив|оди́ть, -ести́; пойти́ (*pf.*) за+*i.*; **they ~ed the doctor** они́ вы́звали врача́. **2.** (*of price*): **his house ~ed £50,000** он вы́ручил 50 000 фу́нтов за свой дом; **it won't ~ more than £20** кра́сная цена́ э́тому — 20 фу́нтов (*coll.*).

fetching ['fetʃɪŋ] *adj.* привлека́тельный, соблазни́тельный.

fête [feɪt] *n.* пра́зднество, пра́здник; **village ~** се́льский пра́здник.

v.t. пра́здновать, от-.

fetid ['fetɪd, 'fi:tɪd] *adj.* воню́чий, злово́нный.

fetish ['fetɪʃ] *n.* (*lit., fig.*) фети́ш.

fetlock ['fetlɒk] *n.* щётка.

fetter ['fetə(r)] *n.* (*pl.*) ножны́е кандал|ы́ (*pl., g.* -ов); (*fig.*) око́в|ы (*pl., g.* —)

v.t. зако́в|ывать, -а́ть в кандалы́; (*of horse*) спу́т|ывать, -ать.

fettle ['fet(ə)l] *n.*: **in good ~** в хоро́шем состоя́нии/настрое́нии.

fetus ['fi:təs] = **foetus**

feud [fju:d] *n.* (*quarrel*) вражда́; **blood ~** кро́вная месть; **be at ~ with** враждова́ть (*impf.*) с+*i.*

v.i. (*carry on a ~*) вести́ (*det.*) вражду́ (*с кем*).

feudal ['fju:d(ə)l] *adj.* феода́льный.

feudalism ['fju:dəl,ız(ə)m] *n.* феодали́зм.

fever ['fi:və(r)] *n.* **1.** (*body temperature*) жар; высо́кая температу́ра; **he has a high ~** у него́ жар. **2.** (*disease*) лихора́дка; **rheumatic ~** ревмати́зм; **scarlet ~** скарлати́на. **3.** (*fig.*): **in a ~ of impatience** сгора́я от нетерпе́ния; **at ~ heat** в си́льном возбужде́нии; в са́мом разга́ре.

fevered ['fi:vəd] *adj.* лихора́дочный, горя́чечный; **a ~ brow** пыла́ющий лоб; **~ imagination** бу́йное воображе́ние.

feverish ['fi:vərıʃ] *adj.* лихора́дочный; **the child is ~** у ребёнка повы́шенная температу́ра.

few [fju:] *n. & adj.* немно́гие (*pl.*); немно́го (*+g.*); ма́ло *+g.*; **~ (people) know the truth** немно́гие зна́ют пра́вду; **a ~ (people)** немно́гие (лю́ди); не́сколько челове́к; **a, some ~** немно́го, не́сколько (*+g.*); **quite a ~, a good ~** дово́льно мно́го *+g.*; **not a ~** нема́ло *+g.*; **his friends are ~** у него́ ма́ло друзе́й; **the ~ books (that) I have** те не́сколько книг, что у меня́ есть; те немно́гие кни́ги, каки́е у меня́ есть; **~ and far between** ре́дкие; **every ~ minutes** ка́ждые не́сколько мину́т; **a man of ~ words** немногосло́вный челове́к.

fewer ['fju:ə(r)] *n. & adj.* ме́нее, ме́ньше.

fez [fez] *n.* фе́ска.

fiancé [fı'ɒnseı, fı'ɑ̃seı] *n.* жени́х.

fiancée [fı'ɒnseı, fı'ɑ̃seı] *n.* неве́ста.

fiasco [fı'æskəʊ] *n.* фиа́ско (*indecl.*), прова́л.

fiat ['faıæt, 'faıət] *n.* декре́т, ука́з.

fib [fıb] *n.* вы́думка, непра́вда.

v.i. выду́мывать, вы́думать; подвира́ть (*impf.*).

fibber ['fıbə(r)] *n.* врун (*fem.* -ья); враль (*m.*).

fibre (*US* **fiber**) ['faıbə(r)] *n.* **1.** (*filament*) волокно́; **~ optics** волоко́нная о́птика. **2.** (*substance made of ~s*) фи́бра (*also fig.*); **moral ~** мора́льные усто́и (*m. pl.*).

cpds. **~-board** *n.* фи́бровый карто́н; **~-glass** *n.* стекловолокно́.

fibrous ['faıbrəs] *adj.* волокни́стый, фибро́зный.

fickle ['fık(ə)l] *adj.* переме́нчивый, непостоя́нный.

fiction ['fıkʃ(ə)n] *n.* **1.** (*invention, pretence*) вы́мысел, вы́думка, фи́кция. **2.** (*novels etc.*) беллетри́стика; **work of ~** худо́жественное произведе́ние; **~ writer** беллетри́ст, романи́ст.

fictional ['fıkʃənəl] *adj.* вы́мышленный; беллетристи́ческий.

fictitious [fık'tıʃəs] *adj.* подло́жный, фикти́вный; **a ~ name** вы́мышленное и́мя.

fiddle ['fıd(ə)l] *n.* **1.** (*violin*) скри́пка; (*fig.*): **fit as a ~** в до́бром здра́вии; **play second ~ to s.o.** игра́ть (*impf.*) втору́ю скри́пку у кого́-н. (*or* при ком-н.). **2.** (*sl., piece of cheating or 'graft'*) жу́льничество.

v.t. (*falsify*) подде́л|ывать, -ать; подтасо́в|ывать, -а́ть.

v.i. **1.** (*play ~*) игра́ть (*impf.*) на скри́пке. **2.** (*fidget, meddle*) верте́ться (*impf.*); крути́ться (*impf.*); вози́ться (*impf.*); **he ~d with his tie** он теребі́л свой га́лстук; **don't ~ with my papers!** не тро́гайте мои́ бума́ги!

cpds. **~-bow** *n.* смычо́к; **~-sticks!** *int.*, *see next.*

fiddle-de-dee [,fıdəldı'di:] *n. & int.* чепуха́, вздор.

fiddler ['fıdlə(r)] *n.* (*musician*) скрипа́ч; (*coll., cheat*) моше́нник, жу́лик.

fidelity [fı'delıtı] *n.* (*loyalty*) ве́рность; (*accuracy*) то́чность.

fidget ['fıdʒıt] *n.* **1.** (*~y person*) непосе́да (*c.g.*), егоза́ (*c.g.*). **2. he's got the ~s** (*coll.*) ему́ на ме́сте не сиди́тся.

v.i. (*make aimless movements*) ёрзать (*impf.*); суети́ться (*impf.*); (*show impatience*) не́рвничать (*impf.*).

fidgety ['fıdʒıtı] *adj.* суетли́вый, непосе́дливый.

field [fi:ld] *n.* **1.** (*piece of ground*) по́ле; **a fine ~ of wheat** прекра́сное пшени́чное по́ле. **2.** (*physical range, area*) по́ле; **~ of vision** по́ле зре́ния. **3.** (*mil.*): **~ of battle** по́ле би́твы/сраже́ния; **~ artillery** полева́я артилле́рия; **~ officer** ста́рший офице́р; **F~ Marshal** фельдма́ршал. **4.: in the ~** (*away from headquarters*) на места́х/ме́стности. **5.** (*area of activity or study*) о́бласть; по́ле/сфе́ра де́ятельности; **an expert in his ~** специали́ст в свое́й о́бласти; **that is outside my ~** э́то не моя́ о́бласть; **in the international ~** на междунаро́дной аре́не.

v.t.: **~ a ball** прин|има́ть, -я́ть мяч; (*fig.*): **~ a difficult question** спр|авля́ться, -а́виться с тру́дным вопро́сом; **~** (*muster*) **a team** выставля́ть, вы́ставить кома́нду.

v.i. (*at cricket etc.*) находи́ться (*impf.*) в по́ле.

cpds. **~-day** *n.* (*fig., day of successful exploits*) знамена́тельный/па́мятный день; **~-glasses** *n.* (*binoculars*) полево́й бино́кль; **~mouse** *n.* полева́я мышь; **~-work** *n.* (*research*) иссле́дование на ме́сте.

fiend [fi:nd] *n.* (*devil*) дья́вол; (*evil person*) злоде́й, и́зверг.

fiendish ['fi:ndıʃ] *adj.* дья́вольский, злоде́йский.

fierce ['fıəs] *adj.* свире́пый, лю́тый; **~ heat** нестерпи́мая жара́; **~ competition** жесто́кая конкуре́нция.

fiery ['faıərı] *adj.* о́гненный, пла́менный; **a ~ temper** вспы́льчивый/горя́чий хара́ктер; **a ~ horse** горя́чая ло́шадь.

fife [faıf] *n.* ду́дка; ма́ленькая фле́йта.

fifteen [fıf'ti:n, 'fıf-] *n.* пятна́дцать; **a girl of ~** пятнадцатиле́тняя де́вушка.

adj. пятна́дцать *+g. pl.*; **~ hundred** ты́сяча пятьсо́т, полторы́ ты́сячи.

fifteenth [fıf'ti:nθ, 'fıf-] *n.* (*date*) пятна́дцатое (число́); (*fraction*) одна́ пятна́дцатая; пятна́дцатая часть.

adj. пятна́дцатый.

fifth [fıfθ] *n.* (*date*) пя́тое (число́); (*fraction*) одна́ пя́тая; пя́тая часть.

adj. пя́тый; **~ column** пя́тая коло́нна.

fiftieth ['fıftııθ] *n.* (*fraction*) одна́ пятидеся́тая; пятидеся́тая часть.

adj. пятидеся́тый.

fift|y ['fıftı] *n.* пятьдеся́т; **the ~ies** пятидеся́тые го́ды; **he is in his ~ies** ему́ за пятьдеся́т (лет); **we shared expenses ~-~** мы раздели́ли расхо́ды попола́м.

adj. пятьдеся́т *+g. pl.*

fig[1] [fıg] *n.* (*fruit*) фи́га, инжи́р, ви́нная я́года; **I don't care a ~** мне наплева́ть.

cpds. **~-leaf** *n.* фи́говый листо́к; **~-tree** *n.* фи́говое де́рево.

fig[2] [fıg] *n.* (*abbr. of* **figure 4.**) рис., (рису́нок).

fight [faıt] *n.* **1.** бой, схва́тка, дра́ка; **stand-up ~** кула́чный бой; **free ~** всео́бщая потасо́вка; сва́лка; **he is spoiling for a ~** он и́щет ссо́ры; **~ to a finish** борьба́ до побе́дного конца́; **he put up a (good) ~** он (упо́рно) сопротивля́лся. **2.** (*boxing-match*) боксёрский поеди́нок/бой. **3.** (*~ing spirit*) задо́р; **he has ~ in him yet** в нём ещё оста́лся боево́й задо́р.

v.t. & i. дра́ться, по-; сра|жа́ться, -зи́ться; (*wage war*) воева́ть (*impf.*); **the boys are ~ing** ма́льчики деру́тся; **Britain fought Germany** Великобрита́ния воева́ла с Герма́нией (*or* выступа́ла про́тив Герма́нии); **~ a battle** вести́ (*det.*) бой; **~ a duel** дра́ться (*impf.*) на дуэ́ли; **~ an election** вести́ (*det.*) предвы́борную борьбу́; **~ a lawsuit** суди́ться (*impf.*); **~ a case** (*leg.*) защища́ть (*impf.*) де́ло в суде́; **he fought his way forward** он пробива́лся/

протáлкивался вперёд; **they fought off the enemy** они́ отби́ли врагá; **they fought it out** (*or* **to a finish**) они́ сражáлись/борóлись до концá; ~ **back** *v.i.* отб|ивáться, -и́ться.

fighter ['faɪtə(r)] *n.* **1.** (*one who fights*) боéц, (*fig.*) борéц. **2.** (~ *aircraft*) истреби́тель (*m.*); ~ **cover** прикры́тие истреби́телями.

cpds. **~-bomber** *n.* истреби́тель-бомбардирóвщик; **~-pilot** *n.* лётчик-истреби́тель (*m.*).

fighting ['faɪtɪŋ] *n.* бой, сражéние.

adj. боевóй.

figment ['fɪgmənt] *n.* вы́мысел; фикция; **a ~ of the imagination** плод воображéния.

figurative ['fɪgjʊrətɪv, 'fɪgər-] *adj.* перенóсный, метафори́ческий; (*pictorial*) изобрази́тельный.

figure ['fɪgə(r)] *n.* **1.** (*numerical sign*) ци́фра; **double ~s** двузнáчные чи́сла; **I bought it at a low ~** я э́то дёшево купи́л. **2.** (*geom.*) фигу́ра, тéло. **3.** (*pl., arithmetic*): **he is good at ~s** он силён в арифмéтике. **4.** (*diagram, illustration*) рису́нок. **5.** (*image, effigy*) óбраз, изображéние, стáтуя, фигу́ра; **lay ~** манекéн. **6.** (*human form*) фигу́ра; **she has a good ~** у неё хорóшая фигу́ра; **a fine ~ of a man** хорошó сложённый мужчи́на. **7.** (*person of importance*) фигу́ра, выдаю́щаяся ли́чность; **he is a great ~ in this town** он извéстная фигу́ра в э́том гóроде. **8.** (~ *of speech*) óбразное выражéние.

v.t. **1.** (*picture, imagine*) вообра|жáть, -зи́ть; предст|авля́ть, -áвить себé. **2.:** ~ **out** (*calculate*) вычисля́ть, вы́числить; (*understand*) пон|имáть, -я́ть; **I can't ~ him out** я не могу́ егó поня́ть; ~ **out how much we owe you** подсчитáйте, скóлько мы вам должны́.

v.i. **1.** (*appear*) фигури́ровать (*impf.*); **this did not ~ in my plans** э́то не входи́ло в мои́ плáны. **2.** (*US coll.*): **it ~s** (*makes sense, is plausible*) э́то похóже на прáвду; **I ~d on seeing him** я рассчи́тывал увидéться с ним.

cpds. **~-head** *n.* носовóе украшéние, фигу́ра на носу́ корабля́; (*fig.*) номинáльный руководи́тель; **~-of-eight** *n.* восьмёрка; **~-skater** *n.* фигури́ст; **~skating** *n.* фигу́рное катáние.

figurine [,fɪgjʊ'ri:n, 'fɪg-] *n.* фигу́рка, статуэ́тка.

filament ['fɪləmənt] *n.* (*animal fibre*) волокнó; (*bot.*) нить; (*elec.*) нить накáла.

filbert ['fɪlbət] *n.* (*tree*) лещи́на; (*nut*) фунду́к.

file[1] [faɪl] *n.* (*tool*) напи́льник; (*nail-~*) пи́лочка для ногтéй.

v.t. подпи́л|ивать, -и́ть; ~ **one's nails** подпи́л|ивать, -и́ть нóгти; **he ~d away the roughness** он отшлифовáл гру́бую повéрхность.

file[2] [faɪl] *n.* **1.** (*for papers*) пáпка, скоросшивáтель (*m.*). **2.** (*set of papers etc.*) дéло, досьé (*indecl.*); **a newspaper ~** подши́вка газéты. **3.** (*comput.*) файл; ~ **server** файл-сéрвер.

v.t. **1.** (*place on ~*) подш|ивáть, -и́ть; регистри́ровать, за-; **the letters were ~d away** пи́сьма бы́ли подши́ты к дéлу. **2.:** ~ (*lodge*) **a complaint** под|авáть, -áть жáлобу; ~ **suit against s.o.** возбу|ждáть, -ди́ть судéбное дéло прóтив когó-н.

file[3] [faɪl] *n.* **1.** (*rank, row*) ряд, шерéнга; колóнна; **in single ~** гуськóм; по одномý; **rank and ~** (*mil.*) рядовы́е (*m. pl.*); (*fig., as adj.*) рядовóй (*рабóтник и т.п.*). **2.** (*chess*) вертикáль.

v.i. идти́ (*det.*) гуськóм/колóнной.

filial ['fɪlɪəl] *adj.* (*pert. to son or daughter*) сынóвний, дочéрний; (*dutiful*) почти́тельный.

filibuster ['fɪlɪ,bʌstə(r)] *n.* (*fig., obstruction*) обстру́кция.

v.i. (*fig.*) тормози́ть (*impf.*) приня́тие закóна путём обстру́кции.

filigree ['fɪlɪ,gri:] *n.* филигрáнь; (*fig.*) филигрáнная рабóта.

filing ['faɪlɪŋ] *n.* (*of papers*) регистрáция бумáг.

cpds. **~-cabinet** *n.* шкаф, сейф; **~-clerk** *n.* делопроизводи́тель (*m.*), регистрáтор.

filings ['faɪlɪŋz] *n. pl.* металли́ческие опи́л|ки (*pl., g.* -ок).

fill [fɪl] *n.*: **he ate his ~** он наéлся дóсыта.

v.t. **1.** (*make full*) нап|олня́ть, -óлнить; зап|олня́ть, -óлнить; **smoke ~ed the room** кóмната напóлнилась ды́мом; **I was ~ed with admiration** я был пóлон восхищéния. **2.** ~ **a tooth** пломбировáть, за-. **3.** (*fig., of office etc.*) зан|имáть, -я́ть; ~ **a vacancy** зап|олня́ть, -óлнить вакáнтную дóлжность; постáвить (*pf.*) когó-н. на вакáнтное мéсто; ~ **s.o.'s place** зан|имáть, -я́ть чьё-н. мéсто. **4.** (*execute*) выполня́ть, вы́полнить.

v.i. **1.** (*become full*) нап|олня́ться, -óлниться.

with advs.: ~ **in** *v.t.* (*complete*) зап|олня́ть, -óлнить; **he ~ed in the form** он запóлнил бланк/анкéту; **he ~ed in his name** он вписáл своё и́мя; (*coll., inform*): **I ~ed him in** я ввёл егó в курс дéла; *v.i.*: **I am ~ing in while X is away** я замещáю X в егó отсу́тствие; ~ **out** *v.t.* (*a form*) зап|олня́ть, -óлнить; *v.i.* попрáвиться (*pf.*); нап|олня́ться,-óлниться; ~ **up** *v.t.* (*make full*) нап|олня́ть, -óлнить; **we ~ed up** (*the car*) **with petrol** мы заправились (бензи́ном); (*a form*) зап|олня́ть, -óлнить; *v.i.* (*become full*) нап|олня́ться, -óлниться.

fillet ['fɪlɪt] *n.* **1.** (*head-band*) лéнта, повя́зка. **2.** (*of meat, fish*) филé (*indecl.*).

v.t. (*of fish, take off bone*) отдел|я́ть, -и́ть мя́со от костéй.

filling ['fɪlɪŋ] *n.* (*in tooth*) плóмба; (*in cake*) начи́нка.

adj. (*of food*) сы́тный.

cpd. **~-station** *n.* автозапрáвочная *or* бензозапрáвочная стáнция; (бензо)заправка.

fillip ['fɪlɪp] *n.* щелчóк, толчóк; (*fig.*) **give a ~ to** да|вáть, -ть толчóк *+d*; стимули́ровать (*pf.*).

filly ['fɪlɪ] *n.* молодáя кобы́ла.

film [fɪlm] *n.* **1.** (*thin coating*) плёнка; **a ~ of dust** налёт пы́ли; **a ~ of mist** ды́мка. **2.** (*photographic material*) фотоплёнка; (*cin.*) киноплёнка; **a roll of ~** кату́шка фотоплёнки. **3.** (*motion picture*) фильм; ~ **clip** отры́вок из фи́льма; ~ **crew** киносъёмочная комáнда; ~ **critic** кинообозревáтель (*m.*); ~ **star** кинозвездá; ~ **studio** киносту́дия; **do you go to (the) ~s?** вы хóдите в кинó?; ~ **projector** киноустанóвка; ~ **set** съёмочная площáдка.

v.t. сн|имáть, -я́ть.

filter ['fɪltə(r)] *n.* (*for liquid*) фильтр, цеди́лка; (*for light*) светофи́льтр.

v.t. (*purify*) фильтровáть (*impf.*); процé|живать, -ди́ть.

v.i. (*fig.*): **the news ~ed out** нóвости просочи́лись.

filth [fɪlθ] *n.* грязь.

filthy ['fɪlθɪ] *adj.* гря́зный.

fin [fɪn] *n.* плавни́к.

final ['faɪn(ə)l] *n.* **1.** (*examination*) выпускнóй экзáмен. **2.** (*match*) финáл; **tennis ~s** финáл по тéннису. **3.** (*newspaper edition*) послéдний вы́пуск.

adj. **1.** (*last in order*) послéдний; завершáющий, заключи́тельный. **2.** (*decisive*) окончáтельный, решáющий.

finale [fɪ'nɑ:lɪ, -leɪ] *n.* (*mus., fig.*) финáл; **grand ~** торжéственный финáл.

finalist ['faɪnəlɪst] *n.* финали́ст.

finality [faɪ'nælɪtɪ] *n.*: **he spoke with (an air of) ~** он говори́л об э́том, как о дéле решённом.

finalize ['faɪnə,laɪz] *v.t.* (*give final form to*) при|давáть, -дáть окончáтельную фóрму *+d.*; (*settle, e.g. arrangements*) (окончáтельно) улáдить (*pf.*).

finance ['faɪnæns, fɪ'næns, faɪ'næns] *n.* финáнсы (*m. pl.*); дохóды (*m. pl.*).

v.t. финанси́ровать (*impf., pf.*).

financial [faɪ'nænʃ(ə)l, fɪ-] *adj.* финáнсовый; **he is in ~ difficulties** у негó дéнежные затруднéния.

financier [faɪ'nænsɪə(r), ˌfɪ-] *n.* финанси́ст.

finch [fɪntʃ] *n.* зя́блик.

find [faɪnd] *n.* (*discovery, esp. valuable*) нахóдка.

v.t. **1.** (*discover, encounter*) на|ходи́ть, -йти́; (*by search*) раз|ыскáть, от- (*both impf.*); **he found his tongue** он обрёл дар рéчи; **a letter was found on him** при нём нашли́ письмó; **pine-trees are found in several countries** соснá растёт/встречáется во мнóгих стрáнах; **I found him waiting for me** он ужé ждал меня́; **the bullet found its mark** пу́ля попáла в цель; **water ~s its own level** водá устанáвливает свой у́ровень; **we found the beds comfortable** мы нашли́ кровáти удóбными; **I found I had forgotten the key** я обнару́жил, что забы́л ключ; **I ~ it hard to understand him** мне тру́дно поня́ть егó; **he found himself in hospital** он оказáлся/очути́лся в больни́це; **I called, but found her out** я зашёл, но не застáл её. **2.** (*compute, ascertain, judge*): **I ~ the total to be £20** у меня́ получáется, что óбщая су́мма составля́ет 20 фу́нтов; **the jury found him guilty** прися́жные признáли егó винóвным. **3.** (*provide*) предост|авля́ть, -áвить; **I will ~ the money for the excursion** я раздобу́ду дéньги на экску́рсию. **4.** (*obtain, achieve*) получ|áть, -и́ть; **I ~ pleasure in reading** я получáю удовóльствие от чтéния; **he found favour with his employer** он снискáл благосклóнность у своегó начáльника; **he found time to read** он улучáл врéмя для чтéния. **5. ~ out** (*detect*) узн|авáть, -áть; (*ascertain*) выясня́ть, вы́яснить; **I found out the answer** я нашёл отвéт; **have you found out (about) the trains?** вы узнáли расписáние поездóв?

finding ['faɪndɪŋ] *n.* (*discovery*) откры́тие, нахóдка, нахождéние; (*conclusion; also pl.*) вы́вод(ы); (*leg.*) постановлéние, решéние.

fine[1] [faɪn] *n.* (*punishment*) штраф.

v.t. штрафовáть, о-; **he was ~d £5** егó оштрафовáли на 5 фу́нтов.

fine[2] [faɪn] *adj.* **1.** (*of weather*) я́сный, хорóший; **it has turned ~** проясни́лось; **one ~ day, one of these ~ days** в оди́н прекрáсный день. **2.** (*pleasant, handsome, excellent*) прекрáсный, замечáтельный; **a ~ view** прекрáсный вид; **a ~ girl** (*looks or character*) прелéстная/чудéсная дéвушка; **we had a ~ time** мы прекрáсно/замечáтельно провели́ врéмя. **3.** (*noble, virtuous*) благорóдный, возвы́шенный. **4.** (*delicate, exquisite*) тóнкий; **~ workmanship** тóнкая рабóта. **5.** (*of small particles*) мéлкий; **~ dust** мéлкая пыль; **~ rain** мéлкий дождь. **6.** (*slender, thin, sharp*) тóнкий, óстрый; **~ thread** тóнкая нить; **a pencil with a ~ point** óстро оттóченный карандáш. **7.** (*refined, subtle*) утончённый, тóнкий; **a ~ distinction** тóнкое разли́чие; **the ~ arts** изобрази́тельные искýсства. **8.** (*elegant, distinguished*) изя́щный.

adv.: **he cut it ~** (*of time*) он остáвил себé врéмени в обрéз; **that suits me ~** (*coll.*) э́то меня́ вполнé устрáивает.

cpds. **~-grained** *adj.* мелкозерни́стый.

fineness ['faɪnnɪs] *n.* (*delicacy*) тóнкость, утончённость, изя́щество.

finery ['faɪnərɪ] *n.* пы́шный наря́д.

finesse [fɪ'nes] *n.* (*delicacy*) деликáтность, тóнкость.

finger ['fɪŋgə(r)] *n.* пáлец (*also of glove*); (*of clock*) стрéлка; **eat sth. with one's ~s** есть что-н. рукáми; **lay a ~ on** (*touch, molest*) тró|гать, -нуть пáльцем; **he put his ~ on it** он попáл в сáмую тóчку; **I will not lift a ~ to help him** я и пáльцем не пошевельну́, чтóбы помóчь емý; **she worked her ~s to the bone** онá рабóтала не поклáдая рук; **the criminal slipped through our ~s** престýпник ускользнýл у нас из-под нóса; **he burnt his ~s in that business** он обжёгся на э́том дéле; **they can be counted on the ~s of one hand** их по пáльцам мóжно сосчитáть.

v.t.: **~ an instrument** (*mus.*) перебирáть (*impf.*) пáльцами клáвиши/стрýны.

cpds. **~-mark** *n.* пятнó от пáльца; **~-nail** *n.* нóготь (*m.*); **~-print** *n.* отпечáток пáльца; дактилоскопи́ческий отпечáток; *v.t.* (*take s.o.'s ~-prints*) сн|имáть, -ять отпечáтки пáльцев у+*g.*; **~-tip** *n.* кóнчик пáльца; **he has the subject at his ~-tips** он знáет э́тот предмéт как свои́ пять пáльцев.

fingering ['fɪŋgərɪŋ] *n.* (*mus.*) аппликатýра.

finicky ['fɪnɪkɪ] *adj.* разбóрчивый, приди́рчивый, привереди́ливый.

finish ['fɪnɪʃ] *n.* **1.** (*conclusion*) окончáние, конéц; **they fought to a ~** они́ би́лись до концá. **2.** (*polish*) отдéлка; **mahogany ~** отдéлка из крáсного дéрева; **the manufacture lacks ~** издéлию не хватáет отдéлки.

v.t. **1.** (*smooth, polish*) отдéл|ывать, -ать. **2.** (*perfect*) совершéнствовать (*impf.*); **~ing touch** послéдний штрих. **3.** (*end*) зак|áнчивать, -óнчить; кончáть, кóнчить; **I ~ed** (*sc. writing, reading*) **the book** я (за)кóнчил кни́гу; **he ~ed (off, up) the pie** он доéл весь пирóг; **we will ~ the job** мы закóнчим рабóту. **4.** (*of manufacture*): **~ed goods** готóвые издéлия. **5.** (*coll., exhaust, kill*) изнур|я́ть, -и́ть; прик|áнчивать, -óнчить; **the climb ~ed me** (*coll.*) э́тот подъём доконáл меня́; **the fever ~ed him off** лихорáдка прикóнчила егó.

v.i. кончáться, кóнчиться; зак|áнчиваться, -óнчиться; **they ~ed (off, up) by singing a song** в заключéние они́ спéли пéсню; **I am ~ed with him** мéжду нáми всё кóнчено; (*in race*) финиши́ровать (*impf., pf.*); **he ~ed fourth** он зáнял четвёртое мéсто; **~ing-post** фи́ниш.

finite ['faɪnaɪt] *adj.* конéчный; (*gram.*): **~ verb** ли́чный глагóл.

Finland ['fɪnlənd] *n.* Финля́ндия.

Finn [fɪn] *n.* фин|н (*fem.* -ка).

Finnish ['fɪnɪʃ] *n.* (*language*) фи́нский язы́к.

adj. фи́нский.

fiord, fjord [fjɔːd] *n.* фьорд, фиóрд.

fir [fɜː(r)] *n.* (*also* **~-tree**) ель; **Scotch ~** соснá.

cpds. **~-cone** *n.* елóвая ши́шка.

fire ['faɪə(r)] *n.* **1.** (*phenomenon of combustion*) огóнь (*m.*); **the house is on ~** дом загорéлся/гори́т; **set on ~, set ~ to** подж|игáть, -éчь; **catch ~** загор|áться, -éться; **there is no smoke without ~** нет ды́ма без огня́; **play with ~** (*fig.*) игрáть (*impf.*) с огнём. **2.** (*burning fuel*) огóнь (*m.*); **camp ~** костёр; **he lit a ~** он разжёг огóнь/ками́н; **lay a ~** расклáдывать, разложи́ть огóнь; **make a ~** (*indoors*) зат|áпливать, -опи́тьками́н; **light a ~** разж|игáть, -éчь ками́н; топи́ть, за- печь; **there is a ~ in the next room** в сосéдней кóмнате тóпится (*or* гори́т ками́н). **3.** (*conflagration*) пожáр; **~!** пожáр!; (*excl. by someone in burning building*) гори́м!; **where's the ~?** где гори́т? **4.** (*of ~arms*) огóнь (*m.*), стрельбá; **open ~** откр|ывáть, -ы́ть огóнь; **cease ~** прекра|щáть, -ти́ть огóнь; **under ~** (*lit., also fig., of criticism etc.*) под огнём; **draw s.o.'s ~** (*fig.*) стать (*pf.*) мишéнью для чьих-н. напáдок; **hold one's ~** (*fig.*) сдéрж|иваться, -áться. **5.** (*ardour*) пыл, огóнь (*m.*); **a speech full of ~** плáменная речь.

v.t. **1.** (*set fire to*) подж|игáть, -éчь; заж|игáть, -éчь; (*fig.*): **it ~d her imagination** э́то воспламени́ло её воображéние. **2.** (*bake, e.g. bricks or pottery*) обж|игáть, -éчь. **3.** (*fuel*): **an oil-~d furnace** тóпка, рабóтающая на жи́дком тóпливе. **4.** (*of ~arms*) стреля́ть (*impf.*) из+*g.*; **~ a rifle** стреля́ть (*impf.*) из ружья́; **~ a shot** вы́стрелить (*pf.*); **he ~d off his ammunition** он израсхóдовал все патрóны.

v.i. **1.** (*of ~arms*) стреля́ть (*impf.*); вы́стрелить (*pf.*); **the troops ~d at the enemy** войскá стреля́ли по врагу́; **they ~d at the target** они́ стреля́ли в цель; **the guns ~d** ору́дия стреля́ли; **~ away!** (*fig., coll.*) валя́й!; выкла́дывай!

cpds. **~-alarm** *n.* (*alert*) пожа́рная трево́га; (*device*) автомати́ческий пожа́рный сигна́л; **~arm** *n.* огнестре́льное ору́жие; **~ball** *n.* (*meteor*) боли́д; (*nucl.*) о́гненный шар; **~-bird** *n.* (*myth.*) жар-пти́ца; **~-bomb** *n.* зажига́тельная бо́мба; **~-brigade** *n.* пожа́рная кома́нда; **~-cracker** *n.* фейерве́рк; **~-drill** *n.* пожа́рное уче́ние; **~-engine** *n.* пожа́рная маши́на; **~-escape** *n.* пожа́рная ле́стница; **~-extinguisher** *n.* огнетуши́тель (*m.*); **~-fighter** *n.* пожа́рник, пожа́рный; **~fly** *n.* светля́к; **~-guard** *n.* (*screen*) ками́нная решётка; **~-hose** *n.* пожа́рный шланг; **~-insurance** *n.* страхова́ние от огня́; **~-irons** *n.* ками́нный прибо́р; **~light** *n.* свет от ками́на; **~-lighter** *n.* расто́пка; **~man** *n.* (*member of ~ brigade*) пожа́рник, пожа́рный; **~place** *n.* ками́н, оча́г; **~-power** *n.* огнева́я мощь; **~proof** *adj.* огнеупо́рный; **a ~proof door** несгора́емая дверь; **~-raiser** *n.* поджига́тель (*m.*); **~-ship** *n.* бра́ндер; **~side** *n.* ме́сто о́коло ками́на; **~-station** *n.* пожа́рное депо́ (*indecl.*); **~wood** *n.* дров|а́ (*pl., g.* —); **~work(s)** *n.* фейерве́рк (*also fig.*); **~work display** фейерве́рк.

firing ['faɪərɪŋ] *n.* (*shooting*) стрельба́.

cpds. **~-line** *n.* ли́ния огня́; **~-party, -squad** *nn.* (*at funeral etc.*) салю́тная кома́нда; (*for execution*) кома́нда, наря́женная для расстре́ла.

firm[1] [fɜ:m] *n.* фи́рма.

firm[2] [fɜ:m] *adj.* **1.** (*physical*) кре́пкий, твёрдый; **~ ground** су́ша. **2.** (*fig.*) усто́йчивый, сто́йкий; **you must be ~ with him** вы должны́ быть с ним постро́же; **a ~ offer** твёрдое предложе́ние.

adv. твёрдо, усто́йчиво; **stand ~** стоя́ть (*impf.*) твёрдо.

v.t. (*make ~; also ~ up*) (*e.g. a mixture*) уплотн|я́ть, -и́ть; (*e.g. a project*) укреп|ля́ть, -и́ть.

v.i. (*also ~ up*) (*become ~*) уплотн|я́ться, -и́ться; укреп|ля́ться, -и́ться.

firmament ['fɜ:məmənt] *n.* небе́сный свод.

firmness ['fɜ:mnɪs] *n.* (*physical*) твёрдость; (*moral*) сто́йкость.

first [fɜ:st] *n.* **1.** (*beginning*): **at ~** снача́ла, сперва́; **from ~ to last** с нача́ла до конца́; **from the ~** с са́мого нача́ла. **2.** (*date*) пе́рвое (число́); **on the ~ of May** пе́рвого ма́я. **3.** (*acad.*) вы́сшая оце́нка/отме́тка; **he got a ~ in physics** он получи́л вы́сшую оце́нку по фи́зике.

adj. **1.** (*in time or place*) пе́рвый; **~ aid** пе́рвая по́мощь; **on the ~ floor** на второ́м этаже́; (*US*) на пе́рвом этаже́; **~ form** пе́рвый класс; **at ~ glance** на пе́рвый взгляд; **hear sth. at ~ hand** узна́ть (*pf.*) что-н. из пе́рвых рук; **~ name** и́мя; **~ night** (*theatr.*) премье́ра; **I asked the ~ person I saw** я спроси́л пе́рвого встре́чного; **~ person singular** пе́рвое лицо́ еди́нственного числа́; **in the ~ place** во-пе́рвых; **I will go there ~ thing tomorrow** за́втра я пе́рвым де́лом зайду́ туда́; **the ~ time I saw him** когда́ я в пе́рвый раз уви́дел его́; **he got it right ~ time** у него́ получи́лось э́то с пе́рвого ра́за; **he would be the ~ to admit that ...** он пе́рвый призна́ет, что... **2.** (*in rank or importance*) пе́рвый; **he travels ~ class** он е́здит пе́рвым кла́ссом; **~ team** (*sport*) основно́й соста́в; **~ cousin** двою́родный брат, двою́родная сестра́. **3.** (*basic*) основно́й; **~ principles** основны́е при́нципы; **he doesn't know the ~ thing about dogs** он ничего́ не понима́ет в соба́ках.

adv. **1.** (*before all; also ~ of all*) пре́жде всего́; в пе́рвую о́чередь; **~ come, ~ served** кто пе́рвым пришёл, того́ пе́рвым и обслу́жат. **2.** (*initially*) сперва́, снача́ла; (*in the ~ place*) во-пе́рвых; (*for the ~ time*) впервы́е; **when they were ~ married** когда́ они́ то́лько пожени́лись.

cpds. **~-aid** *adj.*: **~-aid kit** санита́рная су́мка; **~-aid post** пункт пе́рвой по́мощи; **~-aid room, station** медпу́нкт; **~-born** *n.* пе́рвенец; *adj.* ста́рший; **~-class** *adj.* (*excellent*) первокла́ссный; *adv.* (*of travel*) пе́рвым кла́ссом; **~-floor** *adj.* второ́го этажа́, на второ́м этаже́; (*US*) пе́рвого этажа́, на пе́рвом этаже́; **~-form** *adj.*: **~-form pupil** первокла́ссник; **~-hand** *adj.* из пе́рвых рук; **~-rate** *adj.* первокла́ссный; *int.* прекра́сно!

firstly ['fɜ:stlɪ] *adv.* во-пе́рвых.

firth [fɜ:θ] *n.* зали́в; лима́н.

fiscal ['fɪsk(ə)l] *adj.* фиска́льный, фина́нсовый.

fish [fɪʃ] *n.* ры́ба; **catch ~** лови́ть, пойма́ть ры́бу; **drink like a ~** пить (*impf.*) запо́ем; **neither ~, flesh, nor fowl** ни ры́ба, ни мя́со; **I have other ~ to fry** у меня́ есть дела́ поважне́е; (*fig., creature*): **a cold ~** холо́дный челове́к.

v.t. & i. лови́ть/уди́ть (*impf.*) ры́бу; **~ a river** лови́ть ры́бу в реке́; (*fig.*): **~ for compliments** напра́шиваться (*impf.*) на комплиме́нты; **~ for information** выу́живать, вы́удить све́дения.

with advs.: **~ out** *v.t.* выу́живать, вы́удить; **~ up** *v.t.* выта́скивать, вы́тащить.

cpds. **~bone** *n.* ры́бья кость; **~-cake** *n.* ≃ ры́бная котле́та; **~-farm** *n.* рыборазво́дный садо́к; **~-finger** *n.* ры́бная па́лочка; **~-hook** *n.* рыболо́вный крючо́к; **~monger** *n.* торго́вец ры́бой; **~net** *n.* рыболо́вная сеть; **~net stockings** ажу́рные чулки́; **~-pond** *n.* пруд для разведе́ния ры́бы; ры́бный садо́к.

fisherman ['fɪʃəmən] *n.* рыба́к; (*angler for pleasure*) рыболо́в.

fishery ['fɪʃərɪ] *n.* рыболо́вство; ры́бный про́мысел.

fishing ['fɪʃɪŋ] *n.* ры́бная ло́вля; **the boys have gone ~** ма́льчики ушли́ на рыба́лку.

cpds. **~-line** *n.* леса́, ле́ска; **~-net** *n.* рыболо́вная сеть; **~-rod** *n.* уди́лище; **~-tackle** *n.* рыболо́вные сна́сти (*f. pl.*).

fishy ['fɪʃɪ] *adj.* ры́бий, ры́бный; (*coll., suspect*) нечи́стый, подозри́тельный.

fission ['fɪʃ(ə)n] *n.* (*biol.*) размноже́ние путём деле́ния кле́ток; (*phys.*) расщепле́ние/деле́ние (ядра́); **nuclear ~** а́томный распа́д.

fissure ['fɪʃə(r)] *n.* тре́щина, расще́лина.

fist [fɪst] *n.* кула́к; (*dim., e.g. baby's*) кулачо́к; **shake one's ~ at s.o.** грози́ть, по- кому́-н. кулако́м; **with clenched ~s** сжав кулаки́.

fistful ['fɪstfʊl] *n.* горсть.

fisticuffs ['fɪstɪ,kʌfs] *n.* кула́чный бой.

fistula ['fɪstjʊlə] *n.* (*med.*) фи́стула, свищ.

fit[1] [fɪt] *n.* **1.** (*attack of illness*) при́ступ, припа́док; **apoplectic ~** апоплекси́ческий уда́р; (*fig.*): **she would have a ~ if she knew** она́ закати́ла бы сце́ну е́сли бы узна́ла. **2.** (*outburst*): **~ of coughing** при́ступ ка́шля; **his jokes had us in ~s** от его́ шу́ток мы пока́тывались со́ смеху; **in a ~ of passion** в поры́ве стра́сти. **3.** (*transitory state*): **by ~s and starts** уры́вками.

fit[2] [fɪt] *n.* (*of a garment etc.*): **this jacket is a tight ~** э́тот пиджа́к узкова́т; **six people in the car is a tight ~** шесть челове́к едва́ умеща́ются в маши́не.

adj. **1.** (*suitable*) го́дный, приго́дный, подходя́щий; **this food is not ~ to eat** э́та пи́ща несъедо́бна; **he was passed ~ for military service** его́ призна́ли го́дным к вое́нной слу́жбе; **survival of the ~test** есте́ственный отбо́р; **see, think ~** счита́ть, поче́сть ну́жным; **you are not ~ to be seen** вам нельзя́ показа́ться в тако́м ви́де. **2.** (*ready*) гото́вый, спосо́бный; **he was ~ to drop** он едва́ держа́лся на нога́х; **dressed ~ to kill** разоде́тый в пух и прах. **3.** (*in good health*) здоро́вый; в хоро́шей фо́рме; **fighting ~** здоро́вый как бык; **keep (o.s.) ~** следи́ть (*impf.*) за свои́м здоро́вьем.

v.t. **1.** (*equip: also ~ out; ~ up*) снаря|жа́ть, -ди́ть;

снаб|жа́ть, -ди́ть; обору́довать (*impf., pf.*); **he was ~ted out with a new suit** ему́ вы́дали но́вый костю́м; **he went to the tailors to be ~ted** он пошёл к портно́му на приме́рку; **~ a ship out** снаря|жа́ть, -ди́ть кора́бль. **2.** (*install, fix in place*): **~ted carpet** ковёр во всю ко́мнату; **he ~ted a new lock on the door** он вста́вил но́вый замо́к в дверь; (*fig., accommodate*): **I can ~ you in next week** я могу́ назна́чить вам встре́чу на сле́дующей неде́ле. **3.** (*make suitable, adapt*) приспос|а́бливать, -о́бить; **he is not ~ted for heavy work** он не годи́тся для тяжёлых рабо́т; **I had a suit ~ted** я приме́рил костю́м; **I ~ted in my holiday with his** я подогна́л вре́мя своего́ о́тпуска к его́; (*correspond to in dimensions: also v.i.*) под|ходи́ть, -ойти́ +*d.*; **the dress ~s you** э́то пла́тье хорошо́ на вас сиди́т; **will the letter ~ (into) this envelope?** войдёт письмо́ в э́тот конве́рт?; **a key to ~ this lock** ключ к э́тому замку́; **that ~s in with my plans** э́то вполне́ совпада́ет с мои́ми пла́нами; **his story ~s in with hers** его́ расска́з подтвержда́ет её слова́. **4.** (*insert: also v.i.*): **he ~ted the cigarette into the holder** он вста́вил сигаре́ту в мундшту́к; **tubes that ~ into one another** тру́бки, вставля́ющиеся одна́ в другу́ю. **5.** (*suit*) соотве́тствовать (*impf.*) +*d.*

fitful ['fɪtfʊl] *adj.* неро́вный, преры́вистый.

fitment ['fɪtmənt] *n.* предме́т обстано́вки; часть обору́дования.

fitness ['fɪtnɪs] *n.* (*suitability*) соотве́тствие, приго́дность; (*health*) хоро́шее здоро́вье.

fitter ['fɪtə(r)] *n.* (*tailor's assistant*) портно́й, занима́ющийся приме́ркой; (*mechanic*) монтёр, сбо́рщик.

fitting ['fɪtɪŋ] *n.* **1.** (*of clothes*) приме́рка. **2.** (*fixture in building*) обору́дование; **light ~s** освети́тельные прибо́ры (*m. pl.*). **3.** (*furnishing*) обору́дование, устано́вка.

adj. подходя́щий, го́дный.

cpd. **~-room** *n.* приме́рочная.

five [faɪv] *n.* (число́/но́мер) пять; (*~ people*) пя́теро; пять челове́к; **we ~** нас пя́теро; **~ each** по пяти́; (*figure, thg. numbered 5, group of ~*) пятёрка; (*of things purchased in ~s, e.g. eggs*) пято́к; (*with var. nn. expr. or understood; cf. also examples under* **two**): **~ (o'clock)** пять (часо́в); **chapter ~ (5)** пя́тая (5) глава́; **he is ~** ему́ пять лет; **~ to 4 (o'clock)** без пяти́ четы́ре; **~ past 6** пять мину́т шесто́го; **have you got this dress in a ~?** есть у вас пя́тый разме́р э́того пла́тья.

adj. пять +*g. pl.*; (*for people and pluralia tantum, also*) пя́теро +*g. pl.*; **~ sixes are thirty** пя́тью шесть — три́дцать; **~ eggs** (*as purchase*) пято́к яи́ц; **~ times as good** впя́теро лу́чше.

cpds. **~-day** *adj.*: **~-day week** *n.* пятидне́вная неде́ля, пятидне́вка; **~fold** *adj.* пятикра́тный; *adv.* впя́теро; **~-pound** *adj.*: **~-pound note** пятифунто́вая бума́жка; **~-year** *adj.* пятиле́тний; **~-year plan** пятиле́тний план, пятиле́тка; **~-year-old** *n.* пятиле́тний ребёнок.

fiver ['faɪvə(r)] *n.* пятёрка (*coll.*).

fix [fɪks] *n.* (*coll., dilemma*) затрудни́тельное положе́ние; затрудне́ние; (*determination of position*) определе́ние ме́ста.

v.t. **1.** (*fasten, make firm*) укреп|ля́ть, -и́ть; (*fig.*): **I ~ed him with a glance** я при́стально посмотре́л на него́; **the event was ~ed in his mind** э́то собы́тие запечатле́лось у него́ в мозгу́; **~ the blame on s.o.** взва́л|ивать, -и́ть вину́ на кого́-н. **2.** (*direct steadily*) напр|авля́ть, -а́вить; **~ one's eyes (up)on** остан|а́вливать, -ови́ть взгляд на+*p.*; **~ one's attention on** сосредото́чи|вать, -ть внима́ние на+*p.*; **~ed gaze** при́стальный/засты́вший взгляд. **3.** (*determine, settle: also v.i.*) **let us ~ (on) a date** дава́йте договори́мся о да́те. **4.** (*chem.*) сгу|ща́ть, -сти́ть; свяЗ|ывать, -а́ть. **5.** (*phot.*) фикси́ровать (*impf., pf.*). **6.** (*provide: also* **~ up**) **can you ~ (up) a room for me?** (*or* **~ me up with a room?**) мо́жете ли вы найти́ для меня́ ко́мнату? **7.** (*coll., attend to*): **he ~ed the radio in no time** он в два счёта почини́л радиоприёмник; **I will ~ the drinks** я пригото́влю напи́тки.

fixation [fɪk'seɪʃ(ə)n] *n.* (*phot.*) фикса́ция; (*psych.*) фикса́ция.

fixative ['fɪksətɪv] *n.* фиксати́в, фикса́тор.

fixed ['fɪksd] *adj.* неподви́жный, закреплённый, постоя́нный; **~ idea** навя́зчивая иде́я, иде́я фикс; **~ point** (*geom.*) постоя́нная то́чка; **~ rate** установле́нная ста́вка.

fixedly ['fɪksɪdlɪ] *adv.* при́стально; в упо́р.

fixture ['fɪkstʃə(r)] *n.* **1.** (*fitting in building*) приспособле́ние. **2.** (*tech.*) неподви́жная/закреплённая дета́ль. **3.** (*sporting event*) предстоя́щее спорти́вное состяза́ние/мероприя́тие.

fizz [fɪz] *n.* шипе́ние.

v.i. шипе́ть (*impf.*).

fizzle ['fɪz(ə)l] *v.i.* шипе́ть (*impf.*); **~ out** выдыха́ться, вы́дохнуться; (*fig.*) око́нчиться (*pf.*) ниче́м.

fizzy ['fɪzɪ] *adj.* шипу́чий.

fjord [fjɔːd] = **fiord**

flabbergast ['flæbə,gɑːst] *v.t.* (*coll.*) ошелом|ля́ть, -и́ть; ошара́ши|вать, -ть.

flabbiness ['flæbɪnɪs] *n.* вя́лость, дря́блость.

flabby ['flæbɪ] *adj.* вя́лый, дря́блый.

flaccid ['flæksɪd, 'flæsɪd] *adj.* отви́слый, вя́лый.

flag[1] [flæg] *n.* (*emblem*) флаг, зна́мя (*nt.*); **show the white ~** выве́шивать, вы́весить бе́лый флаг; **hoist, raise, run up the ~** подн|има́ть, -я́ть флаг; **lower, strike the ~** (*naut.*) опус|ка́ть, -ти́ть флаг; **~ of convenience** удо́бный флаг; **keep the ~ flying** (*fig.*) высоко́ держа́ть (*impf.*) зна́мя (*чего*); **put the ~s out** (*fig.*) пра́здновать (*impf.*) побе́ду.

v.t. **1.** (*deck with ~s*) укр|аша́ть, -а́сить фла́гами. **2.** (*signal: also v.i.*) сигнализи́ровать (*impf., pf.*) фла́гом; (*fig.*): **~ (down) a passing car** останови́ть (*pf.*) проезжа́ющую маши́ну.

cpds. **~-day** *n.* день сбо́ра де́нег на благотвори́тельные це́ли; **~man** *n.* сигна́льщик; **~pole** *n.* флагшто́к; **~ship** *n.* фла́гманский кора́бль, фла́гман; **~staff** *n.* флагшто́к.

flag[2] [flæg] *n.* (*~ stone*) ка́менная плита́, плитня́к.

v.t. выстила́ть, вы́стлать пли́тами.

flag[3] [flæg] v.i. (*hang limp*) пон|ика́ть, -и́кнуть; (*grow weary*) ослаб|ева́ть, -е́ть; (*fig.*): **the conversation was ~ging** разгово́р не кле́ился.

flagellate ['flædʒə,leɪt] *v.t.* бичева́ть (*impf.*).

flagellation [,flædʒə'leɪʃ(ə)n] *n.* бичева́ние.

flagrant ['fleɪgrənt] *adj.* вопию́щий, возмути́тельный.

flail [fleɪl] *n.* цеп.

v.t. & i. молоти́ть, с-; (*fig.*) маха́ть (*impf.*).

flair ['fleə(r)] *n.* нюх, чутьё; **a ~ for languages** спосо́бности (*f. pl.*) к языка́м.

flak [flæk] *n.* зени́тный ого́нь; **~ jacket** защи́тная ку́ртка.

flake [fleɪk] *n.* (*pl.*) хло́пья (*pl., g.* -ев); **soap ~s** мы́льная стру́жка.

v.i. (*peel*) шелуши́ться (*impf.*); слои́ться (*impf.*); **the rust ~d off** ржа́вчина отслои́лась.

flaky ['fleɪkɪ] *adj.* слои́стый.

flamboyance [flæm'bɔɪəns] *n.* цвети́стость; я́ркость.

flamboyant [flæm'bɔɪənt] *adj.* цвети́стый; я́рко окра́шенный; (*fig.*) бро́ский, показно́й.

flame [fleɪm] *n.* **1.** (*burning gas; pl., fire*) ого́нь (*m.*), пла́мя (*nt.*); **burst into ~(s)** вспы́х|ивать, -нуть; **the house was in ~s** дом был охва́чен пла́менем; **add fuel to the ~s** (*fig.*) подли́ть (*pf.*) ма́сла в ого́нь. **2.** (*blaze of light or colour*) пла́мя (*nt.*), вспы́шка. **3.** (*coll., sweetheart*) предме́т стра́сти; **she is an old ~**

of mine она́ моя́ ста́рая па́ссия.

v.i. горе́ть, пыла́ть, пламене́ть (*all impf.*).

cpd. **~-thrower** *n.* огнемёт.

flaming ['fleɪmɪŋ] *adj.* **1.** (*ablaze; very hot*) пыла́ющий, горя́щий. **2.** (*fig., violent*): **they had a ~ row** у них произошёл стра́шный сканда́л; **he was in a ~ temper** он был в бе́шенстве.

flamingo [flə'mɪŋgəʊ] *n.* флами́нго (*m. indecl.*).

flammable ['flæməb(ə)l] *adj.* легко́ воспламеня́ющийся.

flan [flæn] *n.* ола́дья.

flange [flændʒ] *n.* фла́нец, кро́мка.

flank [flæŋk] *n.* **1.** (*of the body*) бок. **2.** (*of a building*) торцо́вая сторона́. **3.** (*of an army*) фланг; **~ attack** фла́нговая ата́ка.

v.t. **1.** (*be or go alongside*) находи́ться (*impf.*) (*or* идти́) сбо́ку. **2.** (*menace or cut off by ~ing movement*) угрожа́ть (*impf.*) с фла́нга +*g.*; отр|е́зать, -еза́ть фланг; **he was ~ed by guards** по о́бе его́ стороны́ шла/стоя́ла стра́жа.

flannel ['flæn(ə)l] *n.* **1.** (*kind of cloth*) флане́ль. **2.** (*piece of cloth*) флане́лька; **face ~** махро́вая рукави́чка для лица́. **3.** (*pl., trousers*) флане́левые брю́ки (*pf. g.* —).

adj. флане́левый.

flap[1] [flæp] *n.* **1.** (*hinged piece etc.*): **the table has two ~s** у стола́ две откидны́е доски́; **a jacket with a ~ at the back** пиджа́к с двумя́ разре́зами сза́ди; (*of pocket*) кла́пан; (*aeron.*) закры́лок; **with ~s down** с опу́щенными закры́лками. **2.** (*waving motion*) взмах.

v.t. & i. взма́х|ивать, -ну́ть +*i.*; мах|а́ть, -ну́ть +*i.*; хло́п|ать, -нуть; развева́ть(ся) (*impf.*); **the bird ~ped its wings** пти́ца взмахну́ла кры́льями; **the flags ~ped in the wind** фла́ги развева́лись на ветру́.

flap[2] [flæp] *n.* (*coll., state of alarm*) переполо́х; **don't get into a ~!** не паникуйте!

flare[1] [fleə(r)] *n.* **1.** (*effect of flame*) сверка́ние; вспы́шка; (*illuminating device*) сигна́льная раке́та; освети́тельный патро́н.

v.i. сверк|а́ть, -ну́ть; горе́ть (*impf.*) неро́вным пла́менем; (*fig.*) вспы́х|ивать, -нуть; вспыли́ть (*pf.*); **she ~s up at the least thing** она́ взрыва́ется от ка́ждого пустяка́.

flare[2] [fleə(r)] *v.t. & i.* расш|иря́ться, -и́риться; **~d skirt** ю́бка-клёш.

flash[1] [flæʃ] *n.* **1.** (*burst of light*) вспы́шка, про́блеск; **a ~ of lightning** вспы́шка мо́лнии; **he had a ~ of inspiration** на него́ нашло́ вдохнове́ние. **2.** (*instant*) мгнове́ние, миг; **he answered in a ~** он мгнове́нно отве́тил. **3.: news ~** э́кстренное сообще́ние.

v.t.: **he ~ed the light in my face** он напра́вил свет мне в лицо́; **they were ~ing signals to the enemy** они́ посыла́ли светов́ые сигна́лы врагу́.

v.i. сверк|а́ть, -ну́ть; вспы́х|ивать, -нуть; мельк|а́ть, -ну́ть; **the light ~ed on and off** свет то вспы́хивал, то гас; **the lightning ~ed** сверкну́ла мо́лния; **~ing eyes** сверка́ющие глаза́; **the thought ~ed across my mind** э́та мысль промелькну́ла у меня́ в голове́; **cars ~ed by** маши́ны мча́лись ми́мо.

cpds. **~back** *n.* (*cin.*) ретроспе́кция, обра́тный кадр; **~-bulb** *n.* (*phot.*) ла́мпа-вспы́шка; **~-gun** *n.* ла́мпа для ма́гниевой вспы́шки, «блиц»; **~light** *n.* (*for signalling*) сигна́льный ого́нь; проже́ктор; (*phot.*) вспы́шка (ма́гния); (*torch: also* **~-lamp**) карма́нный/электри́ческий фона́рь.

flashy ['flæʃɪ] *adj.* крича́щий, показно́й.

flask [flɑːsk] *n.* фля́га, фля́жка; ко́лба.

flat [flæt] *n.* **1.** (*apartment*) кварти́ра; **block of ~s** многокварти́рный дом. **2.** (*coll., punctured tyre*) спу́щенная ши́на.

adj. & adv. **1.** (*level*) пло́ский, ро́вный; **he has ~ feet** у него́ плоскосто́пие; **~ racing** ска́чка без препя́тствий; **~ tyre** спу́щенная ши́на; **the battery is ~** батаре́я се́ла; **he fell ~ on his back** он упа́л на́взничь; **my hair won't lie ~** у меня́ во́лосы не лежа́т. **2.** (*uniform, undifferentiated*) однообра́зный; **~ rate** еди́ная ста́вка. **3.** (*unqualified*) прямо́й, категори́ческий; **~ broke** вконе́ц разори́вшийся; **~ out** (*sl. exhausted*) вы́дохшийся; **drive ~ out** (*coll., at top speed*) гнать (*impf.*) во весь опо́р; **in ten seconds ~** ро́вно за де́сять секу́нд. **4.** (*dull, insipid*) ску́чный, вя́лый, бесцве́тный; **the story fell ~** расска́з не вы́звал интере́са. **5.** (*expressionless*) безжи́зненный, уны́лый. **6.** (*mus.*): **she sings ~ on the high notes** она́ фальши́вит (*or* не дотя́гивает) на высо́ких но́тах.

cpds. **~-footed** *adj.* страда́ющий плоскосто́пием; (*fig., clumsy*) неуклю́жий; **~-iron** *n.* утю́г.

flatly ['flætlɪ] *adv.* (*expressionlessly*) безжи́зненно, уны́ло; (*bluntly*) категори́чески, наотре́з, пря́мо.

flatness ['flætnɪs] *n.* пло́скость.

flatten ['flæt(ə)n] *v.t.* **1.** (*make smooth*) выра́внивать, вы́ровнять; разгла́|живать, -дить. **2.** (*reduce thickness of*) расплющи|вать, -ть; **he ~ed himself against the wall** он прижа́лся к стене́. **3.** (*lay low*) повали́ть, примя́ть (*both pf.*); **the gale ~ed the corn** бу́рей примя́ло хлеба́.

v.i. выра́вниваться, вы́ровняться; **the pilot ~ed out at fifty metres** пило́т вы́ровнял самолёт на высоте́ 50 ме́тров.

flatter ['flætə(r)] *v.t.* **1.** (*praise insincerely or unduly*) льсти́ть, по- +*d.* **2.** (*represent too favourably*) приукра́|шивать, -сить. **3.** (*gratify vanity of*): **~ o.s.** те́шить (*impf.*) себя́; льсти́ть (*impf.*) себя́ наде́ждой.

flattering ['flætərɪŋ] *adj.* ле́стный, льсти́вый.

flattery ['flætərɪ] *n.* лесть.

flatulence ['flætjʊləns] *n.* скопле́ние га́зов.

flaunt [flɔːnt] *v.t.* афиши́ровать (*impf.*); щегол|я́ть, -ьну́ть +*i.*; выставля́ть, вы́ставить напока́з.

flautist ['flɔːtɪst] *n.* флейти́ст.

flavour ['fleɪvə(r)] *n.* арома́т, вкус; (*fig.*) при́вкус.

v.t. припр|авля́ть, -а́вить; (*fig.*) прид|ава́ть, -а́ть при́вкус +*d.*

flavouring ['fleɪvərɪŋ] *n.* припра́ва; спе́ции (*f. pl.*); эссе́нция.

flaw [flɔː] *n.* (*crack*) тре́щина; (*defect*) изъя́н, недоста́ток.

v.t. по́ртить, ис-.

flawless ['flɔːlɪs] *adj.* безупре́чный.

flax [flæks] *n.* лён.

flaxen ['flæks(ə)n] *adj.* льняно́й.

cpd. **~-haired** *adj.* с льняны́ми волоса́ми.

flay [fleɪ] *v.t.* свежева́ть, о-; сдира́ть, содра́ть ко́жу с+*g.*; **he will ~ me alive if he finds out** он с меня́ живьём шку́ру сдерёт, е́сли узна́ет.

flea [fliː] *n.* блоха́; **~ market** бараха́лка, толку́чка.

cpds. **~bite** *n.* блоши́ный уку́с; (*coll.*) ме́лочь, була́вочный уко́л.

fleck [flek] *n.* кра́пинка, пятно́; (*of dust*) пыли́нка.

v.t. покр|ыва́ть, -ы́ть пя́тками/кра́пинками.

fledge [fledʒ] *v.t.* (*bird, arrow*) опер|я́ть, -и́ть; **fully ~d** (*lit., fig.*) опери́вшийся.

fledg(e)ling ['fledʒlɪŋ] *n.* птене́ц.

flee [fliː] *v.t.* избе|га́ть, -жа́ть; **~ the country** бежа́ть из страны́.

v.i. бежа́ть, с-; исч|еза́ть, -е́знуть.

fleece [fliːs] *n.* руно́, ове́чья шерсть.

v.t. (*fig.*) об|ира́ть, -обра́ть.

fleecy ['fliːsɪ] *adj.* шерсти́стый; **~ clouds** кудря́вые облака́; **~ lining** мехова́я подкла́дка.

fleet[1] [fliːt] *n.* **1.** (*collection of vessels*) флоти́лия, флот. **2.** (*naval force*) вое́нно-морско́й флот. **3.** (*of vehicles*) парк.

fleet[2] [fliːt] *adj.* (*liter.*) бы́стрый, прово́рный; **~ of foot** быстроно́гий.

fleeting ['fli:tɪŋ] *adj.* бéглый, мимолётный; **a ~ glimpse** бéглый взгляд.

Fleming ['flemɪŋ] *n.* флама́нд|ец (*fem.* -ка).

Flemish ['flemɪʃ] *adj.* флама́ндский.

flesh [fleʃ] *n.* **1.** (*bodily tissue*) плоть, тéло; (*meat*) мя́со; **pig's ~** свини́на; (*surface of body*): **~ tint** телéсный цвет; **~ wound** повéрхностное ранéние; **make s.o.'s ~ creep** (*fig.*) прив|одúть, -ести́ когó-н. в содрогáние. **2.** (*fig.*): **sins of the ~** плóтские грехи́; **see s.o. in the ~** уви́деть (*pf.*) когó-н. во плоти́; **appear in ~ and blood** появи́ться (*pf.*) сóбственной персóной; **my own ~ and blood** (*children*) моя́ плоть и кровь; (*relatives*) моя́ родня́. **3.** (*of plant or fruit*) мя́со, мя́коть.

cpd. **~-coloured** *adj.* телéсного цвéта.

fleshy ['fleʃɪ] *adj.* (*of persons*) тóлстый, тýчный; (*of meat, plant, fruit*) мяси́стый.

flex[1] [fleks] *n.* (ги́бкий) шнур.

flex[2] [fleks] *v.t.* сгибáть, согнýть; **~ one's muscles** напр|ягáть, -я́чь мýскулы.

flexibility [ˌfleksɪ'bɪlɪtɪ] *n.* эласти́чность; (*fig.*) ги́бкость.

flexible ['fleksɪb(ə)l] *adj.* эласти́чный, ги́бкий.

flexitime ['fleksɪˌtaɪm] *n.* свобóдный режи́м рабóчего дня.

flick [flɪk] *n.* (*jerk*) толчóк; **with a ~ of the wrist** взмахнýв ки́стью руки́.

v.t. (*shake with a jerk*) встряхнýть (*pf.*); (*propel with finger end*) щёлкнуть (*pf.*); (*touch e.g. with whip*) стегнýть (*pf.*); хлестнýть (*pf.*).

cpds. **~-knife** *n.* пружи́нный нож.

flicker ['flɪkə(r)] *n.* (*of light*) мерцáние; (*movement*) трепетáние; (*fig.*): **a ~ of hope** прóблеск надéжды.

v.i. (*flutter*) трепетáть (*impf.*); (*burn or shine fitfully*) мерцáть (*impf.*); (*fig.*) мельк|áть, -нýть.

flier ['flaɪə(r)] = **flyer**

flight[1] [flaɪt] *n.* **1.** полёт; **shoot birds in ~** стреля́ть (*impf.*) птиц на летý; (*journey by air*): **a non-stop ~** беспосáдочный полёт; **the next ~ from London to Paris** слéдующий рейс по маршрýту Лóндон-Пари́ж; **~ number** нóмер рéйса; **~ recorder** бортовóй самопи́сец; **~ simulator** лётный тренажёр. **2.** (*fig.*): **~ of fancy** полёт фантáзии. **3. ~ of steps** лéстничный марш. **4. a ~ of birds** стáя птиц.

cpds. **~-deck** *n.* (*of carrier*) полётная пáлуба; (*of aircraft*) каби́на экипáжа; **~-lieutenant** *n.* капитáн авиáции; **~-sergeant** *n.* стáрший сержáнт авиáции.

flight[2] [flaɪt] *n.* бéгство, побéг; **put to ~** обра|щáть, -ти́ть в бéгство; **take (to) ~** обра|щáться, -ти́ться в бéгство.

flighty ['flaɪtɪ] *adj.* вéтреный, капри́зный.

flimsiness ['flɪmzɪnɪs] *n.* тóнкость, непрóчность.

flimsy ['flɪmzɪ] *adj.* тóнкий, непрóчный; **a ~ dress** óчень лёгкое плáтье; **a ~ structure** непрóчная пострóйка; **a ~ excuse** слáбое оправдáние.

flinch [flɪntʃ] *v.i.* (*wince*) вздр|áгивать, -óгнуть.

fling [flɪŋ] *n.* **1.** (*throw*) бросóк. **2.** (*attempt*) попы́тка. **3.: Highland ~** шотлáндский тáнец. **5.: he had his ~** он повесели́лся/нагуля́лся вдóволю.

v.t.: **~ o.s. into a chair** бр|осáться, -óситься в крéсло; **he flung himself into the project** он с головóй окунýлся в осуществлéние проéкта; **he was flung into prison** егó брóсили в тюрьмý; **she flung her arms around me** онá обнялá меня́.

with advs.: **~ o.s. about** разбрáсываться (*impf.*); **~ one's money around** транжи́рить (*impf.*) дéньги; **he flung her aside** он оттолкнýл её в стóрону; **she flung her clothes off** онá сбрóсила с себя́ одéжду; **~ open the window** распáх|ивать, -нýть окнó; **he was flung out** егó вы́швырнули вон; **he flung a few things together** он нáскоро собрáл свои́ вéщи; **she flung up her arms in horror** онá в ýжасе всплеснýла рукáми.

flint [flɪnt] *n.* крéмень (*m.*).

flip [flɪp] *n.* **1.** (*drink*) флип; **egg ~** яи́чный флип. **2.** (*coll., short flight*) корóткий полёт. **3.** (*coll.*): **the ~ side of a record** обрáтная сторонá пласти́нки.

v.t. щёлк|ать, -нуть.

flip-flop ['flɪpflɒp] *n.* **1.** (*noise*) шлёпанье, хлóпанье. **2.** (*backward somersault*) сáльто-мортáле (*indecl.*). **3.** (*footwear*) вьетнáмка.

flippancy ['flɪpənsɪ] *n.* легкомы́слие, вéтреность.

flippant ['flɪpənt] *adj.* легкомы́сленный, вéтреный.

flipper ['flɪpə(r)] *n.* плавни́к, ласт.

flirt [flɜ:t] *n.* кокéтка; люби́тель (*m.*) поухáживать.

v.i. флиртовáть (*impf.*) (с+*i.*); кокéтничать (*impf.*) (с+*i.*); (*fig.*): **~ with danger** игрáть (*impf.*) с огнём.

flirtation [flɜ:'teɪʃ(ə)n] *n.* флирт; кокéтство (*fig.*) игрá.

flirtatious [flɜ:'teɪʃəs] *adj.* кокéтливый.

flit [flɪt] *n.*: **the tenants did a moonlight ~** жильцы́ потихóньку смы́лись (*coll.*).

v.i. (*fly lightly*) порх|áть, -нýть.

float [fləʊt] *n.* **1.** (*for supporting line or net*) поплавóк, буй. **2.** (*cart*) платфóрма на колёсах; **milk ~** электрокáр для развóзки молокá.

v.t. спус|кáть, -ти́ть нá воду; (*comm.*): **~ a company** учре|ждáть, -ди́ть акционéрное óбщество; **~ a loan** разм|ещáть, -сти́ть заём.

v.i. **1.** плáвать (*indet.*), плыть (*det.*); **oil ~s on water** мáсло не тóнет в водé; **the boat ~ed downriver** лóдку неслó течéнием вниз по рекé. **2.** (*in air*) (*aeroplane*) плани́ровать (*impf.*); (*clouds etc.*) плыть (*det.*). **3.** (*fig.*): **his past ~ed before him** егó прóшлое пронеслóсь пéред ним.

floating ['fləʊtɪŋ] *adj.* плáвающий, плавýчий; **~ bridge** понтóнный/наплавнóй мост; **~ capital** оборóтный капитáл; **~ population** текýчее народонаселéние.

flock [flɒk] *n.* (*of birds*) стáя; (*of sheep or goats*) стáдо; (*of people*) толпá; (*relig.*) пáства.

v.i. стекáться (*impf.*); дви́гаться (*impf.*) толпóй.

floe [fləʊ] *n.* плавýчая льди́на.

flog [flɒg] *v.t.* **1.** (*beat*) стегáть, от-; порóть, вы́-; сечь, вы́-. **2.** (*sell*) заг|оня́ть, -нáть; толк|áть, -нýть; (*both coll.*).

flood [flʌd] *n.* **1.** (*tide*) прили́в. **2.** (*inundation*) наводнéние, половóдье; **the F~** (*bibl.*) потóп; **the river is in ~** рекá разлилáсь. **3.** (*torrent of water*) потóк. **4.** (*fig.*): **she burst into ~s of tears** онá разрыдáлась.

v.t. затоп|ля́ть, -и́ть; наводн|я́ть, -и́ть; **the basement was ~ed** подвáл затопи́ло; **he was ~ed with replies** óтклики так и посы́пались на негó.

v.i. разл|ивáться, -и́ться; выходи́ть, вы́йти из берегóв.

cpds. **~-gate** *n.* шлюз; **~light** *n.* прожéктор; *v.t.* осве|щáть, -ти́ть прожéкторами; **~lighting** *n.* прожéкторное освещéние; **~-plain** *n.* заливнóй луг; **~-tide** *n.* прили́в.

flooding ['flʌdɪŋ] *n.* затоплéние.

floor [flɔ:(r)] *n.* **1.** пол; **it fell to the ~** э́то упáло нá пол; **the child was playing on the ~** ребёнок игрáл на полý. **2.: take the ~** (*in public assembly*) брать, взять слóво; (*in dance hall*) вы́ступить (*pf.*) в тáнце. **3.: ground ~** пéрвый этáж. **4.: shop ~** цех; **threshing ~** гумнó.

v.t. **1.** (*provide floor for*) наст|илáть, -лáть пол в+*p.* **2.** (*coll., knock down*) сби|вáть, -ть с ног; (*fig., nonplus*) сра|жáть, -зи́ть; ошелом|ля́ть, -и́ть; **the question ~ed him** вопрóс срази́л егó.

cpds. **~board** *n.* полови́ца; **~-cloth** *n.* половáя тря́пка; **~-polish** *n.* масти́ка (для нати́рки полóв); **~-show** *n.* представлéние в кабарé; **~-space** *n.* плóщадь пóла.

flooring ['flɔ:rɪŋ] *n.* насти́л, пол.

flop [flɒp] *n.* (*motion, sound*) шлепóк, хлопóк; (*coll., failure*) провáл.

v.i. **1.** (*move limply*): **~ down in a chair** плюх|аться, -нуться в кресло; **~ around in slippers** шлёпать (*impf.*) в домашних туфлях. **2.** (*coll., fail*) провал|иваться, -иться.

cpds. **~-eared** *adj.* лопоухий; **~-house** *n.* (*US sl.*) ночлежка.

floppy ['flɒpɪ] *adj.* болтающийся, свисающий; мягкий, обвислый; **~ disk** (*comput.*) гибкий диск.

flora ['flɔːrə] *n.* флора.

floral ['flɔːr(ə)l, 'flɒ-] *adj.* цветочный; **~ tribute** подношение цветов.

floriculture ['flɒrɪ,kʌltʃə(r), 'flɔː-] *n.* цветоводство.

florid ['flɒrɪd] *adj.* (*ornate*) цветистый, витиеватый; (*ruddy*) красный, багровый.

florist ['flɒrɪst] *n.* продавец цветов.

floss [flɒs] *n.* шёлк-сырец; **candy ~** сахарная вата; **dental ~** шёлковая нить для чистки между зубами.

flotilla [flə'tɪlə] *n.* флотилия (мелких судов).

flounce[1] [flaʊns] *v.i.* бр|осаться, -оситься; **~ out (of a room)** вылетать, вылететь из комнаты.

flounce[2] [flaʊns] *n.* (*trimming*) оборка.

v.i. отдел|ывать, -ать оборками.

flounder[1] ['flaʊndə(r)] *n.* (*zool.*) мелкая камбала.

flounder[2] ['flaʊndə(r)] *v.i.* барахтаться (*impf.*); (*fig.*) путаться в словах.

flour ['flaʊə(r)] *n.* мука.

cpds. **~-bin** *n.* банка для муки; **~-mill** *n.* мукомольная мельница; мукомольня.

flourish ['flʌrɪʃ] *n.* **1.** (*wave of hand etc.*) широкий жест; размахивание. **2.** (*embellishment of literary style*) цветистость; (*fanfare*) фанфары (*f. pl.*); (*of penmanship*) росчерк, завитушка.

v.t. размахивать (*impf.*) +*i.*

v.i. (*grow healthily*) пышно расти (*impf.*); (*prosper; be active*) процветать (*impf.*).

flourishing ['flʌrɪʃɪŋ] *adj.* процветающий; **a ~ business** процветающее дело.

floury ['flaʊərɪ] *adj.* (*of potato*) рассыпчатый, мучнистый.

flout [flaʊt] *v.t.* поп|ирать, -рать; (*mock*) насмехаться (*impf.*) над+*i.*

flow [fləʊ] *n.* течение, поток; **ebb and ~** прилив и отлив; (*fig.*) течение; **interrupt the ~ of conversation** прер|ывать, -вать плавное течение разговора; **in full ~** в разгаре.

v.i. **1.** течь, литься (*both impf.*); **the wine ~ed freely** вино лилось рекой; **the Oka ~s into the Volga** Ока впадает в Волгу. **2.** (*fig., proceed, move freely*) литься (*impf.*); течь (*impf.*).

flower ['flaʊə(r)] *n.* цветок; цветковое растение; **in ~** в цвету; **come into ~** расцве|тать, -сти; **~ arrangement** расположение цветов; **~ show** выставка цветов.

v.i. (*blossom; flourish*) цвести (*impf.*).

cpds. **~-bed** *n.* клумба; **~-girl** *n.* цветочница; **~-pot** *n.* цветочный горшок.

flowering ['flaʊərɪŋ] *n.* цветение.

adj. цветущий.

flowery ['flaʊərɪ] *adj.* покрытый цветами; (*fig.*) цветистый.

flowing ['fləʊɪŋ] *adj.*: **~ hair** развевающиеся волосы; **~ lines** мягкие/плавные линии; **~ style** гладкий стиль.

flu [fluː] *n.* (*coll.*) грипп; **go down with ~** слечь (*pf.*) с гриппом.

fluctuate ['flʌktjʊ,eɪt] *v.i.* колебаться (*impf.*).

fluctuation [,flʌktjʊ'eɪʃ(ə)n] *n.* колебание.

flue [fluː] *n.* дымоход.

fluency ['fluːənsɪ] *n.* плавность, беглость.

fluent ['fluːənt] *adj.* плавный, беглый; **he speaks Russian ~ly** он свободно говорит по-русски.

fluff [flʌf] *n.* пух, пушок.

v.t. взби|вать, -ть; распушить (*pf.*); **~ up a cushion** взби|вать, -ть подушку; **the bird ~ed out its feathers** птица распушила перья.

fluffy ['flʌfɪ] *adj.* пушистый, взбитый.

fluid ['fluːɪd] *n.* жидкость; **cleaning ~** жидкость для чистки; **correction ~** белил|а (*pl., g.* —).

adj. жидкий, текучий.

fluidity [,fluː'ɪdɪtɪ] *n.* текучесть.

fluke[1] [fluːk] *n.* (*lucky stroke*) (неожиданная) удача, случайность.

fluke[2] [fluːk] *n.* (*worm*) глист.

flunk [flʌŋk] *v.t. & i.* (*US coll.*): **he ~ed his exam** он провалился/засыпался на экзамене.

flunkey ['flʌŋkɪ] *n.* лакей.

fluoresce [flʊə'res] *v.i.* флюоресцировать (*impf.*).

fluorescence [flʊə'res(ə)ns] *n.* флюоресценция.

fluorescent [flʊə'res(ə)nt] *adj.* флюоресцентный.

fluoride ['flʊəraɪd] *n.* фторид.

fluoridize ['flʊərɪdaɪz] *v.t.* фторировать (*impf., pf.*).

fluorine ['flʊəriːn] *n.* фтор.

fluor|ite ['flʊəraɪt], **-spar** ['flʊəspɑː(r)] *nn.* флюорит; плавиковый шпат.

flurry ['flʌrɪ] *n.* (*gust, squall*) шквал; (*agitation*) волнение, суматоха.

flush[1] [flʌʃ] *n.* (*flow of water*) внезапный прилив; поток; (*flow of blood; blush*) прилив крови; румянец; краска на лице; **hot ~** приступ лихорадки; (*fig.*): **in the ~ of youth** в расцвете юности.

v.t. **1.** (*swill clean*) пром|ывать, -ыть; **~ the lavatory** спус|кать, -тить воду в уборной. **2.: he is ~ed with pride** его распирает гордость.

v.i. краснеть, по-; зал|иваться, -иться краской.

flush[2] [flʌʃ] *n.* (*cards*) карты одной масти; **royal ~** флешь-рояль, коронка.

flush[3] [flʌʃ] *adj.* **1.** (*coll., well supplied with money*): **he is ~** у него денег куры не клюют. **2.** (*on the same level*) заподлицо (*adv.*); (находящийся) на одном уровне (*с чем*).

fluster ['flʌstə(r)] *v.t.* волновать, вз-; будоражить, вз-.

flute[1] [fluːt] *n.* флейта.

fluted ['fluːtɪd] *adj.* гофрированный, рифлёный.

flutter ['flʌtə(r)] *n.* **1.** (*of wings, leaves, flags etc.*) трепетание, дрожь. **2.** (*agitation*) волнение, трепет; **to be in a ~ of expectation** с трепетом ждать (*impf.*). **3.** (*gambling venture*) риск.

v.t. мах|ать, -нуть +*i.*; (*fig., agitate*) прив|одить, -ести в трепет; взволновать (*pf.*).

v.i. трепетать (*impf.*); (*of birds*) переп|архивать, -орхнуть.

flux [flʌks] *n.* **1.** (*succession of changes*) постоянная смена; **everything was in a state of ~** всё было в состоянии непрерывного изменения. **2.** (*metall.*) флюс, плавень (*m.*).

fly[1] [flaɪ] *n.* муха; (*fig.*): **~ in the ointment** ложка дёгтя в бочке мёду.

cpds. **~-blown** *adj.* засиженный мухами; **~-catcher** *n.* (*bird*) мухоловка; **~-paper** *n.* липкая бумага от мух; **~-spray** *n.* аэрозоль (*m.*) от мух; **~-weight** *n.* вес «мухи»; наилегчайший боксёрский вес.

fly[2] [flaɪ] *n.*: (*on trousers*) ширинка; **his ~ is open, undone** у него ширинка расстёгнута.

cpds. **~-button** *n.* пуговица ширинки; **~-leaf** *n.* форзац; **~-wheel** *n.* маховое колесо, маховик.

fly[3] [flaɪ] *v.t.* **~ the Atlantic** перелет|ать, -еть через Атлантический океан; **~ an aircraft** управлять (*impf.*) самолётом; **~ a kite** запус|кать, -тить змея; (*fig., put out feeler or lure*) пус|кать, -тить пробный шар; **~ a flag** вывешивать, вывесить флаг; (*naut.*) носить, нести флаг; **~ the British flag** плавать (*indet.*) под британским флагом.

v.i. **1.** (*move through the air*) летать (*indet.*), лететь, по- (*det.*); **as the crow flies** напрямик; по прямой; **he has never flown** он никогда не летал;

~ **in the face of fortune** искуша́ть (*impf.*) судьбу́. **2.** (*move or pass swiftly*) пролет|а́ть, -е́ть; **I must ~!** ну, я побежа́л!; **the dog flew at him** соба́ка бро́силась за ним; ~ **into a passion** вспыли́ть (*pf.*); ~ **to s.o.'s defence** бро́ситься (*pf.*) на защи́ту кого́-н.; **let ~ (at s.o.)** вы́ругать (*pf.*) кого́-н.; **send ~ing** швыр|я́ть, -ну́ть; (*of pers.*) сби|ва́ть, -ть с ног; **time flies** вре́мя лети́т; **the flag is ~ing** флаг развева́ется. **3.** (*flee*) бежа́ть (*det.*); **the bird has flown** (*fig.*) пти́чка улете́ла.

with advs.: **leaves were ~ing about** повсю́ду кружи́лись ли́стья; ~ **away** улет|а́ть, -е́ть; **the plane flew in to refuel and flew off again** самолёт прилете́л на запра́вку и вновь/сно́ва улете́л; ~ **off at a tangent** сорва́ться (*pf.*); отклон|я́ться, -и́ться; **the door flew open** дверь распахну́лась на́стеж.

cpds. **~over** *n.* (*bridge, overpass*) эстака́да; путепро́вод; **~-past** *n.* возду́шный пара́д.

flyer, flier ['flaɪə(r)] *n.* (*aviator*) лётчик.

flying ['flaɪɪŋ] *n.* полёт; **he likes ~** он лю́бит лета́ть; ~ **instructor** лётчик-инстру́ктор; ~ **school** лётная шко́ла.

adj.: ; **pass with ~ colours** пройти́ (*pf.*) с бле́ском; ~ **leap** прыжо́к с разбе́га; **F~ Officer** ста́рший лейтена́нт авиа́ции; ~ **saucer** лета́ющее блю́дце; **F~ Squad** специа́льный отря́д полице́йских для бы́строго налёта; **off to a ~ start** с ме́ста в карье́р; **pay a ~ visit** нанести́ (*pf.*) мимолётный визи́т.

cpds. **~-fish** *n.* лету́чая ры́ба; **~-machine** *n.* лета́тельный аппара́т.

FM *abbr. of* **1.** ***Field Marshal*** фельдма́ршал. **2.** ***frequency modulation***: ~ **radio** часто́тно-модули́рованное ра́дио.

FO (*abbr. of* ***Foreign Office***) Министе́рство иностра́нных дел, Фо́рин О́фис.

foal [fəʊl] *n.* жеребёнок.

foam [fəʊm] *n.* пе́на; ~ **rubber** по́ристая рези́на; пенопла́ст.

v.i. пе́ниться (*impf.*).

fob [fɒb] *v.t.*: ~ **s.o. off with promises** корми́ть (*impf.*) кого́-н. обеща́ниями; ~ **off a cheap article on s.o.** всучи́ть (*pf.*) кому́-н. каку́ю-н. дешёвку.

focal ['fəʊk(ə)l] *adj.* фо́кусный; ~ **distance, length** фо́кусное расстоя́ние; (*fig.*): **the ~ point in his argument** гла́вный пункт его́ доказа́тельств.

focus ['fəʊkəs] *n.* (*math., phys., phot.*) фо́кус; **bring into ~** поме|ща́ть, -сти́ть в фо́кусе; **out of ~** не в фо́кусе; (*fig.*) центр, средото́чие; **he became the ~ of interest** он оказа́лся в це́нтре внима́ния.

v.t. сосредото́чи|вать, -ть.

fodder ['fɒdə(r)] *n.* корм для скота́; фура́ж.

foe [fəʊ] *n.* враг.

foetal, fetal ['fi:t(ə)l] *adj.* заро́дышевый, эмбриона́льный; ~ **position** положе́ние эмбрио́на (в ма́тке).

foetus, fetus ['fi:təs] *n.* плод, заро́дыш.

fog [fɒg] *n.* тума́н; (*phot.*) вуа́ль; (*fig.*): **in a ~** как в тума́не.

v.t. оку́т|ывать, -ать тума́ном; затума́ни|вать, -ть; (*fig.*): **the windows are ~ged up** о́кна запоте́ли.

cpds. **~-bound** *adj.* оку́танный тума́ном; **~-horn** *n.* тума́нный горн; **~-lamp** *n.* фа́ра с цветны́ми стёклами.

fog(e)y ['fəʊgɪ] *n.* старомо́дный/отста́лый челове́к.

fogg|y ['fɒgɪ] *adj.* тума́нный; (*fig.*): **I haven't the ~iest idea** я не име́ю ни мале́йшего представле́ния.

foible ['fɔɪb(ə)l] *n.* сла́бость; сла́бая стру́нка.

foil[1] [fɔɪl] *n.* (*thin metal*) фольга́, стани́оль (*m.*); (*fig., contrast*) контра́ст, противопоставле́ние.

foil[2] [fɔɪl] *n.* (*fencing sword*) рапи́ра.

foil[3] [fɔɪl] *v.t.* сби|ва́ть, -ть со сле́да; расстр|а́ивать, -о́ить (*or* срыва́ть, сорва́ть) пла́ны +*g.*

foist [fɔɪst] *v.t.* навя́з|ывать, -а́ть (*что кому*).

fold[1] [fəʊld] *n.* скла́дка; **the ~s of a dress** скла́дки пла́тья; **a ~ in the hills** лощи́на.

v.t. **1.** (*double over*) скла́дывать, сложи́ть; св|ёртывать, -ерну́ть; ~ **one's arms** скре́|щивать, -сти́ть ру́ки на груди́; ~ **back the bedclothes** отки́|дывать, -нуть одея́ло; ~ **(up) the newspaper** скла́дывать, сложи́ть газе́ту. **2.** (*embrace*) обн|има́ть, -я́ть; **she ~ed the child in her arms** она́ заключи́ла ребёнка в объя́тия; **the hills were ~ ed in mist** холмы́ бы́ли оку́таны мглой.

v.i. скла́дываться, сложи́ться; (*fig.*): **the play ~ed after a week** пье́са сошла́ (со сце́ны) че́рез неде́лю.

fold[2] [fəʊld] *n.* (*for sheep*) заго́н.

folder ['fəʊldə(r)] *n.* скоросшива́тель (*m.*); па́пка-планше́т.

folding ['fəʊldɪŋ] *adj.* складно́й; ~ **doors** складны́е две́ри.

cpds. **~-bed** *n.* раскладу́шка; **~-chair** *n.* складно́й стул.

foliage ['fəʊlɪɪdʒ] *n.* листва́; ~ **plant** ли́ственное расте́ние.

folio ['fəʊlɪəʊ] *n.* (*book*) фолиа́нт; (*ledger sheet*) лист бухга́лтерской кни́ги.

folk [fəʊk] *n.* **1.** (*sing. or pl., coll., persons*) наро́д, лю́д|и (*pl., g.* -е́й); **the old ~s** старики́; роди́тели (*both m. pl.*); **old ~s' home** дом для престаре́лых. **2.** (*pl., coll., relatives*) родня́, родны́е (*pl.*).

cpds. **~lore** *n.* фолькло́р; **~-music** *n.* наро́дная му́зыка; **~-song** *n.* наро́дная пе́сня.

folklorist ['fəʊk,lɔ:rɪst] *n.* фольклори́ст.

follicle ['fɒlɪk(ə)l] *n.* фолли́кул.

follow ['fɒləʊ] *v.t. & i.* **1.** (*proceed or happen after*) сле́довать, по- за+*i.*; **the dog ~s him about** соба́ка хо́дит за ним по пята́м; **he ~ed (in) his father's footsteps** он пошёл по стопа́м отца́; ~ **the crowd** (*fig.*) плыть (*det.*) по тече́нию; ~ **suit** (*fig.*) сле́довать, по- чьему́-н. приме́ру; **the frost was ~ed by a thaw** моро́з смени́лся о́ттепелью; **as ~s** сле́дующим о́бразом; как сле́дует ни́же; **his plan was as ~s** его́ план был тако́в. **2.** (*as inference*) сле́довать (*impf.*) из+*g.*; **it does not ~ that ...** э́то во́все не зна́чит, что... **3.** (*pursue*) следи́ть (*impf.*) за+*i.*; **he ~ed the ball with his eye** он следи́л за мячо́м; **don't look now, we're being ~ed** не огля́дывайтесь, но за на́ми следя́т; (*fig.*): ~ **one's bent** сле́довать (*impf.*) свои́м накло́нностям. **4.** (*keep to*) приде́рживаться (*impf.*) +*g.*; ~ **this road** сле́дуйте/иди́те по э́той доро́ге; ~ **the policy of one's predecessor** продолжа́ть (*impf.*) поли́тику своего́ предше́ственника; (*fig., engage in*): ~ **a trade** име́ть (*impf.*) профе́ссию; (*fig., be guided by*): ~ **s.o.'s advice/example** сле́довать, по- чьему́-н. сове́ту/приме́ру. **5.** (*fig., keep track of*): ~ **s.o.'s arguments** следи́ть (*impf.*) за хо́дом чьих-н. рассужде́ний; **I don t ~ you** я вас не понима́ю; ~ **the news in the papers** следи́ть (*impf.*) за новостя́ми в газе́тах.

with advs.: ~ **on** *v.t. & i.* сле́довать, по- (за+*i.*); ~ **through** *v.t. & i.* сле́довать (*impf.*) (за+*i.*) до конца́; ~ **up** *v.t.* дов|оди́ть, -ести́ до конца́; ~ **up an advantage** (*mil.*) разв|ива́ть, -и́ть успе́х; (*in general*) по́лностью испо́льзовать (*impf., pf.*) вы́годы положе́ния; ~ **up a clue** рассле́доватьули́ку; ~ **up a suggestion** уч|и́тывать, -е́сть чьё-н. предложе́ние.

follower ['fɒləʊwə(r)] *n.* после́дователь (*m.*); сторо́нник.

following ['fɒləʊwɪŋ] *n.* после́дователи (*m. pl.*); приве́рженцы (*m. pl.*).

adj. **1.** (*ensuing*) сле́дующий; **(on) the ~ day** на сле́дующий день; (*about to be specified*): **we shall need the ~** нам потре́буется сле́дующее. **2.** (*coming behind*) попу́тный; **a ~ tide** попу́тное тече́ние.

folly ['fɒlɪ] *n.* (*foolishness*) безрассу́дство, глу́пость; (*caprice*) причу́да, капри́з.

foment [fə'ment, fəʊ-] *v.t.* класть, положи́ть припа́рку к+*d.*; (*fig.*) подстрек|а́ть, -ну́ть.

fond [fɒnd] *adj.* **1.** (*pred.*, *with* **of**): **he became ~ of her** он привяза́лся к ней; **are you ~ of music?** вы лю́бите му́зыку? **2.** (*loving*) не́жный, лю́бящий. **3.** (*credulous*) дове́рчивый.

fondle ['fɒnd(ə)l] *v.t.* ласка́ть (*impf.*); гла́дить, по-.

font[1] [fɒnt] *n.* (*eccl.*) купе́ль.

font[2] [fɒnt] *n.* (*US*, *typ.*) = **fount 2.**

food [fu:d] *n.* пи́ща, пита́ние; еда́; **~ supplies** продово́льственные припа́сы (*m. pl.*); **~ and drink** еда́ и питьё; **go without ~** голода́ть (*impf.*); **baby ~** де́тское пита́ние; (*fig.*): **~ for thought** пи́ща для размышле́ний.

cpds. **~-processor** *n.* ку́хонный комба́йн; **~-store** *n.* продово́льственный магази́н; **~stuff** *n.* пищево́й проду́кт.

fool [fu:l] *n.* (*simpleton*) дура́к, глупе́ц; **any ~ could do that** э́то ка́ждый дура́к мо́жет; **he is nobody's ~** он совсе́м не дура́к; **like a ~, I told him** я был так глуп, что сказа́л ему́; (*jester*) шут; **~'s cap** шутовско́й колпа́к; **play the ~** дура́читься (*impf.*); валя́ть (*impf.*) дурака́; **April ~** одура́ченный пе́рвого апре́ля; **All F~s' Day** пе́рвое апре́ля; **make a ~ (out) of s.o.** дура́чить, о- кого́-н.; **make a ~ of o.s.** ста́вить, по- себя́ в дура́цкое положе́ние.

v.t. (*delude*, *deceive*) одура́чи|вать, -ть; **he was ~ed into going there** обма́ном его́ убеди́ли пойти́ туда́.

v.i. дура́читься (*impf.*); **~ about, around** валя́ть (*impf.*) дурака́.

cpd. **~proof** *adj.* безотка́зный; несло́жный.

foolhardiness ['fu:l,hɑ:dɪnɪs] *n.* безрассу́дная хра́брость.

foolhardy ['fu:l,hɑ:dɪ] *adj.* безрассу́дно хра́брый.

foolish ['fu:lɪʃ] *adj.* глу́пый; дура́цкий.

foot [fʊt] *n.* **1.** (*extremity of leg*) ступня́, нога́; стопа́ ноги́; (*dim.*) но́жка; (*of an animal*) ла́па; (*of a garment*) низ, подо́л; (*of a chair*) но́жка; (*lowest part*, *bottom*) ни́жняя часть, ни́жний край; **at the ~ of the hill** у подно́жия холма́; **at the ~ of the page** в конце́ страни́цы; **at the ~ of the stairs** внизу́ ле́стницы; **at the ~ of the bed** в нога́х крова́ти.

phrr.: **we came here on ~** мы пришли́ сюда́ пешко́м; **she is on her feet all day** она́ це́лый день на нога́х; **he was on his feet in an instant** он то́тчас вскочи́л на́ ноги; **the business got off on the wrong ~** де́ло с са́мого нача́ла пошло́ не так; **she was swept off her feet** (*fig.*) она́ потеря́ла го́лову; **he fell on his feet** (*fig.*) он сча́стливо отде́лался; **find one's feet** нащу́п|ывать, -ать по́чву под нога́ми; **get, rise to one's feet** подня́ться, вста́ть (*both pf.*); **have one ~ in the grave** стоя́ть (*impf.*) одно́й ного́й в моги́ле; **have both feet on the ground** (*fig.*) кре́пко стоя́ть (*impf.*) на нога́х; **keep one's feet** уде́рживаться (*pf.*) на нога́х; **kneel at s.o.'s feet** пасть (*pf.*) на коле́ни пе́ред кем-н.; **put one's ~ down** (*fig.*) заня́ть (*pf.*) твёрдую пози́цию; (*accelerate*) дать (*pf.*) га́зу; **put one's ~ in it** (*fig.*) дать (*pf.*) ма́ху; **put one's feet up** (*fig.*) отдыха́ть (*impf.*); **set ~ in** вступи́ть (*pf.*) в+*a.*; **stand on one's own (two) feet** стоя́ть (*impf.*) на свои́х нога́х; быть самостоя́тельным; **trample under ~** поп|ира́ть, -ра́ть; **wipe one's feet** вытира́ть, вы́тереть но́ги. **2.** (*unit of length*) фут; **six ~ (*or* feet) tall** шести́ фу́тов ро́стом. **3.** (*infantry*) пехо́та.

v.t.: **~ the bill** опла́|чивать, -ти́ть счёт.

cpds. **~-and-mouth** (*disease*) я́щур; **~ball** *n.* футбо́л; **~ball player** футболи́ст; **~baller** *n.* футболи́ст; **~-brake** *n.* ножно́й то́рмоз; **~bridge** *n.* пешехо́дный мо́стик; **~hills** *n.* предго́рье; **~hold** *n.* то́чка опо́ры; (*mil.*) опо́рный пункт; **~lights** *n.* ра́мпа (*sg.*); **~man** *n.* лаке́й; **~note** *n.* сно́ска; **~path** *n.* тропа́, тропи́нка; **~print** *n.* след ноги́; **~-soldier** *n.* пехоти́нец; **~sore** *adj.* со стёртыми нога́ми; **~step** *n.* шаг, по́ступь; **~stool** *n.* скаме́ечка для ног; **~wear** *n.* о́бувь.

footing ['fʊtɪŋ] *n.* (*foothold*) опо́ра для ног(и́); **lose one's ~** оступи́ться (*pf.*); (*fig.*) потеря́ть (*pf.*) по́чву под нога́ми; **on an equal ~** на ра́вной ноге́; **the army was placed on a war ~** а́рмия была́ введена́ в боеву́ю гото́вность.

footling ['fu:tlɪŋ] *adj.* (*coll.*) пустя́чный, ерундо́вый.

fop [fɒp] *n.* фат, хлыщ, щёголь (*m.*).

foppish ['fɒpɪʃ] *adj.* фатова́тый, щеголева́тый.

for [fə(r), fɔ:(r)] *prep.* **1.** (*with the object or purpose of*) для+*g.*; ра́ди+*g.*; **~ example** наприме́р; **I did it ~ fun** я сде́лал э́то для сме́ху; **~ a laugh** шу́тки ра́ди; **~ the sake of peace** ра́ди ми́ра; **they have gone ~ a walk** они́ отпра́вились гуля́ть; **who's coming ~ dinner?** кто придёт к у́жину?; **what ~?** заче́м?; **a house ~ sale** дом на прода́жу; **save up ~ a house** копи́ть (*impf.*) (де́ньги) на поку́пку до́ма; **he sent ~ the doctor** он посла́л за врачо́м; **I've come ~ the rent** я пришёл получи́ть за кварти́ру; **run ~ a train** бежа́ть (*det.*), по- к по́езду; **run ~ it!** беги́те изо всех сил!; (*destination*) на+*a.*; к+*d.*; **the train ~ Moscow** по́езд на Москву́; **he made ~ the exit** он напра́вился к вы́ходу; **he left ~ home** он отпра́вился домо́й; **where are you ~?** куда́ вы направля́етесь? **you're in ~ a shock** вас ждёт больша́я неприя́тность; (*aspiration*): **who could ask ~ more?** чего́ же ещё жела́ть?; **he begged ~ money** он проси́л де́нег; **a cry ~ help** крик о по́мощи; **oh ~ a drink!** эх, вы́пить бы!; **greed ~ money** жа́дность к деньга́м; **longing ~ home** тоска́ по ро́дине; **demand ~ coal** спрос на у́голь; **prospecting ~ oil** разве́дка на нефть. **2.** (*denoting reason*;*on account of*) ра́ди+*g.*, для+*g.*; **cry ~ joy** пла́кать (*impf.*) от ра́дости; **~ fear of being found out** из боя́зни разоблаче́ния; **grateful ~ help** благода́рный за по́мощь; **you can't move here ~ books** из-за книг здесь не́где поверну́ться; **he can't see the wood ~ trees** он за дере́вьями не ви́дит ле́са; **~ the love of God** ра́ди Бо́га; **~ shame!** как не сты́дно; **but ~ me he would have died** ка́бы не я, он бы у́мер; **he is known ~ his generosity** он изве́стен свое́й ще́дростью; **they married ~ love** они́ жени́лись по любви́; (*accorded to*): **the penalty ~ treason is death** наказа́ние за изме́ну — сме́ртная казнь; **a prize ~ a novel** пре́мия за рома́н; **a decoration ~ bravery** о́рден за отва́гу; (*on the occasion of*): **I gave him a book ~ his birthday** я подари́л ему́ кни́гу на день рожде́ния; **he went abroad ~ his holidays** он пое́хал за грани́цу в о́тпуск; **she wore black ~ the funeral** она́ наде́ла всё чёрное на по́хороны; **the church was decorated ~ Easter** це́рковь была́ укра́шена к Па́схе; **what are we having ~ dinner?** что у нас на у́жин? **3.** (*representative of*): **A ~ Anna** А как в сло́ве «А́нна»; **the member (of parliament) ~ Oxford** член парла́мента из О́ксфорда; **red is ~ danger** кра́сный цвет знамену́ет опа́сность; (*in support*; *in favour of*); **a vote ~ freedom** го́лос за свобо́ду; **I'm all ~ it** я по́лностью за (э́то); **stand up ~ one's rights** отст|а́ивать, -оя́ть свои́ права́; (*denoting purpose*): **they need premises ~ a school** им ну́жно помеще́ние под шко́лу; **a report ~ the director** докладна́я на и́мя дире́ктора; **a candidate ~ the presidium** кандида́т в прези́диум; **the order ~ retreat** прика́з об отступле́нии; **this barrel is meant ~ wine** э́та бо́чка предназна́чена под вино́; **ready ~ departure** гото́в к отъе́зду; (*on behalf of*) за+*a.*, от+*g.*; **speak ~ yourself!** говори́те за себя́!; **see ~ yourself!** смотри́те са́ми!; **pray ~ the sick** моли́ться (*impf.*) за больны́х. **4.** (*denoting intended recipient*): **a dinner ~ 10 people** обе́д на де́сять челове́к; **there is a letter ~ you** вам письмо́; **votes**

~ women пра́во го́лоса для же́нщин. **5.** (*denoting duration or extent*): **~ a time** на вре́мя; **he stayed ~ the night** он оста́лся на́ ночь; **he was away ~ ages** он о́чень до́лго был в отъе́зде; **I haven't seen him ~ (some) days** я не ви́дел его́ не́сколько дней; **the forest stretches ~ miles** лес простира́ется на не́сколько киломе́тров; **a weather report ~ the past week** сво́дка пого́ды за про́шлую неде́лю; (*intended duration*): **~ ever and ever** навсегда́; **I've lost it ~ good** я навсегда́ потеря́л его́/её; **I shan't stay ~ long** я до́лго не задержу́сь; **they are going away ~ a few days** они́ уезжа́ют на не́сколько дней. **6.** (*denoting relationship*; *in respect of*): **I ~ my part ...** со свое́й стороны́, я...; **~ the rest** что каса́ется остально́го; **as ~ me, myself** что каса́ется меня́; **he is hard up ~ money** у него́ пло́хо с деньга́ми; **luckily ~ her** к сча́стью для неё; **~ one thing it's too short, and ~ another I don't like it** во-пе́рвых, э́то о́чень ко́ротко, во-вторы́х, мне э́то не нра́вится; (*responsive to*): **an eye ~ a bargain** намётанный глаз на вы́годную поку́пку; **an ear ~ music** музыка́льный слух; **a weakness ~ sweets** сла́бость к сла́дкому; (*in relation to what is normal or suitable*): **warm ~ the time of year** тепло́ для э́того вре́мени го́да; **cold ~ summer** не по ле́тнему холо́дный; **he is too thoughtful ~ his age** он заду́мчив не по лета́м; **not bad ~ a beginner** для новичка́ непло́хо; **that's no job ~ a woman** э́то не же́нская рабо́та. **7.** (*in return ~*, *instead of*): **an eye ~ an eye** о́ко за о́ко; **new lamps ~ old** но́вые ла́мпы вме́сто ста́рых; **get something ~ nothing** получи́ть (*pf.*) что-н. да́ром; **not ~ the world** ни за что (на све́те); **once (and) ~ all** раз и навсегда́; **seven ~ a pound** семь штук на фунт; **how many books can I buy ~ that money?** ско́лько книг я смогу́ купи́ть на э́ти де́ньги?; **you'll pay ~ this!** вы мне за э́то запла́тите! **8.** (*as being*; *in the capacity of*): **what do you take me ~?** за кого́ вы меня́ принима́ете?; **take sth. ~ granted** приня́ть (*pf.*) что-н. как само́ собо́й разуме́ющееся. **9.** (*up to*; *incumbent upon*): **it's ~ you to decide** вам реша́ть; **it's not ~ me to say** не мне́ об э́том говори́ть. **10.** (*despite*): **~ all that, I still love him** несмотря́ на всё э́то, я его́ люблю́. **11.** (*ethic dative*): **there's gratitude ~ you!** и вот вам благода́рность! **12.** (*with certain expressions of time*): **~ the first time** в пе́рвый раз; **~ the last time, will you shut up!** говорю́ тебе́ в после́дний раз — замолчи́!; **~ once I agree with you** на э́тот раз я с ва́ми согла́сен; **the wedding is arranged ~ June the 1st** сва́дьба назна́чена на пе́рвое ию́ня. **13.** (*with following inf.*): **it will be better ~ us all to leave** бу́дет лу́чше нам всем уйти́; **it was absurd ~ him to do that** э́то бы́ло неле́по с его́ стороны́. **14.**: **~ all I know, he may he there already** почём я зна́ю, мо́жет быть он уже́ там; **~ all his boasting** при всём его́ хвастовстве́; **you can go away ~ all I care** а по мне — хоть сейча́с уходи́те.

conj. так как, и́бо.

forage ['fɒrɪdʒ] *n.* фура́ж, корм.

v.i. (*search*) разы́скивать (*impf.*).

foray ['fɒreɪ] *n.* набе́г.

forbear[1] ['fɔːbeə(r)] *n.* = **forebear**

forbear[2] [fɔː'beə(r)] *v.t. & i.* возде́рж|иваться, -а́ться (*от чего*); быть терпели́вым.

forbearance [fɔː'beərəns] *n.* возде́ржанность, терпели́вость.

forbid [fə'bɪd] *v.t.* запре|ща́ть, -ти́ть (*кому что*); **God ~!** Бо́же упаси́!

forbidden [fə'bɪd(ə)n] *adj.* запрещённый, запре́тный.

forbidding [fə'bɪdɪŋ] *adj.* (*unfriendly*) неприя́зненный; (*threatening*) гро́зный; **a ~ air** непристу́пный вид.

force [fɔːs] *n.* **1.** (*strength*: *lit.*, *fig.*) си́ла; **use ~** приб|ега́ть, -е́гнуть к си́ле; **in full ~** в по́лном соста́ве; **by ~** си́лой, наси́льно; **from ~ of habit** в си́лу привы́чки; **by ~ of circumstance(s)** в си́лу обстоя́тельств; **the ~s of darkness** си́лы тьмы́. **2.** (*body of men*, *usu. armed*) вооружённый отря́д; **he attacked with a small ~** он атакова́л с небольши́м отря́дом; **Air F~** вое́нно-возду́шные си́лы; **(Police) F~** поли́ция; (*pl.*) **the (Armed) F~s** вооружённые си́лы. **3.** (*binding power*, *validity*) де́йственность; **the agreement has the ~ of law** э́то соглаше́ние име́ет си́лу зако́на; **in ~** (*of law etc.*) в си́ле; **come into ~** вступ|а́ть, -и́ть в си́лу; (*significance*, *cogency*) смысл, значе́ние. **4.** (*phys.*) си́ла; **the ~ of gravity** си́ла притяже́ния.

v.t. **1.** (*compel*, *constrain*) заст|авля́ть, -а́вить; прин|ужда́ть, -у́дить; **he was ~ed to sell the house** он был вы́нужден прода́ть дом; **you are not ~d to answer** вы не обя́заны отвеча́ть; **~ s.o.'s hand** прин|ужда́ть, -у́дить кого́-н. к де́йствию; **~d** (*laugh etc.*) принуждённый; **~d labour** принуди́тельный труд; **~d landing** вы́нужденная поса́дка. **2.** (*effect by ~*): **~ an entry** вл|а́мываться, -оми́ться; (*apply ~ to*): **~ (open) the door** выла́мывать, вы́ломать дверь; **~ a lock** взл|а́мывать, -ома́ть замо́к. **3.** (*increase under stress*): **~ the pace** уск|оря́ть, -о́рить шаг; (*produce under stress*): **~ a laugh** смея́ться (*impf.*) че́рез си́лу. **4.** (*cause accelerated growth*): **~ plants** уск|оря́ть, -о́рить рост расте́ний.

cpds. **~-feed** *v.t.* корми́ть (*impf.*) наси́льно; **~-feeding** *n.* наси́льственное кормле́ние.

forceful ['fɔːsfʊl] *adj.* си́льный, убеди́тельный.

forceps ['fɔːseps] *n.* хирурги́ческие щипц|ы́ (*pl.*, *g.* -о́в).

forcible ['fɔːsɪb(ə)l] *adj.* наси́льственный; **~ entry** наси́льственное вторже́ние.

ford [fɔːd] *n.* брод.

v.t. пере|ходи́ть, -йти́ вброд.

fore [fɔː(r)] *n.* **1.**: **he finished the race well to the ~** он зако́нчил бег, намно́го опереди́в други́х; **this subject has recently come to the ~** в после́днее вре́мя э́тот вопро́с оказа́лся в це́нтре внима́ния. **2.** (*naut.*) нос; носова́я часть.

adj. пере́дний; (*naut.*) носово́й; (*as pref.*) пред...

adv. впереди́; **~ and aft** на носу́ и на корме́.

forearm ['fɔːrɑːm] *n.* предпле́чье.

forebear ['fɔːbeə(r)] *n.* пре́док.

forebode [fɔː'bəʊd] *v.t.* предвеща́ть (*impf.*) (дурно́е).

foreboding [fɔː'bəʊdɪŋ] *n.* дурно́е предчу́вствие.

forecast ['fɔːkɑːst] *n.* предсказа́ние; **weather ~** прогно́з пого́ды.

v.t. & i. предска́з|ывать, -а́ть; **weather ~ing** сино́птика.

forecaster ['fɔːkɑːstə(r)] *n.*: **weather ~** сино́птик.

forecastle ['fəʊks(ə)l] *n.* (*naut.*) бак.

forecourt ['fɔːkɔːt] *n.* пере́дний двор.

forefather ['fɔːˌfɑːðə(r)] *n.* пре́док.

forefinger ['fɔːˌfɪŋgə(r)] *n.* указа́тельный па́лец.

forefront ['fɔːfrʌnt] *n.*: **in the ~ of the battle** на передово́й (ли́нии).

forego[1] [fɔː'gəʊ] *v.i.* (*precede*) предше́ствовать (*impf.*) +*d.*; **the ~ing** вышеупомя́нутое; **a ~ne conclusion** предрешённый исхо́д.

forego[2] [fɔː'gəʊ] = **forgo**

foreground ['fɔːgraʊnd] *n.* (*lit.*, *fig.*) пере́дний план.

forehand ['fɔːhænd] *n.* (*tennis*) уда́р спра́ва.

forehead ['fɒrɪd, 'fɔːhed] *n.* лоб.

foreign ['fɒrɪn, 'fɒrən] *adj.* **1.** (*of or pertaining to another country or countries*) иностра́нный, заграни́чный; **~ affairs** междунаро́дные дела́; **Ministry of F~ Affairs** Министе́рство иностра́нных дел; **~ policy** вне́шняя поли́тика; **~ trade** вне́шняя торго́вля; **in ~ parts** в чужи́х края́х. **2.** (*alien*) чужо́й, чу́ждый; **~ soil** чужа́я земля́. **3.** (*med.*) иноро́дный; **~ body** (*lit.*, *fig.*) иноро́дное те́ло.

foreigner [ˈfɒrɪnə(r), ˈfɒrənə(r)] *n.* иностра́н|ец (*fem.* -ка).
foreleg [ˈfɔːleg] *n.* пере́дняя ла́па/нога́.
forelock [ˈfɔːlɒk] *n.* прядь воло́с на лбу; чуб; вихо́р.
foreman [ˈfɔːmən] *n.* ма́стер, деся́тник; прора́б, (производи́тель рабо́т); ~ **of the jury** старшина́ (*m.*) прися́жных.
foremast [ˈfɔːmɑːst, -məst] *n.* фок-ма́чта.
foremost [ˈfɔːməʊst] *adj.* са́мый пере́дний.
adv.: **first and** ~ пре́жде всего́; в пе́рвую о́чередь.
forename [ˈfɔːneɪm] *n.* и́мя (*nt.*).
forenoon [ˈfɔːnuːn] *n.* вре́мя до полу́дня; у́тро.
forensic [fəˈrensɪk] *adj.* суде́бный.
foreordain [ˌfɔːrɔːˈdeɪn] *v.t.* предопредел|я́ть, -и́ть.
forerunner [ˈfɔːˌrʌnə(r)] *n.* предше́ственник.
foresail [ˈfɔːseɪl, -s(ə)l] *n.* фок.
foresee [fɔːˈsiː] *v.t.* предви́деть (*impf.*).
foreseeable [fɔːˈsiːəb(ə)l] *adj.*: **in the** ~ **future** в обозри́мом бу́дущем.
foreshadow [fɔːˈʃædəʊ] *v.t.* предвеща́ть (*impf.*).
foreshorten [fɔːˈʃɔːt(ə)n] *v.t.* черти́ть, на- в ра́курсе.
foresight [ˈfɔːsaɪt] *n.* **1.** (*knowledge of future*) предви́дение. **2.** (*care for future*) предусмотри́тельность.
foreskin [ˈfɔːskɪn] *n.* кра́йняя плоть.
forest [ˈfɒrɪst] *n.* лес; ~ **fire** лесно́й пожа́р.
v.t. заса́|живать, -ди́ть ле́сом; **heavily ~ed country** леси́стая/лесна́я ме́стность.
forestall [fɔːˈstɔːl] *v.t.* предвосх|ища́ть, -ти́ть; предупре|жда́ть, -ди́ть.
forester [ˈfɒrɪstə(r)] *n.* лесни́чий.
forestry [ˈfɒrɪstrɪ] *n.* лесово́дство; **F~ Commission** коми́ссия по охра́не лесо́в.
foretaste [ˈfɔːteɪst] *n.* предвкуше́ние.
foretell [fɔːˈtel] *v.t.* предска́з|ывать, -а́ть.
forethought [ˈfɔːθɔːt] *n.* предусмотри́тельность.
forever [fəˈrevə(r)] *adv.* навсегда́, наве́чно; (*continually*) постоя́нно, ве́чно.
forewarn [fɔːˈwɔːn] *v.t.* предостер|ега́ть, -е́чь; **~ed is forearmed** кто предостережён, тот вооружён.
forewoman [ˈfɔːˌwʊmən] *n.* (же́нщина-)деся́тник/ма́стер; (*of a jury*) (же́нщина-)старшина́ прися́жных.
foreword [ˈfɔːwɜːd] *n.* предисло́вие.
forfeit [ˈfɔːfɪt] *n.* (*penalty*) штраф, конфиска́ция; (*trivial fine, e.g. at games*) фант; **play at ~s** игра́ть в фа́нты.
v.t. теря́ть, по- (пра́во на) +*a.*
forfeiture [ˈfɔːfɪtʃə(r)] *n.* конфиска́ция; лише́ние пра́ва (на+*a*).
forge [fɔːdʒ] *n.* (*workshop*) ку́зница; (*hearth or furnace*) кузне́чный горн.
v.t. & i. **1.** (*shape metal*) кова́ть (*impf.*). **2.** (*fabricate*) изобре|та́ть, -сти́; (*counterfeit*) подде́л|ывать, -ать. **3.**: ~ **ahead** вырыва́ться, вы́рваться вперёд.
forger [ˈfɔːdʒə(r)] *n.* подде́лыватель (*m.*); фальсифика́тор.
forgery [ˈfɔːdʒərɪ] *n.* (*act*) подде́лка, подло́г; (*object*) подде́лка; подло́жный докуме́нт.
forget [fəˈget] *v.t. & i.* заб|ыва́ть, -ы́ть; **his deeds will never be forgotten** его́ дея́ния не забу́дутся; **it is easy to** ~ э́то легко́ забыва́ется; **he drinks to** ~ он пьёт, что́бы забы́ться; ~ **it!** (*coll.*) ла́дно!; бро́сьте!; ~ **o.s.** (*act unselfishly*) забыва́ть (*impf.*) себя́ ра́ди други́х; (*act without decorum*) заб|ыва́ться, -ы́ться.
cpd. **~-me-not** *n.* (*bot.*) незабу́дка.
forgetful [fəˈgetfʊl] *adj.* забы́вчивый.
forgetfulness [fəˈgetfʊlnɪs] *n.* забы́вчивость.
forgivable [fəˈgɪvəb(ə)l] *adj.* прости́тельный.
forgive [fəˈgɪv] *v.t. & i.* про|ща́ть, -сти́ть; **I ~ you for everything** я вам всё проща́ю; ~ **me, I didn't hear what you said** прости́те, я не расслы́шал, что вы сказа́ли.
forgiveness [fəˈgɪvnɪs] *n.* проще́ние.
forgo, forego [fɔːˈgəʊ] *v.t.* отка́з|ываться, -а́ться от+*g.*; возде́рж|иваться, -а́ться от+*g.*
fork [fɔːk] *n.* **1.** (*for cul. or table use*) ви́лка. **2.** (*bifurcation*) разви́лка, разветвле́ние.
v.t. **1.** (*dig or turn with* ~): ~ **over a rose-bed** разрыхл|я́ть, -и́ть ви́лами гря́дку с ро́зами.
v.i. (*bifurcate*) раздв|а́иваться, -о́иться; развет|вля́ться, -и́ться; (*of road-direction*): **you must** ~ **right at the church** у це́ркви (, где доро́га разветвля́ется,) возьми́те напра́во; ~ **out** (*sl., provide money*) раскоше́ли|ваться, -ться.
cpd. **~-lift** *adj.*: **~-lift truck** автопогру́зчик.
forked [fɔːkt] *adj.* раздво́енный, разветвлённый; ~ **lightning** зигзагообра́зная мо́лния.
forlorn [fɔːˈlɔːn] *adj.* забро́шенный, жа́лкий, несча́стный; **he looked** ~ у него́ был жа́лкий вид.
form [fɔːm] *n.* **1.** (*shape, aspect*) фо́рма, вид; (*figure, body*) фигу́ра. **2.** (*species, kind, variant*) вид, фо́рма; ~ **of government** госуда́рственный строй; фо́рма правле́ния; (*gram.*) фо́рма. **3.** (*accepted or expected behaviour*) но́рмы (*f. pl.*) поведе́ния; **that is not good** ~ так вести́ себя́ не при́нято; **that is common** ~ э́то обы́чно; так при́нято. **4.** (*ritual, formality*) тип, вид; **~s of worship** обря́ды (*m. pl.*). **5.** (*of health*) состоя́ние; **in good** ~ в хоро́шей фо́рме; (*of spirits*): **he appeared in great** ~ он был в отли́чной фо́рме. **6.** (*document*) бланк, анке́та. **7.** (*class*) класс. **8.** (*bench*) скамья́. **9.** (*mould*) фо́рма.
v.t. **1.** (*fashion, shape*) формирова́ть, с-; прид|ава́ть, -а́ть фо́рму +*d.*; **he ~ed the clay into a vase** гли́на под его́ рука́ми преврати́лась в ва́зу; **the rocks are ~ed by wave action** ска́лы формиру́ются под возде́йствием волн; **she ~s her letters well** она́ хорошо́ выво́дит бу́квы; **he can ~ simple sentences** она́ уме́ет составля́ть просты́е предложе́ния; (*by discipline, training etc.*) тренирова́ть, на-; дисциплини́ровать (*impf., pf.*); разв|ива́ть, -и́ть; **his character was ~ed at school** его́ хара́ктер сформирова́лся в шко́ле. **2.** (*organize, create*) организ|о́вывать, -ова́ть; образ|о́вывать, -ова́ть; созд|ава́ть, -а́ть; формирова́ть, с-; **they ~ed an alliance** они́ со́здали/образова́ли сою́з; **he was unable to ~ a government** он не смог сформирова́ть прави́тельство. **3.** (*conceive*): **they ~ed a plan** они́ вы́работали план; ~ **an opinion** соста́вить (*pf.*) мне́ние; **I ~ed the conclusion that ...** я пришёл к заключе́нию, что... **4.** (*develop, acquire*): **habits ~ed in childhood** привы́чки, сложи́вшиеся с де́тства. **5.** (*constitute*) сост|авля́ть, -а́вить; представля́ть собо́й, явля́ться (*both impf.*); **this ~s the basis of our discussion** э́то составля́ет осно́ву на́шей диску́ссии; **the room ~s part of the museum** э́та ко́мната составля́ет часть (*or* явля́ется ча́стью) музе́я. **6.** (*gram.*) обра|зо́вывать, -ова́ть. **7.** (*mil. etc.*) стро́ить, по-; **the troops were ~ed (up) into line** солда́т вы́строили в ряд; ~ **a queue** образова́ть (*pf.*) о́чередь.
v.i. (*take shape, appear, come into being*): **mist was ~ing in the valley** в доли́не собира́лся тума́н; **ice ~ed on the window** на окне́ образова́лся моро́зный узо́р; **an idea ~ed in his mind** в его́ мозгу́ возни́кла иде́я; (*mil. etc.*; *also* ~ **up**) стро́иться, по-.
cpds. **~-master** *n.* кла́ссный руководи́тель; **~-mistress** *n.* кла́ссная руководи́тельница; **~-room** *n.* кла́ссная ко́мната.
formal [ˈfɔːm(ə)l] *adj.* **1.** (*in outward form*) вне́шний; форма́льный. **2.** (*conventional*) общепри́нятый; надлежа́щий; ~ **garden** англи́йский сад. **3.** (*official*) официа́льный. **4.** (*ceremonious*) церемо́нный.
formaldehyde [fɔːˈmældɪˌhaɪd] *n.* формальдеги́д.
formalism [ˈfɔːməˌlɪz(ə)m] *n.* формали́зм.

formalist [ˈfɔːməlɪst] *n.* формали́ст.
formalistic [ˌfɔːməˈlɪstɪk] *adj.* формалисти́ческий.
formality [fɔːˈmælɪtɪ] *n.* форма́льность.
formalize [ˈfɔːməˌlaɪz] *v.t.* оф|ормля́ть, -óрмить.
format [ˈfɔːmæt] *n.* форма́т.
v.t. (*comput.*) формати́ровать (*impf.*, *pf.*).
formation [fɔːˈmeɪʃ(ə)n] *n.* **1.** (*creation*) образова́ние, формирова́ние. **2.** (*mil.*) строй, расположе́ние, поря́док; (*aeron.*) боево́й поря́док; строй самолётов в во́здухе. **3.** (*geol.*) форма́ция.
formative [ˈfɔːmətɪv] *adj.* формиру́ющий, образу́ющий; **he spent his ~ years in France** го́ды, когда́ скла́дывался его́ хара́ктер, он провёл во Фра́нции.
former [ˈfɔːmə(r)] *adj.* **1.** (*earlier*) предше́ствующий; **in ~ times** в пре́жние времена́; **my ~ husband** мой бы́вший муж. **2.** (*first mentioned of two*) пе́рвый.
formerly [ˈfɔːməlɪ] *adv.* пре́жде, ра́ньше.
formic [ˈfɔːmɪk] *adj.* муравьи́ный; **~ acid** муравьи́ная кислота́.
formidable [ˈfɔːmɪdəb(ə)l] *adj.* устраша́ющий, гро́зный; (*task*) невероя́тно тру́дный.
formless [ˈfɔːmlɪs] *adj.* бесфо́рменный.
formula [ˈfɔːmjʊlə] *n.* (*set form of words*) выраже́ние, формулиро́вка; (*recipe*) реце́пт; (*math.*, *chem.*) фо́рмула.
formulate [ˈfɔːmjʊˌleɪt] *v.t.* формули́ровать, с-.
formulation [ˌfɔːmjʊˈleɪʃ(ə)n] *n.* формулиро́вка.
fornicate [ˈfɔːnɪˌkeɪt] *v.i.* развра́тничать (*impf.*); вести́ (*det.*) распу́тную жизнь.
fornication [ˌfɔːnɪˈkeɪʃ(ə)n] *n.* развра́т.
forsake [fəˈseɪk, fɔː-] *v.t.* пок|ида́ть, -и́нуть; ост|авля́ть, -а́вить; бр|оса́ть, -о́сить.
forswear [fɔːˈsweə(r)] *v.t.* отр|ека́ться, -е́чься от+*g.*
fort [fɔːt] *n.* форт; **hold the ~** (*fig.*) держа́ть/уде́рживать (*impf.*) пози́цию.
forte[1] [ˈfɔːteɪ] *n.* (*strong point*) си́льная сторона́.
forte[2] [ˈfɔːteɪ] *n.* & *adv.* (*mus.*) фо́рте (*indecl.*).
forth [fɔːθ] *adv.* вперёд, да́льше; **back and ~** взад и вперёд; **and so ~** и так да́лее; **from this day ~** с э́того дня; впредь; **let ~ a yell** изд|ава́ть, -а́ть вопль.
forthcoming [fɔːθˈkʌmɪŋ, *attrib.* ˈfɔːθ-] *adj.* предстоя́щий; (*helpful*) услу́жливый; **the money was not ~** де́ньги не поступа́ли.
forthright [ˈfɔːθraɪt] *adj.* прямо́й, прямолине́йный.
forthwith [fɔːθˈwɪθ, -ˈwɪð] *adv.* неме́дленно, то́тчас.
fortieth [ˈfɔːtɪɪθ] *n.* (*fraction*) одна́ сорокова́я; сорокова́я часть.
adj. сорокову́й.
fortification [ˌfɔːtɪfɪˈkeɪʃ(ə)n] *n.* укрепле́ние, фортифика́ция.
fortif|y [ˈfɔːtɪˌfaɪ] *v.t.* укреп|ля́ть, -и́ть; **~ied wines** крепле́ные ви́на; (*food*) витаминизи́ровать (*impf.*, *pf.*).
fortissimo [fɔːˈtɪsɪˌməʊ] *n.* & *adv.* форти́ссимо (*indecl.*).
fortitude [ˈfɔːtɪˌtjuːd] *n.* сто́йкость; си́ла ду́ха.
fortnight [ˈfɔːtnaɪt] *n.* две неде́ли.
fortnightly [ˈfɔːtˌnaɪtlɪ] *n.* (*publication*) двухнеде́льное изда́ние.
adj. двухнеде́льный.
adv. раз в две неде́ли.
fortress [ˈfɔːtrɪs] *n.* кре́пость.
fortuitous [fɔːˈtjuːɪtəs] *adj.* случа́йный.
fortuit|ousness [fɔːˈtjuːɪtəsnɪs], **-y** [fɔːˈtjuːɪtɪ] *nn.* случа́йность, слу́чай.
fortunate [ˈfɔːtjʊnət, -tʃənət] *adj.* счастли́вый, уда́чный; **he was ~ to escape** ему́ посчастли́вилось убежа́ть; **~ly** к сча́стью.
fortune [ˈfɔːtjuːn, -tʃuːn] *n.* **1.** (*chance*) уда́ча, сча́стье; **by good ~** по сча́стью; **he had ~ on his side** сча́стье бы́ло на его́ стороне́; **try one's ~** попыта́ть (*pf.*) сча́стья. **2.** (*fate*) судьба́; **the Gypsy (woman) told my ~** цыга́нка (по/на)гада́ла мне. **3.** (*prosperity*, *large sum*) состоя́ние, бога́тство; **come into a ~** унасле́довать (*pf.*) состоя́ние; **make a ~** разбогате́ть (*pf.*); нажи́ть (*pf.*) состоя́ние; **I spent a small ~ today** я истра́тил у́йму де́нег сего́дня.
cpd. **~-teller** *n.* гада́лка, ворожея́.
fort|y [ˈfɔːtɪ] *n.* со́рок; **the ~ies** (*decade*) сороковы́е го́ды (*m. pl.*); **they are both in their ~ies** (*age*) им обо́им за со́рок; **the roaring ~ies** (*latitude*) реву́щие сороковы́е.
adj. со́рок +*g. pl.*; **a man of ~y** сорокале́тний челове́к; **have ~y winks** вздремну́ть (*pf.*).
forum [ˈfɔːrəm] *n.* (*hist.*) фо́рум; (*fig.*, *court*) суд; (*fig.*, *discussion*) обсужде́ние; (*meeting*) фо́рум, съезд.
forward [ˈfɔːwəd] *n.* (*sport*) напада́ющий.
adj. (*situated to the fore*) пере́дний; (*progressive*) прогресси́вный; (*precocious*) скороспе́лый, преждевре́менный; (*pert*) наглова́тый, развя́зный.
adv. (*onward*; *towards one*) вперёд; **~, march!** ша́гом марш!; **please come ~** пожа́луйста, вы́йдите вперёд; **carry ~** (*on a ledger*) перен|оси́ть, -ести́ на другу́ю страни́цу; **the meeting has been brought ~ a day** собра́ние перенесли́ на́ день ра́ньше; **walk back(wards) and ~(s)** ходи́ть (*indet.*) взад и вперёд; (*towards the future*): **I look ~ to meeting her** я с нетерпе́нием жду встре́чи с ней; **from this time ~** начина́я с э́того вре́мени; (*naut.*) в носово́й ча́сти; в носову́ю часть.
v.t. (*promote*, *encourage*) продв|ига́ть, -и́нуть; (*send*) пос|ыла́ть, -ла́ть; отпр|авля́ть, -а́вить; (*send on*) перес|ыла́ть, -ла́ть.
cpd. **~-looking** *adj.* предусмотри́тельный, дальнови́дный.
fossil [ˈfɒs(ə)l] *n.* окамене́лость; (*also fig.*) ископа́емое.
adj. окамене́лый, ископа́емый.
fossilize [ˈfɒsɪlaɪz] *v.t.* & *i.* превра|ща́ть(ся), -ти́ть(ся) в окамене́лость; (*fig.*) закосне́ть (*pf.*).
foster [ˈfɒstə(r)] *v.t.* (*tend*) ходи́ть (*indet.*) за (*детьми*); (*rear*) воспи́т|ывать, а́ть; (*fig.*): **~ evil thoughts** вына́шивать (*impf.*) недо́брые мы́сли.
cpds. **~-brother** *n.* моло́чный брат; **~-child** *n.* приёмыш, воспи́танник; **~-father** *n.* приёмный оте́ц; **~-mother** *n.* приёмная мать.
foul [faʊl] *n.* (*sport*) наруше́ние (пра́вил игры́).
adj. гря́зный, отврати́тельный; **a ~ smell** злово́ние; **~ air** загрязнённый во́здух; **~ language** руга́тельства (*nt. pl.*); скверносло́вие; **~ weather** отврати́тельная пого́да; непого́да; **a ~ deed** тёмное де́ло; **~ play** (*sport*) гру́бая игра́; (*violence*) нечи́стое де́ло; **by fair means or ~** любы́ми сре́дствами; **fall ~ of** поссо́риться (*pf.*) с+*i.*
v.t. (*defile*) загрязн|я́ть, -и́ть; па́чкать, за-; **~ one's own nest** (*fig.*) га́дить, на- в своём гнезде́; (*obstruct*) образо́в|ывать, -а́ть зато́р в+*p.*
v.i. (*become entangled*) запу́т|ываться, -аться.
cpds. **~-mouthed** *adj.* сквернословящий; **~-up** *n.* неразбери́ха, заварýха.
found [faʊnd] *v.t.* осно́в|ывать, -а́ть; за|кла́дывать, ложи́ть; **~ a city** за|кла́дывать, -ложи́ть го́род; (*endow*) осно́в|ывать, -а́ть; учре|жда́ть, -ди́ть; (*base*) осно́в|ывать, -а́ть.
foundation [faʊnˈdeɪʃ(ə)n] *n.* **1.** (*establishing*) основа́ние, учрежде́ние; (*endowment*) учрежде́ние; (*founded institution*) учрежде́ние, существу́ющее на поже́ртвованный фонд; (*fund*) фонд. **2.** (*base of building etc.*) фунда́мент; **lay the ~** за|кла́дывать, -ложи́ть фунда́мент/осно́ву; (*fig.*) осно́ва; **the story has no ~ in fact** расска́з не име́ет ни мале́йшего основа́ния.
cpd. **~-stone** *n.* фунда́ментный ка́мень; (*fig.*) краеуго́льный ка́мень, осно́ва.
founder[1] [ˈfaʊndə(r)] *n.* основа́тель (*m.*); учреди́тель (*m.*).
cpd. **~-member** *n.* член-основа́тель (*m.*).

founder[2] ['faʊndə(r)] *n.* (*metall.*) литéйщик, плави́льщик.
founder[3] ['faʊndə(r)] *v.i.* (*collapse*) ос|едáть, -éсть; (*of a horse, go lame*) охромéть (*pf.*); (*from fatigue*) вали́ться, с-; (*of a ship*) идти́ (*det.*) ко дну.
foundling ['faʊndlɪŋ] *n.* подки́дыш, найдёныш.
foundry ['faʊndrɪ] *n.* литéйная; ~ **hand** литéйщик.
fount[1] [faʊnt] *n.* (*source*) истóчник, ключ.
fount[2] [faʊnt] (*US* **font**) *n.* (*typ.*) комплéкт шри́фта.
fountain ['faʊntɪn] *n.* фонтáн; (*fig.*) истóчник; **drinking** ~ фонтáнчик для питья́.
cpd. **~-pen** *n.* автору́чка.
four [fɔ:(r)] *n.* (числó/нóмер) четы́ре; (~ *people*) чéтверо; **we** ~ нас чéтверо; **(the, all)** ~ **of us went** мы пошли́ вчетверóм; ~ **each** по четы́ре; (*figure*; *thg. numbered 4*; *set, team, crew of* ~) четвёрка; **fold in** ~ сложи́ть (*pf.*) вчéтверо; (*with var. nn. expr. or understood*: *cf. also examples under* **two**): **he got down on all ~s** он опусти́лся на четверéньки.
adj. четы́ре *+g. sg.*; (*for people and pluralia tantum, also*) чéтверо *+g. pl.* (*cf. examples under* **two**); **he and** ~ **others** он и ещё чéтверо други́х; ~ **fives are twenty** четы́режды (*or* четы́ре на) пять — двáдцать; ~ **times as big** в четы́ре рáза бóльше; **from the** ~ **corners of the earth** со всех концóв земли́.
cpds. **~-course** *adj.*: **~-course meal** обéд из четырёх блюд; **~fold** *adj.* четырёхкрáтный; *adv.* в четы́ре рáза (бóльше); **~-hundredth** *adj.* четырёхсóтый; **~-lane** *adj.*: **~-lane highway** шоссé с движéнием в четы́ре ря́да; **~-letter** *adj.*: **~-letter word** (*fig.*) ругáтельство; непристóйное слóво; **~-poster (bed)** *n.* кровáть с пóлогом на четырёх стóлбиках; **~-seater** (*car*) *n.* четырёхмéстная маши́на; **~-wheel** *adj.*: **~-wheel drive** (*attr.*) с привóдом на четы́ре колесá.
fourteen [fɔ:'ti:n] *n. & adj.* четы́рнадцать (*+g. pl.*).
fourteenth [fɔ:'ti:nθ] *n.* (*date*) четы́рнадцатое (числó); (*fraction*) однá четы́рнадцатая; четы́рнадцатая часть.
adj. четы́рнадцатый.
fourth [fɔ:θ] *n.* **1.** (*date*) четвёртое (числó). **2.** (*fraction*) однá четвёртая; четвёртая часть; чéтверть. **3.** (*mus.*) квáрта; четвёртая.
adj. четвёртый.
fowl [faʊl] *n.* (*domestic*) домáшняя пти́ца; (*chicken*) ку́рица.
fowler ['faʊlə(r)] *n.* птицелóв.
fox [fɒks] *n.* лисá, лиси́ца; (*fur*) ли́сий мех; (*wily man*) хитрéц; лисá (*c.g.*).
v.t. (*deceive*) обмáн|ывать, -у́ть; (*puzzle*) стáвить, по- в тупи́к; озадáчи|вать, -ть.
cpds. **~glove** *n.* наперстя́нка; **~hole** *n.* ли́сья норá; (*mil.*) стрелкóвая ячéйка; **~hound** *n.* гóнчая; **~-hunting** *n.* (верховáя) охóта на лис; **~-terrier** *n.* фокстерьéр; **~trot** *n.* фокстрóт.
foxy ['fɒksɪ] *adj.* (*crafty*) хи́трый.
foyer ['fɔɪeɪ] *n.* фойé (*indecl.*).
fracas ['frækɑ:] *n.* скандáл, шу́мная ссóра.
fraction ['frækʃ(ə)n] *n.* **1.** (*arith.*) дробь; **decimal** ~ десяти́чная дробь; ~ **of a second** дóля секу́нды. **2.** (*small piece or amount*) части́ца, крупи́ца.
fractional ['frækʃən(ə)l] *adj.* дрóбный, части́чный; **the difference is** ~ рáзница незначи́тельна.
fractious ['frækʃəs] *adj.* капри́зный, раздражи́тельный; неуправля́емый.
fracture ['fræktʃə(r)] *n.* трéщина, разры́в; (*of a bone*) перелóм.
v.t. & i. ломáть(ся), с-; раск|áлывать(ся), -олóть(ся).
fragile ['frædʒaɪl, -dʒɪl] *adj.* лóмкий, хру́пкий.
fragility [frə'dʒɪlɪtɪ] *n.* лóмкость, хру́пкость.
fragment ['frægmənt] *n.* oблóмок, оскóлок; (*of writing or music*) фрагмéнт; **~s of conversation** обры́вки (*m. pl.*) разговóра.
fragmentary ['frægməntərɪ] *adj.* отры́вочный.
fragmentation [,frægmən'teɪʃ(ə)n] *n.* разры́в на мéлкие чáсти; ~ **bomb** оскóлочная бóмба.
fragrance ['freɪgrəns] *n.* аромáт.
fragrant ['freɪgrənt] *adj.* аромáтный.
frail [freɪl] *adj.* хру́пкий, непрóчный; (*in health*) хру́пкий, болéзненный.
frailty ['freɪltɪ] *n.* хру́пкость, непрóчность; (*of health*) хру́пкость, болéзненность.
frame [freɪm] *n.* **1.** (*structural skeleton*) скелéт, костя́к; (*of a ship or aircraft*) кóрпус, óстов. **2.** (*wood or metal surround*) рáма, рáмка; **picture** ~ рáма (для) карти́ны; **window** ~ окóнная рáма. **3.** (*body*): **more than the human** ~ **can bear** свы́ше сил человéческих; **sobs shook her** ~ рыдáния сотрясáли её (тéло). **4.**: ~ **of mind** настроéние; расположéние ду́ха. **5.** (*cin.*) кадр.
v.t. **1.** (*compose, devise*) сост|авля́ть, -áвить; созд|авáть, -áть; ~ **a constitution** сост|авля́ть, -áвить конститу́цию; **he ~d his question carefully** он тóчно сформули́ровал свой вопрóс. **2.** (*surround*): ~ **a picture** вст|авля́ть, -áвить карти́ну в рáм(к)у; обр|амля́ть, -áмить карти́ну; **he was ~d in the doorway** он стоя́л в проёме двéри. **3.** (*sl., concoct case against*) приши́ть (*pf.*) дéло *+d.*
cpds. **~-house** *n.* каркáсный дом; **~-up** *n.* (*sl.*) сфабрикóванное обвинéние; **~work** *n.* каркáс, óстов; (*fig.*): **within the ~work of the constitution** в рáмках конститу́ции.
franc [fræŋk] *n.* франк.
France [frɑ:ns] *n.* Фрáнция.
franchise ['fræntʃaɪz] *n.* (*right of voting*) прáво гóлоса; (*comm.*) привилéгия.
frank[1] [fræŋk] *adj.* откровéнный, и́скренний.
frank[2] [fræŋk] *v.t.* франки́ровать (*impf., pf.*); **~ing machine** франкировáльная маши́на.
frankfurter ['fræŋk,fɜ:tə(r)] *n.* соси́ска.
frankincense ['fræŋkɪn,sens] *n.* лáдан.
frankness ['fræŋknɪs] *n.* откровéнность, и́скренность.
frantic ['fræntɪk] *adj.* нéистовый, безу́мный; **she became** ~ **with grief** онá обезу́мела от гóря; **the noise is driving me** ~ шум вывóдит меня́ из себя́; **he was in a** ~ **hurry** он ужáсно спеши́л.
fraternal [frə'tɜ:n(ə)l] *adj.* брáтский.
fraternity [frə'tɜ:nɪtɪ] *n.* брáтство; (*student association*) студéнческая общи́на.
fraternization [,frætənaɪ'zeɪʃ(ə)n] *n.* братáние.
fraternize ['frætə,naɪz] *v.i.* братáться (*impf.*).
fratricidal [,frætrɪ'saɪd(ə)l] *adj.* братоуби́йственный.
fratricide ['frætrɪ,saɪd] *n.* братоуби́йство.
fraud [frɔ:d] *n.* (*fraudulent act*) обмáн, мошéнничество; (*impostor*) обмáнщик, мошéнник; (*thg. that deceives or disappoints*) фальши́вка, поддéлка.
fraudulence ['frɔ:djʊləns] *n.* обмáнчивость, фальши́вость.
fraudulent ['frɔ:djʊlənt] *adj.* обмáнный, фальши́вый, мошéннический.
fraught [frɔ:t] *adj.* пóлный, преиспóлненный, чревáтый; **the expedition is** ~ **with danger** экспеди́ция чревáта опáсностями; (*tense*) напряжённый.
fray[1] [freɪ] *n.* дрáка; побóище.
fray[2] [freɪ] *v.t. & i.* прот|ирáть(ся), -ерéть(ся); (*fig.*): **her nerves are ~ed** у неё совершéнно истрёпаны нéрвы.
freak [fri:k] *n.* (*unusual occurrence*): **a** ~ **storm** необы́чная бу́ря; (*abnormal pers. or thg.*) урóд, вы́родок; урóдство; (*absurd or fanciful idea*) причу́да; ~ **of nature** оши́бка прирóды; (*enthusiast*) фанáт; **health** ~ помéшанный на здорóвье; **film** ~ киномáн.

freakish ['fri:kɪʃ] *adj.* причу́дливый, чудно́й.

freckle ['frek(ə)l] *n.* весну́шка.

v.t. покр|ыва́ть, -ы́ть весну́шками; **a ~d face** весну́шчатое лицо́.

free [fri:] *adj.* **1.** свобо́дный, во́льный; **you are ~ to leave** вы мо́жете уйти́; **they gave us a ~ hand** они́ да́ли нам по́лную свобо́ду де́йствий; **break ~** вырыва́ться, вы́рваться на во́лю; **set ~** освобо|жда́ть, -ди́ть; **~ of disease** здоро́вый; **~ from blame** неви́нный; **~ composition** сочине́ние на свобо́дную те́му; **~ speech** свобо́да сло́ва; **~ translation** во́льный перево́д; **~ will** свобо́да во́ли; **he left of his own ~ will** он ушёл доброво́льно (*or* по свое́й во́ле). **2.** (*without constraint*) непринуждённый, раско́ванный; **~ and easy** непринуждённый; **make ~ with** свобо́дно распоряжа́ться (*impf.*) +*i.*. **3.** (*without payment*) беспла́тный; **the price is £5 post ~** цена́ 5 фу́нтов с беспла́тной доста́вкой по по́чте; **~ of charge** беспла́тный; **~ gift** полу́ченное да́ром; **~ pass** (*on railway etc.*) беспла́тный прое́зд; (*admission*) про́пуск. **4.** (*unoccupied*) свобо́дный, неза́нятый; **my hands are ~** (*fig.*) у меня́ развя́заны ру́ки. **5.** (*liberal*) ще́дрый; **~ with one's money** ще́дрый, расточи́тельный; **~ with advice** всегда́ гото́вый дава́ть сове́ты. **6.** (*chem.*) несвя́занный.

v.t. (*release, e.g. a rope*) высвобожда́ть, вы́свободить; (*liberate*) освобо|жда́ть, -ди́ть.

cpds. **~-for-all** *n.* (*competition*) откры́тый для всех ко́нкурс; (*fight*) всео́бщая дра́ка/сва́лка; **~hand** *adj.*: **~hand drawing** рису́нок, сде́ланный от руки́; **~hold** *n.* неограни́ченное пра́во со́бственности на недви́жимость; **~holder** *n.* свобо́дный со́бственник; **~lance(r)** *n.* внешта́тник (*coll.*); **F~mason** *n.* масо́н; **F~masonry** *n.* масо́нство; **~-thinker** *n.* вольноду́м|ец (*fem.* -ка); **~-thinking** *adj.* вольноду́мный; **~-wheel** *v.i.* (*lit.*) дви́гаться (*impf.*) свобо́дным хо́дом; **~-wheeling** *adj.* (*fig.*) во́льный, неско́ванный.

freedom ['fri:dəm] *n.* свобо́да; **~ of speech** свобо́да сло́ва.

freez|e [fri:z] *n.* (*period of frost*) замора́живание; хо́лод, моро́з; **wage ~e** замора́живание за́работной пла́ты.

v.t. замор|а́живать, -о́зить; **frozen food** моро́женые проду́кты.

v.i. **1.** (*impers.*) моро́зить (*impf.*); **it's ~ing outside** на дворе́ стра́шный моро́з; **will it ~e tonight?** бу́дет сего́дня но́чью моро́з? **2.** (*congeal with cold*): **the lake is frozen over, across** о́зеро покры́лось льдом; **the pipes are frozen (up)** тру́бы промёрзли; **~ing point** то́чка замерза́ния. **3.** (*fig., become rigid*) заст|ыва́ть, -ы́ть; **he froze where he stood** он засты́л на ме́сте; **his features froze** его́ лицо́ как бу́дто засты́ло; **~e!** (*coll., remain motionless*) замри́! **4.** (*become chilled*) зам|ерза́ть, -ёрзнуть; **he froze to death** он промёрз до косте́й; **I'm ~ing** я замёрз.

freezer ['fri:zə(r)] *n.* морози́льник; **~ compartment** морози́лка.

freight [freɪt] *n.* **1.** (*carriage of goods*) фрахт, груз; **~ charge** сто́имость прово́за. **2.** (*goods carried*) груз.

cpd. **~-train** *n.* (*US*) това́рный по́езд.

freighter ['freɪtə(r)] *n.* (*vessel*) грузово́е су́дно; (*aircraft*) грузово́й самолёт.

French [frentʃ] *n.* (*language*) францу́зский язы́к; **the ~** (*people*) францу́зы (*m. pl.*).

adj. францу́зский; **~ bean** фасо́ль; **~ horn** валто́рна; **~ loaf** (дли́нный) бато́н; **~ polish** политу́ра; **~ window** двуство́рчатое окно́ до по́ла.

cpds. **~man** *n.* францу́з; **~woman** *n.* францу́женка.

frenetic [frə'netɪk] *adj.* нейстовый; лихора́дочный.

frenzied ['frenzɪd] *adj.* нейстовый, взбешённый.

frenzy ['frenzɪ] *n.* нейстовство, бе́шенство.

frequency ['fri:kwənsɪ] *n.* частота́; (*rate*), ча́стность; **~ modulation** часто́тная модуля́ция.

frequent[1] ['fri:kwənt] *adj.* ча́стый.

frequent[2] [frɪ'kwent] *v.t.* ча́сто посеща́ть (*impf.*).

frequently ['fri:kwəntlɪ] *adv.* ча́сто.

fresco ['freskəʊ] *n.* фре́ска.

fresh [freʃ] *adj.* **1.** (*new*) све́жий, но́вый; (*more*): **make some ~ tea** завари́ть (*pf.*) све́жего ча́ю. **2.** (*recent in origin*): **~ bread** све́жий хлеб; **it is still ~ in my memory** э́то ещё свежо́ в мое́й па́мяти. **3.** (*not salt*) пре́сный. **4.** (*cool, refreshing*) све́жий, прохла́дный; **a ~ breeze** све́жий ветеро́к. **5.** (*unspoilt, unsullied*) све́жий, незапя́тнанный; **~ air** све́жий во́здух; **a ~ complexion** све́жий цвет лица́. **6.** (*lively*) бо́дрый, живо́й. **7.** (*US, impudent*) развя́зный, де́рзкий.

cpds. **~man** *n.* новичо́к (в университе́те); первоку́рсник; **~-water** *adj.* пресново́дный.

freshen ['freʃ(ə)n] *v.t.* освеж|а́ть, -и́ть.

v.i. свеже́ть, по-; **the wind is ~ing** ве́тер свеже́ет; **she's gone to ~ up** она́ пошла́ привести́ себя́ в поря́док.

freshly ['freʃlɪ] *adv.* свежо́, бо́дро; (*recently*) неда́вно.

freshness ['freʃnɪs] *n.* (*novelty*) све́жесть, оригина́льность; (*coolness*) све́жесть; (*brightness*) све́жесть, я́ркость; (*US, impudence*) развя́зность, де́рзость.

fret[1] [fret] *n.* (*of a guitar etc.*) лад.

fret[2] [fret] *v.i.* раздража́ться; волнова́ться; му́читься (*all impf.*).

fret[3] [fret] *v.t.* (*decorate by cutting*) укр|аша́ть, -а́сить резьбо́й.

cpds. **~saw** *n.* ло́бзик; **~work** *n.* резно́е украше́ние, резьба́.

fretful ['fretfʊl] *adj.* раздражи́тельный, капри́зный.

Freudian ['frɔɪdɪən] *adj.* фрейди́стский.

FRG (*abbr. of* **Federal Republic of Germany**) ФРГ, (Федерати́вная Респу́блика Герма́нии).

friable ['fraɪəb(ə)l] *adj.* кроша́щийся, ры́хлый.

friar ['fraɪə(r)] *n.* мона́х.

friary ['fraɪərɪ] *n.* мужско́й монасты́рь.

fricassee ['frɪkə,si:, -'si:] *n.* фрикасе́ (*indecl.*).

friction ['frɪkʃ(ə)n] *n.* тре́ние; (*fig.*) тре́ния (*nt. pl.*).

Friday ['fraɪdeɪ, -dɪ] *n.* пя́тница; **Good ~** Страстна́я/Вели́кая Пя́тница.

fridge [frɪdʒ] *n.* холоди́льник.

cpd. **~-freezer** двухсекцио́нный холоди́льник.

friend [frend] *n.* **1.** (*close ~*) друг, прия́тель (*fem.* -ница); (*acquaintance*) знако́м|ый (*fem.* -ая); (*woman's fem. ~*) подру́га; **make ~s** подружи́ться (*pf.*) (*с кем*); **he makes ~s easily** он легко́ схо́дится с людьми́. **2.** (*in addressing or referring to persons in public*) колле́га (*c.g.*); **my honourable ~** мой достопочте́нный колле́га/собра́т. **3.** (*Quaker*) ква́кер; **Society of F~s** се́кта ква́керов.

friendless ['frendlɪs] *adj.* не име́ющий друзе́й.

friendliness ['frendlɪnɪs] *n.* дружелю́бие.

friendly ['frendlɪ] *adj.* дру́жеский, това́рищеский.

friendship ['frendʃɪp] *n.* дру́жба.

frieze [fri:z] *n.* (*decorative band*) бордю́р, фриз.

frigate ['frɪgɪt] *n.* (*hist.*) фрега́т; (*small destroyer*) эска́дренный миноно́сец; сторожево́й кора́бль.

fright [fraɪt] *n.* **1.** (*fear; frightening experience*) страх, испу́г; **I almost died of ~** я чуть не у́мер от стра́ха; **give s.o. a ~** испуга́ть (*pf.*) кого́-н.; напуга́ть (*pf.*) кого́-н.; **I got the ~ of my life** я жу́тко испуга́лся. **2.** (*absurd-looking person*) пу́гало, страши́лище.

frighten ['fraɪt(ə)n] *v.t.* пуга́ть, на-/ис-; устраш|а́ть, -и́ть; **she is ~ed of the dark** она́ бои́тся темноты́; **don't ~ the birds away** не спугни́те птиц; **~ing** *adj.* ужа́сный.

frightful ['fraɪtfʊl] *adj.* (*terrible*) ужа́сный, стра́шный; (*coll., hideous*) безобра́зный; (*coll., very great*) колосса́льный.

frigid ['frɪdʒɪd] *adj.* **1.** (*cold*) холо́дный. **2.** (*unfeeling*) холо́дный, безразли́чный; (*sexually*) холо́дный, фриги́дный.

frigidity [ˌfrɪ'dʒɪdɪtɪ] *n.* хо́лодность, фриги́дность.

frill [frɪl] *n.* обо́рочка; сбо́рки (*f. pl.*); **~s** (*fig.*) выкрута́с|ы (*pl., g.* -ов).

v.t.: **a ~ed skirt** ю́бка с обо́рочками.

frilly ['frɪlɪ] *adj.* с обо́рочками.

fringe [frɪndʒ] *n.* **1.** (*ornamental border*) бахрома́. **2.** (*of hair*) чёлка. **3.** (*fig., edge, margin*) край, кайма́; **~ benefits** дополни́тельные льго́ты (*f. pl.*).

v.t. окайм|ля́ть, -и́ть.

frisk[1] [frɪsk] *v.t.* (*US coll., search*) обы́ск|ивать, -а́ть.

frisk[2] [frɪsk] *v.i.* резви́ться (*impf.*); пры́гать (*impf.*).

frisky ['frɪskɪ] *adj.* ре́звый, игри́вый.

fritter[1] ['frɪtə(r)] *n.* (*cul.*) ≃ ола́дья.

fritter[2] ['frɪtə(r)] *v.t.*: **~ away** транжи́рить, рас-; **~ one's time away** по́пусту тра́тить (*impf.*) вре́мя.

frivolity [ˌfrɪ'vɒlɪtɪ] *n.* легкомы́слие.

frivolous ['frɪvələs] *adj.* (*of object*) пустя́чный; (*of pers.*) легкомы́сленный, пусто́й.

frizz [frɪz] *n.* (*of hair*) ку́дри (*f. pl.*).

v.t. зав|ива́ть, -и́ть.

frizzy ['frɪzɪ] *adj.* вью́щийся, курча́вый.

fro [frəʊ] *adv.*: **to and ~** взад и вперёд.

frock [frɒk] *n.* пла́тье; **party ~** вече́рнее пла́тье.

cpd. **~-coat** сюрту́к.

frog [frɒg] *n.* лягу́шка; **I've got a ~ in my throat** я охри́п.

cpds. **~man** *n.* легководола́з; **~-march** *v.t.* тащи́ть (*impf.*) за́ руки и за́ ноги лицо́м вниз; **~-spawn** *n.* лягуша́чья икра́.

frolic ['frɒlɪk] *n.* ша́лость; весе́лье, ре́звость.

v.i. шали́ть (*impf.*); резви́ться (*impf.*).

frolicsome ['frɒlɪksəm] *adj.* шаловли́вый, ре́звый.

from [frəm, frɒm] *prep.* **1.** (*denoting origin of movement, measurement or distance*): **the train ~ London to Paris** по́езд из Ло́ндона в Пари́ж; **guests ~ the Ukraine** го́сти с Украи́ны; **where is he ~?** отку́да он? (*родом и т.п.*); **10 miles ~ here** в десяти́ ми́лях отсю́да; **we are 2 hours' journey ~ there** мы в двух часа́х пути́ отту́да; **~ the beginning of the book** с нача́ла кни́ги; **~ cradle to grave** от колыбе́ли до моги́лы; **the lamp hung ~ the ceiling** ла́мпа свиса́ла с потолка́; **she rose ~ the piano** она́ вста́ла из-за роя́ля; **extracts ~ a novel** отры́вки из рома́на; **bark ~ a tree** кора́ с де́рева; **~ end to end** от одного́ конца́ до друго́го; **~ the bottom** со дна; **~ the top** све́рху; **~ my point of view** с мое́й то́чки зре́ния; **far ~ it!** отню́дь!; во́все нет! **2.** (*expr. separation*): **I took the key ~ him** я взял у него́ ключ; **part ~ s.o.** расст|ава́ться, -а́ться с кем-н.; **hide ~** пря́таться, с- от+*g.*; **saved ~ death** спасённый от сме́рти; **released ~ prison** вы́пущенный из тюрьмы́. **3.** (*denoting personal origin*): **a letter ~ my son** письмо́ от моего́ сы́на; **tell him ~ me** переда́йте ему́ от меня́. **4.** (*expr. material origin*): **wine is made ~ grapes** вино́ де́лается из виногра́да. **5.** (*expr. origin in time*): **~ the very beginning** с са́мого нача́ла; **blind ~ birth** слепо́й от приро́ды; **~ dusk to dawn** от зари́ до зари́; **~ day to day** изо дня в день; со дня на́ день; **~ February to October** с февраля́ по октя́брь; **~ spring to autumn** с весны́ до о́сени; **~ time to time** вре́мя от вре́мени. **6.** (*expr. source or model*): **I see ~ the papers that ...** я зна́ю из газе́т, что...; **he quoted ~ memory** он цити́ровал по па́мяти; **he spoke ~ the heart** он говори́л от души́; **paint ~ nature** писа́ть (*impf.*) с нату́ры; **change ~ a rouble** сда́ча с рубля́. **7.** (*expr. cause*) от/с+*g.*; **~ grief** с го́ря; **suffer ~ arthritis** страда́ть (*impf.*) артри́том; **die ~ poisoning** ум|ира́ть, -ере́ть от отравле́ния; **~ jealousy** из ре́вности. **8.** (*expr. difference*): **I can't tell him ~ his brother** я не могу́ отличи́ть его́ от его́ бра́та; **they live differently ~ us** они́ живу́т не так как мы. **9.** (*expr. change*): **things went ~ bad to worse** де́ло шло всё ху́же и ху́же. **10.** (*with numbers*): **~ 1 to 10** от одного́ до десяти́; **it will last ~ 10 to 15 days** э́то продли́тся 10-15 дней; **~ 15 August to 10 September** с пятна́дцатого а́вгуста по деся́тое сентября́. **11.** (*with advs.*): **~ above** све́рху; **~ below** сни́зу; **~ inside** изнутри́; **~ outside** снару́жи; **~ afar** издалека́; **~ under the table** из-под стола́.

frond [frɒnd] *n.* ва́йя; ветвь с ли́стьями.

front [frʌnt] *n.* **1.** (*foremost side or part*) перёд; пере́дняя сторона́; **he walked in ~ of the procession** он шёл впереди́ проце́ссии; **in ~ of the house** пе́ред до́мом; **at the ~ of the house** в пере́дней ча́сти до́ма; **back to ~** за́дом наперёд; **in the ~ of the book** в нача́ле кни́ги. **2.** (*archit.*) фаса́д. **3.** (*fighting line*) фронт; **he was sent to the ~** его́ посла́ли на фронт; **on all ~s** на всех фронта́х; **in the ~ line** на передово́й ли́нии. **4.** (*road bordering sea*) на́бережная. **5.** (*meteor.*) фронт. **6.** (*face, in fig. senses*): **put on a bold ~** напус|ка́ть, -ти́ть на себя́ хра́брый вид; **have the ~ to** име́ть (*impf.*) на́глость (*сделать что-н.*). **7.** (*attr.*): **~ door** пара́дная дверь; **~ garden** сад пе́ред до́мом; палиса́дник; **~ page** пе́рвая страни́ца/полоса́; **in the ~ rank** (*fig.*) в пе́рвых ряда́х; **we had ~ seats** мы сиде́ли в пе́рвых ряда́х.

v.t. (*face on to*) выходи́ть (*impf.*) на+*a.*; быть обращённым к+*d.*

frontal ['frʌnt(ə)l] *adj.* лобово́й; (*mil.*) фронта́льный.

frontier ['frʌntɪə(r), -'tɪə(r)] *n.* грани́ца; (*fig.*) грани́ца, преде́л; **~s of knowledge** преде́лы зна́ний.

frontispiece ['frʌntɪsˌpi:s] *n.* фронтиспи́с.

frost [frɒst] *n.* моро́з; **ten degrees of ~** де́сять гра́дусов моро́за; **black ~** моро́з без и́нея; **hard, sharp ~** си́льный моро́з; **hoar, white ~** моро́з с и́неем.

v.t.: **the windows were ~ed over** о́кна замёрзли; (*fig.*): **~ a cake** покр|ыва́ть, -ы́ть торт глазу́рью; **~ed glass** ма́товое стекло́.

cpds. **~-bite** *n.* отмороже́ние, обмороже́ние; **~-bitten** *adj.* обморо́женный.

frosting ['frɒstɪŋ] *n.* (*cul.*) глазу́рь.

frosty ['frɒstɪ] *adj.* моро́зный; (*fig., unfriendly*) холо́дный, ледяно́й.

froth [frɒθ] *n.* пе́на.

v.t. сби|ва́ть, -ть в пе́ну.

v.i. пе́ниться (*impf.*); **~ at the mouth** бры́згать (*impf.*) слюно́й; **the milk ~ed up** молоко́ подняло́сь.

frothy ['frɒθɪ] *adj.* пе́нистый.

frown [fraʊn] *n.* хму́рый взгляд.

v.i. хму́риться, на-; **the authorities ~ on gambling** вла́сти неодобри́тельно отно́сятся к аза́ртным и́грам.

frozen ['frəʊz(ə)n] *adj.* замёрзший, засты́вший; (*icebound*) ско́ванный льдом.

frugal ['fru:g(ə)l] *adj.* (*of pers.*) бережли́вый; **a ~ meal** ску́дная еда́.

frugality [ˌfru:'gælɪtɪ] *n.* бережли́вость.

fruit [fru:t] *n.* **1.** (*class of food*) фрукт; **dried ~** сухофру́кты; **soft ~** я́годы (*f. pl.*); **forbidden ~** (*fig.*) запре́тный плод. **2.** (*bot.*) плод. **3.** (*vegetable products*) плоды́, фру́кты. **4.** (*fig., result, reward*) плод; **this book is the ~ of long research** э́та кни́га — плод дли́тельных иссле́дований; **enjoy the ~s of one's labours** наслажда́ться (*impf.*) плода́ми свои́х трудо́в.

cpds. **~-cake** *n.* фрукто́вый торт; **~-drop** *n.* ледене́ц; **~-juice** *n.* фрукто́вый сок.

fruitful ['fru:tfʊl] *adj.* (*of soil*) плодоро́дный; (*fig.*) плодотво́рный, тво́рческий.

fruition [fru:'ɪʃ(ə)n] *n.* (*realization*) осуществле́ние; **come to ~** осуществ|ля́ться, -и́ться.

fruitless ['fru:tlɪs] *adj.* (*lit.*, *fig.*) бесплóдный.
fruity ['fru:tɪ] *adj.* фруктóвый; напоминáющий фрýкты; (*fig.*) пикáнтный, скандáльный.
frustrate [frʌ'streɪt, 'frʌs-] *v.t.* разочарóв|ывать, -áть; расстр|áивать, -óить (*планы*).
frustration [frʌ'streɪʃ(ə)n] *n.* **1.** (*thwarting*) крушéние (*планов/надежд*). **2.** (*disappointment*) разочаровáние; **sense of ~** чýвство безысхóдности. **3.** (*psych.*) фрустрáция.
fry[1] [fraɪ] *n.* (*fish*) мальк|и́ (*pl.*, *g.* -óв); **small ~** (*fig.*) мелюзгá; мéлкая сóшка.
fry[2] [fraɪ] *v.t.* жáрить, за-/из-; **~ing-pan** сковородá; **out of the ~ing-pan into the fire** из огня́ да в пóлымя.
v.i. жáриться (*impf.*).
fuchsia ['fju:ʃə] *n.* фýксия.
fuck [fʌk] *v.t.* & *i.* (*vulg.*) еть/ети́, у-; **~ off!** иди́ нá хуй!
fudge[1] [fʌdʒ] *n.* & *int.* (*nonsense*) чепухá, вздор.
fudge[2] [fʌdʒ] *n.* (*sweetmeat*) сли́вочная помáдка.
fudge[3] [fʌdʒ] *v.t.* & *i.*: **~ accounts** поддéл|ывать, -ать счетá; **~ up an excuse** вы́думать (*pf.*) предлóг.
fuel ['fju:əl] *n.* тóпливо, горю́чее; **~ gauge** бензинóмéр; **~ oil** мазýт; **~ pump** бензопóмпа; **add ~ to the flames** подл|ивáть, -и́ть мáсла в огóнь.
v.t. снаб|жáть, -ди́ть тóпливом; запр|авля́ть, -áвить горю́чим.
v.i. запр|авля́ться, -áвиться горю́чим.
fugitive ['fju:dʒɪtɪv] *n.* беглéц.
adj. бéглый.
fugue [fju:g] *n.* фýга.
fulcrum ['fʊlkrəm, 'fʌl-] *n.* тóчка опóры; тóчка приложéния си́лы.
fulfil [fʊl'fɪl] *v.t.* выполня́ть, вы́полнить; исп|олня́ть, -óлнить; **~ all expectations** опрáвд|ывать, -áть все ожидáния.
fulfilment [fʊl'fɪl mənt] *n.* выполнéние, исполнéние; осуществлéние.
full [fʊl] *n.* (*limit*): **enjoy sth. to the ~** в пóлной мéре наслаждáться (*impf.*) чем-н.
adj. **1.** (*filled to capacity*) пóлный; **~ to to the brim** пóлный до краёв; **the hotel is ~ (up)** все кóмнаты в гости́нице зáняты; **he ate till he was ~ (up)** он наéлся до отвáла; **~ house** (*theatr.*) все билéты прóданы; аншлáг; (*having plenty*): **~ of ideas** пóлон идéй/зáмыслов; **~ of life** жизнерáдостный; пóлон жи́зни; (*thinking or talking only*): **~ of o.s.** зáнят одни́м собóй. **2.** (*copious*) подрóбный; **he gave ~ details** он сообщи́л все подрóбности. **3.** (*complete*; *whole*; *reaching the limit*): **the radio was going ~ blast** рáдио бы́ло включенó на пóлную мóщность; **in ~ bloom** в пóлном цветý; **~ dress** костю́м для торжéственных слýчаев; парáдная фóрма; **we waited a ~ hour** мы ждáли цéлый час; **he lay at ~ length** он растянýлся во весь рост; **~ moon** полнолýние; **on ~ pay** на пóлной стáвке; **at ~ speed** на пóлной скóрости; **~ stop** тóчка; **in ~ swing** в пóлном разгáре. **4.** (*plump*) пóлный; **~ in the face** круглоли́цый. **5.** (*amply fitting*) ширóкий; **a ~ skirt** пы́шная ю́бка.
adv. **1.** (*completely*): **she turned the radio on ~** онá включи́ла рáдио на пóлную мóщность; **~ out** пóлностью. **2.** (*squarely*) пря́мо; **he took the blow ~ in the face** удáр пришёлся емý пря́мо в лицó.
cpds. **~-back** *n.* защи́тник; **~-blooded** *adj.* полнокрóвный; **~-face** *adv.* анфáс; **~-fledged** *adj.* вполнé опери́вшийся; (*fig.*) полнопрáвный; **~-grown** *adj.* взрóслый; **~-length** *adj.* во всю длинý; **~-length dress** плáтье дó полу; **~-scale** *adj.* в пóлном объёме; **~-time** *adj.* (*of job*) занимáющий всё (рабóчее) врéмя.
ful(l)ness ['fʊlnɪs] *n.* **1.** (*full state*) полнотá. **2.** (*sense of repletion*) сы́тость. **3.**: **in the ~ of time** в надлежáщее врéмя.
fully ['fʊlɪ] *adv.* вполнé, пóлностью, совершéнно; **~ satisfied** пóлностью удовлетворённый.
cpds. **~-clothed** *adj.* пóлностью одéтый.
fulminate ['fʌlmɪˌneɪt, 'fʊl-] *v.i.* (*flash*) сверк|áть, -нýть; (*fig.*, *protest vehemently*) греми́ть (*impf.*); метáть (*impf.*) грóмы и мóлнии.
fulsome ['fʊlsəm] *adj.* чрезмéрный, тошнотвóрный.
fumble ['fʌmb(ə)l] *v.t.* теребúть (*impf.*) в рукáх.
v.i. ры́ться (*impf.*); неумéло обращáться (*impf.*) (*с чем-н.*); **he ~d in his pockets for a key** он ры́лся в кармáнах, ищá ключ.
fume [fju:m] *n.* дым, кóпоть; **he was overcome by ~s** он потеря́л сознáние от удýшливых испарéний.
v.i. (*fig.*): **fuming with rage** кипя́щий гнéвом.
fumigate ['fju:mɪˌgeɪt] *v.t.* окýр|ивать, -и́ть.
fumigation [ˌfju:mɪ'geɪʃ(ə)n] *n.* окýривание.
fumitory ['fju:mɪtərɪ] *n.* дымя́нка.
fun [fʌn] *n.* шýтка, весéлье, забáва; **it was only meant in ~** э́то былá шýтка; **just for the ~ of it** прóсто рáди удовóльствия; **he never has any ~** он никогдá не весели́тся; **make ~ of** насмехáться (*impf.*) над+*i.*; **he is ~ to be with** с ним не соскýчишься; **what ~!** вот здóрово!; как вéсело!; **figure of ~** предмéт насмéшек; **we had ~ at the party** в гостя́х бы́ло вéсело.
cpd. **~-fair** *n.* увесели́тельный парк.
function ['fʌŋkʃ(ə)n] *n.* **1.** (*proper activity*, *purpose*) фýнкция, назначéние. **2.** (*social gathering*) вéчер; приём. **3.** (*math.*) фýнкция.
v.i. функциони́ровать, дéйствовать (*both impf.*).
functional ['fʌŋkʃən(ə)l] *adj.* функционáльный.
functionary ['fʌŋkʃənərɪ] *n.* чинóвник.
fund [fʌnd] *n.* фонд, запáс, резéрв; (*sum of money*) фонд, капитáл; **relief ~** фонд пóмощи; (*pl.*, *resources*) фóнды (*m. pl.*); дéнежные срéдства; **public ~s** госудáрственные срéдства; **he is in ~s** он при деньгáх.
v.t. финанси́ровать (*impf.*, *pf.*).
cpd. **~-raising** *n.* сбор средств; **a ~-raising dinner** (*for charity*) благотвори́тельный банкéт.
fundamental [ˌfʌndə'ment(ə)l] *n.* (*usu. pl.*, *principle*) оснóва, при́нцип; **the ~s of mathematics** оснóвы матемáтики.
adj. (*basic*) основнóй, сущéственный; **~ly** в основнóм; по существý.
funeral ['fju:nər(ə)l] *n.* пóхор|оны (*pl.*, *g.* -óн); **~ march** похорóнный марш; **~ parlour, home** (*US*) бюрó похорóнных процéссий; **~ pyre** погребáльный костёр; **~ rites** похорóнный обря́д.
funereal [fju:'nɪərɪəl] *adj.* мрáчный; трáурный.
fungus ['fʌŋgəs] *n.* грибóк; ни́зший гриб.
funicular [fju:'nɪkjʊlə(r)] *n.* фуникулёр; канáтная (желéзная) дорóга.
adj. канáтный.
funnel ['fʌn(ə)l] *n.* ворóнка; (*of ship*) дымовáя трубá.
funny ['fʌnɪ] *adj.* **1.** (*amusing*) смешнóй, забáвный; **no ~ business!** без фóкусов! **2.** (*strange*) стрáнный; **it's a ~ thing, but ...** э́то óчень стрáнно, но...; **funnily enough ...** как э́то ни стрáнно,...
cpd. **~-bone** *n.* локтевóй сустáв.
fur [fɜ:(r)] *n.* **1.** (*animal hair*) шерсть. **2.** (*as worn*) мех (*pf.* -á); **~ coat** меховóе пальтó; меховáя шýба.
cpd. **~-bearing** *adj.* пушнóй; **~-seal** *n.* кóтик.
furious ['fjʊərɪəs] *adj.* **1.** (*violent*) бýйный, неистóвый; **a ~ struggle** я́ростная схвáтка; **drive at a ~ pace** éхать (*det.*) на бéшеной скóрости. **2.** (*enraged*) взбешённый; **she was ~ with him** онá разозли́лась на негó не на шýтку.
furl [fɜ:l] *v.t.* (*sails*) свёр|тывать, -нýть; (*umbrella*) склáдывать, сложи́ть.
furlong ['fɜ:lɒŋ] *n.* восьмáя часть ми́ли.
furlough ['fɜ:ləʊ] *n.* óтпуск; **on ~** в отпускý, в óтпуске.

furnace ['fɜːnɪs] *n.* горн, печь; **blast ~** до́менная печь.
furnish ['fɜːnɪʃ] *v.t.* **1.** (*provide*) снаб|жа́ть, -ди́ть (*кого чем*); предост|авля́ть, -а́вить (*что кому*). **2.** (*equip with furniture*) обст|авля́ть, -а́вить; **~ed apartment** меблиро́ванная кварти́ра.
furnishings ['fɜːnɪʃɪŋz] *n.* принадле́жности (*f. pl.*); (*furniture*) обстано́вка.
furniture ['fɜːnɪtʃə(r)] *n.* ме́бель; **~ polish** политу́ра/лак для ме́бели.
furore [fjʊə'rɔːrɪ] *n.* фуро́р.
furrier ['fʌrɪə(r)] *n.* меховщи́к, скорня́к.
furrow ['fʌrəʊ] *n.* **1.** (*in the earth etc.*) борозда́, жё-лоб. **2.** (*wrinkle*) глубо́кая морщи́на.
v.t. борозди́ть, вз-; (*fig.*): **~ed brow** морщи́нистый лоб.
furry ['fɜːrɪ] *adj.* покры́тый ме́хом; пушно́й.
further ['fɜːðə(r)] *adj.* (*see also* **farther**) **1.** дальне́йший; (*additional*) доба́вочный, дополни́тельный; **until ~ notice** до дальне́йшего уведомле́ния; **without ~ ado** без ли́шних хлопо́т; **we need a ~ five pounds** нам ну́жно ещё пять фу́нтов. **2.** (*more distant*) да́льний; **on the ~ side** на друго́й стороне́.
adv. **1.** (*additionally*) в дополне́ние; **~ to my last letter** в дополне́ние к моему́ после́днему письму́. **2.** (*to or at a more distant point*) да́лее, да́льше; **I can go no ~** я не могу́ да́льше идти́; **I'll go ~ than that, he's a liar** бо́лее того́, он лгун.
v.t. продв|ига́ть, -и́нуть; соде́йствовать (*impf.*) +*d.*; спосо́бствовать (*impf.*) +*d.*
furtherance ['fɜːðərəns] *n.* продвиже́ние; **in ~ of this plan** для осуществле́ния э́того пла́на.
furthermore [,fɜːðə'mɔː(r)] *adv.* к тому́ же; кро́ме того́.
furthermost ['fɜːðə,məʊst] *adj.* са́мый да́льний.
furthest ['fɜːðɪst] *adj.* са́мый да́льний.
adv. да́льше всего́; **the ~ I can go is to say that ...** са́мое бо́льшее, что я могу́ сказа́ть, э́то то, что...
furtive ['fɜːtɪv] *adj.* (*of movements*) краду́щийся; скры́тый; (*of a pers.*) скры́тный.
fury ['fjʊərɪ] *n.* **1.** (*violence*) неи́стовство, я́рость, бе́шенство; **the ~ of the elements** я́рость стихи́й. **2.** (*fit of anger*) я́рость; **she flew into a ~** она́ пришла́ в я́рость. **3.** (**F~**: *myth.*) фу́рия.
fuse[1] [fjuːz] *n.* (*elec.*) предохрани́тель (*m.*), про́бка.
v. t. & i. **1.** (*make or become liquid*) пла́вить(ся) (*impf.*). **2.** (*join by fusion*) спл|авля́ть(ся), -а́вить(ся); (*fig.*) сли|ва́ть(ся), -ть(ся); (*elec.*): **he ~d the lights** он пережёг про́бки; **the lights ~d** про́бки перегоре́ли.
cpds. **~-box** *n.* коро́бка с про́бками; **~-wire** *n.* про́волока для предохрани́теля.
fuse[2], **fuze** [fjuːz] *n.* (*igniting device*) запа́л, затра́вка, фити́ль (*m.*); (*detonating device*) заря́дная тру́бка; взрыва́тель (*m.*).
fuselage ['fjuːzə,lɑːʒ, -lɪdʒ] *n.* фюзеля́ж.
fusible ['fjuːzɪb(ə)l] *adj.* пла́вкий.
fusillade [,fjuːzɪ'leɪd] *n.* стрельба́.
fusion ['fjuːʒ(ə)n] *n.* **1.** (*melting together*) сплавле́ние, пла́вка; **~ bomb** термоя́дерная бо́мба. **2.** (*blending, coalition*) сплав, слия́ние.
fuss [fʌs] *n.* суета́, шум (из-за пустяко́в); **cause a lot of ~ and bother** причин|я́ть, -и́ть ма́ссу хлопо́т и забо́т; **get into a ~** разволнова́ться (*pf.*); **make a ~ about, over sth.** суети́ться (*impf.*) вокру́г чего́-н.; **make a ~ of s.o.** суетли́во опека́ть (*impf.*) кого́-н.
v.i. суети́ться (*impf.*); **she ~es over her children** она́ ве́чно во́зится со свои́ми детьми́.
cpd. **~-pot** *n.* (*coll.*) хлопоту́н (*fem.* -ья); суетли́вый челове́к.
fussy ['fʌsɪ] *adj.* **1.** (*worrying over trifles*) суетли́вый. **2.** (*coll., fastidious*) разбо́рчивый. **3.** (*of dress, style etc.*) вы́чурный.
fusty ['fʌstɪ] *adj.* (*stale-smelling*) за́тхлый, спёртый; (*fig., old-fashioned*) старомо́дный.
futile ['fjuːtaɪl] *adj.* напра́сный, тще́тный.
futility [,fjuː'tɪlɪtɪ] *n.* тще́тность, бесполе́зность.
future ['fjuːtʃə(r)] *n.* **1.** бу́дущее; **in (the) ~** в бу́дущем; **for the ~** на бу́дущее; **he has a great ~ before him** у него́ большо́е бу́дущее. **2.** (*gram.*) бу́дущее вре́мя.
adj. бу́дущий; **belief in a ~ life** ве́ра в загро́бную жизнь; (*gram.*): **~ tense** бу́дущее вре́мя; **~ perfect tense** бу́дущее соверше́нное вре́мя.
futurism ['fjuːtʃə,rɪz(ə)m] *n.* футури́зм.
futurist ['fjuːtʃərɪst] *n.* футури́ст.
futuristic [,fjuːtʃə'rɪstɪk] *adj.* футуристи́ческий.
fuze [fjuːz] = **fuse**[2]
fuzz [fʌz] *n.* (*fluffy mass*) пух; (*blur*) мгла.
v.t. (*blur*) затемн|я́ть, -и́ть.
fuzzy ['fʌzɪ] *adj.* (*fluffy*) пуши́стый; (*blurred*) расплы́вчатый.

G

G [dʒiː] *n.* (*mus.*) соль (*nt. indecl.*).
g. [græm] *n.* (*abbr. of* **gram(me)(s)**) гм, (грамм).
gab [gæb] (*coll.*) *n.*: **he has the gift of the ~** у него́ язы́к хорошо́ подве́шен.
v.i. трепа́ться (*impf.*); точи́ть (*impf.*) ля́сы (*coll.*).
gabardine ['gæbə,diːn, -'diːn] *n.* (*material*) габарди́н; (*attr.*) габарди́новый.
gabble ['gæb(ə)l] *n.* бормота́ние; (*sl.*) трёп, трепотня́.
v.t. & i. бормота́ть, про-; (*of geese*) гогота́ть (*impf.*).
gabbler ['gæblə(r)] *n.* болту́н.
gabby ['gæbɪ] *adj.* (*coll.*) болтли́вый, трепли́вый.
gable ['geɪb(ə)l] *n.* щипе́ц; **~(d) roof** двуска́тная кры́ша.
gad [gæd] *v.i.* (*also* **~ about**) шля́ться (*impf.*); шата́ться (*impf.*).
gadfly ['gædflaɪ] *n.* о́вод, слепе́нь (*m.*).
gadget ['gædʒɪt] *n.* (*coll.*) шту́чка.
Gaelic ['geɪlɪk, 'gæ-] *n.* (*language*) гэ́льский язы́к.
adj. гэ́льский.
gaff [gæf] *n.*: **blow the ~** (*coll.*) проболта́ться (*pf.*).
gaffe [gæf] *n.* ло́жный шаг, оплო́шность.
gaffer ['gæfə(r)] *n.* стари́к, дед; (*foreman*) ма́стер (це́ха).
gag [gæg] *n.* **1.** (*to prevent speech etc.*) кляп; (*parl.*) прекраще́ние пре́ний; (*fig.*): **a ~ on free speech** подавле́ние свобо́ды сло́ва. **2.** (*joke*) шу́тка, хо́хма.
v.t. вст|авля́ть, -а́вить кляп +*d.*; (*fig.*) зат|ыка́ть, -кну́ть рот +*d.*; **the press was ~ged** пре́ссу заста́вили замолча́ть.
v.i. (*retch, choke*) дави́ться (*impf.*).
gaggle ['gæg(ə)l] *n.* (*of geese*) ста́я, ста́до; (*fig., joc.*) ста́йка, толпа́.
gaiety ['geɪətɪ] *n.* весёлость.
gain [geɪn] *n.* **1.** (*profit*) при́быль; вы́года; вы́игрыш. **2.** (*pl., things ~ed*) дохо́ды (*m. pl.*); нажи́ва; (*achievements*) завоева́ния; **ill-gotten ~s** нече́стно на́житое. **3.** (*increase*) увеличе́ние; **a ~ in weight** приба́вка в ве́се.
v.t. **1.** (*reach*) доб|ира́ться, -ра́ться до+*g.*; дост|ига́ть, -и́гнуть +*g.*; **the swimmer ~ed the shore** пловéц дости́г бе́рега. **2.** (*win, acquire*) овлад|ева́ть, -е́ть;

доб|ива́ться, -и́ться +*g*.; приобре|та́ть, -сти́; ~ **one's living** зараба́тывать (*impf.*) на жизнь; ~ **a victory** одержа́ть (*pf.*) побе́ду; ~ **time** выи́гр|ывать, вы́играть вре́мя; ~ **a friend** приобрести́ (*pf.*) дру́га; **he ~ed 5 pounds in weight** он попра́вился на 5 фу́нтов; **the patient is ~ing strength** пацие́нт наби-ра́ется сил. **3.** (*also* ~ **over**; *persuade, bring on to one's side*) перемани́ть (*pf.*) на свою́ сто́рону; переубеди́ть (*pf.*).

v.i. **1.** (*reap profit, benefit, advantage*) извл|ека́ть, -е́чь по́льзу/вы́году; **how do I stand to ~ from it?** кака́я мне от э́того по́льза/вы́года?; **he has ~ed in experience** он приобрёл о́пыт. **2.** (*move ahead*): **my watch ~s (three minutes a day)** мои́ часы́ спеша́т (на три мину́ты в день); **he ~ ed on his rival** он нагоня́л сопе́рника.

gainer ['geɪnə(r)] *n.*: **he was a ~ by the transaction** он вы́играл на э́той сде́лке.

gainful ['geɪnfʊl] *adj.* при́быльный; дохо́дный; ~ **employment** опла́чиваемая рабо́та.

gainsa|y [geɪn'seɪ] *v.t.* (*liter.*) противоре́чить (*impf.*) +*d.*; **the facts cannot be ~id** фа́кты неопровер-жи́мы.

gait [geɪt] *n.* похо́дка.

gaiter ['geɪtə(r)] *n.* гама́ша; (*pl.*) ге́тр|ы (*pl., g.* —).

gal [gæl] *n.* (*joc.*) = **girl**

gala ['gɑːlə] *n.* пра́зднество; ~ **day** пра́здничный день; ~ **night** (*theatr.*) гала́-представле́ние.

galactic [gə'læktɪk] *adj.* галакти́ческий.

galaxy ['gæləksɪ] *n.* гала́ктика; (*fig.*) плея́да.

gale [geɪl] *n.* бу́ря; шторм; **it is blowing a ~** ду́ет штормово́й ве́тер; (*fig.*): **~s of laughter** взры́вы (*m. pl.*) хо́хота.

gall[1] [gɔːl] *n.* **1.** жёлчь; (*fig., bitterness*) жёлчность. **2.** (*coll., impudence*) на́глость.

cpds. **~-bladder** *n.* жёлчный пузы́рь; **~stone** *n.* жёлчный ка́мень.

gall[2] [gɔːl] *n.* (*swelling; sore*) потёртость; сса́дина.

v.t. (*lit.*) ссади́ть (*pf.*); нат|ира́ть, -ере́ть; (*fig.*) злить, разо-.

gall[3] [gɔːl] *n.* (*bot.*) галл.

cpd. **~-fly** *n.* орехотво́рка.

gallant ['gælənt] *adj.* **1.** (*attentive to ladies*) гала́нт-ный; (*amatory*) любо́вный. **2.** (*brave*) до́блестный; (*of ship*) велича́вый; (*of horse*) лихо́й, рети́вый.

gallantry ['gæləntrɪ] *n.* (*bravery*) до́блесть; (*courtli-ness to women*) гала́нтность.

galleon ['gælɪən] *n.* галео́н.

gallery ['gælərɪ] *n.* **1.** (*walk, passage*) галере́я; **shoot-ing ~** тир. **2.** (*picture ~*) карти́нная галере́я. **3.** (*raised floor or platform*) хо́р|ы (*pl., g.* -ов); **press ~** места́ для представи́телей печа́ти. **4.** (*theatr.*) галёрка.

galley ['gælɪ] *n.* **1.** (*ship*) гале́ра. **2.** (*ship's kitchen*) ка́мбуз; (*in aircraft*) пищебло́к. **3.** (*typ.*) (**~-proof**) гра́нка.

Gallic ['gælɪk] *adj.* га́лльский.

galling ['gɔːlɪŋ] *adj.* (*fig.*) раздража́ющий.

gallivant ['gælɪ,vænt] *v.i.* (*coll.*) шля́ться (*impf.*); слоня́ться (*impf.*).

gallon ['gælən] *n.* галло́н.

gallop ['gæləp] *n.* гало́п; **he rode off at a/full ~** он поскака́л во весь опо́р; **we went for a ~** мы отпра́-вились на верхову́ю прогу́лку.

v.t.: ~ **a horse** пус|ка́ть, -ти́ть ло́шадь гало́пом.

gallows ['gæləʊz] *n.* (*also* **~-tree**) ви́селица.

galore [gə'lɔː(r)] *adv.* (*coll.*) в изоби́лии, ско́лько уго́дно.

galosh [gə'lɒʃ] *n.* гало́ша.

galvanic [gæl'vænɪk] *adj.* гальвани́ческий.

galvanism ['gælvə,nɪz(ə)m] *n.* гальвани́зм.

galvanize ['gælvə,naɪz] *v.t.* гальванизи́ровать (*impf.*, *pf.*); (*fig.*) побу|жда́ть, -ди́ть; возбу|жда́ть, -ди́ть; гальванизи́ровать.

gambit ['gæmbɪt] *n.* (*chess*) гамби́т; (*trick*) ухва́тка.

gamble ['gæmb(ə)l] *n.* аза́ртная игра́; (*risky under-taking*) риско́ванное предприя́тие; **take a ~** пойти́ (*pf.*) на риск.

v.t. & i. игра́ть (*impf.*) в аза́ртные и́гры; ~ **away a fortune** проигра́ть (*pf.*) состоя́ние.

gambler ['gæmblə(r)] *n.* игро́к; картёжник.

gambling ['gæmblɪŋ] *n.* аза́ртные и́гры (*f. pl.*).

cpds. **~-den** *n.* иго́рный прито́н.

gambol ['gæmb(ə)l] *n.* прыжо́к, скачо́к.

v.i. пры́г|ать, -нуть.

game[1] [geɪm] *n.* **1.** игра́; **we had a ~ of golf** мы сыгра́ли па́ртию в гольф; **play the ~** (*fig.*) игра́ть (*impf.*) по пра́вилам; **~s** (*at school*) физкульту́ра; **Olympic G~s** Олимпи́йские и́гры; **what is the state of the ~?** (*score*) како́й счёт?; **we bought the child a ~** мы купи́ли ребёнку насто́льную игру́; **beat s.o. at his own ~** поби́ть (*pf.*) кого́-н. его́ же ору́-жием. **2.** (*scheme, plan, trick*) игра́; **he is playing a deep ~** он ведёт сло́жную игру́; **he gave the ~ away** он раскры́л свои́ ка́рты; **the ~ is up** ста́вка би́та; ко́нчен бал! **3.** (*hunted animal, quarry*) дичь; зверь (*m.*); **big ~** кру́пный зверь; **fair ~** (*fig.*) объе́кт тра́вли.

adj. боево́й; задо́рный; **are you ~ for a ten-mile walk?** у вас есть настрое́ние соверши́ть прогу́лку миль на де́сять?

v.t. & i. игра́ть, сыгра́ть; **gaming-house** иго́рный дом; **gaming-table** иго́рный стол.

cpds. **~-bag** *n.* ягдта́ш; **~keeper** *n.* лесни́к, охра-ня́ющий дичь; **~-preserve** *n.* охо́тничий запове́д-ник; **~s-master/mistress** *nn.* преподава́тель(ница) физкульту́ры; **~-warden** *n.* е́герь/лесни́к, охраня́-ющий дичь.

game[2] [geɪm] *adj.* (*lame*) хромо́й.

gamete ['gæmiːt, gə'miːt] *n.* гаме́та.

gamma ['gæmə] *n.*: ~ **rays** га́мма-лучи́ (*m. pl.*).

gammon ['gæmən] *n.* (*ham, bacon*) о́корок.

gamut ['gæmət] *n.* (*mus.*) га́мма; (*fig.*) диапазо́н, га́мма; **she ran the ~ of the emotions** она́ передала́ всю га́мму чувств.

gander ['gændə(r)] *n.* (*male goose*) гуса́к; (*sl., look*): **take a ~ at** взгля́|дывать, -ну́ть на+*a*.

gang [gæŋ] *n.* (*of workmen*) брига́да; (*of prisoners*) па́ртия (заключённых); (*of criminals*) ша́йка, ба́нда.

v.i.: **they ~ together** они́ собира́ются в ба́нду (*or* ба́ндой); **they ~ed up on me** они́ ополчи́лись про́-тив/на меня́.

cpds. **~land** *n.* престу́пный мир; **~-plank** *n.* схо́д-ни (*f. pl.*); **~way** *n.* (*from ship to shore*) схо́дни (*f. pl.*); (*from aircraft to ground*) трап; (*in theatre etc.*) прохо́д; (*coll. int., clear the way!*) прочь с доро́ги!; сторони́сь!

gangling ['gæŋglɪŋ] *adj.* долговя́зый.

ganglion ['gæŋglɪən] *n.* га́нглий, не́рвный у́зел.

gangrene ['gæŋgriːn] *n.* гангре́на.

gangrenous ['gæŋgrɪnəs] *adj.* гангрено́зный.

gangster ['gæŋstə(r)] *n.* га́нгстер.

gannet ['gænɪt] *n.* (*bird*) о́луша; (*fig., glutton*) обжо́ра.

gantry ['gæntrɪ] *n.* помо́ст; ~ **crane** эстака́дный кран.

gaol [dʒeɪl] *n.* тюрьма́; (*imprisonment*) тюре́мное заключе́ние; **break ~** бежа́ть (*pf.*) из тюрьмы́.

v.t. заключ|а́ть, -и́ть в тюрьму́.

cpds. **~-bird** *n.* аре́стант, рецидиви́ст; **~-break** *n.* побе́г из тюрьмы́.

gaoler ['dʒeɪlə(r)] *n.* тюре́мщик, тюре́мный надзира́-тель (*m.*).

gap [gæp] *n.* **1.** (*in a wall etc.*) брешь, проло́м; (*in defences*) проры́в; (*in ranks*) брешь; **he filled up the ~s in his education** он воспо́лнил пробе́лы в своём образова́нии; **there is a wide ~ between their**

views они́ ре́зко расхо́дятся во взгля́дах; **export ~** э́кспортный дефици́т. **2.** (*gorge, pass*) прохо́д; уще́лье.

gap|e [geɪp] *v.i.* (*stare*) зева́ть (*impf.*) (на+*a.*); глазе́ть (*impf.*) (на+*a.*); **a ~ing wound** зия́ющая ра́на; **the chasm ~ed before him** пе́ред ним зия́ла про́пасть.

garage ['gærɑːdʒ, -rɪdʒ] *n.* гара́ж.

v.t. ста́вить, по- в гара́ж.

cpd. **~-hand** *n.* рабо́чий/меха́ник в гараже́; автосле́сарь (*m.*).

garb [gɑːb] *n.* наря́д.

garbage ['gɑːbɪdʒ] *n.* отбро́сы (*m. pl.*); му́сор.

cpds. **~-can** *n.* му́сорный я́щик; **~-collector** *n.* му́сорщик.

garble ['gɑːb(ə)l] *v.t.* (*distort*) иска|жа́ть, -зи́ть; ковéркать, ис-.

garden ['gɑːd(ə)n] *n.* **1.** (*plot of ground*) сад; **vegetable ~** огоро́д; **lead up the ~ path** (*coll.*) води́ть за́ нос (*indet.*); **everything in the ~'s lovely** (*coll., all is well*) всё в поря́дке. **2.** (*attr.*) садо́вый; огоро́дный; **common or ~** обы́денный; заура́дный; **~ flowers/plants** садо́вые цветы́/расте́ния; **~ city** го́род-сад; **~ party** приём на откры́том во́здухе; **~ suburb** да́чный посёлок. **3.** (*pl., park*) сад; парк; **Zoological G~s** зоологи́ческий сад; зоопа́рк.

v.i. занима́ться (*impf.*) садово́дством; **he is fond of ~ing** он лю́бит садово́дство; **~ing tools** садо́вые инструме́нты.

gardener ['gɑːdnə(r)] *n.* садо́вник; (*horticulturist*) садово́д.

gardenia [gɑː'diːnɪə] *n.* гарде́ния.

gargantuan [gɑː'gæntjʊən] *adj.* гига́нтский, колосса́льный.

gargle ['gɑːg(ə)l] *n.* полоска́ние.

v.i. полоска́ть, про- го́рло.

gargoyle ['gɑːgɔɪl] *n.* горгу́лья.

garish ['geərɪʃ] *adj.* пёстрый, бро́ский, крича́щий.

garishness ['geərɪʃnɪs] *n.* пестрота́, бро́скость.

garland ['gɑːlənd] *n.* гирля́нда; вено́к.

v.t. укр|аша́ть, -а́сить гирля́ндами.

garlic ['gɑːlɪk] *n.* чесно́к; **clove of ~** зубо́к чеснока́.

garment ['gɑːmənt] *n.* одея́ние; (*pl., clothes*) оде́жда; **the ~ industry** (*dressmaking, tailoring*) шве́йная промы́шленность.

garner ['gɑːnə(r)] *v.t.* (*liter.*) сс|ыпа́ть, -ы́пать в амба́р; (*fig.*): **~ experience** нак|а́пливать, -опи́ть о́пыт.

garnet ['gɑːnɪt] *n.* грана́т.

garnish ['gɑːnɪʃ] *n.* отде́лка, украше́ние; (*cul.*) гарни́р.

v.t. (*decorate*) укр|аша́ть, -а́сить; (*cul.*) гарни́ровать (*impf., pf.*).

garret ['gærɪt] *n.* манса́рда; черда́к.

garrison ['gærɪs(ə)n] *n.* гарнизо́н; (*attr.*) гарнизо́нный.

v.t.: **~ a town** ста́вить, по- гарнизо́н в го́роде.

garrulous ['gærʊləs] *adj.* болтли́вый, говорли́вый.

garter ['gɑːtə(r)] *n.* подвя́зка.

gas [gæs] *n.* **1.** газ; **natural ~** приро́дный газ; **put the kettle on the ~** поста́вить ча́йник на газ; **turn the ~ on/off** включи́ть/вы́ключить газ; (*dentist's*) эфи́р; (*poison ~*) ядови́тый газ; отравля́ющее вещество́; (*mining*) грему́чий газ; (*flatulence*) га́зы (*m. pl.*). **2.** (*attr.*) га́зовый; **~ alarm, alert** хими́ческая трево́га; **~ bomb** хими́ческая бо́мба; **~ burner** га́зовая горе́лка; **~ chamber** (*for lethal purposes*) га́зовая ка́мера; **~ cooker** га́зовая плита́; **~ field** месторожде́ние га́за; **~ fire** га́зовый ками́н; **~ lighting** га́зовое освеще́ние; **~ main** газопрово́д; **~ mask** противога́з; **~ meter** га́зовый счётчик; **~ oven** (*domestic*) га́зовая духо́вка; **~ ring** га́зовое кольцо́; **~ shelter** газоубе́жище; **~ stove** га́зовая плита́; *see also cpds.* **3.** (*US, petrol*) бензи́н, горю́чее; **step on the ~** (*coll.*) да|ва́ть, -ть га́зу; **~ station** бензоколо́нка; **~ tank** бензоба́к.

v.t. (*poison with ~*) отрав|ля́ть, -и́ть га́зом; (*kill with ~*) умер|щвля́ть, -тви́ть га́зом.

v.i. (*coll., talk long and emptily*) болта́ть (*impf.*); моло́ть (*impf.*).

cpds. **~bag** *n.* (*coll., chatterer*) пустоме́ля (*c.g.*); **~light** *n.* га́зовое освеще́ние; **~-lit** *adj.* освещённый га́зом; **~man** *n.* (сле́сарь-)газовщи́к; **~works** *n.* га́зовый заво́д.

gaseous ['gæsɪəs] *adj.* га́зовый; газообра́зный.

gash [gæʃ] *n.* разре́з; глубо́кая ра́на.

v.t. разр|еза́ть, -е́зать; полосну́ть (*pf.*).

gasket ['gæskɪt] *n.* прокла́дка; тесьма́.

gasol|ine, -ene ['gæsə,liːn] *n.* газоли́н; (*US, petrol*) бензи́н.

gasp [gɑːsp] *n.* глото́к во́здуха; перехва́т дыха́ния; **at one's last ~** при после́днем издыха́нии.

v.t. & i. зад|ыха́ться, -охну́ться; а́хнуть (*pf.*); **he ~ed out a few words** задыха́ясь, он произнёс не́сколько слов; **he ~ed with astonishment** он задохну́лся от удивле́ния.

gastric ['gæstrɪk] *adj.* желу́дочный; **~ juice** желу́дочный сок; **~ ulcer** я́зва желу́дка.

gastritis [gæ'straɪtɪs] *n.* гастри́т.

gastro-enteritis [,gæstrəʊ,entə'raɪtɪs] *n.* гастроэнтери́т.

gastronome ['gæstrə,nəʊm] *n.* гастроно́м.

gastronomic [,gæstrə'nɒmɪk] *adj.* гастрономи́ческий.

gastronomy [gæ'strɒnəmɪ] *n.* гастроно́мия.

gate [geɪt] *n.* **1.** вор|о́та (*pl., g.* -о́т); кали́тка; (*city ~*) городски́е воро́та; (*garden ~*) садо́вая кали́тка; (*water-~*) шлю́зные воро́та. **2.** (*fig.*) (*size of audience*) коли́чество зри́телей; (*takings*) сбор, вы́ручка.

cpds. **~-crash** *v.t. & i.* приходи́ть, -йти́ незва́ным; про|ходи́ть, -йти́ без биле́та; **~-crasher** *n.* незва́ный гость; (*spectator*) безбиле́тный зри́тель (*m.*), «за́яц»; **~-house** *n.* сторо́жка; **~-keeper** *n.* привра́тник; **~way** *n.* подворо́тня; (*fig.*) подхо́д.

gateau ['gætəʊ] *n.* пиро́жное; торт.

gather ['gæðə(r)] *n.* (*in cloth*) сбо́рки (*f. pl.*).

v.t. **1.** (*pick, cull: e.g. flowers, nuts, harvest; also ~ in*) соб|ира́ть, -ра́ть. **2.** (*collect, also ~ up*) соб|ира́ть, -ра́ть; **things ~ dust** ве́щи собира́ют пыль; **he ~ed his papers together** он собра́л свои́ бума́ги; **~ experience** нака́пливать (*impf.*) о́пыт. **3.** (*receive addition of*) наб|ира́ть, -ра́ть +*a. or g.*; **the ship ~ed way** кора́бль набра́л ход. **4.** (*understand, conclude*) заключ|а́ть, -и́ть; де́лать, с- вы́вод (*pf.*) (*на основании чего-н.*); **I ~ he's abroad** он как бу́дто за грани́цей; **I ~ you don't like him** мне сдаётся, что он вам не нра́вится; **as far as I can ~** наско́лько я могу́ суди́ть. **5.** (*draw, pull together*): **he ~ed his cloak about him** он заверну́лся в плащ; **he ~ed her in his arms** он заключи́л её в объя́тия; **~ one's thoughts** соб|ира́ться, -ра́ться с мы́слями. **6.** (*sewing*) соб|ира́ть, -ра́ть в скла́дки.

v.i. **1.** (*collect*) соб|ира́ться, -ра́ться; **a crowd ~ed** собрала́сь толпа́. **2.** (*increase*) нараст|а́ть, -и́; **the tale ~ed like a snowball** исто́рия разраста́лась как сне́жный ком.

gathering ['gæðərɪŋ] *n.* собра́ние; встре́ча.

gauche [gəʊʃ] *adj.* нело́вкий; неуклю́жий.

gaudy ['gɔːdɪ] *adj.* (*of colour*) крича́щий; безвку́сный.

gauge (*US* **gage**) [geɪdʒ] *n.* **1.** (*thickness, diameter etc.*) разме́р; (*rail.*): **standard ~** станда́ртная колея́; **narrow ~** у́зкая колея́. **2.** (*instrument*) шабло́н; лека́ло; этало́н.

v.t. **1.** (*measure*) изм|еря́ть, -е́рить. **2.** (*fig., estimate*) оце́н|ивать, -и́ть; взве́сить (*pf.*); **~ the strength of the wind** определ|я́ть, -и́ть си́лу ве́тра.

gaunt [gɔ:nt] *adj.* исхуда́лый; измождённый.
gauntlet[1] ['gɔ:ntlɪt] *n.* рукави́ца; (*armoured glove*) ла́тная рукави́ца; **throw down the ~** (*fig.*) бро́сить (*pf.*) перча́тку/вы́зов; **pick up the ~** приня́ть (*pf.*) вы́зов.
gauntlet[2] ['gɔ:ntlɪt] *n.*: **run the ~** про|ходи́ть, -йти́ сквозь строй.
gauze [gɔ:z] *n.* ма́рля, газ.
gavel ['gæv(ə)l] *n.* молото́к.
gawk [gɔ:k] *v.i.* (*also* **gawp**) глазе́ть (*impf.*); пя́лить (*impf.*) глаза́ (на+*a.*).
gawky ['gɔ:kɪ] *adj.* нело́вкий, неуклю́жий.
gawp [gɔ:p] = **gawk** *v.i.*
gay [geɪ] *adj.* весёлый; **~ colours** я́ркие цвета́; (*coll., homosexual*) гомосексуа́льный, голубо́й.
gaz|e [geɪz] *n.* при́стальный взгляд; **a strange sight met his ~e** его́ взо́ру откры́лось стра́нное зре́лище.
v.i. при́стально гляде́ть; **stop ~ing around!** переста́ньте глазе́ть по сторона́м!
gazelle [gə'zel] *n.* газе́ль.
gazette [gə'zet] *n.* (*official journal*) официа́льные ве́домости (*f. pl.*); (*newspaper*) газе́та.
gazetteer [,gæzɪ'tɪə(r)] *n.* географи́ческий спра́вочник; слова́рь географи́ческих назва́ний.
GB (*abbr. of* ***Great Britain***) Великобрита́ния.
GCSE (*abbr. of* ***General Certificate of Secondary Education***) ≃ аттеста́т о сре́днем образова́нии.
GDR (*abbr. of* ***German Democratic Republic***) ГДР, (Герма́нская Демократи́ческая Респу́блика).
gear [gɪə(r)] *n.* **1.** (*apparatus, mechanism*) механи́зм. **2.** (*equipment, utensils, clothing*) принадле́жности (*f. pl.*), аксессуа́ры (*m. pl.*); оде́жда; **hunting ~** охо́тничье снаряже́ние; **household ~** хозя́йственные принадле́жности. **3.** (*of car etc.*) зу́бчатая переда́ча; **top ~** вы́сшая переда́ча; **bottom ~** пе́рвая переда́ча; **reverse ~** за́дний ход; **the car is in ~** маши́на на переда́че; **throw out of ~** (*fig.*) расстр|а́ивать, -о́ить.
v.t.: (*fig., adjust, correlate*) приспос|обля́ть, -о́бить; **production is ~ed to demand** произво́дство приспосо́блено к спро́су.
cpds. **~-box** *n.* коро́бка переда́ч; **~-lever** *n.* рыча́г переключе́ния переда́ч/скоросте́й **~-shift** *n.* переключе́ние переда́ч.
Geiger ['gaɪgə(r)] *n.*: **~ counter** счётчик Ге́йгера.
geisha ['geɪʃə] *n.* ге́йша.
gelatine ['dʒelə,ti:n] *n.* желати́н.
gelatinous [dʒɪ'lætɪnəs] *adj.* желати́новый.
geld [geld] *v.t.* кастри́ровать (*impf., pf.*).
gelding ['geldɪŋ] *n.* ме́рин.
gelignite ['dʒelɪg,naɪt] *n.* гелигни́т.
gem [dʒem] *n.* (*jewel*) драгоце́нный ка́мень; (*fig., outstanding specimen*) жемчу́жина, сокро́вище.
cpd. **~stone** *n.* драгоце́нный ка́мень.
Gemini ['dʒemɪ,naɪ, -,ni:] *n.* Близнецы́ (*m. pl.*).
gendarme ['ʒɒndɑ:m] *n.* жанда́рм.
gendarmerie [ʒɒn'dɑ:mərɪ] *n.* жандарме́рия.
gender ['dʒendə(r)] *n.* род.
gene [dʒi:n] *n.* ген.
genealogical [,dʒi:nɪə'lɒdʒɪk(ə)l] *adj.* родосло́вный; генеалоги́ческий.
genealogist [,dʒi:nɪ'ælədʒɪst] *n.* специали́ст по генеало́гии.
genealogy [,dʒi:nɪ'ælədʒɪ] *n.* генеало́гия.
general ['dʒenər(ə)l] *n.* генера́л.
adj. **1.** (*universal or nearly so*) о́бщий; генера́льный; **~ rule** о́бщее пра́вило; **~ election** всео́бщие вы́боры; **~ strike** всео́бщая забасто́вка; **~ knowledge** о́бщие зна́ния; **~ practitioner** терапе́вт; **~ hospital** больни́ца о́бщего ти́па; **~ reader** ма́ссовый чита́тель; **G~ Assembly** (*of UN*) Генера́льная Ассамбле́я; **a book of ~ interest** неспециализи́рованная кни́га. **2.** (*usual, prevalent*) обы́чный; повсеме́стный; **~ opinion** о́бщее мне́ние; **in ~** вообще́; **as a ~ rule** как пра́вило, обыкнове́нно. **3.** (*approximate; not specific*) о́бщий; **~ resemblance** о́бщее схо́дство; **~ idea** о́бщее представле́ние. **4.** (*chief*) гла́вный; **~ staff** генера́льный штаб; **G~ Post Office** главпочта́мт.
cpd. **~-purpose** *adj.* многоцелево́й; универса́льный.
generalissimo [,dʒenərə'lɪsɪ,məʊ] *n.* генерали́ссимус.
generalit|y [,dʒenə'rælɪtɪ] *n.* **1.** (*majority*) большинство́. **2.** (*general statement*) о́бщее ме́сто, о́бщая фра́за; **he spoke in ~ies** он говори́л о́бщими фра́зами.
generalization [,dʒenərəlaɪ'zeɪʃ(ə)n] *n.* обобще́ние.
generalize ['dʒenərə,laɪz] *v.t. & i.* обобщ|а́ть, -и́ть; (*make general*) распростран|я́ть, -и́ть.
generally ['dʒenərəlɪ] *adv.* **1.** (*usually*) обы́чно. **2.** (*widely*) широко́; бо́льшей ча́стью; **the plan was ~ welcomed** план получи́л всео́бщее одобре́ние; **~ received ideas** общепри́нятые поня́тия. **3.** (*approximately, summarily*) вообще́; **~ speaking** вообще́ говоря́. **4.** (*as a class*): **this is true of Frenchmen ~** э́то отно́сится к францу́зам вообще́.
generat|e ['dʒenə,reɪt] *v.t.* поро|жда́ть, -ди́ть; вызыва́ть, вы́звать; **~e heat** выделя́ть (*impf.*) тепло́; **~e hatred** вызыва́ть (*impf.*) не́нависть; **~ing station** электроста́нция.
generation [,dʒenə'reɪʃ(ə)n] *n.* **1.** (*of heat etc.*) генера́ция. **2.** (*geneal.*) поколе́ние; **from ~ to ~** из поколе́ния в поколе́ние; **a ~ ago** в про́шлом поколе́нии; **the ~ gap** пробле́ма отцо́в и дете́й. **3.** (*fig., of weapons etc.*) эта́п разви́тия.
generator ['dʒenə,reɪtə(r)] *n.* производи́тель (*m.*); (*tech.*) генера́тор.
generic [dʒɪ'nerɪk] *adj.* (*of a class*) родово́й; (*general*) о́бщий; (*of drug*) непатенто́ванный, о́бщего ти́па.
generosity [,dʒenə'rɒsɪtɪ] *n.* великоду́шие; ще́дрость.
generous ['dʒenərəs] *adj.* **1.** (*magnanimous*) великоду́шный. **2.** (*liberal*) ще́дрый. **3.** (*plentiful*) оби́льный; **a ~ helping of meat** ще́драя/соли́дная по́рция мя́са.
genesis ['dʒenɪsɪs] *n.* гене́зис; возникнове́ние; **(Book of) G ~** кни́га Бытия́.
genetic [dʒɪ'netɪk] *adj.* генети́ческий; **~ fingerprinting** ге́нная дактилоскопи́я.
geneticist [dʒɪ'netɪsɪst] *n.* гене́тик.
genetics [dʒɪ'netɪks] *n.* гене́тика.
genial ['dʒi:nɪəl] *adj.* **1.** (*jovial, kindly*) серде́чный, доброду́шный. **2.** мя́гкий; **a ~ climate** мя́гкий/благотво́рный кли́мат.
geniality [,dʒi:nɪ'ælɪtɪ] *n.* раду́шие; доброду́шие.
genie ['dʒi:nɪ] *n.* джинн, дух.
genital ['dʒenɪt(ə)l] *adj.* полово́й; (*pl.*) половы́е о́рганы (*m. pl.*), гени́талии (*f. pl.*).
genitive ['dʒenɪtɪv] *n. & adj.* роди́тельный (паде́ж).
genius ['dʒi:nɪəs] *n.* ге́ний; **a man of ~** гениа́льный челове́к.
genocide ['dʒenə,saɪd] *n.* геноци́д.
genre ['ʒɑ̃rə] *n.* жанр; (*attr.*) жа́нровый, бытово́й.
gent [dʒent] *n.* (*coll.*) тип; **~s** (*lavatory*) мужска́я убо́рная.
genteel [dʒen'ti:l] *adj.* благовоспи́танный; «благоро́дный»; с аристократи́ческими зама́шками; **they live in ~ poverty** они́ живу́т в го́рдой нищете́.
gentian ['dʒenʃ(ə)n, -ʃɪən] *n.* гореча́вка.
gentile ['dʒentaɪl] *n.* неевре́й; (*bibl.*) язы́чник.
adj. неевре́йский; язы́ческий.
gentility [dʒen'tɪlɪtɪ] *n.* благовоспи́танность.
gentle ['dʒent(ə)l] *adj.* (*mild, tender, kind*) мя́гкий, ти́хий, делика́тный; **~ heat** лёгкое тепло́; **a ~ slope** отло́гий склон; **a ~ breeze** лёгкий ветеро́к; **a ~ hint** то́нкий намёк.

cpds. **~folk** *n.* дворя́нство; знать; **~woman** *n.* да́ма; ле́ди (*f. indecl.*).

gentleman ['dʒent(ə)lmən] *n.* джентльме́н; **~'s agreement** джентльме́нское соглаше́ние; **a ~ has called to see you** како́й-то господи́н жела́ет вас ви́деть; **gentlemen!** господа́!

gentlemanly ['dʒent(ə)lmənlɪ] *adj.* джентльме́нский; по-джентльме́нски.

gentleness ['dʒent(ə)lnɪs] *n.* мя́гкость, не́жность.

gently ['dʒentlɪ] *adv.* мя́гко; делика́тно; **hold it ~!** держи́те осторо́жно!

gentry ['dʒentrɪ] *n.* нетитуло́ванное дворя́нство.

genuflect ['dʒenjʊˌflekt] *v.i.* преклон|я́ть, -и́ть коле́но.

genuine ['dʒenjʊɪn] *adj.* настоя́щий; по́длинный; **~ sorrow** и́скренняя печа́ль; **a ~ person** прямо́й/и́скренний челове́к.

genus ['dʒi:nəs, 'dʒenəs] *n.* род.

geocentric [ˌdʒi:əʊ'sentrɪk] *adj.* геоцентри́ческий.

geodesy [dʒi:'ɒdɪsɪ] *n.* геоде́зия.

geodetic [ˌdʒi:əʊ'detɪk] *adj.* геодези́ческий.

geographer [dʒɪ'ɒgrəfə(r)] *n.* гео́граф.

geographic(al) [ˌdʒi:ə'græfɪk(ə)l] *adj.* географи́ческий.

geography [dʒɪ'ɒgrəfɪ] *n.* геогра́фия.

geological [ˌdʒi:ə'lɒdʒɪk(ə)l] *adj.* геологи́ческий.

geologist [dʒɪ'ɒlədʒɪst] *n.* гео́лог.

geology [dʒɪ'ɒlədʒɪ] *n.* геоло́гия.

geometric(al) [ˌdʒɪə'metrɪkəl] *adj.* геометри́ческий.

geometry [dʒɪ'ɒmɪtrɪ] *n.* геоме́трия.

geophysical [ˌdʒi:əʊ'fɪzɪkəl] *adj.* геофизи́ческий.

geophysics [ˌdʒi:əʊ'fɪzɪks] *n.* геофи́зика.

geopolitical [ˌdʒi:əʊpə'lɪtɪk(ə)l] *adj.* геополити́ческий.

geopolitics [ˌdʒi:əʊ'pɒlɪtɪks] *n.* геополи́тика.

geoprobe ['dʒi:əʊˌprəʊb] *n.* геофизи́ческая раке́та.

Georgia ['dʒɔ:dʒɪə] *n.* Гру́зия.

Georgian[1] ['dʒɔ:dʒ(ə)n] *n.* грузи́н (*fem.* -ка). *adj.* грузи́нский.

Georgian[2] ['dʒɔ:dʒ(ə)n] *adj.* (*Br.*): **~ architecture** георгиа́нский стиль в архитекту́ре.

geranium [dʒə'reɪnɪəm] *n.* гера́нь.

geriatric [ˌdʒerɪ'ætrɪk] *adj.* гериатри́ческий.

geriatrics [ˌdʒerɪ'ætrɪks] *n.* гериатри́я.

germ [dʒɜ:m] *n.* микро́б; **~ warfare** бактериологи́ческая война́; (*fig.*) зача́тки (*m. pl.*); **the ~ of an idea** зарожде́ние иде́и.

German ['dʒɜ:mən] *n.* **1.** (*pers.*) не́м|ец (*fem.* -ка); **Swiss ~ (*or* ~ Swiss)** швейца́рский не́мец. **2.** (*language*) неме́цкий язы́к.

adj. неме́цкий; (*esp. pol.*) герма́нский; **~ measles** красну́ха.

germane [dʒɜ:'meɪn] *adj.* уме́стный; подходя́щий.

germanium [dʒɜ:'meɪnɪəm] *n.* герма́ний.

Germany ['dʒɜ:mənɪ] *n.* Герма́ния; **Federal Republic of ~ (FRG)** Федерати́вная Респу́блика Герма́ния (*abbr.* ФРГ).

germicidal [ˌdʒɜ:mɪ'saɪd(ə)l] *adj.* бактерици́дный.

germinal ['dʒɜ:mɪn(ə)l] *adj.* заро́дышевый.

germinate ['dʒɜ:mɪˌneɪt] *v.i.* прораст|а́ть, -и́; (*fig.*) дава́ть (*impf.*) всхо́ды.

germination [ˌdʒɜ:mɪ'neɪʃ(ə)n] *n.* прораста́ние; (*fig.*) зарожде́ние; разви́тие.

gerontocracy [ˌdʒerɒn'tɒkrəsɪ] *n.* правле́ние старе́йших.

gerontology [ˌdʒerɒn'tɒlədʒɪ] *n.* геронтоло́гия.

gerund ['dʒerənd] *n.* геру́ндий.

gerundive [dʒe'rʌndɪv] *n.* герунди́в.

Gestapo [ge'stɑ:pəʊ] *n.* геста́по (*indecl.*); (*attr.*) геста́повский; **~ man** геста́повец.

gestate [dʒe'steɪt] *v.t.* вына́шивать, вы́носить.

gestation [dʒe'steɪʃ(ə)n] *n.* бере́менность; (*fig.*) созрева́ние.

gesticulate [dʒe'stɪkjʊˌleɪt] *v.i.* жестикули́ровать (*impf.*).

gesticulation [dʒeˌstɪkjʊ'leɪʃ(ə)n] *n.* жестикуля́ция.

gesture ['dʒestʃə(r)] *n.* жест.

v.i. жестикули́ровать (*impf.*).

get [get] *v.t.* **1.** (*obtain, receive*) получ|а́ть, -и́ть; **I got your telegram** я получи́л ва́шу телегра́мму; **we got dinner at the hotel** мы поу́жинали в гости́нице; **I got Paris on the radio** я пойма́л по приёмнику Пари́ж; **I've got it!** (*answer to problem etc.*) э́врика!; дошло́!; **I ~ you** (*sl., understand*) по́нял!; **have you got that (down)?** (*e.g. to secretary*) (вы э́то) записа́ли?; гото́во?; **I never ~ time to see him** ника́к не могу́ вы́брать вре́мя повида́ться с ним; **this room ~s a lot of sun** э́та ко́мната о́чень со́лнечная; **he got his own way** он доби́лся своего́; **I ~ 9.5** (*as answer to calculation*) у меня́ получи́лось 9,5; **I got** (*bought*) **a new suit** я приобрёл/купи́л но́вый костю́м. **2.** (*of suffering etc.*): **he got 2 years** (*sentence*) он получи́л 2 го́да (тюрьмы́); **he got the measles** он заболе́л ко́рью; **he got a blow on the head** он получи́л уда́р по голове́; **she got her feet wet** она́ промочи́ла но́ги. **3.** (*procure, fetch, reach, lay hands on*) дост|ава́ть, -а́ть; доб|ыва́ть, -ы́ть; **I got him a chair** я принёс ему́ стул; **the book is not in stock, but we can ~ it for you** э́той кни́ги нет на скла́де, но мы мо́жем её вам доста́ть; **~ me the manager!** мне заве́дующего!; **I got him by telephone** я с ним связа́лся по телефо́ну. **4.** (*bring into a position or state*): **we got him home** мы доста́вили его́ домо́й; **he got the sum right** он пра́вильно реши́л зада́чу; **we got the room tidy** мы прибра́ли ко́мнату; **we got the piano through the door** мы пронесли́ пиани́но че́рез дверь; **I got the clock going** я почини́л часы́; **I've got him where I want him** тепе́рь он у меня́ в рука́х. **5.** (*p.p., expr. possession*): **he has got a book** у него́ есть кни́га. **6.** (*p.p., expr. obligation*): **I have got to go** я до́лжен идти́; (*coll., expr. inference*) **you've got to be joking** вы, коне́чно (*or* должно́ быть), шу́тите. **7.** (*induce, persuade*) заст|авля́ть, -а́вить; **I got him to talk** я заста́вил его́ заговори́ть; **I got the fire to burn** мне удало́сь разже́чь ого́нь. **8.** (*factitive*): **I got my hair cut** я подстри́гся; **I got the table made by the carpenter** я заказа́л стол у столяра́. **9.** (*conquer, captivate*) завоёв|ывать, -а́ть; **there you have got me** вот тут-то вы меня́ и пойма́ли. **10.** (*denoting progress or achievement*): **I got to know him** я его́ узна́л бли́же; **I could not ~ to see him** мне не удало́сь с ним уви́деться; **I got to like travelling** я полюби́л путеше́ствия; **they got to be friends** они́ подружи́лись; **he got to be manager** он стал дире́ктором. **11.** (*see, experience*): **you never ~ working men standing for parliament** вы не встре́тите рабо́чего, кото́рый бы выставля́л свою́ кандидату́ру в парла́мент; **you won't ~ me inviting him again** бу́дьте поко́йны — я его́ никогда́ бо́льше не позову́! **12.** (*sl., kill, 'do for'*) поко́нчить (*pf.*) с+*i*.

v.i. **1.** (*become, be*) ста|нови́ться, -ть; **he got red in the face** он покрасне́л; **he got angry** он разозли́лся; **he got drunk** он напи́лся; **he got married** он жени́лся; **he got ready** он пригото́вился; **he got left behind** он отста́л; **he got killed** его́ уби́ли; он поги́б; **we got talking** мы разговори́лись. **2.** (*arrive*) приб|ыва́ть, -ы́ть; **when did you ~ here?** когда́ вы сюда́ при́были?; **I got to bed at 11** я лёг спать в 11 часо́в; **where has my book got to?** куда́ де́лась/дева́лась моя́ кни́га?; **we cannot ~ home tonight** мы сего́дня не попадём домо́й.

with preps.: **he got above himself** он мно́го о себе́ возомни́л; **the officer got his troops across the river** офице́р перепра́вил свои́ войска́ че́рез ре́ку; **he got ahead of his competitors** он обогна́л свои́х сопе́рников; **I cannot ~ at the books** я не могу́ добра́ться до э́тих книг; **what is he ~ting at?** (*trying to say*) что он хо́чет сказа́ть?; куда́ он гнёт?;

she is always ~ting at me (*criticizing, nagging*) она всегда́ ко мне придира́ется; **he got in(to) the taxi** он сел в такси́; **I cannot ~ into these shoes** я не могу́ влезть в э́ти ту́фли; **he got into a rage** он пришёл в я́рость; **what got into him?** что на него́ нашло́?; **he got into bad habits** у него́ завели́сь дурны́е привы́чки; **he got into bad company** он завёл плоху́ю компа́нию; **he got into the club** его́ при́няли в клуб; **he got into trouble** он попа́л в беду́; **he got it into his head** (*imagined wrongly*) **that ...** он почему́-то реши́л, что...; **~ off the grass!** сойди́те с газо́на!; **she got the ring off her finger** она́ (с трудо́м) сняла́ кольцо́ с па́льца; **he got on his feet** он встал на́ ноги; **I got on to** (*contacted*) **him by telephone** я связа́лся с ним по телефо́ну; **the lion got out of its cage** лев вы́скочил из кле́тки; **I got out of going to the party** я уклони́лся от вечери́нки; **he got out of the habit of seeing her** он переста́л с ней ви́деться; **they got a confession out of him** они́ вы́рвали у него́ призна́ние; **I got £6 out of him** я вы́жал из него́ 6 фу́нтов; **what did you ~ out of his lecture?** что вы вы́несли из его́ ле́кции?; **I cannot ~ over his rudeness** я не могу́ опо́мниться от его́ гру́бости; **he could not ~ over the loss** он не мог пережи́ть э́той утра́ты; **she got over her shyness** она́ преодоле́ла свою́ засте́нчивость; **she got round him** ей удало́сь его́ уговори́ть; **he got through all his money** он истра́тил все свои́ де́ньги; **he got through his exam** он вы́держал экза́мен; **he got her through the exam** он помо́г ей сдать экза́мен; **he got the bill through parliament** он провёл законопрое́кт че́рез парла́мент; **let us ~ to business** дава́йте присту́пим к де́лу; **I cannot ~ to the meeting** я не могу́ яви́ться на собра́ние; **we got to Paris by noon** мы добра́лись до Пари́жа в по́лдень; *see also v.t.* **10.; the children got up to mischief** де́ти расшали́лись; **we got up to 10,000 feet** мы подняли́сь на высоту́ 10 000 (десяти́ ты́сяч) фу́тов.

with advs.: **~ about, ~ around** *v.i.*: **he ~s about a great deal** он мно́го разъезжа́ет; **a car makes it easier to ~ about** с маши́ной ле́гче поспева́ть всю́ду; **the news got about** но́вость распространи́лась; **~ across** *v.t.*: **the speaker got his point across** выступа́ющий чётко изложи́л свою́ то́чку зре́ния; **~ along** *v.i.*: **we can ~ along without him** мы мо́жем обойти́сь без него́; **they ~ along** (*agree*) **very well** они́ отли́чно ла́дят; **~ along/away with you!** брось!; да ну тебя́!; **I must be ~ting along** я до́лжен идти́; **~ around** *v.i.* = **~ about** *or* **~ round; ~ away** *v.t.*: **we got him away to the seaside** мы увезли́ его́ к мо́рю; *v.i.*: **the prisoner got away** заключённый бежа́л; **you cannot ~ away from this fact** от э́того фа́кта не уйдёшь; **the thieves got away with the money** во́ры удра́ли с деньга́ми; **he got away with cheating** ему́ удало́сь сжу́льничать; **~ back** *v.t.*: **he got his books back** он получи́л обра́тно свои́ кни́ги; **he got his own back** (*revenge*) он отомсти́л за себя́; **I got him back to London** я привёз его́ обра́тно в Ло́ндон; *v.i.*: **he got back from the country** он верну́лся из дере́вни; **he got back into bed** он сно́ва лёг в крова́ть; **~ by** *v.i.*: **please let me ~ by** (*pass*) разреши́те мне пройти́, пожа́луйста; **can I ~ by** (*coll., pass muster*) **in a dark suit?** тёмный костю́м сойдёт?; **~ down** *v.t.*: **he got a book down from the shelf** он снял кни́гу с по́лки; **he got his weight down** он сбро́сил (ли́шний) вес; **the secretary got the conversation down** секрета́рша записа́ла разгово́р; **I could not ~ the medicine down** я не мог проглоти́ть лека́рство; **things got him down** его зае́л быт; *v.i.*: **the child got down (from table)** ребёнок встал из-за стола́; **he got down to his work** он засе́л за рабо́ту; **let us ~ down to the facts** дава́йте займёмся фа́ктами; **~ in** *v.t.*: **they got the crops in** они́ убра́ли урожа́й; **we got a plumber in** мы позва́ли водопрово́дчика; **I could not ~ a word in** я не мог вста́вить ни сло́ва; *v.i.*: **the burglar got in through the window** взло́мщик прони́к в дом че́рез окно́; **we didn't ~ in to the concert** мы не попа́ли на конце́рт; **he got in with a bad crowd** он связа́лся с плохо́й компа́нией; **~ off** *v.t.* (*remove*) сн|има́ть, -ять; (*dispatch*): **we got the letters off** мы отпра́вили пи́сьма; **we got the baby off to sleep** мы уложи́ли ребёнка спать; **his lawyer got him off** (*acquitted*) адвока́т доби́лся его́ оправда́ния; *v.i.*: **he got off at the next station** он сошёл (с по́езда) на сле́дующей ста́нции; **I got off (to sleep) early** я ра́но засну́л; **he got off with a fine** он отде́лался штра́фом; **~ on** *v.t.*: **I cannot ~ the lid on** я не могу́ наде́ть кры́шку; **~ your clothes on!** оде́ньтесь!; *v.i.*: **how are you ~ting on?** как дела́?; **she is ~ting on** (*making progress*) она́ де́лает успе́хи; (*growing old*) она́ старе́ет; **~ting on (in years)** в лета́х; **he is ~ting on for 70** ему́ уже́ к семи́десяти идёт; **~ting on for** (*nearly*) почти́; **it is ~ting on for 4 o'clock** уже́ почти́ 4 часа́; **~ on with your work!** займи́тесь свое́й рабо́той; **he is easy to ~ on with** с ним легко́ ла́дить; **~ out** *v.t.*: **the chauffeur got the car out** шофёр вы́вел маши́ну; **he got out his spectacles** он вы́нул очки́; *v.i.*: **~ out!** (*begone!*) убира́йтесь!; **the secret got out** секре́т стал изве́стен; **~ over** *v.t.*: **I got the main point over to him** я внуши́л/ ему́ гла́вное; **I shall be glad to ~ the meeting over (with)** скоре́е бы уж состоя́лось э́то собра́ние!; **~ (a)round** *v.i.*: **I haven't got round to writing to him** я ещё не собра́лся написа́ть ему́; **~ through** *v.t.* (*an exam*) выде́рживать, вы́держать экза́мен; *v.i.* (*of a bill*) про|ходи́ть, -йти́ в парла́мент; **the message got through to him** поруче́ние ему́ переда́ли; (*fig., coll.*) он по́нял в чём де́ло; **~ together** *v.t.*: **he got an army together** он собра́л а́рмию; *v.i.*: **we must ~ together and have a talk** мы должны́ встре́титься и поговори́ть; **~ up** *v.t.*: **they got me up at 7** они́ по́дняли меня́ в 7 часо́в; **they got up a subscription** они́ организова́ли подпи́ску; **the engine-driver got up steam** машини́ст развёл пары́; **she got herself up beautifully** она́ была́ прекра́сно оде́та; **he got himself up as a pirate** он наряди́лся пира́том; *v.i.* (*from bed, chair etc.*) вста|ва́ть, -ть; **the wind is ~ting up** поднима́ется ве́тер.

cpds. **~away** *n.* бе́гство; **make one's ~** бежа́ть (*det.*; *impf, pf.*); **~-together** *n.* (*meeting, gathering*) встре́ча, сбо́рище; (*entertainment*) вечери́нка; **~-up** *n.* (*dress*) наря́д.

geyser ['gaɪzə(r), 'gi:-] *n.* (*hot spring*) ге́йзер; (*apparatus*) коло́нка для нагре́ва воды́.

Ghana ['gɑ:nə] *n.* Га́на

ghastly ['gɑ:stlɪ] *adj.* ужа́сный, отврати́тельный, кошма́рный; **a ~ accident** ужа́сная катастро́фа; **you look ~** у вас жу́ткий вид.

adv. ужа́сно.

gherkin ['gɜ:kɪn] n. корнишо́н.

ghetto ['getəʊ] *n.* ге́тто (*indecl.*).

ghost [gəʊst] *n.* **1.** (*life, spirit*): **give up the ~** испусти́ть (*pf.*) дух; **Holy G~** Свято́й Дух. **2.** (*of dead pers.*) привиде́ние; дух. **3.** (*vestige*): **he hasn't the ~ of a chance** у него́ нет ни мале́йшего ша́нса; **the ~ of a smile** чуть заме́тная улы́бка.

v.t. (*also* **~-write**): **the autobiography was ~ed** автобиогра́фию за него́ написа́л друго́й.

cpds. **~buster** *n.* охо́тник за привиде́ниями; **~-story** *n.* расска́з с привиде́ниями.

ghostly ['gəʊstlɪ] *adj.* похо́жий на привиде́ние.

ghoul [gu:l] *n.* вампи́р.

ghoulish ['gu:lɪʃ] *adj.* наслажда́ющийся у́жасами.

GHQ (*abbr. of* **General Headquarters**) ста́вка, гла́вное кома́ндование.

GI (*abbr. of* ***government issue***; = *US private soldier*) «джи-áй» (*indecl.*); солдáт.

giant ['dʒaɪənt] *n.* **1.** (*fabulous being*) гигáнт. **2.** (*very tall pers. etc.*) великáн, исполи́н. **3.** (*fig.*): **an intellectual ~** гигáнт мы́сли. **4.** (*attr.*) гигáнтский; исполи́нский; **~ cactus** исполи́нский кáктус; **G~ Panda** бамбу́ковый медвéдь.

gibberish ['dʒɪbərɪʃ] *n.* тарабáрщина, лопотáние.

gibbet ['dʒɪbɪt] *n.* ви́селица.

gibbon ['gɪbən] *n.* гиббóн.

gibe, jibe [dʒaɪb] *n.* насмéшка.

v.i.: **~ at** насмехáться над+*i.*

giblets ['dʒɪblɪts] *n.* гуси́ные потрох|á (*pl.*, *g.* -óв).

giddap [gɪ'dæp] *int.* (*US*) но!

giddiness ['gɪdɪnɪs] *n.* головокружéние.

giddy ['gɪdɪ] *adj.* **1.** головокружи́тельный; **I feel ~** у меня́ крýжится головá; **a ~ height** головокружи́тельная высотá. **2.** (*capricious*): **a ~ girl** вéтреная девчóнка.

giddy-up [,gɪdɪ'ʌp] *int.* но!

gift [gɪft] *n.* **1.** (*thg. given*) подáрок; дар; **I would not have it as a ~** я э́то и дáром не возьмý; **~ shop** магази́н подáрков; **~ voucher/token** подáрочный талóн. **2.** (*talent*) даровáние; дар; **he has a ~ for languages** у негó спосóбности (*f. pl.*)/талáнт к языкáм; **a man of many ~s** разносторóнне одарённый человéк.

cpds. **~-horse** *n.*: **you must not look a ~-horse in the mouth** дарёному конéю в зýбы не смóтрят; **~-wrap** *v.t.* завёр|тывать, -нýть в подáрочную упакóвку.

gifted ['gɪftɪd] *adj.* одарённый.

giga- ['gɪgə, 'gaɪgə] *comb. form* гига…; **~byte** гигабáйт; **~watt** гигавáтт.

gigantic [dʒaɪ'gæntɪk] *adj.* гигáнтский.

giggle ['gɪg(ə)l] *n.* хихи́канье; **for a ~** смéха/шýтки рáди.

v.i. хихи́к|ать, -нуть.

gigolo ['ʒɪgə,ləʊ, 'dʒɪg-] *n.* жи́голо (*m. indecl.*).

gild [gɪld] *v.t.* **1.** (*cover or tinge with gold*) золоти́ть, по-. **2.** (*fig.*) укр|ашáть, -áсить; **~ the pill** позолоти́ть (*pf.*) пилю́лю; **~ed youth** золотáя молодёжь.

gilding ['gɪldɪŋ] *n.* позолóта.

gill [gɪl] *n.* (*of fish*) жáбра; **he looks green about the ~s** (*fig.*) он вы́глядит больны́м.

gillyflower ['dʒɪlɪ,flaʊə(r)] *n.* левкóй.

gilt [gɪlt] *n.* позолóта.

cpds. **~-edged** *adj.* (*book etc.*) с золочёным обрéзом; **~-edged securities** первоклáссные (*or* осóбо надёжные) цéнные бумáги.

gimlet ['gɪmlɪt] *n.* бурáв; бурáвчик.

gimmick ['gɪmɪk] *n.* (*coll.*) трюк; финт, ухищрéние.

gimmicky ['gɪmɪkɪ] *adj.* (*coll.*) трюкáческий; с выкрутáсами.

gin[1] [dʒɪn] *n.* (*cotton-~*) джин, волокноотдели́тель (*m.*).

gin[2] [dʒɪn] *n.* (*drink*) джин.

ginger ['dʒɪndʒə(r)] *n.* (*bot.*, *cul.*) имби́рь (*m.*); (*attr.*) имби́рный.

adj. (*colour*) ры́жий.

v.t.: **~ up** подзадóри|вать, -ть.

cpds. **~-ale, ~-beer** *nn.* имби́рное пи́во; **~bread** *n.* имби́рная коври́жка; **~-nut, ~-snap** *nn.* имби́рный пря́ник.

gingerly ['dʒɪndʒəlɪ] *adj.* (крáйне) осторóжный.

adv. осторóжно.

gingery ['dʒɪndʒərɪ] *adj.* **1.** (*like ginger in taste etc.*) имби́рный. **2.** (*colour*) рыжевáтый.

gingham ['gɪŋəm] *n.* пестроткáнный гринсбóн.

gingivitis [,dʒɪndʒɪ'vaɪtɪs] *n.* воспалéние дёсен, гингиви́т.

ginormous [dʒaɪ'nɔːməs] *adj.* (*coll.*) огромáдный.

ginseng ['dʒɪnseŋ] *n.* женьшéнь (*m.*).

Gipsy, Gypsy ['dʒɪpsɪ] *n.* цыгáн (*fem.* -ка).

adj. цыгáнский.

giraffe [dʒɪ'rɑːf, -'ræf] *n.* жирáф(а).

gird [gɜːd] *v.t.* **1.** (*with belt etc.*) опоя́с|ывать, -ать; **~ on one's sword** прикрепи́ть (*pf.*) сáблю к пóясу. **2.** (*encircle, e.g. fortress or island*) окруж|áть, -и́ть.

girder ['gɜːdə(r)] *n.* (*beam*) бáлка; брус; (*span of bridge etc.*) переклáдина; фéрма.

girdle ['gɜːd(ə)l] *n.* **1.** (*belt etc.*) пóяс; кушáк. **2.** (*corset*) корсéт.

v.t. (*encircle*) окруж|áть, -и́ть.

girl [gɜːl] *n.* (*child*) дéвочка; (*young woman*) дéвушка; (*maid-servant*) служáнка; (*sweetheart*) возлю́бленная; **old ~** (*coll., old woman; also as affec. term of address*) старýшка; (*ex-pupil of school*) выпускни́ца (*данной школы*).

cpd. **~-friend** *n.* (*female friend*) подрýга.

girlhood ['gɜːlhʊd] *n.* деви́чество, óтрочество; **in her ~** в деви́честве.

girlish ['gɜːlɪʃ] *adj.* деви́ческий.

girth [gɜːθ] *n.* (*of horse*) подпрýга; (*of tree, person etc.*) обхвáт; размéр.

gist [dʒɪst] *n.* суть.

give [gɪv] *n.* **1.** (*elasticity*) подáтливость, эласти́чность; **there is no ~ in this rope** э́та верёвка не растя́гивается. **2.: ~ and take** взаи́мные устýпки (*f. pl.*).

v.t. **1.** да|вáть, -ть; **~ lessons** давáть урóки; **I ~ you my word** даю́ вам слóво; **I gave the porter my luggage ~** я óтдал свой багáж носи́льщику. **2.** (*imper., expr. preference*): **~ me the good old days!** где нáше дóброе стáрое врéмя?!; **~ me Bach every time** я всем и всегдá предпочитáю Бáха. **3.** (*present, bestow, surrender*) дари́ть, по-; **he was ~n a book** емý подари́ли кни́гу; **he gave him his daughter in marriage** он отдáл емý свою́ дочь в жёны; **she gave herself to him** онá емý отдалáсь. **4.** (*propose*): **I ~ you** (*the toast of*) **the Queen** я предлагáю тост за королéву. **5.** (*~ in exchange*): **I gave a good price for it** я за э́то хорошó заплати́л; **what will you ~ me for this coat?** скóлько вы мне дади́те за э́то пальтó?; **he gave as good as he got** он заплати́л той же монéтой; **I don't ~ a damn!** а мне наплевáть! **6.** (*provide, furnish, impart, inflict*): **the sun ~s light** сóлнце — истóчник свéта; **he ~s me a lot of trouble** он мне доставля́ет мнóго хлопóт; **he has ~n me his cold** я зарази́лся от негó нáсморком; **the place gave its name to the battle** би́тва берёт своё назвáние от мéстности; **he gave** (*cited*) **an example** он привёл примéр; **he gave me to understand that ...** он дал мне поня́ть, что…; **~ him my regards** передáйте емý от меня́ привéт; **~ evidence** (*in court*) да|вáть, -ть показáния; **~ pleasure** дост|авля́ть, -áвить удовóльствие; **the court gave him 6 months** емý дáли 6 мéсяцев; **I gave him a look** я (*сердито и т.п.*) взглянýл на негó; **the noise ~s me a headache** у меня́ головá боли́т от шýма; **he gave no sign of life** он не подавáл при́знаков жи́зни. **7.** (*indicate*): **this book ~s you the answers** отвéты вы найдёте в э́той кни́ге; **he gave no reason for his absence** он не объясни́л своегó отсýтствия. **8.** (*decide*): **the case was ~n against him** дéло реши́ли не в егó пóльзу. **9.** (*devote, sacrifice*) удел|я́ть, -и́ть; посвя|щáть, -ти́ть; **he gave his life for her** он отдáл за неё жизнь; **he gave thought to the question** он мнóго дýмал над э́тим вопрóсом; **he gave me his attention** он внимáтельно меня́ слýшал. **10.** (*allow, estimate*): **I ~ you an hour to get ready** я даю́ вам час приготóвиться; **to ~ him his due, he tried hard** нáдо отдáть емý дóлжное — он óчень старáлся; **I would ~ him** (*estimate his age at*) **50** я бы дал емý лет 50. **11.** (*organize*) устр|áивать, -óить; **they gave a dance** они́ устрóили танцевáльный вéчер. **12.** (*perform action*): **he gave a loud laugh** он грóмко рассмея́лся; **the dog gave a**

bark собáка залáяла. **13.** (*with pronominal object*): **~ it to him!** (*beating etc.*) дай емý!; **I gave him what for** (*coll.*) я зáдал емý трёпку. **14.** (*special uses of* **~n**): **under the ~n** (*existing*) **conditions** в дáнных обстоя́тельствах/услóвиях; **~n time, it can be done** при нали́чии врéмени э́то мóжно сдéлать; **at a ~n** (*specified, agreed, particular*) **time** в определённое врéмя; **~n name** (*forename*) и́мя (*nt.*); **~ that ...** при том, что...

v.i. **1.: he ~s generously** он óчень щедр; **~ of one's best** вложи́ть (*pf.*) дýшу. **2.** (*yield*) подд|авáться, -áться; **his knees gave** егó колéни подкоси́лись; **the ground gave under our feet** земля́ подалáсь под нáшими ногáми; **the rope gave** (*broke*) верёвка оборвалáсь. **3.** (*face*): **the window ~s on to the yard** окнó выхóдит во двор.

with advs.: **~ away** *v.t.* дари́ть, по-; (*distribute, e.g. prizes*) разд|авáть, -áть; **he gave away the secret** он вы́дал секрéт; **don't ~ me away!** не выдавáйте меня́!; **he gave the game away** (*blew the gaff*) он проболтáлся; **~ back** *v.t.* (*restore*) возвра|щáть, -ти́ть; отд|авáть, -áть; **~ forth** *v.t.* (*emit*) изд|авáть, -áть; испус|кáть, -ти́ть; **~ in** *v.t.*: **he gave in his name** он записáлся; **he gave in his** (*exam*) **paper** он сдал свою́ экзаменациóнную рабóту; *v.i.* (*yield*) подд|авáться, -áться; уступ|áть, -и́ть; **he gave in to my persuasion** он поддáлся мои́м уговóрам; **~ off** *v.t.* (*emit, e.g. smell or smoke*) испус|кáть, -ти́ть; изд|авáть, -áть; **~ out** *v.t.* (*distribute*) распредел|я́ть, -и́ть; (*announce*) объяв|ля́ть, -и́ть; *v.i.* кончáться, кóнчиться; **the rations gave out** продовóльствие кóнчилось; **his strength gave out** егó си́лы исся́кли; **~ over** *v.t.* (*hand over*) перед|авáть, -áть; (*abandon*) ост|авля́ть, -áвить; **~ over!** (*coll., desist!*) брóсьте!; (*devote*) **the time was ~n over to discussion** врéмя бы́ло посвящено́ дискýссии; **~ up** *v.t.* ост|авля́ть, -áвить; (*resign, surrender*) откáз|ываться, -áться +*g.*; **he gave up his seat to her** он уступи́л ей мéсто; **the murderer gave himself up** уби́йца сдáлся; (*desist from*) бр|осáть, -óсить; **he gave up smoking** он брóсил кури́ть; (*abandon hope of*): **they gave him up for lost** они́ реши́ли, что он пропáл; **we gave it up as a bad job** (*desisted from hopeless attempt*) мы махнýли рукóй на э́то дéло; **after the quarrel she gave him up** пóсле ссóры онá с ним порвáла; *v.i.* **I ~ up!** сдаю́сь!

gizmo ['gɪzməʊ] *n.* (*US*) штукóвина.

gizzard ['gɪzəd] *n.* вторóй желýдок (*у птиц*); (*fig., coll.*) желýдок.

glacé ['glæseɪ] *adj.*: **~ fruits** засáхаренные фрýкты.

glacial ['gleɪʃ(ə)l, -sɪəl] *adj.* ледóвый; ледянóй; **the ~ era** ледникóвый перио́д.

glacier ['glæsɪə(r)] *n.* ледни́к; глéтчер.

glad [glæd] *adj.* **1.** (*pleased*) довóльный; **I am ~ to meet you** рад с вáми познакóмиться; **I should be ~ of a few pounds** я был бы рад (и) нéскольким фýнтам. **2.** (*happy*) рáдостный.

gladden ['glæd(ə)n] *v.t.* рáдовать, об-.

glade [gleɪd] *n.* поля́на, прогáлина.

gladiator ['glædɪˌeɪtə(r)] *n.* гладиáтор.

gladiolus [ˌglædɪ'əʊləs] *n.* гладиóлус.

gladly ['glædlɪ] *adv.* (*joyfully*) рáдостно; (*willingly, with pleasure*) охóтно.

gladness ['glædnɪs] *n.* рáдость.

glamorous ['glæmərəs] *adj.* очаровáтельный; плени́тельный.

glamour ['glæmə(r)] *n.* очаровáние; шик.

glamo(u)rize ['glæməˌraɪz] *v.t.* приукрá|шивать, -сить.

glanc|e [glɑːns] *n.* **1.** (*quick look*) взгляд; **I took a ~e at the newspaper** я заглянýл в газéту; **I recognised him at a ~e** я узнáл егó с пéрвого взгля́да. **2.** (*flash*) блеск, блик.

v.t. & i. **1.** (*look*) взглянýть (*pf.*); брóсить (*pf.*) взгляд; **he ~ed at the clock** он взглянýл на часы́; **he ~ed round the room** он оглядéл кóмнату; **he ~ed down the page** он пробежáл страни́цу глазáми. **2.: the sword ~ed aside** меч скользнýл (по повéрхности щитá *и т.п.*); **a ~ ing blow** скользя́щий удáр.

gland [glænd] *n.* железá.

glandular ['glændjʊlə(r)] *adj.* желéзистый.

glare [gleə(r)] *n.* (*fierce light*) ослепи́тельный свет/блеск; (*fig.*): **~ of publicity** реклáмная шуми́ха; (*angry look*) свирéпый взгляд.

v.t. & i. ослепи́тельно сверкáть; **the sun ~d down** сóлнце пали́ло; **~ at s.o.** испепел|я́ть, -и́ть когó-н. взгля́дом.

glaring ['gleərɪŋ] *adj.* (*e.g. headlights*) слепя́щий, ослепи́тельный; (*of colour*) кричáщий, я́ркий; (*fierce, angry*) свирéпый; (*of mistake etc.*) грýбый.

glasnost ['glæznɒst, 'glɑːs-] *n.* глáсность.

glass [glɑːs] *n.* **1.** (*substance*) стеклó; **~ eye** стекля́нный глаз; **~ case** стекля́нный колпáк. **2.** (*for drinking*) (*tumbler*) стакáн; (*wine-~*) рю́мка, бокáл; **they clinked ~es** они́ чóкнулись. **3.** (*~ware*) стекля́нная посýда. **4.: tomatoes under ~** (*in ~houses*) помидóры в тепли́це. **5.** (*pl., spectacles*) очк|и́ (*pl., g.* -óв).

cpds. **~-blower** *n.* стеклодýв; **~house** *n.* тепли́ца; **~ware** *n.* стекля́нная посýда.

glassful ['glɑːsfʊl] *n.* стакáн (*чего*).

glassy ['glɑːsɪ] *adj.*: **a ~ stare** тýсклый/засты́вший взгляд; **a ~ lake** зеркáльная гладь óзера.

glaucoma [glɔː'kəʊmə] *n.* глаукóма.

glaze [gleɪz] *n.* (*substance*) муравá, глазýрь.

v.t. (*pottery, paint etc.*) глазуровáть (*impf., pf.*).

v.i.: **his eyes ~d over** егó взгляд потускнéл.

glazier ['gleɪzjə(r)] *n.* стекóльщик.

glazing ['gleɪzɪŋ] *n.* (*material*) глазýрь; (*glasswork*) остеклéние; **double ~** двойны́е рáмы (*f. pl.*).

gleam [gliːm] *n.* прóблеск; **a ~ of hope** прóблеск надéжды; **a dangerous ~ in the eye** опáсный блеск в глазáх.

v.i. поблёскивать (*impf.*); блестéть (*impf.*).

glean [gliːn] *v.t.* (*lit., also v.i.*) подбирáть (*impf.*) (колоски́); (*fig.*) соб|ирáть, -рáть (по крупи́цам).

glee [gliː] *n.* (*delight*) весéлье; ликовáние; **~ club** клуб певцóв-люби́телей.

gleeful ['gliːfʊl] *adj.* ликýющий.

glen [glen] *n.* лощи́на.

glib [glɪb] *adj.* бóйкий на язы́к; **a ~ excuse** благови́дный предлóг.

glide [glaɪd] *n.* скольжéние.

v.i. скольз|и́ть, -нýть; (*in aircraft*) плани́ровать, с-.

glider ['glaɪdə(r)] *n.* планёр; **~ pilot** планери́ст.

gliding ['glaɪdɪŋ] *n.* (*sport*) планери́зм.

glimmer ['glɪmə(r)] *n.* тýсклый свет; мерцáние; **a ~ of hope/intelligence** прóблеск надéжды/умá.

v.i. мерцáть (*impf.*).

glimpse [glɪmps] *n.* прóблеск; **I caught a ~ of him** он промелькнýл у меня́ пéред глазáми.

v.t. уви́деть (*pf.*) мéльком.

glint [glɪnt] *n.* блеск; (*reflection*) óтблеск.

v.i. блестéть (*impf.*); (*flash*) вспы́х|ивать, -нуть.

glisten ['glɪs(ə)n] *v.i.* сверк|áть, -нýть.

glitter ['glɪtə(r)] *n.* блеск, сверкáние.

v.i. блестéть (*impf.*); сверкáть (*impf.*).

gloaming ['gləʊmɪŋ] *n.* сýмер|ки (*pl., g.* -ек).

gloat [gləʊt] *v.i.* злорáдствовать (*impf.*).

global ['gləʊb(ə)l] *adj.* (*total*) всеóбщий; (*world-wide*) глобáльный; **~ warming** глобáльное потеплéние.

globe [gləʊb] *n.* **1.** (*spherical body*) шар; глóбус; **~ artichoke** артишóк. **2.: terrestrial ~** земнóй шар.

cpd. **~-trotter** заядлый тури́ст.

globular ['glɒbjʊlə(r)] *adj.* шарови́дный.

globule ['glɒbjuːl] *n.* шáрик; кáпелька.

gloom [glu:m] *n.* (*dark*) тьма; мрак; (*despondency*) мра́чность; уны́ние; **the news cast a ~ over us** но́вость омрачи́ла нам настрое́ние.
gloominess ['glu:mɪnɪs] *n.* мра́чность.
gloomy ['glu:mɪ] *adj.* (*dark*) мра́чный; (*depressing*) гнету́щий; (*depressed*) хму́рый; уны́лый.
glorification [,glɔ:rɪfɪ'keɪʃ(ə)n] *n.* прославле́ние.
glorify ['glɔ:rɪ,faɪ] *v.t.* **1.** (*worship*) восхваля́ть (*impf.*). **2.** (*honour, extol*) просл|авля́ть, -а́вить.
glorious ['glɔ:rɪəs] *adj.* сла́вный, великоле́пный; **a ~ day** (*weather*) изуми́тельный день.
glory ['glɔ:rɪ] *n.* **1.** (*renown, honour*) сла́ва. **2.** (*splendour*) великоле́пие.
v.i. упива́ться (*impf.*) +*i.*; горди́ться (*impf.*) +*i.*
gloss[1] [glɒs] *n.* (*comment, explanation*) гло́сса, поясне́ние.
gloss[2] [glɒs] *n.* (*lit., fig.*) лоск.
v.t.: **~ over faults** обойти́ (*pf.*) оши́бки молча́нием; зама́з|ывать, -ать недоста́тки.
glossary ['glɒsərɪ] *n.* глосса́рий.
glossy ['glɒsɪ] *adj.* глянцеви́тый; лощёный; **a ~ photograph** гля́нцевая фотогра́фия; **~ magazines** дороги́е иллюстри́рованные журна́лы.
glottal ['glɒt(ə)l] *adj.* относя́щийся к голосово́й щёли; **~ stop** горта́нный взрыв.
glottis ['glɒtɪs] *n.* голосова́я щель.
glove [glʌv] *n.* перча́тка; (*fig.*): **fit like a ~** быть впо́ру; **handle s.o. with kid ~s** церемо́ниться (*impf.*) с кем-н.
glow [gləʊ] *n.* (*of bodily warmth*) жар; (*of fire, sunset etc.*) за́рево; (*of feelings*) пыл.
v.i. (*incandesce*) нака́л|иваться, -и́ться; (*shine*) свети́ться (*impf.*); **~ing metal** раскалённый мета́лл; **a forest ~ing with autumn tints** лес, пыла́ющий осе́нними кра́сками; **he ~ed with pride** его́ распира́ла го́рдость.
cpd. **~-worm** *n.* светля́к.
glower ['glaʊə(r)] *v.i.* серди́то смотре́ть (*impf.*).
glucose ['glu:kəʊs, -kəʊz] *n.* глюко́за.
glue [glu:] *n.* клей.
v.t. прикле́и|вать; (*fig.*): **he ~d his eyes to the floor** он уста́вился в пол.
cpd. **~-sniffing** *n.* токсикома́ния.
gluey ['glu:ɪ] *adj.* кле́йкий.
glum [glʌm] *adj.* угрю́мый.
glumness ['glʌmnɪs] *n.* угрю́мость.
glut [glʌt] *n.* избы́ток.
v.t. нас|ыща́ть, -ы́тить; **~ the market** затова́ри|вать, -ть ры́нок.
gluten ['glu:t(ə)n] *n.* клейкови́на.
glutinous ['glu:tɪnəs] *adj.* кле́йкий, ли́пкий, вя́зкий.
glutton ['glʌt(ə)n] *n.* обжо́ра (*c.g.*); **a ~ for work** жа́дный к рабо́те.
gluttonous ['glʌtənəs] *adj.* прожо́рливый.
gluttony ['glʌtənɪ] *n.* обжо́рство.
glycerin(e) ['glɪsə,ri:n] *n.* глицери́н.
GMT = Greenwich (mean) time
gnarled [nɑ:ld] *adj.* сучкова́тый.
gnash [næʃ] *v.t.*: **~ one's teeth** скрежета́ть (*impf.*) зуба́ми.
gnat [næt] *n.* кома́р.
gnaw [nɔ:] *v.t. & i.* грызть (*impf.*); **the dog ~ed (at) a bone** соба́ка глода́ла кость; **rats ~ed away the woodwork** кры́сы изгры́зли де́рево; **~ing pangs of hunger** мучи́тельные при́ступы го́лода; **~ing anxiety** грызу́щее беспоко́йство.
gneiss [naɪs] *n.* гнейс.
gnome [nəʊm] *n.* (*goblin etc.*) гном.
adj. гности́ческий.
GNP (*abbr. of* ***Gross National Product***) ВНП, (валово́й национа́льный проду́кт).
gnu [nu:, nju:] *n.* гну (*m. indecl.*).
go [gəʊ] *n.* **1.** (*movement, animation*) движе́ние; ход; **she's on the ~ from morning to night** она́ с утра́ до ве́чера на нога́х; **she has no ~ in her** нет в ней изю́минки/огонька́ (*coll.*). **2.** (*turn, attempt, shot*) попы́тка; **now it's my ~** тепе́рь моя́ о́чередь; **why don't you have a ~?** почему́ бы вам не попро́бовать?; **he scored 50 in one ~** он набра́л 50 очко́в в одно́м захо́де. **3.** (*coll., success*) успе́х; **he tried to make a ~ of it** он стара́лся доби́ться успе́ха (в э́том де́ле); **it's no ~** э́то де́ло безнадёжное. **4.**: **let ~ of** отпус|ка́ть, -ти́ть.
v.i. (*see also* **gone**). **1.** (*on foot*) (*det.*) идти́; (*indet.*) ходи́ть; (*ride etc.*) (*det.*) е́хать; (*indet.*) е́здить; (*by train*) е́хать по́ездом; (*by plane*) лете́ть (*det.*) (самолётом); **the clock is ~ing** часы́ иду́т/хо́дят; **this train ~es to London** э́тот по́езд идёт в Ло́ндон; **he went cycling** он пое́хал ката́ться на велосипе́де; **who ~es there?** кто идёт?; **mind how you ~!** осторо́жно! **2.** (*fig., with general idea of motion or direction*): **~!** (*at games*) марш; **from the word ~** (*fig.*) с са́мого нача́ла; **where do we ~ from here?** (*what is next step or development?*) что же да́льше?; **this road ~es to York** э́та доро́га ведёт в Йорк; **he ~es to school** (*is a schoolboy*) он хо́дит в шко́лу; **he went to** (*was educated at*) **Eton** он око́нчил Итон; **he went sick** (*mil.*) он получи́л освобожде́ние по боле́зни; **let me ~!** отпусти́те меня́!; **there you ~ again!** ну вот, опя́ть!; **there is still an hour to ~** ещё час в запа́се; **where do these forks ~?** куда́ положи́ть э́ти ви́лки?; **if you follow me, you can't ~ wrong** де́лайте как я и вы не ошибётесь; **his plans went wrong** с его́ за́мыслами не получи́лось; **the criminal decided to ~ straight** престу́пник реши́л испра́виться. **3.** (*with cognate etc. object*): **he went a long way** он пошёл/ушёл далеко́; **they went halves** они́ раздели́ли всё попола́м; **can Britain ~ it alone?** спра́вится ли Великобрита́ния в одино́чку?; **the balloon went 'pop'** шар ло́пнул. **4.** (*idea of progress or outcome*): **how's it ~ing?** (*health, affairs*) как дела́?; как пожива́ете?; **everything is ~ing well** всё (идёт) хорошо́; **~ easy!** (*slowly, gently*) осторо́жно!; **he is ~ing strong** он по́лон сил; он молоде́ц; **the play went well** пье́са прошла́ хорошо́; **how did the election ~?** (*who won it?*) как прошли́ вы́боры?. **5.** (*idea of extension or distance*): **I will ~** (*offer*) **as high as £100** я гото́в вы́ложить и сто фу́нтов; **his land ~es as far as the river** его́ зе́мли простира́ются до реки́; **£5 will not ~ far** пяти́ фу́нтов надо́лго не хва́тит; **he will ~ far** (*attain distinction*) он далеко́ пойдёт; **I will ~ so far as to say** я бы да́же сказа́л, что...; **this is all right as far as it ~es** пока́ что всё в поря́дке. **6.** (*expr. tenor or tendency*): **how does the poem ~?** как звучи́т э́то стихотворе́ние?; **the story ~es that ...** расска́зывают, что...; **this ~es to show that he is wrong** э́то пока́зывает, что он не прав; **qualities that ~ to make a hero** ка́чества, необходи́мые геро́ю. **7.** (*set out, depart*): **the post ~es at 5 p.m.** по́чта ухо́дит в 5 часо́в дня. **8.** (*pass, come to an end, disappear*): **our holiday went in a flash** на́ши кани́кулы пролете́ли мгнове́нно; **as soon as we buy cheese it ~es** не успе́ем мы купи́ть сыр, как его́ уже́ нет; **it's ~ne 4** (*o'clock*) уже́ бо́льше четырёх; **the Minister must ~** (*be got rid of*) мини́стр до́лжен уйти́ в отста́вку; **I wish this pain would ~** хоть бы прошла́ э́та боль!; **his interest in literature has ~ne** у него́ пропа́л интере́с к литерату́ре; **~ing, ~ne!** (*at auction*) кто бо́льше? про́дано! **9.** (*be in a certain state*): **the children ~ barefoot** де́ти хо́дят босико́м; **I went hungry last night** я не ел вчера́ ве́чером. **10.** (*become*): **the milk went sour** молоко́ прокисло; **she went red in the face** она́ покрасне́ла. **11.** (*function, succeed*): **I can't get my watch to ~** у меня́ не заво́дятся часы́; **this machine ~es by electricity** э́та

машина работает на электричестве. **12.** (*cease to function, die*): **if the bulb ~es, change it** если лампочка перегорит, поменяйте её; **poor old Smith has ~ne** бедного Смита не стало. **13.** (*sound*): **come in when the bell ~es** входите, когда зазвонит звонок. **14.** (*make specified motion*): **~ like this with your left foot** сделайте так левой ногой. **15.** (*be known, accepted, usual*): **what he says ~es** его слово — закон; **anything ~es** всё сойдёт; **it ~es without saying** это само собой разумеется **he ~es by the name of Smith** он известен под именем Смит; **it is cheap as yachts ~** для яхты это недорого. **16.** (*be sold, offered for sale*): **these cakes are ~ing cheap** эти пирожные стоят дёшево (*or* идут по дешёвке). **17.** (*expr. impending or predicted action*): **I'm ~ing to sneeze** я сейчас чихну; **it's ~ing to rain** собирается дождь; **you are ~ing to do as I tell you** вы сделаете то, что я вам скажу; **he's not ~ing to** (*shan't*) **cheat me** меня он не проведёт. **18.** (*expr. intention*): **I am ~ing to ask him** я решил спросить его. **19.** (*emph. v.*): **he went and told his mother** он взял и рассказал матери; **what have you ~ne and done?** ну, что вы там натворили?

with preps.: **how shall I ~ about this?** как мне за это взяться; **he went about his business** он занялся своими делами; **if the price ~es above £50** если цена превысит 50 фунтов; **the dog went after the hare** собака погналась за зайцем; **it ~es against my principles** это противоречит моим принципам; **he went at it like a bull at a gate** он бросился очертя голову; **he went before the magistrates** он предстал перед судом; **he went** (*passed*) **by the window** он прошёл мимо окна; **I ~ by what I hear** я исхожу из того, что слышу; **they went down the river** они поплыли вниз по реке; **the dog went for his legs** собака хватала его за ноги; **I went for** (*fetched*) **him** я пошёл за ним; **he will always ~ for the best** он всегда будет стремиться к лучшему; **I ~ for that** (*like it*: *US coll.*) это мне по душе/вкусу; **he went into the house** он вошёл в дом; **the car went into a wall** машина врезалась в стену; **he had to ~ into hospital** ему пришлось лечь в больницу; **6 into 30 ~es 5 times** шесть содержится в тридцати пять раз; **I will ~ into the matter** я это дело рассмотрю; **he went off his food** он перестал есть; **he went off his head** он сошёл с ума; **I've ~ne off prawns** (*coll.*) я разлюбил креветки; **I am ~ing on a course** я поступаю на курсы; **all his money went on food** все его деньги пошли/уходили на еду; **he went on his way** он пошёл своим путём; **~ out of sight** исч|езать, -езнуть из виду; **he went out of his mind** он сошёл с ума; **she went out of her way to help** она всячески старалась помочь; **the shell went over his head** снаряд пролетел у него над головой; **his words went right over my head** я пропустил его слова мимо ушей; **we have ~ne over** (*discussed*) **that** мы это обсуждали; **we went round the gallery** мы обошли галерею; **my trousers won't ~ round me any longer** на мне уже не сходятся брюки; **~ through the main gate!** проходите через главные ворота!; **the ball went through** (*i.e. broke*) **the window** мяч разбил окно; **he has ~ne through a lot** ему довелось много испытать; **he went through the money in a week** он растратил деньги за неделю; **I'll ~ through the main points again** я хочу повторить главные пункты; **the estate went to her nephew** имущество перешло её племяннику; **the prize went to him** он выиграл приз; **he went to great expense** он пошёл на большие расходы; **~ to it!** за дело!; **the money will ~ towards a new car** деньги пойдут на покупку новой машины; **he went under an assumed name** он жил под чужим именем; **~ up the hill** подниматься (*impf.*)/идти/ехать (*both det.*) в гору; **this tie ~es with your suit** этот галстук подходит к вашему костюму; **crime ~es with poverty** преступность идёт рука об руку с бедностью; **we went without a holiday** мы обошлись без отпуска.

with advs.: **~ about** *v.i.* **the story is ~ing about that ...** ходят слухи, что...; **they ~ about together** они повсюду ходят вместе; **~ ahead!** вперёд!; **~ along** *v.i.*: **I went along to see** я пошёл посмотреть; **will you ~ along to the station with him?** вы доведёте его до станции?; **I cannot ~ along with that** я не могу с этим согласиться; **~ around** *v.i.*: **he went around with a long face** он ходил с кислым видом; **he is ~ing around with my sister** он встречается с моей сестрой; **~ away** *v.i.* уходить, уйти; **~ away!** уходите!; **~ back** *v.i.* идти (*det.*) назад; возвра|щаться, -титься; **to ~ back to what I was saying** возвращаясь к тому, что я сказал; **he went back on his word** он не сдержал своего слова; **~ below** (*deck*) *v.i.*: **when the storm broke they went below** когда разразился шторм, они спустились в каюту; **~ by** *v.i.*: **he let the opportunity ~ by** он упустил случай; **as the years ~ by** с годами; с течением лет; **he has just ~ne by** он только что прошёл мимо; **~ down** *v.i.*: спус|каться, -титься; **he went down on his knees** он опустился на колени; **the sun went down** солнце село; **she went down with 'flu** она слегла с гриппом; **prices are ~ing down** цены падают; **~ing down!** (*of lift*) вниз!; **his story went down well** его рассказ был хорошо принят; **the wind has ~ne down** ветер утих; **~ forth** *v.i.*: **the order went forth** приказ был опубликован; **~ forward** *v.i.*: **the plan went forward** план вступил в действие; **~ in** *v.i.* (*enter*) входить, войти; **the sun went in** солнце зашло; **he ~es in for sport** он занимается спортом; **he went in for the competition** он принял участие в конкурсе **~ off** *v.i.*: **he went off without a word** он ушёл без единого слова; **the servant went off with** (*stole*) **the spoons** слуга украл ложки и скрылся; **the goods went off** (*were sent*) **today** товар отправили сегодня; **the gun went off** ружьё выстрелило; **the alarm clock went off** будильник зазвенел; **the light has ~ne off** свет погас; **the fruit has ~ne off** фрукты погнили; **it went off according to plan** всё прошло согласно плану; **~ on** *v.i.*: **the shoe will not ~ on** этот ботинок не лезет; **the lights went on** загорелся свет; **I can't ~ on any longer** я так больше не могу; **shall we ~ on to the next item?** давайте перейдём к следующему пункту?; **~ on!** (*coll., expr. incredulity*) да ну!; (*urging action*) давайте!; валяйте!; **that is enough to be ~ing on with** этого пока хватит; **he went on to say that ...** затем он сказал, что...; **what is ~ing on here?** что тут происходит?; **~ on at** (*nag*) пилить (*impf.*); **he went on ahead of the others** он опередил/обогнал остальных; **the show must ~ on** что бы ни случилось, спектакль продолжается; **as time ~es on** со временем; **~ out** *v.i.* (*exit*) выходить, выйти; **the light went out** свет погас; **he went out to Australia** он выехал в Австралию; **the tide was ~ing out** шёл отлив; **our hearts ~ out to them** мы всей душой с ними; **~ over** *v.i.*: **~ over to the enemy** перейти (*pf.*) в стан врага; **he went over to France** он переправился во Францию; **~ round** *v.i.*: **I went round to see him** я пошёл его навестить; **we had to ~ round by the park** нам пришлось идти в обход через парк; **is there enough food to ~ round?** хватит ли еды на всех?; **everything's ~ing round** (*describing dizziness*) всё идёт кругом; **~ through** *v.i.*: **I cannot ~ through with the plan** я не могу осуществить этот план; **the deal went through** сделка состоялась; **the bill went through** (*parl.*) проект был принят; **~ together** *v.i.*: **they were ~ing together** (*keeping company*) **for years** они́ встреча́лись мно́гие го́ды; **these colours ~ together** э́ти цвета́ гармони́руют; **~ under** *v.i.*: **it is the poor who ~ under** бе́дному ху́же всех; **the drowning man went under** утопа́ющий пошёл ко дну; **his business went under** его́ де́ло ло́пнуло; **~ up** *v.i.* подн|има́ться, -я́ться; **I went up to town** я пое́хал в го́род; **prices have ~ne up** це́ны повы́сились; **the lights went up** загоре́лся свет; **houses are ~ing up** (*being built*) дома́ стро́ятся; **the house went up in flames** дом сгоре́л; **he ~es up to Oxford next year** он посту́пит в О́ксфордский университе́т на бу́дущий год; **he is ~ing up in the world** он выбива́ется в лю́ди.

cpds. **~-ahead** *n.* разреше́ние, «добро́»; *adj.* предприи́мчивый; **~-between** *n.* посре́дник; **~-cart** *n.* (де́тская) коля́ска; (*for racing, also* **~-kart**) карт; **~-slow** *n.* части́чная забасто́вка.

goad [gəʊd] *n.* кол; (*fig.*) сти́мул.

v.t. погоня́ть (*impf.*); (*prod*) пришпо́ри|вать, -ть; (*tease, torment*) раздража́ть (*impf.*).

goal [gəʊl] *n.* **1.** фи́ниш; (*fig., destination, objective*) цель; **he set himself a difficult ~** он поста́вил себе́ тру́дную зада́чу/цель. **2.** (*sport*) воро́т|а (*pl., g.* —); **keep ~** защи|ща́ть, -ти́ть воро́та; (*point scored*) гол; **our team won by three ~s to one** на́ша кома́нда вы́играла со счётом три — оди́н.

cpds. **~-keeper** *n.* врата́рь (*m.*); **~-post** *n.* шта́нга.

goalie ['gəʊlɪ] *n.* (*coll.*) врата́рь (*m.*).

goat [gəʊt] *n.* коза́; (*male*) козёл; **he gets my ~** (*sl.*) он меня́ раздража́ет.

cpds. **~-herd** *n.* козопа́с; **~-meat** *n.* козля́тина; **~skin** *n.* ко́зья шу́ба.

goatee [gəʊ'tiː] *n.* козли́ная боро́дка.

gobble[1] ['gɒb(ə)l] *v.t.* жрать, по-/со-.

v.i. ло́пать, с-; бы́стро и шу́мно есть (*impf.*).

gobble[2] ['gɒb(ə)l] *v.i.* (*of a turkey*) кулды́кать (*impf.*).

goblet ['gɒblɪt] *n.* ку́бок, бока́л.

goblin ['gɒblɪn] *n.* домово́й.

goby ['gəʊbɪ] *n.* бычо́к.

god [gɒd] *n.* **1.** (*deity*) бог; **in the lap of the ~s** у Христа́ за па́зухой; **ye ~s!** (*joc.*) Бо́же мой!; си́лы небе́сные!; (*fig., revered object or person*) и́дол, куми́р; (**G~**: *supreme being*) Бог; божество́; **act of G~** стихи́йное бе́дствие; **Almighty G~** всемогу́щий Бог; **G~ bless** (*you*)! благослови́ вас Бог; (*after sneeze*) бу́дьте здоро́вы!; **my G~!** Бо́же мой!; Го́споди!; **G~ forbid!** Бо́же сохрани́!; изба́ви Бог!; **G~ knows where he is** Бог зна́ет, где он; **for G~'s sake!** ра́ди Бо́га!; **thank G~ (for that)!** сла́ва Бо́гу!; **G~ willing** даст Бог. **2.** (*pl., theatr.*) галёрка; **a seat in the ~s** ме́сто на галёрке.

cpds. **~child** *n.* кре́стни|к (*fem.* -ца); **~dam** *adj.* (*US sl.*) чёртов; **~daughter** *n.* кре́стница; **~father** *n.* крёстный (оте́ц); **~-fearing** *adj.* богобоя́зненный; **~-forsaken** *adj.* забро́шенный; **~-forsaken place** медве́жий у́гол; **~mother** *n.* крёстная (мать); **~send** *n.* нахо́дка; **~son** *n.* кре́стник.

goddess ['gɒdɪs] *n.* боги́ня.

godless ['gɒdlɪs] *adj.* безбо́жный.

godly ['gɒdlɪ] *adj.* на́божный.

goggle ['gɒg(ə)l] *v.i.* тара́щить (*impf.*) глаза́.

cpds. **~-box** *n.* (*sl.*) те́лик, «я́щик»; **~-eyed** *adj.* пучегла́зый.

goggles ['gɒg(ə)lz] *n.* тёмные/защи́тные очк|и́ (*pl., g.* -о́в).

going ['gəʊɪŋ] *n.* **1.** (*departure*) отъе́зд, ухо́д; **there will be no tears at his ~** по нём пла́кать не бу́дут. **2.** (*state of track*) состоя́ние бегово́й доро́жки; **the next mile is rough ~** сле́дующая ми́ля бу́дет тру́дной. **3.** (*progress, speed*) ско́рость; **fifty miles an hour is good ~** 50 миль в час — э́то хоро́шая ско́рость; **this book is heavy ~** э́та кни́га тру́дно чита́ется; **he is heavy ~** он ну́дный челове́к.

adj. **1.** (*working, flourishing*): **a ~ concern** де́йствующее предприя́тие. **2.** (*to be had*): **one of the best newspapers ~** одна́ из лу́чших ны́нешних газе́т; **there are plenty of sandwiches ~** бутербро́дов ско́лько уго́дно.

cpd. **~-over** *n.* (*coll., scrutiny*) осмо́тр; (*coll., cleaning*) прочи́стка; **~s-on** *n.* (*coll.*) поведе́ние; посту́пки (*m. pl.*); дела́ (*nt. pl.*); **there have been strange ~s-on lately** в после́днее вре́мя творя́тся стра́нные ве́щи.

goitre ['gɔɪtə(r)] *n.* зоб; базе́дова боле́знь.

gold [gəʊld] *n. & adj.* (*metal*) зо́лото; **~ plate** (*tableware*) золота́я посу́да; (*gilding*) позоло́та; **(made of) solid ~** из чи́стого зо́лота; **the ~ standard** золото́й станда́рт; ; **he's as good as ~** он зо́лото, а не ребёнок; **she has a heart of ~** у неё золото́е се́рдце.

cpds. **~-dust** *n.* золото́й песо́к; **~finch** *n.* щего́л; **~fish** *n.* золота́я ры́бка; **~-leaf** *n.* суса́льное зо́лото; **~-mine** *n.* золото́й рудни́к; (*fig.*): **the shop is a ~-mine** э́тот магази́н — золото́е дно; **~-rush** *n.* золота́я лихора́дка; **~smith** *n.* золоты́х дел ма́стер.

golden ['gəʊld(ə)n] *adj.* (*lit., fig.*) золото́й; (*of colour*) золоти́стый; **the ~ age** золото́й век; **~ rod** (*bot.*) золота́рник; **~ syrup** све́тлая па́тока; **receive a ~ handshake on retirement** получи́ть (*pf.*) вознагражде́ние при ухо́де на пе́нсию; **the ~ mean** золота́я середи́на; **miss a ~ opportunity** упусти́ть (*pf.*) редча́йшую возмо́жность.

cpd. **~-haired** *adj.* золотоволо́сый.

Goldilocks ['gəʊldɪˌlɒks] *n.* Златовла́ска.

golf [gɒlf] *n.* гольф.

v.i. игра́ть (*impf.*) в гольф.

cpds. **~-ball** *n.* мяч для игры́ в гольф; **~-club** *n.* (*association*) клуб люби́телей игры в гольф; (*implement*) клю́шка; **~-course** *n.* площа́дка/по́ле для игры́ в гольф.

golfer ['gɒlfə(r)] *n.* игро́к в гольф.

golfing ['gɒlfɪŋ] *n.* игра́ в гольф.

gonad ['gəʊnæd] *n.* гона́да; полова́я железа́.

gondola ['gɒndələ] *n.* (*boat; airship car*) гондо́ла.

gondolier [ˌgɒndə'lɪə(r)] *n.* гондолье́р.

gone [gɒn] *adj.* (*see also* **go**). **1.** (*departed, past*) уе́хавший; уше́дший. **2.** (*dead*) уме́рший.

gong [gɒŋ] *n.* гонг.

gonorrhoea [ˌgɒnə'rɪə] *n.* гоноре́я.

goo [guː] *n.* (*coll.*) что-н. кле́йкое, ли́пкое.

good [gʊd] *n.* **1.** (*~ness, ~ action*) доброта́, добро́; **there is some ~ in everyone** в ка́ждом челове́ке есть что́-то хоро́шее; **he is up to no ~** он заду́мал что́-то недо́брое. **2.** (*benefit*) по́льза; **drink it! it will do you ~** вы́пейте э́то — вам поле́зно; **that will do no ~** э́то не принесёт по́льзы; **what's the ~ of making a fuss?** како́й смысл поднима́ть шум?; **it's all to the ~** всё к лу́чшему; **for the ~ of the cause** для по́льзы де́ла. **3.**: **for ~** (*permanently*) навсегда́. **4.** (*pl., property*) добро́; **~s and chattels** пожи́тк|и (*pl., g.* -ов). **5.** (*pl., merchandise*) това́р(ы); **~s train** това́рный по́езд; **~s vehicle** грузово́й автомоби́ль/фурго́н.

adj. **1.** (*in most senses*) хоро́ший; до́брый; (*of food*) вку́сный; **that shows ~ sense** в э́том ви́ден здра́вый смысл; **~ idea!** прекра́сная мысль!; **very ~** (*expr. acquiescence*) ла́дно; хорошо́; **~ works** до́брые дела́; **lead a ~ life** вести́ (*det.*) досто́йную жизнь; **G~ Friday** Страстна́я Пя́тница; **~ heavens!** Бо́же мой! **2.** (*of health, condition etc.*) хоро́ший; здоро́вый; **I don't feel so ~ today** (*coll.*) я себя́ нева́жно чу́вствую сего́дня; **apples are ~ for you** я́блоки поле́зны для здоро́вья. **3.** (*favourable, fortunate*): **~ luck!** жела́ю успе́ха; **it's a ~ thing we stayed at home** хорошо́, что мы оста́лись до́ма;

he's gone, and a ~ thing too! он ушёл, и сла́ва Бо́гу! **4.** (*kind*) любе́зный, до́брый; **be so ~ as to let me in** бу́дьте добры́, впусти́те меня́; **that's very ~ of you** э́то о́чень ми́ло с ва́шей стороны́. **5.** (*of skill*): **he is ~ at games** он хоро́ший спортсме́н; **he is ~ at French** он силён во францу́зском. **6.** (*suitable*) подходя́щий. **7.** (*well-behaved*) воспи́танный; послу́шный; **be ~!** веди́ себя́ прили́чно!; **be a ~ boy!** веди́ себя́ хорошо́!; будь у́мницей!; **as ~ as gold** (*of child*) зо́лотко; **~ dog!** молоде́ц, соба́ка. **8.** (*var.*): **~ morning!** до́брое у́тро!; **I bade him ~ night** я пожела́л ему́ споко́йной но́чи; **it's ~ to see you** прия́тно вас ви́деть; **~ looks** краси́вая вне́шность; **a ~ deal of noise** мно́го шу́ма; **a ~ way off** дово́льно далеко́; **the jug holds a ~ pint** кувши́н вмеща́ет до́брую пи́нту; **he was as ~ as his word** он сдержа́л своё сло́во; **he as ~ as refused to go** он факти́чески отказа́лся идти́; **the car is ~ for another 5 years** э́тот автомоби́ль прослу́жит ещё лет 5. **9.: make ~** *v.t.* (*fulfil*) исп|олня́ть, -о́лнить; (*substantiate*) обосно́в|ывать, -а́ть; (*recompense for*) возме|ща́ть, -сти́ть.

cpds. **~-for-nothing** *n.* негодя́й, безде́льник; *adj.* никуды́шный; никчёмный; **~-looking** *adj.* краси́вый; хоро́ш/хороша́ собо́й; **~-natured** *adj.* доброду́шный; **~-night** *n.* проща́ние пе́ред сном; *int.* поко́йной но́чи!; **~-neighbourliness** *n.* добрососе́дство; **~will** *n.* (*friendship*) доброжела́тельность; (*willingness*) до́брая во́ля; (*of business*) популя́рность; репута́ция; клиенту́ра.

goodbye [gʊd'baɪ] *n.* проща́ние; **a ~ kiss** проща́льный поцелу́й.

int. до свида́ния!

goodness ['gʊdnɪs] *n.* **1.** (*virtue*) доброта́. **2.** (*kindness*) любе́зность; **please have the ~ to move** бу́дьте любе́зны, подви́ньтесь. **3.** (*quality, nourishment*): **these apples are full of ~** э́ти я́блоки о́чень хороши́. **4.** (*euph., God*): **G~ me!** вот те на́!; **G~ (only) knows** кто его́ зна́ет!; **thank ~!** сла́ва Бо́гу!

goody ['gʊdɪ] *n.* (*coll.*) **1.** (*sweetmeat*) конфе́та. **2.** (*character in film etc.*) положи́тельный геро́й. **3.** (*also ~-~*) па́инька (*c.g.*). **4.** (*int., coll.*) прекра́сно!

gooey ['gu:ɪ] (*coll.*) *adj.* клё́йкий; ли́пкий.

goose [gu:s] *n.* **1.** гусь (*m.*); (*fem., also*) гусы́ня; **he couldn't say boo to a ~** (*fig.*) он боязли́в как лань. **2.** (*simpleton*) простофи́ля (*c.g.*).

cpds. **~berry** *n.* крыжо́вник (*collect.*); я́года крыжо́вника**~-flesh** *n.* гуся́тина; гуси́ная ко́жа; **it gives me ~flesh** у меня́ от э́того мура́шки по те́лу бе́гают.

gopher ['gəʊfə(r)] *n.* го́фер; колумби́йский су́слик.

gore[1] [gɔ:(r)] *n.* (*blood*) проли́тая/запёкшаяся кровь.

gore[2] [gɔ:(r)] *n.* (*gusset*) клин.

gore[3] [gɔ:(r)] *v.t.* бода́ть, за-.

gorge [gɔ:dʒ] *n.* уще́лье.

v.t. & i. объ|еда́ться, -е́сться; **the lion ~ed (itself) on its prey** лев жа́дно поглоща́л свою́ добы́чу.

gorgeous ['gɔ:dʒəs] *adj.* (*magnificent*) великоле́пный; (*richly coloured*) кра́сочный.

gorilla [gə'rɪlə] *n.* гори́лла.

gorse [gɔ:s] *n.* утёсник обыкнове́нный.

gory ['gɔ:rɪ] *adj.* окровавленный; кровопроли́тный.

gosh [gɒʃ] *int.* (*coll.*) Бо́же мой!

goshawk ['gɒshɔ:k] *n.* большо́й я́стреб.

gosling ['gɒzlɪŋ] *n.* гусёнок.

gospel ['gɒsp(ə)l] *n.* ева́нгелие; **preach the ~** пропове́довать (*impf.*) Ева́нгелие; (*fig.*): **~ truth** и́стинная пра́вда; **she takes everything for ~** она́ всё принима́ет на ве́ру.

gossamer ['gɒsəmə(r)] *n.* **1.** (*spider web*) осе́нняя паути́нка. **2.** (*gauzy material*) газ.

gossip ['gɒsɪp] *n.* **1.** (*talk*) спле́тня; **they met to have a good ~** они́ встре́тились, что́бы хороше́нько посплё́тничать. **2.** (*person addicted to ~ing*) спле́тни|к (*fem.* -ца). **3.** (*attr.*): **~ column/writer** коло́нка/репортёр све́тской хро́ники.

v.i. спле́тничать, на-.

Goth [gɒθ] *n.* гот.

Gothic ['gɒθɪk] *n.* **1.** (*language*) го́тский язы́к. **2.** (*archit.*) готи́ческий стиль. **3.** (*script*) готи́ческий шрифт.

adj. (*of style or script*) готи́ческий.

gouache [gʊ'ɑ:ʃ, gwɑ:ʃ] *n.* гуа́шь.

gouge [gaʊdʒ] *n.* полукру́глое долото́.

v.t. выда́лбливать, вы́долбить; **~ s.o.'s eyes out** выка́лывать, вы́колоть кому́-н. глаза́.

goulash ['gu:læʃ] *n.* гуля́ш.

gourd [gʊəd] *n.* (*bot.*) горля́нка, ты́ква буты́лочная; (*vessel*) калеба́са, сосу́д из ты́квы.

gourmet ['gʊəmeɪ] *n.* гурма́н; гастроно́м.

gout [gaʊt] *n.* пода́гра.

govern ['gʌv(ə)n] *v.t.* **1.** (*rule; also v.i.*) пра́вить (*impf.*) +*i.*; **~ing body** (*of hospital, school etc.*) дире́кция, правле́ние; (*control, influence*) руководи́ть (*impf.*) +*i.*; управля́ть (*impf.*) +*i.* **2.** (*apply to*): **the same principle ~s both cases** оди́н и тот же при́нцип примени́м в обо́их слу́чаях. **3.** (*gram.*) управля́ть (*impf.*) +*i.*

governance ['gʌvənəns] *n.* управле́ние (*чем*); руково́дство (*чем*).

governess ['gʌvənɪs] *n.* гуверна́нтка.

government ['gʌvənmənt] *n.* (*rule*) правле́ние; (*system*) фо́рма правле́ния; **local ~** ме́стное самоуправле́ние; (*pol.*) прави́тельство; **~ house** резиде́нция губерна́тора; **~ securities** госуда́рственные це́нные бума́ги.

governmental [,gʌvən'ment(ə)l] *adj.* прави́тельственный.

governor ['gʌvənə(r)] *n.* **1.** (*ruling official*) губерна́тор. **2.** (*member of governing body*) член правле́ния. **3.** (*coll., boss*) хозя́ин; шеф. **4.** (*regulating mechanism*) регуля́тор.

cpd. **~-general** *n.* генера́л-губерна́тор.

gown [gaʊn] *n.* (*woman's*) пла́тье; (*academic or official*) ма́нтия.

GP (*abbr. of* ***general practitioner***) райо́нный врач; терапе́вт широ́кого про́филя.

GPO (*abbr. of* ***General Post Office***) главпочта́мт.

grab [græb] *n.* (*snatch*): **he made a ~ for the money** он попыта́лся схвати́ть де́ньги.

v.t. & i. схва́т|ывать, -и́ть; **he ~bed me by the lapels** он схвати́л меня́ за ла́цканы; **how does that ~ you?** что вы на э́то ска́жете?

grace [greɪs] *n.* **1.** (*elegance*) гра́ция. **2.** (*favour*) благоскло́нность; **act of ~** поми́лование; **by the ~ of God** бо́жьей ми́лостью; **I am not in his good ~s** я у него́ в неми́лости; (*dispensation*) отсро́чка; **the law allows 3 days' ~** зако́н даёт 3 дня отсро́чки; **he fell from ~** он сошёл с пути́ и́стинного; (*fell into disgrace*) он впал в неми́лость; (*sense of the seemly*): **he had the ~ to apologize** он был насто́лько такти́чен, что извини́лся; (*easy or pleasant manner*): **he could lose the game with good ~** он уме́л прои́грывать с досто́инством; (*prayer before meal*) моли́тва; **say ~** моли́ться (*impf.*) пе́ред едо́й. **3.** (*myth.*): **the three G~s** три гра́ции. **4.** (*courtesy title*): **his G~** све́тлость/сия́тельство; (*eccl.*) его́ преосвяще́нство.

v.t. удост|а́ивать, -о́ить; награ|жда́ть, -ди́ть; **he ~d the meeting with his presence** он удосто́ил собра́ние свои́м прису́тствием; **she is ~d with good looks** она́ наделена́ прия́тной вне́шностью.

graceful ['greɪsfʊl] *adj.* грацио́зный; изя́щный.

gracefulness ['greɪsfʊlnɪs] *n.* грацио́зность.

gracious ['greɪʃəs] *adj.* ми́лостивый; любе́зный; **~ living** краси́вая жизнь.

int. **good(ness) ~ (me)!** ба́тюшки!; Бо́же мой!

gradation [grəˈdeɪʃ(ə)n] *n.* градáция.

grade [greɪd] *n.* **1.** (*assessed category*) стéпень; (*of quality*) сорт; **low-~ oil** нефть ни́зкого кáчества (*of rank*) стéпень; класс; (*US, class in school*) класс; **~ school** начáльная шкóла. **2.** (*US, school rating*) отмéтка; оцéнка. **3.** (*fig., coll.*): **on the down ~** на спáде.

v.t. **1.** (*classify*) сорти́ровáть, рас-. **2.** (*reduce slope of*) профили́ровать (*impf.*).

grader [ˈgreɪdə(r)] *n.* (*road-building*) грéйдер.

gradient [ˈgreɪdɪənt] *n.* **1.** (*ratio of slope*) градиéнт; (*up/down*) градиéнт подъёма/уклóна; **a ~ of 1 in 5** уклóн оди́н к пяти́. **2.** (*slope*) подъём; склон.

gradual [ˈgrædjʊəl] *adj.* постепéнный.

graduate¹ [ˈgrædjʊət] *n.* (*of university, school etc.*) выпускни́|к (*fem.* -ца); **he is an Oxford ~** он окóнчил Óксфордский университéт; **~ student** аспирáнт (*fem.* -ка); **~ study** аспирантýра.

graduate² [ˈgrædjʊˌeɪt] *v.t.* **1.** (*mark with degrees*) градуи́ровать, про-. **2.** (*arrange by grade*) распол|агáть, -ожи́ть на шкалé.

v.i. (*from university*) ок|áнчивать, -óнчить университéт/вуз.

graduation [ˌgrædjʊˈeɪʃ(ə)n] *n.* **1.** (*marking with degrees*) градуирóвка. **2.** (*pl., degrees so marked*) делéния (*nt. pl.*). **3.** (*arrangement in grades*) расположéние на шкалé. **4.** (*receiving degree*) получéние диплóма/стéпени; (*US*) окончáние шкóлы.

graffiti [grəˈfiːtiː] *n.* нáдписи (*f. pl.*) (на стéнах/забóрах).

graft¹ [grɑːft] *n.* **1.** (*scion*) черенóк; (*tissue*) пересáженная ткань; (*process applied to trees*) приви́вка. **2.** (*surgery*) оперáция пересáдки. **3.** (*coll.*) (*hard work*) вкáлывание.

v.t. (*surg.*) пересá|живать, -ди́ть; (*hort., also fig.*) прив|ивáть, -и́ть.

graft² [grɑːft] *n.* (*coll., bribery etc.*) взя́точничество; блат.

grain [greɪn] *n.* **1.** (*collect., seed of cereal plants*) зернó; хлéбные злáки (*m. pl.*); (*single seed*) зернó, зёрнышко, крупи́нка. **2.** (*small particle*) зёрнышко; крупи́нка; **~ of sand** песчи́нка; **~ of truth** крупи́ца/ /кáпля прáвды. **3.** (*texture*) волокнó; узелóк. **4.** (*of wood*) тексту́ра; **it goes against the ~ with me** (*fig.*) э́то мне не по душé/нутрý.

gram [græm] = **gram(me)**

grammar [ˈgræmə(r)] *n.* граммáтика; **this sentence is bad ~** э́то неграмóтная фрáза.

cpds. **~-book** *n.* учéбник граммáтики; **~-school** *n.* срéдняя шкóла с гуманитáрным уклóном.

grammatical [grəˈmætɪk(ə)l] *adj.* граммати́ческий; **a ~ sentence** грáмотное (*or* прáвильно состáвленное) предложéние.

gram(me) [græm] *n.* грамм.

gramophone [ˈgræməˌfəʊn] *n.* раммофóн; **~ record** грампласти́нка.

granary [ˈgrænərɪ] *n.* амбáр; зернохрани́лище.

grand [grænd] *n.* (*sl., 1000 dollars, pounds, etc.*) штýка, кося́.

adj. **1.** (*title*) вели́кий; **~ duke** вели́кий князь (*m.*); **~ master** (*chess*) гроссмéйстер. **2.** (*great, important*) вели́кий; грандиóзный; **~ opera** большáя óпера; **~ piano** роя́ль (*m.*). **3.** (*elevated, imposing*) велúчественный; **the ~ style** высóкий стиль. **4.** (*all embracing*): **~ finale** торжéственный финáл; **~ total** óбщая сýмма. **5.** (*coll., very fine*) восхити́тельный; великолéпный; **we had a ~ time** мы потрясáюще провели́ врéмя.

cpds. **~child** *n.* внук; внýчка; **~daughter** *n.* внýчка; **~father** *n.* дéдушка (*m.*); **~mother** *n.* бáбушка; **~parent** *n.* дéдушка; бáбушка; **~son** *n.* внук; **~stand** *n.* трибýна. *For kinship terms see also cpds. of* **great**

grandeur [ˈgrændjə(r), -ndʒə(r)] *n.* великолéпие.

grandiloquence [ˌgrænˈdɪləkwəns] *n.* высокопáрность.

grandiloquent [ˌgrænˈdɪləkwənt] *adj.* высокопáрный.

grandiose [ˈgrændɪˌəʊs] *adj.* грандиóзный.

grange [greɪndʒ] *n.* (*farmstead*) усáдьба.

granite [ˈgrænɪt] *n.* грани́т.

adj. грани́тный.

granny [ˈgrænɪ] *n.* (*coll.*) бáбушка.

grant [grɑːnt] *n.* дотáция; субси́дия; (*to student*) стипéндия.

v.t. **1.** (*bestow*) даровáть (*impf., pf.*); жáловать; **I ~ my consent** я даю́ соглáсие; **~ me this favour!** сдéлайте мне э́то одолжéние! **2.** (*concede*) призн|авáть; -áть; **I ~ you that** в э́том вы прáвы; **~ed, he has done all he could** соглáсен, он сдéлал всё, что мог. **3.**: **he takes my help for ~ed** он принимáет мою́ пóмощь как дóлжное.

granular [ˈgrænjʊlə(r)] *adj.* грануди́рованный.

granulate [ˈgrænjʊˌleɪt] *v.t. & i.* дроби́ть, раз-; **~d sugar** сáхарный песóк.

granule [ˈgrænjuːl] *n.* зернó.

grape [greɪp] *n.*: **a ~** виногрáдина; **the ~, ~s** виногрáд; **bunch of ~s** гроздь виногрáда.

cpds. **~fruit** *n.* грéйпфрут; **~-vine** *n.* виногрáдная лозá; (*fig.*): **I heard on the ~-vine that ...** молвá донеслá до меня́, что...

graph [grɑːf, græf] *n.* грáфик.

cpd. **~-paper** *n.* бумáга в клéтку.

graphic [ˈgræfɪk] *adj.* **1.** (*pertaining to drawing etc.*) изобрази́тельный; **the ~ arts** изобрази́тельные искýсства; грáфика. **2.** (*vivid*) крáсочный; нагля́дный. **3.** (*using diagrams*) графи́ческий.

graphite [ˈgræfaɪt] *n.* графи́т.

adj. графи́товый.

grapnel [ˈgræpn(ə)l] *n.* (*anchor*) шлю́почный я́корь; (*for boarding*) абордáжный крюк.

grappl|e [ˈgræp(ə)l] *v.i.* схвáт|ываться, -и́ться; **~e with the enemy** схвати́ться с врагóм; **~e with a problem** брáться, взя́ться за проблéму; **~ing-iron** крюк.

grasp [grɑːsp] *n.* **1.** (*grip*) хвáтка; (*fig.*): **victory is within our ~** побéда ужé близкá. **2.** (*comprehension*) понимáние; **he has a good ~ of the subject** он хорошó в э́том разбирáется; **it is beyond my ~** э́то вы́ше моегó понимáния.

v.t. (*seize*) схвáт|ывать, -и́ть; **~ the nettle** (*fig.*) взять (*pf.*) быкá за рогá; (*embrace*) обхвáт|ывать, -и́ть; (*comprehend*) схвáт|ывать, -и́ть смысл +*g.*

v.i.: **~ at, for** (*lit., fig.*) ухвати́ться (*pf.*) за+*a.*; **a ~ing person** стяжáтель (*fem.* -ница).

grass [grɑːs] *n.* **1.** травá; **blade of ~** трави́нка; (*pasture*) пáстбище; **~ widow** солóменная вдовá. **2.** (*lawn*) газóн; **'keep off the ~'** «по травé не ходи́ть». **3.** (*sl., police informer*) стукáч.

v.t. зас|евáть, -éять травóй; об|клáдывать, -ложи́ть дёрном.

v.i. (*sl., inform*) стучáть, на-.

cpds. **~hopper** *n.* кузнéчик; **~land** *n.* луг; **~-snake** *n.* уж.

grassy [ˈgrɑːsɪ] *adj.* травянóй; травяни́стый.

grate¹ [greɪt] *n.* (*fireplace*)ками́нная решётка; ками́н.

grate² [greɪt] *v.t.* терéть (*impf.*); **~d cheese** тёртый сыр; **~ one's teeth** скрежетáть (*impf.*) зубáми.

v.i. **1.** (*rub*) терéться (*impf.*); **~ on** (*fig.*) раздражáть (*impf.*); нерви́ровать (*impf.*); **it ~s on my ear** э́то мне рéжет слух. **2.** (*make harsh sound*) скр|ипéть, -и́пнуть.

grateful [ˈgreɪtfʊl] *adj.* благодáрный.

gratefulness [ˈgreɪtfʊlnɪs] *n.* благодáрность.

grater [ˈgreɪtə(r)] *n.* тёрка.

gratification [ˌgrætɪfɪˈkeɪʃ(ə)n] *n.* удовлетворéние.

gratify [ˈgrætɪˌfaɪ] *v.t.* **1.** (*give pleasure to*) дост|авля́ть,

-а́вить удово́льствие +*d*.; **the results were most ~ing** результа́ты бы́ли са́мыми обнадёживающими. **2.** (*indulge*) удовлетвор|я́ть, -и́ть.

grating ['greɪtɪŋ] *n.* решётка.

gratis ['grɑːtɪs, 'greɪ-] *adj.* беспла́тный.
adv. беспла́тно.

gratitude ['grætɪ,tjuːd] *n.* благода́рность.

gratuitous [grə'tjuːɪtəs] *adj.* **1.** (*free*) даровóй; безвозме́здный. **2.** (*unwarranted*) беспричи́нный; **a ~ insult** незаслу́женное оскорбле́ние.

gratuity [grə'tjuːɪtɪ] *n.* (*bounty on retirement etc.*) посо́бие; пре́мия; (*tip*) чаевы́|е (*pl.*, *g.* -х).

grave[1] [greɪv] *n.* моги́ла; **an old man with one foot in the ~** стари́к, стоя́щий одно́й ного́й в моги́ле; **he would turn in his ~ if he heard you** е́сли бы он вас услы́шал, он переверну́лся бы в гробу́; (*death*) смерть; **he went to his ~** он сошёл в моги́лу; **life beyond the ~** загро́бная жизнь.
cpds. **~-digger** *n.* моги́льщик; **~side** *n.*: **at the ~** на краю́ моги́лы; **~stone** *n.* надгро́бный ка́мень; **~yard** *n.* кла́дбище.

grave[2] [greɪv] *adj.* (*of pers.*) серьёзный; (*of events*) серьёзный, тяжёлый; **~ news** трево́жные ве́сти.

grave[3] [greɪv] *adj.* (*gram.*): **~ accent** тупо́е ударе́ние.

gravel ['græv(ə)l] *n.* гра́вий; **a ~ path** доро́жка, посы́панная гра́вием.

gravelly ['grævəlɪ] *adj.* гравии́ный; (*fig.*, *of the voice*) скрипу́чий.

gravitate ['grævɪ,teɪt] *v.i.* прит|я́гиваться, -яну́ться; (*fig.*) тяготе́ть (*impf.*) (*к чему*).

gravitation [,grævɪ'teɪʃ(ə)n] *n.* притяже́ние, тяготе́ние.

gravitational [,grævɪ'teɪʃən(ə)l] *adj.* гравитацио́нный.

gravity ['grævɪtɪ] *n.* **1.** (*force*) си́ла притяже́ния. **2.** (*weight*) тя́жесть; **centre of ~** центр тя́жести; **law of ~** зако́н всеми́рного тяготе́ния. **3.** (*seriousness*) серьёзность; тя́жесть. **4.** (*solemnity*) торже́ственность.

gravy ['greɪvɪ] *n.* подли́вка.
cpd. **~-boat** со́усник.

gray [greɪ] = **grey**

graze[1] [greɪz] *n.* (*abrasion*) цара́пина; сса́дина.
v.t. зад|ева́ть, -е́ть; сса́|живать, -ди́ть; **the bullet ~d his cheek** пу́ля оцара́пала ему́ щёку; **he fell and ~d his knee** он упа́л и ссади́л коле́но.

graze[2] [greɪz] *v.t.* пасти́; **~ sheep** пасти́ ове́ц; **~ (*feed in*) a field** пасти́сь на по́ле/лугу́.

grazing ['greɪzɪŋ] *n.* па́стбище; **~ land** вы́пас.

grease [griːs] *n.* (*fat*) жир; (*lubricant*) сма́зка.
v.t. сма́з|ывать, -ать; (*fig.*): **~ s.o.'s palm** (*with a bribe*) «подма́зать» кого́-н.
cpds. **~-monkey** *n.* (авто)меха́ник; авиамеха́ник; **~-paint** *n.* грим; **~proof** *adj.* жиронепроница́емый; **~-spot** *n.* то́чка сма́зки.

greasy ['griːsɪ, -zɪ] *adj.* жи́рный; (*of a road*) ско́льзкий.

great [greɪt] *adj.* **1.** большо́й, вели́кий; (*famous*) знамени́тый; **they are ~ friends** они́ больши́е друзья́; **a ~ big boy** ро́слый ма́льчик; **a ~ many people** ма́сса наро́ду; **I've a ~ mind to ...** мне бы о́чень хоте́лось...; **he lived to a ~ age** он до́жил до глубо́кой ста́рости; **the ~ majority** подавля́ющее большинство́; **take ~ care!** бу́дьте о́чень осторо́жны; **he shows ~ ignorance** он проявля́ет по́лное неве́жество (*в чём*). **2.** (*enthusiastic*, *assiduous*): **a ~ reader** стра́стный чита́тель; **a ~ walker** завзя́тый ходо́к. **3.** (*coll.*, *splendid*, *marvellous*) замеча́тельный; **we had a ~ time** мы замеча́тельно провели́ вре́мя; **he thinks he's the ~est** (*US sl.*) он мно́го о себе́ вообража́ет; **he is ~ at repairing a car** он великоле́пно ремонти́рует маши́ну. **4.** (*eminent*, *distinguished*) вели́кий; **the G~ Powers** вели́кие держа́вы; **Peter the G~** Пётр Вели́кий; **a ~ occasion** торже́ственное собы́тие. **5.** (*var.*): **the G~ Bear** Больша́я Медве́дица; **G~ Britain** Великобрита́ния.
cpds. **~-aunt** *n.* двою́родная ба́бушка; **~coat** *n.* пальто́ (*indecl.*); **~-granddaughter** *n.* пра́внучка; **~-grandfather** *n.* пра́дед; **~-grandmother** *n.* праба́бушка; **~-grandson** *n.* пра́внук; **~-uncle** *n.* двою́родный дед.

greatly ['greɪtlɪ] *adv.* о́чень, си́льно, значи́тельно; **I was ~ amused** э́то меня́ си́льно позаба́вило; **~ esteemed** глубокоуважа́емый.

greatness ['greɪtnɪs] *n.* вели́чие.

grebe [griːb] *n.* пога́нка (*птица*).

Greece [griːs] *n.* Гре́ция.

greed [griːd], **-iness** ['griːdɪnɪs] *nn.* жа́дность; а́лчность; (*for food*) прожо́рливость.

greedy ['griːdɪ] *adj.* (*for money etc.*) жа́дный; а́лчный; (*for food*) прожо́рливый.

Greek [griːk] *n.* **1.** (*pers.*) гре|к (*fem.* -ча́нка). **2.** (*language*) гре́ческий язы́к; **it's ~ to me** э́то для меня́ кита́йская гра́мота.
adj. гре́ческий.

green [griːn] *n.* **1.** (*colour*) зелёный цвет; зелёное; **dressed in ~** оде́тый в зелёное. **2.** (*pl.*, *vegetables*) зе́лень; **spring ~s** ра́нние о́вощи (*m. pl.*). **3.** (*grassy area*) лужа́йка; (*on golf course*) площа́дка вокру́г лу́нки.
adj. зелёный; **she has ~ fingers** она́ уме́лый садово́д; **~ with envy** зелёный от за́висти; (*unripe*) незре́лый.
cpds. **~-eyed** *adj.* зеленогла́зый; **~finch** *n.* зелену́шка; **~fly** *n.* тля; **~grocer** *n.* зеленщи́к; **~house** *n.* тепли́ца; **~house effect** парнико́вый *or* тепли́чный эффе́кт.

greenery ['griːnərɪ] *n.* зе́лень.

greenish ['griːnɪʃ] *adj.* зеленова́тый.

Greenland ['griːnlənd] *n.* Гренла́ндия.

Greenwich (mean) time ['grenɪtʃ, 'grɪnɪdʒ] *n.* вре́мя по Гри́нвичу.

greet [griːt] *v.t.* (*socially*) здоро́ваться, по- с+*i.*; (*welcome*) приве́тствовать (*impf.*); (*e.g. the dawn*) встр|еча́ть, -е́тить; **a fine view ~ed us at the summit** с верши́ны нам откры́лся прекра́сный вид.

greeting ['griːtɪŋ] *n.* (*on meeting*) приве́тствие; **~s** (*in a letter*) приве́т; **~s!** приве́т!; приве́тствую!; (*on a special occasion*): **birthday ~s** поздравле́ние с днём рожде́ния; **~ card** поздрави́тельная откры́тка.

gregarious [grɪ'geərɪəs] *adj.* ста́дный; (*fig.*, *also*) общи́тельный.

Gregorian [grɪ'gɔːrɪən] *adj.* григориа́нский.

gremlin ['gremlɪn] *n.* (*coll.*) злой дух.

grenade [grɪ'neɪd] *n.* грана́та.

grenadier [,grenə'dɪə(r)] *n.* гренаде́р.

grey, gray [greɪ] *n.* се́рый цвет; се́рое; **dressed in ~** оде́тый в се́рое.
adj. се́рый; **~ area** (*fig.*) о́бласть неопределённости; **~ matter** (*fig.*) «се́рое вещество́»; **he has gone quite ~** он си́льно поседе́л.
cpds. **~-haired, ~-headed** *adjs.* седо́й; **~hound** *n.* гре́йгаунд, англи́йская борза́я.

greyish ['greɪɪʃ] *adj.* серова́тый.

grid [grɪd] *n.* **1.** (*grating*) решётка. **2.** (*map reference squares*) координа́тная се́тка; **~ reference** координа́ты (*f. pl.*). **3.** (*elec.*) сеть электропереда́ч. **5.** (*power supply system*) энергосисте́ма.
cpd. **~iron** *n.* ра́шпер.

griddle ['grɪd(ə)l] *n.* сковоро́дка.
cpd. **~cake** *n.* лепёшка; блин.

grief [griːf] *n.* (*sorrow*) го́ре, печа́ль; (*cause of sorrow*) огорче́ние; (*disaster*): **he will come to ~** он пло́хо ко́нчит.

grievance ['griːv(ə)ns] *n.* прете́нзия; недово́льство.

grieve [griːv] *v.t.* огорч|а́ть, -и́ть; печа́лить, о-; **I am ~d to hear of it** мне бо́льно э́то слы́шать.

v.i. печа́литься, о-; горева́ть (*impf.*); **she ~d for her husband** она́ горева́ла о му́же.
grievous ['gri:vəs] *adj.* го́рестный; печа́льный; **~ harm** тяжёлый уще́рб; **~ pain** мучи́тельная боль.
griffin ['grɪfɪn] *n.* гриф, грифо́н.
grill[1] [grɪl] *n.* (*gridiron*) ра́шпер; (*dish*) жа́реное мя́со; **mixed ~** ассорти́ (*nt. indecl.*) из жа́реного мя́са.
v.t. (*cook*) жа́рить, под-; (*coll. interrogate*) учин|я́ть, -и́ть допро́с +*d.*
v.i. (*of food*) жа́риться, под-.
cpd. **~room** *n.* гриль-ба́р.
grill[2], **-e** [grɪl] *n.* решётка.
grim [grɪm] *adj.* суро́вый, мра́чный, гро́зный; **the prospect is ~** перспекти́вы безра́достные.
grimace ['grɪməs, grɪ'meɪs] *n.* грима́са.
v.i. грима́сничать (*impf.*).
grime [graɪm] *n.* са́жа; грязь.
grimy ['graɪmɪ] *adj.* чума́зый; гря́зный.
grin [grɪn] *n.* усме́шка.
v.i. усмех|а́ться, -ну́ться; ухмыл|я́ться, -ну́ться; ска́лить (*impf.*) зу́бы; **you must ~ and bear it** вы должны́ му́жественно перенести́ э́то.
grind [graɪnd] *n.* (*coll.*) изнури́тельный труд; рабо́та на изно́с; **this work is a fearful ~** э́та рабо́та до у́жаса изнуря́ет.
v.t. **1.** (*crush*) моло́ть, с-; **~ corn** моло́ть, перезерно́; **ground almonds** мо́лотый минда́ль; **ground rice** дроблёный рис; (*fig.*) угнета́ть (*impf.*). **2.** (*wear down*) изн|а́шивать, -оси́ть; **ground glass** ма́товое стекло́; (*sharpen*)точи́ть, на-; (*make smooth*) шлифова́ть, от-. **3. ~ one's teeth** скрежета́ть/скрипе́ть (*impf.*) зуба́ми. **4. ~ one's heel into the earth** вда́в|ливать, -и́ть каблу́к в зе́млю.
v.i. **1.** (*rub, grate*) раст|ира́ть, -ере́ть. **2.** (*coll., work hard*) изм|а́тываться, -ота́ться. **3.: ~ to a halt** остан|а́вливаться, -ови́ться (с ля́згом); засто́пориться (*pf.*).
cpds. **~stone** *n.* точи́ло; **he kept his nose to the ~stone** он труди́лся без о́тдыха.
grinder ['graɪndə(r)] *n.* **1.** (*for crushing*) дроби́лка; (*coffee-~*) кофемо́лка, кофе́йная ме́льница. **2.** (*for abrasive work*) точи́льный ка́мень; шлифова́льный стано́к.
grip [grɪp] *n.* **1.** (*grasp*) схва́тывание; (*fig.*) понима́ние; **he has a powerful ~** у него́ кре́пкая хва́тка; **come to ~s with a problem** вплотну́ю заня́ться (*pf.*) пробле́мой; **take a ~ of yourself!** возьми́те себя́ в ру́ки!; **he got a ~ of the facts** он разобра́лся в фа́ктах; **he is losing his ~** хва́тка у него́ уже́ не та. **2.** (*travelling-bag*) саквоя́ж.
v.t. (*hold tightly*) схва́т|ывать, -и́ть; (*of a disease*) не отпуска́ть, кре́пко держа́ть (*both impf.*); (*hold the attention of*) захва́т|ывать, -и́ть; **a ~ping story** захва́тывающий расска́з.
v.i. схва́т|ываться, -и́ться; **the brakes failed to ~** тормоза́ отказа́ли.
gripe [graɪp] (*coll.*) *n.* **1.** (*pl., colic pains*) ко́лик|и (*pl., g.* —). **2.** (*grumble, complaint*) ворча́ние.
v.i. (*complain*) ворча́ть (*impf.*).
cpd. **~-water** *n.* укро́пная вода́.
grisly ['grɪzlɪ] *adj.* ужаса́ющий.
grist [grɪst] *n.* зерно́ для помо́ла; (*fig.*): **it will bring ~ to the mill** э́то принесёт дохо́д; **all is ~ to his mill** он из всего́ извлека́ет вы́году.
gristle ['grɪs(ə)l] *n.* хрящ.
gristly ['grɪslɪ] *adj.* хрящево́й; с хряща́ми.
grit [grɪt] *n.* **1.** (*small bits of stone*) гра́вий; песо́к; **I've a piece of ~ in my eye** мне в гла́з попа́ла сори́нка. **2.** (*coll., courage and endurance*) вы́держка; му́жество. **3.** (*pl., coarse meal*) овся́нка.
v.t. **1.** (*spread ~ on*): **the streets were ~ted at the first sign of frost** при пе́рвых при́знаках моро́за у́лицы посы́пали песко́м. **2.: ~ one's teeth** скрипе́ть (*impf.*) зуба́ми; (*fig.*) сти́снуть (*pf.*) зу́бы.
grizzly ['grɪzlɪ] *n.* (**~-bear**) гри́зли (*m. indecl.*).
groan [grəʊn] *n.* стон.
v.i. стона́ть, за.
groats [grəʊts] *n.* крупа́.
grocer ['grəʊsə(r)] *n.* бакале́йщик.
grocery ['grəʊsərɪ] *n.* (*trade*) бакале́йное де́ло; (*shop*) бакале́йная ла́вка; магази́н бакале́йных това́ров; (*pl., goods*) бакале́я.
grog [grɒg] *n.* грог; пунш.
groggy ['grɒgɪ] *adj.* нетвёрдый на нога́х.
groin [grɔɪn] *n.* (*anat.*) пах.
groom [gru:m] *n.* (*for horses*) ко́нюх; (*bride~*) жени́х.
v.t. **1. ~ a horse** ходи́ть (*impf.*) за ло́шадью. **2. well-~ed** (*of pers.*) хорошо́ причёсанный и оде́тый.
groove [gru:v] *n.* желобо́к.
grope [grəʊp] *v.t. & i.* идти́ (*det.*) о́щупью; ощу́п|ывать, -ать; **he ~d his way toward the door** он о́щупью добра́лся до две́ри.
gross [grəʊs] *n.* (*number*) гросс.
adj. **1.** (*coarse; flagrant*) гру́бый; вульга́рный. **2.** (*obese*) ту́чный. **3.** (*opp. net*) валово́й; **~ weight** вес бру́тто; **in the ~** (*wholesale*) о́птом, гурто́м.
v.t. (*coll., make a ~ profit*): **we ~ed £1,000** мы получи́ли о́бщую при́быль в 1000 фу́нтов.
grossness ['grəʊsnɪs] *n.* гру́бость; вульга́рность; (*obesity*) ту́чность.
grotesque [grəʊ'tesk] *n. adj.* гроте́сковый; гроте́скный.
grotto ['grɒtəʊ] *n.* грот.
grouch [graʊtʃ] *n.* (*coll.*) ворчу́н; брюзга́ (*c.g.*).
grouchy ['graʊtʃɪ] *adj.* (*coll.*) брюзгли́вый.
ground [graʊnd] *n.* **1.** (*surface of earth*) земля́; грунт; **the tree fell to the ~** де́рево упа́ло на зе́млю; **he cut the ~ from under my feet** он вы́бил у меня́ по́чву из-под ног; **his plan fell to the ~** его́ план ру́хнул; **the plane was a long while getting off the ~** самолёт де́лал большо́й разбе́г пе́ред взлётом; **the plan will never get off the ~** прое́кт так и оста́нется на бума́ге; **he has both feet on the ~** (*fig.*) он про́чно стои́т на нога́х; **it suits me down to the ~** э́то меня́ вполне́ устра́ивает; **from the ~ up** сни́зу до́верху; **~ floor** пе́рвый эта́ж; **~ forces** сухопу́тные войска́; **~ speed** (*aeron.*) путева́я ско́рость; **~ swell** мёртвая зыбь. **2.** (*soil, also fig.*) по́чва; **~ frost** за́морозк|и (*pl., g.* -ов); **this theory breaks fresh ~** э́та тео́рия прокла́дывает но́вые пути́; **you are** (*treading*) **on dangerous ~** вы вступи́ли на ско́льзкую по́чву. **3.** (*position*) положе́ние; **our forces gained ~** на́ши ча́сти продвига́лись вперёд; **this opinion is gaining ~** э́та то́чка зре́ния набира́ет си́лу; **he had to give ~** он до́лжен был уступи́ть; **he stood his ~ like a man** он держа́лся как мужчи́на; **he has shifted his ~ so many times** он сто́лько раз меня́л свою́ пози́цию; **I prefer to meet him on my own ~** я предпочита́ю встреча́ться с ним на свое́й террито́рии; **there is much common ~ between us** у нас мно́го о́бщего. **4.** (*area, distance*) расстоя́ние; **we covered a lot of ~** (*distance*) мы покры́ли большо́е расстоя́ние; (*fig., work*) мы заме́тно продви́нулись вперёд. **5.** (*defined area of activity*) площа́дка; **football ~** футбо́льная площа́дка; **parade ~** плац; **home ~** своё по́ле. **6.** (*pl., estate*) сад, парк, зе́мли (*f. pl.*); **house and ~s** дом и земе́льный уча́сток. **7.** (*pl. dregs*) гу́ща; **coffee ~s** кофе́йная гу́ща. **8.** (*reason*) основа́ние; **I have no ~s for complaint** у меня́ нет основа́ний жа́ловаться; **he has good ~(s) for saying so** у него́ есть все основа́ния так говори́ть. **9.** (*surface for painting, printing etc.*) фон; **a design on a white ~** рису́нок на бе́лом фо́не.

v.t. **1.** (*run aground*) сажа́ть, посади́ть на мель. **2.** (*prevent from flying*) запре|ща́ть, -ти́ть полёты +*g.* **3.** (*base*) обосно́в|ывать, -а́ть; **his fears were well ~ed** его́ опасе́ния бы́ли по́лностью обосно́ваны. **4.** (*give basic instruction to*) подгот|а́вливать, -о́вить. **5.** (*elec., connect to earth*) заземл|я́ть, -и́ть.

v.i. (*of a vessel*) сади́ться, сесть на мель.

cpds. **~-floor** *adj.* на пе́рвом этаже́; **~-hog** *n.* суро́к лесно́й (америка́нский); **~nut** *n.* землянó́й оре́х; **~-rent** *n.* земе́льная ре́нта; **~-work** *n.* фунда́мент, осно́вы (*f. pl.*).

grounding ['graʊndɪŋ] *n.* (*basic instruction*) подгото́вка.

groundless ['graʊndlɪs] *adj.* беспричи́нный, беспо́чвенный, необосно́ванный.

group [gru:p] *n.* **1.** (*assemblage*) гру́ппа; коллекти́в; (*for artistic purposes*) гру́ппа; анса́мбль (*m.*); (*interest ~, e.g. at school*) кружо́к; (*political etc. unit*) группиро́вка; фра́кция. **2.** (*attr.*) группово́й; **~ therapy** группова́я психотерапи́я.

v.t. & i. группирова́ться, с-.

cpd. **~-captain** *n.* полко́вник авиа́ции.

grouping ['gru:pɪŋ] *n.* группиро́вка.

grouse[1] [graʊs] *n.* (*bird*) шотла́ндская куропа́тка.

grouse[2] [graʊs] (*coll.*) (*complaint*) жа́лоба; претéнзия.

v.i. ворча́ть (*impf.*).

grout [graʊt] *n.* (*mortar*) цеме́нтный раство́р.

v.t. зал|ива́ть, -и́ть цеме́нтом.

grove [grəʊv] *n.* ро́ща.

grovel ['grɒv(ə)l] *v.i.* (*fig.*) пресмыка́ться (*impf.*) (*перед кем*); па́|дать, -сть в но́ги.

grow [grəʊ] *v.t.* расти́ть, вы́-; выра́щивать (*impf.*); разводи́ть (*impf.*); **he is ~ing a beard** он отра́щивает бо́роду.

v.i. **1.** (*of vegetable habitat*) расти́, вы́расти; **ivy ~s on walls** плющ растёт на сте́нах. **2.** (*of vegetable or animal development*): **he has ~n tall** он о́чень вы́рос/вы́тянулся; **he grew (by) 5 inches** он вы́рос на 5 дю́ймов; **he is ~ing out of his clothes** он выраста́ет из свое́й оде́жды; **she has ~n into a young lady** она́ преврати́лась в молоду́ю же́нщину; **she is letting her hair ~** она́ отра́щивает во́лосы; **he looks quite ~n up** он вы́глядит совсе́м взро́слым; **~n-ups** взро́слые (*pl.*); **it's a habit I've never ~n out of** э́то привы́чка, от кото́рой я никогда́ не мог изба́виться; **he grew out of his clothes** он вы́рос из оде́жды; **full(y)- ~n** зре́лый; **a ~n man** взро́слый челове́к; (*increase*) увели́чи|ваться, -ться; уси́ли|ваться, -ться; **his influence is ~ing** его́ влия́ние растёт; **he listened with ~ing impatience** он слу́шал с расту́щим нетерпе́нием; **the tune ~s on one** э́тот моти́в начина́ет нра́виться со вре́менем. **3.** (*become*) станови́ться, стать; *also expr. by inchoative pref.*; **it grew suddenly dark** вдруг ста́ло темно́ (*or* стемне́ло); **as he grew older, he ...** с во́зрастом он...; **she grew pale** она́ побледне́ла; **he grew rich** он разбогате́л.

grower ['grəʊə(r)] *n.* (*cultivator*) садово́д.

growl [graʊl] *n.* рыча́ние; (*of thunder*) гро́хот.

v.i. рыча́ть (*impf.*); греме́ть (*impf.*).

growth [grəʊθ] *n.* (*development*) рост; (*increase*) приро́ст; (*path.*) наро́ст.

grub[1] [grʌb] *n.* (*larva*) личи́нка; червь (*m.*); (*food*) жратва́ (*coll.*).

grub[2] [grʌb] *v.t.* выка́пывать, вы́копать; **a hoe for ~bing out weeds** моты́га для прополки сорняко́в.

v.i. ры́ться (*impf.*).

grubby ['grʌbɪ] *adj.* (*dirty*) гря́зный, запа́чканный.

grudg|e [grʌdʒ] *n.* претéнзия, недоброжела́тельность; **I bear him no ~e** я на него́ не в оби́де.

v.t. зави́довать, по- +*d.*; жале́ть, по- (*чего*); **I do not ~e him his success** я не зави́дую его́ успе́ху; **I ~e paying so much** мне жаль плати́ть так мно́го; **~ing praise** скупа́я похвала́; **he obeyed ~ingly** он неохо́тно вы́полнил приказа́ние.

gruel ['gru:əl] *n.* (жи́дкая) ка́шица.

gruelling ['gru:əlɪŋ] *adj.* изнури́тельный.

gruesome ['gru:səm] *adj.* жу́ткий.

gruff [grʌf] *adj.* (*of demeanour*) неприве́тливый; ре́зкий; (*of voice*) хри́плый.

gruffness ['grʌfnɪs] *n.* неприве́тливость; ре́зкость.

grumble ['grʌmb(ə)l] *n.* (*complaint*) ворча́ние; (*rumbling noise*) гро́хот.

v.i. (*complain*) ворча́ть (*impf.*); жа́ловаться, по-; (*rumble*) грохота́ть (*impf.*).

grumbler ['grʌmblə(r)] *n.* ворчу́н.

grumpy ['grʌmpɪ] *adj.* сварли́вый.

grunt [grʌnt] *n.* (*animal*) хрю́канье; (*human*) ворча́ние.

v.i. (*of animals*) хрю́к|ать, -нуть; (*of humans*; *also v.t.*) ворча́ть, про-.

guano ['gwɑ:nəʊ] *n.* гуа́но (*indecl.*).

guarantee [,gærən'ti:] *n.* **1.** (*undertaking*) гара́нтия; поручи́тельство; **this watch carries a ~** э́ти часы́ с гара́нтией. **2.** (*security*) гара́нтия (*чего*). **3.** (*determinant*) зало́г; **money is no ~ of success** де́ньги ещё не гаранти́руют успе́х.

v.t. **1.** (*stand surety*; *undertake, promise*) гаранти́ровать (*impf., pf.*). **2.** (*ensure*) обеспе́чи|вать, -ть. **3.** (*coll., feel sure, wager*) руча́ться, поручи́ться. **4.** (*insure*) страхова́ть, за-; **it is ~d to last 10 years** срок го́дности/гара́нтии — 10 лет; **~d against rust** гаранти́рованный от ржа́вчины.

guarantor [,gærən'tɔ:(r), 'gærəntə(r)] *n.* поручи́тель (*m.*); гара́нт.

guard [gɑ:d] *n.* **1.** (*state of alertness*) насторожённость; **be on your ~ against pickpockets** остерега́йтесь карма́нников; **he was caught off his ~** его́ заста́ли врасплох; (*defence*): **on ~!** (*fencing*) к бо́ю!; (*mil.*): **mount ~** вступ|а́ть, -и́ть в карау́л; **on ~ duty** на часа́х; в карау́ле; **they kept ~ by day and night** они́ стоя́ли на стра́же днём и но́чью; **the soldiers stood ~ over the prisoner** солда́ты охраня́ли заключённого. **2.** (*man appointed to keep ~*) охра́нник, карау́льный; (*collect.*) охра́на, стра́жа; **advance ~** аванга́рд; **a ~ was set on the gates** у воро́т вы́ставили охра́ну; **changing of the ~** сме́на карау́ла; **~ of honour** почётный карау́л. **3.** (*pl., collect.*) гва́рдия; **Brigade of G~s** гварде́йская брига́да. **4.** (*of a train*) проводни́к; **~'s van** бага́жный ваго́н. **5.** (*protective device*) защи́тное устро́йство, предохрани́тель (*m.*); (*of a sword*) эфе́с.

v.t. охраня́ть (*impf.*); бере́чь; **the prisoners were closely ~ed** заключённые находи́лись под уси́ленной охра́ной; **you must ~ your tongue** вам ну́жно быть бо́лее сде́ржанным на язы́к.

v.i. бере́чься (*impf.*), остерега́ться (*impf.*) (**against:** +*g.*); **everything was done to ~ against infection** бы́ли при́няты все ме́ры про́тив инфе́кции.

cpds. **~-house** *n.* карау́льное помеще́ние; **~-rail** *n.* пери́л|а (*pl., g.* —); **~-room** *n.* гауптва́хта; **~sman** *n.* гварде́ец.

guarded ['gɑ:dɪd] *adj.* сде́ржанный; осторо́жный.

guardian ['gɑ:dɪən] *n.* **1.** (*protector*) опеку́н; попечи́тель (*m.*); **~ angel** а́нгел-храни́тель (*m.*); **~ of the public interest** защи́тник обще́ственных интере́сов. **2.** (*leg.*) опеку́н.

guardianship ['gɑ:dɪən,ʃɪp] *n.* опе́ка; опеку́нство.

Guatemala [,gwɑ:tə'mɑ:lə] *n.* Гватема́ла.

guelder-rose ['geldə(r)] *n.* кали́на.

guer(r)illa [gə'rɪlə] *n.* партиза́н; **~ warfare** партиза́нская война́.

guess [ges] *n.* дога́дка; предположе́ние; **at a rough ~** гру́бо/ориентиро́вочно; **my ~ is that ...** мне сдаётся, что...; **it's anybody's ~** никому́ неизве́стно.

v.t. **1.** (*estimate*) прики́|дывать, -нуть; **I would ~ his age at 40** я дал бы ему́ лет 40. **2. ~ a riddle** отга́д|ывать, -а́ть зага́дку. **3.** (*conjecture*) дога́д|ываться, -а́ться (*о чём*); уга́д|ывать, -а́ть. **4.** (*US coll., expect, suppose*) полага́ть (*impf.*); **I ~ you are right** вероя́тно, вы пра́вы.

v.i. гада́ть (*impf.*); **she likes to keep him ~ing** ей нра́вится держа́ть его́ в неве́дении.

cpd. **~work** *n.* дога́дки (*f. pl.*).

guest [gest] *n.* **1.** (*one privately entertained*) гость (*m.*); **paying ~** ≃ жиле́ц; **~ of honour** почётный гость; **~ artist, star** гастроли́рующий арти́ст; звезда́ на гастро́лях. **2.** (*at a hotel etc.*) постоя́лец.

cpds. **~-house** *n.* пансио́н; **~-room** *n.* ко́мната для госте́й.

guffaw [gʌ'fɔ:] *n.* го́гот.

v.i. гогота́ть (*impf.*).

guidance ['gaɪd(ə)ns] *n.* руково́дство.

guide [gaɪd] *n.* **1.** (*leader*) руководи́тель (*m.*); (*for travellers, tourists etc.*) гид, экскурсово́д; (*mil.*) разве́дчик. **2.** (*directing principle*) руково́дство. **3.** **(~-book): ~ to Germany** путеводи́тель (*m.*) по Герма́нии; (*manual*) уче́бник. **4. (Girl) G~** де́вочка-ска́ут.

v.t. **1.** (*lead, take around*) води́ть (*indet.*), вести́, по- (*det.*); руководи́ть (*impf.*) +*i.*; **he ~d them around the city** он поводи́л их по го́роду; **be ~d by principles** руково́дствоваться (*impf.*) при́нципами; **be ~d by circumstances** де́йствовать (*impf.*) по обстоя́тельствам. **2.** (*direct*) напр|авля́ть, -а́вить; **~d missile** управля́емая раке́та.

cpds. **~-book** *n.* путеводи́тель (*m.*); **~-dog** *n.* соба́ка-поводы́рь; **~line** *n.* директи́ва; **~-post** *n.* указа́тель (*m.*).

guild [gɪld] *n.* **1.** (*hist.*) ги́льдия. **2.** ассоциа́ция, сою́з.

cpd. **~hall** *n.* ра́туша.

guilder ['gɪldə(r)] *n.* гу́льден.

guile [gaɪl] *n.* лука́вство, кова́рство.

guillemot ['gɪlɪ,mɒt] *n.* ка́йра.

guillotine ['gɪlə,ti:n] *n.* **1.** гильоти́на. **2.** (*for paper, metal etc.*) ре́зальная маши́на. **3.** (*parl.*) гильотини́рование пре́ний.

v.t. (*execute*) гильотини́ровать (*impf., pf.*); (*pages etc.*) обр|еза́ть, -е́зать.

guilt [gɪlt] *n.* вина́; **~ complex** ко́мплекс вины́.

guiltless ['gɪltlɪs] *adj.* невино́вный (*в чём*).

guilty ['gɪltɪ] *adj.* вино́вный; **he pleaded ~ to the crime** он призна́л себя́ вино́вным в преступле́нии; **he was found ~** он был при́знан вино́вным; **a verdict of not ~** верди́кт невино́вности; **~ conscience** нечи́стая со́весть; **a ~ look** винова́тый вид.

guinea[1] ['gɪnɪ] *n.* гине́я.

Guinea[2] ['gɪnɪ] *n.* Гвине́я.

cpds. **g~-fowl, hen** *nn.* цеса́рка; **g~-pig** *n.* (*lit.*) морска́я сви́нка; (*fig.*) «подо́пытный кро́лик».

guise [gaɪz] *n.* (*dress*) наря́д; (*pretence*) предло́г; **under the ~ of friendship** под ви́дом дру́жбы.

guitar [gɪ'tɑ:(r)] *n.* гита́ра.

guitarist [gɪ'tɑ:rɪst] *n.* гитари́ст.

gulf [gʌlf] *n.* **1.** (*deep bay*) зали́в; **the G~ Stream** Гольфстри́м. **2.** (*abyss*) бе́здна. **3.** (*fig.*) про́пасть.

gull [gʌl] *n.* ча́йка.

gullet ['gʌlɪt] *n.* пищево́д.

gullibility [,gʌlɪ'bɪlɪtɪ] *n.* легкове́рие.

gullible ['gʌlɪb(ə)l] *adj.* легкове́рный.

gully ['gʌlɪ] *n.* лощи́на; волосто́к.

gulp [gʌlp] *n.* большо́й глото́к; **at one ~** за́лпом.

v.t. глот|а́ть, -ну́ть; **don't ~ down your food!** не глота́й еду́/пи́щу!

v.i.: **he ~ed with astonishment** он поперхну́лся от удивле́ния.

gum[1] [gʌm] *n.* (*anat.*) десна́.

gum[2] [gʌm] *n.* (*adhesive*) клей; (*resin*) каме́дь; (*chewing-~*) жева́тельная рези́нка.

v.t. скле́и|вать, -ть.

cpd. **~-boots** *n.* рези́новые сапоги́ (*m. pl.*).

gummy ['gʌmɪ] *adj.* кле́йкий.

gumption ['gʌmpʃ(ə)n] *n.* (*coll.*) смышлённость; нахо́дчивость.

gun [gʌn] *n.* **1.** (*cannon*) пу́шка; (*pistol*) пистоле́т; (*rifle*) ружьё; **heavy ~s** тяжёлая артилле́рия; **he stuck to his ~s** (*fig.*) он не сдал пози́ций; **jump the ~** (*fig.*) сова́ться, су́нуться ра́ньше вре́мени. **2.** (*device resembling ~*) пистоле́т.

v.t. стреля́ть (*impf.*); **the refugees were ~ned down** бе́женцев расстреля́ли.

v.i. охо́титься (*impf.*); **he is ~ning for me** (*sl.*) он то́чит на меня́ нож.

cpds. **~-barrel** *n.* ду́ло; **~-battle, ~-fight** *n.* пере-стре́лка; **~boat** *n.* канонéрская ло́дка, канонéрка; **~-carriage** *n.* лафе́т; **~fire** *n.* ору́дийный ого́нь; **~man** *n.* банди́т; террори́ст; **~-point** *n.*: **at ~-point** угрожа́я ору́жием; под ду́лом пистоле́та; **~powder** *n.* по́рох; **~shot** *n.* да́льность вы́стрела; **out of ~shot** вне досяга́емости ору́дия; **~smith** *n.* оруже́йный ма́стер.

gunner ['gʌnə(r)] *n.* канони́р; артиллери́ст.

gunnery ['gʌnərɪ] *n.* артиллери́йское де́ло.

gunwale ['gʌn(ə)l] *n.* планши́р.

gurgle ['gɜ:g(ə)l] *n.* бу́льканье.

v.i. бу́лькать (*impf.*).

guru ['gʊru:, 'gu:ru:] *n.* гу́ру (*m. indecl.*).

gush [gʌʃ] *n.* пото́к; **a ~ of enthusiasm** вспы́шка энтузиа́зма.

v.i. хлы́нуть (*pf.*); **the water ~ed from the tap** вода́ хлы́нула из кра́на.

gusset ['gʌsɪt] *n.* (*in a garment*) клин.

gust [gʌst] *n.* (*of wind etc.*) поры́в ве́тра; (*fig.*) взрыв.

gustatory ['gʌstətərɪ] *adj.* вкусово́й.

gusto ['gʌstəʊ] *n.* смак; (*zeal*) жар, рве́ние.

gusty ['gʌstɪ] *adj.* бу́рный; поры́вистый; **a ~ day** ве́треный день.

gut [gʌt] *n.* **1.** (*intestine*) кишка́; (*for strings of instrument*) струна́. **2.** (*pl.*) (*intestines, stomach*) ки́шки (*f. pl.*); потрох|а́ (*pl., g.* -о́в); (*fig., gist, essential contents*) су́щность; (*fig., courage and determination*) вы́держка; **he is a man with no ~s** он бесхара́ктерный челове́к; **he hadn't the ~s to tackle the burglar** у него́ не хвати́ло му́жества задержа́ть взло́мщика; **~ reaction** инстинкти́вная реа́кция; **I hate his ~s** я его́ на́ дух не принима́ю.

v.t. **1.** (*eviscerate*) потроши́ть, вы́-. **2.** (*destroy contents of*) опустош|а́ть, -и́ть; **the house was ~ted by fire** дом сгоре́л дотла́.

gutter ['gʌtə(r)] *n.* (*under eaves*) водосто́чный жёлоб; (*at roadside*) сто́чная кана́ва; (*fig.*): **the language of the ~** гру́бый/вульга́рный язы́к; **the ~ press** бульва́рная пре́сса.

cpd. **~-snipe** *n.* у́личный мальчи́шка.

guttural ['gʌtər(ə)l] *adj.* горта́нный; горлово́й.

guy[1] [gaɪ] *n.* **(~-rope)** оття́жка.

guy[2] [gaɪ] *n.* (*effigy*) пу́гало; (*US coll., fellow*) ма́лый; **tough ~** желе́зный ма́лый; **wise ~** у́мник.

Guyana [gaɪ'ænə] *n.* Гайа́на.

guzzle ['gʌz(ə)l] *v.t.* про|еда́ть, -е́сть.

v.i. объ|еда́ться, -е́сться.

guzzler ['gʌzlə(r)] *n.* обжо́ра (*c.g.*).

gym [dʒɪm] *n.* (*coll.*) (*gymnasium*) гимнасти́ческий зал; (*gymnastics*) гимна́стика.

cpds. **~-master, ~-mistress** *nn.* учи́тель (*fem.* -ница) физкульту́ры; **~-shoe** *n.* спорти́вная та́почка; **~-slip, ~-tunic** *nn.* пла́тье-сарафа́н в скла́дку.

gymkhana [dʒɪm'kɑ:nə] *n.* конноспорти́вные состяза́ния (*nt. pl.*).

gymnasium [dʒɪm'neɪzɪəm] *n.* гимнасти́ческий зал.

gymnast ['dʒɪmnæst] *n.* гимна́ст (*fem.* -ка).

gymnastic [dʒɪm'næstɪk] *adj.* гимнасти́ческий.

gymnastics [dʒɪm'næstɪks] *n.* гимна́стика.

gynaecological [ˌgaɪnɪkəˈlɒdʒɪk(ə)l] *adj.* гинекологи́ческий.
gynaecologist [ˌgaɪnɪˈkɒlədʒɪst] *n.* гинеко́лог.
gynaecology [ˌgaɪnɪˈkɒlədʒɪ] *n.* гинеколо́гия.
gypsum [ˈdʒɪpsəm] *n.* гипс.
Gypsy [ˈdʒɪpsɪ] = **Gipsy**
gyrate [ˌdʒaɪəˈreɪt] *v.i.* враща́ться (*impf.*).
gyration [ˌdʒaɪˈreɪʃ(ə)n] *n.* враще́ние.
gyro(scope) [ˈdʒaɪərəˌskəʊp] *n.* гироско́п.
gyroscopic [ˌdʒaɪrəˈskɒpɪk] *adj.* гироскопи́ческий.

H

ha [hɑː] *int.* ага́!; ~, ~ (*expr. laughter*) ха-ха-ха́!
ha. [ˈhekteə(r), -tɑː(r)] *n.* (*abbr. of* **hectare(s)**) га, (гекта́р).
haberdasher [ˈhæbəˌdæʃə(r)] *n.* галантере́йщик.
haberdashery [ˈhæbəˌdæʃərɪ] *n.* (*shop*) галантере́йный магази́н; (*wares*) галантере́я.
habit [ˈhæbɪt] *n.* **1.** (*settled practice*) привы́чка; обыкнове́ние; **get into a ~** прив|ыка́ть, -ы́кнуть (+*inf.*); **get out of a ~** отв|ыка́ть, -ы́кнуть (+*inf. or* от+*g.*); **break (o.s.) of a bad ~** отуч|а́ть(ся), -и́ть(ся) от дурно́й привы́чки; **he got into bad ~s** он усво́ил дурны́е привы́чки; **from force of ~** в си́лу привы́чки; по привы́чке. **2.** (*monk's dress*) ря́са.
habitable [ˈhæbɪtəb(ə)l] *adj.* обита́емый.
habitat [ˈhæbɪˌtæt] *n.* есте́ственная среда́ (*растения, животного*).
habitation [ˌhæbɪˈteɪʃ(ə)n] *n.*: **unfit for ~** неприго́дный для жилья́; (*dwelling-place*) жили́ще.
habitual [həˈbɪtjʊəl] *adj.* привы́чный; обы́чный; **a ~ liar** завзя́тый лгун.
habituate [həˈbɪtjʊˌeɪt] *v.t.* приуч|а́ть, -и́ть (*кого к чему*).
habitué [həˈbɪtjʊˌeɪ] *n.* завсегда́тай.
hack[1] [hæk] *v.t.* разруб|а́ть, -и́ть; руби́ть (*impf.*).
v.i.: **a ~ing cough** си́льный сухо́й ка́шель.
cpd. **~-saw** *n.* ножо́вка.
hack[2] [hæk] *n.* (*horse*) наёмная ло́шадь; (*writer*) халту́рщик.
cpd. **~-work** *n.* халту́ра.
hacker [ˈhækə(r)] *n.* компью́терный взло́мщик.
hackles [ˈhæk(ə)lz] *n. pl.*: (*fig.*) **it makes my ~ rise** э́то приво́дит меня́ в бе́шенство.
hackney [ˈhæknɪ] *v.t.*: **a ~ed expression** затёртое/истаска́нное выраже́ние.
haddock [ˈhædək] *n.* пи́кша.
Hades [ˈheɪdiːz] *n.* Гаде́с.
h(a)ematite [ˈhiːməˌtaɪt] *n.* кра́сный железня́к.
h(a)emoglobin [ˌhiːməˈgləʊbɪn] *n.* гемоглоби́н.
h(a)emophilia [ˌhiːməˈfɪlɪə] *n.* гемофи́лия.
h(a)emorrhage [ˈhemərɪdʒ] *n.* кровотече́ние.
h(a)emorrhoids [ˈheməˌrɔɪdz] *n. pl.* геморро́й.
haft [hɑːft] *n.* рукоя́тка.
hag [hæg] *n.* карга́.
haggard [ˈhægəd] *adj.* измождённый; осу́нувшийся.
haggle [ˈhæg(ə)l] *v.i.* торгова́ться (*impf.*).
hagiography [ˌhægɪˈɒgrəfɪ] *n.* описа́ние жити́й святы́х.
hail[1] [heɪl] *n.* (*frozen rain*) град; (*fig.*) **a ~ of blows** град уда́ров.
v.t. (*fig.*): **he ~ed down curses upon us** он осыпа́л нас прокля́тиями.
v.i.: **it is ~ing** идёт град; (*fig.*) сы́паться гра́дом.
cpds. **~stone** *n.* гра́дина; **~storm** *n.* гроза́ с гра́дом.
hail[2] [heɪl] *v.t.* **1.** (*acclaim*) провозгла|ша́ть, -си́ть; (*praise*) превозноси́ть (*impf.*); **he was ~ed by the critics** кри́тики восто́рженно при́няли его́. **2.** (*greet*) приве́тствовать (*impf.*); окл|ика́ть, -и́кнуть; **he ~ed me in the street** он окли́кнул меня́ на у́лице. **3.** (*summon*) под|зыва́ть, -озва́ть; **he ~ed a taxi** он подозва́л такси́.
v.i. происходи́ть (*impf.*); **he ~s from Scotland** он ро́дом из Шотла́ндии.
hair [heə(r)] *n.* **1.** (*single strand*) во́лос, волосо́к; **he never turned a ~** он и бро́вью не повёл; **that is splitting ~s** э́то спор по пустяка́м. **2.** (*dim., e.g. baby's*) воло́сик(и). **3.** (*head of ~*) во́лосы (*m. pl.*); **have, get one's ~ cut** стри́чься, по-; **lose one's ~** лысе́ть, об-/по-; **let one's ~ down** (*lit.*) распус|ка́ть, -ти́ть во́лосы; (*fig.*) разоткрове́нничаться (*pf.*); **she put her ~ up** она́ подобрала́ во́лосы. **4.** (*of animals*) шерсть, щети́на.
cpds. **~('s)-breadth** *n.*: **within a ~'s breadth of death** на волосо́к от сме́рти; **~-brush** *n.* щётка для воло́с; **~cut** *n.* стри́жка; **have a ~cut** подстри́чься (*pf.*); **~-do** *n.* (*coll.*) причёска; **~dresser** *n.* парикма́хер; **~dresser's** *n.* (*shop, salon*) парикма́херская; **~-dryer** *n.* фен; **~-piece** *n.* накладны́е во́лосы; **~pin** *n.* шпи́лька; **~pin bend** круто́й поворо́т; **~-raising** *adj.* жу́ткий; **~-shirt** *n.* власяни́ца; **~spray** *n.* (*substance*) лак для воло́с; (*container*) аэрозо́ль (*m.*) для воло́с; **~-spring** *n.* волоско́вая пружи́на.
hairy [ˈheərɪ] *adj.* волоса́тый.
hake [heɪk] *n.* хек.
halberd [ˈhælbəd] *n.* алеба́рда.
halcyon [ˈhælsɪən] *adj.* (*fig.*) ти́хий, безмяте́жный.
hale [heɪl] *adj.* кре́пкий; здоро́вый; **~ and hearty** кре́пкий и бо́дрый.
half [hɑːf] *n.* **1.** (*one of two equal parts*) полови́на; пол- (*pref: see examples and cpds.*); **one and a ~** полтора́; **he cut the loaf in ~** он разре́зал хлеб попола́м; **~ an hour** полчаса́; **~ an hour later** получа́сом по́зже; **~ and ~** попола́м, по́ровну; **~ a minute!** (одну́) мину́точку!; **~ past two** полови́на тре́тьего; (*coll.*) полтре́тьего; **they agreed to go halves** они́ согласи́лись подели́ть попола́м; **that's not the ~ of it!** и э́то ещё далеко́ не всё. **2.** (*one of two parts*) часть; **the greater ~ of the audience** бо́льшая часть аудито́рии; **my better ~** моя́ дража́йшая/лу́чшая полови́на. **3.** (*of a game*) тайм; (*of academic year*) семе́стр.
adj. (*see also cpds.*): **he's not one for ~ measures** он не сторо́нник полуме́р.
adv.: **~ asleep** со́нный; **I feel ~ dead** я едва́ жив; **the meat is only ~ done** мя́со недожа́рено; **~ as much** вдво́е ме́ньше; **~ as much again** в полтора́ ра́за бо́льше; **a pound is not ~ enough** одного́ фу́нта ника́к не хва́тит; **I ~ expected it** я почти́ ждал э́того; **not ~!** (*coll.*) ещё бы!; а как же!; **it was ~ raining, ~ snowing** шёл не то дождь, не то снег.
cpds. **~-and-~** *adv.* полови́на на полови́ну; (*fig.*) и да и нет; ни то ни сё; **~-back** *n.* полузащи́тник; **~-baked** *adj.* недопечённый; (*fig.*) непроду́манный; **~-brother** *n.* единокро́вный брат; **~-caste** *n.* мети́с; **~-dozen** *n., also* **~ a dozen** полдю́жины; **~-hearted** *adj.* нереши́тельный; без энтузиа́зма; **~-holiday** *n.* непо́лный рабо́чий/уче́бный день; **~-hour** *n., also* **~ an hour** полчаса́; **every ~-hour** ка́ждые полчаса́; **~-hourly** *adj.* получасово́й; *adv.* ка́ждые полчаса́; **~-light** *n.* полутьма́; **~-mast** *n.*: **at ~-mast** приспу́щенный; **~-moon** *n.* полуме́сяц; **~penny** *n.* полпе́нни (*indecl.*); **~-pound** *n., also* **~ a pound** полфу́нта; *adj.* полуфунто́вый; **~-price**

adj. полцены́; **at ~-price** за полцены́; **children under 5 ~-price** за детей до пяти́ лет пла́тят полови́ну; **~-sister** *n.* единокро́вная сестра́; **~-term** *n.*: **~-term (holiday)** кани́кул|ы (*pl., g.* —) в середи́не триме́стра; **~-time** *n.* коне́ц та́йма; переры́в ме́жду та́ймами; **the teams changed ends at ~-time** кома́нды поменя́лись места́ми по́сле пе́рвого та́йма; (*reduced working hours*): **the men were put on ~-time** рабо́чих перевели́ на непо́лную рабо́чую неде́лю; **~-truth** *n.* полупра́вда; **~-turn** *n.* пол-оборо́та; **~-way** *adj.* лежа́щий на полпути́; **~-way house** (*fig.*) компроми́сс; *adv.* на полпути́; **we met ~-way from the station** мы встре́тились на полпути́ от вокза́ла; **we turned back ~-way** мы верну́лись с полпути́; **I'll meet you ~-way** (*fig.*) я гото́в пойти́ вам навстре́чу; **~-wit** *n.* дура́к; **~-witted** *adj.* слабоу́мный; **~-yearly** *adj.* шестиме́сячный; *adv.* раз в полго́да.

halibut ['hælɪbət] *n.* па́лтус.

halitosis [ˌhælɪ'təʊsɪs] *n.* дурно́й за́пах изо рта́.

hall [hɔːl] *n.* **1.** (*place of assembly*) зал; **town ~** ра́туша. **2.** (*country mansion*) поме́щичий дом. **3.** (*lobby*; *also* **~way**) пере́дняя, прихо́жая.

cpds. **~mark** *n.* проби́рное клеймо́; про́ба; (*fig.*) отличи́тельный при́знак; *v.t.* ста́вить, по- про́бу на+*p*.

halleiujah [ˌhælɪ'luːjə] *n.* & *int.* аллилу́йя.

halloo [hə'luː] *int.* (*in hunting*) ату́!; эй!

v.i. улюлю́кать (*impf.*).

hallow ['hæləʊ] *v.t.* освя|ща́ть, -ти́ть; **in ~ed memory of** све́тлой па́мяти +*g*.

Hallowe'en [ˌhæləʊ'iːn] *n.* кану́н Дня всех святы́х (*31 октября*).

hallucination [həˌluːsɪ'neɪʃ(ə)n] *n.* галлюцина́ция; **have ~s** галлюцини́ровать (*impf.*).

hallucinogenic [həˌluːsɪnə'dʒenɪk] *adj.* вызыва́ющий галлюцина́ции.

halo ['heɪləʊ] *n.* орео́л.

halt[1] [hɒlt, hɔːlt] *n.* (*in march or journey*) остано́вка; **come to a ~** останáвливаться, -ови́ться; **the train came to a ~** по́езд останови́лся; **bring to a ~** оста-н|а́вливать, -ови́ть; **call a ~** де́лать, с- прива́л; (*fig.*) да|ва́ть, -ть отбо́й; (*stopping-place on railway*) полуста́нок.

v.t. остан|а́вливать, -ови́ть; **progress was ~ed** прогре́сс был приостано́влен.

v.i. (*stop*) остан|а́вливаться, -ови́ться.

halt[2] [hɒlt, hɔːlt] *v.i.* (*esp. pres. part.*: *limp, falter*) хрома́ть (*impf.*); зап|ина́ться, -ну́ться; **a ~ing gait** неве́рная похо́дка; **a ~ing voice** запина́ющийся го́лос.

halter ['hɒltə(r), 'hɔːl-] *n.* (*for a horse*) по́вод; недоу́здок; (*for execution*) верёвка; уда́вка.

halve [hɑːv] *v.t.* (*divide in two*) дели́ть, раз- пополáм; (*reduce by half*) ум|еньша́ть, -е́ньшить наполови́ну.

halyard ['hæljəd] *n.* фал.

ham [hæm] *n.* **1.** ветчина́; **~ sandwich** бутербро́д с ветчино́й. **2.** (*sl., poor actor*) безда́рный актёр. **3.** (*sl., amateur radio operator*) радиолюби́тель (*m.*).

v.t. & *i.* (*sl.*) скве́рно игра́ть (*impf.*); **~ it up** пере-и́гр|ывать, -а́ть.

hamburger ['hæmˌbɜːgə(r)] *n.* га́мбургер.

Hamitic [hə'mɪtɪk] *adj.* хами́тский.

hamlet ['hæmlɪt] *n.* дереву́шка.

hammer ['hæmə(r)] *n.* молото́к, мо́лот; **~ and sickle** серп и мо́лот; **throwing the ~** мета́ние мо́лота; **he went at it ~ and tongs** он бро́сил на э́то все си́лы; (*auctioneer's*) молото́к; **the estate came** (*or* **was brought) under the ~** име́ние пошло́ с молотка́.

v.t. (*beat*) уд|аря́ть, -а́рить; бить, по-; **~ in** вби|ва́ть, -ть; вкол|а́чивать, -оти́ть; **he ~ed in the nails** он вбил гвозди́; **the smith ~s the metal into shape** кузне́ц куёт мета́лл; **he was ~ing a box together** он скола́чивал я́щик; **the enemy got a good ~ing** неприя́телю кре́пко доста́лось; **the idea was ~ed into his head** э́ту мысль вби́ли ему́ в го́лову; **we ~ed out a plan** мы разрабо́тали план.

v.i. стуча́ть (*impf.*); колоти́ть (*impf.*); **someone was ~ing on the door** кто́-то колоти́л в дверь; **he ~ed away on the piano** он бараба́нил по роя́лю.

cpds. **~-blow** *n.* (*fig.*) сокруши́тельный/тяжёлый уда́р; **~-head** *n.* голо́вка молотка́; (*shark*) мо́лот-ры́ба.

hammock ['hæmək] *n.* гама́к.

hamper[1] ['hæmpə(r)] *n.* корзи́на с кры́шкой.

hamper[2] ['hæmpə(r)] *v.t.* меша́ть, по- +*d.*; стесня́ть (*impf.*).

hamster ['hæmstə(r)] *n.* хомя́к.

hand [hænd] *n.* **1.** (*lit., fig.*) рука́, кисть; **the ~ of God** перст бо́жий; (*dim., e.g. baby's*) ру́чка; (*attr.*) ручно́й; **~ luggage** ручно́й бага́ж; (*of animal or bird*) ла́па, ла́пка; **he was bound ~ and foot** его́ связа́ли по рука́м и нога́м; **they won ~s down** они́ с лёгкостью победи́ли; **I shall have my ~s full next week** я бу́ду о́чень за́нят на сле́дующей неде́ле; **he was ~ in glove with the enemy** он был в сго́воре с враго́м; **~ in ~** (*lit., fig.*) рука́ о́б руку; **~s up!** ру́ки вверх!; **~s off!** ру́ки прочь (от+*g.*)!; **they fought ~ to ~** они́ би́лись врукопа́шную. **2.** (*vbl. phrr.*): **he asked for her ~** (*in marriage*) он проси́л её руки́; **the money changed ~s** де́ньги перешли́ в други́е ру́ки; **force s.o.'s ~** заста́вить (*pf.*) кого́-н. раскры́ть свои́ ка́рты; **get one's ~ in** наби́ть (*pf.*) ру́ку (*на чём*); осв|а́иваться, -о́иться с рабо́той; **let me give, lend you a ~!** дава́йте я вам помогу́!; **they gave the singer a big ~** (*coll.*) певцу́ бу́рно аплоди́ровали; **he was given a free ~** ему́ предоста́вили по́лную свобо́ду де́йствий; **she had a ~ in his downfall** в его́ паде́нии она́ сыгра́ла не после́днюю роль; **they were holding ~s** они́ держа́лись за́ руки; **keep one's ~ in** подде́рживать (*impf.*) фо́рму; **don't dare to lay a ~ on her** не смей прикаса́ться к ней; **he rules with an iron ~** он пра́вит желе́зной руко́й; **he set his ~ to** (*set about*) **the work** он взя́лся за рабо́ту; **let me shake your ~** позво́льте пожа́ть ва́шу/вам ру́ку; **(let's) shake ~s on it!** по рука́м!; **my ~s are tied** (*fig.*) у меня́ свя́заны ру́ки; **he can turn his ~ to anything** он уме́ет де́лать что уго́дно; **I wash my ~s of it** я умыва́ю ру́ки. **3.** (*prepositional phrr.*): **he lives close at ~** он живёт совсе́м ря́дом; **she suffered at his ~s** она́ натерпе́лась с ним; **he started the car by ~** он завёл маши́ну вручну́ю; **the letter was delivered by ~** письмо́ бы́ло доста́влено с на́рочным; **he died by his own ~** он наложи́л на себя́ ру́ки; **he lives from ~ to mouth** он ко́е-как сво́дит концы́ с конца́ми; **I have enough money in ~** у меня́ при себе́ доста́точно де́нег; **he took the matter in ~** он взял де́ло в свои́ ру́ки; **the matter is no longer in my ~s** я бо́льше э́тим не занима́юсь; **you are playing into his ~s** вы игра́ете ему́ на́ руку; **my eldest daughter is off my ~s** моя́ ста́ршая дочь уже́ пристро́ена; **on ~** в нали́чии; в распоряже́нии; **he has a sick father on his ~s** у него́ на рука́х больно́й оте́ц; **he refused out of ~** он тут же отказа́лся; **things are getting out of ~** собы́тия выхо́дят из-под контро́ля; **news has come to ~** дошли́ ве́сти; есть сведе́ния, что...; **his gun was ready to ~** ружьё бы́ло у него́ под руко́й. **4.** (*member of crew or team*): **all ~s on deck!** все наве́рх; **the ship went down with all ~s** кора́бль затону́л со всем экипа́жем; **factory ~** фабри́чный рабо́чий; **farm ~** рабо́тник на фе́рме. **5.** (*source*): **I heard it at first/second ~** я узна́л э́то из пе́рвых/вторы́х рук. **6.** (*side*): **on the right ~** по пра́вую ру́ку; **at his right ~** по его́ пра́вую ру́ку; **on the one ~ ..., on the other ~** (*fig.*) с одно́й стороны́..., с друго́й стороны́. **7.** (*handwriting*): **he writes**

a good ~ у него́ хоро́ший по́черк. **8.** (*of a clock*) стре́лка. **9.** (*measure*) ладо́нь (*10 сантиметров*). **11.** (*player at cards*) игро́к; (*set of cards*) ка́рты (*f. pl.*); **show one's ~** (*fig.*) раскры́ть ка́рты.

v.t. перед|ава́ть, -а́ть; под|ава́ть, -а́ть; **I ~ it to you** (*coll., acknowledge your skill etc.*) я до́лжен призна́ть — вы (по э́той ча́сти) ма́стер.

with advs.: **he ~ed back the money** он верну́л де́ньги; **~ me down that book from the shelf** сними́те мне э́ту кни́гу с по́лки; **will you ~ in your resignation?** вы подади́те заявле́ние об ухо́де?; **the estate was ~ed on to the heirs** име́ние перешло́ к насле́дникам; **the teacher ~ed out books** учи́тель разда́л кни́ги; **the king ~ed over his authority** коро́ль переда́л свою́ власть.

cpds. **~bag** *n.* да́мская су́мка; **~ball** *n.* ручно́й мяч; (*game*) гандбо́л; **~bill** *n.* рекла́мный листо́к; **~book** *n.* посо́бие; спра́вочник; руково́дство; **~-brake** *n.* ручно́й то́рмоз; **~cart** *n.* ручна́я теле́жка; **~cuff** *n.* нару́чник; *v.t.* над|ева́ть, -е́ть нару́чники *+d.*; **~-grenade** *n.* (*shell*) ручна́я грана́та; **~-made** *adj.* ручно́й рабо́ты; **~-out** *n.* ми́лостыня; подая́ние; **~rail** *n.* пери́л|а (*pl., g.* —); **~saw** *n.* ножо́вка; **~shake** *n.* рукопожа́тие; **~stand** *n.* сто́йка на рука́х; **~-to-~** *adj.* рукопа́шный; **~-to-~ fighting** рукопа́шный бой; **~-to-mouth** *adj.*: **a ~-to-mouth existence** жизнь впро́голодь; **~writing** *n.* по́черк; **~written** *adj.* напи́санный от руки́.

handful ['hændfʊl] *n.* горсть; при́горшня; (*coll.*): **this child is a ~** с э́тим ребёнком хлопо́т не оберёшься.

handicap ['hændɪˌkæp] *n.* **1.** (*hindrance*) поме́ха, препя́тствие. **2.** (*sport*) гандика́п.

v.t. чини́ть (*impf.*) препя́тствия (*кому*); ста́вить, по- в невы́годное положе́ние; **~ped children** де́ти-инвали́ды.

handicraft ['hændɪˌkrɑ:ft] *n.* ремесло́, ручна́я рабо́та; (*attr.*) реме́сленный; куста́рный.

handiwork ['hændɪˌwɜ:k] *n.* ручна́я рабо́та; **this is his ~** э́то сде́лано его́ рука́ми.

handkerchief ['hæŋkətʃɪf, -ˌtʃi:f] *n.* носово́й плато́к.

handle ['hænd(ə)l] *n.* ру́чка, рукоя́тка; (*fig.*): **don't fly off the ~!** (*coll.*) не кипяти́сь!

v.t. **1.** (*take or hold in the hands*) тро́гать (*impf.*); брать, взять рука́ми. **2.** (*manage, deal with, treat*) обраща́ться (*impf.*) с+*i.*; обходи́ться (*impf.*) с+*i.*; спр|авля́ться, -а́виться с+*i.*; **he ~d the affair very well** он прекра́сно спра́вился с э́тим де́лом; **he ~d himself well** (*US*) он хорошо́ держа́лся; **the officer ~d his men well** офице́р уме́ло кома́ндовал свои́ми солда́тами. **3.** (*comm., deal in*) торгова́ть (*impf.*) *+i.*

v.i.: **this car ~s well** э́та маши́на удо́бна в управле́нии.

cpd. **~-bars** *n.* (*of a bicycle*) руль (*m.*).

handsome ['hænsəm] *adj.* (*of appearance*) краси́вый; (*generous*): **a ~ present** ще́дрый пода́рок.

handy ['hændɪ] *adj.* **1.** (*clever with hands*) ло́вкий; ма́стер (на все ру́ки). **2.** (*easy to handle*) удо́бный для по́льзования. **3.** (*to hand, available*) (име́ющийся) под руко́й. **4.** (*convenient*) удо́бный; **it may come in ~** э́то мо́жет пригоди́ться.

cpd. **~-man** *n.* рабо́чий для ра́зных поде́лок.

hang [hæŋ] *n.* (*knack, sense*) смысл; «что к чему́»; **I can't get the ~ of this machine** (*or* **of his argument**) я не могу́ разобра́ться в э́той маши́не (*or* в его́ до́водах)).

v.t. **1.** (*suspend*) ве́шать, пове́сить; **this gate has been hung badly** э́ти воро́та пло́хо подве́шены. **2.** (*let droop*) пове́сить (*pf.*); **she hung her head in shame** она́ опусти́ла го́лову от стыда́. **3.** (*decorate, furnish*) разве́|шивать, -сить; **the hall was hung with flags** зал был уве́шен фла́гами. **4.** (*execute by* **~ing**) ве́шать, пове́сить. **5.** (*as imprecation*): **~ it all!** чёрт возьми́!

v.i. **1.** (*be suspended*) висе́ть (*impf.*); (*fig.*): **his life ~s by a thread** его́ жизнь (виси́т) на волоске́; **the outcome ~s in the balance** ещё нея́сно, чем всё э́то ко́нчится; **the threat of dismissal hung over him** над ним нави́сла угро́за увольне́ния; **everything ~s on his decision** всё упира́ется в его́ реше́ние. **2.** (*lean*) све́шиваться (*impf.*); **don't ~ out of the window** не высо́вывайтесь из окна́. **3.** (*droop*) висе́ть (*impf.*); свиса́ть (*impf.*). **4.** (*be executed*): **he will ~ for it** он попадёт за э́то на ви́селицу. **5.** (*loiter, stay close*): **he hung round the door** он задержа́лся у две́ри; **the children hung about their mother** де́ти льну́ли к ма́тери.

with advs.: **~ about, ~ around** *v.i.* болта́ться (*impf.*); шля́ться (*impf.*); **~ on** *v.i.* (*cling*) держа́ться (*impf.*) (*за что*); цепля́ться (*impf.*); не сдава́ться (*impf.*); **~on!** (*coll.*) погоди́те!; посто́йте!; мину́точку!; **~ out** *v.t.* выве́шивать, вы́весить; *v.i.* (*protrude*): **his shirt was ~ing out** у него́ руба́шка вы́лезла из брюк; (*coll., live*) обита́ть (*impf.*); **~ together** *v.i.* (*stand by one another*) держа́ться (*impf.*) вме́сте; (*make sense*): **the story doesn't ~ together** ≃ концы́ с конца́ми не схо́дятся; **~ up** *v.t.* (*fasten on peg, nail etc.*) пове́сить (*pf.*); *v.i.* (*end telephone conversation*) пове́сить (*pf.*) тру́бку.

cpds. **~-glider** *n.* (*craft*) дельтапла́н; **~-glider** *n.* (*pers.*) дельтапланери́ст; **~-gliding** *n.* дельтаплане́рный спорт; **~man** *n.* пала́ч; **~-nail** *n.* заусе́ница; **~out** *n.* (*sl.*) местожи́тельство; **~over** *n.* (*survival*) пережи́ток; (*from drink*) похме́лье; **I had a ~over** у меня́ разболе́лась голова́ от похме́лья.

hangar ['hæŋə(r)] *n.* анга́р.

hanger ['hæŋə(r)] *n.* ве́шалка.

cpd. **~-on** *n.* прихлеба́тель (*m.*), приспе́шник.

hanging ['hæŋɪŋ] *n.* **1.** висе́ние; (*execution*) пове́шение; **it is not a ~ matter** (*fig.*) э́то не тако́е уж стра́шное преступле́ние. **2.** (*pl., tapestry etc.*) портье́ры (*f. pl.*); драпиро́вки (*f. pl.*).

adj. вися́чий.

hank [hæŋk] *n.* мото́к.

hanker ['hæŋkə(r)] *v.i.*: **~ after** жа́ждать *+g.*

hanky ['hæŋkɪ] (*coll.*) = **handkerchief**

ha'penny ['heɪpnɪ] = **halfpenny**

haphazard [hæp'hæzəd] *adj.* случа́йный.

adv. случайно; науда́чу.

hapless ['hæplɪs] *adj.* несча́стный; злополу́чный.

happen ['hæpən] *v.i.* **1.** (*occur*) случ|а́ться, -и́ться; прои|сходи́ть, -зойти́; получ|а́ться, -и́ться; **accidents will ~** ≃ вся́кое быва́ет; **I hope nothing has ~ed to him** наде́юсь, с ним ничего́ не случи́лось. **2.** (*chance*): **it (so) ~ed that I was there** случи́лось так, что я был там; **as it ~s I can help you ~** я в да́нном слу́чае могу́ вам помо́чь; **do you ~ to know her?** вы случа́йно не зна́ете её?; **I ~ed to be out** меня́ не оказа́лось до́ма; **we ~ed to meet** мы неожи́данно/случа́йно встре́тились; **this ~s to be my birthday** сего́дня как раз мой день рожде́ния. **3.**: **~ on** случа́йно наткну́ться (*pf.*) на*+g.*

happening ['hæpənɪŋ, -pnɪŋ] *n.* слу́чай; собы́тие.

happily ['hæpɪlɪ] *adv.* **1.** (*contentedly*) сча́стливо. **2.** (*fortunately*) к сча́стью.

happiness ['hæpɪnɪs] *n.* сча́стье.

happy ['hæpɪ] *adj.* **1.** (*contented*) счастли́вый. **2.** (*fortunate, felicitous*) счастли́вый, уда́чливый; уда́чный; **by a ~ coincidence** по счастли́вой случа́йности; **~ medium** золота́я середи́на; **~ birthday!** с днём рожде́ния; **~ Christmas!** с Рождество́м (христо́вым). **3.** (*pleased*) дово́льный (*чем*); **we shall be ~ to come** мы с удово́льствием придём.

cpd. **~-go-lucky** *adj.* беззабо́тный; беспе́чный.

hara-kiri [ˌhærə'kɪrɪ] *n.* хараќири (*nt. indecl.*).

v.t. увещева́ть (*impf.*).

harass ['hærəs, *disp.* hə'ræs] *v.t.* изводи́ть (*impf.*);

трави́ть, за-; ~ **the enemy** изма́тывать (*impf.*) врага́.

harassment ['hærəsmənt, hə'ræs-] *n.* тра́вля; изма́тывание.

harbinger ['hɑ:bɪndʒə(r)] *n.* предве́стник.

harbour ['hɑ:bə(r)] *n.* га́вань, порт.

v.t. да|ва́ть, -ть убе́жище +*d.*; укр|ыва́ть, -ы́ть; ~**ing a criminal** укрыва́тельство престу́пника; (*fig.*): **I ~ no grudge against him** я не держу́ на него́ зла.

cpd. ~**-master** *n.* нача́льник по́рта.

hard [hɑ:d] *adj.* **1.** (*firm, resistant, solid*) твёрдый; про́чный; ~ **core** (*fig., nucleus of resistance etc.*) ядро́; ~ **and fast rules** жёсткие пра́вила; ~ **copy** (*comput.*) печа́тная ко́пия; ~ **disk** (*comput.*) жёсткий диск; ~ **hat** защи́тный шлем. **2.** (*of money*): ~ **cash** нали́чные (де́ньги); ~ **currency** твёрдая валю́та. **3.** (*difficult*) тру́дный; **do sth. the ~ way** идти́ тру́дным путём; **you're ~ to please** вам тру́дно угоди́ть; **it's ~ to say yet** пока́ тру́дно сказа́ть; **bargains are ~ to come by** нелегко́ доста́ть ве́щи по дешёвой цене́. **4.:** ~ **of hearing** глухова́тый; туго́й на́ ухо. **5.** (*unsentimental, relentless*): **he drives a ~ bargain** с ним не сторгу́ешься; **a ~ drinker** го́рький пья́ница; **don't be too ~ on her!** не бу́дьте к ней сли́шком строги́. **6.** (*vigorous, harsh*): ~ **times** тяжёлые времена́; **a ~ climate** суро́вый кли́мат; **it's a ~ life** жизнь трудна́; тру́дно живётся; **take a ~ line** заня́ть (*pf.*) жёсткую пози́цию; **a ~ master** стро́гий хозя́ин; (~*-hearted*) жестокосе́рдный; ~ **liquor** кре́пкие напи́тки; ~ **drugs** сильноде́йствующие нарко́тики; ~ **water** жёсткая вода́. **7.** (*intensive*): ~ **work** тяжёлая/тру́дная рабо́та; **a ~ blow** си́льный уда́р; ~ **labour** исправи́тельно-трудовы́е рабо́ты; (*fig.*) ка́торга; **a ~ worker** усе́рдный/приле́жный рабо́тник. **8.** (*coll., unfortunate*): ~ **luck!** как вам (*и т.п.*) не повезло́!; **his parents are ~ up** его́ роди́тели — лю́ди небога́тые.

adv. **1.** (*solid*): **the ground froze ~** земля́ промёрзла. **2.** (*with force*): **it is raining ~** дождь льёт вовсю́; **he had to brake ~** ему́ пришло́сь ре́зко затормози́ть. **3.** (*unremittingly*) усе́рдно; **I was ~ put to it to answer** мне нелегко́ бы́ло найти́ отве́т. **4.** (*adversely*): **it will go ~ with him** ему́ ту́го придётся; ~ **done by** обделённый; пострада́вший. **5.** (*persistently*): **he looked ~ in my direction** он при́стально посмотре́л в мою́ сто́рону; **I looked ~ for the book** я до́лго иска́л кни́гу; **work** (*study*) ~ усе́рдно занима́ться (*impf.*); **we worked ~** мы мно́го рабо́тали; **I tried ~ to make him understand** я изо всех сил стара́лся разъясни́ть ему́ (*что*).

cpds. ~**back** *n.* (*book*) кни́га в жёстком переплёте; ~**-boiled** *adj.* (*lit.*) сва́ренный вкруту́ю; **a ~-boiled egg** круто́е яйцо́; яйцо́ вкруту́ю; (*fig.*) прожжённый; ~**-cover** *adj.* в жёстком переплёте; в твёрдой обло́жке; ~**-earned** *adj.* зарабо́танный тя́жким трудо́м; ~**-headed** *adj.* тре́звый; практи́чный; ~**-hearted** *adj.* жестокосе́рдный; неумоли́мый; ~**ware** *n.* скобяны́е изде́лия/това́ры; (*mil., coll.*) те́хника; (*comput.*) аппара́тное обеспе́чение; ~**-working** *adj.* работя́щий, усе́рдный.

harden ['hɑ:d(ə)n] *v.t.* укреп|ля́ть, -и́ть; прид|ава́ть, -а́ть твёрдость +*d.*; ~**ed steel** закалённая сталь; (*fig.*): **he ~ed his heart** он ожесточи́л своё се́рдце; **a ~ed criminal** закорене́лый престу́пник.

v.i. (*fig.*): **opinion ~ed** мне́ние укрепи́лось.

hardiness ['hɑ:dɪnɪs] *n.* выно́сливость.

hardly ['hɑ:dlɪ] *adv.* **1.** (*with difficulty*) едва́ (ли). **2.** (*only just*): **I had ~ sat down when the phone rang** то́лько я сел, как зазвони́л телефо́н; **I ~ know him** я его́ почти́ не зна́ю. **3.** (*not reasonably*): **he can ~ have arrived yet** вряд ли он уже́ прие́хал; **you can ~ expect her to agree** вы едва́ (*or* вряд) ли мо́жете рассчи́тывать на её согла́сие. **4.** (*almost not*): ~ **ever** почти́ никогда́; **there's ~ any money left** де́нег почти́ не оста́лось; **I need ~ say** само́ собо́й разуме́ется; са́ми понима́ете.

hardness ['hɑ:dnɪs] *n.* твёрдость, жёсткость.

hardship ['hɑ:dʃɪp] *n.* невзго́ды (*f. pl.*); испыта́ние.

hardy ['hɑ:dɪ] *adj.* **1.** (*bold*) отва́жный; де́рзкий. **2.** (*robust*) закалённый; выно́сливый; (*of plants*) морозоусто́йчивый.

hare [heə(r)] *n.* за́яц.

cpds. ~**bell** *n.* колоко́льчик круглоли́стый; ~**-brained** *adj.* опроме́тчивый; шально́й; ~**lip** *n.* за́ячья губа́.

harem ['hɑ:ri:m, hɑ:'ri:m] *n.* гаре́м.

haricot ['hærɪˌkəʊ] *n.* (~ **bean**) фасо́ль (*collect.*).

hark [hɑ:k] *v.i.* **1.** (*listen*) вн|има́ть, -ять +*d.*; **just ~ at him!** вы то́лько его́ послу́шайте! **2.** ~ **back to** (*recall*) упом|ина́ть, -яну́ть; верну́ться (*pf.*) к (*теме и т.п.*); (*date back to*) восходи́ть к+*d.*

harlequin ['hɑ:lɪkwɪn] *n.* арлеки́н.

harlot ['hɑ:lət] *n.* (*arch.*) шлю́ха.

harm [hɑ:m] *n.* вред, уще́рб; **it can do no ~** от э́того вреда́ не бу́дет; **there's no ~ (in) trying** попы́тка не пы́тка; **he will come to no ~** с ним ничего́ не случи́тся; **I meant no ~** я не хоте́л (вас *и т.п.*) оби́деть; **out of ~'s way** от греха́ пода́льше; **there is no ~ done** никто́ не пострада́л.

v.t. вреди́ть, по- +*d.*; причин|я́ть, -и́ть (*or* нан|оси́ть, -ести́) вред +*d.*; **be ~ed** пострада́ть (*pf.*).

harmful ['hɑ:mfʊl] *adj.* вре́дный.

harmless ['hɑ:mlɪs] *adj.* (*not injurious*) безвре́дный; (*innocent*) безоби́дный.

harmonic [hɑ:'mɒnɪk] *adj.* гармони́ческий.

harmonica [hɑ:'mɒnɪkə] *n.* гармо́ника.

harmonious [hɑ:'məʊnɪəs] *adj.* (*lit., fig.*) гармони́чный; (*amicable*) дру́жный; сла́женный; согла́сный.

harmonium [hɑ:'məʊnɪəm] *n.* фисгармо́ния.

harmonize ['hɑ:məˌnaɪz] *v.t.* **1.** (*mus., put chords to melody*) гармонизи́ровать (*impf.*). **2.** (*bring into agreement*) согласо́в|ывать, -а́ть.

v.i.: **these colours ~ well** э́ти цвета́ гармони́руют.

harmony ['hɑ:mənɪ] *n.* **1.** (*mus., theory*) гармо́ния. **2.** (*of sounds, colours*) гармони́чность. **3.** (*agreement*) гармо́ния; сла́женность.

harness ['hɑ:nɪs] *n.* у́пряжь.

v.t. запр|яга́ть, -я́чь; (*fig.*) (*of natural forces*) обу́зд|ывать, -а́ть; покор|я́ть, -и́ть.

harp [hɑ:p] *n.* а́рфа.

v.i. (*fig.*): ~ **on sth.** тверди́ть (*impf.*) о чём-н.

harpist ['hɑ:pɪst] *n.* арфи́ст (*fem.* -ка).

harpoon [hɑ:'pu:n] *n.* гарпу́н.

v.t. бить гарпуно́м; гарпу́нить, за-.

harpsichord ['hɑ:psɪˌkɔ:d] *n.* клавеси́н.

harridan ['hærɪd(ə)n] *n.* ста́рая карга́.

harrow ['hærəʊ] *n.* борона́.

v.t. **1.** (*agric.; also v.i.*) борони́ть (*impf.*). **2.** (*fig., lacerate*) терза́ть, ис-; ра́нить (*impf.*) (*чувства*); **a ~ing tale** душераздира́ющая исто́рия.

harry ['hærɪ] *v.t.* изв|оди́ть, -ести́; му́чить, из-.

harsh [hɑ:ʃ] *adj.* **1.** (*rough*) гру́бый, ре́зкий; **a ~ taste** ре́зкий вкус; ~ **colours** ре́зкие цвета́. **2.** (*severe*) суро́вый.

harshness ['hɑ:ʃnɪs] *n.* ре́зкость, суро́вость.

hart [hɑ:t] *n.* оле́нь-саме́ц.

harvest ['hɑ:vɪst] *n.* (*yield*) урожа́й; (~*ing*) жа́тва, сбор урожа́я; (*garnering*) убо́рка; **the ~ is ripe** урожа́й созре́л; ~ **festival** пра́здник урожа́я.

v.t. & i. соб|ира́ть, -ра́ть (урожа́й).

harvester ['hɑ:vɪstə(r)] *n.* (*reaper*) жн|ец (*fem.* и́ца); (*machine*) убо́рочная маши́на.

hash [hæʃ] *n.* ме́лко наре́занное мя́со; (*fig.*): **he made a ~ of it** он завали́л всё де́ло.

v.t. (*also* ~ **up**) ме́лко ре́зать, на- (*мясо*).

hashish [ˈhæʃiːʃ] *n.* гаши́ш.
hasp [hɑːsp] *n.* засо́в.
hassle [ˈhæs(ə)l] *n.* (*coll.*) тру́дность, препя́тствие.
hassock [ˈhæsək] *n.* поду́шечка для коленопреклоне́ния.
haste [heɪst] *n.* спе́шка, торопли́вость; **he went off in great ~** он поспе́шно ушёл; **make ~!** потора́пливайтесь!; **more ~, less speed** ти́ше е́дешь — да́льше бу́дешь.
hasten [ˈheɪs(ə)n] *v.t.* торопи́ть, по-; уск|оря́ть, -о́рить.
v.i. торопи́ться (*impf.*), спеши́ть (*impf.*); **I ~ to add that ...** спешу́ доба́вить, что...
hasty [ˈheɪstɪ] *adj.* (*hurried*) поспе́шный; торопли́вый; (*quick-tempered*) вспы́льчивый; горя́чий.
hat [hæt] *n.* шля́па; **top ~** цили́ндр; **keep it under your ~** (*coll.*) никому́ об э́том ни сло́ва; **I take off my ~ to him** я преклоня́юсь пе́ред ним; **he's talking through his ~** он несёт ахине́ю (*coll.*); **at the drop of a ~** (*coll.*) неме́дленно, то́тчас же; по мале́йшему по́воду; **old ~** (*sl.*) устаре́лый; старо́!
cpds. **~-band** *n.* ле́нта на шля́пе; **~-pin** *n.* зако́лка для шля́пы; **~rack** *n.* ве́шалка для шляп; **~-stand** *n.* стоя́чая ве́шалка для шляп.
hatch[1] [hætʃ] *n.* (*opening*) люк; отве́рстие; (*cover*) кры́шка; две́рцы (*f. pl.*).
cpd. **~-back** *n.* пятидве́рная маши́на; **~way** *n.* люк.
hatch[2] [hætʃ] *v.t.* (*produce by incubation*; *incubate*) вына́шивать, вы́носить; (*fig.*, *plot*): **what are you ~ing?** что вы там замышля́ете?
v.i. (*also* **~ out**) вылу́пливаться, вы́лупиться.
hatchet [ˈhætʃɪt] *n.* топо́р, топо́рик.
hatching [ˈhætʃɪŋ] *n.* штрих, штрихо́вка.
hate [heɪt] *n.* не́нависть.
v.t. ненави́деть (*impf.*); (*dislike strongly*) не терпе́ть/выноси́ть, о́чень не люби́ть (*all impf.*); **I ~ getting up early** я ненави́жу ра́но встава́ть; **I ~ to trouble you, but ...** мне о́чень не хо́чется вас беспоко́ить, но...
hateful [ˈheɪtfʊl] *adj.* ненави́стный.
hatred [ˈheɪtrɪd] *n.* не́нависть; **have a ~ of sth.** не терпе́ть/выноси́ть чего́-н.; **feel ~ for** пита́ть не́нависть к+*d*.
hatter [ˈhætə(r)] *n.* шля́пник.
haughtiness [ˈhɔːtɪnɪs] *n.* высокоме́рие; зазна́йство.
haughty [ˈhɔːtɪ] *adj.* зано́счивый; высокоме́рный.
haul [hɔːl] *n.* **1.** рейс, пробе́г; **a long ~** (*fig.*) до́лгое де́ло. **2.**: **a ~ of fish** то́ня; (*fig.*, *booty*) добы́ча; «уло́в».
v.t. & i. тяну́ть (*impf.*); тащи́ть (*impf.*).
with advs.: **~ down,** *v.t.*: **the flag was ~ed down** флаг был спу́щен; **~ in** *v.t.* вт|я́гивать, -яну́ть; **~ out** *v.t.* вытя́гивать, вы́тянуть; **~ up** *v.t.* подн|има́ть, -я́ть.
haulage [ˈhɔːlɪdʒ] *n.* транспортиро́вка, перево́зка.
haulier [ˈhɔːlɪə(r)] *n.* перево́зчик.
haunch [hɔːntʃ] *n.* бедро́, ля́жка; **he got down on his ~es** он присе́л на ко́рточки.
haunt [hɔːnt] *n.* излю́бленное ме́сто.
v.t. & i. неотвя́зно пресле́довать (*impf.*); **a ~ed house** дом с привиде́ниями; **a ~ing melody** навя́зчивый моти́в.
have [hæv, həv] *v.t.* **1.** име́ть; (*possess*) облада́ть +*i.*; *often expr. by* у+*g.*; **she has blue eyes** у неё голубы́е глаза́; **I ~ no doubt** у меня́ нет сомне́ний; **he has no equal** он не име́ет себе́ ра́вных; **~ the goodness to ...** бу́дьте добры́; **he had the courage to refuse** он име́л му́жество отказа́ться; **I ~ no idea** поня́тия не име́ю; **they ~ large reserves of oil** они́ владе́ют больши́ми запа́сами не́фти. **2.** (*contain*): **June has 30 days** в ию́не 30 дней. **3.** (*experience*): **~ a good time!** жела́ю вам хорошо́ провести́ вре́мя; (*suffer from*): **he has a cold** у него́ на́сморк; **do you often ~ toothache?** у вас ча́сто боля́т зу́бы? **4.** (*bear*) роди́ть (*impf.*, *pl.*); рожа́ть (*impf.*); **she is having a baby in May** в ма́е у неё бу́дет ребёнок. **5.** (*receive*, *obtain*): **we had news of him yesterday** вчера́ мы получи́ли о нём изве́стие; **you always ~ your own way** ты ве́чно наста́иваешь на своём; **there was nothing to be had** там ничего́ не́ было; **the play had a great success** пье́са име́ла большо́й успе́х; (*tolerate*): **I won't ~ it!** э́того я не потерплю́! **6.** (*show*, *exercise*): **~ pity on** сжа́литься над+*i.*; **~ pity on me** сжа́льтесь надо мно́й; **he had no mercy** он был безжа́лостен. **7.** (*undertake*, *perform*): **~ a game of tennis** сыгра́ть (*pf.*) в те́ннис; **~ a go** (*coll.*) попыта́ться (*pf.*). **8.** (*partake of*, *enjoy*): **~ dinner** у́жинать (*impf.*). **9.** (*puzzle*, *put at a loss*): **you ~ me there** вы меня́ озада́чили. **10.** (*coll.*, *swindle*): **you've been had** вас провели́. **11.** (*cause*, *order*): **~ him come here!** приведи́те/пришли́те его́ сюда́; **I must ~ my shoes mended** мне на́до отда́ть ту́фли в почи́нку; я до́лжен почини́ть ту́фли; **what would you ~ me do?** так что, по-ва́шему, я до́лжен де́лать? **12.** (*with inf.*, *be obliged to*) быть вы́нужденным/обя́занным; **I ~ to** я до́лжен; мне прихо́дится; **it has to be done** э́то необходи́мо сде́лать; **you don't ~ to go** вы не обя́заны идти́; **I didn't want to, but I had to** я не хоте́л, но был вы́нужден. **13.** (*phrr. with it*): **I ~ it!** (*the answer*, *solution*) нашёл!; **let him ~ it!** (*sl.*, *attack him*) дай ему́ хороше́нько!; **rumour has it that ...** хо́дят слу́хи, что...; **as he would ~ it** как он утвержда́ет; **you can't ~ it both ways** (*coll.*) и́ли то, и́ли друго́е; **~ it out with s.o.** объясн|я́ться, -и́ться с кем-н.; **I had it in mind to go there** у меня́ была́ мысль пойти́ туда́.
with advs.: **can I ~ my watch back?** могу́ я получи́ть свои́ часы́ обра́тно?; **may we ~ the blinds down?** мо́жно опусти́ть што́ры?; **we had her parents down** (*to stay*) у нас гости́ли её роди́тели; **we are having the painters in next week** на сле́дующей неде́ле приду́т маляры́; **he had his coat off** он был без пальто́; **she had his coat off** (*took it off him*) **in a moment** она́ сра́зу же сняла́ с него́ пальто́; **she had a red dress on** на ней бы́ло кра́сное пла́тье; **~ you anything on tonight?** у вас есть пла́ны на сего́дняшний ве́чер?; **we ~ a lot of work on at present** у нас сейча́с мно́го рабо́ты; **~ s.o. on** разы́гр|ывать, -а́ть кого́-н.; **I must ~ this tooth out** мне ну́жно удали́ть э́тот зуб; **they had the road up last week** на про́шлой неде́ле э́ту доро́гу ремонти́ровали; **he was had up for speeding** (*coll.*) его́ задержа́ли за превыше́ние ско́рости.
misc. phrr.: **I ~ nothing against it** я ничего́ про́тив э́того не име́ю; **you had better give the book back** вам лу́чше бы верну́ть кни́гу; **~ done with sth.** поко́нчить (*pf.*) с чем-н.; **~ you might as well pay and ~ done with it** заплати́те — и де́лу коне́ц; **it has to do with his work** э́то свя́зано с его́ рабо́той; **it has nothing to do with you** вас э́то не каса́ется; **I'll ~ nothing to do with it** я не жела́ю име́ть никако́го отноше́ния к э́тому.
haven [ˈheɪv(ə)n] *n.* га́вань; (*fig.*) прию́т.
haversack [ˈhævəˌsæk] *n.* рюкза́к.
havoc [ˈhævək] *n.* разгро́м; опустоше́ние; (*fig.*) **play ~ with** вн|оси́ть, -ести́ беспоря́док/хао́с в+*a*.
haw [hɔː] *n.* я́года боя́рышника.
cpd. **~thorn** *n.* боя́рышник.
hawk[1] [hɔːk] *n.* я́стреб (*also fig.*, *pol.*); со́кол.
cpd. **~-eyed** *adj.* зо́ркий.
hawk[2] [hɔːk] *v.t.* (*peddle*) торгова́ть (*impf.*) вразно́с +*i.*; (*fig.*) быть разно́счиком +g.
hawker [ˈhɔːkə(r)] *n.* торго́вец-разно́счик.
hawser [ˈhɔːzə(r)] *n.* (стально́й) трос.
hay [heɪ] *n.* се́но; **~ fever** сенна́я лихора́дка; **hit the ~** (*sl.*, *go to bed*) отпр|авля́ться, -а́виться на бо-

кову́ю; **make** ~ (*lit.*) вороши́ть|загота́вливать (*both impf.*) се́но; **make ~ while the sun shines** ≃ куй желе́зо, пока горячо́.

cpds. **~cock** *n.* копна́; **~-fork** *n.* ви́л|ы (*pl. g.* —); **~making** *n.* сеноко́с, загото́вка се́на; **~rick** *n.* стог се́на; **~stack** *n.* стог се́на.

hazard ['hæzəd] *n.* **1.** (*risk*) риск. **2.** (*danger*) опа́сность; **road ~s** опа́сности на доро́гах.

v.t. **1.** (*endanger*) риск|ова́ть, -ну́ть +*i.*; **he ~ed his life for her** ради неё он рискова́л жи́знью. **2.** (*venture upon*) рискну́ть (*pf.*) +*i.*; отва́ж|иваться, -иться на+*a.*; **he ~ed a remark** он отва́жился вы́сказать замеча́ние.

hazardous ['hæzədəs] *adj.* риско́ванный; опа́сный.

haze [heɪz] *n.* ды́мка.

hazel ['heɪz(ə)l] *n.* (*tree*) лесно́й оре́х; (*colour*) оре́ховый цвет; **~ eyes** ка́рие глаза́.

cpd. **~-nut** *n.* лесно́й оре́х.

hazy ['heɪzɪ] *adj.* подёрнутый ды́мкой; затума́ненный; (*fig.*) сму́тный, тума́нный.

he [hi:, hɪ] *n.* **1.** (*coll.*, *male human*) мужчи́на; (*child*) ма́льчик; (*animal*) саме́ц. **2.** он; тот; (*in children's game*) тот, кто во́дит; вожа́к, водя́щий; (*etc.*, *acc. to game*); **who is '~'?** кто во́дит?; чья о́чередь?; **~ who believes** тот, кто ве́рит.

cpds. **~-bear** *n.* медве́дь-саме́ц; **~-man** *n.* настоя́щий мужчи́на.

head [hed] *n.* **1.** голова́; (*dim.*, *e.g. baby's*) голо́вка; **he was hit on the ~** его́ уда́рили по голове́; **~ first** голово́й вперёд; **he was ~ over heels in love** он был по́ уши влюблён; **covered in dust from ~ to foot, toe** покры́тый пы́лью с головы́ до ног; **a good ~ of hair** густы́е во́лосы; **I could do it standing on my ~** я могу́ э́то сде́лать одно́й ле́вой; **he goes about with his ~ in the air** он задира́ет но́с; **his ~ is in the clouds** он вита́ет в облака́х; **he is keeping his ~ above water** (*fig.*) он де́ржится на пове́рхности; **he will never hold up his ~ again** он бо́льше не смо́жет смотре́ть лю́дям в глаза́; **he hung his ~ for shame** он пове́сил го́лову от стыда́; **shake one's ~** покача́ть (*pf.*) голово́й; **he turned his ~** он поверну́л го́лову; **I cannot make ~ or tail of it** я не могу́ в э́том разобра́ться; **this is all completely over my ~** э́то всё вы́ше моего́ понима́ния; **keep your ~ down** (*lit.*) опусти́те го́лову; (*fig.*) не су́йтесь; **he can talk your ~ off** он вас заговори́т; **bury one's ~ in the sand** (*fig.*) отка́зываться (*impf.*) смотре́ть фа́ктам в лицо́; (*attr.*) головно́й; **a ~ cold** на́сморк; **a ~ wind** встре́чный ве́тер. **2.** (*as measure*): **he gave me a ~ start** он дал мне фо́ру; **he is taller by a ~** он вы́ше на́ голову; **he stands ~ and shoulders above the rest** (*fig.*) он на́ голову вы́ше остальны́х. **3.** (*mind*, *brain*): **two ~s are better than one** ум хорошо́, а два лу́чше; **he has a good ~ for figures** он хорошо́ счита́ет; **he's a bit weak in the ~** у него́ ви́нтика не хвата́ет; **he's off his ~** он спя́тил; **you can do the sum in your ~** вы мо́жете вы́числить э́то в уме́; **it came into my ~** мне э́то пришло́ в го́лову; **I can't keep it in my ~** э́то не де́ржится у меня́ в голове́; **they put their ~s together** они́ ста́ли ду́мать вме́сте; **I made it up out of my ~** я э́то вы́думал; **put it out of your ~!** вы́бросьте э́то из головы́!; **what put that into your ~?** отку́да вы э́то взя́ли?; **he took it into his ~ to invite them** ему́ взбрело́ в го́лову их пригласи́ть; **it went clean out of my ~** э́то у меня́ соверше́нно вы́скочило из головы́; **it never entered my ~** мне э́то никогда́ не приходи́ло в го́лову; (*faculties*); **success went to his ~** успе́х вскружи́л ему́ го́лову; (*balance*, *composure*): **he kept his ~** он сохраня́л прису́тствие ду́ха; **he has no ~ for heights** у него́ кру́жится голова́ от высоты́; (*freedom*, *scope*): **he gave the horse its ~** он дал ло́шади по́лную во́лю. **4.** (*on a coin*): **~s or tails?** орёл и́ли ре́шка?; **~s I win** е́сли орёл, я вы́играл. **5.** (*personage*): **crowned ~s** корони́ванные осо́бы. **6.** (*unit*): **£5 a ~** пять фу́нтов с ка́ждого; **forty ~ of cattle** со́рок голо́в скота́. **7.** (*life*): **it cost him his ~** он поплати́лся за э́то голово́й; **he had a price on his ~** его голова́ была́ оценена́; **on your own ~ be it!** на ваш страх и риск! **8.** (*upper or principal end*): **at the ~ of the table** во главе́ стола́; **at the ~ of the stairs** на ве́рхней площа́дке ле́стницы; **at the ~ of the page** в нача́ле страни́цы; **at the ~ of the procession** во главе́ проце́ссии. **9.** (*principal member*) глава́ (*c.g.*), ста́рший; **~ of state** глава́ госуда́рства; **~ of the family** глава́ семьи́; (*attr.*, *principal*): **~ boy** ста́рший учени́к; ста́роста шко́лы; **~ waiter** метрдоте́ль (*m.*); **~ office** гла́вная конто́ра, центр. **10.** (*culmination*): **things came to a ~** наступи́л перело́мный моме́нт; **he brought the issue to a ~** он поста́вил вопро́с ребро́м. **11.** (*of tool*, *plant*, *vegetable*, *flower*) голо́вка; (*of water*, *steam*) напо́р, давле́ние; (*froth*) пе́на; (*promontory*) мыс.

v.t. **1.** (*steer*, *direct*): **he is ~ed for home** он направля́ется домо́й; **I managed to ~ him off** (*fig.*) мне удало́сь переключи́ть его на другу́ю те́му. **2.** (*strike with head*): **he ~ed the ball into the net** он заби́л мяч голово́й в се́тку. **3.** (*be first in*): **he ~ed the team** он возглавля́л кома́нду; **he ~ed the list** он был пе́рвым в спи́ске.

v.i. (*move*, *steer*) напр|авля́ться, -а́виться.

cpds. **~ache** *n.* головна́я боль; **I have a ~ ache** у меня́ боли́т голова́; **~-band** *n.* головна́я повя́зка; **~dress** *n.* головно́й убо́р; **~gear** *n.* головно́й убо́р; **~lamp, ~-light** *nn.* фа́ра; **~land** *n.* (*promontory*) мыс; **~light** *n.* = **~lamp; ~line** *n.* заголо́вок; **he hit the ~lines** о нём крича́ли все газе́ты; **~long** *adj.* (*fig.*): **~long flight** стреми́тельное бе́гство; *adv.* голово́й вперёд; стремгла́в; **~master, ~mistress** *nn.* дире́ктор шко́лы; **~-on** *adj.* лобово́й, встре́чный; **a ~-on collision** столкнове́ние «но́сом к но́су»; *adv.*: **the wind blew ~-on** ве́тер дул нам в лицо́; **~phone** *n.* нау́шник; **~quarters** *n.* штаб-кварти́ра; (*mil.*) штаб, ста́вка; **~-room** *n.* габари́тная высота́; **~-scarf** *n.* косы́нка; **~set** *n.* (*pair of ~-phones*) нау́шники (*m. pl.*); **~stone** *n.* (*tombstone*) надгро́бный ка́мень; **~strong** *adj.* своево́льный, упря́мый, упо́рный; **~way** *n.* продвиже́ние вперёд; (*fig.*): **we are not making much ~way** мы продвига́емся сли́шком ме́дленно.

header ['hedə(r)] *n.* **1.** (*dive*, *fall*) прыжо́к со вхо́дом в во́ду голово́й; **he took a ~** он нырну́л; он упа́л голово́й вниз. **2.** (*blow with head*) уда́р голово́й.

heading ['hedɪŋ] *n.* заголо́вок; ру́брика.

heady ['hedɪ] *adj.* кре́пкий, хмельно́й; (*fig.*) пьяня́щий.

heal [hi:l] *v.t.* исцел|я́ть, -и́ть; залеч|ивать, -и́ть; **~ing ointment** лече́бная мазь.

v.i. заж|ива́ть, -и́ть; **his wounds ~ed up, over** его́ ра́ны за́жили.

healer ['hi:lə(r)] *n.* ле́карь (*m.*); (ис)цели́тель (*m.*).

health [helθ] *n.* **1.** (*state of body or mind*) здоро́вье; **in good ~** здоро́вый; **he suffers from poor ~** у него́ сла́бое здоро́вье; **mental ~** душе́вное здоро́вье; **~ centre** поликли́никa; **~ service** здравоохране́ние. **2.** (*toast*): **we drank (to) his ~** мы вы́пили за его́ здоро́вье.

healthful ['helθfʊl] *adj.* здоро́вый, целе́бный.

healthy ['helθɪ] *adj.* здоро́вый.

heap [hi:p] *n.* **1.** (*pile*) ку́ча, гру́да. **2.** (*esp. pl.*, *coll.*, *large quantity*) ма́сса, у́йма; **he has ~s of money** у него́ у́йма/ку́ча де́нег.

v.t.: **a ~ed spoonful** ло́жка с ве́рхом; **they ~ed honours on him** его́ осыпа́ли поче́стями; **the table was ~ed with food** стол ломи́лся от яств.

hear [hɪə(r)] *v.t. & i.* **1.** (*perceive with ear*) слы́шать, у-; **I can't ~ a word** я не слы́шу ни сло́ва; **I ~ someone coming** я слы́шу (чьи́-то) шаги́; **I ~d him shout** я слы́шал, как он закрича́л; **the shot was ~d a mile away** вы́стрел бы́ло слы́шно за ми́лю. **2.** (*listen to*): **~ evidence** слу́шать, за- показа́ния свиде́телей; **his prayer was ~d** его́ моли́твы бы́ли услы́шаны; **~ s.o. out** вы́слушать (*pf.*) кого́-н.; **I won't ~ of it!** я и слы́шать об э́том не хочу́! **3.** (*be told*; *learn*) слы́шать, у-; **have you ~d the news?** вы слы́шали но́вости?; **I ~d about it from a friend** я узна́л об э́том от одного́ моего́ дру́га; **I never ~d of such a thing** э́то неслы́ханно; **you will ~ more of this** вам э́то так не пройдёт. **4. ~!, ~!** пра́вильно!; ве́рно ска́зано!

cpd. **~say** *n.* слу́хи (*m. pl.*); то́лки (*m. pl.*).

hearing ['hɪərɪŋ] *n.* **1.** (*perception*) слух; **~ aid** слухово́й аппара́т; **he is hard of ~** он туг на́ ухо. **2.** (*earshot*): **wait till he gets out of ~** да́йте ему́ сперва́ отойти́ (, а то он мо́жет услы́шать); **don't say that in my ~** не говори́те э́того при мне. **3.** (*attention*): **give him a fair ~** вы́слушайте его́; да́йте ему вы́сказаться. **4.** (*leg.*) слу́шание.

hearken ['hɑːkən] *v.i.* вн|има́ть, -ять *+d.*; слу́шать (*impf.*).

hearse [hɜːs] *n.* катафа́лк, похоро́нные дро́ги (*pl.*, *g.* —).

heart [hɑːt] *n.* **1.** (*organ*) се́рдце; **~ attack** серде́чный при́ступ; **~ disease** боле́знь се́рдца; **~ failure** разры́в се́рдца; **his ~ stopped beating** у него́ се́рдце останови́лось; **my ~ was in my mouth** у меня́ душа́ в пя́тки ушла́; **it will break his ~** он бу́дет в отча́янии; **his ~ sank** у него́ се́рдце упа́ло. **2.** (*soul*; *seat of emotions*) се́рдце, душа́; **she has a ~ of gold** у неё золото́е се́рдце; **at ~** по приро́де; в глубине́ души́; **I am sick at ~** у меня́ тяжело́ на душе́; **to one's ~'s content** ско́лько душе́ уго́дно; **bless my ~!** Бо́же мой!; вот те на!; **bless his ~** дай Бог ему́ здоро́вья; **from the bottom of one's ~** из глубины́ души́; **he had a change of ~** он переду́мал; **she cried her ~ out** она́ вы́плакала все глаза́; **have a ~!** (*coll.*) сжа́льтесь!; поми́луйте!; **he lost his ~ to her** он полюби́л её (всем се́рдцем); **with all my ~** всем се́рдцем; **he speaks from his ~** он говори́т от чи́стого се́рдца; **don't take it to ~** не принима́йте э́то бли́зко к се́рдцу; **he won their ~s** он завоева́л их сердца́; (*enthusiasm*): **his ~ is not in his work** он не лю́бит свою́ рабо́ту; (*courage*): **he lost ~** он пал ду́хом; **take ~!** не па́дайте ду́хом!; (*memory*): **I learnt it by ~** я вы́учил э́то наизу́сть. **3.** (*centre*) середи́на; **in the ~ of the forest** в глуши́ ле́са; **this book gets to the ~ of the matter** э́та кни́га затра́гивает са́мую суть де́ла. **4.** (*pl.*, *cards*) че́рв|и (*pl.*, *g.* -е́й); **ace of ~s** черво́нный туз, туз черве́й.

cpds. **~ache** *n.* бо́ль в се́рдце; **~-beat** *n.* сердцеби́ение; **~-breaking** *adj.* душераздира́ющий; **~-broken** *adj.* с разби́тым се́рдцем; **~burn** *n.* изжо́га; **~felt** *adj.* душе́вный, глубоко́ прочу́вствованный; **~-rending** *adj.* душераздира́ющий; **~-sick** *adj.* пода́вленный, удручённый; **~-throb** *n.* (*coll.*) люби́мец; **~-to-~** *adj.*: **a ~-to-~ talk** разгово́р по душа́м; **~-warming** *adj.* ра́достный.

hearten ['hɑːt(ə)n] *v.t.* ободр|я́ть, -и́ть.

hearth [hɑːθ] *n.* оча́г.

heartily ['hɑːtɪlɪ] *adv.* **1.** (*from the heart*) серде́чно, и́скренне; **I am ~ sick of it** мне э́то до́ смерти надое́ло. **2.** (*with relish*, *enthusiasm*) охо́тно, усе́рдно; **he agreed with me ~** он всеце́ло со мной согласи́лся; **the boys ate ~** ма́льчики е́ли с аппети́том.

heartless ['hɑːtlɪs] *adj.* бессерде́чный.

heartlessness ['hɑːtlɪsnɪs] *n.* бессерде́чие.

hearty ['hɑːtɪ] *adj.* **1.** (*cordial*, *sincere*) серде́чный. **2.** (*healthy*, *vigorous*): **he is still hale and ~** он всё ещё здоро́в и бодр; **a ~ appetite** прекра́сный аппети́т. **3.** (*abundant*): **he ate a ~ breakfast** он пло́тно поза́втракал. **4.** (*cheerful*) весёлый.

heat [hiːt] *n.* **1.** (*hotness*) жара́, тепло́, теплота́; **white ~** бе́лое кале́ние; (*hot weather*) жара́; **the ~ of the day** (*lit.*) полдне́вный зной; **he feels the ~** (*badly*) он пло́хо перено́сит жару́; (*heating*): **the ~ was turned on** (*lit.*) отопле́ние бы́ло включено́. **2.** (*warmth of feeling*) теплота́, горя́чность; **he spoke with some ~** он говори́л горячо́; **in the ~ of the moment** сгоряча́. **3.** (*in race etc.*) забе́г, зае́зд; (*in swimming*) заплы́в; **dead ~** мёртвый гит. **4.** (*of animals*) пери́од те́чки; **be on ~** находи́ться (*impf.*) в пери́оде те́чки.

v.t. **1.** (*raise temperature of*) нагр|ева́ть, -е́ть; **the potatoes were ~ed up** карто́шку разогре́ли. **2.** (*inflame*) накал|я́ть, -и́ть; горячи́ть, раз-; **a ~ed argument** жа́ркий спор.

cpds. **~-proof, ~-resistant** *adjs.* жаросто́йкий; **~stroke** *n.* теплово́й уда́р; **~-wave** *n.* полоса́ си́льной жары́.

heater ['hiːtə(r)] *n.* пе́чка, нагрева́тель; батаре́я.

heath [hiːθ] *n.* **1.** (*waste land*) пу́стошь. **2.** (*shrub*) ве́реск.

heathen ['hiːð(ə)n] *n.* язы́чник.

adj. язы́ческий

heathenism ['hiːðən'ɪz(ə)m] *n.* язы́чество.

heather ['heðə(r)] *n.* ве́реск.

heating ['hiːtɪŋ] *n.* обогрева́ние; отопле́ние; **central ~** центра́льное отопле́ние.

heave [hiːv] *n.* (*lifting effort*) подъём; (*throw*) бросо́к.

v.t. (*lift*) подн|има́ть, -я́ть; (*throw*) бр|оса́ть, -о́сить; **~ a sigh** (тяжело́) вздохну́ть (*pf.*).

v.i. **1.** (*pull*): **they ~d on the rope** они́ вы́брали кана́т; **~ ho!** раз-два взя́ли!; эй, у́хнем! **2.** (*retch*) ту́житься (*impf.*) (при рво́те). **3.** (*rise and fall*) вздыма́ться (*impf.*). **4.**: **~ to** (*naut.*) ложи́ться в дрейф.

heaven ['hev(ə)n] *n.* **1.** (*sky*, *firmament*) не́бо, небе́сный свод; **the ~s opened** (*of heavy rain*) небеса́ разве́рзлись; **move ~ and earth** приложи́ть все уси́лия. **2.** (*state of bliss*) блаже́нство; **in the seventh ~** на седьмо́м не́бе. **3.** (*paradise*) рай, ца́рство небе́сное. **4.** (*God*, *Providence*) Бог, провиде́ние; **~ knows where he is** Бог зна́ет, где он; **~ forbid!** Бо́же упаси́!; **thank ~ for that** сла́ва Бо́гу; **for ~'s sake** ра́ди Бо́га.

heavenly ['hevənlɪ] *adj.* **1.** (*in or of heaven*) небе́сный; **~ bodies** небе́сные тела́ (*nt. pl.*). **2.** (*coll.*, *excellent*, *wonderful*) изуми́тельный; ди́вный; **we had a ~ time** мы чуде́сно провели́ вре́мя.

heavily ['hevɪ] *adv.* (*very*, *seriously*) значи́тельно, интенси́вно; **the rain is falling ~** идёт си́льный дождь; **they were ~ defeated** они́ понесли́ тяжёлое пораже́ние.

heaviness ['hevɪnɪs] *n.* тя́жесть.

heavy ['hevɪ] *adj.* тяжёлый; **a ~ blow** (*lit.*, *fig.*) тяжёлый уда́р; **~ breathing** сопе́ние; **a ~ cold** си́льный на́сморк; **there will be a ~ crop this year** в э́том году́ бу́дет оби́льный урожа́й; **he had a ~ day** у него́ был тяжёлый день; **he is a ~ drinker** он челове́к пью́щий; **he had a ~ fall** он си́льно уда́рился при паде́нии; **his book is ~ going** его́ кни́га тру́дно чита́ется; **with a ~ heart** с тяжёлым се́рдцем; **~ industry** тяжёлая промы́шленность; **~ losses** больши́е поте́ри; **a ~ programme** насы́щенная програ́мма; **~ rain** си́льный дождь; **a ~ sea** бу́рное мо́ре; **he is a ~ sleeper** он кре́пко спит; **a ~ sky** хму́рое не́бо; **~ taxes** больши́е нало́ги; **~ traffic** интенси́вное движе́ние.

cpds. **~-handed** *adj.* неуклю́жий; **~-hearted** *adj.* с тяжёлым се́рдцем; **~-laden** *adj.* тяжело нагру́женный (*чем*); **~weight** *n.* & *adj.* (*sport*) (боксёр/борéц) тяжёлого вéса.

Hebrew ['hi:bru:] *n.* **1.** (*Jew*) еврéй. **2.** (*language*) древнееврéйский язы́к; (*modern*) (язы́к) иври́т.
adj. (древне)еврéйский.

heckle ['hek(ə)l] *v.t.* & *i.* (*fig.*) прерывáть (*impf.*) (орáтора) кáверзными вопрóсами.

hectare ['hekteə(r), -tɑ:(r)] *n.* гектáр.

hectic ['hektɪk] *adj.* лихорáдочный, бýрный.

hedge [hedʒ] *n.* живáя и́згородь.
v.t. **1.** (*enclose*) обсá|живать, -ди́ть кустáрником; огор|áживать, -оди́ть. **2.:** **~ one's bets** (*fig.*) перестрахóвываться (*impf.*).
v.i. (*prevaricate*) увíл|ивать, -ьнýть.
cpds. **~hog** *n.* ёж; **~row** *n.* шпалéра, живáя и́згородь; **~-sparrow** *n.* завирýшка леснáя.

hedonism ['hi:dəˌnɪz(ə)m, 'he-] *n.* гедони́зм.

hedonist ['hi:dəˌnɪst, 'he-] *n.* гедони́ст.

hedonistic [ˌhi:də'nɪstɪk, 'he-] *adj.* гедонисти́ческий.

heed [hi:d] *n.* внимáние, внимáтельность; **she paid no ~ to his advice** онá не послýшалась егó совéта.
v.t. уч|и́тывать, -éсть +*d.*

heedless ['hi:dlɪs] *adj.* беззабóтный; беспéчный; **~ of danger** пренебрегáющий опáсностями.

heel[1] [hi:l] *n.* **1.** (*part of foot*) пя́тка; **on the ~s of** вслед за+*i.*; **he took to his ~s** он брóсился наутёк; **he turned on his ~** он крýто повернýлся; **they suffered under the ~ of a tyrant** они́ страдáли под и́гом тирáна. **2.** (*of a shoe*) каблýк; **these shoes are down at ~** у э́тих тýфель сби́лись каблуки́. **3.** (*of a stocking*) пя́тка.
v.t. **1.:** **~ a stocking** вязáть, с- пя́тку чулкá. **2.:** **~ shoes** стáвить, по- каблуки́ на тýфли.

heel[2] [hi:l] *v.i.* **the ship ~ed over** сýдно накрени́лось.

hefty ['heftɪ] *adj.* здоровéнный; рóслый.

hegemony [hɪ'dʒemənɪ, -'gemənɪ] *n.* гегемóния.

heifer ['hefə(r)] *n.* тёлка.

height [haɪt] *n.* **1.** высотá; (*of pers.*) рост; **he was six feet in ~** он был рóстом в 6 фýтов; **a wall six feet in ~** стенá высотóй в 6 фýтов; **he drew himself up to his full ~** он встал во весь рост; **the plane is losing ~** самолёт теря́ет высотý. **2.** (*high ground*) верши́на, верхýшка. **3.** (*utmost degree*) вы́сшая стéпень; **the ~ of folly** верх глýпости; **the ~ of fashion** послéдний крик мóды; **the gale was at its ~** шторм был в разгáре.

heighten ['haɪt(ə)n] *v.t.* (*make higher*) пов|ышáть, -ы́сить; (*increase*) уси́ли|вать, -ть.
v.i. (*fig.*) уси́ливаться (*impf.*).

heinous ['heɪnəs, 'hi:nəs] *adj.* гнýсный.

heir [eə(r)] *n.* наслéдник; **~ apparent** прямóй/непосрéдственный наслéдник.

heiress ['eərɪs] *n.* наслéдница.

heirloom ['eəlu:m] *n.* фами́льная рели́квия.

helicopter ['helɪˌkɒptə(r)] *n.* вертолёт.

heliograph ['hi:lɪəˌgrɑ:f] *n.* гелиóграф.

heliotrope ['hi:lɪəˌtrəʊp, 'hel-] *n.* гелиотрóп.

heliport ['helɪˌpɔ:t] *n.* вертодрóм.

helium ['hi:lɪəm] *n.* гéлий.

helix ['hi:lɪks] *n.* спирáль; завитóк.

hell [hel] *n.* **1.** (*place or state*) ад; **he went through ~** он перенёс мýки áда; **he made her life a ~ (on earth)** он преврати́л её жизнь в сýщий ад; **I gave him ~** (*coll.*) я задáл емý жáру; **he will raise ~** (*coll.*) он подни́мет стрáшный шум. **2.** (*coll. or sl., expr. vexation or emphasis*) **oh ~!** чёрт возьми́!; **go to ~!** иди́ к чёрту; **what the ~ do you want?** что вам нýжно, чёрт возьми́/побери́?; **what the ~!** (*sc. does it matter*) какóго чёрта!; **it hurts like ~** чертóвски бóльно; **to ~ with it!** чёрт с ним/ней!; **they made the ~ of a noise** они́ ужáсно шумéли; **all ~ broke loose** началáсь свистопля́ска; **he rode ~ for leather** он мчáлся сломя́ гóлову; **just for the ~ of it** за здóрово живёшь; **come ~ or high water** будь, что бýдет.
cpds. **~-fire** *n.* áдский огóнь; **~-raiser** *n.* бузотёр, скандали́ст.

hellish ['helɪʃ] *adj.* áдский.

hello [hə'ləʊ] *int.* (*greeting*) здрáсте!; привéт; (*on telephone*) аллó!; (*expr. surprise*) вот те нá!

helm [helm] *n.* (*tiller*) руль, рýмпель (*both m.*); **take the ~** (*lit., fig.*) стать (*pf.*) у штурвáла.
cpd. **~-sman** *n.* рулевóй.

helmet ['helmɪt] *n.* шлем; (*modern soldier's or fireman's*) кáска; **sun ~** тропи́ческий шлем.

help [help] *n.* **1.** (*assistance*) пóмощь; **he walks with the ~ of a stick** он хóдит с пáлкой; **she manages without** (*domestic*) **~** онá обхóдится без прислýги; **can I be of (any) ~?** я могý вам чéм-нибудь помóчь?; **your advice was a great ~ to us** вы óчень помогли́ нам совéтом. **2.** (*remedy*): **there's no ~ for it** ничегó не подéлаешь. **3.** (*domestic servant*) прислýга.
v.t. **1.** (*assist*) пом|огáть, -óчь; **please ~ me up** помоги́те мне, пожáлуйста, подня́ться; **he ~ed her out of the car** он помóг ей вы́йти из маши́ны; **he ~ed her off with her coat** он помóг ей снять пальтó. **2.** (*alleviate*) облегч|áть, -и́ть. **3.** (*serve with food etc.*) уго|щáть, -сти́ть; положи́ть/дать (*pf.*) (*что кому*); **may I ~ you to salad?** могý я положи́ть вам немнóго салáта?; **~ yourself!** угощáйтесь!; бери́те, пожáлуйста!. **4.** (*avoid, prevent; also v.i.*): **I can't ~ it** я не могý ничегó подéлать; от меня́ э́то не зави́сит; **I can't ~ laughing** я не могý удержáться от смéха; я не могý не смея́ться; **don't stay longer than you can ~** не оставáйтесь дóльше, чем нáдо; **it can't be ~ed** ничегó не подéлаешь. **5.:** **so ~ me (God)!** да помóжет мне Бог!
v.i. (*avail, be of use*) быть полéзным; **crying won't ~** слезáми гóрю не помóжешь.

helper ['helpə(r)] *n.* помóщник.

helpful ['helpfʊl] *adj.* полéзный; (*obliging*) услýжливый.

helping ['helpɪŋ] *n.* пóрция; тарéлка (*чего*).
adj.: **she lent a ~ hand** онá протянýла рýку пóмощи.

helpless ['helplɪs] *adj.* беспóмощный, бесси́льный.

helplessness ['helplɪsnɪs] *n.* беспóмощность, бесси́лие.

helter-skelter [ˌheltə'skeltə(r)] *adv.* беспоря́дочно (и поспéшно); врассыпнýю.

hem [hem] *n.* край, каймá.
v.t. **1.** (*sew the edge of*) подш|ивáть, -и́ть; подруб|áть, -и́ть. **2.:** **~ in, ~ about, ~ round** окруж|áть, -и́ть.
cpds. **~-line** *n.* ≃ длинá ю́бки; **~-stitch** *n.* подрýбочный шов; *v.t.* подш|ивáть, -и́ть.

hema-, hemo- ['hi:məʊ] = **h(a)ema-, h(a)emo-**

hemisphere ['hemɪˌsfɪə(r)] *n.* полушáрие.

hemlock ['hemlɒk] *n.* болиголóв, цикýта.

hemp [hemp] *n.* (*plant*) конопля́; (*fibre*) пенькá.

hen [hen] *n.* (*domestic fowl*) кýрица; (*female of bird species*) пти́ца-сáмка.
cpds. **~-bane** *n.* беленá; **~-coop, ~-house** *nn.* куря́тник; **~pecked** *adj.* под каблукóм у жены́.

hence [hens] *adv.* (*from here*) отсю́да; (*from now*): **3 years ~** чéрез три гóда; (*consequently*) отсю́да, слéдовательно.
cpds. **~forth, ~forward** *advs.* впредь, с э́того врéмени.

henchman ['hentʃmən] *n.* приспéшник.

henna ['henə] *n.* хна.
v.t.: **~ed hair** вóлосы, крáшенные хной.

hepatitis [ˌhepə'taɪtɪs] *n.* гепати́т.

her [hɜ:(r), hə(r)] *poss. adj.* её; (*referring to subj. of sentence*) свой.

herald ['her(ə)ld] *n.* (*messenger, forerunner*) геро́льд, ве́стник.
v.t. возве|ща́ть, -сти́ть; предвеща́ть (*impf.*).
heraldic [he'rældɪk] *adj.* геральди́ческий.
heraldry ['herəldrɪ] *n.* гера́льдика.
herb [hɜ:b] *n.* трава́, лека́рственное расте́ние; (*pl., cul.*) коре́н|ья (g. -ев); ку́хонные тра́вы.
herbaceous [hɜ:'beɪʃəs] *adj.* травяно́й; ~ **border** цвето́чный бордю́р
herbal ['hɜ:b(ə)l] *adj.* травяно́й; ~ **medicine** траволече́ние.
herbalist ['hɜ:bəlɪst] *n.* специали́ст по (лека́рственным) тра́вам.
herbicide ['hɜ:bɪˌsaɪd] *n.* гербици́д.
herbivore ['hɜ:bɪˌvɔ:(r)] *n.* травоя́дное живо́тное.
herbivorous [ˌhɜ:'bɪvərəs] *adj.* травоя́дный.
Herculean [ˌhɜ:kjʊ'li:ən, -'kju:lɪən] *adj.* геркуле́сов; (*fig.*): ~ **efforts** титани́ческие уси́лия.
Hercules ['hɜ:kjʊˌli:z] *n.* Геркуле́с.
herd [hɜ:d] *n.* (*animals*) ста́до; (*people*) толпа́; ~ **instinct** ста́дное чу́вство.
v.t. сгоня́ть, согна́ть (вме́сте).
v.i. (*fig.*) ходи́ть (*indet.*) ста́дом/ско́пом.
cpd. **-sman** *n.* пасту́х.
here [hɪə(r)] *n.*: **from ~ to there** отсю́да — туда́/доту́да; **my house is near ~** мой дом ря́дом.
adv. **1.** (*in this place*) здесь; (*coll.*) тут. **2.** (*to this place, in this direction*): **come ~!** иди́те сюда́!; **look ~!** (*lit.*) посмотри́те сюда́; (*expr. emph., impatience etc.*) послу́шайте! **3.** (*demonstrative*): **~ I am!** вот и я!; я тут!; **~ he comes!** вот и он!; **~ we are at last!** наконе́ц-то (мы) пришли́/прие́хали/при́были; **~ goes!** (*coll.*) будь что бу́дет!; **~'s how it happened** вот как э́то случи́лось; **~'s to our victory!** за на́шу побе́ду! **4.** (*with offers*): **~ you are!** пожа́луйста; **~ is my hand!** вот вам моя́ рука́. **5.** (*at this point*): **~ she began to cry** тут она́ запла́кала. **6.** (*for emph.*): **~, take this** вот, возьми́те э́то. **7.**: **same ~!** и я то́же! **8.** (*misc. phrr.*): **he looked ~ and there** он поиска́л там и сям; **I've been ~, there and everywhere** я был повсю́ду; **it's neither ~ nor there** э́то здесь ни при чём.
hereabouts [ˌhɪərə'baʊts] *adv.* побли́зости.
hereafter [hɪər'ɑ:ftə(r)] *n.*: **the ~** загро́бная жизнь.
adv. впосле́дствии.
hereby [hɪə'baɪ] *adv.* э́тим; настоя́щим.
hereditary [hɪ'redɪtərɪ] *adj.* насле́дственный.
heredity [hɪ'redɪtɪ] *n.* насле́дственность.
herein [hɪə'rɪn] *adv.*: **I enclose ~ ...** при сём прилага́ю…
hereinafter [ˌhɪərɪn'ɑ:ftə(r)] *adv.* ни́же, в дальне́йшем.
heresy ['herəsɪ] *n.* е́ресь.
heretic ['herətɪk] *n.* ерети́|к (*fem.* -чка).
heretical [hɪ'retɪk(ə)l] *adj.* ерети́ческий.
hereto [hɪə'tu:] *adv.* к э́тому.
heretofore [ˌhɪətʊ'fɔ:(r)] *adv.* пре́жде; до сих пор.
herewith [hɪə'wɪð, -'wɪθ] *adv.* при сём.
heritage ['herɪtɪdʒ] *n.* насле́дство; (*fig.*) насле́дие.
hermaphrodite [hɜ:'mæfrəˌdaɪt] *n.* гермафроди́т.
hermetic [hɜ:'metɪk] *adj.* гермети́ческий; **~ally sealed** герметизо́ванный.
hermit ['hɜ:mɪt] *n.* отше́льник.
hermitage ['hɜ:mɪtɪdʒ] *n.* оби́тель/прию́т отше́льника; **H~** (*museum*) Эрмита́ж.
hernia ['hɜ:nɪə] *n.* гры́жа.
hero ['hɪərəʊ] *n.* геро́й.
cpd. **~-worship** *n.* преклоне́ние пе́ред геро́ями; (*pej.*) культ ли́чности.
heroic [hɪ'rəʊɪk] *adj.* геро́йский, герои́ческий.
heroics [hɪ'rəʊɪks] *n.* напы́щенность, ходу́льность.
heroin ['herəʊɪn] *n.* герои́н.
heroine ['herəʊɪn] *n.* герои́ня.
heroism ['herəʊˌɪz(ə)m] *n.* герои́зм.
heron ['herən] *n.* ца́пля.
herpes ['hɜ:pi:z] *n.* лиша́й.
herring ['herɪŋ] *n.* сельдь; (*as food*) селёдка.
cpds. **~-bone** *n. & adj.* (*stitch*) «в ёлочку»; (*archit. pattern*) кла́дка «в ёлку».
hers [hɜ:z] *pron.*: **is this handkerchief ~?** э́то её плато́к?; **your dress is prettier than ~** у вас пла́тье краси́вее, чем у неё; **some friends of ~** её друзья́.
herself [hə'self] *pron.* **1.** (*refl.*) себя́, -ся (*suff.*); **she fell down and hurt ~** она́ упа́ла и ушибла́сь. **2.** (*emph.*): **she said so ~** она́ сама́ э́то сказа́ла; **I saw the Queen ~** я ви́дел саму́ короле́ву. **3.** (*after preps.*): **she lives by ~** она́ живёт одна́; **can she do it by ~?** она́ мо́жет сама́ э́то сде́лать?; **she kept it to ~** она́ не дели́лась э́тим ни с кем. **4.** (*her normal state*): **she is not ~ today** сего́дня она́ сама́ не своя́; **she will soon come to ~** она́ ско́ро придёт в себя́.
hesitancy ['hezɪtənsɪ] *n.* колеба́ние.
hesitant ['hezɪt(ə)nt] *adj.* колеблющийся, нереши́тельный.
hesitate ['hezɪˌteɪt] *v.i.* колеба́ться (*imp.*); **don't ~ to ask** проси́те, не смуща́йтесь!; не стесня́йтесь спроси́ть; **I ~ to say this** не зна́ю, сле́дует ли мне об э́том говори́ть.
hesitation [ˌhezɪ'teɪʃ(ə)n] *n.* колеба́ние, сомне́ние.
hessian ['hesɪən] *n.* (*cloth*) мешкови́на; джу́товая ткань.
het [het] *adj.*: **he got ~ up** он распсихова́лся (*sl.*).
heterodox ['hetərəʊˌdɒks] *adj.* неортодокса́льный.
heterogeneous [ˌhetərəʊ'dʒi:nɪəs] *adj.* неодноро́дный, разнохара́ктерный.
heterosexual [ˌhetərəʊ'seksjʊəl] *adj.* гетеросексуа́льный.
hew [hju:] *v.t.* руби́ть (*impf.*); **they ~ed down a tree** они́ сруби́ли де́рево; **a branch had been ~n off** кто́-то сруби́л ве́тку.
hexagon ['heksəgən] *n.* шестиуго́льник.
hexagonal [ˌhek'sægən(ə)l] *adj.* шестиуго́льный.
hey [heɪ] *int.* эй!; **~ presto!** але́-гоп!
heyday ['heɪdeɪ] *n.* расцве́т, зени́т.
hi [haɪ] *int.* **1.** (*to call attention*) эй! **2.** (*US, in greeting, also* **~ there!**) приве́т!; салю́т!
hiatus [haɪ'eɪtəs] *n.* **1.** (*gap*) про́пуск, пробе́л. **2.** (*between vowels*) зия́ние.
hibernate ['haɪbəˌneɪt] *v.i.* находи́ться (*impf.*) в зи́мней спя́чке; **these animals ~** э́ти живо́тные впада́ют в зи́мнюю спя́чку.
hibernation [ˌhaɪbə'neɪʃ(ə)n] *n.* зи́мняя спя́чка.
hibiscus [hɪ'bɪskəs] *n.* гиби́скус.
hicc|up, -ough ['hɪkʌp] *n.* ико́та; (*slight delay*) за́минка.
v.i. ик|а́ть, -ну́ть.
hick [hɪk] *n.* (*US coll.*) дереве́нщина (*c.g.*).
hickory ['hɪkərɪ] *n.* пека́н.
hide[1] [haɪd] *n.* ко́жа, шку́ра; **I'll tan his ~ for him** я дам ему́ взбу́чку; **he lied to save his ~** он солга́л, что́бы спасти́ свою́ шку́ру.
cpd. **~-bound** *adj.* ограни́ченный, с у́зким кругозо́ром.
hide[2] [haɪd] *v.t.* пря́тать, с-; скры|ва́ть, -ть; **~ one's face** закр|ыва́ть, -ы́ть лицо́ рука́ми; **~ one's feelings** скры|ва́ть, -ть свои́ чу́вства; **the house was hidden from the road** дом не́ был ви́ден с доро́ги; **clouds hid the sun** ту́чи закры́ли со́лнце; **a hidden meaning** скры́тый смысл.
v.i. пря́таться, с-.
cpds. **~-and-seek** *n.* пря́т|ки (*pl., g.* -ок); **~away, ~out** *nn.* укры́тие.
hideous ['hɪdɪəs] *adj.* уро́дливый, безобра́зный.
hideousness ['hɪdɪəsnɪs] *n.* уро́дливость, безобра́зие.

hiding[1] ['haɪdɪŋ] *n.* (*coll.*, *thrashing*): **she gave him a good ~** она́ его́ вы́порола как сле́дует.

hiding[2] ['haɪdɪŋ] *n.* (*concealment*) укры́тие; **he went into ~** он скры́лся; он ушёл в подпо́лье; **he is in ~** он скрыва́ется.

cpd. **~-place** *n.* укры́тие.

hierarchical [ˌhaɪəˈrɑːkɪk(ə)l] *adj.* иерархи́ческий.

hierarchy ['haɪəˌrɑːkɪ] *n.* иера́рхия.

hieroglyph ['haɪərəglɪf] *n.* иеро́глиф.

hieroglyphic [ˌhaɪərəˈglɪfɪk] *adj.* иероглифи́ческий.

hieroglyphics [ˌhaɪərəˈglɪfɪks] *n.* иерогли́фика; иерати́ческие письм|ена́ (*pl.*, *g.* -ён).

hi-fi ['haɪfaɪ] *n.* (*coll.*) прои́грыватель (*m.*) с высо́кой то́чностью воспроизведе́ния зву́ка.

higgledy-piggledy [ˌhɪgəldɪˈpɪgəldɪ] *adj.* беспоря́дочный; сумбу́рный.

adv. вперемե́шку; беспоря́дочно.

high [haɪ] *n.* **1.** (*peak*) вы́сшая то́чка; **prices reached a new ~** це́ны дости́гли небыва́ло высо́кого у́ровня. **2.: on ~** на небеса́х; **from on ~** свы́ше.

adj. **1.** (*tall*, *elevated*) высо́кий (*also mus.*); **a ~ building** высо́кое/высо́тное зда́ние; **a ~ chair** высо́кий стул; **ten feet ~** высото́й в 10 фу́тов; **~ jump** прыжо́к в высоту́; **~ tide, water** больша́я вода́, прили́в; **~ and dry** вы́брошенный на бе́рег; (*fig.*) на мели́; **don't get on your ~ horse** (*coll.*) не ва́жничайте. **2.** (*chief*, *important*): **~ altar** гла́вный престо́л; **~ command** вы́сшее кома́ндование; **~ life** све́тская жизнь; **H~ Mass** торже́ственная ме́сса; **~ and mighty** (*coll.*, *arrogant*) надме́нный, вла́стный; **the Most H~** Всевы́шний; **in ~ places** (*fig.*) в верха́х, в вы́сших сфе́рах; **~ priest** первосвяще́нник; **~ school** сре́дняя шко́ла; **~ society** вы́сшее о́бщество; **the ~ spot of the evening** гвоздь програ́ммы; **~ street** гла́вная у́лица; **~ table** почётный стол; **~ treason** госуда́рственная изме́на. **3.** (*greater than average*; *extreme*): **a ~ colour** (*complexion*) я́ркий румя́нец; **in the ~est degree** в вы́сшей сте́пени; **held in ~ esteem** по́льзующийся больши́м уваже́нием; **~ explosive** дробя́щее взры́вчатое вещество́; **in ~ gear** на большо́й ско́рости; **~ jinks** (*coll.*) шу́мное весе́лье; **they are having a ~ old time** они́ веселя́тся вовсю́; **it is a ~ price to pay** сли́шком уж велика́ цена́; **on the ~ seas** в откры́том мо́ре; **in ~ spirits** в припо́днятом настрое́нии; **~ tension** си́льное напряже́ние; **a ~ wind** си́льный ве́тер. **4.** (*at its peak*): **~ noon** по́лдень; **~ summer** середи́на/разга́р ле́та; **it is ~ time I was gone** мне уже́ давно́ пора́ идти́. **5.** (*noble*, *lofty*): **a ~ calling** высо́кое призва́ние. **6.** (*intoxicated*) навеселе́; (*on drugs*) в дурма́не.

adv. **1.** (*aloft*; *at or to a height*): **~ up** высоко́; (*of direction*) ввысь; **the ball rose ~ into the air** мяч взлете́л высоко́ в во́здух; **you must aim ~** (*fig.*) вы должны́ ме́тить вы́ше; **he held his head ~** (*fig.*) он ходи́л с высоко́ по́днятой голово́й; **I searched ~ and low** я иска́л повсю́ду. **2.** (*at a ~ level*): **the seas were running ~** мо́ре бы́ло неспоко́йно; **feelings ran ~** стра́сти разгора́лись.

cpds. **~brow** *n.* интеллектуа́л; *adj.* интеллектуа́льный, серьёзный; **~-class** *adj.* высо́кого кла́сса; **~-fidelity** *adj.* с высокой то́чностью воспроизведе́ния; **~-flown** *adj.* высокопа́рный; витиева́тый; **~-frequency** *adj.* коротково́лновый, высокочасто́тный; **~-grade** *adj.* высокока́чественный; **~-handed** *adj.* вла́стный; своево́льный; бесцеремо́нный; **~land** *adj.* го́рский; **H~lander** *n.* го́р|ец (*fem.* -я́нка); **the H~lands** *n.* се́вер и се́веро-за́пад Шотла́ндии; **~-level** *adj.* на высо́ком у́ровне; **~light** *n.* (*in painting*) блик; (*phot.*) светово́й эффе́кт; (*fig.*) кульминацио́нный моме́нт; *v.t.* (*fig.*, *emphasize*) выделя́ть, вы́делить; заостр|я́ть, -и́ть внима́ние на+*p.*; **~-minded** *adj.* благоро́дный, великоду́шный; **~-pitched** *adj.* высо́кий; **~-powered** *adj.* (*of an engine*) большо́й мо́щности; (*of a pers.*) динами́чный, операти́вный; **~-pressure** *adj.* (*aggressive*) агресси́вный; **~-pressure work** напряжённая рабо́та; **~-priced** *adj.* дорогосто́ящий; **~-ranking** *adj.* высокопоста́вленный; **~-rise** *adj.*: **~-rise apartment blocks** высо́тные многокварти́рные дома́; **~road** *n.* шоссе́ (*indecl.*); **~-sounding** *adj.* напы́щенный; **~-sounding words** гро́мкие слова́; **~-speed** *adj.* сверхскоростно́й; **~-technology** *n.* высокосло́жная техноло́гия; **~-water mark** *n.* у́ровень по́лной воды́; **~way** *n.* шоссе́ (*indecl.*); **H~way Code** n. пра́вила у́личного движе́ния; **~way robbery** (*lit.*) грабёж на большо́й доро́ге; (*fig.*) грабёж, обира́ловка; **~wayman** *n.* разбо́йник (с большо́й доро́ги).

higher ['haɪə(r)] *adj.* (*senior*, *advanced*) вы́сший.

adv.: **~ up the hill** вы́ше на холме́ (*or* по скло́ну); **~ up the road** да́льше по э́той доро́ге/у́лице.

highly ['haɪlɪ] *adv.* весьма́, о́чень; **~ paid** высокоопла́чиваемый; **~ polished** (*lit.*) хорошо́ отполиро́ванный; **he speaks ~ of you** он о вас о́чень хорошо́ отзыва́ется; **~ strung** взви́нченный; нерво́зный; **she is ~ thought of** её о́чень це́нят.

highness ['haɪnɪs] *n.* (*title*) высо́чество; **His Royal H~** Его́ Короле́вское Высо́чество.

hijack ['haɪdʒæk] *n.* уго́н, похище́ние.

v.t. уг|оня́ть, -на́ть; пох|ища́ть, -и́тить.

hijacker ['haɪˌdʒækə(r)] *n.* уго́нщик, похити́тель (*m.*).

hike[1] [haɪk] *n.* (*coll.*, *walk*) экску́рсия пешко́м.

v.i. броди́ть (*impf.*).

hike[2] [haɪk] (*US coll.*) *n.* (*rise*) подъём.

v.t. (*raise*) подн|има́ть, -я́ть.

hiker ['haɪkə(r)] *n.* (*coll.*) путеше́ственник.

hilarious [hɪ'leərɪəs] *adj.* весёлый, умори́тельный.

hilarity [hɪ'lærɪtɪ] *n.* весе́лье, потéха.

hill [hɪl] *n.* холм; **down the ~** с горы́, по́д гору; **as old as the ~s** старо́ как мир; **the village lies just over the ~** дере́вня лежи́т пря́мо за холмо́м; **up the ~** в го́ру; **up ~ and down dale** повсю́ду.

cpds. **~side** *n.* склон холма́; **~top** *n.* верши́на холма́.

hillock ['hɪlək] *n.* хо́лмик, бугóр.

hilly ['hɪlɪ] *adj.* холми́стый.

hilt [hɪlt] *n.* рукоя́тка, эфе́с.

Himalayas [ˌhɪmə'leɪəz] *n.* Гимала́|и (*pl.*, *g.* -ев).

himself [hɪm'self] *pron.* **1.** (*refl.*) себя́, -ся; **I hope he behaves ~** наде́юсь, что он бу́дет вести́ себя́ прили́чно. **2.** (*emph.*) сам; **he did the job ~** он сам сде́лал э́ту рабо́ту. **3.** (*after preps.*): **he lives by ~** он живёт оди́н; **he did it by ~** он сде́лал э́то сам; **he was talking to ~** он разгова́ривал сам с собо́й. **4.** (*in his normal state*): **he will see you when he is ~ again** он повида́ется с ва́ми, когда́ придёт в себя́.

hind[1] [haɪnd] *n.* (*deer*) са́мка оле́ня.

hind[2] [haɪnd] *adj.* за́дний; **the dog stood on its ~ legs** соба́ка вста́ла на за́дние ла́пы.

cpds. **~-quarters** *n.* зад; **~sight** *n.* (*coll.*, *wisdom after the event*): **he spoke with ~sight** он говори́л, зна́я, чем ко́нчилось де́ло.

hinder ['hɪndə(r)] *v.t.* меша́ть, по-; **he ~ed me from working** он меша́л (*or* не дал) мне рабо́тать.

Hindi ['hɪndɪ] *n.* (*language*) хи́нди (*m. indecl.*).

hindrance ['hɪndrəns] *n.* поме́ха.

Hindu ['hɪnduː, -'duː] *n.* инду́с (*fem.* -ка).

adj. инду́сский.

Hinduism ['hɪnduːˌɪz(ə)m] *n.* индуи́зм.

hinge [hɪndʒ] *n.* петля́, шарни́р; (*fig.*) сте́ржень (*m.*).

v.t. наве́|шивать, -сить на пе́тли.

v.i. висе́ть (*impf.*); враща́ться (*impf.*) на пе́тлях; (*fig.*): **it all ~d on this event** всё бы́ло свя́зано с э́тим собы́тием.

hint [hɪnt] *n.* (*suggestion*) намёк; **can't you take a ~?**

намёка не понима́ете?; **he is always dropping ~s** он говори́т намёками; **a broad/gentle ~** я́сный/то́нкий намёк; **there was a ~ of frost** начина́ло подмора́живать; **~ of garlic** чу́точка чеснока́; (*written advice*) сове́т.

v.t. & i. намек|а́ть, -ну́ть на+*a.*; **what are you ~ing (at)?** на что вы намека́ете?

hinterland ['hɪntəˌlænd] *n.* (*inland area*) райо́ны (*m. pl.*), удалённые от побере́жья; (*supply area*) прилега́ющие райо́ны снабже́ния.

hip[1] [hɪp] *n.* бедро́; **he stood with his hands on his ~s** он стоя́л подбоче́нясь; **what do you measure round the ~s?** како́й у вас разме́р бёдер?

cpds. **~-flask** *n.* карма́нная фля́жка; **~-pocket** *n.* за́дний карма́н.

hip[2] [hɪp] *n.* (*fruit*) я́года шипо́вника.

hip[3] [hɪp] *int.*: **~, ~, hooray!** гип-гип, ура́.

hippopotamus [ˌhɪpə'pɒtəməs] *n.* гиппопота́м, бегемо́т.

hire ['haɪə(r)] *n.* (*engagement of person*) наём; (*of thg.*) наём, прока́т; **cars for ~** маши́ны напрока́т; **he let his boat out on ~** он сда(ва́)л свою́ ло́дку напрока́т.

v.t. **1.** (*obtain use of, employ*) нан|има́ть, -я́ть; сн|има́ть, -я́ть; **they ~d the hall for a night** они́ сня́ли зал на ве́чер; **~d help** (*domestic servant*) слуга́ (*m.*); служа́нка, домрабо́тница. **2.** (*let out for hire*) сда|ва́ть, -ть внаём/напрока́т.

cpd. **~-purchase** *n.* поку́пка в рассро́чку.

hireling ['haɪəlɪŋ] *n.* наёмник, найми́т.

hirsute ['hɜːsjuːt] *adj.* волоса́тый, косма́тый.

his [hɪz] *pron.*: **what is ~ by right** то, что принадлежи́т ему́ по пра́ву; **my bicycle is newer than ~** у меня́ велосипе́д нове́е, чем у него́.

poss. adj. его́; (*referring to subj. of sentence*) свой.

Hispanic [hɪ'spænɪk] *adj.* испа́нский; латиноамерика́нский; **~ studies** испани́стика.

hiss [hɪs] *n.* шипе́ние, свист.

v.t. (*an actor*) освист|ывать, -а́ть; **he was ~ed off the stage** его́ освиста́ли.

v.i. шипе́ть, за-/про-.

historian [hɪ'stɔːrɪən] *n.* исто́рик.

historic [hɪ'stɒrɪk] *adj.* истори́ческий; (*significant*) знамена́тельный.

historical [hɪ'stɒrɪk(ə)l] *adj.* истори́ческий.

historicity [ˌhɪstə'rɪsɪtɪ] *n.* истори́чность.

history ['hɪstərɪ] *n.* исто́рия; **make (*or* go down in) ~** войти́ (*pf.*) в исто́рию; **~ is silent on that point** исто́рия об э́том ума́лчивает; **that is ancient ~!** (*fig.*) э́то старо́!

cpd. **~-book** *n.* уче́бник исто́рии.

histrionic [ˌhɪstrɪ'ɒnɪk] *adj.* (*pert. to acting*) актёрский; (*stagy*) театра́льный, наи́гранный.

histrionics [ˌhɪstrɪ'ɒnɪks] *n.* (*performance*) представле́ние; (*behaviour*) театра́льность, наи́гранность.

hit [hɪt] *n.* (*blow*) уда́р, толчо́к; **~ man** профессиона́льный уби́йца; (*strike or shot which reaches target*) попада́ние; (*coll., success*) успе́х; (*popular song*) популя́рная пе́сенка.

v.t. **1.** (*strike*) уд|аря́ть, -а́рить; бить, по-; сту́к|ать, -нуть; **he fell and ~ his head on a stone** он упа́л и уда́рился голово́й о ка́мень; **he was ~ on the head** его́ уда́рили по голове́; **don't ~ a man when he's down** лежа́чего не бьют; **the car ~ a tree** маши́на вре́залась в де́рево; **he ~ the nail on the head** (*fig.*) он попа́л пря́мо в то́чку. **2.** (*fig. uses*): **you've ~ it!** вы попа́ли в то́чку; **the idea suddenly ~ me** меня́ вдруг осени́ло; **the town was ~ by an earthquake** го́род был поражён землетрясе́нием; **~ the trail, road** (*coll.*) выступа́ть, вы́ступить в похо́д.

v.i.: **he ~ on an idea** ему́ пришла́ в го́лову мысль.

with advs.: **~ back** *v.t.*: **he ~ the ball back** он отби́л мяч; **if he ~s you, ~ him back** е́сли он вас уда́рит, да́йте сда́чи; **~ off** *v.t.*: **~ it off** ла́дить (*impf.*); **~ out** *v.i.*: **he ~ out at his opponents** он дал ре́зкий отпо́р свои́м проти́вникам.

cpd. **~-or-miss** *adj.* сде́ланный как попа́ло.

hitch [hɪtʃ] *n.* (*jerk*) рыво́к; (*temporary stoppage; snag*) заде́ржка; **without a ~** гла́дко.

v.t. **1.** (*fasten*) привя́з|ывать, -а́ть; прицеп|ля́ть, -и́ть. **2.** (*lift*): **~ up one's trousers** подтя́|гивать, -ну́ть брю́ки. **3.** (*coll.*): **~ a lift** подъе́хать (*pf.*) на попу́тной маши́не.

v.i. (*coll., travel by getting free rides; also* **~-hike**) е́здить автосто́пом.

cpds. **~-hiker** *n.* (*coll.*) автосто́повец; **~-hiking** *n.* «голосова́ние», езда́ автосто́пом (*or* на попу́тных маши́нах).

hither ['hɪðə(r)] *adv.* сюда́.

cpd. **~to** *adv.* до сих пор.

HIV (*abbr. of med.,* ***human immunodeficiency virus***) ВИЧ, (ви́рус иммунодефици́та челове́ка).

hive [haɪv] *n.* у́лей; (*fig.*): **the office is a ~ of industry** рабо́та в конто́ре кипи́т.

v.t. (*fig.*): **they ~d off and formed a new party** они́ отколо́лись и со́здали но́вую па́ртию; **certain jobs were ~d off to other departments** не́которые ви́ды рабо́т бы́ли пору́чены други́м отде́лам.

hives [haɪvz] *n.* (*med.*) крапи́вница.

hm [hm] *int.* гм!

hoard [hɔːd] *n.* (та́йный) запа́с, склад.

v.t. припря́тывать (*impf.*); ск|а́пливать, -опи́ть больши́е запа́сы.

hoarding ['hɔːdɪŋ] *n.* **1.** (*fence round building site*) забо́р вокру́г стройплоща́дки. **2.** (*for poster display*) рекла́мный щит. **3.** (*stocking up*) накопле́ние.

hoar-frost ['hɔː(r)frɒst] *n.* и́ней, и́зморозь.

hoarse [hɔːs] *adj.* хри́плый, си́плый; **he talked himself ~** он договори́лся до хрипоты́.

hoarseness ['hɔːsnɪs] *n.* хрипота́, си́плость.

hoary ['hɔːrɪ] *adj.* (*grey or white with age*) седо́й; (*ancient*) дря́хлый; **a ~ joke** анекдо́т с бородо́й.

hoax [həʊks] *n.* надува́тельство, ро́зыгрыш.

v.t. над|ува́ть, -у́ть; разыгр|ывать, -а́ть.

hob [hɒb] *n.* по́лка в ками́не/пе́чи.

hobble ['hɒb(ə)l] *v.t.*: **~ a horse** стрено́жить (*pf.*) ло́шадь.

v.i. ковыля́ть (*impf.*); прихра́мывать (*impf.*).

hobby ['hɒbɪ] *n.* (*leisure pursuit*) хо́бби (*nt. indecl.*).

cpd. **~-horse** *n.* игру́шечная лоша́дка; (*fig.*) конёк.

hobgoblin ['hɒbˌgɒblɪn] *n.* чертёнок, бесёнок.

hobnail ['hɒbneɪl] *n.*: **~ed boots** подби́тые гвоздя́ми боти́нки.

hobnob ['hɒbnɒb] *v.i.* води́ться (*impf.*), якша́ться (*impf.*) (*с кем*).

hobo ['həʊbəʊ] *n.* (*US sl.*) бродя́га (*m.*).

hock[1] [hɒk] *n.* (*wine*) рейнве́йн.

hock[2] [hɒk] *n.* (*sl., pawn*): **in ~** в ломба́рде; в закла́де.

v.t. за|кла́дывать, -ложи́ть.

hockey ['hɒkɪ] *n.* (*on field*) травяно́й хокке́й; **ice ~** хокке́й (с ша́йбой).

cpds. **~-player** *n.* хоккеи́ст (*fem.* -ка); **~-stick** *n.* клю́шка.

hocus-pocus [ˌhəʊkəs'pəʊkəs] *n.* фо́кус, трюк.

hod [hɒd] *n.* (строи́тельный) лото́к.

hodge-podge ['hɒdʒpɒdʒ] *n.* (*coll.*) мешани́на.

hoe [həʊ] *n.* моты́га, тя́пка.

v.t. & i. моты́жить (*impf.*); выпа́лывать, вы́полоть.

hog [hɒg] *n.* бо́ров; (*US, also fig.*) свинья́; **go the whole ~** дов|оди́ть, -ести́ де́ло до конца́; идти́ (*det.*) на всё.

v.t. (*coll.*) (*eat greedily*) жрать, со-; (*monopolize*): **he ~ged the conversation** он не дава́л никому́ сло́ва вста́вить.

cpd. **~wash** *n.* (*pig-swill*) по́йло; (*coll.*, *rubbish*) чушь, вздор.

hogmanay ['hɒgmə,neɪ, -'neɪ] *n.* (*Sc.*) кану́н Но́вого го́да.

hoi polloi [,hɔɪ pə'lɔɪ] *n.* простонаро́дье.

hoist [hɔɪst] *n.* подъёмник.

v.t. подн|има́ть, -я́ть; **he was ~ by his own petard** он попа́л в со́бственную лову́шку.

hold [həʊld] *n.* **1.** (*grasp*, *grip*) уде́рживание, захва́т; **he caught ~ of the rope** он ухвати́лся за кана́т; **he kept ~ of the reins** он не выпуска́л пово́дья из рук; **he laid, seized, took ~ of my arm** он схвати́л/взял меня́ за́ руку; **don't lose ~; don't let go your ~** держи́те, не отпуска́йте; (*fig.*); **I got ~ of a plumber** я нашёл водопрово́дчика; **where did you get ~ of that idea?** отку́да вы э́то взя́ли? **2.** (*in boxing or wrestling*) захва́т. **3.** (*means of pressure*): **he has a ~ over him** он де́ржит его́ в рука́х. **4.** (*support*): **his feet could find no ~ on the cliff face** его́ нога́ не могла́ найти́ опо́ры на пове́рхности утёса. **5.** (*ship's*) трюм.

v.t. **1.** (*clasp*, *grip*) держа́ть (*impf.*); **they sat ~ing hands** они́ сиде́ли, держа́сь за́ руки. **2.** (*maintain*, *keep in a certain position*): **~ yourself straight!** держи́сь пря́мо!; **~ it!** (*coll.*) (*don't move*) не дви́гайтесь!; не шевели́тесь!; (*fig.*, *keep*): **he held himself in readiness** он был нагото́ве; **they held the enemy at bay** они́ не подпуска́ли непри́ятеля; **I won't ~ you to your promise** я не тре́бую, что́бы вы сдержа́ли своё сло́во; **~ the line!** (*teleph.*) жди́те у телефо́на!; не клади́те тру́бку! **3.** (*detain*): **he was held prisoner** его́ держа́ли в плену́; **they held him for questioning** его́ задержа́ли для допро́са. **4.** (*contain*): **the hall ~s a thousand** зал вмеща́ет ты́сячу челове́к; **~ one's liquor** переноси́ть (*impf.*) спиртно́е; **his theory will not ~ water** (*fig.*) его́ тео́рия несостоя́тельна. **5.** (*consider*, *believe*) полага́ть (*impf.*), счита́ть (*impf.*); **the court held that ...** суд призна́л, что...; **~ dear** высоко́ цени́ть (*impf.*); **he is held in great esteem** он по́льзуется больши́м уваже́нием; **I don't ~ it against him** я не ста́влю ему́ э́то в вину́. **6.** (*restrain*): **she held her breath** она́ затаи́ла дыха́ние; **~ everything!** (*coll.*) останови́тесь!; **~ your tongue!** молчи́те!; **there's no ~ing him** на него́ (*or* ему́) нет у́держу. **7.** (*have*, *own*): **he ~s the ace** у него́ туз; **all this land is held by one man** всей э́той землёй владе́ет оди́н челове́к; **~ the record** быть рекордсме́ном; **~ shares** быть держа́телем а́кций; **the opinion is widely held** э́то мне́ние широко́ распространено́; **we ~ the same views** мы приде́рживаемся одина́ковых взгля́дов. **8.** (*occupy*, *remain in possession of*): **how long has he held office?** как давно́ он занима́ет э́ту до́лжность; **he held his ground** (*lit.*) он не уступа́л; (*fig.*) он не сдава́лся; **I can ~ my own against anyone** я могу́ потяга́ться с кем уго́дно; **he ~s the rank of sergeant** он име́ет зва́ние сержа́нта. **9.** (*carry on*, *conduct*, *convene*): **they were ~ing a conversation** они́ бесе́довали; **the meeting was held at noon** собра́ние состоя́лось в по́лдень.

v.i. **1.** (*grasp*): **~ tight!** держи́те кре́пче/кре́пко. **2.** (*adhere*): **he ~s firmly to his beliefs** он твёрдо де́ржится свои́х убежде́ний. **3.** (*agree*, *approve*): **I don't ~ with that** я э́того не одобря́ю. **4.** (*remain*): **he held aloof** он держа́лся особняко́м; **~ still!** не дви́гайтесь!; **the argument ~s good** до́вод сохраня́ет си́лу. **5.** (*remain unbroken*, *unchanged*, *intact*): **will the rope ~?** вы́держит ли верёвка?; **how long will the weather ~?** до́лго ли проде́ржится така́я пого́да?

with advs.: **~ back** *v.t.* (*restrain*): **I couldn't ~ him back** я не мог его́ удержа́ть; (*withhold*): **he held back part of their wages** он удержа́л часть их зарпла́ты; (*repress*): **I had to ~ back a smile** мне пришло́сь сдержа́ть улы́бку; *v.i.* (*hesitate*) ме́шкать (*impf.*); (*refrain*): возде́рж|иваться, -а́ться (*от чего*); **~ down** *v.t.* (*lit.*): **~ your head down!** не поднима́йте головы́!; (*fig.*): **do you think you can ~ the job down?** суме́ете ли вы удержа́ться на э́той до́лжности; **~ forth** *v.t.* (*offer*) протя́|гивать, -ну́ть; *v.i.* (*coll.*, *orate*) разглаго́льствовать (*impf.*); **~ in** *v.t.* (*lit.*): **her waist was held in by a belt** её та́лия была́ стя́нута по́ясом; (*fig.*): **I could hardly ~ myself in** я едва́ сдержа́лся; **~ off** *v.t.* (*keep away*, *repel*): **he held his dog off** он придержа́л соба́ку; **they held off the attack** они́ отби́ли ата́ку; *v.i.* (*stay away*): **the rain held off all morning** дождя́ так и не́ было всё у́тро; **~ on** *v.t.* (*keep in position*) прикре-п|ля́ть, -и́ть; **the handle was held on with glue** ру́чка держа́лась на клею́; *v.i.* (*cling*) держа́ться (*за что*); **she held on to the banisters** она́ держа́лась за пери́ла; (*coll.*, *wait*): **~ on a minute till I'm ready** подожди́те — я бу́ду гото́в че́рез мину́ту; (*on the telephone*): **~ on, please!** не ве́шайте тру́бку!; **~ out** *v.t.* (*extend*): **he greeted me and held out his hand** он произнёс приве́тствие и протяну́л мне ру́ку; (*fig.*, *offer*): **I can't ~ out any hope** я не могу́ вас ниче́м обнадёжить; *v.i.* (*endure*, *refuse to yield*): **the men are ~ing out for more money** рабо́чие не уступа́ют, тре́буя повыше́ния зарпла́ты; (*last*): **supplies cannot ~ out much longer** запа́сов надо́лго не хва́тит; **~ over** *v.t.* (*defer*) от|кла́дывать, -ложи́ть; **~ together** *v.t.*: **the box was held together with string** коро́бка была́ перевя́зана бечёвкой; (*fig.*) **the leader held his party together** ли́дер сплоти́л па́ртию; *v.i.* (*fig.*): **his arguments do not ~ together** в его до́водах есть неувя́зка; **~ up** *v.t.* (*lift*, *hold erect*): **the boy held up his hand** ма́льчик по́днял ру́ку; (*fig.*, *display*, *expose*): **he was held up as an example** его́ поста́вили в приме́р; (*delay*) заде́рж|ивать, -а́ть; **we were held up on the way** по доро́ге нас задержа́ли; **traffic was held up by fog** движе́ние останови́лось из-за тума́на; **work is (*or* has been) held up** рабо́та ста́ла; (*waylay*): **the robbers held them up at pistol point** банди́ты огра́били их, угрожа́я пистоле́том; *v.i.*: **do you think the table will ~ up under the weight?** вы ду́маете, стол вы́держит тако́й вес?; (*fig.*): **if the weather ~s up, we can go out** е́сли така́я пого́да проде́ржится, мы мо́жем пойти́ куда́-нибудь.

cpds. **~-all** *n.* вещево́й мешо́к; су́мка; **~-up** *n.* (*stoppage*, *delay*) заде́ржка; **what's the ~-up?** за чем де́ло ста́ло?; (*robbery*) вооружённый грабёж.

holder ['həʊldə(r)] *n.* **1.** (*possessor*, *e.g. of a passport*) владе́лец; облада́тель (*m.*); **~ of an office** занима́ющий до́лжность. **2.** (*device for holding*) держа́тель (*m.*).

holding ['həʊldɪŋ] *n.* **1.** (*of land*) уча́сток (земли́). **2.** (*property*) вкла́ды (*m. pl.*), авуа́ры (*m. pl.*). **3.** (*pl.*) (*stock*) запа́с; (*of library*) фонд.

hole [həʊl] *n.* **1.** (*cavity*) дыра́. **2.** (*opening*) отве́рстие. **3.** (*rent*) щель, про́резь. **4.** (*burrow*) нора́. **5.** (*pej. of a place*) дыра́. **6.** (*predicament*) беда́. **7.** (*in golf*) лу́нка. **8.** (*phrr.*): **he is always picking ~s** он ко всему́ придира́ется; **a square peg in a round ~** челове́к не на своём ме́сте.

v.t. **1.** (*make ~ in*) де́лать отве́рстия в+*p*. **2.** (*make ~ through*) продыря́в|ливать, -ить. **3.** (*golf*) заг|оня́ть, -на́ть (мяч) в лу́нку.

holiday ['hɒlɪ,deɪ, -dɪ] *n.* **1.** (*day off*) выходно́й (день); **church ~** церко́вный пра́здник. **2.** (*annual leave*) о́тпуск, о́тдых; (*school*, *university vacation*) кани́кул|ы (*pl.*, *g.* —); (*leisure time*) о́тдых; **he is on ~** он в отпуску́; у него́ кани́кулы; **I take my ~s in June** я беру́ о́тпуск в ию́не; **where are you spending your ~?** где вы бу́дете отдыха́ть?; **~ camp**

(ле́тний) ла́герь; ~ **home** дом о́тдыха.

cpd. **~-maker** *n.* отдыха́ющий; тури́ст (*fem.* -ка).

holiness ['həʊlɪnɪs] *n.* свя́тость, свяще́нность; **His H~ (the Pope)** его́ Святе́йшество.

holistic [həʊ'lɪstɪk] *adj.* це́лостный.

Holland ['hɒlənd] *n.* Голла́ндия.

holler ['hɒlə(r)] *v.t. & i.* (*US coll.*) ора́ть (*impf.*); вопи́ть (*impf.*).

hollow ['hɒləʊ] *n.* **1.** (*small depression*) вы́емка, впа́дина. **2.** (*dell*) лощи́на, низи́на.

adj. **1.** (*not solid*) пусто́й, по́лый. **2.** (*of sounds*) глухо́й. **3.** (*fig., false, insincere*) фальши́вый, лжи́вый; ~ **laughter** неесте́ственный смех; **a ~ victory** беспло́дная побе́да. **4.** (*sunken*) ввали́вшийся, впа́лый; ~ **cheeks** ввали́вшиеся щёки.

v.t. (*usu.* ~ **out**) выда́лбливать, вы́долбить.

holly ['hɒlɪ] *n.* остроли́ст.

hollyhock ['hɒlɪ,hɒk] *n.* алте́й ро́зовый.

holm-oak [həʊm] *n.* дуб ка́менный.

holocaust ['hɒlə,kɔ:st] *n.* ма́ссовое уничтоже́ние; **the H~** холоко́уст; **nuclear ~** я́дерная катастро́фа.

hologram ['hɒlə,græm] *n.* голограмма.

holster ['həʊlstə(r)] n. кобура́.

holy ['həʊlɪ] *n.*: **the H~ of Holies** (*lit., fig.*) Свята́я Святы́х.

adj. свяще́нный, свято́й; **H~ Communion** Свято́е Прича́стие; **the H~ Father** его́ Святе́йшество; **the H~ Ghost, Spirit** Свято́й Дух; ~ **orders** духо́вный сан; ~ **place** святи́лище; **H~ Russia** Свята́я Русь; **the H~ See** Святе́йший Престо́л; **a ~ war** свяще́нная война́; ~ **water** свята́я вода́; **H~ Week** Страстна́я неде́ля.

homage ['hɒmɪdʒ] *n.* (*fig.*) почте́ние, преклоне́ние; **we pay ~ to his genius** мы преклоня́емся пе́ред его ге́нием.

home [həʊm] *n.* **1.** (*place where one resides or belongs*) дом; (*attr.*) дома́шний; ~ **economics** домово́дство; ~ **help** приходя́щая домрабо́тница; **it was a ~ from ~** там бы́ло как до́ма; **a ~ of one's own** со́бственный дом; **his ~ is in London** жи́тель Ло́ндона; **he made his ~ in Bristol** он посели́лся в Бри́столе; **she left ~** она́ поки́нула (роди́тельский) дом; **at home** (*in one's house*) до́ма; (*on one's ~ ground*) у себя́; (*e.g. football*) на своём по́ле; **make yourself at ~** бу́дьте как до́ма; **I feel at ~ here** я чу́вствую себя́ здесь как до́ма; **he is away from ~** он в отъе́зде. **2.** (*institution*): **a ~ for the disabled** дом инвали́дов; **he put his parents into a ~** он помести́л свои́х роди́телей в дом для престаре́лых. **3.** (*in games*): **the ~ stretch** фи́нишная пряма́я. **4.** (*attr., opp. foreign; native, local*): ~ **affairs** вну́тренние дела́; **H~ Counties** гра́фства, окружа́ющие Ло́ндон; **H~ Guard** отря́ды (*m. pl.*) ме́стной оборо́ны; **the ~ market** вну́тренний ры́нок; **H~ Office** министе́рство вну́тренних дел; ~ **team** кома́нда хозя́ев по́ля; ~ **rule** самоуправле́ние; ~ **town** родно́й го́род.

adv. **1.** (*at or to one's own house*): **is he ~ yet?** он (уже́) до́ма?; **he was on his way ~** он шёл/е́хал домо́й; **nothing to write ~ about** (*fig.*) ничего́ осо́бенного. **2.** (*in or to one's own country*): **things are different back ~** (*coll.*) у нас э́то не так (*or* ина́че); **he came ~ from abroad** он верну́лся из-за грани́цы. **3.** (*to the point aimed at*): **the nails were driven ~** гво́зди бы́ли заби́ты; **bring sth. ~ to s.o.** довести́ (*pf.*) что-н. до чьего́-н. созна́ния; **his remarks struck ~** его́ замеча́ния попа́ли в цель.

v.i.: **homing instinct** тя́га домо́й; **homing pigeon** почто́вый го́лубь.

cpds. **~-baked** *adj.* дома́шней вы́печки; **~-brewed** *adj.* дома́шнего изготовле́ния; **~coming** *n.* возвраще́ние домо́й; **~-grown** *adj.* доморо́щенный; **~land** *n.* ро́дина; **~-lover** *n.* домосе́д (*fem.* -ка); **~-made** *adj.* дома́шнего изготовле́ния; **~sick** *adj.* скуча́ющий/тоску́ющий по до́му/ро́дине; **~sickness** *n.* ностальги́я; **~stead** *n.* уса́дьба; фе́рма; **~work** *n.* дома́шнее зада́ние.

homeless ['həʊmlɪs] *adj.* бездо́мный.

homely ['həʊmlɪ] *adj.* **1.** (*like home*) дома́шний, ую́тный; **a ~ atmosphere** дома́шняя обстано́вка. **2.** (*unpretentious*): **a ~ old lady** ми́лая стару́шка; **a ~ meal** неприхотли́вая еда́. **3.** (*US, unattractive*) некраси́вый.

homeopath ['həʊmɪəʊ,pæθ, 'hɒmɪ-] *n.* гомеопа́т.

homeopathic [,həʊmɪəʊ'pæθɪk, 'hɒmɪ-] *adj.* гомеопати́ческий.

homeopathy [,həʊmɪ'ɒpəθɪ, ,hɒmɪ-] *n.* гомеопа́тия.

homeward ['həʊmwəd] *adj.* иду́щий/веду́щий к до́му; ~ **voyage** обра́тный рейс/путь.

adv. (*also* **~s**) домо́й; восвоя́си.

homicide ['hɒmɪ,saɪd] *n.* (*crime*) уби́йство.

homily ['hɒmɪlɪ] *n.* про́поведь; (*reprimand*) нота́ция.

hominy ['hɒmɪnɪ] *n.* марёная кукуру́за, мамалы́га.

homogeneity [,həʊməʊdʒɪ'ni:ɪtɪ] *n.* одноро́дность.

homogeneous [,həʊməʊ'dʒi:nɪəs, ,hɒməʊ-] *adj.* одноро́дный.

homogenize [hə'mɒdʒɪ,naɪz] *v.t.* гомогенези́ровать (*impf.*).

homonym ['hɒmənɪm] *n.* омо́ним.

homophobia [,həʊməʊ'fəʊbɪə, ,hɒm-] *n.* не́нависть к гомосексуали́стам.

homophone ['hɒmə,fəʊn] *n.* омофо́н.

homo sapiens [,həʊməʊ 'sæpɪenz] *n.* хо́мо са́пиенс (*m. indecl.*).

homosexual [,həʊməʊ'seksjʊəl, ,hɒm-] *n.* гомосексуали́ст.

adj. гомосексуа́льный.

homosexuality [,həʊməʊ,seksjʊ'ælɪtɪ, ,hɒm-] *n.* гомосексуали́зм.

hone [həʊn] *v.t.* точи́ть, за-/на-.

honest ['ɒnɪst] *adj.* (*fair, straightforward*) че́стный; (*sincere*): **an ~ attempt** че́стная попы́тка; (*expressive of honesty*): **an ~ face** откры́тое лицо́; (*candid*): **if you want the ~ truth** е́сли вы хоти́те знать всю/чи́стую пра́вду; **to be ~ (with you)** че́стно говоря́.

cpds. **~-to-goodness** *adj.* настоя́щий; *adv.* че́стно!; ей-Бо́гу!

honestly ['ɒnɪstlɪ] *adv.* **1.** (*straightforwardly*) че́стно. **2.** (*candidly*) чистосерде́чно; **~!** че́стное сло́во!; **~, that's all the money I have** э́то все мои де́ньги, пове́рьте.

honesty ['ɒnɪstɪ] *n.* **1.** (*integrity*) че́стность. **2.** (*candour*) чистосерде́чие, прямота́.

honey ['hʌnɪ] *n.* мёд; (*US coll., darling*) дорого́й, ми́лый.

cpds. **~-bee** *n.* пчела́ медоно́сная; **~comb** *n.* со́т|ы (*pl., g.* -ов); **~-dew** *n.*: **~-dew melon** муска́тная ды́ня; **~moon** *n.* медо́вый ме́сяц; *v.i.* пров|оди́ть, -ести́ медо́вый ме́сяц; **~suckle** *n.* жи́молость.

Hong Kong [hɒŋ'kɒŋ] *n.* Гонко́нг.

honk [hɒŋk] *n.* **1.** (*of goose*) крик (ди́ких гусе́й). **2.** (*of motor horn*) гудо́к.

v.i. **1.** крича́ть (*impf.*). **2.** гуде́ть (*impf.*).

honorary ['ɒnərərɪ] *adj.* (*conferred as honour*) почётный; (*unpaid*) неопла́чиваемый.

honour ['ɒnə(r)] *n.* **1.** (*good character, reputation*) честь; **a man of ~** благоро́дный/че́стный челове́к; **code of ~** ко́декс че́сти; **debt of ~** долг че́сти; **he considered himself in ~ bound to obey** он счёл свои́м до́лгом подчини́ться; **(on my) word of ~!** че́стное сло́во. **2.** (*dignity, credit*): **it's an ~ to work with him** рабо́тать с ним — больша́я честь; **it does you ~** э́то де́лает вам честь; **guard of ~** почётный карау́л; **the reception was held in his ~** приём был устро́ен в его́ честь; **he won ~ in war** он был увéнчан боевóй слáвой; (*in polite formulae*): **will you do me the ~ of accepting this gift?** окажи́те мне честь, приня́в э́тот дар; **I have the ~ to inform you** имéю честь сообщи́ть вам. **3.** (*usu. pl., mark of respect, distinction*): **~s list** спи́сок пожáлованных монáрхом почётных звáний и ти́тулов; **he was buried with military ~s** он был похорóнен с вóинскими пóчестями; **let me do the ~s** я бу́ду за хозя́ина; (*as title*) **your H~** вáша честь. **4.** (*pl., academic distinction*): **~s course** курс, даю́щий прáво на диплóм с отли́чием; **pass with ~s** сдать (*pf.*) экзáмен с отличием.

v.t. **1.** (*respect, do ~ to*) окáз|ывать, -áть честь +*d.* **2.** (*confer dignity on*): **he ~ed me with a visit** он удостóил меня́ визи́том. **3.** (*fulfil obligation*): **he failed to ~ the agreement** он не вы́полнил соглашéния; **will the cheque be ~ed?** бу́дет ли уплáчено по э́тому чéку?

honourable ['ɒnərəb(ə)l] *adj.* **1.** (*upright*) чéстный, достóйный. **2.** (*consistent with honour*): **an ~ peace** почётный мир. **3.** (*title*: *also* **right ~**) достопочтéнный.

hood [hʊd] *n.* **1.** (*headgear*) капюшóн, кáпор. **2.** (*of car or carriage*) складнóй верх; (откиднáя) кры́ша. **3.** (*US, of car engine*) капóт.

hoodlum ['hu:dləm] *n.* (*US sl.*) хулигáн.

hoodwink ['hʊdwɪŋk] *v.t.* одурáчи|вать, -ть; (*coll.*) провести́ (*pf.*).

hoof [hu:f] *n.* копы́то; **on the ~** (*of cattle*) живóй.

v.t. (*sl.*): **~ it** идти́ пёхом (*sl.*).

hook [hʊk] *n.* **1.** (*curved, usu. metal, device*) крючóк (*also for fishing*), крюк; **the receiver was off the ~** трýбка былá снятá; **he swallowed the tale ~, line and sinker** (*fig.*) он попáлся на у́дочку; (*dress fastening*): **~ and eye** крючóк; **by ~ or by crook** всéми прáвдами и непрáвдами. **2.** (*boxing blow*) хук, боковóй удáр.

v.t. (*catch*) поймáть (*pf.*); **she ~ed a rich husband** (*coll.*) онá подцепи́ла богáтого мýжа; **he is ~ed on drugs** (*sl.*) он пристрасти́лся к наркóтикам. **2.** (*usu. with advs., fasten*): **she ~ed up her dress** онá застегнýла плáтье (на крючки́).

v.i. (*fasten*): **the dress ~s (up) at the back** плáтье застёгивается сзáди.

cpds. **~-nosed** *adj.* с крючковáтым нóсом; **~worm** *n.* нематóда.

hookey ['hʊkɪ] *n.*: **play ~** (*US sl.*) прогýливать (*impf.*) (урóки).

hooligan ['hu:lɪgən] *n.* хулигáн.

hooliganism ['hu:lɪgənɪz(ə)m] *n.* хулигáнство.

hoop [hu:p] *n.* **1.** (*of barrel etc.; plaything; in circus*) óбруч. **2.** (*croquet*) ворóт|а (*pl., g.* —).

v.t. (*bind with ~s*) скреп|ля́ть, -и́ть óбручем.

cpds. **~-la** *n.* (*game*) кóльца (*nt. pl.*); **~-skirt** *n.* криноли́н.

hooray! [hʊ'reɪ] *int.* урá.

hoot [hu:t] *n.* **1.** (*derisive noise*) ши́канье, гвалт; (*owl's cry*) ýханье; (*warning note of vessel, car, siren etc.*) гудóк, сигнáл.

v.t. оши́к|ивать, -ать; **they ~ed him off (the stage)** егó оши́кали.

v.i. (*in derision or amusement*) улюлю́кать (*impf.*); **we ~ed with laughter** мы покáтывались сó смеху; (*of an owl*) ýх|ать, -нуть; (*of a vessel, car etc.*) гудéть, про-; да|вáть, -ть гудóк.

hooter ['hu:tə(r)] *n.* (*of factory*) гудóк.

Hoover ['hu:və(r)] *n.* (*propr.*) пылесóс.

v.t. (**h~**) пылесóсить, про-.

hop[1] [hɒp] *n.* **1.** подскóк, скачóк (на однóй ногé); **~, skip and jump** тройнóй прыжóк; **I was caught on the ~** (*coll.*) меня́ застáли врасплóх. **2.** (*dance*) танцýлька (*coll.*). **3.** (*stage of flight*) перелёт.

v.t.: **~ it!** (*sl.*) кати́сь!

v.i. пры́гать, скакáть (*both impf.*); **he ~ped over the ditch** он перепры́гнул чéрез канáву; **where has he ~ped off to?** (*coll.*) кудá э́то он ускакáл?; **he was ~ping mad** (*coll.*) он рассвирепéл.

cpd. **~scotch** *n.* клáссы (*m. pl.*) (*игра*).

hop[2] [hɒp] *n.* (*bot.*) хмель (*m.*).

hop|e [həʊp] *n.* надéжда; **I have high ~es of him** я возлагáю на негó больши́е надéжды; **we live in ~e(s)** мы живём надéждой; **don't raise my ~es in vain** не обнадёживайте меня́ понапрáсну; **his ~es were dashed** егó надéжды рýхнули; **I went in the ~e of finding him** я пошёл в надéжде найти́ егó; **there's not much ~e of that** на э́то мáло надéжды; **things are past all ~e** положéние безнадёжно.

v.t. & i.: **I ~e to see you soon** надéюсь, мы скóро уви́димся; **let's ~e so!** бýдем надéяться!; **I ~e not** надéюсь, что нет; **I am ~ing against ~e** я продолжáю надéяться, несмотря́ ни на что.

hopeful ['həʊpfʊl] *adj.* **1.** (*having hope*): **I am ~ of success** я надéюсь/рассчи́тываю на успéх. **2.** (*inspiring hope*): **a ~ prospect** обнадёживающая перспекти́ва; **a ~ sign** благоприя́тный при́знак.

hopefully ['həʊpfʊlɪ] *adv.* (*in sense 'it is hoped'*): **~ he will arrive soon** нáдо надéяться, он скóро приéдет.

hopeless ['həʊplɪs] *adj.* **1.** (*affording no hope*): **a ~ situation** безнадёжное положéние; **a ~ illness** неизлечи́мая болéзнь. **2.** (*coll., incapable*): **he's quite ~ at science** тóчные нáуки емý совершéнно не даю́тся; **he is a ~ ass** он безнадёжно глуп. **3.: he fell ~ly in love** он влюби́лся пó уши.

hopelessness ['həʊplɪsnɪs] *n.* безнадёжность.

hopper ['hɒpə(r)] *n.* (*for grain*) ворóнка.

horde [hɔ:d] *n.* (*of nomads*) ордá; (*fig.*) пóлчище.

horizon [hə'raɪz(ə)n] *n.* (*lit., fig.*) горизóнт; **over the ~** за горизóнт(ом).

horizontal [,hɒrɪ'zɒnt(ə)l] *n.* горизонтáль.

adj. горизонтáльный.

hormone ['hɔ:məʊn] *n.* гормóн; **~ replacement therapy** гормонáльная терапи́я; (*attr.*) гормóнный.

horn [hɔ:n] *n.* **1.** (*of cattle*) рог; **I took the bull by the ~s** (*fig.*) я взял быкá за рогá; **he drew in his ~s** (*fig.*) он присмирéл/прити́х. **2.** (*hist., drinking-vessel*) рог; **~ of plenty** рог изоби́лия. **3.** (*mus.*): **French ~** валтóрна; (*hunting-~*) рог. **4.** (*warning device*) гудóк, свистóк; (*of a car*) клаксóн, гудóк; **he sounded his ~** он дал сигнáл. **5.** (*substance*) рог. **6.** (*geog.*): **the H~** мыс Горн.

cpds. **~beam** *n.* граб; **~pipe** *n.* хóрнпайп; **~-rimmed** *adj.* в роговóй опрáве.

horned [hɔ:nd] *adj.* рогáтый, с рогáми.

hornet ['hɔ:nɪt] *n.* шéршень (*m.*); **~'s nest** оси́ное гнездó.

horny ['hɔ:nɪ] *adj.* роговóй; **~ hands** мозóлистые рýки.

horoscope ['hɒrə,skəʊp] *n.* гороскóп.

horrendous [hə'rendəs] *adj.* ужáсный, жýткий.

horri|ble ['hɒrɪb(ə)l], **-d** ['hɒrɪd] *adjs.* ужáсный, ужасáющий; (*coll., unpleasant*) ужáсный, отврати́тельный; **you're being ~** ты злой!

horrific [hə'rɪfɪk] *adj.* ужасáющий.

horrif|y ['hɒrɪ,faɪ] *v.t.* (*fill with horror*) ужас|áть, -нýть; (*shock*) потряс|áть, -ти́; **I was ~ied at his behaviour** егó поведéние меня́ ужаснýло.

horror ['hɒrə(r)] *n.* ýжас; **~s!** какóй ýжас!; жуть!; **the ~s of war** ýжасы войны́; **~ film** фильм ýжасов; (*extreme dislike*) **I have a ~ of cats** я терпéть не могý кóшек.

cpd. **~-struck** *adj.* в ýжасе.

hors d'oeuvres [ɔ:'dɜ:vr, -'dɜ:v] *n.* закýски (*f. pl.*).

horse [hɔ:s] *n.* **1.** (*animal*) лóшадь, конь (*m.*); **he backs ~s** он игрáет на скáчках; **he backed the wrong ~** (*fig.*) он просчитáлся; он постáвил не на ту лóшадь; **he drove a ~ and cart** он éхал на телéге;

he eats like a ~ он ест за семеры́х; **you are flogging a dead ~** зря стара́етесь!; ги́блое де́ло!; не рвись!; **he learnt to ride a ~** он научи́лся е́здить верхо́м; **that's a ~ of another colour** (*fig.*) э́то совсе́м друго́й коленко́р; **a dark ~** тёмная лоша́дка; **I had it straight from the ~'s mouth** я зна́ю э́то из первоисто́чника; **he got on his high ~** он стал в по́зу. **2.** (*cavalry*) ко́нница, кавале́рия. **3.** (*in gymnasium*) конь (*m.*).

cpds. **~back** *n.*: **on ~back** верхо́м; **~back riding** (*US*) = **~-riding; ~-box** *n.* тре́йлер, автофурго́н; **~-chestnut** *n.* кашта́н ко́нский; **~flesh** *n.* кони́на; **~-fly** *n.* слепе́нь (*m.*); **~hair** *n.* ко́нский во́лос; *adj.* из ко́нского во́лоса; **~man** *n.* нае́здник, вса́дник; **~manship** *n.* иску́сство верхово́й езды́; **~play** *n.* шу́мная игра́/возня́; **~-power** *n.* лошади́ная си́ла; **~-race, ~-racing** *n.* ска́чки (*f. pl.*); **~-radish** *n.* хрен; **~-riding** *n.* верхова́я езда́; **~shoe** *n.* подко́ва; **~-trading** торги́ (*m. pl.*); **~whip** *n.* хлыст; *v.t.* хлеста́ть; **~-woman** *n.* нае́здница, вса́дница.

horticultural [ˌhɔːtɪˈkʌltʃər(ə)l] *adj.* садово́дческий.

horticultur(al)ist [ˌhɔːtɪˈkʌltʃər(əl)ɪst] *n.* садово́д.

horticulture [ˈhɔːtɪˌkʌltʃə(r)] *n.* садово́дство.

hosanna [həʊˈzænə] *n.* & *int.* оса́нна.

hose [həʊz] *n.* **1.** (*stockings*) чуло́чные изде́лия; (*US*) чулки́ (*m. pl.*). **2.** (*tube, also* **~-pipe**) шланг.

v.t.: **he was hosing down the car** он полива́л маши́ну водо́й из шла́нга.

hosiery [ˈhəʊzɪərɪ, ˈhəʊʒərɪ] *n.* трикота́жные изде́лия (*nt. pl.*).

hospice [ˈhɒspɪs] *n.* (*for terminal patients*) больни́ца для безнадёжных пацие́нтов.

hospitable [ˈhɒspɪtəb(ə)l, hɒˈspɪt-] *adj.* гостеприи́мный.

hospital [ˈhɒspɪt(ə)l] *n.* больни́ца; (*esp. military*) го́спиталь (*m.*); **he went into ~** он лёг в больни́цу; **he is in ~** он лежи́т в больни́це; **~ ship** плаву́чий го́спиталь.

hospitality [ˌhɒspɪˈtælɪtɪ] *n.* гостеприи́мство.

hospitalize [ˈhɒspɪtəˌlaɪz] *v.t.* госпитализи́ровать (*impf., pf.*).

host[1] [həʊst] *n.* хозя́ин (*also zool.*); **he is a good ~** он гостеприи́мный хозя́ин.

v.t.: **the conference was ~ed by the British** хозя́евами конфере́нции бы́ли брита́нцы.

host[2] [həʊst] *n.* (*army, multitude*) мно́жество; **the Heavenly H~** си́лы небе́сные (*f. pl.*); **a ~ of difficulties** ма́сса тру́дностей.

host[3] [həʊst] *n.* (*sacrament*) го́стия.

hostage [ˈhɒstɪdʒ] *n.* зало́жник.

hostel [ˈhɒst(ə)l] *n.* общежи́тие; **youth ~** молодёжная тури́стская ба́за.

hostelry [ˈhɒstəlrɪ] *n.* (*arch., joc.*) постоя́лый двор.

hostess [ˈhəʊstɪs] *n.* хозя́йка; (*on aircraft*) стюарде́сса.

hostile [ˈhɒstaɪl] *adj.* вражде́бный, неприя́зненный; **he is ~ to the idea** он про́тив э́той иде́и.

hostility [hɒˈstɪlɪtɪ] *n.* (*enmity, ill-will*) вражде́бность; (*pl., warlike activity*) вое́нные/вооружённые де́йствия.

hot [hɒt] *adj.* **1.** горя́чий; жа́ркий; **I am ~** мне жа́рко; **he got ~ playing** ему́ ста́ло жа́рко от игры́; **~ air** (*coll.*) бахва́льство; **these goods are selling like ~cakes** э́тот това́р идёт нарасхва́т; **a ~ day** жа́ркий день; **the issue is too ~ to handle** (*fig.*) э́то сли́шком щекотли́вый вопро́с; **you'll get into ~ water** вы попадёте в беду́. **2.** (*spicy*) о́стрый. **3.** (*ardent*) горя́чий, пла́менный; **~ on the scent, trail** по горя́чему следу́. **4.** (*angry*) раздражённый. **5.** (*excited*) взволно́ванный, возбуждённый; **~ under the collar** (*coll.*) распалённый, взбешённый. **6.** (*exciting*) отли́чный, шика́рный; **not so ~** (*coll.*) ничего́ осо́бенного; **~ stuff** (*coll.*) (*something new and exciting*) блеск!; шик! **7.** (*fresh*): **~ news** све́жие но́вости; **~ from the press** то́лько что из типогра́фии. **8.** (*racing etc.*): **~ favourite** всео́бщий фаворит; **a ~ tip** де́льный сове́т. **9.** (*emergency*): **~ line** пряма́я телефо́нная связь.

v.t. (*usu.* **~ up**) нагр|ева́ть, -е́ть; подогр|ева́ть, -е́ть; разогр|ева́ть, -е́ть.

v.i.: **~ up** (*fig.*): **the game ~ted up** игра́ оживи́лась.

cpds. **~bed** *n.* парни́к; (*fig.*) оча́г; **~-blooded** *adj.* пы́лкий, стра́стный; **~foot** *adv.* стремгла́в, поспе́шно; **~head** *n.* бу́йная/бедо́вая голова́; **~-headed** *adj.* вспы́льчивый, горя́чий; **~house** *n.* оранжере́я, тепли́ца; **~-plate** *n.* электри́ческая/га́зовая пли́тка; **~pot** *n.* тушёное мя́со с овоща́ми; **~-water-bottle** *n.* гре́лка.

hotch-potch [ˈhɒtʃpɒtʃ] *n.* мешани́на.

hotel [həʊˈtel] *n.* оте́ль (*m.*), гости́ница.

hotelier [həʊˈtelɪə(r)] *n.* хозя́ин оте́ля.

hotly [ˈhɒtlɪ] *adv.*: **her cheeks flushed ~** её щёки я́рко зарде́лись; **he replied ~** он отве́тил ре́зко.

hound [haʊnd] *n.* (*for hunting*) охо́тничья соба́ка; **he rides to ~s** он охо́тится на лиси́ц (с соба́ками); (*coll., any dog*) пёс, соба́ка.

v.t. (*with advs.*): **~ down** вы́ловить (*pf.*); **~ on** натра́в|ливать, -и́ть.

hour [aʊə(r)] *n.* **1.** (*period*) час; **it will take me an ~** мне потре́буется час; **boats for hire by the ~** прока́т ло́док с почасово́й опла́той; **he works an 8-~ day** у него́ восьмичасово́й рабо́чий день; **~ after ~** час за ча́сом. **2.** (*of clock-time*): **every ~ on the ~** в нача́ле ка́ждого ча́са; **every ~ on the half-~** ка́ждый час в середи́не ча́са; **at the eleventh ~** (*fig.*) в после́дний моме́нт. **3.** (*time of day or night*): **we are open at all ~s** мы откры́ты круглосу́точно; **at an early ~** ра́но; **they keep late ~s** они́ по́здно ложа́тся; **in the small ~s** в предрассве́тные часы́; **regardless of the ~** в любо́е вре́мя (дня и но́чи). **4.** (*specific period of time*): **our working ~s are long** у нас до́лгий рабо́чий день; **I had to work after ~s** мне пришло́сь рабо́тать сверхуро́чно; **in office ~s** в рабо́чее вре́мя; **out of ~s** в нерабо́чее вре́мя; **after ~s** по́сле закры́тия. **5.** (*fig., moment*): **the ~ has come** про́бил час; **in the ~ of danger** в мину́ту опа́сности.

cpds. **~-glass** *n.* песо́чные час|ы́ (*pl., g.* -о́в); **~-hand** *n.* часова́я стре́лка; **~-long** *adj.* одночасово́й; продолжа́ющийся час.

hourly [ˈaʊəlɪ] *adj.* **1.** (*occurring once an hour*) ежеча́сный. **2.** (*constant*) постоя́нный. **3.: an ~ wage** почасова́я пла́та.

adv. (*once every hour*) ежеча́сно; (*at any hour*) с ча́су на час; в любо́е вре́мя.

house[1] [haʊs] *n.* **1.** (*habitation*) дом, зда́ние; **~ arrest** дома́шний аре́ст; **~ guest** гость (живу́щий в до́ме); **~ of cards** (*lit., fig.*) ка́рточный до́мик; **~ of God** дом бо́жий, це́рковь; **they get on like a ~ on fire** они́ прекра́сно ла́дят; **keep ~** вести́ (*det.*) хозя́йство; **put, set one's ~ in order** (*fig.*) прив|оди́ть, -ести́ свои́ дела́ в поря́док; **as safe as ~s** в по́лной безопа́сности; **turn s.o. out of ~ and home** вы́гнать (*pf.*) кого́-н. из дому; (*inn*): **public ~** паб; **have a drink on the ~** вы́пить (*pf.*) за счёт хозя́ина; (*parl.*): **H~ of Commons** пала́та о́бщин; **H~ of Lords** пала́та ло́рдов; **the H~** парла́мент. **2.** (*audience*) зал, аудито́рия; **she brought down the ~** её выступле́ние произвело́ фуро́р; (*performance*) представле́ние; (*cinema*) сеа́нс. **3.** (*dynasty*) дом, дина́стия. **4.** (*business concern*) учрежде́ние, фи́рма.

cpds. **~boat** *n.* плаву́чий дом; **~bound** *adj.* прико́ванный к до́му; **~breaker** *n.* граби́тель-взло́мщик; **~breaking** *n.* грабёж со взло́мом;

~coat *n.* (дома́шний) хала́т; **~-fly** *n.* му́ха ко́мнатная; **~hold** *n.* дом; дома́шний круг; (*attr.*): **~hold appliances** бытовы́е прибо́ры; **~holder** *n.* домовладе́лец; **~-hunting** *n.* по́иски (*m. pl.*) кварти́ры/до́ма; **~husband** *n.* домохозя́ин; **~keeper** *n.* эконо́мка; дома́шняя хозя́йка; **~keeping** *n.* дома́шнее хозя́йство; **~keeping expenses** расхо́ды на хозя́йство; **~-maid** *n.* го́рничная; **~painter** *n.* маля́р; **~-to-~** *adj.*: **a ~-to-~ search** обхо́д всех домо́в подря́д с о́быском; пова́льный о́быск; **~top** *n.* кры́ша, кро́вля; **~-trained** (*adj.*) приу́ченный жить (*or* не па́чкать) в до́ме; **~-warming** *n.* новосе́лье; **~wife** *n.* домохозя́йка; **~work** *n.* рабо́та по до́му.

house[2] [haʊz] *v.t.* **1.** (*provide house(s) for*) предост|авля́ть, -а́вить жильё +*d.*; сели́ть, по-. **2.** (*accommodate*) вме|ща́ть, -сти́ть; **this building ~s the city council** в э́том зда́нии размеща́ется муниципалите́т. **3.** (*store*) храни́ть (*impf.*).

housing [ˈhaʊzɪŋ] *n.* **1.** (*provision of houses*) обеспе́чение жильём; **~ benefit** посо́бие по вы́плате квартпла́ты; **the ~ problem** жили́щная пробле́ма. **2.** (*houses built in quantity*): **~ estate** жило́й микрорайо́н. **3.** (*casing*) ко́рпус, ко́жух.

hovel [ˈhɒv(ə)l] *n.* лачу́га, шала́ш.

hover [ˈhɒvə(r)] *v.i.* пари́ть (*impf.*); **he ~ed between life and death** он был ме́жду жи́знью и сме́ртью.

cpds. **~craft** *n.* су́дно на возду́шной поду́шке; **~train** *n.* аэропо́езд.

how [haʊ] *adv.* **1.** (*in direct and indirect questions*) как; каки́м о́бразом?; **~ come?** (*coll.*) как э́то?; **~ on earth did it happen?** как же э́то случи́лось?; **~ comes it that you are late?** почему́ э́то вы опа́здываете?; **~ are you?** как пожива́ете?; **~ do I know?** почём я зна́ю?; **~ do you know that?** отку́да вы э́то зна́ете?; **~ do you mean?** что вы хоти́те сказа́ть?; в како́м смы́сле?; **~'s that?** (*enquiring reason*) ка́к это?; (*inviting comment*): **~'s that for a jump!** ничего́ себе́ прыжо́к!; **~ about a drink?** не хоти́те ли вы́пить?; **~ about that!** (*coll., expr. admiration etc.*) ну и ну!; **~ so?** почему́ э́то?; то́ есть?; **~ ever does he do it?** как же он э́то де́лает? **2.** (*with adjs. and advs.*): **~ far is it?** как далеко́ э́то нахо́дится?; како́е расстоя́ние (до+*g.*)?; **~ many, much?** ско́лько?; **tell me ~ old she is** скажи́те мне, ско́лько ей лет? **3.** (*in indirect statements or questions*): **I told him ~ I'd been abroad** я рассказа́л ему́, как я съе́здил за грани́цу. **4.** (*in exclamations*): **~ he goes on!** до чего́ он зану́да!; **~ I wish I were there!** как бы мне хоте́лось сейча́с быть там!; **and ~!** (*coll.*) ещё как!; **~ beautifully she plays!** как она́ прекра́сно игра́ет!

however [haʊˈevə(r)] *adv.*: **~ hard he tried** как он ни стара́лся.

conj. одна́ко; и всё же.

howitzer [ˈhaʊɪtsə(r)] *n.* га́убица.

howl [haʊl] *n.* (*cry of pain or grief*) вопль (*m.*), стон; (*cry of derision*) вой, гул; (*of an animal*) вой; (*of the wind*) завыва́ние.

v.t. & i. выть (*impf.*); **the baby was ~ing its head off** ребёнок надрыва́лся от кри́ка; **he was ~ed down** его́ перекрича́ли; **listen to the wolves ~ing!** послу́шайте, как во́ют во́лки; **a ~ing gale** завыва́ющий ве́тер.

howler [ˈhaʊlə(r)] *n.* (*coll., solecism*) грубе́йшая оши́бка, ля́псус.

hoy [hɔɪ] *int.* эй!

h.p. (*abbr. of* **horsepower**) л.с., (лошади́ная си́ла).

HQ (*abbr. of* **headquarters**) штаб, ста́вка.

HRH (*abbr. of* **Her/His Royal Highness**) Её/Его́ Короле́вское Высо́чество.

HRT (*abbr. of* **hormone replacement therapy**) гормона́льная терапи́я.

hub [hʌb] *n.* вту́лка.

hubbub [ˈhʌbʌb] *n.* шум, го́вор, го́мон, гвалт.

huckleberry [ˈhʌkəlbərɪ] *n.* черни́ка (*collect.*); я́года черни́ки.

huckster [ˈhʌkstə(r)] *n.* торго́вец, бары́шник.

huddle [ˈhʌd(ə)l] *n.* **1.** (*disorderly mass*) ку́ча, гру́да, во́рох. **2.: they went into a ~** (*coll.*) они́ ста́ли та́йно совеща́ться.

v.i. толпи́ться, с-; **he lay ~d up** он лежа́л, сверну́вшись кала́чиком; **they ~d together for warmth** они́ прижа́лись друг к дру́гу, что́бы согре́ться.

hue[1] [hjuː] *n.* (*colour*) отте́нок, тон (*pl.* -а́).

hue[2] [hjuː] *n.*: **~ and cry** кри́ки (*m. pl.*); во́згласы (*m. pl.*); **raise a ~ and cry** подн|има́ть, -я́ть крик.

huff [hʌf] *n.* вспы́шка раздраже́ния/оби́ды; **he walked off in a ~** он ушёл вконе́ц разоби́женный.

huffy [ˈhʌfɪ] *adj.* оби́женный, рассе́рженный.

hug [hʌg] *n.* объя́тие.

v.t. **1.** (*embrace*) обн|има́ть, -я́ть. **2.** (*fig., cling to, keep close to*): **the ship ~ged the shore** кора́бль шёл вдоль са́мого бе́рега.

huge [hjuːdʒ] *adj.* огро́мный, грома́дный; **he ate a ~ supper** за у́жином он нае́лся до отва́ла; **a ~ joke** великоле́пный ро́зыгрыш.

hugely [ˈhjuːdʒlɪ] *adv.* весьма́, чрезвыча́йно.

Huguenot [ˈhjuːgəˌnəʊ, -ˌnɒt] *n.* гугено́т.

adj. гугено́тский

hulk [hʌlk] *n.* (*body of dismantled ship*) ко́рпус; (*unwieldy vessel*) неповоро́тливое су́дно; (*large clumsy person*) «медве́дь» (*m.*); у́валень (*m.*).

hulking [ˈhʌlkɪŋ] *adj.* неуклю́жий, неповоро́тливый.

hull[1] [hʌl] *n.* (*of ship*) ко́рпус; (*of aircraft*) фюзеля́ж.

v.t.: **~ a ship** (*strike in ~*) проби́ть (*pf.*) ко́рпус корабля́.

hull[2] [hʌl] *n.* (*shell, pod*) кожура́; скорлупа́.

v.t. лущи́ть (*impf.*), шелуши́ть (*impf.*).

hullabaloo [ˌhʌləbəˈluː] *n.* шум, шуми́ха.

hullo [hʌˈləʊ] *int.* (*greeting*) здра́сте!; приве́т!; (*on telephone*) алло́!; (*expr. surprise*) вот те на́!

hum [hʌm] *n.* жужжа́ние.

v.t. & i. **1.** (*make murmuring sound*): **~ming bird** коли́бри (*m. indecl.*); **~ming-top** волчо́к. **2.** (*sing with closed lips*) напева́ть (*impf.*). **3.: ~and haw** мя́млить (*impf.*). **4.** (*coll., be active*) идти́ (*det.*) по́лным хо́дом; кипе́ть (*impf.*); **he made things ~** у него́ рабо́та кипе́ла.

human [ˈhjuːmən] *n.* челове́к.

adj. челове́ческий; **~ being** челове́к; **~ kind** челове́чество; **~ nature** челове́ческая приро́да; **the ~ race** род людско́й; **~ shield** живо́й щит; **he did all that was ~ly possible** он сде́лал всё, что в челове́ческих си́лах.

humane [hjuːˈmeɪn] *adj.* **1.** (*compassionate*) гума́нный, челове́чный. **2.: ~ studies** гуманита́рные нау́ки (*f. pl.*).

humaneness [hjuːˈmeɪnnɪs] *n.* гума́нность, челове́чность.

humanism [ˈhjuːməˌnɪz(ə)m] *n.* (*classical studies; non-religious ethics*) гумани́зм.

humanist [ˈhjuːmənɪst] *n.* гумани́ст.

humanistic [ˌhjuːməˈnɪstɪk] *adj.* гуманисти́ческий.

humanitarian [hjuːˌmænɪˈteərɪən] *n.* гумани́ст.

adj. гума́нный, челове́чный, человеколюби́вый.

humanity [hjuːˈmænɪtɪ] *n.* **1.** (*human nature*) челове́чность, челове́ческие ка́чества. **2.** (*the human race*) челове́чество; род людско́й. **3.** (*crowd*) ма́сса люде́й, толпа́, наро́д. **4.** (*humaneness*) гума́нность. **5.: the ~ies** гуманита́рные нау́ки (*f. pl.*).

humanize [ˈhjuːməˌnaɪz] *v.t.* очелове́чи|вать, -ть.

humble [ˈhʌmb(ə)l] *adj.* **1.** (*lacking self-importance*) поко́рный, смире́нный; **in my ~ opinion** по моему́ непросвещённому мне́нию; **your ~ servant** ваш поко́рный слуга́. **2.** (*lowly*) просто́й, скро́мный; **of ~ birth** из простонаро́дья.

v.t. смир|я́ть, -и́ть; ун|ижа́ть, -и́зить; ~ **o.s.** унижа́ться (*impf.*).

humbug [ˈhʌmbʌg] *n.* (*deceit, hypocrisy*) надува́тельство; (*hypocrite, fraud*) обма́нщик, очковтира́тель (*m.*); (*nonsense*) чушь, вздо́р; (*boiled sweet*) леденéц.

v.t. над|ува́ть, -у́ть; провести́ (*pf.*).

humdrum [ˈhʌmdrʌm] *adj.* однообра́зный, ну́дный.

humid [ˈhju:mɪd] *adj.* вла́жный.

humidifier [hju:ˈmɪdɪˌfaɪ(ə)r] *n.* увлажни́тель (*m.*) во́здуха.

humidity [hju:ˈmɪdɪtɪ] *n.* вла́жность.

humiliate [hju:ˈmɪlɪˌeɪt] *v.t.* ун|ижа́ть, -и́зить.

humiliation [hju:ˌmɪlɪˈeɪʃ(ə)n] *n.* униже́ние.

humility [hju:ˈmɪlɪtɪ] *n.* смире́ние; скро́мность.

hummock [ˈhʌmək] *n.* бугóр, пригóрок.

humoresque [ˌhju:məˈresk] *n.* юморе́ска.

humorist [ˈhju:mərɪst] *n.* (*facetious person*) остря́к, весельча́к; (*humorous writer etc.*) юмори́ст.

humorous [ˈhju:mərəs] *adj.* юмористи́ческий; **a ~ author** писа́тель-юмори́ст; **a ~ situation** коми́ческое положе́ние.

humour [ˈhju:mə(r)] *n.* **1.** (*disposition*) нрав, душе́вный склад; **in an ill ~** не в ду́хе; в плохо́м настрое́нии; **this will put you in a good ~** э́то подни́мет вам настрое́ние; **he is out of ~** он не в ду́хе; **I am in no ~ for argument** у меня́ нет настрое́ния спо́рить. **2.** (*amusement*) ю́мор; **his speech was full of ~** в его́ ре́чи бы́ло мно́го ю́мора; **he has little sense of ~** у него́ сла́бое чу́вство ю́мора.

v.t. потака́ть (*impf.*) +*d.*; ублаж|а́ть, -и́ть +*d.*

hump [hʌmp] *n.* **1.** (*protuberance on back*) горб. **2.** (*rounded hillock*) бугóр, бугорóк; **we are over the ~ now** (*fig.*) са́мое тру́дное позади́. **3.** (*fit of depression*) пода́вленное состоя́ние, хандра́; **it gives me the ~** э́то наво́дит на меня́ тоску́.

v.t. (*carry, shoulder*) нести́ (*det.*) (на плеча́х); взва́ливать (*impf.*) на́ спину.

cpd. **~-backed** *adj.* горба́тый.

humus [ˈhju:məs] *n.* гу́мус, перегно́й.

Hun [hʌn] *n.* гунн.

hunch [hʌntʃ] *n.* **1.** (*hump*) горб. **2.** (*US coll., intuitive feeling*) чутьё, интуи́ция; **I had a ~ he would come** я предчу́вствовал, что он придёт; **he acted on a ~** он де́йствовал интуити́вно.

v.t.: **he ~ed (up) his shoulders** он сго́рбился.

cpd. **~-back** *n.* горбу́н.

hundred [ˈhʌndrəd] *n.* (число́, но́мер) сто; (*collect*) со́тня; **about 100** о́коло ста; **100 each** по́ сто; **up to 100** до ста; **page 100** со́тая страни́ца; **room 100** со́тая ко́мната, со́тый но́мер; **a ~ and fifty** сто пятьдеся́т, полтора́ста; **~s of people** со́тни люде́й; **sell by the ~** прод|ава́ть, -а́ть по сто штук; **~s of thousands** со́тни ты́сяч; **I have a ~ and one things to do** я до́лжен сде́лать ку́чу дел; **~ per cent** (*as adj.*) стопроце́нтный; (*adv.*) на сто проце́нтов; **I'm one ~ per cent behind you** я целико́м и по́лностью на ва́шей стороне́; **a ~ to one** наверняка́; **he lived to be a ~** он до́жил до ста лет; **at fourteen ~ hours** (*mil.*) в четы́рнадцать (часо́в) ноль-ноль (мину́т); в 14 ч. ро́вно; **the nineteen ~s** в девятисо́тые го́ды.

adj. сто +*g. pl.*; **two** (*etc. to* **nine**) **~** две́сти, три́ста, четы́реста, пятьсо́т, шестьсо́т, семьсо́т, восемьсо́т, девятьсо́т (*all* +*g. pl.*); **a ~ miles away** (*fig.*) за ты́сячу вёрст; далеко́.

cpds. **~fold** *adj.* стокра́тный; *adv.* в сто раз; **~weight** *n.* (*Imperial — approx. 50.8 kilograms*) англи́йский це́нтнер; (*US — approx. 45.4 kilograms*) америка́нский це́нтнер.

hundredth [ˈhʌndrədθ] *n.* (*fraction*) одна́ со́тая.

adj. со́тый.

Hungarian [hʌŋˈgeərɪən] *n.* (*pers.*) венгр, венге́р|ец (*fem.* -ка).

adj. венге́рский.

Hungary [ˈhʌŋgərɪ] *n.* Ве́нгрия.

hunger [ˈhʌŋgə(r)] *n.* го́лод; (*fig., strong desire*) жа́жда.

v.i. (*fig.*) жа́ждать (*impf.*); **she ~ed for excitement** она́ жа́ждала развлече́ний.

cpd. **~-march** *n.* голо́дный похо́д; **~-strike** *n.* голодо́вка.

hungry [ˈhʌŋgrɪ] *adj.* голо́дный; (*fig., avid*) жа́ждущий; (*fig., of soil*) беспло́дный.

hunk [hʌŋk] *n.* большо́й кусо́к; (*of bread*) ломо́ть (*m.*) хле́ба.

hunky-dory [ˌhʌŋkɪˈdɔ:rɪ] *adj.* (*coll.*): **everything's ~** всё в ажу́ре.

hunt [hʌnt] *n.* **1.** (*~ing expedition*) охо́та. **2.** (*search*) охо́та, по́иск|и (*pl., g.* -ов) (*чего*).

v.t. & i. (*e.g. animals*) охо́титься (*impf.*) (на+*a.*); (*persons or things*) охо́титься (*impf.*) за+*i.*; вести́ (*det.*) по́иски +*g.*

with advs.: **the criminal was ~ed down** престу́пника пойма́ли; **she ~ed out some old clothes** она́ отыска́ла где́-то ста́рую оде́жду; **will you ~ up the address for me?** мо́жете разыска́ть для меня́ э́тот а́дрес?

hunter [ˈhʌntə(r)] *n.* охо́тник.

hunting [ˈhʌntɪŋ] *n.* охо́та.

cpds. **~-crop** *n.* охо́тничий хлыст; **~-ground** *n.* охо́тничье уго́дье; **happy ~-ground(s)** (*fig., heaven*) рай; **~-horn** *n.* охо́тничий рог.

huntsman [ˈhʌntsmən] *n.* охо́тник; е́герь (*m.*).

hurdle [ˈhɜ:d(ə)l] *n.* (*fencing*) (перено́сная) загоро́дка; (*in athletics & fig.*) барье́р, препя́тствие.

v.i. (*engage in ~-jumping*) уча́ствовать в бе́ге с барье́рами.

hurdler [ˈhɜ:dlə(r)] *n.* (*athlete*) барьери́ст (*fem.* -ка).

hurl [hɜ:l] *v.t.* бр|оса́ть, -о́сить; швыр|я́ть, -ну́ть; **he ~ed abuse at me** он осыпа́л меня́ оскорбле́ниями.

hurly-burly [ˈhɜ:lɪˌbɜ:lɪ] *n.* переполо́х, сумя́тица.

hurr|ah [hʊˈrɑ:], **-ay** [hʊˈreɪ] *n. & int.* ура́!

v.t. крича́ть (*impf.*) «ура́».

hurricane [ˈhʌrɪkən, -ˌkeɪn] *n.* урага́н; **~ lamp** фона́рь «мо́лния».

hurr|y [ˈhʌrɪ] *n.* спе́шка, поспе́шность; **what's the ~y?** куда́/заче́м спеши́ть?; **there's no ~y!** спеши́ть не́куда; **she is always in a great ~y** она́ ве́чно торо́пится; **he was in no ~y to go** он не спеши́л уходи́ть; **in his ~y, he forgot his brief-case** в спе́шке он забы́л взять портфе́ль.

v.t. & i. **1.** (*perform hastily*): **don't ~y the job** рабо́тайте не спеша́; **he ~ied over his breakfast** он поспе́шно проглоти́л свой за́втрак; **he had a ~ied meal** он на́скоро перекуси́л. **2.** (*move or cause to move hastily*): **if you ~y him, he'll make mistakes** е́сли вы бу́дете его́ торопи́ть/подгоня́ть, он наде́лает оши́бок; **she ~ied down the road** она́ торопли́во (за)шага́ла вдоль у́лицы.

with advs.: **~y along there, please!** торопи́тесь, пожа́луйста!; **you need not ~y back** не спеши́те возвраща́ться; **he ~ied away, off** он бы́стро удали́лся; **the boy was ~ied off to bed** ма́льчика бы́стро уложи́ли спать; **~y up!** торопи́тесь!; **can't you ~ him up?** ра́зве вы не мо́жете его́ поторопи́ть?

hurt [hɜ:t] *v.t. &i.* (*inflict pain on*): **I won't ~ you** я вам не причиню́ бо́ли (*or* не сде́лаю бо́льно); **my arm ~s** у меня́ боли́т/но́ет рука́; **these shoes ~ (me)** э́ти ту́фли мне жмут; **it didn't ~ a bit** ниско́лько не́ было бо́льно; **where does it ~?** что/где у вас боли́т?; (*damage, harm*) ушиб|а́ть, -и́ть; **he fell and ~ his back** он упа́л и ушиб спи́ну; **~ o.s.** ушиби́ться (*pf.*), уда́риться (*pf.*); **it won't ~ this chair to get wet** от воды́ э́тому сту́лу ничего́ не бу́дет; **it wouldn't ~ to try it** (*coll.*) попы́тка не пы́тка; **it won't ~ to wait** не меша́ло бы подожда́ть; (*offend, pain*): **she was deeply ~ by my remark** моё замеча́ние её о́чень оби́дело; **now you've ~ his feelings** ну вот, вы его́ и оби́дели; **a ~ expression** оби́женное/оскорблённое выраже́ние.

hurtful ['hɜ:tfʊl] *adj.* **1.** (*detrimental*) вре́дный, па́губный. **2.**: **a ~ remark** оби́дное замеча́ние.

hurtle ['hɜ:t(ə)l] *v.t. & i.* нести́сь (*impf.*), мча́ться (*impf.*).

husband ['hʌzbənd] *n.* муж (*pl.* -ья́).

v.t. бере́чь (*impf.*); **we must ~ our resources** мы должны́ бере́чь/эконо́мить на́ши ресу́рсы.

husbandry ['hʌzbəndrɪ] *n.* **1.** (се́льское) хозя́йство; **animal ~** скотово́дство. **2.** (*frugality*) бережли́вость.

hush [hʌʃ] *n.* молча́ние, тишь.

v.t.: **she ~ed the baby to sleep** она́ убаю́кала ребёнка; **the scandal was ~ed up** сканда́л замя́ли.

v.i.: **~!** (*as int.*) ти́ше!; молчи́те!

cpds. **~-~** *adj.* (*coll.*) та́йный, засекре́ченный; **~-money** *n.* взя́тка за молча́ние.

husk [hʌsk] *n.* шелуха́, скорлупа́.

v.t. очища́ть (*impf.*); лущи́ть (*impf.*).

huskiness ['hʌskɪnɪs] *n.* (*hoarseness*) хриплова́тость.

husky[1] ['hʌskɪ] *n.* (*Eskimo dog*) эскимо́сская ла́йка.

husky[2] ['hʌskɪ] *adj.* **1.** (*hoarse*) сухо́й, хри́плый. **2.** (*coll., brawny*) ро́слый, здоро́вый.

hussar [hʊ'zɑ:(r)] *n.* гуса́р.

hussy ['hʌsɪ] *n.* (*pert girl*) де́рзкая девчо́нка; (*trollop*) шлю́ха, потаску́шка.

hustings ['hʌstɪŋz] *n.* (*fig.*) вы́боры (*m. pl.*) в парла́мент.

hustle ['hʌs(ə)l] *n.* су́толока, да́вка.

v.t. **1.** (*jostle*) толка́ть (*impf.*); пиха́ть (*impf.*); **he ~d his way through the crowd** он проти́снулся сквозь толпу́. **2.** (*thrust, impel*): **the police ~d him away** его́ забра́ли полице́йские.

v.i. толка́ться (*impf.*); проти́скиваться (*impf.*); (*act strenuously*) пробива́ться (*impf.*).

hustler ['hʌslə(r)] *n.* (*bustler, strenuous person*) пробивно́й челове́к.

hut [hʌt] *n.* (*small building*) хи́жина; (*barrack*) бара́к.

hutch [hʌtʃ] *n.* (*for pets*) кле́тка.

hyacinth ['haɪəsɪnθ] *n.* гиаци́нт.

hybrid ['haɪbrɪd] *n.* гибри́д.

adj. гибри́дный; сме́шанный.

hydra ['haɪdrə] *n.* ги́дра.

hydrangea [haɪ'dreɪndʒə] *n.* горте́нзия.

hydrant ['haɪdrənt] *n.* гидра́нт.

hydrate ['haɪdreɪt] *n.* гидра́т, гидрооки́сь.

v.t. гидрати́ровать.

hydraulic [haɪ'drɔ:lɪk, -'drɒlɪk] *adj.* гидравли́ческий.

hydraulics [haɪ'drɔ:lɪks, -'drɒlɪks] *n.* гидра́влика.

hydrocarbon [ˌhaɪdrəʊ'kɑ:bən] *n.* углеводоро́д.

hydrochloric [ˌhaɪdrə'klɔ:rɪk, -'klɒrɪk] *adj.*: **~ acid** соля́ная кислота́.

hydrodynamic [ˌhaɪdrəʊdaɪ'næmɪk] *adj.* гидродинами́ческий.

hydroelectric [ˌhaɪdrəʊɪ'lektrɪk] *adj.* гидроэлектри́ческий; **~ power station** гидроэлектроста́нция (*abbr.* ГЭС).

hydrofoil ['haɪdrəˌfɔɪl] *n.* су́дно на подво́дных кры́льях (*abbr.* СПК); раке́та.

hydrogen ['haɪdrədʒ(ə)n] *n.* водоро́д; **~ bomb** водоро́дная бо́мба.

hydrolysis [haɪ'drɒlɪsɪs] *n.* гидро́лиз.

hydrometer [haɪ'drɒmɪtə(r)] *n.* гидро́метр, водоме́р.

hydrophobia [ˌhaɪdrə'fəʊbɪə] *n.* водобоя́знь.

hydroplane ['haɪdrəˌpleɪn] *n.* гидросамолёт.

hydroxide [haɪ'drɒksaɪd] *n.* гидрооки́сь.

hyena [haɪ'i:nə] *n.* гие́на.

hygiene ['haɪdʒi:n] *n.* гигие́на.

hygienic [haɪ'dʒi:nɪk] *adj.* гигиени́ческий.

hymen ['haɪmen] *n.* (*anat.*) де́вственная пле́ва.

hymn [hɪm] *n.* (церко́вный) гимн.

v.t.: **he insists on ~ing my praises** он не перестаёт петь мне дифира́мбы.

cpd. **~-book** *n.* (*also* **hymnal**) сбо́рник церко́вных ги́мнов.

hype [haɪp] *n.* крикли́вая рекла́ма.

adj.: **~d-up** ду́тый, ли́повый.

hyperactive [ˌhaɪpə'ræktɪv] *adj.* чрезме́рно акти́вный.

hyperactivity [ˌhaɪpəræk'tɪvɪtɪ] *n.* повы́шенная акти́вность.

hyperbola [haɪ'pɜ:bələ] *n.* (*geom.*) гипе́рбола.

hyperbole [haɪ'pɜ:bəlɪ] *n.* гипе́рбола, преувеличе́ние.

hyperbolical [ˌhaɪpə'bɒlɪk(ə)l] *adj.* гиперболи́ческий, преувели́ченный.

hypercritical [ˌhaɪpə'krɪtɪk(ə)l] *adj.* приди́рчивый.

hypermarket ['haɪpəˌmɑ:kɪt] *n.* кру́пный универса́м (*в пригороде*).

hypersensitive [ˌhaɪpə'sensɪtɪv] *adj.* с повы́шенной чувстви́тельностью.

hyperspace ['haɪpəˌspeɪs] *n.* гиперпростра́нство.

hypertension [ˌhaɪpə'tenʃ(ə)n] *n.* (*med.*) высо́кое кровяно́е давле́ние.

hypertext ['haɪpəˌtekst] *n.* (*comput.*) гиперте́кст.

hyphen ['haɪf(ə)n] *n.* дефи́с, чёрточка.

hyphenate ['haɪfəˌneɪt] *v.t.* писа́ть, на- че́рез дефи́с/чёрточку.

hypnosis [hɪp'nəʊsɪs] *n.* гипно́з.

hypnotic [hɪp'nɒtɪk] *adj.* гипноти́ческий.

hypnotism ['hɪpnəˌtɪz(ə)m] *n.* гипноти́зм.

hypnotist ['hɪpnətɪst] *n.* гипнотизёр.

hypnotize ['hɪpnəˌtaɪz] *v.t.* гипнотизи́ровать, за-.

hypochondria [ˌhaɪpə'kɒndrɪə] *n.* ипохо́ндрия.

hypochondriac [ˌhaɪpə'kɒndrɪˌæk] *n.* ипохо́ндрик.

hypocrisy [hɪ'pɒkrɪsɪ] *n.* лицеме́рие.

hypocrite ['hɪpəkrɪt] *n.* лицеме́р.

hypocritical [ˌhɪpə'krɪtɪk(ə)l] *adj.* лицеме́рный, неи́скренний.

hypodermic [ˌhaɪpə'dɜ:mɪk] *adj.*: **~ injection** подко́жное впры́скивание; подко́жная инъе́кция; **~ syringe/needle** шприц/игла́ для подко́жных инъе́кций.

hypotenuse [haɪ'pɒtəˌnju:z] *n.* гипотену́за.

hypothermia [ˌhaɪpəʊ'θɜ:mɪə] *n.* гипотерми́я.

hypothesis [haɪ'pɒθɪsɪs] *n.* гипо́теза.

hypothesize [haɪ'pɒθɪˌsaɪz] *v.i.* предпол|ага́ть, -ожи́ть; стро́ить (*impf.*) дога́дки.

hypothetical [ˌhaɪpə'θetɪk(ə)l] *adj.* гипотети́ческий.

hyssop ['hɪsəp] *n.* иссо́п.

hysterectomy [ˌhɪstə'rektəmɪ] *n.* удале́ние ма́тки.

hysteria [hɪ'stɪərɪə] *n.* истери́я.

hysterical [hɪ'sterɪk(ə)l] *adj.* истери́чный; в исте́рике.

hysterics [hɪ'sterɪks] *n.* исте́рика.

I

I [aɪ] *pron.* я; **it is ~** э́то я; **he and ~ were there** мы с ним бы́ли там; **~ too** и я то́же; **he is older than ~** он ста́рше меня́.

iambic [aɪ'æmbɪk] *adj.* ямби́ческий.

iambus [aɪ'æmbəs] *n.* ямб.

ibex ['aɪbeks] *n.* ка́менный козёл, козеро́г.

ibid(em) ['ɪbɪˌdem] *adv.* там же, в том же ме́сте.

ibis ['aɪbɪs] *n.* и́бис.

ICBM (*abbr. of* ***intercontinental ballistic missile***) МБР, (межконтинента́льная баллисти́ческая ракета).

ice [aɪs] *n.* **1.** лёд; **black ~** гололе́дица; **he broke the ~** (*lit., fig.*) он слома́л/разби́л лёд; **the proposal was kept on ~** прое́кт заморо́зили; **~ age** леднико́вый пери́од. **2.** (*~-cream*) моро́женое; **do they sell ~s?** продаётся ли моро́женое?

v.t. **1.** (*freeze*; *of wine, coffee etc., chill*) замор|а́живать, -о́зить. **2.** (*cover with ~*): **the pond was soon ~d over** пруд вскоре затяну́ло/скова́ло льдом. **3.** (*cul.*) глазирова́ть (*impf., pf.*)

cpds. **~bound** *adj.* затёртый/ско́ванный льда́ми; **~-box** *n.* ле́дник, холоди́льник; **~breaker** *n.* ледоко́л; **~-bucket** *n.* ведёрко со льдом; **~-cap** *n.* леднико́вый покро́в; **~-cold** *adj.* ледяно́й; **~-cream** *n.* моро́женое; **~-cream man** моро́женщик; **~-cream parlour** кафе́-моро́женое; **~field** *n.* ледяно́е по́ле; **~-floe** *n.* плаву́чая льди́на; **~-hockey** *n.* хокке́й (на льду); **~-lolly** *n.* (*coll.*) моро́женое на па́лочке; **~-pack** *n.* **1.** (*pack~*) ледяно́й пак, торо́систый лёд. **2.** пузы́рь со льдом; **~-rink** *n.* като́к; **~-show** бале́т на льду́; **~-skate** *n.* конёк; *v.i.* ката́ться (*impf.*) на конька́х.

iceberg ['aɪsbɜ:g] *n.* а́йсберг.

Iceland ['aɪslənd] *n.* Исла́ндия.

ichneumon [ɪk'nju:mən] *n.* **1.** (*animal*) ихневмо́н. **2.** (**~-fly**) нае́здник.

ichthyology [,ɪkθɪ'ɒlədʒɪ] *n.* ихтиоло́гия.

icicle ['aɪsɪk(ə)l] *n.* сосу́лька.

icing ['aɪsɪŋ] *n.* (*on cake*) са́харная глазу́рь; (*of surfaces*) глазиро́вка, обледене́ние.

icon, ikon ['aɪkɒn] *n.* ико́на; о́браз (*pl.* -а́); **~ lamp** лампа́д(к)а.

iconoclasm [aɪ'kɒnə,klæz(ə)m] *n.* иконобо́рство.

iconoclast [aɪ'kɒnə,klæst] *n.* иконобо́рец.

iconoclastic [aɪ,kɒnə'klæstɪk] *adj.* (*fig.*) иконобо́рческий.

iconography [,aɪkə'nɒgrəfɪ] *n.* иконогра́фия.

iconostasis [,aɪkə'nɒstəsɪs, aɪ,kɒnə'stæsɪs] *n.* иконоста́с.

icy ['aɪsɪ] *adj.* (*cold, lit., fig.*) ледяно́й; (*covered with ice*) покры́тый льдом.

ID (*abbr. of* **identification**) удостовере́ние ли́чности; **have you got some ~?** у вас есть удостовере́ние ли́чности?

idea [aɪ'dɪə] *n.* **1.** (*mental concept*) иде́я; **fixed ~** навя́зчивая иде́я; **where did you get that ~?** отку́да вы э́то взя́ли? **2.** (*thought*) мысль; **I can't bear the ~ of it** (одна́) мысль об э́том мне проти́вна; **don't put ~s into his head** не внуша́йте ему́ нену́жных иде́й; **the (very) ~ (of it)!** поду́мать то́лько! **3.** (*notion*; *understanding*) поня́тие; **I've no ~** я поня́тия не име́ю; **he has little ~ of physics** у него́ сла́бое представле́ние о фи́зике; **I have a good ~ of his abilities** я прекра́сно представля́ю себе́, на что он спосо́бен; **he gave me a general ~ of the story** он в о́бщих черта́х пересказа́л мне расска́з. **4.** (*scheme*; *plan*) иде́я, за́мысел; **a bright ~** блестя́щая иде́я; **a man (full) of ~s** челове́к, по́лный иде́й; **my ~ is to start afresh** я ду́маю нача́ть всё снача́ла; **what's the big ~?** (*coll.*) в чём смысл всего́ э́того?; **that's the ~!** вот и́менно!; э́то то, что ну́жно!

ideal [aɪ'di:əl] *n.* идеа́л.

adj. идеа́льный; соверше́нный; превосхо́дный.

idealism [aɪ'dɪə,lɪz(ə)m] *n.* идеали́зм.

idealist [aɪ'dɪəlɪst] *n.* идеали́ст.

idealistic [aɪ,dɪə'lɪstɪk] *adj.* идеалисти́ческий.

idealize [aɪ'dɪə,laɪz] *v.t.* идеализи́ровать (*impf., pf.*).

idée fixe [,i:deɪ 'fi:ks] *n.* навя́зчивая иде́я, иде́я фикс.

identical [aɪ'dentɪk(ə)l] *adj.* **1.** (*the same*): **the ~ room where he was born** та са́мая ко́мната, в кото́рой он роди́лся. **2.** (*exactly similar*) тожде́ственный, иденти́чный; **the handwriting in the two manuscripts is ~** по́черк обе́их ру́кописей иденти́чен; **~ twins** однояйцевые близнецы́.

identification [aɪ,dentɪfɪ'keɪʃ(ə)n] *n.* (*recognition*; *establishing identity*): **~ of a body** опозна́ние тру́па; **~ of a prisoner** установле́ние ли́чности аресто́ванного; (*attr.*) опознава́тельный; **~/identity disc** ли́чный знак; **~ marks** опознава́тельные зна́ки; **~ papers** докуме́нты, удостоверя́ющие ли́чность; **~ parade** процеду́ра опозна́ния подозрева́емого (свиде́телем и́ли пострада́вшим).

identif|y [aɪ'dentɪ,faɪ] *v.t.* **1.** (*recognize*; *establish identity of*) опозн|ава́ть, -а́ть; устан|а́вливать, -ови́ть ли́чность +*g.* **2.** (*associate*), *also v.i.* (*coll.*): **he ~ied (himself) with the movement** он солидаризова́лся с э́тим движе́нием.

identity [aɪ'dentɪtɪ] *n.* **1.** (*sameness*) иденти́чность, тожде́ственность. **2.** (*who one is*) ли́чность; **he proved his ~** он предста́вил удостовере́ние свое́й ли́чности; **a case of mistaken ~** (суде́бная/сле́дственная) оши́бка в установле́нии престу́пника *и т.п.*; **~ card** удостовере́ние ли́чности.

ideo|gram ['ɪdɪə,græm], **-graph** ['ɪdɪə,grɑ:f] *nn.* идеогра́мма.

ideological [,aɪdɪə'lɒdʒɪk(ə)l] *adj.* идеологи́ческий, иде́йный.

ideologist [,aɪdɪə'ɒlədʒɪst] *n.* идео́лог.

ideology [,aɪdɪ'ɒlədʒɪ] *n.* идеоло́гия.

Ides [aɪdz] *n.* и́д|ы (*pl., g.* —).

idiocy ['ɪdɪəsɪ] *n.* (*mental condition*) идиоти́зм; (*med.*) слабоу́мие; (*stupidity*; *stupid behaviour*) идио́тство.

idiom ['ɪdɪəm] *n.* (*expression*) идио́ма; (*language*; *way of speaking*) наре́чие, го́вор, язы́к.

idiomatic [,ɪdɪə'mætɪk] *adj.* идиомати́ческий; **he speaks ~ Russian** он свобо́дно владе́ет ру́сским языко́м; он говори́т по-ру́сски как ру́сский.

idiosyncrasy [,ɪdɪəʊ'sɪŋkrəsɪ] *n.* своеобра́зие.

idiosyncratic [,ɪdɪəʊsɪn'krætɪk] *adj.* своеобра́зный.

idiot ['ɪdɪət] *n.* идио́т, дура́к; **a drivelling ~** кру́глый дура́к; **don't be an ~** (*coll.*) не валя́йте дурака́.

idiotic [ɪdɪ'ɒtɪk] *adj.* идио́тский, дура́цкий.

idle ['aɪd(ə)l] *adj.* **1.** (*not working*) нерабо́тающий, безде́йствующий; (*unemployed*) безрабо́тный; **the strike made thousands ~** из-за забасто́вки ты́сячи люде́й оказа́лись без рабо́ты; (*unoccupied*) неза́нятый, свобо́дный; (*inactive*) безде́ятельный; **he stands ~ while others work** он безде́льничает, пока́ други́е рабо́тают; (*of factories etc.*) безде́йствующий; (*of machinery*) простаи́вающий; **the machines stood ~ all week** маши́ны простоя́ли це́лую неде́лю; (*of time*): **in an ~ moment** в свобо́дную мину́ту. **2.** (*lazy*; *slothful*) пра́здный, лени́вый; **he leads an ~ existence** он ведёт пра́здную жизнь. **3.** (*purposeless*): **out of ~ curiosity** из пра́здного/пусто́го любопы́тства; **~ talk** пуста́я болтовня́; (*fruitless*; *vain*): **an ~ attempt** напра́сное уси́лие; **~ hopes** пусты́е/тще́тные наде́жды; **~ dreams** пусты́е мечты́.

v.t.: **he ~d away his life** он растра́тил свою́ жизнь впусту́ю.

v.i. **1.** (*be ~*) безде́льничать (*impf.*); **stop idling about!** переста́ньте безде́льничать! **2.** (*of an engine*): **the motor ~s well** мото́р хорошо́ рабо́тает на холосто́м ходу́.

idleness ['aɪdəlnɪs] *n.* пра́здность; безде́лье.

idler ['aɪdlə(r)] *n.* безде́льник, лентя́й.

idly ['aɪdlɪ] *adv.* лени́во; (*absently*) рассе́янно.

idol ['aɪd(ə)l] *n.* и́дол, куми́р; **the ~ of the public** люби́мец пу́блики.

idolater [aɪ'dɒlətə(r)] *n.* идолопокло́нник.

idolatrous [aɪ'dɒlətrəs] *adj.* идолопокло́ннический.

idolatry [aɪ'dɒlətrɪ] *n.* идолопокло́нство.

idolize ['aɪdə,laɪz] *v.t.* обоготвор|я́ть, -и́ть; (*fig.*)

боготвори́ть (*impf.*); обожа́ть (*impf.*).

idyll [ˈɪdɪl] *n.* иди́ллия.

idyllic [ɪˈdɪlɪk] *adj.* идилли́ческий.

i.e. (*abbr. of* **id est**) т.е., (то есть).

if [ɪf] *n.*: **I want no ~s and buts** (я не хочу́ слы́шать) никаки́х отгово́рок; **there are no ~s about it** никаки́х «е́сли»!; **it is a very big ~** э́то ещё большо́й вопро́с.

conj. **1.** (*condition or supposition*) е́сли, е́сли бы; **~ he is reading** е́сли он чита́ет; **~ he were reading** е́сли бы он чита́л; **~ he comes** е́сли он придёт; **~ I were you** на ва́шем ме́сте; **~ necessary** е́сли необходи́мо; **~ so** е́сли так; **~ anything she is more stupid than he** е́сли уж на то пошло́, она́ глупе́е его́; **hold on, ~ not you'll fall** держи́тесь, а то упадёте; **~ only they arrive in time!** хоть бы они́ прие́хали во́время!; **~ only I had known!** е́сли бы я то́лько знал!; **~ only to please him** хотя́ бы для того́, что́бы доста́вить ему́ удово́льствие; **he talks as ~ he were the boss** он говори́т, как бу́дто он нача́льник; **he stood there as ~ dumb** он стоя́л, бу́дто немо́й; **as ~ by chance** бу́дто бы случа́йно; **as ~ you didn't know!** как бу́дто вы не зна́ли!; **even ~** е́сли да́же. **2.** (*though*) хотя́, пусть; **~ they are poor, they are nevertheless happy** хотя́ они́ и бедны́, они́ всё же сча́стливы; **a pleasant, ~ chilly, day** прия́тный, хотя́ и прохла́дный день. **3.** (*whether*): **do you know ~ he is at home?** вы не зна́ете, он до́ма?; **see ~ the door is locked** посмотри́те, заперта́ ли дверь.

igloo [ˈɪglu:] *n.* и́глу (*nt. indecl.*).

igneous [ˈɪgnɪəs] *adj.* (*of rock*) изве́рженный, пироге́нный; вулкани́ческого происхожде́ния.

ignite [ɪgˈnaɪt] *v.t. & i.* заж|ига́ть(ся), -е́чь(ся); воспламен|я́ть(ся), -и́ть(ся).

ignition [ɪgˈnɪʃ(ə)n] *n.* (*igniting*) зажига́ние, воспламене́ние; (*~ system in engine*) зажига́ние; **~ key** ключ зажига́ния.

ignoble [ɪgˈnəʊb(ə)l] *adj.* (*base*) по́длый, ни́зкий, посты́дный; (*of lowly birth*) ни́зкого происхожде́ния.

ignominious [ˌɪgnəˈmɪnɪəs] *adj.* позо́рный, посты́дный; **an ~ death** бессла́вная смерть.

ignominy [ˈɪgnəmɪnɪ] *n.* (*dishonour*) позо́р, бесче́стье.

ignoramus [ˌɪgnəˈreɪməs] *n.* неве́жда.

ignorance [ˈɪgnərəns] *n.* (*in general*) неве́жество; **he displayed total ~** он обнару́жил по́лное неве́жество; (*of certain facts*) незна́ние, неве́дение; **he did it in ~ of the facts** он сде́лал э́то по незна́нию фа́ктов (*or* по неве́дению); **in a state of blissful ~** в состоя́нии блаже́нного неве́дения.

ignorant [ˈɪgnərənt] *adj.* неве́жественный; **~ of music** несве́дущий в му́зыке; **I was ~ of his intentions** я не знал о его́ наме́рениях.

ignore [ɪgˈnɔ:(r)] *v.t.* игнори́ровать (*impf., pf.*); не обра|ща́ть, -ти́ть внима́ния на+*a*.

iguana [ɪgˈwɑ:nə] *n.* игуа́на.

ikon [ˈaɪkɒn] = **icon**

ilk [ɪlk] *n.*: **and others of his ~** (*coll.*) и други́е того́ же ро́да; и ему́ подо́бные.

ill [ɪl] *n.* **1.** (*evil, harm*) зло; **I meant him no ~** я не жела́л ему́ зла. **2.** (*pl., misfortunes*) бе́ды (*f. pl.*), несча́стья (*nt. pl.*).

adj. **1.** (*unwell*) больно́й, нездоро́вый; **he looks ~** он вы́глядит больны́м; **he was taken** (*or* **fell**) **~ of a fever** он заболе́л лихора́дкой; **I feel ~** мне нехорошо́; я пло́хо себя́ чу́вствую; **the mentally ~** психи́чески больны́е. **2.** (*bad*): **~ effects** па́губные после́дствия; **~ fame, repute** дурна́я сла́ва; плоха́я репута́ция; **~ feeling** неприя́знь, вражде́бность, оби́да; **I did it to show there was no ~ feeling** я сде́лал э́то, что́бы показа́ть, что я не пита́ю оби́ды; **~ fortune** несча́стье, неуда́ча; **~ health** нездоро́вье; **~ humour, temper** (*disposition*) дурно́й нрав/хара́ктер; (*mood*) дурно́е настрое́ние; **as ~ luck would have it** как на зло; по несча́стью; **a run of ~ luck** полоса́ невезе́нья; **~ treatment** дурно́е обраще́ние; **~ will** зла́я во́ля, зло́ба; *see also* **~ feeling; I bear you no ~ will** я не жела́ю вам зла; **it's an ~ wind (that blows nobody any good)** нет ху́да без добра́.

adv. пло́хо, ду́рно; **~ at ease** не по себе́; **I can ~ afford it** я с трудо́м могу́ себе́ э́то позво́лить; **it ~ becomes you** э́то вам не идёт; **he took it ~ that ...** он оби́делся на то, что...; **I have never spoken ~ of him** я никогда́ не отзыва́лся о нём пло́хо.

cpds. **~-advised** *adj.* не(благо)разу́мный; **~-bred, ~-mannered** *adjs.* невоспи́танный, пло́хо воспи́танный; **~-considered, ~-judged** *adjs.* необду́манный; **~-defined** *adj.* неопределённый; **~-disposed** *adj.* (*malicious*) зло́бный; (*unfavourable*) недоброжела́тельный (*к кому*); не располо́жен (*к кому*); **~-fated** *adj.* злосча́стный, рокова́й; **~-favoured** *adj.* (*in appearance*) непривлека́тельный, некраси́вый; **~-gotten** *adj.* нече́стно на́житый; **~-informed** *adj.* пло́хо осведомлённый; **~-intentioned** *adj.* злове́дный, злонаме́ренный; **~judged** *adj.* = **~-considered; ~-mannered** *adj.* = **~-bred; ~-starred** *adj.* злосча́стный; **~-tempered** *adj.* вспы́льчивый, зло́бный; **~-timed** *adj.* несвоевре́менный; **~-treat, ~-use** *v.t.* пло́хо об|ходи́ться, -ойти́сь с+*i.*; пло́хо обраща́ться (*impf.*) с+*i.*; **~-will** *n.* недоброжела́тельность, вражде́бность.

illegal [ɪˈli:g(ə)l] *adj.* незако́нный, нелега́льный.

illegality [ˌɪli:ˈgælɪtɪ] *n.* незако́нность, нелега́льность.

illegibility [ɪˌledʒɪˈbɪlɪtɪ] *n.* неразбо́рчивость.

illegible [ɪˈledʒɪb(ə)l] *adj.* неразбо́рчивый, неудобочита́емый.

illegitimacy [ˌɪlɪˈdʒɪtɪməsɪ] *n.* (*of action*) незако́нность; (*of birth*) незаконнорождённость.

illegitimate [ˌɪlɪˈdʒɪtɪmət] *adj.* (*of action*) незако́нный; (*of pers.*) незаконнорождённый.

illiberal [ɪˈlɪbər(ə)l] *adj.* (*unenlightened*) непросвещённый; (*narrow-minded*) ограни́ченный; (*intolerant*) нетерпи́мый.

illicit [ɪˈlɪsɪt] *adj.* незако́нный, недозво́ленный.

illiteracy [ɪˈlɪtərəsɪ] *n.* негра́мотность.

illiterate [ɪˈlɪtərət] *n.* негра́мотный.

adj. (*esp. of pers.*) негра́мотный; (*esp. of writing*) безгра́мотный.

illness [ˈɪlnɪs] *n.* боле́знь; **he caught a serious ~** он зарази́лся тяжёлой боле́знью; **she had a long ~** она́ перенесла́ дли́тельную боле́знь; **he was absent through ~** он отсу́тствовал по боле́зни; (*ill-health*) нездоро́вье, сла́бое здоро́вье; (*incidence of ~*) заболева́емость; **has there been much ~ in your family?** страда́ли ли чле́ны ва́шей семьи́ серьёзными заболева́ниями?; (*onset of ~*) заболева́ние.

illogical [ɪˈlɒdʒɪk(ə)l] *adj.* нелоги́чный.

illogicality [ɪˌlɒdʒɪˈkælɪtɪ] *n.* нелоги́чность.

illuminat|e [ɪˈlu:mɪˌneɪt, ɪˈlju:-] *v.t.* **1.** (*light*) осве|ща́ть, -ти́ть; **an ~ed sign** светя́щаяся рекла́ма. **2.** (*decorate with lights*) иллюмини́ровать (*impf., pf.*); **the town was ~ed for the festival** к пра́зднику в го́роде устро́или иллюмина́цию. **3.** (*of manuscripts etc.*) иллюмини́ровать (*impf., pf.*); **an ~ed manuscript** заста́вочная ру́копись. **4.** (*shed light on; explain*) осве|ща́ть, -ти́ть; прол|ива́ть, -и́ть свет на+*a.*; **an ~ing talk** поучи́тельная бесе́да.

illumination [ɪˌlu:mɪˈneɪʃ(ə)n, ɪˈlju:-] *n.* **1.** освеще́ние. **2.** иллюмина́ция. **3.** (*of manuscript*) заста́вка.

illusion [ɪˈlu:ʒ(ə)n, ɪˈlju:-] *n.* иллю́зия, обма́н; **optical ~** опти́ческая иллю́зия, обма́н зре́ния; **I was under an ~** я был во вла́сти иллю́зии.

illus|ive [ɪˈlu:sɪv, ɪˈlju:-], **-ory** [ɪˈlu:sərɪ, ɪˈlju:-] *adjs.* иллюзо́рный, при́зрачный.

illustrate [ˈɪləˌstreɪt] *v.t.* **1.** (*decorate with pictures*) иллюстри́ровать (*impf., pf.*). **2.** (*make clear by examples*) иллюстри́ровать; поясн|я́ть, -и́ть; **this ~s the advantages of cooperation** э́то пока́зывает преиму́щества сотру́дничества.

illustration [ˌɪləˈstreɪʃ(ə)n] *n.* иллюстри́рование; иллюстра́ция, поясне́ние.

illustrative [ˈɪləstrətɪv] *adj.* иллюстрати́вный, поясни́тельный.

illustrator [ˈɪləˌstreɪtə(r)] *n.* иллюстра́тор.

illustrious [ɪˈlʌstrɪəs] *adj.* просла́вленный, знамени́тый.

image [ˈɪmɪdʒ] *n.* **1.** (*representation*) изображе́ние. **2.** (*statue*) ста́туя, скульпту́ра; **graven ~** и́дол, куми́р. **3.** (*likeness; counterpart*) ко́пия, портре́т; **he was the ~ of his father** он был то́чной ко́пией своего́ отца́. **4.** (*idea; conception*) о́браз. **5.** (*simile or metaphor*) о́браз. **6.** (*opt.*) изображе́ние; (*reflection*) отраже́ние. **7.** (*impression made on others*) репута́ция, прести́ж.

imagery [ˈɪmɪdʒərɪ] *n.* (*in writing*) о́бразность.

imaginable [ɪˈmædʒɪnəb(ə)l] *adj.* вообрази́мый; **we had the greatest trouble ~** у нас бы́ли невообрази́мые хло́поты.

imaginary [ɪˈmædʒɪnərɪ] *adj.* вообража́емый, вы́мышленный; (*also math.*) мни́мый.

imagination [ɪˌmædʒɪˈneɪʃ(ə)n] *n.* воображе́ние; **use your ~!** напряги́те своё воображе́ние!

imaginative [ɪˈmædʒɪnətɪv] *adj.* с воображе́нием; облада́ющий (бога́тым) воображе́нием; **~ writing** худо́жественная литерату́ра, беллетри́стика.

imagin|e [ɪˈmædʒɪn] *v.t.* **1.** (*form mental picture of*) вообра|жа́ть, -зи́ть; **she is always ~ing things** ей ве́чно что́-то мере́щится. **2.** (*conceive*) предст|авля́ть, -а́вить себе́; **I cannot ~e how it happened** я не могу́ предста́вить себе́ как э́то случи́лось. **3.** (*suppose*) предпол|ага́ть, -ожи́ть; полага́ть (*impf.*); **do you ~e I like it?** неуже́ли вы полага́ете, что мне э́то нра́вится? **4.** (*think*) ду́мать, по-; **I ~ed I heard footsteps** мне показа́лось, что я слы́шал шаги́. **5.** (*fancy*): **~e seeing you here!** кто бы мог поду́мать, что я уви́жу вас здесь? **6.** (*guess*) дога́д|ываться, -а́ться; пон|има́ть, -я́ть; **I cannot ~e what you mean** ума́ не приложу́, что вы име́ете в виду́.

imbalance [ɪmˈbæləns] *n.* отсу́тствие равнове́сия, неусто́йчивость; несоотве́тствие.

imbecile [ˈɪmbɪˌsiːl] *n.* (*person of weak intellect*) крети́н; слабоу́мный; (*fool*) глупе́ц, дура́к (*coll.*).

adj. слабоу́мный; (*stupid*) глу́пый.

imbecility [ˌɪmbɪˈsɪlɪtɪ] *n.* имбеци́льность; слабоу́мие; (*stupidity*) глу́пость.

imbib|e [ɪmˈbaɪb] *v.t.* (*drink*) погло|ща́ть, -ти́ть; пить, вы́-; (*fig., assimilate*) усв|а́ивать, -о́ить; впи́т|ывать, -а́ть; **he ~ed new ideas** он впита́л но́вые иде́и.

imbue [ɪmˈbjuː] *v.t.* **1.** (*lit., saturate*) пропи́т|ывать, -а́ть; (*dye*) окра́|шивать, -сить. **2.** (*fig., inspire*) всел|я́ть, -и́ть (*что в кого*); (*fill*): **~d with hatred** прони́кнутый не́навистью.

imitate [ˈɪmɪˌteɪt] *v.t.* **1.** (*follow example of*) подража́ть (*impf.*) +*d.*. **2.** (*copy; mimic*) копи́ровать (*impf.*); имити́ровать (*impf.*); передра́зн|ивать, -и́ть. **3.** (*make sth. similar to*) имити́ровать (*impf.*); подде́л|ывать, -ать; **fabric made to ~ silk** материа́л, имити́рующий шёлк.

imitation [ˌɪmɪˈteɪʃ(ə)n] *n.* **1.** (*imitating; mimicry*) подража́ние; **in ~ of her teacher** в подража́ние своему́ учи́телю; **(built in) ~ Gothic** постро́енный в псевдоготи́ческом сти́ле; **he does bird ~s** он уме́ет подража́ть пти́цам. **2.** (*copy*) имита́ция, подде́лка; **wood painted in ~ of marble** де́рево, окра́шенное под мра́мор; **beware of ~s!** остерега́йтесь подде́лок; (*attr.*) иску́сственный, подде́льный; **~ leather** иску́сственная ко́жа; **~ antiques** подде́льные антиква́рные изде́лия.

imitative [ˈɪmɪtətɪv] *adj.*: **~ words** звукоподража́тельные слова́; **the ~ arts** изобрази́тельные иску́сства; **~ behaviour** подража́тельное поведе́ние.

imitator [ˈɪmɪˌteɪtə(r)] *n.* подража́тель (*fem.* -ница).

immaculate [ɪˈmækjʊlət] *adj.* **1.** (*pure*) незапя́тнанный; **the I~ Conception** непоро́чное зача́тие. **2.** (*faultless*) безупре́чный, безукори́зненный.

immaterial [ˌɪməˈtɪərɪəl] *adj.* (*not corporeal*) невеще́ственный; (*unimportant*) несуще́ственный; **it is quite ~ to me** мне реши́тельно всё равно́.

immature [ˌɪməˈtjʊə(r)] *adj.* незре́лый.

immaturity [ˌɪməˈtjʊərɪtɪ] *n.* незре́лость.

immeasurable [ɪˈmeʒərəb(ə)l] *adj.* неизмери́мый.

immediacy [ɪˈmiːdɪəsɪ] *n.* **1.** (*directness*) непосре́дственность. **2.** (*in time*) незамедли́тельность; (*urgency*) безотлага́тельность.

immediate [ɪˈmiːdɪət] *adj.* **1.** (*direct, closest possible*) непосре́дственный, прямо́й, ближа́йший; **in the ~ neighbourhood** в непосре́дственной бли́зости; **my ~ neighbours** мои́ ближа́йшие сосе́ди; **on his ~ left** сра́зу нале́во от него́; **in the ~ future** в ближа́йшем бу́дущем. **2.** (*without delay*) неме́дленный, мгнове́нный; **there was an ~ silence** наступи́ла мгнове́нная тишина́.

immediately [ɪˈmiːdɪətlɪ] *adv.* (*directly*) непосре́дственно; (*without delay, at once*) неме́дленно, то́тчас (же), сра́зу, мгнове́нно.

conj.: **~ I heard the news** как то́лько я узна́л но́вости.

immemorial [ˌɪmɪˈmɔːrɪəl] *adj.* незапа́мятный; **from time ~** с незапа́мятных времён.

immense [ɪˈmens] *adj.* (*huge*) огро́мный, грома́дный; (*vast*) безме́рный, необозри́мый; (*coll., very great*): **it was an ~ disappointment** э́то бы́ло огро́мным разочарова́нием; **we enjoyed ourselves ~ly** мы получи́ли огро́мное удово́льствие; **she was ~ly proud of her son** она́ невероя́тно горди́лась свои́м сы́ном.

immensity [ɪˈmensɪtɪ] *n.* безме́рность, необъя́тность.

immerse [ɪˈmɜːs] *v.t.* **1.** погр|ужа́ть, -зи́ть; окун|а́ть, -у́ть; **~d in thought** погружённый в ду́му. **2.** (*fig., entangle*) запу́т|ывать, -ать.

immersion [ɪˈmɜːʃ(ə)n] *n.* (*lit., fig.*) погруже́ние; **~ heater** погружа́емый нагрева́тель.

immigrant [ˈɪmɪɡrənt] *n.* иммигра́нт (*fem.* -ка).

immigrate [ˈɪmɪˌɡreɪt] *v.i.* иммигри́ровать (*impf., pf.*).

immigration [ˌɪmɪˈɡreɪʃ(ə)n] *n.* иммигра́ция; **~ officer** сотру́дник иммиграцио́нного ве́домства (*or* иммиграцио́нной слу́жбы).

imminence [ˈɪmɪnəns] *n.* нави́сшая угро́за, опа́сность.

imminent [ˈɪmɪnənt] *adj.* надвига́ющийся; **a storm was ~** надвига́лась гроза́; (*of danger*) непосре́дственный.

immobile [ɪˈməʊbaɪl] *adj.* неподви́жный.

immobility [ˌɪməʊˈbɪlɪtɪ] *n.* неподви́жность.

immobilization [ɪˌməʊbɪlaɪˈzeɪʃ(ə)n] *n.* (*med.*) дли́тельный посте́льный режи́м; (*of limb etc.*) иммобилиза́ция; (*of troops*) ско́вывание.

immobilize [ɪˈməʊbɪˌlaɪz] *v.t.* иммобилизова́ть (*pf.*); (*mil.*) ско́в|ывать, -а́ть; парализова́ть (*impf., pf.*); **our troops were ~d** на́ши войска́ бы́ли парализо́ваны; **I was ~d by a broken leg** я не мог дви́гаться из-за сло́манной ноги́.

immoderate [ɪˈmɒdərət] *adj.* неуме́ренный.

immodest [ɪˈmɒdɪst] *adj.* нескро́мный; (*indecent*) неприли́чный.

immodesty [ɪˈmɒdɪstɪ] *n.* нескро́мность; (*indecency*) неприли́чие.

immolate [ˈɪməˌleɪt] *v.t.* (*lit., fig.*) прин|оси́ть, -ести́ в же́ртву.

immolation [ˌɪməˈleɪʃ(ə)n] *n.* жертвоприноше́ние.

immoral [ɪ'mɒr(ə)l] *adj.* безнрáвственный; ~ **earnings** сомни́тельные дохóды.
immorality [ˌɪmə'rælɪtɪ] *n.* безнрáвственность.
immortal [ɪ'mɔ:t(ə)l] *n. & adj.* бессмéртный; ~ **fame** неувядáемая слáва.
immortality [ˌɪmɔ:'tælɪtɪ] *n.* бессмéртие.
immortalization [ɪˌmɔ:təlaɪ'zeɪʃ(ə)n] *n.* увековéчение.
immortalize [ɪ'mɔ:təˌlaɪz] *v.t.* увековéчи|вать, -ть; обессмéртить (*pf.*).
immovable [ɪ'mu:vəb(ə)l] *adj.* (*that cannot be moved*; *stationary*; *fixed, e.g. of property*) недви́жимый; (*motionless*) неподви́жный; недви́жимый; (*steadfast*) непоколеби́мый.
immune [ɪ'mju:n] *adj.*: ~ **to disease** невосприи́мчивый к болéзни; ~ **against poison** иммýнный к я́ду; ~ **from criticism** неподвлáстный кри́тике; ~ **from taxes** свобóдный/освобождённый от налóгов.
immunity [ɪ'mju:nɪtɪ] *n.* **1.** (*from disease etc.*) невосприи́мчивость, иммуни́тéт (*к чему*). **2.** (*in law*) неприкосновéнность, иммуни́тéт; **diplomatic** ~ дипломати́ческий иммуни́тéт. **3.** (*from tax*) освобождéние (от налóга).
immunization [ˌɪmju:naɪ'zeɪʃ(ə)n] *n.* иммунизáция.
immunize ['ɪmju:ˌnaɪz] *v.t.* иммунизи́ровать (*impf.*, *pf.*) (*кого к чему*).
immunology [ˌɪmju:'nɒlədʒɪ] *n.* иммунолóгия.
immunotherapy [ˌɪmju:nəʊ'θerəpɪ] *n.* иммунотерапи́я.
immutable [ɪ'mju:təb(ə)l] *adj.* неизмéнный, непрелóжный.
imp [ɪmp] *n.* (*lit.*; *fig., mischievous child*) чертёнок, бесёнок; (*fig. only*) пострéл.
impact ['ɪmpækt] *n.* (*collision*) столкновéние; (*striking force*) удáр, толчóк; (*fig., effect, influence*) воздéйствие, влия́ние; **his words made an immediate** ~ егó словá возымéли немéдленное дéйствие.
impair [ɪm'peə(r)] *v.t.* (*damage*) повре|ждáть, -ди́ть; (*spoil*) пóртить, ис-; (*undermine*) под|рывáть, -орвáть; (*weaken*) осл|абля́ть, -áбить; (*make worse*) ух|удшáть, -ýдшить; **smoking will** ~ **your health** курéние подорвёт вáше здорóвье; **his vision was** ~**ed** егó зрéние пострадáло.
impairment [ɪm'peəmənt] *n.* повреждéние; пóрча; подры́в; ослаблéние; ухудшéние.
impale [ɪm'peɪl] *v.t.* прок|áлывать, -олóть; пронз|áть, -и́ть; (*hist.*) сажáть, посади́ть нá кол; **he** ~**d himself on his sword** он пронзи́л себя́ мечóм.
impart [ɪm'pɑ:t] *v.t.* **1.** (*lend*; *give*) прид|авáть, -áть; **he** ~**ed a serious tone to the conversation** он придáл разговóру серьёзный тон. **2.** (*communicate, e.g. news*) перед|авáть, -áть; сообщ|áть, -и́ть. **3.** (*pass on, e.g. knowledge*) дели́ться, по- +*i.*; **he** ~**ed his skill to** он подели́лся с нáми свои́м умéнием.
impartial [ɪm'pɑ:ʃ(ə)l] *adj.* беспристрáстный.
impartiality [ɪmˌpɑ:ʃɪ'ælɪtɪ] *n.* беспристрáстность.
impassable [ɪm'pɑ:səb(ə)l] *adj.* (*on foot*) непроходи́мый; (*for vehicles*) непроéзжий.
impasse ['æmpæs, 'ɪm-] *n.* (*lit., fig.*) тупи́к; **things reached an** ~ делá зашли́ в тупи́к.
impassioned [ɪm'pæʃ(ə)nd] *adj.* стрáстный, пы́лкий.
impassive [ɪm'pæsɪv] *adj.* (*unmoved*) бесстрáстный; (*serene*) безмятéжный.
impassivity [ˌɪmpæ'sɪvɪtɪ] *n.* бесстрáстие; безмятéжность.
impatience [ɪm'peɪʃəns] *n.* нетерпéние, нетерпели́вость; **he was all** ~ **to begin** емý не терпéлось начáть; (*irritation*) раздражéние.
impatient [ɪm'peɪʃ(ə)nt] *adj.* нетерпели́вый; (*irritable*) раздражи́тельный; **he was growing, getting** ~ он теря́л терпéние, он раздражáлся; **she was** ~ **for a letter** онá нетерпели́во ждалá письмá; **he is** ~ **to begin** емý не тéрпится начáть.
impeach [ɪm'pi:tʃ] *v.t.* **1.** (*accuse*) обвин|я́ть, -и́ть (*кого в чём*); **he was** ~**ed (for treason)** емý предъяви́ли обвинéние в госудáрственной измéне. **2.** (*call in question*) осп|áривать, -óрить; **are you** ~**ing my honour?** неужéли вы стáвите под сомнéние мою честь?
impeachment [ɪm'pi:tʃmənt] *n.* **1.** (*accusation*) обвинéние; (*on charge of treason etc.*) импи́чмент. **2.** (*calling in question*) выражéние сомнéния в+*p.* (*or* недовéрия +*d.*).
impeccable [ɪm'pekəb(ə)l] *adj.* (*without sin*) непогреши́мый; (*faultless*) безупрéчный.
impecunious [ˌɪmpɪ'kju:nɪəs] *adj.* безде́нежный.
impedance [ɪm'pi:d(ə)ns] *n.* (*elec.*) пóлное сопротивлéние; импедáнс.
impede [ɪm'pi:d] *v.t.* (*obstruct*) препя́тствовать (*impf.*) +*d.*; прегра|ждáть, -ди́ть; (*delay*) задéрж|ивать, -áть; (*hinder*) мешáть, по- (*кому/чему*); затрудн|я́ть, -и́ть; **the traffic was** ~**d** ýличное движéние бы́ло задéржано.
impediment [ɪm'pedɪmənt] *n.* **1.** (*obstruction*) препя́тствие, преграда, помéха; (*hindrance, delay*) задéржка; **an** ~ **to progress** препя́тствие на пути́ прогрéсса. **2.** (*speech defect*) заикáние; **he has an** ~ **in his speech** он заикáется.
impel [ɪm'pel] *v.t.* **1.** (*propel*) прив|оди́ть, -ести́ в движéние. **2.** (*drive*; *force*) прин|уждáть, -ýдить; заст|авля́ть, -áвить; побу|ждáть, -ди́ть; **conscience** ~**led him to speak the truth** сóвесть принýдила егó говори́ть прáвду; **I feel** ~**led to say** я вы́нужден сказáть.
impend [ɪm'pend] *v.i.* **1.** (*be imminent*; *approach*) надв|игáться, -и́нуться; прибл|ижáться, -и́зиться; **war was** ~**ing** войнá надвигáлась; **his** ~**ing arrival** егó предстоя́щий приéзд. **2.** (*threaten*) угрожáть (*impf.*); нав|исáть, -и́снуть; ~**ing danger** нави́сшая опáсность.
impenetrability [ɪmˌpenɪtrə'bɪlɪtɪ] *n.* (*lit., fig.*) непроницáемость.
impenetrable [ɪm'penɪtrəb(ə)l] *adj.* непроницáемый; **an** ~ **forest** непроходи́мый лес; **an** ~ **mystery** непостижи́мая тáйна; ~ **darkness** непрогля́дная тьма.
impenitent [ɪm'penɪt(ə)nt] *adj.* нераскáянный, закоснéлый.
imperative [ɪm'perətɪv] *n.* (*gram.*) повели́тельное наклонéние, императи́в.
adj. **1.** (*urgent*; *essential*): **an** ~ **request** настоя́тельное трéбование; **it is** ~ **that you come at once** вам необходи́мо тóтчас яви́ться. **2.** (*gram.*) повели́тельный.
imperceptible [ˌɪmpə'septɪb(ə)l] *adj.* (*that cannot be perceived*) незамéтный; (*very slight, gradual*) незначи́тельный.
imperfect [ɪm'pɜ:fɪkt] *n.* (*gram.*) прошéдшее несовершённое врéмя, имперфéкт.
adj. (*faulty*) несовершéнный; (*incomplete*) непóлный; (*gram.*) прошéдший, несовершéнный.
imperfection [ˌɪmpə'fekʃ(ə)n] *n.* (*incompleteness, faultiness*) несовершéнство, неполнотá; (*fault*) дефéкт, изъя́н; недостáток.
imperfective [ˌɪmpə'fektɪv] *n. & adj.* (*gram.*) несовершéнный (вид).
imperial [ɪm'pɪərɪəl] *adj.* **1.** (*of an empire*) импéрский; ~ **Rome/Russia** Ри́мская/Росси́йская импéрия. **2.** (*of an emperor*) императóрский; **His I~ Majesty** егó императóрское вели́чество. **3.** (*majestic*) великолéпный; **with** ~ **disdain** с цáрственным презрéнием. **4.** (*of British measures*) импéрский.
imperialism [ɪm'pɪərɪəˌlɪz(ə)m] *n.* империали́зм.
imperialist [ɪm'pɪərɪəlɪst] *n.* империали́ст.
imperialist(ic) [ɪmˌpɪərɪə'lɪst(ɪk)] *adj.* империалисти́ческий.
imperil [ɪm'perɪl] *v.t.* подв|ергáть, -éргнуть опáсности; стáвить, по- под угрóзу.

imperious [ɪm'pɪərɪəs] *adj.* (*domineering*) повели́тельный, вла́стный; (*urgent, imperative*) настоя́тельный, императи́вный.

imperishable [ɪm'perɪʃəb(ə)l] *adj.* (*lit.*) непо́ртящийся; (*fig.*) нетле́нный.

impermanence [ɪm'pɜːmənəns] *n.* непостоя́нство.

impermanent [ɪm'pɜːmənənt] *adj.* непостоя́нный.

impermeability [ɪm,pɜːmɪə'bɪlɪtɪ] *n.* непроница́емость.

impermeable [ɪm'pɜːmɪəb(ə)l] *adj.* непроница́емый.

impermissible [,ɪmpə'mɪsɪb(ə)l] *adj.* непозволи́тельный, недозво́ленный.

impersonal [ɪm'pɜːsən(ə)l] *adj.* безли́чный.

impersonate [ɪm'pɜːsə,neɪt] *v.t.* (*act the part of*) игра́ть (*impf.*) роль +*g.*; изобра|жа́ть, -зи́ть; (*pretend to be*) выдава́ть (*impf.*) себя́ за+*a.*

impersonation [ɪm,pɜːsə'neɪʃ(ə)n] *n.* изображе́ние; **he gave an ~ of the professor** он изобрази́л профе́ссора.

impersonator [ɪm'pɜːsə,neɪtə(r)] *n.*: **female ~** эстра́дный арти́ст, изобража́ющий же́нщину.

impertinence [ɪm'pɜːtɪnəns] *n.* де́рзость, на́глость, наха́льство.

impertinent [ɪm'pɜːtɪnənt] *adj.* де́рзкий, на́глый, наха́льный.

imperturbability [,ɪmpə,tɜːbə'bɪlɪtɪ] *n.* невозмути́мость.

imperturbable [,ɪmpə'tɜːbəb(ə)l] *adj.* невозмути́мый.

impervious [ɪm'pɜːvɪəs] *adj.* непроница́емый; **~ to light** све́тонепроница́емый; (*fig.*): **~ to criticism** глух к кри́тике.

impetuosity [ɪm,petjʊ'ɒsɪtɪ] *n.* стреми́тельность, поры́вистость, горя́чность.

impetuous [ɪm'petjʊəs] *adj.* (*moving violently*) стреми́тельный, поры́вистый; (*acting or done with rash energy*) стреми́тельный, поры́вистый; горя́чий; (*impulsive*) импульси́вный; (*unpremeditated*) необду́манный.

impetus ['ɪmpɪtəs] *n.* толчо́к; и́мпульс; (*fig.*) толчо́к, сти́мул; **this will give an ~ to trade** э́то даст торго́вле толчо́к.

impiety [ɪm'paɪətɪ] *n.* не(благо)честй́вость.

impinge [ɪm'pɪndʒ] *v.i.* па́дать (*impf.*) на+*a.*; ударя́ться (*impf.*) о+*a.*

impious ['ɪmpɪəs] *adj.* не(благо)чести́вый.

impish ['ɪmpɪʃ] *adj.* прока́зливый, озорно́й.

implacable [ɪm'plækəb(ə)l] *adj.* неумоли́мый, безжа́лостный.

implant [ɪm'plɑːnt] *v.t.* вв|оди́ть, -ести́; (*fig., instil*) внедр|я́ть, -и́ть; наса|жда́ть, -ди́ть, всел|я́ть, -и́ть.

implausibility [ɪm,plɔːzɪ'bɪlɪtɪ] *n.* неправдоподо́бность, невероя́тность.

implausible [ɪm'plɔːzɪb(ə)l] *adj.* неправдоподо́бный, невероя́тный.

implement[1] ['ɪmplɪmənt] *n.* ору́дие, инструме́нт; **farm ~s** сельскохозя́йственные ору́дия.

implement[2] ['ɪmplɪ,ment] *v.t.* выполня́ть, вы́полнить; осуществ|ля́ть, -и́ть; пров|оди́ть, -ести́ в жизнь; **when the scheme is ~ed** когда́ план бу́дет осуществлён.

implementation [,ɪmplɪmen'teɪʃ(ə)n] *n.* выполне́ние, осуществле́ние.

implicate ['ɪmplɪ,keɪt] *v.t.* вовл|ека́ть, -е́чь; вме́ш|ивать, -а́ть; впу́т|ывать, -ать; **the evidence ~d him** ули́ки пока́зывали на его́ прича́стность; **I refuse to be ~d** я отка́зываюсь быть заме́шанным.

implication [,ɪmplɪ'keɪʃ(ə)n] *n.* (*involvement*) вовлече́ние; (*implying; thg. implied*) скры́тый смысл; намёк; **by ~** ко́свенно; **I do not like your ~** мне не нра́вится ваш намёк; (*significance*) значе́ние.

implicit [ɪm'plɪsɪt] *adj.* **1.** (*implied*) подразумева́емый, недоска́занный; **~ threat** скры́тая угро́за; **~ consent** молчали́вое согла́сие; **~ in his statement was a denial** его́ заявле́ние подразумева́ло отка́з. **2.** (*unquestioning*) безоговóрочный; **I have ~ belief in him** я безоговóрочно ве́рю в него́.

implore [ɪm'plɔː(r)] *v.t.* умол|я́ть, -и́ть; **he ~d my forgiveness** он моли́л меня́ о проще́нии.

impl|y [ɪm'plaɪ] *v.t.* **1.** (*of a pers.: suggest, hint at*) подразумева́ть (*impf.*), намека́ть (*impf.*) на+*a.*; **what are you ~ying by that?** что вы хоти́те э́тим сказа́ть?; **he ~ied that I was wrong** он намека́л на то, что я не прав. **2.** (*of a statement, action etc.*) подразумева́ть (*impf.*); (об)означа́ть (*impf.*); **what do his words ~y?** что означа́ют его́ слова́?; **silence ~ies consent** молча́ние — знак согла́сия.

impolite [,ɪmpə'laɪt] *adj.* неве́жливый.

impoliteness [,ɪmpə'laɪtnɪs] *n.* неве́жливость.

impolitic [ɪm'pɒlɪtɪk] *adj.* не(благо)разу́мный, неполити́чный.

imponderable [ɪm'pɒndərəb(ə)l] *adj.* (*fig.*) неулови́мый.

import[1] ['ɪmpɔːt] *n.* **1.** (*bringing from abroad*) и́мпорт, ввоз; (*pl., goods introduced*) и́мпортные това́ры (*m. pl.*); (*attr.*) и́мпортный, привозно́й; **~ duty** ввозна́я по́шлина. **2.** (*meaning*) значе́ние.

import[2] [ɪm'pɔːt, 'ɪm-] *v.t.* **1.** (*bring in*) импорти́ровать (*impf., pf.*); вв|ози́ть, -езти́; **wheat is ~ed from abroad** пшени́ца вво́зится из-за грани́цы. **2.** (*signify*) означа́ть (*impf.*).

importance [ɪm'pɔːt(ə)ns] *n.* значе́ние, значи́тельность, ва́жность; **attach ~ to sth.** придава́ть (*impf.*) значе́ние чему́-н.; **it is of no ~** э́то не име́ет значе́ния; **a person of some ~** ва́жное лицо́; **of little ~** малова́жный; **a matter of great ~** де́ло огро́мной ва́жности.

important [ɪm'pɔːt(ə)nt] *adj.* значи́тельный, ва́жный; **he went away on ~ business** он уе́хал по ва́жному де́лу; **~ people** ва́жные/влия́тельные лю́ди; **it is ~ for you to realize it** ва́жно, что́бы вы по́няли э́то.

importation [,ɪmpɔː'teɪʃ(ə)n] *n.* и́мпорт, ввоз.

importer [ɪm'pɔːtə(r)] *n.* импортёр.

importunate [ɪm'pɔːtjʊnət] *adj.* назо́йливый, навя́зчивый; **~ demands** настоя́тельные тре́бования.

importune [ɪm'pɔːtjuːn, -'tjuːn] *v.t.* докуча́ть (*impf.*) +*d.*; **he ~d me for a loan** он докуча́л мне про́сьбами о ссу́де.

impose [ɪm'pəʊz] *v.t.* (*obligation*) возл|ага́ть, -ожи́ть (*что на кого*); (*tax, penalty etc.*) нал|ага́ть, -ожи́ть (*что на кого*); обл|ага́ть, -ожи́ть (*кого чем*); **the judge ~d a fine of 20 roubles** судья́ наложи́л штраф в 20 рубле́й; **the government ~d a tax on wealth** госуда́рство обложи́ло бога́тых нало́гом; **this will ~ a heavy burden on the people** э́то ля́жет тя́жким бре́менем на наро́д; **he ~d himself on our company** он навяза́лся к нам в компа́нию; **he ~s his views on everyone** он навя́зывает всем свои́ взгля́ды.

v.i.: **~ on** (*deceive*) обма́н|ывать, -у́ть; **we have been ~d upon** нас обману́ли; (*take advantage of*): **he ~s on his friends** он испо́льзует свои́х друзе́й.

imposing [ɪm'pəʊzɪŋ] *adj.* внуши́тельный, импоза́нтный, представи́тельный.

imposition [,ɪmpə'zɪʃ(ə)n] *n.* **1.** (*imposing of obligation, burden etc.*) возложе́ние, наложе́ние. **2.** (*thg. imposed; tax etc.*) обложе́ние, нало́г. **3.** (*unreasonable demand*) чрезме́рное тре́бование.

impossibility [ɪm,pɒsɪ'bɪlɪtɪ] *n.* невозмо́жность.

impossible [ɪm'pɒsɪb(ə)l] *adj.* невозмо́жный; **don't ask me to do the ~** не тре́буйте от меня́ невозмо́жного; **an ~ person** несно́сный челове́к.

impost ['ɪmpəʊst] *n.* нало́г.

impostor [ɪm'pɒstə(r)] *n.* обма́нщи|к (*fem.* -ца); самозва́н|ец (*fem.* -ка).

impotence ['ɪmpət(ə)ns] *n.* бесси́лие; (*sexual*) импоте́нция.

impotent [ˈɪmpət(ə)nt] *adj.* бесси́льный; **he is ~** (*sexually*) он импоте́нт.
impound [ɪmˈpaʊnd] *v t.* (*cattle etc.*) заг|оня́ть, -на́ть; (*property*) конфискова́ть (*impf., pf.*).
impoverish [ɪmˈpɒvərɪʃ] *v.t.* (*reduce to poverty*) обедн|я́ть, -и́ть; дов|оди́ть, -ести́ до бе́дности; **become ~ed** бедне́ть, о-; нища́ть, об-; **~ed** (*adj.*) бе́дный, обедне́вший; обнища́вший; (*of soil; make barren*) истощ|а́ть, -и́ть; (*of ideas, style etc.*) обедн|я́ть, -и́ть; **an ~ed mind** убо́гий/ску́дный ум.
impoverishment [ɪmˈpɒvərɪʃmənt] *n.* обедне́ние, обнища́ние; истоще́ние.
impracticability [ɪm,præktɪkəˈbɪlɪtɪ] *n.* невыполни́мость, неисполни́мость, неосуществи́мость.
impracticable [ɪmˈpræktɪkəb(ə)l] *adj.*: **an ~ scheme** невыполни́мый/неосуществи́мый план; **~ ideas** неосуществи́мые иде́и.
imprecation [,ɪmprɪˈkeɪʃ(ə)n] *n.* прокля́тие.
imprecise [,ɪmprɪˈsaɪs] *adj.* нето́чный.
imprecision [,ɪmprɪˈsɪʒ(ə)n] *n.* нето́чность.
impregnability [ɪm,pregnəˈbɪlɪtɪ] *n.* непристу́пность.
impregnable [ɪmˈpregnəb(ə)l] *adj.* непристу́пный; (*fig.*): **an ~ argument** неопровержи́мый до́вод.
impregnate [ˈɪmpreg,neɪt] *v.t.* (*fertilize*) оплодотвор|я́ть, -и́ть; (*saturate*) пропи́т|ывать, -а́ть.
impregnation [,ɪmpregˈneɪʃ(ə)n] *n.* оплодотворе́ние; пропи́тывание.
impresario [,ɪmprɪˈsɑːrɪəʊ] *n.* импреса́рио (*m. indecl.*), антрепенёр.
impress [ɪmˈpres] *v.t.* **1.** (*make by imprinting*) отти́с|кивать, -нуть; вытесня́ть, вы́теснить; (*fig., on the mind*) запечатл|ева́ть, -е́ть; внуш|а́ть, -и́ть (*кому*); **the words were ~ed on his memory** слова́ запечатле́лись в его́ па́мяти; **we ~ed on them the need for caution** мы внуши́ли им необходи́мость соблюда́ть осторо́жность. **2.** (*make imprint on*) де́лать, с- отпеча́ток на+*p.*; (*fig., have a strong effect on*) произв|оди́ть, -ести́ впечатле́ние на+*a.* **3.** (*for mil. service*) наси́льно вербова́ть, за-.
impression [ɪmˈpreʃ(ə)n] *n.* **1.** (*imprint*) отпеча́ток, о́ттиск; **his fingers left an ~** его́ па́льцы оста́вили отпеча́тки. **2.** (*typ., copies printed*) тира́ж; (*reprint*) печа́тание, перепеча́тка. **3.** (*effect*) эффе́кт, результа́т; впечатле́ние; **make, create an ~** произв|оди́ть, -ести́ впечатле́ние. **4.** (*notion*) впечатле́ние, представле́ние; **I have, get an ~ (*or* my ~ is) that he is not sincere** у меня́ сложи́лось впечатле́ние, что он нейскренен; **I was under the ~ that ...** я полага́л, что...; **I have a strong ~ that ...** я почти́ уве́рен, что...; **one cannot rely on first ~s** нельзя́ доверя́ть пе́рвому впечатле́нию.
impressionable [ɪmˈpreʃənəb(ə)l] *adj.* впечатли́тельный.
impressionism [ɪmˈpreʃə,nɪz(ə)m] *n.* импрессиони́зм.
impressionist [ɪmˈpreʃənɪst] *n.* **1.** (*art*) импрессиони́ст. **2.** (*mimic*) пароди́ст, имита́тор.
impressionistic [ɪm,preʃəˈnɪstɪk] *adj.* импрессионисти́ческий, импрессиони́стский.
impressive [ɪmˈpresɪv] *adj.* внуши́тельный, впечатля́ющий, си́льный; **an ~ speech** я́ркая речь.
imprint[1] [ˈɪmprɪnt] *n.* (*lit., fig.*) отпеча́ток; (*fig.*) печа́ть; **publisher's ~** выходны́е да́нные (*nt. pl.*).
imprint[2] [ɪmˈprɪnt] *v.t.* отпеча́т|ывать, -ать; вытесня́ть, вы́теснить; (*fig.*) запечатл|ева́ть, -е́ть.
imprison [ɪmˈprɪz(ə)n] *v.t.* заключ|а́ть, -и́ть в тюрьму́.
imprisonment [ɪmˈprɪzənmənt] *n.* тюре́мное заключе́ние; **he was sentenced to life ~** его́ приговори́ли к пожи́зненному заключе́нию.
improbability [ɪm,prɒbəˈbɪlɪtɪ] *n.* неправдоподо́бие, невероя́тность.
improbable [ɪmˈprɒbəb(ə)l] *adj.* неправдоподо́бный, невероя́тный.
improbity [ɪmˈprəʊbɪtɪ] *n.* бесче́стность.
impromptu [ɪmˈprɒmptjuː] *adj.* импровизи́рованный. *adv.* экспро́мтом, без подгото́вки.
improper [ɪmˈprɒpə(r)] *adj.* **1.** (*unsuitable*) неподходя́щий, несоотве́тствующий; неуме́стный; **behaviour ~ to the occasion** поведе́ние, неподходя́щее к слу́чаю; **an ~ question** неуме́стный вопро́с. **2.** (*incorrect*) непра́вильный; **~ fraction** непра́вильная дробь; **put sth. to ~ use** испо́льзовать что-н. не по назначе́нию. **3.** (*unseemly, indecent*) неприли́чный, непристо́йный.
impropriety [,ɪmprəˈpraɪətɪ] *n.* неуме́стность; непра́вильность; непристо́йность, неприли́чие.
improvable [ɪmˈpruːvəb(ə)l] *adj.* поддаю́щийся улучше́нию.
improv|e [ɪmˈpruːv] *v.t.* **1.** (*make better*) ул|учша́ть, -у́чшить; **he ~ed his French** он сде́лал успе́хи во францу́зском языке́. **2.** (*turn to good account*): **~e the occasion** воспо́льзоваться (*pf.*) слу́чаем.
v.i. **1.** (*become better*) ул|учша́ться, -у́чшиться; **he has ~ed in manners** его́ мане́ры улу́чшились; **her looks have ~ed** она́ похороше́ла; **wine ~es with age** вино́ улучша́ется с года́ми; **it will ~e with use** э́то бу́дет улучша́ться по ме́ре по́льзования; **things are ~ing** дела́ нала́живаются; **his health is ~ing** он (*or* его́ здоро́вье) поправля́ется; (*of prices: rise*) подн|има́ться, -я́ться. **2.: ~e on** (*produce sth. better than*): **I can ~e on that** я могу́ предложи́ть не́что лу́чшее; **he ~ed on my ideas** он разви́л да́льше мои́ мы́сли.
improvement [ɪmˈpruːvmənt] *n.* улучше́ние; **there has been an ~ in the weather** пого́да улу́чшилась; **your writing is in need of ~** вам сле́дует испра́вить ваш по́черк; **there is room for ~** могло́ бы быть лу́чше; (*rebuilding etc.*) перестро́йка; перестано́вка; **he is carrying out ~s on his house** он за́нят усоверше́нствованием своего́ до́ма.
improvidence [ɪmˈprɒvɪd(ə)ns] *n.* непредусмотри́тельность; небережли́вость.
improvident [ɪmˈprɒvɪd(ə)nt] *adj.* (*heedless of the future*) непредусмотри́тельный; (*wasteful*) небережли́вый.
improvisation [,ɪmprəvaɪˈzeɪʃ(ə)n] *n.* импровиза́ция.
improvise [ˈɪmprə,vaɪz] *v.t. & i.* (*music, speech etc.*) импровизи́ровать (*impf.*); (*arrange as makeshift*) мастери́ть, с-.
imprudence [ɪmˈpruːd(ə)ns] *n.* неблагоразу́мие, неосторо́жность.
imprudent [ɪmˈpruːd(ə)nt] *adj.* неблагоразу́мный, неосторо́жный.
impudence [ˈɪmpjʊd(ə)nt] *n.* де́рзость; бессты́дство; на́глость.
impudent [ˈɪmpjʊd(ə)nt] *adj.* (*audacious*) де́рзкий; (*shameless*) бессты́дный; (*insolent*) на́глый: **an ~ fellow** нагле́ц.
impugn [ɪmˈpjuːn] *v.t.* осп|а́ривать, -о́рить; **he ~ed my honesty** он подве́рг мою́ че́стность сомне́нию.
impulse [ˈɪmpʌls] *n.* (*lit., phys.*) толчо́к; (*elec.*) и́мпульс; (*fig., impetus, stimulus*): **the war gave an ~ to trade** война́ дала́ толчо́к торго́вле.
impulsive [ɪmˈpʌlsɪv] *adj.* импульси́вный.
impunity [ɪmˈpjuːnɪtɪ] *n.*: **with ~** безнака́занно.
impure [ɪmˈpjʊə(r)] *adj.* нечи́стый, гря́зный.
impurity [ɪmˈpjʊərɪtɪ] *n.* нечистота́, грязь.
imputation [ɪm,pjuːˈteɪʃ(ə)n] *n.* **1.** (*imputing, ascription*) вмене́ние в вину́; обвине́ние, припи́сывание; **he could not avoid the ~ of dishonesty** он не мог избежа́ть подозре́ния в бесче́стности. **2.** (*aspersion*) тень, пятно́; **~s were cast on his character** на его́ репута́цию была́ бро́шена тень.
impute [ɪmˈpjuːt] *v.t.* вмен|я́ть, -и́ть; припи́с|ывать, -а́ть; **the faults ~d to him** недоста́тки, припи́сываемые ему́.
in [ɪn] *n.*: **he knew all the ~s and outs of the affair** он

знал все то́нкости де́ла.

adj. (*coll.*, *fashionable*) популя́рный, мо́дный.

adv. **1.** (*at home*) до́ма; **tell them I'm not ~** скажи́те, что меня́ нет до́ма; (*~ one's office etc.*): **the boss is not ~ yet** нача́льника (в кабине́те) ещё нет; **he has been ~ and out all day** он весь день то приходи́л, то уходи́л. **2.** (*arrived at station, port etc.*): **the train has been ~ (for) 10 minutes** по́езд пришёл 10 мину́т тому́ наза́д. **3.** (*inside*) внутри́, внутрь. **4.** (*harvested*): **the crops were ~** урожа́й был со́бран. **5.** (*available for purchase*): **strawberries are ~** начался́ сезо́н клубни́ки. **6.** (*~ fashion*): **short skirts are ~ again** коро́ткие ю́бки опя́ть в мо́де. **7.** (*~ office*): **which party was ~ then?** кака́я па́ртия была́ тогда́ у вла́сти? **8.** (*burning*): **is the fire still ~?** ками́н ещё гори́т? **9.: day ~, day out** изо дня в день. **10.** (*involved*): **count me ~!** включи́те и меня́!; **he was ~ at the start** он принима́л уча́стие с са́мого нача́ла. **11.** (*with preps.*): **we are ~ for a storm** грозы́ не минова́ть; **he is ~ for a surprise** его́ ожида́ет сюрпри́з; **are you ~ for the next race?** вы уча́ствуете в сле́дующем забе́ге?; **he has got it ~ for me** (*coll.*) он про́тив меня́ что́-то име́ет; **you'll be ~ for it when she finds out** вам доста́нется за э́то, когда́ она́ узна́ет; **are you ~ on his plans?** (*coll.*) вы в ку́рсе его́ пла́нов?; **~ with** (*coll.*, *on good terms with*) вхож в+*a.*, к+*d.*; **he is well ~ with the council** у него́ в сове́те свои́ лю́ди.

prep. **1.** (*position*) в/на+*p.*; (*inhabited places*): **~ Moscow** в Москве́; **he is the best worker ~ the village** он пе́рвый рабо́тник на селе́; (*countries and territories*): **~ France** во Фра́нции; **~ the Crimea** в Крыму́; **~ (the) Ukraine** на Украи́не; (*islands and promontories*): **~ the British Isles** на Брита́нских острова́х; **~ Alaska** на Аля́ске; (*mountainous regions within Russia*): **~ the Caucasus** на Кавка́зе; (*mountainous regions elsewhere*): **~ the Alps** в А́льпах; (*open spaces and flat areas*): **~ the street** на у́лице; **~ the square** на пло́щади; **in the country** в дере́вне; **~ the garden** в саду́; **~ the field** в по́ле; **~ the fields** на поля́х; (*buildings*): **~ the theatre** в теа́тре; (*places of learning*): **~ school** в шко́ле; **~ the university** в университе́те; (*places of work*): **~ the factory** на заво́де; (*activities*): **~ the lesson** на уро́ке; **~ the war** на войне́; во вре́мя войны́; (*groups*): **~ the crowd** в толпе́; (*points of compass*): **~ the (Far) East** на (Да́льнем) Восто́ке; (*vehicles*): **let's go ~ the car** пое́дем на маши́не; (*parts of body*): **hold this ~ your hand** держи́те э́то в руке́; **she had a child ~ her arms** у неё на рука́х был ребёнок; (*natural phenomena*): **~ the sun** на со́лнце; **~ the fresh air** на све́жем во́здухе; **~ darkness** в темноте́; **~ the rain** под дождём; (*books*): **~ the Bible** в Би́блии; (*authors*): **~ Shakespeare** у Шекспи́ра; (*close to*): **she was sitting ~ the window** она́ сиде́ла у окна́. **2.** (*motion*) в (*rarely* на) +*a.*: **they arrived ~ the city** они́ при́были в го́род; **he whispered ~ my ear** он шепта́л мне на́ ухо. **3.** (*time*) (*i*) (*specific centuries, years and decades*): **~ the 20th century** в двадца́том ве́ке; **~ 1975** в ты́сяча девятьсо́т се́мьдесят пя́том году́; **~ May** в Ма́е; **~ future** в бу́дущем; **~ childhood** в де́тстве; **~ old age** на ста́рости лет; **he is ~ his fifties** ему́ за пятьдеся́т; (*ii*) (*ages of history, events, periods*): **~ the Middle Ages** в сре́дние века́; **~ these days** в э́ти дни; **~ our day** в на́ши дни; **~ my time** в моё вре́мя; **injured ~ the explosion** ра́неный во вре́мя взры́ва; **~ the course of** в тече́ние+*g.* (*see also vii*); **3 times ~ one day** три ра́за в оди́н день; (*iii*): **~ the first minute of the game** на пе́рвой мину́те игры́; (*iv*) (*seasons*): **~ spring** весно́й; (*times of day*): **~ the morning** у́тром; **~ the mornings** по утра́м; **~ the afternoon** днём; по́сле полу́дня; (*v*) (*with gerund*): **~ crossing the river** при перехо́де реки́; переходя́ ре́ку; (*of reigns*: *during*): **~ Napoleon's time** при Наполео́не; (*vi*) (*at the end of*): **I shall finish this book ~ 3 days' time** я ко́нчу э́ту кни́гу че́рез три дня; **~ less than 3 weeks** ра́ньше чем че́рез три неде́ли; (*vii*) (*in the course of*): **how many will come ~ one day?** ско́лько приду́т за день?; **I haven't been there ~ the last 3 years** за после́дние три го́да я не́ был там; **he wrote twice ~ one week** он написа́л два́жды за одну́ неде́лю; **he completed it ~ 6 weeks** он зако́нчил э́то в тече́ние шести́ неде́ль. **4.** (*condition, situation*): **~ his absence** в его́ отсу́тствие; **~ these circumstances** при э́тих усло́виях; **~ custody** под аре́стом; **cry out ~ fear** вскри́кнуть (*pf.*) от стра́ха; **~ place** на ме́сте; **~ power** у вла́сти; **~ the wake of** вслед за+*i.*; **~ the way** (*lit.*) поперёк доро́ги; (*fig.*): **these books are ~ my way** э́ти кни́ги мне меша́ют. **5.** (*dress*): **she was ~ white** она́ была́ в бе́лом (пла́тье); **he was dressed ~ ...** на нём был... **6.** (*form*; *mode*; *arrangement*; *quantity*): **~ pairs** па́рами; **~ folds** скла́дками; **they died ~ (their) thousands** они́ умира́ли ты́сячами; **~ writing** в пи́сьменном ви́де; **~ a row** в ряду́; (*successively*) подря́д; **~ a circle** в кругу́; **~ short** в не́скольких слова́х. **7.** (*manner*): **~ a whisper** шёпотом; **~ a businesslike way** делов́ым о́бразом; **~ a loud voice** гро́мким го́лосом; **~ detail** подро́бно; **~ full** по́лностью; **~ part** ча́стью, части́чно; **~ secret** по секре́ту; **~ succession** подря́д, после́довательно; **~ turn** по о́череди; **~ haste** в спе́шке. **8.** (*language*): **~ Russian** по-ру́сски; **~ several languages** на не́скольких языка́х. **9.** (*material*): **a statue ~ marble** ста́туя из мра́мора. **10.** (*medium*): **he paints ~ oils** он пи́шет ма́слом. **11.** (*cul.*): **~ butter** на ма́сле. **12.** (*solvent*; *diluent*): **take the medicine ~ water** лека́рство принима́ть с водо́й. **13.** (*contained ~*; *inherent ~*): **there are 7 days ~ a week** в неде́ле семь дней; **there's no sense ~ complaining** жа́ловаться бессм́ысленно; **there's nothing ~ it** (*coll.*, *it is easy*) па́ра пустяко́в; (*coll.*, *there is no difference*) нет никако́й ра́зницы. **14.** (*consisting ~*): **we have lost a good friend ~ him** в нём (*or* в его́ лице́) мы потеря́ли хоро́шего дру́га. **15.** (*ratio*: *out of*): **only 1 ~ every 10 survived** из ка́ждых десяти́ то́лько оди́н вы́жил; **he has 1 chance ~ 5 of success** его́ ша́нсы на успе́х — оди́н к пяти́; **they had to pay 10p ~ the pound** им пришло́сь плати́ть де́сять пе́нсов с фу́нта. **16.** (*division*): **he broke the plate ~ pieces** он разби́л таре́лку на куски́. **17.** (*~ respect of*): **they differ ~ size but not ~ colour** они́ различа́ются по разме́ру, а не по цвету́; **a lecture ~ anatomy** ле́кция по анато́мии; **strong ~ mathematics** силён (*pred.*) в матема́тике; **broad ~ the shoulders** широ́к (*pred.*) в плеча́х; (*dimension*): **4 feet ~ length** четы́ре фу́та в длину́; (*of bodily defects*): **blind ~ one eye** слеп (*pred.*) на оди́н глаз; (*of physique or natural characteristics*): **slight ~ build** хру́пкого сложе́ния; **poor ~ quality** плохо́го ка́чества; **he is young ~ appearance** он молодо́й на вид; **he is advanced ~ years** ему́ уже́ не ма́ло лет; он уже́ не мо́лод; **they were 7 ~ number** их бы́ло се́меро. **18.** (*according to*): **~ my opinion** по моему́ мне́нию; по-мо́ему. **19.: ~ reply to** в отве́т на+*a.*; **~ honour of** в честь +*g.*; **~ memory of** в па́мять +*g.*; **~ protest** в знак проте́ста. **20.** (*engaged ~*): **~ business** в де́ле; **~ battle** в бою́; **~ search of** в по́исках +*g.*; **~ self-defence** для самооборо́ны. **21.** (*with other parts of speech, forming phrasal conjs.*): **~ that** тем, что; так как; **~ between** ме́жду+*i.*; **something ~ between** не́что сре́днее.

inability [ˌɪnəˈbɪlɪtɪ] *n.* неспосо́бность.

in absentia [ˌɪn æbˈsentɪə] *adv.* зао́чно.

inaccessibility [ˌɪnækˌsesɪ'bɪlɪtɪ] *n.* недосту́пность.
inaccessible [ˌɪnæk'sesɪb(ə)l] *adj.* недосту́пный.
inaccuracy [ɪn'ækjʊrəsɪ] *n.* нето́чность.
inaccurate [ɪn'ækjʊrət] *adj.* нето́чный.
inaction [ɪn'ækʃ(ə)n] *n.* безде́йствие.
inactive [ɪn'æktɪv] *adj.* **1.** безде́йственный, безде́йствующий; **he leads an ~ life** он ведёт безде́ятельный/пасси́вный о́браз жи́зни; **the machines were ~** маши́ны проста́ивали. **2.** (*of chemicals etc.*) ине́ртный, неде́ятельный.
inactivity [ˌɪnæk'tɪvɪtɪ] *n.* безде́йствие.
inadequacy [ɪn'ædɪkwəsɪ] *n.* недоста́точность, неполноце́нность; (*personal*) неспосо́бность.
inadequate [ɪn'ædɪkwət] *adj.* (*insufficient*) недоста́точный; **words are ~ to express my joy** слов недостаёт, что́бы вы́разить мою́ ра́дость; (*less than capable of*) неспосо́бный.
inadmissible [ˌɪnəd'mɪsɪb(ə)l] *adj.* (*unacceptable*) неприе́млемый; (*impermissible*) недопусти́мый.
inadvertence [ˌɪnəd'vɜːt(ə)ns] *n.* (*inattention*) невнима́тельность; (*oversight*) недосмо́тр; (*false step*) неосторо́жность.
inadvertent [ˌɪnəd'vɜːt(ə)nt] *adj.* неумы́шленный, нечаянный, нево́льный.
inadvisability [ˌɪnədvaɪzə'bɪlɪtɪ] *n.* нецелесообра́зность, нежела́тельность.
inadvisable [ˌɪnəd'vaɪzəb(ə)l] *adj.* нецелесообра́зный, нежела́тельный.
inalienable [ɪn'eɪlɪənəb(ə)l] *adj.* неотъе́млемый.
inalterable [ɪn'ɒltərəb(ə)l] *adj.* неизменя́емый, неизме́нный.
inane [ɪ'neɪn] *adj.* глу́пый, пусто́й, неле́пый.
inanimate [ɪn'ænɪmət] *adj.* неодушевлённый, неживо́й; **~ nature** нежива́я приро́да; **an ~ noun** неодушевлённое существи́тельное; (*lifeless*; *also fig.*, *without animation*) безжи́зненный.
inanity [ˌɪn'ænɪtɪ] *n.* глу́пость; пустота́, неле́пость; глу́пое замеча́ние.
inapplicable [ɪn'æplɪkəb(ə)l, ˌɪnə'plɪk-] *adj.* неприме-ни́мый; (*unsuitable*) неподходя́щий.
inappropriate [ˌɪnə'prəʊprɪət] *adj.* неуме́стный, неподходя́щий.
inarticulate [ˌɪnɑː'tɪkjʊlət] *adj.* (*of speech*) невня́тный, нечленоразде́льный; (*of pers.*) косноязы́чный.
inasmuch as [ˌɪnəz'mʌtʃ] *adj.* так как; ввиду́ того́, что; поско́льку.
inattention [ˌɪnə'tenʃ(ə)n] *n.* невнима́ние, невнима́тельность (к+*d.*).
inattentive [ˌɪnə'tentɪv] *adj.* невнима́тельный.
inaudible [ɪn'ɔːdɪb(ə)l] *adj.* неслы́шный; (*indistinct*) невня́тный.
inaugural [ɪ'nɔːgjʊr(ə)l] *n.* торже́ственная речь при вступле́нии в до́лжность.
adj. вступи́тельный.
inaugurate [ɪ'nɔːgjʊˌreɪt] *v.t.* (*install with ceremony*) (торже́ственно) вв|оди́ть, -ести́ в до́лжность; **the President was ~d** президе́нт вступи́л в до́лжность. **2.** (*launch*; *officiate at opening of*) откр|ыва́ть, -ы́ть; (*fig.*): **they ~d many reforms** они́ ввели́ мно́го рефо́рм.
inauguration [ɪˌnɔːgjʊ'reɪʃ(ə)n] *n.* вступле́ние в до́лжность; инаугура́ция.
inauspicious [ˌɪnɔː'spɪʃəs] *adj.* (*of ill omen*) злове́щий; (*unlucky*) несчастли́вый.
inborn ['ɪnbɔːn] *adj.* врождённый, прирождённый.
inbred [ɪn'bred, 'ɪn-] *adj.* (*innate*) = **inborn**
inbreeding [ɪn'briːdɪŋ] *n.* (*of animals*) ро́дственное спа́ривание.
incalculable [ɪn'kælkjʊləb(ə)l] *adj.* неисчисли́мый, бесчи́сленный, несме́тный; **it has done ~ harm** э́то причини́ло неисчисли́мый вред.
in camera [ɪn 'kæmərə] *adv.*: **the trial will be held ~** проце́сс бу́дет закры́тым (*or* бу́дет идти́ при закры́тых дверя́х).
incandescence [ˌɪnkæn'des(ə)ns] *n.* нака́л, кале́ние.
incandescent [ˌɪnkæn'des(ə)nt] *adj.* накалённый, раскалённый; (*of light*) светя́щийся от нагре́ва; **~ lamp** ла́мпа нака́ливания.
incantation [ˌɪnkæn'teɪʃ(ə)n] *n.* заклина́ние, закля́тие.
incapable [ɪn'keɪpəb(ə)l] *adj.* неспосо́бный; **he is ~ of understanding** он неспосо́бен поня́ть (*что*); он неспосо́бен к понима́нию; **~ of speech** невладе́ющий ре́чью; **~ of lying** неспосо́бный на ложь.
incapacitate [ˌɪnkə'pæsɪˌteɪt] *v.t.*: **~ for, from** (*render incapable of or unfit for*) де́лать, с- неспосо́бным/неприго́дным к+*d.*; **his illness ~d him for work** из-за боле́зни он стал нетрудоспосо́бным; (*disable*): **he was ~d for 3 weeks** он вы́был из стро́я на три неде́ли; (*mil.*) выводи́ть, вы́вести из стро́я; **the enemy's tanks were ~d** та́нки проти́вника бы́ли вы́ведены из стро́я.
incapacity [ˌɪnkə'pæsɪtɪ] *n.* неспосо́бность.
incarcerate [ɪn'kɑːsəˌreɪt] *v.t.* заточ|а́ть, -и́ть (в тюрьму́).
incarceration [ɪnˌkɑːsə'reɪʃ(ə)n] *n.* заточе́ние (в тюрьму́).
incarnate[1] [ɪn'kɑːnət] *adj.* (*in bodily form*) воплощённый; **he is the Devil ~** он дья́вол во пло́ти; (*personified*) олицетворённый.
incarnate[2] ['ɪnkɑːˌneɪt, -'kɑːneɪt] *v.t.* вопло|ща́ть, -ти́ть; олицетвор|я́ть, -и́ть.
incarnation [ˌɪnkɑː'neɪʃ(ə)n] *n.* **1.** (*taking on bodily form*): **the I~** воплоще́ние (божества́ в Христе́); (*re-birth*) инкарна́ция; **in a future ~** в но́вом рожде́нии. **2.** (*embodiment*, *personification*) воплоще́ние, олицетворе́ние.
incautious [ɪn'kɔːʃəs] *adj.* неосторо́жный.
incendiary [ɪn'sendɪərɪ] *n.* **1.** (*arsonist*) поджига́тель (*m.*); (*fig.*, *firebrand*) подстрека́тель (*m.*). **2.** (**~ bomb**) зажига́тельная бо́мба.
adj. зажига́тельный; (*fig.*) подстрека́ющий.
incense[1] ['ɪnsens] *n.* ла́дан, фимиа́м (*also fig.*); **they were burning ~** они́ кади́ли ла́даном.
cpd. **~-burner** *n.* (*vessel*) кади́льница.
incense[2] ['ɪnsens] *v.t.* разгне́вать (*pf.*); прив|оди́ть, -ести́ в я́рость; **she was ~d at, by his behaviour** его́ поведе́ние привело́ её в я́рость.
incentive [ɪn'sentɪv] *n.* побужде́ние, сти́мул; **he lacks all ~ to work** у него́ нет никако́го сти́мула для рабо́ты; **~ bonus** поощри́тельная пре́мия.
inception [ɪn'sepʃ(ə)n] *n.* нача́ло, начина́ние.
incertitude [ɪn'sɜːtɪˌtjuːd] *n.* неуве́ренность.
incessant [ɪn'ses(ə)nt] *adj.* непреста́нный, непреры́вный.
incest ['ɪnsest] *n.* кровосмеше́ние.
incestuous [ɪn'sestjʊəs] *adj.* кровосмеси́тельный.
inch [ɪntʃ] *n.* дюйм; **he moved forward by ~es** ма́ло-пома́лу он дви́гался вперёд; **the car missed me by ~es** автомоби́ль едва́ меня́ не задави́л; **he was every ~ a sailor** он был моряко́м с головы́ до пят; **he did not yield an ~** он не уступи́л ни на йо́ту; **he was flogged within an ~ of his life** его́ изби́ли до полусме́рти.
v.i. with advs.: **he was ~ing along** он ме́дленно тащи́лся; **the car began to ~ forward** маши́на ме́дленно тро́нулась с ме́ста.
inchoate [ɪn'kəʊeɪt, 'ɪn-] *adj.* зача́точный.
incidence ['ɪnsɪd(ə)ns] *n.* **1.** (*phys.*, *falling*; *contact*) паде́ние, накло́н; **angle of ~** у́гол паде́ния. **2.** (*range or scope of effect*) охва́т, сфе́ра де́йствия; **the ~ of taxation** охва́т налогообложе́нием; **the ~ of a disease** число́ заболе́вших.
incident ['ɪnsɪd(ə)nt] *n.* слу́чай, собы́тие; происше́ствие, инциде́нт; **without ~** без происше́ствий; (*in play*, *novel etc.*) эпизо́д.

adj. ~ **to** (*connected with*) свя́занный с+*i*.; (*characteristic of*) прису́щий +*d*., сво́йственный +*d*.

incidental [ˌɪnsɪ'dent(ə)l] *adj.* **1.** (*casual*) случа́йный; (*passing*) попу́тный; (*inessential*) несуще́ственный; (*secondary*) побо́чный; ~ **expenses** побо́чные расхо́ды; ~ **music** музыка́льное сопровожде́ние. **2.:** ~ **to** (*accompanying*, *contingent on*) сопряжённый с+*i*.; (*resulting from*) вытека́ющий из+*g*.

incidentally [ˌɪnsɪ'dentəlɪ] *adv.* (*in passing*) попу́тно; (*parenthetically*) ме́жду про́чим; кста́ти.

incinerate [ɪn'sɪnəˌreɪt] *v.t.* испепел|я́ть, -и́ть; сж|ига́ть, -ечь дотла́.

incinerator [ɪn'sɪnəˌreɪtə(r)] *n.* мусоросжига́тельная печь; кремацио́нная печь.

incipient [ɪn'sɪpɪənt] *adj.* зарожда́ющийся.

incise [ɪn'saɪz] *v.t.* (*make cut in*) надр|еза́ть, -е́зать; (*engrave*) выреза́ть, вы́резать.

incision [ɪn'sɪʒ(ə)n] *n.* надре́з.

incisive [ɪn'saɪsɪv] *adj.* ре́жущий; (*fig.*): **an** ~ **tone** ре́зкий тон; **an** ~ **mind** о́стрый/проница́тельный ум.

incisor [ɪn'saɪzə(r)] *n.* (*tooth*) резе́ц.

incite [ɪn'saɪt] *v.t.* (*stir up*) возбу|жда́ть, -ди́ть; (*encourage*, *urge*, *impel*) подстрек|а́ть, -ну́ть; **he** ~**d them to revolt** он подстрека́л их к мятежу́.

incitement [ɪn'saɪtmənt] *n.* (*inciting*) подстрека́тельство; (*spur*, *stimulus*) побужде́ние, сти́мул.

inclement [ɪn'klemənt] *adj.* суро́вый.

inclination [ˌɪnklɪ'neɪʃ(ə)n] *n.* **1.** (*bending*; *slanting*) наклоне́ние, накло́н; **an** ~ **of the head** киво́к; накло́н головы́. **2.** (*tendency*) накло́нность, скло́нность; **an** ~ **to stoutness** скло́нность к полноте́. **3.** (*desire*) охо́та, жела́ние; **he has lost all** ~ **to work** он потеря́л вся́кую охо́ту к рабо́те; **I have no** ~ **to go out** у меня́ нет никако́го жела́ния выходи́ть.

incline[1] ['ɪnklaɪn] *n.* накло́нная пло́скость, накло́н, скат.

incline[2] [ɪn'klaɪn] *v.t.* **1.** (*cause to lean or slant*) наклон|я́ть, -и́ть; ~**d plane** накло́нная пло́скость; (*bend forward or down*) склон|я́ть, -и́ть. **2.** (*turn*, *direct*) напр|авля́ть, -а́вить; **he** ~**d his ear to their plea** он благоскло́нно вы́слушал их про́сьбу. **3.** (*fig.*, *dispose*) склон|я́ть, -и́ть; **his heart** ~**d him to pity** его́ до́брое се́рдце склоня́ло его́ к жа́лости; **I am** ~**d to agree with you** я скло́нен с ва́ми согласи́ться; **if you feel** ~**d (to do so)** е́сли вы располо́жены э́то сде́лать; **favourably** ~**d to** благоскло́нный к+*d*.

v.i. **1.** (*lean*, *slope*) наклон|я́ться, -и́ться; склон|я́ться, -и́ться. **2.** (*tend*) склон|я́ться, -и́ться; **I** ~ **to think that ...** я скло́нен ду́мать, что...

includ|e [ɪn'klu:d] *v.t.* включ|а́ть, -и́ть; (*place on a list*) вн|оси́ть, -ести́; **I** ~**e you among my friends** я включа́ю вас в число́ свои́х друзе́й; **they were all there, wives** ~**ed** все бы́ли в сбо́ре, включа́я жён; **we saw several of them,** ~**ing your brother** мы ви́дели не́которых из них, в том числе́ (и) ва́шего бра́та; **service** ~**ed** включа́я услу́ги; **your work will** ~**e sweeping the floor** в ва́ши обя́занности бу́дет входи́ть подмета́ние поло́в; (*contain*) заключа́ть (*impf.*); содержа́ть (*impf.*) в себе́; **this book** ~**es all his poems** в э́той кни́ге со́браны все его́ стихи́.

inclusion [ɪn'klu:ʒ(ə)n] *n.* включе́ние.

inclusive [ɪn'klu:sɪv] *adj. & adv.* **1.:** ~ **of** (*including*) включа́я; включа́ющий в себя́; содержа́щий в себе́. **2.: from Feb. 2nd to 20th** ~ со второ́го февраля́ по двадца́тое включи́тельно. **3.:** ~ **terms** (*at hotel*) цена́ ко́мнаты с по́лным содержа́нием.

incognito [ˌɪnkɒg'ni:təʊ] *n.*, *adj. & adv.* инко́гнито (*m.*, *nt.*, *indecl.*).

incoherence [ˌɪnkəʊ'hɪərəns] *n.* несвя́зность, бессвя́зность.

incoherent [ˌɪnkəʊ'hɪərənt] *adj.* несвя́зный, бессвя́зный.

incombustible [ˌɪnkəm'bʌstɪb(ə)l] *adj.* негорю́чий, невоспламеня́емый.

income ['ɪnkʌm, 'ɪŋkəm] *n.* дохо́д, прихо́д; **earned** ~ за́работок; **unearned** ~ ре́нта, нетрудовы́е дохо́ды (*m. pl.*); **private** ~ ча́стные дохо́ды; ~ **support** де́нежное посо́бие малоопла́чиваемым; **live on one's** ~ жить на свои́ сре́дства; **live within one's** ~ жить по сре́дствам.

cpd. ~**-tax** *n.* подохо́дный нало́г.

incoming ['ɪnˌkʌmɪŋ] *n.* (*pl.*, *income*) дохо́ды (*m. pl.*).

adj. входя́щий, поступа́ющий; **the** ~ **year** наступа́ющий год; **the** ~ **tide** прили́в; **the** ~ **president** новои́збранный президе́нт; ~ **mail** входя́щая по́чта.

incommensurability [ˌɪnkəˌmenʃərə'bɪlɪtɪ, -sjərə'bɪlɪtɪ] *n.* несоизмери́мость.

incommensurable [ˌɪnkə'menʃərəb(ə)l, -sjərəb(ə)l] *adj.* несоизмери́мый.

incommensurate [ˌɪnkə'menʃərət, -sjərət] *adj.* (*out of proportion*) несоразме́рный (с+*i*.); (*inadequate*) несоотве́тствующий (+*d*.).

incommode [ˌɪnkə'məʊd] *v.t.* (*disturb*, *put out*) беспоко́ить, о-; (*make difficulties for*) стесн|я́ть, -и́ть; (*hinder*) меша́ть, по- +*d*.

incom(m)unicado [ˌɪnkəˌmju:nɪ'kɑ:dəʊ] *adj. & adv.* лишённый пра́ва перепи́ски и сообще́ния; в изоля́ции.

incomparable [ɪn'kɒmpərəb(ə)l] *adj.* (*not comparable to or with*) несравни́мый (с+*i*.); (*matchless*) несравне́нный.

incompatibility [ˌɪnkəmˌpætɪ'bɪlɪtɪ] *n.* несовмести́мость; **a divorce on grounds of** ~ разво́д по причи́не несхо́дства хара́ктеров.

incompatible [ˌɪnkəm'pætɪb(ə)l] *adj.* несовмести́мый.

incompetence [ɪn'kɒmpɪt(ə)ns] *n.* неспосо́бность, некомпете́нтность.

incompetent [ɪn'kɒmpɪt(ə)nt] *adj.* (*lacking ability*) неспосо́бный (*к чему or inf.*); (*lacking qualifications*) некомпете́нтный (*в чём*).

incomplete [ˌɪnkəm'pli:t] *adj.* (*not full*) непо́лный; **an** ~ **set** непо́лный компле́кт; (*defective*, *lacking*) несоверше́нный; (*unfinished*) незако́нченный.

incompleteness [ˌɪnkəm'pli:tnɪs] *n.* неполнота́; несоверше́нство; незако́нченность.

incomprehensibility [ɪnˌkɒmprɪhensɪ'bɪlɪtɪ] *n.* непоня́тность, непостижи́мость.

incomprehensible [ɪnˌkɒmprɪ'hensɪb(ə)l] *adj.* непоня́тный, непостижи́мый.

incomprehension [ɪnˌkɒmprɪ'henʃ(ə)n] *n.* непонима́ние.

incomunicado = **incom(m)unicado**

inconceivable [ˌɪnkən'si:vəb(ə)l] *adj.* (*incomprehensible*) непостижи́мый; (*unimaginable*) невообрази́мый.

inconclusive [ˌɪnkən'klu:sɪv] *adj.* (*of argument etc.*) неубеди́тельный; (*of action*) нереши́тельный.

incongruity ['ɪnkɒŋ'gru:ɪtɪ] *n.* несоотве́тствие; неуме́стность.

incongruous [ɪn'kɒŋgrʊəs] *adj.* (*out of keeping*) несоотве́тствующий, неподходя́щий; (*out of place*, *inappropriate*) неуме́стный.

inconsequential [ɪnˌkɒnsɪ'kwenʃ(ə)l, ˌɪnkɒn-] *adj.* (*disconnected*, *disjointed*) несвя́зный; (*irrelevant*, *immaterial*) несуще́ственный.

inconsiderable [ˌɪnkən'sɪdərəb(ə)l] *adj.* незначи́тельный; **his income was** ~ его́ за́работок был ничто́жным.

inconsiderate [ˌɪnkən'sɪdərət] *adj.* невнима́тельный (к други́м), нечу́ткий; **he is** ~ **of, to everyone** он невнима́телен ко всем; (*thoughtless*, *rash*) необду́манный.

inconsistenc|y [ˌɪnkən'sɪst(ə)nsɪ] *n.* непосле́довательность; противоречи́вость; **there are** ~**ies in his argument** его́ до́воды непосле́довательны.

inconsistent [ˌɪnkən'sɪst(ə)nt] *adj.* (*incompatible, not in agreement*) несовмести́мый (*с чем*); (*inconsequent*) непосле́довательный; (*containing contradictions*) противоречи́вый.

inconsolable [ˌɪnkən'səʊləb(ə)l] *adj.* неуте́шный, безуте́шный.

inconspicuous [ˌɪnkən'spɪkjʊəs] *adj.* незаме́тный.

inconstancy [ɪn'kɒnst(ə)nsɪ] *n.* непостоя́нство, изме́нчивость; неве́рность.

inconstant [ɪn'kɒnst(ə)nt] *adj.* непостоя́нный, изме́нчивый; (*in love or friendship*) неве́рный.

incontestable [ˌɪnkən'testəb(ə)l] *adj.* неоспори́мый.

incontinence [ɪn'kɒntɪnəns] *n.* невозде́ржанность; (*of urine/faeces*) недержа́ние мочи́/ка́ла.

incontinent [ɪn'kɒntɪnənt] *adj.* невозде́ржанный (*esp. sexually*); (*of urine/faeces*): **he was ~** он страда́л недержа́нием (мочи́/ка́ла).

incontrovertible [ˌɪnkɒntrə'vɜ:tɪb(ə)l] *adj.* неоспори́мый.

inconvenience [ˌɪnkən'vi:nɪəns] *n.* неудо́бство, беспоко́йство.

v.t. причин|я́ть, -и́ть неудо́бство +*d.*; беспоко́ить, о-; стесн|я́ть, -и́ть.

inconvenient [ˌɪnkən'vi:nɪənt] *adj.* неудо́бный; **if it is not ~ to you** е́сли э́то вам удо́бно.

inconvertibility [ˌɪnkənvɜ:tɪ'bɪlɪtɪ] *n.* (*fin.*) необрати́мость.

inconvertible [ˌɪnkən'vɜ:tɪb(ə)l] *adj.* (*fin.*) необрати́мый, неконверти́руемый; **~ currency** необрати́мая валю́та.

incorporate [ɪn'kɔ:pəˌreɪt] *v.t.* **1.** (*unite, combine*) объедин|я́ть, -и́ть; **fertilizers should be ~d with the soil** удобре́ния должны́ быть переме́шаны с землёй. **2.** (*include, introduce*) включ|а́ть, -и́ть; **his suggestions were ~d in the plan** его́ предложе́ния бы́ли включены́ в план; **~ in, into** (*annex to*) присоедин|я́ть, -и́ть; **Austria was ~d into Germany** А́встрия была́ включена́ в Герма́нию. **3.** (*form into corporation*) регистри́ровать, за- как корпора́цию.

v.i. соедин|я́ться, -и́ться; **the firm ~d with others** фи́рма слила́сь с други́ми.

incorporation [ɪnˌkɔ:pə'reɪʃ(ə)n] *n.* объедине́ние, включе́ние (в соста́в); инкорпора́ция.

incorporeal [ˌɪnkɔ:'pɔ:rɪəl] *adj.* (*not material*) невеще́ственный; (*without bodily form*) бестеле́сный.

incorrect [ˌɪnkə'rekt] *adj.* (*inaccurate; displaying errors, of style etc.*) непра́вильный; (*untrue; erroneous, of statements etc.*) неве́рный.

incorrectness [ˌɪnkə'rektnɪs] *n.* непра́вильность; неве́рность.

incorrigible [ɪn'kɒrɪdʒɪb(ə)l] *adj.* неисправи́мый.

incorruptibility [ˌɪnkərʌptɪ'bɪlɪtɪ] *n.* неподку́пность.

incorruptible [ˌɪnkə'rʌptɪb(ə)l] *adj.* неподку́пный.

increase[1] ['ɪnkri:s] *n.* (*measurable*) увеличе́ние; **~ of speed** увеличе́ние ско́рости; **~ in value** увеличе́ние сто́имости; (*growth*) рост, возраста́ние; **~ in population** рост населе́ния; **unemployment is on the ~** безрабо́тица растёт/увели́чивается; (*amount of ~*) приро́ст; **we had an ~ (of pay)** мы получи́ли приба́вку.

increase[2] [ɪn'kri:s] *v.t.* увели́чи|вать, -ть; (*extend*): **~ one's influence** расш|иря́ть, -и́рить своё влия́ние; (*raise*): **~ prices** пов|ыша́ть, -ы́сить це́ны; (*quicken*): **~ one's pace** уск|оря́ть, -о́рить шаг; (*multiply*): **~ one's efforts** умн|ожа́ть, -о́жить уси́лия; (*strengthen*): **this merely ~d his determination** э́то то́лько уси́лило его́ реши́мость.

v.t. увели́чи|ваться, -ться; (*grow*) расти́ (*impf.*); возраст|а́ть, -и́ (с+*g.*, до+*g.*); (*intensify*) уси́ли|ваться, -ться; (*expand*) расш|иря́ться, -и́риться; **the pace of life ~s** темп жи́зни ускоря́ется; (*multiply*): **his efforts ~d tenfold** его́ уси́лия возросли́/умно́жились в де́сять раз; (*rise*): **sugar ~d in price** са́хар повы́сился в цене́.

increasingly [ɪn'kri:sɪŋlɪ] *adv.* всё бо́лее; всё бо́льше и бо́льше; **it becomes ~ difficult** стано́вится всё трудне́е.

incredibl|e [ɪn'kredɪb(ə)l] *adj.* (*lit., unbelievable*) неправдоподо́бный, невероя́тный; (*coll., extraordinary*) невероя́тный, неслы́ханный; **he was ~y stupid** он был невероя́тно глуп.

incredulity [ˌɪnkrɪ'dju:lɪtɪ] *n.* недове́рчивость.

incredulous [ɪn'kredjʊləs] *adj.* недове́рчивый.

increment ['ɪnkrɪmənt] *n.* (*increase*) рост, приро́ст; (*profit*) при́быль; (*amount of regular increase*) приба́вка.

incriminate [ɪn'krɪmɪˌneɪt] *v.t.* (*accuse*) обвин|я́ть, -и́ть; (*expose; show to be guilty*) изоблич|а́ть, -и́ть.

incriminatory [ɪn'krɪmɪnətərɪ] *adj.* инкримини́рующий.

incubate ['ɪŋkjʊbeɪt] *v.t.* (*of a bird: hatch out*) выси́живать, вы́сидеть; (*hatch by artificial heat*) инкуби́ровать (*impf., pf.*).

v.i. сиде́ть (*impf.*) на яйца́х.

incubation [ˌɪŋkjʊ'beɪʃ(ə)n] *n.* (*of eggs*) выси́живание, инкуба́ция; (*stage of disease*) инкуба́ция.

incubator ['ɪŋkjʊˌbeɪtə(r)] *n.* инкуба́тор.

inculcate ['ɪnkʌlˌkeɪt] *v.t.* внедр|я́ть, -и́ть; внуш|а́ть, -и́ть.

incumbent [ɪn'kʌmbənt] *n.* **1.** (*eccl.*) приходско́й свяще́нник. **2.** занима́ющий (*какую-н.*) до́лжность.

adj.: **the ~ president** ны́нешний президе́нт; **~ upon** возлежа́щий на+*p.*; возло́женный на+*a.*; **it is ~ upon you to warn them** вы обя́заны предупреди́ть их.

incur [ɪn'kɜ:(r)] *v.t.* (*bring on o.s.*) навл|ека́ть, -е́чь на себя́; **she ~red the blame** она́ навлекла́ на себя́ обвине́ния; **I ~red his displeasure** я навлёк на себя́ его́ неудово́льствие; **he ~red heavy expenses** он понёс больши́е расхо́ды.

incurable [ɪn'kjʊərəb(ə)l] *adj.* (*of sick person*) безнадёжный; (*of disease*) неизлечи́мый.

incursion [ɪn'kɜ:ʃ(ə)n] *n.* вторже́ние, наше́ствие, набе́г.

indebted [ɪn'detɪd] *adj.* (*owing money*) в долгу́, до́лжный; (*owing gratitude*) обя́занный; **to whom am I ~ for this?** кому́ я обя́зан за э́то.

indebtedness [ɪn'detɪdnɪs] *n.* задо́лженность; обя́занность.

indecency [ɪn'di:s(ə)nsɪ] *n.* неприли́чие, непристо́йность.

indecent [ɪn'di:s(ə)nt] *adj.* **1.** (*unseemly*) неподоба́ющий, неблагови́дный. **2.** (*obscene*) неприли́чный, непристо́йный.

indecipherable [ˌɪndɪ'saɪfərəb(ə)l] *adj.* не поддаю́щийся расшифро́вке; (*of handwriting etc.*) неразбо́рчивый.

indecision [ˌɪndɪ'sɪʒ(ə)n] *n.* нереши́тельность, неуве́ренность.

indecisive [ˌɪndɪ'saɪsɪv] *adj.* нереши́тельный.

indeclinable [ˌɪndɪ'klaɪnəb(ə)l] *adj.* несклоня́емый.

indecorous [ɪn'dekərəs] *adj.* (*improper*) неприли́чный; (*unseemly*) неподоба́ющий.

indeed [ɪn'di:d] *adv.* **1.** (*really, actually*) действи́тельно; в са́мом де́ле; **and ~** да и; (*confirmatory, 'to be sure'*) и то́чно; **if ~** е́сли то́лько/вообще́. **2.** (*expr. emphasis*): **yes, ~** ну коне́чно!; ну да!; **very glad ~** о́чень, о́чень рад; **thanks very much ~** премно́го вам благода́рен; **this is generosity ~** вот э́то ще́дрость!; **why ~?** действи́тельно, заче́м?; **"Will you come?" — "I will ~"** «Вы придёте?» — «Непреме́нно/обяза́тельно»; **"Did you have any trouble?" — "We did ~"** «У вас бы́ли неприя́тности?» — «Ещё каки́е!» **3.** (*expr. intensification*) к тому́ же; ма́ло/бо́лее того́; да́же; **she was worried, ~ desperate** она́ была́ озабо́чена, да́же в отча́янии; **I saw him recently, ~ yesterday** я ви́дел его́ неда́вно, не да́лее как вчера́. **4.** (*admittedly*) пра́вда; хотя́ (и); коне́чно; разуме́ется; **there are ~ exceptions** коне́чно, есть и исключе́ния; **I may ~ be wrong** допуска́ю, что я, мо́жет быть, непра́в; **he is ~ rich, but ...** он разуме́ется, бога́т, но... **5.** (*acknowledging information*) пра́вда?; вот как! **6.** (*iron.*): **charity ~!** ничего́ себе́ благотвори́тельность!; **is it ~!** в са́мом де́ле!

indefatigable [ˌɪndɪˈfætɪgəb(ə)l] *adj.* неутоми́мый.

indefensible [ˌɪndɪˈfensɪb(ə)l] *adj.* (*mil.*) неприго́дный для оборо́ны; (*unjustified*) не име́ющий оправда́ния, непрости́тельный.

indefinable [ˌɪndɪˈfaɪnəb(ə)l] *adj.* неопредели́мый.

indefinite [ɪnˈdefɪnɪt] *adj.* **1.** (*not clearly defined*) неопределённый. **2.** (*unlimited*) неограни́ченный. **3.** (*gram.*): **~ article** неопределённый арти́кль.

indelible [ɪnˈdelɪb(ə)l] *adj.* (*lit.*, *fig.*) несмыва́емый; **~ ink** несмыва́емые черни́ла; (*fig.*, *unforgettable*) неизглади́мый.

indelicacy [ɪnˈdelɪkəsɪ] *n.* неделика́тность; беста́ктность.

indelicate [ɪnˈdelɪkət] *adj.* (*unrefined*, *immodest*) неделика́тный; (*tactless*) нетакти́чный, беста́ктный.

indemnification [ɪnˌdemnɪfɪˈkeɪʃ(ə)n] *n.* страхова́ние; возмеще́ние, компенса́ция.

indemnif|y [ɪnˈdemnɪˌfaɪ] *v.t.* **1.** (*insure*, *protect*) страхова́ть, за-; **~y s.o. against loss** застрахова́ть кого́-н. на слу́чай убы́тков. **2.** (*compensate*) возме|ща́ть, -сти́ть (*что кому*); компенси́ровать (*impf.*, *pf.*) (*что кому*); **he was ~ied for all his expenses** ему́ бы́ли возмещены́ все расхо́ды.

indemnity [ɪnˈdemnɪtɪ] *n.* (*security against damage or loss*) гара́нтия возмеще́ния убы́тков; (*compensation*) возмеще́ние.

indent [ɪnˈdent] *v.t.* **1.** (*make notches or recesses in*) зазу́бр|ивать, -и́ть; нас|ека́ть, -е́чь; **an ~ed coastline** изви́листая берегова́я ли́ния. **2.** (*typ.*): **~ed** (напи́санный/напеча́танный) с о́тступом; **the first line of each paragraph is ~ed** ка́ждый абза́ц начина́ется с кра́сной строки́.

indentation [ˌɪndenˈteɪʃ(ə)n] *n.* (*notch*, *cut*) зубе́ц, вы́рез; (*in coastline etc.*) изви́лина.

indention [ɪnˈdenʃ(ə)n] *n.* (*typ.*) абза́ц, о́тступ.

independence [ˌɪndɪˈpend(ə)ns] *n.* незави́симость (от+*g.*), самостоя́тельность; **war of ~** война́ за незави́симость; **I~ Day** День незави́симости.

independent [ˌɪndɪˈpend(ə)nt] *n.* (*pol.*) незави́симый.

adj. незави́симый, самостоя́тельный; **~ proof** объекти́вное доказа́тельство; **an ~ witness** непредубеждённый свиде́тель; (*in adv. sense*): **~ of** незави́симо от+*g.*; **she is an ~ person** у неё незави́симый хара́ктер; **an ~ income** самостоя́тельный дохо́д; **we are travelling ~ly** (*separately*) мы путеше́ствуем врозь/отде́льно.

in-depth [ɪnˈdepθ] *adj.* углублённый.

indescribable [ˌɪndɪˈskraɪbəb(ə)l] *adj.* неопису́емый.

indestructible [ˌɪndɪˈstrʌktɪb(ə)l] *adj.* неразруши́мый.

indeterminate [ˌɪndɪˈtɜːmɪnət] *adj.* (*not fixed*; *indefinite*) неопределённый; (*not settled*; *undecided*) нерешённый; неоконча́тельный; **an ~ result** неоконча́тельный результа́т; (*vague*; *indefinable*) нея́сный, сму́тный.

index [ˈɪndeks] *n.* **1.** (*indicator*, *pointer on instrument*) стре́лка. **2.** (*indicative figure or value*) и́ндекс; **retail price ~** и́ндекс ро́зничных цен; (*fig.*, *indication*) показа́тель (*m.*). **3.** (*alphabetical*) указа́тель (*m.*); **subject ~** предме́тный указа́тель; **card ~** картоте́ка; **~ card** (картоте́чная) ка́рточка. **4.** (*math.*) показа́тель (*m.*) сте́пени. **5.** (*also* **~ finger**) указа́тельный па́лец.

v.t. **1.** (*compile ~ to*) снаб|жа́ть, -ди́ть указа́телем. **2.** (*insert in ~*) зан|оси́ть, -ести́ в указа́тель.

India [ˈɪndɪə] *n.* И́ндия.

Indian [ˈɪndɪən] *n.* **1.** (*native of India*) инди́|ец (*fem.* -анка). **2.** (**American, red ~**) инд|е́ец (*fem.* -иа́нка), краснокóжий. **3.: West ~** вест-и́нд|ец (*fem.* -ка).

adj. **1.** (*of India*) инди́йский; **~ ink** тушь; **~ Ocean** Инди́йский океа́н. **2.** (*North American*) инде́йский; **~ corn** кукуру́за, маи́с; **in i~ file** гусько́м; **~ summer** ба́бье ле́то. **3. West ~** вест-и́ндский.

indicate [ˈɪndɪˌkeɪt] *v.t.* (*point out*) пока́з|ывать, -а́ть; ука́з|ывать, -а́ть (*кого/что or на кого/что*); **he ~d the way** он указа́л/показа́л путь; (*fig.*, *point to*) ука́з|ывать, -а́ть; **he ~d the need for secrecy** он указа́л на необходи́мость соблюде́ния та́йны; (*show*) обозн|ача́ть, -а́чить; **the frontier is ~d in red** грани́ца обозна́чена кра́сным (цве́том); (*state*) выража́ть, вы́разить; **he ~d his intentions** он вы́разил свои́ наме́рения; (*be a sign of*) свиде́тельствовать (*impf.*) о+*p.*; означа́ть (*impf.*); быть при́знаком +*g.*; **rust ~s neglect** ржа́вчина свиде́тельствует о плохо́м ухо́де.

indication [ˌɪndɪˈkeɪʃ(ə)n] *n.* (*pointing out*) указа́ние; (*sign*) знак, указа́тель (*m.*); **~ of a right of way** указа́тель пра́ва прое́зда; (*suggestion*; *intimation*) при́знак, намёк; **he gave no ~ of his feelings** он ниче́м не вы́дал свои́х чувств; (*portent*) при́знак; **~s of trouble** при́знаки неприя́тностей.

indicative [ɪnˈdɪkətɪv] *n.* (*gram.*) изъяви́тельное наклоне́ние.

adj. **1.: ~ of** (*suggesting*, *showing*) ука́зывающий (*на что*); свиде́тельствующий (*о чём*); **this may be ~ of his intentions** э́то, возмо́жно, ука́зывает на его́ наме́рения. **2.** (*gram.*) изъяви́тельный.

indicator [ˈɪndɪˌkeɪtə(r)] *n.* **1.** (*pointer of instrument*) стре́лка; указа́тель (*m.*). **2.** (*other indicating device*) индика́тор; **direction ~s** (*road signs*) доро́жные зна́ки (*m. pl.*); указа́тели направле́ния; **traffic ~s** (*on a vehicle*) указа́тели поворо́тов; **~ board** (*showing train arrivals and departures*) табло́ (*indecl.*). **3.** (*chem.*) индика́тор. **4.** (*fig.*, *sign*, *symptom*) показа́тель (*m.*), при́знак.

indict [ɪnˈdaɪt] *v.t.* предъяв|ля́ть, -и́ть обвине́ние +*d.*; **he was ~ed for theft** он был обвинён в кра́же.

indictable [ɪnˈdaɪtəb(ə)l] *adj.*: **an ~ offence** преступле́ние, пресле́дуемое по обвини́тельному а́кту.

indictment [ɪnˈdaɪtmənt] *n.* (*charge*) обвини́тельный акт; (*action*) предъявле́ние обвине́ния; **bring an ~ against s.o.** предъяв|ля́ть, -и́ть обвине́ние кому́-н.

Indies [ˈɪndɪz] *n. pl.*: **the East ~** Ост-И́ндия; **the West ~** Вест-И́ндия.

indifference [ɪnˈdɪfrəns] *n.* **1.** (*absence of interest*) безразли́чие; равноду́шие; **he regarded the matter with ~** он отнёсся к э́тому де́лу с равноду́шием. **2.** (*absence of feeling*) безразли́чие; равноду́шие; **he showed complete ~ to their sufferings** он прояви́л по́лное равноду́шие к их страда́ниям. **3.** (*small importance*) малова́жность; **it is a matter of ~ to me** мне э́то безразли́чно; э́то для меня́ не име́ет значе́ния.

indifferent [ɪnˈdɪfrənt] *adj.* (*without interest*) безразли́чный; равноду́шный; (*mediocre*) посре́дственный.

indigence [ˈɪndɪdʒ(ə)ns] *n.* нищета́, нужда́.

indigenous [ɪnˈdɪdʒɪnəs] *adj.* тузе́мный; ме́стный; **kangaroos are ~ to Australia** кенгуру́ во́дятся в Австра́лии.

indigent [ˈɪndɪdʒ(ə)nt] *adj.* бе́дный, ни́щий.

indigestible [ˌɪndɪˈdʒestɪb(ə)l] *adj.* неудобовари́мый.

indigestion [ˌɪndɪˈdʒestʃ(ə)n] *n.* несваре́ние, диспепси́я; **the meal has given me ~** э́та еда́ вы́звала у меня́ расстро́йство желу́дка; **he gets ~ after eating** по́сле еды́ у него́ быва́ет изжо́га.

indignant [ɪnˈdɪgnənt] *adj.* возмущённый; негоду́ющий; **I was ~ at his remark** его́ замеча́ние меня́ возмути́ло; **he became ~ with me** он вознегодова́л на меня́.

indignation [ˌɪndɪɡ'neɪʃ(ə)n] *n.* возмуще́ние, негодова́ние; **the sight aroused his ~** э́то зре́лище вы́звало у него́ возмуще́ние.

indignit|y [ɪn'dɪɡnɪtɪ] *n.* униже́ние, оскорбле́ние; **we were subjected to various ~ies** мы подве́рглись вся́ческим униже́ниям.

indigo ['ɪndɪˌɡəʊ] *n.* (*dye*) инди́го (*indecl.*); **~ blue** цвет инди́го; си́не-фиоле́товый цвет.

indirect [ˌɪndaɪ'rekt] *adj.* непрямо́й, ко́свенный; **an ~ route** обходно́й/око́льный путь; **~ tax** ко́свенный нало́г; **an ~ reference** ко́свенная ссы́лка; (*secondary*) побо́чный, втори́чный; **~ effect** побо́чный эффе́кт; (*gram.*): **~ object** ко́свенное дополне́ние; **~ speech** ко́свенная речь.

indiscernible [ˌɪndɪ'sɜːnɪb(ə)l] *adj.* неразличи́мый.

indiscreet [ˌɪndɪ'skriːt] *adj.* (*incautious*) неосторо́жный; неосмотри́тельный; (*tactless*) беста́ктный; **an ~ question** нескро́мный вопро́с.

indiscretion [ˌɪndɪ'skreʃ(ə)n] *n.* (*indiscreetness*) нескро́мность; (*indiscreet act*) неосторо́жный посту́пок; (*revelation of secret*) неосторо́жность в выска́зываниях.

indiscriminate [ˌɪndɪ'skrɪmɪnət] *adj.* **1.** (*undiscriminating*) неразбо́рчивый; **to be ~ in one's friendships** води́ться (*impf.*) с любы́м и ка́ждым. **2.** (*random*) де́йствующий без разбо́ра; **he gives ~ praise** он хва́лит без разбо́ра; **he hit out ~ly** он наноси́л уда́ры куда́ попа́ло. **3.** (*disorderly*; *unselected*) беспоря́дочный.

indispensable [ˌɪndɪ'spensəb(ə)l] *adj.* (*of thg.*) необходи́мый; (*of pers.*) незамени́мый.

indisposed [ˌɪndɪ'spəʊzd] *adj.* (*disinclined*): **I am ~ to believe you** я не скло́нен вам ве́рить; (*unwell*) (немно́го) нездоро́вый.

indisposition [ˌɪndɪspə'zɪʃ(ə)n] *n.* (*disinclination*) нерасположе́ние; (*feeling unwell*) недомога́ние.

indisputabl|e [ˌɪndɪ'spjuːtəb(ə)l] *adj.* неоспори́мый; **his genius is ~e** он бесспо́рно гениа́льный челове́к; **you are ~y correct** вы бесспо́рно пра́вы.

indissoluble [ˌɪndɪ'sɒljʊb(ə)l] *adj.* неразры́вный; неруши́мый; **~ bonds of friendship** неразры́вные у́зы дру́жбы; (*chem.*) нераствори́мый.

indistinct [ˌɪndɪ'stɪŋkt] *adj.* (*of things seen or heard*) нея́сный; невня́тный; **his speech was ~** он говори́л невня́тно; (*vague*; *obscure*) сму́тный; **I have only an ~ memory of him** я по́мню его́ о́чень сму́тно.

indistinguishable [ˌɪndɪ'stɪŋɡwɪʃəb(ə)l] *adj.* (*not recognizably different*) неразличи́мый, неотличи́мый; **he is ~ from his brother** его́ невозмо́жно отличи́ть от бра́та; **the two are ~** э́ти дво́е неразличи́мы.

individual [ˌɪndɪ'vɪdjʊəl] *n.* **1.** (*single being*) ли́чность, индиви́дуум, едини́ца, о́собь; **the rights of the ~** права́ ли́чности. **2.** (*type of person*) челове́к, тип; **an unpleasant ~** неприя́тный тип.

adj. **1.** (*single*, *particular*) отде́льный. **2.** (*of or for one person*) ли́чный, ча́стный. **3.** (*distinctive*) характе́рный, осо́бенный.

individualism [ˌɪndɪ'vɪdjʊəˌlɪz(ə)m] *n.* индивидуали́зм.

individualist [ˌɪndɪ'vɪdjʊəlɪst] *n.* индивидуали́ст.

individuality [ˌɪndɪvɪdjʊ'ælɪtɪ] *n.* индивидуа́льность.

indivisibility [ˌɪndɪˌvɪzɪ'bɪlɪtɪ] *n.* недели́мость.

indivisible [ˌɪndɪ'vɪzɪb(ə)l] *adj.* недели́мый.

Indochina ['ɪndəʊ'tʃaɪnə] *n.* Индокита́й.

indoctrinate [ɪn'dɒktrɪˌneɪt] *v.t.* внуш|а́ть, -и́ть при́нципы *+d.*; подв|ерга́ть, -е́ргнуть идеологи́ческой обрабо́тке.

indoctrination [ɪnˌdɒktrɪ'neɪʃ(ə)n] *n.* идеологи́ческая обрабо́тка.

indolence ['ɪndələns] *n.* ле́ность, вя́лость.

indolent ['ɪndələnt] *adj.* лени́вый, вя́лый.

indomitable [ɪn'dɒmɪtəb(ə)l] *adj.* неукроти́мый.

Indonesia [ˌɪndəʊ'niːzɪə] *n.* Индоне́зия.

indoor ['ɪndɔː(r)] *adj.* ко́мнатный; **~ aerial** вну́тренняя/ко́мнатная анте́нна; **~ games** ко́мнатные и́гры; **~ swimming-pool** закры́тый бассе́йн; **~ work** рабо́та в помеще́нии.

indoors [ɪn'dɔːz] *adv.* (*expr. position*) в до́ме; взаперти́; **we stayed ~ all morning** мы просиде́ли до́ма всё у́тро; (*expr. motion*) в дом.

indubitable [ɪn'djuːbɪtəb(ə)l] *adj.* несомне́нный.

induc|e [ɪn'djuːs] *v.t.* **1.** (*persuade*, *prevail on*) убеж|да́ть, -ди́ть; возде́йствовать (*impf.*, *pf.*) на*+a.*; **nothing will ~e him to change his mind** ничто́ не заста́вит его́ измени́ть реше́ние. **2.** (*bring about*) вызыва́ть, вы́звать; **sleep-~ing drugs** снотво́рные сре́дства; **~e a birth** стимули́ровать (*impf.*, *pf.*) ро́ды. **3.** (*log.*) выводи́ть, вы́вести путём инду́кции.

inducement [ɪn'djuːsmənt] *n.* (*motive*, *incentive*) сти́мул; **there is no ~ for me to stay here** ничто́ не уде́рживает меня́ зде́сь; (*lure*) прима́нка.

induct [ɪn'dʌkt] *v.t.* (*install in post*) вв|оди́ть, -ести́; назн|ача́ть, -а́чить на до́лжность; (*US*, *into armed forces*) приз|ыва́ть, -ва́ть на вое́нную слу́жбу.

induction [ɪn'dʌkʃ(ə)n] *n.* **1.** (*installation in post*) введе́ние в до́лжность; (*US*, *into armed forces*) призы́в на вое́нную слу́жбу. **2.** (*log.*) инду́кция. **3.** (*elec.*) инду́кция. **4.** (*med.*, *of a birth*) стимуля́ция ро́дов.

inductive [ɪn'dʌktɪv] *adj.* индукти́вный.

indulge [ɪn'dʌldʒ] *v.t.* (*gratify*, *give way to*) потво́рствовать (*impf.*, *pf.*) *+d.*; потака́ть (*impf.*) *+d.*; **she ~d all his wishes** она́ потака́ла всем его́ жела́ниям; (*spoil*) по́ртить (*impf.*); балова́ть, из-; **their children have been over-~d** они́ избалова́ли свои́х дете́й.

v.i. (*allow o.s. pleasure*) увлека́ться (*impf.*) (*чем*); не отказа́ть (*pf.*) себе́ в удово́льствии; **he ~s in a cigar** он позволя́ет себе́ вы́курить сига́ру.

indulgence [ɪn'dʌldʒ(ə)ns] *n.* **1.** (*gratification of others*) потво́рство, потака́ние, посла́жка; (*of o.s.*) потво́рство свои́м при́хотям. **2.** (*tolerance*) снисходи́тельность. **3.** (*pleasure indulged in*) удово́льствие; **smoking is his only ~** куре́ние — его́ еди́нственная сла́бость. **4.** (*eccl.*) индульге́нция.

indulgent [ɪn'dʌldʒ(ə)nt] *adj.* (*compliant*) потво́рствующий; (*tolerant*) снисходи́тельный; **~ parents** не сли́шком стро́гие роди́тели.

industrial [ɪn'dʌstrɪəl] *adj.* промы́шленный, индустриа́льный; **~ accident** несча́стный слу́чай на произво́дстве; **~ action** забасто́вочные де́йствия; **~ area** индустриа́льный райо́н; **~ crops** техни́ческие культу́ры; **~ design** промы́шленный диза́йн; **~ disease** профессиона́льное заболева́ние; **~ dispute** трудово́й конфли́кт; **~ training** произво́дственное обуче́ние.

industrialism [ɪn'dʌstrɪəˌlɪz(ə)m] *n.* индустриали́зм.

industrialist [ɪn'dʌstrɪəlɪst] *n.* промы́шленник.

industrialization [ɪnˌdʌstrɪəlaɪ'zeɪʃ(ə)n] *n.* индустриализа́ция.

industrialize [ɪn'dʌstrɪəˌlaɪz] *v.t.* индустриализи́ровать (*impf.*).

industrious [ɪn'dʌstrɪəs] *adj.* трудолюби́вый, усе́рдный.

industr|y ['ɪndəstrɪ] *n.* **1.** (*branch of manufacture*) о́трасль; **home ~ies** о́трасли оте́чественной промы́шленности; **cottage ~** куста́рная промы́шленность. **2.** (*the world of manufacture*) инду́стрия; промы́шленность; **he intends to go into ~y** он хо́чет заня́ться промы́шленной де́ятельностью. **3.** (*diligence*) трудолю́бие; усе́рдие.

inebriate [ɪ'niːbrɪˌeɪt] *v.t.* (*usu. in p.p.*) вызыва́ть, вы́звать опьяне́ние у*+g.*; **he became ~d** он опьяне́л.

inedible [ɪn'edɪb(ə)l] *adj.* несъедо́бный.

ineffable [ɪn'efəb(ə)l] *adj.* неопису́емый, невырази́мый.

ineffective [ˌɪnɪˈfektɪv] *adj.* безрезульта́тный; напра́сный, неэффекти́вный; (*of pers.*, *inefficient*) неуме́лый, неспосо́бный.

ineffectual [ɪnɪˈfektjʊəl, -ʃʊəl] *adj.* безрезульта́тный, неуда́чный; **an ~ person** неуда́чник.

inefficacy [ɪnˈefɪkəsɪ] *n.* бесполе́зность, неэффекти́вность.

inefficiency [ˌɪnɪˈfɪʃ(ə)nsɪ] *n.* неэффекти́вность.

inefficient [ˌɪnɪˈfɪʃ(ə)nt] *adj.* (*of persons*) неуме́лый, неспосо́бный; (*of organizations, measures etc.*) неэффекти́вный; малопроизводи́тельный; (*of machines*) непроизводи́тельный.

inelegant [ɪnˈelɪgənt] *adj.* неэлега́нтный.

ineligible [ɪnˈelɪdʒɪb(ə)l] *adj.* (*for office*) неподходя́щий; (*for military service*) него́дный (к+*d.*).

inept [ɪˈnept] *adj.* (*out of place*) неуме́стный; (*clumsy*) неуме́лый; (*stupid*; *absurd*) глу́пый, неле́пый.

ineptitude [ɪˈneptɪˌtju:d] *n.* неуме́стность, неуме́ние; глу́пая вы́ходка.

inequalit|y [ˌɪnɪˈkwɒlɪtɪ] *n.* **1.** (*lack of equality*) нера́венство; **~ies in wealth** иму́щественное нера́венство. **2.** (*difference*; *dissimilarity*) несхо́дство. **3.** (*pl.*, *variability*) изме́нчивость; **the ~ies in his work** неро́вность его́ работы.

inequitable [ɪnˈekwɪtəb(ə)l] *adj.* несправедли́вый.

inequity [ɪnˈekwɪtɪ] *n.* несправедли́вость.

ineradicable [ˌɪnɪˈrædɪkəb(ə)l] *adj.* неискорени́мый.

inert [ɪˈnɜ:t] *adj.* (*of substance*) ине́ртный; (*of the body, movements etc.*) тяжёлый, неповоро́тливый.

inertia [ɪˈnɜ:ʃə, -ʃɪə] *n.* (*phys.*) ине́рция; (*inertness*, *sloth*) ине́ртность.

inescapable [ˌɪnɪˈskeɪpəb(ə)l] *adj.* неизбе́жный.

inessential [ˌɪnɪˈsenʃ(ə)l] *adj.* незначи́тельный; малова́жный; несуще́ственный.

inestimable [ɪnˈestɪməb(ə)l] *adj.* неоцени́мый.

inevitability [ɪnˌevɪtəˈbɪlɪtɪ] *n.* неизбе́жность.

inevitable [ɪnˈevɪtəb(ə)l] *adj.* неизбе́жный, немину́емый; (*coll.*, *customary*) неизме́нный.

inexact [ˌɪnɪgˈzækt] *adj.* нето́чный.

inexactitude [ˌɪnɪgˈzæktɪtju:d] *n.* нето́чность.

inexcusable [ˌɪnɪkˈskju:zəb(ə)l] *adj.* непрости́тельный.

inexhaustible [ˌɪnɪgˈzɔ:stɪb(ə)l] *adj.* (*unfailing*) неистощи́мый, неисчерпа́емый; **an ~ supply** неисчерпа́емый запа́с; (*untiring*) неутоми́мый.

inexorable [ɪnˈeksərəb(ə)l] *adj.* (*relentless, unyielding*) неумоли́мый, непреклóнный.

inexpedient [ˌɪnɪkˈspi:dɪənt] *adj.* нецелесообра́зный.

inexpensive [ˌɪnɪkˈspensɪv] *adj.* недорого́й.

inexperience [ˌɪnɪkˈspɪərɪəns] *n.* нео́пытность.

inexperienced [ˌɪnɪkˈspɪərɪənsd] *adj.* нео́пытный.

inexpert [ɪnˈekspɜ:t] *adj.* неуме́лый.

inexplicable [ˌɪnɪkˈsplɪkəb(ə)l, ɪnˈeks-] *adj.* необъясни́мый.

inexpressible [ˌɪnɪkˈspresɪb(ə)l] *adj.* невырази́мый, неизъясни́мый.

inexpressive [ˌɪnɪkˈspresɪv] *adj.* невырази́тельный.

inextinguishable [ˌɪnɪkˈstɪŋgwɪʃəb(ə)l] *adj.* (*lit.*, *fig.*) неугаси́мый; (*fig.*) неистреби́мый.

inextricable [ɪnˈekstrɪkəb(ə)l, ˌɪnɪkˈstrɪk-] *adj.* запу́танный, сло́жный; **an ~ situation** безвы́ходное положе́ние; **~ difficulties** неразреши́мые тру́дности.

infallibility [ˌɪnfælɪˈbɪlɪtɪ] *n.* безоши́бочность; **Papal ~** непогреши́мость Па́пы.

infallible [ɪnˈfælɪb(ə)l] *adj.* (*incapable of error*) безоши́бочный, непогреши́мый; (*unfailing*) надёжный; **an ~ method** надёжный/ве́рный спо́соб; **~ proof** неопровержи́мое доказа́тельство.

infamous [ˈɪnfəməs] *adj.* позо́рный, посты́дный.

infamy [ˈɪnfəmɪ] *n.* (*evil repute*) дурна́я сла́ва; (*infamous conduct*) позо́рное поведе́ние; (*shame, disgrace*) позо́р.

infancy [ˈɪnfənsɪ] *n.* младе́нчество; **the child died in ~** ребёнок у́мер во младе́нчестве; **from his earliest ~** с ра́ннего де́тства.

infant [ˈɪnf(ə)nt] *n.* младе́нец; **~ mortality** де́тская сме́ртность; **~ prodigy** вундерки́нд; **~ school** шко́ла для малыше́й.

infanticide [ɪnˈfæntɪˌsaɪd] *n.* детоуби́йство.

infantile [ˈɪnfənˌtaɪl] *adj.* **1.** де́тский, младе́нческий; **~ paralysis** де́тский парали́ч. **2.** (*childish*) инфанти́льный.

infantry [ˈɪnfəntrɪ] *n.* пехо́та; **~ regiment** пехо́тный полк.

cpd. **~man** *n.* пехоти́нец.

infatuate [ɪnˈfætjʊˌeɪt] *v.t.*: **he is ~d with her** она́ ему́ вскружи́ла го́лову; **he was ~d with the idea** иде́я его́ ослепи́ла.

infatuation [ɪnˌfætjʊˈeɪʃ(ə)n] *n.* (*for s.o.*) влюблённость, увлече́ние; (*with sth.*) увлече́ние.

infect [ɪnˈfekt] *v.t.* (*lit.*, *fig.*) зара|жа́ть, -зи́ть; **the wound became ~ed** ра́на загнои́лась.

infection [ɪnˈfekʃ(ə)n] *n.* (*infecting*) инфе́кция; (*infectious disease*) инфекцио́нное заболева́ние; **he caught the ~ from his brother** (*lit.*, *fig.*) он зарази́лся от бра́та.

infectious [ɪnˈfekʃəs] *adj.* (*carrying infection, liable to infect*) инфекцио́нный; (*fig.*) зарази́тельный; **his enthusiasm was ~** энтузиа́зм оказа́лся зарази́тельным.

infelicitous [ˌɪnfɪˈlɪsɪtəs] *adj.* неуда́чный, неуме́стный.

infer [ɪnˈfɜ:(r)] *v.t.* **1.** (*deduce*) заключ|а́ть, -и́ть; **am I to ~ that you disagree?** зна́чит ли э́то, что вы несогла́сны? **2.** (*imply*) подразумева́ть (*impf.*).

inference [ˈɪnfərəns] *n.* (*inferring*) выведе́ние; **by ~** путём выведе́ния; (*conclusion*) вы́вод; заключе́ние.

inferior [ɪnˈfɪərɪə(r)] *n.* (*in rank, social status etc.*) подчинённый.

adj. **1.** (*lower in position, rank etc.*) ни́зший; **he held an ~ position** он занима́л (бо́лее) ни́зкое положе́ние; **the rank of captain is ~ to that of major** капита́н ни́же майо́ра по зва́нию. **2.** (*of poor quality*) плохо́й, скве́рный, низкосо́ртный, низкопро́бный; **an ~ specimen** плохо́й образе́ц. **3.** (*of less importance*) неполноце́нный; **he makes me feel ~** в его́ прису́тствии у меня́ появля́ется ко́мплекс неполноце́нности.

inferiority [ɪnˌfɪərɪˈɒrɪtɪ] *n.* (*of position*) бо́лее ни́зкое положе́ние; (*of rank*) бо́лее ни́зкое зва́ние; (*of quality*) низкосо́ртность; (*of ability*) неполноце́нность; **~ complex** ко́мплекс неполноце́нности.

infernal [ɪnˈfɜ:n(ə)l] *adj.* **1.** (*of hell*) а́дский. **2.** (*devilish, abominable*) а́дский, дья́вольский; **an ~ machine** а́дская маши́на; **~ cruelty** нечелове́ческая жесто́кость. **3.** (*coll.*, *confounded*) черто́вский; **an ~ nuisance** прокля́тье.

inferno [ɪnˈfɜ:nəʊ] *n.* (*lit.*, *fig.*) ад; **the building became a blazing ~** дом преврати́лся в пыла́ющий ад.

infertile [ɪnˈfɜ:taɪl] *adj.* неплодоро́дный, беспло́дный.

infertility [ɪnˌfɜ:ˈtɪlɪtɪ] *n.* неплодоро́дность, беспло́дность.

infest [ɪnˈfest] *v.t.* наводня́ть (*impf.*); **the house is ~ed with rats** дом наводнён кры́сами; **his clothes were ~ed with lice** его́ оде́жда кише́ла вша́ми.

infestation [ˌɪnfeˈsteɪʃ(ə)n] *n.* наводне́ние.

infidel [ˈɪnfɪd(ə)l] *n.* & *adj.* неве́рный.

infidelity [ˌɪnfɪˈdelɪtɪ] *n.* неве́рность, изме́на.

in-fighting [ˈɪnˌfaɪtɪŋ] *n.* (*fig.*) междоусо́бная дра́ка; вну́тренняя борьба́; вну́тренний конфли́кт.

infiltrate [ˈɪnfɪlˌtreɪt] *v.t.* (*permeate*) инфильтрова́ть (*impf.*); пропи́т|ывать, -а́ть; (*fig.*) прон|ика́ть, -и́кнуть; **the enemy ~d our lines** враг прони́к к нам в тыл.

v.i. (*lit.*, *fig.*) прос|а́чиваться, -очи́ться; (*fig.*) инфильтрова́ть (*impf.*).

infiltration [ˌɪnfɪl'treɪʃ(ə)n] *n.* (*lit.*) инфильтра́ция; (*fig., mil. and pol.*) проникнове́ние, инфильтра́ция.
infinite ['ɪnfɪnɪt] *adj.* (*boundless*) бесконе́чный; **the ~ goodness of God** беспреде́льная благода́ть бо́жья; **there are ~ possibilities** возмо́жности неисчерпа́емы; (*very great*) огро́мный.
infinitesimal [ˌɪnfɪnɪ'tesɪm(ə)l] *adj.* бесконе́чно ма́лый.
infinitive [ɪn'fɪnɪtɪv] *n.* инфинити́в.
infinity [ɪn'fɪnɪtɪ] *n.* бесконе́чность.
infirm [ɪn'fɜːm] *adj.* (*physically*) не́мощный, дря́хлый; (*of mind, judgement etc.*) нетвёрдый; **~ of purpose** нереши́тельный.
infirmary [ɪn'fɜːmərɪ] *n.* (*hospital*) лазаре́т; (*sick quarters*) изоля́тор.
infirmity [ɪn'fɜːmɪtɪ] *n.* не́мощь; дря́хлость.
inflame [ɪn'fleɪm] *v.t.* **1.: her eyes were ~d with weeping** от слёз у неё воспали́лись глаза́; **the wound became ~d** ра́на воспали́лась. **2.** (*arouse*) возбу|жда́ть, -ди́ть; **~d with passion** пыла́ющий стра́стью.
inflammable [ɪn'flæməb(ə)l] *adj.* легко́ воспламеня́ющийся, горю́чий.
inflammation [ˌɪnflə'meɪʃ(ə)n] *n.* воспале́ние.
inflammatory [ɪn'flæmətərɪ] *adj.* (*lit.*) воспали́тельный; (*fig.*) зажига́тельный; подстрека́тельный.
inflatable [ɪn'fleɪtəb(ə)l] *n.* надувна́я игру́шка.
adj. надувно́й.
inflate [ɪn'fleɪt] *v.t.* **1.** (*fill with air, gas etc.*) над|ува́ть, -у́ть; нака́ч|ивать, -а́ть; (*fig.*): **~d with pride** наду́тый от ва́жности; **~d importance** разду́тое значе́ние. **2.** (*fin.*): **~d prices** взви́нченные це́ны.
inflation [ɪn'fleɪʃ(ə)n] *n.* (*of balloon, tyre etc.*) надува́ние; (*econ.*) инфля́ция.
inflationary [ɪn'fleɪʃənərɪ] *adj.* инфляцио́нный.
inflect [ɪn'flekt] *v.t.* (*gram.*) склоня́ть, про-; (*modulate*) модули́ровать (*impf.*).
inflection [ɪn'flekʃ(ə)n] *n.* (*gram.*) фле́ксия, склоне́ние; (*of voice*) интона́ция.
inflexibility [ɪnˌfleksɪ'bɪlɪtɪ] *n.* неги́бкость, жёсткость; (*fig.*) непрекло́нность, непоколеби́мость.
inflexible [ɪn'fleksɪb(ə)l] *adj.* неги́бкий, жёсткий; (*fig.*) непрекло́нный, непоколеби́мый.
inflict [ɪn'flɪkt] *v.t.* нан|оси́ть, -ести́ (*удар*); причин|я́ть, -и́ть (*боль*); **he ~ed a mortal blow** он нанёс смерте́льный уда́р; **the judge ~ed a severe penalty** судья́ вы́нес суро́вый пригово́р; **I don't wish to ~ myself upon you** я не хочу́ навя́зываться вам.
infliction [ɪn'flɪkʃ(ə)n] *n.* (*of blow, wound etc.*) причине́ние (*боли*); (*of penalty etc.*) назначе́ние (*наказания*); (*painful or troublesome experience*) страда́ние; наказа́ние.
inflow ['ɪnfləʊ] *n.* наплы́в, прито́к.
influence ['ɪnflʊəns] *n.* (*power to affect or change*) влия́ние, возде́йствие; **she is a good ~ on him** она́ на него́ хорошо́ влия́ет; **he is an ~ for good** он хорошо́ возде́йствует на окружа́ющих; **under the ~ (of drink)** под возде́йствием (алкого́ля); (*power due to position or wealth*) влия́ние; авторите́т; **use your ~ on my behalf** не откажи́те замо́лвить за меня́ слове́чко; **a man of ~** влия́тельный челове́к.
v.t. влия́ть, по- на+*a.*; ока́з|ывать, -а́ть влия́ние на+*a.*; де́йствовать, по- (*or* возде́йствовать *impf., pf.*) на+*a.*; **nothing will ~ me to change my mind** ничто́ не изме́нит моего́ реше́ния.
influential [ˌɪnflʊ'enʃ(ə)l] *adj.* влия́тельный.
influenza [ˌɪnflʊ'enzə] *n.* инфлюэ́нца, грипп.
influx ['ɪnflʌks] *n.* (*fig.*) наплы́в.
inform [ɪn'fɔːm] *v.t.* информи́ровать (*impf.*); сооб|щ|а́ть, -и́ть +*d.*; осв|едомля́ть, -е́домить; ста́вить, по- в изве́стность; **I was not ~ed of the facts** мне не сообщи́ли о фа́ктах; **keep me ~ed** держи́те меня́ в ку́рсе дел; **according to ~ed opinion** согла́сно осведомлённым круга́м; **he is a well ~ed man** он хорошо́ осведомлён; **an ~ed guess** дога́дка, осно́ванная на зна́ниях.
v.i. дон|оси́ть, ести́; **he ~ed against, on his comrades** он доноси́л на свои́х това́рищей.
informal [ɪn'fɔːm(ə)l] *adj.* неофициа́льный; непринуждённый; **~ dress** повседне́вная оде́жда; **an ~ meeting** неофициа́льная встре́ча.
informality [ɪnˌfɔː'mælɪtɪ] *n.* непринуждённость.
informant [ɪn'fɔːmənt] *n.* информа́тор; осведоми́тель (*fem.* -ница); исто́чник/носитель (*m.*) информа́ции.
information [ˌɪnfə'meɪʃ(ə)n] *n.* информа́ция; све́дения (*nt. pl.*); спра́вка; да́нные (*nt. pl.*); **a useful piece of ~** поле́зная информа́ция; **according to my ~** согла́сно мои́м све́дениям; **can you give me any ~ about fares?** не мо́жете ли дать мне спра́вку о сто́имости прое́зда?; **for your ~** к ва́шему све́дению; **~ bureau** спра́вочное бюро́; **~ superhighway** информацио́нная сверхмагистра́ль; **~ technology** информа́тика.
informative [ɪn'fɔːmətɪv] *adj.* информи́рующий; поучи́тельный; **I found him most ~** он снабди́л меня́ о́чень поле́зной информа́цией; **an ~ article** содержа́тельная статья́.
informer [ɪn'fɔːmə(r)] *n.* осведоми́тель (*fem.* -ница); (*against s.o.*) доно́счи|к (*fem.* -ца).
infraction [ɪn'frækʃ(ə)n] *n.* наруше́ние.
infra dig [ˌɪnfrə 'dɪg] *pred. adj.* (*coll.*) унизи́тельно.
infra-red [ˌɪnfrə'red] *adj.* инфракра́сный.
infrastructure ['ɪnfrəˌstrʌktʃə(r)] *n.* инфраструкту́ра.
infrequency [ɪn'friːkwənsɪ] *n.* ре́дкость.
infrequent [ɪn'friːkwənt] *adj.* ре́дкий.
infringe [ɪn'frɪndʒ] *v.t. & i.* нар|уша́ть, -у́шить; посяга́ть (*impf.*) на+*a.*; ущем|ля́ть, -и́ть; **this does not ~ on your rights** э́то не ущемля́ет ва́ших прав.
infringement [ɪn'frɪndʒmənt] *n.* наруше́ние; посяга́тельство; ущемле́ние.
infuriat|e [ɪn'fjʊərɪˌeɪt] *v.t.* прив|оди́ть, -ести́ в я́рость; **an ~ing delay** приводя́щая в бе́шенство заде́ржка; **he became ~ed with me** он разозли́лся на меня́.
infuse [ɪn'fjuːz] *v.t.* (*pour in*) вли|ва́ть, -ть; (*steep in liquid*) зава́р|ивать, -и́ть; наста́ивать (*impf.*); (*inspire*) всел|я́ть, -и́ть; внуш|а́ть, -и́ть.
v.i. наста́иваться (*impf.*); **let the tea ~ for 5 minutes** пусть чай наста́ивается пять мину́т.
infusion [ɪn'fjuːʒ(ə)n] *n.* влия́ние; (*fig.*) внуше́ние; (*liquid made by ~*) насто́йка.
ingenious [ɪn'dʒiːnɪəs] *adj.* изобрета́тельный; остроу́мный; **an ~ solution** остроу́мное/гениа́льное реше́ние; (*of a device, machine etc.*) иску́сный; замыслова́тый.
ingenuity [ˌɪndʒɪ'njuːɪtɪ] *n.* изобрета́тельность.
ingenuous [ɪn'dʒenjʊəs] *adj.* (*sincere; candid*) и́скренний; открове́нный; (*simple, unsophisticated*) просто́й, простоду́шный; (*naive*) простоду́шный.
ingenuousness [ɪn'dʒenjʊəsnɪs] *n.* и́скренность; простоду́шие.
ingest [ɪn'dʒest] *v.t.* глота́ть (*impf.*); прогл|а́тывать, -оти́ть.
inglorious [ɪn'glɔːrɪəs] *adj.* (*ignominious*) бесла́вный; (*obscure*) незаме́тный.
ingot ['ɪŋgɒt, -gət] *n.* сли́ток.
ingrained [ɪn'greɪnd, *attrib.* 'ɪn-] *adj.* **1.** прони́кший; въе́вшийся; **~ dirt** въе́вшаяся грязь. **2.** (*fig.*) закорене́лый, врождённый; **~ prejudice** укорени́вшийся предрассу́док.
ingratiat|e [ɪn'greɪʃɪˌeɪt] *v.t.*: **he ~ed himself with the new manager** он вошёл в дове́рие к но́вому нача́льнику; **an ~ing smile** заи́скивающая улы́бка.
ingratitude [ɪn'grætɪˌtjuːd] *n.* неблагода́рность.
ingredient [ɪn'griːdɪənt] *n.* составна́я часть, ингредие́нт, компоне́нт.
ingrowing ['ɪnˌgrəʊɪŋ] *adj.* враста́ющий; **~ toe-nail** враста́ющий но́готь ноги́.
inhabit [ɪn'hæbɪt] *v.t.* жить (*impf.*) в+*p.*; обита́ть

(*impf.*) в+*p.*; населя́ть (*impf.*); **is the island ~ed?** э́тот о́стров обита́ем; **the house was ~ed by foreigners** дом был населён иностра́нцами; **many birds ~ the forest** в лесу́ во́дится мно́го птиц.

inhabitable [ɪn'hæbɪtəb(ə)l] *adj.* приго́дный для жилья́; жило́й.

inhabitant [ɪn'hæbɪt(ə)nt] *n.* жи́тель (*fem.* -ница); жиле́ц.

inhalation [,ɪnhə'leɪʃ(ə)n] *n.* ингаля́ция.

inhale [ɪn'heɪl] *v.t.* вд|ыха́ть, -охну́ть.

v.i. затя́гиваться (*сигаретой и т.п.*).

inhaler [ɪn'heɪlə(r)] *n.* (*device*) ингаля́тор.

inherent [ɪn'hɪərənt, ɪn'herənt] *adj.* сво́йственный, прису́щий; (*inalienable*) неотъе́млемый.

inherit [ɪn'herɪt] *v.t. & i.* насле́довать (*impf.*, *pf.*; *pf. also* у-); полу|ча́ть, -и́ть насле́дство.

inheritance [ɪn'herɪt(ə)ns] *n.* (*inheriting*) насле́дование; (*sth. inherited*) насле́дство.

inheritor [ɪn'herɪtə(r)] *n.* насле́дни|к (*fem.* -ца).

inhibit [ɪn'hɪbɪt] *v.t.* сде́рж|ивать, -а́ть; подав|ля́ть, -и́ть; ско́в|ывать, -а́ть; **fear ~s his actions** страх ско́вывает его́ де́йствия; **an ~ed person** ско́ванный челове́к.

inhibition [,ɪnhɪ'bɪʃ(ə)n] *n.* сде́рживание/подавле́ние (чувств); (*psych.*) торможе́ние.

inhospitable [,ɪnhɒ'spɪtəb(ə)l, ɪn'hɒsp-] *adj.* негостеприи́мный, неприве́тливый.

inhuman [ɪn'hju:mən] *adj.* бесчелове́чный; античелове́ческий.

inhumane [,ɪnhju:'meɪn] *adj.* негума́нный.

inhumanity [,ɪnhju:'mænɪtɪ] *n.* бесчелове́чность.

inimical [ɪ'nɪmɪk(ə)l] *adj.* (*hostile*; *conflicting*) вражде́бный; недружелю́бный; (*harmful*) вре́дный; **~ to one's health** вре́дный для здоро́вья.

inimitable [ɪ'nɪmɪtəb(ə)l] *adj.* неподража́емый; несравне́нный.

iniquitous [ɪ'nɪkwɪtəs] *adj.* несправедли́вый.

iniquity [ɪ'nɪkwɪtɪ] *n.* несправедли́вость.

initial [ɪ'nɪʃ(ə)l] *n.*: **what are your ~s?** ва́ши инициа́лы?; (*pl.*, *as signature*) пара́ф.

adj. нача́льный; **in the ~ stage** в первонача́льной ста́дии; **~ cost** первонача́льная сто́имость; **~ letter** нача́льная бу́ква.

v.t.: **~ a document** ста́вить, по- инициа́лы под докуме́нтом.

initiate [ɪ'nɪʃɪ,eɪt] *v.t.* **1.** (*set in motion*) нач|ина́ть, -а́ть. **2.** (*introduce*) вв|оди́ть, -ести́; посвяти́ть (*pf.*); **they ~d him into society** они́ ввели́ его́ в о́бщество.

initiation [ɪ,nɪʃɪ'eɪʃ(ə)n] *n.* (*beginning*) основа́ние, установле́ние; (*admission*; *introduction*) введе́ние (в о́бщество); **~ ceremonies** обря́ды посвяще́ния.

initiative [ɪ'nɪʃətɪv, ɪ'nɪʃɪətɪv] *n.* **1.** (*lead*) инициати́ва, почи́н; **he took the ~** он взял на себя́ инициати́ву; **he acted on his own ~** он де́йствовал по со́бственной инициати́ве. **2.** (*enterprise*) инициати́ва, инициати́вность; **a man of ~** инициати́вный челове́к.

initiator [ɪ'nɪʃɪeɪtə(r)] *n.* инициа́тор.

inject [ɪn'dʒekt] *v.t.* вв|оди́ть, -ести́; впры́с|кивать, -нуть; **the drug was ~ed into the blood-stream** лека́рство ввели́ в ве́ну; **he learned to ~ himself with insulin** он научи́лся де́лать себе́ уко́лы инсули́на; (*fig.*): **he will ~ new life into the government** он вдохнёт но́вую жизнь в де́ятельность прави́тельства.

injection [ɪn'dʒekʃ(ə)n] *n.* впры́скивание; инъе́кция; **have you had an ~ for cholera?** вы привива́лись про́тив холе́ры?

injudicious [,ɪndʒu:'dɪʃəs] *adj.* неблагоразу́мный; неразу́мный.

injunction [ɪn'dʒʌŋkʃ(ə)n] *n.* (*command*) прика́з, предписа́ние; (*leg.*) суде́бный запре́т.

injure ['ɪndʒə(r)] *v.t.* (*physically*) ушиб|а́ть, -и́ть; повре|жда́ть, -ди́ть; ра́нить, по-; **he fell and ~d himself** он упа́л и ушиб́ся; (*offend*) ра́нить, по-; об|ижа́ть, -и́деть; оскорб|ля́ть, -и́ть; **you have ~d his feelings** вы ра́нили/оскорби́ли его́ чу́вства.

injured ['ɪndʒəd] *adj.* (*suffering injury*) ра́неный; **the ~ party** пострада́вшая сторона́; (*as n.*): **the dead and ~** уби́тые и ра́неные; (*showing sense of wrong*) оби́женный, оскорблённый; **in an ~ voice** оби́женным то́ном.

injurious [ɪn'dʒʊərɪəs] *adj.* вре́дный, губи́тельный; **~ to health** вре́дный для здоро́вья.

injur|y ['ɪndʒərɪ] *n.* (*to the body*) ра́на, ране́ние, уши́б, тра́вма; **a war ~y** боево́е ране́ние; **his ~ies were superficial** его́ ра́ны бы́ли несерьёзные; **he sustained multiple ~ies** он получи́л мно́жество ране́ний; **he threatened to do me an ~y** он грози́лся меня́ поби́ть; (*wrongful treatment*) оскорбле́ние; **that is adding insult to ~y** э́то равноси́льно но́вому оскорбле́нию; (*fig.*, *damage*) вред, уще́рб; **this will do great ~y to our cause** э́то нанесёт большо́й вред на́шему де́лу.

injustice [ɪn'dʒʌstɪs] *n.* несправедли́вость; **you do him an ~** вы к нему́ несправедли́вы.

ink [ɪŋk] *n.* черни́л|а (*pl.*, *g.* —); **printer's ~** типогра́фская кра́ска; **the ~ came off on my hands** я изма́зался черни́лами; **an ~ drawing** рису́нок ту́шью.

v.t.: **~ one's fingers** па́чкать, за- па́льцы черни́лами.

with advs.: **~ in a drawing** покр|ыва́ть, -ы́ть рису́нок ту́шью; **~ over pencil lines** обв|оди́ть, -ести́ каранда́шные ли́нии черни́лами.

cpds. **~-blot** *n.* черни́льная кля́кса; **~-bottle** *n.* пузырёк для черни́л; **~-jet** *adj.*: **~-jet printer** (*comput.*) (краско)стру́йный при́нтер; **~-pad** *n.* ште́мпельная поду́шечка; **~-stand** *n.* черни́льный прибо́р; **~-well** *n.* черни́льница.

inkling ['ɪŋklɪŋ] *n.* намёк; сла́бое подозре́ние; **I had not the least ~ of their intentions** я не име́л ни мале́йшего представле́ния об их наме́рениях.

inky ['ɪŋkɪ] *adj.* (*stained with ink*) запа́чканный черни́лами; (*black*) чёрный как смоль.

inland ['ɪnlənd, 'ɪnlænd] *adj.* располо́женный внутри́ страны́; **an ~ sea** вну́треннее мо́ре; **the I~ Revenue** управле́ние нало́говых сбо́ров.

adv. (*motion*) внутрь/вглубь страны́; (*place*) внутри́ страны́; **they travelled ~** они́ е́хали вглубь страны́.

in-law ['ɪnlɔ:] *n.* сво́йственник, родня́ со стороны́ му́жа/жены́; **~s** свояки́ (*m. pl.*).

inla|y [ɪn'leɪ] *n.* инкруста́ция; моза́ика.

v.t. покр|ыва́ть, -ы́ть моза́икой; инкрусти́ровать (*impf.*, *pf.*); **an ~id floor** пол, покры́тый моза́икой; парке́тный пол.

inlet ['ɪnlet, -lɪt] *n.* **1.** (*small arm of water*) у́зкий зали́в. **2.**: **~ valve** впускно́й кла́пан.

inmate ['ɪnmeɪt] *n.* (*of house*) жиле́ц; (*of hospital*, *mental home etc.*) обита́тель (*m.*); больно́й, пацие́нт; (*of prison*) заключённый.

inmost ['ɪnməʊst, -məst], **innermost** ['ɪnərməʊst, -məst] *adjs.* глубоча́йший; (*fig.*) сокрове́ннейший.

inn [ɪn] *n.* гости́ница, тракти́р; постоя́лый двор.

cpds. **~keeper** *n.* хозя́ин гости́ницы; **~-sign** *n.* вы́веска придоро́жного тракти́ра.

innards ['ɪnədz] *n.* (*coll.*) вну́тренности (*f. pl.*).

innate [ɪ'neɪt, 'ɪ-] *adj.* врождённый, приро́дный.

inner ['ɪnə(r)] *adj.* (*nearer to centre*) вну́тренний; **an ~ room** вну́тренняя ко́мната; **~ tube** ка́мера ши́ны; (*intimate*) инти́мный, сокрове́нный; **my ~ convictions** мои́ вну́тренние убежде́ния.

innermost ['ɪnəməʊst, -məst] = **inmost**

innings ['ɪnɪŋz] *n.* о́чередь уда́ра (*крикет*); (*fig.*): **the Socialists had a long ~** социали́сты до́лго держа́лись у вла́сти; **he had a good ~** он про́жил до́лгую и счастли́вую жизнь.

innocence [ˈɪnəs(ə)ns] *n.* **1.** (*guiltlessness*) невино́вность; **his ~ was established** его́ невино́вность была́ дока́зана. **2.** (*freedom from sin*) неви́нность; (*chastity*) целому́дрие.

innocent [ˈɪnəs(ə)nt] *adj.* **1.** (*leg.*) невино́вный. **2.** (*harmless*) неви́нный, безоби́дный; **an ~ amusement** неви́нное развлече́ние. **3.** (*without sin*) неви́нный, безгре́шный. **4.** (*naive, simple*) наи́вный, простоду́шный.

innocuous [ɪˈnɒkjʊəs] *adj.* безвре́дный, безоби́дный.

innovate [ˈɪnə,veɪt] *v.i.* вв|оди́ть, -ести́ нововведе́ния/но́вшество.

innovation [,ɪnəˈveɪʃ(ə)n] *n.* нововведе́ние, но́вшество, нова́торство.

innovative [ˈɪnə,veɪtɪv] *adj.* нова́торский.

innovator [ˈɪnə,veɪtə(r)] *n.* нова́тор.

innuendo [,ɪnjʊˈendəʊ] *n.* ко́свенный намёк; недомо́лвка; инсинуа́ция.

innumerable [ɪˈnju:mərəb(ə)l] *adj.* бесчи́сленный, неисчисли́мый, бессчётный.

innumeracy [ɪˈnju:mərəsɪ] *n.* цифрова́я негра́мотность.

innumerate [ɪˈnju:mərət] *adj.* не уме́ющий счита́ть.

inoculate [ɪˈnɒkjʊ,leɪt] *v.t.* де́лать, с- приви́вку; приви|ва́ть, -и́ть; **he was ~d against smallpox** ему́ приви́ли о́спу.

inoculation [ɪ,nɒkjʊˈleɪʃ(ə)n] *n.* приви́вка; **I have to have an ~ for typhoid** мне ну́жно сде́лать приви́вку от ти́фа.

inoffensive [,ɪnəˈfensɪv] *adj.* (*giving no offence*) необи́дный; (*harmless*) безоби́дный.

inoperable [ɪnˈɒpərəb(ə)l] *adj.* (*untreatable by surgery*) неопера́бельный; (*unworkable*) неприменимый.

inoperative [ɪnˈɒpərətɪv] *adj.* неэффекти́вный, неде́йстви́тельный.

inopportune [ɪnˈɒpə,tju:n] *adj.* неуме́стный, несвоевре́менный.

inordinate [ɪnˈɔ:dɪnət] *adj.* чрезме́рный; неуме́ренный.

inorganic [,ɪnɔ:ˈgænɪk] *adj.* неоргани́ческий.

in-patient [ˈɪn,peɪʃ(ə)nt] *n.* стациона́рный/ко́ечный больно́й; **~ treatment** стациона́рное лече́ние.

input [ˈɪnpʊt] *n.* (*to computer*) ввод, пода́ча (информа́ции).

inquest [ˈɪnkwest, ˈɪŋ-] *n.* (*official enquiry*) сле́дствие, дозна́ние; (*investigation*) рассле́дование, разбира́тельство.

inquir|e [ɪnˈkwaɪə(r), ɪŋ-] (*see also* **enquire**) *v.t.* спр|а́шивать, -оси́ть; узн|ава́ть, -а́ть; **may I ~e your name?** могу́ я узна́ть, как вас зову́т?

v.i. спр|авля́ться, -а́виться; нав|оди́ть, -ести́ спра́вку; **we ~ed about the train service** мы спра́вились относи́тельно расписа́ния поездо́в; **has he ~ed for me?** он меня́ спра́шивал?; **we must ~e into the matter** мы должны́ рассле́довать э́то де́ло; **an ~ing mind** пытли́вый ум.

inquir|y [ɪnˈkwaɪərɪ, ɪŋ-] (*see also* **enquiry**) *n.* **1.** (*question*) наведе́ние спра́вок; **I made ~ies** я навёл спра́вки; **on ~y** в отве́т на вопро́с. **2.** (*investigation*) рассле́дование; сле́дствие; **court of ~y** сле́дственная коми́ссия; **the police are making ~ies** поли́ция рассле́дует де́ло.

inquisition [,ɪnkwɪˈzɪʃ(ə)n, ,ɪŋ-] *n.* иссле́дование, изыска́ние; (*hist.*) инквизи́ция.

inquisitive [ɪnˈkwɪzɪtɪv, ɪŋ-] *adj.* любозна́тельный, пытли́вый.

inquisitiveness [ɪnˈkwɪzɪtɪvnɪs, ɪŋ-] *n.* любозна́тельность, пытли́вость.

inquisitor [ɪnˈkwɪzɪtə(r), ɪŋ-] *n.* (*hist.*) инквизи́тор.

inroad [ˈɪnrəʊd] *n.* (*raid*) набе́г; (*encroachment*) посяга́тельство; **the holiday will make a large ~ on my savings** кани́кулы поглотя́т бо́льшую часть мои́х сбереже́ний.

insane [ɪnˈseɪn] *adj.* безу́мный, сумасше́дший; **he went ~** он лиши́лся рассу́дка; он сошёл с ума́; (*as n.*): **the ~** душевнобольны́е; **home for the ~** сумасше́дший дом; психиатри́ческая больни́ца.

insanitary [ɪnˈsænɪtərɪ] *adj.* антисанита́рный, негигиени́чный.

insanity [ɪnˈsænɪtɪ] *n.* **1.** (*madness*) психи́ческая боле́знь; безу́мие; невменя́емость; **the defendant pleaded ~** обвиня́емый сосла́лся на невменя́емость. **2.** (*folly*) безу́мие.

insatiable [ɪnˈseɪʃəb(ə)l] *adj.* ненасы́тный; **his appetite is ~** у него́ ненасы́тный аппети́т.

inscribe [ɪnˈskraɪb] *v.t.* **1.** (*engrave*) выреза́ть, вы́резать; начерта́ть (*pf.*); **the stone was ~d with their names** их имена́ бы́ли вы́сечены на ка́мне. **2.** (*write; sign*) надпи́с|ывать, -а́ть; **please ~ your name in the book** пожа́луйста, распиши́тесь в кни́ге. **3.** (*dedicate*) посвя|ща́ть, -ти́ть. **4.** (*geom.*) впи́с|ывать, -а́ть.

inscription [ɪnˈskrɪpʃ(ə)n] *n.* на́дпись.

inscrutable [ɪnˈskru:təb(ə)l] *adj.* зага́дочный, непроница́емый; (*incomprehensible*) непостижи́мый.

insect [ˈɪnsekt] *n.* насеко́мое; **~ bite** уку́с насеко́мого; **~ powder** порошо́к от насеко́мых.

insecticide [ɪnˈsektɪ,saɪd] *n.* инсектици́д.

insecure [,ɪnsɪˈkjʊə(r)] *adj.* **1.** (*unsafe; unreliable*) ненадёжный, небезопа́сный; **the window was ~ly fastened** окно́ бы́ло непло́тно закры́то; **his position in the firm is ~** у него́ ша́ткое положе́ние в фи́рме. **2.** (*lacking confidence*) неуве́ренный (в себе́); **I feel ~ of the future** я не уве́рен в бу́дущем.

insecurity [,ɪnsɪˈkjʊrɪtɪ] *n.* ненадёжность, небезопа́сность; неуве́ренность.

insemination [ɪn,semɪˈneɪʃ(ə)n] *n.* оплодотворе́ние; **artificial ~** иску́сственное оплодотворе́ние.

insensibility [ɪn,sensɪˈbɪlɪtɪ] *n.* нечувстви́тельность; (*lack of appreciation; indifference*) бесчу́вственность, безразли́чие, равноду́шие.

insensible [ɪnˈsensɪb(ə)l] *adj.* (*without physical sensation*) нечувстви́тельный; (*unaware*) не сознаю́щий; **he was ~ of his danger** он не сознава́л опа́сности; (*without emotion; unsympathetic*) бесчу́вственный.

insensitive [ɪnˈsensɪtɪv] *adj.* нечувстви́тельный; невосприи́мчивый, равноду́шный; **~ to beauty** равноду́шный к красоте́.

insensitivity [ɪn,sensɪˈtɪvɪtɪ] *n.* нечувстви́тельность; (*indifference*) невосприи́мчивость, равноду́шие.

inseparable [ɪnˈsepərəb(ə)l] *adj.* неразде́льный, неразры́вный; **~ companions** неразлу́чные прия́тели; **he was ~ from his books** его́ невозмо́жно бы́ло оторва́ть от книг.

insert[1] [ˈɪnsɜ:t] *n.* вста́вка; (*in book, newspaper etc.*) вкла́дыш, вкла́дка.

insert[2] [ɪnˈsɜ:t] *v.t.* вст|авля́ть, -а́вить; поме|ща́ть, -сти́ть; **he ~ed the key in the lock** он вста́вил ключ в замо́к; **have you ~ed a coin?** вы опусти́ли моне́ту?; **I ~ed an advertisement in the paper** я помести́л объявле́ние в газе́те.

insertion [ɪnˈsɜ:ʃ(ə)n] *n.* (*inserting*) вставле́ние, введе́ние; (*sth. inserted*) вста́вка.

inset[1] [ˈɪnset] *n.* (*in book*) вкла́дка, вкле́йка; (*in dress*) вста́вка.

inset[2] [ɪnˈset] *v.t.* (*insert*) вст|авля́ть, -а́вить; вкла́дывать, вложи́ть; (*indent*) печа́тать, на- с о́тступом.

inshore [ɪnˈʃɔ:(r), ˈɪn-] *adj.* прибре́жный.

adv. (*position*) у бе́рега; (*motion*) к бе́регу, на взмо́рье; **the wind was blowing ~** ве́тер дул по направле́нию к бе́регу.

inside [ɪn'saɪd] *n.* **1.** (*interior*) вну́треннее простра́нство; вну́тренняя часть; **have you seen the ~ of the house?** вы бы́ли внутри́ до́ма?; **the door was bolted on the ~** дверь была́ заперта́ изнутри́; **~ out** наизна́нку; **he knows the subject ~ out** он зна́ет предме́т назубо́к. **2.** (*of a garment*) изна́нка. **3.** (*of circular objects: part nearest centre*) вну́тренняя пове́рхность. **4.** (*stomach; intestines*) вну́тренности (*f. pl.*); **he complained of a pain in his ~** он жа́ловался на боль в желу́дке.

adj. вну́тренний; **~ pocket** вну́тренний карма́н; **he received ~ information** он получи́л секре́тную информа́цию.

adv. **1.** (*in or on the inner surface*) внутрь; **she wore her coat with the fur ~** она́ носи́ла шу́бу ме́хом внутрь. **2.** (*in the interior*) внутри́. **3.** (*indoors*) внутри́, в помеще́нии, до́ма; **stay ~ till the rain stops** остава́йтесь до́ма, пока́ дождь не прекрати́тся. **4.** (*in prison*): **he did 6 weeks ~** (*coll.*) он просиде́л 6 неде́ль (за решёткой).

prep. **1.** (*of place*) внутрь+*g.*; в+*p.*; **she was just ~ the door** она́ стоя́ла пря́мо в дверя́х; **have you seen ~ the house?** вы ви́дели дом изнутри́? **2.** (*of time*) в преде́лах+*g.*; **the job can't be done ~ (of) a month** э́ту рабо́ту невозмо́жно сде́лать в тече́ние ме́сяца; **I shall be back ~ (of) a week** я верну́сь не поздне́е, чем че́рез неде́лю.

insidious [ɪn'sɪdɪəs] *adj.* преда́тельский, кова́рный.

insidiousness [ɪn'sɪdɪəsnɪs] *n.* преда́тельство, кова́рство.

insight ['ɪnsaɪt] *n.* проница́тельность; понима́ние; **he shows great ~ into human character** он прекра́сно понима́ет люде́й; **a man of ~** проница́тельный челове́к.

insignia [ɪn'sɪgnɪə] *n.* (*decorations*) зна́ки (*m. pl.*) отли́чия, ордена́ (*m. pl.*); (*badges of rank etc.*) зна́ки (*m. pl.*) разли́чия, эмбле́мы (*f. pl.*) вла́сти.

insignificance [ˌɪnsɪg'nɪfɪkəns] *n.* малова́жность, ничто́жность.

insignificant [ˌɪnsɪg'nɪfɪkənt] *adj.* малова́жный, ничто́жный.

insincere [ˌɪnsɪn'sɪə(r)] *adj.* нei̇скренний.

insincerity [ˌɪnsɪn'serɪtɪ] *n.* нei̇скренность.

insinuat|e [ɪn'sɪnjʊˌeɪt] *v.t.* **1.** (*introduce*): **he ~ed himself into their company** он втёрся/прони́к в их о́бщество. **2.** (*hint*) намек|а́ть, -ну́ть на+*a.*; (и́сподволь) внуш|а́ть, -и́ть; говори́ть (*impf.*) намёками; **what are you ~ing?** на что вы намека́ете?

insinuation [ɪnˌsɪnjʊ'eɪʃ(ə)n] *n.* (*hint*) намёк; инсинуа́ция.

insipid [ɪn'sɪpɪd] *adj.* безвку́сный, пре́сный; (*fig.*) неинтере́сный; вя́лый.

insist [ɪn'sɪst] *v.t. & i.* наст|а́ивать, -оя́ть на+*p.*; тре́бовать, по- +*g.*; **he ~ed on his rights** он наста́ивал на свои́х права́х; **he ~ed on my accompanying him** он настоя́л на том, что́бы я его́ сопровожда́л; **very well, if you ~!** ну ла́дно, ко́ли вы наста́иваете!

insistence [ɪn'sɪst(ə)ns] *n.* (*quality*) насто́йчивость; (*act*) настоя́ние, насто́йчивое тре́бование.

insistent [ɪn'sɪst(ə)nt] *adj.* (*repeatedly urged*) насто́йчивый; **~ demands** насто́йчивые/настоя́тельные тре́бования.

insofar as [ˌɪnsəʊ'fɑː(r)] *conj.* (посто́льку) поско́льку; в той ме́ре, в како́й...; наско́лько.

insole ['ɪnsəʊl] *n.* сте́лька.

insolence ['ɪnsələns] *n.* (*contempt*) высокоме́рие; (*insulting behaviour*) наха́льство, де́рзость.

insolent ['ɪnsələnt] *adj.* (*contemptuous*) высокоме́рный; (*insulting; disrespectful*) наха́льный, де́рзкий.

insoluble [ɪn'sɒljʊb(ə)l] *adj.* (*of substance*) нераствори́мый; (*of problem*) неразреши́мый.

insolvency [ɪn'sɒlv(ə)nsɪ] *n.* неплатёжеспосо́бность; несостоя́тельность.

insolvent [ɪn'sɒlv(ə)nt] *adj.* неплатёжеспосо́бный; несостоя́тельный.

insomnia [ɪn'sɒmnɪə] *n.* бессо́нница.

inspect [ɪn'spekt] *v.t.* осм|а́тривать, -отре́ть; **the Queen ~ed the troops** короле́ва произвела́ смотр во́йск.

inspection [ɪn'spekʃ(ə)n] *n.* (*examination*) осмо́тр, инспе́кция; **on closer ~** при бо́лее внима́тельном рассмотре́нии; **medical ~** медици́нский осмо́тр; **the house is open to ~** дом откры́т для всео́бщего обозре́ния; **the general held an ~** генера́л произвёл смотр во́йск.

inspector [ɪn'spektə(r)] *n.* (*inspecting official*) инспе́ктор, ревизо́р; (*police officer*) инспе́ктор (поли́ции).

inspiration [ˌɪnspɪ'reɪʃ(ə)n] *n.* **1.** (*source of creative activity; idea*) вдохнове́ние; **I had an ~** меня́ осени́ла мысль. **2.** (*divine guidance*) вдохнове́ние, нае́тие. **3.** (*pers. or thg. that inspires; stimulus*) вдохнове́ние, вдохнови́тель (*m.*).

inspire [ɪn'spaɪə(r)] *v.t.* **1.** (*influence creatively*) вдохнов|ля́ть, -и́ть; **in an ~d moment** в моме́нт вдохнове́ния. **2.** (*instil; imbue*) всел|я́ть, -и́ть; **his work does not ~ me with confidence** его́ рабо́та не вызыва́ет у меня́ дове́рия; **~ s.o. with courage** внуш|а́ть, -и́ть му́жество кому́-н. (*or* в кого́-н.).

instability [ˌɪnstə'bɪlɪtɪ] *n.* неусто́йчивость; (*of character*) неуравнове́шенность.

install [ɪn'stɔːl] *v.t.* **1.** (*place in office; induct*) вв|оди́ть, -ести́ в до́лжность. **2.** (*settle*) устр|а́ивать, -о́ить; поме|ща́ть, -сти́ть; **we are comfortably ~ed in our new home** мы удо́бно устро́ились в но́вом до́ме. **3.** (*fix in position*) устан|а́вливать, -ови́ть.

installation [ˌɪnstə'leɪʃ(ə)n] *n.* (*of pers.*) введе́ние в до́лжность; (*of thg.*) устано́вка; (*equipment etc. installed*) устано́вка, устро́йство; (*buildings etc. for tech. purposes*) сооруже́ния (*nt. pl.*); **a military ~** вое́нные сооруже́ния.

instalment [ɪn'stɔːlmənt] *n.* **1.** (*partial payment*) взнос; **by ~s (*or* on the ~ plan)** в рассро́чку. **2.** (*of published work*) отры́вок, вы́пуск; отде́льная часть.

instance ['ɪnst(ə)ns] *n.* **1.** (*example*) приме́р; **for ~** наприме́р; **let me give you an ~** я вам приведу́ приме́р. **2.** (*particular case*) слу́чай; **in this ~** в э́том/да́нном слу́чае; **in the first ~** в пе́рвую о́чередь.

instant ['ɪnst(ə)nt] *n.* **1.** (*precise moment*) мгнове́ние; **come here this ~!** иди́ сюда́ сию́ же мину́ту!; **he left that very ~** он момента́льно (*or* в то́т же моме́нт) удали́лся; **I recognized him the ~ I saw him** я сра́зу же его́ узна́л. **2.** (*momentary duration*) мгнове́ние, миг; **I shall be back in an ~** я — ми́гом; я верну́сь че́рез мину́ту.

adj. **1.** (*immediate*) неме́дленный; мгнове́нный; **I felt ~ relief** я то́тчас же почу́вствовал облегче́ние; **the book was an ~ success** кни́га име́ла мгнове́нный успе́х. **2.** (*of food preparation*): **~ coffee** раствори́мый ко́фе. **3.** (*abbr.* **inst.**) теку́щий; **your letter of the 5th ~** ва́ше письмо́ от пя́того числа́ сего́ ме́сяца.

instantaneous [ˌɪnstən'teɪnɪəs] *adj.* (*done in an instant*) мгнове́нный; **it was an ~ decision** э́то бы́ло решено́ мгнове́нно; (*immediate*) неме́дленный; **death was ~** смерть наступи́ла мгнове́нно.

instead [ɪn'sted] *adv.* взаме́н (+*g.*); **~ of** вме́сто+*g.*, **let me go ~ (of you)** дава́йте я пойду́ вме́сто вас; **if the steak is off I'll have chicken ~** е́сли бифште́ксов нет, я возьму́ ку́рицу; **why don't you go out ~ of reading?** вме́сто того́, что́бы чита́ть, вы лу́чше бы пошли́ погуля́ть; **we are going by train ~ of by car** мы е́дем по́ездом, а не на маши́не.

instep ['ɪnstep] *n.* подъём (ноги́).

instigate ['ɪnstɪˌgeɪt] *v.t.* подстрека́ть (*impf.*); **they**

were ~d to rebel их подстрека́ли на бунт; **he ~d the murder** он провоци́ровал уби́йство.

instigation [,ɪnstɪ'geɪʃ(ə)n] *n.* подстрека́тельство.

instigator ['ɪnstɪ,geɪtə(r)] *n.* подстрека́тель (*fem.* -ница).

instil [ɪn'stɪl] *v.t.* (*lit.*) вл|ива́ть, -и́ть; (*fig.*) внуш|а́ть, -и́ть; прив|ива́ть, -и́ть; **his love of science was ~led at an early age** с ма́лых лет ему́ внуша́ли любо́вь к нау́ке.

instinct ['ɪnstɪŋkt] *n.* инсти́нкт; **herd ~** ста́дное чу́вство; **he acted by, on ~** он де́йствовал по интуи́ции (*or* инстинкти́вно); (*natural liking or propensity*) спосо́бность, чутьё; **he has an ~ for a bargain** у него́ приро́дное чутьё к вы́годным поку́пкам.

instinctive [ɪn'stɪŋktɪv] *adj.* инстинкти́вный, безотчётный; **I took an ~ dislike to him** у меня́ возни́кла безотчётная неприя́знь к нему́.

institute ['ɪnstɪ,tju:t] *n.* институ́т.

v.t. **1.** (*found; establish*) устан|а́вливать, -ови́ть; учре|жда́ть, -ди́ть; **~ a law** вв|оди́ть, -ести́ зако́н. **2.** (*set on foot*) нач|ина́ть, -а́ть; **the police ~d proceedings** поли́ция возбуди́ла де́ло.

institution [,ɪnstɪ'tju:ʃ(ə)n] *n.* **1.** (*setting up*) установле́ние, учрежде́ние. **2.** (*established custom or practice*) институ́т, учрежде́ние. **3.** (*organization with social purpose*) организа́ция, заведе́ние; **charitable ~** благотвори́тельное учрежде́ние; **mental ~** психиатри́ческая лече́бница.

institutional [,ɪnstɪ'tju:ʃən(ə)l] *adj.* устано́вленный; учреждённый; **~ religion** организо́ванная рели́гия; **she is in need of ~ care** её сле́дует госпитализи́ровать.

instruct [ɪn'strʌkt] *v.t.* **1.** (*teach*) учи́ть, на- (*кого чему*); обуч|а́ть, -и́ть (*кого чему*); **he ~s the class in English** он преподаёт англи́йский язы́к. **2.** (*order; direct*) прика́з|ывать, -а́ть; **I was ~ed to call on you** мне бы́ло ве́лено к вам зайти́; **I shall ~ my solicitor ~** я поручу́ де́ло своему́ адвока́ту.

instruction [ɪn'strʌkʃ(ə)n] *n.* **1.** (*teaching*) обуче́ние; **he received ~ in mathematics** он получи́л математи́ческое образова́ние. **2.** (*direction*) инструкти́рование; руково́дство; **follow the ~s on the packet** сле́дуйте указа́ниям на паке́те; **he had ~s to return** ему́ веле́ли/приказа́ли верну́ться.

cpd. **~-book** *n.* руково́дство.

instructive [ɪn'strʌktɪv] *adj.* поучи́тельный.

instruct|or [ɪn'strʌktə(r)], **-ress** [ɪn'strʌktrɪs] *nn.* инстру́ктор; учи́тель (*fem.* -ница); преподава́тель (*fem.* -ница).

instrument ['ɪnstrəmənt] *n.* **1.** (*implement*) инструме́нт; (*apparatus*) аппара́т, прибо́р; **~ panel** пульт управле́ния; (*machine or device*) ору́дие; **~ of torture** ору́дие пы́тки. **2.** (*musical ~*) (музыка́льный) инструме́нт. **3.** (*fig., means*) ору́дие. **4.** (*formal document*) докуме́нт; акт.

instrumental [,ɪnstrə'ment(ə)l] *n.* (*gram.*) твори́тельный паде́ж.

adj. **1.** (*serving as means*): **~ to our purpose** поле́зный для на́шей це́ли; **he was ~ in obtaining the order** они спосо́бствовал получе́нию зака́за. **2.** (*mus.*) инструмента́льный. **3.** (*gram.*) твори́тельный.

instrumentalist [,ɪnstrə'mentəlɪst] *n.* инструментали́ст.

instrumentality [,ɪnstrəmen'tælɪtɪ] *n.* соде́йствие; **by the ~ of** при соде́йствии +*g.*

insubordinate [,ɪnsə'bɔ:dɪnət] *adj.* неподчиня́ющийся; непоко́рный.

insubordination [,ɪnsə,bɔ:dɪ'neɪʃ(ə)n] *n.* неподчине́ние; непоко́рность.

insubstantial [,ɪnsəb'stænʃ(ə)l, -'stɑ:nʃ(ə)l] *adj.* (*not real*) нереа́льный, иллюзо́рный; (*groundless*) неоснова́тельный.

insufferable [ɪn'sʌfərəb(ə)l] *adj.* несно́сный, невыноси́мый.

insufficiency [,ɪnsə'fɪʃənsɪ] *n.* недоста́точность, недоста́ток, нехва́тка.

insufficient [,ɪnsə'fɪʃ(ə)nt] *adj.* недоста́точный, непо́лный; **our food supply is ~ for a week** нам не хва́тит проду́ктов на неде́лю; **that in itself is ~ excuse** само́ по себе́ э́то недоста́точное оправда́ние.

insular ['ɪnsjʊlə(r)] *adj.* островно́й; (*fig.*) ограни́ченный, у́зкий.

insularity [,ɪnsjʊ'lærɪtɪ] *n.* ограни́ченность, у́зость.

insulat|e ['ɪnsjʊ,leɪt] *v.t.* (*separate; detach*) отдел|я́ть, -и́ть; изоли́ровать (*impf., pf.*); (*protect from escape of heat or electricity*) изоли́ровать (*impf., pf.*); **~ing tape** изоляцио́нная ле́нта; **~e one's roof** утепл|я́ть, -и́ть кры́шу.

insulation [,ɪnsjʊ'leɪʃ(ə)n] *n.* (*insulating*) (тепло)изоля́ция; (*substance*) изоляцио́нный материа́л.

insulator ['ɪnsjʊ,leɪtə(r)] *n.* непроводни́к.

insulin ['ɪnsjʊlɪn] *n.* инсули́н.

insult[1] ['ɪnsʌlt] *n.* оскорбле́ние; оби́да; **he took it as a personal ~** он э́то восприня́л как ли́чное оскорбле́ние; *see also* **injury**

insult[2] [ɪn'sʌlt] *v.t.* оскорб|ля́ть, -и́ть; **I have never been so ~ed** меня́ в жи́зни никто́ так не оскорбля́л; **~ing language** оскорби́тельные выраже́ния.

insuperable [ɪn'su:pərəb(ə)l, ɪn'sju:-] *adj.* непреодоли́мый.

insupportable [,ɪnsə'pɔ:təb(ə)l] *adj.* нестерпи́мый, невыноси́мый, несно́сный.

insurance [ɪn'ʃʊərəns] *n.* страхова́ние, страхо́вка; (*sum insured*) су́мма страхова́ния; **~ company** страхова́я компа́ния; **~ policy** страхово́й по́лис; **life ~** страхова́ние жи́зни; **National I~** госуда́рственное страхова́ние; **take out ~** страхова́ться, за-.

insure [ɪn'ʃʊə(r)] *v.t.* **1.** (*pay for guarantee of*) страхова́ть, за-; **he ~d his house for £20,000** он застрахова́л свой дом на 20 000 фу́нтов; **is your life ~d?** вы застрахова́ли свою́ жизнь?; **the ~d** (*pers.*) застрахо́ванный. **2.** (*guarantee*) гаранти́ровать (*impf.*); страхова́ть.

v.i. страхова́ться; **have you ~d against fire?** вы застрахова́лись от пожа́ра?

insurer [ɪn'ʃʊərə(r)] *n.* страховщи́к.

insurgent [ɪn'sɜ:dʒ(ə)nt] *n.* повста́нец.

adj. восста́вший.

insurmountable [,ɪnsə'maʊntəb(ə)l] *adj.* непреодоли́мый.

insurrection [,ɪnsə'rekʃ(ə)n] *n.* восста́ние.

intact [ɪn'tækt] *adj.* (*untouched*) нетро́нутый, це́лый; (*unharmed*) невреди́мый, нетро́нутый.

intake ['ɪnteɪk] *n.* (*of recruits etc.*) набо́р; (*consumption*) потребле́ние.

intangible [ɪn'tændʒɪb(ə)l] *adj.* **1.** (*non-material*) неосяза́емый; **~ assets** нематериа́льные акти́вы, неосяза́емые це́нности. **2.** (*vague, obscure*): **~ ideas** сму́тные/нея́сные представле́ния.

integer ['ɪntɪdʒə(r)] *n.* це́лое число́.

integral ['ɪntɪgr(ə)l] *adj.* **1.** (*essential*) неотъе́млемый. **2.** (*whole; complete*) по́лный, це́льный. **3.** (*math.*) интегра́льный; **~ calculus** интегра́льное исчисле́ние.

integrate ['ɪntɪ,greɪt] *v.t.* **1.** (*combine into whole*) объедин|я́ть, -и́ть в еди́ное це́лое; **an ~d personality** це́льная ли́чность. **2.** (*complete by adding parts*) прид|ава́ть, -а́ть зако́нченный вид (*чему*). **3.** (*assimilate*) ассимили́ровать (*impf., pf.*); **racially ~d schools** шко́лы совме́стного обуче́ния для дете́й разли́чных рас.

v.i. (*join together*) объедин|я́ться, -и́ться.

integrated ['ɪntɪ,greɪtɪd] *adj.*: **~ circuit** интегра́льная схе́ма.

integration [,ɪntɪ'greɪʃ(ə)n] *n.* объедине́ние, интегри́рование; (*of armed forces, races etc.*) интегра́ция.

integrity [ɪn'tegrɪtɪ] *n.* **1.** (*uprightness; honesty*) че́стность, це́льность; **a man of ~** че́стный/принципиа́льный челове́к. **2.** (*complete state*) це́лостность; **territorial ~** территориа́льная це́лостность.
intellect ['ɪntɪˌlekt] *n.* интелле́кт, ум, рассу́док.
intellectual [ˌɪntɪ'lektjʊəl] *n.* интеллиге́нт (*fem.* -ка), интеллектуа́л; (*pl. collect.*) интеллиге́нция.
adj. интеллектуа́льный; **~ process** мысли́тельный проце́сс; **~ pursuits** у́мственная рабо́та.
intelligence [ɪn'telɪdʒ(ə)ns] *n.* **1.** (*mental power*) ум, интелле́кт; **~ quotient** коэффицие́нт у́мственного разви́тия; **~ test** испыта́ние у́мственных спосо́бностей; **high/low ~** высо́кий/ни́зкий интелле́кт. **2.** (*quickness of understanding; sagacity*) ум, сообрази́тельность; **he has ~** он сообража́ет; **a person of ~** у́мный челове́к. **3.** (*news, information*) изве́стия (*nt. pl.*), све́дения (*nt. pl.*). **4.** (*mil.*) разве́дка; разве́дывательное управле́ние.
intelligent [ɪn'telɪdʒ(ə)nt] *adj.* у́мный, смышлёный, сообрази́тельный.
intelligentsia [ˌɪntelɪ'dʒentsɪə] *n.* интеллиге́нция.
intelligibility [ɪnˌtelɪdʒɪ'bɪlɪtɪ] *n.* поня́тность.
intelligible [ɪn'telɪdʒɪb(ə)l] *adj.* поня́тный, вня́тный, вразуми́тельный; **his words were barely ~** его́ слова́ едва́ мо́жно бы́ло поня́ть.
intemperance [ɪn'tempərəns] *n.* (*immoderation*) невозде́ржанность; (*lack of self-control*) несде́ржанность.
intemperate [ɪn'tempərət] *adj.* (*immoderate*) невозде́ржанный; (*lacking self-control*) несде́ржанный.
intend [ɪn'tend] *v.t.* **1.** (*purpose; have in mind*) хоте́ть, собира́ться, намерева́ться (*all impf.*); **I ~ed him to do it (*or* that he should do it)** я хоте́л, что́бы он э́то сде́лал; **was this ~ed?** э́то бы́ло сде́лано преднаме́ренно? **2.** (*design; mean*) предназн|ача́ть, -а́чить; **a book ~ed for advanced students** кни́га, рассчи́танная на продви́нутый эта́п обуче́ния студе́нтов; **a measure ~ed to secure peace** ме́ра, напра́вленная на укрепле́ние ми́ра.
intended [ɪn'tendɪd] *n.* (*betrothed*) наречённый, жени́х; (*fem.*) наречённая, неве́ста.
intense [ɪn'tens] *adj.* **1.** (*extreme*) си́льный, интенси́вный; **~ cold** си́льный хо́лод; **~ hatred** о́страя не́нависть; **~ly annoyed** кра́йне рассе́рженный. **2.** (*ardent; emotionally charged*) напряжённый; **an ~ expression** напряжённое выраже́ние.
intensification [ɪnˌtensɪfɪ'keɪʃ(ə)n] *n.* усиле́ние, увеличе́ние.
intensif|y [ɪn'tensɪˌfaɪ] *v.t.* уси́ли|вать, -ть; увели́чи|вать, -ть; **he ~ied his efforts** он приложи́л ещё бо́льше уси́лий.
intensity [ɪn'tensɪtɪ] *n.* си́ла, интенси́вность, глубина́.
intensive [ɪn'tensɪv] *adj.* интенси́вный, напряжённый; **~ methods of farming** интенси́вное земледе́лие; **~ care unit** блок интенси́вной терапи́и.
intent[1] [ɪn'tent] *n.* наме́рение, цель; **I did it with good ~** я сде́лал э́то из до́брых побужде́ний; **to all ~s and purposes** на са́мом де́ле; по существу́.
intent[2] [ɪn'tent] *adj.* **1.** (*earnest, eager*) увлечённый; **there was an ~ expression on his face** у него́ бы́ло сосредото́ченное выраже́ние лица́. **2.** (*sedulously occupied*) погружённый (*во что*); поглощённый (*чем*); **he was ~ on his work** он был поглощён свое́й рабо́той. **3.** (*resolved*) по́лный реши́мости; **he was ~ on getting a first** он был по́лон реши́мости получи́ть дипло́м с отли́чием.
intention [ɪn'tenʃ(ə)n] *n.* наме́рение; у́мысел; **it was quite without ~** э́то бы́ло сде́лано/ска́зано без у́мысла; **I have no ~ of going to the party** я во́все не намерева́юсь идти́ на вечери́нку.
intentional [ɪn'tenʃən(ə)l] *adj.* умы́шленный, преднаме́ренный; **my absence was not ~** моё отсу́тствие не́ было преднаме́ренным; **he ignored me ~ly** он умы́шленно меня́ не заме́тил.
inter [ɪn'tɜ:(r)] *v.t.* хорони́ть, по-/за-; погре|ба́ть, -сти́.
inter- ['ɪntə(r)] *comb. form* взаимо..., меж(ду)...
interact [ɪntər'ækt] *v.i.* взаимоде́йствовать (*impf.*).
interaction [ˌɪntər'ækʃ(ə)n] *n.* взаимоде́йствие.
interactive [ˌɪntər'æktɪv] *adj.* интеракти́вный, диало́говый.
intercede [ˌɪntə'si:d] *v.i.* заступ|а́ться, -и́ться (*за кого перед кем*); ходата́йствовать, по- (*о ком/чем перед кем*).
intercept [ˌɪntə'sept] *v.t.* перехва́т|ывать, -и́ть; (*listen in on*) подслу́ш|ивать, -ать.
interception [ˌɪntə'sepʃ(ə)n] *n.* перехва́тывание, перехва́т, подслу́шивание.
intercession [ˌɪntə'seʃ(ə)n] *n.* хода́тайство; засту́пничество.
interchange ['ɪntəˌtʃeɪndʒ] *n.* **1.** (*transposition*) перестано́вка. **2.** (*exchange*) обме́н; **~ of views** обме́н мне́ниями. **3.** (*alternation*) чередова́ние.
v.t. **1.** (*transpose*) перест|авля́ть, -а́вить. **2.** (*exchange*) обме́н|ивать, -я́ть; обме́н|иваться, -я́ться +*i.* **3.** (*alternate*) чередова́ть (*impf.*).
interchangeable [ˌɪntə'tʃeɪndʒəb(ə)l] *adj.* взаимозаменя́емый; (*equivalent*) равноце́нный.
inter-city [ˌɪntə'sɪtɪ] *adj.* межгородско́й.
intercom ['ɪntəˌkɒm] *n.* (*coll.*) перегово́рное устро́йство; селе́ктор.
intercommunicat|e [ˌɪntəkə'mju:nɪˌkeɪt] *v.i.* обща́ться (*impf.*) друг с дру́гом; **~ing bedrooms** сме́жные спа́льни.
intercommunication [ˌɪntəkəˌmju:nɪ'keɪʃ(ə)n] *n.* обще́ние, связь.
interconnect [ˌɪntəkə'nekt] *v.i.* соедин|я́ться, -и́ться.
interconnected [ˌɪntəkə'nektɪd] *adj.* взаимосвя́занный.
interconnecting [ˌɪntəkə'nektɪŋ] *adj.*: **~ rooms** сме́жные ко́мнаты.
interconnection [ˌɪntəkə'nekʃ(ə)n] *n.* взаимосвя́зь.
intercontinental [ˌɪntəˌkɒntɪ'nent(ə)l] *adj.* межконтинента́льный.
intercourse ['ɪntəˌkɔ:s] *n.* (*social*) обще́ние; (*diplomatic or commercial*) сноше́ние, связь; (*sexual*) половы́е сноше́ния.
interdependence [ˌɪntədɪ'pendəns] *n.* взаимозави́симость.
interdependent [ˌɪntədɪ'pendənt] *adj.* взаимозави́симый.
interdiction [ˌɪntə'dɪkʃ(ə)n] *n.* запре́т.
interest ['ɪntrəst, -trɪst] *n.* **1.** (*attention, curiosity, concern*) интере́с; **show, take a great, keen ~ in sth.** прояв|ля́ть, -и́ть большо́й интере́с к чему́-н.; **I have no ~ in games** спорт меня́ не интересу́ет. **2.** (*quality arousing ~*) занима́тельность; **his books lack ~ for me** меня́ его́ кни́ги не занима́ют; **it is of ~ to note that ...** интере́сно заме́тить, что...; **matters of ~ to everybody** вопро́сы, ва́жные для всех. **3.** (*pursuit*) интере́с; **my chief ~s are art and history** я интересу́юсь гла́вным о́бразом иску́сством и исто́рией. **4.** (*oft. pl., advantage, benefit*) по́льза, вы́года; **I acted in your ~s** я де́йствовал в ва́ших интере́сах; **in the ~s of truth** в интере́сах и́стины; **I know where my ~s lie** я зна́ю свою́ вы́году. **5.** (*legal or financial right or share*) до́ля, часть; **he has an ~ in that firm** он име́ет до́лю в э́той фи́рме; **American ~s in Europe** америка́нские капиталовложе́ния в Евро́пе. **6.** (*group having common concern*) заинтересо́ванные круги́ (*m. pl.*); **business ~s** торго́вые предпринима́тели (*m. pl.*). **7.** (*charge on loan*) ссу́дный проце́нт; проце́нтный дохо́д; **pay ~ on a loan** плати́ть (*impf.*) проце́нты по за́йму; **rate of ~** проце́нтная ста́вка; **he lives on the ~ from his investments** он живёт на дохо́д со свои́х капиталовложе́ний.

v.t. интересова́ть (*impf.*); **this will ~ you** вам э́то бу́дет интере́сно; **I shall be ~ed to know what happens** держи́те меня́ в изве́стности о дальне́йшем.

cpds. **~-bearing** *adj.* проце́нтный, принося́щий проце́нт; **~-free** *adj.* беспроце́нтный.

interested ['ɪntrəstɪd, 'ɪntrɪstɪd] *adj.* **1.** (*having or showing interest*) интересу́ющийся; **are you ~ in football?** вы интересу́етесь футбо́лом? **2.** (*not impartial*) заинтересо́ванный; **an ~ party** заинтересо́ванная сторона́.

interesting ['ɪntrəstɪŋ, -trɪstɪŋ] *adj.* интере́сный.

interethnic [,ɪntə'eθnɪk] *adj.* межнациона́льный.

interface ['ɪntə,feɪs] *n.* стык; (*comput.*) интерфе́йс; (*fig.*) взаимосвя́зь, взаимоде́йствие.

interfer|e [,ɪntə'fɪə(r)] *v.i.* **1.** (*meddle*) вме́ш|иваться, -а́ться; **she is an ~ing old lady** она́ назо́йливая стару́ха; **don't ~e with this machine** не тро́гайте э́ту маши́ну; **my papers have been ~ed with** кто́-то тро́гал мои́ бума́ги. **2.** (*come in the way*; *present an obstacle*) меша́ть, по- *+d.*; **I am going to London tomorrow if nothing ~es** я за́втра пое́ду в Ло́ндон, е́сли ничто́ не помеша́ет.

interference [,ɪntə'fɪərəns] *n.* вмеша́тельство, поме́ха; (*radio*) поме́хи (*f. pl.*).

interim ['ɪntərɪm] *n.* промежу́ток вре́мени; **in the ~** тем вре́менем.

adj. вре́менный, промежу́точный; **~ report** предвари́тельный докла́д.

interior [ɪn'tɪərɪə(r)] *n.* **1.** (*inside*) вну́тренность. **2.** (*of building*) интерье́р; **~ decorator** худо́жник по интерье́ру. **3.** (*inland areas*) глуби́нные райо́ны (*m. pl.*); **he made a journey into the ~ of Brazil** он соверши́л путеше́ствие вглубь Брази́лии. **5.** (*home affairs*): **Minister of the I~** мини́стр вну́тренних дел.

adj. вну́тренний.

interject [,ɪntə'dʒekt] *v.t.* вст|авля́ть, -а́вить; (*coll.*) ввверну́ть (*pf.*) (*замечание*).

interjection [,ɪntə'dʒekʃ(ə)n] *n.* восклица́ние; (*gram.*) междоме́тие.

interlace [,ɪntə'leɪs] *v.t. & i.* перепле|та́ть(ся), -сти́(сь); спле|та́ть(ся), -сти́(сь).

interlard [,ɪntə'lɑːd] *v.t.*: **his prose is ~ed with foreign words** его́ про́за пересы́пана иностра́нными слова́ми.

interlocutor [,ɪntə'lɒkjʊtə(r)] *n.* собесе́дник.

interloper ['ɪntə,ləʊpə(r)] *n.* тре́тий ли́шний; незва́ный гость.

interlude ['ɪntə,luːd, -,ljuːd] *n.* (*interval of play*) антра́кт; (*mus. & fig.*) интерлю́дия.

intermarriage [,ɪntə'mærɪdʒ] *n.* брак ме́жду людьми́ ра́зных рас/национа́льностей *и т.п.*

intermarry [,ɪntə'mærɪ] *v.i.* сме́ш|иваться, -а́ться; родни́ться, по- путём бра́ка.

intermediary [,ɪntə'miːdɪərɪ] *n.* посре́дник.

adj. (*acting as go-between*) посре́днический; (*intermediate*) промежу́точный, посре́дствующий.

intermediate [,ɪntə'miːdɪət] *adj.* промежу́точный; **at an ~ stage** на перехо́дной ста́дии.

interment [ɪn'tɜːmənt] *n.* погребе́ние.

intermezzo [,ɪntə'metsəʊ] *n.* интерме́ццо (*indecl.*).

interminable [ɪn'tɜːmɪnəb(ə)l] *adj.* бесконе́чный, нескончáемый.

intermingle [,ɪntə'mɪŋg(ə)l] *v.t. & i.* сме́ш|ивать(ся), -а́ть(ся).

intermission [,ɪntə'mɪʃ(ə)n] *n.* переры́в, па́уза; (*US, theatr.*) антра́кт.

intermittent [,ɪntə'mɪt(ə)nt] *adj.* преры́вистый.

intern[1] ['ɪntɜːn] *n.* (*US*) студе́нт медици́нского ко́лледжа; молодо́й врач (*работающий в больнице и живущий при ней*).

intern[2] [ɪn'tɜːn] *v.t.* интерни́ровать (*impf., pf.*).

internal [ɪn'tɜːn(ə)l] *adj.* вну́тренний; **~ injuries** пораже́ния вну́тренних о́рганов; **~ combustion engine** дви́гатель (*m.*) вну́треннего сгора́ния.

internally [ɪn'tɜːn(ə)lɪ] *adv.* изнутри́, вну́тренне.

international [,ɪntə'næʃən(ə)l] *n.* (*sporting event*) междунаро́дные состяза́ния (*nt. pl.*).

adj. междунаро́дный, интернациона́льный.

Internationale [,ɪntə,næʃjə'nɑːl] *n.* Интернациона́л.

internecine [,ɪntə'niːsaɪn] *adj.* междоусо́бный; смертоно́сный.

Internet ['ɪntə,net] *n.* (*comput.*) интерне́т.

internment [ɪn'tɜːnmənt] *n.* интерни́рование; **~ camp** ла́герь (*m.*) для интерни́рованных (лиц).

interplanetary [,ɪntə'plænɪtərɪ] *adj.* межплане́тный.

interplay ['ɪntə,pleɪ] *n.* взаимоде́йствие, взаимосвя́зь.

interpolate [ɪn'tɜːpə,leɪt] *v.t.* интерполи́ровать (*impf., pf.*); вст|авля́ть, -а́вить.

interpolation [ɪn,tɜːpə'leɪʃ(ə)n] *n.* интерполя́ция.

interpose [,ɪntə'pəʊz] *v.t.* **1.** (*insert*; *cause to intervene*; *also v.i.*) вме́ш|иваться, -а́ться; вст|авля́ть, -а́вить; **~ an objection** выдвига́ть, вы́двинуть возраже́ние. **2.** (*interrupt*) переб|ива́ть, -и́ть.

interpret [ɪn'tɜːprɪt] *v.t.* **1.** (*expound meaning of*) толкова́ть (*impf.*); истолк|о́вывать, -ова́ть; интерпрети́ровать (*impf.*); **this passage has been ~ed in various ways** э́тот отры́вок истолко́вывали по-ра́зному; (*of an actor*) трактова́ть (*impf.*). **2.** (*understand*) истолко́в|ывать, -а́ть; **I ~ed his silence as a refusal** я истолкова́л его́ молча́ние как отка́з.

v.i. перев|оди́ть, -ести́ (у́стно); **he ~ed for the President** он был перево́дчиком президе́нта.

interpretation [ɪn,tɜːprɪ'teɪʃ(ə)n] *n.* (*expounding*; *exposition*) интерпрета́ция, толкова́ние; (*by an actor*) тракто́вка, интерпрета́ция; (*understanding, construction*) толкова́ние; **he puts a different ~ on the facts** он ина́че истолко́вывает э́ти фа́кты; (*oral translation*) (у́стный) перево́д.

interpreter [ɪn'tɜːprɪtə(r)] *n.* перево́дчи|к (*fem.* -ца).

interregnum [,ɪntə'regnəm] *n.* междуца́рствие.

interrelate [,ɪntərɪ'leɪt] *v.t.* взаимосвя́зывать (*impf.*).

interrelation(ship) [,ɪntərɪ'leɪʃ(ə)nʃɪp] *n.* взаимоотноше́ние.

interrogate [ɪn'terə,geɪt] *v.t.* допр|а́шивать, -оси́ть.

interrogation [ɪn,terə'geɪʃ(ə)n] *n.* допро́с.

interrogative [,ɪntə'rɒgətɪv] *adj.* вопроси́тельный.

interrogator [ɪn'terə,geɪtə(r)] *n.* сле́дователь (*m.*).

interrupt [,ɪntə'rʌpt] *v.t.* **1.** (*break in on*; *also v.i.*) прер|ыва́ть, -ва́ть; переб|ива́ть, -и́ть; **he ~ed me as I was reading** он прерва́л моё чте́ние. **2.** (*disturb*) нар|уша́ть, -у́шить; меша́ть, по- *+d.*; **my sleep was ~ed by the noise of trains** шум поездо́в то и де́ло меня́ буди́л. **3.** (*obstruct*) заслон|я́ть, -и́ть; препя́тствовать (*impf.*) *+d.*; **these trees ~ the view** э́ти дере́вья заслоня́ют вид.

interruption [,ɪntə'rʌpʃ(ə)n] *n.* переры́в; поме́ха; наруше́ние; **he continued to speak despite ~s** он продолжа́л говори́ть, невзира́я на поме́хи; **~ of communications** наруше́ние свя́зи.

intersect [,ɪntə'sekt] *v.t. & i.* перес|ека́ть(ся), -е́чь(ся); перекр|е́щивать(ся), -ести́ть(ся).

intersection [,ɪntə'sekʃ(ə)n] *n.* (*intersecting*) пересече́ние; (*point of ~*) то́чка пересече́ния; (*crossroads*) перекрёсток.

intersperse [,ɪntə'spɜːs] *v.t.* разбр|а́сывать, -оса́ть; расс|ыпа́ть, -ы́пать; **his talk was ~d with anecdotes** он пересыпа́л своё выступле́ние анекдо́тами.

intertwine [,ɪntə'twaɪn] *v.t. & i.* спле|та́ть(ся), -сти́(сь); **their arms were ~d** их ру́ки бы́ли сплетены́.

interval ['ɪntəv(ə)l] *n.* **1.** (*of time*) промежу́ток, отре́зок вре́мени; **we see each other at ~s** вре́мя от вре́мени мы ви́димся; **at ~s of an hour** ка́ждый час. **2.** (*of place*) расстоя́ние; **the posts were set at ~s of 10 feet** столбы́ бы́ли расста́влены на расстоя́нии десяти́ фу́тов. **3.** (*theatr.*) антра́кт. **4.** (*mus.*) интерва́л.

intervene [ˌıntə'vi:n] *v.i.* **1.** (*of an event*): **we were to have met, but his death ~d** мы должны́ бы́ли встре́титься, но его́ смерть э́тому помеша́ла; **if nothing ~s** е́сли ничего́ не случи́тся; **some years ~d** с тех пор прошло́ не́сколько лет. **2.** (*interpose one's influence*) вме́ш|иваться, -а́ться; **the government ~d in the dispute** прави́тельство вмеша́лось в конфли́кт.

intervention [ˌıntə'venʃ(ə)n] *n.* вмеша́тельство; интерве́нция.

interview ['ıntəˌvju:] *n.* делова́я встре́ча; собесе́дование; интервью́ (*nt. indecl.*); **I am having an ~ for the job** у меня́ собесе́дование в связи́ с но́вой рабо́той.

v.t. & i. интервьюи́ровать (*impf., pf.*); взять (*pf.*) интервью́ у+*g.*; **he ~s well** (*conducts an ~*) он хоро́ший интервьюе́р.

interviewer ['ıntəˌvju:ə(r)] *n.* интервьюе́р.

interweave [ˌıntə'wi:v] *v.t.* впле|та́ть, -сти́; (*insert*) вст|авля́ть, -а́вить.

intestate [ın'testət] *adj.* уме́рший без завеща́ния.

intestinal [ˌınte'staın(ə)l] *adj.* кише́чный.

intestine [ın'testın] *n.* кише́чник.

intimacy ['ıntıməsı] *n.* инти́мность, бли́зость.

intimate[1] ['ıntımət] *adj.* **1.** (*close, familiar*) закады́чный; **~ friends** закады́чные/задуше́вные друзья́; **they are on ~ terms** они́ в бли́зких отноше́ниях. **2.** (*private, personal*) инти́мный, ли́чный; **the ~ details of his life** подро́бности его́ ли́чной жи́зни. **3.** (*detailed*) основа́тельный, глубо́кий, доскона́льный; **he has an ~ knowledge of the subject** он доскона́льно зна́ет предме́т.

intimate[2] ['ıntımeıt] *v.t.* (*convey*) ув|едомля́ть, -е́домить; (*hint, imply*) намек|а́ть, -ну́ть на+*a.*.

intimation [ˌıntı'meıʃ(ə)n] *n.* намёк, уведомле́ние.

intimidate [ın'tımıˌdeıt] *v.t.* запу́г|ивать, -а́ть; угрожа́ть (*impf.*) +*d.*

intimidation [ınˌtımı'deıʃ(ə)n] *n.* запу́гивание; угро́зы (*f. pl.*).

into ['ıntʊ, 'ıntə] *prep.* **1.** (*expr. motion to a point within*) в+*a.*; **I was going ~ the theatre** я входи́л в теа́тр. **2.** (*expr. extent*) до; **far ~ the night** до по́здней но́чи. **3.** (*expr. change or process*) *usu.* в+*a.*; **the rain turned ~ snow** дождь перешёл в снег; **translate ~ French** перев|оди́ть, -ести́ на францу́зский. **4.** (*coll., devotee*): **I'm not ~ Shakespeare** я не увлека́юсь Шекспи́ром; **he's ~ jazz** он увлека́ется джа́зом.

intolerable [ın'tɒlərəb(ə)l] *adj.* невыноси́мый, несно́сный.

intolerance [ın'tɒlərəns] *n.* нетерпи́мость.

intolerant [ın'tɒlərənt] *n.* нетерпи́мый; **~ of** (*unable to bear*) не выновся́щий +*g.*

intonation [ˌıntə'neıʃ(ə)n] *n.* интона́ция.

intone [ın'təʊn] *v.t.* интони́ровать; модули́ровать; чита́ть нараспе́в (*all impf.*).

intoxicat|e [ın'tɒksıˌkeıt] *v.t.* (*lit., fig.*) опьян|я́ть, -и́ть; **~ing liquor** опьяня́ющий напи́ток; **become ~ed** опьяне́ть (*pf.*).

intoxication [ınˌtɒksı'keıʃ(ə)n] *n.* опьяне́ние.

intra- ['ıntrə] *pref.* внутри...

intractable [ın'træktəb(ə)l] *adj.* непоко́рный, несгово́рчивый; (*of thgs.*) непода́тливый, трудноуправля́емый; **~ pain** неустрани́мая боль.

intransigence [ın'trænsıdʒ(ə)ns, -zıdʒ(ə)ns] *n.* непрекло́нность.

intransigent [ın'trænsıdʒ(ə)nt, -zıdʒ(ə)nt] *adj.* непрекло́нный.

intransitive [ın'trænsıtıv, ın'trɑ:n-, -zıtıv] *adj.* неперехо́дный.

intravenous [ˌıntrə'vi:nəs] *adj.* внутриве́нный.

intrepid [ın'trepıd] *adj.* неустраши́мый, бесстра́шный.

intricacy ['ıntrıkəsı] *n.* запу́танность, сло́жность.

intricate ['ıntrıkət] *adj.* запу́танный, сло́жный.

intrigu|e [ın'tri:g, 'ın-] *n.* интри́га; про́иски (*m. pl.*).

v.t. интригова́ть, за-; интересова́ть, за-; **I was ~ed to learn** мне бы́ло интере́сно узна́ть; **an ~ing prospect** зама́нчивая перспекти́ва; **they ~ed against the king** они́ интригова́ли про́тив короля́.

intrinsic [ın'trınzık] *adj.* прису́щий, сво́йственный, по́длинный; **~ value** вну́тренняя це́нность.

introduce [ˌıntrə'dju:s] *v.t.* **1.** (*insert*): **he ~d the key into the lock** он вста́вил ключ в замо́к. **2.** (*bring in*) вв|оди́ть, -ести́; (при)вн|оси́ть, -ести́; **many improvements have been ~d** ввели́ мно́го усоверше́нствований; **tobacco was ~d from America** впервы́е таба́к был завезён из Аме́рики; **~ a bill** вв|оди́ть, -ести́ законопрое́кт. **3.** (*present*) предст|авля́ть, -а́вить; знако́мить, по- (*кого с кем*); **may I ~ my fiancée?** разреши́те мне предста́вить мою́ неве́сту; **have we been ~d (to each other)?** мы знако́мы?; **my father ~d me to chess** мой оте́ц научи́л меня́ игра́ть в ша́хматы.

introduction [ˌıntrə'dʌkʃ(ə)n] *n.* **1.** (*inserting*) ввод, введе́ние, включе́ние. **2.** (*bringing in, instituting*) введе́ние, установле́ние. **3.** (*sth. brought in*) но́вшество; **a recent ~ from abroad** заграни́чная нови́нка. **4.** (*presentation*) представле́ние; **the hostess made ~s all round** хозя́йка всех перезнако́мила; **letter of ~** рекоменда́тельное письмо́. **5.** (*title of book*): **An I~ to Nuclear Physics** «Введе́ние в я́дерную фи́зику». **6.** (*preliminary matter in book, speech etc.*) введе́ние, вступле́ние.

introductory [ˌıntrə'dʌktərı] *adj.* вступи́тельный, вво́дный.

introspection [ˌıntrə'spekʃ(ə)n] *n.* интроспе́кция, самоана́лиз.

introspective [ˌıntrə'spektıv] *adj.* интроспекти́вный.

introvert ['ıntrəˌvɜ:t] *n.* челове́к, сосредото́ченный на само́м себе́; ро́бкий, засте́нчивый челове́к.

v.t.: **an ~ed nature** за́мкнутая нату́ра.

intrud|e [ın'tru:d] *v.t.*: **he ~ed himself into our company** он навяза́л нам своё о́бщество; **I don't wish to ~e my opinions on you** я не хочу́ вам навя́зывать свои́ мне́ния.

v.i. вт|орга́ться, -о́ргнуться; **I hope I'm not ~ing** наде́юсь, я вам не помеша́ю.

intruder [ın'tru:də(r)] *n.* (*burglar*) граби́тель (*m.*).

intrusion [ın'tru:ʒ(ə)n] *n.* вторже́ние; **an ~ on my privacy** наруше́ние моего́ уедине́ния/поко́я; вторже́ние в мою́ ли́чную жизнь.

intrusive [ın'tru:sıv] *adj.* незва́ный; назо́йливый.

intuition [ˌıntju:'ıʃ(ə)n] *n.* интуи́ция; чутьё.

intuitive [ın'tju:ıtıv] *adj.* интуити́вный.

inundate ['ınənˌdeıt] *v.t.* затоп|ля́ть, -и́ть; наводн|я́ть, -и́ть; **floods ~d the valley** доли́на была́ залита́ в результа́те наводне́ний; (*fig.*) наводн|я́ть, -и́ть; **I was ~d with letters** меня́ засы́пали пи́сьмами; **the town was ~d with tourists** го́род был наводнён тури́стами.

inundation [ˌınən'deıʃ(ə)n] *n.* наводне́ние.

inure [ı'njʊə(r)] *v.t.* приуч|а́ть, -и́ть; прив|ива́ть, -и́ть на́вык (*к чему*).

invade [ın'veıd] *v.t.* захва́т|ывать, -и́ть; **Germany ~d France** Герма́ния вто́рглась во (*or* напа́ла на) Фра́нцию; (*fig.*) охва́т|ывать. -и́ть; наводн|я́ть, -и́ть; овлад|ева́ть, -е́ть +*i.*; **crowds of tourists ~d the restaurants** то́лпы тури́стов наводни́ли рестора́ны.

invader [ın'veıdə(r)] *n.* захва́тчик.

invalid[1] ['ınvəˌli:d, -lıd] *n.* (*sick person*) больно́й.

invalid[2] [ın'valıd] *adj.* (*groundless*) несостоя́тельный, неприго́дный; (*having no legal force*) недействи́тельный, не име́ющий зако́нной си́лы.

invalidate [ın'vælıˌdeıt] *v.t.* де́лать, с- неполноце́нным; лиш|а́ть, -и́ть зако́нной си́лы; аннули́ровать (*impf., pf.*).

invaluable [ɪn'væljʊəb(ə)l] *adj.* неоцени́мый, бесце́нный.

invariable [ɪn'veərɪəb(ə)l] *adj.* неизме́нный, постоя́нный.

invasion [ɪn'veɪʒ(ə)n] *n.* вторже́ние, наше́ствие; **the ~ of Europe** вторже́ние в Евро́пу; **~ of privacy** наруше́ние поко́я/уедине́ния; вторже́ние в (*чью-н.*) ли́чную жизнь.

invective [ɪn'vektɪv] *n.* инвекти́ва, брань.

inveigh [ɪn'veɪ] *v.i.*: **~ against** я́ростно нап|ада́ть, -а́сть на+*a.*; де́лать, с- вы́пады про́тив+*g.*

inveigle [ɪn'veɪg(ə)l, -'vi:g(ə)l] *v.t.* соблазн|я́ть, -и́ть; оболь|ща́ть, -сти́ть.

invent [ɪn'vent] *v.t.* (*devise, originate*) изобре|та́ть, -сти́; (*think up*) приду́м|ывать, -ать; выду́мывать, вы́думать.

invention [ɪn'venʃ(ə)n] *n.* (*designing; contrivance*) изобрете́ние; (*inventiveness*) изобрета́тельность, нахо́дчивость; (*fabrication*) вы́думка; **his story is pure ~** его́ расска́з — сплошна́я вы́думка.

inventive [ɪn'ventɪv] *adj.* изобрета́тельный, нахо́дчивый.

inventor [ɪn'ventə(r)] *n.* изобрета́тель (*m.*).

inventory ['ɪnvəntərɪ] *n.* инвента́рь (*m.*).

inverse ['ɪnvɜ:s, -'vɜ:s] *adj.* обра́тный, противополо́жный; **in ~ ratio, proportion to** в обра́тной пропорциона́льности к+*d.*

inversion [ɪn'vɜ:ʃ(ə)n] *n.* (*turning upside down*) перестано́вка; перевёртывание; (*reversing order or relation*) измене́ние поря́дка/после́довательности; (*gram.*) инве́рсия.

invert [ɪn'vɜ:t] *v.t.* (*turn upside down*) перев|ора́чивать, -ерну́ть; **~ed commas** кавы́чки (*f. pl.*); (*reverse order or relation*) перест|авля́ть, -а́вить.

invertebrate [ɪn'vɜ:tɪbrət, -ˌbreɪt] *n.* беспозвоно́чное (живо́тное).

adj. беспозвоно́чный.

invest [ɪn'vest] *v.t.* **1.** (*clothe, usu. fig.*) од|ева́ть, -е́ть; облач|а́ть, -и́ть; **he was ~ed with full authority** его́ облекли́ все́ми полномо́чиями. **2.** (*lay out as ~ment*) поме|ща́ть, сти́ть; вкла́дывать, вложи́ть.

v.i. поме|ща́ть, -сти́ть де́ньги/капита́л; (*coll., spend money usefully*): **I must ~ in a new hat** мне придётся потра́титься на но́вую шля́пу.

investigate [ɪn'vestɪˌgeɪt] *v.t.* рассле́довать (*impf., pf.*); иссле́довать (*impf., pf.*).

investigation [ɪnˌvestɪ'geɪʃ(ə)n] *n.* рассле́дование, сле́дствие; иссле́дование.

investigative [ɪn'vestɪgətɪv] *adj.*: **~ journalism** журнали́стика рассле́дований.

investigator [ɪn'vestɪˌgeɪtə(r)] *n.* сле́дователь (*m.*).

investiture [ɪn'vestɪˌtjʊə(r)] *n.* инвеститу́ра.

investment [ɪn'vestmənt] *n.* (*investing*) капиталовложе́ние, помеще́ние капита́ла; **a wise ~** разу́мное испо́льзование де́нег; (*sum invested*) инвести́ция; вклад; (*lucrative acquisition*) уда́чное приобрете́ние.

investor [ɪn'vestə(r)] *n.* вкла́дчик.

inveterate [ɪn'vetərət] *adj.* закорене́лый, зая́длый.

invidious [ɪn'vɪdɪəs] *adj.* оскорби́тельный; оби́дный.

invigilate [ɪn'vɪdʒɪˌleɪt] *v.t. & i.* надзира́ть (*impf.*) за (*кем*); следи́ть (*impf.*) за экзамену́ющимися.

invigilator [ɪn'vɪdʒɪˌleɪtə(r)] *n.* следя́щий/надзира́ющий за экзамену́ющимися.

invigorat|e [ɪn'vɪgəˌreɪt] *v.t.* укреп|ля́ть, -и́ть; прид|ава́ть, -а́ть си́лу +*d.*; (*fig.*) вдохнов|ля́ть, -и́ть.

invincibility [ɪnˌvɪnsɪ'bɪlɪtɪ] *n.* непобеди́мость.

invincible [ɪnˌvɪnsɪb(ə)l] *adj.* непобеди́мый.

inviolability [ɪnˌvaɪələ'bɪlɪtɪ] *n.* неруши́мость; неприкоснове́нность.

inviolable [ɪn'vaɪələb(ə)l] *adj.* неруши́мый; неприкоснове́нный.

inviolate [ɪn'vaɪələt] *adj.* нена́рушенный; нетро́нутый.

invisibility [ɪnˌvɪzɪ'bɪlɪtɪ] *n.* неви́димость.

invisible [ɪn'vɪzɪb(ə)l] *adj.* неви́димый, незри́мый; **~ ink** симпати́ческие черни́ла; **~ repair** худо́жественная што́пка.

invitation [ˌɪnvɪ'teɪʃ(ə)n] *n.* приглаше́ние; **an ~ to lunch** приглаше́ние на обе́д; **I came at your ~** я пришёл по ва́шему приглаше́нию.

invit|e [ɪn'vaɪt] *v.t.* **1.** (*request to come*) пригла|ша́ть, -си́ть; **she ~ed him into her flat** она́ пригласи́ла его́ к себе́ на кварти́ру; **~e o.s.** напроси́ться (*pf.*) в го́сти. **2.** (*request*) предл|ага́ть, -ожи́ть; проси́ть, по-; **I ~ed him to reconsider** я предложи́л ему́ пересмотре́ть своё реше́ние; **we were ~ed to choose** нам был предоста́влен вы́бор. **3.** (*encourage*) привл|ека́ть, -е́чь; распол|ага́ть, -ожи́ть; **his manner ~es confidence** его́ обраще́ние вызыва́ет дове́рие; (*tend to provoke*) вызыва́ть (*impf.*), спосо́бствовать (*impf.*) +*d.* **4.** (*attract*) привл|ека́ть, -е́чь; **the water looks ~ing** вода́ ма́нит.

invocation [ˌɪnvə'keɪʃ(ə)n] *n.* взыва́ние (к Бо́гу); моли́тва.

invoice ['ɪnvɔɪs] *n.* (счёт-)факту́ра.

v.t.: **~ goods to s.o.** выпи́сывать, вы́писать счёт/факту́ру кому́-н. на това́ры.

invoke [ɪn'vəʊk] *v.t.* **1.** (*call on*) приз|ыва́ть, -ва́ть; **~ the law** взыва́ть, воззва́ть к зако́ну. **2.** (*call for*) взыва́ть, воззва́ть (*о чём*), моли́ть (*impf.*); **~ God's blessing** моли́ть Бо́га о благослове́нии.

involuntary [ɪn'vɒləntərɪ] *adj.* (*forced*) вы́нужденный; (*accidental*) случа́йный; (*unintentional*) ненаме́ренный; (*uncontrollable*) нево́льный, непроизво́льный.

involve [ɪn'vɒlv] *v.t.* **1.** (*entangle; implicate*) вовл|ека́ть, -е́чь; впу́т|ывать, -ать; **I don't want to get ~d in this business** я не хочу́ впу́тываться в э́то де́ло; **he was ~d in debt** он запу́тался в долга́х; **it will not ~ you in any expense** э́то не введёт вас в расхо́ды. **2.** (*have as consequence; entail*) влечь (*impf.*) за собо́й; вызыва́ть, вы́звать; **it would ~ my living in London** в тако́м слу́чае мне бы пришло́сь жить в Ло́ндоне; **I want to know what is ~d** я хочу́ знать, с чем э́то сопряжено́.

involved [ɪn'vɒlvd] *adj.* сло́жный, запу́танный.

involvement [ɪn'vɒlvmənt] *n.* (*participation*) прича́стность; (*complicated situation*) сло́жное положе́ние; (*financial*) де́нежное затрудне́ние; (*personal*) связь, вовлечённость.

invulnerability [ɪnˌvʌlnərə'bɪlɪtɪ] *n.* неуязви́мость.

invulnerable [ɪn'vʌlnərəb(ə)l] *adj.* неуязви́мый.

inward ['ɪnwəd] *adj.* (*lit., fig.*) вну́тренний; **I was ~ly relieved** в душе́ я вздохну́л с облегче́нием.

adv. = **inward(s)**

inward(s) ['ɪnwədz] *adv.* вну́тренне; (*expr. motion*) внутрь.

iodine ['aɪəˌdi:n, -ɪn] *n.* йод.

ion ['aɪən] *n.* ио́н.

Ionic [aɪ'ɒnɪk] *adj.* ioни́ческий.

ionization [ˌaɪənaɪ'zeɪʃ(ə)n] *n.* иониза́ция.

ionize ['aɪəˌnaɪz] *v.t.* ионизи́ровать (*impf.*).

ionosphere [aɪ'ɒnəˌsfɪə(r)] *n.* ионосфе́ра.

iota [aɪ'əʊtə] *n.* (*lit., fig.*) йо́та; **we will not yield one ~** мы не отсту́пим ни на йо́ту; **I don't care one ~** мне реши́тельно всё равно́.

IOU [ˌaɪəʊ'ju:] *n.* (*coll.*) долгова́я распи́ска.

IQ (*abbr. of* ***intelligence quotient***) коэффицие́нт у́мственного разви́тия.

IRA (*abbr. of* ***Irish Republican Army***) Ирла́ндская республика́нская а́рмия.

Iran [ɪ'rɑ:n] *n.* Ира́н.

Iranian [ɪ'reɪnɪən] *n.* ира́н|ец (*fem.* -ка).

adj. ира́нский.

Iraq [ɪ'rɑ:k] *n.* Ира́к.

Iraqi [ɪ'rɑ:kɪ] *n.* ира́кец, жи́тель (*fem.* -ница) Ира́ка.

irascibility [ɪˌræsɪ'bɪlɪtɪ] *n.* раздражи́тельность, вспы́льчивость.

irascible [ɪ'ræsɪb(ə)l] *adj.* раздражи́тельный, вспы́льчивый.

irate [aɪ'reɪt] *adj.* серди́тый, гне́вный.

ire ['aɪə(r)] *n.* (*liter.*) гнев, зло́ба.

Ireland ['aɪələnd] *n.* Ирла́ндия.

iridescence [ˌɪrɪ'des(ə)ns] *n.* ра́дужность.

iridescent [ˌɪrɪ'des(ə)nt] *adj.* ра́дужный, перели́вчатый.

iridium [ɪ'rɪdɪəm] *n.* ири́дий.

iris ['aɪərɪs] *n.* **1.** (*plant*) и́рис. **2.** (*of eye*) ра́дужная оболо́чка.

Irish ['aɪərɪʃ] *adj.* ирла́ндский.

cpds. **~man** ирла́ндец; **~woman** *n.* ирла́ндка.

irk [ɜːk] *v.t.* надоеда́ть (*impf.*) +*d.*; раздража́ть (*impf.*).

irksome ['ɜːksəm] *adj.* раздражи́тельный, надое́дливый.

irksomeness ['ɜːksəmnɪs] *n.* раздражи́тельность, надое́дливость.

iron ['aɪən] *n.* **1.** (*metal*) желе́зо; **the I~ Age** желе́зный век; **his muscles are of ~** у него́ стальны́е му́скулы; **strike while the ~ is hot** (*prov.*) куй желе́зо, пока́ горячо́. **2.** (*flat- or smoothing ~*) утю́г; **electric ~** электри́ческий утю́г; **run the ~ over my trousers, please** погла́дьте мне, пожа́луйста, брю́ки. **3.** (*pl.*, **fire-~s**) ками́нный прибо́р; **he has too many ~s in the fire** он берётся за сли́шком мно́го дел сра́зу. **4.** (*pl.*, *fetters*) око́в|ы (*pl.*, *g.* —); (*handcuffs*) нару́чники (*m. pl.*).

adj. (*lit.*, *fig.*) желе́зный; **the I~ Curtain** желе́зный за́навес; **~ lung** иску́сственное лёгкое; **~ rations** неприкоснове́нный запа́с; **he ruled with an ~ hand** он управля́л/пра́вил желе́зной руко́й; **an ~ will** желе́зная во́ля.

v.t. & i. (*smooth with flat-~*) утю́жить, вы-; гла́дить, по-/вы́-; **she spent the whole evening ~ing** она́ гла́дила бельё весь ве́чер; **~ out** (*fig.*) сгла́|живать, -дить; **the difficulties have all been ~ed out** все осложне́ния устранены́.

cpds. **~-age** *adj.* принадлежа́щий желе́зному ве́ку; **~-foundry** *n.* чугунолите́йный цех; **~monger** *n.* торго́вец скобяны́м това́ром; **~-ware** *n.* скобяно́й това́р; **~work** *n.* чугу́нные украше́ния; **~-works** *n.* чугунолите́йный заво́д.

ironic(al) [aɪ'rɒnɪkəl] *adj.* ирони́ческий.

ironing ['aɪənɪŋ] *n.* **1.** (*action*) утю́жка, гла́женье; **~-board** глади́льная доска́. **2.** (*linen*) бельё для гла́женья.

irony ['aɪrənɪ] *n.* иро́ния; **the ~ of fate** иро́ния судьбы́; **the ~ of it is that ...** иро́ния в том, что...

irradiate [ɪ'reɪdɪˌeɪt] *v.t.* (*subject to light rays*) осве|ща́ть, -ти́ть; бр|оса́ть, -о́сить свет на+*a.*; (*subject to radiation*) излуч|а́ть, -и́ть; облуч|а́ть, -и́ть.

irradiation [ɪˌreɪdɪ'eɪʃ(ə)n] *n.* освеще́ние; иррадиа́ция.

irrational [ɪ'ræʃən(ə)l] *adj.* (*not endowed with reason*) неразу́мный; (*illogical*; *absurd*) иррациона́льный, нелоги́чный; (*math*) иррациона́льный.

irrationality [ɪˌræʃə'nælɪtɪ] *n.* неразу́мность, иррациона́льность, нелоги́чность.

irreconcilability [ɪˌrekənˌsaɪlə'bɪlɪtɪ] *n.* непримири́мость; несовмести́мость.

irreconcilable [ɪ'rekənˌsaɪləb(ə)l] *adj.* (*of persons*) непримири́мый; (*of ideas etc.*) несовмести́мый.

irrecoverable [ˌɪrɪ'kʌvərəb(ə)l] *adj.* невозмести́мый; (*irremediable*) непоправи́мый.

irredeemable [ˌɪrɪ'diːməb(ə)l] *adj.* непоправи́мый; (*of currency*) неразме́нный; (*of an annuity*) не подлежа́щий вы́купу.

irreducible [ˌɪrɪ'djuːsɪb(ə)l] *adj.* преде́льный, минима́льный; **the ~ minimum** преде́льный ми́нимум.

irrefutable [ɪ'refjʊtəb(ə)l, ˌɪrɪ'fjuː-] *adj.* неопровержи́мый.

irregular [ɪ'regjʊlə(r)] *n.* (*usu. pl.*, *mil.*) нерегуля́рные войска́.

adj. **1.** (*contrary to rule or norm*) непра́вильный; необы́чный; непри́нятый; **~ proceeding** де́йствие, наруша́ющее заведённый поря́док. **2.** (*variable in occurrence*) нерегуля́рный; **he keeps ~ hours** он встаёт и ложи́тся когда́ попа́ло. **3.** (*unsymmetrical*) непра́вильный, несимметри́чный. **4.** (*uneven*) неро́вный; **an ~ surface** неро́вная пове́рхность. **5.** (*unequal*; *heterogeneous*) неравноме́рный, неодина́ковый; **at ~ intervals** с неодина́ковыми интерва́лами. **6.** (*not straight*) неро́вный. **7.** (*gram.*) непра́вильный.

irregularity [ɪˌregjʊ'lærɪtɪ] *n.* (*of conduct*, *procedure*) беспоря́док; незако́нность; (*of occurrence*) непра́вильность, нерегуля́рность; (*of form*) несимметри́чность, непра́вильность, неро́вность.

irrelevanc|e [ɪ'relɪv(ə)ns], **-y** [ɪ'relɪv(ə)nsɪ] *nn.* неуме́стность; (*remark*) неуме́стное замеча́ние.

irrelevant [ɪ'relɪv(ə)nt] *adj.* неуме́стный, неподходя́щий; **~ to the matter in hand** не относя́щийся к де́лу.

irreligious [ˌɪrɪ'lɪdʒəs] *adj.* неве́рующий.

irremediable [ˌɪrɪ'miːdɪəb(ə)l] *adj.* непоправи́мый.

irremovable [ˌɪrɪ'muːvəb(ə)l] *adj.* неустрани́мый.

irreparable [ɪ'repərəb(ə)l] *adj.*: **an ~ mistake** непоправи́мая оши́бка; **an ~ loss** безвозвра́тная поте́ря/утра́та.

irreplaceable [ˌɪrɪ'pleɪsəb(ə)l] *adj.* незамени́мый.

irrepressible [ˌɪrɪ'presɪb(ə)l] *adj.* неугомо́нный, неудержи́мый; **an ~ child** неугомо́нный ребёнок; **~ optimism** нестреби́мый оптими́зм.

irreproachable [ˌɪrɪ'prəʊtʃəb(ə)l] *adj.* безукори́зненный, безупре́чный.

irresistible [ˌɪrɪ'zɪstɪb(ə)l] *adj.* непреодоли́мый, неотрази́мый; **an ~ impulse** безу́держный поры́в; **an ~ argument** неопровержи́мый до́вод; **her smile was ~** у неё была́ покоря́ющая улы́бка.

irresolute [ɪ'rezəˌluːt, -ˌljuːt] *adj.* нереши́тельный.

irrespective [ˌɪrɪ'spektɪv] *adj.*: **~ of** невзира́я/несмотря́ на+*a.*

irresponsibility [ˌɪrɪˌspɒnsɪ'bɪlɪtɪ] *n.* безотве́тственность.

irresponsible [ˌɪrɪ'spɒnsɪb(ə)l] *adj.* безотве́тственный.

irretrievable [ˌɪrɪ'triːvəb(ə)l] *adj.* (*unrecoverable*) невозмести́мый; (*beyond rescue*) безнадёжный; (*irreparable*) непоправи́мый.

irreverence [ɪ'revərəns] *n.* непочти́тельность, неуваже́ние.

irreverent [ɪ'revərənt] *adj.* непочти́тельный, неуважи́тельный.

irreversible [ˌɪrɪ'vɜːsɪb(ə)l] *adj.* (*e.g. process*) необрати́мый; (*e.g. decision*) неотменя́емый.

irrevocable [ɪ'revəkəb(ə)l] *adj.* (*unalterable*) неотменя́емый; (*gone beyond recall*) бесповоро́тный.

irrigate ['ɪrɪˌgeɪt] *v.t.* оро|ша́ть, -си́ть.

irrigation [ˌɪrɪ'geɪʃ(ə)n] *n.* ороше́ние, ирригáция; **~ canal** ирригацио́нный кана́л.

irritability [ˌɪrɪtə'bɪlɪtɪ] *n.* раздражи́тельность.

irritable ['ɪrɪtəb(ə)l] *adj.* раздражи́тельный.

irritant ['ɪrɪt(ə)nt] *n.* раздражи́тель (*m.*).

irritat|e ['ɪrɪˌteɪt] *v.t.* **1.** (*annoy*) раздража́ть (*impf.*); **he was in an ~ing mood** он был соверше́нно невозмо́жен. **2.** (*cause discomfort to*) раздража́ть (*impf.*); **the smoke ~es one's eyes** дым ест глаза́.

irritation [ˌɪrɪ'teɪʃ(ə)n] *n.* раздраже́ние.

isinglass ['aɪzɪŋˌglɑːs] *n.* ры́бий желати́н/клей.

Islam ['ɪzlɑːm, -læm, -'lɑːm] *n.* исла́м, мусульма́нство.

Islamic [ɪz'læmɪk] *adj.* мусульма́нский, исламистский.

island ['aɪlənd] *n.* о́стров; **traffic ~** острово́к безопа́сности.

islander ['aɪləndə(r)] *n.* островитя́н|ин (*fem.* -ка).

isle [aɪl] *n.* о́стров; **the British I~s** Брита́нские острова́.

isobar [ˈaɪsəʊ,bɑː(r)] *n.* изоба́ра.

isolate [ˈaɪsə,leɪt] *v.t.* **1.** изоли́ровать (*impf.*, *pl.*) (*also med.*); разобщ|а́ть, -и́ть; **an ~d village** отдалённая дере́вня; **an ~d occasion** ча́стный/отде́льный слу́чай. **2.** (*chem.*) выделя́ть, вы́делить.

isolation [,aɪsəˈleɪʃ(ə)n] *n.* (*separation*) изоля́ция, разобще́ние; **a policy of ~** поли́тика изоля́ции; (*detachment*) уедине́ние; **a case considered in ~** отде́льно взя́тый слу́чай; (*med.*) изоля́ция; **~ hospital** инфекцио́нная больни́ца.

isolationism [,aɪsəˈleɪʃə,nɪz(ə)m] *n.* изоляциони́зм.

isolationist [,aɪsəˈleɪʃə,nɪst] *n.* изоляциони́ст.

isometric [,aɪsəʊˈmetrɪk] *adj.* изометри́ческий.

isosceles [aɪˈsɒsɪ,liːz] *adj.* равнобе́дренный.

isotope [ˈaɪsə,təʊp] *n.* изото́п.

Israel [ˈɪzreɪl] *n.* (*bibl.*, *pol.*) Изра́иль (*m.*).

Israeli [ɪzˈreɪlɪ] *n.*, **Israelite** [ˈɪzrɪə,laɪt, -rə,laɪt] *n.* (*bibl.*) израильтя́н|ин (*fem.* -ка).

adj. изра́ильский.

issue [ˈɪʃuː, ˈɪsjuː] *n.* **1.** (*outflowing*; *emergence*) вытека́ние; (*place of emergence*) вы́ход. **2.** (*putting out*, *publication*, *production*) вы́пуск; **an ~ of stamps** вы́пуск ма́рок; (*sth. published or produced*) вы́пуск, изда́ние; **recent ~s of a magazine** после́дние номера́ журна́ла; **an ~ of winter clothing** компле́кт зи́мней оде́жды. **3.** (*question*, *topic*) вопро́с; предме́т обсужде́ния; **the point at ~** предме́т спо́ра; **I don't want to make an ~ of it** я не хочу́ де́лать из э́того исто́рию; **join, take ~ with s.o. on sth.** нач|ина́ть, -а́ть спо́рить с кем-н. о чём-н. **4.** (*outcome*) исхо́д; ито́г; **I await the ~** я жду результа́та. **5.** (*leg.*, *offspring*) пото́мство.

v.t. **1.** (*utter*, *publish*) изд|ава́ть, -а́ть; выпуска́ть, вы́пустить; **he ~d a solemn warning** он сде́лал серьёзное предупрежде́ние. **2.** (*supply*) выдава́ть, вы́дать; снаб|жа́ть, -ди́ть; **everyone was ~d with ration cards** всем вы́дали продово́льственные ка́рточки.

v.i. **1.** (*go*, *come out*) выходи́ть, вы́йти; вытека́ть (*impf.*); **smoke ~d from the chimney** дым шёл/вали́л из трубы́; **no sound ~d from his lips** он не пророни́л ни зву́ка. **2.** (*proceed*, *emanate*) проис|ходи́ть, -зойти́.

isthmus [ˈɪsməs, ˈɪsθ-] *n.* перешéек, перемы́чка.

it [ɪt] *pron.* **1.** он (она́, оно́); э́то; *often untranslated, see examples*: **he loved his country and died for ~** он люби́л свою́ страну́ и поги́б за неё; **who is it?** кто э́то?; **~'s the postman** э́то почтальо́н; **I don't speak Russian but I understand ~** я не говорю́ по-ру́сски, но понима́ю; **the shed has no roof over ~** сара́й не име́ет кры́ши; **that's just ~** то́-то и оно́; в то́м-то и де́ло; **that's not ~** э́то не то; не в том де́ло. **2.** (*impersonal or indefinite*): **~ is winter** (стои́т) зима́; **~ was in winter** де́ло бы́ло зимо́й; **~ is cold** хо́лодно; **~ is 6 o'clock** (сейча́с) шесть часо́в; **~ is raining** идёт дождь; **~ is 5 miles to Oxford** до О́ксфорда пять миль; **run for ~!** беги́те изо всех сил!; **he had a bad time of ~** ему́ здо́рово доста́лось; **if ~ were not for him** е́сли бы не он; не будь его́; **how goes ~?** как дела́?; **~ is said** говоря́т; **~ is no use going there** не́зачем идти́ туда́. **3.** (*anticipating logical subject*): **~ is hard to imagine** тру́дно себе́ предста́вить; **I thought ~ best to inform you** я почёл за лу́чшее сообщи́ть вам; **~ appears I was wrong** выхо́дит, что я был непра́в. **4.** (*emph. another word*): **~ was John who said that** э́то сказа́л Джон; **~ is to him you must write** э́то ему вы должны́ написа́ть; **~ is here that the trouble lies** вот в чём беда́; **~ was here that I met her** здесь-то мы с ней и встре́тились. **5.** (*other emph. uses*): **he thinks he's ~** (*coll.*) он (поря́дком) зазнаётся; **that's ~** (*the problem*) вот и́менно; (*right*) (вот) и́менно, ве́рно; (*coll.*, *the end*) вот и всё; и то́чка; **this is ~** (*expected event*) наконе́ц-то. **6.:** '**~**' (*at children's games*) водя́щий (*etc.*, *depending on game*; *see also* **he**): **who is ~?** кто во́дит?

Italian [ɪˈtæljən] *n.* (*pers.*) италья́н|ец (*fem.* -ка); (*language*) италья́нский язы́к.

adj. италья́нский.

italicize [ɪˈtælɪ,saɪz] *v.t.* выделя́ть, вы́делить курси́вом.

italics [ɪˈtælɪks] *n.* курси́в; **in ~** курси́вом.

Italy [ˈɪtəlɪ] *n.* Ита́лия.

itch [ɪtʃ] *n.* **1.** (*irritation of skin*) зуд. **2.** (*disease*) чесо́тка. **3.** (*hankering*) стремле́ние; зуд.

v.i. **1.** (*irritate*) чеса́ться (*impf.*). **2.** (*feel a longing*) испы́тывать (*impf.*) зуд; **I was ~ing to strike him** у меня́ рука́ так и зуде́ла/чеса́лась уда́рить его́.

itchy [ˈɪtʃɪ] *adj.* зудя́щий.

item [ˈaɪtəm] *n.* пункт, но́мер; **~s on the agenda** пу́нкты пове́стки дня; **the first ~ on the programme** (*entertainment*) пе́рвый но́мер програ́ммы; **~ of expenditure** статья́ расхо́да; **news ~** (коро́ткое) сообще́ние.

itemize [ˈaɪtə,maɪz] *v.t.* переч|исля́ть, -и́слить; сост|авля́ть, -а́вить пе́речень +*g.*; **an ~d account** подро́бный счёт.

itinerant [aɪˈtɪnərənt, ɪ-] *adj.* стра́нствующий; **~ musicians** стра́нствующие/бродя́чие музыка́нты; **an ~ judge** судья́, объезжа́ющий свой о́круг.

itinerary [aɪˈtɪnərərɪ, ɪ-] *n.* (*route*) маршру́т, путь (*m.*).

its [ɪts] *poss. adj.* его́, её; (*pert. to subject of sentence*) свой; **the horse broke ~ leg** ло́шадь слома́ла (себе́) но́гу.

itself [ɪtˈself] *n.* **1.** (*refl.*) себя́; -ся (*suff.*); **the cat was washing ~** кот мы́лся; **the monkey saw ~ in the mirror** обезья́на уви́дела себя́ в зе́ркале. **2.** (*emph.*) сам; **she is kindness ~** она́ сама́ доброта́; **the house ~ is not worth much** дом сам по себе́ мно́гого не сто́ит; **by ~** (*alone*) оди́н, одино́ко, в отдале́нии; (*automatically*) самостоя́тельно; **in ~** сам по себе́; **of ~** сам (по себе́); **the house looked ~ again** дом сно́ва приобрёл пре́жний вид.

ITV (*abbr. of* ***Independent Television***) незави́симое (комме́рческое) телеви́дение.

ivory [ˈaɪvərɪ] *n.* **1.** (*substance*) слоно́вая кость. **2.** (*colour*) цвет слоно́вой ко́сти.

adj. (*made of ~*) из слоно́вой ко́сти; (*of the colour of ~*) ма́товый, кре́мовый; **~ skin** ма́товая ко́жа.

ivy [ˈaɪvɪ] *n.* плющ.

J

jab [dʒæb] *n.* **1.** (*sharp blow*) тычо́к; **he gave me a ~ in the ribs with his elbow** он ткнул меня́ ло́ктем в бок; (*with foot or knee*) пино́к. **2.** (*coll.*, *injection*) уко́л; **they gave him a ~** ему́ сде́лали уко́л; **have you had your smallpox ~?** вам уже́ сде́лали приви́вку от о́спы?

v.t. **1.** (*poke*) ты́кать, ткнуть; (*pierce*) кол|о́ть, -ну́ть; пырну́ть (*pf.*) (ножо́м); **he was ~bed with a bayonet** его́ проткну́ли штыко́м. **2.** (*thrust*) втыка́ть, воткну́ть; **they ~bed a needle into his arm** они́ воткну́ли иго́лку ему́ в ру́ку.

v.i.: **he ~bed at my chin** он ткнул меня́ в подборо́док.
jabber ['dʒæbə(r)] *n.* трескотня́, тарабарщина.
v.t. & i. треща́ть (*impf.*); тарато́рить, про-.
jack [dʒæk] *n.* **1.** (*name*): **J~ Frost** Моро́з Кра́сный Нос; **before you could say J~ Robinson** момента́льно; в два счёта; **J~ Tar** матро́с; **every man ~** все до еди́ного; **~ of all trades** ма́стер на все ру́ки; **~ rabbit** (*US*) кро́лик-саме́ц. **2.** (*card*) вале́т; **~ of spades** пи́ковый вале́т. **3.** (*flag*) гюйс; **Union J~** госуда́рственный флаг Соединённого Короле́вства. **4.** (*lifting device*) домкра́т.
v.t.: **~ up** (*of car etc.*) подн|има́ть, -я́ть домкра́том; (*fig.*, *of prices etc.*) пов|ыша́ть, -ы́сить.
cpds. **~ass** *n.* осёл; **~daw** *n.* га́лка; **~-in-the-box** *n.* я́щик с выска́кивающей фигу́ркой; **~pot** *n.* (*at cards*) банк при «пра́зднике»; **he hit the ~pot** (*fig.*) ему́ кру́пно повезло́.
jackal ['dʒæk(ə)l] *n.* шака́л.
jacket ['dʒækɪt] *n.* **1.** ку́ртка; (*part of suit*) пиджа́к; (*woman's*) жаке́т. **2.** (*tech.*, *insulating cover*) ко́жух; обши́вка. **3.** (*of book*) супероблóжка. **4.** (*skin of potato*) кожура́; **potatoes in their ~s** карто́фель в мунди́ре.
jade[1] [dʒeɪd] *n.* **1.** (*min.*) нефри́т; гага́т; (*attr.*) нефри́товый. **2.** (**~ green**) цвет нефри́та.
jade[2] [dʒeɪd] *v.t.* (*esp. p.p.*): **you look ~d** у вас утомлённый вид; **a ~d appetite** вя́лый аппети́т.
jag [dʒæg] *n.* (*sharp projection*) о́стрый вы́ступ; зубе́ц; (*notch*) зазу́брина.
jagged ['dʒægɪd] *adj.* (*notched*) зазу́бренный; (*unevenly cut, torn*) неро́вно наре́занный/ото́рванный.
jaguar ['dʒægjʊə(r)] *n.* ягуа́р.
jail [dʒeɪl] = **gaol**
jailer ['dʒeɪlə(r)] = **gaoler**
jalopy [dʒə'lɒpɪ] *n.* (*sl.*) драндуле́т.
jam[1] [dʒæm] *n.* джем; варе́нье; **~ tart** пиро́г с варе́ньем.
cpds. **~-jar, ~-pot** *nn.* ба́нка для джéма; (*empty*) ба́нка из-под джéма.
jam[2] [dʒæm] *n.* **1.** (*crush*) да́вка; **traffic ~** зато́р, про́бка. **2.** (*stoppage*) останóвка. **3.** (*dilemma*) нело́вкое положе́ние.
v.t. **1.** (*cram*) наб|ива́ть, -и́ть; вти́с|кивать, -нуть; **she ~med everything into the cupboard** она́ всё запихну́ла в шка́ф; **he ~med his foot into the doorway** он просу́нул но́гу в дверь; **they were ~med in like sardines** они́ наби́лись (туда́) как се́льди в бо́чке; (*force*): **he ~med the brakes on** он ре́зко затормози́л. **2.** (*trap*) прищем|ля́ть, -и́ть; **the child ~med its fingers in the door** ребёнок прищеми́л себе́ па́льцы две́рью. **3.** (*cause to stick or stop*): **the machine got ~med** стано́к засто́порило; (*wedge*): **~ the door open!** закрепи́те дверь откры́той! **4.** (*obstruct*; *crowd*) заб|ива́ть, -и́ть; **the crowds ~med every exit** толпа́ заби́ла все вы́ходы; **the roads were ~med with cars** доро́ги бы́ли запру́жены маши́нами; (*radio*) глуши́ть, за-.
v.i. (*get stuck*) застр|ева́ть, -я́ть; за|еда́ть, -е́сть; **the door ~med** дверь зае́ло.
cpd. **~-packed** *adj.* битко́м наби́тый.
Jamaica [dʒə'meɪkə] *n.* Яма́йка; **~ rum** яма́йский ром.
jamb [dʒæm] *n.* (*of door, window*) кося́к.
jamboree [,dʒæmbə'riː] *n.* **1.** (*of Scouts etc.*) слёт. **2.** (*celebration*) пра́зднество; (*spree*) весе́лье.
jangl|e ['dʒæŋg(ə)l] *n.* ре́зкий звук.
v.t. & i. издава́ть (*impf.*) ре́зкий звук; бренча́ть (*impf.*); **their voices ~ed my nerves** их голоса́ де́йствовали мне на не́рвы.
janitor ['dʒænɪtə(r)] *n.* привра́тник, швейца́р; (*US*) убо́рщик; дво́рник.
January ['dʒænjʊərɪ] *n.* янва́рь (*m.*); (*attr.*) янва́рский.
Japan [dʒə'pæn] *n.* Япо́ния
Japanese [,dʒæpə'niːz] *n.* (*pers.*) япо́н|ец (*fem.* -ка); (*language*) япо́нский язы́к.
adj. япо́нский.
jar[1] [dʒɑː(r)] *n.* (*vessel*) ба́нка.
jar[2] [dʒɑː(r)] *n.* (*shock, vibration*) сотрясе́ние; (*on nerves or feelings*) неприя́тный эффе́кт.
v.t. (*shake*) сотряс|а́ть, -ти́; (*fig.*, *shock*) потряс|а́ть, -ти́.
v.i. **1.** (*emit harsh sound*) изд|ава́ть, -а́ть ре́зкий звук; (*sound discordantly*) дисгармони́ровать (*impf.*). **2.**: **~on, against** (*strike with grating sound*) скрежета́ть (*impf.*) по+*d.*; **~ on** (*irritate, annoy*) раздраж|а́ть, -и́ть.
jargon ['dʒɑːgən] *n.* жарго́н.
jasmine ['dʒæsmɪn, 'dʒæz-] *n.* жасми́н.
jasper ['dʒæspə(r)] *n.* я́шма.
jaundice ['dʒɔːndɪs] *n.* желту́ха.
v.t. (*usu. p.p.*): **a ~d complexion** жёлтый цвет лица́; **he took a ~d view of the affair** он ко́со смотре́л на э́то де́ло.
jaunt [dʒɔːnt] *n.* увеселн́тельная пое́здка/прогу́лка.
jaunty ['dʒɔːntɪ] *adj.* (*sprightly*) бо́йкий, лихо́й; (*carefree*) беспе́чный, небре́жный.
Java ['dʒɑːvə] *n.* Я́ва.
javelin ['dʒævəlɪn, -vlɪn] *n.* мета́тельное копьё; **(throwing) the ~** (*contest*) мета́ние копья́.
cpd. **~-thrower** *n.* мета́тель (*fem.* -ница) копья́.
jaw [dʒɔː] *n.* че́люсть; (*pl.*, *mouth*) рот; (*of animal*) пасть; **the dog held the bird in its ~s** соба́ка держа́ла пти́цу в зуба́х; **in the ~s of death** в когтя́х сме́рти.
cpd. **~bone** *n.* челюстна́я кость.
jay [dʒeɪ] *n.* со́йка.
cpds. **~-walk** *v.i.* неосторо́жно пере|ходи́ть, -йти́ у́лицу; **~-walker** *n.* неосторо́жный пешехо́д.
jazz [dʒæz] *n.* джаз; (*attr.*), джа́зовый.
v.t.: **~ up** (*fig.*, *enliven*) ожив|ля́ть, -и́ть.
cpds. **~-band** *n.* джаз-орке́стр; **~-player** *nn.* джази́ст; уча́стник джаз-орке́стра.
jazzy ['dʒæzɪ] *adj.* (*like jazz*) джа́зовый; (*showy*) бро́ский, я́ркий.
jealous ['dʒeləs] *adj.* **1.** (*of affection etc.*) ревни́вый; **she was ~ of her husband's secretary** она́ ревнова́ла му́жа к секрета́рше. **2.** (*vigilant in defence*): **he is ~ of his rights** он ревни́во оберега́ет свои́ права́. **3.** (*envious*) зави́стливый; **I am ~ of his success!** я зави́дую его́ успе́ху.
jealousy ['dʒeləsɪ] *n.* ре́вность, ревни́вость.
jeans [dʒiːnz] *n.pl.* джи́нс|ы (*pl.*, *g.* -ов).
jeep [dʒiːp] *n.* джип, вездехо́д.
jeer [dʒɪə(r)] *n.* насме́шка; (*taunt*) издёвка.
v.t. & i. глуми́ться (*impf.*) (над+*i.*); насмеха́ться (*impf.*) (над+*i.*); **he was ~ed off the stage** он ушёл со сце́ны под улюлю́канье.
Jehovah [dʒə'həʊvə] *n.* Игова́ (*m.*).
jell [dʒel] *v.i.* (*coll.*, *set into jelly*) заст|ыва́ть, -ы́ть; (*fig.*) формирова́ться, с-.
jellied ['dʒelɪd] *adj.* засты́вший; **~ eels** заливно́е из угре́й.
jelly ['dʒelɪ] *n.* желе́ (*indecl.*); (*aspic*) сту́день (*m.*).
cpd. **~fish** *n.* меду́за.
jeopardize ['dʒepə,daɪz] *v.t.* (*endanger*) подв|ерга́ть, -е́ргнуть опа́сности; (*put at risk*) рискова́ть (*impf.*) +*i.*; **he ~d his chances of success** он рискова́л свои́ми ша́нсами на успе́х.
jeopardy ['dʒepədɪ] *n.* (*danger*) опа́сность; (*risk*) риск; **his life was in ~** его́ жизнь была́ в опа́сности.
jerk [dʒɜːk] *n.* **1.** (*pull*) рыво́к; (*jolt*; *shock*) уда́р; **the train stopped with a ~** по́езд ре́зко затормози́л. **2.** (*twitch*) су́дорожное вздра́гивание; **with a ~ of his head** дёрнув голово́й. **3.**: (*US sl.*, *despicable person*) подо́нок.

v.t. (*push*) ре́зко толк|а́ть, -ну́ть; (*pull, twitch*) дёр|гать, -нуть; **he ~ed his head back** он вски́нул го́лову.

v.i.: **the train ~ed to a halt** по́езд ре́зко останови́лся.

jerkin ['dʒɜːkɪn] *n.* ку́ртка-безрука́вка.

jerk|y ['dʒɜːkɪ] *adj.* (*moving in jerks*) дви́гающийся ре́зкими толчка́ми; **~y movements** су́дорожные движе́ния; **he spoke ~ily** он говори́л отры́висто.

jerry ['dʒerɪ] *n.* (**J~:** *German*) фриц (*coll.*).

cpds. **~-builder** *n.* подря́дчик, возводя́щий постро́йки из плохо́го материа́ла; **~-built** *adj.* постро́енный ко́е-как.

jersey ['dʒɜːzɪ] *n.* (*fabric, garment*) дже́рси (*nt. indecl.*); **football ~** футбо́лка.

jest [dʒest] *n.* шу́тка; **in ~** в шу́тку.

v.i. шути́ть, по-; **~ at** шути́ть над+*i.*

jester ['dʒestə(r)] *n.* (*hist.*) шут; **court ~** придво́рный шут.

jesting ['dʒestɪŋ] *adj.* шутли́вый.

Jesuit ['dʒezjʊɪt] *n.* иезуи́т; (*attr.*) иезуи́тский.

Jesus ['dʒiːzəs] *n.* Иису́с.

jet[1] [dʒet] *n.* (*min.*) гага́т.

adj. гага́товый; (**~-black**) чёрный как смоль.

jet[2] [dʒet] *n.* **1.** (*stream of water etc.*) струя́. **2.** (*spout, nozzle*) со́пло. **3.** (**~ engine**) реакти́вный дви́гатель; (**~ aircraft**) реакти́вный самолёт.

v.i. (*spurt, gush*) бить (*impf.*) струёй; (*coll., fly by ~*) лета́ть (*indet.*) на реакти́вном самолёте.

cpds. **~-fighter** *n.* реакти́вный истреби́тель; **~-lag** *n.* наруше́ние су́точного ри́тма; **~-propelled** *adj.* реакти́вный.

jetsam ['dʒetsəm] *n.* груз, вы́брошенный за́ борт при угро́зе ава́рии.

jettison ['dʒetɪs(ə)n, -z(ə)n] *v.t.* (*lit., fig.*) выбра́сывать, вы́бросить (за́ борт).

jetty ['dʒetɪ] *n.* при́стань, мол.

Jew [dʒuː] *n.* евре́й (*fem.* -ка).

jewel ['dʒuːəl] *n.* (*precious stone*) драгоце́нный ка́мень; (*in watch*) ка́мень; (*ornament containing ~*) ювели́рное изде́лие; драгоце́нность; (*fig., of pers. or thg.*) сокро́вище.

v.t. (*esp. p.p.*): **a ~led watch** час|ы́ (*pl., g.* -о́в) на камня́х; **a ~led sword** меч, укра́шенный драгоце́нными камня́ми.

cpd. **~-box, ~-case** *nn.* футля́р/шкату́лка для ювели́рных изде́лий.

jeweller ['dʒuːələ(r)] *n.* ювели́р.

jewel|lery, -ry ['dʒuːəlrɪ] *n.* ювели́рные изде́лия; драгоце́нности (*f. pl.*).

Jewess ['dʒuːes] *n.* евре́йка.

Jewish ['dʒuːɪʃ] *adj.* евре́йский.

Jewry ['dʒʊərɪ] *n.* (*collect., Jews*) евре́йство.

jib[1] [dʒɪb] *n.* **1.** (*naut.*) кли́вер. **2.** (*of crane*) стрела́.

cpd. **~-boom** *n.* утлега́рь (*m.*).

jib[2] [dʒɪb] *v.i.* (*of horse or person*) уп|ира́ться, -ере́ться; **~ at sth.** уклоня́ться (*impf.*) от чего́-н.

jibe[1] [dʒaɪb] (*mock*) = **gibe**

jibe[2] [dʒaɪb] (*US, fit, agree*) соотве́тствовать (+*d.*), согласова́ться (с+*i.*) (*both impf.*).

jiffy ['dʒɪfɪ] *n.* (*coll.*) миг; **wait a ~!** подожди́те мину́тку; **in a ~** одни́м ми́гом.

jig[1] [dʒɪg] *n.* (*dance*) джи́га.

v.i. (*dance*) танцева́ть (*impf.*) джи́гу; (*move jerkily; fidget*): **~ about** припля́сывать (*impf.*); **~ up and down** пры́гать (*impf.*).

jig[2] [dʒɪg] *n.* (*tech.*) зажи́мное приспособле́ние.

cpds. **~-saw** *n.* (*tool*) ажу́рная пила́; (*puzzle*) (составна́я) карти́нка-зага́дка.

jiggery-pokery [ˌdʒɪgərɪ'pəʊkərɪ] *n.* (*coll.*) ко́зн|и (*pl., g.* -ей); плу́тни (*f. pl.*).

jiggle ['dʒɪg(ə)l] *v.t.* пока́ч|ивать, -а́ть.

jilt [dʒɪlt] *v.t.* бр|оса́ть, -о́сить.

jingle ['dʒɪŋg(ə)l] *n.* (*ringing sound*) звя́канье.

v.t. & i. звя́к|ать, -нуть (+*i.*); **he ~d the keys** он позвя́кивал/звя́кнул ключа́ми; **the bell ~d** колоко́льчик звя́кнул.

jingoism ['dʒɪŋgəʊˌɪz(ə)m] *n.* шовини́зм.

jingoistic [ˌdʒɪŋgəʊ'ɪstɪk] *adj.* шовинисти́ческий.

jink [dʒɪŋk] *n.* (*coll.*): **high ~s** (шу́мное/бу́рное) весе́лье.

jinx [dʒɪŋks] *n.* (*coll.*) злы́е ча́ры (*f. pl.*); **put a ~ on** сгла́зить (*pf.*).

jitter ['dʒɪtə(r)] *n.* (*coll.*): **have the ~s** не́рвничать (*impf.*); **it gave me the ~s** меня́ о́торопь взяла́.

v.i. не́рвничать (*impf.*).

jittery ['dʒɪtərɪ] *adj.* (*coll.*) не́рвный.

jive [dʒaɪv] *v.i.* танцева́ть (*impf.*) под джа́зовую му́зыку.

Jnr. ['dʒuːnɪə(r)] *n.* (*abbr. of* **Junior**) мл., (мла́дший).

job [dʒɒb] *n.* **1.** (*piece of work; task*) рабо́та; зада́ние; **he does a good ~ (of work)** он хорошо́ рабо́тает; **my ~ is to wash the dishes** моя́ обя́занность — мыть посу́ду; **odd ~s** случа́йная рабо́та; **payment by the ~** сде́льная опла́та; **he is on the ~ by 8 o'clock** он прихо́дит на рабо́ту в во́семь часо́в; (*difficult task*): **we had a ~ finding them** мы наси́лу их отыска́ли. **2.** (*product of work*): **you've made a good ~ of that** вы сде́лали э́то хорошо́; **just the ~** (*coll.*) то, что на́до. **3.** (*employment; position*) рабо́та; ме́сто; **what is your ~?** кака́я у вас рабо́та?; кем/где вы рабо́таете?; **he has a good ~** он име́ет хоро́шую рабо́ту; **look for a ~** иска́ть (*impf.*) рабо́ту; **out of a ~** без рабо́ты. **4.** (*coll., crime, esp. theft*) воровство́, «де́ло». **5.** (*transaction*): **a put-up ~** махина́ция; **it's a good ~ you stayed at home** хорошо́, что вы оста́лись до́ма; **he's gone, and a good ~ too!** он ушёл — и сла́ва Бо́гу!; **make the best of a bad ~** переби́ться (*pf.*), обойти́сь (*pf.*); не унывать; **give up as a bad ~** махну́ть (*pf.*) руко́й на+*a.*

v.i. (*do ~s*): **~bing gardener** наёмный садо́вник; (*deal in stocks*) быть ма́клером.

jobber ['dʒɒbə(r)] *n.* (*broker*) ма́клер.

jobless ['dʒɒblɪs] *adj.* безрабо́тный.

jockey ['dʒɒkɪ] *n.* жоке́й.

v.i.: **~ for position** (*fig.*) оттира́ть (*impf.*) друг дру́га (*в борьбе за выгодное положение и т.п.*).

jock-strap ['dʒɒkstræp] *n.* суспензо́рий.

jocose [dʒə'kəʊs] *adj.* игри́вый.

jocular ['dʒɒkjʊlə(r)] *adj.* (*merry*) весёлый; (*humorous*) шутли́вый, заба́вный.

jocularity [ˌdʒɒkjʊ'lærɪtɪ] *n.* весёлость, шутли́вость.

jocund ['dʒɒkənd] *adj.* (*cheerful*) весёлый; (*lively*) живо́й.

jodhpurs ['dʒɒdpəz] *n.* галифе́ (*nt. pl., indecl.*).

jog [dʒɒg] *n.* **1.** (*push; nudge*) толчо́к. **2.** (*trot*) рысь; бег трусцо́й; оздорови́тельный бе́г.

v.t.: **~ up and down** подбра́сывать (*impf.*); **~ s.o.'s elbow** толк|а́ть, -ну́ть кого́-н. под ло́коть; **~ s.o.'s memory** освеж|а́ть, -и́ть чью-н. па́мять.

v.i. **1.** (*coll., run slowly*) бе́гать (*indet.*) трусцо́й; **he ~ged along (on horseback)** он труси́л (на ло́шади); **business is ~ging along** дела́ иду́т свои́м чередо́м. **2.: ~ up and down** подпры́гивать (*impf.*).

cpd. **~-trot** *n.*: **at a ~-trot** ры́сью, рысцо́й.

jogger ['dʒɒgə(r)] *n.* люби́тель (*m.*) оздорови́тельного бе́га, джо́ггер.

jogging ['dʒɒgɪŋ] *n.* (*trot*) бег трусцо́й; (*sport*) оздорови́тельный бе́г; джо́ггинг.

joie de vivre [ˌʒwɑː də 'viːvrə] *n.* жизнера́достность.

join [dʒɔɪn] *n.* связь, соедине́ние.

v.t. **1.** (*connect*) соедин|я́ть, -и́ть; **the towns are ~ed by a railway** э́ти города́ соединя́ет желе́зная доро́га; **~ hands** взя́ться (*pf.*) за́ руки; (*fasten*) свя́з|ывать, -а́ть (*что с чем*); (*unite*) объедин|я́ть,

-и́ть; **they ~ed forces** они́ объедини́ли уси́лия; **~ in marriage** венча́ть, об-. **2.** (*enter*) вступ|а́ть, -и́ть в+*a.*; **he ~ed the party** (*pol.*) он вступи́л в па́ртию; **~ battle** вступ|а́ть, -и́ть в бой; нача́ть (*pf.*) сраже́ние; **~ a club** стать (*pf.*) чле́ном клу́ба; **~ the army** вступи́ть/пойти́ (*pf.*) в а́рмию; **~** (*sc. rejoin*) **one's regiment (***or* **ship)** верну́ться (*pf.*) в полк (*or* на кора́бль). **3.** (*enter s.o.'s company*) присоедин|я́ться, -и́ться к+*d.*; (*side with*) прим|ыка́ть, -кну́ть к+*d.*; (*meet*) встр|еча́ться, -е́титься с+*i.*; **may I ~ you?** (*at table*) разреши́те мне присе́сть? **4.** (*flow or lead into*) соедин|я́ться, -и́ться с+*i.*; сл|ива́ться, -и́ться с+*i.*; **where the Cherwell ~s the Thames** где река́ Че́рвелл впада́ет в Те́мзу; **there is a restaurant where you ~ the motorway** у въе́зда на автостра́ду есть рестора́н.

v.i. **1.** (*be connected, fastened, united; come or flow together*) соедин|я́ться, -и́ться; свя́з|ываться, -а́ться; сходи́ться, сойти́сь; сл|ива́ться, -и́ться; (*border on each other*) грани́чить (*impf.*) друг с дру́гом. **2.** (*take part*): **may I ~ in the game?** мо́жно мне поигра́ть с ва́ми?; **they all ~ed in the chorus** все пе́ли припе́в хо́ром. **3.** (*become a member*) стать (*impf.*) чле́ном (*чего*).

with advs.: **~ in** *v.i.* (*take part*) прин|има́ть, -я́ть уча́стие; (*in conversation*) вступ|а́ть, -и́ть в бесе́ду; **~ on** *v.t. & i.* присоедин|я́ть(ся), -и́ть(ся); **~ together** *v.t.* свя́з|ывать, -а́ть; соедин|я́ть, -и́ть; **~ up** *v.t. & i.* соедин|я́ть(ся), -и́ть(ся); *v.i.* (*coll., enlist*) поступ|а́ть, -и́ть на вое́нную слу́жбу.

joiner ['dʒɔɪnə(r)] *n.* (*woodworker*) столя́р; **~'s shop** столя́рная мастерска́я.

joinery ['dʒɔɪnərɪ] *n.* столя́рная рабо́та; **do, practise ~** столя́рничать (*impf.*).

joint [dʒɔɪnt] *n.* **1.** (*place of juncture; means of joining*) соедине́ние; стык; **the pipe is leaking at the ~s** труба́ течёт в сты́ке; **ball and socket ~** шарни́р; шарово́е соедине́ние. **2.** (*anat.*) суста́в, сочлене́ние; **out of ~** (*pred.*) вы́вихнут; (*fig.*) не в поря́дке; **my ~s ache** у меня́ ло́мит в суста́вах. **3.: a ~ of meat** кусо́к мя́са (к обе́ду).

adj. **1.** (*combined; shared*) совме́стный; **~ action** совме́стное де́йствие; **take ~ action** де́йствовать (*impf.*) сообща́; (*common*) о́бщий; **~ account** о́бщий счёт; (*united*) соединённый; **~ venture** совме́стное предприя́тие. **2.** (*sharing*): **~ owner** совладе́лец; **~ author** соа́втор.

cpd. **~-stock** *n.* (*attr.*) акционе́рный.

joist [dʒɔɪst] *n.* ба́лка.

jok|e [dʒəʊk] *n.* шу́тка; (*story*) анекдо́т; (*witticism*) остро́та; (*laughing-stock*) посме́шище; **it's no ~e** э́то не шу́тка!; **crack, make a ~e** шути́ть, по-; **make a ~e of sth.** оберну́ть (*pf.*) что-н. в шу́тку; **play a ~e on s.o.** сыгра́ть (*pf.*) шу́тку с кем-н.; подшу́|чивать, -ти́ть над кем-н.; **can't you take a ~e?** вы что, шу́ток не понима́ете?; **practical ~e** ро́зыгрыш; **the ~e was on him** э́то он в дурака́х оста́лся.

v.i. шути́ть, по-; **I was only ~ing** я всего́ лишь пошути́л; **~ing apart** шу́тки в сто́рону.

joker ['dʒəʊkə(r)] *n.* (*one who jokes*) шутни́к; (*coll., fellow*) па́рень (*m.*); (*cards*) джо́кер.

jollity ['dʒɒlɪtɪ] *n.* весе́лье, увеселе́ние.

jolly ['dʒɒlɪ] *adj.* (*cheerful*) весёлый; (*festive; entertaining*) пра́здничный; (*pred.*) навеселе́; (*coll., pleasant*) прия́тный.

adv. (*coll., very*) о́чень; **~ well** (*coll., definitely*) вправь; **you'll ~ well have to do it** всё-таки придётся э́то сде́лать.

v.t.: **~ s.o. along** ума́сл|ивать, -ить кого́-н.

jolt [dʒəʊlt, dʒɒlt] *n.* толчо́к; (*fig.*) уда́р, потрясе́ние.

v.t. & i. трясти́(сь) (*impf.*); **we were ~ed about** нас швыря́ло во все сто́роны; **the cart ~ed along** теле́гу подбра́сывало; (*fig.*) потряс|а́ть, -ти́; пора|жа́ть, -зи́ть; **it ~ed him out of his routine** э́то вы́било его́ из коле́й.

jonquil ['dʒɒnkwɪl] *n.* жонки́лия.

Jordan ['dʒɔːd(ə)n] *n.* (*river*) Иорда́н; (*country*) Иорда́ния.

jostle ['dʒɒs(ə)l] *v.t.* толк|а́ть, -ну́ть; отт|ира́ть, -ере́ть; **I was ~d from every side** меня́ толка́ли со всех сторо́н.

v.i. толка́ться (*impf.*); **he ~d against me** он оттира́л меня́.

jot[1] [dʒɒt] *n.* (*small amount*) йо́та; **he was not one ~ the worse for it** э́то ему́ ничу́ть не повреди́ло.

jot[2] [dʒɒt] *v.t.*: **~ down** кра́тко запи́с|ывать, -а́ть.

jotter ['dʒɒtə(r)] *n.* (*pad*) блокно́т.

jottings ['dʒɒtɪŋz] *n.* за́писи (*f. pl.*).

joule [dʒuːl] *n.* джо́уль (*m.*).

journal ['dʒɜːn(ə)l] *n.* (*newspaper*) газе́та; (*periodical*) журна́л; (*bookkeeping*) журна́л.

journalism ['dʒɜːnəˌlɪz(ə)m] *n.* журнали́стика.

journalist ['dʒɜːnəlɪst] *n.* журнали́ст.

journalistic [ˌdʒɜːnə'lɪstɪk] *adj.* журнали́стский.

journey ['dʒɜːnɪ] *n.* (*expedition; trip*) путеше́ствие, пое́здка; рейс; **(under)take a ~** предприн|има́ть, -я́ть путеше́ствие; **break one's ~** прер|ыва́ть, -ва́ть пое́здку; **be, go on a ~** путеше́ствовать (*impf.*); **he did the ~ on foot** он соверши́л путеше́ствие пешко́м; **the bus makes 6 ~s a day** авто́бус соверша́ет шесть ре́йсов в день; (*travel; travelling time*): **on the return ~** на обра́тном пути́; **will there be any refreshments on the ~?** бу́дут ли в пути́ дава́ть лёгкие заку́ски?; **London is 6 hours' ~ from here** отсю́да до Ло́ндона шесть часо́в езды́; **it was a wasted ~** путеше́ствие бы́ло напра́сным.

v.i. путеше́ствовать (*impf.*).

joust [dʒaʊst] *n.* (ры́царский) турни́р.

v.i. состяза́ться (*impf.*) на турни́ре.

jovial ['dʒəʊvɪəl] *adj.* весёлый.

joviality [ˌdʒəʊvɪ'ælɪtɪ] *n.* весёлость.

jowl [dʒaʊl] *n.* (*jaw*) че́люсть; (*dewlap*) подгру́док; (*chin*): **a heavy ~** тяжёлый подборо́док.

joy [dʒɔɪ] *n.* **1.** (*gladness*) ра́дость; (*pleasure*) удово́льствие; **jump for ~** скака́ть (*impf.*) от ра́дости. **2.** (*coll., success, response*): **I kept phoning but got no ~** я звони́л-звони́л, но никако́го то́лку.

cpds. **~ride** *n.* пое́здка ра́ди заба́вы на чужо́й автомаши́не (без разреше́ния); **~rider** *n.* автово́рлиха́ч; **~stick** *n.* (*aeron., sl.*) рыча́г/ру́чка управле́ния; (*comput.*) джо́йстик.

joyful ['dʒɔɪfʊl] *adj.* ра́достный, счастли́вый.

joyless ['dʒɔɪlɪs] *adj.* безра́достный.

joyous ['dʒɔɪəs] *adj.* ра́достный; (*happy*) весёлый.

JP (*abbr. of* ***Justice of the Peace***) мирово́й судья́.

jubilant ['dʒuːbɪlənt] *adj.* лику́ющий; **be ~** ликова́ть (*impf.*).

jubilation [ˌdʒuːbɪ'leɪʃ(ə)n] *n.* ликова́ние.

jubilee ['dʒuːbɪˌliː] *n.* **1.** (*anniversary*) юбиле́й; (*attr.*) юбиле́йный. **2.** (*rejoicing*) пра́зднество.

Judaic [dʒuː'deɪɪk] *adj.* иуде́йский.

Judaism ['dʒuːdeɪˌɪz(ə)m] *n.* иудаи́зм.

Judas ['dʒuːdəs] *n.* (*bibl.*) Иу́да (*m.*); (*fig.*) преда́тель (*m.*).

judder ['dʒʌdə(r)] *v.i.* вибри́ровать (*impf.*) с гро́хотом.

judge [dʒʌdʒ] *n.* **1.** (*legal functionary*) судья́ (*m.*). **2.** (*arbiter*) арби́тр; **let me be the ~ of that** оста́вьте мне суди́ть об э́том; **the ~s** (*of a contest*) жюри́ (*nt. indecl.*); **he is one of the ~s** он в соста́ве жюри́. **3.** (*expert, connoisseur*) экспе́рт, знато́к; **a ~ of art** цени́тель (*m.*) иску́сства.

v.t. **1.** (*pass ~ment on*) суди́ть (*impf.*) о+*i.*; **don't ~ him by appearances!** не суди́те о нём по вне́шности!; **who ~d the race?** кто суди́л на э́том состяза́нии?; (*assess*) оце́н|ивать, -и́ть. **2.** (*consider*) считáть (*impf.*); **he was ~d to be innocent** егó сочли́ невинóвным; (*suppose*) полагáть (*impf.*); **I ~d him to be about 50** я полагáл, что емý óколо пяти́десяти. **3.** (*hear and try*): **the case was ~d in secret** дéло слýшалось в закры́том судé.

v.i. **1.** (*make an appraisal or decision*) суди́ть (*impf.*); **to ~ from what you say** сýдя по томý, что вы сказáли. **2.** (*act as ~; arbitrate*) быть арби́тром, суди́ть (*impf.*).

judgement ['dʒʌdʒmənt] *n.* **1.** (*sentence*) приговóр; **pass ~ (on)** выноси́ть, вы́нести приговóр *+d.*; суди́ть (*impf.*) о*+p.*; **a reserved ~** отсрóченное решéние; **the ~ was in his favour** решéние судá бы́ло в егó пóльзу; (*act or process of judging*): **sit in ~** (*fig.*) суди́ть (*impf.*) други́х свысокá; **J~ Day** Сýдный день; **the Last J~** Стрáшный суд. **2.** (*opinion; estimation*) мнéние; суждéние; **in my ~** по моемý мнéнию; **against one's better ~** вопреки́ гóлосу рáзума; **an error of ~** оши́бка в суждéнии. **3.** (*criticism*) осуждéние. **4.** (*discernment*) рассуди́тельность; **he shows good ~** он здрáво сýдит.

judicial [dʒu:'dɪʃ(ə)l] *adj.* **1.** судéбный; **~ proceedings** судéбный процéсс. **2.** (*critical; impartial*) рассуди́тельный; беспристрáстный.

judiciary [dʒu:'dɪʃɪərɪ] *n.* сýдьи (*m. pl.*).

judicious [dʒu:'dɪʃəs] *adj.* здравомы́слящий, рассуди́тельный.

judo ['dʒu:dəʊ] *n.* дзюдó (*indecl.*).

judoist ['dʒu:dəʊɪst] *n.* дзюдои́ст (*fem.* -ка).

jug [dʒʌg] *n.* кувши́н.

juggernaut ['dʒʌgə,nɔ:t] *n.* многотóнный грузови́к.

juggle ['dʒʌg(ə)l] *v.t. & i.* (*lit., fig.*) жонгли́ровать (*impf.*) *+i.*

juggler ['dʒʌglə(r)] *n.* жонглёр.

jugular ['dʒʌgjʊlə(r)] *n.* **(~ vein)** ярéмная вéна.

juice [dʒu:s] *n.* сок; (*fruit* **~**) фрýктóвый сок.

juicer ['dʒu:sə(r)] *n.* (*cul.*) соковыжимáлка.

juiciness ['dʒu:sɪnɪs] *n.* сóчность.

juicy ['dʒu:sɪ] *adj.* сóчный; (*coll., racy, scandalous*) смáчный.

ju-jitsu [dʒu:'dʒɪtsu:] *n.* джи́у-джи́тсу (*nt. indecl.*).

juke-box ['dʒu:kbɒks] *n.* автомáт-проигрыватель (*m.*).

Julian ['dʒu:lɪən] *adj.*: **~ calendar** юлиáнский календáрь.

July [dʒu:'laɪ] *n.* ию́ль (*m.*); (*attr.*) ию́льский.

jumble ['dʒʌmb(ə)l] *n.* (*untidy heap*) беспоря́дочная кýча; (*disorder, muddle*) беспоря́док, пýтаница; (*coll., unwanted articles*) хлам; **~ sale** дешёвая распродáжа (на благотвори́тельном базáре).

v.t. (*also* **~ up**) перемéш|ивать, -áть.

jumbo ['dʒʌmbəʊ] *n.* (*coll., elephant*) слон; (*attr., very large*) гигáнтский; большýщий; **~ jet** реакти́вный лáйнер.

jump [dʒʌmp] *n.* прыжóк, скачóк; **long/high ~** прыжóк в длинý/высотý; (*obstacle in steeplechase*) препя́тствие; **water ~** ров с водóй; (*fig., abrupt rise*): **there was a big ~ in the temperature** температýра си́льно подскочи́ла; (*fig., start, shock*) вздрáгивание; **you gave me a ~** вы меня́ напугáли.

v.t. **1.** (**~** *over, across*) перепры́г|ивать, -нуть чéрез*+a.* **2.** (*cause to* **~**): **he ~ed his horse at the fence** он послáл свою́ лóшадь чéрез забóр. **3.** (*var. fig. uses*): **~ the gun** (*coll.*) начáть (*pf.*) скáчки до сигнáла; начáть что-н. до полóженного врéмени; **~ the queue** пройти́ (*pf.*) без óчереди; **the train ~ed the rails** пóезд сошёл с рéльсов; **~ ship** бежáть, с- с корабля́ до истечéния срóка слýжбы; дезерти́ровать (*impf., pf.*) с сýдна; **you've ~ed a few lines** вы пропусти́ли (*or* перескочи́ли чéрез) нéсколько строк.

v.i. **1.** пры́г|ать, -нуть; (*on horseback*) вск|áкивать, -очи́ть; (*with parachute*) пры́г|ать, -нуть с парашю́том. **2.** (*fig.*): **he ~ed from one topic to another** он перескáкивал с однóй тéмы на другýю. **3.** (*start*): **the noise made me ~** звук застáвил меня́ вздрóгнуть. **4.** (*make sudden movement*): **shares ~ed to a new level** áкции подскочи́ли. **5.** (*fig. uses*): **he ~ed at my offer** он ухвати́лся за моё предложéние; **~ for joy** пры́гать/скакáть (*impf.*) от рáдости; **~ on s.o.** (*attack*) набрóситься (*pf.*) на когó-н.; (*rebuke*) рéзко осади́ть (*pf.*) когó-н.; **~ to conclusions** дéлать (*impf.*) поспéшные вы́воды; **he ~ed to his feet** он вскочи́л нá ноги.

with advs.: **they ~ed about to keep warm** они́ пры́гали, чтóбы согрéться; **he ~ed back in surprise** он отпря́нул в удивлéнии; **she ~ed down from the fence** онá соскочи́ла с забóра; **he took off his clothes and ~ed in** он раздéлся и пры́гнул в вóду; **don't ~ off before the bus stops!** не спры́гивайте на ходý; **as the train began to move I ~ed on** я впры́гнул в пóезд, когдá он ужé трóнулся; **~ up from one's chair** вск|áкивать, -очи́ть со стýла; **~ up and down** пры́гать/подпры́гивать (*impf.*) вверх и вниз.

cpd. **~-suit** *n.* комбинезóн.

jumper ['dʒʌmpə(r)] *n.* (*garment*) джéмпер; (*US, pinafore dress*) сарафáн.

jumpy ['dʒʌmpɪ] *adj.* нéрвный.

junction ['dʒʌŋkʃ(ə)n] *n.* **1.** (*joining*) соединéние. **2.** (*meeting point: of railways*) ýзел; узловóй пункт; (*of roads*) скрещéние (дорóг), перекрёсток; (*of rivers*) слия́ние. **3.** (*elec.*): **~ box** соедини́тельная мýфта.

juncture ['dʒʌŋktʃə(r)] *n.* (*joining*) соединéние; **at a critical ~** в крити́ческий момéнт; **at this ~** в э́тот момéнт, сейчáс.

June [dʒu:n] *n.* ию́нь (*m.*); (*attr.*) ию́ньский.

jungle ['dʒʌŋg(ə)l] *n.* джýнгл|и (*pl., g.* -ей); **the law of the ~** закóн джýнглей.

junior ['dʒu:nɪə(r)] *n. & adj.* млáдший; **John Jones ~** Джон Джонс млáдший; **he is 6 years my ~** он молóже меня́ на шесть лет; **~ partner** млáдший партнёр; **~ school** начáльная шкóла.

juniper ['dʒu:nɪpə(r)] *n.* можжевéльник.

junk[1] [dʒʌŋk] *n.* (*rubbish*) рýхлядь, хлам, ути́ль (*m.*); **~ food** неполноцéнная пи́ща.

v.t. (*sl., discard*) вы́бросить (*pl.*) в ути́ль.

cpds. **~-heap** *n.*: **it is only fit for the ~-heap** э́то порá сдать в ути́ль; **~-shop** *n.* лáвка старьёвщика.

junk[2] [dʒʌŋk] *n.* (*sailing vessel*) джóнка.

Junker ['jʊŋkə(r)] *n.* ю́нкер.

junket ['dʒʌŋkɪt] *n.* **1.** (*dish*) слáдкий творóг со сли́вками. **2.** (*also* **~ing**) пирýшка.

junkie ['dʒʌŋkɪ] *n.* (*sl., drug addict*) наркомáн.

junta ['dʒʌntə] *n.* хýнта.

Jupiter ['dʒu:pɪtə(r)] *n.* (*myth., astron.*) Юпи́тер.

Jurassic [dʒʊə'ræsɪk] *adj.* ю́рский.

juridical [dʒʊə'rɪdɪk(ə)l] *adj.* юриди́ческий.

jurisdiction [,dʒʊərɪs'dɪkʃ(ə)n] *n.* (*legal authority*) юрисди́кция; **have ~ over** имéть (*impf.*) юрисди́кцию над*+i.*; **it does not lie within my ~** э́то не вхóдит в мою́ компетéнцию.

jurisprudence [,dʒʊərɪs'pru:d(ə)ns] *n.* юриспрудéнция.

jurist ['dʒʊərɪst] *n.* юри́ст.

juror ['dʒʊərə(r)] *n.* член жюри́, прися́жный (заседáтель).

jury ['dʒʊərɪ] *n.* жюри́ (*nt. indecl.*); прися́жные (заседáтели) (*m. pl.*); **grand ~** (*US hist.*) большóе жюри́.

just [dʒʌst] *adj.* (*equitable*) справедли́вый; **act ~ly to(wards) s.o.** быть справедли́вым по отношéнию к комý-н.; (*deserved*) заслýженный; **receive one's ~ deserts** получи́ть (*pf.*) по заслýгам; (*well-grounded*) обоснóванный, справедли́вый.

adv. тóчно, как раз; **it was ~ 3 o'clock** бы́ло рóвно три часá; **~ then** как раз тогдá; **that's ~ the trouble** в тóм-то и бедá; **~ how did you do it?** как (же) и́менно вам удало́сь э́то сде́лать?; ~ **like, as** (*expr. comparison*) так же как (и); **that's ~ it** вот и́менно; **that's ~ the point** в то́м-то и де́ло; ~ **the thing** и́менно то, что на́до; **the hat is ~ my size** шля́па мне в са́мую по́ру; ~ **so** то́чно/и́менно так; ~ **as much** сто́лько же; **it's ~ as well I warned you** хорошо́, что я вас предупреди́л. **3.:** ~ **about** (*approximately*): ~ **about right** почти́ пра́вильно; (*almost*): **I've ~ about finished** я почти́ ко́нчил. **4.** (*expr. time*) то́лько что; (*very recently*): **I saw him ~ now** я то́лько что ви́дел его́; ~ **as** (*expr. time*) (как) то́лько; (*at this moment*): **I'm ~ off** я ухожу́ сию́ мину́ту; **the show is ~ beginning** представле́ние как раз начина́ется. **5.** (*barely, no more than*) едва́; **I ~ caught the train** я едва́ успе́л на по́езд; **I've got ~ enough for my fare** у меня́ де́нег то́лько-то́лько хва́тит на биле́т; **(wait) ~ a minute!** (одну́) мину́т(к)у! **6.** (*merely, simply*) то́лько; ~ **listen to this!** вы то́лько послу́шайте!; ~ **fancy!** поду́мать то́лько!; ~ **you wait!** ну, погоди́!; ~ **for fun** шу́тки ра́ди; ~ **in case** на вся́кий слу́чай. **7.** (*positively, absolutely*) так и; про́сто(-на́просто); **the coffee ~ would not boil** ко́фе ника́к не закипа́л; **it's ~ splendid!** э́то про́сто великоле́пно!; **don't I ~!** ещё бы!; **not ~ yet** ещё не/нет.

justice [ˈdʒʌstɪs] *n.* **1.** (*fairness; equity*) справедли́вость; **do ~ to** отд|ава́ть, -а́ть до́лжное *+d.*; **to do him ~** к че́сти его́ сказа́ть. **2.** (*system of institutions*) юсти́ция; (*judicial proceedings*) правосу́дие; **administer ~** отправля́ть (*impf.*) правосу́дие; **bring s.o. to ~** отд|ава́ть, -а́ть кого́-н. под суд; **Court of J~** суд. **3.** (*magistrate; judge*) судья́ (*m.*); **J~ of the Peace** мирово́й судья́.

justifiable [ˈdʒʌstɪˌfaɪəb(ə)l] *adj.* опра́вданный.

justification [ˌdʒʌstɪfɪˈkeɪʃ(ə)n] *n.* оправда́ние; **he objected, and with ~** он возрази́л и не без основа́ний.

justif|y [ˈdʒʌstɪˌfaɪ] *v.t.* опра́вд|ывать, -а́ть; **I was ~ied in suspecting ...** я име́л все основа́ния подозрева́ть...; **~y o.s.** опра́вд|ываться, -а́ться.

jut [dʒʌt] *v.i.* (*usu.* **~ out**) выступа́ть (*impf.*); выдава́ться (*impf.*).

jute [dʒuːt] *n.* джут.

juvenile [ˈdʒuːvəˌnaɪl] *n.* подро́сток (*fem.* де́вочка-подро́сток).

adj. ю́ный, ю́ношеский; ~ **delinquent** малоле́тний престу́пник; ~ **delinquency** де́тская престу́пность; ~ **court** суд по дела́м несовершенноле́тних.

juxtapose [ˌdʒʌkstəˈpəʊz] *v.t.* поме|ща́ть, -сти́ть бок о́ бок; (*for comparison*) сопост|авля́ть, -а́вить (*кого с кем or что с чем*).

juxtaposition [ˌdʒʌkstəpəˈzɪʃ(ə)n] *n.* сосе́дство, бли́зость; (*for comparison*) сопоставле́ние.

K

K *abbr. of* **1. kilobyte** килоба́йт. **2. £1,000** ты́сяча фу́нтов, коса́я (*sl.*); **he earns 35K a year** он зараба́тывает 35 косы́х в год.

k (*abbr. of* **kilometre(s)**) км, (киломе́тр).

Kaiser [ˈkaɪzə(r)] *n.* ка́йзер.

kale [keɪl] *n.* листова́я капу́ста.

kaleidoscope [kəˈlaɪdəˌskəʊp] *n.* (*lit., fig.*) калейдоско́п.

kaleidoscopic [kəˌlaɪdəˈskɒpɪk] *adj.* калейдоскопи́ческий.

Kampuchea [ˌkæmpʊˈtʃɪə] *n.* Кампучи́я.

kangaroo [ˌkæŋgəˈruː] *n.* кенгуру́ (*m. indecl.*).

kaolin [ˈkeɪəlɪn] *n.* каоли́н.

kapok [ˈkeɪpɒk] *n.* капо́к.

karat [ˈkærət] (*US*) = **carat**

karate [kəˈrɑːtɪ] *n.* карате́ (*nt. indecl.*).

kayak [ˈkaɪæk] *n.* кая́к.

Kazakh [kəˈzɑːk, kɑː-] *n.* (*pers.*) каза́|х (*fem.* -шка); (*language*) каза́хский язы́к.

Kazakhstan [ˌkɑːzɑːkˈstæn, -ˈstɑːn] *n.* Казахста́н.

kebab [kɪˈbæb] *n.* кеба́б, шашлы́к; ~ **house** кеба́бная, шашлы́чная.

keel [kiːl] *n.* (*of ship*) киль (*m.*); **on an even ~** не кача́ясь; (*fig.*) усто́йчивый, стаби́льный.

v.i.: ~ **over** опроки́|дываться, -нуться.

keen [kiːn] *adj.* (*lit., fig.: sharp, acute*) о́стрый; ~ **eyesight** о́строе зре́ние; **a ~ intellect** о́стрый/проница́тельный ум; (*piercing*) пронзи́тельный; **a ~ wind** ре́зкий ве́тер; (*strong, intense*) си́льный; ~ **desire** си́льное/о́строе жела́ние; ~ **interest** живо́й интере́с; (*eager; energetic*) ре́вностный; энерги́чный; **a ~ businessman** энерги́чный деле́ц; **a ~ pupil** усе́рдный учени́к; ~ **competition** тру́дное соревнова́ние; **a ~ demand for sth.** большо́й спрос на что-н.; (*enthusiastic*) стра́стный; **a ~ sportsman** стра́стный спортсме́н; **be ~ on** си́льно/стра́стно увл|ека́ться, -е́чься *+i.*; **I am not ~ on chess** я не осо́бенно увлека́юсь ша́хматами.

keenness [ˈkiːnnɪs] *n.* (*sharpness*) острота́; (*of cold etc.*) си́ла, интенси́вность; (*eagerness, enthusiasm*) усе́рдие; энтузиа́зм.

keep[1] [kiːp] *n.* (*tower*) гла́вная ба́шня (за́мка).

keep[2] [kiːp] *n.* **1.** (*maintenance*) содержа́ние. **2.** (*sustenance*) прокo̍рм, пропита́ние; **earn one's ~** зараб|а́тывать, -о́тать себе́ на пропита́ние. **3.: for ~s** насовсе́м (*coll.*).

v.t. **1.** (*retain possession of*) держа́ть (*impf.*), не отдава́ть (*impf.*); ост|авля́ть, -а́вить (себе́ *or* при себе́); ~ **the change!** сда́чи не на́до!; (*preserve*) храни́ть (*impf.*); сохран|я́ть, -и́ть; (*save, put by*): **I shall ~ this paper to show my mother** я сохраню́ э́ту газе́ту, что́бы показа́ть ма́тери; **I'm ~ing this for a rainy day** я берегу́ э́то на чёрный день; **he ~s all her letters** он храни́т все её пи́сьма; (*hold on to*): **she kept the book a long time** она́ до́лго держа́ла кни́гу; (*appropriate*) присв|а́ивать, -о́ить себе́. **2.** (*cause to remain*): **the traffic kept me awake** у́личное движе́ние не дава́ло мне спать; **the garden ~s me busy** сад не даёт мне сиде́ть сложа́ ру́ки; **this will ~ him quiet for a bit** всё э́то отвлечёт его́ немно́жко; ~ **sth. safe** храни́ть (*impf.*) что-н. в безопа́сности; ~ **o.s. alive** подде́рживать (*impf.*) свою́ жизнь (*чем*); ~ **the house clean** содержа́ть (*impf.*) дом в чистоте́; ~ **your mouth shut!** держи́те язы́к за зуба́ми!; **I'm ~ing my ears open** я держу́ у́шки на маку́шке; ~ **the grass cut** регуля́рно стричь (*impf.*) траву́; ~ **s.o. in the dark** держа́ть кого́-н. в неве́дении; ~ **it to yourself** пома́лкивайте об э́том; ~ **an eye on sth.** пригля́дывать (*impf.*) за чем-н.; ~ **sth. in mind, view** име́ть (*impf.*) что-н. в виду́; ~ **sth. in order** держа́ть что-н. в поря́дке; ~ **s.o. in order** держа́ть кого́-н. в узде́; **where do you ~ the salt?** где вы храни́те соль? **3.** (*cause to continue*): **he kept me standing for an hour** он продержа́л меня́ на нога́х це́лый час; **they kept him working late** они́ заде́рживали его́ на рабо́те допоздна́. **4.** (*remain in, on*): ~ **one's seat** (*remain sitting*) не встава́ть (*impf.*); ~ **one's feet** удержа́ться на нога́х, устоя́ть (*both pf.*); (*retain, preserve*): ~ **one's balance** сохраня́ть (*impf.*) равнове́сие; ~ **one's distance** соблю|да́ть, -сти́ расстоя́ние; **she has kept**

her figure она́ сохрани́ла стро́йность; (*for phrr. of the kind* '**~ company**'; '**~ guard**'; '**~ order**'; '**~ time**' *etc. see under nn.*). **5.** (*have charge of*; *manage*, *own*; *rear*, *maintain*) име́ть, держа́ть, содержа́ть (*all impf.*); **who ~s the keys?** у кого́ храня́тся ключи́?; **the shop was kept by an Italian** владе́льцем ла́вки был италья́нец; **he wants to ~ pigs** он хо́чет держа́ть свине́й; **I have a wife and family to ~** у меня́ на иждиве́нии жена́ и де́ти; **~ house** вести́ (*det.*) (дома́шнее) хозя́йство; **a well-kept garden** хорошо́ ухо́женный сад. **6.** (*maintain*, *~ entries in*) вести́ (*det.*); **~ books/accounts** вести́ счета́; **do you ~ a diary?** ведёте ли вы дневни́к?; **are you ~ing the score?** вы ведёте счёт? **7.** (*detain*) заде́рж|ивать, -а́ть; **I won't ~ you** я вас не задержу́; **there was nothing to ~ me there** меня́ там ничто́ не держа́ло. **8.** (*stock*; *have for sale*): **we do not ~ such goods** таки́х това́ров мы не де́ржим. **9.** (*defend*, *protect*): **~ goal** защища́ть (*impf.*) воро́та; **God ~ you!** да храни́т вас Госпо́дь! **10.** (*observe*; *be faithful to*; *fulfil*) сде́рж|ивать, -а́ть; соблю|да́ть, -сти́; **~ the law** соблюда́ть зако́н; **~ one's word** держа́ть, с- сло́во; **~ faith** сохран|я́ть, -и́ть ве́рность; **I can't ~ the appointment** я не могу́ прийти́ на встре́чу. **11.** (*celebrate*) пра́здновать, от-; отм|еча́ть, -е́тить. **12.** (*guard*, *not divulge*) храни́ть (*impf.*); сохран|я́ть, -и́ть.

v.i. **1.** (*remain*) держа́ться (*impf.*); остава́ться (*impf.*); **if it ~s fine** е́сли проде́ржится хоро́шая пого́да; **I can't ~ warm here** я здесь не могу́ согре́ться; **~ cool** (*fig.*) не теря́ть (*impf.*) головы́: **please ~ quiet!** пожа́луйста, не шуми́те!; **I exercise to ~ fit** я занима́юсь гимна́стикой/спо́ртом, что́бы быть в фо́рме; **we still ~ in touch** мы всё ещё подде́рживаем отноше́ния/связь; **~ in step** шага́ть (*impf.*) в но́гу. **2.** (*continue*) продолжа́ть (*impf.*) +*inf.*; **she ~s giggling** она́ всё хихи́кает; **~ going!** продолжа́йте идти́!; **~ straight on!** иди́те/поезжа́йте пря́мо вперёд! **3.** (*remain fresh*): **the food will ~ in the refrigerator** еда́ в холоди́льнике не испо́ртится.

with preps.: (*for phrr. with* **in** *or* **on** *+n. see under v.t.* **2.** *or v.i.* **1.** *or under n.*): **~ after** (*continue to pursue*) продолжа́ть (*impf.*) пого́ню за+*i.*; (*chivvy*) пристава́ть (*impf.*) к+*d.*; **we are ~ing ahead of schedule** мы продолжа́ем опережа́ть гра́фик; **he ~s his pupils at it** он заставля́ет ученико́в труди́ться; **I kept at him to start the job** я наста́ивал, что́бы он на́чал рабо́ту; **he kept his hands behind his back** он держа́л ру́ки за спино́й; **he kept behind me all the way** он шёл позади́ меня́ всю доро́гу; **his brothers kept his share from him** его́ бра́тья удержа́ли его́ до́лю; **what are you trying to ~ from me?** что вы скрыва́ете от меня́?; **I kept him from hurting himself** я не дал ему́ ушиби́ться; '**~ off the grass**' «по газо́нам не ходи́ть»; **I have to ~ off sugar** мне на́до избега́ть са́хара; **I couldn't ~ my eyes off her** ~ я не мог отвести́ от неё глаз; **they tried to ~ me out of the room** они́ пыта́лись не пуска́ть меня́ в ко́мнату; **I kept the sweets out of his reach** я держа́л конфе́ты пода́льше от него́; **~ out of s.o.'s way** (*avoid him*) избега́ть (*impf.*) кого́-н.; (*not hinder him*) не меша́ть (*impf.*) кому́-н.; **I kept him to his promise** я заста́вил его́ вы́полнить обеща́ние; **he ~s his feelings to himself** он скрыва́ет свои́ чу́вства; **he ~s himself to himself** он замыка́ется в себе́; **~ to one's bed** остава́ться (*impf.*) в посте́ли; **~ to the path** держа́ться (*impf.*) тропи́нки; **~ to the point** не отклон|я́ться, -и́ться от те́мы; **he ~s to his former opinion** он приде́рживается пре́жнего мне́ния; **~ s.o. under observation** следи́ть (*impf.*) за кем-н.

with advs.: **~ away** *v.t.*: **the rain kept people away** дождь отпугну́л наро́д; **she kept her daughter away from school** она́ не пуска́ла дочь в шко́лу; **we could not ~ him away from books** мы не могли́ удержа́ть его́ от чте́ния; *v.i.*: **he tried to ~ away from them** он стара́лся их избега́ть; **~ back** *v.t.* (*restrain*) сде́рж|ивать, -а́ть; (*retain*): **they ~ back £1 from my wages** из мое́й зарпла́ты уде́рживают оди́н фунт; (*repress*): **she could hardly ~ back her tears** она́ с трудо́м сде́рживала слёзы; (*conceal*): **he kept back the sad news from her** он скрыва́л от неё печа́льные изве́стия; *v.i.* держа́ться (*impf.*) в стороне́; **~ down** *v.t.*: **~ your head down!** не поднима́йте головы́!; **~ your voice down!** не повыша́йте го́лоса!; (*limit*, *control*): **they tried to ~ down expenses** они́ стара́лись ограни́чить расхо́ды; **unemployment was kept down** безрабо́тице не дава́ли разраста́ться; (*oppress*) держа́ть (*impf.*) в подчине́нии; (*suppress*) подав|ля́ть, -и́ть; (*digest*): **he can't ~ anything down** у него́ желу́док ничего́ не принима́ет; **~ in** *v.t.* (*confine*): **I ~ the children in when it rains** когда́ идёт дождь, я держу́ дете́й до́ма; **he was kept in after school** его́ оста́вили по́сле уро́ков; (*maintain*): **we ~ the fire in overnight** мы подде́рживаем ого́нь всю ночь; **I practise to ~ my eye, hand in** я трениру́юсь, что́бы не отвы́кнуть; *v.i.* (*stay indoors*) ост|ава́ться, -а́ться до́ма; **~ in with s.o.** подде́рживать (*impf.*) хоро́шие отноше́ния с кем-н.; **~ off** *v.t.* (*restrain*): **they kept the hounds off till the signal was given** го́нчих не подпуска́ли, пока́ не да́ли сигна́л; (*ward off*, *repel*): **I kept his blows off with my stick** я отрази́л его́ уда́ры па́лкой; **my hat will ~ the rain off** моя́ шля́па защити́т меня́ от дождя́; *v.i.* (*stay at a distance*): **I hope the rain ~s off** я наде́юсь, что дождь не начнётся; **the crowd kept off till the very end** толпа́ до са́мого конца́ держа́лась в отдале́нии; **~ on** *v.t.* (*continue to wear*): **women ~ their hats on in church** в це́ркви же́нщины не снима́ют шляп; (*continue to employ*, *educate*): **they kept the workers on** они́ оста́вили рабо́чих; **they won't ~ you on after 60** они́ уво́лят вас, когда́ вам испо́лнится 60 лет; **I'm ~ing my boy on (at school) for another year** я оставля́ю сы́на в шко́ле ещё на́ год; (*leave in place*): **~ the lid on** не снима́йте кры́шку; *v.i.* (*with pres. part.*, *continue*): **he kept on reading** он продолжа́л чита́ть; **she kept on glancing out of the window** она́ беспреста́нно выгля́дывала из окна́; **he kept on falling** он постоя́нно па́дал; (*continue*, *persist*): **the rain kept on all day** дождь шёл весь день; (*continue talking*): **he will ~ on about his dogs** он как зала́дит (*coll.*) о соба́ках; **~ out** *v.t.* (*exclude*): **this coat ~s out the cold very well** э́то пальто́ хорошо́ защища́ет от хо́лода; (*leave in view*): **I kept these papers out to show you** я оста́вил э́ти бума́ги, что́бы показа́ть их вам; *v.i.*: '**Private — ~ out**' (*notice*) «посторо́нним вход запрещён»; **~ together** *v.t.*: **this folder will ~ your papers together** в э́ту па́пку вы смо́жете сложи́ть все докуме́нты; **he has hardly enough to ~ body and soul together** он едва́ сво́дит концы́ с конца́ми; *v.i.*: **the mountaineers kept together for safety** для безопа́сности альпини́сты держа́лись вме́сте; **~ under** *v.t.* держа́ть (*impf.*) в подчине́нии; **~up** *v.t.* (*prevent from falling or sinking*): **he could not ~ his trousers up** у него́ всё вре́мя сва́ливались брю́ки; **the wall was kept up by a buttress** стена́ держа́лась на подпо́рке; (*fig.*, *sustain*, *maintain*): **~ up one's spirits** не па́дать (*impf.*) ду́хом; **~ one's strength up** подкрепля́ть (*impf.*) си́лы; **~ up appearances** соблюда́ть (*impf.*) ви́димость прили́чий; **the house is expensive to ~ up** э́тот дом до́рого содержа́ть; (*continue*): **~ up the good work!** продолжа́йте в том же ду́хе!; **he could not ~ up the payments** он не мог регуля́рно плати́ть; **the custom** has been kept up for centuries э́тот обы́чай сохраня́лся столе́тия; **I wish I had kept up my Latin** жаль, что я забро́сил латы́нь; (*prevent from going to bed*): **the baby kept us up half the night** ребёнок не дава́л нам спать полно́чи; *v.i.* (*stay high*, *e.g. a kite*; *temperature*) держа́ться (*impf.*); (*continue*): **if the weather ~s up we will have a picnic** е́сли хоро́шая пого́да продержи́тся, мы устро́им пикни́к; (*stay level*): **we kept up with them the whole way** всю доро́гу мы не отстава́ли от них; **stop! I can't ~ up** подожди́те! я за ва́ми не поспева́ю; **~ up with the times** не отстава́ть (*impf.*) от собы́тий; **~ up with the Joneses** быть не ху́же други́х; (*remain in touch*): **I try to ~ up with the news** я стара́юсь следи́ть за собы́тиями; **I ~ up with several old friends** я подде́рживаю отноше́ния ко́е с кем из ста́рых друзе́й.

cpd. **~-fit** *adj.*: **~-fit exercises** заря́дка.

keeper [ˈkiːpə(r)] *n.* (*guardian*) храни́тель (*m.*), сто́рож; (*in zoo*) служи́тель (*m.*) (зоопа́рка); (*lighthouse-~*, *museum-~*) смотри́тель (*m.*); (*of shop*, *restaurant etc.*) владе́лец; хозя́ин; (*goal-~*) врата́рь (*m.*).

keeping [ˈkiːpɪŋ] *n.* **1.: in safe ~** в надёжных рука́х; в по́лной сохра́нности. **2.: be in ~ with** соотве́тствовать (*impf.*) +*d.*; **that remark is out of ~ with his character** э́то замеча́ние для него́ не типи́чно.

keepsake [ˈkiːpseɪk] *n.* сувени́р; **as a ~** на па́мять.

keg [keg] *n.* бочо́нок.

ken [ken] *n.*: **beyond my ~** за преде́лами мои́х позна́ний.

kennel [ˈken(ə)l] *n.* **1.** конура́. **2.** (*pl.*, *for hounds*) пса́рня.

Kenya [ˈkenjə] *n.* Ке́ния.

kerb [kɜːb] *n.* обо́чина.

cpd. **~stone** *n.* бордю́рный ка́мень.

kerchief [ˈkɜːtʃiːf, -tʃɪf] *n.* плато́к, косы́нка.

kerfuffle [kəˈfʌf(ə)l] *n.* шум, заваруха.

kernel [ˈkɜːn(ə)l] *n.* (*of nut or fruit-stone*) ядро́; (*of seed*, *e.g. wheat grain*) зерно́.

keros|ene, -ine [ˈkerəˌsiːn] *n.* кероси́н; (*attr.*) кероси́новый.

kestrel [ˈkestr(ə)l] *n.* пустельга́.

ketchup [ˈketʃʌp] *n.* ке́тчуп.

kettle [ˈket(ə)l] *n.* ча́йник; (*pot for boiling*, *e.g. fish*) котело́к; **here's a pretty ~ of fish!** вот так но́мер!

cpd. **~-drum** *n.* лита́вра.

key [kiː] *n.* **1.** ключ; **~ to the door** ключ от две́ри. **2.** (*fig.*, *sth. providing access or solution*) ключ; **the ~ to a mystery** разга́дка та́йны; **the ~ to success is hard work** зало́г успе́ха — упо́рная рабо́та; (*to foreign text*) подстро́чник; (*to map*) леге́нда. **3.** (*attr.*, *important*, *essential*) ва́жный, важне́йший; веду́щий; **~ position** ключева́я пози́ция; **~ question** стержнево́й вопро́с; **a ~ man** незамени́мый рабо́тник. **4.** (*of piano or typewriter*) кла́виш, кла́виша; (*pl.*) клавиату́ра; (*of wind instrument*) кла́пан. **5.** (*mus.*) ключ, тона́льность.

v.t.: **~ up** взви́н|чивать, -ти́ть.

cpds. **~board** *n.* клавиату́ра; **~board instrument** кла́вишный инструме́нт; **~boarder** *n.* опера́тор клавиату́ры; **~hole** *n.* замо́чная сква́жина; **~note** *n.* (*mus.*) основна́я но́та ключа́; (*fig.*) лейтмоти́в; основна́я мысль; **~note address** програ́ммная речь; **~-ring** *n.* кольцо́ для ключе́й.

kg. [ˈkɪləˌgræm] *n.* (*abbr. of* **kilogram(me)(s)**) кг, (килогра́мм).

KGB (*abbr. of Russ.*) КГБ, (*Комитет государственной безопасности*); **~ agent** кагебе́шник.

khaki [ˈkɑːkɪ] *n.* защи́тный цвет, ха́ки (*nt. indecl.*).

adj.: **a ~ shirt** руба́шка цве́та ха́ки.

khan [kɑːn, kæn] *n.* хан.

khanate [ˈkɑːneɪt, ˈkæneɪt] *n.* ха́нство.

kibbutz [kɪˈbʊts] *n.* киб(б)у́ц.

kick [kɪk] *n.* **1.** уда́р, пино́к; **give s.o. a ~** уд|аря́ть, -а́рить кого́-н. ного́й; **give a ~** (*of horse*) ляг|а́ться, -ну́ться; (*football*): **the referee gave a free ~** судья́ объяви́л штрафно́й уда́р. **2.** (*recoil*) отда́ча. **3.** (*coll.*, *stimulus*): **get a ~ out of sth.** получ|а́ть, -и́ть удово́льствие от чего́-н.; **he does it for ~s** (*sl.*) он де́лает э́то из озорства́.

v.t. уд|аря́ть, -а́рить ного́й; **he ~ed me on the shin** он уда́рил меня́ по го́лени; **I could have ~ed myself** я рвал на себе́ во́лосы; **he ~ed the ball** он уда́рил по мячу́; **he ~ed a goal** он заби́л гол; **~ one's heels** ждать (*impf.*) с нетерпе́нием; **~ the habit** (*sl.*, *give up drug-taking*) бро́сить (*pf.*) нарко́тики.

v.i. (*of animals*) ляга́ться (*impf.*); брыка́ться (*impf.*); (*fig.*): **~ at, against sth.** протестова́ть (*impf.*) про́тив чего́-н.; **he is still alive and ~ing** он всё ещё жив-здоро́в.

with advs.: **~ about, around** *v.t.*: **they were ~ing a ball about** они́ гоня́ли мяч; (*treat badly*): **he felt he had been ~ed around too long** он чу́вствовал, что его́ сли́шком уж шпыня́ют; *v.i.* (*coll.*): **is his father still ~ing around?** его́ оте́ц ещё жив?; **there are plenty of jobs ~ing around** круго́м мест ско́лько уго́дно; **~ back** *v.i.* (*retaliate*) соверши́ть (*pf.*) отве́тный уда́р; (*recoil*) отдава́ть (*impf.*); **~ in** *v.t.*: **~ the door in** взл|а́мывать, -ома́ть дверь; **~ s.o.'s teeth in** выбива́ть, вы́бить кому́-н. зу́бы; **~ off** *v.t.* (*e.g. shoes*) сбр|а́сывать, -о́сить; *v.i.* (*football*) нач|ина́ть, -а́ть игру́; (*coll.*, *begin*) нач|ина́ть, -а́ть; **~ out** *v.t.* (*eject*, *expel*) выгоня́ть, вы́гнать; *v.i.* выбра́сывать, вы́бросить но́ги; ляга́ться (*impf.*); **~ over** *v.t.* опроки́|дывать, -нуть; **~ up** *v.t.*: **the horse ~ed up its heels** ло́шадь взбрыкну́ла; **he ~ed up a stone** он подбро́сил ка́мень ного́й; (*coll.*, *create*): **~ up a row** устр|а́ивать, -о́ить сканда́л; **~ up a din** подн|има́ть, -я́ть шум.

cpds. **~-off** *n.* нача́ло (игры́); **~-start** *v.t.* (*lit. and fig.*): **to ~-start the economy** дать толчо́к эконо́мике.

kid[1] [kɪd] *n.* **1.** (*young goat*) козлёнок. **2.** (*leather*) шевро́ (*indecl.*); (*attr.*) шевро́вый; (*for gloves*) ла́йка; **~ glove** ла́йковая перча́тка; **use, wear ~ gloves** (*fig.*) осторо́жно/мя́гко обраща́ться (*impf.*) (*с кем*). **3.** (*coll.*, *child*) малы́ш; **he's just a ~** он всего́ лишь ребёнок; **my ~ brother** мой мла́дший брат.

kid[2] [kɪd] *v.t.* **1.** (*coll.*, *deceive*) над|ува́ть, -у́ть; **who are you ~ding?** кого́ вы хоти́те обману́ть?; **don't ~ yourself!** не обма́нывайте себя́! **2.** (*tease*) дразни́ть (*impf.*); **~ s.o. on, along** води́ть (*impf.*) кого́-н. за́ нос.

v.i. (*tease with untruths*): **you're ~ding!** врёшь!

kidnap [ˈkɪdnæp] *v.t.* пох|ища́ть, -и́тить.

kidnapper [ˈkɪdnæpə(r)] *n.* похити́тель (*m.*).

kidney [ˈkɪdnɪ] *n.* по́чка; **~ machine** аппара́т «иску́сственная по́чка»; **~ transplant** переса́дка по́чек.

cpds. **~-bean** *n.* фасо́ль (*collect.*); **~-shaped** *adj.* почкови́дный; **~-stone** *n.* га́лька.

kill [kɪl] *n.* **1.** (*of hunted animal*) отстре́л; (*of enemy aircraft etc.*) уничтоже́ние; **be in at the ~** (*fig.*) прибы́ть (*pf.*) к дележу́ добы́чи. **2.** (*animal(s) ~ed*) добы́ча; **a good ~** бога́тая добы́ча.

v.t. **1.** уб|ива́ть, -и́ть; (*rats etc.*) мори́ть, вы́-; **he was ~ed in an accident** он поги́б при ава́рии; **~ed in action** уби́т в бою́; **~ o.s.** (*lit.*) ко́нчить самоуби́йством; **the villain gets ~ed in the end** злоде́й в конце́ концо́в погиба́ет; **my feet are ~ing me** я без за́дних ног; **the frost ~ed my roses** мои́ ро́зы поги́бли от моро́за. **2.** (*animals for food*) ре́зать, за-; (*esp. in quantity*) заб|ива́ть, -и́ть. **3.** (*destroy*, *put an end to*) уничт|ожа́ть, -о́жить; разб|ива́ть, -и́ть; **this drug ~s the pain** э́то лека́рство утоля́ет боль;

~ **a proposal** провалить (*pf.*) предложение. **4.** (*neutralize, e.g. colours*) нейтрализовать (*impf., pf.*); **cigarettes ~ the appetite** папиросы портят аппетит; **~ time** уб|ивать, -ить время. **5.** (*overwhelm*): **~ s.o. with kindness** погубить кого-н. чрезмерной добротой; **your jokes are ~ing me!** ваши шутки меня уморили!; **dressed to ~** разодетый в пух и прах.

v.i.: **thou shalt not ~!** не убий!; **~ or cure** ≃ рискованное средство.

with adv.: **~ off** *v.t.* переб|ивать, -ить.

cpd. **~joy** *n.* брюзга (*c.g.*).

killer ['kɪlə(r)] *n.* (*murderer*) убийца (*c.g.*); **~ whale** косатка; (*fatal disease*): **typhus is a ~** тиф — смертельная болезнь.

killing ['kɪlɪŋ] *n.* (*murder*) убийство; (*slaughter of animals*) убой, забой; (*fig., coll.*): **he made a ~** он сорвал большой куш.

adj. (*exhausting*) убийственный; (*amusing*) уморительный.

kiln [kɪln] *n.* печь.

kilo ['ki:ləʊ] *n.* кило (*indecl.*).

kilobyte ['kɪlə,baɪt] *n.* килобайт.

kilogram(me) ['kɪlə,græm] *n.* килограмм.

kilohertz ['kɪlə,hɜ:ts] *n.* килогерц.

kilometre ['kɪlə,mi:tə(r)] *n.* километр.

kiloton ['kɪlə,tʌn] *n.* килотонна.

kilowatt ['kɪlə,wɒt] *n.* киловатт.

cpd. **~-hour** *n.* киловатт-час.

kilt [kɪlt] *n.* (шотландская) юбка.

kimono [kɪ'məʊnəʊ] *n.* кимоно (*indecl.*).

kin [kɪn] *n.* (*family*) семья; (*relations*) родня (*collect.*); родственники (*m. pl.*); **kith and ~** родные и близкие; **next of ~** ближайший родственник, ближайшая родственница.

kind [kaɪnd] *n.* **1.** (*race*) род; **human ~** род человеческий. **2.** (*class, sort, variety*) род, сорт, разновидность; **all ~s of goods** всякие товары; **something of the ~** что-то в этом роде; **of a different ~** другого рода; **nothing of the ~** ничего подобного; **he is a ~ of actor** он в своём роде актёр; **one of a ~** уникум; уникальный; **what ~ of?** что за?; какой?; **what ~ of box do you want?** какого рода коробка вам нужна?; **that ~ of person is never satisfied** такой человек всегда чем-то недоволен; **that ~ of thing** такие вещи; всё в таком роде. **3.**: **~ of** (*coll., to some extent*): **I ~ of expected it** я вроде бы ожидал этого; **I felt ~ of sorry for him** мне его было как-то жаль. **4.** (*natural character*) качество; **differ in ~** отличаться по качеству; различаться по своей природе. **5.**: **in ~** натурой; **pay in ~** платить, за- натурой; **repay in ~** (*fig.*) отпла|чивать, -тить той же монетой.

adj. добрый, любезный; **be so ~ as to close the door** будьте любезны, закройте дверь; **with ~ regards** с сердечным приветом.

cpds. **~-hearted** *adj.* добросердечный; **~heartedness** *n.* доброта.

kindergarten ['kɪndə,gɑ:t(ə)n] *n.* детский сад.

kindle ['kɪnd(ə)l] *v.t.* разж|игать, -ечь; (*fig., arouse*) возбу|ждать, -дить.

v.i. загор|аться, -еться; (*fig.*) вспых|ивать, -нуть.

kindliness ['kaɪndlɪnɪs] *n.* доброта.

kindling ['kɪndlɪŋ] *n.* (*firewood*) растопка.

kindly ['kaɪndlɪ] *adj.* добрый, добродушный; (*fig., of climate etc.*) благоприятный, мягкий.

adv. **1.** (*in a kind manner*) любезно, мило. **2.** (*please*): **~ ring me tomorrow** будьте добры, позвоните мне завтра. **3.**: **he took ~ to my suggestion** он хорошо отнёсся к моему предложению; **he does not take ~ to criticism** он не любит критики.

kindness ['kaɪndnɪs] *n.* **1.** (*benevolence, kind nature*) доброта; **he did it out of (the) ~ (of his heart)** он сделал это по доброте (сердечной). **2.** (*kind act; service*) любезность; одолжение; **do s.o. a ~** ока|з|ывать, -ать кому-н. любезность; делать, с- кому-н. одолжение.

kindred ['kɪndrɪd] *adj.* (*lit., fig.*) родственный; **~ ideas** родственные идеи; **a ~ spirit** родная душа.

kinetic [kɪ'netɪk, kaɪ-] *adj.* кинетический.

kinetics [kɪ'netɪks, kaɪ-] *n.* кинетика.

king [kɪŋ] *n.* **1.** король (*m.*); (*anc. and bibl.*) царь (*m.*); **the K~'s English** правильный английский язык. **2.** (*fig.*): **~ of beasts/birds** царь зверей/птиц; (*chess*): **White K~** белый король; (*draughts, checkers*) дамка.

cpds. **~fisher** *n.* (голубой) зимородок; **~pin** *n.* (*bolt*) шкворень (*m.*); (*fig.*) главное лицо; **~-size(d)** *adj.* крупный; большего размера.

kingdom ['kɪŋdəm] *n.* королевство; **the United K~** Соединённое Королевство; **the animal ~** животное царство; **the ~ of heaven** царство небесное.

king|like ['kɪŋlaɪk], **-ly** ['kɪŋlɪ] *adjs.* королевский, царский; (*fig.*) величественный.

kink [kɪŋk] *n.* (*in rope etc.*) перегиб; (*in metal*) изгиб; (*fig., in character*) причуда.

kinky ['kɪŋkɪ] *adj.* (*twisted*) кручёный; (*coll., perverted*) извращённый; со странностями.

kinsfolk ['kɪnzfəʊk] *n.* родня (*collect.*).

kinship ['kɪnʃɪp] *n.* (*relationship*) родство; (*similarity*) сходство.

kinsman ['kɪnzmən] *n.* родственник.

kinswoman ['kɪnz,wʊmən] *n.* родственница.

kiosk ['ki:ɒsk] *n.* киоск; **telephone ~** телефонная будка, автомат.

kip [kɪp] *n.* (*coll.*) (*sleep*) сон.

v.i. **1.**: **~ down for the night** устроиться (*pf.*) на ночь. **2.** (*sleep*) кемарить, по- (*coll.*).

kipper ['kɪpə(r)] *n.* копчёная селёдка.

Kirghizia [kɜ:'gi:zɪə] *n.* Киргизия.

kiss [kɪs] *n.* поцелуй; **blow s.o. a ~** послать (*pf.*) кому-н. воздушный поцелуй; **steal a ~** сорвать (*pf.*) поцелуй; **give her a ~ from me!** поцелуй её за меня!; **~ of life** искусственное дыхание.

v.t. целовать, по-; **he ~ed away her tears** поцелуями он осушил её слёзы; **they ~ed each other goodbye** они поцеловались на прощанье; **you can ~ goodbye to the inheritance** вы можете распрощаться с наследством; **he ~ed his hand to me** он послал мне воздушный поцелуй.

v.i. целоваться, по-.

kisser ['kɪsə(r)] *n.* (*mouth*) варежка (*sl.*).

kit [kɪt] *n.* (*personal equipment, esp. clothing*) снаряжение; **a soldier's ~** солдатское снаряжение; (*workman's tools*) набор инструментов; (*for particular sport or activity*) набор/комплект (спортивных) принадлежностей; **survival ~** набор самого необходимого.

v.t. & i. (*usu.* **~ out, up**) снаря|жать(ся), -дить(ся).

cpd. **~bag** *n.* вещевой мешок/ранец; вещмешок.

kitchen ['kɪtʃɪn, -tʃ(ə)n] *n.* кухня; **~ garden** огород.

kite [kaɪt] *n.* **1.** (*bird*) (красный) коршун. **2.** (*toy*) (воздушный/бумажный) змей; **fly a ~** запус|кать, -тить змея.

kith [kɪθ] *see* **kin**

kitsch [kɪtʃ] *n.* китч, дешёвка.

kitten ['kɪt(ə)n] *n.* котёнок; **our cat has had ~s** наша кошка окотилась; у нашей кошки котята.

kittiwake ['kɪtɪ,weɪk] *n.* моёвка.

kitty ['kɪtɪ] *n.* (*at cards etc.*) пулька, банк; (*cat*) киска.

kiwi ['ki:wi:] *n.* (*bird*) киви (*f. indecl.*).

kleptomania [,kleptəʊ'meɪnɪə] *n.* клептомания.

kleptomaniac [,kleptəʊ'meɪnɪ,æk] *n.* клептоман (*fem.* -ка).

km. ['kɪlə,mi:tə(r)(z)] *n.* (*abbr. of* **kilometre(s)**) км, (километр).

knack [næk] *n.* (*skill, faculty*) сноро́вка, уме́ние; **have the ~ of** име́ть (*impf.*) сноро́вку (*в чём*); **there's a ~ to it** де́ло тре́бует сноро́вки.

knacker ['nækə(r)] *n.* ску́пщик ста́рых лошаде́й; **~'s yard** живодёрня.

knapsack ['næpsæk] *n.* ра́нец.

knave [neɪv] *n.* **1.** (*arch., rogue*) плут, моше́нник. **2.** (*cards*) вале́т; **~ of hearts** вале́т черве́й.

knavish ['neɪvɪʃ] *adj.* плутовско́й.

knead [ni:d] *v.t.* (*e.g. dough or clay*) меси́ть, за-/с-; (*massage*) масси́ровать (*impf., pf.*).

knee [ni:] *n.* коле́н|о (*pl.* и); **he was on his ~s** он стоя́л на коле́нях; **go down on one's ~s** стать/упа́сть (*pf.*) на коле́ни.; **bring s.o. to his ~s** ста́вить, по- кого́-н. на коле́ни; **I went weak at the ~s** у меня́ задрожа́ли поджи́лки (*or* подкоси́лись но́ги); **I learnt it at my mother's ~** я впита́л э́то с молоко́м ма́тери; **they were up to their ~s in mud** они́ бы́ли по коле́но в грязи́.

v.t. уд|аря́ть, -а́рить коле́ном.

cpds. **~-cap** *n.* коле́нная ча́шка; **~-deep** *pred. adj. & adv.*: **he stood ~-deep in water** он стоя́л по коле́но в воде́; **~-jerk** *adj.* автомати́ческий, непроизво́льный; **~-length** *adj.* до коле́н.

kneel [ni:l] *v.i.* **1.** (*also* **~ down:** *go down on one's knees*) ста|нови́ться, -ть на коле́ни; **~ to s.o.** преклон|я́ть, -и́ть коле́на пе́ред кем-н. **2.** (*be in ~ing position*) стоя́ть (*impf.*) на коле́нях; **they knelt in prayer** они́ моли́лись на коле́нях.

knell [nel] *n.* похоро́нный звон.

knickerbockers ['nɪkə,bɒkə(r)z] *n.* бри́дж|и (*pl., g.* -ей).

knickers ['nɪkəz] *n.* (*fem. undergarment*) пантало́н|ы (*pl., g.* —).

(k)nick-(k)nack ['nɪknæk] *n.* безделу́шка.

knife [naɪf] *n.* но́ж; (*pocket ~*) но́жик; **he has his ~ into me** (*fig.*) он име́ет зуб на меня́; **hold a ~ to s.o.'s throat** прист|ава́ть, -а́ть с ножо́м к го́рлу к кому́-н..

v.t. зак|а́лывать, -оло́ть ножо́м.

cpds. **~-edge** *n.* (*blade*) остриё ножа́; **on a ~-edge** (*fig.*) вися́щий на волоске́; **~-point** *n.*: **at ~-point** угрожа́я ножо́м.

knight [naɪt] *n.* **1.** (*hist.*) ры́царь (*m.*). **2.** (*member of order*) кавале́р; **K~ of the Garter** кавале́р о́рдена Подвя́зки. **3.** (*chess*) конь (*m.*).

v.t. (*hist.*) возв|оди́ть, -ести́ в ры́царское досто́инство; (*mod.*) ≃ присв|а́ивать, -о́ить (*кому*) ненасле́дственное дворя́нское зва́ние.

cpd. **~-errant** *n.* стра́нствующий ры́царь.

knighthood ['naɪthʊd] *n.* ры́царство; **he was recommended for a ~** его́ предста́вили к ры́царскому зва́нию.

knit [nɪt] *v.t.* **1.:** **~ wool into stockings (*or* stockings from wool)** вяза́ть, с- чулки́ из ше́рсти; **hand-/machine-~ted garments** вя́заная/трикота́жная оде́жда; вя́занки (*f. pl.*). **2.** (*fasten*; *also* **~ together**) скреп|ля́ть, -и́ть; (*unite*) соедин|я́ть, -и́ть. **3.:** **~ one's brows** хму́рить, на- бро́ви; хму́риться, на-.

v.i. **1.** (*do ~ting*) вяза́ть (*impf.*). **2.** (*of bones*) сраст|а́ться, -и́сь.

cpd. **~wear** *n.* трикота́жные изде́лия.

knitting ['nɪtɪŋ] *n.* (*action*) вяза́ние; (*fig.*) скрепле́ние, соедине́ние; (*material being knitted*) вяза́нье.

cpds. **~-machine** *n.* вяза́льная маши́на; **~-needle** *n.* вяза́льная спи́ца; **~-yarn** *n.* трикота́жная пря́жа.

knob [nɒb] *n.* **1.** (*protuberance*) вы́пуклость; ши́шка. **2.** (*handle*) ру́чка; (*button*) кно́пка. **3.** (*of butter etc.*) кусо́чек.

knobbly ['nɒblɪ] *adj.* шишкова́тый.

knock [nɒk] *n.* **1.** (*rap, rapping sound*) стук; **give a ~ on the door** стуча́ть, по- в дверь; **there came a loud ~** разда́лся гро́мкий стук. **2.** (*sound of ~ing in engine*) (детонацио́нный) стук. **3.** (*blow*) уда́р; **he got a nasty ~ on the head** он си́льно уда́рился голово́й.

v.t. **1.** (*hit*) удар|я́ть, -а́рить; **the blow ~ed him flat** уда́р сбил его́ с ног; **he ~ed the ball into the net** он заби́л мяч в се́тку; **he ~ed the table with his hammer** он уда́рил по́ столу молотко́м; **she ~ed her arm against the chair** она́ сту́кнулась руко́й о стул; **he ~ed a nail into the wall** он вбил гвоздь в сте́ну; **he ~ed a hole in, through the wall** он проби́л ды́рку в стене́; **he ~ed the glass off the table** он смахну́л стака́н со стола́; **~ s.o. on, over the head** уда́рить (*pf.*) кого́-н. по голове́; **I ~ed the gun out of his hand** я вы́бил из его́ руки́ пистоле́т. **2.** (*fig. uses*): **the idea was ~ed on the head** э́тому предложе́нию не да́ли хо́ду; **I tried to ~ some sense into his head** я пыта́лся впра́вить ему́ мо́зги; **~ into shape** прив|оди́ть, -ести́ в поря́док; **I'll ~ a pound off the price** я сбро́шу фунт с цены́; **he ~ed five seconds off the record time** он поби́л реко́рд на пять секу́нд. **3.** (*criticize*) хая́ть (*impf.*) (*sl.*).

v.i. **1.** (*rap*) стуча́ть; **~ at the door** стуча́ть(ся), по- в дверь; **'~ before entering'** (*notice*) «без сту́ка не входи́ть». **2.:** **~ against** (*collide with*) нат|ыка́ться, -кну́ться на+*a.* **3.** (*of engine*) стуча́ть (*impf.*).

with advs.: **~ about** *v.t.* (*treat roughly*) помя́ть/намя́ть (*pf.*) бока́ (*кому*); *v.i. also* **~ (a)round** (*travel, wander*): **he's ~ed about a bit in his time** он в своё вре́мя побroди́л/пое́здил по све́ту; (*coll., keep company*): **she's ~ing around with a married man** она́ связа́лась с жена́тым челове́ком; **~ back** *v.t.* (*disconcert*): **the news ~ed me back** изве́стие привело́ меня́ в замеша́тельство; (*coll., consume*): **he can ~ back 5 pints in as many minutes** он за пять мину́т мо́жет опроки́нуть пять пинт (пи́ва); **~ down** *v.t.* (*strike to ground*) сби|ва́ть, -ть с ног; вали́ть, с-; **he was ~ed down by a car** его́ сби́ла маши́на; (*demolish*) сн|оси́ть, -ести́; (*dismantle*) раз|бира́ть, -обра́ть; (*reduce*) сн|ижа́ть, -и́зить; **~ in** *v.t.*: **~ a nail in** вби|ва́ть, -ть (*or* заб|ива́ть, -и́ть) гвоздь; **~ off** *v.t.* (*lit.*) сби|ва́ть, -ть; сма́х|ивать, -ну́ть; (*coll. uses*): (*deduct from price*) сб|авля́ть, -а́вить; (*compose or complete rapidly*): **he can ~ off an article in half-an-hour** он мо́жет состря́пать (*sl.*) статью за полчаса́; (*steal*) сти́брить (*pf.*) (*sl.*); *v.i.* (*stop work*) шаба́шить, по- (*sl.*); **~ out** *v.t.* (*lit.*): **he ~ed a pane out** он вы́бил стекло́ из ра́мы; **he ~ed two of my teeth out** он вы́бил мне два зу́ба; (*make unconscious*) оглуш|а́ть, -и́ть; **the blow on his head ~ed him out** он был оглушён уда́ром по голове́; (*boxing*) нокаути́ровать (*impf., pf.*); (*overwhelm*) потряс|а́ть, -ти́; (*eliminate from contest*): **he was ~ed out in the first round** он вы́был в пе́рвом ту́ре; **~ over** *v.t.* опроки́|дывать, -нуть; **~ together** *v.t.*: **he ~ed together a cupboard** он на́спех сколоти́л шкаф; **~ up** *v.t.* (*lit.*): **she ~ed up the ball with her racket** она́ подбро́сила мяч ракёткой; (*prepare*): **I can soon ~ up a meal** я бы́стренько пригото́влю еду́; (*waken*) буди́ть, раз-; *v.i.* (*tennis*) разм|ина́ться, -я́ться (*coll.*).

cpds. **~down** *adj.*: **at a ~down price** по дешёвке (*coll.*); **~-kneed** *adj.* с вывернутыми внутрь коле́нями; **~out** *n.* (*boxing*) нока́ут; (*competition*) соревнова́ния (*nt. pl.*) по олимпи́йской систе́ме; (*fig., sth. striking*) не́что сногшиба́тельное; (*attr.*): **~out blow** сокруши́тельный уда́р; **~-up** *n.* (*tennis*) разми́нка.

knocker ['nɒkə(r)] *n.* (*on door*) (дверно́й) молото́к.

knocking ['nɒkɪŋ] *n.* (*noise*) стук.

knoll [nəʊl] *n.* хо́лмик, буго́р, бугоро́к.

knot [nɒt] *n.* **1.** (*in rope etc.; in wood; measure of speed*) у́зел; **tie a ~ in a rope** завя́з|ывать, -а́ть у́зел на верёвке; **tie sth. in a ~** завя́з|ывать, -а́ть что-н. узло́м; **tie o.s. (up) in(to) ~s** (*fig.*) запу́таться (*pf.*); **a vessel of 20 ~s** сýдно со скóростью двáдцать узлóв; **we are flying at 500 ~s** мы летúм со скóростью 500 узлóв в час. **2.** (*group, cluster*) кýчка.

v.t. & i. завя́з|ывать(ся), -áть(ся).

cpd. **~-hole** *n.* дырá от сучкá.

knotted ['nɒtɪd] *adj.* **1.** (*also* **knotty:** *gnarled*) узловáтый, сучковáтый. **2.: a ~ed rope** верёвка с узлáми; верёвка, завя́занная узлóм.

knotty ['nɒtɪ] *adj.* **1.** = **knotted 1.. 2.: a ~ problem** запýтанная/трýдная проблéма.

knout [naʊt, nu:t] *n.* кнут.

know [nəʊ] *n.*: **be in the ~** быть в кýрсе дéла.

v.t. **1.** (*be aware, have knowledge of*) знать (*impf.*): **I ~ nothing about it** я об э́том ничегó не знáю; **as far as I ~** наскóлько мне извéстно; **who ~s?** как знать?; **I wouldn't ~** откýда мне знать?; **he let it be ~n that ...** он дал поня́ть, что...; **never let it be ~n** никогдá в э́том не признавáйтесь; **you (should) ~ best** вам лýчше знать; **before I knew it we had arrived** я не успéл оглянýться, как мы прúбыли; **before you ~ where you are** не успéешь оглянýться; **I knew it!** (я) так и знал!; **I don't ~ that I like this** я не увéрен, что мне э́то нрáвится; **he ~s what's what** он знáет, что к чемý; **he ~s his own mind** он знáет, чегó (он) хóчет; **he doesn't ~ his own mind** он сам не знáет, чегó хóчет; **he ~s a thing or two** он кóе в чём разбирáется; **he has been ~n to be wrong** у негó бывáли ошúбки; **I ~ what!** вот что!; знáете что?; **you ~ what?** (*US* **you ~ something?**) знáете что?; **not if I ~ it!** я э́того не допущý; **you ~ what he is** (ну, да) вы егó знáете; **he ~s what he is about** он своё дéло знáет. **2.** (*recognize, distinguish*) знать, у-; узн|авáть, -áть; отлич|áть, -úть; **I ~ him by sight** я знáю егó в лицó; **he knew her at once** он её срáзу узнáл; **I shouldn't ~ him from his brother** я егó не отличúл бы от брáта; **I knew him for a liar** я знал, что он лжец; **I'd ~ him anywhere** я узнáю егó дáже во сне; **he is ~n to his friends as Jumbo** друзья́ клúчут егó Слонóм; **he ~s a good thing when he sees it** он понимáет, что хорошó и что плóхо. **3.** (*be acquainted, familiar with*) знать (*impf.*); быть знакóмым с+*i.*; **get to ~ s.o.** знакóмиться, по- с кем-н.; **I have ~n him since childhood** я с ним знакóм с дéтства; **I don't ~ him to speak to** я с ним недостáточно знакóм, чтóбы вступáть в разговóр; **make o.s. ~n to s.o.** предст|авля́ться, -áвиться комý-н. **4.** (*be versed in; understand; have experience in*) знáть, понимáть (*impf.*), разбирáться (*impf.*) в+*p.*; **he ~s Russian** он знáет рýсский язы́к; **~ by heart** знать наизýсть (*coll.*) назубóк; **~ how to** умéть, с-. **5.** (*experience*): **he ~s no peace** он не знáет покóя; **he has ~n many privations** он пережúл мнóго лишéний; **I have ~n worse to happen** мне извéстны слýчаи и похýже. **6.** (*be subject to*): **he ~s no shame** он не вéдает стыдá; **her happiness knew no bounds** её счáстье не знáло границ. *See also* **known**

v.i.: **let s.o. ~** сообщ|áть, -úть (*or* да|вáть, -ть знать) комý-н.; **will you let me ~?** вы сообщúте мне?; **(the) Lord only ~s!** Бог егó знáет!; **how should I ~?** почём я знáю?; **what do you ~ (about that)?** подýмайте (тóлько)!; ишь ты!; **you never ~** как знать?; **he doesn't want to ~** (*refuses to take notice, interest*) он (и) знать не хóчет; **I ~ better than to ...** я не так прост, чтóбы...; **(do) you ~** (*in parenthesis*) знáете ли; понимáете; **it's too hot to work, you ~** жáрко рабóтать-то; **I don't ~ him but I ~ of him** лúчно я с ним незнакóм, но наслы́шал о нём; **he ~s about cars** он разбирáется в машúнах. *See also* **known**

cpds. **~-all** *n.* всезнáйка (*c.g.*); **~-how** *n.* умéние; óпыт; ýровень (*m.*) знáний; секрéты (*m. pl.*) произвóдства; технолóгия; **have the ~-how** обладáть (*impf.*) умéнием; (*body of experience*): **professional/technical ~-how** профессионáльные/технúческие нáвыки (*m. pl.*).

knowing ['nəʊɪŋ] *n.*: **there's no ~ what may happen** невозмóжно предвúдеть, что мóжет случúться; **I did it without ~** я сдéлал э́то бессознáтельно.

adj. (*intelligent*) ýмный; (*shrewd*) проницáтельный; (*understanding*) понимáющий; (*significant*): **a ~ look** многозначúтельный взгляд.

knowingly ['nəʊɪŋlɪ] *adv.* (*significantly*) многозначúтельно; (*intentionally, consciously*) нарóчно, сознáтельно.

knowledge ['nɒlɪdʒ] *n.* знáние; **field, branch of ~** óбласть знáния; óтрасль наýки; (*understanding*): **our ~ of the subject is as yet limited** нáши познáния в э́той óбласти покá ограничены; (*experience*) óпыт; (*information*) извéстия (*nt. pl.*), свéдения (*nt. pl.*); **I have no ~ of that** я не имéю об э́том свéдений; (*range of information or experience*): **to the best of my ~** наскóлько мне извéстно; **it came to my ~ that ...** мне стáло извéстно, что...; **not to my ~** мне э́то неизвéстно; наскóлько я знáю — нет; **without s.o.'s ~** без чьегó-н. вéдома.

knowledgeable ['nɒlɪdʒəb(ə)l] *adj.* хорошó осведомлённый.

known [nəʊn] *adj.*: **it is a ~ fact that ...** извéстно, что; **a scene ~ to him from childhood** картúна, знакóмая емý с дéтства; **everything gets ~** всё станóвится извéстным. *See also* **know** *v.t.*

knuckle ['nʌk(ə)l] *n.* **1.** (*anat.*) сустáв; **rap s.o. over the ~s** (*fig.*) дать (*pf.*) нагоня́й комý-н. **2.** (*joint of meat*) нóжка, голя́шка.

v.i.: **~ down to one's work** прин|имáться, -я́ться за дéло; **~ under (to)** уступ|áть, -úть (*+d.*); покор|я́ться, -úться (*+d.*).

koala [kəʊ'ɑ:lə] *n.* **(~ bear)** коáла (*m.*).

kohlrabi [kəʊl'rɑ:bɪ] *n.* кольрáби (*f. indecl.*)

kolkhoz ['kɒlkɒz, kʌlk'hɔ:z] *n.* колхóз.

Komsomol ['kɒmsə,mɒl] *n.* (*association*) комсомóл; (*member*) комсомóл|ец (*fem.* -ка); (*attr.*) комсомóльский.

kopeck ['kəʊpek, 'kɒpek] = **copeck**

Koran [kɔ:'rɑ:n, kə-] *n.* корáн.

Korea [kə'ri:ə] *n.* Корéя.

Korean [kə'ri:ən] *m.* (*pers.*) корé|ец (*fem.* -я́нка); (*language*) корéйский язы́к.

adj. корéйский.

kosher ['kəʊʃə(r), 'kɒʃ-] *adj.* кошéрный.

koumiss ['ku:mɪs] *n.* кумы́с.

ko(w)tow [kaʊ'taʊ] *n.* нúзкий поклóн.

v.i. дéлать, с- нúзкий поклóн; (*fig.*) раболéпствовать (*impf.*), пресмыкáться (*impf.*) (*перед кем*).

kremlin ['kremlɪn] *n.* кремль (*m.*); **the K~** Кремль; (*attr.*) кремлёвский.

Kremlinologist [,kremlɪn'ɒlədʒɪst] *n.* кремлевéд, кремлинóлог.

Kremlinology [,kremlɪn'ɒlədʒɪ] *n.* кремлевéдение, кремлинолóгия.

krill [krɪl] *n.* криль (*m.*).

krypton ['krɪptɒn] *n.* криптóн.

kudos ['kju:dɒs] *n.* слáва.

Ku-Klux-Klan [,ku:klʌks'klæn, ,kju:-] *n.* ку-клукс-клáн.

kulak ['ku:læk] *n.* (*hist.*) кулáк.

kumquat ['kʌmkwɒt] *n.* кумквáт.

kung fu [kʊŋ 'fu:, kʌŋ] *n.* кун-фý (*nt. indecl.*).

kvass [kvɑ:s] *n.* квас.

kW ['kɪlə,wɒt] *n.* (*abbr. of* **kilowatt(s)**) кВт, (киловáтт).

L

L (*abbr. of* **learner**): **~-plate** ≃ щиток с на́дписью «уче́бная» (*на машине*).
l. ['li:tə(r)(z)] *n.* (*abbr. of* **litre(s)**) л, (литр).
la [lɑ:] *n.* (*mus.*) ля (*nt. indecl.*).
lab [læb] (*coll.*) = **laboratory**
label ['leɪb(ə)l] *n.* ярлы́к, этике́тка; (**stick-on ~**) накле́йка; (*tag*) би́рка; **pin, stick a ~ on** (*lit., fig.*) прикле́и|вать, -ть ярлы́к/этике́тку +*d.*; (*gram. or stylistic ~, gloss*) поме́та.
v.t. (*stick ~ on*) накле́и|вать, -ть ярлы́к на+*a.*; (*fasten ~ to*) привя́з|ывать, -а́ть ярлы́к/би́рку к+*d.*
labial ['leɪbɪəl] *adj.* губно́й.
laboratory [lə'bɒrətərɪ] *n.* лаборато́рия; (*in school*) кабине́т; **in ~ conditions** в лаборато́рных усло́виях; **~ assistant** лабора́нт (*fem.* -ка).
laborious [lə'bɔ:rɪəs] *adj.* **1.** (*difficult*) тру́дный, тяжёлый; (*toilsome*) трудоёмкий; (*wearying*) утоми́тельный. **2.** (*of style, forced*) вы́мученный; (*involved*) тяжёлый.
labour ['leɪbə(r)] *n.* **1.** (*toil, work*) труд, рабо́та; **manual ~** физи́ческий труд; **~ camp** исправи́тельно-трудово́й ла́герь. **2.** (*pol., workers*) трудя́щиеся; **Ministry of L~** министе́рство труда́. **3.** (*workforce*) рабо́чие (*pl.*), рабо́чая си́ла; **skilled ~** квалифици́рованные рабо́чие; **shortage of ~** нехва́тка рабо́чей си́лы; **~ dispute** трудово́й конфли́кт; **~ exchange** би́ржа труда́; **~ relations** трудовы́е отноше́ния. **4. (L~ Party)** лейбори́стская па́ртия, лейбори́сты (*m. pl.*); **Vote L~!** голосу́йте за лейбори́стскую па́ртию! **5.** (*childbirth*) ро́д|ы (*pl., g.* -ов); **~ pains** родовы́е схва́тки (*f. pl.*); **~ ward** роди́льная пала́та; **she went into ~** у неё начали́сь ро́ды.
v.t.: **~ a point** входи́ть (*impf.*) в изли́шние подро́бности; распространя́ться (*impf.*) о чём-н.
v.i. **1.** (*toil, work*) труди́ться (*impf.*), рабо́тать (*impf.*); **a ~ing man** рабо́чий. **2.** (*strive, exert o.s.*): **he is ~ing to finish his book** он прилага́ет все уси́лия, что́бы ко́нчить кни́гу. **3.** (*move, work etc. with difficulty*): **~ for breath** дыша́ть (*impf.*) с трудо́м; **the car ~ed up the hill** маши́на с трудо́м взбира́лась в го́ру **3.**: **~ under** (*suffer from*): **you are ~ing under a delusion** вы нахо́дитесь в заблужде́нии.
cpds. **~-intensive** *adj.* трудоёмкий; **~-saving** *adj.* рационализа́торский; трудосберега́ющий.
laboured ['leɪbəd] *adj.* **1.** (*difficult*): **~ breathing** затруднённое дыха́ние. **2.** (*forced*): **~ style/compliment** вы́мученный стиль/комплиме́нт.
labourer ['leɪbərə(r)] *n.* рабо́чий.
labourite ['leɪbə,raɪt] *n.* лейбори́ст (*fem.* -ка).
adj. лейбори́стский.
Labrador ['læbrə,dɔ:(r)] *n.* (*dog*) лабрадо́р.
laburnum [lə'bɜ:nəm] *n.* золото́й дождь.
labyrinth ['læbərɪnθ] *n.* (*lit., fig.*) лабири́нт.
lace [leɪs] *n.* **1.** (*open-work fabric*) кру́жево, кружева́ (*nt. pl.*); **~ collar** кружевно́й воротни́к. **2.** (*of shoe etc.*) шнуро́к.
v.t. **1.** (*fasten or tighten with ~*) шнурова́ть, за-; зашнуро́в|ывать, -а́ть. **2.** (*interlace*) сплет|та́ть, -сти́. **3.** (*trim with ~*) отде́л|ывать, -ать кружева́ми. **4.** (*fortify*): **~ coffee with rum** подл|ива́ть, -и́ть ром в ко́фе.
cpd. **~-maker** *n.* (*fem.*) кружевни́ца.
lacerate ['læsə,reɪt] *v.t.* (*lit., fig.*) терза́ть, рас-/ис-; расте́рз|ывать, -а́ть; (*wound*) ра́нить (*impf., pf.*).
laceration [,læsə'reɪʃ(ə)n] *n.* (*tearing*) терза́ние, разрыва́ние; (*wound*) рва́ная ра́на.
lachrymal ['lækrɪm(ə)l] *adj.* слёзный.
lachrymose ['lækrɪ,məʊs] *adj.* слезли́вый.
lack [læk] *n.* недоста́ток; **for ~ of money** из-за недоста́тка (*or* за неиме́нием) де́нег; **for ~ of evidence** за отсу́тствием ули́к; **there was no ~ of water** воды́ бы́ло вполне́ доста́точно.
v.t. & i.: **he ~s sth.** ему́ чего́-то недостаёт; **he ~s in courage** у него́ не хвата́ет хра́брости; **we ~ money** мы нужда́емся в деньга́х; **a week ~ing in incident** неде́ля, бе́дная собы́тиями; **he ~s for nothing** у него́ ни в чём нет недоста́тка.
cpd. **~lustre** *adj.* ту́склый, без бле́ска.
lackadaisical [,lækə'deɪzɪk(ə)l] *adj.* апати́чный; **in a ~ manner** спустя́ рукава́, без воодушевле́ния.
lackey ['lækɪ] *n.* (*lit., fig.*) лаке́й; (*fig.*) подхали́м.
laconic [lə'kɒnɪk] *adj.* (*of pers.*) неразгово́рчивый, немногосло́вный; (*of speech etc.*) лакони́чный.
lacquer ['lækə(r)] *n.* политу́ра (*no pl.*); лак.
v.t. лакирова́ть (*impf.*).
cpd. **~-ware** *n.* лакиро́ванные изде́лия.
lacrosse [lə'krɒs] *n.* лакро́сс.
lactate [læk'teɪt] *v.i.* выделя́ть (*impf.*) молоко́.
lactation [læk'teɪʃ(ə)n] *n.* лакта́ция.
lactic ['læktɪk] *adj.* моло́чный.
lacuna [lə'kju:nə] *n.* пробе́л, лаку́на.
lad [læd] *n.* (*boy*) ма́льчик; (*fellow, youth*) па́рень (*m.*), ма́лый; (*pl.*) ребя́т|а (*pl., g.* —); **good ~!** молоде́ц!
ladder ['lædə(r)] *n.* **1.** ле́стница; **folding/extending ~** складна́я/выдвижна́я ле́стница; (*fig.*): **~ of success** путь к успе́ху; **climb the social ~** поднима́ться (*impf.*) по обще́ственной ле́стнице. **2.** (*on a ship*) трап. **3.** (*in stocking*) спусти́вшаяся петля́.
v.t. & i.: **I have ~ed my stocking** у меня́ спусти́лась петля́ на чулке́; **you have ~ed my stocking** вы мне порва́ли чуло́к.
lade [leɪd] *v.t.* (*usu. p.p.*) грузи́ть, на-; нагру|жа́ть, -зи́ть; **he returned ~n with books** он верну́лся нагру́женный кни́гами; **the table was ~n with food** стол ломи́лся от еды́/яств.
ladies ['leɪdɪs] *n. see* **lady** *n.* **6.**
ladle ['leɪd(ə)l] *n.* ковш; **soup ~** разлива́тельная ло́жка.
v.t. че́рпать (*impf.*); отче́рп|ывать, -а́ть; **~ out soup** разл|ива́ть, -и́ть суп.
lady ['leɪdɪ] *n.* **1.** (*woman of social status*) да́ма; **society ~** све́тская да́ма; **first ~** (*US*) супру́га президе́нта; (*as title*) ле́ди (*f. indecl.*). **2.** (*relig.*): **Our L~** Богоро́дица. **3.** (*courteous or formal for woman*) да́ма, госпожа́; **Ladies and Gentlemen** да́мы и господа́; **ladies first!** доро́гу да́мам; **old ~** пожила́я же́нщина; (*sweetheart*) возлю́бленная; (*fiancée*) неве́ста; **leading ~** (*theatr.*) веду́щая актри́са. **4.** (*attr.*): **~ doctor** же́нщина-врач. **5.** (*wife*): **your good ~; your ~ wife** ва́ша супру́га. **6.**: **the ladies'** (*or* **ladies**) (*coll., lavatory*) же́нская убо́рная.
cpds. **~bird,** (*US*) **~bug** *nn.* бо́жья коро́вка; **~-in-waiting** *n.* фре́йлина; **~-killer** *n.* сердцее́д; **~like** *adj.* (*refined, elegant*) изя́щный, делика́тный, благоро́дный; **~-love** *n.* возлю́бленная; да́ма се́рдца; **~'s-maid** *n.* камери́стка.
lag[1] [læg] *n.* (*delay*) запа́здывание.
v.i. отст|ава́ть, -а́ть; **the children were ~ging (behind)** де́ти тащи́лись сза́ди.
lag[2] [læg] *n.* (*coll., convict*) каторжа́нин, ка́торжник; **old ~** рецидиви́ст.

lag[3] [læg] *v.t.* (*wrap in felt etc.*) покрыва́ть (*impf.*) (во́йлоком); (*encase with boards*) обш|ива́ть, -и́ть до́сками.
lager ['lɑːgə(r)] *n.* све́тлое пи́во.
laggard ['lægəd] *n.* ло́дырь (*m.*); отстаю́щий.
lagging ['lægɪŋ] *n.* (*for pipes etc.*) терми́ческая изоля́ция, обши́вка.
lagoon [lə'guːn] *n.* лагу́на.
laid-back [leɪd'bæk] *adj.* непринуждённый, споко́йный.
lair [leə(r)] *n.* ло́говище; (*of bear*) берло́га; (*fig.*): **thieves' ~** воровско́й прито́н.
laity ['leɪɪtɪ] *n.* миря́не (*m. pl.*).
lake [leɪk] *n.* о́зеро; (*attr.*): **L~ District** Озёрный край; **L~ Superior** Ве́рхнее о́зеро.
cpd. **~side** *n.* бе́рег о́зера.
lama ['lɑːmə] *n.* ла́ма (*m.*).
Lamaism ['lɑːməˌɪz(ə)m] *n.* ламаи́зм.
lamasery ['lɑːməsərɪ, lə'mɑːsərɪ] *n.* ламаи́стский монасты́рь.
lamb [læm] *n.* ягнёнок, бара́шек; **L~ of God** А́гнец Бо́жий; **Persian ~** кара́куль (*m.*); (*fig., of child or mild pers.*) ягнёнок, ове́чка; (*meat*) (молода́я) бара́нина; **leg of ~** бара́нья нога́.
v.i. (*of ewe*) ягни́ться, о(б)-; **the ~ing season** вре́мя ягне́ния.
cpds. **~skin** *n.* овчи́на; бара́шек; мерлу́шка; **~'s-wool** *n.* поя́рок.
lambast(e) [læm'beɪst] *v.t.* дуба́сить, от- (*coll.*).
lame [leɪm] *adj.* **1.** хромо́й; **be ~** хрома́ть (*impf.*); **he is ~ in one leg** он хрома́ет на одну́ но́гу. **2.** (*fig., of argument, speech etc.*) сла́бый; **a ~ excuse** сла́бая отгово́рка.
cpds. **~-brain** *n.* тугоду́м, тупи́ца; **~-brained** *adj.* тупо́й, бестолко́вый.
lamé ['lɑːmeɪ] *n.* ламе́ (*indecl.*).
lament [lə'ment] *n.* (*expression of grief*) се́тование, причита́ние; (*in music or verse*) плач; эле́гия.
v.t.: **~ one's fate** се́товать, по- (*or* ропта́ть, воз-) на судьбу́; **~ one's youth** опла́к|ивать, -ать свою́ мо́лодость; **late ~ed** поко́йный, незабве́нный.
v.i. се́товать, по-; причита́ть (*impf.*) (по+*p.*).
lamentable ['læməntəb(ə)l] *adj.* плаче́вный; приско́рбный, жа́лкий.
lamentation [ˌlæmən'teɪʃ(ə)n] *n.* (*lamenting*) се́тование, причита́ние; (*lament*) плач, жа́лобы (*f. pl.*).
laminate[1] ['læmɪnət] *adj.* (*in plates*) пласти́нчатый; (*in layers*) расслоённый, слои́стый.
laminate[2] ['læmɪˌneɪt] *v.t.* (*roll into plates*) прока́т|ывать, -а́ть в листы́; (*split into layers*) рассл|а́ивать, -ои́ть.
lamp [læmp] *n.* ла́мпа; **standard ~** торше́р; **table ~** насто́льная ла́мпа; (*on vehicle*) фа́ра; (*lantern*; *street ~*) фона́рь (*m.*); (*icon-~*) лампа́да.
cpds. **~light** *n.* (*indoors*) свет ла́мпы; (*in street*) фона́рный свет; **~lighter** *n.* фона́рщик; **~-post, ~-standard** *nn.* у́личный фона́рь; **~shade** *n.* абажу́р.
lampoon [læm'puːn] *n.* па́сквиль (*m.*).
v.t. писа́ть, на- па́сквиль на+*a.*
lamprey ['læmprɪ] *n.* мино́га.
lance [lɑːns] *n.* (*for throwing*) копьё; (*cavalry weapon*) пи́ка.
v.t. (*pierce with ~*) коло́ть, за- пи́кой; (*med.*) вскры|ва́ть, -ть ланце́том.
cpd. **~-corporal** *n.* мла́дший капра́л.
lancer ['lɑːnsə(r)] *n.* ула́н; (*pl., regiment*) ула́нский полк; (*pl., dance*) лансье́ (*indecl.*).
lancet ['lɑːnsɪt] *n.* (*surg.*) ланце́т; (*archit.*): **~ arch** стре́льчатая а́рка; **~ window** стре́льчатое окно́.
land [lænd] *n.* **1.** земля́; **~ mass** земе́льный масси́в; (*dry ~*) су́ша; **they sighted ~** они́ уви́дели су́шу/зе́млю; **travel by ~** е́хать (*det.*) су́шей (*or* по су́ше); **~ forces** (*mil.*) сухопу́тные войска́; **reach, make ~** дост|ига́ть, -и́гнуть бе́рега; **see how the ~ lies** (*fig.*) пров|еря́ть, -е́рить как обстоя́т дела́. **2.** (*ground, soil*) грунт, по́чва; **he works on the ~** он рабо́тает на земле́; **work the ~** обраба́тывать (*impf.*) зе́млю; **good farming ~** плодоро́дная по́чва; **a house with some ~** дом с земе́льным уча́стком; **~ tax** позе-ме́льный нало́г. **3.** (*country*) земля́, страна́; (*state*) госуда́рство; **in the ~ of the living** в живы́х; **no man's ~** ничья́ земля́; (*mil.*) ниче́йная полоса́. **4.** (*property*) земля́, име́ние; **he owns ~** он владе́ет землёй; **his ~s extend for several miles** его́ владе́ния простира́ются на не́сколько миль.
v.t. **1.** (*bring to shore*): **~ a vessel** прив|оди́ть, -ести́ су́дно к бе́регу; **~ cargo** выгружа́ть, вы́грузить груз; **~ passengers** выса́живать, вы́садить пассажи́ров. **2.**: **~ an aircraft** сажа́ть, посади́ть самолёт. **3.**: **~ a fish** выта́скивать, вы́тащить ры́бу на бе́рег. **4.** (*win*) выи́грывать, вы́играть; (*secure*): **he ~ed himself a good job** он пристро́ился на хоро́шую рабо́ту. **5.** (*get, involve*): **that will ~ you in gaol** э́то доведёт вас до тюрьмы́; **he ~ed himself in trouble** он навлёк на себя́ беду́.
v.i. **1.** (*of passengers*) выса́живаться, вы́садиться; сходи́ть, сойти́ (на бе́рег). **2.** (*of aircraft*) призе-мл|я́ться, -и́ться; де́лать, с- поса́дку; (*on water*) приводн|я́ться, -и́ться; (*space-craft on moon*) прилун|я́ться, -и́ться. **3.** (*of athlete, after jump*) приземл|я́ться, -и́ться. **4.** (*fall, lit. or fig.*): **she ~ed in trouble** она́ попа́ла в беду́; **we ~ed in a bog** мы угоди́ли в боло́то. **5.**: **~ up** (*coll., arrive*) приб|ыва́ть, -ы́ть; **I ~ed up in the wrong street** я очути́лся не на той у́лице.
cpds. **~holder** *n.* землевладе́лец; **~lady** *n.* хозя́йка; **~-locked** *adj.* окружённый су́шей; без вы́хода к мо́рю; **~lord** *n.* хозя́ин; (*owner of ~*) землевладе́лец; (*of building*) до́мовладе́лец; **~mark** *n.* (*boundary marker*) межево́й столб; (*prominent feature*) заме́тный предме́т на ме́стности; (*mil.*) (назе́мный) ориенти́р; (*turning-point in history etc.*) ве́ха; **~-mine** *n.* фуга́с; **~owner** *n.* землевладе́лец; **~slide** *n.* (*of hill etc.*) обва́л; (*subsidence*) о́ползень (*m.*); (*pol.*): **they won by a ~slide** они́ одержа́ли реши́тельную побе́ду.
landed ['lændɪd] *adj.* (*possessing land*) землевладе́льческий; **~ gentry** поме́щики (*m. pl.*).
landing ['lændɪŋ] *n.* **1.** (*bringing or coming to earth*) поса́дка, приземле́ние; **forced ~** вы́нужденная поса́дка. **2.** (*on water*) приводне́ние; (*on the moon*) прилуне́ние. **3.** (*putting ashore*; *depositing by air*) вы́садка; (*of goods*) вы́грузка. **4.** (*mil.*) деса́нт, вы́садка деса́нта. **5.** (*on stairs*) (ле́стничная) площа́дка.
cpds. **~-craft** *n.* деса́нтное су́дно; **~-field** *n.* лётное по́ле; **~-gear** *n.* шасси́ (*nt. indecl.*); **~-ground** *n.* взлётно-поса́дочная площа́дка; **~-party** *n.* деса́нтная гру́ппа; **~-stage** *n.* дебаркаде́р, при́стань; **~-strip** *n.* поса́дочная полоса́.
landscape [ˌlændskeɪp, 'læns-] *n.* (*picture*) пейза́ж; (*scenery*) ландша́фт.
cpds. **~-gardening** *n.* садо́во-па́рковая архитекту́ра; **~-painter** *n.* пейзажи́ст.
landward ['lændwəd] *n.*: **to ~** к бе́регу.
adj.: **on the ~ side** со стороны́ су́ши.
adv. (*also* **~s**) к бе́регу.
lane [leɪn] *n.* **1.** (*narrow street*) переу́лок, у́зкая у́лочка; (*country road*) доро́жка. **2.** (*between rows of people*) прохо́д; **form a ~** вы́строиться (*pf.*). **3.** (*of traffic*) ряд; **get into ~** вста|ва́ть, -ть в ряд; **four-~ highway** автостра́да с четырьмя́ ряда́ми движе́ния. **4.** (*air route*) тра́сса. **5.** (*for shipping*) морско́й путь. **6.** (*on race-track, swimming-pool*) доро́жка.
language ['læŋgwɪdʒ] *n.* язы́к; (*esp. spoken*) речь; **~ and literature** (*as subj. of study*) филоло́гия; **in a**

foreign ~ на иностра́нном языке́; (*words*, *expressions*): **he has a great command of** ~ он прекра́сно владе́ет языко́м; **bad** ~ скверносло́вие; **strong** ~ си́льные выраже́ния; **native** ~ родно́й язы́к; ~ **student** (*at university*) фило́лог; ~ **laboratory** лингафо́нный кабине́т.

languid ['læŋgwɪd] *adj.* то́мный, вя́лый.

languish ['læŋgwɪʃ] *v.i.* томи́ться (*impf.*); изныва́ть (*impf.*); **a ~ing look** то́мный взгляд.

languor ['læŋgə(r)] *n.* то́мность, вя́лость; (*pleasant*) исто́ма.

languorous ['læŋgərəs] *adj.* то́мный; по́лный исто́мы.

lank [læŋk] *adj.* **1.** (*tall and lean*) поджа́рый, худоща́вый. **2.**: ~ **hair** гла́дкие/прямы́е во́лосы.

lanky ['læŋkɪ] *adj.* долговя́зый.

lanolin ['lænəlɪn] *n.* ланоли́н.

lantern ['lænt(ə)n] *n.* **1.** фона́рь (*m.*). **2.** (*of lighthouse*) светова́я ка́мера.

lanyard ['lænjəd, -jɑːd] *n.* (*cord*) реме́нь (*m.*); (*for securing sail*) та́лреп; (*mil.*) вытяжно́й шнур.

Laos [lauz, laʊs] *n.* Лао́с.

lap[1] [læp] *n.* **1.**: **the boy sat on his mother's** ~ ма́льчик сиде́л у ма́тери на коле́нях; (*fig.*): **in the ~ of the gods** в руце́ бо́жьей; **he lives in the ~ of luxury** ≃ он живёт как у Христа́ за па́зухой. **2.** (*of garment*) пола́, фа́лда, подо́л.

cpds. **~-dog** *n.* боло́нка; **~top** *adj.*: **~top computer** наколе́нный компью́тер.

lap[2] [læp] *n.* (*circuit of race-track*) круг; **he won by 3 ~s** он победи́л, обойдя́ проти́вника на 3 кру́га; **I'm on the last** ~ (*fig.*, *have almost finished*) я закругля́юсь; я почти́ ко́нчил.

v.t. (*sport*: *be a ~ ahead of*) об|ходи́ть, -ойти́ (*or* об|гоня́ть, -огна́ть) (*кого*) на круг.

lap[3] [læp] *n.* (*sound of waves*) плеск.

v.t. (*drink with tongue*) лака́ть, вы́-.

v.i. (*of waves*) плеска́ться (*impf.*); **waves ~ on the beach** во́лны пле́щутся о бе́рег.

lapel [lə'pel] *n.* ла́цкан, отворо́т.

lapidary ['læpɪdərɪ] *n.* (*gem cutter*) грани́льщик; (*polisher*) шлифова́льщик; (*engraver*) гравёр.

adj. грани́льный.

lapis lazuli [ˌlæpɪs 'læzjuːlɪ, -ˌlaɪ] *n.* ля́пис-лазу́рь.

Lapland ['læplænd] *n.* Лапла́ндия.

Laplander ['læpˌlændə(r)] *n.* лапла́нд|ец (*fem.* -ка).

Lapp [læp] *n.* **1.** (*pers.*) саа́м (*fem.* -ка); лопа́р|ь (*fem.* -ка). **2.** (*also* **~ish**: *language*) саа́мский/лопа́рский язы́к; язы́к саа́ми.

adj. **1.** (*also* **~ish**) лопа́рский, саа́мский. **2.** (*of Lapland*) лапла́ндский.

lapse [læps] *n.* **1.** (*slight mistake*, *slip*) упуще́ние, оплошность; (*of memory*) прова́л па́мяти; (*of the pen*) опи́ска; (*of the tongue*) обмо́лвка, оговорка. **2.** (*moral deviation*) просту́пок; (*decline*) паде́ние. **3.** (*leg.*, *ending of right etc.*) прекраще́ние; недействи́тельность. **4.** (*passage of time*) тече́ние; (*interval*) промежу́ток.

v.i. **1.** (*decline morally*; *slip back*) пасть (*pf.*); **they ~d into heresy** они́ впа́ли в е́ресь; ~ **into idleness** облени́ться (*pf.*); ~ **into silence** зам|олка́ть, -о́лкнуть; **a ~d Catholic** бы́вший като́лик. **2.** (*leg.*, *become void*) теря́ть, по- си́лу. **3.** (*of time*) про|ходи́ть, -йти́; минова́ть (*impf.*, *pf.*).

lapwing ['læpwɪŋ] *n.* чи́бис, пи́галица.

larcenous ['lɑːsənəs] *adj.*: **with ~ intent** с наме́рением соверши́ть кра́жу.

larceny ['lɑːsənɪ] *n.* кра́жа; **petty** ~ ме́лкая кра́жа.

larch [lɑːtʃ] *n.* ли́ственница.

lard [lɑːd] *n.* топлёное свино́е са́ло.

v.t. (*cul.*) шпигова́ть, на-; (*fig.*) усна|ща́ть, -сти́ть.

larder ['lɑːdə(r)] *n.* кладова́я.

large [lɑːdʒ] *n.*: **at** ~ (*free*) на во́ле, на свобо́де; **set at** ~ освобо|жда́ть, -ди́ть; (*in general*) целико́м; во всём объёме; **the public at** ~ широ́кая пу́блика; **ambassador at** ~ (*US*) посо́л по осо́бым поруче́ниям.

adj. большо́й, кру́пный; **on a ~ scale** в большо́м/кру́пном масшта́бе; ~ **handwriting** кру́пный по́черк; **in ~ type** кру́пным шри́фтом; **a ~ population** многочи́сленное/большо́е населе́ние; (*spacious*) просто́рный; (*considerable*) значи́тельный (*copious*) оби́льный; (*extensive*) широ́кий; (*fat*) по́лный; **as ~ as life** (*fig.*) во всей красе́; **he turned up as ~ as life** он яви́лся со́бственной персо́ной; **~r than life** бо́лее, чем в натура́льную величину́; (*fig.*) преувели́ченный.

adv.: **by and** ~ вообще́ говоря́.

cpd. **~-scale** *adj.* крупномасшта́бный.

largely ['lɑːdʒlɪ] *adv.* (*to a great extent*) по бо́льшей ча́сти; в значи́тельной сте́пени.

largess(e) [lɑː'ʒes] *n.* щедро́ты (*f. pl.*).

largo ['lɑːgəʊ] *n.*, *adj.* & *adv.* ла́рго (*indecl.*).

lark[1] [lɑːk] *n.* (*bird*) жа́воронок; **rise with the** ~ вста|ва́ть, -ть с петуха́ми.

cpd. **~spur** *n.* жи́вокость, шпо́рник.

lark[2] [lɑːk] *n.* (*coll.*), (*prank*) прока́за; (*amusement*) заба́ва; **for a** ~ шу́тки ра́ди; **what a ~!** вот потёха!

v.i.: ~ **about** резви́ться (*impf.*).

larva ['lɑːvə] *n.* личи́нка.

laryngeal [lə'rɪndʒɪəl] *adj.* горта́нный.

laryngitis [ˌlærɪn'dʒaɪtɪs] *n.* ларинги́т.

larynx ['lærɪŋks] *n.* горта́нь.

lascivious [lə'sɪvɪəs] *adj.* похотли́вый.

lasciviousness [lə'sɪvɪəsnɪs] *n.* похотли́вость.

laser ['leɪzə(r)] *n.* ла́зер; (*attr.*) ла́зерный; ~ **printer** (*comput.*) ла́зерный при́нтер.

lash[1] [læʃ] *n.* (**eye** ~) ресни́ца.

lash[2] [læʃ] *n.* **1.** (*thong*) реме́нь (*m.*); **he got the** ~ он был нака́зан плетью. **2.** (*stroke*) уда́р (пле́тью); **he got fifty ~es** он получи́л пятьдеся́т уда́ров пле́тью.

v.t. **1.** (*with whip*; *also of wind*, *rain*) хлест|а́ть, -ну́ть. **2.** (*wave about*): **the dog ~ed its tail** соба́ка би́ла хвосто́м. **3.** (*fasten with rope etc.*) свя́з|ывать, -а́ть; привя́з|ывать, -а́ть.

v.i.: **the rain ~ed against the window** ве́тер хлеста́л в окно́; **he ~ed into his opponent** он набро́сился на своего́ проти́вника.

with advs.: ~ **down** *v.t.* привя́з|ывать, -а́ть (*что к чему*); ~ **out** *v.i.* (*with fists*) наки́|дываться, -нуться (*на кого*); (*verbally*) разра|жа́ться, -зи́ться бра́нью; (*coll.*, *spend lavishly*) сори́ть (*impf.*) деньга́ми; ~ **together** *v.i.* свя́з|ывать, -а́ть.

lashing ['læʃɪŋ] *n.* (*whipping*) по́рка; (*pl.*, *coll.*, *plenty*): **~s of cream** ма́сса сли́вок.

lass [læs] *n.* (*child*) де́вочка; (*young woman*) де́вушка.

lassitude ['læsɪˌtjuːd] *n.* уста́лость, вя́лость.

lasso [læ'suː, 'læsəʊ] *n.* арка́н, лассо́ (*indecl.*).

v.t. арка́нить, за-.

last[1] [lɑːst] *n.* (*shoemaker's*) коло́дка; **stick to your ~!** (*fig.*) занима́йся свои́м де́лом!

last[2] [lɑːst] *n.* (*final or most recent person or thg.*): **he was the ~ of his line** он был после́дним в роду́; **he was the ~ to go** он ушёл после́дним; **our house is the ~ in the road** наш дом после́дний/кра́йний на у́лице; **the ~ of the wine** оста́тки (*m. pl.*) вина́; **on the ~ of the month** в после́дний день ме́сяца; **breathe one's** ~ испусти́ть (*pf.*) после́дний вздох; **we have seen the ~ of him** мы его́ бо́льше не уви́дим; **he remained impenitent to the** ~ он не раска́ялся до са́мого конца́; **at** ~ наконе́ц; (*as excl.*) наконе́ц-то!; **at long** ~ в конце́ концо́в, наконе́ц.

adj. **1.** (*latest*; *final*; ~ *of series*) после́дний; **in the ~ 7 years** в после́дние 7 лет; **at the very ~ moment** в са́мый после́дний моме́нт; **the L~ Judgement** Стра́шный суд; Су́дный день; ~ **rites, sacrament** причаще́ние пе́ред сме́ртью; ~ **name** фами́лия; ~ **but not least** после́дний по счёту, но не по ва́жности; ~ **but one** предпосле́дний; ~ **thing at night** по́здно ве́чером; пре́жде, чем лечь спать; пе́ред сном. **2.** (*preceding, of time*) про́шлый; **in the ~ century/year/month** в про́шлом столе́тии/году́/ме́сяце; ~ **week** на про́шлой неде́ле; ~ **night we got home late** вчера́ ве́чером мы по́здно верну́лись; ~ **night I slept badly** про́шлой но́чью я пло́хо спал; **the week before** ~ позапро́шлая неде́ля; **the night before** ~ позавчера́ ве́чером. **3.** (*least likely or suitable*): **he is the ~ person I expected to see** вот кого́ ме́ньше всего́ я ожида́л уви́деть; **she is the ~ person to help** от неё ме́ньше всего́ мо́жно ожида́ть по́мощи; **that's the ~ thing I would have expected** э́того я ника́к не ожида́л.

adv. **1.** (*in order*) по́сле всех; **he finished ~** он ко́нчил после́дним. **2.** (*for the ~ time*) в после́дний раз. **3.** (*~ly, in the ~ place*) на после́днем ме́сте.

v.i. **1.** (*go on, continue*) дли́ться, про-; прод|олжа́ться, -о́лжиться; **winter ~s six months** зима́ дли́тся шесть ме́сяцев; **the rain won't ~ long** дождь ско́ро пройдёт. **2.** (*hold out*) выде́рживать, вы́держать; **as long as my health ~s (out)** пока́ у меня́ хва́тит здоро́вья; (*be preserved, survive*) сохра|ня́ться, -и́ться. **3.** (*of clothes*): **this suit has ~ed well** э́тому костю́му сно́су нет. **4.** (*of the dying*): **he won't ~ long** он до́лго не протя́нет (*coll.*). **5.** (*be sufficient for*) хват|а́ть, -и́ть на+*a.*; **£30 ~s me a week** 30 фу́нтов мне хвата́ет на неде́лю; **the bread won't ~ us today** хле́ба нам на сего́дня не хва́тит.

cpds. **~-minute** *adj.* (сде́ланный) в после́днюю мину́ту; **~-named** *adj.* после́дний (из упомя́нутых).

lasting ['lɑːstɪŋ] *adj.* (*durable, enduring*) про́чный, продолжи́тельный; ~ **peace** про́чный мир; **a ~ monument** ве́чный па́мятник; (*persistent, permanent*) постоя́нный; ~ **regrets** постоя́нное чу́вство сожале́ния; **leave a ~ impression** произв|оди́ть, -ести́ неизглади́мое впечатле́ние.

lastly ['lɑːstlɪ] *adv.* в заключе́ние; наконе́ц.

latch [lætʃ] *n.* (*bar*) щеко́лда; (*lock*) защёлка; **on the ~** на щеко́лде/защёлке.

v.t. (*put on ~*) закр|ыва́ть, -ы́ть на щеко́лду.

v.i.: ~ **on to** смекну́ть (*pf.*) (*coll.*).

cpd. **~-key** *n.* ключ (от америка́нского замка́).

late [leɪt] *adj.* **1.** (*far on in time*) по́здний; **it is ~** по́здно; **it's getting ~** де́ло идёт к но́чи; **in the ~ evening** по́здним ве́чером; **in ~ summer** к концу́ ле́та; **in ~ May** к концу́ ма́я; **the ~ 19th century** коне́ц 19 ве́ка; ~ **edition** вече́рний вы́пуск; **keep ~ hours** по́здно ложи́ться (*impf.*) спать; **it is ~ in the day for that** для э́того позднова́то; **at, by 2 o'clock at the ~st** са́мое по́зднее в 2 часа́. **2.** (*behind time*): **be ~ for the train** оп|а́здывать, -озда́ть на по́езд (**for the theatre** в теа́тр; **for dinner** к у́жину); **he was an hour ~** он опозда́л на ча́с; **the train is running an hour ~** по́езд идёт с опозда́нием в (оди́н) час; **I was ~ in replying** я опозда́л отве́тить (*or* с отве́том); **he is a ~ riser** он по́здно встаёт. **3.** (*recent*) неда́вний; после́дний; **his ~st book** его́ после́дняя кни́га; **~st news** после́дние изве́стия. **4.** (*former*) пре́жний; (*immediately preceding*) бы́вший. **5.** (*deceased*) поко́йный. **6.** (*belated*) запозда́лый.

adv. по́здно; **better ~ than never** лу́чше по́здно, чем никогда́; **sooner or ~r** ра́но и́ли по́здно; **stay up ~** по́здно ложи́ться (*impf.*); ~ **in life** в пожило́м во́зрасте; на ста́рости лет; **a year ~r** спустя́ год; **see you ~r!** уви́димся!; пока́!; ~ **into the night** до по́здней но́чи; **of ~** (в/за) после́днее вре́мя.

cpd. **~-night** *adj.* ночно́й (*сеанс и т.п.*).

latecomer ['leɪtˌkʌmə(r)] *n.* опозда́вший.

lately ['leɪtlɪ] *adv.* (в/за) после́днее вре́мя; **have you seen him ~?** ви́дели ли вы его́ в после́днее вре́мя?; **I've been working hard ~** после́днее вре́мя я мно́го рабо́тал.

lateness ['leɪtnɪs] *n.*: **the ~ of the train** опозда́ние по́езда; **despite the ~ of the hour** несмотря́ на по́здний час.

latent ['leɪt(ə)nt] *adj.* скры́тый, лате́нтный; (*chem.*) свя́занный.

lateral ['lætər(ə)l] *adj.* боково́й, горизонта́льный; ~ **section** попере́чный разре́з.

latest ['leɪtɪst] *adj.* после́дний; са́мый но́вый; **the ~ thing** после́днее сло́во, но́вость, нови́нка; *see also* **late**

latex ['leɪteks] *n.* ла́текс.

lath [lɑːθ] *n.* ре́йка, пла́нка.

lathe [leɪð] *n.* тока́рный стано́к.

lather ['lɑːðə(r), 'læðə(r)] *n.* (мы́льная) пе́на; **in a ~** в мы́ле; (*fig., agitated*) в запа́рке.

v.t. мы́лить (*impf.*); намы́ли|вать, -ть.

v.i. (*of soap*) мы́литься.

Latin ['lætɪn] *n.* **1.** (*language*) латы́нь; лати́нский язы́к. **2.** (*Frenchman, Italian etc.*) челове́к рома́нского происхожде́ния.

adj. лати́нский; ~ **America** Лати́нская Аме́рика; ~ **languages/nations** рома́нские языки́/наро́ды; ~ **scholar** латини́ст.

cpd. **~-American** *adj.* латиноамерика́нский.

latitude ['lætɪˌtjuːd] *n.* **1.** (*distance from equator; pl., regions*) широта́; ~ **25° N** 25° се́верной широты́. **2.** (*freedom of action*) свобо́да (де́йствий); (*liberality*) широта́ (взгля́дов). **3.** (*breadth, extent*) обши́рность.

latrine [lə'triːn] *n.* убо́рная, отхо́жее ме́сто.

latter ['lætə(r)] *pron. & adj.* после́дний, второ́й; **in the ~ half of June** во второ́й полови́не ию́ня; **the former ... the ~** пе́рвый… второ́й/после́дний; **the ~** то, после́дний.

latterly ['lætəlɪ] *adv.* (*of late*) (в/за) после́днее вре́мя; (*towards the end*) к концу́, под коне́ц.

lattice ['lætɪs] *n.* решётка; (*attr.; also* **~d**) решётчатый.

Latvia ['lætvɪə] *n.* Ла́твия.

Latvian ['lætvɪən] *n.* (*pers.*) латви́|ец (*fem.* -йка); латы́ш (*fem.* -ка); (*language*) латы́шский язы́к.

adj. латви́йский, латы́шский.

laud [lɔːd] *v t.* восхвал|я́ть, -и́ть; сла́вить (*impf.*).

laudable ['lɔːdəb(ə)l] *adj.* похва́льный.

laudatory ['lɔːdətərɪ] *adj.* хвале́бный.

laugh [lɑːf] *n.* смех; **it was a ~** сме́ху-то бы́ло; **we had a good ~ over it** мы от души́ посмея́лись над э́тим; **he had the last ~** в конце́ концо́в посмея́лся он; **the ~ was on him** он оста́лся в дурака́х; **he joined in the ~** он присоедини́лся к о́бщему сме́ху; **he gave a loud ~** он гро́мко рассмея́лся.

v.t. ~ **to scorn** высме́ивать, вы́смеять; **he was ~ed out of court** он был осме́ян; **he was ~ing his head off** он хохота́л как безу́мный.

v.i. смея́ться (*impf.*); хохот|а́ть, -ну́ть; (*begin ~ing*) засмея́ться (*pf.*); **burst out ~ing** рассмея́ться (*pf.*); **he who ~s last, ~s longest** хорошо́ смеётся тот, кто смеётся после́дним; **he ~s at my jokes** он смеётся, когда́ я шучу́; **who/what are you ~ing at?** над чем/кем вы смеётесь?; **it's nothing to ~ at** ничего́ смешно́го; **I ~ed till I cried** я смея́лся до слёз; **make s.o. ~** смеши́ть, рас- кого́-н.; **don't make me ~!** (*iron.*) не смеши́те (меня́); **I couldn't help ~ing** я не мог удержа́ться от сме́ха.

with advs.: ~ **off** *v.t.*: ~ **it off** отшу́|чиваться, -ти́ться; ~ **sth. off** отде́л|ываться, -аться от чего́-н. шу́ткой.

laughable ['lɑːfəb(ə)l] *adj.* смешно́й, смехотво́рный.

laughing ['lɑːfɪŋ] *n.* смех; **I was in no mood for ~**

мне бы́ло не до сме́ху; **I couldn't speak for ~** от сме́ха я не мог произнести́ ни сло́ва; **it is no ~ matter** э́то не шу́точное де́ло; **he burst out ~** он рассмея́лся/расхохота́лся.

cpds. **~-gas** *n.* веселя́щий газ; **~-stock** *n.* посме́шище; **make a ~-stock of s.o.** выставля́ть, вы́ставить кого́-н. на посме́шище.

laughter ['lɑ:ftə(r)] *n.* смех; (*loud*) хо́хот; **die of, with ~** ум|ира́ть, -ере́ть со́ смеху; **roar with ~** хохота́ть (*impf.*) во всё го́рло.

launch[1] [lɔ:ntʃ] *n.* (*motor-boat*) ка́тер.

launch[2] [lɔ:ntʃ] *n.* (*of ship*) спуск (на́ воду); (*of rocket or spacecraft*) за́пуск; (*of torpedo*) вы́пуск.

v.t. (*set afloat*): **~ a ship** спус|ка́ть, -ти́ть кора́бль на́ воду; (*send into air*): **~ a rocket** запус|ка́ть, -ти́ть раке́ту; (*aircraft from flight deck*) катапульти́ровать (*impf., pf.*); (*hurl, discharge*): **~ a spear** мет|а́ть, -ну́ть копьё; **~ a torpedo** выпуска́ть, вы́пустить торпе́ду; (*initiate*): **~ an attack** нач|ина́ть, -а́ть ата́ку; **~ an enterprise** пус|ка́ть, -ти́ть предприя́тие.

v.i. пус|ка́ться, -ти́ться; **we are ~ing (out) on, into a new enterprise** мы начина́ем но́вое де́ло.

cpds. **~(ing)-pad** *n.* ста́ртовая площа́дка; **~(ing)-site** *n.* ста́ртовая пози́ция; **~-vehicle** *n.* раке́та-носи́тель (*m.*).

launder ['lɔ:ndə(r)] *v.t. & i.* **1.** стира́ть(ся), вы́-; **this cloth ~s well** э́та мате́рия хорошо́ стира́ется. **2.** (*fig.*): **~ money** отмы́ть де́ньги.

laund(e)rette [lɔ:n'dret] *n.* пра́чечная самообслу́живания.

laundress ['lɔ:ndrɪs] *n.* пра́чка.

laundry ['lɔ:ndrɪ] *n.* **1.** (*establishment*) пра́чечная; **send to the ~** отд|ава́ть, -а́ть в сти́рку (*or* в пра́чечную). **2.** (*clothes*) бельё (для сти́рки *or* из сти́рки).

laureate ['lɒrɪət, 'lɔ:-] *n.*: **Poet L~** поэ́т-лауреа́т.

laurel ['lɒr(ə)l] *n.* лавр; (*attr.*) лавро́вый; (*fig., pl.*): **reap, win ~s** пожина́ть (*impf.*) ла́вры; **rest on one's ~s** поч|ива́ть, -и́ть на ла́врах.

lava ['lɑ:və] *n.* ла́ва; **~ bed** пласт ла́вы; **~ flow** пото́к ла́вы.

lavatory ['lævətərɪ] *n.* (*WC*) убо́рная, туале́т; (*washroom*) умыва́льная (ко́мната); **~ paper** туале́тная бума́га.

lavender ['lævɪndə(r)] *n.* лава́нда; **~ water** лава́ндовая вода́; **a ~ gown** пла́тье бле́дно-лило́вого цве́та.

lavish ['lævɪʃ] *adj.* **1.** (*generous*) ще́дрый; (*prodigal*) расточи́тельный; **he is ~ in his praise** он щедр на похвалы́; **a ~ reception** бога́тый приём. **2.** (*abundant*) оби́льный.

v.t.: **~ money on sth.** расточа́ть (*impf.*) де́ньги на что-н.; **~ praise on s.o.** расточа́ть (*impf.*) похвалы́ кому́-н.; **~ care on s.o.** окружа́ть (*impf.*) кого́-н. чрезме́рными забо́тами.

law [lɔ:] *n.* **1.** (*rule or body of rules for society*) зако́н; **the bill became ~** законопрое́кт был при́нят; **above the ~** вы́ше зако́на; **by ~** по зако́ну; **within the ~** в ра́мках (*or* без наруше́ния) зако́на; **break, violate the ~** нар|уша́ть, -у́шить зако́н; **keep, observe the ~** соблюда́ть (*impf.*) зако́н; **pass a ~** прин|има́ть, -я́ть зако́н; **the ~ of supply and demand** зако́н спро́са и предложе́ния; **the ~s of the game** пра́вила (*nt. pl.*) игры́. **2.** (*as subject of study, profession, system*) пра́во, юсти́ция; **civil ~** гражда́нское пра́во; **declare martial ~** объяв|ля́ть, -и́ть вое́нное положе́ние; **~ and order** правопоря́док; **~ school** юриди́ческая шко́ла; **read, study ~** изуч|а́ть, -и́ть пра́во; **go in for the ~** учи́ться, вы- на юри́ста; **follow, practise ~** быть юри́стом; **court of ~** суд. **3.** (*process of ~; ~suit*) суде́бный проце́сс; **go to ~** возбу|жда́ть, -ди́ть суде́бное де́ло; **take the ~ into one's own hands** поступ|а́ть, -и́ть само́чи́нно. **4.** (*phys. etc.*): **~ of gravity** зако́н тяготе́ния; **~ of probability** тео́рия вероя́тностей.

cpds. **~-abiding** *adj.* законопослу́шный; **~-breaker** *n.* правонаруши́тель (*m.*); **~-enforcement** *attr.*: **~-enforcement agencies** правоохрани́тельные о́рганы; **~-maker** *n.* законода́тель (*m.*); **~suit** *n.* суде́бный проце́сс.

lawful ['lɔ:fʊl] *adj.* зако́нный.

lawless ['lɔ:lɪs] *adj.* (*of country etc.*) ди́кий, анархи́чный; (*of pers.*) непоко́рный, мяте́жный.

lawlessness ['lɔ:lɪsnɪs] *n.* беззако́ние; непоко́рность, мяте́жность.

lawn[1] [lɔ:n] *n.* (*area of grass*) газо́н; **~ tennis** те́ннис.

cpds. **~-mower** *n.* газо́нокоси́лка.

lawn[2] [lɔ:n] *n.* (*linen*) бати́ст.

lawyer ['lɔɪə(r), 'lɔ:jə(r)] *n.* юри́ст; (*advocate, barrister*) адвока́т.

lax [læks] *adj.* (*negligent, inattentive*) небре́жный; (*not strict*) нестро́гий; **~ discipline** сла́бая дисципли́на; **~ morals** распу́щенные нра́вы.

laxative ['læksətɪv] *n.* слаби́тельное (сре́дство).

adj. слаби́тельный.

lax|ity ['læksɪtɪ], **-ness** ['læksnɪs] *nn.* небре́жность; (*of morals*) распу́щенность.

lay[1] [leɪ] *n.* (*liter.*) пе́сня, балла́да.

lay[2] [leɪ] *v.t.* **1.** (*put down, deposit*) класть, положи́ть; **~ a child to sleep** укла́дывать, уложи́ть ребёнка (спать); **~ to rest** (*bury*) хорони́ть, по-; **~ an egg** нести́, с- яйцо́; (*set in position*): **~ bricks** класть (*impf.*) кирпичи́; **~ a foundation** (*lit., fig.*) за|кла́дывать, -ложи́ть фунда́мент; **~ a carpet** стлать, по- ковёр; **~ pipes** про|кла́дывать, -ложи́ть тру́бы; **~ rails** укла́дывать, уложи́ть ре́льсы; **~ an ambush** устр|а́ивать, -о́ить заса́ду; **~ a trap** ста́вить, по- лову́шку. **2.** (*fig., place*): **~ a bet** держа́ть (*impf.*) пари́; **~ £10 on a horse** ста́вить, по- 10 фу́нтов на ло́шадь; **~ the facts before s.o.** дов|оди́ть, -ести́ фа́кты до све́дения кого́-н.; **~ a charge** предъяв|ля́ть, -и́ть обвине́ние (*кому в чём*); **the scene is laid in London** де́йствие происхо́дит в Ло́ндоне. **3.** (*prepare*): **~ the table for dinner** накр|ыва́ть, -ы́ть стол к обе́ду; **~ plans** сост|авля́ть, -а́вить пла́ны. **4.** (*cause to subside*): **~ the dust** приб|ива́ть, -и́ть пыль; **~ a ghost** изг|оня́ть, -на́ть ду́ха. **5.** (*cover*) укла́дывать, уложи́ть; покр|ыва́ть, -ы́ть. **6.** (*cause to be*): **~ bare** (*lit.*) обнаж|а́ть, -и́ть; (*fig., reveal*) раскр|ыва́ть, -ы́ть; **~ low** (*knock over*) вали́ть, с-; (*overthrow*) низл|ага́ть, -ожи́ть; **he was laid low with a fever** он слёг с лихора́дкой; **~ o.s. open to attack** подст|авля́ть, -а́вить себя́ под уда́р; **~ o.s. open to suspicion** навл|ека́ть, -е́чь на себя́ подозре́ние; **~ waste** опустош|а́ть, -и́ть.

v.i. **1.** (*sc. eggs*) нести́сь (*impf.*). **2.** (*sc. the table*): **she laid for six** она́ накры́ла на шестеры́х. **3.** (*strike*): **~ about s.o.** колоти́ть, по- кого́-н.; **~ into s.o.** нап|ада́ть, -а́сть на кого́-н.

with advs.: **~ aside** (*also* **~ by**) *v.t.* (*lit.*) от|кла́дывать, -ложи́ть; (*relinquish, abandon*) ост|авля́ть, -а́вить; **you must ~ aside your prejudices** на́до оста́вить/(от)бро́сить предрассу́дки; (*save*) от|кла́дывать, -ложи́ть; **~ back** *v.t.*: **the dog laid back its ears** соба́ка прижа́ла у́ши; **~ by** *v.t.* = **~ aside; ~ down** *v.t.* (*on ground, bed etc.*) укла́дывать, уложи́ть; **~ down one's arms** (*surrender*) скла́дывать, сложи́ть ору́жие; (*formulate, prescribe*): **~ down conditions/rules** устан|а́вливать, -ови́ть усло́вия/пра́вила; **this is laid down in the regulations** э́то предпи́сано пра́вилами; **he is fond of ~ing down the law** он лю́бит диктова́ть/распоряжа́ться; (*sacrifice*): **~ down one's life for one's friends** же́ртвовать, по- жи́знью за друзе́й; (*begin to build*): **~ down a ship** за|кла́дывать, -ложи́ть кора́бль; **~ in** *v.t.* (*stock up with*) запас|а́ть, -ти́; запас|а́ться, -ти́сь +*i.*; **~ off** *v.t.* (*suspend from work*) ув|ольня́ть, -о́лить (со слу́жбы); отстран|я́ть, -и́ть (от рабо́ты); (*coll.*, *desist from*) перест|ава́ть, -а́ть; *v.i.*: ~ **off!** (*coll.*) бро́сь(те)!; отста́нь(те)!; ~ **on** *v.t.* (*provide supply of*) пров|оди́ть, -ести́; **is water laid on here?** здесь есть водопрово́д?; (*coll.*): **he promised to ~ on some drinks** он обеща́л поста́вить вы́пивку; (*arrange*) устр|а́ивать, -о́ить; **it's all laid on** всё устро́ено; ~ **out** *v.t.* (*arrange for display etc.*) выставля́ть, вы́ставить; ~ **out clothes** выкла́дывать, вы́ложить оде́жду; (*design*) плани́ровать, рас-; (*for burial*): ~ **out a corpse** уб|ира́ть, -ра́ть поко́йника; (*spend*) тра́тить, ис-; (*knock down*) сби|ва́ть, -ть (с ног); ~ **to** *v.i.* (*of ship*) ложи́ться, лечь в дрейф (*or* на курс); ~ **up** *v.t.* (*save, store*) копи́ть, на-; запас|а́ть, -ти́; (*make inactive*): **my car was laid up all winter** всю зи́му моя́ маши́на простоя́ла; **he was laid up with a broken leg** он был прико́ван к посте́ли из-за сло́манной ноги́.

cpds. **~about** *n.* (*coll.*) тунея́дец; безде́льник; **~-by** *n.* придоро́жная площа́дка для стоя́нки автомоби́лей; **~-off** *n.* (*of workers*) сокраще́ние ка́дров; **~out** *n.* (*arrangement*) расположе́ние; (*of town etc.*) планиро́вка; (*of garden etc.*) разби́вка; (*plan*) чертёж, план.

lay[3] [leɪ] *adj.* **1.** (*opp. clerical*) мирско́й. **2.** (*opp. professional*): ~ **opinion** мне́ние неспециали́стов.

cpd. **~man** *n.* миря́нин; непрофессиона́л, неспециали́ст; **~woman** *n.* мироя́нка, непрофессиона́лка.

layer[1] ['leɪə(r)] *n.* (*thickness, stratum*) слой, пласт; (*of ice on road*) ледяна́я ко́рка; (*inserted* ~) прокла́дка; ~ **cake** слоёный пиро́г.

v.t. (*lay or cut in ~s*) пластова́ть (*impf.*); насл|а́ивать, -ои́ть.

layer[2] ['leɪə(r)] *n.* (*laying hen*) несу́шка; **these hens are good ~s** э́ти ку́ры хорошо́ несу́тся.

layette [leɪ'et] *n.* прида́ное новорождённого.

laying [leɪɪŋ] *n.* (*of eggs*) кла́дка; (*of cable*) прокла́дка; (*of bricks*) укла́дка; (*of carpet*) расстила́ние; (*of turf*) дерно́вка; (*of rails, pipes*) укла́дка.

laze [leɪz] *v.t.* & *i.*: ~ **about** слоня́ться (*impf.*) без де́ла; ~ **away the time** безде́льничать (*impf.*).

laziness ['leɪzɪnɪs] *n.* лень, ле́ность.

lazy ['leɪzɪ] *adj.* лени́вый; **be** ~ лени́ться (*impf.*); **I was too ~ to write to him** я лени́лся ему́ писа́ть.

cpds. **~bones** *n.* лентя́й (*fem.* -ка); (*coll.*) лежебо́ка (*c.g.*).

lb. [paʊnd(z)] *n.* (*abbr. of* **libra**) фунт.

LCD (*abbr. of* **liquid-crystal display**) ЖКИ, (жидкокристалли́ческий индика́тор).

LEA (*abbr. of* **local education authority**) ме́стные о́рганы образова́ния.

leach [li:tʃ] *v.t.* выщела́чивать, вы́щелочить.

lead[1] [led] *n.* **1.** (*metal*) свине́ц; (*attr.*) свинцо́вый; ~ **poisoning** отравле́ние свинцо́м. **2.** (*black* ~) графи́т; ~ **pencil** (графи́товый) каранда́ш; **the ~ keeps breaking** гри́фель постоя́нно лома́ется. **3.** (*on fishing line*) грузи́ло; (*as ammunition*) дробь; (*bullets*) пу́ли (*f. pl.*).

cpd. **~-free** *adj.* неэтили́рованный.

lead[2] [li:d] *n.* **1.** (*direction, guidance; initiative*) руково́дство; инициати́ва; **give a ~ to s.o.** под|ава́ть, -а́ть приме́р кому́-н.; **take the ~** брать, взять на (себя́) руково́дство/инициати́ву; **follow s.o.'s ~** (*lit., fig.*) сле́довать, по- за кем-н. **2.** (*first place*): **be in the ~** стоя́ть (*impf.*) во главе́; (*sport*) быть впереди́; вести́ (*det.*); (*fig.*) стоя́ть (*impf.*) во главе́, пе́рвенствовать (*impf.*); **take the ~** (*sport*) выходи́ть, вы́йти вперёд. **3.** (*clue*): **give s.o. a ~ on sth.** наво|ди́ть, -ести́ кого́-н. на след чего́-н.; **the police are looking for a ~** поли́ция пыта́ется напа́сть на след. **4.** (*cord, strap*) поводо́к, при́вязь; **'dogs must be kept on a ~'** (*notice*) «соба́к держа́ть на поводке́». **5.** (*elec.*) про́вод (*pl.* -а́). **6.** (*theatr.*) гла́вная роль; актёр, игра́ющий гла́вную роль. **7.** (*cards*) ход; **your ~!** ваш ход!

v.t. **1.** (*conduct*) води́ть (*indet.*), вести́, по- (*det.*), ~ **by the hand** вести́ за́ руку; ~ **astray** сбива́ть (*impf.*) с пути́ и́стинного; **he led his troops into battle** он повёл солда́т в бой; ~ **the way** идти́ (*det.*) во главе́. **2.** (*fig., bring, incline, induce*): **what led you to this idea?** что навело́ вас на э́ту мысль?; ~ **s.o. to believe** созда́ть (*pf.*) впечатле́ние у кого́-н., что...; **he led us to expect much** он пробуди́л у нас больши́е наде́жды. **3.** (*cause to go, e.g. water*) пров|оди́ть, -ести́. **4.** (*be in charge of*): ~ **an expedition/orchestra** руководи́ть (*impf.*) экспеди́цией/орке́стром; (*direct*) управля́ть (*impf.*) +*i.*; (*command*) кома́ндовать (*impf.*) +*i.*; (*act as chief or head of*) возгл|авля́ть, -а́вить; (*be in the forefront of*): **the choir ~s the procession** хор идёт во главе́ проце́ссии. **5.** (*pass, spend*): ~ **an idle life** вести́ (*det.*) пра́здную жизнь; ~ **a wretched existence** влачи́ть (*impf.*) жа́лкое существова́ние. **6.** (*cards*): ~ **trumps** ходи́ть, пойти́ с ко́зыря.

v.i. **1.** (*of a road etc.*) вести́ (*det.*): **all roads ~ to Rome** все доро́ги веду́т в Рим; (*fig.*) вести́; прив|оди́ть, -ести́. **2.** (*be first or ahead*) быть впереди́; вести́ (*det.*); **our team is ~ing by 5 points** на́ша кома́нда впереди́ на пять очко́в. **3.** (*cards*) ходи́ть, пойти́.

with advs.: ~ **away** *v.t.* отв|оди́ть, -ести́; ув|оди́ть, -ести́; ~ **in** *v.t.* вв|оди́ть, -ести́; ~ **off** *v.t.* (*take away*) ув|оди́ть, -ести́; (*start*): **they led off the dance** они́ откры́ли та́нец; *v.i.*: **he led off with an apology** он на́чал с извине́ния; ~ **on** *v.t.* (*lit.*): **he led his troops on to victory** он вёл свои́ войска́ к побе́де; (*encourage*) поощр|я́ть, -и́ть; (*deceive*) обма́н|ывать, -у́ть; (*flirt with*): **she is ~ing him on** она́ его́ завлека́ет; *v.i.*: ~ **on!** вперёд!; ~ **up** *v.i.*: ~ **up to** (*lit.*) подв|оди́ть, -ести́ к+*d.*; (*precede, form preparation for*) подгот|овля́ть, -о́вить; **the events that led up to the war** собы́тия, приве́дшие к войне́; (*direct conversation towards*) нав|оди́ть, -ести́ разгово́р на+*a.*; **what are you ~ing up to?** куда́ вы кло́ните?

cpd. **~-in** *n.* (*introduction*) введе́ние, ввод; (*elec.*) ввод.

leaden ['led(ə)n] *adj.* (*lit., fig.*) свинцо́вый.

leader ['li:də(r)] *n.* **1.** (*pol.*) руководи́тель (*m.*), ли́дер; (*rhet.*) вождь (*m.*). **2.** (*of group*) вожа́к; (*of gang*) глава́рь (*m.*). **3.** (*mil.*) команди́р. **4.** (*of orchestra*) пе́рвая скри́пка; (*US, conductor*) дирижёр. **5.** (*leading article*) передова́я (статья́).

leadership ['li:dərʃɪp] *n.* (*role of leader; group of leaders*) руково́дство; (*pre-eminence*) пе́рвенство; (*qualities of a leader*) ли́дерство, инициати́вность.

leading ['li:dɪŋ] *adj.* (*foremost*) веду́щий; (*outstanding*) выдаю́щийся; ~ **article** передова́я (статья́); ~ **lady** исполни́тельница гла́вной ро́ли; ~ **light** (*of art, science etc.*) свети́ло, корифе́й; ~ **question** наводя́щий вопро́с; ~ **seaman** ста́рший матро́с.

cpd. **~-rein** *n.* по́вод.

leaf [li:f] *n.* **1.** (*of tree or plant*) лист (*pl.* -ья); **in ~** покры́тый листво́й; **come into ~** распус|ка́ться, -ти́ться; **tobacco ~** листово́й таба́к. **2.** (*of book*) лист (*pl.* -ы́); (*fig.*): **take a ~ out of s.o.'s book** брать, взять приме́р с кого́-н.; **turn over a new ~** нач|ина́ть, -а́ть но́вую жизнь, испра́виться (*pl.*). **3.** (*of metal etc.*) лист (*pl.* -ы́); **gold ~** листово́е зо́лото. **4.** (*of table etc.*) откидна́я доска́; (*inserted section*) вставна́я доска́. **5.** (*of shutter*) ство́рка.

v.t.: ~ **over, through** перелист|ывать, -а́ть.

cpds. **~-green** *adj.* цве́та зелёной листвы́; **~-mould** *n.* ли́ственный перегно́й.

leaflet ['li:flɪt] *n.* **1.** (*bot.*) листо́к. **2.** (*printed*) брошю́рка; (*fold-out*) букле́т; (*pol.*) листо́вка.

leafy ['li:fɪ] *adj.* густоли́ственный.

league [li:g] *n.* ли́га; **L~ of Nations** Ли́га на́ций; **in ~ with** в сою́зе с+*i.*; (*pej.*) в сго́воре с+*i.*

leak [li:k] *n.* (*hole*) течь; **spring a ~** да|ва́ть, -ть течь; **stop a ~** остан|а́вливать, -ови́ть течь; (*escape of fluid*) уте́чка; (*fig., of information*) уте́чка/проса́чивание информа́ции.

v.t. (*fig.*) выдава́ть, вы́дать.

v.i. (*lit.*) течь (*impf.*); протека́ть (*impf.*); прос|а́чиваться, -очи́ться; (*fig.*): **the affair ~ed out** де́ло вы́плыло нару́жу.

cpd. **~-proof** *adj.* непроница́емый, гермети́ческий.

leakage ['li:kɪdʒ] *n.* (*lit., fig.*) уте́чка.

leaky ['li:kɪ] *adj.* дыря́вый, име́ющий течь; **a ~ pipe** протека́ющая труба́; **these barrels are ~** э́ти бо́чки теку́т.

lean[1] [li:n] *n.* (*of meat*) по́стная часть.

adj. **1.** (*thin*) то́щий; (*fig.*): **~ years** ску́дные го́ды; **a ~ harvest** ску́дный/плохо́й урожа́й. **2.** (*of meat*) нежи́рный, по́стный.

lean[2] [li:n] *n.* (*inclination*) укло́н, накло́н.

v.t. прислон|я́ть, -и́ть (*что к чему*); оп|ира́ть, -ере́ть (*что обо что*): **~ the ladder against the wall!** прислони́те ле́стницу к стене́!; **he was ~ing his arm on the table** он опира́лся руко́й о стол.

v.i. **1.** (*incline from vertical*) наклон|я́ться, -и́ться; **the tower ~s slightly** ба́шня слегка́ наклони́лась; **the trees are ~ing in the wind** дере́вья кло́нятся от ве́тра; **the L~ing Tower of Pisa** Па́дающая ба́шня в Пи́зе; **sit ~ing backward/forward** сиде́ть (*impf.*), пода́вшись наза́д/вперёд; **he ~s over backwards to help** (*fig.*) он из ко́жи вон ле́зет, что́бы помо́чь; **~ out of the window** высо́вываться, вы́сунуться из окна́; **he ~ed over to her** он наклони́лся к ней; **he was ~ing over my shoulder** он загля́дывал мне че́рез плечо́. **2.** (*support o.s.*) прислон|я́ться, -и́ться; оп|ира́ться, -ере́ться; **he was ~ing against a tree** он стоя́л, прислони́вшись к де́реву; **he walked ~ing on a stick** он шёл, опира́ясь на трость; (*fig.*): **he ~s** (*depends*) **on his wife for support** он опира́ется на подде́ржку жены́.

cpd. **~-to** *n.* односка́тная пристро́йка.

leaning ['li:nɪŋ] *n.* (*inclination*) скло́нность; (*tendency*) пристра́стие.

leanness ['li:nnɪs] *n.* худоба́, истоще́ние.

leap [li:p] *n.* прыжо́к, скачо́к; **take a ~** пры́гнуть (*pf.*); (*fig.*): **a ~ in the dark** прыжо́к в неизве́стность; **by ~s and bounds** стреми́тельно.

v.t. (*~ over*) переск|а́кивать, -очи́ть (*or* перепры́г|ивать, -нуть) че́рез+*a.*

v.i. пры́г|ать, -нуть; **my heart ~t for joy** у меня́ се́рдце подскочи́ло от ра́дости; **~ to one's feet** вск|а́кивать, -очи́ть; **he ~t** (*fig.*) **at my offer** он так и ухвати́лся за моё предложе́ние.

cpds. **~-frog** *n.* чехарда́; *v.t.* перепры́г|ивать, -нуть че́рез+*a.*; **~-year** *n.* високо́сный год.

learn [lɜ:n] *v.t.* **1.** (*get knowledge of*) учи́ться, на- +*d. or inf.*; изуч|а́ть, -и́ть; (*study*) занима́ться +*i.*; **he ~ed (how) to ride** он научи́лся е́здить верхо́м; (*~ a trade*) обуч|а́ться, -и́ться +*d. or inf.*; **he is ~ing to be an interpreter** он у́чится на перево́дчика; (*~ off or by heart*) учи́ть, вы́-; вы́учиться (*pf.*) +*d.*; **he ~t French** он вы́учился францу́зскому языку́; **she is ~ing her part** она́ у́чит/разу́чивает свою́ роль; **he ~t the prayer by heart** он вы́учил моли́тву наизу́сть; **he ~t his lesson** (*fig.*) он получи́л хоро́ший уро́к. **2.** (*be informed*) узн|ава́ть, -а́ть.

v.i.: **he ~s slowly** нау́ки ему́ даю́тся тру́дно; он у́чится с трудо́м; **you can ~ from his mistakes** учи́тесь на его́ оши́бках; **I was sorry to ~ of your illness** я с сожале́нием узна́л о ва́шей боле́зни.

learned ['lɜ:nɪd] *adj.* учёный; **my ~ friend** (*Counsel*) мой учёный колле́га; **a ~ society** нау́чное о́бщество.

learner ['lɜ:nə(r)] *n.* начина́ющий; **he is a good ~** он хорошо́ у́чится; (*~-driver*) води́тель-учени́|к (*fem.* -ца).

learning ['lɜ:nɪŋ] *n.* (*process*) уче́ние; изуче́ние; **~ did not come easily to him** уче́ние ему́ дава́лось нелегко́; (*possession of knowledge*) учёность, эруди́ция; (*body of knowledge*) нау́ка.

lease [li:s] *n.* аре́нда; **long ~** долгосро́чная аре́нда; **the ~ is running out** срок аре́нды истека́ет; **we took the house on a 20-year ~** мы взя́ли дом в аре́нду на 20 лет; (*fig.*): **he took on a new ~ of life** он сло́вно за́ново роди́лся.

v.t. (*of lessee*) арендова́ть (*impf., pf.*); брать, взять в аре́нду; (*of lessor*) сд|ава́ть, -ать в аре́нду.

cpds. **~hold** *n.* аре́нда; владе́ние на права́х аре́нды; **~hold property** арендо́ванная со́бственность; **~holder** *n.* аренда́тор.

leash [li:ʃ] *n.* при́вязь, поводо́к; **let off the ~** (*lit.*) спус|ка́ть, -ти́ть с поводка́; (*fig.*) развяза́ть (*pf.*) ру́ки +*d.*; **strain at the ~** (*fig.*) рва́ться (*impf.*) в бой.

v.t. брать, взять на поводо́к.

least [li:st] *n.*: **to say the ~** мя́гко говоря́; **the ~ he could do is to pay for the damage** он мог бы по кра́йней ме́ре возмести́ть уще́рб; **at ~** по кра́йней ме́ре; са́мое ме́ньшее; не ме́ньше +*g.*; **at the very ~** по ме́ньшей ме́ре; **give me ten at the (very) ~** да́йте мне ми́нимум де́сять; **at ~ once a year** не ре́же, чем раз в год; **you should at ~ have warned me** вы бы хоть предупреди́ли меня́; **not in the ~** ни в мале́йшей сте́пени, ничу́ть, ниско́лько; **not in the ~ interested** совсе́м не заинтересо́ван (*pred.*).

adj. (*smallest*) наиме́ньший; минима́льный; **that's the ~ of my worries** э́то меня́ ме́ньше всего́ волну́ет; (*slightest*) мале́йший; **he hasn't the ~ idea about it** он об э́том не име́ет ни мале́йшего поня́тия.

adv. ме́ньше всего́; **I like this the ~ of all his plays** э́та его́ пье́са мне нра́вится ме́ньше всех други́х; **it is the ~ successful of his books** э́то наиме́нее уда́чная из его́ книг; **with the ~ possible trouble** с наиме́ньшими хло́потами; **not ~** не в после́днюю о́чередь.

leather ['leðə(r)] *n.* **1.** ко́жа; **patent ~** лакиро́ванная ко́жа; **imitation ~** кожими́т. **2.** (*wash-~*) за́мша; бархо́тка. **3.** (*~ thong*) реме́нь (*m.*).

adj. **1.** (*made of ~*) ко́жаный. **2.** (*pert. to ~*) коже́венный; **~ goods** коже́венный това́р.

leatherette [,leðə'ret] *n.* кожими́т.

leathery ['leðərɪ] *adj.* (*tough*) жёсткий; **~ skin** загрубе́вшая ко́жа.

leave [li:v] *n.* **1.** (*permission*) позволе́ние, разреше́ние; **who gave you ~ to go?** кто дал вам разреше́ние уйти́?; **I take ~ to remark** я позво́лю себе́ заме́тить; **by your ~** с ва́шего разреше́ния; **without (so much as) a 'by your ~'** без спро́са/спро́су. **2.** (*~ of absence*) о́тпуск; **he is on ~** он в отпуску́; **when are you going on ~?** когда́ вы ухо́дите в о́тпуск?; **sick ~** о́тпуск по боле́зни; **compassionate ~** (*mil.*) увольне́ние по семе́йным обстоя́тельствам; **~ pass** увольни́тельная запи́ска; отпускно́е свиде́тельство. **3.** (*farewell*): **take (one's) ~ (of s.o.)** про|ща́ться, -сти́ться (с кем-н.); **take ~ of one's senses** с ума́ сойти́ (*pf.*).

v.t. **1.** (*allow or cause to remain*) ост|авля́ть, -а́вить; **the wound left a scar** от ра́ны оста́лся шрам; **his words left a deep impression** его́ слова́ произвели́ большо́е впечатле́ние; **I was left with the feeling that ...** у меня́ оста́лось чу́вство, что...; **let us ~ it at that** пусть так; **you can take it or ~ it!** ва́ша во́ля!; **has anyone left a message?** никто́ ничего́ не передава́л?; **he left a wife and three children** по́сле его́ сме́рти жена́ оста́лась одна́ с тремя́ детьми́; **two from five ~s three** пять ми́нус два равня́ется трём; (*with indication of state or circumstances*): **~ me alone!** оста́вьте меня́ (в поко́е)!; **~ my books alone!** не тро́гайте мои́ кни́ги; **it ~s me cold** (*fig.*) э́то меня́ не тро́гает; **I left him in no doubt as to my intention** я ему́ я́сно объясни́л своё наме́рение; **they left him in the lurch** они́ бро́сили его́ в беде́; **it ~s much to be desired** э́то оставля́ет жела́ть мно́го лу́чшего; **~ the door open!** оста́вьте дверь откры́той!; **she was left a widow** она́ оста́лась вдово́й; (*past p., remaining*): **I have no money left** у меня́ не оста́лось де́нег; **how much milk is there left?** ско́лько оста́лось молока́? **2.** (*~ behind by accident*) заб|ыва́ть, -ы́ть; **I left my umbrella at home** я забы́л зо́нтик до́ма. **3.** (*bequeath*) завеща́ть (*impf., pf.*); ост|авля́ть, -а́вить в насле́дство. **4.** (*abandon*) бр|оса́ть, -о́сить; пок|ида́ть, -и́нуть; **he left his wife for another woman** он бро́сил свою́ жену́ ра́ди друго́й же́нщины. **5.** (*relinquish*): **~ hold, go of** выпуска́ть, вы́пустить из рук. **6.** (*commit, entrust*) предост|авля́ть, -а́вить; **I ~ the decision to you** предоставля́ю реше́ние вам; **it was left to him to decide** реша́ть до́лжен был он; **~ it to him** пусть он э́то сде́лает; **~ it to me** я э́тим займу́сь; **he was left to himself** он был предоста́влен самому́ себе́. **7.** (*go away from*) выходи́ть, вы́йти из+*g.*; (*by vehicle*) выезжа́ть, вы́ехать из+*g.*; (*by air*) вылета́ть, вы́лететь из+*g.*; (*for vv. used when subj. is a mode of transport, see v.i.*); **I ~ the house at eight** я выхожу́ и́з дому в во́семь часо́в; **~ the room!** вы́йдите из ко́мнаты; (*come off*): **the train left the rails** по́езд сошёл с ре́льсов; (*rise from*): **~ the table** вст|ава́ть, -ать из-за стола́; (*~ for good, quit*) бр|оса́ть, -о́сить; пок|ида́ть, -и́нуть; **he left his job** он бро́сил свою́ рабо́ту; **our typist left us** на́ша машини́стка уво́лилась; **has he left the country for good?** он навсегда́ поки́нул страну́?; **he left home at 16** в 16 лет он ушёл и́з дому; **he ~s school this year** он конча́ет шко́лу в э́том году́.

v.i. **1.** (*of pers. on foot*) уходи́ть, уйти́; (*by transport*) уезжа́ть, уе́хать; (*by air*) улет|а́ть, -е́ть; (*~ for good*): **she left** (*her job*) **without giving notice** она́ ушла́ с рабо́ты, не уве́домив нача́льства. **2.** (*of train*) от|ходи́ть, -ойти́; (*of boat*) от|ходи́ть, -ойти́; отпл|ыва́ть, -ы́ть; (*of aircraft*) вылета́ть, вы́лететь.

with advs.: **~ about, ~ around** *v.t.*: **don't ~ your money around** не оставля́йте де́ньги где попа́ло; **~ aside** *v.t.* ост|авля́ть, -а́вить в стороне́; **~ behind** *v.t.* ост|авля́ть, -а́вить по́сле себя́; (*forget to take*): **he left his hat behind** он забы́л свою́ шля́пу; (*abandon*): **he was left behind on the island** его́ поки́нули на о́строве; (*bequeath*): **he left behind a tidy sum** он оста́вил изря́дную су́мму; (*outstrip*): **we left him far behind** мы его́ оста́вили далеко́ позади́; **~ in** *v.t.*: **we ~ the fire in overnight** у нас ками́н гори́т всю ночь; **he left in all the quotations** он сохрани́л все цита́ты; **~ off** *v.t.* (*stop*) перест|ава́ть, -а́ть +*inf*; конча́ть, ко́нчить +*a.*; **~ off smoking** бр|оса́ть, -о́сить кури́ть; *v.i.* (*halt*) остан|а́вливаться, -ови́ться; **where did we ~ off?** на чём мы останови́лись?; **~ on** *v.t.*: **I left the light on** я оста́вил свет включённым; **~ out** *v.t.*; (*omit*) пропус|ка́ть, -ти́ть; **~ me out of this!** не втя́гивайте меня́ в э́то!; **I felt left out** я почу́вствовал себя́ ли́шним; **~ over** *v.t.* (*defer*) от|кла́дывать, -ложи́ть; (*pass., remain*) ост|ава́ться, -а́ться.

cpd. **~-taking** *n.* проща́ние, расстава́ние.

leaven ['lev(ə)n] *n.* (*lit., fig.*) заква́ска.

v.t. (*lit.*) заква́|шивать, -сить.

leavings ['li:vɪŋz] *n.* оста́тки (*m. pl.*).

Lebanon ['lebə,nən] *n.*: **(the) ~** Лива́н.

lecher ['letʃə(r)] *n.* развра́тник, распу́тник.

lecherous ['letʃərəs] *adj.* развра́тный, распу́тный.

lechery ['letʃərɪ] *n.* развра́т.

lectern ['lektɜ:n, -t(ə)n] *n.* анало́й; (*in lecture-room*) пюпи́тр.

lector ['lektɔ:(r)] *n.* доце́нт, преподава́тель (*m.*).

lecture ['lektʃə(r)] *n.* **1.** (*dissertation*) ле́кция; **attend a ~** слу́шать, про- ле́кцию; **give a ~** чита́ть, про- (*or* проче́сть) ле́кцию. **2.** (*reproof*) нота́ция; **give s.o. a ~** чита́ть, про- нота́цию кому́-н.

v.t. чита́ть, про- ле́кцию/нота́цию +*d.*

v.i.: **he ~s in Russian** он чита́ет ле́кции по ру́сскому языку́; **he ~s in Roman law** он преподаёт ри́мское пра́во.

cpd. **~-room** *n.* аудито́рия.

lecturer ['lektʃərə(r)] *n.* (*speaker*) докла́дчик; (*professional ~*) ле́ктор; (*univ.*) преподава́тель (*m.*).

LED (*abbr. of* **light-emitting diode**) СИД, (светоизлуча́ющий дио́д).

ledge [ledʒ] *n.* (*shelf*) пла́нка, по́лочка; (*projection*) вы́ступ; (*edge*) край; (*under water*) шельф, бар.

ledger ['ledʒə(r)] *n.* (*book*) гроссбу́х; (гла́вная) учётная кни́га.

lee [li:] *n.* (*shelter*): **under the ~ of** под защи́той +*g.*; (*~ side*) подве́тренная сторона́.

cpd. **~way** *n.* дрейф; **make up ~way** (*fig.*) навёрст|ывать, -а́ть упу́щенное; **he has much ~way to make up** ему́ предстои́т мно́гое наверста́ть.

leech [li:tʃ] *n.* пия́вка.

leek [li:k] *n.* лук-поре́й.

leer [lɪə(r)] *n.* ухмы́лка.

v.i. ухмыл|я́ться, -ьну́ться; **~ at** хитро/зло́бно смотре́ть, по- на+*a.*

leery ['lɪərɪ] *adj.* (*sl.*) хи́трый; (*wary*) недове́рчивый.

lees [li:z] *n.* (*lit., fig.*) подо́нки (*m. pl.*); **drain to the ~** (*lit.*) вы́пить (*pf.*) до дна.

leeward ['li:wəd, *naut.* 'lu:əd] *n.* подве́тренная сторона́; **to ~ (of)** на подве́тренной стороне́ (от+*g.*).

adj. подве́тренный.

adv. под ве́тром.

left [left] *n.* **1.** (*side, direction*): **from the ~** сле́ва; **from ~ to right** сле́ва напра́во; **on the ~ of the street** по ле́вой стороне́ у́лицы; **on, to my ~** (*location or motion*) нале́во от меня́; **on, from my ~** сле́ва от меня́; **he turned to the ~** он поверну́л нале́во. **2.** (*pol.*): **the L~** ле́вые (*pl.*) (па́ртии).

adj. ле́вый; **~ turn** ле́вый поворо́т.

adv. нале́во; **turn ~** св|ора́чивать, -ерну́ть нале́во; **~ turn!** (*mil.*) нале́во!

cpds. **~-hand** *adj.* ле́вый; **car with ~-hand drive** маши́на с левосторо́нним управле́нием (*or* с рулём сле́ва); **~-handed** *adj.* де́лающий всё ле́вой руко́й; **~-handed person** левша́ (*c.g.*); **~-wing** *adj.* ле́вый.

leftist ['leftɪst] *n.* лева́|к (*fem.* -чка).

adj. ле́вый.

leftovers ['left,əʊvəz] *n. pl.* оста́тк|и (*pl. g.* -ов); (*food*) объе́дк|и (*pl. g.* -ов).

leg [leg] *n.* **1.** нога́; (*dim.*) но́жка; (*of bird*) ла́па, ла́пка; **with one's ~s in the air** вверх нога́ми; **he is on his ~s again** (*after illness*) он встал на́ ноги; **I've been on my ~s all day** я был на нога́х це́лый день; **he is on his last ~s** (*dying*) он ды́шит на ла́дан; **the car is on its last ~s** маши́на вот-во́т разва́лится; **get on one's hind ~s** (*of dog etc.*) вста|ва́ть, -ть на за́дние ла́пы; **give s.o. a ~ up** (*lit.*) помо́чь (*pf.*) кому́-н. взобра́ться; (*fig., assist*) ока́з|ывать, -а́ть по́мощь кому́-н.; **pull s.o.'s ~** подшу́|чивать, -ти́ть над кем-н.; **be run off one's ~s** сб|ива́ться, -и́ться с ног; **he hasn't a ~ to stand on** ему́ нет оправда́ния; его́ до́воды не выде́рживают (ни мале́йшей) кри́тики; **stretch one's ~s** размя́ть (*pf.*) но́ги. **2.** (*meat*): **~ of mutton** бара́нья нога́; ~ **of pork** о́корок. **3.** (*of furniture etc.*) но́жка. **4.** (*of garment*): **trouser** ~ штани́на. **5.** (*stage of journey etc.*) эта́п.

v.t.: ~ **it** (*coll.*) идти́ (*det.*) пешко́м.

cpds. ~**-pull** *n.* (*coll.*) ро́зыгрыш; ~**-room** *n.* ме́сто для ног.

legacy ['legəsɪ] *n.* насле́дство, насле́дие.

legal ['li:g(ə)l] *adj.* **1.** (*pert. to or based on law*) юриди́ческий, правово́й; ~ **aid bureau** юриди́ческая консульта́ция; ~ **obligation** правово́е обяза́тельство; ~ **practitioner** адвока́т; ~ **adviser** юриско́нсульт; **the** ~ **profession** профе́ссия юри́ста; (*lawyers*) юри́сты, адвока́ты (*both m. pl.*); **take** ~ **advice** консульти́роваться, про- с юри́стом. **2.** (*permitted or ordained by law*) зако́нный. лега́льный; ~ **tender** зако́нное платёжное сре́дство; ~ **offence** правонаруше́ние; **within one's** ~ **rights** в зако́нном пра́ве. **3.** (*involving court proceedings*) суде́бный; ~ **action** суде́бный иск; суде́бное де́ло; **take** ~ **action against** возбу|жда́ть, -ди́ть де́ло про́тив+*g.*; ~ **costs** суде́бные изде́ржки.

legality [lɪ'gælɪtɪ, li:'g-] *n.* зако́нность, лега́льность.

legalization [ˌli:gəˌlaɪ'zeɪʃ(ə)n] *n.* узаконе́ние, легализа́ция.

legalize ['li:gəˌlaɪz] *v.t.* узако́ни|вать, -ть; легализи́ровать (*impf., pf.*).

legation [lɪ'geɪʃ(ə)n] *n.* представи́тельство, ми́ссия.

legato [lɪ'gɑ:təʊ] *n. & adv.* лега́то (*indecl.*).

legend ['ledʒ(ə)nd] *n.* **1.** леге́нда. **2.** (*inscription, explanatory matter*) на́дпись, леге́нда.

legendary ['ledʒəndərɪ] *adj.* легенда́рный.

legerdemain [ˌledʒədə'meɪn] *n.* (*sleight of hand*) ло́вкость рук; (*trickery*) надува́тельство; (*trick*) уло́вка.

leggings ['legɪŋz] *n.* (*cloth*) гама́ши (*f. pl.*); (*leather*) кра́ги (*f. pl.*)

leggy ['legɪ] *adj.* длинноно́гий.

legibility [ˌledʒɪ'bɪlɪtɪ] *n.* разбо́рчивость.

legible ['ledʒɪb(ə)l] *adj.* разбо́рчивый.

legion ['li:dʒ(ə)n] *n.* **1.** (*body of soldiers*) легио́н; **Foreign L**~ иностра́нный легио́н; **L**~ **of Honour** о́рден Почётного легио́на. **2.** (*multitude*) легио́н, тьма.

legionnaire [ˌli:dʒə'neə(r)] *n.* легионе́р.

legislate ['ledʒɪsˌleɪt] *v.i.* изд|ава́ть, -а́ть зако́ны.

legislation [ˌledʒɪs'leɪʃ(ə)n] *n.* законода́тельство.

legislative ['ledʒɪslətɪv] *adj.* законода́тельный.

legislator ['ledʒɪsˌleɪtə(r)] *n.* законода́тель (*m.*).

legislature ['ledʒɪsˌleɪtʃə(r), -lətʃə(r)] *n.* (*authority*) законода́тельная власть; (*assembly*) законода́тельный о́рган; (*institutions*) законода́тельные учрежде́ния.

legitimacy [lɪ'dʒɪtɪməsɪ] *n.* зако́нность.

legitimate [lɪ'dʒɪtɪmət] *adj.* **1.** (*lawful*) зако́нный; (*justifiable*): ~ **demands** справедли́вые тре́бования; (*reasonable, admissible*) обосно́ванный. **2.** (*by birth*) законнорождённый.

legitimize [lɪ'dʒɪtɪˌmaɪz] *v.t.* узако́ни|вать, -ть.

legless ['leglɪs] *adj.* безно́гий.

legume ['legju:m] *n.* (*pod*) стручо́к; (*pl., crops*) бобо́вые (*pl.*).

leguminous [lɪ'gju:mɪnəs] *adj.* бобо́вый, стручко́вый.

leisure ['leʒə(r)] *n.* свобо́дное вре́мя; досу́г; **at** ~ на досу́ге; **at one's** ~ (*in free time*) в свобо́дное вре́мя; (*unhurriedly*) не спеша́; **in one's** ~ **hours** в свобо́дное вре́мя; ~ **time** досу́жее вре́мя.

leisured ['leʒəd] *adj.* досу́жий, пра́здный; **the** ~ **classes** нетрудовы́е кла́ссы.

leisurely ['leʒəlɪ] *adj.* неспе́шный, неторопли́вый; **at a** ~ **pace** споко́йным ша́гом.

adv. не спеша́, ме́дленно.

leitmotif ['laɪtməʊˌti:f] *n.* лейтмоти́в.

lemming ['lemɪŋ] *n.* ле́мминг.

lemon ['lemən] *n.* **1.** (*fruit, tree*) лимо́н; (*attr.*) лимо́нный; ~ **drop** лимо́нный леденец. **2.** (*colour*) лимо́нный цвет.

lemonade [ˌlemə'neɪd] *n.* лимона́д.

lemur ['li:mə(r)] *n.* лему́р.

lend [lend] *v.t.* **1.** да|ва́ть, -ть взаймы́; од|а́лживать, -олжи́ть; ссу|жа́ть, -ди́ть (*кого чем or что кому*); ~ **me £5** одолжи́те мне (*or* да́йте мне взаймы́) пять фу́нтов; ~ **me the book for a while** да́йте мне кни́гу на вре́мя. **2.** (*impart*) прид|ава́ть, -а́ть. **3.** (*proffer*): ~ **an ear to** выслу́шивать, вы́слушать; ~ **a hand** (*help*) ока́з|ывать, -а́ть по́мощь (*кому*); (*cooperate*) ока́з|ывать, -а́ть соде́йствие (*кому*). **4.**: ~ **o.s. to** (*agree to*) позво́лить (*pf.*) себе́ согласи́ться на+*a.*; **the novel** ~**s itself to filming** рома́н подхо́дит для экраниза́ции; (*allow of*) допус|ка́ть, -ти́ть; **the affair** ~**s itself to many interpretations** де́ло мо́жно толкова́ть по-ра́зному; (*be serviceable for*) годи́ться (*impf.*) на+*a.* (*or* для+*g.*).

with advs.: ~ **out** *v.t.* (*of library etc.*) выдава́ть, вы́дать на́ дом.

lender ['lendə(r)] *n.* заимода́вец, кредито́р.

lending ['lendɪŋ] *n.* ссу́да; (*of money*) да́ча взаймы́; **he does not approve of** ~ он не одобря́ет долго́в; ~ **library** библиоте́ка (с вы́дачей книг на́ дом).

length [leŋθ, leŋkθ] *n.* **1.** (*dimension, measurement*) длина́; **2 metres in** ~ 2 ме́тра длино́й; **this material is sold by** ~ э́та мате́рия продаётся на ме́тры/я́рды; **he lay at full** ~ он лежа́л вы́тянувшись во всю длину́; **he travelled the** ~ **and breadth of Europe** он изъе́здил Евро́пу вдоль и поперёк. **2.** (*racing etc.*): **the horse won by a** ~ ло́шадь опереди́ла други́х на ко́рпус. **3.** (*of time*) продолжи́тельность, дли́тельность, срок; **the** ~ **of the visit was excessive** визи́т затяну́лся; **the chief fault of this film is its** ~ гла́вный недоста́ток э́того фи́льма — его́ растя́нутость; **he objected to the** ~ **of the play** он счита́л, что пье́са сли́шком дли́нная; **seniority by** ~ **of service** старшинство́ по вы́слуге лет; **I shall be away for a certain** ~ **of time** меня́ не бу́дет не́которое вре́мя; ~ **of the course** (*of study*) срок обуче́ния; **at** ~ (*finally*) наконе́ц; (*in detail*) во всех подро́бностях; (*for a long time*) до́лго; **he spoke at great** ~ он говори́л о́чень до́лго. **4.** (*distance, extent*) расстоя́ние; **keep s.o. at arm's** ~ (*fig.*) держа́ть (*impf.*) кого́-н. на почти́тельном расстоя́нии. **5.** (*extent, degree*): **go to any** ~**(s)** идти́ (*det.*) на всё; **he went to great** ~**s not to offend them** он сде́лал всё возмо́жное, что́бы их не оби́деть; **she went to all** ~**s to get her own way** она́ из ко́жи ле́зла, что́бы доби́ться своего́. **6.** (*piece of material*) кусо́к; отре́з.

lengthen ['leŋθ(ə)n, 'leŋkθ(ə)n] *v.t. & i.* удлин|я́ть(ся), -и́ть(ся).

lengthening ['leŋθənɪŋ, 'leŋkθənɪŋ] *n.* удлине́ние.

lengthiness ['leŋθɪnɪs, 'leŋkθɪnɪs] *n.* растя́нутость; длинно́ты (*f. pl.*).

length|ways ['leŋθweɪz, 'leŋkθ-], **-wise** ['leŋθwaɪz, 'leŋkθ-] *adv.* (*along its length*): **fold the blanket** ~ сложи́те одея́ло вдоль; (*in length*): **this piece measures 3 feet** ~ в длину́ в э́том куске́ три фу́та.

lengthy ['leŋθɪ, 'leŋkθɪ] *adj.* дли́нный, затя́нутый; (*in time*) дли́тельный; (*of speech etc.*) растя́нутый.

leniency ['li:nɪənsɪ] *n.* снисхожде́ние; мя́гкость.

lenient ['li:nɪənt] *adj.* (*of pers.*) снисходи́тельный; (*of punishment etc.*) мя́гкий.

Leningrad ['lenɪnˌgræd] *n.* Ленингра́д; *attr.* ленингра́дский.

Leningrader ['lenɪnˌgrædə(r)] *n.* ленингра́д|ец (*fem.* -ка).

Leninism ['lenɪˌnɪz(ə)m] *n.* ленини́зм.

Leninist ['lenɪˌnɪst] *n.* ле́нинец.

adj. ле́нинский.

lens [lenz] *n.* (*anat., opt.*) ли́нза; (*anat.*) хруста́лик гла́за; (*phot.*) объекти́в.

Lent [lent] *n.* вели́кий пост.
Lenten ['lent(ə)n] *adj.* (*of Lent*) великопо́стный.
lentil ['lentıl] *n.* чечеви́ца; ~ **soup** чечеви́чная похлёбка.
lento ['lentəʊ] *adv.* ле́нто (*indecl.*).
Leo ['li:əʊ] *n.* (*astr., hist.*) Лев.
leopard ['lepəd] *n.* леопа́рд.
leotard ['li:ə,tɑ:d] *n.* трико́ (*indecl.*), леота́рд
leper ['lepə(r)] *n.* прокажённый.
leprechaun ['leprə,kɔ:n] *n.* гном.
leprosy ['leprəsı] *n.* прока́за.
leprous ['leprəs] *adj.* (*infected by leprosy*) прокажённый.
lesbian ['lezbıən] *n.* лесбия́нка.
adj. лесби́йский.
lesion ['li:ʒ(ə)n] *n.* поврежде́ние, пораже́ние.
less [les] *n.* ме́ньшее коли́чество; **you should eat** ~ вам сле́дует ме́ньше есть; **I cannot accept ~ than £50** ме́ньше, чем на 50 фу́нтов я не соглашу́сь; **no ~ than £500** не ме́нее пятисо́т фу́нтов; **no more and no ~ than ...** не бо́лее и не ме́нее, как...; **in ~ than no time** в одно́ мгнове́ние; **in ~ than an hour** ме́ньше чем за час; **the ~ said, the better** чем ме́ньше слов, тем лу́чше.
adj. **1.** (*smaller*) ме́ньший; **of ~ importance** ме́ньшей ва́жности; **of ~ magnitude** ме́ньшего разме́ра; **in a ~(er) degree** в ме́ньшей сте́пени; **grow** ~ ум|еньша́ться, -е́ньшиться. **2.** (*not so much*) ме́ньше; **eat ~ meat!** е́шьте ме́ньше мя́са!; ~ **noise!** поти́ше!
adv. ме́ньше, ме́нее; не так, не сто́лько; **he is ~ intelligent than his sister** он не так умён, как его́ сестра́; **the ~ you think about it the better** чем ме́ньше об э́том ду́мать, тем лу́чше; ~ **and** ~ всё ме́ньше и ме́ньше; **none the** ~ тем не ме́нее.
prep. ми́нус; **I paid him his wages, ~ what he owed me** я вы́дал ему́ зарпла́ту, вы́чтя из неё су́мму, кото́рую он мне задолжа́л.
lessee [le'si:] *n.* (*of house etc.*) съёмщик; (*of land*) аренда́тор, нанима́тель (*m.*).
lessen ['les(ə)n] *v.t. & i.* ум|еньша́ть(ся), -е́ньшить(ся).
lesser ['lesə(r)] *adj.* ме́ньший; (*of plants, animals*) ма́лый; **the ~ of two evils** ме́ньшее из двух зол.
lesson ['les(ə)n] *n.* **1.** уро́к, заня́тие; **English ~s** уро́ки англи́йского языка́; **give ~s in physics** да|ва́ть, -ть уро́ки фи́зики; **~s begin on 1 September** заня́тия начина́ются пе́рвого сентября́; **take ~s** брать (*impf.*) уро́ки; **teach s.o. a** ~ (*rebuke, punish*) дать (*pf.*) уро́к кому́-н.; проучи́ть (*pf.*) кого́-н.; **let that be a ~ to you!** да бу́дет э́то вам нау́кой! **2.** (*eccl.*) чте́ние.
lest [lest] *conj.* что́бы не; **I fear ~ he should see her** я бою́сь, как бы он её не уви́дел.
let[1] [let] *n.* (*of property*) аре́нда; **take a house on a long** ~ снять (*pf.*) дом на дли́тельный срок.
v.t. (*also* ~ **out**) сда|ва́ть, -ть в наём; **the flat is already** ~ кварти́ра уже́ сдана́; **'house to ~ furnished'** (*notice*) «сдаётся дом с ме́белью».
v.i.: **this house would ~ easily** э́тот дом сни́мут бы́стро.
let[2] [let] *v.t.* **1.** (*allow*) позв|оля́ть, -о́лить +*d.*; разреш|а́ть, -и́ть +*d.*; ~ **me help you** позво́льте вам помо́чь; **why not ~ him try?** да́йте ему́ возмо́жность попро́бовать; **he won't ~ me work** он не даёт мне рабо́тать; ~ **s.o. be** ост|авля́ть, -а́вить кого́-н. в поко́е; ~ **sth. be** не тро́|гать, -нуть чего́-н.; ~ **drop, fall** роня́ть, урони́ть; ~ **fly at** (*go for*) **s.o.** напус|ка́ться, -ти́ться на кого́-н.; ~ **go** (*relax grip on*) выпуска́ть, вы́пустить из рук; отпус|ка́ть, -ти́ть; ~ **go (of) my hand** отпусти́те мою́ ру́ку; ~ **o.s. go** увл|ека́ться, -е́чься; (*set free*) выпуска́ть, вы́пустить; (*sell*): **he ~ the chair go for a song** он про́дал стул по дешёвке; (*ignore*): **this was untrue but I ~ it go, pass** э́то бы́ло непра́вдой, но я не стал возража́ть; ~ **one's hair grow** отпус|ка́ть, -ти́ть во́лосы; ~ **slide** пусти́ть (*pf.*) на самотёк (*see also* ~ **go**); ~ **slip** (*chance etc.*) упус|ка́ть, -ти́ть. **2.** (*cause to*): ~ **s.o. have it** (*coll., punish*) суро́во наказа́ть (*pf.*) кого́-н.; ~ **s.o. know** да|ва́ть, -ть кому́-н. знать; **I ~ him see he was in the wrong** я дал ему́ поня́ть, что он непра́в. **3.** (*in imper. or hortatory sense*): ~ **me see** (*reflect*) погоди́те; да́йте поду́мать; ~ **him do it** пусть он э́то сде́лает; **just ~ him try it!** пусть то́лько попро́бует!; ~ **us drink** вы́пьем(те); дава́й(те) вы́пьем/пить; ~ **us pray** помо́лимся; ~ **them come in** пусть войду́т; ~ **there be light** да бу́дет свет. **4.** (~ *come or go*): **he ~ me into the room** он впусти́л меня́ в ко́мнату; **shall I ~ you into a secret?** хоти́те я раскро́ю вам та́йну?; **he was ~ out of prison** его́ вы́пустили из тюрьмы́.
with advs.: ~ **alone** *v.t.* ост|авля́ть, -а́вить (*кого*) в поко́е; не тро́|гать, -нуть (*чего*); ~ **him alone to finish it** не меша́йте ему́ зако́нчить э́то; ~ **alone** (*not to mention*) не говоря́ уже́ о+*p.*; **they haven't got a radio, ~ alone television** у них и ра́дио нет, не то, что телеви́зора; ~ **well alone** не вме́шиваться без нужды́; ~ **down** *v.t.* (*lower*) опус|ка́ть, -ти́ть; ~ **one's hair down** (*lit.*) распус|ка́ть, -ти́ть во́лосы; (*fig.*) разоткрове́нничаться (*pf.*); (*disappoint*) разочаро́в|ывать, -а́ть; **I feel ~ down** я разочаро́ван; (*fail to support*) подв|оди́ть, -ести́ (*coll.*); **I was badly ~ down** меня́ здо́рово подвели́; (*deflate*): ~ **down tyres** спус|ка́ть, -ти́ть ши́ны; (*lengthen*): ~ **down a dress** выпуска́ть, вы́пустить пла́тье; ~ **in** *v.t.* (*admit*) впус|ка́ть, -ти́ть; **the window doesn't ~ in much light** че́рез э́то окно́ проника́ет ма́ло све́та; **what have I ~ myself in for?** во что я ввяза́лся?; **we ~ him in on the secret** мы посвяти́ли его́ в та́йну; (*insert*) вст|авля́ть, -а́вить; (*engage*): ~ **the clutch in** включ|а́ть, -и́ть сцепле́ние; ~ **off** *v.t.* (*discharge*) разря|жа́ть, -ди́ть; ~ **off fireworks** запуска́ть (*impf.*) фейерве́рк; (*emit*): ~ **off steam** (*lit., fig.*) выпуска́ть, вы́пустить пары́; (*allow to dismount*): ~ **me off at the next stop** ссади́те меня́ на сле́дующей остано́вке; (*acquit; not punish*) не нака́зывать (*impf.*); **he was ~ off lightly** он легко́ отде́лался; (*excuse*) про|ща́ть, -сти́ть +*d.*; (*liberate*) освобо|жда́ть, -ди́ть; *v.i.* (*fire*) вы́стрелить (*pf.*); ~ **on** *v.t. & i.* (*coll., divulge*) прогов|а́риваться, -ори́ться; **don't ~ on about it** ни сло́ва об э́том!; ~ **out** *v.t.* выпуска́ть, вы́пустить; ~ **the water out of the bath** вы́пустить/спусти́ть (*both pf.*) во́ду из ва́нны; ~ **out a scream** завизжа́ть (*pf.*); взви́згнуть (*pf.*); ~ **out a secret** прогов|а́риваться, -ори́ться; **he ~ out the whole story** он вы́болтал всю исто́рию; ~ **the fire out** да|ва́ть, -ть поту́хнуть огню́; ~ **past** *v.t.* да|ва́ть, -ть пройти́; ~ **through** *v.t.* пропус|ка́ть, -ти́ть; ~ **up** *v.i.* (*weaken, diminish*) ослаб|ева́ть, -е́ть; (*relax, take a rest*) перед|ыха́ть, -охну́ть; **he never ~s up in his work** он рабо́тает без переды́шки.
cpds. **~-down** *n.* (*disappointment, anticlimax*) разочарова́ние; **~-up** *n.* (*respite*) переды́шка; остано́вка.
lethal ['li:θ(ə)l] *adj.* (*fatal*) смерте́льный; **a ~ dose** смерте́льная до́за; (*designed to kill*) смертоно́сный.
lethargic [lı'θɑ:dʒık] *adj.* вя́лый; (*med.*) летарги́ческий.
lethargy ['leθədʒı] *n.* вя́лость; летерги́я.
Lett [let] *n.* латы́ш (*fem.* -ка).
letter ['letə(r)] *n.* **1.** (*of alphabet*) бу́ква; **capital** ~ прописна́я бу́ква; **the word is written with a capital** ~ э́то сло́во пи́шется с прописно́й бу́квы; **small** ~ строчна́я бу́ква; **it was written in small ~s** э́то бы́ло напи́сано строчны́ми бу́квами; (*fig., precise detail*): **to the** ~ буква́льно; **the ~ of the law** бу́ква зако́на; **he follows the law to the** ~ он соблюда́ет зако́н до

после́дней запято́й. **2.** (*written communication*) письмо́; **registered ~** заказно́е письмо́; **~ of introduction** рекоменда́тельное письмо́. **3.** (*pl.*, *literature*) литерату́ра; **man of ~s** литера́тор.

v.t. **1.** (*impress title on*) отти́с|кивать, -нуть загла́вие на+*a.*; **the title was ~ed in gold** загла́вие бы́ло вы́теснено золоты́ми бу́квами. **2.** (*classify by means of ~s*) пом|еча́ть, -е́тить бу́квами.

cpds. **~-box** *n.* почто́вый я́щик; **~-head(ing)** *n.* (*heading*) ша́пка на фи́рменном бла́нке; (*paper*) фи́рменный бланк.

lettering ['letərɪŋ] *n.* (*inscription*) на́дпись; (*impressing of title*) тисне́ние (бу́квами); (*script*) шрифт.

Lettish ['letɪʃ] *n.* латы́шский язы́к.

adj. латы́шский.

lettuce ['letɪs] *n.* (*plant*, *dish*) сала́т; (*plant*) лату́к.

leucocyte ['lu:kəˌsaɪt] *n.* лейкоци́т.

leuk(a)emia [lu:'ki:mɪə] *n.* белокро́вие, лейкеми́я.

level ['lev(ə)l] *n.* **1.** (*instrument*) ватерпа́с; у́ровень (*m.*); **spirit ~** спиртово́й у́ровень. **2.** (*horizontal plane or line*) у́ровень; **on a ~ with** на одно́м у́ровне с+*i.*; **at eye ~** на у́ровне гла́за; (*fig.*, *coll.*): **on the ~!** че́стно!; **is he on the ~?** мо́жно ли ему́ ве́рить? **3.** (*social etc.*, *standing*): **subsistence ~** прожи́точный ми́нимум; **talks at Cabinet ~** перегово́ры на у́ровне прави́тельства.

adj. (*even*) ро́вный; (*flat*) пло́ский; (*horizontal*) горизонта́льный; **~ crossing** (железнодоро́жный) перее́зд; **the room was ~ with the street** ко́мната была́ на одно́м у́ровне с у́лицей; **the water was ~ with the banks** вода́ была́ вро́вень с берега́ми; **draw ~ with** наг|оня́ть, -на́ть; **keep a ~ head** сохраня́ть (*impf.*) споко́йствие; **do one's ~ best** че́стно стара́ться (*impf.*).

v.t. **1.** (*make ~*) ур|а́внивать, -овня́ть; выра́внивать, вы́ровнять. **2.** (*raze to ground*) ср|а́внивать, -овня́ть с землёй. **3.** (*geol.*) нивели́ровать (*impf.*, *pf.*). **4.** (*direct*, *aim*) нав|оди́ть, -ести́; наце́ли|вать, -ть; **she ~led a gun at his head** она́ прице́лилась ему́ в го́лову.

with advs.: **~ off, ~ out** *vv.t.* (*smooth out*) сгла́|живать, -дить; *v.i.* (*of aircraft*) выра́вниваться, вы́ровняться; **~ up** *v.t.* ур|а́внивать, -овня́ть.

cpd. **~-headed** *adj.* тре́звый, рассуди́тельный.

lever ['li:və(r)] *n.* (*lit.*, *fig.*) рыча́г.

v.t.: **~ sth. out** высвобожда́ть, вы́свободить что-н. рычаго́м; **~ sth. up** подн|има́ть, -я́ть что-н. рычаго́м; **he ~ed the stone into position** он установи́л ка́мень с по́мощью рычага́.

leverage ['li:vərɪdʒ] *n.* (*action*) де́йствие/уси́лие рычага́; **use ~ on s.o.** (*fig.*) повлия́ть (*pf.*) на кого́-н.

leviathan [lɪ'vaɪəθ(ə)n] *n.* (*bibl.*, *fig.*) левиафа́н.

levitate ['levɪˌteɪt] *v.t. & i.* подн|има́ть(ся), -я́ть(ся) в во́здух.

levitation [ˌlevɪ'teɪʃ(ə)n] *n.* левита́ция.

levity ['levɪtɪ] *n.* легкомы́слие.

levy ['levɪ] *n.* **1.** (*collection of taxes etc.*) сбор; (*imposition*) обложе́ние; (*raising*) взима́ние; **capital ~** нало́г на капита́л. **2.** (*of recruits*) набо́р.

v.t. **1.** (*raise*) взима́ть (*impf.*) (*что с кого*). **2.** (*recruit*) наб|ира́ть, -ра́ть.

lewd [lju:d] *adj.* (*of pers.*) развра́тный; (*of thg.*) са́льный.

lexical ['leksɪk(ə)l] *adj.* лекси́ческий.

lexicographer [ˌleksɪ'kɒgrəfə(r)] *n.* лексико́граф.

lexicographical [ˌleksɪkə'græfɪk(ə)l] *adj.* лексикографи́ческий.

lexicography [ˌleksɪ'kɒgrəfɪ] *n.* лексикогра́фия.

lexicon ['leksɪkən] *n.* (*dictionary*) слова́рь, лексико́н; (*vocabulary of writer etc.*) ле́ксика.

liabilit|y [ˌlaɪə'bɪlɪtɪ] *n.* **1.** (*responsibility*) отве́тственность; **admit ~y for sth.** призн|ава́ть, -а́ть себя́ отве́тственным за что-н. **2.** (*obligation*) обяза́тельство; **meet one's ~ies** выполня́ть, вы́полнить обяза́тельства; (*pl.*, *debts*) долги́ (*m. pl.*). **3.** (*burden*, *handicap*): **this is a terrible ~y** э́то нам стра́шно меша́ет; **I shall only be a ~y** я бу́ду то́лько поме́хой.

liable ['laɪəb(ə)l] *adj.* **1.** (*answerable*) отве́тственный (за+*a.*). **2.** (*subject*): **he is ~ to a heavy fine** его́ мо́гут подве́ргнуть большо́му штра́фу. **3.** (*apt*, *likely*): **difficulties are ~ to arise** мо́гут возни́кнуть тру́дности; **she is ~ to forget it** она́ скло́нна забыва́ть об э́том.

liaise [lɪ'eɪz] *v.i.* (*coll.*) устана́вливать/подде́рживать (*impf.*) связь (с+*i.*).

liaison [lɪ'eɪzɒn] *n.* **1.** (*mil. etc.*) связь; **~ officer** офице́р свя́зи. **2.** (*love affair*) (любо́вная) связь.

liar ['laɪə(r)] *n.* лгун (*fem.* -ья); врун (*fem.* -ья).

Lib [lɪb] *n.* (*coll.*): **Women's ~** фемини́стское движе́ние (*за уравнение женщин в правах с мужчинами*).

libation [laɪ'beɪʃ(ə)n, lɪ-] *n.* возлия́ние.

libel ['laɪb(ə)l] *n.* клевета́; **~ action** де́ло по обвине́нию в клевете́; **law of ~** зако́н о диффама́ции.

v.t. клевета́ть, о- (*кого*), на- (*на кого*).

libellous ['laɪbələs] *adj.* клеветни́ческий.

liberal ['lɪbər(ə)l] *n.* либера́л.

adj. **1.** (*generous*, *open-handed*) ще́дрый; (*abundant*) оби́льный. **2.** (*open or broadminded*): **a man of ~ views** челове́к широ́ких взгля́дов; (*progressive*) передово́й; (*non-specialist*): **a ~ education** гуманита́рное образова́ние; **the ~ arts** гуманита́рные нау́ки. **3.** (*pol.*) либера́льный; **the L~s** либера́льная па́ртия.

liberalism ['lɪbərəlˌɪz(ə)m] *n.* либерали́зм.

liberality [ˌlɪbə'rælɪtɪ] *n.* ще́дрость; широта́ взгля́дов.

liberalization [ˌlɪbərəlaɪ'zeɪʃ(ə)n] *n.* демократиза́ция, либерализа́ция.

liberalize ['lɪbərəˌlaɪz] *v.t.*: **~ trade** облегч|а́ть, -и́ть усло́вия торго́вли; (*ideas*, *regime*) либерализи́ровать (*impf.*, *pf.*).

liberate ['lɪbəˌreɪt] *v.t.* освобо|жда́ть, -ди́ть.

liberation [ˌlɪbə'reɪʃ(ə)n] *n.* освобожде́ние.

liberator ['lɪbəˌreɪtə(r)] *n.* освободи́тель (*fem.* -ница).

Liberia [laɪ'bɪərɪə] *n.* Либе́рия.

libertarian [ˌlɪbə'teərɪən] *n.* боре́ц за демократи́ческие свобо́ды.

libertine ['lɪbəˌti:n, -tɪn, -ˌtaɪn] *n.* распу́тник.

adj. распу́щенный.

libert|y ['lɪbətɪ] *n.* **1.** (*freedom*) свобо́да; **~y of action** свобо́да де́йствий; **at ~y** находя́щийся на свобо́де; **you are at ~y to go** вы вольны́ уйти́; **set at ~y** выпуска́ть, вы́пустить на во́лю/свобо́ду; **regain one's ~y** (*be released*) быть вы́пущенным на свобо́ду. **2.** (*licence*) во́льность; **take ~ies** позв|оля́ть, -о́лить себе́ во́льности; **take the ~y** осме́ли|ваться, -ться +*inf.*; позв|оля́ть, -о́лить себе́ +*inf.*; **may I take the ~y of asking your name?** позво́льте спроси́ть, как вас зову́т?

libidinous [lɪ'bɪdɪnəs] *adj.* похотли́вый.

libido [lɪ'bi:ˌdəʊ, lɪ'baɪdəʊ] *n.* либи́до (*indecl.*).

Libra ['li:brə, 'lɪb-, 'laɪb-] *n.* (*astron.*) Вес|ы́ (*pl.*, *g.* -о́в).

librarian [laɪ'breərɪən] *n.* библиоте́карь (*m.*).

librarianship [laɪ'breərɪənʃɪp] *n.* библиоте́чное де́ло, библиотекове́дение.

library ['laɪbrərɪ] *n.* библиоте́ка; **reference ~** спра́вочная библиоте́ка; (*attr.*) библиоте́чный; **~ ticket** чита́тельский биле́т.

librettist [lɪ'bretɪst] *n.* либретти́ст.

libretto [lɪ'bretəʊ] *n.* либре́тто (*indecl.*).

Libya ['lɪbɪə, 'lɪbjə] *n.* Ли́вия.

licence ['laɪs(ə)ns] (*US also* **license**) *n.* **1.** (*permission*) разреше́ние; (*for trade*) лице́нзия; **grant s.o. a ~** выдава́ть, вы́дать лице́нзию кому́-н. **2.** (*permit*, *certificate*) свиде́тельство; **driving ~** води́тельские правá. **3.** (*freedom*): **poetic ~** поэти́ческая во́льность.

cpds. **~-holder** *n.* = **licensee; ~-plate** *n.* (*US*) номерно́й знак.

license ['laɪs(ə)ns] (*US also* **licence**) *v.t.* **1.** (*permit, authorize*) разреш|а́ть, -и́ть (*что*); да|ва́ть, -ть разреше́ние на (*что*). **2.** (*grant permit, permission to*) разреш|а́ть, -и́ть +*d.*; **a shop ~d to sell tobacco** ла́вка, облада́ющая лице́нзией на прода́жу таба́чных изде́лий; **~d premises** (*inn*) заведе́ние, в кото́ром разреша́ется прода́жа спиртны́х напи́тков.

licensee [,laɪsən'si:] (*also* **license-holder**) *n.* облада́тель (*fem.* -ница) разреше́ния/лице́нзии; (*of public house*) хозя́|ин (*fem.* -йка) ба́ра.

licensing ['laɪsənsɪŋ] *n.* лицензи́рование; **~ hours** часы́ прода́жи спиртны́х напи́тков; **~ system** лицензио́нная систе́ма.

licentious [laɪ'senʃəs] *adj.* распу́щенный.

licentiousness [laɪ'senʃəsnɪs] *n.* распу́щенность.

lichee, lychee ['laɪtʃɪ, 'lɪ-] *n.* личжи́ (*indecl.*), кита́йский крыжо́вник (*collect.*).

lichen ['laɪkən, 'lɪtʃ(ə)n] *n.* лиша́йник.

lick [lɪk] *v.t.* **1.** лиз|а́ть, -ну́ть; (*~ all over*) обли́з|ывать, -а́ть; **~ one's lips/**(*coll.*) **chops** обли́з|ываться, -а́ться; (*fig.*): **~ s.o.'s boots** лиза́ть (*impf.*) сапоги́ кому́-н.; **~ one's wounds** зали́з|ывать, -а́ть ра́ны. **2.** (*coll., defeat*) поб|ива́ть, -и́ть.

v.t.: **~ off, ~ up** слиз|ывать, -а́ть (*or* -ну́ть).

cpd. **~spittle** *n.* подхали́м.

licking ['lɪkɪŋ] *n.* (*coll.*): **he took a ~** (*thrashing*) ему́ доста́лась взбу́чка; (*was defeated*) он был разби́т в пух и прах.

licorice ['lɪkərɪs, -rɪʃ] = **liquorice**

lid [lɪd] *n.* кры́шка; (*fig.*): **take the ~ off** (*disclose*) вы́тащить (*pf.*) на свет бо́жий.

lido ['li:dəʊ, 'laɪ-] *n.* (обще́ственный) пляж.

lie[1] [laɪ] *n.* (*falsehood*) ложь; **white ~** ложь во спасе́ние; **tell a ~** лгать, со-.

v.t.: **he ~d his way out** он вы́путался с по́мощью лжи.

v.i. лгать, со-; врать, со-/на-; **he ~d to me** он мне солга́л.

cpd. **~-detector** *n.* дете́ктор лжи.

lie[2] [laɪ] *n.*: **the ~ of the land** хара́ктер ме́стности; обстано́вка.

v.i. **1.** (*repose*) лежа́ть, по-; **she lay on the grass all morning** она́ всё у́тро пролежа́ла на траве́; **here ~s ...** здесь поко́ится прах +*g.*; (*remain*): **~ in wait for s.o.** выжида́ть (*impf.*) кого́-н. в заса́де; **~ low** притаи́ться (*pf.*); **~ idle** (*of machinery etc.*) прост|а́ивать, -оя́ть. **2.** (*be; be situated*) находи́ться (*impf.*); быть располо́женным; **~ at anchor** стоя́ть (*impf.*) на я́коре; **London ~s on the Thames** Ло́ндон стои́т на Те́мзе; **the town lay in ruins** го́род лежа́л в руи́нах; **see how the land ~s** (*fig.*) узн|ава́ть, -а́ть, как обстои́т де́ло. **3.** (*fig., reside, rest*): **the choice ~s with you** вы́бор зави́сит от вас; вам выбира́ть; **do you know what ~s behind it all?** вы зна́ете, что за э́тим кро́ется?; **do your interests ~ in that direction?** э́та о́бласть вас интересу́ет?; **she knows where her interests ~** она́ зна́ет свою́ вы́году; **the blame ~s at his door** вина́ на нём; **I will do all that ~s in my power** сде́лаю всё, что в мои́х си́лах. **4.** (*~ down*) ложи́ться, лечь; приле́чь (*pf.*).

with advs.: **~ about, ~ around** валя́ться (*impf.*); (*idle*) болта́ться (*impf.*); **~ ahead** предстоя́ть (*impf.*); **~ back** (*in chair etc.*) отки́|дываться, -нуться; (*take things easy*) сиде́ть (*impf.*) сложа́ ру́ки; **~ down** ложи́ться, лечь; **I shall ~ down for an hour** я приля́гу на час; **take an insult lying down** безро́потно прин|има́ть, -я́ть оскорбле́ние; **~ down on the job** (*fig., slack*) лени́ться (*impf.*); **~ in** остава́ться (*impf.*) в посте́ли; не встава́ть (*impf.*).

lieu [lju:] *n.*: **in ~ of** вме́сто+*g.*

lieutenant [lef'tenənt] *n.* **1.** (*mil.*) лейтена́нт; **first, second ~**: *corresponding to these two Br. Army ranks are the three Russ. Army ranks of* ста́рший лейтена́нт, лейтена́нт *and* мла́дший лейтена́нт. **2.** (*civilian*) замести́тель (*m.*).

cpds. **~-colonel** *n.* подполко́вник; **~-commander** *n.* (*nav.*) капита́н-лейтена́нт; **~-general** *n.* генера́л-лейтена́нт.

life [laɪf] *n.* **1.** (*being alive*) жизнь; **a matter of ~ and death** вопро́с жи́зни и сме́рти; **bring back to ~** (*from the dead*) воскре|ша́ть, -си́ть; возвра|ща́ть, -ти́ть к жи́зни; **escape with one's ~** вы́жить (*pf.*), уцеле́ть (*pf.*); **give (or lay down) one's ~ for s.o.** отда́ть/положи́ть (*both pf.*) жизнь за кого́-н.; **lose one's ~** ги́бнуть, по-; **many lives were lost** мно́гие поги́бли; мно́го наро́ду поги́бло; **run for one's ~** бежа́ть (*det.*) сломя́ го́лову; **take one's (own) ~** конча́ть, (по)ко́нчить с собо́й; **take one's ~ in one's hands** рискова́ть (*impf.*) жи́знью; **take s.o.'s ~** лиши́ть (*pf.*) кого́-н. жи́зни; **not on your ~!** ни за что!; **I couldn't for the ~ of me ...** хоть убе́й, я не мог (бы)...; (*existence*): **this (earthly) ~** земно́е бытие́; **the next ~, ~ beyond the grave** загро́бная/жизнь; **~ everlasting** ве́чная жизнь; **that's ~!** такова́ жизнь!; **what a ~!** (*pej.*) ра́зве э́то жизнь?; **make ~ easy for s.o.** облегча́ть (*impf.*) кому́-н. жизнь; (*way or style of ~*) быт; житьё-бытьё; **family ~** дома́шний быт; **village ~** дереве́нская жизнь; **this is the ~!** вот э́то жизнь! **2.** (*period, span of ~*): **at my time of ~** в моём во́зрасте; **get the fright of one's ~** перепуга́ться (*pf.*) на́смерть; **have the time of one's ~** прекра́сно проводи́ть (*impf.*) вре́мя; **he has had a quiet ~** он про́жил споко́йную жизнь; **he got ~; he is in for ~** (*coll.*) он получи́л пожи́зненное заключе́ние; **~ sentence** пригово́р к пожи́зненному заключе́нию; (*of inanimate things, durability*) долгове́чность; срок слу́жбы; **these machines have an average ~ of 10 years** сре́дний срок слу́жбы э́тих маши́н 10 лет. **3.** (*animation*) жи́вость, оживле́ние; **put some ~ into it!** живе́е!; пошеве́ливайтесь!; **the ~ and soul of the party** душа́ о́бщества; **the child is full of ~** ребёнок о́чень живо́й; **come to ~** (*recover senses*) очну́ться (*pf.*). **4.** (*living things*) жизнь; **is there ~ on Mars?** есть ли жизнь на Ма́рсе?; **animal ~** живо́тный мир; **still ~** натюрмо́рт; **draw from ~** рисова́ть, на- с нату́ры. **5.** (*actuality*): **true to ~** реалисти́чный; **as large as ~** как живо́й; со́бственной персо́ной. **6.** (*biography*) жизнь, биогра́фия; **lives of the saints ~** жития́ святы́х; **the ~ history of a plant** жи́зненный цикл расте́ния.

cpds. **~-and-death** *adj.*: **a ~-and-death struggle** борьба́ не на жизнь, а на́ смерть; **~belt** *n.* спаса́тельный круг; **~boat** *n.* спаса́тельная ло́дка; **~-buoy** *n.* спаса́тельный круг; **~-cycle** *n.* жи́зненный цикл; цикл разви́тия; **~-guard, ~-saver** *nn.* спаса́тель (*fem.* -ница) (на пля́же); **~jacket** *n.* спаса́тельная ку́ртка; **~like** *adj.* реалисти́чный; **~long** *adj.* пожи́зненный; **~-saver** *n.* = **~-guard; ~-saving** *n.* спасе́ние; *adj.* спаса́тельный; **~-size(d)** *adj.* в натура́льную величину́; **~-span** *n.* продолжи́тельность жи́зни; **~-style** *n.* о́браз жи́зни; **~time** *n.* жизнь; **in s.o.'s ~time** при жи́зни кого́-н.; **the chance of a ~time** ре́дкий/исключи́тельный слу́чай.

lifeless ['laɪflɪs] *adj.* (*dead*) мёртвый; (*inanimate*) неживо́й; (*inert, without animation*) безжи́зненный.

lifelessness ['laɪflɪsnɪs] *n.* безжи́зненность.

lift [lɪft] *n.* **1.** (*act of raising*) подъём; (*extent of rise*) высота́ подъёма. **2.** (*transport by air*) возду́шные перево́зки (*f. pl.*). **3.** (*transport of passenger in car etc.*): **give s.o. a ~** подв|ози́ть, -езти́ кого́-н.; (*coll.*)

подки́|дывать, -нуть кого́-н. **4.** (*fig.*, *of spirits*): **the news gave her a ~** от э́той но́вости она́ воспря́ла ду́хом. **5.** (*apparatus*) лифт; (*tech.*) подъёмник; **~ attendant** лифтёр (*fem.* -ша); **take the ~** подн|има́ться, -я́ться ли́фтом (*or* на ли́фте).

v.t. **1.** (*raise*) подн|има́ть, -я́ть; **he barely ~ed his eyes to her** он едва́ взгляну́л на неё; **he did not ~ a finger** (*fig.*) он и па́льцем не пошевельну́л. **2.** (*dig up*): **~ potatoes** выка́пывать, вы́копать карто́фель. **3.** (*transport by air*): **the troops were ~ed to Africa** войска́ бы́ли доста́влены в А́фрику по во́здуху. **4.** (*steal*) спере́ть (*pf.*) (*coll.*); (*of a plagiarist*) спи́с|ывать, -а́ть. **5.** (*remove*): **~ a ban** сн|има́ть, -ять запре́т.

v.i. (*rise*) подн|има́ться, -я́ться; (*disperse*) рассе́|иваться, -яться; (*cease*) прекра|ща́ться, -ти́ться.

with advs.: **~ down** *v.t.* снять (*pf.*) и поста́вить (*pf.*) на́ пол (*or* на зе́млю); **~ off** *v.t.* сн|има́ть, -ять; *v.i.* (*of rocket*) от|рыва́ться, -орва́ться от земли́; **~ out** *v.t.* вынима́ть, вы́нуть; **~ up** *v.t.* подн|има́ть, -я́ть; **~ up one's voice** (*sing*) запе́ть (*pf.*); (*speak*) заговори́ть (*pf.*).

cpds. **~boy, ~man** *nn.* лифтёр; **~-off** *n.* отры́в от земли́; (*of rocket*) моме́нт схо́да.

ligament ['lɪgəmənt] *n.* свя́зка.

ligature ['lɪgətʃə(r)] *n.* (*med.*, *typ.*) лигату́ра.

light[1] [laɪt] *n.* **1.** свет; **in the ~** на свету́; **in the ~ of day** при дневно́м све́те; **in artificial ~** при иску́сственном освеще́нии; **at first ~** на рассве́те; (*attr.*) светово́й; (*fig.*): **see the ~ (of day)** (*be made public*) быть обнаро́дованным, уви́деть (*pf.*) свет; **see the ~** (*realize truth*) прозр|ева́ть, -е́ть; **in the ~ of experience** исходя́ из о́пыта; **bring to ~** раскр|ыва́ть, -ы́ть; **come to ~** обнару́жи|ваться, -ться; выплыва́ть, вы́плыть; **throw ~ on sth.** прол|ива́ть, -и́ть свет на что-н.; (*brightness*): **northern ~s** се́верное сия́ние; **there was a ~ in his eyes** у него́ блесте́ли глаза́; (*lighting*) освеще́ние; **electric ~** электри́ческое освеще́ние; (*fig.*): **this book shows him in a bad ~** э́та кни́га пока́зывает его́ в невы́годном све́те; **put on the ~** заж|ига́ть, -е́чь свет; (*point of ~*): **the ~s of the town** огни́ го́рода. **2.** (*lamp*) ла́мпа; **~ bulb** ла́мпочка; **'L~s out!'** «погаси́ть ого́нь/свет!»; (*of car*) фа́ра; **dip the ~s** переключ|а́ть, -и́ть на бли́жний свет; **traffic ~s** светофо́р; **give s.o. the green ~** (*fig.*) да|ва́ть, -ть зелёную у́лицу кому́-н.; **see the red ~** (*fig.*) зам|еча́ть, -е́тить опа́сность; (*fig.*): **a leading ~** (*in society*) свети́ло, знамени́тость. **3.** (*flame*) ого́нь (*m.*); **strike a ~** (*with match*) заж|ига́ть, -е́чь спи́чку; **have you a ~?** нет ли у вас огонька́?; **give me a ~** да́йте прикури́ть.

adj. **1.** (*opp. dark*) све́тлый; **get ~** рассве|та́ть, -сти́. **2.** (*in colour*) све́тлый; све́тлого цве́та; **a ~ green** светло-зелёный цвет.

v.t. (*also* **~ up**) **1.** (*kindle*) заж|ига́ть, -е́чь; **~ a fire** разв|оди́ть, -ести́ ого́нь; **~ (up) a cigarette** заку́р|ивать, -и́ть папиро́су. **2.** (*illuminate*) осве|ща́ть, -ти́ть; **the house is lit by electricity** в до́ме электри́ческое освеще́ние; **~ the way for s.o.** свети́ть, по- кому́-н.; (*fig.*): **a smile lit up his face** улы́бка озари́ла его́ лицо́.

v.i.: **~ up** (*switch on ~s*) включ|а́ть, -и́ть свет; **~ing-up time** вре́мя для включе́ния фар; (*of the face*) свети́ться, за-; (*start smoking*) заку́р|ивать, -и́ть.

cpds. **~house** *n.* мая́к; **~house keeper** смотри́тель (*m.*) маяка́; **~-meter** *n.* экспоно́метр; **~ship** *n.* плаву́чий мая́к; **~-year** *n.* светово́й год.

light[2] [laɪt] *adj.* (*opp. heavy*) лёгкий; **a ~ blow** лёгкий уда́р; **our casualties were light** на́ши поте́ри бы́ли незначи́тельны; **with a ~ heart** с лёгким се́рдцем; **~ industry** лёгкая промы́шленность; **a ~ meal** непло́тная еда́; **we had a ~ meal** мы перекуси́ли; **~ music** лёгкая му́зыка; **~ rain** ме́лкий дождь; **~ reading** лёгкое чте́ние; **a ~ sentence** мя́гкий пригово́р; **I am a ~ sleeper** я чу́тко сплю; **traffic is ~ today** сего́дня неинтенси́вное движе́ние; **he made ~ work of it** он легко́ спра́вился с э́тим де́лом; **he made ~ of the difficulties** он преуменьша́л тру́дности.

adv.: **travel ~** путеше́ствовать (*impf.*) налегке́.

cpds. **~-fingered** *adj.* нечи́стый на́ руку; **~-footed** *adj.* проворный, легконо́гий; **~-headed** *adj.*: **she felt ~-headed** у неё закружи́лась голова́; **~-hearted** *adj.* (*carefree*) беспе́чный; весёлый; (*thoughtless*) легкомы́сленный; **~-weight** *n.* легкове́с; боре́ц/боксёр лёгкого ве́са; *adj.* легкове́сный.

light[3] [laɪt] *v.i.*: **~ on** (*encounter*) набрести́ (*pf.*) на+*a.*; **his eyes ~ed on her face** его́ взгляд упа́л на её лицо́.

lighten[1] ['laɪt(ə)n] *v.t.* (*make less heavy or easier*) облегч|а́ть, -и́ть; (*mitigate*): **~ a sentence** смягч|а́ть, -и́ть пригово́р.

v.i.: **his heart ~ed** у него́ ста́ло ле́гче на душе́.

lighten[2] ['laɪt(ə)n] *v.t.* (*illuminate, make brighter*) осве|ща́ть, -ти́ть; просвет|ля́ть, -и́ть.

v.i. **1.** (*grow brighter*) светле́ть, про-; проясн|я́ться, -и́ться. **2.** (*of lightning*) сверк|а́ть, -ну́ть; **it is ~ing** сверка́ет мо́лния.

lighter ['laɪtə(r)] *n.* зажига́лка.

lighting ['laɪtɪŋ] *n.* освеще́ние.

lightly ['laɪtlɪ] *adv.* легко́; **tread ~** легко́/осторо́жно ступа́ть (*impf.*); **he touched ~ on the past** он слегка́ косну́лся про́шлого; **he jumped ~ to the ground** он ло́вко спры́гнул на зе́млю; **it's not a thing to enter upon ~** за таки́е дела́ не сле́дует бра́ться необду́манно; **he takes everything ~** он ничего́ не принима́ет всерьёз; **you have got off ~** вы легко́ отде́лались; **the accused got off ~** обвиня́емый отде́лался лёгким наказа́нием.

lightness ['laɪtnɪs] *n.* (*of weight*) лёгкость; (*mildness*) мя́гкость; (*of colour*) све́тлость, светлота́.

lightning ['laɪtnɪŋ] *n.* мо́лния; **forked ~** зигзагообра́зная мо́лния; **sheet, summer ~** зарни́ца; **he was struck by ~** в него́ уда́рила мо́лния.

adj.: **with ~ speed** молниено́сно; **a ~ attack** молниено́сная ата́ка.

cpds. **~-conductor, ~-rod** *nn.* громоотво́д.

lights [laɪts] *n.* (*animal's lungs*) лёгкие (*nt. pl.*).

lignite ['lɪgnaɪt] *n.* лигни́т.

likable ['laɪkəb(ə)l] = **lik(e)able**

like[1] [laɪk] *n.* (*sth. equal or similar*) подо́бное; **did you ever hear the ~ (of it)?** слы́шали ли вы что́-нибудь подо́бное?; **music, dancing and the ~** му́зыка, та́нцы и тому́ подо́бное; (*pers.*) подо́бный; **we shall not look upon his ~ again** тако́го (челове́ка) мы никогда́ бо́льше не встре́тим.

adj. подо́бный, похо́жий; **in ~ manner** подо́бным о́бразом; **as ~ as two peas** похо́жи как две ка́пли воды́; **~ father, ~ son** я́блоко от я́блони недалеко́ па́дает; (*equal*) ра́вный. *See also prep. uses.*

adv. **1.** (*probably*): **~ enough, very ~** весьма́ возмо́жно; **(as) ~ as not** верне́е всего́. **2.** (*coll.*, *as it were*) вро́де, похо́же.

prep. **1.** (*similar to*, *characteristic of*) похо́жий на +*a.*; **she is ~ her mother** она́ похо́жа на мать; **that's just ~ him!** э́то похо́же на него́!; **what's she ~?** что она́ за челове́к?; кака́я она́?; **I don't care for films ~ that** я не люблю́ подо́бных фи́льмов; **a house ~ yours** дом вро́де ва́шего; **there's nothing ~ walking to keep you fit** для здоро́вья нет ничего́ поле́знее, чем ходьба́; **that is nothing ~ enough** э́того не мо́жет хвати́ть; **£500 would be more ~ it** скоре́е фу́нтов 500; **they sold something ~ 1,000 copies** они́ про́дали (что́-то) о́коло 1000 экземпля́ров; **look ~** *see* **look** *v.i.* **3.**; **it smells ~ something burning** па́хнет горе́лым; **it sounds ~ thun-**

der как бу́дто греми́т гром; **it sounds ~ a good idea** э́то, пожа́луй, хоро́шая иде́я; **he drinks ~ a fish** он пьёт как бо́чка; **don't talk ~ that!** не на́до так говори́ть; **a person ~ that** тако́й челове́к; **it's ~ nothing on earth** э́то ни на что не похо́же. **2.** (*inclined towards*): **do you feel ~ going for a walk?** вам (не) хо́чется пройти́сь?; **I don't feel ~ it** мне (что́-то) не хо́чется; **I felt ~ crying** мне хоте́лось пла́кать; **I feel ~ an ice-cream** я бы не прочь съесть моро́женое.

conj. (*coll.*): **he talks ~ I do** он говори́т так же, как я.

cpd. **~-minded** *adj.* приде́рживающийся тех же взгля́дов; **~-minded person** единомы́шленник.

like² [laɪk] *n.*: **~s and dislikes** симпа́тии и антипа́тии (*both f. pl.*); **she has her ~s and dislikes** у неё о́чень определённый вкус.

v.t. (*take pleasure in*) люби́ть (*impf.*); **he ~s living in Paris** ему́ нра́вится жить в Пари́же; **she ~d dancing** она́ люби́ла танцева́ть; **I ~ him** он мне нра́вится; **we ~d the play** пье́са нам понра́вилась; **how do you ~ that?** как вам э́то нра́вится?; **I ~ his impudence** вот э́то наха́льство!; **what don't you ~ about it?** что вас в э́том не устра́ивает?; **I don't ~** (*am reluctant*) **to disturb you** прости́те, что беспоко́ю вас; **whether you ~ it or not** во́лей-нево́лей; **would you ~ a drink?** хоти́те вы́пить (чего́-нибудь)?; **if you ~** е́сли хоти́те; **I should ~ to meet him** мне хоте́лось бы познако́миться с ним; **he would ~ to come** он хоте́л бы прийти́; **I would have ~d to** (*or* **would like to have**) **come** я жале́ю, что не мог прийти́; **I ~ to think he values my advice** мне хоте́лось бы ду́мать (*or* я наде́юсь), что он це́нит мой сове́т; **I ~ to be sure** я предпочита́ю знать наверняка́; **as you ~** как уго́дно; **come whenever you ~** приходи́те в любо́е вре́мя; **he was outspoken if you ~, but not rude** он был, е́сли хоти́те, открове́нен, но ника́к не груб.

lik(e)able ['laɪkəb(ə)l] *adj.* симпати́чный.

likelihood ['laɪklɪ,hʊd] *n.* вероя́тность; **in all ~** по всей вероя́тности.

likely ['laɪklɪ] *adj.* **1.** (*probable*) вероя́тный; (*plausible*) правдоподо́бный. **2.** (*suitable*) подходя́щий; (*promising*) многообеща́ющий. **3.** (*to be expected*): **he is ~ to come** он вероя́тно придёт; **that is never ~ to happen** э́то вряд ли когда́-нибудь случи́тся.

adv. вероя́тно; **most, very ~** наве́рно; скоре́е всего́; **not ~!** (на)вря́д ли!; как бы не так!; **as ~ as not** вполне́ вероя́тно/возмо́жно.

liken ['laɪkən] *v.t.* упод|obля́ть, -о́бить (*кого/что кому/чему*); сра́вн|ивать, -и́ть (*кого, что с чем*).

likeness ['laɪknɪs] *n.* **1.** (*resemblance*) схо́дство, подо́бие; **a family ~** фами́льное схо́дство. **2.** (*guise*) обли́чие; **in the ~ of** в ви́де +*g.*; под личи́ной +*g.* **3.** (*representation, portrait*) изображе́ние, портре́т.

likewise ['laɪkwaɪz] *adv.* подо́бно.

conj. таки́м же о́бразом.

liking ['laɪkɪŋ] *n.* симпа́тия (*к кому*); расположе́ние (*к чему*); **I took a ~ to him** я почу́вствовал к нему́ симпа́тию; **she has no ~ for this work** э́та рабо́та ей не по душе́.

lilac ['laɪlək] *n.* сире́нь.

adj. (*~-coloured*) сире́невый.

lilt [lɪlt] *n.* (*tune*) напе́в; (*rhythm*) ритм.

v.i.: **a ~ing melody** мелоди́чный напе́в.

lily ['lɪlɪ] *n.* ли́лия; **~ of the valley** ла́ндыш.

cpd. **~-white** *adj.* лиле́йный.

limb [lɪm] *n.* **1.** (*of body*; *also fig.*). член; коне́чность; **tear s.o. ~ from ~** раз|рыва́ть, -орва́ть кого́-н. на ча́сти. **2.** (*branch of tree*) сук, ветвь; **out on a ~** (*fig.*) в невы́годном/опа́сном положе́нии.

limber ['lɪmbə(r)] *adj.* (*flexible, pliable*) ги́бкий, пода́тливый; (*nimble*) прово́рный.

v.i.: **~ up** разм|ина́ться, -я́ться.

limbo ['lɪmbəʊ] *n.* **1.** (*relig.*) лимб; предде́рие а́да. **2.** (*fig.*): **our plans are in ~** неизве́стно, что из на́ших пла́нов полу́чится.

lime¹ [laɪm] *n.* (*fruit*) лайм; **~ juice** сок ла́йма.

lime² [laɪm] *n.* (*tree*) ли́па; (*attr.*) ли́повый.

lime³ [laɪm] *n.* (*calcium oxide*) и́звесть; **slaked/quick ~** гашёная/негашёная и́звесть.

v.t. (*soil*) известкова́ть (*impf., pf.*); уд|обря́ть, -о́брить и́звестью.

cpds. **~light** *n.* (*lit.*) свет ра́мпы; (*fig.*): **be in the ~light** быть знамени́тостью; быть в це́нтре внима́ния; быть на виду́; **come into the ~light** ста|нови́ться, -ть знамени́тостью; **~stone** *n.* известня́к; (*attr.*) известняко́вый.

limit ['lɪmɪt] *n.* **1.** (*terminal point*) преде́л; (*comm.*) лими́т; **the ~s of endurance** преде́лы выно́сливости; **he exceeded the speed ~** он превы́сил устано́вленную ско́рость; **set, fix a ~ to sth.** устан|а́вливать, -ови́ть преде́л чему́-н.; **lower/upper ~** ми́нимум/ма́ксимум; **that's the ~!** э́то перехо́дит все грани́цы; **without ~** без конца́; (*endlessly*) бесконе́чно. **2.** (*border, boundary*) грани́ца; **city ~s** городска́я черта́; **'off ~s to military personnel'** (*US*) «вход военнослу́жащим запрещён». **3.** (*time ~*) (преде́льный) срок; **age ~** преде́льный во́зраст.

v.t. ограни́чи|вать, -ть (*кого/что чем*); **~ed edition** изда́ние, вы́пущенное ограни́ченным тиражо́м; **~ed liability company** компа́ния с ограни́ченной отве́тственностью.

limitation [,lɪmɪ'teɪʃ(ə)n] *n.* (*limiting, being limited*) ограниче́ние; (*condition*) огово́рка; (*drawback*) недоста́ток; **he has his ~s** он не лишён недоста́тков.

limitless ['lɪmɪtlɪs] *adj.* безграни́чный, беспреде́льный; (*of time*) бесконе́чный.

limousine ['lɪmʊ,zi:n, ,lɪmʊ'zi:n, 'lɪmə,zi:n] *n.* лимузи́н.

limp¹ [lɪmp] *n.* хромота́; **he has a ~** он хрома́ет.

v.i. хрома́ть (*impf.*); (*fig.*): **the plane ~ed back to base** самолёт с трудо́м добра́лся до ба́зы.

limp² [lɪmp] *adj.* **1.** (*flexible*) мя́гкий; **a book in ~ covers** кни́га в мя́гком переплёте. **2.** (*without energy; flabby*) вя́лый; **I feel ~** я совсе́м без сил; **go ~** обм|яка́ть, -я́кнуть.

limpet ['lɪmpɪt] *n.* блю́дечко (*моллюск*); **stick like a ~** приста́ть (*pf.*) как ба́нный лист.

limpid ['lɪmpɪd] *adj.* прозра́чный.

linchpin, lynchpin ['lɪntʃpɪn] *n.* чека́; (*fig., of pers. or thg.*) тот/то, на ком/чём всё де́ржится; незамени́мый челове́к; опо́ра.

linctus ['lɪŋktəs] *n.* миксту́ра.

linden ['lɪnd(ə)n] *n.* ли́па.

line¹ [laɪn] *n.* **1.** (*cord*) верёвка; **hang washing on the ~** разве́сить (*pf.*) бельё на верёвке; (*fishing-~*) ле́ска; (*plumb-~*) отве́с. **2.** (*wire, cable for communication*) ли́ния (свя́зи); ка́бель (*m.*); про́вод; **direct ~** пряма́я ли́ния; **hot ~** (*coll.*) прямо́й про́вод; **the ~ is bad** пло́хо слы́шно; **the ~ is engaged** (*US, busy*) ли́ния занята́; **he is on the ~** он говори́т по телефо́ну; он у телефо́на; **give me a ~ to the Ministry** соедини́те меня́ с министе́рством; **an outside ~, please** да́йте го́род, пожа́луйста; **hold the ~!** подожди́те у телефо́на!; не ве́шайте тру́бку! **3.** (*rail.*) ли́ния; **~s of communication** (*mil.*) коммуника́ции (*f. pl.*); **main ~** гла́вный путь, магистра́ль; **branch ~** (железнодоро́жная) ве́тка; (*track*) полотно́; ре́льсы (*m. pl.*). **4.** (*transport system*) ли́ния; **air ~s** возду́шные ли́нии. **5.** (*long narrow mark*) ли́ния, черта́; (*geom.*, geog. *etc.*): **~s of force** силовы́е ли́нии; **date ~** ли́ния су́точного вре́мени; (*imagined straight ~*): **~ of fire** направле́ние стрельбы́. **6.** (*on face etc.*) скла́дка, морщи́ны. **7.** (*drawn, painted etc.*) штрих; **~ drawing** штрихово́й/

карандáшный рисýнок; **in broad ~s** в óбщих чертáх; (*pl., contour, outline, shape*) кóнтур, очертáние; **~s of a ship** обвóды (*m. pl.*) корабля́. **8.** (*boundary, limit*) грани́ца, предéл, чертá; **dividing ~** раздели́тельная чертá; (*fig.*): **draw a ~ between** различ|áть, -и́ть; **draw the ~** пров|оди́ть, -ести́ грани́цу; **one must draw the ~ somewhere** всемý есть предéл; **I draw the ~ at that** на э́то я уж не соглáсен; (*sport*): **the ball went over the ~** мяч перешёл чертý; **at the starting ~** на стáрте. **9.** (*row*) ряд, ли́ния; **stand in ~** стоя́ть (*impf.*) в ряд; (*US, queue*) стоя́ть (*impf.*) в óчереди; (в)стать (*pf.*) в óчередь; **in ~ with** в однý ли́нию (*or* в ряд) с+*i.*; (*fig.*) в соглáсии/соотвéтствии с+*i.*; **bring into ~** (*fig.*) привлéчь (*pf.*) (*когó*) на свою стóрону; соглacóв|ывать, -áть (*что*); **come, fall into ~** согла|шáться, -си́ться; (*fig.*) согласовáться (*impf., pf.*); **be out of ~** (*fig.*) не соотвéтствовать (*impf.*) нóрме; (*mil.*): **in ~** в развёрнутом строю́; **draw up in ~** стрóить, по- в ряд. **10.** (*mil., entrenched position*): **front ~** ли́ния фрóнта; **in the front ~** на передовóй; **behind the enemy~s** за расположéнием проти́вника; **he was beaten all along the ~** (*fig.*) он потерпéл поражéние на всех фронтáх. **11.** (*mil., nav.: main formation*): **~ regiment** линéйный полк; **ship of the ~** линéйный корáбль (*abbr.* линкóр). **12.** (*of print or writing*) строкá; **on ~ 10** на строкé деся́той; **begin a new ~!** начни́те с нóвой строки́!; **read between the ~s** (*fig.*) читáть (*impf.*) мéжду строк; **send** (*coll. drop*) **s.o. a ~** (*or* **a few ~s**) черкнýть (*pf.*) комý-н. нéсколько слов; (*pl., verse*) стихи́ (*m. pl.*); (*pl., actor's part*) роль. **13.** (*lineage*) ли́ния; **in direct ~ of descent** по прямóй ли́нии; **in the male ~** по мужскóй ли́нии. **14.** (*course, direction, track*) направлéние, ли́ния; **~ of action** ли́ния поведéния/дéйствия; **take a firm, hard ~** зан|имáть, -я́ть твёрдую пози́цию; стрóго об|ходи́ться, -ойти́сь (*с кем*); **take a different ~** зан|имáть, -я́ть инýю пози́цию; **get a ~ on sth.** навести́ (*pf.*) спрáвки о чём-нибудь; **on similar ~s** аналоги́чным óбразом; **on different ~s** по-другóму; (*principle*): **the business is run on co-operative ~s** предприя́тие дéйствует на кооперати́вных начáлах. **15.** (*province, sphere of activity*): **cards are not in my ~** кáрточная игрá — не по моéй чáсти; **in the ~ of duty** при исполнéнии служéбных обя́занностей; **what's your ~?** чем вы занимáетесь?; какáя у вас профéссия? **16.** (*class of goods*) сорт, род, модéль (товáра); **consumer ~s** потреби́тельские товáры (*m. pl.*). **17.** (*pl., coll., fortune*): **it was hard ~s on him** (ужáсно) не повезлó емý; **hard ~s!** бедня́га! (*c.g.*).

v.t. **1.** (*mark with ~s*) линовáть, раз-; **~d paper** линóванная бумáга. **2.** (*form a ~ along*) стоя́ть (*impf.*) (*or* быть расстáвленными) вдоль+*g.*; **police ~d the street** полицéйские стоя́ли по обéим сторонáм ýлицы; **the road was ~d with trees** дорóга былá обсáжена дерéвьями.

with adv.: **~ up** *v.t.* (*align*) выстрáивать, вы́строить в ряд/ли́нию; (*coll., arrange*): **I have something ~d up for you** я для вас кóе-что устрóил; *v.i.* выстрáиваться, вы́строиться в ряд/ли́нию; (*queue up*) ста|нови́ться, -ть в óчередь.

cpds. **~sman** *n.* (*sport*) боковóй судья́; **~-up** *n.* (*arrangement, grouping*) расположéние, строй.

line[2] [laɪn] *v.t.* **1.** (*put lining into*) стáвить, по- на подклáдку; подб|ивáть, -и́ть; **her coat is ~d with silk** у неё пальтó на шёлковой подклáдке. **2.** (*fig.*) заст|авля́ть, -áвить; **the wall was ~d with books** стенá былá застáвлена кни́гами; (*fig., fill*): **~ one's pockets** наб|ивáть, -и́ть себé кармáны. **3.** (*tech., of walls etc.*) облиц|óвывать, -евáть.

lineage [ˈlɪnɪɪdʒ] *n.* (*ancestry*) происхождéние; (*genealogy*) родослóвная.

lineal [ˈlɪnɪəl] *adj.* происходя́щий по прямóй ли́нии (*от когó*).

linear [ˈlɪnɪə(r)] *adj.* линéйный.

linen [ˈlɪnɪn] *n.* **1.** (*material: smooth*) полотнó; (*coarse*) холст. **2.** (*~ articles*) бельё; (*clothing*) (носи́льное) бельё; (*bed-~*) постéльное бельё.

adj. **1.** (*pert. to flax*) льнянóй; **~ cloth** льнянóе полотнó. **2.** (*made of ~*) полотня́ный.

liner [ˈlaɪnə(r)] *n.* (*ship*) лáйнер; **air ~** воздýшный лáйнер.

linger [ˈlɪŋgə(r)] *v.i.* (*take one's time*) мéдлить (*impf.*); мéшкать (*impf.*); **she ~ed over her dressing** онá дóлго одевáлась; **a ~ing death** мéдленная смерть; (*stay on*) задéрж|иваться, -áться; **~ing disease** затяжнáя болéзнь; **I have ~ing doubts** мои сомнéния не рассéялись; **the guests ~ed over their coffee** гóсти засидéлись за кóфе; (*of time: drag*) затя́гиваться (*impf.*); (*continue to live*): **the old man ~ed for another week** стари́к протянýл ещё однý недéлю.

with advs.: **~ about, ~ around** *v.i.* болтáться (*impf.*); **~ on** *v.i.* (*of doubt etc.: remain*) ост|авáться, -áться; (*of customs; be preserved*) сохраня́ться (*impf.*).

lingerie [ˈlæ̃ʒərɪ] *n.* дáмское бельё.

lingo [ˈlɪŋgəʊ] *n.* (*pej.*) (инострáнный) язы́к; (*jargon*) жаргóн.

linguist [ˈlɪŋgwɪst] *n.* (*speaker of foreign languages*): **he is a good ~** емý легкó даю́тся языки́; (*philologist*) лингви́ст, языковéд.

linguistic [lɪŋˈgwɪstɪk] *adj.* лингвисти́ческий, языковéдческий; **~ problems** проблéмы языкá.

linguistics [lɪŋˈgwɪstɪks] *n.* лингви́стика, языкознáние, языковéдение.

liniment [ˈlɪnɪmənt] *n.* мазь.

lining [ˈlaɪnɪŋ] *n.* (*of garment*) подклáдка; (*of walls etc.*) облицóвка; **brake ~** тормознáя проклáдка; **every cloud has a silver ~** нет хýда без добрá.

link [lɪŋk] *n.* **1.** (*of chain; also fig.*) звенó; **missing ~** недостаю́щее звенó. **2.** (*connection*) связь.

v.t. (*unite*) соедин|я́ть, -и́ть; (*join*) свя́з|ывать, -áть; (*tech., couple*) сцеп|ля́ть, -и́ть; **~ arms with s.o.** идти́ (*det.*) пóд руку с кем-н.; **~ one's arm through another's** взять когó-н. пóд руку.

v.i.: **~ on to sth.** прим|ыкáть, -кнýть к чемý-н.; **~ with** (*fit in with*) **sth.** вязáться (*impf.*) с чем-н.

with advs.: **~ together** *v.t.* свя́з|ывать, -áть; **~ up** *v.t. & i.* соедин|я́ться, -и́ться.

linkage [ˈlɪŋkɪdʒ] *n.* (*chem.*) связь; (*pol.*) **a ~ policy** поли́тика «увя́зок».

links [lɪŋks] *n.* (*golf-~*) пóле для игры́ в гольф.

linnet [ˈlɪnɪt] *n.* коноплЯ́нка.

linoleum [lɪˈnəʊlɪəm] *n.* линóлеум.

linotype [ˈlaɪnəʊˌtaɪp] *n.* линоти́п.

linseed [ˈlɪnsiːd] *n.* льнянóе сéмя; **~ oil** льнянóе мáсло.

lint [lɪnt] *n.* **1.** (*med.*) кóрпия; (*gauze*) мáрля. **2.** (*fluff*) пух.

lintel [ˈlɪnt(ə)l] *n.* при́толока.

lion [ˈlaɪən] *n.* лев; **~'s share** (*fig.*) льви́ная дóля.

cpds. **~-cub** *n.* львёнок; **~-hunter** *n.* охóтник на львов.

lioness [ˈlaɪənɪs] *n.* льви́ца.

lionize [ˈlaɪəˌnaɪz] *v.t.*: **~ s.o.** носи́ться (*impf.*) с кéм-нибудь, как со знамени́тостью.

lip [lɪp] *n.* **1.** губá (*dim.* гýбка); **bite one's ~** (*in vexation*) кусáть (*impf.*) гýбы; (*in thought*) закýс|ывать, -и́ть губý; **not a word escaped his ~s** он не пророни́л ни слóва; **keep a stiff upper ~** сохран|я́ть, -и́ть самообладáние; **lick one's ~s** обли́з|ываться, -нýться; **smack one's ~s** чмóк|ать, -нуть; **I heard it from his own ~s** я слы́шал э́то от негó самогó; **the news is on everyone's ~s** нóвость у всех на устáх. **2.** (*edge of cup etc.*) край; (*of ladle*) нóсик.

3. (*coll.*, *impudence*) де́рзость; **none of your ~!** не дерзи́!; **I won't take any ~ from him!** я ему́ покажу́ дерзи́ть!

cpds. **~-read** *v.t.* & *i.* чита́ть (*impf.*) с губ; **~-reading** *n.* чте́ние с губ; **~-salve** *n.* мазь для смягче́ния губ; **~-service** *n.*: **pay ~-service to sth.** призн|ава́ть, -а́ть что-н. то́лько на слова́х; **~stick** *n.* (*substance*) губна́я пома́да.

liquefaction [ˌlɪkwɪˈfækʃ(ə)n] *n.* расплавле́ние; сжиже́ние.

liquefy [ˈlɪkwɪˌfaɪ] *v.t.* & *i.* (*of metals etc.*) распл|авля́ть(ся), -а́вить(ся); (*of gas*) сжи́|жа́ть(ся), -ди́ть(ся).

liqueur [lɪˈkjʊə(r)] *n.* ликёр.

liquid [ˈlɪkwɪd] *n.* жи́дкость.

adj. **1.** (*in ~ form*) жи́дкий. **2.** (*translucent*): **~ eyes** я́сные глаза́; **a ~ sky** прозра́чное не́бо. **3.**: **~ assets** ликви́дные акти́вы.

liquidate [ˈlɪkwɪˌdeɪt] *v.t.* (*all senses*) ликвиди́ровать (*impf.*, *pf.*).

liquidation [ˌlɪkwɪˈdeɪʃ(ə)n] *n.* ликвида́ция; **go into ~** ликвиди́роваться (*impf.*, *pf.*); **~ of debts** погаше́ние долго́в.

liquidator [ˈlɪkwɪˌdeɪtə(r)] *n.* ликвида́тор.

liquidity [lɪˈkwɪdɪtɪ] *n.* (*fin.*) ликви́дность.

liquidize [ˈlɪkwɪˌdaɪz] *v.t.* (*cul.*) разжи|жа́ть, -ди́ть.

liquidizer [ˈlɪkwɪˌdaɪzə(r)] *n.* (*cul.*) разжижи́тель (*m.*).

liquor [ˈlɪkə(r)] *n.* (*alcoholic drink*) (спиртно́й) напи́ток; **~ store** ви́нный магази́н.

liqu|orice, lic- [ˈlɪkərɪs, -rɪʃ] *n.* (*plant*) соло́дка, лакри́чник; (*substance*) лакри́ца.

lira [ˈlɪərə] *n.* ли́ра.

lisp [lɪsp] *n.* шепеля́вость; **he has** (*or* **speaks with**) **a ~** он шепеля́вит.

v.i. шепеля́вить (*impf.*); сюсю́кать (*impf.*).

lissom(e) [ˈlɪsəm] *adj.* ги́бкий.

list[1] [lɪst] *n.* (*roll*, *inventory*, *enumeration*) спи́сок, пе́речень (*m.*); **black ~** чёрный спи́сок; **casualty ~** спи́сок поте́рь; **~ price** цена́ по прейскура́нту.

v.t. (*make a ~ of*) сост|авля́ть, -а́вить спи́сок +*g.*; (*enter on a ~*) вн|оси́ть, -ести́ в спи́сок; (*enumerate*) переч|исля́ть, -и́слить; **~ed building** зда́ние, находя́щееся под охра́ной госуда́рства.

list[2] [lɪst] *n.* (*leaning*) крен; накло́н; **have a ~** крени́ться (*impf.*).

v.i. (*of ship*) накреня́ться (*impf.*); крени́ться, на-.

listen [ˈlɪs(ə)n] *v.i.* слу́шать, по-; **~ to** слу́шать, по- +*a.*; **do you ~ (in) to the radio?** слу́шаете ли вы ра́дио?; (*pay attention*; *heed to*) прислу́ш|иваться, -аться к+*d.*; **don't ~ to him!** не обраща́йте на него́ внима́ния!; (*hear out*) выслу́шивать, вы́слушать; **~ to me and then decide** вы́слушайте меня́, а пото́м реша́йте!; (*for a certain time*) прослу́ш|ивать, -ать; **the doctor ~ed to his heart** врач прослу́шал его́ се́рдце; (*overhear*, *eavesdrop on*) подслу́ш|ивать, -ать; **~ing-post** пост подслу́шивания.

listener [ˈlɪsənə(r)] *n.* слу́шатель (*m.*); **he is a good ~** он уме́ет слу́шать; (*to radio*) радиослу́шатель (*m.*).

listless [ˈlɪstlɪs] *adj.* апати́чный, вя́лый.

listlessness [ˈlɪstlɪsnɪs] *n.* апа́тия, вя́лость.

litany [ˈlɪtənɪ] *n.* екте́нья.

liter [ˈliːtə(r)] = **litre**

literacy [ˈlɪtərəsɪ] *n.* гра́мотность.

literal [ˈlɪtər(ə)l] *adj.* **1.** (*of, or expr. in, letters*) бу́квенный; **~ error** опеча́тка, бу́квенная оши́бка. **2.** (*following the text exactly*; *taking words in primary sense*) буква́льный; **he has a ~ mind** у него́ педанти́чный/прозаи́ческий ум.

literary [ˈlɪtərərɪ] *adj.* **1.** (*pert. to literature, books, writing*) литерату́рный; (*of ~ studies*) литературове́дческий; **a ~ man** литера́тор. **2.** (*of style or vocabulary*) кни́жный.

literate [ˈlɪtərət] *adj.* гра́мотный.

literature [ˈlɪtərətʃə(r), ˈlɪtrə-] *n.* литерату́ра.

lithe [laɪð] *adj.* ги́бкий.

lithium [ˈlɪθɪəm] *n.* ли́тий.

lithograph [ˈlɪθəˌgrɑːf, ˈlaɪθə-] *n.* литогра́фия; **~ print** литогра́фский о́ттиск.

v.t. литографи́ровать (*impf.*, *pf.*).

lithographer [lɪˈθɒgrəfə(r)] *n.* лито́граф.

lithographic [ˌlɪθəˈgræfɪk] *adj.* литогра́фский.

lithography [lɪˈθɒgrəfɪ] *n.* литогра́фия.

Lithuania [ˌlɪθjuːˈeɪnɪə, ˌlɪθuː-] *n.* Литва́.

Lithuanian [ˌlɪθjuːˈeɪnɪən, ˌlɪθuː-] *n.* (*pers.*) лито́в|ец (*fem.* -ка); (*language*) лито́вский язы́к.

adj. лито́вский.

litigant [ˈlɪtɪgənt] *n.* тя́жущаяся сторона́.

litigate [ˈlɪtɪˌgeɪt] *v.i.* суди́ться (*impf.*)

litigation [ˌlɪtɪˈgeɪʃ(ə)n] *n.* тя́жба; суде́бный проце́сс.

litmus [ˈlɪtməs] *n.* ла́кмус; **~ paper** ла́кмусовая бума́га.

litre [ˈliːtə(r)] (*US* **liter**) *n.* литр.

litter [ˈlɪtə(r)] *n.* **1.** (*refuse*) сор, отбро́с|ы (*pl.*, *g.* -ов). **2.** (*straw etc. for animals*) подсти́лка. **3.** (*newly-born animals*) помёт. **4.** (*stretcher*) носи́л|ки (*pl.*, *g.* -ок).

v.t. сори́ть, на-; **he ~ed the room with paper** он разброса́л бума́гу по всей ко́мнате; **the table is ~ed with books** стол зава́лен кни́гами.

cpds. **~-basket** *n.* му́сорная корзи́на; **~-bin** *n.* му́сорный я́щик.

little [ˈlɪt(ə)l] *n.* (*not much*) ма́ло, немно́го, немно́жко +*g.*; **there was ~ left** оста́лось ма́ло/немно́го; **it had ~ to do with me** э́то де́ло меня́ ма́ло каса́лось; **he makes ~ of physical pain** он не бои́тся физи́ческой бо́ли; **it takes ~ to make him angry** его́ нетру́дно рассерди́ть; **I see ~ of him now** я тепе́рь ре́дко ви́жу его́; **~ or nothing** почти́ ничего́; ма́ло что; (*small amount*): **I did what ~ I could** я сде́лал то немно́гое, что мог; **I'd like a ~ of that salad** я бы хоте́л немно́го/чу́точку э́того сала́та; **he knows a ~ Japanese** он немно́го зна́ет япо́нский; **he knows a ~ of everything** он зна́ет обо всём понемно́гу; (*short time or distance*): **after a ~ he returned** вско́ре он верну́лся; **won't you stay (for) a ~?** побу́дьте/посиди́те ещё немно́го!; **~ by ~** ма́ло-пома́лу; постепе́нно.

adj. **1.** (*small*) ма́ленький, небольшо́й; **~ finger** мизи́нец; **~ toe** мизи́нец ноги́; (*expr. by dim.*, *e.g.*); **~ house** до́мик; **~ man** челове́чек. **2.** (*young*): **~ boy** (ма́ленький) ма́льчик; **~ girl** (ма́ленькая) де́вочка; **~ ones** (*children*) де́т|и (*pl.*, *g.* -е́й); малыши́ (*m. pl.*); (*animals*) детёныши (*m. pl.*). **3.** (*trivial, unpretentious*) ме́лкий; незначи́тельный; **the ~ things of life** жите́йские ме́лочи (*f. pl.*). **4.** (*not tall or long*) невысо́кий; недли́нный; **he was a ~ man** он был челове́к небольшо́го ро́ста; **I went a ~ way with him** я с ним прошёл не́сколько шаго́в; **wait here for a ~ while** подожди́те здесь немно́жко. **5.** (*small, of quantity*) ма́ло, немно́го, немно́жко +*g.*; **there is ~ butter left** ма́сла оста́лось ма́ло; **he knows ~ Japanese** он пло́хо зна́ет япо́нский. **6.** (*in var. emotive senses*): **that poor ~ girl!** бедня́жка!; **he's quite the ~ gentleman** э́тот ма́льчик — настоя́щий джентльме́н; **so that's your ~ game!** так вы вон что заду́мали!; **I know your ~ ways** я зна́ю ва́ши шту́чки.

adv. **1.** (*not much*) ма́ло; **I see him very ~** я ма́ло/ре́дко с ним ви́жусь; **~ more** ненамно́го/немно́гим бо́льше; **he is ~ better than a thief** он про́сто-на́просто вор; **~ short of madness** су́щее безу́мие; (*not at all*): **~ did he know I was following him** он и не подозрева́л, что я иду́ за ним; **we ~ thought he would go to those lengths** мы ника́к не ожида́ли, что он дойдёт до тако́й кра́йности. **2.** (**a ~**: *slightly, somewhat*) немно́го, немно́жко; **this hat is a ~ too**

big for me э́та шля́па мне немно́го велика́; **I was a ~ afraid you would not come** я немно́го боя́лся, что вы не придёте; **I am a ~ happier now** я тепе́рь не́сколько успоко́ился; **she is a ~ over 40** ей немно́гим бо́льше сорока́.

liturgical [lɪ'tɜːdʒɪk(ə)l] *adj.* литурги́ческий.

liturgy ['lɪtədʒɪ] *n.* (*eccl.*) литурги́я.

livable ['lɪvəb(ə)l] = **liv(e)able**

live[1] [laɪv] *adj.* **1.** (*living*) живо́й; (*pert. to living person or thg.*): **~ birth** рожде́ние живо́го ребёнка; (*fig.*): **a ~ issue** актуа́льный вопро́с. **2.** (*burning*): **~ coals** горя́щие у́гли. **3.** (*not spent or exploded*): **~ ammunition** боевы́е патро́ны; **~ rail** токопроводя́щий рельс; **a ~ wire** (*lit.*) про́вод под то́ком/напряже́нием; (*fig.*) челове́к с изю́минкой. **4.** (*not recorded*): **~ broadcast** пряма́я переда́ча; **the game was broadcast ~** матч трансли́ровался непосре́дственно со стадио́на.

cpd. **~stock** *n.* дома́шний скот.

live[2] [lɪv] *v.t.* (*spend, experience*) пров|оди́ть, -ести́; прож|ива́ть, -и́ть; **he ~d his whole life there** он там про́жил всю жизнь; **he is living a double life** он ведёт двойну́ю жизнь; **he ~s life to the full** он живёт по́лной жи́знью; **life is not worth living** жить не сто́ит.

v.i. **1.** (*be alive*) жить (*impf.*); (*of habitat*) води́ться, обита́ть (*both impf.*). **2.** (*subsist*): **they ~ on vegetables** они́ пита́ются овоща́ми; **they ~ off the land** они́ живу́т на подно́жном корму́; **they ~ from hand to mouth** они́ перебива́ются с хле́ба на во́ду. **3.** (*depend for one's living*) жить (*impf.*); **he ~s on his earnings** он живёт на свой за́работки; **they ~ quietly, within their income** они́ живу́т скро́мно, по сре́дствам; **he ~s on, off his friends** он живёт за счёт друзе́й. **4.** (*conduct o.s.*) жить (*impf.*); **he ~s up to his principles** он стро́го приде́рживается свои́х при́нципов; **he ~d up to my expectations** он не обману́л мои́х ожида́ний; (*arrange one's diet, habits etc.*): **he ~s well** он живёт хорошо́; **two can ~ as cheaply as one** вдвоём жить не доро́же, чем одному́; **~ like a lord** ката́ться (*impf.*) как сыр в ма́сле. **5.** (*enjoy life*): **now at last I'm really living** вот э́то я называ́ю жи́знью!; **if you've never been to Paris, you haven't ~d** кто в Пари́же не быва́л, тот жи́зни не вида́л. **6.** (*continue alive*): **the doctors think he won't ~** врачи́ ду́мают, что он не вы́живет; **he ~d to a great** (*or* **ripe old) age** он дожи́л до глубо́кой ста́рости; **he ~d to regret it** впосле́дствии он об э́том жале́л; **he will ~ to see his grandchildren married** он успе́ет вну́ков жени́ть; **long ~ the Queen!** да здра́вствует короле́ва!; **she has ~d through a great deal** она́ мно́го пережила́; **you, we ~ and learn** век живи́ — век учи́сь; **~ and let ~** сам живи́ и други́м не меша́й; **he ~s for his work** он живёт свое́й рабо́той; (*fig., survive*): **his fame will ~ for ever** сла́ва его́ не умрёт. **7.** (*reside*) жить, прожива́ть (*both impf.*); обита́ть (*impf.*); **where do you ~?** где вы живёте; **they are living apart** (*of married couple*) они́ живу́т врозь; они́ разъе́хались; **~ with** (*fig. tolerate*) мири́ться, при- с+*i.*

with advs.: **~ down** *v.t.* загла́|живать, -дить; **he will never ~ down the scandal** ему́ никогда́ не уда́стся загла́дить сканда́л; **~ on** *v.i.*: **his memory ~s on** па́мять о нём жива́; **~ together** *v.i.*: **are they married or only living together?** они́ жена́ты и́ли так живу́т (*or* сожи́тельствуют)?; **France and Germany have learnt to ~ together** Фра́нция и Герма́ния научи́лись жить в ми́ре; **~ up** *v.t.*: **~ it up** (*coll.*) жить (*impf.*) широко́.

liv(e)able ['lɪvəb(ə)l] *adj.* **1.** (*of house etc.*) го́дный для жилья́. **2.** (*of life*) сно́сный. **3.: ~-with** (*of pers.*) тако́й, с кото́рым мо́жно ужи́ться.

livelihood ['laɪvlɪ,hʊd] *n.* сре́дства (*nt. pl.*) к существова́нию; **earn one's ~** зараба́тывать (*impf.*) на жизнь.

liveliness ['laɪvlɪnɪs] *n.* жи́вость, оживлённость.

lively ['laɪvlɪ] *adj.* (*lit., fig.*) живо́й; **take a ~ interest in sth.** проявля́ть (*impf.*) живо́й интере́с к чему́-н.; (*animated*) оживлённый; **trade was ~** торго́вля шла бо́йко; (*energetic*) живо́й, де́ятельный; (*bright*): **~ colours** я́ркие кра́ски; (*brisk*): **we walked at a ~ pace** мы шли бы́стрым ша́гом; **look ~!** быстре́е!; жи́во!

liven ['laɪv(ə)n] *v.t. & i.* (*also* **~ up**) ожив|ля́ть(ся), -и́ть(ся).

liver[1] ['lɪvə(r)] *n.* (*anat.*) пе́чень; (*food*) печёнка; **~ sausage** ли́верная колбаса́.

liver[2] ['lɪvə(r)] *n.*: **loose ~** распу́тник; **fast ~** прожига́тель (*m.*) жи́зни.

liveried ['lɪvərɪd] *adj.* ливре́йный.

liverish ['lɪvərɪʃ] *adj.* (*fig., peevish*) жёлчный.

livery ['lɪvərɪ] *n.* (*of servants*) ливре́я; (*of a guild etc.*) фо́рма; **~ stable** пла́тная коню́шня.

livid ['lɪvɪd] *adj.* (*of colour*) серова́то-си́ний; мёртвенно-бле́дный; (*coll., of temper*): **be ~** черне́ть, по-; **I was ~** я был взбешён.

living ['lɪvɪŋ] *n.* **1.** (*process, manner of ~*): **~ conditions** усло́вия жи́зни; **a ~ wage** прожи́точный ми́нимум; **cost of ~** сто́имость жи́зни; **standard of ~** жи́зненный у́ровень. **2.** (*livelihood*) сре́дства (*nt. pl.*) к жи́зни; **earn one's ~** зараб|а́тывать, -о́тать себе́ на жизнь; **he makes his ~ by teaching** он зараба́тывает преподава́нием. **3.** (*fare*): **good, high ~** бога́тый стол; **plain ~** просто́й стол. **4.** (*eccl.*) бенефи́ций.

adj. **1.** (*alive*) живо́й; **a ~ language** живо́й язы́к; **within ~ memory** на па́мяти живу́щих; **not a ~ soul** (*as obj.*) ни (одно́й) живо́й души́; (*as n.*) **the ~** живы́е (*pl.*); **he is in the land of the ~** он ещё жив. **2.** (*true to life*): **he is the ~ image of his father** он вы́литый оте́ц. **3.** (*contemporary*): **he is the greatest of ~ writers** он крупне́йший из совреме́нных писа́телей.

cpds. **~-room** *n.* гости́ная; **~space** *n.* жи́зненное простра́нство.

lizard ['lɪzəd] *n.* я́щерица.

llama ['lɑːmə] *n.* ла́ма.

lo [ləʊ] *int.* (*arch.*): **~ and behold** и вдруг, о чу́до.

load [ləʊd] *n.* **1.** (*what is carried; burden*) но́ша; груз, нагру́зка; тя́жесть; (*fig.*) бре́мя; **a ~ of worries** бре́мя забо́т; **that was a ~ off my mind** у меня́ как гора́ с плеч; **you have taken a ~ off my mind** от ва́ших слов мне ста́ло ле́гче. **2.** (*amount carried by vehicle etc.*) груз; (*fig., coll.*): **it's a ~ of rubbish** э́то сплошна́я чепуха́. **3.** (*pl., coll., large amount*) у́йма, ма́сса.

v.t. **1.** (*cargo etc.*) грузи́ть, по-; **the goods were ~ed on to the ship** това́ры погрузи́ли на кора́бль. **2.** (*ship, vehicle etc.*) грузи́ть, на-; нагру|жа́ть, -зи́ть (*что чем*). **3.** (*fig., with cares etc.*) обремен|я́ть, -и́ть (*кого чем*); **don't ~ yourself with extra work** не взва́ливайте на себя́ ли́шнюю рабо́ту. **4.** (*with gifts, praises etc.*) ос|ыпа́ть, -ы́пать (*кого чем*). **5.** (*firearm, camera etc.*) заря|жа́ть, -ди́ть; **he ~ed the camera with film** он заряди́л аппара́т (плёнкой). **6.** (*weight with lead*) нал|ива́ть, -и́ть свинцо́м; **~ed dice** на́литые свинцо́м ко́сти; **the dice were ~ed against him** (*fig.*) все ша́нсы бы́ли про́тив него́; (*fig.*): **a ~ed question** провокацио́нный вопро́с. **7.** (*fill to capacity*): **the bus was ~ed with people** авто́бус был перепо́лнен. **8.** (*sl.*): **he's ~ed** (*rich*) у него́ де́нег ку́ры не клюю́т; (*US drunk*) он нагрузи́лся.

v.i. грузи́ться, на-.

with advs.: **~ down** *v.t.* обремен|я́ть, -и́ть; **~ up**

v.t. нагру|жа́ть, -зи́ть; *v.i.* грузи́ться, на-
loader ['ləʊdə(r)] *n.* (*pers.*) гру́зчик.
loading ['ləʊdɪŋ] *n.* **1.** (*of cargo*) погру́зка. **2.** (*of ship, vehicle etc.*) нагру́зка. **3.** (*of gun, camera etc.*) заря́дка.
loaf[1] [ləʊf] *n.* буха́нка; **cottage ~** карава́й; **small ~** бу́лка; (~*shaped food*): **meat ~** мясно́й руле́т.
loaf[2] [ləʊf] *v.i.* (*coll.*; *also* **~ about**) ло́дырничать (*impf.*); шата́ться (*impf.*) без де́ла.
loafer ['ləʊfə(r)] *n.* ло́дырь (*m.*).
loam [ləʊm] *n.* сугли́нок.
loamy ['ləʊmɪ] *adj.* сугли́нистый.
loan [ləʊn] *n.* **1.** (*sum lent*) заём, ссу́да; **he asked for a ~ of £10** он попроси́л 10 фу́нтов взаймы́. **2.** (*lending or being lent*): **take on ~; have the ~ of** (*of money*) брать, взять взаймы́; (*of objects*) брать, взять на вре́мя.
v.t. одолж|а́ть, -и́ть; да|ва́ть, -ть взаймы́.
cpds. **~-translation** *n.* ка́лька; **~-word** *n.* заимствованное сло́во.
lo(a)th [ləʊθ] *pred. adj.*: **he was ~ to do anything** он ничего́ не хоте́л де́лать.
loathe [ləʊð] *v.t.* (*detest*) ненави́деть (*impf.*); (*feel disgust for*) испы́тывать (*impf.*) отвраще́ние к+*d.*; (*be unable to bear*) быть не в состоя́нии терпе́ть.
loathing ['ləʊðɪŋ] *n.* отвраще́ние; **feel ~ for** испы́тывать (*impf.*) отвраще́ние к+*d.*
loathsome ['ləʊðsəm] *adj.* отврати́тельный, омерзи́тельный.
lob [lɒb] *n.* (*high-pitched ball*) свеча́.
v.t.: **~ a ball** под|ава́ть, -а́ть свечу́.
lobby ['lɒbɪ] *n.* вестибю́ль (*m.*); (*theatr.*) фойе́ (*indecl.*); (*in Parliament*) кулуа́р|ы (*pl.*, *g.* -ов).
v.t. агити́ровать, (*impf.*) (в кулуа́рах).
lobbying ['lɒbɪɪŋ] *n.* агита́ция (в кулуа́рах).
lobbyist ['lɒbɪɪst] *n.* лобби́ст.
lobe [ləʊb] *n.* (*of brain etc.*) до́ля; (*of ear*) мо́чка.
lobotomy [lə'bɒtəmɪ] *n.* лоботоми́я.
lobster ['lɒbstə(r)] *n.* ома́р.
cpd. **~-pot** *n.* ве́рша для ома́ров.
local ['ləʊk(ə)l] *n.* (*inhabitant*) ме́стный жи́тель; (*paper*) ме́стная газе́та; (*train*) ме́стный по́езд; (*public house*) ме́стный паб, ме́стная пивна́я.
adj. ме́стный; зде́шний; **~ anaesthetic** ме́стный нарко́з; **~ authority** ме́стные вла́сти; **~ colour** ме́стный колори́т; **~ population** коренно́е населе́ние; **2 o'clock ~ time** два часа́ по ме́стному вре́мени.
locale [ləʊ'kɑːl] *n.* ме́сто (де́йствия); ме́стность.
locality [ləʊ'kælɪtɪ] *n.* ме́стность; (*neighbourhood*): **there is no cinema in the ~** нигде́ побли́зости нет кино́.
localization [ˌləʊkəlaɪ'zeɪʃ(ə)n] *n.* локализа́ция.
localize ['ləʊkəˌlaɪz] *v.t.* локализова́ть (*impf.*, *pf.*).
locally ['ləʊkəlɪ] *adv.*: **he is well-known ~** он изве́стен в э́тих края́х; **he works ~** он рабо́тает побли́зости.
locate [ləʊ'keɪt] *v.t.* **1.** (*establish in a place*) поме|ща́ть, -сти́ть; (*designate place of*) назн|ача́ть, -а́чить ме́сто (*чему or для чего*); **be ~d** (*situated*) находи́ться (*impf.*). **2.** (*determine position of*) определ|я́ть, -и́ть ме́сто/местоположе́ние +*g.*; **has the fault been ~d?** нашли́ поврежде́ние?; (*discover*) обнару́жи|вать, -ть; **he ~d the source of the Nile** он нашёл исто́ки Ни́ла.
location [ləʊ'keɪʃ(ə)n] *n.* **1.** (*determining of place*) определе́ние (ме́ста). **2.** (*position, situation*) местонахожде́ние, местоположе́ние. **3.**: **on ~** (*cin.*) на нату́ре.
locative ['lɒkətɪv] *n.* & *adj.* (*gram.*) ме́стный (паде́ж).
loch [lɒk, lɒx] *n.* о́зеро (*в Шотландии*); **L~ Ness** о́зеро Лох-Не́сс.
lock[1] [lɒk] *n.* (*of hair*) ло́кон, прядь.
lock[2] [lɒk] *n.* **1.** (*on door or firearm*) замо́к; **under ~ and key** под замко́м; **~, stock and barrel** целико́м и по́лностью; (*on door or gate*) запо́р. **2.** (*of vehicle's wheels*) у́гол поворо́та; **full ~** до упо́ра. **3.** (*wrestling hold*) захва́т. **4.** (*on canal*) шлюз.
v.t. **1.** (*secure; restrict movement of*) зап|ира́ть, -ере́ть (на замо́к); **is the door ~ed?** дверь заперта́? **2.** (*cause to stop moving or revolving*) тормози́ть, за-; **he ~ed the steering** он за́пер руль. **3.** (*engage, interlace*) сцепл|та́ть, -сти́; **his fingers were ~ed together** он сцепи́л ру́ки; **they were ~ed in an embrace** они́ сжима́ли друг дру́га в объя́тиях.
v.i. **1.**: **does this chest ~?** э́тот сунду́к запира́ется? **2.** (*interlace*) сцеп|ля́ться, -и́ться; **the parts ~ into each other** дета́ли взаи́мно блоки́руются.
with advs.: **~ away** *v.t.* спря́тать (*pf.*) под замо́к; **~ in** *v.t.* зап|ира́ть, -ере́ть (*кого*) в ко́мнате/до́ме *и т.п.*; **he ~ed himself in** он за́перся́ на ключ; **~ out** *v.t.* зап|ира́ть, -ере́ть дверь и не впуска́ть; **the workers were ~ed out** рабо́чих подве́ргли лока́уту; **~ up** *v.t.* зап|ира́ть, -ере́ть на замо́к; (*imprison*) сажа́ть, посади́ть.
cpds. **~-gate** *n.* шлю́зные воро́та; **~jaw** *n.* тризм че́люсти; **~out** *n.* лока́ут; **~smith** *n.* сле́сарь (*m.*); **~-up** *n.* аре́стантская ка́мера; (*shed*) сара́й.
locker ['lɒkə(r)] *n.* (*cupboard*) шка́фчик.
cpd. **~-room** *n.* раздева́лка.
locket ['lɒkɪt] *n.* медальо́н.
locomotion [ˌləʊkə'məʊʃ(ə)n] *n.* передвиже́ние.
locomotive [ˌləʊkə'məʊtɪv] *n.* локомоти́в; (*steam*) парово́з; (*electric*) электрово́з; (*diesel*) ди́зель (*m.*), теплово́з; **~ shed** депо́ (*indecl.*).
adj. дви́жущий, дви́гательный; **~ engine** = *n.*
locum (tenens) [ˌləʊkəm 'tiːnenz, 'tenenz] *n.* (*doctor or clergyman*) вре́менный замести́тель (*m.*).
locus ['ləʊkəs, 'lɒkəs] *n.* (*math.*) траекто́рия; **~ of points** геометри́ческое ме́сто то́чек.
locust ['ləʊkəst] *n.* саранча́ (*also collect.*).
locution [lək'juːʃ(ə)n] *n.* оборо́т (ре́чи), идио́ма.
lode [ləʊd] *n.* ру́дная жи́ла.
cpds. **~star** *n.* (*fig.*) путево́дная звезда́; **~stone** *n.* магни́тный железня́к; (*fig.*) магни́т.
lodge [lɒdʒ] *n.* **1.** (*cottage e.g. at entrance to park*) дом привра́тника. **2.** (*porter's apartment*) сторо́жка. **3.** (*hunting ~*) охо́тничий до́мик. **4.** (*freemason's ~*) масо́нская ло́жа.
v.t. **1.** (*accommodate*) да|ва́ть, -ть помеще́ние +*d.*; поме|ща́ть, -сти́ть. **2.** (*fig.*, *enter*): **~ a complaint/appeal** обра|ща́ться, -ти́ться с жа́лобой/апелля́цией; **~ a claim** предъяв|ля́ть, -и́ть прете́нзию; **~ an objection** заяв|ля́ть, -и́ть проте́ст.
v.i. **1.** (*reside*) жить (*impf.*); **he ~s with us** он наш жиле́ц. **2.** (*become embedded, stuck*) застр|ева́ть, -я́ть; **a bone ~d in his throat** кость застря́ла у него́ в го́рле.
lodger ['lɒdʒə(r)] *n.* жил|е́ц (*fem.* -и́ца).
lodging ['lɒdʒɪŋ] *n.* наёмная кварти́ра; (*pl.*) меблиро́ванные ко́мнаты (*f. pl.*); **he lives in ~s** он снима́ет ко́мнату.
loft [lɒft] *n.* (*room in roof*) черда́к; (*hay-~*) сенова́л; (*organ-~*) хо́р|ы (*pl.*, *g.* -ов).
loftiness ['lɒftɪnɪs] *n.* (больша́я) высота́; возвы́шенность.
lofty ['lɒftɪ] *adj.* высо́кий; возвы́шенный.
log[1] [lɒg] *n.* **1.** (*of wood*) бревно́, чурба́н; (*for fire*) поле́но; **he slept like a ~** он спал как уби́тый; **~ cabin** (бреве́нчатая) хи́жина.
cpd. **~jam** *n.* зато́р; (*fig.*) засто́й, тупи́к.
log[2] [lɒg] *n.* (*~-book*) ва́хтенный журна́л; (*of aircraft*) бортово́й журна́л; формуля́р; (*of lorry or car*) формуля́р.
v.t. (*record*) занос|и́ть, -ести́ в ва́хтенный журна́л; регистри́ровать (*impf.*, *pf.*).
cpd. **~-book** *n.* = *n.*

logarithm ['lɒgə,rɪð(ə)m] *n.* логари́фм.
logarithmic [,lɒgə'rɪðmɪk] *adj.* логарифми́ческий.
loggerhead ['lɒgə,hed] *n.*: **they are at ~s** они́ в ссо́ре (*or* не в лада́х) друг с дру́гом.
logging ['lɒgɪŋ] *n.* (*cutting into logs*) лесозаготóвка.
logic ['lɒdʒɪk] *n.* ло́гика.
logical ['lɒdʒɪk(ə)l] *adj.* логи́ческий; (*consistent*) логи́чный, после́довательный.
logician [lə'dʒɪʃ(ə)n] *n.* ло́гик.
logistics [lə'dʒɪstɪks] *n.* (*mil.*) материа́льно-техни́ческое обеспе́чение.
logo ['ləʊgəʊ, 'lɒgəʊ] *n.* эмбле́ма.
loin [lɔɪn] *n.* **1.** (*pl.*) поясни́ца. **2.** (*joint of meat*) филе́ (*indecl.*).
cpd. **~-cloth** *n.* набе́дренная повя́зка.
loiter ['lɔɪtə(r)] *v.i.* (*dawdle*) ме́шкать (*impf.*); заме́шкаться (*pf.*); (*hang about*) слоня́ться (*impf.*) (без де́ла).
loiterer ['lɔɪtərə(r)] *n.* праздношата́ющийся.
loll [lɒl] *v.i.* **1.** (*sit or stand in lazy attitude*) сиде́ть/стоя́ть (*impf.*) разваля́сь. **2.** (*of tongue etc.*: *hang loose*) выва́ливаться (*impf.*).
lollipop ['lɒlɪ,pɒp] *n.* ледене́ц на па́лочке.
lolly ['lɒlɪ] *n.* **1.** (*coll.*) = **lollipop. 2.** (*sl.*, *money*) гро́ш|и (*pl.*, *g.* -ей).
London ['lʌnd(ə)n] *n.* Ло́ндон; (*attr.*) ло́ндонский.
Londoner ['lʌndənə(r)] *n.* ло́ндон|ец (*fem.* -ка).
lone [ləʊn] *adj.* одино́кий, уединённый.
loneliness ['ləʊnlɪnɪs] *n.* одино́чество.
lonely ['ləʊnlɪ] *adj.* **1.** (*solitary*, *alone*) одино́кий; **lead a ~ existence** вести́ (*det.*) одино́кий о́браз жи́зни; жить (*impf.*) уединённо. **2.** (*isolated*) уединённый.
loner ['ləʊnə(r)] *n.* (*coll.*) бирю́к, одино́чка (*c.g.*).
lonesome ['ləʊnsəm] *adj.* одино́кий; **feel ~** тоскова́ть (*impf.*); томи́ться (*impf.*) одино́чеством.
long[1] [lɒŋ] *n.* **1.** (*a ~ time*): **I shan't be away for ~** я уезжа́ю ненадо́лго; я ско́ро верну́сь; **it won't take ~** э́то не займёт мно́го вре́мени; **will you take ~ over it?** вы ско́ро ко́нчите?; **it is ~ since he was here** он давно́ здесь не́ был; **at the ~est** са́мое бо́льшее. **2.: the ~ and the short of it is that ...** сло́вом, де́ло в том, что...
adj. **1.** (*of space*, *measurement*) дли́нный; **the table is 2 metres ~** э́тот стол длино́й в 2 ме́тра; **how ~ is this river?** какова́ длина́ э́той реки́?; **~ form** (*of Russian adj.*) по́лная фо́рма; **~ jump** прыжо́к в длину́; **in the ~ run** в коне́чном ито́ге/счёте; с тече́нием вре́мени; **on the ~ wave** на дли́нной волне́. **2.** (*of distance*) да́льний; **a ~ journey** да́льний/до́лгий путь; **a ~ way off** далеко́; **from a ~ way off** издалека́. **3.** (*of time*) до́лгий; **a ~ life** до́лгая жизнь; **a ~ memory** хоро́шая па́мять; **my holiday is 2 weeks ~** мой о́тпуск дли́тся две неде́ли; **a quarrel of ~ standing** да́вняя/многоле́тняя ссо́ра; **for a ~ time** до́лго, давно́; надо́лго; **a ~ time ago** мно́го вре́мени тому́ наза́д; давны́м-давно́; **a ~ time before the war** задо́лго до войны́; **I had not seen him for many a ~ day** я его́ це́лую ве́чность не ви́дел. **4.** (*prolonged*) дли́тельный; **a ~ illness** затяжна́я боле́знь.
adv. **1.** (*a ~ time*): **I shan't be ~** я ско́ро верну́сь; я не задержу́сь; **she is ~ since dead** она́ давно́ умерла́; **it was ~ past midnight** бы́ло далеко́ за́ полночь; **~ after** (*prep.*) до́лгое вре́мя по́сле+*g.*; **~ before** (*prep.*) задо́лго до+*g.*; **~ after(wards)** до́лгое вре́мя спустя́; **~ before** (*adv.*) давно́, гора́здо ра́ньше; **these events are ~ past** всё э́то случи́лось давно́; **~ ago** (давны́м-)давно́; **before ~** вско́ре, ско́ро. **2.** (*for a ~ time*): **I have ~ thought so** я давно́ так ду́маю; **how ~ have you been here?** вы здесь давно́?; **~ live the Queen!** да здра́вствует короле́ва! **3.** (*throughout*): **all day ~** це́лый день; **all night ~** всю ночь напролёт. **4.: as ~ as I live** пока́ я жив; **stay as ~ as you like** остава́йтесь, ско́лько хоти́те; **as ~ as you don't mind** е́сли вы не возража́ете. **5.: so ~!** пока́! (*coll.*). **6.: no ~er** бо́льше не; **I can't wait much ~er** мно́го до́льше ждать я не могу́.
cpds. **~-awaited** *adj.* долгожда́нный; **~boat** *n.* барка́с; **~bow** *n.* большо́й лук; **~-distance** *adj.*: **~-distance call** междугоро́дный вы́зов; **~-distance train** по́езд да́льнего сле́дования; **~-distance runner** бегу́н на дли́нные диста́нции; **~-haired** *adj.* длинноволо́сый; **~hand** *n.* обы́чное письмо́ (от руки́); **~-legged** *adj.* длинноно́гий; **~-lived** *adj.* долгове́чный; **~-lost** *adj.* давно́ поте́рянный/утра́ченный; **~-playing** *adj.* долгоигра́ющий; **~-range** *adj.* (*of gun*) дальнобо́йный; (*of aircraft*) да́льнего де́йствия; (*of forecast*, *policy etc.*) долгосро́чный; **~shoreman** *n.* порто́вый гру́зчик; **~-sighted** *adj.* дальнозо́ркий; **~-standing** *adj.* стари́нный, долголе́тний; **a ~-standing promise** да́внее обеща́ние; **~-suffering** *adj.* многострада́льный; **~-term** *adj.* долгосро́чный; (*of plans etc.*) перспекти́вный; **~-wave** *adj.* длинново́лновый; **~-winded** *adj.* (*prolix*) многосло́вный.
long[2] [lɒŋ] *v.i.*: **~ for sth.** жа́ждать (*impf.*) чего́-н.; **we are ~ing for your return** мы ждём не дождёмся ва́шего возвраще́ния; **I ~ed for a drink** я ужа́сно хоте́л пить; **~ for s.o.** тоскова́ть (*impf.*) по кому́-н.; **~ to do sth.** мечта́ть (*impf.*) что́-то де́лать.
longevity [lɒn'dʒevɪtɪ] *n.* (*of pers.*) долголе́тие; (*of thg.*) долгове́чность.
longing ['lɒŋɪŋ] *n.* жа́жда (*чего*); тоска́ (*по чему*).
adj. тоску́ющий; **he looked at the books with ~ eyes** он смотре́л на кни́ги с вожделе́нием.
longitude ['lɒŋgɪ,tju:d, 'lɒndʒ-] *n.* долгота́; **at 20° West** на двадца́том гра́дусе за́падной долготы́.
longitudinal [,lɒŋgɪ'tju:dɪn(ə)l, ,lɒndʒ-] *adj.* (*of longitude*) долго́тный; (*lengthwise*) продо́льный.
longw|ays ['lɒŋweɪz], **-ise** ['lɒŋwaɪz] *adv.* в длину́.
loo [lu:] *n.* (*lavatory*) сорти́р (*coll.*); **I need (to use) the ~** мне на́до ко́е-куда́ сбе́гать.
look [lʊk] *n.* **1.** (*glance*) взгляд; **he gave me a ~** он бро́сил взгляд (*or* взгляну́л) на меня́; **give s.o. a black ~** зло́бно посмотре́ть/взгляну́ть (*pf.*) на кого́-н.; **may I have a ~ at your paper?** позво́льте просмотре́ть ва́шу газе́ту. **2.: have, take a ~ at** (*examine*) осм|а́тривать, -отре́ть; рассм|а́тривать, -отре́ть; **the doctor had a good ~ at his throat** до́ктор внима́тельно посмотре́л его́ го́рло. **3.: have a ~ for** (*search for*) иска́ть, по-. **4.** (*expression*) выраже́ние; **there was a ~ of horror on his face** его́ лицо́ выража́ло у́жас. **5.** (*appearance*) вид; **he had an odd ~ about him** у него́ был стра́нный вид; **I don't like the ~ of things** пло́хо де́ло!; (*pl.*, *personal appearance*) нару́жность, вне́шность; **~s don't count** по вне́шности не су́дят; **she has good ~s** она́ хороша́ собо́й; **lose one's (good) ~s** дурне́ть, по-.
v.t. **1.** (*inspect*, *scrutinize*): **~ s.o. in the face, eye** смотре́ть, по- в глаза́ кому́-н.; **don't ~ a gift horse in the mouth** дарёному коню́ в зу́бы не смо́трят; **~ s.o. up and down** сме́рить (*pf.*) кого́-н. глаза́ми/взгля́дом. **2.** (*express with eyes*): **she ~ed daggers at him** она́ зло́бно посмотре́ла на него́. **3.** (*have the appearance of*; *see also v.i.* **3.**) вы́глядеть (*impf.*) +*i.*: **he ~s an old man** он вы́глядит старико́м; **he ~s his age** ему́ вполне́ дашь его́ го́ды; **he is not ~ing himself** на нём лица́ нет; **you are ~ing yourself again** тепе́рь вы сно́ва ста́ли похо́жи на себя́; **I ~ my best after breakfast** я лу́чше всего́ вы́гляжу по́сле за́втрака. **4.** (*with ind. questions*: *observe*) смотре́ть, по-; **~ who's here!** кого́ я ви́жу!; **now ~ what you've done!** смотри́те, что вы наде́лали!
v.i. **1.** (*use one's eyes*; *pay attention*) смотре́ть,

по-; **he ~ed out of the window to see if she was coming** он посмотре́л в окно́, не идёт ли она́; **~ over there!** посмотри́те/взгляни́те туда́!; **~ here!** послу́шайте; (*fig.*, *consider*) вду́маться (*impf.*); **when one ~s more closely** при ближа́йшем рассмотре́нии; (*search*) иска́ть, по-. **2.** (*face*) выходи́ть (*impf.*); **the windows ~ on to the garden** о́кна выхо́дят в сад. **3.** (*appear*; *see also v.i.* **3.**) вы́глядеть (*impf.*) +*i.*; **she is ~ing well** она́ хорошо́ вы́глядит; **everybody ~ed tired** у всех был уста́лый вид; **that ~s tasty** у э́того блю́да аппети́тный вид; **he made me ~ small** он меня́ уни́зил; **things ~ black** пло́хо де́ло; **the situation ~s promising** ситуа́ция как бу́дто благоприя́тная; **that ~s suspicious** э́то подозри́тельно; **it ~s as if ...** ка́жется (, что)...; похо́же на то, что...; **~ like** (*resemble*) вы́глядеть (*impf.*) +*i.* походи́ть (*impf.*) на+*a.*; **the old man ~s like a tramp** у старика́ вид бродя́ги; **he ~s like his father** он похо́ж на отца́; **she ~s like nothing on earth** она́ Бог зна́ет на что похо́жа; (*give expectation of*): **it ~s like rain** собира́ется (*or* похо́же, что бу́дет) дождь; **it ~s like a fine day** день обеща́ет быть хоро́шим; **he ~s like winning** он, ка́жется, вы́йдет победи́телем.

with preps.: **~ about one** огля́д|ываться, -е́ться; **he ~ed about the room** он обвёл глаза́ми ко́мнату; **~ after** (*follow with eye*) следи́ть (*impf.*) глаза́ми за+*i.*; (*care for*) смотре́ть (*impf.*) за+*i.*; присма́тривать (*impf.*) за+*i.*; уха́живать (*impf.*) за+*i.*; **he needs ~ing after** он нужда́ется в ухо́де; **he had to ~ after himself** ему́ приходи́лось всё де́лать самому́; **~ after yourself!** (*in leave-taking*) береги́те себя́!; (*keep safe*) храни́ть (*impf.*); (*be responsible for*) вести́ (*det.*); занима́ться (*impf.*) +*i.*; **a lawyer is ~ing after my affairs** мои́ми дела́ми ве́дает юри́ст; **don't worry, I'll ~ after the bill** не беспоко́йтесь, я займу́сь счётом; **~ at** (*direct gaze on*) смотре́ть, по- на+*a.*; **he was ~ing at a book** он смотре́л на кни́гу; **just ~ at the time!** поду́майте, как по́здно!; **to ~ at him, you would think ...** су́дя по его́ ви́ду, мо́жно поду́мать, что...; (*inspect*, *examine*) смотре́ть, по- на+*a.*; осм|а́тривать, -отре́ть; **the doctor ~ed at the patient** врач осмотре́л больно́го; **I must get my car ~ed at** на́до, что́бы посмотре́ли мою́ маши́ну; (*fig.*, *consider*) вду́маться (*impf.*) в+*a.*; обра|ща́ть, -ти́ть внима́ние на+*a.*, **we must ~ at the matter carefully** на́до как сле́дует поду́мать об э́том де́ле; **I ~ed down the street** я оки́нул взгля́дом у́лицу; **he ~ed down the page** он пробежа́л страни́цу глаза́ми; **~ for** (*seek*) иска́ть, по-; **he is ~ing for a job** он и́щет ме́ста; **he is ~ing for trouble** он рвётся в бой; (*hope for*, *expect*) наде́яться (*impf.*) на+*a.*; ожида́ть (*impf.*) +*g.*; **I ~ed for better things from him** я ожида́л от него́ лу́чшего; **we obtained the ~ed-for result** мы доби́лись жела́емого результа́та; **~ in the mirror** смотре́ться, по- в зе́ркало; **~ into** (*lit.*) смотре́ть, по- в+*a.*; (*investigate*, *examine*) иссле́довать (*impf.*); рассм|а́тривать, -отре́ть; **I shall ~ into the matter** я займу́сь э́тим вопро́сом; **~ on** (*regard*) счита́ть (*impf.*); **I ~ on him as my son** я счита́ю его́ свои́м сы́ном; **he ~ed on the remark as an insult** он восприня́л замеча́ние как оскорбле́ние; **~ on the bright side** смотре́ть (*impf.*) оптимисти́чески; **~ on to** (*face*) *see v.i.* **2.**; **he ~ed out of the window** он посмотре́л в окно́; **he ~ed over the wall** он посмотре́л че́рез стену́; **~ over one's shoulder** огля́|дываться, -ну́ться; **~ over s.o.'s shoulder** смотре́ть, по- кому́-н. че́рез плечо́; **~ round** (*inspect*) осм|а́тривать, -отре́ть; **he ~ed through the window** он посмотре́л в окно́; **he ~ed right through** (*ignored*) **me** он смотре́л ми́мо меня́; **they ~ed through** (*examined*) **our papers** они́ просмотре́ли на́ши бума́ги; **he quickly ~ed through the newspaper** он бы́стро пробежа́л глаза́ми газе́ту; **~ to** (*turn to*) обра|ща́ться, -ти́ться к+*d.*; **we ~ed to him for help** мы рассчи́тывали на его́ по́мощь; (*heed*): **he should ~ to his manners** ему́ сле́дует обрати́ть внима́ние на свои́ мане́ры; **~ upon** *see* **~ at, on**

with advs.: **~ about, ~ around** *v.i.* осм|атриваться, -отре́ться; **~ ahead** *v.i.* (*lit.*, *fig.*) смотре́ть (*impf.*) вперёд; **~ around** *see* **~ about, ~ round;** **~ aside** *v.i.* смотре́ть (*impf.*) в сто́рону; **~ away** *v.i.* отв|ора́чиваться, -ерну́ться; **~ back** *v.i.* (*lit.*, *fig.*) огл|я́дываться, -яну́ться; **once started, there was no ~ing back** раз уж мы на́чали, отступа́ть бы́ло по́здно; **~ back on** вспомина́ть (*impf.*); припомина́ть (*impf.*); **~ behind** *v.i.* смотре́ть, поназа́д; **~ down** *v.i.* (*lower one's gaze*) опус|ка́ть, -ти́ть глаза́; **~ down on** смотре́ть (*impf.*) свысока́ на+*a.*; презира́ть (*impf.*); **~ forward** смотре́ть (*impf.*) вперёд; **~ forward to** предвкуша́ть (*impf.*); ждать (*impf.*) +*g.* с нетерпе́нием; **I am so ~ing forward to it** я так жду э́того; **~ in** *v.i.*: **~ in** (*call*) **on s.o.** загля́|дывать, -ну́ть к кому́-н.; **~ on** *v.i.* наблюда́ть, смотре́ть (*both impf.*); **~ out** *v.t.* (*select*): **I must ~ out some old dresses** мне на́до отобра́ть каки́е-то ста́рые пла́тья; **he ~ed out some examples** он подыска́л не́сколько приме́ров; *v.i.* (*from a window*) смотре́ть, по- в окно́; (*be careful*) быть настороже́; **~ out!** осторо́жно!; (*keep one's eyes open*): **she stood at the door ~ing out for the postman** она́ стоя́ла в дверя́х, высма́тривая почтальо́на; **we are ~ing out for a house** мы присма́триваем дом; **~ over** *v.t.* (*scrutinize*) просм|а́тривать, -отре́ть; **~round, ~ around** *v.i.* (*turn one's head*) огля́|дываться, -ну́ться; (*make an inspection*) осм|а́триваться, -отре́ться; **~ round for** (*seek*) поды́скивать (*impf.*); **~ up** *v.t.* (*visit*) наве|ща́ть, -сти́ть; (**~** *for*, *seek information on*) оты́ск|ивать, -а́ть; **~ up trains** посмотре́ть (*pf.*) расписа́ние; *v.i.* (*raise one's eyes*) подн|има́ть, -я́ть глаза́ (**at s.o.:** на кого́-н.); (*improve*) ул|учша́ться, -у́чшиться; **things are ~ing up** дела́ иду́т на попра́вку; **~ up to** (*respect*) уважа́ть (*impf.*); **he is ~ed up to by everybody** все его́ уважа́ют.

cpds. **~-alike** *n.* двойни́к; **a Prince Charles ~-alike** вы́литый принц Чарлз; **~-in** *n.*: **I didn't get a ~-in** меня́ не подпусти́ли к пирогу́; **~-out** *n.* (*watchman*) наблюда́тель (*m.*); (*post*) наблюда́тельный пункт; (*watch*): **be on the ~-out** быть настороже́; **be on the ~-out for the enemy** подстерега́ть (*impf.*) неприя́теля; (*concern*): **that's his ~-out** э́то его́ де́ло/забо́та.

looking-glass ['lʊkɪŋ,glɑ:s] *n.* зе́ркало.

loom[1] [lu:m] *n.* тка́цкий стано́к.

loom[2] [lu:m] *v.i.* **1.** (*appear indistinctly*; *also* **~ up**) нея́сно вырисо́вываться (*impf.*); ма́ячить (*impf.*). **2.** (*impend*) нав|иса́ть, -и́снуть; **~ large** (*threateningly*) прин|има́ть, -я́ть угрожа́ющие разме́ры.

loony ['lu:nɪ] *n.* & *adj.* рехну́вшийся; чо́кнутый (*coll.*).

cpd. **~-bin** *n.* (*sl.*) психбольни́ца

loop [lu:p] *n.* **1.** петля́. **2.** (*aeron.*) мёртвая петля́.

v.t. **1.** (*form into* **~**) де́лать, с- пе́тлю из+*g.* **2.** (*fasten with* **~**) закреп|ля́ть, -и́ть петлёй. **3.** **~ the ~** (*aeron.*) де́лать, с- мёртвую пе́тлю.

loophole ['lu:phəʊl] *n.* (*fig.*) лазе́йка.

loose [lu:s] *n.*: **on the ~** на свобо́де; на во́ле.

adj. **1.** (*free*, *unconfined*, *unrestrained*) свобо́дный; **break ~** вы́рваться (*pf.*) на свобо́ду; (*of a dog*) сорва́ться с цепи́; **let ~** (*e.g. a dog*) спус|ка́ть, -ти́ть с цепи́; (*e.g. lion*, *maniac*) выпуска́ть, вы́пустить. **2.** (*not fastened or held together*): **~ papers** отде́льные листы́; **~ cover** (*on armchair etc.*) чехо́л; **he carries his change ~ in his pocket** ме́лочь у него́ пря́мо в карма́не; **she wears her hair ~** она́ хо́дит с распу́щенными волоса́ми; (*not packed*) без упако́вки. **3.** (*not secure or firm*): **a ~ end** (*of rope*) свобо́дный коне́ц; **at a ~ end** (*fig.*) без де́ла; **he was at a ~ end** он не знал за что приня́ться; **I have a ~ tooth** у меня́ зуб шата́ется; **the button is ~** пу́говица болта́ется; **the string came ~** верёвка развяза́лась; **hang ~** болта́ться (*impf.*). **4.** (*slack*) сла́бо натя́нутый; **~ bowels** поно́с; **he has a ~ tongue** он сли́шком болтли́в; **~ clothes** широ́кая оде́жда; **a ~ collar** свобо́дный во́рот. **5.** (*not compact or dense*): **~ soil** ры́хлая по́чва; **~ weave** ре́дкая ткань. **6.** (*imprecise*): **a ~ translation** приблизи́тельный/во́льный перево́д. **7.** (*morally lax*) распу́щенный; **~ living** распу́тство.

v.t. (*release*) освобо|жда́ть, -ди́ть; отпус|ка́ть, -ти́ть; (*undo*) развя́з|ывать, -а́ть; (*relax*) распус|ка́ть, -ти́ть.

cpds. **~fitting** *adj.* широ́кий, просто́рный; **~-leaf** *adj.* со вкладны́ми листка́ми; **~-leaf binder** скоросшива́тель (*m.*).

loosen ['lu:s(ə)n] *v.t.* (*tongue*) развя́з|ывать, -а́ть; (*screw*) отви́н|чивать, -ти́ть; (*by shaking or pulling*) расша́т|ывать, -а́ть; (*soil*) разрыхл|я́ть, -и́ть; (*tie, rope, belt etc.*) осл|абля́ть, -а́бить; **~ one's grip** осла́бить (*pf.*) хва́тку; **~ one's hold on sth.** выпуска́ть, вы́пустить что-н. из рук.

looseness ['lu:snɪs] *n.* (*slackness*) сла́бость; (*of morals*) распу́щенность.

loot [lu:t] *n.* добы́ча, награ́бленное добро́.

v.t. гра́бить, раз-.

v.i. ун|оси́ть, -ести́ добы́чу.

looter ['lu:tə(r)] *n.* граби́тель (*m.*).

looting ['lu:tɪŋ] *n.* грабёж.

lop [lɒp] *v.t.* (*also* **~ off**) руби́ть (*impf*); отруб|а́ть, -и́ть.

lope [ləʊp] *v.i.* бежа́ть (*det.*) вприпры́жку.

lop-eared ['lɒp,ɪəd] *adj.* вислоу́хий.

lop-sided [lɒp'saɪdɪd] *adj.* кривобо́кий; (*fig.*) неравноме́рный, односторо́нний.

loquacious [lɒ'kweɪʃəs] *adj.* словоохо́тливый, болтли́вый.

lord [lɔ:d] *n.* **1.** (*ruler; also fig.*) власти́тель (*m.*), властели́н; **~ of the manor** владе́лец поме́стья; **live like a ~** жить (*impf.*) припева́ючи; **drunk as a ~** пьян в сте́льку. **2.** (*nobleman*) лорд; **House of L~s** пала́та ло́рдов; **My ~!** мило́рд! **3.** (*God*) Госпо́дь; **Our L~** (*Christ*) Госпо́дь; **L~ have mercy!** Го́споди, поми́луй!; **(the) L~ only knows** Бог (его́) зна́ет; **L~'s Prayer** О́тче наш.

v.t.: **~ it over s.o.** кома́ндовать (*impf.*) кем-н.

lordly ['lɔ:dlɪ] *adj.* (*magnificent*) пы́шный; (*haughty*) надме́нный.

lordship ['lɔ:dʃɪp] *n.*: **Your L~** ва́ша све́тлость.

lore [lɔ:(r)] *n.* (специа́льные) зна́ния (*nt. pl.*); (*traditions*) преда́ния (*nt. pl.*).

lorgnette [lɔ:'njet] *n.* лорне́т.

lorry ['lɒrɪ] *n.* грузови́к.

los|e [lu:z] *v.t.* **1.** теря́ть, по-; утра́|чивать, -тить; лиш|а́ться, -и́ться *+g.*; **give sth. up for ~t** счита́ть (*impf.*) что-н. (безвозвра́тно) пропа́вшим; **the goods were ~t in transit** това́ры пропа́ли в пути́; **I ~t count of his mistakes** я потеря́л счёт его́ оши́бкам; **he ~t his head** (*fig.*) он потеря́л го́лову; **~e heart** па́|дать, -сть ду́хом; **~e patience** выходи́ть, вы́йти из терпе́ния; **~e one's place** (*job*) быть уво́ленным; **~e one's reason** лиш|а́ться, -и́ться рассу́дка; **~e** (*forfeit*) **one's rights** утра́|чивать, -тить свои́ права́; **~e sight of** (*lit.*) упус|ка́ть, -ти́ть и́з виду; (*fig.*) не уч|и́тывать, -е́сть; **~e one's sight** потеря́ть (*pf.*) зре́ние; **~e one's temper** рассерди́ться (*pf.*); **have you ~t your tongue?** вы что — язы́к проглоти́ли?; **I ~t touch with him** я потеря́л связь с ним; **he ~t his voice** он потеря́л/сорва́л го́лос; **~e one's way** заблуди́ться (*pf.*); **I am trying to ~e weight** я стара́юсь похуде́ть; **I am ~t without her** без неё я как без рук. **2.** (**~e by death**): **~e an old friend** лиши́ться (*pf.*) ста́рого дру́га; **he ~t his wife** у него́ умерла́ жена́; **be ~t** (*perish, die*) ги́бнуть (*impf.*); пог|иба́ть, -и́бнуть; **the ship was ~t with all hands** су́дно со всем экипа́жем поги́бло. **3.: be, get ~t** (**~e one's way**) заблуди́ться (*pf.*); **get ~t!** кати́сь! (*coll.*); (*fig.*): **~t in thought** заду́мавшись; **~e o.s. in sth.** погру|жа́ться, -зи́ться во что́-н. **4.** (*cease to see, understand etc.*): **you've ~t me** (*coll., I can't follow you*) я потеря́л нить (ва́шей мы́сли); **be ~t** (*disappear*) исч|еза́ть, -е́знуть; проп|ада́ть, -а́сть; **the church was ~t in the fog** це́рковь скры́лась в тума́не. **5.** (*fail to use; waste*): **~e an opportunity** упус|ка́ть, -ти́ть возмо́жность; **he ~t no opportunity** он по́льзовался вся́кой возмо́жностью; **~e time** теря́ть, по- вре́мя; **there is not a moment to be ~t** нельзя́ теря́ть ни мину́ты (вре́мени); **make up for ~t time** навёрст|ывать, -а́ть упу́щенное вре́мя. **6.** (*in contest, sport, gambling*) проигр|ывать, -а́ть; **the motion was ~t** предложе́ние не прошло́; **they ~t the match** они́ проигра́ли. **7.** (*of a clock*) отст|ава́ть, -а́ть на*+a.*; **my watch ~es 5 minutes a day** мои́ часы́ отстаю́т на 5 мину́т в день.

v.i. **1.** прои́гр|ывать, -а́ть; теря́ть, по-; **fight a ~ing battle** вести́ (*det.*) безнадёжную борьбу́; **they ~t by 3 points** они́ недобра́ли трёх очко́в. **2.** (*of a clock*): **my watch is ~ing** мои́ часы́ отстаю́т.

loser ['lu:zə(r)] *n.* (*at a game*) проигра́вший; (*person who habitually fails*) неуда́чник; **come off (***or* **be) a ~** оста́ться (*pf.*) в про́игрыше.

loss [lɒs] *n.* **1.** поте́ря; **~ of sight** поте́ря зре́ния; **~ of life** поте́ри уби́тыми; **suffer heavy ~es** понести́ (*pf.*) больши́е поте́ри. **2.** (*detriment*) утра́та; **his death was a great ~** его́ смерть была́ большо́й утра́той; **it's your ~, not mine** э́то ва́ша беда́, не моя́. **3.** (*monetary*) убы́ток; **incur ~es** терпе́ть, поубы́тки; **meet a ~** нести́ (*det.*) убы́ток; **sell at a ~** прод|ава́ть, -а́ть с убы́тком; **gambling ~es** про́игрыши (*m. pl.*) (в ка́ртах, на бега́х *и т.п.*). **4.** (*destruction, wreck*) ги́бель. **5.: I am at a ~ to answer** я затрудня́юсь отве́тить; **he was at a ~ what to say** он не нашёлся, что сказа́ть.

lot [lɒt] *n.* **1.: decide by ~** реш|а́ть, -и́ть жеребьёвкой; **draw ~s** тяну́ть (*impf.*) жре́бий; (*fig., destiny*) судьба́, у́часть; **cast in one's ~ with s.o.** свя́з|ывать, -а́ть свою́ судьбу́ с кем-н.; **it fell to his ~ to go** ему́ вы́пал жре́бий (*or* пришло́сь) идти́. **2.** (*plot of land*) уча́сток; **parking ~** (*US*) стоя́нка для маши́н. **3.** (*coll., of persons*) наро́д; **our/your ~** наш/ваш брат. **4.** (*in auction*) па́ртия. **5.: the ~** (*coll., everything*) всё; **that's the ~!** вот и всё! **6. (a ~, ~s:** *a large number, amount*) мно́го; ма́ло ли что; **a ~ of people** мно́го наро́ду; мно́гие; ма́ло ли кто (*+sg. vb.*); **what a ~ of people there were!** ско́лько бы́ло наро́ду!; **I have seen a ~ in my time** на своём веку́ я мно́гое повида́л; **he has ~s of friends** у него́ мно́го друзе́й; **there were ~s of apples left** оста́лась у́йма я́блок; **he plays a ~ of football** он мно́го игра́ет в футбо́л.

adv. **(a ~) 1.** (*often*) ча́сто; **we went to the theatre a ~** мы ча́сто ходи́ли в теа́тр. **2.** (*with comps.: much*) гора́здо, си́льно; **a ~ worse** гора́здо ху́же; **a ~ better** куда́ лу́чше; **the patient became a ~ worse** больно́му ста́ло намно́го ху́же.

lotion ['ləʊʃ(ə)n] *n.* приmо́чка; (*cosmetic*) лосьо́н.

lottery ['lɒtərɪ] *n.* лотере́я; **~ ticket** лотере́йный биле́т.

lotto ['lɒtəʊ] *n.* лото́ (*indecl.*).

lotus ['ləʊtəs] *n.* (*bot., myth.*) ло́тос.

loud [laʊd] *adj.* гро́мкий; (*noisy*) шу́мный; (*fig.*): **~ colours** крича́щие/крикли́вые кра́ски/цвета́.

adv. гро́мко; **out ~** вслух.

cpds. **~-hailer** *n.* ру́пор; **~-mouthed** *adj.* крикли́вый; **~speaker** *n.* громкоговори́тель (*m.*), дина́мик.

loudness ['laʊdnɪs] *n.* гро́мкость.

lounge [laʊndʒ] *n.* (*in hotel*) фойе́ (*indecl.*); (*at airport*) зал ожида́ния.

v.i. (*sit in relaxed position*) сиде́ть (*impf.*) развали́сь (*or* вразва́лку); (*sit or stand, leaning against sth.*) сиде́ть/стоя́ть (*impf.*) прислоня́сь (*к чему*); **~ about** (*idly*) безде́льничать (*impf.*); слоня́ться (*impf.*); **~ suit** костю́м, пиджа́чная па́ра.

lour ['laʊə(r)], **lower** ['ləʊə(r)] *v.i.* (*lit., fig.*) насу́п|ливаться, -иться; **he ~ed at me** он смотре́л на меня́ насу́пившись; **a ~ing expression** угрю́мое выраже́ние.

louse [laʊs] *n.* вошь; (*sl., of pers.*) гни́да.

v.t. **~ up** (*sl.*) испо́ртить, испога́нить (*both pf.*).

lousy ['laʊzɪ] *adj.* **1.** (*infested with lice*) вши́вый. **2.** (*sl., disgusting, rotten*) парши́вый, отврати́тельный; **he played a ~ trick on me** он мне сде́лал га́дость; **I feel ~ today** я сего́дня чу́вствую себя́ отврати́тельно.

lout [laʊt] *n.* хам.

loutish ['laʊtɪʃ] *adj.* ха́мский; неотёсанный.

lovable ['lʌvəb(ə)l] *adj.* ми́лый, обая́тельный.

love [lʌv] *n.* **1.** любо́вь; **he has a ~ of adventure** он большо́й люби́тель приключе́ний; **feel ~ for, towards s.o.** испы́тывать (*impf.*) любо́вь к кому́-н.; **show ~ to s.o.** прояв|ля́ть, -и́ть любо́вь к кому́-н.; **for ~ of** из любви́ к+*d.*; ра́ди+*g.*; **for the ~ of God** ра́ди Бо́га; **he sent you his ~** он проси́л переда́ть вам серде́чный приве́т; **not for ~ or money** ни за что на све́те; **they married for ~** они́ жени́лись по любви́; **be in ~ (with s.o.)** быть влюблённым в кого́-н.; **fall in ~ with s.o.** влюб|ля́ться, -и́ться в кого́-н.; **make ~** (*have sexual intercourse*) быть бли́зкими; **unrequited ~** неразделённая любо́вь; **~ affair** рома́н; **~ story** рома́н про любо́вь; (*in address*): **(my) ~!** (мой) ми́лый!; (моя́) ми́лая! **2.** (*delightful person, esp. child*) пре́лесть; (*sweetheart, mistress*) люби́мая, возлю́бленная. **3.** (*zero score*) ноль (*m.*); **~ all** счёт ноль-ноль.

v.t. люби́ть (*impf.*); **I ~ the way he smiles** мне ужа́сно нра́вится, как он улыба́ется; **I ~ walking in the rain** я обожа́ю гуля́ть под дождём; **I'd ~ to go to Italy** мне о́чень хоте́лось бы съе́здить в Ита́лию; **I'd ~ you to come** я был бы сча́стлив, е́сли бы вы пришли́; **'Will you come?' — 'Yes. I'd ~ to'** «Вы придёте?» — «Да, с удово́льствием».

cpds. **~-letter** *n.* любо́вная запи́ска; **~-lorn** *adj.* безнадёжно влюблённый; **~-making** *n.* (*intimacy*) физи́ческая бли́зость; **~-match** *n.* брак по любви́; **~sick** *adj.* снеда́емый любо́вью; **~-song** *n.* любо́вная пе́сня.

loveless ['lʌvlɪs] *adj.* нелю́бящий, без любви́.

loveliness ['lʌvlɪnɪs] *n.* (*beauty*) красота́; (*attractiveness*) очарова́ние.

lovely ['lʌvlɪ] *adj.* (*beautiful*) краси́вый, прекра́сный; (*charming, attractive*) преле́стный; **we had a ~ time** мы прекра́сно провели́ вре́мя; **~!** (*excellent!*) замеча́тельно!; отли́чно!

lover ['lʌvə(r)] *n.* любо́вни|к (*fem.* -ца); (*pl.*) влюблённые. **2.** (*devotee*) люби́тель (*m.*); покло́нник.

loving ['lʌvɪŋ] *n.*: **the child needs a lot of ~** ребёнок нужда́ется в любви́ и ла́ске.

adj. лю́бящий; **from your ~ father** от лю́бящего тебя́ отца́; (*tender*) не́жный.

low[1] [ləʊ] *n.* **1.** (*meteor.*) цикло́н. **2.** (**~** *point or level*): **the pound fell to an all-time ~** фунт дости́г небыва́ло ни́зкого у́ровня.

adj. **1.** ни́зкий, невысо́кий; **the chair is too ~** стул сли́шком ни́зкий/ни́зок; **of ~ stature** невысо́кого ро́ста; **~ dress** (*with ~ neck*) пла́тье с ни́зким/глубо́ким вы́резом; **~ gear** пе́рвая ско́рость; **the sun was ~ in the sky** со́лнце стоя́ло ни́зко (над горизо́нтом); **~ blood pressure** пони́женное кровяно́е давле́ние; **~ tide** отли́в; **~ visibility** пони́женная/плоха́я ви́димость; (*geog.*, **~**-*lying*) ни́зкий, ни́зменный; (*of pitch of sound*) ни́зкий; (*of volume of sound*) негро́мкий, ти́хий; **he spoke in a ~ voice** он говори́л, пони́зив го́лос (*or* ти́хим го́лосом); **keep a ~ profile** вести́ себя́ сде́ржанно; **I have a ~ opinion of him** я невысо́кого/нева́жного мне́ния о нём. **2.** (*vulgar, common*): **~ life** жизнь низо́в; **~ language** ни́зменный/вульга́рный язы́к. **3.** (*base*) ни́зкий, по́длый; **a ~ trick** по́длая уло́вка. **4.** (*nearly empty; scanty*): **the river is ~** река́ мелка́/обмеле́ла; **a ~ attendance** ма́лая/плоха́я посеща́емость; **we are getting ~ on sugar** у нас остаётся малова́то са́хару. **5.** (*poor, depressed*): **in ~ spirits** в пода́вленном настрое́нии; **I was feeling ~** я чу́вствовал себя́ нева́жно.

adv. ни́зко; **bow ~** ни́зко кла́няться, поклони́ться; **lay ~** (*fig.*) низв|ерга́ть, -е́ргнуть; **lie ~** (*fig.*) зата́|иваться, -и́ться; **stocks are running ~** запа́сы конча́ются.

cpds. **~-alcohol** *adj.* слабоалкого́льный; **~-born** *adj.* ни́зкого происхожде́ния; **~-calorie** *adj.* малокалори́йный; **~-down** *n.* (*information*) подного́тная (*coll.*); *adj.* по́длый, скве́рный; **~-fat** маложи́рный; **~-frequency** *adj.* низкочасто́тный; **~-grade** *adj.* низкосо́ртный; **~-key** *adj.* (*fig.*) сде́ржанный; **~land** *n.* (*usu. pl.*) ни́зменность, низи́на; *adj.* низи́нный; **~-lying** *adj.* ни́зменный; **~-lying areas** ни́зменности (*f. pl.*); **~-necked** *adj.* с ни́зким вы́резом; **~-paid** малооплачиваемый; **~-powered** *adj.* маломо́щный; **~-spirited** *adj.* уны́лый, пода́вленный; **~-water** *adj.*: **~-water mark** отме́тка у́ровня ни́зкой воды́.

low[2] [ləʊ] *v.i.* (*of cattle*) мыча́ть, за-.

lower[1] ['ləʊə(r)] *adj.* ни́жний; **~ case** (*typ.*) стро́чные бу́квы (*f. pl.*); **the L~ Chamber, House** ни́жняя пала́та; пала́та о́бщин; **~ deck** ни́жняя па́луба; **the ~ orders** ни́зшие сосло́вия; **~ school** мла́дшие кла́ссы.

cpd. **~-class** *adj.* принадлежа́щий к ни́зшему сосло́вию.

v.t. **1.** (*e.g. boat, flag*) спус|ка́ть, -ти́ть; (*eyes*) опус|ка́ть, -ти́ть; (*price*) сн|ижа́ть, -и́зить; (*voice*) пон|ижа́ть, -и́зить. **2.** (*decrease*) ум|еньша́ть, -е́ньшить. **3.** (*debase*) ун|ижа́ть, -и́зить.

lower[2] ['ləʊə(r)] = **lour**

lowly ['ləʊlɪ] *adj.* (*humble*) скро́мный; (*primitive*) ни́зший.

loyal ['lɔɪəl] *adj.* (*faithful*) ве́рный; **he is ~ to his comrades** он ве́рен това́рищам: (*devoted*) пре́данный; **~ supporters of the local team** постоя́нные боле́льщики ме́стной кома́нды.

loyalist ['lɔɪəlɪst] *n.* лояли́ст.

loyalty ['lɔɪəltɪ] *n.* ве́рность, пре́данность, лоя́льность; **political ~** полити́ческая благонадёжность.

lozenge ['lɒzɪndʒ] *n.* табле́тка, лепёшка, пасти́лка.

cpd. **~-shaped** *adj.* ромбови́дный.

LP (*abbr. of* **long-playing record**) долгоигра́ющая пласти́нка.

LSD (*pharm. abbr. of* **lysergic acid diethylamide**) ЛСД, (диэтилами́д лизерги́новой кислоты́).

Lt [lef'tenənt] *n.* (*abbr. of* **Lieutenant**) л-т, (лейтена́нт).

Ltd. ['lɪmɪtɪd] *adj.* (*comm., abbr. of* **limited liability company**) с ограни́ченной отве́тственностью.

lubricant ['lu:brɪkənt] *n.* сма́зка, мазь.

lubricat|e ['lu:brɪ,keɪt] *v.t.* сма́з|ывать, -ать; **~ing oil** сма́зочное ма́сло.

lubrication [,lu:brɪ'keɪʃ(ə)n] *n.* сма́зывание.

lubricator [ˈluːbrɪˌkeɪtə(r)] *n.* (*pers.*) сма́зчик; (*oil*) сма́зка; (*machine component*) лубрика́тор.
lucerne [luːˈsɜːn] *n.* люце́рна.
lucid [ˈluːsɪd] *adj.* я́сный; **he has a ~ mind** у него́ я́сная голова́; **a ~ interval** све́тлый промежу́ток; про́блеск созна́ния.
lucidity [ˌluːˈsɪdɪtɪ] *n.* я́сность.
luck [lʌk] *n.*: **good/bad ~** сча́стье/несча́стье; уда́ча/неуда́ча; **good ~!; the best of ~!** жела́ю уда́чи/успе́ха!; **bad, hard ~!** не повезло́!; **what rotten ~!** како́е невезе́ние!; **worse ~!** к несча́стью/сожале́нию; **as ~ would have it** по/к сча́стью; (*unfortunately*) по/к несча́стью; как назло́; (*in neutral sense*) получи́лось так, что…; **just my ~!** тако́е уж у меня́ везе́ние!; **I had the (good) ~ to be selected** мне посчастли́вилось попа́сть в число́ и́збранных; **he had the bad ~ to break his leg** как на грех, он слома́л себе́ но́гу; **we're in ~ ('s way)** нам везёт; **we're out of ~** (нам) не везёт; **I did it by sheer ~** мне про́сто повезло́; **try one's ~** пыта́ть, по- сча́стья; **he wears a mascot for ~** он но́сит талисма́н на сча́стье.
luckily [ˈlʌkɪlɪ] *adv.* к сча́стью.
luckless [ˈlʌklɪs] *adj.* несчастли́вый, незада́чливый.
lucky [ˈlʌkɪ] *adj.* **1.** (*of pers.*) счастли́вый, уда́чливый; (*of things, actions, events*) уда́чный; **a ~ person** счастли́вец, уда́чник; **he's ~ in everything** ему́ во всём везёт; **he's ~ in business** он уда́члив в дела́х; **~ for you he's not here** ва́ше сча́стье, что его́ здесь нет. **2.** (*bringing luck*): **a ~ charm** счастли́вый талисма́н.
lucrative [ˈluːkrətɪv] *adj.* (*profitable*) при́быльный; (*remunerative*) дохо́дный.
lucre [ˈluːkə(r)] *n.* нажи́ва; **filthy ~** презре́нный мета́лл.
ludicrous [ˈluːdɪkrəs] *adj.* (*absurd*) неле́пый; (*laughable*) смехотво́рный, смешно́й.
lug[1] [lʌg] *n.* (*projection*) ушко́; (*sl., ear*) у́хо.
lug[2] [lʌg] *v.t.* (*coll.*) волочи́ть (*impf.*); тащи́ть (*impf.*).
luggage [ˈlʌgɪdʒ] *n.* бага́ж; **piece of ~** вещь, ме́сто; **left ~ office** ка́мера хране́ния.
cpds. **~-label** *n.* бага́жный ярлы́к; **~-rack** *n.* (*in train*) се́тка/по́лка для багажа́; **~-trolley** *n.* бага́жная теле́жка; **~-van** *n.* бага́жный ваго́н.
lugubrious [luːˈguːbrɪəs, lʊ-] *adj.* (*mournful*) ско́рбный; (*dismal*) мра́чный.
lukewarm [luːkˈwɔːm, ˈluːk-] *adj.* теплова́тый, чуть тёплый; (*fig., indifferent*) прохла́дный.
lull [lʌl] *n.* (*in storm, fighting etc.*) зати́шье; (*in conversation*) па́уза, переры́в.
v.t. (**~** *to sleep*) убаю́к|ивать, -ать; (*allay*) усып|ля́ть, -и́ть.
lullaby [ˈlʌləˌbaɪ] *n.* колыбе́льная (пе́сня).
lumbago [lʌmˈbeɪgəʊ] *n.* люмба́го (*indecl.*); простре́л.
lumbar [ˈlʌmbə(r)] *adj.* поясни́чный.
lumber[1] [ˈlʌmbə(r)] *n.* (*disused furniture etc.*) ру́хлядь, хлам; (*US, timber*) пиломатериа́лы (*m. pl.*).
v.t. (*make untidy with* **~**) завал|ивать, -и́ть (*что чем*); (*encumber*) обременя́ть (*impf.*); **I'm ~ed with my mother-in-law** тёща у меня́ на шее́.
v.i. (*work on tree-felling etc.*) руби́ть/вали́ть (*impf.*) дере́вья; распи́ливать/загота́вливать (*impf.*) лес.
cpds. **~jack** *n.* лесору́б; **~-jacket** *n.* (коро́ткая) рабо́чая ку́ртка; **~-room** *n.* чула́н; **~-yard** *n.* склад пиломатериа́лов.
lumber[2] [ˈlʌmbə(r)] *v.i.* (*also* **~ along**) дви́гаться (*impf.*) тяжело́; перева́ливаться (*impf.*).
lumbering[1] [ˈlʌmbərɪŋ] *n.* лесозаготó́вка.
lumbering[2] [ˈlʌmbərɪŋ] *adj.* (*of pers.*) дви́гающийся тяжело́/неуклю́же; (*of cart etc.*) громыха́ющий.
luminary [ˈluːmɪnərɪ] *n.* (*lit., fig.*) свети́ло.
luminescence [ˌluːmɪˈnes(ə)ns] *n.* свече́ние, люминисце́нция.
luminescent [ˌluːmɪˈnes(ə)nt, ˌljuː-] *adj.* светя́щийся, люминисце́нтный.
luminosity [ˌluːmɪˈnɒsɪtɪ, ˈljuː-] *n.* освещённость.
luminous [ˈluːmɪnəs, ˈljuː-] *adj.* светя́щийся.
lump [lʌmp] *n.* **1.** (*of earth, dough etc.*) ком; **~ of clay** ком гли́ны; (*large piece*) (кру́пный) кусо́к; **~ of sugar** кусо́к са́хара; **~ sugar** кускобо́й са́хар; **~ of ice/snow** глы́ба льда/сне́га; **~ of wood** чурба́н; **~ in the throat** комо́к в го́рле. **2.** (*swelling*) ши́шка, о́пухоль. **3.: ~ sum** пауша́льная су́мма; **they get paid a ~ sum** им пла́тят акко́рдно.
v.t. **1. ~ together** (*collect into heap*) вали́ть (*impf.*), сва́л|ивать, -и́ть в ку́чу; (*treat alike; place in single category*) ста́вить (*impf.*) на одну́ до́ску. **2.: ~ it** (*coll., put up with it*) примири́ться (*pf.*) (*с чем*); **you must ~ it** нра́вится — не нра́вится, а придётся проглоти́ть.
lumpy [ˈlʌmpɪ] *adj.* комкова́тый.
lunacy [ˈluːnəsɪ] *n.* безу́мие, сумасше́ствие.
lunar [ˈluːnə(r), ˈljuː-] *adj.* лу́нный.
lunatic [ˈluːnətɪk] *n.* сумасше́дший; душевнобольно́й.
adj. (*mad*) сумасше́дший; **~ asylum** сумасше́дший дом; психиатри́ческая больни́ца; (*foolish, senseless*) безу́мный; (*eccentric*) чуда́ческий.
lunch [lʌntʃ] *n.* (*midday meal*) обе́д; (второ́й) за́втрак, ленч.
v.i. обе́дать, по-; за́втракать, по-.
cpds. **~-break, ~-hour, ~-time** *nn.* обе́денный переры́в.
luncheon [ˈlʌntʃ(ə)n] *n.* обе́д.
cpds. **~-meat** *n.* мясно́й руле́т; **~-voucher** *n.* тало́н на обе́д.
lung [lʌŋ] *n.* лёгкое; **~ cancer** рак лёгк|ого, -их.
lunge [lʌndʒ, ljuː-] *n.* (*forward movement*) бросо́к; (*in fencing*) вы́пад.
v.i. **~ (out) at** (*fencing, boxing etc.*) сде́лать (*pf.*) вы́пад на+*a.*
lupin [ˈluːpɪn] *n.* люпи́н.
lurch[1] [lɜːtʃ] *n.*: **leave s.o. in the ~** пок|ида́ть, -и́нуть кого́-н. в беде́; подв|оди́ть, -ести́ кого́-н.
lurch[2] [lɜːtʃ] *n.*: (*stagger*) **the ship gave a ~** кора́бль дал крен (*or* накрени́лся).
v.i. шата́ться (*impf.*); поша́т|ываться, -ну́ться; **the drunken man ~ed across the street** пья́ный, поша́тываясь, перешёл у́лицу.
lure [ljʊə(r), lʊə(r)] *n.* (*decoy*) прима́нка; (*fig., enticement*) собла́зн; **the ~ of foreign travel** зама́нчивость заграни́чных путеше́ствий.
v.t. (*fish*) прима́н|ивать, -и́ть; (*persons*) зама́н|ивать, -и́ть; завле|ка́ть, -е́чь; **I was ~d (on) by the promise of a reward** меня́ соблазни́ла перспекти́ва награ́ды; **they were ~d on to destruction** их замани́ли на (по)ги́бель.
lurid [ˈljʊərɪd, ˈlʊə-] *adj.* (*gaudy*) крича́щий; (*sensational*): **a ~ novel** бульва́рный рома́н; **~ details** жу́ткие подро́бности.
lurk [lɜːk] *v.i.* прита́|иваться, -и́ться; **~ about** ждать (*impf.*) притаи́вшись.
luscious [ˈlʌʃəs] *adj.* (*succulent*) со́чный; (*ripe, also fig.*) наливно́й.
lush[1] [lʌʃ] *n.* (*US, drunkard*) пьянчу́жка (*c.g.*).
lush[2] [lʌʃ] *adj.* пы́шный, роско́шный.
lust [lʌst] *n.* **1.** (*sexual passion*) по́хоть, вожделе́ние. **2.** (*craving*): **~ for power** жа́жда вла́сти.
v.i.: **~ for, after s.o.** испы́т|ывать, -а́ть вожделе́ние к кому́-н.; жела́ть (*impf.*) кого́-н.
lustful [ˈlʌstfʊl] *adj.* похотли́вый.
lustre [ˈlʌstə(r)] *n.* (*glaze*) глазу́рь; (*gloss, brilliance*) блес, гля́нец; (*bright light*) сия́ние; (*splendour, glory*) сла́ва; **add ~ to sth.** прид|ава́ть, -а́ть блеск чему́-н.
lustrous [ˈlʌstrəs] *adj.* (*brilliant*) блестя́щий; (*glossy*) глянцеви́тый.

lusty [ˈlʌstɪ] *adj.* (*healthy*) здоро́вый; (*robust*) здоровенный; (*vigorous*) бо́дрый.
lute [lu:t, lju:t] *n.* (*mus.*) лю́тня.
Lutheran [ˈlu:θərən, ˈlju:-] *n.* лютера́н|ин (*fem.* -ка).
adj. лютера́нский.
Lutheranism [ˈlu:θərənˌɪz(ə)m, ˈlju:-] *n.* лютера́нство.
Luxemburg [ˈlʌksəmˌbɜ:g] *n.* Люксембу́рг.
luxuriance [lʌgˈzjʊərɪəns, lʌkˈsj-, lʌgˈʒʊə-] *n.* изоби́лие; бога́тство; пы́шность.
luxuriant [lʌgˈzjʊərɪənt, lʌkˈsj-, lʌgˈʒʊə-] *adj.* (*profuse*) оби́льный; (*of imagination etc.*) бога́тый; (*splendid*) пы́шный; (*of growth*) бу́йный.
luxuriate [lʌgˈzjʊərɪˌeɪt, lʌkˈsj-, lʌgˈʒʊə-] *v.i.* (*enjoy o.s.*): ~ **in sth.** наслажда́ться (*impf.*) чем-н.
luxurious [lʌgˈzjʊərɪəs, lʌkˈsj-, lʌgˈʒʊə-] *adj.* (*sumptuous*) роско́шный; (*splendid*) пы́шный; (*self-indulgent*) расточи́тельный.
luxury [ˈlʌkʃərɪ] *n.* **1.** (*luxuriousness*) ро́скошь; **live in the lap of** ~ жить (*impf.*) в ро́скоши; (*pleasure*) удово́льствие. **2.** (*object of* ~) предме́т ро́скоши; ~ **apartment** роско́шная кварти́ра; но́мер-люкс.
lycée [ˈli:seɪ] *n.* лице́й.
lye [laɪ] *n.* щёлок.
lying[1] [ˈlaɪɪŋ] *n.* (*telling lies*) ложь, враньё.
adj. ло́жный, лжи́вый.
lying[2] [ˈlaɪɪŋ] *n.*: ~ **in state** до́ступ к те́лу имени́того поко́йника.
lymph [lɪmf] *n.* (*physiol.*) ли́мфа.
lymphatic [lɪmˈfætɪk] *adj.* лимфати́ческий; (*fig., of pers.*) вя́лый.
lynch [lɪntʃ] *n.*: ~ **law** суд/зако́н Ли́нча; самосу́д.
v.t. линчева́ть (*impf., pf.*).
lynx [lɪŋks] *n.* рысь.
lyre [ˈlaɪə(r)] *n.* ли́ра.
lyric [ˈlɪrɪk] *n.* **1.** (~ *poem*) лири́ческое стихотворе́ние; (~ *poetry*) ли́рика. **2.** (*pl., theatr., words of song*) слова́ (*nt. pl.*)/текст пе́сни.
adj. лири́ческий.
lyrical [ˈlɪrɪk(ə)l] *adj.* лири́ческий; **he was ~ in his praise of the play** он с воодушевле́нием расхва́ливал пье́су.
lyricism [ˈlɪrɪˌsɪz(ə)m] *n.* лири́зм.

M

m. [ˈmi:tə(r)(z)] *n.* (*abbr. of* **metre(s)**) м, (метр).
MA (*abbr. of* ***Master of Arts***) маги́стр гуманита́рных нау́к.
ma'am [mæm, mɑ:m, məm] *n.* суда́рыня.
mac [mæk] (*coll.*) = **mac(k)intosh**
macabre [məˈkɑ:br] *adj.* мра́чный, жу́ткий.
macadam [məˈkædəm] *n.* макада́м, щебёночное покры́тие.
macadamize [məˈkædəmaɪz] *v.t.*: ~**d road** доро́га с щебёночным покры́тием.
macaroni [ˌmækəˈrəʊnɪ] *n.* макаро́н|ы (*pl., g.* —)
macaroon [ˌmækəˈru:n] *n.* минда́льное пече́нье.
macaw [məˈkɔ:] *n.* а́ра (*m. indecl.*).
mace[1] [meɪs] *n.* (*club; staff of office*) булава́; жезл.
mace[2] [meɪs] *n.* (*spice*) муска́т.
macedoine [ˈmæsɪˌdwɑ:n] *n.* (*cul.*) маседуа́н.
machete [məˈtʃetɪ, məˈʃetɪ] *n.* маче́те (*indecl.*).
Machiavellian [ˌmækɪəˈvelɪən] *adj.* макиаве́ллевский.
machination [ˌmækɪˈneɪʃ(ə)n, ˌmæʃ-] *n.* (*usu. pl.*) махина́ции; ко́зни (*f. pl.*).
machine [məˈʃi:n] *n.* **1.** (*mechanical device, apparatus*) маши́на, механи́зм; **the ~ age** век маши́н; ~ **shop** механи́ческий цех; (~-*tool*) стано́к; **grinding** ~ шлифова́льный стано́к. **2.** (*means of transport*) маши́на. **3.** (*controlling organization*) аппара́т; **party** ~ парти́йный аппара́т.
v.t. (*on lathe etc.*) обраб|а́тывать, -о́тать (на станке́ *or* механи́ческим спо́собом); (*on sewing-*~) шить, с- на маши́не.
cpds. ~**-gun** *n.* пулемёт; *v.t.* (*fire at*) обстре́л|ивать, -я́ть; (*shoot down*) расстре́л|ивать, -я́ть; ~**-gunner** *n.* пулемётчик; ~**-made** *adj.*: ~**-made goods** това́р фабри́чного произво́дства.
machinery [məˈʃi:nərɪ] *n.* (*collect., machines*) маши́ны (*f. pl.*), те́хника; (*mechanism*) механи́зм; (*fig.*): **the ~ of government** прави́тельственная структу́ра.
machinist [məˈʃi:nɪst] *n.* машини́ст; (*sewing-machine operator*) шве́йник, (*fem.*) швея́.
mackerel [ˈmækr(ə)l] *n.* макре́ль, ску́мбрия.
mac(k)intosh [ˈmækɪnˌtɒʃ] *n.* непромока́емый плащ, макинто́ш.
macro [ˈmækrəʊ] *n.* (*comput.*) макрокома́нда.
macrocosm [ˈmækrəʊˌkɒz(ə)m] *n.* макроко́см.
mad [mæd] *adj.* **1.** (*insane*) сумасше́дший; **go** ~ сходи́ть, сойти́ с ума́; **drive s.o.** ~ св|оди́ть, -ести́ кого́-н. с ума́. **2.** (*of animals*) бе́шеный. **3.** (*wildly foolish*) шально́й; **a ~ escapade** безрассу́дная вы́ходка; ~**ly in love** безу́мно влюблённый; ~**ly expensive** безу́мно дорого́й. **4.** (*coll., angry, annoyed*) серди́тый; ~ **with anger** вне себя́ от гне́ва; **be, get** ~ вы́йти (*pf.*) из себя́; **be, get ~ with s.o.** серди́ться, рас- на кого́-н. **5.**: ~ **about** (*infatuated with, enthusiastic for*) в восто́рге (*or* без па́мяти) от+*g.*; **she was ~ about him** она́ была́ от него́ без ума́; **his wife was ~ about cats** его́ жена́ была́ поме́шана на ко́шках. **6.**: **like** ~ безу́держно; **I rushed like** ~ я помча́лся как угоре́лый.
cpds. ~**cap** *n.* сорвиголова́ (*c.g.*); *adj.* сумасбро́дный; ~**house** *n.* сумасше́дший дом; ~**man** *n.* сумасше́дший; ~**woman** *n.* сумасше́дшая.
Madagascar [ˌmædəˈgæskə(r)] *n.* Мадагаска́р.
madam [ˈmædəm] *n.* (*form of address*) мада́м, суда́рыня.
madden [ˈmæd(ə)n] *v.t.* (*persons*) раздраж|а́ть, -и́ть; (*animals*) беси́ть, вз-.
maddening [ˈmædənɪŋ] *adj.* несно́сный.
madder [ˈmædə(r)] *n.* (*plant*) маре́на.
Madeira [məˈdɪərə] *n.* Маде́йра; (*wine*) маде́ра.
mademoiselle [ˌmædəmwəˈzel] *n.* мадемуазе́ль.
made-to-measure [ˈmeɪdtəˈmeʒə(r)]*adj.* сде́ланный (как) на зака́з.
madness [ˈmædnɪs] *n.* (*insanity*) сумасше́ствие; (*of animals*) бе́шенство; (*folly*) безу́мие.
madonna [məˈdɒnə] *n.* мадо́нна; ~ **lily** бе́лая ли́лия.
madrigal [ˈmædrɪg(ə)l] *n.* мадрига́л.
maelstrom [ˈmeɪlstrəm] *n.* водоворо́т; (*fig.*) вихрь (*m.*).
maestro [ˈmaɪstrəʊ] *n.* маэ́стро (*m. indecl.*).
Mafia [ˈmæfɪə, ˈmɑ:-] *n.* ма́фия; (*fig.*) кли́ка.
magazine[1] [ˌmægəˈzi:n] *n.* **1.** (*mil. store*) по́греб боеприпа́сов. **2.** (*cartridge chamber*) магази́нная коро́бка; (*attr.*) магази́нный.
magazine[2] [ˌmægəˈzi:n] *n.* (*periodical*) журна́л; (*attr.*) журна́льный.
magenta [məˈdʒentə] *n.* фукси́н.
adj. краснова́то-лило́вого цве́та.
maggot [ˈmægət] *n.* личи́нка.
maggoty [ˈmægətɪ] *adj.* черви́вый.
Magi [ˈmeɪdʒaɪ] *n.*: **the** ~ волхвы́ (*m. pl.*).
magic [ˈmædʒɪk] *n.* (*lit., fig.*) ма́гия, волшебство́; **as if by** ~ как по волшебству́.
adj. волше́бный, маги́ческий; ~ **lantern** волше́бный

фона́рь; ~ **wand** волше́бная па́лочка.

magical ['mædʒɪk(ə)l] *adj.* феери́ческий, волше́бный.

magician [mə'dʒɪʃ(ə)n] *n.* (*sorcerer*) волше́бник; (*conjurer*) фо́кусник.

magisterial [ˌmædʒɪ'stɪərɪəl] *adj.* (*of a magistrate*) суде́йский; (*authoritative*) авторите́тный.

magistracy ['mædʒɪstrəsɪ] *n.* магистрату́ра.

magistrate ['mædʒɪstrət] *n.* судья́ (*m.*).

Magna C(h)arta [ˌmægnə 'kɑːtə] *n.* Вели́кая ха́ртия во́льностей.

magnanimity [ˌmægnə'nɪmɪtɪ] *n.* великоду́шие.

magnanimous [mæg'nænɪməs] *adj.* великоду́шный.

magnate ['mægneɪt, -nɪt] *n.* магна́т.

magnesia [mæg'niːʒə, -ʃə, -zjə] *n.* магне́зия, о́кись ма́гния; **milk of** ~ молочко́ магне́зии.

magnesium [mæg'niːzɪəm] *n.* ма́гний.

magnet ['mægnɪt] *n.* (*lit.*, *fig.*) магни́т.

magnetic [mæg'netɪk] *adj.* магни́тный; ~ **tape** магнитоле́нта; (*fig.*): ~ **personality** притяга́тельная/магнети́ческая ли́чность.

magnetism ['mægnɪˌtɪz(ə)m] *n.* магнети́зм; (*fig.*) притяга́тельность.

magnetize ['mægnɪˌtaɪz] *v.t.* намагни́|чивать, -тить.

magneto [mæg'niːtəʊ] *n.* магне́то (*indecl.*).

magnification [ˌmægnɪfɪ'keɪʃ(ə)n] *n.* увеличе́ние; (*of a radio signal*) усиле́ние; (*exaggeration*) преувеличе́ние.

magnificence [mæg'nɪfɪs(ə)ns] *n.* великоле́пие.

magnificent [mæg'nɪfɪs(ə)nt] *adj.* великоле́пный.

magnify ['mægnɪˌfaɪ] *v.t.* (*cause to appear larger*) увели́чи|вать, -ть; ~**ing-glass** увеличи́тельное стекло́, лу́па; (*exaggerate*) преувели́чи|вать, -ть.

magnitude ['mægnɪˌtjuːd] *n.* (*size*) величина́; (*importance*) ва́жность; **a matter of the first** ~ де́ло первостепе́нной ва́жности.

magnolia [mæg'nəʊlɪə] *n.* магно́лия.

magpie ['mægpaɪ] *n.* соро́ка.

Magyar ['mægjɑː(r)] *n.* **1.** (*pers.*) мадья́р (*fem.* -ка); венг|р (*fem.* -е́рка). **2.** (*language*) венге́рский язы́к.

adj. мадья́рский, венге́рский.

Maharaja(h) [ˌmɑːhə'rɑːdʒə] *n.* магара́джа (*m.*).

mahogany [mə'hɒgənɪ] *n.* (*wood*, *tree*) кра́сное де́рево; (*colour*) цвет кра́сного де́рева.

maid [meɪd] *n.* **1.** (*girl*, *unmarried woman*) де́ва, деви́ца; **old** ~ ста́рая де́ва. **2.** (*domestic servant*) домрабо́тница; (*in hotel*) го́рничная.

cpd. ~**servant** *n.* прислу́га, служа́нка.

maiden ['meɪd(ə)n] *n.* де́ва.

adj. **1.** (*of a girl*) де́ви́чий; ~ **name** де́вичья фами́лия. **2.** (*unmarried*): ~ **aunt** незаму́жняя тётка. **3.** (*first*): ~ **speech** пе́рвая речь (новои́збранного члéна парла́мента); ~ **voyage** пе́рвый рейс.

cpds. ~**head** *n.* де́вственность; ~**ly** *adj.* де́ви́чий.

mail[1] [meɪl] *n.* **1.** (*postal system*) по́чта; ~ **order** почто́вый зака́з/перево́д. **2.** (~*-train*) почто́вый по́езд. **3.** (*letters*) по́чта, пи́сьма (*nt. pl.*); **has the** ~ **come?** по́чта была́?

v.t. отпр|авля́ть, -а́вить (по по́чте); **the firm has me on its** ~**ing-list** я состою́ в спи́ске подпи́счиков фи́рмы.

cpds. ~**bag** *n.* мешо́к для почто́вой корреспонде́нции; ~**box** *n.* (*US*) почто́вый я́щик; ~**-order** *adj.* торгу́ющий по почто́вым зака́зам; ~**-order firm** торго́во-посы́лочная фи́рма; ~**-van** *n.* (*road*) автомоби́ль, собира́ющий и развозя́щий по́чту; (*rail*) почто́вый ваго́н.

mailed [meɪld] *adj.*: ~ **fist** (*fig.*) брони́рованный кула́к.

maim [meɪm] *v.t.* кале́чить, ис-; **he was** ~**ed for life** он оста́лся кале́кой на всю жизнь.

main [meɪn] *n.* **1.**: **in the** ~ в основно́м. **2.**: **with might and** ~ изо всех сил. **3.** (*sg. and pl.*, *principal supply line*) магистра́ль; (*sewerage*) канализа́ция; (*water*) водопрово́д; водопрово́дная магистра́ль; **turn the water off at the** ~**(s)!** перекро́йте водопрово́д; (*gas*) газопрово́д; (*electricity*) ка́бель (*m.*); ~**s supply** электроснабже́ние; **the** ~**s voltage is 250** напряже́ние электросе́ти 250 вольт.

adj. гла́вный, основно́й; ~ **course** (*of meal*) жарко́е; ~ **line** (*rail*) железнодоро́жная магистра́ль; **the** ~ **point** основно́й/гла́вный пункт, суть; ~ **road** магистра́ль; ~ **street** гла́вная у́лица.

cpds. ~**land** *n.* (*continent*) матери́к; (*opp. island*): **they live on the** ~**land** они́ живу́т на большо́й земле́; ~**mast** *n.* грот-ма́чта; ~**sail** *n.* грот; ~**spring** *n.* (*of watch*) ходова́я пружи́на; (*fig.*) гла́вная дви́жущая си́ла; ~**stay** *n.* (*fig.*) опо́ра; ~**stream** *n.* (*fig.*) госпо́дствующая тенде́нция.

mainly ['meɪnlɪ] *adv.* гла́вным о́бразом.

maintain [meɪn'teɪn] *v.t.* **1.** (*keep up*) подде́рживать (*impf.*); (*preserve*) сохран|я́ть, -и́ть; (*continue*) продолжа́ть (*impf.*); **if prices are** ~**ed** е́сли це́ны уде́ржатся на пре́жнем у́ровне; **law and order must be** ~**ed** законопоря́док до́лжен соблюда́ться; **he** ~**ed his ground** он стоя́л на своём; **he** ~**ed silence** он храни́л молча́ние. **2.** (*support*) содержа́ть (*impf.*); **he has a wife and child to** ~ ему́ прихо́дится содержа́ть жену́ и ребёнка. **3.** (*keep in repair*): **he** ~**s his car himself** он ремонти́рует свою́ маши́ну сам. **4.** (*defend*) отст|а́ивать, -оя́ть; **he** ~**ed his rights** он отста́ивал свои́ права́. **5.** (*assert as true*) утвержда́ть (*impf.*); **he** ~**ed his innocence** он наста́ивал на свое́й невино́вности.

maintenance ['meɪntənəns] *n.* **1.** (*maintaining*) подде́ржа́ние; сохране́ние. **2.** (*payment in support of dependants*) содержа́ние. **3.** (*care or repair of machinery etc.*) техни́ческое обслу́живание; ~ **crew** ремо́нтная брига́да; ~ **manual** руково́дство по ухо́ду и обслу́живанию.

maison(n)ette [ˌmeɪzə'net] *n.* двухэта́жная кварти́ра.

maître d'hôtel [ˌmetrə dəʊ'tel, ˌmeɪt-] *n.* метрдоте́ль (*m.*).

maize [meɪz] *n.* кукуру́за, ма́ис.

Maj. ['meɪdʒə(r)] *n.* (*abbr. of* **Major(-)**) м, (майо́р).

majestic [mə'dʒestɪk] *adj.* вели́чественный.

majesty ['mædʒɪstɪ] *n.* (*stateliness*) вели́чественность; (*title*): **His/Her M**~ его́/её вели́чество.

major ['meɪdʒə(r)] *n.* (*rank*) майо́р; (*mus.*: ~ **key**) мажо́р.

adj. **1.** (*greater*) бо́льший; **the** ~ **part** бо́льшая часть; (*principal*, *more important*) гла́вный; ~ **road** гла́вная доро́га; **the** ~ **part in a play** гла́вная роль в пье́се. **2.** (*significant*) кру́пный; **a** ~ **success** кру́пный успе́х; ~ **advances in science** значи́тельные успе́хи в нау́ке; **a** ~ **operation** кру́пная опера́ция; **a** ~ **war** больша́я война́. **3.** (*elder*): **Smith M**~ Смит ста́рший. **4.** (*mus.*) мажо́рный.

v.i.: **he** ~**ed in physics** (*US*) он специализи́ровался в фи́зике.

cpds. ~**-domo** *n.* мажордо́м; ~**-general** *n.* генера́л-майо́р.

Majorca [mə'jɔːkə, -'dʒɔː-] *n.* Мальо́рка, Майо́рка.

majority [mə'dʒɒrɪtɪ] *n.* **1.** (*greater part or number*) бо́льшая часть; большинство́; (*in elections etc.*): **they gained a** ~ **of 30** они́ получи́ли на 30 голосо́в бо́льше; **he won by a large** ~ он победи́л значи́тельным большинство́м (голосо́в). **2.** (*full age*) совершенноле́тие.

make [meɪk] *n.* (*product of particular firm or person*): **a good** ~ **of car** автомоби́ль хоро́шей ма́рки; **is this jam your own** ~**?** э́то варе́нье ва́шего со́бственного изготовле́ния?

v.t. **1.** (*fashion*, *create*, *construct*) де́лать, с-; (*build*) стро́ить, по-; **what is this made of?** из чего́ э́то сде́лано?; **you must think I'm made of money** вы, наве́рно, ду́маете, что я де́нежный мешо́к; **this chair is made to last** э́тот стул сде́лан про́чно; **they were made for each other** они́ бы́ли со́зданы друг для дру́га. **2.** (*sew together*) шить, с-; **a suit made to order** костю́м, сши́тый на зака́з. **3.** (*utter*) произн|оси́ть, -ести́; **he made a speech** он вы́ступил с ре́чью; **she made a remark** она́ сде́лала замеча́ние; **don't ~ a noise** не шуми́те. **4.** (*compile, compose*) сост|авля́ть, -а́вить; **~ a list!** соста́вьте спи́сок!; **have you made your will?** вы соста́вили завеща́ние? **5.** (*bodily movements, etc.: execute*) де́лать, с-; *see also under n. obj.* **6.** (*manufacture, produce*) изгот|овля́ть, -о́вить; произв|оди́ть, -ести́; **the factory ~s shoes** заво́д изготовля́ет о́бувь; **paper is made here** зде́сь произво́дится бума́га; **he made a good impression** он произвёл хоро́шее впечатле́ние; **~ a film** сн|има́ть, -ять фильм. **7.** (*prepare*) гото́вить, при-; вари́ть, с-; **she made breakfast** она́ пригото́вила за́втрак; **is the coffee made?** ко́фе гото́в?; **~ a fire** разв|оди́ть, -ести́ ого́нь; **~ a bed** (*prepare it for sleeping*) стлать, по- посте́ль; (*tidy it after use*) уб|ира́ть, -ра́ть посте́ль. **8.** (*establish, create*): **~ a rule** устан|а́вливать, -ови́ть пра́вило. **9.** (*equal, result in*) равня́ться (*impf.*) *+d.*; **four plus two ~s six** четы́ре плюс два равня́ется шести́; **it ~s no difference** всё равно́; (*constitute*) **he ~s a good chairman** он хоро́ший председа́тель; **it ~s (good) sense** э́то разу́мно; (*become, turn out to be*): **she will ~ a good pianist** из неё вы́йдет хоро́шая пиани́стка. **10.** (*construe, understand*) пон|има́ть, -я́ть; **what do you ~ of this sentence?** как вы понима́ете э́то предложе́ние?; (*estimate, consider to be*): **what do you ~ the time?** кото́рый час на ва́ших часа́х? **11.:** **~ much of: the author ~s much of his childhood** а́втор придаёт большо́е значе́ние своему́ де́тству; **~ little of** не придава́ть (*impf.*) большо́го значе́ния *+d.*; **~ the best of a bad job** де́лать, с- хоро́шую ми́ну при плохо́й игре́; **~ the most of** испо́льзовать (*impf., pf.*) максима́льно. **12.** (*reach*) дост|ига́ть, -и́чь *+g.*; **we made the bridge by dusk** мы добра́лись до моста́, когда́ ста́ло смерка́ться; **we just made the train** мы е́ле поспе́ли на по́езд; **he made it** (*succeeded*) **after three years** он дости́г успе́ха че́рез три го́да; (*gain*) получ|а́ть, -и́ть; **he made a clear profit** он получи́л чи́стую при́быль; (*earn*) зараб|а́тывать, -о́тать; **he ~s a good living** он хорошо́ зараба́тывает; (*ensure*) обеспе́чи|вать, -ть; **this success made his career** э́тот успе́х обеспе́чил ему́ карье́ру. **13.** (*cause to be*) де́лать, с- *+a. and i.*; **the rain ~s the road slippery** от дождя́ доро́га де́лается ско́льзкой; **she made his life miserable** она́ отрави́ла ему́ жизнь; **~ s.o. angry** серди́ть, рас- кого́-н.; (*appoint, elect*): **they made him a general** его́ произвели́ в генера́лы; **they made him chairman** его́ вы́брали председа́телем. **14.** (*compel, cause to*) заст|авля́ть, -а́вить; побу|жда́ть, -ди́ть; **he was made to kneel** его́ заста́вили стать на коле́ни; **I'll ~ you pay for this!** вы у меня́ за э́то запла́тите!; **don't ~ me laugh!** не смеши́те меня́!; **it ~s you think** э́то заставля́ет заду́маться; **look what you made me do!** ≃ всё из-за вас!; смотри́, до чего́ ты меня́ довёл!; **she made believe she was crying** она́ сде́лала вид, бу́дто пла́чет; **~ sth. do, ~ do with sth.** об|ходи́ться, -ойти́сь с чем-н.; **we must ~ do on our pension** мы должны́ обойти́сь одно́й пе́нсией.

v.i. **1.** (*with certain preps.: move, proceed*): **~ for** (*head towards*) напр|авля́ться, -а́виться на*+a. or* к*+d.*; (*depart for*) отпр|авля́ться, -а́виться в/на*+a.*; (*conduce to*) спосо́бствовать (*impf.*) *+d.* **2.** (*act, behave*): **he made as if to go** он сде́лал вид, что хо́чет уйти́; **may I ~ so bold as to come in?** позво́льте мне взять на себя́ сме́лость войти́. **3.** (*~ a profit*): **did you ~ on the deal?** ну как, кре́пко нагре́ли ру́ки на э́той сде́лке? (*coll.*).

with advs.: **~ away** *v.i.* = **~ off; ~ away with** (*get rid of*) изб|авля́ться, -а́виться от*+g.*; (*kill*) прик|а́нчивать, -о́нчить; **~ away with o.s.** (*or* **one's life**) поко́нчить (*pf.*) с собо́й; **~ off** *v.i.* (*hurry away*) сбе|га́ть, -жа́ть; **he made off with all speed** он пусти́лся бежа́ть со всех ног; (*escape, abscond*) скр|ыва́ться, -ы́ться; **~ out** *v.t.* (*write out*): **~ out a cheque** выпи́сывать, вы́писать чек; **~ out a report** сост|авля́ть, -а́вить отчёт; (*assert, maintain*) утвержда́ть (*impf.*); **you ~ me out to be a liar** по-ва́шему выхо́дит, что я лгу; (*conclude*): **how do you ~ that out?** как э́то у вас получа́ется?; (*understand*) раз|бира́ться, -обра́ться в*+p.*; **I can't ~ him out** я не могу́ его́ поня́ть; (*discern, distinguish*) различ|а́ть, -и́ть; *v.i.* (*coll., get on*): **how did he ~ out?** как он спра́вился (с э́той зада́чей)?; **~ over** *v.t.* (*refashion*) переде́л|ывать, -ать; (*transfer*) перев|оди́ть, -ести́; **~ up** *v.t.* (*complete*): **~ up the complement** сост|авля́ть, -а́вить кома́нду, гру́ппу *и т.п.*; (*pay; pay the residue of*) допла́|чивать, -ти́ть; (*repay*) возме|ща́ть, -сти́ть; (*recover*) навёрст|ывать, -а́ть; (*prepare, ~ ready*) гото́вить, при-/из-; **ask the chemist to ~ up this prescription** попроси́те фармаце́вта пригото́вить лека́рство по э́тому реце́пту; **~ up a bed** заст|ила́ть, -ла́ть (*or* -ели́ть) посте́ль; **~ up a road** асфальти́ровать (*impf., pf.*) доро́гу; (*typ.: set up*) наб|ира́ть, -ра́ть; (*sew together*) шить, с-; (*fig.*): **~ up one's mind** реш|а́ть, -и́ть; **my mind is made up** я при́нял реше́ние; (*form, compose; compile*) сост|авля́ть, -а́вить; **life is made up of disappointments** жизнь полна́ разочарова́ний; (*concoct, invent*) выду́мывать; сочин|я́ть, -и́ть; (*assemble*) соб|ира́ть, -ра́ть; (*settle*) ула́|живать, -дить; **~ (it) up** (*be reconciled*) мири́ться, по-; **let's ~ it up and be friends** дава́йте помири́мся; (*for a stage performance*) гримирова́ть, за-; (*with cosmetics*) кра́сить, по-; **she was heavily made up** она́ была́ си́льно накра́шена; *v.i.* (*be reconciled*) мири́ться, по-; (*for the stage*) гримирова́ться, за-; (*use cosmetics*) кра́ситься, на-; **~ up for** (*compensate for*) возме|ща́ть, -сти́ть; **this will ~ up for everything** э́тим всё бу́дет компенси́ровано; **~ up to** (*curry favour with*) подли́з|ываться, -а́ться к*+d.*

cpds. **~-believe** *n.*: **he lives in a world of ~-believe** он живёт в ми́ре грёз; **it's all ~-believe** э́то — сплошна́я фанта́зия; **~shift** *n.* вре́менное приспособле́ние; (*attr.*): **a ~shift dinner** на́скоро пригото́вленный обе́д; **~-up** *n.* (*composition*): **there is some cowardice in his ~-up** он не́сколько трусова́т; (*theatr.*) грим; **put on ~-up** гримирова́ться, за-; (*cosmetics*) космети́ческие това́ры (*m. pl.*); **~-up (room)** (*theatr., etc.*) грими́рная; **~weight** *n.* дове́сок; противове́с.

maker ['meɪkə(r)] *n.* (*manufacturer*) производи́тель (*m.*), изготови́тель (*m.*); (*relig., creator*): **the M~ of the universe** творе́ц вселе́нной.

making ['meɪkɪŋ] *n.* **1.** (*that which makes s.o. successful etc.; decisive influence*): **this incident was the ~ of him** благодаря́ э́тому собы́тию, он вы́шел в лю́ди. **2.** (*pl., potential qualities*): **he has all the ~s of a general** у него́ есть все зада́тки, что́бы стать генера́лом. **3.** (*construction*) стро́йка, построе́ние; (*creation*) созда́ние; (*compilation*) составле́ние; (*manufacture, production*) изготовле́ние, произво́дство; (*preparation*) приготовле́ние.

malachite ['mæləˌkaɪt] *n.* малахи́т; (*attr.*) малахи́товый.

maladjusted [ˌmælə'dʒʌstɪd] *adj.* (*fig., of pers.*) пло́хо приспосо́бленный; **~ children** трудновоспиту́емые де́ти.

maladjustment [ˌmælə'dʒʌstmənt] *n.* плоха́я приспосо́бляемость.

maladministration [ˌmælədˌmɪnɪ'streɪʃ(ə)n] *n.* плохо́е управле́ние.
maladroit [ˌmælə'drɔɪt, 'mæl-] *adj.* (*clumsy*) нело́вкий; (*tactless*) беста́ктный.
malady ['mælədɪ] *n.* (*lit.*, *fig.*) неду́г, боле́знь.
malaise [mə'leɪz] *n.* (*bodily discomfort*) недомога́ние; (*disquiet*) беспоко́йство.
malapropos [ˌmælæprə'pəʊ] *adv.* некста́ти.
malaria [mə'leərɪə] *n.* маляри́я.
malarial [mə'leərɪəl] *adj.* маляри́йный.
Malawi [mə'lɑːwɪ] *n.* Мала́ви (*nt. indecl.*).
Malaya [mə'leɪə] *n.* Мала́йя.
Malaysia [mə'leɪzɪə, -ʒə] *n.* Мала́йзия.
malcontent ['mælkənˌtent] *n.* & *adj.* недово́льный.
male [meɪl] *n.* (*pers.*) мужчи́на (*m.*); (*animal etc.*) саме́ц.
adj. мужско́й; ~ **animal** саме́ц; ~ **model** манеке́нщик; ~ **nurse** санита́р.
malediction [ˌmælɪ'dɪkʃ(ə)n] *n.* прокля́тие.
malefactor ['mælɪˌfæktə(r)] *n.* злоде́й.
maleficent [mə'lefɪs(ə)nt] *adj.* (*hurtful*) па́губный; (*criminal*) престу́пный.
malevolence [mə'levələns] *n.* недоброжела́тельность, злора́дство.
malevolent [mə'levələnt] *adj.* недоброжела́тельный, злора́дный.
malfeasance [mæl'fiːz(ə)ns] *n.* должностно́е преступле́ние.
malformation [ˌmælfɔː'meɪʃ(ə)n] *n.* уро́дство.
malformed [mæl'fɔːmd] *adj.* уро́дливый.
malfunction [mæl'fʌŋkʃ(ə)n] *n.* неиспра́вная рабо́та, отка́з.
v.i. неиспра́вно де́йствовать (*impf.*).
malice ['mælɪs] *n.* **1.** (*ill-will*) зло́ба; **bear ~ to(wards), against s.o.** таи́ть, за- зло́бу на кого́-н. (*or* про́тив кого́-н.); **I bear you no ~** я не пита́ю к вам зло́бы. **2.** (*leg.*, *wrongful intent*): **with ~ aforethought** злоумы́шленно.
malicious [mə'lɪʃəs] *adj.* (*of pers.*) злой; (*of thought, act etc.*) зло́бный; ~ **intent** престу́пное наме́рение.
malign [mə'laɪn] *adj.* па́губный.
v.t. (*slander*) клевета́ть, на- на+*a.*; (*defame*) поро́чить, о-; **much-~ed** оклеве́танный.
malignancy [mə'lɪgnənsɪ] *n.* зло́бность; (*med.*) злока́чественность.
malignant [mə'lɪgnənt] *adj.* злой, зло́бный; (*med.*) злока́чественный.
malinger [mə'lɪŋgə(r)] *v.i.* симули́ровать (*impf.*, *pf.*) боле́знь.
malingerer [mə'lɪŋgərə(r)] *n.* симуля́нт (*fem.* -ка).
mall [mæl, mɔːl] *n.* алле́я; (*shopping precinct*) торго́вый центр.
mallard ['mælɑːd] *n.* кря́ква.
malleability [ˌmælɪə'bɪlɪtɪ] *n.* ко́вкость; (*fig.*) пода́тливость.
malleable ['mælɪəb(ə)l] *adj.* (*of metal etc.*) ко́вкий; (*of pers.*) пода́тливый.
mallet ['mælɪt] *n.* деревя́нный молото́к; колоту́шка.
mallow ['mæləʊ] *n.* ма́льва, просвирня́к.
malnutrition [ˌmælnjuː'trɪʃ(ə)n] *n.* недоеда́ние.
malodorous [mæl'əʊdərəs] *adj.* злово́нный.
malpractice [mæl'præktɪs] *n.* (*wrongdoing*) противозако́нное де́йствие; (*leg.*, *of physician*) престу́пная небре́жность (врача́).
malt [mɔːlt, mɒlt] *n.* со́лод; ~ **liquor** со́лодовый напи́ток.
Malta ['mɔːltə, 'mɒltə] *n.* Ма́льта.
maltreat [mæl'triːt] *v.t.* ду́рно обраща́ться (*impf.*) с+*i.*
maltreatment [mæl'triːtmənt] *n.* дурно́е обраще́ние (*с кем*).
mama ['mæmə, mə'mɑː], **mamma** ['mæmə] *n.* ма́ма, ма́мочка; **~'s boy** ма́менькин сыно́к.
mammal ['mæm(ə)l] *n.* млекопита́ющее (живо́тное).
mammary ['mæmərɪ] *adj.*: ~ **gland** моло́чная железа́.
mammogram ['mæməˌgræm] *n.* маммогра́мма.
mammoth ['mæməθ] *n.* ма́монт.
adj. (*huge*) гига́нтский, грома́дный.
mammy ['mæmɪ] = **mama**
man [mæn] *n.* **1.** (*person, human being*) челове́к (*pl.* лю́ди); **what can a ~ do?** что (тут) поде́лаешь?; **as one ~** все как оди́н; **to a ~** все до одного́; **any ~ = anybody; no ~ = nobody; ~ about town** све́тский челове́к; **~ in the street** сре́дний челове́к; **a ~ in a thousand** ре́дкостный челове́к; **~ of action** челове́к де́йствия/де́ла; **~ of character** челове́к с хара́ктером; **~ of letters** литера́тор; **~ of means** состоя́тельный челове́к; **~ of principle** принципиа́льный челове́к; **~ of property** состоя́тельный челове́к; **~ of his word** челове́к сло́ва; **~ of few words** немногосло́вный челове́к; **~ of the world** быва́лый челове́к; **he is an Oxford ~** он выпускни́к О́ксфорда; **he is his own ~** он сам себе́ хозя́ин; **he's just the ~ for the job** он со́здан для э́того; **I'm your ~** я и́менно тот, кто вам ну́жен. **2.** (*mankind*) челове́к, челове́чество; **the rights of ~** права́ челове́ка. **3.** (*adult male*) мужчи́на (*m.*); **they talked ~ to ~** они́ говори́ли как мужчи́на с мужчи́ной; **old ~** стари́к; **young ~** молодо́й челове́к; (*implying virility or fortitude*): **it will make a ~ of him** э́то сде́лает из него́ настоя́щего мужчи́ну; **be a ~!** бу́дьте мужчи́ной! **4.** (*in address*): **speak up, ~!** говори́те же!; **tell me, my (good) ~ ...** скажи́те мне, дружо́к... **5.** (*husband*) муж; **they lived as ~ and wife** они́ жи́ли как муж и жена́. **6.: best ~** (*at wedding*) ша́фер. **7.** (*servant, esp. valet*) слуга́ (*m.*). **8.** (*pl., soldiers*) солда́ты; (*sailors*) матро́сы; (*employees*) рабо́чие. **9.** (*piece in chess*) фигу́ра; (*in draughts*) ша́шка; (*in other games*) фи́шка.
v.t. **1.** (*mil., equip*) укомплекто́в|ывать, -а́ть ли́чным соста́вом. **2.** (*occupy*) зан|има́ть, -я́ть; **~ the guns** обслу́живать (*impf.*) ору́дия; **a ~ned spacecraft** пилоти́руемый косми́ческий кора́бль.
cpds. **~handle** *v.t.* (*move by manual effort*) та|ска́ть (*indet.*), -щи́ть (*det.*) (вручну́ю); (*treat roughly*) изб|ива́ть, -и́ть; **~hole** *n.* (*inspection well*) смотрово́й коло́дец; (*naut.*) люк; **~-hour** *n.* челове́ко-час; **~-hunt** *n.* ро́зыск, полице́йская обла́ва; **~kind** *n.* челове́чество; **~-made** *adj.* иску́сственный; (*text.*) синтети́ческий; **~-of-war, ~-o'-war** *nn.* вое́нный кора́бль; **~power** *n.* рабо́чая си́ла; **~servant** *n.* слуга́; **~slaughter** *n.* непредумы́шленное уби́йство; уби́йство по неосторо́жности.
manacle ['mænək(ə)l] *n.* нару́чник.
v.t. над|ева́ть, -е́ть нару́чники +*d.*
manag|e ['mænɪdʒ] *v.t.* **1.** (*control, conduct*) управля́ть, руководи́ть, заве́довать (*all impf.* +*i.*); **they ~ed the business between them** они́ вдвоём управля́ли предприя́тием; **the estate was ~ed by his brother** име́нием управля́л его́ брат; **~e a household** вести́ (*det.*) (дома́шнее) хозя́йство; **~ing director** дире́ктор-распоряди́тель (*m.*). **2.** (*handle*) владе́ть (*impf.*) +*i.*; **she can ~e a bicycle** она́ уме́ет е́здить на велосипе́де; **can you ~e the car by yourself?** вы мо́жете са́ми спра́виться с маши́ной?; **I can't ~e it** э́то мне не по си́лам. **3.** (*be ~er of*): **he has ~ed the team for 10 years** он руководи́л кома́ндой в тече́ние десяти́ лет; **who ~es this department?** кто заве́дует э́тим отде́лом? **4.** (*cope with*) спр|авля́ться, -а́виться с+*i.*; **I can't ~e this work** я не спра́влюсь с э́той рабо́той. **5.** (*contrive*) суме́ть (*pf.*); умудр|я́ться, -и́ться; **he ~ed to answer** он суме́л отве́тить; **I ~ed to convince him** мне удало́сь убеди́ть его́; **he ~ed to break his neck** он умудри́лся слома́ть себе́ ше́ю.
v.i. (*cope*) спр|авля́ться, -а́виться; **you will never ~e on your pension** вы ни за что не проживёте на

свою пе́нсию; (*get by, make do*) об|ходи́ться, -ойти́сь; **we must ~e without bread today** сего́дня нам придётся обойти́сь без хле́ба.
manageable ['mænɪdʒəb(ə)l] *adj.* (*of task etc.*) выполни́мый; **of ~ dimensions** удо́бных разме́ров; (*of pers.*) сгово́рчивый.
management ['mænɪdʒmənt] *n.* **1.** (*control, controlling*) управле́ние (*чем*), руково́дство, организа́ция. **2.** (*handling pers. or thg.*) обраще́ние; уме́ние владе́ть +*i.*; **staff ~** обраще́ние с ли́чным соста́вом. **3.** (*governing body*) правле́ние; (*managerial staff*) администра́ция; (*senior staff*) дире́кция.
manager ['mænɪdʒə(r)] *n.* **1.** (*controller of business etc.*) заве́дующий (*чем*); нача́льник, дире́ктор, ме́неджер; (*sport*) ста́рший тре́нер; ме́неджер; **sales ~** заве́дующий отде́лом сбы́та. **2.** (*person with administrative skill*) администра́тор.
manageress [,mænɪdʒə'res] *n.* заве́дующая.
managerial [,mænɪ'dʒɪərɪəl] *adj.* администрати́вный; управле́нческий.
manatee [,mænə'tiː] *n.* ламанти́н.
mandarin[1] ['mændərɪn] *n.* **1.** (*official*) мандари́н; (*bureaucrat*) чино́вник. **2.** (*language*) мандари́нское наре́чие кита́йского языка́.
mandarin[2] ['mændərɪn] *n.* (*orange*) мандари́н.
mandate ['mændeɪt] *n.* (*authority*) полномо́чие; (*to govern territory*) манда́т; (*given by voters*) нака́з.
mandatory ['mændətərɪ] *adj.* (*compulsory*) обяза́тельный.
mandible ['mændɪb(ə)l] *n.* ни́жняя че́люсть.
mandolin [,mændə'lɪn] *n.* мандоли́на.
mandrake ['mændreɪk] *n.* мандраго́ра.
mandrill ['mændrɪl] *n.* мандри́л.
mane [meɪn] *n.* гри́ва.
manège [mæ'neɪʒ] *n.* мане́ж.
maneuver [mə'nuːvə(r)], **-ability** [mə,nuːvrə'bɪlɪtɪ], **-able** [mə'nuːvrəb(ə)l] = **manoeuvre** *etc.*
manganese ['mæŋgə,niːz] *n.* ма́рганец.
adj. ма́рганцевый.
mange [meɪndʒ] *n.* парша́.
mangel(-wurzel) ['mæŋg(ə)l] *n.* кормова́я свёкла.
manger ['meɪndʒə(r)] *n.* я́сл|и (*pl., g.* -е́й); **dog in the ~** соба́ка на се́не.
mangle[1] ['mæŋg(ə)l] *n.* (отжи́мный) като́к.
mangle[2] ['mæŋg(ə)l] *v.t.* (*mutilate*) уро́довать, из-; (*cut to pieces*) кромса́ть, ис-; (*fig.*) иска|жа́ть, -зи́ть.
mango ['mæŋgəʊ] *n.* ма́нго (*indecl.*).
mangy ['meɪndʒɪ] *adj.* парши́вый.
manhood ['mænhʊd] *n.* **1.** (*state of being a man; adult status*) возмужа́лость; взро́слость, совершенноле́тие. **2.** (*manly qualities*) му́жественность.
mania ['meɪnɪə] *n.* ма́ния.
maniac ['meɪnɪ,æk] *n.* маньяк; (*fig.*): **football ~** зая́длый футболи́ст.
adj. (*also* **~al, manic**) маниака́льный.
manic-depressive ['mænɪk] *adj.* страда́ющий маниака́льно-депресси́вным психо́зом.
manicure ['mænɪ,kjʊə(r)] *n.* маникю́р; (*attr.*) маникю́рный.
v.t. де́лать, с- маникю́р +*d.*
manicurist ['mænɪ,kjʊərɪst] *n.* (*fem.*) маникю́рша.
manifest ['mænɪ,fest] *adj.* я́вный, очеви́дный.
v.t. (*show clearly*) я́сно пока́з|ывать, -а́ть; (*exhibit*) проявл|я́ть, -и́ть; (*prove*) дока́з|ывать, -а́ть.
manifestation [,mænɪfe'steɪʃ(ə)n] *n.* проявле́ние.
manifesto [,mænɪ'festəʊ] *n.* манифе́ст.
manifold ['mænɪ,fəʊld] *adj.* (*numerous*) многочи́сленный; (*various*) разнообра́зный.
manikin ['mænɪkɪn] *n.* (*artist's dummy*) манеке́н.
manioc ['mænɪ,ɒk] *n.* маниока.
manipulate [mə'nɪpjʊ,leɪt] *v.t.* (*lit., fig.; also pej.*) манипули́ровать (*impf.*) +*i.*
manipulation [mə,nɪpjʊ'leɪʃ(ə)n] *n.* манипуля́ция.
manipulator [mə'nɪpjʊ,leɪtə(r)] *n.* манипуля́тор.
manlike ['mænlaɪk] *adj.* мужско́й; (*of a woman*) мужеподо́бная; (*of animal*) похо́жий на челове́ка.
manliness ['mænlɪnɪs] *n.* му́жественность.
manly ['mænlɪ] *adj.* му́жественный.
manna ['mænə] *n.* ма́нна; **like ~ from heaven** ма́нна небе́сная.
mannequin ['mænɪkɪn] *n.* (*pers.*) манеке́нщица; (*dummy*) манеке́н.
manner ['mænə(r)] *n.* **1.** (*way, fashion, mode*) о́браз; **in, after this ~** таки́м о́бразом; **in a ~ of speaking** в не́котором смы́сле; **~ of proceeding** при́нятый поря́док (*чего*). **2.** (*pl., ways of life; customs*) обы́чаи (*m. pl.*); нра́вы (*m. pl.*); **comedy of ~s** коме́дия нра́вов. **3.** (*personal bearing, style of behaviour*) мане́ра; **he has a strange ~ of speaking** у него́ стра́нная мане́ра говори́ть; (*style in literature or art*): **after the ~ of Dickens** в сти́ле Ди́ккенса. **4.** (*pl., behaviour*) мане́ры (*f. pl.*); **good, bad ~s** хоро́шие/плохи́е мане́ры; **it is bad ~s to yawn** зева́ть неприли́чно; (*polite behaviour*): **have you no ~s?** где ва́ши мане́ры?; **have you forgotten your ~s?** вы забы́ли, как на́до себя́ вести́? **5.** (*kind*): **what ~ of man is he?** что он за челове́к?; **all ~ of things** вся́кого ро́да ве́щи; **by no ~ of means** нико́им о́бразом.
mannered ['mænəd] *adj.* (*showing mannerism*) мане́рный.
mannerism ['mænə,rɪz(ə)m] *n.* мане́ра, мане́рность.
mannerly ['mænəlɪ] *adj.* ве́жливый.
mannish ['mænɪʃ] *adj.* (*of a woman*) мужеподо́бная.
manœuvrability [mə,nuːvrə'bɪlɪtɪ] (*US* **maneuverability**) *n.* манёвренность.
manœuvrable [mə'nuːvrəb(ə)l] (*US* **maneuverable**) *adj.* манёвренный.
manœuvre [mə'nuːvə(r)] (*US* **maneuver**) *n.* **1.** (*mil.*) манёвр; **on ~s** на манёврах; **the Army is holding ~s** сухопу́тные войска́ прово́дят манёвры. **2.** (*adroit management*) манёвр, махина́ция.
v.t. маневри́ровать (*impf.*) +*i.*; **I ~d him to his chair** мне удало́сь подвести́ его́ к сту́лу.
v.i. (*lit., fig.*) маневри́ровать (*impf.*).
manometer [mə'nɒmɪtə(r)] *n.* мано́метр.
manor ['mænə(r)] *n.* (*estate*) поме́стье; **lord of the ~** поме́щик; (*~-house*) уса́дьба, поме́щичий дом.
manorial [mə'nɔːrɪəl] *adj.* манориа́льный.
mansard ['mænsɑːd] *n.* (*~ roof*) манса́рдная кры́ша; (*garret*) манса́рда.
mansion ['mænʃ(ə)n] *n.* особня́к; **country ~** за́городный дом; (*pl., house of flats*) многокварти́рный дом.
mantel(piece) ['mænt(ə)l,piːs] *n.* ками́нная по́лка.
mantilla [mæn'tɪlə] *n.* манти́лья.
mantis ['mæntɪs] *n.* **(praying ~)** богомо́л.
mantissa [mæn'tɪsə] *n.* манти́сса
mantle ['mænt(ə)l] *n.* **1.** (*cloak*) ма́нтия. **2.** (*fig., covering*) покро́в. **3.** (*for gas-jet*) кали́льная се́тка.
manual ['mænjʊəl] *n.* (*handbook*) руково́дство; (*textbook*) уче́бник; (*aid*) посо́бие.
adj. (*operated by hand*) ручно́й; **~ly** ручны́м спо́собом; (*performed by hand*): **~ labour** физи́ческий труд.
manufactur|e [,mænjʊ'fæktʃə(r)] *n.* изготовле́ние; (*on large scale*) произво́дство.
v.t. **1.** (*produce*) изгот|овля́ть, -о́вить; **~ed goods** промтова́ры (*m. pl.*); **~ing industry** обраба́тывающая промы́шленность; **~ing town** промы́шленный го́род. **2.** (*make up, invent*) фабрикова́ть, с-.
manure [mə'njʊə(r)] *n.* наво́з.
v.t. унаво́|живать, -зить.
manuscript ['mænjʊskrɪpt] *n.* ру́копись.
many ['menɪ] *adj.* мно́гие; **a good, great ~** большо́е коли́чество +*g.*; **~ people** мно́го люде́й; мно́гие

(люди); ~ **years passed** прошло много лет; ~ **a time,** ~ **times** много раз; ~**'s the time** очень часто; **half as** ~ вдвое меньше; **twice as** ~ вдвое больше; **I haven't seen him for** ~ **a day** я его давно не видел; **as, so** ~ **(as)** столько(, сколько); **not as** ~ **as** не так много, как; **there were as** ~ **as forty people there** там было целых сорок человек; **not** ~ немного, не так уж много; ~ **more** гораздо больше +*g.*; **one too** ~ (*not wanted*; *in the way*) третий лишний; **he's had one too** ~ (*coll.*) он выпил лишнего.

cpds. много...; ~**-coloured** *adj.* пёстрый, многоцветный; ~**-sided** *adj.* (*lit.*, *fig.*) многосторонний.

Maoism ['maʊɪz(ə)m] *n.* маоизм.

Maoist ['maʊɪst] *adj.* маоистский.

Maori ['maʊrɪ] *n.* (*pers.*) маори (*c.g.*, *indecl.*); (*language*) маорийский язык.

adj. маорийский.

map [mæp] *n.* карта; (*e.g. of rail system*) схема; **town** ~ план города.

v.t.: (*make* ~ *of*): **this district was first** ~**ped a hundred years ago** карта этого района была впервые составлена сто лет назад; **he** ~**ped out his route before leaving** он составил маршрут перед отъездом.

cpds. ~**-maker** *n.* картограф; ~**-reading** *n.* чтение карт.

maple ['meɪp(ə)l] *n.* клён; ~ **sugar/syrup** кленовый сахар/сироп.

mar [mɑ:(r)] *v.t.* портить, ис-.

marabou ['mærəˌbu:] *n.* марабу (*m. indecl.*).

maraschino [ˌmærə'ski:nəʊ] *n.* мараскин.

marathon ['mærəθ(ə)n] *n.* (~ **race**) марафонский бег; ~ **runner** марафонец; (*attr.*): **a** ~ **effort** гигантское усилие.

maraud [mə'rɔ:d] *v.i.* мародёрствовать (*impf.*, *pf.*).

marauder [mə'rɔ:də(r)] *n.* мародёр.

marble ['mɑ:b(ə)l] *n.* **1.** (*substance*) мрамор. **2.** (*in child's game*) стеклянный шарик; **play** ~**s** играть (*impf.*) в шарики.

adj. (*lit.*, *fig.*) мраморный.

v.t. раскра|шивать, -сить под мрамор; ~**d paper** мраморная бумага.

cpd. ~**-topped** *adj.* с мраморным верхом.

March[1] [mɑ:tʃ] *n.* март; (*attr.*) мартовский.

march[2] [mɑ:tʃ] *n.* (*mil.*) марш; **on the** ~ в походе; ~ **past** торжественный марш; **quick** ~ быстрый марш; (*mus.*): **in** ~ **time** в темпе марша; (*pol.*) поход, демонстрация; **peace** ~ поход за мир; (*fig.*, *distance*): **it was a long day's** ~ был длинный переход; (*fig.*, *progress*): ~ **of events** ход событий; **the** ~ **of time** поступь времени.

v.t. **1.** (*cause to* ~) водить (*indet.*), вести, построем. **2.** (*cover by* ~**ing**) про|ходить, -йти.

v.i. **1.** (*mil.*) маршировать (*impf.*, *pf.*); **German troops** ~**ed into Austria** немецкие войска вступили в Австрию; **we watched them** ~ **past** мы смотрели, как они прошли строем; **quick** ~! шагом марш! **2.** (*walk determinedly*): **he** ~**ed into the room** он смело вошёл в комнату.

with advs.: ~ **along** *v.i.*: **they were** ~**ing along singing** они маршировали с песнями; ~ **back** *v.t.*: **I caught him running off and** ~**ed him back** я поймал его, когда он убегал, и препроводил обратно; *v.i.*: **they** ~**ed back to barracks** они строем вернулись в казармы; ~ **by** *v.i.* прошагать (*pf.*) мимо; ~ **in** *v.t.*: **he was** ~**ed in to see the Head** его ввели в кабинет начальника; *v.i.*: **when the soldiers** ~**ed in** когда солдаты вступили (в город *и т.п.*); ~ **off** *v.t.*: **he was** ~**ed off to prison** его препроводили в тюрьму; *v.i.*: **she** ~**ed off in disgust** ей стало противно и она вышла; ~ **out** *v.t.*: выводить, вывести *v.i.*: **the workers** ~**ed out on strike** рабочие вышли на забастовку; ~ **up** *v.i.*: **they** ~**ed up to the wall** они прошагали к стене; **he** ~**ed up and hit her** он решительно подошёл к ней и ударил её.

marcher ['mɑ:tʃə(r)] *n.* демонстрант (*fem.* -ка).

marching ['mɑ:tʃɪŋ] *n.* походное движение; **in** ~ **order** в походном порядке; ~ **orders** (*mil.*) приказ о выступлении; (*fig.*): **get one's** ~ **orders** получ|ать, -ить расчёт; **they gave him his** ~ **orders** они уволили его.

marchioness [ˌmɑ:ʃə'nes, 'mɑ:-] *n.* маркиза.

Mardi Gras [ˌmɑ:dɪ 'grɑ:] *n.* масленица.

mare [meə(r)] *n.* кобыла.

margarine [ˌmɑ:dʒə'ri:n, ˌmɑ:gə-, 'mɑ:-] *n.* маргарин.

marge [mɑ:dʒ] (*coll.*) = **margarine**

margin ['mɑ:dʒɪn] *n.* **1.** (*edge, border*) край; (*of page*) поле (*usu. pl.*); **in the** ~ на полях. **2.** (*extra amount*) запас; коэффициент; **safety** ~ запас прочности; **he won by a narrow** ~ он победил с небольшим преимуществом; ~ **of error** допустимая погрешность; **profit** ~ прибыль, размер прибыли.

marginal ['mɑ:dʒɪn(ə)l] *adj.* **1.** (*written in margin*) (написанный) на полях; ~ **notes** заметки (*f. pl.*) (на полях). **2.** (*pert. to an edge or limit*) краевой; предельный; ~ **land** малоплодородная земля; ~ **question** второстепенный вопрос. **3.** (*minimal*; *barely adequate or perceptible*) минимальный.

marginalia [ˌmɑ:dʒɪ'neɪlɪə] *n.* заметки (*f. pl.*) на полях.

marigold ['mærɪˌgəʊld] *n.* ноготки (*m. pl.*).

mari|juana, -huana [ˌmærɪ'hwɑ:nə] *n.* марихуана.

marina [mə'ri:nə] *n.* марина (*пристань для яхт*).

marinade [ˌmærɪ'neɪd, 'mæ-] *n.* маринад.

v.t. (*also* **marinate**) мариновать, за-.

marine [mə'ri:n] *n.* **1.** (*fleet*): **merchant** ~ торговый флот. **2.** (*naval infantryman*) солдат морской пехоты; **the M**~**s** морская пехота.

adj. морской; ~ **engineer** судовой механик.

mariner ['mærɪnə(r)] *n.* мореплаватель (*m.*); **master** ~ капитан, шкипер; ~**'s compass** морской компас.

marionette [ˌmærɪə'net] *n.* марионетка.

marital ['mærɪt(ə)l] *adj.* (*of marriage*): ~ **union** брачный союз; (*of husband or wife*): ~ **rights** супружеские права.

maritime ['mærɪˌtaɪm] *adj.* (*of the sea*): ~ **law** морское право; (*situated by the sea*) приморский.

marjoram ['mɑ:dʒərəm] *n.* майоран, душица.

mark[1] [mɑ:k] *n.* **1.** (*surface imperfection*; *stain, spot etc.*) пятно; (*scratch*) царапина; (*cut*) порез; (*scar*) рубец, шрам; **there were** ~**s of smallpox on his face** его лицо было изрыто оспой. **2.** (*trace*) след; **tyre** ~**s** следы шин. **3.** (*sign, symbol*) знак; **punctuation** ~**s** знаки препинания; **question** ~ вопросительный знак; **as a** ~ **of goodwill** в знак расположения; (*indication, feature, symptom*) признак; **politeness is the** ~ **of a gentleman** вежливость — отличительная черта джентльмена. **4.** (*for purpose of distinction or identification*) метка; (*fig.*): **make one's** ~ выдвигаться, выдвинуться; (*as signature*): **he could not write his name but made his** ~ он вместо подписи поставил крест; (*on an industrial product*) фабричная марка; (*fig.*, *stamp*): **it bears the** ~ **of hurried work** видно, что это делалось в спешке. **5.** (*reference point*) метка; **the** ~**s show the depth of water in feet** отметки показывают глубину воды в футах; (*fig.*, *standard*): **I'm not quite up to the** ~ **today** я сегодня не совсем в форме; **come up to the** ~ оправд|ывать, -ать ожидания; **overstep the** ~ (*fig.*) выходить, выйти за границы дозволенного. **6.** (*starting-line*) старт; **get off the** ~ стартовать (*impf.*, *pf.*); **quick/slow off the** ~ (*fig.*) лёгкий/тяжёлый на подъём; **on your** ~**s; get set; go!** на старт; внимание; марш! **7.** (*assessment of performance*) отметка; **he always gets good** ~**s** он всегда́ получа́ет хоро́шие отме́тки; **she got top ~s in the exam** она́ сдала́ (экза́мен) на «отли́чно». **8.** (*target*) цель; **hit the ~** (*lit., fig.*) поп|ада́ть, -а́сть в цель; **miss (*or* fall wide of) the ~** прома́х|иваться, -ну́ться; **you're way off the ~** вы попа́ли па́льцем в не́бо (*coll.*).

v.t. **1.** (*stain, scar, scratch etc.*): **a tablecloth ~ed with coffee stains** ска́терть, забры́зганная ко́фе; **the table was badly ~ed** стол был си́льно запа́чкан; **features ~ed by grief** черты́ лица́, отме́ченные го́рем. **2.** (*for recognition purposes*) ме́тить, по-; **~ed cards** краплёные ка́рты; **~ing-ink** маркиро́вочные черни́ла; (*with price*): **all the goods are ~ed** на всех това́рах проста́влена цена́. **3.** (*distinguish*): **his reign was ~ed by great victories** его́ ца́рствование бы́ло ознамено́вано вели́кими побе́дами; **he called for champagne to ~ the occasion** он заказа́л шампа́нское, что́бы отме́тить (э́то) собы́тие. **4.** (*indicate*) отм|еча́ть, -е́тить; **is our village ~ed on this map?** на́ша дере́вня нанесена́ на э́ту ка́рту?; **to ~ his displeasure he remained silent** он храни́л молча́ние в знак недово́льства. **5.** (*record*) запи́с|ывать, -а́ть; (*football etc.: follow closely*) закр|ыва́ть, -ы́ть; (*notice; pay heed to*) зам|еча́ть, -е́тить; **~ you, I don't agree with all he says** заме́тьте, я согла́сен не со всем, что он говори́т; **~ my words!** помяни́те моё сло́во! **6.** (*assign ~s to; assess*): **~ an exercise** пров|еря́ть, -е́рить упражне́ние; **the judges ~ed his performance very high** су́дьи высоко́ оцени́ли его́ выступле́ние. **7.: ~ time** (*mil.*) обознача́ть (*impf.*) шаг на ме́сте; (*fig.*) топта́ться (*impf.*) на ме́сте.

with advs.: **~ down** *v.t.* (*reduce price of*): **all the goods were ~ed down for the sale** для распрода́жи це́ны на все това́ры бы́ли сни́жены; (*give low ~ to*): **he was ~ed down for bad spelling** ему́ сни́зили оце́нку за орфографи́ческие оши́бки; **~ off** *v.t.* отм|еча́ть, -е́тить; **an area was ~ed off for the guests** часть мест *и т.п.* была́ отведена́ для госте́й; **~ out** *v.t.*: **a tennis court had been ~ed out** те́ннисный корт был расче́рчен/разме́чен; (*preselect, destine*): **he was ~ed out for promotion** его́ реши́ли повы́сить в до́лжности; **~ up** *v.t.* (*raise; raise price of*): **prices were ~ed up every month** це́ны повыша́ли ка́ждый ме́сяц; (*record*): **who will ~ up the score?** кто бу́дет запи́сывать счёт?; (*raise ~s of*) зав|ыша́ть, -ы́сить оце́нку +*d*.

cpd. **~-up** *n.* наце́нка.

mark² [mɑːk] *n.* (*currency*) ма́рка.

marked [mɑːkt] *adj.* (*distinct, noticeable*) заме́тный; **they were ~ly different** они́ суще́ственно отлича́лись друг от дру́га.

marker ['mɑːkə(r)] *n.* (*recorder of score*) маркёр; (*indicator*) индика́тор; (*flag*) сигна́льный флажо́к; (*beacon*) ма́ркерный (ра́дио)мая́к; (*buoy*) буёк; (*bookmark*) закла́дка; (*pen*) флома́стер.

market ['mɑːkɪt] *n.* **1.** (*gathering; event; place of business*) ры́нок, база́р; (*attr.*) ры́ночный, база́рный; **~ hall** ры́ночный павильо́н/зал; (*fig., area of sale*): **world ~** мирово́й ры́нок; **the Common M~** О́бщий ры́нок. **2.** (*trade*) торго́вля; **the ~ in wool** торго́вля ше́рстью; (*opportunity for sale*) сбыт; **there is no ~ for these goods** на э́ти това́ры нет спро́са; **they will find a ready ~** они́ легко́ найду́т сбыт. **3.** (*rates of purchase and sale; share prices*) це́ны (*f. pl.*); **the ~ is falling** це́ны па́дают; **the coffee ~ is steady** цена́ на ко́фе стаби́льна; **play the ~** спекули́ровать (*impf.*) на би́рже; **~ value** ры́ночная сто́имость. **4.: in the ~ for** (*ready to buy*) обду́мывающий поку́пку (*чего*). **5. on the ~** (*available for purchase*): **he put his house on the ~** он вы́ставил свой дом на прода́жу; **his estate will soon come on to the ~** его́ име́ние ско́ро посту́пит в прода́жу.

v.t. (*sell in ~*) продава́ть (*impf.*); (*put up for sale*) пус|ка́ть, -ти́ть в прода́жу.

cpds. **~-day** *n.* база́рный день; **~-garden** *n.* огоро́д (для выра́щивания овоще́й на прода́жу); **~-gardening** *n.* това́рное овощево́дство; **~-place** *n.* база́рная пло́щадь; **~ town** *n.* го́род, в кото́ром есть ры́нок.

marketable ['mɑːkɪtəb(ə)l] *adj.* (*produced for sale*) това́рный; (*selling quickly*) хо́дкий.

marketing ['mɑːkɪtɪŋ] *n.* (*trade*) торго́вля; (*sale*) сбыт.

marking ['mɑːkɪŋ] *n.* **1.** (*coloration of animals etc.*) окра́ска. **2.** (*for identification*): **aircraft ~s** опознава́тельные зна́ки (*m. pl.*) самолёта. **3.** (*assessment*) оце́нка.

marksman ['mɑːksmən] *n.* стрело́к; **a good ~** ме́ткий стрело́к.

marksmanship ['mɑːksmən,ʃɪp] *n.* ме́ткая стрельба́; стрелко́вое мастерство́.

marl [mɑːl] *n.* ме́ргель (*m.*).

marmalade ['mɑːmə,leɪd] *n.*: **orange ~** апельси́новое/апельси́нное варе́нье.

Marmara ['mɑːmərə] *n.*: **Sea of ~** Мра́морное мо́ре.

marmoreal [mɑː'mɔːrɪəl] *adj.* мра́морный.

marmoset ['mɑːmə,zet] *n.* марты́шка.

marmot ['mɑːmət] *n.* суро́к.

maroon¹ [mə'ruːn] *n.* & *adj.* (*colour*) тёмно-бордо́вый цвет.

maroon² [mə'ruːn] *v.t.* выса́живать, вы́садить на необита́емый о́стров *и т.п.*; (*fig., pass.*) застр|ева́ть, -я́ть; **we were ~ed by the tide** мы бы́ли отре́заны прили́вом.

marquee [mɑː'kiː] *n.* (больша́я) пала́тка.

marqu|is ['mɑːkwɪs], **-ess** ['mɑːkwɪs] *n.* марки́з.

marquise [mɑː'kiːz] *n.* марки́за.

marriage ['mærɪdʒ] *n.* **1.** (*ceremony*) сва́дьба; бракосочета́ние. **2.** (*contraction of ~ by man*) жени́тьба; **his ~ to Liza** его́ жени́тьба на Ли́зе; **he made her an offer of ~** он сде́лал ей предложе́ние; **he took her in ~** он взял её в жёны; (*by woman*) вы́ход за́муж; **he gave his daughter in ~** он вы́дал дочь за́муж. **3.** (*married state*) брак, супру́жество; (*of woman, also*) заму́жество; **~ of convenience** брак по расчёту; **their ~ broke up** их брак распа́лся; **relative by ~** сво́йственни|к (*fem.* -ца). **4.** (*attr.*) бра́чный; **~ bureau** бракопосре́дническое аге́нтство; **~ certificate** свиде́тельство о бра́ке; **~ licence** разреше́ние на брак.

cpd. **~-broker** *n.* сват; (*fem.*) сва́ха.

married ['mærɪd] *adj.* **1.** (*of man*) жена́тый; (*of woman*) заму́жняя, (*pred.*) за́мужем (за+*i.*); **they are ~** (*to each other*) они́ жена́ты. **2.** (*pert. to marriage*) супру́жеский; **a ~ couple** супру́жеская па́ра; **~ life** супру́жеская жизнь; (*n.pl.*) **young ~s** молодожёны.

marrow ['mærəʊ] *n.* **1.** (*anat.*) (ко́стный) мозг. **2.** **(vegetable ~)** кабачо́к.

marr|y ['mærɪ] *v.t.* **1.** (*of man*) жени́ться (*impf., pf.*) на+*p.*. **2.** (*of woman*) выходи́ть, вы́йти за́муж за+*a.* **3.** (*of parent; give daughter in marriage*) выдава́ть, вы́дать за́муж (*за кого*); (*give son in marriage*) жени́ть (*на ком*). **4.** сочета́ть бра́ком; (*of priest*) венча́ть, об-.

v.i. (*of man*) жени́ться (*impf., pf.*); (*of woman*) выходи́ть, вы́йти за́муж; (*of couple*) пожени́ться (*pf.*); вступ|а́ть, -и́ть в брак; (*relig.*) венча́ться, об-.

Mars [mɑːz] *n.* (*myth., astron.*) Марс.

Marsala [mɑː'sɑːlə] *n.* марсала́.

Marseillaise [,mɑːseɪ'jeɪz, ,mɑːsə'leɪz] *n.* Марселье́за.

marsh [mɑːʃ] *n.* боло́то; (*attr.*) боло́тный.

cpds. **~land** *n.* боло́тистая ме́стность; топь; **~mallow** *n.* (*plant*) лека́рственный алте́й; (*confection*) пастила́; **~-marigold** *n.* боло́тная калу́жница.

marshal ['mɑːʃ(ə)l] *n.* **1.** (*mil.*) ма́ршал; **air ~** ма́ршал авиа́ции. **2.** (*organizer of ceremonies*) оберцеремонийме́йстер.

v.t. **1.** (*draw up in order*): **~ troops** выстра́ивать, вы́строить войска́; (*fig.*): **~ one's forces** соб|ира́ть, -ра́ть си́лы; **~ facts, arguments** прив|оди́ть, -ести́ фа́кты/до́воды в систе́му. **2.** (*direct*): **~ a crowd** напр|авля́ть, -а́вить толпу́. **3.** (*rail.*) сортирова́ть (*impf.*); **~ling-yard** сортиро́вочная (ста́нция).

marshy ['mɑːʃɪ] *adj.* боло́тистый, то́пкий.

marsupial [mɑː'suːpɪəl] *n.* су́мчатое живо́тное.

adj. су́мчатый.

marten ['mɑːtɪn] *n.* куни́ца.

martial ['mɑːʃ(ə)l] *adj.* (*military*) вое́нный; **~ arts** спорти́вная борьба́; **~ law** вое́нное положе́ние.

Martian ['mɑːʃ(ə)n] *n.* марсиа́н|ин (*fem.* -ка).

martin ['mɑːtɪn] *n.*: **house-~** городска́я ла́сточка.

martyr ['mɑːtə(r)] *n.* му́чени|к (*fem.* -ца); **be a ~ to, for a cause** страда́ть, по- за де́ло.

v.t. му́чить, за-.

martyrdom ['mɑːtədəm] *n.* му́ченичество; (*ordeal*) муче́ние; **suffer ~** (*lit., fig.*) быть му́чеником.

marvel ['mɑːv(ə)l] *n.* чу́до; **he's a ~** он чуде́сный челове́к; **it's a ~ that he escaped** э́то су́щее чу́до, что ему́ удало́сь спасти́сь.

v.t. & i. (*wonder*) диви́ться (*impf.*) +*d.*; удив|ля́ться, -и́ться +*d.* **he ~led that ...** он порази́лся тому́, что...; **~ at** (*be surprised at*) изум|ля́ться, -и́ться +*d.*

marvellous ['mɑːvələs] *adj.* (*astonishing*) изуми́тельный; (*splendid*) чуде́сный.

Marxism ['mɑːksɪz(ə)m] *n.* маркси́зм.

Marxist ['mɑːksɪst] *n.* маркси́ст (*fem.* -ка).

adj. маркси́стский.

marzipan ['mɑːzɪˌpæn, -'pæn] *n.* марципа́н.

mascara [mæ'skɑːrə] *n.* тушь для ресни́ц.

mascot ['mæskɒt] *n.* талисма́н.

masculine ['mæskjʊlɪn, 'mɑːs-] *n.* **(~ gender)** мужско́й род; **(~ noun)** существи́тельное мужско́го ро́да.

adj. мужско́й; (*manly*) му́жественный.

masculinity [ˌmæskjʊ'lɪnɪtɪ] *n.* му́жественность.

mash [mæʃ] *n.* (*for brewing*) су́сло; (*animal fodder*) ме́сиво, болту́шка из отрубе́й; (*potato etc.*) пюре́ (*indecl.*).

v.t. (*brewing*): **~ malt** зава́р|ивать, -и́ть со́лод; (*cul.*): **~ turnips** де́лать, с- пюре́ из ре́пы; **~ed potatoes** карто́фельное пюре́.

mask [mɑːsk] *n.* ма́ска; **under the ~ of friendship** под личи́ной дру́жбы.

v.t. над|ева́ть, -е́ть ма́ску на+*a.*; **~ed men** лю́ди в ма́сках; **~ed ball** маскара́д; (*fig.*) **she ~ed her feelings** она́ скрыва́ла свои́ чу́вства.

masochism ['mæsəˌkɪz(ə)m] *n.* мазохи́зм.

masochist ['mæsə'kɪst] *n.* мазохи́ст.

masochistic [ˌmæsə'kɪstɪk] *adj.* мазохи́стский.

mason ['meɪs(ə)n] *n.* (*builder*) ка́менщик; (*stonedresser*) каменотёс; **(M~, Free~)** масо́н.

Masonic [mə'sɒnɪk] *adj.* масо́нский.

masonry ['meɪsənrɪ] *n.* (*stonework*) ка́менная кла́дка; **(M~, Free~)** масо́нство.

masquerad|e [ˌmɑːskə'reɪd, ˌmæs-] *n.* (*lit., fig.*) маскара́д.

v.i.: **he ~ed as a general** он выдава́л себя́ за генера́ла; **he is ~ing under an assumed name** он скрыва́ется под вы́мышленной фами́лией.

mass[1] [mæs] *n.* (*relig.*) ме́сса, литурги́я; (*in Orthodox church*) обе́дня; **high ~** торже́ственная ме́сса; **low ~** ме́сса без пе́ния.

mass[2] [mæs] *n.* **1.** (*phys. etc.*) ма́сса; **his body is a ~ of bruises** он весь в синяка́х; **his story was a ~ of lies** его́ расска́з был сплошно́й ло́жью; **a ~ of earth** гру́да земли́. **2.** (*large number*) мно́жество; **~es of people** ма́сса наро́ду; **the ~es** (наро́дные/широ́кие) ма́ссы; (*pl., coll., a large amount*): **there's ~es of food** полно́ еды́. **3.** (*greater part*) бо́льшая часть. **4.** (*attr.*) ма́ссовый; **~ destruction** ма́ссовое уничтоже́ние; **the ~ media** сре́дства ма́ссовой информа́ции; **~ meeting** ма́ссовый ми́тинг; **~ production** ма́ссовое произво́дство.

v.t. соб|ира́ть, -ра́ть; **~ troops** масси́ровать (*impf., pf.*) войска́; **the flowers were ~ed for effect** для созда́ния эффе́кта цветы́ бы́ли со́браны вме́сте.

v.i. соб|ира́ться, -ра́ться.

cpd. **~-produce** *v.t.*: **these toys are ~-produced** э́ти игру́шки ма́ссового произво́дства.

massacre ['mæsəkə(r)] *n.* бо́йня.

v.t. переб|ива́ть, -и́ть.

massage ['mæsɑːʒ, -sɑːdʒ] *n.* масса́ж.

v.t. масси́ровать (*impf., pf.*).

masseur [mæ'sɜː(r)] *n.* массажи́ст.

masseuse [mæ'sɜːz] *n.* массажи́стка.

massive ['mæsɪv] *adj.* масси́вный; (*very considerable, substantial*): **he received ~ support** он получи́л огро́мную подде́ржку.

mast [mɑːst] *n.* (*ship's ~, flagpole, radio ~*) ма́чта.

cpd. **~head** *n.* топ ма́чты; (*of newspaper*) заголо́вок газе́ты.

master ['mɑːstə(r)] *n.* **1.** (*one in control, boss*) хозя́ин; (*owner*) владе́лец; **~ of the house** хозя́ин до́ма; **be one's own ~** ни от кого́ не зави́сеть; **I will show you who's ~** посмо́трим, кто здесь гла́вный; **be ~ of o.s.** владе́ть (*impf.*) собо́й; **~ of ceremonies** церемонийме́йстер; **~ of the situation** хозя́ин положе́ния; (*of a ship*) капита́н; **~ mariner** капита́н, шки́пер. **2.** (*teacher*) учи́тель (*m.*); **maths ~** учи́тель матема́тики; (*in university*); **M~ of Arts** маги́стр гуманита́рных нау́к. **3.** (*skilled craftsman, expert*) ма́стер; **~ builder** строи́тель-подря́дчик; **old ~s** (*artists*) ста́рые мастера́; **grand ~** (*chess*) гроссме́йстер; **he made himself ~ of the language** он овладе́л языко́м. **4.** (*original*) по́длинник, моде́ль, оригина́л. **5.** (*attr.*): **~ bedroom** гла́вная спа́льня; **~ plan** генера́льный план; **~ switch** гла́вный выключа́тель.

v.t. **1.** (*gain control of; deal with*) спр|авля́ться, -а́виться с+*i.* **2.** (*acquire knowledge of, skill in*) овлад|ева́ть, -е́ть +*i.*; **it is a language which can be ~ed in 6 months** э́тим языко́м мо́жно овладе́ть за шесть ме́сяцев. **3.** (*overcome*) овлад|ева́ть, -е́ть +*i.*; **~ one's feelings** владе́ть, о- свои́ми чу́вствами.

cpds. **~-key** *n.* отмы́чка; **~-mind** *n.* (*genius*) ге́ний; *v.t.*: **he ~-minded the plan** он разрабо́тал весь план; **~piece** *n.* шеде́вр; **~-stroke** *n.* гениа́льный ход.

masterful ['mɑːstəˌfʊl] *adj.* (*imperious*) вла́стный; (*skilful*) мастерско́й.

masterly ['mɑːstəlɪ] *adj.* мастерско́й; **in (a) ~ fashion** мастерски́.

mastery ['mɑːstərɪ] *n.* **1.** (*authority*) власть; (*supremacy*) госпо́дство; **gain the ~ of** доб|ива́ться, -и́ться госпо́дства над+*i.* **2.** (*skill*) мастерство́. **3.** (*knowledge*) владе́ние; **~ of a subject** основа́тельное зна́ние предме́та.

mastic ['mæstɪk] *n.* (*resin*) масти́ка; (*tree*) масти́ковое де́рево.

masticate ['mæstɪˌkeɪt] *v.t. & i.* жева́ть, раз-.

mastication [ˌmæstɪ'keɪʃ(ə)n] *n.* жева́ние.

mastiff ['mæstɪf, 'mɑːs-] *n.* масти́фф.

mastitis [mæ'staɪtɪs] *n.* масти́т.

mastodon ['mæstəˌdɒn] *n.* мастодо́нт.

masturbate ['mæstəˌbeɪt] *v.i.* онани́ровать (*impf.*), мастурби́ровать (*impf.*).

masturbation [ˌmæstə'beɪʃ(ə)n] *n.* онани́зм, мастурба́ция.

mat[1] [mæt] *n.* **1.** (*floor covering*) ко́врик; **(door-~)**

полови́к; **wipe your feet on the ~** вы́трите но́ги о полови́к. **2.** (*placed under an object to protect surface*) подста́вка.

mat[2] [mæt] *n.* (*tangled mass of hair etc.*) колту́н, клубо́к.

v.t.: **his hair was ~ted with blood** его́ во́лосы сли́плись от кро́ви.

mat[3] [mæt] *adj.* = **mat(t)**

match[1] [mætʃ] *n.* (*for producing flame*) спи́чка; **box of ~es** коро́бка спи́чек; **put a ~ to** заж|ига́ть, -е́чь; **strike a ~** заж|ига́ть, -е́чь спи́чку.

cpds. **~box** *n.* спи́чечная коро́бка; **~stick** *n.*: **he's as thin as a ~stick** он худо́й как ще́пка; **he drew ~stick figures** он рисова́л па́лочных челове́чков; **~wood** *n.* (*splinters*) спи́чечная соло́мка; **make ~wood of** разб|ива́ть, -и́ть вдре́безги.

match[2] [mætʃ] *n.* **1.** (*equal in strength or ability*) па́ра, ро́вня; **he's no ~ for her** он ей не па́ра; куда́ ему́ с ней равня́ться; **he found, met his ~** он нашёл/встре́тил досто́йного проти́вника; **he was more than a ~ for me** он был сильне́е меня́. **2.** (*thg. resembling or suiting another*): **these curtains are a good ~ for the carpet** э́ти занаве́ски подхо́дят к ковру́; **a perfect ~ of colours** прекра́сное сочета́ние цвето́в; **I can't find a ~ for this glove** я не могу́ подобра́ть па́ру к э́той перча́тке; (*of man and woman*): **they are, make a good ~** они́ хоро́шая па́ра. **3.** (*matrimonial alliance*) па́ртия; **she wants to make a good ~ for her daughter** она́ и́щет хоро́шей па́ртии свое́й до́чери; (*person eligible for marriage*): **he would be an excellent ~** он соста́вит отли́чную па́ртию. **4.** (*contest*; *game*) соревнова́ние, состяза́ние; матч, игра́; **wrestling ~** состяза́ние по борьбе́; **football ~** футбо́льный матч; **doubles ~** па́рная игра́.

v.t. **1.** (*equal*) сравня́ться (*impf.*) с+*i.* **2.** (*pit, oppose*) противопост|авля́ть, -а́вить (*кого/что кому/чему*); **the contestants were well ~ed** уча́стники состяза́ния бы́ли уда́чно подо́браны. **3.** (*suit*; *correspond to*) под|ходи́ть, -ойти́ к+*d.*; гармони́ровать с+*i.*; **her hat doesn't ~ her dress** у неё шля́па не подхо́дит к пла́тью; (*find a ~ for*): **can you ~ this button?** мо́жете ли вы подобра́ть таку́ю же пу́говицу?

v.i. (*correspond*: *be identical*): **the handbag and gloves don't ~** су́мочка и перча́тки не гармони́руют друг с дру́гом.

cpd. **~-maker** *n.* сват; (*fem.*) сва́ха.

matchless ['mætʃlɪs] *adj.* несравне́нный.

mate[1] [meɪt] *n.* **1.** (*companion*; (*coll.*) *form of address*) брат, друг; (*fellow-worker*) напа́рник; (*schoolfellow*) соучени́к. **2.** (*one of a pair of animals or birds*) саме́ц; (*fem.*) са́мка; (*marriage partner*) супру́г (*fem.* -а). **3.** (*assistant*) помо́щник. **4.** (*ship's ~*) помо́щник капита́на.

v.t. & i. спа́ри|вать(ся), -ть(ся).

mate[2] [meɪt] *n.* (*chess*) мат; **~!** шах и мат!

v.t. де́лать, с- мат +*d.*

material [mə'tɪərɪəl] *n.* **1.** (*substance*) материа́л; **raw ~(s)** сырьё; (*fig., of pers.*): **he is good officer ~** из него́ вы́йдет хоро́ший офице́р; (*subject matter*): **there is good ~ there for a novel** там есть хоро́ший материа́л для рома́на. **2.** (*fabric, stuff*) мате́рия; **dress ~** платяна́я ткань; **made of waterproof ~** сде́ланный из непромока́емого материа́ла. **3.** (*pl.*): **writing ~s** пи́сьменные принадле́жности.

adj. **1.** (*pert. to matter or material*; *physical*; *bodily*) материа́льный; **~ needs** физи́ческие потре́бности; **the ~ world** материа́льный мир; **~ pleasures** земны́е ра́дости. **2.** (*important*, *essential*) суще́ственный; **a ~ witness** ва́жный свиде́тель; **~ evidence** веще́ственные доказа́тельства.

materialism [mə'tɪərɪə,lɪz(ə)m] *n.* материали́зм.

materialist [mə'tɪərɪə,lɪst] *n.* материали́ст.

materialistic [mə,tɪərɪə'lɪstɪk] *adj.* материалисти́ческий.

materialize [mə'tɪərɪə,laɪz] *v.i.* материализова́ться; (*come to pass, be fulfilled*) осуществ|ля́ться, -и́ться.

matériel [mə,tɪərɪ'el] *n.* (*mil.*) материа́льная часть.

maternal [mə'tɜ:n(ə)l] *adj.* (*motherly*) матери́нский; (*on mother's side*): **~ uncle** дя́дя с матери́нской стороны́ (*or* по ма́тери).

maternity [mə'tɜ:nɪtɪ] *n.* матери́нство; (*attr.*): **~ benefit** посо́бие роже́нице; **~ dress** пла́тье для бере́менных; **~ hospital** роди́льный дом; **~ leave** декре́тный о́тпуск.

mat(e)y ['meɪtɪ] *adj.* общи́тельный, компане́йский.

math [mæθ] *n.* (*US coll., abbr.*) = **mathematics**

mathematical [,mæθɪ'mætɪk(ə)l] *adj.* математи́ческий.

mathematician [,mæθɪmə'tɪʃ(ə)n] *n.* матема́тик.

mathematics [,mæθɪ'mætɪks] *n.* матема́тика.

maths [mæθs] *n.* (*coll., abbr.*) = **mathematics**

matinée ['mætɪ,neɪ] *n.* дневно́е представле́ние.

matins ['mætɪnz] *n.* (за)у́треня.

matriarchy ['meɪtrɪ,ɑ:kɪ] *n.* матриарха́т.

matricide ['meɪtrɪ,saɪd] *n.* матереуби́йство.

matriculate [mə'trɪkjʊ,leɪt] *v.i.* быть при́нятым в вы́сшее уче́бное заведе́ние.

matriculation [mə,trɪkjʊ'leɪʃ(ə)n] *n.* зачисле́ние в вы́сшее уче́бное заведе́ние.

matrimonial [,mætrɪ'məʊnɪəl] *adj.* супру́жеский; бра́чный.

matrimony ['mætrɪmənɪ] *n.* брак.

matrix ['meɪtrɪks] *n.* (*typ. etc.*, *mould*) ма́трица.

matron ['meɪtrən] *n.* **1.** (*elderly married woman*) матро́на. **2.** (*in hospital*) ста́ршая сестра́; сестра́-хозя́йка. **3.** (*in school*) эконо́мка.

matronly ['meɪtrənlɪ] *adj.* подоба́ющий почте́нной же́нщине.

mat(t) [mæt] *adj.* ма́товый; **~ paint** ма́товая кра́ска.

matter ['mætə(r)] *n.* **1.** (*phys., phil*) мате́рия; (*substance*) вещество́. **2.** (*physiol.*): **grey ~** се́рое вещество́; (*pus*) гной. **3.** (*content, opp. form or style*) содержа́ние. **4.** (*material for reading*) материа́лы (*m. pl.*); **printed ~** печа́тный материа́л. **5.** (*material for discussion*) те́ма, предме́т; (*question*; *issue*) вопро́с; де́ло; **that's quite another ~** э́то совсе́м друго́е де́ло; **a ~ of common knowledge** общеизве́стный факт; **it is a ~ of course** само́ собо́й разуме́ется; **as a ~ of fact** (*to tell the truth*) по пра́вде сказа́ть; (*in reality*) на са́мом де́ле; (*incidentally*) со́бственно (говоря́); **a ~ of some importance** ва́жный вопро́с; **it's no laughing ~** э́то де́ло не шу́точное; **a ~ of life and death** вопро́с жи́зни и сме́рти; **that's a ~ of opinion** э́то вопро́с мне́ния; **a ~ of taste** де́ло вку́са; (*pl., affairs*) дела́; **money ~s** де́нежные дела́; **to make ~s worse** в доверше́ние ко всем бе́дам. **6.: the ~** (*wrong, amiss*): **what's the ~?** в чём де́ло?; **what's the ~ with him?** что с ним?; **there's nothing the ~ (with me)** (у меня́) всё в поря́дке. **7.** (*importance*): **(it's) no ~** э́то нева́жно; **he could not do it, no ~ how he tried** как он ни стара́лся, он не мог э́того сде́лать. **8.: a ~ of** (*about*): **a ~ of £5** о́коло пяти́ фу́нтов; (*a few*): **he was back again in a ~ of hours** он верну́лся че́рез не́сколько часо́в. **9.: for that ~** е́сли уж на то пошло́. **10.: in the ~ of** в отноше́нии +*g.*; относи́тельно+*g.*; что каса́ется +*g.*

v.i. име́ть (*impf.*) значе́ние; **it doesn't ~ to me** э́то не име́ет для меня́ значе́ния; **does it ~ if I come late?** ничего́, е́сли я опозда́ю? **it doesn't ~ much if you come late** ничего́ стра́шного, е́сли вы опозда́ете.

cpd. **~-of-fact** *adj.* приземлённый, лишённый фанта́зии; сухо́й, делово́й.

matting ['mætɪŋ] *n.* рого́жка, цино́вка.

mattock ['mætək] *n.* моты́га.

mattress ['mætrɪs] *n.* матра́ц; **air ~** надувно́й матра́ц.

maturation [ˌmætjʊ'reɪʃ(ə)n] *n.* созрева́ние.

mature [mə'tjʊə(r)] *adj.* **1.** (*of fruit etc., ripe*) спе́лый; (*lit., fig., ripe, developed*) зре́лый. **2.** (*ready, prepared*) гото́вый. **3.** (*comm., ready for payment*) подлежа́щий опла́те; (*of debt*) подлежа́щий погаше́нию.

v.t. (*crops, wine etc.*) выде́рживать, вы́держать.

v.i. **1.** (*lit., fig., ripen, develop*) созр|ева́ть, -е́ть; **the grapes ~d in the sun** виногра́д созре́л на со́лнце; **his plans have not yet ~d** его́ пла́ны ещё не созре́ли/офо́рмились. **2.** (*become due for payment*): **the policy ~s next year** в бу́дущем году́ наступа́ет срок вы́платы по страхово́му по́лису.

maturity [məˌtjʊər'ɪtɪ] *n.* зре́лость; **reach ~** дост|ига́ть, -и́чь зре́лости; **bring to ~** заверши́ть (*pf.*).

matzo ['mɑːtsəʊ] *n.* маца́.

maudlin ['mɔːdlɪn] *adj.* слюня́во сентимента́льный.

maul [mɔːl] *v.t.* **1.** (*of pers.*) изб|ива́ть, -и́ть; **stop ~ing me about!** переста́ньте меня́ терза́ть!; (*of animal*) терза́ть, рас-. **2.** (*fig., by criticism*) громи́ть, раз-.

Maundy Thursday ['mɔːndɪ] *n.* Страстно́й Четве́рг.

mausoleum [ˌmɔːsə'liːəm] *n.* мавзоле́й.

mauve [məʊv] *n., adj.* розова́то-лило́вый (цвет).

maverick ['mævərɪk] *n.* (*calf*) неклеймёный телёнок; (*fig., dissenter; outsider*) диссиде́нт; (*attr.*) неприка́янный.

mawkish ['mɔːkɪʃ] *adj.* при́торный.

maxim ['mæksɪm] *n.* (*aphorism*) афори́зм; (*principle*) при́нцип.

maximize ['mæksɪˌmaɪz] *v.t.* максима́льно увели́чи|вать, -ть.

maximum ['mæksɪməm] *n.* ма́ксимум.

adj. максима́льный.

May[1] [meɪ] *n.* **1.** (*month*) май; **~ Day** Пе́рвое мая; пра́здник Пе́рвого ма́я. **2.** (*attr.*) ма́йский. **3. (m~)** (*hawthorn*) боя́рышник.

cpds. **~day** (*distress signal*) сигна́л бе́дствия; **~fly** *n.* подёнка; **~pole** *n.* ма́йское де́рево.

may[2] [meɪ] *v.aux.* **1.** (*expr. possibility*) мо́жет быть; пожа́луй; **it ~ be true** возмо́жно, э́то пра́вда; **it ~ not be true** возмо́жно, э́то не так; **he ~, might lose his way** он мо́жет заблуди́ться; **he might have lost his way without my help** без моей по́мощи он мог бы заблуди́ться; **I was afraid he might have lost his way** я боя́лся, как бы он не заблуди́лся; **you ~ well be right** вполне́ возмо́жно, вы и пра́вы; **we ~, might as well stay** почему́ бы нам не оста́ться; **and who ~, might you be?** а кто вы тако́й?; **that's as ~ be** э́то ещё вопро́с; **be that as it ~** как бы то ни́ было. **2.** (*expr. permission*): **~ I come and see you?** мо́жно мне (*or* могу́ я) к вам зайти́?; **you ~ go if you wish** е́сли хоти́те, мо́жете идти́; **you ~ not smoke** нельзя́ кури́ть. **3.** (*expr. suggestion*): **you might call at the butcher's** вы бы зашли́ к мяснику́. **4.** (*expr. reproach*): **you might offer to help!** вы могли́ бы предложи́ть свою́ по́мощь!; **you might have asked my permission** мо́жно бы́ло бы спроси́ть моего́ согла́сия. **5.** (*in subord. clauses, expr. purpose, fear, wish, hope*): **I wrote (so) that you might know** я вам написа́л, что́бы вы зна́ли; **I fear he ~ be dead** я бою́сь, что он у́мер; **I hope he ~ come** наде́юсь, он придёт; **I hoped he might come** я наде́ялся, что он придёт. **6.** (*in main clause, expr. wish or hope*): **~ you live long!** жела́ю вам до́лгой жи́зни!; **~ the best man win!** да победи́т сильне́йший! **7.** (*be able*): **try as I ~, I shall never learn to speak Russian well** как бы я ни стара́лся, я никогда́ не научу́сь хорошо́ говори́ть по-ру́сски.

cpds. **~be** *adv.* мо́жет быть.

mayhem ['meɪhem] *n.* нанесённые уве́чья; (*fig.*) разгро́м; **cause, create ~** нан|оси́ть, -ести́ уве́чье (*кому*).

mayonnaise [ˌmeɪə'neɪz] *n.* майоне́з.

mayor [meə(r)] *n.* мэр.

mayoress ['meərɪs] *n.* (*mayor's wife*) жена́ мэ́ра; (*female mayor*) же́нщина-мэр.

maze [meɪz] *n.* лабири́нт; (*fig.*) пу́таница.

mazurka [mə'zɜːkə] *n.* мазу́рка.

Mb ['megəˌbaɪt(z)] *n.* (*comput., abbr. of* **megabyte(s)**) мегаба́йт.

MBE (*abbr. of* ***Member of the Order of the British Empire***) кавале́р о́рдена Брита́нской импе́рии 5-й сте́пени.

MC (*abbr. of* ***Master of Ceremonies***) конферансье́.

MD *abbr. of* **1. *Doctor of Medicine*** до́ктор медици́ны. **2. *Managing Director*** дире́ктор-распоряди́тель.

ME (*abbr. of* ***myalgic encephalomyelitis***) миальги́ческий энцефаломиели́т.

mead [miːd] *n.* мёд.

meadow ['medəʊ] *n.* луг.

cpd. **~-sweet** *n.* та́волга; лаба́зник.

meagre ['miːgə(r)] *adj.* **1.** (*of pers., thin*) худо́й, то́щий. **2.** (*poor, scanty*) ску́дный; **~ fare** по́стная еда́.

meal[1] [miːl] *n.* (*ground grain*) мука́ (гру́бого помо́ла).

meal[2] [miːl] *n.* еда́; **have a good ~** пло́тно пое́сть (*pf.*); **have a light ~** заку́с|ывать, -и́ть; **it's a long time since I had a square ~** я давно́ не ел сы́тно; **don't make a ~ of it** (*coll., fig.*) не раздува́йте из э́того це́лую исто́рию; **we have 3 ~s a day** мы еди́м три ра́за в день; **let's have a ~ out this evening** дава́йте сего́дня поу́жинаем в рестора́не; **evening ~** у́жин; **midday ~** обе́д.

cpds. **~-ticket** *n.* тало́н на обе́д; **~time** *n.*: **at ~times** за едо́й.

mealy ['miːlɪ] *adj.* (*consisting of meal*) мучни́стый; (*resembling meal, floury*): **~ potatoes** рассы́пчатый карто́фель.

cpd. **~-mouthed** *adj.* чрезме́рно делика́тный.

mean[1] [miːn] *n.* (*intermediate or average point, condition etc.*) середи́на; **the golden ~** золота́я середи́на; (*math.*) сре́дняя величина́; (*pl., method, resources*) *see* **means**

adj. сре́дний; **Greenwich ~ time** сре́днее вре́мя по Гри́нвичу.

cpds. **~time** *n.*: **in the ~time** ме́жду тем; **~while** *adv.* ме́жду тем, тем вре́менем.

mean[2] [miːn] *adj.* **1.** (*lowly*) ни́зкий. **2.** (*inferior*): **he is a man of no ~ abilities** он челове́к незауря́дных спосо́бностей. **3.** (*shabby, squalid*): **~ streets** убо́гие у́лицы (*f. pl.*). **4.** (*niggardly*) скупо́й. **5.** (*ignoble; discreditable*) ни́зкий, по́длый. **6.** (*ill-natured, spiteful*) зло́бный; **don't be ~ to him** не обижа́йте его́.

mean[3] [miːn] *v.t.* **1.** (*intend*) име́ть (*impf.*) в виду́; намерева́ться (*impf.*); **I ~ to solve this problem** я наме́рен реши́ть э́тот вопро́с; **he ~s business** он берётся за де́ло всерьёз; **he ~s mischief** у него́ дурны́е наме́рения; **he ~s well by you** он жела́ет вам добра́; **I ~t no harm** я не жела́л зла; **I ~t it as a joke** я хоте́л пошути́ть; **I ~t to leave yesterday, but couldn't** я собира́лся вчера́ уе́хать, но не смог. **2.** (*design, destine*) предназн|ача́ть, -а́чить; **his parents ~t him to be a doctor** роди́тели про́чили его́ в доктора́; **they were ~t for each other** они́ бы́ли со́зданы друг для дру́га; **this letter is ~t for you** э́то письмо́ предназнача́ется вам. **3.** (*of person, intend to convey*) хоте́ть (*impf.*) сказа́ть; **what do you ~?** что вы э́тим хоти́те сказа́ть; **he ~s what he says** он говори́т то, что ду́мает; **what do you ~, 'finished'?** как так, зако́нчил?; **what do you ~ by it?** (*how dare you?*) как вы сме́ете? **4.** (*of words etc., signify*) зна́чить (*impf.*), означа́ть (*impf.*); **this sentence ~s nothing to me** э́то предложе́ние ничего́ мне не говори́т; **what is ~t by this word?** как на́до понима́ть э́то сло́во?; **modern music ~s nothing to me** совреме́нная му́зыка мне соверше́нно непоня́тна; **this ~s we can't go** зна́чит, мы не смо́жем пойти́; (*entail, involve*): **organizing a fête ~s a lot of hard work** подгото́вка к пра́зднику тре́бует мно́го уси́лий; (*portend*): **this ~s war** э́то приведёт к войне́; зна́чит, бу́дет война́.

meander [mɪ'ændə(r)] *v.i.* (*of streams, roads etc.*) извива́ться (*impf.*); **a ~ing river** изви́листая река́; (*of person, wander along*) броди́ть (*impf.*).

meaning ['mi:nɪŋ] *n.* значе́ние; **what is the ~ of this word?** что э́то сло́во означа́ет; **get the ~ of** пон|има́ть, -я́ть смысл +*g.*; **what is the ~ of this?** (*querying another's action*) что э́то зна́чит?

meaningful ['mi:nɪŋfʊl] *adj.* (*full of meaning*) многозначи́тельный; (*making sense*) содержа́тельный, толко́вый.

meaningless ['mi:nɪŋlɪs] *adj.* бессмы́сленный.

meanness ['mi:nnɪs] *n.* по́длость, ни́зость; ску́пость.

means [mi:nz] *n.* **1.** (*instrument, method*) спо́соб; **a ~ to an end** сре́дство для достиже́ния це́ли; **we shall find ways and ~ of persuading him** мы найдём спо́соб убеди́ть его́; **by ~ of** посре́дством+*g.*; с по́мощью +*g.*; **by all (manner of) ~** все́ми сре́дствами; **by all ~** (*US, without fail*) непреме́нно; (*expr. permission*) коне́чно; пожа́луйста; **by no ~** нико́им о́бразом; **it was by no ~ easy** э́то бы́ло отню́дь не легко́. **2.** (*facilities*): **~ of communication** (*transport*) сре́дства сообще́ния; (*telecommunication*) сре́дства свя́зи. **3.** (*resources*) сре́дства; **~ of existence** сре́дства к существова́нию; **a man of ~** челове́к со сре́дствами; **live beyond one's ~** жить (*impf.*) не по сре́дствам.

measles ['mi:z(ə)lz] *n.* корь; **German ~** красну́ха.

measly ['mi:zlɪ] *adj.* (*coll., miserably small*) жа́лкий.

measurable ['meʒərəb(ə)l] *adj.* измери́мый; **within ~ limits** в изве́стных преде́лах.

measure ['meʒə(r)] *n.* **1.** (*calculated quantity, size etc.; system of ~ment*) ме́ра; **dry ~** ме́ра сыпу́чих тел; **linear ~** лине́йная ме́ра; **liquid ~** ме́ра жи́дкостей; **clothes made to ~** оде́жда, сши́тая на зака́з. **2.** (*degree, extent*) сте́пень; **in some ~** до не́которой сте́пени; (*prescribed limit, extent*) преде́л; **set ~s to** ограни́чи|вать, -ть. **3.** (*measuring device*): **metre ~** метр; **litre ~** литро́вый ме́рный сосу́д. **4.** (*proceeding, step*) ме́ра, мероприя́тие; **take ~s against** прин|има́ть, -я́ть ме́ры про́тив+*g.*; **adopt severe ~s** примен|я́ть, -и́ть стро́гие ме́ры. **5.** (*law*) зако́н; **pass a ~** приня́ть (*pf.*) зако́н. **6.** (*verse rhythm*) разме́р; (*mus.*) такт.

v.t. **1.** (*find size etc. of*) ме́рить, с-; изм|еря́ть, -е́рить; **he was ~d for a suit** с него́ сня́ли ме́рку для костю́ма; (*fig.*): **I ~d him up and down** я сме́рил его́ взгля́дом. **2.** (*amount to when ~d*): **the room ~s 12 ft. across** ко́мната ширино́й в двена́дцать фу́тов.

with advs.: **~ off, ~ out** *vv.t.* отм|еря́ть, -е́рить; **the football pitch had been ~d out** футбо́льное по́ле бы́ло уже́ разме́чено; **~ up** *v.i.*: **the team has not ~d up to our expectations** кома́нда не оправда́ла на́ших ожида́ний.

measured ['meʒəd] *adj.* **1.** (*rhythmical*) разме́ренный; **~ tread** ме́рная по́ступь. **2.** (*of speech, moderate*) уме́ренный; (*carefully considered*) обду́манный.

measurement ['meʒəmənt] *n.* (*measuring*) измере́ние; (*dimension*) разме́р; **take s.o.'s ~s** снять (*pf.*) ме́рку с кого́-н.; **waist ~** объём та́лии.

meat [mi:t] *n.* мя́со; **one man's ~ is another man's poison** что поле́зно одному́, то друго́му вре́дно.

cpds. **~-ball** *n.* фрикаде́лька; **~-eating** *adj.* плотоя́дный; **~-pie** *n.* пиро́г с мя́сом.

meaty ['mi:tɪ] *adj.* мяси́стый; (*fig., pithy*) содержа́тельный.

Mecca ['mekə] *n.* (*lit., fig.*) Ме́кка.

mechanic [mɪ'kænɪk] *n.* меха́ник.

mechanical [mɪ'kænɪk(ə)l] *adj.* **1.** (*pert. to machines*) механи́ческий; **~ engineering** машинострое́ние; **a ~ failure** механи́ческое поврежде́ние; **~ly operated** с механи́ческим управле́нием. **2.** (*of pers. or movements: automatic*) машина́льный.

mechanics [mɪ'kænɪks] *n.* (*lit., fig.*) меха́ника.

mechanism ['mekə‚nɪz(ə)m] *n.* механи́зм.

mechanization [‚mekənaɪ'zeɪʃ(ə)n] *n.* механиза́ция.

mechanize ['mekə‚naɪz] *v.t. & i.* механизи́ровать(ся) (*impf., pf.*).

medal ['med(ə)l] *n.* меда́ль; (*mil. award*) о́рден (*pl.* -а́).

medallion [mɪ'dæljən] *n.* медальо́н.

medallist ['medəlɪst] *n.* (*recipient*) медали́ст (*fem.* -ка).

meddle ['med(ə)l] *v.i.*: **~ in** (*interfere in*) вме́ш|иваться, -а́ться в+*a.*; **~ with** (*touch, tamper with*) тро́|гать, -нуть.

meddlesome ['medəlsəm] *adj.* назо́йливый; **he is a ~ person** он всё вре́мя вме́шивается не в свои́ дела́.

media ['mi:dɪə] *see* **medium** *n.* **5.**

mediaeval [‚medɪ'i:v(ə)l] = **medieval**

median ['mi:dɪən] *n.* (*math., stat.*) медиа́на.

adj. среди́нный.

mediate ['mi:dɪ‚eɪt] *v.t.*: **the settlement was ~d by Britain** соглаше́ние бы́ло дости́гнуто при посре́дничестве Великобрита́нии.

v.i. выступа́ть, вы́ступить посре́дником; посре́дничать (*impf.*).

mediation [‚mi:dɪ'eɪʃ(ə)n] *n.* посре́дничество.

mediator ['mi:dɪ‚eɪtə(r)] *n.* посре́дник.

medical ['medɪk(ə)l] *n.* (*coll., ~ examination*): **have a ~** про|ходи́ть, -йти́ медици́нский осмо́тр (*abbr.* медосмо́тр).

adj. медици́нский; (*opp. surgical*) терапевти́ческий; **~ certificate** спра́вка от врача́; **~ history** исто́рия боле́зни; **~ man, practitioner** врач, терапе́вт; **~ officer** офице́р медици́нской слу́жбы; **~ orderly** санита́р; **~ service** медици́нское обслу́живание; **~ unit** санита́рная часть; санча́сть.

medicament [mɪ'dɪkəmənt, 'medɪkəmənt] *n.* лека́рство, медикаме́нт.

medication [‚medɪ'keɪʃ(ə)n] *n.* лече́ние.

medicinal [mɪ'dɪsɪn(ə)l] *adj.* (*of medicine*) лека́рственный; (*curative*) целе́бный.

medicine ['medsɪn, -dɪsɪn] *n.* **1.** (*science, practice*) медици́на; **practise ~** рабо́тать (*impf.*) врачо́м. **2.** (*substance*) лека́рство; медикаме́нт, миксту́ра; **he is taking ~ for a cough** он принима́ет лека́рство от ка́шля; **I gave him a taste of his own ~** (*fig.*) я ему́ отплати́л той же моне́той.

cpds. **~-chest** *n.* апте́чка; **~-man** *n.* зна́харь (*m.*).

medieval [‚medɪ'i:v(ə)l] *adj.* средневеко́вый.

mediocre [‚mi:dɪ'əʊkə(r)] *adj.* посре́дственный.

mediocrity [‚mi:dɪ'ɒkrɪtɪ] *n.* (*quality; person*) посре́дственность.

meditate ['medɪ‚teɪt] *v.i.* размышля́ть (*impf.*) (**on:** о+*p.*).

meditation [‚medɪ'teɪʃ(ə)n] *n.* размышле́ние.

meditative ['medɪtətɪv] *adj.* заду́мчивый.

Mediterranean [‚medɪtə'reɪnɪən] *n.* **(~ Sea)** Средизе́мное мо́ре.

adj. средиземномо́рский.

medium ['mi:dɪəm] *n.* **1.** (*middle quality*) середи́на; **he strikes a happy ~** он приде́рживается золото́й середи́ны. **2.** (*phys., intervening substance*) среда́. **3.** (*means, agency*) сре́дство; **through the ~ of** посре́дством+*g.* **4.** (*spiritualist*) ме́диум. **5.** (*means or channel of expression*) сре́дство; **the media** (*sc. of communication*) сре́дства ма́ссовой информа́ции.

adj. (*average*) сре́дний; **a man of ~ height** челове́к сре́днего ро́ста.

cpds. **~-sized** *adj.* сре́днего разме́ра; **~-wave** *adj.* среднево́лновый.
medley ['medlɪ] *n.* смесь; (*mus.*) попурри́ (*nt. indecl.*).
medusa [mɪ'dju:sə] *n.* (*zool.*) меду́за.
meek [mi:k] *adj.* кро́ткий.
meekness ['mi:knɪs] *n.* кро́тость.
meerschaum ['mɪəʃəm] *n.* (*clay*) морска́я пе́нка; (*pipe*) пе́нковая тру́бка.
meet[1] [mi:t] *n.* (*of sportsmen, etc.*) сбор.
v.t. **1.** (*encounter*) встр|еча́ть, -е́тить; **fancy ~ing you!** ну и встре́ча!; **~ s.o. halfway** (*fig.*) идти́, пойти́ навстре́чу кому́-н.; **a bus ~s all trains** к прихо́ду ка́ждого по́езда подаю́т авто́бус; (*make acquaintance of*) знако́миться, по- с+*i.*; **I met your sister in Moscow** я познако́мился с ва́шей сестро́й в Москве́; **(I want you to) ~ my fiancée** я хочу́ познако́мить вас с мое́й неве́стой. **2.** (*reach point of contact with*): **where the river ~s the sea** там, где река́ впада́ет в мо́ре; **there is more in this than ~s the eye** здесь де́ло не так про́сто. **3.** (*face*): **they advanced to ~ the enemy** они́ продви́нулись навстре́чу проти́внику; **I am ready to ~ your challenge** я гото́в приня́ть ваш вы́зов. **4.** (*experience, suffer*): **~ one's death** поги́бнуть (*pf.*); **he met misfortune with a smile** он му́жественно переноси́л невзго́ды. **5.** (*satisfy, answer, fulfil*): **I cannot ~ your wishes** я не могу́ вы́полнить (*pf.*) ва́ши тре́бования; **I'm afraid your offer does not ~ the case** я бою́сь, ва́ше предложе́ние не отвеча́ет тре́бованиям; **how can I ~ my commitments?** как мне вы́полнить свои́ обя́занности? **6.** (*pay, settle*): **~ a bill** упла́|чивать, -ти́ть по счёту; **this will barely ~ my expenses** э́то с трудо́м покро́ет мои́ расхо́ды.
v.i. **1.** (*of pers., come together*) встр|еча́ться, -е́титься; **haven't we met before?** мы с ва́ми не знако́мы?; **till we ~ again** до сле́дующей встре́чи; (*become acquainted*) знако́миться, по-; **we met at a dance** мы познако́мились на та́нцах. **2.** (*assemble*) соб|ира́ться, -ра́ться. **3.** (*of things, qualities etc.: come into contact, unite*) сходи́ться (*impf.*); **this belt won't ~ round his waist** э́тот по́яс на нём не схо́дится; **there are traffic lights where the roads ~** на перекрёстке — светофо́р; **the rivers Oka and Volga ~ at Nizhniy Novgorod** Ни́жний Но́вгород — ме́сто слия́ния рек Оки́ и Во́лги; **make (both) ends ~** (*fig.*) св|оди́ть, -ести́ концы́ с конца́ми. **4. ~ with: ~ with difficulties** испы́т|ывать, -а́ть затрудне́ния; **I met with much opposition** я натолкну́лся на си́льное сопротивле́ние; **he met with an accident** с ним произошёл несча́стный слу́чай.
with advs.: **~ together** *v.i.* соб|ира́ться, -ра́ться; **~ up** *v.i.* (*coll.*): **we met up (*or* I met up with him) in London** мы встре́тились в Ло́ндоне.
meeting ['mi:tɪŋ] *n.* **1.** (*encounter*) встре́ча; **our ~ was purely accidental** мы встре́тились соверше́нно случа́йно; (*by arrangement*) свида́ние. **2.** (*gathering*) собра́ние; **address a ~** выступа́ть, вы́ступить на собра́нии; (*political ~*) ми́тинг; (*session*) заседа́ние. **3.** (*sports ~*) (спорти́вное) состяза́ние; (*race-~*) ска́чки (*f. pl.*).
cpd. **~-house** *n.* моли́твенный дом.
megabyte ['megə,baɪt] *n.* (*comput.*) мегаба́йт.
megacycle ['megə,saɪk(ə)l] *n.* мегаге́рц.
megalith ['megəlɪθ] *n.* мегали́т.
megalithic [,megə'lɪθɪk] *n.* мегалити́ческий.
megalomania [,megələ'meɪnɪə] *n.* мегалома́ния, ма́ния вели́чия.
megalomaniac [,megələ'meɪnɪ,æk] *n.* страда́ющий ма́нией вели́чия.
megaphone ['megə,fəʊn] *n.* мегафо́н.
megaton ['megə,tʌn] *n.* мегато́н.
megawatt ['megə,wɒt] *n.* мегава́тт.
melancholia [,melən'kəʊlɪə] *n.* меланхо́лия.
melancholy ['melənkəlɪ] *n.* уны́ние.
adj. (*of pers.*) уны́лый; (*of things: saddening*) гру́стный, печа́льный.
mélange [meɪ'lɑ̃ʒ] *n.* смесь.
mêlée ['meleɪ] *n.* сва́лка.
mellifluous [mɪ'lɪflʊəs] *adj.* медоточи́вый.
mellow ['meləʊ] *adj.* **1.** (*of fruit*) спе́лый; (*of wine*) вы́держанный. **2.** (*of voice, sound, colour, light*) со́чный. **3.** (*of character: softened*) подобре́вший; (*genial*) доброду́шный.
v.t.: **fruit ~ed by the sun** плод, созре́вший на со́лнце; **age has ~ed him** го́ды смягчи́ли его́ хара́ктер.
v.i. (*of fruit*) созр|ева́ть, -е́ть; посп|ева́ть, -е́ть; (*of pers.*) смягч|а́ться, -и́ться; добре́ть, по-.
melodic [mɪ'lɒdɪk] *adj.* мелоди́чный.
melodious [mɪ'ləʊdɪəs] *adj.* мелоди́чный; **~ voice** певу́чий го́лос.
melodiousness [mɪ'ləʊdɪəsnɪs] *n.* мелоди́чность, певу́честь.
melodrama ['melə,drɑ:mə] *n.* (*lit., fig.*) мелодра́ма.
melodramatic [,melədrə'mætɪk] *adj.* мелодрамати́ческий.
melody ['melədɪ] *n.* мело́дия.
melon ['melən] *n.* ды́ня; **(water-~)** арбу́з.
melt [melt] *v.t.* **1.** (*reduce to liquid: of ice, snow, butter, wax*) раст|а́пливать, -опи́ть; (*of metal*) пла́вить, рас-. **2.** (*dissolve*) раствор|я́ть, -и́ть. **3.** (*fig., soften*) размягч|а́ть, -и́ть.
v.i. **1.** (*become liquid: of ice, snow, butter, wax*) та́ять, рас-; (*of metal*) пла́виться, рас-. **2.** (*dissolve*) раствор|я́ться, -и́ться. **3.** (*fig., soften*) смягч|а́ться, -и́ться; та́ять, от-; **her heart ~ed at the sight** её се́рдце смягчи́лось при ви́де э́того. **4.** (*change slowly; merge*): **one colour ~ed into another** оди́н цвет переходи́л в друго́й. **5.** (*coll., suffer from heat*): **I'm ~ing!** я весь распла́вился (от жары́).
with advs.: **~ away** *v.i.* (*lit., fig., disappear*) та́ять, рас-; (*fig., disperse*) рассе́|иваться, -яться; **~ down** *v.t.* распл|авля́ть, -а́вить.
melting [meltɪŋ] *n.* плавле́ние.
cpds. **~-point** *n.* температу́ра плавле́ния; **~-pot** *n.* ти́гель (*m.*).
member ['membə(r)] *n.* член, уча́стни|к (*fem.* -ца) (о́бщества *и т.п.*); **full ~** полнопра́вный член.
membership ['membəʃɪp] *n.* (*being a member*) чле́нство; (*collect., members*) чле́ны (*m. pl.*); (*number of members*) число́ чле́нов; (*composition*) соста́в; **admission to ~** приня́тие (*в клуб и т.п.*); **~ card** чле́нский биле́т.
membrane ['membreɪn] *n.* перепо́нка, мембра́на.
memento [mɪ'mentəʊ] *n.* сувени́р; **as a ~** на па́мять.
memo ['meməʊ] = **memorandum**
memoir ['memwɑ:(r)] *n.* (*brief biography*) (биографи́ческая) заме́тка; (*pl., autobiography*) воспомина́ния (*nt. pl.*), мемуа́р|ы (*pl., g.* -ов).
memorable ['memərəb(ə)l] *adj.* достопа́мятный.
memorandum [,memə'rændəm] *n.* (*written reminder*) запи́ска; (*record of events, facts, transactions etc.*) докладна́я запи́ска; (*dipl.*) мемора́ндум; **memo(randum) book, pad** записна́я кни́жка; блокно́т.
memorial [mɪ'mɔ:rɪəl] *n.* (*commemorative object, custom etc.*) па́мятник.
adj.: **~ plaque** мемориа́льная доска́; **~ service** помина́льная слу́жба.
memorialize [mɪ'mɔ:rɪə,laɪz] *v.t.* (*commemorate*) увекове́чи|вать, -ть.
memorize ['memə,raɪz] *v.t.* (*commit to memory*) зап|омина́ть, -о́мнить; (*learn by heart*) зау́ч|ивать, -и́ть (наизу́сть).
memory ['memərɪ] *n.* **1.** (*faculty; its use*) па́мять; **I have a bad ~ for faces** у меня́ плоха́я па́мять на ли́ца; **search, rack one's ~** ры́ться, по- в па́мяти; **play by, from ~** игра́ть (*impf.*) на па́мять; **lose one's**

~ лиш|а́ться, -и́ться па́мяти; **loss of ~** потеря па́мяти; **may I refresh, jog your ~?** позво́льте вам напо́мнить; **in ~ of** в па́мять +*g.*; **within living ~** на па́мяти живу́щих. **2.** (*recollection*) воспомина́ние; **I have a clear ~ of what happened** я я́сно по́мню, что случи́лось. **3.** (*comput.*): **~ bank, store** маши́нная па́мять; запомина́ющее устро́йство.

menace ['menɪs] *n.* (*threat*) угро́за; (*obnoxious person*) (*coll.*) зану́да (*c.g.*).

v.t. угрожа́ть (*impf.*) +*d.*

menagerie [mɪ'nædʒərɪ] *n.* (*lit.*, *fig.*) звери́нец.

mend [mend] *n.* **1.** (*patch*) запла́та; (*darn*) што́пка. **2. be on the ~** идти́ (*det.*) на попра́вку.

v.t. **1.** (*repair*; *make sound again*) чини́ть, по-; заш|ива́ть, -и́ть; **~ socks** што́пать, за- носки́. **2.** (*improve*, *reform*) испр|авля́ть, -а́вить; **~ one's ways** испр|авля́ться, -а́виться.

v.i. (*regain health*) выздора́вливать, вы́здороветь; **his leg is ~ing nicely** его́ нога́ заживáет хорошо́.

mendacious [men'deɪʃəs] *adj.* лжи́вый.

mendacity [men'dæsɪtɪ] *n.* лжи́вость.

mendicancy ['mendɪkənsɪ] *n.* ни́щенство.

mendicant ['mendɪkənt] *n.* & *adj.* ни́щий.

mending ['mendɪŋ] *n.* (*of clothes*) почи́нка, што́пка; **invisible ~** худо́жественная што́пка.

menfolk ['menfəʊk] *n.* мужчи́ны (*m. pl.*).

menial ['mi:nɪəl] *adj.* лаке́йский; **~ work** чёрная рабо́та.

meningitis [,menɪn'dʒaɪtɪs] *n.* менинги́т.

menopause ['menə,pɔ:z] *n.* кли́макс.

Menshevik ['menʃəvɪk] *n.* меньшеви́к; (*attr.*) меньшеви́стский.

menstrual ['menstrʊəl] *adj.* менструа́льный.

menstruate ['menstrʊ,eɪt] *v.i.* менструи́ровать (*impf.*).

menstruation [,menstrʊ'eɪʃ(ə)n] *n.* менструа́ция.

menswear ['menzweə(r)] *n.* мужска́я оде́жда.

mental ['ment(ə)l] *adj.* **1.** (*of the mind*) у́мственный; **~ powers** у́мственные спосо́бности; **~ deficiency** слабоу́мие; **~ly defective** у́мственно отста́лый. **2.** (*pert. to ~ illness*) психи́ческий; **~ disease** психи́ческая боле́знь; **~ home, hospital** психиатри́ческая больни́ца; **~ patient** душевнобольно́й. **3.** (*carried out in the mind*) мы́сленный; **~ reservation** мы́сленная огово́рка; **he made a ~ note of the number** он отме́тил но́мер в уме́; **~ arithmetic** у́стный счёт.

mentality [men'tælɪtɪ] *n.* (*capacity*) у́мственные спосо́бности (*f. pl.*); (*level*) у́мственное разви́тие; (*attitude*) пси́хика.

menthol ['menθɒl] *n.* ментóл, мя́та.

mentholated ['menθə,leɪtɪd] *adj.* ментóловый.

mention ['menʃ(ə)n] *n.* упомина́ние; **there was a ~ of him in the paper** в газе́те упомина́лось его́ и́мя; **he made no ~ whatever of your illness** он ни сло́вом не обмо́лвился о ва́шей боле́зни.

v.t. упом|ина́ть, -яну́ть (*кого/что or о ком/чём*); **I shall ~ it to him** я скажу́ ему́ об э́том; **~ s.o.'s name** наз|ыва́ть, -ва́ть чьё-н. и́мя; **forgive me for ~ing it, but ...** прости́те, что я говорю́ об э́том, но...; **don't ~ it!** не́ за что!; ничего́; не сто́ит!; **not to ~** не говоря́ уж о+*p.*; не то́лько что.

mentor ['mentɔ:(r)] *n.* наста́вник, ме́нтор.

menu ['menju:] *n.* меню́ (*nt. indecl.*).

mercantile ['mɜ:kən,taɪl] *adj.* торго́вый; **~ marine** торго́вый флот.

mercenary ['mɜ:sɪnərɪ] *n.* наёмник.

adj. (*hired*) наёмный; (*motivated by money*) коры́стный.

merchandise ['mɜ:tʃən,daɪz] *n.* това́ры (*m. pl.*).

merchant ['mɜ:tʃ(ə)nt] *n.* (*trader*) купе́ц; (*attr.*) купе́ческий; (*with qualifying word*: *dealer*, *tradesman*) торго́вец; **wine ~** торго́вец ви́нами; (*attr.*) торго́вый; **~ ship** торго́вое су́дно; **~ marine, navy** торго́вый флот; **~ bank** комме́рческий банк.

merciful ['mɜ:sɪ,fʊl] *adj.* милосе́рдный, сострада́тельный; **his death was a ~ release** смерть была́ для него́ бла́гом; **we were ~ly spared the details** к сча́стью, нас не посвяти́ли во все подро́бности.

merciless ['mɜ:sɪlɪs] *adj.* беспоща́дный, безжа́лостный.

mercurial [mɜ:'kjʊərɪəl] *adj.* **1.** (*of mercury*) рту́тный. **2.** (*of pers.*, *lively*) живо́й; (*volatile*) непостоя́нный, изме́нчивый.

mercuric [mɜ:'kjʊərɪk] *adj.*: **~ chloride** суле́ма; **~ oxide** о́кись рту́ти.

Mercury[1] ['mɜ:kjʊrɪ] *n.* (*myth.*, *astron.*) Мерку́рий.

mercury[2] ['mɜ:kjʊrɪ] *n.* (*metal*) ртуть; **~ column** (*of barometer*) рту́тный столб.

mercy ['mɜ:sɪ] *n.* **1.** (*compassion*, *forbearance*, *clemency*) милосе́рдие; поща́да; **beg for ~** проси́ть (*impf.*) поща́ды; **show ~ to** (*or* **have ~ on**) щади́ть, по-; **they were given no ~** им не́ было поща́ды; **throw o.s. on s.o.'s ~** сда́ться (*pf.*) на ми́лость кого́-н.; **act of ~** акт милосе́рдия; **~ killing** эйтана́зия, умерщвле́ние неизлечи́мых больны́х; **God's ~** ми́лость Бо́жья; **Lord, have ~ upon us!** Го́споди, поми́луй! **2.** (*power*): **at the ~ of** во вла́сти +*g.* **3.** (*blessing*): **it's a ~ he wasn't drowned** сча́стье, что он не утону́л.

mere [mɪə(r)] *adj.* **1.** (*simple*; *pure*) просто́й; чи́стый; (*absolute*) су́щий; (*no more than*, *nothing but*) не бо́лее чем; всего́ лишь; то́лько; **~ coincidence** просто́е совпаде́ние; **by the ~st chance** по чи́стой случа́йности; **it's a ~ trifle** э́то су́щая ме́лочь; **he is a ~ child** он всего́ лишь ребёнок; **they received a ~ pittance** они́ получа́ли су́щие гроши́. **2.** (*single*; *...alone*) оди́н (то́лько); **at the ~ thought** при одно́й мы́сли; **the ~ sight of him disgusts me** оди́н его́ вид вызыва́ет у меня́ отвраще́ние.

merely ['mɪəlɪ] *adv.* (*simply*) про́сто; (*only*) то́лько.

meretricious [,merɪ'trɪʃəs] *adj.* мишу́рный.

merge [mɜ:dʒ] *v.t.* & *i.* сл|ива́ть(ся), -и́ть(ся).

merger ['mɜ:dʒə(r)] *n.* слия́ние; (*comm.*) объедине́ние.

meridian [mə'rɪdɪən] *n.* (*geog.*) меридиа́н; (*astr. and fig.*) зени́т.

meringue [mə'ræŋ] *n.* мере́нга.

merino [mə'ri:nəʊ] *n.* (*sheep*) мерино́с; (*wool*) мерино́совая шерсть.

merit ['merɪt] *n.* (*deserving quality*, *worth*) досто́инство; **there is some ~ in the suggestion** в э́том предложе́нии есть свои́ плю́сы; (*action etc. deserving recognition*) заслу́га; **he was rewarded according to his ~s** он был вознаграждён по заслу́гам; (*pl.*, *rights and wrongs*): **one must decide each question on its ~s** на́до реша́ть ка́ждый вопро́с по существу́.

v.t. заслу́ж|ивать, -и́ть.

meritocracy [,merɪ'tɒkrəsɪ] *n.* о́бщество, управля́емое людьми́ с наибо́льшими спосо́бностями.

meritorious [,merɪ'tɔ:rɪəs] *adj.* похва́льный.

mermaid ['mɜ:meɪd] *n.* руса́лка.

merman ['mɜ:mæn] *n.* водяно́й трито́н.

merriment ['merɪmənt] *n.* весе́лье.

merry ['merɪ] *adj.* **1.** (*happy*, *full of gaiety*) весёлый; **make ~** (*have fun*) весели́ться, по-; **M~ Christmas!** с Рождество́м (Христо́вым)!

cpds. **~-go-round** *n.* карусе́ль; **~-making** *n.* весе́лье, потéха.

mesh [meʃ] *n.* **1.** (*space in net etc.*) яче́йка; **~ bag** аво́ська. **2.** (*pl.*, *network*) сеть; (*fig.*, *snares*) се́ти (*f. pl.*). **3.: in ~** (*mech.*) сце́пленный.

v.i. (*interlock*) зацеп|ля́ться, -и́ться.

mesmeric [mez'merɪk] *adj.* гипноти́ческий.

mesmerism ['mezmə,rɪz(ə)m] *n.* гипноти́зм.

mesmerist ['mezmərɪst] *n.* гипнотизёр.

mesmerize ['mezmə,raɪz] *v.t.* (*lit.*, *fig.*) гипнотизи́ровать, за-.

mesolithic [ˌmezəʊ'lɪθɪk] *adj.* мезоли́тический; **~ age** сре́дний ка́менный век.
Mesozoic [ˌmesəʊ'zəʊɪk] *adj.* мезозо́йский.
mess[1] [mes] *n.* **1.** (*disorder*) беспоря́док; **the room was in a complete ~** ко́мната была́ в соверше́нном беспоря́дке; **make a ~ of** (*spoil*; *bungle*) прова́л|ивать, -и́ть; **he made a ~ of his life** он загуби́л свою́ жизнь. **2.** (*dirt*) грязь; **make a ~ of** (*soil*) па́чкать, за-. **3.** (*confusion*) пу́таница. **4.** (*trouble*) неприя́тность, беда́, го́ре.
v.t. (*make dirty, esp. with excrement*): **Johnny's ~ed his pants** Джо́нни замара́л штани́шки.
v.i.: **~ with** (*interfere with*) вме́шиваться (*impf.*) в+*a.*
with advs.: **~ about** *v.t.* (*inconvenience*) причиня́ть (*impf.*) неудо́бство +*d.*; *v.i.* (*work half-heartedly or without plan*) ковыря́ться (*impf.*); (*potter, idle about*) канители́ться (*impf.*); **~ about with** (*fiddle with*) вози́ться (*impf.*) с+*i.*; **~ up** *v.t.* (*make dirty*) па́чкать, пере-; (*bungle*) прова́л|ивать, -и́ть; (*put into confusion*) перепу́т|ывать, -ать.
mess[2] [mes] *n.* (*eating-place*) столо́вая; **officers' ~** офице́рский клуб.
cpds. **~-kit** *n.* столо́вый набо́р; **~-tin** *n.* котело́к.
message ['mesɪdʒ] *n.* **1.** (*formal*) сообще́ние; (*informal*) запи́ска, за́пись; **I received a ~ by telephone** мне переда́ли по телефо́ну; **can I take a ~ for him?** что ему́ переда́ть?; **have you got the ~?** (*understood*) до вас дошло́?; поня́тно? **2.** (*writer's theme*) иде́йное содержа́ние; (*prophet's teaching*) уче́ние.
messenger ['mesɪndʒə(r)] *n.* курье́р, посы́льный.
cpd. **~-boy** *n.* ма́льчик на посы́лках.
Messiah [mɪ'saɪə] *n.* Мессия (*m.*).
Messianic [ˌmesɪ'ænɪk] *adj.* мессиа́нский.
Messrs ['mesəz] *n. pl.* (*abbr. of* ***Messieurs***) господ|а́ (*pl. g.* —).
messy ['mesɪ] *adj.* (*untidy*) неу́бранный; (*dirty*) гря́зный; (*slovenly*) неря́шливый.
metabolic [ˌmetə'bɒlɪk] *adj.*: **~ disease** наруше́ние обме́на веще́ств.
metabolism [mɪ'tæbəˌlɪz(ə)m] *n.* обме́н веще́ств.
metacarpus [ˌmetə'kɑ:pəs] *n.* пясть.
metal ['met(ə)l] *n.* мета́лл; **ferrous/non-ferrous ~s** чёрные/цветны́е мета́ллы.
adj. металли́ческий.
cpds. **~-detector** металлоиска́тель (*m.*); **~work** *n.* металлообрабо́тка; **~worker** *n.* сле́сарь (*m.*).
metallic [mɪ'tælɪk] *adj.* металли́ческий.
metalliferous [ˌmetə'lɪfərəs] *adj.* рудоно́сный.
metallurgic(al) [ˌmetə'lɜ:dʒɪk(ə)l] *adj.* металлурги́ческий.
metallurgist [me'tælədʒɪst] *n.* металлу́рг.
metallurgy [mɪ'tælədʒɪ, 'metəˌlɜ:dʒɪ] *n.* металлу́ргия.
metamorphose [ˌmetə'mɔ:fəʊz] *v.t.* превра|ща́ть, -ти́ть.
metamorphosis [ˌmetə'mɔ:fəsɪs, ˌmetəmɔ:'fəʊsɪs] *n.* метаморфо́за.
metaphor ['metəˌfɔ:(r)] *n.* мета́фора.
metaphorical [ˌmetə'fɒrɪk(ə)l] *adj.* метафори́ческий; **~ly speaking** о́бразно говоря́.
metaphysical [ˌmetə'fɪzɪk(ə)l] *adj.* метафизи́ческий; **~ poet** поэ́т метафизи́ческой шко́лы.
metaphysics [ˌmetə'fɪzɪks] *n.* метафи́зика.
metatarsal [ˌmetə'tɑ:səl] *n.* **(~ bone)** плюснева́я кость.
adj. плюснево́й.
metatarsus [ˌmetə'tɑ:səs] *n.* плюсна́.
mete (out) [mi:t] *v.t.* назн|ача́ть, -а́чить; выделя́ть, вы́делить.
meteor ['mi:tɪə(r)] *n.* метео́р.
meteoric [ˌmi:tɪ'ɒrɪk] *adj.* **1.** (*of meteors*) метеори́ческий; (*fig.*): **a ~ career** метеори́ческая карье́ра. **2.** (*of the atmosphere*) метеорологи́ческий.
meteorite ['mi:tɪəˌraɪt] *n.* метеори́т.
meteorological [ˌmi:tɪərə'lɒdʒɪk(ə)l] *adj.* метеорологи́ческий; **~ centre, office** слу́жба пого́ды.
meteorologist [ˌmi:tɪə'rɒlədʒɪst] *n.* метеоро́лог.
meteorology [ˌmi:tɪə'rɒlədʒɪ] *n.* метеороло́гия.
meter[1] ['mi:tə(r)] *n.* (*apparatus*) счётчик; **gas ~** га́зовый счётчик; **a man came to read the ~** слу́жащий пришёл снять показа́ния счётчика.
v.t. изм|еря́ть, -е́рить; зам|еря́ть, -е́рить.
meter[2] ['mi:tə(r)] = **metre**
methane ['meθeɪn, 'mi:θeɪn] *n.* мета́н.
method ['meθəd] *n.* (*mode, way*) ме́тод, спо́соб; (*system*) систе́ма, мето́дика.
methodical [mɪ'θɒdɪk(ə)l] *adj.* (*systematic*) системати́ческий; (*of regular habits*) методи́чный.
Methodism ['meθəˌdɪz(ə)m] *n.* методи́зм.
Methodist ['meθədɪst] *n.* методи́ст; (*attr.*) методи́стский.
methodological [ˌmeθədə'lɒdʒɪk(ə)l] *adj.* методологи́ческий.
meths [meθs] (*coll.*) = **methylated spirit**
methyl ['meθɪl, 'mi:θaɪl] *n.* мети́л; (*attr.*): **~ alcohol** мети́ловый спирт.
methylated ['meθɪˌleɪtɪd] *adj.*: **~ spirit** денатура́т.
meticulous [mə'tɪkjʊləs] *adj.* тща́тельный, педанти́чный.
meticulousness [mə'tɪkjʊləsnɪs] *n.* тща́тельность, педанти́чность.
métier ['metjeɪ] *n.* (*profession*) профе́ссия; (*trade*) ремесло́.
met|re ['mi:tə(r)] (*US* **-er**) *n.* (*unit of length*) метр; (*verse rhythm*) разме́р.
metric ['metrɪk] *adj.* метри́ческий.
metrication [ˌmetrɪ'keɪʃ(ə)n] *n.* введе́ние метри́ческой систе́мы.
metrics ['metrɪks] *n.* ме́трика.
Metro ['metrəʊ] *n.* метро́ (*indecl.*).
metronome ['metrəˌnəʊm] *n.* метроно́м.
metropolis [mɪ'trɒpəlɪs] *n.* столи́ца.
metropolitan [ˌmetrə'pɒlɪt(ə)n] *n.* (*eccl.*) митрополи́т.
adj. (*of capital*) столи́чный.
mettle ['met(ə)l] *n.* (*strength of character*) хара́ктер; **show one's ~** прояви́ть (*pf.*) свой хара́ктер; (*spirit, combativeness*) боево́е настрое́ние.
mew [mju:] *n.* (*of cat*) мяу́канье.
v.i. мяу́к|ать, -нуть.
mews [mju:z] *n.* коню́шни (*f. pl.*) (переде́ланные в жило́е помеще́ние).
Mexico ['meksɪˌkəʊ] *n.* Ме́ксика.
mezzanine ['metsəˌni:n, 'mez-] *n.* антресо́ль, полуэта́ж.
mezzo ['metsəʊ] *adv.* по́лу-; **~ forte** дово́льно гро́мко.
cpd. **~-soprano** *n.* ме́ццо-сопра́но (*indecl.*).
mg. ['mɪlɪˌgræm(z)] *n.* (*abbr. of* **milligram(me)(s)**) мг, (миллигра́м).
miaou, miaow [mɪ'aʊ] n. мяу́канье; (*onomat.*) мя́у!
v.i. мяу́кать (*impf.*).
miasma [mɪ'æzmə, maɪ-] *n.* миа́зм|ы (*pl., g.* —).
mica ['maɪkə] *n.* слюда́; (*attr.*) слюдяно́й.
Michaelmas ['mɪkəlməs] *n.* Миха́йлов день; **~ term** (*acad.*) осе́нний триме́стр.
mickey ['mɪkɪ] *n.* (*sl.*): **take the ~ out of s.o.** издева́ться (*impf.*) над кем-н.
microbe ['maɪkrəʊb] *n.* микро́б.
microbiologist [ˌmaɪkrəʊbaɪ'ɒlədʒɪst] *n.* микробио́лог.
microbiology [ˌmaɪkrəʊbaɪ'ɒlədʒɪ] *n.* микробиоло́гия.
microcircuit ['maɪkrəʊˌsɜ:kɪt] *n.* микросхе́ма.
microcomputer ['maɪkrəʊkəm'pju:tə(r)] *n.* микрокомпью́тер.
microcosm ['maɪkrəˌkɒz(ə)m] *n.* микроко́см.
microcomponent [ˌmaɪkrəʊkəm'pəʊnənt] *n.* микроэлеме́нт.
micro-electronics [ˌmaɪkrəʊɪlek'trɒnɪks] *n.* микроэлектро́ника.

microfiche ['maɪkrəʊ,fi:ʃ] *n.* микрофи́ша.
microfilm ['maɪkrəʊfɪlm] *n.* микрофи́льм.
micrometer [maɪ'krɒmɪtə(r)] *n.* микро́метр.
micron ['maɪkrɒn] *n.* микро́н.
microphone ['maɪkrə,fəʊn] *n.* микрофо́н.
microscope ['maɪkrə,skəʊp] *n.* микроско́п.
microscopic [,maɪkrə'skɒpɪk] *adj.* микроскопи́ческий.
microsurgery ['maɪkrəʊ,sɜ:dʒərɪ] *n.* микрохирурги́я.
microwave ['maɪkrəʊ,weɪv] *n.* микроволна́; (*attr.*) микрово́лновый; ~ **oven** высокочасто́тная печь.
mid [mɪd] *adj. & pref*: **in ~ air** (высоко́) в во́здухе; **in ~ Channel** посреди́ Ла-Ма́нша; **in ~ course** посреди́не пути́; **from ~ June to ~ July** с середи́ны ию́ня до середи́ны ию́ля; **she interrupted him in ~ sentence** она́ прервала́ его́ на полусло́ве.

cpds. **~day** *n.* по́лдень (*m.*); *adj.*: **the ~day sun** полу́денное со́лнце; **the M~lands** центра́льные гра́фства А́нглии; **~night** *n.* по́лночь; **during the ~night hours** в полночь; **he was burning the ~night oil** он рабо́тал по ноча́м; **~summer** *n.* середи́на ле́та; **at ~summer** среди́ ле́та; *adj.* **M~summer Day** Ива́нов день; **~way** *adv.* на полпути́; **~winter** *n.* середи́на зимы́.
middle ['mɪd(ə)l] *n.* **1.** середи́на; (*of time*): **in the ~ of the night** посреди́ но́чи; **I was in the ~ of getting ready** в тот моме́нт я как раз собира́лся. **2.** (*waist*) та́лия; **he caught her round the ~** он о́бнял/схвати́л её за та́лию.

adj. сре́дний; **in ~ age** в сре́днем во́зрасте; **the M~ Ages** сре́дние века́; **the ~ classes** сре́дние сло́и о́бщества; буржуази́я; **~ distance** сре́дний план; **M~ East** Бли́жний Восто́к; **M~ English** средне-англи́йский язы́к; **~ finger** сре́дний па́лец; **his ~ name is George** его́ второ́е и́мя — Гео́ргий; **~ school** сре́дняя шко́ла.

cpds. **~-aged** *adj.* сре́дних лет; **~-class** *adj.* буржуа́зный; **~man** *n.* посре́дник; **~-of-the-road** *adj.* уме́ренных (полити́ческих) взгля́дов; **~weight** *n. & adj.* (боксёр) сре́днего ве́са.
middling ['mɪdlɪŋ] *adj.* сре́дний, второсо́ртный; **fair to ~** так себе́.

adv. сно́сно; ничего́, так себе́.
midge [mɪdʒ] *n.* кома́р, мо́шка.
midget ['mɪdʒɪt] *n.* ка́рлик; (*attr.*) ка́рликовый.
midpoint ['mɪd,pɔɪnt] *n.* сре́дняя то́чка.
midshipman ['mɪdʃɪpmən] *n.* ми́чман, гардемари́н.
midst [mɪdst] *n.* середи́на; **in the ~ of** среди́, в разга́р +*g.*, ме́жду+*i.*; **in our ~** среди́ нас.
midwife ['mɪdwaɪf] *n.* акуше́рка; повива́льная ба́бка.
midwifery ['mɪd,wɪfərɪ] *n.* акуше́рство.
mien [mi:n] *n.* (*liter.*) вид, нару́жность.
miff [mɪf] *v.t.* (*coll.*): **he was ~ed by my remark** моё замеча́ние его́ оби́дело.
might[1] [maɪt] *n.* **1.** (*power to enforce will*) мощь; **~ is right** кто силён, тот и прав. **2.** (*strength*) си́ла; **with (all his) ~ and main** изо всей мо́чи.
might[2] [maɪt] *v. aux. see* **may**
mighty ['maɪtɪ] *adj.* **1.** (*powerful*) мо́щный; (*great*) вели́кий; **high and ~** (*pompous, arrogant*) зано́счивый. **2.** (*massive*) грома́дный.

adv. (*US coll.*) о́чень.
mignonette [,mɪnjə'net] *n.* резеда́.
migraine ['mi:greɪn, 'maɪ-] *n.* мигре́нь.
migrant ['maɪgrənt] *n.* переселе́нец.

adj. кочу́ющий; перелётный.
migrate [maɪ'greɪt] *v.i.* пересел|я́ться, -и́ться; мигри́ровать (*impf.*); (*of birds*) соверш|а́ть, -и́ть перелёт.
migration [maɪ'greɪʃ(ə)n] *n.* мигра́ция; перелёт.
migratory [maɪ'greɪtərɪ] *adj.* перелётный.
mike [maɪk] (*coll.*) = **microphone**
milch [mɪltʃ] *adj.*: **~ cow** до́йная коро́ва.
mild [maɪld] *adj.* мя́гкий; (*of pers.*) кро́ткий, ти́хий; **a ~ reproof** мя́гкий упрёк; **to put it ~ly** мя́гко говоря́; **a ~ cheese** нео́стрый/мя́гкий сыр; **~ steel** мя́гкая сталь; **~ tobacco** сла́бый таба́к.
mildew ['mɪldju:] *n.* ми́лдью (*nt. indecl.*), ложномучни́стая роса́.
mildness ['maɪldnɪs] *n.* мя́гкость; (*of food etc.*) пре́сность.
mile [maɪl] *n.* ми́ля; **for ~s around** на мно́го миль вокру́г; **30 ~s an hour** 30 миль в час; (*fig.*): **I am feeling ~s better** мне намно́го лу́чше; **I was ~s away** я замечта́лся; **it sticks out a ~** э́то ви́дно за версту́.

cpd. **~stone** *n.* ка́мень с указа́нием расстоя́ния; (*fig.*) ве́ха.
mileage ['maɪlɪdʒ] *n.* **1.** (*distance in miles*) расстоя́ние в ми́лях; (*of car*) пробе́г автомоби́ля в ми́лях; **~ indicator** счётчик про́йденного пути́. **2.** (*travel expenses*) проездны́е (*pl.*). **3.** (*coll., benefit*) по́льза, вы́года.
milieu [mɪ'ljɜ:, 'mi:ljɜ:] *n.* окруже́ние, среда́.
militancy ['mɪlɪt(ə)nsɪ] *n.* вои́нственность.
militant ['mɪlɪt(ə)nt] *n.* бо́ец, бо́рец; активи́ст (*fem.* -ка).

adj. вои́нствующий; **~ students** вои́нственно настро́енные студе́нты.
militarism ['mɪlɪtə,rɪz(ə)m] *n.* милитари́зм.
militarist ['mɪlɪtərɪst] *n.* милитари́ст.
militarize ['mɪlɪtə,raɪz] *v.t.* милитаризи́ровать (*impf., pf.*).
military ['mɪlɪtərɪ] *n.*: **the ~** военнослу́жащие (*m. pl.*), войска́ (*nt. pl.*).

adj. вое́нный; **of ~ age** призывно́го во́зраста; **a ~ man** военнослу́жащий, вое́нный; **~ service** вое́нная слу́жба; (*as liability*) во́инская пови́нность.
militate ['mɪlɪ,teɪt] *v.i.*: **~ against** препя́тствовать (*impf.*) +*d.*; говори́ть (*impf.*) про́тив+*g.*; **his age ~s against him** ему́ меша́ет во́зраст.
militia [mɪ'lɪʃə] *n.* мили́ция.

cpd. **~man** *n.* милиционе́р.
milk [mɪlk] *n.* молоко́; **it's no good crying over spilt ~** слеза́ми го́рю не помо́жешь; (*attr.*) моло́чный; **~ pudding** моло́чный пу́динг.

cpds. **~-bar** *n.* кафе́-моло́чная; **~-churn** *n.* маслобо́йка; **~-float** *n.* теле́жка для разво́зки молока́; **~maid** *n.* доя́рка; **~man** *n.* моло́чник; **~-powder** *n.* порошко́вое молоко́; **~-shake** *n.* моло́чный кокте́йль; **~sop** *n.* тря́пка; **~-white** *adj.* моло́чно-бе́лый.

v.t. доить, по-.
milky ['mɪlkɪ] *adj.* моло́чный; **the M~ Way** Мле́чный путь.
mill [mɪl] *n.* (*for grinding corn*) ме́льница; **they put him through the ~** (*fig.*) они́ подве́ргли его́ тяжёлым испыта́ниям; (*factory*) фа́брика.

v.t. **1.** (*grind*) моло́ть, пере-. **2.** (*cut with ~ing-machine*) фрезерова́ть (*impf.*).

v.i. (*coll.*): **a crowd was ~ing around the entrance** лю́ди толпи́лись у вхо́да.

cpds. **~-pond** *n.* ме́льничный пруд; **~-race** *n.* (*trough*) ме́льничный лото́к; **~stone** *n.* жёрнов; (*fig.*) ка́мень (*m.*) на ше́е; **~-wheel** *n.* ме́льничное колесо́.
millennium [mɪ'lenɪəm] *n.* тысячеле́тие.
miller ['mɪlə(r)] *n.* ме́льник.
millet ['mɪlɪt] *n.* про́со.
milligram(me) ['mɪlɪ,græm] *n.* миллигра́м.
millilitre ['mɪlɪ,li:tə(r)] *n.* миллили́тр.
millimetre ['mɪlɪ,mi:tə(r)] *n.* миллиме́тр.
milliner ['mɪlɪnə(r)] *n.* (*fem.*) моди́стка.
millinery ['mɪlɪnərɪ] *n.* (*trade*) произво́дство/прода́жа да́мских шляп; (*stock-in-trade*) да́мские шля́пки (*f. pl.*).
million ['mɪljən] *n. & adj.* миллио́н (+*g.*); **thanks a ~** (*coll.*) огро́мное спаси́бо.
millionaire [,mɪljə'neə(r)] *n.* миллионе́р.

millionairess [ˌmɪljəˈneərɪs] *n.* миллионе́рша.

millionth [ˈmɪljənθ] *n.* миллио́нная часть.

adj. миллио́нный.

millipede [ˈmɪlɪˌpi:d] *n.* многоно́жка.

milometer [maɪˈlɒmɪtə(r)] *n.* счётчик про́йденных миль.

mime [maɪm] *n.* (*drama; performer*) мим; (*dumb-show*) пантоми́ма.

v.t. (*act by miming*) изобра|жа́ть, -зи́ть мими́чески; (*mimic*) подража́ть (*impf.*) +*d.*; передра́зн|ивать, -и́ть; имити́ровать (*impf.*).

mimeograph [ˈmɪmɪəˌgrɑ:f] *n.* мимео́граф.

v.t. печа́тать на мимео́графе.

mimic [ˈmɪmɪk] *n.* имита́тор; мими́ст (*fem.* -ка); **he is a good ~** он облада́ет да́ром подража́ния.

v.t. передра́зн|ивать, -и́ть; пароди́ровать (*impf.*).

mimicry [ˈmɪmɪkrɪ] *n.* (*imitation*) имити́рование; подража́ние (+*d.*); (*zool.*) мимикри́я.

mimosa [mɪˈməʊzə] *n.* мимо́за.

min. [ˈmɪnɪt(z)] *n.* (*abbr. of* **minute(s)**) мин., (мину́та).

minaret [ˌmɪnəˈret] *n.* минаре́т.

mince [mɪns] *n.* (*chopped meat*) фарш.

v.t. (*chop small*) руби́ть (*impf.*); пропус|ка́ть, -ти́ть че́рез мясору́бку; **~d beef** фарш из говя́дины; **mincing-machine** мясору́бка; (*fig.*): **he does not ~ matters** он говори́т без обиняко́в.

v.i. (*behave affectedly*) жема́ниться (*impf.*); (*of walk*) семени́ть (*impf.*).

cpds. **~meat** *n.* сла́дкая начи́нка для пирожко́в; **they made ~meat of our team** (*fig.*) они́ разгроми́ли на́шу кома́нду в пух и прах.

mincer [ˈmɪnsə(r)] *n.* мясору́бка.

mind [maɪnd] *n.* **1.** (*intellect*) ум, ра́зум; **he has a very good ~** он о́чень спосо́бный; **you must be out of your ~** вы с ума́ сошли́ **he has lost his ~** он не в своём уме́; **great ~s** вели́кие умы́. **2.** (*remembrance*): **bear in ~** зап|омина́ть, -о́мнить; **bring to ~** нап|омина́ть, -о́мнить о+*p.*; **I called his words to ~** я вспо́мнил его́ слова́; **it puts me in ~ of something** э́то мне что́-то напомина́ет; **the tune went clean out of my ~** я на́чисто забы́л э́ту мело́дию; **out of sight, out of ~** с глаз доло́й — из се́рдца вон. **3.** (*opinion*) мне́ние; **he spoke his ~ on the subject** он открове́нно вы́сказался на э́ту те́му; **we are of one ~** мы одина́кового мне́ния; **he doesn't know his own ~** он сам не зна́ет, чего́ он хо́чет; **try to keep an open ~!** попыта́йтесь сохрани́ть объекти́вный подхо́д. **4.** (*intention*) наме́рение; **I have a good ~ not to go** я скло́нен не пойти́; **he changed his ~** он переду́мал; **my ~ is made up** я твёрдо реши́л; **I was in two ~s whether to accept the invitation** я колеба́лся, приня́ть мне приглаше́ние или нет. **5.** (*direction of thought or desire*): **she set her ~ on a holiday abroad** ей о́чень хоте́лось провести́ кани́кулы заграни́цей. **6.** (*thought*) мы́сли (*f. pl.*); **my ~ was on other things** я ду́мал о друго́м; **I had something on my ~** меня́ что́-то трево́жило; **I set his ~ at rest** я его́ успоко́ил; **I cannot read his ~** я не могу́ разгада́ть его́ мы́сли; **I can see him in my ~'s eye** он стои́т у меня́ пе́ред глаза́ми. **7.** (*way of thinking*) настрое́ние; **in his present frame, state of ~** в его́ ны́нешнем состоя́нии; **to my ~** на мой взгляд; мне ка́жется, что. **8.** (*attention*): **he turned his ~ to his work** он сосредото́чился на свое́й рабо́те; **if you set your ~ to your work** е́сли вы настро́итесь на рабо́ту; **keep your ~ on what you are doing** не отвлека́йтесь; **absence of ~** рассе́янность; **he showed great presence of ~** он проявля́л огро́мное прису́тствие ду́ха.

v.t. **1.** (*take care, charge of*) присм|а́тривать, -отре́ть за+*i.*; **~ your own business!** не вме́шивайтесь не в своё де́ло! **2.** (*worry about*) забо́титься (*impf.*) о+*p.*; беспоко́иться о+*p.*; **never ~ the expense** не ду́майте о расхо́дах; **~ your head!** осторо́жнее, не ушиби́те го́лову. **3.** (*object to*) возра|жа́ть, -зи́ть на+*a.*; име́ть (*impf.*) что-н. про́тив+*g.*; **I don't ~ the cold** я не бою́сь хо́лода; **would you ~ opening the door?** откро́йте, пожа́луйста, дверь; **I wouldn't ~ going for a walk** я не прочь прогуля́ться; **I don't ~ going alone** мне всё равно́, я могу́ пойти́ оди́н. **4.** (*heed, note*) прислу́ш|иваться, -аться к+*d.*; слу́шаться (*impf.*) +*g.*; **if I had ~ed his advice** е́сли бы я прислу́шался к его́ сове́ту; **~ you lock the door!** не забу́дьте запере́ть/закры́ть дверь!

v.i. **1.** (*worry*) беспоко́иться (*impf.*); трево́житься (*impf.*); **we're rather late, but never ~** мы немно́го опа́здываем, ну, ничего́!; **but I do ~!** но мне не всё равно́!; **'Where have you been?' — 'Never you ~!'** «Где вы бы́ли? — «Не ва́ше де́ло!». **2.** (*object*) возра|жа́ть, -зи́ть; **if you don't ~** с ва́шего разреше́ния. **3.** (*bear sth. in ~*) не заб|ыва́ть, -ы́ть; **~ you, I don't altogether approve** заме́тьте, что я э́то не совсе́м одобря́ю; **not a word, ~!** смотри́те, нико́му ни сло́ва!

cpds. **~-reader** *n.* отга́дчик мы́слей; ясновидя́щий; **~-reading** *n.* чте́ние/уга́дывание мы́слей, ясновиде́ние.

minded [ˈmaɪndɪd] *adj.* (*as suff. expr. interest*) скло́нный к+*d.*; проявля́ющий интере́с к+*d.*; **mathematically-~** с математи́ческими накло́нностями.

mindful [ˈmaɪndfʊl] *adj.* забо́тливый; **we must be ~ of the children** мы должны́ ду́мать о де́тях; **I was ~ of his advice** я по́мнил его́ сове́т; **he was ~ of his duty** он сознава́л свой долг.

mindless [ˈmaɪndlɪs] *adj.* **1.** (*without care*) беззабо́тный; **~ of danger** не сознава́я опа́сности. **2.** (*not requiring intelligence*): **~ drudgery** механи́ческий труд. **3.** (*without intelligence*) глу́пый.

mindlessness [ˈmaɪndlɪsnɪs] *n.* (*unconcern*) беззабо́тность; (*stupidity*) глу́пость, безмо́зглость.

mine[1] [maɪn] *n.* **1.** (*excavation*) ша́хта; рудни́к; копь; **(gold-~)** (золото́й) при́иск; **the men went down the ~** рабо́чие спусти́лись в ша́хту; (*fig.*) сокро́вищница; **he is a ~ of information** он неиссяка́емый исто́чник информа́ции. **2.** (*explosive device*) ми́на.

v.t. **1.** (*excavate*); **~ coal/ore** добыва́ть (*impf.*) у́голь/руду́. **2.** (*mil.*) мини́ровать, за-; под|рыва́ть, -орва́ть; **they ~d the approaches to the harbour** они́ замини́ровали подхо́ды к га́вани; **the vessel was ~d** су́дно подорва́ли.

v.i. разраб|а́тывать, -о́тать рудни́к; **they were mining for gold** они́ добыва́ли зо́лото; **the mining industry** го́рная промы́шленность; **a mining town** шахтёрский го́род; **mining engineer** го́рный инжене́р.

cpds. **~-detector** *n.* миноиска́тель (*m.*); **~field** *n.* ми́нное по́ле; **~layer** *n.* ми́нный загради́тель; **~sweeper** *n.* ми́нный тра́льщик.

mine[2] [maɪn] *pron.*: **that book is ~** э́то моя́ кни́га; **a friend of ~** (оди́н) мой друг.

miner [ˈmaɪnə(r)] *n.* (*coal-~*) шахтёр; (*gold-~*) золотоиска́тель (*m.*).

mineral [ˈmɪnər(ə)l] *n.* минера́л, руда́.

adj. минера́льный; **~ oil** нефть.

mineralogist [ˌmɪnəˈrælədʒɪst] *n.* минерало́г.

mineralogy [ˌmɪnəˈrælədʒɪ] *n.* минерало́гия.

minestrone [ˌmɪnɪˈstrəʊnɪ] *n.* италья́нский овощно́й суп.

mingle [ˈmɪŋg(ə)l] *v.i.* сме́шиваться (*impf.*); **~ with** (*frequent*) обща́ться (*impf.*) с+*i.*; враща́ться (*impf.*) среди́+*g.*

mingy [ˈmɪndʒɪ] *adj.* (*coll.*) скупо́й, прижи́мистый.

mini [ˈmɪnɪ] *n.* (*garment*) ми́ни (*юбка и т.д.*); (*car*) малолитра́жный автомоби́ль.

miniature [ˈmɪnɪtʃə(r)] *n.* (*portrait*) миниатю́ра; (*small-scale model*) маке́т.

adj. миниатю́рный; ~ **camera** малоформа́тный фотоаппара́т.
minibus ['mɪnɪ,bʌs] *n.* микроавто́бус.
minicab ['mɪnɪ,kæb] *n.* микротакси́ (*nt. indecl.*).
minim ['mɪnɪm] *n.* (*mus.*) полови́нная но́та
minimal ['mɪnɪm(ə)l] *adj.* (*least possible*) минима́льный; (*minute*) о́чень ма́ленький, наиме́ньший.
minimize ['mɪnɪ,maɪz] *v.t.* (*reduce to minimum*) дов|оди́ть, -ести́ до ми́нимума; (*make light of*) преум|еньша́ть, -е́ньшить.
minimum ['mɪnɪməm] *n.* ми́нимум; (*attr.*) минима́льный; ~ **wage** минима́льная за́работная пла́та.
mining ['maɪnɪŋ] *n.* го́рное де́ло; *see also* **mine** *v.t.*
minion ['mɪnjən] *n.* (*favourite*) фаво́рит, люби́мец; (*servant*) приспе́шник.
miniskirt ['mɪnɪ,skɜ:t] *n.* мини-ю́бка.
minister ['mɪnɪstə(r)] *n.* **1.** (*head of government dept.*) мини́стр; **Prime M~** премье́р-мини́стр. **2.** (*in dipl. service*) посла́нник. **3.** (*clergyman*) па́стор.
v.i.: ~ **to** служи́ть (*impf.*) +*d.*; прислу́живать (*impf.*) +*d.*; **he ~ed to her wants** он ей прислу́живал.
ministerial [,mɪnɪ'stɪərɪəl] *adj.* министе́рский.
ministration [,mɪnɪ'streɪʃ(ə)n] *n.* (*pl., services*) по́мощь; обслу́живание; (*of a priest*) отправле́ние свяще́нником свои́х обя́занностей.
ministry ['mɪnɪstrɪ] *n.* **1.** (*department of state*) министе́рство. **2.** (*relig.*): **he entered the ~** он при́нял духо́вный сан.
mink [mɪŋk] *n.* но́рка; (*attr.*) но́рковый.
minnow ['mɪnəʊ] *n.* песка́рь (*m.*).
minor ['maɪnə(r)] *n.* (*person under age*) несовершенноле́тний.
adj. **1.** (*of lesser importance*) второстепе́нный; малозначи́тельный, ме́лкий, небольшо́й; ~ **repairs** ме́лкий ремо́нт. **2.** (*younger*) ме́ньший, мла́дший. **3.** (*mus.*) мино́рный.
minority [maɪ'nɒrɪtɪ] *n.* **1.** (*being under age*) несовершенноле́тие. **2.** (*smaller number of votes etc.*) меньшинство́, ме́ньшая часть; **you are in the ~** вы в меньшинстве́. **3.** (~ *nationality*) национа́льное меньшинство́.
minster ['mɪnstə(r)] *n.* кафедра́льный собо́р.
minstrel ['mɪnstr(ə)l] *n.* менестре́ль (*m.*).
mint[1] [mɪnt] *n.* (*bot.*) мя́та; ~ **sauce** со́ус из мя́ты.
mint[2] [mɪnt] *n.* (*fin.*) моне́тный двор; **he made a ~ of money** он сколоти́л (*coll.*) состоя́ние; (*attr., lit., fig.*) но́венький, но́вый.
v.t. чека́нить (*impf.*).
minuet [,mɪnjʊ'et] *n.* менуэ́т.
minus ['maɪnəs] *n.* ми́нус; **two ~es make a plus** (*in multiplication*) ми́нус на ми́нус даёт плюс.
adj. отрица́тельный; ~ **sign** (знак) ми́нус.
prep. ми́нус; без+*g.*; ~ **1** ми́нус едини́ца.
minuscule ['mɪnə,skju:l] *adj.* минуска́льный; о́чень ма́ленький.
minute[1] ['mɪnɪt] *n.* **1.** (*fraction of hour or degree*) мину́та; **the train left several ~s ago** по́езд отошёл не́сколько мину́т наза́д. **2.** (*moment*) мгнове́ние, моме́нт, миг; **I'll come in a ~** я сейча́с/ми́гом приду́; **come here this ~!** сейча́с же иди́ сюда́!; **just a ~** одну́ мину́тку!; **I won't be a ~** сейча́с верну́сь!; **I'll tell him the ~ he arrives** как то́лько он придёт, я ему́ скажу́; **they left at 2 o'clock to the ~** они́ ушли́ в 2 часа́ ро́вно; **he is always up to the ~ with his news** он всегда́ в ку́рсе после́дних новосте́й. **3.** (*usu. pl., record*) протоко́л; (*memorandum*) (делова́я) запи́ска.
v.t. вести́ протоко́л +*g.*; запис|ывать, -а́ть.
cpds. **~-book** *n.* кни́га протоко́лов; **~-hand** *n.* мину́тная стре́лка.
minute[2] [maɪ'nju:t] *adj.* (*tiny*) ме́лкий, кро́хотный; (*detailed*) подро́бный, дета́льный.
minutiae [maɪ'nju:ʃɪ,i:, mɪ-] *n.* ме́лочи (*f. pl.*).
minx [mɪŋks] *n.* озорни́ца; (*coquette*) коке́тка.
miracle ['mɪrək(ə)l] *n.* чу́до; **he escaped by a ~** он чу́дом уцеле́л.
miraculous [mɪ'rækjʊləs] *adj.* (*surprising*) чуде́сный; (*miracle-working*) чудотво́рный.
mirage ['mɪrɑ:ʒ] *n.* (*lit., fig.*) мира́ж.
mire ['maɪə(r)] *n.* тряси́на; боло́то.
mirror ['mɪrə(r)] *n.* зе́ркало; ~ **image** (*lit., fig.*) (зерка́льное) отображе́ние.
v.t. отра|жа́ть, -зи́ть; (*fig.*) отобра|жа́ть, -зи́ть.
mirth [mɜ:θ] *n.* (*gladness*) весе́лье; (*laughter*) смех.
mirthful ['mɜ:θfʊl] *adj.* весёлый.
misadventure [,mɪsəd'ventʃə(r)] *n.* несча́стье, несча́стный слу́чай.
misanthrope ['mɪzən,θrəʊp, 'mɪs-] *n.* мизантро́п.
misanthropic [,mɪzən'θrɒpɪk, 'mɪs-] *adj.* мизантропи́ческий, человеконенави́стнический.
misanthropy [mɪ'zænθrəpɪ] *n.* мизантро́пия.
misapply [,mɪsə'plaɪ] *v.t.* непра́вильно испо́льзовать (*impf., pf.*); злоупотреб|ля́ть, -и́ть +*i.*
misapprehension [,mɪsæprɪ'henʃ(ə)n] *n.* превра́тное понима́ние; недоразуме́ние; **I was under a ~** я заблужда́лся.
misappropriate [,mɪsə'prəʊprɪ,eɪt] *v.t.* (незако́нно) присв|а́ивать, -о́ить; соверш|а́ть, -и́ть растра́ту +*g.*
misappropriation [,mɪsə,prəʊprɪ'eɪʃ(ə)n] *n.* незако́нное присвое́ние; растра́та.
misbehave [,mɪsbɪ'heɪv] *v.i.* ду́рно себя́ вести́ (*det.*).
misbehaviour [,mɪsbɪ'heɪvɪə(r)] *n.* дурно́е поведе́ние.
miscalculate [,mɪs'kælkjʊ,leɪt] *v.t.* пло́хо рассчи́т|ывать, -а́ть.
v.i. просчи́т|ываться, -а́ться.
miscalculation [,mɪskælkjʊ'leɪʃ(ə)n] *n.* просчёт.
miscarriage ['mɪs,kærɪdʒ, mɪs'kærɪdʒ] *n.* **1.** (*biol.*) вы́кидыш; **she had a ~** у неё произошёл вы́кидыш. **2.**: ~ **of justice** суде́бная оши́бка.
miscarr|y [mɪs'kærɪ] *v.i.* **1.** (*of a woman*) име́ть (*impf.*) вы́кидыш. **2.** (*fail*) терпе́ть (*impf.*) неуда́чу; **his plans ~ied** его́ пла́ны провали́лись.
miscast [mɪs'kɑ:st] *v.t.* да|ва́ть, -ть неподходя́щую роль +*d.*; **he was ~ as Falstaff** ему́ не сле́довало поруча́ть роль Фальста́фа.
miscellaneous [,mɪsə'leɪnɪəs] *adj.* сме́шанный; разнообра́зный, разношёрстный.
miscellany [mɪ'selənɪ] *n.* смесь, вся́кая вся́чина; **literary ~** литерату́рный сбо́рник.
mischance [mɪs'tʃɑ:ns] *n.* неуда́ча; невезе́ние; **by ~** к несча́стью.
mischief ['mɪstʃɪf] *n.* **1.** (*harm, damage*) вред. **2.** (*discord, ill-feeling*) раздо́р; **he is out to make ~ between us** он хо́чет нас поссо́рить. **3.** (*naughtiness*) озорство́; прока́зы (*f. pl.*); **he is always getting into ~** он всегда́ прока́зничает/шали́т. **4.** (*mockery*) **his eyes were full of ~** его́ глаза́ бы́ли полны́ лука́вства. **5.** (*coll., mischievous child*) озорни́к; прока́зник.
cpds. **~-maker** *n.* интрига́н, смутья́н.
mischievous ['mɪstʃɪvəs] *adj.* (*harmful*) вре́дный; (*spiteful, malicious*) злой, зло́бный; (*given to pranks*) озорно́й, шаловли́вый.
misconception [,mɪskən'sepʃ(ə)n] *n.* непра́вильное представле́ние/понима́ние.
misconduct [mɪs'kɒndʌkt] *n.* **1.** (*mismanagement*) плохо́е веде́ние (дел). **2.** (*improper conduct*) дурно́е поведе́ние; **professional ~** наруше́ние профессиона́льной э́тики; должностно́е преступле́ние.
misconstruction [,mɪskən'strʌkʃ(ə)n] *n.* непра́вильное/неве́рное толкова́ние; **his words were open to ~** его́ слова́ могли́ быть истолко́ваны превра́тно.
misconstrue [,mɪskən'stru:] *v.t.* непра́вильно истолко́в|ывать, -а́ть.
miscount [mɪs'kaʊnt] *n.* непра́вильный подсчёт.
v.t. & i. обсчи́т|ываться, -а́ться.

miscreant ['mɪskrɪənt] *n.* подле́ц, негодя́й.
misdeal [mɪs'di:l] *n.* непра́вильная сда́ча.
v.i. ошиб|а́ться, -и́ться при сда́че карт.
misdeed [mɪs'di:d] *n.* преступле́ние.
misdemeanour [ˌmɪsdɪ'mi:nə(r)] *n.* просту́пок.
misdirect [ˌmɪsdaɪ'rekt, -dɪ'rekt] *v.t.* неве́рно напр|а-вля́ть, -а́вить; **the letter was ~ed** письмо́ бы́ло непра́вильно адресо́вано; **his efforts were ~ed** его́ уси́лия бы́ли напра́влены по ло́жному пути́.
miser ['maɪzə(r)] *n.* скря́га (*c.g.*), скупе́ц.
miserable ['mɪzərəb(ə)l] *adj.* **1.** (*wretched*; *unhappy*) жа́лкий, несча́стный. **2.** (*causing wretchedness*) плохо́й, скве́рный; **what ~ weather!** кака́я скве́рная пого́да!; **a ~ hovel** жа́лкая хиба́рка. **3.** (*mean*; *contemptible*) **a ~ sum (of money)** ничто́жная/ми́зерная су́мма.
miserliness ['maɪzəlɪnɪs] *n.* ску́пость.
miserly ['maɪzəlɪ] *adj.* скупо́й.
misery ['mɪzərɪ] *n.* **1.** (*suffering*; *wretchedness*) страда́ние; муче́ние; **he put the dog out of its ~** он положи́л коне́ц страда́ниям соба́ки. **2.** (*extreme poverty*) нищета́, бе́дность. **3.** (*coll.*, *person who complains*) зану́да (*c.g.*), ны́тик.
misfire [mɪs'faɪə(r)] *n.* осе́чка.
v.i. да|ва́ть, -ть осе́чку; (*fig.*) не состоя́ться (*impf.*); **his plans ~d** его́ план сорва́лся.
misfit ['mɪsfɪt] *n.* (*pers.*) неприспосо́бленный челове́к; (*failure*) неуда́чник.
misfortune [mɪs'fɔ:tʃu:n, -tju:n] *n.* беда́, несча́стье.
misgiving [mɪs'gɪvɪŋ] *n.* опасе́ние; дурно́е предчу́вствие.
misguided [mɪs'gaɪdɪd] *adj.*: **I was ~ enough to trust him** я име́л неосторо́жность ему́ дове́рить; **~ enthusiasm** энтузиа́зм, досто́йный лу́чшего примене́ния.
mishandle [mɪs'hænd(ə)l] *v.t.* (*ill-treat*) пло́хо/ду́рно обраща́ться (*impf.*) с+*i.*; (*manage inefficiently*) пло́хо вести́ (*det.*) (де́ло).
mishap ['mɪshæp] *n.* неуда́ча; неприя́тное происше́ствие.
mishear [mɪs'hɪə(r)] *v.t.* нето́чно рассл́ышать (*pf.*).
mishit ['mɪshɪt] *n.* про́мах.
mishmash ['mɪʃmæʃ] *n.* (*coll.*) пу́таница, мешани́на.
misinform [ˌmɪsɪn'fɔ:m] *v.t.* непра́вильно информи́ровать (*impf.*, *pf.*).
misinformation [ˌmɪsɪnfə'meɪʃ(ə)n] *n.* неве́рная информа́ция.
misinterpret [ˌmɪsɪn'tɜ:prɪt] *v.t.* непра́вильно пон|има́ть, -я́ть; непра́вильно истолко́в|ывать, -а́ть.
misinterpretation [ˌmɪsɪnˌtɜ:prɪ'teɪʃ(ə)n] *n.* непра́вильное понима́ние/толкова́ние.
misjudge [mɪs'dʒʌdʒ] *v.t.* неве́рно оце́н|ивать, -и́ть; **he ~d the distance and fell** он не рассчита́л расстоя́ние и упа́л.
misjudg(e)ment [mɪs'dʒʌdʒmənt] *n.* непра́вильное мне́ние/сужде́ние.
mislay [mɪs'leɪ] *v.t.* (*lose*) затеря́ть (*pf.*); (*put in wrong place*) положи́ть (*pf.*) не на ме́сто.
mislead [mɪs'li:d] *v.t.* (*fig.*, *cause to do wrong*) сби|ва́ть, -ть с пути́; (*fig.*, *give wrong impression to*) вв|оди́ть, -ести́ в заблужде́ние; **a ~ing statement** заявле́ние, вводя́щее в заблужде́ние.
mismanage [mɪs'mænɪdʒ] *v.t.* пло́хо управля́ть (*impf.*) +*i.*; пло́хо руководи́ть (*impf.*) +*i.*
mismanagement [mɪs'mænɪdʒmənt] *n.* плохо́е управле́ние/руково́дство.
misnomer [mɪs'nəʊmə(r)] *n.* непра́вильное назва́ние.
misogynist [mɪ'sɒdʒɪnɪst] *n.* женоненави́стник.
misogyny [mɪ'sɒdʒɪnɪ] *n.* женоненави́стничество.
misplace [mɪs'pleɪs] *v.t.* положи́ть (*pf.*) не на ме́сто.
misplaced [mɪs'pleɪsd] *adj.* (*out of place*) неуме́стный; (*unfounded*) безоснова́тельный.
misprint ['mɪsprɪnt] *n.* опеча́тка.
mispronounce [ˌmɪsprə'naʊns] *v.t.* непра́вильно произн|оси́ть, -ести́.
mispronunciation [ˌmɪsprəˌnʌnsɪ'eɪʃ(ə)n] *n.* непра́вильное произноше́ние.
misquotation [mɪsˌkwəʊ'teɪʃ(ə)n] *n.* нето́чная цита́та.
misquote [mɪs'kwəʊt] *v.t.* нето́чно цити́ровать, про-; **I have been ~d** мои́ слова́ искази́ли.
misread [mɪs'ri:d] *v.t.* (*read incorrectly*) чита́ть, про-непра́вильно; (*misinterpret*) непра́вильно истолко́в|ывать, -а́ть.
misrepresent [ˌmɪsreprɪ'zent] *v.t.* иска|жа́ть, -зи́ть.
misrepresentation [ˌmɪsreprɪzen'teɪʃ(ə)n] *n.* искаже́ние (фа́ктов).
misrule [mɪs'ru:l] *n.* (*bad government*) плохо́е правле́ние; (*lawlessness*) беспоря́док, ана́рхия.
miss[1] [mɪs] *n.* (*failure to hit etc.*) про́мах; **near ~** (*lit.*) попада́ние вблизи́ це́ли; (*fig.*) бли́зкая дога́дка *и т.п.*
v.t. **1.** (*fail to hit or catch*): **he ~ed the ball** он пропусти́л мяч; **he ~ed the target** он не попа́л в цель; **the bullet ~ed him by inches** пу́ля чуть-чуть его́ не заде́ла; **he ~ed the bus** он опозда́л на авто́бус. **2.** (*fig.*, *fail to grasp*) не пон|има́ть, -я́ть; не улови́ть (*pf.*); **you have ~ed the point** вы не по́няли су́ти. **3.** (*fail to secure*): **he ~ed his footing and fell** он оступи́лся и упа́л. **4.** (*fail to hear or see*) не услы́шать (*pf.*); пропус|ка́ть, -ти́ть; **I ~ed your last remark** я прослу́шал ва́ше после́днее замеча́ние; **you must not ~ this film** не пропусти́те э́тот фильм; **it's the corner house; you can't ~ it** э́то углово́й дом — вы его́ не мо́жете не заме́тить. **5.** (*fail to meet*): **you've just ~ed him!** вы с ним чуть-чу́ть размину́лись! **6.** (*escape by chance*) избе|га́ть, -жа́ть; **we just ~ed having an accident** мы чуть не попа́ли в катастро́фу. **7.** (*discover or regret absence of*): **when did you ~ your purse?** когда́ вы обнару́жили, что у вас нет кошелька́?; **she ~es her husband** она́ скуча́ет по му́жу; **we ~ed you** нам вас недостава́ло; **he won't be ~ed** его́ отсу́тствия не заме́тят; **I ~ his talks** я скуча́ю по его́ ле́кциям.
v.i. прома́х|иваться, -ну́ться; не поп|ада́ть, -а́сть в цель.
with adv.: **~ out** *v.t.* упус|ка́ть, -ти́ть; пропус|ка́ть, -ти́ть; **I shall ~ out the first course** я не бу́ду есть пе́рвое; *v.i.* (*coll.*): **he ~ed out on all the fun** он пропусти́л са́мое весёлое.
miss[2] [mɪs] *n.* (*young girl*; *also voc.*) де́вушка; (**M~**: *as title*, *abbr. of* **mistress**) мисс.
misshapen [mɪs'ʃeɪpən] *adj.* уро́дливый.
missile ['mɪsaɪl] *n.* **1.** (*object thrown*) мета́тельный предме́т. **2.** (*weapon thrown or fired*) снаря́д. **3.** (*rocket weapon*) ракета; **guided ~** управля́емая раке́та; **~ site** ста́ртовый ко́мплекс.
missing ['mɪsɪŋ] *adj.* недостаю́щий; потеря́вшийся; **there is a page ~** не хвата́ет страни́цы; **he was ~ing for a whole day** он где́-то пропада́л це́лый день; **he went ~** он пропа́л (бе́з вести); **the ~ link** недостаю́щее звено́.
mission ['mɪʃ(ə)n] *n.* **1.** (*errand*) поруче́ние; команди-ро́вка. **2.** (*vocation*) ми́ссия, призва́ние; **his ~ in life** цель его́ жи́зни. **3.** (*mil.*, *sortie or task*) зада́ние. **4.** (*dipl.*) ми́ссия, (*to UN*) делега́ция. **5.** (*relig.*) ми́ссия.
missionary ['mɪʃənərɪ] *n.* миссионе́р (*fem.* -ка).
adj. миссионе́рский.
missive ['mɪsɪv] *n.* посла́ние.
misspell [mɪs'spel] *v.t. & i.* непра́вильно написа́ть (*pf.*); сде́лать (*pf.*) орфографи́ческую оши́бку.
misspelling [mɪs'spelɪŋ] *n.* непра́вильное написа́ние.
misspen|d [mɪs'spend] *v.t.* (*of funds*) тра́тить, рас-; **a ~t youth** (напра́сно) растра́ченная мо́лодость.
misstate [mɪs'steɪt] *v.t.* де́лать, с- ло́жное заявле́ние

o+p.; предст|авля́ть, -а́вить в ло́жном све́те.
misstatement [mɪs'steɪtmənt] *n.* ло́жное заявле́ние.
mist [mɪst] *n.* (*lit., fig.*) тума́н, ды́мка, мгла.
v.t. & i. затума́ни|вать(ся), -ть(ся); **my glasses have ~ed over** у меня́ запоте́ли очки́.
mistak|e [mɪ'steɪk] *n.* оши́бка; **by ~e** по оши́бке; **make no ~e (about it)** бу́дьте уве́рены.
v.t. (*misunderstand*) ошиб|а́ться, -и́ться в+*p.*; (*misrecognize*): **he mistook me for my brother** он при́нял меня́ за моего́ бра́та.
mistaken [mɪ'steɪkən] *adj.* **1.** (*in error*): **if I am not ~** е́сли я не ошиба́юсь. **2.** (*ill-judged; erroneous*) неосмотри́тельный; оши́бочный, непра́вильный.
mister ['mɪstə(r)] *n.* (*coll., as voc.*) ми́стер; господи́н.
mistime [mɪs'taɪm] *v.t.* (*action*) сде́лать (*pf.*) не во́время; (*speech*) сказа́ть (*pf.*) не во́время; **a ~d remark** неуме́стное замеча́ние.
mistiness ['mɪstɪnɪs] *n.* тума́нность.
mistletoe ['mɪs(ə)l,təʊ] *n.* оме́ла бе́лая.
mistranslate [,mɪstrænz'leɪt, ,mɪstrɑ:-, -s'leɪt] *v.t.* непра́вильно перев|оди́ть, -ести́.
mistranslation [,mɪstrænz'leɪʒ(ə)n, ,mɪstrɑ:-] *n.* непра́вильный перево́д.
mistress ['mɪstrɪs] *n.* **1.** (*of household etc.*) хозя́йка. **2.** (*schoolteacher*) учи́тельница. **3.** (*lover*) любо́вница.
mistrial [mɪs'traɪəl] *n.* непра́вильное суде́бное разбира́тельство.
mistrust [mɪs'trʌst] *n.* недове́рие.
v.t. не доверя́ть (*impf.*) +*d.*
mistrustful [mɪs'trʌstfʊl] *adj.* недове́рчивый.
misty ['mɪstɪ] *adj.* тума́нный; (*fig.*) сму́тный.
misunderstand [,mɪsʌndə'stænd] *v.t.* непра́вильно пон|има́ть, -я́ть.
misunderstanding [,mɪsʌndə'stændɪŋ] *n.* недоразуме́ние.
misuse[1] [mɪs'ju:s] *n.* непра́вильное употребле́ние; злоупотребле́ние (*чем*).
misuse[2] [mɪs'ju:z] *v.t.* (*use improperly*) непра́вильно употреб|ля́ть, -и́ть; (*treat badly*) ду́рно обраща́ться (*impf.*) с+*i.*
mite[1] [maɪt] *n.* (*fig., small contribution*) ле́пта; (*bit*) чу́точка, ка́пелька; **he was not a ~ ashamed** ему́ не́ было ни ка́пельки сты́дно; (*small child*) малю́тка (*c.g.*), кро́шка.
mite[2] [maɪt] *n.* (*insect*) клещ.
mitigat|e ['mɪtɪ,geɪt] *v.t.* смягч|а́ть, -и́ть; **~ing circumstances** смягча́ющие обстоя́тельства.
mitre[1] ['maɪtə(r)] *n.* (*headgear*) ми́тра.
mitre[2] ['maɪtə(r)] *n.* (*joint*) соедине́ние в ус.
v.t. соедин|я́ть, -и́ть в ус.
mitten ['mɪt(ə)n] *n.* рукави́ца, ва́режка.
mix [mɪks] *n.* смесь; соста́в.
v.t. **1.** (*mingle*) сме́ш|ивать, -а́ть; (*combine*) сочета́ть (*impf.*); **I like to ~ business with pleasure** я люблю́ сочета́ть прия́тное с поле́зным. **2.** (*prepare by ~ing*) сме́ш|ивать, -а́ть; переме́ш|ивать, -а́ть; **~ me a cocktail** пригото́вьте мне кокте́йль.
v.i. (*mingle*) сме́шиваться (*impf.*); (*combine*) сочета́ться (*impf.*); (*of persons*) обща́ться (*impf., pf.*); **she won't ~ with her neighbours** она́ не хо́чет обща́ться с сосе́дями.
with advs.: **~ in** *v.t.* заме́|шивать, -си́ть; **beat the eggs and ~ in the flour** взбе́йте я́йца и смеша́йте с муко́й; **~ up** *v.t.* (*~ thoroughly*) (хорошо́) переме́|шивать, -си́ть; (*confuse*) перепу́т|ывать, -ать; **a ~ed-up child** (*coll.*) тру́дный ребёнок; (*involve*) впу́т|ывать, -ать; **I don't want to become ~ed up in the affair** я не хочу́ вввя́зываться в э́то де́ло.
cpds. **~-up** *n.* недоразуме́ние.
mixed [mɪkst] *adj.* сме́шанный; **(place for) ~ bathing** о́бщий пляж; (*of people*) разношёрстная компа́ния; **~ doubles** сме́шанная па́рная игра́; **~ farming** сме́шанное хозя́йство; **I have ~ feelings about it** у меня́ на э́тот счёт разноречи́вые чу́вства; **~ grill** ассорти́ (*nt. indecl.*) из жа́реного мя́са; **~ marriage** сме́шанный брак; **~ school** шко́ла совме́стного обуче́ния.
mixer ['mɪksə(r)] *n.* **1.** (*machine*) меша́лка, ми́ксер. **2.** (*sociable person*): **he is a good ~** он общи́тельный челове́к.
mixture ['mɪkstʃə(r)] *n.* смесь; **cough ~** миксту́ра от ка́шля.
miz(z)en ['mɪz(ə)n] *n.* **(~-sail)** биза́нь.
cpd. **~-mast** *n.* биза́нь-ма́чта.
ml. *n. abbr. of* **1. millilitre(s)** ['mɪlɪ,li:tə(r)(z)] мл, (миллили́тр). **2. mile(s)** [maɪl(z)] ми́ля.
mm. ['mɪlɪ,mi:tə(r)(z)] *n.* (*abbr. of* **millimetre(s)**) мм, (миллиме́тр).
mnemonic [nɪ'mɒnɪk] *n.* (*aid to memory*) мнемони́ческая па́мять.
adj. мнемони́ческий.
moan [məʊn] *n.* стон; (*coll., complaint*) стон, нытьё.
v.t. & i. стона́ть (*impf.*); (*coll., complain*) ныть (*impf.*); (*fig.*) выть (*impf.*); завыва́ть (*impf.*).
moat [məʊt] *n.* ров с водо́й.
mob [mɒb] *n.* **1.** (*rabble, crowd*) толпа́. **2.: the ~** (*common people*) толпа́; чернь; **~ rule** самосу́д.
v.t. нап|ада́ть, -а́сть на+*a.*; **the singer was ~bed by his fans** певца́ осажда́ли покло́нники.
mobile ['məʊbaɪl] *n.* подвесна́я констру́кция, «моба́йл».
adj. передвижно́й, перено́сный; **~ canteen** автола́вка; **~ phone** портати́вный телефо́н; **~ troops** подвижны́е войска́.
mobility [mə'bɪlɪtɪ] *n.* подви́жность, моби́льность.
mobilization [,məʊbɪlaɪ'zeɪʃ(ə)n] *n.* мобилиза́ция.
mobilize ['məʊbɪ,laɪz] *v.t.* мобилизова́ть (*impf., pf.*).
v.i. мобилизова́ться (*impf., pf.*).
mobster ['mɒbstə(r)] *n.* банди́т.
moccasin ['mɒkəsɪn] *n.* мокаси́н.
mocha ['mɒkə] *n.* ко́фе (*m.*) мо́кко (*indecl.*).
mock [mɒk] *adj.* подде́льный, фальши́вый; **~ battle** уче́бный бой; **~ examination** предэкзаменацио́нная прове́рка.
v.t. **1.** (*ridicule*) насмеха́ться (*impf.*) над+*i.*; издева́ться (*impf.*) над+*i.*; высме́ивать, вы́смеять. **2.** (*mimic*) передра́зни|вать, -ть; **~ing-bird** пересме́шник.
cpd. **~up** *n.* маке́т.
mockery ['mɒkərɪ] *n.* (*ridicule*) издева́тельство, осмея́ние; **he was held up to ~** над ним издева́лись; (*parody*) паро́дия; **the trial was a ~ of justice** суд был паро́дией на правосу́дие.
modal ['məʊd(ə)l] *adj.* (*logic, gram.*) мода́льный.
mode [məʊd] *n.* **1.** (*manner*) ме́тод, спо́соб; **~ of operation** спо́соб рабо́ты; **~ of life** о́браз жи́зни. **2.** (*fashion*) мо́да; обы́чай.
model ['mɒd(ə)l] *n.* **1.** (*representation*) моде́ль, маке́т, схе́ма; **working ~** де́йствующая моде́ль; **~ aircraft** моде́ль самолёта. **2.** (*pattern*) образе́ц, станда́рт; **he is a ~ of gallantry** он образе́ц гала́нтности; **a ~ husband** идеа́льный муж. **3.** (*person posing for artist*) нату́рщи|к (*fem.* -ца); **life ~** жива́я моде́ль. **4.** (*woman displaying clothes etc.*) манеке́нщица; **male ~** манеке́нщик. **5.** (*dress*) моде́ль. **6.** (*design*) моде́ль, тип; **sports ~** (*car*) спорти́вный автомоби́ль.
v.t. де́лать, с- моде́ль +*g.*; **he ~led her face in wax** он вы́лепил из во́ска её лицо́; **she ~led the dress** (*wore it as a ~*) она́ демонстри́ровала пла́тье; **clay ~ling** ле́пка из гли́ны; (*fig.*): **he ~s himself upon his father** он сле́дует приме́ру своего́ отца́; **she ~s for a living** она́ рабо́тает манеке́нщицей.
modem ['məʊdem] *n.* моде́м.
moderate[1] ['mɒdərət] *n.* уме́ренный челове́к; челове́к, приде́рживающийся уме́ренных взгля́дов.

adj. умéренный; срéдний; **~ly well dressed** довóльно хорошó одéтый.
moderat|e[2] ['mɒdə,reɪt] *v.t.* ум|ерять, -éрить; смягч|áть, -ить; **~e your language** выбирáйте выражéния.
v.i. **1.** (*become less violent*) смягч|áться, -иться. **2.** (*preside*) председáтельствовать (*impf.*).
moderation [,mɒdə'reɪʃ(ə)n] *n.* (*moderating*) сдéрживание; регулирование; (*moderateness*) умéренность, сдéржанность; **in ~** умéренно.
moderator ['mɒdə,reɪtə(r)] *n.* (*mediator*) арбитр, посрéдник; (*chairman*) председáтель (*m.*).
modern ['mɒd(ə)n] *adj.* совремéнный; **~ languages** нóвые языки; **~ history** нóвая истóрия.
modernism ['mɒdə,nɪz(ə)m] *n.* модернизм.
modernist ['mɒdə,nɪst] *n.* модернист.
modernistic [,mɒdə'nɪstɪk] *adj.* модернистский.
modernity [mɒ'dɜ:nɪtɪ] *n.* совремéнность.
modernization [,mɒdənaɪ'zeɪʃ(ə)n] *n.* модернизáция.
modernize ['mɒdə,naɪz] *v.t.* модернизировать (*impf.*, *pf.*).
modest ['mɒdɪst] *adj.* **1.** (*unassuming*, *indifferent*) скрóмный, застéнчивый. **2.** (*not excessive*) скрóмный, умéренный.
modesty ['mɒdɪstɪ] *n.* **1.** скрóмность, застéнчивость. **2.** сдéржанность, умéренность.
modicum ['mɒdɪkəm] *n.* óчень мáлое количество.
modification [,mɒdɪfɪ'keɪʃ(ə)n] *n.* модификáция; видоизменéние.
modif|y ['mɒdɪ,faɪ] *v.t.* *1.* (*make changes in*) модифицировать (*impf.*); видоизмен|ять, -ить. **2.** (*make less severe*, *violent etc.*) смягч|áть, -ить. **3.** (*gram.*) определ|ять, -ить.
modish ['məʊdɪʃ] *adj.* мóдный.
modulate ['mɒdjʊ,leɪt] *v.t.* (*vary pitch of*; *also radio*) модулировать (*impf.*).
modulation [,mɒdjʊ'leɪʃ(ə)n] *n.* модуляция.
modular ['mɒdjʊlə(r)] *adj.* блóчный.
module ['mɒdju:l] *n.* (*independent unit*) блок, сéкция; (*spacecraft*) мóдульный отсéк; **command ~** комáндный отсéк; **lunar ~** лýнная кáпсула.
mogul ['məʊg(ə)l] *n.* (*fig.*, *tycoon*) магнáт.
mohair ['məʊheə(r)] *n.* мохéр; (*attr.*) мохéровый.
Mohammed [mə'hæməd] *n.* Мухáммед, Магомéт.
Mohammedan [mə'hæməd(ə)n] *n.* магометáн|ин (*fem.* -ка).
adj. магометáнский.
Mohammedanism [mə'hæmədən,ɪz(ə)m] *n.* магометáнство.
moire [mwɑ:(r)] *n.* муáр.
moiré ['mwɑ:reɪ] *adj.* муáровый.
moist [mɔɪst] *adj.* влáжный, сырóй.
moisten ['mɔɪs(ə)n] *v.t.* увлажн|ять, -ить; см|áчивать, -очить; **he ~ed his lips** он облизнýл гýбы.
moisture ['mɔɪstʃə(r)] *n.* влáжность, влáга.
moisturize ['mɔɪstʃə,raɪz] *v.t.* увлажн|ять, -ить.
moisturizer ['mɔɪstʃə,raɪzə(r)] *n.* увлажняющий крем.
molar ['məʊlə(r)] *n.* моляр, кореннóй зуб.
molasses [mə'læsɪz] *n.* мелáсса, чёрная пáтока.
mold [məʊld], **-er** ['məʊldə(r)], **-ing** ['məʊldɪŋ], **-y** ['məʊldɪ] = **mould** *etc.*
Moldavia [mɒl'deɪvɪə] *n.* Молдáвия.
Moldavian [mɒl'deɪvɪən] *n.* молдавáн|ин (*fem.* -ка); *adj.* молдáвский.
mole[1] [məʊl] *n.* (*blemish*) рóдинка, бородáвка.
mole[2] [məʊl] *n.* (*zool.*) крот; (*secret agent*) «крот».
cpds. **~-hill** *n.* кротóвина.
molecular [mə'lekjʊlə(r)] *adj.* молекулярный.
molecule ['mɒlɪ,kju:l] *n.* молéкула.
molest [mə'lest] *v.t.* прист|авáть, -áть к+*d.*
molestation [,mɒle'steɪʃ(ə)n, ,məʊl-] *n.* приставáние.
mollify ['mɒlɪ,faɪ] *v.t.* смягч|áть, -ить; успок|áивать, -óить.
mollusc ['mɒləsk] *n.* моллюск.
mollycoddle ['mɒlɪ,kɒd(ə)l] *n.* нéженка.
v.t. нéжить (*impf.*); баловáть, из-.
Molotov cocktail ['mɒlə'tɒf] *n.* бутылка с зажигáтельной смéсью.
molt [məʊlt] = **moult**
molten ['məʊlt(ə)n] *adj.* расплáвленный, литый.
molybdenum [mə'lɪbdɪnəm] *n.* молибдéн.
moment ['məʊmənt] *n.* **1.** (*instant*; *short period of time*) момéнт, миг; **this ~ (at once)** сию минýту; **at the right ~** в подходящий момéнт; **at the last ~** в послéднюю минýту; **half, just a ~!** один момéнт; минýточку!; **it was all done in a ~** всё было сдéлано в миг; **I am busy at the ~** я сейчáс зáнят; **at this ~** в дáнную минýту; **at odd ~s** мéжду дéлом; **I would not agree to that for a ~** я никáк не могý с этим согласиться; **the ~** (*as soon as*) **I saw him** как тóлько я егó увидел. **2.** (*importance*) вáжность, значéние; **affairs of (great) ~** вáжные делá.
momentary ['məʊməntərɪ, -trɪ] *adj.* (*lasting a moment*) моментáльный.
momentous [mə'mentəs] *adj.* вáжный, знаменáтельный.
momentum [mə'mentəm] *n.* (*phys.*) инéрция; (*fig.*, *impetus*) движущая сила; импульс; **the conspiracy gathered ~** зáговор разрастáлся.
monarch ['mɒnək] *n.* монáрх.
monarchic(al) [mə'nɑ:kɪk(ə)l] *adj.* монархический.
monarchism ['mɒnə,kɪz(ə)m] *n.* монархизм.
monarchist ['mɒnəkɪst] *n.* монархист.
adj. монархистский.
monarchy ['mɒnəkɪ] *n.* монáрхия.
monastery ['mɒnəstərɪ, -strɪ] *n.* монастырь (*m.*).
monastic [mə'næstɪk] *adj.* монáшеский.
monasticism [mə'næstɪ,sɪz(ə)m] *n.* монáшество.
Monday ['mʌndeɪ, -dɪ] *n.* понедéльник.
monetarism ['mʌnɪtə,rɪz(ə)m] *n.* монетаризм.
monetarist ['mʌnɪtə,rɪst]*n.* монетарист.
adj. монетаристский.
monetary ['mʌnɪtərɪ] *adj.* дéнежный; монéтный; **~ unit** дéнежная единица; **~ fund** валютный фонд.
money ['mʌnɪ] *n.* дéн|ьги (*pl. g.* -ег); **ready ~** наличные (*pl.*); **for my ~** (*fig.*) на мой взгляд; **I got my ~'s worth** я получил сполнá за свои дéньги; **make ~** (*become rich*) разбогатéть (*pf.*); **he put his ~ into the business** он вложил свой капитáл в дéло; **there's ~ in it for you** вы́годное для вас дéло; **~ talks** с деньгáми всегó мóжно добиться.
cpds. **~-box** *n.* копилка; **~-changer** *n.* меняла (*m.*); **~lender** *n.* ростовщик; **~-market** *n.* дéнежный рынок; **~-order** *n.* почтóвый перевóд; **~-spinner** *n.* (*coll.*) дéнежное дéло.
Mongol ['mɒŋg(ə)l] *n.* (*racial type*) монгóл (*fem.* -ка); (**m~:** *sufferer from ~ism*) монголóид.
adj. (*racial*) монгóльский; (*path.*) монголóидный.
Mongolia [mɒŋ'gəʊlɪə] *n.* Монгóлия.
Mongolian [mɒŋ'gəʊlɪən] *n.* (*pers.*) монгóл (*fem.* -ка); (*language*) монгóльский язык.
adj. монгóльский.
mongolism ['mɒŋgə,lɪz(ə)m] *n.* монголизм.
mongoose ['mɒŋgu:s] *n.* мангýста.
mongrel ['mʌŋgr(ə)l, 'mɒŋ-] *n.* дворняжка, пóмесь; (*fig.*) метис (*fem.* -ка).
adj. нечистокрóвный, беспорóдный.
monitor ['mɒnɪt(ə)r] *n.* **1.** (*in school*) стáроста (*c.g.*). **2.** (*of broadcasts*) сотрýдник слýжбы радиопрослýшивания. **3.** (*detector apparatus*) устанóвка для радиоперехвáта. **4.** (*computer etc*) монитóр.
v.t. проверять, контролировать (*both impf.*); **~ a treaty** наблюдáть (*impf.*) за исполнéнием договóра.
monk [mʌŋk] *n.* монáх.
monkey ['mʌŋkɪ] *n.* обезьяна; **~ business, tricks**

ша́лости (*f. pl.*), проде́лки (*f. pl.*); **he made a ~ out of me** (*fig.*) он вы́ставил меня́ на посме́шище; **you young ~!** ах ты, прока́зник/озорни́к!

v.i. дура́читься (*impf.*); **stop ~ing about with the radio!** переста́ньте копа́ться в приёмнике!

cpds. **~-jacket** *n.* матро́сская ку́ртка; **~-nut** *n.* ара́хис; **~-wrench** *n.* разводно́й га́ечный ключ.

monochrome ['mɒnə,krəʊm] *adj.* монохро́мный.

monocle ['mɒnək(ə)l] *n.* моно́кль (*m.*).

monogamous [mə'nɒgəməs] *adj.* монога́мный, единобра́чный.

monogamy [mə'nɒgəmɪ] *n.* монога́мия, единобра́чие.

monogram ['mɒnə,græm] *n.* моногра́мма.

monograph ['mɒnə,grɑ:f] *n.* моногра́фия.

monolith ['mɒnəlɪθ] *n.* моноли́т.

monolithic [,mɒnə'lɪθɪk] *adj.* (*lit.*, *fig.*) моноли́тный.

monologue ['mɒnə,lɒg] *n.* моноло́г.

monomania [,mɒnə'meɪnɪə] *n.* монома́ния.

monomaniac [,mɒnə'meɪnɪæk] *n.* монома́н.

monoplane ['mɒnə,pleɪn] *n.* монопла́н.

monopolist [mə'nɒpəlɪst] *n.* монополи́ст.

monopolistic [mə,nɒpə'lɪstɪk] *adj.* монополисти́ческий.

monopolize [mə'nɒpə,laɪz] *v.t.* монополизи́ровать (*impf.*, *pf.*).

monopoly [mə'nɒpəlɪ] *n.* монопо́лия.

monorail ['mɒnəʊ,reɪl] *n.* одноре́льсовая подвесна́я желе́зная доро́га.

monosyllabic [,mɒnəsɪ'læbɪk] *adj.* односло́жный.

monosyllable ['mɒnə,sɪləb(ə)l] *n.* односло́жное сло́во.

monotheism ['mɒnə,θi:ɪz(ə)m] *n.* монотеи́зм, единобо́жие.

monotheistic [,mɒnəʊθi:'ɪstɪk] *adj.* монотеисти́ческий.

monotone ['mɒnə,təʊn] *n.*: **in a ~** без вся́кого выраже́ния, моното́нно.

monotonous [mə'nɒtənəs] *adj.* моното́нный.

monotony [mə'nɒtənɪ] *n.* моното́нность, однообра́зие.

monotype ['mɒnə,taɪp] *n.* моноти́п.

monsoon [mɒn'su:n] *n.* (*wind*) муссо́н; (*season*) сезо́н дожде́й.

monster ['mɒnstə(r)] *n.* (*misshapen creature*) уро́д; (*imaginary animal*) чудо́вище; (*person of exceptional cruelty etc.*) чудо́вище, и́зверг; (*sth. abnormally large*) грома́дина; (*attr.*) чудо́вищный.

monstrosity [mɒn'strɒsɪtɪ] *n.* (*quality*) уро́дство, чудо́вищность; (*object*) чудо́вище.

monstrous ['mɒnstrəs] *adj.* (*monster-like*) ужа́сный; (*huge*) грома́дный; (*outrageous*) чудо́вищный.

montage [mɒn'tɑ:ʒ] *n.* (*cinema*) монта́ж; (*composite picture*) фо́томонта́ж.

month [mʌnθ] *n.* ме́сяц; **the last six ~s** после́дние полго́да.

monthly ['mʌnθlɪ] *n.* (*periodical*) ежеме́сячник.

adj. ме́сячный.

adv. ежеме́сячно.

monument ['mɒnjʊmənt] *n.* па́мятник.

monumental [,mɒnjʊ'ment(ə)l] *adj.* увекове́чивающий, монумента́льный; (*fig.*) колосса́льный; **a ~ achievement** колосса́льное достиже́ние.

moo [mu:] *n.* мыча́ние.

v.i. мыча́ть, про-.

mooch [mu:tʃ] *v.i.* (*coll.*) слоня́ться (*impf.*) (без де́ла).

mood[1] [mu:d] *n.* (*state of mind*) настрое́ние; **I am not in the ~ for conversation** я не располо́жен к разгово́ру; **he works as the ~ takes him** он рабо́тает по настрое́нию; **she is in one of her ~s** она́ опя́ть не в ду́хе.

mood[2] [mu:d] *n.* (*gram.*) наклоне́ние.

moodiness ['mu:dɪnɪs] *n.* угрю́мость; капри́зность.

moody ['mu:dɪ] *adj.* (*gloomy*) угрю́мый; (*subject to changes of mood*) капри́зный; переме́нчивого настрое́ния.

moon[1] [mu:n] *n.* луна́; (*astron.*) Луна́; (*esp. poet.*) ме́сяц; **is there a ~ tonight?** ночь сего́дня лу́нная?; **new ~** молодо́й ме́сяц, новолу́ние; **the ~ was full** бы́ло полнолу́ние; (*satellite*) спу́тник; **the ~s of Jupiter** спу́тники Юпи́тера; (*month*): **many ~s ago** давны́м-давно́; **once in a blue ~** раз в год по обеща́нию.

cpds. **~beam** *n.* луч луны́; **~-landing** *n.* прилуне́ние; **~light** *n.* лу́нный свет; **by ~light** при луне́; **~lighter** *n.* (*coll.*) халту́рщик; **~lighting** *n.* (*coll.*) халту́ра; **~lit** *adj.* зали́тый лу́нным све́том; **~scape** *n.* лу́нный ландша́фт; **~-shot** *n.* за́пуск на Луну́; **~stone** *n.* лу́нный ка́мень.

moon[2] [mu:n] *v.t.* & *i.*: **stop ~ing around the house!** переста́ньте слоня́ться/болта́ться по до́му!

moonless ['mu:nlɪs] *adj.* безлу́нный.

moor[1] [mʊə(r), mɔ:(r)] *n.* ме́стность, поро́сшая ве́реском.

cpd. **~land** *n.* ве́ресковая пу́стошь.

Moor[2] [mʊə(r), mɔ:(r)] *n.* мавр; (*fem.*) маврита́нка.

moor[3] [mʊə(r), mɔ:(r)] *v.t.* ста́вить, по- на прича́л; швартова́ть, при-.

v.i.: **they ~ed in the harbour** они́ пришвартова́лись в га́вани.

mooring|s ['mʊərɪŋz, 'mɔ:rɪŋz] *n.* (*gear*) мёртвые якоря́; (*place*) ме́сто стоя́нки; прича́л.

cpd. **~-rope** *n.* швартóв.

Moorish ['mʊərɪʃ, 'mɔ:rɪʃ] *adj.* маврита́нский.

moose [mu:s] *n.* америка́нский лось.

moot [mu:t] *adj.*: **a ~ point** спо́рный пункт.

mop [mɒp] *n.* шва́бра; **~ of hair** копна́ воло́с.

v.t. прот|ира́ть, -ере́ть; вытира́ть, вы́тереть; **he ~ped his brow** он вы́тер лоб.

with adv.: **~ up** *v.t.* & *i.* (*fig.*): **~ping-up operations** (*mil.*) прочёсывание райо́на; очи́стка захва́ченной террито́рии от проти́вника.

mope [məʊp] *v.i.* хандри́ть (*impf.*).

moped ['məʊped] *n.* мопе́д.

moraine [mə'reɪn] *n.* море́на.

moral ['mɒr(ə)l] *n.* **1.** мора́ль; **the ~ of this story is ...** мора́ль сей ба́сни такова́...; **the book points a ~** в кни́ге соде́ржится нравоуче́ние. **2.** (*pl.*) нра́в|ы (*pl.*, *g.* -ов); **loose ~s** свобо́дные нра́вы; **a man without ~s** безнра́вственный челове́к.

adj. **1.** (*ethical*) мора́льный; нра́вственный; **~ sense** уме́ние отлича́ть добро́ от зла; **~ philosophy** э́тика. **2.** (*virtuous*) нра́вственный. **3.** (*capable of ~ action*): **man is a ~ agent** челове́к — носи́тель эти́ческого нача́ла. **4.** (*conducive to ~ behaviour*) нравоучи́тельный; **a ~ tale** нравоучи́тельный расска́з. **5.** (*non-physical*) мора́льный, духо́вный; **he won a ~ victory** он одержа́л мора́льную побе́ду; **I gave him ~ support** я оказа́л ему́ мора́льную подде́ржку.

morale [mə'rɑ:l] *n.* мора́льное состоя́ние.

moralist ['mɒrəlɪst] *n.* (*teacher of morality*) морали́ст.

morality [mə'rælɪtɪ] *n.* **1.** (*moral conduct*) мора́ль. **2.** (*system of morals*) нра́вственность, э́тика.

moralize ['mɒrə,laɪz] *v.i.* морализи́ровать (*impf.*).

morass [mə'ræs] *n.* боло́то; тряси́на.

moratorium [,mɒrə'tɔ:rɪəm] *n.* морато́рий.

morbid ['mɔ:bɪd] *adj.* боле́зненный, нездоро́вый.

morbidity [mɔ:'bɪdɪtɪ] *n.* боле́зненность.

mordant ['mɔ:d(ə)nt] *adj.* ко́лкий; язви́тельный.

more [mɔ:(r)] *n.* & *adj.* (*greater amount or number*) бо́льше, бо́лее; **a little ~** побо́льше; **he received ~ than I did** он получи́л бо́льше меня́; **~ than enough** предоста́точно; **you thanked her, which is ~ than I did** вы поблагодари́ли её, чего́ я не сде́лал; (*additional amount or number*) ещё; бо́льше; **~ tea** ещё ча́ю; **I hope to see ~ of you** я наде́юсь ви́деться с ва́ми поча́ще; **and what is ~** а кро́ме того́; и бо́льше того́; **have you any ~ matches?** у вас ещё оста́лись спи́чки?; **there is no ~ soup** бо́льше нет су́па; **twice ~** ещё два ра́за.

adv. бо́льше, бо́лее; (*rather*) скоре́е; **~ or less** бо́лее и́ли ме́нее; **I like beef ~ than mutton** я предпочита́ю говя́дину бара́нине; **he is no ~ a professor than I am** он тако́й же профе́ссор как я; **~ ridiculous** бо́лее смехотво́рный; **she is ~ beautiful than her sister** она́ краси́вее свое́й сестры́; **~ and ~** всё бо́лее и бо́лее; **I became ~ and ~ tired** я всё бо́льше устава́л; **the ~ the better** чем бо́льше, тем лу́чше; **~ than once** не раз; **once ~** сно́ва, опя́ть, ещё раз; **I saw him no ~** я его́ бо́льше не ви́дел; **he is no ~** его́ уже́ нет с на́ми (*or* нет в живы́х); **all the ~ because ...** тем бо́лее, что...

moreover [mɔːˈrəʊvə(r)] *adv.* кро́ме того́; сверх того́.

mores [ˈmɔːreɪz, -riːz] *n.* нра́вы (*m. pl.*).

morganatic [ˌmɔːgəˈnætɪk] *adj.* морганати́ческий.

morgue [mɔːg] *n.* морг, мертве́цкая.

moribund [ˈmɒrɪˌbʌnd] *adj.* умира́ющий.

Mormon [ˈmɔːmən] *n.* мормо́н (*fem.* -ка).

Mormonism [ˈmɔːmənˌɪz(ə)m] *n.* мормони́зм.

morning [ˈmɔːnɪŋ] *n.* **1.** у́тро; **in the ~** у́тром; **on Monday ~** в понеде́льник у́тром; **next ~** на (сле́дующее) у́тро; **three o'clock in the ~** три часа́ но́чи; **this ~** сего́дня у́тром; **from ~ till night** с утра́ до ве́чера; **one ~** одна́жды у́тром; **good ~!** до́брое у́тро! **2.** (*attr.*) у́тренний; **~ coat** визи́тка; **~ sickness** тошнота́ и рво́та бере́менных по утра́м; **~ star** у́тренняя звезда́, Вене́ра.

Morocco [məˈrɒkəʊ] *n.* Маро́кко (*indecl.*); (**m~**: *leather*) сафья́н, (*attr.*) сафья́новый.

moron [ˈmɔːrɒn] *n.* слабоу́мный.

moronic [məˈrɒnɪk] *adj.* слабоу́мный, идио́тский.

morose [məˈrəʊs] *adj.* мра́чный.

moroseness [məˈrəʊsnɪs] *n.* мра́чность.

morph|ia [ˈmɔːfɪə], **-ine** [ˈmɔːfiːn] *n.* мо́рфий.

morphological [ˌmɔːfəˈlɒdʒɪk(ə)l] *adj.* морфологи́ческий.

morphology [mɔːˈfɒlədʒɪ] *n.* морфоло́гия.

morse [mɔːs] *n.* (**~ code**) а́збука Мо́рзе.

morsel [ˈmɔːs(ə)l] *n.* кусо́чек.

mortal [ˈmɔːt(ə)l] *n.* сме́ртный.

adj. **1.** (*subject to death*) сме́ртный; **in this ~ life** в э́той преходя́щей жи́зни. **2.** (*leading to death*) смерте́льный; **a ~ wound** смерте́льная ра́на; **~ combat** сме́ртный бой. **3.** (*extreme*) смерте́льный, ужа́сный; **~ fear** смерте́льный страх.

mortality [mɔːˈtælɪtɪ] *n.* (*being mortal*; *number or rate of deaths*) сме́ртность.

mortar[1] [ˈmɔːtə(r)] *n.* (*building material*) известко́вый раство́р.

cpd. **~-board** (*used in building*) со́кол; (*cap*) акаде́мическая ша́почка.

mortar[2] [ˈmɔːtə(r)] *n.* (*bowl*) сту́п(к)а.

mortar[3] [ˈmɔːtə(r)] *n.* (*mil.*) миномёт.

cpd. **~-fire** *n.* миномётный ого́нь.

mortgage [ˈmɔːgɪdʒ] *n.* закла́д; ипоте́ка; (*deed*) закладна́я; **pay off the ~** вы́купить (*pf.*) зало́женный дом; **raise a ~** получ|а́ть, -и́ть заём под закладну́ю.

v.t. за|кла́дывать, -ложи́ть.

mortician [mɔːˈtɪʃ(ə)n] *n.* (*US*) похоро́нных дел ма́стер.

mortification [ˌmɔːtɪfɪˈkeɪʃ(ə)n] *n.* **1.** (*hurt, humiliation, grief*) оби́да, униже́ние. **2.** (*subduing*) подавле́ние, укроще́ние; **~ of the flesh** умерщвле́ние пло́ти.

mortify [ˈmɔːtɪˌfaɪ] *v.t.* **1.** (*cause shame or humiliation to*) об|ижа́ть, -и́деть; ун|ижа́ть, -и́зить. **2.** (*cause grief to*) оскорб|ля́ть, -и́ть; **a ~ing defeat** унизи́тельное пораже́ние. **3.** (*subdue*) под|авля́ть, -ави́ть; укро|ща́ть, -ти́ть; умерщв|ля́ть, -и́ть.

mortise [ˈmɔːtɪs] *n.* гнездо́; **~ lock** врезно́й замо́к.

mortuary [ˈmɔːtjʊərɪ] *n.* морг, поко́йницкая.

adj. похоро́нный, погреба́льный.

mosaic [məʊˈzeɪɪk] *n.* моза́ика.

adj. мозаи́чный.

Moscow [ˈmɒskəʊ] *n.* Москва́; (*attr.*) моско́вский; **in the ~ area** под Москво́й.

Moslem [ˈmɒzləm] = **Muslim**

mosque [mɒsk] *n.* мече́ть.

mosquito [mɒsˈkiːtəʊ] *n.* кома́р.

cpd. **~-net** *n.* противомоски́тная се́тка.

moss [mɒs] *n.* мох.

cpds. **~-green** *adj.* тёмно-зелёный; **~-grown** *adj.* поро́сший мхом.

mossy [ˈmɒsɪ] *adj.* мши́стый.

most [məʊst] *n.* (*greatest part*) бо́льшая часть; (*greatest amount*) наибо́льшее коли́чество; **who scored the ~?** кто получи́л наибо́льшее коли́чество очко́в?; **at (the) ~** са́мое бо́льшее; ма́ксимум; не бо́льше (+*g.*, *or* чем...); **£5 at the ~** ма́ксимум 5 фу́нтов; **you must make the ~ of your chances** вам ну́жно наилу́чшим о́бразом испо́льзовать свои́ возмо́жности.

adj.: **the play was boring for the ~ part** в основно́м пье́са была́ ску́чная; **~ people** большинство́ люде́й; **~ of us** большинство́ из нас; **who has the ~ money?** у кого́ бо́льше всех де́нег?

adv. **1.** (*expr. comparison*): **what I ~ desire** чего́ я бо́льше всего́ хочу́; **the ~ beautiful** са́мый краси́вый. **2.** (*very*) о́чень, весьма́, в вы́сшей сте́пени.

mostly [ˈməʊstlɪ] *adv.* гла́вным о́бразом; **the weather was ~ dull** в основно́м пого́да стоя́ла па́смурная.

MOT (*abbr. of **Ministry of Transport***) Министе́рство тра́нспорта; **~ (test)** ≃ листо́к техосмо́тра.

mote [məʊt] *n.* (*speck*) пыли́нка.

motel [məʊˈtel] *n.* моте́ль (*m.*).

moth [mɒθ] *n.* мотылёк, ночна́я ба́бочка; **(clothes) ~** (платяна́я) моль.

cpds. **~ball** *n.* нафтали́новый ша́рик; **in ~balls** (*fig.*) на хране́нии; *v.t.* (*fig.*): **the ship was ~balled** кора́бль поста́вили на консерва́цию; **~-eaten** *adj.* (*lit.*) изъе́денный мо́лью; (*fig.*) устаре́вший.

mother [ˈmʌðə(r)] *n.* **1.** мать; (*dim.*) ма́ма; **she was like a ~ to him** она́ была́ ему́ как родна́я мать; **unmarried ~** мать-одино́чка. **2.** (*attr.*) матери́нский; **~ country** ро́дина; **~ ship** плаву́чая ба́за; **~ tongue** родно́й язы́к. **3.** (*head of religious community*): **M~ Superior** мать-игу́менья.

v.t. относи́ться (*impf.*) по-матери́нски к+*d.*; уха́живать (*за кем*) как за ребёнком; **she ~ed a family of ten** она́ вы́растила десятеры́х дете́й; **a child needs ~ing** ребёнку нужна́ матери́нская забо́та; **M~ing Sunday** матери́нское воскресе́нье.

cpds. **~-in-law** *n.* (*wife's mother*) тёща; (*husband's mother*) свекро́вь; **~land** *n.* ро́дина, оте́чество; **~-of-pearl** *n.* перламу́тр; *adj.* перламу́тровый.

motherhood [ˈmʌðəhʊd] *n.* матери́нство.

motherless [ˈmʌðəlɪs] *adj.* лишённый ма́тери.

motherly [ˈmʌðəlɪ] *adj.* не́жный, забо́тливый.

motif [məʊˈtiːf] *n.* (*in music, literature*) лейтмоти́в; гла́вная мысль; (*in painting*) моти́в; (*ornament on dress*) вы́шитое украше́ние.

motion [ˈməʊʃ(ə)n] *n.* **1.** (*movement*), движе́ние; **the car was in ~** маши́на дви́галась; **he put the machine in ~** он привёл маши́ну в де́йствие; **~ picture** кинофи́льм. **2.** (*gesture*) телодвиже́ние; жест. **3.** (*proposal*) предложе́ние; **the ~ was carried** предложе́ние бы́ло при́нято.

v.t. & i.: **he ~ed to them to leave** он показа́л же́стом, что́бы они́ ушли́; **he ~ed to the auctioneer** он дал знак аукциони́сту.

motionless [ˈməʊʃənlɪs] *adj.* неподви́жный.

motivate [ˈməʊtɪˌveɪt] *v.t.* побу|жда́ть, -ди́ть; толк|а́ть, -ну́ть.

motivation [ˌməʊtɪˈveɪʃ(ə)n] *n.* побужде́ние, сти́мул; (*interest*) заинтересо́ванность.

motive ['məʊtɪv] *n.* по́вод, моти́в, побужде́ние.
adj. дви́жущий; ~ **power/force** дви́жущая си́ла.
motley ['mɒtlɪ] *adj.* (*multi-coloured*) разноцве́тный, пёстрый; (*varied*): **a ~ crowd** разношёрстная толпа́.
motor ['məʊtə(r)] *n.* **1.** (*engine*) дви́гатель (*m.*), мото́р; **electric ~** электродви́гатель (*m.*); **~ oil** авто́л; **~ vehicle** автомоби́ль (*m.*). **2.** **(~-car)** (легково́й) автомоби́ль (*m.*); **~ show** автосало́н. **3.** (*anat.*): **~ nerve** дви́гательный нерв.
v.i. **they ~ed down to the country** они́ пое́хали на автомоби́ле за́ город.
cpds. **~-bike** *n.* мотоци́кл; **~-boat** *n.* мото́рная ло́дка; **~-car** *n.* автомоби́ль (*m.*); **~-cycle** *n.* мотоци́кл; **~-cycle racing** мотого́нки (*f. pl.*); **~-cyclist** *n.* мотоцикли́ст; **~man** *n.* води́тель (*m.*); (*of train*) машини́ст; **~-racing** *n.* автомоби́льные го́нки (*f. pl.*); **~scooter** *n.* моторо́ллер; **~-ship** *n.* теплохо́д; **~way** *n.* автостра́да, автомагистра́ль.
motorcade ['məʊtəˌkeɪd] *n.* (*US*) автоколо́нна; корте́ж автомоби́лей.
motorist ['məʊtərɪst] *n.* автомобили́ст (*fem.* -ка).
motorize ['məʊtəˌraɪz] *v.t.* моторизова́ть (*impf., pf.*).
mottled ['mɒtəld] *adj.* пятни́стый, кра́пчатый.
motto ['mɒtəʊ] *n.* **1.** (*inscription*) эпи́граф; (*her.*) на́дпись на гербе́. **2.** (*maxim*) деви́з; ло́зунг.
moujik, muzhik ['mu:ʒɪk] *n.* мужи́к.
mould[1] [məʊld] (*US* **mold**) *n.* (*hollow form for casting etc.*) лите́йная фо́рма; (*for making jellies etc.*) фо́рмочка, фо́рма.
v.t. отлива́ть (*impf.*); формова́ть (*impf.*): **she ~ed the dough into loaves** она́ формова́ла буха́нки из те́ста; **the head was ~ed in clay** голова́ была́ вы́леплена в гли́не; (*fig.*) формирова́ть (*impf.*).
mould[2] [məʊld] (*US* **mold**) *n.* (*fungus*) пле́сень.
mould[3] [məʊld] (*US* **mold**) *n.* (*loose earth*) взрыхлённая земля́.
moulder[2] ['məʊldə(r)] (*US* **molder**) *v.i.* расс|ыпа́ться, -ы́паться; **~ing ruins** ве́тхие разва́лины.
moulding ['məʊldɪŋ] (*US* **molding**) *n.* **1.** (*shaping*) формо́вка; отли́вка. **2.** (*archit.*) лепно́е украше́ние.
mouldy ['məʊldɪ] (*US* **moldy**) *adj.* (*affected by mould*) запле́сневелый; (*stale*) чёрствый; (*coll., unwell*) нездоро́вый.
moult [məʊlt] (*US* **molt**) *n.* ли́нька.
v.i. линя́ть (*impf.*); меня́ть (*impf.*) опере́ние.
mound [maʊnd] *n.* на́сыпь; курга́н.
mount [maʊnt] *n.* **1.** (*mountain; hill*) возвы́шенность; **M~ Everest** гора́ Эвере́ст. **2.** (*horse*) (верхова́я) ло́шадь. **3.** (*of a picture*) паспарту́ (*nt. indecl.*). **4.** (*of a jewel*) опра́ва.
v.t. **1.** (*ascend, get on to*) вз|бира́ться, -обра́ться на+*a.*; подн|има́ться, -я́ться на+*a.*; **he ~ed his horse** он сел на ло́шадь; **he ~ed the throne** он взошёл на престо́л; **the stallion ~ the mare** жеребе́ц покры́л кобы́лу. **2.** (*provide with horse*): **~ed police** ко́нная поли́ция. **3.** (*put, fix on a ~*) вст|авля́ть, -а́вить в опра́ву; опр|авля́ть, -а́вить. **4.** (*set up*): **they ~ed guard over the jewels** они́ охраня́ли драгоце́нности; **the enemy ~ed an offensive** враг предпри́нял наступле́ние. **5.** (*present on stage or for display*) ста́вить, по-.
v.i. **1.** (*increase*) расти́ (*impf.*); (*also* **~ up**) нак|а́пливаться, -опи́ться. **2.: he ~ed and rode off** он вскочи́л в седло́ и ускака́л.
mountain ['maʊntɪn] *n.* **1.** гора́; **he is making a ~ out of a molehill** он де́лает из му́хи слона́. **2.** (*attr.*) го́рный; **~ range** го́рная цепь; **~ ash** ряби́на; **~ lion** пу́ма, кугуа́р. **3.** (*fig.*) ма́сса, ку́ча; **a butter ~** (*glut*) избы́ток ма́сла.
mountaineer [ˌmaʊntɪ'nɪə(r)] *n.* альпини́ст.
mountaineering [ˌmaʊntɪ'nɪərɪŋ] *n.* альпини́зм.
mountainous ['maʊntɪnəs] *adj.* гори́стый; (*huge*) грома́дный.

mountebank ['maʊntɪˌbæŋk] *n.* (ле́карь-)шарлата́н.
mourn [mɔ:n] *v.t.* опла́кивать (*impf.*); **he ~ed the loss of his wife** он скорбе́л по по́воду сме́рти свое́й жены́.
v.i. скорбе́ть (*impf.*); печа́литься (*impf.*).
mourner ['mɔ:nə(r)] *n.* прису́тствующий на похорона́х.
mournful ['mɔ:nfʊl] *adj.* ско́рбный, тра́урный.
mourning ['mɔ:nɪŋ] *n.* **1.** (*grief; respect for the dead*) скорбь; тра́ур; **day of ~** тра́урный день. **2.** (*black clothes*) тра́ур; **she was in deep ~** она́ была́ в глубо́ком тра́уре.
cpd. **~-band** *n.* тра́урная повя́зка.
mouse [maʊs] *n.* (*zool.*) мышь; (*comput.*) мышь.
cpd. **~-trap** *n.* мышело́вка.
mousse [mu:s] *n.* мусс.
moustache [mə'stɑ:ʃ] (*US* **mustache**) *n.* ус|ы́ (*pl.*, g. -о́в).
mousy ['maʊsɪ] *adj.* (*colour*) мыши́ный.
mouth[1] [maʊθ] *n.* рот; (*dim., e.g. baby's*) ро́тик; **I shouldn't have opened my ~** мне не сле́довало говори́ть; **keep your ~ shut!** молчи́!; пома́лкивай!; **the word passed from ~ to ~** но́вость передава́лась из уст в уста́; **by word of ~** у́стно; **they live from hand to ~** они́ е́ле сво́дят концы́ с конца́ми; **don't put words into my ~** не припи́сывайте мне того́, что я не говори́л; **you have taken the words out of my ~** я и́менно э́то хоте́л сказа́ть; (*fig.*): **~ of a bottle** го́рлышко; **~ of a cave** вход в пеще́ру; **~ of a river** у́стье реки́.
cpds. **~-organ** *n.* губна́я гармо́ника; **~piece** *n.* (*of instrument, pipe etc.*) мундшту́к; (*fig., spokesman*) ру́пор; **~-wash** *n.* полоска́ние для рта; **~-watering** *adj.* вку́сный, аппети́тный.
mouth[2] [maʊð] *v.t.*: **the actor ~ed his words** актёр напы́щенно деклами́ровал; **he ~ed the words 'Go away'** «Уйди́те», сказа́л он одни́ми губа́ми.
mouthful ['maʊθfʊl] *n.* кусо́к, глото́к; (*fig., long word*) тру́дно произноси́мое сло́во.
movable ['mu:vəb(ə)l] *adj.* (*portable*) подвижно́й, портати́вный; (*varying in date*): **~ feast** переходя́щий.
movables ['mu:vəb(ə)lz] *n.* (*furniture etc.*) дви́жимое иму́щество.
move [mu:v] *n.* **1.** (*in games*) ход; **it's your ~** ваш ход!; (*fig.*) посту́пок; ход, шаг. **2.** (*initiation of action or motion*) движе́ние; **it's time we made a ~** нам пора́ дви́гаться; **get a ~ on!** дви́гайтесь!, поторáпливайтесь!; **the enemy is on the ~** враг на ма́рше. **3.** (*change of residence*) перее́зд; **when does your ~ take place?** когда́ вы переезжа́ете?
v.i. **1.** (*change position of; put in motion*) дви́гать (*impf.*); передв|ига́ть, -и́нуть; **he ~d his chair nearer the fire** он пододви́нул стул к ками́ну; **~ your books out of the way!** убери́те свои́ кни́ги!; **do you mind moving your car?** бу́дьте любе́зны, переста́вьте свою́ маши́ну; **he never ~d a muscle** он не шевельну́л ни одни́м му́скулом; (*fig.*) он и бро́вью не повёл. **2.** (*affect, provoke*) тро́гать (*impf.*); волнова́ть (*impf.*); **the play ~d me deeply** пье́са меня́ глубоко́ взволнова́ла; **the sight ~d him to tears** зре́лище тро́нуло его́ до слёз; **he is easily ~d to anger** его́ легко́ рассерди́ть. **3.** (*prompt, induce*) побу|жда́ть, -ди́ть; заст|авля́ть, -а́вить. **4.** (*propose*) вн|оси́ть, -ести́ предложе́ние; **I ~ that the meeting be adjourned** я предлага́ю отложи́ть заседа́ние.
v.i. **1.** (*change position; be in motion*) дви́гаться (*impf.*); шевел|и́ться, -ьну́ться; **the lever won't ~** рыча́г не сдвига́ется; **don't ~!** не дви́гайтесь! **2.** (*in games*) ходи́ть (*impf.*); **whose turn is it to ~?** чей ход? **3.** (*change one's residence*) пере|езжа́ть, -е́хать. **4.** (*make progress*) развива́ться (*impf.*);

work ~s slowly рабо́та идёт ме́дленно; **one must ~ with the times** на́до шага́ть в но́гу со вре́менем. **5.** (*stir*) шевели́ться (*impf.*). **6.** (*go about*) враща́ться (*impf.*); **he ~s in exalted circles** он враща́ется в вы́сших сфе́рах.

with advs.: **~ about, ~ around** *v.t.* перест|авля́ть, -а́вить; **he was ~d about a lot** его́ ча́сто переводи́ли с одно́й до́лжности на другу́ю; *v.i.* пере|езжа́ть, -е́хать; разъезжа́ть (*impf.*); **he ~s about a lot** он мно́го разъезжа́ет; **~ along** *v.i.*: **~ along there, please!** проходи́те, пожа́луйста!; **~ around** *v.t.* = **~ about, ~ round; ~ aside** *v.t. & i.* отодв|ига́ть(ся), -и́нуть(ся); **~ away** *v.t. & i.* удал|я́ть(ся), -и́ть(ся); **~ your hand away!** убери́те ру́ку!; **they ~d away from here** они́ перее́хали отсю́да; **~ back** *v.t.*: **he ~d the books back** (*away from him*) он отодви́нул кни́ги; (*to where they had been*) он поста́вил кни́ги наза́д; *v.i.*: **he ~d** (*stepped*) **back** он отошёл; **they ~d back** (*to where they had lived*) они́ верну́лись (на ста́рую кварти́ру *и т.п.*); **~ forward** *v.t. & i.* дви́|гать(ся), -нуть(ся) вперёд; **~ in** *v.t.*: **troops were ~d in** бы́ли введены́ войска́; *v.i.* (*take up abode*): **they ~d in next door** они́ посели́лись в сосе́днем до́ме; **~ off** *v.i.*: **the train was moving off** по́езд на́чал отходи́ть; **~ on** *v.t.* продв|ига́ть, -и́нуть; **he ~d the hands** (*of the clock*) **on** он переста́вил стре́лки вперёд; **the police ~d the crowd on** поли́ция заста́вила толпу́ отойти́; *v.i.* продв|ига́ться, -и́нуться; идти́ (*det.*) да́льше; **~ out** *v.t.*: **the squatters were ~d out** скваттеров вы́селили; *v.i.*: **we have to ~ out tomorrow** мы должны́ съе́хать за́втра; **~ over** *v.t.* отодв|ига́ть, -и́нуть; *v.i.* (*e.g. in bed*) передв|ига́ться, -и́нуться; **~ round** *v.t.* = **~ about**; *v.i.*: **the sails of the windmill ~d round** кры́лья ме́льницы враща́лись; **~ together** *v.t.* сдв|ига́ть, -и́нуть; *v.i.* сходи́ться, сойти́сь; съ|езжа́ться, -е́хаться; **~ up** *v.t.*: **~ up a chair!** пододви́ньте стул!; **he was ~d up into the next class** его́ перевели́ в сле́дующий класс; *v.i.*: **~ up and let me sit down!** подви́ньтесь и да́йте мне сесть; **they ~d up in the world** они́ вы́шли в лю́ди.

movement ['mu:vmənt] *n.* **1.** (*state of moving, motion*) движе́ние, перемеще́ние. **2.** (*of the body or part of it*) жест, телодвиже́ние. **3.** (*mil. evolution*) передвиже́ние. **4.** (*from one place to another*) переселе́ние; **~ of populations** переселе́ние наро́дов. **5.** (*mus., section of composition*) часть; **slow ~** ме́дленная часть. **6.** (*moving parts*) ход; механи́зм; **a clock's ~** ход часо́в. **7.** (*group united by common purpose*) движе́ние; **the labour ~** рабо́чее движе́ние; **peace ~** движе́ние за мир.

mover ['mu:və(r)] *n.* **1.** (*initiator of idea etc.*) инициа́тор. **2.** (*of proposal*) а́втор предложе́ния. **3. prime ~** перви́чный дви́гатель.

movie ['mu:vɪ] *n.* (*coll.*) фильм, кинокарти́на; **he's gone to the ~s** он пошёл в кино́.

cpds. **~-goer** *n.* люби́тель (*fem.* -ница) кино́; **~-maker** *n.* режиссёр.

moving ['mu:vɪŋ] *adj.* волну́ющий, тро́гательный.

mow [məʊ] *v.t. & i.* коси́ть, с-; **he ~ed the lawn** он подстри́г траву́.

with adv.: **~ down** (*fig.*) ск|а́шивать, -оси́ть.

Mozambique [,məʊzæm'bi:k] *n.* Мозамби́к.

MP (*abbr. of* ***Member of Parliament***) чле́н парла́мента.

mpg (*abbr. of* ***miles per gallon***) ми́ли на галло́н бензи́на.

mph (*abbr. of* ***miles per hour***) (*столько-то*) миль в час.

Mr ['mɪstə(r)] *n.* (*abbr. of* **mister**) (*pl.* **Messrs.**) г-н, (господ|и́н, *pl.* -а́); ми́стер.

Mrs ['mɪsɪz] *n.* (*abbr. of* **mistress**) (*pl. as sg.*) г-жа, (госпожа́).

MS *abbr. of* **1. manuscript** ['mænjʊskrɪpt] ру́копись. **2.** ***multiple sclerosis*** рассе́янный склеро́з.

Ms [mɪz, məz] *n.* (*pl. as sg.*) миз, г-жа, (госпожа́).

M.Sc. (*abbr. of* ***Master of Science***) маги́стр (есте́ственных) нау́к.

Mt. [maʊnt] *n.* (*abbr. of* **Mount**) г, (гора́).

much [mʌtʃ] *n. & adj.* мно́гое; мно́го +*g.*; **~ of what you say is true** мно́гое из того́, что вы говори́те, справедли́во; **I will say this ~** сто́лько (и не бо́льше) я гото́в сказа́ть; **his work is not up to ~** в его́ рабо́те нет ничего́ осо́бенного; **too ~** сли́шком (мно́го); мно́го; **it was too ~ for me** э́то бы́ло для меня́ (уж) сли́шком; **he thinks too ~ of himself** он сли́шком высо́кого мне́ния о себе́; **I couldn't make ~ of the lecture** ле́кция была́ мне не о́чень поня́тна; **I don't see ~ of him** я его́ ре́дко ви́жу; **he doesn't read ~** он ма́ло чита́ет; **he is not ~ of an actor** он актёр о́чень нева́жный; **she is not ~ to look at** она́ далеко́ не краса́вица; **I don't think ~ of this cheese** мне не о́чень нра́вится э́тот сыр; **how ~** ско́лько +*g.*; **very ~** о́чень (мно́го); о́чень си́льно; **as ~ again** ещё сто́лько же; **I thought as ~** я так и ду́мал; **as ~ as to say** как бы говоря́; **it is as ~ my idea as yours** э́то сто́лько же моя́ иде́я, ско́лько ва́ша; **so ~** сто́лько +g..

adv. **1.** (*by far*) гора́здо; **~ better** гора́здо лу́чше; **~ the best** гора́здо лу́чше други́х/остальны́х. **2.** (*greatly*) о́чень; нема́ло; **it doesn't ~ matter** э́то не име́ет большо́го значе́ния; **it does not differ ~** э́то немно́гим отлича́ется; **so ~ the better** тем лу́чше; **he was not ~ the worse** он не о́чень пострада́л; **~ to my surprise** к моему́ вели́кому удивле́нию; **~ as I should like to go** как бы я ни хоте́л пойти́; **not ~!** (*coll., very ~*) о́чень да́же!; а как же! **3.** (*about*) приме́рно, почти́; **they are ~ of a size** они́ почти́ одного́ разме́ра.

mucilage ['mju:sɪlɪdʒ] *n.* (*US*) клей.

muck [mʌk] (*coll.*) *n.* **1.** (*manure*) наво́з. **2.** (*dirt*) грязь; (*fig., anything disgusting*) дрянь.

with advs.: **~ about** *v.t.* (*inconvenience*) причин|я́ть, -и́ть неудо́бство +*d.*; *v.i.*: **he was ~ing about with the radio** он вози́лся с ра́дио; **~ in** *v.i.*: **if we all ~ in we shall soon get it done** е́сли мы вме́сте за э́то возьмёмся, мы э́то бы́стро сде́лаем; **~ out** *v.t.*: **he ~ed out the stables** он почи́стил коню́шни; **~ up** *v.t.* (*make dirty*) загрязн|я́ть, -и́ть; па́чкать, ис-; (*spoil, bungle*) испо́ртить (*pf.*); напорта́чить (*pf.*); **I ~ed up my exam** я завали́л экза́мен.

cpds. **~-heap** *n.* наво́зная ку́ча; **~-raker** *n.* (*fig.*) выгреба́тель (*m.*) му́сора; **~-raking** *n.* копа́ние в грязи́; **~-up** *n.* пу́таница.

mucky ['mʌkɪ] *adj.* (*coll.*) гря́зный; пога́ный.

mucus ['mju:kəs] *n.* слизь.

mud [mʌd] *n.* грязь; сля́коть; **his name was ~** (*fig.*) он был опозо́рен; (*attr.*): **~ flat** вя́зкое дно, обнажа́ющееся при отли́ве; **~ hut** земля́нка.

cpds. **~-bath** *n.* грязева́я ва́нна; **~guard** *n.* крыло́; **~-slinging** *n.* (*fig.*) клевета́.

muddle ['mʌd(ə)l] *n.* **1.** (*mess; disorder*) беспоря́док; неразбери́ха; **you have made a ~ of it** вы всё перепу́тали; **things have got into a ~** всё перепу́талось/смеша́лось. **2.** (*confusion of mind*) пу́таница; **I was in a ~ over the dates** я запу́тался в да́тах.

v.t. **1.** (*bring into disorder*) перепу́т|ывать, -ать; вн|оси́ть, -ести́ беспоря́док в+*a.*; **you have ~d (up) my papers** вы смеша́ли мои́ бума́ги. **2.** (*confuse*) пу́тать, на-; сби|ва́ть, -ть с то́лку; **don't ~ me (up)** не сбива́йте меня́ с то́лку.

v.i. **~ along, ~ through** вози́ться (*impf.*); **they ~ed along** они́ де́йствовали наобу́м; **we shall ~ through somehow** мы ко́е-как спра́вимся.

cpds. **~-headed** *adj.* бестолко́вый.

muddy ['mʌdɪ] *adj.* **1.** (*covered or soiled with mud*) гря́зный, запа́чканный; ~ **boots** забры́зганные гря́зью боти́нки. **2.** (*of liquids*) му́тный.

v.t. обры́зг|ивать, -ать гря́зью.

muff[1] [mʌf] *n.* (*for hands*; *also tech.*) му́фта.

muff[2] [mʌf] *v.t.* (*coll.*) ма́зать, про-; пропус|ка́ть, -ти́ть; (*spoil*) по́ртить, ис-; **the actor ~ed his lines** актёр перепу́тал ре́плики.

muffin ['mʌfɪn] *n.* ≃ горя́чая бу́лочка.

muffle ['mʌf(ə)l] *v.t.* **1.** (*wrap up*) ку́тать, за-; **he was ~d up in an overcoat** он заку́тался в пальто́. **2.** (*of sound*) глуши́ть, за-; **~ed voices** приглушённые голоса́.

muffler ['mʌflə(r)] *n.* (*scarf*) кашне́ (*indecl.*), шарф; (*silencer*) глуши́тель (*m.*).

mufti ['mʌftɪ] *n.* (*civilian clothes*) шта́тское пла́тье; **in ~** в шта́тском.

mug[1] [mʌg] *n.* (*vessel*) кру́жка; (*sl.*, *face*) мо́рда.

mug[2] [mʌg] *n.* (*simpleton*) балбе́с; **it's a ~'s game** э́то для дурако́в; безнадёжное де́ло.

mug[3] [mʌg] *v.t.*: **~ up** (*sl.*, *study hard*) зубри́ть, вы́-.

mug[4] [mʌg] *v.t.* (*sl.*, *attack*) напада́ть, -а́сть на+*a.*; (*rob*) гра́бить, о-; **~ging** у́личный грабёж.

mugger ['mʌgə(r)] *n.* у́личный граби́тель.

muggy ['mʌgɪ] *adj.* (*damp and warm*) сыро́й и тёплый; (*close*) уду́шливый.

mulberry ['mʌlbərɪ] *n.* (*tree*) ту́товое де́рево, шелкови́ца; (*fruit*) ту́товая я́года.

mulch [mʌltʃ, mʌlʃ] *n.* му́льча.

v.t. мульчи́ровать (*impf.*, *pf.*).

mule[1] [mju:l] *n.* мул; (*fig.*, *of pers.*) упря́мый осёл.

cpd. **~-driver** *n.* пого́нщик му́лов.

mule[2] [mju:l] *n.* (*slipper*) шлёпанец.

muleteer [ˌmju:lɪ'tɪə(r)] *n.* пого́нщик му́лов.

mull[1] [mʌl] *v.t.* **~ wine** вари́ть, с- глинтве́йн.

mull[2] [mʌl] *v.t.*: **~ over** (*ponder*) размышля́ть (*impf.*) над+*i.*; обду́м|ывать, -ать.

mullah ['mʌlə] *n.* мулла́ (*m.*).

mullet ['mʌlɪt] *n.* кефа́ль.

multi- ['mʌltɪ] *comb. form* много..., мульти...

multicoloured ['mʌltɪˌkʌləd] *adj.* многоцве́тный, кра́сочный.

multifaceted [ˌmʌltɪ'fæsɪtɪd] *adj.* многогра́нный.

multifarious [ˌmʌltɪ'feərɪəs] *adj.* разнообра́зный.

multiform ['mʌltɪˌfɔ:m] *adj.* многообра́зный.

multilateral [ˌmʌltɪ'lætər(ə)l] *adj.* многосторо́нний.

multilingual [ˌmʌltɪ'lɪŋgw(ə)l] *adj.* многоязы́чный, разноязы́чный.

multimedia ['mʌltɪˌmi:dɪə] *n.* (*comput.*) мультиме́диа *f. indecl.*

multimillionaire [ˌmʌltɪˌmɪljə'neə(r)] *n.* мультимиллионе́р.

multinational [ˌmʌltɪ'næʃən(ə)l] *n.* междунаро́дная корпора́ция.

adj. многонациона́льный.

multipartite [ˌmʌltɪ'pɑ:taɪt] *adj.* многосторо́нний.

multiple ['mʌltɪp(ə)l] *n.* кра́тное число́; **lowest common ~** о́бщее наиме́ньшее кра́тное.

adj. составно́й; многочи́сленный; **~ sclerosis** рассе́янный склеро́з; **~ store** фи́рменный магази́н; **~ warhead** многозаря́дная боеголо́вка.

multiplication [ˌmʌltɪplɪ'keɪʃ(ə)n] *n.* умноже́ние; **~ table** табли́ца умноже́ния.

multiplicity [ˌmʌltɪ'plɪsɪtɪ] *n.* многочи́сленность.

multiplier ['mʌltɪˌplaɪə(r)] *n.* мно́житель (*m.*).

multipl|y ['mʌltɪˌplaɪ] *v.t.* **1.** (*math.*) умн|ожа́ть, -о́жить; **seven ~ied by two** два́жды семь; **66 ~ied by 36** 66 помно́женное на 36. **2.** (*increase*) увели́чи|вать, -ть; мно́жить, по-/у-.

v.i. размн|ожа́ться, -о́житься.

multi-purpose [ˌmʌltɪ'pɜ:pəs] *adj.* многоцелево́й.

multiracial [ˌmʌltɪ'reɪʃ(ə)l] *adj.* многонациона́льный, многора́совый.

multi-storey [ˌmʌltɪ'stɔ:rɪ] *adj.* многоэта́жный.

multitasking [ˌmʌltɪ'tɑ:skɪŋ] *n.* (*comput.*) многозада́чный режи́м (рабо́ты).

multitude ['mʌltɪˌtju:d] *n.* (*great number*) мно́жество, ма́сса; **the ~** (*mass of people*) толпа́; ма́сса.

multitudinous [ˌmʌltɪ'tju:dɪnəs] *adj.* многочи́сленный.

mum[1] [mʌm] *n.* (*coll.*, *mother*) маму́ля, ма́ма.

mum[2] [mʌm] *adj.* (*coll.*, *quiet*): **I kept ~ about it** я об э́том пома́лкивал; **~'s the word** ни сло́ва!

mumble ['mʌmb(ə)l] *n.* бормота́ние.

v.t. & i. (*mutter*) бормота́ть, про-.

mummer ['mʌmə(r)] *n.* ря́женый.

mummify ['mʌmɪˌfaɪ] *v.t.* мумифици́ровать (*impf.*, *pf.*).

mummy[1] ['mʌmɪ] *n.* (*embalmed corpse*) му́мия.

mummy[2] ['mʌmɪ] *n.* (*coll.*, *mother*) ма́ма, ма́мочка.

mumps [mʌmps] *n.* сви́нка.

munch [mʌntʃ] *v.t. & i.* ча́вкать (*impf.*).

mundane [mʌn'deɪn] *adj.* земно́й, мирско́й.

municipal [mju:'nɪsɪp(ə)l] *adj.* муниципа́льный, городско́й.

municipality [mju:ˌnɪsɪ'pælɪtɪ] *n.* муниципалите́т.

munificence [mju:'nɪfɪs(ə)ns] *n.* ще́дрость.

munificent [mju:'nɪfɪs(ə)nt] *adj.* ще́дрый.

munitions [mju:'nɪʃ(ə)ns] *n.* снаряже́ние, вооруже́ние; (*attr.*) **~ factory** вое́нный заво́д.

mural ['mjʊər(ə)l] *n.* фре́ска, стенна́я ро́спись.

adj. стенно́й.

murder ['mɜ:də(r)] *n.* уби́йство; **~ weapon** ору́дие уби́йства; (*fig.*): **the traffic was (sheer) ~** (*coll.*) движе́ние бы́ло стра́шное.

v.t. уб|ива́ть, -и́ть; **a man was ~ed** уби́ли челове́ка; (*fig.*, *of a bad performance*) по́ртить (*impf.*); **he ~s the language** он кове́ркает язы́к.

murderer ['mɜ:dərə(r)] *n.* уби́йца (*c.g.*).

murderous ['mɜ:dərəs] *adj.* смертоно́сный, уби́йственный.

murky ['mɜ:kɪ] *adj.* мра́чный, тёмный; **his ~ past** его́ тёмное про́шлое.

murmur ['mɜ:mə(r)] *n.* **1.** (*low sound*) бормота́ние, шёпот; **his voice sank to a ~** его́ го́лос пони́зился до шёпота; **a ~ of conversation** ти́хая бесе́да; **the ~ of bees** жужжа́ние пчёл; **the ~ of the waves** ро́пот волн; **a heart ~** (*med.*) шумы́ (*m. pl.*) в се́рдце. **2.** (*fig.*, *complaint*) ро́пот, ворча́ние; **~s of discontent** выраже́ние (*nt. pl.*) недово́льства; **he paid up without a ~** он заплати́л без зву́ка.

v.t. & i. бормота́ть, про-; шепта́ть, про-; (*complain*) ропта́ть (*impf.*); ворча́ть (*impf.*).

muscatel [ˌmʌskə'tel] *n.* (*wine*) муска́т.

muscle ['mʌs(ə)l] *n.* мы́шца, му́скул; **he didn't move a ~** (*remained motionless*) он не (по)шевельну́лся.

v.i. (*coll.*): **he ~d in on the conversation** он ввяза́лся в разгово́р.

Muscovite ['mʌskəˌvaɪt] *n.* москви́ч (*fem.* -ка).

adj. моско́вский.

Muscovy ['mʌskəvɪ] *n.* Моско́вия.

muscular ['mʌskjʊlə(r)] *adj.* (*pert. to muscle*) мы́шечный; (*with strong muscles*; *robust*) му́скули́стый.

muse[1] [mju:z] *n.* (*myth.*) му́за.

muse[2] [mju:z] *v.i.* размышля́ть (*impf.*); заду́мываться (*impf.*).

museum [mju:'zɪəm] *n.* музе́й; **~ piece** (*lit.*, *fig.*) музе́йная ре́дкость.

mush [mʌʃ] *n.* ка́ша, ка́шица.

mushroom ['mʌʃrʊm, -ru:m] *n.* гриб; **~ cloud** грибови́дное о́блако.

v.i. (*pick ~s*) собира́ть (*impf.*) грибы́; (*fig.*, *grow rapidly*) бы́стро распространя́ться (*impf.*); расти́ (*impf.*) как грибы́ под дождём.

mushy ['mʌʃɪ] *adj.* мя́гкий; (*fig.*) слаща́вый.

music ['mju:zɪk] *n.* **1.** му́зыка; **the lines were put, set to ~ by Brahms** Брамс положи́л стихи́ на му́зыку; **you will have to face the ~** (*criticism*, *outcry*) вам придётся за э́то распла́чиваться. **2.** (*attr.*) **~ centre**

музыкальный комбайн; ~ **teacher** учитель (*m.*) музыки. **3.** (*sheet* ~, ~*al score*) ноты (*f. pl.*).

cpds. **~-hall** *n.* (*place, entertainment*) мюзик-холл; **~-hall artist** эстрадный артист (*fem.* -ка); **~-stand** *n.* пюпитр.

musical ['mju:zık(ə)l] *n.* (~ *comedy*) музыкальная комедия; музыкальное ревю (*indecl.*), оперетта.

adj. (*pert. to, fond of music*) музыкальный; ~ **box** музыкальная шкатулка; **a ~ voice** мелодичный голос; ~ **talent** музыкальность.

musician [mju:'zıʃ(ə)n] *n.* музыкант.

musicologist [,mju:zı'kɒlədʒıst] *n.* музыковед.

musicology [,mju:zı'kɒlədʒı] *n.* музыковедение.

musk [mʌsk] *n.* мускус.

cpds. **~-deer** *n.* мускусный олень; **~-ox** *n.* овцебык; **~-rat** *n.* ондатра; **~-rose** *n.* мускусная роза.

musket ['mʌskıt] *n.* мушкет.

musketeer [,mʌskı'tıə(r)] *n.* мушкетёр.

Muslim ['mʊzlım, 'mʌ-], **Moslem** ['mɒzləm] *n.* мусульман|ин (*fem.* -ка).

adj. мусульманский.

muslin ['mʌzlın] *n.* муслин, кисея.

adj. муслиновый, кисейный.

musquash ['mʌskwɒʃ] *n.* (*fur*) мех ондатры.

mussel ['mʌs(ə)l] *n.* мидия.

must [mʌst] *n.* (*coll., necessary item*): **the Tower of London is a ~ for visitors** туристы должны непременно посмотреть Лондонский Тауэр.

v. aux. **1.** (*expr. necessity*): **one ~ eat to live** чтобы жить, нужно есть; ~ **you go so soon?** неужели вам надо уже уходить?; **if you ~, you ~** в конце концов, нужно значит нужно; ~ **you behave like that?** неужели вы иначе не можете?; (*expr. obligation*): **you ~ do as you're told** нужно слушаться; **we ~ not be late** нам нельзя опаздывать; **I ~ ask you to leave** я вынужден попросить вас уйти; **I ~ admit** я должен признать. **2.** (*with neg., expr. prohibition*): **cars ~ not be parked here** стоянка машин запрещена. **3.** (*expr. certainty or strong probability*): **you ~ be tired** вы, наверно, устали; **you ~ have known that** не может быть, чтобы вы этого не знали.

mustache [mə'stɑ:ʃ] = **moustache**

mustang ['mʌstæŋ] *n.* мустанг.

mustard ['mʌstəd] *n.* (*plant; relish*) горчица; ~ **gas** горчичный газ, иприт.

cpds. **~-plaster** *n.* горчичник.

muster ['mʌstə(r)] *n.* **1.** (*mil., assembly*) сбор, смотр. **2.** (*numbers attending a function*) общее число. **3.** (*inspection; roll-call*) поверка; перекличка; **will his work pass ~?** (*fig.*) его работа годится?

v.t. (*summon together*) соз|ывать, -вать; соб|ирать, -рать; (*fig.*) **he ~ed up all his courage** он собрался с духом.

v.i. (*assemble*) соб|ираться, -раться.

mustiness ['mʌstınıs] *n.* затхлость; косность, отсталость.

musty ['mʌstı] *adj.* (*smelling of mould or age*) затхлый; (*fig., ancient; out-of-date*) косный, устарелый.

mutant ['mju:t(ə)nt] *adj.* мутантный.

mutate [mju:'teıt] *v.i.* (*biol.*) видоизменяться (*impf.*).

mutation [mju:'teıʃ(ə)n] *n.* изменение; (*biol.*) мутация.

mute [mju:t] *n.* **1.** (*dumb person*) немой. **2.** (*mus.*) сурдин(к)а.

adj. **1.** (*silent*) безмолвный; **he made a ~ appeal** он бросил молящий взгляд. **2.** (*dumb*) немой.

v.t. приглуш|ать, -ить; **they played with ~d strings** они играли под сурдинку.

mutilate ['mju:tı,leıt] *v.t.* увечить, из-; калечить, ис-.

mutilation [,mju:tı'leıʃ(ə)n] *n.* увечье.

mutineer [,mju:tı'nıə(r)] *n.* мятежник.

mutinous ['mju:tınəs] *adj.* мятежный.

mutiny ['mju:tını] *n.* мятеж.

v.i. бунтовать, взбунтоваться; под|ымать, -нять мятеж.

mutter ['mʌtə(r)] *n.* бормотание.

v.t. & i. бормотать (*impf.*); говорить (*impf.*) невнятно; **he ~ed an apology** он пробормотал извинение.

mutton ['mʌt(ə)n] *n.* баранина; ~ **chop** баранья отбивная.

mutual ['mju:tʃʊəl, -tjʊəl] *adj.* взаимный; **our ~ friend** наш общий друг.

muzhik ['mu:ʒık] = **moujik**

muzzle ['mʌz(ə)l] *n.* **1.** (*animal's*) морда, рыло. **2.** (*guard for this*) намордник. **3.** (*of firearm*) дуло.

v.t. над|евать, -еть намордник на+*a.*; (*fig.*) заст|авлять, -авить молчать.

MW ['megə,wɒt(z)] *n.* (*abbr. of* **megawatt(s)**) МВт, (мегаватт).

my [maı] *poss. adj.* мой; (*belonging to speaker*) свой; **I lost ~ pen** я потерял свою ручку; **for ~ part** что касается меня; (*with words of address*): ~ **dear** дорогой; ~ **dear fellow** дорогой мой; (*in exclamations*): ~ **goodness!; oh, ~!** Боже мой!; ~, ~! ну и ну! подумать только!

mycology [maı'kɒlədʒı] *n.* микология.

myna(h) ['maınə] *n.* майна.

myopia [maı'əʊpıə] *n.* миопия, близорукость.

myopic [maı'ɒpık] *adj.* миопический, близорукий.

myriad ['mırıəd] *n.* мириад|ы (*pl., g.* —).

adj. несчётный.

myrrh [mɜ:(r)] *n.* (*resin*) мирра.

myrtle ['mɜ:t(ə)l] *n.* мирт.

myself [maı'self] *pron.* **1.** (*refl.*) себя; **I said to ~** я себе сказал; **I felt pleased with ~** я был доволен собой. **2.** (*emph.*) сам; **I ~ did it** это я сделал; **I did it ~** я сам это сделал; **I did it by ~** (*without help*) я это сделал сам; **I am not ~ today** я сегодня немного не в форме. **3.** (*after preps.*): **for ~, I prefer tea** что касается меня, я предпочитаю чай.

mysterious [mı'stıərıəs] *adj.* таинственный, загадочный.

mystery ['mıstərı] *n.* **1.** (*secret, secrecy; obscurity*) тайна, загадка; **their origins are wrapped in ~** их происхождение покрыто мраком неизвестности. **2.** (*relig.*) таинство, тайные обряды (*m. pl.*); ~ **play** мистерия. **3.** (*novel etc.*) детектив.

mystic ['mıstık] *n.* мистик.

adj. (*also* **~al**) мистический.

mysticism ['mıstı,siz(ə)m] *n.* мистицизм, мистика.

mystification [,mıstıfı'keıʃ(ə)n] *n.* мистификация.

mystify ['mıstı,faı] *v.t.* мистифицировать (*impf., pf.*); озадачи|вать, -ть.

mystique [mı'sti:k] *n.* таинственность, загадочность.

myth [mıθ] *n.* (*lit., fig.*) миф.

mythic(al) ['mıθık(ə)l] *adj.* мифический.

mythological [,mıθə'lɒdʒık(ə)l] *adj.* мифологический.

mythology [mı'θɒlədʒı] *n.* мифология.

N

nab [næb] *v.t.* (*arrest*) накр|ывать, -ыть (*coll.*); (*catch in wrong-doing*) заст|игать, -игнуть.

nadir ['neıdıə(r), 'næd-] *n.* (*astron.*) надир; (*fig.*) низшая точка.

nag[1] [næg] *n.* лоша́дка; (*pej.*) кля́ча.

nag[2] [næg] *v.t.* пили́ть (*impf.*).

v.i. брюзжа́ть (*impf.*); ~ **at s.o.** пили́ть (*impf.*) кого́-н.

nagger ['nægə(r)] *n.* брюзга́ (*c.g.*).

nagging ['nægɪŋ] *n.* брюзжа́ние; постоя́нные приди́рки (*f. pl.*).

adj. приди́рчивый; (*quarrelsome*) сварли́вый; **a ~ pain** но́ющая боль.

nail [neɪl] *n.* **1.** (*on finger or toe*) но́готь (*m.*); **bite one's ~s with impatience** куса́ть (*impf.*) но́гти от нетерпе́ния. **2.** (*metal spike*) гвоздь (*m.*); **you've hit the ~ on the head** вы попа́ли в то́чку; **he pays on the ~** он распла́чивается неме́дленно.

v.t. **1.** пригво|жда́ть, -зди́ть; приб|ива́ть, ~и́ть (*что к чему*); **he ~ed the picture (on) to the wall** он приби́л карти́ну к стене́; **the windows were ~ed up** о́кна бы́ли заколо́чены; (*fig.*): **he stood ~ed to the ground** он стоя́л как вко́панный. **2.** (*fig., catch, get hold of*): **he ~ed me as I was leaving** он перехвати́л меня́ на вы́ходе; (*pin down*): **he tried to evade the issue but I ~ed him down** он пыта́лся уйти́ от пробле́мы, но я его́ прижа́л к сте́нке; (*confute*): **that lie must be ~ed** э́ту ложь на́до разоблачи́ть.

cpds. **~-brush** *n.* щёт(оч)ка для ногте́й; **~-file** *n.* пи́лка (для ногте́й); **~-scissors** *n.* но́жниц|ы (*pl., g.* —) для ногте́й; **~-varnish** *n.* лак для ногте́й.

naive [nɑː'iːv, naɪ'iːv] *adj.* наи́вный, простоду́шный.

naïvety [nɑː'iːvtɪ, naɪ-] *n.* наи́вность, простоду́шие.

naked ['neɪkɪd] *adj.* го́лый; **strip ~** разд|ева́ть(ся), -е́ть(ся) (догола́); **~ flame, light** откры́тый ого́нь; (*of natural objects: bare*) го́лый; (*plain, undisguised, unadorned*) просто́й; **the ~ truth** го́лая и́стина; **with the ~ eye** невооружённым гла́зом.

nakedness ['neɪkɪdnɪs] *n.* нагота́, обнажённость.

namby-pamby [,næmbɪ'pæmbɪ] *adj.* мягкоте́лый; слаща́вый, сентимента́льный.

name [neɪm] *n.* **1.** (*esp.* **fore~**) и́мя (*nt.*); (*surname*) фами́лия; (*of pet*) кли́чка; **what is his ~?** как его́ зову́т/фами́лия?; **a man by the ~ of ...** челове́к по и́мени/фами́лии...; **a certain doctor, Crippen by ~** не́кий до́ктор по и́мени Кри́ппен; **they are known to me by ~** я зна́ю их понаслы́шке; **he goes by, under the ~ of Smith** он изве́стен под и́менем Смит; **in heaven's ~** ра́ди Бо́га; **in the ~** (*on behalf*) **of** от и́мени +*g.*; **in the ~ of the law** и́менем зако́на; **he kept the money in his own ~** он держа́л де́ньги на своё и́мя; **he published the book in his own ~** он изда́л кни́гу под свои́м и́менем; **she was his wife in ~ only** она́ была́ его́ жено́й лишь номина́льно; **he lent his ~ to their petition** он поддержа́л пети́цию свои́м авторите́том; **I put my ~ down for a flat** я записа́лся в о́чередь на кварти́ру; **she hasn't a penny to her ~** у неё за душо́й ни гроша́; **he has £500 to his ~** он мо́жет похва́статься пятьюста́ми фу́нтами; **you may use my ~** мо́жете сосла́ться на меня́. **2.** (*of a thg.*) назва́ние; **what is the ~ of your school?** как называ́ется ва́ша шко́ла?; **this street has changed its ~** э́ту у́лицу переименова́ли. **3.** (*personage*): **the great ~s of history** вели́кие истори́ческие ли́чности (*f. pl.*)/де́ятели (*m. pl.*). **4.** (*reputation*) и́мя, репута́ция; **he made a ~ for himself** он со́здал/сде́лал себе́ и́мя; **he has a bad ~** у него́ дурна́я сла́ва; **this firm has a ~ for honesty** э́та фи́рма изве́стна свое́й че́стностью. **5.: call s.o. ~s** руга́ть (*impf.*) кого́-н.

v.t. **1.** (*give ~ to*) наз|ыва́ть, -ва́ть; да|ва́ть, -ть и́мя +*d.*; **he was ~d Andrew after his grandfather** его́ назва́ли Андре́ем по де́ду (*or* в честь де́да); **the street is ~d after Napoleon** у́лица но́сит и́мя Наполео́на; **Cape Kennedy was ~d in honour of the President** назва́ние «Мыс Ке́ннеди» бы́ло дано́ в честь президе́нта. **2.** (*recite*): **the pupil ~d the chief cities of Europe** учени́к перечи́слил гла́вные города́ Евро́пы; (*state, mention*) наз|ыва́ть, -ва́ть; **~ your price!** назна́чьте це́ну!; (*identify*): **how many stars can you ~?** ско́лько звёзд вы мо́жете определи́ть?; (*appoint*): **he asked her to ~ the day** он проси́л её назна́чить день (сва́дьбы); (*nominate*): **he was ~d for the professorship** он был назна́чен профе́ссором; (*as an example*) прив|оди́ть, -ести́ (что) в ка́честве приме́ра.

cpds. **~-day** *n.* имени́н|ы (*pl., g.* —); **~-plate** *n.* доще́чка/табли́чка с и́менем; **~sake** *n.* тёзка (*c.g.*).

nameless ['neɪmlɪs] *adj.* (*without a name*) безымя́нный; (*unnamed, unmentioned*) нена́званный; **someone who shall be ~** не́кто, кого́ мы не ста́нем называ́ть по и́мени.

namely ['neɪmlɪ] *adv.* и́менно; то есть.

Namibia [nə'mɪbɪə] *n.* Нами́бия.

nanny ['nænɪ] *n.* ня́ня.

cpd. **~-goat** *n.* коза́.

nap[1] [næp] *n.* (*short sleep*) коро́ткий сон; **have, take a ~** вздремну́ть (*pf.*); **catch s.o. ~ping** заста́ть/засти́гнуть (*pf.*) кого́-н. врасплох.

nap[2] [næp] *n.* ворс, начёс.

napalm ['neɪpɑːm] *n.* напа́лм; (*attr.*) напа́лмовый.

nape [neɪp] *n.* загри́вок.

naphtha ['næfθə] *n.* лигрои́н.

naphthalene ['næfθə,liːn] *n.* нафтали́н.

napkin ['næpkɪn] *n.* **(table-~)** салфе́тка.

nappy ['næpɪ] *n.* (*coll.*) пелёнка.

narcissism ['nɑːsɪ,sɪz(ə)m, nɑː'sɪs-] *n.* нарцисси́зм.

narcissistic [,nɑːsɪ'sɪstɪk] *adj.* самовлюблённый.

narcissus [nɑː'sɪsəs] *n.* нарци́сс.

narcotic [nɑː'kɒtɪk] *n.* нарко́тик.

adj. наркоти́ческий.

nark [nɑːk] *n.* (*police decoy or spy; informer*) лега́вый (*coll.*); стука́ч (*coll.*).

narrate [nə'reɪt] *v.t.* расска́з|ывать, -а́ть.

narration [nə'reɪʃ(ə)n] *n.* (*action, story*) расска́з, повествова́ние; (*story*) по́весть.

narrative ['nærətɪv] *n.* расска́з, по́весть.

adj. повествова́тельный.

narrator [nə'reɪtə(r)] *n.* расска́зч|ик (*fem.* -ица).

narrow ['nærəʊ] *adj.* (*lit., fig.*) **1.** у́зкий; **a ~ circle of acquaintances** те́сный круг знако́мых; **a ~ mind** ограни́ченный ум; **take a ~ view of sth.** у́зко под|ходи́ть, -ойти́ к чему́-н. **2.** (*with little margin*): **a ~ majority** незначи́тельное большинство́; **a ~ victory** побе́да с небольши́м преиму́ществом; **he had a ~ escape from death** он чу́дом избежа́л сме́рти; **he ~ly escaped drowning** он чуть не утону́л.

v.t. сужа́ть, су́|живать, -зить; **~ one's eyes, gaze** сощу́ри|ваться, -ться; (*limit*) ограни́чи|вать, -ть; **the choice was ~ed down to two candidates** вы́бор свёлся к двум кандидату́рам.

v.i. (*of river etc.*) су́|живаться, -зиться; **his eyes ~ed** он прищу́рился; он сощу́рил глаза́.

cpds. **~-gauge** *adj.* узкоколе́йный; **~-minded** *adj.* у́зкий; с предрассу́дками; **~-mindedness** *n.* у́зость взгля́дов.

narrowness ['nærəʊnɪs] *n.* у́зость, теснота́.

narwhal ['nɑːw(ə)l] *n.* нарва́л.

NASA ['næsə] *n.* (*abbr. of* ***National Aeronautics and Space Administration***) НАСА, (Национа́льное управле́ние по аэрона́втике и иссле́дованию косми́ческого простра́нства).

nasal ['neɪz(ə)l] *adj.* (*of, for the nose*) носово́й; (*of the voice*) гнуса́вый; **speak in a ~ voice** говори́ть (*impf.*) в нос; гнуса́вить (*impf.*).

nascent ['næs(ə)nt, 'neɪs-] *adj.* (на)рожда́ющийся.

nastiness ['nɑːstɪnɪs] *n.* гну́сность, проти́вность.

nasturtium [nə'stɜːʃəm] *n.* насту́рция.

nasty ['nɑːstɪ] *adj.* **1.** (*offensive*, *e.g. smell or taste*) неприя́тный, проти́вный; (*repellent*, *sickening*) отврати́тельный. **2.** (*morally offensive*) ме́рзкий, га́дкий; **he has a ~ mind** у него́ гря́зное воображе́ние. **3.** (*unkind*, *spiteful*, *unpleasant*) злой; **a ~ remark** зло́е замеча́ние; **a ~ temper** тяжёлый хара́ктер; **he played a ~ trick on me** он сыгра́л со мной злу́ю шу́тку; **turn ~** обозли́ться (*pf.*); (*of the elements*): **~ weather** скве́рная пого́да. **4.** (*threatening*) опа́сный. **5.** (*troublesome*): **a ~ bout of bronchitis** тяжёлый при́ступ бронхи́та. **6.** (*difficult*): **it's a ~ situation to be in** очути́ться в тако́м положе́нии неприя́тно; **that's a ~ one!** (*question*) тру́дный вопро́с!; (*insult*) э́то уж чересчу́р!

nation ['neɪʃ(ə)n] *n.* на́ция; (*people*) наро́д; (*state*) госуда́рство; (*country*) страна́.

cpd. **~-wide** *adj.*: **a ~-wide search** ро́зыск/по́иски по всей стране́; (*in former USSR*) всесою́зный ро́зыск; **~-wide poll** всенаро́дный опро́с.

national ['næʃən(ə)l] *n.* (*citizen*) гражд|ани́н (*fem.* -а́нка); (*subject*) по́дданн|ый (*fem.* -ая).

adj. (*of the state*) госуда́рственный; (*of the country or population as a whole*) наро́дный, всенаро́дный; (*central*; *opp. provincial*) центра́льный; (*pert. to a particular nation or ethnic group*) национа́льный; **~ anthem** госуда́рственный гимн; **~ economy** наро́дное хозя́йство; **~ genius, spirit** дух наро́да; **~ government** центра́льное прави́тельство; **~ newspapers** центра́льные газе́ты; **~ park** запове́дник, национа́льный парк; **~ service** во́инская пови́нность.

nationalism ['næʃənə,lɪz(ə)m] *n.* национали́зм.

nationalist ['næʃənə,lɪst] *n.* национали́ст (*fem.* -ка).

adj. (*also* **-ic**) националисти́ческий.

nationality [,næʃə'nælɪtɪ] *n.* (*membership of a nation*, *country*) по́дданство; гражда́нство; **(of) what ~ are you?** како́го вы по́дданства?; (*ethnic group*, *e.g. within former USSR*) национа́льность.

nationalization [,næʃənəlaɪ'zeɪʃ(ə)n] *n.* национализа́ция.

nationalize ['næʃənə,laɪz] *v.t.* национализи́ровать (*impf.*, *pf.*).

native ['neɪtɪv] *n.* **1.** (*indigenous inhabitant*) тузе́м|ец (*fem.* -ка); коренно́й жи́тель (*fem.* коренна́я жи́тельница). **2.: a ~ of** (*born in*) уроже́н|ец (*fem.* -ка) +*g.*; (*living in*) жи́тель (*fem.* -ница) +*g.* **3.** (*of plant*): **the eucalyptus is a ~ of Australia** ро́дина эвкали́пта — Австра́лия.

adj. **1.** (*of one's birth*) родно́й; **~ language** родно́й язы́к; **~ land** ро́дина, оте́чество; **he returned to his ~ haunts** он возврати́лся в родны́е края́. **2.** (*indigenous*) тузе́мный; **~ population** тузе́мное/коренно́е/ме́стное населе́ние.

nativity [nə'tɪvɪtɪ] *n.* (*birth of Christ*) Рождество́ Христо́во; (*of Virgin etc.*) рожде́ние.

NATO ['neɪtəʊ] *n.* (*abbr. of* ***North Atlantic Treaty Organization***) НАТО, (Организа́ция Се́вероатланти́ческого догово́ра); **~ member** на́товец.

adj. на́товский.

natter ['nætə(r)] (*coll.*) *n.*: **I came in for a ~** я зашёл поболта́ть.

v.i. болта́ть (*impf.*).

natt|y ['nætɪ] *adj.* (*coll.*, *spruce*, *trim*) элега́нтный; **he is ~ily dressed** он одет с иго́лочки.

natural ['nætʃər(ə)l] *n.* **1.** (*mus. sign*) бека́р. **2.: he's a ~ for the part** он рождён/со́здан для э́той ро́ли.

adj. **1.** (*found in*, *established by*, *conforming or pertaining to nature*) есте́ственный, приро́дный; стихи́йный; **~ death** есте́ственная смерть; **she died a ~ death** она́ умерла́ свое́й сме́ртью; **~ forces** си́лы приро́ды; **~ gas** приро́дный газ; **~ history** естествозна́ние; **~ phenomena** явле́ния приро́ды; **~ resources** приро́дные бога́тства; **~ sciences** есте́ственные нау́ки; **~ selection** есте́ственный отбо́р. **2.** (*normal*, *ordinary*, *not surprising*) есте́ственный, норма́льный; **he spoke in his ~ voice** он говори́л свои́м обы́чным го́лосом. **3.** (*unforced*, *spontaneous*) непринуждённый; (*simple*, *unaffected*) просто́й; простоду́шный. **4.** (*innate*) врождённый, приро́дный; **~ gifts** приро́дные дарова́ния. **5.** (*destined by nature*): **he is a ~ linguist** он прирождённый лингви́ст. **6.** (*mus.*): **B ~** си-бека́р.

cpd. **~-born** *adj.*: **a ~-born Englishman** англича́нин по рожде́нию.

naturalism ['nætʃərə,lɪz(ə)m] *n.* натурали́зм.

naturalist ['nætʃərəlɪst] *n.* **1.** (*student of animals etc.*) естествоиспыта́тель (*m.*). **2.** (*in art*) натурали́ст.

naturalistic [,nætʃərə'lɪstɪk] *adj.* натуралисти́ческий.

naturalization [,nætʃərəlaɪ'zeɪʃ(ə)n] *n.* натурализа́ция; акклиматиза́ция.

naturalize ['nætʃərə,laɪz] *v.t.* (*admit to citizenship*) натурализова́ть (*impf.*, *pf.*); (*of animals*, *plants*: *introduce to another country*) акклиматизи́ровать (*impf.*, *pf.*).

naturally ['nætʃərəlɪ] *adv.* **1.** (*not surprisingly*) есте́ственно; (*of course*) коне́чно. **2.** (*spontaneously*, *without affectation*) есте́ственно. **3.** (*by nature*) от рожде́ния; по приро́де (свое́й); (*as by instinct*): **he took ~ to swimming** пла́вание дало́сь ему́ легко́.

naturalness ['nætʃərəlnɪs] *n.* (*absence of affectation*) непринуждённость.

nature ['neɪtʃə(r)] *n.* **1.** (*force*, *natural phenomena*) приро́да; **N~'s laws** зако́ны приро́ды; **~ reserve** запове́дник; **~ study** природове́дение, естествозна́ние; **paint from ~** писа́ть (*impf.*) с нату́ры. **2.** (*of humans or animals*: *character*, *temperament*) хара́ктер, нату́ра; **a generous ~** ще́дрый хара́ктер; **she was cautious by ~** она́ была́ от приро́ды осторо́жна; **human ~** челове́ческая приро́да; **second ~** втора́я нату́ра; **it was his ~ to be proud** он был го́рдым по нату́ре. **3.** (*of things*: *essential quality*) хара́ктер; **by, in the (very) ~ of things** по приро́де веще́й; **the ~ of gases** сво́йства (*nt. pl.*) га́зов; (*sort*, *kind*) род; **things of this ~** тако́го ро́да ве́щи; **something in the ~ of a disappointment** не́что вро́де разочарова́ния.

naturism ['neɪtʃə,rɪz(ə)m] *n.* (*nudism*) нуди́зм.

naturist ['neɪtʃərɪst] *n.* (*nudist*) нуди́ст.

naturopath [,neɪtʃərə'pæθ] *n.* натуропа́т.

naturopathy [,neɪtʃə'rɒpəθɪ] *n.* натуропа́тия.

naught [nɔːt] *n.* (*arch. exc. in phrr.*): **come to ~** св|оди́ться, -ести́сь к нулю́; ни к чему́ не прив|оди́ть, -ести́; **set at ~** ни во что не ста́вить (*impf.*); *see also* **nought**

naughty ['nɔːtɪ] *adj.* **1.** (*e.g. child's behaviour*) озорно́й, капри́зный; **be ~** озорнича́ть (*impf.*); капри́зничать (*impf.*); **you were ~ today** ты сего́дня пло́хо себя́ вёл; **that is ~ of you** (*to adult*) э́то нехорошо́ с ва́шей стороны́; **don't be ~!** не шали́! **2.** (*risqué*) риско́ванный.

nausea ['nɔːzɪə, -sɪə] *n.* тошнота́; **I was overcome by ~** меня́ затошни́ло/стошни́ло.

nauseat|e ['nɔːzɪ,eɪt, -sɪ,eɪt] *v.t.* **1.** (*physically*) вызыва́ть, вы́звать тошноту́ у+*g.*; **~ing** тошнотво́рный; **I find rich food ~ing** меня́ тошни́т от жи́рной пи́щи. **2.** (*fig.*, *disgust*) вызыва́ть, вы́звать отвраще́ние у+*g.*; **I am ~ed by hypocrisy** мне проти́вно лицеме́рие; **~ing** отврати́тельный.

nauseous ['nɔːzɪəs, -sɪəs] *adj.* тошнотво́рный; (*fig.*) отврати́тельный.

nautical ['nɔːtɪk(ə)l] *adj.* морско́й; **~ mile** морска́я ми́ля.

nautilus ['nɔːtɪləs] *n.* наути́лус, кора́блик.

naval ['neɪv(ə)l] *adj.* **1.** морско́й; (*of the navy*) вое́нно-морско́й; (*of a fleet*) фло́тский; **~ officer** морско́й офице́р; **~ stores** шки́персое иму́щество.

2. (*pert. to ships*) корабе́льный, судово́й; ~ **architect** инжене́р-судострои́тель (*m.*); ~ **yard** вое́нная верфь; судострои́тельный заво́д.

nave [neɪv] *n.* (*of church*) кора́бль (*m.*), неф.

navel ['neɪv(ə)l] *n.* пуп, пупо́к.

navigability [ˌnævɪgə'bɪlɪtɪ] *n.* судохо́дность.

navigable ['nævɪgəb(ə)l] *adj.* судохо́дный.

navigate ['nævɪˌgeɪt] *v.t.* **1.** (*of pers.*): ~ **a ship/aircraft** управля́ть (*impf.*) кораблём/самолётом; ~ **a river/sea** пл|а́вать, -ыть по реке́/мо́рю; (*fig.*): **he ~d the difficulties with skill** он уме́ло обходи́л тру́дности. **2.** (*of vessel*): **the yacht easily ~d the locks** я́хта легко́ прошла́ шлю́зы.

v.i. (*in ship*) пла́вать (*indet.*), плыть (*det.*); (*in aircraft*) лета́ть (*indet.*), лете́ть (*det.*).

navigation [ˌnævɪ'geɪʃ(ə)n] *n.* **1.** (*process*) управле́ние (кораблём, самолётом *и т.п.*). **2.** (*skill*) навига́ция; ~ **lights** навигацио́нные огни́. **3.** (*passage of ships*) судохо́дство.

navigator ['nævɪˌgeɪtə(r)] *n.* (*naut.*, *aeron.*) шту́рман, навига́тор; (*hist.*, *explorer*) морепла́ватель (*m.*).

navvy ['nævɪ] *n.* землеко́п; чернорабо́чий.

navy ['neɪvɪ] *n.* **1.** (*naval forces*) вое́нно-морски́е си́лы (*f. pl.*); (*ships of war*) вое́нно-морско́й флот; **merchant** ~ торго́вый флот. **2.** (*department of naval affairs*) морско́е ве́домство. **3.** (~ *blue*) тёмно-си́ний цвет

cpd. **~-blue** *adj.* тёмно-си́ний.

nay [neɪ] *adv.* (*arch.*) нет; **he asked,** ~ **begged us to stay** он проси́л, верне́е, умоля́л нас оста́ться.

Nazi ['nɑːtsɪ, 'nɑːzɪ] *n.* наци́ст (*fem.* -ка).

adj. наци́стский.

Nazism ['nɑːtsɪz(ə)m] *n.* наци́зм.

NB (*abbr. of* **nota bene**) нотабе́не.

NCO *n.* = **non-commissioned officer**

Neanderthal [nɪ'ændəˌtɑːl] *n.* (~ **man**) неандерта́лец.

near [nɪə(r)] *adj.* **1.** (*close at hand, in space or time*) бли́зкий; **how ~ is the sea?** (как) бли́зко/далеко́ отсю́да мо́ре?; **the station is quite ~ (to) our house** ста́нция совсе́м бли́зко от на́шего до́ма; **which is the ~est way to the stadium?** как бли́же всего пройти́ к стадио́ну?; **in the ~ future** в ближа́йшем бу́дущем; **spring is ~** бли́зится весна́; **the N~ East** Бли́жний Восто́к; ~ **sight** близору́кость. **2.** (*closely connected*) бли́зкий; **a ~ relative** бли́зкий ро́дственник; **his ~est and dearest** его́ бли́зкие (*pl.*). **3. the ~ side** (*of road or vehicle in Britain*) ле́вая сторона́. **4.** (*narrowly achieved*): **he had a ~ escape** он едва́ избежа́л (*чего*); **a ~ miss** непрямо́е попада́ние; **we won, but it was a ~ thing** мы победи́ли, но с трудо́м.

adv. **1.** (*of place or time*) бли́зко; **he was standing ~ at hand** (*or* ~ **by)** он стоя́л бли́зко/ря́дом; **they looked far and ~** они́ иска́ли повсю́ду; **people came from far and ~** лю́ди прибыва́ли отовсю́ду; **the procession drew ~** проце́ссия приближа́лась; **it is ~ (up)on midnight** почти́ по́лночь; **come a little ~er** подойди́те побли́же. **2.** (*fig.*): **I came ~ to believing him** я чуть бы́ло ему́ не пове́рил; **as ~ as I can guess** наско́лько я могу́ суди́ть; **the bus was nowhere ~ full** авто́бус был далеко́ не по́лон.

v.t. прибл|ижа́ться, -и́зиться к+*d.*; **he is ~ing his end** ему́ ско́ро придёт коне́ц; он при́ смерти.

prep. у, о́коло, близ, бли́зко от (*all +g.*); **she sat ~ the door** она́ сиде́ла у две́ри; **there are woods ~ the town** о́коло го́рода есть лес; **he lives ~ us** он живёт бли́зко от нас; ~ **here** недалеко́ отсю́да; **is there a hotel ~ here?** есть здесь побли́зости гости́ница; **I'm getting ~ the end of the book** я зака́нчиваю кни́гу; **it must be ~ dinner-time** ско́ро должно́ быть обе́д; **we are no ~er a solution** мы ничу́ть не бли́же к реше́нию.

cpds. **~by** *adj.* располо́женный побли́зости; близлежа́щий, сосе́дний; **~-side** *adj.* (*in Britain*) ле́вый; **~-sighted** *adj.* близору́кий.

nearly ['nɪəlɪ] *adv.* почти́; **we are ~ there** мы почти́ прие́хали/пришли́; **I was ~ run over** меня́ чуть не задави́ли; **he ~ fell** он чуть бы́ло не упа́л; **there is not ~ enough to eat** еды́ далеко́ не доста́точно.

nearness ['nɪənɪs] *n.* бли́зость.

neat [niːt] *adj.* **1.** (*of appearance: tidy*) опря́тный, аккура́тный. **2.** (*clear, precise, e.g. of handwriting, style*) чёткий. **3.** (*of liquor etc., undiluted*) неразба́вленный; **drink one's whisky ~** пить (*impf.*) чи́стое ви́ски. **4.** (*skilful*) иску́сный, ло́вкий; **he made a ~ job of it** он э́то здо́рово сде́лал.

neatness ['niːtnɪs] *n.* опря́тность; аккура́тность.

nebula ['nebjʊlə] *n.* (*astron.*) тума́нность.

nebulous ['nebjʊləs] *adj.* (*cloudy*) о́блачный; (*fig.*) тума́нный, нея́сный, сму́тный.

necessarily ['nesəsərɪlɪ, -'serɪlɪ] *adv.* обяза́тельно.

necessary ['nesəsərɪ] *n.*: **I did the ~** я сде́лал (всё), что ну́жно.

adj. (*inevitable, inescapable*) неизбе́жный; **a ~ evil** неизбе́жное зло; (*indispensable*) необходи́мый; **food is ~ to life** пи́ща необходи́ма для жи́зни; (*compulsory, obligatory*) необходи́мый, обяза́тельный; **it is ~ to eat in order to live** что́бы жить, необходи́мо пита́ться.

necessitate [nɪ'sesɪˌteɪt] *v.t.* вынужда́ть, вы́нудить; **the weather ~s a change of plan** из-за пого́ды прихо́дится меня́ть пла́ны.

necessity [nɪ'sesɪtɪ] *n.* **1.** (*compulsion, need*) нужда́, необходи́мость; **physical ~** физи́ческая необходи́мость; **of ~** по необходи́мости; **in case of ~** в слу́чае необходи́мости. **2.** (*necessary thg.*): **the telephone is a ~** телефо́н не ро́скошь, а предме́т пе́рвой необходи́мости.

neck [nek] *n.* **1.** ше́я; (*dim.*) ше́йка; **he got it in the ~** ему́ да́ли по ше́е; **he's a pain in the ~** он ужа́сная зану́да (*coll.*); **risk one's ~** риск|ова́ть, -ну́ть голово́й; **stick one's ~ out** (*coll.*) ста́вить, по- себя́ под уда́р; **he was up to his ~ in water** он стоя́л по ше́ю в воде́; **he is up to his ~ in work** у него́ рабо́ты по го́рло; **the horse won by a ~** ло́шадь опереди́ла други́х на го́лову; ~ **and ~** голова́ в го́лову. **2.** (*geog.*, *promontory*) мыс; (*isthmus*) переше́ек. **3.** (*of var. objects*): ~ **of a bottle** го́рлышко буты́лки; ~ **of a violin** гриф скри́пки; ~ **of a shirt** во́рот руба́шки; **grab s.o. by the ~** хвата́ть, схвати́ть кого́-н. за ши́ворот.

v.i. не́жничать (*impf.*); обжима́ться (*impf.*) (*sl.*).

cpds. **~lace** *n.* ожере́лье; **~line** *n.* вы́рез (пла́тья); **low ~line** декольте́ (*indecl.*); **~tie** *n.* га́лстук.

necrosis [ne'krəʊsɪs] *n.* омертве́ние, некро́з.

nectar ['nektə(r)] *n.* (*myth.*, *bot.*) некта́р.

nectarine ['nektərɪn, -ˌriːn] *n.* нектари́н.

née [neɪ] *adj.* урождённая.

need [niːd] *n.* (*want, requirement*) нужда́; **be in ~ of** нужда́ться (*impf.*) в+*p.*; **the house is in ~ of repair** дом нужда́ется в ремо́нте; **I have ~ of a rest** мне ну́жен о́тдых; **she feels a ~ for company** ей не хвата́ет о́бщества; **my ~s are few** у меня́ потре́бности скро́мные; (*emergency*) нужда́; **in one's** (*hour of*) ~ в нужде́; **a friend in ~ is a friend indeed** друзья́ познаю́тся в беде́; (*necessity*) необходи́мость; **if ~ be** в слу́чае необходи́мости; **is there any ~ to hurry?** ра́зве ну́жно торопи́ться?; **there's no ~ to get upset** не́зачем расстра́иваться.

v.t. **1.** (*want, require*) нужда́ться (*impf.*) в+*p.*; **the grass ~s cutting** газо́н сле́дует подстри́чь; **he ~s a haircut** ему́ пора́ (под)стри́чься; **we shall ~ every penny** нам потре́буется/пона́добится ка́ждая копе́йка; **what he ~s is a good hiding** его́ сле́дует хороше́нько вы́пороть. **2.** (*with inf., be obliged, under necessity*): **~ I come today?** мне ну́жно приходи́ть сего́дня?; **you ~n't do it all tomorrow** вам не обяза́тельно ко́нчить всю рабо́ту за́втра; **it ~s to be done** э́то ну́жно сде́лать; **don't be away longer than you ~** не заде́рживайтесь там до́льше, чем необходи́мо; **~ she have come at all?** на́до ли бы́ло ей приходи́ть вообще́?; **you ~ not have bothered** напра́сно вы беспоко́ились; **I ~ not** (*have no reason to*) мне не́зачем.

v.i. (*be in want*) нужда́ться (*impf.*).

needle ['ni:d(ə)l] *n.* **1.** (*for sewing etc.*) игла́, иго́лка; **thread a ~** вд|ева́ть, -еть ни́тку в иго́лку; **eye of a ~** (иго́льное) ушко́; **look for a ~ in a haystack** иска́ть (*impf.*) иго́лку в сто́ге се́на; (*for knitting*) спи́ца; (*instrument pointer*) стре́лка. **2.** (*leaf of conifer*): **pine/fir ~** сосно́вая/ело́вая игла́; (*pl.*) хво́я (*collect.*).

v.t. (*irritate, tease*) подд|ева́ть, -е́ть.

cpds. **~craft** *n.* рукоде́лие; **~woman** *n.* швея́; (*non-professional*) рукоде́льница; **~work** *n.* рукоде́лие, шитьё, вышива́ние.

needless ['ni:dlɪs] *adj.* (*unnecessary*) нену́жный; (*superfluous*) ли́шний; (*inappropriate, uncalled for*) неуме́стный; **~ to say** (само́ собо́й) разуме́ется.

needs [ni:dz] *adv.* (*liter.*): **I ~ must go** я до́лжен идти́.

needy ['ni:dɪ] *adj.* нужда́ющийся; (*as n.*): **the poor and ~** беднота́.

ne'er [neə(r)] *adv.* (*arch.*) никогда́.

cpd. **~-do-well** *n.* безде́льник, него́дник.

nefarious [nɪ'feərɪəs] *adj.* злоде́йский, бесче́стный.

negate [nɪ'geɪt] *v.t.* (*nullify*) св|оди́ть, -ести́ на нет; (*be opposite of; contradict*) опроверга́ть (*impf.*).

negation [nɪ'geɪʃ(ə)n] *n.* (*denial*) отрица́ние; (*nullification*) опроверже́ние.

negative ['negətɪv] *n.* **1.** (*statement, reply, word*) отрица́ние; **he answered in the ~** он дал отрица́тельный отве́т. **2.** (*elec.*) отрица́тельный по́люс. **3.** (*phot.*) негати́в.

adj. отрица́тельный; **take a ~ attitude** отрица́тельно отн|оси́ться, -ести́сь к (*чему*); **~ sign** (*math.*) знак ми́нус; **~ voice** (*vote*) го́лос про́тив.

negativism ['negətɪ,vɪz(ə)m] *n.* негативи́зм.

neglect [nɪ'glekt] *n.* **1.** (*failure to attend to*) пренебреже́ние +*i.*. **2.** (*lack of care*) запу́щенность; **~ of one's children** отсу́тствие забо́ты о со́бственных де́тях. **3.** (*failure to notice; disregard*) невнима́ние. **4.** (*uncared-for state*) запу́щенность, забро́шенность; **the house was in a state of ~** дом был запу́щен/забро́шен.

v.t. **1.** (*leave undone, let slip*) запус|ка́ть, -ти́ть; забр|а́сывать, -о́сить; **you ~ed your duty** вы не вы́полнили свой долг. **2.** (*leave uncared for*): **he ~s his family** он не забо́тится о семье́; **~ed children** забро́шенные де́ти; **a ~ed garden** запу́щенный/забро́шенный сад. **3.** (*with inf., fail, forget*) заб|ыва́ть, -ы́ть.

neglectful [nɪ'glektfʊl] *adj.* (*careless, inattentive*) небре́жный, невнима́тельный; **he is ~ of his interests** он не забо́тится о со́бственных интере́сах.

negligée ['neglɪ,ʒeɪ] *n.* неглиже́ (*indecl.*); пеньюа́р.

negligence ['neglɪdʒ(ə)ns] *n.* небре́жность, хала́тность; **criminal ~** престу́пная небре́жность.

negligent ['neglɪdʒ(ə)nt] *adj.* (*careless*) небре́жный; **he is ~ of his duties** он отно́сится небре́жно/хала́тно к свои́м обя́занностям; (*inattentive*) невнима́тельный.

negligible ['neglɪdʒɪb(ə)l] *adj.* незначи́тельный.

negotiable [nɪ'gəʊʃəb(ə)l] *adj.* **1.: ~ conditions, terms** усло́вия, кото́рые мо́гут служи́ть предме́том перегово́ров. **2.** (*of securities, cheques etc.*) с пра́вом переда́чи; **~ securities** оборо́тные це́нные бума́ги. **3.** (*navigable*) проходи́мый; (*of roads*) прое́зжий.

negotiate [nɪ'gəʊʃɪ,eɪt] *v.t.* **1.** (*arrange*) догов|а́риваться, -ори́ться о+*p.*; (*conduct negotiations over*) вести́ (*impf.*) перегово́ры о+*p.*; (*conclude agreement on*) прийти́ (*pf.*) к соглаше́нию о+*p.* **2.** (*get over or through*) проб|ира́ться, -ра́ться че́рез+*a.*; **~ a corner** брать, взять поворо́т; (*fig., surmount*): **~ an obstacle** преодол|ева́ть, -е́ть препя́тствие.

v.i. догов|а́риваться, -ори́ться.

negotiation [nɪ,gəʊʃɪ'eɪʃ(ə)n, nɪ,gəʊsɪ'eɪʃ(ə)n] *n.* **1.: ~ of terms** обсужде́ние усло́вий; **conduct ~s** вести́ перегово́ры. **2.** (*fig.*): **~ of difficulties** преодоле́ние тру́дностей.

negotiator [nɪ'gəʊʃɪ,eɪtə(r)] *n.* уча́стник перегово́ров.

Negress ['ni:grɪs] *n.* негритя́нка.

Negro ['ni:grəʊ] *n.* негр.

adj. негритя́нский.

Negroid ['ni:grɔɪd] *adj.* негро́идный.

neigh [neɪ] *n.* ржа́ние.

v.i. ржать, за-.

neighbour ['neɪbə(r)] *n.* сосе́д (*fem.* -ка); **my next-door ~** мой ближа́йший сосе́д (по у́лице); **this house and its ~s** э́тот и сосе́дние с ним дома́; **love of one's ~** любо́вь к бли́жнему.

v.i.: **~ on** прилега́ть (*impf.*) к+*d.*; сосе́дствовать (*impf.*) +*i.*; **~ing countries** сосе́дние стра́ны.

neighbourhood ['neɪbə,hʊd] *n.* **1.** (*locality*) ме́стность, окре́стность; (*district*) райо́н; (*vicinity*) сосе́дство; **in the ~ of the park** о́коло (*or* недалеко́ от) па́рка; **in the ~ of 20 tons** приблизи́тельно/приме́рно два́дцать тонн. **2.** (*neighbours; community*) сосе́ди (*m. pl.*); окружа́ющие (*pl.*).

neighbourly ['neɪbəlɪ] *adj.* добрососе́дский; **in a ~ fashion** по-сосе́дски.

neither ['naɪðə(r), 'ni:ð-] *pron. & adj.* ни тот ни друго́й; **~ of them knows** ни оди́н (*or* никто́) из них не зна́ет; они́ о́ба не зна́ют.

adv. **1.: ~ ...** ни... ни; **~ one thing nor the other** ни ры́ба, ни мя́со; **he ~ knows nor cares** он не зна́ет и не хо́чет знать; **that's ~ here nor there** э́то тут ни при чём; **~ he nor I went** ни он ни я не пошли́. **2.** (*after neg. clause*): **if you don't go, ~ shall I** е́сли вы не пойдёте, то и я не пойду́; **he didn't go and ~ did I** он не пошёл, я то́же.

Nemesis ['nemɪsɪs] *n.* (*retribution*) возме́здие, ка́ра.

neoclassical [,ni:əʊ'klæsɪk(ə)l] *adj.* неоклассический.

neolithic [,ni:ə'lɪθɪk] *adj.* неолити́ческий.

neologism [ni:'ɒlədʒ,ɪz(ə)m] *n.* неологи́зм.

neon ['ni:ɒn] *n.* нео́н.

adj. нео́новый; **~ sign** нео́новая рекла́ма.

neophyte ['ni:ə,faɪt] *n.* неофи́т.

Nepal [nɪ'pɔ:l] *n.* Непа́л.

nephew ['nevju:, 'nef-] *n.* племя́нник.

nephrite ['nefraɪt] *n.* нефри́т.

nephritis [nɪ'fraɪtɪs] *n.* нефри́т.

nepotism ['nepə,tɪz(ə)m] *n.* непоти́зм, кумовство́.

Neptune ['neptju:n] *n.* (*myth., astron.*) Непту́н.

nerd [nɜ:d] *n.* зану́да.

nerve [nɜ:v] *n.* **1.** нерв; **~ gas** отравля́ющее вещество́ не́рвно-паралити́ческого де́йствия; (*pl.*): **he has ~s of steel** у него́ желе́зные не́рвы; **he's just a bundle of ~s** он про́сто комо́к не́рвов; **he suffers from ~s** у него́ не́рвы не в поря́дке; **he gets on my ~s** он де́йствует мне на не́рвы. **2.** (*courage, assurance*) сме́лость; **lose one's ~** оробе́ть (*pf.*); (*coll., impudence*): **have the ~ to ...** име́ть на́глость +*inf.*; **he's got a ~** ну и нагле́ц! **3.** (*sinew*) жи́ла; **strain every ~ to ...** напр|яга́ть, -я́чь все си́лы, что́бы...

cpds. **~-centre** *n.* не́рвный центр; **~-racking** *adj.* де́йствующий на не́рвы; изма́тывающий.

nervous ['nɜ:vəs] *adj.* **1.** (*pert. to nerves*) не́рвный; **~ system** не́рвная систе́ма; **he had a ~ breakdown** у него́ бы́ло не́рвное расстро́йство. **2.** (*highly strung*) не́рвный. **3.** (*agitated*) взволно́ванный; **he**

was ~ before making his speech он волнова́лся пе́ред выступле́нием. **4.** (*apprehensive*) не́рвный; **I am ~ of asking him** я не реша́юсь спроси́ть его́.
nervousness ['nɜːvəsnɪs] *n.* не́рвность, нерво́зность.
nervy ['nɜːvɪ] *adj.* не́рвный, нерво́зный; **feel ~** не́рвничать (*impf.*).
nest [nest] *n.* гнездо́; (*fig.*) **feather one's ~** ≃ наби́ть (*pf.*) себе́ карма́н; **foul one's own ~** па́костить (*impf.*) в со́бственном до́ме.
v.i. гнезди́ться (*impf.*).
cpds. **~-egg** *n.* (*fig., savings*) сбереже́ния (*nt. pl.*).
nestle ['nes(ə)l] *v.t. & i.*: **~ (one's head/face) against s.o./sth.** приж|има́ться, -а́ться (голово́й/лицо́м) к кому́/чему́-н.; **~ up to s.o.** льну́ть, при- к кому́-н.
nestling ['neslɪŋ, 'nest-] *n.* птене́ц.
net[1] [net] *n.* **1.** (*fruit-~, mosquito-~ etc.*) се́тка; (*snare for birds, fishing-~ and fig.*) сеть, се́ти (*f. pl.*); (*hair-~, tennis, cricket-~ etc.*) се́тка; (*butterfly-~*) сачо́к. **2.** (*fabric*) тюль (*m.*); **~ curtains** тю́левые занаве́ски. **3.** (*network, of communications etc.*) сеть.
v.t. **1.** (*fish, birds etc.*) лови́ть, пойма́ть в сеть/се́ти. **2. he ~ted the ball** он заки́нул мяч в се́тку; (*at football*) он заби́л гол.
cpds. **~ball** *n.* баскетбо́л; **~work** *n.* сеть.
net[2], **nett** [net] *adj.* чи́стый; **~ income** чи́стый дохо́д; **~ weight** чи́стый вес; вес не́тто.
v.t. (*obtain as profit*) срыва́ть, сорва́ть.
nether ['neðə(r)] *adj.* ни́жний; **~ world** преиспо́дняя.
cpd. **~most** *adj.* са́мый ни́жний.
Netherlander ['neðələndə(r)] *n.* голла́нд|ец (*fem.* -ка).
Netherlands ['neðələndz] *n.* Нидерла́нды (*pl., g.* -ов).
nett [net] = **net**[2]
netting ['netɪŋ] *n.* се́тка.
nettle ['net(ə)l] *n.* крапи́ва.
v.t. (*fig.*) зад|ева́ть, -е́ть; раздраж|а́ть, -и́ть.
neural ['njʊər(ə)l] *adj.* не́рвный.
neuralgia [njʊə'rældʒə] *n.* невралги́я.
neuralgic [njʊə'rældʒɪk] *adj.* невралги́ческий.
neuritis [njʊə'raɪtɪs] *n.* неври́т.
neurologist [njʊə'rɒlədʒɪst] *n.* невро́лог.
neurology [njʊə'rɒlədʒɪ] *n.* неврологи́я.
neuron ['njʊərɒn] *n.* нейро́н.
neurosis [njʊə'rəʊsɪs] *n.* невро́з.
neurotic [njʊə'rɒtɪk] *n.* невро́тик.
adj. невроти́ческий.
neuter ['njuːtə(r)] *n.* (*gram., gender*) сре́дний род.
adj. (*gram.*) сре́дний; сре́днего ро́да; (*zool.*) кастри́рованный.
v.t. кастри́ровать (*impf:, pf.*).
neutral ['njuːtr(ə)l] *n.* (*of gears*) холосто́й ход; **in ~** в сре́днем положе́нии.
adj. **1.** (*of state or pers.*) нейтра́льный; **be ~** зан|има́ть, -я́ть нейтра́льную пози́цию. **2.** (*of colour etc., indeterminate*) неопределённый, нейтра́льный. **3.** (*elec.*) нулево́й, нейтра́льный.
neutrality [njuː'trælɪtɪ] *n.* нейтралите́т.
neutralization [ˌnjuːtrəlaɪ'zeɪʃ(ə)n] *n.* нейтрализа́ция.
neutralize ['njuːtrəˌlaɪz] *v.t.* нейтрализова́ть (*impf., pf.*); (*paralyse*) парализова́ть (*impf., pf.*).
neutron ['njuːtrɒn] *n.* нейтро́н.
Neva ['niːvə] *n.* Нева́.
never ['nevə(r)] *adv.* **1.** никогда́ (... не); (*not once*) ни ра́зу (... не); **~ a dull moment!** не соску́чишься!; **you ~ know** как знать?; **~ before** никогда́ ра́ньше; **I have ~ before (*or* in my life) seen such tomatoes** в жи́зни не ви́дел таки́х помидо́ров; **I believed him once, but ~ again** одна́жды я ему́ пове́рил, но бо́льше никогда́ не пове́рю; (*emphatic for not*) так и не; **that will ~ do** э́то никуда́ не годи́тся; **he ~ even tried** он да́же не попро́бовал; (*expr. incredulity*) **~!** не мо́жет быть!; (*with imper.*): **~ fear!** не бо́йтесь!; не беспоко́йтесь!; **~ say die!** не отча́ивайтесь!; **~ mind** (*don't trouble yourself*) не беспоко́йтесь!; (*in answer to apology*) ничего́! **2.** (*expr. surprise*): **surely you ~ told him!** неуже́ли вы ему́ сказа́ли?; **well, I ~ (did)!** не мо́жет быть!
cpds. **~-ending** *adj.* бесконе́чный; **it's a ~-ending job** э́той рабо́те конца́ нет; **~more** *adv.* никогда́ бо́льше/впредь; **~-~** *n.*: **~-~ land** (*sc. of plenty*) ска́зочная страна́ изоби́лия; **he bought his car on the ~-~** (*coll.*) он купи́л маши́ну в рассро́чку; **~theless** *adv.* одна́ко; *conj.* тем не ме́нее; **~-to-be-forgotten** *adj.* незабве́нный.
new [njuː] *adj.* **1.** но́вый; **the N~ World** Но́вый Свет; **the N~ Testament** Но́вый заве́т; **N~ Year** Но́вый год; *see also* **Year; as good as ~** совсе́м как но́вый; **what's ~?** что но́вого?; **he became a ~ man** он стал други́м челове́ком. **2.** (*fresh*) молодо́й; **~ potatoes** молодо́й карто́фель; **~ moon** молодо́й ме́сяц, новолу́ние; **~ wine** молодо́е вино́. **3.** (*unaccustomed*): **I am ~ to this work** я в э́том де́ле нови́чо́к; (*unfamiliar*) **this work is ~ to me** э́та рабо́та для меня́ непривы́чна.
cpds. **~-born** *adj.* новорождённый; **~comer** *n.* нович́ок; **~-fangled** *adj.* новомо́дный; **N~foundland** *n.* Ньюфа́ундле́нд; (*dog*) ньюфа́ундленд, водола́з; **~-laid** *adj.* све́жий; **~-year** *adj.* нового́дний.
New Guinea [njuː 'gɪnɪ] *n.* Но́вая Гвине́я.
newly ['njuːlɪ] *adv.* **1.** (*recently*) неда́вно; **~ arrived** неда́вно прибы́вший. **2.** (*anew*) вновь.
cpds. **~-built** *adj.* неда́вно вы́строенный; **~-wed** *n.*: **the ~-weds** молодожён|ы (*pl., g.* -ов); *adj.* новобра́чный.
newness ['njuːnɪs] *n.* новизна́.
news [njuːz] *n.* **1.** но́вости (*f. pl.*); (*piece of ~*) но́вость; **is there any (*or* what's the) ~?** что но́вого?; **what ~ of him?** что слы́шно о нём?; **that's good ~!** рад слы́шать!; вот здо́рово!; **that's no ~ to me!** я э́то и ра́ньше знал; **no ~ is good ~** отсу́тствие весте́й — хоро́шая весть; **we had ~ from him** мы получи́ли от него́ ве́сточку. **2.** (*in press or radio*) после́дние изве́стия; **he is in the ~** о нём пи́шут в газе́тах; **~ agency** аге́нтство печа́ти; **~ bulletin** информацио́нный бюллете́нь; **~ conference** пресс-конфере́нция; **~ flash** э́кстренное сообще́ние.
cpds. **~agent** *n.* продав|е́ц (*fem.* -щи́ца) газе́т; (газе́тный) киоскёр (*fem.* -ша); **~boy** *n.* газе́тчик; **~cast** *n.* после́дние изве́стия (по ра́дио/телеви́дению); **~caster** *n.* ди́ктор; радиокомментáтор; **~-girl** *n.* газе́тчица; **~-letter** *n.* информацио́нный бюллете́нь; **~paper** *n.* газе́та; (*attr.*) газе́тный; **~print** *n.* газе́тная бума́га; **~-reader** *n.* ди́ктор (после́дних изве́стий); **~reel** *n.* кинохро́ника; **~room** *n.* отде́л новосте́й; **~stand** *n.* газе́тный кио́ск.
newt [njuːt] *n.* трито́н.
New York [njuː'jɔːk] *n.* Нью-Йо́рк; (*attr.*) нью-йо́ркский.
New Zealand [njuː 'ziːlənd] *n.* Но́вая Зела́ндия; (*attr.*) новозела́ндский.
next [nekst] *n.* (*in order*): **the week after ~** че́рез неде́лю; **~, please!** сле́дующий!; **~ of kin** ближа́йший ро́дственник.
adj. **1.** (*of place: nearest*) ближа́йший; (*adjacent*) сосе́дний; **in the ~ house** в сосе́днем до́ме; **the house ~ to ours** дом ря́дом с на́шим; **he lives ~ door** он живёт ря́дом; **he lives ~ door but one to us** он живёт че́рез дом от нас; **the chair was ~ to the fire** стул стоя́л у ками́на. **2. ~ to** (*fig., almost*) почти́; **it was ~ to impossible** бы́ло почти́ невозмо́жно; **I got it for ~ to nothing** я купи́л э́то за бесце́нок. **3.** (*in a series*) очередно́й; (*past or future*) сле́дующий; (*future*) сле́дующий, бу́дущий; **~ day** на друго́й/сле́дующий день; **~ Friday** в (сле́дующую) пя́тницу; **~ October** в октябре́ э́того/

бу́дущего го́да; ~ **week** на бу́дущей/той неде́ле; ~ **year** в бу́дущем году́; ~ **time** в сле́дующий раз; **he is ~ in line** он пе́рвый на о́череди; он сле́дующий; **the ~ world** друго́й/потусторо́нний мир.

adv.: **he stood ~ to the fire** он стоя́л во́зле ками́на; **he placed his chair ~ to hers** он поста́вил свой стул ря́дом с её (сту́лом); **what ~?** ещё что!; э́того ещё не хвата́ло!; **what will he do ~?** а тепе́рь что он наду́мает?; **when I ~ saw him** когда́ я его́ уви́дел в сле́дующий раз; **~ we come to the library** зате́м мы подхо́дим к библиоте́ке.

prep. ря́дом с+*i*

cpd. **~-door** *adj.* сосе́дний; **~-door neighbour** ближа́йший сосе́д.

NHS (*abbr. of* ***National Health Service***) Национа́льная слу́жба здравоохране́ния.

nib [nɪb] *n.* перо́.

nibble ['nɪb(ə)l] *n.*: **have, take a ~ at sth.** надку́с|ывать, -и́ть что-н.

v.t. поку́сывать (*impf.*); (*at grass*) щипа́ть (*impf.*); пощи́пывать (*impf.*); (*of fish*) кл|ева́ть, -ю́нуть.

v.i.: **~ at sth.** грызть (*impf.*) что-н.

Nicaragua [ˌnɪkə'rægjʊə] *n.* Никара́гуа (*indecl.*).

nice [naɪs] *adj.* **1.** (*agreeable*) прия́тный, ми́лый; (*good*) хоро́ший; (*of pers.*) ми́лый, симпати́чный, любе́зный; **they have a ~** (*comfortable*) **home** у них ую́тный дом; **this soup tastes ~** э́то вку́сный суп; **the house was ~ and big** дом был просто́рный; **get the room ~ and tidy!** хороше́нько убери́те ко́мнату!; **the soup was ~ and hot** суп был по-настоя́щему горя́чий; (*iron.*): **a ~ state of affairs!** хороше́нькое де́ло! **2.** (*fastidious, scrupulous*) разбо́рчивый; (*subtle*) то́нкий; **a ~ shade of meaning** то́нкий смыслово́й отте́нок; **~ distinctions** то́нкие разли́чия.

cpd. **~-looking** *adj.* краси́вый, симпати́чный.

nicely ['naɪslɪ] *adv.* (*well, satisfactorily*) хорошо́; **he is getting along ~** у него́ дела́ иду́т хорошо́; (*of progress*) он де́лает успе́хи; (*agreeably*) прия́тно; (*kindly*) ми́ло; **that will suit me ~** э́то мне вполне́ подойдёт; (*aptly*): **~ put** ме́тко ска́зано.

nicety ['naɪsɪtɪ] *n.* **1.** (*exactness*) то́чность; (*accuracy*) аккура́тность. **2.** (*subtle quality*) то́нкость; **a point of great ~** о́чень то́нкий вопро́с.

niche [nɪtʃ, niːʃ] *n.* ни́ша.

nick [nɪk] *n.* **1.** (*notch*) зару́бка. **2.** (*prison*) куту́зка (*sl.*). **3.: in the ~ of time** в (са́мый) после́дний моме́нт; как раз во́время.

v.t. **1.** (*cut notch in*) де́лать, с- зару́бку на+*p.*; **he ~ed his chin shaving** он поре́зал себе́ подборо́док во вре́мя бритья́. **2.** (*sl., arrest*) задержа́ть, схвати́ть (*both pf.*). **3.** (*steal*) сти́брить (*pf.*) (*sl.*).

nickel ['nɪk(ə)l] *n.* (*metal*) ни́кель (*m.*); (*US coin*) пятице́нтовик.

adj. ни́келевый.

nickname ['nɪkneɪm] *n.* про́звище, кли́чка.

v.t. проз|ыва́ть, -ва́ть +*a.* & *i.*

nicotine ['nɪkəˌtiːn] *n.* никоти́н.

cpd. **~-stained** *adj.* жёлтый от табака́.

niece [niːs] *n.* племя́нница.

nifty ['nɪftɪ] *adj.* (*sl.*) (*adept*) ло́вкий; (*stylish*) сти́льный.

Nigeria [naɪ'dʒɪərɪə] *n.* Ниге́рия.

niggardly ['nɪgədlɪ] *adj.* скупо́й.

nigger ['nɪgə(r)] *n.* (*pej.*) черномա́зый (*coll.*).

niggle ['nɪg(ə)l] *v.t.* (*irritate*) задева́ть (*impf.*).

v.i. (*fuss over detail*) мелочи́ться (*impf.*).

niggling ['nɪglɪŋ] *adj.* (*petty*) ме́лочный; **~ criticism** ме́лочная кри́тика, придира́ки (*f. pl.*).

nigh [naɪ] (*arch.*) = **near**

night [naɪt] *n.* **1.** ночь; (*waking hours of darkness*) ве́чер; **black as ~** чёрный как смоль; **all ~ (long)** всю ночь (напролёт); **last ~** вчера́ ве́чером; **tomorrow ~** за́втра ве́чером; **at, by ~** но́чью; **at ~s** по ноча́м; **at dead of ~** в глуху́ю ночь; **~ and day** днём и но́чью; **on Saturday ~** в суббо́ту ве́чером; **good ~!**; споко́йной но́чи!; **have a good ~ (~'s sleep)** хорошо́ спать (*impf.*); **it's my ~ off** э́то мой свобо́дный ве́чер; **stay the ~** ночева́ть, пере-; **work ~s** рабо́тать (*impf.*) по ноча́м. **2.** (*attr.*) ночно́й; **~ life** ночна́я жизнь (го́рода); **~ shift** ночна́я сме́на.

cpds. **~-bird** *n.* (*fig.*) полуно́чник, сова́; **~-blindness** *n.* кури́ная слепота́; **~cap** *n.* (*clothing*) ночно́й колпа́к; (*beverage*) стака́н (*чего*) на́ ночь; **~-club** *n.* ночно́й клуб; **~-dress** *n.* ночна́я соро́чка/руба́шка; **~fall** *n.* су́мер|ки (*pl., g.* -ек); **by ~fall** к ве́черу; **~-gown** *n.* ночна́я руба́шка; **~-light** *n.* ночни́к; **~mare** *n.* кошма́р; (*fig.*) у́жас; **he had ~s all through the night** всю ночь ему́ сни́лись кошма́ры; **~marish** *adj.* кошма́рный; **~-owl** *n.* (*fig.*) = **~-bird**; **~-school** *n.* вече́рняя шко́ла; **~shade** *n.* паслён; **deadly ~shade** со́нная о́дурь; **~-shirt** *n.* ночна́я руба́шка; **~-time** *n.* ночно́е вре́мя; **~-watchman** *n.* ночно́й сто́рож.

nightie ['naɪtɪ] *n.* ночна́я соро́чка.

nightingale ['naɪtɪŋˌgeɪl] *n.* солове́й.

nightly ['naɪtlɪ] *adj.* ежено́щный.

adv. ежено́щно; ка́ждую ночь.

nihilism ['naɪɪˌlɪz(ə)m, 'naɪhɪˌlɪz(ə)m] *n.* нигили́зм.

nihilist ['naɪɪlɪst, 'naɪhɪlɪst] *n.* нигили́ст (*fem.* -ка).

nihilistic [ˌnaɪɪ'lɪstɪk, ˌnaɪhɪ'lɪstɪk] *adj.* нигилисти́ческий.

nil [nɪl] *n.* нуль (*m.*); **his influence is ~** его́ влия́ние равно́ нулю́.

nimble ['nɪmb(ə)l] *adj.* (*agile*) прово́рный; (*lively*) живо́й; (*swift*) бы́стрый; (*dextrous*) ло́вкий; (*mentally quick, sharp*) бо́йкий, нахо́дчивый.

cpds. **~-footed** *adj.* быстроно́гий; **~-witted** *adj.* нахо́дчивый, остроу́мный; **he is ~-witted** он за сло́вом в карма́н не поле́зет.

nimbus ['nɪmbəs] *n.* нимб.

nincompoop ['nɪŋkəmˌpuːp] *n.* дура́к, болва́н.

nine [naɪn] *n.* (число́/но́мер) де́вять; (**~** *people*) де́вятеро, де́вять челове́к; (*figure; thg. numbered 9; group of* **~**) девя́тка; (*with var. nn. expr. or understood: cf. examples under* **five**); **dressed (up) to the ~s** разоде́тый в пух и прах.

adj. де́вять +*g. pl.*; **~ twos are eighteen** де́вять на два — восемна́дцать; **~ times out of ten** в девяти́ слу́чаях из десяти́.

cpd. **~pins** *n.* ке́гл|и (*pl., g.* -ей).

nineteen [naɪn'tiːn] *n.* девятна́дцать; **in the 1920s** в двадца́тые го́ды 20-го ве́ка; **talk ~ to the dozen** тарато́рить (*impf.*); треща́ть (*impf.*) без у́молку.

adj. девятна́дцатый.

nineteenth [naɪn'tiːnθ] *adj.* девятна́дцатый.

ninetieth ['naɪntɪɪθ] *adj.* девяно́стый.

ninet|y ['naɪntɪ] *n.* девяно́сто; **he is in his ~ies** ему́ за девяно́сто; **in the ~ies** (*decade*) в девяно́стых года́х.

adj. девяно́сто +*g. pl.*; **~y-nine times out of a hundred** в девяно́ста девяти́ слу́чаях из ста.

ninny ['nɪnɪ] *n.* дурачо́к.

ninth [naɪnθ] *adj.* девя́тый.

nip [nɪp] *n.* **1.** (*pinch*) щипо́к. **2.** (*small bite*) уку́с. **3.** (*of frost*): **there's a ~ in the air today** сего́дня (моро́з) пощи́пывает. **4.** (*of liquor etc.*) рю́мочка.

v.t. **1.** (*pinch*) щип|а́ть, -ну́ть. **2.** (*bite*) покуса́ть, укуси́ть, кусану́ть (*all pf.*). **3.** (*of frost etc.*) щип|а́ть, -ну́ть; **~ sth. in the bud** (*fig.*) задуши́ть/подави́ть (*pf.*) что-н. в заро́дыше. **4. ~ off** отку́с|ывать, -и́ть.

v.i. **1.** (*pinch*) щипа́ться (*impf.*). **2.** (*strike cold*) щипа́ть (*impf.*). **3.** (*usu. with advs., move smartly*): **I must ~ along to the shop** мне ну́жно сбе́гать в магази́н; **he ~ped in just ahead of me** он заскочи́л как раз пе́редо мной; **I'll (just) ~ on ahead** я побегу́ вперёд.

nipper ['nɪpə(r)] *n.* (*claw*) клешня́; (*pl., pincers*) клещ|и́ (*pl., g.* -е́й); (*sl., child*) малы́ш, кро́шка.
nipple ['nɪp(ə)l] *n.* (*of breast*) сосо́к; (*of feeding-bottle*) со́ска; (*tech.*) ни́ппель (*m.*).
nippy ['nɪpɪ] *adj.* **1.** (*nimble*) прово́рный. **2.** (*chilly*): **a ~ wind** ре́зкий ве́тер; **the weather is ~** моро́зит.
nirvana [nɜː'vɑːnə, nɪə-] *n.* нирва́на.
nisi ['naɪsaɪ] *conj.*: **decree ~** усло́вный разво́д.
nit [nɪt] *n.* гни́да; (*sl., fool*) дурачо́к.
cpd. **~-pick** *v.i.* (*sl.*) придира́ться (*impf.*) к мелоча́м; **~-picking** *adj.* приди́рчивый.
nitrate ['naɪtreɪt] *n.* соль азо́тной кислоты́; нитра́т.
nitre ['naɪtə(r)] *n.* сели́тра.
nitric ['naɪtrɪk] *adj.* азо́тный; **~ acid** азо́тная кислота́; **~ oxide** о́кись азо́та.
nitrogen ['naɪtrədʒ(ə)n] *n.* азо́т.
nitroglycerine [ˌnaɪtrəʊ'glɪsərɪn] *n.* нитроглицери́н.
nitrous ['naɪtrəs] *adj.* азо́тистый; **~ acid** азо́тистая кислота́; **~ oxide** за́кись азо́та.
nitwit ['nɪtwɪt] *n.* о́лух (*coll.*).
no [nəʊ] *n.* (*refusal*) отка́з; (*vote against*) го́лос про́тив; **the ~es have it** большинство́ про́тив.
adj. **1.** (*not any*) никако́й; **there's ~ food in the house** в до́ме нет еды́; **it's ~ use complaining** нет (никако́го) смы́сла жа́ловаться; **~ doubt** несомне́нно; **~ end of sth.** о́чень мно́го чего́-н.; **in ~ way** ничу́ть; нисколько; **~ way** (*coll., certainly not*) нико́им о́бразом; **~ words can describe ...** слова́ бесси́льны описа́ть...; **there is ~ question of that** об э́том не мо́жет быть и ре́чи; **~ man, ~ one** никто́; **I spoke to ~ one** я ни с кем не говори́л; **~ one was there** там никого́ не́ было; *see also* **nobody. 2.** (*not a; quite other than*) не; **he's ~ fool** он (во́все) не дура́к; **he's ~ friend of mine** он мне отню́дь не друг; **it's ~ distance at all** э́то совсе́м недалеко́; э́то в двух шага́х; **in ~ time** в два счёта. **3.** (*expr. refusal or prohibition*): **~ children!** то́лько без дете́й!; **~ smoking** кури́ть воспреща́ется; **~ entry** нет вхо́да.
adv. **1.** (*with comps., not at all, in no way*) не; **~ better than before** ничу́ть не лу́чше, чем ра́ньше; **he gave him ~ less than 10,000** он дал ему́ це́лых де́сять ты́сяч; **we met the president, ~ less** мы да́же ви́дели самого́ президе́нта; **he ~ longer lives there** он бо́льше там не живёт; **there is ~ more bread** хле́ба бо́льше нет; **~ sooner said than done!** ска́зано — сде́лано! **2. whether or ~** так и́ли ина́че; в любо́м слу́чае; **whether he comes or ~** придёт он и́ли нет.
particle **1.** (*in replies*) нет; **he can never say ~ to an invitation** он никогда́ не отка́жется от приглаше́ния; **he will not take ~ for an answer** он не при́мет отка́за; (*after negative statement or question, sometimes*) да; **"You don't like him, do you?" — "No, I don't"** «Вам ведь он не нра́вится?» — «Да, не нра́вится»; **"He's not a nice man" — "No, he isn't"** «Он челове́к нева́жный» — «Да, нева́жный». **2.** (*expr. incredulity*) **~**! не мо́жет быть!
cpds. **~-go** *adj.*: **a ~-go area** запре́тная о́бласть; **~-man's-land** *n.* ничья́ земля́; нейтра́льная зо́на; **~-one** *pron.*: *see* **no** *adj.* **1., nobody**
No. ['nʌmbə(r)] *n.* (*abbr. of* **number**) №.
Nobel prize ['nəʊbel, -'bel] *n.* Но́белевская пре́мия.
nobility [nəʊ'bɪlɪtɪ] *n.* (*quality*) благоро́дство; (*titled class*) дворя́нство.
noble ['nəʊb(ə)l] *n.* двор|яни́н (*fem.* -я́нка).
adj. **1.** (*of character or conduct*) благоро́дный. **2.** (*belonging to the nobility*) дворя́нский; **of ~ birth** дворя́нского происхожде́ния.
cpds. **~man** *n.* дворяни́н; **~-minded** *adj.* великоду́шный, благоро́дный; **~woman** *n.* дворя́нка.
nobody ['nəʊbədɪ] *n.* ничто́жный челове́к, ничто́жество.
pron. (*also* **no(-)one**) никто́ (... не); **~ knows** никто́ не зна́ет; **there was ~ present** никого́ не́ было; **it's ~'s business but his own** э́то его́ (со́бственное) де́ло; *see also* **no** *adj.* **1.**
nocturnal [nɒk'tɜːn(ə)l] *adj.* ночно́й.
nocturne ['nɒktɜːn] *n.* ноктю́рн.
nod [nɒd] *n.* киво́к; **give a ~ of the head to s.o.** кив|а́ть, -ну́ть голово́й кому́-н.; **the land of ~** (*joc.*) со́нное ца́рство.
v.t.: **~ one's head** кив|а́ть, -ну́ть голово́й; **~ assent** кивну́ть (*pf.*) в знак согла́сия.
v.i. **1.** кив|а́ть, -ну́ть; **a ~ding acquaintance** шапо́чное знако́мство. **2.** (*become drowsy*) клева́ть (*impf.*) но́сом (*coll.*); **he ~ded off during the lecture** он задрема́л на ле́кции.
node [nəʊd] *n.* (*bot., phys.*) у́зел.
nodule ['nɒdjuːl] *n.* узело́к.
noise [nɔɪz] *n.* **1.** (*din*) шум; **make a ~** шуме́ть, за-. **2.** (*sound*) звук. **3.: a big ~** (*coll.*) ши́шка.
noiseless ['nɔɪzlɪs] *adj.* бесшу́мный.
noisome ['nɔɪsəm] *adj.* (*harmful*) вре́дный; (*fetid*) зловонный; (*offensive*) отврати́тельный.
noisy ['nɔɪzɪ] *adj.* (*of thg.*) шу́мный; **your engine sounds ~** мото́р у вас что́-то шуми́т; (*of pers.*) шумли́вый; **~ laughter** гро́мкий смех.
nomad ['nəʊmæd] *n.* коче́вник; (*attr.*) кочево́й.
nomadic [nəʊ'mædɪk] *adj.* кочево́й; **lead a ~ life** кочева́ть (*impf.*).
nomenclature [nəʊ'menklətʃə(r), 'nəʊmənˌkleɪtʃə(r)] *n.* номенклату́ра.
nominal ['nɒmɪn(ə)l] *adj.* номина́льный.
nominate ['nɒmɪˌneɪt] *v.t.* (*appoint, e.g. date, place, pers.*) назн|ача́ть, -а́чить; (*propose, e.g. candidate*) выставля́ть, вы́ставить кандидату́ру +*g.*
nomination [ˌnɒmɪ'neɪʃ(ə)n] *n.* назначе́ние; выставле́ние кандидату́ры; **how many ~s are there for chairman?** ско́лько вы́ставлено кандида́тов на пост председа́теля?
nominative ['nɒmɪnətɪv] *n.* **(~ case)** имени́тельный паде́ж.
adj. имени́тельный.
nominee [ˌnɒmɪ'niː] *n.* кандида́т.
non- [nɒn] *pref.* не...
non-aggression [ˌnɒnə'greʃ(ə)n] *n.*: **~ pact** догово́р о ненападе́нии.
non-alcoholic [ˌnɒnælkə'hɒlɪk] *adj.* безалкого́льный.
non-aligned [ˌnɒnə'laɪnd] *adj.* (*pol.*) неприсоедини́вшийся (к бло́кам).
non-alignment [ˌnɒnə'laɪnmənt] *n.* поли́тика неприсоедине́ния.
non-attendance [ˌnɒnə'tend(ə)ns] *n.* непосеще́ние, нея́вка.
non-believer [ˌnɒnbɪ'liːvə(r)] *n.* неве́рующий.
non-belligerent [ˌnɒnbə'lɪdʒərənt] *n. & adj.* невою́ющий.
nonchalance ['nɒnʃələns] *n.* беззабо́тность.
nonchalant ['nɒnʃələnt] *adj.* (*carefree*) беспе́чный, беззабо́тный; **a ~ manner** развя́зная мане́ра.
non-combatant [nɒn'kɒmbət(ə)nt] *n.* (*non-fighting soldier*) нестроево́й солда́т.
adj. небоево́й; (*of units*) нестроево́й.
non-commissioned [ˌnɒnkə'mɪʃ(ə)nd] *adj.*: **~ officer** сержа́нт; военнослу́жащий сержа́нтского соста́ва.
non-committal [ˌnɒnkə'mɪt(ə)l] *adj.* (*evasive*) уклончивый.
non-compliance [ˌnɒnkəm'plaɪəns] *n.*: **~ with regulations** несоблюде́ние пра́вил.
non-conductor [ˌnɒnkən'dʌktə(r)] *n.* непроводни́к.
nonconformist [ˌnɒnkən'fɔːmɪst] *n.* своеобы́чный челове́к; (*pol.*) диссиде́нт, инакомы́слящий; (*relig.*) секта́нт, раско́льник.
adj. своеобы́чный; диссиде́нтский; секта́нтский.
nonconformity [ˌnɒnkən'fɔːmɪtɪ] *n.* несоблюде́ние

(пра́вил), неподчине́ние; (*relig.*) секта́нтство, раско́л.
non-cooperation [ˌnɒnkəʊˌɒpəˈreɪʃ(ə)n] *n.* нежела́ние совме́стно рабо́тать; отка́з от сотру́дничества.
non-dairy [ˌnɒnˈdeərɪ] *adj.* безмоло́чный.
nondescript [ˈnɒndɪskrɪpt] *adj.* невзра́чный; неопределённого ви́да.
none [nʌn] *pron.* (*pers.*) никто́; **I saw ~ of the people I wanted to** я не ви́дел никого́ из тех, кого хоте́л повида́ть; **it was ~ other than Smith himself** э́то был никто́ ино́й, как Смит; **~ of the people died** ни оди́н челове́к не у́мер; (*thg.*) ничто́; **there is ~ of it left** из э́того ничего́ не оста́лось; **~ of this is mine** всё э́то не моё; **~ of the houses collapsed** ни оди́н дом не ру́хнул; **it's better than ~ at all** э́то лу́чше, чем ничего́; **he would have ~ of it** он и слу́шать не хоте́л; **~ of that!** э́то не пойдёт!; дово́льно!; **it's ~ of your business** э́то не ва́ше де́ло; **you have money and I have ~** у вас есть де́ньги, а у меня́ нет.
adv.: **I feel ~ the better for seeing the doctor** врач мне ниче́м не помо́г; **the pay is ~ too high** пла́та отню́дь не высо́кая; **~ the less** тем не ме́нее.
nonentity [nɒˈnentɪtɪ] *n.* (*pers.*) ничто́жество.
non-essential [ˌnɒnɪˈsenʃ(ə)l] *n.* несуще́ственная вещь.
adj. несуще́ственный.
non-event [ˌnɒnɪˈvent] *n.* собы́тие сомни́тельной ва́жности.
non-existence [ˌnɒnɪgˈzɪst(ə)ns] *n.* небытие́.
non-existent [ˌnɒnɪgˈzɪst(ə)nt] *adj.* несуществу́ющий.
non-ferrous [nɒnˈferəs] *adj.*: **~ metals** цветны́е мета́ллы.
non-fiction [nɒnˈfɪkʃ(ə)n] *adj.* документа́льный.
non-flammable [nɒnˈflæməb(ə)l] *adj.* невоспламеня́ющийся.
non-fulfilment [ˌnɒnfʊlˈfɪlmənt] *n.* невыполне́ние.
non-interference [ˌnɒnɪntəˈfɪərəns] *n.* невмеша́тельство.
non-intervention [ˌnɒnɪntəˈvenʃ(ə)n] *n.* невмеша́тельство.
non-iron [nɒnˈaɪən] *adj.* (*of clothes*) немну́щийся.
non-member [nɒnˈmembə(r)] *n.* нечле́н.
non-negotiable [ˌnɒnnɪˈgəʊʃəb(ə)l] adj. (*comm.*) непередава́емый, необраща́ющийся; (*not for discussion*) не подлежа́щий осужде́нию.
non-nuclear [nɒnˈnjuːklɪə(r)] *adj.* нея́дерный; (*pol.*) не применя́ющий я́дерное ору́жие.
no-nonsense [ˌnəʊˈnɒns(ə)ns] *adj.* серьёзный, делово́й; стро́гий.
non-payment [nɒnˈpeɪmənt] *n.* неупла́та, неплатёж.
nonplus [nɒnˈplʌs] *v.t.* прив|оди́ть, -ести́ в замеша́тельство; сму|ща́ть, -ти́ть.
non-political [ˌnɒnpəˈlɪtɪk(ə)l] *adj.* неполити́ческий.
non-productive [ˌnɒnprəˈdʌktɪv] *adj.* непроизводи́тельный.
non-proliferation [ˌnɒnprəˌlɪfəˈreɪʃ(ə)n] *n.* нераспростране́ние (я́дерного ору́жия).
non-recognition [ˌnɒnrekəgˈnɪʃ(ə)n] *n.* непризна́ние.
non-renewable [ˌnɒnrɪˈnjuːəb(ə)l] *adj.* невозобновля́емый.
non-resident [nɒnˈrezɪd(ə)nt] *n.* & *adj.* непроживаю́щий (где-н.); прие́зжий.
non-resistant [ˌnɒnrɪˈzɪst(ə)nt] *adj.* не ока́зывающий сопротивле́ния; неусто́йчивый.
non-sectarian [ˌnɒnsekˈteərɪən] *adj.* включа́ющий все рели́гии.
nonsense [ˈnɒns(ə)ns] *n.* (*sth. without meaning*) бессмы́слица; (*rubbish*) ерунда́, чепуха́, вздор; **talk ~** говори́ть (*impf.*) ерунду́. **2.** (*foolish conduct*) глу́пость; **let's have no more ~!** хва́тит валя́ть дурака́!; **what ~ is this?** э́то что за глу́пости!
nonsensical [nɒnˈsensɪk(ə)l] *adj.* бессмы́сленный, неле́пый, глу́пый.
non-slip [nɒnˈslɪp] *adj.* нескользкий.
non-smoker [nɒnˈsməʊkə(r)] *n.* (*pers.*) некуря́щий.
non-smoking [nɒnˈsməʊkɪŋ] *adj.*: **~ compartment** купе́ (*indecl.*) для некуря́щих.
non-stick [nɒnˈstɪk] *adj.*: **a ~ saucepan** неподгора́ющая кастрю́ля.
non-stop [nɒnˈstɒp] *adj.* **1.** (*of train or coach*) безостано́вочный; (*of aircraft or flight*) беспоса́дочный. **2.** (*continuous*) непреры́вный.
adv. **1.** безостано́вочно; беспоса́дочно; без остано́вок. **2.**: **he talks ~** он говори́т без у́молку.
non-swimmer [nɒnˈswɪmə(r)] *n.* не уме́ющий пла́вать.
non-transferable [ˌnɒntrænsˈfɜːrəb(ə)l] *adj.* не подлежа́щий переда́че (друго́му).
non-union [nɒnˈjuːnɪən] *adj.*: **he employs ~ labour** он принима́ет на рабо́ту нечле́нов профсою́за.
non-violence [nɒnˈvaɪələns] *n.* отка́з от примене́ния наси́льственных ме́тодов.
non-violent [nɒnˈvaɪələnt]*adj.* ненаси́льственный.
non-white [nɒnˈwaɪt] *n.* & *adj.* (*of race*) цветно́й.
noodles [ˈnuːd(ə)lz] *n. pl.* (*cul.*) лапша́.
nook [nʊk] *n.* уголо́к; **I searched every ~ and cranny** я обша́рил ка́ждый уголо́к.
noon [nuːn] *n.* (*also* **~day, ~tide**) по́лдень (*m.*); **at ~** в по́лдень; **12 ~** двена́дцать часо́в дня; (*attr.*) полу́денный, полдне́вный.
noose [nuːs] *n.* (*loop*) петля́; (*lasso*) арка́н.
nor [nɔː(r), nə(r)] *conj.*: **they had neither arms ~ provisions** у них не́ было ни ору́жия, ни провиа́нта; **he can't do it, ~ can I** он не мо́жет э́то сде́лать, да и я то́же; **you are not well, ~ am I** вам нездоро́вится, и мне то́же; **I said I had not seen him, ~ had I** я сказа́л, что не ви́дел его́, и э́то пра́вда; **~ will I deny that ...** не ста́ну та́кже отрица́ть, что...; **~ is this all** и э́то ещё не всё.
norm [nɔːm] *n.* но́рма, пра́вило.
normal [ˈnɔːm(ə)l] *adj.* (*regular, standard*) норма́льный; (*usual*) обы́чный; **I ~ly use the bus** обы́чно я е́ду авто́бусом; (*sane, well-balanced*) норма́льный.
normal|cy [ˈnɔːməlsɪ], **-ity** [nɔːˈmælɪtɪ] *nn.* норма́льность; обы́чное состоя́ние.
normalization [ˌnɔːməlaɪˈzeɪʃ(ə)n] *n.* нормализа́ция.
normalize [ˈnɔːməˌlaɪz] *v.t.* нормализова́ть (*impf., pf.*).
v.i. нормализова́ться (*impf., pf.*).
Norman [ˈnɔːmən] *n.* норма́ндец.
adj. норма́ндский; **the ~ Conquest** Норма́ндское завоева́ние А́нглии.
normative [ˈnɔːmətív] *adj.* нормати́вный.
Norse [nɔːs] *adj.* норма́ннский.
cpd. **~man** *n.* норма́нн; (*Russ. hist.*) варя́г.
north [nɔːθ] *n.* се́вер; **the far ~** кра́йний се́вер; **in the ~** на се́вере; **from the ~** с се́вера; **to the ~** на се́вер; **to the ~ of** к се́веру от+*g*..
adj. се́верный; **the ~ country** се́верная А́нглия; **N~ Pole** Се́верный по́люс; **N~ star** Поля́рная звезда́.
adv.: **we went ~** мы пое́хали на се́вер.
cpds. **~bound** *adj.* иду́щий/дви́жущийся на се́вер; **~-east** *n.* се́веро-восто́к; *adj.* (*also* **~-easterly, ~-eastern**) се́веро-восто́чный; **~-east wind** (*also* **~-easter** *n.*) норд-о́ст; *adv.* (*also* **~-easterly, ~-eastward**) к се́веро-восто́ку; на се́веро-восто́к; **~-west** *n.* се́веро-за́пад; *adj.* (*also* **~-westerly, ~-western**) се́веро-за́падный; **~-west wind** (*also* **~-wester(ly)** *nn.*) норд-ве́ст; *adv.* (*also* **~-westerly, ~-westward**) к се́веро-за́паду; на се́веро-за́пад.
northerly [ˈnɔːðəlɪ] *n.* (*wind*) се́верный ве́тер.
adj. се́верный.
northern [ˈnɔːð(ə)n] *adj.* се́верный; **~ lights** се́верное сия́ние.
northerner [ˈnɔːðənə(r)] *n.* северя́н|ин (*fem.* -ка).
northernmost [ˈnɔːðənˌməʊst] *adj.* са́мый се́верный.
northward [ˈnɔːθwəd] *n.*: **to ~** к се́веру.

adj. се́верный.
adv. на се́вер.

Norway ['nɔːweɪ] *n.* Норве́гия.

Norwegian [nɔː'wiːdʒ(ə)n] *n.* (*pers.*) норве́ж|ец (*fem.* -ка); (*language*) норве́жский язы́к.
adj. норве́жский.

nose [nəʊz] *n.* **1.** нос; (*dim.*) но́сик; **his ~ is running** у него́ на́сморк/со́пли; **I have a stuffy ~** у меня́ заложи́ло нос; **with one's ~ in the air** (*fig.*) задра́в нос; **as plain as the ~ on your face** я́сно как два́жды два — четы́ре; **blow one's ~** сморка́ться, вы-; **follow one's ~** (*go straight ahead*) идти́ (*det.*) пря́мо (вперёд); (*be guided by instinct*) руководствоваться (*impf.*) интуи́цией/чутьём; **hold one's ~** заж|има́ть, -а́ть нос; **keep your ~ out of my business!** не су́йте нос не в своё де́ло!; **keep one's ~ to the grindstone** не отрыва́ться (*impf.*) от де́ла; рабо́тать (*impf.*) не покладая рук; **keep s.o.'s ~ to the grindstone** не дава́ть (*impf.*) кому́-н. ни о́тдыху ни сро́ку; **lead s.o. by the ~** вести́ (*det.*) кого́-н. на поводу́; **look down one's ~ at s.o.** смотре́ть, по- свысока́ на кого́-н.; **pay through the ~** плати́ть, за- втри́дорога; **poke one's ~ into sth.** сова́ть, су́нуть нос во что-н.; **he can see no further than his ~** он да́льше своего́ но́са не ви́дит; **talk through one's ~** говори́ть (*impf.*) в нос; **turn up one's ~ at sth.** вороти́ть (*impf.*) нос от чего́-н.; **under one's ~** под са́мым но́сом; **he stole the purse from under my ~** он укра́л кошелёк из-под моего́ но́са. **2.** (*sense of smell*; *also fig.*, *flair*) чутьё; **my dog has a good ~** у мое́й соба́ки хоро́шее чутьё; **he has a ~ for gossip** у него́ како́й-то нюх на спле́тни. **3.** (*of car*, *aircraft etc.*) нос; **they were driving ~ to tail** они́ е́хали вплотну́ю друг за дру́гом.
v.t. **1.** (*of animals*, *smell*) чу́ять (*impf.*). **2.** (*nuzzle*) ты́каться, ткну́ться но́сом в+*a.* **3. ~ one's way** проб|ира́ться, -ра́ться. **4. ~ into** (*pry*, *meddle*) сова́ться (*or* сова́ть нос) (*impf.*) в+*a.*
with advs.: **~ about** *v.i.* (*sniff*, *smell*) ню́хать (*impf.*); **the dog ~d about the room** соба́ка обню́хивала ко́мнату; **~ out** *v.t.* (*of animals*) учу́ять (*impf.*); оты́ск|ивать, -а́ть чутьём; (*fig.*) разню́х|ивать, -ать.
cpds. **~-bleed** *n.*: **he has frequent ~-bleeds** у него́ ча́сто идёт но́сом кровь; **~-cone** *n.* (*of rocket etc.*) носово́й ко́нус; **~-dive** *n.* пики́рование, пике́ (*indecl.*); **prices took a ~-dive** це́ны ре́зко упа́ли; *v.i.* пики́ровать (*impf.*, *pf.*).

nosey ['nəʊzɪ] = **nosy**

nosh [nɒʃ] *n.* шамо́вка, жратва́ (*sl.*).

nostalgia [nɒ'stældʒɪə, -dʒə] *n.* ностальги́я; (*for old times*) тоска́ по про́шлому.

nostalgic [nɒ'stældʒɪk] *adj.* (*pers.*) тоску́ющий; (*thg.*) ностальги́ческий, вызыва́ющий воспомина́ния.

nostril ['nɒstrɪl] *n.* ноздря́.

nos|y,-ey ['nəʊzɪ] *adj.* (*coll.*) любопы́тный.

not [nɒt] *adv.* **1.** не; **it is my book, ~ yours** э́то моя́ кни́га, а не ва́ша; **~ till after dinner** то́лько по́сле обе́да; **she is ~ here** её здесь нет. **2.** (*elliptical phrr.*): **guilty or ~, he is my son** вино́вен — невино́вен, а всё равно́ он мой сын; **if it's fine, we'll go, but if ~ we'll stay here** е́сли бу́дет хоро́шая пого́да, мы пое́дем, а нет — (так) оста́немся здесь; **whether or ~** так и́ли ина́че; **I hope ~** наде́юсь, что нет. **3.** (*~ even*): **~ one of them moved** ни оди́н из них не подви́нулся; **there's ~ a drop left** не оста́лось ни (еди́ной) ка́пли; **~ a day passed without ...** и дня не проходи́ло без (того́, что́бы)... **4.** (*litotes*): **~ a few** мно́гие, дово́льно мно́го; **~ infrequently** дово́льно ча́сто; **~ unconnected with ...** име́ющий не́которую связь с+*i.*; **'Was he annoyed?' — 'N~ half!'** «Он рассерди́лся?» — «Ещё как!». **5.** (*~ at all*): **'Do you mind if I smoke?' — 'N~ at all!'** «Вы не возража́ете, е́сли я закурю́?» — «Ниско́лько/ничу́ть»; **'Many thanks!' — 'N~ at all!'** «Большо́е спаси́бо!» — «Не сто́ит! (*or* Пожа́луйста!)»; **it's ~ at all clear** совсе́м/во́все не я́сно. **6.** (*introducing concession*): **it's ~ that I don't want to, I can't** не то что я не хочу́, не могу́. **7.** (*var. phrr.*): **~ for the world** ни за что на све́те; **~ on your life** ни в ко́ем слу́чае; **~ really!** да нет!; не мо́жет быть!; **~ in the least** ничу́ть; ниско́лько; **he's ~ much of an actor** он нева́жный (*or* так себе́) актёр.

notable ['nəʊtəb(ə)l] *adj.* (*worthy of note*, *remarkable*) замеча́тельный; (*eminent*, *outstanding*) выда́ющийся; (*well-known*) изве́стный; (*celebrated*) знамени́тый; (*famed*, *renowned*) сла́вящийся (*чем*).

notably ['nəʊtəblɪ] *adv.* осо́бенно; в осо́бенности; (*perceptibly*) заме́тно.

notary ['nəʊtərɪ] *n.* нота́риус.

notation [nəʊ'teɪʃ(ə)n] *n.* нота́ция; **musical ~** но́тное письмо́.

notch [nɒtʃ] *n.* зару́бка.
v.t. **1.** (*mark with ~*) де́лать, с- зару́бку на+*p.* **2.: ~ up a point** (*in game*) выи́грывать, вы́играть очко́.

note [nəʊt] *n.* **1.** (*mus.*, *as written*, *sounded or sung*) но́та; (*key of instrument*) кла́виша; **strike the ~s** брать, взять но́ты; ударя́ть (*impf.*) по кла́вишам; (*fig.*): **he sounded a ~ of warning** он вы́разил опасе́ние; **strike the right ~** попа́сть (*pf.*) в тон; **strike a false ~** не попа́сть в тон; взять (*pf.*) неве́рный тон. **2.** (*distinction*): **a family of ~** изве́стная семья́; **a man of ~** ва́жное лицо́. **3.** (*attention*, *notice*) внима́ние; **take ~ of** (*observe*) прин|има́ть, -я́ть во внима́ние; **worthy of ~** заслу́живающий внима́ния. **4.** (*written record*) за́пись; **make a ~ of sth.** запи́с|ывать, -а́ть что-н.; **he made, took ~s of the lecture** он законспекти́ровал ле́кцию; **he spoke from ~s** он говори́л по конспе́кту; **compare ~s** (*fig.*) обме́н|иваться, -я́ться впечатле́ниями. **5.** (*annotation*) примеча́ние; (*in paper*, *book etc.*) заме́тка. **6.** (*communication*) запи́ска; **diplomatic ~** дипломати́ческая но́та. **7.** (*currency*) банкно́т; ба́нковый биле́т.
v.t. **1.** (*observe*, *notice*) зам|еча́ть, -е́тить; (*heed*) обра|ща́ть, -ти́ть внима́ние на+*a.* **2. ~ down** (*in writing*) запи́с|ывать, -а́ть.
cpds. **~book** *n.* (*pad*) блокно́т, (*exercise-book*) тетра́дь; **~book (computer)** *n.* но́утбук; **~case** *n.* бума́жник; **~paper** *n.* пи́счая бума́га; **~worthy** *adj.* досто́йный внима́ния; (*of thg.*) достопримеча́тельный.

noted ['nəʊtɪd] *adj.* изве́стный, знамени́тый.

nothing ['nʌθɪŋ] *n.* (*trifle*) ме́лочь, пустя́к; **sweet ~s** ми́лый вздор; (*zero*) нуль (*m.*).
pron. ничто́, ничего́; **~ came of it** из э́того ничего́ не вы́шло; **~ I did was right** что бы я ни де́лал, всё (бы́ло) не так; **~ whatever** ро́вно ничего́; **~ worries him** ничто́ не забо́тит его́; **he's a politician and ~ more** он поли́тик и ничего́ бо́лее; **I heard ~ but reproaches** я слы́шал одни́ упрёки; **in ~ but a shirt** в одно́й руба́шке; **she is ~ to me** она́ мне безразли́чна; **it's ~ to him to work all night** ему́ ничего́ не сто́ит прорабо́тать всю ночь; **it's ~ to him what I say** мои́ слова́ для него́ — ничто́; **there's ~ to do (*or* be done)** не́чего де́лать; **there's ~ to be ashamed of** в э́том ничего́ нет посты́дного; **there was ~ for it but to tell the truth** пришло́сь сказа́ть пра́вду; **there's ~ (*no difficulty*) to it** э́то пустяки́; **there's ~ (*no truth*) in it** э́то (сплошна́я) вы́думка; **there's ~ (*no advantage*) in it for me** мне э́то ничего́ не да́ст; **there's ~ like a hot bath** нет ничего́ лу́чше горя́чей ва́нны; **~ much** ма́ло; **what's wrong? ~ much!** что случи́лось? Ничего́ осо́бенного!; **there's ~ wrong with that** ничего́ в э́том плохо́го нет; **bring to ~** св|оди́ть, -ести́ на нет; **our efforts came to ~**

из на́ших уси́лий ничего́ не вы́шло; **that music does ~ for me** э́та му́зыка меня́ не тро́гает; **he did ~ to help** он ниче́м не помо́г; **you knew, and did ~ about it** вы зна́ли и ничего́ не сде́лали; **I feel like ~ on earth** я чу́вствую себя́ отврати́тельно; **I have ~ to do** мне не́чего де́лать; **it has ~ to do with me** э́то меня́ не каса́ется; я здесь ни при чём; э́то от меня́ не зави́сит; **they had ~ to eat** у них не́ было никако́й еды́; **I had ~ to do with him** я с ним ника́к не́ был свя́зан (*or* не име́л никаки́х дел); **he had ~ on** (*was naked*) он был нагишо́м (*or* соверше́нно го́лый); **our investigations led to ~** на́ши иссле́дования ни к чему́ не привели́; **I like ~ better than ...** я бо́льше всего́ люблю́...; **he looks like ~ on earth** он вы́глядит соверше́нным пу́галом; **he made ~ of his illness** он не придава́л значе́ния свое́й боле́зни; **~ of the kind** ничего́ подо́бного; **to say ~ of the expense** не говоря́ о расхо́дах; **he started from ~** он на́чал с нуля́; **he will stop at ~** он ни пе́ред чем не остано́вится; **think ~ of it!** (*replying to thanks etc.*) э́то пустяки́!; ничего́!; **for ~** (*without cause*) ни за́ что, ни про́ что; (*to no purpose*) зря, напра́сно, да́ром; (*free of charge*) (за)да́ром, беспла́тно; **he was not his father's son for ~** неда́ром он был сы́ном своего́ отца́; **she wants for ~** она́ ни в чём не нужда́ется.

adv.: **she is ~ like her sister** она́ совсе́м не похо́жа на сестру́; **this exam is ~ like as hard as the last** э́тот экза́мен гора́здо/куда́ ле́гче предыду́щего; **it is ~ short of scandalous** э́то настоя́щее/су́щее/про́сто безобра́зие.

nothingness ['nʌθɪŋnɪs] *n.* (*non-existence*) небытие́; (*insignificance*) ничто́жество.

notice ['nəʊtɪs] *n.* **1.** (*intimation*) предупрежде́ние; **give ~ of sth. to s.o.** предупре|жда́ть, -ди́ть кого́-н. о чём-н.; **~ is hereby given** настоя́щим сообща́ется. **2.** (*time-limit*): **he gave me a week's ~** (*of dismissal*) он предупреди́л меня́ об увольне́нии за неде́лю; **I have to give my employer a month's ~** (*of resignation*) я до́лжен предупреди́ть хозя́ина за ме́сяц (об ухо́де с рабо́ты); **the employees were all given ~** всем слу́жащим объяви́ли об увольне́нии; **at short ~** в после́днюю мину́ту; в сро́чном поря́дке; **at a moment's ~** то́тчас, незамедли́тельно; **till further ~** впредь до дальне́йшего уведомле́ния. **3.** (*written or printed announcement*) объявле́ние; **obituary ~** (*reporting death*) объявле́ние о сме́рти. **4.** (*attention*) внима́ние; **it has come to my ~ that ...** мне ста́ло изве́стно, что...; до меня́ дошли́ све́дения о том, что...; **he took no ~ of me** он не обраща́л на меня́ внима́ния. **5.** (*critique*) реце́нзия, о́тзыв; **the play got good ~s** газе́ты да́ли положи́тельные о́тзывы о пье́се.

v.t. (*observe*) зам|еча́ть, -е́тить; **I couldn't help but ~ what she was wearing** я нево́льно обрати́л внима́ние на её наря́д; **I ~d fear in his voice** я почу́вствовал страх в его́ го́лосе; **he ~s things** он всё замеча́ет.

cpd. **~-board** *n.* доска́ объявле́ний.

noticeable ['nəʊtɪsəb(ə)l] *adj.* заме́тный.

notification [ˌnəʊtɪfɪ'keɪʃ(ə)n] *n.* (*announcement*) объявле́ние, извеще́ние, предупрежде́ние; (*official registration*) регистра́ция.

notif|y ['nəʊtɪˌfaɪ] *v.t.* **1.** (*give notice of, announce*) объяв|ля́ть, -и́ть о+*p.*; **he ~ied the loss of his wallet to the police** он заяви́л в поли́цию о пропа́же бума́жника; (*register*) регистри́ровать (*impf.*, *pf.*); **all births must be ~ied** все рожде́ния подлежа́т регистра́ции. **2.** (*inform*) изве|ща́ть, -сти́ть; сооб|ща́ть, -и́ть +*d.*; **I was ~ied of your arrival** меня́ извести́ли о ва́шем (предстоя́щем) прие́зде.

notion ['nəʊʃ(ə)n] *n.* **1.** (*idea, conception*) поня́тие, представле́ние; (*opinion*) мне́ние, взгляд; **I haven't the slightest ~** не име́ю ни мале́йшего поня́тия; **his head is full of stupid ~s** голова́ его́ наби́та дура́цкими иде́ями; **such is the common ~** таково́ общепри́нятое мне́ние. **2.** (*pl., US, small wares*) галантере́я.

notional ['nəʊʃən(ə)l] *adj.* (*ostensible, imaginary*) вообража́емый, мни́мый.

notoriety [ˌnəʊtə'raɪətɪ] *n.* дурна́я сла́ва.

notorious [nəʊ'tɔːrɪəs] *adj.* (*well-known*) (обще)изве́стный; **a ~ criminal** изве́стный престу́пник; (*pej.*) пресловýтый; печа́льно изве́стный.

notwithstanding [ˌnɒtwɪθ'stændɪŋ] *adv.* всё-таки.

prep. несмотря́ на+*a.*

conj.: **~ that ...** несмотря́ на то, что...

nougat ['nuːgɑː] *n.* нуга́.

nought [nɔːt] *n.* **1.** (*nothing*) = **naught. 2.** (*zero*) нуль (*m.*); **6 from 6 leaves ~** шесть ми́нус шесть равня́ется нулю́. **3.** (*figure 0*) ноль (*m.*); **add a ~** приба́вить (*pf.*) ноль; **~ point one (0.1)** ноль це́лых и одна́ деся́тая.

noun [naʊn] *n.* (и́мя) существи́тельное.

nourish ['nʌrɪʃ] *v.t.* (*lit., fig.*) пита́ть (*impf.*); **~ing food** пита́тельная еда́.

nourishment ['nʌrɪʃmənt] *n.* пита́ние; **he is able to take ~ again** он сно́ва мо́жет принима́ть пи́щу.

nouveau riche [ˌnuːvəʊ 'riːʃ] *n.* нувори́ш.

nova ['nəʊvə] *n.* но́вая звезда́.

novel ['nɒv(ə)l] *n.* рома́н.

adj. (*new*) но́вый; (*unusual*) необы́чный.

novelist ['nɒvəlɪst] *n.* писа́тель (*fem.* -ница); романи́ст (*fem.* -ка).

novella [nə'velə] *n.* по́весть, нове́лла.

novelt|y ['nɒvəltɪ] *n.* (*newness*) новизна́; (*new thg.*) нови́нка; но́вшество; **it was a ~y for him to travel by plane** бы́ло ему́ в нови́нку путеше́ствовать самолётом; **the shops were full of Christmas ~ies** магази́ны ломи́лись от но́вых рожде́ственских това́ров.

November [nə'vembə(r)] *n.* ноя́брь (*m.*); (*attr.*) ноя́брьский; **on ~ the fifth** пя́того ноября́.

novice ['nɒvɪs] *n.* **1.** (*relig.*) по́слушни|к (*fem.* -ца). **2.** (*beginner*) новичо́к.

now [naʊ] *adv.* **1.** (*at the present time*) тепе́рь, сейча́с; (*opp. previously*): **I'm married ~** я уже́ жена́т; **(it's) ~ or never** тепе́рь и́ли никогда́; **~ and again** вре́мя от вре́мени; **(every) ~ and then** поро́й; **~ he's cheerful, ~ he's sad** он то ве́сел, то гру́стен; (*with preps.*): **before ~** (*hitherto*) до сих пор; **by ~** к э́тому вре́мени; **he should be here by ~** он до́лжен бы уже́ быть здесь; **from ~ on** впредь; отны́не; **till (or up to) ~** до сих пор. **2.** (*this time*): **~ you've broken it!** ну, вот вы и слома́ли его́/её!; **~ you're talking!** (*coll.*) э́то друго́е де́ло. **3.** (*at once; at this moment*) сейча́с; **I must go ~** мне пора́ (уходи́ть); **he was here just ~** он то́лько что был здесь; **only ~** то́лько тепе́рь. **4.** (*in historic narrative*) тепе́рь; тогда́; (*by then*) к тому́ вре́мени; (*next*) по́сле э́того. **5.** (*introducing new factor or aspect; summing up*) а; так вот; и вот; **~ it turned out that** и вот оказа́лось, что. **6.** (*emphatic*) ну, так, ита́к; **~ don't get upset** вы то́лько не расстра́ивайтесь; **~ what do you mean by that?** что вы, со́бственно, хоти́те э́тим сказа́ть?; **~ then** ну́-ка; ну-ну́; послу́шайте!

conj. (*also* **~ that**) по́сле того́, как; **~ you mention it, I do remember** тепе́рь, когда́ вы упомяну́ли об э́том, я вспомина́ю; **~ (that) he has come** раз/поско́льку он пришёл.

nowadays ['naʊəˌdeɪz] *adv.* ны́нче; в на́ше вре́мя; в ны́нешние времена́.

nowhere ['nəʊweə(r)] *adv.* нигде́; (*motion*) никуда́; **the house was ~ near the park** дом стоя́л о́чень далеко́ от па́рка; **he was ~ near 60** ему́ ещё бы́ло далеко́ до шести́десяти (лет); **this conversation is getting us ~** э́тот разгово́р нас ни к чему́ не приведёт; **a bottle of vodka appeared from ~** отку́да ни возми́сь, возни́кла буты́лка во́дки; **there's ~ to sit** не́где сесть; **he has ~ to go** ему́ не́куда идти́; **in the middle of ~** у чёрта на кули́чках.

noxious ['nɒkʃəs] *adj.* вре́дный, па́губный.

nozzle ['nɒz(ə)l] *n.* со́пло; **fire ~** брандспо́йт.

NSPCC (*abbr. of* ***National Society for the Prevention of Cruelty to Children***) Национа́льное о́бщество защи́ты дете́й от жесто́кого обраще́ния.

nth [enθ] *adj.* э́нный; **to the ~ degree** (*fig.*) в вы́сшей сте́пени.

nuance ['nju:ɑ̃s] *n.* отте́нок, нюа́нс.

nub [nʌb] *n.* (*fig.*, *point*, *gist*) суть.

nuclear ['nju:klɪə(r)] *adj.* **1.** (*phys.*) я́дерный; **~ bomb** термоя́дерная бо́мба; **~ fallout** радиоакти́вные оса́дки (*m. pl.*); **~ reactor** а́томный реа́ктор; **~ test** испыта́ние термоя́дерного ору́жия; **~ weapons** я́дерное ору́жие. **2.: ~ family** ма́лая/нуклеа́рная семья́.

nucleus ['nju:klɪəs] *n.* (*phys.*, *fig.*) ядро́; (*biol.*) заро́дыш.

nude [nju:d] *n.* **1.** (*art*) обнажённая (фигу́ра). **2.: in the ~** нагишо́м.

adj. го́лый, обнажённый, наго́й.

nudge [nʌdʒ] *n.* толчо́к ло́ктем; **give s.o. a ~** (*lit.*, *fig.*) подт|а́лкивать, -олкну́ть кого́-н.

v.t. подт|а́лкивать, -олкну́ть.

nudist ['nju:dɪst] *n.* нуди́ст.

nudity ['nju:dɪtɪ] *n.* нагота́.

nugget ['nʌgɪt] *n.* саморо́док.

nuisance ['nju:s(ə)ns] *n.* (*annoyance*) доса́да; (*inconvenience*) неудо́бство; **what a ~!** кака́я доса́да!; **that boy is a perfect ~** э́тот мальчи́шка — су́щее наказа́ние; **go away, you are a ~!** уходи́, ты мне меша́ешь!; **make a ~ of o.s. to s.o.** надо|еда́ть, -е́сть кому́-н.; **he makes a ~ of himself** он тако́й надое́дливый.

null [nʌl] *adj.* недействи́тельный; **become ~ and void** утра́|чивать, -тить (зако́нную) си́лу.

nullification [ˌnʌlɪfɪ'keɪʃ(ə)n] *n.* аннули́рование.

nullify ['nʌlɪˌfaɪ] *v.t.* (*annul*) аннули́ровать (*impf.*, *pf.*); (*bring to nothing*) св|оди́ть, -ести́ к нулю́.

numb [nʌm] *adj.* **1.** (*of body*) онеме́лый, онеме́вший; (*of extremities*: *~ with cold*) окочене́лый; **go ~** онеме́ть (*pf.*). **2.** (*of mind*, *senses*) оцепене́вший; **go ~** оцепене́ть (*pf.*).

v.t.: **my hand was ~ed with cold** моя́ рука́ окочене́ла от хо́лода; **my senses were ~ed with terror** я оцепене́л от у́жаса.

number ['nʌmbə(r)] *n.* **1.** (*numeral*) число́, ци́фра; **odd and even ~s** чётные и нечётные чи́сла; **in round ~s** в кру́глых ци́фрах; приме́рно. **2.** (*quantity*, *amount*, *total*) число́, коли́чество; **the average ~ in a class is 30** сре́дняя чи́сленность кла́сса — 30 челове́к/ученико́в; **we were 20 in ~** нас бы́ло два́дцать (челове́к); **there were a large ~ of people there** там бы́ло мно́го наро́ду; **a ~ of professors attended the lecture** не́сколько профессоро́в слу́шали ле́кцию; **a small ~ of children** небольша́я гру́ппа дете́й; (*company*): **among our ~ there were several students** среди́ нас бы́ло не́сколько уча́щихся; **times without ~** несчётное число́ раз. **3.** (*identifying*) но́мер; **he was ~ 3 on the list** он шёл тре́тьим но́мером в спи́ске; **look after ~ one** (*fig.*) забо́титься (*impf.*) о со́бственной персо́не; **he lives at ~ 5** он живёт в до́ме но́мер 5; **telephone ~** но́мер телефо́на; **you have the wrong ~** вы не туда́ звони́те/попа́ли; **a car's (registration) ~** но́мер автомоби́ля; **catalogue ~** шифр по катало́гу; **he drew a ~ in a raffle** он вы́тащил биле́т в лотере́е; **when your ~ comes up** (*fig.*) когда́ придёт ваш черёд (*or* ва́ша о́чередь); (*issue of magazine*): **the current ~** после́дний/очередно́й но́мер; **back ~** ста́рый но́мер; (*song or item in stage performance*) но́мер. **4.** (*gram.*) число́.

v.t. **1.** (*count*) переч|исля́ть, -и́слить; **his days are ~ed** его́ дни сочтены́. **2.** (*give ~ to*) нумерова́ть, за-/пере-; **all the seats are ~ed** все места́ нумеро́ваны. **3.** (*amount to*) насчи́тываться (*impf.*); **they ~ed sixty all told** их в о́бщей сло́жности насчи́тывалось шестьдеся́т (челове́к). **4.** (*include*) включ|а́ть, -и́ть; **I ~ him among my friends** я счита́ю его́ свои́м дру́гом.

v.i. (*mil.*, *also* **~ off**) рассчи́т|ываться, -а́ться (по поря́дку номеро́в).

cpd. **~-plate** *n.* номерно́й знак.

numberless ['nʌmbəlɪs] *adj.* бесчи́сленный.

numbness ['nʌmnɪs] *n.* оцепене́ние.

numbskull ['nʌmskʌl] = **numskull**

numeracy ['nju:mərəsɪ] *n.* элемента́рное зна́ние арифме́тики.

numeral ['nju:mər(ə)l] *n.* **1.** ци́фра; **Arabic/Roman ~s** ара́бские/ри́мские ци́фры. **2.** (*gram.*) (и́мя) числи́тельное.

numerate ['nju:mərət] *adj.* облада́ющий элемента́рным зна́нием арифме́тики.

numeration [ˌnju:mə'reɪʃ(ə)n] *n.* нумера́ция.

numerator ['nju:məˌreɪtə(r)] *n.* числи́тель (*m.*).

numerical [nju:'merɪk(ə)l] *adj.* чи́сленный, числово́й; **~ superiority** чи́сленное превосхо́дство; **~ value** числово́е значе́ние.

numerous ['nju:mərəs] *adj.* многочи́сленный.

numismatics [ˌnju:mɪz'mætɪks] *n.* нумизма́тика.

numismatist [ˌnju:'mɪzmətɪst] *n.* нумизма́т.

numskull, numbskull ['nʌmskʌl] *n.* тупи́ца (*c.g.*), о́лух.

nun [nʌn] *n.* мона́хиня, мона́шенка.

nuncio ['nʌnʃɪəʊ, -sɪəʊ] *n.* па́пский ну́нций.

nunnery ['nʌnərɪ] *n.* (же́нский) монасты́рь.

nuptial ['nʌpʃ(ə)l] *adj.* сва́дебный.

nuptials ['nʌpʃəlz] *n. pl.* сва́дьба.

nurse [nɜ:s] *n.* **1.** (*~maid*) ня́ня. **2.** (*of the sick*) санита́рка, сиде́лка; (*senior ~*) медсестра́; **male ~** санита́р, медбра́т.

v.t. **1.** (*suckle*) корми́ть (*impf.*) (гру́дью); **nursing mother** кормя́щая мать. **2.** (*take charge of*; *attend to*) уха́живать (*impf.*) за+*i.* **3.** (*hold in one's arms*) держа́ть (*impf.*) на рука́х. **4.** (*fig.*): **~ hopes** леле́ять (*impf.*) наде́жду; **~ a grudge against s.o.** таи́ть (*impf.*) оби́ду про́тив кого́-н.; **~ a cold** (сиде́ть (*impf.*) до́ма и) лечи́ться (*impf.*) от на́сморка.

v.i. (*US*, *feed at the breast*) соса́ть (*impf.*) грудь.

nursery ['nɜ:sərɪ] *n.* **1.** (*room*) де́тская. **2.** (*institution etc. for care of young*): **day ~** (дневны́е) я́сл|и (*pl.*, *g.* -е́й). **3.: ~ school** де́тский сад, детса́д; **~ rhyme** де́тские стишки́ (*m. pl.*); де́тская пе́сенка; **~ slopes** (*skiing*) спу́ски для начина́ющих лы́жников. **3.** (*hort.*) расса́дник, пито́мник.

cpd. **~man** *n.* (*proprietor*) владе́лец пито́мника; (*employee*) рабо́тник пито́мника.

nursing ['nɜ:sɪŋ] *n.* (*career*) профе́ссия сре́днего медици́нского персона́ла; **take up ~** учи́ться (*impf.*) на медсестру́; **~ sister** медсестра́; **~ home** (ча́стная) лече́бница, (ча́стный) санато́рий.

nurture ['nɜ:tʃə(r)] *n.* (*nourishment*) пита́ние; (*training*) воспита́ние; (*care*) ухо́д.

v.t. (*nourish*) пита́ть (*impf.*); (*rear*, *train*) воспи́т|ывать, -а́ть.

nut [nʌt] *n.* **1.** оре́х; **crack ~s** раск|а́лывать, -оло́ть (*or* щёлкать, *impf.*) оре́хи; **a hard ~ to crack** (*fig.*) кре́пкий оре́шек. **2.** (*sl.*, *head*) башка́; **he is off his ~** он спя́тил; **do one's ~** беси́ться, вз-. **3.** (*pl.*, *coll.*, *crazy*): **he is ~s** у него́ не все до́ма; **he is ~s about**

motor-cycles он помéшан на мотоци́клах. **4.** (*for securing bolt*) гáйка.

cpds. **~-case** *n.* (*sl.*) псих; **~crackers** *n.* щипц|ы́ (*pl.*, *g.* -óв) для орéхов; **~hatch** *n.* пóползень (*m.*); **~shell** *n.* орéховая скорлупá; **in a ~shell** (*fig.*) крáтко; в двух словáх; **~-tree** *n.* орéх(овое дéрево); (*hazel tree*) орéшник.

nutmeg ['nʌtmeg] *n.* мускáтный орéх.

nutria ['nju:trɪə] *n.* нýтрия.

nutrient ['nju:trɪənt] *n.* питáтельное веществó.

nutrition [nju:'trɪʃ(ə)n] *n.* питáние; (*food*) пи́ща.

nutritional [nju:'trɪʃən(ə)l] *adj.* питáтельный; диéтный.

nutritionist [nju:'trɪʃənɪst] *n.* диетóлог.

nutritious [nju:'trɪʃəs] *adj.* питáтельный.

nutritive ['nju:trɪtɪv] *adj.* питáтельный.

nutter ['nʌtə(r)] *n.* (*sl.*) псих.

nutty ['nʌtɪ] *adj.* **1.** (*of taste*) с при́вкусом орéха. **2.** (*crazy*) чóкнутый (*coll.*).

nuzzle ['nʌz(ə)l] *v.t.* & *i.*: **~ (against, into) s.o./sth.** ты́каться, (у)ткнýться нóсом в когó-н./что-н.

nylon ['naɪlɒn] *n.* нейлóн; (*pl.*, **~** *stockings*) нейлóновые чулки́ (*m. pl.*).

adj. нейлóновый.

nymph [nɪmf] *n.* **1.** (*myth.*) ни́мфа. **2.** (*zool.*) ни́мфа.

nymphomania [ˌnɪmfə'meɪnɪə] *n.* нимфомáния.

nymphomaniac [ˌnɪmfə'meɪnɪæk] *n.* нимфомáнка.

O

O [əʊ] *n.* (*nought*) нуль (*m.*).

oaf [əʊf] *n.* (*awkward lout*) ýвалень (*m.*); (*stupid person*) дýрень (*m.*).

oafish ['əʊfɪʃ] *adj.* неуклю́жий; придурковáтый.

oak [əʊk] *n.* (*tree*; *wood*) дуб; (*attr.*) дубóвый.

oakum ['əʊkəm] *n.* пáкля.

OAP (*abbr. of* **old-age pensioner**) пенсионéр (*fem.* -ка) (по стáрости).

oar [ɔ:(r)] *n.* **1.** веслó; **strain at the ~s** налегáть (*impf.*) на вёсла. **2.** (*rower*) гребéц; **he is a good ~** он хорóший гребéц; он хорошó гребёт.

cpds. **~lock** *n.* уклю́чина; **~sman** *n.* гребéц.

oasis [əʊ'eɪsɪs] *n.* оáзис.

oasthouse [əʊsthaʊs] *n.* суши́лка для хмéля.

oat [əʊt] *n.* (*in pl.*) овёс.

adj. овся́ный.

cpds. **~-cake** *n.* овся́ная лепёшка; **~meal** *n.* толокнó; овся́ная мукá.

oath [əʊθ] *n.* **1.** прися́га; **on, under ~** под прися́гой; **~ of allegiance** прися́га на вéрность; **take, swear an ~** да|вáть, -ть кля́тву; присяг|áть, -нýть. **2.** (*profanity*) прокля́тие, ругáтельство.

obduracy ['ɒbdjʊrəsɪ] *n.* упря́мство.

obdurate ['ɒbdjʊrət] *adj.* (*stubborn*) упря́мый; (*hard-headed*) ожесточённый, чёрствый.

OBE (*abbr. of* **Officer of the Order of the British Empire**) кавалéр óрдена Британской импéрии 4-й стéпени.

obedience [əʊ'bi:dɪəns] *n.* послушáние, покóрность; **~ to rules** повиновéние прáвилам; **in ~ to the law** соглáсно закóну; в соотвéтствии с закóном.

obedient [əʊ'bi:dɪənt] *adj.* послýшный, покóрный.

obeisance [əʊ'beɪs(ə)ns] *n.* (*bow*) поклóн; (*curtsey*) реверáнс; (*fig.*, *homage*) почтéние, уважéние.

obelisk ['ɒbəlɪsk] *n.* обели́ск.

obese [əʊ'bi:s] *adj.* тýчный, пóлный.

obesity [əʊ'bi:sɪtɪ] *n.* тýчность, полнотá; ожирéние.

obey [əʊ'beɪ] *v.t.* (*comply with*): **~ the laws** подчин|я́ться, -и́ться закóнам; (*be obedient to*): **~ one's parents** слýшаться, по- роди́телей; (*execute*): **~ an order** выполня́ть, вы́полнить комáнду/прикáз.

v.i. повиновáться (*impf.*, *pf.*).

obfuscate ['ɒbfʌˌskeɪt] *v.t.* (*darken*, *obscure*) затемн|я́ть, -и́ть; (*confuse*) сму|щáть, -ти́ть.

obfuscation [ˌɒbfʌs'keɪʃ(ə)n] *n.* затемнéние.

obituary [ə'bɪtjʊərɪ] *n.* некролóг.

object[1] ['ɒbdʒɪkt] *n.* **1.** (*material thg.*) предмéт, вещь; **~ lesson** (*lit.*) нагля́дный урóк; (*fig.*): **he is an ~ lesson in courtesy** он образéц вéжливости. **2.** (*focus of feeling*, *effort etc.*) предмéт, объéкт; **an ~ of curiosity** предмéт любопы́тства; **a suitable ~ for study** объéкт, подходя́щий для изучéния. **3.** (*purpose*, *aim*) цель; **what was your ~ in writing?** с какóй цéлью вы писáли?; **I had no particular ~ in view** я никакóй определённой цéли не преслéдовал; **his one ~ in life** цель всей егó жи́зни. **4.** (*consideration*): **money/time is no ~** дéньги/врéмя не в счёт. **5.** (*gram.*) дополнéние; **a transitive verb takes a direct ~** перехóдный глагóл трéбует прямóго дополнéния.

object[2] [əb'dʒekt] *v.t.* & *i.* возра|жáть, -зи́ть; выдвигáть, вы́двинуть возражéния (прóтив+*g.*); **I ~ to being treated like this** я не желáю, чтóбы со мной так обращáлись; **I'll open a window if you don't ~** с вáшего разрешéния я открóю oкнó.

objection [əb'dʒekʃ(ə)n] *n.* возражéние; **raise (an) ~ to, against sth.** возра|жáть, -зи́ть прóтив чегó-н.; **are there any ~s?** есть возражéния?; **~ overruled/sustained** возражéние отклоня́ется/принимáется.

objectionable [əb'dʒekʃənəb(ə)l] *adj.* нежелáтельный; неприя́тный.

objective [əb'dʒektɪv] *n.* **1.** (*aim*) цель. **2.** (*mil.*) объéкт, цель.

adj. (*var. senses*) объекти́вный.

objectivity [ˌɒbdʒek'tɪvɪtɪ] *n.* объекти́вность.

objector [əb'dʒektə(r)] *n.* возражáющий; **conscientious ~** человéк, откáзывающийся от воéнной слýжбы по принципиáльным соображéниям.

obligate ['ɒblɪˌgeɪt] *v.t.* обя́з|ывать, -áть.

obligation [ˌɒblɪ'geɪʃ(ə)n] *n.* (*promise*, *engagement*) обязáтельство; (*duty*, *responsibility*) обя́занность; **be under an ~ to s.o.** быть обя́занным комý-н.; **fulfil an ~** выполня́ть, вы́полнить обязáтельство; **meet one's ~s** покр|ывáть, -ы́ть свои́ обязáтельства; **you are under no ~ to reply** вы не обя́заны отвечáть.

obligatory [ə'blɪgətərɪ] *adj.* обязáтельный.

oblige [ə'blaɪdʒ] *v.t.* **1.** (*bind by promise etc.*; *require*) обя́з|ывать, -áть. **2.** (*compel*) вынуждáть, вы́нудить; **we are ~d to remind you** мы вы́нуждены напóмнить вам; **I am ~d to say** я дóлжен (вам) сказáть; **if you do not leave I shall be ~d to call the police** éсли вы не поки́нете помещéние, мне придётся вы́звать поли́цию. **3.** (*do favour to*) обя́з|ывать, -áть; **I am much ~d to you** я вам óчень обя́зан/благодáрен; **can you ~ me with a pen?** не мóжете ли вы одолжи́ть мне рýчку?

v.i.: **he ~d with a song** он любéзно спел пéсню.

obliging [ə'blaɪdʒɪŋ] *adj.* услýжливый, любéзный.

oblique [ə'bli:k] *adj.* **1.** (*slanting*) косóй. **2.** (*gram. and fig.*) кóсвенный.

obliterate [ə'blɪtəˌreɪt] *v.t.* (*lit.*, *fig.*, *erase*) ст|ирáть, -ерéть; (*destroy*) уничт|ожáть, -óжить.

obliteration [əˌblɪtə'reɪʃ(ə)n] *n.* стирáние; уничтожéние.

oblivion [ə'blɪvɪən] *n.* забве́ние; **fall, sink into ~** быть забы́тым (*or* пре́данным забве́нию).

oblivious [ə'blɪvɪəs] *adj.* (*forgetful*) забы́вчивый; **he was ~ of the time** он (соверше́нно) забы́л о вре́мени; **he was ~ to her objections** он был глух к её возраже́ниям.

oblong ['ɒblɒŋ] *n.* продолгова́тая фигу́ра.
adj. продолгова́тый.

obloquy ['ɒbləkwɪ] *n.* (*defamation*) клевета́; (*reproach*) поноше́ние.

obnoxious [əb'nɒkʃəs] *adj.* (*offensive*) проти́вный; (*intolerable*) несно́сный.

oboe ['əʊbəʊ] *n.* гобо́й.

oboist ['əʊbəʊɪst] *n.* гобои́ст (*fem.* -ка).

obscene [əb'si:n] *adj.* непристо́йный, неприли́чный.

obscenit|y [əb'senɪtɪ] *n.* непристо́йность; **he was shouting ~ies** он гро́мко выкри́кивал нецензу́рные слова́.

obscurantism [ˌɒbskjʊə'ræntɪz(ə)m] *n.* мракобе́сие, обскуранти́зм.

obscurantist [ˌɒbskjʊə'ræntɪst] *n.* мракобе́с, обскура́нт.
adj. обскуранти́стский.

obscure [əb'skjʊə(r)] *adj.* **1.** (*not easily understood or clearly expressed*) непоня́тный; нея́сный; невня́тный. **2.** (*remote; hidden*) уединённый; скры́тый; **an ~ village** глуха́я дереву́шка; (*inconspicuous; little-known*) малоизве́стный; безве́стный. **3.** (*dark, sombre, dim, dull*) тёмный, сму́тный.
v.t. (*darken; also fig., make less noticeable or clear*) затемн|я́ть, -и́ть; (*dim the glory of; eclipse*) затм|ева́ть, -и́ть.

obscurity [əb'skjʊərɪtɪ] *n.* (*vagueness, lack of clarity*) нея́сность; (*unintelligibility*) непоня́тность; (*being unknown or unheard of*) неизве́стность, безве́стность.

obsequious [əb'si:kwɪəs] *adj.* подобостра́стный, раболе́пный.

obsequiousness [əb'si:kwɪəsnɪs] *n.* подобостра́стие, раболе́пие.

observable [əb'zɜ:vəb(ə)l] *adj.* заме́тный, различи́мый.

observance [əb'zɜ:v(ə)ns] *n.* **1.** (*of rule, law, custom etc.*) соблюде́ние. **2.** (*rite, ceremony*) обря́д, пра́зднование.

observant [əb'zɜ:v(ə)nt] *adj.* наблюда́тельный; внима́тельный.

observation [ˌɒbzə'veɪʃ(ə)n] *n.* **1.** (*observing, surveillance*) наблюде́ние; **keep s.o. under ~** держа́ть (*impf.*) кого́-н. под наблюде́нием; **he was sent to hospital for ~** его́ положи́ли в больни́цу на обсле́дование; **~ post** наблюда́тельный пункт. **2.** (*remark*) замеча́ние, выска́зывание.

observatory [əb'zɜ:vətərɪ] *n.* обсервато́рия.

observe [əb'zɜ:v] *v.t.* **1.** (*notice*) зам|еча́ть, -е́тить; (*see*) ви́деть, у-. **2.** (*watch*) наблюда́ть (*impf.*) за+*i.*; следи́ть (*impf.*) за+*i.* **3.** (*keep, adhere to*) соблю|да́ть, -сти́. **4.** (*remark, comment*) зам|еча́ть, -е́тить. **5.** (*commemorate*) отм|еча́ть, -е́тить. **6.** (*celebrate*) пра́здновать, от-.

observer [əb'zɜ:və(r)] *n.* наблюда́тель (*m.*).

obsess [əb'ses] *v.t.* завлад|ева́ть, -е́ть (чьим-н.) умо́м; (*haunt*) му́чить (*impf.*); **he was ~ed by the thought of failure** он был одержи́м мы́слью о неуда́че; **he is ~ed by money** он поме́шан на деньга́х.

obsession [əb'seʃ(ə)n] *n.* (*being obsessed*) одержи́мость; (*fixed idea*) навя́зчивая иде́я.

obsessive [əb'sesɪv] *adj.* навя́зчивый.

obsolescence [ˌɒbsə'les(ə)ns] *n.* устарева́ние; **planned, built-in ~** заплани́рованная устаре́лость.

obsolescent [ˌɒbsə'les(ə)nt] *adj.* устарева́ющий; выходя́щий из употребле́ния.

obsolete ['ɒbsəˌli:t] *adj.* устаре́лый; вы́шедший из употребле́ния; **become ~** выходи́ть, вы́йти из употребле́ния; отж|ива́ть, -и́ть.

obstacle ['ɒbstək(ə)l] *n.* (*physical obstruction*) препя́тствие; **clear an ~** взять (*pf.*) препя́тствие; (*hindrance*) препя́тствие, поме́ха.

obstetric(al) [əb'stetrɪk(əl)] *adj.* акуше́рский.

obstetrician [ˌɒbstə'trɪʃ(ə)n] *n.* акуше́р (*fem.* -ка).

obstetrics [əb'stetrɪks] *n.* акуше́рство.

obstinacy ['ɒbstɪnəsɪ] *n.* упря́мство; насто́йчивость.

obstinate ['ɒbstɪnət] *adj.* (*stubborn*) упря́мый; (*persistent*) насто́йчивый.

obstreperous [əb'strepərəs] *adj.* (*unruly*) бу́йный; (*noisy*) шу́мный.

obstruct [əb'strʌkt] *v.t.* меша́ть (*impf.*) +*d.*, препя́тствовать (*impf.*) +*d.*; **~ the road** загра|жда́ть, -ди́ть доро́гу; **~ the view** заслон|я́ть, -и́ть вид; **~ the light** загор|а́живать, -оди́ть свет.

obstruction [əb'strʌkʃ(ə)n] *n.* загражде́ние, поме́ха; (*hindrance*) препя́тствие; (*parl.*) обстру́кция.

obstructive [əb'strʌktɪv] *adj.* препя́тствующий; загора́живающий; обструкцио́нный.

obtain [əb'teɪn] *v.t.* **1.** (*receive*) получ|а́ть, -и́ть; **have you ~ed permission?** вы получи́ли разреше́ние. **2.** (*procure*) доб|ыва́ть, -ы́ть; (*acquire*) приобре|та́ть, -сти́. **3.** (*attain*) дост|ига́ть, -и́гнуть +*g.*; **they ~ed good results** они́ дости́гли/доби́лись хоро́ших результа́тов.
v.i. (*be current, prevalent*) примен|я́ться, -и́ться; **these views no longer ~** э́ти взгля́ды уже́ устаре́ли.

obtrude [əb'tru:d] *v.t.* навя́з|ывать, -а́ть.
v.i. навя́з|ываться, -а́ться.

obtrusive [əb'tru:sɪv] *adj.* (*importunate*) навя́зчивый, назо́йливый; (*conspicuous*) броса́ющийся в глаза́.

obtuse [əb'tju:s] *adj.* (*lit., fig.*) тупо́й.

obtuseness [əb'tju:snɪs] *n.* ту́пость.

obverse ['ɒbvɜ:s] *n.* (*of a coin etc.*) лицева́я сторона́.

obviate ['ɒbvɪˌeɪt] *v.t.* (*evade, circumvent*) избе|га́ть, -жа́ть +*g.*; (*remove*) устран|я́ть, -и́ть.

obvious ['ɒbvɪəs] *adj.* очеви́дный, я́сный; **for an ~ reason** по вполне́ поня́тной причи́не.

occasion [ə'keɪʒ(ə)n] *n.* **1.** слу́чай; **on many ~s** во мно́гих слу́чаях; ча́сто; **on ~** (*when the ~ arises*) при слу́чае; (*now and then*) вре́мя от вре́мени, иногда́; **on the ~ of his marriage** по слу́чаю его́ бра́ка; **today is a special ~** сего́дня осо́бый день; **profit by the ~** воспо́льзоваться (*pf.*) слу́чаем; **choose one's ~** вы́брать (*pf.*) подходя́щий моме́нт; **rise to the ~** оказа́ться (*pf.*) на высоте́ положе́ния. **2.** (*reason, ground*) причи́на, основа́ние; **give ~ to** служи́ть, по- причи́ной/основа́нием для+*g.*; **I had no ~ to meet him** у меня́ не́ было по́вода встреча́ться с ним.
v.t. (*cause*) причин|я́ть, -и́ть; вызыва́ть, вы́звать; **his behaviour ~ed his parents much anxiety** его́ поведе́ние доставля́ло роди́телям мно́го волне́ний; (*be reason for*) служи́ть (*impf.*) по́водом к+*d.*

occasional [ə'keɪʒən(ə)l] *adj.* случа́йный; (*infrequent*) ре́дкий; **~ table** сто́лик.

occasionally [ə'keɪʒən(ə)lɪ] *adv.* (*at times*) поро́й, иногда́; вре́мя от вре́мени; случа́йно.

Occident ['ɒksɪd(ə)nt] *n.* за́пад.

occidental [ˌɒksɪ'dent(ə)l] *adj.* за́падный.

occult[1] [ɒ'kʌlt, 'ɒkʌlt] *n.*: **the ~** окку́льтные нау́ки (*f. pl.*).
adj. (*secret*) та́йный, сокрове́нный; (*magical*) маги́ческий.

occupancy ['ɒkjʊpənsɪ] *n.* заня́тие; (*taking, holding possession*) завладе́ние.

occupant ['ɒkjʊpənt] *n.* **1.** (*inhabitant*) жи́тель (*fem.* -ница). **2.** (*tenant, lessee*) жиле́ц, аренда́тор, нанима́тель (*m.*). **3.** (*one who has taken possession, conqueror*) оккупа́нт; захва́тчик. **4.: the ~s of the car** е́хавшие в маши́не.

occupation [ˌɒkjʊ'peɪʃ(ə)n] *n.* **1.** (*taking possession*) завладе́ние; **the house is ready for immediate ~**

дом гото́в для неме́дленного вселе́ния; (*forcible ~ of building etc.*) захва́т. **2.** (*mil.*) оккупа́ция; **army of ~** оккупацио́нная а́рмия. **3.** (*holding, inhabiting as owner or tenant*) прожива́ние (в до́ме *и т.п.*). **4.** (*way of spending time*) заня́тие. **5.** (*employment*) заня́тие; профе́ссия; **what is his ~?** чем он занима́ется?; кто он по профе́ссии?

occupational [ˌɒkjʊˈpeɪʃən(ə)l] *adj.* профессиона́льный; **~ hazard** риск, свя́занный с хара́ктером рабо́ты; профессиона́льный риск; **~ therapy** трудотерапи́я.

occup|y [ˈɒkjʊˌpaɪ] *v.t.* **1.** (*be in possession of; hold*) занима́ть (*impf.*); (*mil.*) оккупи́ровать (*impf., pf.*); **all the rooms are ~ied** все ко́мнаты за́няты. **2.** (*take up*): **the bed ~ies most of the room** крова́ть занима́ет бо́льшую часть ко́мнаты; **the work ~ies my whole attention** рабо́та целико́м поглоща́ет меня́. **3.** (*employ*): **my day is fully ~ied** мой день по́лностью за́нят; **~y o.s. with sth.** занима́ться (*impf.*) чем-н.

occur [əˈkɜː(r)] *v.i.* **1.** (*be met, found*) встр|еча́ться, -е́титься. **2.** (*take place*) случа́ться, -и́ться; прои|сходи́ть, -зойти́. **3.** (*of thought, ideas*) при|ходи́ть, -йти́ на ум; **it ~red to me that ...** мне пришло́ в го́лову, что...

occurrence [əˈkʌrəns] *n.* (*incident, event*) происше́ствие, слу́чай; (*phenomenon*) явле́ние.

ocean [ˈəʊʃ(ə)n] *n.* океа́н; (*attr.*) океа́нский.
cpd. **~-going** *adj.* океа́нский.

oceanic [ˌəʊʃɪˈænɪk, ˌəʊsɪ-] *adj.* океа́нский.

oceanographer [ˌəʊʃənˈɒgrəfə(r)] *n.* океано́граф.

oceanographic [ˌəʊʃənəˈgræfɪk] *adj.* океанографи́ческий.

oceanography [ˌəʊʃəˈnɒgrəfɪ] *n.* океаногра́фия.

ocelot [ˈɒsɪˌlɒt] *n.* оцело́т.

ochre [ˈəʊkə(r)] *n.* о́хра.

o'clock [əˈklɒk] *adv.*: **two ~** два часа́.

octagon [ˈɒktəgən] *n.* восьмиуго́льник.

octagonal [ˌɒkˈtægən(ə)l] *adj.* восьмиуго́льный.

octahedral [ˌɒktəˈhiːdrəl] *adj.* восьмигра́нный.

octahedron [ˌɒktəˈhiːdrəl, -ˈhedrəl] *n.* восьмигра́нник.

octane [ˈɒkteɪn] *n.* окта́н.

octave [ˈɒktɪv] *n.* окта́ва.

octet [ɒkˈtet] *n.* октéт.

October [ɒkˈtəʊbə(r)] *n.* октя́брь (*m.*); (*attr.*) октя́брьский; **the ~ Revolution** Октя́брьская револю́ция.

octogenarian [ˌɒktəʊdʒɪˈneərɪən] *adj.* восьмидесятиле́тний.

octopus [ˈɒktəpəs] *n.* осьмино́г, спру́т.

ocular [ˈɒkjʊlə(r)] *adj.* глазно́й.

oculist [ˈɒkjʊlɪst] *n.* окули́ст.

odd [ɒd] *adj.* **1.** (*not even*) нечётный; **~ numbers** нечётные чи́сла. **2.** (*not matching*) непа́рный; **I was wearing ~ socks** я был в ра́зных носка́х. **3.** (*not in a set*) разро́зненный. **4.** (*with some remainder or excess*) с ли́шним; **40 ~** со́рок с ли́шним (*or* с чем-то); **£12 ~** двена́дцать с ли́шним фу́нтов; **~ change** сда́ча; (*small coins*) ме́лочь. **5.** (*spare, extra*) доба́вочный. **6.** (*occasional, casual*) случа́йный; **~ jobs** случа́йная рабо́та; **at ~ times** (*now and then*) поро́й; **he made the ~ mistake** (*coll.*) ему́ случа́лось ошиба́ться; (*unoccupied*): **in an ~ moment** ме́жду де́лом. **7.** (*strange, queer, unusual*) стра́нный, необы́чный, чудно́й; **his behaviour was very ~** он о́чень стра́нно себя́ вёл.
cpds. **~ball** *n.* (*sl.*) чуда́к, оригина́л; **~job** *n.* (*attr.*): **~-job man** разнорабо́чий.

oddity [ˈɒdɪtɪ] *n.* (*quality*) стра́нность; (*pers.*) чуда́|к, (*fem.* -чка); (*thg. or event*) причу́дливая вещь; стра́нное явле́ние.

oddly [ˈɒdlɪ] *adv.*: **~ enough** как (э́то) ни стра́нно.

oddment [ˈɒdmənt] *n.* (*left-over piece*) оста́ток, обре́зок; (*misc. article*) шту́ка.

odds [ɒdz] *n. pl.* **1.** (*difference*) ра́зница; **it makes no ~** нева́жно, всё равно́; **what's the ~?** кака́я ра́зница? **2.** (*balance of advantage*): **the ~ are in our favour** переве́с на на́шей стороне́; **the ~ were against his winning** ша́нсы (*m. pl.*) на вы́игрыш бы́ли про́тив него́; **by long ~** намно́го, значи́тельно. **3.** (*chances, likelihood*): **the ~ are that he will do so** вероя́тнее всего́, что он и́менно так посту́пит. **4.** (*betting*): **lay, give ~ of 10 to 1** ста́вить (*impf.*) де́сять про́тив одного́; **long ~** нера́вные ша́нсы (*m. pl.*); **short ~** почти́ ра́вные ша́нсы; **over the ~** (*fig., excessive*) чересчу́р. **5.** (*variance*): **be at ~ with s.o.** не ла́дить (*impf.*) с кем-н. **6.**: **~ and ends** (*leftovers*) оста́тки (*m. pl.*); (*sundries*) вся́кая вся́чина; (*of material*) обре́зки (*m. pl.*).

ode [əʊd] *n.* о́да.

odious [ˈəʊdɪəs] *adj.* (*hateful*) ненави́стный; (*foul, vile*) гну́сный; (*repulsive*) отврати́тельный.

odium [ˈəʊdɪəm] *n.* (*hatred*) не́нависть; (*disgust*) отвраще́ние; (*reprobation*) осужде́ние, позо́р.

odometer [əʊˈdɒmɪtə(r)] *n.* одо́метр.

odour [ˈəʊdə(r)] *n.* (*smell*) за́пах; (*aroma*) арома́т; (*fig., savour, trace*) при́вкус; (*fig., repute, reputation*): **be in good/bad ~ with s.o.** быть в ми́лости/неми́лости у кого́-н.

odourless [ˈəʊdəlɪs] *adj.* без за́паха.

odyssey [ˈɒdɪsɪ] *n.* одиссе́я, приключе́ния (*nt. pl.*).

oedema [ɪˈdiːmə] *n.* отёк.

o'er [ˈəʊə(r)] = **over**

oesophagus [iːˈsɒfəgəs] *n.* пищево́д.

oestrogen [ˈiːstrədʒ(ə)n] *n.* эстроге́н.

oeuvre [ˈɜːvr] *n.* труды́ (*m. pl.*); произведе́ния (*nt. pl.*).

of [ɒv, əv] *prep., expr. by g. and/or var. preps.*: **1.** (*origin*): **he is ~ noble descent** он благоро́дного происхожде́ния; **there was one child ~ that marriage** от э́того бра́ка роди́лся оди́н ребёнок; **Lawrence ~ Arabia** Ло́уренс Арави́йский; **what will become ~ us?** что с на́ми бу́дет? **2.** (*cause*): **he died ~ fright** он у́мер от испу́га (*or* со стра́ху); **he did it ~ necessity** он сде́лал э́то по необходи́мости; **~ one's own accord** доброво́льно; по со́бственному жела́нию; **it happened ~ itself** э́то произошло́ само́ по себе́. **3.** (*authorship*): **the works ~ Shakespeare** произведе́ния Шекспи́ра. **4.** (*material*): **what is it made ~?** из чего́ э́то сде́лано?; **a house ~ cards** ка́рточный до́мик. **5.** (*composition*): **a bunch ~ keys** свя́зка ключе́й; **a family ~ 8** семья́ из восьми́ челове́к (*or* в во́семь челове́к); **a work ~ 250 pages** рабо́та в 250 страни́ц; **a loan ~ £20** заём в 20 фу́нтов. **6.** (*contents*): **a bottle ~ milk** буты́лка молока́. **7.** (*qualities, characteristics*): **a man ~ strong character** челове́к си́льного хара́ктера (*or* с си́льным хара́ктером); **a man ~ ability** спосо́бный челове́к. **8.** (*description*): **a case ~ smallpox** слу́чай (чёрной) о́спы; **an accusation ~ theft** обвине́ние в кра́же; **a vow ~ friendship** кля́тва в дру́жбе; **an act ~ violence** акт наси́лия; **a man ~ 80** челове́к восьми́десяти лет. **9.** (*identity, definition*): **the name ~ George** и́мя Гео́ргий; **the city ~ Rome** (го́род) Рим; **that fool ~ a driver** э́тот глу́пый води́тель; **a letter ~ introduction** рекоменда́тельное письмо́; **your letter ~ the 14th** ва́ше письмо́ от 14-го (числа́). **10.** (*objective*): **a lover ~ music** люби́тель (*m.*) му́зыки; **love ~ study** любо́вь к заня́тиям; **the use ~ a car** по́льзование маши́ной; **a view ~ the river** вид на́ реку. **11.** (*subjective*): **the love ~ a mother** любо́вь ма́тери; матери́нская любо́вь. **12.** (*possession, belonging*): **the property ~ the state** госуда́рственная со́бственность; **a thing ~ the past** де́ло про́шлого. **13.** (*partitive*): **some ~ us** не́которые/ко́е-кто из нас; **a quarter ~ an hour** че́тверть ча́са; **most ~ all** осо́бенно; бо́льше всего́/всех; **a friend ~ ours** оди́н из на́ших знако́мых; **a great friend ~ ours** большо́й наш друг; **he is ~ the same opinion** он того́ же мне́ния. **14.** (*concerning*): **we talked ~ politics** мы говори́ли о поли́тике; **what ~ it?** что из того́?; ну и что? **15.** (*during*): **~ an evening** ве́чером; по вечера́м; **~ late years** в после́дние го́ды. **16.** (*separation, distance, direction*): **within 10 miles ~ London** в десяти́ ми́лях от Ло́ндона; **north ~** к се́веру от+*g.*; се́вернее +*g.* **17.** (*on the part ~*): **it was good ~ you** бы́ло о́чень ми́ло с ва́шей стороны́.

off [ɒf] *adj.* **1.** (*nearer to centre of road*): **on the ~ side** (*in Britain*) на пра́вой стороне́ доро́ги. **2.** (*improbable*): **I went on the ~ chance of finding him in** я пошёл туда́ на аво́сь — вдруг заста́ну (его́). **3.** (*spare*): **during an ~ moment** ме́жду де́лом. **4.** (*substandard*): **it was one of my ~ days** в тот день я был не в са́мой лу́чшей фо́рме. **5.** (*inactive*): **the ~ season** мёртвый сезо́н. **6.**: **~ licence** пате́нт на прода́жу спиртны́х напи́тков на вы́нос.

adv. (*for phrasal vv. with* **off** *see relevant v. entries*) **1.** (*away*): **two miles ~** в двух ми́лях отту́да/отсю́да; **the elections are still two years ~** до вы́боров ещё два го́да; **~ with you!** пойди́те прочь!; **he's ~ to France tomorrow** он за́втра уезжа́ет во Фра́нцию; **it's time I was ~** мне пора́ (уходи́ть); **~ we go!** пошли́!; **they're ~!** (*racing*) старту́ют!; **~ with his head!** го́лову с плеч! **2.** (*removed*): **hats ~!** (*fig.*) ша́пки доло́й; **he is going to have his beard ~** он собира́ется сбрить бо́роду. **3.** (*disconnected*; *not available*): **the light is ~** свет отключён; **the electricity was ~** электри́чество бы́ло отключено́; **are the brakes ~?** вы отпусти́ли тормоза́?; **the ice-cream is ~** моро́женое ко́нчилось; **the ~ position** (*of switch etc.*) «отключено́». **4.** (*ended, cancelled*): **their engagement is ~** их помо́лвка расто́ргнута; **the match is ~** матч отменён. **5.** (*not working*): **day ~** выходно́й (день); **today is my day ~** я (*or* у меня́) сего́дня выходно́й; **night ~** свобо́дный ве́чер; **he was ~ sick** он не́ был на рабо́те по боле́зни; **I'm ~ now till Monday** меня́ не бу́дет до понеде́льника. **6.** (*of food: not fresh*; *tainted*): **the fish is ~** ры́ба испо́ртилась. **7.** (*theatr.*): **noises ~** шум за сце́ной. **8.** (*supplied*): **they are quite well ~** они́ вполне́ обеспе́чены; **how are you ~ for money?** как у вас с деньга́ми? **9.**: **~ and on** (*intermittently*) с переры́вами; вре́мя от вре́мени.

prep. (*from*; *away from*; *up or down from*): **the car went ~ the road** маши́на съе́хала с доро́ги; **just ~ the High Street** неподалёку от гла́вной у́лицы; **~ balance** несбаланси́рованный; **~ work** не на рабо́те; **~ colour** (*out of sorts*) нездоро́вый; не в фо́рме; **he fell ~ the ladder** он упа́л с ле́стницы; **he took 50p ~ the price** он сни́зил це́ну на пятьдеся́т пенсов; **I picked it up ~ the floor** я по́днял э́то с по́лу; **they were eating ~ the same plate** они́ е́ли из одно́й таре́лки; **the ship lay ~ the coast** су́дно стоя́ло неподалёку от бе́рега; **I broke the spout ~ the teapot** я отби́л но́сик у ча́йника; **I was run ~ my feet** я сби́лся с ног; **he was ~ his game** он был не в лу́чшей фо́рме; **he must be ~ his head** он, должно́ быть, спя́тил; **he got ~ the point** он сби́лся с те́мы; (*disinclined for*): **he is ~ his food** он потеря́л аппети́т; **I'm ~ smoking** (*have given it up*) я бро́сил кури́ть.

offal ['ɒf(ə)l] *n.* (*of meat*) потроха́ (*m. pl.*); (*entrails*) требуха́.

off-beat ['ɒfbi:t] *n.* (*mus.*) неуда́рная но́та.

adj. (*fig.*) необы́чный; оригина́льный.

off-centre [ɒf'sentə(r)] *adj.* смещённый от це́нтра.

offence [ə'fens] (*US* **offense**) *n.* **1.** (*wrong-doing*) просту́пок; (*crime*) преступле́ние; **an ~ against the law** наруше́ние зако́на; **commit an ~** соверш|а́ть, -и́ть правонаруше́ние. **2.** (*affront*; *wounded feeling*; *annoyance*) оби́да; **cause, give ~ to** оскорб|ля́ть, -и́ть; **take ~ at** об|ижа́ться, -и́деться на+*a.*; **no ~ (meant)!** не в оби́ду бу́дет ска́зано! **3.** (*attack*) нападе́ние.

offend [ə'fend] *v.t.* **1.** (*give offence to*; *wound*) об|ижа́ть, -и́деть; **are you ~ed with me?** вы на меня́ (не) оби́делись? **2.** (*outrage*) оскорб|ля́ть, -и́ть.

v.i. греши́ть (*impf.*); **~ against the law** нар|уша́ть, -у́шить зако́н; **he deleted the ~ing words** он вы́черкнул слова́, вы́звавшие возраже́ния.

offender [ə'fendə(r)] *n.* (*against law*) правонаруши́тель (*m.*); престу́пник.

offense [ə'fens] = **offence**

offensive [ə'fensɪv] *n.* нападе́ние; (*mil.*) наступле́ние; **take (*or* go over to) the ~** пере|ходи́ть, -йти́ в наступле́ние.

adj. **1.** (*causing offence*) оскорби́тельный; (*of pers.*) проти́вный. **2.** (*repulsive*) отврати́тельный. **3.** (*mil.*) наступа́тельный; **~ weapon** наступа́тельное ору́жие.

offer ['ɒfə(r)] *n.* **1.** предложе́ние; **make an ~** де́лать, с- предложе́ние; **decline an ~** отклон|я́ть, -и́ть предложе́ние. **2.**: **on ~** в прода́же.

v.t. предл|ага́ть, -ожи́ть; **~ one's hand** протя́|гивать, -ну́ть ру́ку; **he ~ed me a drink** он предложи́л мне вы́пить; **I was ~ed a lift** меня́ предложи́ли подвезти́; **the job ~s good prospects** э́то перспекти́вная рабо́та; **they are ~ing a reward** объя́влено вознагражде́ние; **may I ~ my congratulations?** позво́льте вас поздра́вить?; **~ an opinion** выража́ть, вы́разить своё мне́ние; **~ an apology** прин|оси́ть, -ести́ извине́ния; **~ resistance** ока́з|ывать, -а́ть сопротивле́ние; **~ prayers** возн|оси́ть, -ести́ моли́твы.

v.i.: **as opportunity ~s** как предста́вится слу́чай.

offering ['ɒfərɪŋ] *n.* **1.** предложе́ние. **2.** (*of a sacrifice*) жертвоприноше́ние. **3.** (*contribution*) поже́ртвование.

offertory ['ɒfətərɪ, -trɪ] *n.* (*collection*) церко́вные поже́ртвования (*nt. pl.*).

off-hand [ɒf'hænd, 'ɒfhænd] *adj.* (*also* **off-handed**) развя́зный, бесцеремо́нный.

adv. сра́зу, без подгото́вки.

office ['ɒfɪs] *n.* **1.** (*position of responsibility*; *service*) до́лжность, слу́жба; **the party in ~** па́ртия, находя́щаяся у вла́сти; **he held ~ for 10 years** он занима́л пост де́сять лет; **take ~** вступ|а́ть, -и́ть в до́лжность; **run for ~** (*US*) выставля́ть, вы́ставить свою́ кандидату́ру; **term of ~** срок полномо́чий. **2.** (*premises*) конто́ра, канцеля́рия; (*private ~, also doctor's or dentist's*) кабине́т; **~ block** администрати́вное зда́ние; **~ equipment** оргте́хника; **~ hours** часы́ рабо́ты; рабо́чее/служе́бное вре́мя. **3.** (*department, agency*) бюро́ (*indecl.*); отде́л; управле́ние, ве́домство; **Foreign O~** Министе́рство иностра́нных дел; **Record O~** Госуда́рственный архи́в; **booking ~** биле́тная ка́сса; **editorial ~** реда́кция; **enquiry ~** спра́вочное бюро́; **lost property ~** бюро́ нахо́док; **branch ~** филиа́л, отделе́ние. **4.** (*usu. pl., service, assistance*) услу́га; **through his good ~s** благодаря́ его́ посре́дничеству. **5.** (*rite*) обря́д; **the last ~s** погреба́льный обря́д.

cpds. **~-boy** *n.* рассы́льный; посы́льный; **~-work** *n.* канцеля́рская рабо́та; **~-worker** *n.* (конто́рский) слу́жащий; канцеля́рский рабо́тник.

officer ['ɒfɪsə(r)] *n.* **1.** (*in armed forces*) офице́р; (*pl., collect.*) офице́рский соста́в; **commanding ~** команди́р; **first ~** (*naval*) пе́рвый помо́щник капита́на. **2.** (*official*) должностно́е лицо́, чино́вник; **medical ~ of health** санита́рный инспе́ктор; **customs ~** тамо́женник; **~s of a club** руково́дство клу́ба.

official [ə'fɪʃ(ə)l] *n.* должностно́е лицо́, чино́вник, слу́жащий; **government ~s** прави́тельственные чино́вники; госуда́рственные слу́жащие.

adj. (*relating to an office*) служе́бный, должностно́й; **~ duties** служе́бные обя́занности; (*formal*):

an ~ style формáльный стиль; (*authoritative*) официáльный; **~ language** официáльная терминолóгия; (*of a country*) госудáрственный язы́к.

officialdom [ə'fɪʃəldəm] *n.* чинóвничество.

officialese [ə,fɪʃə'li:z] *n.* бюрократи́ческий жаргóн.

officiate [ə'fɪʃɪ,eɪt] *v.i.*: **~ at a wedding** совершáть (*impf.*) обря́д бракосочетáния; **~ as host** быть за хозя́ина; **~ as chairman** председáтельствовать (*impf.*).

officious [ə'fɪʃəs] *adj.* навя́зчивый, назóйливый.

offing ['ɒfɪŋ] *n.*: в перспекти́ве.

off-key [ɒf'ki:] *adj.* (*lit., fig.*) фальши́вый.

off-load ['ɒfləʊd, ɒf'ləʊd] *v.t.* разгру|жáть, -зи́ть.

off-peak ['ɒfpi:k] *adj.* непи́ковый; **~ hours** часы́ зати́шья.

offprint ['ɒfprɪnt] *n.* óттиск.

off-putting ['ɒfpʊtɪŋ] *adj.* (*coll.*) оттáлкивающий.

off-season ['ɒfsi:z(ə)n] *n.* межсезóнье.

adj. несезóнный.

offset ['ɒfset] *n.* (*typ.*) офсéт.

v.i. (*compensate for*) возме|щáть, -сти́ть; (*typ.*) печáтать, на- офсéтным спóсобом.

offshoot ['ɒfʃu:t] *n.* побéг; (*fig.*) óтрасль; боковáя ветвь.

offshore ['ɒfʃɔ:(r)] *adj.* (*close to shore*) прибрéжный; **~ wind** береговóй вéтер.

off-side [ɒf'saɪd] *n.* (*football*) вне игры́; офсáйд.

offspring ['ɒfsprɪŋ] *n.* потóмок, óтпрыск; (*pl.*) потóмство.

off-stage [ɒf'steɪdʒ] *adj.*: **~ whisper** шёпот за кули́сами.

off-the-cuff [,ɒfðə'kʌf] *adj.* импровизи́рованный.

off-the-peg [,ɒfðə'peg] *adj.* готóвый (*об одежде*).

off-the-record [,ɒfðə'rekɔ:d] *adj.* неофициáльный.

off-the-shelf [,ɒfðə'ʃelf] *adj.* стандáртный, типовóй.

off-white ['ɒfwaɪt] *adj.* сéровáто-бéлый.

often ['ɒf(ə)n, 'ɒft(ə)n] *adv.* чáсто; **every so ~** врéмя от врéмени; **as ~ as not** нерéдко; **more ~ than not** бóльшей чáстью, в большинствé слýчаев.

ogle ['əʊg(ə)l] *v.t.* стрóить (*impf.*) глáзки +*d.*

ogre ['əʊgə(r)] *n.* великáн-людоéд.

oh [əʊ] *int.* о!, ах!; (*expr. surprise, fright, pain*) ой!; **~ yes, ~ really?** (нет,) прáвда; неужéли?; да?

ohm [əʊm] *n.* ом.

oho [əʊ'həʊ] *int.* огó.

oil [ɔɪl] *n.* **1.** мáсло; **mineral/vegetable ~** минерáльное/расти́тельное мáсло; **fixed/volatile ~s** жи́рные/эфи́рные маслá; **cod-liver ~** ры́бий жир; **engine ~** маши́нное мáсло; **fuel ~** мазýт; **burn the midnight ~** рабóтать (*impf.*) по ночáм; **pour ~ on troubled waters** успок|áивать, -óить волнéния. **2.** (*petroleum*) нефть. **3.** (*painting*) мáсляная крáска; **paint in ~s** писáть (*impf.*) мáслом.

v.t. (*lubricate*) смáз|ывать, -ать; **~ the wheels** (*fig.*) улáдить дéло; (*treat with ~*) пропи́т|ывать, -áть мáслом.

cpds. **~-can** *n.* маслёнка; **~cloth** *n.* клеёнка; (*linoleum*) линóлеум; **~-colour** *n.* мáсляная крáска; **~field** *n.* месторождéние нéфти; **~-fired** *adj.*: **~-fired central heating** нефтянóе центрáльное отоплéние; **~-heater** *n.* парафи́новая пéчка; **~-lamp** *n.* кероси́новая лáмпа; **~-paint** *n.* мáсляная крáска; **~-rig** *n.* нефтянáя вы́шка; **~skin** *n.* (*material*) клеёнка; (*garment*) непромокáемый костю́м; **~-slick** *n.* плёнка нéфти на водé; **~-tanker** *n.* (*ship*) тáнкер; (*vehicle*) нефтевóз; **~-well** *n.* нефтянáя сквáжина.

oily ['ɔɪlɪ] *adj.* **1.** мáсляный; **~ cheese** масляни́стый сыр. **2.** (*fig., fawning, unctuous*) елéйный.

ointment ['ɔɪntmənt] *n.* мазь.

OK, okay [əʊ'keɪ] (*coll.*) *n.* одобрéние, разрешéние, «добрó».

adj.: **it's ~** ничегó; годи́тся; **it's ~ by me** я соглáсен; **it looks ~ to me** по-мóему, ничегó.

adv.: **the meeting went off ~** собрáние прошлó благополýчно.

v.t.: **he ~ed the proposal** он одóбрил э́то предложéние.

int. лáдно!; хорошó!; идёт!; слýшаюсь.

okay [əʊ'keɪ] = **OK**

okra ['əʊkrə, 'ɒkrə] *n.* óкра.

old [əʊld] *n.* **1.: the ~** (*people*) старики́ (*m. pl.*); **young and ~** (*everyone*) стар и млад. **2.: of ~** в прéжнее врéмя; **in days of ~** в старинý.

adj. **1.** стáрый, стари́нный; **~ age** стáрость; **~ age pension** пéнсия по стáрости; **~ man** стари́к; **~ woman** старýха; **~ folk** старики́; **~ folk's home** дом для престарéлых; **grow ~** стáриться, со-. **2.** (*expr. age in years etc.*): **how ~ is he?** скóлько емý лет?; **he is ~ enough to know better** в егó вóзрасте порá бы понимáть, что к чемý; **my son is 4 years ~** моемý сы́ну четы́ре гóда; **he could read at 4 years ~** в четы́ре гóда он ужé читáл; **a four-year-~** четырёхлéтний ребёнок; **this newspaper is two weeks ~** э́та газéта двухнедéльной дáвности. **3.** (*practised, experienced*) óпытный; (*inveterate*) закоренéлый; **he is an ~ hand at such things** он в таки́х делáх мáстер. **4.** (*coll., expr. familiarity*): **~ man, chap, fellow** старинá (*m.*), стари́к; **~ boy, thing** дружóк, дружи́ще (*m.*); **we had a high ~ time** мы хорошó/здóрово провели́ врéмя. **5.** (*coll., whatever*): **any ~ time** когдá угóдно; **he dresses any ~ how** он одевáется, как попáло. **6.** (*dating from the past; ancient; longstanding*) стари́нный, давни́шний; **an ~ family** стари́нный род; **that story is as ~ as the hills** э́тот расскáз стар как мир; **they are ~ friends** они́ стари́нные/дáвние друзья́; **the O~ World** Стáрый Свет; **the O~ Testament** Вéтхий завéт. **7.** (*former*) бы́вший, прéжний; **an ~ boy** (*of school*) бы́вший учени́к; выпускни́к; **the good ~ days** дóброе стáрое врéмя; **the ~ country** рóдина (отцóв); **O~ English** (*language*) древнеанглийский (язы́к); **~ ways** стари́нные обы́чаи; **see the ~ year out** встр|ечáть, -éтить Нóвый год. **8.** (*worn, shabby*) понóшенный, потрёпанный.

cpds. **~-fashioned** *adj.* старомóдный; (*obsolete*) устарéлый; **~-time** *adj.* стари́нный; **~-timer** *n.* старожи́л; **~-world** *adj.* (*ancient*) стари́нный; (*belonging to former days*) старосвéтский.

olden ['əʊld(ə)n] *adj.* (*arch.*) стáрый, былóй; **in ~ days, times** в было́е временá.

olde-worlde ['əʊldɪ] *adj.* (*coll.*) стилизóванный под старинý.

oleaginous [,əʊlɪ'ædʒɪnəs] *adj.* (*oily*) масляни́стый; (*yielding oil*) мáсличный.

oleander [,əʊlɪ'ændə(r)] *n.* олеáндр.

O level ['əʊ lev(ə)l] *n.* (*Br.*) экзáмен (по прогрáмме срéдней шкóлы) на обы́чном ýровне.

olfactory [ɒl'fæktərɪ] *adj.* обоня́тельный.

oligarch ['ɒlɪ,gɑ:k] *n.* олигáрх.

oligarchic(al) [,ɒlɪ'gɑ:kɪk((ə)l)] *adj.* олигархи́ческий.

oligarchy ['ɒlɪ,gɑ:kɪ] *n.* олигáрхия.

olive ['ɒlɪv] *n.* **1.** (*tree*) масли́на; оли́вковое дéрево; (*fruit*) масли́на, оли́вка. **2.** (*colour*) оли́вковый цвет.

adj. оли́вковый.

Olympiad [ə'lɪmpɪ,æd] *n.* олимпиáда.

Olympian [ə'lɪmpɪən] *adj.* олимпи́йский.

Olympic [ə'lɪmpɪk] *adj.* олимпи́йский; **~ games, ~s** Олимпи́йские и́гры.

ombudsman ['ɒmbʊdzmən] *n.* óмбудсман (*чиновник, рассматривающий претензии граждан к правительственным служащим*).

omega ['əʊmɪgə] *n.* омéга.

omelet(te) ['ɒmlɪt] *n.* омлéт.

omen ['əʊmən, -men] *n.* предзнаменовáние; (*sign*) знак.

ominous ['ɒmɪnəs] *adj.* злове́щий.
omission [ə'mɪʃ(ə)n] *n.* **1.** про́пуск. **2.** упуще́ние.
omit [ə'mɪt] *v.t.* **1.** (*leave out*) пропус|ка́ть, -ти́ть. **2.** (*neglect*) упус|ка́ть, -ти́ть.
omnibus ['ɒmnɪbəs] *n.* **1.** (*obs.*) авто́бус. **2.** (~ *volume*) однoто́мник; сбо́рник.
omnipotence [ɒm'nɪpət(ə)ns] *n.* всемогу́щество.
omnipotent [ɒm'nɪpət(ə)nt] *adj.* всемогу́щий.
omnipresent [ˌɒmnɪ'prez(ə)nt] *adj.* вездесу́щий.
omniscience [ɒm'nɪsɪəns, -ʃɪəns] *n.* всеве́дение.
omniscient [ɒm'nɪsɪənt, -ʃɪənt] *adj.* всеве́дущий.
omnivorous [ɒm'nɪvərəs] *adj.* (*lit., fig.*) всея́дный.
on [ɒn] *adv.* (*for phrasal vv. with* **on,** *see relevant v. entries*). **1.** (*expr. continuation*): **straight ~** пря́мо; **and so ~** и так да́лее; **from now ~** (начина́я) с э́того дня; **read ~!** чита́йте да́льше!; **he looked at me and then walked ~** он взгляну́л на меня́ и пошёл да́льше; **we walked ~ and ~** мы всё шли и шли; **he went ~ (and ~) about his dog** он без конца́ говори́л о свое́й соба́ке; **he was ~ at me to lend him my bicycle** он (всё) пристава́л ко мне, что́бы я одолжи́л ему́ мой велосипе́д; (*expr. extension*): **further ~** да́льше; **later ~** по́зже. **2.** (*placed, fixed, spread etc.* ~ *sth.*): **the kettle is ~** ча́йник поста́влен; **the light-switch is ~** свет включён; **he had his glasses ~** он был в очка́х. **3.** (*arranged, available*): **what's ~ this week?** (*at theatre*) что идёт/даю́т на э́той неде́ле?; **what's ~ tonight?** (*TV*) что сего́дня пока́зывают?; **he is ~** (*performing*) **tonight** он выступа́ет сего́дня (ве́чером); **have you anything ~ next week?** у вас что́-нибудь наме́чено на бу́дущей неде́ле?; **is the match still ~?** матч не отмени́ли/отменён? **4.** (*turned, switched* ~): **the radio was ~ full blast** ра́дио бы́ло включено́ на всю мощь; **the tap was left ~** кран был не вы́ключен; забы́ли вы́ключить кран; **leave the light ~!** не гаси́те свет!; **is the brake ~?** то́рмоз включён? **5.** (~ *stage*): **you're ~ next!** сле́дующий вы́ход — ваш! **6.** (*expr. contact*): **I've been ~ to him this morning** (*by telephone*) я говори́л с ним (по телефо́ну) сего́дня у́тром; **he's ~ to a good thing** (*coll.*) ему́ повезло́. **7.: you're ~!** (*coll., I accept your offer, bet etc.*) идёт!; **it's not ~** (*coll., feasible*) не вы́йдет/пройдёт.

prep. (*for some senses see also* **upon**) **1.** (*expr. position*): **~ the table** на столе́; **Rostov-~-Don** Ростов-на-Дону́; (*supported by*): **he walks ~ crutches** он хо́дит на костыля́х; **the look ~ his face** выраже́ние его́ лица́; (*as means of transport*): **~ horseback** верхо́м; **~ foot** пешко́м; **I came ~ the bus** я прие́хал авто́бусом; (~ *one's person*): **I have no money ~ me** у меня́ нет при себе́ де́нег; (*over the surface of; along*): **the fly was crawling ~ the ceiling** му́ха по́лзала по потолку́; **the boat floated ~ the current** ло́дка плыла́ по тече́нию; (*expr. relative position, with* **left, right, side, hand** *etc.*): **~ all sides** со всех сторо́н; повсю́ду; **~ my left** сле́ва от меня́; **~ my part** с мое́й стороны́; **~ the one hand ... ~ the other (hand)** с одно́й стороны́... с друго́й (стороны́); **~ either side of the street** по о́бе сто́роны у́лицы; **he walked ~ the other side of the street** он шёл по противополо́жной стороне́ у́лицы. **2.** (*expr. final position of movement or action*): **she threw her gloves ~(to) the floor** она́ бро́сила перча́тки на́ пол; **the windows open ~ (to) the garden** о́кна выхо́дят в сад. **3.** (*expr. point of contact*): **he hit me ~ the head** он уда́рил меня́ по голове́; **I hit my head ~ a stone** я уда́рился голово́й о ка́мень; **he kissed her ~ the lips** он поцелова́л её в гу́бы; **he knocked ~ the door** он постуча́л в дверь; **her dress caught ~ a nail** она́ зацепи́лась пла́тьем за гвоздь. **4.** (*of musical instrument*): **he played a tune ~ the fiddle** он сыгра́л мело́дию на скри́пке. **5.** (*of a medium of communication*): **~ the radio/telephone/television** по ра́дио/телефо́ну/телеви́зору. **6.** (*expr. membership*): **she is ~ the committee** она́ член комите́та; **~ our staff** у нас в шта́те. **7.** (*expr. time*): **~ that same day** в тот же день; **~ Tuesday** во вто́рник; **~ time** во́время; своевре́менно; **~ this occasion** на э́тот раз; **~ the 8th of May** восьмо́го ма́я; **~ the morning of the 8th of May** у́тром восьмо́го ма́я; **~ Tuesdays** по вто́рникам; **~ the occasion of his death** по слу́чаю его́ сме́рти. **8.** (*at the time of; immediately after*): **~ his arrival** по его́ прие́зде; **cash ~ delivery** опла́та по доста́вке; **~ seeing him she ran off** уви́дев его́, она́ убежа́ла; **~ his father's death** по сме́рти отца́; (*during*): **~ my way home** по доро́ге домо́й; **~ examination** при осмо́тре. **9.** (*concerning*): **an article ~ Pushkin** статья́ о Пу́шкине; **decisions ~ reparations** реше́ния по репара́циям; **~ that subject** на э́ту те́му, по э́той те́ме, над э́той те́мой. **10.** (*on the strength, basis of*): **he was acquitted ~ my evidence** он был опра́вдан на осно́ве мои́х показа́ний; **~ easy terms** на льго́тных усло́виях. **11.** (*expr. direction of effort*): **work ~ a book** рабо́та над кни́гой; **work ~ building a house** рабо́та по постро́йке до́ма; **I spent two hours ~ that job** я потра́тил на э́ту рабо́ту два часа́. **12.** (*at the expense of*): **drinks are ~ me** я угоща́ю; **the joke was ~ me** шу́тка оберну́лась про́тив меня́; **he lives ~ his friends** он живёт за счёт друзе́й. **13.** (*by means of*): **he lives ~ slender means** он живёт на ску́дные сре́дства; **he lives ~ fish** он пита́ется ры́бой; **the machine runs ~ oil** маши́на рабо́тает на ма́сле. **14.** (*imposed* ~): **a tax ~ tobacco** по́шлина на таба́чные изде́лия.
on-board ['ɒnbɔ:d] *adj.* бортово́й.
once [wʌns] *adv.* **1.** (оди́н) раз; **~ is enough** одного́ ра́за (вполне́) доста́точно; **~ six is six** одина́жды шесть — шесть; **more than ~** не раз; **~ a day** (оди́н) раз в день; **~ every 6 weeks** ка́ждые шесть неде́ль; **just (for) this ~** хотя́ бы на э́тот раз; **for ~** на сей раз; в ви́де исключе́ния; **~ again, more** ещё раз; **(every) ~ in a while** (*occasionally*) и́зредка; вре́мя от вре́мени; **~ (and) for all** (*finally*) раз (и) навсегда́; **~ or twice** не́сколько раз; **not ~** ни ра́зу, никогда́. **2.** (*whenever, as soon as*): **~ he understands this** как то́лько он поймёт э́то. **3.** (*at one time, formerly*) не́когда; одно́ вре́мя; одна́жды; когда́-то; **~ upon a time there was** (давны́м-давно́) жил-был; (*on one occasion in the past*) одна́жды. **4.: at ~** (*immediately*) сейча́с же; неме́дленно; (*simultaneously*) в то же вре́мя; **don't all talk at ~!** не говори́те все сра́зу/вме́сте!; **all at ~** (*suddenly*) внеза́пно/вдруг.

conj. see adv. **2.**

cpd. **~-over** *n.* (*coll.*): **give s.o./sth. the ~-over** бе́гло осм|а́тривать, -отре́ть кого́/что-н.
oncology [ɒŋ'kɒlədʒɪ] *n.* онколо́гия.
oncoming ['ɒnˌkʌmɪŋ] *adj.* приближа́ющийся, наступа́ющий.
on-duty ['ɒndju:tɪ] *adj.* дежу́рный.
one [wʌn] *n.* **1.** (*number*) оди́н; (*in counting*): **~, 2, 3** раз/оди́н, два, три; (*figure 1*) едини́ца; число́ оди́н; **minus ~** ми́нус едини́ца; **a row of ~s** ряд едини́ц; **they came in, by ~s and twos** они́ входи́ли по одино́чке и по́ двое; **5 ~s are 5** пя́тью оди́н — пять; **~ or two** (*several*) не́сколько; (*a few*) немно́го; **~ in 10** оди́н из десяти́; **he's ~ in a thousand** таки́х, как он — оди́н на ты́сячу; **last but ~** предпосле́дний; **~ and a half** полтора́ +*g.* **2.** (*in a series*): **Part O~** часть пе́рвая, I часть (*read as* пе́рвая часть); **room ~** ко́мната (но́мер) оди́н; пе́рвый но́мер; **he looks after number ~** (*i.e. himself*) он забо́тится (лишь) о само́м себе́. **3.** (*hour*) час; **I'll**

see you at ~ я вас увижу в час; **it was past ~** шёл второй час; **half past ~** половина второго; **at a quarter to ~** без четверти час; **~ o'clock** (*a.m.*) час ночи; (*p.m.*) час дня. **4.** (*age*): **he's only ~** ему всего/только год. **5.** (*expr. unity or identity*): **we are at ~ in thinking ...** мы согласны в том, что...; **it's all ~ to me** мне безразлично (*or* всё равно). **6.** (*being, person, creature*): **the Evil O~** чёрт, дьявол; **little ~s** дети; **our loved ~s** наши близкие; **he is not ~ to refuse** он не таков, чтобы отказаться; **he is ~ who never complains** он не из тех, кто жалуется. **7.** (*member of a group*) один; **~ of my friends** один из моих друзей; **he was ~ of the first to arrive** он пришёл одним из первых; **many a ~** многие; **the ~ with the beard** тот(, который) с бородой; **which ~ of you did it?** кто из вас это сделал?; **~ and all** все как один; **not ~ of them** ни один из них; никто из них; **~ another** друг друга; **~ after the other; ~ by ~** один за другим; **(the) ~ ... the other ...** один/тот... другой...; **~ each** по одному; **~ at a time** по очереди; не все разом; **~ of a kind** (*unique specimen*) уникум; (*unique*) уникальный. **8.** (*referring to category specified or understood*): **which book do you want, the red or the green ~?** какую книгу вы хотите, красную или зелёную?; **'Take my pen!' — 'Thanks, I have ~'** «Возьмите мою ручку!» — «Спасибо, у меня есть»; **this pencil is better than that ~** этот карандаш лучше того; **I gave him ~** (*blow*) **on the chin** я дал ему по челюсти; **we had ~** (*drink*) **for the road** мы выпили на дорожку; **he had ~ too many** он выпил лишнего.

pron.: **~ never knows** никогда не знаешь; кто его знает?; **~ doesn't say that in Russian** по-русски так не говорят; **~ can say anything nowadays** в наше время можно всё говорить; **how can ~ do it?** как это сделать?; **~ gets used to anything** человек ко всему привыкает; **~'s own** свой (собственный).

adj. **1.** один; (*sometimes untranslated, e.g.*) **price ~ rouble** цена рубль; (*with pluralia tantum*) одни; **~ watch** одни часы; **~ hundred and ~** сто один; **I have ~ or two things to do** у меня есть кое-какие дела. **2.** (*only*) единственный; **the ~ thing I detest is ...** больше всего я ненавижу...; (*single*): **no ~ man can lift it** одному это никак не поднять; **with ~ accord** единодушно; **they spoke with ~ voice** они говорили в один голос. **3.** (*the same*) тот же самый; **at ~ and the same time** в одно и то же время. **4.** (*particular but unspecified*): **at ~ time** когда-то; некогда; **~ evening** однажды вечером; **~ day** (*in past*) однажды; (*in future*) когда-нибудь; **~ fine day** в один прекрасный день. **5.** (*a certain*) некий; **we bought the house from ~ Jones** мы купили дом у некоего Джонса. **6.** (*opp. other*): **I'll go ~ way and you go the other** я пойду одной дорогой, а вы — другой; **neither ~ thing nor the other** ни то ни сё; **(just) ~ thing after another** не одно, так другое; **for ~ thing, I'm not ready** во-первых, я не готов.

cpds. **~-armed** *adj.* однорукий; **~-eyed** *adj.* одноглазый; **~-legged** *adj.* одноногий; **~-man** *adj.*: **~-man business** единоличное предприятие; **~-night** *adj.*: **~-night stand** (*theatr.*) единственное представление; **~-off, ~-shot** *adjs.* (*coll.*) уникальный, единственный; разовый; **~-sided** *adj.* (*prejudiced*) однобокий, односторонний; **~-time** *adj.* бывший; былой; *see also* **~-off**; **~-track** *adj.* (*fig.*): **~-track mind** узкий кругозор; **~-way** *adj.*: **~-way traffic** одностороннее движение; **~-way ticket** билет в один конец.

oneness ['wʌnnɪs] *n.* единство.

onerous ['ɒnərəs, 'əʊn-] *adj.* обременительный, тягостный, хлопотный.

oneself [wʌn'self] *pron.* (*refl.*) себя, ...ся; **talk to ~** говорить (*impf.*) с самим собой; **sit by ~** сидеть (*impf.*) в стороне/одиночестве; **for ~** самостоятельно; **cooking for ~ is a bore** скучно готовить для одного/самого себя; **see for ~** убедиться самому лично.

ongoing ['ɒn,gəʊɪŋ] *adj.* текущий; проходящий сейчас.

onion ['ʌnjən] *n.* луковица; (*pl., collect.*) лук (репчатый); **spring ~s** зелёный лук; (*attr.*) луковый.

on-line [ɒn'laɪn] *adj.* (*comput.*) неавтономный.

onlooker ['ɒn,lʊkə(r)] *n.* зритель (*m.*); наблюдатель (*m.*); (*witness*) свидетель (*m.*).

only ['əʊnlɪ] *adj.* единственный; **one and ~** один единственный; **she was an ~ child** она была единственным ребёнком; **she is not the ~ one** она не исключение; **I was the ~ one there** кроме меня там никого не было; **he was the ~ one to object** он один возражал; **~ women attended the meeting** на заседании были одни женщины; **~ a month ago** не далее как месяц тому назад; **the ~ thing is, I can't afford it** дело лишь в том, что мне это не по средствам.

adv. только; всего; **I have ~ just arrived** я только что прибыл; **he was ~ just in time** он чуть (было) не опоздал; он едва успел; **if ~ you knew** если бы вы только знали; **the engine started, ~ to stop again** мотор завёлся, но тут же заглох; **not ~ that!** мало того!; **the soup was ~ warm** суп был только что тёплый.

conj. но; **I would go myself, ~ I'm tired** я пошёл бы сам, но я устал; **he's a good speaker, ~ he shouts a lot** он хороший оратор, только вот слишком кричит.

on-off ['ɒn'ɒf] *adj.*: **~-off switch** выключатель (*m.*).

onomatopoeia [,ɒnə,mætə'pi:ə] *n.* звукоподражание.

onomatopoeic [,ɒnə,mætə'pi:ɪk] *adj.* звукоподражательный.

onrush ['ɒnrʌʃ] *n.* натиск; (*attack*) атака.

on-screen [ɒn'skri:n] *adj.* (*comput.*) экранный; **~ graphics** экранная графика.

onset ['ɒnset] *n.* начало, наступление.

onshore ['ɒnʃɔ:(r)] *adj.*: **~ wind** морской ветер.

on-site ['ɒnsaɪt] *adj.* на местах/месте.

onslaught ['ɒnslɔ:t] *n.* стремительная атака.

onto ['ɒntu:] = **on** *prep.* **2.**

ontological [,ɒntə'lɒdʒɪk(ə)l] *adj.* онтологический.

ontology [ɒn'tɒlədʒɪ] *n.* онтология.

onus ['əʊnəs] *n.* бремя, ответственность.

onward ['ɒnwəd] *adj.* продвигающийся; **~ movement** движение вперёд.

adv. (*also* **~s**) вперёд; **from now ~** впредь, отныне; **from then ~** с тех пор; с той поры.

onyx ['ɒnɪks] *n.* оникс.

oodles ['u:d(ə)lz] *n.* (*coll.*) масса, уйма; **~ of money** куча денег.

ooze [u:z] *n.* (*slime*) ил, тина; (*wet mud*) липкая грязь.

v.t. (*emit*): **the wound ~d blood** из раны сочилась кровь.

v.i. (*flow slowly*) медленно течь (*impf.*); (*in drops*) сочиться (*impf.*).

opacity [ə'pæsɪtɪ] *n.* **1.** непрозрачность. **2.** (*obscurity of meaning*) неясность; (*of thought*) смутность.

opal ['əʊp(ə)l] *n.* опал.

adj. опаловый.

opalescent [,əʊpə'les(ə)nt] *adj.* опаловый.

opaque [əʊ'peɪk] *adj.* непрозрачный; (*dark, obscure*) тёмный; (*obtuse, dull-witted*) тупой, глупый.

open ['əʊpən] *n.* **1.** (**~** *space*; **~** *air*) открытое пространство; **in the ~** под открытым небом; на открытом воздухе. **2.** (*fig.*): **bring sth. into the ~** выводить, вывести что-н. на чистую воду; **come into the ~** выявляться, выявиться; (*be frank*) быть откровенным.

adj. **1.** откры́тый; **in the ~ air** на откры́том во́здухе; **receive, welcome with ~ arms** (*fig.*) встр|ечáть, -éтить тепло́/раду́шно; **~ boat** беспáлубное су́дно; **~ car/carriage** откры́тая маши́на/карéта; **~ competition** откры́тое состязáние; **~ contempt** я́вное презрéние; **in ~ country** в непересечённой мéстности; **~ day** (*at school*) день откры́тых двeрéй; **keep one's ears ~** навостри́ть (*pf.*) у́ши; **with one's eyes ~** с откры́тыми глазáми; (*fig.*) сознáтельно; **~ flower** распусти́вшийся цветóк; **~ ground** незащищённый грунт; **~ hostility** откры́тая враждá; **have an ~ mind on sth.** не имéть предвзя́того мнéния по дáнному вопрóсу; **~ prison** тюрьмá откры́того ти́па; **an ~ question** откры́тый/нерешённый вопрóс; **on the ~ road** на большóй дорóге; **on the ~ sea** в откры́том мóре; **~ season** охóтничий сезóн; **~ secret** секрéт полишинéля; **~ space** незагорóженное мéсто; **~ ticket** билéт без ограничéния срóка пóльзования; **~ warfare** откры́тая войнá; **~ wound** откры́тая/незажи́вшая рáна; **break ~** (*v.t.*) вскры|вáть, -ть; распечáт|ывать, -ать; взл|áмывать, -омáть; **the door flew ~** дверь распахну́лась; **he threw the window ~** он распахну́л oкнó. **2.** (*accessible, available*) досту́пный; **the chairman threw the debate ~** председáтель объяви́л прéния откры́тыми; **the post is still ~** мéсто ещё не зáнято; **~ to attack** уязви́мый; **~ to question** спóрный; **~ to misinterpretation** спосóбный вы́звать непрáвильное толковáние; **~ to offer** готóвый рассмотрéть предложéние. **3.** (*generous*) щéдрый; (*hospitable*) гостеприи́мный. **4.** (*frank*) откровéнный.

v.t. **1.** откр|ывáть, -ы́ть; (*unseal*) распечáт|ывать, -ать; (*unwrap*) разв|орáчивать, -ернýть; (*book, newspaper*) раскр|ывáть, -ы́ть; (*vein; parcel at customs etc.*) вскр|ывáть, -ыть; (*bottle*) откупóри|вать, -ть; **~ wide** (*e.g. door*) распáх|ивать, -нýть; **he ~ed his mouth wide** он широкó откры́л рот. **2.** (*fig.*): **she ~ed her heart to me** онá откры́ла мне ду́шу; **I ~ed his eyes to the situation** я откры́л емý глазá на положéние дел; **we ~ed negotiations** мы приступи́ли к переговóрам; **a new business has been ~ed** оснóвано нóвое предприя́тие. **3.: a road was ~ed through the forest** чéрез лес проложи́ли дорóгу; **they are planning to ~ a mine** они́ собирáются заложи́ть шáхту.

v.i. **1.** откр|ывáться, -ы́ться; (*unfold, ~ wide*) раскр|ывáться, -ы́ться; **the heavens ~ed** (*fig.*) дождь поли́л, как из ведрá. **2.** (*fig., begin*) нач|инáться, -áться; **the new play ~s on Saturday** нóвая пьéса идёт с суббóты; **I shall ~ by reading the minutes** я начнý с чтéния протокóла. **3.** (*of door, room etc.*): **the study ~s into the drawing-room** кабинéт сообщáется с гости́ной; **the windows ~ on to a courtyard** óкна выхóдят во двор.

with advs.: **~ out** *v.i.*: **the roses ~ed out** рóзы распусти́лись; **~ up** *v.t.*: **~ up!** (*command to open*) открóйте дверь!; **his stories ~ up a new world** егó расскáзы раскрывáют нóвый мир; *v.i.*: **he ~ed up about his visit** он откровéнно рассказáл о своéй поéздке; **a machine-gun ~ed up** нáчал стреля́ть пулемёт.

cpds. **~-air** *adj.*: **~-air life** жизнь на откры́том вóздухе; **~cast** *adj.*: **~cast mining** откры́тые гóрные рабóты; **~ended** *adj.* (*fig.*) бессрóчный; **~-handed** *adj.* щéдрый; **~-hearted** *adj.* чистосердéчный; **~-hearth** *adj.*: **~-hearth furnace** мартéновская печь; **~-minded** *adj.* непредубеждённый; **~-mouthed** *adj.* рази́нувший рот от удивлéния; **~-work** *n.* ажу́рная рабóта/стрóчка; мерéжка.

opener ['əʊpənə(r), 'əʊpnə(r)] *n.* (*for cans etc.*) консéрвный нож; (*coll.*) открывáлка (*also for bottles*).

opening ['əʊpənɪŋ, 'əʊpnɪŋ] *n.* **1.** (*vbl. senses*) откры́тие, раскры́тие. **2.** (*aperture*) отвéрстие; прохóд. **3.** (*beginning*) начáло, вступлéние. **4.** (*job*) мéсто, вакáнсия. **5.** (*favourable opportunity*) удóбный слу́чай. **6.** (*chess*) дебю́т.

adj. (*initial*) начáльный, пéрвый; (*introductory*) вступи́тельный; **~ night** премьéра; (*working*): **~ hours** рабóчие часы́; часы́ рабóты.

openly ['əʊpənlɪ] *adv.* откры́то; (*frankly*) откровéнно; (*publicly*) публи́чно, откры́то.

openness ['əʊpənnɪs] *n.* откры́тость; глáсность; (*frankness*) откровéнность.

opera ['ɒpərə] *n.* óпера.

cpds. **~-glass(es)** *n.* (театрáльный) бинóкль; **~-house** *n.* óперный теáтр; **~-singer** *n.* óперный певéц, óперная певи́ца.

operate ['ɒpə,reɪt] *v.t.* **1.** (*control work of*) управля́ть (*impf.*) +*i.*; эксплуати́ровать (*impf.*); **he ~s a lathe** он рабóтает на токáрном станкé; **the machine is ~d by electricity** э́та маши́на рабóтает на электри́честве. **2.** (*bring into motion*) прив|оди́ть, -ести́ в движéние. **3.** (*put into effect*): **we ~ a simple system** мы применя́ем простýю систéму.

v.i. **1.** (*work, act*) рабóтать (*impf.*); дéйствовать (*impf.*); **the brakes failed to ~** тормозá отказáли. **2.** (*produce effect or influence*) окáз|ывать, -áть влия́ние (на+*a.*); дéйствовать, по-. **3.: ~ on** (*surg.*) опери́ровать (*impf., pf.*) (**for:** по пóводу +*g.*).

operatic [,ɒpə'rætɪk] *adj.* óперный.

operating ['ɒpə,reɪtɪŋ] *adj.* **1.** (*surg.*): **~ room, theatre** операциóнная; **~ table** операциóнный стол. **2.: ~ costs** эксплуатациóнные расхóды.

operation [,ɒpə'reɪʃ(ə)n] *n.* **1.** (*action, effect*) дéйствие; рабóта; **bring into ~** прив|оди́ть, -ести́ в дéйствие; **go out of ~** выходи́ть, вы́йти из стрóя. **2.** (*force, validity*) си́ла. **3.** (*process*) процéсс, операция. **4.** (*control, making work*) управлéние, эксплуатáция. **5.** (*business transaction*) операция. **6.** (*mil.*) операция, дéйствие; **combined ~s** совмéстные дéйствия; **~s room** комáндный пункт. **7.** (*med.*) операция; **an ~ for cancer** операция (по пóводу) рáка; **perform an ~** дéлать, с- операцию.

operational [,ɒpə'reɪʃən(ə)l] *adj.* **1.** (*mil.*) операти́вный; **~ unit** боевóе подразделéние. **2. the fleet is ~** флот в состоя́нии боевóй готóвности; **the factory is fully ~** завóд пóлностью готóв к эксплуатáции.

operative ['ɒpərətɪv] *n.* (*machine operator*) квалифици́рованный рабóчий, станóчник, механик.

adj. **1.** (*working, operating*) дéйствующий; (*having force*) действи́тельный; (*effective*) дéйственный; **become ~** (*of law etc.*) входи́ть, войти́ в си́лу. **2.** (*practical*) операти́вный.

operator ['ɒpə,reɪtə(r)] *n.* **1.** (*one who works a machine*) управля́ющий (маши́ной); оперáтор. **2.** (*telephonist*) телефони́ст (*fem.* -ка). **3.** (*comm.*) делéц.

operetta [,ɒpə'retə] *n.* оперéтта.

ophthalmologist [,ɒfθæl'mɒlɒdʒɪst] *n.* офтальмóлог.

ophthalmology [,ɒfθæl'mɒlədʒɪ] *n.* офтальмолóгия.

opiate ['əʊpɪət] *n.* опиáт; (*fig.*) óпиум.

opine [əʊ'paɪn] *v.t.* выскáзывать, вы́сказать мнéние, что...

opinion [ə'pɪnjən] *n.* (*judgement, belief*) мнéние; (*view*) взгляд; **in the ~ of** по мнéнию +*g.*; **in my ~** по моéму мнéнию, по-мóему, на мой взгляд; **be of the ~ that ...** держáться (*impf.*) тогó мнéния, что...; полагáть (*impf.*) что...; **change one's ~** меня́ть (*impf.*), перемени́ть (*pf.*) мнéние; **form an ~** сост|авля́ть, -áвить себé мнéние; **that is a matter of ~** э́то зави́сит от тóчки зрéния; **~ poll** опрóс общéственного мнéния; (*estimate*): **have a high/low ~ of** быть высóкого/невысóкого мнéния о+*p.*; (*conviction*) убеждéние; (*expert judgment*) заключéние.

opinionated [ə'pɪnjə,neɪtɪd] *adj.* догмати́чный.

opium ['əʊpɪəm] *n.* óпиум; ~ **den** притóн курúльщиков óпиума.
opossum [ə'pɒsəm] *n.* опóссум.
opponent [ə'pəʊnənt] *n.* оппонéнт, протúвник.
opportune ['ɒpə,tju:n] *adj.* (*timely*) своеврéменный, умéстный; (*suitable*) подходя́щий.
opportunism [,ɒpə'tju:nɪz(ə)m, 'ɒpə-] *n.* оппортунúзм.
opportunist [,ɒpə'tju:nɪst] *n.* оппортунúст.
adj. оппортунистúческий.
opportunit|y [,ɒpə'tju:nɪtɪ] *n.* (*favourable circumstance*) удóбный слу́чай; (*good chance*) благоприя́тная возмóжность; **as ~y offers** при слу́чае; **I had no ~y to thank him** у меня́ нé было возмóжности поблагодарúть егó; **ring me up if you get the ~y!** позвонúте, éсли бу́дет возмóжность (*or* предстáвится слу́чай); **he seized, took the ~y to ...** он воспóльзовался слу́чаем, чтóбы....
oppos|e [ə'pəʊz] *v.t.* **1.** (*set against or in contrast to*) противопост|авля́ть, -áвить (*что чему*); **two ~ed ideas** две противоположные идéи; **as ~ed to** в отлúчие от+*g.*; **I am firmly ~ed to the idea** я решúтельно прóтив э́той идéи. **2.** (*set o.s. against*) возра|жáть, -зúть (*or* выступáть, вы́ступить) прóтив+*g.*; **the ~ing side** протúвная сторонá; (*sport*) комáнда протúвника; (*show opposition to*) окáз|ывать, -áть сопротивлéние +*d.*; (*reject*; *propose rejection of*) отклон|я́ть, -úть; **he ~ed my request** он отклонúл мою́ прóсьбу.
opposite ['ɒpəzɪt] *n.* противоположность; **just the ~** прямáя/пóлная противоположность; как раз наоборóт.
adj. противоположный; **his house is ~ ours** егó дом (стоúт) напрóтив нáшего; **in the ~ direction** в обрáтном направлéнии; **~ poles** (*elec.*) разноимённые пóлюсы; **~ number** лицó, занимáющее такýю же дóлжность в другóм вéдомстве *и т.п.*
adv. напрóтив.
prep. (на)прóтив+*g.*
opposition [,ɒpə'zɪʃ(ə)n] *n.* **1.** (*placing or being placed opposite*) противопоставлéние; **they found themselves in ~ (to each other)** онú оказáлись в противополóжных лагеря́х. **2.** (*resistance, contrary action*) сопротивлéние, противодéйствие, оппозúция; **the infantry encountered heavy ~** пехóта встрéтила сúльное сопротивлéние; **he acted in ~ to my wishes** он поступúл вопрекú моúм желáниям. **3.** (*pol.*) оппозúция; **the Leader of the O~** лúдер оппозúции. **5.** (*astron.*) противостоя́ние.
oppress [ə'pres] *v.t.* **1.** (*of a ruler or government*) угнетáть (*impf.*); притесн|я́ть, -úть. **2.** (*weigh down*; *weary*) удруч|áть, -úть; томúть (*impf.*); **feel ~ed with the heat** томúться (*impf.*) от жары́.
oppression [ə'preʃ(ə)n] *n.* (*oppressing*) угнетéние, гнёт, притеснéние, тирания; (*being oppressed*) угнетённость.
oppressive [ə'presɪv] *adj.* угнетáющий; (*tyrannical*) деспотúческий; (*burdensome*) тя́гостный; (*wearisome*) утомúтельный; **~ weather** угнетáющая/ду́шная погóда.
oppressor [ə'presə(r)] *n.* угнетáтель (*m.*).
opprobrious [ə'prəʊbrɪəs] *adj.* (*injurious*) оскорбúтельный; (*shameful*) позóрный.
opprobrium [ə'prəʊbrɪəm] *n.* (*reproach*) напáдки (*m. pl.*); возмущéние; (*shame, disgrace*) позóр.
opt [ɒpt] *v.i.*: **~ for** выбирáть, вы́брать; **~ out of** уклон|я́ться, -úться от+*g.*; (добровóльно) выбывáть, вы́быть из+*g.*
optic ['ɒptɪk] *adj.* зрúтельный, оптúческий, глазнóй; **~ nerve** зрúтельный нерв.
optical ['ɒptɪk(ə)l] *adj.* оптúческий, зрúтельный; **~ illusion** оптúческий обмáн; обмáн зрéния.
optician [ɒp'tɪʃ(ə)n] *n.* óптик.
optics ['ɒptɪks] *n.* óптика.
optimism ['ɒptɪ,mɪz(ə)m] *n.* оптимúзм.
optimist ['ɒptɪmɪst] *n.* оптимúст (*fem.* -ка).
optimistic [,ɒptɪ'mɪstɪk] *adj.* оптимистúческий.
optimum ['ɒptɪməm] *adj.* оптимáльный.
option ['ɒpʃ(ə)n] *n.* **1.** (*choice*) вы́бор; **soft ~** лёгкий вы́бор; **I have no ~ but to ...** у меня́ нет другóго вы́бора, как...; **keep one's ~s open** ост|авля́ть, -áвить вы́бор за собóй. **2.** (*right of choice*) прáво вы́бора. **3.** (*stock exchange etc.*) опциóн.
optional ['ɒpʃən(ə)l] *adj.* необязáтельный, факультатúвный.
optometrist [ɒp'tɒmɪtrɪst] *n.* óптик.
opulence ['ɒpjʊləns] *n.* богáтство, изобúлие.
opulent ['ɒpjʊlənt] *adj.* (*wealthy*) богáтый; (*abundant*) обúльный.
opus ['əʊpəs, 'ɒp-] *n.* **1.** (*mus.*) óпус. **2.: magnum ~** сáмое крýпное произведéние (áвтора *и т.п.*).
or [ɔ:(r), ə(r)] *conj.* **1.** úли; **will you be here ~ not?** вы здесь бу́дете úли нет?; **he came for a day ~ two** он приéхал на день-другóй; **two ~ three** два-три. **2.** (**~ *else***) úли, инáче; úли же; а (не) то; **wear your coat ~ you'll catch cold** надéньте пальтó, инáче (*or* а то) просту́дитесь; **do as I say ~ else!** дéлай, что скáзано úли пеня́й на себя́! **3.: there were 20 ~ so people present** там бы́ло человéк 20 (*or* óколо двадцатú человéк). **4.: storm ~ no storm, I shall go** грозá не грозá, пойду́.
oracle ['ɒrək(ə)l] *n.* орáкул.
oral ['ɔ:r(ə)l] *n.* у́стный экзáмен.
adj. у́стный.
orange ['ɒrɪndʒ] *n.* **1.** (*fruit*) апельсúн; (*attr.*) апельсúновый (*see also cpds.*); **Seville ~** померáнец. **2.** (*tree*) апельсúновое дéрево. **3.** (*colour*) орáнжевый цвет.
adj. (*colour*) орáнжевый.
cpds. **~-blossom** *n.* флёрдорáнж; померáнцевые цветы́ (*m. pl.*); **~juice** *n.* апельсúновый сок; **~-peel** *n.* апельсúнная кóрка; (*candied*) апельсúнный цукáт; **~-pip** *n.* зёрнышко апельсúна.
orangeade [,ɒrɪndʒ'eɪd] *n.* оранжáд.
orang-utan [ɔ:,ræŋu:'tæn] *n.* орангутáнг.
orate [ɔ:'reɪt] *v.i.* орáторствовать (*impf.*).
oration [ɔ:'reɪʃ(ə)n, ə-] *n.* речь.
orator ['ɒrətə(r)] *n.* орáтор.
oratorical [,ɒrə'tɒrɪk(ə)l] *adj.* орáторский.
oratorio [,ɒrə'tɔ:rɪəʊ] *n.* оратóрия.
oratory ['ɒrətərɪ] *n.* (*rhetoric*) краснорéчие, ритóрика.
orb [ɔ:b] *n.* (*globe, sphere*) шар, сфéра; (*heavenly body*) небéсное светúло; (*part of regalia*) держáва.
orbit ['ɔ:bɪt] *n.* **1.** (*of planet etc.*) орбúта; (*circuit completed by space vehicle*) витóк. **2.** (*fig., sphere of action*) сфéра дéятельности, орбúта.
v.t. (*put into ~*) выводúть, вы́вести на орбúту.
v.i. (*move in ~*) вращáться (*impf.*) по орбúте.
orbital ['ɔ:bɪt(ə)l] *adj.* (*astron.*) орбитáльный; (*of road*) окружнóй.
orchard ['ɔ:tʃəd] *n.* (фруктóвый) сад.
orchestra ['ɔ:kɪstrə] *n.* оркéстр; **full ~** симфонúческий оркéстр; **~ pit** оркестрóвая я́ма; **~ stalls** партéр.
orchestral [,ɔ:'kestr(ə)l] *adj.* оркестрóвый.
orchestrate ['ɔ:kɪ,streɪt] *v.t.* оркестровáть (*impf., pf.*); (*fig.*) организовáть, с-.
orchestration [,ɔ:kɪ'streɪʃ(ə)n] *n.* оркестрóвка.
orchid ['ɔ:kɪd] *n.* орхидéя.
ordain [ɔ:'deɪn] *v.t.* **1.** (*eccl.*) посвя|щáть, -тúть в духóвный сан. **2.** (*destine, decree*) предпúс|ывать, -áть.
ordeal [ɔ:'di:l] *n.* мытáрство; тяжёлое испытáние.
order ['ɔ:də(r)] *n.* **1.** (*arrangement*) поря́док; (*sequence, succession*) послéдовательность; **in alphabetical ~** в алфавúтном поря́дке; **in ~ of size** по размéру; **in ~ of importance** по стéпени вáжности; **out of ~, not in the right ~** не по поря́дку; не в поря́дке; не на (том) мéсте; **put sth. in ~** при-

в|одить, -ести что-н. в порядок. **2.** (*mil. formation*) строй; **battle ~** боевой порядок. **3.** (*result of arrangement or control*): **everything is in ~** всё в порядке; (*settled state*): **keep ~** поддерживать (*impf.*) порядок; **restore ~** восстан|авливать, -овить порядок; **law and ~** правопорядок; (*efficient state*) порядок, исправность; **out of ~** неисправный, в плохом состоянии; **the bell is out of ~** звонок не работает; **he got the typewriter into working ~** он починил машинку; (*healthy state*) порядок; хорошее состояние. **4.** (*procedure*) порядок; **call s.o. to ~** приз|ывать, -вать кого-н. к порядку; **call a meeting to ~** открыть (*pf.*) заседание; **maintain, keep ~** следить (*impf.*) за порядком; **O~!** к порядку!; **out of ~** в нарушение процедуры. **5.** (*command, instruction*) приказ, распоряжение; **by ~ of the president** по приказу президенту; **give an, the ~** отд|авать, -ать приказ; **obey ~s** подчин|яться, -иться приказу; **under s.o.'s ~s** под командой кого-н.; **get one's marching ~s** (*dismissal*) (*fig.*) получить (*pf.*) отставку; (*warrant*) ордер (*pl.* -а). **6.** (*direction to supply*) заказ (на+*a.*); **on ~** по заказу; **is on ~** заказан; **put in an ~ for** заказ|ывать, -ать; **fill, fulfil an ~** выполнять, выполнить заказ; **I am having a suit made to ~** я шью себе костюм на заказ. **7.** (*direction to bank*): **standing ~** приказ о регулярных платежах; (*pl., parl.*) правила (*nt. pl.*) процедуры. **8.** (*direction to Post Office*): **money/postal ~** денежный/почтовый перевод. **9.** (*social group, stratum*) социальная группа; слой; **lower ~s** простой народ. **10.** (*pl., eccl.*): **holy ~s** духовный сан; **take ~s** ста|новиться, -ть духовным лицом. **11.** (*distinction; insignia*) орден (*pl.* -а); **O~ of Lenin** орден Ленина; **he was awarded the O~ of the Garter** его наградили орденом Подвязки. **12.** (*kind, sort, category*) сорт, род; (*biol.*) отряд. **13.** (*of chivalry or relig.*) орден (*pl.* -ы). **14.**: **in ~ to** (для того,) чтобы +*inf.*; **in ~ that** (для того,) чтобы +*past tense*.

v.t. **1.** (*arrange, regulate*) прив|одить, -ести в порядок. **2.** (*command*) приказ|ывать, -ать; **he ~ed the soldiers to leave** он приказал солдатам разойтись; **he was ~ed home** ему приказали вернуться домой. **3.** (*prescribe*) пропис|ывать, -ать. **4.** (*reserve; request; arrange for supply of*) заказ|ывать, -ать. **5.**: **~ s.o. about** командовать (*impf.*) +*i.*

cpds. **~-book** *n.* книга заказов; **~-form** *n.* бланк заказа.

orderliness ['ɔːdəlɪnɪs] *n.* (*order*) порядок; (*methodical nature*) аккуратность.

orderly ['ɔːdəlɪ] *n.* (*mil., runner*) ординарец; (*in hospital*) санитар.

adj. **1.** (*tidy*) аккуратный, опрятный. **2.** (*quiet; well-behaved*) тихий, послушный. **3.** (*organized*) организованный. **4.** (*mil.*): **~ officer** дежурный офицер.

ordinal ['ɔːdɪn(ə)l] *n.* (*~ number*) порядковое числительное.

ordinance ['ɔːdɪnəns] *n.* указ; (*decree*) декрет.

ordinary ['ɔːdɪnərɪ] *n.*: **out of the ~** необычный, незаурядный.

adj. (*usual*) обычный; (*average, common*) обыкновенный; (*simple*) простой; (*commonplace*) заурядный; **~ seaman** младший матрос.

ordination [,ɔːdɪ'neɪʃ(ə)n] *n.* (*eccl.*) рукоположение.

ordnance ['ɔːdnəns] *n.* артиллерия.

ore [ɔː(r)] *n.* руда.

cpd. **~-bearing** *adj.* рудоносный.

organ ['ɔːgən] *n.* **1.** (*mus.*) орган, (*attr.*) органный; **mouth ~** губная гармоника; **street ~** шарманка. **2.** (*biol., pol. etc.*) орган.

cpd. **~-grinder** *n.* шарманщик.

organd|ie, -y ['ɔːgəndɪ, -'gændɪ] *n.* органди (*f. indecl.*); (грубая) кисея.

organic [ɔː'gænɪk] *adj.* органический; **~ whole** единое целое.

organism ['ɔːgə,nɪz(ə)m] *n.* организм.

organist ['ɔːgənɪst] *n.* органист.

organization [,ɔːgənaɪ'zeɪʃ(ə)n] *n.* организация.

organize ['ɔːgə,naɪz] *v.t.* организов|ывать, -ать; устр|аивать, -оить.

organizer ['ɔːgə,naɪzə(r)] *n.* организатор.

orgasm ['ɔːgæz(ə)m] *n.* оргазм.

orgiastic [,ɔːdʒɪ'æstɪk] *adj.* (*fig.*) разнузданный.

orgy ['ɔːdʒɪ] *n.* оргия; (*fig.*) разгул.

orient ['ɔːrɪənt] *n.* восток.

v.t. = **orient(ate)**

oriental [,ɔːrɪ'ent(ə)l, ,ɒr-] *adj.* восточный; **~ studies** востоковедение.

orientalist [,ɔːrɪ'entəlɪst, ,ɒr-] *n.* востоковед.

orient(ate) ['ɒrɪen,teɪt, 'ɔːr-] *v.t.* (*determine position of*) определ|ять, -ить местонахождение +*g.*; **~ o.s.** ориентироваться (*impf., pf.*).

orientation [,ɒrɪen'teɪʃ(ə)n, ,ɔːr-] *n.* (*lit., fig.*) ориентировка, ориентация.

orienteering [,ɔːrɪen'tɪərɪŋ, ,ɒr-] *n.* ориентирование на местности.

orifice ['ɒrɪfɪs] *n.* отверстие.

origin ['ɒrɪdʒɪn] *n.* (*beginning, source*) начало, источник; (*derivation, extraction*) происхождение.

original [ə'rɪdʒɪn(ə)l] *n.* **1.** подлинник; **a copy of the ~** копия с подлинника/оригинала. **2.** (*eccentric*) оригинал, чудак.

adj. **1.** (*first, earliest*) первоначальный; **~ sin** первородный грех; **the ~ inhabitants** исконные жители. **2.** (*archetypal; genuine*) подлинный. **3.** (*constructive, inventive*) оригинальный; **an ~ mind** изобретательный/самобытный ум. **4.** (*novel, fresh*) новый, свежий; своеобразный.

originality [ə,rɪdʒɪ'nælɪtɪ] *n.* подлинность; оригинальность, изобретательность, самобытность.

originally [ə'rɪdʒɪnəlɪ] *adv.* (*in the first place*) первоначально, исходно; (*in origin*) по происхождению.

originate [ə'rɪdʒɪ,neɪt] *v.t.* **1.** (*cause to begin, initiate*) причин|ять, -ить; дав|ать, -ть начало +*d.* **2.** (*create*) созд|авать, -ать; поро|ждать, -дить.

v.i. брать, взять начало; (*arise*) возн|икать, -икнуть; **the quarrel ~d in a remark of mine** ссора возникла из-за моего замечания.

origination [ə,rɪdʒɪ'neɪʃ(ə)n] *n.* (*source, origin*) начало, происхождение; (*creation*) источник, создание.

originator [ə'rɪdʒɪ,neɪtə(r)] *n.* (*initiator*) инициатор; (*author*) автор; (*creator*) создатель (*m.*).

Orion [ə'raɪən] *n.* (*astron.*) Орион.

ornament[1] ['ɔːnəmənt] *n.* **1.** (*adornment, embellishment*) украшение. **2.** (*decorative feature*) орнамент.

ornament[2] ['ɔːnə,ment] *v.t.* укр|ашать, -асить.

ornamental [,ɔːnə'ment(ə)l] *adj.* орнаментальный; (*decorative*) декоративный.

ornamentation [,ɔːnəmen'teɪʃ(ə)n] *n.* украшение.

ornate [ɔː'neɪt] *adj.* богато украшенный; (*of style*) витиеватый, цветистый.

ornithological [,ɔːnɪθə'lɒdʒɪk(ə)l] *adj.* орнитологический.

ornithologist [,ɔːnɪ'θɒlədʒɪst] *n.* орнитолог.

ornithology [,ɔːnɪ'θɒlədʒɪ] *n.* орнитология.

orphan ['ɔːf(ə)n] *n.* сирота (*c.g.*).

adj. сиротский.

v.t. лиш|ать, -ить (*кого*) родителей; делать, с-сиротой; **an ~ed child** осиротевший ребёнок.

orphanage ['ɔːfənɪdʒ] *n.* приют для сирот.

orthodox ['ɔːθə,dɒks] *adj.* ортодоксальный, правоверный; (*relig.*): **the O~ Church** православная церковь.

orthodoxy ['ɔːθə,dɒksɪ] *n.* ортодоксальность, правоверность; (*relig.*) православие.

orthographic(al) [,ɔːθə'græfɪk((ə)l)] *adj.* орфографический.

orthography [ɔːˈθɒgrəfɪ] *n.* правописа́ние, орфогра́фия.

orthopaedic [ˌɔːθəˈpiːdɪk] *adj.* ортопеди́ческий.

orthopaedics [ˌɔːθəˈpiːdɪks] *n.* ортопе́дия.

orthopaedist [ˌɔːθəˈpiːdɪst] *n.* ортопе́д.

oryx [ˈɒrɪks] *n.* сернобы́к.

Oscar [ˈɒskə(r)] *n.* (*cin.*) пре́мия О́скара.
cpds. **~-winner** *n.* лауреа́т пре́мии О́скара.

oscillate [ˈɒsɪˌleɪt] *v.t.* кача́ть (*impf.*).
v.i. кача́ться (*impf.*); колеба́ться (*impf.*).

oscillation [ˌɒsɪˈleɪʃ(ə)n] *n.* колеба́ние; (*elec.*) осцилля́ция.

oscillator [ˈɒsɪˌleɪtə(r)] *n.* осцилля́тор; (*radio*) генера́тор.

oscillograph [əˈsɪləˌgrɑːf] *n.* осцилло́граф.

oscilloscope [əˈsɪləˌskəʊp] *n.* осциллоско́п.

osier [ˈəʊzɪə(r)] *n.* (*plant*) и́ва; (*shoot*) лоза́.

osmosis [ɒzˈməʊsɪs] *n.* о́смос.

osprey [ˈɒspreɪ, -prɪ] *n.* (*zool.*) скопа́.

osseous [ˈɒsɪəs] *adj.* (*of bone*) костяно́й; (*bony*) кости́стый.

ossification [ˌɒsɪfɪˈkeɪʃ(ə)n] *n.* окостене́ние.

ossify [ˈɒsɪˌfaɪ] *v.t.* & *i.* превра|ща́ть(ся), -ти́ть(ся) в кость; (*fig.*) заст|ыва́ть, -ы́ть; окостене́ть (*pf.*).

ostensibl|e [ɒˈstensɪb(ə)l] *adj.* (*for show*) показно́й; (*professed*) мни́мый; **he called ~y to thank me** он пришёл я́кобы для того́, что́бы поблагодари́ть меня́.

ostentation [ˌɒstenˈteɪʃ(ə)n] *n.* (*display*) выставле́ние напока́з; (*boasting*) хвастовство́, бахва́льство.

ostentatious [ˌɒstenˈteɪʃəs] *adj.* показно́й, хвастли́вый.

osteoarthritis [ˌɒstɪəʊɑːˈθraɪtɪs] *n.* остеоартри́т.

osteopath [ˈɒstɪəˌpæθ] *n.* остеопа́т.

osteopathy [ˌɒstɪˈɒpəθɪ] *n.* остеопа́тия.

ostler [ˈɒslə(r)] *n.* ко́нюх.

ostracism [ˈɒstrəˌsɪz(ə)m] *n.* (*hist.*, *fig.*) остраки́зм; (*fig.*) изгна́ние (из о́бщества).

ostracize [ˈɒstrəˌsaɪz] *v.t.* подв|ерга́ть, -е́ргнуть острраки́зму; изг|оня́ть, -на́ть.

ostrich [ˈɒstrɪtʃ] *n.* (*also fig.*) стра́ус; (*attr.*) стра́усовый.

other [ˈʌðə(r)] *pron.* друго́й, ино́й; **the ~** (*liter.*, *person referred to*) тот; **one (thing) or the ~** одно́ из двух; **~s may disagree with you** ины́е мо́гут с ва́ми не согласи́ться; **as an example to ~s** в приме́р други́м/про́чим; **'~s'** (*in classification*) про́чие; **one after the ~** оди́н за други́м; **we talked of this, that and the ~** мы говори́ли о том, о сём; **someone or ~** кто́-то; **some day or ~** когда́-нибудь, ка́к-нибудь; **somehow or ~** ка́к-нибудь; **I want this book and no ~** я хочу́ и́менно э́ту кни́гу; **it was none ~ than Mr. Brown** э́то был не кто ино́й, как сам г-н Бра́ун; **no one ~ than he** никто́, кро́ме него́; (*expr. reciprocity*): **they were in love with each ~** они́ бы́ли влюблены́ друг в дру́га; **they got in each ~'s way** они́ друг дру́гу меша́ли; (*pl.*, *additional ones*; *more*) ещё +*g.*; **let me see some ~s** покажи́те ещё каки́е-нибудь!; **there are no ~s** други́х нет; (*remaining ones*): **the ~s had already gone** остальны́е уже́ ушли́; **why this day of all ~s?** почему́ и́менно сего́дня?
adj. **1.** друго́й; **on the ~ hand** с друго́й стороны́; **on the ~ side of the road** на той стороне́ доро́ги; **the ~ side of the moon** обра́тная сторона́ луны́; **we must find some ~ way** мы должны́ изыска́ть друго́й спо́соб; **there was no ~ place to go** бо́льше идти́ бы́ло не́куда; **some ~ time** в друго́й раз. **2.** (*additional*) ещё +*g.*; **how many ~ children have you?** ско́лько у вас ещё дете́й? **3.** (*remaining*) остально́й; **~ things being equal** при про́чих ра́вных усло́виях. **4.:** **the ~ day** на днях; **every ~** ка́ждый второ́й; **every ~ day** че́рез день.
adv.: see **otherwise** *adv.* **1.**

otherwise [ˈʌðəˌwaɪz] *adv.* **1.** (*in a different way*) по-друго́му, други́м спо́собом, ина́че; **I was ~ engaged** я был за́нят други́м (де́лом); **~ known as ...** та́кже имену́емый +*i.*; он же; **I could do no ~** (*or* **other**) я не мог поступи́ть ина́че. **2.** (*in other respects or circumstances*): в други́х отноше́ниях; **the house is cold but ~ comfortable** дом холо́дный, но в остально́м удо́бный. **3.** (*if not*; *or else*): **I went, ~ I would have missed them** я пошёл, ина́че я бы их не заста́л; **shut the windows, ~ the rain will come in** закро́йте о́кна, а то дождём намо́чит.

otter [ˈɒtə(r)] *n.* вы́дра; **sea ~** морско́й бобр.

Ottoman[1] [ˈɒtəmən] *adj.* оттома́нский.

ottoman[2] [ˈɒtəmən] *n.* (*sofa*) оттома́нка, тахта́.

ouch [aʊtʃ] *int.* ой!, ай!

ought [ɔːt] *v. aux.* **1.** (*expr. duty*): **you ~ to go there** вы должны́ (*or* вам сле́дует) туда́ пойти́; **you ~ to have gone yesterday** вам сле́довало пойти́ туда́ вчера́. **2.** (*expr. desirability*): **you ~ to see that film** вы должны́ посмотре́ть э́тот фильм; **you ~ to have seen his face** на́до бы́ло ви́деть его́ лицо́; **I told him the house ~ to be painted** я сказа́л ему́, что сле́дует покра́сить дом. **3.** (*expr. probability*) вероя́тно; **it ~ not to take you long** э́то не должно́ заня́ть у вас мно́го вре́мени.

ounce [aʊns] *n.* (*weight*) у́нция; (*fig.*): **he hasn't an ~ of sense** у него́ нет ни ка́пли здра́вого смы́сла.

our [ˈaʊə(r)] *poss. adj.* наш; **O~ Father** О́тче наш; **in ~ midst** среди́ нас, в на́шей среде́; **in ~ opinion** (*i.e. of the writer*, *editor*) по на́шему мне́нию.

ours [ˈaʊəz] *pron.* & *pred. adj.* наш; **~ is a blue car** на́ша маши́на си́няя; **this tree is ~** э́то де́рево на́ше (*or* принадлежи́т нам); **this government of ~** э́то на́ше прави́тельство.

ourselves [aʊəˈselvz] *pron.* **1.** (*refl.*) себя́; **we washed ~** мы умы́лись; (*after preps.*): **we can only depend on ~** мы мо́жем полага́ться то́лько на себя́ (сами́х); **we were not satisfied with ~** мы бы́ли недово́льны собо́й. **2.** (*emph.*) са́ми; **we ~ were not present** са́ми мы не прису́тствовали. **3.:** **by ~** (*alone*) са́ми по себе́; **we can't do it by ~** (*without aid*) мы не мо́жем сде́лать э́то са́ми/одни́.

oust [aʊst] *v.t.* вытесня́ть, вы́теснить; (*expel*) выгоня́ть, вы́гнать.

out [aʊt] *pred. adj.* & *adv.* (*for phrasal vv. see relevant v. entries*) **1.** (*away from home*, *office*, *room*, *usual place etc.*): **he is ~** его́ нет до́ма; **he is, was ~ for lunch** он ушёл обе́дать; **let's have dinner ~!** пойдёмте обе́дать в рестора́н!; **it was the maid's night ~** у прислу́ги был свобо́дный ве́чер; **the book was ~** (*of the library*) кни́га была́ вы́дана (*or* на рука́х); **the children are ~** (*of school*) **early today** сего́дня дете́й ра́но отпусти́ли; (*of expulsion*): **the crowd were shouting 'Stevens ~!'** толпа́ крича́ла: «доло́й Сти́венса!» (*or* «Сти́венса вон!»); **the workers are ~** (*on strike*) рабо́чие басту́ют; **~!** (*at tennis*) нет! **2.** (**~** *of doors*) на дворе́; на у́лице; **he was ~ and about all day** он был на нога́х весь день; (*fig.*, *intent*): **they are ~ to get him** они́ наме́рены его́ пойма́ть; **he is ~ for my blood** он жа́ждет мое́й кро́ви. **3.** (*open*): **the blossom is ~** цветы́ распусти́лись; (*visible*): **the moon came ~** луна́ показа́лась; вы́плыла луна́; **the stars are ~** звёзды вы́сыпали; **the sun will be ~ this afternoon** по́сле полу́дня пока́жется со́лнце; (*revealed*): **the secret is, was ~** секре́т раскры́лся; **~ with it!** отвеча́йте!; говори́те же, что́ у вас на душе́!; (*published*, *issued*): **my book is ~ at last** моя́ кни́га вы́шла, наконе́ц, из печа́ти; **when will the results be ~?** когда́ объя́вят результа́ты?; **there is a warrant ~ for his arrest** име́ется о́рдер на его́ аре́ст. **4.** (*at departure*): **will you see me ~?** вы меня́ прово́дите (до двере́й)?; **on the voyage ~** на пути́ туда́; **he stumbled on the way ~** выходя́, он споткну́лся; (*at a distance*): **~ at sea** в откры́том мо́ре; **when they were four days ~** на четвёртый день пла́вания; **the tide is ~** сейча́с отли́в. **5.** (*coll.*, *~ of favour*, *fashion*): **short hair is ~** коро́ткая стри́жка не в мо́де; (*inadmissible*): **that idea is ~ for a start** э́та иде́я исключа́ется с са́мого нача́ла; (*astray*, *wrong*): **be ~ in one's calculations** ошиб|а́ться, -и́ться в расчётах; **I wasn't far ~** я не на мно́го оши́бся; **my watch is 10 minutes ~** мои́ часы́ отстаю́т/спеша́т на де́сять мину́т. **6.** (*ended*, *over*): **before the week is ~** до оконча́ния неде́ли; (*extinguished*): **the fire is ~** ого́нь поту́х; (*conflagration*) пожа́р ко́нчился; **lights ~!** гаси́те свет!; (*unconscious*) без созна́ния. **7.**: **~ and ~** соверше́нно, по́лностью; **~ and away** безусло́вно, несравне́нно. **8.**: **~ of** (*movement*): **as they came ~ of the theatre** когда́ они́ вы́шли из теа́тра; **he leapt ~ of bed** он вскочи́л с посте́ли; (*material*): **made ~ of silk** (сши́тый) из шёлка, шёлковый; (*from among*): **2 students ~ of 40** два студе́нта из сорока́; (*motive*): **~ of pity/love** из жа́лости/любви́ (*к кому/чему*); **~ of grief/joy** с го́ря/ра́дости; **~ of boredom** от/со ску́ки; (*outside*): **~ of danger** вне опа́сности; **~ of doors** на у́лице, на во́здухе; **~ of (its) place** не на ме́сте; **it's ~ of the question** об э́том не мо́жет быть и ре́чи; **~ of town** за́ городом; **he is ~ of town** его́ нет в го́роде; он уе́хал; **feel ~ of it** чу́вствовать (*impf.*) себя́ чужи́м (*or* ни при чём); (*not conforming or amenable to*): **~ of condition** не в фо́рме; **~ of control** вне контро́ля; **~ of fashion** не в мо́де; **~ of sorts** не в свое́й таре́лке; не в ду́хе/настрое́нии; **~ of step** не в но́гу; **~ of tune** расстро́енный; не в тон; (*without*): **~ of breath** запыха́вшийся; **~ of work** безрабо́тный; **we are ~ of sugar** у нас ко́нчился са́хар; (*origin*): **a scene ~ of a play** сце́на из пье́сы.

outage ['aʊtɪdʒ] *n.* переры́в, безде́йствие.

out-and-out [ˌaʊtənd'aʊt] *adj.* соверше́нный, по́лный, отъя́вленный.

outback ['aʊtbæk] *n.* глушь.

outbid [aʊt'bɪd] *v.t.* (*at auction*): **~ s.o.** предл|ага́ть, -ожи́ть бо́лее высо́кую це́ну, чем кто-н.

outboard ['aʊtbɔːd] *adj.*: **~ motor** подвесно́й мото́р.

outbound ['aʊtbaʊnd] *adj.* выходя́щий/уходя́щий в рейс.

outbreak ['aʊtbreɪk] *n.* (*of disease*, *anger etc.*) вспы́шка; **~ of hostilities** нача́ло вое́нных де́йствий.

outbuilding ['aʊtˌbɪldɪŋ] *n.* надво́рная постро́йка.

outburst ['aʊtbɜːst] *n.* вспы́шка, взрыв.

outcast ['aʊtkɑːst] *n.* изгна́нник, отве́рженный.
adj. и́згнанный, отве́рженный.

outclass [aʊt'klɑːs] *v.t.* прев|осходи́ть, -зойти́.

outcome ['aʊtkʌm] *n.* (*result*) результа́т; (*issue*) исхо́д; (*consequence*) (по)сле́дствие.

outcrop ['aʊtkrɒp] *n.* (*geol.*) обнаже́ние поро́д.

outcry ['aʊtkraɪ] *n.* (*noise*) крик, вы́крик; (*protest*) проте́ст; (обще́ственное) негодова́ние.

outdated [aʊt'deɪtɪd] *adj.* устаре́лый, устаре́вший.

outdistance [aʊt'dɪst(ə)ns] *v.t.* перег|оня́ть, -на́ть.

outdo [aʊt'duː] *v.t.* прев|осходи́ть, -зойти́.

outdoor ['aʊtdɔː(r)] *adj.*: **~ games** и́гры на откры́том во́здухе; подвижны́е и́гры; **~ clothes** ве́рхнее пла́тье.

outdoors [aʊt'dɔːz] *adv.* на откры́том во́здухе, на дворе́; (*expr. motion*) на во́здух.

outer ['aʊtə(r)] *adj.* (*external*) вне́шний; (*turned to the outside*) нару́жный; (*further away*): **~ space** ко́смос; **the ~ suburbs** да́льние предме́стья.

outermost ['aʊtəˌməʊst] *adj.* са́мый да́льний от це́нтра.

outfit ['aʊtfɪt] *n.* **1.** (*set of equipment*) снаряже́ние, компле́кт; (*of clothes*) костю́м. **2.** (*organized group*) ба́нда (*coll.*); (*mil. unit*) (воен)ча́сть.

outfitter ['aʊtˌfɪtə(r)] *n.*: **gentlemen's ~** владе́лец магази́на мужско́й оде́жды.

outflank [aʊt'flæŋk] *v.t.* об|ходи́ть, -ойти́ фланг +*g.*

outflow ['aʊtfləʊ] *n.* истече́ние; (*e.g. of gold*) уте́чка.

outfox [aʊt'fɒks] *v.t.* (*coll.*) перехитри́ть (*pf.*).

outgoing ['aʊtˌgəʊɪŋ] *adj.* **1.** (*departing*): **~ ship** уходя́щее су́дно; **~ mail** исходя́щая по́чта; **the ~ president** президе́нт, чей срок на посту́ истека́ет. **2.** (*sociable*): **an ~ personality** общи́тельный хара́ктер; ужи́вчивый челове́к.

outgoings ['aʊtˌgəʊɪŋz] *n.* расхо́ды (*m. pl.*), изде́ржки (*f. pl.*).

outgrow [aʊt'grəʊ] *v.t.* **1.** (*grow taller than*) перераст|а́ть, -и́; (*grow too large for*) выраста́ть, вы́расти из+*g.* **2.** (*discard with time*) отде́л|ываться, -аться от (*чего*) с во́зрастом.

outgrowth ['aʊtgrəʊθ] *n.* **1.** (*of plants etc.*) наро́ст. **2.** (*result*, *development*) проду́кт, результа́т. **3.** (*offshoot*) о́тпрыск.

outhouse ['aʊthaʊs] *n.* надво́рное строе́ние; (*US*) убо́рная во дворе́.

outing ['aʊtɪŋ] *n.* прогу́лка, экску́рсия; (*on foot*) похо́д; (*picnic*) пикни́к.

outlandish [aʊt'lændɪʃ] *adj.* дико́винный, чудно́й.

outlast [aʊt'lɑːst] *v.t.* (*outlive*) переж|ива́ть, -и́ть.

outlaw ['aʊtlɔː] *n.* лицо́, объя́вленное вне зако́на.
v.t. объяв|ля́ть, -и́ть вне зако́на.

outlay ['aʊtleɪ] *n.* (*expenses*) изде́ржки (*f. pl.*), затра́ты (*f. pl.*).

outlet ['aʊtlet, -lɪt] *n.* **1.** (*lit.*) выходно́е/выпускно́е отве́рстие. **2.** (*fig.*, *comm.*) сбыт. **3.** (*for energies etc.*) отду́шина, вы́ход. **4.** (*elec.*) ште́псельная розе́тка.

outline ['aʊtlaɪn] *n.* **1.** (*contour*) очерта́ние, ко́нтур; (*attr.*) ко́нтурный; **in ~** в о́бщих черта́х. **2.** (*draft*, *sketch*, *summary*) набро́сок, эски́з. **3.** (*scheme*; *schedule*) схе́ма, конспе́кт.
v.t. **1.** (*drawing*) нарисова́ть (*pf.*) ко́нтур (*чего*). **2.** (*give an ~ of*) нам|еча́ть, -е́тить в о́бщих черта́х.

outlive [aʊt'lɪv] *v.t.* переж|ива́ть, -и́ть.

outlook ['aʊtlʊk] *n.* **1.** (*prospect*, *lit.*, *fig.*) вид, перспекти́ва; **the ~ for trade is good** перспекти́вы для торго́вли хоро́шие; (*weather etc.*) прогно́з. **2.** (*point of view*) то́чка зре́ния; (*mental horizon*) кругозо́р.

outlying ['aʊtˌlaɪɪŋ] *adj.* отдалённый, удалённый.

outmoded [aʊt'məʊdɪd] *adj.* старомо́дный.

outnumber [aʊt'nʌmbə(r)] *v.t.* прев|осходи́ть, -зойти́ (*кого, что*) чи́сленно.

out-of-date [ˌaʊtəv'deɪt] *adj.* устаре́лый.

out-of-fashion [ˌaʊtəv'fæʃən] *adj.* старомо́дный.

out-of-the-way [ˌaʊtəvˌðə'weɪ] *adj.* **1.** (*remote*) отдалённый. **2.** (*obscure*) малоизве́стный.

out-of-work [ˌaʊtəv'wɜːk] *adj.* безрабо́тный.

outpace [aʊt'peɪs] *v.t.* об|гоня́ть, -огна́ть.

out-patient ['aʊtˌpeɪʃ(ə)nt] *n.* амбулато́рный больно́й; **~ department** поликли́ника.

outplay [aʊt'pleɪ] *v.t.* обы́гр|ывать, -а́ть.

outpost ['aʊtpəʊst] *n.* (*mil.*) аванпо́ст; (*settlement*) отдалённое поселе́ние.

outpouring ['aʊtˌpɔːrɪŋ] *n.* излия́ние.

output ['aʊtpʊt] *n.* **1.** (*production*) вы́пуск, проду́кция, произво́дство; **literary ~** литерату́рная проду́кция; (*of mine*) добы́ча; (*of power station*) мо́щность. **2.** (*productivity*) производи́тельность.

outrage ['aʊtreɪdʒ] *n.* безобра́зие, оскорбле́ние; наруше́ние прили́чий.
v.t. (*offend*, *insult*) оскорб|ля́ть, -и́ть.

outrageous [aʊt'reɪdʒəs] *adj.* безобра́зный, возмути́тельный, вопию́щий; **an ~ remark** возмути́тельное замеча́ние.

outrider ['aʊtˌraɪdə(r)] *n.* (*usu. pl.*) полице́йский эско́рт.

outright ['aʊtraɪt] *adj.* (*open*, *direct*) прямо́й, откры́тый; (*positive*) соверше́нный; **he gave an ~ denial**

он категори́чески отрица́л (свою́ вину́ *и т.п.*).

adv. (*openly*, *right out*) пря́мо, откры́то; (*at once*) сра́зу; (*once and for all*) раз (и) навсегда́; **own sth.** ~ владе́ть (*impf.*) чем-н. по́лностью.

outrun [aʊt'rʌn] *v.t.* (*outstrip*) опере|жа́ть, -ди́ть; (*run farther than*) перег|оня́ть, -на́ть.

outsell [aʊt'sel] *v.t.*: ~ **s.o.** прод|ава́ть, -а́ть бо́льше, чем кто-н.

outset ['aʊtset] *n.* нача́ло; **at the** ~ внача́ле; **from the** ~ с са́мого нача́ла.

outshine [aʊt'ʃaɪn] *v.t.* (*lit.*, *fig.*) затм|ева́ть, -и́ть.

outside [aʊt'saɪd, 'aʊtsaɪd] *n.* нару́жная сторона́; (*outer surface*) вне́шняя пове́рхность; **from** ~ извне́; **from, on the** ~ снару́жи; **the** ~ **of the house needs painting** нару́жные сте́ны до́ма нужда́ются в покра́ске; **at the (very)** ~ са́мое бо́льшее.

adj. **1.** (*external*, *exterior*) нару́жный, вне́шний; ~ **broadcast** внестуди́йная переда́ча. **2.** (*extreme*) кра́йний; ~ **chance** небольшо́й шанс. **3.** (*not belonging*) посторо́нний, вне́шний; ~ **help** посторо́нняя по́мощь; **the** ~ **world** вне́шний мир.

adv. снару́жи; извне́; (*to the* ~) нару́жу; (*out of doors*) на у́лице; на дворе́.

prep. **1.** вне+*g.*; (*beyond bounds of*) за преде́лами +*g.*; ~ **the door/window** за две́рью/окно́м; **he went** ~ **the house** он вы́шел и́з дому во двор. **2.** (*apart from*) за исключе́нием +*g.*; **he has no interests** ~ **his work** вне/кро́ме рабо́ты его ничего́ не интересу́ет.

outsider [aʊt'saɪdə(r)] *n.* посторо́нний; (*in contest*, *lit.*, *fig.*) аутса́йдер.

outsize ['aʊtsaɪz] *n.* разме́р бо́льше станда́ртного.

adj. нестанда́ртный; больши́х разме́ров.

outskirts ['aʊtskɜːts] *n.* (*of town*) окра́ина.

outspoken [aʊt'spəʊkən] *adj.* прямо́й, открове́нный.

outspread [aʊt'spred, 'aʊtspred] *adj.* распростёртый.

outstanding [aʊt'stændɪŋ] *adj.* (*prominent*, *eminent*) выдаю́щийся; (*still to be done*) невы́полненный; (*unpaid*): ~ **accounts** невы́плаченные счета́.

outstay [aʊt'steɪ] *v.t.*: ~ **one's welcome** загости́ться (*pf.*); злоупотреб|ля́ть, -и́ть гостеприи́мством.

outstretched ['aʊtstretʃd, aʊt'stretʃd] *adj.* протя́нутый, растяну́вшийся.

outstrip [aʊt'strɪp] *v.t.* (*lit.*, *fig.*) опере|жа́ть, -ди́ть; об|гоня́ть, -огна́ть.

out-tray ['aʊttreɪ] *n.* корзи́нка для исходя́щих бума́г.

outvote [aʊt'vəʊt] *v.t.*: ~ **s.o.** наб|ира́ть, -ра́ть бо́льше голосо́в, чем кто-н.

outward ['aʊtwəd] *adj.* (*external*) нару́жный, вне́шний; ~ **form** вне́шность; **to all** ~ **appearances** су́дя по вне́шности; (*superficial*) пове́рхностный.

adv.: ~ **bound** выходя́щий/уходя́щий в пла́вание.

outwardly ['aʊtwədlɪ] *adv.* вне́шне, снару́жи; (*at sight*) на вид.

outwards ['aʊtwədz] *adv.* нару́жу.

outweigh [aʊt'weɪ] *v.t.* переве́|шивать, -сить.

outwit [aʊt'wɪt] *v.t.* перехитри́ть (*pf.*).

outworn [aʊt'wɔːn] *adj.* (*of ideas etc.*) устаре́лый, изби́тый.

oval ['əʊv(ə)l] *n.* ова́л.

adj. ова́льный.

ovarian [ə'veərɪən] *adj.* яи́чниковый.

ovary ['əʊvərɪ] *n.* яи́чник.

ovation [əʊ'veɪʃ(ə)n] *n.* ова́ция.

oven ['ʌv(ə)n] *n.* духо́вка; (*baker's*, *industrial*) печь.

cpd. ~**ware** *n.* огнеупо́рная посу́да.

over[1] ['əʊvə(r)] *n.* (*cricket*) се́рия броско́в.

over[2] ['əʊvə(r)] *adv.* (*for phrasal vv. with* **over** *see relevant v.*) **1.** (*across*; *to*, *on the other side*): ~ **there** (вон) там; ~ **against** (*opposite*) про́тив/напро́тив+*g.*; **I asked him** ~ я пригласи́л его́ (к себе́); **he's** ~**!** (*has jumped clear*) он перепры́гнул!; он взял высоту́!; ~ **(to you)!** (*said by radio operator*) перехожу́ на приём!; (*to the ground*): **one push and** ~ **I went!** толчо́к — и я растяну́лся на земле́! **2.** (*covering surface*): **all** ~ (*everywhere*) повсю́ду; **hills covered** ~ **with trees** холмы́, сплошь покры́тые дере́вьями; **your shoes are all** ~ **mud** ва́ши ту́фли все в грязи́; **the whole world** ~ по всему́ ми́ру; во всём ми́ре; **that's John all** ~ э́то типи́чный Джон; **John is his father all** ~ Джон — вы́литый оте́ц. **3.** (*at an end*): **the meeting is** ~ собра́ние ко́нчилось; **the holidays are half** ~ уже́ прошла́ полови́на кани́кул; **it's all** ~ **with their marriage** с их супру́жеской жи́знью поко́нчено; **the doctor could see it was all** ~ **with him** врачу́ бы́ло я́сно, что он безнадёжен. **4.** (*also* ~ **again:** *for a second time*; *once more*) опя́ть, сно́ва, ещё раз; ~ **and** ~ **again** ты́сячу раз; **he read it three times** ~ он три́жды э́то перечита́л; **if I had my life** ~ **again** е́сли б мне довело́сь прожи́ть жизнь за́ново. **5.** (*in excess*): **sums of £5 and** ~ су́ммы в 5 фу́нтов и вы́ше; **the parcel weighs 2 pounds or** ~ посы́лка ве́сит два фу́нта, е́сли не бо́льше; **I had £3 (left)** ~ у меня́ ещё остава́лось три фу́нта.

prep. **1.** (*above*): **a roof** ~ **one's head** кры́ша над голово́й; **a seagull flew** ~ **us** над на́ми пролете́ла ча́йка; (*expr. division*): **five** ~ **two** (*math.*) пять дробь два; **1** ~ **2** одна́ втора́я; (*fig.*): **the lecture was** ~ **their heads** ле́кция была́ вы́ше их понима́ния; **his voice was heard** ~ **the crowd** его́ го́лос раздава́лся над толпо́й. **2.** (*to the far side of*): **a bridge** ~ **the river** мост че́рез ре́ку; **he climbed** ~ **the fence** он переле́з че́рез забо́р; ~ **the sea** за́ море; ~ **the hills** за го́ры; **he swam** ~ **the river** он переплы́л ре́ку; **he looked** ~ **his shoulder** он огляну́лся; (*down from*): **he fell** ~ **the cliff** он упа́л со скалы́; (*against*): **he tripped** ~ **a stone** он споткну́лся о ка́мень. **3.** (*on the far side of*): **he lives** ~ **the ocean** он живёт по ту сто́рону океа́на (*or* за океа́ном); **he lives** ~ **the way** он живёт че́рез у́лицу; **she is** ~ **the operation** опера́ция у неё прошла́ благополу́чно. **4.** (*resting on*; *covering*): **he carried a raincoat** ~ **his arm** он шёл, переки́нув плащ че́рез ру́ку; **crossing one leg** ~ **the other** переки́нув но́гу за́ ногу; **a change came** ~ **him** с ним произошла́ переме́на; **what has come** ~ **you?** что с ва́ми случи́лось?; (*across*, ~ *the surface of*): ~ **the whole country** по всей стране́; **a flush spread** ~ **her face** кра́ска разлила́сь по её лицу́; **all** ~ **the world** во всём ми́ре; по всему́ све́ту; **the news was all** ~ **town** но́вость разошла́сь по го́роду. **5.** (*more than*): ~ **a year ago** бо́льше/свы́ше го́да тому́ наза́д; **he can't be** ~ **60** ему́ (ника́к) не бо́льше шести́десяти (лет); ~ **and above his wages** в добавле́ние к его́ зарпла́те; ~ **and above that** (*moreover*) к тому́ же; **children** ~ **5** де́ти ста́рше пяти́ лет. **6.** (*in command*, *charge*, *control of*): **he was ruler** ~ **several tribes** он был вождём не́скольких племён; **I have two people** ~ **me** на́до мной ещё два нача́льника. **7.** (*as long as*): **can you stay** ~ **the whole week?** мо́жете ли вы оста́ться на всю/це́лую неде́лю?; (*during*): **much has happened** ~ **the past two years** за после́дние два го́да мно́го чего́ произошло́. **8.** (*near*; *leaning*, *bending* ~): **they were sitting** ~ **the fire** они́ сиде́ли у ками́на; **I stood** ~ **him while he finished it** я не отходи́л от него́, пока́ он не ко́нчил. **9.** (*while engaged in*): **he takes too long** ~ **his work** он сли́шком до́лго во́зится со свое́й рабо́той; **he fell asleep** ~ **the job** он засну́л за рабо́той; (*while consuming*): **we chatted** ~ **a bottle of wine** мы болта́ли за буты́лкой вина́. **10.** (*on the subject of*; *because of*): **he laughed** ~ **our misfortune** он смея́лся над на́шей бедо́й; **he gets angry** ~ **nothing** он зли́тся из-за пустяко́в; **a quarrel** ~ **money** ссо́ра из-за де́нег. **11.** (*through the medium of*): **I heard it** ~ **the radio** я слы́шал э́то по ра́дио.

over-abundance [ˌəʊvərə'bʌnd(ə)ns] *n.* избы́ток.
over-abundant [ˌəʊvərə'bʌnd(ə)nt] *adj.* избы́точный.
overact [ˌəʊvər'ækt] *v.t. & i.* переигр|ывать, -а́ть.
over-active [ˌəʊvər'æktɪv] *adj.* сверхакти́вный.
over-activity [ˌəʊvəræk'tɪvɪtɪ] *n.* повы́шенная акти́вность.
overall ['əʊvərˌɔːl] *n.* рабо́чий хала́т; (*pl.*) комбинезо́н.
adj. (*total*) по́лный; (*general*) (все)о́бщий.
adv. (*taken as a whole*) в це́лом.
overawe [ˌəʊvər'ɔː] *v.t.* внуш|а́ть, -и́ть благогове́йный страх +*d.*
overbalance [ˌəʊvə'bæləns] *v.t.* (*knock over*) опроки́|дывать, -нуть; (*capsize*) перев|ора́чивать, -ерну́ть.
v.i. теря́ть, по- равнове́сие.
overbear [ˌəʊvə'beə(r)] *v.t.*: **an ~ing manner** вла́стная мане́ра.
overblown [ˌəʊvə'bləʊn] *adj.* разду́тый.
overboard ['əʊvəˌbɔːd] *adv.*: **man ~!** челове́к за борто́м!; **throw ~** (*lit.*) выки́дывать, вы́кинуть за́ борт; (*fig.*) бр|оса́ть, -о́сить.
overburden [ˌəʊvə'bɜːd(ə)n] *v.t.* перегру|жа́ть, -зи́ть.
over-careful [ˌəʊvə'keəfʊl] *adj.* чрезме́рно осторо́жный.
overcast ['əʊvəˌkɑːst] *adj.* (*of sky*) покры́тый облака́ми; (*of weather*) хму́рый.
overcharge [ˌəʊvə'tʃɑːdʒ] *v.t. & i.* запр|а́шивать, -оси́ть чрезме́рную це́ну у (*кого*); (*elec.*) перезаря|жа́ть, -ди́ть; (*fig.*) перегру|жа́ть, -зи́ть.
overcoat ['əʊvəˌkəʊt] *n.* пальто́ (*indecl.*); (*mil.*) шине́ль.
overcome [ˌəʊvə'kʌm] *v.t. & i.* (*prevail over, get the better of*) преодол|ева́ть, -е́ть; (*be victorious over*) побе|жда́ть, -ди́ть; (*of emotion*) охва́т|ывать, -и́ть; **he was ~ by rage** он был охва́чен я́ростью; (*of heat*) изнур|я́ть, -и́ть; (*of hunger*) истощ|а́ть, -и́ть.
over-confidence [ˌəʊvə'kɒnfɪd(ə)ns] *n.* самонаде́янность, самоуве́ренность.
over-confident [ˌəʊvə'kɒnfɪd(ə)nt] *adj.* самонаде́янный, самоуве́ренный; **he was ~ of success** он был сли́шком уве́рен в успе́хе.
overcook [ˌəʊvə'kʊk] *v.t.* пережа́р|ивать, -ить; перева́р|ивать, -и́ть.
over-critical [ˌəʊvə'krɪtɪk(ə)l] *adj.* чрезме́рно суро́вый.
overcrowd [ˌəʊvə'kraʊd] *v.t.* переп|олня́ть, -о́лнить.
overdevelop [ˌəʊvədɪ'veləp] *v.t.* (*phot.*) передержи|ивать, -а́ть (при проявле́нии); **~ed** чрезме́рно ра́звитый; преувели́ченный.
overdo [ˌəʊvə'duː] *v.t.* (*overcook*) пережа́ри|вать, -ть; **~ it** переб|а́рщивать, -орщи́ть; переусе́рдствовать (*pf.*) (*в чём*); **don't ~ it** (*work too hard*) не перенапряга́йтесь/переутомля́йтесь.
overdose ['əʊvəˌdəʊs] *n.* передозиро́вка; **she died of an ~** она́ умерла́ от чрезме́рной до́зы.
overdraft ['əʊvəˌdrɑːft] *n.* превыше́ние креди́та.
overdraw [ˌəʊvə'drɔː] *v.t.*: **~ one's account** прев|ыша́ть, -ы́сить креди́т; **I am £100 ~n** у меня́ на счету́ 100 фу́нтов дефици́та.
overdress [ˌəʊvə'dres] *v.t. & i.*: **she ~es (or is ~ed)** она́ одева́ется/оде́та сли́шком наря́дно.
overdue [ˌəʊvə'djuː] *adj.* запозда́лый; **the train is ~** по́езд запа́здывает; **the baby is 2 weeks ~** ребёнок до́лжен был роди́ться две неде́ли тому́ наза́д; (*of payment*) просро́ченный.
overeat [ˌəʊvər'iːt] *v.i.* пере|еда́ть, -е́сть; объ|еда́ться, -е́сться.
over-emphasize [əʊvər'emfəˌsaɪz] *v.t.* изли́шне подчёрк|ивать, -ну́ть.
over-enthusiastic [ˌəʊvərɪnˌθjuːzɪ'æstɪk, -θuːzɪ'æstɪk] *adj.* с изли́шним энтузиа́змом; **he was not ~** он не́ был в восто́рге.
overestimate[1] [ˌəʊvər'estɪˌmeɪt] *n.* переоце́нка.
overestimate[2] [ˌəʊvər'estɪˌmeɪt] *v.t.* переоце́н|ивать, -и́ть.
over-excite [ˌəʊvərɪk'saɪt] *v.t.* кра́йне возбу|жда́ть, -ди́ть.
over-excitement [ˌəʊvərɪk'saɪtmənt] *n.* перевозбужде́ние.
over-exert [ˌəʊvərɪg'zɜːt] *v.t.* перенапр|яга́ть, -я́чь.
over-exertion [ˌəʊvərɪg'zɜːʃ(ə)n] *n.* пернапряже́ние.
over-expose [ˌəʊvərɪk'spəʊz] *v.t.* (*phot.*) переде́рж|ивать, -а́ть.
over-exposure [ˌəʊvərɪk'spəʊzjə(r)] *n.* переде́ржка.
overfeed [ˌəʊvə'fiːd] *v.t.* перек|а́рмливать, -орми́ть.
overfish [ˌəʊvə'fɪʃ] *v.i.* истощ|а́ть, -и́ть запа́сы ры́бы.
overflow ['əʊvəˌfləʊ] *n.* (*flowing ~*) разли́в; (*superfluity*) избы́ток; (*outlet*) сливно́е отве́рстие.
v.t. & i. перел|ива́ться, -и́ться (*через что*); **the river ~s its banks** река́ выхо́дит из берего́в; **~ing with** перепо́лненный +*i.*
overfulfil [ˌəʊvəfʊl'fɪl] (*US* **-l**) *v.t.* перев|ыполня́ть, -ы́полнить.
overfulfilment [ˌəʊvəfʊl'fɪlmənt] (*US* **-ll-**) *n.* перевыполне́ние.
overfull [ˌəʊvə'fʊl] *adj.* перепо́лненный (+*i.*).
overground ['əʊvəˌgraʊnd] *adj.* надзе́мный.
overgrow [ˌəʊvə'grəʊ] *v.t.* зараст|а́ть, -и́; **the garden was ~n with nettles** сад заро́с крапи́вой.
overhang ['əʊvəˌhæŋ] *n.* вы́ступ.
v.t. & i. выступа́ть (*impf.*) над+*i.*; (*fig.*) нав|иса́ть, -и́снуть над+*i.*
overhaul ['əʊvəˌhɔːl] *n.* (*reconditioning*) восстановле́ние; (*thorough repair*) капита́льный ремо́нт.
v.t. **1.** осм|а́тривать, -отре́ть; восстан|а́вливать, -ови́ть; ремонти́ровать, от-. **2.** (*overtake*) дог|оня́ть, -на́ть.
overhead ['əʊvəˌhed] *n.* (*usu. pl.*) накладны́е расхо́ды (*m. pl.*).
adj. **1.** (*above ground level*): **~ projector** графопрое́ктор; **~ railway** надзе́мная желе́зная доро́га; **~ wires, lines** возду́шные провода́. **2.** (*comm.*): **~ charges, costs** накладны́е расхо́ды.
adv. наверху́; (*above one's head*) над голово́й.
overhear [ˌəʊvə'hɪə(r)] *v.t.* (*intentionally*) подслу́ш|ивать, -ать; (*accidentally*) неча́янно услы́шать (*pf.*).
overheat [ˌəʊvə'hiːt] *v.t. & i.* перегр|ева́ть(ся), -е́ть(ся).
over-indulge [ˌəʊvərɪn'dʌldʒ] *v.t.* (*spoil*) сли́шком балова́ть, из-.
v.i.: **~ in sth.** злоупотребля́ть (*impf.*) чем-н.
over-indulgence [ˌəʊvərɪn'dʌldʒəns] *n.* чрезме́рное баловство́; злоупотребле́ние (+*i*).
over-indulgent [ˌəʊvərɪn'dʌldʒənt] *adj.* потака́ющий; сли́шком снисходи́тельный.
overjoyed [ˌəʊvə'dʒɔɪd] *adj.* вне себя́ от ра́дости.
overkill ['əʊvəkɪl] *n.* многокра́тное уничтоже́ние.
overladen [ˌəʊvə'leɪd(ə)n] *adj.* перегру́женный.
overland ['əʊvəˌlænd] *adj.* сухопу́тный.
adv. по су́ше.
overlap ['əʊvəˌlæp] *v.t.* покр|ыва́ть, -ы́ть части́чно.
v.i. заходи́ть (*impf.*) (оди́н на друго́й); (*coincide*) (части́чно) совпада́ть (*impf.*).
overlay ['əʊvəˌleɪ] *n.* покры́тие.
v.i. покр|ыва́ть, -ы́ть.
overleaf [ˌəʊvə'liːf] *adv.* на оборо́те страни́цы.
overload ['əʊvəˌləʊd] *n.* перегру́зка.
v.t. перегру|жа́ть, -зи́ть.
over-long [ˌəʊvə'lɒŋ] *adj.* сли́шком дли́нный/до́лгий.
adv. сли́шком до́лго.
overlook [ˌəʊvə'lʊk] *v.t.* **1.** (*look down on*) смотре́ть, по- све́рху на+*a.*; (*tower above*): **the mountains ~ the sea** го́ры возвыша́ются над мо́рем. **2.** (*open on to*) выходи́ть (*impf.*) на+*a.*; **a view ~ing the lake** вид на о́зеро. **3.** (*fail to notice*) просмотре́ть (*pl.*); пропус|ка́ть, -ти́ть; **the mistake was completely ~ed** никто́ не заме́тил оши́бки. **4.** (*excuse*) про|ща́ть, -сти́ть; **I will ~ his mistakes** я не бу́ду задéрживаться на его́ оши́бках.

overly ['əʊvəlɪ] *adv.* сли́шком, чересчу́р.
over-much [ˌəʊvə'mʌtʃ] *adv.* сли́шком мно́го; чрезме́рно.
overnight [ˌəʊvə'naɪt] *adj.*: ~ **preparations** подгото́вка накану́не; **an ~ stay** ночёвка, ночле́г.
adv.(*through the night*) всю ночь; (*during the night*) за́ ночь; **stay ~** ночева́ть, за-; (*fig.*) **he rose to fame ~** сла́ва пришла́ к нему́ внеза́пно.
overpass ['əʊvəˌpɑːs] *n.* эстака́да.
overpay [ˌəʊvə'peɪ] *v.t.* перепла́|чивать, -ти́ть.
overpayment [ˌəʊvə'peɪmənt] *n.* перепла́та.
overplay [ˌəʊvə'pleɪ] *v.t.* (*overact*) переигр|ывать, -а́ть; (*overemphasize*) прид|ава́ть, -а́ть чрезме́рное значе́ние +*d.*; ~ **one's hand** (*fig.*) переоце́н|ивать, -и́ть свои́ возмо́жности.
overpopulated [ˌəʊvə'pɒpjʊˌleɪtɪd] *adj.* перенаселённый.
overpopulation [ˌəʊvəpɒpjʊ'leɪʃ(ə)n] *n.* перенаселе́ние.
overpower [ˌəʊvə'paʊə(r)] *v.t.* одол|ева́ть, -е́ть; **~ing grief** сокруша́ющее го́ре; **I found the heat ~ing** я изнемога́л от жары́.
over-production [ˌəʊvəprə'dʌkʃ(ə)n] *n.* перепроизво́дство.
overrate [ˌəʊvə'reɪt] *v.t.* переоце́н|ивать, -и́ть.
over-react [ˌəʊvərɪ'ækt] *v.i.* реаги́ровать (*impf.*) чрезме́рно ре́зко.
over|ride [ˌəʊvə'raɪd] *v.t.*: **he ~rode my objections** он отве́рг мои́ возраже́ния; **~riding** первостепе́нный; реша́ющий; **an ~riding objection** неопровержи́мое возраже́ние.
over-ripe [ˌəʊvə'raɪp] *adj.* перезре́лый.
overrule [ˌəʊvə'ruːl] *v.t.* (*annul*) аннули́ровать (*impf.*, *pf.*); отмен|я́ть, -и́ть; ~ **a claim** отв|ерга́ть, -е́ргнуть прете́нзию; **I was ~d** моё возраже́ние отве́ргли.
overrun [ˌəʊvə'rʌn] *v.t.* **1.** (*of enemy*) соверш|а́ть, -и́ть набе́г на+*a.* **2.** (*of vermin, weeds etc.*: *infest*): **the garden is ~ with weeds** сад заро́с сорняка́ми; **the house is ~ with rats** дом киши́т кры́сами. **3.** (*go beyond*): **the speaker overran his time** выступа́ющий превы́сил регла́мент.
overseas ['əʊvəˌsiːz] *adj.* замо́рский; (*foreign*) заграни́чный; **~ trade** вне́шняя торго́вля.
adv. за́ мо́рем; **go ~** е́хать (*det.*), по- за́ мо́ре.
oversee [ˌəʊvə'siː] *v.t.* надзира́ть (*impf.*) за+*i.*
overseer ['əʊvəˌsiːə(r)] *n.* надсмо́трщик, надзира́тель (*m.*).
overshadow [ˌəʊvə'ʃædəʊ] *v.t.* (*lit.*, *fig.*) заслон|я́ть, -и́ть; затм|ева́ть, -и́ть.
overshoe ['əʊvəˌʃuː] *n.* гало́ша.
overshoot ['əʊvəˌʃuːt] *v.t.*: **~ the mark** (*lit.*) взять (*pf.*) вы́ше це́ли; (*fig.*) преувели́чи|вать, -ть.
v.i.: **the plane overshot on landing** самолёт перелете́л при поса́дке.
oversight ['əʊvəˌsaɪt] *n.* (*failure to notice*) недосмо́тр, упуще́ние; (*supervision*) надзо́р.
over-simplification [ˌəʊvəsɪmplɪfɪ'keɪʃ(ə)n] *n.* сли́шком большо́е упроще́ние; вульгариза́ция.
over-simplify [ˌəʊvə'sɪmplɪˌfaɪ] *v.t.* сли́шком упро|ща́ть, -сти́ть.
oversize(d) ['əʊvəˌsaɪzd] *adj.* о́чень/сли́шком большо́го разме́ра.
oversleep [ˌəʊvə'sliːp] *v.i.* проспа́ть (*pf.*).
overspill ['əʊvəspɪl] *n.* (*of population*) избы́ток населе́ния; **~ town** го́род-спу́тник.
overstate [ˌəʊvə'steɪt] *v.t.* преувели́ч|ивать, -ить.
overstatement ['əʊvəˌsteɪtmənt] *n.* преувеличе́ние.
overstay [ˌəʊvə'steɪ] *v.t.*: **~ one's welcome** загости́ться (*pf.*).
overstep [ˌəʊvə'step] *v.t.* преступ|а́ть, -и́ть (*что or грани́цы чего*).
overt [əʊ'vɜːt, 'əʊvɜːt] *adj.* (*open*) откры́тый; (*obvious, evident*) я́вный, очеви́дный.
overtak|e [ˌəʊvə'teɪk] *v.t.* (*catch up with*) дог|оня́ть, -на́ть; (*outstrip*) об|гоня́ть, -огна́ть; **'no ~ing!'** «обго́н запрещён!»; **misfortune overtook him** его́ пости́гло несча́стье.
overtax [ˌəʊvə'tæks] *v.t.* (*lit.*) обремен|я́ть, -и́ть чрезме́рными нало́гами; (*strength, patience etc.*) истощ|а́ть, -и́ть.
over-the-top [ˌəʊvəðə'tɒp] *adj.* чрезме́рный.
overthrow[1] ['əʊvəˌθrəʊ] *n.* (*ruin, destruction*) ниспроверже́ние; (*defeat*) пораже́ние.
overthrow[2] [ˌəʊvə'θrəʊ] *v.t.* (*lit.*, *fig.*) ниспров|ерга́ть, -е́ргнуть; пора|жа́ть, -зи́ть.
overtime ['əʊvəˌtaɪm] *n.* сверхуро́чное вре́мя; (*work*) сверхуро́чная рабо́та, перерабо́тка.
adv. сверхуро́чно.
overtired [ˌəʊvə'taɪəd] *adj.* переутомлённый.
overtone ['əʊvəˌtəʊn] *n.* оберто́н; (*fig.*, *also*) отте́нок.
overture ['əʊvəˌtjʊə(r)] *n.* **1.** (*mus.*) увертю́ра. **2.** (*pl.*): **peace ~s** ми́рные предложе́ния.
overturn [ˌəʊvə'tɜːn] *v.t. & i.* опроки́|дывать(ся), -нуть(ся).
overvalue [ˌəʊvə'væljuː] *v.t.* ста́вить, по- завы́шенную це́ну на+*a.*
overview ['əʊvəˌvjuː] *n.* обзо́р.
overweening [ˌəʊvə'wiːnɪŋ] *adj.* (*arrogant*) высокоме́рный; **~ ambition** чрезме́рное тщесла́вие.
overweight ['əʊvəˌweɪt] *adj.* ве́сящий бо́льше но́рмы; **he is several pounds ~** он ве́сит на не́сколько фу́нтов бо́льше но́рмы; **~ luggage** (опла́чиваемый) изли́шек багажа́.
overwhelm [ˌəʊvə'welm] *v.t.* (*weigh down*) подав|ля́ть, -и́ть; (*in battle*) сокруш|а́ть, -и́ть; (*fig.*): **his kindness ~ed me** я был ошеломлён его́ доброто́й; **~ing majority** подавля́ющее большинство́.
overwind [ˌəʊvə'waɪnd] *v.t.*: **~ a watch** перекрути́ть (*pf.*) пружи́ну у часо́в.
overwork [ˌəʊvə'wɜːk] *n.* (*overstrain*) перенапряже́ние, переутомле́ние.
v.t. & i. переутом|ля́ть(ся), -и́ть(ся).
overwrought [ˌəʊvə'rɔːt] *adj.* сли́шком возбуждённый, не́рвничающий; **she is ~** у неё не́рвное истоще́ние.
oviduct ['əʊvɪˌdʌkt] *n.* яйцево́д.
ovulate ['ɒvjʊˌleɪt] *v.i.* овули́ровать (*impf.*, *pf.*).
ovulation [ˌɒvjʊ'leɪʃ(ə)n] *n.* овуля́ция.
ovum ['əʊvəm] *n.* яйцо́.
owe [əʊ] *v.t. & i.* **1.** (*be under obligation to pay*) быть до́лжным +*d.*; **I ~d him a large sum** я был до́лжен ему́ большу́ю су́мму; **I ~ you for the ticket** я вам до́лжен за́ биле́т; **he ~s 4 roubles** за ним оста́лось четы́ре рубля́; **he still ~s for last year** у него́ ещё задо́лженность за про́шлый год. **2.** (*be indebted for*) быть обя́занным (*кому чем*); **I ~ it to you that I am still alive** я обя́зан вам жи́знью; **he ~s his success to hard work** свои́м успе́хом он обя́зан неуста́нной рабо́те.
owing ['əʊɪŋ] *adj.* **1.** (*yet to be paid*) причита́ющийся; **there is 2 roubles ~ to you from me** вам причита́ется два рубля́ с меня́. **2.**: **~ to** (*attributable to*; *caused by*) по причи́не +*g.*; всле́дствие+*g.*; (*thanks to*) благодаря́+*d.*; (*on account of, because of*) из-за+*g.*; **~ to fog we were late** из-за тума́на мы опозда́ли.
owl [aʊl] *n.* сова́; **barn ~** сипу́ха; **tawny ~** нея́сыть.
own [əʊn] *pron.*: **come into one's ~** доби́ться (*pf.*) призна́ния; **get one's ~ back on s.o.** поквита́ться (*pf.*) с кем-н.; **hold one's ~** стоя́ть (*impf.*) на своём; **on one's ~** (*alone*) в одино́честве; (*unaided, independently*) самостоя́тельно, незави́симо, сам (по себе́).
adj. со́бственный, свой; **my ~ house** мой со́бственный дом; **this house is not my ~** э́тот дом мне не принадлежи́т; **my time is my ~** я хозя́ин своего́ вре́мени; **may I have it for my ~?** мо́жно мне взять э́то насовсе́м?; **can I have a room of my ~?** мо́жно

получи́ть отде́льную ко́мнату?; **a flavour all its ~** осо́бенный арома́т; **with one's ~ hand** собственнору́чно; **he died by his ~ hand** он поко́нчил с собо́й; **he had reasons of his ~** у него́ бы́ли свои́ причи́ны; **he has nothing of his ~** он ничего́ не име́ет; **I love truth for its ~ sake** я люблю́ пра́вду ра́ди пра́вды; **of one's ~ accord** по со́бственному побужде́нию; доброво́льно; **he is his ~ master** он сам себе́ хозя́ин; **my ~ father** мой родно́й оте́ц.

v.t. **1.** (*have as property*) владе́ть +*i.*; **who ~s this bag?** чья э́то су́мка; **the land was ~ed by my father** (э́та) земля́ принадлежа́ла моему́ отцу́. **2.** (*acknowledge*, *admit*) призн|ава́ть, -а́ть.

v.i.: **~ to sth.; ~ up** призн|ава́ться, -а́ться в чём-н.; **I ~ to having told a lie** я призна́юсь, что солга́л.

owner [ˈəʊnə(r)] *n.* владе́лец; хозя́|ин (*fem.* -йка); **at ~'s risk** на отве́тственность владе́льца.

cpd. **~-occupier** *n.* домо... *or* квартировладе́лец.

ownership [ˈəʊnəʃɪp] *n.* со́бственность; владе́ние; **joint ~** о́бщая со́бственность.

ox [ɒks] *n.* бык; (*castrated*) вол.

cpds. **~tail** *n.* воло́вий/бы́чий хвост; **~-tongue** *n.* воло́вий/бы́чий язы́к.

oxalic [ɒkˈsælɪk] *adj.* щаве́левый.

oxide [ˈɒksaɪd] *n.* о́кись.

oxidization [ˌɒksɪˌdaɪˈzeɪʃ(ə)n] *n.* окисле́ние.

oxidize [ˈɒksɪˌdaɪz] *v.t.* окисл|я́ть, -и́ть.

oxyacetylene [ˌɒksɪəˈsetɪˌliːn] *adj.* кислоро́дно-ацетиле́новый.

oxygen [ˈɒksɪdʒ(ə)n] *n.* кислоро́д; **~ mask** кислоро́дная ма́ска; **~ tent** кислоро́дная пала́тка.

oyster [ˈɔɪstə(r)] *n.* у́стрица.

cpds. **~-bed** *n.* у́стричный садо́к; **~-catcher** *n.* (*zool.*) кули́к-соро́ка.

oz. [aʊns(ɪz)] *n.* (*abbr. of* **ounce(s)**) у́нция.

ozone [ˈəʊzəʊn] *n.* озо́н; **~ layer** озо́нный слой.

cpd. **~-friendly** *adj.* не разруша́ющий слой озо́на.

P

p. *n. abbr. of* **1. penny** [ˈpenɪ] (*pl.* ***pence***) пе́нни (*nt. indecl.*), пенс. **2. page** [peɪdʒ] стр, (страни́ца).

PA (*abbr. of* ***personal assistant***) ли́чный секрета́рь.

pa [pɑː] *n.* (*coll.*) па́па (*m.*).

p.a. (*abbr. of* ***per annum***) в год.

pace[1] [peɪs] *n.* **1.** (*step*) шаг. **2.** (*speed of progression*): **mend, quicken one's ~** уск|оря́ть, -о́рить шаг; **keep ~ with** посп|ева́ть, -е́ть за+*i.*; **at a snail's ~** с черепа́шьей ско́ростью.

v.t. **1.** (*measure out*, *traverse in ~s*) шага́ть (*impf.*); **he ~d the floor** он расха́живал по ко́мнате; **I ~d out the distance ~** я изме́рил расстоя́ние шага́ми. **2.** (*set the ~ for*) за|дава́ть, -а́ть темп +*d.*

v.i. ходи́ть (*indet.*); расха́живать (*impf.*); **he ~d up and down** он ходи́л взад и вперёд.

cpd. **~-maker** *n.* ли́дер, задаю́щий темп; (*cardiac aid*) ритмиза́тор се́рдца.

pacific [pəˈsɪfɪk] *n.*: **the P~ (Ocean)** Ти́хий океа́н; (*attr.*) тихоокеа́нский; **the P~ Islands** Океа́ния.

adj. (*peaceful*, *calm*) споко́йный; (*promoting peace*) миролюби́вый.

pacification [ˌpæsɪfɪˈkeɪʃ(ə)n] *n.* умиротворе́ние.

pacifier [ˈpæsɪˌfaɪə(r)] *n.* (*bringer of peace*) миротво́рец; (*US*, *child's dummy*) со́ска, пусты́шка.

pacifism [ˈpæsɪˌfɪz(ə)m] *n.* пацифи́зм.

pacifist [ˈpæsɪfɪst] *n.* пацифи́ст; (*attr.*) пацифи́стский.

pacify [ˈpæsɪˌfaɪ] *v.t.* (*soothe*; *appease*) успок|а́ивать, -о́ить; умиротвор|я́ть, -и́ть; (*rebels etc.*) усмир|я́ть, -и́ть.

pack [pæk] *n.* **1.** (*bundle*) тюк; (*carried on back*) вьюк, у́зел. **2.** (*packet*; *packaged quantity of goods*) па́чка, паке́т. **3.** (*collection*) набо́р; **it's all a ~ of lies** э́то сплошна́я ложь; **a ~ of thieves** ша́йка воро́в. **4.** (*animals*): **~ of hounds** сво́ра го́нчих; **~ of wolves** ста́я волко́в. **5.** (*cards*) коло́да.

v.t. **1.** (*put into container*) упако́в|ывать, -а́ть; укла́дывать, уложи́ть; **~ed lunch** за́втрак в паке́те, кото́рый беру́т с собо́й. **2.** (*put into small space*) наб|ива́ть, -и́ть; **they were ~ed like sardines** они́ наби́лись как се́льди в бо́чке. **3.** (*cover for protection in transit etc.*) уплотн|я́ть, -и́ть; **the glass is ~ed in cotton wool** стекло́ упако́вано в ва́ту. **4.** (*fill*) зап|олня́ть, -о́лнить; **the hall was ~ed** зал был наби́т. **5.: he ~s a punch** (*coll.*) у него́ си́льный уда́р.

v.i. **1. (~ one's clothes)** упако́в|ываться, -а́ться. **2.** (*crowd together*): **they ~ed into the car** они́ вти́снулись в автомоби́ль. **3.: send s.o. ~ing** прогна́ть (*pf.*) кого́-н.

with advs.: **~ away** *v.t.* от|кла́дывать, -ложи́ть; **I ~ed my overcoat away for the summer** я убра́л своё пальто́ на ле́то; **~ down** *v.t.* уплотн|я́ть, -и́ть; **~ in** *v.t.*: (*coll.*, *stop*, *give up*) прекра|ща́ть, -ти́ть; **he's ~ing in his job** он броса́ет рабо́ту; **~ it in, will you!** бро́сьте, пожа́луйста; **~ off** *v.t.* (*dispatch*) отгру|жа́ть, -зи́ть; отпр|авля́ть, -а́вить; **she ~ed the children off to school** она́ отпра́вила дете́й в шко́лу; **~ out** *v.t.*: **the hall was ~ed out** зал был запо́лнен до отка́за; **~ up** *v.t.* (*coll.*, *stop*): **I ~ed up smoking last year** я бро́сил кури́ть в про́шлом году́; *v.i.*: **we spent the day ~ing up** мы це́лый день скла́дывались; (*coll.*, *stop working*): **the workmen ~ed up at 5** рабо́чие смота́лись в 5 часо́в; **the engine ~ed up** мото́р отказа́л.

cpds. **~-horse** *n.* вью́чная ло́шадь; **~-ice** *n.* пак; па́ковый лёд; **~-saddle** *n.* вью́чное седло́.

package [ˈpækɪdʒ] *n.* посы́лка, паке́т; (*fig.*): **~ deal** ко́мплексная сде́лка.

v.t. упак|о́вывать, -ова́ть; (*fig.*): **a ~ tour** организо́ванная тури́стская пое́здка.

packer [ˈpækə(r)] *n.* (*person*; *firm*) упако́вщик.

packet [ˈpækɪt] *n.* **1.** (*small parcel*; *carton*) па́чка; паке́т. **2.** (*coll.*, *large sum of money*): **that must have cost him a ~** э́то, наве́рное, ему́ сто́ило у́йму де́нег.

packing [ˈpækɪŋ] *n.* **1.** (*action*, *process*) упако́вка. **2.** (*material*) упако́вочный материа́л.

cpd. **~-case** *n.* я́щик для упако́вки.

pact [pækt] *n.* пакт.

pad [pæd] *n.* **1.** (*small cushion*) поду́шечка; (*for protection*) прокла́дка; **he played with ~s on his shins** он игра́л в щитка́х. **2.** (*block of paper*) блокно́т.

v.t. **1.** (*provide with padding*): **~ded cell** пала́та, оби́тая во́йлоком; **~ shoulders** подкладны́е пле́чики (*nt. pl.*). **2.** (*fig.*, *also* **~ out**) перегру|жа́ть, -зи́ть; разб|авля́ть, -а́вить.

padding [ˈpædɪŋ] *n.* наби́вка, подби́вка.

paddle[1] [ˈpæd(ə)l] *n.* (*oar*) гребо́к; байда́рочное весло́.

v.t. & i. грести́ (*impf.*).

cpds. **~-steamer** *n.* колёсный парохо́д; **~-wheel** *n.* гребно́е колесо́.

paddl|e[2] [ˈpæd(ə)l] *n.*: **the children have gone for a ~e** де́ти пошли́ поплеска́ться в воде́.

v.i. (*walk in shallow water*) шлёпать (*impf.*) по

водé; **~ing-pool** дéтский бассéйн-лягушáтник.

paddock ['pædək] *n.* (*small field, esp. for horses*) вы́гул, пáстбище; (*at racecourse*) пáддок.

paddy ['pædɪ] *n.*: **~-field** *n.* (заливнóе) ри́совое пóле.

padlock ['pædlɒk] *n.* вися́чий замóк.

v.t. вéшать, повéсить замóк на+*a.*

paean ['pi:ən] *n.* пеáн.

paediatric [,pi:dɪ'ætrɪk] *adj.* педиатри́ческий.

paediatrician [,pi:dɪə'trɪʃ(ə)n] *n.* педиáтр.

paediatrics [,pi:dɪ'ætrɪks] *n.* педиатри́я.

paedophile ['pi:dəfaɪl] *n.* педофи́л.

paedophilia [,pi:də'fɪlɪə] *n.* педофили́я.

paella [paɪ'elə] *n.* (*cul.*) паэ́лья.

pagan ['peɪgən] *n.* язы́чник.

adj. язы́ческий.

paganism ['peɪgən,ɪz(ə)m] *n.* язы́чество.

page[1] [peɪdʒ] *n.* (*of a book etc.*; *also fig.*) страни́ца.

page[2] [peɪdʒ] *n.* (*boy servant, attendant*) паж.

v.t.: **please have Mr. Smith ~d** пожáлуйста, вы́зовите господи́на Сми́та.

pageant ['pædʒ(ə)nt] *n.* (*sumptuous spectacle*) церемóния, процéссия; (*open-air enactment of historical events*) представлéние.

pageantry ['pædʒəntrɪ] *n.* пы́шность, парáдность.

paginate ['pædʒɪ,neɪt] *v.t.* нумеровáть, пере- страни́цы +*g.*

pagination [,pædʒɪ'neɪʃ(ə)n] *n.* пагинáция.

pagoda [pə'gəʊdə] *n.* пáгода.

pail [peɪl] *n.* ведрó.

pain [peɪn] *n.* **1.** (*suffering*) боль; **he is in great ~** у негó си́льная боль; **he cried out in ~** он вскри́кнул от бóли; (*particular or localized*): **he had severe stomach ~s** у негó бы́ли óстрые бóли в желýдке; **he is a ~ in the neck** (*coll.*) он дéйствует на нéрвы. **2.** (*pl., trouble, effort*) старáния (*nt. pl.*), хлóп|оты (*pl., g.* -óт); **he takes great ~s over every picture** он мýчится над кáждой карти́ной; **he was at ~s to show us everything** он позабóтился о том, чтóбы показáть нам всё. **3.** (*penalty*): **he goes there on ~ of death** он идёт тудá под стрáхом смéрти.

v.t. причин|я́ть, -и́ть боль +*d.*; **it ~s me to have to say this** мне бóльно э́то говори́ть; **a ~ed expression** оби́женное выражéние лицá.

cpds. **~-killer** *n.* болеутоля́ющее (срéдство).

painful ['peɪnfʊl] *adj.* (*to body or mind*) болéзненный, мучи́тельный, причиня́ющий боль.

painless ['peɪnlɪs] *adj.* безболéзненный.

painstaking ['peɪnz,teɪkɪŋ] *adj.* старáтельный, усéрдный.

paint [peɪnt] *n.* крáска; **'wet ~!'** «осторóжно, окрáшено!»; **that door could do with a touch of ~** э́ту дверь хорошó бы подкрáсить; (*cosmetic*) космéтика; (*theatr.*) грим.

v.t. & i. **1.** (*portray in colours*) рисовáть (*impf.*); писáть, на- крáсками; **he ~s** он худóжник; (*fig., in words*) распи́с|ывать, -áть; **he's not as black as he is ~ed** не так уж он плох, как егó изображáют. **2.** (*cover or adorn with ~*) крáсить, по-; **the house is ~ed white** дом вы́крашен в бéлый цвет; **she never ~s her face** онá никогдá не крáсится.

with advs.: **~ in** *v.t.* впи́с|ывать, -áть; **~ out** *v.t.* закрá|шивать, -сить.

cpds. **~-box** *n.* набóр крáсок; **~-brush** *n.* кисть; **~-remover** *n.* раствори́тель (*m.*), смы́вка.

painter[1] ['peɪntə(r)] *n.* (*artist*) худóжник; (*decorator*) маля́р.

painter[2] ['peɪntə(r)] *n.* (*rope*) фáлинь (*m.*).

painting ['peɪntɪŋ] *n.* **1.** (*profession*) жи́вопись; **he took up ~** он заня́лся́ жи́вописью. **2.** (*work of art*) карти́на.

pair [peə(r)] *n.* пáра; **I have found one boot, but its ~ is missing** я нашёл оди́н боти́нок, а пáрного нет; **they walked along in ~s** они́ шли пáрами; **a ~ of scissors** нóжниц|ы (*pl., g.* —); **one ~ of scissors** одни́ нóжницы; **a ~ of spectacles** очк|и́ (*pl., g.* -óв); **two ~s of trousers** двóе (*or* две пáры) брюк.

v.t. (*unite*) спáри|вать, -ть; (*mate*) случ|áть, -и́ть.

with adv.: **~ off** *v.t. & i.* разб|ивáть(ся), -и́ть(ся) на пáры.

pajamas [pɪ'dʒɑ:məz, pə-] = **pyjamas**

Pakistan [,pɑ:kɪ'stɑ:n, ,pækɪ-] *n.* Пакистáн.

Pakistani [,pɑ:kɪ'stɑ:nɪ, ,pækɪ-] *n.* пакистáн|ец (*fem.* -ка).

adj. пакистáнский.

pal [pæl] (*coll.*) *n.* кóреш, корешóк; **he was a real ~ to me** он был мне настоя́щим дрýгом.

v.i.: **~ up** подружи́ться (*pf.*).

palace ['pælɪs] *n.* дворéц.

palaeographer [,pælɪ'ɒgrəfə(r)] *n.* палеóграф.

palaeographic [,pælɪə'græfɪk] *adj.* палеографи́ческий.

palaeography [,pælɪ'ɒgrəfɪ] *n.* палеогрáфия.

palaeolithic [,pælɪəʊ'lɪθɪk] *adj.* палеолити́ческий.

palaeontologist [,pælɪɒn'tɒlədʒɪst, ,peɪlɪ-] *n.* палеонтóлог.

paleontology [,pælɪɒn'tɒlədʒɪ, ,peɪlɪ-] *n.* палеонтолóгия.

Palaeozoic [,pælɪəʊ'zəʊɪk] *adj.* палеозóйский.

palatable ['pælətəb(ə)l] *adj.* вкýсный; (*fig.*) приéмлемый.

palatalization [,pælətəlaɪ'zeɪʃ(ə)n] *n.* палатализáция, смягчéние.

palatalize ['pælətə,laɪz] *v.t.* палатализи́ровать (*impf.*); смягч|áть, -и́ть.

palate ['pælət] *n.* (*roof of mouth*) нёбо; (*lit., fig. taste*) вкус.

palatial [pə'leɪʃ(ə)l] *adj.* роскóшный, великолéпный.

palaver [pə'lɑ:və(r)] *n.* (*coll.*) переговóры (*pl., g.* -ов).

pale[1] [peɪl] *n.* (*stake*) кол; (*boundary*) чертá; **his conduct puts him beyond the ~** (*fig.*) егó поведéние перехóдит все грани́цы; **~ of settlement** (*hist.*) чертá осéдлости.

pale[2] [peɪl] *adj.* **1.** (*of complexion*) блéдный; **she turned ~** онá побледнéла; (*of colours*) свéтлый; **~ blue** свéтло-голубóй. **2.** (*dim*) блéдный, тýсклый.

v.i. бледнéть, по-; (*fig.*) тускнéть, по-.

cpd. **~faced** *adj.* бледноли́цый.

paleness ['peɪlnɪs] *n.* блéдность.

Palestine ['pælɪ,staɪn] *n.* Палести́на.

palette ['pælɪt] *n.* (*lit., fig.*) пали́тра.

cpd. **~-knife** *n.* мастихи́н.

paling ['peɪlɪŋ] *n.* палисáд, частокóл.

palisade [,pælɪ'seɪd] *n.* частокóл.

pall[1] [pɔ:l] *n.* покрóв; **a ~ of smoke hung over the city** óблако ды́ма висéло над гóродом.

cpd. **~-bearer** *n.* несýщий гроб.

pall[2] [pɔ:l] *v.i.* при|едáться, -éсться (+*d.*); **~ on** наскýчи|вать, -ть +*d.*

pallet ['pælɪt] *n.* (*straw bed*) солóменный тюфя́к.

palliate ['pælɪ,eɪt] *v.t.* (*alleviate*) облегч|áть, -и́ть; (*extenuate*) смягч|áть, -и́ть.

palliative ['pælɪətɪv] *n.* паллиати́в.

adj. паллиати́вный; смягчáющий.

pallid ['pælɪd] *adj.* блéдный.

pallor ['pælə(r)] *n.* блéдность.

pally ['pælɪ] *adj.* (*coll.*) свóйский, обходи́тельный.

palm[1] [pɑ:m] *n.* (*tree*) пáльма; (*branch, symbol of victory*) пáльмовая ветвь; **P~ Sunday** вéрбное воскресéнье.

cpd. **~-oil** *n.* пáльмовое мáсло.

palm[2] [pɑ:m] *n.* (*of hand*) ладóнь; **he greased the doorman's ~** (*bribed him*) он подмáзал портьé.

v.t.: **~ sth. off on s.o.** (*or* **s.o. off with sth.**) подс|óвывать, -ýнуть что-н. комý-н.

palmist ['pɑ:mɪst] *n.* хиромáнт (*fem.* -ка).

palmistry ['pɑ:mɪstrɪ] *n.* хиромáнтия.

palpable ['pælpəb(ə)l] *adj.* ощути́мый; **a ~ error** я́вная оши́бка.

palpate [pæl'peɪt] *v.t.* пальпи́ровать (*impf.*).

palpitate ['pælpɪ,teɪt] *v.i.* (*pulsate*) пульси́ровать (*impf.*); (*tremble*) трепета́ть (*impf.*).

palpitation [,pælpɪ'teɪʃ(ə)n] *n.* сердцебие́ние.

palsy ['pɔ:lzɪ, 'pɒl-] *n.* парали́ч.

paltry ['pɔ:ltrɪ, 'pɒl-] *adj.* (*worthless*) ничто́жный; (*petty, mean*) ме́лкий; (*contemptible*) презре́нный.

pampas ['pæmpəs] *n.* пампа́с|ы (*pl., g.* -ов).
cpd. **~-grass** *n.* трава́ пампа́сная.

pamper ['pæmpə(r)] *v.t.* балова́ть, из-; **she ~ed herself and stayed in bed all morning** она́ не́жилась в посте́ли всё у́тро.

pamphlet ['pæmflɪt] *n.* (*treatise*) памфле́т; (*printed leaflet*) брошю́ра.

pamphleteer [,pæmflɪ'tɪə(r)] *n.* памфлети́ст.

pan[1] [pæn] *n.* **1.** (*kitchen utensil; sauce~*) кастрю́ля; **(frying-~)** сковорода́. **2.** (*of scales*) ча́шка. **3.** (*of water-closet*) унита́з.
v.t. **1.** (*coll., criticize severely*) разн|оси́ть, -ести́. **2.** (*also* **~ out:** *wash gravel etc.*) пром|ыва́ть, -ы́ть.
v.i. (*fig.*): **everything ~ned out well** де́ло вы́шло как нельзя́ лу́чше.
cpds. **~cake** *n.* блин; ола́дья; **~handle** *v.t. & i.* (*US*) попроша́йничать (*impf.*); **~-lid** *n.* кры́шка (кастрю́ли).

pan[2] [pæn] *v.t.* панорами́ровать (*impf.*).
v.i. (*of camera*) повора́чиваться (*impf.*).

panacea [,pænə'si:ə] *n.* панаце́я.

panache [pə'næʃ] *n.* (*fig.*) рисо́вка.

Panama ['pænə,mɑ:] *n.* Пана́ма; **~ hat** пана́ма.

panchromatic [,pænkrəʊ'mætɪk] *adj.* панхромати́ческий.

pancreas ['pæŋkrɪəs] *n.* поджелу́дочная железа́.

pancreatic ['pæŋkrɪ'ætɪk] *adj.* панкреати́ческий.

panda ['pændə] *n.* па́нда.

pandemic [pæn'demɪk] *n.* пандеми́я.
adj. всео́бщий.

pandemonium [,pændɪ'məʊnɪəm] *n.* (*uproar, confusion*) смяте́ние, шум, столпотворе́ние.

pander ['pændə(r)] *v.i.* (*procure*) сво́дничать (*impf.*); (*minister*) потво́рствовать (*impf.*).

pane [peɪn] *n.* око́нное стекло́.

panegyric [,pænɪ'dʒɪrɪk] *n.* панеги́рик.

panel ['pæn(ə)l] *n.* **1.** (*of door etc.*) пане́ль. **2.** (*of cloth*) вста́вка. **3.** (*register*) спи́сок. **4.** (*group of speakers*) коми́ссия, жюри́ (*nt. indecl.*); **~ game** виктори́на. **5.** (*for instruments*) пульт; **control ~** пульт управле́ния.

panelling ['pænəlɪŋ] *n.* пане́льная обши́вка; филёнка.

panellist ['pænəlɪst] *n.* уча́стник диску́ссии; член жюри́.

pang [pæŋ] *n.* **1.** (*physical*) боль; **~s of hunger** му́ки го́лода; **birth ~s** родовы́е схва́тки (*f. pl.*). **2.** (*mental*) му́ки (*f. pl.*); **a ~ of conscience** угрызе́ние со́вести.

panic ['pænɪk] *n.* па́ника.
v.t. (*coll.*): **they were ~ked into surrender** они́ впа́ли в па́нику и сдали́сь.
v.i. впа|да́ть, -сть в па́нику; паникова́ть (*impf.*).
cpds. **~-monger** *n.* паникёр; **~-stricken** *adj.* охва́ченный па́никой.

panicky ['pænɪkɪ] *adj.* (*coll.*) пани́ческий.

pannier ['pænɪə(r)] *n.* корзи́на.

panoply ['pænəplɪ] *n.* доспе́х|и (*pl., g.* -ов).

panorama [,pænə'rɑ:mə] *n.* (*lit., fig.*) панора́ма.

panoramic [,pænə'ræmɪk] *adj.* панора́мный.

pansy ['pænzɪ] *n.* (*flower*) аню́тины гла́з|ки (*pl., g.* -ок).

pant [pænt] *v.i.* тяжело́ дыша́ть (*impf.*); пыхте́ть (*impf.*); зад|ыха́ться, -охну́ться.

pantaloon [,pæntə'lu:n] *n.* (*pl., hist.*) панталóн|ы (*pl., g.* —); (*coll., trousers*) штан|ы́ (*pl., g.* -о́в).

pantheism ['pænθɪ,ɪz(ə)m] *n.* пантеи́зм.

pantheist ['pænθɪst] *n.* пантеи́ст.

pantheistic [,pænθɪ'ɪstɪk] *adj.* пантеисти́ческий.

pantheon ['pænθɪən] *n.* (*lit., fig.*) пантео́н.

panther ['pænθə(r)] *n.* панте́ра; (*US*) пу́ма.

panties ['pæntɪz] *n.* (*children's*) штани́ш|ки (*pl., g.* -ек); (*women's*) тру́сик|и (*pl., g.* -ов).

pantomime ['pæntə,maɪm] *n.* пантоми́ма; фее́рия.

pantry ['pæntrɪ] *n.* кладова́я.

pants [pænts] *n.* (*underwear*) трус|ы́ (*pl., g.* -о́в); (*long*) кальсо́н|ы (*pl., g.* —); (*coll. or US, trousers*) брю́к|и (*pl., g.* —); штан|ы́ (*pl., g.* -о́в).

pantyhose ['pæntɪ,həʊz] *n.* колго́т|ки (*pl., g.* -ок).

pap [pæp] *n.* (*soft food*) каши́ца.

papa [pə'pɑ:] *n.* па́па (*m.*).

papacy ['peɪpəsɪ] *n.* па́пство.

papal ['peɪp(ə)l] *adj.* па́пский.

papaw, pawpaw [pə'pɔ:] *n.* **1.** (*Carica papaya*) папа́йя. **2.** (*Asimina*) азими́на.

paper ['peɪpə(r)] *n.* **1.** бума́га; (*attr.*): **~ bag** бума́жный мешо́к; **~ napkin** бума́жная салфе́тка. **2.** **(news~)** газе́та; **what do the ~s say?** что пи́шут газе́ты?; (*attr.*): **~ round** доста́вка газе́т на́ дом; **~ shop** газе́тный кио́ск. **3.** (*currency*) банкно́ты (*f. pl.*), бума́жные де́н|ьги (*pl., g.* -ег). **4.** (*pl., documents*) докуме́нты (*m. pl.*), бума́ги (*f. pl.*). **5.** **(examination ~)** экзаменацио́нная рабо́та; сочине́ние. **6.** (*essay, lecture*) докла́д. **7.** **(wall~)** обо́|и (*pl., g.* -ев).
v.t. (*put wall~ on*) окле́и|вать, -ть обо́ями.
with adv.: **~ over** *v.t.* заклеи́|вать, -ть бума́гой.
cpds. **~back** *n.* кни́га в бума́жном/мя́гком переплёте; **~-boy** *n.* разно́счик газе́т; **~-clip** *n.* скре́пка; **~-hanger** *n.* обо́йщик; **~-knife** *n.* листоре́з; **~-weight** *n.* пресс-папье́ (*indecl.*); **~-work** *n.* канцеля́рская рабо́та.

papier mâché [,pæpjeɪ 'mæʃeɪ] *n.* папье́-маше́ (*indecl.*).

papist ['peɪpɪst] *n.* (*pej.*) папи́ст; като́лик.

papistry ['peɪpɪstrɪ] *n.* (*pej.*) папи́зм; католици́зм.

papoose [pə'pu:s] *n.* инде́йский ребёнок.

paprika ['pæprɪkə, pə'pri:kə] *n.* кра́сный/стручко́вый пе́рец, па́прика.

papyrus [pə'paɪərəs] *n.* папи́рус.

par [pɑ:(r)] *n.* **1.** (*equality*) ра́венство; **this is on a ~ with his other work** э́то на у́ровне други́х его́ рабо́т. **2.** (*recognized or face value*) цена́; **above ~** вы́ше номина́льной цены́; **below ~** ни́же номина́льной цены́. **3.** (*standard, normal condition*) норма́льное состоя́ние; **I feel below ~ today** я себя́ сего́дня нева́жно чу́вствую; **~ for the course** (*fig., coll.*) сре́дняя но́рма.

parable ['pærəb(ə)l] *n.* при́тча.

parabola [pə'ræbələ] *n.* пара́бола.

parabolic [,pærə'bɒlɪk] *adj.* (*math.*) параболи́ческий.

parachute ['pærə,ʃu:t] *n.* парашю́т; (*attr.*): **~ jump/landing** прыжо́к/приземле́ние с парашю́том; **~ troops** возду́шно-деса́нтные войска́.
v.t.: **the stores were ~d to the ground** припа́сы бы́ли сбро́шены с парашю́том.
v.i.: **the pilot ~d out of the aircraft** пило́т вы́бросился из самолёта с парашю́том.

parachutist ['pærə,ʃu:tɪst] *n.* парашюти́ст.

parade [pə'reɪd] *n.* **1.** (*display*) пока́з; **fashion ~** пока́з мод. **2.** (*muster of troops*) пара́д. **3.** (*public promenade*) промена́д.
v.t. (*display*) выставля́ть, вы́ставить напока́з.
v.i. ше́ствовать (*impf.*); марширова́ть (*impf.*).
cpds. **~-dress** *n.* пара́дное пла́тье; **~-ground** *n.* плац.

paradigm ['pærə,daɪm] *n.* паради́гма.

paradise ['pærə,daɪs] *n.* рай; **bird of ~** ра́йская пти́ца; **a ~ on earth** рай земно́й.

paradox ['pærə,dɒks] *n.* парадо́кс.
paradoxical [,pærə'dɒksɪk(ə)l] *adj.* парадокса́льный.
paraffin ['pærəfɪn] *n.* **1.** (**~** *oil*) кероси́н; **~ lamp** кероси́новая ла́мпа. **2.** (**~** *wax*) парафи́н; **liquid ~** парафи́новое ма́сло.
paragon ['pærəgən] *n.* образе́ц.
paragraph ['pærə,grɑ:f] *n.* абза́ц.
Paraguay ['pærə,gwaɪ] *n.* Парагва́й.
parakeet ['pærə,ki:t] *n.* длиннохво́стый попуга́й.
parallax ['pærə,læks] *n.* паралла́кс.
parallel ['pærə,lel] *n.* **1.** (*line or direction*) паралле́льная ли́ния; **in ~** паралле́льно; (*of latitude*) паралле́ль. **2.** (*fig., similar thg.; comparison*) паралле́ль; **draw a ~** пров|оди́ть, -ести́ паралле́ль.
adj. паралле́льный; **~ bars** (паралле́льные) бру́с|я (*pl., g.* -ев); (*analogous, similar*) аналоги́чный.
v.t. (*correspond to*) соотве́тствовать (*impf.*) +*d.*
parallelism ['pærəlel,ɪz(ə)m] *n.* (*lit., fig.*) параллели́зм.
parallelogram [,pærə'lelə,græm] *n.* параллелогра́мм.
paralyse ['pærə,laɪz] *v.t.* (*lit., fig.*) парализова́ть (*impf., pf.*).
paralysis [pə'rælɪsɪs] *n.* (*lit., fig.*) парали́ч.
paralytic [,pærə'lɪtɪk] *n.* парали́тик.
adj. (*lit.*) паралити́ческий, парализо́ванный.
paramedic [,pærə'medɪk] *n.* медрабо́тник без вы́сшего образова́ния.
parameter [pə'ræmɪtə(r)] *n.* (*math.; also fig.*) пара́метр.
paramilitary [,pærə'mɪlɪtərɪ] *adj.* полувое́нный.
paramount ['pærə,maʊnt] *adj.* первостепе́нный; **his influence was ~** он име́л огро́мное влия́ние.
paramour ['pærə,mʊə(r)] *n.* любо́вни|к (*fem.* -ца).
paranoia [,pærə'nɔɪə] *n.* парано́йя.
paranoi|d ['pærə,nɔɪd], **-ac** [,pærə'nəʊɪk, -'nɔɪɪk] *nn.* парано́ик.
adjs. параноические.
paranormal [,pærə'nɔ:m(ə)l] *adj.* паранорма́льный.
parapet ['pærəpɪt] *n.* (*low wall*) парапе́т; (*trench defence*) бру́ствер.
paraphernalia [,pærəfə'neɪlɪə] *n.* (*belongings*) ли́чные ве́щи (*f. pl.*), принадле́жности (*f. pl.*).
paraphrase ['pærə,freɪz] *n.* переска́з.
v.t. переска́з|ывать, -а́ть.
paraplegia [,pærə'pli:dʒə] *n.* параплеги́я.
paraplegic [,pærə'pli:dʒɪk] *adj.* парализо́ванный.
parasite ['pærə,saɪt] *n.* парази́т; (*fig.*) парази́т; туне́ядец.
parasitic [,pærə'sɪtɪk] *adj.* (*lit., fig.*) паразити́ческий.
parasol ['pærə,sɒl] *n.* зо́нтик (от со́лнца).
paratrooper ['pærə,tru:pə(r)] *n.* парашюти́ст-деса́нтник.
paratroops ['pærə,tru:ps] *n.* парашю́тно-деса́нтные войска́ (*nt. pl.*).
paratyphoid [,pærə'taɪfɔɪd] *n.* парати́ф.
parcel ['pɑ:s(ə)l] *n.* **1.** (*package*) паке́т, посы́лка. **2.** (*arch., portion*): **a ~ of land** уча́сток земли́; **part and ~** составна́я/неотъе́млемая часть (*чего*).
v.t. (*pack up; also* **~ up**) пакова́ть, у-; (*divide; also* **~ out**) дроби́ть, раз-.
parch [pɑ:tʃ] *v.t.* иссуш|а́ть, -и́ть; перес|ыха́ть, -о́хнуть; **the ground was ~ed** земля́ вы́сохла; **his throat was ~ed with thirst** у него́ от жа́жды пересо́хло в го́рле; **my lips are ~ed** у меня́ запекли́сь гу́бы.
parchment ['pɑ:tʃmənt] *n.* перга́мент.
pardon ['pɑ:d(ə)n] *n.* **1.** извине́ние, проще́ние; **I beg your ~** (*apology*) прошу́ проще́ния; (*request for repetition*) повтори́те, пожа́луйста! **2.** (*leg.*) поми́лование.
v.t. (*forgive*) про|ща́ть, -сти́ть; (*excuse*) извин|я́ть, -и́ть; (*leg.*) поми́ловать (*pf.*).
pardonable ['pɑ:dənəb(ə)l] *adj.* прости́тельный.
pare [peə(r)] *v.t.* (*trim*) стричь, обо-; (*peel*) чи́стить, по-; (*reduce; also* **~ down**) ур|е́зывать, -еза́ть, (*pf.*) -е́зать.
parent ['peərənt] *n.* (*father or mother*) роди́тель (*fem.* -ница); (*attr., original*) первонача́льный; **~ firm** компа́ния-учреди́тель.
parentage ['peərəntɪdʒ] *n.* происхожде́ние; **he is of mixed ~** он происхо́дит от сме́шанного бра́ка.
parental [pə'rent(ə)l] *adj.* роди́тельский.
parenthes|is [pə'renθəsɪs] *n.* вво́дное сло́во/предложе́ние; (*pl.*) кру́глые ско́бки (*f. pl.*); **in ~es** в ско́бках.
parenthetic(al) [,pærən'θetɪkəl] *adj.* вво́дный.
parenthetically [,pærən'θetɪkəlɪ] *adv.* ме́жду про́чим, в ви́де отступле́ния.
parenthood ['peərənthʊd] *n.*: **planned ~** (иску́сственное) ограниче́ние соста́ва семьи́.
pariah [pə'raɪə, 'pærɪə] *n.* (*lit. fig.*) па́рия (*c.g.*).
paring ['peərɪŋ] *n.* (*peeling*) очище́ние; (*trimming: of nails etc.*) стри́жка; (*slicing: of cheese etc.*) нареза́ние; **nail ~s** обре́зки (*m. pl.*) ногте́й.
Paris ['pærɪs] *n.* (*geog.*) Пари́ж; (*myth.*) Пари́с.
parish ['pærɪʃ] *n.* (*eccles.*) прихо́д; (*civil*) о́круг; **~ council** прихо́дский сове́т.
parishioner [pə'rɪʃənə(r)] *n.* прихожа́н|ин (*fem.* -ка).
Parisian [pə'rɪzɪən] *n.* парижа́н|ин (*fem.* -ка).
adj. пари́жский.
parity ['pærɪtɪ] *n.* ра́венство; парите́т.
park [pɑ:k] *n.* **1.** (*public garden*) парк. **2.** (*protected area of countryside*) запове́дник; национа́льный парк. **3.** (*grounds of country mansion*) уго́д|ья (*pl., g.* -ий). **4.** (*for vehicles etc.*) стоя́нка, парк.
v.t. паркова́ть, за~; ост|авля́ть, -а́вить; (*coll., stow, dispose*) скла́дывать, сложи́ть; **you can ~ your things in my room** вы мо́жете бро́сить свои́ ве́щи в мое́й ко́мнате; **he ~ed himself in the best chair** он усе́лся в лу́чшее кре́сло.
v.i. паркова́ться, за~; ста́вить, по- маши́ну (на стоя́нку); (*coll.*) расположи́ться (*pf.*).
cpd. **~-keeper** *n.* сто́рож (при па́рке).
parka ['pɑ:kə] *n.* па́рка.
parking ['pɑ:kɪŋ] *n.* (авто)стоя́нка; **'no ~!'** «стоя́нка запрещена́!»
cpds. **~-light** *n.* подфа́рник; **~-lot** *n.* стоя́нка; ме́сто стоя́нки; **~-meter** *n.* стоя́ночный счётчик.
Parkinson's disease ['pɑ:kɪns(ə)nz] *n.* боле́знь Паркинсо́на.
parlance ['pɑ:ləns] *n.* язы́к; **in common ~** в простоко́речии.
parley ['pɑ:lɪ] *n.* перегово́р|ы (*pl., g.* -ов).
v.i. догова́риваться (*impf.*).
parliament ['pɑ:ləmənt] *n.* парла́мент; **P~ is sitting** парла́мент заседа́ет.
parliamentarian [,pɑ:ləmen'teərɪən] *n.* (*member of parliament*) парламента́рий.
parliamentary [,pɑ:lə'mentərɪ] *adj.* парла́ментский, парламента́рный.
parlour ['pɑ:lə(r)] *n.* (*in house*) гости́ная; **beauty ~** космети́ческий кабине́т; **funeral ~** похоро́нное бюро́ (*indecl.*); **ice-cream ~** кафе́-моро́женое.
cpds. **~-game** *n.* фа́нт|ы (*pl., g.* -ов).
parlous ['pɑ:ləs] *adj.* (*arch., joc.*) стра́шный.
Parmesan [,pɑ:mɪ'zæn, 'pɑ:-] *n.* (**~ cheese**) сыр пармеза́н.
parochial [pə'rəʊkɪəl] *adj.* прихо́дский; (*fig.*) ограни́ченный, у́зкий.
parodist ['pærədɪst] *n.* пароди́ст.
parody ['pærədɪ] *n.* паро́дия.
v.t. пароди́ровать (*impf., pf.*).
parole [pə'rəʊl] *v.t.* освобо|жда́ть, -ди́ть под че́стное сло́во (*or* на пору́ки).
paroxysm ['pærək,sɪz(ə)m] *n.* пароксизм; (*of anger, laughter*) при́ступ.
parquet ['pɑ:kɪ, -keɪ] *n.* парке́т.
parrot ['pærət] *n.* (*lit., fig.*) попуга́й.
v.t. повтор|я́ть, -и́ть как попуга́й.

cpd. **~-fashion** *adv.* как попуга́й.

parry ['pærɪ] *v.t.* отра|жа́ть, -зи́ть (уда́р).

parsimonious [ˌpɑːsɪ'məʊnɪəs] *adj.* скупо́й.

parsimony ['pɑːsɪmənɪ] *n.* ску́пость.

parsley ['pɑːslɪ] *n.* петру́шка.

parsnip ['pɑːsnɪp] *n.* пастерна́к.

parson ['pɑːs(ə)n] *n.* па́стор.

parsonage ['pɑːsənɪdʒ] *n.* пастора́т.

part [pɑːt] *n.* **1.** часть; (*portion*) до́ля; **the greater ~** (*majority*) бо́льшая часть; **for the most ~** бо́льшей ча́стью; **in ~** части́чно, отча́сти; **this book is good in ~s** э́та кни́га хороша́ места́ми; **~ and parcel** *see* **parcel** *n.* **2.**; (*equal division*): **he received a fifth ~ of the estate** он получи́л пя́тую до́лю состоя́ния; (*instalment*): **the journal comes out in weekly ~s** журна́л выхо́дит еженеде́льными вы́пусками; (*component*): **spare ~s** запасны́е ча́сти; (*gram.*): **~s of speech** ча́сти ре́чи; **principal ~s of a verb** основны́е фо́рмы (*f. pl.*) глаго́ла. **2.** (*share, contribution*) уча́стие; **take ~ in** прин|има́ть, -я́ть уча́стие в+*p.*; **I have done my ~** я сде́лал своё де́ло. **3.** (*actor's role or lines*) роль; **he is only playing a ~** он про́сто игра́ет. **4.** (*side in dispute etc.*) сторона́; **take s.o.'s ~** вст|ава́ть, -ать на чью-н. сто́рону; **for my ~** с мое́й стороны́, что каса́ется меня́; **he took my criticism in good ~** он не оби́делся на мою́ кри́тику. **5.** (*region*) места́ (*nt. pl.*), край; **in our ~ of the world** в на́ших края́х; **I'm a stranger in these ~s** я в э́тих места́х чужо́й. **6.** (*mus.*) па́ртия; **it is a difficult ~ to sing** э́ту па́ртию тру́дно спеть. **7.** (*pl., abilities*) спосо́бности (*f. pl.*); **a man of ~s** спосо́бный челове́к. **8.** (*pl., genitals*): **private ~s** половы́е о́рганы (*m. pl.*).

adv. части́чно, ча́стью, отча́сти.

v.t. раздел|я́ть, -и́ть; **he ~ed the fighters** он разня́л драчуно́в; **he ~s his hair at the side** он но́сит пробо́р сбо́ку; **we ~ed company** (*went different ways*) мы разошли́сь/разъе́хались; (*ended our relationship*) мы расста́лись.

v.i. расст|ава́ться, -а́ться; **they ~ed friends** они́ расста́лись друзья́ми; **she has ~ed from her husband** она́ разошла́сь с му́жем.

cpds. **~-owner** *n.* совладе́лец; **~-time** *adj., adv.* на непо́лной ста́вке.

partake [pɑː'teɪk] *v.i.* (*take a share*) прин|има́ть, -я́ть уча́стие; **they partook of our meal** они́ пое́ли с на́ми.

parthenogenesis [ˌpɑːθɪnəʊ'dʒenɪsɪs] *n.* партеногене́з

partial ['pɑːʃ(ə)l] *adj.* **1.** (*opp. total*) части́чный; **~ eclipse** непо́лное затме́ние. **2.** (*biased*) пристра́стный. **3.**: **~ to** (*fond of*) неравноду́шный к+*d.*

partiality [ˌpɑːʃɪ'ælɪtɪ] *n.* (*bias*) пристра́стность; (*fondness*) скло́нность (*к кому/чему*).

participant [pɑː'tɪsɪpənt] *n.* уча́стник.

participate [pɑː'tɪsɪˌpeɪt] *v.i.* (*take part*) уча́ствовать (*impf.*).

participation [pɑːˌtɪsɪ'peɪʃ(ə)n] *n.* уча́стие.

participle ['pɑːtɪˌsɪp(ə)l] *n.* прича́стие.

particle ['pɑːtɪk(ə)l] *n.* **1.** части́ца, крупи́ца; **a ~ of dust** пыли́нка. **2.** (*gram.*) неизменя́емая части́ца.

particular [pə'tɪkjʊlə(r)] *n.* ча́стность; **in ~** в ча́стности; (*pl.*) да́нные (*pl.*); **let me take down your ~s** разреши́те мне записа́ть ва́ши да́нные; **they sent me ~s of the house** они́ присла́ли мне (подро́бное) описа́ние до́ма.

adj. **1.** (*specific, special*) осо́бенный, осо́бый; **for no ~ reason** без осо́бой причи́ны. **2.** (*detailed*) обстоя́тельный. **3.** (*fastidious*) привере́дливый; **she is not ~ about her dress** ей всё равно́, что наде́ть.

particularity [pəˌtɪkjʊ'lærɪtɪ] *n.* специ́фика.

particularly [pə'tɪkjʊləlɪ] *adv.* осо́бенно.

parting ['pɑːtɪŋ] *n.* **1.** (*leave-taking*) проща́ние; **a kiss at ~** поцелу́й на проща́ние; **a ~ gift** проща́льный пода́рок. **2.** (*separation*) расстава́ние; проща́ние. **3.** (*of the hair*) пробо́р.

partisan ['pɑːtɪˌzæn] *n.* **1.** (*zealous supporter*) приве́рженец. **2.** (*resistance fighter*) партиза́н (*fem.* -ка).

partisanship ['pɑːtɪˌzænʃɪp] *n.* приве́рженность.

partition [pɑː'tɪʃ(ə)n] *n.* (*division*) разде́л; **the ~ of Poland** разде́л По́льши; (*dividing structure*) перегоро́дка; (*compartment*) отделе́ние, се́кция.

v.t. дели́ть, раз-/по-; **~ off** отгор|а́живать, -оди́ть.

partitive ['pɑːtɪtɪv] *adj.* (*gram.*) раздели́тельный.

partly ['pɑːtlɪ] *adv.* части́чно, отча́сти.

partner ['pɑːtnə(r)] *n.* (*cards, dancing etc.*) партнёр (*fem.* -ша); (*comm.*): **senior ~ in the firm** гла́вный компаньо́н фи́рмы; (*in marriage*) супру́г (*fem.* -а).

v.t. (*be ~ to*) быть партнёром +*g.*

partnership ['pɑːtnəʃɪp] *n.* това́рищество; компа́ния; партнёрство.

partridge ['pɑːtrɪdʒ] *n.* куропа́тка.

party ['pɑːtɪ] *n.* **1.** (*political group*) па́ртия; **~ politics** парти́йная поли́тика. **2.** (*group with common interests or pursuits*) компа́ния, гру́ппа; **we travelled abroad in a ~** мы пое́хали за грани́цу гру́ппой. **3.** (*social gathering*) вечери́нка, приём; **~ dress** вече́рнее пла́тье. **4.** (*outing*) экску́рсия. **5.** (*participant in contract etc.*) сторона́; **the wife was the injured ~** жена́ была́ пострада́вшей стороно́й; **I won't be ~ to such a scheme** я не приму́ уча́стия в э́той зате́е. **6.** (*attr., shared*): **~ line** (*telephone*) о́бщий телефо́нный про́вод.

paschal ['pæsk(ə)l] *adj.* пасха́льный.

pas de deux [pɑː də 'dɜː] *n.* па-де-де́ (*m., nt. indecl.*).

pass [pɑːs] *n.* **1.** (*qualifying standard in exam*) сда́ча экза́мена; **he got a ~ in French** он сдал францу́зский. **2.** (*situation*) положе́ние; **things reached a pretty ~** дела́ при́няли скве́рный оборо́т. **3.** (*permit, document*) про́пуск (*pl.* -а́); **free ~** свобо́дный вход; контрама́рка. **4.** (*transfer of ball in game*) пас, переда́ча. **5.** (*lunge, thrust*) вы́пад; (*coll., amorous approach*): **he made a ~ at her** он к ней пристава́л. **7.** (*passage in mountains*) уще́лье, перева́л. **8.** (*at cards*) пас.

v.t. **1.** (*go by*) про|ходи́ть, -йти́ ми́мо +*g.* **2.** (*overtake*) об|гоня́ть, -огна́ть. **3.** (*go, get through*) про|ходи́ть, -йти́; **not a word ~ed his lips** он не произнёс ни сло́ва; **~ an exam** сдать/вы́держать (*pf.*) экза́мен. **4.** (*spend*) пров|оди́ть, -ести́. **5.** (*surpass, exceed*) прев|ыша́ть, -ы́сить; **it ~es all reason** э́то выхо́дит за преде́лы разу́много. **6.** (*examine and accept*) пропус|ка́ть, -ти́ть; **only one candidate was ~ed by the board** коми́ссия утверди́ла то́лько одного́ кандида́та; (*approve, sanction*) од|обря́ть, -о́брить. **7.** (*hand over*) перед|ава́ть, -а́ть. **8.** (*utter*) произн|оси́ть, -ести́; **he refrained from ~ing judgement** он воздержа́лся выноси́ть сужение; **the judge ~ed sentence** судья́ вы́нес пригово́р. **9.** (*cause to go, move*): **he ~ed his eye over the goods** он просмотре́л това́ры; **he ~ed a rope round her waist** он обвяза́л её та́лию верёвкой; **~ a ball** перед|ава́ть, -а́ть мяч. **10.** (*excrete*) испус|ка́ть, -ти́ть; **he could not ~ water** он не мог мочи́ться.

v.i. **1.** (*proceed, move*) про|ходи́ть, -йти́; **he ~ed by the window** он прошёл ми́мо окна́; **he ~ed through the door** он прошёл в/че́рез дверь; **~ along (down) the car!** проходи́те да́льше; **she ~ed out of sight** она́ исче́зла и́з виду; (*get through*): **let me ~!** да́йте мне пройти́; (*circulate*) перед|ава́ться, -а́ться; (*in opposite directions*) минова́ть (*impf., pf.*). **2.** (*overtake*) об|гоня́ть, -огна́ть. **3.** (*go by, elapse*) про|ходи́ть, -йти́; **the procession ~ed** проце́ссия прошла́ ми́мо; **six years have ~ed since then** с тех пор прошло́ шесть лет. **4.** (*be said or done*) прои|сходи́ть, -зойти́; **did you hear what ~ed between them?** вы зна́ете, что произошло́ ме́жду ни́ми? **5.** (*go without comment*): **his words ~ed unnoticed** его́ словá прошли́ незамéченными; **let it ~!** не нáдо об э́том говори́ть! **6.** (*come to an end*) про|ходи́ть, -йти́; прекра|щáться, -ти́ться; **the pain will ~** боль проидёт. **7.** (*qualify in exam etc.*; *be accepted*, *recognized*) про|ходи́ть, -йти́; **he ~es for an expert** он считáется специали́стом. **8.** (*at cards*) пасовáть, с-.

with advs.: **~ along** *v.i.* про|ходи́ть, -йти́; **~ away** *v.i.* (*die*) скончáться (*pf.*); **~ by** *v.t. & i.* про|ходи́ть, -йти́ ми́мо; **~ down** *v.t.* перед|авáть, -áть; *v.i.* пере|ходи́ть, -йти́; **~ off** *v.t.* (*dismiss*): **he ~ed off the whole affair as a joke** он обрати́л всё дéло в шу́тку; (*palm off*, *get rid of*) подс|óвывать, -у́нуть; (*falsely represent*): **he ~es himself off as a foreigner** он выдаёт себя́ за инострáнца; *v.i.* (*go away*) прекра|щáться, -ти́ться; **the pain was slow to ~ off** боль проходи́ла мéдленно; (*be carried through*) про|ходи́ть, -йти́; **the wedding ~ed off without a hitch** свáдьба прошлá без сучкá, без задóринки; **~ on** *v.t.* перед|авáть, -áть; *v.i.* про|ходи́ть, -йти́; (*euph.*, *die*) скончáться (*pf.*); **~ out** *v.i.* (*qualify*, *graduate*) про|ходи́ть, -йти́; **~ing-out parade** парáд выпускникóв; (*coll.*, *lose consciousness*) терять, по-сознáние; **~ over** *v.t.* (*hand over*) перед|авáть, -áть; (*omit*; *overlook*, *ignore*) пропус|кáть, -ти́ть; **he was ~ed over for a younger man** они́ емý предпочли́ бóлее молодóго человéка; *v.i.* про|ходи́ть, -йти́; **the storm ~ed over** буря́ пронеслáсь (и ушлá); **~ round** *v.t.* перед|авáть, -áть; **~ through** *v.t.* прод|евáть, -éть; **~ up** *v.t.* (*hand up*) под|авáть, -áть; (*coll.*, *refuse*) откáз|ываться, -áться от +*g*.

cpds. **~-book** *n.* бáнковская кни́жка; **~-key** *n.* отмы́чка; **P~over** *n.* еврéйская пáсха; **~word** *n.* парóль (*m.*).

passable [ˈpɑːsəb(ə)l] *adj.* (*affording passage*) проходи́мый, проéзжий; (*tolerable*) снóсный.

passage [ˈpæsɪdʒ] *n.* **1.** (*going by*) прохóд; **the ~ of time** течéние врéмени; (*going across*, *over*) переéзд; перелёт; **a bird of ~** перелётная пти́ца; (*transition*, *change*) перехóд; (*going through*, *way through*) прохóд. **2.** (*crossing by ship etc.*) рейс; **have you booked your ~?** вы заказáли билéт на парохóд?; **work one's ~** отраб|áтывать, -óтать свой проéзд. **3.** (*passing of law etc.*) проведéние. **4.** (*corridor*) коридóр. **5.** (*alley*) прохóд. **6.** (*coll.*, *duct in body*): **back ~** (*rectum*) зáдний прохóд. **7.** (*literary excerpt*) отры́вок, текст; (*mus.*) пассáж.

cpd. **~-way** *n.* коридóр; прохóд.

passenger [ˈpæsɪndʒə(r)] *n.* пассажи́р; **~ train** пассажи́рский пóезд; **~ seat** мéсто ря́дом с води́телем.

passer-by [ˌpɑːsəˈbaɪ] *n.* прохóжий.

passing [ˈpɑːsɪŋ] *n.* **1.** (*going by*) прохождéние; **I just called in ~** я зашёл мимохóдом; **I will mention in ~** я замéчу попу́тно. **2.** (*death*) смерть, кончи́на.

adj. (*transient*): **a ~ fancy** мимолётное увлечéние; **the ~ fashion** преходя́щая мóда.

passion [ˈpæʃ(ə)n] *n.* **1.** (*strong emotion*; *sexual feeling*) страсть; **his ~s were quickly aroused** егó бы́ло нетру́дно разъяри́ть; (*burst of anger*) взрыв; **fly into a ~** при|ходи́ть, -йти́ в я́рость; (*enthusiasm*) пыл; **she has a ~ for Bach** онá стрáстно увлеченá му́зыкой Бáха. **2.** (*relig.*): **the P~** стрáсти Госпóдни (*f. pl.*); крéстные му́ки (*f. pl.*).

passionate [ˈpæʃənət] *adj.* (*having strong emotions*) стрáстный, пы́лкий; (*sexually ardent*) стрáстный; (*impassioned of language etc.*) пы́лкий, стрáшный.

passionately [ˈpæʃənətlɪ] *adv.* стрáстно, пы́лко.

passive [ˈpæsɪv] *n.* (*gram.*) пасси́вная фóрма, страдáтельный залóг.

adj. пасси́вный; (*gram.*) пасси́вный, страдáтельный.

passivity [pæˈsɪvɪtɪ] *n.* пасси́вность.

passport [ˈpɑːspɔːt] *n.* (*lit.*) пáспорт; (*fig.*) ключ, путёвка; **hard work is the ~ to success** усéрдие — залóг успéха.

past [pɑːst] *n.* **1.** прóшлое; **in the ~** в прóшлом; **one cannot undo the ~** нельзя́ зачеркну́ть прóшлое. **2.** (*gram.*) прошéдшее врéмя.

adj. **1.** (*bygone*) мину́вший, прóшлый; **that is all ~ history** всё э́то ужé истóрия; (*pred.*, *gone by*) ми́мо; **the time for that is ~** врéмя для э́того давнó минoвáло; **that is all ~ and done with** с э́тим покóнчено; **what's ~ is ~** дéло прóшлое. **2.** (*preceding*) прóшлый; **for the ~ few days** за послéдние нéсколько дней; **during the ~ week** за э́ту недéлю. **3.** (*gram.*) прошéдший. **4.**: **a ~ master** непревзойдённый мáстер.

adv. ми́мо; **the soldiers marched ~** солдáты прошли́ ми́мо; **he pushed ~** он протолкáлся/проби́лся.

prep. **1.** (*after*) пóсле +*g.*; **it is ~ eight o'clock** тепéрь девя́тый час; **ten ~ one** дéсять мину́т вторóго. **2.** (*by*) ми́мо+*g.*; **he drove ~ the house** он проéхал ми́мо дóма. **3.** (*to or on the far side of*) за+*a./i.*; **you've gone ~ the turning** вы проéхали поворóт. **4.** (*beyond*, *exceeding*) свы́ше+*g.*, сверх+*g.*; **I am ~ caring** тепéрь мне ужé всё равнó; **this is ~ a joke** э́то перехóдит грани́цы шу́ток.

pasta [ˈpæstə] *n.* макарóн|ы (*pl.*, *g.* —).

paste [peɪst] *n.* (*soft dough*) тéсто; (*malleable mixture*; *savoury preparation*) пáста; (*adhesive*) клей.

v.t. **1.** (*stick*) наклé|ивать, -ить; **the notice was ~ed up on the wall** объявлéние бы́ло приклéено к стенé; **she ~d the pictures into her album** онá вклéила карти́нки в альбóм. **2.** (*sl.*, *beat*) устр|áивать, -óить взбу́чку +*d.*

cpd. **~board** *n.* картóн.

pastel [ˈpæst(ə)l] *n.* (*crayon*) пастéль; **~ shades** пастéльные крáски; (*drawing in ~*) рису́нок пастéлью.

pasteurization [ˌpɑːstjəraɪˈzeɪʃ(ə)n] *n.* пастеризáция.

pasteurize [ˈpɑːstjəˌraɪz] *v.t.* пастеризовáть (*impf.*, *pf.*).

pastiche [pæˈstiːʃ] *n.* (*literary imitation*) стилизáция (под+*a.*); поддéлка.

pastille [ˈpæstɪl] *n.* пасти́лка.

pastime [ˈpɑːstaɪm] *n.* (прия́тное) время(пре)провождéние.

pastor [ˈpɑːstə(r)] *n.* пáстор.

pastoral [ˈpɑːstər(ə)l] *n.* пасторáль.

adj. (*pert. to country life*) пасторáльный; (*pert. to clergy*) пáсторский.

pastry [ˈpeɪstrɪ] *n.* (*baked dough*) конди́терские издéлия; (*tart*, *cake*) пирóжное.

cpd. **~-cook** *n.* конди́тер.

pasturage [ˈpɑːstʃərɪdʒ] *n.* (*grazing*) пáстбище; (*herbage for cattle etc.*) поднóжный корм; (*grazing land*) вы́пас.

pasture [ˈpɑːstjə(r)] *n.* = **pasturage; the sheep were put out to ~** овéц вы́гнали на пáстбище.

v.t. (*put to graze*) пасти́ (*impf.*).

pasty[1] [ˈpæstɪ] *n.* пирожóк, расстегáй.

pasty[2] [ˈpeɪstɪ] *adj.* (*like paste*) тестообрáзный; (*palefaced*) блéдный.

pat[1] [pæt] *n.* **1.** (*light touch or sound*) хлопóк; шлепóк; **he deserves a ~ on the back** (*fig.*) он заслу́живает похвалы́. **2.** (*small mass*): **the butter was served in ~s** мáсло пóдали крóхотными кусóчками.

v.t. подхлóп|ывать, -ать; (*a dog*) глáдить, по-.

pat[2] [pæt] *adv.* (*appositely*) кстáти; **he had his lesson off ~** он знал урóк назубóк; **stand ~** (*stick to one's decision or bet*) стоя́ть (*impf.*) на своём.

patch [pætʃ] *n.* **1.** (*covering over hole*) заплáта; (*over wound*) плáстырь (*m.*); (*over eye*) повя́зка; (*fig.*, *coll.*): **the film is not a ~ on the book** фильм — ничтó по сравнéнию с кни́гой. **2.** (*superficial mark or stain*) пятнó; (*distinctive area*) клочóк; **~es of blue sky** клочки́ голубóго нéба; **we ran into a fog**

~ мы попáли в тумáн; **there were ~es of ice on the road** на дорóге местáми былá гололéдица. **4.** (*piece of ground*) учáсток. **5.** (*scrap*, *remnant*) отрéзок.

v.t. (*mend*) латáть, за-.

with advs.: ~ **over** *v.t.* латáть, за-; ~ **up** *v.t.* (*lit.*) чини́ть, по-; (*fig.*) мири́ть, по-; **the quarrel was soon ~ed up** ссóра былá вскóре улáжена.

cpds. **~-pocket** *n.* накладнóй кармáн; **~work** *n.* лоскýтное шитьё; **~work quilt** лоскýтное одея́ло; (*lit.*) латáние; (*fig.*) мешани́на.

patchy ['pætʃɪ] *adj.* (*fig.*, *of uneven quality*) неоднорóдный, разнорóдный, нерóвный.

pâté ['pæteɪ] *n.* паштéт.

patent ['peɪt(ə)nt, 'pæt-] *n.* патéнт.

adj. **1.** (*protected by ~*) патентóванный; ~ **leather** лакирóванная кóжа, лак. **2.** (*coll.*, *well-contrived*, *ingenious*) изобретáтельный. **3.** (*obvious*) очеви́дный.

v.t. патентовáть, за-.

paternal [pə'tɜːn(ə)l] *adj.* **1.** (*fatherly*) отцóвский, отéческий. **2.** (*related through father*) рóдственный по отцý; ~ **grandmother** бáбушка со стороны́ отцá.

paternity [pə'tɜːnɪtɪ] *n.* отцóвство.

path [pɑːθ] *n.* (*track for walking*) тропá, тропи́нка; дорóжка; ~ **through the woods** леснáя тропá/тропи́нка; (*fig.*) путь (*m.*); **on our ~ through life** на нáшем жи́зненном пути́; **our ~s diverged** нáши дорóги разошли́сь.

cpd. **~way** *n.* тропá, путь (*m.*).

pathetic [pə'θetɪk] *adj.* печáльный, жáлкий, трóгательный.

pathological [,pæθə'lɒdʒɪk(ə)l] *adj.* патологи́ческий.

pathologist [pə'θɒlədʒɪst] *n.* патóлог.

pathology [pə'θɒlədʒɪ] *n.* паталóгия.

pathos ['peɪθɒs] *n.* пáфос.

patience ['peɪʃ(ə)ns] *n.* **1.** терпéние; **I have no ~ with him** он меня́ вывóдит из терпéния; **my ~ is exhausted** моё терпéние кóнчилось. **2.** (*card game*) пасья́нс.

patient ['peɪʃ(ə)nt] *n.* пациéнт, больнóй.

adj. терпели́вый.

patina ['pætɪnə] *n.* пати́на.

patio ['pætɪəʊ] *n.* пáтио (*indecl.*), двóрик.

patois ['pætwɑː] *n.* мéстный гóвор.

patriarch ['peɪtrɪ,ɑːk] *n.* патриáрх.

patriarchal [,peɪtrɪ'ɑːk(ə)l] *adj.* патриархáльный.

patriarchate ['peɪtrɪ,ɑːkət] *n.* (*eccl.*) патриáршество.

patriarchy ['peɪtrɪ,ɑːkɪ] *n.* патриáрхия, патриархáт.

patrician [pə'trɪʃ(ə)n] *n.* (*Roman noble*) патри́ций; (*aristocrat*) аристокрáт.

adj. патрициáнскии; аристократи́ческий.

patrimony ['pætrɪmənɪ] *n.* (*inheritance from father*) отцóвское наслéдие; (*fig.*) наслéдие.

patriot ['peɪtrɪət, 'pæt-] *n.* патриóт.

patriotic [,peɪtrɪ'ɒtɪk, ,pæt-] *adj.* патриоти́ческий.

patriotism ['peɪtrɪət,ɪz(ə)m, 'pæt-] *n.* патриоти́зм.

patrol [pə'trəʊl] *n.* **1.** (*action*) патрули́рование; **on ~** в дозóре; ~ **car** (полицéйская) патрýльная маши́на; ~ **vessel** сторожевóе сýдно. **2.** (*~ling body*) патрýль (*m.*); (*~ling official*) патрýльный.

cpds. **~man** *n.* (*road scout*) патрýльный; (*US*, *policeman*) полицéйский.

v.t. & i. патрули́ровать (*impf.*).

patron ['peɪtrən] *n.* **1.** (*supporter*, *protector*) покрови́тель (*m.*); **a ~ of the arts** покрови́тель искýсств, меценáт; ~ **saint** святóй застýпник, святáя застýпница. **2.** (*customer*) (постоя́нный) клиéнт, покупáтель (*m.*).

patronage ['pætrənɪdʒ] *n.* (*support*, *sponsorship*) покрови́тельство; (*right of appointment*) прáво назначéния на дóлжность; (*customer's support*) постоя́нная клиентýра.

patroniz|e ['pætrə,naɪz] *v.t.* (*support*, *encourage*) покрови́тельствовать (*impf.*) +*d.*; (*visit as customer*) постоя́нно посещáть (*impf.*); (*treat condescendingly*) отн|оси́ться, -ести́сь свысокá к+*d.*; **~ing airs** покрови́тельственные манéры (*f. pl.*).

patronymic [,pætrə'nɪmɪk] *n.* (*Russ.*) óтчество.

patter[1] ['pætə(r)] *n.* (*of salesman etc.*) скороговóрка.

v.i. (*talk glibly*) таратóрить (*impf.*).

patter[2] ['pætə(r)] *n.* (*tapping sound*) постýкивание; тóпот, стук.

v.i. барабáнить (*impf.*), топотáть (*impf.*); **her footsteps ~ed down the hall** её шаги́ простучáли по зáлу.

pattern ['pæt(ə)n] *n.* **1.** (*laudable example*) образéц; (*attr.*) образцóвый. **2.** (*model for production*) вы́кройка; **dress ~** вы́кройка (плáтья). **3.** (*design*) модéль. **4.** (*arrangement*, *system*) óбраз, манéра; **new ~s of behaviour** нóвые нóрмы (*f. pl.*) поведéния.

v.t. **1.** (*model*) копи́ровать, с-; **he ~ed himself on his father** он брал примéр со своегó отцá. **2.** (*decorate with design*) укр|ашáть, -áсить; **a ~ed dress** плáтье в узóрах (*or* с узóрами).

patty ['pætɪ] *n.* пирожóк; котлéта.

paucity ['pɔːsɪtɪ] *n.* нехвáтка, скýдость.

paunch [pɔːntʃ] *n.* брюшкó, пýзо.

paunchy ['pɔːntʃɪ] *adj.* пузáтый.

pauper ['pɔːpə(r)] *n.* бедня́к.

pause [pɔːz] *n.* (*intermission*, *temporary halt*) переры́в; передышка; (*in speaking*, *mus. etc.*) пáуза.

v.i. остан|áвливаться, -ови́ться; **she scarcely ~d for breath** онá не переводи́ла дыхáния; **if you ~ to think** éсли задýматься.

pave [peɪv] *v.t.* мости́ть, вы́-; **~d road** мощёная дорóга; (*fig.*): **his proposal ~d the way for an understanding** егó предложéние откры́ло путь к взаимопонимáнию.

pavement ['peɪvmənt] *n.* тротуáр.

pavilion [pə'vɪljən] *n.* (*building for sport or tournament*) павильóн; (*large tent*) шатёр.

paving ['peɪvɪŋ] *n.* (*paved way*) мостовáя; (*act of ~*) мощéние ýлиц.

cpd. **~-stone** *n.* брусчáтка, булы́жник.

paw [pɔː] *n.* лáпа; (*coll.*): **take your ~s off!** рýки прочь!

v.t. (*touch with ~*) трóгать, по- лáпой; **the horse ~ed the ground** конь бил копы́тами; (*handle*, *fondle clumsily*) лáпать (*impf.*, *pf.*).

pawn[1] [pɔːn] *n.* (*chessman*, *also fig.*) пéшка.

pawn[2] [pɔːn] *n.* (*pledge*) залóг, заклáд; **in ~** заложенный; **he took his watch out of ~** он вы́купил часы́ из ломбáрда.

v.t. за|клáдывать, -ложи́ть.

cpds. **~broker** *n.* ростовщи́к; **~shop** *n.* ломбáрд.

pawpaw ['pɔːpɔː] = **papaw**

pay [peɪ] *n.* плáта, (*coll.*) зарплáта; жáлование; **a ~ cut** снижéние зарплáты; **a ~ increase** повышéние зарплáты; **on half ~** на полови́нной стáвке.

v.t. **1.** (*give in return for sth.*) плати́ть, за-, у-; **she always ~s cash** онá всегдá плáтит нали́чными; (*contribute*): **everyone must ~ his share** кáждый дóлжен внести́ свою́ дóлю; **I'll ~ the difference** я доплачý; ~ **one's fare** оплá|чивать, -ти́ть проéзд. **2.** (*remunerate*, *recompense*) оплá|чивать, -ти́ть +*d.*; **they are paid by the hour** они́ получáют почасовýю оплáту; **there will be the devil to ~** бýдет грандиóзный скандáл. **3.** (*settle*, *~ for*) уплá|чивать, -ти́ть; **the defendant must ~ costs** обвиня́емый дóлжен уплати́ть судéбные издéржки. **4.** (*bestow*, *render*): ~ **attention to me!** послýшайте меня́!; ~ **s.o. a compliment** дéлать, с- комý-н. комплимéнт; ~ **heed to** обра|щáть, -ти́ть внимáние на+*a.*; ~ **one's respects to** свидéтельствовать, за- своё почтéние +*d.*; ~ **s.o. a visit** наве|щáть, -сти́ть когó-н. **5.** (*benefit*, *profit*): **it will ~ you to wait** вам стóит подождáть.

v.i. **1.** (*give money*) расплá|чиваться, -ти́ться; **he**

~s on the nail он пла́тит неме́дленно; **I paid through the nose for it** я заплати́л за э́то бе́шеные де́ньги. **2.** (*suffer*) поплати́ться (*pf.*); **you'll ~ dearly for this** вы за э́то до́рого запла́тите. **3.** (*yield a return*) окуп|а́ться, -и́ться; дава́ть (*impf.*) при́быль; (*fig.*) име́ть смысл; опра́вд|ывать, -а́ть себя́; **it ~s to advertise** рекла́ма окупа́ется.

with advs.: **~ back** *v.t.* (*return*) возвра|ща́ть, -ти́ть (*also* верну́ть); (*have revenge on*): **I'll ~ you back for this** я вам за э́то отплачу́; **~ in** *v.t.* вн|оси́ть, -ести́; **~ off** *v.t.* рассчи́т|ываться, -а́ться с+*i.*; **the workers were paid off** с рабо́чими рассчита́лись; **I have paid off my debts** я расплати́лся со свои́ми долга́ми; (**~** *wages and discharge*) рассчи́т|ывать, -а́ть; *v.i.* (*bring profit*) окуп|а́ться, -и́ться; **~ out** *v.t.* (*expend, make payment of*) выпла́чивать, вы́платить; **~ up** *v.t.* (*settle*) выпла́чивать, вы́платить; **a paid-up account** закры́тый счёт; *v.i.* (**~** *amount due*) рассчи́т|ываться, -а́ться сполна́.

cpds. **~-day** *n.* платёжный день; **~-desk** *n.* ка́сса; **~load** *n.* (*of vehicle*) поле́зный груз; (*of missile*) поле́зная нагру́зка; **~master** *n.* касси́р; казначе́й; **~-off** *n.* (*settlement*) вы́плата; (*profit, reward*) награ́да; (*bribe*) взя́тка; (*coll., climax, e.g. of a joke*) развя́зка; **~-packet** *n.* за́работок, (*coll.*) полу́чка; **~roll** *n.* платёжная ве́домость; **there are 500 men on the ~roll** в платёжной ве́домости (*or* в шта́те) чи́слится 500 челове́к.

payable ['peɪəb(ə)l] *adj.* опла́чиваемый; подлежа́щий упла́те.

payee [peɪ'i:] *n.* получа́тель (*fem.* -ница) (де́нег).

payer ['peɪə(r)] *n.* плате́льщи|к (*fem.* -ца).

payment ['peɪmənt] *n.* (*paying, sum paid*) опла́та; платёж; (*of debt etc.*) упла́та; **prompt ~ is requested** про́сят неме́дленно уплати́ть.

PC *abbr. of* **1.** ***Police Constable*** полице́йский. **2.** ***personal computer*** ПК, (персона́льный компью́тер). **3.** ***politically correct*** полити́чески корре́ктный.

PE (*abbr. of* ***physical education***) физкульту́ра.

pea [pi:] *n.* горо́шина; (*pl., collect.*) горо́х; **~ soup** горохово́й суп; **split ~s** лущёный горо́х.

cpds. **~nut** *n.* земляно́й оре́х, ара́хис; **~nut butter** па́ста из тёртого ара́хиса; **~nuts** *n.* (*US sl., trifling amount*) гроши́ (*m. pl.*).

peace [pi:s] *n.* **1.** (*freedom from war*) мир; **~ talks** ми́рные перегово́ры; (*fig.*): **make one's ~ with s.o.** помири́ться (*pf.*) с кем-н. **2.** (*freedom from civil disorder*) споко́йствие; поря́док; **breach of the ~** наруше́ние обще́ственного поря́дка; **Justice of the P~** мирово́й судья́. **3.** (*rest, quiet*) споко́йствие, поко́й; **may he rest in ~** мир пра́ху его́; **she found ~** (*died*) **at last** она́, наконе́ц, отпра́вилась на поко́й; **can we have some ~ and quiet?** нельзя́ ли поти́ше?; **~ of mind** споко́йствие ду́ха.

cpds. **~-keeping** *adj.*: **~-keeping force** войска́ (*nt. pl.*) по поддержа́нию ми́ра; **~-loving** *adj.* миролюби́вый; **~maker** *n.* миротво́рец; **~offering** *n.* (*fig.*) зада́бривание; **~time** *n.* ми́рное вре́мя.

peaceable ['pi:səb(ə)l] *adj.* миролюби́вый, ми́рный.

peaceful ['pi:sfʊl] *adj.* ми́рный; **~ coexistence** ми́рное сосуществова́ние.

peach [pi:tʃ] *n.* **1.** (*fruit*) пе́рсик. **2.** (*tree*) пе́рсиковое де́рево.

peacock ['pi:kɒk] *n.* павли́н.

peahen ['pi:hen] *n.* са́мка павли́на, па́ва.

peajacket ['pi:,dʒækɪt] *n.* бушла́т, тужу́рка.

peak [pi:k] *n.* **1.** (*mountain top*) пик, верши́на. **2.** (*of cap*) козырёк. **3.** (*fig., highest point, maximum*) пик; **~ load** (*elec.*) максима́льная нагру́зка; **his excitement reached its ~** его́ возбужде́ние дости́гло преде́ла; **~ viewing hours** наибо́лее популя́рные часы́ для пока́за телепереда́ч.

v.i.: **demand ~ed** спрос дости́г вы́сшей то́чки.

peaked [pi:kd] *adj.* **1.** остроконе́чный; **~ cap** (фо́рменная) фура́жка. **2.** (*haggard; also* **peaky**) осу́нувшийся; измождённый.

peaky ['pi:kɪ] *adj.* = **peaked 2.**

peal [pi:l] *n.* (*of bells*) звон, трезво́н; (*of thunder*) гро́хот, раска́т; (*of laughter*) взрыв.

v.i. (*of bells*) трезво́нить (*impf.*); (*of thunder*) греме́ть, про-; (*of laughter*) разд|ава́ться, -а́ться.

pear [peə(r)] *n.* **1.** (*fruit*) гру́ша. **2.** (*tree*) гру́шевое де́рево, гру́ша.

pearl [pɜ:l] *n.* жемчу́жина; (*pl., collect.*) же́мчуг.

cpds. **~-barley** *n.* перло́вая крупа́.

pearly ['pɜ:lɪ] *adj.* похо́жий на же́мчуг; жемчу́жного цве́та, жемчу́жный.

peasant ['pez(ə)nt] *n.* крестья́н|ин (*fem.* -ка).

peasantry ['pezəntrɪ] *n.* крестья́нство.

pease pudding [pi:z] *n.* горо́ховый пу́динг, горо́ховая запека́нка.

peat [pi:t] *n.* торф.

cpd. **~-bog** *n.* торфяно́е боло́то.

pebble ['peb(ə)l] *n.* голы́ш; га́лька; булы́жник.

pebbly ['peblɪ] *adj.* покры́тый га́лькой.

pecan ['pi:kən] *n.* оре́х-пека́н.

peccadillo [,pekə'dɪləʊ] *n.* грешо́к.

peck [pek] *n.* (*made by beak*) клево́к; (*fig., hasty kiss*): **he gave her a ~ on the cheek** он чмо́кнул её в щёку.

v.t. клева́ть, клю́нуть; поклева́ть (*pf.*).

v.i. (*fig.*): **she ~ed at her food** она́ едва́ дотро́нулась до еды́; **~ing order** ≃ неофициа́льная иера́рхия.

peckish ['pekɪʃ] *adj.* (*coll.*) голо́дный.

pectoral ['pektər(ə)l] *adj.* грудно́й.

peculiar [pɪ'kju:lɪə(r)] *adj.* **1.** (*exclusive, distinctive*) осо́бенный, своеобра́зный; **this custom is ~ to the English** э́то чи́сто англи́йский обы́чай. **2.** (*particular*) осо́бенный; **a building of ~ interest** зда́ние, представля́ющее осо́бый интере́с. **3.** (*strange*) стра́нный.

peculiarity [pɪ,kju:lɪ'ærɪtɪ] *n.* (*characteristic*) сво́йство; осо́бенность; (*oddity*) стра́нность.

pecuniary [pɪ'kju:nɪərɪ] *adj.* де́нежный.

pedagogic(al) [,pedə'gɒgɪk((ə)l), -'gɒdʒɪk((ə)l)] *adj.* педагоги́ческий.

pedagogue ['pedə,gɒg] *n.* педаго́г.

pedagogy ['pedə,gɒdʒɪ, -,gɒgɪ] *n.* педаго́гика.

pedal ['ped(ə)l] *n.* педа́ль.

v.t. & i. (*of cyclist*) е́хать (*det.*) (на велосипе́де); (*of organist*) наж|има́ть, -а́ть (на) педа́ль.

pedant ['ped(ə)nt] *n.* педа́нт.

pedantic [pɪ'dæntɪk] *adj.* педанти́чный.

pedantry ['ped(ə)ntrɪ] *n.* педанти́чность.

peddle ['ped(ə)l] *v.t.* торгова́ть (*impf.*) вразно́с.

peddler ['pedlə(r)] = **pedlar**

pe|derast, pae- ['pedə,ræst] *n.* педера́ст.

pe|derasty, pae- ['pedə,ræstɪ] *n.* педера́стия.

pedestal ['pedɪst(ə)l] *n.* (*of column or statue*) пьедеста́л; (*of desk etc.*) основа́ние.

pedestrian [pɪ'destrɪən] *n.* пешехо́д.

adj. **1.** (*of or for walking*) пешехо́дный; **~ crossing** перехо́д; **~ footpath** пешехо́дная доро́жка. **2.** (*fig., prosaic*) прозаи́чный, ску́чный.

pedestrianization [pɪ,destrɪə,naɪ'zeɪʃ(ə)n] *n.* созда́ние пешехо́дных зон.

pedestrianize [pɪ'destrɪə,naɪz] *v.t.* запре|ща́ть, -ти́ть автомоби́льное движе́ние.

pedicure ['pedɪ,kjʊə(r)] *n.* педикю́р.

pedigree ['pedɪ,gri:] *n.* (*genealogical table*) родосло́вная; (*line of descent*) происхожде́ние; (*attr.*): **~ cattle** племенно́й скот.

pediment ['pedɪmənt] *n.* фронто́н.

pedlar ['pedlə(r)] (*US* **peddler**) *n.* разно́счик, коробе́йник.

pedometer [pɪ'dɒmɪtə(r)] *n.* шагоме́р.

peek [pi:k] (*coll.*) *n.* взгляд укра́дкой.
v.i. взгля́|дывать, -ну́ть; **~ in** загля́|дывать, -ну́ть; **~ out** выгля́дывать, вы́глянуть.

peel [pi:l] *n.* (*thin skin e.g. of apple or potato*) кожура́, шелуха́; (*rind of orange etc.*) ко́рка.
v.t. **1.** (*remove skin from*) оч|ища́ть, -и́стить; (*fig.*): **he kept his eyes ~ed** (*coll.*) он смотре́л в о́ба. **2.** (*remove from surface*) сн|има́ть, -я́ть; **he ~ed the stamp off the envelope** он откле́ил ма́рку от конве́рта.
v.i. **1.** (*lose skin, bark etc.*) шелуши́ться (*impf.*); **the sun makes my arms ~** у меня́ шелуша́тся пле́чи от со́лнца. **2.** (*come away from surface; also* **~ away, ~ off**) слез|а́ть, -ть; обл|еза́ть, -е́зть; **the paint has begun to ~ (off)** кра́ска начала́ сходи́ть.
with advs.: **~ away** *v.t.* сн|има́ть, -ять; *v.i.* = **peel** *v.i.* **2.**; **~ off** *v.t.*: **he ~ed off his clothes and dived in** он сбро́сил с себя́ оде́жду и нырну́л; *v.i.* (*lit.*) = **peel** *v.i.* **2.**

peeler ['pi:lə(r)] *n.* (*device for peeling*) шелуши́тель (*m.*).

peeling ['pi:lıŋ] *n.* кожура́, шелуха́; **potato ~s** карто́фельные очи́стки (*f. pl.*).

peep[1] [pi:p] *n.* (*furtive or hasty look*) взгляд укра́дкой; **~ing Tom** ≃ любопы́тная Варва́ра; **take, have a ~ at** взгляну́ть (*pf.*) на+*a.*
v.i. погля́д|ывать, -е́ть; **he ~ed in at the window** он загляну́л в окно́.
cpd. **~-hole** *n.* глазо́к.

peep[2] [pi:p] *n.* (*chirp*) писк, чири́канье.
v.i. пища́ть, пи́скнуть; чири́к|ать, -нуть.

peer[1] [pıə(r)] *n.* **1.** (*equal*) ро́вня; **you will not find his ~** вы не найдёте ему́ ра́вного; **~ group** гру́ппа све́рстников. **2.** (*noble*) лорд, пэр; **he was made a ~** его́ возвели́ в ло́рды.

peer[2] [pıə(r)] *v.i.* (*look closely*) всм|а́триваться, -отре́ться (в+*a.*).

peerage ['pıərıdʒ] *n.* (*body of peers*) сосло́вие пэ́ров; (*rank*) пэ́рство, ти́тул пэ́ра.

peerless ['pıərlıs] *adj.* несравне́нный.

peeve [pi:v] (*coll.*) *v.t.*: **he looks ~d** у него́ недово́льный вид.

peevish ['pi:vıʃ] *adj.* брюзгли́вый; капри́зный.

peg [peg] *n.* ко́лышек; **(clothes-~)** крючо́к; **(hat-, coat-~)** ве́шалка; **he buys his clothes off the ~** он покупа́ет гото́вую оде́жду; (*fig.*): **he is a square ~ in a round hole** он не на своём ме́сте; **he should be taken down a ~** с него́ на́до сбить спесь.
v.t. (*fasten*) прикреп|ля́ть, -и́ть; (*comm., fix level of*): **~ prices** замор|а́живать, -о́зить це́ны.
with advs.: **~ down** *v.t.* (*lit.*) укреп|ля́ть, -и́ть; **~ out** *v.t.* (*hang out with* **~s**): **~ out the clothes** разве́|шивать, -сить оде́жду; *v.i.* (*sl., expire*) выдыха́ться, вы́дохнуться.
cpd. **~-leg** *n.* деревя́нная нога́.

peignoir ['peınwɑ:(r)] *n.* пеньюа́р.

pejorative [pı'dʒɒrətıv, 'pi:dʒə-] *adj.* унижи́тельный, пренебрежи́тельный.

Pekin(g)ese [,pi:kı'ni:z] *n.* (*dog*) кита́йский мопс, пекине́с.

pelican ['pelıkən] *n.* пелика́н.

pellet ['pelıt] *n.* ша́рик; (*small shot*) пу́лька.

pell-mell [pel'mel] *adv.* впереме́шку; беспоря́дочно.

pellucid [pı'lu:sıd, -'lju:sıd] *adj.* прозра́чный.

pelmet ['pelmıt] *n.* ламбреке́н.

pelt[1] [pelt] *n.* (*skin*) ко́жа, шку́ра.

pelt[2] [pelt] *n.*: **at full ~** по́лным хо́дом.
v.t. (*assail*) швыр|я́ть, -ну́ть; забр|а́сывать, -о́сить.
v.i. стуча́ть, по-; бараба́нить (*impf.*); **the rain was ~ing down** дождь бараба́нил вовсю́.

pelvic ['pelvık] *adj.* та́зовый; **~ girdle** та́зовый по́яс.

pelvis ['pelvıs] *n.* таз.

pen[1] [pen] *n.* (*writing instrument*) перо́ (*strictly* 'nib, quill'), ру́чка (*strictly* '**~-holder**'); **he never puts ~ to paper** он никогда́ не берётся за перо́.
v.t. писа́ть, на-; сочин|я́ть, -и́ть.
cpds. **~-friend** *n.* корреспонде́нт (*fem.* -ка); **~holder** *n.* ру́чка; **~knife** *n.* перочи́нный но́ж(ик); **~-name** *n.* (литерату́рный) псевдони́м.

pen[2] [pen] *n.* (*enclosure*) заго́н.
v.t. (*also* **~ in, ~ up**) зап|ира́ть, -ере́ть.

penal ['pi:n(ə)l] *adj.*: **~ code** уголо́вный ко́декс; **~ colony** штрафна́я коло́ния; **~ servitude** ка́торжные рабо́ты.

penalize ['pi:nə,laız] *v.t.* штрафова́ть, о-; нака́з|ывать, -а́ть; **he was ~d for a foul** он был нака́зан за гру́бую игру́.

penalty ['penəltı] *n.* (*lit., fig.*) наказа́ние; **on, under ~ of death** под стра́хом сме́ртной ка́зни; (*sport*) штрафно́е очко́; **~ kick** штрафно́й уда́р.

penance ['penəns] *n.* покая́ние.

pence [pens] *n. see* **penny**

penchant ['pɑ̃ʃɑ̃] *n.* скло́нность (*к чему*).

pencil ['pensıl] *n.* каранда́ш; **coloured ~** цветно́й каранда́ш; **eyebrow ~** каранда́ш для брове́й; **a ~ drawing** рису́нок карандашо́м.
v.t. рисова́ть, на-; **~led eyebrows** подрисо́ванные бро́ви.

pendant ['pend(ə)nt] *n.* подве́ска; брело́к.

pending ['pendıŋ] *adj.* рассма́триваемый; нерешённый; **~ tray, file** я́щик для бума́г, отло́женных для рассмотре́ния; па́пка «К рассмотре́нию».
prep. **1.** (*during*) во вре́мя+*g.*; в тече́ние+*g.* **2.** (*until*) до+*g.*; в ожида́нии+*g.*

pendulous ['pendjʊləs] *adj.* подвесно́й.

pendulum ['pendjʊləm] *n.* ма́ятник.

penetrate ['penı,treıt] *v.t.* **1.** (*pierce, find access to*) прон|ика́ть, -и́кнуть в+*a.*; **they ~d the enemy's defences** они́ прорвали́сь че́рез оборо́ну проти́вника; (*see through*): **our eyes could not ~ the darkness** мы не могли́ ничего́ разгляде́ть в темноте́. **2.** (*pervade*) прон|ика́ть, -и́кнуть; прони́з|ывать, -а́ть; **the smell ~d the whole house** за́пах распространи́лся по всему́ до́му.
v.i. **1.** (*make one's way*) вт|орга́ться, -о́ргнуться; **Livingstone ~d into the interior of Africa** Ливингсто́н прони́к вглубь А́фрики. **2.** (*be heard clearly*): **his voice ~d into the next room** его́ го́лос доноси́лся в сосе́днюю ко́мнату.

penetrating ['penı,treıtıŋ] *adj.* си́льный; о́стрый; **a ~ mind** проница́тельный ум; **a ~ voice** пронзи́тельный го́лос.

penetration [,penı'treıʃ(ə)n] *n.* (*penetrating*) проника́ние; проникнове́ние; (*mil., breach of defences*) проры́в; (*mental acumen*) проница́тельность.

penguin ['peŋgwın] *n.* пингви́н.

penicillin [,penı'sılın] *n.* пеницилли́н.

peninsula [pı'nınsjʊlə] *n.* полуо́стров.

peninsular [pı'nınsjʊlə(r)] *adj.* полуостровно́й.

penis ['pi:nıs] *n.* пе́нис, (мужско́й) член.

penitence ['penıt(ə)ns] *n.* раска́яние.

penitent ['penıt(ə)nt] *adj.* раска́ивающийся.

penitentiary [,penı'tenʃərı] *n.* (*house of correction*) исправи́тельный дом; (*prison*) тюрьма́.

pennant ['penənt] *n.* флажо́к, вы́мпел.

penniless ['penılıs] *adj.* без гроша́.

penny ['penı] *n.* пе́нни (*nt. indecl.*), пенс; (*US coin*) цент; **a ~ for your thoughts** о чём вы заду́мались?; **that cost a pretty ~** э́то влете́ло в копе́ечку; **at last the ~ has dropped!** (*coll.*) наконе́ц-то дошло́; **I must (go and) spend a ~** (*coll.*) мне ну́жно кой-куда́.
cpds. **~-farthing** *n.* (*bicycle*) велосипе́д-пау́к; **~-in-the-slot machine** *n.* автома́т.

pension ['penʃ(ə)n] *n.* пе́нсия; **old-age ~** пе́нсия по ста́рости; **war ~** вое́нная пе́нсия.

with adv.: **~ off** *v.t.* ув|ольня́ть, -о́лить на пе́нсию.
pension [pɑ̃'sjɔ̃] *n.* (*boarding-house*) пансио́н.
pensionable ['penʃənəb(ə)l] *adj.*: **he is a ~ employee** он име́ет пра́во на пе́нсию; **his job is ~** э́то рабо́та даёт ему́ пра́во на пе́нсию.
pensioner ['penʃənə(r)] *n.* пенсионе́р.
pensive ['pensɪv] *adj.* заду́мчивый.
pensiveness ['pensɪvnɪs] *n.* заду́мчивость.
pent [pent] *adj.*: **~-up feelings** пода́вленные чу́вства.
pentagon ['pentəgən] *n.* пятиуго́льник; **the P~** (*U.S. War Dept.*) Пентаго́н.
pentameter [pen'tæmɪtə(r)] *n.* пента́метр.
Pentateuch ['pentəˌtju:k] *n.* пятикни́жие.
pentathlete [pen'tæθli:t] *n.* пятибо́рец.
pentathlon [pen'tæθlən] *n.* пятибо́рье.
Pentecost ['pentɪˌkɒst] *n.* пятидеся́тница.
penthouse ['penthaʊs] *n.* (*US*, *apartment on roof*) особня́к, вы́строенный на кры́ше небоскрёба.
penultimate [pɪ'nʌltɪmət] *adj.* предпосле́дный.
penumbra [pɪ'nʌmbrə] *n.* полуте́нь.
penurious [pɪ'njʊərɪəs] *adj.* бе́дный; ску́дный.
penury ['penjʊrɪ] *n.* нужда́; ску́дность.
peony ['pi:ənɪ] *n.* пио́н.
people ['pi:p(ə)l] *n.* **1.** (*race*, *nation*) наро́д; **~'s republic** наро́дная респу́блика. **2.** (*proletariat*) наро́д; **the common ~** просто́й наро́д; **a man of the ~** челове́к из наро́да. **3.** (*inhabitants*) жи́тели (*m. pl.*); (*citizens*) гра́ждане (*m. pl.*). **4.** (*persons grouped by class*, *place etc.*): **poor ~** бедняки́ (*m. pl.*); **country ~** се́льские жи́тели; **young ~** молодёжь; **old ~** старики́ (*m. pl.*); **our ~** на́ши. **5.** (*relatives*, *parents*) родны́е (*pl.*). **6.** (*persons in general*) лю́ди (*pl.*, *g.* -е́й); **few ~** ма́ло люде́й; **four ~** четы́ре челове́ка; че́тверо; **there were 20 ~ present** прису́тствовало 20 челове́к; **~ say he's mad** говоря́т, что он сумасше́дший.
v.t. засел|я́ть, -и́ть; **a thickly-~d district** густонаселённый райо́н.
pep [pep] (*coll.*) *n.* бо́дрость ду́ха; **put some ~ into it!** живе́е!; **~ pill** стимуля́тор, стимули́рующая пилю́ля (*наркотик*); **~ talk** «нака́чка».
v.t. (*usu.* **~ up**) подбодр|я́ть, -и́ть.
pepper ['pepə(r)] *n.* (*condiment*) пе́рец; (*capsicum plant or pod*) стручко́вый пе́рец.
v.t. **1.** (*sprinkle or season with ~*) пе́рчить, на-/по-. **2.** (*fig.*, *sprinkle*) усе́|ивать, -ять. **3.** (*fig.*, *pelt*) забр|а́сывать, -о́сить.
cpds. **~corn** *n.* пе́речное зерно́, перчи́нка; **~-mill** *n.* ме́льница (для пе́рца); **~mint** *n.* (*plant*; *its essence*) мя́та пе́речная; (*flavoured sweet*) мя́тный ледене́ц; **~-pot** *n.* пе́речница.
peppery ['pepərɪ] *adj.* (*of food*) напе́рченный; (*fig.*, *irascible*) вспы́льчивый.
pepsin ['pepsɪn] *n.* пепси́н.
peptic ['peptɪk] *adj.* пепти́ческий, пищевари́тельный; **~ ulcer** я́зва желу́дка.
per [pɜ:(r)] *prep.* **1.** (*for each*) в+*a.*; на+*a.*; с+*g.*; **60 miles ~ hour** 60 миль в час; **grams ~ square centimetre** гра́ммы на оди́н квадра́тный сантиме́тр; **they collected 20 pence ~ man** они́ собра́ли по 20 пе́нсов с челове́ка. **2.**: **as ~ usual** (*coll.*) по обыкнове́нию.
per annum [pər 'ænəm] *adv.* в год.
per capita [pə 'kæpɪtə] *adv.* на ду́шу.
perceivable [pə'si:vəb(ə)l] *adj.* ощути́мый.
perceive [pə'si:v] *v.t.* (*with mind*) пон|има́ть, -я́ть; пост|ига́ть, -и́гнуть, -и́чь; (*through senses*) чу́вствовать, по-; ощу|ща́ть, -ти́ть.
per cent, percent [pə 'sent] *n.* проце́нт; **three ~** три проце́нта.
adv. проце́нт, на со́тню.
percentage [pə'sentɪdʒ] *n.* (*rate per cent*) проце́нтное содержа́ние; (*proportion*) проце́нтное отноше́ние, проце́нт; (*share in profits*) до́ля, часть.
perceptibl|e [pə'septɪb(ə)l] *adj.* ощути́мый; **he was ~y moved** он был заме́тно растро́ган.
perception [pə'sepʃ(ə)n] *n.* (*process or faculty of perceiving*) восприя́тие, ощуще́ние; (*quality of discernment*) осозна́ние; понима́ние.
perceptive [pə'septɪv] *adj.* восприи́мчивый; проница́тельный.
perch[1] [pɜ:tʃ] *n.* (*zool.*) о́кунь (*m.*).
perch[2] [pɜ:tʃ] *n.* (*of bird*) насе́ст.
v.t. & i. сади́ться (*impf.*) на насе́ст; устр|а́иваться, -о́иться; **he ~ed (himself) on a stool** он присе́л на табуре́т.
perchance [pə'tʃɑ:ns] *adv.* (*arch. or joc.*) случа́йно.
percolate ['pɜ:kəˌleɪt] *v.t.* про|ходи́ть, -йти́ че́рез+*a.*
v.i. прос|а́чиваться, -очи́ться; **water ~s through sand** вода́ прохо́дит сквозь песо́к; **I'm waiting for the coffee to ~** я жду, пока́ ко́фе профильтру́ется.
percolator ['pɜ:kəˌleɪtə(r)] *n.* (*cul.*) кофе́йник, перколя́тор, кофева́рка.
percussion [pə'kʌʃ(ə)n] *n.* **1.** (*striking*) уда́р; **~ cap** уда́рный писто́н. **2.** (**~ instruments**) уда́рные инструме́нты (*m. pl.*).
percussionist [pə'kʌʃ(ə)nɪst] *n.* уда́рник.
per diem [pə 'di:em, 'daɪem] *adv.* в день.
perdition [pə'dɪʃ(ə)n] *n.* ги́бель.
peregrination [ˌperɪgrɪ'neɪʃ(ə)n] *n.* стра́нствование.
peregrine ['perɪgrɪn] *n.* (**~ falcon**) со́кол; сапса́н.
peremptory [pə'remptərɪ, 'perɪm-] *adj.* (*imperious*) повели́тельный; непререка́емый.
perennial [pə'renɪəl] *n.* (*plant*) многоле́тнее расте́ние; **hardy ~** (*lit.*) выно́сливый многоле́тник.
adj. (*lasting throughout year*) для́щийся кру́глый год; (*enduring*) (веко)ве́чный; (*regularly repeated*) регуля́рно повторя́ющийся.
perestroika [ˌpere'strɔ:kə]*n.* перестро́йка.
perfect[1] ['pɜ:fɪkt] *n.* (*gram.*) перфе́кт; **the future ~** бу́дущее соверше́нное вре́мя.
adj. **1.** (*entire*, *complete*; *absolute*) соверше́нный, по́лный; **that is ~ nonsense** э́то абсолю́тная чепуха́; **a ~ stranger** совсе́м чужо́й (челове́к); **I am ~ly sure of it** я соверше́нно уве́рен в э́том. **2.** (*faultless*) соверше́нный; безупре́чный; **he speaks ~ English** он в соверше́нстве говори́т по-англи́йски; (*thoroughly accomplished*) соверше́нный; (*corresponding to an ideal*) соверше́нный, идеа́льный; (*corresponding to definition*; *archetypal*): **a ~ circle** то́чный круг; **he committed the ~ murder** он соверши́л класси́ческое уби́йство. **3.** (*exact*, *precise*) абсолю́тный; **~ pitch** (*mus.*) абсолю́тный слух; (*corresponding to requirements*) безупре́чный; **the dress is a ~ fit** пла́тье прекра́сно сиди́т. **4.** (*gram.*) перфе́ктный, соверше́нный; **~ tense** перфе́кт.
perfect[2] [pə'fekt] *v.t.* (*complete*; *accomplish*, *achieve*) заверш|а́ть, -и́ть; выполня́ть, вы́полнить; (*bring to highest standard*) соверше́нствовать, у-.
perfection [pə'fekʃ(ə)n] *n.* **1.** (*perfecting*) заверше́ние, соверше́нствование. **2.** (*faultlessness*, *excellence*) соверше́нство. **3.** (*ideal or its embodiment*) зако́нченность.
perfectionist [pə'fekʃənɪst] *n.* взыска́тельный челове́к; добива́ющийся соверше́нства.
perfective [pə'fektɪv] *n.* (*gram.*) соверше́нный вид.
adj. соверше́нный; в соверше́нном ви́де.
perfidious [ˌpɜ:'fɪdɪəs] *adj.* вероло́мный, кова́рный.
perfid|iousness [ˌpɜ:'fɪdɪəsnɪs], **-y** ['pɜ:fɪdɪ] *nn.* вероло́мство, кова́рность.
perforate ['pɜ:fəˌreɪt] *v.t.* перфори́ровать (*impf.*); **a ~d appendix** прободно́й аппе́ндикс.
perforation [ˌpɜ:fə'reɪʃ(ə)n] *n.* (*piercing*) перфора́ция; (*row of pierced holes*) перфори́рованный ряд.
perform [pə'fɔ:m] *v.t.* **1.** (*carry out*) выполня́ть, вы́полнить; исп|олня́ть, -о́лнить. **2.** (*enact*) исп|ол-

ня́ть, -о́лнить; **Hamlet will be ~ed next week** «Га́млета» даю́т на сле́дующей неде́ле; **he ~ed conjuring tricks** он показа́л фо́кусы.

v.i. **1.** (*act, play instrument etc.*) игра́ть, сыгра́ть; (*execute tricks*): **~ing seal** дрессиро́ванный тюле́нь. **2.** (*function*): **my car ~s well on hills** моя́ маши́на хорошо́ идёт в го́ру.

performance [pə'fɔ:məns] *n.* **1.** (*execution*) исполне́ние, выполне́ние; **in the ~ of his duty** при исполне́нии до́лга. **2.** (*achievement, feat*) де́йствие. **3.** (*of a machine, vehicle etc.*) ход, характери́стика. **4.** (*public appearance*) выступле́ние. **5.** (*of play etc.*) представле́ние; постано́вка; спекта́кль (*m.*); (*of music*) исполне́ние.

performer [pə'fɔ:mə(r)] *n.* исполни́тель (*m.*).

perfume ['pɜ:fju:m] *n.* (*odour*) благоуха́ние; (*fluid*) дух|и́ (*pl., g.* -о́в).

v.t. (*impart odour to*) де́лать, с- благоуха́нным; (*apply scent to*) души́ть, на-.

perfumer [pə'fju:mə(r)] *n.* парфюме́р.

perfumery [pə'fju:mərɪ] *n.* парфюме́рия.

perfunctory [pə'fʌŋktərɪ] *adj.* пове́рхностный; небре́жный.

pergola ['pɜ:gələ] *n.* пе́ргола.

perhaps [pə'hæps] *adv.* мо́жет быть; возмо́жно; пожа́луй; **~ not** мо́жет быть и нет.

peril ['perɪl] *n.* опа́сность; риск; **he goes in ~ of his life** его́ жизнь в постоя́нной опа́сности.

perilous ['perɪləs] *adj.* опа́сный; риско́ванный.

perimeter [pə'rɪmɪtə(r)] *n.* (*of a geom. figure*) пери́метр; (*of an airfield etc.*) вне́шняя грани́ца.

period ['pɪərɪəd] *n.* **1.** пери́од; **he will be away for a long ~** его́ не бу́дет до́лгое вре́мя. **2.** (*previous age*) эпо́ха; **~ furniture** сти́льная ме́бель. **3.** (*session of instruction*) уро́к. **4.** (*menses*) ме́сячные (*pl.*). **5.** (*full stop*) то́чка; коне́ц.

periodic [,pɪərɪ'ɒdɪk] *adj.* периоди́ческий, очередно́й; **~ table** (*chem.*) периоди́ческая табли́ца.

periodical [,pɪərɪ'ɒdɪk(ə)l] *n.* периоди́ческое изда́ние; (*pl.*) перио́дика.

adj. = **periodic**

peripatetic [,perɪpə'tetɪk] *adj.* (*itinerant*) бродя́чий.

peripheral [pə'rɪfər(ə)l] *n.* (*comput.*) перифери́йное устро́йство.

adj. (*lit.*) перифери́йный; (*fig., not central to a subject*) несуще́ственный; побо́чный.

periphery [pə'rɪfərɪ] *n.* (*lit., fig.*) перифери́я.

periscope ['perɪ,skəʊp] *n.* периско́п.

periscopic [,perɪ'skɒpɪk] *adj.* перископи́ческий; **~ sight** периско́пный приме́л.

perish ['perɪʃ] *v.t.*: **we were ~ed with cold** мы про́сто погиба́ли от хо́лода; **strong sun will ~ rubber** си́льные со́лнечные лучи́ разруша́ют рези́ну.

v.i. **1.** пог|иба́ть, -и́бнуть; **~ the thought!** Бо́же упаси́! **2.**: **the rubber has ~ed** рези́на пришла́ в него́дность.

perishable ['perɪʃəb(ə)l] *adj.* тле́нный, непро́чный, скоропо́ртящийся; (*pl., as n.*) скоропо́ртящийся това́р.

perishing ['perɪʃɪŋ] *adj.* (*coll.*) (*cold*): **it's ~ here** здесь а́дский хо́лод.

peritoneum [,perɪtə'ni:əm] *n.* брюши́на.

peritonitis [,perɪtə'naɪtɪs] *n.* перитони́т.

periwinkle ['perɪ,wɪŋk(ə)l] *n.* (*mollusc*) litори́на; (*plant*) барви́нок.

perjure ['pɜ:dʒə(r)] *v.t.*: **~ o.s.** да|ва́ть, -ть ло́жное показа́ние под прися́гой.

perjurer ['pɜ:dʒərə(r)] *n.* лжесвиде́тель (*fem.* -ница).

perjury ['pɜ:dʒərɪ] *n.* лжесвиде́тельство; **commit ~** = **perjure o.s.**

perk[1] [pɜ:k] *n.* (*coll.*) = **perquisite**

perk[2] [pɜ:k] *v.t.* **1.** (*move smartly*): **the dog ~ed up its tail** соба́ка задрала́ хвост. **2.**: **~ up** (*smarten*) приукра́|шивать, -сить; ожив|ля́ть, -и́ть.

v.i.: **I hope the weather ~s up** (*coll.*) наде́юсь, что пого́да нала́дится.

perky ['pɜ:kɪ] *adj.* живо́й, бо́йкий; весёлый.

perm [pɜ:m] *n.* (*coll., permanent wave*) переманент.

v.t.: **she had her hair ~ed** она́ сде́лала себе́ пермане́нтную зави́вку.

permafrost ['pɜ:mə,frɒst] *n.* ве́чная мерзлота́.

permanence ['pɜ:mənəns] *n.* неизме́нность.

permanent ['pɜ:mənənt] *adj.* постоя́нный; **~ wave** зави́вка «пермане́нт».

permanganate [pɜ:'mæŋgə,neɪt, -nət] *n.* перманганат; **~ of potash** марганцовоки́слый ка́лий.

permeability [,pɜ:mɪə'bɪlɪtɪ] *n.* проница́емость.

permeable ['pɜ:mɪəb(ə)l] *adj.* проница́емый.

permeate ['pɜ:mɪ,eɪt] *v.t. & i.* пропи́т|ывать, -а́ть; прос|а́чиваться, -очи́ться в+*a.*

permissible [pə'mɪsɪb(ə)l] *adj.* допусти́мый, позволи́тельный.

permission [pə'mɪʃ(ə)n] *n.* позволе́ние, разреше́ние; **with your ~ I'll leave** с ва́шего позволе́ния я ухожу́.

permissive [pə'mɪsɪv] *adj.*: **~ society** о́бщество вседозво́ленности.

permissiveness [pə'mɪsɪvnɪs] *n.* вседозво́ленность.

permit[1] ['pɜ:mɪt] *n.* разреше́ние, про́пуск (*pl.* -а́); **work ~** разреше́ние на рабо́ту; **residence ~** вид на жи́тельство.

permit[2] [pə'mɪt] *v.t.* разреш|а́ть, -и́ть; **if I may be ~ted to speak** е́сли мне бу́дет позво́лено вы́сказаться.

v.i.: **if circumstances ~** е́сли обстоя́тельства позво́лят; **weather ~ting** е́сли пого́да позво́лит.

permutation [,pɜ:mjʊ'teɪʃ(ə)n] *n.* пермута́ция.

pernicious [pə'nɪʃəs] *adj.* па́губный, вре́дный; **~ anaemia** злока́чественное малокро́вие.

peroxide [pə'rɒksaɪd] *n.* пе́рекись; **hydrogen ~** пе́рекись водоро́да.

perpendicular [,pɜ:pən'dɪkjʊlə(r)] *n.* перпендикуля́р.

adj. (*at right angles*) перпендикуля́рный; (*vertical*) вертика́льный.

perpetrate ['pɜ:pɪ,treɪt] *v.t.* соверш|а́ть, -и́ть.

perpetration [,pɜ:pɪ'treɪʃ(ə)n] *n.* соверше́ние.

perpetrator ['pɜ:pɪ,treɪtə(r)] *n.* вино́вный; престу́пник.

perpetual [pə'petjʊəl] *adj.* ве́чный; **~ motion** ве́чное движе́ние.

perpetuate [pə'petjʊ,eɪt] *v.t.* увекове́чи|вать, -ть.

perpetuation [pə,petjʊ'eɪʃ(ə)n] *n.* увекове́чение.

perpetuity [,pɜ:pɪ'tju:ɪtɪ] *n.* ве́чность; **in ~** (на)ве́чно.

perplex [pə'pleks] *v.t.* озада́чи|вать, -ть.

perplexity [pə'pleksɪtɪ] *n.* (*bewilderment*) озада́ченность, недоуме́ние.

perquisite ['pɜ:kwɪzɪt] *n.* льго́та; (*pl.*) побо́чные преиму́щества.

per se [pɜ: 'seɪ] *adv.* само́ по себе́.

persecute ['pɜ:sɪ,kju:t] *v.t.* пресле́довать (*impf.*).

persecution [,pɜ:sɪ'kju:ʃ(ə)n] *n.* пресле́дование.

persecutor ['pɜ:sɪ,kju:tə(r)] *n.* пресле́дователь (*m.*).

perseverance [,pɜ:sɪ'vɪərəns] *n.* упо́рство; насто́йчивость.

persever|e [,pɜ:sɪ'vɪə(r)] *v.i.*: **you must ~e in (at, with) your work** вы должны́ упо́рно продолжа́ть свою́ рабо́ту; **he is very ~ing** он о́чень стара́телен.

Persia ['pɜ:ʃə] *n.* Пе́рсия.

Persian ['pɜ:ʃ(ə)n] *n.* (*pers.*) перс (*fem.* -ия́нка); (*language*) перси́дский язы́к.

adj. перси́дский; **~ Gulf** Перси́дский зали́в.

persimmon [pɜ:'sɪmən] *n.* хурма́.

persist [pə'sɪst] *v.i.* **1.** (*resist dissuasion*) упо́рствовать (*impf.*). **2.** (*continue to exist, remain*) сохран|я́ться, -и́ться; **fog will ~ all day** тума́н продержи́тся весь день.

persistence [pə'sɪst(ə)ns] *n.* (*obstinacy*) упо́рство; (*continuation*) продолже́ние.

persistent [pə'sɪst(ə)nt] *adj.* **1.** (*obstinate*) упо́рный.

2. (*slow to go or change*) устóйчивый, постоя́нный.

person ['pɜ:s(ə)n] *n.* **1.** (*individual*) человéк; осóба; **a young ~** молода́я осóба; **not a single ~ was injured** ра́неных нé было совсéм; (*of particular category*) лицó; **a very important ~** óчень ва́жное лицó. **2.** (*body*) лицó; **an offence against the ~** преступлéние прóтив ли́чности; **the great man appeared in ~** вели́кий человéк яви́лся сóбственной персóной. **3.** (*gram.*) лицó; **first ~** пéрвое лицó.

persona [pɜ:'səʊnə] *n.* внéшняя сторона́ ли́чности; **~ (non) grata** персóна (нон) гра́та (*indecl.*).

personable ['pɜ:sənəb(ə)l] *adj.* привлека́тельный.

personage ['pɜ:sənɪdʒ] *n.* (*important person*) ли́чность; (*in a play*) персона́ж.

personal ['pɜ:sən(ə)l] *adj.* ли́чный; **she is a ~ acquaintance of mine** я её ли́чно зна́ю; **~ estate** (*leg.*) дви́жимое иму́щество; **~ pronoun** ли́чное местоимéние; **~ stereo** плéер; **don't make ~ remarks!** не переходи́те на ли́чности!

personality [,pɜ:sə'nælɪtɪ] *n.* **1.** (*character*) ли́чность; **a strong ~** си́льная ли́чность; **~ cult** культ ли́чности. **3.** (*public figure*) дéятель (*m.*), извéстная ли́чность. **4.** (*pl.*, *offensive remarks*) вы́пады (*m. pl.*).

personalize ['pɜ:sənə,laɪz] *v.t.* прин|има́ть, -я́ть на свой счёт; вноси́ть, -ести́ ли́чный элемéнт в+*a.*; **~d stationery** именна́я пи́счая бума́га.

personally ['pɜ:sənəlɪ] *adv.* ли́чно; **don't take it ~!** не принима́йте э́то на свой счёт!

personification [pə,sɒnɪfɪ'keɪʃ(ə)n] *n.* олицетворéние.

personif|y [pə'sɒnɪ,faɪ] *v.t.* (*give personal attributes to*) олицетвор|я́ть, -и́ть; (*exemplify*) вопло|ща́ть, -ти́ть; **she was kindness ~ied** она́ была́ воплощéнием доброты́.

personnel [,pɜ:sə'nel] *n.* персона́л; штат; ка́дры (*m. pl.*); **~ department** отдéл ка́дров.

perspective [pə'spektɪv] *n.* **1.** (*system of representation*) перспекти́ва; **the roof is out of ~** (*in a drawing*) кры́ша изображена́ вне перспекти́вы; (*fig.*): **you must get things in ~** на́до ви́деть вéщи в их и́стинным свéте. **2.** (*vista*) вид; (*fig.*) перспекти́вы (*f.pl.*).
adj. перспекти́вный.

perspex ['pɜ:speks] *n.* плексигла́с.

perspicacious [,pɜ:spɪ'keɪʃəs] *adj.* проница́тельный.

perspicacity [,pɜ:spɪ'kæsɪtɪ] *n.* проница́тельность.

perspiration [,pɜ:spɪ'reɪʃ(ə)n] *n.* (*sweating*) потéние; (*sweat*) пот.

perspire [pə'spaɪə(r)] *v.i.* потéть, вс-.

persuade [pə'sweɪd] *v.t.* **1.** (*convince*) убе|жда́ть, -ди́ть; **I ~d him of my innocence** я убеди́л егó в моéй невинóвности. **2.** (*induce*) угов|а́ривать, -ори́ть.

persuasion [pə'sweɪʒ(ə)n] *n.* (*persuading*) убеждéние; (*persuasiveness*) убеди́тельность; (*conviction*) убеждéние; (*denomination*) вероисповéдание.

persuasive [pə'sweɪsɪv] *adj.* убеди́тельный.

persuasiveness [pə'sweɪsɪvnɪs] *n.* убеди́тельность.

pert [pɜ:t] *adj.* дéрзкий, наха́льный.

pertain [pə'teɪn] *v.i.* относи́ться (*impf.*) (*к кому/чему*).

pertinacious [,pɜ:tɪ'neɪʃəs] *adj.* упря́мый, неусту́пчивый.

pertinence ['pɜ:tɪnəns] *n.* умéстность.

pertinent ['pɜ:tɪnənt] *adj.* умéстный; подходя́щий.

perturb [pə'tɜ:b] *v.t.* тревóжить, вс-; волнова́ть, вз-.

perturbation [,pɜ:tə'beɪʃ(ə)n] *n.* встревóженность; волнéние.

Peru [pə'ru:] *n.* Перу́ (*f. indecl.*).

perusal [pə'ru:zəl] *n.* (внима́тельное) чтéние.

peruse [pə'ru:z] *v.t.* внима́тельно чита́ть, про-; (*examine*) рассм|а́тривать, -отрéть.

Peruvian [pə'ru:vɪən] *n.* перуа́н|ец, (*fem.* -ка).
adj. перуа́нский.

pervade [pə'veɪd] *v.t.* наполня́ть (*impf.*); пропи́тывать (*impf.*).

pervasive [pə'veɪsɪv] *adj.* прони́зывающий, распространённый.

perverse [pə'vɜ:s] *adj.* (*unreasonable*) превра́тный; (*persistent in wrongdoing*) порóчный.

pervers|eness [pə'vɜ:snɪs], **-ity** [pə'vɜ:sɪtɪ] *nn.* превра́тность; извращённость.

perversion [pə'vɜ:ʃ(ə)n] *n.* (*distortion*, *misrepresentation*) искажéние; (*corruption*, *leading astray*) извращéние.

pervert[1] ['pɜ:vɜ:t] *n.* (*sexual deviant*) извращéнец.

pervert[2] [pə'vɜ:t] *v.t.* (*misapply*) извра|ща́ть, -ти́ть; (*corrupt*) развра|ща́ть, -ти́ть.

peseta [pə'seɪtə] *n.* песéта.

pesky ['peskɪ] *adj.* (*US coll.*) доку́чливый, зану́дливый.

peso ['peɪsəʊ] *n.* пéсо (*indecl.*).

pessary ['pesərɪ] *n.* песса́рий.

pessimism ['pesɪ,mɪz(ə)m] *n.* пессими́зм.

pessimist ['pesɪmɪst] *n.* пессими́ст.

pessimistic [,pesɪ'mɪstɪk] *adj.* пессимисти́ческий.

pest [pest] *n.* (*harmful creature*) вреди́тель (*m.*); **insect ~s** врéдные насекóмые; (*of pers.*) зану́да (*c.g.*).

pester ['pestə(r)] *v.t.* докуча́ть (*impf.*); **he keeps ~ing me for money** он всё пристаёт ко мне насчёт дéнег.

pesticide ['pestɪ,saɪd] *n.* пестици́д.

pestilence ['pestɪləns] *n.* чума́.

pestilential [,pestɪ'lenʃ(ə)l] *adj.* чумнóй; па́губный.

pestle ['pes(ə)l] *n.* пéстик.

pet [pet] *n.* **1.** (*animal*, *bird etc.*) дома́шнее/кóмнатное/люби́мое живóтное; **~ food** корм для дома́шних живóтных; **~ shop** зоомагази́н. **2.** (*favourite*) люби́м|ец (*fem.* -ица), ба́ловень (*m.*); **his ~ subject** егó излю́бленная тéма; **~ name** ласка́тельное/уменьши́тельное и́мя.
v.t. (*fondle*) ласка́ть, при-.
v.i. (*coll.*, *fondle each other*) обжима́ться (*impf.*).

petal ['pet(ə)l] *n.* лепестóк.

petard [pɪ'tɑ:d] *n.* петáрда.

peter ['pi:tə(r)] *v.i.*: **~ out** (*run dry*, *low*) исс|яка́ть, -я́кнуть; **the track ~ed out** след постепéнно исчéз.

petit bourgeois [,pətɪ 'bʊəʒwɑ:] *adj.* мелкобуржуа́зный.

petite [pə'ti:t] *adj.* ма́ленькая (*f.*), миниатю́рная (*f.*).

petite bourgeoisie [pə'ti:t ,bʊəʒwɑ:'zi:] *n.* мéлкая буржуази́я.

petit four [,petɪ 'fɔ:(r)] *n.* петифу́р.

petition [pɪ'tɪʃ(ə)n] *n.* пети́ция; (*application to court*) хода́тайство.
v.t. & i. хода́тайствовать, по-.

petitioner [pɪ'tɪʃənə(r)] *n.* проси́тель (*m.*).

petits pois [,petɪ 'pwɑ:] *n.* мéлкий горóшек.

petrel ['petr(ə)l] *n.* буревéстник; **stormy ~** качу́рка ма́лая.

petrif|y ['petrɪ,faɪ] *v.t.* (*lit.*) превра|ща́ть, -ти́ть в ка́мень; (*fig.*) прив|оди́ть, -ести́ в оцепенéние; **I was ~ied** я остолбенéл/оцепенéл.

petrochemicals [,petrəʊ'kemɪk(ə)ls] *n. pl.* хими́ческие продýкты (*m. pl.*) из нефтянóго сырья́.

petrodollar ['petrəʊ,dɒlə(r)] *n.* нефтедóллар.

petrol ['petr(ə)l] *n.* бензи́н; **fill up with ~** запр|авля́ться, -а́виться бензи́ном; **~ bomb** буты́лка с зажига́тельной смéсью; **~ can** кани́стра для бензи́на; **~ pump** бензонасóс; **~ station** бензоколóнка; **~ tank** бензоба́к; **~ tanker** бензовóз.

petroleum [pɪ'trəʊlɪəm] *n.* нефть; **the ~ industry** нефтяна́я промы́шленность; **~ jelly** вазели́н.

petticoat ['petɪ,kəʊt] *n.* ни́жняя ю́бка.

pettifogging ['petɪ,fɒgɪŋ] *n.* сутя́жничество, крючкотвóрчество.
adj. сутя́жнический.

pettiness ['petɪnɪs] *n.* мéлочность.

petty ['petɪ] *adj.* **1.** (*trivial*) мéлкий, малова́жный. **2.** (*small-minded*) мéлочный. **3.** (*of small amounts*):

~ **cash** де́ньги на ме́лкие расхо́ды; ~ **theft** ме́лкая кра́жа. **4.:** ~ **officer** (*nav.*) старшина́ (*m.*).
petulance [ˈpetjʊləns] *n.* раздражи́тельность.
petulant [ˈpetjʊlənt] *adj.* раздражи́тельный.
petunia [pɪˈtjuːnɪə] *n.* пету́ния.
pew [pjuː] *n.* отгоро́женное ме́сто в це́ркви.
pewter [ˈpjuːtə(r)] *n.* (*alloy*) сплав о́лова с други́м мета́ллом; (*vessels made of* ~) оловя́нная посу́да.
adj. оловя́нный.
pfennig [ˈpfenɪg, ˈfenɪg] *n.* пфе́нниг.
phalanx [ˈfælæŋks] *n.* фала́нга.
phallic [ˈfælɪk] *adj.* фалли́ческий.
phallus [ˈfæləs] *n.* фа́ллос.
phantasm [ˈfænˌtæz(ə)m] *n.* (*ghost*) фанто́м, при́зрак.
phantasmagoria [ˌfæntæzməˈgɔːrɪə] *n.* фантасмаго́рия.
phantom [ˈfæntəm] *n.* при́зрак, фанто́м; (*attr.*) при́зрачный.
Pharaoh [ˈfeərəʊ] *n.* фарао́н.
Pharisaical [ˌfærɪˈseɪɪk(ə)l] *adj.* (*fig.*) фарисе́йский; (*fig.*) ха́нжеский.
Pharisee [ˈfærɪˌsiː] *n.* фарисе́й; (*fig.*) ханжа́ (*c.g.*).
pharmaceutical [ˌfɑːməˈsjuːtɪk(ə)l] *adj.* фармацевти́ческий; ~ **chemist** фармаце́вт, апте́карь (*m.*).
pharmaceutics [ˌfɑːməˈsjuːtɪks] *n.* фарма́ция.
pharmacist [ˈfɑːməsɪst] *n.* фармаце́вт.
pharmacologist [ˌfɑːməˈkɒlədʒɪst] *n.* фармако́лог.
pharmacology [ˌfɑːməˈkɒlədʒɪ] *n.* фармаколо́гия.
pharmacopoeia [ˌfɑːməkəˈpiːə] *n.* фармакопе́я.
pharmacy [ˈfɑːməsɪ] *n.* (*dispensary*) апте́ка.
pharyng(e)al [ˌfærɪŋˈdʒiːəl] *adj.* гло́точный.
pharynx [ˈfærɪŋks] *n.* зев; гло́тка.
phase [feɪz] *n.* фа́за; (*stage*) ста́дия.
v.t.: **a** ~**d withdrawal** поэта́пный вы́вод; ~ **out** (*e.g. weapons, bases*) сн|има́ть, -я́ть с вооруже́ния (по эта́пам); ликвиди́ровать (*impf., pf.*).
Ph.D. (*abbr. of* ***Doctor of Philosophy***) сте́пень кандида́та нау́к.
pheasant [ˈfez(ə)nt] *n.* фаза́н.
phenomenal [fɪˈnɒmɪn(ə)l] *adj.* феномена́льный.
phenomenon [fɪˈnɒmɪnən] *n.* (*object of perception*) фено́мен, явле́ние; (*remarkable pers. or thg.*) фено́мен, чу́до.
phew [fjuː] *int.* (*expr. astonishment*) ну и ну!; ~, **what a crowd!** ну и толпа́!; (*discomfort*): ~, **isn't it hot!** уф, ну и жара́!; (*disgust*): ~, **that meat's bad!** фу, э́то мя́со испо́рчен!
phial [ˈfaɪəl] *n.* пузырёк.
philander [fɪˈlændə(r)] *v.i.* флиртова́ть (*impf.*).
philanderer [fɪˈlændərə(r)] *n.* волоки́та (*c.g.*).
philanthropic [ˌfɪlənˈθrɒpɪk] *adj.* филантропи́ческий.
philanthropist [fɪˈlænθrəpɪst] *n.* филантро́п.
philanthropy [fɪˈlænθrəpɪ] *n.* филантро́пия.
philatelic [ˌfɪləˈtelɪk] *adj.* филателисти́ческий.
philatelist [ˌfɪˈlætəlɪst] *n.* филатели́ст.
philately [fɪˈlætəlɪ] *n.* филатели́я.
philharmonic [ˌfɪlhɑːˈmɒnɪk] *n.* (~ *society*) филармо́ния.
adj. филармони́ческий.
Philippine [ˈfɪlɪˌpiːn] *adj.* филиппи́нский; **the** ~**s** (*islands*) Филиппи́н|ы (*pl., g.* —).
Philistine [ˈfɪlɪˌstaɪn] *n.* (*fig.*) фили́стер, обыва́тель (*m.*).
adj. обыва́тельский.
Philistinism [ˈfɪlɪstɪˌnɪz(ə)m] *n.* фили́стерство.
philological [ˌfɪləˈlɒdʒɪk(ə)l] *adj.* филологи́ческий.
philologist [fɪˈlɒlədʒɪst] *n.* языкове́д; фило́лог.
philology [fɪˈlɒlədʒɪ] *n.* языкове́дение; филоло́гия.
philosopher [fɪˈlɒsəfə(r)] *n.* фило́соф.
philosophic(al) [ˌfɪləˈsɒfɪk(ə)l] *adj.* филосо́фский.
philosophize [fɪˈlɒsəˌfaɪz] *v.i.* филосо́фствовать (*impf.*).
philosophy [fɪˈlɒsəfɪ] *n.* филосо́фия.
phlebitis [flɪˈbaɪtɪs] *n.* флеби́т.
phlegm [flem] *n.* (*secretion*) мокро́та; (*fig.*) флегмати́чность.
phlegmatic [flegˈmætɪk] *adj.* флегмати́чный.
phobia [ˈfəʊbɪə] *n.* фо́бия, страх.
phoenix [ˈfiːnɪks] *n.* фе́никс.
phone [fəʊn] (*see also* **telephone**) *n.* телефо́н; (*attr.*) телефо́нный; ~ **card** ка́рточка для телефо́нного автома́та.
v.t. & i. звони́ть, по- (*кому*).
with advs.: ~ **back** *v.t. & i.* сде́лать (*pf.*) отве́тный телефо́нный звоно́к; перезвони́ть (*pf.*); ~ **up** *v.t. & i.* позвони́ть (*pf.*) (*кому*).
phoneme [ˈfəʊniːm] *n.* фоне́ма.
phonetic [fəˈnetɪk] *adj.* фонети́ческий.
phonetics [fəˈnetɪks] *n.* фоне́тика.
phon(e)y [ˈfəʊnɪ] (*sl.*) *n.* (*pers.*) шарлата́н, обма́нщик; (*thg.*) подде́лка, фальши́вка, ли́па.
adj. подде́льный, фальши́вый, ли́повый.
phonology [fəˈnɒlədʒɪ] *n.* фоноло́гия.
phosgene [ˈfɒzdʒiːn] *n.* фосге́н.
phosphate [ˈfɒsfeɪt] *n.* фосфа́т.
phosphorescence [ˌfɒsfəˈres(ə)ns] *n.* фосфоресце́нция.
phosphorescent [ˌfɒsfəˈres(ə)nt] *adj.* фосфоресци́рующий.
phosphoric [ˌfɒsˈfɒrɪk] *adj.* фосфори́ческий.
phosphorous [ˈfɒsfərəs] *adj.* фо́сфористый.
phosphorus [ˈfɒsfərəs] *n.* фо́сфор.
photo [ˈfəʊtəʊ] *n.* (*coll.*) фо́то (*indecl.*), сни́мок.
cpds. ~**copier** *n.* фотокопирова́льный аппара́т; ~**-copy** *n.* фотоко́пия; *v.t.* сн|има́ть, -ять фотоко́пию +*g*; ~**-finish** *n.* фотофи́ниш; ~**fit** *n.* фотокомпозицио́нный портре́т.
photoelectric [ˌfəʊtəʊɪˈlektrɪk] *adj.* фотоэлектри́ческий.
photogenic [ˌfəʊtəʊˈdʒenɪk, -ˈdʒiːnɪk] *adj.* фотогени́чный.
photograph [ˈfəʊtəˌgrɑːf] *n.* фотогра́фия.
v.t. фотографи́ровать, с-.
v.i.: **she** ~**s well** она́ хорошо́ выхо́дит на фотогра́фиях.
photographer [fəˈtɒgrəfə(r)] *n.* фото́граф.
photographic [ˌfəʊtəˈgræfɪk] *adj.* фотографи́ческий.
photography [fəˈtɒgrəfɪ] *n.* фотогра́фия.
photogravure [ˌfəʊtəʊgrəˈvjʊə(r)] *n.* фотогравю́ра.
photostat [ˈfəʊtəʊˌstæt] *n.* фотоко́пия.
v.t. сн|има́ть, -ять фотоко́пию +*g*.
phototypesetter [ˌfəʊtəʊˈtaɪpˌsetə(r)] *n.* (*phototypesetting machine*) фотонабо́рный аппара́т.
phrase [freɪz] *n.* фра́за; (*expression*) оборо́т, словосочета́ние; **empty** ~**s** пусты́е слова́.
v.t. формули́ровать, с-.
cpd. ~**-book** *n.* разгово́рник.
phraseological [ˌfreɪzɪəˈlɒdʒɪk(ə)l] *adj.* фразеологи́ческий.
phraseology [ˌfreɪzɪˈɒlədʒɪ] *n.* фразеоло́гия.
phrenetic [frɪˈnetɪk] *adj.* исступлённый.
phrenology [frɪˈnɒlədʒɪ] *n.* френоло́гия.
phylum [ˈfaɪləm] *n.* (*biol.*) фи́люм.
physical [ˈfɪzɪk(ə)l] *adj.* физи́ческий; **the** ~ **universe** материа́льный мир; **it is a** ~ **impossibility** э́то физи́чески невозмо́жно; (*relating to the body*): ~ **education** физкульту́ра; ~ **exercises** гимнасти́ческие упражне́ния; заря́дка; ~**ly handicapped** физи́чески неполноце́нный; **have you had your** ~ **(examination)?** вы бы́ли на медици́нском осмо́тре?
physician [fɪˈzɪʃ(ə)n] *n.* врач.
physicist [ˈfɪzɪsɪst] *n.* фи́зик.
physics [ˈfɪzɪks] *n.* фи́зика.
physiognomy [ˌfɪzɪˈɒnəmɪ] *n.* физионо́мия.
physiological [ˌfɪzɪəˈlɒdʒɪk(ə)l] *adj.* физиологи́ческий.
physiologist [ˌfɪzɪˈɒlədʒɪst] *n.* физио́лог.
physiology [ˌfɪzɪˈɒlədʒɪ] *n.* физиоло́гия.

physiotherapist [ˌfɪzɪəʊ'θerəpɪst] *n.* физиотерапе́вт.
physiotherapy [ˌfɪzɪəʊ'θerəpɪ] *n.* физиотерапи́я.
physique [fɪ'zi:k] *n.* телосложе́ние.
pi [paɪ] *n.* (*geom.*) число́ «пи».
pianissimo [ˌpɪə'nɪsɪˌməʊ] *n., adj. & adv.* пиани́ссимо (*indecl.*).
pianist ['pɪənɪst] *n.* пиани́ст (*fem.* -ка).
piano[1] [pɪ'ænəʊ] *n.* фортепья́но (*indecl.*), роя́ль (*m.*); (*upright*) пиани́но (*indecl.*); ~ **accordion** аккордео́н; ~ **lessons** уро́ки игры́ на фортепья́но.

cpds. **~forte** *n.* фортепья́но (*indecl.*); **~-tuner** *n.* настро́йщик.

piano[2] [pɪ'ænəʊ] *adj. & adv.* (*mus.*) пиа́но (*indecl.*).
pica ['paɪkə] *n.* (*typ.*) ци́церо (*m. indecl.*).
picaresque [ˌpɪkə'resk] *adj.* авантю́рно-плутовско́й.
piccolo ['pɪkəˌləʊ] *n.* пи́kkоло (*indecl.*).
pick [pɪk] *n.* **1.** (*~axe*) кирка́, кайло́. **2.** (*probing instrument, e.g. dentist's*) про́бник. **3.** (*selection*) отбо́р, вы́бор; **take your ~!** выбира́йте!; **the ~ of the bunch** са́мое лу́чшее/отбо́рное.

v.t. **1.** (*pluck, gather*) соб|ира́ть, -ра́ть; **don't ~ the flowers!** не рви́те цветы́!; **she ~ed the thread from her dress** она́ сняла́ ни́тку с пла́тья. **2.** (*extract contents of*): **he is ~ing your brains** он испо́льзует ва́ши иде́и/позна́ния; **his pocket was ~ed in the crowd** в толпе́ ему́ зале́зли в карма́н. **3.** (*remove flesh from*) обгл|а́дывать, -ода́ть. **4.** (*probe*) ковыря́ть (*impf.*); **it's not nice to ~ one's teeth** ковыря́ть в зуба́х некраси́во; **stop ~ing your nose!** не ковыря́й в носу́!; (*probe to open*) откр|ыва́ть, -ы́ть отмы́чкой; **the lock has been ~ed** замо́к взло́ман. **5.** (*make by ~ing*): **he ~ed a hole in the cloth** он продыря́вил мате́рию; **he ~s holes in everything I say** он придира́ется ко вся́кому моему́ сло́ву. **6.** (*select*) выбира́ть, вы́брать; **he ~ed his words carefully** он тща́тельно подбира́л слова́; **can you ~ the winner?** мо́жете ли вы зара́нее угада́ть победи́теля?; **he's trying to ~ a quarrel** он и́щет по́вода для ссо́ры.

v.i. (*select*) выбира́ть, вы́брать.

with preps.: **the invalid ~ed at** (*trifled with*) **his food** инвали́д поковыря́л еду́ ви́лкой; **why do you always ~ on** (*single out*) **the same boy?** почему́ вы всегда́ выбира́ете одного́ и того́ же ма́льчика?

with advs.: ~ **off** *v.t.* (*pluck*) срыва́ть, сорва́ть; (*shoot by deliberate aim*) подстрели́ть (*pf.*); ~ **out** *v.t.* (*select*): **he ~ed out the best for himself** са́мое лу́чшее он вы́брал для себя́; (*distinguish*): **I ~ed him out in the crowd** я узна́л его́ в толпе́; **the pattern was ~ed out in red** кра́сный узо́р выделя́лся (на фо́не); (*play note by note*): **she can ~ out tunes by ear** она́ подбира́ет мело́дии по слу́ху; ~ **over** *v.t.* (*examine*) переб|ира́ть, -ра́ть; ~ **up** *v.t.* (*lift*) подн|има́ть, -я́ть; **he ~ed himself up off the ground** он подня́лся́ с земли́; **he ~ed up his bag** он взял свою́ су́мку; (*acquire, gain*) приобре|та́ть, -сти́; **he went there to ~ up information** он пошёл туда́ раздобы́ть све́дения; **I ~ed up a bargain at the sale** я сде́лал вы́годную поку́пку на распрода́же; **where can I have ~ed up this germ?** где я мог подцепи́ть э́ту инфе́кцию?; **the car began to ~ up speed** маши́на начала́ набира́ть ско́рость; **can you ~ up Moscow on your radio?** вы мо́жете пойма́ть Москву́ на своём приёмнике?; (*provide transport for*) брать (*impf.*), под|бира́ть, -обра́ть; (*collect*): **I ~ her up from school** я забира́ю её из шко́лы; (*apprehend*) заде́рж|ивать, -а́ть; **the culprit was ~ed up by the police** престу́пник был заде́ржан поли́цией; *v.i.* (*recover health*) попр|авля́ться, -а́виться; **he soon ~ed up after his illness** он бы́стро опра́вился по́сле боле́зни; (*improve*) ул|учша́ться, -у́чшиться ; **trade is ~ing up** торго́вля оживля́ется; (*gain speed*): **after a slow start the engine ~ed up** по́сле ме́дленного ста́рта мото́р зарабо́тал как сле́дует.

cpds. **~axe** *n.* киркомоты́га; **~pocket** *n.* вор-карма́нник; **~-up** *n.* (*microphone*) да́тчик; (*of record-player*) ада́птер; (*van*) пика́п; (*acceleration*) ускоре́ние.

picker ['pɪkə(r)] *n.* (*of fruit etc.*) сбо́рщи|к (*fem.* -ца).
picket ['pɪkɪt] *n.* **1.** (*pointed stake*) кол; ~ **fence** частоко́л. **2.** (*also* **picquet:** *small body of troops*) заста́ва, карау́л. **3.** (*of strikers*) пике́т; (*individual*) пике́тчик.

v.t. **1.** (*secure with stakes*) обн|оси́ть, -ести́ частоко́лом. **2.** (*guard*): **the camp was securely ~ed** ла́герь надёжно охраня́лся. **3.** (*deploy as guards*): **he ~ed his men round the house** он вы́ставил свои́х люде́й охраня́ть дом. **4.** (*mount guards on*): **the enemy has ~ed the bridge** враг вы́ставил карау́л у моста́. **5.** (*deny entry to*) пикети́ровать (*impf.*).

picking ['pɪkɪŋ] *n.* **1.** (*gathering*) собира́ние, сбор. **2.** (*pl., remains*) оста́тки (*m. pl.*); объе́дки (*m. pl.*).
pickle ['pɪk(ə)l] *n.* **1.** (*preservative*) марина́д; рассо́л. **2.** (*usu. pl., preserved vegetables*) соле́нья (*pl.*). **3.** (*coll., predicament, mess*) беда́.

v.t. маринова́ть, за-; **~d herrings** марино́ванная селёдка.

picky ['pɪkɪ] *adj.* (*US coll.*) разбо́рчивый, придирчивый.
picnic ['pɪknɪk] *n.* пикни́к.

v.i. за́втракать, по- на траве́.

cpds. **~-basket** *n.* корзи́нка для пикника́; **~-flask** *n.* фля́жка для пикника́.

picquet ['pɪkɪt] = **picket** *n.* **2.**
pictograph ['pɪktəˌgrɑ:f] *n.* пиктогра́мма.
pictorial [pɪk'tɔ:rɪəl] *adj.* изобрази́тельный; (*illustrated*) иллюстри́рованный.
picture ['pɪktʃə(r)] *n.* **1.** (*depiction; pictorial composition*) карти́на; **~s** (*in general*) жи́вопись; ~ **postcard** откры́тка с ви́дом; (*illustration*) изображе́ние; (*portrait*) портре́т, ко́пия; (*drawing*) рису́нок; (*image on TV screen*) карти́н(к)а. **2.** (*beautiful object*) карти́нка. **3.** (*embodiment*) олицетворе́ние; **he looks the ~ of health** он олицетворе́ние здоро́вья. **4.** (*coll., of information*): **he will soon put you in the ~** он вско́ре объясни́т вам, что к чему́; **don't fail to keep me in the ~** не забу́дьте держа́ть меня́ в ку́рсе де́ла. **5.** (*film*) (кино)фи́льм, карти́на; (*pl., cinema show, cinema*) кино́ (*indecl.*).

v.t. (*depict*) опи́с|ывать, -а́ть; изобра|жа́ть, -зи́ть; ~ **to yourself** вообрази́те/предста́вьте себе́.

cpds. **~-book** *n.* кни́жка с карти́нками; **~-gallery** *n.* карти́нная галлере́я.

picturesque [ˌpɪktʃə'resk] *adj.* живопи́сный.
pidgin ['pɪdʒɪn], **pigeon** ['pɪdʒɪn, -dʒ(ə)n] *n.*: **that's not my ~** э́то не моя́ забо́та; ~ **English** упрощённый гибри́дный вариа́нт англи́йского языка́.
pie [paɪ] *n.* (*pastry with filling*) пиро́г, пирожо́к; (*fig.*): **it's as easy as ~** э́то плёвое де́ло (*coll.*).

cpd. **~-crust** *n.* ко́рочка (пирога́).

piebald ['paɪbɔ:ld] *adj.* пе́гий.
piece [pi:s] *n.* **1.** (*portion, fragment, bit*) кусо́к; **a ~ of cake** (*lit.*) кусо́к то́рта; (*coll., sth. easily accomplished*) ле́гче лёгкого; **a ~ of paper** листо́к бума́ги; **(all) of a ~ with** в соотве́тствии с+*i.*; **all in one ~** неразо́бранный; (*fig., unharmed*) це́лый и невреди́мый; **the dish lay in ~s** блю́до разби́лось на куски́; **the record was smashed to ~s** пласти́нка разби́лась вдре́безги; **he took the watch to ~s** он разобра́л часы́; **he went to ~s after his wife's death** он совсе́м рассы́пался по́сле сме́рти жены́. **2.** (*small area*) уча́сток; **a ~** (*plot*) **of land** уча́сток земли́. **3.** (*example, instance*) образе́ц; **a ~ of news** но́вость; **here's a ~ of luck!** вот э́то уда́ча!; **may I give you a ~ of advice?** мо́жно дать вам сове́т?; **I gave him a ~ of my mind** я его́ отчита́л. **4.** (*unit of*

material) штýка, кусóк; **this cloth is sold by the ~** э́тот материáл продаётся отрéзами. **5.** (*single composition*) произведéние; **a ~ of music** пьéса; **a ~ of verse** стихотворéние. **6.** (*object of art or craft*) произведéние искýсства; вещь; **~ of furniture** мéбель; **three-~ suite** дивáн с двумя́ крéслами; **museum ~** (*fig.*) музéйная рéдкость; **a beautiful ~ of work** великолéпная рабóта. **7.** (*one of a set*): **he set out the ~s on the chessboard** он расстáвил фигýры на шáхматной доскé; **a 52-~ dinner service** обéденный сервиз из пятидесяти́ двух предмéтов. **8.** (*coin*) монéта; **a ten-cent ~** монéта в дéсять цéнтов. **9.** (*instrument*) инструмéнт; **a six-~band** секстéт.

with adv.: **~ together** *v.t.* соедин|я́ть, -и́ть; (*fig.*) свя́з|ывать, -áть.

cpds. **~meal** *adj.* части́чный; *adv.* по частя́м; урывками; **~-work** *n.* сдéльщина; **~-worker** *n.* сдéльщик.

pièce de résistance [ˌpjes də reɪˈziːstɑ̃s] *n.* (*cul.*) глáвное блю́до; (*fig.*) достопримечáтельность.

pied [paɪd] *adj.* пёстрый.

pier [pɪə(r)] *n.* **1.** (*structure projecting into sea*) пирс; (*landing stage*) мол. **2.** (*bridge support*) бык. **3.** (*masonry between windows*) простéнок.

pierc|e [pɪəs] *v.t.* прок|áлывать, -олóть; **she had her ears ~ed** ей прокололи ýши; **~ing cold** прони́зывающий хóлод; **a ~ing cry** пронзи́тельный крик; **a ~ing gaze** проницáтельный взгляд.

v.i. прон|икáть, -и́кнуть; проб|ивáться, -и́ться.

piety [ˈpaɪɪtɪ] *n.* нáбожность.

pig [pɪg] *n.* свинья́; **he bought a ~ in a poke** он купи́л котá в мешкé; (*greedy or disagreeable person*): **he made a ~ of himself** он нажрáлся, как свинья́.

cpds. **~-headed** *adj.* тупóй; **~-iron** *n.* чугýн в чýшках; **~skin** *n.* свинáя кóжа; **~sty** *n.* (*lit., fig.*) свинáрник; **~tail** *n.* коси́чка.

pigeon[1] [ˈpɪdʒɪn, -dʒ(ə)n] *n.* гóлубь (*m.*); **carrier, homing ~** почтóвый гóлубь; **clay ~** гли́няная летáющая мишéнь.

cpds. **~hole** *n.* отделéние для бумáг; **~-toed** *adj.* косолáпый.

pigeon[2] [ˈpɪdʒɪn, -dʒ(ə)n] = **pidgin**

piggy [ˈpɪgɪ] *n.* (*piglet; greedy child*) поросёнок.

cpds. **~-back** *adv.* на спинé; на закóрках; **~-bank** *n.* копи́лка.

piglet [ˈpɪglɪt] *n.* поросёнок.

pigment [ˈpɪgmənt] *n.* пигмéнт.

pigmentation [ˌpɪgmənˈteɪʃ(ə)n] *n.* пигментáция.

pigmented [ˈpɪgməntɪd] *adj.* пигменти́рованный.

pike [paɪk] *n.* **1.** (*weapon*) копьё. **2.** (*fish*) щýка.

pila|ff [pɪˈlæf], **-u** [pɪˈlaʊ] *n.* пилáв, плов.

pilaster [pɪˈlæstə(r)] *n.* пиля́стр(а).

pilau [pɪˈlaʊ] = **pilaff**

pilchard [ˈpɪltʃəd] *n.* сарди́н(к)а.

pile[1] [paɪl] *n.* (*stake, post*) свáя.

cpd. **~-driver** *n.* копёр.

pile[2] [paɪl] *n.* **1.** (*heap*) кýча, грýда; (*coll., of money*): **he made his ~** он нáжил состоя́ние; (*coll., any large quantity*) кýча, мáсса. **2.** (*elec.*) батарéя.

v.t. **1.** (*heap up*) свал|ивать, -и́ть в кýчу; **he ~d coal on to the fire** он подбрóсил ýгля́ вками́н. **2.** (*load*) нагру|жáть, -зи́ть.

with advs.: **~ in** *v.i.* (*coll., crowd into a vehicle etc.*) наб|ивáться, -и́ться; **~ on** *v.t.* навáл|ивать, -и́ть; (*fig.*) преувели́чи|вать, -ть; **~ up** *v.t.* накоп|ля́ть, -и́ть; *v.i.* (*accumulate*) нагромо|ждáться, -зди́ться; **work keeps piling up** рабóта всё врéмя прибавля́ется.

cpd. **~-up** *n.* (*crash*) столкновéние нéскольких маши́н.

pile[3] [paɪl] *n.* (*down, soft hair*) шерсть, вóлос; (*nap on cloth, carpet etc.*) ворс.

pile[4] [paɪl] *n.* (*usu. pl. haemorrhoid*) геморрóй.

pilfer [ˈpɪlfə(r)] *v.t. & i.* ворovать (*impf.*), таскáть (*impf.*).

pilfer|age [ˈpɪlfərɪdʒ], **-ing** [ˈpɪlfərɪŋ] *nn.* мéлкая крáжа.

pilgrim [ˈpɪlgrɪm] *n.* пилигри́м, палóмник.

pilgrimage [ˈpɪlgrɪmɪdʒ] *n.* палóмничество.

pill [pɪl] *n.* пилю́ля, таблéтка; **contraceptive ~** противозачáточная пилю́ля; **she is on the ~** онá принимáет (противозачáточные) таблéтки.

cpd. **~box** *n.* (*receptacle*) корóбочка для таблéток; (*mil., emplacement*) долговрéменное огневóе сооружéние (*abbr.* ДОС).

pillage [ˈpɪlɪdʒ] *n.* мародёрство, грабёж.

v.t. & i. мародёрствовать (*impf.*); грáбить.

pillar [ˈpɪlə(r)] *n.* (*column*) столб; (*support*) опóра; (*fig.*) столп; **~s of society** столпы́ óбщества.

cpd. **~-box** *n.* (стоя́чий) почтóвый я́щик.

pillion [ˈpɪljən] *n.* (*on motor-cycle*) зáднее сидéнье; **she rode ~** онá éхала на зáднем сидéнье мотоци́кла.

pillory [ˈpɪlərɪ] *n.* позóрный столб.

v.t. (*fig.*) пригво|ждáть, -зди́ть к позóрному столбý.

pillow [ˈpɪləʊ] *n.* подýшка.

cpds. **~-case, ~-slip** *nn.* нáволочка.

pilot [ˈpaɪlət] *n.* **1.** (*of vessel*) лóцман; (*of aircraft*) лётчик, пилóт; **~ officer** лейтенáнт авиáции. **2.** (*attr., fig.*) прóбный, óпытный; **~ scheme** эксперимéнт.

v.t. (*lit., fig.*) пилоти́ровать (*impf.*); напр|авля́ть, -áвить.

cpds. **~-boat** *n.* лóцманское сýдно; **~-fish** *n.* ры́ба-лóцман; **~-light** *n.* (*for gas indicator*) гáзовая горéлка; контрóльная/сигнáльная лáмпа.

pim(i)ento [ˌpɪmɪˈentəʊ, pɪmˈjentəʊ] *n.* (*sweet pepper*) пимéнт, пéрец души́стый.

pimp [pɪmp] *n.* свóдник.

v.i. свóдничать (*impf.*).

pimpernel [ˈpɪmpəˌnel] *n.* óчный цвет.

pimple [ˈpɪmp(ə)l] *n.* прыщ, пры́щик.

pimply [ˈpɪmplɪ] *adj.* прыщáвый.

PIN [pɪn] *n.* (*abbr. of* ***personal identification number***) персонáльный код.

pin [pɪn] *n.* **1.** булáвка; шпи́лька; **you could have heard a ~ drop** мóжно бы́ло услы́шать, как мýха пролети́т; **I've got ~s and needles in my leg** у меня́ ногá затеклá. **2.** (*securing peg*) прищéпка.

v.t. **1.** (*fasten*) прик|áлывать, -олóть; (*fig.*): **~ accusation, blame on s.o.** свáл|ивать, -и́ть винý на когó-н.; **I ~ my faith on the captain** я возлагáю все надéжды на капитáна. **2.** (*immobilize*) приж|имáть, -áть; **he was ~ned beneath the vehicle** егó придави́ло маши́ной; **his arms were ~ned behind him** емý связáли рýки за спинóй.

with advs.: **~ down** *v.t.* (*lit.*) прик|áлывать, -олóть; (*fig., commit to an action or opinion*) прип|ирáть, -ерéть к стéнке; **~ on** *v.t.* прик|áлывать, -олóть; **~ together** *v.t.* ск|áлывать, -олóть; скреп|ля́ть, -и́ть; **~ up** *v.t.* повéсить (*pf.*); **she ~ned up her hair** онá заколóла вóлосы.

cpds. **~ball, ~-table** *nn.* (*game, machine*) пинбóл, китáйский бильярд; **~ball machine** бильярд-автомáт; **~cushion** *n.* подýшечка для игóлок и булáвок; **~-money** *n.* дéньги на мéлкие расхóды; **~point** *v.t.* (*fig.*) тóчно определ|я́ть, -и́ть; укáз|ывать, -áть пáльцем; **~-prick** *n.* (*lit.*) булáвочный укóл; (*fig.*) «шпи́лька», мéлкий укóл; **~-table** *n.* = **~ball; ~-up** *n.* фотогрáфия красóтки в журнáле; **~-up girl** красóтка.

pinafore [ˈpɪnəˌfɔː(r)] *n.* фáртук, передник; **~ dress** плáтье-сарафáн.

pince-nez [ˈpænsneɪ, pæsˈneɪ] *n.* пенснé (*indecl.*).

pincer ['pɪnsə(r)] *n.* **1.** (*of crustacean*) клешня́. **2.** (*pl.*) щипц|ы́ (*pl., g.* -о́в); клещ|и́ (*pl., g.* -е́й); **~ movement** (*mil.*) захва́т в кле́щи.

pinch [pɪntʃ] *n.* **1.** (*nip*) щипо́к; **he gave her a ~ on the cheek** он ущипну́л её за щёку; (*fig., constraint*) сжа́тие; **at a ~** в кра́йнем слу́чае. **2.** (*small amount*) щепо́тка; **a ~ of snuff** поню́шка табаку́; **you must take that with a ~ of salt** (*fig.*) вы не должны́ э́тому ве́рить.

v.t. **1.** (*nip, squeeze*) прищем|ля́ть, -и́ть; ущипну́ть (*pf.*); **his fingers were ~ed in the door** он прищеми́л па́льцы две́рью; (*fig.*): **his face was ~ed with cold** моро́з щипа́л ему́ лицо́. **2.** (*steal*) стяну́ть (*pf.*), стащи́ть (*pf.*) (*coll.*).

v.i. (*be niggardly*) скупи́ться, по-; отка́зывать (*impf.*) себе́ (*в чём*); **she had to ~ and scrape to make ends meet** ей приходи́лось эконо́мить на всём для того́, что́бы своди́ть концы́ с конца́ми.

pine[1] [paɪn] *n.* сосна́.

cpds. **~apple** *n.* анана́с; **~-cone** *n.* сосно́вая ши́шка; **~-needle** *n.* хво́я; **~wood** *n.* сосно́вая древеси́на.

pine[2] [paɪn] *v.i.* **1.** (*languish, waste*) ча́хнуть, за-; томи́ться (*impf.*). **2.** (*long*): **~ for** жа́ждать +*g*; **I ~ for sea air** так хо́чется подыша́ть морски́м во́здухом.

ping [pɪŋ] *n.* свист, писк.

v.i. св|исте́ть, -и́стнуть; пи́скнуть (*pf.*).

ping-pong ['pɪŋpɒŋ] *n.* пинг-по́нг.

pinion[1] ['pɪnjən] *v.t.* (*bind arms of*) свя́з|ывать, -а́ть ру́ки +*g.*

pinion[2] ['pɪnjən] *n.* (*cog-wheel*) шестерня́.

pink[1] [pɪŋk] *n.* (*flower*) гвозди́ка; (*colour*) ро́зовый цвет; (*perfection*): **he is in the ~ (of health)** он пы́шет здоро́вьем.

adj. (*of colour*) ро́зовый.

pink[2] [pɪŋk] *v.i.* (*of engine*) стуча́ть (*impf.*).

pinnacle ['pɪnək(ə)l] *n.* (*of building*) шпиц; (*fig.*) верши́на.

pint [paɪnt] *n.* пи́нта.

cpd. **~-sized** *adj.* (*fig.*) ма́ленький, кро́хотный.

pioneer [,paɪə'nɪə(r)] *n.* пионе́р, нова́тор, первооткрыва́тель (*m.*); (*mil.*) сапёр; **P~ Corps** сапёрно-строи́тельные ча́сти.

v.t. & i. быть пионе́ром (*в чём*); про|кла́дывать, -ложи́ть путь; **~ing** *adj.* нова́торский; первопроходческий.

pious ['paɪəs] *adj.* на́божный.

pip [pɪp] *n.* **1.** (*fruit seed*) се́мечко; зёрнышко. **2.** (*high-pitched sound*) писк; (*teleph.*) гудо́к, сигна́л.

v.t. (*sl., defeat*) прова́л|ивать, -и́ть; **he was ~ped at the post** его́ обогна́ли в после́днюю мину́ту.

cpd. **~-squeak** *n.* (*coll.*) ничто́жество.

pipe [paɪp] *n.* **1.** (*conduit*) труба́. **2.** (*mus. instrument*) свире́ль; ду́дка. **3.** (*shrill voice or sound*) вопль (*m.*); писк; (*note of bird*) свист; пе́ние. **4.** (*for smoking*) тру́бка; **he lit a ~ and smoked it** он закури́л тру́бку; **~ of peace** тру́бка ми́ра.

v.t. **1.** (*also v.i.*) (*play on ~*) игра́ть, сыгра́ть на свире́ли/ду́дке. **2.** (*lead, summon by piping*) свиста́ть (*impf.*); **he ~d all hands on deck** он свиста́л всех наве́рх. **3.** (*utter in shrill voice*) пища́ть, пи́скнуть. **4.** (*ornament dress*) отде́л|ывать, -ать ка́нтом. **5.** (*convey by ~s*) пус|ка́ть, -ти́ть по тру́бам; **a ~d water supply** водопрово́д.

with advs.: **~ down** *v.i.* (*restrain o.s.*) сба́вить (*pf.*) тон (*coll.*); **~ up** (*coll., start to sing, play, speak*) запе́ть (*pf.*); пода́ть (*pf.*) го́лос.

cpds. **~-dream** *n.* пуста́я/несбы́точная мечта́; **~line** *n.* трубопрово́д, нефтепрово́д; **in the ~line** (*fig.*) на подхо́де; **~-rack** *n.* подста́вка для тру́бок; **~-tobacco** *n.* тру́бочный таба́к.

piper ['paɪpə(r)] *n.* ду́дочник; (*bag ~*) волы́нщик; **he who pays the ~ calls the tune** кто пла́тит, тот и распоряжа́ется.

pipette [pɪ'pet] *n.* пипе́тка.

piping ['paɪpɪŋ] *n.* (*system of pipes*) трубопрово́д; (*ornamental cord*) кант; (*cake decoration*) глазу́рь, крем; (*playing of pipes*) игра́ свире́ли *и т.п.*

adj. (*of voice etc.*) пронзи́тельный.

adv.: **~ hot** с пы́лу, с жа́ру.

piquancy ['pi:kənsɪ, -kɑ:nsɪ] *n.* (*lit., fig.*) пика́нтность.

piquant ['pi:kənt, -kɑ:nt] *adj.* (*lit., fig.*) пика́нтный.

pique [pi:k] *n.* доса́да; **in a fit of ~** в поры́ве раздраже́ния.

v.t. (*hurt the pride of*) уязв|ля́ть, -и́ть; (*stimulate*) возбу|жда́ть, -ди́ть.

piqué ['pi:keɪ] *n.* пике́ (*indecl.*).

piracy ['paɪrəsɪ] *n.* пира́тство; (*infringement of copyright*) наруше́ние а́вторского пра́ва.

pirate ['paɪərət] *n.* пира́т; **~ ship** пира́тский кора́бль; (*infringer of copyright*) наруши́тель (*m.*) а́вторского пра́ва.

v.t. (*literary etc. work*) публикова́ть, о- в наруше́ние а́вторских прав.

piratical [,paɪə'rætɪk(ə)l] *adj.* пира́тский.

pirouette [,pɪrʊ'et] *n.* пируэ́т.

v.i. де́лать (*impf.*) пируэ́ты; сде́лать (*pf.*) пируэ́т.

Pisces ['paɪsi:z, 'pɪski:z] *n.* Ры́бы (*f. pl.*).

piss [pɪs] *n.* (*vulg.*) моча́; **take the ~ (out of)** насмеха́ться (над+*i.*) (*impf.*).

v.t.: **~ the bed** мочи́ться, по- в крова́ть.

v.i. мочи́ться (*impf.*); **~ off!** отцепи́сь!; прова́ливай!

cpds. **~-taker** *n.* насме́шник; **~-up** *n.* выпиво́н.

pissed [pɪsd] *adj.* (*vulg., drunk*) пья́ный в сте́льку.

pistachio [pɪ'stɑ:ʃɪəʊ] *n.* фиста́шка.

pistil ['pɪstɪl] *n.* пе́стик.

pistol ['pɪst(ə)l] *n.* пистоле́т.

cpd. **~-shot** *n.* пистоле́тный вы́стрел.

piston ['pɪst(ə)n] *n.* по́ршень (*m.*); (*mus.*) писто́н.

cpds. **~-engine** *n.* поршнево́й дви́гатель; **~-ring** *n.* поршнево́е кольцо́; **~-rod** *n.* поршнево́й шток.

pit[1] [pɪt] *n.* **1.** (*excavation*) я́ма; **gravel from the ~** гра́вий из карье́ра. **2.** (*coal-mine*) ша́хта; **he works down the ~** он на подзе́мных рабо́тах в ша́хте. **3.** (*covered hole, trap*) западня́, лову́шка. **4.** (*depression*) углубле́ние, я́мка; **~ of the stomach** подло́жечная я́мка. **5.** (*theatr.*) оркестро́вая я́ма. **6.** (*on motor-racing circuit*) ремо́нтная я́ма, смотрова́я кана́ва.

v.t. (*scar*): **his face was ~ted by smallpox** его́ лицо́ бы́ло изры́то о́спой.

cpds. **~fall** *n.* (*lit., fig.*) западня́, капка́н; **~head** *n.* надша́хтное зда́ние.

pit[2] [pɪt] (*US*) *n.* (*fruit-stone*) ко́сточка.

v.t. (*remove stones from*) вынима́ть, вы́нуть ко́сточки из+*g.*

pit-a-pat ['pɪtə,pæt] *n.* бие́ние, тре́пет.

adv. с бие́нием/тре́петом; **her heart went ~** её се́рдце затрепета́ло.

pitch[1] [pɪtʃ] *n.* **1.** (*plunging motion of ship*) (килева́я) ка́чка; (*lurch forward*) бросо́к. **2.** (*throw*) бросо́к; (*delivery of ball*) пода́ча. **3.** (*area for games*) по́ле, площа́дка. **4.** (*spot where trader or entertainer operates*) (постоя́нное/обы́чное) ме́сто. **5.** (*of voice or instrument*) высота́. **6.** (*height, intensity, degree*) у́ровень (*m.*), сте́пень; **excitement reached fever ~** всех трясло́ от возбужде́ния. **7.** (*slope of roof*) укло́н, скат.

v.t. **1.** (*set up, erect*): **they ~ed camp for the night** они́ разби́ли ла́герь на́ ночь; **a ~ed battle** генера́льное сраже́ние. **2.** (*throw*) бр|оса́ть, -о́сить; (*fig.*): **he was ~ed into the centre of events** он очути́лся в са́мом це́нтре собы́тий. **3.** (*mus.*): **the song is ~ed too high for me** пе́сня сли́шком высока́ для моего́ го́лоса.

v.i. (*of ship*): **the ship was ~ing** кора́бль кача́ло; (*of pers.*, *fall forwards*) па́дать, упа́сть; (*fig.*) на-бр|а́сываться, -о́ситься; **he ~ed into the work** он окуну́лся в рабо́ту.

with adv.: **~ in** *v.i.* (*join in with vigour*) горячо́/энерги́чно взя́ться (*pf.*) (*за что*).

cpd. **~fork** *n.* (се́нные) ви́л|ы (*pl.*, *g.* —).

pitch[2] [pɪtʃ] *n.* (*bituminous substance*) смола́; **~ darkness** тьма кроме́шная.

cpds. **~-black** *adj.* чёрный как смоль; **~-dark** *adj.*: **it is ~-dark here** здесь темны́м-темно́.

pitcher [ˈpɪtʃə(r)] *n.* (*jug*) кувши́н; (*at baseball*) подаю́щий.

piteous [ˈpɪtɪəs] *adj.* жа́лкий; жа́лобный.

pith [pɪθ] *n.* сердцеви́на.

pithy [ˈpɪθɪ] *adj.* (*fig.*) сжа́тый; содержа́тельный.

pitiable [ˈpɪtɪəb(ə)l] *adj.* несча́стный; (*contemptible*) жа́лкий.

pitiful [ˈpɪtɪˌfʊl] *adj.* (*arousing pity*) жа́лостный; (*contemptible*) жа́лкий.

pitiless [ˈpɪtɪlɪs] *adj.* безжа́лостный.

pittance [ˈpɪt(ə)ns] *n.* «жа́лкие гроши́» (*m. pl.*).

pitter-patter [ˈpɪtəˌpætə(r)] *n.* & *adv.* топ-то́п, тук-ту́к.

v.i. посту́кивать (*impf.*).

pituitary [pɪˈtju:ɪtərɪ] *n.* (**~ gland**) мозгово́й прида́ток; гипо́физ.

pit|y [ˈpɪtɪ] *n.* **1.** (*compassion*) жа́лость; **have, take ~y on** сжа́литься (*pf.*) над+*i.*; **I feel ~y for him** мне его́ о́чень жа́лко; **for ~y's sake!** (*expr. impatience*) Го́споди Бо́же мой! **2.** (*cause for regret*) жаль; **what a ~y!** как жа́лко!; **more's the ~y** тем ху́же; **it's a great ~y** о́чень, о́чень жаль.

v.t. жале́ть, по-; **she is much to be ~ied** её о́чень жаль.

pivot [ˈpɪvət] *n.* то́чка враще́ния; (*fig.*) то́чка опо́ры.

v.i. враща́ться (*impf.*); верте́ться (*impf.*).

pivotal [ˈpɪvətəl] *adj.* осево́й; центра́льный; (*fig.*) основно́й.

pixel [ˈpɪks(ə)l]*n.* (*comput.*) элеме́нт изображе́ния.

pix|y, -ie [ˈpɪksɪ] *n.* эльф.

pizza [ˈpi:tsə] *n.* пи́цца; **~ parlour** пиццери́я.

pizzeria [ˌpi:tsəˈri:ə] *n.* пиццери́я.

pizzicato [ˌpɪtsɪˈkɑ:təʊ] *n. adj.* & *adv.* пиццика́то (*indecl.*).

placard [ˈplækɑ:d] *n.* плака́т; афи́ша.

placate [pləˈkeɪt, ˈplæ-, ˈpleɪ-] *v.t.* умиротвор|я́ть, -и́ть; успок|а́ивать, -о́ить.

placatory [pləˈkeɪtərɪ] *adj.* зада́бривающий; умиротворя́ющий.

place [pleɪs] *n.* **1.** ме́сто; **all over the ~** (*everywhere*) повсю́ду; (*in confusion*) повсю́ду, в беспоря́дке; (*correct*, *appropriate* **~**): **everything is in ~** всё на ме́сте; **there's a time and a ~ for everything** всему́ своё вре́мя и ме́сто; **her hair was out of ~** её приче́ска растрепа́лась; **your laughter is out of ~** ваш смех неуме́стен; **that put him in his ~** э́то поста́вило его́ на ме́сто; (*reserved*, *occupied* **~**): **he took his ~ in the queue** он за́нял ме́сто в о́череди; (*seat*): **he gave up his ~ to a lady** он уступи́л своё ме́сто да́ме; **take your ~s!** займи́те свои́ места́!; (*fig.*, *position*): **put yourself in my ~** поста́вьте себя́ на моё ме́сто; (*at table*): **six ~s were laid** стол был накры́т на шесть персо́н; (*fig.*): **take ~** (*occur*) име́ть (*impf.*) ме́сто; **when will the race take ~?** когда́ состоя́тся го́нки?; **take the ~ of** (*replace*) замен|я́ть, -и́ть; **give ~ to** смен|я́ться, -и́ться +*i.*; **in ~ of** вме́сто+*g.* **2.** (*locality*; *specific area or point*) ме́сто; **in ~s** (*here and there*) места́ми; **small ~s are not marked on the map** ме́лкие пу́нкты не обозна́чены на ка́рте; **there's no ~ like home** в гостя́х хорошо́, а до́ма лу́чше. **3.** (*building*; *domicile*) дом; жили́ще; **~ of worship** моли́твенный дом; **come round to my ~!** заходи́те ко мне! **4.** (*employment*) ме́сто, слу́жба. **5.** (*point or passage in book etc.*) ме́сто, страни́ца; **I put in a pencil to mark my ~** я заложи́л страни́цу карандашо́м. **6.** (*position in race or contest*): **our team took first ~** на́ша кома́нда заняла́ пе́рвое ме́сто; (*stage*, *position in series*): **in the first ~** во-пе́рвых. **7.** (*math.*): **correct to three ~s of decimals** с то́чностью до тре́тьего десяти́чного зна́ка.

v.t. **1.** (*stand*) ста́вить, по-; (*lay*) класть, положи́ть; (*set*) сажа́ть, посади́ть; (*dispose*) разме|ща́ть, -сти́ть. **2.** (*appoint*) поме|ща́ть, -сти́ть. **3.** (*comm.*) поме|ща́ть, -сти́ть (*деньги и т.п.*); **I ~d an order with them** я помести́л у них зака́з. **4.** (*repose*) возл|ага́ть, -ожи́ть (*надежды и т.п.*). **5.** (*identify*) определ|я́ть, -и́ть.

cpd. **~-name** *n.* географи́ческое назва́ние.

placebo [pləˈsi:bəʊ] *n.* (*med.*) безвре́дное (не ока́зывающее де́йствия) лека́рство.

placement [ˈpleɪsmənt] *n.* размеще́ние; (*seating order*) расса́дка.

placenta [pləˈsentə] *n.* плаце́нта.

placid [ˈplæsɪd] *adj.* споко́йный, безмяте́жный.

plagiarism [ˈpleɪdʒəˌrɪz(ə)m] *n.* плагиа́т.

plagiarist [ˈpleɪdʒərɪst] *n.* плагиа́тор.

plagiarize [ˈpleɪdʒəˌraɪz] *v.t.* & *i.* занима́ться (*impf.*) плагиа́том; **he ~d my book** его́ рабо́та целико́м спи́сана с мое́й кни́ги.

plague [pleɪg] *n.* **1.** (*pestilence*) чума́. **2.** (*infestation*) бе́дствие; **a ~ of rats** наше́ствие крыс.

v.t. (*afflict*) нас|ыла́ть, -ла́ть чуму́/бе́дствие на+*a.*; (*pester*) докуча́ть (*impf.*) +*d.*

plaice [pleɪs] *n.* ка́мбала.

plaid [plæd] *n.* (*garment*) плед.

plain [pleɪn] *n.* равни́на.

adj. **1.** (*clear*, *evident*) я́сный, я́вный; **it is as ~ as the nose on one's face** э́то я́сно как день; **it was ~ sailing from then on** с тех пор всё пошло́ как по ма́слу. **2.** (*easy to understand*) я́сный, поня́тный; **why can't you speak ~ English?** почему́ вы не говори́те просты́м языко́м? **3.** (*straightforward*, *candid*) прямо́й; **I am a ~ man** я челове́к просто́й; **I will be ~ with you** я бу́ду с ва́ми открове́нен. **4.** (*simple*, *unembellished*, *not coloured*) просто́й, скро́мный, неприхотли́вый; **~ clothes** (*opp. to uniform*) шта́тское (пла́тье); **~ food** проста́я пи́ща; **~ living** скро́мная жизнь. **5.** (*unattractive*) некраси́вый.

adv. я́сно, про́сто.

cpds. **~-clothes** *adj.* оде́тый в шта́тское; **~-clothes man** сы́щик, переоде́тый полице́йский; **~-spoken** *adj.* открове́нный.

plaintiff [ˈpleɪntɪf] *n.* исте́ц.

plaintive [ˈpleɪntɪv] *adj.* печа́льный, гру́стный.

plait [plæt] *n.* коса́.

v.t. запле|та́ть, -сти́.

plan [plæn] *n.* план; (*drawing*, *diagram*) чертёж; **~s were drawn up** бы́ли соста́влены пла́ны; (*map*) ка́рта; **a ~ of the city** план го́рода; (*schedule*): **all went according to ~** всё прошло́ по пла́ну; (*project*) прое́кт; **five-year ~** пятиле́тний план; **master ~** генера́льный план; **on the instalment ~** в рассро́чку; **an open-~ house** дом откры́той планиро́вки.

v.t. **1.** (*make a ~ of*) плани́ровать, за-. **2.** (*arrange*, *design*) проекти́ровать (*impf.*); **~ned economy** пла́новая эконо́мика.

v.i. намерева́ться (*impf.*); **we must ~ ahead** на́до ду́мать о бу́дущем.

plane[1] [pleɪn] *n.* (*tree*) плата́н.

plane[2] [pleɪn] *n.* (*tool*) руба́нок, струг.

v.t. & *i.* строга́ть, вы́-.

with advs.: **~ away, ~ down** *v.t.* состру́г|ивать, -а́ть.

plane[3] [pleɪn] *n.* **1.** (*flat surface*) пло́скость. **2.** (*aeroplane*) самолёт. **3.** (*fig., level*) у́ровень (*m.*); **her thoughts are on a higher ~** у неё бо́лее высо́кий строй мы́слей.

adj. пло́ский, плоскостно́й.

planet ['plænɪt] *n.* плане́та.

planetarium [ˌplænɪ'teərɪəm] *n.* планета́рий.

planetary ['plænɪtərɪ] *adj.* планета́рный, плане́тный.

plank [plæŋk] *n.* доска́.

planking ['plæŋkɪŋ] *n.* обши́вка доска́ми; насти́л; (*planks*) до́ски (*f. pl.*).

plankton ['plæŋkt(ə)n] *n.* планкто́н.

planner ['plænə(r)] *n.* планови́к; проектиро́вщик.

planning ['plænɪŋ] *n.* плани́рование; **long-term ~** перспекти́вное плани́рование; **family ~** (иску́сственное) ограниче́ние соста́ва семьи́; **~ permission** разреше́ние на строи́тельство.

plant [plɑ:nt] *n.* **1.** (*vegetable organism*) расте́ние; **house ~** ко́мнатное расте́ние. **2.** (*industrial fixtures or machinery*) обору́дование. **3.** (*factory*) заво́д.

v.t. **1.** (*put in ground*) сажа́ть, посади́ть; се́ять; **I have ~ed out the cabbages** я вы́садил капу́сту в грунт. **2.** (*furnish with ~s*) заса́|живать, -ди́ть. **3.** (*fig.*): **he ~ed a doubt in my mind** он посе́ял во мне сомне́ние; **he ~ed himself in front of the fire** он стал пе́ред са́мымками́ном; **~ evidence** подстр|а́ивать, -о́ить ули́ки.

plantain ['plæntɪn] *n.* (*herb*) подоро́жник; (*tropical tree*) ди́кий бана́н.

plantation [plæn'teɪʃ(ə)n, plɑ:n-] *n.* (*area of planted trees*) насажде́ния (*pl.*); (*estate*) планта́ция.

planter ['plɑ:ntə(r)] *n.* (*plantation owner*) планта́тор; (*agric. machine*) се́ялка.

plaque [plæk, plɑ:k] *n.* (*tablet*) табли́чка, доще́чка; (*badge*) значо́к, бля́ха.

plasm(a) ['plæzmə] *n.* (*fluid*) пла́зма; **blood ~** кровяна́я пла́зма.

plaster ['plɑ:stə(r)] *n.* **1.** (*for coating walls etc.*) штукату́рка; **~ cast** ги́псовый сле́пок; **~ of Paris** гипс. **2.** (*med.*) пла́стырь (*m.*).

v.t. **1.** (*coat with ~*) штукату́рить, о(т)-; (*fig.*) па́чкать, за-; **his boots were ~ed with mud** его́ боти́нки бы́ли обле́плены гря́зью. **2.** (*fig.*): **the trunk was ~ed with labels** сунду́к был весь обле́плен накле́йками. **3.: get ~ed** (*sl., drunk*) упи́ться (*pf.*).

plasterer ['plɑ:stərə(r)] *n.* штукату́р.

plastic ['plæstɪk] *n.* пла́стик, пластма́сса.

adj. **1.** (*made of ~*) пластма́ссовый; **~ bomb** пла́стиковая бо́мба. **2.** (*pert. to moulding; sculptural*) лепно́й; скульпту́рный; **the ~ arts** пласти́ческие иску́сства; **~ surgery** пласти́ческая хирурги́я. **3.** (*malleable*) пласти́чный.

plasticine ['plæstɪˌsi:n] *n.* пластили́н.

plate [pleɪt] *n.* **1.** (*shallow dish*) таре́лка; **side ~** таре́лка для хле́ба; **a ~ of cold meat** блю́до с холо́дным мя́сом; (*fig.*): **he has a lot on his ~** у него́ дел по го́рло (*coll.*). **2.** (*collect., metal tableware*) посу́да; **silver ~** сере́бряная посу́да. **3.** (*sheet of metal, glass etc.*) лист, полоса́; **a ~ on the door gave the doctor's name** на двери́ была́ табли́чка с фами́лией до́ктора; (*metal in this form*) броня́; **armour ~** броневы́е пли́ты (*f. pl.*). **4.** (*phot.*) фотопласти́нка. **5.** (*illustration*) вкладна́я иллюстра́ция. **6.** (*typ.*) стереоти́п. **7. (dental ~)** (зубно́й) проте́з.

v.t. **1.** (*cover with metal ~s*) плакирова́ть (*impf.*). **2.** (*coat with layer of metal*) покр|ыва́ть, -ы́ть мета́ллом; **silver-~d spoons** посеребрённые ло́жки.

cpds. **~-glass** *adj.* из зерка́льного стекла́; **~-rack** *n.* суши́лка для посу́ды.

plateau ['plætəʊ] *n.* плато́ (*indecl.*).

platen ['plæt(ə)n] *n.* (*of typewriter*) ва́лик.

platform ['plætfɔ:m] *n.* **1.** (*at station*) платфо́рма, перро́н; **at ~ No. 3** на платфо́рме № 3; **~ ticket** перро́нный биле́т. **2.** (*for speakers*) трибу́на; (*fig., pol.*) (полити́ческая) платфо́рма.

plating ['pleɪtɪŋ] *n.* покры́тие, обши́вка.

platinum ['plætɪnəm] *n.* пла́тина; *attr.* пла́тиновый.

platitude ['plætɪˌtju:d] *n.* пло́скость, бана́льность.

platitudinous [ˌplætɪ'tju:dɪnəs] *adj.* пло́ский, бана́льный.

Platonic [plə'tɒnɪk] *adj.* платони́ческий.

platoon [plə'tu:n] *n.* взвод.

platter ['plætə(r)] *n.* блю́до; **cold ~** холо́дное ассорти́ (*indecl.*).

platypus ['plætɪpəs] *n.* утконо́с.

plaudit ['plɔ:dɪt] *n.* (*usu. pl.*) аплодисме́нт|ы (*pl., g.* -ов); похвала́ (*sg.*).

plausibility [ˌplɔ:zɪ'bɪlɪtɪ] *n.* вероя́тность, правдоподо́бие.

plausible ['plɔ:zɪb(ə)l] *adj.* правдоподо́бный.

play [pleɪ] *n.* **1.** (*recreation, amusement*) игра́; **the children were at ~** де́ти игра́ли; **mathematics is child's ~ to him** матема́тика для него́ — де́тские игру́шки; **~ on words** игра́ слов. **2.** (*conduct of game etc.*) игра́; мане́ра игры́; **there was a lot of rough ~** бы́ло мно́го гру́бой игры́; **the police suspect foul ~** поли́ция подозрева́ет, что де́ло нечи́сто. **3.** (*state of being played with*): **the ball was out of ~** мяч был вне игры́. **4.** (*fig., action*) де́йствие, де́ятельность; **all his strength was brought into ~** он моболизова́л все свои́ си́лы; **the ~ of market forces** возде́йствие фа́кторов ры́нка. **5.** (*dramatic work*) пье́са, спекта́кль (*m.*). **6.** (*visual effect*) игра́; перели́вы (*m. pl.*); **the ~ of light on the water** игра́ све́та на воде́. **7.** (*free movement*) люфт, свобо́дный ход. **8.** (*fig., scope*) во́ля; просто́р.

v.t. **1.** (*perform, take part in*) игра́ть, сыгра́ть в+*a.*; **~ football** игра́ть (*impf.*) в футбо́л; **~ the game!** (*fig., abide by the rules*) игра́йте по пра́вилам!; **he wouldn't ~ ball** (*coll., cooperate*) он не хоте́л сотру́дничать. **2.** (*perform on*) игра́ть, сыгра́ть на+*p.*; **can you ~ the piano?** вы игра́ете на роя́ле? **3.** (*cause to be heard*) исп|олня́ть, -о́лнить; **they ~ed records** они́ поста́вили/проигра́ли пласти́нки; **he ~ed it by ear** (*fig., of extempore action*) он де́йствовал по интуи́ции. **4.** (*perpetrate*): **he is always ~ing tricks on me** он всегда́ надо мно́й подшу́чивает; **my memory ~s tricks** па́мять меня́ подво́дит. **5.** (*enact role of*) игра́ть, сыгра́ть; **I ~ed Horatio** я игра́л Гора́цио; **stop ~ing the fool!** переста́ньте валя́ть дурака́!; **~ truant** прогу́л|ивать, -я́ть заня́тия. **6.** (*enact drama of*) дава́ть (*impf.*); дава́ть представле́ние +*g.*; **they are ~ing Othello** (в теа́тре) даю́т/идёт «Оте́лло». **7.** (*cards*): **he ~ed the ace** он пошёл с туза́; **he ~ed his cards well** (*fig.*) он де́йствовал уме́ло.

v.i. **1.** игра́ть, сыгра́ть; (*amuse o.s., have fun*) забавля́ться (*impf.*); **they were ~ing at soldiers** они́ игра́ли в войну́; **what are you ~ing at?** что за игру́ вы ведёте?; **she ~ed on his vanity** она́ сыгра́ла на его́ тщесла́вие; **he is fond of ~ing on words** он лю́бит каламбу́ры; **don't ~ with fire!** (*fig.*) не игра́йте с огнём!; **run away and ~!** пойди́ поигра́й!; (*take part in game or sport*): **they ~ed to win** они́ игра́ли с аза́ртом; **I have always ~ed fair with you** я всегда́ поступа́л с ва́ми че́стно; (*gamble*) **what shall we ~ for?** по ско́льку бу́дем игра́ть/ста́вить?; (*perform music*): **it's an old instrument but it ~s well** э́то ста́рый инструме́нт, но у него́ хоро́ший звук; (*on stage etc.*): **they ~ed to full houses** они́ игра́ли при по́лном за́ле; (*move, be active*): **a smile ~ed on her lips** улы́бка игра́ла на её губа́х. **2.** (*be directed*): **searchlights ~ed on the aircraft** проже́кторы бы́ли напра́влены на самолёт. **3.** (*strike ball*) де́лать, с- бросо́к; (*fig.*): **he ~ed into my hands** он сыгра́л мне на́ руку.

with advs.: ~ **about,** ~ **around** *v.i.* игра́ть (*impf.*); резви́ться (*impf.*); ~ **back** *v.t.* воспроизв|оди́ть, -ести́; прослу́ш|ивать, -ать; **the tape was ~ed back** плёнку проигра́ли; ~ **down** *v.t.* (*fig., minimize*) преум|еньша́ть, -е́ньшить; ~ **off** *v.t.* (*replay*): **the drawn game must be ~ed off next week** ничья́ должна́ быть перейграна на сле́дующей неде́ле; (*set in opposition*) натра́в|ливать, -и́ть (*кого на кого*); ~ **out** *v.t.* (~ *to the end, to a result*) доигр|ывать, -а́ть; ~ **through** *v.t.* сыгра́ть (*pf.*) (целико́м); ~ **up** *v.t.* (*give emphasis, importance to*) обы́гр|ивать, -а́ть; (*coll., give trouble to*) му́чить, за-; **my car is ~ing up again** моя́ маши́на опя́ть барахли́т; *v.i.* (*misbehave*) распус|ка́ться, -ти́ться; ~ **up to** (*humour*) подда́кивать (*impf.*); (*give flattering attention to*) подли́зываться (*impf.*) к+*d.*

cpds. **~-acting** *n.* (*fig.*) притво́рство, на́игрыш; **~back** *n.* воспроизведе́ние; **~bill** *n.* (*poster*) театра́льная афи́ша; **~boy** *n.* пове́са (*m.*), донжуа́н; **~fellow,** **~mate** *nn.*: **the child needs a ~fellow** ребёнку на́до с ке́м-то игра́ть; **~goer** *n.* театра́л; **~ground** *n.* (*at school*) площа́дка для игр; (*fig.*) излю́бленное ме́сто развлече́ния; **~group** *n.* дошко́льная гру́ппа (малыше́й); **~house** *n.* теа́тр; **~mate** *n.* = **~fellow**; **~-off** *n.* реша́ющая встре́ча; повто́рная встре́ча после ничье́й; **~-pen** *n.* де́тский мане́ж; **~school** *n.* де́тский сад; **~-suit** *n.* спорти́вный костю́м; **~thing** *n.* (*lit., fig.*) игру́шка; **~time** *n.* вре́мя о́тдыха; шко́льная переме́на; **~wright** *n.* драмату́рг.

player ['pleɪə(r)] *n.* **1.** (*of game*) игро́к; спортсме́н. **2.** (*actor*) актёр. **3.** (*musician*): **a ~ on the clarinet** кларнети́ст. **4.** (*record-~*) проигрыватель (*m.*).

playful ['pleɪfʊl] *adj.* игри́вый, шаловли́вый.

playfulness ['pleɪfʊlnɪs] *n.* игри́вость.

playing ['pleɪɪŋ] *n.* игра́.

cpds. **~-card** *n.* игра́льная ка́рта; **~-field** *n.* спорти́вное по́ле.

plaza ['plɑːzə] *n.* пло́щадь.

PLC, plc (*abbr. of* **public limited company**) обще́ственная компа́ния с ограни́ченной отве́тственностью.

plea [pliː] *n.* **1.** (*leg.*) заявле́ние в суде́, возраже́ние; **he entered a ~ of guilty** он призна́л себя́ вино́вным. **2.** (*excuse*) предло́г; **on the ~ of ill-health** под предло́гом боле́зни. **3.** (*request, appeal*) про́сьба.

plead [pliːd] *v.t.* **1.** (*argue for*) защи|ща́ть, -ти́ть; **he had a lawyer to ~ his case** его́ де́ло вёл адвока́т. **2.** (*offer as excuse*) ссыла́ться, сосла́ться на+*a.*; **I must ~ ignorance of the facts** к сожале́нию, я не в ку́рсе де́ла. **3.** (*declare o.s.*): **my client ~s (not) guilty** мой клие́нт (не) признаёт себя́ вино́вным.

v.i. **1.** (*address court as advocate*) выступа́ть, вы́ступить в суде́. **2.** (*appeal, entreat*) приз|ыва́ть, -ва́ть; умоля́ть (*impf.*); **the prisoners ~ed for mercy** заключённые проси́ли о поми́ловании.

pleading ['pliːdɪŋ] *n.* выступле́ние защи́ты; хода́тайство.

pleasant ['plez(ə)nt] *adj.* прия́тный.

pleasantness ['plezəntnɪs] *n.* любе́зность.

pleasantry ['plezəntrɪ] *n.* (*joke*) шу́тка; (*amiable interchange*) любе́зность.

please [pliːz] *v.t.* нра́виться, по- +*d.*; дост|авля́ть, -а́вить удово́льствие +*d.*; **it ~s the eye** э́то ра́дует глаз; **I was not very ~d at, by, with the results** я был не о́чень дово́лен результа́тами; **I feel better, I'm ~d to say** рад сообщи́ть, что я чу́вствую себя́ лу́чше; **I was ~d to note** мне бы́ло прия́тно отме́тить; **I shall be ~d to attend** я бу́ду рад приня́ть уча́стие; ~ **God** дай Бог; ~ **yourself** как вам бу́дет уго́дно; **he ~s himself what he does** он поступа́ет, как ему́ заблагорассу́дится.

v.i. **1.** (*give pleasure*) уго|жда́ть, -ди́ть. **2.** (*think fit*) изво́лить (*impf.*); **do as you ~** де́лайте, как хоти́те; **he comes just when he ~s** он прихо́дит, когда́ ему́ взду́мается. **3.** (*polite request*): ~ **shut the door** пожа́луйста, закро́йте дверь; ~ **do try the jam** прошу́ вас, попро́буйте варе́нья; ~ **forgive our long silence** о́чень про́сим извини́ть нас за до́лгое молча́ние; **if you ~** е́сли вам уго́дно; о́чень вас прошу́; (*iron.*) предста́вьте себе́!; поду́майте то́лько!

pleasing ['pliːzɪŋ] *adj.* прия́тный.

pleasurable ['pleʒərəb(ə)l] *adj.* доставля́ющий удово́льствие.

pleasure ['pleʒə(r)] *n.* **1.** (*enjoyment*) удово́льствие; **it's a ~!** (*sc. to oblige*) рад служи́ть!; **it gives me great ~ to see you** мне о́чень прия́тно вас ви́деть; **may I have the ~ (of a dance)?** разреши́те пригласи́ть вас (на та́нец)? **2.** (*will, desire*) жела́ние; **at your ~** по ва́шему жела́нию; **we await your ~** к ва́шим услу́гам.

cpds. **~-boat** *n.* прогу́лочный ка́тер; **~-ground** *n.* сад, парк.

pleat [pliːt] *n.* скла́дка.

v.t. плиссирова́ть (*impf.*); **~ed skirt** ю́бка в скла́дку.

plebeian [plɪ'biːən] *n.* плебе́й.

adj. плебе́йский.

plebiscite ['plebɪsɪt, -ˌsaɪt] *n.* плебисци́т.

plectrum ['plektrəm] *n.* плектр.

pledge [pledʒ] *n.* **1.** (*thg. left as earnest of intent; token*) зало́г. **2.** (*promise*) обе́т, обеща́ние; **he has signed the** (*temperance*) ~ он дал заро́к не пить.

v.t. **1.** (*give as security*) отд|ава́ть, -а́ть в зало́г; (*pawn*) за|кла́дывать, -ложи́ть; ~ **o.s.** обя́з|ываться, -а́ться; руча́ться, поручи́ться; **I ~ my word** даю́ сло́во; руча́юсь. **2.** (*enjoin*): **I ~d him to secrecy** я взял с него́ сло́во не говори́ть (об э́том).

Pleiades ['plaɪəˌdiːz] *n.* Плея́д|ы (*pl., g.* —).

Pleistocene ['pleɪstəˌsiːn] *n.* плейстоце́н.

plenary ['pliːnərɪ] *adj.*: ~ **powers** неограни́ченные полномо́чия; ~ **session** плена́рное заседа́ние.

plenipotentiary [ˌplenɪpə'tenʃərɪ] *n.* полномо́чный представи́тель.

adj. полномо́чный, неограни́ченный.

plentiful ['plentɪˌfʊl] *adj.* изоби́льный, оби́льный.

plenty ['plentɪ] *n.* **1.** (*abundance*) изоби́лие; **there was food in ~** еда́ была́ в изоби́лии. **2.** (*large quantity or number*) мно́жество; **he has ~ of money** у него́ по́лно де́нег. **3.** (*sufficient*) доста́ток.

adv. (*coll., amply*) впо́лне́.

plenum ['pliːnəm] *n.* пле́нум.

plethora ['pleθərə] *n.* (*med.*) полнокро́вие; (*fig., overabundance*) избы́ток.

pleurisy ['plʊərɪsɪ] *n.* плеври́т.

plexus ['pleksəs] *n.* сплете́ние; **solar ~** со́лнечное сплете́ние.

pliability [ˌplaɪə'bɪlɪtɪ] *n.* ги́бкость.

pliable ['plaɪəb(ə)l] *adj.* ги́бкий.

pliant ['plaɪənt] *adj.* ги́бкий.

pliers ['plaɪəz] *n.* щипц|ы́ (*pl., g.* -о́в); клещ|и́ (*pl., g.* -е́й).

plight [plaɪt] *n.* незави́дное положе́ние.

plimsoll ['plɪms(ə)l] *n.* **1.** (*light shoe*): **~s** парусиновые ту́фли (*f. pl.*); та́почки (*f. pl.*). **2.**: **P~ line** грузова́я ма́рка.

plinth [plɪnθ] *n.* пли́нтус.

plod [plɒd] *v.t. & i.* тащи́ться (*impf.*); (*fig.*): ~ **away at sth.** корпе́ть (*impf.*) над чем-н.

plodder ['plɒdə(r)] *n.* (*fig.*) трудя́га (*c.g.*); работя́га (*c.g.*).

plonk [plɒŋk] *v.t.* (*coll., put down heavily*) гро́х|ать, -нуть; ба́х|ать, -нуть; **he ~ed himself in an armchair** он плю́хнулся в кре́сло.

plop [plɒp] *n.* бульк.

adv.: **fall ~** булты́хну́ться (*pf.*).

v.t. & i. шлёпнуть(ся) (*pf.*).
int. бух!

plot [plɒt] *n.* **1.** (*piece of ground*) участок (земли́). **2.** (*outline of play etc.*) фа́була, сюже́т. **3.** (*conspiracy*) за́говор.
v.t. **1.** (*make plan of*) плани́ровать, за-. **2.** (*record*) нан|оси́ть, -ести́. **3.** (*measure out*: *also* ~ **out**) разб|ива́ть, -и́ть. **4.** (*conspire to achieve*): **they ~ted his ruin** они́ гото́вили ему́ ги́бель.
v.i. (*conspire*) вына́шивать (*impf.*) за́говор.

plough [plaʊ] (*US* **plow**) *n.* **1.** плуг; **we have 100 acres under** ~ у нас 100 а́кров па́шни. **2.**: **the P~** (*astron.*) Больша́я Медве́дица.
v.t. **1.** паха́ть, вс-; **he ~s a lonely furrow** (*fig.*) он де́йствует в одино́чку. **2.** (*coll., fail*) прова́л|ивать, -и́ть.
v.i. **1.** (*fig.*) продв|ига́ться, -и́нуться; **the ship ~ed through the waves** кора́бль рассека́л во́лны; **I ~ed through the book** я с трудо́м оси́лил кни́гу. **2.** (*coll., fail in exam*) прова́л|иваться, -и́ться.
with advs.: ~ **back** *v.t.*: **profits are ~ed back** при́быль вкла́дывается в де́ло; ~ **in** *v.t.* запа́х|ивать, -а́ть.
cpds. **~land** *n.* па́хотная земля́; **~man** *n.* па́харь (*m.*); **~share** *n.* плу́жный ле́мех.

plover ['plʌvə(r)] *n.* ржа́нка.

plow [plaʊ] = **plough**

ploy [plɔɪ] *n.* (*manoeuvre*) уло́вка.

pluck [plʌk] *n.* (*coll., courage*) сме́лость, отва́га.
v.t. **1.** (*pull off, pick*) срыва́ть, сорва́ть; соб|ира́ть, -ра́ть. **2.** (*strip of feathers*) ощи́п|ывать, -а́ть. **3.** (*cause to vibrate by twitching*) щипа́ть (*pf.*). **4.** (*twitch, pull at*; *also v.i.*) дёр|гать, -нуть.
with advs.: ~ **off** *v.t.* выдёргивать, вы́дернуть; ~ **out** *v.t.* выщи́пывать, вы́щипать; ~ **up** *v.t.*: ~ **up courage** собра́ться (*pf.*) с ду́хом.

plucky ['plʌkɪ] *adj.* (*coll.*) сме́лый, отва́жный.

plug [plʌg] *n.* **1.** (*stopper, e.g. of bath*) про́бка, заты́чка, сто́пор; **(wax) ear-~** заты́чка для уше́й. **2.** (*elec. connector*) ви́лка; (*socket*) розе́тка. **3.** (*spark-~*) запа́льная свеча́. **4.** (*of WC*): **he pulled the** ~ он спусти́л во́ду. **5.** (*of tobacco*) жева́тельный таба́к. **6.** (*coll., advertisement*) рекла́ма.
v.t. (*stop up*) заку́пори|вать, -ть; (*coll., boost*) реклами́ровать (*impf., pf.*).
with advs.: ~ **away** *v.i.* (*coll., persevere*) корпе́ть (*impf.*); ~ **in** *v.t.* включ|а́ть, -и́ть; ~ **up** *v.t.* заку́пори|вать, -ть.

plum [plʌm] *n.* **1.** (*fruit, tree*) сли́ва. **2.** (*fig., prized object or possession*) «жи́рный кусо́к»; ла́комый кусо́чек; **a ~ job** тёплое месте́чко.

plumage ['plu:mɪdʒ] *n.* опере́ние.

plumb [plʌm] *n.* отве́с, грузи́ло.
adj. (*vertical*) вертика́льный.
adv. (*exactly*) то́чно.
v.t. (*sound*) изм|еря́ть, -е́рить ло́том; (*fig.*) прон|ика́ть, -и́кнуть в+*a.*
cpd. **~-line** *n.* отве́с, отве́сная ли́ния.

plumber ['plʌmə(r)] *n.* водопрово́дчик.

plumbing ['plʌmɪŋ] *n.* (*occupation*) слеса́рно-водопрово́дное де́ло; (*installation*) водопрово́д, санте́хника.

plume [plu:m] *n.* **1.** (*feather*) перо́; **a ~ of smoke** стру́йка ды́ма. **2.** (*in headdress*) султа́н, плюма́ж.

plummet ['plʌmɪt] *v.i.* об|рыва́ться, -орва́ться; (*fig.*): **shares ~ed** а́кции ре́зко упа́ли.

plummy ['plʌmɪ] *adj.* (*coll., of voice*) со́чный.

plump[1] [plʌmp] *adj.* (*rounded, chubby*) пу́хлый, окру́глый; (*fattish*) по́лный.
v.t.: ~ **up 1.** (*fatten*) вск|а́рмливать, -орми́ть. **2.**: **she ~ed up the cushions** она́ взби́ла поду́шки.
v.i.: ~ **out** разд|ава́ться, -а́ться; толсте́ть, рас-; **her cheeks have ~ed out** у неё округли́лись щёки.

plump[2] [plʌmp] *v.i.* (*fall heavily*; *usu.* ~ **down**) шлёп|аться, -нуться; (*make one's choice*) реш|а́ть, -и́ть; **I ~ for the roast beef** я — за ро́стбиф.

plunder ['plʌndə(r)] *n.* (*looting*) грабёж; (*loot*) добы́ча.
v.t. & i. гра́бить, о-; расх|ища́ть, -и́тить.

plunge [plʌndʒ] *n.* **1.** (*dive*) ныря́ние. **2.** (*violent movement*) бросо́к.
v.t. погру|жа́ть, -зи́ть; **the room was ~d into darkness** ко́мната погрузи́лась во мрак; **he ~d his hands into water** он опусти́л ру́ки в во́ду.
v.i. **1.** (*dive*) окун|а́ться, -у́ться; (*fig.*): **a plunging neckline** глубо́кий вы́рез на пла́тье. **2.** (*lunge forward*) бр|оса́ться, -о́ситься (вперёд); **the horse ~d forward** ло́шадь рвану́лась вперёд; (*fig.*) погру|жа́ться, -зи́ться.

plunger ['plʌndʒə(r)] *n.* плу́нжер.

pluperfect [plu:'pɜ:fɪkt] *n.* давнопроше́дшее вре́мя.
adj. давнопроше́дший.

plural ['plʊər(ə)l] *n.* мно́жественное число́.
adj. **1.** (*gram.*) мно́жественный. **2.** (*multiple*) многочи́сленный; неодноро́дный.

pluralism ['plʊərə,lɪz(ə)m] *n.* плюрали́зм.

plurality [plʊə'rælɪtɪ] *n.* (*plural state*) мно́жественность; (*large number*) мно́жество; (*pluralism*) совмести́тельство; (*relative majority*) относи́тельное большинство́.

plus [plʌs] *n.* **1.** (*symbol*) знак плюс. **2.** (*additional or positive quantity*) доба́вочное коли́чество.
adj. (*additional, extra*) доба́вочный; (*math., elec.*) положи́тельный.
prep. плюс; ~ **or minus** плюс-ми́нус.
cpd. **~-fours** *n.* брю́к|и (*pl., g.* —) гольф.

plush [plʌʃ] *n.* плюш.
adj. (*made of* ~) плю́шевый; (*sl., sumptuous*; *also* **plushy**) шика́рный.

Pluto ['plu:təʊ] *n.* (*myth., astron.*) Плуто́н.

plutocracy [plu:'tɒkrəsɪ] *n.* плутокра́тия.

plutocrat ['plu:tə,kræt] *n.* плутокра́т.

plutocratic [,plu:tə'krætɪk] *adj.* плутократи́ческий.

plutonium [plu:'təʊnɪəm] *n.* плуто́ний.

ply[1] [plaɪ] *n.* (*layer*) слой, пласт; (*strand*) слой; **three-~ cable** трёхсло́йный/трёхжи́льный ка́бель.
cpd. **~wood** *n.* фане́ра; *adj.* фане́рный.

ply[2] [plaɪ] *v.t.* **1.** (*manipulate*): **she plied her needle** она́ занима́лась шитьём; **they plied the oars** они́ налега́ли на вёсла. **2.** (*work at*): **he plies an honest trade** он зараба́тывает на хлеб че́стным трудо́м. **3.** (*keep supplied*) по́тчевать (*impf.*); **I was plied with food** меня́ усе́рдно корми́ли; **they plied him with questions** они́ засы́пали его́ вопро́сами.
v.i. курси́ровать (*impf.*).

PM (*abbr. of* ***Prime Minister***) премье́р-мини́стр.

p.m. (*abbr. of* ***post meridiem***) пополу́дни; **at 5 p.m.** в 5 ч. дня.

PMT (*abbr. of* ***premenstrual tension***) предменструа́льный невро́з.

pneumatic [nju:'mætɪk] *adj.* пневмати́ческий.

pneumonia [nju:'məʊnɪə] *n.* воспале́ние лёгких.

PO *abbr. of* **1.** ***Post Office*** по́чта. **2.** ***postal order*** почто́вый перево́д. **3.** ***Petty Officer*** старшина́ (во фло́те).

poach[1] [pəʊtʃ] *v.t.*: ~ **eggs** вари́ть, с- (яйцо́-)пашо́т.

poach[2] [pəʊtʃ] *v.t. & i.*: ~ **game** браконье́рствовать (*impf.*); охо́титься (*or* уди́ть ры́бу) (*both impf.*) в чужи́х владе́ниях; **you are ~ing on my preserves** (*lit., fig.*) вы вме́шиваетесь в мои́ дела́; вы вторга́етесь в мои́ владе́ния.

poacher ['pəʊtʃə(r)] *n.* браконье́р.

pocket ['pɒkɪt] *n.* **1.** (*in clothing*) карма́н; **he has the chairman in his** ~ председа́тель у него́ в рука́х. **2.** (*money resources*): **your ~ will suffer** э́то уда́рит по ва́шему карма́ну; **he was in ~ at the end of the**

day под конéц дня он был в вы́игрыше; **I shall be out of ~** я бу́ду в прóигрыше; **out-of-~ expenses** расхóды, оплáчиваемые нали́чными. **3.** (*at billiards*) лу́за. **4.** (*small area*): **~ of resistance** очáг сопротивлéния. **5.: air ~** возду́шная я́ма. **6.** (*attr., miniature*) кармáнный; **~ edition** кармáнное издáние.

v.t. **1.** класть, положи́ть в кармáн; (*fig., appropriate*) прикармáни|вать, -ть. **2.: he ~ed the ball** (*billiards*) он загнáл шар в лу́зу.

cpds. **~-book** *n.* (*notebook*) записнáя кни́жка; (*wallet*) бумáжник; **~-handkerchief** *n.* носовóй платóк; **~-knife** *n.* кармáнный нóж(ик); **~-money** *n.* кармáнные дéн|ьги (*pl., g.* -ег); **~-size(d)** *adj.* кармáнного формáта; миниатю́рный.

pocketful ['pɒkɪt,fʊl] *n.* пóлный кармáн (*чего*).

pock-marked ['pɒkmɑ:kt] *adj.* рябóй.

pod [pɒd] *n.* (*seed vessel*) стручóк.

v.t. (*shell*) лущи́ть (*impf.*).

podgy ['pɒdʒɪ] *adj.* тóлстенький; (*of face*) пу́хлый, толстощёкий.

podium ['pəʊdɪəm] *n.* (*archit.*) пóдиум, пóдий; (*rostrum*) трибу́на.

poem ['pəʊɪm] *n.* стихотворéние; (*long narrative*) поэ́ма.

poet ['pəʊɪt] *n.* поэ́т.

poetess ['pəʊɪtɪs] *n.* поэтéсса.

poetic [pəʊ'etɪk] *adj.* поэти́ческий; **~ licence** поэти́ческая вóльность; **~ justice** справедли́вое возмéздие.

poetical [pəʊ'etɪk(ə)l] *adj.* поэти́ческий, поэти́чный.

poetry ['pəʊɪtrɪ] *n.* (*also fig.*) поэ́зия; (*poetical work*) стих|и́ (*pl., g.* -óв).

pogrom ['pɒgrəm, -rɒm] *n.* погрóм.

poignancy ['pɔɪnjənsɪ] *n.* остротá, рéзкость.

poignant ['pɔɪnjənt] *adj.* (*of taste etc.*) óстрый; (*painfully moving*) óстрый, рéзкий, гóрький.

point [pɔɪnt] *n.* **1.** (*sharp end*) остриё; **not to put too fine a ~ on it** (*fig.*) без обинякóв; не делика́тничая. **2.** (*tip*) кóнчик. **3.** (*promontory*) мыс. **4.** (*dot*) тóчка; **decimal ~** (*in Russian usage*) запятáя (*отделяющая десятичную дробь от целого числа*); **two ~ five (2.5)** две цéлых и пять деся́тых; **36.6** (*human temperature Centigrade*) три́дцать шесть и шесть. **5.** (*mark, position*) мéсто, пункт; **~ of contact** (*lit., fig.*) тóчка соприкосновéния; **~ of departure** отправнáя/исхóдная тóчка; **~ of view** тóчка зрéния; **they have reached the ~ of no return** возврáта назáд для них ужé нет. **6.** (*moment*) момéнт; **I was on the ~ of leaving** я ужé собрáлся уходи́ть; **at the ~ of death** при́ смерти; **when it came to the ~, he refused** в решáющий момéнт он отказáлся. **7.** (*mark on scale*) отмéтка, делéние; (*unit*) едини́ца; **boiling-~** тóчка кипéния; **up to a ~** до извéстной стéпени. **8.** (*of the compass*) странá свéта. **9.** (*unit of evaluation, score*) пункт, очкó; **they won on ~s** они́ вы́играли по очкáм. **10.** (*chief idea, meaning, purpose*) суть, дéло, вопрóс, смысл; **that is beside the ~** не в э́том суть/дéло; **come to the ~** дойти́ (*pf.*) до глáвного/су́ти дéла; **that's just the ~** вот и́менно; в тóм-то и дéло; **you have a ~ there** тут вы прáвы; **a case in ~** нагля́дный примéр; **in ~ of fact** в действи́тельности; факти́чески; **I made a ~ of seeing him** я счёл необходи́мым повидáться с ним; **you missed the ~** вы не пóняли су́ти дéла; **there was no ~ in staying** не имéло смы́сла оставáться; **that's not the ~** не в э́том суть; **off the ~** некстáти; **I see your ~** я вас понимáю; **what's the ~ of it?** какóй в э́том смысл? **11.** (*item*) пункт; **I explained the theory ~ by ~** я разъясни́л теóрию по пу́нктам; **~ of order** вопрóс к поря́дку ведéния; **that is a ~ in his favour** э́то говори́т в егó пóльзу. **12.** (*quality, trait*) чертá; **the plan has its good ~s** э́тот план не лишён достóинств; **singing is not my strong ~** я не силён в пéнии. **13.** (*pl., rail.*) стрéлочный перевóд; стрéлки (*f. pl.*). **14.** (*typ.*) пункт.

v.t. **1.** (*aim*) укáз|ывать, -áть; покáз|ывать, -áть; **he ~ed a gun at her** он навёл на неё пистолéт. **2.** (*fill with mortar*): **~ brickwork** расш|ивать, -и́ть швы клáдки.

v.i. укáз|ывать, -áть; **the sign ~ed to the station** дорóжный знак укáзывал направлéние к стáнции.

with adv.: **~ out** *v.t.* укáз|ывать, -áть на+*a.*; подч|ёркивать, -еркну́ть.

cpd. **~-blank** *adj.* (*lit.*) прямóй; (*fig.*) категори́ческий; *adv.* пря́мо, в упóр.

pointed ['pɔɪntɪd] *adj.* **1.** (*e.g. a stick*) остроконéчный. **2.** (*significant, directed against s.o.*) óстрый, кóлкий; подчёркнутый; **she gave me a ~ look** онá на меня́ многозначи́тельно посмотрéла.

pointer ['pɔɪntə(r)] *n.* **1.** (*rod*) укáзка. **2.** (*of balance etc.*) стрéлка, указáтель (*m.*). **3.** (*indication, hint*) намёк. **4.** (*dog*) пóйнтер.

pointing ['pɔɪntɪŋ] *n.* (*of wall etc.*) расши́вка швов.

pointless ['pɔɪntlɪs] *adj.* бессмы́сленный.

poise [pɔɪz] *n.* (*equilibrium*) равновéсие; (*self-possession*) уравновéшенность, самообладáние.

v.t. удéрж|ивать, -áть в равновéсии; **he is ~d to attack** он готóв к нападéнию.

poison ['pɔɪz(ə)n] *n.* яд, отрáва.

v.t. (*lit., fig.*) отрав|ля́ть, -и́ть; **he has food ~ing** он отрави́лся.

cpds. **~-gas** *n.* ядови́тый газ; **~-ivy** *n.* сумáх ядонóсный; **~-pen** *adj.*: **~-pen letter** анони́мка.

poisoner ['pɔɪzənə(r)] *n.* отрави́тель (*fem.* -ница).

poisonous ['pɔɪzənəs] *adj.* ядови́тый; (*fig.*) врéдный; (*coll., repulsive*) проти́вный.

poke [pəʊk] *n.* (*prod*) толчóк; **he gave me a ~ in the ribs** он толкну́л меня́ в бок.

v.t. **1.** (*prod*) ты́кать, ткнуть. **2.** (*thrust*) пихáть (*impf.*); совáть (*impf.*); **he ~d his stick through the fence** он просу́нул пáлку чéрез забóр; **he ~d his tongue out** он вы́сунул язы́к; **he ~s his nose into other people's business** он суёт нос не в своё дéло; **he ~d fun at me** он насмехáлся надо мнóй.

v.i.: **he ~d about among the rubbish** он ры́лся в му́соре.

poker ['pəʊkə(r)] *n.* **1.** (*for a fire*) кочергá; **gas ~** гáзовая зажигáлка. **2.** (*game*) пóкер.

cpd. **~-faced** *adj.* с кáменным выражéнием лицá.

poky ['pəʊkɪ] *adj.* (*coll.*) тéсный, убóгий.

Poland ['pəʊlənd] *n.* Пóльша.

polar ['pəʊlə(r)] *adj.* **1.** (*of or near either Pole*) поля́рный; **~ bear** бéлый медвéдь. **2.** (*elec.*) поля́рный, пóлюсный. **3.** (*geom.*) поля́рный.

polarity [pə'lærɪtɪ] *n.* (*lit., fig.*) поля́рность.

polarization [,pəʊləraɪ'zeɪʃ(ə)n] *n.* (*lit., fig.*) поляризáция.

polarize ['pəʊlə,raɪz] *v.t. & i.* (*lit., fig.*) поляризовáть(ся) (*impf.*).

pole[1] [pəʊl] *n.* (*of the earth; also elec. and fig.*) пóлюс.

cpd. **~-star** *n.* Поля́рная звездá.

pole[2] [pəʊl] *n.* (*post, rod etc.*) столб, шест.

cpds. **~-vault** *n.* прыжк|и́ (*m. pl.*) с шестóм; **~-vaulter** *n.* шестови́к.

Pole[3] [pəʊl] *n.* (*pers.*) поля́к (*fem.* пóлька).

pole-axe ['pəʊlæks] *n.* (*old weapon*) секи́ра; (*butcher's implement*) топóр.

v.t. заб|ивáть, -и́ть (*скот*).

polecat ['pəʊlkæt] *n.* леснóй хорёк.

polemic [pə'lemɪk] *n.* полéмика; спор.

adj. (*also* **~al**) полеми́ческий, спóрный.

polemicist [pə'lemɪsɪst] *n.* полеми́ст; спóрщик.

police [pə'li:s] *n.* поли́ция, (*in former USSR*) мили́ция; **~ constable** полицéйский; **~ force** поли́ция; **a ~ state** полицéйское госудáрство.

v.t. соблюда́ть (*impf.*) поря́док и дисципли́ну в+*p.*
cpds. **~man** *n.* полисме́н, полице́йский; (*in former USSR*) милиционе́р; **~-officer** *n.* полице́йский; **~-station** *n.* (полице́йский) уча́сток; отделе́ние мили́ции; **~woman** *n.* же́нщина-полице́йский/милиционе́р.

policy ['pɒlɪsɪ] *n.* (*planned course of action*) поли́тика, курс; (*insurance*) страхово́й по́лис.
cpd. **~-holder** *n.* держа́тель (*m.*) страхово́го по́лиса.

polio(myelitis) [ˌpəʊlɪəʊˌmaɪɪ'laɪtɪs] *n.* полиомиели́т.

polish[1] ['pɒlɪʃ] *n.* **1.** (*smoothness, brightness*) полиро́вка. **2.** (*substance used for ~ing*) политу́ра. **3.** (*act of ~ing*) полиро́вка; **I must give my shoes a ~** я до́лжен почи́стить ту́фли. **4.** (*fig., refinement*) то́нкость; лоск.
v.t. полирова́ть, от-; (*fig.*) шлифова́ть, от-; **~ed** (*behaviour etc.*) све́тский, ве́жливый.
with advs.: **~ off** *v.t.* (*coll., finish*) разде́латься (*pf.*) с+*i.*; **I must ~ off this letter** я до́лжен поко́нчить с э́тим письмо́м; **~ up** *v.t.* (*lit., give gloss to*) прид|ава́ть, -а́ть лоск +*d.*; **she ~ed up the silver** она́ почи́стила серебро́; (*fig., improve*) соверше́нствовать, у-; **I must ~ up my French** мне ну́жно освежи́ть (в па́мяти) францу́зский язы́к.

Polish[2] ['pəʊlɪʃ] *n.* (*language*) по́льский язы́к.
adj. по́льский.

polisher ['pɒlɪʃə(r)] *n.* (*workman*) полиро́вщик; (*machine*) полирова́льная маши́на.

Politburo ['pɒlɪtˌbjʊərəʊ] *n.* политбюро́ (*indecl.*).

polite [pə'laɪt] *adj.* ве́жливый, учти́вый; **~ society** хоро́шее/культу́рное о́бщество.

politeness [pə'laɪtnɪs] *n.* ве́жливость.

politic ['pɒlɪtɪk] *adj.* **1.** (*prudent*) благоразу́мный. **2.: the body ~** госуда́рство, полити́ческая систе́ма.

political [pə'lɪtɪk(ə)l] *adj.* полити́ческий; **~ correctness** полити́ческая корре́ктность.

politician [ˌpɒlɪ'tɪʃ(ə)n] *n.* поли́тик.

politics ['pɒlɪtɪks] *n.* поли́тика; (*political views*) полити́ческие взгля́ды (*m. pl.*); **what are his ~?** каковы́ его́ полити́ческие убежде́ния?

polka ['pɒlkə, 'pəʊlkə] *n.* по́лька.
cpd. **~-dot** *n.* (*pattern*) узо́р в горо́шек; (*attr.*): **~-dot dress** пла́тье в горо́шек.

poll [pəʊl] *n.* (*voting process*) голосова́ние; **the country will go to the ~s in May** в стране́ бу́дут вы́боры в ма́е; **he came head of the ~** он получи́л наибо́льшее коли́чество/число́ голосо́в; (*number of votes*) коли́чество по́данных голосо́в; (*opinion canvass*) опро́с.
v.t. **1.** (*receive*): **he ~ed 60,000 votes** он получи́л 60 000 голосо́в. **2.** (*take votes of*): **they ~ed the meeting** они́ поста́вили вопро́с на голосова́ние.
cpd. **~-tax** *n.* поду́шный нало́г.

pollard ['pɒləd] *n.* подстри́женное де́рево; (*attr.*) подстри́женный.
v.t. подстр|ига́ть, -и́чь (*дерево*).

pollen ['pɒlən] *n.* цвето́чная пыльца́.

pollinate ['pɒlɪˌneɪt] *v.t.* опыл|я́ть, -и́ть.

pollination [ˌpɒlɪ'neɪʃ(ə)n] *n.* опыле́ние.

polling ['pəʊlɪŋ] *n.* голосова́ние.
cpds. **~-booth** *n.* каби́на для голосова́ния; **~-day** *n.* день вы́боров; **~-station** *n.* избира́тельный уча́сток.

pollutant [pə'lu:tənt]*n.* загрязни́тель (*m.*); поллюта́нт.

pollute [pə'lu:t] *v.t.* загрязн|я́ть, -и́ть.

pollution [pə'lu:ʃ(ə)n] *n.* загрязне́ние; **environmental ~** загрязне́ние окружа́ющей среды́.

polo ['pəʊləʊ] *n.* по́ло (*indecl.*).
cpd. **~-neck** (*sweater*) *n.* сви́тер с закры́тым высо́ким воротнико́м; «водола́зка».

polonaise [ˌpɒlə'neɪz] *n.* полоне́з.

polonium [pəl'əʊnɪəm] *n.* поло́ний.

poltergeist ['pɒltəˌgaɪst] *n.* полтерге́йст.

polyanthus [ˌpɒlɪ'ænθəs] *n.* при́мула высо́кая.

polyclinic ['pɒlɪˌklɪnɪk] *n.* поликли́ника.

polygamist [pə'lɪgəmɪst] *n.* полигами́ст.

polygamous [pə'lɪgəməs] *adj.* полига́мный.

polygamy [pə'lɪgəmɪ] *n.* полига́мия, многобра́чие.

polyglot ['pɒlɪˌglɒt] *n.* полигло́т.
adj. многоязы́чный.

polygon ['pɒlɪgən, -ˌgɒn] *n.* многоуго́льник.

polygonal [pə'lɪgən(ə)l] *adj.* многоуго́льный.

polymath ['pɒlɪˌmæθ] *n.* эруди́т; всесторо́нне осведомлённый челове́к.

polymer ['pɒlɪmə(r)] *n.* полиме́р.

polyp ['pɒlɪp] *n.* (*zool., med.*) поли́п.

polystyrene [ˌpɒlɪ'staɪəˌri:n] *n.* полистиро́л.

polysyllabic [ˌpɒlɪsɪ'læbɪk] *adj.* многосло́жный.

polytechnic [ˌpɒlɪ'teknɪk] *n.* полите́хникум.
adj. политехни́ческий.

polytheism ['pɒlɪθi:ˌɪz(ə)m] *n.* политеи́зм.

polytheist ['pɒlɪˌθi:ɪst] *n.* политеи́ст.

polytheistic [ˌpɒlɪθi:'ɪstɪk] *adj.* политеисти́ческий.

polythene ['pɒlɪˌθi:n] *n.* полиэтиле́н; (*attr.*) полиэтиле́новый.

polyunsaturated [ˌpɒlɪʌn'sætʃəˌreɪtɪd] *adj.*: **~ fats** полиненасы́щенные жиры́.

pomade [pə'mɑ:d] *n.* пома́да.
v.t. пома́дить, на-.

pomander [pə'mændə(r)] *n.* ша́рик с ароматическими тра́вами.

pomegranate ['pɒmɪˌgrænɪt] *n.* грана́т.

pommel ['pʌm(ə)l] *n.* (*of saddle*) лука́.
v.t. = **pummel**

pomp [pɒmp] *n.* пы́шность, по́мпа.

pompon ['pɒmpɒn] *n.* (*tuft*) помпо́н.

pomposity [pɒm'pɒsɪtɪ] *n.* помпёзность; (*of pers.*) напы́щенность.

pompous ['pɒmpəs] *adj.* помпёзный; (*of pers.*) напы́щенный.

poncho ['pɒntʃəʊ] *n.* наки́дка «по́нчо», (*indecl.*).

pond [pɒnd] *n.* пруд.
cpds. **~-life** *n.* прудова́я фа́уна; **~weed** *n.* рдест.

ponder ['pɒndə(r)] *v.t.* обду́м|ывать, -ать.
v.i. размышля́ть (*impf.*).

ponderous ['pɒndərəs] *adj.* (*heavy*) тяжёлый; (*of style etc.*) тяжелове́сный.

pong [pɒŋ] *n.* (*coll.*) вонь, злово́ние.

pontiff ['pɒntɪf] *n.* (*high priest*) первосвяще́нник; (*bishop*) епи́скоп; **supreme ~** (*the Pope*) па́па ри́мский.

pontifical [pɒn'tɪfɪk(ə)l] *adj.* епи́скопский, епископа́льный; (*fig.*) догмати́ческий.

pontificate [pɒn'tɪfɪkət] *n.* (*office*) понтифика́т.
v.i. (*fig., lay down the law*) веща́ть (*impf.*).

pontoon [pɒn'tu:n] *n.* **1.** (*boat*) понто́н; **~ bridge** понто́нный мост. **2.** (*card game*) два́дцать одно́.

pony ['pəʊnɪ] *n.* (*horse*) по́ни (*m. indecl.*).
cpd. **~-tail** *n.* «ко́нский хвост».

poodle ['pu:d(ə)l] *n.* пу́дель (*m.*).

pooh [pu:] *int.* фу!; уф!

pooh-pooh [pu:'pu:] *v.t.* фы́ркать (*impf.*) на+*a.*; относи́ться (*impf.*) пренебрежи́тельно к+*d.*

pool[1] [pu:l] *n.* (*small body of water*) пруд; (*puddle*) лу́жа; **(swimming-~)** бассе́йн.

pool[2] [pu:l] *n.* **1.** (*total of staked money*) пу́лька; совоку́пность ста́вок; **football ~s** футбо́льный тотализа́тор. **2.** (*common reserve*) о́бщий фонд. **3.** (*billiards game*) пул. **4.: typing ~** машинопи́сное бюро́ (*indecl.*).
v.t. объедин|я́ть, -и́ть в о́бщий фонд.
cpd. **~-room** *n.* билья́рдная.

poop [pu:p] *n.* (*of ship*) корма́.

poor [pʊə(r)] *n.* (*collect.*: **the ~**) бедняки́ (*m. pl.*), бе́дные (*pl.*).

adj. **1.** (*indigent*) бéдный. **2.** (*unfortunate, deserving of sympathy*) бéдный, несчáстный; **~ fellow** бедня́га; **~ little chap!** бедня́жка! **3.** (*small, scanty*) скýдный; плохóй; **a ~ supply** плохóе снабжéние; **a ~ harvest** ни́зкий урожáй; **a ~ response** слáбый óтклик. **4.** (*of low quality*) плохóй; **~ soil** бéдная, неплодорóдная пóчва; **~ health** слáбое здорóвье. **5.** (*miserable, spiritless*) несчáстный, жáлкий.

cpds. **~-box** *n.* крýжка для сбóра в пóльзу бéдных; **~-house** *n.* богадéльня.

poorly ['puəlı] *adj.* нездорóвый; **are you feeling ~?** вам нездорóвится?

adv. бéдно; плóхо; **his parents are ~ off** егó роди́тели живýт бéдно.

poorness ['puənıs] *n.* (*poor quality*) бéдность; недостáточность; **the ~ of the soil** скýдость/неплодорóдность пóчвы.

pop[1] [pɒp] *n.* (*explosive sound*) щёлк, треск; (*coll., gaseous drink*) шипýчий напи́ток.

adv.: **the balloon went ~** шáрик лóпнул.

v.t. **1.** (*cause to explode*): **~ a balloon** прокол|óть (*pf.*) шáрик. **2.** (*put suddenly*) совáть, сýнуть; **he ~ped his head through the window** он вы́сунул гóлову из окнá; **~ the question** (*coll., propose*) сдéлать (*pf.*) предложéние.

v.i. (*make explosive sound*) трéскаться (*impf.*); (*shoot*) стрельнýть (*pf.*); **they were ~ping away at the target** они́ пали́ли по мишéни.

with advs. (*coll.*): **they ~ped in for a drink** они́ заскочи́ли/забежáли вы́пить; **I am ~ping off home now** ну, я побежáл домóй; **his eyes ~ped out** он вы́лупил глазá; **I'll ~ over to the shop** я сбéгаю в магази́н.

cpds. **~corn** *n.* пóпкорн; воздýшная кукурýза; **~-gun** *n.* пугáч.

pop[2] [pɒp] *n.* (*coll., abbr. of* **popular 2.**) (*music*) поп-мýзыка.

adj.: **~ concert** поп-концéрт; **~ singer** поп-пев|éц (*fem.* -и́ца); исполни́тель (*fem.* -ница) поп-мýзыки.

pop[3] [pɒp] *n.* (*US coll., father*) пáпка (*m.*).

pope [pəup] *n.* (*bishop of Rome*) пáпа (*m.*); (*Orthodox priest*) поп.

poplar ['pɒplə(r)] *n.* тóполь (*m.*).

poplin ['pɒplın] *n.* попли́н.

poppet ['pɒpıt] *n.* (*as term of endearment*) крóшка, малы́шка; **she is a ~** онá прéлесть.

poppy ['pɒpı] *n.* мак; (*attr.*) мáковый.

cpd. **~-seed** *n.* мак.

poppycock ['pɒpı,kɒk] *n.* чепухá (*coll.*).

populace ['pɒpjuləs] *n.* (*the masses*) мáссы (*f. pl.*).

popular ['pɒpjulə(r)] *adj.* **1.** (*of the people*) нарóдный; **~ front** нарóдный фронт. **2.** (*suited to the needs, tastes etc. of the people*): **the ~ press** мáссовая прéсса/печáть; **~ prices** общедостýпные цéны; **~ song** популя́рная пéсня. **3.** (*generally liked*) пользýющийся óбщей симпáтией; **she is ~ at school** её лю́бят в шкóле; **he is ~ with the ladies** он имéет успéх у жéнщин.

popularity [,pɒpju'lærıtı] *n.* популя́рность; успéх.

popularization [,pɒpjulərai'zeıʃ(ə)n] *n.* популяризáция.

popularize ['pɒpjulə,raız] *v.t.* популяризи́ровать (*impf.*).

popularly ['pɒpjuləlı] *adv.*: **he was ~ supposed to be a magician** в нарóде егó считáли волшéбником.

populate ['pɒpju,leıt] *v.t.* насел|я́ть, -и́ть; засел|я́ть, -и́ть.

population [,pɒpju'leıʃ(ə)n] *n.* населéние.

populism ['pɒpjulız(ə)m] *n.* (*Russ. hist.*) нарóдничество.

populist ['pɒpjulıst] *n.* (*Russ. hist.*) нарóдник.

adj. попули́стский, нарóднический.

populous ['pɒpjuləs] *adj.* многолю́дный, густонаселённый.

porcelain ['pɔ:səlın] *n.* фарфóр; (*attr.*) фарфóровый.

porch [pɔ:tʃ] *n.* (*covered entrance*) подъéзд, пóртик; (*US, verandah*) верáнда, балкóн.

porcupine ['pɔ:kju,paın] *n.* дикобрáз.

pore[1] [pɔ:(r)] *n.* пóра.

pore[2] [pɔ:(r)] *v.i.*: **he likes to ~ over old books** он лю́бит сидéть над стáрыми кни́гами.

pork [pɔ:k] *n.* свини́на; **~ chop** свинáя отбивнáя котлéта; **~ pie** пирóг со свини́ной.

cpd. **~-butcher** *n.* свинобóец.

pornographer [pɔ:'nɒgrəfə(r)] *n.* человек, распространя́ющий порногрáфию.

pornographic [,pɔ:nə'græfık] *adj.* порнографи́ческий.

pornography [pɔ:'nɒgrəfı] *n.* порногрáфия.

porosity [pɔ:'rɒsıtı] *n.* пóристость.

porous ['pɔ:rəs] *adj.* пóристый.

porphyry ['pɔ:fırı] *n.* порфи́р.

porpoise ['pɔ:pəs] *n.* морскáя свинья́.

porridge ['pɒrıdʒ] *n.* (овся́ная) кáша.

port[1] [pɔ:t] *n.* (*harbour*) порт, гáвань; **P~ of London** Лóндонский порт; **~ of call** порт захóда; **free ~** вóльная гáвань.

port[2] [pɔ:t] *n.* (*left side*) лéвый борт; **hard to ~!** лéво рулю́!; **on the ~ bow** слéва пó носу.

port[3] [pɔ:t] *n.* (*wine*) портвéйн.

portable ['pɔ:təb(ə)l] *adj.* портати́вный.

portage ['pɔ:tıdʒ] *n.* перенóска, перевóз; переправа вóлоком.

v.t. перепр|авля́ть, -áвить вóлоком.

portal ['pɔ:t(ə)l] *n.* портáл.

portcullis [pɔ:t'kʌlıs] *n.* опускнáя решётка.

portend [pɔ:'tend] *v.t.* предвещáть(*impf.*).

portent ['pɔ:tent, -t(ə)nt] *n.* (*omen*) предзнаменовáние; (*marvel*) чýдо.

portentous [pɔ:'tentəs] *adj.* (*prophetic*) вéщий; (*significant*) многозначи́тельный; (*pompous*) напы́щенный.

porter ['pɔ:tə(r)] *n.* **1.** (*carrier of luggage etc.*) носи́льщик. **2.** (*US, sleeping car attendant*) проводни́к. **3.** (*door-keeper*) швейцáр.

portfolio [pɔ:t'fəulıəu] *n.* **1.** (*case*) портфéль (*m.*), пáпка. **2.** (*of investments*) пéречень (*m.*) цéнных бумáг. **3.** (*ministerial office*) портфéль (*m.*); **minister without ~** мини́стр без портфéля.

porthole ['pɔ:thəul] *n.* иллюминáтор.

portico ['pɔ:tı,kəu] *n.* пóртик.

portion ['pɔ:ʃ(ə)n] *n.* (*part, share*) часть; дóля; (*of food*) пóрция.

v.t. (*divide*) дели́ть, раз-; **~ out** (*distribute*) произв|оди́ть, -ести́ раздéл +*g*.

portly ['pɔ:tlı] *adj.* дорóдный, пóлный, тýчный.

portrait ['pɔ:trıt] *n.* портрéт.

portray [pɔ:'treı] *v.t.* (*depict, describe*) рисовáть, нарисовать портрéт +*g.*; (*act part of*) игрáть, сыгрáть; создáть (*pf.*) óбраз +*g*.

portrayal [pɔ:'treıəl] *n.* изображéние, óбраз.

Portugal ['pɔ:tjug(ə)l] *n.* Португáлия.

Portuguese [,pɔ:tju'gi:z, ,pɔ:tʃ-] *n.* **1.** (*pers.*) португáл|ец (*fem.* -ка). **2.** (*language*) португáльский язы́к.

adj. португáльский.

pose [pəuz] *n.* (*of body or mind*) пóза.

v.t. (*put forward, propound*) предл|агáть, -ожи́ть; изл|агáть, -ожи́ть; **this ~s an awkward problem** э́то создаёт серьёзную проблéму.

v.i. (*take up a position or attitude*) пози́ровать (*impf.*); **he ~s as an expert** он выдаёт себя́ за знатокá/специали́ста.

posh [pɒʃ] *adj.* (*coll.*) шикáрный, фешенéбельный.

position [pə'zıʃ(ə)n] *n.* **1.** (*place occupied by s.o. or sth.*) мéсто; **he took up his ~ by the door** он зáнял своё мéсто у двéри; (*mil.*) пози́ция; **the enemy's ~s were stormed** пози́ции врагá бы́ли взя́ты штýрмом. **2.** (*situation, circumstances*) положéние; **the**

~ is desperate положе́ние отча́янное; **I am not in a ~ to say** я не в состоя́нии сказа́ть. **3.** (*posture*) по́за; **he assumed a sitting ~** он при́нял сидя́чую по́зу. **4.** (*mental attitude, line of argument*) пози́ция; **allow me to state my ~** разреши́те мне вы́сказать свою́ то́чку зре́ния. **5.** (*place in society, status*) положе́ние. **6.** (*post, employment*) до́лжность, ме́сто.

v.t. (*place in ~*) ста́вить, по-; поме|ща́ть, -сти́ть.

positive ['pɒzɪtɪv] *n.* (*phot.*) позити́в.

adj. **1.** (*definite, explicit*) несомне́нный, определённый. **2.** (*convinced, certain*) уве́ренный, убеждённый; **are you ~ you saw him?** вы уве́рены, что ви́дели его́? **3.** (*assertive*) самоуве́ренный. **4.** (*practical, helpful*) положи́тельный; **a ~ suggestion** де́льное предложе́ние. **5.** (*gram., math., elec.*) положи́тельный; **the ~ sign** знак плюс. **6.** (*phot.*) позити́вный.

positively ['pɒzɪtɪvlɪ] *adv.* несомне́нно, я́сно, абсолю́тно; положи́тельно; **she was ~ rude to me** она́ была́ со мно́й про́сто груба́.

positivism ['pɒzɪtɪ,vɪz(ə)m] *n.* позитиви́зм.

positron ['pɒzɪ,trɒn] *n.* позитро́н.

posse ['pɒsɪ] *n.* отря́д полице́йских.

possess [pə'zes] *v.t.* **1.** (*own, have*) владе́ть (*impf.*) +*i.*; облада́ть (*impf.*) +*i.*. **2.** (*dominate, influence*) овлад|ева́ть, -е́ть; захва́т|ывать, -и́ть; **he is ~ed by one idea** он одержи́м одно́й иде́ей; **whatever ~ed him to do that?** что его́ заста́вило поступи́ть таки́м о́бразом?

possession [pə'zeʃ(ə)n] *n.* **1.** (*ownership, occupation*) владе́ние; **they took ~ of the house** они́ ста́ли владе́льцами до́ма; **the documents are in my ~** докуме́нты в мои́х рука́х; **he is in full ~ of his senses** он в здра́вом уме́. **2.** (*pl., property*) иму́щество, со́бственность. **3.** (*pl., territory*) владе́ния (*nt. pl.*).

possessive [pə'zesɪv] *adj.* **1.** (*gram.*) притяжа́тельный. **2.** (*of pers.*) со́бственнический; (*jealous*) ревни́вый; **she is a ~ mother** она́ вла́стная мать.

possessor [pə'zesə(r)] *n.* (*owner*) владе́лец, облада́тель (*m.*).

possibilit|y [,pɒsɪ'bɪlɪtɪ] *n.* возмо́жность; (*likelihood*) вероя́тность; **it is within the bounds of ~y** э́то в преде́лах возмо́жности; (*pl., potentiality*) возмо́жности (*f. pl.*); перспекти́вы (*f. pl.*).

possible ['pɒsɪb(ə)l] *n.* (*~ choice*) возмо́жное.

adj. возмо́жный; (*achievable*) осуществи́мый; **as soon as ~** как мо́жно скоре́е; **I have done everything ~ to help** я сде́лал всё возмо́жное, что́бы помо́чь.

possibly ['pɒsɪblɪ] *adv.* **1.** (*in accordance with what is possible*) возмо́жно; вероя́тно; **how can I ~ do that?** как же я могу́ э́то сде́лать? **2.** (*perhaps*) возмо́жно; мо́жет быть.

post[1] [pəʊst] *n.* (*of wood, metal etc.*) столб; **starting ~** ста́ртовый столб; **winning ~** столб у фи́ниша.

v.t. (*display publicly*) выве́шивать, вы́весить; объяв|ля́ть, -и́ть.

post[2] [pəʊst] *n.* (*mail*) по́чта; **by ~** по́чтой; по по́чте; **by return of ~** с обра́тной по́чтой; **parcel ~** почто́во-посы́лочная слу́жба; **if you hurry you will catch the ~** е́сли вы поспеши́те, то успе́ете до отпра́вки по́чты; **has the ~ come yet?** по́чта уже́ была́?

v.t. **1.** (*dispatch by mail*) отпр|авля́ть, -а́вить по по́чте. **2.** (*book-keeping*) перен|оси́ть, -ести́ в гроссбу́х; (*fig.*) изве|ща́ть, -сти́ть; **keep me ~ed (of events)** держи́те меня́ в ку́рсе (дел)!

cpds. **~-bag** *n.* су́мка почтальо́на; **~-box** *n.* почто́вый я́щик; **~card** *n.* откры́тка; **~code** *n.* почто́вый и́ндекс; **~-haste** *adv.* о́чень бы́стро; **~man** *n.* почтальо́н; **~mark** *n.* почто́вый ште́мпель; *v.t.* ста́вить, по- почто́вый ште́мпель на+*a./p.*; **~master** *n.* почтме́йстер; **~mistress** *n.* нача́льница почто́вого отделе́ния; **~-office** *n.* по́чта; (*branch office*) отделе́ние свя́зи; (*main office*) почта́мт; **~-paid** *adj.* с опла́ченными почто́выми расхо́дами; *adv.* опла́чено.

post[3] [pəʊst] *n.* **1.** (*place of duty*) пост; **at one's ~** на посту́. **2.** (*fort*) форт. **3.** (*trading station*) торго́вый пост. **4.** (*appointment, job*) до́лжность.

v.t. **1.** (*assign to place of duty*) назн|ача́ть, -а́чить на до́лжность. **2.** (*mil.*) прикомандиро́в|ывать, -а́ть.

postage ['pəʊstɪdʒ] *n.* почто́вые расхо́ды (*m. pl.*).

cpd. **~-stamp** *n.* почто́вая ма́рка.

postal ['pəʊst(ə)l] *adj.* почто́вый; **~ order** де́нежный почто́вый перево́д; **~ tuition** зао́чное обуче́ние.

post-date [pəʊst'deɪt] *v.t.* дати́ровать (*impf.*) пере́дним (*or* бо́лее по́здним) число́м.

poster ['pəʊstə(r)] *n.* (*placard*) афи́ша, плака́т.

cpd. **~-paint** *n.* плака́тная кра́ска.

poste restante [,pəʊst re'stɑ̃t] *n.* до востре́бования.

posterior [pɒ'stɪərɪə(r)] *n.* зад.

adj. (*subsequent*) после́дующий; (*behind*) за́дний.

posterity [pɒ'sterɪtɪ] *n.* (*descendants*) пото́мство; **go down to ~** войти́ (*pf.*) в века́.

post-graduate [pəʊst'grædjʊət] *n.*: **~ student** аспира́нт (*fem.* -ка); **~ studies** аспиранту́ра.

posthumous ['pɒstjʊməs] *adj.* посме́ртный.

postil(l)ion [pɒ'stɪljən] *n.* форе́йтор.

post-mortem [pəʊst'mɔːtəm] *n.* (*on dead body*) вскры́тие тру́па, аутопси́я; (*coll., on game etc.*) разбо́р (*игры/матча и т.п.*).

post-natal [pəʊst'neɪt(ə)l] *adj.* послеродово́й.

postpone [pəʊst'pəʊn, pə'spəʊn] *v.t.* отсро́чи|вать, -ть; от|кла́дывать, -ложи́ть.

postponement [pəʊst'pəʊnmənt, pə'spəʊnmənt] *n.* отсро́чка, откла́дывание.

postscript ['pəʊstskrɪpt, 'pəʊskrɪpt] *n.* постскри́птум.

post-traumatic [,pəʊs(t)trɔː'mætɪk, -traʊ-] *adj.*: **~ stress disorder** посттравмати́ческий стресс.

postulate[1] ['pɒstjʊlət] *n.* постула́т.

postulate[2] ['pɒstjʊ,leɪt] *v.t.* постули́ровать (*impf.*).

posture ['pɒstʃə(r)] *n.* (*physical attitude*) по́за; (*carriage of body*) оса́нка; (*situation, condition*) положе́ние.

post-war [pəʊst'wɔː(r), 'pəʊst-] *adj.* послевое́нный.

posy ['pəʊzɪ] *n.* буке́т цвето́в.

pot[1] [pɒt] *n.* **1.** (*vessel*) горшо́к; **a ~ of jam** ба́нка варе́нья; **~s and pans** ку́хонная посу́да; **a ~ of tea** ча́йник с зава́ренным ча́ем; **~ plant** горшо́чное расте́ние; **~ roast** тушёное мя́со; (*fig.*): **his work is going to ~** (*coll.*) его́ рабо́та идёт насма́рку. **2.** (*coll., usu. pl., large sum*): **~s of money** ку́ча де́нег.

v.t. **1.** (*e.g. preserves*) консерви́ровать, за-; **~ted meat** консерви́рованное мя́со. **2.** (*e.g. plants*) сажа́ть, посади́ть в горшо́к; **~ting shed** помеще́ние для переса́дки расте́ний. **3.** (*fig., abridge*): **~ted history** кра́ткая исто́рия. **4.** (*billiards*) заг|оня́ть, -на́ть в лу́зу.

cpds. **~-bellied** *adj.* пуза́тый; **~-belly** *n.* брю́хо, пу́зо; **~-boiler** *n.* (*book etc.*) халту́ра; **~hole** *n.* (*in road surface*) вы́боина, ры́твина; (*in rocks*) котлови́на, му́льда; **~-holer** *n.* (спортсме́н-)спелео́лог; **~-holing** *n.* спелеоло́гия; **~-roast** *v.t.* туши́ть, с-; **~-shot** *n.* неприце́льный вы́стрел.

pot[2] [pɒt] *n.* (*coll., marijuana*) тра́вка, анаша́; **~ smoker** анаши́ст.

potash ['pɒtæʃ] *n.* пота́ш.

potassium [pə'tæsɪəm] *n.* ка́лий; (*attr.*) ка́лиевый.

potato [pə'teɪtəʊ] *n.* (*collect., and pl.*) карто́фель (*m.*), (*coll.*) карто́шка; (*single ~*) карто́фелина; **mashed ~es** карто́фельное пюре́ (*indecl.*); **~ crisps** хрустя́щий карто́фель.

potency ['pəʊt(ə)nsɪ] *n.* си́ла; власть; эффекти́вность.

potent ['pəʊt(ə)nt] *adj.* (*powerful*) си́льный, могу́щественный; (*efficacious*) эффекти́вный.

potentate ['pəʊtən,teɪt] *n.* повели́тель (*m.*), власте́ли́н.

potential [pə'tenʃ(ə)l] *n.* потенциа́л.

adj. потенциа́льный.
potentiality [pə,tenʃɪ'ælɪtɪ] *n.* потенциа́льность; возмо́жности (*f. pl.*).
potion ['pəʊʃ(ə)n] *n.* насто́йка; зе́лье; **love ~** любо́вный напи́ток.
potpourri [pəʊ'pʊərɪ, -'riː] *n.* (*lit., fig.*) попурри́ (*nt. indecl.*).
pottage ['pɒtɪdʒ] *n.* (*arch.*) похлёбка.
potter[1] ['pɒtə(r)] *n.* гонча́р; **~'s wheel** гонча́рный круг.
potter[2] ['pɒtə(r)] *v.i.* (*e.g. in garden*) копа́ться (*impf.*), ковыря́ться (*impf.*); **he ~ed along the road** он плёлся по доро́ге.
pottery ['pɒtərɪ] *n.* (*ware*) кера́мика; (*craft*) гонча́рное де́ло; (*workshop*) гонча́рня.
potty[1] ['pɒtɪ] *n.* (*coll., chamber-pot*) горшо́чек.
potty[2] ['pɒtɪ] *adj.* (*trifling*) ме́лкий, пустяко́вый; (*crazy*) чо́кнутый (*coll.*).
pouch [paʊtʃ] *n.* су́мка, мешо́чек; **tobacco ~** кисе́т; **diplomatic ~** (*US*) дипломати́ческая по́чта; (*kangaroo's*) су́мка.
pouf(fe) [puːf] *n.* (*seat*) пуф.
poulterer ['pəʊltərə(r)] *n.* торго́вец пти́цей и ди́чью.
poultice ['pəʊltɪs] *n.* припа́рка.
poultry ['pəʊltrɪ] *n.* дома́шняя пти́ца (*collect.*).
cpds. **~-farm** *n.* птицефе́рма; **~-farmer** *n.* птицево́д; **~farming** *n.* птицево́дство; **~-run** *n.* пти́чий волье́р.
pounce [paʊns] *n.* (*swoop*) налёт, прыжо́к.
v.i. набр|а́сываться, -о́ситься; **the cat ~d on the mouse** ко́шка бро́силась на мышь; (*fig.*) кида́ться, наки́нуться (*на кого/что*).
pound[1] [paʊnd] *n.* **1.** (*weight*) фунт; **butter is 60p a ~** ма́сло сто́ит 60 пе́нсов за фунт. **2.** (*money*) фунт (сте́рлингов); **a five-~ note** банкно́та в 5 фу́нтов сте́рлингов.
pound[2] [paʊnd] *n.* (*enclosure*) заго́н.
pound[3] [paʊnd] *v.t.* **1.** (*crush*) бить, раз-; **the ship was ~ed on the rocks** кора́бль уда́рило о ска́лы. **2.** (*thump*) колоти́ть (*impf.*).
v.i. **1.** (*thump*): **the guns were ~ing away** ору́дия пали́ли вовсю́; **he ~ed at the door** он колоти́л в дверь; **his feet ~ed on the stairs** он то́пал по ле́стнице; **her heart was ~ing with excitement** её се́рдце колоти́лось от волне́ния. **2.** (*run heavily*) мча́ться/нести́сь (*both impf.*) с гро́хотом.
poundage ['paʊndɪdʒ] *n.* (*payment per lb.*) по́шлина с ве́са.
pour [pɔː(r)] *v.t.* лить (*impf.*); нал|ива́ть, -и́ть; **who will ~ (the tea)?** кто бу́дет разлива́ть чай?; (*fig.*): **he ~ed scorn on the idea** он вы́смеял э́ту иде́ю; **he ~ed cold water on my suggestion** он раскритикова́л моё предложе́ние.
v.i. ли́ться (*impf.*); **water ~ed from the roof** вода́ струи́лась с кры́ши; **sweat ~ed off his brow** с него́ кати́лся пот; (*fig.*): **the crowd ~ed out of the theatre** толпа́ повали́ла из теа́тра; (*of rain*) лить (*impf.*) как из ведра́; **it's going to ~** бу́дет ли́вень; **it was ~ing with rain** шёл проливно́й дождь.
with advs. (*fig.*): **letters ~ed in** пи́сьма так и посы́пались; **she ~ed out a tale of woe** она́ излила́ своё го́ре; **his words ~ed out in a flood** слова́ лили́сь из него́ пото́ком.
pout [paʊt] *n.* наду́тые гу́бы (*f. pl.*).
v.i. над|ува́ть, -у́ть гу́бы; ду́ться, на-.
pouter ['paʊtə(r)] *n.* (*pigeon*) зоба́стый го́лубь.
poverty ['pɒvətɪ] *n.* бе́дность, нищета́; **on the ~ line** на гра́ни нищеты́; (*fig.*) отсу́тствие; **~ of ideas** ску́дость мы́слей.
cpd. **~-stricken** *adj.* (*lit.*) ни́щий; (*fig.*) убо́гий.
POW (*abbr. of **prisoner of war***) военнопле́нный.
powder ['paʊdə(r)] *n.* (*chem., med. etc.*) порошо́к; (*cosmetic*) пу́дра; (*explosive*) по́рох; **keep your ~ dry** (*fig.*) держи́те по́рох сухи́м.
v.t. **1.** (*reduce to ~*) превра|ща́ть, -ти́ть в порошо́к; **~ed milk** порошко́вое/сухо́е молоко́. **2.** (*apply ~ to*) пу́дрить, на-.
cpds. **~-magazine** *n.* порохово́й по́греб; **~-puff** *n.* пухо́вка; **~-room** *n.* да́мская (туале́тная) ко́мната.
powdery ['paʊdərɪ] *adj.* порошкообра́зный.
power ['paʊə(r)] *n.* **1.** (*ability, capacity*) си́ла, мощь; **I will do all in my ~** я сде́лаю всё, что в мои́х си́лах; **it is not within my ~** э́то не в моéй вла́сти; **purchasing ~** покупа́тельная спосо́бность; **the ~ to express one's thoughts** спосо́бность выража́ть свои́ мы́сли. **2.** (*pl., faculties*): **he is a man of considerable ~s** он наделён больши́ми спосо́бностями; **he was at the height of his ~s** он был в расцве́те сил. **3.** (*vigour, strength*) эне́ргия; **more ~ to your elbow!** (*coll.*) жела́ю уда́чи! **4.** (*energy, force*) эне́ргия; **electric ~** электроэне́ргия; **there was a ~ cut** электроэне́ргию вре́менно отключи́ли; **the machine is on full ~** маши́на рабо́тает на по́лную мо́щность. **5.** (*authority, control*) власть; **France was at the height of her ~** Фра́нция находи́лось в расцве́те своего́ могу́щества; **in ~** у вла́сти; **the party in ~** пра́вящая па́ртия; **balance of ~** равнове́сие сил; **~ politics** поли́тика с пози́ции си́лы. **6.** (*right, authorization*) пра́во; **the judge exceeded his ~s** судья́ превы́сил свои́ полномо́чия. **7.** (*influential person or organization*) си́ла; **he is a great ~ for good** его́ влия́ние весьма́ благотво́рно; **the ~s that be** си́льные (*pl.*) ми́ра сего́. **8.** (*state*) держа́ва; **the Great P~s** вели́кие держа́вы. **9.** (*supernatural force*) си́ла; **the ~s of darkness** си́лы тьмы. **10.** (*math.*) сте́пень; **two to the ~ of ten** два в деся́той сте́пени.
v.t. (*supply with energy*) снаб|жа́ть, -ди́ть силовы́м дви́гателем.
cpds. **~-boat** *n.* мото́рный ка́тер; **~-driven** *adj.* с механи́ческим приво́дом; **~-plant, ~-station** *nn.* электроста́нция; **~-point** *n.* электроввóд, ште́псельная розе́тка.
powerful ['paʊə,fʊl] *adj.* си́льный, мо́щный; **a ~ argument** мо́щный/убеди́тельный до́вод; **a ~ nation** могу́щественный наро́д.
powerless ['paʊəlɪs] *adj.* бесси́льный; **I was ~ to move** я был не в состоя́нии дви́нуться.
pox [pɒks] *n.* (*coll.*) си́филис.
pp. ['peɪdʒɪz] *n.* (*abbr. of **pages***) стр, (страни́цы).
PR *abbr. of **public relations** see* **public** *adj.* **1.**
practicability [,præktɪkə'bɪlɪtɪ] *n.* целесообра́зность.
practicable ['præktɪkəb(ə)l] *adj.* (*feasible*) осуществи́мый, реа́льный.
practical ['præktɪk(ə)l] *adj.* **1.** (*concerned with practice*) практи́ческий; **a ~ joke** ро́зыгрыш, шу́тка; **play a ~ joke on** разы́гр|ывать, -а́ть; **he is a ~ man** он практи́ческий челове́к. **2.** (*useful in practice, workable, feasible*) осуществи́мый; **this is not a ~ suggestion** э́то предложе́ние нереа́льно. **3.** (*virtual*) факти́ческий, настоя́щий; **it is a ~ impossibility** э́то практи́чески невозмо́жно.
practicality [,præktɪ'kælɪtɪ] *n.* практи́чность.
practically ['præktɪkəlɪ] *adv.* **1.** (*in a practical manner*) практи́чески; **look at a question ~** смотре́ть на вопро́с с практи́ческой то́чки зре́ния. **2.** (*almost*) практи́чески, факти́чески; почти́.
practice ['præktɪs] *n.* **1.** (*performance*) пра́ктика; **the idea will not work in ~** э́та иде́я на пра́ктике неосуществи́ма; **he put his plan into ~** он осуществи́л свой план. **2.** (*regular or habitual performance*) обы́чай, обыкнове́ние; **he makes a ~ of early rising** он взял себе́ за пра́вило ра́но встава́ть; **this ~ must stop** э́ту пра́ктику на́до прекрати́ть; **sharp ~** моше́нничество. **3.** (*repeated exercise*) упражне́ние, трениро́вка; **~ makes perfect** на́вык ма́стера

ста́вит; **your game needs more ~** вам на́до бо́льше трени́роваться; **I am badly out of ~** я давно́ не упражня́лся/практикова́лся. **4.** (*work of doctor, lawyer etc.*) пра́ктика; **he is in ~ in York** он име́ет пра́ктику в Йо́рке.

v.t. & i.: = **practise**

practis|e ['præktɪs] (*US* **practice**) *v.t.* **1.** (*perform habitually*) де́лать, с- по привы́чке; (*sport game etc.*) упражня́ться (*impf.*) в+*p.*; (*instrument*): **she was ~ing the piano** она́ упражня́лась на роя́ле. **2.** (*a profession etc.*) практикова́ть (*impf.*); **a ~ing physician** практику́ющий врач.

v.i. упражня́ться (*impf.*); тренирова́ться (*impf.*).

practitioner [præk'tɪʃənə(r)] *n.* (*med.*) практику́ющий врач; **general ~** участко́вый врач.

pragmatic(al) [præg'mætɪk(əl)] *adj.* прагмати́ческий.

pragmatism ['prægmə,tɪz(ə)m] *n.* прагмати́зм.

pragmatist ['prægmətɪst] *n.* прагма́тик.

prairie ['preərɪ] *n.* пре́рия.

praise [preɪz] *n.* похвала́; **his work is beyond ~** его́ рабо́та вы́ше вся́кой похвалы́; **he was loud in her ~s** он осыпа́л её похвала́ми; **~ be (to God)!** сла́ва Бо́гу!

v.t. (*voice approval, admiration of*) хвали́ть, по-; (*give glory to*) восхвал|я́ть, -и́ть.

cpd. **~worthy** *adj.* похва́льный.

pram [prɑːm] *n.* де́тская коля́ска.

prance [prɑːns] *n.* (*leap*) скачо́к.

v.i. (*of horse*) гарцева́ть (*impf.*); (*of pers.*) (*coll.*) форси́ть (*impf.*).

prang [præŋ] *n.* ава́рия, столкнове́ние.

prank [præŋk] *n.* вы́ходка, проде́лка; **play ~s on** разы́грывать (*impf.*); **play a ~ on** разыгра́ть (*pf.*).

prankster ['præŋkstə(r)] *n.* шутни́к, прока́зник.

prat [præt] *n.* дурале́й.

prate [preɪt] *v.i.* трепа́ться (*impf.*).

prattle ['præt(ə)l] *n.* болтовня́; ле́пет.

v.i. болта́ть (*impf.*); лепета́ть, про-.

prawn [prɔːn] *n.* креве́тка.

pray [preɪ] *v.t.* (*supplicate*) моли́ть (*impf.*); умол|я́ть, -и́ть; **~ God he comes in time** дай Бог, что́бы он пришёл во́время.

v.i. моли́ться, по-; **the farmers ~ed for rain** фе́рмеры моли́лись о дожде́; **we will ~ for the Queen** мы бу́дем моли́ться за короле́ву.

prayer ['preə(r)] *n.* **1.** (*act of praying*) моле́ние. **2.** (*formula, petition*) моли́тва; **the Lord's P~** О́тче наш; **say one's ~s** моли́ться, по-. **3.** (*entreaty*) про́сьба, мольба́.

cpds. **~-book** *n.* моли́твенник; **~-meeting** *n.* моли́твенное собра́ние.

preach [priːtʃ] *v.t.* пропове́довать (*impf.*); **go out and ~ the gospel!** иди́те и неси́те лю́дям Ева́нгелие!

v.i. (*deliver sermon*) чита́ть про́поведь; (*give moral advice*) поуча́ть (*impf.*).

preacher ['priːtʃə(r)] *n.* пропове́дник.

preamble [priː'æmb(ə)l, 'priː-] *n.* преа́мбула.

pre-arrange [,priːə'reɪndʒ] *v.t.* организо́в|ывать, -а́ть зара́нее; **at a ~d signal** по усло́вленному сигна́лу.

precarious [prɪ'keərɪəs] *adj.* **1.** (*uncertain*) ненадёжный; **a ~ foothold** ненадёжная опо́ра; **he makes a ~ living** он едва́ зараба́тывает на жизнь. **2.** (*dangerous, risky*) опа́сный, риско́ванный.

precaution [prɪ'kɔːʃ(ə)n] *n.* предосторо́жность; **it is wise to take ~s against fire** разу́мно приня́ть ме́ры предосторо́жности про́тив (*or* на слу́чай) пожа́ра.

precautionary [prɪ'kɔːʃənərɪ] *adj.*: **~ measures** ме́ры предосторо́жности.

preced|e [prɪ'siːd] *v.t.* (*take ~ence of, come before*) предше́ствовать (*impf.*) +*d.*; (*walk ahead of*): **he was ~ed by his wife** жена́ шла впереди́ его́.

v.i.: **in the ~ing sentence** в предыду́щем предложе́нии.

precedence ['presɪd(ə)ns] *n.* **1.** (*priority, superiority*) приорите́т; **this question takes ~** э́тот вопро́с до́лжен рассма́триваться в пе́рвую о́чередь. **2.** (*right of preceding others*) старшинство́.

precedent ['presɪd(ə)nt] *n.* прецеде́нт; **there is no ~ for this** э́то не име́ет прецеде́нта; **create, set a ~** созд|ава́ть, -а́ть прецеде́нт.

precept ['priːsept] *n.* наставле́ние; предписа́ние.

precinct ['priːsɪŋkt] *n.* **1.** (*enclosed space*) двор. **2.** (*pl., environs*) окре́стности (*f. pl.*). **3.** (*area of restricted access*): **pedestrian ~** уча́сток у́лицы то́лько для пешехо́дов; **shopping ~** торго́вый пасса́ж. **4.** (*US, police or electoral district*) уча́сток.

precious ['preʃəs] *adj.* **1.** (*of great value*) драгоце́нный; **~ stones** драгоце́нные ка́мни (*m. pl.*); (*as endearment*) люби́мый; **my ~** мой ненагля́дный. **2.** (*affected, over-refined*) мане́рно-изы́сканный.

adv. (*coll.*) о́чень, здо́рово; **I got ~ little for the ring** я получи́л за кольцо́ о́чень ма́ло; **there is ~ little hope** наде́жды почти́ нет.

precipice ['presɪpɪs] *n.* про́пасть, обры́в; **fall over a ~** сорва́ться (*pf.*) с обры́ва.

precipitate[1] [prɪ'sɪpɪtət] *adj.* (*headlong*) стреми́тельный; (*rash*) опроме́тчивый.

precipitate[2] [prɪ'sɪpɪ,teɪt] *v.t.* **1.** (*throw down*) низв|ерга́ть, -е́ргнуть; (*fig.*) вв|ерга́ть, -е́ргнуть; **the country was ~d into war** страну́ вве́ргнули в войну́. **2.** (*bring on rapidly*) уск|оря́ть, -о́рить. **3.** (*chem.*) оса|жда́ть, -ди́ть.

precipitation [prɪ,sɪpɪ'teɪʃ(ə)n] *n.* (*rain etc.*) оса́д|ки (*pl., g.* -ов).

precipitous [prɪ'sɪpɪtəs] *adj.* (*steep*) обры́вистый, крутой; (*hasty*) поспе́шный.

precipitousness [prɪ'sɪpɪtəsnɪs] *n.* (*steepness*) обры́вистость, крутизна́; (*haste*) поспе́шность.

précis ['preɪsiː] *n.* кра́ткое изложе́ние, конспе́кт.

precise [prɪ'saɪs] *adj.* (*exact*) то́чный, аккура́тный; (*punctilious*) тща́тельный.

precisely [prɪ'saɪslɪ] *adv.* то́чно; (*with numbers or quantities*) ро́вно; **at ~ two o'clock** ро́вно в два часа́; (*as reply: 'quite so'*) соверше́нно ве́рно; вот и́менно.

precision [prɪ'sɪʒ(ə)n] *n.* то́чность; аккура́тность; **~ bombing** прице́льное бомбомета́ние; **~ instrument** то́чный прибо́р.

preclude [prɪ'kluːd] *v.t.* предотвра|ща́ть, -ти́ть; исключ|а́ть, -и́ть.

precocious [prɪ'kəʊʃəs] *adj.* ра́но разви́вшийся.

precoci|ousness [prɪ'kəʊʃəsnɪs], **-ty** [prɪ'kɒsɪtɪ] *nn.* ра́ннее разви́тие.

preconceived [,priːkən'siːvd] *adj.* предвзя́тый.

preconception [,priːkən'sepʃ(ə)n] *n.* предвзя́тое мне́ние.

pre-condition [,priːkən'dɪʃ(ə)n] *n.* предвари́тельное усло́вие.

precursor [priː'kɜːsə(r)] *n.* предше́ственник, предве́стник.

pre-date [priː'deɪt] *v.t.* (*antedate*) дати́ровать за́дним число́м; (*precede*) предше́ствовать +*d.*

predator ['predətə(r)] *n.* хи́щник.

predatory ['predətərɪ] *adj.* хи́щный, граби́тельский.

predecessor ['priːdɪ,sesə(r)] *n.* предше́ственник.

predestination [priː,destɪ'neɪʃ(ə)n] *n.* предопределе́ние.

predestine [priː'destɪn] *v.t.* предопредел|я́ть, -и́ть.

predetermination [,priːdɪtɜːmɪ'neɪʃ(ə)n] *n.* предопределе́ние.

predetermine [,priːdɪ'tɜːmɪn] *v.t.* предреш|а́ть, -и́ть.

predicament [prɪ'dɪkəmənt] *n.* тру́дная ситуа́ция.

predicate[1] ['predɪkət] *n.* (*gram.*) сказу́емое; (*log.*) предика́т.

predicate[2] ['predɪ,keɪt] *v.t.* утвер|жда́ть, -ди́ть.

predicative [prɪ'dɪkətɪv] *adj.* предикати́вный.

predict [prɪ'dɪkt] *v.t.* предска́з|ывать, -а́ть.

predictable [prɪˈdɪktəb(ə)l] *adj.* предсказу́емый.
prediction [prɪˈdɪkʃ(ə)n] *n.* предсказа́ние.
predilection [ˌpriːdɪˈlekʃ(ə)n] *n.* пристра́стие, скло́нность (**for:** к+*d.*).
predispose [ˌpriːdɪˈspəʊz] *v.t.* предраспол|ага́ть, -ожи́ть; **I am ~d in his favour** я предраспо́ложен к нему́.
predisposition [ˌpriːdɪspəˈzɪʃ(ə)n] *n.* предрасположе́ние, скло́нность (*к чему*).
predominance [prɪˈdɒmɪnəns] *n.* (*control*; *superiority*) превосхо́дство; (*preponderance*) преоблада́ние.
predominant [prɪˈdɒmɪnənt] *adj.* (*without rival*) преоблада́ющий; (*preponderant*) домини́рующий.
predominate [prɪˈdɒmɪˌneɪt] *v.i.* преоблада́ть (*impf.*); домини́ровать (*impf.*).
pre-eminence [priːˈemɪnəns] *n.* превосхо́дство.
pre-eminent [priːˈemɪnənt] *adj.* выдаю́щийся.
pre-empt [priːˈempt] *v.t.* (*appropriate*) присв|а́ивать, -о́ить; (*forestall*) предупре|жда́ть, -ди́ть.
pre-emptive [priːˈemptɪv] *adj.* опережа́ющий; **~ strike** упрежда́ющий уда́р.
preen [priːn] *v.t.* (*of bird*): **~ one's feathers** чи́стить (*impf.*) пе́рья/пёрышки; (*of pers.*) прихор|а́шиваться, -оши́ться.
pre-existence [ˌpriːɪgˈzɪstəns] *n.* предсуществова́ние.
pre-existent [ˌpriːɪgˈzɪstənt] *adj.* предсуществу́ющий.
prefabricate [priːˈfæbrɪˌkeɪt] *v.t.*; **~d house** сбо́рный дом.
preface [ˈprefəs] *n.* предисло́вие.
v.t. де́лать, с- вступле́ние к+*d.*; предпос|ыла́ть, -ла́ть.
prefatory [ˈprefətərɪ] *adj.* вступи́тельный, вво́дный.
prefect [ˈpriːfekt] *n.* **1.** (*official*) префе́кт. **2.** (*at school*) ста́рший учени́к, ста́роста (*c.g.*).
prefecture [ˈpriːfektjʊə(r)] *n.* префекту́ра.
prefer [prɪˈfɜː(r)] *v.t.* **1.** (*like better*) предпоч|ита́ть, -е́сть; **I ~ fish to meat** я предпочита́ю ры́бу мя́су. **2.** (*submit*): **~ charges** выдвига́ть, вы́двинуть обвине́ния.
preferable [ˈprefərəb(ə)l] *adj.* предпочти́тельный.
preference [ˈprefərəns] *n.* предпочте́ние; **have you any ~?** что вы предпочита́ете?; **I chose this in ~ to the other** я предпочёл э́то тому́; (*preferred thg.*) вы́бор.
preferential [ˌprefəˈrenʃ(ə)l] *adj.* предпочти́тельный; льго́тный.
prefix [ˈpriːfɪks] *n.* (*at beginning of word*) приста́вка, пре́фикс; (*title such as* 'Mr') обраще́ние, ти́тул.
v.t. присоедин|я́ть, -и́ть (*приставку к слову*).
pregnancy [ˈpregnənsɪ] *n.* бере́менность.
pregnant [ˈpregnənt] *adj.* бере́менная; **become ~** забере́менеть (*pf.*).
prehensile [priːˈhensaɪl] *adj.* хвата́тельный.
prehistoric [ˌpriːhɪˈstɒrɪk] *adj.* доистори́ческий.
prehistory [ˌpriːˈhɪstərɪ] *n.* предысто́рия.
prejudge [priːˈdʒʌdʒ] *v.i.* предреш|а́ть, -и́ть.
prejudice [ˈpredʒʊdɪs] *n.* **1.** (*preconceived opinion*) предубежде́ние, предрассу́док. **2.** (*detriment*) уще́рб, вред. **3.** (*prejudgement*): **without ~** без уще́рба (для+*g.*).
v.t. **1.** (*cause to have a ~*) предубе|жда́ть, -ди́ть; **you are ~d against him** вы предубеждены́ про́тив него́. **2.** (*impair validity of*) нан|оси́ть, -ести́ уще́рб +*d.*
prejudicial [ˌpredʒʊˈdɪʃ(ə)l] *adj.* (*detrimental*) вре́дный; ущемля́ющий; нанося́щий уще́рб +*d.*
prelate [ˈprelət] *n.* прела́т.
preliminary [prɪˈlɪmɪnərɪ] *n.* подготови́тельное мероприя́тие.
adj. предвари́тельный.
prelude [ˈpreljuːd] *n.* (*mus.*) прелю́дия.
v.t. (*serve as ~ to*) служи́ть (*impf.*) вступле́нием к+*d.*
premarital [priːˈmærɪt(ə)l] *adj.* добра́чный.
premature [ˈpreməˌtjʊə(r), -ˈtjʊə(r)] *adj.* преждевре́менный; **~ birth** преждевре́менные ро́д|ы (*pl.*, *g.* -ов); **~ baby** недоно́шеный младе́нец; **~ decision** поспе́шное реше́ние.
premeditate [priːˈmedɪˌteɪt] *v.t.*: **~d murder** преднаме́ренное уби́йство.
premeditation [priːˌmedɪˈteɪʃ(ə)n] *n.* преднаме́ренность.
premenstrual [priːˈmenstrʊəl] *adj.* предменструа́льный.
premier [ˈpremɪə(r)] *n.* премье́р-мини́стр.
adj. пе́рвый; гла́вный.
première [ˈpremɪˌeə(r)] *n.* премье́ра.
premise [ˈpremɪs] *n.* **1.** посы́лка. **2.** (*pl.*, *house and land*) помеще́ние; **drinks are to be consumed on the ~s** напи́тки продаю́тся распи́вочно; **licensed ~s** помеще́ние, в кото́ром разрешена́ прода́жа спиртны́х напи́тков.
premium [ˈpriːmɪəm] *n.* **1.** (*reward*) награ́да. **2.** (*amount paid for insurance*) (страхова́я) пре́мия. **3.** (*additional charge or payment*) припла́та. **4.**: **at a ~** вы́ше номина́ла; с при́былью; (*in demand*) по́льзующийся спро́сом.
premonition [ˌpreməˈnɪʃ(ə)n, ˌpriː-] *n.* предчу́вствие.
pre-natal [priːˈneɪt(ə)l] *adj.* предродово́й.
preoccupation [priːˌɒkjʊˈpeɪʃ(ə)n] *n.* (*mental absorption*) озабо́ченность, поглощённость; (*absorbing subject*) забо́та.
preoccup|y [priːˈɒkjʊˌpaɪ] *v.t.* забо́тить, о-; **~ied** поглощённый; **the match ~ied his thoughts** матч занима́л все его́ мы́сли.
pre-ordain [ˌpriːɔːˈdeɪn] *v.t.* предназн|ача́ть, -а́чить.
prep [prep] *n.* (*coll.*, *school work set*) ≃ уро́к(и) на́ дом.
adj. (*coll.*): **~ school** (ча́стная) приготови́тельная шко́ла.
pre-packed [priːˈpækd] *adj.* расфасо́ванный.
preparation [ˌprepəˈreɪʃ(ə)n] *n.* **1.** (*process of preparing or being prepared*) приготовле́ние; **a second edition is in ~** гото́вится второ́е изда́ние; (*pl.*, *preparatory measures*): **~s are well under way** подгото́вка идёт вовсю́; **he made ~s to leave** он стал гото́виться к отъе́зду. **2.** (**medicine**) лека́рство.
preparatory [prɪˈpærətərɪ] *adj.* подготови́тельный.
adv.: **~ to** пре́жде чем (+*inf.*).
prepare [prɪˈpeə(r)] *v.t.* гото́вить (*impf.*); пригот|а́вливать, -о́вить; подгот|а́вливать, -о́вить; **I was ~d for the worst** я был гото́в к са́мому ху́дшему; **the tutor ~d him for his exams** учи́тель гото́вил его́ к экза́менам.
v.i. подгот|а́вливаться, -о́виться; пригот|а́вливаться, -о́виться.
preparedness [prɪˈpeərɪdnɪs] *n.* гото́вность.
prepa|y [priːˈpeɪ] *v.t.* опла́|чивать, -ти́ть зара́нее; **~id** опла́ченный зара́нее.
preponderance [prɪˈpɒndərəns] *n.* переве́с, преиму́щество.
preponderant [prɪˈpɒndərənt] *adj.* преоблада́ющий.
preposition [ˌprepəˈzɪʃ(ə)n] *n.* предло́г.
prepositional [ˌprepəˈzɪʃənəl] *adj.* предло́жный.
prepossess [ˌpriːpəˈzes] *v.t.* предраспол|ага́ть, -ожи́ть; **his appearance is not ~ing** у него́ нерасполага́ющая вне́шность.
preposterous [prɪˈpɒstərəs] *adj.* неле́пый.
prerequisite [priːˈrekwɪzɪt] *n.* предпосы́лка.
pre-revolutionary [ˌpriːˌrevəˈluːʃənərɪ] *adj.* дореволюцио́нный.
prerogative [prɪˈrɒgətɪv] *n.* (*of ruler*, *etc.*) прерогати́ва; (*privilege*) привиле́гия.
presage [ˈpresɪdʒ] *v.t.* (*portend*) предвеща́ть (*impf.*); (*forebode*) предчу́вствовать (*impf.*).
Presbyterian [ˌprezbɪˈtɪərɪən] *n.* пресвитериа́н|ин (*fem.* -ка).

adj. пресвитериа́нский.

prescience ['presɪəns] *n.* предви́дение.

prescient ['presɪənt] *adj.* предви́дящий.

prescribe [prɪ'skraɪb] *v.t.* **1.** (*lay down, impose*) предпи́с|ывать, -а́ть; **penalties ~d by the law** ме́ры наказа́ния, предусмо́тренные зако́ном. **2.** (*med.*) пропи́с|ывать, -а́ть.

prescription [prɪ'skrɪpʃ(ə)n] *n.* **1.** (*prescribing*) предпи́сывание. **2.** (*doctor's direction*) реце́пт. **3.** (*leg.*) пра́во да́вности.

prescriptive [prɪ'skrɪptɪv] *adj.* **1.** (*giving directions*) предпи́сывающий. **2.** (*leg.*): **~ right** пра́во, осно́ванное на да́вности.

presence ['prez(ə)ns] *n.* **1.** (*being present*) прису́тствие; **~ of mind** прису́тствие ду́ха; **I was summoned to his ~** я был вы́зван к нему́; **a military ~** вое́нное прису́тствие. **2.** (*carriage, bearing*) оса́нка.

present[1] ['prez(ə)nt] *n.* **1.** (*time now at hand*) настоя́щее (вре́мя); **there's no time like the ~** ≃ лови́ моме́нт; **at ~** сейча́с; **for the ~** пока́. **2.** (*gram.*, **~ tense**) настоя́щее вре́мя.

adj. **1.** (*at hand*) прису́тствующий; **no one else was ~** никого́ бо́льше не́ было; **all ~ and correct** все налицо́; всё в поря́дке. **2.** (*in question, under consideration*) да́нный, настоя́щий; **in the ~ case** в да́нном слу́чае. **3.** (*existent, prevalent*) настоя́щий, тепе́решний; (*available, to hand*) име́ющийся; **at the ~ time** в настоя́щее вре́мя; сейча́с; **the ~ holder of the title** ны́нешний облада́тель ти́тула; **under ~ circumstances** в ны́нешних усло́виях; **~ value** (*of an object*) тепе́решняя цена́. **4.** (*gram.*) настоя́щий.

cpd. **~-day** *adj.* совреме́нный, ны́нешний.

present[2] ['prez(ə)nt] *n.* (*gift*) пода́рок, дар; **I will make you a ~ of this shawl** я вам подарю́ э́ту шаль.

present[3] [prɪ'zent] *v.t.* **1.** (*tender, offer, put forward*) дари́ть, по-; вруч|а́ть, -и́ть; **the waiter ~ed the bill** официа́нт предста́вил счёт; **he ~ed his case well** он хорошо́ изложи́л свои́ до́воды; **he ~ed himself for duty** он яви́лся на слу́жбу; **as soon as an opportunity ~s itself** как то́лько предста́вится слу́чай; (*give, furnish*): **I was ~ed with a choice** мне предоста́вили вы́бор. **2.** (*introduce*) предст|авля́ть, -а́вить; **may I ~ my wife?** разреши́те предста́вить мою́ жену́. **3.** (*put on stage*) пока́з|ывать, -а́ть. **4.** (*mil.*): **~ arms** брать, взять на карау́л; (*as command*) на карау́л!

presentable [prɪ'zentəb(ə)l] *adj.* прили́чный, респекта́бельный.

presentation [,prezən'teɪʃ(ə)n] *n.* **1.** (*making a present*) вруче́ние. **2.** (*introduction*) представле́ние; **sales ~** презента́ция това́ра. **3.** (*theatr.*) пока́з, постано́вка. **4.** (*production, submission*) предъявле́ние. **5.** (*exposition*) пода́ча.

presentiment [prɪ'zentɪmənt] *n.* предчу́вствие.

presently ['prezəntlɪ] *adv.* (*soon*) вско́ре; (*US, at present*) сейча́с, в настоя́щее вре́мя.

preservation [,prezə'veɪʃ(ə)n] *n.* **1.** (*act of preserving*) сохране́ние, консерви́рование; (*of monuments, etc.*) охра́на. **2.** (*state of being preserved*) сохра́нность; **the building is in a fine state of ~** э́то зда́ние прекра́сно сохрани́лось.

preservative [prɪ'zɜːvətɪv] *n.* (*in food*) консерва́нт.

preserve [prɪ'zɜːv] **1.** (*jam*) варе́нье. **2.** (*area for protection of game, etc.*) запове́дник.

v.t. **1.** (*save; protect from harm*) сохран|я́ть, -и́ть; **God ~ us!** упаси́ нас Бог/Госпо́дь! **2.** (*keep from decomposition, etc.*) консерви́ровать, за-. **3.** (*of game, etc.*) охраня́ть (*impf.*) от браконье́рства. **4.** (*keep alive, youthful etc.*) сохран|я́ть, -и́ть; **his name will be ~d for ever** его́ и́мя оста́нется в века́х; **she is well ~d** она́ хорошо́ сохрани́лась. **5.** (*maintain*) подде́рж|ивать, -а́ть; храни́ть, со-; **she ~d a discreet silence** она́ благоразу́мно храни́ла молча́ние.

preside [prɪ'zaɪd] *v.i.* председа́тельствовать (*impf.*).

presidency ['prezɪdənsɪ] *n.* президе́нтство.

president ['prezɪd(ə)nt] *n.* (*of State etc.*) президе́нт; (*of college*) ре́ктор, дире́ктор; (*US, of company, bank etc.*) дире́ктор, глава́ (*c.g.*).

presidential [,prezɪ'denʃ(ə)l] *adj.* президе́нтский.

presidium [prɪ'sɪdɪəm, -'zɪdɪəm] *n.* прези́диум.

press [pres] *n.* **1.** (*act of ~ing*): **he gave her hand a ~** он пожа́л ей ру́ку; **she gave his trousers a ~** она́ погла́дила ему́ брю́ки. **2.** (*machine for ~ing*) пресс. **3.** (*printing-machine*) печа́тный стано́к; **we go to ~ tomorrow** за́втра но́мер идёт в печа́ть; **stop ~ (news)** э́кстренное сообще́ние. **4.** (*printing or publishing house*) изда́тельство. **5.** (*newspaper world*) печа́ть, пре́сса; **~ agency** аге́нство печа́ти; **~ agent** аге́нт по дела́м печа́ти; **~ campaign** камп́ания в печа́ти; **~ conference** пресс-конфере́нция; **~ release** сообще́ние для печа́ти; (*newspaper reaction*) о́тклик, реце́нзия. **6.** (*cupboard*) шкаф.

v.t. **1.** (*exert physical pressure on*) наж|има́ть, -а́ть; нада́в|ливать, -и́ть; **~ the trigger/button** нажа́ть (*pf.*) куро́к/кно́пку. **2.** (*push*) приж|има́ть, -а́ть. **3.** (*compress, etc.*) гла́дить, по-; утю́жить, от-; **my suit needs ~ing** мой костю́м нужда́ется в утю́жке; **the villagers are ~ing the grapes** жи́тели дере́вни да́вят виногра́д. **4.** (*clasp, embrace*) приж|има́ть, -а́ть; **he ~ed her hand** он пожа́л ей ру́ку. **5.** (*fig., sustain vigorously*): **he ~ed his claim** он наста́ивал на своём тре́бовании. **6.** (*fig., harry, exert pressure on*) тесни́ть (*impf.*); **our forces were hard ~ed** враг си́льно тесни́л на́ши войска́; **he was hard ~ed for an answer** он не нашёл, что отве́тить; **I was ~ed for time** у меня́ бы́ло вре́мени в обре́з. **7.** (*urge, importune*): **they ~ed me to stay** они́ угова́ривали меня́ оста́ться. **8.** (*urge acceptance of*) навя́зывать (*impf.*); **he ~ed money on me** он уси́ленно предлага́л мне де́ньги. **9.** (*recruit forcibly*) наси́льно вербова́ть, за-.

v.i.: **if you ~ too hard, the pencil will break** е́сли сли́шком нажима́ть, каранда́ш слома́ется; (*fig.*): **time ~es** вре́мя не те́рпит.

with advs.: **~ down** *v.t.* приж|има́ть, -а́ть; прида́в|ливать, -и́ть; **~ forward** *v.i.* прот|а́лкиваться, -олкну́ться (вперёд); **~ on** *v.i.* потора́пливаться (*impf.*); **~ out** *v.t.* выжима́ть, вы́жать.

cpds. **~-button** *n.* нажи́мная кно́пка; **~-cutting** *n.* газе́тная вы́резка; **~-gallery** *n.* места́ для представи́телей пре́ссы/печа́ти; **~-gang** *n.* (*hist.*) отря́д вербо́вщиков во флот; *v.t.* наси́льно вербова́ть во флот; (*fig.*) ока́з|ывать, -а́ть давле́ние на+*a.*; **~man** *n.* журнали́ст; **~-stud** *n.* кно́пка (*одёжная*); **~-up** *n.* отжи́м; **do ~-ups** отжима́ться (*impf.*) (на полу́).

pressing[1] ['presɪŋ] *n.* (*of clothing*) гла́жка, утю́жка.

pressing[2] ['presɪŋ] *adj.* (*urgent*) спе́шный, неотло́жный; (*insistent*) настоя́тельный, насто́йчивый.

pressure ['preʃə(r)] *n.* **1.** давле́ние; **~ suit** пневмокостю́м; (*fig.*) напряже́ние; **they are working at high ~** они́ рабо́тают о́чень напряжённо. **2.** (*compulsive influence*) давле́ние, возде́йствие; **bring ~ to bear on** прин|ужда́ть, -у́дить; **put ~ on** наж|има́ть, -а́ть на+*a.*; **the police put ~ on him** поли́ция оказа́ла нажи́м на него́; **~ group** ≃ инициати́вная гру́ппа.

cpds. **~-cooker** *n.* скорова́рка; **~-gauge** *n.* мано́метр.

pressurize ['preʃə,raɪz] *v.t.* **1.** герметизи́ровать (*impf.*); **~d cabin** гермети́ческая каби́на. **2.** (*fig.*) ока́з|ывать, -а́ть давле́ние на+*a.*.

prestige [pre'stiːʒ] *n.* прести́ж.

prestigious [pre'stɪdʒəs] *adj.* влия́тельный, авторите́тный, уважа́емый.

presto ['prestəʊ] *int.*: **(hey) ~!** гопля́!

presumably [prɪ'zjuːməblɪ] *adv.* веро́ятно; на́до полага́ть, что...

presume [prɪ'zju:m] *v.t.* **1.** (*assume, take for granted*) полага́ть (*impf.*). **2.** (*with inf.*: *venture*) позв|оля́ть, -о́лить себе́; осме́ли|ваться, -ться.

v.i.: ~ **on** (*take liberties with*): **he ~d on my good nature** он злоупотреби́л мое́й доброто́й.

presumption [prɪ'zʌmpʃ(ə)n] *n.* **1.** (*assumption*) предположе́ние, (*leg.*) презу́мпция; ~ **of innocence** презу́мпция невино́вности; **the ~ is that he is lying** на́до исходи́ть из того́, что он врёт. **2.** (*arrogance, boldness*) самонаде́янность.

presumptive [prɪ'zʌmptɪv] *adj.* предположи́тельный.

presumptuous [prɪ'zʌmptjʊəs] *adj.* самонаде́янный.

presuppose [ˌpri:sə'pəʊz] *v.t.* (зара́нее) предпол|ага́ть, -ожи́ть; допус|ка́ть, -ти́ть.

presupposition [pri:ˌsʌpə'zɪʃ(ə)n] *n.* предположе́ние, допуще́ние.

pre-tax [pri:'tæks] *adj.* начи́сленный до вы́чета нало́гов; ~ **profits** при́быль до нало́га.

pretence [prɪ'tens] (*US* **pretense**) *n.* **1.** (*pretending, make-believe*) притво́рство; **he obtained money by false ~s** он раздобы́л де́ньги обма́нным путём. **2.** (*pretext, excuse*) предло́г, отгово́рка. **3.** (*claim*) прете́нзия; **I make no ~ to scholarship** я не претенду́ю на учёность.

pretend [prɪ'tend] *v.t. & i.* **1.** (*make believe*) притворя́ться (*impf.*); де́лать вид; **let's ~ to be pirates!** дава́йте игра́ть в пира́тов! **2.** (*claim*) претендова́ть (*impf.*); **they both ~ed to the throne** они́ о́ба претендова́ли на престо́л.

pretender [prɪ'tendə(r)] *n.* претенде́нт.

pretense [prɪ'tens] = **pretence**

pretension [prɪ'tenʃ(ə)n] *n.* (*claim*) притяза́ние, прете́нзия; **I make no ~ to literary style** я во́все не претенду́ю на литерату́рный стиль.

pretentious [prɪ'tenʃəs] *adj.* претенцио́зный.

pretentiousness [prɪ'tenʃəsnɪs] *n.* претенцио́зность.

preternatural [ˌpri:tə'nætʃər(ə)l] *adj.* сверхъесте́ственный.

pretext ['pri:tekst] *n.* предло́г; **on, under the ~ of** под предло́гом +*g.*

prettiness ['prɪtɪnɪs] *n.* милови́дность; пре́лесть, привлека́тельность.

pretty ['prɪtɪ] *n.*: **my ~!** моя́ пре́лесть!

adj. **1.** (*attractive*) краси́вый, хоро́шенький. **2.** (*pleasant*) прия́тный, хоро́ший. **3.** (*iron.*) хоро́шенький; **a ~ mess you have made of it!** ну и ка́шу вы навари́ли! **4.** (*considerable*) значи́тельный; изря́дный.

adv. **1.** (*fairly*) доста́точно, дово́льно; ~ **much** о́чень, в значи́тельной сте́пени; почти́. **2.**: **he is sitting ~** он непло́хо устро́ился.

pretzel ['prets(ə)l] *n.* кренделёк.

prevail [prɪ'veɪl] *v.i.* **1.** (*win*) торжествова́ть (*impf.*); **truth will ~** пра́вда восторжеству́ет; ~ **over** одол|ева́ть, -е́ть. **2.** (*be widespread*) преоблада́ть (*impf.*), госпо́дствовать (*impf.*): **~ing winds** преоблада́ющие ве́тры. **3.**: ~ **on** (*persuade*) убе|жда́ть, -ди́ть.

prevalence ['prevələns] *n.* распростране́ние.

prevalent ['prevələnt] *adj.* распространённый.

prevaricate [prɪ'værɪˌkeɪt] *v.i.* уклоня́ться (*impf.*) от отве́та; увил|ивать, -ьну́ть.

prevarication [prɪˌværɪ'keɪʃ(ə)n] *n.* уклоне́ние от отве́та; увилива́ние.

prevent [prɪ'vent] *v.t.* предотвра|ща́ть, -ти́ть; меша́ть, по- +*d.*; препя́тствовать, вос- +*d.*; не дать (*pf.*) +*d.*; **illness ~ed him from coming** боле́знь помеша́ла ему́ прийти́.

prevention [prɪ'venʃ(ə)n] *n.* предотвраще́ние, предохране́ние; ~ **is better than cure** предупрежде́ние — лу́чше лече́ния.

preventive [prɪ'ventɪv] *adj.* предупреди́тельный; ~ **detention** превенти́вное заключе́ние; ~ **medicine** профилакти́ческая медици́на, профила́ктика.

preview ['pri:vju:] *n.* (предвари́тельный) просмо́тр.

v.t. предвари́тельно просм|а́тривать, -отре́ть.

previous ['pri:vɪəs] *adj.* предыду́щий; **on a ~ occasion** в предыду́щем слу́чае; **on the ~ day** за́ день до э́того.

adv.: ~ **to** пре́жде+*g.*, до+*g.*

previously ['pri:vɪəslɪ] *adv.* **1.** (*earlier*) зара́нее, ра́ньше. **2.** (*formerly*): ~ **he had lived with his brother** до э́того он жил со свои́м бра́том.

pre-war [pri:'wɔ:(r)] *adj.* предвое́нный, довое́нный.

prey [preɪ] *n.* добы́ча; **bird of ~** хи́щная пти́ца; (*fig.*) же́ртва; **she was a ~ to anxiety** её мучи́ло беспоко́йство.

v.i. охо́титься (*impf.*); **owls ~ on mice** со́вы охо́тятся на мыше́й; (*fig.*): **the crime ~ed upon his mind** (совершённое) преступле́ние не дава́ло ему́ поко́я.

price [praɪs] *n.* **1.** цена́; **he bought it at cost ~** он купи́л э́то по себесто́имости; **what is the ~ of eggs?** ско́лько сто́ят я́йца?; **they wanted peace at any ~** им ну́жен был мир любо́й цено́й. **2.** (*value*) це́нность. **3.** (*betting odds*) ша́нсы (*m. pl.*); **what ~ the favourite?** какова́ вы́плата за фавори́та?

v.t. **1.** (*fix ~ of*) назн|ача́ть, -а́чить цену́ на+*a.* **2.** (*enquire ~ of*) прице́н|иваться, -и́ться к+*d.*

cpds. **~-list** *n.* прейскура́нт; **~-tag** *n.* ярлы́к (с указа́нием цены́).

priceless ['praɪslɪs] *adj.* (*invaluable*) бесце́нный.

pricey ['praɪsɪ] *adj.* (*coll.*) дорого́й.

prick [prɪk] *n.* **1.** шип; колю́чка; (*puncture*) проко́л; (*fig.*): **the ~s of conscience** угрызе́ния (*nt. pl.*) со́вести. **2.** (*mark made by ~ing*) уко́л.

v.t. коло́ть, у-; (*fig.*) терза́ть (*impf.*).

v.i. коло́ться, у-.

with advs.: ~ **off**, ~ **out** *v.t.* пикирова́ть (*impf.*); перес|а́живать, -ади́ть; ~ **up** *v.t.*: ~ **up one's ears** (*of animal or person*) навостри́ть (*pf.*) у́ши.

prickle ['prɪk(ə)l] *n.* (*thorn*) колю́чка, шип; (*of hedgehog etc.*) игла́.

v.t. & i. коло́ть(ся), у-.

prickly ['prɪklɪ] *adj.* (*having spines or thorns*) колю́чий; (*causing a prickling sensation*) ко́лкий.

pride [praɪd] *n.* **1.** (*self-esteem, conceit*) го́рдость; **swallow one's ~** поступи́ться (*pf.*) свои́м самолю́бием. **2.** (*consciousness of worth; dignity*) чу́вство со́бственного досто́инства; **false ~** ло́жная го́рдость; **he takes ~ in his work** он горди́тся свое́й рабо́той. **3.** (*object of satisfaction*): **the yacht was his ~ and joy** э́та я́хта была́ его́ го́рдостью и ра́достью.

v.t.: ~ **o.s. on** горди́ться (*impf.*) +*i.*.

priest [pri:st] *n.* (*of Christian church*) свяще́нник.

priestess ['pri:stɪs] *n.* жри́ца.

priestly ['pri:stlɪ] *adj.* свяще́ннический.

prig [prɪg] *n.* педа́нт; (*hypocrite*) ханжа́ (*c.g.*).

priggish ['prɪgɪʃ] *adj.* педанти́чный; ха́нжеский.

prim [prɪm] *adj.* (*also* ~ **and proper**) чо́порный.

prima [ˌpri:mə] *adj.*: ~ **ballerina** при́ма-балери́на; ~ **donna** (*lit.*) примадо́нна, ди́ва; (*fig.*) примадо́нна.

primacy ['praɪməsɪ] *n.* (*pre-eminence*) главе́нство.

primaeval [praɪ'mi:v(ə)l] = **primeval**

prima facie [ˌpraɪmə 'feɪʃi:] *adj.*: ~ **evidence** доказа́тельство, доста́точное при отсу́тствии опроверже́ния.

primarily ['praɪmərɪlɪ, -'meərɪlɪ] *adv.* (*originally*) первонача́льно; (*principally, essentially*) в основно́м; гла́вным о́бразом.

primary ['praɪmərɪ]*adj.* **1.** (*original*) первонача́льный; ~ **school** нача́льная шко́ла. **2.** (*fundamental, basic, principal*) основно́й; ~ **colours** основны́е цвета́; **of ~ importance** первостепе́нной ва́жности.

primate ['praɪmeɪt] *n.* (*archbishop*) прима́с; (*mammal*) прима́т.

prime [praɪm] *n.* (*perfection, best part*) расцве́т; **in the ~ of life** в расцве́те сил.

adj. **1.** (*principal*) гла́вный; **~ minister** премье́р-мини́стр. **2.** (*excellent*) первокла́ссный. **3.** (*fundamental*) основно́й; **~ cost** себесто́имость; **~ number** просто́е число́.

v.t. **1.** (*firearm*) заря|жа́ть, -ди́ть; (*engine, pump*) запр|авля́ть, -а́вить. **2.** (*supply with facts etc.*) ната́ск|ивать, -а́ть. **3.** (*fill with food or drink*) накорми́ть (*pf.*); напои́ть (*pf.*). **4.** (*cover with first coat of paint etc.*) грунтова́ть (*impf.*).

primer ['praɪmə(r)] *n.* **1.** (*school-book*) буква́рь (*m.*). **2.** (*for igniting*) запа́л, ка́псюль (*m.*). **3.** (*paint*) грунто́вка.

prim|eval, -aeval [praɪ'mi:v(ə)l] *adj.* первобы́тный.

primitive ['prɪmɪtɪv] *adj.* (*earliest*) первобы́тный; **~ man** первобы́тный челове́к; (*unsophisticated, simple*) примити́вный.

primogeniture [ˌpraɪməʊ'dʒenɪtʃə(r)] *n.* перворо́дство.

primordial [praɪ'mɔ:dɪəl] *adj.* перви́чный, иско́нный, первобы́тный.

primrose ['prɪmrəʊz] *n.* при́мула.

Primus ['praɪməs] *n.* (*propr.*) **(~ stove)** при́мус.

prince [prɪns] *n.* **1.** князь (*m.*); (*son of royalty*) принц; **~ consort** принц-супру́г. **2.** (*fig.*): **the P~ of Peace** Христо́с; **the ~ of darkness** сатана́ (*m.*).

princely ['prɪnslɪ] *adj.* кня́жеский; (*generous*) благоро́дный.

princess [prɪn'ses] *n.* (*wife of non-royal prince*) княги́ня; (*their daughter*) княжна́; (*daughter or daughter-in-law of sovereign*) принце́сса.

principal ['prɪnsɪp(ə)l] *n.* **1.** (*head of college etc.*) дире́ктор, ре́ктор. **2.** (*sum of money*) капита́л.

adj. гла́вный, основно́й.

principality [ˌprɪnsɪ'pælɪtɪ] *n.* кня́жество.

principally ['prɪnsɪpəlɪ] *adv.* гла́вным о́бразом; преиму́щественно.

principle ['prɪnsɪp(ə)l] *n.* при́нцип, нача́ло; **the first ~s of geometry** осно́вы (*f. pl.*) геоме́трии; **~** в при́нципе; **on ~** из при́нципа; **a man of ~** принципиа́льный челове́к.

print [prɪnt] *n.* **1.** (*mark made on surface by pressure*) след; отпеча́ток. **2.** (*letters, etc.*) шрифт; печа́ть; **~ run** тира́ж; **the book is in ~** кни́га ещё в прода́же; **the book is out of ~** кни́га распро́дана. **3.** (*picture*) гравю́ра, эста́мп, репроду́кция. **4.** (*phot.*) отпеча́ток. **5.** (*cotton fabric*) си́тец.

v.t. **1.** (*impress*) печа́тать, на-/от-; (*fig.*) запечатл|ева́ть, -е́ть. **2.** (*produce by ~ing process; copy photographically*) печа́тать, на-/от-. **3.** (*write in imitation of ~*) писа́ть, на- печа́тными бу́квами. **4.** (*mark with coloured design*) наб|ива́ть, -и́ть.

with advs.: **~ off, ~ out** *v.t.* (*phot.*) де́лать, с- фотоотпеча́тки +*g.*

cpd. **~-out** *n.* (*by computer*) распеча́тка (с) ЭВМ.

printer ['prɪntə(r)] *n.* (*operator of press*) печа́тник, типо́граф; (*type-setter*) набо́рщик; (*owner of printing business*) типо́граф; (*comput.*) при́нтер; (*teleprinter*) телепри́нтер.

printing ['prɪntɪŋ] *n.* (*act or process*) печа́тание; (*trade*) печа́тное де́ло; (*material printed in one operation*) печа́тное изда́ние.

cpds. **~-office** *n.* типогра́фия; **~-press** *n.* печа́тный стано́к.

prior[1] ['praɪə(r)] *n.* (*eccl.*) прио́р, настоя́тель (*m.*).

prior[2] ['praɪə(r)] *adj.* (*earlier*) пре́жний; (*more important*) первоочередно́й.

adv.: **~ to** до+*g.*

prioress ['praɪərɪs] *n.* настоя́тельница.

prioritize [praɪ'ɒrɪtaɪz] *v.t.* устан|а́вливать, -ови́ть очерёдность; распредел|я́ть, -и́ть приорите́ты.

priorit|y [praɪ'ɒrɪtɪ] *n.* приорите́т; **safety is our first, highest, top ~y** безопа́сность — на́ша са́мая неотло́жная забо́та; **have you got your ~ies right?** пра́вильно ли вы оцени́ли, что бо́лее и что ме́нее ва́жно?

priory ['praɪərɪ] *n.* монасты́рь (*m.*).

pri|se, -ze [praɪz] *v.t.* взл|а́мывать, -ома́ть; **the box was ~d open** я́щик взлома́ли.

prism ['prɪz(ə)m] *n.* при́зма.

prismatic [prɪz'mætɪk] *adj.* призмати́ческий.

prison ['prɪz(ə)n] *n.* **1.** тюрьма́; **he was sent to ~ for a year** его́ посади́ли в тюрьму́ на́ год. **2.** (*attr.*) тюре́мный; **~ camp** исправи́тельно-трудово́й ла́герь; **~ sentence** тюре́мный срок.

prisoner ['prɪznə(r)] *n.* **1.** (*detained by civil authorities*) заключённый; **~ at the bar** подсуди́мый; (*fig.*) пле́нник. **2.** (*~ of war*) военнопле́нный; **they were all taken ~** их всех взя́ли в плен.

pristine ['prɪsti:n, 'prɪstaɪn] *adj.* (*former*) пре́жний, было́й; (*fresh, pure*) чи́стый, нетро́нутый.

privacy ['prɪvəsɪ, 'praɪ-] *n.* (*seclusion*) уедине́ние; **this is an invasion of my ~** э́то — вмеша́тельство в мою́ ли́чную/ча́стную жизнь; (*avoidance of publicity*) секре́тность.

private ['praɪvət, -vɪt] *n.* **1.** (*soldier*) рядово́й. **2.**: **in ~** в у́зком кругу́; в ча́стной жи́зни; **can we discuss this in ~?** мо́жно нам поговори́ть об э́том с глазу на глаз?

adj. **1.** (*personal*) ча́стный, ли́чный; **~ enterprise** ча́стное предпринима́тельство; **in ~ life** в ли́чной жи́зни; **~ property** ча́стная со́бственность; **for ~ reasons** по ли́чным причи́нам. **2.** (*not open to the general public*) закры́тый. **3.** (*secret*) та́йный, секре́тный; **~ parts** полові́е о́рганы. **4.** (*without official status*) ча́стный; неофициа́льный; **in one's ~ capacity** как ча́стное лицо́; **~ eye** (*coll.*) ча́стный сы́щик, детекти́в; **a doctor in ~ practice** ча́стный врач.

privation [praɪ'veɪʃ(ə)n] *n.* (*loss*) утра́та; лише́ние; (*hardship*) лише́ние; нужда́.

privatization [ˌpraɪvəˌtaɪ'zeɪʃ(ə)n] *n.* приватиза́ция.

privatize ['praɪvəˌtaɪz] *v.t.* приватизи́ровать.

privet ['prɪvɪt] *n.* бирючи́на.

privilege ['prɪvɪlɪdʒ] *n.* привиле́гия.

v.t. да|ва́ть, -ть привиле́гию +*d.*; **I was ~d to be there** я име́л сча́стье/честь там быть.

privileged ['prɪvɪlɪdʒd] *adj.* привилегиро́ванный.

privy ['prɪvɪ] *n.* (*latrine*) убо́рная.

adj. **1.** (*secret*) ча́стный, прива́тный, скры́тый. **2.**: **~ to** посвящённый в+*a.*; **he was ~ to her intentions** он был посвящён в её пла́ны.

prize[1] [praɪz] *n.* **1.** (*reward for merit etc.*) приз; (*esp. monetary*) пре́мия; награ́да. **2.** (*attr., awarded as prize*) призово́й; (*~-winning*) премиро́ванный; (*coll., egregious*) отъя́вленный; **he is a ~ idiot** он патенто́ванный дура́к.

v.t. высоко́ цени́ть (*impf.*).

cpds. **~-fight** *n.* матч боксёров-профессиона́лов; **~fighter** *n.* боксёр-профессиона́л; **~-ring** *n.* ринг; **~-winner** *n.* призёр (*fem. coll.* -ша).

prize[2] [praɪz] = **prise**

pro[1] [prəʊ] *n.* (*point in favour*): **~s and cons** до́воды «за» и «про́тив».

pro[2] [prəʊ] *n.* (*coll., professional actor, sportsman etc.*) профессиона́л (*fem.* -ка).

PRO[3] (*abbr. of* **public relations officer**) *see* **public** *adj.* **1.**

proactive [prəʊ'æktɪv] *adj.* де́йственный.

probability [ˌprɒbə'bɪlɪtɪ] *n.* вероя́тность; **in all ~** по всей вероя́тности.

probable ['prɒbəb(ə)l] *adj.* вероя́тный.

probate ['prəʊbeɪt, -bət] *n.* (*proving of will*) утвержде́ние завеща́ния.

probation [prə'beɪʃ(ə)n] *n.* **1.** (*testing of candidate etc.*) испыта́ние; (*period of test*) испыта́тельный срок.

2. (*leg.*) усло́вное освобожде́ние; **he was put on ~** он получи́л усло́вный пригово́р; **~ officer** должностно́е лицо́, осуществля́ющее надзо́р за усло́вно осуждённым.

probationer [prəˈbeɪʃənə(r)] *n.* (*trainee*) стажёр; практика́нт; (*offender on probation*) усло́вно осуждённый.

probe [prəʊb] *n.* (*instrument*) зонд; (*fig., investigation*) рассле́дование; (*space exploration*): **moon ~** испыта́тельный полёт на Луну́.

v.t. & i. зонди́ровать (*impf.*); (*fig., also*) иссле́довать (*impf., pf.*).

probity [ˈprəʊbɪtɪ, ˈprɒ-] *n.* че́стность.

problem [ˈprɒbləm] *n.* пробле́ма, вопро́с; **~ child** тру́дный ребёнок; (*math. etc.*) зада́ча.

problematic(al) [ˌprɒbləˈmætɪk(əl)] *adj.* проблемати́чный.

proboscis [prəʊˈbɒsɪs] *n.* (*of elephant etc.*) хо́бот; (*of insect*) хобото́к.

procedural [prəˈsiːdjərəl, -dʒərəl] *adj.* процеду́рный.

procedure [prəˈsiːdjə(r), -dʒə(r)] *n.* процеду́ра; **rules of ~** пра́вила процеду́ры, регла́мент.

proceed [prəˈsiːd, prəʊ-] *v.i.* **1.** (*go on*) прод|олжа́ть, -о́лжить. **2.** (*start*): **she ~ed to lay the table** она́ приняла́сь накрыва́ть на стол; **shall we ~ to business?** перейдём к де́лу? **3.** (*make one's way*) отпр|авля́ться, -а́виться. **4.** (*originate*) исходи́ть (*impf.*). **5.** (*take legal action*): **will you ~ against him?** вы собира́етесь возбуди́ть де́ло про́тив него́?

proceeding [prəˈsiːdɪŋ] *n.* **1.** (*pl., conduct*) поведе́ние; (*pl., activity*) де́ятельность. **2.** (*pl., records of society etc.*) труды́ (*m. pl.*), запи́ски (*f. pl.*). **3.** (*pl., legal action*) суде́бное де́ло; **he took ~s against his employer** он возбуди́л (суде́бное) де́ло про́тив своего́ работода́теля.

proceeds [ˈprəʊsiːdz] *n.* вы́ручка, дохо́д.

process[1] [ˈprəʊses] *n.* **1.** проце́сс. **2.** (*course*) тече́ние, ход; **the house is in ~ of construction** дом стро́ится. **3.** (*method of manufacture etc.*) проце́сс; спо́соб.

v.t. **1.** (*treat in special way*) обраб|а́тывать, -о́тать; **~ed cheese** пла́вленый сыр. **2.** (*subject to routine handling*) оф|ормля́ть, -о́рмить.

procession [prəˈseʃ(ə)n] *n.* проце́ссия, ше́ствие.

processor [ˈprəʊsesə(r)] *n.* (*comput.*) проце́ссор.

proclaim [prəˈkleɪm] *v.t.* провозла|ша́ть, -си́ть.

proclamation [ˌprɒkləˈmeɪʃ(ə)n] *n.* провозглаше́ние.

proclivity [prəˈklɪvɪtɪ] *n.* скло́нность, накло́нность.

proconsul [prəʊˈkɒns(ə)l] *n.* замести́тель (*m.*) ко́нсула.

procrastinate [prəʊˈkræstɪˌneɪt] *v.i.* ме́длить (*impf.*); тяну́ть (*impf.*) вре́мя.

procrastination [prəʊˌkræstɪˈneɪʃ(ə)n] *n.* промедле́ние.

procreate [ˈprəʊkrɪˌeɪt] *v.t. & i.* произв|оди́ть, -ести́ (пото́мство).

procreation [ˌprəʊkrɪˈeɪʃ(ə)n] *n.* (*of people*) деторожде́ние; (*of animals*) размноже́ние.

proctor [ˈprɒktə(r)] *n.* **1.** (*university official*) про́ктор, надзира́тель (*m.*). **2.** (*leg.*) адвока́т.

procurator [ˈprɒkjʊˌreɪtə(r)] *n.* **1.** (*magistrate*) пове́ренный; **public ~** прокуро́р. **2.** (*proxy*) дове́ренное лицо́.

procure [prəˈkjʊə(r)] *v.t.* **1.** (*obtain*) дост|ава́ть, -а́ть. **2.** (*bring about*): **he ~d her dismissal** он доби́лся того́, что её уво́лили.

procurement [prəˈkjʊəmənt] *n.* приобрете́ние, получе́ние; (*of equipment etc.*) поста́вка.

procurer [prəˈkjʊərə(r)] *n.* (*pimp*) сво́дник.

prod [prɒd] *n.* тычо́к.

v.t. ты́кать (*impf.*); (*fig.*) подстрека́ть (*impf.*).

prodigal [ˈprɒdɪg(ə)l] *adj.* (*wasteful*) расточи́тельный; **the P~ Son** блу́дный сын.

prodigality [ˌprɒdɪˈgælɪtɪ] *n.* расточи́тельность, мотовство́; ще́дрость.

prodigious [prəˈdɪdʒəs] *adj.* (*amazing*) потряса́ющий; (*enormous*) огро́мный.

prodigy [ˈprɒdɪdʒɪ] *n.* чу́до; **infant ~** вундерки́нд.

produce[1] [ˈprɒdjuːs] *n.* проду́кты (*m. pl.*).

produce[2] [prəˈdjuːs] *v.t.* **1.** (*make, manufacture*) произв|оди́ть, -ести́; выпуска́ть, вы́пустить. **2.** (*bring about*) прин|оси́ть, -ести́; **this method ~s good results** э́тот ме́тод даёт хоро́шие результа́ты. **3.** (*bring forward*) предст|авля́ть, -а́вить. **4.** (*bring out, into view*) предъяв|ля́ть, -и́ть; дост|ава́ть, -а́ть. **5.** (*also v.i., yield, bear*) прин|оси́ть, -ести́; произв|оди́ть, -ести́; **France ~s the best wine** Фра́нция произво́дит лу́чшее вино́; **this soil ~s good crops** э́то по́чва даёт хоро́ший урожа́й; **his wife ~d an heir** его́ жена́ родила́ насле́дника. **6.** (*compose, write*) созд|ава́ть, -а́ть. **7.** (*bring before public*) ста́вить, по-; (*cin.*) выпуска́ть, вы́пустить.

producer [prəˈdjuːsə(r)] *n.* **1.** (*of goods*) производи́тель (*m.*). **2.** (*stage, TV*) режиссёр, постано́вщик. **3.** (*film*) продю́сер.

product [ˈprɒdʌkt] *n.* (*article produced*) проду́кт; (*result*) результат, плод; (*math.*) произведе́ние.

production [prəˈdʌkʃ(ə)n] *n.* **1.** (*manufacture*) проду́кция; **~ line** пото́чная ли́ния. **2.** (*yield*) производи́тельность. **3.** (*composing; composition*) произведе́ние. **4.** (*stage, film*) постано́вка.

productive [prəˈdʌktɪv] *adj.* (*tending to produce*) производи́тельный; (*yielding well, fertile*) плодоро́дный; **a ~ author** плодови́тый а́втор; (*efficient*) продукти́вный.

productivity [ˌprɒdʌkˈtɪvɪtɪ] *n.* производи́тельность; (*productiveness, efficiency*) продукти́вность.

profanation [ˌprɒfəˈneɪʃ(ə)n] *n.* профана́ция, оскверне́ние.

profane [prəˈfeɪn] *adj.* (*secular*) мирско́й; (*heathen*) язы́ческий; (*irreverent*) богоху́льный.

v.t. оскверн|я́ть, -и́ть.

profanity [prəˈfænɪtɪ] *n.* (*irreverence*) богоху́льство; (*swearing*) скверносло́вие.

profess [prəˈfes] *v.t.* **1.** (*claim to have or feel*) откры́то заяв|ля́ть, -и́ть. **2.** (*claim, admit, pretend*) претендова́ть (*impf.*); **he ~es to be an expert at chess** он выдаёт себя́ за первокла́ссного шахмати́ста. **3.** (*affirm belief in*) испове́довать (*impf.*).

professed [prəˈfest] *adj.* **1.** (*self-declared*) откры́тый, я́вный. **2.** (*alleged, ostensible*) мни́мый.

profession [prəˈfeʃ(ə)n] *n.* **1.** (*occupation*) профе́ссия; **he is a teacher by ~** он по профе́ссию учи́тель. **2.** (*declaration; admission*) заявле́ние; завере́ние; **~s of love** завере́ния любви́.

professional [prəˈfeʃən(ə)l] *n.* профессиона́л.

adj. профессиона́льный.

professionalism [prəˈfeʃənəˌlɪz(ə)m] *n.* профессионали́зм.

professor [prəˈfesə(r)] *n.* профе́ссор.

professorial [ˌprɒfɪˈsɔːrɪəl] *adj.* профе́ссорский.

professorship [prəˈfesəʃɪp] *n.* профе́ссорство.

proffer [ˈprɒfə(r)] *v.t.* предл|ага́ть, -ожи́ть; **he ~ed his hand** он протяну́л ру́ку.

proficiency [prəˈfɪʃ(ə)nsɪ] *n.* мастерство́, уме́ние.

proficient [prəˈfɪʃ(ə)nt] *adj.* уме́лый; **she is ~ at typing** она́ хорошо́ печа́тает.

profile [ˈprəʊfaɪl] *n.* (*side view, esp. of face*) про́филь (*m.*); **seen in ~** в про́филь; (*fig.*) пози́ция; **to adopt a low/high ~** де́йствовать сде́ржанно/акти́вно; (*biographical sketch*) биографи́ческий о́черк.

profit [ˈprɒfɪt] *n.* **1.** (*advantage*) по́льза, вы́года; **there is no ~ in further discussion** продолжа́ть диску́ссию бесполе́зно; **with ~** вы́годно. **2.** (*pecuniary gain*) при́быль; **he sold the land at a ~** он про́дал зе́млю с вы́годой; **the ~ motive** пого́ня за при́былью; **~ and loss account** счёт при́былей и убы́тков.

v.t. прин|оси́ть, -ести́ по́льзу +*d.*; **what will it ~ him?** что э́то ему́ даст?

v.i. по́льзоваться, вос- (+*i.*); извле|ка́ть, -е́чь по́льзу (из+*g.*); **I ~ed by your advice** ваш сове́т пошёл мне на по́льзу.

cpd. **~-sharing** *n.* уча́стие в при́были.

profitability [ˌprɒfɪtəˈbɪlɪtɪ] *n.* дохо́дность, при́быльность, рента́бельность.

profitable [ˈprɒfɪtəb(ə)l] *adj.* (*advantageous*) поле́зный, вы́годный; (*lucrative*) дохо́дный, при́быльный, рента́бельный.

profiteer [ˌprɒfɪˈtɪə(r)] *n.* спекуля́нт.

v.i. спекули́ровать (*impf.*).

profiteering [ˌprɒfɪˈtɪərɪŋ] *n.* спекуля́ция.

profligacy [ˈprɒflɪgəsɪ] *n.* распу́тство; расточи́тельность.

profligate [ˈprɒflɪgət] *n.* развра́тник; расточи́тель (*m.*).

adj. (*dissolute*) распу́тный; (*extravagant*) расточи́тельный.

pro forma [prəʊ ˈfɔːmə] *adj.*: **~ invoice** приме́рная/ предвари́тельная факту́ра.

adv. phr. для профо́рмы.

profound [prəˈfaʊnd] *adj.* глубо́кий; **~ ignorance** по́лное неве́жество; **a ~ subject** сло́жный предме́т.

profundity [prəˈfʌndɪtɪ] *n.* глубина́; (*fig.*) серьёзность.

profuse [prəˈfjuːs] *adj.* (*plentiful*) оби́льный; (*lavish*) ще́дрый, расточи́тельный; **he apologized ~ly** он рассы́пался в извине́ниях.

profusion [prəˈfjuːʒ(ə)n] *n.* изоби́лие.

progenitor [prəʊˈdʒenɪtə(r)] *n.* прароди́тель (*m.*).

progeny [ˈprɒdʒɪnɪ] *n.* пото́мство.

prognosis [prɒgˈnəʊsɪs] *n.* прогно́з.

prognosticate [prɒgˈnɒstɪˌkeɪt] *v.t.* предска́з|ывать, -а́ть; предвеща́ть (*impf.*).

prognostication [prɒgˌnɒstɪˈkeɪʃ(ə)n] *n.* предсказа́ние; (*omen*) предзнаменова́ние.

program(me) [ˈprəʊgræm] *n.* **1.** програ́мма; (*radio, TV*) переда́ча; (*plan*) план; **he has a full ~ tomorrow** за́втра он по́лностью за́нят. **2.** (*computer instructions*) программи́рование.

v.t. программи́ровать, за-.

progress[1] [ˈprəʊgres] *n.* **1.** (*forward movement*) движе́ние вперёд. **2.** (*advance, development*) прогре́сс; **~ report** докла́д о хо́де рабо́ты; **the invalid is making good ~** больно́й поправля́ется; **a meeting is in ~** идёт заседа́ние.

progress[2] [prəˈgres] *v.i.* прогресси́ровать (*impf.*); **how are things ~ing?** как иду́т дела́?; **he has hardly ~ed at all with his studies** он не сде́лал почти́ никаки́х успе́хов в учёбе.

progression [prəˈgreʃ(ə)n] *n.* (*progress*) продвиже́ние; (*math.*) прогре́ссия.

progressive [prəˈgresɪv] *adj.* **1.** (*favouring progress*) прогресси́вный. **2.** (*gradual*) поступа́тельный, постепе́нный. **3.** (*of disease etc.*) прогресси́рующий.

prohibit [prəˈhɪbɪt] *v.t.* запре|ща́ть, -ти́ть; **'smoking ~ed'** «кури́ть воспреща́ется».

prohibition [ˌprəʊhɪˈbɪʃ(ə)n, ˌprəʊɪˈb-] *n.* запреще́ние; (*of sale of intoxicants*) сухо́й зако́н.

prohibitive [prəʊˈhɪbɪtɪv] *adj.* запрети́тельный; **~ prices** недосту́пные це́ны.

project[1] [ˈprɒdʒekt] *n.* прое́кт, план.

project[2] [prəˈdʒekt] *v.t.* **1.** (*devise*) проекти́ровать, за-. **2.** (*throw, impel*) выбра́сывать, вы́бросить. **3.** (*of light*) испус|ка́ть, -ти́ть. **4.** (*with projector; also math.*) проекти́ровать, с-.

v.i. (*protrude*) выдава́ться (*impf.*); выступа́ть (*impf.*).

projectile [prəˈdʒektaɪl] *n.* снаря́д.

projection [prəˈdʒekʃ(ə)n] *n.* **1.** (*planning*) проекти́рование. **2.** (*throwing, propulsion*) отбра́сывание. **3.** (*cin.*) прое́кция (изображе́ния); **~ room** (кино)-проекцио́нная каби́на. **4.** (*psych., geom.*) прое́кция. **5.** (*protrusion*) вы́ступ.

projectionist [prəˈdʒekʃənɪst] *n.* киномеха́ник.

projector [prəˈdʒektə(r)] *n.* кинопрое́ктор.

prolapse [ˈprəʊlæps] *n.* прола́пс, выпаде́ние.

proletarian [ˌprəʊlɪˈteərɪən] *n.* пролета́рий.

adj. пролета́рский.

proletariat [ˌprəʊlɪˈteərɪət] *n.* пролетариа́т.

proliferate [prəˈlɪfəˌreɪt] *v.i.* размн|ожа́ться, -о́житься; (*fig.*) распростран|я́ться, -и́ться.

proliferation [prəˌlɪfəˈreɪʃ(ə)n] *n.* распростране́ние.

prolific [prəˈlɪfɪk] *adj.* (*lit.*) плодоро́дный; (*fig.*) плодови́тый.

prolix [ˈprəʊlɪks, prəˈlɪks] *adj.* многосло́вный.

prolixity [ˌprəʊˈlɪksɪtɪ, prəˈlɪksɪtɪ] *n.* многосло́вие.

prologue [ˈprəʊlɒg] *n.* проло́г.

prolong [prəˈlɒŋ] *v.t.* продл|ева́ть, -и́ть; **a ~ed argument** затяну́вшийся спор.

prolongation [ˌprəʊlɒŋˈgeɪʃ(ə)n] *n.* продле́ние.

prom [prɒm] (*coll.*) = **promenade** *n.* **2.**

promenade [ˌprɒməˈnɑːd] *n.* **1.** (*walk for pleasure etc.*) прогу́лка. **2.** (*place of pedestrian resort*) ме́сто для гуля́ния.

v.i. гуля́ть, по-; прогу́л|иваться, -я́ться.

prominence [ˈprɒmɪnəns] *n.* (*importance*) ви́дное положе́ние.

prominent [ˈprɒmɪnənt] *adj.* **1.** (*projecting*) выступа́ющий. **2.** (*conspicuous*) заме́тный. **3.** (*important, distinguished*) выдаю́щийся.

promiscuity [ˌprɒmɪˈskjuːɪtɪ] *n.* неразбо́рчивость; распу́щенность.

promiscuous [prəˈmɪskjʊəs] *adj.* неразбо́рчивый; (*sexually*) распу́щенный.

promise [ˈprɒmɪs] *n.* **1.** (*assurance*) обеща́ние; **he kept his ~** он сдержа́л своё обеща́ние. **2.** (*ground for expectation*) наде́жда; **he shows ~** он подаёт наде́жды; **a writer of ~** многообеща́ющий писа́тель.

v.t. & i. **1.** (*undertake, assure*) обеща́ть, по-; **it will not be easy, I ~ you** уверя́ю вас, что э́то бу́дет нелегко́; **the P~d Land** (*bibl.*) земля́ обетова́нная. **2.** (*give grounds for expecting*): **it ~s to be a warm day** день обеща́ет быть тёплым; **the boy ~s well** ма́льчик подаёт больши́е наде́жды.

promising [ˈprɒmɪsɪŋ] *adj.* перспекти́вный; многообеща́ющий, подаю́щий наде́жды.

promissory [ˈprɒmɪsərɪ] *adj.*: **~ note** долгово́е обяза́тельство.

promontory [ˈprɒməntərɪ] *n.* мыс.

promote [prəˈməʊt] *v.t.* **1.** (*raise to higher rank*) продв|ига́ть, -и́нуть; пов|ыша́ть, -ы́сить в чи́не; **he was ~d (to the rank of) sergeant** ему́ присво́или зва́ние сержа́нта. **2.** (*encourage, support*) поощр|я́ть, -и́ть; подде́рж|ивать, -а́ть; соде́йствовать, по- +*d.* **3.** (*publicize to boost sales*) реклами́ровать (*impf.*); соде́йствовать прода́же +*g.*

promoter [prəˈməʊtə(r)] *n.* (*patron*) покрови́тель (*m.*).

promotion [prəˈməʊʃ(ə)n] *n.* (*in rank*) продвиже́ние, повыше́ние; (*encouragement, support*) поощре́ние, подде́ржка, соде́йствие; (*publicizing*) рекла́ма.

prompt[1] [prɒmpt] *n.* (*theatr.*) подска́зка.

v.t. & i. **1.** (*assist memory of*) подска́з|ывать, -а́ть +*d.*; (*theatr.*) суфли́ровать +*d.* **2.** (*impel, induce*) побу|жда́ть, -ди́ть; **he was ~ed by mercy** он де́йствовал из жа́лости.

prompt[2] [prɒmpt] *adj.* бы́стрый; **he arrived ~ly at 9** он прие́хал то́чно в де́вять; **a ~ answer** неме́дленный отве́т; **~ payment** своевре́менная упла́та.

prompter [ˈprɒmptə(r)] *n.* суфлёр.

promptness [ˈprɒmptnɪs] *n.* быстрота́, гото́вность.

promulgate [ˈprɒməlˌgeɪt] *v.t.* обнаро́довать (*impf.*); провозгла|ша́ть, -си́ть.

promulgation [ˌprɒməlˈgeɪʃ(ə)n] *n.* обнаро́дование, провозглаше́ние.

prone [prəʊn] *adj.* **1.** (*face downwards*) лежа́щий ничко́м. **2.:** ~ **to** (*disposed, liable to*) скло́нный к+*d.*; **he is ~ to make mistakes** ему́ сво́йственно ошиба́ться; **I am ~ to accidents** со мной ве́чно что́-то случа́ется.

prong [prɒŋ] *n.* зубе́ц.

pronominal [prəʊ'nɒmɪn(ə)l] *adj.* местоиме́нный.

pronoun ['prəʊnaʊn] *n.* местоиме́ние.

pronounc|e [prə'naʊns] *v.t.* **1.** (*declare*) объявл|я́ть, -и́ть; **~e judgement** (*leg.*) выноси́ть, вы́нести суде́бное реше́ние. **2.** (*utter*) произн|оси́ть, -ести́; выгова́ривать (*impf.*); **how is this word ~ed?** как произно́сится э́то сло́во?

v.i. **1.** (*give one's opinion*) выска́зываться, вы́сказаться; **the jury ~ed for the defendant** прися́жные оправда́ли подсуди́мого. **2.: a ~ing dictionary** слова́рь произноше́ния, орфоэпи́ческий слова́рь.

pronounced [prə'naʊnst] *adj.* (*decided*) я́вный; **he walks with a ~ limp** он си́льно/заме́тно хрома́ет.

pronouncement [prə'naʊnsmənt] *n.* заявле́ние; выска́зывание.

pronunciation [prə,nʌnsɪ'eɪʃ(ə)n] *n.* произноше́ние.

proof [pru:f] *n.* **1.** доказа́тельство; **as ~ of his good intentions** в доказа́тельство его́ до́брых наме́рений. **2.** (*demonstration*): **is it capable of ~?** э́то доказу́емо? **3.** (*test, trial*) испыта́ние; прове́рка. **4.** (*of alcoholic liquor*) кре́пость. **5.** (*typ.*) корректу́ра.

adj. **1.** (*of tried or prescribed strength*) устано́вленной кре́пости. **2.** (*impenetrable, resistant*): ~ **against bullets** пуленепроница́емый; ~ **against weather** непромока́емый, погодоусто́йчивый.

v.t. (*waterproof*) де́лать, с- непроница́емым.

cpds. **~-read** *v.t. & i.* чита́ть, про- (*or* держа́ть) корректу́ру; **~-reader** *n.* корре́ктор; **~-reading** *n.* чте́ние корректу́ры; **~-sheet** *n.* корректу́ра.

prop[1] [prɒp] *n.* (*support*) сто́йка; подпо́рка.

v.t. **1.** подп|ира́ть, -ере́ть; **he sat ~ped up in bed** он сиде́л в крова́ти, опира́ясь на поду́шки; ~ **the ladder against the wall!** приста́вьте ле́стницу к стене́! **2.** (*fig.*) подде́рж|ивать, -а́ть.

prop[2] [prɒp] *n.* (*theatr.*) бутафо́рия, реквизи́т.

propaganda [,prɒpə'gændə] *n.* пропага́нда; (*attr.*) пропага́ндный, пропаганди́ческий.

propagandist [,prɒpə'gændɪst] *n.* пропаганди́ст.

propagandize [,prɒpə'gændaɪz] *v.t.* пропаганди́ровать (*impf.*).

propagate ['prɒpə,geɪt] *v.t.* (*multiply by reproduction*) размн|ожа́ть, -о́жить; разв|оди́ть, -ести́; (*disseminate*) распростран|я́ть, -и́ть.

v.i. размн|ожа́ться, -о́житься.

propagation [,prɒpə'geɪʃ(ə)n] *n.* размноже́ние; (*fig.*) распростране́ние.

propane ['prəʊpeɪn] *n.* пропа́н.

propel [prə'pel] *v.t.* прив|оди́ть, -ести́ в движе́ние; **~ling pencil** автокаранда́ш.

propellant [prə'pelənt] *n.* дви́жущая си́ла; (*fuel*) раке́тное то́пливо.

propeller [prə'pelə(r)] *n.* (*of ship*) винт (корабля́); (*of aircraft*) пропе́ллер, (возду́шный) винт.

propensity [prə'pensɪtɪ] *n.* предрасполо́женность, скло́нность.

proper ['prɒpə(r)] *adj.* **1.** (*belonging especially*) сво́йственный; прису́щий. **2.** (*suitable, appropriate*) подходя́щий, ну́жный; **at the ~ time** в своё вре́мя. **3.** (*decent, respectable*) (благо)присто́йный, прили́чный. **4.** (*correct, accurate*) пра́вильный; **in the ~ sense of the word** в прямо́м смы́сле сло́ва. **5.** (*gram.*): ~ **noun** и́мя со́бственное. **6.** (*strictly so called*): **within the sphere of architecture ~** в о́бласти со́бственно архитекту́ры. **7.** (*coll. thorough*) соверше́нный, по́лный; **his room was in a ~ mess** в его́ ко́мнате цари́л по́лный беспоря́док.

properly ['prɒpəlɪ] *adv.* (*correctly*) подоба́юще; как сле́дует; ~ **speaking** со́бственно говоря́; **you must be ~ dressed** вы должны́ оде́ться подоба́ющим о́бразом.

propertied ['prɒpətɪd] *adj.* име́ющий со́бственность; иму́щий; **the ~ classes** землевладе́льцы.

property ['prɒpətɪ] *n.* **1.** (*possession(s)*) со́бственность; иму́щество; **a man of ~** со́бственник; **the news is common ~** но́вость изве́стно всем. **2.** (*house; estate*) дом; име́ние. **3.** (*attribute, quality*) сво́йство. **4.** (*theatr.*) бутафо́рия, реквизи́т.

cpds. **~man, ~-master** *nn.* реквизи́тор.

prophecy ['prɒfɪsɪ] *n.* предсказа́ние, проро́чество.

prophesy ['prɒfɪ,saɪ] *v.t. & i.* предска́з|ывать, -а́ть; проро́чить, на-.

prophet ['prɒfɪt] *n.* проро́к, предсказа́тель (*m.*).

prophetic [prə'fetɪk] *adj.* проро́ческий.

prophylactic [,prɒfɪ'læktɪk] *n.* профилакти́ческое сре́дство.

adj. профилакти́ческий.

prophylaxis [,prɒfɪ'læksɪs] *n.* профила́ктика.

propinquity [prə'pɪŋkwɪtɪ] *n.* (*closeness*) бли́зость, сосе́дство; (*kinship*) родство́.

propitiate [prə'pɪʃɪ,eɪt] *v.t.* (*appease*) умиротвор|я́ть, -и́ть; ут|еша́ть, -е́шить.

propitious [prə'pɪʃəs] *adj.* (*benevolent*) благожела́тельный; (*favourable*) благоприя́тный.

proponent [prə'pəʊnənt] *n.* побо́рник (*чего*).

proportion [prə'pɔ:ʃ(ə)n] *n.* **1.** (*comparative part*) пропо́рция, часть. **2.** (*ratio*) пропо́рция, соотноше́ние; **in ~** пропорциона́льно, соразме́рно. **3.** (*math., equality of ratios*) пропо́рция. **4.** (*due relation*) соразме́рность; **keep a sense of ~** сохрани́ть (*impf.*) чу́вство ме́ры; **his ambitions are out of all ~** его́ честолю́бие выхо́дит за вся́кие ра́мки. **5.** (*pl., dimensions*) разме́р, разме́ры (*m. pl.*).

v.t. соразм|еря́ть, -е́рить.

proportional [prə'pɔ:ʃən(ə)l] *adj.* пропорциона́льный.

proportionate [prə'pɔ:ʃənət] *adj.* соразме́рный; **payment will be ~ to effort** опла́та бу́дет соотве́тствовать затра́ченным уси́лиям.

proposal [prə'pəʊz(ə)l] *n.* предложе́ние.

propose [prə'pəʊz] *v.t.* **1.** (*offer suggestion or plan of*) предл|ага́ть, -ожи́ть; **he ~d (marriage) to her** он сде́лал ей предложе́ние. **2.** (*nominate, put forward*) выдвига́ть, вы́двинуть; **his name was ~d for secretary** его́ выдвига́ли на пост секретаря́. **3.** (*offer as toast*): **his health was ~d** провозгласи́ли тост за его́ здоро́вье. **4.** (*intend*) предпол|ага́ть, -ожи́ть; **I ~ to leave tomorrow** я собира́юсь е́хать за́втра.

v.i. (*make plans*) намерева́ться (*impf.*).

proposition [,prɒpə'zɪʃ(ə)n] *n.* **1.** (*statement*) заявле́ние. **2.** (*proposed scheme*) предложе́ние. **3.** (*coll., undertaking, problem etc.*) де́ло; **he is a tough ~** с ним тру́дно име́ть де́ло.

propound [prə'paʊnd] *v.t.* предл|ага́ть, -ожи́ть на обсужде́ние.

proprietary [prə'praɪətərɪ] *adj.* со́бственнический; (*pert. to a firm*) фи́рменный; ~ **medicines** патенто́ванные лека́рства; ~ **rights** пра́во со́бственности.

proprietor [prə'praɪətə(r)] *n.* владе́лец, хозя́ин.

proprietress [prə'praɪətrɪs] *n.* владе́лица, хозя́йка.

propriet|y [prə'praɪɪtɪ] *n.* (*fitness*) уме́стность; (*correctness of behaviour or morals*) пра́вильность; (*pl., rules of behaviour*) **the ~ies must be observed** на́до соблюда́ть пра́вила прили́чия.

propulsion [prə'pʌlʃ(ə)n] *n.* движе́ние вперёд; **jet ~** реакти́вное движе́ние.

pro rata [prəʊ 'rɑ:tə, 'reɪtə] *adv.* пропорциона́льно.

prorogation [,prərəʊ'geɪʃ(ə)n] *n.* пророга́ция (парла́мента).

prorogue [prə'rəʊg] *v.t.* назн|ача́ть, -а́чить переры́в в рабо́те (*парламента и т.п.*).

prosaic [prə'zeɪɪk, prəʊ-] *adj.* прозаи́ческий.

proscenium [prəˈsiːnɪəm, prəʊ-] *n.* просце́ниум.
proscribe [prəˈskraɪb] *v.t.* объяв|ля́ть, -и́ть вне зако́на.
proscription [prəˈskrɪpʃ(ə)n] *n.* объявле́ние вне зако́на.
prose [prəʊz] *n.* **1.** про́за; (*attr.*) прозаи́ческий; ~ **writers** проза́ики; ~ **poem** стихотворе́ние в про́зе. **2.** (*piece set for translation*) отры́вок для перево́да.
prosecute [ˈprɒsɪˌkjuːt] *v.t.* **1.** (*carry on*) занима́ться (*impf.*) +*i.*; **he ~d the inquiry with vigour** он энерги́чно повёл рассле́дование. **2.** (*leg.*) возбу|жда́ть, -ди́ть де́ло про́тив+*g.*; **trespassers will be ~d** наруши́тели бу́дут пресле́доваться по зако́ну.
prosecution [ˌprɒsɪˈkjuːʃ(ə)n] *n.* **1.** (*pursuit*) веде́ние. **2.** (*carrying on legal proceedings*) обвине́ние; предъявле́ние и́ска. **3.** (*prosecuting party*) обвине́ние; **counsel for the ~** обвини́тель (*m.*).
prosecutor [ˈprɒsɪˌkjuːtə(r)] *n.* обвини́тель (*m.*); **Public P~** прокуро́р.
proselytize [ˈprɒsɪlɪˌtaɪz] *v.t.* (*convert*) обра|ща́ть, -ти́ть в другу́ю ве́ру.
prosodic [prəˈsɒdɪk] *adj.* просоди́ческий.
prosody [ˈprɒsədɪ] *n.* просо́дия.
prospect[1] [ˈprɒspekt] *n.* **1.** (*extensive view*) вид, панора́ма; (*fig.*, *mental scene*) перспекти́ва. **2.** (*expectation, hope*) перспекти́ва; **there is no ~ of success** нет наде́жды на успе́х. **3.** (*coll.*, *possible customer*) потенциа́льный покупа́тель/зака́зчик.
prospect[2] [prəˈspekt] *v.t.* иссле́довать (*impf.*); разве́д|ывать, -ать.
v.i.: **they were ~ing for gold** они́ иска́ли зо́лото.
prospective [prəˈspektɪv] *adj.* **1.** (*applicable to future*) бу́дущий; предпологае́мый. **2.** (*expected*) ожида́емый. **3.** (*future*) бу́дущий.
prospector [prəˈspektə(r)] *n.* разве́дчик, стара́тель (*m.*).
prospectus [prəˈspektəs] *n.* проспе́кт.
prosper [ˈprɒspə(r)] *v.i.* процвета́ть (*impf.*).
prosperity [prɒˈsperɪtɪ] *n.* процвета́ние.
prosperous [ˈprɒspərəs] *adj.* процвета́ющий, зажи́точный.
prostate [ˈprɒsteɪt] *n.* проста́та; ~ **disease** боле́знь предста́тельной железы́.
prosthesis [ˈprɒsθɪsɪs, -ˈθiːsɪs] *n.* проте́з.
prosthetic [prɒsˈθetɪk] *adj.* проте́зный.
prostitute [ˈprɒstɪˌtjuːt] *n.* проститу́тка.
v.t.: ~ **o.s.** зан|има́ться, -я́ться проститу́цией; (*fig.*) торгова́ть (*impf.*) собо́й.
prostitution [ˌprɒstɪˈtjuːʃ(ə)n] *n.* (*lit.*, *fig.*) проститу́ция.
prostrate[1] [ˈprɒstreɪt] *adj.* **1.** (*lying face down*) распростёртый; лежа́щий ничко́м. **2.** (*overcome, overthrown*) пове́рженный. **3.** (*exhausted*) измождённый.
prostrate[2] [prɒˈstreɪt, prə-] *v.t.* **1.** (*lay flat on ground*) опроки́|дывать, -нуть; **he ~d himself before the altar** он пал ниц пе́ред алтарём. **2.** (*overcome*) изнур|я́ть, -и́ть.
prostration [prɒˈstreɪʃ(ə)n, prə-] *n.* (*exhaustion*) изможе́ние; простра́ция.
protagonist [prəʊˈtægənɪst] *n.* протагони́ст.
protect [prəˈtekt] *v.t.* **1.** (*keep safe, guard*) охран|я́ть, -и́ть; предохран|я́ть, -и́ть; **the house is well ~ed against fire** дом хорошо́ защищён от огня́. **2.** (*fit with safety device*) обезопа́сить (*pf.*). **3.** (*shelter*) защи|ща́ть, -ти́ть; огра|жда́ть, -ди́ть.
protection [prəˈtekʃ(ə)n] *n.* **1.** (*defence*) защи́та; ~ **money** о́ткуп от вымога́телей. **2.** (*shelter*) огражде́ние. **3.** (*care*) попече́ние; **under my ~** на моём попече́нии. **4.** (*patronage*) покрови́тельство. **5.** (*assurance, security*) обеспе́чение.
protectionism [prəˈtekʃ(ə)ˌnɪz(ə)m] *n.* протекциони́зм.
protective [prəˈtektɪv] *adj.* защи́тный; ~ **custody** содержа́ние под стра́жей.
protector [prəˈtektə(r)] *n.* защи́тник.
protectorate [prəˈtektərət] *n.* протектора́т.
protégé [ˈprɒtɪˌʒeɪ, ˈprəʊ-] *n.* протеже́ (*c.g.*, *indecl.*).
protein [ˈprəʊtiːn] *n.* протеи́н; бело́к.
protest[1] [ˈprəʊtest] *n.* проте́ст; возраже́ние; **without ~** не протесту́я; ~ **march** марш проте́ста; ~ **vote** го́лос, по́данный в знак проте́ста.
protest[2] [prəˈtest] *v.t.* **1.** (*affirm*) утвержда́ть (*impf.*); **he continued to ~ his innocence** он продолжа́л отста́ивать свою́ невино́вность. **2.** (*US*, *object to*) возража́ть/протестова́ть (*impf.*) про́тив+*g.*
v.i.: ~ **against** протестова́ть (*impf.*) про́тив+*g.*
Protestant [ˈprɒtɪst(ə)nt] *n.* протеста́нт.
adj. протеста́нтский.
Protestantism [ˈprɒtɪstənˌtɪz(ə)m] *n.* протеста́нтство.
protestation [ˌprɒtɪˈsteɪʃ(ə)n] *n.* (*affirmation*) (торже́ственное) заявле́ние; (*protest*) проте́ст.
protester [prəʊˈtestə(r)] *n.* протесту́ющий.
protocol [ˌprəʊtəˈkɒl] *n.* протоко́л.
proton [ˈprəʊtɒn] *n.* прото́н.
protoplasm [ˈprəʊtəˌplæz(ə)m] *n.* протопла́зма.
prototype [ˈprəʊtəˌtaɪp] *n.* прототи́п; о́пытный образе́ц.
protozoa [ˌprəʊtəˈzəʊə] *n.* протозо́а (*pl. indecl.*), простéйшие (*nt. pl.*).
protract [prəˈtrækt] *v.t.* затя́|гивать, -ну́ть; **a ~ed war** затяжна́я война́.
protractor [prəˈtræktə(r)] *n.* транспорти́р, угломе́р.
protrud|e [prəˈtruːd] *v.t.* высо́вывать, вы́сунуть.
v.i. выдава́ться (*impf.*); **~ing teeth** торча́щие зу́бы.
protrusion [prəˈtruːʒ(ə)n] *n.* высо́вывание; вы́ступ.
protuberance [prəˈtjuːbərəns] *n.* вы́пуклость, о́пухоль, ши́шка.
protuberant [prəˈtjuːbərənt] *adj.* вы́пуклый.
proud [praʊd] *adj.* го́рдый; **he is a ~ man** он горде́ц; **he was ~ of his garden** он горди́лся свои́м са́дом; **he was the ~ father of twins** он был счастли́вым отцо́м двойни́; (*arrogant*) надме́нный.
adv.: **it was a sumptuous meal: they did us ~** они́ нас угости́ли на сла́ву.
prove [pruːv] *v.t.* **1.** (*demonstrate*) дока́з|ывать, -а́ть; **he ~d his worth** он показа́л себя́ досто́йным челове́ком; **he needs to ~ himself to others** ему́ надо утверди́ть себя́ в глаза́х други́х. **2.** (*put to the test*) испы́т|ывать, -а́ть; **the exception ~s the rule** исключе́ние подтвержда́ет пра́вило; **proving-ground** (*mil.*) испыта́тельный полиго́н.
v.i. (*turn out*) ока́з|ываться, -а́ться; **the alarm ~d (to be) a hoax** трево́га оказа́лась ло́жной; **the play ~d a success** пье́са име́ла успе́х; **the report ~d true** сообще́ние подтверди́лось.
proven [ˈpruːv(ə)n, ˈprəʊ-] *adj.* дока́занный.
provenance [ˈprɒvɪnəns] *n.* происхожде́ние.
provender [ˈprɒvɪndə(r)] *n.* фура́ж.
proverb [ˈprɒvɜːb] *n.* посло́вица; **(the Book of) P~s** Кни́га при́тчей Соломо́новых.
proverbial [prəˈvɜːbɪəl] *adj.* **1.** (*pert. to provs.*) провербиа́льный; ~ **wisdom** наро́дная му́дрость. **2.** (*notorious*) общеизве́стный.
provide [prəˈvaɪd] *v.t.* **1.** ~ **s.o. with sth.** обеспе́чи|вать, -ть кого́-н. чем-н.; снаб|жа́ть, -ди́ть кого́-н. чем-н.; **who will ~ the food?** кто позабо́тится о пи́ще?; **they are well ~d with money** у них доста́точно де́нег. **2.** (*prescribe*) предусм|а́тривать, -отре́ть.
v.i. (*prepare o.s.*) пригот|а́вливаться, -о́виться; ~ **against one's old age** обеспе́чить (*pf.*) себя́ к ста́рости; **she had three children to ~ for** на её содержа́нии бы́ло тро́е дете́й.
provid|ed [prəˈvaɪdɪd], **-ing** [prəˈvaɪdɪŋ] *conjs.* при усло́вии, что; е́сли.
providence [ˈprɒvɪd(ə)ns] *n.* **1.** (*foresight, thrift*) предусмотри́тельность. **2.** (*divine care*) провиде́ние.

provident ['prɒvɪd(ə)nt] *adj.* предусмотри́тельный; расчётливый.
provider [prə'vaɪdə(r)] *n.* снабже́нец; поставщи́к; **her husband is a good ~** её муж хорошо́ обеспе́чивает семью́.
providing [prə'vaɪdɪŋ] = **provided**
province ['prɒvɪns] *n.* **1.** (*division of country*) о́бласть, прови́нция. **2.: the ~s** прови́нция; перифе́рия. **3.** (*sphere, department*) компете́нция; о́бласть.
provincial [prə'vɪnʃ(ə)l] *n.* провинциа́л (*fem.* -ка).
adj. (*lit., fig.*) провинциа́льный.
provision [prə'vɪʒ(ə)n] *n.* **1.** (*supplying*) снабже́ние. **2.** (*pl., supplies, food*) прови́зия. **3.** (*preparation*) обеспе́чение; **their father had made ~ for them** оте́ц обеспе́чил их на бу́дущее. **4.** (*item of agreement, law etc.*) усло́вие; положе́ние.
provisional [prə'vɪʒən(ə)l] *adj.* вре́менный; (*approximate*) ориентиро́вочный; **he gave ~ consent** он дал предвари́тельное согла́сие; **~ government** вре́менное прави́тельство.
proviso [prə'vaɪzəʊ] *n.* усло́вие, огово́рка; **with the ~ that ...** с усло́вием (*or* с огово́ркой), что.
provocation [,prɒvə'keɪʃ(ə)n] *n.* **1.** (*challenge, incitement*) вы́зов; **at the slightest ~** по мале́йшему по́воду. **2.** (*ruse*) провока́ция.
provocative [prə'vɒkətɪv] *adj.* вызыва́ющий; провокацио́нный.
provoke [prə'vəʊk] *v.t.* (*cause, arouse; challenge*) вызыва́ть, вы́звать; провоци́ровать, с-. **2.** (*impel*) побу|жда́ть, -ди́ть. **3.** (*anger*) серди́ть, рас-; раздраж|а́ть, -и́ть.
provost ['prɒvəst] *n.* ре́ктор; (*Sc. dignitary*) мэр; **~-marshal** нача́льник вое́нной поли́ции.
prow [praʊ] *n.* нос (*судна*).
prowess ['praʊɪs] *n.* до́блесть; (*skill*) мастерство́.
prowl [praʊl] *v.t.*: **thieves ~ the streets** во́ры шныря́ют по у́лицам.
v.i. кра́сться (*impf.*); **wolves were ~ing outside the tent** во́лки ры́скали вокру́г пала́тки.
proximity [prɒk'sɪmɪtɪ] *n.* бли́зость; **in (close) ~ to** вблизи́/поблизо́сти от+*g.*, ря́дом с+*i.*
proxy ['prɒksɪ] *n.* **1.** (*authorization*) полномо́чие, дове́ренность; **they voted by ~** они́ голосова́ли по дове́ренности. **2.** (*substitute*) замести́тель (*m.*); (*attr.*): **~ vote** голосова́ние по дове́ренности.
prude [pru:d] *n.* ханжа́ (*c.g.*).
prudence ['pru:d(ə)ns] *n.* благоразу́мие; предусмотри́тельность.
prudent ['pru:d(ə)nt] *adj.* благоразу́мный; предусмотри́тельный.
prudish ['pru:dɪʃ] *adj.* стыдли́вый; ха́нжеский.
prune[1] [pru:n] *n.* чернosли́в.
prun|e[2] [pru:n] *v.t.* **1.** (*trim*) обр|еза́ть, -е́зать; подр|еза́ть, -е́зать; **~ing-shears** сека́тор; садо́вые но́жницы. **2.** (*simplify*) упро|ща́ть, -сти́ть.
prurient ['prʊərɪənt] *adj.* похотли́вый.
Prussia ['prʌʃə] *n.* Пру́ссия.
Prussian ['prʌʃ(ə)n] *n.* прусса́|к (*fem.* -чка).
adj. пру́сский; **~ blue** берли́нская лазу́рь.
prussic ['prʌsɪk] *adj.*: **~ acid** сини́льная кислота́.
pry [praɪ] *v.i.* (*peer*) подсм|а́тривать, -отре́ть; (*interfere*) вме́шиваться (*impf.*).
PS (*abbr. of* **postscript**) постскри́птум.
psalm [sɑ:m] *n.* псало́м.
psalter ['sɔ:ltə(r), 'sɒl-] *n.* псалты́рь (*f. or m.*).
pseud [sju:d] *n.* позёр.
pseudo ['sju:dəʊ] *adj.* фальши́вый.
pseudonym ['sju:dənɪm] *n.* псевдони́м.
psoriasis [sə'raɪəsɪs] *n.* псориа́з.
psyche ['saɪkɪ] *n.* душа́; дух.
psychiatric [,saɪkɪ'ætrɪk] *adj.* психиатри́ческий.
psychiatrist [saɪ'kaɪətrɪst] *n.* психиа́тр.
psychiatry [saɪ'kaɪətrɪ] *n.* психиатри́я.
psychic ['saɪkɪk] *n.* экстрасе́нс.
adj. **1.** = **psychical. 2.** (*susceptible to occult influence*) ≃ ясновидящий.
psychical ['saɪkɪk(ə)l] *adj.* душе́вный; психи́ческий.
psychoanalyse [,saɪkəʊ'ænə,laɪz] *v.t.* психоанализи́ровать (*impf., pf.*).
psychoanalysis [,saɪkəʊə'nælɪsɪs] *n.* психоана́лиз.
psychoanalyst [,saɪkəʊ'ænəlɪst] *n.* психоанали́тик.
psychoanalytic [,saɪkəʊ,ænə'lɪtɪk] *adj.* психоаналити́ческий.
psychological [,saɪkə'lɒdʒɪk(ə)l] *adj.* психологи́ческий.
psychologist [saɪ'kɒlədʒɪst] *n.* психо́лог.
psychology [saɪ'kɒlədʒɪ] *n.* психоло́гия.
psychopath ['saɪkə,pæθ] *n.* психопа́т (*fem.* -ка).
psychopathic [,saɪkə'pæθɪk] *adj.* психопати́ческий.
psychosis [saɪ'kəʊsɪs] *n.* психо́з.
psychosomatic [,saɪkəʊsə'mætɪk] *adj.* психосомати́ческий.
psychotherapist [,saɪkəʊ'θerəpɪst] *n.* психотерапе́вт.
psychotherapy [,saɪkəʊ'θerəpɪ] *n.* психотерапи́я.
psychotic [saɪ'kɒtɪk] *adj.* психоти́ческий.
pt. [paɪnt(z)] *n.* (*abbr. of* **pint(s)**) пи́нта.
ptarmigan ['tɑ:mɪgən] *n.* шотла́ндский те́терев.
pterodactyl [,terə'dæktɪl] *n.* птерода́ктиль (*m.*).
PTO (*abbr. of* **please turn over**) см. на об., (смотри́ на оборо́те).
pub [pʌb] *n.* (*coll.*) пивна́я; бар; каба́к.
puberty ['pju:bətɪ] *n.* полова́я зре́лость.
pubic ['pju:bɪk] *adj.* лобко́вый, ло́нный; **~ hair** во́лосы на лобке́.
public ['pʌblɪk] *n.* **1.** (*community*) обще́ственность; наро́д; **the British ~** англи́йский наро́д; **the library is open to the ~** вход в библиоте́ку свобо́дный; **members of the ~** представи́тели обще́ственности. **2.** (*section of community*) пу́блика. **3.** (*audience*) пу́блика; **I have never spoken in ~** я никогда́ не выступа́л публи́чно.
adj. **1.** (*pert. to people in general*) обще́ственный; **~ opinion** обще́ственное мне́ние; **he is in the ~ eye** он нахо́дится в по́ле зре́ния обще́ственности; **~ health** здравоохране́ние; **it is ~ knowledge** э́то общеизве́стно; **~ relations** взаимоотноше́ние (организа́ции) с клиенту́рой (и о́бществом в це́лом); **~ relations officer** нача́льник/сотру́дник отде́ла информа́ции; **in the ~ interest** в интере́сах о́бщества; **~ enemy** враг наро́да. **2.** (*pert. to politics or the state*) обще́ственный, госуда́рственный; **a ~ figure** обще́ственный де́ятель; **~ prosecutor** обще́ственный прокуро́р. **3.** (*accessible to all; shared by the community*) публи́чный, общедосту́пный; **~ convenience** обще́ственная убо́рная; **~ holiday** устано́вленный зако́ном пра́здник. **4.** (*done openly, in view of others*) публи́чный, гла́сный; откры́тый; **~ inquiry** публи́чное рассле́дование; **~ speaking** ора́торское иску́сство; **~ address system** систе́ма трансляцио́нного радиовеща́ния; **~ protest** откры́тый проте́ст.
cpd. **~-house** *n.* пивна́я, бар.
publican ['pʌblɪkən] *n.* содержа́тель (*m.*) ба́ра.
publication [,pʌblɪ'keɪʃ(ə)n] *n.* (*of news etc.*) публика́ция, опубликова́ние; (*issuing of written work, photograph etc.*) изда́ние, вы́пуск; (*published work*) изда́ние; произведе́ние.
publicist ['pʌblɪsɪst] *n.* (*writer on current topics*) публици́ст.
publicity [pʌb'lɪsɪtɪ] *n.* **1.** (*public notice*) гла́сность; **an actress seeking ~** актри́са, добыва́ющаяся рекла́мы; **the report was given full ~** сообще́ние получи́ло широ́кую огла́ску. **2.** (*advertisement*) реклами́рование; **~ agent** аге́нт по рекла́ме; **~ campaign** рекла́мная кампа́ния.
publicize ['pʌblɪ,saɪz] *v.t.* реклами́ровать (*impf.*); огла|ша́ть, -си́ть.

publish ['pʌblɪʃ] *v.t.* **1.** (*make generally known*) публикова́ть, о-; огла|ша́ть, -си́ть. **2.** (*issue copies of*) печа́тать, на-; изд|ава́ть, -а́ть; **be ~ed** выходи́ть, вы́йти (из печа́ти).

publisher ['pʌblɪʃə(r)] *n.* изда́тель (*m.*).

publishing ['pʌblɪʃɪŋ] *n.* изда́тельское де́ло; **~ house** изда́тельство.

puck [pʌk] *n.* (*in ice-hockey*) ша́йба.

pucker ['pʌkə(r)] *v.t. & i.* мо́рщить(ся), на-; **his brow was ~ed** он насу́пился.

pudding ['pʊdɪŋ] *n.* пу́динг, запека́нка; (*sweet course*) сла́дкое; **black ~** кровяна́я колбаса́.

puddle ['pʌd(ə)l] *n.* (*pool*) лу́жа.

puerile ['pjʊəraɪl] *adj.* де́тский, инфанти́льный.

puerility [pjʊə'rɪlɪtɪ] *n.* инфанти́льность.

puff [pʌf] *n.* **1.** (*of breath*) вы́дох. **2.** (*of smoke, steam etc.*) дымо́к, клуб; **he took a ~ at his cigar** он затяну́лся сига́рой. **3.** (*sound*) пыхте́ние. **4.** (*of air or wind*) струя́ во́здуха. **5.** (*cake*) сло́йка; слоёный пирожо́к.

v.t. **1.** (*breathe out*) выдыха́ть, вы́дохнуть; **he ~ed smoke in my face** он пусти́л дым мне в лицо́. **2.** (*make out of breath*): **I was ~ed after the climb** у меня́ сде́лалась оды́шка по́сле подъёма. **3.: ~ out, up** над|ува́ть, -у́ть; расп|уха́ть, -у́хнуть; **he ~ed out his chest with pride** он го́рдо вы́пятил грудь.

v.i. **1.** (*come out in ~s*) клуби́ться (*impf.*). **2.** (*breathe quickly*): **he was ~ing and panting** он пыхте́л. **3.** (*emit smoke*) дыми́ться (*impf.*); **he ~ed away at his pipe** он попы́хивал тру́бкой.

puffer(-train) ['pʌfə(r)] *n.* (*coll.*) ту-ту́ (*nt. indecl.*).

puffin ['pʌfɪn] *n.* ту́пик, топо́рик.

puffy ['pʌfɪ] *adj.* (*swollen*) одутлова́тый.

pugnacious [pʌg'neɪʃəs] *adj.* драчли́вый.

pugnacity [pʌg'næsɪtɪ] *n.* драчли́вость.

puke [pju:k] *v.i.* блева́ть (*impf.*); **he ~d** его́ вы́рвало.

pull [pʊl] *n.* **1.** (*tug*) тя́га; дёрганье; **he gave a ~ on the rope** он дёрнул (за) верёвку. **2.** (*force, effort*) напряже́ние; **the tide exerts a strong ~** прили́в облада́ет большо́й си́лой; **it was a long hard ~ up the hill** взобра́ться на́ гору сто́ило больши́х уси́лий. **3.** (*coll., influence*) блат; **he has a lot of ~** у него́ больши́е свя́зи.

v.t. **1.** (*draw towards one, tug, jerk*) тяну́ть, по-; тащи́ть, под-; **the boy ~ed his sister's hair** ма́льчик дёрнул сестру́ за́ волосы; **he ~ed me by the sleeve** он потяну́л меня́ за рука́в. **2.** (*obtain by ~ing*): **the barman ~ed a glass of beer** барме́н нацеди́л стака́н пива. **3.** (*fig.*): **he is good at ~ing strings** он ма́стер нажима́ть на кно́пки; **~ s.o.'s leg** разы́гр|ивать, -а́ть кого́-н.; **she ~ed a face at him** она́ ско́рчила ему́ грима́су. **4.** (*extract, pluck*) выта́скивать, вы́тащить; выдёргивать, вы́дернуть; **~ a tooth** вырыва́ть, вы́рвать зуб; **he ~ed a gun on me** он вы́хватил пистоле́т и навёл его́ на меня́. **5.** (*propel by ~ing*) тяну́ть, по-; **the carriage was ~ed by horses** каре́та была́ запряжена́ лошадьми́; **he is not ~ing his weight** (*fig.*) он рабо́тает вполси́лы. **6.** (*strain, e.g. muscle*) растя́|гивать, -ну́ть.

v.i. **1.** (*exert drawing force*) тяну́ть, по-; **they ~ed on the rope** они́ потяну́ли за верёвку; **the boatman ~ed hard on the oars** ло́дочник усе́рдно налега́л на вёсла. **2.** (*suck*) тяну́ть, по-; **he ~ed on his pipe** он потя́гивал тру́бку. **3.** (*propel boat, car etc.*) е́хать, про-; **he had to ~ across the road** ему́ на́до бы́ло перее́хать на другу́ю сто́рону; **~ for the shore!** греби́те к бе́регу! **4.** (*move under propulsion*) дви́гаться (*impf.*); **the train ~ed out of the station** по́езд отошёл от ста́нции.

with advs.: **~ about** *v.t.* таска́ть (*impf.*) туда́ и сюда́; **the dog ~ed the cushion about** соба́ка тереби́ла поду́шку; **~ apart** *v.t.* (*also* **~ to pieces**) раз|рыва́ть, -орва́ть на куски́; (*fig., criticize severely*) разн|оси́ть, -ести́ в пух и прах; **~ aside** *v.t.* оття́|гивать, -ну́ть; **~ away** *v.t.*: **he ~ed his hand away** он убра́л ру́ку; *v.i.* (*move off*) от|рыва́ться, -орва́ться; **the boat ~ed away from the quay** ло́дка отплыла́ от при́стани; **~ back** *v.t.* отта́|скивать, -щи́ть; оття́|гивать, -ну́ть; **~ back the curtains!** откро́йте занаве́ски!; **~ down** *v.t.* (*lower by ~ing*) спус|ка́ть, -ти́ть; **~ down the blinds!** опусти́те што́ры!; **he was attacked and ~ed down** на него́ напа́ли и повали́ли его́ на зе́млю; (*demolish*) сн|оси́ть, -ести́; **~ in** *v.t.* (*retract*) втя́|гивать, -ну́ть; (*haul on, draw towards one*) тащи́ть, вы́-; тяну́ть, по-; **the rope was ~ed in** верёвку натяну́ли; *v.i.* (*drive or move to a standstill*) остан|а́вливаться, -ови́ться; **the train ~ed in** по́езд подошёл к перро́ну; **he ~ed in to the kerb** он подъе́хал к тротуа́ру; (*drive or move towards near side of road*): **he ~ed in to avoid a collision** он прижа́лся к обо́чине, что́бы избежа́ть столкнове́ние; **~ off** *v.t.* (*remove, detach*) стя́|гивать, -ну́ть; сн|има́ть, -ять; **he ~ed the buttons off** он оторва́л пу́говицы; **he ~ed his shoes off** он стащи́л ту́фли; (*coll., achieve*) успе́шно заверш|а́ть, -и́ть; *v.i.* тро́гаться (*impf.*); **the car ~ed off in a hurry** маши́на бы́стро отъе́хала; **~ on** *v.t.* натя́|гивать, -ну́ть; **~ out** *v.t.* (*extract*) выта́скивать, вы́тащить; **he ~ed out the drawer** он вы́двинул я́щик; (*withdraw*) выводи́ть, вы́вести; **the troops should be ~ed out** войска́ сле́дует вы́вести; *v.i.* (*drive or move away*) от|ходи́ть, -ойти́; **he caught the train as it was ~ing out** он вскочи́л в по́езд на ходу́; (*of driving manœuvres*) отъ|езжа́ть, -е́хать; **he ~ed out to overtake** он вы́шел на обго́н; (*withdraw*): **the troops had to ~ out** войска́м пришло́сь вы́йти из бо́я; **the drawer won't ~ out** я́щик не выдвига́ется; **~ round** *v.t.* выле́чивать, вы́лечить; **the brandy will soon ~ you round** конья́к ско́ро приведёт вас в чу́вство; *v.i.* (*recover*) попр|авля́ться, -а́виться; **he will ~ round in a day or so** он придёт в себя́ че́рез день-друго́й; **~ through** *v.t.* (*lit.*) прота́|скивать, -щи́ть; (*fig.*) спас|а́ть, -ти́; *v.i.* (*recover from illness*) попр|авля́ться, -а́виться; (*surmount difficulties, survive*): **we shall ~ through in the end** в конце́ концо́в мы вы́крутимся; **~ together** *v.t.*: **~ yourself together!** возьми́те себя́ в ру́ки!; *v.i.* (*fig.*) сраб|а́тываться, -о́таться; **if we all ~ together, we shall win** объедини́вшись, мы победи́м; **~ up** *v.t.* (*uproot*) вырыва́ть, вы́рвать; (*raise*) вытя́гивать, вы́тянуть; **he ~ed himself up to his full height** он вы́прямился во весь рост; (*draw nearer*) придв|ига́ть, -и́нуть; (*reprimand*) отчи́т|ывать, -а́ть; *v.i.* (*come to a halt*) остан|а́вливаться, -ови́ться; **don't get off the bus until it ~s up** не выходи́те из авто́буса до по́лной остано́вки.

pulley ['pʊlɪ] *n.* шкив; блок.

pullover ['pʊl,əʊvə(r)] *n.* пуло́вер.

pulmonary ['pʌlmənərɪ] *adj.* лёгочный.

pulp [pʌlp] *n.* **1.** (*of fruit*) мя́коть. **2.** (*of animal tissue*) пу́льпа. **3.** (*of wood etc. for making paper*) древе́сная ма́сса. **4.** (*fig.*) каши́ца; бесфо́рменная ма́сса; **his arm was crushed to a ~** ему́ раздроби́ло ру́ку.

v.t. (*make into ~*) превра|ща́ть, -ти́ть в пу́льпу.

pulpit ['pʊlpɪt] *n.* амво́н, ка́федра.

pulpy ['pʌlpɪ] *adj.* мяси́стый.

pulsar ['pʌlsɑ:(r)] *n.* пульса́р.

pulsate [pʌl'seɪt, 'pʌl-] *v.i.* пульси́ровать (*impf.*).

pulsation [pʌl'seɪʃ(ə)n] *n.* пульса́ция.

pulse[1] [pʌls] *n.* пульс; **the doctor took his ~** врач пощу́пал ему́ пульс; **what is your ~ rate?** како́й у вас пульс?; (*fig.*) пульса́ция, бие́ние; (*of music*) ритм.

v.i. пульси́ровать (*impf.*); би́ться (*impf.*).

pulse[2] [pʌls] *n.* (*collect., legumes*) бобо́вые (расте́ния).

pulverize ['pʌlvə,raɪz] *v.t.* **1.** (*reduce to powder*) размельч|а́ть, -и́ть; (*fig., smash, demolish*) сокруш|а́ть,

-и́ть. **2.** (*divide into spray*) распыл|я́ть, -и́ть.

v.i. распыля́ться (*impf.*).

puma ['pju:mə] *n.* пу́ма, кугуа́р.

pumice ['pʌmɪs] *n.* **(~-stone)** пе́мза.

pummel ['pʌm(ə)l] *v.t.* колоти́ть, по-; тузи́ть, от-.

pump[1] [pʌmp] *n.* насо́с, по́мпа.

v.t. **1.** (*transfer by ~ing*) кача́ть, на-; **they ~ed water out of the hold** они́ вы́качали во́ду из трю́ма; **the tyre needs more air ~ing into it** ши́ну на́до подкача́ть; (*fig.*): **I had maths ~ed into me at school** в меня́ вда́лбливали матема́тику в шко́ле. **2.** (*affect or empty by ~ing*) выка́чивать, вы́качать; **the well had been ~ed dry** коло́дец по́лностью осуши́ли; (*fig.*): **I ~ed him for information** я его́ выспра́шивал. **3.** (*agitate as in ~ing*): **he ~ed my arm up and down** он до́лго тряс мне ру́ку. **4.** (*also* **~ up**: *inflate*) нака́ч|ивать, -а́ть.

pump[2] [pʌmp] *n.* (*shoe*) ту́фля-ло́дочка.

pumpernickel ['pʌmpəˌnɪk(ə)l, 'pʊ-] *n.* неме́цкий ржано́й хлеб.

pumpkin ['pʌmpkɪn] *n.* ты́ква.

pun [pʌn] *n.* игра́ слов, каламбу́р.

v.i. игра́ть слова́ми, каламбу́рить (*impf.*).

punch[1] [pʌntʃ] *n.* **1.** (*blow with fist*) уда́р кулако́м; **I gave him a ~ on the nose** я дал ему́ по́ носу. **2.** (*fig., energy*) эне́ргия; **his performance lacked ~** его́ игре́ недостава́ло огня́. **3.** (*tool for perforating e.g. paper*) перфора́тор, компо́стер.

v.t. **1.** (*hit with fist*) уд|аря́ть, -а́рить кулако́м; **he was ~ed on the chin** он получи́л кулако́м в че́люсть. **2.** (*perforate*) компости́ровать (*impf.*); **~ holes** проб|ива́ть, -и́ть отве́рстия; **~ed card** перфока́рта.

cpds. **~-ball** *n.* пенчингбо́л; **~-line** *n.* кульминацио́нный пункт; **~-up** *n.* дра́ка, потасо́вка.

punch[2] [pʌntʃ] *n.* (*beverage*) пунш.

Punch[3] [pʌntʃ] *n.* (*puppet character*) Панч, Петру́шка (*m.*); **~ and Judy show** ку́кольное (я́рмарочное) представле́ние; **he was as pleased as ~** он расплыва́лся от удово́льствия.

punctilious [pʌŋk'tɪlɪəs] *adj.* скрупулёзный.

punctiliousness [pʌŋk'tɪlɪəsnɪs] *n.* скрупулёзность.

punctual ['pʌŋktjʊəl] *adj.* пунктуа́льный, то́чный.

punctuality [ˌpʌŋktjʊ'ælɪtɪ] *n.* пунктуа́льность, то́чность.

punctuate ['pʌŋktjʊˌeɪt] *v.t.* (*insert punctuation marks in*) ста́вить, по- зна́ки препина́ния в+*a.*; (*fig., interrupt, intersperse*) прер|ыва́ть, -ва́ть.

punctuation [ˌpʌŋktjʊ'eɪʃ(ə)n] *n.* пунктуа́ция; **~ mark** знак препина́ния.

puncture ['pʌŋktʃə(r)] *n.* проко́л; **his bicycle had a ~** он проткну́л ши́ну своего́ велосипе́да.

v.t. прок|а́лывать, -оло́ть.

pundit ['pʌndɪt] *n.* знато́к, специали́ст.

pungency ['pʌndʒ(ə)nsɪ] *n.* острота́; е́дкость.

pungent ['pʌndʒ(ə)nt] *adj.* о́стрый.

punish ['pʌnɪʃ] *v.t.* **1.** (*inflict penalty on*) нака́з|ывать, -а́ть; **the thief was ~ed by a fine** на во́ра наложи́ли штраф. **2.** (*inflict penalty for*): **theft was severely ~ed** за кра́жу суро́во кара́ли. **3.** (*tax strength of*) изнур|я́ть, -и́ть; изм|а́тывать, -ота́ть; **he set a ~ing pace** он за́дал уби́йственный темп.

punishable ['pʌnɪʃəb(ə)l] *adj.*: **treason is ~ by death** изме́на кара́ется сме́ртной ка́знью.

punishment ['pʌnɪʃmənt] *n.* (*penalty*) взыска́ние; наказа́ние.

punitive ['pju:nɪtɪv] *adj.* кара́тельный.

punk [pʌŋk] *n.* (*admirer of ~ rock*) панк.

adj. па́нковый.

punnet ['pʌnɪt] *n.* корзи́н(оч)ка.

punt[1] [pʌnt] *n.* (*boat*) плоскодо́нный я́лик.

v.i. плыть (*impf.*), отта́лкиваясь шесто́м.

punter ['pʌntə(r)] *n.* (*at races*) игро́к.

puny ['pju:nɪ] *adj.* тщеду́шный; хи́лый.

pup [pʌp] *n.* (*young dog*) щено́к; **you've been sold a ~** (*fig., coll.*) вас провели́.

pupa ['pju:pə] *n.* ку́колка.

pupate [pju:'peɪt] *v.i.* оку́кли|ваться, -ться.

pupil ['pju:pɪl, -p(ə)l] *n.* **1.** (*one being taught*) учени́к. **2.** (*of eye*) зрачо́к.

puppet ['pʌpɪt] *n.*: **glove ~** ку́кла; **string ~** марионе́тка; (*fig.*) марионе́тка; **~ state** марионе́точное госуда́рство.

cpd. **~-play, ~-show** *nn.* ку́кольное представле́ние, ку́кольный спекта́кль.

puppy ['pʌpɪ] *n.* (*young dog*) щено́к; **~ fat** де́тская пу́хлость; **~ love** де́тская любо́вь.

purblind ['pɜ:blaɪnd] *adj.* подслеповáтый; (*fig.*) недальнови́дный.

purchase ['pɜ:tʃɪs, -tʃəs] *n.* **1.** (*buying*) ку́пля; **~ price** покупна́я цена́. **2.** (*thing bought*) поку́пка. **3.** (*lever, leverage*) рыча́г; зажи́м, захва́т.

v.t. (*buy*) покупа́ть, купи́ть; приобре|та́ть, -сти́; **purchasing power** покупа́тельная спосо́бность.

cpd. **~-tax** *n.* нало́г на поку́пку.

purchaser ['pɜ:tʃɪsə(r), -tʃəsə(r)] *n.* покупа́тель (*fem.* -ница).

pure [pjʊə(r)] *adj.* (*in var. senses*) чи́стый; (*unmixed*) беспри́месный; **it was a ~ accident** э́то была́ чи́стая случа́йность.

cpd. **~-bred** *adj.* чистокро́вный.

purée ['pjʊəreɪ] *n.* пюре́ (*indecl.*).

purely ['pjʊəlɪ] *adv.* (*blamelessly*) чи́сто; (*entirely*) чи́сто, соверше́нно.

purgative ['pɜ:gətɪv] *n.* слаби́тельное сре́дство.

adj. (*aperient*) слаби́тельный, очисти́тельный.

purgatory ['pɜ:gətərɪ] *n.* чисти́лище; (*fig.*) ад.

purge [pɜ:dʒ] *n.* (*clearance; cleansing*) очище́ние; очи́стка; (*pol.*) чи́стка; репре́ссии (*f. pl.*).

v.t. оч|ища́ть, -и́стить; **he was ~d of his sins** ему́ отпусти́ли грехи́; **he ~d himself of all suspicion** он очи́стил себя́ от всех подозре́ний; **the party was ~d of its rebels** па́ртию очи́стили от бунтовщико́в.

purification [ˌpjʊərɪfɪ'keɪʃ(ə)n] *n.* очи́стка, очище́ние.

purify ['pjʊərɪˌfaɪ] *v.t.* оч|ища́ть, -и́стить.

purist ['pjʊərɪst] *n.* пури́ст.

puritan ['pjʊərɪt(ə)n] *n.* (*lit., fig.*) пурита́н|ин (*fem.* -ка).

adj. пурита́нский.

puritanical [ˌpjʊərɪ'tænɪk(ə)l] *adj.* пурита́нский.

puritanism ['pjʊərɪtənˌɪz(ə)m] *n.* пурита́ни́зм.

purity ['pjʊərɪtɪ] *n.* (*var. senses*) чистота́; (*absence of adulteration*) беспри́месность.

purl[1] [pɜ:l] *n.* (*knitting*) оборо́тное двухлицево́е вяза́ние.

v.i. вяза́ть (*impf.*) пе́тлей наизна́нку.

purloin [pə'lɔɪn] *v.t.* пох|ища́ть, -и́тить.

purple ['pɜ:p(ə)l] *n.* пу́рпур; фиоле́товый цвет.

adj. пу́рпу́рный; фиоле́товый; багро́вый; **he turned ~ with rage** он побагрове́л от я́рости.

purport[1] ['pɜ:pɔ:t] *n.* смысл; суть.

purport[2] [pə'pɔ:t] *v.t.* подразумева́ть (*impf.*); **this book is not all it ~s to be** э́та кни́га не совсе́м така́я, како́й она́ претенду́ет быть.

purpose ['pɜ:pəs] *n.* **1.** (*design, aim, intention*) цель, наме́рение; **what was your ~ in coming?** с како́й це́лью вы пришли́?; **this tool will serve my ~** э́тот инструме́нт мне подойдёт; **for practical ~s the war is over** война́ практи́чески око́нчена; **on ~** наро́чно, специа́льно; **I went there to no ~** я напра́сно туда́ ходи́л; **she went out with the ~ of buying clothes** она́ вы́шла с наме́рением купи́ть оде́жду. **2.** (*determination, resolve*) целеустремлённость.

purposeful ['pɜ:pəsˌfʊl] *adj.* целеустремлённый.

purposely ['pɜ:pəslɪ] *adv.* нарo̒чно, наме́ренно, специа́льно.

purr [pɜ:(r)] *n.* мурлы́канье.

v.i. (*of cat; also fig.*) мурлы́кать (*impf.*).

purse [pɜ:s] *n.* **1.** (*bag for money*) кошелёк; (*US, handbag*) су́м(оч)ка. **2.** (*fig., monetary resources*) де́н|ьги (*pl., g.* -ег); **the public ~** казна́. **3.** (*prize money*) де́нежный приз.

v.t. мо́рщить, с-; **he ~d (up) his lips** он поджа́л гу́бы.

purser ['pɜ:sə(r)] *n.* судово́й казначе́й.

pursuance [pə'sju:əns] *n.* выполне́ние; **in ~ of one's duties** по до́лгу слу́жбы.

pursuant [pə'sju:ənt] *adj.*: **~ to** в соотве́тствии с+*i.*; **~ to your instructions** согла́сно ва́шим указа́ниям.

pursue [pə'sju:] *v.t.* (*hunt, chase, beset*) пресле́довать (*impf.*). **2.** (*strive after, aim at*) добива́ться (*impf.*) +*g.* **3.** (*carry out, engage in*) сле́довать (*impf.*) +*d.*; **the policy ~d by the government** поли́тика, проводи́мая прави́тельством. **4.** (*continue*) прод|олжа́ть, -о́лжить.

pursuer [pə'sju:ə(r)] *n.* пресле́дователь (*m.*).

pursuit [pə'sju:t] *n.* **1.** (*chase*) пресле́дование; пого́ня. **2.** (*following, seeking*) по́иск|и (*pl., g.* -ов). **3.** (*profession or recreation*) заня́тие.

purvey [pə'veɪ] *v.t.* (*supply*) снаб|жа́ть, -ди́ть (*кого чем*).

v.i. (*supply provisions*) пост|авля́ть, -а́вить продово́льствие.

purveyor [pə'veɪə(r)] *n.* поставщи́|к (*fem.* -ца).

purview ['pɜ:vju:] *n.* (*range, scope*) сфе́ра; о́бласть де́йствия; **these matters fall within my ~** э́ти дела́ вхо́дят в мою́ компете́нцию.

pus [pʌs] *n.* гной.

push [pʊʃ] *n.* **1.** (*act of propulsion*) толчо́к; **he closed the door with a ~** он захло́пнул дверь. **2.** (*coll., dismissal*) увольне́ние; **they have given me the ~** меня́ вы́гнали. **3.**: **at a ~** (*coll.*) на худо́й коне́ц.

v.t. **1.** (*propel; exert pressure to move*) толк|а́ть, -ну́ть; пих|а́ть, -ну́ть; **he ~es all the dirty jobs on to me** он всю гря́зную рабо́ту спи́хивает на меня́. **2.** (*fig., urge, impel*) подт|а́лкивать, -олкну́ть. **3.** (*force*) прот|а́лкивать, -олкну́ть; **he ~ed his fist through the window** он просу́нул кула́к в окно́; **I ~ed my way through the crowd** я проти́снулся сквозь толпу́. **4.** (*press*) наж|има́ть, -а́ть; **~ the button and the bell will ring** нажми́те кно́пку, и звоно́к зазвони́т. **5.** (*put under pressure*) ока́з|ывать, -а́ть давле́ние на+*a.*; **I am ~ed for time** у меня́ вре́мени в обре́з. **6.** (*promote, advertise*) реклами́ровать (*impf.*); прота́лкивать (*impf.*).

v.i. **1.** (*exert force*) толка́ться (*impf.*); **~ hard at the door!** толкни́те дверь посильне́е!; **don't ~!** не толка́йтесь! **2.** (*force one's way*) прот|а́лкиваться, -олкну́ться; **he ~ed between us** он проти́снулся ме́жду на́ми; **they all ~ed into the room** они́ все ввали́лись в ко́мнату.

with advs.: **~ about** *v.t.* (*coll.*) потрепа́ть (*pf.*); помя́ть (*pf.*); **~ along** *v.t.* (*lit.*): **the boy was ~ing his barrow along** ма́льчик кати́л та́чку; (*fig.*) спеши́ть, по-; пот|ора́пливать, -ороп́ить; **~ around** *v.t.* переставля́ть (*impf.*); передвига́ть (*impf.*); (*fig.*) кома́ндовать (*impf.*) (*кем*); **I won't be ~ed around** я не позво́лю кома́ндовать над собо́й; **~ aside** *v.t.* отт|а́лкивать, -олкну́ть; **~ away** *v.t.* = **~ aside;** *v.i.*: **they ~ed away from the shore** они́ отплы́ли от бе́рега; **~ back** *v.t.* (*repulse*) отбр|а́сывать, -о́сить; (*move away*) отодв|ига́ть, -и́нуть; **she ~ed back the bedclothes** она́ отки́нула одея́ло; **~ down** *v.t.* вали́ть, по-; **~ forward** *v.t.* толк|а́ть, -ну́ть вперёд; *v.i.* (*make progress*) продв|ига́ться, -и́нуться (вперёд); **~ in** *v.t.* вт|а́лкивать, -олкну́ть; *v.i.* втира́ться, вотере́ться; **don't ~ in!** (*intrude*) не ле́зьте; **~ off** *v.t.* отт|а́лкивать, -олкну́ть; **in the struggle his hat was ~ed off** в потасо́вке ему́ сби́ли шля́пу; *v.i.* (*in a boat*) отт|а́лкиваться, -олкну́ться от бе́рега; (*coll., leave*) см|ыва́ться, -ы́ться; **~ on** *v.i.* продв|ига́ться, -и́нуться вперёд; **next day they ~ed on again** на сле́дующий день они́ продолжа́ли путь; **~ out** *v.t.*: **plants are ~ing out new leaves** у расте́ний распуска́ются но́вые ли́стья; **he opened the door and ~ed me out** он откры́л дверь и вы́толкнул меня́; *v.i.* выдава́ться (*impf.*) вперёд; **they ~ed out to sea** они́ вы́шли в мо́ре; **~ over** *v.t.* опроки́|дывать, -нуть; **I was nearly ~ed over in the rush** в толкотне́ меня́ чуть не сби́ли с ног; **~ past** *v.i.* прот|а́лкиваться, -олкну́ться; **~ through** *v.t.* (*lit., fig.*) прот|а́лкивать, -олкну́ть; *v.i.* проти́|скиваться, -снуться; **~ to** *v.t.* (*close*) закр|ыва́ть, -ы́ть; **~ together** *v.t.* (*e.g. books on a shelf*) сдв|ига́ть, -и́нуть; **~ up** *v.t.* сдв|ига́ть, -и́нуть; подн|има́ть, -я́ть кве́рху; (*increase*) увели́чи|вать, -ть; *v.i.*: **he ~ed up against me** он прижа́лся ко мне.

cpds. **~-bike** *n.* (*coll.*) велосипе́д; **~-button** *n.* нажи́мная кно́пка; **~-cart** *n.* ручна́я теле́жка; **~-chair** *n.* прогу́лочная коля́ска; **~over** *n.* (*sl., something easily accomplished*) па́ра пустяко́в; **~-up** *n.* (*exercise*): **do ~-ups** отжима́ться (*impf.*) на рука́х.

pusher ['pʊʃə(r)] *n.* (*sl., drug ~*) наркоделе́ц.

pushy ['pʊʃɪ] *adj.* насты́рный, назо́йливый.

pusillanimous [,pju:sɪ'lænɪməs] *adj.* малоду́шный.

puss [pʊs] *n.* ко́шечка, ки́ска; **~, ~!** кис-ки́с!

pussy ['pʊsɪ] *n.* ки́са, ки́ска, ко́ш(еч)ка.

cpds. **~-cat** *n.* ко́шечка; **~foot** *v.i.* (*coll., behave cautiously*) виля́ть (*impf.*); темни́ть (*impf.*); **~-willow** *n.* и́ва-шелю́га кра́сная, ве́рба.

pustule ['pʌstju:l] *n.* пу́стула; прыщ.

put [pʊt] *v.t.* **1.** (*move into a certain position*) класть, положи́ть; (*stand*) ста́вить, по-; (*set*) сажа́ть, посади́ть; **~ the glasses on the tray!** поста́вьте стака́ны на подно́с; **~ the money in your pocket!** положи́те де́ньги в карма́н; **he ~ his hands in his pockets** он засу́нул ру́ки в карма́ны; **~ a nail in the wall** вбить (*pf.*) гвоздь в сте́ну; **~ some milk in my tea!** нале́йте мне молока́ в чай!; **don't ~ sugar in my tea!** не клади́те са́хару в чай; **he was ~ in prison** его́ посади́ли в тюрьму́; **~ yourself in my place!** поста́вьте себя́ на моё ме́сто; **I ~ him in his place** (*fig.*) я поста́вил его́ на ме́сто; **I ~ the matter into the hands of my lawyer** я поручи́л э́то де́ло своему́ адвока́ту; **he ~ me on my way** он показа́л мне доро́гу; **she ~ the clothes on the line** она́ разве́сила бельё; **she ~ a cloth on the table** она́ накры́ла стол ска́тертью; **he ~ a shawl round her shoulder** он накры́л её пле́чи ша́лью; **the postman ~ a letter through the box** почтальо́н опусти́л письмо́ в я́щик; **she ~ the children to bed** она́ уложи́ла дете́й; **he ~ the glass to his lips** он поднёс стака́н к губа́м; **where did I ~ that book** куда́ я дел ту кни́гу? **2.** (*move with force; thrust*) вонз|а́ть, -и́ть; **he ~ a bullet through his head** он пусти́л себе́ пу́лю в лоб; **he ~ his fist through the window** он проби́л окно́ кулако́м. **3.** (*bring into a certain state or relationship*): **that ~s me at a disadvantage** э́то ста́вит меня́ в невы́годное положе́ние; **the dinner ~ him in a good mood** обе́д привёл его́ в хоро́шее расположе́ние ду́ха; **you ~ me in mind of your mother** вы напомина́ете мне ва́шу мать; **the least thing ~s him in a rage** любо́й пустя́к приво́дит его́ в я́рость; **that ~s us level** (*at game etc.*) тепе́рь мы кви́ты; **his antics ~ me off my game** его́ проде́лки меша́ли мне игра́ть; **he was ~ on oath** его́ привели́ к прися́ге; **he ~ the poor creature out of its misery** он изба́вил бедня́гу от страда́ний; **he ~ me right on this point** в э́том он меня́ попра́вил; **the boiler needs to be ~ right** на́до почини́ть коло́нку; **he ~ my suggestion to the test** он подве́рг моё предложе́ние испыта́нию; **he was ~ to death** его казни́ли; **let's ~ it to the**

vote поста́вим вопро́с на голосова́ние; **I was ~ to great expense** меня́ ввели́ в огро́мный расхо́д; **your generosity ~s me to shame** ва́ша ще́дрость заставля́ет меня́ красне́ть; **the villagers were ~ to the sword** жи́телей дере́вни пре́дали мечу́; (*impose, bring in*): **the tax ~s a heavy burden on the rich** нало́г ложи́тся тяжёлым бре́менем на бога́тых; **~ an end to** прекра|ща́ть, -ти́ть; положи́ть (*pf.*) коне́ц +*d.*; **he ~ the blame on me** он свали́л вину́ на меня́; **the government ~ a tax on wealth** прави́тельство ввело́ нало́г на состоя́ние; (*set, arrange*): **~ in order** прив|оди́ть, -ести́ в поря́док; **he tried to ~ matters right** он стара́лся попра́вить дела́; (*appoint, set*) назн|ача́ть, -а́чить; **~ s.o. in charge of** ста́вить, по- кого́-н. во главе́ +*g.*; (*apply*): **if you ~ your mind to it** е́сли вы займётесь э́тим всерьёз; (*offer, present*): **they ~ their house on the market** они́ объяви́ли о прода́же до́ма; (*instil, inspire*) всел|я́ть, -и́ть; вдохну́ть (*pf.*); (*stake*) ста́вить, по-; (*invest*) вкла́дывать, вложи́ть; поме|ща́ть, -сти́ть; **I should ~ the money into property** я бы помести́л де́ньги в недви́жимость; (*make s.o. succumb or resort to*): **he ~ his opponent to flight** он обрати́л своего́ проти́вника в бе́гство; **the dog had to be ~ to sleep** соба́ку пришло́сь усыпи́ть. **4.** (*write; mark*) писа́ть, на-; ста́вить, по- (*знак и т.п.*); **I cannot ~ my name to that document** я не могу́ подписа́ть тако́й докуме́нт; **this ~ paid to his ambitions** э́то положи́ло коне́ц его́ наде́ждам. **5.** (*of price etc.*): **he ~s a high value on courtesy** он высоко́ це́нит ве́жливость; **I would ~ her (age) at about 65** я бы дал ей лет 65. **6.** (*submit, propound*) выдвига́ть, вы́двинуть; зад|ава́ть, -а́ть; **may I ~ a suggestion?** мо́жно мне внести́ предложе́ние? **7.** (*express; present*) изл|ага́ть, -ожи́ть; **how can I ~ it?** как бы э́то сказа́ть?; **will you ~ that in writing?** вы мо́жете подтверди́ть э́то на бума́ге?; **I can't ~ it into words** я не могу́ вы́разить э́то слова́ми; **how would you ~ that in English?** как вы э́то ска́жете (*or* как э́то бу́дет) по-англи́йски?; **that's ~ting it mildly!** мя́гко говоря́! **8.** (*translate*) перев|оди́ть, -ести́. **9.** (*mus., set*): **his poems have been ~ to music many times** его́ стихи́ бы́ли мно́го раз поло́жены на му́зыку. **10.** (*hurl*): **~ting the shot** толка́ние ядра́.

v.i. **1.** (*impose*): **don't let him ~ upon you** смотри́те, что́бы он вам на ше́ю не сел. **2. ~ to sea** (*of vessel or crew*) уходи́ть, уйти́ в мо́ре.

with advs.: **~ about** *v.t.* (*spread*) распростран|я́ть, -и́ть; (*turn round*): **he ~ the boat about** он разверну́л ло́дку; *v.i.* пов|ора́чиваться, -ерну́ться; **~ across** *v.t.* (*make clear, communicate*) объясн|я́ть, -и́ть; **he failed to ~ his idea across** ему́ не удало́сь поясни́ть свою́ иде́ю; **~ aside** *v.t.* (*lay to one side; save*) от|кла́дывать, -ложи́ть; (*ignore*): **these objections cannot be ~ aside** мы обя́заны приня́ть во внима́ние э́ти возраже́ния; **~ away** *v.t.* (*tidy*) уб|ира́ть, -ра́ть; (*save*) от|кла́дывать, -ложи́ть; (*renounce*) отка́з|ываться, -а́ться от+*g.*; **~ back** *v.t.* (*replace, restore*) класть, положи́ть на ме́сто; (*move backwards*) передв|ига́ть, -и́нуть наза́д; (*of clock*) перев|оди́ть, -ести́ наза́д; (*retard, delay*) заде́рж|ивать, -а́ть; **heavy rains ~ back the harvest** си́льные дожди́ задержа́ли созрева́ние (*or* убо́рку) урожа́я; (*postpone*) от|кла́дывать, -ложи́ть; *v.i.* возвра|ща́ться, -ти́ться; **~ by** *v.t.* (*save*) от|кда́дывать, -ложи́ть; **~ down** *v.t.* (*place on ground etc.*) класть, положи́ть на зе́млю; **~ your gun down!** бро́сьте ору́жие!; **~ one's foot down** (*be firm*) стоя́ть (*impf.*) на своём; (*accelerate*) нажа́ть (*pf.*) на газ; (*allow to alight*): **the bus stopped to ~ down passengers** авто́бус останови́лся, что́бы вы́садить пассажи́ров; (*make deposit of*) вн|оси́ть, -ести́ (*задаток*); (*lower, reduce*) сн|ижа́ть, -и́зить; (*bring in to land*): **the pilot ~ his machine down safely** пило́т благополу́чно посади́л маши́ну; (*repress*) подав|ля́ть, -и́ть; (*write down*) запи́с|ывать, -а́ть; **you may ~ me down for £5** я даю́ 5 фу́нтов; (*consider*) счита́ть (*impf.*); (*attribute*) припи́с|ывать, -а́ть; (*kill, of animals*) усып|ля́ть, -и́ть; **~ forth** *v.t.* (*exert*) напр|яга́ть, -я́чь; (*produce*): **the trees are ~ting forth new leaves** на дере́вьях распуска́ются но́вые ли́стья; **~ forward** *v.t.* (*advance*): **the clocks are ~ forward in spring** весно́й часы́ перево́дят вперёд; (*propose*) выдвига́ть, вы́двинуть; **his name was ~ forward** была́ вы́двинута его́ кандидату́ра; (*bring nearer*) передв|ига́ть, -и́нуть вперёд; **the meeting has been ~ forward to Tuesday** собра́ние перенесли́ на вто́рник; **~ in** *v.t.* (*cause to enter; insert*) вст|авля́ть, -а́вить; **he ~ his head in at the window** он всу́нул го́лову в окно́; (*instal*) вст|авля́ть, -а́вить; **they are ~ting in the telephone** они́ ста́вят себе́ телефо́н; (*submit, present*) под|ава́ть, -а́ть; **he is ~ting in a claim for damages** он предъявля́ет иск об убы́тках; **I ~ in an application** я по́да́л заявле́ние; **~ in an appearance** появ|ля́ться, -и́ться; (*work*): **I ~ in 6 hours today** я сего́дня отрабо́тал 6 часо́в; *v.i.* (*of boat or crew*) за|ходи́ть, -йти́ в порт; **~ off** *v.t.* (*postpone*) от|кла́дывать, -ложи́ть; (*cancel engagement with*) отмен|я́ть, -и́ть встре́чу с+*i.*; (*deter*) отпу́г|ивать, -ну́ть; **we were ~ off by the weather** мы переду́мали из-за пого́ды; (*repel*) отт|а́лкивать, -олкну́ть; **I was ~ off by his tactlessness** меня́ оттолкну́ла его́ беста́ктность; (*distract*): **I can't recite if you keep ~ting me off** я не могу́ деклами́ровать, когда́ вы меня́ отвлека́ете; (*allow to alight*): **will you ~ me off at the next stop?** вы мо́жете вы́садить меня́ на сле́дующей остано́вке?; **~ on** *v.t.* (*clothes etc.*) над|ева́ть, -е́ть; **you should ~ more clothes on** вы должны́ потепле́е оде́ться; (*place in position*): **~ the potatoes on (to boil)!** поста́вьте (вари́ть) карто́шку!; (*add*) приб|авля́ть, -а́вить; **he ~ more coal on** он подбро́сил у́гля; (*assume*): **he ~ on an air of innocence** он напусти́л на себя́ неви́нный вид; **she is fond of ~ting on airs** она́ лю́бит ва́жничать; (*increase*) увели́чи|вать, -ть; **you're ~ting on weight** вы полне́ете; (*light, radio etc.*) включ|а́ть, -и́ть; (*make available*) примен|я́ть, -и́ть; (*present*) ста́вить, по-; **the children are ~ting on a play** де́ти ста́вят пье́су; **she ~ on a first-class meal** она́ пригото́вила отли́чный обе́д/у́жин; (*advance*) передв|ига́ть, -и́нуть вперёд; **watches should be ~ on an hour** часы́ на́до перевести́ на час вперёд; (*stake*) ста́вить, по-; **~ out** *v.t.*: (*thrust out, eject*): **his family was ~ out into the street** его́ семью́ вы́бросили на у́лицу; (*extend, protrude*): **~ your tongue out!** покажи́те язы́к!; **he ~ out his hand in welcome** он протяну́л ру́ку для приве́тствия; **she opened the window and ~ her head out** она́ откры́ла окно́ и вы́сунула го́лову; **the snail ~ out its horns** ули́тка вы́пустила ро́жки; (*arrange so as to be seen*) выкла́дывать, вы́ложить; **the shopkeeper ~ out his best wares** ла́вочник вы́ложил/вы́ставил свой лу́чший това́р; (*hang up outside*) выве́шивать, вы́весить; **she ~ the washing out to dry** она́ разве́сила бельё суши́ться; (*produce*) выпуска́ть, вы́пустить; (*issue*) выпуска́ть, вы́пустить; **they ~ out invitations** они́ разосла́ли приглаше́ния; (*extinguish*) туши́ть, по-; гаси́ть, по-; **~ the lights out!** потуши́те свет!; **~ your cigarette out!** погаси́те сигаре́ту!; (*inconvenience*) наруш|а́ть, -и́ть пла́ны +*g.*; **would it ~ you out to come at 3?** вас не затрудни́т прийти́ в 3 часа́?; (*vex*) раздраж|а́ть, -и́ть; (*allow to alight*) опус|ка́ть, -ти́ть; **I asked the driver to ~ me out at the station** я попроси́л шофёра вы́садить меня́ у ста́нции; *v.i.*: **the lifeboat ~ out to sea** спаса́тельная шлю́пка вы́шла в мо́ре; **~ over** *v.t.* (*convey*) перед|ава́ть, -а́ть; **he ~ over his meaning effectively** он хорошо́ изложи́л свою́ мысль; **~ through** *v.t.* (*transact*) осуществ|ля́ть, -и́ть; выполня́ть, вы́полнить; (*connect by telephone*) соедин|я́ть, -и́ть; **~ together** *v.t.* (*bring close or into contact*) соедин|я́ть, -и́ть; (*assemble*) сост|авля́ть, -а́вить; (*construct from components*) соб|ира́ть, -ра́ть; (*collect*) соб|ира́ть, -ра́ть; **~ your things together ready for the journey!** соберите ве́щи в доро́гу!; **~ up** *v.t.* (*raise, hold up*) подн|има́ть, -я́ть; **~ up your hand if you know the answer!** кто зна́ет отве́т, подними́те ру́ку!; **~ your hands up!** (*coll.*) ру́ки вверх!; **~ one's feet up** полёживать (*impf.*); **he ~s my back up** (*coll.*) он меня́ раздража́ет; (*display*) выставля́ть, вы́ставить; (*erect*) возд|вига́ть, -и́гнуть; стро́ить, по-; **this house was ~ up in six weeks** э́тот дом постро́или за шесть неде́ль; (*increase*) пов|ыша́ть, -ы́сить; (*offer*) выдвига́ть, вы́двинуть; **he ~ up no resistance** он не оказа́л сопротивле́ния; **the house was ~ up for sale** объяви́ли о прода́же до́ма; (*propose*) выдвига́ть, вы́двинуть (в кандида́ты); (*supply*) вн|оси́ть, -ести́; **I will ~ up £1,000** я внесу́ ты́сячу фу́нтов; (*accommodate*): **he ~ me up for the night** я переночева́л у него́; *v.i.* (*stay*) остан|а́вливаться, -ови́ться; ночева́ть, пере-; (*tolerate*) мири́ться, при- (*с кем/чем*); **I won't ~ up with any nonsense** я не потерплю́ никаки́х глу́постей.

putative ['pju:tətɪv] *adj.* мни́мый, предполага́емый.

putrefaction [,pju:trɪ'fækʃ(ə)n] *n.* гние́ние; разложе́ние.

putrefy ['pju:trɪ,faɪ] *v.i.* гнить, с-.

putrid ['pju:trɪd] *adj.* (*decomposed*) гнило́й; (*coll., unpleasant*) отврати́тельный.

putsch [pʊtʃ] *n.* путч.

putty ['pʌtɪ] *n.* зама́зка; шпаклёвка.

puzzle ['pʌz(ə)l] *n.* зага́дка; головоло́мка.

v.t. озада́чи|вать, -ть; прив|оди́ть, -ести́ в недоуме́ние.

v.i.: **he ~d over the problem all night** он всю ночь би́лся над э́той зада́чей.

with adv.: **~ out** *v.t.* разгада́ть (*pf.*).

PVC (*abbr. of* ***polyvinyl chloride***) ПХВ, (полихлорвини́л).

pygmy ['pɪgmɪ] *n.* пигме́й.

pyjamas [pɪ'dʒɑ:məz, pə-] (*US* **pajamas**) *n.* пижа́ма.

pylon ['paɪlən, -lɒn] *n.* столб, пило́н.

pyramid ['pɪrəmɪd] *n.* (*lit., fig.*) пирами́да.

pyramidal [pɪ'ræmɪd(ə)l] *adj.* пирамида́льный.

pyre ['paɪə(r)] *n.* погреба́льный костёр.

Pyrenees [,pɪrə'ni:z] *n.* Пирене́|и (*pl., g.* -ев).

pyromaniac [,paɪərəʊ'meɪnɪ,æk] *n.* пирома́н.

pyrotechnics [,paɪərəʊ'teknɪks] *n.* пироте́хника.

Pyrrhic ['pɪrɪk] *adj.*: **a ~ victory** пи́ррова побе́да.

Pythagoras [paɪ'θægərəs] *n.*: **~' theorem** теоре́ма Пифаго́ра.

python ['paɪθ(ə)n] *n.* пито́н.

Q

QC (*abbr. of* ***Queen's Counsel***) адвока́т вы́сшего ра́нга.

QED (*abbr. of* ***quod erat demonstrandum***) что и тре́бовалось доказа́ть.

quack[1] [kwæk] *n.* (*sound*) кря́канье.

v.i. кря́кать (*impf.*).

quack[2] [kwæk] *n.* (*bogus doctor etc.*) шарлата́н.

quackery ['kwækərɪ] *n.* шарлата́нство.

quadrangle ['kwɒd,ræŋg(ə)l] *n.* (*courtyard*) четырёхуго́льный дво́р.

quadrant ['kwɒdrənt] *n.* квадра́нт.

quadratic [kwɒ'drætɪk] *adj.* квадра́тный.

quadrilateral [,kwɒdrɪ'lætər(ə)l] *n.* четырёхуго́льник.

adj. четырёхсторо́нный.

quadruped ['kwɒdrʊ,ped] *n.* четвероно́гое (живо́тное).

quadruple ['kwɒdrʊp(ə)l] *adj.* (*fourfold*) учетверённый; **his income is ~ mine** его́ дохо́д бо́льше моего́ в четы́ре ра́за.

v.t. учетвер|я́ть, -и́ть.

v.i. увели́|чиваться, -ться в четы́ре ра́за.

quadruplets ['kwɒdrʊplɪts, 'kwɒ'dru:plɪts] *n.* четверня́.

quaff [kwɒf, kwɑ:f] *v.t. & i.* пить, вы́- за́лпом.

quagmire ['kwɒg,maɪə(r), 'kwæg-] *n.* боло́то.

quail[1] [kweɪl] *n.* пе́репел.

quail[2] [kweɪl] *v.i.* тру́сить, с-; па́дать (*impf.*) ду́хом.

quaint [kweɪnt] *adj.* причу́дливый, чудно́й, курьёзный.

quak|e [kweɪk] *n.* (*coll., earth~*) землетрясе́ние.

v.i. дрожа́ть (*impf.*); содрог|а́ться, -ну́ться.

Quaker ['kweɪkə(r)] *n.* ква́кер (*fem.* -ша); (*attr.*) ква́керский.

qualification [,kwɒlɪfɪ'keɪʃ(ə)n] *n.* **1.** (*modification, limiting factor*) ограниче́ние, огово́рка; **without ~** безогово́рочно. **2.** (*required quality*) квалифика́ция.

qualif|y ['kwɒlɪ,faɪ] *v.t.* **1.** (*render fit*) де́лать, с- приго́дным; **I am not ~ied to advise you ~** я недоста́точно компете́нтен, что́бы дава́ть вам сове́ты; **~ying examination** отбо́рочный экза́мен; **he is a ~ied doctor** он дипломи́рованный врач. **2.** (*limit, modify*) ум|еньша́ть, -е́ньшить; ум|еря́ть, -е́рить; **I must ~y my statement** я до́лжен сде́лать огово́рку. **3.** (*describe*) определ|я́ть, -и́ть; **adjectives ~y nouns** прилага́тельные определя́ют существи́тельные.

v.i.: **he will ~y after three years** че́рез три го́да он полу́чит дипло́м; **will you ~y for a pension?** бу́дет ли вам причита́ться пе́нсия?

qualitative ['kwɒlɪtətɪv, -,teɪtɪv] *adj.* ка́чественный.

quality ['kwɒlɪtɪ] *n.* **1.** (*degree of merit*) ка́чество; **of poor ~** ни́зкого ка́чества; (*excellence*) доброка́чественность; **~ goods** высокока́чественные това́ры. **2.** (*faculty, characteristic, attribute*) ка́чество, сво́йство; **he has the ~ of inspiring confidence** он облада́ет сво́йством внуша́ть дове́рие; **he has many good qualities** у него́ мно́го це́нных ка́честв.

adj. (высоко)ка́чественный; **~ newspapers** «соли́дные» газе́ты.

qualm [kwɑ:m, kwɔ:m] *n.* сомне́ние, колеба́ние; **~s of conscience** угрызе́ния (*nt. pl.*) со́вести.

quandary ['kwɒndərɪ] *n.* затрудни́тельное положе́ние.

quango ['kwæŋgəʊ] *n.* полуавтоно́мная организа́ция.

quantify ['kwɒntɪ,faɪ] *v.t.* (*determine quantity of*) определ|я́ть, -и́ть коли́чество *+g.*; (*express as quantity*) выража́ть, вы́разить коли́чественно.

quantitative ['kwɒntɪtətɪv, -,teɪtɪv] *adj.* коли́чественный.

quantit|y ['kwɒntɪtɪ] *n.* **1.** (*measurable property*) коли́чество. **2.** (*thg. having ~y*) величина́; число́; **unknown ~y** (*math.*) неизве́стное; (*pers.*) челове́к-зага́дка. **3.** (*sum or amount*) до́ля; часть; **she buys in small ~ies** она́ покупа́ет понемно́гу; (*considerable sum or amount*) большо́е коли́чество.

quantum ['kwɒntəm] *n.* (*phys.*) квант; **~ leap** ква́нтовый скачо́к; **~ theory** ква́нтовая тео́рия.

quarantine ['kwɒrən,ti:n] *n.* каранти́н.

v.t. содержа́ть (*impf.*) в каранти́не.

quarrel ['kwɒr(ə)l] *n.* **1.** (*altercation*, *contention*) ссо́ра. **2.** (*cause for complaint*) по́вод для ссо́ры; **I have no ~ with him on that score** у меня́ нет к нему́ прете́нзии по э́тому по́воду.

v.t. (*contend*, *dispute*) ссо́риться, по-; (*take issue*) спо́рить, по-.

quarrelsome ['kwɒrəlsəm] *adj.* сварли́вый.

quarry[1] ['kwɒrɪ] *n.* (*object of pursuit*; *prey*) добы́ча.

quarry[2] ['kwɒrɪ] *n.* (*for stone etc.*) каменоло́мня.

v.t. (*extract*) доб|ыва́ть, -ы́ть.

cpd. **~man** *n.* каменобо́ец, каменотёс.

quart [kwɔːt] *n.* ква́рта.

quarter ['kwɔːtə(r)] *n.* **1.** (*fourth part*) че́тверть; (*of hour*): **a ~ to six** без че́тверти шесть; **a ~ past six** че́тверть седьмо́го; **an hour and a ~** час с че́твертью; **a ~ of an hour later** на пятна́дцать мину́т по́зже; (*of year*) кварта́л. **2.** (*part of animal*) часть; **fore/hind ~s** пере́дняя/за́дняя часть; **the dog got up on its hind ~s** соба́ка вста́ла на за́дние ла́пы. **3.** (*US coin*) два́дцать пять це́нтов. **4.** (*fig.*, *direction*, *place*) ме́сто; **the boys came running from every ~** ма́льчики бежа́ли со всех сторо́н; **there is a belief in certain ~s that ...** в не́которых круга́х счита́ется, что... **5.** (*district of town*) кварта́л; **residential ~** жило́й кварта́л. **6.** (*pl.*, *lodgings*) каза́рмы (*f. pl.*); кварти́ры (*f. pl.*); **the army went into winter ~s** а́рмия перешла́ на зи́мние кварти́ры. **7.**: **at close ~s** в те́сном сосе́дстве, вблизи́; **they were fighting at close ~s** они́ вели́ бли́жный бой. **8.** (*mercy*) поща́да; **no ~ was asked and none was given** никто́ поща́ды не проси́л, никто́ поща́ды не дава́л.

v.t. **1.** (*divide into four*) дели́ть, раз- на четы́ре ча́сти. **2.** (*put into lodgings*) расквартиро́в|ывать, -а́ть.

cpds. **~-deck** *n.* квартерде́к; **~-final** *n.* четвертьфина́л; **~master** *n.* квартирме́йстер.

quarterly ['kwɔːtəlɪ] *n.* (*periodical*) ежекварта́льное изда́ние.

adj. кварта́льный; **~ payment** поквarта́льная вы́плата; вы́плата раз в три ме́сяца.

adv. ежекварта́льно; раз в три ме́сяца.

quartet(te) [kwɔː'tet] *n.* кварте́т.

quarto ['kwɔːtəʊ] *n.* (*size of paper*) (ин-)ква́рто (*indecl.*).

quartz [kwɔːts] *n.* кварц; (*attr.*) ква́рцевый.

quasar ['kweɪzɑː(r), -sɑː(r)] *n.* кваза́р.

quash [kwɒʃ] *v.t.* (*cancel*) отмен|я́ть, -и́ть; аннули́ровать (*impf.*, *pf.*); (*crush*) подав|ля́ть, -и́ть.

quatrain ['kwɒtreɪn] *n.* четверости́шие.

quaver ['kweɪvə(r)] *n.* **1.** (*trembling tone*) дрожа́ние. **2.** (*mus.*) восьма́я но́та.

v.i. дрожа́ть (*impf.*); вибри́ровать (*impf.*).

quay [kiː] *n.* прича́л; на́бережная.

cpd. **~side** *n.* при́стань.

queasiness ['kwiːzɪnɪs] *n.* тошнота́.

queasy ['kwiːzɪ] *adj.* подве́рженный тошноте́; **my stomach feels a little ~** меня́ немно́го тошни́т.

queen [kwiːn] *n.* **1.** короле́ва; **~ consort** супру́га пра́вящего короля́; **~ dowager** вдо́вствующая короле́ва; **~ mother** короле́ва-мать. **2.** (*fig.*) боги́ня, короле́ва, цари́ца; **beauty ~** короле́ва красоты́. **3.** (**~ *bee***, **~ *wasp***, **~ *ant***) ма́тка. **4.** (*at chess*) ферзь (*m.*); **~'s pawn** фе́рзевая пе́шка. **5.** (*at cards*) да́ма; **~ of hearts** черво́нная да́ма. **6.**: **Q~'s Counsel** адвока́т вы́сшего ра́нга; **he can't speak the Q~'s English** он не уме́ет пра́вильно говори́ть по-англи́йски; *see also* **king**

queer [kwɪə(r)] *n.* (*sl.*, *pej.*, *homosexual*) педера́ст, (*coll.*) пе́дик.

adj. (*strange*, *odd*) стра́нный; чудакова́тый; **he's a ~ customer** он стра́нный тип; (*causing suspicion*) подозри́тельный, сомни́тельный; (*unwell*) недомога́ющий; **the heat is making me feel ~** мне нехорошо́ от жары́; (*homosexual*) гомосексуа́льный.

quell [kwel] *v.t.* подав|ля́ть, -и́ть.

quench [kwentʃ] *v.t.* (*extinguish*) гаси́ть, по-; туши́ть, по-; (*slake*): **~ one's thirst** утол|я́ть, -и́ть жа́жду.

querulous ['kwerʊləs] *adj.* ворчли́вый.

quer|y ['kwɪərɪ] *n.* вопро́с.

v.t. **1.** (*ask*, *inquire*) осв|едомля́ться, -е́домиться. **2.** (*call in question*) выража́ть, вы́разить сомне́ние в+*p.*; **he ~ied my reasons for coming** он усомни́лся в причи́нах моего́ прихо́да.

quest [kwest] *n.* по́иски (*m. pl.*); **the ~ for happiness** пого́ня за сча́стьем; **he went in ~ of food** он отпра́вился на по́иски еды́.

question ['kwestʃ(ə)n] *n.* **1.** (*interrogation*; *problem*) вопро́с; **I put the ~ to him** я за́дал ему́ вопро́с; **a leading ~** наводя́щий вопро́с; **a good ~!** зако́нный/толко́вый вопро́с!; **a holiday is out of the ~** об о́тпуске не мо́жет быть и ре́чи; **that's not the ~** не в э́том де́ло; **the man in ~** челове́к, о кото́ром идёт речь; **his wishes do not come into ~** его́ жела́ния тут ни при чём. **2.** (*doubt*, *objection*) сомне́ние; **his veracity is open to ~** его́ правди́вость ещё под вопро́сом; **without, beyond ~** бесспо́рно; **there is no ~ of his not succeeding** его́ успе́х не подлежи́т сомне́нию

v.t. **1.** (*interrogate*) допр|а́шивать, -оси́ть; **I ~ed him closely on his theory** я подро́бно расспра́шивал его́ о его́ тео́рии. **2.** (*cast doubt on*) сомнева́ться (*impf.*) в+*p.*; осп|а́ривать, -о́рить.

cpds. **~-mark** *n.* вопроси́тельный знак; **~-master** *n.* веду́щий виктори́ну (*or* в виктори́не).

questionable ['kwestʃənəb(ə)l] *adj.* (*doubtful*) сомни́тельный; ненадёжный; (*disreputable*) сомни́тельный, подозри́тельный.

questioner ['kwestʃənə(r)] *n.* интервьюе́р.

questionnaire [ˌkwestʃə'neə(r)] *n.* анке́та, вопро́сник.

queue [kjuː] *n.* о́чередь.

v.i. (*also* **~ up**) станови́ться (*impf.*) в о́чередь.

quibble ['kwɪb(ə)l] *n.* увёртка.

v.i. уви́л|ивать, -ьну́ть; **I won't ~ over 20p** я не бу́ду пререка́ться из-за двадцати́ пе́нсов.

quick [kwɪk] *n.*: **he bit his nails to the ~** он искуса́л но́гти до кро́ви; **his words cut me to the ~** его́ слова́ заде́ли меня́ за живо́е.

adj. **1.** (*rapid*) бы́стрый, ско́рый; **this is the ~est way home** э́то са́мая коро́ткая доро́га домо́й; **be ~ about it!** потороп́итесь!; **~ march!** ша́гом — марш!; **we got there in double ~ time** мы добрали́сь туда́ в два счёта. **2.** (*lively*, *prompt*) бы́стрый; живо́й; (*of mind*) сообрази́тельный; **he has a ~ temper** он вспы́льчив; **she is ~ to take offence** она́ о́чень оби́дчива.

adv. бы́стро; **~, get a doctor!** скоре́е позови́те врача́!; **I'll come as ~ as I can** я приду́, как то́лько смогу́.

cpds. **~lime** *n.* негашёная и́звесть; **~sand(s)** *n.* зыбу́чий песо́к; **~silver** *n.* ртуть; **~step** *n.* (*dance*) куик-сте́п; **~-tempered** *adj.* вспы́льчивый; **~-witted** *adj.* смышлёный, нахо́дчивый.

quicken ['kwɪkən] *v.t.* (*make quicker*) уск|оря́ть, -о́рить; **he ~ed his pace** он приба́вил ша́гу; (*stimulate*) возбу|жда́ть, -ди́ть.

v.i. уск|оря́ться, -о́риться; **her pulse ~ed** её пульс уско́рился/участи́лся.

quickness ['kwɪknɪs] *n.* быстрота́; (*of eye*, *ear etc.*) острота́; (*of mind*) сообрази́тельность.

quid [kwɪd] *n.* (*coll.*, *£1*) фунт (сте́рлингов).

quid pro quo [ˌkwɪd prəʊ 'kwəʊ] *n.* услу́га за услу́гу.

quiescence [kwɪ'es(ə)ns] *n.* неподви́жность; безде́йствие.

quiescent [kwɪ'es(ə)nt] *adj.* неподви́жный; безде́йствующий.

quiet ['kwaɪət] *n.* (*stillness, silence*) тишинá; **absolute ~ reigned** царúло пóлное спокóйствие; (*repose*) покóй, спокóйствие; **there is peace and ~ in the countryside** в дерéвне тишинá и покóй.

adj. **1.** (*making little or no sound*) тúхий; бесшýмный; **a ~ room** тúхий нóмер; **be ~!** помолчúте!; **can't you keep ~?** не мóжете ли вы помолчáть?; **the baby was ~ at last** наконéц младéнец утúх. **2.** (*undisturbed*) спокóйный; мúрный; **we had a ~ night** ночь прошлá спокóйно. **3.** (*of gentle or inactive disposition*) спокóйный; тúхий. **4.** (*private; concealed*) тáйный; скры́тый; **keep it ~!** об э́том молчóк!; **on the ~** (*secretly*) тайкóм; (*in confidence*) под секрéтом. **5.** (*informal, unostentatious*) скрóмный.

v.t. успок|áивать, -óить.

int. тúше!

quieten ['kwaɪət(ə)n] *v.t. & i.* (*also* **~ down**) успок|áивать(ся), -óить(ся).

quietness ['kwaɪətnɪs] *n.* (*stillness*) тишинá; (*repose*) покóй; (*of manner, character*) невозмутúмость.

quietude ['kwaɪɪ,tju:d] *n.* (*liter.*) покóй, спокóйствие.

quiff [kwɪf] *n.* чёлка; (*tuft*) зачёс.

quill [kwɪl] *n.* (*feather*) птúчье перó; (**~ pen**) гусúное перó; (*of porcupine*) иглá (дикобрáза).

quilt [kwɪlt] *n.* стёганое одея́ло.

v.t. стегáть, вы-/про-; **a ~ed dressing-gown** стёганый халáт.

quince [kwɪns] *n.* (*fruit, tree*) айвá; (*attr.*) айвóвый.

quinine ['kwɪni:n, -'ni:n] *n.* хинúн.

quintessence [kwɪn'tes(ə)ns] *n.* квинтэссéнция.

quintet(te) [kwɪn'tet] *n.* квинтéт.

quintuplet ['kwɪntjʊplɪt, -'tju:plɪt] *n.* одúн из пятú близнецóв.

quip [kwɪp] *n.* остротá, крáсное словцó.

v.i. острúть, с-.

quire ['kwaɪə(r)] *n.* (*of paper*) десть.

quirk [kwɜ:k] *n.* (*oddity*) причýда; **through some ~ of fate** по капри́зу судьбы́.

quirky ['kwɜ:kɪ] *adj.* с причýдами.

quisling ['kwɪzlɪŋ] *n.* квúслинг, предáтель (*m.*).

quit [kwɪt] *v.t.* **1.** (*leave*) ост|авля́ть, -áвить. **2.** (*coll., stop*) прекра|щáть, -тúть; бр|осáть, -óсить; (*US*): **~ grumbling!** брóсьте ворчáть!

v.i. **1.** (*leave premises, job etc.*): **the tenant was asked to ~** жильцá попросúли съéхать с квартúры; **the maid was given notice to ~** гóрничную предупредúли об увольнéнии. **2.** (*leave off*) перест|авáть, -áть.

quite [kwaɪt] *adv.* **1.** (*entirely*) совсéм, совершéнно, вполнé; **I ~ agree** я вполнé соглáсен; **~ right!** совершéнно вéрно!; **~!** безуслóвно!, несомнéнно!, вéрно!; **that is ~ another matter** э́то совсéм другóе дéло; **I am not ~ myself today** я немнóго не в себé сегóдня. **2.** (*to a certain extent*) довóльно, вполнé; **it is ~ cold here** здéсь довóльно хóлодно; **~ a few** довóльно мнóго; немáло.

quits [kwɪts] *pred. adj.*: **I will be ~ with you yet** я ещё с вáми расквитáюсь; **now we are ~** тепéрь мы квúты; **he decided to cry ~** он решúл пойтú на мировýю.

quiver[1] ['kwɪvə(r)] *n.* (*for arrows*) колчáн.

quiver[2] ['kwɪvə(r)] *n.* (*vibration*) дрожь.

v.i. дрожáть, за-; трястúсь, за-.

quixotic [kwɪk'sɒtɪk] *adj.* донкихóтский.

quiz [kwɪz] *n.* (*interrogation*) опрóс; (*test of knowledge*) сéрия вопрóсов; (*entertainment*) викторúна.

v.t. (*interrogate*) выспрáшивать, вы́спросить.

cpd. **~-master** *n.* ведýщий викторúну.

quizzical ['kwɪzɪk(ə)l] *adj.* насмéшливый, иронúческий.

quoit [kɔɪt] *n.* метáтельное кольцó; **~s** (*game*) метáние колéц в цель.

quorum ['kwɔ:rəm] *n.*квóрум.

quota ['kwəʊtə] *n.* квóта, нóрма.

quotation [kwəʊ'teɪʃ(ə)n] *n.* **1.** (*quoting*) цитúрование; **~ marks** кавы́ч|ки (*pl., g.* -ек); (*passage quoted*) цитáта. **2.** (*estimate of cost*) ценá, расцéнка.

quot|e [kwəʊt] *n.* **1.** (*coll., quotation*) цитáта. **2.** (*pl., coll., quotation marks*) кавы́ч|ки (*pl., g.* -ек).

v.t. **1.** (*repeat words of*) цитúровать, про-; **can I ~e you on that?** могý ли я сослáться на вáши словá?. **2.** (*adduce*) ссылáться, сослáться на+*a.*; **can you ~ an instance?** мóжете ли вы привестú примéр? **3.**: **~ a price** назн|ачáть, -áчить цéну.

quotient ['kwəʊʃ(ə)nt] *n.* чáстное; **intelligence ~** коэффициéнт врождённых ýмственных спосóбностей.

q.v. (*abbr. of* ***quod vide***) см., (смотрú) (*там-то*).

R

R [ɑ:(r)] *n.*: **the three ~s** ≃ азы́ (*m. pl.*) наýки.

rabbi ['ræbaɪ] *n.* раввúн.

rabbinical [rə'bɪnɪk(ə)l] *adj.* раввúнский.

rabbit ['ræbɪt] *n.* **1.** крóлик. **2.**: **Welsh ~** (*also* **rarebit**) гренóк с сы́ром.

v.i. **1.** (*hunt ~s*) охóтиться (*impf.*) на зáйцев. **2.** (*babble*) трепáться (*impf.*) (*coll.*).

cpds. **~-hole** *n.* крóличья норá; **~-hutch** *n.* крóличья клéтка; **~-warren** *n.* крольчáтник; (*fig.*) лабиpúнт.

rabble ['ræb(ə)l] *n.* сброд, чернь.

rabid ['ræbɪd, 'reɪ-] *adj.* **1.** (*affected with rabies*) бéшеный. **2.** (*furious, violent*) бéшеный, я́ростный. **3.** (*extremist*): **a ~ socialist** оголтéлый социалúст.

rabies ['reɪbi:z] *n.* бéшенство, водобоя́знь.

RAC (*abbr. of* ***Royal Automobile Club***) Королéвский автомобúльный клуб.

race[1] [reɪs] *n.* **1.** (*contest*) бег на скóрость, гóнка; забéг; **(horse-)~s** скáчки (*f. pl.*); **let's have a ~** давáйте побежúм наперегóнки; **it was a ~ against time** врéмени бы́ло в обрéз. **2.** (*swift current*) бы́стрый потóк.

v.t. **1.** (*compete in speed with*): **I'll ~ you to the corner** посмóтрим, кто быстрée добежúт до углá. **2.** (*cause to move fast*): **they ~d the bill through** онú в спéшном поря́дке протащúли билль чéрез парлáмент; **~ an engine** перегру|жáть, -зúть мотóр.

v.i. **1.** (*compete in speed*) состязáться (*impf.*) в скóрости. **2.** (*participate in horse-racing*) учáствовать (*impf.*) в скáчках. **3.** (*move at speed*) нестúсь (*impf.*); мчáться, по-.

cpds. **~course** *n.* ипподрóм; **~horse** *n.* скаковáя лóшадь; **~-meeting** *n.* день (*m.*) скáчек; **~-track** *n.* трéк; автомотодрóм.

race[2] [reɪs] *n.* плéмя (*nt.*), род; **the human ~** род людскóй; (*descent*) происхождéние; (*ethnic*) рáса; (*attr.*) рáсовый.

raceme [rə'si:m] *n.* гроздь (*m.*), кисть.

racer ['reɪsə(r)] *n.* (*pers.*) гóнщик, (*rider*) наéздник; (*horse*) скаковáя лóшадь; (*car, yacht etc.*) гóночная машúна/я́хта *и т.п.*

racial ['reɪʃ(ə)l] *adj.* рáсовый.

raci|alism ['reɪʃə,lɪz(ə)m], **-sm** ['reɪsɪz(ə)m] *nn.* раси́зм.
raci|alist ['reɪʃə,lɪst], **-st** ['reɪsɪst] *nn.* раси́ст.
rack[1] [ræk] *n.* **1.** (*frame*) сто́йка с по́лками; стелла́ж; (*plate-~*) подста́вка для посу́ды; (*hat-~*) ве́шалка; (*luggage-~ for travellers*) се́тка. **2.** (*toothed bar*) зубча́тая ре́йка.
rack[2] [ræk] *n.* (*instrument of torture*) ды́ба.
v.t. (*torture*) му́чить, и́з-; терза́ть, ис-; **he was ~ed with pain** он ко́рчился от бо́ли; (*fig.*): **I ~ed my brains for an answer** я лома́л го́лову над отве́том.
rack[3] [ræk] *n.* (*destruction*): **everything went to ~ and ruin** всё пошло́ пра́хом.
racket ['rækɪt] *n.* (*for tennis etc.*) раке́тка.
racket[2] ['rækɪt] *n.* **1.** (*din, uproar*) шум, гам. **2.** (*coll., dishonest scheme or system*) жу́льническое предприя́тие, надува́тельство; (*extortion*) вымога́тельство.
racketeer [,rækɪ'tɪə(r)] *n.* афери́ст, рэкети́р.
raconteur [,rækɒn'tɜ:(r)] *n.* хоро́ший расска́зчик.
rac|oon, -coon [rə'ku:n] *n.* ено́т.
racy ['reɪsɪ] *adj.* (*piquant, lively*) о́стрый, пря́ный; **a ~ style** бо́йкий/я́ркий стиль.
RADA ['rɑ:də] *n.* (*abbr. of* ***Royal Academy of Dramatic Art***) Короле́вская акаде́мия театра́льного иску́сства.
radar ['reɪdɑ:(r)] *n.* (*system*) радиолока́ция; (*apparatus*) радиолока́тор; (*attr.*) радиолокацио́нный.
radial ['reɪdɪəl] *adj.* радиа́льный; (*anat.*) лучево́й.
radiance ['reɪdɪəns] *n.* сия́ние, блеск; **the sun's ~** со́лнечное сия́ние.
radiant ['reɪdɪənt] *adj.* **1.** (*lit., fig.*) сия́ющий; **she was ~ with happiness** она́ сия́ла от сча́стья; **he is in ~ health** он пы́шет здоро́вьем. **2.** (*transmitted by radiation*) лучи́стый; **~ heat** теплово́е излуче́ние.
radiate ['reɪdɪ,eɪt] *v.t. & i.* излуч|а́ть(ся), -и́ть(ся); (*fig.*): **his face ~d happiness** его́ лицо́ свети́лось ра́достью.
radiation [,reɪdɪ'eɪʃ(ə)n] *n.* радиа́ция, излуче́ние; **~ treatment** радиотерапи́я; **~ sickness** лучева́я боле́знь.
radiator ['reɪdɪ,eɪtə(r)] *n.* батаре́я, радиа́тор.
radical ['rædɪk(ə)l] *n.* (*math., philol.*) ко́рень (*m.*); (*pol.*) радика́л.
adj. (*fundamental*) коренно́й; (*pol.*) радика́льный.
radicalism ['rædɪkə,lɪz(ə)m] *n.* радикали́зм.
radio ['reɪdɪəʊ] *n.* (*means of communication*) ра́дио (*indecl.*); (*broadcasting system*) радиовеща́ние; (*receiving apparatus*) радиоприёмник; **~ car** радиофици́рованный автомоби́ль; **~ cassette (recorder)** магнито́ла; **~ ham** радиолюби́тель (*m.*); **~ programme** радиопереда́ча.
v.t. **1.** (*send by ~*) перед|ава́ть, -а́ть (по ра́дио). **2.** (*contact by ~*) ради́ровать (*pf.*) +*d.*
radioactive [,reɪdɪəʊ'æktɪv] *adj.* радиоакти́вный.
radioactivity [,reɪdɪəʊæk'tɪvɪtɪ] *n.* радиоакти́вность.
radiocarbon [,reɪdɪəʊ'kɑ:bən] *n.* радиоакти́вный углеро́д; **~ dating** дати́ровка радиоуглеро́дным ме́тодом.
radiogram ['reɪdɪəʊ,græm] *n.* (*picture*) рентгеногра́мма; (*gramophone with radio*) радио́ла.
radiography [,reɪdɪ'ɒgrəfɪ] *n.* радиогра́фия.
radiologist [,reɪdɪ'ɒlədʒɪst] *n.* радио́лог, рентгено́лог.
radiotherapy [,reɪdɪəʊ'θerəpɪ] *n.* лучева́я терапи́я.
radish ['rædɪʃ] *n.* реди́ска.
radium ['reɪdɪəm] *n.* ра́дий.
radius ['reɪdɪəs] *n.* ра́диус; (*anat.*) лучева́я кость; **within a ~ of** в ра́диусе +*g.*
RAF (*abbr. of* ***Royal Air Force***) ВВС (*f. pl.*) (вое́нно-возду́шные си́лы) Великобрита́нии.
raffia ['ræfɪə] *n.* ра́ффия.
raffle ['ræf(ə)l] *n.* лотере́я.
v.t. (*also* **~ off**) разы́гр|ывать, -а́ть в лотере́е.
raft [rɑ:ft] *n.* (сплавно́й) плот.
rag[1] [ræg] *n.* **1.** (*small, esp. torn, piece of cloth*) тря́пка, лоску́т; **they tore his shirt to ~s** они́ разорва́ли его́ руба́шку в кло́чья; (*pl., torn or tattered clothing*) лохмо́ть|я (*pl., g.* -ев); отре́пья (*nt. pl.*). **2.** (*pej. or joc., garment*) тря́пки (*f. pl.*); **the ~ trade** (*coll.*) шве́йная промы́шленность; **glad ~s** (*coll.*) пара́дное облаче́ние. **3.** (*pej., newspaper*) газетёнка.
cpds. **~-(and-bone-)man** *n.* старьёвщик; **~bag** *n.* (*fig.*) вся́кая вся́чина; **~-doll** *n.* тряпи́чная ку́кла; **~time** *n.* ре́гтайм.
rag[2] [ræg] *n.* (*students' prank*) подтру́нивание, прока́зы (*f. pl.*).
v.t. (*play prank on; tease*) разы́гр|ывать, -а́ть; изводи́ть (*impf.*).
ragamuffin ['rægə,mʌfɪn] *n.* оборва́нец.
rag|e [reɪdʒ] *n.* **1.** (*violent anger*) я́рость, гнев; **he flew into a ~e** он пришёл в я́рость. **2.** (*dominant fashion*) после́дний крик мо́ды.
v.i.: **he ~ed at his wife** он наки́нулся на свою́ жену́; **the wind ~ed all day** ве́тер бушева́л весь день; **a ~ing torrent** бушу́ющий пото́к; **a ~ing thirst** мучи́тельная жа́жда.
ragged ['rægɪd] *adj.* **1.** (*torn, frayed*) рва́ный, потрёпанный; (*wearing torn clothes*) обо́рванный. **2.** (*rough or uneven in outline*): **a ~ beard** косма́тая борода́; **~ clouds** рва́ные облака́.
raglan ['ræglən] *n.*: **~ sleeve** рука́в регла́н.
ragout [ræ'gu:] *n.* рагу́ (*nt. indecl.*).
raid [reɪd] *n.* налёт, набе́г, рейд; **the police made a ~ on the club** поли́ция нагря́нула в клуб; **there was a ~ on sterling** была́ сде́лана попы́тка подорва́ть курс фу́нта.
v.t.: **our bombers ~ed Hamburg** на́ши бомбардиро́вщики соверши́ли налёт на Га́мбург; **the flat was ~ed in his absence** в его́ отсу́тствие кварти́ру огра́били.
raider ['reɪdə(r)] *n.* (*criminal*) налётчик, граби́тель (*m.*).
rail[1] [reɪl] *n.* **1.**(*bar for protection, support etc.*) перекла́дина; (*of staircase*) пери́л|а (*pl., g.* —); **~ fence** огра́да. **2.** (*of railway or tram track*) рельс; **the train ran off the ~s** по́езд сошёл с ре́льсов; (*railway transport*): **by ~** по́ездом.
v.t.: **~ in** огор|а́живать, -оди́ть; **~ off** отгор|а́живать, -оди́ть.
cpds. **~car** *n.* дрези́на; **~road** *n.* (*US*) желе́зная доро́га; *v.t.* (*coll.*): **they were ~roaded into agreement** их с хо́ду втяну́ли в соглаше́ние; **~way** *n.* (*track, system, company*) желе́зная доро́га; (*attr.*) железнодоро́жный; **~wayman** *n.* железнодоро́жник.
rail[2] [reɪl] *v.i.* (*liter.*) руга́ться (*impf.*); **he ~ed at me** он стал на меня́ ора́ть; **it's no use ~ing against the system** како́й смы́сл поноси́ть систе́му?
railing(s) ['reɪlɪŋs] *n.* и́згородь, огра́да.
rain [reɪn] *n.* дождь (*m.*); **I was caught in the ~** я попа́л под дождь; **I think I felt a drop of ~** вро́де начина́ет накра́пывать; **a shower of ~** ли́вень (*m.*); **a light ~ was falling** мороси́л до́ждик; **~ or shine** в любу́ю пого́ду; **as right as ~** в по́лном поря́дке; **a ~ of bullets** град пуль.
v.t.: **it is ~ing cats and dogs** льёт как из ведра́; (*fig.*): **she ~ed blows on his head** она́ колоти́ла его́ по голове́.
v.i.: **it is ~ing** дождь идёт; **it was ~ing hard** шёл си́льный/проливно́й дождь.
with adv.: **~ off** *v.t.*: **the match was ~ed off** матч был со́рван из-за́ дождя́.
cpds. **~bow** *n.* ра́дуга; **~-cloud** *n.* ту́ча; **~coat** *n.* плащ; **~drop** *n.* ка́пля дождя́; **~fall** *n.* оса́дк|и (*pl., g.* -ов); **~proof** *adj.* непромока́емый; **~storm** *n.* гроза́; **~-water** *n.* дождева́я вода́; **~wear** *n.* непромока́емая оде́жда и о́бувь.

rainforest ['reɪn,fɒrɪst] *n.* тропи́ческий лес.

rainy ['reɪnɪ] *adj.* дождли́вый; **you should save for a ~ day** вы должны́ откла́дывать на чёрный день.

raise [reɪz] *n.* (*US, rise in salary*) приба́вка; (*increase in stake or bid*) повыше́ние.

v.t. **1.** (*lift; cause to rise*) подн|има́ть, -я́ть; **the anchor was ~d** я́корь был по́днят; **he ~d his hat** он припо́днял шля́пу; (*make higher*) пов|ыша́ть, -ы́сить; **the news ~d my hopes** изве́стие укрепи́ло мои́ наде́жды; (*make louder*): **don't ~ your voice** не повыша́йте го́лос; (*cause to stand*): **I ~d him from his knees** я помо́г ему́ подня́ться с коле́н; (*arouse*): **the heat ~d blisters on his skin** от жары́ он весь покры́лся волдыря́ми; **the carriage ~d a cloud of dust** каре́та подняла́ о́блако пы́ли; (*fig.*): **he ~d hell** он устро́ил стра́шный сканда́л; (*elevate*): **he was ~d to the peerage** его́ произвели́ в пэ́ры; (*erect*): **a monument was ~d to his memory** ему́ был воздви́гнут па́мятник. **2.** (*bring up*): **may I ~ one question?** мо́жно мне зада́ть вопро́с?; **several objections were ~d** бы́ло сде́лано не́сколько возраже́ний; (*evoke*): **you ~d a doubt in my mind** вы зарони́ли мне в ду́шу сомне́ние; (*summon up*): **I couldn't ~ a smile** я не мог себя́ заста́вить улыбну́ться; **he could hardly ~ the energy to get up** он е́ле собра́лся с си́лами, что́бы встать. **3.** (*give voice to*): **she ~d the alarm** она́ подняла́ трево́гу. **4.** (*collect, procure*): **she ~d money for charity** она́ собрала́ де́ньги на благотвори́тельные це́ли; **I tried to ~ a loan** я попыта́лся взять де́ньги в долг; **he couldn't ~ enough money for a meal** он не смог раздобы́ть доста́точно де́нег, что́бы пое́сть; (*levy*): **the king ~d an army** коро́ль собра́л а́рмию. **5.** (*rear*): **they ~d a family** они́ вы́растили дете́й; **sheep are ~d on the downs** ове́ц разво́дят в холми́стых райо́нах. **6.** (*siege etc.*) сн|има́ть, -ять.

raisin ['reɪz(ə)n] *n.* изю́минка; (*pl., collect.*) изю́м.

raison d'être [,reɪzɔ̃ 'detr] *n.* смысл, разу́мное основа́ние.

raj [rɑːdʒ] *n.* (*hist.*) брита́нское правле́ние в И́ндии.

rajah ['rɑːdʒə] *n.* ра́джа (*m.*).

rake[1] [reɪk] *n.* (*implement*) гра́бл|и (*pl., g.* -ей); **as thin as a ~** худо́й как ще́пка.

v.t.: **he ~d the soil level** он разрыхли́л грунт; **the paths were ~d clean** доро́жки бы́ли расчи́щены.

v.i. (*fig.*): **he ~d among his papers** он перевороши́л свои́ бума́ги.

with advs.: **~ in** *v.t.*: **he ~d in the money** (*fig.*) он загреба́л де́ньги лопа́той; **~ out** *v.t.* выгреба́ть, вы́грести; **~ together** *v.t.* сгре|ба́ть, -сти́ в ку́чу; **~ up** *v.t.* сгре|ба́ть, -сти́; (*fig.*): **why ~ up an old quarrel?** заче́м вороши́ть ста́рую ссо́ру?

rake[2] [reɪk] *n.* (*arch., dissolute person*) пове́са (*m.*), распу́тни|к (*fem.* -ца).

rakish ['reɪkɪʃ] *adj.* (*jaunty*) щеголева́тый; у́харский.

rall|y ['rælɪ] *n.* **1.** (*assembly*) сбор, слёт, ми́тинг. **2.** (*recovery, revival*) восстановле́ние сил; попра́вка. **3.** (*at tennis etc.*) переки́дка. **4.** (*motor race*) автора́лли; **~y driver** авторалли́ст.

v.t. **1.** (*reassemble*) соб|ира́ть, -ра́ть (в строй); спл|а́чивать, -оти́ть. **2.** (*revive*): **his words ~ied their spirits** его́ слова́ воодушеви́ли их.

v.i. **1.** (*reassemble*) соб|ира́ться, -ра́ться; спл|а́чиваться, -оти́ться; **they ~ied round the leader** они́ сплоти́лись вокру́г вождя́; **they ~ied to the cause** де́ло сплоти́ло их. **2.** (*revive*): **he ~ied from his illness** он опра́вился от боле́зни; **the market ~ied** ры́нок воспря́нул.

RAM [ræm] *n.* (*comput.*) (*abbr. of* ***random-access memory***) ЗУПВ, (запомина́ющее устро́йство с произво́льной вы́боркой).

ram [ræm] *n.* **1.** (*male sheep*) бара́н. **2.** (*battering-~*) тара́н.

v.t. **1.** (*drive or compress by force*): **stakes were ~med into the ground** ко́лья бы́ли вби́ты в зе́млю; **the soil was ~med down** грунт был утрамбо́ван; (*fig.*): **he ~med the point home** он вдолби́л им свою́ мысль. **2.** (*strike with force*): **the ship ~med the bridge** (*by accident*) кора́бль наскочи́л на мост; **he ~med the enemy flagship** он протара́нил фла́гман проти́вника.

cpd. **~rod** *n.* шо́мпол.

Ramadan ['ræmə,dæn] *n.* (*relig.*) рамаза́н.

rambl|e ['ræmb(ə)l] *n.* прогу́лка.

v.i. **1.** (*walk for pleasure*) прогу́л|иваться, -я́ться. **2.** (*fig., of speech or writing*) болта́ть (*impf.*) языко́м; **a ~ing speaker** раски́дчивый ора́тор; (*of sick person*) загова́риваться (*impf.*).

rambler ['ræmblə(r)] *n.* (*hiker*) люби́тель пешехо́дного тури́зма; (*kind of rose*) выо́щаяся ро́за.

rambling ['ræmblɪŋ] *n.* пешехо́дный тури́зм.

ramification [,ræmɪfɪ'keɪʃ(ə)n] *n.* разветвле́ние.

ramif|y ['ræmɪ,faɪ] *v.t. & i.* развет|вля́ть(ся), -и́ть(ся); **a ~ied system of railways** разветвлённая систе́ма желе́зных доро́г.

ramp [ræmp] *n.* (*slope*) скат, укло́н.

rampage ['ræmpeɪdʒ] *n.* бу́йство, разгу́л.

v.i. бу́йствовать, буя́нить (*both impf.*).

rampant ['ræmpənt] *adj.* **1.** (*unchecked, widespread*) свире́пствующий, безу́держный; **disease was ~** боле́знь свире́пствовала. **2.** (*rank, luxuriant*) бу́йный, пы́шный.

rampart ['ræmpɑːt] *n.* крепостно́й вал; парапе́т.

ramshackle ['ræm,ʃæk(ə)l] *adj.* (*e.g. house*) обветша́лый; (*e.g. car*) разби́тый.

ranch [rɑːntʃ] *n.* ра́нчо (*indecl.*), фе́рма.

v.t. разв|оди́ть, -ести́.

rancher ['rɑːntʃə(r)] *n.* владе́лец ра́нчо; скотово́д.

rancid ['rænsɪd] *adj.* прого́рклый, ту́хлый.

rancorous ['ræŋkərəs] *adj.* озло́бленный, злопа́мятный.

rancour ['ræŋkə(r)] *n.* зло́ба; злопа́мятство.

random ['rændəm] *n.*: **at ~** наобу́м, науга́д, науда́чу; **shoot at ~** стреля́ть (*impf.*) не це́лясь.

adj. случа́йный; сде́ланный на аво́сь; **~ bullet** шальна́я пу́ля; **~ remark** случа́йное замеча́ние.

range [reɪndʒ] *n.* **1.** (*row, line, series*) цепь, ряд; **a ~ of mountains** го́рная цепь; **a ~ of buildings** ряд зда́ний. **2.** (*grazing area*) неогоро́женое па́стбище. **3.** (*area for firing, bombing etc.*) полиго́н; **rifle ~** стре́льбище; тир. **4.** (*operating distance*) да́льность, ра́диус; **the missile has a ~ of 1,000 miles** ра́диус де́йствия раке́ты — 1000 миль; **~ of an aircraft** да́льность полёта самолёта; **the enemy was out of ~ of our guns** враг был вне досяга́емости на́ших ору́дий. **6.** (*distance to target*) расстоя́ние, да́льность; **they fired at close ~** они́ стреля́ли с бли́зкого расстоя́ния. **7.** (*limit of audibility or visibility*) преде́л; **beyond the ~ of vision** вне преде́лов ви́димости. **8.** (*extent; distance between limits*) диапазо́н; **her voice has a remarkable ~** у неё замеча́тельный диапазо́н. **9.** (*selection*) набо́р; (*assortment*) ассортиме́нт; **this fabric comes in a wide ~ of colours** э́та ткань выпуска́ется са́мых разли́чных цвето́в. **10.** (*scope*): **the subject is outside my ~** э́тот вопро́с — не по мое́й ча́сти. **11.** (*cooking-stove*) ку́хонная плита́.

v.t. **1.** (*place in row*) распол|ага́ть -ожи́ть (*or* выстра́ивать, вы́строить) в ряд; **they ~d themselves against the wall** они́ вы́строились вдоль стены́. **2.** (*traverse*): **wolves ~d the prairie** во́лки ры́скали по сте́пи.

v.i. **1.** (*wander, roam*): **tigers ~d through the jungle** ти́гры броди́ли по джу́нглям. **2.** (*extend*) простира́ться (*impf.*); **my research ~s over a wide field** мои́ иссле́дования охва́тывают широ́кую о́бласть. **3.** (*vary between limits*) колеба́ться (*impf.*). **4.** (*of guns etc., carry*): **the gun ~s over 5 miles** дальнобо́йность пу́шки — 5 миль.

cpd. **~-finder** *n.* дальноме́р.

ranger [ˈreɪndʒə(r)] *n.* (*guard of forest etc.*) лесни́к, объе́здчик; (*pl., mounted troops*) ко́нная охра́на.

rank[1] [ræŋk] *n.* **1.** (*row*) ряд; (*taxi-~*) стоя́нка такси́. **2.** (*line of soldiers*) шере́нга; **in the front ~** (*lit.*) в пе́рвой шере́нге; (*fig., pre-eminent*) в пе́рвых ряда́х; **the men broke ~(s)** солда́ты нару́шили строй; **an artist of the first ~** первокла́ссный худо́жник. **3.** (*usu. pl., common soldiers*): **~ and file** (*mil. etc.*) рядовы́е; **he rose from the ~s** он вы́служился из рядовы́х. **4.** (*in armed forces*) зва́ние, чин; **he has the ~ of captain** он име́ет чин капита́на. **5.** (*official position*) служе́бное положе́ние; (*social position*): **persons of ~** высокопоста́вленные лю́ди; **people of all ~s of society** представи́тели всех слоёв о́бщества.

v.t. (*class, assess*) классифици́ровать (*impf., pf.*); **he was ~ed among the great poets** его́ причисля́ли к вели́ким поэ́там.

v.i. (*have a place*): **a major ~s above a captain** майо́р — вы́ше капита́на по чи́ну; **a high-~ing officer** ста́рший офице́р; **France ~s among the great powers** Фра́нция вхо́дит в число́ вели́ких держа́в.

rank[2] [ræŋk] *adj.* **1.** (*too luxuriant*) бу́йный, пы́шный; **a garden ~ with weeds** сад, заро́сший сорняка́ми. **2.** (*foul to smell or taste*): **the skunk gives off a ~ odour** от ску́нса исхо́дит злово́ние. **3.** (*loathsome, corrupt*) гну́сный. **4.** (*gross*) чрезме́рный; **~ indecency** ди́кая непристо́йность; **~ injustice** вопию́щая несправедли́вость; **~ nonsense** су́щая чепуха́.

rank-and-file [ˈræŋkəndˌfaɪl] *adj.* рядово́й.

rankle [ˈræŋk(ə)l] *v.i.* (*fester*) гнои́ться (*impf.*); (*give pain*) боле́ть (*impf.*).

ransack [ˈrænsæk] *v.t.* **1.** (*search*) обша́ри|вать, -ть; переры́ть (*pf.*). **2.** (*plunder*) гра́бить, раз-.

ransom [ˈrænsəm] *n.* вы́куп; **he was held to ~** (*lit.*) за него́ тре́бовали вы́куп; (*fig.*) его́ шантажи́ровали.

v.t. (*pay ~ for*) плати́ть, за- вы́куп за+*a.*

rant [rænt] *v.i.* вити́йствовать; разглаго́льствовать (*both impf.*).

rap [ræp] *n.* **1.** (*light blow*) лёгкий уда́р, стук; **he received a ~ on the knuckles** (*fig., reproof*) ему́ да́ли по рука́м. **2.** (*blame*): **who will take the ~ for this?** кто бу́дет за э́то отдува́ться? (*coll.*).

v.t. слегка́ уд|аря́ть, -а́рить по+*d.*

v.i. ст|уча́ть, -у́кнуть; посту́|кивать, -ча́ть.

with adv.: **~ out** *v.t.* (*utter brusquely*) говори́ть (*impf.*) отры́висто; **he ~ped out his orders** он выкри́кивал свои́ приказа́ния.

rapacious [rəˈpeɪʃəs] *adj.* жа́дный, ненасы́тный.

rape[1] [reɪp] *n.* изнаси́лование.

v.t. наси́ловать, из-.

rape[2] [reɪp] *n.* (*bot.*) рапс.

rapid [ˈræpɪd] *n.* (*pl.*) речно́й поро́г; **shoot ~s** преодол|ева́ть, -е́ть поро́ги.

adj. (*swift*) бы́стрый, ско́рый.

rapidity [rəˈpɪdɪtɪ] *n.* быстрота́, ско́рость.

rapier [ˈreɪpɪə(r)] *n.* рапи́ра.

rapist [ˈreɪpɪst] *n.* наси́льник.

rapport [ræˈpɔː(r)] *n.* взаимопонима́ние, конта́кт.

rapprochement [ræˈprɒʃmɑ̃] *n.* сближе́ние.

rapt [ræpt] *adj.* (*enraptured*) восхищённый; (*absorbed*) поглощённый.

rapture [ˈræptʃə(r)] *n.* восто́рг; **she went into ~s over the play** она́ была́ в (ди́ком) восто́рге от пье́сы.

rapturous [ˈræptʃərəs] *adj.* восто́рженный.

rare[1] [reə(r)] *adj.* **1.** (*uncommon*) ре́дкий; **it is ~ for him to smile** он ре́дко улыба́ется; **this flower is ~ in Britain** э́тот цвето́к ре́дко встреча́ется в Великобрита́нии. **2.** (*remarkably good*): ре́дкостный; **he has a ~ wit** он на ре́дкость остроу́мен.

rare[2] [reə(r)] *adj.* (*undercooked*) недожа́ренный; **a ~ steak** бифште́кс с кро́вью.

rarebit [ˈreəbɪt] = **rabbit** *n.* **2.**

rarefy [ˈreərɪˌfaɪ] *v.t.* разре|жа́ть, -ди́ть.

v.i. разре|жа́ться, -ди́ться.

rarely [ˈreəlɪ] *adv.* ре́дко, и́зредка.

rarity [ˈreərɪtɪ] *n.* (*uncommonness, infrequency*) ре́дкость; (*thg. valued for this*) (больша́я) ре́дкость.

rascal [ˈrɑːsk(ə)l] *n.* (*rogue*) моше́нник, плут; (*mischievous child*) шалу́н.

rash[1] [ræʃ] *n.* сыпь; **he broke out in a ~** у него́ вы́ступила сыпь.

rash[2] [ræʃ] *adj.* опроме́тчивый, необду́манный.

rasher [ˈræʃə(r)] *n.* ло́мтик (беко́на).

rasp [rɑːsp] *n.* (*file*) тёрка, ра́шпиль (*m.*); (*grating sound*) скре́жет.

v.t. (*scrape*) скрести́, тере́ть (*all impf.*).

v.i. скрежета́ть (*impf.*); **a ~ing voice** скрипу́чий го́лос.

raspberry [ˈrɑːzbərɪ] *n.* **1.** (*fruit*) мали́на (*collect.*); **a ~** я́года мали́ны; **~ cane** куст мали́ны; **~ jam** мали́новое варе́нье. **2.** (*sl, sound or gesture of derision*): **he blew me a ~** он показа́л мне нос.

Rastafarian [ˌræstəˈfeərɪən] *n.* растафа́ри (*c.g. indecl.*).

adj. растафа́ри.

rat [ræt] *n.* **1.** (*rodent*) кры́са; (*fig.*) **I smell a ~** я чу́ю подво́х; здесь что́-то нечи́сто. **2.** (*traitor to cause*) изме́нник, ренега́т.

v.i. **1.** (*hunt ~s*) лови́ть (*impf.*) крыс. **2.: ~ on** (*break faith with*) **s.o.** измен|я́ть, -и́ть кому́-н.

cpds. **~-catcher** *n.* крысоло́в; **~-trap** *n.* крысоло́вка.

ratchet [ˈrætʃɪt] *n.* (*toothed mechanism*) храпово́й механи́зм, храпови́к; (**~-wheel**) храпово́е колесо́.

rate[1] [reɪt] *n.* **1.** (*numerical proportion*) но́рма, разме́р; ста́вка; **~ of exchange** курс обме́на; **~ of interest** проце́нтная ста́вка; **bank ~** учётная ста́вка ба́нка; **birth ~** рожда́емость; **death ~** сме́ртность. **2.** (*speed*) ско́рость; **we shall never get there at this ~** при таки́х те́мпах мы туда́ никогда́ не доберёмся. **3.** (*price*) расце́нка, тари́ф. **4.** (*tax on property etc.*) ме́стный нало́г; **water ~** пла́та за водоснабже́ние. **5.: at any ~** (*in any case*) во вся́ком слу́чае.

v.t. **1.** (*estimate, consider*) оце́н|ивать, -и́ть; **do you ~ him among your friends?** счита́ете ли вы его́ свои́м дру́гом? **2.** (*assess for purposes of levy*) оце́н|ивать, -и́ть в це́лях налогообложе́ния. **3.** (*deserve*): **he ~s a prize** он заслу́живает награ́ды.

v.i.: **~ as** (*be considered*) счита́ться (*impf.*) +*i.*; **he ~s high in my esteem** я его́ о́чень ценю́/уважа́ю.

cpd. **~payer** *n.* плате́льщик ме́стных нало́гов.

rat(e)able [ˈreɪtəb(ə)l] *adj.* подлежа́щий обложе́нию нало́гом/нало́гами.

rather [ˈrɑːðə(r)] *adv.* **1.** (*by preference or choice*): **I would ~ die than consent** я скоре́е умру́, чем соглашу́сь; **I'd ~ have coffee** я предпочёл бы ко́фе; **I'd ~ not say** я лу́чше промолчу́; **~ than annoy him, she agreed** она́ согласи́лась, что́бы не серди́ть его́. **2.** (*more truly or precisely*) скоре́е, верне́е; **last night, or ~ this morning** вчера́ ве́чером, и́ли, верне́е/точне́е (сказа́ть), сего́дня у́тром. **3.** (*somewhat*) дово́льно, не́сколько; **the result was ~ surprising** результа́т был дово́льно неожи́данным; **he is ~ taller than his brother** он немно́го вы́ше своего́ бра́та; **it is ~ a pity** а жаль всё же; **I ~ think you are mistaken** а мне сдаётся, что вы ошиба́етесь; **the effect was ~ spoiled** эффе́кт был не́сколько подпо́рчен. **4.** (*coll., assuredly*) ещё бы!

ratification [ˌrætɪfɪˈkeɪʃ(ə)n] *n.* ратифика́ция.

ratify [ˈrætɪˌfaɪ] *v.t.* ратифици́ровать (*impf., pf.*).

rating ['reɪtɪŋ] *n.* **1.** (*of property etc.*) оце́нка; (*assessment of worth*) определе́ние сто́имости. **2.** (*sailor*) матро́с, специали́ст рядово́го и́ли старши́нского соста́ва.

ratio ['reɪʃɪəʊ] *n.* отноше́ние, соотноше́ние.

ration ['ræʃ(ə)n] *n.* рацио́н, паёк; ~ **card** продово́льственная ка́рточка; **iron ~s** неприкоснове́нный запа́с; **they were on short ~s** они́ бы́ли на ску́дном пайке́; (*pl.*, *food*) продово́льствие.

v.t.: **they were ~ed to one loaf a week** их паёк своди́лся к одно́й буха́нке в неде́лю; **meat was severely ~ed** мя́со бы́ло стро́го нормиро́вано.

rational ['ræʃən(ə)l] *adj.* (*based on reason*) разу́мный; (*endowed with reason*) разу́мный, мы́слящий; (*math.*) рациона́льный.

rationale [,ræʃə'nɑːl] *n.* основна́я причи́на.

rationalism ['ræʃənə,lɪz(ə)m] *n.* рационали́зм.

rationalist ['ræʃənəlɪst] *n.* рационали́ст.

rationalistic [,ræʃənə'lɪstɪk] *adj.* рационалисти́ческий.

rationality [,ræʃə'nælɪtɪ] *n.* разу́мность, рациона́льность.

rationalization [,ræʃənəlaɪ'zeɪʃ(ə)n] *n.* (*explanation*) разу́мное объясне́ние; (*justification*) оправда́ние; (*improvement*) рационализа́ция.

rationalize ['ræʃənə,laɪz] *v.t.* (*give or find reasons for*) разу́мно объясн|я́ть, -и́ть; опра́вд|ывать, -а́ть; (*make more efficient*) рационализи́ровать (*impf.*, *pf.*).

rattan [rə'tæn] *n.* (*material*) рота́нг; (*cane*) трость.

rattle ['ræt(ə)l] *n.* **1.** (*sound*) треск, гро́хот; **the ~ of machine-guns** пулемётная дробь; (*of crockery*) гро́хот. **2.** (*child's toy*) погрему́шка. **3.** (*for sports fans etc.*) трещо́тка.

v.t. **1.** (*cause to* ~): **he ~d the money-box** он встряхну́л копи́лку; **the wind ~d the windows** о́кна дребезжа́ли от ве́тра. **2.** (*coll.*, *agitate*): **he is not easily ~d** его́ нелегко́ вы́вести из равнове́сия.

v.i.: **the hail ~d on the roof** град бараба́нил по кры́ше; **the car ~d over the stones** маши́на громыха́ла по камня́м.

with advs.: **he ~d off a list of names** он вы́палил це́лый спи́сок фами́лий.

cpd. **~snake** *n.* грему́чая змея́.

raucous ['rɔːkəs] *adj.* ре́зкий, хри́плый.

raunchy ['rɔːntʃɪ] *adj.* (*US coll.*) распу́тный.

ravage ['rævɪdʒ] *n.* (*usu. pl.*) разруше́ние, опустоше́ние; (*fig.*): **the ~s of time** следы́ (*m. pl.*) вре́мени.

v.t. & i. опустош|а́ть, -и́ть; (*fig.*): **her face was ~d by suffering** на её лице была́ печа́ть страда́ния.

rave [reɪv] *adj.* (*coll.*, *enthusiastic*) ~ **review** восто́рженный о́тзыв.

v.i. (*in delirium*) бре́дить (*impf.*); (*in delight*): **they ~d about the play** они́ бы́ли в восто́рге от пье́сы (*see also* **raving**).

ravel ['ræv(ə)l] *v.t. & i.* спу́т|ывать(ся), -ать(ся).

with advs.: ~ **up** *v.t.* пу́тать (*or* запу́тывать), за-.

raven ['reɪv(ə)n] *n.* во́рон.

ravenous ['rævənəs] *adj.* прожо́рливый; **a ~ appetite** во́лчий аппети́т; **I am** ~ я го́лоден как волк.

raver ['reɪvə(r)] *n.* (*pleasure-seeker*) гуля́ка (*c.g.*).

ravine [rə'viːn] *n.* овра́г, лощи́на.

raving ['reɪvɪŋ] *n.* бред; **the ~s of an idiot** бред сумасше́дшего.

adj. & adv. **1.** (*insane*): **a ~ lunatic** бу́йно поме́шанный; **you must be ~ mad** ты совсе́м спя́тил. **2.**: **a ~ beauty** сногсшиба́тельная краса́вица.

ravioli [,rævɪ'əʊlɪ] *n.* равио́ли (*nt. and pl. indecl.*).

ravish ['rævɪʃ] *v.t.* (*enchant*) восхи|ща́ть, -ти́ть; **a ~ing view** восхити́тельный вид.

raw [rɔː] *n.*: **my remarks touched him on the** ~ мои́ слова́ заде́ли его́ за живо́е.

adj. **1.** (*uncooked*) сыро́й, све́жий; **I prefer my fruit** ~ я предпочита́ю све́жие фру́кты. **2.** (*in natural state*, *unprocessed*) необрабо́танный; ~ **data** необрабо́танные да́нные; ~ **material(s)** сырьё; ~ **sugar** нерафини́рованный са́хар. **3.** (*callow*, *inexperienced*) зелёный, нео́пытный. **4.** (*unprotected by skin*, *sensitive*): **a ~ wound** незажи́вшая ра́на; **the wind has made my face** ~ у меня́ обве́трилось лицо́. **5.** (*of weather*) сыро́й; холо́дный и вла́жный. **6.** (*harsh*) суро́вый; **he got a ~ deal** (*coll.*) с ним суро́во обошли́сь.

ray[1] [reɪ] *n.* (*lit.*, *fig.*) луч; **the sun's ~s** со́лнечные лучи́; **a ~ of hope** луч/про́блеск наде́жды.

ray[2] [reɪ] *n.* (*fish*) скат.

rayon ['reɪɒn] *n.* иску́сственный шёлк, виско́за.

raze [reɪz] *v.t.* **1.** (*demolish*) разр|уша́ть, -у́шить до основа́ния; **the city was ~d to the ground** го́род сравня́ли с землёй. **2.** (*efface*) ст|ира́ть, -ере́ть.

razor ['reɪzə(r)] *n.* бри́тва; **electric** ~ электробри́тва.

cpd. **~-blade** *n.* ле́звие.

RC (*abbr. of* ***Roman Catholic***) като́лик.

Rd. [rəʊd] *n.* (*abbr. of* **Road**) ул., (у́лица).

RE (*abbr. of* ***Religious Education***) религио́зное обуче́ние.

re[1] [reɪ, riː] *n.* (*mus.*) ре (*indecl.*).

re[2] [riː, rɪ, re] *prep.* по де́лу +*g.*, каса́тельно+*g.*

reach [riːtʃ] *n.* **1.** (*extent of stretching movement*) разма́х/длина́ руки́; **the apples were beyond their** ~ они́ не могли́ дотяну́ться до я́блок; (*fig.*): **we are within easy ~ of London** от нас легко́ добра́ться до Ло́ндона. **2.** (*stretch of river etc.*): **the upper ~es of the Thames** верхо́вья (*nt. pl.*) Те́мзы.

v.t. **1.** (*attain*, *fetch with outstretched hand*) дотя́|гиваться, -ну́ться до+*g.*; **please ~ me that book** доста́ньте мне, пожа́луйста, э́ту кни́гу. **2.** (*arrive at*) дост|ига́ть, -и́гнуть +*g.*; **the ladder will not ~ the window** ле́стница не доста́нет до окна́; **your letter ~ed me only yesterday** ва́ше письмо́ дошло́ до меня́ то́лько вчера́; ~ **agreement** прийти́ (*pf.*) к соглаше́нию. **3.** (*make contact with*): **can I ~ you by telephone?** с ва́ми мо́жно связа́ться по телефо́ну? **4.** (*rise or sink to*): **his genius ~ed new heights** его́ ге́ний дости́г небыва́лых высо́т; **the pound ~ed a new low** курс фу́нта (сте́рлингов) упа́л ещё ни́же, чем когда́-нибудь пре́жде.

v.i. **1.** (*stretch out hand*) тяну́ться, по- руко́й. **2.** (*extend*) простира́ться, тяну́ться (*both impf.*); **the park ~es from here to the river** парк тя́нется отсю́да до реки́.

with advs.: ~ **down** *v.t.* (*fetch down*) дост|ава́ть, -а́ть; сн|има́ть, -ять; *v.i.*: **he ~ed down and picked up the coin** он нагну́лся и по́днял моне́ту; ~ **out** *v.i.*: **he ~ed out to catch the ball** он протяну́л ру́ки, что́бы пойма́ть мяч; ~ **up** *v.i.* (*stretch hand up*) протяну́ть (*pf.*) ру́ку вверх; (*rise*) **the tree ~es up to the sky** де́рево тя́нется к не́бу.

react [rɪ'ækt] *v.i.* реаги́ровать (*impf.*, *pf.*); (*chem.*): **acids ~ together** кисло́ты вступа́ют в реа́кцию; (*respond*) отв|еча́ть, -е́тить (на+*a.*); **she ~ed by bursting into tears** в отве́т она́ распла́калась; (*act in opposition*) проти́виться, вос-; сопротивля́ться (*impf.*).

reaction [rɪ'ækʃ(ə)n] *n.* (*var. senses*) реа́кция; **my first ~ was one of disbelief** снача́ла э́то вы́звало у меня́ недове́рие; **chain** ~ цепна́я реа́кция.

reactionary [rɪ'ækʃənərɪ] *n.* реакционе́р.

adj. реакцио́нный.

reactivate [rɪ'æktɪ,veɪt] *v.t.* реактиви́ровать (*impf.*, *pf.*); вдохну́ть (*pf.*) но́вую жизнь в+*a.*

reactive [rɪ'æktɪv] *adj.* реакти́вный.

reactor [rɪ'æktə(r)] *n.* (*tech.*) реа́ктор.

read [riːd] *n.* чте́ние; **a good** ~ (*book*) интере́сная/захва́тывающая кни́га.

v.t. **1.** (*peruse*) чита́ть, про- *or* проче́сть; **have you ~ this book?** вы чита́ли э́ту кни́гу?; **he ~ the letter to himself** он прочёл письмо́ про себя́; **this**

author is widely ~ э́того а́втора мно́го чита́ют; **can you** ~ **music?** вы уме́ете игра́ть по но́там?; **Johnny learnt to** ~ **the time** Джо́нни научи́лся понима́ть вре́мя по часа́м; **the bill was** ~ (*parl.*) ≃ билль был обсуждён. **2.** (*discern, make out*): **he** ~ **my thoughts** он чита́л мои́ мы́сли; **he can** ~ **shorthand** он уме́ет расшифро́вывать стеногра́ммы; **she had her hand** ~ ей погада́ли по руке́. **3.** (*interpret*): **do not** ~ **my silence as consent** не прими́те моё молча́ние за согла́сие. **4.** (*study*) изуча́ть (*impf.*); **he is ~ing law** он у́чится на юриди́ческом факульте́те. **5.** (*examine*): ~ **a meter** сн|има́ть, -ять показа́ния счётчика; ~ **proofs** пра́вить, вы- вёрстку.

v.i. **1.: he can neither** ~ **nor write** он не уме́ет ни чита́ть, ни писа́ть; **have you** ~ **of him before?** вы чита́ли о нём ра́ньше?; **you must** ~ **between the lines** (*fig.*) сле́дует чита́ть ме́жду срок. **2.** (*consist of specified words etc.*): **the letter ~s ...** в письме́ говори́тся/ска́зано...; **how does the sentence** ~ **now?** как тепе́рь звучи́т э́то предложе́ние; **the thermometer ~s 20° below** термо́метр пока́зывает ми́нус 20°. **3.** (*produce effect when read*): **this ~s like a threat** э́то звучи́т как угро́за; **the play ~s well** пье́са хорошо́ чита́ется.

with advs.: ~ **back** *v.t.* повтор|я́ть, -и́ть; ~ **off** *v.t.* (*e.g. list*) прочи́т|ывать, -а́ть; (*from dial etc.*) сн|има́ть, -ять (*показания*); ~ **out** *v.t.* прочи́т|ывать, -а́ть; огла|ша́ть, -си́ть; ~ **over** *v.t.* перечи́т|ывать, -а́ть; прочи́т|ывать, -а́ть; ~ **through** *v.t.* прочи́т|ывать, -а́ть; ~ **up** *v.t.* подчита́ть (*pf.*); чита́ть (*impf.*) для подгото́вки; **he** ~ **up the subject** он подчита́л ко́е-что по э́тому предме́ту.

cpd. **~-out** *n.* вы́вод/вы́дача да́нных.

readable ['ri:dəb(ə)l] *adj.* **1.** (*legible*) разбо́рчивый, удобочита́емый. **2.** (*enjoyable*) (*coll.*) интере́сный; **this is a** ~ **novel** э́тот рома́н хорошо́ чита́ется.

readdress [ˌri:ə'dres] *v.t.* переадресо́в|ывать, -а́ть.

reader ['ri:də(r)] *n.* **1.** (*of books etc.*) чита́тель (*fem.* -ница); **he is a fast** ~ он бы́стро чита́ет. **2.** (*university teacher*) ≃ ста́рший преподава́тель; доце́нт. **3.** (*textbook*) хрестома́тия; кни́га для чте́ния.

readership ['ri:dəʃɪp] *n.* круг чита́телей.

readily ['redɪlɪ] *adv.* (*willingly*) охо́тно; (*without difficulty*) легко́, без труда́.

readiness ['redɪnɪs] *n.* гото́вность, охо́та.

reading ['ri:dɪŋ] *n.* **1.** (*act or pursuit*) чте́ние. **2.** (*interpretation*) толкова́ние; **what is your** ~ **of events?** как вы оце́ниваете собы́тия? **3.** (*of instrument*) показа́ние. **4.** (*stage in passage of bill*) чте́ние; **on the second** ~ при второ́м чте́нии.

cpds. **~-desk** *n.* пюпи́тр; **~-lamp** *n.* насто́льная ла́мпа; **~-room** *n.* чита́льный зал, чита́льная.

readjust [ˌri:ə'dʒʌst] *v.t.* попр|авля́ть, -а́вить; приспос|а́бливать, -о́бить; **they had to** ~ **their attitude** им пришло́сь пересмотре́ть свои́ пози́ции.

v.i.: **after the war he found it hard to** ~ по́сле войны́ ему́ тру́дно бы́ло приспосо́биться.

readjustment [ˌri:ə'dʒʌstmənt] *n.* приспособле́ние, перестро́йка; **the war brought about a complete** ~ война́ вы́звала по́лную перестро́йку жи́зни.

ready ['redɪ] *n.*: **he held his rifle at the** ~ он держа́л винто́вку в положе́нии для стрельбы́.

adj. (*prepared; in a fit state*) гото́вый (*к чему*); пригото́вленный, подгото́вленный; **I'm just getting** ~ я почти́ гото́в; **~! go!** внима́ние — марш!; (*willing*) гото́вый, проявля́ющий гото́вность; **he is** ~ **for anything** он гото́в ко всему́ (*or* на всё); (*quick, facile*) скло́нный; **he is always** ~ **with an excuse** у него́ всегда́ найдётся отгово́рка; **a** ~ **wit** нахо́дчивость; (*available*) (име́ющийся) нагото́ве; ~ **money** нали́чные де́ньги.

cpds. **~-made** *adj.* гото́вый; (*fig.*) избі́тый, шабло́нный; **~-to-wear** *adj.* гото́вый.

reaffirm [ˌri:ə'fɜ:m] *v.t.* (вновь) подтвер|жда́ть, -ди́ть.

reagent [ri:'eɪdʒ(ə)nt] *n.* (*chem.*) реакти́в.

real [ri:l] *n.*: **for** ~ (*coll.*) по-настоя́щему; всерьёз.

adj. (*actual*) реа́льный; настоя́щий; (*genuine*) по́длинный; (*sincere*) и́скренний, неподде́льный; (*substantial, fundamental*) реа́льный, суще́ственный; **in** ~ **life** в жи́зни; ~ **silver** чи́стое серебро́; **that is not the** ~ **reason** настоя́щая причи́на не в том; **a** ~ **gentleman** настоя́щий джентльме́н; **he has a** ~ **grievance** его́ прете́нзии обосно́ваны; **the** ~ **point is ...** суть вопро́са в том, что...; (*leg.*): ~ **estate** недви́жимость.

adv. (*US coll.*): **we had a** ~ **nice time** мы здо́рово провели́ вре́мя.

realign [ˌri:ə'laɪn] *v.t.* перестр|а́ивать, -о́ить.

realignment [ˌri:ə'laɪnmənt] *n.* перестро́йка.

realism ['ri:əˌlɪz(ə)m] *n.* реали́зм.

realist ['rɪəlɪst] *n.* реали́ст (*fem.* -ка)

realistic [rɪə'lɪstɪk] *adj.* (*practical*) реалисти́чный, практи́чный; (*in art etc.*) реалисти́ческий.

reality [rɪ'ælɪtɪ] *n.* реа́льность, действи́тельность; **in** ~ в/на са́мом де́ле; в действи́тельности.

realization [ˌrɪəlaɪ'zeɪʃ(ə)n] *n.* (*recognition*) осозна́ние; (*achievement*) осуществле́ние.

realize ['rɪəlaɪz] *v.t.* **1.** (*be aware of*) осозн|ава́ть, -а́ть; (*grasp mentally*) сообра|жа́ть, -зи́ть; **I** ~ **what you must think of me** представля́ю, что вы обо мне ду́маете; **do you** ~ **what you have done?** вы понима́ете, что вы сде́лали?; **I didn't** ~ **you wanted it** до меня́ не дошло́, что э́то вам ну́жно. **2.** (*convert into fact*) осуществ|ля́ть, -и́ть; **her worst fears were ~d** оправда́лись её са́мые ху́дшие опасе́ния. **3.** (*convert into money*) реализо́в|ывать, -а́ть. **4.** (*fetch*) выруча́ть, вы́ручить; **the sale ~d over £5,000** при прода́же бы́ло вы́ручено бо́лее пяти́ ты́сяч фу́нтов. **5.** (*amass, gain*) получ|а́ть, -и́ть.

really ['rɪəlɪ] *adv.* действи́тельно; в/на са́мом де́ле; **do you** ~ **mean it?** вы серьёзно?; **did that** ~ **happen last year?** ра́зве э́то случи́лось в про́шлом году́?; **I am** ~ **sorry for you** мне вас и́скренне жаль; **~?** (*expr. surprise*) серьёзно?, неуже́ли?; (*acknowledging information*) да?, пра́вда?; **~!** (*expr. indignation*) ну, зна́ете!

realm [relm] *n.* короле́вство; (*fig.*) сфе́ра; **coin of the** ~ ходя́чая моне́та; (*fig.*): **you are entering the ~s of fancy** вы вступа́ете в ца́рство фанта́зии.

realtor ['ri:əltə(r)] *n.* (*US*) аге́нт по прода́же недви́жимости.

ream [ri:m] *n.* (*quantity of paper*) стопа́; (*fig.*): **he wrote ~s of nonsense** он написа́л бе́здну вся́кой чепухи́.

reap [ri:p] *v.t. & i.* жать, с-; пож|ина́ть, -а́ть ; (*fig.*): **he is ~ing the fruits of his folly** он пожина́ет плоды́ свое́й глу́пости.

reaper ['ri:pə(r)] *n.* **1.** (*labourer*) жн|ец (*fem.* -и́ца). **2.** (*machine*) жа́тка.

reappear [ˌri:ə'pɪə(r)] *v.i.* сно́ва появ|ля́ться, -и́ться.

reappearance [ˌri:ə'pɪərəns] *n.* но́вое появле́ние.

reappraisal [ˌri:ə'preɪzəl] *n.* переоце́нка.

reappraise [ˌri:ə'preɪz] *v.t.* пересм|а́тривать, -отре́ть; переоце́н|ивать, -и́ть.

rear[1] [rɪə(r)] *n.* **1.** за́дняя ча́сть, сторона́; **the kitchen is at the** ~ **of the house** ку́хня — в за́дней ча́сти до́ма. **2.** (*of army etc.*) тыл; хвост коло́нны; **he was a slow runner and always brought up the** ~ он пло́хо бежа́л и всегда́ ока́зывался в хвосте́. **3.** (*coll., buttocks*) зад, за́дница.

adj.: ~ **entrance** чёрный ход; ~ **wheel** за́днее колесо́.

cpds. **~-admiral** *n.* контр-адмира́л; **~guard** *n.* арьерга́рд; **~guard action** арьерга́рдный бой.

rear[2] [rɪə(r)] *v.t.* **1.** (*raise, erect*) возд|ига́ть, -и́гнуть; **jealousy ~ed its head** (в нём *и т.п.*) зашевели́лась ре́вность. **2.** (*bring up*) расти́ть, вы́-; воспи́т|ывать, -а́ть; (*breed*) разв|оди́ть, -ести́.

v.i. (*also* ~ **up**) ста|нови́ться, -ть на дыбы́.

rearm [ri:'ɑ:m] *v.t. & i.* перевоору́ж|а́ть(ся), -и́ть(ся).

rearmament [ri:'ɑ:məmənt] *n.* перевооруже́ние.

rearrange [ˌri:ə'reɪndʒ] *v.t.* перест|авля́ть, -а́вить.

rearrangement [ˌri:ə'reɪndʒmənt] *n.* перестано́вка.

rearward ['rɪəwəd] *adj.* тылово́й, за́дний.

rearwards ['rɪəwədz] *adv.* наза́д; в тыл.

reason ['ri:z(ə)n] *n.* **1.** (*cause, ground*) причи́на; **he refused to give his ~s** он отказа́лся объясни́ть; **there is ~ to believe that ...** есть основа́ния полага́ть, что...; **with ~** обосно́ванно; **for no good ~** без уважи́тельной причи́ны; **for the simple ~ that ...** по той просто́й причи́не, что.... **2.** (*intellectual faculty*) ра́зум, рассу́док; **he lost his ~** он лиши́лся рассу́дка. **3.** (*good sense, moderation*) благоразу́мие; **he will not listen to ~** он не прислу́шивается к го́лосу ра́зума; **it stands to ~** разуме́ется; **I will do anything in ~** я сде́лаю всё в преде́лах разу́много; **there is ~ in what you say** то, что вы говори́те, разу́мно.

v.t. **1.** (*argue, contend*) дока́зывать (*impf.*). **2.** (*express logically*): **a ~ed argument** обосно́ванный до́вод. **3.: ~ out** (*solve by ~ing*) разга́д|ывать, -а́ть.

v.i.: **it is useless to ~ with him** его́ бесполе́зно убежда́ть; ло́гика на него́ не де́йствует.

reasonable ['ri:zənəb(ə)l] *adj.* **1.** (*sensible, amenable to reason*) (благо)разу́мный. **2.** (*moderate*) уме́ренный, прие́млемый; **he has a ~ chance of success** у него́ неплохи́е ша́нсы на успе́х. **3.** (*of price*) недорого́й; **the shoes are quite ~** ту́фли сто́ят недо́рого.

reasoning ['ri:zənɪŋ] *n.* рассужде́ние, аргумента́ция; **powers of ~** спосо́бность рассужда́ть.

reassemble [ˌri:ə'semb(ə)l] *v.t.* сно́ва соб|ира́ть, -ра́ть.

v.i. сно́ва соб|ира́ться, -ра́ться; сно́ва встр|еча́ться, -е́титься.

reassembly [ˌri:ə'semb(ə)lɪ] *n.* (*of committee etc.*) возобновлённое заседа́ние (по́сле переры́ва).

reassess [ˌri:ə'ses] *v.t.* переоце́н|ивать, -и́ть.

reassessment [ˌri:ə'sesmənt] *n.* переоце́нка.

reassign [ˌri:ə'saɪn] *v.t.* назн|ача́ть, -а́чить на друго́е ме́сто.

reassignment [ˌri:ə'saɪnmənt] *n.* перево́д.

reassurance [ˌri:ə'ʃʊərəns] *n.* (повто́рное) завере́ние, подтвержде́ние.

reassure [ˌri:ə'ʃʊə(r)] *v.t.* успок|а́ивать, -о́ить; подбодр|я́ть, -и́ть; **I can ~ you on that point** я могу́ успоко́ить вас на э́тот счёт.

reawaken [ˌri:ə'weɪkən] *v.t.* возро|жда́ть, -ди́ть.

reawakening [ˌri:ə'weɪkənɪŋ] *n.* возрожде́ние.

rebate ['ri:beɪt] *n.* (*discount*) ски́дка; вы́чет.

rebel[1] ['reb(ə)l] *n.* (*against government*) повста́нец, мяте́жник; бунтовщи́|к (*fem.* -ца), бунта́рь (*m.*); (*attr.*) повста́нческий; бунта́рский.

rebel[2] [rɪ'bel] *v.i.* восст|ава́ть, -а́ть; бунтова́ть.

rebellion [rɪ'beljən] *n.* восста́ние, мяте́ж, бунт.

rebellious [rɪ'beljəs] *adj.* (*in revolt*) восста́вший, мяте́жный; (*disobedient*) непоко́рный.

rebelliousness [rɪ'beljəsnɪs] *n.* непоко́рность.

rebind [ri:'baɪnd] *v.t.* за́ново перепле|та́ть, -сти́.

rebirth [ri:'bɜ:θ, 'ri:-] *n.* возрожде́ние.

reborn [ri:'bɔ:n] *adj.* возрождённый.

rebound[1] [rɪ'baʊnd] *n.* рикоше́т; **on the ~** рикоше́том.

rebound[2] [rɪ'baʊnd] *v.i.* отск|а́кивать, -очи́ть.

rebuff [rɪ'bʌf] *n.* отпо́р, ре́зкий отка́з.

v.t.: **the enemy's attack was ~ed** ата́ка неприя́теля была́ отби́та.

rebuild [ri:'bɪld] *v.t.* сно́ва стро́ить, по-; перестр|а́ивать, -о́ить; реконструи́ровать (*impf., pf.*).

rebuke [rɪ'bju:k] *n.* упрёк; вы́говор, замеча́ние.

v.t. упрек|а́ть, -ну́ть; де́лать, с- замеча́ние/вы́говор +*d.*

rebut [rɪ'bʌt] *v.t.* опров|ерга́ть, -е́ргнуть

rebuttal [rɪ'bʌtəl] *n.* опроверже́ние.

recalcitrance [rɪ'kælsɪtrəns] *n.* непоко́рность.

recalcitrant [rɪ'kælsɪtrənt] *adj.* непоко́рный.

recalculate [ri:'kælkjʊˌleɪt] *v.t.* пересчи́т|ывать, -а́ть.

recall ['ri:kɔl] *n.* **1.** (*summons to return*) отзы́в; (*bringing back*): **the letters are lost beyond ~** э́ти пи́сьма бессле́дно исче́зли. **2.** (*recollection*) па́мять; **total ~** по́лное восстановле́ние в па́мяти.

v.t. **1.** (*summon back*) от|зыва́ть, -озва́ть; **the ambassador was ~ed** посла́ отозва́ли. **2.** (*bring back to mind*) нап|омина́ть, -о́мнить; **this ~s my childhood to me** э́то напомина́ет мне де́тство; **I ~ed his words** я вспо́мнил его́ слова́. **3.** (*revoke*) отмен|я́ть, -и́ть.

recant [rɪ'kænt] *v.t. & i.* публи́чно ка́яться, рас- (*в чём*); отр|ека́ться, -е́чься (*от чего*).

recapitulate [ˌri:kə'pɪtjʊˌleɪt] *v.t.* повтор|я́ть, -и́ть; резюми́ровать (*impf., pf.*).

recapitulation [ˌri:kəˌpɪtjʊ'leɪʃ(ə)n] *n.* резюме́ (*indecl.*); сумми́рование.

recapture [ri:'kæptʃə(r)] *v.t.* взять (*pf.*) обра́тно; пойма́ть (*pf.*); **the prisoner was ~d** заключённого пойма́ли.

recast [ri:'kɑ:st] *v.t.* **1.** (*cast again, e.g. a gun*) отл|ива́ть, -и́ть за́ново. **2.** (*rewrite, rephrase*) перераб|а́тывать, -о́тать. **3.** (*remodel, refashion*) переде́л|ывать, -ать.

reced|e [rɪ'si:d] *v.i.* **1.** (*move back*) отступ|а́ть, -и́ть; **the tide was ~ing** вода́ спада́ла; **~ing hair** реде́ющие во́лосы. **2.** (*slope back*) отклоня́ться (*impf.*) наза́д; **a ~ing chin** сре́занный подборо́док.

receipt [rɪ'si:t] *n.* **1.** (*receiving*) получе́ние; **on ~ of the news** по получе́нии изве́стия. **2.** (*pl., money received*) де́нежные поступле́ния. **3.** (*written acknowledgement*) распи́ска, квита́нция.

receive [rɪ'si:v] *v.t.* **1.** (*get, be given*) получ|а́ть, -и́ть; **your letter will ~ attention** ва́ше письмо́ бу́дет рассмо́трено; **he ~d a warm welcome** ему́ оказа́ли тёплый приём; **he ~d severe punishment** он подве́ргся суро́вому наказа́нию; **information has not yet been ~d** све́дения ещё не поступи́ли. **2.** (*admit*) прин|има́ть, -я́ть; допус|ка́ть, -ти́ть; **I am not receiving guests** я не принима́ю госте́й; (*give reception to, greet*) прин|има́ть, -я́ть; **he was ~d with open arms** его́ встре́тили с распростёртыми объя́тиями; **how did he ~ the news?** как он воспри́нял э́ту но́вость? **3.** (*accept as true, accurate etc.*) призн|ава́ть, -а́ть пра́вильным; **~d pronunciation** нормати́вное произноше́ние. **4.** (*obtain signals from*): **are you receiving me?** вы меня́ слы́шите?; **can you ~ the third programme?** ваш приёмник берёт тре́тью програ́мму?.

receiver [rɪ'si:və(r)] *n.* **1.** получа́тель (*m.*). **2. (telephone ~)** (телефо́нная) тру́бка. **3. (radio ~)** (радио)приёмник.

recent ['ri:s(ə)nt] *adj.* **1.** (*occurring lately*) неда́вний; **within ~ memory** за после́днее вре́мя. **2.** (*modern*) совреме́нный.

recently ['ri:səntlɪ] *adv.* неда́вно, на днях, за после́днее вре́мя; **until quite ~** ещё совсе́м неда́вно.

receptacle [rɪ'septək(ə)l] *n.* вмести́лище.

reception [rɪ'sepʃ(ə)n] *n.* **1.** (*of guests etc.*) приём; **they are having a ~** они́ даю́т приём; **~ centre** приёмник; **~ clerk** (*in hotel, hospital*) (*also* **~ist**) регистра́тор, дежу́рный; (*in a business firm*) секрета́р|ь (*fem.* -ша) по приёму посети́телей; **~ desk** (*in hotel*) регистра́ция, конто́рка портье́; (*in hospital*) регистрату́ра; **~ room** приёмная. **2.** (*greeting, display of feeling*) встре́ча, приём; **he was given a great ~** ему́ устро́или великоле́пный приём. **3.** (*of ideas etc.*) восприя́тие. **4.** (*of radio signals*) приём.

receptionist [rɪˈsepʃənɪst] *see* **reception 1.**
receptive [rɪˈseptɪv] *adj.* восприи́мчивый.
receptivity [ˌri:sepˈtɪvɪtɪ] *n.* восприи́мчивость.
recess [rɪˈses, ˈri:ses] *n.* **1.** (*vacation*) переры́в; **Parliament has gone into ~** парла́мент распу́щен на кани́кулы. **2.** (*alcove, niche*) ни́ша. **3.** (*secret place*) тайни́к; **in the ~es of the heart** в глубине́ души́.
v.t. (*set back*) отодв|ига́ть, -и́нуть наза́д.
v.i. (*adjourn*): **the court ~ed** был объя́влен переры́в в заседа́нии суда́.
recession [rɪˈseʃ(ə)n] *n.* спад.
recharge [ri:ˈtʃɑ:dʒ] *v.t.* перезаря|жа́ть, -ди́ть.
recidivism [rɪˈsɪdɪvˌɪz(ə)m] *n.* рециди́в.
recidivist [rɪˈsɪdɪvɪst] *n.* рецидиви́ст.
recipe [ˈresɪpɪ] *n.* (*lit., fig.*) реце́пт; **a ~ for happiness** секре́т сча́стья.
recipient [rɪˈsɪpɪənt] *n.* получа́тель (*fem.* -ница).
reciprocal [rɪˈsɪprək(ə)l] *adj.* (*mutual*) взаи́мный (*also gram.*), обою́дный.
reciprocate [rɪˈsɪprəˌkeɪt] *v.t.* отв|еча́ть, -е́тить взаи́мностью; **she ~ed his feelings** она́ отвеча́ла ему́ взаи́мностью.
v.i. **1.** (*move back and forth*) дви́гаться (*impf.*) взад и вперёд; **~ing engine** поршнево́й дви́гатель. **2.** (*make a return*) отпла́|чивать, -ти́ть.
reciprocation [rɪˌsɪprəˈkeɪʃ(ə)n] *n.* отве́тное де́йствие; обме́н.
reciprocity [ˌresɪˈprɒsɪtɪ] *n.* взаи́мность; взаимоде́йствие; обме́н.
recital [rɪˈsaɪt(ə)l] *n.* (*narration*) изложе́ние; (*entertainment*) со́льный конце́рт.
recitation [ˌresɪˈteɪʃ(ə)n] *n.* деклама́ция; **there is to be a ~ from Shakespeare** бу́дут чита́ть отры́вки из Шекспи́ра.
recite [rɪˈsaɪt] *v.t.* (*declaim from memory*) деклами́ровать, про-; (*enumerate*) переч|исля́ть, -и́слить.
reckless [ˈreklɪs] *adj.* безрассу́дный; **he drove ~ly** он неосторо́жно вёл маши́ну.
recklessness [ˈreklɪsnɪs] *n.* безрассу́дность.
reckon [ˈrekən] *v.t.* **1.** (*calculate*) счита́ть, вы́-; **he never ~s the cost** он никогда́ не учи́тывает расхо́дов. **2.** (*consider, rate*) счита́ть (*impf.*). **3.** (*coll., opine*) полага́ть (*impf.*); **I ~ he will win** я ду́маю, что он победи́т.
v.i. **1.** (*count*) счита́ть (*impf.*); **he is a man to be ~ed with** с таки́м челове́ком, как он, ну́жно счита́ться; **he ~ed without the English climate** он не взял в расчёт англи́йский кли́мат. **2.** (*rely, depend*) рассчи́тывать (*impf.*) (*на кого/что*). **3.** (*settle account*) (*lit., fig.*) рассчи́т|ываться, -а́ться; (*fig.*) расквита́ться (*pf.*).
reckoning [ˈrekənɪŋ] *n.* **1.** (*calculation*) счёт, вычисле́ние; **dead ~** (*nav., aeron.*) навигацио́нное счисле́ние. **2.** (*account*) распла́та; **day of ~** (*fig.*) час распла́ты.
reclaim [rɪˈkleɪm] *n.* **beyond ~** неисправи́мый.
v.t. **1.** (*bring under cultivation*) осв|а́ивать, -о́ить. **2.** (*demand return of*) тре́бовать, по- обра́тно.
reclamation [ˌrekləˈmeɪʃ(ə)n] *n.* освое́ние.
reclassify [ri:ˈklæsɪˌfaɪ] *v.t.* перев|оди́ть, -ести́ в другу́ю катего́рию; переклассифици́ровать (*impf., pf.*).
recline [rɪˈklaɪn] *v.t.* отки́|дывать, -и́нуть ; **she ~d her head on his shoulder** она́ склони́ла го́лову ему́ на плечо́.
v.i. (полу)лежа́ть (*impf.*); **they ~d on the ground** они́ разлегли́сь на земле́.
recluse [rɪˈklu:s] *n.* затво́рник, отше́льник.
recognition [ˌrekəgˈnɪʃ(ə)n] *n.* **1.** (*knowing again*) опознава́ние; **he changed beyond ~** он измени́лся до неузнава́емости. **2.** (*acknowledgement*) призна́ние; **he received a cheque in ~ of his services** он получи́л чек в знак призна́ния его́ услу́г.
recognizable [ˈrekəgˌnaɪzəb(ə)l] *adj.* опознава́емый.
recognize [ˈrekəgˌnaɪz] *v.t.* **1.** (*know again*) узн|ава́ть, -а́ть; **I could barely ~ him** я его́ е́ле узна́л. **2.** (*acknowledge*) призн|ава́ть, -а́ть; **he was ~d as the lawful heir** он был при́знан зако́нным насле́дником.
recoil [ˈri:kɔɪl] *n.* отско́к; отда́ча.
v.i. **1.** (*shrink back*) отпря́нуть (*pf.*); отша́т|ываться, -ну́ться; **the sight made him ~ with horror** зре́лище заста́вило его́ отпря́нуть в у́жасе. **2.** (*of gun*) отка́т|ываться, -и́ться; (*of rifle*) отд|ава́ть, -а́ть.
recollect [ˌrekəˈlekt] *v.t.* всп|омина́ть, -о́мнить; прип|омина́ть, -о́мнить.
recollection [ˌrekəˈlekʃ(ə)n] *n.* па́мять; воспомина́ние; **to the best of my ~** наско́лько я по́мню.
recommence [ˌri:kəˈmens] *v.t.* возобнов|ля́ть, -и́ть; нач|ина́ть, -а́ть сно́ва.
v.i. возобнов|ля́ться, -и́ться.
recommend [ˌrekəˈmend] *v.t.* **1.** (*speak well of; suggest as suitable*) рекомендова́ть (*impf., pf.*), от-/по- (*pf.*); сове́товать, по-; **he was ~ed for promotion** его́ вы́двинули на повыше́ние. **2.** (*advise*) рекомендова́ть, по- *+d.*; сове́товать, по- *+d.*
recommendation [ˌrekəˌmenˈdeɪʃ(ə)n] *n.* рекоменда́ция; **I bought the shares on your ~** я купи́л а́кции по ва́шей рекоменда́ции.
recompense [ˈrekəmˌpens] *n.* компенса́ция; **in ~ for your help** в вознагражде́ние за ва́шу по́мощь.
v.t. компенси́ровать (*impf., pf.*); **he was amply ~d for his trouble** его́ ще́дро вознагради́ли за его́ уси́лия.
reconcilable [ˈrekənˌsaɪləb(ə)l] *adj.* (*compatible*) совмести́мый (*с чем*).
reconcile [ˈrekənˌsaɪl] *v.t.* **1.** (*make friendly*) мири́ть, по-; **they finally became ~d** они́, наконе́ц, помири́лись. **2.** (*settle, compose*) ула́|живать, -дить; **their differences were ~d** они́ ула́дили свои́ разногла́сия. **3.** (*cause to agree, make compatible*) совме|ща́ть, -сти́ть; согласо́в|ывать, -а́ть. **4.** (*resign*): **~ o.s.** смир|я́ться, -и́ться (*с чем*); примир|я́ться, -и́ться (*с чем*).
reconciliation [ˌrekənˌsɪlɪˈeɪʃ(ə)n] *n.* примире́ние; ула́живание.
recondite [ˈrekənˌdaɪt, rɪˈkɒn-] *adj.* зау́мный, малоизве́стный.
recondition [ˌri:kənˈdɪʃ(ə)n] *v.t.* ремонти́ровать, от-.
reconnaissance [rɪˈkɒnɪs(ə)ns] *n.* разве́дка; **~ party** разве́дывательный отря́д.
reconnoitre [ˌrekəˈnɔɪtə(r)] *v.t. & i.* разве́дывать (*impf.*); производи́ть (*impf.*) разве́дку.
reconsider [ˌri:kənˈsɪdə(r)] *v.t.* пересм|а́тривать, -отре́ть.
v.i. переду́мать (*pf.*).
reconsideration [ˌri:kənˌsɪdəˈreɪʃ(ə)n] *n.* пересмо́тр; измене́ние реше́ния.
reconstitute [ri:ˈkɒnstɪˌtju:t] *v.t.* воспроизв|оди́ть, -ести́.
reconstruct [ˌri:kənˈstrʌkt] *v.t.* перестр|а́ивать, -о́ить; реконструи́ровать (*impf., pf.*); (*fig.*) воспроизв|оди́ть, -ести́.
reconstruction [ˌri:kənˈstrʌkʃ(ə)n] *n.* перестро́йка, реконстру́кция; (*of acts etc.*) воспроизведе́ние.
reconvene [ˌri:kənˈvi:n] *v.t.* соз|ыва́ть, -ва́ть вновь.
v.i. соб|ира́ться, -ра́ться вновь.
record[1] [ˈrekɔ:d] *n.* **1.** (*written note, document*) за́пись, учёт; **the teacher keeps a ~ of attendance** учи́тель ведёт учёт посеща́емости; **R~ Office** госуда́рственный архи́в. **2.** (*state of being recorded, esp. as evidence*) за́пись; **it is a matter of ~** э́то зарегистри́ровано; **it is on ~ that you lost every game** изве́стно, что вы проигра́ли все ма́тчи; **it was the hottest day on ~** э́то был са́мый жа́ркий день из ра́нее зафикси́рованных; **I went on ~ as opposing the plan** в протоко́ле бы́ло отме́чено,

что я про́тив э́того пла́на; **this is off the ~** э́то не должно́ быть пре́дано огла́ске. **3.** (*relic of past*) па́мятник. **4.** (*chronicle*) ле́топись; **the film provides an interesting ~ of the war** э́тот фильм интере́сен как ле́топись войны́. **5.** (*past achievement*): **attendance ~** посеща́емость; **he has an honourable ~ of service** у него́ безупре́чный послужно́й спи́сок; **his ~ is against him** его́ про́шлое говори́т про́тив него́; **the defendant had a (criminal) ~** у обвиня́емого ра́нее име́лись суди́мости. **6.** (*sound recording*) (грам)пласти́нка; **long-playing ~** долгоигра́ющая пласти́нка; **they made a new ~ of the song** вы́пустили ещё одну́ за́пись э́той пе́сни. **7.** (*best performance*) реко́рд; **world ~** реко́рд ми́ра; **she set up a new ~ for the mile** она́ установи́ла но́вый реко́рд в бе́ге на одну́ ми́лю; **he will easily beat the ~** он легко́ побьёт реко́рд; **equal a ~** повтор|я́ть, -и́ть реко́рд; (*attr.*) реко́рдный, небыва́лый; **cars have had ~ sales** про́дано реко́рдное коли́чество маши́н.

cpds. **~-breaking** *adj.* реко́рдный; **~-holder** *n.* рекордсме́н (*fem.* -ка); **~-player** *n.* проигрыватель (*m.*).

record[2] [rɪ'kɔːd] *v.t.* **1.** (*set down in writing, or fig.*) запи́с|ывать, -а́ть; **the book ~s his early years** в кни́ге отражены́ его́ молоды́е го́ды. **2.** (*on tape, film etc.*) запи́с|ывать, -а́ть (на плёнку); **the camera ~ed his features** фотоаппара́т запечатле́л его́ черты́. **3.** (*of instrument: register*) регистри́ровать, за-; **the thermometer ~ed zero** термо́метр пока́зывал ноль.

recorder [rɪ'kɔːdə(r)] *n.* (*magistrate*) реко́рдер; (*apparatus*) магнитофо́н; (*mus.*) (англи́йская) фле́йта.

recording [rɪ'kɔːdɪŋ] *n.* (*putting on record*) за́пись, регистра́ция; (*registering of sound or TV*) звукоза́пись; видеоза́пись; (*recorded performance etc.*) за́пись.

recount[1] [riː'kaʊnt] *n.* (*second count*) пересчёт.

v.t. пересчи́т|ывать, -а́ть.

recount[2] [rɪ'kaʊnt] *v.t.* (*narrate*) расска́з|ывать, -а́ть.

recoup [rɪ'kuːp] *v.t.* (*recover*): **~ one's losses** возвраща́ть, верну́ть поте́рянное.

recourse [rɪ'kɔːs] *n.* прибе́жище; вы́ход; **have ~ to** приб|ега́ть, -е́гнуть к+*d.*

recover[1] [rɪ'kʌvə(r)] *v.t.* **1.** (*regain, retrieve*) получ|а́ть, -и́ть обра́тно; верну́ть (*pf.*); **he quickly ~ed his health** он бы́стро вы́здоровел; **she never ~ed consciousness** она́ так и не пришла́ в созна́ние; **he ~ed his appetite** к нему́ возврати́лся аппети́т; **she was badly shocked, but ~ed herself** она́ была́ си́льно потрясена́, но пото́м пришла́ в себя́; (*win back*) отвоёв|ывать, -а́ть; **much land has been ~ed from the sea** мно́го су́ши отвоёвано у мо́ря. **2.** (*secure by legal process*) взы́ск|ивать, -а́ть в суде́бном поря́дке; **an action to ~ damages** иск о возмеще́нии уще́рба.

v.i. **1.** (*revive*) попр|авля́ться, -а́виться; опр|авля́ться, -а́виться; **I have quite ~ed** я по́лностью вы́здоровел; **it took me some time to ~ from my astonishment** я до́лго не мог прийти́ в себя́ от удивле́ния. **2.** (*leg.*) возме|ща́ть, -сти́ть по суду́.

recover[2] [riː'kʌvə(r)] *v.t.* перекр|ыва́ть, -ы́ть; **the chair needs ~ing** стул на́до оби́ть на́ново.

recovery [rɪ'kʌvərɪ] *n.* **1.** (*regaining possession; reclamation*) возвра́т; возмеще́ние; **the ~ of marshland** осуше́ние боло́т. **2.** (*revival; restoration to health*) выздоровле́ние; **he made a rapid ~** он бы́стро попра́вился; **his business made a ~** его́ дела́ пошли́ на попра́вку. **3.** (*rehabilitation; restoration to use*) восстановле́ние; **~ vehicle** авари́йный автомоби́ль.

re-create [ˌriːkrɪ'eɪt] *v.t.* вновь созд|ава́ть, -а́ть; воссозд|ава́ть, -а́ть.

recreation [ˌrekrɪ'eɪʃ(ə)n] *n.* о́тдых; развлече́ние; **he plays chess for ~** он отдыха́ет, игра́я в ша́хматы; **~ ground** спортплоща́дка; площа́дка для игр.

recrimination [rɪˌkrɪmɪ'neɪʃ(ə)n] *n.* встре́чное обвине́ние.

recruit [rɪ'kruːt] *n.* (*mil.*) новобра́нец; **raw ~** (*fig.*) новичо́к; (*new member*) но́вый член/уча́стник.

v.t. вербова́ть, за-; наб|ира́ть, -ра́ть; **~ing sergeant** сержа́нт по вербо́вке на вое́нную слу́жбу.

recruitment [rɪ'kruːtmənt] *n.* вербо́вка.

rectangle ['rekˌtæŋɡ(ə)l] *n.* прямоуго́льник.

rectangular [rek'tæŋɡʊlə(r)] *adj.* прямоуго́льный.

rectification [ˌrektɪfɪ'keɪʃ(ə)n] *n.* исправле́ние.

rectify ['rektɪˌfaɪ] *v.t.* испр|авля́ть, -а́вить.

rectilinear [ˌrektɪ'lɪnɪə(r)] *adj.* прямоли́не́йный.

rectitude ['rektɪˌtjuːd] *n.* че́стность, прямота́.

rector ['rektə(r)] *n.* (*clergyman*) ≃ прихо́дский свяще́нник; (*of university*) ре́ктор.

rectory ['rektərɪ] *n.* дом прихо́дского свяще́нника.

rectum ['rektəm] *n.* пряма́я кишка́.

recumbent [rɪ'kʌmbənt] *adj.* лежа́чий, лежа́щий.

recuperate [rɪ'kuːpəˌreɪt] *v.i.* попр|авля́ться, -а́виться.

recuperation [rɪˌkuːpə'reɪʃ(ə)n] *n.* выздоровле́ние.

recur [rɪ'kɜː(r)] *v.i.* **1.** (*occur repeatedly*) повтор|я́ться, -и́ться; **a ~ring headache** хрони́ческие головны́е бо́ли (*f. pl.*); **it is a ~ring problem** э́то постоя́нно возника́ющая пробле́ма. **2.** (*return*) возвра|ща́ться, -ти́ться.

recurrence [rɪ'kʌrəns] *n.* повторе́ние; возвра́т.

recurrent [rɪ'kʌrənt] *adj.* повторя́ющийся.

recycle [riː'saɪk(ə)l] *v.t.* рециркули́ровать (*impf., pf.*); **~d paper** бума́га из ути́ля.

recycling [riː'saɪklɪŋ] *n.* повто́рное испо́льзование, перерабо́тка.

red [red] *n.* **1.** кра́сный цвет; **the article made me see ~** (*fig.*) статья́ привела́ меня́ в бе́шенство; (*of clothes*): **~ doesn't suit her** кра́сное ей не идёт. **2.** (*debit side of account*) долг, задо́лженность; **my account is in the ~** у меня́ задо́лженность в ба́нке. **3.** (*coll., Communist*) «кра́сный».

adj. **1.** кра́сный; а́лый; **she went ~ in the face** она́ покрасне́ла; **he was ~ with anger** он покрасне́л от гне́ва; **R~ Cross** Кра́сный Крест; **~ deer** благоро́дный оле́нь; **R~ Indian** краснoко́жий, инде́ец; (*adj.*) краснoко́жий; **~ lead** (*min.*) свинцо́вый су́рик; **~ light** (*warning signal*) сигна́л опа́сности; **~ meat** чёрное мя́со; **it was like a ~ rag to a bull** э́то поде́йствовало, как кра́сная тря́пка на быка́; **the R~ Sea** Кра́сное мо́ре; **~ tape** (*fig.*) канцеля́рская волоки́та. **2.** (*coll., Soviet*): **the R~ Air Force** сове́тские вое́нно-возду́шные си́лы.

cpds. **~-blooded** *adj.* (*fig.*) энерги́чный; му́жественный; **~breast** *n.* мали́новка; **~currant** *n.* кра́сная сморо́дина; **~-eyed** *adj.* (*from weeping*) с глаза́ми, кра́сными от слёз; **~-haired** *adj.* рыжево-ло́сый; **~-handed** *adj.*: **he was caught ~-handed** его́ пойма́ли с поли́чным; **~head** *n.* ры́жий (челове́к); **~-headed** *adj.* ры́жий; **~-hot** *adj.* раскалённый докрасна́; (*fig.*) (*fervent*) горя́чий, пы́лкий; (*exciting*): **~-hot news** сенсацио́нное сообще́ние; **~-letter** *adj.* пра́здничный; **it was a ~-letter day for me** э́то бы́ло для меня́ пра́здником; **~skin** *n.* (*coll.*) краснoко́жий.

redden ['red(ə)n] *v.i.* красне́ть, по-.

redecorate [riː'dekəˌreɪt] *v.t.* отде́л|ывать, -ать.

redecoration [riːˌdekə'reɪʃ(ə)n] *n.* отде́лка; ремо́нт.

redeem [rɪ'diːm] *v.t.* **1.** (*get back, recover*) выкупа́ть, вы́купить; **the mortgage was ~ed** зало́г был вы́плачен. **2.** (*fulfil*) выполня́ть, вы́полнить; **he ~ed his promise** он вы́полнил обеща́ние. **3.** (*purchase freedom of*) выкупа́ть, вы́купить; **Christ came to ~ sinners** Христо́с пришёл искупи́ть грехи́ люде́й. **4.** (*compensate*) искуп|а́ть, -и́ть; компенси́ровать (*impf., pf.*); **he has one ~ing feature** у него́ есть одно́ положи́тельное ка́чество.

redeemer [rɪ'di:mə(r)] *n.* спаси́тель, искупи́тель (*both m.*).

redefine [,ri:dɪ'faɪn] *v.t.* определ|я́ть, -и́ть за́ново.

redefinition [,ri:defɪ'nɪʃ(ə)n] *n.* но́вое определе́ние.

redemption [rɪ'dempʃ(ə)n] *n.* **1.** (*repurchase*) вы́куп. **2.** (*fulfilment*): ~ **of a promise** выполне́ние обеща́ния. **3.** (*deliverance*) искупле́ние; **past** ~ без наде́жды на спасе́ние.

redeploy [,ri:dɪ'plɔɪ] *v.t. & i.* передислоци́ровать(ся) (*impf., pf.*); (*of resources*) перераспредел|я́ть, -и́ть.

redeployment [,ri:dɪ'plɔɪmənt] *n.* передислока́ция; перераспределе́ние.

re-design [,ri:dɪ'zaɪn] *v.t.* за́ново (с)конструи́ровать (*pf.*).

redevelop [,ri:dɪ'veləp] *v.t.* перестр|а́ивать, -о́ить.

redevelopment [,ri:dɪ'veləpmənt] *n.* перестро́йка.

redirect [,ri:daɪ'rekt, -dɪ'rekt] *v.t.* (*e.g. letters*) переадресо́в|ывать, -а́ть; (*re-route*): **the traffic was ~ed** тра́нспорт был напра́влен по друго́му маршру́ту.

rediscover [,ri:dɪ'skʌvə(r)] *v.t.* откр|ыва́ть, -ы́ть за́ново.

redistribute [,ri:dɪ'strɪ,bju:t] *v.t.* перераспредел|я́ть, -и́ть.

redistribution [,ri:dɪ,strɪ'bju:ʃ(ə)n] *n.* перераспределе́ние.

redo [ri:'du:] *v.t.* переде́л|ывать, -а́ть.

redolent ['redələnt] *adj.*: ~ (*fig., suggestive*) **of** отдаю́щий (*чем*), напомина́ющий (*что*).

redouble [ri:'dʌb(ə)l] *v.t. & i.* удв|а́ивать(ся), -о́ить(ся); **he ~d his efforts** он удво́ил свои́ уси́лия.

redoubt [rɪ'daʊt] *n.* реду́т.

redoubtable [rɪ'daʊtəb(ə)l] *adj.* гро́зный; устраша́ющий.

redress [rɪ'dres] *n.* возмеще́ние; **I shall seek** ~ я бу́ду добива́ться компенса́ции.

v.t. возме|ща́ть, -сти́ть; **their victory ~ed the balance of forces** их побе́да восстанови́ла равнове́сие сил; **her grievances were ~ed** её жа́лобы бы́ли удовлетворены́.

reduce [rɪ'dju:s] *v.t.* **1.** (*make less or smaller*) ум|еньша́ть, -е́ньшить; сокра|ща́ть, -ти́ть; **we must ~ our expenditure** мы должны́ сократи́ть расхо́ды; **in ~d circumstances** в стеснённых обстоя́тельствах; **exercise will ~ your weight** заря́дка помо́жет вам сба́вить вес; (*lower*) сн|ижа́ть, -и́зить; сб|авля́ть, -а́вить; **'~ speed now'** «води́тель, притормози́!»; **all prices are ~d** все це́ны сни́жены; (*shorten*) сокра|ща́ть, -ти́ть; **his sentence was ~d to 6 months** ему́ сократи́ли пригово́р до шести́ ме́сяцев; (*make narrower*) сужа́ть, су́зить. **2.** (*bring, compel*) дов|оди́ть, -ести́ (*до чего*); **the film ~d her to tears** фильм расстро́гал её до слёз; **I was ~d to silence** мне пришло́сь промолча́ть; **this ~s your argument to absurdity** э́то лиша́ет ваш до́вод вся́кого смы́сла. **3.** (*convert*) превра|ща́ть, -ти́ть; **all fractions can be ~d to decimals** все дро́би мо́жно перевести́ в десяти́чные; **the logs were ~d to ashes** поле́нья сгоре́ли дотла́; **he was ~d to a skeleton** он преврати́лся в скеле́т.

v.i. **1.** (*become less*) сн|ижа́ться, -и́зиться; ум|еньша́ться, -е́ньшиться; **interest is paid at a reduced rate** проце́нт выпла́чивается по пони́женной ста́вке. **2.** (*lose weight*) худе́ть (*impf.*); **a reducing diet** дие́та для поте́ри ве́са. **3.** (*be equivalent*) равня́ться (*impf.*).

reduction [rɪ'dʌkʃ(ə)n] *n.* **1.** (*decrease*) сокраще́ние; сниже́ние; **a ~ in numbers** коли́чественное сокраще́ние; **price ~s** сниже́ние цен; **is there a ~ for children?** есть ли ски́дка для дете́й?; ~ **of armaments** сокраще́ние вооруже́ний; ~ **of temperature** сниже́ние температу́ры; (*shortening*) сокраще́ние; (*narrowing*) суже́ние; (*demotion*) пониже́ние; ~ **to the ranks** разжа́лование (в солда́ты). **2.** (*conversion*) перево́д; превраще́ние.

redundancy [rɪ'dʌnd(ə)nsɪ] *n.* (*superfluity*) изли́шек, избы́точность; (*in work-force*) безрабо́тица.

redundant [rɪ'dʌnd(ə)nt] *adj.* изли́шний, избы́точный; **the last sentence is** ~ после́днее предложе́ние изли́шне; **many workers were made** ~ мно́гих рабо́чих уво́лили.

reduplicate [rɪ'dju:plɪ,keɪt] *v.t.* удв|а́ивать, -о́ить.

reduplication [rɪ,dju:plɪ'keɪʃ(ə)n] *n.* удвое́ние.

reed [ri:d] *n.* **1.** (*bot.*) тростни́к, камы́ш. **2.** (*mus. instrument*) свире́ль; (*vibrating piece*) язычо́к; ~ **instruments** язычко́вые инструме́нты (*m. pl.*).

re-educate [ri:'edjʊ,keɪt] *v.t.* перевоспи́т|ывать, -а́ть.

re-education [ri:,edjʊ'keɪʃ(ə)n] *n.* перевоспита́ние.

reedy ['ri:dɪ] *adj.* **1.** (*full of reeds*) тростнико́вый. **2.** (*of sounds*) пронзи́тельный.

reef [ri:f] *n.* (*geog.*) риф; подво́дная скала́.

reek [ri:k] *n.* вонь.

v.i. воня́ть, про-; **his clothes ~ed of tobacco** от его́ оде́жды несло́ табако́м; (*fig.*) попа́хивать, па́хнуть (*both impf.*); **the affair ~s of corruption** де́ло па́хнет корру́пцией.

reel[1] [ri:l] *n.* (*winding device*) кату́шка; руло́н; **a ~ of thread, cotton** кату́шка ни́ток; **a ~ of film for a camera** кату́шка плёнки для фотоаппара́та.

v.t. нам|а́тывать, -ота́ть.

with advs.: **the fisherman ~ed in the line** рыба́к смота́л у́дочку; **the guide ~ed off a lot of dates** гид вы́палил це́лый ряд истори́ческих дат.

reel[2] [ri:l] *v.i.* кружи́ться (*impf.*); верте́ться (*impf.*); **he ~ed under the blow** он зашата́лся от уда́ра; **the drunkard went ~ing home** шата́ясь, пья́ница поплёлся домо́й.

re-elect [,ri:ɪ'lekt] *v.t.* переизб|ира́ть, -ра́ть.

re-election [,ri:ɪ'lekʃ(ə)n] *n.* переизбра́ние.

re-emerge [,ri:ɪ'mɜ:dʒ] *v.i.* вновь появ|ля́ться, -и́ться.

re-emergence [,ri:ɪ'mɜ:dʒəns] *n.* появле́ние вновь.

re-emphasize [ri:'emfə,saɪz] *v.t.* подчёрк|ивать, -ну́ть сно́ва (*or* ещё раз).

re-enact [,ri:ɪ'nækt] *v.t.* вновь вв|оди́ть, -ести́ в де́йствие.

re-enlist [,ri:ɪn'lɪst] *v.i.* поступ|а́ть, -и́ть на сверхсро́чную слу́жбу.

re-enter [ri:'entə(r)] *v.i.* сно́ва входи́ть, войти́ в+*a.*

re-entry [ri:'entrɪ] *n.* вхожде́ние/вступле́ние за́ново; ~ **module** возвраща́емый отсе́к; ~ **into the atmosphere** возвра́т в атмосфе́ру.

re-equip [,ri:ɪ'kwɪp] *v.t.* переосна|ща́ть, -сти́ть.

re-establish [,ri:ɪ'stæblɪʃ] *v.t.* восстан|а́вливать, -ови́ть.

re-establishment [,ri:ɪ'stæblɪʃmənt] *n.* восстановле́ние.

re-examine [,ri:ɪg'zæmɪn] *v.t.* вновь рассм|а́тривать, -отре́ть; пересм|а́тривать, -отре́ть; (*acad.*) втори́чно экзаменова́ть, про-.

refectory [rɪ'fektərɪ] *n.* тра́пезная; столо́вая.

refer [rɪ'fɜ:(r)] *v.t.* (*pass on, direct*) от|сыла́ть, -осла́ть; напр|авля́ть, -а́вить; **the clerk ~red me to the manager** слу́жащий отосла́л меня́ к нача́льнику.

v.i. **1.** (*have recourse*) спр|авля́ться, -а́виться; **he ~red to the dictionary** он спра́вился со словарём; **the speaker ~red to his notes** ора́тор загляну́л в конспе́кт. **2.** (*allude*): ~ **to** упом|ина́ть, -яну́ть; **all his writings ~ to the war** все его́ произведе́ния посвящены́ войне́; **are you ~ring to me?** вы име́ете в виду́ меня́?

referee [,refə'ri:] *n.* **1.** (*arbitrator*) арби́тр. **2.** (*at games*) судья́ (*m.*); рефери́ (*m. indecl.*). **3.** (*person supplying testimonial*) поручи́тель (*m.*).

v.t. & i.: **he agreed to ~ the match** он согласи́лся суди́ть матч; **~ing** суде́йство.

reference ['refərəns] *n.* **1.** (*referring for decision, consideration etc.*) отсы́лка; **terms of** ~ компете́нция, круг полномо́чий. **2.** (*relation*) отноше́ние; **with ~ to your letter** в связи́ с ва́шим письмо́м. **3.** (*allusion*) упомина́ние, ссы́лка; **he made frequent ~ to our agreement** он ча́сто ссыла́лся на на́ше соглаше́ние. **4.** (*in text*) ссы́лка, сно́ска. **5.** (*referring for information*) спра́вка; **you should make ~ to a dictionary** вам сле́дует обрати́ться к словарю́; **~ book** спра́вочник; **~ library** спра́вочная библиоте́ка. **6.** (*testimonial*) о́тзыв, рекоменда́ция; (*person supplying ~*) поручи́тель (*m.*).

referendum [ˌrefəˈrendəm] *n.* рефере́ндум.

referral [rɪˈfɜːr(ə)l] *n.* направле́ние.

refill [riːˈfɪl] *v.t.* нап|олня́ть, -о́лнить вновь; **may I ~your glass?** позво́льте подли́ть?

v.i. запр|авля́ться, -а́виться.

refine [rɪˈfaɪn] *v.t.* **1.** (*purify*) оч|ища́ть, -и́стить; **~d sugar** са́хар-рафина́д. **2.** (*make more elegant or cultured*) соверше́нствовать, у-; **~d manners** утончённые/изы́сканные мане́ры.

refinement [rɪˈfaɪnmənt] *n.* **1.** (*purification*) очище́ние. **2.** (*of feeling, taste etc.*) утончённость, то́нкость; (*of breeding or manners*) благовоспи́танность; **lack of ~** неотёсанность. **3.** (*subtle or ingenious manifestation*) утончённость.

refinery [rɪˈfaɪnərɪ] *n.* (*oil*) нефтеочисти́тельный заво́д.

refit[1] [ˈriːfɪt] *n.* ремо́нт, переоборудование.

refit[2] [riːˈfɪt] *v.t.* чини́ть, по-; переобору́довать (*impf., pf.*); ремонти́ровать, от-.

reflate [riːˈfleɪt] *v.i.* (*econ.*) пров|оди́ть, -ести́ рефля́цию.

reflect [rɪˈflekt] *v.t.* **1.** (*light, heat etc.*) отра|жа́ть, -зи́ть; **light is ~ed from a white surface** свет отража́ется от бе́лой пове́рхности; (*fig., express, reveal*): **her thoughts were ~ed in her face** все её мы́сли отража́лись на её лице́. **2.** (*consider*) размышля́ть (*impf.*); **I ~ed how fortunate I had been** я поду́мал о том, как мне повезло́.

v.i. **1.** (*produce a reflection*) отра|жа́ться, -зи́ться; (*fig., bring discredit*): **your behaviour ~s on us all** ва́ше поведе́ние кладёт пятно́ на нас всех; **I do not wish to ~ on your honesty** я не хочу́ броса́ть тень на ва́шу честь. **2.** (*ponder*) заду́маться (*pf.*) (над+*i.*).

reflection [rɪˈflekʃ(ə)n] *n.* **1.** (*of light, heat etc.*) отраже́ние. **2.** (*consideration*) размышле́ние; **he acts without ~** он де́йствует неосмотри́тельно; **she was lost in ~** она́ была́ погружена́ в свои́ мы́сли. **3.** (*expression of idea*) соображе́ние; замеча́ние. **4.** (*expression of blame*) порица́ние; **I intended no ~ on you** я не собира́лся вас порица́ть. **5.** (*cause of credit or discredit*): **it is a ~ on my honour** э́то задева́ет мою́ честь.

reflective [rɪˈflektɪv] *adj.* (*of a surface*) отража́ющий; (*thoughtful*) мы́слящий; заду́мчивый.

reflector [rɪˈflektə(r)] *n.* рефле́ктор.

reflex [ˈriːfleks] *n.* (**~ action**) рефле́кс.

adj. рефлекто́рный; **~ camera** зерка́льный фотоаппара́т.

reflexive [rɪˈfleksɪv] *adj.* возвра́тный.

refloat [riːˈfləʊt] *v.t.* подн|има́ть, -я́ть (*затонувшее судно*); сн|има́ть, -ять с ме́ли.

reforestation [riːˌfɒrɪˈsteɪʃ(ə)n] *n.* восстановле́ние лесны́х масси́вов.

reform [rɪˈfɔːm] *n.* (*improvement, correction*) рефо́рма.

v.t. **1.** (*change for the better*) реформи́ровать (*impf., pf.*); **he is a ~ed character** он соверше́нно испра́вился. **2.** (*correct*) испр|авля́ть, -а́вить; **~ abuses** устран|я́ть, -и́ть злоупотребле́ния.

re-form [riːˈfɔːm] *v.t.* (*reshape, form again*) переформиро́в|ывать, -а́ть.

v.i. перестр|а́иваться, -о́иться; **the soldiers ~ed into two ranks** солда́ты перестро́ились в две шере́нги.

reformation [ˌrefəˈmeɪʃ(ə)n] *n.* (*change, improvement*) преобразова́ние; **the R~** Реформа́ция.

reformatory [rɪˈfɔːmətərɪ] *n.* исправи́тельное заведе́ние.

reformer [rɪˈfɔːmə(r)] *n.* реформа́тор; преобразова́тель (*m.*).

refract [rɪˈfrækt] *v.t.* прелом|ля́ть, -и́ть.

refraction [rɪˈfrækʃ(ə)n] *n.* преломле́ние; рефра́кция.

refractor [rɪˈfræktə(r)] *n.* рефра́ктор.

refractory [rɪˈfræktərɪ] *adj.* **1.** (*of pers.*) упря́мый, непослу́шный. **2.** (*of illness*) упо́рный. **3.** (*fire-resisting*) огнеупо́рный.

refrain[1] [rɪˈfreɪn] *n.* рефре́н, припе́в.

refrain[2] [rɪˈfreɪn] *v.i.* сде́рж|иваться, -а́ться; возде́рж|иваться, -а́ться; **I could hardly ~ from laughing** я е́ле сде́рживался от сме́ха.

refresh [rɪˈfreʃ] *v.t.* освеж|а́ть, -и́ть; **I woke ~ed** сон освежи́л меня́; **~ o.s.** (*with food and drink*) подкреп|ля́ться, -и́ться; **let me ~ your memory** позво́льте напо́мнить вам.

refresher [rɪˈfreʃə(r)] *n.* (**~ course**) курс переподгото́вки (*or* повыше́ния квалифика́ции).

refreshing [rɪˈfreʃɪŋ] *adj.* освежа́ющий.

refreshment [rɪˈfreʃmənt] *n.* **1.** (*reinvigoration*) восстановле́ние сил. **2.** (*food or drink*) еда́; питьё; **won't you take some ~?** не хоти́те ли подкрепи́ться/закуси́ть?; **~s are served on the train** в по́езде мо́жно перекуси́ть; **~ room** буфе́т.

refrigerate [rɪˈfrɪdʒəˌreɪt] *v.t.* замор|а́живать, -о́зить.

refrigeration [rɪˌfrɪdʒəˈreɪʃ(ə)n] *n.* замора́живание.

refrigerator [rɪˈfrɪdʒəˌreɪtə(r)] *n.* холоди́льник.

refuel [riːˈfjuːəl] *v.i.* поп|олня́ть, -о́лнить запа́сы то́плива; дозапра́виться (*pf.*).

refuge [ˈrefjuːdʒ] *n.* убе́жище; приста́нище; **the cat took ~ beneath the table** кот спря́тался под столо́м; (*fig.*) утеше́ние; **take ~ in lies** приб|ега́ть, -е́гнуть ко лжи.

refugee [ˌrefjʊˈdʒiː] *n.* бе́жен|ец (*fem.* -ка); **political ~** политэмигра́нт.

refund[1] [ˈriːfʌnd] *n.* возмеще́ние убы́тков; **they gave me a ~** мне верну́ли де́ньги.

refund[2] [rɪˈfʌnd] *v.t.* (*pay back*) возвраща́ть, верну́ть (*деньги*); (*reimburse*) возме|ща́ть, -сти́ть.

refurbish [riːˈfɜːbɪʃ] *v.t.* отде́л|ывать, -ать.

refusal [rɪˈfjuːz(ə)l] *n.* отка́з; **he would take no ~** он не при́нял отка́за.

refuse[1] [ˈrefjuːs] *n.* му́сор; **~ collection** убо́рка му́сора; **~ dump** сва́лка.

refuse[2] [rɪˈfjuːz] *v.t. & i.* (*decline to give or grant*) отка́з|ывать, -а́ть (*кому в чём*); (*reject*) отв|ерга́ть, -е́ргнуть; (*decline sth. offered*) отка́з|ываться, -а́ться от+*g.*; **the invitation was ~d** приглаше́ние не бы́ло при́нято; **children were ~d admittance** дете́й не впусти́ли; **it is an offer not to be ~d** тако́е предложе́ние не сле́дует отклоня́ть.

refusenik [rɪˈfjuːznɪk] *n.* отка́зни|к (*fem.* -ца).

refutation [ˌrefjʊˈteɪʃ(ə)n] *n.* опроверже́ние.

refute [rɪˈfjuːt] *v.t.* опров|ерга́ть, -е́ргнуть.

regain [rɪˈgeɪn] *v.t.* **1.** (*recover*) получ|а́ть, -и́ть обра́тно; **he never ~ed consciousness** он так и не пришёл в созна́ние; (*mil., recapture*) отвоёв|ывать, -а́ть. **2.** (*reach again*) сно́ва дост|ига́ть, -и́гнуть; **they ~ed the shore** они́ вновь дости́гли бе́рега.

regal [ˈriːg(ə)l] *adj.* короле́вский.

regale [rɪˈgeɪl] *v.t.* уго|ща́ть, -сти́ть; по́тчевать (*impf.*).

regalia [rɪˈgeɪlɪə] *n.* рега́ли|и (*pl., g.* -й).

regard [rɪˈgɑːd] *n.* **1.** (*gaze*) взгляд. **2.** (*point of attention, respect*) отноше́ние; **in this ~** в э́том отноше́нии; **in, with ~ to your request** что каса́ется ва́шей про́сьбы. **3.** (*heed*) внима́ние; **he pays no ~ to my warnings** он не прислу́шивается к мои́м предупрежде́ниям. **4.** (*consideration*) внима́ние, забо́та; **he paid no ~ to her feelings** он не счита́лся с её чу́вствами. **5.** (*esteem*) уваже́ние (к+*g.*); **he**

holds your opinion in high ~ он óчень высокó цéнит вáше мнéние. **6.** (*pl., greetings*) привéт; (*formula at end of letter*) с привéтом; **give him my warmest ~s** передáйте емý от меня сердéчный привéт.

v.t. **1.** (*look at*) разгля́д|ывать, -éть; **he ~ed me with hostility** он разгля́дывал меня́ с неприя́знью. **2.** (*view mentally, consider*) сч|итáть, -есть; **I ~ his behaviour with suspicion** я отношýсь к егó постýпкам с подозрéнием; **he was ~ed as a hero** егó считáли герóем. **3.** (*respect, esteem*) уважáть (*impf.*); **we all ~ him highly** мы все егó óчень уважáем. **4.** (*concern*): **this does not ~ me** э́то меня́ не касáется; **as ~s, ~ing** относи́тельно+*g.*; что касáется +*g.*; насчёт+*g.*

regardless [rɪ'gɑ:dlɪs] *adj.* невнимáтельный (к+*d.*); **~ of expense** не считáясь с расхóдами; **he pressed on ~** (*coll.*) он рвáлся вперёд, невзирáя ни на что.

regatta [rɪ'gætə] *n.* регáта.

regency ['ri:dʒənsɪ] *n.* рéгентство.

regenerate [rɪ'dʒenə,reɪt] *v.t. & i.* возро|ждáть(ся), -ди́ть(ся).

regeneration [rɪ,dʒenə'reɪʃ(ə)n] *n.* перерождéние, возрождéние.

regent ['ri:dʒ(ə)nt] *n.* рéгент; **Prince R~** принц-рéгент.

reggae ['regeɪ] *n.* рéгги (*m. indecl.*).

regime [reɪ'ʒi:m] *n.* режи́м, строй.

regimen ['redʒɪ,men] *n.* (*set of rules*) режи́м; порядок; (*med., esp. diet*) режи́м, диéта.

regiment[1] ['redʒɪmənt] *n.* полк.

regiment[2] ['redʒɪ,ment] *v.t.* муштровáть (*impf.*).

regimental [,redʒɪ'ment(ə)l] *adj.* полковóй.

regimentation [,redʒɪmən'teɪʃ(ə)n] *n.* региментáция, стрóгая регламентáция; муштрá.

region ['ri:dʒ(ə)n] *n.* райóн, óбласть; региóн; (*of body*) пóлость; **the abdominal ~** брюшнáя пóлость; **in the ~ of the heart** в óбласти сéрдца; (*fig.*) óбласть, сфéра.

regional ['ri:dʒənəl] *adj.* райóнный, областнóй; регионáльный; **a ~ accent** мéстный акцéнт.

register ['redʒɪstə(r)] *n.* **1.** (*record, list*) реéстр; зáпись; (*in school*) журнáл; **hotel ~** регистрациóнная кни́га; **~ of voters** спи́сок избирáтелей; **parish ~** прихóдская кни́га; **~ office = registry 2.. 2.** (*compass of voice or instrument*) реги́стр. **3.** (*mechanical recording device*) счётчик; **cash ~** кáсса.

v.t. **1.** (*enter on official record*) регистри́ровать, за-; оф|ормля́ть, -óрмить; **~ed letter** заказнóе письмó. **2.** (*make mental note of*) отм|ечáть, -éтить; зап|оминáть, -óмнить; **his mind did not ~ the fact** э́тот факт не запечатлéлся у негó в умé. **3.** (*of an instrument: record*) покáз|ывать, -áть; отм|ечáть, -éтить. **4.** (*express*) выражáть, вы́разить; **the audience ~ed their disapproval** пýблика вы́разила своё недовóльство.

v.i. **1.** (*record one's name*) регистри́роваться, за-. **2.** (*coll., correspond to sth. known*): **your name doesn't ~ with him** вáше и́мя ничегó емý не говори́т.

registrar [,redʒɪs'trɑ:(r), 'redʒ-] *n.* (*keeper of records*) рабóтник регистратýры; (*head of register office*) завéдующий (райóнного) отдéления зáгса; (*of university etc.*) регистрáтор, секретáрь (*m.*).

registration [,redʒɪ'streɪʃ(ə)n] *n.* регистрáция; **~ number of a car** (регистрациóнный) нóмер маши́ны.

registry ['redʒɪstrɪ] *n.* **1.** (*registration*) регистрáция. **2.** (*office for keeping records*) регистратýра; **they were married at a ~** они расписáлись в зáгсе.

regress [rɪ'gres] *v.i.* дви́гаться (*impf.*) в обрáтном направлéнии.

regression [rɪ'greʃ(ə)n] *n.* возвращéние (к+*d.*); (*decline*) упáдок.

regressive [rɪ'gresɪv] *adj.* регресси́вный.

regret [rɪ'gret] *n.* сожалéние; **I found to my ~ that I was late** я обнаружи́л, к своемý сожалéнию, что опоздáл; **I have no ~s** я ни о чём не жалéю.

v.t. **1.** (*feel sorrow for*) сожалéть (*impf.*); **I ~ losing my temper** я сожалéю, что вы́шел из себя́; **I ~ to say ...** к сожалéнию, я дóлжен сказáть... **2.** (*feel loss of*): **he ~s his lost opportunities** он (со)жалéет об утрáченных возмóжностях.

regretful [rɪ'gretfʊl] *adj.* пóлный сожалéния.

regrettable [rɪ'gretəb(ə)l] *adj.* прискóрбный; достóйный сожалéния.

regroup [ri:'gru:p] *v.t. & i.* перегруппирóв|ывать(ся), -áть(ся).

regular ['regjʊlə(r)] *n.* **1.** (**~ soldier**) солдáт регуля́рной áрмии. **2.** (*coll.*, **~ customer**) завсегдáтай; постоя́нный посети́тель.

adj. **1.** (*orderly in appearance, symmetrical*) прáвильный, регуля́рный. **2.** (*steady, unvarying, systematic*) регуля́рный, нормáльный; **~ breathing** спокóйное дыхáние; **a ~ pulse** ритми́чный пульс; **I have no ~ work** у меня́ нет постоя́нной рабóты; **he keeps ~ hours** у негó чёткий режи́м; (*in order*) очереднóй. **3.** (*conventional, proper*) при́нятый, установлéнный. **4.** (*gram.*) прáвильный. **5.** (*properly appointed*) регуля́рный; кáдровый. **6.** (*coll., thorough, real*) сýщий, настоя́щий. **7.** (*US, ordinary, standard*) регуля́рный, обы́чный. **8.** (*US, likeable*): **a ~ guy** (*coll.*) слáвный мáлый.

regularity [,regjʊ'lærɪtɪ] *n.* (*symmetry*) прáвильность; (*systematic occurrence*) регуля́рность.

regulate ['regjʊ,leɪt] *v.t.* регули́ровать (*impf.*).

regulation [,regjʊ'leɪʃ(ə)n] *n.* **1.** (*control*) регули́рование. **2.** (*rule*) прáвило; **the ~s say we must wear black** соглáсно/по прáвилам мы должны́ ходи́ть в чёрном. **3.** (*attr., standard*) установлéнный.

regulator ['regjʊ,leɪtə(r)] *n.* регуля́тор, стабилизáтор.

regurgitate [rɪ'gɜ:dʒɪ,teɪt] *v.t.* отры́г|ивать, -нýть.

rehabilitate [,ri:hə'bɪlɪ,teɪt] *v.t.* перевоспи́т|ывать, -áть; реабилити́ровать (*impf., pf.*).

rehabilitation [,ri:hə,bɪlɪ'teɪʃ(ə)n] *n.* перевоспитáние; реабилитáция.

rehearsal [rɪ'hɜ:s(ə)l] *n.* репети́ция; **dress ~** генерáльная репети́ция.

rehearse [rɪ'hɜ:s] *v.t.* репети́ровать, от-.

rehouse [ri:'haʊz] *v.t.* пересел|я́ть, -и́ть.

Reich [raɪx] *n.* рейх.

reign [reɪn] *n.* цáрствование, власть; **in the ~ of Peter the Great** в цáрствование Петрá Вели́кого; (*fig.*) власть, господство.

v.i. цáрствовать (*impf.*); (*fig.*) цари́ть (*impf.*); **silence ~ed** цари́ла тишинá.

reimburse [,ri:ɪm'bɜ:s] *v.t.* возме|щáть, -сти́ть (*что кому*); оплá|чивать, -ти́ть (*что кому*).

reimbursement [,ri:ɪm'bɜ:smənt] *n.* возмещéние.

rein [reɪn] *n.* пóвод (*pl.* -á *or* повóдья), вожжá; **he gave his horse the ~(s)** он отпусти́л повóдья; (*fig.*): **you are giving ~ to your imagination** у вас разыгрáлось воображéние; **we must keep a tight ~ on our spending** мы должны́ стрóго контроли́ровать нáши расхóды.

v.t. (*fig.*) держáть (*impf.*) в уздé; **~ in a horse** придéрж|ивать, -áть лóшадь.

reincarnate [,ri:ɪn'kɑ:neɪt] *v.t.* перевопло|щáть, -ти́ть.

reincarnation [,ri:ɪnkɑ:'neɪʃ(ə)n] *n.* перевоплощéние.

reindeer ['reɪndɪə(r)] *n.* сéверный олéнь.

reinforce [,ri:ɪn'fɔ:s] *v.t.* усили|вать, -ть; **this ~s my argument** э́то подкрепля́ет мои́ дóводы; **~d concrete** железобетóн.

reinforcement [,ri:ɪn'fɔ:smənt] *n.* усилéние; (*pl., troops*) подкреплéние.

reinstate [,ri:ɪn'steɪt] *v.t.* восстан|áвливать, -ови́ть в правáх/дóлжности.

reinstatement [,ri:ɪn'steɪtmənt] *n.* восстановлéние в правáх/дóлжности.

reinterpret [ˌriːɪnˈtɜːprɪt] *v.t.* интерпрети́ровать (*pf.*) по-но́вому.

reinterpretation [ˌriːɪnˌtɜːprɪˈteɪʃ(ə)n] *n.* но́вая интерпрета́ция.

reinvest [ˌriːɪnˈvest] *v.t. & i.* сно́ва поме|ща́ть, -сти́ть (капита́л).

reissue [riːˈɪʃuː, -sjuː] *n.* переизда́ние.

v.t. переизд|ава́ть, -а́ть.

reiterate [riːˈɪtəˌreɪt] *v.t.* повтор|я́ть, -и́ть.

reiteration [riːˌɪtəˈreɪʃ(ə)n] *n.* повторе́ние.

reject[1] [ˈriːdʒekt] *n.* брак.

reject[2] [rɪˈdʒekt] *v.t.* **1.** (*throw away*) отбр|а́сывать, -о́сить. **2.** (*refuse to accept*) отв|ерга́ть, -е́ргнуть; отклон|я́ть, -и́ть; **my offer was ~ed out of hand** моё предложе́ние сра́зу же отклони́ли; **I ~ your accusation** я не принима́ю ва́ше обвине́ние; **a ~ed suitor** отве́ргнутый покло́нник.

rejection [rɪˈdʒekʃ(ə)n] *n.* (*refusal to accept*) отка́з, отклоне́ние.

rejoice [rɪˈdʒɔɪs] *v.i.* ра́доваться, об- (*чему*).

rejoicing [rɪˈdʒɔɪsɪŋ] *n.* весе́лье, ра́дость.

rejoin [riːˈdʒɔɪn] *v.t.* **1.** (*join together again*) вновь присоедин|я́ть, -и́ть. **2.** (*return to*) присоедин|я́ться, -и́ться вновь +*d.*; **he ~ed his regiment** он верну́лся в свой полк.

rejoinder [rɪˈdʒɔɪndə(r)] *n.* отве́т; возраже́ние.

rejuvenate [rɪˈdʒuːvɪˌneɪt] *v.t.* омол|а́живать, -оди́ть.

rejuvenation [rɪˌdʒuːvɪˈneɪʃ(ə)n] *n.* омоложе́ние.

relapse [rɪˈlæps] *n.* рециди́в; **she suffered a ~** она́ сно́ва заболе́ла.

v.i. сно́ва преда́ться (*pf.*) (*чему*); сно́ва впасть (*pf.*) (*в какое-н. состояние*); **he ~d into bad ways** он сно́ва сби́лся с пути́; **she ~d into silence** она́ (сно́ва) замолча́ла.

relate [rɪˈleɪt] *v.t.* **1.** (*narrate*) расска́з|ывать, -а́ть о+*p.*; **strange to ~** как э́то ни стра́нно. **2.** (*establish relation between*) свя́з|ывать, -а́ть (*что с чем*); *see also* **related**

v.i. **1.** (*be relevant*) относи́ться (*impf.*) (к+*d.*). **2.** (*establish contact*): **he does not ~ well to people** он пло́хо схо́дится с людьми́.

related [rɪˈleɪtɪd] *adj.* **1.** (*logically connected*) (взаи́мно) свя́занный (с+*i.*). **2.** (*by blood or marriage*): **he and I are ~** мы с ним ро́дственники; **we are distantly ~** мы в да́льнем родстве́.

relation [rɪˈleɪʃ(ə)n] *n.* **1.** (*connection, correspondence*) отноше́ние, зави́симость; **in, with ~ to** что каса́ется +*g.*; относи́тельно+*g.* **2.** (*pl., dealings*) отноше́ния (*nt. pl.*); **international ~s** междунаро́дные отноше́ния; **public ~s officer** сотру́дник отде́ла информа́ции и рекла́мы; **sexual ~s** половы́е сноше́ния. **3.** (*kinsman, kinswoman*) ро́дственни|к (*fem.* -ца); **~s by marriage** ро́дственники по му́жу/жене́; сво́йственники.

relationship [rɪˈleɪʃənʃɪp] *n.* (*relevance*) связь, отноше́ние; (*kinship*) родство́.

relative [ˈrelətɪv] *n.* (*kinsman, kinswoman*) ро́дственни|к (*fem.* -ца).

adj. **1.** (*comparative*) относи́тельный; **he is a ~ newcomer** он здесь относи́тельно неда́вно; (*not absolute*) относи́тельный, усло́вный; **~ly speaking** вообще́ говоря́. **2.:** **~ to** (*having reference to*) каса́ющийся +*g.*; относя́щийся к+*d.*; **the facts ~ to the situation** обстоя́тельства, относя́щиеся к де́лу. **3.** (*gram.*): **~ pronoun** относи́тельное местоиме́ние.

relativity [ˌreləˈtɪvɪtɪ] *n.* относи́тельность; **theory of ~** тео́рия относи́тельности.

relax [rɪˈlæks] *v.t.* рассл|абля́ть, -а́бить; **he ~ed his grip** он разжа́л ру́ку; **we must not ~ our efforts** мы не должны́ ослабля́ть уси́лий; **a ~ing climate** кли́мат, де́йствующий расслабля́юще.

v.i. (*weaken*) осл|абева́ть, -а́бнуть; (*rest*) рассл|абля́ться, -а́биться; отдыха́ть (*impf.*); **I like to ~ in the sun** я люблю́ посиде́ть/поваля́ться на со́лнце; **the atmosphere ~ed** атмосфе́ра разряди́лась.

relaxation [ˌriːlækˈseɪʃ(ə)n] *n.* **1.** (*slackening*) уменьше́ние; смягче́ние; **~ of discipline** ослабле́ние дисципли́ны. **2.** (*recreation*) о́тдых, развлече́ние; **take one's ~** отдыха́ть (*impf.*). **3.** (*relief of tension*) разря́дка.

relay [ˈriːleɪ] *n.* **1.** (*fresh team*) сме́на; (*pl.*): **they worked in ~s** они́ рабо́тали посме́нно. **2.** (**~ race**) эстафе́тный бег. **3.** (*elec.*) реле́ (*indecl.*). **4.:** **~ station** ретрансляцио́нная ста́нция.

v.t. (*retransmit*) ретрансли́ровать (*impf., pf.*).

re-lay [riːˈleɪ] *v.t.* пере|кла́дывать, -ложи́ть.

relearn [riːˈlɜːn] *v.t.* вы́учить (*pf.*) за́ново.

release [rɪˈliːs] *n.* **1.** (*liberation, deliverance*) освобожде́ние; **~ from prison** освобожде́ние из тюрьмы́. **2.** (*device for doing this*) спуск; **carriage ~** (*of typewriter*) освобожде́ние каре́тки; **~ button** спускова́я кно́пка. **3.** (*publication, issue*) вы́пуск; **press ~** сообще́ние для печа́ти; **the latest ~s** (*films*) нови́нки (*f. pl.*) экра́на; **this film is on general ~** э́тот фильм в широ́ком прока́те.

v.t. **1.** (*liberate*) освобо|жда́ть, -ди́ть. **2.** (*unfasten, let go*) отпус|ка́ть, -ти́ть; выпуска́ть, вы́пустить; **he ~d her hand** он отпусти́л её ру́ку. **3.** (*make over, surrender*) отд|ава́ть, -а́ть. **4.** (*issue for circulation*) выпуска́ть, вы́пустить; **the news was ~d** сообще́ние бы́ло пре́дано огла́ске; **the film was ~d** фильм был вы́пущен (на экра́ны).

relegate [ˈrelɪˌgeɪt] *v.t.* от|сыла́ть, -осла́ть; **the team was ~d to the second division** кома́нду перевели́ во второ́й разря́д.

relegation [ˌrelɪˈgeɪʃ(ə)n] *n.* пониже́ние, перево́д (в бо́лее ни́зкий класс *и т.п.*).

relent [rɪˈlent] *v.i.* смягч|а́ться, -и́ться.

relentless [rɪˈlentlɪs] *adj.* (*merciless*) безжа́лостный; (*implacable*) неумоли́мый; **~ persecution** жесто́кие гоне́ния; (*persistent*) упо́рный, неукло́нный.

relevance [ˈrelɪv(ə)ns] *n.* отноше́ние к де́лу; уме́стность.

relevant [ˈrelɪv(ə)nt] *adj.* относя́щийся к де́лу; уме́стный; **~ to** относя́щийся к+*d.*

reliability [rɪˌlaɪəˈbɪlɪtɪ] *n.* надёжность; достове́рность.

reliable [rɪˈlaɪəb(ə)l] *adj.* надёжный; (*of a source, statement etc.*) достове́рный.

reliance [rɪˈlaɪəns] *n.* (*trust*) дове́рие; **I place great ~ upon him** я ему́ о́чень доверя́ю; я о́чень на него́ наде́юсь/полага́юсь.

reliant [rɪˈlaɪənt] *adj.* (*dependent*) зави́симый, зави́сящий; **they are completely ~ on their pension** они́ по́лностью зави́сят от свое́й пе́нсии.

relic [ˈrelɪk] *n.* **1.** (*of saint etc.*) рели́квия. **2.** (*survival from past*) рели́квия; (*custom etc.*) пережи́ток. **3.** (*pl., residue*) оста́ток.

relief [rɪˈliːf] *n.* **1.** (*alleviation, deliverance*) облегче́ние; **it was a great ~ to me** у меня́ отлегло́ от се́рдца. **2.** (*abatement*) сниже́ние, смягче́ние; **~ road** вспомога́тельная доро́га. **3.** (*assistance to poor, distressed etc.*) посо́бие; **~ agency** организа́ция по оказа́нию по́мощи; **famine ~** по́мощь голода́ющим. **4.** (*replacement*) сме́на (дежу́рных); (*pers.*) сме́на. **5.** (*sculpture etc.*) релье́ф; **~ map** релье́фная ка́рта.

relieve [rɪˈliːv] *v.t.* **1.** (*alleviate*) облегч|а́ть, -и́ть; **it ~s the monotony** э́то вно́сит разнообра́зие. **2.** (*bring assistance to*) при|ходи́ть, -йти́ на по́мощь +*d.*; выруча́ть, вы́ручить. **3.** (*unburden*) освобо|жда́ть, -ди́ть (*кого от чего*); **he ~d himself** (*urinated*) **against the wall** он помочи́лся у сте́нки; **may I ~ you of your bags?** позво́льте мне взять ва́ши чемода́ны. **4.** (*replace on duty*) смен|я́ть, -и́ть; **you will be ~d at 10 o'clock** вас сме́нят в 10 часо́в.

religion [rɪˈlɪdʒ(ə)n] *n.* рели́гия; вероисповеда́ние.

religious [rɪ'lɪdʒəs] *adj.* **1.** религио́зный. **2.** (*fig.*, *scrupulous*): **he attended every meeting ~ly** он добросо́вестно посеща́л все собра́ния.

relinquish [rɪ'lɪŋkwɪʃ] *v.t.* (*give up*, *abandon*) ост|авля́ть, -а́вить; **I ~ed the habit** я бро́сил э́ту привы́чку; (*surrender*) сд|ава́ть, а́ть; **he ~ed his claims** он отказа́лся от свои́х тре́бований; (*let go*) разж|има́ть, -а́ть; **the dog ~ed its hold** соба́ка разжа́ла зу́бы.

relish ['relɪʃ] *n.* **1.** (*fig.*, *attractive quality*) пре́лесть, привлека́тельность; (*zest*, *liking*) смак, пристра́стие; **he ate with ~** он ел с аппети́том. **3.** (*sauce*, *garnish*) припра́ва.

v.t. получ|а́ть, -и́ть удово́льствие от+*g.*; **you will not ~ what I have to say** то, что я скажу́, не придётся вам по вку́су.

relive [ri:'lɪv] *v.t.* переж|ива́ть, -и́ть вновь.

reload [ri:'ləʊd] *v.t.* (*a vehicle etc.*) нагру|жа́ть, -зи́ть за́ново; (*a weapon*) перезаря|жа́ть, -ди́ть.

relocate [ˌri:ləʊ'keɪt] *v.t.* & *i.* переме|ща́ть(ся), -сти́ть(ся).

relocation [ˌri:ləʊ'keɪʃən] *n.* перемеще́ние.

reluctance [rɪ'lʌkt(ə)ns] *n.* нежела́ние; неохо́та.

reluctant [rɪ'lʌkt(ə)nt] *adj.* неохо́тный; **she was ~ to leave home** ей не хоте́лось покида́ть дом.

rely [rɪ'laɪ] *v.i.* полага́ться (*impf.*); наде́яться (*impf.*) (*both* на+*a.*); **you can ~ on me** вы мо́жете на меня́ положи́ться.

remain [rɪ'meɪn] *v.i.* ост|ава́ться, -а́ться; **that ~s to be seen** поживём — уви́дим; (*stay*) пребыва́ть (*impf.*); **he ~ed a week in Paris** он про́был неде́лю в Пари́же; **he ~ed silent** он храни́л молча́ние; **these things ~ the same** э́ти ве́щи не меня́ются; **please ~ seated!** пожа́луйста, не встава́йте!; **one thing ~s certain** одно́ безусло́вно я́сно; **I ~ yours truly** остаю́сь пре́данный Вам.

remainder [rɪ'meɪndə(r)] *n.* оста́т|ок, -ки; (*of people*) остальны́е (*pl.*).

remains [rɪ'meɪnz] *n.* оста́тки (*m. pl.*), оста́нк|и (*pl.*, *g.* -ов); (*ruins*) разва́лин|ы (*pl.*, *g.* —); (*corpse*): **the ~s were cremated** оста́нки бы́ли сожжены́.

remake ['ri:meɪk] *n.* переде́лка.

v.t. переде́л|ывать, -ать.

remand [rɪ'mɑ:nd] *v.t.*: **he was ~ed in custody** его́ отосла́ли обра́тно под стра́жу.

remark [rɪ'mɑ:k] *n.* **1.** (*notice*) наблюде́ние; **it is worthy of ~** э́то досто́йно внима́ния. **2.** (*spoken observation*) замеча́ние.

v.t. **1.** (*observe*) отм|еча́ть, -е́тить. **2.** (*comment*) зам|еча́ть, -е́тить.

v.i. выска́зываться, вы́сказаться; **he ~ed upon your absence** он отме́тил ва́ше отсу́тствие.

remarkable [rɪ'mɑ:kəb(ə)l] *adj.* удиви́тельный; замеча́тельный.

remarry [ri:'mærɪ] *v.i.* вступ|а́ть, -и́ть в но́вый брак.

remedial [rɪ'mi:dɪəl] *adj.* исправля́ющий, лече́бный; (*educ.*) корректи́вный.

remedy ['remɪdɪ] *n.* сре́дство, лека́рство; **a ~ for warts** сре́дство про́тив бородо́вок.

v.t. выле́чивать, вы́лечить; испр|авля́ть, -а́вить; **this cannot ~ the situation** э́то не попра́вит положе́ния.

remember [rɪ'membə(r)] *v.t.* **1.** (*keep in the memory*) по́мнить (*impf.*); уде́рживать (*impf.*) в па́мяти; **I ~ her as a girl** я по́мню её де́вочкой. **2.** (*recall*) всп|омина́ть, -о́мнить; прип|омина́ть, -о́мнить; **not that I can ~** наско́лько я по́мню, нет; **he ~ed himself in time** он во́время опо́мнился. **3.** (*not forget*; *be mindful of*) не забыва́ть/забы́ть, име́ть (*impf.*) в виду́; **~ to turn out the light** не забу́дьте погаси́ть свет; **~ you are still a young man** не забыва́йте, что вы ещё мо́лоды. **4.** (*implying gift or gratuity*): **~ the waiter!** не забу́дьте дать официа́нту на чай!; **he ~ed her in his will** он упомяну́л её в своём завеща́нии. **5.** (*convey greetings*): **~ me to your mother** переда́йте приве́т ва́шей ма́тери.

remembrance [rɪ'membrəns] *n.* **1.** (*memory*; *recollection*) па́мять; воспомина́ние; **in ~ of** в па́мять о+*p.*; **it put me in ~ of my youth** э́то напо́мнило мне мо́лодость; **a service in ~ of the dead** помина́льная слу́жба; **R~ Day** день па́мяти поги́бших (в пе́рвую и втору́ю мировы́е во́йны). **2.** (*memento*) сувени́р.

remind [rɪ'maɪnd] *v.t.* нап|омина́ть, -о́мнить (*кому что or о чём or inf.*); **he ~s me of my father** он напомина́ет мне отца́; **that ~s me!** кста́ти!; **visitors are ~ed that there is no admission after 6** посети́телей про́сят име́ть в виду́, что впуск прекраща́ется в 6 часо́в.

reminder [rɪ'maɪndə(r)] *n.* напомина́ние; **he needs a gentle ~** ему́ на́до осторо́жно напо́мнить.

reminisce [ˌremɪ'nɪs] *v.i.* пред|ава́ться, -а́ться воспомина́ниям.

reminiscence [ˌremɪ'nɪs(ə)ns] *n.* воспомина́ние; **he wrote ~s of the war** он написа́л вое́нные мемуа́ры.

reminiscent [ˌremɪ'nɪs(ə)nt] *adj.* **1.** (*recalling the past*) вспомина́ющий, напомина́ющий. **2.**: **~** (*suggestive*) **of** напомина́ющий; **his music is ~ of Brahms** его́ му́зыка напомина́ет Бра́мса.

remiss [rɪ'mɪs] *adj.* хала́тный; неради́вый.

remission [rɪ'mɪʃ(ə)n] *n.* **1.** (*forgiveness*) проще́ние; **~ of sins** отпуще́ние грехо́в. **2.** (*abatement*, *decrease*) уменьше́ние; **the noise went on without ~** шум не умолка́л.

remit[1] ['ri:mɪt, rɪ'mɪt] *n.* (*terms of reference*) зада́чи (*f. pl.*), компете́нция.

remit[2] [rɪ'mɪt] *v.t.* **1.** (*forgive*) про|ща́ть, -сти́ть; отпус|ка́ть, -ти́ть (*грехи*). **2.** (*slacken*, *mitigate*) ум|еньша́ть, -е́ньшить; осл|абля́ть, -а́бить. **3.** (*send*, *transfer*) перес|ыла́ть, -ла́ть; перев|оди́ть, -ести́ (*деньги*).

remittance [rɪ'mɪt(ə)ns] *n.* (*sending of money*) перево́д де́нег; (*money sent*) де́нежный перево́д.

remnant ['remnənt] *n.* (*remains*) оста́ток; (*of cloth*) оста́ток; (*survival*) пережи́ток.

remodel [ri:'mɒd(ə)l] *v.t.* переде́л|ывать, -ать.

remonstrate ['remənˌstreɪt] *v.i.* протестова́ть (*impf.*); возра|жа́ть, -зи́ть; (*urge*): **he ~d with me** он увещева́л меня́.

remorse [rɪ'mɔ:s] *n.* **1.** (*repentance*; *regret*) угрызе́ния (*nt. pl.*) со́вести; **do you feel no ~ for what you did?** вас не му́чит со́весть, что вы так поступи́ли? **2.** (*compunction*) жа́лость; **without ~** безжа́лостно.

remorseful [rɪ'mɔ:sfʊl] *adj.* по́лный раска́яния.

remorseless [rɪ'mɔ:slɪs] *adj.* безжа́лостный.

remote [rɪ'məʊt] *adj.* отдалённый, глухо́й; **a ~ village** глухо́е село́; **a ~ ancestor** далёкий пре́док; **~ control** дистанцио́нное управле́ние; **there is a ~ possibility of its happening** не совсе́м исключено́, что э́то случи́тся; **he was not even ~ly interested** он не прояви́л ни мале́йшего интере́са (к+*d.*).

cpd. **~-controlled** *adj.* радиоуправля́емый.

remount[2] [ri:'maʊnt] *v.t.* **1.** (*climb again*): **he ~ed the ladder** он сно́ва подня́лся на ле́стницу; **he ~ed his horse** он сно́ва сел на ло́шадь. **2.** (*a photograph etc.*) переклéить (*pf.*) на друго́е паспарту́.

v.i. сно́ва сади́ться/сесть на ло́шадь.

removable [rɪ'mu:vəb(ə)l] *adj.* (*detachable*) съёмный; (*from office*) устрани́мый, сменя́емый.

removal [rɪ'mu:v(ə)l] *n.* (*taking away*) удале́ние; (*from office etc.*) смеще́ние, отстране́ние; (*of obstacles etc.*) устране́ние; (*of furniture*) перево́зка; **~ firm** трансаге́нтство; **~ men** перево́зчики ме́бели.

remove [rɪ'mu:v] *v.t.* **1.** (*take away*, *off*) уб|ира́ть, -ра́ть; ун|оси́ть, -ести́; **how can I ~ these stains?** как мо́жно вы́вести э́ти пя́тна?; **the boy was ~d**

from school ма́льчика забра́ли из шко́лы; **he ~d his hat** он снял шля́пу. **2.** (*dismiss*) сме|ща́ть, -сти́ть; **he was ~d from office** его́ сня́ли с рабо́ты. **3.** (*eliminate*) устран|я́ть, -и́ть.

remunerate [rɪˈmju:nəˌreɪt] *v.t.* (*pers.*) вознагра|жда́ть, -ди́ть; (*work*) опла́|чивать, -ти́ть.

remuneration [rɪˌmju:nəˈreɪʃ(ə)n] *n.* вознагражде́ние; опла́та.

remunerative [rɪˈmju:nərətɪv] *adj.* вы́годный, хорошо́ опла́чиваемый.

renaissance [rɪˈneɪs(ə)ns, rəˈn-, -sɑ̃s] *n.* (*hist.*) Возрожде́ние; (*revival*) возрожде́ние.

renal [ˈri:n(ə)l] *adj.* по́чечный.

rename [ri:ˈneɪm] *v.t.* переимено́в|ывать, -а́ть.

rend [rend] *v.t.* **1.** (*tear apart*) раз|рыва́ть, -орва́ть; раз|дира́ть, -одра́ть; **an explosion rent the air** взрыв сотря́с во́здух. **2.** (*tear away*) от|рыва́ть, -орва́ть; от|дира́ть, -одра́ть.

render [ˈrendə(r)] *v.t.* **1.** (*give when required or due*) возд|ава́ть, -а́ть; отд|ава́ть, -а́ть; **doctors ~ valuable service** врачи́ де́лают поле́зное де́ло; **I was called on to ~ assistance** меня́ попроси́ли оказа́ть по́мощь. **2.** (*present, submit*) предст|авля́ть, -а́вить; **you must ~ an account of your expenditure** вы должны́ отчита́ться в свои́х расхо́дах. **3.** (*perform, portray*) исп|олня́ть, -о́лнить; **the sonata was beautifully ~ed** сона́та была́ прекра́сно испо́лнена. **4.** (*translate*) перев|оди́ть, -ести́. **5.** (*cause to be*): **he was ~ed speechless** он онеме́л; **the car accident ~ed him helpless** в результа́те автомоби́льной катастро́фы он оста́лся инвали́дом. **6.** (*melt and clarify*) топи́ть, пере-. **7.** (*cover with plaster*) штукату́рить, от-.

rend|ering [ˈrendərɪŋ], **-ition** [renˈdɪʃ(ə)n] *nn.* (*performance*) исполне́ние; (*translation*) перево́д.

rendezvous [ˈrɒndɪˌvu:, -deɪˌvu:] *n.* (*meeting*) свида́ние; (*place*) ме́сто свида́ния.

v.i. встр|еча́ться, -е́титься.

rendition [renˈdɪʃ(ə)n] = **rendering**

renegade [ˈrenɪˌgeɪd] *n.* ренега́т, отсту́пник.

adj. ренега́тский, отсту́пнический.

reneg(u)e [rɪˈni:g, -ˈneg, -ˈneɪg] *v.i.*: **he ~d on his promise** он нару́шил своё обеща́ние.

renew [rɪˈnju:] *v.t.* **1.** (*replace*) обн|овля́ть, -о́вить; замен|я́ть, -и́ть; **she ~ed the water in his glass** она́ поменя́ла ему́ во́ду в стака́не. **2.** (*restore, mend*) восстан|а́вливать, -ови́ть; **with ~ed vigour** с но́выми си́лами. **3.** (*repeat, continue*) возобнов|ля́ть, -и́ть; **your subscription needs ~ing** вам ну́жно возобнови́ть/продли́ть перепи́ску.

renewal [rɪˈnju:əl] *n.* (*replacement*) обновле́ние; заме́на; (*restoration*) восстановле́ние; (*resumption*) возобновле́ние, продле́ние.

rennet [ˈrenɪt] *n.* сычу́жный ферме́нт.

renounce [rɪˈnaʊns] *v.t.* отка́з|ываться, -а́ться от+*g.*; отр|ека́ться, -е́чься от+*g.*

renouncement [rɪˈnaʊnsmənt] *n.* (*surrender*) отрече́ние, отка́з; (*repudiation*) отрица́ние.

renovate [ˈrenəˌveɪt] *v.t.* обнов|ля́ть, -ови́ть; восстан|а́вливать, -ови́ть; (*repair*) ремонти́ровать, от-.

renovation [ˌrenəˈveɪʃ(ə)n] *n.* обновле́ние; восстановле́ние; (*repair*) реконстру́кция; ремо́нт.

renown [rɪˈnaʊn] *n.* сла́ва; изве́стность; **he won ~ on the battlefield** он завоева́л сла́ву на по́ле боя́.

renowned [rɪˈnaʊnd] *adj.* просла́вленный, изве́стный; **he is ~ for his eloquence** он сла́вится свои́м красноре́чием.

rent[1] [rent] *n.* (*tear, split*) дыра́; проре́ха.

rent[2] [rent] *n.* (*for premises*) наёмная пла́та; (*of land*) аре́ндная пла́та; (*of a flat*) квартпла́та; (*of telephone*) пла́та за телефо́н; **I shall charge you ~ for the use of my car** я бу́ду брать с вас пла́ту за по́льзование мои́м автомоби́лем.

v.t. **1.** (*occupy or use for ~*) арендова́ть (*impf.*); сн|има́ть, -ять в наём. **2.** (*let out for ~*) сд|ава́ть, -ать в наём; **~ed accommodation** сня́тое жильё. **3.** (*be let*): **these old houses ~ cheap** э́ти ста́рые дома́ сдаю́тся дёшево.

cpds. **~-book** *n.* кни́га учёта аре́ндной пла́ты; **~-collector** *n.* сбо́рщик кварти́рной пла́ты; **~-free** *adj.* & *adv.* освобождённый от кварти́рной пла́ты.

rental [ˈrent(ə)l] *n.* (*income from rents*) ре́нтный дохо́д; (*rate of rent*) разме́р аре́ндной пла́ты.

renter [ˈrentə(r)] *n.* (*payer*) нанима́тель (*m.*), аренда́тор; (*payee*) наймода́тель (*m.*), арендода́тель (*m.*).

renunciation [rɪˌnʌnsɪˈeɪʃ(ə)n] *n.* (*surrender*) отка́з, отрече́ние.

reopen [ri:ˈəʊpən] *v.t.* вновь/сно́ва откр|ыва́ть, -ы́ть; возобнов|ля́ть, -и́ть; **the discussion was ~ed** диску́ссия возобнови́лось.

v.i.: **the shops will ~ after the holidays** по́сле пра́здников магази́ны откро́ются сно́ва.

reorder [ri:ˈɔ:də(r)] *n.* повто́рный зака́з.

v.t. (*rearrange*) перестр|а́ивать, -о́ить; (*renew order for*) повтор|я́ть, -и́ть зака́з на+*a.*

reorganization [ri:ˌɔ:gəˌnaɪˈzeɪʃ(ə)n] *n.* реорганиза́ция.

reorganize [ri:ˈɔ:gəˌnaɪz] *v.t.* реорганизо́в|ывать, -а́ть.

repaint [ri:ˈpeɪnt] *v.t.* перекра́|шивать, -сить.

repair[1] [rɪˈpeə(r)] *n.* **1.** (*restoring to sound condition*) ремо́нт; **minor/running ~s** ме́лкий/теку́щий ремо́нт; **the shop is closed for ~s** магази́н закры́т на ремо́нт; **the road is under ~** доро́гу ремонти́руют; **my shoes need ~** мне ну́жно почини́ть ту́фли; **~ shop** ремо́нтная мастерска́я. **2.** (*good condition*) го́дность, испра́вность; **the house is in good ~** дом в хоро́шем состоя́нии.

v.t. (*mend, renovate*) ремонти́ровать, от-; (*restore*) восстан|а́вливать, -ови́ть.

repair[2] [rɪˈpeə(r)] *v.i.* (*go*) напр|авля́ться, -а́виться.

repairman [rɪˈpeərmæn] *n.* ма́стер, ремо́нтник.

reparable [ˈrepərəb(ə)l] *adj.* исправи́мый.

reparation [ˌrepəˈreɪʃ(ə)n] *n.* компенса́ция; возмеще́ние уще́рба; (*pl.*, *compensation for war damage*) (вое́нные) репара́ции (*f. pl.*).

repatriate[1] [ri:ˈpætrɪˌeɪt] *n.* репатриа́нт (*fem.* -ка).

repatriate[2] [ri:ˈpætrɪˌeɪt] *v.t.* репатрии́ровать (*impf.*, *pf.*).

repatriation [ri:ˌpætrɪˈeɪʃ(ə)n] *n.* репатриа́ция.

repay [ri:ˈpeɪ] *v.t.* выпла́чивать, вы́платить; отпла́|чивать, -ти́ть; **how can I ~ you?** как я могу́ вас отблагодари́ть?; **I shall ~ him in kind** я отплачу́ ему́ тем же (*or* той же моне́той); **I repaid his visit** я нанёс ему́ отве́тный визи́т.

repayable [ri:ˈpeɪəb(ə)l] *adj.* подлежа́щий упла́те.

repayment [ri:ˈpeɪmənt] *n.* вы́плата.

repeal [rɪˈpi:l] *n.* отме́на, аннули́рование.

v.t. аннули́ровать (*impf.*, *pf.*).

repeat [rɪˈpi:t] *n.* повторе́ние; **~ order** повто́рный зака́з.

v.t. **1.** (*say or do again*) повтор|я́ть, -и́ть; **after ~ed attempts** по́сле неоднокра́тных попы́ток; **don't ~ what I have told you** не говори́те никому́ того́, что я вам сказа́л. **2.** (*recite*) говори́ть (*impf.*) наизу́сть; деклами́ровать (*impf.*).

v.i. **1.** (*recur*) повтор|я́ться, -и́ться. **2.** (*of food*): **onions ~ on me** (*coll.*) у меня́ отры́жка от лу́ка. **3.**: **~ing rifle** магази́нная винто́вка.

repeatedly [rɪˈpi:tɪdlɪ] *adv.* неоднокра́тно, многокра́тно, то и де́ло.

repel [rɪˈpel] *v.t.* **1.** (*phys.*) отт|а́лкивать, -олкну́ть. **2.** (*repulse*) от|гоня́ть, -огна́ть; отб|ива́ть, -и́ть; **measures to ~ the enemy** ме́ры для оказа́ния отпо́ра врагу́; **she ~led his advances** она́ отве́ргла его́ уха́живания. **3.** (*be repulsive to*) отта́лкивать (*impf.*); вызыва́ть, вы́звать отвраще́ние у+*g.*

repellent [rɪˈpelənt] *n.*: **insect ~** сре́дство от насеко́мых.

adj. (*repulsive*) отта́лкивающий.
repent [rɪ'pent] *v.t. & i.* ка́яться (*impf.*); раска́|иваться, -яться (*в чём*).
repentance [rɪ'pəntəns] *n.* раска́яние.
repentant [rɪ'pəntənt] *adj.* ка́ющийся, раска́ивающийся.
repercussion [ˌri:pə'kʌʃ(ə)n] *n.* (*usu. pl.*) после́дствия (*nt. pl.*).
repertoire ['repəˌtwɑ:(r)] *n.* репертуа́р.
repertory ['repətərɪ] *n.* **1.** (*repertoire*) репертуа́р. **2.**: ~ **company** постоя́нная гру́ппа с определённым репертуа́ром; ~ **theatre** репертуа́рный теа́тр. **3.** (*fig., store*) запа́с.
repetition [ˌrepɪ'tɪʃ(ə)n] *n.* повторе́ние; **let there be no ~ of this** что́бы э́того бо́льше не́ было.
repetiti|ous [ˌrepɪ'tɪʃəs], **-ve** [rɪ'petɪtɪv] *adjs.* повторя́ющийся.
rephrase [ri:'freɪz] *v.t.* перефрази́ровать (*impf., pf.*).
replace [rɪ'pleɪs] *v.t.* **1.** (*put back, return*) класть, положи́ть (*or* ста́вить, по-) на ме́сто; возвра|ща́ть, -ти́ть; ~ **the receiver** положи́ть телефо́нную тру́бку. **2.** (*provide substitute for*) замен|я́ть, -и́ть. **3.** (*take the place of; succeed*) заме|ща́ть, -сти́ть; **he ~d me as secretary** он замеща́л/смени́л меня́ в до́лжности секретаря́.
replaceable [rɪ'pleɪsəb(ə)l] *adj.* замени́мый.
replacement [rɪ'pleɪsmənt] *n.* (*restitution*) возмеще́ние; (*provision of substitute or successor*) замеще́ние; (*substitute, successor*) заме́на.
replant [ri:'plɑ:nt] *v.t.* сно́ва заса́|живать, -ди́ть; переса́|живать, -ди́ть.
replay[1] ['ri:pleɪ] *n.* (*of a game*) переигро́вка; (*of a record etc.*) (повто́рное) проигрывание, повто́р.
replay[2] [ri:'pleɪ] *v.t.* переигр|ывать, -а́ть.
replenish [rɪ'plenɪʃ] *v.t.* поп|олня́ть, -о́лнить.
replenishment [rɪ'plenɪʃmənt] *n.* пополне́ние.
replete [rɪ'pli:t] *adj.* напо́лненный; сы́тый; ~ **with food** нае́вшийся вдо́воль.
replica ['replɪkə] *n.* то́чная ко́пия.
reply [rɪ'plaɪ] *n.* отве́т; **in (or by way of) ~** в отве́т (на+*a.*); **I rang but there was no ~** я звони́л, но никто́ не отве́тил; ~ **paid** с опла́ченным отве́том.
v.i. отв|еча́ть, -е́тить.
report [rɪ'pɔ:t] *n.* **1.** (*account, statement*) докла́д, отчёт; **newspaper ~** сообще́ние; **school ~** отчёт об успева́емости; **progress ~** отчёт о хо́де выполне́ния; **the policeman made a full ~** полице́йский соста́вил подро́бный протоко́л. **2.** (*rumour*) молва́, слух; **by all ~s, he is doing well** по всем све́дениям он процвета́ет. **3.** (*sound of explosion or shot*) звук взры́ва/вы́стрела.
v.t. **1.** (*give news or account of*) сообщ|а́ть, -и́ть; сост|авля́ть, -а́вить отчёт о+*p.*; перед|ава́ть, -а́ть; **it has been ~ ed that ...** сообща́лось, что...; **he was ~ed missing** он счита́лся пропа́вшим бе́з ве́сти; **he ~ed having lost the money** он заяви́л о поте́ре де́нег; **the trial was ~ed in the press** проце́сс освеща́лся в печа́ти; (*gram.*): **~ed** (*indirect*) **speech** ко́свенная речь. **2.** (*inform against, make known*) жа́ловаться, по- на+*a.*
v.i. **1.** (*give information*) до|кла́дывать, -ложи́ть; де́лать, с- докла́д; предст|авля́ть, -а́вить отчёт. **2.** (*present o.s.*) яв|ля́ться, -и́ться (*куда-н.*); приб|ыва́ть, -ы́ть (*куда-н.*).
reportedly [rɪ'pɔ:tɪdlɪ] *adv.* по сообще́ниям; (*allegedly*) я́кобы.
reporter [rɪ'pɔ:tə(r)] *n.* репортёр.
repose [rɪ'pəʊz] *n.* (*rest, sleep*) о́тдых, переды́шка; (*restfulness, tranquillity*) поко́й, безмяте́жность.
v.t. (*fig., place*): **he ~s confidence in her** он ей целико́м доверя́ет.
v.i. **1.** (*take one's rest*) отд|ыха́ть, -охну́ть; лечь (*pf.*) отдохну́ть. **2.** (*lie*) лежа́ть (*impf.*); поко́иться (*impf.*); **his remains ~ in the churchyard** его́ прах поко́ится на кла́дбище.
repository [rɪ'pɒzɪtərɪ] *n.* (*receptacle*) храни́лище; (*store*) склад; (*fig.*): **he is a ~ of information** он неиссяка́емый исто́чник информа́ции.
repossess [ˌri:pə'zes] *v.t.* из|ыма́ть, -ъя́ть за неплатёж.
repossession [ˌri:pə'zeʃ(ə)n] *n.* (*in hire-purchase*) изъя́тие иму́щества, взя́того в рассро́чку.
reprehensible [ˌreprɪ'hensɪb(ə)l] *adj.* досто́йный осужде́ния; предосуди́тельный.
represent [ˌreprɪ'zent] *v.t.* **1.** (*portray*) изобра|жа́ть, -зи́ть; **what does this picture ~?** что изображено́ на э́той карти́не? **2.** (*symbolize, correspond to*) символизи́ровать (*impf., pf.*), изобража́ть (*impf.*), обознача́ть (*impf.*); **one inch on the map ~s a mile** оди́н дюйм на ка́рте равня́ется одно́й ми́ле. **3.** (*make out*): **he ~ed himself as an expert** он выдава́л себя́ за знатока́. **4.** (*speak or act for*) представля́ть (*impf.*); **he ~s Britain at the UN** он представля́ет Великобрита́нию в ООН; **who ~s the defendant?** кто явля́ется защи́тником обвиня́емого?
representation [ˌreprɪzen'teɪʃ(ə)n] *n.* **1.** (*portrayal*) изображе́ние. **2.** (*statement of one's case*): **diplomatic ~s** дипломати́ческие представле́ния. **3.** (*delegation, deputizing*) представи́тельство; **proportional ~** пропорциона́льное представи́тельство.
representative [ˌreprɪ'zentətɪv] *n.* представи́тель (*m.*), **House of R~s** пала́та представи́телей.
adj. показа́тельный, типи́чный; ~ **government** представи́тельное прави́тельство; **he is ~ of his age** он типи́чный представи́тель свое́й эпо́хи.
repress [rɪ'pres] *v.t.* **1.** (*put down, curb*) подав|ля́ть, -и́ть; угнета́ть (*impf.*); **the revolt was ~ed** восста́ние бы́ло пода́влено. **2.** (*restrain*) сде́рж|ивать, -а́ть; **I could not ~ my laughter** я не мог удержа́ться от сме́ха; **a ~ed personality** пода́вленная ли́чность.
repression [rɪ'preʃ(ə)n] *n.* (*suppression*) подавле́ние; репре́ссия.
repressive [rɪ'presɪv] *adj.* репресси́вный.
reprieve [rɪ'pri:v] *n.* (*leg.*): отсро́чка приведе́ния в исполне́ние (сме́ртного) пригово́ра; (*fig.*) переды́шка, вре́менное облегче́ние.
v.t.: **the murderer was ~ed** казнь уби́йцы отсро́чили.
reprimand ['reprɪˌmɑ:nd] *n.* вы́говор, замеча́ние.
v.t. де́лать, с- вы́говор/замеча́ние +*d.*
reprint[1] ['ri:prɪnt] *n.* перепеча́тка; репри́нт.
reprint[2] [ri:'prɪnt] *v.t.* перепеча́т|ывать, -ать.
v.i.: **the book is ~ing** кни́га переиздаётся.
reprisal [rɪ'praɪz(ə)l] *n.* отве́тное де́йствие, отме́стка; **by way of ~** в отме́стку.
reproach [rɪ'prəʊtʃ] *n.* **1.** (*rebuke*) упрёк, уко́р; **his honesty is above ~** он безупре́чно че́стен; **he gave me a look of ~** он посмотре́л на меня́ с укори́зной. **2.** (*disgrace*) позо́р; **he brought ~ on himself** он себя́ опозо́рил.
v.t. упрек|а́ть, -ну́ть; укоря́ть (*impf.*); **I have nothing to ~ myself for** мне не́ в чем себя́ упрекну́ть.
reproachful [rɪ'prəʊtʃfʊl] *adj.* укори́зненный.
reprobate ['reprəˌbeɪt] *n.* негодя́й, нечести́вец.
adj. нечести́вый; безнра́вственный.
reprobation [ˌreprə'beɪʃ(ə)n] *n.* порица́ние.
reproduce [ˌri:prə'dju:s] *v.t.* **1.** (*copy, imitate*) воспроизв|оди́ть, -ести́; (*of pictures*) репродуци́ровать (*impf., pf.*). **2.** (*beget*): **living things ~ their kind** живы́е существа́ размножа́ются.
v.i. размн|ожа́ться, -о́житься.
reproduction [ˌri:prə'dʌkʃ(ə)n] *n.* воспроизведе́ние; (*of picture*) репроду́кция; (*begetting of offspring*) размноже́ние.
reproductive [ˌri:prə'dʌktɪv] *adj.* воспроизводи́тельный; (*biol.*) полово́й; ~ **organs** о́рганы размноже́ния.

reproof [rɪ'pru:f] *n.* порица́ние; вы́говор; **the teacher administered a sharp ~** учи́тель сде́лал ре́зкое замеча́ние.

reproval [rɪ'pru:vəl] *n.* вы́говор, порица́ние.

reprove [rɪ'pru:v] *v.t.* де́лать, с- вы́говор +*d.*

reptile ['reptaɪl] *n.* пресмыка́ющееся.

republic [rɪ'pʌblɪk] *n.* респу́блика; **People's R~** наро́дная респу́блика; **R~ of South Africa** Ю́жно-Африка́нская Респу́блика.

republican [rɪ'pʌblɪkən] *n.* республика́нец.

adj. республика́нский.

republicanism [rɪ'pʌblɪkənɪz(ə)m] *n.* республикани́зм.

republication [ˌrɪpʌblɪ'keɪʃ(ə)n] *n.* переизда́ние.

republish [ri:'pʌblɪʃ] *v.t.* переизд|ава́ть, -а́ть.

repudiate [rɪ'pju:dɪˌeɪt] *v.t.* отв|ерга́ть, -е́ргнуть; отр|ека́ться, -е́чься от+*g.*; **I ~ your accusation** я отверга́ю ва́ше обвине́ние; **he ~s the authority of the law** он не признаёт вла́сти зако́на.

repudiation [rɪˌpju:dɪ'eɪʃ(ə)n] *n.* отрече́ние; отрица́ние; отка́з.

repugnance [rɪ'pʌgnəns] *n.* отвраще́ние.

repugnant [rɪ'pʌgnənt] *adj.* отврати́тельный.

repulse [rɪ'pʌls] *n.* отпо́р, отраже́ние.

v.t. (*drive back*) отб|ива́ть, -и́ть; (*rebuff, refuse*) отт|а́лкивать, -олкну́ть; отв|ерга́ть, -е́ргнуть.

repulsion [rɪ'pʌlʃ(ə)n] *n.* отвраще́ние.

repulsive [rɪ'pʌlsɪv] *adj.* отврати́тельный.

repurchase [ri:'pɜ:tʃɪs] *v.t.* вновь покупа́ть, купи́ть (ра́нее про́данный това́р).

reputable ['repjʊtəb(ə)l] *adj.* почте́нный, уважа́емый.

reputation [ˌrepjʊ'teɪʃ(ə)n] *n.* **1.** (*name*) репута́ция; **he has a ~ for courage** он сла́вится хра́бростью. **2.** (*respectability*) до́брое и́мя; **persons of ~** почте́нные лю́ди.

repute [rɪ'pju:t] *n.* (*reputation*) репута́ция; **I know him by ~** я зна́ю о нём понаслы́шке; (*good reputation, renown*) до́брое и́мя; **an artist of ~** худо́жник с и́менем.

v.t.: **he is ~d to be rich** он счита́ется бога́тым; говоря́т, что он бога́т; **the ~d father** предполага́емый оте́ц.

reputedly [rɪ'pju:tɪdlɪ] *adv.* по о́бщему мне́нию.

request [rɪ'kwest] *n.* про́сьба; **at my ~** по мое́й про́сьбе; **~ stop** остано́вка по тре́бованию; **I have a ~ to make of you** у меня́ к вам про́сьба; **put in a ~ for** пода́ть (*pf.*) заявле́ние/зая́вку на+*a.*; **this book is in great ~** на э́ту кни́гу большо́й спрос.

v.t. проси́ть, по-; **that is all I ~ of you** э́то всё, чего́ я от вас прошу́; **passengers are ~ed not to smoke** пассажи́ров про́сят не кури́ть; **may I ~ the pleasure of a dance?** разреши́те пригласи́ть вас на та́нец.

requiem ['rekwɪˌem] *n.* ре́квием, панихи́да.

require [rɪ'kwaɪə(r)] *v.t.* **1.** (*need*) нужда́ться (*impf.*) в+*p.*; тре́бовать (*impf.*) +*g.*; **when do you ~ the job to he done?** к како́му сро́ку должна́ быть заверше́на рабо́та?; **it ~d all his skill to ...** ему́ пона́добилось примени́ть всё своё уме́ние, что́бы...; **all that is ~d is a little patience** всё, что тре́буется, э́то немно́го терпе́ния. **2.** (*demand, order*) тре́бовать, по- +*g.*; прика́з|ывать, -а́ть; **my attendance is ~d by law** по зако́ну я обя́зан прису́тствовать; **what do you ~ of me?** что вы от меня́ хоти́те?; **I have done all that is ~d** я сде́лал всё, что тре́буется.

requirement [rɪ'kwaɪəmənt] *n.* **1.** (*need*) нужда́; потре́бность; **I have few ~s** мои́ потре́бности невелики́. **2.** (*demand*) тре́бование; усло́вие.

requisite ['rekwɪzɪt] *n.* необходи́мая вещь.

adj. необходи́мый.

requisition [ˌrekwɪ'zɪʃ(ə)n] *n.* (*official demand*) тре́бование; (*mil.*) реквизи́ция.

v.t. реквизи́ровать (*impf., pf.*).

requital [rɪ'kwaɪtəl] *n.* воздая́ние, вознагражде́ние; **in ~ of his services** в вознагражде́ние за его́ услу́ги.

requite [rɪ'kwaɪt] *v.t.* вознагра|жда́ть, -ди́ть; отпла́|чивать, -ти́ть; **his kindness was ~d with ingratitude** за доброту́ ему́ отплати́ли неблагода́рностью.

re-read [ri:'ri:d] *v.t.* перечи́т|ывать, -а́ть.

resale [ri:'seɪl] *n.* перепрода́жа.

reschedule [ri:'ʃedju:l, -'ske-] *v.t.* (*change time of*) перен|оси́ть, -ести́.

rescind [rɪ'sɪnd] *v.t.* аннули́ровать (*impf., pf.*); отмен|я́ть, -и́ть.

rescue ['reskju:] *n.* спасе́ние; **he came to my ~** он пришёл мне на по́мощь; **a ~ attempt** попы́тка спасти́ (*кого/что*); **~ vessel** спаса́тельная ло́дка.

v.t. спас|а́ть, -ти́; **all the crew were ~d** всю кома́нду спасли́.

rescuer ['reskju:ə(r)] *n.* спаси́тель (*fem.* -ница).

research [rɪ'sɜ:tʃ] *n.* иссле́дование, изыска́ние; **~ and development** нау́чно-иссле́довательская рабо́та; **~ library** нау́чно-техни́ческая библиоте́ка; **~ assistant** нау́чный сотру́дник; **~ satellite** иссле́довательский спу́тник.

v.t. & i. иссле́довать (*impf., pf.*); **he is ~ing the subject** он изуча́ет/разраба́тывает э́ту те́му.

researcher [rɪ'sɜ:tʃə(r)] *n.* иссле́дователь (*fem.* -ница).

resell [ri:'sel] *v.t.* перепрод|ава́ть, -а́ть.

resemblance [rɪ'zembləns] *n.* схо́дство; **he bears a strong ~ to his father** он о́чень похо́ж на своего́ отца́.

resemble [rɪ'zemb(ə)l] *v.t.* походи́ть (*impf.*) на+*a.*; име́ть (*impf.*) схо́дство с+*i.*

resent [rɪ'zent] *v.t.* возму|ща́ться, -ти́ться +*i.*; негодова́ть (*impf.*) на+*a.*.

resentful [rɪ'zentfʊl] *adj.* возмущённый.

resentment [rɪ'zentmənt] *n.* возмуще́ние; **I bear no ~ against him** я на него́ не в оби́де.

reservation [ˌrezə'veɪʃ(ə)n] *n.* **1.** (*limitation, exception*) огово́рка. **2.** (*booking*) (предвари́тельный) зака́з; зака́занное/заброни́рованное ме́сто. **3.** (*for tribes etc.*) резерва́ция; (*for game*) запове́дник.

reserve [rɪ'zɜ:v] *n.* **1.** (*store*) запа́с, резе́рв; **he has great ~s of energy** у него́ большо́й запа́с эне́ргии; **he has a little money in ~** у него́ припасено́ немно́го де́нег; **~ bank** резе́рвный банк. **2.** (*mil.*) резе́рв; **the R~** резе́рвные ча́сти (*f. pl.*). **3.** (**~ *player***) запасно́й (игро́к). **4.** (*area*): **game ~** охо́тничий запове́дник. **5.** (*limitation, restriction*) огово́рка; **I accept your statement without ~** я принима́ю ва́ше заявле́ние без огово́рок. **6.** (*reticence*) сде́ржанность.

v.t. **1.** (*hold back, save*) бере́чь, с-; прибер|ега́ть, -е́чь. **2.**: **~ judgement** (*leg.*) от|кла́дывать, -ложи́ть реше́ние; **I prefer to ~ judgement** я предпочита́ю пока́ не выска́зываться; **~ a right** сохран|я́ть, -и́ть пра́во. **3.** (*set aside*) резерви́ровать, за-; (*book*) зака́з|ывать, -а́ть; брони́ровать, за-.

reserved [rɪ'zɜ:vd] *adj.* **1.** (*booked, set aside*) зака́занный (зара́нее); **~ seats** (*in train*) плацка́ртные места́. **2.** (*reticent, uncommunicative*) сде́ржанный, за́мкнутый.

reservist [rɪ'zɜ:vɪst] *n.* резерви́ст.

reservoir ['rezəˌvwɑ:(r)] *n.* (*for water*) водохрани́лище; (*for other fluids*) резервуа́р, бачо́к.

reset [ri:'set] *v.t.* **1.** (*e.g. a watch*) перест|авля́ть, -а́вить; (*trap etc.*) сно́ва ста́вить, по-. **2.** (*place in position again*) впр|авля́ть, -а́вить; вновь вст|авля́ть, -а́вить; **the doctor ~ his arm** врач впра́вил ему́ ру́ку.

resettle [ri:'set(ə)l] *v.t.* пересел|я́ть, -и́ть.

v.i. пересел|я́ться, -и́ться.

resettlement [ri:'setəlmənt] *n.* переселе́ние.

reshuffle [ri:'ʃʌf(ə)l] *n.* (*cards*) перетасо́вка; (*fig.*) перестано́вка, перетря́ска.

v.t. перетасо́в|ывать, -а́ть; (*fig.*) произвести́ (*pf.*)

перестано́вку/перетря́ску в+*p*.
reside [rɪ'zaɪd] *v.i.* **1.** (*live*) прожива́ть (*impf.*). **2.:** ~ (*inhere, be vested*) **in** принадлежа́ть (*impf.*) +*d.*; быть прису́щим +*d.*; **supreme authority ~s in the President** президе́нт облечён вы́сшей вла́стью.
residence ['rezɪd(ə)ns] *n.* **1.** (*residing*) прожива́ние; **take up ~** въ|езжа́ть, -е́хать (в официа́льную резиде́нцию); **the students are in ~ again** студе́нты верну́лись в общежи́тие. **2.** (*home, mansion*) дом, резиде́нция.
resident ['rezɪd(ə)nt] *n.* (*permanent inhabitant*) (постоя́нный) жи́тель; (*in hotel*) постоя́лец.
adj. (*residing*) постоя́нно прожива́ющий; **the ~ population** постоя́нное населе́ние.
residential [ˌrezɪ'denʃ(ə)l] *adj.*: **a ~ area** жило́й райо́н.
residual [rɪ'zɪdjʊəl] *adj.* оста́точный, оста́вшийся.
residue ['rezɪˌdju:] *n.* оста́ток.
resign [rɪ'zaɪn] *v.t.* **1.** (*give up*) отка́з|ываться, -а́ться от+*g.*; **he ~ed his post as Chancellor** он по́дал в отста́вку с поста́ ка́нцлера; **they ~ed all hope** они́ оста́вили вся́кую наде́жду. **2.** (*reconcile*): **he ~ed himself to defeat** он смири́лся с пораже́нием.
v.i. под|ава́ть, -а́ть (*or* уходи́ть, уйти́) в отста́вку.
resignation [ˌrezɪg'neɪʃ(ə)n] *n.* **1.** (*resigning of office*) отста́вка; **he handed in his ~** он по́дал заявле́ние об отста́вке/ухо́де. **2.** (*acceptance of fate*) поко́рность, смире́ние.
resigned [rɪ'zaɪnd] *adj.* поко́рный, смири́вшийся (с+*i.*).
resilience [rɪ'zɪlɪəns] *n.* эласти́чность, упру́гость.
resilient [rɪ'zɪlɪənt] *adj.* эласти́чный, упру́гий.
resin ['rezɪn] *n.* смола́.
resinous ['rezɪnəs] *adj.* смоли́стый.
resist [rɪ'zɪst] *v.t.* **1.** (*oppose*) сопротивля́ться (*impf.*) +*d.*; проти́виться (*impf.*) +*d.*; **all their attacks were ~ed** все их ата́ки бы́ли отби́ты. **2.** (*be proof against*) не поддава́ться (*impf.*) +*d.* **3.** (*refrain from*) воздéрж|иваться, -а́ться от+*g.*; **I could not ~ the temptation to smile** я не мог удержа́ться от улы́бки.
resistance [rɪ'zɪst(ə)ns] *n.* **1.** (*opposition*) сопротивле́ние; **he took the line of least ~** он пошёл по ли́нии наиме́ньшего сопротивле́ния; **(~ movement)** движе́ние сопротивле́ния. **2.** (*power to withstand*) сопротивля́емость. **3.** (*elec.*) сопротивле́ние.
resistant [rɪ'zɪst(ə)nt] *adj.* сопротивля́ющийся; сто́йкий; **~ to heat** жаросто́йкий.
re-sit [ri:'sɪt] *v.t.*: **~ an examination** пересдава́ть (*impf.*) экза́мен.
resolute ['rezəˌlu:t, -ˌlju:t] *adj.* реши́тельный; по́лный реши́мости.
resolution [ˌrezə'lu:ʃ(ə)n, -'lju:ʃ(ə)n] *n.* **1.** (*firmness of purpose*) реши́тельность, реши́мость. **2.** (*vow*): **New Year ~** новогó́дний заро́к; новогó́днее обеща́ние самому́ себе́. **3.** (*expression of opinion or intent*) резолю́ция; **they passed a ~ to go on strike** они́ при́няли реше́ние нача́ть забасто́вку. **4.** (*of doubt, discord etc.*) (раз)реше́ние.
resolve [rɪ'zɒlv] *n.* (*determination*) реши́тельность, реши́мость; (*vow, intention*) реше́ние; наме́рение.
v.t. & i. **1.** (*decide, determine*) реш|а́ть, -и́ть; прин|има́ть, -я́ть реше́ние; **it was ~d** бы́ло решено́. **2.** (*settle*) (раз)реша́ть, -и́ть; **their quarrel was ~d** их спор разреши́лся.
resonance ['rezənəns] *n.* резона́нс, гул.
resonant ['rezənənt] *adj.* звуча́щий, зво́нкий.
resort [rɪ'zɔ:t] *n.* **1.** (*recourse*): **without ~ to force** не прибега́я к наси́лию; **in the last ~** в кра́йнем слу́чае. **2.** (*expedient*) наде́жда; спаси́тельное сре́дство. **3.** (*frequented place*): **holiday ~** куро́рт; **seaside ~** морско́й куро́рт.
v.i. приб|ега́ть, -е́гнуть (к+*d.*).
resound [rɪ'zaʊnd] *v.i.* звуча́ть (*impf.*); **the hall ~ed with voices** в за́ле раздава́лись голоса́; (*fig.*) греме́ть, про-; **a ~ing success** шу́мный успе́х.
resource [rɪ'sɔ:s, -'zɔ:s] *n.* запа́сы (*m. pl.*); ресу́рсы (*m. pl.*); **the country's natural ~s** есте́ственные ресу́рсы страны́; **he was left to his own ~s** он мог положи́ться то́лько на самого́ себя́.
resourceful [rɪ'sɔ:sfʊl, -'zɔ:sfʊl] *adj.* изобрета́тельный, нахо́дчивый.
resourcefulness [rɪ'sɔ:sfʊlnɪs, -'zɔ:sfʊlnɪs] *n.* изобрета́тельность, нахо́дчивость.
respect [rɪ'spekt] *n.* **1.** (*esteem, deference*) уваже́ние; **he is held in great ~** его́ о́чень уважа́ют; **I have the greatest ~ for his opinion** я о́чень счита́юсь с его́ мне́нием. **2.** (*consideration, attention*): **we must have, pay ~ to public opinion** нам на́до счита́ться с обще́ственным мне́нием. **3.** (*reference, relation*) отноше́ние; **in ~ of, with ~ to** что каса́ется +*g.* **4.** (*pl., polite greetings*) приве́т; **give my ~s to her** переда́йте ей от меня́ приве́т; **he came to pay his ~s** он пришёл засвиде́тельствовать своё почте́ние.
v.t. **1.** (*treat with consideration or esteem; defer to*) уважа́ть (*impf.*); почита́ть (*impf.*); **my wishes were ~ed** мои́ пожела́ния бы́ли учтены́. **2.** (*relate to*): **the law ~ing young persons** зако́н, каса́ющийся молодёжи.
respectability [rɪˌspektə'bɪlɪtɪ] *n.* респекта́бельность.
respectable [rɪ'spektəb(ə)l] *adj.* **1.** (*estimable*) досто́йный уваже́ния. **2.** (*qualifying for social approval*) респекта́бельный; **your clothes are not quite ~** вы не о́чень прили́чно оде́ты; **he comes of a ~ family** он из хоро́шей/прили́чной семьи́. **3.** (*of some merit, size or importance*) прили́чный; **he earns a ~ salary** он зараба́тывает прили́чные де́ньги.
respectful [rɪ'spektfʊl] *adj.* почти́тельный; **they kept (at) a ~ distance** они́ держа́лись на почти́тельном расстоя́нии; **yours ~ly** с уваже́нием.
respective [rɪ'spektɪv] *adj.* соотве́тственный; **we went off to our ~ rooms** мы разошли́сь по свои́м ко́мнатам.
respiration [ˌrespɪ'reɪʃ(ə)n] *n.* дыха́ние; **he was given artificial ~** ему́ сде́лали иску́сственное дыха́ние.
respirator ['respɪˌreɪtə(r)] *n.* респира́тор; (*med.*) прибо́р для дли́тельного иску́сственного дыха́ния.
respiratory [rɪ'spɪrətərɪ, 'respəˌreɪtərɪ] *adj.* респира́торный, дыха́тельный.
respite ['respaɪt, -pɪt] *n.* **1.** (*relief, rest*) переды́шка; **they gave us no ~** они́ не дава́ли нам передохну́ть. **2.** (*temporary reprieve*) отсро́чка.
resplendent [rɪ'splend(ə)nt] *adj.* блиста́тельный.
respond [rɪ'spɒnd] *v.i.* **1.** (*reply*) отв|еча́ть, -е́тить (на+*a.*). **2.** (*react*) реаги́ровать, от- (на+*a.*); от|зыва́ться, -озва́ться (на+*a.*); **his illness is ~ing to treatment** его́ боле́знь поддаётся лече́нию.
respondent [rɪ'spɒnd(ə)nt] *n.* (*leg.*) отве́тчи|к (*fem.* -ца).
response [rɪ'spɒns] *n.* **1.** (*reply*) отве́т; **he made no ~** он ничего́ не отве́тил. **2.** (*reaction*) реа́кция, о́тклик; **there was little ~ from the audience** аудито́рия реаги́ровало сла́бо.
responsibilit|y [rɪˌspɒnsɪ'bɪlɪtɪ] *n.* **1.** (*being responsible*) отве́тственность; **he acted on his own ~y** он де́йствовал на свой страх и риск; **he has a position of great ~y** он занима́ет о́чень отве́тственную до́лжность. **2.** (*charge, duty*) обя́занность, отве́тственность; **he was relieved of his ~ies** он был освобождён от исполне́ния обя́занностей.
responsible [rɪ'spɒnsɪb(ə)l] *adj.* **1.** (*accountable*) отве́тственный; **he is ~ to me for keeping the accounts** в вопро́сах бухгалте́рии он подчиня́ется мне; **she is ~ for cleaning my room** убо́рка мое́й ко́мнаты вхо́дит в её обя́занности; (*to blame*): **he was held ~ for the loss** его́ обвини́ли в э́той пропа́же. **2.** (*trustworthy*) надёжный. **3.** (*involving responsibility*) ва́жный; **a ~ post** отве́тственный пост.

responsive [rɪ'spɒnsɪv] *adj.* отзы́вчивый.

rest[1] [rest] *n.* **1.** (*sleep; relaxation in bed*) сон; о́тдых; **you need a good night's ~** вам на́до как сле́дует вы́спаться. **2.** (*inactive, immobile or undisturbed state*) поко́й; **day of ~** де́нь о́тдыха; **I set his mind at ~** я его́ успоко́ил; **the ball came to ~** мяч останови́лся; **he was laid to ~** (*buried*) его́ похорони́ли. **3.** (*intermission of work, activity etc.*) переды́шка; **he gave his horse a ~** он дал коню́ отдохну́ть. **4.** (*prop, support*) опо́ра; (*for telephone*) рыча́г; (*for billiard cue*) сто́йка. **5.** (*mus.*) па́уза.

v.t. **1.** (*give ~ to*) да|ва́ть, -ть о́тдых *+d.*; **are you quite ~ed?** вы хорошо́ отдохну́ли? **2.** (*place for support*) класть, положи́ть (на*+a.*); прислон|я́ть, -и́ть (*что к чему*); **he ~ed his chin on his hand** он подпира́л подборо́док руко́й; **~ the ladder against the wall!** прислони́те ле́стницу к сте́нке; (*fig., base*) обосно́в|ывать, -а́ть; **he is ~ing his hopes on fine weather** он наде́ется на хоро́шую пого́ду.

v.i. **1.** (*relax; take repose*) лежа́ть (*impf.*); отд|ыха́ть, -охну́ть; **may he ~ in peace!** мир пра́ху его́!; **I could not ~ until I'd told you the news** я не мог успоко́иться, пока́ не подели́лся с ва́ми но́востью. **2.** (*fig., remain*) ост|ава́ться, -а́ться; **the matter cannot ~ there** э́то де́ло нельзя́ так оста́вить. **3.** (*be supported*) опира́ться (*impf.*) (*на что*); поко́иться (*impf.*) (*на чём*); **there was a bicycle ~ing against the wall** у стены́ стоя́л велосипе́д; (*fig.*) осно́вываться (*impf.*). **4.** (*linger; alight*) поко́иться (*impf.*); ост|ава́ться, -а́ться.

cpds. **~-day** *n.* выходно́й/нерабо́чий день; **~-home** *n.* санато́рий, дом о́тдыха.

rest[2] [rest] *n.* (*remainder*) оста́ток; (*remaining things, people*) остальны́е (*pl.*); **and all the ~ of it** и всё про́чее; **for the ~** в остально́м.

restate [ri:'steɪt] *v.t.* (*repeat*) вновь заяв|ля́ть, -и́ть.

restaurant ['restəˌrɒnt, -ˌrɔ̃] *n.* рестора́н.

restaurateur [ˌrestərə'tɜ:(r)] *n.* владе́лец рестора́на.

restful ['restfʊl] *adj.* успокои́тельный, успока́ивающий; **a ~ light** мя́гкий свет.

restitution [ˌrestɪ'tju:ʃ(ə)n] *n.* возвраще́ние, возмеще́ние; **~ of conjugal rights** восстановле́ние супру́жеских прав.

restive ['restɪv] *adj.* (*of horse*) норови́стый; (*of pers.*) стропти́вый; (*restless*) беспоко́йный.

restless ['restlɪs] *adj.* беспоко́йный, непосе́дливый; **she spent a ~ night** она́ провела́ беспоко́йную/бессо́нную ночь.

restlessness ['restlɪsnɪs] *n.* беспоко́йство, непосе́дливость.

restock [ri:'stɒk] *v.i.* поп|олня́ть, -о́лнить запа́сы.

restoration [ˌrestə'reɪʃ(ə)n] *n.* **1.** (*return*) восстановле́ние; **~ of property** возвраще́ние иму́щества. **2.** (*refurbishment; renewal*) реставра́ция.

restore [rɪ'stɔ:(r)] *v.t.* **1.** (*give, bring or put back*) возвра|ща́ть, -ти́ть (*or* верну́ть); восстан|а́вливать, -ови́ть; **he was ~d to his former post** его́ восстанови́ли на пре́жней рабо́те; **it ~s my confidence** э́то вселя́ет в меня́ но́вую уве́ренность; **order was ~d** поря́док был восстано́влен. **2.** (*reconvert to original state*) реставри́ровать (*impf., pf.*); восстан|а́вливать, -ови́ть; **the text has been ~d** текст восстано́влен.

restorer [rɪ'stɔ:rə(r)] *n.* реставра́тор.

restrain [rɪ'streɪn] *v.t.* сде́рж|ивать, -а́ть; обу́зд|ывать, -а́ть; **it needed four men to ~ him** пона́добилось четы́ре челове́ка, что́бы удержа́ть его́; **his manner was ~ed** он был сде́ржан.

restraint [rɪ'streɪnt] *n.* **1.** (*self-control*) сде́ржанность, самооблада́ние. **2.** (*physical*) ограниче́ние свобо́ды движе́ния. **3.** (*constraint*) ограниче́ние; **without ~** без ограниче́ний; свобо́дно.

restrict [rɪ'strɪkt] *v.t.* ограни́чи|вать, -ть; **free travel is ~ed to pensioners** беспла́тный прое́зд распространя́ется то́лько на пенсионе́ров; **speed is ~ed to 30 mph** ско́рость ограни́чена до тридцати́ миль в час.

restriction [rɪ'strɪkʃ(ə)n] *n.* ограниче́ние.

restrictive [rɪ'strɪktɪv] *adj.* ограничи́тельный; **~ practices in industry** ме́ры по ограниче́нию конкуре́нции и́ли произво́дства.

result [rɪ'zʌlt] *n.* результа́т, сле́дствие; **he died as a ~ of his injuries** он у́мер от ран; **his efforts were without ~** его́ уси́лия бы́ли безрезульта́тны.

v.i. **1.** (*arise, come about*) сле́довать (*impf.*) (*из чего*); **this ~s from negligence** э́то сле́дствие небре́жности. **2.** (*issue, end*) конча́ться, ко́нчиться (*+i.*); **the quarrel ~ed in bloodshed** ссо́ра ко́нчилась кровопроли́тием.

resume [rɪ'zju:m] *v.t.* (*renew*) возобнов|ля́ть, -и́ть; (*continue*) прод|олжа́ть, -о́лжить; **to ~ my story** я продо́лжу свой расска́з; (*take again*) вновь обре|та́ть, -сти́; **he ~d his seat** он верну́лся на своё ме́сто; **he ~d command** он сно́ва при́нял кома́ндование (*чем*).

v.i.: **let us ~ after lunch** продо́лжим по́сле обе́да.

résumé ['rezjʊˌmeɪ] *n.* резюме́ (*indecl.*).

resumption [rɪ'zʌmpʃ(ə)n] *n.* (*renewal*) возобновле́ние; (*continuation*) продолже́ние; (*reacquisition*) возвраще́ние.

resurface [ri:'sɜ:fɪs] *v.i.* (*of a submarine*) всплы|ва́ть, -ть.

resurgence [rɪ'sɜ:dʒ(ə)ns] *n.* возрожде́ние.

resurgent [rɪ'sɜ:dʒ(ə)nt] *adj.* возрожда́ющийся.

resurrect [ˌrezə'rekt] *v.t.* **1.** (*raise from the dead*) воскр|еса́ть, -е́снуть. **2.** (*fig., rediscover, revive*) возро|жда́ть, -ди́ть; воскре|ша́ть, -си́ть.

resurrection [ˌrezə'rekʃ(ə)n] *n.* воскресе́ние; (*fig.*) возрожде́ние, воскреше́ние.

resuscitate [rɪ'sʌsɪˌteɪt] *v.t.* прив|оди́ть, -ести́ в созна́ние.

resuscitation [rɪˌsʌsɪ'teɪʃ(ə)n] *n.* приведе́ние в созна́ние.

retail ['ri:teɪl] *n.* ро́зничная прода́жа; **~ prices** ро́зничные це́ны.

v.t. (*sell by ~*) прод|ава́ть, -а́ть в ро́зницу.

v.i. продава́ться (*impf.*) в ро́зницу.

retailer ['ri:teɪlə(r)] *n.* ро́зничный торго́вец.

retain [rɪ'teɪn] *v.t.* **1.** (*keep, continue to have*) уде́рживать (*impf.*); сохран|я́ть, -и́ть. **2.** (*keep in place*) подде́рж|ивать, -а́ть; **~ing wall** подпо́рная стена́. **3.** (*secure services of*) нан|има́ть, -я́ть.

retainer [rɪ'teɪnə(r)] *n.* **1.** (*servant*) слуга́ (*m.*). **2.** (*fee*) предвари́тельный гонора́р.

retake[1] ['ri:teɪk] *n.* (*cin.*) повто́рная съёмка.

retake[2] [ri:'teɪk] *v.t.* **1.** (*recapture*) сно́ва брать, взять. **2.** (*film etc.*) пересн|има́ть, -я́ть.

retaliate [rɪ'tælɪˌeɪt] *v.i.* отпла́|чивать, -ти́ть той же моне́той; мстить, ото- (*кому за что*).

retaliation [rɪˌtælɪ'eɪʃ(ə)n] *n.* отпла́та, возме́здие.

retaliatory [rɪ'tæljətərɪ] *adj.* отве́тный.

retard [rɪ'tɑ:d] *v.t.* зам|едля́ть, -е́длить; **a ~ed child** у́мственно отста́лый ребёнок.

retch [retʃ, ri:tʃ] *v.i.* ту́житься (*impf.*) при рво́те.

retell [ri:'tel] *v.t.* переска́з|ывать, -а́ть.

retention [rɪ'tenʃ(ə)n] *n.* уде́рживание, сохране́ние.

retentive [rɪ'tentɪv] *adj.*: **a ~ memory** це́пкая па́мять.

rethink [ri:'θɪŋk] *v.t.* пересм|а́тривать, -отре́ть.

reticence ['retɪs(ə)ns] *n.* молчали́вость; скры́тность.

reticent ['retɪs(ə)nt] *adj.* молчали́вый; скры́тный.

retina ['retɪnə] *n.* сетча́тка.

retinue ['retɪˌnju:] *n.* сви́та.

retir|e [rɪ'taɪə(r)] *v.t.* ув|ольня́ть, -о́лить; **he was ~ed on a pension** его́ отпра́вили на пе́нсию.

v.i. **1.** (*withdraw*) удал|я́ться, -и́ться; **in company he ~es into himself** когда́ круго́м лю́ди, он ухо́дит в себя; **she ~ed (to bed) early** она́ ра́но легла́ (спать); **he has a ~ing disposition** он засте́нчивый челове́к; (*mil.*) отступ|а́ть, -и́ть. **2.** (*from employment*) уходи́ть, уйти́ в отста́вку.

retired [rɪ'taɪəd] *adj.* (находя́щийся) на пе́нсии; в отста́вке; **a ~ officer** отставно́й офице́р.

retirement [rɪ'taɪəmənt] *n.* (*withdrawal*) отхо́д; (*seclusion*) уедине́ние; (*end of employment*) отста́вка, вы́ход на пе́нсию; **in ~** в отста́вке; **~ age** пенсио́нный во́зраст.

retort [rɪ'tɔ:t] *n.* (*reply*) возраже́ние; ре́зкий отве́т.

v.t. & i. отв|еча́ть, -е́тить ре́зко.

retouch [ri:'tʌtʃ] *v.t.* ретуши́ровать, от-/под-.

retrace [rɪ'treɪs] *v.t.* просле́|живать, -ди́ть; **~ one's steps** возвраща́ться, верну́ться тем же путём; (*reconstruct, rehearse*) переч|исля́ть, -и́слить.

retract [rɪ'trækt] *v.t.* **1.** (*draw in*) втя́|гивать, -ну́ть. **2.** (*withdraw*) отка́з|ываться, -а́ться от+*g.*; **I ~ my statement** я беру́ наза́д своё заявле́ние.

v.i. втя́|гиваться, -ну́ться.

retraction [rɪ'trækʃ(ə)n] *n.* (*drawing in*) втя́гивание; (*withdrawal*) отрече́ние, отка́з (от+*g.*).

retrain [ri:'treɪn] *v.t.* переподгот|а́вливать, -о́вить.

retreat [rɪ'tri:t] *n.* **1.** (*withdrawal*) отступле́ние, отхо́д; **the army was in full ~** а́рмия отступа́ла по всему́ фро́нту; **they sounded the ~** они́ да́ли сигна́л к отхо́ду. **2.** (*secluded place*) убе́жище.

v.i. (*withdraw*) удал|я́ться, -и́ться.

retrench [rɪ'trentʃ] *v.t.* сокра|ща́ть, -ти́ть.

v.i. (*economize*) эконо́мить, с-.

retrenchment [rɪ'trentʃmənt] *n.* сокраще́ние расхо́дов.

retrial [ri:'traɪəl] *n.* повто́рное слу́шание де́ла.

retribution [ˌretrɪ'bju:ʃ(ə)n] *n.* возме́здие.

retrieval [rɪ'tri:vəl] *n.* **1.** (*recovery, getting back*) возвраще́ние; **the money is lost beyond ~** де́ньги потеря́ны безвозвра́тно; (*tech., of information*) по́иск. **2.** (*recollection, restoration, revival*) восстановле́ние. **3.** (*making good, repair*) исправле́ние.

retrieve [rɪ'tri:v] *v.t.* **1.** (*get back, recover*) брать, взять обра́тно; доста́ть (*pf.*), верну́ть (*pf.*). **2.** (*restore*) восстан|а́вливать, -ови́ть. **3.** (*put right, make amends for*) испр|авля́ть, -а́вить.

retriever [rɪ'tri:və(r)] *n.* охо́тничья по́иско́вая соба́ка.

retroactive [ˌretrəʊ'æktɪv] *adj.* име́ющий обра́тное де́йствие (*or* обра́тную си́лу).

retrograde ['retrəˌgreɪd] *adj.* дви́жущийся в обра́тном направле́нии; **~ motion** обра́тное движе́ние.

retrogress [ˌretrə'gres] *v.i.* регресси́ровать (*impf.*).

retrogression [ˌretrə'greʃ(ə)n] *n.* регре́сс.

retrogressive [ˌretrə'gresɪv] *adj.* регресси́рующий.

retro-rocket ['retrəʊˌrɒkɪt] *n.* тормозна́я ракéта.

retrospect ['retrəˌspekt] *n.*: **in ~** ретроспекти́вно.

retrospection [ˌretrə'spekʃ(ə)n] *n.* размышле́ния (*nt. pl.*) о про́шлом; ретроспе́кция.

retrospective [ˌretrə'spektɪv] *adj.* (*regarding the past*) ретроспекти́вный; **a ~ law** зако́н, име́ющий обра́тную си́лу.

re-try [ri:'traɪ] *v.t.* (*leg., case*) слу́шать (*impf.*) за́ново; (*pers.*) суди́ть (*impf.*) сно́ва.

return [rɪ'tɜ:n] *n.* **1.** (*coming or going back*) возвраще́ние; **there was no ~ of the symptoms** симпто́мы не повтори́лись; **by ~ (of post)** обра́тной по́чтой; **many happy ~s (of the day)!** с днём рожде́ния!; **~ fare** сто́имость обра́тного прое́зда. **2.** (**~ ticket**) обра́тный биле́т. **3.** (*turnover*) оборо́т; (*profit*) при́быль; **he got a good ~ on his investment** он получи́л хоро́ший дохо́д от вло́женных де́нег. **4.** (*giving, sending, putting, paying back*) отда́ча, возвра́т, опла́та; **the ~ of a ball** возвра́т мяча́; **~ match** отве́тный матч. **5.** (*reciprocation*): **in ~ (for)** взаме́н (+*g.*); (*in response to*) в отве́т (на+*a.*). **6.** (*report*) отчёт; **income tax ~** нало́говая деклара́ция; **election ~s** результа́т вы́боров.

v.t. **1.** (*give, send, put, pay back*) возвра|ща́ть, -ти́ть (*or* верну́ть); **I ~ed the book to the shelf** я поста́вил кни́гу обра́тно на по́лку; **he ~ed the ball accurately** он хорошо́ отби́л мяч; **she ~ed my compliment** она́ сде́лала мне отве́тный комплиме́нт; **he was ~ed by a narrow majority** он прошёл (в парла́мент) с незначи́тельным большинство́м. **2.** (*say in reply*) отв|еча́ть, -е́тить; возра|жа́ть, -зи́ть. **3.** (*declare*) до|кла́дывать, -ложи́ть; **the jury ~ed a verdict of guilty** прися́жные призна́ли обвиня́емого вино́вным.

v.i. возвра|ща́ться, -ти́ться (*or* верну́ться).

returnable [rɪ'tɜ:nəb(ə)l] *adj.* подлежа́щий возвра́ту.

reunion [ri:'ju:njən, -nɪən] *n.* (*reuniting*) воссоедине́ние; (*meeting of old friends etc.*) встре́ча; **family ~** сбор всей семьи́.

reunite [ˌri:ju:'naɪt] *v.t. & i.* воссоедин|я́ть(ся), -и́ть(ся).

reusable [ri:'ju:zəb(ə)l] *adj.* многокра́тного по́льзования.

re-use[1] [ri:'ju:s] *n.* повто́рное испо́льзование.

re-use[2] [ri:'ju:z] *v.t.* сно́ва испо́льзовать (*impf., pf.*).

Rev.[1] ['revərənd] *n.* = **Reverend**

rev[2] [ˌrevə'lu:ʃ(ə)n] *n.* (*coll.*) = **revolution 2.**

v.t. & i. (*also* **~ up**) увели́чи|вать, -ть оборо́ты (мото́ра).

revaluation [ri:ˌvælju:'eɪʃ(ə)n] *n.* (*of currency*) ревальва́ция.

revalue [ri:'vælju:] *v.t.* ревальви́ровать (*impf., pf.*).

revamp [ri:'væmp] *v.t.* (*fig.*) поднов|ля́ть, -и́ть.

revanchist [rɪ'væntʃɪst] *n.* реванши́ст.

adj. реванши́стский.

reveal [rɪ'vi:l] *v.t.* обнару́жи|вать, -ть; пока́з|ывать, -а́ть; **he would not ~ his name** он не хоте́л назва́ть своё и́мя; **he ~ed himself to be the father** он объяви́л себя́ отцо́м; **this account is very ~ing** э́тот отчёт о́чень показа́телен; **she wore a ~ing dress** она́ была́ в откры́том пла́тье.

reveille [rɪ'vælɪ, rɪ'velɪ] *n.* у́тренняя заря́; побу́дка.

revel ['rev(ə)l] *n.*: **the ~s went on all night** гуля́нка шла всю ночь.

v.i. **1.** (*make merry*) пирова́ть (*impf.*); кути́ть (*impf.*). **2.** (*take delight in*) наслажда́ться (*impf.*) (+*i.*); упива́ться (*impf.*) (+*i.*).

revelation [ˌrevə'leɪʃ(ə)n] *n.* откры́тие, открове́ние (*also fig., surprise*); (*bibl.*, **R~(s)**) апока́липсис.

reveller ['revələ(r)] *n.* кути́ла (*m.*), гуля́ка (*m.*).

revelry ['revəlrɪ] *n.* попо́йка, разгу́л.

revenge [rɪ'vendʒ] *n.* **1.** (*retaliatory action*) месть; **he took his ~ on me** он мне отомсти́л. **2.** (*vindictive feeling*) мсти́тельность; **I acted out of ~** я э́то сде́лал из ме́сти. **3.** (*in games*) рева́нш.

v.t. мстить, ото- (*кому за кого/что*); **he ~d the wrong done him** он отомсти́л за нанесённую ему́ оби́ду; **he ~d himself on his enemies** он отомсти́л свои́м врага́м.

revengeful [rɪ'vendʒfʊl] *adj.* мсти́тельный.

revenue ['revəˌnju:] *n.* дохо́д; **Inland R~** фина́нсовое/нало́говое управле́ние.

reverberate [rɪ'vɜ:bəˌreɪt] *v.i.* отра|жа́ться, -зи́ться.

reverberation [rɪˌvɜ:bə'reɪʃ(ə)n] *n.* ревербера́ция.

revere [rɪ'vɪə(r)] *v.t.* почита́ть (*impf.*); чтить (*impf.*).

reverence ['revərəns] *n.* **1.** (*awe, respect*) почита́ние, почте́ние. **2.**: **your R~** ва́ше преподо́бие.

reverend ['revərənd] *adj.*: **the R~ John Smith** его́ преподо́бие Джон Смит.

reverent(ial) [ˌrevə'renʃ(ə)l] *adj.* почти́тельный, благогове́йный.

reverie ['revərɪ] *n.* мечта́ние, мечта́; **she was lost in ~** она́ погрузи́лась в мечта́ния.

reversal [rɪ'vɜ:səl] *n.* (*annulment*) отме́на; (*conversion into opposite*) по́лная переме́на; переворо́т; **a ~ of fortune** превра́тность судьбы́.

reverse [rɪ'vɜ:s] *n.* **1.** (*opposite*) противополо́жность;

the ~ is true дéло обстои́т как раз наоборóт; **I am not ill, quite the ~** я не бóлен — совсéм наоборóт. **2. (~ gear): he put the car into ~** он включи́л зáдний ход. **3.** (*of coin*) обрáтная сторонá; рéшка. **4.** (*misfortune*; *defeat*) неудáча; поражéние.

adj. обрáтный, противополóжный; **in ~ order** в обрáтном поря́дке; **in ~ gear** зáдним хóдом.

v.t. **1.** (*turn round*, *invert*) пов|орáчивать, -ернýть обрáтно; **the situation was ~d** ситуáция крýто измени́лась. **2.** (*annul*) отмен|я́ть, -и́ть; **he ~d his decision** он пересмотрéл своё решéние. **3.** (*drive backwards*): **he ~d (the car) into a wall** он дал зáдний ход и врéзался в стéну.

v.i. **1.** (*of driver*) да|вáть, -ть зáдний ход. **2.** (*of vehicle*): **the car ~s well** маши́на хорошó идёт зáдним хóдом; **reversing light** фонáрь (*m.*) зáднего хóда.

reversible [rɪˈvɜːsɪb(ə)l] *adj.* (*of process etc.*) обрати́мый; (*that can be turned inside out*) двусторóнний.

reversion [rɪˈvɜːʃ(ə)n] *n.* возвращéние (к прéжнему состоя́нию).

revert [rɪˈvɜːt] *v.i.* возвра|щáться, -ти́ться; **the fields have ~ed to scrub** поля́ вновь поросли́ кустáрником; **he ~ed to his old ways** он взя́лся за стáрое; (*of property*, *rights etc.*) пере|ходи́ть, -йти́ (*к прéжнему владéльцу*).

review [rɪˈvjuː] *n.* **1.** (*re-examination*, *survey*, *revision*) пересмóтр, просмóтр; **the decision is subject to ~** решéние подлежи́т пересмóтру; **the matter is under constant ~** к э́тому вопрóсу постоя́нно возвращáются. **2.** (*retrospect*) пересмóтр; **a ~ of the year's events** обзóр собы́тий гóда. **3.** (*of mil. forces etc.*) парáд. **4.** (*of book etc.*) рецéнзия, óтзыв. **5.** (*periodical*) периоди́ческое издáние, обозрéние.

v.t. **1.** (*reconsider*, *re-examine*) пересм|áтривать, -отрéть. **2.** (*survey mentally*) мы́сленно обозр|евáть, -éть; **he ~ed his chances of success** он взвéсил свои́ шáнсы на успéх. **3.** (*inspect*) просм|áтривать, -отрéть. **4.** (*write critical account of*) рецензи́ровать, от-/про-; **the film was well ~ed** фильм получи́л хорóшие рецéнзии.

v.i.: **he ~s for the Times** он рецензéнт газéты «Таймс».

reviewer [rɪˈvjuːə(r)] *n.* рецензéнт, кри́тик.

revile [rɪˈvaɪl] *v.t.* оскорб|ля́ть, -и́ть; понoси́ть (*impf.*).

revise [rɪˈvaɪz] *v.t.* пересм|áтривать, -отрéть; испр|авля́ть, -áвить; перераб|áтывать, -óтать; **~d edition** испрáвленное издáние; **I ~d my opinion of him** я измени́л своё мнéние о нём.

v.i.: **I must ~ for the exams** я дóлжен повтори́ть материáл (*or* готóвиться) к экзáменам.

revision [rɪˈvɪʒ(ə)n] *n.* пересмóтр; (*checking*) провéрка, переработка; (*for exams*) повторéние.

revisionism [rɪˈvɪʒəˌnɪz(ə)m] *n.* ревизиони́зм.

revisionist [rɪˈvɪʒənɪst] *n.* ревизиони́ст.

revisit [riːˈvɪzɪt] *v.t.* посе|щáть, -ти́ть снóва.

revitalize [riːˈvaɪtəˌlaɪz] *v.t.* (вновь) ожив|ля́ть, -и́ть.

revival [rɪˈvaɪv(ə)l] *n.* (*return to consciousness*, *health etc.*) возвращéние сознáния; восстановлéние здорóвья; **a sudden ~ in spirits** внезáпный подъём дýха; **a ~ of interest** оживлéние интерéса; (*return to use*, *knowledge*, *popularity*) возрождéние; (*of play*) возобновлéние.

revivalism [rɪˈvaɪvəˌlɪz(ə)m] *n.* евангели́зм.

revivalist [rɪˈvaɪvəlɪst] *n.* евангели́ст (*fem.* -ка).

revive [rɪˈvaɪv] *v.t.* возро|ждáть, -ди́ть; ожив|ля́ть, -и́ть; **a glass of brandy ~d her** рю́мка коньякý привелá её в чýвство; **the opera was recently ~d** э́ту óперу недáвно постáвили снóва.

v.i. возро|ждáться, -ди́ться; (*regain vigour*) ожив|áть, -и́ть; **his spirits ~d** он приободри́лся; (*regain consciousness*) при|ходи́ть, -йти́ в себя́/чýвство.

revocation [ˌrevəˈkeɪʃ(ə)n] *n.* отмéна, аннули́рование.

revoke [rɪˈvəʊk] *v.t.* отмен|я́ть, -и́ть; аннули́ровать (*impf.*, *pf.*).

revolt [rɪˈvəʊlt] *n.* восстáние; бунт; **the peasants were in ~** крестья́не восстáли.

v.t. вызывáть, вы́звать отвращéние у+*g.*; **a ~ing sight** отврати́тельное зрéлище.

v.i. восст|авáть, -áть; бунтовáть(ся), взбунтовáться.

revolution [ˌrevəˈluːʃ(ə)n] *n.* **1.** (*revolving*) вращéние. **2.** (*one complete rotation*) оборóт; **at 60 ~s per minute** при шести́десяти оборóтах в минýту. **3.** (*pol.*, *fig.*) революция.

revolutionary [ˌrevəˈluːʃənərɪ] *n.* революционéр.

adj. революциóнный.

revolutionize [ˌrevəˈluːʃəˌnaɪz] *v.t.* (*stir up to revolution*, *transform*) революционизи́ровать (*impf.*, *pf.*).

revolv|e [rɪˈvɒlv] *v.i.* вращáться (*impf.*); **~ing doors** вращáющиеся двéри.

revolver [rɪˈvɒlvə(r)] *n.* револьвéр.

revue [rɪˈvjuː] *n.* обозрéние, ревю́ (*nt. indecl.*).

revulsion [rɪˈvʌlʃ(ə)n] *n.* отвращéние.

reward [rɪˈwɔːd] *n.* **1.** (*recompense*) нагрáда (за+*a.*); **without thought of ~** не дýмая о вознаграждéнии. **2.** (*sum offered*) прéмия; дéнежное вознаграждéние.

v.t. (воз)награ|ждáть, -ди́ть; **it was a ~ing task** дéло стóило тогó; **our patience was ~ed** нáше терпéние бы́ло вознагражденó.

rewind [riːˈwaɪnd] *v.t.* перем|áтывать, -отáть.

re-wire [riːˈwaɪə(r)] *v.t.*: **~ a house** обнов|ля́ть, -и́ть провóдку в дóме.

reword [riːˈwɜːd] *v.t.* выражáть, вы́разить други́ми словáми; переформули́ровать (*impf.*, *pf.*).

rewrite [riːˈraɪt] *v.t.* перепи́с|ывать, -áть.

rhapsody [ˈræpsədɪ] *n.* (*mus.*) рапсóдия.

rheostat [ˈriːəˌstæt] *n.* реостáт.

rhesus [ˈriːsəs] *n.* **(~ monkey)** рéзус; **R~ factor** рéзус-фáктор; **R~-negative** рéзус-отрицáтельный.

rhetoric [ˈretərɪk] *n.* ритóрика; орáторское искýсство; (*pej.*) краснобáйство.

rhetorical [rɪˈtɒrɪk(ə)l] *adj.* ритори́ческий; **~ question** ритори́ческий вопрóс.

rheumatic [ruːˈmætɪk] *n.* ревмáтик; (*pl.*, *coll.*, *rheumatism*) ревмати́зм.

adj. ревмати́ческий; **~ fever** ревмати́зм.

rheumatism [ˈruːməˌtɪz(ə)m] *n.* ревмати́зм.

rheumatoid [ˈruːməˌtɔɪd] *adj.*: **~ arthritis** ревмати́ческий полиартри́т, суставнóй ревмати́зм.

rhinestone гóрный хрустáль.

rhinoceros [raɪˈnɒsərəs] *n.* носорóг.

rhizome [ˈraɪzəʊm] *n.* ризóма.

Rhodesia [rəʊˈdiːʃə] *n.* Родéзия.

rhododendron [ˌrəʊdəˈdendrən] *n.* рододéндрон.

rhomboid [ˈrɒmbɔɪd] *n.* (*geom.*) ромбóид.

adj. (*also* **-al**) ромбови́дный.

rhombus [ˈrɒmbəs] *n.* (*geom.*) ромб.

rhubarb [ˈruːbɑːb] *n.* ревéнь (*m.*).

rhyme [raɪm] *n.* ри́фма; **he wrote the greeting in ~** он написáл привéтствие в стихáх; **there is no ~ or reason in it** в э́том нет никакóго смы́сла; (*poem*) стих; **nursery ~** дéтский стишóк.

v.t. & i. рифмовáть(ся) (*impf.*); **you can't ~ those two words** э́ти два слóва не рифмýются.

rhythm [ˈrɪð(ə)m] *n.* ритм; **~ section** (*of a band*) удáрные инструмéнты.

rhythmic(al) [ˈrɪðmɪk(əl)] *adj.* ритми́чный, ритми́ческий; **rhythmic gymnastics** худóжественная гимнáстика.

rib [rɪb] *n.* (*anat.*) ребрó; **he dug me in the ~s** он толкнýл меня́ в бок; **spare ~s** (*of meat*) рёбрышки (*nt. pl.*).

v.t. (*sl.*, *tease*) разыгр|ывать, -áть.

ribald [ˈrɪb(ə)ld] *adj.* непристóйный, скабрёзный.

ribaldry [ˈrɪbəldrɪ] *n.* непристóйность, скабрёзность.

ribbed [rɪbd] *adj.*: **~ cloth** рýбчатая ткань.
ribbon ['rɪbən] *n.* лéнта, тесьмá; **hair ~** лéнта; (*fig.*): **his clothes were torn to ~s** егó одéжда былá разóрвана в клóчья.
rice [raɪs] *n.* рис; **boiled ~** рúсовая кáша.
cpds. **~field** *n.* рúсовое пóле; **~-paper** *n.* рúсовая бумáга.
rich [rɪtʃ] *n.* (*collect.*, **the ~**) богáтые (*pl.*).
adj. **1.** (*wealthy*) богáтый. **2.** (*fertile*, *abundant*) плодорóдный; **he struck it ~** (*coll.*) он напáл на жúлу. **3.** (*valuable*, *plentiful*) обúльный; **a ~ harvest** богáтый урожáй. **4.** (*costly*, *splendid*) цéнный, богáтый. **5.** (*of food*) жúрный. **6.** (*of colours*) густóй. **7.** (*of sounds or voices*) густóй, сóчный.
riches ['rɪtʃɪz] *n.* богáтство, обúлие.
richly ['rɪtʃlɪ] *adv.*: **she was ~ dressed** онá былá богáто одéта; **his punishment was ~ deserved** он вполнé заслужúл такóе наказáние.
richness ['rɪtʃnɪs] *n.* богáтство; (*of food*) жúрность.
Richter scale ['rɪktə] *n.* шкалá Рúхтера.
rick[1] [rɪk] *n.* (*stack*) стог.
rick[2] [rɪk] (*also* **wrick**) *v.t.* растя́|гивать, -нýть; **I ~ed my neck** я нелóвко повернýл шéю.
rickets ['rɪkɪts] *n.* рахúт.
rickety ['rɪkɪtɪ] *adj.* шáткий, неустóйчивый.
rickshaw ['rɪkʃɔ:] *n.* рúкша.
ricochet ['rɪkə,ʃeɪ, -,ʃet] *n.* рикошéт.
v.i. рикошетúровать (*impf.*).
rid [rɪd] *v.t.* освобо|ждáть, -дúть; изб|авля́ть, -áвить; **get ~ of** изб|авля́ться, -áвиться от+*g.*; **we were glad to be ~ of him** мы бы́ли рáды от негó избáвиться.
riddance ['rɪd(ə)ns] *n.* избавлéние; устранéние; **good ~ to him!** ≃ скáтертью дорóга!
riddle[1] ['rɪd(ə)l] *n.* загáдка; (*mystery*) тáйна; **he set me a ~ to solve** он зáдал мне загáдку.
riddle[2] ['rɪd(ə)l] *n.* (*sieve*) решетó.
v.t. (*pierce all over*) решетúть, из-; **he was ~d with bullets** пýли изрешетúли егó тéло; (*fig.*): **~d with disease** насквóзь больнóй; **the manuscript is ~d with errors** рýкопись пестрúт оши́бками.
ride [raɪd] *n.* **1.** (*journey on horseback*) прогýлка верхóм; (*by vehicle*) поéздка, ездá; **it is only a 5-minute ~ to the station** до стáнции всегó 5 минýт езды́. **2.** (*excursion*) прогýлка; **he took me for a ~** (*lit.*) он прокатúл меня́; (*coll.*, *cheated*) он меня́ разыгрáл.
v.t. & i. **1.** (*on horseback*) éздить (*indet.*), éхать, по- (верхóм) (на+*p.*); (*gallop*) скакáть (*impf.*); **he rode his horse at the fence** он напрáвил лóшадь к барьéру; **he rode his horse over the fence** он перемахнýл на лóшади чéрез забóр; **the jockey rode a good race** жокéй хорошó скакáл; **he ~s to hounds** он охóтится верхóм с собáками. **2.** (*on a vehicle*) éздить (*indet.*), éхать, по- (на+*p.*); **I ~ a bicycle to work** я éзжу на рабóту на велосипéде. **3.** (*of ships etc.*) плыть (*impf.*) (по+*d.*); **the ship rode the waves** корáбль рассекáл вóлны; **the ship was riding at anchor** корáбль стоя́л на я́коре; **let it ~** (*fig.*) ну и пусть! **4.** (*of a horse or vehicle*) катúться (*impf.*); идтú (*det.*).
with advs.: **~ away** *v.i.* отъ|езжáть, -éхать; уезжáть, уéхать; **~ down** *v.t.* (*pursue and catch up with*) дог|оня́ть, -нáть; (*knock down by riding at s.o.*) давúть (*impf.*); топтáть (*impf.*); **~ out** *v.t.*: **the ship rode out the storm** корáбль вы́держал нáтиск бýри; **we shall ~ out our present troubles** мы переживём ны́нешние трýдности; **~ up** *v.i.* (*approach on horseback*) подъ|езжáть, -éхать верхóм; (*of clothing*) лезть (*impf.*) вверх.
rider ['raɪdə(r)] *n.* **1.** (*horseman*) всáдни|к (*fem.* -ца), наéздни|к (*fem.* -ца). **2.** (*clause*) дополнéние; добавлéние.
ridge [rɪdʒ] *n.* **1.** край; спúнка; **the ~ of a roof** конёк кры́ши. **2.** (*of soil*) грéбень (*m.*). **3.** (*of high land*) гóрный хребéт/кряж.
ridicule ['rɪdɪ,kju:l] *n.* осмея́ние, насмéшка; **he was an object of ~** он был предмéтом насмéшек; **I don't like being held up to ~** не люблю́, когдá из меня́ дéлают посмéшище.
v.t. осмéивать (*impf.*); подн|имáть, -я́ть нá смех.
ridiculous [rɪ'dɪkjʊləs] *adj.* смехотвóрный; нелéпый; **don't be ~!** не говорúте глýпостей!
riding ['raɪdɪŋ] *n.* верховáя ездá.
cpds. **~-breeches** *n.* брúдж|и (*pl.*, *g.* -ей) для верховóй езды́; **~-habit** *n.* амазóнка; **~-master** *n.* берéйтор; **~-school** *n.* шкóла верховóй езды́.
rife [raɪf] *adj.* распространённый; **the country was ~ with rumours** в странé ходúло мнóжество слýхов.
riffraff ['rɪfræf] *n.* подóнки (*m. pl.*) óбщества; сброд.
rifle ['raɪf(ə)l] *n.* винтóвка; **~ regiment** пехóтный/стрелкóвый полк.
v.t. **1.** (*cut grooves in*) нарезáть (*impf.*) канáл (*ствола*). **2.** (*plunder*) грáбить, о-.
cpds. **~man** *n.* стрелóк; **~-range** *n.* (*for shooting practice*) тир, стрéльбище; **~-shot** *n.* вы́стрел из винтóвки.
rift [rɪft] *n.* **1.** трéщина, щель. **2.** (*fig.*) разлáд.
cpd. **~-valley** *n.* рúфтовая долúна.
rig [rɪg] *n.* **1.** (*naut.*) оснáстка. **2.** (*for drilling*) буровáя вы́шка.
v.t. **1.** (*fit out*) осна|щáть, -стúть **2.** (*manipulate, conduct fraudulently*): **the elections were ~ged** результáты вы́боров бы́ли подтасóваны; **a ~ged match** договóрный матч.
with advs.: **~ out** *v.t.* снаря|жáть, -дúть; наря|жáть, -дúть; **~ up** (нáскоро) *v.t.* соору|жáть, -дúть.
cpd. **~-out** *n.* наря́д.
rigging ['rɪgɪŋ] *n.* такелáж, оснáстка.
right [raɪt] *n.* **1.** (*what is just, fair*) правотá; справедлúвость; **the child must learn the difference between ~ and wrong** ребёнка слéдует научúть отличáть добрó от злá; **I know I am in the ~** я знáю, что я прав. **2.** (*entitlement*) прáво; **as of ~** как полагáющийся по прáву; **in one's own ~** сам; сам по себé; **stand on one's ~s** наст|áивать, -оя́ть на своúх правáх; **stand up for one's ~s** отст|áивать, -оя́ть своú правá; **the house is hers by ~** дом принадлежúт ей по закóну; **by ~s** по справедлúвости; чéстно говоря́; **~ of way** прáво прохóда/проéзда; **bill of ~s** билль (*m.*) о правáх. **3.** (*pl.*, *correct state*): **he put the engine to ~s** он привёл мотóр в поря́док; **he tried to set the world to ~s** он пытáлся передéлать мир. **4.** (*~-hand side etc.*) прáвая сторонá; **on, to the ~** напрáво; **on, from the ~** спрáва; **most countries drive on the ~** в большинствé стран правосторóнное движéние. **5.** (*pol.*): **the R~** прáвые (*pl.*).
adj. **1.** (*just, morally good*) прáвый, справедлúвый; **I try to do what is ~** я старáюсь поступáть чéстно; **you were ~ to refuse** вы сдéлали прáвильно, что отказáлись; **it is only ~ to tell you ...** я считáю своúм дóлгом сказáть вам, что...; **that is only ~ and proper** так томý и слéдует быть. **2.** (*correct, true, required*) прáвильный, вéрный, нýжный; **the ~ road** прáвильный путь; **that's not the ~ way to do it** э́то дéлается не так; **what is the ~ time?** вы мóжете сказáть тóчное врéмя?; **he tried to keep on the ~ side of the teacher** он старáлся не пóртить отношéния с учúтелем; **~ side up** в прáвильном положéнии; **he is on the ~ side of forty** емý ещё нет сорокá; **that's ~!** прáвильно!; вéрно!; **let's get it ~, are you on my side or not?** давáйте разберёмся, на моéй вы сторонé илú нет?; **I tried to put him ~** я пытáлся вы́вести егó из заблуждéния; **I set him ~ on a few points** я емý кóе-что разъяснúл. **3.** (*in order, good health*) испрáвный; здорóвый; **can you put my watch ~?** вы мóжете

почини́ть мои́ часы́?; **these matters must be put ~** э́ти дела́ ну́жно ула́дить; **I feel as ~ as rain** я себя́ прекра́сно чу́вствую; **he's not quite ~ in the head** у него́ не все до́ма; **he was not in his ~ mind** он был не в своём уме́; **everything will turn out ~ in the end** всё в конце́ концо́в ула́дится; **are you all ~?** всё в поря́дке?; (*expr. doubt*) вам нехорошо́?; **all ~, I'll come with you!** ла́дно, я пойду́ с ва́ми!; **it's all ~ with me** я не возража́ю; **~!** (*expr. agreement or consent*) ве́рно!; хорошо́!; **~ you are** хорошо́!; (*coll.*) идёт! **4.** (*opp. left*) пра́вый; **on my ~ hand** напра́во от меня́; **he is my ~ arm** (*fig.*) он моя́ пра́вая рука́; **he made a ~ turn** он поверну́л напра́во. **5.: ~ angle** прямо́й у́гол; **at ~ angles to** под прямы́м у́глом к+*d.*

adv. **1.** (*straight*) пря́мо; **he went ~ to the point** он сра́зу перешёл к де́лу; **the plane flew ~ overhead** самолёт пролете́л пря́мо над голово́й. **2.** (*exactly*) то́чно; **the shot was ~ on target** уда́р попа́л пря́мо в цель; **I was there ~ on the stroke of one** я пришёл ро́вно в час, мину́та в мину́ту; **~ now** (*US*) сейча́с; в да́нный моме́нт. **3.** (*immediately*) сра́зу (же); **~ away** сра́зу (же), неме́дленно. **4.** (*all the way, completely*) по́лностью; **he turned ~ round** он поверну́лся круго́м; **they climbed ~ to the top** они́ взобрали́сь на са́мую верши́ну; **I went ~ back to the beginning** я верну́лся к са́мому нача́лу; **he came ~ up to me** он подошёл ко мне вплотну́ю. **5.** (*justly; correctly, properly*) справедли́во; пра́вильно; **he can do nothing ~** у него́ ничего́ не ла́дится; **have I guessed ~?** я угада́л?; **if I remember ~** е́сли мне не изменя́ет па́мять; **it serves you ~** так вам и на́до. **6.** (*in titles*): **R~ Honourable** достопочте́нный. **7.** (*of direction*) напра́во; **eyes ~!** равне́ние напра́во!; **he owes money ~ and left** он круго́м в долга́х; **~, left and centre** круго́м, всю́ду.

v.t. (*restore to correct position*) выра́внивать, вы́ровнять; **the boat ~ed itself** ло́дка вы́ровнялась; (*fig., correct*) испр|авля́ть, -а́вить; **the fault will ~ itself** э́то испра́вится само́ собо́й.

cpds. **~about** *adj. & adv.*: **~about turn** поворо́т круго́м; **~-angled** *adj.* прямоуго́льный; **~-hand** *adj.* пра́вый; **~-hand drive** правосторо́ннее управле́ние; **~-hand man** (*fig.*) ве́рный помо́щник; **~-hand turn** пра́вый поворо́т; **~-handed** *adj.* де́лающий всё пра́вой руко́й; **~-wing** *adj.* (*pol.*) пра́вых взгля́дов.

righteous [ˈraɪtʃəs] *adj.* пра́ведный; **~ indignation** справедли́вое негодова́ние.

righteousness [ˈraɪtʃəsnɪs] *n.* пра́ведность.

rightful [ˈraɪtfʊl] *adj.* зако́нный, правоме́рный.

rightist [ˈraɪtɪst] *n. & adj.* пра́вый; (челове́к) пра́вых взгля́дов.

rightly [ˈraɪtlɪ] *adv.* **1.** (*correctly, properly*) пра́вильно. **2.** (*justly*) справедли́во; **he was punished, and ~ so** он был нака́зан, и подело́м.

rightness [ˈraɪtnɪs] *n.* справедли́вость.

righto [ˈraɪtəʊ, raɪˈtəʊ] (*int.*) хорошо́!; ла́дно!

rigid [ˈrɪdʒɪd] *adj.* жёсткий, негну́щийся; (*fig.*) неги́бкий; **~ discipline** стро́гая дисципли́на.

rigidity [ˌrɪˈdʒɪdɪtɪ] *n.* жёсткость; (*fig.*) неги́бкость.

rigor [ˈrɪgə(r), ˈraɪgɔː(r)] *n.*: **~ mortis** тру́пное окочене́ние.

rigorous [ˈrɪgərəs] *adj.* (*strict*) стро́гий; (*severe, harsh*) суро́вый.

rigour [ˈrɪgə(r)] *n.* стро́гость; суро́вость; **with all the ~ of the law** по всей стро́гости зако́на; **the ~s of winter** суро́вость зимы́.

rile [raɪl] *v.t.* (*coll.*) серди́ть, рас-; раздраж|а́ть, -и́ть; **it ~d him to lose the game** его́ зли́ло, что он проигра́л.

rim [rɪm] *n.* о́бод; край; **~ of a wheel** о́бод колеса́; **~ of a cup** край ча́шки; **spectacles with steel ~s** очки́ в стально́й опра́ве.

rime [raɪm] *n.* (*frost*) и́ней, и́зморозь.

rind [raɪnd] *n.* (*bark*) кора́; (*of melon, cheese*) ко́рка; (*of bacon*) кожура́, шку́рка.

ring[1] [rɪŋ] *n.* **1.** (*ornament, implement*) кольцо́; (*with stone; signet-~*) пе́рстень (*m.*); **engagement ~** кольцо́, пода́ренное при помо́лвке; **wedding ~** обруча́льное кольцо́. **2.** (*circle*) кольцо́, круг; **~s of a tree** годовы́е ко́льца де́рева; **they stood in a ~** они́ ста́ли в круг; **he had ~s under his eyes** у него́ бы́ли тёмные круги́ под глаза́ми. **3.** (*conspiracy*) ша́йка, ба́нда; **spy ~** шпио́нская организа́ция. **4.** (*of circus, boxing etc.*) аре́на, ринг. **5.** (*of cooker*) конфо́рка.

v.t. **1.** (*encompass*) окруж|а́ть, -и́ть. **2.** (*put ~ on*): **the birds have been ~ed** птиц око́льцевали. **3.** (*put ~ around*): **his name was ~ed in pencil** его́ и́мя бы́ло обведено́ карандашо́м.

cpds. **~-finger** *n.* безымя́нный па́лец; **~leader** *n.* глава́рь (*m.*), зачи́нщик; **~master** *n.* инспе́ктор мане́жа; **~-road** *n.* кольцева́я доро́га; **~side** *n.* пе́рвые ряды́ (*m. pl.*) (вокру́г аре́ны); **~worm** *n.* стригу́щий лиша́й.

ring[2] [rɪŋ] *n.* **1.** звон; звук; (*fig.*): **it has the ~ of truth** э́то звучи́т правдоподо́бно. **2.** (*sound of bell*) звоно́к; **there was a ~ at the door** в дверь позвони́ли. **3.** (*telephone call*) звоно́к; **give me a ~ tomorrow** позвони́те мне за́втра.

v.t. **1.** звони́ть, по- в+*a.*; **the postman rang the bell** почтальо́н позвони́л в дверь; **that ~s a bell** да, да, припомина́ю. **2.** (*telephone, also ~ up*) звони́ть, по- +*d.*; **will you ~ me when you get home?** вы мне позвони́те, когда́ прибу́дете домо́й?

v.i. **1.** звони́ть, по-; **the bells are ~ing** звоня́т колокола́; **the bell rang for dinner** позвони́ли к обе́ду; **the telephone rang** зазвони́л телефо́н; **my ears are ~ing** у меня́ звени́т в уша́х; **his voice was still ~ing in my ears** его́ го́лос всё ещё звуча́л у меня́ в уша́х; (*fig.*): **his words ~ true** его́ слова́ звуча́т правдоподо́бно. **2.** (*telephone*) звони́ть, по-; **we must ~ for the doctor** мы должны́ вы́звать врача́ (по телефо́ну). **3.** (*resound*) огла|ша́ться, -си́ться; разноси́ться (*impf.*); **the house rang with the sound of children's voices** де́тские голоса́ разноси́лись по всему́ до́му.

with advs.: **they rang down/up the curtain** за́навес опусти́ли/по́дняли; **~ off** пове́сить (*pf.*) тру́бку; **the bells rang out the old year and rang in the new** колоко́льным зво́ном проводи́ли ста́рый год и встре́тили но́вый; **a shot rang out** разда́лся вы́стрел; **someone rang (up) for you this morning** вам кто-то звони́л у́тром.

ringlet [ˈrɪŋlɪt] *n.* (*curl*) ло́кон, завито́к.

rink [rɪŋk] *n.* като́к.

rinse [rɪns] *n.* (*action of rinsing*) полоска́ние; (*hair-dye*) сре́дство для подкра́шивания воло́с.

v.t. полоска́ть, вы́-; спол|а́скивать, -осну́ть; **~ out your mouth!** прополощи́те рот!

riot [ˈraɪət] *n.* **1.** (*brawl*) беспоря́дки (*m. pl.*); **there was a ~ in the theatre** в теа́тре разрази́лся сканда́л. **2.** (*revolt*) мяте́ж, бунт; **the R~ Act** зако́н об охра́не обще́ственного поря́дка; (*fig.*): **the teacher read the ~ act to his class** учи́тель сде́лал вы́говор всему́ кла́ссу. **3.** (*fig.*): **she allowed her fancy to run ~** она́ дала́ по́лную во́лю воображе́нию; **the weeds are running ~** сорняки́ бу́йно разраста́ются; **the garden was a ~ of colour** сад пестре́л все́ми кра́сками.

v.i. (*brawl, rebel*) бесчи́нствовать (*impf.*); бу́йствовать (*impf.*); **the crowd ~ed in the streets** толпа́ бесчи́нствовала на у́лицах.

rioter [ˈraɪətə(r)] *n.* бунта́рь (*m.*), мяте́жник.

riotous [ˈraɪətəs] *adj.* (*rebellious*) мяте́жный; (*wildly enthusiastic*) безу́держный, шу́мный; **~ laughter**

безу́держный смех; ~ **living** разгу́льная жизнь.

RIP (*abbr. of* ***rest in peace***) мир пра́ху (*кого*).

rip [rɪp] *n.* (*tear*) разре́з, проре́ха.

v.t. рвать, разо-; **he ~ped his trousers on a nail** он разорва́л брю́ки о гвоздь; **he ~ped off the lid** он сорва́л кры́шку; **they ~ped out his appendix** ему́ удали́ли аппе́ндикс; ~ **off** (*coll.*, *steal*) об|ди-ра́ть, -одра́ть.

v.i. **1.** (*tear*) рва́ться, разо-; **the cloth ~ped right across** мате́рия разорва́лась попола́м. **2.** (*rush along*) мча́ться, про-; **let her ~!** жми на всю кату́шку! (*coll.*).

cpds. **~-cord** *n.* вытяжно́й трос; **~-off** *n.* (*sl.*) воровство́; **it's a ~-off** э́то обдира́ловка; **~-saw** *n.* продо́льная пила́.

ripe [raɪp] *adj.* **1.** (*ready for gathering, eating or use*) спе́лый, зре́лый; **the corn is** ~ зерно́ созре́ло; ~ **cheese** вы́держанный сыр; (*fig.*): **he lived to a ~ old age** он до́жил до глубо́кой ста́рости. **2.** (*ready, suitable*) гото́вый, созре́вший; **the time is ~ for action** пришло́ вре́мя де́йствовать.

ripen ['raɪpən] *v.i.* зреть (*or* созрева́ть), со-.

ripeness ['raɪpnɪs] *n.* спе́лость, зре́лость.

riposte [rɪ'pɒst] *n.* (*fencing*) отве́тный уда́р; (*verbal*) нахо́дчивый отве́т.

ripple ['rɪp(ə)l] *n.* рябь, зыбь, круг; (*fig.*): **his words caused a ~ of laughter** его́ слова́ вы́звали лёгкий смешо́к.

v.t. & i. покр|ыва́ть(ся), -ы́ть(ся) ря́бью.

rise [raɪz] *n.* **1.** (*upward slope*) подъём. **2.** (*area of higher ground*) холм, возвы́шенность. **3.** (*fig.*, *ascent*) подъём; восхожде́ние. **4.** (*increase*) повыше́ние, увеличе́ние; **they asked for a ~** они попроси́ли об увеличе́нии зарпла́ты; **a ~ in the cost of living** удорожа́ние жи́зни; **unemployment is on the ~** безрабо́тица растёт. **5.** (*origin*): **give ~ to** вызыва́ть, вы́звать.

v.i. **1.** (*get up from bed*) вста|ва́ть, -ть (на́ ноги); **I rose at 6** я встал в 6; (*from seated or kneeling position*) вста|ва́ть, -ть; подн|има́ться, -я́ться; **they rose from the table** они́ подняли́сь из-за стола́; **he rose to his full height** он встал во весь рост; **the horse rose (up) on its hind legs** ло́шадь вста́ла на дыбы́; (*into the air*) подн|има́ться, -я́ться; (*above the horizon*) восходи́ть, взойти́; **when the sun ~s** когда́ восхо́дит со́лнце; (*fig.*, *appear*) возн|ика́ть, -и́кнуть; **the rising generation** подраста́ющее поколе́ние; (*to the surface*) выходи́ть, вы́йти на пове́рхность; (*fig.*): **he will always ~ to the occasion** он не растеря́ется в любо́й ситуа́ции. **2.** (*slope upwards*) подн|има́ться, -я́ться; **on rising ground** на скло́не/возвыше́нии; (*tower*): **the cliffs rose sheer above them** над ни́ми кру́то возвыша́лись ска́лы. **3.** (*increase in amount*) возраста́ть (*impf.*); увели́чи|ваться, -ться; (*in level*): **the waters are rising** вода́ прибыва́ет; **rising tide** нараста́ющий прили́в; **the temperature is rising** температу́ра повыша́ется; (*in price*) пов|ыша́ться, -ы́ситься в цене́; **his voice rose in anger** в гне́ве он повы́сил го́лос; (*in intensity or animation*) увели́чи|ваться, -ться; **the wind is rising** ве́тер поднима́ется; **her colour rose** она́ покрасне́ла; **his spirits rose** его́ настрое́ние улу́чшилось; (*in importance or rank*) продв|ига́ться, -и́нуться; **he rose from the ranks** (*mil.*) он вы́служился из рядовы́х; **he rose to international fame** он приобрёл мирову́ю изве́стность; (*in age*): **he is rising 40** ему́ под со́рок. **4.** (*spring, originate*) брать, взять нача́ло; возн|ика́ть, -и́кнуть. **5.** (*rebel*) восст|ава́ть, -а́ть; **the people rose (up) in arms** наро́д восста́л с ору́жием в рука́х.

riser ['raɪzə(r)] *n.*: **he is an early ~** он встаёт с петуха́ми.

rising ['raɪzɪŋ] *n.* **1.** (*getting up*) подъём; **I believe in early ~** я счита́ю, что встава́ть на́до ра́но. **2.** (*of the sun, moon etc.*) восхо́д. **3.** (*rebellion*) восста́ние.

risk [rɪsk] *n.* риск; **he takes many ~s** он лю́бит рискова́ть; **at the ~ of one's life** риску́я жи́знью; **at owner's ~** на риск владе́льца; **you go at your own ~** вы идёте туда́ на свой страх и риск.

v.t. **1.** (*expose to* ~) рискова́ть (*impf.*); **he ~ed his life to save her** он спас её, риску́я жи́знью. **2.** (*take the chance of*) риск|ова́ть, -ну́ть (*чем*); **shall we ~ it?** ну что, рискнём?

risky ['rɪskɪ] *adj.* риско́ванный, опа́сный.

risotto [rɪ'zɒtəʊ] *n.* ризо́тто (*m. indecl.*).

risqué ['rɪskeɪ, -'keɪ] *adj.* риско́ванный, сомни́тельный.

rissole ['rɪsəʊl] *n.* ру́бленая котле́та.

rite [raɪt] *n.* обря́д, ритуа́л, церемо́ния; **the ~s of hospitality** обы́чаи гостеприи́мства; **last ~s** (*extreme unction*) соборова́ние.

ritual ['rɪtjʊəl] *n.* ритуа́л.

adj. ритуа́льный; (*fig.*, *invariable*) неизме́нный.

ritzy ['rɪtzɪ] *adj.* (*coll.*) (*US*) шика́рный.

rival ['raɪv(ə)l] *n.* сопе́рник; **~s in love** сопе́рники в любви́; **he has many business ~s** у него́ мно́го конкуре́нтов; **he was without a ~ as chef** он был непревзойдённым по́варом.

adj. сопе́рничающий; **the ~ team** кома́нда проти́вника.

v.t. сопе́рничать (*impf.*) с+*i.*

rivalry ['raɪvəlrɪ] *n.* сопе́рничество, конкуре́нция; **let us not enter into ~** заче́м нам сопе́рничать?

river ['rɪvə(r)] *n.* река́; (*attr.*) речно́й; **up/down ~** вверх/вниз по реке́.

cpds. **~-basin** *n.* бассе́йн реки́; **~-bed** *n.* ру́сло реки́; **~side** *n.* прибре́жная полоса́; *adj.* прибре́жный, стоя́щий на берегу́ реки́.

rivet ['rɪvɪt] *n.* заклёпка.

v.t. клепа́ть (*impf.*); склёп|ывать, -а́ть; (*fig.*) устрем|ля́ть, -и́ть (*взгляд/внимание*); **his eyes were ~ed on her** его́ взгляд был прико́ван к ней.

riveting ['rɪvɪtɪŋ] *adj.* (*coll.*) захва́тывающий.

rivulet ['rɪvjʊlɪt] *n.* руче́й.

RN (*abbr. of* ***Royal Navy***) англи́йский ВМФ, (вое́нно-морско́й флот).

roach [rəʊtʃ] *n.* (*fish*) плотва́; (**cock~**) тарака́н.

road [rəʊd] *n.* **1.** (*thoroughfare*) доро́га; (*attr.*) доро́жный (*see also cpds.*); **main ~** гла́вная доро́га; **~ accident** автомоби́льная/доро́жная катастро́фа; **~ junction** пересече́ние доро́г, перекрёсток; **~ works** доро́жные-ремо́нтные рабо́ты; **my car is parked off the ~** я поста́вил маши́ну на обо́чине; **we have been on the ~ for hours** мы е́дем уже́ мно́го часо́в; **he is on the ~** (*of a salesman*) он в отъе́зде; (*of an actor*) он на гастро́лях; **the ~ has been up since Sunday** доро́гу ремонти́руют с воскресе́нья. **2.** (*fig.*) путь (*m.*), доро́га; **he is on the ~ to recovery** он на пути́ к выздоровле́нию. **3.** (*coll.*, *way*): **get out of my ~!** прочь с доро́ги!; **you are getting in my ~** вы мне меша́ете.

cpds. **~-block** *n.* загражде́ние на доро́ге; **~-hog** *n.* плохо́й води́тель, лиха́ч; **~-map** *n.* доро́жная ка́рта; **~side** *n.* обо́чина доро́ги; **~stead** *n.* рейд; **~-test** (*of a car*) доро́жное испыта́ние; **~way** *n.* доро́га, прое́зжая часть; **~worthy** *adj.* приго́дный для езды́ по доро́гам.

roam [rəʊm] *v.t. & i.* броди́ть, стра́нствовать (*both impf.*); **he ~ed the streets** он броди́л по у́лицам.

roar [rɔː(r)] *n.* (*of animal*) рёв, рык; (*loud human cry*) крик; вопль (*m.*); **he gave a ~ of anger** он изда́л я́ростный вопль; **there were ~s of laughter** разда́ли́сь взры́вы хо́хота; (*of wind or sea*) рёв; (*of engine*) гро́хот, гул.

v.t. & i. реве́ть (*impf.*); рыча́ть (*impf.*); **the audience ~ed approval** пу́блика реве́ла от восто́рга; **they ~ed themselves hoarse** они́ охри́пли от кри́ка;

he ~ed his head off он ора́л изо всей мо́чи; **the lion ~ed** лев зарыча́л; **he ~ed with laughter** он хохота́л во всё го́рло; **shops are doing a ~ing trade** в магази́нах това́ры иду́т нарасхва́т.

roast [rəʊst] *n.* жарко́е.

v.t. жа́рить, под-; **~ beef** жа́реная говя́дина; **~ed coffee beans** поджа́ренные кофе́йные зёрна; **he ~ed himself in front of the fire** он гре́лся у ками́на.

v.i. жа́риться (*impf.*).

roaster ['rəʊstə(r)] *n.* (*oven*) жаро́вня.

rob [rɒb] *v.t.* красть, обо-; гра́бить, о-; **the bank was ~bed** банк огра́били; **they ~bed him of his watch** они́ укра́ли у него́ часы́; (*fig., deprive*) лиш|а́ть, -и́ть.

robber ['rɒbə(r)] *n.* граби́тель (*m.*), вор.

robbery ['rɒbərɪ] *n.* грабёж; **~ with violence** грабёж с наси́лием; **there has been a ~** произошло́ ограбле́ние.

robe [rəʊb] *n.* ма́нтия; (*US, dressing-gown*; *also* **bath-~**) (купа́льный) хала́т.

v.t.: **~d in black** облачённый в чёрное.

v.i. облач|а́ться, -и́ться.

robin (redbreast) ['rɒbɪn] *n.* мали́новка.

robot ['rəʊbɒt] *n.* (*lit., fig.*) ро́бот; (*attr.*) автомати́ческий.

robotics [rəʊ'bɒtɪks] *n.* робо(то)те́хника.

robust [rəʊ'bʌst] *adj.* (*of pers., physique*) кре́пкий, си́льный; (*of health*) хоро́ший, кре́пкий; (*of appetite*) здоро́вый; (*of an object etc.*) про́чный.

rock[1] [rɒk] *n.* (*solid part of earth's crust*) го́рная поро́да; **a house built on ~** дом, постро́енный на скале́ (*or* ска́льном гру́нте); (*large stone*) скала́, утёс; (*boulder*) валу́н; **the ship ran upon the ~s** кора́бль наскочи́л на ска́лы; **the firm is on the ~s** (*coll.*) фи́рма прогоре́ла; (*US, stone, pebble*) ка́мень (*m.*); **whisky on the ~s** (*coll.*) ви́ски со льдом.

cpds. **~-bottom** *n.* (*fig.*): **at ~-bottom prices** по са́мым ни́зким це́нам; **~-climber** *n.* скалола́з; **~-climbing** *n.* скалола́зание; **~-crystal** *n.* го́рный хруста́ль; **~-garden** *n.* (*also* **~ery**) альпина́рий; **~-plant** *n.* альпи́йское расте́ние; **~-salmon** *n.* нали́м; **~-salt** *n.* ка́менная соль.

rock[2] [rɒk] *n.* (*music*) рок.

v.t. (*sway gently*) кач|а́ть, -ну́ть; ука́ч|ивать, -а́ть; **the nurse ~ed the baby to sleep** ня́ня укача́ла/убаю́кала ребёнка; **the boat was ~ed by the waves** ло́дка покача́лась на во́лна́х; (*shake*) трясти́, по-; **the earthquake ~ed the house** дом шата́лся от землетрясе́ния.

v.i. (*sway gently*) кача́ться (*impf.*); **~ing-chair** кача́лка; **~ing-horse** конь(*m.*)-кача́лка.

cpd. **~-'n'-roll** *n.* рок-н-ро́лл.

rocker ['rɒkə(r)] *n.* **1.** (*of cradle etc.; chair*) кача́лка. **2.**: **go off one's ~** рехну́ться (*pf.*) (*coll.*).

rockery ['rɒkərɪ] = **rock-garden**

rocket ['rɒkɪt] *n.* **1.** (*projectile*) раке́та. **2.** (*reprimand*): **he got a ~ from the boss** он получи́л взбу́чку (*coll.*) от нача́льника.

v.i. (*fig.*): **prices ~ed (up)** це́ны ре́зко подскочи́ли.

rocketry ['rɒkɪtrɪ] *n.* раке́тная те́хника.

rocky ['rɒkɪ] *adj.* **1.** (*of or like rock; full of rocks*) скали́стый, камени́стый; **the R~ Mountains** (*coll.*) Скали́стые го́ры (*f. pl.*). **2.** (*shaky, unsteady*) неусто́йчивый, ша́ткий.

rococo [rə'kəʊkəʊ] *n.* рококо́ (*indecl.*).

adj. в сти́ле рококо́.

rod [rɒd] *n.* **1.** (*slender stick*) прут; (*fishing-~*) у́дочка; **he fished with ~ and line** он лови́л ры́бу у́дочкой; (*instrument of chastisement*) ро́зга, хлыст; **he ruled the people with a ~ of iron** он пра́вил желе́зной руко́й. **2.** (*metal bar*) сте́ржень (*m.*).

rodent ['rəʊd(ə)nt] *n.* грызу́н.

roe[1] [rəʊ] *n.* (*hard ~*) икра́; (*soft ~*) моло́к|и (*pl., g.* —).

roe[2] [rəʊ] *n.* (*deer*) косу́ля.

cpd. **~buck** *n.* косу́ля-саме́ц.

rogue [rəʊg] *n.* **1.** (*dishonest person*) жу́лик, моше́нник. **2.** (*mischievous person*) прока́зник, озорни́к.

roguish ['rəʊgɪʃ] *adj.* жуликова́тый.

role [rəʊl] *n.* (*lit., fig.*) роль; **he played (in) the ~ of Hamlet** он исполня́л роль Га́млета; **title ~** загла́вная роль; **he assumed the ~ of leader** он взял на себя́ роль ли́дера; **~ model** приме́р.

roll [rəʊl] *n.* **1.** (*of cloth, paper, film etc.*) руло́н. **2.** (*register, list*) рее́стр, спи́сок; **~ of honour** спи́сок уби́тых на войне́; **the sergeant called the ~** сержа́нт сде́лал перекли́чку. **3.** (*of bread*) бу́лочка. **4.** (*swaying or revolving motion*) враще́ние; пока́чивание; **the ~ of the ship** пока́чивание корабля́. **5.** (*rumbling sound*) раска́т; бой бараба́на; **a ~ of thunder** раска́т гро́ма; **a ~ of drums** бараба́нная дробь.

v.t. **1.** (*move by revolving*) ката́ть (*indet.*), кати́ть (*det.*), по-; **the logs were ~ed down the hill** брёвна скати́ли с холма́; (*wind*) завёр|тывать, -ну́ть; (*rotate*) враща́ть (*impf.*); **~ one's eyes** враща́ть (*impf.*) глаза́ми. **2.** (*flatten by use of cylinder*) ката́ть, рас-; раска́тывать (*impf.*); **she was ~ing pastry** она́ раска́тывала те́сто; **~ing-mill** прока́тный стан; **~ing-pin** ска́лка. **3.** (*shape into cylinder or sphere*) свёр|тывать, -ну́ть; свора́чивать (*impf.*); (*e.g. cigarette*) скру́|чивать, -ти́ть; **the hedgehog ~ed itself (up) into a ball** ёж сверну́лся в клубо́к; **help me ~ this ball of wool** помоги́те мне смота́ть э́тот клубо́к ше́рсти.

v.i. **1.** (*move by revolving; revolve*) кати́ться (*impf.*); ска́тываться (*impf.*); **the coin ~ed under the table** моне́та закати́лась под стол; **tears ~ed down her cheeks** слёзы кати́лись по её щека́м; **set, start the ball ~ing** (*fig.*) откры́ть (*pf.*) диску́ссию; **~ing stock** подвижно́й соста́в. **2.** (*tumble about, wallow*) валя́ться (*impf.*); **porpoises were ~ing in the waves** дельфи́ны кувы́ркались в во́лна́х; **he is ~ing in money** он купа́ется в деньга́х. **3.** (*sway, rock*) кача́ться (*impf.*); **the ship began to ~** парохо́д на́чало кача́ть; **~ing gait** похо́дка вразва́лку. **4.** (*undulate*): **waves were ~ing on to the shore** во́лны накатыва́лись на бе́рег; **~ing countryside** холми́стая ме́стность. **5.** (*make deep vibrating sound*) греме́ть (*impf.*); грохота́ть (*impf.*); **thunder ~ed in the hills** по холма́м прокати́лся гром.

with advs.: **~ about** *v.i.* валя́ться; **~ along** *v.i.*: **we were ~ing along at 30 m.p.h.** маши́на кати́лась со ско́ростью 30 миль в час; **~ back** *v.t.* отка́т|ывать, -и́ть наза́д; **let's ~ back the carpet and dance!** дава́йте свернём/ската́ем ковёр и потанцу́ем!; **~ by** *v.i.*: **the bus ~ed by** авто́бус прое́хал ми́мо; **how the years ~ by!** как бы́стро ка́тятся го́ды!; **~ down** *v.t.* ска́т|ывать, -и́ть вниз; **~ down the blinds!** опусти́те жалюзи́!; **~ in** *v.i.*: **contributions began to ~ in** на́чали поступа́ть взно́сы; **~ off** *v.i.* ска́т|ываться, -и́ться; **he ~ed off the bed** он скати́лся с крова́ти; **~ on** *v.t.*: **she ~ed on her stockings** она́ натяну́ла чулки́; *v.i.*: **~ on summer!** (*coll.*) скоре́й бы наступи́ло ле́то!; **~ out** *v.t.* (*e.g. carpet, pastry*) раска́т|ывать, -а́ть; *v.i.*: **she dropped her basket and everything ~ed out** она́ урони́ла корзи́нку, и всё из неё вы́катилось; **~ over** *v.t.* перев|ора́чивать, -ерну́ть; *v.i.* воро́чаться (*impf.*); **he ~ed over and went to sleep again** он переверну́лся на друго́й бок и сно́ва засну́л; **~ up** *v.t.* свёр|тывать, -ну́ть; **~ up the curtain** подня́ть (*pf.*) за́навес; **he ~ed himself up in a blanket** он заверну́лся в одея́ло; *v.i.*: **he ~ed up to me** (*fig.*) он подкати́л ко мне.

cpds. **~-call** *n.* перекли́чка; **~-neck (pullover)** *n.* водола́зка.

roller ['rəʊlə(r)] *n.* **1.** ро́лик; като́к; **garden ~** садо́вый като́к. **2.** (*wave*) волна́, вал.

cpds. **~-bearing** *n.* ро́ликовый подши́пник; **~-coaster** *n.* америка́нские го́ры (*f. pl.*); **~-skate** *n.* ро́лик; *v.i.* ката́ться (*indet.*) на ро́ликах.
rollick ['rɒlɪk] *v.i.* резви́ться (*impf.*); весели́ться (*impf.*); **we had a ~ing time** мы здо́рово повесели́лись.
roly-poly [ˌrəʊlɪ'pəʊlɪ] *n.* пу́динг с варе́нием; (*fig., plump child*) пу́хлый ребёнок.
ROM [rɒm] *n. comput.* (*abbr. of* ***read only memory***) ПЗУ, (постоя́нное запомина́ющее устро́йство).
Roman ['rəʊmən] *n.* ри́млян|ин (*fem.* -ка).
adj. **1.** (*of Rome*) ри́мский; **the ~ alphabet** лати́нский алфави́т; **the ~ Empire** Ри́мская импе́рия. **2.** (*relig.*) католи́ческий; **~ Catholicism** католи́чество.
romance [rəʊ'mæns] *n.* **1.: R~ languages** рома́нские языки́. **2.** (*tale, episode, love affair*) рома́н. **3.** (*romantic atmosphere, glamour*) рома́нтика.
Romania, R(o)umania [rəʊ'meɪnɪə] *n.* Румы́ния.
Romanian, R(o)umanian [rəʊ'meɪnɪən] *n.* (*pers.*) румы́н (*fem.* -ка); (*language*) румы́нский язы́к.
adj. румы́нский.
romantic [rəʊ'mæntɪk] *n.* рома́нтик.
adj. романти́ческий, романти́чный.
romanticism [rəʊ'mæntɪˌsɪz(ə)m] *n.* романти́зм.
romanticist [rəʊ'mæntɪsɪst] *n.* рома́нтик.
romanticize [rəʊ'mæntɪˌsaɪz] *v.i.* романтизи́ровать (*impf., pf.*).
Romany ['rɒmənɪ, 'rəʊ-] *n.* (*Gypsy*) цыга́н (*fem.* -ка); (*language*) цыга́нский язы́к.
adj. цыга́нский.
Rome [rəʊm] *n.* **1.** (*city or state*) Рим. **2.** (*Church of ~*) ри́мско-католи́ческая це́рковь.
romp [rɒmp] *n.* (*boisterous play*) возня́.
v.i. резви́ться (*impf.*); **he ~ed through his exams** он шутя́ сдал экза́мены.
rompers ['rɒmpəs] *n.* (*also* **romper suit**) ползунк|и́ (*pl., g.* -о́в); де́тский комбинезо́н.
rondo ['rɒndəʊ] *n.* ро́ндо (*indecl.*).
roof [ru:f] *n.* кры́ша; **the water-tank is in the ~** бак для воды́ стои́т под кры́шей; **~ of the mouth** нёбо.
v.t. крыть, по-; наст|ила́ть, -ла́ть кры́шу на+*p.*; **~ed with slates** кры́тый ши́фером; **~ing-felt** кро́вельный карто́н.
cpd. **~-rack** *n.* бага́жник (на кры́ше автомоби́ля).
rook [rʊk] *n.* (*bird*) грач; (*chess piece*) тура́, ладья́.
v.t. (*swindle*) обма́н|ывать, -у́ть.
rookery ['rʊkərɪ] *n.* грачо́вник; (*of seals etc.*) ле́жбище.
room [ru:m, rʊm] *n.* **1.** ко́мната; **a four-~(ed) flat** четырёхко́мнатная кварти́ра; **~ service** обслу́живание в но́мере; **~ and board** по́лный пансио́н; (*pl., apartments*) кварти́ра, ко́мнаты (*f. pl.*). **2.** (*space*) ме́сто; **there's plenty of ~** полно́ ме́ста; **there was no ~ to turn round in** не́где бы́ло поверну́ться; **is there ~ for one more?** ещё оди́н челове́к уся́дется? **3.** (*scope, opportunity*) возмо́жность; **it leaves no ~ for doubt** э́то не оставля́ет никаки́х сомне́ний; **there is ~ for improvement in your work** ва́ша рабо́та могла́ бы быть и лу́чше.
v.i.: **we ~ed together in Paris** в Пари́же мы жи́ли в одно́й кварти́ре; **~ing-house** меблиро́ванные ко́мнаты (*f. pl.*).
cpd. **~-mate** *n.* това́рищ по ко́мнате.
roomy ['ru:mɪ] *adj.* просто́рный, вмести́тельный.
roost [ru:st] *n.* куря́тник, насе́ст; **go to ~** сади́ться, сесть на насе́ст; (*fig.*): **he rules the ~ here** он тут верхово́дит.
v.i. (*of birds*) ус|а́живаться, -е́сться на насе́ст.
rooster ['ru:stə(r)] *n.* пету́х.
root [ru:t] *n.* **1.** (*of plant*) ко́рень (*m.*); **the tree was torn up by the ~s** де́рево вы́рвали с ко́рнем; **take, strike ~** пус|ка́ть, -ти́ть ко́рни; **poverty must be removed ~ and branch** нищету́ ну́жно искорени́ть. **2.** (*cul., med.*): **~s** коре́нь|я (*pl., g.* -ев); **~ crop** корнепло́дная культу́ра. **3.** (*of tooth, tongue, hair etc.*) ко́рень (*m.*). **4.** (*fig., source, basis*) причи́на; **~ cause** основна́я причи́на; **money is the ~ of all evil** де́ньги — ко́рень зла; **he got to the ~ of the problem** он добра́лся до су́ти де́ла; **the quarrel had its ~s deep in the past** конфли́кт уходи́л корня́ми в далёкое про́шлое. **5.** (*math., philol.*) ко́рень (*m.*); **square ~** квадра́тный ко́рень (из+*g.*).
v.t. **1.: the seedling ~ed itself** са́женец приви́лся. **2.** (*fig.*): **he is a man of deeply ~ed prejudices** он челове́к с укорени́вшимися предрассу́дками. **3.** (*transfix*): **he stood ~ed to the ground** он стоя́л как вко́панный.
v.i. **1.** (*take ~*) укорен|я́ться, -и́ться. **2.** (*of pigs etc., also* **rootle**) ры́ться (*impf.*); рыть (*impf.*) зе́млю. **3.: ~ for** (*US, support*) боле́ть (*impf.*) за+*a.* (*coll.*).
with advs.: **~ about** *v.i.* (*lit., fig.*) ры́ться (*impf.*); **~ out** *v.t.* (*lit., fig., extirpate*) вырыва́ть, вы́рвать с ко́рнем; (*fig., also*) уничт|ожа́ть, -о́жить; **~ up** *v.t.* вырыва́ть, вы́рвать с ко́рнем.
rootle ['ru:t(ə)l] = **root** *v.i.* **2.**
rope [rəʊp] *n.* (*cord, cable*) верёвка, кана́т; (*fig.*): **money for old ~** лёгкая нажи́ва; **he knows the ~s** он зна́ет все ходы́ и вы́ходы; он зна́ет, что к чему́; (*string, skein*) ни́тка, вя́зка.
v.t. привя́з|ывать, -а́ть (*что к чему*).
with advs.: **~ in** *v.t.* (*coll., enlist*) втя́|гивать, -ну́ть; **~ off** *v.t.* отгор|а́живать, -оди́ть верёвкой; **~ together** *v.t.*: **the climbers were ~d together** альпини́сты бы́ли свя́заны верёвкой.
cpd. **~-ladder** *n.* верёвочная ле́стница.
ropy ['rəʊpɪ] *adj.* (*sl., of poor quality*) никуды́шный.
ro-ro ['rəʊrəʊ] *adj.*: **~ ship** су́дно «ро-ро́», ро́лкер.
rosary ['rəʊzərɪ] *n.* чёт|ки (*pl., g.* -ок).
rose [rəʊz] *n.* **1.** ро́за; (*fig.*): **her path was strewn with ~s** её путь был усы́пан ро́зами; **life was no bed of ~s for him** у него́ была́ отню́дь не сла́дкая жизнь; **this will put the ~s back into your cheeks** э́то вернёт вам здоро́вье и све́жесть. **2.** (*colour*) ро́зовый цвет. **3.** (*sprinkler*) спри́нклерная розе́тка.
cpds. **~-bed** *n.* клу́мба с ро́зами; **~bud** *n.* буто́н ро́зы; **~-bush** *n.* ро́зовый куст; **~-coloured** *adj.* ро́зовый; **he sees the world through ~-coloured spectacles** он смо́трит на мир че́рез ро́зовые очки́; **~-garden** *n.* роза́рий; **~-tree** *n.* штамбо́вая ро́за; **~-water** *n.* ро́зовая вода́; **~wood** *n.* палиса́ндровое/ро́зовое де́рево.
rosé ['rəʊzeɪ] *n.* (*wine*) ро́зовое вино́.
rosemary ['rəʊzmərɪ] *n.* ро́змари́н.
rosette [rəʊ'zet] *n.* розе́тка.
rosin ['rɒzɪn] *n.* канифо́ль.
roster ['rɒstə(r)] *n.* гра́фик; рее́стр; расписа́ние.
rostrum ['rɒstrəm] *n.* трибу́на; ка́федра.
rosy ['rəʊzɪ] *adj.* ро́зовый; **~ cheeks** румя́ные щёки; (*fig.*) ра́достный, ра́дужный.
rot [rɒt] *n.* **1.** (*decay*) гние́ние; гниль; (*fig., deterioration*): **the ~ set in** начался́ разла́д; **stop the ~** пресе́чь (*pf.*) зло в ко́рне. **2.** (*coll., nonsense*) вздор, чушь; **don't talk ~!** бро́сьте чепуху́ моло́ть!
v.t. по́ртить, ис-.
v.i. гнить, с-; по́ртиться, ис-; **the tree was ~ting away** де́рево гни́ло.
rota ['rəʊtə] *n.* гра́фик; рее́стр; (шта́тное) расписа́ние.
rotary ['rəʊtərɪ] *adj.* враща́ющийся; **~ motion** враща́тельное движе́ние; **~ press** ротацио́нная печа́тная маши́на.
rotate [rəʊ'teɪt] *v.t. & i.* **1.** (*revolve*) враща́ть(ся) (*impf.*). **2.** (*arrange or recur in rotation*) чередова́ть(ся) (*impf.*); **the duties (were) ~d every six weeks** дежу́рства чередова́лись ка́ждые шесть неде́ль.
rotation [rəʊ'teɪʃ(ə)n] *n.* **1.** (*revolving*) враще́ние; оборо́т. **2.** (*regular succession*) чередова́ние; **~ of crops** севооборо́т; **they did guard duty in ~** они́

поочерёдно несли́ карау́льную слу́жбу.

rote [rəʊt] *n.*: **he learnt the poem by ~** он вы́учил/вы́зубрил стихотворе́ние наизу́сть; **perform duties by ~** механи́чески выполня́ть обя́занности.

rotor ['rəʊtə(r)] *n.* ро́тор.

rotten ['rɒt(ə)n] *adj.* (*decayed, putrid*) гнило́й; **~ eggs** ту́хлые я́йца; (*morally corrupt*) разложи́вшийся; испо́рченный; (*worthless*) никуды́шный; **a ~ idea** дура́цкая иде́я; (*very disagreeable, unfortunate*) отврати́тельный; **what a ~ shame!** э́то про́сто безобра́зие!; **I'm feeling ~** я себя́ пога́но чу́вствую.

rotter ['rɒtə(r)] *n.* (*sl.*) подле́ц, подо́нок.

rotund [rəʊ'tʌnd] *adj.* (*spherical*) округлённый; (*corpulent, plump*) по́лный.

rotunda [rəʊ'tʌndə] *n.* рото́нда.

r(o)uble ['ru:b(ə)l] *n.* рубль (*m.*).

roué ['ru:eɪ] *n.* пове́са (*m.*).

rouge [ru:ʒ] *n.* (*cosmetic*) румя́н|а (*pl., g.* —).

v.t. & i. румя́нить(ся), на-.

rough [rʌf] *n.* **1.** (~ *things or circumstances*) тру́дности (*f. pl.*); **you must take the ~ with the smooth** на́до сто́йко переноси́ть превра́тности судьбы́. **2.** (~ *ground, esp. on golfcourse*) неро́вная пове́рхность. **3.** (*unfinished state*): **I saw the poem in the ~** я ви́дел поэ́му в черновике́.

adj. **1.** (*opp. smooth, even, level*) шерохова́тый, неро́вный; **his skin was ~ to the touch** у него́ была́ шерша́вая на о́щупь ко́жа. **2.** (*opp. calm, gentle, orderly*) бу́рный; **~ water** бу́рные во́ды; **the wind is getting ~** ве́тер крепча́ет; **their team played a ~ game** их кома́нда игра́ла гру́бо; **a ~ crowd** хамова́тая пу́блика; **the students were ~ly handled by the police** поли́ция гру́бо обраща́лась со студе́нтами; **the bill had a ~ passage** законопрое́кт прошёл с трудо́м. **3.** (*uncomfortable, arduous*) тру́дный; **he had a ~ time** ему́ пришло́сь ту́го. **4.** (*crude*) гру́бый; **they meted out ~ justice** наказа́ние вы́несли суро́вое; **a ~ and ready meal** еда́, пригото́вленная на ско́рую ру́ку. **5.** (*unfinished, rudimentary*) чернов́ой; **a ~ sketch** черново́й набро́сок. **6.** (*inexact, approximate*) приблизи́тельный; **at a ~ guess** по приблизи́тельной оце́нке; **this will give you a ~ idea** э́то даст вам о́бщее представле́ние; **~ly speaking** гру́бо говоря́.

adv.: **they treated him ~** (*coll.*) с ним гру́бо обраща́лись.

v.t.: **~ it** (*coll.*) жить (*impf.*) без удо́бств.

with advs.: **~ out** *v.t.* (*e.g. a plan*) набр|а́сывать, -оса́ть; **~ up** *v.t.*: **don't ~ up my hair!** не еро́шьте мне во́лосы!

cpds. **~-and-tumble** *n.* дра́ка; сумато́ха; **~-hew** *v.t.* гру́бо обтёс|ывать, -а́ть; **~-hewn** *adj.* (*fig.*) неотёсанный, некульту́рный; **~-neck** *n.* (*coll.*) хулига́н; **~shod** *adj.* подко́ванный на шипы́; *adv.* (*fig.*): **he rode ~shod over their feelings** он гру́бо попира́л их чу́вства; **~-spoken** *adj.* гру́бый; гру́бо выража́ющийся.

roughage ['rʌfɪdʒ] *n.* гру́бая пи́ща.

roughen ['rʌf(ə)n] *v.t. & i.* де́лать(ся), с- гру́бым.

roughness ['rʌfnɪs] *n.* **1.** (*to touch*) шерохова́тость. **2.** (*unevenness*) неро́вность. **3.** (*crudity, coarseness*) гру́бость.

roulette [ru:'let] *n.* руле́тка; **~ wheel** колесо́ руле́тки.

Roumania [ru:'meɪnɪə], **-n** [ru:'meɪnɪən] = **Romania, -n**

round [raʊnd] *n.* **1.** (*regular circuit or cycle*) цикл; обхо́д; круговоро́т; **the daily ~** повседне́вные дела́; **the doctor is on his ~s** до́ктор нахо́дится на обхо́де; **the news went the ~ of the village** но́вость обошла́ всю дере́вню; **a ~ of golf** па́ртия го́льфа. **2.** (*stage in contest*) тур, эта́п, ра́унд; **he was knocked out in the third ~** он получи́л нока́ут в тре́тьем ра́унде; **the team got through to the final ~** кома́нда вы́шла в фина́л. **3.** (*set, series, burst*): **he bought a ~ of drinks** он поста́вил по стака́нчику всем прису́тствующим; **a ~ of applause** взрыв аплодисме́нтов. **4.** (*of ammunition*) патро́н; компле́кт вы́стрела; **dummy ~** уче́бный/холосто́й патро́н.

adj. **1.** (*circular, spherical, convex*) кру́глый; **~ shoulders** суту́лые пле́чи. **2.** (*involving circular motion*) кругово́й; **~ dance** хорово́д; **~ trip** пое́здка в о́ба конца́. **3.** (*of numbers*) кру́глый; **a ~ dozen** це́лая дю́жина; **in ~ numbers** в кру́глых ци́фрах. **4.** (*considerable*) кру́пный, значи́тельный; **a good ~ sum** поря́дочная су́мма.

adv. (*for phrasal vv. with* **round** *see relevant v. entries*): **all the year ~** кру́глый год; **he slept the clock ~** он проспа́л весь день; **the tree is six feet ~** э́то де́рево шесть фу́тов в окру́жности; **better all ~** лу́чше во всех отноше́ниях; **taking it all ~** принима́я во внима́ние всё; **he went a long way ~** он сде́лал изря́дный крюк; **he was ~ at our house** он зашёл к нам.

v.t. **1.** (*make ~*) округл|я́ть, -и́ть; **a well-~ed phrase** гла́дкая фра́за. **2.** (*go ~*) огиба́ть, обогну́ть; об|ходи́ть, -ойти́ круго́м; **we ~ed the corner** мы заверну́ли за́ угол; **the ship ~ed the Cape** кора́бль обогну́л мыс До́брой Наде́жды.

v.i. (*turn aggressively*): **he ~ed on me with abuse** он обру́шился на меня́ с бра́нью; **he ~ed on his pursuers** он набро́сился на свои́х пресле́дователей.

with advs.: **~ off** *v.t.* (*smooth*) выра́внивать, вы́ровнять; (*bring to a conclusion*) заверш|а́ть, -и́ть; **~ out** *v.t.* закругл|я́ть, -и́ть; заверш|а́ть, -и́ть; *v.i.*: **her figure was beginning to ~ out** её фигу́ра начала́ округля́ться; **~ up** *v.t.* сгоня́ть, согна́ть; **the courier ~ed up the party** гид собра́л свою́ гру́ппу; (*arrest*) арест|о́вывать, -ова́ть.

prep. **1.** (*encircling*) вокру́г, круго́м, о́коло (*all +g.*); **~ the world** вокру́г све́та; **they sat ~ the table** они́ сиде́ли вокру́г стола́; **he worked ~ the clock** он рабо́тал круглосу́точно (*or* кру́глые су́тки). **2.** (*to or at all points of*): **he looked ~ the room** он осмотре́л (всю) ко́мнату; **we walked ~ the garden** мы гуля́ли по са́ду; **they went ~ the galleries** они обошли́ карти́нные галере́и. **3. ~ the corner** за угло́м, (*of motion*) за́ угол. **4.** (*approximately*) о́коло+*g.*; **he got there ~ (about) midday** он добра́лся туда́ о́коло полу́дня.

cpds. **~about** *n.* (*merry-go-round*) карусе́ль; (*traffic island*) кольцева́я тра́нспортная развя́зка; *adj.* око́льный, кру́жный; (*fig.*) ко́свенный, обхо́дный; **~-shouldered** *adj.* суту́лый; **~-the-clock** *adj.* круглосу́точный; **~-up** *n.* (*of news*) сво́дка новосте́й; (*of cattle*) заго́н скота́; (*raid*) обла́ва.

rounders ['raʊndəs] *n.* англи́йская лапта́.

rouse [raʊz] *v.t.* **1.** (*wake*) буди́ть, раз-. **2.** (*stimulate to action, interest etc.*) подстрека́ть (*impf.*); побу|жда́ть, -ди́ть; **he ~d himself and went to work** он взял себя́ в ру́ки и пошёл на рабо́ту; **a rousing chorus** волну́ющий припе́в. **3.** (*provoke to anger*) возбу|жда́ть, -ди́ть; выводи́ть, вы́вести из себя́.

v.i. пробу|жда́ться, -ди́ться.

rout [raʊt] *n.* (*defeat*) разгро́м; (*disorderly retreat*) бе́гство.

v.t. разб|ива́ть, -и́ть на́голову; разгроми́ть (*pf.*); обра|ща́ть, -ти́ть в бе́гство.

route [ru:t, *mil. also* raʊt] *n.* маршру́т; тра́сса.

v.t. отпр|авля́ть, -а́вить по маршру́ту.

cpd. **~-march** *n.* похо́дный марш.

routine [ru:'ti:n] *n.* **1.** (*regular course of action*) заведённый поря́док; режи́м; пра́ктика; (*attr.*) регуля́рный; очередно́й; повседне́вный. **2.** (*artiste's act*) но́мер, выступле́ние; **a dance ~** танцева́льный но́мер.

rov|e [rəʊv] *v.i.* скита́ться (*impf.*); **he has a ~ing**

disposition он любит стра́нствовать; **a ~ing correspondent** разъездно́й корреспонде́нт.
rover ['rəʊvə(r)] *n.* (*wanderer*) бродя́га (*m.*); скита́лец.
row[1] [rəʊ] *n.* (*line*) ряд; **they stood in a ~** они стоя́ли в ряд; **the houses were built in ~s** дома́ бы́ли постро́ены ряда́ми; **seats in the front ~** места́ в пе́рвом ряду́.
row[2] [rəʊ] *n.* (*by boat*) прогу́лка на ло́дке; **we went (out) for a ~** мы пошли́ поката́ться на ло́дке.
v.t.: **he ~ed the boat in to shore** он привёл ло́дку к бе́регу; **we were ~ed across the river** нас перевезли́ че́рез ре́ку на ло́дке.
v.i. грести́ (*impf.*); **~ out** грести́ (*impf.*) от бе́рега; **~(ing)-boat** гребна́я шлю́пка.
row[3] [raʊ] *n.* **1.** (*noise, commotion*) шум; **don't make (such) a ~!** не шуми́те!; **the tenants kicked up a ~** (*made a noise; protested*) жильцы́ по́дняли шум. **2.** (*argument, quarrel*) ссо́ра; спор; **I had a ~ with the neighbours** я поруга́лся с сосе́дями. **3.** (*disgrace*): **I shall get into a ~ if I'm late** мне здо́рово доста́нется, е́сли я опозда́ю.
v.i. (*quarrel*) ссо́риться, по-; руга́ться (*impf.*).
rowan ['rəʊən, 'raʊ-] *n.* ряби́на.
rowdiness ['raʊdɪnɪs] *n.* бесчи́нство; хулига́нство.
rowdy ['raʊdɪ] *n.* буя́н, скандали́ст; хулига́н.
adj. гру́бый, шу́мный.
rowlock ['rɒlək, 'rʌlək] *n.* уклю́чина.
royal ['rɔɪəl] *n.* (*coll., member of a ~ family*) член короле́вской семьи́.
adj. (*of the reigning family; kingly*) короле́вский, ца́рский; **of the blood ~** короле́вской кро́ви; **His R~ Highness** его́ короле́вское высо́чество; **the R~ Navy** англи́йский вое́нно-морско́й флот; **~ blue** я́рко-си́ний цвет.
royalism ['rɔɪəlɪz(ə)m] *n.* рояли́зм.
royalist ['rɔɪəlɪst] *n.* рояли́ст (*fem.* -ка).
adj. рояли́стский.
royalty ['rɔɪəltɪ] *n.* **1.** (*royal person or persons*) чле́н(ы) короле́вской семьи́. **2.** (*payment to owner of patent or copyright*) а́вторский гонора́р; отчисле́ния (*pl.*) а́втору пье́сы *и т.п.*
rpm (*abbr. of* **revolutions per minute**) оборо́ты (*m. pl.*) в мину́ту.
RSPCA (*abbr. of* **Royal Society for the Prevention of Cruelty to Animals**) Короле́вское о́бщество защи́ты живо́тных от жесто́кого обраще́ния.
RSVP (*abbr. of* **répondez, s'il vous plaît**) бу́дьте любе́зны отве́тить.
Rt. Hon. [raɪt 'ɒnərəb(ə)l] *n.* (*abbr. of* **Right Honourable**) высокочти́мый.
rub [rʌb] *n.* **1.** (*act of ~bing*) натира́ние; **she gave the mirror a ~ with a cloth** она́ протёрла зе́ркало тря́пкой. **2.** (*snag*): **there's the ~!** в то́м-то и загво́здка!
v.t. тере́ть (*impf.*); пот|ира́ть, -ере́ть; **the dog ~bed its head against my legs** соба́ка тёрлась голово́й о мои́ но́ги; **he ~bed the skin off his knees** он стёр ко́жу на коле́нях; **he ~bed himself (dry) with a towel** он до́суха вы́терся полоте́нцем; **he ~bed his hands with satisfaction** он потира́л ру́ки от удово́льствия; **there is no need to ~ my nose in it** (*fig.*) не́зачем ты́кать меня́ но́сом; **he ~s shoulders with the great** он обща́ется с больши́ми людьми́; **~ the oil well into your skin** на́до хороше́нько втере́ть ма́сло в ко́жу.
v.i. тере́ться (*impf.*).
with advs.: **~ along** *v.i.* ла́дить (*impf.*); уж|ива́ться, -и́ться; **~ down** *v.t.* обт|ира́ть, -ере́ть; **~ in** *v.t.* вт|ира́ть, -ере́ть; **the liniment should be ~bed in** мазь сле́дует втира́ть; **it was my fault; don't ~ it in!** моя́ вина́! но ско́лько мо́жно упрека́ть?; **~ off** *v.t.* ст|ира́ть, -ере́ть; **all the shine was ~bed off** весь блеск стёрся; *v.i.*: **her happiness ~bed off on those around her** её сча́стье передава́лось тем, кто её окружа́л; **~ on** *v.t.* (*e.g. ointment*) на|кла́дывать, -ложи́ть; **~ out** *v.t.* ст|ира́ть, -ере́ть; *v.i.*: **this ink will not ~ out** э́ти черни́ла не стира́ются; **~ over** *v.t.* прот|ира́ть, -ере́ть; **~ through** *v.i.* **his trousers had ~bed through at the knees** его́ брю́ки протёрлись на коле́нях; **~ together** *v.t.*: **he lit the fire by ~bing two sticks together** он развёл костёр, добы́в ого́нь тре́нием; **~ up** *v.t.* нач|ища́ть, -и́стить; **she ~bed up the silver** она́ начи́стила серебро́; **you ~bed him up the wrong way** вы к нему́ не так подошли́.
rubber ['rʌbə(r)] *n.* **1.** (*substance*) рези́на; **~ band** рези́нка; **~ plant** каучуконо́с; фи́кус каучуконо́сный. **2.** (*eraser*) ла́стик, рези́нка.
cpd. **~-stamp** *v.t.* (*coll.*) подпи́с|ывать, -а́ть не гля́дя.
rubberized ['rʌbəˌraɪzd] *adj.* прорези́ненный, обло́женный рези́ной.
rubbing ['rʌbɪŋ] *n.* (*tracing*) копиро́вка притира́нием.
rubbish ['rʌbɪʃ] *n.* (*refuse, trash*) му́сор; хлам; (*nonsense*) чепуха́, вздор.
cpds. **~-bin** *n.* му́сорное ведро́; **~-cart** *n.* мусорово́з; **~-dump, ~-tip** *nn.* му́сорная я́ма.
rubbishy ['rʌbɪʃɪ] *adj.* никуда́ не го́дный; дрянно́й.
rubble ['rʌb(ə)l] *n.* булы́жник, ще́бень (*m.*).
rubella [ru:'belə] *n.* красну́ха.
rubicund ['ru:bɪˌkʌnd] *adj.* румя́ный.
ruble ['ru:b(ə)l] = **r(o)uble**
rubric ['ru:brɪk] *n.* заголо́вок; ру́брика.
ruby ['ru:bɪ] *n.* руби́н; (*attr.*) руби́новый.
rucksack ['rʌksæk, 'rʊk-] *n.* рюкза́к.
rudder ['rʌdə(r)] *n.* руль (*m.*), штурва́л.
ruddy ['rʌdɪ] *adj.* **1.** (*glowing, reddish*) румя́ный; **a ~ face** румя́ное лицо́; **a ~ glow** я́рко-кра́сный цвет. **2.** (*as expletive*) прокля́тый, чо́ртов.
rude [ru:d] *adj.* **1.** (*impolite, offensive*) гру́бый; невоспи́танный; **don't make ~ remarks!** не груби́те!; **he was ~ to the teacher** он нагруби́л учи́теля. **2.** (*indecent*) гру́бый, непристо́йный. **3.** (*startling, violent*) ре́зкий; **I had a ~ awakening** (*fig.*) меня́ пости́гло го́рькое разочарова́ние. **4.** (*vigorous*) кре́пкий, си́льный; **in ~ health** кре́пкого здоро́вья.
rudeness ['ru:dnɪs] *n.* (*impoliteness*) гру́бость, невоспи́танность.
rudiment ['ru:dɪmənt] *n.* **1.** (*in pl., elements, first principles*) элемента́рные зна́ния; (*beginnings, first trace*) зача́тки (*m. pl.*). **2.** (*imperfectly developed organ*) рудимента́рный о́рган.
rudimentary [ˌru:dɪ'mentərɪ] *adj.* (*elementary*) элемента́рный; (*undeveloped*) рудимента́рный, зача́точный.
rue [ru:] *v.t.* (*liter.*) сожале́ть (*impf.*); **you will ~ it** вы об э́том пожале́ете; **he lived to ~ the day** пришло́ вре́мя, когда́ он про́клял тот день.
rueful ['ru:fʊl] *adj.* печа́льный, удручённый.
ruff [rʌf] *n.* (*frill*) жабо́ (*indecl.*); (*on bird's neck*) кольцо́ пе́рьев вокру́г ше́и пти́цы.
ruffian ['rʌfɪən] *n.* головоре́з, банди́т.
ruffle ['rʌf(ə)l] *n.* (*ornamental frill*) обо́рка.
v.t.: **a breeze ~d the surface of the lake** от ве́тра о́зеро покры́лось ря́бью; **she ~d his hair** она́ взъеро́шила ему́ во́лосы; **the bird ~d up its feathers** пти́ца взъеро́шила пе́рья; **he never gets ~d** он всегда́ невозмути́м.
rug [rʌg] *n.* **1.** (*mat*) ковёр. **2.** (*wrap*) плед.
Rugby (football) ['rʌgbɪ] *n.* ре́гби (*nt. indecl.*).
rugged ['rʌgɪd] *adj.* **1.** (*rough, uneven*) неро́вный; **a ~ coast** скали́стый бе́рег. **2.** (*irregular, strongly-marked*) гру́бый; **~ features** ре́зкие черты́. **3.** (*austere, harsh*) тяжёлый, тру́дный. **4.** (*sturdy*) кре́пкий, твёрдый.
ruggedness ['rʌgɪdnɪs] *n.* неро́вность; гру́бость; твёрдость.

rugger ['rʌgə(r)] (*coll.*) = **Rugby (football)**

ruin ['ru:ɪn] *n.* **1.** (*downfall*) ги́бель, круше́ние; **~ stared him in the face** ему́ грози́ло разоре́ние. **2.** (*collapsed or destroyed state*; *building in this state*) разва́лины, руи́ны (*both f. pl.*); **the house fell into ~** дом соверше́нно развали́лся; **ancient ~s** дре́вние руи́ны (*f. pl.*); **his life lay in ~s** его́ жизнь была́ загу́блена.

v.t. разр|уша́ть, -у́шить; губи́ть, по-; **he was ~ed** (*in business*) он разори́лся; **this will ~ my chances** э́то подорвёт мои́ ша́нсы; **the rain ~ed my suit** дождь испо́ртил мой костю́м; **a ~ed building** разру́шенное зда́ние.

ruination [ˌru:ɪ'neɪʃ(ə)n] *n.* ги́бель; разоре́ние.

ruinous ['ru:ɪnəs] *adj.* (*disastrous*) губи́тельный; (*expensive*) разори́тельный.

rule [ru:l] *n.* **1.** (*regulation*; *recognized principle*) пра́вило; **keep, stick to the ~s of the game** соблюда́ть (*impf.*) пра́вила игры́; **~ of the road** пра́вила (*pl.*) у́личного движе́ния; **smoking is against the ~s** кури́ть не разреша́ется. **2.** (*normal practice*; *custom*) привы́чка, обы́чай; **my ~ is never to start an argument** мой при́нцип — никогда́ не затева́ть спор; **as a ~** как пра́вило; **he makes it a ~ to rise early** он взял за пра́вило встава́ть ра́но. **3.** (*government*, *sway*) правле́ние, госпо́дство; **~ of law** власть зако́на. **4.** (*measuring-stick*) лине́йка.

v.t. **1.** (*govern*) управля́ть (*impf.*) +*i.*; руководи́ть (*impf.*) +*i.*; **don't be ~d by prejudice** не поддава́йтесь предрассу́дкам. **2.** (*decree*, *decide*) постан|а́вливать, -ови́ть; **the umpire ~d that the ball was not out** судья́ объяви́л, что мяч не́ был в а́уте. **3.**: **a ~d exercise book** тетра́дь в лине́йку; **~d paper** лино́ванная бума́га.

v.i. (*hold sway*) пра́вить (*impf.*); управля́ть (*impf.*); **ruling classes** пра́вящие кла́ссы.

with adv.: **~ out** *v.t.* (*exclude*) исключ|а́ть, -и́ть.

ruler ['ru:lə(r)] *n.* (*reigning person*) пра́витель (*m.*); (*measuring-stick*) лине́йка.

ruling ['ru:lɪŋ] *n.* (*decree*; *decision*) постановле́ние; реше́ние.

rum[1] [rʌm] *n.* ром.

rum[2] [rʌm] *adj.* (*coll.*) чудно́й; **he is a ~ customer** он стра́нный тип.

Rumania [ru:'meɪnɪə], **-n** [ru:'meɪnɪən] = **Romania, -n**

rumba ['rʌmbə] *n.* ру́мба.

v.i. танцева́ть, про- ру́мбу.

rumbl|e ['rʌmb(ə)l] *n.* громыха́ние, гул.

v.i. громыха́ть (*impf.*); греме́ть, за-/про-; **thunder was ~ing in the distance** вдалеке́ греме́л гром.

ruminant ['ru:mɪnənt] *n.* жва́чное живо́тное.

adj. жва́чный.

ruminate ['ru:mɪˌneɪt] *v.i.* (*chew the cud*) жева́ть (*impf.*) жва́чку; (*ponder*) разду́мывать (*impf.*).

rumination [ˌru:mɪ'neɪʃ(ə)n] *n.* (*fig.*) размышле́ние.

rummage ['rʌmɪdʒ] *n.* (*search*) о́быск; **~ sale** барахо́лка; распрода́жа подержанных веще́й.

v.i. ры́ться (*impf.*).

rumour ['ru:mə(r)] *n.* слух; **~ has it that ...** хо́дят слу́хи, что...

v.t.: **it was ~ed that ...** ходи́ли слу́хи, что...; **the ~ed visit** визи́т, о кото́ром прошёл слух.

rump [rʌmp] *n.* кресте́ц.

cpd. **~-steak** *n.* ромште́кс; вы́резка.

rumple ['rʌmp(ə)l] *v.t.* мять, по-; трепа́ть, по-; **her dress was ~d** её пла́тье помя́лось; **don't ~ my hair!** не трепи́те мне во́лосы!

rumpus ['rʌmpəs] *n.* шум, гам; сканда́л; **~ room** ко́мната для игр и развлече́ний.

run [rʌn] *n.* **1.** (*action of ~ning*) бег, пробе́г; **he went for a ~ before breakfast** он сде́лал пробе́жку перед за́втраком; **he started off at a ~** он побежа́л (с ме́ста); **the prisoner made a ~ for it** заключённый бежа́л/удра́л; **the general had the enemy on the ~** генера́л обрати́л проти́вника в бе́гство; **the prisoner is on the ~** заключённый нахо́дится в бега́х; **she has been on the ~ all morning** она́ была́ в бега́х всё у́тро. **2.** (*trip*, *journey*, *route*) пое́здка, рейс, маршру́т; **we went for a ~ in the country** мы съе́здили за́ город; **the driver was not on his usual ~** води́тель рабо́тал не на своём обы́чном маршру́те; **the train did the ~ in 3 hours** по́езд дошёл за три часа́; **the ship was on a trial ~** кора́бль находи́лся в испыта́тельном ре́йсе. **3.** (*continuous stretch*) пери́од; отре́зок вре́мени; **he had a ~ of good luck** у него́ была́ полоса́ везе́ния; **the play had a long ~** пье́са шла до́лго; **in the long ~** в коне́чном счёте. **4.** (*score at cricket etc.*) очко́. **5.** (*demand*) спрос; **there is a ~ on this book** э́та кни́га по́льзуется больши́м спро́сом. **6.** (*ordinary kind*): **his talents are out of the common ~** он незауря́дно тала́нтлив; **~ of the mill** обы́чный/сре́дний сорт. **7.** (*for fowls etc.*) заго́н. **8.** (*use*, *access*): **he gave me the ~ of his library** он предоста́вил мне всю свою́ библиоте́ку.

v.t. **1.** (*cause to ~*): **he ran a horse in the Derby** он вы́ставил свою́ ло́шадь на Де́рби; **he nearly ran me off my legs** он меня́ так загна́л, что я на нога́х не стоя́л. **2.** (*execute*, *perform*): **he ran a good race** он хорошо́ пробежа́л (диста́нцию); **the heats were ~ yesterday** забе́ги состоя́лись вчера́. **3.** (*cover*, *traverse*) бежа́ть (*det.*), про-; **he can ~ the mile in under a minute** он мо́жет пробежа́ть ми́лю ме́ньше, чем за мину́ту; **the illness has to ~ its course** боле́знь должна́ пройти́ все эта́пы. **4.** (*expose o.s. to*) подв|ерга́ться, -е́ргнуться +*d.*; **he ~s the risk of being caught** он риску́ет быть по́йманным. **5.** (*hunt*, *pursue*) пресле́довать (*impf.*); трави́ть (*impf.*); **the hounds ran the fox to earth** соба́ки загна́ли лису́ в но́ру. **6.** (*convey in car*) подв|ози́ть, -езти́ (на маши́не); **shall I ~ you home?** хоти́те, я подвезу́ вас домо́й? **7.** (*cause to go*): **they ran the ship aground** они́ посади́ли кора́бль на мель; **he ran the car into the garage** он загна́л маши́ну в гара́ж; **he ran the car into a tree** он вре́зался в де́рево; **he ran his eye over the page** он пробежа́л глаза́ми страни́цу; **I shall ~ the bath** я напущу́ воды́ в ва́нну; я пригото́влю ва́нну; **he ran a sword through his enemy's body** он пронзи́л врага́ мечо́м. **9.** (*operate*) управля́ть (*impf.*) +*i.*; эксплуати́ровать (*impf.*); **who is ~ning the shop?** кто ве́дает ла́вкой?; **he ~s a small business** у него́ своё небольшо́е де́ло; **she ~s the house single-handed** она́ сама́ ведёт хозя́йство; **he ran the engine for a few minutes** он завёл мото́р на не́сколько мину́т; **can you afford to ~ a car?** вы в состоя́нии держа́ть маши́ну?; **he thinks he ~s the show** (*fig.*) он ду́мает, что он здесь гла́вный.

v.i. **1.** (*move quickly*, *hurry*) бе́гать (*indet.*); бежа́ть (*det.*), по-; **I ran after him** я побежа́л за ним; **he ran for his life** он удира́л изо всех сил; **~ for it!** беги́!; **he came ~ning to my aid** он бро́сился ко мне на по́мощь; **~ and see who's at the door!** сбе́гай посмотри́, кто пришёл! **2.** (*compete*) соревнова́ться (*impf.*); **he is ~ning in the 100 metres** он бежи́т стометро́вку; (*fig.*): **he ran for president** он баллоти́ровался в президе́нты. **3.** (*come by chance*) столкну́ться (*pf.*) (с+*i.*); натолкну́ться (*pf.*) (на+*a.*); **I ran into an old friend** я случа́йно встре́тил ста́рого това́рища. **4.** (*of ship etc.*): **the vessel ran ashore** су́дно вы́бросило на бе́рег; **they were ~ning before the wind** они́ плы́ли с попу́тным ве́тром; **they had to ~ into port** им пришло́сь зайти́ в порт. **5.** (*of public transport*) ходи́ть (*indet.*); **there are no trains ~ning** поезда́ не хо́дят. **6.** (*of machines etc.*: *function*) де́йствовать (*impf.*); **most cars ~ on petrol** большинство́ маши́н рабо́тает/хо́дит на бензи́не; **leave the engine ~ning!** не выключа́йте мото́р! **7.** (*of objects in motion*): **it ~s on wheels** э́то дви́гается на колёсах. **8.** (*of liquid, sand etc.*: *flow*) течь, протека́ть, струи́ться (*all impf.*); **the water is ~ning** кран откры́т; **the floor was ~ning with water** пол был зали́т водо́й; **tears/sweat ran down his face** слёзы кати́лись (*or* пот струи́лся) по его́ щека́м; **the river is ~ning high** вода́ в реке́ подняла́сь; **my eyes are ~ning** у меня́ слезя́тся глаза́; **his nose was ~ning** у него́ текло́ и́з носу; (*fig.*): **feelings ran high** стра́сти разгоре́лись. **9.** (*become, grow*) станови́ться (*impf.*); **the well ran dry** коло́дец вы́сох; **supplies were ~ning low** запа́сы бы́ли на исхо́де; **he ran short of money** у него́ не остава́лось де́нег; **his blood ran cold** у него́ кровь засты́ла в жи́лах. **10.** (*develop unchecked*): **the garden is ~ning wild** сад бу́рно разраста́ется; **she lets her children ~ wild** её де́ти расту́т без присмо́тра. **11.** (*of colour, ink etc.*: *spread*) линя́ть, по-; **if you wash this dress the dye will ~** е́сли вы постира́ете э́то пла́тье, оно́ полиня́ет. **12.** (*of emotions, thought etc.*: *travel*): **the news ran like wildfire** но́вость распространи́лась с молниено́сной быстрото́й; **a tremor ran through the crowd** толпа́ затрепета́ла; **the thought ran through his head** у него́ промелькну́ла мысль; **the tune kept ~ning through my head** э́та мело́дия всё вре́мя звуча́ла у меня́ в уша́х. **13.** (*extend, stretch*) тяну́ться (*impf.*); простира́ться (*impf.*); **a road ~ning along the river** доро́га, иду́щая вдоль реки́; **a fence ~s round the field** по́ле огоро́жено забо́ром; **it will ~ to a lot of money** э́то бу́дет сто́ить больши́х де́нег; **our funds will not ~ to it** на́ших де́нег на э́то не хва́тит. **14.** (*continue; remain in operation*) быть действи́тельным; **the play has been ~ning for five years** пье́са идёт пять лет; **it ~s in their family** э́то у них насле́дственное. **15.** (*become unwoven*) спуска́ться (*impf.*); **these stockings will not ~** на э́тих чулка́х пе́тли не спуска́ются. **16.** (*of narrative or verse*) гласи́ть (*impf.*); **I forget how the line (of poetry) ~s** я забы́л, как звучи́т э́та строка́; **so the story ~s** так говоря́т.

further phrr. with preps.: **~ into** (*collide with*) налете́ть (*impf.*) на+*a.*; столкну́ться (*pf.*) с+*i.*; **he ran into a lamp-post** он налете́л на фона́рный столб; (*encounter, incur*): **he ran into debt** он залёз в долги́; **if you ~ into danger** е́сли вам бу́дет угрожа́ть опа́сность; **the plan ran into difficulties** план натолкну́лся на тру́дности; **~ over, through** (*review; rehearse*) повтор|я́ть, -и́ть; **I will ~ over the main points** я повторю́ гла́вные пу́нкты; **shall I ~ over the part with you?** дава́йте пройдём ва́шу роль вме́сте; **~ through** (*spend*) тра́тить, по-.

with advs.: **~ about** *v.i.* бе́гать (*indet.*); **~ along** *v.i.*: **I must ~ along** мне на́до бежа́ть; **~ along and play!** иди́ поигра́й!; **~ around** *v.i.*: **he had me ~ning around in circles** он меня́ соверше́нно сбил с то́лку; **~ away, ~ off** *v.i.* убе|га́ть, -жа́ть; уд|ира́ть, -ра́ть; **he ran away with his employer's daughter** он сбежа́л с хозя́йской до́чкой; **don't ~ away with the idea that I am against you** не внуша́йте себе́, что я име́ю что-ли́бо про́тив вас; **the horse ran away with him** ло́шадь его́ понесла́; **he lets his tongue ~ away with him** он сли́шком распуска́ет язы́к; **~ back** *v.i.*: **he ran back to apologize** он прибежа́л наза́д, что́бы извини́ться; **the car ran back down the hill** маши́на откати́лась наза́д по́д гору; **~ down** *v.t.*: **the cyclist was ~ down by a lorry** грузови́к сбил велосипеди́ста; **don't ~ your battery down** не тра́тьте батере́ю; **she is always ~ning down her neighbours** она́ ве́чно поно́сит сосе́дей; **you look very ~ down** у вас о́чень утомлённый вид; **it is their policy to ~ down production** их поли́тика напра́влена к свёртыванию произво́дства; *v.i.* остан|а́вливаться, -ови́ться; **~ in** *v.t.*: **he is ~ning in his car** он обка́тывает свою́ маши́ну; **~ off** *v.t.*: **I ran off the water from the tank** я вы́пустил во́ду из ба́ка; **he can ~ off an article in half an hour** он мо́жет настрочи́ть статью́ за полчаса́; **can you ~ off 100 more copies?** вы мо́жете отпеча́тать ещё 100 экземпля́ров?; *v.i.* убе|га́ть, -жа́ть; уд|ира́ть, -ра́ть; **he ran off with the jewels** он сбежа́л с драгоце́нностями; (*see also* **~ away**); **~ on** *v.i.* прод|олжа́ться, -о́лжиться; **~ out** *v.t.*: **he ran the rope out** он протяну́л верёвку; **he was ~ out of the country** его́ изгна́ли из страны́; *v.i.* (*lit.*) выбега́ть, вы́бежать; (*come to an end*) конча́ться, ко́нчиться; **he will soon ~ out of money** у него́ ско́ро ко́нчатся де́ньги; **our tea ran out** у нас вы́шел чай; **time is ~ning out** вре́мя истека́ет; **~ over** *v.t.* задави́ть (*pf.*); **he was ~ over by a car** его́ задави́ла маши́на; *v.i.*: **the bath ran over** ва́нна перели́лась че́рез край; **the (boiling) milk ran over** молоко́ убежа́ло; **~ through** *v.t.*: **the teacher ran my mistakes through with his pencil** учи́тель зачеркну́л мои́ оши́бки карандашо́м; **~ up** *v.t.*: **~ up the flag** подня́ть (*pf.*) флаг; **she ran up a dress** она́ (бы́стро) смастери́ла пла́тье; **he ran up a bill at the tailor's** он задолжа́л портно́му; *v.i.*: **she ran up to tell me the news** она́ прибежа́ла, что́бы сообщи́ть мне но́вость; **he ran up against a snag** он натолкну́лся на препя́тствие.

cpds. **~about** *n.* (*car*) небольшо́й автомоби́ль; малолитра́жка; **~around** *n.* (*coll., excuses*) отгово́рки (*f. pl.*); **~away** *n.* (*fugitive*) бегле́ц; (*attr.*): **~away inflation** безу́держная инфля́ция; **~-down** *n.* (*reduction*) сокраще́ние; (*summary*) кра́ткое изложе́ние; конспе́кт; **give me a ~-down on events** скажи́те мне кра́тко, что произошло́; **~-off** *n.* (*deciding heat*) дополни́тельная игра́; (*diversion of water*) сток; **~-up** *n.* (*run preparatory to action*) разбе́г; (*fig.*): **the ~-up to the election** предвы́борная пора́/кампа́ния; **~way** *n.* (*aeron.*) взлётно-поса́дочная полоса́.

rune [ru:n] *n.* ру́на.

rung [rʌŋ] *n.* ступе́нька.

runic ['ru:nɪk] *adj.* руни́ческий.

runner ['rʌnə(r)] *n.* **1.** (*athlete*) бегу́н; **front ~** ли́дер; **long-distance ~** ста́йер; **marathon ~** марафо́нец. **2.** (*horse*) (бегова́я) ло́шадь. **3.** (*messenger; scout*) посы́льный курье́р. **4.** (*part which assists sliding motion*): **curtain ~** кольцо́ для занаве́ски; **sledge ~** по́лоз. **5.** (*narrow cloth; strip of carpet*) доро́жка. **6.** (*bot., shoot*) побе́г; **~ bean** фасо́ль о́гненная.

cpd. **~-up** *n.* уча́стник/кандида́т, заня́вший второ́е ме́сто.

running ['rʌnɪŋ] *n.* **1.** (*sport, exercise*) бе́ганье, бег; **I shall take up ~** я займу́сь бе́гом. **2.** (*pace*) ход; **the favourite made all the ~** фавори́т вёл бег. **3.** (*contest*) состяза́ние; **they are out of the ~ for the Cup** они́ вы́были из соревнова́ний на кубо́к; **he is in the ~ for Prime Minister** он мо́жет стать премье́р-мини́стром.

adj. **1.** (*performed while ~*) бегу́щий; **~ jump** прыжо́к с разбе́га. **2.** (*performed while events proceed*) теку́щий; **~ commentary** репорта́ж (по хо́ду де́йствия). **3.** (*continuous*) непреры́вный. **4.** (*in succession*) подря́д, кря́ду; **he won three times ~** он вы́играл три ра́за подря́д. **5.** (*flowing*): **~ water** (*in nature*) прото́чная вода́; (*domestic*) водопрово́д; **a ~ sore** гноя́щаяся боля́чка; **a ~ nose** сопли́вый нос, на́сморк.

cpd. **~-board** *n.* подно́жка.

runny ['rʌnɪ] *adj.* теку́чий, жи́дкий; **a ~ egg** жи́дкое яйцо́; **a ~ nose** мо́крый нос, на́сморк.

runt [rʌnt] *n.* (*undersized animal*) низкоро́слое живо́тное; (*of pers., pej.*) ка́рлик.

rupee [ruːˈpiː] *n.* ру́пия.

rupture [ˈrʌptʃə(r)] *n.* **1.** (*breaking, bursting*) проры́в. **2.** (*hernia*) гры́жа. **3.** (*breach, quarrel*) разры́в.

v.t. **1.** (*burst, break*) прор|ыва́ть, -ва́ть; **he ~d a blood-vessel** он повреди́л кровено́сный сосу́д. **2.** **~ o.s.** над|рыва́ться, -орва́ться.

v.i. раз|рыва́ться, -орва́ться.

rural [ˈrʊər(ə)l] *adj.* се́льский.

ruse [ruːz] *n.* уло́вка.

rush[1] [rʌʃ] *n.* (*bot.*) тростни́к.

rush[2] [rʌʃ] *n.* (*precipitate movement*) стреми́тельное движе́ние; **the ~ of water** пото́к воды́; **a ~ of blood to the head** прили́в кро́ви к голове́; (*bustle*) спе́шка; (*increase in activity, buying etc.*): **the Christmas ~** предрожде́ственская суета́/су́толока; **the gold ~** золота́я лихора́дка; **a ~ job** спе́шная рабо́та; **in the ~ hour** в часы́ пик.

v.t. **1.** (*speed, hurry*) торопи́ть, по-; **troops were ~ed to the front** войска́ бы́ли сро́чно перебро́шены на фронт; **I refuse to be ~ed into a decision** я отка́зываюсь принима́ть реше́ние в спе́шке; **I was ~ed off my feet** (*exhausted*) я сби́лся с ног; **I must ~ off a letter** я до́лжен бы́стренько настрочи́ть письмо́. **2.** (*charge*) брать, взять шту́рмом; **the audience ~ed the platform** пу́блика хлы́нула на эстра́ду.

v.i. мча́ться, по-; бр|оса́ться, -о́ситься; **she is always ~ing about** она́ ве́чно в бега́х; **he ~ed after me** он бро́сился за мной; **the train ~ed by** по́езд промча́лся ми́мо; **he ~ed in and out** он заскочи́л на мину́тку; **the blood ~ed to her face** кровь бро́силась ей в лицо́; **don't ~ to conclusions** не де́лайте поспе́шных вы́водов; **a ~ing wind** поры́вистый ве́тер.

rusk [rʌsk] *n.* суха́рь (*m.*).

russet [ˈrʌsɪt] *adj.* краснова́то-кори́чневый.

Russia [ˈrʌʃə] *n.* Росси́я.

Russian [ˈrʌʃ(ə)n] *n.* **1.** (*person of Russ. nationality*) ру́сск|ий (*fem.* -ая); (*person of Russ. citizenship*) россия́н|ин (*fem.* -ка); **the ~s** ру́сские (*pl.*). **2.** (*language*) ру́сский язы́к; **do you speak ~?** вы говори́те по-ру́сски?

adj. ру́сский; (*pol., hist.*) росси́йский.

Russification [ˌrʌsɪfɪˈkeɪʃ(ə)n] *n.* русифика́ция.

Russify [ˈrʌsɪˌfaɪ] *v.t.* русифици́ровать (*impf., pf.*).

Russophile [ˈrʌsəʊˌfaɪl] *n.* русофи́л (*fem.* -ка).

Russophobia [ˌrʌsəʊˈfəʊbɪə] *n.* русофо́бия.

rust [rʌst] *n.* (*on metal; plant disease*) ржа́вчина.

v.i. ржа́веть, за-.

cpd. **~-proof** *adj.* нержаве́ющий.

rustic [ˈrʌstɪk] *n.* дереве́нщина (*c.g.*).

adj. (*countrified*) дереве́нский, се́льский; (*unrefined*) неотёсанный, гру́бый; **a ~ bridge** мост из нетёсаного ле́са.

rusticate [ˈrʌstɪˌkeɪt] *v.t.* вре́менно исключа́ть (*impf.*).

rustiness [ˈrʌstɪnɪs] *n.* ржа́вчина; (*fig.*) отста́лость.

rustle [ˈrʌs(ə)l] *n.* ше́лест, шо́рох.

v.t. **1.** (*cause to ~*) шелесте́ть (*impf.*) +*i.*; шурша́ть (*impf.*) +*i.*; **don't ~ the newspaper** не шелести́те газе́той. **2.** (*US sl., steal*) красть, у-. **3.**: **~ up** (*coll.*) разы́ск|ивать, -а́ть; **can you ~ up some food?** вы мо́жете раздобы́ть чего́-нибу́дь пое́сть?

v.i. шелесте́ть (*impf.*); шурша́ть (*impf.*).

rustler [ˈrʌslə(r)] *n.* (*US*) конокра́д; вор, угоня́ющий скот.

rusty [ˈrʌstɪ] *adj.* ржа́вый, заржа́вленный; (*fig.*): (*out of practice*): **my German is ~** я подзабы́л неме́цкий.

rut [rʌt] *n.* (*wheel-track*) колея́; (*fig.*) рути́на; **it is easy to get into a ~** легко́ погря́знуть в рути́не.

ruthless [ˈruːθlɪs] *adj.* безжа́лостный, жесто́кий.

ruthlessness [ˈruːθlɪsnɪs] *n.* безжа́лостность, жесто́кость.

rye [raɪ] *n.* рожь; **~ bread** ржано́й хлеб.

S

sabbath [ˈsæbəθ] *n.* (*Jewish*) суббо́та; (*Christian*) воскресе́нье.

sabbatical [səˈbætɪk(ə)l] *n.* (*~ year, term*) *see adj.*

adj.: **~ leave** тво́рческий/академи́ческий о́тпуск.

sable [ˈseɪb(ə)l] *n.* (*zool.*) со́боль (*m.*); (*fur*) со́боль, собо́лий мех.

adj. собо́лий, соболи́ный.

sabotage [ˈsæbəˌtɑːʒ] *n.* сабота́ж, диве́рсия; **acts of ~** диверсио́нные а́кты.

v.t. саботи́ровать (*impf., pf.*); (*damage*) повре|жда́ть, -ди́ть; (*fig., disrupt*) срыва́ть, сорва́ть.

saboteur [ˌsæbəˈtɜː(r)] *n.* сабота́жник, диверса́нт.

sabre [ˈseɪbə(r)] *n.* са́бля; (*fencing*) эспадро́н.

cpds. **~-rattling** *n.* (*fig.*) бряца́ние ору́жием; **~-toothed** *adj.* саблезу́бый.

sac [sæk] *n.* мешо́чек.

saccharin [ˈsækərɪn] *n.* сахари́н.

saccharine [ˈsækəˌriːn] *adj.* са́харный, сахари́стый; (*fig.*) слаща́вый, при́торный.

sacerdotal [ˌsækəˈdəʊt(ə)l] *adj.* свяще́ннический.

sachet [ˈsæʃeɪ] *n.* саше́ (*indecl.*).

sack[1] [sæk] *n.* **1.** (*bag*) мешо́к. **2.** (*coll., dismissal*): **get the ~** быть уво́ленным; получ|а́ть, -и́ть расчёт; **give s.o. the ~** ув|ольня́ть, -о́лить кого́-н.

v.t. (*coll., dismiss*) рассчи́т|ывать, -а́ть.

cpd. **~cloth** *n.* мешкови́на; (*hair shirt*) власяни́ца.

sack[2] [sæk] *v.t.* гра́бить, раз-; пред|ава́ть, -а́ть разграбле́нию.

sackful [ˈsækfʊl] *n.* по́лный мешо́к (*чего*); **by the ~** (це́лыми) мешка́ми.

sacking [ˈsækɪŋ] *n.* (*text.*) мешкови́на, дерю́га.

sacrament [ˈsækrəmənt] *n.* **1.** (*sacred act or rite*) та́инство. **2.** (*Eucharist*): **the Holy S~** свято́е прича́стие; **take, receive the ~** прича|ща́ться, -сти́ться.

sacramental [ˌsækrəˈment(ə)l] *adj.* сакромента́льный; **~ wine** вино́ для прича́стия.

sacred [ˈseɪkrɪd] *adj.* свяще́нный, свято́й; **~ books** свяще́нные кни́ги; **~ music** духо́вная му́зыка; **~ duty** свяще́нный долг; **~ to the memory of my wife** незабве́нной па́мяти мое́й супру́ги.

sacredness [ˈseɪkrɪdnɪs] *n.* свя́тость.

sacrifice [ˈsækrɪˌfaɪs] *n.* (*lit., fig.*) же́ртва; (*act of relig. ~*) жертвоприноше́ние; **make a ~ of sth.** прин|оси́ть, -ести́ что-н. в же́ртву; **they made ~s for their children** они́ мно́гим же́ртвовали ра́ди дете́й; **at the ~ of his health** же́ртвуя здоро́вьем; **at the ~ of one's principles** поступи́вшись свои́ми при́нципами.

v.t. (*lit., at altar*) прин|оси́ть, -ести́ (*кого/что*) в же́ртву; (*give up, surrender*) же́ртвовать, по- +*i.*; **he ~d truth to his own interests** он принёс и́стину в же́ртву свои́м интере́сам.

sacrificial [ˌsækrɪˈfɪʃ(ə)l] *adj.* же́ртвенный.

sacrilege [ˈsækrɪlɪdʒ] *n.* святота́тство, кощу́нство.

sacrilegious [ˌsækrɪˈlɪdʒəs] *adj.* святота́тственный, кощу́нственный.

sacristan [ˈsækrɪst(ə)n] *n.* ри́зничий.

sacristy [ˈsækrɪstɪ] *n.* ри́зница.

sacrosanct [ˈsækrəʊˌsæŋkt] *adj.* свяще́нный, неприкоснове́нный.

sad [sæd] *adj.* **1.** гру́стный, печа́льный; **I feel ~** мне гру́стно; **with a ~ heart** с тяжёлым се́рдцем; (*regrettable, lamentable*) прискорбный; **a ~ mistake** доса́дная оши́бка; **he came to a ~ end** он пло́хо ко́нчил. **2.: you are ~ly mistaken** вы жесто́ко ошиба́етесь; **the garden was ~ly neglected** сад был доне́льзя запу́щен.

sadden ['sæd(ə)n] *v.t.* печа́лить, о-.

saddle ['sæd(ə)l] *n.* седло́.

v.t. **1.** седла́ть, о-. **2.** (*fig., burden with task, guilt etc.*): **~ s.o. with sth.** взва́л|ивать, -и́ть что-н. на кого́-н; **he was ~d with his relatives** он был обременён ро́дственниками.

cpds. **~-bag** *n.* седе́льный вьюк; **~-cloth** *n.* потни́к; чепра́к; **~-horse** *n.* верхова́я ло́шадь.

saddler ['sædlə(r)] *n.* седе́льник, шо́рник.

saddlery ['sædlərɪ] *n.* (*activity*) шо́рное де́ло; (*workshop*) шо́рная мастерска́я.

sadism ['seɪdɪz(ə)m] *n.* сади́зм.

sadist ['seɪdɪst] *n.* сади́ст (*fem.* -ка).

sadistic [sə'dɪstɪk] *adj.* сади́стский.

sadness ['sædnɪs] *n.* грусть, печа́ль; **a look of ~** печа́льный вид.

s.a.e. (*abbr. of* **stamped addressed envelope**) конве́рт с ма́ркой и обра́тным а́дресом.

safari [sə'fɑːrɪ] *n.* сафа́ри (*nt. indecl.*); охо́тничья экспеди́ция; **on ~** на охо́те; **~ park** «сафа́ри» зоопа́рк.

safe[1] [seɪf] *n.* сейф.

safe[2] [seɪf] *adj.* **1.** (*affording security, not dangerous*) безопа́сный; (*reliable*) надёжный; **in ~ custody** под надёжной охра́ной; **in s.o.'s ~ keeping** у кого́-н. на сохране́нии; **is it ~ to leave him (alone)?** не опа́сно его́ оставля́ть одного́?; **to be on the ~ side** на вся́кий слу́чай, для (бо́льшей) ве́рности; **is the dog ~ with children?** де́тям не опа́сно игра́ть с э́той соба́кой? **2.** (*free from danger*): **we are ~ from attack** мы мо́жем не опаса́ться нападе́ния; **we are ~ as houses here** мы здесь как за ка́менной стено́й; **perfectly ~** в по́лной сохра́нности; **~ area** (*mil.*) зо́на безопа́сности; (*unhurt, undamaged*): **we saw them home ~ and sound** мы доста́вили их домо́й це́лыми и невреди́мыми. **3.** (*cautious, moderate*) осторо́жный; **I decided to play ~** я реши́л не рискова́ть. **4.** (*certain*): **he is a ~ winner** он наверняка́ вы́играет; **it's a ~ bet** мо́жно быть уве́ренным.

cpds. **~-conduct** *n.* (*document*) охра́нная гра́мота; **~-deposit** *n.* храни́лище с се́йфами; **~guard** *n.* охра́на, гара́нтия (от+*g.*); *v.t.* гаранти́ровать (*impf., pf.*); охран|я́ть, -и́ть.

safely ['seɪflɪ] *adv.* **1.** (*unharmed*) благополу́чно, в сохра́нности. **2.** (*for safety*): **I put the bottle ~ away** я убра́л буты́лку от беды́. **3.** (*with confidence*): **I can ~ say that ...** я могу́ с уве́ренностью сказа́ть, что...

safety ['seɪftɪ] *n.* безопа́сность; **our ~ was threatened** на́ша безопа́сность была́ под угро́зой; **~ first** осторо́жность пре́жде всего́; **road ~** безопа́сность у́личного движе́ния; **~ glass** безоско́лочное стекло́; **~ lamp** (*mining*) ру́дничная ла́мпа; **~ measures, precautions** ме́ры безопа́сности; **~ net** страхо́вочная се́тка; **~ razor** безопа́сная бри́тва.

cpds. **~-belt** *n.* привязно́й реме́нь; **~-catch** *n.* (*on gun etc.*) предохрани́тель (*m.*); **~-pin** *n.* англи́йская була́вка; **~-valve** *n.* предохрани́тельный кла́пан.

saffron ['sæfrən] *n.* шафра́н.

adj. шафра́нный, шафра́новый.

sag [sæg] *n.* проги́б.

v.i. (*of gate etc.*) ос|еда́ть, -е́сть; (*of rope, curtain*) пров|иса́ть, -и́снуть; (*of ladder, ceiling*) прог|иба́ться, -ну́ться; (*of garment*) отв|иса́ть, -и́снуть; (*of cheeks, breasts*) обв|иса́ть, -и́снуть; **a ~ging chin** отви́слый подборо́док.

saga ['sɑːgə] *n.* са́га; (*fig.*): **he told me the ~ of his escape** он пове́дал мне исто́рию своего́ побе́га.

sagacious [sə'geɪʃ(ə)s] *adj.* **1.** (*of pers.*) му́дрый; (*of animal*) у́мный. **2.** (*perspicacious*) проница́тельный, прозорли́вый; (*of action: far-sighted*) дальнови́дный, му́дрый.

sagacity [sə'gæsɪtɪ] *n.* му́дрость, ум; проница́тельность, прозорли́вость.

sage[1] [seɪdʒ] *n.* (*bot.*) шалфе́й.

sage[2] [seɪdʒ] *n.* (*wise man*) мудре́ц.

adj. му́дрый.

Sagittarius [ˌsædʒɪ'teərɪəs] *n.* Стреле́ц.

sago ['seɪgəʊ] *n.* са́го (*indecl.*).

Sahara [sə'hɑːrə] *n.* Саха́ра.

sail [seɪl] *n.* **1.** па́рус; **hoist ~** ста́вить, по- паруса́; **lower the ~s** спус|ка́ть, -ти́ть паруса́; **under ~** под паруса́ми; **in full ~** на всех паруса́х; **get under** (*or* **set**) **~** вы́йти (*pf.*) в пла́вание; **set ~ for** отпр|авля́ться, -а́виться к+*d.* (*or* в+*a.*). **2.** (*ship*): **there wasn't a ~ in sight** не́ было ви́дно ни одного́ су́дна/корабля́. **3.** (*voyage or excursion on water*) пла́вание; **go for a ~** отпр|авля́ться, -а́виться в пла́вание; **it is 7 days' ~ from here** э́то в семи́ днях пла́вания отсю́да. **4.** (*of windmill*) крыло́.

v.t. **1.** (*of pers. or ship, travel over*) пла́вать (*indet.*); плыть, про- (*det.*) по+*d.*; **he has ~ed the seven seas** он исходи́л все моря́ (и океа́ны). **2.** (*control navigation of*) управля́ть (*impf.*) +*i.*

v.i. **1.** пл|а́вать (*indet.*), -ыть (*det.*), поплы́ть (*pf.*); **the new yacht ~s well** у но́вой я́хты хоро́ший ход; **~ close to the wind** (*lit.*) идти́/плыть (*det.*) кру́то к ве́тру; (*fig.*) вступ|а́ть, -и́ть на опа́сный путь; **the ship ~ed into harbour** кора́бль вошёл в га́вань; **we ~ed out to sea** мы вы́шли в мо́ре. **2.** (*start a voyage*) отпл|ыва́ть, -ы́ть. **3.** (*fig., move gracefully, smoothly*) плыть (*impf.*); пропл|ыва́ть, -ы́ть; **he ~ed through** (*made light work of*) **the exams** он с лёгкостью вы́держал экза́мены. **4.** (*of birds*) пари́ть (*impf.*); (*of clouds*) нести́сь (*det.*).

cpds. **~cloth** *n.* паруси́на; **~plane** *n.* планёр.

sailboard ['seɪlbɔːd] *n.* виндсёрфер.

sailboarding ['seɪlbɔːdɪŋ] *n.* виндсёрфинг.

sailing ['seɪlɪŋ] *n.* **1.** (*act of ~*) (море)пла́вание; (*navigation*) судохо́дство; (*as sport*) па́русный спорт. **2.** (*departure*) отхо́д, отплы́тие; (*voyage*) рейс; **list of ~s** расписа́ние парохо́дного движе́ния. **3.** (*fig., progress*): **it was plain ~** всё шло как по ма́слу.

cpds. **~-boat** *n.* па́русная ло́дка; **~-ship** *n.* па́русное су́дно, па́русник.

sailor ['seɪlə(r)] *n.* **1.** (*seaman*) моря́к, матро́с; **~'s cap** (матро́сская) бескозы́рка; **~ jacket** матро́ска. **2.: he is a bad ~** он пло́хо перено́сит ка́чку (на мо́ре).

saint [seɪnt, sənt] *n.* свято́й, пра́ведник; **my ~'s day** мой имени́н|ы (*pl., g.* —); **patron ~** свято́й покрови́тель (*fem.* свята́я покрови́тельница); **S~ Bernard** (*dog*) сенберна́р; **S~ Lawrence river** река́ свято́го Лавре́нтия; **S~ Louis** (*city*) Сент-Лу́ис; **S~ Petersburg** Санкт-Петербу́рг; **S~ Valentine's Day** день свято́го Валенти́на; **S~ Vitus's dance** пля́ска свято́го Ви́та; **All S~s (Day)** пра́здник всех святы́х.

cpd. **~like** *adj.* свято́й, а́нгельский.

sainthood ['seɪnthʊd] *n.* свя́тость.

saintly ['seɪntlɪ] *adj.* свято́й; безгре́шный.

St Petersburg [sənt' piːtəzˌbɜːg] *n.* Санкт-Петербу́рг; *attr.* (санкт-)петербу́ргский.

St Petersburger [sənt' piːtəzˌbɜːgə(r)] *n.* (санкт-)петербу́рж|ец (*fem.* -а́нка).

sake [seɪk] *n.*: **for the ~ of** ра́ди+*g.*; **for God's, heaven's, goodness ~** ра́ди Бо́га; **for one's own ~** для себя́; **he was persecuted for the ~ of his opinions** его́ пресле́довали за убежде́ния; **art for art's ~**

иску́сство для иску́сства; **for old times' ~** в па́мять про́шлого.

salacious [sə'leɪʃəs] *adj.* (*indecent*) непристо́йный.

salad ['sæləd] *n.* **1.** сала́т; **fruit ~** фру́кты в сиро́пе. **2.** (*fig.*): **in my ~ days** когда́ я был зелёным юнцо́м.

cpds. **~-bowl** *n.* сала́тница; **~-dressing** *n.* запра́вка (к сала́ту).

salamander ['sælə,mændə(r)] *n.* салама́ндра.

salami [sə'lɑːmɪ] *n.* копчёная колбаса́; саля́ми (*f. indecl.*).

sal ammoniac [,sæl ə'məʊnɪ,æk] *n.* нашаты́рь (*m.*).

salaried ['sælərɪd] *adj.* (*pers.*) слу́жащий; (*post*) опла́чиваемый.

salary ['sælərɪ] *n.* окла́д, зарпла́та.

sale [seɪl] *n.* **1.** прода́жа, сбыт; **be on, for ~** име́ться (*impf.*) в прода́же; **'house for ~'** (*as notice*) «продаётся дом»; **put up for ~** выставля́ть, вы́ставить на прода́жу; **the ~s were enormous** спрос был колосса́льный; **~s clerk** (*US, shop assistant*) продав|е́ц (*fem.* -щи́ца); **~s department** отде́л сбы́та; **~s manager** ме́неджер по сбы́ту; **~s talk** рекла́ма, реклами́рование; **~s tax** нало́г на про́данный това́р. **2.** (*clearance ~*) распрода́жа; **~** (*reduced*) **price** сни́женная цена́, цена́ со ски́дкой.

cpds. **~-room** *n.* аукцио́нный зал; **~sgirl** *n.* = **~swoman; ~sman** *n.* (*in shop*) продаве́ц; (*travelling door-to-door*) коммивояжёр; торго́вый аге́нт; **~smanship** *n.* уме́ние/иску́сство продава́ть; **~swoman, ~sgirl** *nn.* (*in shop*) продавщи́ца.

salient ['seɪlɪənt] *n.* (*in fortifications*) вы́ступ; (*in line of attack or defence*) вы́ступ, клин.

adj. (*jutting out*) выдаю́щийся; (*fig.*) выдаю́щийся, я́ркий.

saline ['seɪlaɪn] *adj.* солёный, соляно́й; **~ spring** солёный исто́чник; **~ solution** соляно́й раство́р.

salinity [sə'lɪnɪtɪ] *n.* солёность.

saliva [sə'laɪvə] *n.* слюна́.

salivary [sə'laɪvərɪ, 'sælɪvərɪ] *adj.* слю́нный.

salivate ['sælɪ,veɪt] *v.i.* выделя́ть, вы́делить слюну́.

salivation [,sælɪ'veɪʃ(ə)n] *n.* слюнотече́ние.

sallow ['sæləʊ] *adj.* боле́зненно-жёлтый; оли́вковый.

sally ['sælɪ] *n.* **1.** (*mil.*) вы́лазка. **2.** (*witty remark*) острота́, ре́плика.

v.i.: **~ forth, out** (*mil.*) де́лать, с- вы́лазку; (*fig.*) отпр|авля́ться, -а́виться.

salmon ['sæmən] *n.* лосо́сь (*m.*); сёмга.

adj. **1.** лососёвый. **2.** (*colour*) ора́нжево-ро́зовый.

salmonella [,sælmə'nelə] *n.* сальмоне́лла.

salon ['sælɒn, -lɔ̃] *n.* сало́н, ателье́ (*indecl.*).

saloon [sə'luːn] *n.* (*on ship*) сало́н, каю́т-компа́ния; **billiard ~** бильа́рдная; **~ (bar)** бар; **~ (car)** седа́н.

salt [sɔːlt, sɒlt] *n.* соль; **bath ~s** аромати́ческие со́ли (*f. pl.*) для ва́нны; **cooking ~** пова́ренная соль; **smelling ~s** ню́хательная соль; **table ~** столо́вая соль; **in ~** (*pickled*) солёный; **take sth. with a grain of ~** отн|оси́ться, -ести́сь скепти́чески к чему́-н.; **rub ~ into s.o.'s wounds** (*fig.*) растрав|ля́ть, -и́ть (*or* сы́пать (*impf.*) соль на) чьи-н. ра́ны; **the ~ of the earth** соль земли́.

adj. солёный; **~ water** морска́я вода́; **~ beef** солони́на.

v.t. **1.** (*cure in brine*) соли́ть, за-; **~ed meat** солони́на. **2.** (*sprinkle with ~*) соли́ть, по-. **3. ~ away** (*fig., coll., put in safe keeping*) копи́ть, на-; класть/скла́дывать (*impf.*) в кубы́шку.

cpds. **~-cellar** *n.* соло́нка; **~-marsh** *n.* солонча́к; **~-mine** *n.* соляна́я ша́хта; **~-water** *adj.*: **~-water fish** морска́я ры́ба; **~-works** *n.* солева́рня.

saltiness ['sɔːltɪnɪs, 'sɒl-] *n.* солёность.

saltpetre [,sɒlt'piːtə(r), ,sɔːlt-] *n.* сели́тра.

salty ['sɔːltɪ, 'sɒl-] *adj.* (*lit., fig.*) солёный; **too ~** пересо́ленный.

salubrious [sə'luːbrɪəs, sə'ljuː-] *adj.* (*healthy*) здоро́вый; (*curative*) целе́бный, цели́тельный.

salutary ['sæljʊtərɪ] *adj.* (*beneficial*) благотво́рный; **a ~ warning** поле́зное предупрежде́ние.

salutation [,sæljuː'teɪʃ(ə)n] *n.* приве́тствие.

salute [sə'luːt, -'ljuːt] *n.* (*mil., naut.*) отда́ние че́сти; во́инское приве́тствие; **give, make a ~** отд|ава́ть, -а́ть честь; **take the ~** прин|има́ть, -я́ть пара́д; (*with guns*) салю́т; **a ~ of 6 guns** салю́т из шести́ за́лпов.

v.t. **1.** отд|ава́ть, -а́ть честь (*кому*); салютова́ть (*impf., pf.*) (*кому/чему*). **2.** (*greet*) приве́тствовать (*impf., pf.*).

v.i. отд|ава́ть, -а́ть честь.

salvage ['sælvɪdʒ] *n.* **1.** (*saving ship or property*) спасе́ние (иму́щества); (*what is saved*) спасённое иму́щество; спасённый груз *и т.п.*; (*~ money*) вознагражде́ние/награ́да за спасённое иму́щество. **2.** (*saving waste paper, metal etc.*) сбор утиля.

v.t. (*also* **salve**) спас|а́ть, -ти́; сохран|я́ть, -и́ть.

salvation [sæl'veɪʃ(ə)n] *n.* спасе́ние (души́), избавле́ние; **S~ Army** А́рмия спасе́ния; (*pers. or thg. that saves*) спаси́тель (*m.*), избави́тель (*m.*); спасе́ние; **you have been the ~ of him** вы его́ спасли́.

salve[2] [sælv, sɑːv] = **salvage** *v.t.*

salver ['sælvə(r)] *n.* (серебряный) подно́с.

salvo ['sælvəʊ] *n.* (*of guns*) залп; **fire a ~** да|ва́ть, -ть залп; (*of bombs*) бо́мбовый уда́р.

Samaritan [sə'mærɪt(ə)n] *n.*: **good ~** до́брый самаритя́нин.

same [seɪm] *pron. & adj.* **1.** тот же (са́мый); тако́й же; оди́н (и тот же); (*unvarying*) одина́ковый, неизме́нный; **not the ~** друго́й; **this ~** э́тот са́мый/же; **I lived in the ~ house as he** я жил в одно́м до́ме с ним; **we are the ~ age** мы одни́х лет (*or* одного́ во́зраста); **in the ~ way** таки́м/подо́бным же о́бразом; **at the ~ time** в то же вре́мя, одновре́ме́нно, вме́сте; (*however*) ме́жду тем; **it's all the ~ to me** мне всё равно́; **it comes to the ~ thing** э́то одно́ и то же; э́то всё равно́/едино́; **I'd do the ~ again** я бы то́чно так поступи́л и тепе́рь; **~ again, please!** то же са́мое, пожа́луйста!; **... and the ~ to you!** ... и вам та́кже (*or* того́ же)!

adv.: **I don't feel the ~ towards him** я стал к нему́ ина́че относи́ться; **all the ~** (*nevertheless*) всё-таки; всё равно́; всё же; **just the ~** (*despite that*) тем не ме́нее; **~ here!** я то́же!

sameness ['seɪmnɪs] *n.* (*identity*) то́ждество; (*uniformity*) единообра́зие; (*monotony*) однообра́зие.

Samoa [sə'məʊə] *n.* Само́а (*nt. indecl.*).

samovar ['sæmə,vɑː(r)] *n.* самова́р.

sample ['sɑːmp(ə)l] *n.* (*comm., fig.*) образе́ц, обра́зчик, приме́р; (*med.*) про́ба; **take a ~ of sth.** *see v.t.*

v.t. брать, взять образе́ц *+g.*; (*wine, food etc.*) про́бовать, по-; (*try out*) испро́бовать (*pf.*).

sampler ['sɑːmplə(r)] *n.* (*embroidery*) ≃ вы́шивка.

sampling ['sɑːmplɪŋ] *n.* (*in statistics*) вы́борка.

samurai ['sæmʊ,raɪ, -jʊ,raɪ] *n.* самура́й.

sanatorium [,sænə'tɔːrɪəm] (*US* **sanitarium**) *n.* санато́рий.

sanctification [,sæŋktɪfɪ'keɪʃ(ə)n] *n.* освяще́ние.

sanctify ['sæŋktɪ,faɪ] *v.t.* освя|ща́ть, -ти́ть.

sanctimonious [,sæŋktɪ'məʊnɪəs] *adj.* ха́нжеский; **~ person** ханжа́ (*c.g.*).

sanctimoniousness [,sæŋktɪ'məʊnɪəsnɪs] *n.* ха́нжество.

sanction ['sæŋkʃ(ə)n] *n.* **1.** (*authorization, permission*) са́нкция; (*approval*) одобре́ние. **2.** (*penalty*) ме́ра наказа́ния. **3.** (*moral, relig., pol.*) са́нкция.

v.t. (*authorize*) санкциони́ровать (*impf., pf.*); (*approve*) од|обря́ть, -о́брить.

sanctity ['sæŋktɪtɪ] *n.* (*holiness, saintliness*) свя́тость; (*inviolability*) неприкоснове́нность.

sanctuary ['sæŋktjʊərɪ] *n.* **1.** (*holy place*) святи́лище. **2.** (*part of church*) алта́рь (*m.*). **3.** (*asylum, refuge*)

убе́жище. **4.** (*for wild life*) запове́дник.
sanctum ['sæŋktəm] *n.* святи́лище; (*fig.*) прибе́жище.
sand [sænd] *n.* **1.** песо́к; **grain of ~** песчи́нка. **2.** (*pl., beach*) (песча́ный) пляж.
v.t. (*sprinkle with ~*) пос|ыпа́ть, -ы́пать песко́м; (*polish with ~*) прот|ира́ть, -ере́ть песко́м.
cpds. **~bag** *n.* мешо́к с песко́м; **~bank** *n.* песча́ная о́тмель; **~-box** (*rail.*) *n.* песо́чница; **~boy** *n.*: **happy as a ~boy** беззабо́тный; **~-castle** *n.* за́мок из песка́ (*or* на песке́); **~-dune** *n.* дю́на; **~-martin** *n.* берегова́я ла́сточка; **~paper** *n.* шку́рка, нажда́чная бума́га; *v.t.* шлифова́ть, от- шку́ркой; **~-pit** *n.* (*quarry*) песча́ный карье́р; (*for children*) песо́чница; **~stone** *n.* песча́ник; **~storm** *n.* песча́ная бу́ря.
sandal ['sænd(ə)l] *n.* (*footwear*) санда́лия.
sandalwood ['sænd(ə)l,wʊd] *n.* санда́л.
sandwich ['sænwɪdʒ, -wɪtʃ] *n.* бутербро́д; **ham ~** бутербро́д с ветчино́й; **~ bar** бутербро́дная.
v.t. (*insert*) вти́с|кивать, -нуть; (*squeeze*) сти́с|кивать, -нуть; вти́с|кивать, -нуть; заж|има́ть, -а́ть; **his car was ~ed between two lorries** его́ маши́на была́ зажа́та ме́жду двумя́ грузовика́ми.
cpds. **~-boards** *n.* рекла́мные щиты́ (*m. pl.*); **~course** *n.* курс обуче́ния, чреду́ющий тео́рию с пра́ктикой; **~-man** *n.* челове́к-рекла́ма.
sandy ['sændɪ] *adj.* **1.** (*consisting of sand*) песча́ный; (*resembling sand*) песо́чный. **2.** (*~ hair*) рыжева́тый.
sane [seɪn] *adj.* (*opp. mad*) норма́льный, психи́чески здоро́вый; (*sensible*) здра́вый; разу́мный.
sang-froid [sɑ̃'frwɑː] *n.* хладнокро́вие, невозмути́мость.
sanguinary ['sæŋgwɪnərɪ] *adj.* крова́вый; (*bloodthirsty*) кровожа́дный.
sanguine ['sæŋgwɪn] *adj.* **1.** (*of complexion etc.*) румя́ный. **2.** (*optimistic*) оптимисти́ческий; **I am ~ that we shall succeed** я уве́рен в успе́хе.
sanitarium [,sænɪ'teərɪəm] = **sanatorium**
sanitary ['sænɪtərɪ] *adj.* санита́рный, гигиени́ческий; **~ engineering** санте́хника; **~ towel** гигиени́ческая (ма́рлевая) поду́шка; **~ ware** унита́зы (*m. pl.*).
sanitation [,sænɪ'teɪʃ(ə)n] *n.* (*conditions*) санита́рные усло́вия; (*sewage system*) канализацио́нная систе́ма; **the houses had no indoor ~** в дома́х не́ было канализа́ции.
sanity ['sænɪtɪ] *n.* (*mental health*) психи́ческое здоро́вье; (*reasonableness*) здравомы́слие.
Sanskrit ['sænskrɪt] *n.* санскри́т; **in ~** на санскри́те.
adj. санскри́тский.
Santa Claus ['sæntə ,klɔːz] *n.* ≃ Дед Моро́з.
sap[1] [sæp] *n.* (*of plants*) сок.
v.t. (*fig.*): **~ s.o.'s strength** под|рыва́ть, -орва́ть (*or* истощ|а́ть, -и́ть) чьи-н. си́лы.
cpd. **~wood** *n.* за́болонь.
sap[2] [sæp] *n.* (*mil, trench*) са́па; кры́тая транше́я.
v.t. (*mil.*) подк|а́пывать, -опа́ть; (*fig., undermine*) под|рыва́ть, -орва́ть.
sap[3] [sæp] *n.* (*US sl., simpleton*) проста́к.
sapience ['seɪpɪəns] *n.* му́дрость.
sapient ['seɪpɪənt] *adj.* (*wise*) му́дрый.
sapling ['sæplɪŋ] *n.* (*tree*) молодо́е де́ревце.
sapper ['sæpə(r)] *n.* (*mil.*) сапёр; (*pl.*) инжене́рные войска́.
sapphire ['sæfaɪə(r)] *n.* (*stone*) сапфи́р; (*colour*) лазу́рь.
adj. сапфи́рный; лазу́рный, сапфи́ровый.
Saracen ['særəs(ə)n] *n.* сараци́н (*fem.* -ка).
adj. сараци́нский.
sarcasm ['sɑː,kæz(ə)m] *n.* сарка́зм.
sarcastic [sɑː'kæstɪk] *adj.* саркасти́ческий.
sarcoma [sɑː'kəʊmə] *n.* сарко́ма.
sarcophagus [sɑː'kɒfəgəs] *n.* саркофа́г.
sardine [sɑː'diːn] *n.* сарди́н(к)а; **packed like ~s** (наби́ты) как се́льди в бо́чке.
sardonic [sɑː'dɒnɪk] *adj.* сардони́ческий.
sari ['sɑriː] *n.* са́ри (*f. indecl.*).
sartorial [sɑː'tɔːrɪəl] *adj.* (*pert. to tailoring*) портня́жный; **~ elegance** изя́щество в оде́жде.
SAS (*abbr. of* ***Special Air Service***) спецслу́жба ВВС.
sash[1] [sæʃ] *n.* (*round waist*) куша́к, по́яс.
sash[2] [sæʃ] *n.* (*of window*) скользя́щая ра́ма (окна́).
cpd. **~-window** *n.* подъёмное окно́.
Satan ['seɪt(ə)n] *n.* сатана́ (*m.*).
Satanic [sə'tænɪk] *adj.* satани́нский.
satchel ['sætʃ(ə)l] *n.* су́мка, ра́нец.
sate [seɪt] *v.t.* (*liter.*) нас|ыща́ть, -ы́тить; **~d with pleasure** пресы́щенный наслажде́ниями.
sateen [sæ'tiːn] *n.* сати́н.
satellite ['sætə,laɪt] *n.* **1.** (*moon, artefact*) спу́тник; **manned ~** обита́емый спу́тник; **~ dish** спу́тниковая анте́нна; **~ town** го́род-спу́тник; **~ (radio) link-up** радиомо́ст; **~ (TV) link-up** телемо́ст; **~ television broadcasting** косми́ческое телеви́дение. **2.** (*fig.*) сателли́т.
satiate ['seɪʃɪ,eɪt] *v.t.* нас|ыща́ть, -ы́тить.
satiety [sə'taɪɪtɪ] *n.* насыще́ние, сы́тость; (*over abundance*) пресыще́ние.
satin ['sætɪn] *n.* а́тлас.
adj. атла́сный.
cpd. **~wood** *n.* атла́сное де́рево.
satire ['sætaɪə(r)] *n.* сати́ра.
satiric(al) [sə'tɪrɪk(ə)l] *adj.* сатири́ческий.
satirist ['sætərɪst] *n.* сати́рик.
satirize ['sætɪ,raɪz] *v.t.* высме́ивать, вы́смеять.
satisfaction [,sætɪs'fækʃ(ə)n] *n.* **1.** удовлетворе́ние, удовлетворённость; (*pleasure*) удово́льствие; **the work was done to my entire ~** я был по́лностью удовлетворён вы́полненной рабо́той; **I wanted to know for my own ~** я про́сто хоте́л удостове́риться. **2.** (*payment of debt*) упла́та; (*fig.*) распла́та. **3.** (*compensation*) компенса́ция.
satisfactory [,sætɪs'fæktərɪ] *adj.* удовлетвори́тельный, хоро́ший; (*successful*) уда́чный; (*convincing*) убеди́тельный.
satisf|y ['sætɪs,faɪ] *v.t.* **1.** удовлетвор|я́ть, -и́ть; **~y one's hunger** утол|я́ть, -и́ть го́лод; **nothing ~ies him** ниче́м ему́ не угоди́шь; **he ~ied the examiners** он вы́держал экза́мен; **a ~ied customer** дово́льный клие́нт. **2.** (*justify*): **the result ~ied our expectations** результа́т оправда́л на́ши ожида́ния. **3.** (*convince*) убе|жда́ть, -ди́ть; **I ~ied myself of his honesty** я убеди́лся в его́ че́стности. **4.** (*pay*): **~y a debt** пога|ша́ть, -си́ть долг. **5.** (*fulfil*): **~y an obligation** выполня́ть, вы́полнить обяза́тельство. **6.** (*meet*): **~y s.o.'s objections** отв|оди́ть, -ести́ чьи-н. возраже́ния. **7.** (*of food*): **a ~ying lunch** сы́тный обе́д.
saturate ['sætʃə,reɪt, -tjʊ,reɪt] *v.t.* нас|ыща́ть, -ы́тить; **the carpet became ~d with water** ковёр пропита́лся водо́й; **I was ~d** (*wet through*) я весь промо́к.
saturation [,sætʃə'reɪʃ(ə)n, -tjʊ'reɪʃ(ə)n] *n.* насыще́ние, насы́щенность; **~ bombing** площадно́е бомбомета́ние со сплошны́м пораже́нием.
Saturday ['sætə,deɪ, -dɪ] *n.* суббо́та; (*attr.*) суббо́тний; **on ~ evening** в суббо́ту ве́чером.
Saturn ['sæt(ə)n] *n.* (*astron., myth.*) Сату́рн; **~'s rings** ко́льца (*nt. pl.*) Сату́рна.
saturnalia [,sætə'neɪlɪə] *n.* сатурна́лии (*f. pl.*).
saturnine ['sætə,naɪn] *adj.* мра́чный, угрю́мый.
satyr ['sætə(r)] *n.* сати́р.
sauce [sɔːs] *n.* (*cul.*) со́ус; (*coll., impertinence*) де́рзость; **none of your ~!** не дерзи́!
cpds. **~-boat** *n.* со́усник; **~pan** *n.* кастрю́ля.
saucer ['sɔːsə(r)] *n.* блю́дце; **cup and ~** ча́шка с блю́дцем; **flying ~** летя́щее блю́дце.
saucy ['sɔːsɪ] *adj.* де́рзкий, озорно́й; **a ~ little hat** коке́тливая шля́пка.

Saudi Arabia ['saʊdɪ] *n.* Саудовская Аравия.
sauerkraut ['saʊə,kraʊt] *n.* ки́слая/ква́шеная капу́ста.
sauna ['sɔːnə] *n.* са́уна, фи́нская (парна́я) ба́ня.
saunter ['sɔːntə(r)] *n.* прогу́лка.
v.i. идти́ (*det.*) не торопя́сь; ~ **up and down** проха́живаться, прогу́ливаться (*both impf.*).
sausage ['sɒsɪdʒ] *n.* соси́ска; (*large Continental type*) колбаса́.
cpds. **~-meat** *n.* колба́сный фарш; **~-roll** *n.* соси́ска, запечённая в бу́лочке.
sauté ['səʊteɪ] *n.* & *adj.* соте́ (*indecl.*).
savage ['sævɪdʒ] *n.* дика́р|ь (*fem.* -ка).
adj. **1.** (*primitive*) ди́кий, первобы́тный. **2.** (*of animals*: *fierce*) свире́пый. **3.** (*of attack, blow etc.*) жесто́кий, я́ростный.
v.t. (жесто́ко) искуса́ть (*pf.*); (*fig.*) растерза́ть (*pf.*).
savagery ['sævɪdʒrɪ] *n.* ди́кость; свире́пость; жесто́кость.
savanna(h) [sə'vænə] *n.* сава́нна.
savant ['sæv(ə)nt, sæ'vɑ̃] *n.* (кру́пный) учёный.
sav|e [seɪv] *n.* (*football etc.*): **the goalkeeper made a brilliant ~e** врата́рь блестя́ще отби́л уда́р.
v.t. **1.** (*rescue, deliver*) спас|а́ть, -ти́; изб|авля́ть, -а́вить; **he ~ed my life** он спас мне жизнь; **she was ~ed from drowning** её во́время вы́тащили из воды́; **he ~ed the situation** он спас положе́ние; (*protect, preserve*): **God ~e the Queen!** Бо́же, храни́ короле́ву!; **~e face** сохрани́ть/спасти́ (*pf.*) лицо́. **2.** (*put by*) бере́чь, с-; от|кла́дывать, -ложи́ть; копи́ть, на-; **~e me something to eat!** оста́вьте мне что́-нибудь пое́сть!; (*collect*) соб|ира́ть, -ра́ть; (*avoid using or spending*) эконо́мить, с-; **~e expense** избе|га́ть, -жа́ть затра́т; (*obviate need for, expense of etc.*): **that will ~e me £100** я сэконо́млю на э́том сто фу́нтов; **it ~ed me a lot of time** э́то мне сберегло́ мно́го вре́мени; **I ~ed him the trouble of replying** я изба́вил его́ от необходи́мости отвеча́ть.
v.i. эконо́мить, с-; **he is ~ing up for a bicycle** он откла́дывает/ко́пит де́ньги на велосипе́д.
prep. (*liter.*) кро́ме+*g.*; без+*g.*; **all the men ~e one** все кро́ме одного́ (челове́ка).
saver ['seɪvə(r)] *n.* (*investor*) вкла́дчик.
saving ['seɪvɪŋ] *n.* **1.** (*salvation, rescue*) спасе́ние. **2.** (*economy*) эконо́мия; **a ~ of millions of pounds** эконо́мия в миллио́ны фу́нтов. **3.** (*pl., money laid by*) сбереже́ния (*nt. pl.*); **~s bank** сберега́тельная ка́сса; **he had to draw on his ~s** ему́ пришло́сь прибе́гнуть к свои́м сбереже́ниям.
adj. (*salutary*) спаси́тельный; ~ **grace** (*fig.*) положи́тельное/спаси́тельное сво́йство.
saviour ['seɪvjə(r)] *n.* спаси́тель (*m.*).
savoir-faire [,sævwɑː 'feə(r)] *n.* сметли́вость.
savour ['seɪvə(r)] *n.* (*lit., fig.*) при́вкус.
v.t. (*enjoy*) смакова́ть (*impf., pf.*).
savoury ['seɪvərɪ] *adj.* пика́нтный, о́стрый; (*fig.*): **a not very ~ district** неприглядный райо́н.
savoy [sə'vɔɪ] *n.*: ~ **(cabbage)** саво́йская капу́ста.
savvy ['sævɪ] *n.* смека́лка (*coll.*).
v.i.: **~?** поня́тно?; дошло́?
saw[1] [sɔː] *n.* (*tool*) пила́.
v.t. пили́ть (*impf.*); распи́л|ивать, -и́ть.
v.i. пили́ть (*impf.*); **this wood ~s easily** э́то де́рево хорошо́ пи́лится.
with advs.: ~ **off** *v.t.* отпи́л|ивать, -и́ть; **~n-off shotgun** обре́з; ~ **up** *v.t.* распи́л|ивать, -и́ть.
cpds. **~-blade** *n.* полотно́ пилы́; **~dust** *n.* опи́л|ки (*pl., g.* -ок); **~mill** *n.* лесопи́лка; лесопи́льный заво́д.
saw[2] [sɔː] *n.* (*maxim*) посло́вица, поговорка.
sawyer ['sɔːjə(r)] *n.* пи́льщик.
saxifrage ['sæksɪ,freɪdʒ] *n.* камнело́мка.
Saxon ['sæks(ə)n] *n.* (*hist.*) сакс.
adj. саксо́нский.
saxophone ['sæksə,fəʊn] *n.* саксофо́н.
say [seɪ] *n.* (*expression of opinion*): **let s.o. have his ~** да|ва́ть, -ть кому́-н. вы́сказаться; **he likes to have a ~** он хо́чет, что́бы счита́лись с его́ мне́нием.
v.t. & *i.* **1.** говори́ть, сказа́ть; **would you ~ I was right?** как по-ва́шему, я прав?; ~ **a good word for** замо́лвить (*pf.*) слове́чко за+*a.*; **as much as to ~** как бы говоря́; **he said as much** он приме́рно так и сказа́л; **how do you ~ this in English?** как э́то сказа́ть по-англи́йски?; **I'll have something to ~ to you about this** на э́тот счёт я име́ю вам ко́е-что сказа́ть; **she is said to he rich** говоря́т, она́ бога́та; **there is much to be said on both sides** здесь мо́жно мно́го сказа́ть и за и про́тив; **there is no more to be said** бо́льше не́чего сказа́ть; ~ **no more!, enough said!** (*coll.*) (всё) поня́тно!; я́сно!; **what have you got to ~ for yourself?** что вы мо́жете сказа́ть в своё оправда́ние?; **he has plenty to ~ for himself** у него́ хорошо́ подве́шен язы́к; **there's no ~ing where they might be** кто зна́ет, где они́ (нахо́дятся); **I dare ~** пожа́луй, наве́рное; **how can you ~ such a thing?** как вы мо́жете так(о́е) говори́ть?; **I wouldn't (go so far as to) ~ that** э́того я бы не сказа́л; **didn't I ~ so?** а я что сказа́л?; **I'll ~!** (*coll.*) (*yes indeed*) ещё бы!; **you said it!; you can ~ that again!** (*coll.*) вот и́менно!; ещё бы!; **you don't ~ (so)!** (*coll.*) неуже́ли?; не мо́жет быть!; ~ **when!** скажи́те, когда́ дово́льно!; **when all is said and done** в конце́ концо́в, в коне́чном счёте; **it ~s something for him that he apologized** то, что он извини́лся, говори́т в его́ по́льзу; ~ **you are sorry!** проси́ прощения!; ~ **good-morning to s.o.** здоро́ваться, по- с кем-н.; **that is to ~** (*in other words*) то есть; ина́че говоря́; **so to ~** так сказа́ть; **I ~!** (**US ~!**) (*attracting attention*) послу́шай(те)!; зна́ете что?; (*expr. surprise*) смотри́те!; поду́майте!; **so he ~s** е́сли ему́ ве́рить; **it goes without ~ing** (само́ собо́й) разуме́ется; слов нет; **to ~ nothing of** (*not to mention*) не говоря́ (уж) о+*p.*; **well said!** хорошо́ ска́зано!. **2.** (*suppose, assume*): **(let's) ~; shall we ~** ска́жем; допу́стим; (*for instance*) наприме́р; к приме́ру; ~ **it were true** предполо́жим, что так. **3.** (*of inanimate objects*: *state, indicate*): **what does it ~ in the instructions?** как говори́тся в инстру́кции?; **the Bible ~s** в би́блии говори́тся/напи́сано; **the signpost ~s London** на указа́теле напи́сано «Ло́ндон»; **the clock ~s 5 o'clock** часы́ пока́зывают пять; **the notice ~s the museum is closed** объявле́ние гласи́т, что музе́й закры́т. **4.** (*formulate, express*): ~ **a prayer** произнести́ (*pf.*) моли́тву; ~ **mass** служи́ть, от- обе́дню. **5.** (*of reactions*): ~ **yes** (*agree*) **to sth.** согла|ша́ться, -си́ться на что-н.; ~ **yes** (*accept invitation*) приня́ть (*pf.*) приглаше́ние; (*grant request*) дать (*pf.*) согла́сие; ~ **no** (*refuse invitation*) отказа́ться (*pf.*) от приглаше́ния; (*refuse request*) отказа́ть(ся) (*pf.*); **what do you ~ to a glass of beer?** как насчёт кру́жечки пи́ва?; **what would you ~ to a game of cards?** а не сыгра́ть ли нам в ка́рты?
saying ['seɪɪŋ] *n.* (*adage*) погово́рка; **as the ~ goes** как говори́тся; (*utterance*): **the ~s of Confucius** выска́зывания (*nt. pl.*) Конфу́ция.
sc. ['saɪlɪ,set, 'skiːlɪ,ket] = **scilicet**
scab [skæb] *n.* струп; (*coll., blackleg*) штрейкбре́хер.
scabbard ['skæbəd] *n.* но́ж|ны (*pl., g.* -ен).
scabby ['skæbɪ] *adj.* (*covered with scabs*) покры́тый стру́пьями.
scabies ['skeɪbiːz] *n.* чесо́тка.
scaffold ['skæfəʊld, -f(ə)ld] *n.* **1.** эшафо́т; **die on the ~** пог|иба́ть, -и́бнуть на эшафо́те. **2.** = **~ing**
v.t. обстр|а́ивать, -о́ить леса́ми.
scaffolding ['skæfəʊldɪŋ, -fəldɪŋ] *n.* лес|а́ (*pl., g.* -о́в).
scald [skɔːld, skɒld] *n.* ожо́г.

v.t. **1.** ошпа́ри|вать, -ть; **~ing water** круто́й кипято́к; **the tea was ~ing hot** чай был обжига́юще горя́чий. **2. ~ milk** подогр|ева́ть, -е́ть молоко́, не доводя́ до кипе́ния.

scale[1] [skeɪl] *n.* **1.** (*of fish, reptile etc.*) чешу́йка; (*pl., collect.*) чешуя́. **2.** (*on teeth*) ка́мень (*m.*).

v.t.: **~ a fish** чи́стить, по- ры́бу.

cpd. **~-armour** *n.* пласти́нчатая броня́.

scale[2] [skeɪl] *n.* **1.** (*of balance*) ча́ш(к)а (весо́в); **turn the ~** (*lit.*); **he turned the ~ at 80 kg** он ве́сил во́семьдесят килогра́ммов; (*fig.*): **this battle turned the ~ in our favour** э́то сраже́ние склони́ло ча́шу весо́в в на́шу сто́рону. **2.** (*pl., weighing machine*) вес|ы́ (*pl., g.* -о́в).

scale[3] [skeɪl] *n.* **1.** (*grading*) шкала́; **~ of charges** шкала́ расце́нок; **centigrade ~** шкала́ Це́льсия; **social ~** обще́ственная ле́стница. **2.** (*of map, and fig.*) масшта́б; **draw sth. to ~** черти́ть, на- что-н. в масшта́бе; **~ drawing** масшта́бный чертёж; **on a large/small ~** в большо́м/ма́лом масшта́бе. **3.** (*size*) разме́р. **4.** (*mus.*) га́мма; **practise one's ~s** разы́гр|ывать, -а́ть га́ммы.

v.t. **1.** (*climb*): **~ a wall** влез|а́ть, -ть на сте́ну; **~ a mountain** вз|бира́ться, -обра́ться на́ гору.

with advs.: **~ down** *v.t.* пон|ижа́ть, -и́зить; ум|еньша́ть, -е́ньшить; **~ up** *v.t.* пов|ыша́ть, -ы́сить; увели́чи|вать, -ть.

scalene ['skeɪli:n] *adj.* неравносторо́нний.

scallion ['skæljən] *n.* лук-шало́т.

scallop ['skæləp, 'skɒl-] *n.* (*mollusc*) гребешо́к; (*ornamental edging*) фесто́н.

v.t. отде́л|ывать, -ать фесто́нами.

cpd. **~-shell** *n.* ра́ковина гребешка́.

scallywag ['skælɪ,wæg] *n.* негодя́й; озорни́к.

scalp [skælp] *n.* ко́жа головы́; (*American Indian trophy*) скальп.

v.t. скальпи́ровать (*impf., pf.*).

scalpel ['skælp(ə)l] *n.* ска́льпель (*m.*).

scalper ['skælpə(r)] *n.* спекуля́нт.

scaly ['skeɪlɪ] *adj.* чешу́йчатый.

scam [skæm] *n.* (*sl.*) обма́н.

scamp [skæmp] *n.* шалу́н, пове́са (*m.*).

scamper ['skæmpə(r)] *n.* (*quick run*) поспе́шное бе́гство.

v.i. бе́гать (*indet.*); **the dog ~ed off** соба́ка отскочи́ла.

scampi ['skæmpɪ] *n.* креве́тки (*f. pl.*).

scan [skæn] *v.t.* **1.** (*survey*) обв|оди́ть, -ести́ взгля́дом; (*stare at*) при́стально смотре́ть (*impf.*) на+*a.*; (*glance through*) пробе|га́ть, -жа́ть (глаза́ми). **2.** (*comput., med.*) скани́ровать (*impf.*).

v.i. (*pros.*) сканди́роваться (*impf.*).

scandal ['skænd(ə)l] *n.* (*disgrace*) сканда́л, безобра́зие; (*malicious gossip*) спле́тни (*f. pl.*); **create a ~, give rise to ~** вызыва́ть, вы́звать возмуще́ние; **it is a ~** э́то безобра́зие; **talk ~** спле́тничать (*impf.*).

scandalize ['skændə,laɪz] *v.t.* шоки́ровать (*impf.*).

scandalmonger ['skænd(ə)l,mʌŋgə(r)] *n.* спле́тни|к (*fem.* -ца).

scandalous ['skændələs] *adj.* позо́рный, безобра́зный, возмути́тельный.

Scandinavia [,skændɪ'neɪvɪə] *n.* Скандина́вия.

Scandinavian [,skændɪ'neɪvɪən] *n.* скандина́в (*fem.* -ка).

adj. скандина́вский.

scanner ['skænə(r)] *n.* (*comput., med.*) ска́нер.

scant [skænt] *adj.* (*inadequate*) недоста́точный; (*meagre*) ску́дный; **with ~ regard for my feelings** не счита́ясь с мои́ми чу́вствами.

scanty ['skæntɪ] *adj.* ску́дный (*see also* **scant**); **~ attire** ску́дная оде́жда; **~ attendance** плоха́я посеща́емость.

scapegoat ['skeɪpgəʊt] *n.* козёл отпуще́ния.

scar [skɑ:(r)] *n.* шрам, рубе́ц; (*fig.*) след.

v.t. (*mark with ~*) ра́нить, из-; **a face ~red with smallpox** лицо́, изры́тое о́спой.

v.i. (*form ~*) зарубц|о́вываться, -ева́ться.

scarab ['skærəb] *n.* скарабе́й.

scarce [skeəs] *adj.* (*insufficient*) недоста́точный; (*scanty*) ску́дный; (*rare*) ре́дкий; **coal is ~ here** у́голь здесь в дефици́те; **butter was ~ during the war** во вре́мя войны́ не хвата́ло ма́сла; **make o.s. ~** (*coll., make off*) уб|ира́ться, -ра́ться.

scarcely ['skeəslɪ] *adv.* **1.** (*barely*) едва́; почти́ не; **I ~ know him** я его́ почти́ не зна́ю; (*only just*) то́лько; **I had ~ entered the room when the bell rang** то́лько я вошёл в ко́мнату, как зазвони́л телефо́н. **2.** (*surely not*): **you can ~ believe her** неуже́ли вы ей ве́рите?; **I ~ know what to say** пра́во, я не зна́ю, что сказа́ть.

scarcity ['skeəsɪtɪ] *n.* **1.** (*insufficiency, dearth*) недоста́ток, нехва́тка, дефици́т. **2.** (*rarity*) ре́дкость.

scare [skeə(r)] *n.* (*fright*) испу́г; **give s.o. a ~** пуга́ть, ис- кого́-н.; (*alarm, panic*) па́ника; **the news created a ~** но́вость вы́звала па́нику.

v.t. пуга́ть, ис-; **I felt ~d** я боя́лся; **they were ~ stiff** они́ до́ смерти перепуга́лись.

v.i. пуга́ться.

with advs.: **~ away, ~ off** *vv.t.* спугну́ть (*pf.*).

cpds. **~crow** *n.* пу́гало, (огоро́дное) чу́чело; **~monger** *n.* пани́кёр (*fem.* -ша).

scarf [skɑ:f] *n.* шарф.

scarify ['skeərɪ,faɪ] *v.t.* (*surg., agric.*) скарифици́ровать (*impf., pf.*); (*fig., criticize*) жесто́ко раскритикова́ть (*pf.*).

scarlet ['skɑ:lɪt] *n.* а́лый цвет.

adj. а́лый; **turn ~** (*blush*) гу́сто покрасне́ть (*pf.*); **~ fever** скарлати́на.

scarper ['skɑ:pə(r)] *v.i.* (*coll.*) = **scram**

scary ['skeərɪ] *adj.* (*coll.*) (*frightening*) жу́ткий.

scathing ['skeɪðɪŋ] *adj.* ре́зкий, е́дкий, язви́тельный.

scatter ['skætə(r)] *v.t.* **1.** (*throw here and there*) разбр|а́сывать, -оса́ть; (*sprinkle*) расс|ыпа́ть, -ы́пать; **toys were ~ed all over the room** игру́шки бы́ли разбро́саны по всей ко́мнате. **2.** (*pass.*): **the area is ~ed with small hamlets** по э́той ме́стности полно́ ма́леньких дереву́шек; **~ed villages** раски́данные (там и тут) сёла. **3.** (*lit., fig., drive away, disperse*) раз|гоня́ть, -огна́ть; рассе́|ивать, -ять; **a shot ~ed the birds** вы́стрел распуга́л птиц; **a thinly ~ed population** ре́дкое населе́ние.

v.i. (*disperse*) расс|ыпа́ться, -ы́паться; рассе́|иваться, -яться; (*move off*) ра|сходи́ться, -зойти́сь; **the crowd ~ed** толпа́ разбежа́лась.

cpds. **~-brain** *n.* вертопра́х; **~-brained** *adj.* ве́треный.

scavenge ['skævɪndʒ] *v.i.* ры́ться (*impf.*) в отбро́сах; ходи́ть (*impf.*) по помо́йкам.

scavenger ['skævɪndʒə(r)] *n.* (*animal*) живо́тное, пита́ющееся па́далью; (*bird*) стервя́тник; (*pers.*) му́сорщик.

scenario [sɪ'nɑ:rɪəʊ, -'neərɪəʊ] *n.* сцена́рий; **a worst-case ~** наиху́дший вариа́нт *or* сцена́рий.

scene [si:n] *n.* **1.** (*stage*) сце́на; (*fig.*): **appear on the ~** появ|ля́ться, -и́ться; **quit the ~** сойти́ (*pf.*) со сце́ны. **2.** (*place of action*) ме́сто де́йствия; **the ~ is laid in London** де́йствие происхо́дит в Ло́ндоне. **3.** (*place*) ме́сто; **the ~ of the crime** ме́сто преступле́ния; **~ of operations** (*mil.*) теа́тр вое́нных де́йствий; **change of ~** переме́на обстано́вки. **4.** (*subdivision of play*) сце́на; (*fig., episode, incident*): **~s of country life** сце́ны из се́льской жи́зни; **make a ~** устр|а́ивать, -о́ить сце́ну (*кому*). **5.** (*set, décor*) декора́ция; (*fig.*): **behind the ~s** за кули́сами. **6.** (*view, landscape*): **a ~ of destruction** карти́на разруше́ния. **7.** (*milieu*): **(on) the pop music ~** в ми́ре поп-му́зыки.

scenery ['si:nərɪ] *n.* (*theatr.*) декора́ции (*f. pl.*); (*landscape*) пейза́ж, вид.

scenic ['si:nɪk] *adj.* сцени́ческий, театра́льный; живопи́сный; ~ **beauty** живопи́сность (ландша́фта).

scent [sent] *n.* **1.** (*odour*) за́пах, арома́т. **2.** (*perfume*) дух|и́ (*pl.*, *g.* -о́в); **use, apply** ~ души́ться, на-. **3.** (*sense of smell*; *lit.*, *fig.*) чутьё, нюх. **4.** (*trail*) след; **pick up the** ~ нап|ада́ть, -а́сть на след; (*fig.*): **he threw the police off the** ~ он сбил поли́цию со сле́да.

v.t. **1.** (*discern by smell*; *also fig.*) чу́ять, по-. **2.** (*impart odour to*): **roses** ~ **the air** ро́зы распространя́ют благоуха́ние; **a** ~**ed rose** благоуха́нная ро́за; ~**ed soap** души́стое мы́ло.

cpds. ~**-bottle** *n.* пузырёк/флако́н (для) духо́в; ~**-spray** *n.* духи́-спре́й (*indecl.*), духи́ в аэрозо́ле.

sceptic ['skeptɪk] (*US* **skeptic**) *n.* ске́птик.

sceptical ['skeptɪk(ə)l] (*US* **skeptical**) *adj.* скепти́ческий; скепти́чески настро́енный (к+*d.*).

scepticism ['skeptɪˌsɪz(ə)m] (*US* **skepticism**) *n.* скептици́зм.

sceptre ['septə(r)] *n.* ски́петр.

schadenfreude ['ʃɑ:dənˌfrɔɪdə] *n.* злора́дство.

schedule ['ʃedju:l, 'ske-] *n.* **1.** (*list*) спи́сок, пе́речень (*m.*); ~ **of charges** тари́ф ста́вок. **2.** (*plan, timetable*) план, расписа́ние; **work** ~ гра́фик рабо́ты; **according to** ~ соотве́тственно пла́ну; **a full** ~ больша́я програ́мма; **be behind** ~ зап|а́здывать, -озда́ть; **be ahead of** ~ опере|жа́ть, -ди́ть гра́фик; **before** ~ ра́ньше вре́мени; **on** ~ во́время/то́чно.

v.t. **1.** (*tabulate*) сост|авля́ть, -а́вить спи́сок +*g.*; **a** ~**d flight** регуля́рный рейс. **2.** (*time*; *plan*) рассчи́т|ывать, -а́ть; **we are** ~**d to finish by May** по пла́ну мы должны́ ко́нчить к ма́ю; **the train is** ~**d to leave at noon** (по расписа́нию) по́езд отхо́дит в по́лдень.

schematic [skɪ'mætɪk, ski:-] *adj.* схемати́ческий.

schem|e [ski:m] *n.* **1.** (*arrangement*) поря́док; **in the** ~**e of things** в поря́дке веще́й; **colour** ~**e** сочета́ние кра́сок. **2.** (*plan*) прое́кт, план. **3.** (*plot*) про́иск|и (*pl.*, *g.* -ов), за́мысел.

v.i. интригова́ть (*impf.*); **they were** ~**ing for power** они́ плели́ интри́ги, что́бы пробра́ться к вла́сти.

schemer ['ski:mə(r)] *n.* интрига́н (*fem.* -ка).

scherzo ['skeəˌtsəʊ] *n.* ске́рцо (*indecl.*).

schism ['sɪz(ə)m, 'skɪ-] *n.* раско́л; схи́зма.

schismatic [sɪz'mætɪk, skɪz-] *adj.* раско́льнический.

schist [ʃɪst] *n.* сла́нец.

schizoid ['skɪtsɔɪd] *n.* шизо́ид.

adj. шизо́идный.

schizophrenia [ˌskɪtsə'fri:nɪə] *n.* шизофрени́я.

schizophrenic [ˌskɪtsə'frenɪk, -'fri:nɪk] *n.* шизофре́н|ик (*fem.* -и́чка).

adj. шизофрени́ческий.

schnitzel ['ʃnɪtz(ə)l] *n.* шни́цель (*m.*).

scholar ['skɒlə(r)] *n.* **1.** (*learned person*) учёный-гуманита́р. **2.** (*learner*) учени́к. **3.** (*holder of* ~*ship*) стипендиа́т (*fem.* -ка).

scholarly ['skɒləlɪ] *adj.* учёный, академи́ческий; **he has a** ~ **mind** у него́ нау́чный склад ума́.

scholarship ['skɒləʃɪp] *n.* (*erudition*) учёность, эруди́ция; (*scholarly method or outlook*) нау́чный подхо́д; (*grant*) стипе́ндия.

scholastic [skə'læstɪk] *adj.* академи́ческий; ~ **institution** учёбное заведе́ние.

school[1] [sku:l] *n.* **1.** (*place of education*) шко́ла; (*incl. higher education*) учёбное заведе́ние; **at** ~ в шко́ле; **go to** ~ ходи́ть (*indet.*) в шко́лу; учи́ться (*impf.*) в шко́ле; **start** ~ поступ|а́ть, -и́ть в шко́лу; **leave** ~ (*complete course*) конча́ть, ко́нчить шко́лу; **where were you at** ~? где вы учи́лись?; **of** ~ **age** шко́льного во́зраста; ~ **fees** пла́та за обуче́ние; ~ **report** шко́льный та́бель; **boarding** ~ шко́ла-интерна́т; **public** ~ (*in UK*) ча́стная шко́ла; (*in US*) (бесплатная) сре́дняя шко́ла; **nursery** ~ де́тский сад; **primary** ~ нача́льная шко́ла; **secondary** ~ сре́дняя шко́ла; **evening, night** ~ вече́рняя шко́ла; **military** ~ вое́нное учи́лище; **vocational** ~ профессиона́льно-техни́ческое учи́лище; (*department of university, branch of study*): ~ **of law** юриди́ческий факульте́т. **2.** (*lessons*) заня́тия (*nt. pl.*); **there will be no** ~ **today** сего́дня уро́ков не бу́дет; ~ **finishes at 4** заня́тия/уро́ки конча́ются в 4. **3.** (*range of classes*): **the lower/middle/upper** ~ мла́дшие/сре́дние/ста́ршие кла́ссы (*m. pl.*). **4.** (*of art, manners etc.*): **the Impressionist** ~ импрессионисти́ческая шко́ла; **he is one of the old** ~ он челове́к ста́рой шко́лы (*or* ста́рого зака́ла); **there is a** ~ **of thought which says ...** существу́ет тече́ние, согла́сно кото́рому.... **5.** (*attr.*) шко́льный, учёбный. *See also cpds.*

v.t. обуч|а́ть, -и́ть.

cpds. ~**-book** *n.* учёбник; ~**boy** *n.* шко́льник; ~**certificate** *n.* аттеста́т зре́лости; ~**children** *n.* шко́льники (*m. pl.*); ~**fellow,** ~**mate** *nn.* соучени́|к (*fem.* -ца); ~**girl** *n.* шко́льница; ~**-leaver** *n.* выпускни́|к (*fem.* -ца); ~**-leaving** *adj.* ~**leaving age** во́зраст, до кото́рого обуче́ние обяза́тельно; ~**master** *n.* учи́тель (*m.*); ~**mate** *n.* = ~**fellow;** ~**mistress** *n.* учи́тельница; ~**pupil** *n.* учени́|к (*fem.* -ца); шко́льни|к (*fem.* -ца); ~**room** *n.* класс; кла́ссная ко́мната; ~**teacher** *n.* учи́тель (*fem.* -ница); ~**teaching** *n.* (*as profession*) педаго́гика; (*activity*) преподава́ние; ~**-time** *n.* (*lesson-time*) учёбное вре́мя.

school[2] [sku:l] *n.* (*of fish etc.*) кося́к.

schooling ['sku:lɪŋ] *n.* (*education*) (об)уче́ние; (*training*) подгото́вка; **he had little** ~ ему́ не довело́сь мно́го учи́ться.

schooner ['sku:nə(r)] *n.* (*naut.*) шху́на; (*glass*) бока́л.

sciatic [saɪ'ætɪk] *adj.* седа́лищный.

sciatica [saɪ'ætɪkə] *n.* и́шиас.

science ['saɪəns] *n.* **1.** (*systematic knowledge*) нау́ка; **pure/applied** ~ чи́стая/прикладна́я нау́ка; **social** ~ обще́ственные нау́ки. **2.** (*natural* ~*s*) есте́ственные нау́ки; ~ **fiction** нау́чная фанта́стика.

scientific [ˌsaɪən'tɪfɪk] *adj.* нау́чный; ~ **calculator** компью́тер-калькуля́тор.

scientist ['saɪəntɪst] *n.* учёный(-есте́ственник).

scilicet ['saɪlɪˌset, 'ski:lɪˌket] *adv.* (*abbr. of* ***scire licet***) т.е., (то есть).

scimitar ['sɪmɪtə(r)] *n.* ятага́н.

scintilla [sɪn'tɪlə] *n.* (*fig.*) чу́точка, ка́пля; **there is not a** ~ **of evidence** нет никаки́х доказа́тельств.

scintillat|e ['sɪntɪˌleɪt] *v.i.* (*lit., fig.*) и́скри́ться (*impf.*); блиста́ть (*impf.*).

scion ['saɪən] *n.* (*descendant*) о́тпрыск, пото́мок.

scissor|s ['sɪzəz] *n.* но́жниц|ы (*pl.*, *g.* —).

sclerosis [sklɪə'rəʊsɪs] *n.* склеро́з; **multiple** ~ рассе́янный склеро́з.

sclerotic [sklɪə'rɒtɪk] *adj.* склероти́ческий.

scoff[1] [skɒf] *v.i.* смея́ться (*impf.*); ~ **at** издева́ться/насмеха́ться (*both impf.*) над+*i.*; **be** ~**ed at** быть подверга́ться (*impf.*) насме́шкам; **he was** ~**ed at** над ним смея́лись.

scoff[2] [skɒf] *n.* (*food*) жратва́ (*sl.*).

v.t. & i. жрать, со-.

scold [skəʊld] *v.t.* брани́ть, вы́-; руга́ть, об-.

v.i. брани́ться, ворча́ть, брюзжа́ть (*all impf.*).

scolding ['skəʊldɪŋ] *n.* брань; **I gave him a good** ~ я дал ему́ хоро́ший нагоня́й.

scone [skɒn, skəʊn] *n.* ≃ бу́лочка.

scoop [sku:p] *n.* **1.** (*for grain etc.*) сово́к; (*for liquids*) ковш; (*for food*) ло́жка. **2.** (*journ.*) ≃ сенса́ция.

v.t. **1.** (*lift with* ~) че́рп|ать, -ну́ть; заче́рп|ывать, -ну́ть; вычёрпывать, вы́черпать. **2.** (*make by* ~*ing*) выда́лбливать, вы́долбить; **he ~ed out a hole in the sand** он вы́рыл я́му в песке́. **3.** (*make a profit of*) срыва́ть, сорва́ть куш. **4.** (*journ.*) обст|авля́ть, -а́вить.

scoot [sku:t] *v.i.* уд|ира́ть, -ра́ть (*coll.*).

scooter ['sku:tə(r)] *n.* самока́т; (*motor* ~) моторо́ллер.

scope [skəʊp] *n.* **1.** (*range, sweep*) разма́х, охва́т; **this is beyond the ~ of our enquiry** э́то выхо́дит за преде́лы/ра́мки на́шего рассле́дования. **2.** (*outlet, vent*): **the game offers ~ for the children's imagination** э́та игра́ даёт просто́р де́тскому воображе́нию; **the project provided ~ for his abilities** э́тот прое́кт дал ему́ возмо́жность разверну́ть свои́ спосо́бности.

scorch [skɔ:tʃ] *v.t.* (*burn, dry up*) жечь, с-; **~ed earth policy** страте́гия вы́жженной земли́; (*clothes etc.*) подпа́л|ивать, -и́ть.

cpd. **~-mark** *n.* подпа́лина, ожо́г.

score [skɔ:(r)] *n.* **1.** (*notch*) зару́бка; (*deep scratch*) глубо́кая цара́пина; (*weal on skin*) рубе́ц. **2.** (*arch., account*) счёт; **pay off old ~s** (*fig.*) св|оди́ть, -ести́ ста́рые счёты. **3.** (*in games*) счёт; **what's the ~?** како́й счёт?; **keep the ~** вести́ (*det.*) счёт; **know the ~** (*fig., coll.*) быть в ку́рсе; знать (*impf.*), что к чему́. **4.** (*mus.*): **(full) ~** партиту́ра; **piano ~** па́ртия фортепиа́но. **5.** (*twenty*) два́дцать; **~s of people** мно́жество наро́ду. **6.** (*grounds*) причи́на, по́вод; **you need have no fear on that ~** на э́то счёт вы мо́жете не беспоко́иться.

v.t. **1.** (*notch*) изре́з|ывать, -ать; (*incise*): **~ a line** провести́ (*pf.*) ли́нию (ножо́м *и т.п.*); **~ out, through** вычёркивать, вы́черкнуть; (*preparatory to cutting*) разм|еча́ть, -е́тить. **2.** (*win*) выи́грывать, вы́играть; **~ a goal** (*football*) заб|ива́ть, -и́ть гол; **a goal ~s six points** за оди́н гол засчи́тывается 6 очко́в. **4.** (*mus., orchestrate*) оркестрова́ть (*impf., pf.*).

v.i. **1.** (*keep score*) вести́ (*impf.*) счёт; (*win point*) выи́грывать, вы́играть очко́. **2.** (*secure advantage; have good luck*) выи́грывать, вы́играть.

cpds. **~-keeper** *n.* судья́-секрета́рь (*m.*); **~-sheet** *n.* суде́йский протоко́л.

scorer ['skɔ:rə(r)] *n.* **1.** (*keeper of score*) счётчик. **2.**: **the captain was the ~ of that goal** тот гол заби́л капита́н.

scorn [skɔ:n] *n.* презре́ние.

v.t. презира́ть (*impf.*); пренебр|ега́ть, -е́чь +*i.*

scornful ['skɔ:nfʊl] *adj.* (*of pers.*) надме́нный; **he was ~ of the idea** он отнёсся к э́той иде́е с презре́нием; (*of glance etc.*) презри́тельный.

Scorpio ['skɔ:pɪəʊ] *n.* Скорпио́н.

scorpion ['skɔ:pɪən] *n.* скорпио́н.

Scot [skɒt] *n.* шотла́нд|ец (*fem.* -ка).

Scotch[1] [skɒtʃ] *n.* (*whisky*) шотла́ндское ви́ски (*indecl.*).

adj. шотла́ндский; ~ (*propr.*) **tape** кле́йкая ле́нта, скотч.

scotch[2] [skɒtʃ] *v.t.* (*fig.*): **he ~ed the rumour** он опрове́рг слух.

scot-free ['skɒtfri:] *adv.*: **go ~** (*unpunished*) ост|ава́ться, -а́ться безнака́занным.

Scotland [ˌskɒtlənd] *n.* Шотла́ндия.

Scots [skɒts] *n. adj.* шотла́ндский.

cpds. **~man** *n.* шотла́ндец; **~woman** *n.* шотла́ндка.

Scottish ['skɒtɪʃ] *adj.* шотла́ндский.

scoundrel ['skaʊndr(ə)l] *n.* подле́ц, мерза́вец.

scour[1] ['skaʊə(r)] *n.* (*cleansing*) чи́стка; **give sth. a good ~** вы́чистить (*pf.*) что-н. хороше́нько.

v.t. **1.** (*cleanse*): **~ a saucepan** чи́стить, вы́- кастрю́лю; **~ a dish** нач|ища́ть, -и́стить блю́до. **2.** (*remove by ~ing; also* **~ away, off**) отт|ира́ть, -ере́ть.

scour[2] ['skaʊə(r)] *v.t.* (*range in search or pursuit*) ры́скать, об-; **he ~ed the town for his daughter** он обе́гал весь го́род в по́исках до́чери.

scourer ['skaʊrə(r)] *n.* (*for saucepans etc.*) металли́ческая моча́лка.

scourge [skɜ:dʒ] *n.* бич.

v.t. (*flog*) сечь, вы́-; (*chastise*) кара́ть, по-.

scout [skaʊt] *n.* **1.** (*mil.*) разве́дчик (*also ship, aircraft*); **~ car** разве́дывательный автомоби́ль. **2.** (*Boy S~*) бойска́ут.

v.i. (*reconnoitre*) разве́дывать (*impf.*); **he is out ~ing** он в разве́дке; (*coll., search*) разы́скивать (*impf.*); (*belong to S~ movement*): **my son is keen on ~ing** мой сын увлека́ется бойска́утской де́ятельностью.

cpd. **~master** *n.* нача́льник отря́да бойска́утов.

scowl [skaʊl] *n.* серди́тый/хму́рый взгляд.

v.i.: **he ~ed at me** он свире́по посмотре́л на меня́; **a ~ing face** хму́рое лицо́; хму́риться, на-.

Scrabble[1] ['skræb(ə)l] *n.* (*propr.*) скрэбл (≃ Эруди́т).

scrabble[2] ['skræb(ə)l] *v.i.*: **~ about** ша́рить (*impf.*); **~ about for sth.** разы́скивать (*impf.*) что-н.

scram [skræm] *v.i.* (*sl.*): **I told him to ~** я веле́л ему́ убира́ться; **~!** прова́ливай!; кати́сь!

scramble ['skræmb(ə)l] *n.* **1.** (*climb with hands and feet*) кара́бканье. **2.** (*motor cycle race*) мотокро́сс. **3.** (*struggle to get sth.*) сва́лка; (*fig.*) борьба́, схва́тка; **there was a ~ for the ball** произошла́ схва́тка/борьба́ за мяч.

v.t.: **~ eggs** жа́рить, под- я́ичницу-болту́нью.

v.i. **1.** (*clamber*) кара́бкаться, вс-; вз|бира́ться, -обра́ться; **the boys ~d over the wall** ма́льчики переле́зли че́рез забо́р. **2.** (*fig.*) боро́ться (*impf.*).

scrap[1] [skræp] *n.* **1.** (*small piece*) кусо́чек; (*of metal*) обло́мок; (*of cloth*) обре́зок; лоску́т; (*fragment*) обры́вок; **~s of paper** клочки́ (*m. pl.*) бума́ги. **2.** (*pl., waste food*) объе́дк|и (*pl., g.* -ов); **they found a few ~s of food** они́ нашли́ ко́е-каки́е оста́тки пи́щи. **3.** (*waste material, refuse*) ути́ль (*m.*); утильсырьё; (*~ metal*) металлоло́м.

v.t. **1.** (*make into ~*) обра|ща́ть, -ти́ть в лом; (*machines etc.*) отд|ава́ть, -а́ть на слом. **2.** (*coll., discard*) выбра́сывать, вы́бросить.

cpds. **~-book** *n.* альбо́м для вы́резок; **~-heap** *n.* сва́лка; **~-iron** *n.* желе́зный лом; **~-merchant** *n.* старьёвщик; торго́вец ути́лем; **~-yard** *n.* склад ло́ма; пункт приёма металлоло́ма/ути́ля.

scrap[2] [skræp] *n.* (*coll., fight*) дра́ка, потасо́вка; **have a ~** дра́ться, по-; вздо́рить, по-.

v.i. дра́ться (*impf.*).

scrape [skreɪp] *n.* **1.** (*action*) скобле́ние, чи́стка; (*of pen*) скрип; (*of foot*) ша́рканье. **2.** (*coll., awkward predicament*) переде́лка.

v.t. **1.** (*abrade*) скобли́ть, вы́-; (*graze*) сса́|живать, -ди́ть. **2.** (*clean*) выска́бливать, вы́скоблить; **~ one's shoes** соск|а́бливать, -обли́ть грязь с подо́шв; **he ~d his plate clean** он подчи́стил всю таре́лку. **3.**: **~ one's feet** ша́ркать (*impf.*) нога́ми. **4.**: **~ a living** ко́е-как своди́ть (*impf.*) концы́ с конца́ми.

v.i. **1.** (*rub*): **my hand ~d against the wall** я ссади́л себе́ ру́ку о сте́ну; **his car ~d against a tree** он поцара́пал маши́ну о де́рево. **2.** (*get through*): **she just ~d into the final** ей едва́ удало́сь вы́йти в фина́л.

with advs.: **~ along, ~ by** *v.i.* (*get by*) проб|ива́ться, -и́ться; **~ off** *v.t.* соск|а́бливать, -обли́ть; **~ out** *v.t.* выскреба́ть, вы́скрести; (*hollow or carve out*) выда́лбливать, вы́долбить; (*bowl etc.*) выска́бливать, вы́скоблить; **~ through** *v.i.* проти́с|киваться, -нуться; **she ~d through (her exam)** она́ с трудо́м вы́держала экза́мен; **~ together** *v.t.* (*money etc.*) наскре|ба́ть, -сти́; **~ up** *v.t.*: **he ~d up enough money for the concert** он наскрёб де́ньги на конце́рт.

scraper ['skreɪpə(r)] *n.* (*implement*) скребо́к; (*for cleaning shoes*) скоба́.

scrappy ['skræpɪ] *adj.* **1.** (*uncoordinated*; *miscellaneous*) разро́зненный; **a ~ education** пове́рхностное образова́ние. **2.** (*fragmentary*) отры́вочный. **3.** (*meagre*) ску́дный.

scratch [skrætʃ] *n.* **1.** (*mark*) цара́пина. **2.** (*noise*) цара́панье. **3.** (*wound*) цара́пина, ссади́на. **4.** (*act of ~ing*): **give one's head a ~** почеса́ть (*pf.*) го́лову. **5.** (*fig.*): **come up to ~** быть на высоте́ (положе́ния); **start from ~** нач|ина́ть, -а́ть с нача́ла/нуля́.

v.t. **1.** цара́п|ать, о-; **~ o.s.** поцара́паться (*pf.*); **he merely ~ed the surface of the problem** он затро́нул вопро́с весьма́ пове́рхностно. **2.** (*to relieve itching*) чеса́ть, по-; **he was ~ing his head over the problem** (*fig.*) он лома́л го́лову над э́той зада́чей; **you ~ my back and I'll ~ yours** (*fig.*) ты — мне, я — тебе́; рука́ ру́ку мо́ет. **3.** (*erase*) вычёркивать, вы́черкнуть; (*withdraw*): **~ a horse** сн|има́ть, -ять ло́шадь с соревнова́ния.

v.i. **1.** (*of pers.*, **~ o.s.**) чеса́ться, по-. **2.** (*of animal*): **does your cat ~?** ва́ша ко́шка цара́пается? **3.** (*of pen*) цара́пать (*impf.*). **4.** (*coll.*, *withdraw from race*) отка́з|ываться, -а́ться от уча́стия в бега́х.

with advs.: **~ about, ~ around** *vv.i.*: **the chickens ~ed around for food** ку́ры копоши́лись в земле́ в по́исках пи́щи; **he had to ~ around for evidence** ему́ с трудо́м удало́сь наскрести́ доказа́тельства/ули́ки; **~ out** *v.t.* (*erase*) вычёркивать, вы́черкнуть; (*with knife*) выреза́ть, вы́резать; **~ s.o.'s eyes out** вы́царапать (*pf.*) глаза́ кому́-н.

cpd. **~-pad** *n.* блокно́т для заме́ток.

scratchy ['skrætʃɪ] *adj.* (*of pen*: *squeaky*) скрипу́чий; (*catching in paper*) цара́пающий.

scrawl [skrɔ:l] *n.* кара́кули (*f. pl.*).

v.t. черк|а́ть, -ну́ть.

v.i. писа́ть (*impf.*) кара́кулями; **a ~ing hand** неразбо́рчивый по́черк.

scrawny ['skrɔ:nɪ] *adj.* костля́вый.

scream [skri:m] *n.* **1.** пронзи́тельный крик; (*shriek*) вопль (*m.*); (*high-pitched ~*) визг; **~s of laughter** взры́вы (*m. pl.*) хо́хота/сме́ха. **2.** (*coll.*, *funny affair*): **it was a ~!** (э́то была́) умо́ра, да и то́лько!

v.t.: **the sergeant ~ed an order** сержа́нт вы́крикнул кома́нду; **the baby was ~ing its head off** ребёнок надрыва́лся от кри́ка.

v.i. **1.** вопи́ть (*impf.*); **he was ~ing for help** он взыва́л о по́мощи; **he made us ~** он заста́вил нас буква́льно визжа́ть от сме́ха; **the film is ~ingly funny** фильм умори́тельно смешно́й. **2.** (*of bird*) (пронзи́тельно) крича́ть, за-.

scree [skri:] *n.* камени́стая о́сыпь.

screech [skri:tʃ] *n.* пронзи́тельный крик, визг; скрип.

v.i. пронзи́тельно крича́ть, за-/про-; (*of gears, tyres etc.*) скрежета́ть (*impf.*); скрипе́ть (*impf.*).

screed [skri:d] *n.* дли́нное, ску́чное посла́ние.

screen [skri:n] *n.* **1.** (*partition*) перегоро́дка. **2.** (*furniture*) ши́рма. **3.** (*shelter, protection*) прикры́тие; (*cover*) покро́в. **4.** (*on window*) се́тка. **5.** (*cin., TV*) экра́н; **~ adaptation** экраниза́ция.

v.t. **1.** (*shelter*) прикр|ыва́ть, -ы́ть; (*protect*) защи|ща́ть, -ти́ть; огра|жда́ть, -ди́ть. **2.** (*hide*) укр|ыва́ть, -ы́ть. **3.** (*separate*) отгор|а́живать, -оди́ть. **4.** (*fig., investigate*): **they were ~ed before going abroad** пе́ред отъе́здом за грани́цу они́ прошли́ прове́рку (на благонадёжность). **5.** (*show on ~*) пока́з|ывать, -а́ть.

cpds. **~-play** *n.* сцена́рий; **~-writer** *n.* сценари́ст.

screw [skru:] *n.* винт, болт, шуру́п; **he has a ~ loose** у него́ ви́нтика не хвата́ет (*coll.*); **put the ~s on** (*fig.*) наж|има́ть, -а́ть на+*a.*

v.t. **1.** зави́н|чивать, -ти́ть; **the cupboard was ~ed to the wall** шкаф был приви́нчен к стене́; **I ~ed the bolt into the post** я ввинти́л болт в столб. **2.** (*fig., turn*): **I had to ~ my neck round to see him** я чуть не вы́вернул ше́ю, что́бы уви́деть его́. **3.** (*copulate with*) тра́х|ать, -нуть (*sl.*).

v.i.: **this piece ~s on to that** э́тот кусо́к привинчивается к тому́.

with advs.: **~ down** *v.t. & i.* приви́н|чивать(ся), -ти́ть(ся); **~ off** *v.t. & i.* отви́н|чивать(ся), -ти́ть(ся); **~ on** *v.t. & i.* нави́н|чивать(ся), -ти́ть(ся); **~ together** *v.t.*: **he ~ed the boards together** он скрепи́л до́ски винта́ми; **~ up** *v.t.* зави́н|чивать, -ти́ть; (*crumple*) ко́мкать, с-; **~ up one's eyes** щу́рить, со-/пригла́за́; **~ up one's courage** собра́ться (*pf.*) с ду́хом; (*sl., spoil*) напорта́чить (*pf.*); зава́л|ивать, -и́ть.

cpds. **~ball** *n.* (*sl.*) чо́кнутый, сумасбро́д; **~-cap, ~-top** *nn.* нави́нчивающаяся кры́шка; **~driver** *n.* отвёртка; **~-propeller** *n.* винт; **~-top** *n.* = **~-cap**

screwy ['skru:ɪ] *adj.* (*sl., crazy*) тро́нутый, чо́кнутый.

scribbl|e ['skrɪb(ə)l] *n.* кара́кули (*f. pl.*).

v.t. & i. **1.** (*make marks* (*on*)) черка́ть, ис-. **2.** (*write hastily*) черка́ть, на-; (*write untidily*) каля́кать, на-; **~ing-pad, block** блокно́т для заме́ток.

scribe [skraɪb] *n.* (*hist.*) писе́ц; (*bibl.*) кни́жник.

scrimmage ['skrɪmɪdʒ] (*also* **scrum(mage)**) *n.* **1.** (*tussle*) сва́лка. **2.** (*Rugby football*) схва́тка вокру́г мяча́.

scrimp [skrɪmp] = **skimp**

script [skrɪpt] *n.* **1.** (*handwriting*) ру́копись; (*writing system*) письмо́, пи́сьменность; **in Cyrillic ~** кири́ллицей. **2.** (*text*) текст, сцена́рий.

v.t.: **~ed discussion** зара́нее подгото́вленная диску́ссия.

cpd. **~-writer** *n.* сценари́ст.

scriptural ['skrɪptʃər(ə)l, -tʃʊər(ə)l] *adj.* библе́йский.

scripture ['skrɪptʃə(r)] *n.* писа́ние; **Holy S~** свяще́нное писа́ние; **in the ~s** в би́блии.

scroll [skrəʊl] *n.* сви́ток.

Scrooge [skru:dʒ] *n.* скря́га (*c.g.*); **don't be such a ~!** не будь таки́м скря́гой!

scrotum ['skrəʊtəm] *n.* мошо́нка.

scroung|e [skraʊndʒ] *v.t.* (*cadge*) стрел|я́ть, -ьну́ть (*coll.*).

v.i. **1.** (*search about*) ры́скать (*impf.*); **they were ~ing for food** они́ ры́скали в по́исках пи́щи. **2.** (*cadge*) попроша́йничать (*impf.*).

scrounger ['skraʊndʒə(r)] *n.* попроша́йка (*c.g.*).

scrub[1] [skrʌb] *n.* (*brushwood*) куста́рник; (*area*) за́росли (*f. pl.*).

scrub[2] [skrʌb] *v.t.* **1.** (*rub hard*) скрести́ (*impf.*); тере́ть (*impf.*); чи́стить, по-; **~ the floor** мыть, вы́пол; **~ paint off one's hands** сч|ища́ть, -и́стить кра́ску с рук; **~bing brush** жёсткая щётка. **2.** (*sl., cancel*) отмен|я́ть, -и́ть.

with advs.: **~ down** *v.t.*: **he ~bed down the walls** он вы́мыл сте́ны; **~ off** *v.t.* отм|ыва́ть, -ы́ть; **~ out** *v.t.*: **she ~bed out the kitchen** она́ вы́скребла ку́хню до́чиста.

scruff[1] [skrʌf] *n.*: **take s.o. by the ~ of the neck** хвата́ть, схвати́ть кого́-н. за ши́ворот/загри́вок.

scruff[2] [skrʌf] *n.* неря́ха, растрёпа

scruffy ['skrʌfɪ] *adj.* (*coll.*) неопря́тный, парши́вый.

scrum(mage) ['skrʌmɪdʒ] = **scrimmage**

scrumptious ['skrʌmpʃəs] *adj.* (*coll.*) о́чень вку́сный.

scruple ['skru:p(ə)l] *n.* (*usu. pl.*) сомне́ния (*nt. pl.*) (нра́вственного хара́ктера); **have no ~s** не стесня́ться (*impf.*) ниче́м.

v.i. стесня́ться (*impf.*); со́веститься, по-.

scrupulous ['skru:pjʊləs] *adj.* (*of sensitive conscience*) щепети́льный, добросо́вестный; (*accurate, punctilious*) тща́тельный, скрупулёзный; **~ cleanliness** абсолю́тная чистота́; **~ honesty** безупре́чная че́стность.

scrutinize ['skru:tɪ,naɪz] *v.t.* рассм|а́тривать, -отре́ть; (*stare at*) при́стально смотре́ть (*impf.*) на+*a.*

scrutiny ['skru:tɪnɪ] *n.* **1.** (*searching gaze*) внима́тельный взгляд. **2.** (*close investigation*) тща́тельное рассле́дование/рассмотре́ние.
scuba ['sku:bə, 'skju:-] *n.* ску́ба, акваланг; ~ **diver** плове́ц со ску́бой.
scud [skʌd] *v.i.* нести́сь, про-; (*naut.*) идти́ (*det.*) под ве́тром.
scuff [skʌf] *v.t.*: ~ (*wear away*) **one's shoes** истрё-п|ывать, -а́ть о́бувь.
scuffle ['skʌf(ə)l] *n.* потасо́вка, схва́тка.
v.i. дра́ться (*impf.*); схва́т|ываться, -и́ться.
scull [skʌl] *n.* (*oar*) па́рное весло́; (*at stern of boat*) кормово́е весло́; (*boat*) па́рная ло́дка.
v.t. & i.: ~ **a boat** грести́ (*impf.*) па́рными вёслами; (*with stern-oar*) грести́ кормовы́м весло́м.
scullery ['skʌlərɪ] *n.* судомо́йня.
sculpt [skʌlpt] *v.t. & i.* (*coll.*) = **sculpture** *v.t.*, *v.i.*
sculptor ['skʌlptə(r)] *n.* ску́льптор.
sculptural ['skʌlptʃərəl] *adj.* скульпту́рный.
sculpture ['skʌlptʃə(r)] *n.* скульпту́ра.
v.t. (*also* **sculpt**) ва́ять, из-; (*model in clay etc.*) лепи́ть, вы́-; (*in stone*) высека́ть, вы́сечь; (*in wood*) ре́зать, вы́-.
v.i. быть/рабо́тать (*impf.*) ску́льптором.
scum [skʌm] *n.* на́кипь, пе́на; (*fig.*) подо́нки (*m. pl.*).
scupper ['skʌpə(r)] *v.t.* (*sink*) потопи́ть (*pf.*); (*fig., coll.*) разби́ть (*pf.*) (в пух и прах); разгроми́ть (*pf.*); **we're ~ed** мы поги́бли.
scurf [skɜ:f] *n.* пе́рхоть.
scurrilous ['skʌrɪləs] *adj.* (*indecent*) непристо́йный; (*abusive*) оскорби́тельный.
scurry ['skʌrɪ] *n.* суета́, спе́шка; **there was a ~ towards the exit** все бро́сились к вы́ходу; **the ~ of mice under the floor** возня́ мыше́й по́д полом.
v.i. (*also* ~ **about**) суетли́во бе́гать (*impf.*); снова́ть (*impf.*).
with advs.: ~ **away,** ~ **off** *vv.i.* убе|га́ть, -жа́ть; (*disperse*) разбе|га́ться, -жа́ться.
scurvy ['skɜ:vɪ] *n.* цинга́.
scuttle[1] ['skʌt(ə)l] *n.* (*for coal*) ведёрко для у́гля́.
scuttle[2] ['skʌt(ə)l] *n.* стреми́тельное бе́гство.
v.i. бе́гать (*impf.*); ю́ркнуть (*pf.*); снова́ть (*impf.*).
scuttle[3] ['skʌt(ə)l] *v.t.* (*sink*) затоп|ля́ть, -и́ть.
scythe [saɪð] *n.* коса́.
v.t. коси́ть, с-.
sea [si:] *n.* мо́ре; **at** ~ (*lit.*) в мо́ре; **he is at** ~ он нахо́дится в пла́вании; **(all) at** ~ (*fig.*) озада́чен, растéрян (*pred.*); в недоуме́нии; **beyond the** ~ за́ морем; **by** ~ мо́рем; **by the** ~ у мо́ря, на мо́ре; **go to** ~ (*become a sailor*) идти́ (*det.*), пойти́ (*pf.*) в моряки́; **ships sail on the** ~ корабли́ пла́вают по́ морю; **put to** ~ (*of ship*) выходи́ть, вы́йти в мо́ре; **on the high ~s** в откры́том мо́ре; **inland** ~ закры́тое мо́ре; **a heavy** ~ си́льное волне́ние.
attr.: ~ **air** морско́й во́здух; ~ **voyage, trip** морско́е путеше́ствие; морска́я прогу́лка; ~ **mile** морска́я ми́ля; ~ **power** морска́я мощь.
cpds. **~-anemone** *n.* акти́ния; **~-bed** *n.* морско́е дно; **~-bird** *n.* морска́я пти́ца; **~board** *n.* примо́рье, (*attr.*) примо́рский; **~-breeze** *n.* ве́тер с мо́ря; **~-change** *n.* (радика́льное) преображе́ние; **~-chest** *n.* матро́сский сундучо́к; **~-coast** *n.* морско́й бе́рег; **~-cow** *n.* морж; **~-dog** *n.* (*old sailor*) (ста́рый) морско́й волк; **~-elephant** *n.* морско́й слон; **~farer** *n.* морепла́ватель (*m.*); **~faring** *n.* морепла́вание; *adj.* мореходный; **~food** *n.* проду́кты мо́ря, морски́е проду́кты (*m. pl.*); **~-front** *n.* примо́рский бульва́р, на́бережная; **~going** *adj.* (*of ship*) мореходный; **~gull** *n.* ча́йка; **~-horse** *n.* морско́й конёк; **~-lane** *n.* морско́й путь; (*pl.*) морски́е коммуника́ции (*f. pl.*); **~-legs** *n.*: **find, get one's ~legs** прив|ыка́ть, -ы́кнуть к ка́чке; **~-level** *n.* у́ровень (*m.*) мо́ря; **~-lion** *n.* морско́й лев; **~man** *n.* моря́к, матро́с; **~manship** *n.* иску́сство морепла́вания; **~plane** *n.* гидросамолёт; **~port** *n.* морско́й порт; порто́вый го́род; **~scape** *n.* морско́й пейза́ж, мари́на; **~-scout** *n.* морско́й бойска́ут; **~-shell** *n.* морска́я ра́ковина; **~-shore** *n.* морско́й бе́рег, взмо́рье; **~sick** *adj.*: **I was ~sick** меня́ укача́ло; **~sickness** *n.* морска́я боле́знь; **~side** *n.* морско́е побере́жье; **he likes the ~side** он лю́бит е́здить на мо́ре; *adj.* примо́рский; **a ~side resort** морско́й куро́рт; **~-trout** *n.* океани́ческая сельдь; **~-urchin** *n.* морско́й ёж; **~-wall** *n.* да́мба; сте́нка на́бережной; **~-water** *n.* морска́я вода́; **~-way** *n.* (*inland waterway*) судохо́дное ру́сло; фарва́тер; **~weed** *n.* морска́я во́доросль; **~worthy** *adj.* мореходный, го́дный к пла́ванию.
seal[1] [si:l] *n.* (*zool.*) тюле́нь (*m.*); **(fur-~)** ко́тик.
cpd. **~skin** *n.* тюле́ний/ко́тиковый мех.
seal[2] [si:l] *n.* **1.** (*on document etc.*) печа́ть; **wax** ~ сургу́чная печа́ть; **leaden** ~ пло́мба; **affix, set one's ~ to sth.** ста́вить, по- свою́ печа́ть на что-н.; **set the ~ on** заверш|а́ть, -и́ть; **he set the ~ of approval on our action** он одо́брил на́ши де́йствия. **2.** (*gem, stamp etc. for ~ing*) печа́тка.
v.t. **1.** (*affix ~ to*) при|кла́дывать, -ложи́ть печа́ть к+*d.*; **the treaty has been signed and ~ed** догово́р подпи́сан и скреплён печа́тями; **~ed orders** секре́тный прика́з; **~ing-wax** сургу́ч. **2.** (*confirm*): ~ **a bargain** закреп|ля́ть, -и́ть сде́лку. **3.** (*close securely; stop up*) запеча́т|ывать, -ать; пло́тно закр|ыва́ть, -ы́ть; **a ~ed envelope** запеча́танный конве́рт; **they ~ed (up) all the windows** они́ зама́зали/заде́лали все о́кна; **the police ~ed off all exits from the square** поли́ция оцепи́ла пло́щадь; **my lips are ~ed** у меня́ запеча́таны уста́. **4.** (*set mark on; destine*) нал|ага́ть, -ожи́ть печа́ть на+*a.*; **his fate is ~ed** его́ у́часть решена́.
seam [si:m] *n.* шов; **burst at the ~s** ло́п|аться, -нуть по шву; **come apart at the ~s** (*lit., fig.*) треща́ть (*impf.*) по швам; (*geol.*) пласт.
seamless ['si:mlɪs] *adj.* без шва; из одного́ куска́; ~ **stockings** чулки́ без шва.
seamstress, sempstress ['semstrɪs] *n.* швея́.
seamy ['si:mɪ] *adj.*: **the ~ side of life** изна́нка жи́зни.
seance ['seɪɑ̃s] *n.* спирити́ческий сеа́нс.
sear [sɪə(r)] *v.t.* (*scorch*) опал|я́ть, -и́ть; (*cauterize*) приж|ига́ть, -е́чь.
search [sɜ:tʃ] *n.* **1.** (*quest*) по́иск (*usu. pl.*); **make a ~ for s.o./sth.** иска́ть (*impf.*) кого́-н./что-н. **2.** (*examination*) о́быск; **the police carried out a ~ of the house** поли́ция произвела́ о́быск в до́ме.
v.t. **1.** (*examine*) обы́ск|ивать, -а́ть; **we were ~ed at the airport** мы прошли́ осмо́тр в аэропорту́; (*rummage through*) обша́ри|вать, -ть. **2.** (*peer at, scan*) обв|оди́ть, -ести́ взгля́дом. **3.** (*fig., scrutinize*): ~ **one's heart** загляну́ть (*pf.*) себе́ в ду́шу; **I ~ed my conscience** я спроси́л свою́ со́весть. **4.** (*penetrate*) прон|ика́ть, -и́кнуть; **~ing questions** подро́бные вопро́сы; **a ~ing enquiry** тща́тельное рассле́дование.
v.i. иска́ть (*impf.*); пров|оди́ть, -ести́ о́быск; ~ **for** разы́скивать (*impf.*); ~ **out** (*find*) отыска́ть, разыска́ть (*both pf.*); ~ **through** просм|а́тривать, -отре́ть; **I ~ed through my desk for the letter** я переры́л весь пи́сьменный стол в по́исках письма́.
cpds. **~light** *n.* проже́ктор; **~-party** *n.* поиско́вая гру́ппа; **~-warrant** *n.* о́рдер на о́быск.
season ['si:z(ə)n] *n.* **1.** сезо́н; **the four ~s** четы́ре вре́мени го́да; **in the rainy** ~ в сезо́н дожде́й; **compliments of the ~!** с пра́здником!; **blackberries are out of** ~ сейча́с ежеви́ке не сезо́н; **at the height of the** ~ в разга́р сезо́на; **holiday** ~ сезо́н отпуско́в.
attr.: ~ **ticket** сезо́нный/проездно́й (биле́т); (*for concerts etc.*) абонеме́нт.

v.t. **1.** (*mature*: *of timber*, *wine etc.*) выдéрживать, вы́держать. **2.** (*acclimatize*, *inure*) приуч|áть, -и́ть; **~ed troops** óпытные войскá. **3.** (*spice*) припр|а-влять, -áвить.

seasonal ['si:zən(ə)l] *adj.* сезóнный.

seasoning ['si:zənɪŋ] *n.* (*cul.*) припрáва; (*of timber*, *wine*) выдéрживание.

seat [si:t] *n.* **1.** сидéнье; (*chair*) стул; (*bench*) скамья́. **2.** (*place in vehicle*, *theatre etc.*) мéсто; **take one's ~** зан|имáть, -я́ть мéсто; **please take a ~!** сади́тесь, пожáлуйста!; **keep one's ~** ост|авáться, -áться на мéсте; **he booked a ~** он заказáл билéт; **take a back ~** (*fig.*) от|ходи́ть, -ойти́ на зáдний план. **3.** (*of chair*) сидéнье. **4.** (*backside*) зад; (*of trousers*) зад (у) брюк. **5.** (*site*, *location*, *headquarters*): **~ of government** местопребывáние прави́тельства; **~ of war** теáтр воéнных дéйствий; **~ of learning** нау́чный центр. **6.** (*parl.*) мéсто в парлáменте; **have a ~ in parliament** быть члéном парлáмента.

v.t. **1.** (*make sit*) сажáть, посади́ть; **~ o.s.** сади́ться, сесть; **be ~ed!** сади́тесь!; **he remained ~ed** он продолжáл сидéть. **2.** (*provide with ~s*) вме|щáть, -сти́ть.

cpd. **~-belt** *n.* (привязнóй) ремéнь.

seating ['si:tɪŋ] *n.* **1.** (*allocation of places*) рассáживание; (*placing at table*) размещéние гостéй за столóм. **2.** (*seats*) (сидя́чие) местá; **~ capacity** числó сидя́чих мест.

sebaceous [sɪ'beɪʃəs] *adj.* сáльный.

sec. [sɪ'kɒnd(z)] *n.* (*abbr. of* **second(s)**) сек., (секу́нда).

secant ['si:kənt, 'se-] *n.* сéканс.

secateurs [ˌsekə'tɜ:z] *n. pl.* садóвые нóжниц|ы (*pl.*, *g.* —); секáтор.

secede [sɪ'si:d] *v.i.* выходи́ть, вы́йти (из+*g.*).

secession [sɪ'seʃ(ə)n] *n.* вы́ход (из+*g.*).

seclude [sɪ'klu:d] *v.t.*: **~ o.s. from society** удал|я́ться, -и́ться от óбщества; **a ~d life** уединённая жизнь; **a ~d spot** укрóмный уголóк.

seclusion [sɪ'klu:ʒ(ə)n] *n.* уединéние, изоля́ция; **to live in ~** жить (*impf.*) в одинóчестве.

second[1] ['sekənd] *n.* **1.** вторóй; **~ in command** замести́тель (*m.*) команди́ра; **on the ~ of May** вторóго мáя. **2.** (*in duel*, *boxing etc.*) секундáнт. **3.** (*pl.*, *imperfect goods*) второсóртный товáр; **these plates are ~s** э́ти тарéлки бракóванные. **4.** (*measure of time or angle*, *also mus.*) секу́нда; **wait a ~!** однý секу́нду!

adj. вторóй, другóй; **Charles the S~** Карл Вторóй; **on the ~ (US third) floor** на трéтьем этажé; **the ~ largest city** вторóй по величинé гóрод; **he came in ~** он зáнял вторóе мéсто; **in the ~ place** во-вторы́х; **for the ~ time** втори́чно, вторóй раз; (*additional*) добáвочный; **~ chamber** вéрхняя палáта; **~ helping** добáвка; **France was a ~ home to him** Фрáнция былá емý вторóй рóдиной; **~ name** фами́лия; **he has ~ sight** он яснови́дец; **have ~ thoughts** раздýмать (*pf.*); **I am having ~ thoughts** я начинáю колебáться; **on ~ thoughts** поразмы́слив; по зрéлом размышлéнии; **get one's ~ wind** обрести́ (*pf.*) вторóе дыхáние; (*subordinate*; *comparable*): **~ to none** непревзойдённый; **he is ~ to none** он никомý не устýпит; **~ cousin** троюродный брат (*fem.* троюродная сестрá); **learn sth. at ~ hand** узнáть (*pf.*) что-н. понаслы́шке; **~ lieutenant** млáдший лейтенáнт; **~ officer** помóщник капитáна.

v.t. (*support*) поддéрж|ивать, -áть.

cpds. **~-best** *adj.* не сáмый лýчший; (*inferior*) второсóртный; **~-class** *n.* (*degree*) диплóм вторóй стéпени; (*of travel*) вторóй класс; *adj.* второклáссный; **~-floor, ~-storey** *adjs.* на трéтьем этажé; **~-hand** *adj.* (*previously used*) подéржанный; **~-hand bookshop** букинисти́ческий магази́н; **~-rate** *adj.* (*of goods*) второсóртный; **~-storey** *n.* = **~-floor**

second[2] [sɪ'kɒnd] *v.t.* (*mil.*, *admin.*) откомандирóв|ывать, -áть.

secondary ['sekəndərɪ] *adj.* **1.** (*opp. primary*) втори́чный; **~ school** срéдняя шкóла. **2.** (*subordinate*) второстепéнный.

secondly ['sekəndlɪ] *adv.* во-вторы́х.

secrecy ['si:krɪsɪ] *n.* тáйна; (*of document*) секрéтность; **he swore me to ~** он взял с меня́ кля́тву/ слóво молчáть.

secret ['si:krɪt] *n.* тáйна; (*in personal relations*) секрéт; **keep a ~** храни́ть, со- секрéт; **let s.o. into a ~** посвя|щáть, -ти́ть когó-н. в тáйну; **I make no ~ of it** я э́того не скрывáю; **in ~** в тáйне, по секрéту.

adj. **1.** тáйный; **top ~** (*as inscription*) совершéнно секрéтно; **keep sth. ~** держáть (*impf.*) что-н. в тáйне; **~ agent** развéдчик, шпиóн; **~ police** тáйная поли́ция; **~ service** секрéтная слýжба; развéдка; **~ sign** услóвный знак; (*hidden*) потайнóй, скры́тый; **~ staircase** потайнáя лéстница; (*undisclosed*): **my ~ ambition** моя́ сокровéнная мечтá; **I was ~ly glad to see him** в глубинé души́ я был рад егó ви́деть.

secretarial [ˌsekrɪ'teərɪəl] *adj.* секретáрский.

secretariat [ˌsekrə'teərɪət] *n.* секретариáт.

secretary ['sekrɪtərɪ, 'sekrətrɪ] *n.* секретáр|ь (*fem.* -ша); **S~-General** Генерáльный Секретáрь; **S~ of State** (*UK*) мини́стр; (*US*) государственный секретáрь, мини́стр инострáнных дел.

secrete [sɪ'kri:t] *v.t.* **1.** (*physiol. etc.*) выделя́ть, вы́делить. **2.** (*conceal*) укр|ывáть, -ы́ть; **~ o.s.** укр|ывáться, -ы́ться.

secretion [sɪ'kri:ʃ(ə)n] *n.* выделéние, секрéция.

secretive ['si:krɪtɪv] *adj.* скры́тный, зáмкнутый.

secretiveness ['si:krɪtɪvnɪs] *n.* скры́тность.

sect [sekt] *n.* сéкта.

sectarian [sek'teərɪən] *n.* сектáнт (*fem.* -ка).

adj. сектáнтский.

section ['sekʃ(ə)n] *n.* **1.** (*separate or distinct part*) сéкция; **built in ~s** сбóрный, разбóрный; (*severed portion*) кусóк; **~ of the population** часть населéния; **~ of a journey** этáп пути́; **~ of a book** раздéл кни́ги; (*mil.*) отделéние; (*department*) отдéл. **2.** (*geom. etc.*) разрéз; сечéние. **3.** (*microscopic ~*) срез. **4.** (*surg.*) сечéние.

sectional ['sekʃən(ə)l] *adj.* **1.** секциóнный. **2.** (*made in parts*) сбóрный, разбóрный, составнóй. **3.**: **~ arrangement of material** распределéние материáла по отдéлам. **4.** (*of drawings*, *plans etc.*) в разрéзе; **~ elevation** разрéз.

sector ['sektə(r)] *n.* **1.** (*geom.*) сéктор. **2.** (*mil. etc.*) учáсток. **3.** (*econ.*): **the private ~** чáстный сéктор.

secular ['sekjʊlə(r)] *adj.* (*this-worldly*) мирскóй; **~ affairs** мирски́е делá; (*non-ecclesiastical*, *lay*) свéтский.

secularization [ˌsekjʊləraɪ'zeɪʃ(ə)n] *n.* секуляризáция.

secularize ['sekjʊləˌraɪz] *v.t.* секуляризовáть (*impf.*, *pf.*).

secure [sɪ'kjʊə(r)] *adj.* **1.** (*free from care*) спокóйный; **feel ~ about sth.** не беспокóиться (*impf.*) о чём-н. **2.** (*safe*): **the doors are ~** двéри зáперты как слéдует; **the ladder is ~** лéстница стои́т прóчно; **the town was ~ against attack** гóрод был хорошó защищён от нападéния; (*reliable*) надёжный; **make ~** закреп|ля́ть, -и́ть; (*assured*): **a ~ income** обеспéченный дохóд; (*well-founded*): **a ~ assumption** обоснóванное предположéние.

v.t. **1.** (*make safe or fast*) закреп|ля́ть, -и́ть; **~ a town against assault** укрепи́ть (*pf.*) оборóну гóрода от нападéния; **~ a prisoner** свя́з|ывать, -áть плéнного. **2.** (*guarantee*, *insure*) страховáть, за-; **he ~d himself against every risk** он застраховáл себя́ от вся́кого ри́ска. **3.** (*obtain*) заруч|áться, -и́ться +*i.*

security [sɪ'kjʊərɪtɪ] *n.* **1.** (*safety*) безопáсность; **~ against attack** безопáсность от нападéния; **~ de-**

vice предохрани́тель (*m.*); **S~ Council** Сове́т Безопа́сности; **~ guard** охра́нник; **he is a ~ risk** он неблагонадёжен. **2.** (*safeguard, guarantee*) гара́нтия. **3.** (*pledge, promise*) зало́г, гара́нтия; **~ for a loan** гара́нтия за́йма. **4.** (*pl., bonds*) це́нные бума́ги (*f. pl.*).

sedan [sɪ'dæn] *n.* **(~ chair)** паланки́н; (*US, saloon car*) седа́н.

sedate[1] [sɪ'deɪt] *adj.* степе́нный, уравнове́шенный.

sedate[2] [sɪ'deɪt] *v.t.* да|ва́ть, -ть успокои́тельное *+d.*

sedation [sɪ'deɪʃ(ə)n] *n.* успокое́ние; **under ~** под де́йствием успокои́тельных.

sedative ['sedətɪv] *n.* успокои́тельное (сре́дство); (*sleeping drug*) снотво́рное (сре́дство).

sedentary ['sedəntərɪ] *adj.* (*of posture etc.*) сидя́чий; **a ~ way of life** сидя́чий о́браз жи́зни.

sedge [sedʒ] *n.* осо́ка.

sediment ['sedɪmənt] *n.* оса́док, отсто́й.

sedimentary [ˌsedɪ'mentərɪ] *adj.* оса́дочный.

sedimentation [ˌsedɪmen'teɪʃ(ə)n] *n.* (*process*) осажде́ние; отложе́ние оса́дка; (*sediment*) оса́док.

sedition [sɪ'dɪʃ(ə)n] *n.* подстрека́тельство к мятежу́.

seditious [sɪ'dɪʃəs] *adj.* мяте́жный, подстрека́тельский.

seduce [sɪ'dju:s] *v.t.* **1.** (*lead astray*) соблазн|я́ть, -и́ть; оболь|ща́ть, -сти́ть. **2.** (*a woman*) совра|ща́ть, -ти́ть.

seducer [sɪ'dju:sə(r)] *n.* соблазни́тель (*m.*); обольсти́тель (*m.*), соврати́тель (*m.*).

seduction [sɪ'dʌkʃ(ə)n] *n.* обольще́ние.

seductive [sɪ'dʌktɪv] *adj.* соблазни́тельный; **~ smile** обольсти́тельная улы́бка.

seductress [sɪ'dʌktrɪs] *n.* обольсти́тельница.

sedulous ['sedjʊləs] *adj.* (*diligent*) приле́жный; (*assiduous*) усе́рдный; (*painstaking*) стара́тельный.

see[1] [si:] *n.* (*territory*) епа́рхия; (*office*) ка́федра; **the Holy S~** па́пский престо́л.

see[2] [si:] *v.t.* **1.** ви́деть; **nothing could be ~n** ничего́ не́ было ви́дно; **nothing was ~n of him** о нём не́ было ни слу́ху ни ду́ху; **I saw her arrive** я ви́дел, как она прибыла́; **I have never ~n such a thing** ничего́ подо́бного я не вида́л/ви́дел; **I never saw such rudeness** я в жи́зни не встреча́лся с тако́й гру́бостью; **~ red** (*coll.*) взбеси́ться (*pf.*); **I thought I was ~ing things** мне каза́лось, что я бре́жу; **I ~ things differently now** я тепе́рь ина́че смотрю́ на ве́щи. **2.** (*look at, watch*) смотре́ть, по- на*+a.*; осм|а́тривать, -отре́ть; **~ p. 4** см. стр. 4; **let me ~ that** да́йте мне на э́то взгляну́ть; **let me ~ your letter** покажи́те мне ва́ше письмо́; **the film is worth ~ing** э́тот фильм сто́ит посмотре́ть; **~ what you've done!** смотри́те, что вы наде́лали!; **~ the sights** осм|а́тривать, -отре́ть достопримеча́тельности. **3.** (*experience*): **he has ~n life (*or* the world)** он вида́л/ви́дывал ви́ды; **the house has ~n many changes** дом претерпе́л/повида́л мно́го переме́н; **he has ~n five reigns** он пережи́л пять ца́рствований. **4.** (*imagine*) предст|авля́ть, -а́вить себе́ (*что*). **5.** (*ascertain by looking; find out*) посмотре́ть, узна́ть, вы́яснить (*all pf.*); **~ for o.s.** убеди́ться (*pf.*) самому́; **(go and) ~ who it is** посмотри́те, кто там; **I'll ~ if I can get tickets** я постара́юсь доста́ть биле́ты; **that remains to be ~n** э́то ещё неизве́стно. **6.** (*discern, comprehend*) пон|има́ть, -я́ть; **as I ~ it** помо́ему; на мой взгляд; **he saw his mistake at once** он сра́зу же по́нял свою́ оши́бку; **I ~ how it is** мне поня́тно, как обстоя́т дела́; **as far as I can ~** наско́лько я понима́ю; **(do) you ~?** (вы) понима́ете?; **don't you ~?** неуже́ли вы не понима́ете?; **from this it can be ~n** из э́того сле́дует; **so I ~** сам ви́жу; понима́ю. **7.** (*consider*) ду́мать, по-; **I'll ~** я поду́маю; посмо́трим; **let me ~!** погоди́те/посто́йте!; **~ing that ...** ввиду́ того́, что...; поско́льку... **8.** (*come across, meet*) ви́деть, у-; встр|еча́ть, -е́тить; (*associate*) ви́деться (*impf.*), встреча́ться (*impf.*) (с кем); **they stopped ~ing each other** они́ разошли́сь (*or* переста́ли встреча́ться); (*visit*) посе|ща́ть, -ти́ть; наве|ща́ть, -сти́ть; **we went to ~ our friends** мы сходи́ли/съе́здили к на́шим друзья́м; **come and ~ me, us sometime** заходи́те ка́к-нибудь; **(I'll) be ~ing you!** до ско́рого!; пока́! (*coll.*); **~ you on Tuesday!** до вто́рника! **9.** (*interview, consult*): **I went to ~ him about a job** я зашёл к нему́ поговори́ть о рабо́те; **can I ~ you for a moment?** мо́жно вас на мину́тку?; **you should ~ a doctor** вам сле́дует обрати́ться к врачу́; **he went to ~ a lawyer** он пошёл посове́товаться с адвока́том; (*receive; grant interview to*) прин|има́ть, -я́ть. **10.** (*escort, conduct*) прово|жа́ть, -ди́ть; **I saw her across the road** я перевёл её че́рез у́лицу; (*provide for*): **£5 should ~ you to the end of the week** пяти́ фу́нтов должно́ хвати́ть вам до конца́ неде́ли. **11.** (*ensure*) следи́ть, про-; **~ that it is done** смотри́те, что́бы э́то бы́ло сде́лано.

v.i. ви́деть, у-; **can you ~ from where you are?** вам отту́да ви́дно?; **he cannot ~** (*is blind*) он не ви́дит; он слеп; **~ing is believing** пока́ не уви́жу, не пове́рю; **go and ~ for yourself!** пойди́те и убеди́тесь са́ми!; **~ if you can ...** попро́буйте...; **may I ~ inside?** мо́жно загляну́ть внутрь?; **they asked to ~ round the house** они́ проси́ли позво́лить им осмотре́ть дом; **he could not ~ over the hedge** и́згородь заслоня́ла ему́ вид; **~ through s.o.** раску́с|ывать, -и́ть кого́-н. **2.** (*imper., look*): **~, here he comes!** вот и он! **3.** (*make provision; take care; give attention*) забо́титься, по- (*о чём*); (*arrange, organize*) ста́вить, по-; **she ~s to the laundry** она́ ве́дает сти́ркой; **I have to ~ to the children** мне прихо́дится смотре́ть за детьми́; **the garden needs ~ing to** са́дом сле́дует заня́ться;; **I saw to it that ...** я устро́ил так, что...

with advs.: **~ back** *v.t.*: **as it was late I offered to ~ her back** так как бы́ло по́здно, я предложи́л проводи́ть её (домо́й *и т.п.*); **~ in** *v.t.*: **we saw the New Year in** мы встре́тили Но́вый год; **~ off** *v.t.*: **we saw them off at the station** мы проводи́ли их на по́езд; **~ out** *v.t.* пров|оди́ть, -ести́ до вы́хода; **~ through** *v.t.*: **who will ~ the job through?** кто доведёт де́ло до конца́?

cpd. **~-through** *adj.* прозра́чный.

seed [si:d] *n.* **1.** (*lit., fig.*) се́мя (*nt.*), зерно́; зёрнышко, се́мечко; (*collect.*) семена́ (*nt. pl.*); **sow ~(s) in the ground** се́ять, по- семена́ в грунт; **go, run to ~** (*lit.*) идти́, пойти́ в семена́; (*fig., of pers.*) опусти́ться (*pf.*). **2.** (*sport*: **~ed player**) просе́янный игро́к; **he is number 3 ~** он просе́ян за № 3.

v.t. **1.** (*sow or sprinkle with ~*) се́ять, по-; зас|ева́ть, -е́ять. **2.** (*sport*) отбира́ть (*impf.*); **~ed player = seed** *n.* **2.**

cpds. **~-bed** *n.* гряда́ с расса́дой; (*fig.*) расса́дник, оча́г; **~-box** *n.* я́щик для расса́ды; **~-cake** *n.* пече́нье/кекс с тми́ном; **~-corn** *n.* посевно́е зерно́; **~-potatoes** *n.* семенно́й карто́фель; **~sman** *n.* торго́вец семена́ми.

seedless ['si:dlɪs] *adj.* бессемя́нный.

seedling ['si:dlɪŋ] *n.* се́янец; (*pl.*) расса́да (*collect.*).

seedy ['si:dɪ] *adj.* (*shabby*) потрёпанный; (*sleazy*) захуда́лый; (*out of sorts*) не в фо́рме; **I feel ~** я себя́ нева́жно чу́вствую.

seek [si:k] *v.t.* **1.** (*look for*) иска́ть (*impf.*) *+a./g. of concrete/abstract object*; **~ one's fortune** пыта́ть (*impf.*) сча́стья; **~ing a better position** в по́исках лу́чшего ме́ста; **~ out** разыска́ть (*pf.*) (*enquire into*) иска́ть (*impf.*); (*ask for*): **~ advice** проси́ть (*impf.*) сове́та; обра|ща́ться, -ти́ться за сове́том; **~ an explanation** тре́бовать, по- объясне́ния; **~ pardon** добива́ться/проси́ть (*impf.*) проще́ния. **2.** (*attempt*) стара́ться, по-; пыта́ться, по-.

v.i.: **~ after sth.** стреми́ться (*impf.*) к чему́-н.; **a**

sought-after person (чрезвыча́йно) популя́рная ли́чность; ~ **for sth.** иска́ть (*impf.*) что-н./чего́-н.
seeker ['si:kə(r)] *n.*: **an earnest ~ after truth** ре́вностный иска́тель и́стины.
seem [si:m] *v.i.* каза́ться, по-; предст|авля́ться, -а́виться; **it ~s to me** мне ка́жется; по-мо́ему; **I ~ed to hear a voice** мне послы́шался чей-то го́лос; **it ~s like yesterday** как бу́дто э́то бы́ло вчера́; **he is not what he ~s** он не тако́й, как ка́жется; **she ~s young** она́ вы́глядит мо́лодо; **it ~s cold today** сего́дня, ка́жется, хо́лодно; **he and I can't ~ to get on together** мы с ним что́-то ника́к не пола́дим; **it would ~** по-ви́димому; каза́лось бы; **so it ~s** на́до полага́ть; как бу́дто так; **so we are to get nothing, it ~s** ита́к, выхо́дит, мы ничего́ не полу́чим.
seeming ['si:mɪŋ] *adj.* ка́жущийся, вне́шний; **a ~ friend** мни́мый друг; **~ly** по-ви́димому; как бу́дто.
seemly ['si:mlɪ] *adj.* прили́чный, присто́йный.
seep [si:p] *v.i.* (*also* **~ out, through**) прос|а́чиваться, -очи́ться; (*leak*) прот|ека́ть, -е́чь.
seepage ['si:pɪdʒ] *n.* уте́чка, проса́чивание.
seer ['si:ə(r), sɪə(r)] *n.* провидец, проро́к.
seersucker ['sɪə,sʌkə(r)] *n.* лёгкая кре́повая ткань.
seesaw ['si:sɔ:] *n.* (доска́-)качéл|и (*pl.*, *g.* -ей).
v.i. (*play on* ~) кача́ться, по- на доске́/каче́лях; (*fig.*, *oscillate*) колеба́ться (*impf.*).
seeth|e [si:ð] *v.i.* (*of liquids*, *and fig.*) бурли́ть (*impf.*); **he ~ed with anger** он кипе́л негодова́нием; **the streets were ~ing with people** у́лицы кише́ли наро́дом.
segment ['segmənt] *n.* сегме́нт, отре́зок.
v.t. & *i.* дели́ть(ся), раз- на сегме́нты.
segregate ['segrɪgət] *v.t.* отдел|я́ть, -и́ть; раздел|я́ть, -и́ть; изоли́ровать (*impf.*, *pf.*).
segregation [,segrɪ'geɪʃ(ə)n] *n.* (*separation*) отделе́ние, изоля́ция; (*racial*) (ра́совая) сегрега́ция.
seismic ['saɪzmɪk] *adj.* сейсми́ческий.
seismograph ['saɪzmə,grɑ:f] *n.* сейсмо́граф.
seismological [saɪzmə'lɒdʒɪk(ə)l] *adj.* сейсмологи́ческий.
seismometer [saɪz'mɒmɪtə(r)] *n.* сейсмо́метр.
seize [si:z] *v.t.* **1.** (*grasp*; *lay hold of*) хвата́ть, схвати́ть; **they ~d the thief** они́ пойма́ли во́ра; (*fig.*, *comprehend*): **he ~d the point at once** он сра́зу схвати́л суть де́ла; (*fig.*, *make use of*): **~ an opportunity** ухвати́ться (*pl.*) за возмо́жность; по́льзоваться, вос- слу́чаем. **2.** (*take possession of*) захва́т|ывать, -и́ть; **~ power** захва́т|ывать, -и́ть власть; (*fig.*, *strike*, *affect*) охва́т|ывать, -и́ть; **he was ~d by a feeling of remorse** его́ охвати́ло раска́яние. **3.** (*impound*, *arrest*) нал|ага́ть, -ожи́ть аре́ст на+*a.*; конфискова́ть (*impf.*, *pf.*).
v.i. **1.** **~ (up)on** ухвати́ться за+*a.*; **he ~d upon my remark** он прицепи́лся к мои́м слова́м. **2.** (*jam*; *also* **~ up**) за|еда́ть, -е́сть; застр|ева́ть, -я́ть.
seizure ['si:ʒə(r)] *n.* (*capture*) захва́т; (*confiscation*) конфиска́ция; (*attack of illness*) припа́док; (*stroke*) уда́р; серде́чный при́ступ.
seldom ['seldəm] *adv.* ре́дко; **~ if ever** кра́йне ре́дко.
select [sɪ'lekt] *adj.* и́збранный, изы́сканный; **~ circles** и́збранные круги́; **~ committee** осо́бый комите́т.
v.t. выбира́ть, вы́брать; от|бира́ть, -обра́ть; изб|ира́ть, -ра́ть; **~ed works** и́збранные сочине́ния.
selection [sɪ'lekʃ(ə)n] *n.* **1.** (*choice*) вы́бор; **make a ~ of** выбира́ть, вы́брать (ме́жду+*i.*); **there was a wide, great ~** был большо́й вы́бор; (*biol.*): **natural ~** есте́ственный отбо́р. **2.** (*assortment*) подбо́р; набо́р; **a ~ of summer clothes** ассортиме́нт ле́тней оде́жды.
selective [sɪ'lektɪv] *adj.* разбо́рчивый; (*radio*) селекти́вный; избира́тельный; **~ service** (*US*) во́инская пови́нность для отде́льных гра́ждан (по отбо́ру).
selectivity [,sɪlek'tɪvɪtɪ, ,sel-, ,si:l-] *n.* разбо́рчивость.
selenium [sɪ'li:nɪəm] *n.* селе́н.
self [self] *n.* **1.** (*individuality*, *essence*) су́щность; (*personality*) ли́чность; (*ego*) (со́бственное) «я» (*indecl.*); **his own, very ~** он сам; **I am not my former ~** я уже́ не тот, что пре́жде; **my other ~** моё второ́е «я». **2.** (*one's own interest*): **he has no thought of ~** он не ду́мает о себе́.
self-absorbed [,selfəb'zɔ:bd] *adj.* поглощённый собо́й.
self-addressed [,selfə'drest] *adj.* адресо́ванный на со́бственное и́мя; **~ envelope** конве́рт с обра́тным а́дресом отправи́теля.
self-adhesive [,selfəd'hi:sɪv] *adj.* самозакле́ивающийся.
self-analysis [,selfə'næləsɪs] *n.* самоана́лиз.
self-appointed [,selfə'pɔɪntɪd] *adj.* самозва́нный.
self-assertive [,selfə'sɜ:tɪv] *adj.* самоутвержда́ющийся.
self-assurance [,selfə'ʃʊərəns] *n.* уве́ренность (в себе́); (*pej.*) самоуве́ренность; самонаде́янность.
self-assured [,selfə'ʃʊəd] *adj.* (само)уве́ренный; самонаде́янный.
self-centred [self'sentəd] *adj.* эгоцентри́ческий.
self-coloured [self'kʌləd] *adj.* одноцве́тный.
self-confessed [,selfkən'fest] *adj.* открове́нный.
self-confidence [self'kɒnfɪd(ə)ns] *n.* уве́ренность (в себе́); (*pej.*) самоуве́ренность; самонаде́янность.
self-confident [self'kɒnfɪd(ə)nt] *adj.* уве́ренный (в себе́); (*pej.*) самоуве́ренный; самонаде́янный.
self-conscious [self'kɒnʃəs] *adj.* (*awkward*) нело́вкий; (*shy*) засте́нчивый; (*embarrassed*) смущённый.
self-consciousness [self'kɒnʃəsnɪs] *n.* нело́вкость, засте́нчивость.
self-contained [,selfkən'teɪnd] *adj.* (*independent*, *of pers.*) самостоя́тельный, незави́симый; (*of accommodation*) отде́льный, изоли́рованный.
self-control [,selfkən'trəʊl] *n.* самооблада́ние; **he regained his ~** к нему́ верну́лось самооблада́ние.
self-controlled [,selfkən'trəʊld] *adj.* с самооблада́нием.
self-critical [self'krɪtɪk(ə)l] *adj.* самокрити́чный.
self-criticism [self'krɪtɪ,sɪz(ə)m] *n.* самокри́тика.
self-deception [,selfdɪ'sepʃ(ə)n] *n.* самообма́н.
self-defeating [,selfdɪ'fi:tɪŋ] *adj.* сам себя́ сводя́щий на нет.
self-defence [,selfdɪ'fens] *n.* самооборо́на, самозащи́та; **in ~** в поря́дке самозащи́ты.
self-denial [,selfdɪ'naɪəl] *n.* самоотрече́ние.
self-destruction [,selfdɪ'strʌkʃ(ə)n] *n.* самоуничтоже́ние; (*suicide*) самоуби́йство.
self-determination [,selfdɪ,tɜ:mɪ'neɪʃ(ə)n] *n.* самоопределе́ние.
self-discipline [self'dɪsɪplɪn] *n.* вну́тренняя дисципли́на.
self-doubt [self'daʊt] *n.* неве́рие в себя́.
self-drive [self'draɪv] *n.*: **~ car hire** прока́т автомаши́н.
self-educated [self'edju:,keɪtɪd] *adj.*: **a ~ man, woman** самоу́чка (*c.g.*)
self-effacing [,selfɪ'feɪsɪŋ] *adj.* держа́щийся в тени́.
self-employed [,selfɪm'plɔɪd] *adj.* рабо́тающий не по на́йму; обслу́живающий своё со́бственное предприя́тие.
self-esteem [,selfɪ'sti:m] *n.* самолю́бие.
self-evident [self'evɪd(ə)nt] *adj.* очеви́дный; само́ собо́й разуме́ющийся.
self-explanatory [,selfɪk'splænətərɪ] *adj.* не тре́бующий разъясне́ний.
self-expression [,selfɪk'spreʃ(ə)n] *n.* самовыраже́ние.
self-governing [self'gʌvənɪŋ] *adj.* самоуправля́ющийся.
self-government [self'gʌvənmənt] *n.* самоуправле́ние.
self-help [self'help] *n.* самопо́мощь.
self-image [self'ɪmɪdʒ] *n.* со́бственное представле́ние о себе́.

self-immolation [ˌselfɪmə'leɪʃ(ə)n] *n.* самосожже́ние.
self-importance [ˌselfɪm'pɔːt(ə)ns] *n.* самомне́ние.
self-important [ˌselfɪm'pɔːt(ə)nt] *adj.* ва́жный.
self-improvement [ˌselfɪm'pruːvmənt] *n.* самосоверше́нствование.
self-indulgence [ˌselfɪn'dʌldʒ(ə)ns] *n.* избало́ванность; потво́рство свои́м жела́ниям.
self-indulgent [ˌselfɪn'dʌldʒ(ə)nt] *adj.* избало́ванный; потво́рствующий свои́м жела́ниям.
self-inflicted [ˌselfɪn'flɪktɪd] *adj.* нанесённый самому́ себе́.
self-interest [self'ɪntrəst, -trɪst] *n.* со́бственный интере́с; коры́сть; **he acted from ~** он де́йствовал из коры́стных побужде́ний.
selfish ['selfɪʃ] *adj.* эгоисти́ческий, эгоисти́чный, коры́стный; **~ person** эгои́ст (*fem.* -ка).
selfishness ['selfɪʃnɪs] *n.* эгоисти́чность, эгои́зм.
self-justification [selfˌdʒʌstɪfɪ'keɪʃ(ə)n] *n.* самооправда́ние.
selfless ['selflɪs] *adj.* самоотве́рженный, беззаве́тный.
selflessness ['selflɪsnɪs] *n.* самоотве́рженность, беззаве́тность.
self-loading [self'ləʊdɪŋ] *adj.* (*of weapon*) самозаря́дный.
self-made ['selfmeɪd] *adj.*: **a ~ man** челове́к, вы́бившийся из низо́в.
self-pity [self'pɪtɪ] *n.* жа́лость к себе́.
self-portrait [self'pɔːtrɪt] *n.* автопортре́т.
self-possessed [ˌselfpə'zest] *adj.* наделённый самооблада́нием; невозмути́мый; со́бранный.
self-preservation [selfˌprezə'veɪʃ(ə)n] *n.* самосохране́ние.
self-propelled [ˌselfprə'peld] *adj.* самохо́дный.
self-reliance [ˌselfrɪ'laɪəns] *n.* самостоя́тельность.
self-reliant [ˌselfrɪ'laɪənt] *adj.* полага́ющийся на себя́.
self-reproach [ˌselfrɪ'prəʊtʃ] *n.* самоосужде́ние.
self-respect [ˌselfrɪ'spekt] *n.* самоуваже́ние; чу́вство со́бственного досто́инства.
self-restraint [ˌselfrɪ'streɪnt] *n.* сде́ржанность.
self-righteous [self'raɪtʃəs] *adj.* ха́нжеский.
self-righteousness [self'raɪtʃəsnɪs] *n.* ха́нжество.
self-sacrifice [self'sækrɪˌfaɪs] *n.* самопоже́ртвование.
selfsame ['selfseɪm] *adj.* тот же са́мый.
self-satisfaction [selfˌsætɪs'fækʃ(ə)n] *n.* самодово́льство.
self-satisfied [self'sætɪsˌfaɪd] *adj.* самодово́льный.
self-seeking ['selfˌsiːkɪŋ] *adj.* своекоры́стный.
self-service [self'sɜːvɪs] *n.* самообслу́живание; **~ store** магази́н самообслу́живания.
self-starter [self'stɑːtə(r)] *n.* самопу́ск.
self-styled ['selfstaɪld] *adj.* самозва́ный.
self-sufficiency [ˌselfsə'fɪʃənsɪ] *n.* (*of pers.*) самостоя́тельность; (*econ.*) самообеспе́ченность.
self-sufficient [ˌselfsə'fɪʃ(ə)nt] *adj.* самостоя́тельный; (*econ.*) самообеспе́ченный.
self-supporting [ˌselfsə'pɔːtɪŋ] *adj.* самостоя́тельный.
self-taught [self'tɔːt] *adj.*: **a ~ man, woman** самоу́чка (*c.g.*).
self-will [self'wɪl] *n.* своево́лие.
self-willed [self'wɪld] *adj.* своево́льный.
sell [sel] *v.t.* **1.** прод|ава́ть, -а́ть; торгова́ть (*impf.*) +*i.*; **~ing price** прода́жная цена́; **this shop ~s stamps** в э́том магази́не продаю́тся почто́вые ма́рки; (*offer dishonourably for gain*): **he sold himself to the highest bidder** он прода́лся тому́, кто бо́льше заплати́л. **2.: ~ o.s.** (*present o.s. to advantage*) прод|ава́ть, -а́ть себя́. **3.: he is sold on the idea** (*coll.*) он твёрдо де́ржится за э́ту иде́ю.
v.i. **1.** (*of pers.*): **you were wise to ~ when you did** вы во́время про́дали свой това́р. **2.** (*of goods*): **the house sold for £9,000** за дом вы́ручили 9000 фу́нтов; **the record is ~ing like hot cakes** э́ту пласти́нку покупа́ют нарасхва́т; **his book ~s well** кни́га хорошо́ идёт; **wheat is not ~ing** пшени́ца пло́хо продаётся; **these pens ~ at 30p each** э́ти ру́чки сто́ят 30 пе́нсов шту́ка.
with advs.: **~ off** *v.t.* прод|ава́ть, -а́ть со ски́дкой; **they sold off the goods at a reduced price** они́ распро́дали това́р по сни́женной цене́; **~ out** *v.i.* **the book sold out** э́та кни́га разошла́сь; **they have sold out of tickets** все биле́ты про́даны; **they were accused of ~ing out to the enemy** их обвиня́ли в том, что они́ продали́сь врагу́; **~ up** *v.i.* (**~** *one's possessions*) распрода́ть (*pf.*) своё иму́щество.
cpds. **~-by** *adj.*: **~ date** срок го́дности; **~-out** *n.* распрода́жа; **the play was a ~-out** пье́са прошла́ с аншла́гом.
seller ['selə(r)] *n.* продав|е́ц (*fem.* -щи́ца); торго́в|ец (*fem.* -ка).
Sellotape ['seləˌteɪp] *n.* (*propr.*) липу́чка (*coll.*), скотч.
selvage ['selvɪdz] *n.* кро́мка.
semantic [sɪ'mæntɪk] *adj.* семанти́ческий, смыслово́й.
semantics [sɪ'mæntɪks] *n.* сема́нтика.
semaphore ['seməˌfɔː(r)] *n.* семафо́р.
semblance ['sembləns] *n.* (*appearance*) вид; ви́димость; **under the ~ of** под ви́дом +*g.*; **the ~ of victory** ви́димость побе́ды; (*likeness*) подо́бие.
semelfactive [ˌseməl'fæktɪv] *adj.* (*gram.*) однокра́тный.
semen ['siːmən] *n.* се́мя (*nt.*), спе́рма.
semester [sɪ'mestə(r)] *n.* семе́стр.
semi ['semɪ] *n.* (*coll.*) = **~-detached house.**
pref. полу...
cpds. **~-automatic** *adj.* полуавтомати́ческий; **~breve** *n.* це́лая но́та; **~-circle** *n.* полукру́г; **~-circular** *adj.* полукру́глый; **~colon** *n.* то́чка с запято́й; **~-conductor** *n.* полупроводни́к; **~-conscious** *adj.* в полузабытьи́; **~-consciousness** *n.* полузабытьё; **~-darkness** *n.* полутьма́; **~-detached** *n.*: **~-detached house** (*coll., abbr.* **semi**) оди́н из двух особняко́в, име́ющих о́бщую сте́ну; **~-final** *n.* полуфина́л; **~-finalist** *n.* полуфинали́ст (*fem.* -ка); **~-literate** *adj.* полугра́мотный; **~-precious** *adj.*: **~-precious stone** самоцве́т; **~quaver** *n.* шестна́дцатая но́та; **~-skilled** *adj.* полуквалифици́рованный; **~tone** *n.* полуто́н.
seminal ['semɪn(ə)l] *adj.* **1.** семенно́й; **~ fluid** семенна́я жи́дкость. **2.** (*fig.*) плодотво́рный.
seminar ['semɪˌnɑː(r)] *n.* семина́р.
seminarist ['semɪnərɪst] *n.* семинари́ст.
seminary ['semɪnərɪ] *n.* семина́рия.
Semite ['siːmaɪt, 'sem-] *n.* семи́т (*fem.* -ка).
Semitic [sɪ'mɪtɪk] *adj.* семити́ческий.
semolina [ˌsemə'liːnə] *n.* ма́нная крупа́.
sempstress ['semstrɪs] = **seamstress**
Sen. ['senətə(r)] *n.* (*abbr. of* **Senator**) сена́тор.
senate ['senɪt] *n.* сена́т; (*univ.*) сове́т.
senator ['senətə(r)] *n.* сена́тор.
senatorial [ˌsenə'tɔːrɪəl] *adj.* сена́торский.
send [send] *v.t.* **1.** (*dispatch*) пос|ыла́ть, -ла́ть; отпр|авля́ть, -а́вить; **they ~ their goods all over the world** они́ рассыла́ют свои́ това́ры по всему́ све́ту; **he sent me a book** он присла́л мне кни́гу; **I shall ~ you to bed** я отпра́влю тебя́ спать; **the teacher sent him out of the room** учи́тель вы́гнал его́ из кла́сса; **he was sent to a good school** его́ помести́ли в хоро́шую шко́лу. **2.** (*cause to move*; *propel*): **~ the ball to s.o.** под|ава́ть, -а́ть мяч кому́-н.; **he sent a stone through the window** он запусти́л ка́мнем в окно́; **the blow sent him flying** уда́р сбил его́ с ног; (*fig., drive*): **~ s.o. mad** св|оди́ть, -ести́ кого́-н. с ума́.
v.i.: **I sent for a catalogue** я заказа́л катало́г; **he sent for a doctor** он вы́звал врача́; **~ to us for details** обраща́йтесь за подро́бностями к нам.
with advs.: **~ away** *v.t.* от|сыла́ть, -осла́ть; *v.i.*: **~ away for sth.** выпи́сывать, вы́писать что-н. (из

друго́го ме́ста); ~ **in** *v.t.*: **he sent in his bill** он посла́л счёт; ~ **in one's name** (*enrol*) запи́с|ываться, -а́ться; ~ **in a report** предст|авля́ть, -а́вить отчёт; ~ **off** *v.t.* (*dispatch*) отпр|авля́ть, -а́вить; **he was sent off by the referee** судья́ удали́л его́ с по́ля; **we went to the airport to ~ him off** мы отпра́вились в аэропо́рт проводи́ть его́; ~ **on** *v.t.* (*forward*) перес|ыла́ть, -ла́ть; ~ **out** *v.t.* высыла́ть, вы́слать; (*distribute*) ра|ссыла́ть, -зосла́ть; (*emit*): ~ **out heat** выделя́ть, вы́делить тепло́; ~ **out signals** посыла́ть (*impf.*) сигна́лы; ~ **up** *v.t.*: ~ **up a rocket** запус|ка́ть, -ти́ть раке́ту; (*coll.*, *ridicule*) высме́ивать, вы́смеять.

cpds. **~-off** *n.* про́воды (*pl. g.* -ов); **~-up** *n.* (*coll.*, *parody*, *satire*) паро́дия, па́сквиль (*m.*).

sender ['sendə(r)] *n.* отправи́тель (*m.*).

senile ['si:naɪl] *adj.* ста́рческий; (*of pers.*) дря́хлый; ~ **dementia** ста́рческое слабоу́мие; **become ~** впасть (*pf.*) в ста́рческое слабоу́мие.

senility [sɪ'nɪlɪtɪ] *n.* дря́хлость; ста́рческое слабоу́мие.

senior ['si:nɪə(r)] *n.*: **he is my ~ by 5 years** он на пять лет ста́рше меня́; (*pl.* ~ *pupils*, *students*) старшекла́ссники, старшеку́рсники (*both m. pl.*).

adj. ста́рший (во́зрастом, чи́ном); **I am several years ~ to him** я на не́сколько лет ста́рше его́; ~ **citizen** челове́к пенсио́нного во́зраста; ~ **partner** гла́вный компаньо́н; **Johnson ~** Джо́нсон-ста́рший; Джо́нсон-оте́ц.

seniority [ˌsi:nɪ'ɒrɪtɪ] *n.* старшинство́.

sensation [sen'seɪʃ(ə)n] *n.* **1.** (*feeling*) ощуще́ние; **lose all ~** по́лностью потеря́ть (*pf.*) чувстви́тельность. **2.** (*exciting event*; *excitement*) сенса́ция.

sensational [sen'seɪʃən(ə)l] *adj.* сенсацио́нный.

sensationalism [sen'seɪʃənəˌlɪz(ə)m] *n.* (*pursuit of sensation*) пого́ня за сенса́циями.

sense [sens] *n.* **1.** (*faculty*) чу́вство; **the five ~s** пять чувств; **a dull ~ of smell** приту́пленное обоня́ние; **a keen ~ of hearing** о́стрый слух. **2.** (*feeling*; *perception*; *appreciation*) чу́вство, ощуще́ние; **have you no ~ of shame?** у вас стыда́ нет?; ~ **of beauty** эстети́ческое чу́вство; ~ **of honour** чу́вство че́сти; ~ **of proportion** чу́вство ме́ры; ~ **of direction** уме́ние ориенти́роваться; ~ **of humour** чу́вство ю́мора. **3.** (*pl.*, *sanity*) ум; **take leave of one's ~s** сходи́ть, сойти́ с ума́; **bring s.o. to his ~s** наст|авля́ть, -а́вить кого́-н. на ум; **come to one's ~s** бра́ться, взя́ться за ум. **4.** (*pl.*, *consciousness*): **come to one's ~s** при|ходи́ть, -йти́ в себя́. **5.** (*common ~*) здра́вый смысл; **a man of ~** (благо)разу́мный челове́к; **talk ~** говори́ть (*impf.*) де́ло; **he had the ~ to call the police** у него́ хвати́ло ума́ вы́звать поли́цию; **what would be the ~ of going any further?** како́й смысл продолжа́ть? **6.** (*meaning*) смысл, значе́ние; **in a ~** в не́котором смы́сле; до не́которой сте́пени; **in every ~** во всех отноше́ниях; **in no ~** нико́им о́бразом; **make ~ of** пон|има́ть, -я́ть; раз|бира́ться, -обра́ться в+*p.*; **it makes ~** э́то разу́мно; **it makes no ~** э́то бессмы́сленно; (*cannot be true*) э́то(го) не мо́жет быть.

v.t. чу́вствовать, по-; ощу|ща́ть, -ти́ть.

senseless ['senslɪs] *adj.* **1.** (*foolish*) бессмы́сленный, бестолко́вый. **2.** (*unconscious*) бесчу́вственный; **knock s.o. ~** оглуш|а́ть, -и́ть кого́-н.

senselessness ['senslɪsnɪs] *n.* бессмы́сленность.

sensibilit|y [ˌsensɪ'bɪlɪtɪ] *n.* чувстви́тельность (*e.g. to kindness* к доброте́); **offend, wound s.o.'s ~ies** ра́нить (*impf.*, *pf.*) чьё-н. самолю́бие; оскорб|ля́ть, -и́ть чью-н. чувстви́тельность.

sensible ['sensɪb(ə)l] *adj.* **1.** (*showing good sense*) (благо)разу́мный; **that was ~ of you** вы хорошо́ сде́лали; ~ **shoes** практи́чная о́бувь. **2.: be ~ of** (*be aware of*, *recognize*, *appreciate*) (о)сознава́ть (*impf.*).

sensitive ['sensɪtɪv] *adj.* чувстви́тельный; **don't be so ~!** вы сли́шком оби́дчивы!; (*sharp*): ~ **ears** о́стрый слух; (*of instruments*): ~ **balance** то́чные весы́; (*tender*): ~ **skin** не́жная ко́жа; (*potentially embarrassing*): **a ~ topic** делика́тная те́ма; (*phot.*): ~ **paper** светочувстви́тельная бума́га.

sensitivity [ˌsensɪ'tɪvɪtɪ] *n.* чувстви́тельность.

sensor ['sensə(r)] *n.* (*tech.*) да́тчик.

sensory ['sensərɪ] *adj.* сенсо́рный.

sensual ['sensjʊəl, 'senʃʊəl] *adj.* чу́вственный (*also of mouth etc.*); сладостра́стный.

sensuality [ˌsensjʊ'ælɪtɪ, ˌsenʃʊ-] *n.* чу́вственность, сладостра́стие.

sensuous ['sensjʊəs] *adj.* чу́вственный.

sentence ['sent(ə)ns] *n.* **1.** (*gram.*) предложе́ние. **2.** (*leg.*) пригово́р; ~ **of death** сме́ртный пригово́р.

v.t. пригов|а́ривать, -ори́ть.

sententious [sen'tenʃəs] *adj.* сентенцио́зный.

sentient ['senʃ(ə)nt] *adj.* наделённый чувстви́тельностью.

sentiment ['sentɪmənt] *n.* **1.** (*feeling*) чу́вство; **have friendly ~s towards s.o.** пита́ть (*impf.*) дру́жеские чу́вства к кому́-н.; (*tendency to be swayed by feeling*): **appeal to ~** взыва́ть (*impf.*) к эмо́циям/чу́вствам. **2.** (*opinion*) мне́ние; то́чка зре́ния; **those are my ~s** таково́ моё мне́ние (по э́тому по́воду).

sentimental [ˌsentɪ'ment(ə)l] *adj.* сентимента́льный; **of ~ value** дорого́й как па́мять.

sentimentality [ˌsentɪmen'tælɪtɪ] *n.* сентимента́льность.

sentinel ['sentɪn(ə)l] *n.* (*guard*) часово́й; (*outpost*) сторожево́й пост; **stand ~ over sth.** (*fig.*) стоя́ть (*impf.*) на стра́же чего́-н.; охраня́ть (*impf.*) что-н.

sentry ['sentrɪ] *n.* (*guard*) часово́й; (*post*) карау́льный пост; **stand ~** стоя́ть (*impf.*) на часа́х; ~ **duty** карау́льная слу́жба.

cpd. **~-box** *n.* бу́дка часово́го.

sepal ['sep(ə)l, 'si:-] *n.* чашели́стик.

separate[1] ['sepərət] *adj.* отде́льный, осо́бый; **under ~ cover** отде́льно; **a ~ peace** сепара́тный мир; **two ~ questions** два ра́зных вопро́са; **they are living ~ly** они́ живу́т вро́зь/разде́льно.

separate[2] ['sepəˌreɪt] *v.t.* (*set apart*) отдел|я́ть, -и́ть; (*disunite*, *part*) разлуч|а́ть, -и́ть; **he is ~d from his family** он разлучён со свое́й семьёй; (*distinguish*): ~ **truth from error** отлича́ть (*impf.*) и́стину от заблужде́ния.

v.i. **1.** (*become detached*) отдел|я́ться, -и́ться; (*come untied*) развя́з|ываться, -а́ться. **2.** (*part company*) расст|ава́ться, -а́ться; разлуч|а́ться, -и́ться. **3.** (*of man and wife*) ра|сходи́ться, -зойти́сь.

separation [ˌsepə'reɪʃ(ə)n] *n.* отделе́ние, разделе́ние; разлу́ка; (*of spouses*) разде́льное жи́тельство супру́гов.

separatist ['sepərətɪst] *n.* сепарати́ст (*fem.* -ка).

separator ['sepəˌreɪtə(r)] *n.* (*machine*) сепара́тор.

sepia ['si:pɪə] *n.* се́пия.

sepsis ['sepsɪs] *n.* се́псис; заража́ние кро́ви.

September [sep'tembə(r)] *n.* сентя́брь (*m.*).

adj. сентя́брьский.

septic ['septɪk] *adj.* септи́ческий; **the wound has gone ~** ра́на загнои́лась; ~ **tank** перегнива́тель (*m.*).

septic(a)emia [ˌseptɪ'si:mɪə] *n.* зараже́ние кро́ви.

sepulchral [sɪ'pʌlkr(ə)l] *adj.* (*of a tomb*): ~ **stone** моги́льный ка́мень; ~ **voice** замоги́льный го́лос.

sepulchre ['sepəlkə(r)] *n.* гробни́ца, моги́ла.

sequel ['si:kw(ə)l] *n.* **1.** (*result*, *consequence*) (по)сле́дствие. **2.** (*of novel etc.*) продолже́ние (+*g.*).

sequence ['si:kwəns] *n.* **1.** (*succession*) после́довательность; поря́док; **in rapid ~** оди́н за други́м; ~ **of events** ход собы́тий; ~ **of the seasons** сме́на времён го́да. **2.** (*part of film*) эпизо́д. **3.** (*mus.*) секве́нция.

sequester [sɪ'kwestə(r)] *v.t.* **1.** (*isolate, detach*) изоли́ровать (*impf., pf.*); ~ **o.s. from the world** удал|я́ться, -и́ться от ми́ра; **he leads a ~ed life** он ведёт уединённый о́браз жи́зни. **2.** (*leg. etc.: seize, confiscate*) секвестрова́ть (*impf., pf.*).

sequestration [ˌsi:kwɪ'streɪʃ(ə)n] *n.* секвестра́ция; ~ **of property** аре́ст иму́щества.

sequin ['si:kwɪn] *n.* блёстка.

sequoia [sɪ'kwɔɪə] *n.* секво́йя.

seraglio [se'rɑ:lɪəʊ, sɪ-] *n.* сера́ль (*m.*).

seraph ['serəf] *n.* серафи́м.

Serb [sɜ:b] *n.* серб (*fem.* -ка).

Serbia ['sɜ:bɪə] *n.* Се́рбия.

Serbian ['sɜ:bɪən] *n.* (*native*) серб (*fem.* -ка); (*language*) се́рбский язы́к.

adj. се́рбский.

Serbo-Croat(ian) [ˌsɜ:bəʊkrəʊ'eɪʃ(ə)n] *n.* серб(ск)охорва́тский язы́к.

adj. серб(ск)охорва́тский.

serenade [ˌserə'neɪd] *n.* серена́да.

v.t. & i. петь, с- серена́ду (*кому*).

serene [sɪ'ri:n, sə'ri:n] *adj.* **1.** (*of sky*) я́сный; (*of weather*) ти́хий; (*of sea*) безмяте́жный; (*of pers.: behaviour, appearance*) споко́йный. **2.: His S~ Highness** его́ све́тлость.

serenity [sɪ'renɪtɪ, sə'r-] *n.* споко́йствие; тишина́; безмяте́жность.

serf [sɜ:f] *n.* крепостно́й.

serfdom ['sɜ:fdəm] *n.* крепостни́чество; крепостно́е пра́во.

serge [sɜ:dʒ] *n.* са́ржа.

sergeant ['sɑ:dʒ(ə)nt] *n.* сержа́нт.

cpd. **~-major** *n.* старшина́ (*m.*).

serial ['sɪərɪəl] *n.* (*publication*) периоди́ческое изда́ние; (*story etc.*) рома́н, выходя́щий отде́льными вы́пусками; (*TV*) сериа́л.

adj. **1.** (*forming series*) поря́дковый; ~ **number** поря́дковый но́мер. **2.** (*issued in instalments*): ~ **story** по́весть с продолже́ниями; ~ **film** фильм в не́скольких се́риях.

serialization [ˌsɪərɪəlaɪ'zeɪʃ(ə)n] *n.* сериализа́ция.

serialize ['sɪərɪəˌlaɪz] *v.t.* (*publish, screen etc. in successive parts*) изд|ава́ть, -а́ть вы́пусками/се́риями.

series ['sɪəri:z, -rɪz] *n.* **1.** (*set; succession*) се́рия; **a ~ of lectures** цикл ле́кций; **in ~** по поря́дку; (*number*) ряд; **a ~ of questions** ряд вопро́сов. **2.** (*math., chem.*) ряд. **3.** (*elec.*) после́довательное соедине́ние; **the lamps are connected in ~** ла́мпы соединя́ются после́довательно. **5.** (*TV*) многосери́йная програ́мма.

serious ['sɪərɪəs] *adj.* **1.** (*thoughtful, earnest*) серьёзный; **a ~ child** заду́мчивый ребёнок; **I am ~ about this** я э́то говорю́ всерьёз; **you can't be ~** вы шу́тите; **take sth. ~ly** прин|има́ть, -я́ть что-н. всерьёз; **to be ~; ~ly** (*joking apart*) шу́тки в сто́рону. **2.** (*important; not slight*) серьёзный, суще́ственный, ва́жный; **a ~ charge** серьёзное/тя́жкое обвине́ние; **he is ~ly ill** он серьёзно/тяжело́ бо́лен.

seriousness ['sɪərɪəsnɪs] *n.* серьёзность, ва́жность; **in all ~** без шу́ток; со всей серьёзностью.

sermon ['sɜ:mən] *n.* про́поведь; **the S~ on the Mount** Наго́рная про́поведь.

sermonize ['sɜ:məˌnaɪz] *v.t. & i.* чита́ть (*impf.*) про́поведь/мора́ль (*кому*).

serpent ['sɜ:pənt] *n.* змея́.

serpentine ['sɜ:pənˌtaɪn] *adj.* (*snake-like*) змееви́дный; (*sinuous*) изви́листый, извива́ющийся.

serrated [se'reɪtɪd] *adj.* зу́бчатый, зазу́бренный.

serried ['serɪd] *adj.*: **in ~ ranks** со́мкнутыми ряда́ми; плечо́м к плечу́.

serum ['sɪərəm] *n.* сы́воротка.

servant ['sɜ:v(ə)nt] *n.* (*male, also fig.*) слуга́ (*m.*); (*maid ~*) служа́нка, прислу́га; **civil ~** госуда́рственный слу́жащий; **public ~s** должностны́е ли́ца.

cpd. **~-girl** *n.* служа́нка.

serve [sɜ:v] *n.* (*at tennis*) пода́ча.

v.t. **1.** (*be servant to; give service to*) служи́ть (*impf.*) +*d.*; **one cannot ~ two masters** нельзя́ служи́ть двум господа́м; **if my memory ~s me correctly** е́сли па́мять мне не изменя́ет. **2.** (*meet needs of, satisfy, look after*): **~ a purpose** служи́ть (*impf.*) це́ли; **it ~d his interests to keep quiet** ему́ бы́ло вы́годно молча́ть; **these tools will ~ my needs** э́ти инструме́нты вполне́ мне подхо́дят; (*provide service to*) обслу́ж|ивать, -и́ть. **3.** (*supply with food, goods etc.*) под|ава́ть, -а́ть +*d.*; **the waiter ~d us with vegetables** официа́нт по́дал (нам) о́вощи; **are you being ~d?** вас кто́-нибудь обслу́живает? **4.** (*proffer*) под|ава́ть, -а́ть; **fish is ~d with sauce** ры́ба подаётся с со́усом; **dinner is ~d** обе́д по́дан; **~ a ball** под|ава́ть, -а́ть мяч; **~ a summons** вруч|а́ть, -и́ть (*кому*) (суде́бную) пове́стку. **5.** (*fulfil, go through*): **~ one's sentence** отб|ыва́ть, -ы́ть срок. **6.** (*treat*): **he ~d me badly** он ду́рно со мной обошёлся; **it ~s him right** так ему́ и на́до.

v.i. служи́ть (*impf.*); **he ~d in the First World War** он воева́л в пе́рвую мирову́ю войну́; **~ on a jury** быть прися́жным; **she ~s in a shop** она́ рабо́тает в магази́не; **he ~d at table** он прислу́живал за столо́м; **the plank ~d as a bench** доска́ служи́ла ла́вкой/скамьёй; **a tool which ~s several purposes** инструме́нт, слу́жащий для разли́чных це́лей; **it will ~ to remind him of his obligations** э́то послу́жит ему́ напомина́нием о его́ обяза́тельствах.

with advs.: **~ out** *v.t.* (*distribute*) разд|ава́ть, -а́ть; **~ up** *v.t.* под|ава́ть, -а́ть.

server ['sɜ:və(r)] *n.* (*at tennis*) подаю́щий.

service ['sɜ:vɪs] *n.* **1.** (*employment*) слу́жба; **take s.o. into one's ~** нан|има́ть, -я́ть кого́-н.; **she went into domestic ~** она́ пошла́ в прислу́ги; **length of ~** стаж. **2.** (*branch of public work*): **public, civil ~** госуда́рственная слу́жба; **he entered the diplomatic ~** он поступи́л на дипломати́ческую слу́жбу; **medical ~** слу́жба здравоохране́ния; (*mil.*) медици́нская слу́жба; **intelligence, secret ~** разве́дка; **military ~** вое́нная слу́жба; **do one's military ~** отб|ыва́ть, -ы́ть во́инскую пови́нность; **the (fighting) ~s** вооружённые си́лы (*f. pl.*); **long ~** сверхсро́чная слу́жба. **3.** (*person's disposal*) услу́га; **at your ~** к ва́шим услу́гам. **4.** (*work done for s.o. or sth.*): **will you do me a ~?** мо́жно вас попроси́ть об услу́ге; **offer one's ~s** предложи́ть (*pf.*) свои́ услу́ги; **I need the ~s of a lawyer** мне нужна́ юриди́ческая по́мощь; (*by hotel staff etc.*): **the ~ is poor in that restaurant** в (э́)том рестора́не обслу́живание никуда́ не годи́тся; **~ charge** пла́та за обслу́живание; **~ station** автосе́рвис. **5.** (*assistance*) по́льза; **can I be of ~ to you?** могу́ я быть вам поле́зен?; **what ~ will that be to you?** кака́я вам от э́того по́льза? **6.** (*system to meet public need*): **postal ~** почто́вая слу́жба; **bus ~** авто́бусное обслу́живание; **municipal ~s** коммуна́льные услу́ги (*f. pl.*); **a frequent train ~ to London** ча́стые поезда́ в Ло́ндон. **7.** (*attention to, maintenance of*) техобслу́живание; **~ station** бензозапра́вочная ста́нция. **8.** (*eccl.*) слу́жба; **divine ~** богослуже́ние. **9.** (*set of dishes*) серви́з. **10.** (*in tennis*) пода́ча. **11.** (*leg.*): **~ of a writ** вруче́ние суде́бного предписа́ния.

v.t.: **~ a vehicle** пров|оди́ть, -ести́ осмо́тр и теку́щий ремо́нт маши́ны.

cpd. **~man** *n.* военнослу́жащий.

serviceable ['sɜ:vɪsəb(ə)l] *adj.* (*useful*) поле́зный, го́дный; (*durable*) про́чный.

serviette [ˌsɜ:vɪ'et] *n.* салфе́тка.

servile ['sɜ:vaɪl] *adj.* (*of pers. or behaviour*) раболе́пный, подобостра́стный.

servility [ˌsɜːˈvɪlɪtɪ] *n.* ра́бство; подобостра́стие.

serving [ˈsɜːvɪŋ] *n.* по́рция.

servitude [ˈsɜːvɪˌtjuːd] *n.* ра́бство; **penal ~** ка́торжные рабо́ты (*f. pl.*).

sesame [ˈsesəmɪ] *n.* кунжу́т, сеза́м; **open ~!** сеза́м, откро́йся!

session [ˈseʃ(ə)n] *n.* **1.** заседа́ние; (*period*) се́ссия; **the House is in ~** пала́та сейча́с заседа́ет. **2.** (*University year*) уче́бный год; (*term*) семе́стр.

set [set] *n.* **1.** (*collection*; *outfit*) набо́р; компле́кт; колле́кция; (*number of persons or things*) ряд; се́рия; (*of accessories*) принадле́жности (*f. pl.*); **~ of tools** набо́р инструме́нтов; **complete ~ of stamps** по́лный компле́кт ма́рок; **chess ~** ша́хмат|ы (*pl.*, *g.* —); **~ of furniture** ме́бельный гарниту́р; **dinner ~** столо́вый серви́з; **~ of rules** свод пра́вил; **~ of questions** се́рия вопро́сов; **~ of ideas** систе́ма иде́й. **2.** (*receiving apparatus*): **television ~** телеви́зор. **3.** (*tennis*) сет, па́ртия; **~ point** сет-бо́л. **4.** (*math.*) мно́жество; **theory of ~s** тео́рия мно́жеств. **5.** (*coterie*) круг, кружо́к; компа́ния; **the racing ~** завсегда́таи (*m. pl.*) бего́в. **6.** (*tendency*): **mental ~** скла́д ума́. **7.** (*theatr.*) декора́ция. **8.** (*cin.*): **on the ~** на съёмочной площа́дке.

adj. **1.** (*fixed*): **a ~ stare** неподви́жный взгляд; **a ~ smile** засты́вшая улы́бка; **a man of ~ purpose** целеустремлённый челове́к; **he is ~ in his ways** он закосне́л в свои́х привы́чках; **~ phrase** клише́ (*indecl.*), шабло́нное выраже́ние; **the weather is ~ fair** (хоро́шая) пого́да установи́лась; (*prearranged*): **at the ~ time** в устано́вленное вре́мя; **~ piece** (*literary etc.*) образцо́вое произведе́ние; (*prescribed*): **~ books** обяза́тельная литерату́ра; (*prepared*): **a ~ speech** подгото́вленная ре́чь. **2.** (*coll.*, *ready*): **all ~?** гото́вы?; **we were all ~ to go** мы совсе́м уже собра́лись идти́. **3.** (*resolved*): **he is ~ on going to the cinema** он настро́ился идти́ в кино́; **he was dead ~ against the idea** он на́мертво встал про́тив э́того предложе́ния.

v.t. **1.** (*lay*) класть, положи́ть; (*place*) распол|ага́ть, -ожи́ть; (*arrange*; **~ out**) расст|авля́ть, -а́вить; **12 chairs were ~ round the table** вокру́г стола́ бы́ло расста́влено двена́дцать сту́льев; **~ eyes on** посмотре́ть (*pf.*) на+*a.*; **I have never ~ eyes on him since** с тех пор я его́ бо́льше не ви́дел; **~ one's face against** ни за что не соглаша́ться (*impf.*) на+*a.*; **~ fire to** подж|ига́ть, -е́чь; **~ foot on** наступ|а́ть, -и́ть на+*a.*; **~ one's hand to** приня́ться (*pf.*) за+*a.*; **~ (a) light to** заж|ига́ть, -е́чь спи́чкой; **~ one's name to a document** расписа́ться (*pf.*) на докуме́нте; **as I was ~ting pen to paper** то́лько я на́чал писа́ть; **~ in the ground** сажа́ть, посади́ть; **a safe was ~ in the wall** в сте́ну был встро́ен сейф. **2.** (*adjust*, *prepare*) ста́вить, по-; **~ sail** подн|има́ть, -я́ть па́рус; (*start a voyage*) отпл|ыва́ть, -ы́ть; **~ the table** накр|ыва́ть, -ы́ть (на) стол. **3.** (*make straight or firm*): **~ a bone** впр|авля́ть, -а́вить кость; **~ s.o.'s hair** укла́дывать, уложи́ть кому́-н. во́лосы; **~ting lotion** жи́дкость для укла́дки воло́с. **4.** (*fig.*, *apply*): **~ one's heart on** стра́стно жела́ть (*impf.*) +*g.*; настро́иться (*pf.*) на+*a.*; **~ one's mind on, to sth.** сосредото́читься (*pf.*) на чем-н,; **~ one's hopes on** возл|ага́ть, -ожи́ть наде́жды на+*a.*; **~ the seal on** (*fig.*) оконча́тельно реши́ть/утверди́ть (*pf.*); **~ store by** (высоко́) цени́ть (*impf.*). **5.** (*make or put into specified state*) прив|оди́ть, -ести́; **he will ~ things right** он приведёт всё в поря́док; **he ~ the boat in motion** он привёл ло́дку в движе́ние; **~ at liberty** освобо|жда́ть, -ди́ть; **~ s.o. at ease; ~ s.o.'s mind at ease, rest** успок|а́ивать, -о́ить кого́-н.; **~ s.o. on his feet** (*lit.*, *fig.*) поста́вить (*pf.*) кого́-н. на́ ноги; **~ on fire** подж|ига́ть, -е́чь; (*incite*): **he ~ his dog on me** он натрави́л на меня́ соба́ку; **he ~ the police on to the criminal** он донёс в поли́цию на престу́пника; **she is trying to ~ me against you** она́ стара́ется настро́ить меня́ про́тив вас; (*weigh*): **against the cost can be ~ the advantage** при всей дороговизне (э́того) сле́дует по́мнить и вы́году. **6.** (*cause*; *compel*): **I ~ him to sweeping the floor** я веле́л ему́ подмести́ пол; **he ~ them to work at Greek** он усади́л их за гре́ческий язы́к; **I ~ him to copy the picture** я поручи́л ему́ скопи́ровать карти́ну. **7.** (*start*): **his remarks ~ them laughing** его́ замеча́ния рассмеши́ли их; **I ~ him talking about Russia** я навёл его́ на разгово́р о Росси́и. **8.** (*present*, *pose*) зад|ава́ть, -а́ть; **you have ~ me a difficult task** вы поста́вили передо мной тру́дную зада́чу. **9.** (*establish*): **~ the pace** зад|ава́ть, -а́ть темп; **he is ~ting his children a bad example** он подаёт свои́м де́тям дурно́й приме́р. **10.** (*compile*): **~ an exam paper** сост|авля́ть, -а́вить вопро́сы для пи́сьменного экза́мена. **11.: ~ sth. to music** класть, положи́ть что-н. на му́зыку. **12.** (*insert for adornment etc.*) вст|авля́ть, -а́вить (*во что*). **13.** (*situate*): **he ~ the scene in Paris** ме́стом де́йствия он избра́л Пари́ж; **the scene is ~ in London** де́йствие происхо́дит в Ло́ндоне. **14.: ~ a jewel** опр|авля́ть, -а́вить драгоце́нный ка́мень. **15.** (*typ.*) наб|ира́ть, -ра́ть.

v.i. **1.** (*of sun*) сади́ться, сесть; **we saw the sun ~ting** мы ви́дели зака́т со́лнца; (*of stars*; *also fig.*) за|ходи́ть, -йти́. **2.** (*become firm or solid*) затверд|ева́ть, -е́ть; (*of jelly*) заст|ыва́ть, -ы́ть; (*of cement*, *concrete etc.*) схва́т|ываться, -и́ться. **3.** (*of face or eyes*) заст|ыва́ть, -ы́ть.

with preps.: **~ about (doing) sth.** приступи́ть (*pf.*) к чему́-н.; заня́ться (*pf.*) чем-н.; **~ about** (*beat up*) **s.o.** отде́лать (*pf.*) кого́-н.; **~ (up)on s.o.** нап|ада́ть, -а́сть на кого́-н.; **~ s.o. to work** усади́ть (*pf.*) кого́-н. за рабо́ту.

with advs.: **~ apart, ~ aside** *vv.t.* (*allocate*) выделя́ть, вы́делить; (*reserve*, *save*) от|кла́дывать, -ложи́ть; (*disregard*): **I ~ aside personal feelings** я отбро́сил все ли́чные чу́вства; (*quash*) отмен|я́ть, -и́ть; **the court's verdict was ~ aside** реше́ние суда́ бы́ло отменено́; **~ back** *v.t.* (*lit.*) отодв|ига́ть, -и́нуть; **a house ~ back from the road** дом, стоя́щий в стороне́ от доро́ги; **~ the clock back** перев|оди́ть, -ести́ часы́ наза́д; (*hinder*, *delay*, *damage*) заме́длить (*pf.*); (*coll.*, *cost*): **the trip ~ him back a few pounds** пое́здка обошла́сь ему́ в не́сколько фу́нтов; **~ down** *v.t.* (*put down*) класть, положи́ть; ста́вить, по-; (*allow to alight*) выса́живать, вы́садить; (*make statement or record*): **he ~ down his complaint in writing** он изложи́л свою́ жа́лобу в пи́сьменном ви́де; **she ~ down her impressions in a diary** она́ запи́сывала свои́ впечатле́ния в дневни́к; **~ forth** *v.t.* (*propound*, *declare*) изл|ага́ть, -ожи́ть; *v.i.* (*leave*) отпр|авля́ться, -а́виться; **~ in** *v.t.* (*insert*) вст|авля́ть, -а́вить; **~ in a sleeve** вш|ива́ть, -и́ть рука́в; *v.i.* (*take hold*): **winter is ~ting in** наступа́ет зима́; **the rain ~ in early** до́ждь начался́ ра́но; **~ off** *v.t.* (*cause to explode*): **they were ~ting off fireworks** они́ пуска́ли фейерве́рк; (*cause*, *stimulate*): **his arrest ~ off a wave of protest** его́ аре́ст вы́звал волну́ проте́стов; (*enhance*): **the ribbon will ~ off your complexion** ле́нт оттени́т цвет ва́шего лица́; (*cause to start*): **the story ~ them off laughing** э́тот расска́з заста́вил их расхохота́ться; *v.i.* (*leave*) пойти́, пое́хать (*both pf.*); **we are ~ting off on a journey** мы отправля́емся в путеше́ствие; **the horse ~ off at a gallop** ло́шадь пусти́лась гало́пом; **they ~ off in pursuit** они́ ки́нулись вдого́нку; **~ out** *v.t.* (*arrange*, *display*) выставля́ть, вы́ставить (на обозре́ние); (*expound*) изл|ага́ть, -ожи́ть; *v.i.* (*leave*) пойти́, пое́хать (*both pf.*); отпр|авля́ться, -а́виться;

(*attempt*): **he ~ out to conquer Europe** он вознамерился покорить (всю) Европу; **~ to** *v.i.* (*make a start*) прин|иматься, -яться; (*begin to fight or argue*) сцепиться (*pf.*); **~ up** *v.t.* (*erect*) устан|авливать, -овить; (*form*): **~ up a committee** организовать (*impf., pf.*) комитет; (*found, establish*): **~ up a school** учре|ждать, -дить школу; **he ~ up a new record** он установил новый рекорд; **they ~ up house together** они стали жить вместе; *v.i.* **he ~ up as a butcher** он открыл мясную лавку; **~ up in business** организовать (*impf., pf.*) своё дело.

cpds. **~back** *n.* (*delay*) задержка; (*reverse*) неудача; (*difficulty*) затруднение; **~-square** *n.* угольник; **~-to** *n.* (*fight*) схватка; **have a ~-to** сцеп|ляться, -иться; **~up** *n.* (*coll., arrangement*) устройство; обстановка.

settee [se'ti:] *n.* (небольшой) диван.

setter ['setə(r)] *n.* (*dog*) сеттер.

setting ['setɪŋ] *n.* **1.** (*of sun etc.*) заход. **2.** (*of gems*) оправа. **3.** (*background*) обстановка, окружение. **4.** (*at table*) прибор.

settle ['set(ə)l] *v.t.* **1.** (*place securely; put to rest*): **~ o.s. in an armchair** (удобно) ус|аживаться, -есться в кресло; **~ children for the night** укладывать, уложить детей на ночь. **2.** (*install, establish*) поме|щать, -стить; устр|аивать, -оить. **3.** (*calm*) успок|аивать, -оить; **he gave me sth. to ~ my stomach** он дал мне желудочное лекарство. **4.** (*reconcile*) ула|живать, -дить. **5.** (*dispel*): **he ~d their doubts** он рассеял их сомнения. **6.** (*decide*) реш|ать, -ить; **that ~s it** это решает дело; **let's ~ the matter** давайте кончим с этим делом; **nothing is ~d yet** ещё ничего (окончательно) не решено. **7.** (*put in order*) прив|одить, -ести в порядок. **8.** (*pay*): **~ a bill** заплатить (*pf.*) по счёту; **~ old scores** (*fig.*) св|одить, -ести старые счёты. **9.** (*bestow legally*) закреп|лять, -ить (*что за кем*); (*bequeath*) завещать (*pf.*). **10.** (*colonize*) засел|ять, -ить; (*transport to new home*) посел|ять, -ить.

v.i. **1.** (*sink down; come to rest*) ос|едать, -есть; **the excitement ~d** страсти утихли; (*alight*) ус|аживаться, -есться; **the butterfly ~d on a leaf** бабочка села на лист; **dust ~d on everything** повсюду осела пыль. **2.** (*become fixed, established*) устан|авливаться, -овиться. **3.** (*become comfortable, accustomed; also* **~ down**): **the dog ~d in its basket** собака улеглась в своей корзинке; **he never ~s to anything for long** он ни на чём подолгу не может задержаться. **4.** (*make one's home*) посел|яться, -иться. **5.** (*pay*) распла|чиваться, -титься; (*come to terms*) догов|ариваться, -ориться. **6.** (*decide*) остан|авливаться, -овиться (*на чём*); **have you ~d where to go?** вы решили, куда ехать?

with advs.: **~ down** *v.t.*: **the nurse ~d the patient down for the night** нянечка приготовила больного ко сну; *v.i.* (*in home, job etc.*) устр|аиваться, -оиться; (*at school*) привыкнуть (*pf.*) к школе; (*become quiet*) успок|аиваться, -оиться; **we ~d down for the night** мы улеглись спать; (*give full attention*): **now we can ~ down to our game** теперь можно заняться нашей игрой; **he ~d down to write letters** он уселся писать письма; **~ in** *v.t. & i.* всел|ять(ся), -ить(ся); **~ up** *v.t.* упла|чивать, -тить; *v.i.* распла|чиваться, -титься (*с кем*).

settled ['setəld] *adj.* (*fixed, stable*) устойчивый; (*permanent*) постоянный; (*determined*) определённый; (*staid*) степенный; (*composed*) спокойный.

settlement ['setəlmənt] *n.* **1.** (*settling people*) поселение; (*populating country*) заселение. **2.** (*colony*) поселение; (*settled place*) посёлок. **3.** (*solution*) урегулирование; решение; (*agreement*) соглашение; **reach a ~** дост|игать, -ичь соглашения. **5.** (*leg.*): **~ of one's estate** (*making will*) составление завещания. **6.** (*payment*) уплата, расчёт; **~ of an account** уплата по счёту.

settler ['setlə(r)] *n.* поселенец.

seven ['sev(ə)n] *n.* (число/номер) семь; (**~** *people*) семеро, семь человек; **~ each** по семи; (*figure; thg. numbered 7; group of ~*) семёрка; (*with var. nn. expr. or understood: cf. examples under* **five**).

adj. семь +*g. pl.*; (*for people and pluralia tantum, also*) семеро +*g. pl.*; **~ twos are fourteen** семью (*or* семь на) два — четырнадцать.

cpd. **~fold** *adj.* семикратный; *adv.* в семь раз.

seventeen [ˌsevən'ti:n] *n. & adj.* семнадцать +*g. pl.*

seventeenth [ˌsevən'ti:nθ] *adj.* семнадцатый.

seventh ['sev(ə)nθ] *n.* **1.** (*date*) седьмое (число). **2.** (*fraction*) седьмая часть; одна седьмая.

adj. седьмой; **in the ~ heaven** на седьмом небе.

seventieth ['sevəntɪɪθ] *adj.* семидесятый.

sevent|y ['sevəntɪ] *n.* семьдесят; **he is in his ~ies** ему за семьдесят; **in the ~ies** (*decade*) в семидесятых годах; в семидесятые годы; (*temperature*) за семьдесят градусов.

sever ['sevə(r)] *v.t.* отдел|ять, -ить; **~ a rope** пере|р|езать, -езать верёвку; **~ one's connection with** пор|ывать, -вать связь с+*i.*; **~ diplomatic relations** раз|рывать, -орвать дипломатические отношения.

several ['sevr(ə)l] *pron.*: **~ of my friends** некоторые из моих друзей.

adj. **1.** (*quite a few*) несколько +*g. pl.*; **myself and ~ others** я и кое-кто ещё. **2.** (*separate*) отдельный; **they all go their ~ ways** каждый из них идёт своим путём.

severance ['sevərəns] *n.* разрыв; **~ pay** выходное пособие.

severe [sɪ'vɪə(r)] *adj.* **1.** (*stern, strict, austere*) строгий, суровый. **2.** (*violent*) сильный; **a ~ frost** сильный/жестокий мороз. **3.** (*exacting*): **a ~ test** суровая проверка; **~ competition** жестокая/острая конкуренция. **4.** (*serious*) тяжёлый; серьёзный; **a ~ shortage of water** острая нехватка воды. **5.** (*unadorned*) строгий, суровый.

severity [sɪ'verɪtɪ] *n.* строгость, суровость.

sew [səʊ] *v.t. & i.* шить, с-; **~ a button on to a dress** приш|ивать, -ить пуговицу к платью.

with adv.: **~ up** *v.t.* заш|ивать, -ить.

sewage ['su:ɪdʒ, 'sju:-] *n.* сточные воды (*f. pl.*); нечистоты (*f. pl.*); **~ farm** поля (*nt. pl.*) орошения.

sewer ['su:ə(r), 'sju:-] *n.* (*conduit*) сточная труба; **main ~** магистральная канализационная труба.

sewerage ['su:ərɪdʒ, 'sju:-] *n.* канализация.

sewing ['səʊɪŋ] *n.* (*process, material*) шитьё; (*attr.*) швейный; **~ needle** швейная игла.

cpd. **~-machine** *n.* швейная машина.

sex [seks] *n.* **1.** пол; **without distinction of age or ~** без различия пола и возраста; (*attr.*) половой; **~ appeal** физическая привлекательность; **~ life** половая жизнь. **2.** (*sexual activity*) секс; (*sexual intercourse*) половое сношение; **have ~ with s.o.** (*coll.*) иметь (*impf.*) сношение с кем-н.

sexiness ['seksɪnɪs] *n.* сексуальность.

sexism ['seksɪz(ə)m] *n.* дискриминация женщин; пренебрежительное отношение к женщине.

sexist ['seksɪst] *adj.* женоненавистнический.

sexless ['sekslɪs] *adj.* бесполый.

sextant ['sekst(ə)nt] *n.* секстант.

sextet [sek'stet] *n.* секстет.

sexton ['sekst(ə)n] *n.* пономарь (*m.*); церковный сторож.

sexual ['seksjʊəl, -ʃʊəl] *adj.* половой.

sexuality [ˌseksjʊ'ælɪtɪ, -ʃʊ'ælɪtɪ] *n.* сексуальность.

sexy ['seksɪ] *adj.* (*coll.*) сексуальный, эротический.

shabbiness ['ʃæbɪnɪs] *n.* изношенность; убогость.

shabby ['ʃæbɪ] *adj.* **1.** (*of clothes*) поношенный; потрёпанный; (*of furniture*) вытертый; (*of personal* *appearance*): **he looks ~** у него́ потёртый вид; (*of buildings, streets etc.*) убо́гий, захуда́лый. **2.** (*of behaviour*) ни́зкий, по́длый.

cpd. **~-genteel** *adj.* ≃ стара́ющийся замаскирова́ть свою́ бе́дность.

shack [ʃæk] *n.* лачу́га.

shackle [ˈʃæk(ə)l] *n.* (*pl., fetters*) око́в|ы (*pl., g.* —).

v.t. (*lit., fetter*) зако́в|ывать, -а́ть в кандалы́; (*impede*) ско́в|ывать, -а́ть; стесня́ть (*impf.*).

shade [ʃeɪd] *n.* **1.** (*unilluminated area*) тень; (*partial darkness*) полумра́к. **2.** (*tint, nuance*) отте́нок. **3.** (*slight amount*): **a ~ better** немно́го лу́чше. **4.** (*of lamp*) абажу́р. **5.** (*eye-~*) козырёк. **6.** (*US, blind*) што́ра.

v.t. **1.** (*screen from light*) затен|я́ть, -и́ть; (*shield from light etc.*) заслон|я́ть, -и́ть; **he ~d his eyes with his hand** он заслони́л глаза́ руко́й (от све́та). **2.** (*restrict light of*) прикр|ыва́ть, -ы́ть. **3.** (*drawing*) тушева́ть, за-.

shading [ˈʃeɪdɪŋ] *n.* (*in drawing*) тушёвка.

shadow [ˈʃædəʊ] *n.* тень; **he was a ~ of his former self** от него́ оста́лась одна́ тень; **cast a ~ on** отбр|а́сывать, -о́сить тень на+*a.*; (*fig.*) омрач|а́ть, -и́ть; **there is not a ~ of doubt** нет ни те́ни сомне́ния.

v.t. (*watch and follow secretly*) (та́йно) следи́ть/сле́довать (*impf.*) за+*i.*

shadowy [ˈʃædəʊɪ] *adj.* (*shady*) тени́стый; (*dim*) нея́сный; (*vague*) сму́тный.

shady [ˈʃeɪdɪ] *adj.* **1.** (*affording shade*) тени́стый; (*in shadow*) теново́й. **2.** (*suspect*) сомни́тельный, тёмный; **~ enterprise** сомни́тельное/тёмное де́ло.

shaft [ʃɑːft] *n.* **1.** (*of lance or spear*) дре́вко. **2.** (*arrow*) стрела́. **3.** (*of light*) луч. **4.** (*of tool*) черено́к, ру́чка, рукоя́тка. **5.** огло́бля; ды́шло. **6.** (*tech., rod*) вал; (*axle*) ось. **7.** (*of mine*) ша́хта; ствол ша́хты.

shaggy [ˈʃægɪ] *adj.* косма́тый, лохма́тый.

shah [ʃɑː] *n.* шах.

shake [ʃeɪk] *n.* **1.** встря́ска; **give s.o./sth. a ~** встря́х|ивать, -ну́ть кого́-н./что-н.; **he answered with a ~ of the head** в отве́т он покача́л голово́й. **2.** (*tremble*): **with a ~ in his voice** с дро́жью в го́лосе. **3.** (*coll., moment*): **in a brace of ~s** вмиг, в оди́н миг.

v.t. **1.** тря|сти́, -хну́ть; сотряс|а́ть, -ти́ (*что, чем*); **I shook his hand** (*in greeting*) я пожа́л ему́ ру́ку; **they shook hands** они́ пожа́ли друг дру́гу ру́ки; **he shook the cocktail** он сбил кокте́йль; **he shook his head** он покача́л голово́й; **she shook the duster** она́ вы́тряхнула тря́пку; **the blast shook the windows** от взры́ва задрожа́ли стёкла; **~ one's fist at s.o.** грози́ть, по- кому́-н. кулако́м. **2.** (*shock*) потряс|а́ть, -ти́; **she was ~n by the news** э́та но́вость её потрясла́; (*morally*) колеба́ть, по-; **his faith was ~n** его́ ве́ра была́ поколе́блена; **my confidence in him was ~n** моё дове́рие к нему́ бы́ло подо́рвано.

v.i. **1.** (*vibrate*) трясти́сь (*impf.*); сотряса́ться (*impf.*). **2.** (*tremble*) дрожа́ть, за-; **he was shaking with cold** он дрожа́л от хо́лода; **he shook with laughter** он (за)тря́сся от сме́ха.

with advs.: **~ down** *v.t.*: **he shook down the apples from the tree** он сбил я́блоки с де́рева; (*cause to settle*) утряс|а́ть, -ти́; *v.i.* (*settle, of grain etc.*) утряс|а́ться, -ти́сь; **~ off** *v.t.* (*lit.*) стря́х|ивать, -ну́ть; (*fig., of pursuers, illness, habit etc.*) отде́л|ываться, -аться от+*g.*; изб|авля́ться, -а́виться от+*g.*; **~ out** *v.t.*: **~ out a blanket** вытря́хивать, вы́тряхнуть одея́ло; **~ up** *v.t.* встря́х|ивать, -ну́ть; (*mix by shaking*): **~ up a medicine** взболта́ть (*pf.*) лека́рство; (*coll., rouse*): **he decided to ~ up his staff** он реши́л расшевели́ть свои́х подчинённых.

cpd. **~-up** *n.* встря́ска; перемеще́ние должностны́х лиц; коренны́е переме́ны (*f. pl.*).

shaky [ˈʃeɪkɪ] *adj.* ша́ткий, нетвёрдый; **he is on ~ ground** (*fig.*) у него́ под нога́ми зы́бкая по́чва; **a ~ voice** дрожа́щий го́лос; **his English is ~** он нетвёрд в англи́йском.

shale [ʃeɪl] *n.* сла́нец.

shall [ʃæl, ʃ(ə)l] *v. aux.* (*see also* **should**) **1.** (*in 1st pers.*) *usu. translated by future tense*: **I ~ go** я пойду́. **2.** (*interrog.*): **~ I wait?** мне подожда́ть?; **~ we have dinner now?** не пообе́дать ли нам сейча́с? **3.** (*mandatory*): **I say you ~ go** я прика́зываю вам пойти́; **thou shalt not kill** не убий.

shallot [ʃəˈlɒt] *n.* (лук-)шало́т.

shallow [ˈʃæləʊ] *n.* (*~ place*) ме́лкое ме́сто; (*shoal*) мель; **in the ~s** на мели́/о́тмели.

adj. ме́лкий; (*fig.*): **~ mind** пове́рхностный ум; **~ talk** пусто́й разгово́р.

sham [ʃæm] *n.* **1.** (*pretence*) притво́рство; **his illness is only a ~** он то́лько притворя́ется больны́м. **2.** (*counterfeit*) подде́лка; (*deceit*) обма́н.

adj. **1.** (*feigned*) притво́рный. **2.** (*counterfeit*) подде́льный.

v.t. (*feign, simulate*) притвор|я́ться, -и́ться +*i.*

v.i.: **he is ~ming** он притворя́ется.

shaman [ˈʃæmən] *n.* шама́н.

shamanism [ˈʃæməˌnɪz(ə)m] *n.* шама́нство.

shamble [ˈʃæmb(ə)l] *v.i.*: **~ along** тащи́ться (*impf.*); **~ in** притащи́ться (*pf.*).

shambles [ˈʃæmb(ə)lz] *n.* (*coll., mess*) беспоря́док; **he made a ~ of the job** он завали́л всё де́ло.

shame [ʃeɪm] *n.* **1.** (*sense of guilt; capacity for this*) стыд; **put to ~** пристыди́ть (*pf.*); **for ~!; ~ on you!** стыди́(те)сь! **2.** (*disgrace*) позо́р; **bring ~ on** опозо́рить (*pf.*); **it's a ~ to laugh at him** сты́дно/нехорошо́ над ним смея́ться. **3.** (*sth. regrettable*) жа́лость, доса́да; **what a ~!** как жаль!

v.t. **1.** (*cause to feel ashamed*) сму|ща́ть, -ти́ть. **2.** (*disgrace*) позо́рить, о-.

cpd. **~faced** *adj.* пристыжённый.

shameful [ˈʃeɪmfʊl] *adj.* позо́рный, посты́дный.

shameless [ˈʃeɪmlɪs] *adj.* бессты́дный; (*unscrupulous*) бессо́вестный; (*indecent*) непристо́йный.

shammy [ˈʃæmɪ] *n.*: **~ leather** за́мша.

shampoo [ʃæmˈpuː] *n.* шампу́нь (*m.*).

v.t. мыть, вы́- (*голову*).

shamrock [ˈʃæmrɒk] *n.* бе́лый кле́вер; трили́стник.

shandy [ˈʃændɪ] *n.* смесь пи́ва с лимона́дом; смесь просто́го пи́ва с имби́рным.

shank [ʃæŋk] *n.* **1.** (*leg*) нога́; **on S~s's pony** (*coll.*) на свои́х (на) двои́х. **2.** (*shin*) го́лень.

shanty [ˈʃæntɪ] *n.* (*hut*) хиба́рка; **~ town** трущо́бный посёлок.

shape [ʃeɪp] *n.* **1.** (*configuration, outward form*) фо́рма; **take ~** (*become clear*) проясн|я́ться, -и́ться; **lose one's ~** (*figure*) распл|ыва́ться, -ы́ться; **give ~ to** прид|ава́ть, -а́ть фо́рму +*d.*; (*appearance, guise*) вид, о́браз; **a cloud in the ~ of a bear** о́блако в ви́де медве́дя. **2.** (*order*) поря́док; **put** (*coll., knock*) **sth. into ~** прив|оди́ть, -ести́ что-н. в поря́док; (*condition*) состоя́ние; **he was in poor ~** он был в плохо́м состоя́нии (*or* плохо́й фо́рме); **in good ~** в по́лном поря́дке; в фо́рме. **3.** (*mould*) фо́рма.

v.t. прид|ава́ть, -а́ть фо́рму +*d.*; **~d like a heart** сердцеви́дный; **~d like a cone** конусообра́зный; (*fig.*): **~ s.o.'s character** формирова́ть, с- чей-н. хара́ктер; **~ a plan** созд|ава́ть, -а́ть план; (*adapt*) приспос|а́бливать, -о́бить (*что к чему*).

with adv.: **~ up** *v.i.* (*take ~*) скла́дываться, сложи́ться.

shapeless [ˈʃeɪplɪs] *adj.* бесфо́рменный.

shapely [ˈʃeɪplɪ] *adj.* хорошо́ сложённый; стро́йный.

share [ʃeə(r)] *n.* **1.** (*part*) часть; (*portion, received or held*) до́ля; **have, take a ~ in sth.** уча́ствовать (*impf.*) в чём-н.; **go ~s with s.o.** входи́ть, войти́ в пай с кем-н. **2.** (*contribution*) вклад; **he had no ~ in the plot** он не́ был прича́стен к за́говору. **3.** (*of* *capital*) а́кция; ~ **certificate** акционе́рное свиде́тельство.

v.t. дели́ть, раз- (*что с кем*); **he ~s all his secrets with me** он де́лится со мной все́ми свои́ми та́йнами; ~ **an office with s.o.** рабо́тать (*impf.*) с кем-н. в одно́й ко́мнате; (~ *in*) раздел|я́ть, -и́ть; **he ~s my opinion** он разделя́ет моё мне́ние.

v.i.: **I ~ in your grief** я разделя́ю ва́ше го́ре.

with adv.: ~ **out** *v.t.* (*divide*) раздел|я́ть, -и́ть; (*allocate*) распредел|я́ть, -и́ть; разд|ава́ть, -а́ть.

cpds. **~-cropper** *n.* издо́льщик; **~holder** *n.* акционе́р; **~-out** *n.* делёж.

shark [ʃɑ:k] *n.* (*also fig.*) аку́ла; (*swindler*) моше́нник, шу́лер.

sharp [ʃɑ:p] *n.* (*mus.*) дие́з.

adj. **1.** (*edged, pointed, clear-cut; also fig., of senses, sensations etc.*) о́стрый, ре́зкий; ~ **knife** о́стрый нож; (*keen, alert*): ~ **eyes** о́строе зре́ние; ~ **ears** то́нкий слух; ~ **wits** о́стрый ум; **he is** ~ он хитёр; **keep a ~ look-out** смотре́ть (*impf.*) в о́ба; (*of sounds*): ~ **voice** ре́зкий го́лос; (*severe*): **a ~ remark** ко́лкое замеча́ние; ~ **temper** ре́зкий хара́ктер; ~ **tongue** злой/о́стрый язы́к; ~ **frost** си́льный моро́з; ~ **pain** о́страя боль; (*to the taste*): ~ **dish** о́строе блю́до. **2.** (*abrupt*) круто́й, ре́зкий. **3.** (*artful*) хи́трый; ~ **practice** моше́нничество. **5.** (*mus.*): **F ~** фа (*nt. indecl.*) дие́з.

adv. **1.** (*at a ~ angle*): **turn ~ right** кру́то поверну́ть (*pf.*) напра́во. **2.** (*punctually*): **at four o'clock ~** то́чно/ро́вно в четы́ре (часа́).

cpds. **~-eyed** *adj.* зо́ркий; **~shooter** *n.* ме́ткий стрело́к; сна́йпер; **~-sighted** *adj.* зо́ркий; **~-witted** *adj.* с о́стрым умо́м.

sharpen ['ʃɑ:pən] *v.t.* (*knife etc.*) заостр|я́ть, -и́ть; точи́ть, от-/на-; (*pencil*) точи́ть, от-.

sharpener ['ʃɑ:pənə(r)] *n.* (*whetstone*)точи́ло; (**pencil-~**) точи́лка.

sharpness ['ʃɑ:pnɪs] *n.* острота́; (*of voice etc.*) ре́зкость; (*of outline, photograph etc.*) чёткость.

shatter ['ʃætə(r)] *v.t.* разб|ива́ть, -и́ть (вдре́безги); **the explosion ~ed the house** от взры́ва дом разлете́лся в щепки; (*of health or nerves*) расстр|а́ивать, -о́ить; **I was ~ed by the news** (*coll.*) я был потрясён э́той но́востью.

shattering ['ʃætərɪŋ] *adj.* (*coll.*) потряса́ющий.

shave [ʃeɪv] *n.* **1.** бритьё; **give s.o. a ~** бри́ть, по- кого́-н.; **have a ~** побри́ться (*pf.*). **2.** (*coll., escape*): **we had a close ~** мы бы́ли на волосо́к от ги́бели.

v.t. **1.** ~ **one's chin/beard** вы́брить (*pf.*) подборо́док; брить (*impf.*) бо́роду; ~ **o.s.** бри́ться, по-; **~n** (*of chin*) бри́тый; (*of monk*) постри́женный. **2.** (*pare, of wood etc.*) строга́ть, вы-.

v.i.: **he does not ~ every day** он бре́ется не ка́ждый день.

shaver ['ʃeɪvə(r)] *n.* бри́тва; **electric ~** электробри́тва.

shaving ['ʃeɪvɪŋ] *n.* **1.** (*action*) бритьё. **2.** (**~s**, *of wood or metal*) стру́жка.

cpds. **~-brush, ~-cream, ~-soap** *nn.* ки́сточка/крем/мы́ло для бритья́.

shawl [ʃɔ:l] *n.* шаль; **head ~** головно́й плато́к.

she [ʃi:] *pron.* она́; та; **it was ~ who did it** э́то она́ сде́лала; ~ **and I** мы с ней.

sheaf [ʃi:f] *n.* (*of corn*) сноп; ~ **of arrows** пук/пучо́к стрел; ~ **of papers** па́чка/свя́зка бума́г.

shear [ʃɪə(r)] *n.* (*pl., pair of ~s*) (садо́вые) но́жниц|ы (*pl., g.* —).

v.t. ре́зать, раз-/от-; (*sheep*) стричь, о-.

with adv.: ~ **off** *v.t.* отр|еза́ть, -е́зать.

shearing ['ʃɪərɪŋ] *n.* стри́жка.

sheath [ʃi:θ] *n.* (*of weapon*) но́жны (*pl., g.* но́жен); (*condom*) презервати́в.

cpd. **~-knife** *n.* фи́нка; охо́тничий нож.

sheathe [ʃi:ð] *v.t.*: ~ **one's sword** вкла́дывать, вложи́ть меч в но́жны.

shed[1] [ʃed] *n.* сара́й; (*railway*) депо́ (*indecl.*); (*for aircraft*) анга́р.

shed[2] [ʃed] *v.t.* **1.** сбр|а́сывать, -о́сить; **trees ~ their leaves** дере́вья роня́ют ли́стья; (*of animals*) ~ **hair, feathers, skin** линя́ть (*impf.*). **2.** (*cause to flow*) прол|ива́ть, -и́ть. **3.** (*diffuse*): ~ **light on** (*lit., fig.*) бр|оса́ть, -о́сить свет на+*a*.

sheen [ʃi:n] *n.* (*gloss*) лоск; (*brightness*) блеск.

sheep [ʃi:p] *n.* овца́; **keep ~** держа́ть (*impf.*) ове́ц; **the black ~ of the family** вы́родок (в семье́); **lost ~** заблу́дшая овца́.

cpds. **~-dog** *n.* овча́рка; **~-farmer** *n.* овцево́д; **~-farming** *n.* овцево́дство; **~-fold** *n.* овча́рня; **~-pen** *n.* заго́н (для ове́ц); **~skin** *n.* овчи́на; ове́чья шку́ра; бара́нья ко́жа; **~skin coat** дублёнка.

sheepish ['ʃi:pɪʃ] *adj.* сконфу́женный; глупова́тый.

sheer [ʃɪə(r)] *adj.* **1.** (*mere, absolute*) соверше́нный, су́щий, я́вный; ~ **accident** чи́стая случа́йность; **from ~ habit** про́сто по привы́чке; **it is ~ madness** э́то про́сто сумасше́ствие. **2.** (*precipitous*) отве́сный; **a ~ drop** круто́й обры́в. **3.** (*text., diaphanous*) прозра́чный; (*lightweight*) лёгкий.

sheet [ʃi:t] *n.* **1.** (*bed-linen*) простыня́; **as white as a ~** бле́дный как полотно́. **2.** (*flat piece*): лист (*pl.* -ы́); ~ **of notepaper** листо́к пи́счей бума́ги; ~ **of snow** пелена́ сне́га; ~ **of water/ice** полоса́ воды́/льда; ~ **metal** листово́й мета́лл; ~ **music** но́ты (*f. pl.*).

sheeting ['ʃi:tɪŋ] *n.* (*text.*) просты́нное полотно́.

sheik(h) [ʃeɪk] *n.* шейх.

shelf [ʃelf] *n.* **1.** по́лка; **set of shelves** по́лки. **2.** (*ledge of rock etc.*) вы́ступ; (*reef*) риф; (*sandbank*) о́тмель.

cpds. **~-life** *n.* срок хране́ния *or* го́дности; **~-room** *n.* (свобо́дное) ме́сто на по́лках.

shell [ʃel] *n.* **1.** (*of mollusc etc.*) ра́ковина, раку́шка; (*of tortoise*) щит, па́нцырь (*m.*); (*of egg, nut*) скорлупа́; **come out of one's ~** (*fig.*) выходи́ть, вы́йти из свое́й скорлупы́; (*pod of pea etc.*) кожура́. **2.** (*outer walls of building, ship*) кожура́. **3.** (*explosive case, cartridge*) ги́льза; (*of bomb*) оболо́чка; (*missile*) снаря́д.

v.t. **1.**: ~ **peas** лущи́ть, об- горо́х. **2.** (*bombard*) обстре́л|ивать, -я́ть (артиллери́йскими снаря́дами).

cpds. **~fire** *n.* артиллери́йский ого́нь; **~fish** *n.* (*mollusc*) моллю́ск; (*crustacean*) ракообра́зное; **~-shocked** *adj.* конту́женный; страда́ющий вое́нным невро́зом.

shellac [ʃə'læk] *n.* шелла́к.

shelter ['ʃeltə(r)] *n.* **1.** (*protection*) укры́тие, защи́та; **under, in the ~ of a tree** под защи́той де́рева; **take ~ from** укр|ыва́ться, -ы́ться от+*g.*. **2.** (*building etc. providing ~*) прию́т, приста́нище, убе́жище; (*bomb-~*) (бомбо)убе́жище.

v.t. **1.** (*provide refuge for*) приюти́ть (*pf.*); (*screen from above*) укр|ыва́ть, -ы́ть; (*from side*) прикр|ыва́ть, -ы́ть. **2.** (*protect, defend*) обер|ега́ть, -е́чь; **he led a ~ed life** он жил без забо́т и трево́г.

v.i. укр|ыва́ться, -ы́ться.

shelve [ʃelv] *v.t.* **1.** (*put on shelf*) класть, положи́ть (*or, standing*: ста́вить, по-) на по́лку; ~ **books** расст|авля́ть, -а́вить кни́ги по по́лкам. **2.** (*fig., put aside*): ~ **a plan** от|кла́дывать, -ложи́ть прое́кт (в до́лгий я́щик).

shepherd ['ʃepəd] *n.* пасту́х; **~'s crook** по́сох.

v.t. **1.** (*tend*) пасти́ (*impf.*). **2.** (*marshal*): **she~ed the children across the road** она́ перевела́ дете́й че́рез доро́гу; **the tourists were ~ed into the museum** тури́стов повели́ в музе́й.

shepherdess ['ʃepədɪs] *n.* пасту́шка.

sherbet ['ʃɜ:bət] *n.* шербе́т.

sheriff ['ʃerɪf] *n.* шери́ф.

sherry ['ʃerɪ] *n.* хе́рес.

shield [ʃi:ld] *n.* щит.

v.t. заслон|я́ть, -и́ть; защи|ща́ть, -ти́ть; (*fig.*) огра|жда́ть, -ди́ть; покр|ыва́ть, -ы́ть.

shift [ʃɪft] *n.* **1.** (*change of position etc.*) сдвиг, перемеще́ние; **there was a ~ in public opinion** в общественном мне́нии произошёл сдвиг. **2.** (*of workers*) сме́на; **work (in) ~s** рабо́тать (*impf.*) посме́нно; **he is on the night ~** он (рабо́тает) в ночно́й сме́не. **3.** (*liter., device, scheme*) уло́вка, хи́трость; **make ~ without sth.** об|ходи́ться, -ойти́сь, без чего́-н. **4.** (*type of dress*) пла́тье «руба́шка». **5.** (*US, gear-change*) переключе́ние (ско́рости).

v.t. (*move*) дви́|гать, -нуть; (*transfer*) переме|ща́ть, -сти́ть; **~ the furniture** перест|авля́ть, -а́вить ме́бель; **~ the scene** (*theatr.*) меня́ть (*impf.*) декора́ции; (*remove*) уб|ира́ть, -ра́ть; **this rubbish has to be ~ed** э́тот му́сор на́до убра́ть отсю́да; (*change*) меня́ть (*impf.*); **he ~ed his weight to the other foot** он перенёс вес на другу́ю но́гу; **~ one's ground** (*in argument*) (из)меня́ть (*impf.*) пози́цию.

v.i. **1.** переме|ща́ться, -сти́ться; (*change seat*) перес|а́живаться, -е́сть; (*move house*) пере|езжа́ть, -е́хать; **~ from one foot to another** перемина́ться (*impf.*) с ноги́ на́ ногу; **the cargo is ~ing in the hold** груз скользи́т по трю́му; **~ing sands** дви́жущиеся пески́. **2.** (*manage*): **I can ~ for myself** я обойду́сь без посторо́нней по́мощи.

cpd. **~-work** *n.* сме́нная рабо́та.

shiftless [ˈʃɪftlɪs] *adj.* беспо́мощный, неуме́лый.

shifty [ˈʃɪftɪ] *adj.*: **a ~ fellow** ско́льзкий тип; хи́трый ма́лый; **~ eyes** бе́гающие гла́зки (*m. pl.*).

Shiite [ˈʃiːaɪt] *n.* шии́т; **~ Muslim** мусульма́нин-шии́т.

adj. шии́тский.

shillela(g)h [ʃɪˈleɪlə, -lɪ] *n.* дуби́нка.

shilling [ˈʃɪlɪŋ] *n.* ши́ллинг.

shimmer [ˈʃɪmə(r)] *v.i.* мерца́ть (*impf.*).

shin [ʃɪn] *n.* го́лень; **he barked his ~s** он уда́рился ного́й.

v.t. (*coll.*): **~ up a tree** вскара́бк|иваться, -аться на де́рево; **~ over a wall** перел|еза́ть, -е́зть че́рез сте́ну.

cpd. **~-bone** *n.* большеберцо́вая кость.

shindy [ˈʃɪndɪ] *n.* шум, сканда́л, сва́лка; **kick up a ~** подн|има́ть, -я́ть шум.

shin|e [ʃaɪn] *n.* **1.** (*brightness*) блеск; (*gloss, lustre*) гля́нец, лоск; **give the silver a ~e** чи́стить, посеребро́; **put a ~e on one's shoes** нав|оди́ть, -ести́ гля́нец на ту́фли. **2.: rain or ~e** в любу́ю пого́ду. **3.** (*US coll.*): **take a ~e to s.o.** увле́чься (*pf.*) кем-н.

v.t. **1.** (*polish*) чи́стить, вы́-; **~e shoes** чи́стить, по- ту́фли. **2.: ~e a light in s.o.'s face** осве|ща́ть, -ти́ть фонарём чьё-н. лицо́.

v.i. **1.** (*emit, radiate light*) свети́ть(ся) (*impf.*); (*brightly*) сия́ть (*impf.*); **the sun ~es** со́лнце сия́ет; **a lamp was ~ing in the window** в окне́ горе́ла ла́мпа; (*fig.*): **his face shone with happiness** его́ лицо́ сия́ло от сча́стья. **2.** (*glitter, glisten*) блиста́ть (*impf.*). **3.** (*fig., excel*) блиста́ть (*impf.*); блесте́ть (*impf.*).

shingle[1] [ˈʃɪŋg(ə)l] *n.* (*pebbles*) га́лька.

shingle[2] [ˈʃɪŋg(ə)l] *n.* **1.** (*wooden tile*) (кро́вельная) дра́нка (*s.g. or collect.*); (*pl.*) гонт (*collect.*). **2.** (*US, sign-board*) вы́веска.

shingles [ˈʃɪŋg(ə)lz] *n.* (*med.*) опоя́сывающий лиша́й.

shiny [ˈʃaɪnɪ] *adj.* **1.** (*polished, glistening*) начи́щенный, блестя́щий. **2.** (*through wear*) лосня́щийся.

ship [ʃɪp] *n.* кора́бль (*m.*); су́дно; **~'s company, crew** экипа́ж корабля́; **~'s papers** судовы́е докуме́нты.

v.t. **1.** (*dispatch*) отпр|авля́ть, -а́вить. **2.: ~ oars** класть, положи́ть вёсла в ло́дку.

cpds. **~builder** *n.* судострои́тель (*m.*), кораблестрои́тель (*m.*); **~building** *n.* судострое́ние, кораблестрое́ние; (*attr.*) судострои́тельный; **~-canal** *n.* кана́л для морски́х судо́в; **~mate** *n.* това́рищ (по пла́ванию); **~-owner** *n.* судовладе́лец; **~shape** *adj. & adv.* аккура́тный; в по́лном поря́дке; **~wreck** *n.* кораблекруше́ние; *v.t.*: **be ~wrecked** терпе́ть, по- кораблекруше́ние; **~yard** *n.* верфь; судострои́тельный заво́д.

shipment [ˈʃɪpmənt] *n.* **1.** (*loading*) погру́зка; (*dispatch*) отпра́вка. **2.** (*goods shipped*) па́ртия това́ра.

shipper [ˈʃɪpə(r)] *n.* грузоотправи́тель (*m.*).

shipping [ˈʃɪpɪŋ] *n.* **1.** = **shipment 1.. 2.** (*transport*) перево́зка. **3.** (*collect., ships*) тонна́ж; **unsuitable for ~** неподходя́щий для судохо́дства.

cpd. **~-company** *n.* судохо́дная компа́ния.

shire [ˈʃaɪə(r)] *n.* гра́фство.

shirk [ʃɜːk] *v.t.* уклон|я́ться, -и́ться от+*g.*

v.i. ло́дырничать (*impf.*); гоня́ть (*impf.*) ло́дыря.

shirker [ˈʃɜːkə(r)] *n.* ло́дырь (*m.*).

shirt [ʃɜːt] *n.* руба́шка; соро́чка (*also* = **undershirt**); (*woman's, also*) блу́зка; (*fig.*): **keep your ~ on!** (*coll.*) споко́йно!; успоко́йтесь!

cpds. **~-front** *n.* мани́шка; **~-sleeve** *n.*: **in ~-sleeves** без пиджака́; **~-tail** *n.* низ/подо́л руба́шки.

shish kebab [ˌʃɪʃ kɪˈbæb] *n.* шиш-кеба́б.

shit [ʃɪt] *n.* говно́ (*vulg.*).

v.i. срать, по- (*vulg.*).

shiver [ˈʃɪvə(r)] *n.* дрожь; **it sent a ~ down my back** у меня́ от э́того мура́шки пробежа́ли по спине́.

v.i. дрожа́ть (*impf.*); **he was ~ing with cold** он дрожа́л от хо́лода.

shivery [ˈʃɪvərɪ] *adj.*: **I feel ~** меня́ зноби́т.

shoal[1] [ʃəʊl] *n.* мелково́дье; (*sandbank*) мель, о́тмель.

shoal[2] [ʃəʊl] *n.* (*of fish*) ста́я, кося́к (ры́бы).

shock[1] [ʃɒk] *n.* **1.** (*violent jar or blow*) толчо́к, уда́р; **I got an electric ~** меня́ уда́рило то́ком; **~ wave** взрывна́я волна́. **2.: ~ troops** уда́рные войска́. **3.** (*disturbing impression*) потрясе́ние; **the news gave him a ~** но́вость потрясла́ его́; (*distressing surprise*): **his death was a great ~ to her** его́ смерть яви́лась для неё больши́м уда́ром. **4.** (*med.*) шок; **he is suffering from ~** он нахо́дится в шо́ковом состоя́нии.

v.t. **1.** (*by electricity etc.*) уд|аря́ть, -а́рить. **2.** (*distress, outrage*): **I was ~ed to hear of the disaster** я был потрясён сообще́нием о катастро́фе. **3.** (*offend sense of decency*) шоки́ровать (*impf.*); **he is not easily ~ed** его́ ниче́м не удиви́шь.

cpd. **~-absorber** *n.* амортиза́тор.

shock[2] [ʃɒk] *n.* (*of hair*) копна́ воло́с.

shocking [ˈʃɒkɪŋ] *adj.* (*disturbing*) потряса́ющий; (*disgusting*) возмути́тельный; (*scandalous*) сканда́льный; (*coll., very bad*) ужа́сный; **he has a ~ temper** он ужа́сно вспы́льчивый.

shoddy [ˈʃɒdɪ] *adj.* дрянно́й, низкопро́бный.

shoe [ʃuː] *n.* **1.** ту́фля; полуботи́нок; (*US*) боти́нок; **she never wore ~s** она́ всегда́ ходи́ла босико́м; (*fig.*): **he is ready to step into my ~s** он гото́в заня́ть моё ме́сто; **I wouldn't be in his ~s** я бы не хоте́л быть на его́ ме́сте. **2. (horse~)** подко́ва; (*of brake*) коло́дка.

v.t. (*horse*) подко́в|ывать, -а́ть; **shod** (*of pers.*) обу́тый.

cpds. **~-brush** *n.* сапо́жная щётка; **~horn** *n.* рожо́к (для о́буви); **~-lace** *n.* шнуро́к; **~maker** *n.* сапо́жник; **~-shop** *n.* обувно́й магази́н; **~-string** *n.* шнуро́к; **live on a ~-string** ко́е-как перебива́ться (*impf.*); **~-tree** *n.* коло́дка.

shoo [ʃuː] *v.t.*: **~ away, ~ off** отпу́г|ивать, -ну́ть.

int. (*to birds*) кыш!; (*to cats*) брысь!

shoot [ʃuːt] *n.* **1.** (*bot.*) росто́к, побе́г. **2.** (*~ing expedition*) охо́та.

v.t. **1.** (*discharge, fire*): **he shot an arrow from his bow** он пусти́л стрелу́ из лу́ка; **these guns ~ rubber bullets** э́ти ру́жья стреля́ют рези́новыми пу́лями; (*fig.*): **~ a glance at s.o.** бро́сить (*pf.*) взгляд на кого́-н. **2.** (*kill*) застрели́ть (*pf.*); (*wound*) ра́нить (*impf., pf.*); ~ **s.o. in the back** вы́стрелить (*pf.*) кому́-н. в спи́ну; ~ **s.o. through the leg** простре́л|ивать, -и́ть кому́-н. но́гу; **he was shot in the head** пу́ля попа́ла ему́ в го́лову; (*execute*) расстре́л|ивать, -я́ть; **he will be shot for treason** его́ расстреля́ют за изме́ну. **3.** (*propel*): ~ **the ball into the net** пос|ыла́ть, -ла́ть мяч в се́тку; ~ **a bolt** (*on door*) задв|ига́ть, -и́нуть засо́в. **4.** (*cin.*): ~ **a film** сн|има́ть, -ять фильм.

v.i. **1.** (*fire, of pers. or weapon*) стрел|я́ть, -ьну́ть; вы́стрелить (*pf.*); **the police shot to kill** полице́йские стреля́ли, не щадя́ жи́зни; **he is out ~ing** он на охо́те. **2.** (*dart*) прон|оси́ться, -ести́сь; **the car shot ahead** маши́на рвану́лась вперёд; **he shot out of the doorway** он вы́скочил из подъе́зда; **a ~ing pain** стреля́ющая боль; **a ~ing star** па́дающая звезда́; **the flames shot upward** пла́мя взмы́ло вверх. **3.** (*of plants*) пус|ка́ть, -ти́ть побе́ги. **4.** (*football etc.*): бить (*impf.*) по мячу́; **~!** бей! **5.** (*cin.*): **they were ~ing all morning** они́ всё у́тро снима́ли.

with advs.: ~ **down** *v.t.*: **we shot down five enemy aircraft** мы сби́ли пять самолётов проти́вника; **the prisoners were shot down** пле́нных расстреля́ли; ~ **off** *v.i.* (*coll., leave hurriedly*) вы́лететь (*pf.*) (пу́лей); ~ **out** *v.t.* (*extend*): **he shot out his hand** он стреми́тельно протяну́л ру́ку; *v.i.* вырыва́ться, вы́рваться; **a car shot out of a side-street** из переу́лка вы́летела маши́на; ~ **up** *v.i.* (*grow rapidly*) бы́стро расти́, вы́-; (*of child*) вытя́гиваться, вы́тянуться; (*of prices etc.*) подск|а́кивать, -очи́ть.

shooting [ˈʃuːtɪŋ] *n.* (*marksmanship*) стрельба́; (*sport*) охо́та.

cpds. **~-gallery** *n.* тир; **~-party** *n.* гру́ппа охо́тников; **~-range** *n.* тир; (*outdoor*) стре́льбище, полиго́н; **~-stick** *n.* трость-табуре́т.

shop [ʃɒp] *n.* **1.** магази́н; (*small* ~) ла́вка; **keep (a)** ~ держа́ть (*impf.*) ла́вку; **all over the** ~ (*everywhere*) повсю́ду; (*in confusion*) в беспоря́дке; **talk** ~ говори́ть (*impf.*) о (свои́х профессиона́льных) дела́х. **2.** (*work*~) мастерска́я, цех; **on the ~ floor** в цеха́х; ~ **steward** цехово́й ста́роста.

v.i. де́лать, с- поку́пки; **we go ~ping in the market** мы хо́дим за поку́пками на ры́нок.

cpds. **~-assistant** *n.* продав|е́ц (*fem.* -щи́ца); **~keeper** *n.* ла́вочни|к (*fem.* -ца); **~-lifter** *n.* магази́нный вор; **~-lifting** *n.* воровство́ в магази́нах; **~-soiled** *adj.* лежа́лый; **~-window** *n.* витри́на.

shopper [ˈʃɒpə(r)] *n.* покупа́тель (*fem.* -ница).

shopping [ˈʃɒpɪŋ] *n.* поку́пки (*f. pl.*); **do one's** ~ де́лать, с- поку́пки; ~ **centre** торго́вый центр.

cpds. **~-bag** *n.* хозя́йственная су́мка.

shore[1] [ʃɔː(r)] *n.* бе́рег; **on the** ~ на берегу́; **in** ~ у бе́рега; ~ **leave** о́тпуск/вольне́ние на бе́рег.

shore[2] [ʃɔː(r)] *v.t.*: ~ **up** подп|ира́ть, -ере́ть.

short [ʃɔːt] *n.* **1.** (~ *film*) короткометра́жный фильм. **2.** (~ *circuit*) коро́ткое замыка́ние. **3.** (~ *drink*) рю́мочка пе́ред едо́й. **4.** (*pl.*, ~ *trousers*) тру́сик|и (*pl., g.* -ов), шо́рт|ы (*pl., g.* -ов).

adj. **1.** коро́ткий; (*of* ~ *duration*) кра́ткий; (*of stature*) невысо́кого ро́ста; (*small*) небольшо́й; **a** ~ **distance away** недалеко́, неподалёку; **this dress is too** ~ э́то пла́тье сли́шком коротко́; ~ **steps** ме́лкие шаги́; **the days are getting ~er** дни стано́вятся коро́че; **the ~est distance** кратча́йшее расстоя́ние; **for a** ~ **time** на коро́ткое вре́мя; **a** ~ **time ago** неда́вно; **a** ~ **life** недо́лгая/коро́ткая жизнь; **time is** ~ вре́мени ма́ло; ~ **cut** (*route*) кратча́йший путь; ~ **list** спи́сок наибо́лее подходя́щих кандида́тов; **in** ~ **order** (*US, at once*) то́тчас; ~ **story** расска́з; **be on** ~ **time** рабо́тать (*impf.*) непо́лную неде́лю (*or* на полста́вке); **make** ~ **work of sth.** бы́стро распр|авля́ться, -а́виться с чем-н.; **I want my hair cut** ~ я хочу́ ко́ротко постри́чься. **2.** (*concise, brief*): **in** ~ коро́че говоря́; **for** ~ сокращённо; для кра́ткости. **3.** (*curt, sharp*) ре́зкий; **he has a** ~ **temper** он вспы́льчив. **4.** (*insufficient*): **in** ~ **supply** дефици́тный; **give s.o.** ~ **change** обсчи́т|ывать, -а́ть кого́-н.; **I am 2 pounds** ~ у меня́ не хвата́ет двух фу́нтов. **5.: be** ~ **of sth.** (*lacking*) испы́тывать (*impf.*) недоста́ток в чём-н.; **be** ~ **of breath** запыха́ться (*impf.*); **they are** ~ **of bread** у них не хвата́ет хле́ба. **6.:** ~ **of** (*except*) кро́ме+*g.*

adv. **1.** (*abruptly*): **he stopped** ~ он вдруг останови́лся; (*while speaking*) он вдруг замолча́л; **he tried to cut me** ~ он стара́лся прерва́ть меня́ на полусло́ве. **2.** (*not far enough*): **the ball fell** ~ мяч не долете́л. **3.** ~ **of** (*without reaching*): **fall** ~ **of a target** не дост|ига́ть, -и́чь це́ли; **the play fell** ~ **of my expectations** пье́са не оправда́ла мои́х наде́жд; **we ran** ~ **of potatoes** у нас вы́шла (вся) карто́шка.

cpds. **~bread, ~cake** *nn.* песо́чное пече́нье; **~-change** *v.t.* (*coll.*) обсчи́т|ывать, -а́ть; **~-circuit** *v.t.* зам|ыка́ть, -кну́ть на́коротка; **~coming** *n.* недоста́ток; **~fall** *n.* недоста́ток, дефици́т; **~hand** *n.* стеногра́фия; **~hand typist** (машини́стка)-стенографи́стка; **take down in ~hand** стенографи́ровать, за-; **~-handed** *adj.*: **we are ~-handed** у нас не хвата́ет рабо́тников; **~-list** *v.t.* зан|оси́ть, -ести́ в спи́сок наибо́лее подходя́щих кандида́тов; **~-lived** *adj.* недолгове́чный; **~-range** *adj.* (*of missile*) бли́жнего де́йствия; (*of forecast*) краткосро́чный; **~-sighted** *adj.* (*lit., fig.*) близору́кий; **~-sightedness** *n.* близору́кость; **~-tempered** *adj.* вспы́льчивый; **~-term** *adj.* краткосро́чный; **~-wave** *adj.* коротково́лновый.

shortage [ˈʃɔːtɪdʒ] *n.* недоста́ток, нехва́тка, дефици́т.

shorten [ˈʃɔːt(ə)n] *v.t. & i.* укор|а́чивать(ся), -оти́ть(ся); сокра|ща́ть(ся), -ти́ть(ся).

shortening [ˈʃɔːtənɪŋ] *n.* (*cul.*) жир.

shortly [ˈʃɔːtlɪ] *adv.* (*soon*) ско́ро; ~ **before** незадо́лго до+*g.*; ~ **after** вско́ре по́сле+*g.*

shortness [ˈʃɔːtnɪs] *n.* коро́ткость; ~ **of breath** оды́шка.

shot [ʃɒt] *n.* **1.** (*missile*): **putting the** ~ (*sport*) толка́ние ядра́; (*pellet*) дроби́нка; (*collect.*) дробь. **2.** (*discharge of firearm*) вы́стрел; **fire a** ~ де́лать, с- вы́стрел; **take a** ~ **at** стрельну́ть (*pf.*) по+*d.*; **like a** ~ (*rapidly*) в одну́ мину́ту; **he was off like a** ~ он вы́бежал стреми́тельно/пу́лей; **have a** ~ попыта́ться (*pf.*); **a** ~ **in the dark** случа́йная дога́дка; **not by a long** ~ нико́им о́бразом. **3.** (*stroke, at games etc.*) уда́р; **(good) ~!** молоде́ц! **4.** (*of pers.*) стрело́к; **he's a good** ~ он хоро́ший стрело́к. **5.** (*phot.*) сни́мок; (*cin.*) кадр. **6.** (*small dose*) небольша́я до́за; ~ **of liquor** глото́к спиртно́го; (*injection*) уко́л.

cpd. **~gun** *n.* дробови́к.

should [ʃud, ʃəd] *v. aux.* **1.** (*conditional*): **I** ~ **say** я бы сказа́л; **I** ~ **have thought so** каза́лось бы; ~ **he die** е́сли он умрёт; **I ~n't think so** не ду́маю; **if I were you I ~n't ...** на ва́шем ме́сте я не стал бы... **2.** (*expr. duty*): **you** ~ **tell him** вам сле́дует ему́ сказа́ть; **there is no reason why you** ~ **do that** у вас нет никаки́х основа́ний так поступа́ть. **3.** (*expr. probability or expectation*): **we** ~ **be there by noon** мы должны́ бы поспе́ть туда́ к полу́дню; **they** ~ **be there by now** они́, ве́рно, уже́ при́были; **how** ~ **I know?** а я почём зна́ю?; отку́да мне знать? **why** ~ **you think that?** почему́ вы так ду́маете? **4.** (*expr. future in the past*): **I told him I** ~ (*would*) **be going** я ему́ сказа́л, что пойду́. **5.** (*expr. purpose*): **I am anxious that it** ~ **be done at once** мне ва́жно, что́бы э́то бы́ло сде́лано сра́зу; **he suggested that I** ~ **go** он предложи́л мне уйти́. **6.** (*subjunctive use*): **I am surprised that he** ~ **be so foolish** не ожида́л я, что он ока́жется столь неразу́мен.

shoulder [ˈʃəʊldə(r)] *n.* плечо́; **shrug one's ~s** пож|има́ть, -а́ть плеча́ми; **slung across the ~** перебро́шенный че́рез плечо́; **~ to ~** плечо́м к плечу́; **have round ~s** быть суту́лым; **have broad ~s** име́ть (*impf.*) широ́кие пле́чи; **I gave it to him straight from the ~** я рубану́л ему́ пря́мо сплеча́; **give s.o. the cold ~** встр|еча́ть, -е́тить кого́-н. хо́лодно. **2.** (*of road*) обо́чина.

v.t. (*lit.*): **~ a heavy load** взва́л|ивать, -и́ть на себя́ тяжёлый груз; **~ a rifle** брать, взять винто́вку на плечо́; **~ arms!** на плечо́! к плечу́!; (*fig.*): **~ responsibility** брать, взять на себя́ отве́тственность.

cpds. **~-blade** *n.* лопа́тка; **~-high** *adj.*: **the grass was ~-high** трава́ была́ (*кому*) по плечо́; *adv.*: **carry s.o. ~-high** носи́ть, нести́ кого́-н. на плеча́х; **~-pad** *n.* пле́чико, подкладно́е плечо́; **~-strap** *n.* (*mil.*) пого́н; (*of knapsack*) реме́нь (*m.*); (*of undergarment*) брете́лька.

shout [ʃaʊt] *n.* крик.

v.t. выкри́кивать, вы́крикнуть.

v.i. кр|ича́ть, за-, -и́кнуть; **he ~ed with laughter** он надрыва́лся от сме́ха; **don't ~ at me** не кричи́те на меня́; **~ for s.o.** гро́мко звать, по- кого́-н.; **~ for help** звать, по- на по́мощь.

with advs.: **~ down** *v.t.* перекрича́ть (*pf.*); **~ out** *v.t.*: **he ~ed out our names** он вы́крикнул на́ши фами́лии; *v.i.* закрича́ть (*pf.*).

shove [ʃʌv] *n.* толчо́к.

v.t. толк|а́ть, -ну́ть; **~ sth. into one's pocket** сова́ть/су́нуть что-н. себе́ в карма́н; **he ~d his way forward** он проти́снулся вперёд.

with advs.: **~ aside, ~ away** *vv.t.* отт|а́лкивать, -олкну́ть; отпи́х|ивать, -ну́ть; **~ down** *v.t.* ст|а́лкивать, -олкну́ть; **~ off** *v.i.* (*naut.*) отт|а́лкиваться, -олкну́ться от бе́рега.

shovel [ˈʃʌv(ə)l] *n.* лопа́та.

v.t.: **~ coal into a cellar** сбр|а́сывать, -о́сить у́голь в подва́л; **~ snow off a path** сгре|ба́ть, -сти́ снег с доро́жки.

show [ʃəʊ] *n.* **1.** (*manifestation*): **a ~ of hands** голосова́ние подня́тием рук; **make a ~ of learning** пока́з|ывать, -а́ть свою́ учёность; **~ trial** показа́тельный проце́сс; (*semblance*) ви́димость. **2.** (*exhibition*) пока́з, вы́ставка; **be on ~** быть вы́ставленным; **dog/flower ~** вы́ставка соба́к/цвето́в; **do sth. for ~** де́лать, с- что-н. напока́з; (*ostentation*) пара́дность. **3.** (*entertainment*) представле́ние; **~ business** театра́льное де́ло; **let's go to a ~** пойдёмте в теа́тр; **good ~!** здо́рово! **4.** (*concern*) де́ло; **run the ~** вести́ (*det.*) де́ло.

v.t. **1.** (*disclose, reveal, offer for inspection*) пока́з|ывать, -а́ть; **he ~ed his true colours** он показа́л своё и́стинное лицо́; **this dress will not ~ the dirt** на э́том пла́тье грязь не бу́дет заме́тна; **he has nothing to ~ for his efforts** у него́ ничего́ не получи́лось; **have sth. to ~ for one's money** тра́тить, по- де́ньги не впусту́ю; **he ~ ed signs of tiring** он на́чал заме́тно устава́ть; **~ o.s.** (*appear*) появ|ля́ться, -и́ться; **he ~ed himself unfit to govern** он прояви́л свою́ неспосо́бность управля́ть. **2.** (*exhibit publicly*) выставля́ть (*impf.*); (*a film*) демонстри́ровать (*impf.*, *pf.*); **what are they ~ing at the theatre?** что идёт в теа́тре? **3.** (*display, manifest*) ока́з|ывать, -а́ть; **he ~ed a preference** он оказа́л предпочте́ние; **~ willing** (*coll.*) прояви́ть (*pf.*) гото́вность. **4.** (*point out*) ука́з|ывать, -а́ть на+*a.*; (*reach by precept*): **he ~ed me how to play** он показа́л мне, как игра́ть; (*demonstrate, prove*) дока́з|ывать, -а́ть; (*explain, illustrate*) объясн|я́ть, -и́ть. **5.** (*conduct*) прово|жа́ть, -ди́ть; **he ~ed me to the door** он проводи́л меня́ до двере́й; **I ~ed him round the garden** я поводи́л его́ по са́ду.

v.i. **1.** (*be visible*) видне́ться (*impf.*); **the stain will not ~** пятно́ не бу́дет заме́тно; **the light ~ed through the curtain** свет просве́чивал сквозь занаве́ску. **2.** (*be exhibited*): **what films are ~ing?** каки́е иду́т фи́льмы?

with advs.: **~ in** *v.t.* вв|оди́ть, -ести́ в ко́мнату/дом; **~ off** *v.t.* (*display to advantage*): **the frame ~s off the picture** в э́той ра́мке карти́на хорошо́ смо́трится; (*boastfully*) щеголя́ть, по- +*i.*; *v.i.*: **the child is ~ing off** ребёнок рису́ется; **~ out** *v.t.* пров|оди́ть, -ести́ к вы́ходу; **~ through** *v.i.*: **light ~s through** свет проника́ет; **~ up** *v.t.* (*make conspicuous*) сде́лать (*pf.*) заме́тным; *v.i.* (*coll., appear*) появ|ля́ться, -и́ться; (*be conspicuous*): **the flowers ~ed up against the white background** цветы́ выделя́лись на бе́лом фо́не.

cpds. **~-boat** *n.* плаву́чий теа́тр; **~-business** *n.* театра́льное де́ло; **~-case** *n.* витри́на; **~-down** *n.* про́ба сил; **~-ground** *n.* ме́сто, вы́деленное для я́рмарок; **~man** *n.* антрепренёр; **~-room** *n.* демонстрацио́нный зал.

shower [ˈʃaʊə(r)] *n.* **1.** (*of rain/snow*) кратковре́менный дождь/снег; **heavy ~** проливно́й дождь. **2.** (*of hail, also fig.*) град. **3.** (**~-bath**) душ; **take a ~** прин|има́ть, -я́ть душ.

v.t. **1.** (*with water etc.*) залива́ть (*impf.*). **2.** (*with bullets etc.*) ос|ыпа́ть, -ы́пать гра́дом (пуль *и т. п.*); **he ~ed me with questions** он засы́пал меня́ вопро́сами.

v.i. **1.** (*of rain etc.*) лить(ся) (*impf.*). **2.** (*fig.*) сы́паться (*impf.*). **3.** (*have a ~-bath*) прин|има́ть, -я́ть душ.

cpds. **~-cap** *n.* рези́новая ша́почка; **~-room** *n.* душева́я.

showery [ˈʃaʊərɪ] *adj.* дождли́вый.

showing [ˈʃəʊɪŋ] *n.*: **he made a poor ~** он произвёл нева́жное впечатле́ние; **on present ~** ; согла́сно име́ющимся показа́ниям; **on your own ~** по ва́шему со́бственному призна́нию.

showy [ˈʃəʊɪ] *adj.* показно́й.

shrapnel [ˈʃræpn(ə)l] *n.* шрапне́ль.

shred [ʃred] *n.* **1.** (*of cloth*) клочо́к; **tear to ~s** раз|рыва́ть, -орва́ть в клочки́/кло́чья; (*small piece*) кусо́к; **cut into ~s** разр|еза́ть, -е́зать на куски́. **2.** (*fig., scrap, bit*): **there is not a ~ of truth in what he says** в том, что он говори́т, (нет) ни ка́пли пра́вды.

v.t. (*tear*) разр|ыва́ть, -орва́ть; (*cut*) разр|еза́ть, -е́зать; **~ cabbage** шинкова́ть (*impf.*) капу́сту.

shrew [ʃru:] *n.* (*zool.*) землеро́йка; (*woman*) сварли́вая же́нщина.

shrewd [ʃru:d] *adj.* проница́тельный, ло́вкий.

shrewdness [ˈʃru:dnɪs] *n.* проница́тельность, ло́вкость.

shriek [ʃri:k] *n.* визг; **~s of laughter could be heard** раздава́лись взры́вы сме́ха.

v.t. визгли́во выкри́кивать, вы́крикнуть.

v.i. визжа́ть, взви́згнуть.

shrift [ʃrɪft] *n.*: **they gave him short ~** они́ с ним бы́стро распра́вились.

shrill [ʃrɪl] *adj.* пронзи́тельный.

shrimp [ʃrɪmp] *n.* креве́тка; (*fig., undersized pers.*) коροты́шка (*c.g.*).

shrine [ʃraɪn] *n.* (*casket with relics*) ра́ка; (*chapel*) часо́вня; (*lit., fig., hallowed place*) святы́ня, храм.

shrink [ʃrɪŋk] *v.t.*: **hot water will ~ this fabric** от горя́чей воды́ э́тот материа́л ся́дет.

v.i. **1.** (*of clothes*) сади́ться, сесть; **my shirt has shrunk** моя́ руба́шка се́ла. **2.** (*grow smaller*) сокра|ща́ться, -ти́ться. **3.** (*recoil, retreat*) отпря́нуть (*pf.*); **he shrank (back) from the fire** он отпря́нул от огня́; **he will not ~ from danger** он не отсту́пит пе́ред опа́сностью.

shrinkage [ˈʃrɪŋkɪdʒ] *n.* уса́дка.

shrivel [ˈʃrɪv(ə)l] *v.t.* (*dry up*) высу́шивать, вы́сушить;

(*wrinkle*) мóрщить, с-.

v.i. (*dry up*) высыхáть, вы́сохнуть; (*wrinkle up*) смóрщи|ваться, -ться; (*wither*) ув|ядáть, -я́нуть.

shroud [ʃraʊd] *n.* сáван.

v.t. (*obscure, lit. & fig.*) окýт|ывать, -ать.

Shrovetide ['ʃrəʊvtaɪd] *n.* мáсленица.

Shrove Tuesday [ʃrəʊv] *n.* втóрник на мáсленой недéле.

shrub [ʃrʌb] *n.* (*bot.*) куст.

shrubbery ['ʃrʌbərɪ] *n.* кустáрник.

shrug [ʃrʌg] *n.* пожимáние плечáми; **with a ~ (of the shoulders)** пожáв плечáми.

v.t. & i.: **~ (one's shoulders)** пож|имáть, -áть плечáми; **~ sth. off** отстран|я́ть, -и́ть что-н. от себя́.

shudder ['ʃʌdə(r)] *n.* дрожь; **he gave a ~** он вздрóгнул.

v.i. дрожáть, за-; содрог|áться, -нýться; **I ~ to think of it** содрогáюсь при однóй мы́сли об э́том.

shuffle ['ʃʌf(ə)l] *n.* **1.** (*movement*) шáркание. **2.** (*of cards*) тасóвка.

v.t. **1. ~ one's feet** шáркать (*impf.*) ногáми. **2.: ~ cards** тасовáть, с- кáрты.

v.i.: **~ along, about** волочи́ть (*impf.*) нóги.

shun [ʃʌn] *v.t.* избегáть (*impf.*) +*g.*

shunt [ʃʌnt] *v.t.* **1.** (*rail.*, *fig.*) перев|оди́ть, -ести́; **~-line** запáсный путь. **2.** (*postpone*, *shelve*) класть, положи́ть под сукнó.

v.i. маневри́ровать (*impf.*).

shush [ʃʊʃ, ʃʌʃ] *v.t.* ши́к|ать, -нуть на+*a.*

v.i. (*be silent*) замолчáть (*pf.*); (*call for silence*) шипéть.

int. шш!

shut [ʃʌt] *v.t.* **1.** (*close*) закр|ывáть, -ы́ть; **the door was ~ tight** дверь былá плóтно закры́та; **~ a drawer** задв|игáть, -и́нуть я́щик; **~ one's mind to** игнори́ровать (*impf.*); **he learnt to keep his mouth ~** он научи́лся держáть язы́к за зубáми; (*lock*) зап|ирáть, -ерéть; (*keep by force*): **he was ~ out of the room** егó не пускáли в кóмнату. **2.** (*trap*): **my raincoat got ~ in the door** мой плащ прищеми́ло двéрью.

v.i. закр|ывáться, -ы́ться.

with advs.: **~ down** *v.t. & i.* закр|ывáть(ся), -ы́ть(ся); **~ in** *v.t.* (*surround*) окруж|áть, -и́ть; **I got ~ in** я оказáлся взаперти́; **~ off** *v.t.* (*stop supply of*) отключ|áть, -и́ть; (*switch off*) выключáть, вы́ключить; (*isolate*) изоли́ровать (*impf.*, *pf.*); **~ out** *v.t.* (*exclude*) исключ|áть, -и́ть; (*fence off*) загор|áживать, -оди́ть; **those trees ~ out the view** э́ти дерéвья заслоня́ют вид; **~ out light/noise** не пропус|кáть, -ти́ть свéта/шýма; **~ up** *v.t.* (*close*) зап|ирáть, -ерéть; (*silence*): **they soon ~ him up** они́ скóро застáвили егó замолчáть; *v.i.* (*be, become silent*) молчáть, за-; **~ up!** заткни́сь!

shutter ['ʃʌtə(r)] *n.* **1.** (*on window*) стáвень (*m.*). **2.** (*phot.*) затвóр.

v.t. закр|ывáть, -ы́ть стáвнями.

shuttle ['ʃʌt(ə)l] *n.* (*for weaving*) челнóк; (*fig.*) **~ service** движéние (поездóв, автóбусов *и т п*) в óба концá; **~ diplomacy** челнóчная дипломáтия; **space ~** косми́ческий челнóк.

v.i. сновáть (*impf.*).

cpd. **~cock** *n.* волáн.

shy[1] [ʃaɪ] *n.* (*coll.*) (*throw*) бросóк; **have a ~ at sth.** запус|кáть, -ти́ть кáмнем (*и т п*) во что-н.

v.t. (*coll.*) бр|осáть, -óсить.

shy[2] [ʃaɪ] *adj.* (*bashful*) застéнчивый; (*timid*) рóбкий; **be ~ of s.o.** робéть (*impf.*) пéред кем-н.; **fight ~ of** избегáть (*impf.*) +*g.*

v.i. **1.** (*of horse*) отпря́|дывать, -нуть; **~ at a fence** откáз|ываться, -áться пéред препя́тствием. **2.** (*of pers.*): **~ away from sth.** робéть, о- пéред чем-н.

shyness ['ʃaɪnɪs] *n.* застéнчивость, рóбость.

Siamese [ˌsaɪə'miːz] *adj.* сиáмский; **~ twins** сиáмские близнецы́ (*m. pl.*).

Siberia [saɪ'bɪərɪə] *n.* Сиби́рь.

Siberian [saɪ'bɪərɪən] *n.* сибиря́|к (*fem.* -чка).

adj. сиби́рский.

sibilant ['sɪbɪlənt] *n.* свистя́щий звук.

adj. свистя́щий.

sibling ['sɪblɪŋ] *n.* роднóй брат, роднáя сестрá; **~s** дéти одни́х роди́телей.

sic [sɪk] *adv.* так!

Sicily ['sɪsɪlɪ] *n.* Сици́лия.

sick [sɪk] *n.* (*collect.*: **the ~**) больны́е (*pl.*).

adj. **1.** (*unwell*) больнóй; **fall ~** забол|евáть, -éть; **he is off ~** он на бюллетéне; (*fig.*): **he ~ at heart** тосковáть (*impf.*). **2.** (*nauseated*): **I feel ~** меня́ тошни́т; **I am going to be ~** меня́ сейчáс вы́рвет; **he was ~** егó вы́рвало. **3.: ~ of: I am ~ to death of her** онá мне надоéла дó смéрти; **he was ~ of the sight of food** он не мог смотрéть на едý без отвращéния. **4.: ~ at: he was ~ at being beaten** он был удручён свои́м поражéнием; **I am ~ at the thought of having to leave home** у меня́ сéрдце щеми́т от однóй мы́сли о расставáнии с дóмом. **5.: ~ joke** мрáчная шýтка; **~ humour** чёрный ю́мор.

v.t.: **~ up** (*coll.*): **he ~ed up the onions** егó вы́рвало лýком.

cpds. **~-bay** *n.* лазарéт; **~-bed** *n.* постéль больнóго; **~-leave** *n.* óтпуск по болéзни; **he is on ~-leave** он на бюллетéне; **~-pay** *n.* оплáта по бюллетéню; **~-room** *n.* кóмната больнóго.

sicken ['sɪkən] *v.t.* (*lit.*): **the sight of blood ~s me** меня́ тошни́т от ви́да крóви; (*fig.*, *disgust*, *repel*) вызывáть, вы́звать отвращéние у (*когo*); **~ing** отврати́тельный, проти́вный.

v.i. (*become ill*) забол|евáть, -éть.

sickle ['sɪk(ə)l] *n.* серп; **a ~ moon** серп луны́.

sickly ['sɪklɪ] *adj.* (*unhealthy*) болéзненный; (*puny*) хи́лый; (*mawkish*) слащáвый.

sickness ['sɪknɪs] *n.* (*ill-health*) нездорóвье; (*disease*) болéзнь.

side [saɪd] *n.* **1.** сторонá; **on this ~** на э́той сторонé; **on (along) both ~s** по обéим сторонáм; **on either ~** с обéих сторóн; **on all ~s** со всех сторóн; **from every ~** отовсю́ду; **on the right/left ~** спрáва/слéва; **put on one ~** (*defer*, *shelve*) от|клáдывать, -ложи́ть; **stand to one ~** сторони́ться, по-; **take s.o. to one ~** отвести́ (*pf.*) когó-н. в сторóнку; **on the ~** (*coll.*, *additionally*) по совмести́тельству; (*illicitly*) налéво; **get, keep on the right ~ of s.o.** быть на хорóшем счетý у когó-н.; **he is on the wrong ~ of 50** емý за 50. **2.** (*edge*) край; **by the ~ of the lake** на берегý óзера; **on the ~ of the mountain** на склóне горы́; **~ of a ship** борт корабля́. **3.** (*of room, table*) конéц. **4.** (*of the body*) бок; **at my ~** ря́дом со мной; **he sat by her ~** он сидéл вóзле/пóдле неё; **they were standing ~ by ~** они́ стоя́ли ря́дом/рядкóм. **5.** (*of meat*) край; **a ~ of beef/pork** полови́на говя́жьей/свинóй тýши. **6.** (*of a building*) боковáя стенá; **he went round the ~ of the house** он обогнýл дом. **7.** (*of cloth*): **right ~** лицевáя сторонá; **wrong ~ out** наизнáнку; (*of packages etc.*): **this ~ up** э́той сторонóй вверх; **wrong ~ up** вверх ногáми; (*of paper*) страни́ца. **8.** (*aspect*): **I can see the funny ~ of the affair** я ви́жу смешнýю стóрону дéла; **hear both ~s (of the case)** вы́слýшивать, вы́слушать обе тóчки зрéния. **9.: on the long/short ~** длиноватый/коротковáтый; **the weather is on the cool ~** погóда довóльно прохлáдная. **10.** (*party*, *faction*) сторонá; **which ~ are you on?** вы на чьей сторонé?; **take ~s with s.o.** прин|имáть, -я́ть чью-н. стóрону. **11.** (*team*) комáнда; **let the ~ down** (*fig.*) подв|оди́ть, -ести́ товáрищей. **12.** (*lineage*): **on the mother's/father's ~** с матери́нской/отцóвской стороны́. **13.** (*attr.*) боковóй; *see also cpds.*

v.i.: ~ **with s.o.** прин|имáть, -я́ть чью-н. стóрону.

cpds. ~**board** *n.* буфéт, сервáнт; ~**boards,** ~**burns** *nn.* (*coll.*) бáк|и (*pl.*, *g.* —); ~**-car** *n.* коля́ска; ~**-dish** *n.* гарни́р, салáт; ~**-effect** *n.* побóчное дéйствие; ~**kick** *n.* (*US*, *coll.*) прия́тель (*m.*), кóреш; ~**light** *n.* боковóй фонáрь; ~**line** *n.* (*work*) побóчная рабóта; (*goods*) неосновнóй товáр; (*football*) боковáя ли́ния пóля; ~**long** *adv.* и́скоса; ~**-plate** *n.* мáленькая тарéлка; ~**-road** *n.* просёлочная дорóга; ~**-step** *v.t.* (*fig.*) уклон|я́ться, -и́ться от+*g.*; об|ходи́ть, -ойти́; ~**-street** *n.* переýлок; ~**-track** *n.* запáсный путь; *v.t.* (*postpone*) от|клáдывать, -ложи́ть; (*distract*): **I meant to finish the job, but I was** ~**-tracked** я собирáлся закóнчить рабóту, да меня́ отвлекли́; ~**-view** *n.* вид сбóку, прóфиль (*m.*); ~**walk** *n.* (*US*) тротуáр; ~**ways** *adj.* боковóй; *adv.* (*to one* ~) вбок; (*of motion*) бóком; ~**-whiskers** *n.* бакенбáрд|ы (*pl.*, *g.* —).

siding ['saɪdɪŋ] *n.* запáсный путь.

sidle ['saɪd(ə)l] *v.i.*: ~ **up to s.o.** под|ходи́ть, -ойти́ к комý-н. бочкóм.

siege [siːdʒ] *n.* осáда, блокáда; **lay** ~ **to** оса|ждáть, -ди́ть; **raise a** ~ сн|имáть, -ять осáду.

sienna [sɪ'enə] *n.* сиéна.

sierra [sɪ'erə] *n.* гóрная цепь.

siesta [sɪ'estə] *n.* сиéста.

sieve [sɪv] *n.* си́то; **he has a memory like a** ~ у негó головá дыря́вая.

v.t. просé|ивать, -ять.

sift [sɪft] *v.t.* просé|ивать, -ять; ~ **sugar on to a cake** пос|ыпáть, -ы́пать печéнье сáхаром; (*fig.*): ~ **the facts** рассм|áтривать, -отрéть фáкты.

sigh [saɪ] *n.* вздох; **heave a** ~ **of relief** взд|ыхáть, -охнýть с облегчéнием.

v.i. взд|ыхáть, -охнýть.

sight [saɪt] *n.* **1.** (*faculty*) зрéние; **long** ~ дальнозóркость; **short** ~ (*lit.*, *fig.*) близорýкость; **second** ~ яснови́дение; **lose one's** ~ теря́ть, по- зрéние; **I know her by** ~ я знáю её в лицó. **2.** (*seeing, being seen*) вид; **I can't bear the** ~ **of him** я егó ви́деть не могý; **catch** ~ **of** замéтить (*pf.*); **I kept him in** ~ я не спускáл с негó глаз; **lose** ~ **of** теря́ть, по- из ви́ду; **at first** ~ с пéрвого взгля́да; на пéрвый взгляд; **he can read music at** ~ он умéет игрáть с листá; (*range of vision*): **come into** ~ появ|ля́ться, -и́ться; **the end is in** ~ ви́ден конéц; **put out of** ~ уб|ирáть, -рáть; **he would not let her out of his** ~ он её с глаз не спускáл; **out of** ~**, out of mind** с глаз долóй, из сéрдца вон; **they were ordered to shoot on** ~ им приказáли стреля́ть без предупреждéния. **3.** (*spectacle*) вид, зрéлище; **a** ~ **for sore eyes** прия́тное зрéлище; **see the** ~**s** осм|áтривать, -отрéть достопримечáтельности. **4.** (*aiming device*) прицéл; **he set his** ~**s on becoming a professor** он мéтил в профессорá. **5.** (*attr.*): ~ **unseen** не гля́дя; за глазá; ~ **translation** перевóд с листá.

v.t. (*spot after searching*): **they** ~**ed game** они́ вы́смотрели дичь; **I** ~**ed her amidst the crowd** я замéтил её в толпé; **the sailors** ~**ed land** матрóсы уви́дели зéмлю.

cpds. ~**-reading** *n.* (*mus.*) игрá с листá; ~**seeing** *n.* осмóтр достопримечáтельностей; ~**seer** *n.* тури́ст (*fem.* -ка); экскурсáнт (*fem.* -ка).

sighted ['saɪtɪd] *adj.* (*not blind*) зря́чий.

sign [saɪn] *n.* **1.** (*mark; gesture*) знак; **make the** ~ **of the cross** крести́ться, пере-; ~**s of the zodiac** знáки (*m. pl.*) зодиáка; ~ **language** ручнáя/дакти́льная áзбука; (*symbol*) си́мвол; **plus/minus** ~ плюс/ми́нус; **equals** ~ знак рáвенства. **2.** (*indication*) при́знак; **there's still no** ~ **of him** егó всё нет и нет; ~ **of the times** знáмение врéмени; (*trace*) след. **3.** (*portent*) примéта. **4.** (~*-board*) вы́веска; **inn** ~ вы́веска тракти́ра; **neon** ~ неóновая реклáма.

v.t. & i. **1.** подпи́с|ывать(ся), -áть(ся); распи́с|ываться, -áться; **I** ~**ed for the parcel** я расписáлся в получéнии пакéта. **2.** (*communicate by* ~) под|авáть, -áть знак; **she** ~**ed to the others to leave** онá подалá остальны́м знак уйти́.

with advs.: ~ **off** *v.i.* (*at end of broadcast*) дать (*pf.*) знак окончáния передáчи; ~ **on** *v.i.* (*as unemployed*) регистри́роваться, за- в кáчестве безрабóтного; ~ **up** *v.t. & i.* нан|имáть(ся), -я́ть(ся); **the club** ~**ed up a new goalkeeper** клуб нáнял нóвого вратаря́.

cpds. ~**board** *n.* вы́веска; ~**-painter** *n.* живопи́сец вы́весок; ~**post** *n.* указáтель (*m.*).

signal[1] ['sɪgn(ə)l] *n.* **1.** (*conventional sign, official message*) сигнáл; **distress** ~ сигнáл бéдствия; **the driver gave a hand** ~ води́тель (*m.*) дал ручнóй сигнáл; (*rail.*) семафóр; **the** ~**s are against us** семафóр закры́т; (*for road traffic*) светофóр. **2.** (*pl.*, *mil.*): ~**s troops** войскá свя́зи.

v.t.: ~ **an order** перед|авáть, -áть прикáз; **the ship** ~**led its position** сýдно сигнализи́ровало своё местонахождéние; **I** ~**ed** (*motioned to*) **him to come nearer** я пóдал емý знак подойти́ побли́же.

v.i. сигнализи́ровать (*impf.*, *pf.*).

cpds. ~**-box** *n.* сигнáльная бýдка; ~**man** *n.* (*rail.*) стрéлочник; (*mil.*) связи́ст; (*nav.*) сигнáльщик.

signal[2] ['sɪgn(ə)l] *adj.*: ~ **success** блестя́щий успéх; ~ **failure** полнéйший провáл.

signalize ['sɪgnə,laɪz] *v.t.* ознаменóв|ывать, -áть; отм|ечáть, -éтить.

signatory ['sɪgnətərɪ] *n.* подписáвшийся.

adj.: ~ **powers** держáвы, подписáвшие договóр.

signature ['sɪgnətʃə(r)] *n.* **1.** пóдпись. **2.** (*mus.*): ~ **tune** музыкáльная шáпка. **3.** (*typ.*) сигнатýра.

signet ['sɪgnɪt] *n.* печáтка; ~ **ring** кольцó с печáткой.

significance [sɪg'nɪfɪkəns] *n.* (*meaning, import*) значéние; (*sense*) смысл.

significant [sɪg'nɪfɪkənt] *adj.* значи́тельный; (*important*) вáжный; ~ **changes** существéнные изменéния.

signif|y ['sɪgnɪ,faɪ] *v.t.* **1.** (*make known*) выражáть, вы́разить; **we** ~**ied our approval** мы вы́разили своё одобрéние. **2.** (*portend*) предвещáть (*impf.*). **3.** (*mean*) означáть (*impf.*).

Sikh [siːk, sɪk] *n.* сикх.

adj. си́кхский.

silage ['saɪlɪdʒ] *n.* си́лос.

silence ['saɪləns] *n.* молчáние; тишинá; **in** ~ мóлча; ~! ти́хо!; молчáть!; **break** ~ нар|ушáть, -ýшить молчáние; **keep** ~ храни́ть (*impf.*) молчáние.

v.t. (*pers.*) заст|авля́ть, -áвить замолчáть; (*thg.*) заглуш|áть, -и́ть.

silencer ['saɪlənsə(r)] *n.* глуши́тель (*m.*).

silent ['saɪlənt] *adj.* (*saying nothing*) безмóлвный; **the** ~ **majority** молчали́вое большинствó; **keep** ~ молчáть (*impf.*); **keep** ~ **about sth.** ум|áлчивать, -олчáть о чём-н.; **fall, become** ~ замолчáть (*pf.*); (*taciturn*) молчали́вый; ~ **film** немóй фильм; (*not pronounced*) непроизноси́мый; (*noiseless*) бесшýмный.

silhouette [,sɪluː'et] *n.* силуэ́т.

silica ['sɪlɪkə] *n.* кремнезём; (*quartz*) кварц.

silicate ['sɪlɪ,keɪt] *n.* силикáт.

silicon ['sɪlɪkən] *n.* крéмний; ~ **chip** крéмневая микропласти́нка.

silicone ['sɪlɪ,kəʊn] *n.* силоксáн.

silicosis [,sɪlɪ'kəʊsɪs] *n.* силикóз.

silk [sɪlk] *n.* **1.** шёлк; (*attr.*) шёлковый; ~ **hat** цили́ндр. **2.** (*pl.*, *for embroidery*) шёлк; шёлковые ни́тки (*f. pl.*).

cpds. ~**-growing** *n.* шелковóдство; ~**worm** *n.* тýтовый шелкопря́д; шелкови́чный червь; ~**-screen** *adj.*: ~**-screen printing** шёлкогрáфия.

silken ['sɪlkən] *adj.* (*made of silk*) шёлковый; (*resembling* ~) шелкови́стый; (*fig.*) = **silky**

silky ['sɪlkɪ] *adj.* шелкови́стый.

sill [sɪl] *n.* (*of window*) подоко́нник; (*of door*) поро́г.

silliness ['sɪlɪnɪs] *n.* глу́пость.

silly ['sɪlɪ] *n.* глупы́ш (*coll., fem.* -ка, глу́пенькая).
adj. глу́пый; **do/say sth. ~** сде́лать/сказа́ть (*pf.*) глу́пость.

silo ['saɪləʊ] *n.* (*tower; pit*) си́лосная ба́шня/я́ма; (*for missile*) ста́ртовая ша́хта.

silt [sɪlt] *n.* ил.
v.t. & i. (*usu.* **~ up**) зайли|ва́ть(ся), -ть(ся).

silver ['sɪlvə(r)] *n.* **1.** (*metal*; **~ware**; **~ coins**) серебро́. **2.** (*colour*) сере́бряный цвет.
adj. (*made of* **~**) сере́бряный; (*resembling* **~**) серебри́стый; **~ birch** бе́лая берёза; **~ fox** черно-бу́рая лиси́ца; **~ jubilee** сере́бряный юбиле́й; двадцатипятиле́тие; **~ paper** фо́льга; **~ wedding** сере́бряная сва́дьба.
cpds. **~-haired** *adj.* седо́й; **~-plated** *adj.* серебрёный, посеребрённый; **~smith** *n.* сере́бряных дел ма́стер; **~ware** *n.* серебро́; изде́лия (*nt. pl.*) из серебра́.

silvery ['sɪlvərɪ] *adj.* серебри́стый.

silviculture ['sɪlvɪˌkʌltʃə(r)] *n.* лесово́дство.

similar ['sɪmɪlə(r)] *adj.* **1.** (*alike*) схо́дный; **the hats are ~ in appearance** шля́пы с ви́ду о́чень похо́жи. **2.**: **~ to** похо́жий на+*a.*; подо́бный +*d.*; **~ triangles** подо́бные треуго́льники.

similarity [ˌsɪmɪ'lærɪtɪ] *n.* схо́дство; **points of ~** черты́ (*f. pl.*) схо́дства; о́бщие черты́.

similarly ['sɪmɪləlɪ] *adv.* так же; таки́м же о́бразом.

simile ['sɪmɪlɪ] *n.* сравне́ние.

simmer ['sɪmə(r)] *v.t.* кипяти́ть (*impf.*) на ме́дленном огне́.
v.i. слегка́ кипе́ть (*impf.*); (*fig.*): **~ with indignation** кипе́ть (*impf.*) негодова́нием; **~ down** (*fig.*) успок|а́иваться, -о́иться; ост|ыва́ть, -ы́ть; **his rage ~ed down** его́ гнев осты́л.

simper ['sɪmpə(r)] *v.i.* жема́нно улыб|а́ться, -ну́ться.

simple ['sɪmp(ə)l] *adj.* **1.** просто́й; **as ~ as ABC** про́ще просто́го; **it's as ~ as that** то́лько и всего́; вот и всё. **2.** (*easy*) лёгкий; **the dress is ~ to make** э́то пла́тье легко́ сшить. **3.** (*math.*): **~ equation** уравне́ние пе́рвой сте́пени.
cpds. **~-hearted** *adj.* простоду́шный; **~-minded** *adj.* (*unsophisticated*) бесхи́тростный; (*feeble-minded*) глу́пый, глупова́тый.

simpleton ['sɪmp(ə)lt(ə)n] *n.* проста́|к (*fem.* -чка).

simplicity [sɪm'plɪsɪtɪ] *n.* простота́; (*easiness*) лёгкость.

simplification [ˌsɪmplɪfɪ'keɪʃ(ə)n] *n.* упроще́ние.

simplify ['sɪmplɪˌfaɪ] *v.t.* упро|ща́ть, -сти́ть.

simplistic [sɪm'plɪstɪk] *adj.* (чрезме́рно) упрощённый.

simply ['sɪmplɪ] *adv.* про́сто; **the weather was ~ dreadful** пого́да была́ пря́мо ужа́сная; **I ~ couldn't manage to come** я ника́к не мог прийти́.

simulate ['sɪmjʊˌleɪt] *v.t.* (*feign*) симули́ровать (*impf., pf.*); (*pretend to be*) притвор|я́ться, -и́ться +*i.*; (*imitate for training purposes*) воспроизв|оди́ть, -ести́; моделúровать (*impf., pf.*).

simulated ['sɪmjʊˌleɪtɪd] *adj.* подде́льный, иску́ственный; **~ flight** модели́рованный/усло́вный полёт.

simulation [ˌsɪmjʊ'leɪʃ(ə)n] *n.* симуля́ция; воспроизведе́ние; модели́рование.

simulator ['sɪmjʊˌleɪtə(r)] *n.* (*device*) модели́рующее/имити́рующее устро́йство.

simultaneity [ˌsɪməltə'neɪtɪ] *n.* одновре́ме́нность.

simultaneous [ˌsɪməl'teɪnɪəs] *adj.* одновре́ме́нный, синхро́нный; **~ interpreting** синхро́нный перево́д.

sin [sɪn] *n.* **1.** грех; **forgiveness of ~s** отпуще́ние грехо́в; **live in ~** жить (*impf.*) в незако́нном бра́ке; **for my ~s** за грехи́ мои́; **as ugly as ~** стра́шен как сме́ртный грех. **2.** (*offence*): **~ against propriety** наруше́ние прили́чий; **it's a ~ to stay indoors** грешно́ сиде́ть до́ма.
v.i. греши́ть, со-.

since [sɪns] *adv.* **1.** (*from that time*) с тех пор; **he has been here ever ~** с той поры́ он здесь так и оста́лся. **2.** (*in the intervening time*): **the theatre has ~ been rebuilt** с тех пор (*or* поздне́е) теа́тр перестро́или.
prep. с+*g.*; **nothing has happened ~ Christmas** с Рождества́ ничего́ не произошло́; **~ our talk** по́сле на́шего разгово́ра; **~ yesterday** со вчера́шнего дня; **~ when have you been fond of music?** с каки́х пор вы ста́ли люби́ть му́зыку?
conj. **1.** (*from, during the time when*): **how long is it ~ we last met?** ско́лько вре́мени прошло́ с на́шей после́дней встре́чи?; **I have moved house ~ I saw you** я перее́хал с тех пор, как мы с ва́ми ви́делись. **2.** (*seeing that*) так как, поско́льку.

sincere [sɪn'sɪə(r)] *adj.* и́скренний; **he was ~ in what he said** он э́то говори́л и́скренне; **yours ~ly** и́скренне Ваш.

sincerity [sɪn'serɪtɪ] *n.* и́скренность.

sine [saɪn] *n.* си́нус.

sinecure ['saɪnɪˌkjʊə(r), 'sɪn-] *n.* синеку́ра.

sinew ['sɪnjuː] *n.* (*tendon*) сухожи́лие; (*pl., muscles*) жи́лы (*f. pl.*).

sinewy ['sɪnjuːɪ] *adj.*: **~ arms** му́скулистые/жи́листые ру́ки.

sinful ['sɪnfʊl] *adj.* гре́шный, грехо́вный.

sing [sɪŋ] *v.t.* петь, с-/про-; (*fig.*): **~ s.o.'s praises** восхваля́ть (*impf.*) кого́-н.
v.i. петь, с-; **~ in tune** петь (*impf.*) пра́вильно; **~ out of tune** петь (*impf.*) фальши́во; **she sang to the guitar** она́ пе́ла под гита́ру; **my ears are ~ing** у меня́ звени́т в уша́х.
cpd. **~-song** *n.* **1.** (*impromptu* **~ing**): **we had a ~-song** мы попе́ли. **2.**: **in a ~-song voice** певу́чим го́лосом.

Singapore [ˌsɪŋə'pɔː(r), ˌsɪŋgə-] *n.* Сингапу́р.

singe [sɪndʒ] *n.* ожо́г.
v.t. пали́ть (*or* опа́ливать), о-; **have one's hair ~d** подпали́ть (*pf.*) во́лосы.
v.i.: **something is ~ing** что́-то гори́т; па́хнет палёным.

singer ['sɪŋə(r)] *n.* пев|е́ц (*fem.* -и́ца).
cpd. **~-songwriter** шансонье́ (*m. indecl.*).

singing ['sɪŋɪŋ] *n.* пе́ние.

single ['sɪŋg(ə)l] *n.* (*ticket*) биле́т в оди́н коне́ц; (*pl., of tennis etc.*) одино́чная игра́.
adj. **1.** (*one*) оди́н; (*only one*) еди́нственный, еди́ный; **I haven't met a ~ soul** я ни еди́ной ду́ши не встре́тил; **he didn't say a ~ word** он не пророни́л ни (одного́) сло́ва; **in ~ file** гусько́м; (*for or involving one person*): **~ bed** односпа́льная крова́ть; **~ room** одино́чный но́мер; **~ combat** единобо́рство; (*taken individually*): **every ~ one of his pupils passed** все его́ учени́ки до еди́ного прошли́. **2.** (*unmarried*) холосто́й; неза́мужняя; **lead a ~ life** вести́ (*det.*) холосту́ю жизнь; **~ father** оте́ц-одино́чка; **~ mother** мать-одино́чка.
v.t.: **~ out**: **he was ~d out** его́ вы́делили.
cpds. **~-breasted** *adj.* однобо́ртный; **~-decker** *n.* (*bus*) одноэта́жный авто́бус; **~-handed** *adj. & adv.* (*unaided*) без посторо́нней по́мощи; **~-line** *adj.*: **~-line traffic** движе́ние в оди́н ряд; **~-minded** *adj.* пре́данный одному́ де́лу; целеустремлённый; **~-sex** *adj.*: **~-sex school** шко́ла разде́льного обуче́ния; **~-track** *adj.* (*rail.*) одноколе́йный.

singleness ['sɪŋgəlnɪs] *n.*: **~ of purpose** целеустремлённость.

singlet ['sɪŋglɪt] *n.* ма́йка.

singly ['sɪŋglɪ] *adv.* (*separately*) врозь; в отде́льности; **these articles are sold ~** э́ти ве́щи продаю́тся пошту́чно.

singular ['sɪŋgjʊlə(r)] *n.* (*gram.*) еди́нственное число́.
adj. **1.** (*gram.*) еди́нственный. **2.** (*rare, unusual*) необыча́йный. **3.** (*outstanding*) чрезвыча́йный; **she was ~ly beautiful** она́ была́ необыча́йно хороша́.

singularity [,sɪŋgjʊ'lærɪtɪ] *n.* (*peculiarity*) осо́бенность; (*uncommonness*) необы́чность.

sinister ['sɪnɪstə(r)] *adj.* злове́щий; **a ~ plot** кова́рный за́говор; **a ~ character** тёмная ли́чность.

sink [sɪŋk] *n.* (*in kitchen etc.*) ра́ковина.
v.t. **1.: ~ a ship** топи́ть, по- су́дно; **we're sunk** (*coll.*) мы поги́бли!; (*immerse*): **sunk in thought** погружённый в размышле́ния. **2.** (*lower*) опус|ка́ть, -ти́ть; **he sank his voice to a whisper** он пони́зил го́лос до шёпота. **3.** (*drive, plunge*): **~ a post six feet into the earth** вк|а́пывать, -опа́ть столб в зе́млю на шесть фу́тов; (*fig.*): **the dog sank its teeth into his leg** соба́ка вонзи́ла зу́бы в его́ но́гу. **4.** (*invest*) вкла́дывать, вложи́ть. **5.** (*excavate*): **~ a well** рыть, вы́- коло́дец; **~ a shaft** про|ходи́ть, -йти́ ша́хтный ствол.
v.i. **1.** (*in water etc.*) тону́ть, за-; погру|жа́ться, -зи́ться; идти́ (*det*), пойти́ ко дну; **he sank to his knees in mud** он по коле́но провали́лся в грязь; **the bather sank like a stone** купа́льщик ка́мнем пошёл ко дну. **2.** (*disappear*) исч|еза́ть, -е́знуть; (*below the horizon*) за|ходи́ть, -йти́; **the sun ~s in the west** со́лнце захо́дит на за́паде. **3.** (*subside, of water*) спа|да́ть, -сть; (*of building or soil*) ос|еда́ть, -е́сть. **4.** (*get lower*) па́дать, упа́сть; **prices were ~ing** це́ны (ре́зко) снижа́лись. **5.** (*fall*): **his head sank back on the pillow** его́ голова́ отки́нулась на поду́шку; **I sank into a deep sleep** я погрузи́лся в глубо́кий сон; (*fig.*): **he has sunk in my estimation** он упа́л в мои́х глаза́х; **my heart sank** у меня́ упа́ло се́рдце; **his spirits sank** он пал ду́хом; **they sank into poverty** они́ впа́ли в нищету́. **6.** (*percolate, penetrate*) впи́т|ываться, -а́ться; **the dye ~s into the fabric** кра́ска впи́тывается в ткань; **the rain sank into the dry ground** дождь пропита́л суху́ю зе́млю; (*fig.*): **the lesson sank into his mind** уро́к ему́ хорошо́ запо́мнился; **his words sank in** его́ слова́ не прошли́ да́ром.

sinker ['sɪŋkə(r)] *n.* (*lead weight*) грузи́ло.

sinking ['sɪŋkɪŋ] *n.* (*of ship*) потопле́ние; (*of debt*) погаше́ние; **~ fund** фонд погаше́ния.

sinner ['sɪnə(r)] *n.* гре́шни|к (*fem.* -ца).

Sino- ['saɪnəʊ] *comb. form* кита́йско-...

sinologist [saɪ'nɒlədʒɪst, sɪ-] *n.* китаи́ст, сино́лог.

sinology [saɪ'nɒlədʒɪ, sɪ-] *n.* китаеве́дение.

sinuous ['sɪnjʊəs] *adj.* (*serpentine*) изви́листый; (*undulating*) волни́стый.

sinus ['saɪnəs] *n.* (*anat.*) па́зуха.

sinusitis [,saɪnə'saɪtɪs] *n.* синуси́т.

sip [sɪp] *n.* глото́к; **have, take a ~ of** глотну́ть (*pf.*); вы́пить (*pf.*) глото́к *+g.*
v.t. потя́гивать (*impf.*).

siphon ['saɪf(ə)n] *n.* сифо́н.
v.t. **~ off, out** выка́чивать, вы́качать сифо́ном.

sir [sɜː(r)] *n.* (*form of address; title*) сэр, су́дарь (*m.*).

sire ['saɪə(r)] *n.* **1.** (*stallion etc.*) производи́тель (*m.*). **2.** (*Your Majesty*) ва́ше вели́чество.
v.t. произвести́ (*pf.*) на свет; **the stallion ~d twenty foals** от э́того жеребца́ родило́сь 20 жеребя́т; **~d by** рождённый от*+g.*

siren ['saɪərən] *n.* (*myth., fig.*) сире́на; (*hooter*) сире́на, гудо́к.

sirloin ['sɜːlɔɪn] *n.* филе́ (*indecl.*).

sirocco [sɪ'rɒkəʊ] *n.* сиро́кко (*m. indecl.*).

sisal ['saɪs(ə)l] *n.* сиза́ль (*m.*).

sissy ['sɪsɪ] *n.* (*coll.*) «девчо́нка», не́женка (*c.g.*).
adj. изне́женный, женоподо́бный.

sister ['sɪstə(r)] *n.* сестра́; (*nursing ~*) (ста́ршая) медици́нская сестра́.
cpd. **~-in-law** *n.* (*brother's wife*) неве́стка; (*husband's sister*) золо́вка; (*wife's sister*) своя́ченица.

sit [sɪt] *v.t.* **1.** (*seat*) сажа́ть, посади́ть; уса́|живать, -ди́ть; **~ yourself down!** (*coll.*) сади́тесь! **2.** (*undergo*): **~ an examination** держа́ть/сдава́ть (*impf.*) экза́мен.
v.i. **1.** (*take a seat*) сади́ться, сесть. **2.** (*be seated*) сиде́ть (*impf.*); **he can't ~ still** ему́ не сиди́тся (на ме́сте); **~** (*stay*) **at home** сиде́ть (*impf.*) до́ма; **~ tight** (*stick to one's position*) не сдава́ться (*impf.*); не уступа́ть (*impf.*); **~ on a committee** бы́ть чле́ном комите́та; **~ on sth.** (*shelve it*) класть (*impf.*) что-н. под сукно́; **~ting duck, target** (*fig.*) лёгкая мише́нь. **3.** (*pose*): **~ to an artist** пози́ровать (*impf.*) худо́жнику; **~ for one's photograph** фотографи́роваться (*impf*). **4.** (*hold meeting; be in session*) заседа́ть (*impf.*); **the committee ~s at 10** заседа́ние комите́та начина́ется в 10 часо́в. **5.** (*be candidate*): **~ for an exam** держа́ть (*impf.*) экза́мен; **~ for a constituency** представля́ть (*impf.*) о́круг в парла́менте. **6.** (*of clothes: fit, hang*): **his coat does not ~ properly on his shoulders** его́ пиджа́к пло́хо сиди́т в плеча́х.
with advs.: **~ back** *v.i.* (*lit.*) отки́|дываться, -нуться; (*fig., relax effort*) безде́йствовать (*impf.*); **~ down** *v.t.* сажа́ть, посади́ть; уса́|живать, -ди́ть; *v.i.* сади́ться, сесть; (*for a moment*) прис|а́живаться, -е́сть; **~ in** *v.i.* (*deputize*): **~ in for s.o.** замеща́ть (*impf.*) кого́-н.; **~ in on a meeting** прису́тствовать (*impf.*) на собра́нии; **~ out** *v.t.* (*stay to end of*) выси́живать, вы́сидеть; *v.i.* (**~** *outdoors*) сиде́ть (*impf.*) на во́здухе; **~ through** *v.t.*: **we sat through the concert** мы вы́сидели весь конце́рт; **~ up** *v.i.* (*from lying position*): **he sat up in bed** он приподня́лся (и сел) в посте́ли; (*straighten one's back*) сиде́ть (*impf.*) пря́мо; вы́прямиться (*pf.*); (*not go to bed*) заси́|живаться, -де́ться; **we sat up all night with the invalid** мы просиде́ли всю ночь с больны́м; **don't ~ up for me** не жди́те меня́, ложи́тесь спать.
cpds. **~-down** *adj.*: **a ~-down strike** сидя́чая забасто́вка; **~-in** *n.* демонстрати́вное заня́тие помеще́ния.

sitcom ['sɪtkɒm] *n.* (*coll.*) коме́дия положе́ний.

site [saɪt] *n.* (*place*) ме́сто; (*position*) положе́ние; (*location*) местоположе́ние; **building ~** строи́тельный уча́сток.
v.t. **1.** (*arrange, dispose*) распол|ага́ть, -ожи́ть. **2.** (*choose ~ of*) выбира́ть, вы́брать ме́сто для*+g.* **3.** (*locate*): **the house is ~d on a slope** дом располо́жен на скло́не горы́/холма́.

sitting ['sɪtɪŋ] *n.* **1.** сиде́ние. **2.** (*session*) заседа́ние; **at one ~** в оди́н присе́ст. **3.** (*posing*) пози́рование; **two ~s** два сеа́нса.
cpd. **~-room** *n.* гости́ная.

situate ['sɪtjʊ,eɪt] *v.t.* распол|ага́ть, -ожи́ть.

situated ['sɪtjʊ,eɪtɪd] *adj.* **1.** (*of buildings etc.*) располо́женный. **2.** (*of pers.*): **I am awkwardly ~** я нахожу́сь в затрудни́тельном положе́нии.

situation [,sɪtjʊ'eɪʃ(ə)n] *n.* **1.** (*place*) ме́сто; (*position*) местоположе́ние. **2.** (*circumstances*) обстано́вка, положе́ние; **what is the ~?** каково́ положе́ние дел?; какова́ обстано́вка? **3.** (*job*) ме́сто; **~s vacant** (*as column heading*) вака́нтные до́лжности; тре́буется рабо́чая си́ла.

six [sɪks] *n.* (число́/но́мер) шесть; (**~** *people*) ше́стеро, шесть челове́к; **~ each** по шести́; (*figure; thg. numbered 6; group of ~*) шестёрка; (*with var. nn. expr. or understood: cf. also examples under* **five**): **it is ~ of one and half a dozen of the other** э́то одно́ и то же; **everything is at ~es and sevens** всё вверх дном; **he threw a ~** (*dice*) у него́ вы́пала шестёрка.
adj. шесть *+g. pl.*; **~ feet high** шесть фу́тов

высото́й; (*for people and pluralia tantum also*) ше́стеро +*g. pl.*; ~ **fives are thirty** ше́стью (*or* шесть на) пять — три́дцать.
cpds. ~**fold** *adj.* шестикра́тный; *adv.* в шесть раз; ~**-foot** *adj.* шестифу́товый; ~**-shooter** *n.* шестизаря́дный револьве́р.
sixteen [ˌsɪks'tiːn, 'sɪks-] *n. & adj.* шестна́дцать (+*g. pl.*).
sixteenth [ˌsɪks'tiːnθ, 'sɪks-] *adj.* шестна́дцатый.
sixth [sɪksθ] *n.* **1.** (*date*) шесто́е (число́). **2.** (*fraction*) шеста́я часть; одна́ шеста́я; **five ~s** пять шесты́х.
adj. шесто́й; **in the ~ form** в ста́ршем кла́ссе; **~ sense** шесто́е чу́вство.
sixtieth ['sɪkstɪɪθ] *adj.* шестидеся́тый.
sixt|y ['sɪkstɪ] *n.* шестьдеся́т; **he is in his ~ies** ему́ за шестьдеся́т (лет); **in the ~ies** (*decade*) в шестидеся́тых года́х; в шестидеся́тые го́ды.
adj. шестьдеся́т +*g. pl.*
size[1] [saɪz] *n.* **1.** (*dimension, magnitude*) разме́р; величина́; **what ~ will the army be?** какова́ бу́дет чи́сленность а́рмии?; **these books are all the same ~** э́ти кни́ги все одного́ форма́та; **a wave the ~ of a house** волна́, величино́й/высото́й с дом; **that's about the ~ of it** (*coll.*) та́к-то обстои́т де́ло. **2.** (*of clothes etc.*): **~ 4** четвёртый разме́р/но́мер; **what ~ do you take?** како́й у вас но́мер?; **the dress is just her ~** э́то пла́тье как раз её разме́ра.
v.t. **1.** сорти́ровать, рас- по разме́ру. **2.: ~ s.o. up** сост|авля́ть, -а́вить о ком-н. мне́ние; **~ up the situation** определи́ть/взве́сить (*pf.*) обстано́вку.
size[2] [saɪz] *n.* (*for glazing paper, walls etc.*) клей, грунт; (*for textile*) шли́хта.
v.t.: **~ a wall** окле́и|вать, -ть сте́ну; **~ paper** прокле́и|вать, -ть бума́гу; **~ cloth** шлихтова́ть (*impf.*) сукно́; **~ canvas** грунтова́ть, за- холст.
siz(e)able ['saɪzəb(ə)l] *adj.* значи́тельного разме́ра; поря́дочный.
sizzle ['sɪz(ə)l] *n.* шипе́ние.
v.i. шипе́ть (*impf.*).
skate[1] [skeɪt] *n.* (*ice-~*) конёк; **get one's ~s on** (*fig., hurry*) потора́пливаться (*impf.*); **(roller-~)** ро́лик.
v.i. **1.** (*on ice*) ката́ться/бе́гать (*both indet.*) на конька́х; (*on roller-~s*) ката́ться (*indet.*) на ро́ликах; **~ over, round sth.** (*fig.*) каса́ться, косну́ться чего́-н. вскользь; об|ходи́ть, -ойти́ что-н. **2.** (*slide, skid*) скользи́ть (*impf.*) (по пове́рхности).
cpd. ~**board** *n.* ро́ликовая доска́.
skate[2] [skeɪt] *n.* (*fish*) скат.
skater ['skeɪtə(r)] *n.* конькобе́ж|ец (*fem. also* -ка).
skating ['skeɪtɪŋ] *n.* ката́ние на конька́х; конькобе́жный спорт.
cpd. ~**-rink** *n.* като́к.
skedaddle [skɪ'dæd(ə)l] *v.i.* улепёт|ывать, -ну́ть (*coll.*); **~!** кати́сь! (*coll.*)
skein [skeɪn] *n.* (*of wool etc.*) мото́к (пря́жи).
skeletal ['skelɪtəl] *adj.* скеле́тный.
skeleton ['skelɪt(ə)n] *n.* **1.** скеле́т, костя́к; **~ in the cupboard** (*fig.*) семе́йная та́йна. **2.** (*fig., outline*) костя́к, схе́ма. **3.** (*framework*) о́стов, карка́с. **4.** (*emaciated person*) ко́жа да ко́сти. **5.** (*attr.*): **~ staff** минима́льный штат; **~ key** отмы́чка.
sketch [sketʃ] *n.* **1.** (*artistic*) эски́з, набро́сок, зарисо́вка. **2.** (*verbal account*) (бе́глый) о́черк. **3.** (*play*) скетч.
v.t. (*draw, lit., fig.*) набр|а́сывать, -оса́ть; **he ~ed out his plans** он обрисова́л свои́ пла́ны в о́бщих черта́х.
v.i. рисова́ть (*impf.*).
cpds. ~**-block**, ~**-book** *nn.* альбо́м; блокно́т; ~**-map** *n.* схемати́ческая ка́рта.
sketchy ['sketʃɪ] *adj.* (*in outline*) схемати́ческий; (*superficial*) пове́рхностный.
skew [skjuː] *n.*: **on the ~** кри́во, ко́со, на́искось.
adj. косо́й; (*math.*) асимметри́чный.
skewer ['skjuːə(r)] *n.* ве́ртел.
v.t. наса́|живать, -ди́ть на ве́ртел.
ski [skiː] *n.* лы́жа.
v.i. ходи́ть (*indet.*) на лы́жах.
cpds. ~**-boots** *n.* лы́жные боти́нки (*m. pl.*); ~**-jump** *n.* лы́жный трампли́н; ~**-lift** *n.* подъёмник; ~**-pants** *n.* лы́жные брю́к|и (*pl., g.* —); ~**-run**, ~**-track** *nn.* лыжня́.
skid [skɪd] *n.* (*of car*) зано́с; юз; **the car went into a ~** маши́ну занесло́.
v.i. (*of wheels*) буксова́ть, за-; (*of car*) пойти́ (*pf.*) ю́зом.
skier ['skiːə(r)] *n.* лы́жник.
skiff [skɪf] *n.* я́лик, скиф-одино́чка.
skiing ['skiːɪŋ] *n.* лы́жный спорт.
skilful ['skɪlfʊl] (*US* **skillful**) *adj.* иску́сный, уме́лый.
skill [skɪl] *n.* иску́сство; (*competence*) уме́ние; (*dexterity*) ло́вкость; (*technique*) мастерство́.
skilled [skɪld] *adj.* иску́сный; (*highly-trained*) квалифици́рованный.
skillet ['skɪlɪt] *n.* (*US*) сковорода́.
skim [skɪm] *adj.*: **~ milk** снято́е молоко́.
v.t. **1.: ~ a liquid** сн|има́ть, -ять на́кипь с жи́дкости; **~ milk** сн|има́ть, -ять сли́вки (с молока́). **2.** (*remove*): **~ the grease from, off the soup** сн|има́ть, -ять жир с су́па. **3.** (*move lightly over*): **~ the ground** лете́ть (*det.*) над са́мой землёй. **4.** (*scan through*) пробе|га́ть, -жа́ть; (*book etc.*) чита́ть (*impf.*) «по диагона́ли».
skimmer ['skɪmə(r)] *n.* **1.** (*ladle*) шумо́вка. **2.** (*for milk*) сепара́тор.
skimp [skɪmp] *v.t.* скупи́ться (*impf.*) на+*a.*
v.i. эконо́мничать (*impf.*).
skimpy ['skɪmpɪ] *adj.* (*meagre*) ску́дный; (*of clothes: short or tight*) те́сный, у́зкий.
skin [skɪn] *n.* **1.** ко́жа; **clear ~** чи́стая ко́жа; **dark ~** сму́глая/тёмная ко́жа; **~ disease** ко́жная боле́знь; **take the ~ off one's knees** сдира́ть, содра́ть ко́жу на коле́нях; **he has a thick ~** (*fig.*) у него́ то́лстая ко́жа; **I got soaked to the ~** я промо́к до ни́тки; **I nearly jumped out of my ~** я так и подскочи́л от неожи́данности; **save one's ~** спас|а́ть, -ти́ свою́ шку́ру; **escape by the ~ of one's teeth** чу́дом спасти́сь (*pf.*); **he was all ~ and bone** от него́ оста́лась одна́ ко́жа да ко́сти. **2.** (*of animal: hide*) шку́ра; (*fur*) мех (*pl.* -а́). **3.** (*for wine etc.*) мех (*pl.* -и́). **4.** (*of fruit*) кожура́; (*of grape*) ко́жица; (*of sausage*) ко́жица; **lemon ~** лимо́нная ко́рка. **5.** (*on liquid etc.*) пе́нка.
v.t. **1.** (*remove ~ from*) сн|има́ть, -ять шку́ру с+*g.*; свежева́ть, о-. **2.** (*remove peel, rind from*) сн|има́ть, -ять кожуру́ с+*g.*; чи́стить, о-. **3.** (*graze*) об|дира́ть, -одра́ть; **she ~ned her knee** она́ ободра́ла/ссади́ла себе́ коле́но.
cpds. ~**-deep** *adj.* пове́рхностный; ~**-diver** *n.* аквалангист; ~**-diving** *n.* подво́дное пла́вание (с аквала́нгом); ~**flint** *n.* скря́га (*c.g.*); ~**-graft** *n.* ко́жный транспланта́т; ~**-tight** *adj.* в обтя́жку.
skinny ['skɪnɪ] *adj.* то́щий.
skip [skɪp] *n.* скачо́к, прыжо́к.
v.t. (*fig.*) пропус|ка́ть, -ти́ть; **he ~ped the class** он пропусти́л/прогуля́л уро́к; **he ~ped a class** (*went up 2 classes*) он перескочи́л че́рез класс.
v.i. **1.** (*use ~ping-rope*) скака́ть (*impf.*) (че́рез верёвочку); **~ping rope** скака́лка; (*jump*): **she ~ped for joy** она́ подпры́гнула от ра́дости; **he ~ped across the brook** он перескочи́л (че́рез) руче́й. **2.** (*coll., go quickly or casually*): **he ~ped off without telling anyone** он ускака́л, никому́ ничего́ не сказа́в; **I ~ped through the preface** я пробежа́л предисло́вие (глаза́ми).
skipper ['skɪpə(r)] *n.* (*captain*) шки́пер, капита́н.

skirmish ['skɜ:mɪʃ] *n.* (*mil.*, *fig.*) сты́чка; (коро́ткая) перестре́лка, схва́тка.
v.i. (*mil.*) перестре́ливаться (*impf.*).

skirt [skɜ:t] *n.* ю́бка.
v.t. (*pass along edge of*): **we ~ed the crowd** мы обошли́ толпу́; **the ship ~ed the coast** су́дно шло вдоль бе́рега; (*form border of*): **the road ~s the forest** доро́га огиба́ет лес; **~ing-board** пли́нтус.
v.i.: **~ round** (*fig.*, *avoid*) об|ходи́ть, -ойти́.

skit [skɪt] *n.* скетч, сати́ра (на+*a.*).

skittish ['skɪtɪʃ] *adj.* норови́стый.

skittle ['skɪt(ə)l] *n.* ке́гля; (*pl.*, *game*) ке́гли (*f. pl.*).
cpd. **~-alley** *n.* кегельба́н.

skive [skaɪv] *v.i.* (*evade duty*) сачкова́ть (*impf.*) (*sl.*).

skivvy ['skɪvɪ] *n.* (*coll.*, *pej.*) служа́нка.

skuld|uggery, skulld- [skʌl'dʌgərɪ] надува́тельство.

skulk [skʌlk] *v.i.* (*lurk*) зата́иваться (*impf.*); (*slink*) кра́сться (*impf.*).

skull [skʌl] *n.* че́реп; **~ and cross bones** че́реп со скре́щенными костя́ми.
cpd. **~-cap** *n.* ермо́лка; (*Central Asian*) тюбете́йка; (*worn by Orthodox priests*) скуфья́.

skunk [skʌŋk] *n.* воню́чка, скунс; (*coll.*, *pers.*) подле́ц, подо́нок.

sky [skaɪ] *n.* не́бо; **there wasn't a cloud in the ~** на не́бе не́ было ни о́блачка; **praise s.o. to the skies** превозн|оси́ть, -ести́ кого́-н. до небе́с.
cpds. **~-high** *adv.* высо́ко́ в во́здух; (*fig.*) до небе́с; **~lark** *n.* полево́й жа́воронок; **~light** *n.* ве́рхний свет; фона́рь (*m.*); **~line** *n.* горизо́нт; силуэ́т; **~-rocket** *v.i.* (*fig.*) стреми́тельно подня́ться (*pf.*); **~scraper** *n.* небоскрёб.

skywards ['skaɪwədz] *adv.* к не́бу; вверх.

slab [slæb] *n.* (*of stone etc.*) плита́; **~ of concrete** бето́нная плита́; (*of cake etc.*) кусо́к.

slack [slæk] *n.* **1.** (*loose part of rope*, *sail*) слабина́; **pull in** (*or* **take in, up**) **the ~** подтя́|гивать, -ну́ть слабину́. **2.** (*pl.*, *trousers*) (широ́кие) брю́к|и (*pl.*, *g.* —).
adj. **1.** (*sluggish*, *slow*): **trade is ~** торго́вля идёт вя́ло; в торго́вле засто́й; **demand is ~** спрос небольшо́й; **at a ~ speed** (*of machine*) ти́хим хо́дом. **2.** (*of pers.*, *lax*) расхля́банный; (*negligent*) небре́жный; **be ~ in one's work** хала́тно относи́ться (*impf.*) к рабо́те. **3.** (*loose*; *not taut*): **~ rope** прови́сшая верёвка; **~ muscles** дря́блые мы́шцы. **4.** (*quiet*, *inactive*): **~ season, period** мёртвый сезо́н; зати́шье.
v.i. **1.** (*also* **~ off**) = **slacken** *v.i.* **2.** (*be indolent*) ло́дырничать (*impf.*).

slacken ['slækən] *v.t.* **1.** (*rope*, *rein*) отпус|ка́ть, -ти́ть; (*screw*) осл|абля́ть, -а́бить. **2.** (*diminish*): **~ one's efforts** осл|абля́ть, -а́бить уси́лия.
v.i. **1.** (*also* **slack**) (*of rope*) пров|иса́ть, -и́снуть; (*of sail*) обв|иса́ть, -и́снуть; (*of screw*, *nut*) ослабе́ть (*pf.*); (*of knot*) развя́з|ываться, -а́ться. **2.** (*die down*): **demand is ~ing** спрос уменьша́ется.

slacker ['slækə(r)] *n.* ло́дырь (*m.*); безде́льни|к (*fem.* -ца).

slag [slæg] *n.* шлак.
cpd. **~-heap** *n.* гру́да шла́ка.

slake [sleɪk] *v.t.* **1.** (*liter.*): **~ one's thirst** утол|я́ть, -и́ть жа́жду. **2.**: **~ lime** гаси́ть, по- и́звесть.

slalom ['slɑ:ləm] *n.* сла́лом.

slam [slæm] *n.* **1.**: **I heard the ~ of a door** я слы́шал, как хло́пнула дверь. **2.** (*cards*): **grand ~** большо́й шлем.
v.t. **1.** (*shut with a bang*): **~ a door** хло́пнуть (*pf.*) две́рью; **he ~med the door to** он захло́пнул дверь. **2.** (*other violent or sudden action*): **he ~med the brakes on** он ре́зко затормози́л; **he ~med the box down on the table** он швырну́л коро́бку на стол.
v.i. **1.** (*of door etc.*) захло́п|ываться, -нуться. **2.**: **he ~med out of the room** он вы́скочил из ко́мнаты.

slander ['slɑ:ndə(r)] *n.* клевета́.
v.t. клевета́ть, на- на+*a.*

slanderer ['slɑ:ndərə(r)] *n.* клеветни́|к (*fem.* -ца).

slanderous ['slɑ:ndərəs] *adj.* клеветни́ческий.

slang [slæŋ] *n.* жарго́н; сленг; **~ word** жарго́нное сло́во.
v.t. обруга́ть (*pf.*); **~ing match** перебра́нка.

slangy ['slæŋɪ] *adj.* жарго́нный, вульга́рный.

slant [slɑ:nt] *n.* **1.** (*oblique position*): **he wears his hat on the ~** он но́сит шля́пу набекре́нь. **2.** (*coll.*, *point of view*) то́чка зре́ния; **my trip gave me a new ~ on things** по́сле пое́здки я на всё взгляну́л поно́вому.
adj. косо́й.
v.t. **1.** (*incline*) наклон|я́ть, -и́ть. **2.** (*fig.*, *distort*) иска|жа́ть, -зи́ть.
v.i.: **his handwriting ~s to the right** он пи́шет с накло́ном впра́во; **the ~ing rays of the sun** косы́е лучи́ со́лнца.
cpd. **~-eyed** *adj.* с раско́сыми глаза́ми.

slantwise ['slɑ:ntwaɪz] *adv.* вкось, ко́со, накло́нно.

slap [slæp] *n.* шлепо́к; **~ in the face** (*lit.*, *fig.*) пощёчина.
adv.: **the ball hit me ~ in the eye** мяч попа́л мне пря́мо в глаз; **he hit the target ~ in the middle** он попа́л в са́мое я́блоко мише́ни.
v.t. **1.** (*smack*) шлёпать, от-; **~ s.o.'s face** дать (*pf.*) кому́-н. пощёчину; **~ s.o. on the back** хло́п|ать, -нуть кого́-н. по спине́. **2.** (*apply with force or carelessly*): **the paint was ~ped on** кра́ска была́ нало́жена ко́е-как. **3.**: **~ down** бр|оса́ть, -о́сить; (*rebuke*) оса|жда́ть, -ди́ть.
cpds. **~-bang** *adv.* со всего́ разма́ха; очертя го́лову; **~dash** *adj.* (*of pers.*) бесшаба́шный; (*of work*) поспе́шный, небре́жный; *adv.* (*hastily*) поспе́шно; (*anyhow*) ко́е-как; **~stick** *n.*: **~stick comedy** (дешёвый) фарс.

slash [slæʃ] *n.* (*slit*) разре́з; (*wound*) ра́на; (*stroke*): **he made a ~ with his sword** он взмахну́л са́блей.
v.t. **1.** (*wound with knife etc.*) ра́нить, по-; (*with sword*) руби́ть (*impf.*). **2.** (*cut slits in*) разр|еза́ть, -е́зать. **3.** (*reduce*): **~ prices** ре́зко сн|ижа́ть, -и́зить це́ны; **~ a budget** ре́зко сокра|ща́ть, -ти́ть бюдже́т.

slat [slæt] *n.* пла́нка; (*of blind*) пласти́нка.

slate [sleɪt] *n.* **1.** (*material*) сла́нец; **~ quarry** сла́нцевый карье́р. **2.** (*piece of ~ for roofing*) ши́ферная пли́тка; **a house roofed with ~s** дом, кры́тый ши́фером. **3.** (*for schoolwork*) гри́фельная доска́; (*fig.*): **start with a clean ~** нач|ина́ть, -а́ть с нача́ла; **wipe the ~ clean** поко́нчить (*pf.*) с про́шлым.
v.t. **1.** (*US*, *nominate*) занести́ (*pf.*) в спи́сок кандида́тов. **2.** (*scold*, *criticize*) разн|оси́ть, -ести́.
cpd. **~-coloured** *adj.* синева́то-се́рый.

slattern ['slæt(ə)n] *n.* неря́ха, грязну́ля (*both c.g.*).

slaughter ['slɔ:tə(r)] *n.* избие́ние, резня́; ма́ссовое уби́йство; (*of animals*) убо́й.
v.t. **1.** (*pers.*) изб|ива́ть, -и́ть; (*coll.*, *defeat heavily*) разб|ива́ть, -и́ть впух и впрах. **2.** (*animals*) ре́зать, за-.
cpd. **~house** *n.* (ското)бо́йня.

slaughterer ['slɔ:tərə(r)] *n.* мясни́к (на бо́йне); (*fig.*) живодёр, пала́ч.

Slav [slɑ:v] *n.* слав|яни́н (*fem.* -я́нка); **the ~s** славя́не.
adj. славя́нский.

slave [sleɪv] *n.* раб (*fem.* -ы́ня); **he works like a ~** он рабо́тает, как вол; **~ labour** ра́бский труд.
v.i.: **~ at sth.** корпе́ть (*impf.*) над чем-н.; **~ away** тяну́ть (*impf.*) ля́мку.
cpds. **~-driver** *n.* (*fig.*) безжа́лостный нача́льник; **~-trade** *n.* работорго́вля.

slaver ['slævə(r)] *n.* (*spittle*) слю́ни (*f. pl.*).

v.i. пуска́ть (*impf.*) слю́ни.
slavery ['sleɪvərɪ] *n.* ра́бство.
Slavic ['slɑ:vɪk] *adj.* славя́нский.
slavish ['sleɪvɪʃ] *adj.* ра́бский.
Slavist ['slɑ:vɪst] *n.* слави́ст.
Slavonic [slə'vɒnɪk] *n.* славя́нский язы́к; **Church ~** церковнославя́нский язы́к; **~ studies** слави́стика.
adj. славя́нский.
Slavophil(e) ['slɑ:vəʊfɪl; -,faɪl] *n.* славянофи́л.
slay [sleɪ] *v.t.* (*liter.*) уб|ива́ть, -и́ть.
slayer ['sleɪə(r)] *n.* уби́йца (*c.g.*).
sleazy ['sli:zɪ] *adj.* (*squalid*) захуда́лый, убо́гий.
sled(ge) [sledʒ] = **sleigh**
sledgehammer ['sledʒ,hæmə(r)] *n.* кува́лда; кузне́чный мо́лот.
sleek [sli:k] *adj.* (*of animal or its coat, fur*) гла́дкий, лосня́щийся; (*of person's hair*) прили́занный.
v.t. (*also* **~ down**) пригла́|живать, -дить; прили́з|ывать, -а́ть.
sleep [sli:p] *n.* сон; **have a ~** поспа́ть (*pf.*); **have a good night's ~** высыпа́ться, вы́спаться; **go** (*coll., drop off*) **to ~** зас|ыпа́ть, -ну́ть; **I couldn't get to ~** я не мог усну́ть; **put a child to ~** укла́дывать, уложи́ть ребёнка (спать); **we had our dog put to ~** нам пришло́сь соба́ку усыпи́ть; **he talks in his ~** он говори́т во сне.
v.t. (*provide ~ing room for*): **you can ~ ten people here** здесь мо́жно уложи́ть де́сять челове́к; **the hotel ~s 200** гости́ница рассчи́тана на 200 челове́к.
v.i. спать (*impf.*); (*spend the night*) ночева́ть (*impf.*); **~ well!** (жела́ю вам) споко́йной но́чи!; **I don't ~ well** у меня́ плохо́й сон; **I can't ~** я не могу́ засну́ть; **he slept through the alarm** он проспа́л всю трево́гу.
with advs.: **~ away** *v.t.*: **he slept the time away** он проспа́л всё э́то вре́мя; **~ in** *v.i.* (*intentionally*) поспа́ть (*pf.*) всласть; (*oversleep*) прос|ыпа́ть, -па́ть; заспа́ться (*pf.*); **~ off** *v.t.*: **~ off a hangover** проспа́ться (*pf.*) (по́сле попо́йки); **~ on** *v.i.*: **he is tired, let him ~ on** он уста́л, пусть спит.
cpds. **~-walker** *n.* луна́тик; **~-walking** *n.* лунати́зм.
sleeper ['sli:pə(r)] *n.* (*pers.*): **he is a light/heavy ~** он чу́тко/кре́пко спит; (*rail support*) шпа́ла; (*sleeping-car*) спа́льный ваго́н.
sleepiness ['sli:pɪnɪs] *n.* сонли́вость.
sleeping ['sli:pɪŋ] *n.*: **~ accommodation** ночле́г; ме́сто для ночёвки.
cpds. **~-bag** *n.* спа́льный мешо́к; **~-car** *n.* спа́льный ваго́н; **~-pill** *n.* снотво́рная табле́тка; **~-quarters** *n.* спа́льное помеще́ние; **~-sickness** *n.* со́нная боле́знь.
sleepless ['sli:plɪs] *adj.* бессо́нный.
sleepy ['sli:pɪ] *adj.* (*lit., fig.*) со́нный; сонли́вый; **I feel ~** мне хо́чется спать.
cpd. **~head** *n.* со́ня (*c.g.*).
sleet [sli:t] *n.* дождь (*m.*) со сне́гом; крупа́.
v.i.: **it is ~ing** сы́плет крупа́.
sleeve [sli:v] *n.* **1.** рука́в; **roll up one's ~s** (*lit., fig.*) засу́ч|ивать, -и́ть рукава́; **have, keep sth. up one's ~** (*fig.*) име́ть (*impf.*) что-н. про запа́с. **2.** (*record cover*) конве́рт.
sleeveless ['sli:vlɪs] *adj.* безрука́вный; **~ vest** безрука́вка.
sleigh [sleɪ], **sled(ge)** [sledʒ] *nn.* (*children's*) са́н|ки (*pl., g.* -ок); сала́з|ки (*pl., g.* -ок); (*for transport*) са́н|и (*pl., g.* -е́й).
v.i. ката́ться (*indet.*) в/на саня́х (*or* на са́нках/сала́зках).
cpd. **~-bell** *n.* бубе́нчик, колоко́льчик.
sleight-of-hand [slaɪt] *n.* ло́вкость рук.
slender ['slendə(r)] *adj.* **1.** (*thin; narrow*) то́нкий; (*of pers., slim*) стро́йный. **2.** (*scanty*) ску́дный; **~ means** ску́дные сре́дства; **~ hope** сла́бая наде́жда.
sleuth [slu:θ] *n.* сы́щик.
slice [slaɪs] *n.* **1.** (*of bread*) ломо́ть (*m.*); **cut bread into ~s** нар|еза́ть, -е́зать хлеб ломтя́ми; (*of meat*) ло́мтик; (*of fruit*) кусо́к, до́ля. **2.** (*portion, share*) часть, до́ля.
v.t. **1.** нар|еза́ть, -е́зать ло́мтиками; **~d bread** (предвари́тельно) наре́занный хлеб. **2.** (*golf*): **~ the ball** ср|еза́ть, -е́зать мяч.
with adv.: **~ off** *v.t.* отр|еза́ть, -е́зать.
slick [slɪk] *n.* (*patch of oil etc.*) плёнка.
adj. (*skilful; smart*) ло́вкий, бо́йкий; (*smooth, also fig.*) гла́дкий; (*slippery*) ско́льзкий.
slid|e [slaɪd] *n.* **1.** (*act of ~ing*) скольже́ние. **2.** (*track on ice*) като́к; (*on snow-covered hill*) ледяна́я го́рка. **3.** (*chute*) спуск, жёлоб. **4.** (*of microscope*) предме́тное стекло́. **5.** (*for projection on screen*) диапозити́в, слайд. **6.** (*hair-~e*) зако́лка.
v.t.: **~e a drawer into place** задв|ига́ть, -и́нуть я́щик; **~e sth. into s.o.'s hand** сова́ть, су́нуть что-н. кому́-н. в ру́ку.
v.i. **1.** скользи́ть (*impf.*); **~ing door** задвижна́я дверь; (*down or off*): **the papers ~ off my lap** бума́ги соскользну́ли у меня́ с коле́н; **the book ~ out of my hand** кни́га вы́скользнула из мои́х рук; **his trousers ~ to the ground** у него́ спусти́лись брю́ки. **2.** ката́ться (*indet.*); **the boy ~ down the banisters** ма́льчик скати́лся по пери́лам. **3.** (*fig.*): **let sth. ~e** пус|ка́ть, -ти́ть что-н. на самотёк; **~ing scale** скользя́щая шкала́.
cpds. **~e-controls** *n.pl.* движко́вые регуля́торы; **~e-rule** *n.* логарифми́ческая лине́йка.
slight[1] [slaɪt] *n.* (*disrespect*) неуваже́ние; (*offence, injury*) оби́да.
v.t. об|ижа́ть, -и́деть; выка́зывать, вы́казать неуваже́ние +*d.*; трети́ровать (*impf.*).
slight[2] [slaɪt] *adj.* **1.** (*frail*) хру́пкий; (*slender*) то́нкий. **2.** (*light; not serious*) лёгкий; **she has a ~ cold** у неё небольшо́й на́сморк; **~ concussion** лёгкая конту́зия. **3.** (*inconsiderable*) незначи́тельный; (*small*): **there is a ~ risk of infection** есть не́которая опа́сность зарази́ться; **the risk is ~** опа́сность невелика́. **4.**: **~est** мале́йший; **not in the ~est** ничу́ть; **he is not to blame in the ~est** он ни в мале́йшей сте́пени не винова́т.
slightly ['slaɪtlɪ] *adv.* слегка́; **I know them ~** я с ни́ми немно́го знако́м; **he was ~ injured** он слегка́ пострада́л; **~ younger** немно́го/чуть моло́же.
slim [slɪm] *adj.* (*slender*) то́нкий; (*small*): **a ~ chance of success** сла́бая наде́жда на успе́х.
v.i. худе́ть, по-; сбра́сывать (*impf.*) (ли́шний) вес.
slime [slaɪm] *n.* (*mud*) ил; (*viscous substance*) слизь.
slimy ['slaɪmɪ] *adj.* **1.** сли́зистый; (*sticky*) вя́зкий; (*slippery*) ско́льзкий. **2.** (*fig., of pers.*) гну́сный.
sling [slɪŋ] *n.* **1.** (*for missile*) праща́. **2.** (*bandage*) пе́ревязь; **his arm was in a ~** у него́ рука́ была́ на пе́ревязи. **3.** (*of rifle*) руже́йный реме́нь.
v.t. **1.** (*throw*) швыр|я́ть, -ну́ть. **2.** (*cast by means of ~*) мет|а́ть, -ну́ть. **3.** (*suspend*) подве́|шивать, -сить; **he slung the rifle over his shoulder** он переки́нул винто́вку че́рез плечо́.
cpd. **~-shot** *n.* (*US*) рога́тка.
slink [slɪŋk] *v.i.*: **~ off, away** потихо́ньку от|ходи́ть, -ойти́; уйти́ (*pf.*), поджа́вши хвост.
slip [slɪp] *n.* **1.** (*landslip*) обва́л. **2.** (*mishap, error*) оши́бка (по небре́жности); **I made a ~** я оши́бся; **~ of the tongue/pen** огово́рка/опи́ска. **3.**: **he gave his pursuers the ~** он ускользну́л от пресле́дователей. **4.** (*loose cover*) чехо́л; **pillow ~** на́волочка. **5.** (*petticoat*) комбина́ция. **6.** (*of paper*) ка́рточка; поло́ска бума́ги.
v.t. **1.** (*slide; pass covertly*): **she ~ped her little hand into mine** она́ вложи́ла свою́ ру́чку в мою́; **he ~ped the ring on to her finger** он наде́л ей на

пáлец кольцó; **I ~ped the waiter a coin** я сýнул официáнту монéтку. **2.** (*slide out of*; *escape from*): **the dog ~ped its collar** собáка вы́тащила гóлову из ошéйника; **it ~ped my mind** э́то у меня́ вы́скочило из головы́.

v.i. **1.** (*fall*; *slide*): **she ~ped on the ice** онá поскользнýлась на льду; **the blanket ~ped off the bed** одеяло соскользнýло с постéли; **~ped disc** смещённый межпозвонкóвый диск; **she let the plate ~** онá уронúла тарéлку (нá пол); (*fig.*): **he let the opportunity ~** он упустúл возмóжность; **the remark ~ped out** э́то замечáние случáйно сорвалóсь у негó (*и т.п.*) с языкá; **he is ~ping** (*losing his grip*) у негó слабéет хвáтка. **2.** (*move quickly and/or unnoticed*): **he ~ped away** он незамéтно ушёл; **I'll ~ across to the pub** я сбéгаю в пивнýю; **the years are ~ping by** гóды ухóдят; **an error ~ped in** вкралáсь ошúбка; **I'll ~ into another dress** я (бы́стренько) переодéнусь; **~ through** проскользнýть (*pf.*) (чéрез+*a.*).

with adv.: **~ up** *v.i.*: **I ~ped up in my calculations** я ошúбся в подсчётах; (*fig.*) я просчитáлся; **I ~ped up there** я дал мáху.

cpds. **~-knot** *n.* скользя́щий ýзел; **~shod** *adj.* (*fig.*) небрéжный, неря́шливый; **~-stream** *n.* (*aeron.*) спýтная струя́ за винтóм; **~-up** *n.* ошúбка, прóмах; **~way** *n.* стáпель (*m.*).

slipper ['slɪpə(r)] *n.* (домáшняя) тýфля; тáпочка; (*step-in*) шлёпанец.

slippery ['slɪpərɪ] *adj.* **1.** скóльзкий. **2.** (*fig.*, *evasive*, *shifty*) увёртливый, скóльзкий.

slit [slɪt] *n.* (*cut*) прорéз; (*slot*) щель; **~ trench** щель; **a ~ skirt** юбка с разрéзом.

v.t.: **~ open an envelope** вскрыть (*pf.*) конвéрт; **~ s.o.'s throat** перерéзать (*pf.*) комý-н. глóтку.

slither ['slɪðə(r)] *v.i.*: **~ about in the mud** скользúть (*impf.*) по грязи; **they ~ed down the hill** онú скатúлись с холмá.

sliver ['slɪvə(r), 'slaɪvə(r)] *n.* (*of wood*) щéпка, лучúна.

slob [slɒb] *n.* (*sl.*) недотёпа (*c.g.*).

slobber ['slɒbə(r)] *v.i.* (*lit.*, *fig.*) распускáть (*impf.*) слю́ни.

sloe [sləʊ] *n.* тёрн.

slog [slɒg] *n.* (*hit*) сúльный удáр; (*arduous work*) тяжёлая/утомúтельная рабóта.

v.t.: **~ s.o. in the jaw** дать (*pf.*) комý-н. в зýбы.

v.i.: **he was ~ging along the road** он упóрно шагáл по дорóге; **he is ~ging away at Latin** он корпúт над латы́нью (*coll.*).

slogan ['sləʊgən] *n.* (*motto*, *watchword*) лóзунг, девúз; (*in advertising*) реклáмная фóрмула.

sloop [slu:p] *n.* шлюп.

slop [slɒp] *n.* (*pl.*, *waste liquid*) помó|и (*pl.*, *g.* -ев).

v.t. **1.** (*spill*, *splash*): **~ beer over the table** расплёск|ивать, -áть пúво по столý. **2.**: **~ out a prison cell** выносúть, вы́нести парáшу.

v.i.: **~ about** плескáться (*impf.*).

cpds. **~-basin** *n.* полоскáтельница.

slope [sləʊp] *n.* наклóн, склон, уклóн; (*upward*) подъём; (*downward*) спуск, скат; **mountain ~s** гóрные склóны; **the house was on the ~ of the hill** дом стоя́л на склóне горы́.

v.t.: **~ arms!** на плечó!

v.i. **1.**: **~ back(wards)/forwards** покосúться (*pf.*) назáд/вперёд; **her handwriting ~s backwards** у неё пóчерк с наклóном влéво; **~ down** спускáться (*impf.*); **~ up(wards)** поднимáться (*impf.*); **a sloping roof** покáтая кры́ша. **2.**: **~ off** см|áтываться, -отáться; уд|ирáть, -рáть (*coll.*).

sloppiness ['slɒpɪnɪs] *n.* (*untidiness*) неря́шливость.

sloppy ['slɒpɪ] *adj.* **1.** (*of food*) жúдкий. **2.** (*of road*: *muddy*, *slushy*) грязный, сля́котный. **3.** (*careless*; *slovenly*) неря́шливый. **4.** (*sentimental*) сентиментáльный.

slosh [slɒʃ] *v.t.* (*pour clumsily*) плеснýть (*pf.*).

v.i. **~** (*splash*) **about** плескáться (*impf.*).

sloshed [slɒʃt] *adj.* (*drunk*) в ды́мину пья́ный (*sl.*).

slot [slɒt] *n.* **1.** отвéрстие; **put a coin in the ~** опус|кáть, -тúть монéту в автомáт. **2.** (*coll.*, *suitable place or job*): **we found a ~ for him as junior editor** мы подыскáли емý мéсто млáдшего редáктора.

v.t. **1.**: **~ together** спл|áчивать, -отúть в паз. **2.**: **~ one part into another** вдв|игáть, -úнуть однý часть в другýю; **we ~ted a song recital into the programme** мы встáвили в прогрáмму исполнéние пéсен.

v.i. **~ in** вст|авля́ться, -áвиться.

cpds. **~-machine** *n.* (торгóвый/игóрный) автомáт; **~-meter** *n.* (*e.g. for gas*) счётчик(-автомáт).

sloth [sləʊθ] *n.* **1.** (*zool.*) ленúвец. **2.** (*idleness*) лéность.

slothful ['sləʊθfʊl] *adj.* ленúвый.

slouch [slaʊtʃ] *n.* (*of walk*) развúнченная похóдка; (*stoop*) сутýлость.

v.i. (*stoop*) сутýлиться (*impf.*); **~ about the house** слоня́ться (*impf.*) по дóму.

slough [slʌf] *v.t.* (*of snake etc.*): **~ its skin** сбр|áсывать, -óсить кóжу; (*fig.*): **~ (off)** изб|авля́ться, -áвиться от+*g.*

Slovak ['sləʊvæk] *n.* (*pers.*) словá|к (*fem.* -чка); (*language*) словáцкий язы́к.

adj. словáцкий.

Slovakia ['sləʊvækɪə] *n.* Словáкия.

sloven ['slʌv(ə)n] *n.* неря́ха (*c.g.*).

Sloven|e ['sləʊvi:n], **-ian** [sləʊ'vi:nɪən] *nn.* (*pers.*) словéн|ец (*fem.* -ка); (*language*) словéнский язы́к.

adj. словéнский.

Slovenia [sləʊ'vi:nɪə, slə'vi:nɪə] *n.* Словéния.

slovenly ['slʌvənlɪ] *adj.* неря́шливый.

slow [sləʊ] *adj.* **1.** мéдленный; **in ~ motion** замéдленной съёмкой; **in a ~ oven** на мéдленном огнé; **be ~ over sth.** мéдлить (*impf.*) с чем-н.; **~ly but surely** мéдленно, но вéрно; **he is ~ in the uptake** он тýго соображáет. **2.** (*of clock*): **my watch is 10 minutes ~** мой часы́ отстаю́т на дéсять минýт. **3.** (*dull-witted*) тупóй. **4.** (*not lively*): **the film was rather ~** фильм был довóльно скýчным; **business is ~** делá идýт вя́ло.

adv. мéдленно; **go ~** (*of workers*) устрáивать (*impf.*) италья́нскую забастóвку.

v.t. (*also* **~ down, ~ up**) зам|едля́ть, -éдлить; **he ~ed (the car) down** он сбáвил скóрость.

v.i. (*also* **~ down, ~ up**) зам|едля́ться, -éдлиться; (*of car or driver*) сб|авля́ть, -áвить скóрость; зам|едля́ть, -éдлить ход.

cpds. **~coach** *n.* копýн, копýша (*c.g.*); **~-down** *n.* замедлéние; **~-witted** *adj.* тупóй; **~-worm** *n.* слепозмéйка.

slowness ['sləʊnɪs] *n.* мéдленность.

sludge [slʌdʒ] *n.* (*mud*) грязь; (*sediment*) осáдок; (*sewage*) нечистóт|ы (*pl.*, *g.* —).

slug [slʌg] *n.* (*zool.*) слизня́к; (*bullet*) пýля; (*US sl.*, *short drink*) глотóк, рю́мочка.

sluggard ['slʌgəd] *n.* лентя́й, лежебóка (*c.g.*).

sluggish ['slʌgɪʃ] *adj.* **1.** вя́лый; **~ market** вя́лый ры́нок; (*slow-moving*) мéдленный. **2.** (*lazy*) ленúвый.

sluice [slu:s] *n.* (*floodgate*) шлюз.

v.t. (*flood with water*) зал|ивáть, -úть; (*rinse, wash down*) опол|áскивать, -оснýть.

v.i.: (*of water*: *pour out*) течь (*or* вытекáть), вы́-; **rain was sluicing down** шёл проливнóй дождь.

cpds. **~-gate, ~-valve** *nn.* шлюз.

slum [slʌm] *n.* трущóба; **~ clearance** расчúстка трущóб; снос вéтхих здáний.

cpd. **~-dweller** *n.* трущóбный жúтель, обитáтель (*m.*) трущóбы.

slumber ['slʌmbə(r)] *n.* дремо́та; **disturb s.o.'s ~s** нар|уша́ть, -у́шить чей-н. сон.
v.i. дрема́ть, за-.

slump [slʌmp] *n.* (*fall in prices etc.*) паде́ние; (*trade recession*) засто́й; ре́зкое паде́ние цен.
v.i. **1.** (*of pers., fall, sink*) сва́л|иваться, -и́ться. **2.** (*of price, output, trade*) ре́зко па́дать, упа́сть.

slur [slɜː(r)] *n.* **1.** (*mus. sign*) ли́га. **2.** (*stigma*) пятно́; **put, cast a ~ on s.o.** очерн|я́ть, -и́ть кого́-н..
v.t. (*pronounce indistinctly*) говори́ть (*impf.*) невня́тно; бормота́ть (*impf.*).

slurry ['slʌrɪ] *n.* жи́дкое цеме́нтное те́сто; жи́дкий строи́тельный раство́р.

slush [slʌʃ] *n.* сля́коть.

slushy ['slʌʃɪ] *adj.* сля́котный; сентимента́льный.

slut [slʌt] *n.* (*sloven*) неря́ха; (*loose woman*) потаску́ха.

sly [slaɪ] *adj.* хи́трый; **on the ~** укра́дкой; потихо́ньку.

smack[1] [smæk] *n.* **1.** (*sound*) хлопо́к; **he brought his hand down with a ~ on the table** он (гро́мко) хло́пнул руко́й по́ столу; **~ of the lips** чмо́канье. **2.** (*blow, slap*) шлепо́к; **~ in the face** пощёчина; **~ in the eye** (*fig.*) (неожи́данный) уда́р; пощёчина.
adv. пря́мо; **he went ~ into the wall** он вре́зался пря́мо в сте́ну.
v.t. **1.** (*slap*) хло́п|ать, -нуть; шлёпать, от-. **2.: ~ one's lips** чмо́к|ать, -нуть (губа́ми).

smack[2] [smæk] *n.* (*taste, tinge, trace*) при́вкус.
v.i.: **~ of** (*lit., fig.*) отдава́ть (*impf*) +*i.*.

smack[3] [smæk] *n.* (*naut.*) смак, рыболо́вный шлюп.

small [smɔːl] *n.*: **1.: ~ of the back** поясни́ца. **2.** (*pl., coll., articles of laundry*) ме́лочь.
adj. **1.** ма́лый, ма́ленький, небольшо́й; (*of eggs, berries, jewels etc.*) ме́лкий; **~ change** ме́лкие де́ньги; **~ claims court** суд ме́лких тяжб; **~ craft** (*vessels*) ме́лкие суда́/ло́дки; **~ print** ме́лкий шрифт; **~ handwriting** ме́лкий по́черк; **~ intestine** то́нкая кишка́; (*not big enough*): **this coat is too ~ for me** э́то пальто́ мне мало́; (*of stature*) невысо́кий; невысо́кого ро́ста; **he is the ~est** он ни́же всех ро́стом; **make s.o. look ~** (*fig.*) ун|ижа́ть, -и́зить кого́-н.; (*of age*): **~ boy** ма́ленький ма́льчик; (*of time*): **in the ~ hours** под у́тро. **2.** (*unimportant, of ~ value*) ме́лкий, незначи́тельный; **~ beer** (*fig.*) ме́лочи (*f. pl.*); пустяки́ (*m. pl.*); **~ fry** (*fig.*) ме́лкая со́шка, мелюзга́; **one must be thankful for ~ mercies** бу́дем благода́рны (и) за ма́лое; **~ talk** све́тский разгово́р. **3.** (*modest, humble*) скро́мный; **he rose from ~ beginnings** он на́чал с ма́лого; **great and ~ alike** вели́кие и ма́лые равно́.
adv.: **chop sth. up ~** ме́лко наруби́ть (*pf.*) что-н.
cpds. **~-arms** *n.* стрелко́вое ору́жие; **~-bore** *adj.* малокали́берный; **~holder** *n.* (*tenant*) ме́лкий аренда́тор; **~holding** *n.* небольшо́е земе́льное владе́ние; **~-minded** *adj.* ме́лочный; **~pox** *n.* о́спа; **~-scale** *adj.* ме́лкий; в ма́леньком масшта́бе.

smart[1] [smɑːt] *v.i.* **1.** (*of wound or part of body*) жечь (*impf.*); са́днить (*impf.*); **my eyes are ~ing** у меня́ глаза́ щи́плет. **2.** (*of pers.*): **he ~ed under, from the insult** он испы́тывал о́строе чу́вство оби́ды.

smart[2] [smɑːt] *adj.* **1.** (*sharp, severe*) ре́зкий, суро́вый, о́стрый; **a ~ rebuke** ре́зкая о́тповедь; **he got a ~ rap on the knuckles** (*lit., fig.*) его́ как сле́дует уда́рили по рука́м (*or* проучи́ли). **2.** (*brisk, prompt*): **he walked off at a ~ pace** он удали́лся бы́стрым ша́гом; **he saluted ~ly** он бра́во о́тдал честь. **3.** (*bright, alert*): **a ~ lad** шу́стрый ма́лый. **4.** (*clever, ingenious, cunning*) ло́вкий, бо́йкий; **he was too ~ for me** он меня́ перехитри́л. **5.** (*neat, tidy*) опря́тный. **6.** (*elegant, stylish*): **a ~ hat** элега́нтная шля́пка; **the ~ set** фешене́бельное о́бщество; **you look ~** у вас о́чень изя́щный вид.
cpd. **~-alec(k)** *n.* самоуве́ренный нагле́ц; наха́л (*fem.* -ка).

smarten ['smɑːt(ə)n] *v.t.* (*also* **~ up**): **~ o.s. up** прихора́шиваться (*impf.*); (*a room, house etc.*) прив|оди́ть, -ести́ в поря́док; нав|оди́ть, -ести́ блеск в+*p.*
v.i.: **~ up** (*in appearance or dress*): **he has ~ed up** он привёл себя́ в поря́док.

smash [smæʃ] *n.* **1.** (*crash, collision*): **the vase fell with a ~** ва́за с гро́хотом упа́ла; **he gave his head an awful ~ on the pavement** он си́льно уда́рился голово́й о тротуа́р; **there has been a ~ on the motorway** на автостра́де произошло́ столкнове́ние. **2.** (*blow with fist*) си́льный уда́р. **3.: ~ hit** (*coll., play, film etc.*) боеви́к; (*song*) мо́дная пе́сенка; шля́гер.
v.t. **1.** (*shatter*) разб|ива́ть, -и́ть; **the bowl was ~ed to bits** ва́за разби́лась вдре́безги; **his theory was ~ed** его́ тео́рия была́ разби́та в пух и прах. **2.** (*drive with force*): **he ~ed his fist into my face** он с си́лой уда́рил меня́ кулако́м по лицу́; **he ~ed the ball over the net** си́льным уда́ром он посла́л мяч че́рез се́тку.
v.i. **1.** (*be broken*) разб|ива́ться, -и́ться. **2.** (*crash, collide*) вр|еза́ться, -е́заться; **the car ~ed into a wall** маши́на вре́залась в сте́ну; **the ship ~ed against the rocks** су́дно наскочи́ло на ска́лы.
with advs.: **~ down** *v.t.* (*e.g. a wall*) сн|оси́ть, -ести́; **~ in** *v.t.* прол|а́мывать, -оми́ть; **I'll ~ your face in** я тебе́ мо́рду разобью́; **~ up** *v.t.*: **~ up the furniture** разлома́ть (*pf.*) всю ме́бель; **~ up one's car** (*in collision*) разби́ть (*pf.*) маши́ну.
cpd. **~-and-grab** *adj.*: **~-and-grab (raid)** (граби́тельский) налёт на витри́ну магази́на.

smashing ['smæʃɪŋ] *adj.* **1.: ~ blow** сокруши́тельный уда́р; **~ defeat** тяжёлое пораже́ние. **2.** (*coll.*): **a ~ film** замеча́тельный/потряса́ющий фильм; **we had a ~ time** мы изуми́тельно провели́ вре́мя.

smattering ['smætərɪŋ] *n.*: **he has a ~ of German** он чуть-чуть зна́ет неме́цкий.

smear [smɪə(r)] *n.* **1.** (*blotch*) пятно́; (*microscope specimen*) мазо́к. **2.** (*coll., slander*) клевета́; **~ campaign** клеветни́ческая кампа́ния.
v.t. **1.** (*daub*) ма́зать, на-; разма́з|ывать, -ать; **he ~ed grease paint on his face** он наложи́л грим (себе́) на лицо́; **I ~ed my trousers with paint** я испа́чкал брю́ки кра́ской. **2.** (*defame*) поро́чить, о-.

smell [smel] *n.* **1.** (*faculty*) обоня́ние; **a keen sense of ~** то́нкое обоня́ние/чутьё; (*in animals*) чутьё. **2.** (*odour*) за́пах; **what a** (*sc. bad*) **~!** ну и вонь!; **this flower has no ~** э́тот цвето́к не име́ет за́паха (*or* не па́хнет); **garlic has a pungent ~** у чеснока́ е́дкий за́пах; **there was a ~ of burning** па́хло горе́лым. **3.** (*inhalation*): **have, take a ~ of, at** поню́хать (*pf.*).
v.t. **1.** (*perceive ~ of; also fig.*) чу́ять (*impf.*); **can you ~ onions?** вы чу́вствуете за́пах лу́ка?; **I can't ~ anything** я не чу́вствую никако́го за́паха; **I ~ a rat** чу́ю недо́брое. **2.** (*sniff*) ню́хать, по-; **just ~ this rose** то́лько поню́хайте э́ту ро́зу; **~ing salts** ню́хательная соль. **3.: ~ out** (*lit., fig.*) проню́х|ивать, -ать.
v.i. **1.** (*sniff*): **the dog was ~ing at the lamp-post** соба́ка (об)ню́хала фона́рь. **2.** (*emit ~*) па́хнуть (*impf.*); **the soup ~s good** суп хорошо́/вку́сно па́хнет; **his breath ~s** у него́ ду́рно па́хнет изо рта; **the fish began to ~** ры́ба ста́ла попа́хивать.

smelly ['smelɪ] *adj.* ду́рно па́хнущий; воню́чий.

smelt[1] [smelt] *n.* (*fish*) ко́рюшка.

smelt[2] [smelt] *v.t.* (*ore*) пла́вить (*impf.*); (*metal*) выплавля́ть, вы́плавить.

smidgen ['smɪdʒ(ə)n] *n.* (*US coll.*) чуто́к.

smile [smaɪl] *n.* улы́бка; **he greeted me with a ~** он встре́тил меня́ улы́бкой; **give s.o. a ~** улыбну́ться (*pf.*) кому́-н.; **force a ~** вы́давить (*pf.*) из себя́ улы́бку; **she was all ~s** у неё был сия́ющий вид.

v.t. (*express by* ~): **she ~d her approval** она́ улыбну́лась в знак одобре́ния.

v.i. улыб|а́ться, -ну́ться; **her ignorance made him ~** её неве́жество вы́звало у него́ улы́бку; **keep smiling!** не унывай́!; **~ on** (*fig.*): **fortune ~ed on him** сча́стье ему́ улыба́лось.

smirk [smɜ:k] *n.* жема́нная/самодово́льная улы́бка.

v.i. ухмыля́ться (*impf.*).

smit|e [smaɪt] *v.t.* (*afflict*) пора|жа́ть, -зи́ть; **~ten with the plague** поражённый чумо́й; **he was ~ten with remorse** его́ охвати́ло раска́яние; **he was ~ten by her charms** он был покорён её ча́рами.

smith [smɪθ] *n.* **(black~)** кузне́ц.

smithereens [ˌsmɪðəˈri:nz] *n.* (*coll.*): **to ~** вдре́безги.

smithy [ˈsmɪðɪ] *n.* ку́зница.

smock [smɒk] *n.* (*child's*) де́тский хала́тик; (*woman's*) ко́фта; (*peasant's*) (крестья́нская) блу́за.

smog [smɒg] *n.* смог.

smoke [sməʊk] *n.* **1.** дым; **clouds of ~** клубы́ (*m. pl.*) ды́ма; **emit ~** дыми́ть (*impf.*); **the ~ gets in my eyes** дым разъеда́ет мне глаза́; **~ was pouring out** дым (так и) вали́л; **go up in ~** (*lit.*) сгор|а́ть, -е́ть. **2.: have a ~** покури́ть (*pf.*); **they broke off for a ~** они́ устро́или переку́р.

v.t. **1.** (*preserve or darken with* ~) копти́ть, за-; **~d fish** копчёная ры́ба. **2.: ~ out** (*wasps etc.*) выку́ривать, вы́курить. **3.** (*tobacco etc.*) кури́ть, вы́-.

v.i. **1.** (*emit* ~; *of chimney, fireplace etc.*) дыми́ть (*impf.*); (*of fire or burning substance*) дыми́ться (*impf.*); кури́ться (*impf.*). **2.** (*of pers.*: ~ *tobacco etc.*) кури́ть (*impf.*).

cpds. **~-bomb** *n.* дымова́я бо́мба; **~-screen** *n.* (*lit., fig.*) дымова́я заве́са; **~-stack** *n.* труба́.

smokeless [ˈsməʊklɪs] *adj.* безды́мный; **~ zone** безды́мная городска́я зо́на.

smoker [ˈsməʊkə(r)] *n.* **1.** (*pers.*) куря́щий; кури́льщи|к (*fem.* -ца); **a heavy ~** зая́длый кури́льщик. **2.** (*coll., carriage*) ваго́н для куря́щих.

smoking [ˈsməʊkɪŋ] *n.* (*of food*) копче́ние; (*of tobacco etc.*) куре́ние; **'No S~'** «кури́ть воспреща́ется»; **I gave up ~** я бро́сил кури́ть.

cpds. **~-carriage, ~-compartment** *nn.* ваго́н/купе́ (*indecl.*) для куря́щих; **~-room** *n.* кури́тельная (ко́мната).

smoky [ˈsməʊkɪ] *adj.* ды́мный; (*of colour*) ды́мчатый; (*blackened by smoke*) закопте́лый.

smooth [smu:ð] *adj.* **1.** (*even, level*) гла́дкий, ро́вный; **a ~ road** ро́вная доро́га; **a ~ sea** споко́йное мо́ре; **a ~ paste** те́сто без комко́в; **we had a ~ ride in the train** по́езд шёл ро́вно; **everything went off ~ly** всё прошло́ без сучка́ и задо́ринки. **2.** (*not harsh to ear or taste*): **~ breathing** ро́вное дыха́ние; **~ vodka** мя́гкая во́дка; **~ wine** нете́рпкое вино́. **3.** (*of pers.*: *equable, unruffled*): **~ manners** мя́гкие мане́ры; **he has a ~ tongue** он говори́т гла́дко; он ма́стер говори́ть.

v.t. **1.** (*make level*) выра́внивать, вы́ровнять. **2.** (*arrange neatly, flatten*) пригла́|живать, -дить. **3.** (*make easy*) смягч|а́ть, -и́ть; **he ~ed the way for his successor** он облегчи́л путь для своего́ прее́мника.

with advs.: **~ away** *v.t.*: **he ~ed away our difficulties** он устрани́л на́ши затрудне́ния; **~ down** *v.t.*: **~ down one's dress** одёр|гивать, -нуть пла́тье; **he ~ed his hair down** он пригла́дил во́лосы; **~ off** *v.t.*: **~ off sharp edges** обт|а́чивать, -очи́ть о́стрые края́; **~ out** *v.t.*: **she ~ed out the folds in the tablecloth** она́ разгла́дила скла́дки на ска́терти; **~ over** *v.t.* смягч|а́ть, -и́ть; **~ things over** ула́|живать, -дить де́ло.

cpds. **~-bore** *adj.* гладкоство́льный; **~-tongued** *adj.* сладкоречи́вый, льсти́вый.

smoothness [ˈsmu:ðnɪs] *n.* гла́дкость.

smorgasbord [ˈsmɔ:gəsˌbɔ:d] *n.* «шве́дский» стол.

smother [ˈsmʌðə(r)] *v.t.* **1.** (*suffocate*) души́ть, за-; **he was ~ed by fumes** он задохну́лся от испаре́ний. **2.** (*cover*): **the furniture was ~ed in dust** ме́бель была́ покры́та густы́м сло́ем пы́ли; **she ~ed the child with kisses** она́ осы́пала ребёнка поцелу́ями. **3.** (*suppress, conceal*) подав|ля́ть, -и́ть; **they ~ed his cries** они́ заглуши́ли его́ кри́ки.

v.i. задо|ыха́ться, -охну́ться.

smoulder [ˈsməʊldə(r)], (*US*) **smolder** *v.i.* (*lit., fig.*) тлеть (*impf.*); **~ing leaves** тле́ющие ли́стья; **~ing hatred** затаённая не́нависть.

smudge [smʌdʒ] *n.* пятно́; **you have a ~ on your cheek** вы че́м-то вы́мазали щёку.

v.t. (*blur*) сма́з|ывать, -ать; (*smear*) ма́зать, вы́-.

v.i.: **the drawing ~s easily** рису́нок легко́ сма́зывается.

smug [smʌg] *adj.* самодово́льный.

smuggle [ˈsmʌg(ə)l] *v.t.* пров|ози́ть, -езти́ контраба́ндой; (*fig.*) **he was ~d into the house** его́ тайко́м провели́ в дом.

smuggler [ˈsmʌglə(r)] *n.* контрабанди́ст (*fem.* -ка).

smuggling [ˈsmʌglɪŋ] *n.* контраба́нда.

smugness [ˈsmʌgnɪs] *n.* самодово́льство.

smut [smʌt] *n.* **1.** (*of soot etc.*) са́жа. **2.: talk ~** нести́ (*det.*) поха́бщину.

smutty [ˈsmʌtɪ] *adj.*: **~ face** запа́чканное лицо́; **~ joke** похá́бный анекдо́т.

snack [snæk] *n.* заку́ска; **have a ~** заку́с|ывать, -и́ть.

cpd. **~-bar** *n.* заку́сочная, буфе́т.

snaffle [ˈsnæf(ə)l] *n.* уздéчка, тре́нзель (*m.*).

v.t. (*appropriate, steal*) стяну́ть, сти́брить (*both pf.*) (*sl.*).

snag [snæg] *n.* (*obstacle*) препя́тствие; (*difficulty*) затрудне́ние; (*hidden*) загво́здка.

v.t. (*catch against*) зацепи́ться (*pf.*) за+*a.*

snail [sneɪl] *n.* ули́тка; **go at a ~'s pace** тащи́ться (*impf.*) как черепа́ха.

snake [sneɪk] *n.* змея́; **grass ~** уж; **~ in the grass** (*fig.*) змея́ подколо́дная.

v.i.: **the road ~s through the mountains** доро́га вьётся меж гор.

cpds. **~bite** *n.* уку́с змеи́; **~-charmer** *n.* заклина́тель (*m.*) змей.

snap [snæp] *n.* **1.** (*noise*) щелчо́к; **the box shut with a ~** коро́бка защёлкнулась; (*of sth. breaking*) треск; (*bite*): **the dog made a ~ at him** соба́ка пыта́лась его́ укуси́ть. **2.** (*fastener*) кно́пка. **3.** (*coll., photograph*) сни́мок; **take a ~ of** сн|има́ть, -ять. **4.** (*spell*): **a cold ~** внеза́пное похолода́ние.

adj.: **~ decision** скоропали́тельное реше́ние.

v.t. **1.** (*make ~ping noise with*) щёлк|ать, -нуть +*i.*; **he ~ped his fingers in my face** он щёлкнул па́льцами пе́ред мои́м но́сом. **2.** (*break*) разл|а́мывать, -ома́ть; **he ~ped the stick in two** он разлома́л па́лку на́двое. **3.** (*coll., photograph*) сн|има́ть, -ять.

v.i. **1.** (*make biting motion*): **~ at** отгрыз|а́ться, -ну́ться на+*a.*; (*speak sharply*) набро́ситься (*pf.*) на+*a.*; **don't ~ at me!** не кричи́те на меня́! **2.** (*make ~ping sound*) щёлк|ать, -нуть; (*of fastener*) защёлк|иваться, -нуться. **3.** (*break*) тре́снуть (*pf.*); **the rope ~ped** верёвка оборвала́сь. **4.** (*move smartly*): **~ to attention** вы́тянуться (*pf.*) во фронт; **~ out of it!** (*coll.*) брось!

with advs.: **~ down** *v.t.*: **he ~ped the lid down** он защёлкнул кры́шку; **~ off** *v.t. & i.* (*break off*) отл|а́мывать(ся), -ома́ть(ся), -оми́ть(ся); **~ s.o.'s head off** (*coll.*) об|рыва́ть, -орва́ть кого́-н.; **~ up** *v.t.* (*snatch*) сца́пать (*pf.*); (*buy eagerly*) расхва́т|ывать,

-áть; **the tickets were ~ped up straight away** билéты тут же расхвата́ли.

cpds. **~dragon** *n.* льви́ный зев; **~-fastener** *n.* кно́пка; **~shot** *n.* сни́мок.

snappy ['snæpɪ] *adj.* (*brisk*) живо́й; **make it ~!** (по)живе́е!; (*coll., neat, elegant*) шика́рный.

snare [sneə(r)] *n.* (*noose*) сило́к; (*trap*) западня́, лову́шка.

v.t. лови́ть, пойма́ть в западню́/лову́шку.

cpd. **~-drum** *n.* бараба́н со стру́нами.

snarl[1] [snɑ:l] *n.* (*growl*) рыча́ние.

v.t. & i. рыча́ть, за-.

snarl[2] [snɑ:l] *n.* (*tangle*) спу́танный клубо́к.

v.t. запу́т|ывать, -ать; (*fig.*): **the arrangements were ~ed up** всё бы́ло перепу́тано.

snatch [snætʃ] *n.* **1.** (*act of ~ing*): **make a ~ at sth.** хвата́ться (*pf.*) за что-н. **2.** (*short spell*): **sleep in ~es** спать (*impf.*) уры́вками. **3.** (*fragment*) обры́вок.

v.t. **1.** (*seize*) хвата́ть, схвати́ть; **~ sth. out of s.o.'s hands** выхва́тывать, вы́хватить (*or* вырыва́ть, вы́рвать) что-н. у кого́-н. (из рук); **don't ~!** не хвата́й!; **~ an opportunity** воспо́льзоваться (*pf.*) слу́чаем. **2.** (*obtain with difficulty*) ур|ыва́ть, -ва́ть; **we ~ed a hurried meal** мы на́скоро перекуси́ли.

v.i.: **~ at sth.** хвата́ться, схвати́ться за что-н.

snazzy ['snæzɪ] *adj.* (*coll.*) шика́рный, эффе́ктный.

sneak [sni:k] *n.* подле́ц; (*in school*) я́беда (*c.g.*).

v.t. стащи́ть (*pf.*); **~ a look at sth.** взгляну́ть (*pf.*) на что-н. укра́дкой.

v.i. **1.** (*creep, move silently*) кра́сться (*impf.*); **~ into a room** прокра́|дываться, -сться в ко́мнату; **~ out of a room** выска́льзывать, вы́скользнуть из ко́мнаты. **2.** (*tell tales*): **~ on s.o.** я́бедничать, на- на кого́-н.

cpd. **~-thief** *n.* ме́лкий вор, вори́шка (*m.*).

sneakers ['sni:kəz] *n.* (*coll.*) полуке́д|ы (*pl., g.* -ов/—).

sneaking ['sni:kɪŋ] *adj.* (*furtive*): **he gave her a ~ glance** он укра́дкой взгляну́л на неё; (*persistent, lingering*): **~ feeling** та́йное подозре́ние.

sneer [snɪə(r)] *n.* презри́тельная усме́шка.

v.i. усмех|а́ться, -ну́ться; **~ at** насмеха́ться (*impf.*) над+*i.*; (*in words*) глуми́ться (*impf.*) над+*i.*.

sneeze [sni:z] *n.* чиха́нье; (*coll.*) чих.

v.i. чих|а́ть, -ну́ть.

snick [snɪk] *n.* (*notch*) зару́бка; (*cut*) надре́з.

snicker ['snɪkə(r)] *n.* хихи́канье.

v.i. хихи́к|ать, -нуть.

snide [snaɪd] *adj.* ехи́дный.

sniff [snɪf] *n.* (*inhalation*) вдох; **take a ~ at, of sth.** поню́хать (*pf.*) что-н.; **give a ~** (*to stop nose running etc.*) шмы́г|ать, -ну́ть (но́сом).

v.t. (*inhale*) вд|ыха́ть, -охну́ть; (*smell at*) ню́хать, по-.

v.i. **1.** шмы́г|ать, -ну́ть (но́сом). **2.: ~ at** ню́хать, по-.

sniffle ['snɪf(ə)l] *n.* сопе́ние; (*pl.*) на́сморк.

v.i. шмы́г|ать, -ну́ть (но́сом).

snigger ['snɪgə(r)] *n.* хихи́канье.

v.i. хихи́к|ать, -нуть.

snip [snɪp] *n.* (*act of ~ping*) ре́зание; (*piece cut off*) обре́зок; кусо́к; (*coll., bargain*) (больша́я) уда́ча.

v.t. (*clip, trim*) подр|еза́ть, -е́зать; (*cut*): **~ off a bud** ср|еза́ть, -е́зать по́чку.

snipe[1] [snaɪp] *n.* (*bird*) бека́с.

snipe[2] [snaɪp] *v.i.* (*mil.*) стреля́ть (*impf.*) из укры́тия.

sniper ['snaɪpə(r)] *n.* сна́йпер.

snippet ['snɪpɪt] *n.* (*of material*) лоску́т; (*pl., of news etc.*) обры́вки (*m. pl.*).

snivel ['snɪv(ə)l] *v.i.* (*run at the nose*) распус|ка́ть, -ти́ть со́пли; (*whine*) хны́кать (*impf.*); распус|ка́ть, -ти́ть ню́ни.

snob [snɒb] *n.* сноб.

snobbery ['snɒbərɪ] *n.* сноби́зм.

snobbish ['snɒbɪʃ] *adj.* сноби́стский.

snooker ['snu:kə(r)] *n.* сну́кер.

v.t. (*sl., defeat*) разби́ть (*pf.*), разгроми́ть (*pf.*).

snoop [snu:p] *v.i.* (*coll.*) подгля́дывать/подсма́тривать (*impf.*) чужи́е та́йны.

snooty ['snu:tɪ] *adj.* (*coll.*) задира́ющий нос, вообража́ющий.

snooze [snu:z] (*coll.*) *n.*: **have, take a ~** вздремну́ть (*pf.*).

v.i. дрема́ть (*impf.*).

snore [snɔ:(r)] *n.* храп.

v.i. храпе́ть, за-.

snorer ['snɔ:rə(r)] *n.* храпу́н (*fem.* -ья).

snorkel ['snɔ:k(ə)l] *n.* шно́ркель (*m.*).

snort [snɔ:t] *n.* фы́ркание.

v.i. фы́рк|ать, -нуть.

snot [snɒt] *n.* (*vulg.*) со́пли (*f. pl.*).

snotty ['snɒtɪ] *adj.* (*vulg., ~-nosed*) сопли́вый; (*sl., annoyed*) серди́тый; раздражённый.

snout [snaʊt] *n.* мо́рда; (*of pig*) ры́ло.

snow [snəʊ] *n.* снег; **there was a fall of ~** вы́пал снег; **the roads are deep in ~** все доро́ги в сугро́бах; **S~ Maiden** Снегу́рочка.

v.i.: **it is ~ing** снег идёт.

with advs.: **~ in, ~ up** *vv.t.*: **the road is ~ed up** доро́гу занесло́ сне́гом; **we were ~ed in** наш дом занесло́ сне́гом; **~ under** *v.t.* (*fig.*): **I was ~ed under with letters** я был зава́лен пи́сьмами.

cpds. **~ball** *n.* снежо́к; *v.i.* игра́ть (*impf.*) в снежки́; (*fig., increase*) расти́ (*impf.*), как сне́жный ком; **~-bound** *adj.* занесённый сне́гом; **~-capped, ~-clad, ~-covered** *adjs.* покры́тый сне́гом; **~-drift** *n.* сугро́б; **~drop** *n.* подсне́жник; **~fall** *n.* снегопа́д; **~flake** *n.* снежи́нка; (*pl.*) (сне́жные) хло́пья; **~-leopard** *n.* сне́жный барс, и́рбис; **~-line** *n.* снегова́я ли́ния; **~man** *n.* сне́жная ба́ба; **~-mobile** *n.* снегохо́д; **~-plough** *n.* снегоочисти́тель (*m.*); **~-shoes** *n.* снегосту́пы (*m. pl.*); **~storm** *n.* мете́ль, вью́га; **~-white** *adj.* белосне́жный; **S~-White** Снегу́рочка.

snowy ['snəʊɪ] *adj.* **1.: ~ roofs** заснéженные кры́ши; **~ weather** сне́жная пого́да. **2.** (*white*): **~ hair** белосне́жные во́лосы; **~ owl** бе́лая сова́.

snub[1] [snʌb] *n.* (*rebuff, slight*) афро́нт.

v.t. оса́|живать, -ди́ть.

snub[2] [snʌb] *adj.*: **~ nose** вздёрнутый нос.

cpd. **~-nosed** *adj.* курно́сый.

snuff[1] [snʌf] *n.* ню́хательный таба́к; **he is up to ~** (*shrewd*) его́ (на мяки́не) не проведёшь (*coll.*).

cpd. **~-box** *n.* табаке́рка.

snuff[2] [snʌf] *v.t.* (*also* **~ out**) туши́ть, по-; (*fig.*) гаси́ть, по-.

snuffle ['snʌf(ə)l] *n.* сопе́ние; **I have the ~s** (*coll.*) у меня́ из носу течёт.

v.i. сопе́ть (*impf.*).

snug [snʌg] *adj.* (*cosy*) ую́тный; (*close-fitting*): **a ~ jacket** облега́ющая ку́ртка.

snuggle ['snʌg(ə)l] *v.i.*: **~ down in bed** свёр|тываться, -ну́ться в посте́ли; **~ up to s.o.** приж|има́ться, -а́ться к кому́-н.

so[1] [səʊ] *n.* (*mus.*) = **so(h)**

so[2] [səʊ] *adv.* **1.** так; **is that ~?** пра́вда?; **~ it is (~ I am etc.)!** действи́тельно!; (и) в са́мом де́ле; **isn't that ~?** не так ли?; **that being ~** раз так; **would you be ~ kind as to visit her?** бу́дьте так добры́, навести́те её; **he is not ~ silly as to ask her** он не насто́лько глуп, что́бы проси́ть её; **he was ~ overworked that ...** он был до тако́й сте́пени перегружён, что...; **not ~ very ...** не так уж...; **it is ever ~ easy** э́то про́ще просто́го (*or* о́чень легко́); **every ~ often** вре́мя от вре́мени; **~ be it!** пусть так!; ~

far (*up to now*) до сих пор; ~ **far as I know** насколько я знаю; ~ **far** ~ **good** пока всё хорошо; **and** ~ **forth, on** и так далее; **just** ~ вот именно!; (*in good order*) в ажуре; ~ **long!** (*au revoir*) пока! (*coll.*); ~ **long as** (*provided that*) если только; ~ **many** столько +*g.*; **thank you** ~ **much!** большое спасибо!; ~ **much** ~ **that** настолько, что; ~ **much the worse/better** тем хуже/лучше; ~ **to say, speak** так сказать; ~ **what** ну и что (же)? **2.** (*also*) тоже; **(and)** ~ **do I** и я тоже. **3.** (*consequently, accordingly*) итак, поэтому; значит; ~ **you did see him after all** итак, вы всё-таки его видели; **it was late,** ~ **I went home** было поздно, и (поэтому) я пошёл домой. **4.** (*that the foregoing is true or will happen*): **I suppose** ~ я думаю, что да; **do you think** ~**?** вы так думаете? **5.:** ~ **as to** (*in order to*) (с тем), чтобы +*inf.*; (*in such a way as to*) так, чтобы. **6.** (*thereabouts*): **there were 100 or** ~ **people there** там было примерно сто человек (*or* около ста человек).

cpds. ~**-and-**~ *pron.* такой-то; ~**-called** *adj.* так называемый; ~**-so** *adj. & adv.* ничего; так себе.

soak [səʊk] *n.* (~*ing*): **give the clothes a thorough** ~**!** пусть бельё подольше помокнет!

v.t. **1.** (*steep*) вымачивать, вымочить; **she** ~**s the laundry overnight** она замачивает бельё на ночь. **2.** (*wet through*): **the shower** ~**ed me to the skin** дождь промочил меня до нитки.

v.i. **1.** (*remain immersed*) мокнуть (*impf.*). **2.** (*drain, percolate*) впит|ываться, -аться; прос|ачиваться, -очится; **the rain** ~**ed into the ground** дождь пропитал почву.

with advs.: ~ **off** *v.t.*: ~ **off dirt** отм|ачивать, -очить грязь; ~ **up** *v.t.* (*lit., fig.*) впит|ывать, -ать.

soaking ['səʊkɪŋ] *n.*: **he got a** ~ он здорово промок.

adj. & adv.: **you are** ~ **(wet)** вы промокли насквозь.

soap [səʊp] *n.* мыло; **cake, tablet of** ~ кусок мыла.

v.t. мылить, на-; ~ **o.s.** намыли|ваться, -ться.

cpds. ~**-bubble** *n.* мыльный пузырь; ~**-dish** *n.* мыльница; ~**-flakes** *n.* мыльные хлопь|я (*pl.*, *g.* -ев); ~**-opera** *n.* «мыльная опера», телесериал; ~**-powder** *n.* стиральный порошок; ~**stone** *n.* мыльный камень; ~**-suds** *n.* мыльная пена; ~**-works** *n.* мыловаренный завод.

soapy ['səʊpɪ] *adj.* **1.** (*covered with soap*): ~ **face** намыленное лицо. **2.** (*resembling, containing, consisting of soap*) мыльный.

soar [sɔ:(r)] *v.i.* **1.** (*of birds*) парить, вос-; высоко взлет|ать, -еть; взмы|вать, -ть. **2.** (*fig., rise, tower*) возн|оситься, -естись. **3.** (*of prices*) (резко) пов|ышаться, -ыситься. **4.** (*of glider*) планировать, с-.

s.o.b. (*abbr. of* **son of a bitch**) (*US*) сукин сын (*coll.*).

sob [sɒb] *n.* всхлип, всхлипывание.

v.t.: ~ **one's heart out** (отчаянно) рыдать (*impf.*); **she** ~**bed herself to sleep** она плакала, пока не уснула.

v.i. всхлип|ывать, -нуть.

cpds. ~**-story** *n.* (*coll.*) жалкие слова; душещипательная история.

sober ['səʊbə(r)] *adj.* **1.** (*not drunk, temperate*) трезвый. **2.** (*not fanciful*) здравый. **3.** (*of colour*) спокойный; ~**ly dressed** носящий неброскую одежду.

v.t. (*usu.* ~ **up**) отрезв|лять, -ить; вытрезвлять, вытрезвить; **this had a** ~**ing effect on them** это подействовало на них отрезвляюще; ~**ing-up station** (*in former USSR*) вытрезвитель (*m.*).

v.i. отрезв|ляться, -иться; ~ **up** протрезвиться (*pf.*).

sobriety [sə'braɪɪtɪ] *n.* трезвость.

sobriquet ['səʊbrɪˌkeɪ] *n.* прозвище, кличка.

soccer ['sɒkə(r)] *n.* футбол; ~ **fan** футбольный болельщик; ~ **player** футболист.

sociability [ˌsəʊʃə'bɪlɪtɪ] *n.* общительность.

sociable ['səʊʃəb(ə)l] *adj.* общительный, компанейский.

social ['səʊʃ(ə)l] *n.* вечеринка.

adj. **1.** (*pert. to the community*) общественный, социальный; **S**~ **Democrat** социал-демократ; ~ **sciences** общественные науки; ~ **security** социальное обеспечение; ~ **services** система социального обслуживания; ~ **worker** работни|к (*fem.* -ца) сферы социальных проблем. **2.** (*convivial*): ~ **gathering** дружеская встреча; ~ **evening** вечеринка.

cpd. ~**-democratic** *adj.* социал-демократический.

socialism ['səʊʃəˌlɪz(ə)m] *n.* социализм.

socialist ['səʊʃəlɪst] *n.* социалист (*fem.* -ка).

adj. социалистический.

socialization [ˌsəʊʃəlaɪ'zeɪʃ(ə)n] *n.* социализация, обобществление.

socialize ['səʊʃəˌlaɪz] *v.t.* обобществ|лять, -ить; ~**d medicine** государственное медицинское обслуживание.

v.i. (*coll., go about socially*) вести (*impf.*) светский образ жизни; (*maintain social relations*) поддерживать (*impf.*) светское общение (с кем-н.).

society [sə'saɪətɪ] *n.* общество; (*association*) общество, организация; (*e.g. students'*) клуб, кружок; **high** ~ высшее общество; **S**~ **of Friends** «Общество друзей», квакеры (*m. pl.*).

sociological [ˌsəʊsɪə'lɒdʒɪk(ə)l, ˌsəʊʃɪ-] *adj.* социологический.

sociologist [ˌsəʊsɪ'ɒlədʒɪst, ˌsəʊʃɪ-] *n.* социолог.

sociology [ˌsəʊsɪ'ɒlədʒɪ, ˌsəʊʃɪ-] *n.* социология.

sock[1] [sɒk] *n.* **1.** (*short stocking*) носок; **ankle** ~**s** короткие носочки (*m. pl.*). **2.** (*inner sole*) стелька.

sock[2] [sɒk] (*sl.*) *n.* (*blow*) удар; **give s.o. a** ~ **on the nose** да|вать, -ть кому-н. по носу.

v.t.: **I** ~**ed him in the jaw** я дал ему в морду.

socket ['sɒkɪt] *n.* **1.** (*anat.*) впадина; **eye** ~ глазная впадина, глазница. **2.** (*for plug*) розетка; (*for bulb*) патрон.

sod[1] [sɒd] *n.* дёрн.

sod[2] [sɒd] *n.* (*sl.*) сволочь (*f.*); **silly** ~ идиот; **S**~**'s Law** закон подлости, закон бутерброда.

soda ['səʊdə] *n.* **1.** сода; **baking** ~ сода для печения; **washing** ~ стиральная сода. **2. (**~**-water)** содовая/газированная вода; газировка.

cpds. ~**-bread** *n.* хлеб, выпеченный на соде; ~**-fountain** *n.* стойка, где продаётся газировка; ~**-siphon** *n.* сифон для газированной воды; ~**water** *n.* содовая/газированная вода; газировка.

sodden ['sɒd(ə)n] *adj.* (*drenched*) промокший; (*steeped*) пропитанный.

sodium ['səʊdɪəm] *n.* натрий.

sodomite ['sɒdəˌmaɪt] *n.* педераст; скотоложец.

sodomy ['sɒdəmɪ] *n.* педерастия; (*bestiality*) скотоложство.

sofa ['səʊfə] *n.* диван.

soft [sɒft] *adj.* **1.** мягкий; ~ **colour** неяркий цвет; ~ **cover** (*of book*) мягкий переплёт; ~ **furnishings** драпировки (*f. pl.*); **a** ~ **light** мягкий свет; ~ **palate** мягкое нёбо; ~ **toy** мягконабивная игрушка; ~ **water** мягкая вода; ~ **drink** безалкогольный напиток; ~ **fruit** ягода; ~ (*gentle*) **voice** мягкий/нежный голос; ~ (*low-pitched*) **voice** тихий голос; ~ **sign** (*gram.*) мягкий знак. **2.** (*gentle, compassionate*) мягкий; отзывчивый; **have a** ~ **spot for s.o.** питать (*impf.*) слабость к кому-н.; (*indulgent*) нестрогий. **3.** (*flabby*) дряблый. **4.** (*coll., easy*): **he has a** ~ **job** у него лёгкая работа.

cpds. ~**-boiled** *adj.*: ~**-boiled egg** яйцо всмятку; ~**-hearted** *adj.* мягкосердечный; ~**-spoken** *adj.* с мягким голосом; ~**ware** *n.* (*comput.*) программное обеспечение; ~**wood** *n.* мягкая древесина.

soften ['sɒf(ə)n] *v.t.* смягч|ать, -ить; (*of voice*) пон|ижать, -изить.

v.i. смягч|аться, -иться.

with adv.: ~ **up** *v.t.*: ~ **s.o. up** (*fig.*) осл|аблять,

-áбить чьё-н. сопротивлéние.

softness ['sɒftnɪs] *n.* мя́гкость.

soggy ['sɒgɪ] *adj.*: ~ **bread** плóхо пропечённый хлеб; ~ **ground** сырáя/отсырéвшая земля́.

so(h) [səʊ] *n.* (*mus.*) соль (*nt. indecl.*).

soil[1] [sɔɪl] *n.* **1.** (*earth*) пóчва; ~ **science** почвовéдение. **2.** (*fig.*, *country*) земля́; **on foreign** ~ на чужóй землé.

soil[2] [sɔɪl] *v.t.* пáчкать, за-/ис-/вы́-; ~**ed linen** гря́зное бельё.

v.i.: **this fabric ~s easily** э́то óчень мáркий материáл.

cpd. ~**-pipe** *n.* канализациóнная трубá.

soirée ['swɑːreɪ] *n.* (звáный) вéчер.

sojourn ['sɒdʒ(ə)n, -dʒɜːn, 'sʌ-] (*liter.*) *n.* (врéменное) пребывáние.

v.i. пребывáть, жить, проживáть (*all impf.*).

solace ['sɒləs] *n.* утешéние.

solar ['səʊlə(r)] *adj.* сóлнечный; ~ **plexus** сóлнечное сплетéние; ~ **system** сóлнечная систéма.

solarium [sə'leərɪəm] *n.* соля́рий.

solder ['səʊldə(r), 'sɒ-] *n.* припóй.

v.t. пая́ть (*impf.*); ~ **together** спá|ивать, -я́ть; ~**ing-iron** пая́льник.

soldier ['səʊldʒə(r)] *n.* солдáт; **play at ~s** игрáть (*impf.*) в солдáтики; ~ **of fortune** (*mercenary*) наёмный солдáт, кондотьéр; **private** ~ рядовóй, боéц; **a great** ~ вели́кий полковóдец.

v.i. служи́ть (*impf.*) (в áрмии); ~ **on** (*fig.*, *persevere doggedly*) не сдавáться (*impf.*).

soldierly ['səʊldʒəlɪ] *adj.* воéнный; по-солдáтски.

sole[1] [səʊl] *n.* (*fish*) морскóй язы́к, соль (*f.*).

sole[2] [səʊl] *n.* (*of foot*) ступня́, подóшва; (*of shoe*) подóшва, подмётка.

v.t. подш|ивáть, -и́ть; ~ **a shoe** стáвить, по- подмётку.

sole[3] [səʊl] *adj.* (*only*) еди́нственный; ~ **agent** еди́нственный представи́тель; (*exclusive*) исключи́тельный.

solecism ['sɒlɪˌsɪz(ə)m] *n.* солеци́зм.

solely ['səʊllɪ] *adv.* тóлько, еди́нственно, исключи́тельно.

solemn ['sɒləm] *adj.* торжéственный; (*serious*) серьёзный, вáжный; **he put on a ~ face** он сдéлал серьёзное лицó.

solemnity [sə'lemnɪtɪ] *n.* торжéственность; (*gravity*) вáжность; (*of appearance*) серьёзность.

sol-fa ['sɒlfɑː] *n.* сольфéджио (*indecl.*).

solicit [sə'lɪsɪt] *v.t.* **1.** (*petition*, *importune*): ~ **s.o.'s help** проси́ть, по- когó-н. о пóмощи. **2.** (*ask for*): ~ **favours of s.o.** выпрáшивать (*impf.*) у когó-н. ми́лости. **3.** (*accost*) прист|авáть, -áть к+*d.*

v.i. (*of prostitute*) приставáть (*impf.*) к мужчи́нам.

solicitation [səˌlɪsɪ'teɪʃ(ə)n] *n.* прóсьба, ходáтайство.

solicitor [sə'lɪsɪtə(r)] *n.* адвокáт, юрискóнсульт.

solicitous [sə'lɪsɪtəs] *adj.* забóтливый, внимáтельный; **she is ~ for, about your safety** онá забóтится о вáшей безопáсности.

solicitude [sə'lɪsɪˌtjuːd] *n.* забóтливость.

solid ['sɒlɪd] *n.* (*phys.*) твёрдое тéло; (*pl.*, *food*) твёрдая пи́ща.

adj. **1.** (*not liquid or fluid*) твёрдый; ~ **food** твёрдая пи́ща; ~ **fuel** твёрдое тóпливо; **become** ~ твердéть, за-. **2.** (*not hollow*) масси́вный; ~ **sphere** масси́вный шар. **3.** (*homogeneous*): ~ **silver** чи́стое серебрó. **4.** (*unbroken*): **12 hours' ~ sleep** 12 часóв непреры́вного сна; **a ~ line** сплошнáя чертá; **it rained for 3 ~ days** дождь лил три дня подря́д; **I waited for a ~ hour** я прождáл цéлый/би́тый час. **5.** (*firmly built*, *substantial*) прóчный; **a man of ~ build** человéк крéпкого телосложéния. **6.** (*sound*, *reliable*) соли́дный; надёжный. **7.** (*unanimous*, *united*) единоду́шный; **the meeting was ~(ly) against him** собрáние единоду́шно вы́ступило прóтив негó. **8.** (*pert. to ~s*): ~ **geometry** стереомéтрия; ~**(-state) physics** фи́зика твёрдых тел.

solidarity [ˌsɒlɪ'dærɪtɪ] *n.* солидáрность; ~ **of purpose** еди́нство цéлей; ~ **of feeling** единоду́шие.

solidify [sə'lɪdɪˌfaɪ] *v.t.* дéлать, с- твёрдым.

v.i. твердéть, за-; заст|ывáть, -ы́ть.

solidity [sə'lɪdɪtɪ] *n.* твёрдость; (*sturdiness*) прóчность; (*reliability*) надёжность.

soliloquize [sə'lɪləkwaɪz] *v.t.* произноси́ть (*impf.*) монолóг.

soliloquy [sə'lɪləkwɪ] *n.* монолóг.

solitaire ['sɒlɪˌteə(r)] *n.* (*gem*) солитéр; (*US*, *card game*) солитéр, пасья́нс.

solitary ['sɒlɪtərɪ] *adj.* (*secluded*) уединённый; (*lonely*) одинóкий; ~ **confinement** одинóчное заключéние; (*single*) едини́чный, еди́ный; **a ~ instance** едини́чный слу́чай.

solitude ['sɒlɪˌtjuːd] *n.* (*being alone*; *lonely place*) уединéние; (*loneliness*) одинóчество.

solo ['səʊləʊ] *n.* (*mus.*) сóло (*indecl.*), сóльный нóмер, сóльное выступлéние.

adj. сóльный; (*aeron.*) одинóчный.

adv. (*alone*): **fly** ~ выполня́ть, вы́полнить одинóчный полёт.

soloist ['səʊləʊɪst] *n.* соли́ст (*fem.* -ка).

solstice ['sɒlstɪs] *n.* солнцестоя́ние.

solubility [ˌsɒljʊ'bɪlɪtɪ] *n.* раствори́мость.

soluble ['sɒljʊb(ə)l] *adj.* (*dissolvable*) раствори́мый; (*solvable*) разреши́мый.

solution [sə'luːʃ(ə)n, -'ljuːʃ(ə)n] *n.* **1.** (*dissolving*) растворéние; (*result of this*) раствóр; **rubber** ~ рези́новый клей. **2.** (*solving*; *answer*) решéние, вы́ход, отвéт.

solve [sɒlv] *v.t.*: ~ **an problem** реш|áть, -и́ть задáчу; ~ **a mystery** распу́т|ывать, -ать тáйну; ~ **a difficulty** на|ходи́ть, -йти́ вы́ход из затруднéния.

solvency ['sɒlv(ə)nsɪ] *n.* платежеспосóбность.

solvent ['sɒlv(ə)nt] *n.* раствори́тель (*m.*); ~ **abuse** токсикомáния; ~ **abuser** токсикомáн.

adj. (*chem.*) растворя́ющий; (*fin.*) платежеспосóбный.

Somalia [sə'mɑːlɪə] *n.* Сомали́ (*nt.*); Сомали́йская Респу́блика.

sombre ['sɒmbə(r)] *adj.* (*gloomy*) угрю́мый; (*dismal*) мрáчный; (*overcast*) пáсмурный.

sombrero [sɒm'breərəʊ] *n.* сомбрéро (*indecl.*).

some [sʌm] *pron.* **1.** (*of persons*): ~ **say yes,** ~ **say no** одни́ говоря́т да, други́е — нет; ~ **(people) were late** кóе-кто опоздáл; ~ **one way,** ~ **the other** кто кудá; ~ **of these girls** коé-кто/нéкоторые из э́тих дéвушек. **2.** (*of thgs.*, *an indefinite quantity or number*): **I have ~ already** у меня́ ужé есть; **have ~ more!** возьми́те ещё! **3.** (*a part*) часть; **I have ~ of the documents** часть докумéнтов у меня́ есть; **I agree with ~ of what you said** я соглáсен кóе с чем из тогó, что вы сказáли. **4.** (*coll.*): **and then ~!** (*more than that*) ещё как!

adj. **1.** (*definite though unspecified*) какóй-то; ~ **fool has locked the door** какóй-то дурáк зáпер дверь; **one must make ~ (sort of) attempt** нáдо сдéлать хоть каку́ю-нибудь попы́тку; ~ **day,** ~ **time** когдá-нибудь; **is this ~ kind of joke?** э́то что — своегó рóда шу́тка? **2.** (*no matter what*) какóй-нибудь, какóй-либо; **he is looking for ~ work** он и́щет (каку́ю-нибудь) рабóту. **3.** (*one or two*) кóе-каки́е (*pl.*); (*a certain amount or number of*: *may be untranslated or expr. by g.*): **I bought ~ envelopes** я купи́л конвéртов; ~ **more** ещё (+*g.*); ~ **distance away** на нéкотором расстоя́нии; **for ~ time now** с нéкоторого врéмени; ~ **books** нéсколько книг; **it takes ~ courage to ...** трéбуется немáло му́жества, чтóбы...; **that takes ~ doing** э́то не тáк-то легкó;

~ **work is pleasant** бывáет/встречáется приятная рабóта. **4.** (*in ~ sense or degree*; *to a certain extent*): **that is ~ proof** это в какóй-то стéпени мóжет служи́ть доказáтельством. **5.** (*approximately*) примéрно, óколо; **we waited ~ 20 minutes** мы ждáли минýт двáдцать. **6.** (*coll.*, *expr. admiration etc.*) вот это; вот так; ~ **speed!** вот это скóрость!; **he's ~ doctor!** это настоя́щий врач!

somebody ['sʌmbədɪ] *n.*: **a ~** вáжная персóна.
pron. (*also* **someone**) (*in particular*) ктó-то; нéкто; **there is ~ in the cellar** в пóгребе ктó-то есть; (*no matter who*) ктó-нибудь, ктó-либо; ~ **else** ктó-нибудь другóй, ктó-то другóй.

somehow ['sʌmhaʊ] *adv.* кáк-нибудь; так и́ли ина́че; **we shall manage ~** мы кáк-нибудь спрáвимся; (*for some reason*): ~ **I never liked him** он мне почемý-то никогдá не нрáвился.

someone ['sʌmwʌn] = **somebody** *pron.*

someplace ['sʌmpleɪs] (*US*) = **somewhere**

somersault ['sʌmə,sɒlt] *n.* сáльто (*indecl.*).
v.i. кувырк|áться, -нýться.

something ['sʌmθɪŋ] *pron.* (*definite*) чтó-то, нéчто; (*indefinite*) чтó-нибудь, чтó-либо; **she lectures in ~ or other** онá читáет лéкции по какóму-то (там) предмéту; **I have seen ~ of his work** я ви́дел кóе-каки́е из егó рабóт; **there is ~ about him** в нём чтó-то такóе есть; **it is ~ of an improvement** это нéкоторый прогрéсс; **you have ~ there** в этом вы прáвы; **we managed to see ~ of each other** нам удавáлось врéмя от врéмени встречáться; **I think I'm on to ~** кáжется, я нащýпал путь; **she has a cold or ~** у неё то ли простýда, то ли ещё чтó-то; **he is a surgeon or ~** он хирýрг и́ли чтó-то в этом рóде.
adv.: **he left ~ like a million** он остáвил чтó-то поря́дка миллиóна; **his house looks ~ like a prison** егó дом смáхивает на тюрьмý.

sometime ['sʌmtaɪm] *adv.* когдá-то, когдá-нибудь, когдá-либо; ~ **soon** скóро; **come and see us ~** приходи́те к нам кáк-нибудь.

sometimes ['sʌmtaɪmz] *adv.* иногдá; ~ ... ~ ... то... то...

somewhat ['sʌmwɒt] *adv.* кáк-то, нéсколько, довóльно; **he is ~ off-hand** он дéржится кáк-то небрéжно; **he was ~ hard to follow** егó бы́ло довóльно трýдно понимáть.

somewhere ['sʌmweə(r)] *adv.* **1.** (*US also* **someplace**) гдé-то, гдé-нибудь, гдé-либо; ~ **else** гдé-то в другóм мéсте; гдé-то ещё; (*motion*) кудá-то; **I am going ~ tomorrow** я зáвтра кóе-кудá идý. **2.** (*approximately*) óколо+*g.*; **it is ~ about 6 o'clock** сейчáс чтó-то óколо шести́.

somnambulism [sɒm'næmbjʊ,lɪz(ə)m] *n.* лунати́зм.

somnambulist [sɒm'næmbjʊlɪst] *n.* лунáт|ик (*fem.* -и́чка).

somnolence ['sɒmnələns] *n.* сонли́вость.

somnolent ['sɒmnələnt] *adj.* (*drowsy*) сóнный, сонли́вый; (*inducing sleep*) снотвóрный.

son [sʌn] *n.* сын (*pl.* -овья́, (*rhet.*) -ы́); ~ **of a bitch** (*sl.*) сýкин сын; (*as form of address*): (**my**) ~ сынóк.
cpd. **~-in-law** *n.* зять (*m.*).

sonar ['səʊnə(r)] *n.* гидролокáтор.

sonata [sə'nɑːtə] *n.* сонáта.

song [sɒŋ] *n.* **1.** (*singing*) пéние; **burst into ~** запéть (*pf.*). **2.** (*words set to music*; *also bird's ~*) пéсня; **he bought it for a ~** он это купи́л за бесцéнок.
cpds. **~-bird** *n.* пéвчая пти́ца; **~-book** *n.* пéсенник; **~writer** *n.* пéсенник.

sonic ['sɒnɪk] *adj.* звуковóй; ~ **bang, boom** сверхзвуковóй хлопóк.

sonnet ['sɒnɪt] *n.* сонéт.

sonny ['sʌnɪ] *n.* (*coll.*) сынóк.

sonorous ['sɒnərəs, sə'nɔːrəs] *adj.* звýчный.

soon [suːn] *adv.* **1.** (*in a short while*) скóро, вскóре; ~ **after** чéрез корóткое врéмя; **write ~!** напиши́те поскорée!; **as ~ as possible** как мóжно скорée. **2.** (*early*) рáно; **we arrived too ~** мы при́были сли́шком рáно; **how ~ can you come?** когдá вы мóжете прибы́ть?; **the ~er the better** чем рáньше, тем лýчше; **~er or later** рáно и́ли пóздно. **3.**: **as ~ as** как тóлько; **no ~er said than done** скáзано — сдéлано. **4.** (*willingly*): **I would as ~ stay at home** я предпочёл бы остáться дóма; **I would ~er die than permit it** я скорée умрý, чем допущý это.

soot [sʊt] *n.* сáжа, кóпоть.

sooth|e [suːð] *v.t.* (*calm, pacify*) успок|áивать, -óить; **in a ~ing tone** успокáивающе.

soothsayer ['suːθ,seɪə(r)] *n.* предсказáтель (*fem.* -ница).

sooty ['sʊtɪ] *adj.* (*blackened with soot*) закопчённый, закоптéлый; покры́тый кóпотью.

sop [sɒp] *n.* (*fig.*) подáчка, взя́тка; **as a ~ to his pride** чтóбы потéшить егó самолю́бие.
v.t.: ~ **up** (*mop up*) подт|ирáть, -ерéть.
v.i.: **the shirt was ~ping wet** рубáшка промóкла насквóзь; **we got ~ping wet** мы промóкли до ни́тки.

sophism ['sɒfɪz(ə)m] *n.* софи́зм, софи́стика.

sophist ['sɒfɪst] *n.* софи́ст.

sophistic(al) [sə'fɪstɪk(ə)l] *adj.* софи́стский.

sophisticated [sə'fɪstɪ,keɪtɪd] *adj.* **1.** (*advanced*): ~ **techniques** слóжная/изощрённая тéхника; ~ **weapons** совремéнные ви́ды орýжия. **2.** (*refined*) ~ **taste** утончённый/изощрённый вкус; ~ **manners** изы́сканные манéры.

sophistication [sə,fɪstɪ'keɪʃ(ə)n] *n.* (*refinement*) утончённость, искушённость.

sophistry ['sɒfɪstrɪ] *n.* софи́стика.

sophomore ['sɒfə,mɔː(r)] *n.* (*US*) студéнт-второкýрсник.

soporific [,sɒpə'rɪfɪk] *adj.* снотвóрный, усыпля́ющий.

soppy ['sɒpɪ] *adj.* (*coll.*) (*sentimental*) сентиментáльный, слюня́вый.

soprano [sə'prɑːnəʊ] *n.* (*voice, singer, part*) сопрáно (*f. & nt. indecl.*); (*attr.*) сопрáнный; **boy ~** ди́скант.

sorbet ['sɔːbeɪ, -bɪt] *n.* шербéт.

sorcerer ['sɔːsərə(r)] *n.* колдýн, волшéбник.

sorceress ['sɔːsərɪs] *n.* колдýнья, волшéбница.

sorcery ['sɔːsərɪ] *n.* колдовствó, волшебствó.

sordid ['sɔːdɪd] *adj.* (*squalid, poor*) убóгий, жáлкий; (*filthy*) гря́зный; **a ~ affair** гнýсная истóрия.

sordidness ['sɔːdɪdnɪs] *n.* убóгость, убóжество; грязь; пóдлость; (*meanness*) ни́зость.

sore [sɔː(r)] *n.* боля́чка, я́зва.
adj. **1.** (*painful*): **a ~ tooth** больнóй зуб; **I have a ~** (*grazed*) **knee** я ссади́л себé колéно; **he has a ~ throat** у негó боли́т гóрло; **I woke up with a ~ head** я проснýлся с головнóй бóлью; **it is a ~ point with him** это у негó больнóе мéсто. **2.** (*coll.*, *aggrieved*) раздражённый, оби́женный; **he was ~ at not being invited** он оби́делся, что егó не позвáли. **3.** (*acute, extreme*) крáйний; **I was ~ly tempted** у меня́ бы́ло си́льное искушéние.

soreness ['sɔːnɪs] *n.* боль.

sorghum ['sɔːgəm] *n.* сóрго (*indecl.*).

sorrel ['sɒr(ə)l] *n.* (*bot.*) щавéль (*m.*).

sorrow ['sɒrəʊ] *n.* (*sadness, grief*) печáль; (*extreme ~*) скорбь; (*regret*) сожалéние; **express ~ for** выражáть, вы́разить сожалéние о+*p.*; **to my ~** к моемý огорчéнию; (*sad experience*) гóре.

sorrowful ['sɒrəʊ,fʊl] *adj.* печáльный, скóрбный.

sorry ['sɒrɪ] *adj.* **1.** (*regretful*): **be ~ for sth.** сожалéть (*impf.*) о чём-н.; **I was ~ I had to do it** я (со)жалéл, что пришлóсь так поступи́ть; **aren't you ~ for what you've done?** вы не раскáиваетесь в том, что надéлали?; **say you're ~!** попроси́ прощéния!; **we were ~ to hear of your father's death** с грýстью узна́ли мы о сме́рти ва́шего отца́; **~!** винова́т!; прости́те!; извини́те! **2.** (*expr. pity, sympathy*): **feel ~ for s.o.** испы́тывать (*impf.*) жа́лость к кому́-н.; жале́ть (*impf.*) кого́-н.; сочу́вствовать (*impf.*) кому́-н.; **it's the children I feel ~ for** кого́ мне жаль — э́то дете́й; **feel ~ for o.s.** быть испо́лненным жа́лости к себе́. **3.** (*wretched, pitiful*) жа́лкий; **in a ~ state** в жа́лком состоя́нии.

sort [sɔːt] *n.* **1.** (*kind, class, category, species*) род, сорт, вид; **we have all ~s of books** у нас вся́кого ро́да кни́ги; **people of that ~** тако́го ро́да лю́ди; **a new ~ of bicycle** но́вый тип велосипе́да; **what ~ of man is he?** что он за челове́к?; **a good ~** хоро́ший челове́к; **what ~ of music do you like?** каку́ю му́зыку вы лю́бите?; **nothing of the ~** ничего́ подо́бного; **a ~ of war** своего́ ро́да война́; **a novel of a ~** не́что вро́де рома́на; **different ~s of goods** това́ры ра́зного ро́да; **people of all ~s** лю́ди вся́кого разбо́ра; **what ~ of people does he think we are?** за кого́ он нас принима́ет? **2.: ~ of** (*coll.*) вро́де, как бы; в о́бщем-то; **he ~ of suggested I took him with me** он как бы дал мне поня́ть, что хо́чет пойти́ со мной. **3.: out of ~s** не в ду́хе.

v.t. раз|бира́ть, -обра́ть; (*grain, coal etc.*) сортирова́ть (*impf., pf.*).

with adv.: **~ out** *v.t.* (*select*) от|бира́ть, -обра́ть; (*separate*) отдел|я́ть, -и́ть; (*arrange, classify*) раз|бира́ть, -обра́ть; (*fig., put in order*): **I have to go home to ~ things out** мне ну́жно пойти́ домо́й и во всём разобра́ться; **everything will ~ itself out** всё нала́дится.

sorter ['sɔːtə(r)] *n.* сортиро́вщик.

sortie ['sɔːtɪ] *n.* (*sally*) вы́лазка; (*flight*) вы́лет.

SOS *n.* (ра́дио)сигна́л бе́дствия.

sot [sɒt] *n.* пья́ница (*c.g.*).

soufflé ['suːfleɪ] *n.* суфле́ (*indecl.*).

soul [səʊl] *n.* **1.** душа́; **throw o.s. body and ~ into sth.** всей душо́й отд|ава́ться, -а́ться чему́-н.; **he puts his heart and ~ into his work** он всю ду́шу вкла́дывает в свою́ рабо́ту; **upon my ~!** ей-Бо́гу! **2.** (*animating spirit*): **he was the life and ~ of the party** он был душо́й о́бщества. **3.** (*personification*): **he is the ~ of honour** э́то/он воплощённая че́стность. **4.** (*pers.*): **there wasn't a ~ in sight** не ви́дно бы́ло ни души́; **a simple ~** проста́я душа́; **the poor ~ lost her way** бедня́жка заблуди́лась. **5.** (*music*) со́ул.

cpds. **~-destroying** *adj.* иссуша́ющий ду́шу; **~-mate** *n.* задуше́вный друг; задуше́вная подру́га.

sound[1] [saʊnd] *n.* **1.** звук; (*of rain, sea, wind etc.*) шум; **not a ~ was heard** не́ было слы́шно ни зву́ка; **~ barrier** звуково́й барье́р; **~ effects** шумовы́е эффе́кты; **~ engineer** звукоопера́тор. **2.: I don't like the ~ of it** мне э́то (что́-то) не нра́вится.

v.t. **1.** (*cause to ~*) звони́ть, по- +*a.*; **they ~ed the bell** они́ позвони́ли в ко́локол; **~ a trumpet** труби́ть, по-; **~ the horn** (*of a car*) да|ва́ть, -ть гудо́к. **2.** (*play on trumpet etc.*): **~ the retreat** труби́ть, за-/про- отступле́ние; **~ the alarm** бить, за- трево́гу. **3.** (*pronounce*) произн|оси́ть, -ести́; **the 'K' is not ~ed** «K» не произно́сится. **4.** (*test*): **the doctor ~ed his chest** до́ктор прослу́шал его́ лёгкие/се́рдце.

v.i. **1.** (*emit sound; convey effect by sound*) звуча́ть, про-; **the trumpets ~ed** раздали́сь зву́ки труб. **2.** (*give impression*) каза́ться, по-; **his voice ~s as if he has a cold** по го́лосу ка́жется, что он просту́жен; **it ~s like thunder** похо́же на гром; **the statement ~s improbable** э́то заявле́ние ка́жется маловероя́тным.

with adv.: **~ off** *v.i.* (*coll., of pers.*) шуме́ть (*impf.*).

cpds. **~-man** *n.* аку́стик; **~-proof** *adj.* звуконепроница́емый; **~-recording** *n.* звукоза́пись; **~-track** *n.* звуково́е сопровожде́ние; **~-wave** *n.* звукова́я волна́.

sound[2] [saʊnd] *n.* (*strait*) проли́в.

sound[3] [saʊnd] *n.* (*probe*) зонд.

v.t. (*measure*) изм|ер́ять, -е́рить. **2.** (*fig.*): **~ (out) s.o.** (*or* **s.o.'s intentions, opinions**) зонди́ровать, по- кого́-н.

sound[4] [saʊnd] *adj.* **1.** (*healthy*) здоро́вый; **~ in body and mind** здоро́вый те́лом и душо́й; **of ~ mind** в здра́вом уме́; (*in good condition*) испра́вный. **2.** (*correct, logical*) здра́вый; **a ~ argument** убеди́тельный до́вод. **3.** (*financially stable*) соли́дный; (*solvent*) платёжеспосо́бный. **4.** (*thorough*) хоро́ший; **he slept ~ly** он кре́пко спал; **he was ~ly thrashed** он был здо́рово изби́т.

sounding-board ['saʊndɪŋ,bɔːd] *n.* наве́с ка́федры; де́ка, резона́тор.

soundless ['saʊndlɪs] *adj.* беззву́чный.

soundness ['saʊndnɪs] *n.* здоро́вье; про́чность; обосно́ванность; разу́мность.

soup[1] [suːp] *n.* суп; **beetroot ~** борщ; **cabbage ~** щи (*pl., g.* щей).

cpds. **~-kitchen** *n.* беспла́тная столо́вая для нужда́ющихся; **~-plate** *n.* глубо́кая таре́лка; **~-spoon** *n.* столо́вая ло́жка; **~-tureen** *n.* су́пница.

soupçon ['suːpsɔ̃] *n.* чу́точка, при́вкус; намёк.

sour ['saʊə(r)] *adj.* **1.** (*of fruit etc.*) ки́слый; **~ grapes!** (*fig.*) зе́лен виногра́д! **2.** (*of milk*) проки́сший, ски́сший; **go, turn ~** ск|иса́ть, -и́снуть; **~ cream** смета́на. **3.** (*of pers.*) мра́чный, озло́бленный.

v.t.: **disappointments ~ed his temper** от постоя́нных неуда́ч у него́ испо́ртился хара́ктер.

v.i. ск|иса́ть, -и́снуть; свёр|тываться, -ну́ться; (*fig.*) по́ртиться, ис-.

source [sɔːs] *n.* **1.** (*of stream etc.*) исто́к. **2.** (*fig.*) исто́чник; **reliable ~s of information** надёжные исто́чники информа́ции.

sourness ['saʊənɪs] *n.* кислота́; ки́слый вкус.

souse [saʊs] *v.t.* **1.** (*put in pickle*) соли́ть, за-; **~d herrings** солёная/марино́ванная сельдь. **2.** (*plunge or soak in liquid*) мочи́ть, на-/за-; окун|а́ть, -у́ть. **3.** (*p.p., sl., drunk*) пья́ный в сте́льку.

south [saʊθ] *n.* юг; **in the ~** на ю́ге; **to the ~ of** к ю́гу от (*or* ю́жнее) +*g.*; **from the ~** с ю́га.

adj. ю́жный; **~ wind** ю́жный ве́тер; ве́тер с ю́га; **S~ Africa** Ю́жная А́фрика; **Republic of S~ Africa** Ю́жно-Африка́нская Респу́блика; **S~ America** Ю́жная Аме́рика; **S~ American** (*n.*) южноамерика́н|ец (*fem.* -ка); (*adj.*) южноамерика́нский; **S~ Pole** Ю́жный по́люс; **the S~ Seas** ю́жная часть Ти́хого океа́на; **S~ Sea Islands** Океа́ния.

adv.: **the ship sailed due ~** су́дно шло пря́мо на юг; **our village is ~ of London** на́ша дере́вня нахо́дится к ю́гу от Ло́ндона.

cpds. **~-east** *n.* юго-восто́к; *adj.* (*also* **~-easterly, ~-eastern**) юго-восто́чный; *adv.* (*also* **~-easterly**) на юго-восто́к; **~-west** *n.* юго-за́пад; *adj.* (*also* **~-westerly, ~-western**) юго-за́падный; *adv.* (*also* **~-westerly**) на юго-за́пад.

southerly ['sʌðəlɪ] *n.* (*wind*) ю́жный ве́тер.

adj. ю́жный.

southern ['sʌð(ə)n] *adj.* ю́жный; **~most** са́мый ю́жный.

southerner ['sʌðənə(r)] *n.* южа́н|ин (*fem.* -ка).

southward ['saʊθwəd] *adj.* ю́жный.

adv. (*also* **~s**) на юг; к ю́гу, в ю́жном направле́нии.

souvenir [,suːvə'nɪə(r)] *n.* сувени́р; **as a ~** на па́мять.

sou'wester [saʊ'westə(r)] *n.* (*wind*) ю́жный ве́тер; (*hat*) зюйдве́стка, клеёнчатая ша́пка.

sovereign ['sɒvrɪn] *n.* (*ruler*) госуда́р|ь (*fem.* -ыня); (*coin*) совере́н.

adj. **1.** (*supreme*) верхо́вный. **2.** (*having ~ power*) сувере́нный; **a ~ state** сувере́нное госуда́рство.

sovereignty ['sɒvrɪntɪ] *n.* суверенитéт.

Soviet ['səʊvɪət, 'sɒ-] *n.* совéт; **the Supreme ~** Верхóвный Совéт.

adj. совéтский; **the ~ Union** Совéтский Союз.

sow[1] [saʊ] *n.* (*pig*) свинья́; **breeding ~** свиномáтка.

sow[2] [səʊ] *v.t.* **1.** (*seed*) сéять, по-; (*fig.*): **he is ~ing dissension** он сéет раздóр. **2.** (*ground*): зас|éивать (*or* -евáть), -éять; **a field ~n with maize** пóле, засéянное кукурýзой.

sower ['səʊə(r)] *n.* сéятель (*m.*).

sowing ['səʊɪŋ] *n.* посéв, засéв.

soya ['sɔɪə] *n.* (*also* (*US*) **soy**) сóя.

adj. сóевый; **~ bean** сóевый боб.

spa [spɑː] *n.* вóды (*f. pl.*); курóрт с минерáльными истóчниками.

space [speɪs] *n.* **1.** (*expanse*) прострáнство, простóр; **he was staring into ~** он смотрéл в однý тóчку; **vanish into ~** (*fig.*) испар|я́ться, -и́ться. **2.** (*cosmic, outer ~*) кóсмос; (*attr.*) косми́ческий; **~ shuttle** косми́ческий челнóк; **~ travel, flight** косми́ческий полёт; *see also cpds.* **3.** (*distance, interval*) расстоя́ние; (*typ.*) интервáл. **4.** (*of time, distance*): **after a short ~** чéрез нéкоторое врéмя; **for the ~ of a mile** на протяжéнии ми́ли; **in the ~ of a hour** за час; в течéние чáса. **5.** (*area; room*) мéсто; **in the ~ provided** на укáзанном мéсте.

v.t. (*also* **~ out**): **the posts were ~d six feet apart** столбы́ бы́ли располóжены на расстоя́нии шести́ фýтов друг от дрýга; **payments can be ~d** вы́плату мóжно производи́ть в рассрóчку.

cpds. **~-bar** *n.* клáвиша для интервáла; **~craft** (*also* **~-ship**) *nn.* косми́ческий корáбль; **~man** *n.* космонáвт; **~-probe** *n.* косми́ческий полёт; **~-ship** *n.* = **~craft; ~-suit** *n.* скафáндр (космонáвта); **~woman** *n.* жéнщина-космонáвт.

spacious ['speɪʃəs] *adj.* (*roomy*) простóрный; (*vast, extensive*) обши́рный; (*capacious*) вмести́тельный.

spaciousness ['speɪʃəsnɪs] *n.* простóрность, простóр; обши́рность, вмести́тельность.

spade [speɪd] *n.* **1.** (*tool*) лопáта; **call a ~ a ~** назывáть (*impf.*) вéщи свои́ми имен́ами. **2.** (*cards*) пи́ка; **queen of ~s** пи́ковая дáма.

cpd. **~-work** *n.* (*fig.*) подготови́тельная рабóта.

spaghetti [spə'getɪ] *n.* спагéтти (*nt. indecl.*).

Spain [speɪn] *n.* Испáния.

span [spæn] *n.* **1.** (*distance between supports*): **~ of an arch of a bridge** пролёт áрки/мостá. **2.** (*of time*) промежýток врéмени. **3.: wing ~** размáх кры́льев. **4.** (*distance between thumb and finger*) пядь.

v.t. **1.** (*extend across*) перекр|ывáть, -ы́ть; **the bridge ~s the river** мост переки́нут чéрез рéку; (*fig.*): **the movement ~s almost two centuries** э́то движéние охвáтывает почти́ два столéтия.

spangle ['spæŋg(ə)l] *n.* блёстка.

v.t. укр|ашáть, -áсить блёстками.

Spaniard ['spænjəd] *n.* испáн|ец (*fem.* -ка).

spaniel ['spænj(ə)l] *n.* спаниéль (*m.*).

Spanish ['spænɪʃ] *n.* (*language*) испáнский (язы́к).

adj. испáнский.

spank [spæŋk] *n.* шлепóк.

v.t. шлёп|ать, -нуть (*or* пошлёпать).

spanking ['spæŋkɪŋ] *adj.*: **go at a ~ pace** нести́сь/мчáться (*impf.*) (во всю).

spanner ['spænə(r)] *n.* (гáечный) ключ; **throw a ~ into the works** (*fig.*) ≃ вставля́ть (*impf.*) пáлки в колёса.

spar[1] [spɑː(r)] *n.* **1.** (*naut.*) рангóутное дéрево. **2.** (*aeron.*) лонжерóн.

spar[2] [spɑː(r)] *n.* (*min.*) шпат.

spar[3] [spɑː(r)] *v.i.* **1.** дрáться (*impf.*) на кулакáх; бокси́ровать (*impf.*); **~ring-match** тренирóвочный матч; **~ring partner** партнёр для тренирóвки. **2.** (*fig., argue*) спóрить (*impf.*); препирáться (*impf.*).

spare [speə(r)] *n.* **1.** (**~ part**) запасна́я часть, запчáсть. **2.** (**~ *wheel***) запаснóе колесó.

adj. (*excess, extra*) ли́шний; **~ room** кóмната для гостéй; **~ time** свобóдное врéмя; **~ cash** ли́шние дéньги; (*additional, reserve*) запаснóй; **~ parts** запасны́е чáсти, запчáсти; **~ tyre** запасна́я ши́на; (*coll., of fat*) брюшкó.

v.t. **1.** (*withhold use of*) жалéть, по-; **he ~d no pains to ...** он не жалéл уси́лий, чтóбы... **2.** (*dispense with, do without*) об|ходи́ться, -ойти́сь без+*g.*; **we cannot ~ him** мы не мóжем обойти́сь без негó. **3.** (*afford*): **can you ~ a cigarette?** нет ли у вас ли́шней сигарéты?; **I can ~ you only a few minutes** я могý удели́ть вам тóлько нéсколько минýт. **4. to ~** (*available, left over*): **I have no time to ~** у меня́ нет ли́шнего врéмени; **we got there with an hour to ~** когдá мы при́были, у нас оказáлся цéлый час в запáсе; **three yards to ~** три я́рда ли́шних. **5.** (*show mercy, leniency to*) щади́ть, по-; **~ s.o.'s life** сохрани́ть (*pf.*) комý-н. жизнь; **if I am ~d** éсли бýду жив. **6.** (*save from*) изб|авля́ть, -áвить (*когó от чегó*); **I will ~ you the trouble of replying** я избáвлю вас от необходи́мости отвечáть.

cpd. **~-ribs** *n.* свины́е рёбрышки (*nt. pl.*).

sparing ['speərɪŋ] *adj.* (*moderate*) умéренный; (*frugal*) скупóй; **~ of words** скупóй на словá.

spark [spɑːk] *n.* **1.** и́скра; **he showed not a ~ of interest** он не прояви́л ни малéйшего интерéса; **he hasn't a ~ of intelligence** у негó нет ни кáпли соображéния. **2.** (*pl., coll., ship's radio operator*) ради́ст.

v.t. (*also* **~ off:** *cause*) вызывáть, вы́звать.

v.i. искри́ть (*impf.*); дать (*pf.*) и́скру.

cpd. **~(ing)-plug** *n.* запáльная свечá.

sparkle ['spɑːk(ə)l] *n.* сверкáние, блеск; блёстка, и́скорка; **a ~ came into his eyes** у негó глазá заблестéли; (*of wine etc.*) шипéние, искрéние; **the wine lost its ~** винó утрáтило искри́стость.

v.i. сверкáть, за-; и́скри́ться (*impf.*); (*flash*) блестéть, за-; **sparkling wine** шипýчее/игри́стое винó.

sparkler ['spɑːklə(r)] *n.* (*coll., diamond*) алмáз.

sparrow ['spærəʊ] *n.* воробéй.

cpd. **~-hawk** *n.* я́стреб-перепеля́тник.

sparse [spɑːs] *adj.* рéдкий; (*scattered*) разбрóсанный; **~ly populated** малонаселённый; **~ vegetation** скýдная расти́тельность.

spars|eness ['spɑːsnɪs], **-ity** ['spɑːsɪtɪ] *nn.* скýдость.

Spartan ['spɑːt(ə)n] *n.* спартáн|ец (*fem.* -ка).

adj. спартáнский.

spasm ['spæz(ə)m] *n.* (*of muscles*) спáзм(а), сýдорога; (*mental or physical reaction*) поры́в, при́ступ, припáдок; **a ~ of coughing** при́ступ кáшля; **~s of grief** взры́вы отчáяния.

spasmodic [spæz'mɒdɪk] *adj.* **1.** (*med.*) спазмати́ческий. **2.** (*intermittent*) преры́вистый.

spastic ['spæstɪk] *adj.* спасти́ческий.

spat[1] [spæt] *n.* (*US coll.*) размóлвка; лёгкая ссóра.

v.i. брани́ться, по-.

spat[2] [spæt] *n.* (*pl.*) корóткие гéтры (*f. pl.*).

spate [speɪt] *n.* разли́в; (*fig.*) потóк; **the river is in ~** рекá вздýлась.

spatial ['speɪʃ(ə)l] *adj.* прострáнственный.

spatter ['spætə(r)] (*also* **splatter**) *v.t.* бры́згать, за-; **~ed with mud** забры́зганный гря́зью.

spatula ['spætjʊlə] *n.* шпáтель (*m.*).

spawn [spɔːn] *n.* (*of fish etc.*) икрá; **mushroom ~** грибни́ца.

v.t. (*of fish etc.*) метáть (*impf.*); (*fig., pej.*) поро|ждáть, -ди́ть.

v.i. (*reproduce*) метáть (*impf.*) икрý; (*pej., multiply*) плоди́ться, рас-.

spay [speɪ] *v.t.* удал|я́ть, -и́ть яи́чники у+*g.*

speak [spiːk] *v.t.* **1.** (*say, pronounce, utter*) говори́ть, сказа́ть; произн|оси́ть, -ести́; **he didn't ~ a word** он не произнёс ни сло́ва; (*give utterance to*, *express*) выска́зывать, вы́сказать; **~ the truth** говори́ть, сказа́ть пра́вду; **~ one's mind** открове́нно выска́зывать, вы́сказать своё мне́ние; *see also* **spoken. 2.** (*converse in*): **he ~s Russian well** он хорошо́ говори́т по-ру́сски; **they were ~ing French** они́ разгова́ривали/говори́ли по-францу́зски.

v.i. говори́ть, по-; (*converse*) разгова́ривать (*impf.*); вести́ (*indet.*) разгово́р; **I was ~ing to him yesterday** я говори́л с ним вчера́; **they are not on ~ing terms** они́ бо́льше не разгова́ривают; (*make a speech*) произн|оси́ть, -ести́ речь; **I am not used to ~ing in public** я не привы́к публи́чно выступа́ть; **'Smith ~ing'** (*on telephone*) «(с ва́ми) говори́т Смит»; «Смит у телефо́на»; **'~ing'** (*on telephone*) «э́то я»; «слу́шаю»; **this calls for some plain ~ing** сле́дует, ви́дно, объясни́ться начистоту́; **so to ~** так сказа́ть; **roughly, broadly ~ing** в о́бщих черта́х; **strictly ~ing** стро́го говоря́; **in a manner of ~ing** е́сли мо́жно так вы́разиться; **~ing for myself** что каса́ется меня́; **~ for yourself!** не говори́те за други́х!; **let him ~ for himself** не подска́зывайте!; пусть сам ска́жет!; **he is well spoken of** о нём хорошо́ отзыва́ются; **~ of** (*mention*, *refer to*) упом|ина́ть, -яну́ть о (*ком/чём*); каса́ться, косну́ться (*чего*); **nothing to ~ of** ничего́ осо́бенного; **the flat is too small, not to ~ of the noise** э́та кварти́ра сли́шком мала́, и к тому́ же ещё здесь о́чень шу́мно.

with advs.: **~ out** *v.i.* (*express o.s. plainly*) выска́зываться, вы́сказаться открове́нно; **~ up** *v.i.* (**~** *louder*) говори́ть (*impf.*) погро́мче; (*express support*): **~ up for s.o.** подде́рж|ивать, -а́ть кого́-н.

speaker ['spi:kə(r)] *n.* **1.**: **the ~ was a man of about 40** говоря́щему бы́ло лет со́рок. **2.**: **a Russian ~** челове́к, владе́ющий ру́сским языко́м; **he is a native Russian ~** его́ родно́й язы́к — ру́сский. **3.** (*public ~*) ора́тор, докла́дчик, выступа́ющий. **4.** (*parl.*) спи́кер. **5.** (**loud-~**) громкоговори́тель (*m.*).

spear ['spɪə(r)] *n.* копьё; (*for fish*) гарпу́н, острога́.

v.t. пронз|а́ть, -и́ть копьём; **~ fish** бить (*impf.*) ры́бу острого́й.

cpds. **~head** *n.* (*lit.*) наконе́чник/остриё копья́; (*fig.*) передово́й отря́д; аванга́рд; *v.t.*: **~head a movement** возгл|авля́ть, -а́вить движе́ние; **~mint** *n.* (*bot.*) мя́та колоси́стая/курча́вая.

spec[1] [spek] *n.* (*coll.*): **he went there on ~** он пошёл туда́ науда́чу.

spec[2] [spek] *n.* (*coll.*, *specification*) специфика́ция.

special ['speʃ(ə)l] *adj.* **1.** осо́бый, осо́бенный, специа́льный; **this book is of ~ interest to me** э́та кни́га представля́ет осо́бый интере́с для меня́; **for a ~ purpose** со специа́льной це́лью; **~ agent** аге́нт по осо́бым поруче́ниям; **a ~ case** осо́бый слу́чай; **~ course** специа́льный курс; **~ correspondent** специа́льный корреспонде́нт. **2.** (*specific*, *definite*) определённый. **3.** (*extraordinary*) э́кстренный; **~ edition** э́кстренный вы́пуск; **~ delivery** сро́чная доста́вка.

cpd. **~-purpose** *adj.* специа́льного назначе́ния.

specialist ['speʃəlɪst] *n.* специали́ст (*fem.* -ка) (по+*d.*).

speciality [,speʃɪ'ælɪtɪ] (*US* **specialty**) *n.* **1.** (*characteristic*) осо́бенность, специ́фика. **2.** (*pursuit*) о́бласть специализа́ции; **what is his ~?** кто он по специа́льности? **3.** (*product*, *recipe etc.*): **~ of the house** фи́рменное блю́до.

specialization [,speʃəlaɪ'zeɪʃ(ə)n] *n.* специализа́ция.

specialize ['speʃə,laɪz] *v.t.*: **~d knowledge** специа́льные позна́ния.

v.i. (*be or become specialist*) специализи́роваться (*impf.*, *pf.*) (по+*d.*; в+*p.*).

specially ['speʃəlɪ] *adv.* **1.** (*individually*) осо́бо; **he was ~ mentioned** о нём упомяну́ли осо́бо. **2.** (*for specific purpose*): специа́льно; **~ selected** специа́льно отобранный. **3.** (*exceptionally*): осо́бенно, исключи́тельно; **be ~ careful** быть осо́бенно осторо́жным.

specialty ['speʃəltɪ] = **speciality**

species ['spi:ʃɪz, -ʃi:z, 'spi:s-] *n.* вид; **our** (*or* **the** (**human**)) **~** челове́ческий род; **origin of ~** происхожде́ние ви́дов.

specific [spɪ'sɪfɪk] *adj.* **1.** (*definite*) определённый, конкре́тный; **he has no ~ aim** у него́ нет никако́й определённой це́ли; **a ~ statement** конкре́тное утвержде́ние. **2.** (*distinct*) специфи́ческий, осо́бый. **3.** (*phys.*): **~ gravity** уде́льный вес. **4.** (*med.*) специфи́ческий. **5.** (*peculiar*) характе́рный.

specification [,spesɪfɪ'keɪʃ(ə)n] *n.* специфика́ция; техни́ческие усло́вия.

specif|y ['spesɪ,faɪ] *v.t.* **1.** (*name expressly*) определ|я́ть, -и́ть; уточн|я́ть, -и́ть; **unless otherwise ~ied** е́сли нет ины́х указа́ний. **2.** (*include in specification*) специфици́ровать (*impf.*, *pf.*).

specimen ['spesɪmən] *n.* (*example*; *sample*) экземпля́р; образе́ц; (*individual of species*) о́собь; **a museum ~** музе́йный экспона́т; **~ page** про́бная страни́ца; **~ of urine** моча́ для ана́лиза.

specious ['spi:ʃəs] *adj.* благови́дный.

speck [spek] *n.* (*dot*) кра́пинка; (*of dirt or decay*) пя́тнышко; **~ of dust** пя́тнышко.

speckle ['spek(ə)l] *v.t.* покр|ыва́ть, -ы́ть кра́пинками.

speckled ['spek(ə)ld] *adj.* кра́пчатый; пятни́стый; **~ hen** пёстрая/ряба́я ку́рица.

specs [speks] *n.* (*coll.*) = **spectacle 2.**

spectacle ['spektək(ə)l] *n.* **1.** (*public show*; *sight*) зре́лище; **he made a ~ of himself** он вы́ставил себя́ на посме́шище. **2.** (*pl.*, *glasses*) очк|и́ (*pl.*, *g.* -о́в).

spectacular [spek'tækjʊlə(r)] *n.* эффе́ктное зре́лище.

adj. эффе́ктный, импоза́нтный.

spectator [spek'teɪtə(r)] *n.* зри́тель (*fem.* -ница).

spectral ['spektr(ə)l] *adj.* при́зрачный; (*phys.*) спектра́льный.

spectre ['spektə(r)] *n.* привиде́ние, при́зрак.

spectroscope ['spektrə,skəʊp] *n.* спектроско́п.

spectroscopic [,spektrə'skɒpɪk] *adj.* спектроскопи́ческий.

spectrum ['spektrəm] *n.* **1.** (*phys.*) спектр. **2.** (*fig.*) диапазо́н.

speculate ['spekjʊ,leɪt] *v.i.* **1.** (*meditate*) размышля́ть (*impf.*) (*о чем*); (*conjecture*) де́лать (*impf.*) предположе́ния, гада́ть (*impf.*). **2.** (*risk*, *invest money*) спекули́ровать (*impf.*), игра́ть (*impf.*) на би́рже.

speculation [,spekjʊ'leɪʃ(ə)n] *n.* (*conjecture*) предположе́ние; дога́дка; (*investment*) спекуля́ция.

speculative ['spekjʊlətɪv] *adj.* (*meditative*) умозри́тельный; (*conjectural*) предположи́тельный; (*risky*) риско́ванный; (*comm.*) спекуляти́вный.

speculator ['spekjʊ,leɪtə(r)] *n.* спекуля́нт (*fem.* -ка).

speech [spi:tʃ] *n.* **1.** (*faculty*, *act of speaking*; *also gram.*) речь; **lose the power of ~** лиш|а́ться, -и́ться да́ра ре́чи; **freedom of ~** свобо́да сло́ва; **direct/indirect ~** пряма́я/ко́свенная речь; **parts of ~** ча́сти ре́чи; **figure of ~** о́бразное выраже́ние. **2.** (*manner of speaking*) речь, го́вор; (*pronunciation*) произноше́ние, вы́говор; **~ therapy** логопе́дия. **3.** (*public address*) речь; **make a ~** произн|оси́ть, -ести́ речь; выступа́ть, вы́ступить с ре́чью.

cpds. **~-day** *n.* акт; а́ктовый день; **~-writer** *n.* «речеви́к».

speechless ['spi:tʃlɪs] *adj.* (*wordless*) немо́й; (*temporarily unable to speak*) онеме́вший; **I was ~ with surprise** я онеме́л от удивле́ния.

speed [spi:d] *n.* (*rapidity*) быстрота́, ско́рость; (*rate of motion*) ско́рость; **with all possible ~** как мо́жно скоре́е; **at full, top ~** по́лным хо́дом; **gain, gather ~** наб|ира́ть, -ра́ть ско́рость; **lose ~** теря́ть, поскóрость; **my bicycle has four ~s** мой велосипéд имéет четы́ре скóрости; **~ limit** дозвóленная скóрость; предéл скóрости.

v.t. (*also* **~ up:** *accelerate*) уск|оря́ть, -óрить; **measures to ~ production** мéры по повышéнию тéмпа произвóдства.

v.i. мчáться, про-; нести́сь, про-; **he was fined for ~ing** егó оштрафовáли за превышéние скóрости.

cpds. **~-boat** *n.* быстрохóдный кáтер; **~way** *n.* гóночный трек; **~way racing** скоростны́е мотогóнки (*f. pl.*); **~way rider** мотогóнщик.

speedometer [spi:ˈdɒmɪtə(r)] *n.* спидóметр.

speedy [ˈspi:dɪ] *adj.* (*rapid*) скóрый, бы́стрый; (*hasty*) поспéшный; **he wished me a ~ return** он пожелáл мне скóрого возвращéния.

spell[1] [spel] *n.* **1.** (*magical formula*; *its effect*) чáр|ы (*pl.*, *g.* —); колдовствó; **cast a ~ over** околдóв|ывать, -áть; заколдóв|ывать, -áть; **break the ~** разр|ушáть, -ýшить чáры. **2.** (*fascination*) обая́ние, очаровáние.

cpd. **~-bound** *adj.* очарóванный, зачарóванный.

spell[2] [spel] *n.* **1.** (*bout, turn*) смéна, перúод; **a ~ of work** перúод рабóты. **2.** (*interval*) перúод; промежýток врéмени; **I slept for a ~** я поспáл нéкоторое врéмя; **we're in for a ~ of fine weather** ожидáется полосá хорóшей погóды.

spell[3] [spel] *v.t.* **1.** (*write or name letters in sequence*) произн|оси́ть, -ести́ (*or* писáть, на-) (*что*) по бýквам; **how do you ~ your name?** как пи́шется вáша фами́лия?; **I wish you would learn to ~** когдá вы наýчитесь писáть без оши́бок? **2.** (*usu.* **~ out:** *decipher slowly*) с трудóм раз|бирáть, -обрáть (по бýквам); (*fig.*, *make explicit*) разжёв|ывать, -áть. **3.** (*of letters*: *make up*) сост|авля́ть, -áвить (по бýквам); **what do these letters ~?** какóе слóво составля́ют э́ти бýквы? **4.** (*fig.*, *signify*) означáть (*impf.*).

v.i. писáть (*impf.*) прáвильно/грáмотно.

cpd. **~-checker** *n.* коррéктор орфогрáфии.

spelling [ˈspelɪŋ] *n.* правописáние, орфогрáфия.

cpd. **~-bee** *n.* состязáние по орфогрáфии.

spen|d [spend] *v.t.* **1.** (*pay out*) трáтить, ис-; **she ~ds too much on clothes** онá сли́шком мнóго трáтит на наря́ды; **~d a penny** (*coll.*, *use lavatory*) пойти́ (*pf.*) кóе-кудá. **2.** (*consume, expend, exhaust*) истощ|áть, -и́ть; **he is completely ~t** он вы́мотался вконéц; **a ~t bullet** пýля на излёте. **3.** (*pass*) пров|оди́ть, -ести́; **we ~t some hours looking for a hotel** у нас ушлó (*or* мы потрáтили) нéсколько часóв на пóиски гости́ницы; **she ~t her life in good works** онá всю свою́ жизнь посвяти́ла дóбрым делáм; **how do you ~d your leisure?** как вы провóдите свой досýг?

v.i. (**~ *money***) трáтиться, по-; **~ding-money** кармáнные дéньги.

cpd. **~dthrift** *n.* мот (*fem.* -óвка); транжи́р (*fem.* -ка); расточи́тель (*fem.* -ница); *adj.* расточи́тельный.

sperm [spɜ:m] *n.* спéрма; (**~ whale**) кашалóт.

spew [spju:] *v.t.* выблёвывать, вы́блевать; (*lit.*, *fig.*) изрыг|áть, -нýть.

v.i. блевáть, сблевнýть.

sphere [sfɪə(r)] *n.* **1.** сфéра; (*globe*) шар, глóбус. **2.** (*fig.*) сфéра, óбласть (дéятельности); **outside my ~** вне моéй компетéнции; **~ of influence** сфéра влия́ния.

spherical [ˈsferɪk(ə)l] *adj.* сфери́ческий, шарообрáзный.

spheroid [ˈsfɪərɔɪd] *n.* сферóид.

spheroidal [sfɪəˈrɔɪd(ə)l] *adj.* сфероидáльный.

sphinx [sfɪŋks] *n.* сфинкс.

spice [spaɪs] *n.* **1.** спéция, пря́ность. **2.** (*fig.*, *smack, dash*) при́вкус; при́месь; **his story lacked ~** егó расскáзу не хватáло изю́минки.

v.t. припр|авля́ть, -áвить; **highly-~d dishes** óстрые/пря́ные блю́да.

spick [spɪk] *adj.*: **~ and span** (*clean, tidy*) сверкáющий чистотóй.

spicy [ˈspaɪsɪ] *adj.* пря́ный; (*fig.*) пикáнтный, солёный.

spider [ˈspaɪdə(r)] *n.* паýк; **~'s web** паути́на.

spidery [ˈspaɪdərɪ] *adj.*: **~ writing** тóнкий витиевáтый пóчерк; **~ legs** дли́нные, тóнкие нóги.

spigot [ˈspɪgət] *n.* прóбка, втýлка.

spike [spaɪk] *n.* остриё, косты́ль (*m.*); (*on fence*) зубéц; (*for papers etc.*) накóлка; (*on shoe*) шип, гвоздь (*m.*).

v.t. **1.** (*fasten with ~s*) приб|ивáть, -и́ть гвоздя́ми. **2.** (*furnish with ~s*) снаб|жáть, -ди́ть гвоздя́ми/шипáми; **~d boots** боти́нки (*m. pl.*) на шипáх.

spiky [ˈspaɪkɪ] *adj.* **1.** (*set with spikes*) усáженный остриями. **2.** (*in form of spike*) остроконéчный; заострённый. **3.** (*fig.*, *of pers.*) колю́чий.

spill [spɪl] *n.*: **have a ~** (*fall, e.g. from a horse*) упáсть (*pf.*); свали́ться (*pf.*).

v.t. **1.** (*accidentally*) прол|ивáть, -и́ть; **I spilt a glass of water on her dress** я проли́л стакáн воды́ на её плáтье; **without ~ing a drop** не расплескáв ни кáпли; **~ salt** расс|ыпáть, -ы́пать соль. **2.** (*intentionally*) прол|ивáть, -и́ть; (*fig.*): **~ the beans** (*coll.*) разб|áлтывать, -олтáть секрéт; **~ s.o.'s blood** прол|ивáть, -и́ть чью-н. кровь.

v.i. (*of liquids*) разл|ивáться, -и́ться; (*of salt etc.*) расс|ыпáться, -ы́паться; прос|ыпáться, -ы́паться.

with advs.: **~ out** *v.i.* вы́ливáться, вы́литься; **~ over** *v.i.* перел|ивáться, -и́ться (чéрез край).

spillage [ˈspɪlɪdʒ] *n.* утéчка, утрýска.

spin [spɪn] *n.* **1.** (*whirl, twisting motion*) кружéние; **go into a ~** завертéться (*pf.*); **his head was in a ~** у негó головá шла крýгом. **2.** (*aeron.*) штóпор; **go into a ~** войти́ (*pf.*) в штóпор. **3.** (*outing*) корóткая прогýлка; **go for a ~ in the car** прокати́ться (*pf.*) на маши́не.

v.t. **1.** (*yarn, wool etc.*) прясть, с-; **~ning-wheel** пря́лка; **~ning-machine** пряди́льная маши́на; **~ a yarn** (*fig.*) расскáз|ывать, -áть истóрию; **the spider ~s its web** паýк плетёт паути́ну; *see also* **spun. 2.** (*cause to revolve*) вертéть, за-; кружи́ть, за-; **~ a coin** подбр|áсывать, -óсить монéтку; **~ a top** пус|кáть, -ти́ть волчóк.

v.i. вертéться, за-; кружи́ться, за-; (*of compass needle or suspended object*) вращáться (*impf.*); (*of pers.*): **my head is ~ning** у меня́ головá идёт крýгом.

with advs.: **~ out** *v.t.*: **~ out a story** растя́|гивать, -нýть расскáз; **~ round** *v.t. & i.* бы́стро пов|орáчивать(ся), -ернýть(ся) (кругóм).

cpds. **~-drier** *n.* центрифýга; **~-off** *n.* (*coll.*) побóчный результáт.

spina bifida [ˌspaɪnə ˈbɪfɪdə] *n.* расщеплéние ости́стых отрóстков позвонóчника.

spinach [ˈspɪnɪdʒ, -ɪtʃ] *n.* шпинáт.

spinal [ˈspaɪn(ə)l] *adj.* спиннóй; **~ column** позвонóчный столб, позвонóчник, спиннóй хребéт; **~ cord** спиннóй мозг; **~ injury** повреждéние позвонóчника.

spindle [ˈspɪnd(ə)l] *n.* (*of spinning-wheel*) веретенó; (*axis, rod*) ось, шпи́ндель (*m.*).

cpd. **~-shanks** *n.* голенáстый (человéк) (*coll*).

spindly [ˈspɪndlɪ] *adj.* дли́нный и тóнкий.

spine [spaɪn] *n.* **1.** (*backbone*) позвонóчник, спиннóй хребéт. **2.** (*of hedgehog etc.*) иглá, колю́чка. **3.** (*of plant*) иглá, колю́чка, шип. **4.** (*of book*) корешóк.

cpd. **~-chilling** *adj.* жýткий; вызывáющий ýжас.

spineless [ˈspaɪnlɪs] *adj.* (*fig.*) бесхребéтный, бесхарáктерный.

spinet [spɪˈnet, ˈspɪnɪt] *n.* спинéт.

spinnaker [ˈspɪnəkə(r)] *n.* спи́накер.

spinner ['spɪnə(r)] *n.* (*pers.*) пряди́льщи|к (*fem.* -ца); пря́ха; (*machine*) пряди́льная маши́на.
spinney ['spɪnɪ] *n.* за́росль, ро́ща.
spinster ['spɪnstə(r)] *n.* (*old maid*) ста́рая де́ва; (*leg., unmarried woman*) незаму́жняя же́нщина.
spiny ['spaɪnɪ] *adj.* (*covered with spines*) покры́тый и́глами/шипа́ми/колю́чками; (*prickly*) колю́чий.
spiral ['spaɪər(ə)l] *n.* спира́ль.
adj. спира́льный; ~ **staircase** винтова́я ле́стница.
v.i.: **the plane ~led down to earth** самолёт произвёл спира́льный спуск на зе́млю.
spire ['spaɪə(r)] *n.* (*of church etc.*) шпиль (*m.*), шпиц.
spirit ['spɪrɪt] *n.* **1.** (*soul, immaterial part of man*) душа́; **I shall be with you in ~** душо́й я бу́ду с ва́ми. **2.** (*immoral, incorporeal being*) дух; **the Holy S~** Свято́й Дух; **evil ~** злой дух; (*apparition, ghost*) привиде́ние. **3.** (*living being*) ум, ли́чность; **leading ~** душа́, руководи́тель (*m.*). **4.** (*mental or moral nature*) хара́ктер; **a man of unbending ~** челове́к непрекло́нного хара́ктера. **5.** (*courage*) хра́брость; **show some ~** прояв|ля́ть, -и́ть му́жество/хара́ктер; **a man of ~** челове́к с хара́ктером; (*vivacity*) жи́вость. **6.** (*mental, moral attitude*) дух, смысл; **take sth. in the wrong ~** не так восприн|има́ть, -я́ть что-н.; **enter into the ~ of Christmas** прон|ика́ться, -и́кнуться ду́хом Рождества́. **7.** (*real meaning, essence*) су́щность, суть; **the ~ of the law** дух зако́на; **I followed the ~ of his instructions** я де́йствовал в ду́хе его́ указа́ний. **8.** (*mental or moral tendency, influence*) дух, тенде́нция; **the ~ of the age** дух вре́мени. **9.** (*pl., humour*) настрое́ние; **he was in high ~s** он был в припо́днятом настрое́нии; **his ~s are low** он в пода́вленном настрое́нии; **keep one's ~s up** не па́дать (*impf.*) ду́хом; **raise s.o.'s ~s** подн|има́ть, -я́ть дух у кого́-н. **10.** (*industrial alcohol*) спирт, алкого́ль (*m.*); (*pl., alcoholic drink*) спиртно́й напи́ток; **he never touches ~s** он не пьёт спиртно́го.
v.t. **~ away, off** (та́йно) похи́тить (*pf.*).
cpds. **~-gum** *n.* театра́льный клей; гримирова́льный лак; **~-lamp** *n.* спирто́вка; **~-level** *n.* ватерпа́с.
spirited ['spɪrɪtɪd] *adj.* живо́й, оживлённый; энерги́чный, жизнера́достный; **a ~ reply** бо́йкий отве́т.
spiritual ['spɪrɪtjʊəl] *n.* (*song*) спи́ричуэл.
adj. **1.** (*pert. to soul, spirit*) духо́вный. **2.** (*inspired by Holy Spirit*): **~ gift** боже́ственный дар; **~ songs** духо́вные пе́сни.
spiritualism ['spɪrɪtjʊəˌlɪz(ə)m] *n.* спирити́зм.
spiritualist ['spɪrɪtjʊəlɪst] *n.* спири́т (*fem.* -ка).
spirituality [ˌspɪrɪtjʊ'ælɪtɪ] *n.* одухотворённость.
spit[1] [spɪt] *n.* (*for roasting*) ве́ртел; (*of land*) коса́, стре́лка.
spit[2] [spɪt] *n.* **1.** (*spittle*) слюна́. **2.: the ~ and** (*or* **~ting) image of his father** то́чная ко́пия своего́ отца́; вы́литый оте́ц.
v.t. (*also* **~ out**) выплёвывать, вы́плюнуть; **~ blood** ха́ркать (*impf.*) кро́вью.
v.i. **1.** пл|ева́ть, -ю́нуть; (*habitually*) плева́ться (*impf.*); **he spat in my face** он плю́нул мне в лицо́; (*of cat etc.*) фы́рк|ать, -нуть. **2.** (*coll., rain*) мороси́ть (*impf.*).
spite [spaɪt] *n.* **1.** (*ill-will*) зло́ба; **out of ~** назло́; по зло́бе. **2.: in ~ of** несмотря́ на+*a.*; **I smiled in ~ of myself** я нево́льно улыбну́лся.
v.t.: **he does it to ~ me** он де́лает э́то мне назло́.
spiteful ['spaɪtfʊl] *adj.* зло́бный, злора́дный.
spitefulness ['spaɪtfʊlnɪs] *n.* зло́бность, злора́дство.
spittle ['spɪt(ə)l] *n.* плево́к; слюна́.
spittoon [spɪ'tu:n] *n.* плева́тельница.
spiv [spɪv] *n.* (*sl.*) ме́лкий спекуля́нт; жу́лик.
splash [splæʃ] *n.* **1.** (*action, effect*) плеск, всплеск; бры́зг|и (*pl., g.* —); **the stone made a huge ~** ка́мень упа́л с гро́мким пле́ском; **make a ~** (*fig., attract attention*) произв|оди́ть, -ести́ сенса́цию. **2.** (*sound*) плеск, всплеск. **3.** (*liquid*): **I felt a ~ of rain** на меня́ упа́ли ка́пли дождя́. **4.** (*of blood, mud etc.*) пятно́; **a ~ of colour** кра́сочное пятно́.
v.t. **1.** бры́з|гать, -нуть (*чем на что*); забры́зг|ивать, -ать (*что чем*); **he ~ed paint on her dress** он забры́згал её пла́тье кра́ской; **she was ~ing her feet in the water** она́ плеска́лась нога́ми в воде́; **they were ~ing water at one another** они́ бры́згали друг в дру́га водо́й. **2.** (*coll., fig.*): **the news was ~ed in all the papers** все газе́ты раструби́ли э́ту но́вость; **he likes to ~ his money about** он лю́бит броса́ться деньга́ми.
v.i. **1.** (*of liquid etc.*) плеска́ться (*impf.*); **the mud ~ed up her legs** гря́зью забры́згало ей все но́ги. **2.** (*move or fall with ~*): **he ~ed into the water** он бултыхну́лся; **the ducks ~ed about in the pond** у́тки плеска́лись в пруду́; **the capsule ~ed down in the Pacific** ка́псула приводни́лась в Ти́хом океа́не.
int. плюх!
cpd. **~-down** *n.* приводне́ние.
splay [spleɪ] *v.t.* (*spread wide*): **~ one's legs** раски́|дывать, -нуть но́ги.
spleen [spli:n] *n.* (*anat.*) селезёнка; (*fig., ill-temper, spite*) зло́ба; **vent one's ~ on s.o.** срыва́ть, сорва́ть зло́бу на ком-н.
splendid ['splendɪd] *adj.* (*magnificent*) великоле́пный; (*luxurious*) роско́шный; (*excellent*) отли́чный; (*impressive, remarkable*) удиви́тельный, замеча́тельный; **~!** замеча́тельно!; **what a ~ idea** замеча́тельная/прекра́сная мысль!
splendour ['splendə(r)] *n.* (*brilliance*) блеск; (*grandeur, magnificence*) великоле́пие, пы́шность.
splenetic [splɪ'netɪk] *adj.* **1.** (*med.*) селезёночный. **2.** (*of pers.*) брюзгли́вый, жёлчный.
splice [splaɪs] *v.t.* **1.** (*rope*) ср|а́щивать, -асти́ть. **2.: get ~d** (*sl., marry*) пожени́ться (*pf.*).
splint [splɪnt] *n.* (*for broken bone*) лубо́к, ши́на.
splinter ['splɪntə(r)] *n.* **1.** (*of wood*) лучи́на, ще́пка, зано́за; (*of stone, metal, glass*) оско́лок; **get a ~ in one's finger** занози́ть (*pf.*) па́лец. **2.** (*fig.*): **~ group** отколо́вшаяся (полити́ческая) группиро́вка.
v.t. & i. расщеп|ля́ть(ся), -и́ть(ся).
split [splɪt] *n.* **1.** раска́лывание; (*crack, fissure*) тре́щина. **2.** (*fig., schism, disunion*) раско́л. **3.: do the ~s** де́лать, с- шпага́т.
v.t. **1.** коло́ть, рас-; расщеп|ля́ть, -и́ть; **~ting the atom** расщепле́ние а́тома; (*crack open, rupture*) раск|а́лывать, -оло́ть; (*fig.*): **~ one's sides** над|рыва́ться, -орва́ться от сме́ха; **~ hairs** спо́рить (*impf.*) о мелоча́х. **2.** (*divide*) раздел|я́ть, -и́ть; (*share*) дели́ть, по-; **they ~ the money into three** они́ раздели́ли де́ньги на́ три ча́сти. **3.** (*cause dissension in*) разъедин|я́ть,-и́ть; **the party was ~ by factions** па́ртия расколо́лась на фра́кции; **~ personality** раздвое́ние ли́чности; **~ second** мгнове́ние.
v.i. **1.** (*of hard substance*) раск|а́лываться, -оло́ться; расщеп|ля́ться, -и́ться; тре́снуть (*pf.*); (*divide*) раздел|я́ться, -и́ться; **the wood ~** де́рево тре́снуло; **~ open** взл|а́мываться, -ома́ться; (*of soft, thin substance*) раз|рыва́ться, -орва́ться; **my head is ~ting** (*fig.*) у меня́ голова́ раска́лывается. **2.** (*become disunited*) раск|а́лываться, -оло́тся.
with advs.: **~ off** *v.t. & i.* отк|а́лывать(ся), -оло́ть(ся); **~ up** *v.t. & i.* (*lit.*) раск|а́лывать(ся), -оло́ть(ся); (*separate*) ра|сходи́ться, -зойти́сь; **we ~ up into two groups** мы разби́лись на две гру́ппы; **he and his wife ~ up** они́ с жено́й разошли́сь.
splotch [splɒtʃ] (*coll.*) *n.* (гря́зное) пятно́, мазо́к.
splurge [splɜ:dʒ] *v.i.* (*coll.*) броса́ться (*impf.*) деньга́ми.
splutter ['splʌtə(r)] *n.* (*noise*) треск, треща́ние.
v.t. & i. говори́ть (*impf.*) захлёбываясь (*or* бы́стро и сби́вчиво).

spoil [spɔɪl] *n.* (*usu. pl.*, *booty*) добы́ча; **~s of war** трофе́и (*m. pl.*); вое́нная добы́ча.

v.t. **1.** (*impair*, *injure*, *ruin*) по́ртить, ис-; **the rain ~t our holiday** дождь испо́ртил нам о́тпуск; **eating sweets will ~ your appetite** конфе́ты испо́ртят вам аппети́т; **~ s.o.'s plans** срыва́ть, сорва́ть чьи-н. пла́ны. **2.** (*over-indulgence*) балова́ть, из-; **a ~t child** избало́ванный ребёнок.

v.i. **1.** (*deteriorate*) ух|удша́ться, -у́дшиться; (*go bad*, *rotten etc.*) по́ртиться, ис-. **2.** (*be eager*): **he is ~ing for a fight** он так и ле́зет в дра́ку.

cpd. **~-sport** *n.* тот, кто по́ртит удово́льствие други́м.

spoilage ['spɔɪlɪdʒ] *n.* (*of food*) испо́рченные проду́кты (*m. pl.*).

spoke [spəʊk] *n.* **1.** (*of wheel*) спи́ца. **2.** (*fig.*): **put a ~ in s.o.'s wheel** вст|авля́ть, -а́вить кому́-н. па́лки в колёса.

spoken ['spəʊkən] *adj.* у́стный; **the ~ word** у́стная речь; **the ~ language** разгово́рный язы́к.

spokesman ['spəʊksmən] *n.* представи́тель (*m.*); **~ for defence** докла́дчик по вопро́сам оборо́ны; **act as ~ for s.o.** выступа́ть, вы́ступить от и́мени кого́-н.

spokeswoman ['spəʊksˌwʊmən] *n.* представи́тельница.

sponge [spʌndʒ] *n.* (*zool.*; *toilet article*) гу́бка; **throw in, up the ~** (*fig.*) призн|ава́ть, -а́ть себя́ побеждённым.

v.t.: **~ a child's face** обт|ира́ть, -ере́ть ребёнку лицо́ гу́бкой; **~ o.s. down** обт|ира́ться, -ере́ться гу́бкой.

v.i. (*fig.*) жить (*impf.*) на чужо́й счёт.

cpds. **~-bag** *n.* су́мка для туале́тных принадле́жностей; **~-cake** *n.* бискви́т; **~-rubber** *n.* рези́новая гу́бка.

sponger ['spʌndʒə(r)] *n.* нахле́бник, прижива́льщик.

spongy ['spʌndʒɪ] *adj.* гу́бчатый; (*porous*) по́ристый; (*e.g. moss, carpet*) мя́гкий; (*of ground*) то́пкий.

sponsor ['spɒnsə(r)] *n.* **1.** (*guarantor*) поручи́тель (*fem.* -ница); (*of new member etc.*) рекоменда́тель (*fem.* -ница). **2.** (*TV etc.*) рекламода́тель (*m.*).

v.t. руча́ться, поручи́ться за+*a.*; рекомендова́ть (*impf.*, *pf.*); (*e.g. a law or resolution*) вн|оси́ть, -ести́; (*on TV etc.*) финанси́ровать (*impf.*, *pf.*).

sponsorship ['spɒnsəʃɪp] *n.* поручи́тельство, пору́ка, гара́нтия.

spontaneity [ˌspɒntə'niːɪtɪ, -'neɪɪtɪ] *n.* стихи́йность, непосре́дственность.

spontaneous [spɒn'teɪnɪəs] *adj.* спонта́нный, стихи́йный; (*unaffected*) непосре́дственный; **~ combustion** самовозгора́ние; **~ generation** самозарожде́ние.

spoof [spuːf] (*sl.*) *n.* (*hoax*) ро́зыгрыш; (*parody*) паро́дия.

v.t. разы́гр|ивать, -а́ть; пароди́ровать, с-.

spook [spuːk] *n.* (*joc.*) привиде́ние, при́зрак.

spooky ['spuːkɪ] *adj.* (*frightening*) жу́ткий; (*sinister*) злове́щий.

spool [spuːl] *n.* шпу́лька, кату́шка.

v.t. нам|а́тывать, -ота́ть на кату́шку.

spoon [spuːn] *n.* ло́жка; **they fed him with a ~** его́ корми́ли с ло́жки.

v.t. (*also* **~ up**) че́рпать, вы́-.

cpds. **~-bait** *n.* блесна́; **~bill** *n.* колпи́ца; **~feed** *v.t.* (*lit.*) корми́ть (*impf.*) с ло́жки; (*fig.*): **~-feed a pupil** всё разжёвывать (*impf.*) ученику́.

sporadic [spə'rædɪk] *adj.* споради́ческий.

spore [spɔː(r)] *n.* спо́ра.

sport [spɔːt] *n.* **1.** (*outdoor pastime(s)*) спорт; (*pl.*) спорт, ви́ды (*m. pl.*) спо́рта; **go in for ~** зан|има́ться, -я́ться спо́ртом; **~s car** спорти́вный автомоби́ль. **2.** (*pl.*, *athletic events*) спорти́вные и́гры (*f. pl.*); **~s day** день спорти́вных состяза́ний. **3.** (*jest*, *fun*) шу́тка, заба́ва; (*ridicule*) насме́шка; **say sth. in ~** сказа́ть (*pf.*) что-н. в шу́тку; **make ~ of** подшу́|чивать, -ти́ть над+*i.* **4.** (*coll.*, *good fellow*) молодчи́на (*m.*); **be a ~!** будь челове́ком!

v.t.: **~ a rose in one's button-hole** щеголя́ть (*impf.*) ро́зой в петли́це; **everyone ~ed their medals** все нацепи́ли свои́ меда́ли.

v.i. (*frolic*) резви́ться (*impf.*).

cpds. **~sman** *n.* спортсме́н; **~smanlike** *adj.* че́стный, поря́дочный; **~smanship** *n.*: **he showed ~smanship** он прояви́л себя́ настоя́щим спортсме́ном; **~swoman** *n.* спортсме́нка.

sporting ['spɔːtɪŋ] *adj.* **1.** (*addicted to sport*) спорти́вный; **he was not a ~ man** он не́ был спортсме́ном. **2.** (*sportsmanlike*) че́стный, поря́дочный; (*enterprising*) предприи́мчивый; **that's very ~ of you** э́то с ва́шей стороны́ благоро́дно; **a ~ chance** наде́жда, не́который шанс.

sportive ['spɔːtɪv] *adj.* весёлый, игри́вый.

sporty ['spɔːtɪ] *adj.* (*rakish*) лихо́й, удало́й.

spot [spɒt] *n.* **1.** (*patch*, *speck*) пятно́, пя́тнышко, кра́пинка; **a white dog with brown ~s** бе́лая соба́ка с кори́чневыми пя́тнами; **come out in ~s** (*rash*) покры́ться (*pf.*) сы́пью. **2.** (*stain*) пятно́; **there were ~s of blood on his shirt** на его́ руба́шке бы́ли пя́тна кро́ви. **3.** (*pimple*) пры́щ(ик). **4.** (*place*) ме́сто; **he was killed on the ~** он был уби́т на ме́сте (*or* сра́зу); **running on the ~** бег на ме́сте; **his question put me on the ~** (*coll.*) его́ вопро́с поста́вил меня́ в затрудни́тельное положе́ние; **~ check** вы́борочная прове́рка; **sore ~** (*lit.*, *fig.*) больно́е ме́сто; **weak ~** сла́бое ме́сто; **he has a soft ~ for her** он пита́ет к ней сла́бость. **5.** (*coll.*, *small amount*): **I must have a ~ to eat** мне ну́жно перекуси́ть; **I have a ~ of work to do** мне ну́жно немно́го порабо́тать; **~ of bother** небольша́я неприя́тность. **6.**: **~ on** (*coll.*, *exactly right*) в са́мую то́чку.

v.t. **1.** (*mark*, *stain*) запа́чкать (*pf.*); зака́пать (*pf.*); **his books were ~ted with ink** его́ кни́ги бы́ли запа́чканы черни́лами; (*p.p.*, *covered*, *decorated with ~s*) пятни́стый, кра́пчатый; **a ~ted tie** га́лстук в кра́пинку. **2.** (*coll.*, *notice*) зам|еча́ть, -е́тить; (*recognize*) узн|ава́ть, -а́ть; (*catch sight of*) уви́деть (*pf.*); **I ~ted my friend in the crowd** я (вдруг) уви́дел в толпе́ своего́ прия́теля.

v.i. **1.**: **this silk ~s easily** э́тот шёлк о́чень ма́ркий. **2.**: **it is ~ting with rain** накра́пывает (дождь).

cpd. **~light** *n.* освети́тельный проже́ктор; (*fig.*): **turn the ~light on sth.** привле́чь (*pf.*) внима́ние к чему́-н.; **be in the ~light** быть в це́нтре (*or* це́нтром) внима́ния; *v.t.* (*lit.*, *fig.*) осве|ща́ть, -ти́ть.

spotless ['spɒtlɪs] *adj.* сверка́ющий чистото́й; **the room was ~** ко́мната сверка́ла чистото́й; (*fig.*) незапя́тнанный, безупре́чный.

spotty ['spɒtɪ] *adj.* (*of colour*) пятни́стый; (*pimply*) прыщева́тый.

spouse [spaʊz, spaʊs] *n.* супру́г (*fem.* -а).

spout [spaʊt] *n.* **1.** (*of vessel*) но́сик; (*of pump*) рука́в; (*for rain-water*) водосто́чная труба́; жёлоб. **2.** (*jet of water etc.*) струя́; столб воды́; (*of whale*) ды́хало.

v.t. **1.**: **a whale ~s water** кит выбра́сывает струю́ воды́; **a volcano ~ing lava** вулка́н, изверга́ющий ла́ву. **2.** (*coll.*, *declaim*) разглаго́льствовать (*impf.*); **~ poetry** деклами́ровать, про- стихи́.

v.i. **1.** струи́ться (*impf.*); бить (*impf.*); ли́ться (*impf.*) пото́ком; (*of whale*) выбра́сывать, вы́бросить струю́ воды́. **2.** (*fig.*, *coll.*, *make speeches*) ора́торствовать (*impf.*).

sprain [spreɪn] *n.* растяже́ние.

v.t.: **~ one's ankle** растяну́ть (*pf.*) щи́колотку.

sprat [spræt] *n.* шпро́та, ки́лька.

sprawl [sprɔːl] *n.* небре́жная по́за; **urban ~** рост городо́в за счёт се́льской ме́стности.

v.i. **1.** растяну́ться (*pf.*); **send s.o. ~ing** сбить (*pf.*)

кого́-н. с ног. **2.** (*straggle*) разва́л|иваться, -и́ться; раскоря́читься (*pf.*).

spray[1] [spreɪ] *n.* (*bot.*) ве́тка, побе́г.

spray[2] [spreɪ] *n.* **1.** (*water droplets*) бры́зг|и (*pl.*, *g.* —). **2.** (*liquid preparation*) жи́дкость для пульвериза́ции; **chemical ~** ядохимика́т для опры́скивания. **3.** (*device for ~ing; also ~er*) разбры́згиватель (*m.*); распыли́тель (*m.*); пульвериза́тор; **~ can** аэрозо́льный балло́н.

v.t. (*apply ~ to*) опры́ск|ивать, -ать; (*apply in the form of ~*) распыл|я́ть, -и́ть.

cpd. **~-gun** *n.* распыли́тель (*m.*).

sprayer ['spreɪə(r)] = **spray** *n.* **3.**

spread [spred] *n.* **1.** (*extension*) протяже́ние, протяжённость; (*expansion*) распростране́ние; (*increase*) увеличе́ние; **~ of wings** разма́х кры́льев. **2.** (*dissemination*) распростране́ние. **3.** (*difference between prices etc.*) ра́зница, разры́в. **4.** (*coll.*, *feast*) пир. **5.** (*cul.*) па́ста. **6.** (*typ.*) разворо́т.

v.t. **1.** (*extend*) распростран|я́ть, -и́ть; (*unfold*) ра|скла́дывать, -зложи́ть; (*cover*) расст|ила́ть, -ели́ть (*or* разостла́ть); **she ~ a cloth on the table** она́ расстели́ла ска́терть на столе́; **~ butter on bread (*or* bread with butter)** нама́з|ывать, -ать ма́сло на хлеб (*or* хлеб ма́слом); **~ manure over a field** разбр|а́сывать, -оса́ть наво́з по́ полю; **the tree ~ its branches** де́рево раски́нуло свои́ ве́тви; **the bird ~ its wings** пти́ца распростёрла кры́лья; **~ (out) a map** ра|скла́дывать, -зложи́ть ка́рту. **2.** (*diffuse*) распростран|я́ть, -и́ть; **he ~ the rumour** он распространи́л слух. **3.: ~ o.s.** (*lounge*) раски́|дываться, -нуться.

v.i. **1.** распростран|я́ться, -и́ться; расстила́ться (*impf.*); **the news soon ~** но́вость бы́стро распространи́лась; **a valley ~s out behind the hill** за холмо́м расстила́ется доли́на; **his name ~ throughout the land** его́ сла́ва разошла́сь по всей стране́; **the fire is ~ing** пожа́р разраста́ется; **a flush ~ over her face** кра́ска залила́ её лицо́; **a smile ~ over his face** его́ рот растяну́лся в улы́бке. **2.** (*disperse*) рассе́|иваться, -яться.

cpd. **~sheet** *n.* (*comput.*) (крупноформа́тная) электро́нная табли́ца.

spreading ['spredɪŋ] *adj.* (*branchy*) разве́систый.

spree [spri:] *n.* (*coll.*) весе́лье, кутёж; **have a ~, go on the ~** кути́ть (*impf.*).

sprig [sprɪg] *n.* (*twig*, *shoot*) ве́точка, побе́г.

sprightly ['spraɪtlɪ] *adj.* живо́й, бо́йкий, ре́звый.

spring[1] [sprɪŋ] *n.* (*season*) весна́; **in ~** весно́й; (*attr.*) весе́нний; **~ onion** зелёный лук.

cpds. **~-clean** *n.* генера́льная (*обычно весенняя*) убо́рка; *v.t. & i.* произв|оди́ть, -ести́ генера́льную убо́рку; **~time** *n.* весна́, весе́нняя пора́.

spring[2] [sprɪŋ] *n.* **1.** (*leap*) прыжо́к, скачо́к; **make, take a ~** пры́гнуть (*pf.*); скакну́ть (*pf.*). **2.** (*elasticity*) упру́гость, эласти́чность. **3.** (*elastic device*) пружи́на; (*attr.*) пружи́нный; **~ balance** пружи́нные весы́; **~ mattress** пружи́нный матра́ц; (*of vehicle*) рессо́ра. **4.** (*of water*) исто́чник, ключ, родни́к; **hot ~s** горя́чие исто́чники; **~ water** ключева́я вода́.

v.t. **1.** (*cause to act*): **~ a trap** захло́пнуть (*pf.*) лову́шку; (*produce suddenly*): **~ a surprise on s.o.** заст|ига́ть, -и́чь кого́-н. враспло́х. **2.: ~ a leak** да|ва́ть, -ть течь. **3.** (*provide with ~s*): **the carriage is well sprung** у каре́ты хоро́шие рессо́ры.

v.i. **1.** (*leap*) пры́г|ать, -нуть; скак|а́ть, -ну́ть; **~ to one's feet** вск|а́кивать, -очи́ть на́ ноги; **~ to s.o.'s help** бр|оса́ться, -о́ситься кому́-н. на по́мощь; **~ into action** энерги́чно приня́ться (*pf.*) за де́ло; **the lid sprang open** кры́шка внеза́пно откры́лась; **where did you ~ from?** (*coll.*) отку́да вы взяли́сь? **2.** (*of liquid*) бить (*impf.*); **water ~s from the earth** из земли́ бьёт ключ. **3.** (*come into being*) появ|ля́ться, -и́ться; возн|ика́ть, -и́кнуть; **he ~s from an old family** он происхо́дит из стари́нного ро́да; **a breeze sprang up** подня́лся лёгкий ветеро́к; **a belief sprang up that …** появи́лось мне́ние, что…

cpd. **~board** *n.* (*lit.*, *fig.*) трампли́н.

springy ['sprɪŋɪ] *adj.* упру́гий, пружи́нистый.

sprinkle ['sprɪŋk(ə)l] *n.*: **a ~ of rain** до́ждик; небольшо́й дождь; **a ~ of snow** (лёгкий) снежо́к; **with a ~ of salt** слегка́ подсо́ленный.

v.t.: **~ sth. with water, ~ water on sth.** бры́згать, по- что-н. водо́й; **~ sth. with salt/sand, ~ salt/sand on sth.** пос|ыпа́ть, -ы́пать что-н. со́лью/песко́м.

sprinkler ['sprɪŋklə(r)] *n.* разбры́згиватель (*m.*).

sprinkling ['sprɪŋklɪŋ] *n.* (*fig.*): **there was a ~ of children in the audience** в аудито́рии находи́лось небольшо́е коли́чество дете́й.

sprint [sprɪnt] *n.* спринт.

v.t. & i. спринтова́ть (*impf.*); бежа́ть (*det.*) с максима́льной ско́ростью.

sprinter ['sprɪntə(r)] *n.* спри́нтер.

sprite [spraɪt] *n.* эльф, фе́я.

sprocket ['sprɒkɪt] *n.* (цепна́я) звёздочка.

cpd. **~-wheel** *n.* цепно́е/зубча́тое колесо́.

sprout [spraʊt] *n.* (*shoot*) росто́к, побе́г, отро́сток; (*pl.*, **Brussels ~s**) брюссе́льская капу́ста.

v.t. отра́|щивать, -сти́ть.

v.i. (*of plant*) пус|ка́ть, -ти́ть ростки́; (*of seed*) прораст|а́ть, -и́.

spruce[1] [spru:s] *n.* (*tree*) ель.

spruce[2] [spru:s] *adj.* аккура́тный, опря́тный, наря́дный; **he looked ~** у него́ был щеголева́тый вид.

v.t.: **~ up** нав|оди́ть, -ести́ красоту́/блеск на+*a.*; прив|оди́ть, -ести́ в поря́док; **~ o.s. up** прихора́шиваться (*pf.*).

spry [spraɪ] *adj.* живо́й, подви́жный, прово́рный.

spud [spʌd] *n.* (*sl.*, *potato*) карто́шка, карто́фелина.

spume [spju:m] *n.* пе́на, на́кипь.

spun [spʌn] *adj.* пря́деный; **~ yarn** кручёная пря́жа; **~ gold** кани́тель; **~ glass** стекля́нная нить.

spunk [spʌŋk] *n.* (*coll.*, *mettle*) отва́га, му́жество.

spunky ['spʌŋkɪ] *adj.* (*coll.*) му́жественный, отва́жный.

spur [spɜ:(r)] *n.* **1.** (*on rider's heel*, *cock's leg*) шпо́ра. **2.** (*fig.*) побужде́ние, сти́мул; **on the ~ of the moment** под влия́нием мину́ты. **3.** (*of mountain range*) отро́г. **4.** (*branch road etc.*) (подъездна́я) ве́тка.

v.t. **1.** (*prick with ~s*) пришпо́ри|вать, -ть. **2.** (*fig.*, *stimulate*) побу|жда́ть, -ди́ть; **her words ~red him (on) to action** её слова́ побуди́ли/подстрекну́ли его́ к де́йствию.

v.i.: **~ on, forward** спеши́ть (*impf.*); мча́ться (*impf.*).

spurious ['spjʊərɪəs] *adj.* подде́льный, фальши́вый, подло́жный.

spurn [spɜ:n] *v.t.* (*repel*) отт|а́лкивать, -олкну́ть; (*refuse with disdain*) отв|ерга́ть, -е́ргнуть.

spurt[1] [spɜ:t] *n.* (*sudden effort*) поры́в; (*in race*) рыво́к; **put on a ~** рвану́ться (*pf.*).

v.i. рвану́ться (*pf.*); **~ into the lead** вырыва́ться, вы́рваться вперёд.

spurt[2] [spɜ:t] *n.* (*jet*) струя́.

v.t. пус|ка́ть, -ти́ть струёй.

v.i. бить (*impf.*) струёй; хлы́нуть (*pf.*); **the water ~ed into the air** вода́ заби́ла струёй.

sputnik ['spʊtnɪk, 'spʌt-] *n.* (иску́сственный) спу́тник.

sputter ['spʌtə(r)] *v.t. & i.* **1.** = **splutter. 2.** (*crackle*) треща́ть (*impf.*); (*sizzle, hiss*) шипе́ть (*impf.*); **the candle ~ed out** свеча́ с шипе́нием пога́сла.

sputum ['spju:təm] *n.* слюна́, мокро́та.

spy [spaɪ] *n.* шпио́н; **police ~** шпик.

v.t. (*liter.*, *discern*) разгля́д|ывать, -е́ть; **~ land** уви́деть (*pf.*) зе́млю; **~ out the land** (*fig.*) зонди́ровать (*impf.*) по́чву.

v.i. (*engage in espionage*) шпио́нить (*impf.*); ~

on s.o. подгля́дывать (*impf.*) за кем-н.

cpds. **~glass** *n.* подзо́рная труба́; **~hole** *n.* глазо́к.

spying ['spaɪɪŋ] *n.* шпиона́ж; подгля́дывание.

Sq. [skweə(r)] *n.* (*abbr. of* **Square**) пл., (пло́щадь).

squabble ['skwɒb(ə)l] *n.* перебра́нка, препрека́ние.

v.i. препрека́ться (*impf.*) (*с кем*); вздо́рить, по-.

squad [skwɒd] *n.* **1.** (*mil.*) гру́ппа, кома́нда, отделе́ние. **2.** (*gang, group*) отря́д; рабо́чая брига́да; **flying ~** (*of police*) лету́чий отря́д.

squadron ['skwɒdrən] *n.* (*mil.*) эскадро́н; (*nav.*) эска́дра; (*aeron.*) эскадри́лья; **fighter ~** эскадри́лья истреби́телей.

cpd. **~-leader** *n.* майо́р авиа́ции.

squalid ['skwɒlɪd] *adj.* гря́зный, ни́щенский, убо́гий.

squall [skwɔ:l] *n.* (*gust, storm*) шквал, гроза́; **encounter a ~** поп|ада́ть, -а́сть в бу́рю.

v.i. вопи́ть, за-; пронзи́тельно крича́ть, за-.

squalor ['skwɒlə(r)] *n.* убо́жество; ни́зость.

squander ['skwɒndə(r)] *v.t.* пром|а́тывать, -ота́ть; растра́|чивать, -тить.

squanderer ['skwɒndərə(r)] *n.* расточи́тель (*fem.* -ница).

square [skweə(r)] *n.* **1.** квадра́т. **2.** (*on chessboard etc.*) кле́тка, по́ле; **we are back to ~ one** (*fig.*) мы верну́лись в исхо́дное положе́ние. **3.** (*open space in town*) пло́щадь; **Red S~** Кра́сная пло́щадь; (*with central garden*) сквер; (*barrack-~*) учёбный плац. **4.** (*US, block of buildings*) кварта́л. **5.** (*drawing instrument*) уго́льник, науго́льник; **out of ~** ко́со, неро́вно. **6.** (*math.*) квадра́т; **find the ~ of 72** возвести́ (*pf.*) 72 в квадра́т(ную сте́пень).

adj. **1.** (*geom., math.*) квадра́тный; **~ metre** квадра́тный метр; **~ number** квадра́т це́лого числа́; **~ root** квадра́тный ко́рень (из+*g.*); (*right-angled*) прямоуго́льный; **with ~ corners** с прямы́ми угла́ми; (*of shape*) квадра́тный, углова́тый. **2.** (*even, balanced*) то́чный; в поря́дке; **get one's accounts ~** прив|оди́ть, -ести́ свои́ счета́ в поря́док; **all ~** (*in order*) всё в поря́дке; (*even scoring*) с ра́вным счётом; **we are all ~** мы кви́ты. **3.** (*thorough*) по́лный, реши́тельный; **a ~ meal** оби́льная еда́. **4.** (*fair, honest*) че́стный, прямо́й, справедли́вый; **~ dealing** че́стное веде́ние дел.

adv. **1.** (*at right angles*) перпендикуля́рно. **2.** (*straight*) пря́мо. **3.** (*honestly*) че́стно, пря́мо, непосре́дственно. **4.: ten feet ~** де́сять фу́тов в ширину́ и де́сять в длину́.

v.t. **1.** (*math.*) возв|оди́ть, -ести́ в квадра́т (*or* во втору́ю сте́пень); **3 ~d is 9** квадра́т трёх ра́вен (*or* три в квадра́те равно́) девяти́; **A ~d** А квадра́т; А в квадра́те; А во второ́й сте́пени. **4.** (*straighten*) выпрямля́ть, вы́прямить; **~ one's shoulders** распр|авля́ть, -а́вить пле́чи. **5.** (*settle*) ула́|живать, -дить; **~ accounts** св|оди́ть, -ести́ счёты. **6.** (*reconcile*) согласо́в|ывать, -а́ть (*что с чем*).

v.i. **1.** (*agree*) согласо́в|ываться, -а́ться; **~ with** вяза́ться/сходи́ться (*both impf.*) с+*i.*; **this statement does not ~ with the facts** э́то заявле́ние не соотве́тствует фа́ктам. **2.: ~ up** (*settle accounts*) **with s.o.** поквита́ться (*pf.*) с кем-н.

squash[1] [skwɒʃ] *n.* (*crush*) да́вка, толчея́; (*drink*) фрукто́вый напи́ток; (**~ rackets)** сквош, ракетбо́л.

v.t. **1.** (*crush*) дави́ть, раз-; разда́в|ливать, -и́ть; сплю́щи|вать, -ть; **the tomatoes were ~ed** помидо́ры подави́лись. **2.** (*crowd*): **the conductor ~ed us into the bus** конду́ктор вти́снул нас в авто́бус; **we were ~ed so tightly, we couldn't move** бы́ло так те́сно, что мы шевельну́ться не могли́. **3.** (*quash*): **we must ~ this rumour** на́до ликвиди́ровать (*impf., pf.*) э́тот слух; **the rebellion was ~ed** мяте́ж был пода́влен.

v.i. (*crowd*) потесни́ться (*pf.*); **they ~ed up to make room for me** они́ потесни́лись, что́бы дать мне ме́сто.

squash[2] [skwɒʃ] *n.* (*bot.*) ты́ква, кабачо́к.

squat [skwɒt] *n.* (*posture*) сиде́нье на ко́рточках; (*coll., unauthorized occupation*) незако́нное вселе́ние.

adj. призе́мистый.

v.i. **1.** (*of pers.*) сиде́ть (*impf.*) на ко́рточках; **~ down** сади́ться (*impf.*) на ко́рточки; присе́сть (*pf.*); (*of animals*) прип|ада́ть, -а́сть к земле́. **2.** (*of unauthorized occupation*) сели́ться, по- самово́льно.

squatter ['skwɒtə(r)] *n.* (*illegal occupant*) скв́аттер.

squaw [skwɔ:] *n.* же́нщина, жена́ (*у индейцев*).

squawk [skwɔ:k] *n.* пронзи́тельный крик.

v.i. пронзи́тельно крича́ть, за-.

squeak [skwi:k] *n.* **1.** (*of mouse etc.*) писк, взвизг. **2.** (*of hinge etc.*) скрип, визг.

v.i. **1.** (*of pers. or animal*) пища́ть, за-. **2.** (*of object*) скрипе́ть (*impf.*), скри́пнуть (*pf.*).

squeaker ['skwi:kə(r)] *n.* (*device*) пища́лка.

squeaky ['skwi:kɪ] *adj.* пискли́вый; скрипу́чий.

squeal [skwi:l] *n.* визг.

v.i. визжа́ть, за-; (*turn informer*) стуча́ть, на- (*sl.*).

squealer ['skwi:lə(r)] (*informer*) стука́ч (*sl.*).

squeamish ['skwi:mɪʃ] *adj.* **1.** (*easily nauseated*) подве́рженный тошноте́; **feel ~** чу́вствовать, по- тошноту́; **blood makes me feel ~** меня́ тошни́т от кро́ви. **2.** (*sensitive, scrupulous*) щепети́льный, брезгли́вый.

squeamishness ['skwi:mɪʃnɪs] *n.* щепети́льность.

squeegee ['skwi:dʒi:] *n.* рези́новая шва́бра.

squeeze [skwi:z] *n.* **1.** (*pressure*) сжа́тие; **he gave the sponge a ~** он вы́жал гу́бку; **he gave her a ~** он кре́пко обня́л её; **he gave my hand a ~** он пожа́л мне ру́ку. **2.** (*sth. ~d out*): **a ~ of lemon** не́сколько ка́пель лимо́нного со́ка. **3.** (*crowding, crush*) теснота́, да́вка. **4.** (*fin.*) нажи́м; ограниче́ние креди́та.

v.t. **1.** (*compress*) сж|има́ть, -ать; сда́в|ливать, -и́ть; **he ~d his fingers in the door** он прищеми́л па́льцы две́рью; (*to extract moisture etc.*) выжима́ть, вы́жать; **he ~d the lemon dry** он вы́жал лимо́н; (*fig.*) (*extort*): **~ money out of s.o.** вымога́ть (*impf.*) де́ньги у кого́-н.; **~ a confession from s.o.** вынужда́ть, вы́нудить кого́-н. призна́ться. **2.** (*force, crowd, cram*) вти́с|кивать, -нуть.

v.i. проти́с|киваться, -каться (*or* -нуться).

squeezer ['skwi:zə(r)] *n.* (соко)выжима́лка.

squelch [skweltʃ] *n.* хлю́панье.

v.i. хлю́п|ать, -нуть.

squib [skwɪb] *n.* (*firework*) пета́рда, шути́ха; **damp ~** (*fig.*) прова́л.

squid [skwɪd] *n.* кальма́р.

squiggle ['skwɪg(ə)l] *n.* загогу́лина; кара́куля.

squiggly ['skwɪglɪ] *adj.* волни́стый, изо́гнутый.

squint [skwɪnt] *n.* **1.** косогла́зие; **she has a ~ in her right eye** она́ коси́т на пра́вый глаз. **2.** (*coll., glance*) взгляд (и́скоса/укра́дкой); **let's have a ~ at the paper** дава́йте посмо́трим, что там в газе́те.

v.i. **1.** коси́ть (*impf.*). **2.** (*half-shut eyes*) щу́риться (*impf.*); прищу́ри|ваться, -ться. **3.: ~ at sth.** смотре́ть, по- и́скоса/укра́дкой на что-н.

cpd. **~-eyed** *adj.* косо́й, косогла́зый.

squire ['skwaɪə(r)] *n.* поме́щик, сквайр.

squirm [skwɜ:m] *n.* извива́ться (*impf.*); ко́рчиться (*impf.*); **the child was ~ing on its seat** ребёнок верте́лся/ёрзал на сту́ле.

squirrel ['skwɪr(ə)l] *n.* бе́лка; (**~ fur)** бе́личий мех.

squirt [skwɜ:t] *n.* **1.** (*jet*) струя́. **2.** (*coll., of pers.*) ничто́жество.

v.t. пры́с|кать, -нуть; **~ water in the air** пус|ка́ть, -ти́ть струю́ воды́ в во́здух; **~ scent from atomizer** бры́згать, по- духа́ми из пульвериза́тора.

v.i. бить (*impf.*) струёй.

Sri Lanka [ʃri: 'læŋkə, ʃrɪ'læŋkə, ˌsr-] *n.* Шри Ла́нка́.

SS *abbr. of* **1. steamship** парохо́д. **2.** (*hist.*) ***Schutz-***

Staffel: **~ man** эсэ́совец.

St. *abbr. of* **1. street** ул., (у́лица). **2. Saint** св., (Свят|о́й, -а́я).

stab [stæb] *n.* **1.** уда́р (о́стрым ору́жием); **~ in the back** (*fig.*) нож/уда́р в спи́ну. **2.** (*fig., sharp pain*) внеза́пная о́страя боль; уко́л. **3.** (*coll., attempt*): **I'll have a ~ at it** попро́бую.

v.t. **1.** (*wound*): **~ s.o. in the chest with a knife** нан|оси́ть, -ести́ кому́-н. уда́р в грудь ножо́м. **2.** (*plunge*): **he ~bed a knife into the table** он всади́л/вонзи́л нож в стол. **3.** (*fig.*): **her reproaches ~bed him to the heart** её упрёки пронзи́ли его́ в са́мое се́рдце.

v.i. **1.: ~ at s.o.** бро́ситься (*pf.*) на кого́-н. с ножо́м. **2.** (*of pain etc.*) стреля́ть (*impf.*).

stability [stəˈbɪlɪtɪ] *n.* стаби́льность, усто́йчивость.

stabilization [ˌsteɪbɪˌlaɪˈzeɪʃ(ə)n] *n.* стабилиза́ция.

stabilize [ˈsteɪbɪˌlaɪz] *v.t.* стабилизи́ровать (*impf., pf.*).

stabilizer [ˈsteɪbɪˌlaɪzə(r)] *n.* стабилиза́тор.

stable[1] [ˈsteɪb(ə)l] *n.* **1.** коню́шня. **2.** (*racing*) скаковы́е ло́шади одного́ владе́льца.

v.t. ста́вить, по- в коню́шню; содержа́ть (*impf.*) в коню́шне.

cpds. **~-boy, ~-lad** *nn.* помо́щник ко́нюха; **~man** *n.* ко́нюх.

stable[2] [ˈsteɪb(ə)l] *adj.* (*firm, strong, fixed*) про́чный, кре́пкий; (*of currency*) стаби́льный, усто́йчивый, сто́йкий; **a ~ job** постоя́нная рабо́та.

staccato [stəˈkɑːtəʊ] *n. & adv.* стакка́то (*indecl.*).

adj. отры́вистый.

stack [stæk] *n.* **1.** (*of hay etc.*) стог; скирда́. **2.** (*pile*): **~ of wood** шта́бель (*m.*) дров, поле́нница; **~ of papers** ки́па бума́г; **~ of plates** стопа́ таре́лок. **3.** (*coll., usu. pl., large amount*) ма́сса, ку́ча; **he has ~s of money** у него́ ку́ча де́нег; **a ~ of work** ма́сса рабо́ты; **we have ~s of time** у нас полно́ вре́мени. **4.** (*chimney*) дымова́я труба́.

v.t. **1.: ~ hay** мете́ть (*impf.*) се́но в стог; скирдова́ть (*impf.*) се́но; **~ books on the floor** ста́вить, по- кни́ги сто́пками на полу́. **2.: ~ the cards** подтасо́в|ывать, -а́ть ка́рты; **the cards were ~ed against him** (*fig.*) всё бы́ло про́тив него́.

stadium [ˈsteɪdɪəm] *n.* стадио́н.

staff [stɑːf] *n.* **1.** (*for walking etc.*) по́сох, па́лка; (*pole*) столб. **2.** (*emblem of office*) жезл. **3.** (*shaft, handle*) дре́вко. **4.** (*body of assistants, employees*) штат; ли́чный соста́в; **editorial ~** сотру́дники реда́кции; **teaching ~** преподава́тельский соста́в; **~ room** (*at school*) учи́тельская; **~ meeting** педагоги́ческий сове́т. **5.** (*mil.*) штаб; **General S~** генера́льный штаб; **~ officer** штабно́й офице́р; **~ sergeant** штаб-сержа́нт. **6.** (*mus.*) но́тный стан.

v.t. укомплекто́в|ывать, -а́ть (*что or* штат *чего*).

stag [stæg] *n.* (*deer*) оле́нь(*m.*)-саме́ц.

cpds. **~-beetle** *n.* жук-оле́нь (*m.*); **~-party** *n.* (*coll.*) мальчи́шник.

stage [steɪdʒ] *n.* **1.** (*theatr.*) сце́на, эстра́да; **front of the ~** авансце́на; (*as profession*) теа́тр, сце́на; **go on the ~** идти́, пойти́ на сце́ну; **put a play on the ~** ста́вить, по- пье́су; **he writes for the ~** он пи́шет для теа́тра. **2.** (*attr.*): **~ direction** рема́рка; **~ door** служе́бный/актёрский вход (в теа́тр); **~ effect** сцени́ческий эффе́кт; **~ fright** страх пе́ред пу́бликой. **3.** (*fig., scene of action*) аре́на, по́прище, сце́на; **he quit the political ~** он поки́нул полити́ческую аре́ну. **4.** (*phase, point*) пери́од, ста́дия, эта́п; **the war reached a critical ~** война́ вступи́ла в крити́ческую фа́зу; **at this ~ he was interrupted** на э́том ме́сте его́ переби́ли; **she was in the last ~ of consumption** она́ находи́лась в после́дней ста́дии чахо́тки; **the baby has reached the talking ~** ребёнок на́чал говори́ть; **negotiations reached their final ~** наступи́л заверша́ющий эта́п перегово́ров; **I shall do it in ~s** я сде́лаю э́то постепе́нно. **7.** (*section of route or journey*) перего́н. **8.** (*of rocket*) ступе́нь.

v.t.: **~ a play** ста́вить, по- пье́су; (*organize*) устр|а́ивать, -о́ить; организова́ть (*impf., pf.*).

cpds. **~-coach** *n.* почто́вый дилижа́нс; **~-hand** *n.* рабо́чий сце́ны; **~-manage** *v.t.* ста́вить, по- (*спекта́кль*); режисси́ровать, с-; **~-manager** *n.* режиссёр, постано́вщик.

stagger [ˈstægə(r)] *v.t.* **1.** (*cause to ~*): **a ~ing blow** сокруши́тельный уда́р. **2.** (*disconcert*) потряс|а́ть, -ти́; пора|жа́ть, -зи́ть; ошелом|ля́ть, -и́ть; **~ing success** потряса́ющий успе́х. **3.** (*arrange in zigzag order*) распол|ага́ть, -ожи́ть в ша́хматном поря́дке. **4.: ~ working hours, holidays etc.** распределя́ть (*impf.*) часы́ рабо́ты, отпуска́ *и т.п.*

v.i. шата́ться (*impf.*); пошáтываться (*impf.*); **they ~ed down the street** они́ шли по у́лице поша́тываясь.

staging [ˈsteɪdʒɪŋ] *n.* **1.** (*platform*) подмо́стк|и (*pl., g.* -ов). **2.** (*of play*) постано́вка. **3.: ~ post** (*aeron.*) промежу́точный аэродро́м.

stagnant [ˈstægnənt] *adj.* **1.** (*of water*) стоя́чий. **2.** (*sluggish*) засто́йный, вя́лый, ко́сный.

stagnate [stægˈneɪt] *v.i.* **1.** (*of water*) заст|а́иваться, -оя́ться. **2.** (*fig.*) косне́ть, за-.

stagnation [stægˈneɪʃ(ə)n] *n.* засто́й.

stagy [ˈsteɪdʒɪ] *adj.* театра́льный; аффекти́рованный.

staid [steɪd] *adj.* степе́нный; положи́тельный.

stain [steɪn] *n.* **1.** пятно́; **remove a ~** выводи́ть, вы́вести пятно́. **2.** (*for colouring wood etc.*) протра́ва, краси́тель (*m.*); **wood ~** протра́ва, мори́лка.

v.t. **1.** (*discolour, soil*) пятна́ть, за-; па́чкать, за-/ис-. **2.** (*colour with dye etc.*) окра́|шивать, -сить; протра́в|ливать (*or* протрав|ля́ть), -и́ть; **~ed glass** цветно́е стекло́; **~ed-glass window** витра́ж; **~ wood** мори́ть, за- де́рево.

v.i. (*cause ~s*) оставля́ть (*impf.*) пя́тна; (*be subject to ~ing*) па́чкаться (*impf.*); быть ма́рким.

stainless [ˈsteɪnlɪs] *adj.* **1.** (*unblemished*) чи́стый; (*fig.*) безупре́чный. **2.: ~ steel** нержаве́ющая сталь.

stair [steə(r)] *n.* **1.** (*step*) ступе́нька. **2.** (*pl.*, **~case**) ле́стница; **flight of ~s** ле́стничный марш.

cpds. **~case, ~way** *nn.* ле́стница; **~-well** *n.* ле́стничная кле́тка.

stake [steɪk] *n.* **1.** (*post*) столб, кол (*pl.* ко́лья); **row of ~s** частоко́л; **the plants were tied to ~s** расте́ния бы́ли подвя́заны к ко́лышкам; **he was burnt at the ~** его́ сожгли́ на костре́; **pull up ~s** (*fig.*) сня́ться (*pf.*) с ме́ста. **2.** (*wager; money deposited*) ста́вка, закла́д; (*pl.* **~** *race*) ска́чки (*f. pl.*) на приз; **hold the ~s** прин|има́ть, -я́ть закла́д; **play for high ~s** игра́ть (*impf.*) по большо́й; (*fig.*) поста́вить (*pf.*) всё на ка́рту. **3.** (*interest, share*) интере́с, до́ля; **he has a ~ in the country** он кро́вно заинтересо́ван в процвета́нии страны́. **4.: his reputation was at ~** его́ репута́ция была́ поста́влена на ка́рту.

v.t. **1.** (*support with ~*) укреп|ля́ть, -и́ть коло́м. **2.** (*wager*) ста́вить, по-; (*risk, gamble*) рискова́ть (*impf.*) +*i.*

with advs.: **~ off** *v.t.* отгор|а́живать, -оди́ть; **~ out** *v.t.*: **~ out a boundary** отм|еча́ть, -е́тить ве́хами грани́цу; **~ (out) one's claim** (*lit.*) застолби́ть (*pf.*) уча́сток.

stalactite [ˈstæləkˌtaɪt, stəˈlæk-] *n.* сталакти́т.

stalagmite [ˈstæləgˌmaɪt] *n.* сталагми́т.

stale [steɪl] *adj.* **1.** (*not fresh*) несве́жий; **~ bread** чёрствый хлеб; (*of air*) спёртый; **the room smells ~** в ко́мнате за́тхлый во́здух. **2.** (*lacking novelty, tedious*) изби́тый, устаре́вший; **a ~ joke** изби́тая шу́тка; **~ news** устаре́вшая но́вость.

v.i.: **pleasures that never ~** ра́дости, кото́рые никогда́ не приеда́ются.

stalemate ['steɪlmeɪt] *n.* (*chess*) пат; (*fig.*, *impasse*) тупи́к, безвы́ходное положе́ние.

v.t. де́лать, с- пат +*d.*; (*fig.*) загна́ть (*pf.*) в тупи́к.

Stalinism ['stɑːlɪ,nɪz(ə)m] *n.* сталини́зм.

Stalinist ['stɑːlɪnɪst] *n.* сталини́ст (*fem.* -ка).

adj. сталини́стский.

stalk[1] [stɔːk] *n.* (*stem*) сте́бель (*m.*).

stalk[2] [stɔːk] *v.t.* (*game*, *pers.*) высле́живать, вы́следить; **~ing-horse** (*fig.*) личи́на, предло́г.

v.i. (*stride*) ше́ствовать (*impf.*); го́рдо выступа́ть (*impf.*); **he ~ed up to me** он церемо́нно подошёл ко мне; (*fig.*): **famine ~ed the land** го́лод ше́ствовал по стране́.

stall[1] [stɔːl] *n.* **1.** (*for animal*) сто́йло. **2.** (*in market etc.*) ларёк, пала́тка; **book ~** киоск; **flower ~** цвето́чный ларёк; **newspaper ~** газе́тный киоск. **3.** (*pl.*, *theatr.*) парте́р, кре́сла (*nt. pl.*).

v.t. **1.** (*place in ~*) ста́вить, по- в сто́йло; (*keep in ~*) содержа́ть (*impf.*) в сто́йле. **2.**: **~ an engine** (нечаянно) заглуш|а́ть, -и́ть мото́р.

v.i. **1.** (*get stuck*) застр|ева́ть, -я́ть. **2.** (*of engine*) гло́хнуть, за-.

cpd. **~-holder** *n.* владе́лец ларька́.

stall[2] [stɔːl] *v.t.* (*block*, *delay*) заде́рж|ивать, -а́ть.

v.i. (*play for time*) тяну́ть, кани́телить (*both impf.*).

stallion ['stæljən] *n.* жеребе́ц.

stalwart ['stɔːlwət] *n.* (*pol.*) активи́ст (*fem.* -ка).

adj. (*robust*) ро́слый, дю́жий; (*staunch*) отва́жный, до́блестный.

stamen ['steɪmən] *n.* тычи́нка.

stamina ['stæmɪnə] *n.* выно́сливость.

stammer ['stæmə(r)] *n.* заика́ние; **person with a ~** заи́ка (*c.g.*); **speak with a ~** заика́ться (*impf.*).

v.t. произн|оси́ть, -ести́ (*что*), заика́ясь.

v.i. заика́ться (*impf.*).

stammerer ['stæmərə(r)] *n.* заи́ка (*c.g.*).

stamp [stæmp] *n.* **1.** (*of foot*) то́пот, то́панье. **2.** (*instrument*) ште́мпель (*m.*), штамп, печа́ть, клеймо́. **3.** (*impress*, *mark*) печа́ть, клеймо́; отпеча́ток; (*postage etc.*) ма́рка. **4.** (*characteristic*, *mark*) печа́ть, отпеча́ток.

v.t. **1.** (*imprint*) штампова́ть (*impf.*); штемпелева́ть (*impf.*); клейми́ть, за-; отти́с|кивать, -нуть; **the maker's name is ~ed on the goods** на това́ре проста́влено фабри́чное клеймо́. **2.** (*affix ~ to*): **~ an envelope** накле́и|вать, -ть ма́рку на конве́рт; **~ a receipt** ста́вить, по- печа́ть на квита́нции. **3.** (*beat on ground*): **~ one's feet** то́пать (*impf.*) нога́ми; **~ the snow from one's shoes** сби|ва́ть, -ть снег с боти́нок.

v.i. (*feet*) то́п|ать, -нуть.

with adv.: **~ out** *v.t.*: (*lit.*): **~ out a fire** затопта́ть (*pf.*) ого́нь; (*exterminate*, *destroy*) уничт|ожа́ть, -о́жить; (*suppress*) подав|ля́ть, -и́ть; **the revolt was quickly ~ed out** восста́ние бы́ло ско́ро пода́влено; **~ out an epidemic** искорени́ть (*pf.*) эпиде́мию.

cpds. **~-album** *n.* альбо́м для ма́рок; **~-collecting** *n.* филатели́я; **~-collector** *n.* филатели́ст (*fem.* -ка); **~-dealer** *n.* торго́вец ма́рками; **~-duty** *n.* ге́рбовый сбор; **~-machine** *n.* автома́т по прода́же почто́вых ма́рок.

stampede [stæm'piːd] *n.* (*of cattle*) бе́гство врассыпну́ю; (*of people*) ма́ссовое (пани́ческое) бе́гство.

v.t. обра|ща́ть, -ти́ть в бе́гство.

v.i. (*of cattle*) разбе|га́ться, -жа́ться врассыпну́ю; (*of people*) обра|ща́ться, -ти́ться в (пани́ческое) бе́гство.

stance [stɑːns, stæns] *n.* пози́ция; **take up a ~** зан|има́ть, -я́ть пози́цию.

stanch, staunch [stɑːntʃ, stɔːntʃ] *v.t.*: **~ a wound** остан|а́вливать, -ови́ть кровотече́ние из ра́ны.

stanchion ['stɑːnʃ(ə)n] *n.* сто́йка.

stand [stænd] *n.* **1.** (*support*, *e.g. for teapot*) подста́вка. **2.** (*stall*) ларёк, сто́йка; (*for display*) стенд, щит. **3.** (*raised structure*, *e.g. for spectators*) трибу́на. **4.** (*for taxis etc.*) стоя́нка. **5.** (*halt*) остано́вка; **bring, come to a ~** остан|а́вливать(ся), -ови́ть(ся). **6.** (*position*) ме́сто; **take one's ~ on the platform** зан|има́ть, -я́ть ме́сто на сце́не; (*fig.*): **take a firm ~** зан|има́ть, -я́ть твёрдую пози́цию; **make a ~ against s.o.** ока́з|ывать, -а́ть сопротивле́ние кому́-н. **7.** (*theatr.*, *stop for performance*): **one-night ~** однодне́вные гастро́ли (*f. pl.*).

v.t. **1.** (*place*, *set*) ста́вить, по-; **he stood the ladder against the wall** он приста́вил ле́стницу к стене́. **2.** (*bear*, *tolerate*, *endure*) терпе́ть, вы́-; выноси́ть, вы́нести; **she can't ~ him** она́ его́ не выно́сит (*or* терпе́ть не мо́жет); **I can't ~ cold** я не выношу́ хо́лода; (*withstand*) выде́рживать, вы́держать; **his plays have stood the test of time** его́ пье́сы вы́держали испыта́ние вре́менем. **3.** (*not yield*): **~ one's ground** не уступ|а́ть, -и́ть. **4.** (*undergo*) подв|ерга́ться +*d.*; **~ trial** отв|еча́ть, -е́тить пе́ред судо́м. **5.**: **he doesn't ~ a chance** у него́ нет никако́й наде́жды.

v.i. **1.** (*be or stay in upright position*) стоя́ть (*impf.*); **she was too weak to ~** она́ не держа́лась на нога́х от сла́бости; **he kept me ~ing** он не предложи́л мне сесть; **~ing room only** (*theatr.*) сидя́чих мест нет; **a ~ing ovation** бу́рная ова́ция; **the sight of the corpse made my hair ~ on end** при ви́де тру́па у меня́ во́лосы ста́ли ды́бом; **he is old enough to ~ on his own feet** он доста́точно взро́слый, что́бы быть самостоя́тельным; **I shan't ~ in your way** я вам не ста́ну меша́ть; **~ still!** не дви́гайтесь! **2.** (*with indication of height*): **he ~s six feet tall** рост у него́ шесть фу́тов. **3.** (*continue*, *remain*): **our house will ~ for another fifty years** наш дом простои́т ещё пятьдеся́т лет; **~ fast, firm** держа́ться (*impf.*) непоколеби́мо/твёрдо; *see also* **standing.** **4.** (*hold good*) ост|ава́ться, -а́ться в си́ле. **5.** (*be situated*) стоя́ть (*impf.*); находи́ться; (*impf.*); **a house once stood here** когда́-то здесь стоя́л дом. **6.** (*find o.s.*, *be*): **he stood convicted of murder** суд призна́л его́ вино́вным в уби́йстве; **we ~ in need of help** мы нужда́емся в по́мощи; **I ~ corrected** я признаю́ свою́ оши́бку; **this is how matters ~** вот как обстои́т де́ло; **as matters ~** при да́нном положе́нии веще́й; **how do we ~ for money?** как у нас (обстои́т) с деньга́ми?; **the umbrella stood me in good stead** зо́нтик мне весьма́ пригоди́лся. **7.** (*rise to one's feet*) вста|ва́ть, -ть. **8.** (*come to a halt*) остан|а́вливаться, -ови́ться; **~ still** не дви́гаться (*impf.*); **~ and deliver!** кошелёк и́ли жизнь! **9.** (*assume or move to specified position*): **we had to ~ in a queue** нам пришло́сь постоя́ть в о́череди; **he stood on tiptoe** он встал на цы́почки; **I (went and) stood by the table** я стал у стола́; **~ back!** (пода́йтесь) наза́д!; отойди́те!; **the soldiers stood to attention** бойцы́ вста́ли в сто́йку «сми́рно»; **~ at ease!** во́льно! **10.** (*remain motionless*): **the machinery is ~ing idle** станки́ проста́ивают; **let the tea ~!** да́йте ча́ю отстоя́ться!

with preps.: **we will ~ by** (*support*) **you** мы вас подде́ржим; **I ~ by what I said** я не отступа́юсь от свои́х слов; **~ for office** выставля́ть, вы́ставить свою́ кандидату́ру; **~ for Parliament** баллоти́роваться (*impf.*) в парла́мент; **we ~ for freedom** мы стои́м за свобо́ду; **'Mg' ~s for magnesium** «Mg» обознача́ет ма́гний; **I will not ~ for such impudence** я не потерплю́ тако́й де́рзости; **don't ~ on ceremony** не стесня́йтесь!; пожа́луйста, без церемо́ний!; **it ~s to reason** (само́ собо́й) разуме́ется; **he ~s to win/lose £1,000** его́ ждёт вы́игрыш/про́игрыш в ты́сячу фу́нтов; **how do you ~ with your boss?** как к вам отно́сится ваш нача́льник?

with advs.: ~ **about,** ~ **around** *vv.i.* (*of one person*) болтáться (*impf.*); (*of a group*) стоя́ть (*impf.*) кругóм; ~ **aside** *v.i.* (*remain aloof*) стоя́ть (*impf.*) в сторонé; (*move to one side*) посторони́ться (*pf.*); ~ **back** *v.i.*: **he stood back to admire the picture** он отошёл назáд, чтóбы полюбовáться карти́ной; **he ~s back in favour of others** он уступáет мéсто други́м; ~ **by** *v.i.* (*be ready*) быть/стоя́ть (*impf.*) наготóве; ~ **by to fire!** приготóвиться к стрельбé!; (*be spectator*): **I could not ~ by and see her ill-treated** я не мог смотрéть безучáстно, как над нéю издевáются; ~ **down** *v.i.* (*of candidate*): **he stood down in favour of his brother** он снял свою́ кандидатýру в пóльзу брáта; ~ **in** *v.i.* (*substitute*): ~ **in for s.o. else** замен|я́ть, -и́ть когó-н. другóго; ~ **off** *v.t.*: ~ **off workers** врéменно ув|ольня́ть, -óлить рабóчих; ~ **out** *v.i.* (*be prominent, conspicuous*) выделя́ться (*impf.*); **his work ~s out from the others'** егó рабóта рéзко выделя́ется среди́ прóчих; **his mistakes ~ out a mile** (*coll.*) егó оши́бки бросáются в глазá; (*show resistance*): ~ **out against tyranny** сопротивля́ться (*impf.*) деспоти́зму; ~ **up** *v.t.*: **he stood his bicycle up against the wall** он прислони́л свой велосипéд к стенé; *v.i.*: **he stood up as I entered** он встал, когдá я вошёл; **he ~s up for his rights** он отстáивает свои́ правá; **he stood up bravely to his opponent** он мýжественно сопротивля́лся проти́внику; **this steel ~s up to high temperatures** э́та сталь выдéрживает высóкие температýры.

cpds. **~by** *n.* (*state of readiness*) готóвность; (*dependable thg. or pers.*) надёжная опóра; испы́танное срéдство; **~by generator** резéрвный генерáтор; **~-in** *n.* замести́тель (*fem.* -ница); **~-offish** *adj.* (*aloof*) сдéржанный, зáмкнутый; **~point** *n.* тóчка зрéния; **~still** *n.* останóвка, бездéйствие; **come to a ~still** останови́ться (*pf.*); застóпориться (*pf.*); **at a ~still** на мёртвой тóчке; **bring to a ~still** останови́ть (*pf.*); застóпорить (*pf.*); **trade is at a ~still** торгóвля нахóдиться в застóе.

standard ['stændəd] *n.* **1.** (*flag*) знáмя, штандáрт. **2.** (*norm, model*) стандáрт, нóрма; **come up to ~** соотвéтствовать (*impf.*) трéбуемому ýровню; **set a high ~** устан|áвливать, -ови́ть высóкие трéбования; **~ of education** ýровень (*m.*) образовáния; **~ of living** жи́зненный ýровень; **by American ~s** по америкáнским критéриям; **by any ~** по любы́м нóрмам; **below ~** ни́же нóрмы; **gold ~** золотóй стандáрт.

adj. **1.** стандáртный, нормáльный; **of ~ size** стандáртного размéра. **2.** (*model, basic*) нормати́вный, образцóвый; (*general*) типовóй; **~ English** литератýрный/нормати́вный англи́йский язы́к; **a ~ reference work** авторитéтный спрáвочник. **3.**: **~ lamp** стоя́чая лáмпа, торшéр.

cpd. **~-bearer** *n.* знаменóсец.

standardization [,stændədaɪ'zeɪʃ(ə)n] *n.* стандартизáция, нормализáция.

standardize ['stændə,daɪz] *v.t.* стандартизи́ровать (*impf., pf.*); нормировáть (*impf., pf.*).

standing ['stændɪŋ] *n.* **1.** (*rank, reputation*) положéние, репутáция; **a person of high ~** высокопостáвленное лицó. **2.** (*duration*): **a custom of long ~** стари́нный обы́чай. **3.** (*length of service*) стаж.

adj.: **~ army** постоя́нная áримя; **~ invitation** приглашéние приходи́ть в любóе врéмя; **~ joke** дежýрная шýтка; **~ order** (*to banker*) прикáз о регуля́рных платежáх; (*to newsagent etc.*) постоя́нный закáз; **~ orders** прáвила процедýры.

stanza ['stænzə] *n.* строфá; станс.

staple[1] ['steɪp(ə)l] *n.* (*metal bar or wire*) скобá; (*for papers*) скрéпка; (*on door*) скобá, пробóй.

v.t.: **~ papers together** скреп|ля́ть, -и́ть бумáги скрéпкой.

staple[2] ['steɪp(ə)l] *n.* **1.** (*principal commodity*) основнóй продýкт; **the ~s of that country** основнáя продýкция э́той страны́. **2.** (*chief material*) оснóва; **~ of diet** оснóва питáния; **~ of conversation** глáвная тéма разговóра. **3.** (*raw material*) сырьё.

adj. основнóй, глáвный.

stapler ['steɪplə(r)] *n.* (*for paper*) стáплер.

star [stɑ:(r)] *n.* **1.** звездá; **North, Pole S~** Поля́рная звездá; **we slept under the ~s** мы спáли под откры́тым нéбом; **thank one's lucky ~s** благодари́ть (*impf.*) судьбý (*or* свою́ звездý). **2.** (*famous actor etc.*) звездá, свети́ло; **film ~** кинозвездá; **~ turn** гвоздь прогрáммы; **~ pupil** звездá клáсса. **3.** (*fig.*): **I saw ~s** у меня́ и́скры из глаз посы́пались.

v.t. **1.** (*adorn with ~s*) укр|ашáть, -áсить звёздами. **2.** (*mark with asterisk*) отм|ечáть, -éтить звёздочкой.

v.i.: **~ in a film** игрáть (*impf.*) глáвную роль в фи́льме.

cpds. **~fish** *n.* морскáя звездá; **~light** *n.* свет звёзд; **by ~light** при свéте звёзд; **~lit** *adj.* освещённый свéтом звёзд; **~-spangled** *adj.* усéянный звёздами.

starboard ['stɑ:bəd] *n.* прáвый борт.

adj. прáвый; **~ side** прáвый борт.

starch [stɑ:tʃ] *n.* крахмáл.

v.t. крахмáлить, на-.

starchiness ['stɑ:tʃɪnɪs] *n.* мучни́стость; (*fig.*) чóпорность, церемóнность.

starchy ['stɑ:tʃɪ] *adj.* (*containing starch*) мучни́стый, крахмáлистый; (*stiffened*) накрахмáленный.

stardom ['stɑ:dəm] *n.*: **rise to ~** сдéлаться/стать (*pf.*) звездóй.

stare [steə(r)] *n.* при́стальный взгляд; **vacant ~** пустóй взгляд.

v.t.: **~ s.o. in the face** смотрéть, по- на когó-н. в упóр; **ruin ~s him in the face** он нахóдится на краю́ ги́бели; **the letter was staring me in the face** письмó лежáло у меня́ под нóсом; **~ s.o. up and down** смéрить (*pf.*) когó-н. взгля́дом.

v.i. глазéть (*impf.*); широкó раскры́ть (*pf.*) глазá; **~ at s.o.** при́стально смотрéть/глядéть (*impf.*) на когó-н.; **~ into s.o.'s face** устáвиться на когó-н.; **~ into space** устрем|ля́ть, -и́ть взор в пространство; смотрéть (*impf.*) неви́дящим взгля́дом.

staring ['steərɪŋ] *adj.* (*of eyes*) при́стальный; широкó раскры́тый.

stark [stɑ:k] *adj.* **1.** (*desolate, bare*) гóлый, пусты́нный; **a ~ winter landscape** сурóвый зи́мний пейзáж. **2.** (*sharply evident*) я́вный; **in ~ contrast** в вопию́щем противорéчии. **3.** (*sheer*) пóлный, абсолю́тный.

adv. совершéнно; **~ staring mad** абсолю́тно сумасшéдший; **~ naked** совершéнно гóлый.

starless ['stɑ:lɪs] *adj.* беззвёздный.

starling ['stɑ:lɪŋ] *n.* скворéц.

starry ['stɑ:rɪ] *adj.* **1.**: **~ night** звёздная ночь; **~ sky** усéянное звёздами нéбо. **2.**: **~ eyes** лучи́стые глазá.

cpd. **~-eyed** *adj.* (*fig.*) романти́чный, увлекáющийся; ви́дящий всё в рóзовом свéте.

start [stɑ:t] *n.* **1.** (*sudden movement*) вздрáгивание; **give a ~ of surprise** вздрóгнуть (*pf.*) от удивлéния; **give s.o. a ~** испугáть (*pf.*) когó-н.; **he woke with a ~** он вздрóгнул и проснýлся; **he works by fits and ~s** он рабóтает уры́вками. **2.** (*beginning*) начáло; (*of journey*) отправлéние; (*of race*) старт; **make a ~ on sth.** нач|инáть, -áть что-н.; **we made an early ~** мы рáно вы́ступили в путь; **make a fresh ~** нач|инáть, -áть сы́знова; **at the (very) ~** в (сáмом) начáле; **for a ~** для начáла; **from ~ to finish** с начáла до концá; **false ~** (*sport*) фальстáрт; **get off to a good ~** удáчно начáть (*pf.*). **3.** (*advantage in race etc.*): **he was given 10 yards' ~** емý дáли фóру в 10 я́рдов.

v.t. **1.** (*begin*) нач|ина́ть, -а́ть; **it is ~ing to rain** начина́ется дождь; **when does she ~ school?** когда́ она́ пойдёт в шко́лу?; **we ~ed our journey** мы пусти́лись в путь; **she ~ed crying** она́ распла́калась; *with many vv., the pf. formed with* за- *means 'to start ...ing'*. **2.** (*set in motion*): **~ a clock** зав|оди́ть, -ести́ часы́; **~ an engine** запус|ка́ть, -ти́ть (*or* зав|оди́ть, -ести́) мото́р. **3.** (*in race*): **~ the runners** да|ва́ть, -ть старт бегуна́м. **4.** (*initiate*): **~ a business** осно́в|ывать, -а́ть предприя́тие; **he ~ed business in a small way** он завёл небольшо́е де́ло; **~ a school** откр|ыва́ть, -ы́ть шко́лу; **~ a fire** (*arson*) устро́ить (*pf.*) пожа́р; (*for warmth etc.*) развести́ (*pf.*) костёр/ого́нь; **~ a movement** положи́ть (*pf.*) нача́ло (како́му-н.) движе́нию; **~ a rumour** (рас)пус|ка́ть, -ти́ть слух. **5.** (*broach*): **~ a bottle of wine** поч|ина́ть, -а́ть буты́лку вина́; **~ a subject (of conversation)** завести́ (*pf.*) разгово́р о чём-н. **6.** (*cause to begin*): **the wine ~ed him talking** вино́ развяза́ло емý язы́к; **this ~ed me thinking** э́то заста́вило меня́ заду́маться.

v.i. **1.** (*make sudden movement*) вздр|а́гивать, -о́гнуть; **~ from one's chair** вскочи́ть (*pf.*) со сту́ла; **tears ~ed from his eyes** у него́ слёзы бры́знули из глаз. **2.** (*begin*) нач|ина́ться, -а́ться; (*come into being, arise*) появ|ля́ться, -и́ться; возн|ика́ть, -и́кнуть; **it ~ed raining** пошёл/начался́ дождь; **we had to ~ again from scratch** пришло́сь нача́ть всё снача́ла; **there were 12 of us to ~ with** снача́ла/сперва́ нас бы́ло 12 челове́к; **to ~ with, you should write to him** пре́жде всего́ (*or* во-пе́рвых,) вы должны́ написа́ть ему́; **what will you have** (*eat*) **to ~ with?** что вы возьмёте на заку́ску? **3.** (*set out*) отпр|авля́ться, -а́виться; **he ~ed back the next day** на сле́дующий день он пусти́лся в обра́тный путь; **~ing point** (*of journey*) отправно́й пункт; (*of race*) старт; (*fig.*) исхо́дная то́чка. **4.** (*in race*) стартова́ть (*impf., pf.*); **~ing-pistol** ста́ртовый пистоле́т. **5.** (*of engine etc.*): **the car ~ed without any trouble** маши́на завела́сь без труда́; **you should always ~ in first gear** стартова́ть всегда́ сле́дует на пе́рвой ско́рости.

with advs.: **~ off** *v.i.* (*leave*) пойти́, пое́хать (*both pf.*); **he ~ed off with a general introduction** он на́чал с о́бщего вступле́ния; **he ~ed off in second gear** он стартова́л на второ́й ско́рости; **~ out** *v.i.* (*leave*) отпр|авля́ться, -а́виться; пойти́, пое́хать (*both pf.*); (*intend*) соб|ира́ться, -ра́ться; **he ~ed out to reform society** он собира́лся измени́ть о́бщество; **~ up** *v.t.*: **~ up an engine** запус|ка́ть, -ти́ть мото́р; **~ up a conversation** завести́ (*pf.*) разгово́р; **~ up a business** основа́ть/учреди́ть (*pf.*) предприя́тие/де́ло; *v.i.* (*spring to one's feet*) вск|а́кивать, -очи́ть; (*come into being*) появ|ля́ться, -и́ться; **a new firm is ~ing up in the town** в го́роде открыва́ется но́вая фи́рма.

starter [ˈstɑːtə(r)] *n.* **1.** (*giving signal for race*) ста́ртер. **2.** (*competitor*) уча́стник состяза́ния; (*horse*) уча́стник забе́га. **3.** (*device for starting engine etc.*) ста́ртер. **4.** (*pl., coll., first course*) заку́ска.

startle [ˈstɑːt(ə)l] *v.t.* (*alarm*) трево́жить, вс-; (*scare*) вспу́г|ивать, -ну́ть; **I was ~d when you shouted** я так и вздро́гнул, когда́ вы закрича́ли; **you ~d me** вы меня́ испуга́ли.

startling [ˈstɑːtlɪŋ] *adj.* порази́тельный; (*staggering*) потряса́ющий; (*alarming*) пуга́ющий.

starvation [stɑːˈveɪʃ(ə)n] *n.* го́лод, голода́ние; **die of ~** ум|ира́ть, -ере́ть от го́лода (*or* с го́лоду); **~ diet** голо́дная дие́та; **~ wage** ни́щенский за́работок.

starv|e [stɑːv] *v.t.* мори́ть, у-/за- (го́лодом); **~e s.o. into submission** взять (*pf.*) кого́-н. измо́ром; (*fig.*): **the child was ~ed of affection** ребёнок страда́л от отсу́тствия любви́.

v.i. **1.** (*go hungry*) голода́ть (*impf.*); **a ~ing child** голода́ющий ребёнок; **I'm ~ing** я ужа́сно проголода́лся!; я го́лоден как волк!; **~e to death** ум|ира́ть, -ере́ть с го́лоду.

stash [stæʃ] *v.t.* (*coll.*): **he has £1,000 ~ed away** у него́ припря́тана ты́сяча фу́нтов.

state[1] [steɪt] *n.* **1.** (*condition*) состоя́ние, положе́ние; **in a poor ~ of health** в плохо́м состоя́нии здоро́вья; **~ of affairs** положе́ние дел; **~ of mind** настрое́ние; душе́вное состоя́ние; **in an untidy ~** в беспоря́дке; **what is the ~ of play?** како́й счёт?; (*fig.*) как обстоя́т дела́? **2.** (*country, community, government*) госуда́рство; **affairs, matters of ~** госуда́рственные дела́; **United S~s** Соединённые Шта́ты (Аме́рики); **~ control** госуда́рственный контро́ль. **3.**: **lie in ~** быть вы́ставленным для торже́ственного проща́ния; **the Queen drove in ~ through London** короле́ва торже́ственно прое́хала по Ло́ндону; **~ coach** пара́дная каре́та; **~ visit** госуда́рственный визи́т; **~ ball** торже́ственный бал.

cpds. **~-aided** *adj.* получа́ющий дота́цию от госуда́рства; **state-of-the-art** *adj.* совреме́нный, нове́йший; **~room** *n.* (*on ship*) каю́та; **~sman** *and cpds., see separate entries.*

state[2] [steɪt] *v.t.* (*declare; say clearly*) заяв|ля́ть, -и́ть; сообщ|а́ть, -и́ть о+*p.*; **he ~d his intentions** он заяви́л о свои́х наме́рениях; (*indicate*) ука́з|ывать, -а́ть; **as ~d above** как ука́зано вы́ше; (*specify*): **at the ~d time** в озна́ченное вре́мя; (*announce*) объяв|ля́ть, -и́ть; (*expound*) изл|ага́ть, -ожи́ть; **the plaintiff ~d his case** исте́ц изложи́л своё де́ло.

statehood [ˈsteɪthʊd] *n.* госуда́рственность.

stateless [ˈsteɪtlɪs] *adj.* не име́ющий гражда́нства.

stately [ˈsteɪtlɪ] *adj.* вели́чественный, велича́вый.

statement [ˈsteɪtmənt] *n.* (*declaration*) заявле́ние; **make, publish a ~** сде́лать/опубликова́ть (*pf.*) заявле́ние; (*exposition*) изложе́ние; (*communication*) сообще́ние; (*fin.*) отчёт, бала́нс; **~ of account** вы́писка счёта; **~ of expenses** отчёт о расхо́дах.

statesman [ˈsteɪtsmən] *n.* госуда́рственный де́ятель.

statesmanlike [ˈsteɪtsmənlaɪk] *adj.* досто́йный госуда́рственного де́ятеля.

statesmanship [ˈsteɪtsmənʃɪp] *n.* иску́сство управле́ния госуда́рством; госуда́рственная му́дрость.

static [ˈstætɪk] *n.* **1.** (*~ electricity*) стати́ческое электри́чество. **2.** (*as radio interference*) (атмосфе́рные) поме́хи (*f. pl.*).

adj. **1.** (*stationary*) неподви́жный, стациона́рный. **2.** (*opp. dynamic*) стати́ческий, стати́чный.

statics [ˈstætɪks] *n.* ста́тика.

station [ˈsteɪʃ(ə)n] *n.* **1.** (*assigned place*) пост; **take up one's ~** зан|има́ть, -я́ть пост. **2.** (*establishment, base, headquarters*) ста́нция; **broadcasting ~** радиоста́нция; **bus ~** авто́бусная ста́нция; **filling ~** запра́вочный пункт, бензоколо́нка; **fire ~** пожа́рное депо́ (*indecl.*); **naval ~** вое́нно-морска́я ба́за; **police ~** полице́йский уча́сток; (*in former USSR*) отделе́ние мили́ции; **power ~** электроста́нция. **3.** (*rail.*) ста́нция; (*large, mainline ~*) вокза́л; (*attr.*) станцио́нный. **4.** (*position in life, rank*) положе́ние; зва́ние; **a man of humble ~** челове́к ни́зкого зва́ния; **the duties of his ~** обя́занности, свя́занные с его́ положе́нием.

v.t. распол|ага́ть, -ожи́ть; **she ~ed herself at a window** она́ расположи́лась у окна́; **~ a guard at the gate** выставля́ть, вы́ставить карау́л у воро́т; (*mil.*) разме|ща́ть, -сти́ть; дислоци́ровать (*impf., pf.*); **the regiment is ~ed in the south** полк стои́т на ю́ге.

cpd. **~-master** *n.* нача́льник ста́нции.

stationary [ˈsteɪʃənərɪ] *adj.* **1.** (*not moving; at rest*) неподви́жный. **2.** (*fixed*) закреплённый, стациона́рный; **~ troops** ме́стные войска́.

stationer ['steɪʃənə(r)] *n.* торго́вец писчебума́жными/канцеля́рскими принадле́жностями.

stationery ['steɪʃənərɪ] *n.* писчебума́жные/канцеля́рские принадле́жности (*f. pl.*).

statistical [stə'tɪstɪk(ə)l] *adj.* статисти́ческий.

statistician [ˌstætɪ'stɪʃ(ə)n] *n.* стати́стик.

statistics [stə'tɪstɪks] *n.* статисти́ческие да́нные; (*science*) стати́стика.

statue ['stætju:, 'stætʃu:] *n.* ста́туя.

statuesque [ˌstætjʊ'esk, ˌstætʃʊ'esk] *adj.* велича́вый, вели́чественный.

statuette [ˌstætjʊ'et, ˌstætʃʊ'et] *n.* статуэ́тка.

stature ['stætʃə(r)] *n.* **1.** (*height*) рост. **2.** (*fig.*) масшта́б, кали́бр.

status ['steɪtəs] *n.* **1.** (*position, rank*) положе́ние, ста́тус; **civil ~** гражда́нское состоя́ние; (*superior position*): **~ symbol** показа́тель положе́ния в о́бществе. **2. ~ quo** ста́тус-кво́ (*indecl.*).

statute ['stætju:t] *n.* стату́т; (*law*) зако́н; (*regulations, ordinance*) уста́в; **~ law** пи́саный зако́н; **~ of limitations** зако́н о да́вностных сро́ках.

cpd. **~-book** *n.* свод зако́нов.

statutory ['statjʊtərɪ] *adj.* устано́вленный зако́ном; **~ minimum** определённый зако́ном ми́нимум; **~ offence** дея́ние, кара́емое по зако́ну.

staunch[1] [stɔ:ntʃ, stɑ:ntʃ] *adj.* (*faithful, trusty*) ве́рный; (*loyal*) лоя́льный; (*reliable*) надёжный; (*devoted*): **a ~ socialist** убеждённый социали́ст.

sta(u)nch[2] [stɔ:ntʃ, stɑ:ntʃ] *v.t.* = **stanch**

stave [steɪv] *n.* (*of cask*) клёпка; (*mus.*) но́тный стан.

v.t. **1.** (*also* **~ in:** *break in*): **~ in a door** проб|ива́ть, -и́ть дыру́ в две́ри. **2.: ~ off** предотвра|ща́ть, -ти́ть.

stay[1] [steɪ] *n.* **1.** (*sojourn*) пребыва́ние; **I am making a short ~ in London** я задержу́сь ненадо́лго в Ло́ндоне; **I enjoyed my ~ with you** я прекра́сно провёл вре́мя у вас. **2.** (*suspension*) отсро́чка; **~ of execution** отсро́чка исполне́ния.

v.t. **1.** (*check*) остан|а́вливать, -ови́ть; препя́тствовать, вос- *+d.*; (*restrain*) сде́рж|ивать, -а́ть; **~ one's hand** возде́рж|иваться, -а́ться от де́йствий. **2.** (*last out*): **~ the course** выде́рживать, вы́держать до конца́.

v.i. **1.** (*stop, put up*) остан|а́вливаться, -ови́ться; (*as guest*) гости́ть (*impf.*); **we are** (*sc. at present*) **~ing with friends** мы останови́лись/гости́м у друзе́й; **we ~ed in Vienna for 3 weeks** мы про́были в Ве́не три неде́ли. **2.** (*remain*) ост|ава́ться, -а́ться; **I ~ed awake all night** я всю ночь не спал; **~ at home** сиде́ть (*impf.*) до́ма; **~ in bed** не встава́ть (*impf.*) (с посте́ли); **the children ~ed away from school** де́ти прогуля́ли шко́лу; **I ~ed away from work** я не пошёл на рабо́ту; **can you ~ for, to tea?** вы мо́жете оста́ться к ча́ю?; **he ~ed for the night** он оста́лся ночева́ть; **if you want to lose weight, ~ off starchy foods** е́сли хоти́те похуде́ть, возде́рживайтесь от мучно́го; **my hat won't ~ on** у меня́ шля́па не де́ржится (на голове́); **he ~ed to dinner** он оста́лся обе́дать; **if we ~ together we shan't get lost** е́сли мы бу́дем держа́ться вме́сте, не заблу́димся; **~ up late** не ложи́ться (*impf.*) (спать) допоздна́. **3.** (*endure in race etc.*): **he has no ~ing-power** у него́ нет никако́й выно́сливости.

cpd. **~-at-home** *n.* домосе́д (*fem.* -ка).

stay[2] [steɪ] *n.* **1.** (*naut.*) штаг. **2.** (*prop, support*) опо́ра, подпо́рка; (*moral support*) опо́ра, подде́ржка. **3.** (*pl., corset*) корсе́т.

stead [sted] *n.* (*liter.*): **stand s.o. in good ~** сослужи́ть (*pf.*) кому́-н. хоро́шую слу́жбу; **in s.o.'s ~** вме́сто кого́-н.

steadfast ['stedfɑ:st, 'stedfəst] *adj.* (*firm, stable*): **~ in danger** сто́йкий в опа́сности; **~ policy** твёрдая поли́тика; (*faithful*): **~ in love** ве́рный в любви́; (*reliable*) надёжный; (*unwavering*) непоколеби́мый.

steadfastness ['stedfɑ:stnɪs, 'stedfəstnɪs] *n.* сто́йкость; ве́рность; непоколеби́мость; надёжность.

steady ['stedɪ] *adj.* **1.** (*firmly fixed, balanced, supported*) про́чный, усто́йчивый, твёрдый; **the ladder must be held ~** на́до кре́пко держа́ть ле́стницу; **he has a ~ hand** у него́ твёрдая рука́; (*unfaltering*): **~ in one's principles** непреклонный в свои́х при́нципах; **a ~ gaze** при́стальный взгляд. **2.** (*uniform*) равноме́рный; (*even*) ро́вный; (*constant*) постоя́нный; (*uninterrupted*) непреры́вный; **at a ~ pace** ро́вным ша́гом; **he works steadily** он упо́рно рабо́тает; **~ demand** постоя́нный спрос; **a ~ flow of water** непреры́вный пото́к воды́. **3.** (*of pers., staid, sober*) степе́нный. **4.** (*in exhortation*): **~!** осторо́жно!

v.t. **1.** (*strengthen, secure*) укрепл|я́ть, -и́ть; **the doctor gave him sth. to ~ his nerves** до́ктор дал ему́ лека́рство для успокое́ния не́рвов. **2.: ~ a boat** прив|оди́ть, -ести́ ло́дку в равнове́сие.

v.i. **1.** (*regain equilibrium*) выра́вниваться, вы́ровняться. **2.** (*become fixed, firm*): **the market is ~ing** це́ны на ры́нке стано́вятся усто́йчивыми.

steak [steɪk] *n.* (*of beef*) бифште́кс (натура́льный); **fillet ~** вы́резка.

cpd. **~-house** *n.* бифште́ксная.

steal [sti:l] *v.t.* **1.** ворова́ть, с-; красть, у-; **I had my handbag stolen** у меня́ укра́ли су́мку. **2.** (*fig.*): **~ a glance at s.o.** взгляну́ть(*pf.*) укра́дкой на кого́-н.; **~ s.o.'s heart (away)** похи́тить (*pf.*) чьё-н. се́рдце.

v.i. **1.** (*thieve*) ворова́ть (*impf.*); **he accused me of ~ing** он обвини́л меня́ в воровстве́; **he was caught ~ing** его́ пойма́ли с поли́чным. **2.** (*move secretly or silently*) кра́сться (*impf.*); **he stole round to the back door** он прокра́лся к за́дней две́ри; **he stole up to her** он подкра́лся к ней.

stealth [stelθ] *n.*: **by ~** тайко́м, укра́дкой.

stealthy ['stelθɪ] *adj.*: **~ glance** взгляд укра́дкой; **~ tread** кра́дущаяся похо́дка.

steam [sti:m] *n.* пар; **full ~ ahead!** по́лный вперёд!; **get up ~** (*lit.*) разв|оди́ть, -ести́ пары́; (*fig.*) набра́ться (*pf.*) сил; **let off ~** (*fig.*) дать (*pf.*) вы́ход чу́вствам; **run out of ~** (*fig.*) выдыха́ться, вы́дохнуться; **under one's own ~** (*fig.*) сам, свои́ми си́лами; **~ iron** парово́й утю́г; **~ train** по́езд с парово́й тя́гой.

v.t. **1.** (*cook with ~*) па́рить (*impf.*); **~ed fish** па́реная ры́ба. **2.** (*treat with ~*): **the envelope had been ~ed open** кто́-то откле́ил конве́рт над па́ром. **3.** (*cover with ~*): **the carriage windows were ~ed up** ваго́нные о́кна запоте́ли.

v.i. **1.** (*give out ~ or vapour*) выделя́ть (*impf.*) пар/испаре́ния; пус|ка́ть, -ти́ть пар; **the kettle is ~ing on the stove** ча́йник кипи́т на плите́; **he wiped his ~ing brow** он вы́тер вспоте́вший лоб. **2.** (*move by ~*): **the boat ~ed into the harbour** кора́бль вошёл в га́вань; **the train ~ed out** парово́з отошёл от ста́нции. **3.: ~ up** запот|ева́ть, -е́ть.

cpds. **~-bath** *n.* парова́я ба́ня; **~boat** *n.* парохо́д; **~-engine** *n.* парова́я маши́на; **~-heat** *n.* отдава́емое па́ром тепло́; **~-roller** *n.* парово́й като́к; *v.t.* (*lit.*) уплотн|я́ть -и́ть; ука́т|ывать, -а́ть; (*fig.*) сокруш|а́ть, -и́ть; **~ship** *n.* парохо́д; **~-shovel** *n.* парово́й экскава́тор.

steamer ['sti:mə(r)] *n.* парохо́д.

steamy ['sti:mɪ] *adj.* (*saturated with steam*) насы́щенный пара́ми; (*covered with steam*) запоте́лый, запоте́вший.

stearin ['stɪərɪn] *n.* стеари́н.

steed [sti:d] *n.* (*poet.*) конь (*m.*).

steel [sti:l] *n.* сталь; (*attr.*) стально́й; **~ foundry** сталелите́йный заво́д; (*fig.*): **nerves of ~** стальны́е/

железные нервы.

v.t. (*fig.*, *harden*): ~ **o.s.** ожесточ|а́ться, -и́ться.

cpds. **~-plated** *adj.* бронированный; обшитый ста́лью; **~-works** *n.* сталелите́йный заво́д; **~yard** *n.* безме́н.

steely ['sti:lɪ] *adj.* (*fig.*, *unyielding*) непрекло́нный; (*stern*) суро́вый.

steep[1] [sti:p] *adj.* **1.** круто́й; **the stairs were ~** ле́стница была́ крута́я; **the ground fell ~ly away** земля́ кру́то обрыва́лась; (*fig.*): **there has been a ~ decline in trade** в торго́вле произошёл круто́й спад. **2.** (*coll.*, *excessive*) чрезме́рный, непоме́рный; **we had to pay a ~ price** нам э́то ста́ло в копе́ечку.

steep[2] [sti:p] *v.t.* **1.** (*soak*) мочи́ть (*impf.*); зам|а́чивать, -очи́ть. **2.** (*fig.*, *pass. or refl.*, *be immersed*) погру|жа́ться, -зи́ться (*во что*) **he ~ed himself in the study of the classics** он погрузи́лся в изуче́ние кла́ссиков; **~ed in ignorance** погря́зший в неве́жестве.

steeple ['sti:p(ə)l] *n.* колоко́льня; шпиль (*m.*).

cpds. **~chase** *n.* стипл-че́з; **~jack** *n.* верхола́з.

steepness ['sti:pnɪs] *n.* крутизна́.

steer[1] [stɪə(r)] *n.* (*animal*) вол, вычо́к.

steer[2] [stɪə(r)] *v.t.* **1.** (*ship*, *vehicle etc.*) пра́вить (*impf.*) +*i.*; управля́ть (*impf.*) +*i.* **2.**: **~ a course** держа́ть (*impf.*) курс. **3.** (*pers.*, *activity etc.*) вести́ (*det.*); напр|авля́ть, -а́вить; **he ~ed the visitors to their seats** он провёл госте́й на их места́; **~ing committee** руководя́щий комите́т.

v.i. **1.** (*of steersman*) пра́вить (*impf.*) рулём; (*of ship*, *vehicle etc.*): **the car ~s well** э́ту маши́ну легко́ вести́. **2.** (*of pers.*): **~ clear of** избега́ть (*impf.*) +*g.*; сторони́ться (*impf.*) +*g.*

steerage ['stɪərɪdʒ] *n.* (*steering*) рулево́е управле́ние; (*part of ship*) четвёртый класс.

steering ['stɪərɪŋ] *n.* управле́ние (*чем*); управля́ющий механи́зм.

cpds. **~-column** *n.* рулева́я коло́нна; **~-wheel** *n.* (*of car*) руль (*m.*); (*naut.*) штурва́л.

steersman ['stɪəzmən] *n.* рулево́й, шту́рман.

stellar ['stelə(r)] *adj.* звёздный.

stem[1] [stem] *n.* **1.** (*bot.*) сте́бель (*m.*); (*of shrub or tree*) ствол. **2.** (*of wine-glass*) но́жка; (*of tobacco-pipe*) черено́к. **3.** (*gram.*) осно́ва. **4.**: **from ~ to stern** от но́са до кормы́.

v.i. прои|сходи́ть, -зойти́ (*от/из чего*).

stem[2] [stem] *v.t.* **1.** (*lit.*, *fig.*, *check*, *stop*) остан|а́вливать, -ови́ть; (*fig.*, *arrest*, *delay*) заде́рж|ивать, -а́ть. **2.** (*make headway against*) идти́ (*det.*) про́тив+*g.*; сопротивля́ться (*impf.*) +*d.*

stench [stentʃ] *n.* вонь (*no pl.*), смрад (*no pl.*); злово́ние.

stencil ['stensɪl] *n.* (*~-plate*) трафаре́т, шабло́н; (*pattern*) трафаре́т; узо́р по трафаре́ту.

v.t. **1.**: **~ a pattern** рисова́ть, на- узо́р по трафаре́ту; **~ letters** нан|оси́ть, -ести́ бу́квы по трафаре́ту. **2.** (*ornament by ~ling*) трафаре́тить (*impf.*).

stenographer [ste'nɒgrəfə(r)] *n.* стено́граф (*fem.* -и́стка).

stenographic [ˌstenə'græfɪk] *adj.* стенографи́ческий.

stenography [ste'nɒgrəfɪ] *n.* стеногра́фия.

stentorian [ˌsten'tɔ:rɪən] *adj.* громово́й, зы́чный.

step [step] *n.* **1.** (*movement*, *distance*, *sound*, *manner of ~ping*) шаг; **take a ~ forward/back** сде́лать (*pf.*) шаг вперёд/наза́д; **at every ~** на ка́ждом шагу́; **~ by ~** шаг за ша́гом; **within a few ~s of the hotel** в двух шага́х от гости́ницы; **watch your ~!** (*lit.*, *fig.*) осторо́жно!. **2.** (*fig.*, *action*) шаг, ме́ра; **take ~s towards** приня́ть (*pf.*) ме́ры к+*d.*; **my first ~ will be to cut prices** я пе́рвым де́лом добью́сь сниже́ния цен; **what's the next ~?** а тепе́рь что сле́дует де́лать? **3.** (*trace of foot*) след; (*fig.*): **I followed in his ~s** я сле́довал по его́ стопа́м; **retrace one's ~s** возвраща́ться, верну́ться по про́йденному пути́. **4.** (*rhythm of ~*): **keep in ~ with** (*lit.*, *fig.*) идти́ (*det.*) в но́гу с+*i.*; **fall into ~** (*fig.*, *conform*) подчин|я́ться, -и́ться; **fall, get out of ~** сби́ться (*pf.*) с ноги́; **he is out of ~** (*lit.*, *fig.*) он идёт не в но́гу. **5.** (*raised surface*) ступе́нь; **mind the ~!** осторо́жно — ступе́нька!; (*of staircase etc.*) ступе́нька; (*of vehicle*) подно́жка; **flight of ~s** марш (ле́стницы); (*in front of house*) крыльцо́; **fall/run down the ~s** скати́ться/сбежа́ть (*pf.*) по ступе́нькам. **6.** (*pl.*, **~-ladder**; *also* **pair of ~s**) стремя́нка. **7.** (*stage*, *degree*) ста́дия, ступе́нь. **8.** (*dance ~*) па (*nt. indecl.*).

v.t.: **~ a few yards** де́лать, с- не́сколько шаго́в.

v.i. шаг|а́ть, -ну́ть; ступ|а́ть, -и́ть; **~ this way, please** пройди́те сюда́, пожа́луйста!; **~ping-stone** ка́мень для перехо́да (*через ручей и т. п.*); (*fig.*): **a ~ping-stone to success** ступе́нь к успе́ху; **he ~ped into his car** он сел в маши́ну; **~ into the breach** (*fig.*) ри́нуться (*pf.*) на по́мощь; **he ~ped off the train** он сошёл с по́езда; **someone ~ped on my foot** кто́-то наступи́л мне на́ ногу; **~ on it!** (*coll.*) жми!; пошеве́ливайся!; **I ~ped out of his way** я уступи́л ему́ доро́гу; **he ~ped over the threshold** он перешагну́л через поро́г.

with advs.: **~ aside** *v.i.* посторони́ться (*pf.*); (*fig.*) уступи́ть (*pf.*) (доро́гу) друго́му; **~ back** *v.i.* отступ|а́ть, -и́ть; **~ down** *v.i.*: **he ~ped down off the ladder** он спусти́лся с ле́стницы; **he ~ped down in favour of a more experienced man** он уступи́л ме́сто бо́лее о́пытному челове́ку; **~ in** *v.i.*: **won't you ~ in for a moment?** мо́жет, зайдёте на мину́тку?; (*intervene*) вме́ш|иваться, -а́ться; **~ off** *v.i.*: **~ off with the left foot** сде́лать (*pf.*) шаг с ле́вой ноги́; **he ~ped off on the wrong foot** (*fig.*) он с са́мого нача́ла де́йствовал не так; **~ out** *v.i.* вы́йти (*pf.*) (ненадо́лго); **~ up** *v.t.* (*increase*) пов|ыша́ть, -ы́сить; уси́ли|вать, -ть; *v.i.*: **he ~ped up to the platform** он подошёл к трибу́не.

cpds. **~-by-~** *adj.* постепе́нный; (*pol.*, *mil.*) поэта́пный; **~-ladder** *n.* = **~** *n.* **6.**

step- [step] *comb. form*: **~brother** *n.* сво́дный брат; **~child** *n.* (*boy*) па́сынок; (*girl*) па́дчерица; **~daughter** *n.* па́дчерица; **~father** *n.* о́тчим; **~mother** *n.* ма́чеха; **~sister** *n.* сво́дная сестра́; **~son** *n.* па́сынок.

steppe [step] *n.* степь; (*attr.*) степно́й.

stereo ['sterɪəʊ, 'stɪə-] *n.* (*~phonic system*) стереофони́ческая систе́ма; **personal ~** пле́йер.

stereophonic [ˌsterɪəʊ'fɒnɪk, ˌstɪə-] *adj.* стереофони́ческий.

stereoscope ['sterɪəˌskəʊp, 'stɪə-] *n.* стереоско́п.

stereoscopic [ˌsterɪə'skɒpɪk, ˌstɪə-] *adj.* стереоскопи́ческий.

stereotype ['sterɪəʊˌtaɪp, 'stɪə-] *n.* (*typ.*) стереоти́п; (*fig.*) шабло́н; (*attr.*) стереоти́пный.

v.t. стереотипи́ровать (*impf.*, *pf.*); (*fig.*) **~d phrase** шабло́нная фра́за.

sterile ['steraɪl] *adj.* **1.** (*barren*, *unproductive*, *lit.*, *fig.*) беспло́дный; (*fig.*) безрезульта́тный. **2.** (*free from germs*) стери́льный, стерилизо́ванный.

sterility [stə'rɪlɪtɪ] *n.* (*lit.*, *fig.*, *unfruitfulness*) беспло́дие; (*freedom from germs*) стери́льность.

sterilization [ˌsterɪlaɪ'zeɪʃ(ə)n] *n.* стерилиза́ция.

sterilize ['sterɪˌlaɪz] *v.t.* стерилизова́ть (*impf.*, *pf.*).

sterilizer ['sterɪˌlaɪzə(r)] *n.* стерилиза́тор.

sterlet ['stɜ:lɪt] *n.* сте́рлядь.

sterling ['stɜ:lɪŋ] *n.* сте́рлинг; фунт сте́рлингов.

adj. **1.** (*of coin*, *metal etc.*) сте́рлинговый; **pound ~** фунт сте́рлингов; **~ silver** серебро́ устано́вленной про́бы. **2.** (*fig.*, *of solid worth*): **a ~ person** челове́к по́длинного благоро́дства.

stern[1] [stɜ:n] *n.* (*of ship*) корма́; (*attr.*) кормово́й.

stern[2] [stɜ:n] *adj.* (*strict*, *harsh*) стро́гий; (*severe*) суро́вый; (*inflexible*) непрекло́нный.

sternness ['stɜːnnɪs] *n.* стро́гость, суро́вость.

sternum ['stɜːnəm] *n.* груди́на.

steroid ['stɪərɔɪd, 'ste-] *n.* стеро́ид.

stethoscope ['steθə,skəʊp] *n.* стетоско́п.

stevedore ['stiːvə,dɔː(r)] *n.* до́кер; порто́вый гру́зчик.

stew [stjuː] *n.* **1.** (*cul.*) тушёное мя́со. **2.** (*coll.*): **get into a ~** разволнова́ться (*pf.*).

v.t. (*meat, fish, vegetables*) туши́ть, по-; (*fruit*) вари́ть (*impf.*); **~ed fruit** компо́т.

v.i. (*of meat, fish, vegetables*) туши́ться (*impf.*); (*of fruit*) вари́ться (*impf.*).

cpds. **~-pan, ~-pot** *nn.* (ме́лкая) кастрю́ля.

steward ['stjuːəd] *n.* (*of estate, club etc.*) управля́ющий, эконо́м; (*of race-meeting, show etc.*) распоряди́тель (*m.*); (*on ship*) стю́ард; (*on plane*) стю́ард, бортпроводни́к.

stewardess [,stjuːə'des, 'stjuːədɪs] *n.* (*on ship*) стюарде́сса; (*on plane*) стюарде́сса, бортпроводни́ца.

stick[1] [stɪk] *n.* **1.** (*for support, punishment*) па́лка; **(walking-~)** трость; (*pl., for kindling*) хво́рость; **(hockey-~ *etc.*)** клю́шка; (*baton*) (дирижёрская) па́лочка; (*fig.*): **they live in the ~s** (*sl.*) они́ живу́т в захолу́стье; **get hold of the wrong end of the ~** превра́тно поня́ть (*pf.*) что-н.; **the big ~** (*fig.*) поли́тика большо́й дуби́нки. **2.** (*~shaped object*): **~ of chalk** мело́к; **~ of shaving-soap** мы́льная па́лочка; **~ of celery** сте́бель (*m.*) сельдере́я; **~ of dynamite** па́лочка динами́та.

stick[2] [stɪk] *v.t.* **1.** (*insert point of*) втыка́ть, воткну́ть; **I stuck a pin in the map** я воткну́л була́вку в ка́рту. **2.** (*cause to adhere*) приклéи|вать, -ть (*что к чему*); наклéи|вать, -ть (*что на что*); **the stamp was stuck on upside down** ма́рка была́ накле́ена вверх нога́ми; (*affix*): **~ a notice on the door** ве́шать, пове́сить объявле́ние на дверь. **3.** (*coll., put*): **~ that book on the shelf** су́ньте э́ту кни́гу на по́лку; **he stuck his head round the door** он просу́нул го́лову в дверь. **4.** (*coll., endure*) терпе́ть, вы́-; выноси́ть, вы́нести; **I couldn't ~ it any longer** я бо́льше не мог терпе́ть. **5.: be stuck, get stuck** *see v.i.* **5.. 6.** (*coll. uses of pass. with preps.*): **get stuck into** (*make serious start on*) всерьёз за что-н. прин|има́ться, -я́ться; **be stuck with** (*unable to get rid of*) быть не в состоя́нии отде́латься от чего́-н.

v.i. **1.** (*be implanted*): **a dagger ~ing in his back** кинжа́л, торча́щий у него́ в спине́; **there's a nail ~ing into my heel** гвоздь впива́ется мне в пя́тку. **2.** (*remain attached, adhere*) прил|ипа́ть, -и́пнуть (*к чему*); приклéи|ваться, -ться; **this envelope won't ~** э́тот конве́рт не закле́ивается; **these pages have stuck (together)** э́ти страни́цы сли́плись; **~ing-plaster** ли́пкий пла́стырь; **the nickname stuck** э́то про́звище так и удержа́лось (за ним *и т.п.*). **3.** (*cling, cleave*): **~ to a task** рабо́тать не поклада́я рук; **~ to the point** держа́ться (*impf.*) бли́же к де́лу; **~ to one's principles** ост|ава́ться, -а́ться ве́рным свои́м при́нципам; **~ to one's word** держа́ть, с- сло́во; **~ by s.o.** подде́рж|ивать, -а́ть кого́-н. **4.** (*coll., stay*): **are you going to ~ at home all day?** вы собира́етесь торча́ть до́ма весь день? **5.** (*also* **be stuck, get stuck:** *become embedded, fixed, immobilized*) застр|ева́ть, -я́ть; **~ in the mud** зав|яза́ть, -я́знуть в грязи́; **the drawer ~s** я́щик не выдвига́ется.

with advs.: **~ around** *v.i.* (*coll.*) не уходи́ть (*impf.*); **~ down** *v.t.* (*seal*): **have you stuck the envelope down?** вы закле́или конве́рт?; **~ on** *v.t.* (*affix*) приклéи|вать, -ть; **~ out** *v.t.*: **~ one's tongue out** высо́вывать, вы́сунуть язы́к; **~ one's head out** высо́вываться, вы́сунуться; **~ one's neck out** (*fig.*) выска́кивать (*impf.*); (*endure*): **how long can they ~ it out?** как до́лго они́ продéржатся?; *v.i.* (*project*) торча́ть (*impf.*); **a nail is ~ing out of the wall** в стене́ гвоздь торчи́т; **~ together** *v.t.* (*with glue*) склéи|вать, -ть; *v.i.*: **good friends ~ together** настоя́щие друзья́ стоя́т друг за дру́га; **~ up** (*coll.*) *v.t.* (*place on end*) ста́вить, по- торчко́м (*or* на попа́); **our neighbours stuck up a fence** на́ши сосе́ди поста́вили забо́р; **~ up a notice** ве́шать, пове́сить объявле́ние; (*raise*): **~ 'em up!** (*coll.*) ру́ки вверх!; *v.i.* (*protrude upwards*) торча́ть (*impf.*); **his hair was ~ing up** у него́ во́лосы торча́ли во все сто́роны; **~ up for** (*coll.*) (*support*) подде́рж|ивать, -а́ть; (*defend*) заступ|а́ться, -и́ться за (*кого*).

cpds. **~-in-the-mud** *n.* рутинёр; ко́сный челове́к; **~-up** *n.* (*coll.*) налёт, ограбле́ние.

sticker ['stɪkə(r)] *n.* накле́йка, этике́тка.

stickleback ['stɪk(ə)l,bæk] *n.* ко́люшка.

stickler ['stɪklə(r)] *n.* побо́рник.

sticky ['stɪkɪ] *adj.* кле́йкий, ли́пкий; (*viscous*) вя́зкий, тягу́чий; **come to a ~ end** (*coll.*) пло́хо ко́нчить (*pf.*).

stiff [stɪf] *adj.* **1.** (*not flexible or soft*) жёсткий, неги́бкий; **~ collar** жёсткий воротничо́к. **2.** (*not working smoothly*) туго́й; **~ hinges** туги́е пе́тли. **3.** (*of pers. or parts of body*) онеме́лый, окостене́лый; **I have a ~ neck** мне наду́ло в шéю; **he has a ~ leg** у него́ нога́ пло́хо сгиба́ется; **I was ~ with cold** я соверше́нно окочене́л. **4.** (*forceful*) си́льный; **the garrison put up a ~ resistance** гарнизо́н отча́янно сопротивля́лся; **a ~ breeze** кре́пкий ве́тер; **a ~ drink** хоро́ший глото́к спиртно́го. **5.** (*hard to stir or mould*) густо́й. **6.** (*difficult, severe*): **a ~ examination** тру́дный экза́мен; **a ~ climb** тяжёлый подъём; **a ~ price** непоме́рно высо́кая цена́; **he got a ~ sentence** ему́ вы́несли суро́вый пригово́р. **7.** (*formal, constrained*) натя́нутый, чо́порный. **8.** (*pred., coll.*): **he was scared ~** он перепуга́лся на́смерть; **I was bored ~** я чуть не у́мер со ску́ки.

stiffen ['stɪf(ə)n] *v.t.* (*make rigid*) прид|ава́ть, -а́ть жёсткость *+d.*; **collars ~ed with starch** накрахма́ленные воротнички́. **2.** (*make resolute*) прид|ава́ть, -а́ть твёрдость *+d.* **3.** (*strengthen*) укреп|ля́ть, -и́ть.

v.i. (*become rigid*) де́латься, с- жёстким; кочене́ть, о-; костене́ть, о-; (*become stronger*) кре́пнуть (*impf.*); де́латься, с- кре́пче; **opposition is ~ing** сопротивле́ние кре́пнет.

stiffness ['stɪfnɪs] *n.* жёсткость; су́хость; чо́порность; принуждённость.

stifl|e ['staɪf(ə)l] *v.t.* (*smother, suffocate*) души́ть, за-; **it is ~ing in here** здесь ду́шно; **~ing heat** удуша́ющая жара́. **2.** (*e.g. rebellion, feelings, hopes, sobs*) подав|ля́ть, -и́ть; **~e one's laughter** сде́рж|ивать, -а́ть смех.

stigma ['stɪgmə] *n.* **1.** (*imputation, stain*) позо́р, пятно́. **2.** (*relig., med.*) сти́гма, стигма́т. **3.** (*bot.*) ры́льце.

stigmatize ['stɪgmə,taɪz] *v.t.* клейми́ть, за-.

stiletto [stɪ'letəʊ] *n.* стиле́т; **~ heels** гво́здики (*m. pl.*).

still[1] [stɪl] *n.* (*for distilling*) перего́нный куб; виноку́ренная устано́вка.

still[2] [stɪl] *n.* **1.** (*liter.*): **in the ~ of night** в ночно́й тиши́. **2.** (*cin.*) (рекла́мный) кадр.

adj. **1.** (*quiet, hushed, calm*) ти́хий, безмо́лвный; **a ~ evening** ти́хий/безве́тренный ве́чер; **become ~** ум|олка́ть, -о́лкнуть. **2.** (*motionless*) неподви́жный; **sit/stand ~** сиде́ть/стоя́ть (*impf.*) споко́йно; **keep ~!** не шевели́тесь!; споко́йно!; (*US*) (за)молчи́те!; (*to a child*) не верти́сь!; сиди́ ти́хо!; **~ life** (*art*) натюрмо́рт. **3.** (*of wine*) неигри́стый. **4.** (*of water*) гла́дкий, споко́йный.

adv. **1.** (*even now, then; as formerly*) (всё) ещё; и сейча́с; по-пре́жнему; **he ~ doesn't understand** он до сих пор не понима́ет. **2.** (*nevertheless*) тем не ме́нее, всё-таки, всё равно́. **3.** (*with comp.: even, yet*) ещё.

v.t. (*calm*) успок|áивать, -óить.

cpds. **~-birth** *n.* рождéние мёртвого плодá; **~-born** *adj.* мертворождённый.

stillness ['stɪlnɪs] *n.* тишинá.

stilt [stɪlt] *n.* **1.** ходýля; **walk on ~s** ходи́ть (*indet.*) на ходýлях. **2.** (*supporting building*) сваяя.

stilted ['stɪltɪd] *adj.* (*of style etc.*) напы́щенный.

stimulant ['stɪmjʊlənt] *n.* побуди́тель (*m.*), сти́мул; (*med.*) стимуля́тор, стимули́рующее срéдство.

adj. возбуждáющий, стимули́рующий.

stimulat|e ['stɪmjʊˌleɪt] *v.t.* **1.** (*rouse, incite*) побу|ждáть, -ди́ть (*кого + inf. or к чему*); стимули́ровать (*impf., pf.*). **2.** (*excite, arouse*) возбу|ждáть, -ди́ть; **light ~es the optic nerve** свет раздражáет зри́тельный нерв. **3.** (*increase*): **this ~es the action of the heart** э́то уси́ливает сердéчную дéятельность.

stimulation [ˌstɪmjʊ'leɪʃ(ə)n] *n.* (*urging*) побуждéние; поощрéние; (*excitement*) возбуждéние.

stimulus ['stɪmjʊləs] *n.* сти́мул, толчóк; (*incentive*) побуждéние; (*motive force*) дви́жущая си́ла.

sting [stɪŋ] *n.* **1.** (*organ of insect etc.*) жáло. **2.** (*of plant*) жгýчий волосóк; (*of nettle*) ожóг. **3.** (*by insect*) укýс; **I got a ~ on my leg** меня́ чтó-то ужáлило/укуси́ло в нóгу.

v.t. **1.** (*of insect etc.*) жáлить, у-; **he was stung by a bee** егó ужáлила пчелá; (*of plant*) жечь (*impf.*); **the nettles stung his feet** крапи́ва жгла емý нóги; **~ing-nettle** (жгýчая) крапи́ва. **2.** (*of pain, smoke etc.*) обж|игáть, -éчь. **3.** (*pain mentally*) терзáть (*impf.*); **the reproaches stung him** упрёки уязви́ли егó; **~ing words** язви́тельные словá.

v.i. **1.** (*of insect etc.*) жáлиться (*impf.*); (*of plant*) жéчься (*impf.*). **2.** (*feel pain or irritation*) жечь (*impf.*); **the blow made his hand ~** емý жгло рýку от удáра.

cpd. **~-ray** *n.* скат.

stingy ['stɪndʒɪ] *adj.* **1.** (*of pers.*) скупóй; (*coll.*) скáредный. **2.** (*meagre*) скýдный.

stink [stɪŋk] *n.* вонь, зловóние.

v.t.: **~ out** выкýривать, вы́курить.

v.i. воня́ть (*impf.*); смердéть (*impf.*); **the room ~s of onions** в кóмнате воня́ет лýком; **a ~ing cellar** воню́чий подвáл.

stint [stɪnt] *n.* **1.** (*liter., restriction*): **without ~** без предéла; неограни́ченно. **2.** (*fixed amount of work*) урóк; **do one's daily ~** выполня́ть, вы́полнить дневнóй урóк.

v.t. ограни́чи|вать, -ть (*кого в чем*); скупи́ться, по- на+*a.*; **he ~s himself for his children** он откáзывает себé рáди детéй.

stipend ['staɪpend] *n.* (*of clergyman*) жáлованье; (*of student*) стипéндия.

stipendiary [staɪ'pendjərɪ, stɪ-] *adj.* получáющий жáлованье/стипéндию.

stipple ['stɪp(ə)l] *v.t.* гравировáть, на- в пункти́рной манéре; изобра|жáть, -зи́ть пункти́ром.

stipulate ['stɪpjʊˌleɪt] *v.t.* обуслóв|ливать, -ить; огов|áривать, -ори́ть; **at the ~d time** в обуслóвленное врéмя.

stipulation [ˌstɪpjʊ'leɪʃ(ə)n] *n.* (*condition*) услóвие.

stir [stɜː(r)] *n.* **1.** (*act of ~ring*) помéшивание; **give one's tea a ~** помешáть (*pf.*) чай. **2.** (*commotion; movement*) волнéние, движéние; **there was a ~ in the crowd** толпá заволновáлась. **3.** (*sensation*) шум, сенсáция; **the news caused a ~** э́то извéстие надéлало мнóго шýму.

v.t. **1.** (*cause to move*): **the wind ~s the trees** вéтер колы́шет дерéвья; **~ the fire** шуровáть, по- ýголь вками́не; **~ one's tea** размéш|ивать, -áть чай; **~ the soup** мешáть, по- суп. **2.** (*arouse, affect, agitate*) возбу|ждáть, -ди́ть; пробу|ждáть, -ди́ть; волновáть, вз-; **he made a ~ring speech** он вы́ступил с волнýющей рéчью.

v.i.: **something ~red in the undergrowth** чтó-то (за)шевели́лось в кустáх; **the wind ~red in the trees** вéтер шелестéл в дерéвьях.

with adv.: **~ up** *v.t.* (*mix*) смéш|ивать, -áть; (*arouse*): **~ up an interest in sth.** пробу|ждáть, -ди́ть интерéс к чемý-н..

stirrup ['stɪrəp] *n.* стрéмя (*nt.*).

cpds. **~-cup** *n.* прощáльный кýбок; **~-pump** *n.* ручнóй огнетуши́тель.

stitch [stɪtʃ] *n.* **1.** (*sewing etc.*) стежóк; (*med.*) шов; **she learnt a new ~** онá освóила нóвую вя́зку; **put ~es in a wound** на|клáдывать, -ложи́ть швы на рáну. **2.** (*knitting*) пéтля́. **3.** (*pain in side*) колотьё в бокý; **he had us in ~es** (*coll.*) он нас чуть не уморил сó смеху.

v.t. (*sew together*) сши|вáть, -ть; (*esp. med.*) заш|ивáть, -и́ть.

with advs.: **~ on** *v.t.* приш|ивáть, -и́ть; **~ up** *v.t.* (*a garment*) сши|вáть, -ть.

stoat [stəʊt] *n.* горностáй (в лéтнем мехý).

stock [stɒk] *n.* **1.** (*handle, base etc.*): **~ of a rifle** ружéйная лóжа. **2.** (*lineage*) семья́, род, происхождéние; **he comes of good ~** он из хорóшей семьи́. **3.** (*resources, store, supply*) запáс, инвентáрь (*m.*); **in ~** в ассортимéнте; **have sth. in ~** имéть чтó-н. в нали́чии; **take ~** (*lit.*) инвентаризовáть (*impf., pf.*); **take ~ of** (*fig., appraise*) крити́чески оцéн|ивать, -и́ть. **4.** (*of farm*): **(live)~** скот. **5.** (*raw material*) сырьё; **paper ~** бумáжное сырьё. **6.** (*cul.*) (крéпкий) бульóн. **8.** (*comm.*) áкции (*f. pl.*); фóнды (*m. pl.*); **S~ Exchange** би́ржа. **7.** (*pl., for confining offenders*) колóдки (*f. pl.*).

adj. **1.** (*kept in ~, available*) имéющийся в нали́чии. **2.** (*regularly used, hackneyed*) изби́тый, шаблóнный.

v.t. **1.** (*equip, furnish with ~*) снаб|жáть, -ди́ть (*что чем*); оборýдовать (*impf., pf.*). **2.** (*keep in ~*) держáть (*impf.*); имéть (*impf.*) в нали́чии.

v.i.: **~ up: we ~ed up with fuel for the winter** мы запасли́сь тóпливом нá зиму.

cpds. **~-account, ~-book** *nn.* счёт капитáла/товáра; **~broker** *n.* (биржевóй) мáклер; **~-farmer** *n.* скотовóд; **~-farming** *n.* скотовóдство; **~fish** *n.* вя́леная трескá; **~holder** *n.* акционéр; **~-in-trade** *n.* запáс товáров; **promises are the politician's ~-in-trade** обещáния — непремéнный арсенáл политикáна; **~list** *n.* спи́сок товáров в ассортимéнте; **~man** *n.* скотовóд; **~-market** *n.* фóндовая би́ржа; **~pile** *n.* материáльный резéрв, запáс; *v.t.* запас|áть, -ти́ +*a. or g.*; **~-still** *adv.* неподви́жно; **~-taking** *n.* инвентаризáция; **closed for ~-taking** закры́то на учёт; (*fig.*) обзóр, оцéнка, крити́ческий анáлиз; **~yard** *n.* скотопригóнный двор.

stockade [stɒ'keɪd] *n.* частокóл.

stocking ['stɒkɪŋ] *n.* чулóк (*also of horse*); **in one's ~(ed) feet** в одни́х чулкáх/носкáх.

stockist ['stɒkɪst] *n.* рóзничный продавéц (*определённых товаров*).

stocky ['stɒkɪ] *adj.* коренáстый, приземи́стый.

stodgy ['stɒdʒɪ] *adj.* (*of food*) тяжёлый; (*coll., of pers., style etc.*) тяжеловéсный, нýдный.

stoic ['stəʊɪk] *n.* (*of either sex*) стóик.

stoical ['stəʊɪk(ə)l] *adj.* стои́ческий.

stoicism ['stəʊɪˌsɪz(ə)m] *n.* стоици́зм.

stoke [stəʊk] *v.t.* (*also* **~ up**) шуровáть (*impf.*); (*put more fuel on*) загру|жáть, -зи́ть (*топку*).

v.i. **1.** (*act as ~r*) топи́ть (*impf.*). **2.**: **~ up** поддéрж|ивать, -áть огóнь; шуровáть (*impf.*); (*coll., eat heavily*) наж|ирáться, -рáться.

stoker ['stəʊkə(r)] *n.* кочегáр, истопни́к.

stole [stəʊl] *n.* паланти́н.

stolid ['stɒlɪd] *adj.* (*impassive*) бесстрáстный; (*dull*) тупóй.

stomach ['stʌmək] *n.* **1.** (*internal organ*) желу́док; **a pain in the ~** боль в животе́; **on a full ~** сра́зу по́сле еды́; на по́лный желу́док; **on an empty ~** натоща́к; на пусто́й желу́док; **it turns my ~** меня́ тошни́т от э́того. **2.** (*external part of body; belly*) живо́т; **someone kicked me in the ~** кто́-то пнул меня́ в живо́т; **he is getting a large ~** у него́ на́чало появля́ться брюшко́. **3.** (*appetite*): **I have no ~ for rich food** я не люблю́ жи́рного. **4.** (*fig., desire*) жела́ние, охо́та; (*spirit, courage*) дух, хра́брость.

v.t. **1.** (*digest*) перева́р|ивать, -и́ть. **2.** (*fig., tolerate*): **~ an insult** прогл|а́тывать, -оти́ть оби́ду; **I can't ~ him** я его́ не переношу́.

cpds. **~-ache** *n.* ко́лик|и (*pl., g.* —) в животе́; **~-pump** *n.* желу́дочный зонд.

stomp [stɒmp] *v.i.* (*coll., tread heavily*) то́пать, про-.

stone [stəʊn] *n.* **1.** ка́мень (*m.*) (*pl.* ка́мни, каме́нья); **throw a ~ at s.o.** бр|оса́ть, -о́сить ка́мнем в кого́-н.; **I have a ~ in my shoe** у меня́ в боти́нке ка́мешек; **leave no ~ unturned** (*fig.*) испо́льзовать (*impf., pf.*) все возмо́жные сре́дства; **his house is within a ~'s throw of here** до его́ до́ма отсю́да руко́й пода́ть. **2.** (*gem*): **precious ~** драгоце́нный ка́мень (*pl.* ка́мни). **3.** (*rock, material*): **built of local ~** постро́енный из ме́стного ка́мня; **he has a heart of ~** у него́ не се́рдце, а ка́мень; **S~ Age** ка́менный век. **4.** (*of plum etc.*) ко́сточка. **5.** (*med.*) ка́мень (*m., pl.* ка́мни). **6.** (*weight*) сто́ун, стон (*6,35 кг.*).

adj. ка́менный.

v.t. (*pelt with ~s*) поб|ива́ть, -и́ть камня́ми.

cpds. **~-deaf** *adj.* соверше́нно глухо́й; **~mason** *n.* ка́менщик; **~wall** *v.i.* (*fig., refuse to be drawn*) отма́лчиваться (*impf.*); **~work** *n.* (*masonry*) ка́менная кла́дка.

stony ['stəʊnɪ] *adj.* камени́стый; (*fig., unfeeling*) ка́менный; из ка́мня.

stooge [stu:dʒ] (*sl.*) *n.* (*comedian's foil*) партнёр ко́мика; (*deputy of low standing*) подставно́е лицо́.

stool [stu:l] *n.* **1.** (*seat*) табуре́т(ка); **fall between two ~s** оказа́ться (*pf.*) ме́жду двух сту́льев. **2.** (**foot~**) скаме́ечка (для ног). **3.** (*faeces*) стул.

cpd. **~-pigeon** *n.* стука́ч (*fem.* -ка) (*coll.*).

stoop [stu:p] *n.* суту́лость; **he walks with a ~** он суту́лится при ходьбе́.

v.t.: **~ one's shoulders** суту́лить (*impf.*) пле́чи.

v.i. **1.** (*of posture*) суту́литься, с-; **walk with a ~ing gait** суту́литься при ходьбе́; (*bend down*) наг|иба́ться, -ну́ться. **2.** (*condescend*) сни|сходи́ть, -зойти́; (*lower o.s.*) ун|ижа́ться, -и́зиться; **he never ~ed to lying** он никогда́ не унижа́лся до лжи.

stop [stɒp] *n.* **1.** (*halt, halting-place*) остано́вка; **come to a ~** останови́ться (*pf.*); **put a ~ to** положи́ть (*pf.*) коне́ц +*d.*; **bus ~** авто́бусная остано́вка. **2.** (кра́ткое) пребыва́ние; **we made a short ~ in Paris** мы останови́лись ненадо́лго в Пари́же. **3.** (*in telegram*) то́чка (*abbr.* тчк); (*fig.*): **come to a full ~** прийти́ (*pf.*) к концу́. **4.** (*mus., on string*) лад; (*of organ*) реги́стр; **pull out all the ~s** (*fig.*) нажа́ть (*pf.*) на все кно́пки.

v.t. **1.** (*also* **~ up**: *close, plug, seal*) закр|ыва́ть, -ы́ть; зат|ыка́ть, -кну́ть; заде́л|ывать, -ать; **he ~ped his ears when I spoke** он заткну́л у́ши, когда́ я говори́л; **the dentist ~ped three of my teeth** зубно́й врач запломбирова́л мне три зу́ба; **~ a gap** (*fig.*) зап|олня́ть, -о́лнить пробе́л. **2.** (*arrest motion of*) остан|а́вливать, -ови́ть; **he ~ped the car** он останови́л маши́ну; **the thief was ~ped by a policeman** вор был заде́ржан полице́йским; **~ thief!** держи́ во́ра!. **3.** (*arrest progress of; bring to an end*) остан|а́вливать, -ови́ть; заде́рж|ивать, -а́ть; прекра|ща́ть, -ти́ть; **rain ~ped play** дождь сорва́л игру́; **it ought to be ~ped** э́тому на́до положи́ть коне́ц; (*suspend*) приостан|а́вливать, -ови́ть; **I ~ped the cheque** я приостанови́л платёж по э́тому че́ку; (*cancel*) отмен|я́ть, -и́ть; **all leave has been ~ped** все отпуска́ отменены́; (*cut off, disallow, ~ provision of*): **my father ~ped my allowance** оте́ц переста́л выделя́ть мне де́ньги. **4.** (*prevent, hinder*): **~ s.o. from** уде́рж|ивать, -а́ть кого́-н. от+*g.*; не дать (*pf.*) (*кому +inf*); **what is to ~ me going?** что мне помеша́ет пойти́? **5.** (*with gerund: discontinue, leave off*) перест|ава́ть, -а́ть +*inf.*; прекра|ща́ть, -ти́ть +*n. obj.*; **~ teasing the cat!** переста́ньте дразни́ть ко́шку!; **~ telling me what to do!** хва́тит учи́ть меня́ жить!

v.i. **1.** (*come to a halt*) остан|а́вливаться, -ови́ться; **a ~ping train** по́езд, иду́щий с остано́вками; **~!** сто́йте!; **~ a minute!** погоди́те мину́ту! **2.** (*in speaking*) зам|олка́ть, -о́лкнуть; **he ~ped talking** он замолча́л; **he ~ped to light his pipe** он сде́лал па́узу, что́бы раскури́ть тру́бку. **3.** (*cease activity*) перест|ава́ть, -а́ть; конча́ть, ко́нчить; **~ that!** переста́нь!; хва́тит!; дово́льно! **4.** (*come to an end*) прекра|ща́ться, -ти́ться; конча́ться, ко́нчиться; **the rain ~ped** дождь ко́нчился/переста́л/прошёл. **5.** (*stay*): **~ at a hotel** остан|а́вливаться, -ови́ться в гости́нице; **~ at home** ост|ава́ться, -а́ться до́ма; **don't ~ out too long** не заде́рживайтесь надо́лго.

with advs.: **~ by** *v.i.* за|ходи́ть, -йти́; (*in a vehicle*) за|езжа́ть, -е́хать; **~ off** *v.i.* остан|а́вливаться, -ови́ться; **~ up** *v.t.* = **~** *v.t.* **1.**

cpds. **~-cock** *n.* запо́рный кран; **~gap** *n.* (*pers.*) вре́менно заменя́ющий; (*thg.*) вре́менная ме́ра; **it will serve as a ~gap** э́то сойдёт на вре́мя; **~-light** *n.* (*on vehicle*) стоп-сигна́л; **~-light** (*of traffic lights*) кра́сный свет; **~-press** *n.* «в после́днюю мину́ту»; э́кстренное сообще́ние (*в газете*); **~-watch** *n.* секундоме́р.

stoppage ['stɒpɪdʒ] *n.* **1.** (*of work etc.*) прекраще́ние, остано́вка. **2.** (*obstruction*) засоре́ние, заку́порка.

stopper ['stɒpə(r)] *n.* (*of bottle etc.*) про́бка.

stopping ['stɒpɪŋ] *n.* (*in tooth*) пло́мба.

storage ['stɔ:rɪdʒ] *n.* (*storing*) хране́ние; (*method*): **in cold ~** в холоди́льнике; **put into cold ~** (*fig.*) отложи́ть (*pf.*) в до́лгий я́щик (*or* под сукно́); (*space*): **put sth. in(to) ~** сда|ва́ть, -ть что-н. на хране́ние; **take sth. out of ~** брать, взять что-н. со скла́да.

cpds. **~-battery** *n.* аккумуля́торная батаре́я; **~-tank** *n.* запасно́й резервуа́р|бак.

store [stɔ:(r)] *n.* **1.** (*stock, reserve*) запа́с, резе́рв, припа́с; **a great ~ of information** огро́мный запа́с све́дений. **2.** (*pl., supplies*): **military ~s** вое́нное иму́щество; **naval ~s** корабе́льные припа́с|ы (*pl., g.* -ов). **3.** (*warehouse*) склад, храни́лище; **put furniture in ~** сда|ва́ть, -ть ме́бель на хране́ние. **4.** (*US, shop*) магази́н, ла́вка; **department, multiple ~(s)** универма́г; **general ~(s)** магази́н сме́шанных това́ров. **5.** (*value, significance*) значе́ние; **set ~ by** прид|ава́ть, -а́ть значе́ние +*d.*

v.t. **1.** (**~ up**, *set aside*) запас|а́ть, -ти́; нак|а́пливать (*or* нак|опля́ть), -опи́ть. **2.** (*deposit in ~*) сда|ва́ть, -ть на хране́ние. **3.** (*hold*) вме|ща́ть, -сти́ть.

cpds. **~house** *n.* склад, кладова́я, амба́р; **~keeper** *n.* (*mil., nav.*) кладовщи́к; (*shopkeeper*) ла́вочник; **~-room** *n.* кладова́я.

storey ['stɔ:rɪ] *n.* (*US* **story**) эта́ж; **a house of 5 ~s** пятиэта́жный дом; **top ~** ве́рхний эта́ж.

stork [stɔ:k] *n.* а́ист.

storm [stɔ:m] *n.* **1.** бу́ря; (*thunder ~*) гроза́; (*snow ~*) мете́ль, вью́га, бура́н; **~ in a teacup** (*fig.*) бу́ря в стака́не воды́. **2.** (*naut.*) (жесто́кий) шторм. **3.** (*fig., hail, shower, volley*) град, ли́вень (*m.*), залп; **a ~ of arrows** град стрел; (*of emotion etc.*): **~ of applause** взрыв аплодисме́нтов; **~ of abuse** град оскорбле́ний. **5.** (*assault*) штурм; **take a town by ~**

брать, взять го́род штýрмом.

v.t. (*mil.*) штурмова́ть (*impf.*); брать, взять при́ступом.

v.i. (*of wind etc.*) бушева́ть (*impf.*); (*fig.*, *rage*) бушева́ть (*impf.*); ~ **at s.o.** крича́ть, на- на кого́-н.; **he ~ed out of the room** он вы́бежал из ко́мнаты в гне́ве.

cpds. **~-cloud** *n.* грозова́я ту́ча; **~-trooper** *n.* штурмови́к; **~-troops** *n.* штурмовы́е войска́.

stormy ['stɔ:mɪ] *adj.* бу́рный (*also fig.*); ~ **wind** штормово́й ве́тер; ~ **weather** непого́да; **a ~ sky** грозово́е не́бо.

story[1] ['stɔ:rɪ] *n.* **1.** (*tale*, *account*, *history*) ска́зка, расска́з, исто́рия; **tell a ~** расска́з|ывать, -а́ть ска́зку; **short ~** расска́з, нове́лла; **funny ~** анекдо́т; **a good ~** заба́вная исто́рия; **it's a long ~** э́то до́лгая пе́сня; **to cut a long ~ short** коро́че говоря́; **that's quite another ~** э́то совсе́м друго́е де́ло; **the ~ goes** говоря́т. **2.** (*newspaper report*) отчёт, статья́. **3.** (*plot*) фа́була, сюже́т. **4.** (*coll.*, *untruth*) исто́рия, вы́думка, ложь; **tell a ~** врать, на-.

cpds. **~-book** *n.* сбо́рник расска́зов; **~-line** *n.* фа́була; **~-teller** *n.* расска́зчи|к (*fem.* -ца).

story[2] ['stɔ:rɪ] *n.* = **storey**

stout [staʊt] *n.* (*beer*) кре́пкий по́ртер.

adj. **1.** (*strong*) кре́пкий, про́чный. **2.** (*resolute*) реши́тельный; (*sturdy*) си́льный; (*staunch*) сто́йкий; **offer ~ resistance** ока́з|ывать, -а́ть упо́рное сопротивле́ние. **3.** (*corpulent*) по́лный, доро́дный; **get, grow ~** полне́ть, по-/рас-.

cpd. **~-hearted** *adj.* сто́йкий, му́жественный.

stove [stəʊv] *n.* печь, пе́чка; (*for cooking*) ку́хонная плита́.

cpd. **~-pipe** *n.* дымохо́д.

stow [stəʊ] *v.t.* укла́дывать, уложи́ть; **I ~ed the trunk (away) in the attic** я убра́л сунду́к на черда́к.

v.i. ~ **away** (*on ship*) е́хать (*det.*) за́йцем.

cpd. **~away** *n.* безбиле́тный пассажи́р, «за́яц».

strabismus [strə'bɪzməs] *n.* страби́зм, косогла́зие.

straddle ['stræd(ə)l] *v.t.* охва́т|ывать, -и́ть; **~ a fence** сиде́ть (*impf.*) верхо́м на забо́ре.

v.i. (*stand/sit with feet apart*) стоя́ть/сиде́ть (*impf.*), широко́ расста́вив но́ги.

strafe [strɑ:f, streɪf] *v.t.* обстре́л|ивать, -я́ть.

straggl|e ['stræg(ə)l] *v.i.*: **the children ~ed home from school** де́ти бре́ли/тащи́лись из шко́лы домо́й; **a wisp of hair ~ed** небольша́я прядь воло́с вы́билась из приче́ски; **a ~ing line of houses** беспоря́дочный ряд домо́в; **a bush with ~ing shoots** куст с торча́щими побе́гами.

straggler ['stræglə(r)] *n.* отста́вший.

straggly ['stræglɪ] *adj.* беспоря́дочный, растрёпанный.

straight [streɪt] *n.* (*of racecourse*): **the ~** (после́дняя) пряма́я.

adj. **1.** прямо́й; **in a ~ line** пря́мо в ряд; **she had ~ hair** у неё бы́ли прямы́е во́лосы; **I couldn't keep a ~ face** я не мог удержа́ться от улы́бки. **2.** (*level*) ро́вный; **are the pictures ~?** карти́ны вися́т ро́вно?; (*neat*, *in order*) в поря́дке; **he never puts his room ~** он никогда́ не убира́ет свою́ ко́мнату; **put one's hat ~** попр|авля́ть, -а́вить шля́пу; **put the record ~** (*fig.*) внести́ (*pf.*) попра́вку; **let's get this ~** дава́йте внесём определённость по э́тому вопро́су. **3.** (*direct*, *honest*) прямо́й, че́стный; **~ fight** че́стный бой. **4.** (*undiluted*) неразба́вленный; (*unbroken*; *in a row*): **ten ~ wins** де́сять вы́игрышей подря́д.

adv. **1.** пря́мо; **he can't walk ~** он не мо́жет идти́ по прямо́й; **sit (up) ~!** сиди́(те); **keep ~ on!** иди́те пря́мо!; (*directly*): **I am going ~ to Paris** я е́ду пря́мо в Пари́ж; **I told him ~ (out)** я сказа́л ему́ пря́мо. **2.** (*in the right direction or manner*): **he can't shoot ~** он не уме́ет (ме́тко) стреля́ть; **he promised to go ~ in future** он обеща́л впредь вести́ себя́ че́стно; **I can't think ~** я не могу́ сосредото́читься. **3.**: **~ away, off** сра́зу, то́тчас.

cpds. **~forward** *adj.* прямо́й; (*honest*) че́стный; (*uncomplicated*) просто́й; **~forwardness** *n.* прямота́; че́стность; простота́.

straighten ['streɪt(ə)n] *v.t.* **1.** выпрямля́ть, вы́прямить; **he ~ed his back** он вы́прямился; он распрями́л спи́ну. **2.** (*put in order*) прив|оди́ть, -ести́ в поря́док; ула́|живать, -дить; **I will try to ~ things out** я постара́юсь всё ула́дить.

v.i. выпрямля́ться, вы́прямиться; распрям|ля́ться, -и́ться; ула́|живаться, -диться.

strain [streɪn] *n.* **1.** (*tension*) натяже́ние; **the ~s of modern life** напряжённость/стресс совреме́нной жи́зни; (*nervous fatigue*): **he is suffering from ~** у него́ не́рвное переутомле́ние; (*muscular ~*) растяже́ние (жил); (*effort*, *exertion*) напряже́ние. **2.** (*of music*) напе́в, мело́дия; **we heard the ~s of a waltz** до нас доноси́лись зву́ки ва́льса. **3.** (*breed*, *stock*) род, происхожде́ние; (*of animals*, *plants*) поро́да; **a hardy ~ of rose** выно́сливый сорт роз.

v.t. **1.** (*exert*) напр|яга́ть, -я́чь; **I ~ed my ears to catch his words** я напря́г слух, что́бы улови́ть его́ слова́; **we must ~ every nerve** нам сле́дует напря́чь все си́лы. **2.** (*over-exert*): **~ one's eyes** по́ртить (*impf.*) зре́ние; **~ a tendon** растя́|гивать, -ну́ть сухожи́лие; **don't ~ yourself** смотри́те, не надорви́тесь. **3.** (*overtax*, *presume too much on*): **~ s.o.'s patience** испы́тывать (*impf.*) чьё-н. терпе́ние; **~ed relations** натя́нутые отноше́ния. **4.** (*filter*, *also ~ off*) проце́|живать, -ди́ть; отце́|живать, -ди́ть.

v.i. (*exert o.s.*) напр|яга́ться, -я́чься; **~ at a rope** тяну́ть (*impf.*) верёвку изо всех сил; **~ at the leash** (*of hound*) рва́ться (*impf.*) с поводка́; **plants ~ towards the light** расте́ния тя́нутся к све́ту.

strainer ['streɪnə(r)] *n.* си́то, си́течко, цеди́лка.

strait [streɪt] *n.* **1.** (*of water*) проли́в; **S~ of Dover** Ду́врский проли́в. **2.** (*pl.*, *liter.*, *difficult situation*; *need*) затрудни́тельное положе́ние; **in dire ~s** в отча́янном положе́нии.

cpds. **~-jacket** *n.* смири́тельная руба́шка; **~-laced** *adj.* (*fig.*) пурита́нский.

straitened ['streɪtənd] *adj.*: **~ circumstances** стеснённые обстоя́тельства.

strand[1] [strænd] *n.* (*shore*) побере́жье, пляж.

v.t. (*ship or person*) сажа́ть, посади́ть на мель; **I was ~ed in Paris** я очути́лся в Пари́же соверше́нно на мели́.

v.i. (*of ship*) сади́ться, сесть на мель.

strand[2] [strænd] *n.* (*fibre*, *thread*) прядь, нить.

strange [streɪndʒ] *adj.* **1.** (*unfamiliar*, *unknown*) незнако́мый. **2.** (*foreign*, *alien*) чужо́й. **3.** (*remarkable*, *unusual*) стра́нный, необыкнове́нный, необы́чный; **how ~ that you should ask that** как стра́нно, что вы (и́менно) об э́том спроси́ли!; **~ to say (*or* ~ly enough) he loves her** как (э́то) ни стра́нно, он лю́бит её; **she wears the ~est clothes** она́ чудно́ одева́ется.

strangeness ['streɪndʒnɪs] *n.* стра́нность.

stranger ['streɪndʒə(r)] *n.* **1.** (*unknown person*) незнако́м|ец (*fem.* -ка); посторо́нний (челове́к); **you're quite a ~** вы совсе́м пропа́ли! **2.**: **a ~ to** (*unfamiliar with*) незнако́мый с+*i.* **3.** (*alien*, *foreigner*): **I am a ~ here** я здесь чужо́й.

strangle ['stræŋg(ə)l] *v.t.* души́ть, за-; удави́ть (*pf.*).

cpd. **~hold** *n.* (*lit.*, *fig.*): **have a ~ hold on s.o.** держа́ть (*impf.*) кого́-н. мёртвой хва́ткой.

strangulation [,stræŋgjʊ'leɪʃ(ə)n] *n.* удуше́ние; (*med.*) ущемле́ние.

strap [stræp] *n.* **1.** реме́нь (*m.*), ремешо́к; (*of dress*) брете́лька. **2.** (*thrashing*): **give s.o. the ~** поро́ть, вы́- кого́-н. ремнём; **get the ~** получ|а́ть, -и́ть по́рку (ремнём).

v.t. **1.** (*secure with ~*) стя́|гивать, -ну́ть ремнём; **he was ~ped to a chair** он был привя́зан к сту́лу ремня́ми; (*bind wound etc.*): бинтова́ть, за-. **2.** (*beat with ~*) поро́ть, вы́- ремнём.

strapping ['stræpɪŋ] *adj.* ро́слый, здоро́вый.

stratagem ['strætədʒəm] *n.* уло́вка; (вое́нная) хи́трость.

strategic [strə'ti:dʒɪk] *adj.* стратеги́ческий.

strategist ['strætɪdʒɪst] *n.* страте́г.

strategy ['strætɪdʒɪ] *n.* страте́гия.

stratification [ˌstrætɪfɪ'keɪʃ(ə)n] *n.* стратифика́ция, расслое́ние, напластова́ние, наслое́ние.

stratify ['strætɪˌfaɪ] *v.t.* (*arrange in strata*) насл|а́ивать, -ои́ть; (*deposit in strata*) напласто́в|ывать, -а́ть.

stratosphere ['strætəˌsfɪə(r)] *n.* стратосфе́ра.

stratospheric [ˌstrætə'sferɪk] *adj.* стратосфе́рный.

strat|um ['strɑ:təm, 'streɪ-] *n.* **1.** (*geol.*) пласт, слой, напластова́ние. **2.: social ~a** слой о́бщества.

straw [strɔ:] *n.* **1.** (*collect.*) соло́ма; (*attr.*) соло́менный; **~ hat** соло́менная шля́п(к)а. **2.** (*single ~*) соло́мин(к)а; **drink lemonade through a ~** пить (*impf.*) лимона́д че́рез соло́минку; **catch, clutch at a ~** (*fig.*) хвата́ться, схвати́ться за соло́минку; **that was the last ~** э́то бы́ло после́дней ка́плей.

strawberry ['strɔ:bərɪ] *n.* (*pl.*, *collect.*) клубни́ка; (*wild*) земляни́ка; **a ~** я́года клубни́ки/земляни́ки; (*attr.*) клубни́чный, земляни́чный.

cpd. **~-mark** *n.* роди́мое пятно́.

stray [streɪ] *adj.* **1.** (*wandering*, *lost*) заблуди́вшийся, бездо́мный; **~ dog** бродя́чая соба́ка; (*as n.*): **waifs and ~s** беспризо́рники (*m. pl.*). **2.** (*sporadic*): **a ~ bullet** шальна́я пу́ля.

v.i. **1.** (*wander*, *deviate*) заблуди́ться (*pf.*); сби́ться (*pf.*) с пути́; **the sheep ~ed on to the road** о́вцы забрели́ на доро́гу. **2.** (*roam*, *rove*) броди́ть (*impf.*); стра́нствовать (*impf.*). **3.** (*of thoughts*, *affections*) блужда́ть (*impf.*); **~ from the subject** отклон|я́ться, -и́ться от те́мы.

streak [stri:k] *n.* **1.** поло́ска, прожи́лка; **~ of lightning** вспы́шка мо́лнии; **like a ~ of lightning** (*fig.*) с быстрото́й мо́лнии. **2.** (*fig.*, *trace*, *tendency*) черта́, накло́нность; **he has a cruel ~** в его́ хара́ктере есть жесто́кая жи́лка.

v.t.: **~ed with red** с кра́сными поло́сками.

v.i. (*coll.*, *move rapidly*) прон|оси́ться, -ести́сь.

streaky ['stri:kɪ] *adj.* полоса́тый; с просло́йками.

stream [stri:m] *n.* **1.** (*rivulet*, *brook*) руче́й, ре́чка. **2.** (*flow*) пото́к, тече́ние; **~ of blood/water** пото́к кро́ви/воды́; **in a ~ (*or* ~s)** пото́ком, ручья́ми (*m. pl.*); (*fig.*) пото́к; **a ~ of people** людско́й пото́к; **~ of abuse** пото́к руга́тельств (*nt. pl.*). **3.** (*lit.*, *fig.*, *current*, *direction of flow*): **with the ~** по тече́нию; **against the ~** про́тив тече́ния. **4.** (*in school*): **he was put in the A ~** он попа́л в класс «А».

v.t. **1.: his wounds ~ed blood** из его́ ран струи́лась кровь. **2.: the pupils were ~ed** ученико́в распредели́ли по кла́ссам (в зави́симости от спосо́бностей); **~ing** *n.* систе́ма пото́ков.

v.i. **1.** (*flow*) течь, струи́ться, ли́ться (*all impf.*); **blood was ~ing from his nose** и́з носу у него́ текла́ кровь; **refugees were ~ing over the fields** бе́женцы нескончае́мым пото́ком шли по поля́м; **he had a ~ing cold** у него́ был стра́шный на́сморк. **2.: with hair ~ing in the wind** с развева́ющимися на ветру́ (*or* по ве́тру) волоса́ми.

cpds. **~line** *v.t.* прид|ава́ть, -а́ть обтека́емую фо́рму +*d.*; (*fig.*) упро|ща́ть, -сти́ть; **~lined** *adj.* стро́йный; упрощённый; **~lined car** автомоби́ль (*m.*) обтека́емой фо́рмы.

streamer ['stri:mə(r)] *n.* вы́мпел; ле́нта.

street [stri:t] *n.* **1.** у́лица; **don't play in the ~** (*roadway*) не игра́й на мостово́й; **man in the ~** обыва́тель (*m.*); просто́й челове́к; **they were turned out on to the ~** их вы́селили и́з дому; **this is just up your ~** э́то как раз по ва́шей ча́сти. **2.** (*attr.*) у́личный; **~ arab** беспризо́рник; **at ~ level** на пе́рвом этаже́.

cpds. **~car** *n.* (*US*) трамва́й; **~-lamp** *n.* у́личный фона́рь; **~sweeper** подмета́льщик; (*machine*) маши́на для подмета́ния у́лиц; **~-walker** *n.* проститу́тка; **~wise** *adj.* до́шлый, у́шлый.

strength [streŋθ, streŋkθ] *n.* **1.** си́ла; **~ of mind/will** си́ла ду́ха/во́ли; **~ of purpose** реши́мость: **the ~ of a fortress** мощь/непристу́пность кре́пости; (*of structure or solution*): **~ of a beam/wine** кре́пость ба́лки/вина́; (*of material*) про́чность; **I haven't the ~ to go on** я не в си́лах да́льше идти́; **recover, regain one's ~** восстан|а́вливать, -ови́ть си́лы; **acquire new ~, build up one's ~** наб|ира́ться, -ра́ться сил. **2.** (*basis*): **on the ~ of** в си́лу +*g.*; на основа́нии +*g.* **3.** (*numerical ~*) чи́сленность; **in full ~** в по́лном соста́ве; **bring up to ~** (до)укомплекто́вать (*pf.*).

strengthen ['streŋθ(ə)n, -ŋkθ(ə)n] *v.t.* укреп|ля́ть, -и́ть; уси́ли|вать, -ть; **~ s.o.'s hand** укреп|ля́ть, -и́ть чью-н. пози́цию; поддержа́ть (*pf.*) кого́-н.

v.i. укреп|ля́ться, -и́ться; уси́ли|ваться, -ться.

strenuous ['strenjʊəs] *adj.* (*of effort*) напряжённый, уси́ленный; (*of work*) тру́дный.

streptococcus [ˌstreptə'kɒkəs] *n.* стрептоко́кк.

stress [stres] *n.* **1.** (*tension*) напряже́ние; (*pressure*) давле́ние; нажи́м; **time of ~** тяжёлое вре́мя; **subject s.o. to ~** ока́з|ывать, -а́ть на кого́-н. давле́ние; (*psych.*) стресс; **a situation of ~** стре́ссовая ситуа́ция. **2.** (*emphasis*) ударе́ние; **lay ~ on** (*lit.*, *fig.*) де́лать, с- ударе́ние на+*p.*; **the ~ is on the second syllable** ударе́ние па́дает на второ́й слог.

v.t. **1.** (*subject to ~*) подв|ерга́ть, -е́ргнуть напряже́нию. **2.** (*emphasize*) подчёрк|ивать, -ну́ть; де́лать, с- упо́р на+*a.* **3.** (*accentuate*) ста́вить, поударе́ние на+*a.*

stressful ['stresfʊl] *adj.* напряжённый; стре́ссовый.

stretch [stretʃ] *n.* **1.** (*extension*) вытя́гивание, растя́гивание; **the cat woke and gave a ~** ко́шка просну́лась и потяну́лась. **2.** (*elasticity*) растяжи́мость; **the rubber has no ~ in it** рези́на не тя́нется; **~ fabric** эласти́чная мате́рия; **~ socks** безразме́рные носки́. **3.** (*expanse*, *tract*) протяже́ние, простра́нство; **a dusty ~ of road** пы́льный отре́зок доро́ги. **4.** (*of time*): **he works 8 hours at a ~** он рабо́тает во́семь часо́в подря́д. **5.** (*interval of time*) срок.

v.t. **1.** (*lengthen*) вытя́гивать, вы́тянуть; (*broaden*) растя́|гивать, -ну́ть. **2.** (*pull to fullest extent*): **~ a rope between two posts** натя́|гивать, -ну́ть верёвку ме́жду двумя́ столба́ми; **~ o.s.** потя́|гиваться, -ну́ться; **~ one's legs** разм|ина́ть, -я́ть но́ги; **I found him ~ed (out) on the floor** я заста́л его́ распростёртым на полу́. **3.** (*strain*, *exert*): **~ a point** де́лать, с- натя́жку; **~ the truth** преувели́чи|вать, -ть.

v.i. **1.** (*be elastic*) растя́|гиваться, -ну́ться. **2.** (*extend*) прост|ира́ться, -ере́ться; (*of time*) дли́ться, про-. **3.** (*reach*): **the rope will not ~ to the post** верёвку не дотяну́ть до столба́; **a rainbow ~ed across the sky** ра́дуга простёрлась по не́бу.

stretcher ['stretʃə(r)] *n.* носи́л|ки (*pl.*, *g.* -ок); **~ case** лежа́чий/носи́лочный ра́неный.

cpd. **~-bearer** *n.* санита́р-носи́льщик.

strew [stru:] *v.t.* **1.** (*scatter*) разбр|а́сывать, -оса́ть. **2.** (*cover by scattering*) пос|ыпа́ть, -ы́пать; ус|ыпа́ть, -ы́пать.

stricken ['strɪkən] *adj.* (*lit.*, *fig.*) ра́неный; поражённый; **~ with fear** поражённый у́жасом; **~ with paralysis** разби́тый параличо́м.

strict [strɪkt] *adj.* **1.** (*precise*) стро́гий, то́чный; **~ accuracy** абсолю́тная то́чность. **2.** (*stringent*): **in**

~ confidence в строжа́йшей та́йне. **3.** (*rigorous, stern*) стро́гий, взыска́тельный.

stricture ['strɪktʃə(r)] *n.* осужде́ние.

stride [straɪd] *n.* (*long pace, step*) (широ́кий) шаг; (*fig.*): **science has made great ~s** нау́ка сде́лала больши́е успе́хи; **he took the exam in his ~** он с лёгкостью одоле́л экза́мен; **he took the news in his ~** он споко́йно при́нял э́ту но́вость; **get into one's ~** входи́ть, войти́ в колею́.

v.i. шага́ть (*impf.*); **he strode across the ditch** он шагну́л че́рез (*or* перешагну́л) кана́ву.

stridency ['straɪd(ə)nsɪ] *n.* ре́зкость, пронзи́тельность.

strident ['straɪd(ə)nt] *adj.* ре́зкий, пронзи́тельный.

strife [straɪf] *n.* борьба́, вражда́, спор.

strike [straɪk] *n.* **1.** (*of workers*) забасто́вка; **general ~** всео́бщая забасто́вка; **~ committee** ста́чечный комите́т; **~ pay** посо́бие басту́ющим; **be on ~** бастова́ть (*impf.*); **go (out) on ~** забастова́ть (*pf.*); объяв|ля́ть, -и́ть забасто́вку. **2.** (*of gold, oil etc.*) нахо́дка/откры́тие месторожде́ния. **3.** (*attack; blow*) нападе́ние; уда́р; налёт.

v.t. **1.** (*hit*) уд|аря́ть, -а́рить (*чем по чему; что обо что; кого чем*); **he struck the table with his hand** он уда́рил руко́й по́ столу; **he struck his head on the table** он уда́рился голово́й об стол; **the bullet struck the tree** пу́ля попа́ло в де́рево; **the ship struck a rock** кора́бль наскочи́л на скалу́; **she struck the knife out of his hand** она́ вы́била нож у него́ из руки́. **2.** (*deliver*): **~ a blow** нан|оси́ть, -ести́ уда́р (*кому*); **who struck the first blow?** кто на́чал (дра́ку/ссо́ру)? **3.** (*fig., instil*) всел|я́ть, -и́ть; **the lion's roar struck panic into them** льви́ный рёв вы́звал у них пани́ческий страх. **4.** (*fig., impress*) пора|жа́ть, -зи́ть; каза́ться, по- *+d.*; **he was struck by her beauty** он был поражён её красото́й; **the idea ~s me as a good one** э́та мысль ка́жется мне хоро́шей; **an idea struck me** мне пришла́ в го́лову мысль. **5.** (*fig., come upon, find, discover*) напада́ть, напа́сть на*+a.*; нат|ыка́ться, -кну́ться на*+a.*; на|ходи́ть, -йти́; откр|ыва́ть, -ы́ть; **I struck a serious difficulty** я столкну́лся с серьёзным затрудне́нием; **they struck oil** они откры́ли нефтяно́е месторожде́ние; **~ gold** на|ходи́ть, -йти́ зо́лото; **~ it rich** (*coll.*) напа́сть (*pf.*) на жи́лу. **6.**: **~ a match** чи́ркнуть (*pf.*) спи́чкой; **~ a coin** выбива́ть, вы́бить (*or* чека́нить, от-) моне́ту; **~ a chord** (*fig.*): **his name ~s a chord** его́ и́мя мне что́-то напомина́ет; **~ a note** (*lit.*) уда́рить (*pf.*) по кла́више/струне́; (*fig.*) взять (*pf.*) тон; **~ root** пус|ка́ть, -ти́ть ко́рни. **7.** (*of bell, clock etc.*) бить (*impf.*), отбива́ть (*impf.*); **the clock struck midnight** часы́ уда́рили по́лночь. **8.** (*arrive at*): **~ a bargain** заключ|а́ть, -и́ть сде́лку; **~ a balance** (*fig.*) на|ходи́ть, -йти́ компроми́сс; **~ a happy medium** найти́ (*pf.*) золоту́ю середи́ну. **9.** (*suddenly make*): **~ s.o. blind** ослеп|ля́ть, -и́ть кого́-н; **~ s.o. dumb** (*fig.*) ошара́шить (*pf.*) кого́-н.; **he was struck dumb** у него́ язы́к прли́п к го́ртани; он онеме́л; **~ s.o. dead** порази́ть (*pf.*) кого́-н. на́ смерть. **10.** (*assume*): **~ an attitude** вста|ва́ть, -ть в по́зу. **11.** (*lower, take down*): **~ one's flag** спус|ка́ть, -ти́ть флаг; **~ camp** сн|има́ться, -я́ться с ла́геря.

v.i. **1.** (*hit*) уд|аря́ть, -а́рить; **~ while the iron is hot** (*prov.*) куй желе́зо, пока́ горячо́; **~** (*aim a blow*) **at s.o.** зама́х|иваться, -ну́ться на кого́-н.; (*fig.*): **~ at the root of the trouble** искорен|я́ть, -и́ть исто́чник зла. **2.**: **~ against** (*collide with*) уд|аря́ться, -а́риться о*+a.* **3.** (*direct one's course; penetrate*): **damp ~s through the walls** сы́рость проника́ет сквозь стены́; **the insult struck home** оскорбле́ние заде́ло его́ за живо́е. **4.** (*take root*) прин|има́ться, -я́ться. **5.** (*of clock etc.*) бить, про-. **6.**: **the match won't ~** спи́чка не зажига́ется. **7.** (*go on ~*) бастова́ть, за-.

with advs.: **~ back** *v.i.* (*retaliate*) нанести́ (*pf.*) отве́тный уда́р; **~ down** *v.t.* (*fell*) сби|ва́ть, -ть с ног; сра|жа́ть, -зи́ть; (*of illness etc.*) сра|жа́ть, -зи́ть; **~ off** *v.t.* отруб|а́ть, -и́ть; **~ s.o. (or s.o.'s name) off (list etc.)** вычёркивать, вы́черкнуть кого́-н. (*or* чьё-н. и́мя) (из спи́ска); **~ out** *v.t.* (*delete*): **~ out a word** вычёркивать, вы́черкнуть сло́во; *v.i.* (*aim blow*) нан|оси́ть, -ести́ уда́р; (*fig.*): **~ out on one's own** пойти́ (*pf.*) свои́м путём; **~ up** *v.t. & i.*: **~ up a song** затя́|гивать, -ну́ть пе́сню; **~ up an acquaintance** завя́з|ывать, -а́ть знако́мство; *v.i.* (*begin playing/singing*) заигра́ть, запе́ть (*both pf.*).

cpd. **~-breaker** *n.* штрейкбре́хер.

striker ['straɪkə(r)] *n.* (*person on strike*) забасто́вщи|к (*fem.* -ца).

striking ['straɪkɪŋ] *adj.* **1.** (*forceful*) порази́тельный; **~ resemblance** рази́тельное схо́дство; (*remarkable*) замеча́тельный. **2.**: **~ distance** досяга́емость, расстоя́ние возмо́жного уда́ра; **~ force** (*mil.*) уда́рная гру́ппа.

string [strɪŋ] *n.* **1.** верёвка, бечёвка; **ball of ~** клубок бечёвки/верёвки; **~ bag** се́тка, (*coll.*) аво́ська; **~ vest** се́тка; (*of apron etc.*) завя́зка, шнуро́к; (*fig.*): **have s.o. on a ~** держа́ть (*impf.*) кого́-н. на поводу́; **pull ~s** наж|има́ть, -а́ть на все кно́пки; **with no ~s attached** (*fig.*) без каки́х бы то ни́ было усло́вий. **2.** (*of mus. instrument, racket*) струна́; **the ~s** (*of orchestra*) стру́нные инструме́нты (*m. pl.*). **3.** (*~y substance, fibre e.g. in bean*) волокно́; **~ bean** (стручко́вая) фасо́ль; (*in meat*) жи́ла. **4.** (*set of objects*): **~ of beads** бу́с|ы (*pl., g.* —); **~ of pearls** ни́тка же́мчуга; **~ of onions** свя́зка лу́ка; **~ of boats/medals** ряд ло́док/меда́лей; **~ of cars/tourists** верени́ца автомоби́лей/тури́стов; **~ of oaths** пото́к руга́тельств.

v.t. **1.** (*furnish with ~*): **~ a racket** натя́|гивать, -ну́ть стру́ны на раке́тку. **2.** (*thread on ~*) низа́ть (*or* нани́зывать), на-.

with advs.: **~ along** *v.t.* (*coll., deceive*) води́ть (*impf.*) за́ нос; **~ out** *v.t. & i.* (*extend*) растя́|гивать(ся), -ну́ть(ся); **~ together** *v.t.* низа́ть, на-; **~ up** *v.t.* (*coll., execute by hanging*) ве́шать, пове́сить; вздёрнуть (*pf.*) на ви́селицу; (*make tense*): **I am all strung up** я в большо́м напряже́нии.

stringed [strɪŋd] *adj.* стру́нный.

stringency ['strɪndʒ(ə)nsɪ] *n.* стро́гость.

stringent ['strɪndʒ(ə)nt] *adj.* (*strict, precise*) стро́гий, то́чный.

stringy ['strɪŋɪ] *adj.* **1.** (*fibrous*) волокни́стый; жили́стый мя́со. **2.** (*of glue*) тягу́чий, вя́зкий.

strip[1] [strɪp] *n.* полоса́; (*of cloth*) поло́ска, ле́нта; **~ of land** поло́ска земли́; **a ~ of wood** деревя́нная пла́нка/ре́йка; **~ cartoon** расска́з в карти́нках; **~ lighting** нео́новое освеще́ние.

strip[2] [strɪp] *v.t.* (*tear off*) сдира́ть, содра́ть; **the bark was ~ped from the tree** с де́рева содра́ли кору́; **she ~ped the blankets off the bed** она́ сняла́ одея́ла с крова́ти; **a tool for ~ping paint** инструме́нт для соска́бливания кра́ски. **2.** (*denude*) разд|ева́ть, -е́ть; **he was ~ped of his clothes** с него́ сорва́ли/сня́ли оде́жду; его́ разде́ли; **the room was ~ped bare** из ко́мнаты вы́несли всю ме́бель; **~ (down) a machine/weapon** раз|бира́ть, -обра́ть маши́ну/ору́жие; (*fig., deprive*) лиш|а́ть, -и́ть (*кого чего*); **he was ~ped of his rank** его́ лиши́ли зва́ния.

v.i.: **~ (naked), ~ off** разд|ева́ться, -е́ться (донага́).

cpds. **~-club** *n.* клуб с пока́зом стрипти́за; **~-tease** *n.* стрипти́з.

stripe [straɪp] *n.* **1.** полоса́, поло́ска. **2.** (*mil.*) наши́вка, шевро́н; **get a ~** получ|а́ть, -и́ть очере́дное зва́ние.

striped [straɪpt] *adj.* (*e.g. tiger*) полоса́тый; **~ fabric**

матéрия в полóску, полосáтая матéрия.

stripling ['strɪplɪŋ] *n.* юнéц.

stripper ['strɪpə(r)] *n.* (*solvent*) раствóр для удалéния крáски; (*artiste*) исполни́тельница стрипти́за.

stripy ['straɪpɪ] *adj.* полосáтый, в полóску.

strive [straɪv] *v.i.* стреми́ться (*impf.*) (**after, for:** к+*d.*); **they strove for victory** они́ стреми́лись к побéде; **I strove to understand what he said** я старáлся поня́ть, что он говори́т.

stroke[1] [strəʊk] *n.* **1.** удáр; **six ~s of the cane** шесть удáров пáлкой; **at a ~** (*fig.*) одни́м удáром/мáхом **2.** (*of clock*) удáр, бой; **on the ~ of 9** рóвно в дéвять. **3.** (*paralytic attack*) парали́ч; удáр; **he had a ~** егó хвати́л удáр; **he died of a ~** он ýмер от удáра. **4.** (*single movement of series*): **~ of a piston** ход пóршня; **~ of an oar** взмах веслá, гребóк. **5.** (*in swimming*) стиль (*m.*); **what ~ does she use?** каки́м сти́лем онá плáвает? **6.** (*single action or instance*): **he has not done a ~ (of work)** он пáльцем о пáлец не удáрил; **~ of genius** гениáльная мысль; **~ of luck** (неожи́данная) удáча; везéние. **7.** (*with pen, pencil etc.*) штрих; **with, at a ~ of the pen** (*lit., fig.*) одни́м рóсчерком перá; (*with brush*) мазóк. **8.** (*typ., oblique ~*) дробь. **9.** (*oarsman*) загребнóй.

stroke[2] [strəʊk] *n.*: **he gave her hand a ~** он поглáдил её по рукé.

v.t. глáдить (*or* поглáживать), по-; **she ~d the horse's head** онá поглáдила лóшадь по головé.

stroll [strəʊl] *n.* прогýлка; **have, take, go for a ~** идти́ (*det.*) на прогýлку (*or* прогуля́ться).

v.i. гуля́ть (*impf.*); прогýл|иваться, -я́ться.

strong [strɒŋ] *adj.* **1.** (*powerful, forceful*) си́льный, крéпкий; **~ man** силáч; **~ character** си́льная натýра; **~ wind** си́льный/крéпкий вéтер; **~ attraction** большáя привлекáтельность; **~ measures** круты́е мéры; **~ argument** вéский аргумéнт; **~ evidence** убеди́тельное доказáтельство; **~ protest** энерги́чный протéст; **~ suspicion** си́льное подозрéние; **~ language** брань. **2.** (*stout, tough; durable*) крéпкий; прóчный; **~ foundations** прóчные основáния. **3.** (*robust, healthy*) крéпкий, здорóвый; **~ constitution** крéпкое здорóвье; **she is feeling ~er** онá чýвствует себя́ лýчше. **4.** (*firm*) твёрдый, крéпкий; **~ conviction** твёрдое убеждéние. **5.** (*of faculties*): **~ mind** хорóшая головá; **he is ~ in Latin** он силён в латы́ни. **6.** (*of smell, taste etc.*): **~ flavour** óстрый/рéзкий при́вкус; **~ cheese** óстрый сыр. **7.** (*concentrated*): **~ drink** крéпкий напи́ток; **a ~ cup of tea** чáшка крéпкого чáя. **8.** (*sharply defined*) рéзкий; **~ light** рéзкий свет; **~ colour** я́ркий цвет; **~ accent** (*in speech*) си́льный акцéнт; **~ likeness** большóе схóдство. **9.** (*well-supported*): **~ candidate** кандидáт, обладáющий больши́м шáнсом на успéх; **a ~** (*well-chosen*) **team** си́льная/отбóрная комáнда. **10.** (*numerous*) чи́сленный; **a ~ contingent** многочи́сленный контингéнт; **a company 200 ~** рóта чи́сленностью в 200 человéк.

adv.: **going ~** в прекрáсной фóрме.

cpds. **~-arm** *adj.*: **~-arm tactics** тáктика применéния си́лы; **~box** *n.* сейф; **~hold** *n.* крéпость, тверды́ня; **~-minded** *adj.* твёрдый, реши́тельный; **~-room** *n.* стальнáя кáмера; **~-willed** *adj.* реши́тельный, волевóй.

strontium ['strɒntɪəm] *n.* стрóнций.

strop [strɒp] *n.* ремéнь (*m.*) для прáвки бритв.

stroppy ['strɒpɪ] *adj.* (*coll.*) несговóрчивый, сварли́вый.

structural ['strʌktʃər(ə)l] *adj.*: **~ linguistics** структýрная лингви́стика; **~ defects** дефéкты в констрýкции; **~ engineer** инженéр-строи́тель (*m.*); **~ engineering** строи́тельная тéхника.

structure ['strʌktʃə(r)] *n.* **1.** (*abstr.*) структýра, стрóй, строéние; **~ of a building** архитектóника здáния; **~ of rocks, of a cell** структýра скал/клéтки; **~ of a language** строй языкá. **2.** (*concr.*) строéние, сооружéние; (*building*) здáние.

v.t. стрóить, по-; организовáть (*impf., pf.*).

struggle ['strʌg(ə)l] *n.* (*lit., fig.*) борьбá; **~ for existence** борьбá за существовáние; (*tussle*) схвáтка, потасóвка; **without a ~** без бóя/сопротивлéния.

v.i. **1.** (*fight*) борóться (*impf.*); би́ться (*impf.*). **2.** (*fig., grapple*) би́ться (*impf.*) (*над чем*); **we ~d with this problem for a long time** мы дóлго би́лись над э́той проблéмой. **3.** (*move convulsively*) би́ться (*impf.*); **the child ~d and kicked** ребёнок вырывáлся и бил ногáми. **4.** (*make strenuous efforts*) борóться (*impf.*); старáться (*impf.*) изо всех сил; (*fig., move with difficulty*): **he ~d to his feet** он с трудóм поднялся нá ноги.

strum [strʌm] *v.t. & i.* бренчáть, трéнькать (*both impf.*) (на+*p.*).

strumpet ['strʌmpɪt] *n.* (*arch.*) потаскýха, шлю́ха.

strut[1] [strʌt] *n.* (*gait*) вáжная похóдка.

v.i. ходи́ть (*indet.*) с вáжным ви́дом.

strut[2] [strʌt] *n.* (*support*) стрóйка, подкóс.

strychnine ['strɪkni:n] *n.* стрихни́н.

stub [stʌb] *n.* (*of pencil*) огры́зок; (*of cigarette*) окýрок; (*of cheque etc.*) корешóк.

v.t. **1. ~ (out) a cigarette** гаси́ть, по- папирóсу. **2.: ~ one's toe on sth.** спот|ыкáться, -кнýться о(бо) что-н.

stubble ['stʌb(ə)l] *n.* жнивьё, стерня́; (*of beard*) щети́на.

stubbly ['stʌblɪ] *adj.*: **~ chin** щети́нистый подборóдок.

stubborn ['stʌbən] *adj.* (*obstinate*) упря́мый; (*tenacious*) упóрный; **a ~ fight** упóрный бой.

stubbornness ['stʌbənnɪs] *n.* упря́мство; упóрство.

stucco ['stʌkəʊ] *n.* штукатýрка; (*attr.*) лепнóй.

v.t. штукатýрить, о-.

stuck-up ['stʌk'ʌp] *adj.* (*coll., haughty, conceited*) чванли́вый, занóсчивый.

stud[1] [stʌd] *n.* (*of horses*) кóнный завóд; коню́шня.

cpd. **~-farm** *n.* кóнный завóд.

stud[2] [stʌd] *n.* **1.** (*nail, boss etc.*) гвоздь (*m.*) с большóй шля́пкой; кнóпка. **2.** (*collar-~*) зáпонка.

v.t.: **~ded boots** боти́нки на шипáх; **a dress ~ded with jewels** плáтье, усы́панное драгоцéнными камня́ми.

student ['stju:d(ə)nt] *n.* студéнт (*fem.* -ка); (*attr.*) студéнческий; (*pupil*) учени́к, учáщийся.

studied ['stʌdɪd] *adj.* (*deliberate*): **~ indifference** дéланное равнодýшие; **~ insult** умы́шленное оскорблéние.

studio ['stju:dɪəʊ] *n.* **1.** (*of artist, photographer etc.*) мастерскáя, стýдия, ательé (*indecl.*). **2.** (*broadcasting ~*) радиостýдия; телестýдия. **3.** (*cin.*) съёмочный павильóн; киностýдия.

studious ['stju:dɪəs] *adj.* **1.** (*fond of study*) лю́бящий наýку. **2.** (*deliberate*): **~ politeness** нарочи́тая вéжливость; **he ~ly ignored me** он старáтельно меня́ игнори́ровал. **3.** (*zealous*) усéрдный, старáтельный.

stud|y ['stʌdɪ] *n.* **1.** (*learning, investigation*) изучéние, учёба, наýка; **~ies** заня́тия (*nt. pl.*); **make a ~y of** (тщáтельно) изуч|áть, -и́ть; **my ~ies have convinced me** мои́ исслéдования убеди́ли меня́. **2.** (*room*) кабинéт.

v.t. **1.** (*learn, investigate*) изуч|áть, -и́ть; исслéдовать (*impf., pf.*); **Greek is not ~ied** не изучáют грéческий (язы́к) (*or* не занимáются грéческим (языкóм)). **2.** (*scrutinize*) (внимáтельно) рассм|áтривать, -отрéть. **3.** (*commit to memory*): **~y a part** учи́ть (*impf.*) роль.

v.i. учи́ться (*impf.*).

stuff [stʌf] *n.* **1.** (*material, substance*) материáл, веществó, вещь; **there's some good ~ in this book** в э́той кни́ге есть кóе-что полéзное/хорóшее;

green ~ (*vegetables*) зе́лень, о́вощ|и (*pl.*, *g.* -е́й). **2.** (*coll.*, *things*) ве́щи (*f. pl.*); (*pej.*, *rubbish*): **what shall I do with this ~ from the cupboard?** что мне де́лать с э́тим хла́мом из шка́фа?; **do you call this ~ beer?** (и) вы э́ту дрянь называ́ете пи́вом?; **~ and nonsense!** чепуха́! **3.** (*coll.*, *business*): **do one's ~** де́лать, с- своё де́ло; **know one's ~** знать (*impf.*) своё де́ло; **that's the ~ (to give 'em)!** вот то, что на́до!; **I don't want any rough ~** пожа́луйста, без дра́ки.

v.t. **1.** (*pack*, *fill*) наби|ва́ть, -и́ть (*что чем*); **a ~ed eagle** чу́чело орла́; (*cul.*) фарширова́ть, за-; начин|я́ть, -и́ть; **he ~ed his head with useless facts** он заби́л себе́ го́лову вся́кими нену́жными све́дениями; **~ o.s.** (*overeat*) объ|еда́ться, -е́сться; **get ~ed!** (*slang*) иди́ ты!; фиг тебе́!; **my nose is ~ed up** у меня́ нос зало́жен. **2.** (*cram*, *push*) запи́х|ивать, -а́ть/-ну́ть (*что во что*); **he ~ed the note behind a cushion** он засу́нул запи́ску за поду́шку.

stuffiness ['stʌfɪnɪs] *n.* духота́, спёртость; (*of pers.*) чо́порность.

stuffing ['stʌfɪŋ] *n.* **1.** (*of cushion*, *doll etc.*) наби́вка. **2.** (*cul.*) начи́нка, фарш.

stuffy ['stʌfɪ] *adj.* (*of room*) ду́шный; (*of atmosphere*) ду́шный, спёртый; (*of pers.*) чо́порный.

stumbl|e ['stʌmb(ə)l] *v.i.* **1.** (*miss one's footing*) осту-п|а́ться, -и́ться; спот|ыка́ться, -кну́ться; **he ~ed over a stone** он споткну́лся о ка́мень; **~ing-block** ка́мень (*m.*) преткнове́ния. **2.** (*speak haltingly*) за-п|ина́ться, -ну́ться; **he ~es over his words** он запина́ется на ка́ждом сло́ве. **3.**: **~e across, upon** (*find by chance*) нат|а́лкиваться, -олкну́ться на+*a.*; на-т|ыка́ться, -кну́ться на+*a.*

stump [stʌmp] *n.* **1.** (*of tree*) пень (*m.*), обру́бок; (*of limb*) культя́; (*of cigar*) оку́рок; (*of pencil*) огры́зок. **2.** (*cricket*) сто́лбик.

v.t. (*floor*) ста́вить, по- в тупи́к; озада́чи|вать, -ть; **I was ~ed by the question** э́тот вопро́с поста́вил меня́ впроса́к.

v.i. (*walk clumsily*) то́пать (*impf.*), тяжело́ ступа́ть (*impf.*).

with adv.: **~ up** *v.t.* & *i.* (*coll.*) выкла́дывать, вы́ложить (де́ньги); **I had to ~ up for the meal** мне пришло́сь заплати́ть за еду́.

stun [stʌn] *v.t.* **1.** (*knock unconscious*) оглуш|а́ть, -и́ть. **2.** (*amaze*, *astound*) пора|жа́ть, -зи́ть; ошело-м|ля́ть, -и́ть; **a ~ning dress** потряса́ющее пла́тье.

stunt [stʌnt] *n.* трюк, но́мер; **~ man** (*cin.*) каскадёр.

v.t.: **~ growth** заде́рж|ивать, -а́ть рост; **~ed trees** низкоро́слые дере́вья.

stupefaction [ˌstju:pɪ'fækʃ(ə)n] *n.* оглуше́ние, ошеломле́ние, оцепене́ние.

stupefy ['stju:pɪˌfaɪ] *v.t.* оглуш|а́ть, -и́ть; (*amaze*) ошелом|ля́ть, -и́ть.

stupendous [stju:'pendəs] *adj.* изуми́тельный; (*in size*) колосса́льный.

stupid ['stju:pɪd] *adj.* глу́пый, тупо́й; **~ person** глу́пый челове́к; глупе́ц; тупи́ца (*c.g.*).

stupidity [ˌstju:'pɪdɪtɪ] *n.* глу́пость.

stupor ['stju:pə(r)] *n.* остолбене́ние, оцепене́ние.

sturdiness ['stɜ:dɪnɪs] *n.* кре́пость, си́ла.

sturdy ['stɜ:dɪ] *adj.* кре́пкий, си́льный.

sturgeon ['stɜ:dʒ(ə)n] *n.* осётр; (*as food*) осетри́на.

stutter ['stʌtə(r)] *n.* заика́ние; **he has a terrible ~** он ужа́сно заика́ется.

v.i. заика́ться (*impf.*).

stutterer ['stʌtərə(r)] *n.* заи́ка (*c.g.*).

sty[1] [staɪ] *n.* (**pig ~**; *lit. fig.*) хлев, свина́рник.

sty[2], **stye** [staɪ] *n.* (*on eye*) ячме́нь (*m.*).

style [staɪl] *n.* **1.** (*manner*) стиль (*m.*), мане́ра; (*of writing*) стиль; **the ~ in which they live** их о́браз жи́зни; **the ~ of Rubens** мане́ра Ру́бенса; **flattery is not his ~** лесть не в его́ ду́хе/сти́ле; **cramp s.o.'s ~** меша́ть (*impf.*) кому́-н.; **in fine ~** с бле́ском. **2.** (*elegance*, *taste*, *luxury*): **she has ~** у неё есть вкус; **in ~** с ши́ком; **live in ~** жить (*impf.*) широко́ (*or* на широ́кую но́гу). **3.** (*fashion*) мо́да, фасо́н; **in the latest ~** по после́дней мо́де. **4.** (*sort*, *kind*) род, тип, сорт; **what ~ of house do you require?** како́го ти́па дом вы хоте́ли бы приобрести́? **5.** (*of dates*): **Old/New S~** (*adv.*) по ста́рому/но́вому сти́лю.

v.t. **1.** (*designate*) наз|ыва́ть, -ва́ть; **self-~d** самозва́нный. **2.** (*design*): **she had her hair ~d** она́ сде́лала себе́ причёску.

stylish ['staɪlɪʃ] *adj.* (*fashionable*) мо́дный; **a coat of ~ cut** пальто́ мо́дного покро́я; (*smart*) элега́нтный.

stylist ['staɪlɪst] *n.*: **hair ~** парикма́хер-модельéр.

stylistic [staɪ'lɪstɪk] *adj.* стилисти́ческий.

stylize ['staɪlaɪz] *v.t.* стилизова́ть (*impf.*, *pf.*).

stylus ['staɪləs] *n.* **1.** (*engraving tool*) гравирова́льная игла́. **2.** (*for records*) (грамофо́нная) иго́лка.

stymie ['staɪmɪ] *v.t.* (*fig.*) меша́ть (*impf.*) +*d.*

suave [swɑ:v] *adj.* гла́дкий, лощёный, обходи́тельный.

sub [sʌb] *n.* (*coll.*) *abbr. of* **1. submarine** подло́дка. **2. substitute** заме́на; врио́ (*m. indecl.*) (вре́менно исполня́ющий обя́занности). **3. subscription** подпи́ска; *see also* **sub-edit, sub-editor**

subaltern ['sʌbəlt(ə)n] *n.* мла́дший офице́р.

subcommittee ['sʌbkəˌmɪtɪ] *n.* подкоми́ссия; подкомите́т.

subconscious [sʌb'kɒnʃəs] *n.* (*the ~*) подсозна́тельное.

adj. подсозна́тельный.

subcontinent ['sʌbˌkɒntɪnənt] *n.* субконтине́нт.

subcontract [ˌsʌbkən'trækt] *v.i.* заключ|а́ть, -и́ть субдогово́р.

subcontractor [ˌsʌbkən'træktə(r)] *n.* субподря́дчик.

subdivide ['sʌbdɪˌvaɪd, -'vaɪd] *v.t.* & *i.* подраздел|я́ть(ся), -и́ть(ся).

subdivision ['sʌbdɪˌvɪʒ(ə)n, -'vɪʒ(ə)n] *n.* подразделе́ние.

subdue [səb'dju:] *v.t.* **1.** (*conquer*, *subjugate*) подав|ля́ть, -и́ть; **~ one's enemies** покор|я́ть, -и́ть враго́в. **2.** (*soften*) смягч|а́ть, -и́ть; **~d light** мя́гкий свет; (*sound etc.*) приглуш|а́ть, -и́ть; **in ~d voices** приглушёнными голоса́ми. **3.** (*restrain*): **he seems ~d today** он сего́дня что-то прити́х.

sub-edit [sʌb'edɪt] *v.t.* де́лать, с- техни́ческое редакти́рование +*g.*; гото́вить (*impf.*) к набо́ру.

sub-editor [sʌb'edɪtə(r)] *n.* помо́щник реда́ктора; техни́ческий реда́ктор (*abbr.* техре́д).

subgroup ['sʌbgru:p] *n.* подгру́ппа.

subheading ['sʌbhedɪŋ] *n.* подзаголо́вок.

subhuman [sʌb'hju:mən] *n.* недочелове́к.

adj. нечелове́ческий.

subject[1] ['sʌbdʒɪkt] *n.* **1.** (*pol.*) по́дданный. **2.** (*gram.*) подлежа́щий. **3.** (*theme*, *matter*) те́ма, предме́т; **the ~ of the book** те́ма кни́ги; **he was made the ~ of an experiment** его́ сде́лали объе́ктом о́пыта; **change the ~** перев|оди́ть, -ести́ разгово́р на другу́ю те́му; **a painter who treats biblical ~s** худо́жник, пи́шущий библе́йские сюже́ты; **you are treating the ~ very lightly** вы недоста́точно серьёзно отно́ситесь к э́тому вопро́су; **while we're on the ~** раз уж мы заговори́ли об э́том (*or* на э́ту те́му). **4.** (*branch of study*) предме́т, дисципли́на; **he passed in four ~s** он прошёл по четырём предме́там. **5.** (*cause*, *occasion*) по́вод; **a ~ of rejoicing** по́вод для весе́лья.

adj. **1.** (*subordinate*) подчинённый; зави́симый; **all citizens are ~ to the law** зако́н распространя́ется на всех гра́ждан; **bodies are ~ to gravity** тела́ подчиня́ются зако́ну тяготе́ния. **2.** (*liable*, *prone*, *inclined*): **he is ~ to changes of mood** он подве́ржен (бы́стрым) сме́нам настрое́ния; **trains are ~ to delay** возмо́жны опозда́ния поездо́в. **3.**: **~ to** (*conditional upon*) подлежа́щий +*d.*; **the fare is ~ to alteration** сто́имость прое́зда мо́жет быть изменена́;

the price is ~ to market fluctuations цена́ зави́сит от колеба́ний ры́нка.

adv.: **~ to** при усло́вии (*чего*); **~ to the following provision** с соблюде́нием нижесле́дующего положе́ния; **~ to your approval** е́сли вы одо́брите; **~ to your rights** поско́льку э́то допуска́ют ва́ши права́.

cpds. **~-heading** *n.* ру́брика, (под)заголо́вок; **~-matter** *n.* содержа́ние, предме́т (*чего*).

subject[2] [səb'dʒekt] *v.t.* **1.** (*make subordinate*) подчин|я́ть, -и́ть. **2.** (*expose, make liable*) подв|ерга́ть, -е́ргнуть (*кого/что чему*); **the machine was ~ed to tests** маши́ну подве́ргли испыта́ниям; **he was ~ed to insult** его́ подве́ргли оскорбле́нию.

subjection [səb'dʒekʃ(ə)n] *n.* подчине́ние.

subjective [səb'dʒektɪv] *adj.* субъекти́вный.

subjectivism [səb'dʒektɪˌvɪz(ə)m] *n.* субъективи́зм.

subjectivist [səb'dʒektɪvɪst] *n.* субъективи́ст.

subjectivity [ˌsʌbdʒek'tɪvɪtɪ] *n.* субъекти́вность.

sub judice [sʌb 'dʒu:dɪsɪ] *adj.* находя́щийся на рассмотре́нии (суда́).

subjugate ['sʌbdʒʊˌgeɪt] *v.t.* (*subdue*) покор|я́ть, -и́ть; (*subject*) подчин|я́ть, -и́ть.

subjugation [ˌsʌbdʒʊ'geɪʃ(ə)n] *n.* покоре́ние; подчине́ние.

subjunctive [səb'dʒʌŋktɪv] *n.* (**~ mood**) сослага́тельное наклоне́ние.

adj. сослага́тельный.

sublease ['sʌbli:s] *n.* субаре́нда.

v.t. **1.** (*of lessor*; *also* **sublet**) перед|ава́ть, -а́ть в субаре́нду. **2.** (*of lessee*) брать, взять в субаре́нду.

sublet ['sʌblet] = **sublease** *v.t.* **1.**

sublieutenant [ˌsʌblef'tenənt] *n.* мла́дший лейтена́нт.

sublimate[1] ['sʌblɪmət] *n.* сублима́т, возго́н; **corrosive ~** сулема́.

sublimate[2] ['sʌblɪˌmeɪt] *v.t.* (*chem.*) сублими́ровать (*impf.*, *pf.*; *also fig.*); воз|гоня́ть, -огна́ть.

sublimation [ˌsʌblɪ'meɪʃ(ə)n] *n.* сублима́ция, возго́нка.

sublime [sə'blaɪm] *n.* (*the ~*) вели́кое, возвы́шенное; **it is only a step from the ~ to the ridiculous** от вели́кого до смешно́го оди́н шаг.

adj. (*majestic*) вели́чественный; (*lofty*) возвы́шенный; **a ~ genius** велича́йший ге́ний; **~ ignorance** великоле́пное неве́дение.

subliminal [səb'lɪmɪn(ə)l] *adj.* подсозна́тельный; де́йствующий на подсозна́ние.

sub-machine gun [ˌsʌbmə'ʃi:n gʌn] *n.* пистоле́т-пулемёт; автома́т.

submarine [ˌsʌbmə'ri:n, 'sʌb-] *n.* подво́дная ло́дка.

adj. подво́дный.

submerge [səb'mɜ:dʒ] *v.t.* & *i.* погру|жа́ть(ся), -зи́ть(ся).

submersion [səb'mɜ:ʃ(ə)n] *n.* погруже́ние в во́ду.

submission [səb'mɪʃ(ə)n] *n.* **1.** (*subjection*) подчине́ние; (*obedience*) повинове́ние; (*humility*) смире́ние; (*submissiveness*) поко́рность; **starve into ~** го́лодом довести́ (*pf.*) до капитуля́ции. **2.** (*presentation*) представле́ние, предъявле́ние; **~ of proof** представле́ние доказа́тельств.

submissive [səb'mɪsɪv] *adj.* поко́рный, смире́нный, послу́шный.

submit [səb'mɪt] *v.t.* **1.** (*yield*) подчин|я́ть, -и́ть; **~ o.s. to s.o.'s authority** покор|я́ться, -и́ться чьей-н. вла́сти. **2.** (*present, e.g. a dissertation*) предст|авля́ть, -а́вить. **3.** (*suggest, maintain*): **I ~ that your proposal is contrary to the statutes** я сме́ю утвержда́ть, что ва́ше предложе́ние противоре́чит уста́ву.

v.i. подчин|я́ться, -и́ться; покор|я́ться, -и́ться.

subnormal [sʌb'nɔ:m(ə)l] *adj.* ни́же норма́льного; **a ~ child** дефекти́вный (*or* у́мственно отста́лый) ребёнок.

subordinate[1] [sə'bɔ:dɪnət] *n.* подчинённый.

adj. **1.** (*in rank or importance*) подчинённый; ни́зший по чи́ну; (*secondary*) второстепе́нный. **2.** (*gram.*) прида́точный; **~ clause** прида́точное предложе́ние.

subordinate[2] [sə'bɔ:dɪˌneɪt] *v.t.* (*make subservient*) подчин|я́ть, -и́ть; (*place in less important position*) ста́вить, по- в подчинённое/зави́симое положе́ние.

subordination [səˌbɔ:dɪ'neɪʃ(ə)n] *n.* подчине́ние, подчинённость.

suborn [sə'bɔ:n] *v.t.* подкуп|а́ть, -и́ть.

subpoena [səb'pi:nə, sə'pi:nə] *n.* пове́стка в суд.

v.t. вызыва́ть, вы́звать в суд.

subscribe [səb'skraɪb] *v.i.* **1.** (*pay or take out subscription*): **~ to a journal** подпи́с|ываться, -а́ться на журна́л; **~ to a library** запи́с|ываться, -а́ться в пла́тную библиоте́ку. **2.** (*agree, assent*) присоедин|я́ться, -и́ться; **I cannot ~ to that view** я не могу́ согласи́ться с э́тим мне́нием.

subscriber [səb'skraɪbə(r)] *n.* подпи́счик; (*telephone ~*) абоне́нт.

subscription [səb'skrɪpʃ(ə)n] *n.* (*to library etc.*) абонеме́нт в+*a.*; (*fee*) взнос, поже́ртвование; **~ to a society** чле́нский взнос в о́бщество; **~ to a newspaper** подпи́ска на газе́ту; **take out a ~** подпи́с|ываться, -а́ться (на+*a.*); **~ form** подписно́й лист.

subsection ['sʌbˌsekʃ(ə)n] *n.* подсе́кция.

subsequent ['sʌbsɪkwənt] *adj.* после́дующий, сле́дующий; **~ to his death** (име́ющий ме́сто) по́сле его́ сме́рти; **~ly** впосле́дствии; зате́м.

subservience [səb'sɜ:vɪəns] *n.* раболе́пие, послуша́ние.

subservient [səb'sɜ:vɪənt] *adj.* раболе́пный, послу́шный.

subside [səb'saɪd] *v.i.* **1.** (*of liquid*) пон|ижа́ться, -и́зиться. **2.** (*of ground or building*) ос|еда́ть, -е́сть; **the ground ~d** земля́ осе́ла. **3.** (*of water*) спа|да́ть, -сть; **the floods ~d** наводне́ние спа́ло; (*of blister*) оп|ада́ть, -а́сть. **4.** (*of fever*) па́дать, упа́сть; (*of wind, storm etc.*) ут|иха́ть, -и́хнуть; **the laughter ~d** смех ути́х; **passions ~d** стра́сти улегли́сь.

subsidence [səb'saɪd(ə)ns, 'sʌbsɪd(ə)ns] *n.* (*of ground*) оседа́ние, оса́дка.

subsidiary [səb'sɪdɪərɪ] *n.* (*comm.*) филиа́л.

adj. вспомога́тельный, подсо́бный; **~ company** доче́рняя компа́ния.

subsidize ['sʌbsɪˌdaɪz] *v.t.* субсиди́ровать (*impf.*, *pf.*).

subsidy ['sʌbsɪdɪ] *n.* субси́дия, посо́бие, дота́ция.

subsist [səb'sɪst] *v.i.* (*exist*) существова́ть (*impf.*); (*survive*) жить, про-.

subsistence [səb'sɪst(ə)ns] *n.* (*existence*) существова́ние; бытие́; (*means of supporting life*) сре́дства (*nt. pl.*) к существова́нию; пропита́ние; **~ farming** натура́льное хозя́йство; **~ wage** прожи́точный ми́нимум.

subsoil ['sʌbsɔɪl] *n.* подпо́чва.

subsonic [sʌb'sɒnɪk] *adj.* дозвуково́й.

subspecies ['sʌbˌspi:ʃi:z, -ʃɪz] *n.* подви́д.

substance ['sʌbst(ə)ns] *n.* **1.** (*essence, reality*) субста́нция, реа́льность. **2.** (*essential elements*) суть, содержа́ние, су́щность, существо́; **he told me the ~ of his speech** он пересказа́л мне основно́е содержа́ние свое́й ре́чи; **in ~** по существу́. **3.** (*piece, type of matter*) вещество́. **4.** (*solidity*) пло́тность, содержа́ние; **a piece of writing that lacks ~** сочине́ние, лишённое содержа́ния; **there is no ~ in the rumour** э́тот слух лишён како́го то ни́ было основа́ния. **5.** (*possessions*) состоя́ние; **a man of ~** состоя́тельный челове́к.

substandard [sʌb'stændəd] *adj.* низкока́чественный; (*of language*) нелитерату́рный, просторе́чный.

substantial [səb'stænʃ(ə)l] *adj.* **1.** (*solid, stout, sturdy*) кре́пкий; **a man of ~ build** челове́к кре́пкого телосложе́ния; **a ~ building** соли́дное зда́ние; **a ~**

dinner сы́тный обе́д. **2.** (*considerable*): **a ~ sum** поря́дочная су́мма; **a ~ contribution** ва́жный вклад; **a ~ improvement** значи́тельное/суще́ственное улучше́ние. **3.** (*essential, overall*) по существу́/су́ти; **I am in ~ agreement** я согла́сен по существу́ (*or* в основно́м).

substantiate [səb'stænʃɪˌeɪt] *v.t.* обосно́в|ывать, -а́ть.

substantiation [səbˌstænʃɪ'eɪʃ(ə)n] *n.* обоснова́ние.

substantive [səb'stæntɪv] *n.* и́мя существи́тельное.

adj. **1.** (*existing independently*) субстанти́вный, незави́симый. **2.** (*pert. to subject matter*): **I have no ~ comments** у меня́ нет замеча́ний по существу́ (де́ла, вопро́са *и т.п.*); **~ provisions** резолюти́вная/операти́вная часть (*документа и т.п.*).

substation ['sʌbˌsteɪʃ(ə)n] *n.* (*elec.*) подста́нция.

substitute ['sʌbstɪˌtjuːt] *n.* заме́на; (*pers.*) замести́тель (*m.*); (*thg.*) замени́тель (*m.*), суррога́т.

v.t. испо́льзовать (*impf., pf.*) (*что*) вме́сто (*чего*); **~ one word for another** замен|я́ть, -и́ть одно́ сло́во други́м; подст|авля́ть, -а́вить одно́ сло́во вме́сто друго́го.

v.i.: **~ for** заме|ща́ть, -сти́ть; подмен|я́ть, -и́ть (*кого*).

substitution [ˌsʌbstɪ'tjuːʃ(ə)n] *n.* заме́на, замеще́ние, подме́на; (*math.*) подстано́вка.

substratum ['sʌbˌstrɑːtəm, -ˌstreɪtəm] *n.* основа́ние; ни́жний слой; (*geol.*) подпо́чва, субстра́т.

subsume [səb'sjuːm] *v.t.* включ|а́ть, -и́ть в каку́ю-н. катего́рию.

subterfuge ['sʌbtəˌfjuːdʒ] *n.* уло́вка, хи́трость.

subterranean [ˌsʌbtə'reɪnɪən] *adj.* подзе́мный.

subtitle ['sʌbˌtaɪt(ə)l] *n.* подзаголо́вок; (*cin.*) субти́тр.

subtle ['sʌt(ə)l] *adj.* **1.** (*fine, elusive*) то́нкий; (*refined*) утончённый; **~ perfume** не́жный/то́нкий за́пах/арома́т; **~ distinction** то́нкое разли́чие. **2.** (*perceptive*) то́нкий; (*acute*) о́стрый; **~ remark** то́нкое замеча́ние; **~ mind** о́стрый ум. **3.** (*ingenious, deft*): **~ fingers** ло́вкие па́льцы; **~ device** иску́сный трюк; **~ argument** хитроу́мный до́вод. **4.** (*crafty, cunning*) иску́сный, хи́трый.

subtlety ['sʌtəltɪ] *n.* то́нкость; острота́; хи́трость; то́нкое разли́чие.

subtract [səb'trækt] *v.t.* вычита́ть, вы́честь.

subtraction [səb'trækʃ(ə)n] *n.* вычита́ние.

subtropical [sʌb'trɒpɪk(ə)l] *adj.* субтропи́ческий.

sub-unit ['sʌbjuːnɪt] *n.* (*mil.*) подразделе́ние.

suburb ['sʌbɜːb] *n.* при́город, предме́стье.

suburban [sə'bɜːbən] *adj.* при́городный; (*fig.*) меща́нский, провинциа́льный.

suburbanite [sə'bɜːbənaɪt] *n.* жи́тель (*fem.* -ница) при́города.

suburbia [sə'bɜːbɪə] *n.* (*pej.*) ≃ меща́нство, провинциали́зм.

subversion [səb'vɜːʃ(ə)n] *n.* подрывна́я де́ятельность.

subversive [səb'vɜːsɪv] *adj.* подрывно́й.

subvert [səb'vɜːt] *v.t.* под|рыва́ть, -орва́ть.

subway ['sʌbweɪ] *n.* (*passage under road*) подзе́мный перехо́д; (*US, railway*) подзе́мка, метро́ (*indecl.*).

subzero [sʌb'zɪərəʊ] *adj.*: **~ temperatures** ми́нусовые температу́ры.

succeed [sək'siːd] *v.t.* **1.** (*follow*) сле́довать (*impf.*) за+*i.*; **night ~s day** ночь сменя́ет день. **2.** (*as heir*) насле́довать (*impf., pf.*) +*d.*; **Mary was ~ed by Elizabeth I** по́сле Мари́и воцари́лась Елизаве́та I; (*as replacement*) смен|я́ть, -и́ть; **who ~ed him as President?** кто был сле́дующим президе́нтом?

v.i. **1.** (*follow*) после́довать (*pf.*) (за+*i.*). **2.** (*as heir etc.*): **he ~ed to his father's estate** он унасле́довал име́ние отца́; **he ~ed to the premiership** он за́нял пост премье́р-мини́стра. **3.** (*be, become successful*) доб|ива́ться, -и́ться успе́ха/своего́; **he ~ed as a lawyer** он име́л успе́х в ка́честве адвока́та; **the attack ~ed beyond all expectation** ата́ка удала́сь сверх вся́ких ожида́ний; **he ~ed in tricking us all** ему́ удало́сь всех нас обману́ть.

success [sək'ses] *n.* успе́х, уда́ча; **his efforts were crowned with ~** его́ уси́лия увенча́лись успе́хом; **I tried to get in, but without ~** я пыта́лся туда́ попа́сть, но безуспе́шно; **I have had no ~ so far** пока́мест я не мог дости́гнуть це́ли; **my holidays were not a ~ this year** мои́ кани́кулы в э́том году́ бы́ли неуда́чными.

successful [sək'sesfʊl] *adj.* успе́шный, уда́чный; **a ~ attempt** успе́шная попы́тка; **a ~ speech** уда́чная речь; **I tried to persuade him, but was not ~** я пыта́лся убеди́ть его́, но мне э́то не удало́сь; (*fortunate*) преуспева́ющий; уда́чливый; **he was ~ in business** он был уда́члив в дела́х.

succession [sək'seʃ(ə)n] *n.* **1.** (*sequence*) последова́тельность; **in ~** подря́д; **they rode past in rapid ~** они промча́лись оди́н за други́м. **2.** (*series*) ряд, цепь; **a ~ of victories** цепь побе́д. **3.** (*succeeding to office etc.*) насле́дство, насле́дование; **the king's right of ~ was disputed** пра́во престолонасле́дия короля́ оспа́ривалось; **the ~ was broken** прее́мственность была́ нару́шена.

successive [sək'sesɪv] *adj.* после́довательный; **on three ~ occasions** три ра́за подря́д.

successor [sək'sesə(r)] *n.* прее́мни|к (*fem.* -ца), насле́дни|к (*fem.* -ца).

succinct [sək'sɪŋkt] *adj.* сжа́тый; кра́ткий.

succour ['sʌkə(r)] (*liter.*) *n.* по́мощь.

v.t. при|ходи́ть, -йти́ на по́мощь +*d.*

succulence ['sʌkjʊləns] *n.* со́чность.

succulent ['sʌkjʊlənt] *adj.* со́чный; (*bot.*) мяси́стый.

succumb [sə'kʌm] *v.i.* уступ|а́ть, -и́ть; подд|ава́ться, -а́ться; **she did not ~ to temptation** она́ не поддала́сь искуше́нию; (*die*) сконча́ться (*pf.*); **he ~ed to his injuries** он сконча́лся от (полу́ченных) ран.

such [sʌtʃ] *pron.* **1.** (*that*) э́то; **~ being the case** в тако́м слу́чае; **he is a good scholar and is recognised as ~** он хоро́ший учёный и при́знан тако-вы́м. **2.: as ~** (*without qualification*) вообще́; как таково́й. **3. ~** (*people*) **as** те, кото́рые.

adj. **1.** (*of the kind mentioned; of this, that kind*) тако́й; **I said no ~ thing** я ничего́ подо́бного не говори́л; **some ~ thing** что́-то в э́том ро́де; **no ~ luck!** увы́!; е́сли бы!; **how could you do ~ a thing?** как вы могли́ так поступи́ть? **2.: ~ as** (*of a kind …*): **~ grapes as you never saw** тако́й виногра́д, како́го вы в жи́зни не ви́дывали; **I am not ~ a fool as to believe him** я не тако́й дура́к, что́бы пове́рить ему́; (*like*): **people ~ as these** таки́е лю́ди; лю́ди, подо́бные э́тим; **small objects ~ as diamonds** ме́лкие предме́ты, как наприме́р бриллиа́нты; **you can share my meal, ~ as it is** вы мо́жете раздели́ть со мно́ю мой у́жин, како́в он ни на есть. **3.** (*pred.*) тако́в; **~ was the force of the gale** такова́ была́ си́ла урага́на; **~ is life!** такова́ жизнь!

cpds. **~-and-~** *adj.* тако́й-то, (*pl.*) ко́е-каки́е; **~like** *pron. & adj.* подо́бный; **theatres, cinemas and ~like** теа́тры, кино́ и тому́ подо́бное.

suck [sʌk] *n.* соса́ние; **take a ~ at** пососа́ть (*pf.*); **give ~ to a child** корми́ть (*impf.*) ребёнка гру́дью.

v.t. **1.** соса́ть (*impf.*); **he was ~ing (at) an orange** он поса́сывал апельси́н; (**~** *in, imbibe*) вс|а́сывать, -оса́ть; **bees ~ nectar** пчёлы втя́гивают некта́р; **he was ~ing fruit juice through a straw** он тяну́л фрукто́вый сок че́рез соло́минку; (**~** *out*) выса́сывать, вы́сосать. **2.** (*squeeze or dissolve in mouth*) соса́ть (*impf.*); поса́сывать (*impf.*); **the baby likes to ~ its thumb** младе́нец лю́бит соса́ть па́лец.

v.i. соса́ть (*impf.*); **~ at, on a pipe** поса́сывать/потя́гивать (*impf.*) тру́бку; **~ing-pig** моло́чный поросёнок.

with advs.: **~ in** *v.t.* вс|а́сывать, -оса́ть; (*engulf*) зас|а́сывать, -оса́ть; ~ **out** *v.t.* выса́сывать, вы́сосать; ~ **up** *v.t.* выса́сывать, вы́сосать; *v.i.*: ~ **up to s.o.** (*coll.*) подли́з|ываться, -а́ться к кому́-н.

sucker ['sʌkə(r)] *n.* **1.** (*organ, device*) присо́сок, присо́ска. **2.** (*bot.*) отро́сток, боково́й побе́г. **3.** (*sl., gullible person*) проста́|к (*fem.* -чка).

suckl|e ['sʌk(ə)l] *v.t.* вск|а́рмливать, -орми́ть; (*of pers.*) корми́ть (*impf.*) гру́дью; **the cow was ~ing the calf** телёнок соса́л ма́тку.

suckling ['sʌklɪŋ] *n.* сосу́н, сосуно́к; ~ **pig** (*US*) моло́чный поросёнок.

sucrose ['su:krəuz, 'sju:-] *n.* сахаро́за.

suction ['sʌkʃ(ə)n] *n.* вса́сывание; ~ **pump** вса́сывающий насо́с.

Sudan [su:'dɑ:n, -'dæn] *n.* Суда́н.

Sudanese [,su:də'ni:z] *n.* суда́н|ец (*fem.* -ка).

adj. суда́нский.

sudden ['sʌd(ə)n] *n.*: **(all) of a** ~ внеза́пно, вдруг.

adj. (*unexpected*) внеза́пный, неожи́данный; ~ **death** скоропости́жная смерть.

suddenly ['sʌd(ə)nlɪ] *adv.* внеза́пно, вдруг.

suddenness ['sʌd(ə)nnɪs] *n.* внеза́пность, неожи́данность.

suds [sʌdz] *n. pl.* мы́льная пе́на.

sue [su:, sju:] *v.t.* возбу|жда́ть, -ди́ть иск/де́ло про́тив+*g.*; под|ава́ть, -а́ть в суд на+*a.*; (**for libel** за клевету́; **for damages** о возмеще́нии убы́тков).

v.i. **1.** (*take legal action*) под|ава́ть, -а́ть в суд (на+*a.*). **2.** (*make entreaties*): ~ **for peace** проси́ть (*impf.*) ми́ра.

suede [sweɪd] *n.* за́мша.

adj. за́мшевый.

suet ['su:ɪt, 'sju:ɪt] *n.* нутряно́е са́ло; по́чечный жир.

Suez ['su:ɪz] *n.* Суэ́ц; ~ **Canal** Суэ́цкий кана́л.

suffer ['sʌfə(r)] *v.t.* **1.** (*experience*) испы́т|ывать, -а́ть; терпе́ть, по-; **she did not ~ much pain** она́ недо́лго му́чилась; **he ~ed many hardships** он перенёс мно́жество лише́ний. **2.** (*permit*) позв|оля́ть, -о́лить; (*tolerate*) терпе́ть, по-/с-; **he does not ~ fools gladly** он не выно́сит дурако́в.

v.i. страда́ть (*impf.*) (от+*g.*); **he ~s from shyness** он (о́чень) засте́нчив; **he is ~ing from measles** он боле́ет ко́рью; у него́ корь; **his reputation will ~ greatly** его́ репута́ция си́льно пострада́ет; **he ~ed for his folly** он был нака́зан за свою́ глу́пость; **I ~ed for it** я за э́то поплати́лся.

sufferance ['sʌfərəns] *n.*: **on** ~ из ми́лости; с молчали́вого согла́сия.

sufferer ['sʌfrə(r)] *n.* страде́лец.

suffering ['sʌfrɪŋ] *n.* страда́ние.

suffice [sə'faɪs] *v.t.* удовлетвор|я́ть, -и́ть; **one meal a day ~s her** ей доста́точно есть оди́н раз в день.

v.i. быть доста́точным; хват|а́ть, -и́ть; **a brief statement will ~ for my purpose** мне потре́буется лишь кра́ткое заявле́ние; ~ **it to say that ...** доста́точно сказа́ть, что...

sufficiency [sə'fɪʃənsɪ] *n.* доста́точность, доста́ток.

sufficient [sə'fɪʃ(ə)nt] *n.*: **have you had ~ (to eat)?** вы сы́ты?

adj. доста́точный, подходя́щий; **the sum is ~ for the journey** э́тих де́нег хва́тит на доро́гу; **lack ~ food** испы́тывать (*impf.*) недоста́ток в пи́ще.

suffix ['sʌfɪks] *n.* су́ффикс.

suffocat|e ['sʌfə,keɪt] *v.t.* души́ть, за-; **he was ~ed by poisonous fumes** он задохну́лся/задо́хся в ядови́том ды́ме; **~ing heat** уду́шливая жара́.

v.i. зад|ыха́ться, -охну́ться.

suffocation [,sʌfə'keɪʃ(ə)n] *n.* удуше́ние, уду́шье.

suffrage ['sʌfrɪdʒ] *n.* избира́тельное пра́во; **universal** ~ всео́бщее избира́тельное пра́во.

suffragette [,sʌfrə'dʒet] *n.* (*hist.*) суфражи́стка.

suffuse [sə'fju:z] *v.t.* зал|ива́ть, -и́ть.

sugar ['ʃʊgə(r)] *n.* са́хар; **granulated/caster** ~ (са́харный) песо́к; **icing** ~ са́харная пу́дра; **brown** ~ неочи́щенный са́харный песо́к; **lump** ~ кускова́й са́хар, (са́хар-)рафина́д.

v.t. **1.** (*lit., fig., sweeten*) подсла́|щивать, -сти́ть. **2.** (*sprinkle with* ~) пос|ыпа́ть, -ы́пать са́харом.

cpds. **~-basin, ~-bowl** *nn.* са́харница; **~-beet** *n.* са́харная свёкла; **~-cane** *n.* са́харный тростни́к; **~-coated** *adj.* обса́харенный; **~-loaf** *n.* са́харная голова́; **~-refinery** *n.* рафина́дный заво́д.

sugary ['ʃʊgərɪ] *adj.* **1.** са́харный, сахари́стый. **2.** (*fig., of tone, smile etc.*) сла́дкий, слаща́вый.

suggest [sə'dʒest] *v.t.* **1.** (*propose*) пред|лага́ть, -ожи́ть; сове́товать, по-; **I ~ you try again** я сове́тую вам попро́бовать ещё раз; **all sorts of plans were ~ed** предлага́лись всевозмо́жные пла́ны; (*with inanimate subject*): **what ~ed that idea to you?** что навело́ вас на э́ту мысль? **2.** (*evoke, call to mind*) вызыва́ть, вы́звать; **what does this shape ~?** что напомина́ет э́та фо́рма?; **does the name ~ nothing to you?** э́то и́мя вам ничего́ не говори́т? **3.** (*imply, indicate*) говори́ть (*impf.*) о+*p.*; **his skill ~s long practice** его́ мастерство́ говори́т о дли́тельной пра́ктике; **his tone ~ed impatience** в его́ то́не чу́вствовалось нетерпе́ние. **4.** (*advance as possible or likely*): **I ~ that the calculation is (*or* may be) wrong** по-мо́ему, здесь оши́бка в расчёте; **I ~ that you knew all the time** я утвержда́ю, что вы с са́мого нача́ла зна́ли об э́том; **do you ~ that I am lying?** вы хоти́те сказа́ть, что я лгу?

suggestion [sə'dʒestʃ(ə)n] *n.* **1.** (*proposal*) предложе́ние, сове́т; **make a ~** внести́ (*pf.*) предложе́ние; **I acted on his ~** я воспо́льзовался его́ сове́том/иде́ей. **2.** (*implication*) намёк; (*tinge*) отте́нок; **there was a ~ of regret in his voice** в его́ го́лосе звуча́ла но́тка сожале́ния. **3.** (*hypnotic etc.*) внуше́ние.

suggestive [sə'dʒestɪv] *adj.* **1.** ~ **of** напомина́ющий. **2.** (*improper*) непристо́йный, риско́ванный.

suicidal [,su:ɪ'saɪd(ə)l, ,sju:-] *adj.* **1.** (*pert. to suicide*) самоуби́йственный. **2.** (*leading to suicide*): ~ **tendencies** скло́нность к самоуби́йству. **3.** (*of pers.*) скло́нный к самоуби́йству. **4.** (*fig., fatal*) губи́тельный, ги́бельный; ~ **policy** па́губная поли́тика.

suicide ['su:ɪ,saɪd, 'sju:-] *n.* (*also fig.*) самоуби́йство; **commit ~** конча́ть, (по)ко́нчить с собо́й, ко́нчить, по- (жизнь) самоуби́йством.

suit [su:t, sju:t] *n.* **1.** (*leg.*) иск, де́ло; **civil/criminal ~** гражда́нский/уголо́вный иск; **bring (a) ~ against s.o.** предъяв|ля́ть, -и́ть иск кому́-н. **2.** (*of clothes*) костю́м; **two-piece ~** костю́м-дво́йка; (*woman's*) костю́м, ю́бка с жаке́том; ~ **of armour** доспе́хи (*m. pl.*), ла́т|ы (*pl., g.* —). **3.** (*of cards*) масть; **follow ~** ходи́ть (*indet.*) в масть.

v.t. **1.** (*accommodate, adapt*) приспос|а́бливать, -о́бить (*что к чему*); согласо́в|ывать, -а́ть (*что с чем*); **he is not ~ed to be an engineer** он не годи́тся в инжене́ры; **they are ~ed to one another** они́ подхо́дят друг дру́гу. **2.** (*be satisfactory, convenient to*): **the plan ~s me** э́тот план меня́ устра́ивает; **will it ~ you to finish now?** удо́бно ли вам ко́нчить на э́том?; **he tries to ~ everybody** он стара́ется всем угоди́ть; ~ **yourself!** как хоти́те! **3.** (*be good for, agree with*): **coffee does not ~ me** мне от ко́фе де́лается нехорошо́; **the English climate does not ~ everyone** не всем подхо́дит англи́йский кли́мат. **4.** (*befit*) под|ходи́ть, -ойти́ +*d.*; **the role does not ~ him** э́та роль ему́ не подхо́дит; **that hat ~s her** э́та шля́па ей идёт (*or* ей к лицу́).

cpd. **~case** *n.* чемода́н.

suitability [,su:tə'bɪlɪtɪ, ,sju:-] *n.* го́дность, приго́дность.

suitable ['su:təb(ə)l, 'sju:-] *adj.* подходя́щий, го́дный, соотве́тствующий; **he is ~ for the job** он подхо́дит для э́той до́лжности; **clothes ~ to the occasion** оде́жда, подходя́щая к (*or* соотве́тствующая) слу́чаю;

reading ~ to her age чте́ние, соотве́тствующее её во́зрасту.
suitably ['su:təblɪ, 'sju:-] *adv.* соотве́тственно, пра́вильно; как сле́дует.
suite [swi:t] *n.* **1.** (*retinue*) сви́та. **2.** (*set*): **~ of furniture** гарниту́р ме́бели; **bedroom ~** спа́льный гарниту́р; **~ of rooms** апарта́менты (*m. pl.*); (*in hotel*) (но́мер-)люкс. **3.** (*mus.*) сюи́та.
suitor ['su:tə(r), 'sju:-] *n.* жени́х, покло́нник.
sulf- ['sʌlf] = **sulph-**
sulk [sʌlk] *n.* дурно́е настрое́ние.
v.i. быть в дурно́м настрое́нии; **~ at s.o.** ду́ться (*impf.*) на кого́-н.
sulky ['sʌlkɪ] *adj.* наду́тый, оби́женный.
sullen ['sʌlən] *adj.* (*morose*) угрю́мый; (*sombre*) мра́чный.
sullenness ['sʌlənnɪs] *n.* угрю́мость; мра́чность.
sully ['sʌlɪ] *v.t.* (*liter.*) пятна́ть, за-.
sulphate ['sʌlfeɪt] *n.* сульфа́т; **copper/iron/zinc ~** ме́дный/желе́зный/ци́нковый купоро́с.
sulphide ['sʌlfaɪd] *n.* сульфи́д; **copper ~** серни́стая медь.
sulphite ['sʌlfaɪt] *n.* сульфи́т; **copper ~** сернистоки́слая медь.
sulphur ['sʌlfə(r)] (*US* **sulfur**) *n.* се́ра; **flowers of ~** се́рный цвет.
sulphuric [sʌl'fjʊərɪk] *adj.* се́рный; **~ acid** се́рная кислота́.
sulphurous ['sʌlfərəs] *adj.* серни́стый.
sultan ['sʌlt(ə)n] *n.* султа́н.
sultana [sʌl'tɑ:nə] *n.* изю́минка, (*collect.*) кишми́ш.
sultanate ['sʌltə,neɪt] *n.* султана́т.
sultry ['sʌltrɪ] *adj.* **1.** (*of atmosphere, weather*) зно́йный, ду́шный; **~ heat** зной. **2.** (*of temper or person*) зно́йный, стра́стный.
sum [sʌm] *n.* **1.** (*total*) ито́г; **~ total** о́бщая су́мма, о́бщий ито́г. **2.** (*amount*) су́мма. **3. ~** (*liter. substance, essence*) су́щность, суть; **in ~** (одни́м) сло́вом; **the ~ of all my wishes** ито́г/верши́на мои́х стремле́ний. **4.** (*problem*) (арифмети́ческая) зада́ча; **he did the ~ in his head** он реши́л зада́чу в уме́; **he is good at ~s** он силён в арифме́тике.
v.t. (*usu.* **~ up**) **1.** (*reckon up*) подсчи́т|ывать, -а́ть; скла́дывать, сложи́ть. **2.** (*summarize*) сумми́ровать (*impf.*); подв|оди́ть, -ести́ ито́г *+g./d.*; резюми́ровать (*impf., pf.*); (*form judgement of*): **he ~med up the situation at a glance** он оцени́л положе́ние с пе́рвого взгля́да.
v.i.: **~ up** сумми́ровать (*impf., pf.*); резюми́ровать (*impf., pf.*); **the judge's ~ming-up** заключи́тельная речь судьи́; **to ~ up, ...** сло́вом,...
summarily ['sʌmərɪlɪ] *adv.* бесцеремо́нно.
summarize ['sʌmə,raɪz] *v.t.* сумми́ровать (*impf., pf.*); резюми́ровать (*impf., pf.*).
summary ['sʌmərɪ] *n.* резюме́ (*indecl.*), сво́дка.
adj. **1.** (*brief*) сумма́рный, кра́ткий; **~ account** кра́ткий отчёт. **2.** (*rapid, sweeping*) бесцеремо́нный. **3.** (*leg.*) ускор́енный.
summation [sə'meɪʃ(ə)n] *n.* резюме́ (*indecl.*).
summer ['sʌmə(r)] *n.* ле́то; **in ~** ле́том; **Indian ~** ба́бье ле́то.
adj. ле́тний; **~ dress** ле́тнее пла́тье; **dressed in ~ clothes** одетый по-ле́тнему; **~ lightning** зарни́ца; **~ school** ле́тний университе́т; **~ time** (*daylight saving*) ле́тнее вре́мя.
v.i. (*spend ~*) пров|оди́ть, -ести́ ле́то.
cpds. **~house** *n.* бесе́дка; **~time** *n.* ле́тняя пора́.
summery ['sʌmərɪ] *adj.*: **~ weather** ле́тняя/тёплая пого́да; **~ clothes** лёгкая/ле́тняя оде́жда.
summit ['sʌmɪt] *n.* (*lit., fig.*) верши́на, верх; **the ~ of his ambition** верши́на его́ честолю́бия; **~ (conference, talks)** совеща́ние на вы́сшем у́ровне.
summon ['sʌmən] *v.t.* **1.** (*send for*) приз|ыва́ть, -ва́ть; (*also leg.*) вызыва́ть, вы́звать. **2.** (*order*) приз|ыва́ть, -ва́ть; **she ~ed the children to dinner** она́ позвала́ дете́й обе́дать. **3.: ~ a meeting** соз|ыва́ть, -ва́ть собра́ние; **~ up one's energy/courage** соб|ира́ться, -ра́ться с си́лами/ду́хом.
summons ['sʌmənz] *n.* вы́зов; (*leg.*) суде́бная пове́стка, вы́зов в суд; **answer a ~** яв|ля́ться, -и́ться по пове́стке.
v.t. вызыва́ть, вы́звать в суд.
sump [sʌmp] *n.* (*for sewage etc.*) выгребна́я я́ма; (*for engine oil*) маслосбо́рник; поддо́н ка́ртера.
sumptuous ['sʌmptjʊəs] *adj.* роско́шный, великоле́пный.
sun [sʌn] *n.* со́лнце; **the ~ rises** со́лнце восхо́дит/всхо́дит; **the ~ sets** со́лнце захо́дит/сади́тся; **before the ~ goes down** до захо́да со́лнца; **the ~ is up** со́лнце вста́ло; **the ~ is out** (*shining*) со́лнце све́тит; **when the ~ comes out** когда́ вы́йдет со́лнце; **when the ~ goes in** когда́ скро́ется со́лнце; **lie in the ~** лежа́ть (*impf.*) на со́лнце; **everything under the ~** всё на све́те; **you have caught the ~** (*become sunburnt*) вы загоре́ли.
v.t.: **~ o.s.** гре́ться (*impf.*) на со́лнце.
cpds. **~bathe** *v.i.* загора́ть (*impf.*); принима́ть (*impf.*) со́лнечные ва́нны; **~bather** *n.* загора́ющий; **~beam** *n.* со́лнечный луч; **~burn** *n.* (*tan*) зага́р; (*inflammation*) со́лнечный ожо́г; **~burn lotion** крем для зага́ра; **~burnt** *adj.* загоре́лый; **get ~burnt** загоре́ть (*pf.*); **S~day** *see separate entry*; **~dial** *n.* со́лнечные часы́ (*m. pl.*); **~down** *n.* захо́д со́лнца; **~-dress** *n.* сарафа́н; **~flower** *n.* подсо́лнечник; **~flower oil** подсо́лнечное ма́сло; **~flower seed** се́мечки (*nt. pl.*); **~-glasses** *n.* очки́ от со́лнца; **~-lamp** *n.* ква́рцевая ла́мпа; **~light** *n.* со́лнечный свет; **~lit** *adj.* освещённый/за́литый со́лнцем; **~rise** *n.* восхо́д (со́лнца); **at ~rise** на заре́; **~set** *n.* захо́д со́лнца, зака́т; **at ~set** на зака́те; **~shade** *n.* (*parasol*) (со́лнечный) зо́нтик; (*awning*) наве́с; **~shine** *n.* со́лнечный свет; (*fig., cheer*) ра́дость; **~spot** *n.* пятно́ на со́лнце; **~stroke** *n.* со́лнечный уда́р; **~-tan** *n.* зага́р; **~-tan lotion** крем для зага́ра.
sundae ['sʌndeɪ, -dɪ] *n.* моро́женое с фру́ктами/оре́хами (*u m.n.*).
Sunday ['sʌndeɪ, -dɪ] *n.* воскресе́нье; **on ~s** по воскресе́ньям.
sunder ['sʌndə(r)] *v.t.* (*liter.*) разлуч|а́ть, -и́ть.
sundries ['sʌndrɪz] *n.* ра́зное.
sundry ['sʌndrɪ] *adj.* ра́зный, разли́чный; **all and ~** всё и вся; все без исключе́ния.
sunken ['sʌŋkən] *adj.* (*of eyes etc.*) впа́лый, запа́вший; (*submerged*) подво́дный, зато́пленный.
sunny ['sʌnɪ] *adj.* со́лнечный; **look on the ~ side of things** ви́деть (*impf.*) све́тлую сто́рону веще́й; **a ~ disposition** жизнера́достный хара́ктер; **a ~ smile** сия́ющая улы́бка.
super ['su:pə(r), 'sju:-] (*coll.*) *n.* = **superintendent**
adj. замеча́тельный, превосхо́дный; **~!** здо́рово!
superabundance [,su:pərə'bʌnd(ə)ns, ,sju:-] (чрезме́рное) изоби́лие.
superabundant [,su:pərə'bʌnd(ə)nt, ,sju:-] *adj.* изоби́льный; избы́точный.
superannuate [,su:pər'ænjʊ,eɪt, ,sju:-] *v.t.* перев|оди́ть, -ести́ на пе́нсию по ста́рости; **~d** (*fig.*) преста-ре́лый; (*of thg.*) устаре́лый.
superannuation [,su:pər,ænjʊ'eɪʃ(ə)n, ,sju:-] *n.* (*payment*) пе́нсия по ста́рости.
superb [su:'pɜ:b, sju:-] *adj.* превосхо́дный, великоле́пный.
supercharger ['su:pə,tʃɑ:dʒə(r), 'sju:-] *n.* нагнета́тель (*m.*); компре́ссор надду́ва.
supercilious [,su:pə'sɪlɪəs, ,sju:-] *adj.* высокоме́рный, надме́нный.
supercomputer [,su:pəkəm'pju:tə(r)] *n.* су́пер-ЭВМ,

су́пер-компьютер.

superficial [ˌsu:pəˈfɪʃ(ə)l, ˌsju:-] *adj.* (*lit.*, *fig.*) пове́рхностный.

superficiality [ˌsu:pəfɪʃɪˈælɪtɪ, ˌsju:-] *n.* пове́рхностность.

superfluity [ˌsu:pəˈflu:ɪtɪ, ˌsju:-] *n.* изли́шек.

superfluous [su:ˈpɜ:fluəs, sju:-] *adj.* изли́шний.

superhuman [ˌsu:pəˈhju:mən, ˌsju:-] *adj.* сверхчелове́ческий.

superimpose [ˌsu:pərɪmˈpəʊz, ˌsju:-] *v.t.* на|кла́дывать, -ложи́ть (*что на что*).

superintend [ˌsu:pərɪnˈtend, ˌsju:-] *v.t. & i.* заве́довать (*impf.*) (*чем*); управля́ть (*impf.*) (*кем/чем*); (*impf.*) надзира́ть за (*кем/чем*).

superintendent [ˌsu:pərɪnˈtend(ə)nt, ˌsju:-] *n.* заве́дующий, управля́ющий, нача́льник.

superior [su:ˈpɪərɪə(r), sju:-, sʊ-] *n.* **1.** (*person of higher rank*) ста́рший, нача́льник. **2.** (*relig.*) настоя́тель (*fem.* -ница); **father ~** (оте́ц-)игу́мен; **mother ~** (мать-)игу́менья.

adj. **1.** (*of higher rank or status*) ста́рший, вы́сший; **~ officer** ста́рший офице́р. **2.** (*of better quality*, *better*) превосхо́дный, превосходя́щий; вы́сшего ка́чества; **~ skill** вы́сшее мастерство́; **this cloth is ~ to that** э́то сукно́ лу́чше того́ (*or* бо́лее высо́кого ка́чества, чем то). **3.** (*conscious of superiority*, *supercilious*): **a ~ smile** презри́тельная улы́бка; улы́бка превосхо́дства; **don't look so ~!** бро́сьте э́ту ва́шу высокоме́рную мане́ру! **4.** (*greater in number*) превосходя́щий.

superiority [su:ˌpɪərɪˈɒrɪtɪ, sju:-, sʊ-] *n.* превосхо́дство.

superlative [su:ˈpɜ:lətɪv, sju:-] *n.* (*gram.*) превосхо́дная сте́пень.

adj. **1.** (*excellent*) велича́йший, высоча́йший. **2.** (*gram.*) превосхо́дный.

superman [ˈsu:pəˌmæn, ˈsju:-] *n.* сверхчелове́к.

supermarket [ˈsu:pəˌmɑ:kɪt, ˈsju:-] *n.* универса́м.

supernatural [ˌsu:pəˈnætʃər(ə)l, ˌsju:-] *n.*: **a belief in the ~** ве́ра в сверхъестесте́ственное.

adj. сверхъесте́ственный.

supernova [ˌsu:pəˈnəʊvə, ˌsju:-] *n.* сверхно́вая (звезда́).

supernumerary [ˌsu:pəˈnju:mərərɪ, ˌsju:-] *n.* сверхшта́тный рабо́тник; (*actor*) стати́ст (*fem.* -ка).

adj. сверхшта́тный.

superpower [ˈsu:pəˌpaʊə(r), ˈsju:-] *n.* сверхдержа́ва.

supersaturate [ˌsu:pəˈsætʃəˌreɪt, ˌsju:-, -tjʊˌreɪt] *v.t.* перес|ыща́ть, -ы́тить.

superscript [ˈsu:pəskrɪpt, ˈsju:-] *adj.* надстро́чный.

supersede [ˌsu:pəˈsi:d, ˌsju:-] *v.t.* смен|я́ть, -и́ть; замен|я́ть, -и́ть.

supersensitive [ˌsu:pəˈsensɪtɪv] *adj.* сверхчувстви́тельный.

supersonic [ˌsu:pəˈsɒnɪk, ˌsju:-] *adj.* сверхзвуково́й.

superstar [ˈsu:pəˌstɑ:(r)] *n.* суперзвезда́.

superstition [ˌsu:pəˈstɪʃ(ə)n, ˌsju:-] *n.* суеве́рие.

superstitious [ˌsu:pəˈstɪʃəs, ˌsju:-] *adj.* суеве́рный.

superstructure [ˈsu:pəˌstrʌktʃə(r), ˈsju:-] *n.* надстро́йка.

supertanker [ˈsu:pəˌtæŋkə(r), ˈsju:-] *n.* суперта́нкер.

supervise [ˈsu:pəˌvaɪz, ˈsju:-] *v.t.* надзира́ть (*impf.*) за+*i.*; наблюда́ть (*impf.*) за+*i.*

supervision [ˌsu:pəˈvɪʒ(ə)n, ˌsju:-] *n.* надсмо́тр/надзо́р (за+*i.*).

supervisor [ˈsu:pəˌvaɪzə(r), ˈsju:-] *n.* надсмо́трщи|к (*fem.* -ца); надзира́тель (*fem.* -ница); (*acad.*) (нау́чный) руководи́тель (*fem.* -ница).

supervisory [ˈsu:pəˌvaɪzərɪ, ˈsju:-] *adj.* контро́льный, надзира́ющий; **~ council** контро́льный сове́т.

supine [ˈsu:paɪn, ˈsju:-] *adj.* (*face up*) лежа́щий на́взничь; (*fig.*) безде́ятельный, ине́ртный.

supper [ˈsʌpə(r)] *n.* у́жин; **have ~** у́жинать, по-.

supplant [səˈplɑ:nt] *v.t.* (*replace*) вытесня́ть, вы́теснить; (*oust*) выжива́ть, вы́жить.

supple [ˈsʌp(ə)l] *adj.* ги́бкий; **~ limbs** ги́бкие чле́ны; (*soft*) мя́гкий; **~ leather** мя́гкая ко́жа.

supplement[1] [ˈsʌplɪmənt] *n.* **1.** (*addition*) дополне́ние. **2.** (*of book etc.*) приложе́ние.

supplement[2] [ˈsʌplɪmənt, ˌsʌplɪˈment] *v.t.* доп|олня́ть, -о́лнить; поп|олня́ть, -о́лнить.

supplementary [ˌsʌplɪˈmentərɪ] *adj.* дополни́тельный, доба́вочный.

suppliant [ˈsʌplɪənt] *n.* проси́тель (*fem.* -ница).

adj. проси́тельный, умоля́ющий.

supplicate [ˈsʌplɪˌkeɪt] *v.t.* моли́ть, умоля́ть (*impf.*).

supplication [ˌsʌplɪˈkeɪʃ(ə)n] *n.* мольба́, про́сьба.

supplier [səˈplaɪə(r)] *n.* поставщи́|к (*fem.* -ца).

suppl|y [səˈplaɪ] *n.* **1.** (*providing*) снабже́ние (*чем*). **2.** (*thg. supplied*, *stock*) запа́с; **have you a good ~y of food?** у вас доста́точно продово́льствия?; **water ~y** водоснабже́ние; **take, lay in a ~y of sth.** запа|са́ться, -ти́сь чем-н.; **bread is in short ~y** хлеб в дефици́те; **a commodity in short ~y** дефици́тный това́р; (*pl.*, *mil.*) (бое)припа́сы (*m. pl.*). **3.** (*econ.*): **~y and demand** спро́с и предложе́ние. **4. ~y teacher** вре́менный учи́тель.

v.t. **1.** (*furnish*, *equip*) снаб|жа́ть, -ди́ть; обеспе́чи|вать, -ть (*all кого/что чем*); **the farm ~ies us with potatoes** фе́рма обеспе́чивает/снабжа́ет нас карто́фелем; **arteries ~y the heart with blood** арте́рии доставля́ют кро́вь к се́рдцу. **2.** (*give*, *yield*) да|ва́ть, -ть; дост|авля́ть, -а́вить (*что кому/чему*); **cows ~y milk** коро́вы даю́т молоко́; **catalogue ~ied on request** катало́г выдаётся по тре́бованию. **3.** (*meet need*): **~y a deficiency** возме|ща́ть, -сти́ть недоста́ток.

support [səˈpɔ:t] *n.* **1.** (*aid*) подде́ржка; **walk without ~** ходи́ть (*indet.*) без подде́ржки; **give, lend ~** ока́з|ывать, -а́ть подде́ржку +*d.*; **in ~ of** в подде́ржку +*g.*; **without visible means of ~** без определённых средств к существова́нию. **2.** (*lit.*, *fig.*, *prop*) опо́ра; **shelf ~** кронште́йн для по́лки; **the sole ~ of his family** еди́нственная опо́ра семьи́.

v.t. **1.** (*hold up*, *prop up*) подде́рж|ива́ть, -а́ть; подп|ира́ть, -ере́ть; **~ o.s. with a stick** оп|ира́ться, -ере́ться на па́лку; (*fig.*, *assist by deed or word*): **which party do you ~?** каку́ю па́ртию вы подде́рживаете?; **~ing actor** актёр на вторы́х роля́х; (*sustain*): **air is necessary to ~ life** во́здух необходи́м для поддержа́ния жи́зни. **2.** (*provide subsistence for*) содержа́ть (*impf.*); **he cannot ~ a family** он не в состоя́нии содержа́ть семью́. **3.** (*confirm*) подкреп|ля́ть, -и́ть; **his theory is not ~ed by the facts** его́ тео́рия не подкрепля́ется фа́ктами. **4.** (*endure*) выде́рживать, вы́держать; **I cannot ~ his insolence** я не выношу́ его́ высокоме́рия.

supporter [səˈpɔ:tə(r)] *n.* (*of cause*, *motion etc.*) сторо́нни|к (*fem.* -ца); (*of sports team*) боле́льщи|к (*fem.* -ца).

supportive [səˈpɔ:tɪv] *adj.* подде́рживающий, лойя́льный.

suppose [səˈpəʊz] *v.t.* **1.** (*assume*) предпол|ага́ть, -ожи́ть; допус|ка́ть, -ти́ть; **let us ~ what you say is true** предполо́жим, что вы говори́те пра́вду; **supposing he came, what would you say?** е́сли бы он пришёл, что бы вы сказа́ли?; **~ it rains?** а что е́сли пойдёт до́ждь?; **~ they find out?** а вдруг они узна́ют?; **everyone is ~d to know the rules** предполага́ется, что все знако́мы с пра́вилами. **2.** (*imagine*, *believe*): **I ~ him to be about sixty** я полага́ю, что ему́ лет шестьдеся́т; **he is ~d to be rich** говоря́т, что он бога́т; **I ~ you like Moscow** вам, наве́рное, нра́вится Москва́; **I don't ~ he will mind that** не ду́маю, что он бу́дет про́тив э́того; **what do you ~ he meant?** как по-ва́шему, что́ он име́л в виду́?; **I ~ so** наве́рное; должно́ быть. **3.** (*expr. suggestion*): **~ we take a holiday?** дава́йте возьмём о́тпуск? **4.** (*pass.*, *be expected*, *required*): **this is ~d to help you sleep** э́то должно́ помо́чь вам засну́ть; **he is ~d to wash the dishes** ему́ поло́жено мыть посу́ду; **he was ~d to lock the door** он должен был запере́ть дверь; **you are ~d to hold the cup like this** ча́шку сле́дует держа́ть (вот) так; **how was I ~d to know?** отку́да мне бы́ло знать? **5.** (*p.p.*, *presumed*) предпола́гаемый, мни́мый.

supposition [ˌsʌpəˈzɪʃ(ə)n] *n.* предположе́ние, гипо́теза, дога́дка.

suppository [səˈpɒzɪtərɪ] *n.* суппозито́рий.

suppress [səˈpres] *v.t.* **1.** подав|ля́ть, -и́ть; сдéрж|ивать, -а́ть; **the rebellion was ~ed** восста́ние бы́ло пода́влено; **she could hardly ~ a smile** она́ с трудо́м подави́ла/сдержа́ла улы́бку; **~ing a yawn** подавля́я зево́ту. **2.** (*stop publication of*) запре|ща́ть, -ти́ть. **3.** (*conceal*) скры|ва́ть, -ть; зам|а́лчивать, -олча́ть; **they succeeded in ~ing the truth** им удало́сь скры́ть/замолча́ть пра́вду.

suppression [səˈpresʃ(ə)n] *n.* (*restraining*) подавле́ние, сде́рживание; (*banning*) запреще́ние; (*silencing*) зама́лчивание.

suppurate [ˈsʌpjəˌreɪt] *v.i.* гнои́ться, за-/на-.

suppuration [ˌsʌpjəˈreɪʃ(ə)n] *n.* нагное́ние.

supremacist [suːˈpreməsɪst, sjuː-] *n.*: **white ~** сторо́нник госпо́дства бе́лых.

supremacy [suːˈpreməsɪ, sjuː-] *n.* госпо́дство; превосхо́дство.

supreme [suːˈpriːm, sjuː-] *adj.* **1.** (*of authority*) верхо́вный; **~ power** верхо́вная власть; **he reigned ~** он вла́ствовал безразде́льно. **2.** (*utmost*, *greatest*, *highest*): **the ~ sacrifice** же́ртва со́бственной жи́знью; **~ test of fidelity** вы́сшее испыта́ние ве́рности; **he was ~ly confident** он был в вы́сшей сте́пени (само)уве́рен; **~ly happy** на верху́ блаже́нства.

supremo [suːˈpriːməʊ, sjuː-] *n.* верхо́вный глава́; дикта́тор.

Supt. [ˌsuːpərɪnˈtend(ə)nt, ˌsjuː-] *n.* (*abbr. of* **Superintendent**) коменда́нт, управля́ющий.

surcharge [ˈsɜːtʃɑːdʒ] *n.* **1.** (*extra fee*) допла́та, припла́та. **2.** (*penalty*) штраф.

sure [ʃʊə(r), ʃɔː(r)] *adj.* **1.** (*convinced*, *certain*, *confident*) уве́ренный, убеждённый; **he is ~** (*confident*) **of success** он уве́рен в (своём) успе́хе; **you can be ~ of one thing ...** одно́ несомне́нно; **he is very ~ of himself** он о́чень самоуве́рен; **I'm not ~ whether to go or not** я не зна́ю, пойти́ и́ли нет; **how can I be ~ he is honest?** отку́да я зна́ю, что он че́стен? **2.** (*safe*, *reliable*, *trusty*, *unfailing*) ве́рный, надёжный; **a ~ way to break one's neck** ве́рный спо́соб слома́ть себе́ ше́ю; **there can be no ~ proof** абсолю́тных доказа́тельств не мо́жет быть. **3.** (*with inf*, *certain*, *to be relied on*): **he is ~ to come** он непреме́нно придёт; **be ~ to lock the door** не забу́дьте запере́ть дверь!; **be ~ and write to me** смотри́те напиши́те мне!; **it is ~ to be wet** наверняка́ бу́дет дождли́во; **~ thing!** (*coll.*) коне́чно!; ещё бы! **4.** (*undoubtedly true*) несомне́нный, уве́ренный; **one thing is ~** в одно́м мо́жно не сомнева́ться. **5.: for ~** несомне́нно; то́чно, наверняка́; **to be ~** (*concessive*) коне́чно, разуме́ется; (*confirmatory*) в са́мом де́ле. **6.: make ~** (*convince*, *satisfy o.s.*) убе|жда́ться, -ди́ться; удостов|еря́ться, -е́риться (*both* в чём); **you must make ~ of your facts** вы должны́ прове́рить все фа́кты. **7.: I made ~** (*ensured*) **that he would come** я позабо́тился о том, что́бы он (непреме́нно) пришёл; **we must make ~ of a house before winter** мы должны́ обеспе́чить себе́ жильё до наступле́ния зимы́.

adv.: **~ enough** действи́тельно, коне́чно; **he will come ~ enough** он придёт, не беспоко́йтесь; **it ~ was cold!** (*US*) до чего́ же бы́ло хо́лодно!

cpds. **~-footed** *adj.* стоя́щий твёрдо на нога́х; с уве́ренной похо́дкой.

surely [ˈʃʊəlɪ] *adv.* **1.** (*securely*) надёжно; **slowly but ~** ме́дленно, но ве́рно. **2.** (*without doubt*) несомне́нно, ве́рно, наверняка́. **3.** (*expr. strong hope or belief*): **it ~ cannot have been he** не мо́жет быть, что́бы э́то был он; **~ I have met you before** я уве́рен, что (где́-то) ви́дел вас пре́жде; **~ you saw him?** неуже́ли вы его́ не ви́дели. **4.** (*as answer*, *certainly*) коне́чно, непреме́нно.

surety [ˈʃʊərɪtɪ, ˈʃʊətɪ] *n.* **1.** (*pledge*) зало́г. **2.** (*pers.*) поручи́тель (*fem.* -ница); **stand ~ for s.o.** руча́ться, поручи́ться за кого́-н.; брать, взять кого́-н. на пору́ки.

surf [sɜːf] *n.* прибо́й, буруны́ (*m. pl.*).

v.i. занима́ться (*impf.*) сёрфингом.

cpds. **~-board** *n.* доска́ для сёрфинга.

surface [ˈsɜːfɪs] *n.* **1.** пове́рхность; **beneath the ~** (*lit.*) под пове́рхности; (*fig.*) за вне́шностью; **come to the ~** (*lit.*) всплы|ва́ть, -ть (на пове́рхность); (*fig.*) обнару́жи|ваться, -ться. **2.** (*attr.*) пове́рхностный, вне́шний; **~ mail** обы́чная по́чта; **~ tension** пове́рхностное натяже́ние; **~ vessel** надво́дное су́дно.

v.t. **1.: ~ a road** покр|ыва́ть, -ы́ть доро́гу асфа́льтом (*u m.n.*). **2.: ~ a submarine** подн|има́ть, -я́ть подво́дную ло́дку на пове́рхность.

v.i. (*of submarine*, *swimmer etc.*) вспл|ыва́ть, -ыть на пове́рхность.

surfeit [ˈsɜːfɪt] *n.* (*excess of eating etc.*) изли́шество, избы́ток; (*repletion*, *satiety*; *also fig.*) пресыще́ние.

v.t. (*satiate*) прес|ыща́ть, -ы́тить.

surfer [ˈsɜːfə(r)] *n.* сёрфинги́ст.

surfing [ˈsɜːfɪŋ] *n.* сёрфинг.

surge [sɜːdʒ] *n.* (*of waves*, *water*) во́лны (*f. pl.*); вал; (*of crowd*, *emotion etc.*) волна́, прили́в.

v.i. **1.** (*of waves*, *water*) вздыма́ться (*impf.*). **2.** (*of crowd*) волнова́ться (*impf.*); **the crowd ~d forward** толпа́ подала́сь вперёд. **3.** (*of emotions*) нахлы́нуть (*pf.*).

surgeon [ˈsɜːdʒ(ə)n] *n.* хиру́рг; **dental ~** зубно́й врач.

surgery [ˈsɜːdʒərɪ] *n.* **1.** (*treatment*) хирурги́я; **minor/major ~** ма́лая/больша́я хирурги́я; (*operation*) опера́ция. **2.** (*office*) приёмная/кабине́т (врача́); **in ~ hours** в приёмные часы́; **the doctor holds a ~ every morning** врач принима́ет ка́ждое у́тро.

surgical [ˈsɜːdʒɪk(ə)l] *adj.* хирурги́ческий; **~ spirit** медици́нский спирт.

surly [ˈsɜːlɪ] *adj.* неприве́тливый, хму́рый, угрю́мый.

surmise [səˈmaɪz] *n.* (*conjecture*) дога́дка; (*supposition*) предположе́ние.

v.t. предпол|ага́ть, -ожи́ть.

v.i. дога́д|ываться, -а́ться.

surmount [səˈmaʊnt] *v.t.* **1.** (*overcome*) преодол|ева́ть, -е́ть. **2.: peaks ~ed with snow** го́рные верши́ны, уве́нчанные сне́гом.

surmountable [səˈmaʊntəb(ə)l] *adj.* преодоли́мый.

surname [ˈsɜːneɪm] *n.* фами́лия.

surpass [səˈpɑːs] *v.t.* прев|осходи́ть, -зойти́; **he ~ed everyone in strength** он превосходи́л всех си́лой; **a woman of ~ing beauty** же́нщина непревзойдённой красоты́.

surplice [ˈsɜːplɪs] *n.* стиха́рь (*m.*).

surplus [ˈsɜːpləs] *n.* (*excess*) изли́шек; (*residue*) оста́ток; **in ~** в избы́тке.

adj. **1.** (*excess*) изли́шний, избы́точный; **~ food** изли́шки (*m. pl.*) продово́льствия; **~ to our requirements** бо́льше, чем (нам) тре́буется. **2.** (*remaining*) оста́точный; **~ value** приба́вочная сто́имость.

surprise [səˈpraɪz] *n.* **1.** (*wonder*, *astonishment*) удивле́ние; **show ~** удив|ля́ться, -и́ться; **to my ~** к моему́ удивле́нию. **2.** (*unexpected events*, *news*, *gift etc.*) неожи́данность, сюрпри́з; **his arrival was a ~ to us all** его́ прие́зд был для нас всех неожи́данность; **I had the ~ of my life** я был совершéнно поражён; **give s.o. a ~** устрóить (*pf.*) комý-н. сюрприз. **3.** (*unexpected action*): **catch, take s.o. by ~** застичь (*pf.*) когó-н. врасплóх. **4.** (*attr.*) неожиданный, внезáпный; **~ visit** неожиданный визит; **~ package, packet** сюрприз.

v.t. **1.** (*astonish*) удив|лять, -ить; пора|жáть, -зить; **I'm ~d at you!** вы меня удивляете!; я этого от вас не ожидáл; **it's nothing to be ~d at** в этом нет ничегó удивительного; **I shouldn't be ~d if ...** я (нискóлько) не удивлюсь, éсли... **2.** (*by unexpected gift etc.*) сдéлать/устрóить (*pf.*) сюрприз +*d.* **3.** (*capture by ~*) захват|ывать, -ить врасплóх; (*liter., take by ~*) заст|игáть, -ичь (*or* заст|авáть, -áть) (врасплóх); **we ~d him in the act of stealing** мы егó поймáли с поличным.

surprising [sə'praɪzɪŋ] *adj.* удивительный, порази-тельный; **~ though it may seem** как ни удиви-тельно; **he eats ~ly little** он удивительно мáло ест.

surrealism [sə'rɪəˌlɪz(ə)m] *n.* сюрреализм.

surrealist [sə'rɪəlɪst] *n.* сюрреалист.

adj. сюрреалистический.

surrender [sə'rendə(r)] *n.* (*handing over*) сдáча; (*giving up*) откáз (от+*g.*); (*capitulation*) капитуляция; **no ~!** не сдавáться!; **unconditional ~** безоговóроч-ная капитуляция.

v.t. **1.** (*yield*) сда|вáть, -ть; **the fort was ~ed to the enemy** крéпость былá сданá неприятелю. **2.** (*give up*) отказ|ывáться, -áться от+*g.* **3. ~ o.s.: he ~ed himself to justice** он отдáлся в рýки право-сýдия.

v.i. сд|авáться, -áться; капитулировать (*impf., pf.*).

surreptitious [ˌsʌrəp'tɪʃəs] *adj.* тáйный; сдéланный исподтишкá.

surrogate ['sʌrəgət] *n.* суррогáт.

surround [sə'raʊnd] *n.* бордюр, окаймлéние.

v.t. окруж|áть, -ить; обступ|áть, -ить; **the ~ing countryside** окружáющая мéстность; окрéстности (*f. pl.*); **the troops were ~ed** войскá были окруже-ны.

surroundings [sə'raʊndɪŋz] *n.* (*material environment*) мéстность, окрéстности (*f. pl.*); обстанóвка; (*intellectual environment*) средá, окружéние.

surtax ['sɜ:tæks] *n.* добáвочный подохóдный налóг.

surveillance [sɜ:'veɪləns] *n.* надзóр; **under ~** под надзóром (полиции).

survey[1] ['sɜ:veɪ] *n.* **1.** (*general view*) обзóр, обозрéние; (*inspection, investigation*) обслéдование, опрóс; **we are carrying out a ~ on the dangers of smoking** мы провóдим исслéдование по вопрóсу о вредé курé-ния. **2.** (*of land*) съёмка, промéр; **they are making a ~ of our village** произвóдится (топографическая/землемéрная) съёмка нáшего селá. **3.** (*plan, map*) план, кáрта.

survey[2] [sə'veɪ] *v.t.* **1.** (*view*) обозр|евáть, -éть. **2.** (*review, consider*) обслéдовать (*impf., pf.*); рассм|á-тривать, -отрéть. **3.** (*inspect*) осм|áтривать, -отрéть. **4.** (*land etc.*) межевáть (*impf.*); произв|одить, -ести съёмку +*g.*; **the house was ~ed and valued** были произведены осмóтр и оцéнка дóма.

surveying [sɜ:'veɪɪŋ] *n.* (топографическая) съёмка; съёмка; **photographic ~** фотосъёмка.

surveyor [sə'veɪə(r)] *n.* **1.** (*official inspector*) инспéк-тор, контролёр. **2.** (*of land etc.*) землемéр.

survival [sə'vaɪv(ə)l] *n.* **1.** (*living on*) выживáние; **~ of the fittest** выживáние наиболее приспосóблен-ных; **their ~ depended on us** их жизнь зависéла от нас; **~ rate** выживáемость. **2.** (*relic*) пережиток.

survive [sə'vaɪv] *v.t.* **1.** (*outlive*) переж|ивáть, -ить; **he will ~ us all** он нас всех переживёт. **2.** (*come alive through*): **~ an illness** перен|осить, -ести болéзнь; **they ~d the shipwreck** они остáлись в живых пóсле кораблекрушéния.

v.i. (*continue to live*) выживáть, выжить; **not one of the family has ~d** из всей семьи никогó не остáлось (в живых); (*be preserved*): сохраниться, уцелéть (*both pf.*); **the custom still ~s** этот обычай ещё сохранился.

survivor [sə'vaɪvə(r)] *n.* уцелéвший; **he was the sole ~** он один остáлся в живых.

susceptibility [səˌseptɪ'bɪlɪtɪ] *n.* (*to disease etc.*) вос-приимчивость (к болéзни *и т. п.*).

susceptible [sə'septɪb(ə)l] *adj.* **1.** (*impressionable*) впечатлительный, восприимчивый. **2.: ~ to** вос-приимчивый к+*d.*; пáдкий на+*a.*; **he is ~ to colds** он подвéржен простýде; **he is ~ to flattery** он пáдок на лесть.

suspect[1] ['sʌspekt] *n.* подозревáемый.

adj. подозрительный; не внушáющий довéрия.

suspect[2] [sə'spekt] *v.t.* **1.** подозревáть; (*apprehend*) предчýвствовать (*impf.*); предпол|агáть, -ожить; **I ~ it will rain before long** я подозревáю, что скóро пойдёт дождь; **you, I ~, don't care** вам, я полагáю/подозревáю, всё равнó; **I ~ed him to be lying** я подозревáл, что он лжёт. **2.** (*disbelieve, doubt*) сомневáться; **I ~ed (the truth of) his story** я сом-невáлся в истинности егó расскáза.

suspend [sə'spend] *v.t.* **1.** (*hang up*) подвé|шивать, -сить; **the cage was ~ed from the ceiling** клéтка былá подвéшена к потолкý (*or* свисáла с потол-кá); **the balloon was ~ed in mid-air** воздýшный шар повис в вóздухе; **particles of dust ~ed in the air** частицы пыли, взвéшенные в вóздухе. **2.** (*postpone, delay, stop for a time*) врéменно прекра|щáть, -тить; приостан|áвливать, -овить; **~ a meeting** пре-р|ывáть, -вáть собрáние; **~ judgement** (*fig.*) воз-дéрж|иваться, -áться от суждéния; **~ hostilities** приостановить (*pf.*) воéнные дéйствия; **state of ~ed animation** состояние бесчýвствия; **~ed sentence** услóвный приговóр. **3.** (*debar temporarily from office etc.*) врéменно отстран|ять, -ить; **the player was ~ed for three months** игрокá отстра-нили на три мéсяца.

suspender [sə'spendə(r)] *n.* **1.** (*for hose*) подвязка. **2.** (*US, pl., braces*) подтяжки (*pl., g.* -ек); пóмочи (*pl., g.* -éй).

cpd. **~-belt** *n.* (жéнский) пóяс с подвязками.

suspense [sə'spens] *n.* напряжéние, напряжённость; **keep s.o. in ~** держáть (*impf.*) когó-н. в неизвéст-ности; **I can't stand the ~** я не в состоянии вынести напряжéние/неизвéстность/неопределённость.

suspension [sə'spenʃ(ə)n] *n.* **1.** (*hanging*) подвéши-вание; **~ bridge** подвеснóй/висячий мост. **2.** (*of vehicle etc.*) подвéс. **3.** (*stoppage*) приостановлéние; **~ of nuclear tests** врéменное прекращéние испы-тáний ядерного орýжия. **6.** (*debarring from office etc.*) отстранéние; **their goalkeeper faces ~** их вра-тарю грозит (врéменное) исключéние из комáн-ды.

suspicion [sə'spɪʃ(ə)n] *n.* **1.** подозрéние; **I had no ~ he was there** я не подозревáл, что он там; **he was looked upon with ~** к немý относились подозри-тельно (*or* с подозрéнием); **arouse ~** возбу|ждáть, -дить подозрéния; **above ~** выше/вне подозрéний; **under ~** под подозрéнием; **on ~ of murder** по подо-зрéнию в убийстве. **2.** (*trace, nuance*) привкус, оттéнок; **a ~ of garlic** зáпах/привкус чеснокá; **a ~ of irony** тень ирóнии.

suspicious [sə'spɪʃəs] *adj.* **1.** (*mistrustful*) подозри-тельный, недовéрчивый (к+*d.*); **his silence made me ~** егó молчáние застáвило меня насторо-житься. **2.** (*arousing suspicion*) подозрительный.

sustain [sə'steɪn] *v.t.* **1.** (*lit., fig.: support*) поддéр-ж|ивать, -áть; **hope alone ~ed him** он жил однóй надéждой. **2.** (*bear, endure*): **the bridge will not ~ heavy loads** мост не выдéрживает больших нагру́зок; **they ~ed the attack** они́ вы́держали ата́ку. **3.** (*undergo, suffer*) потерпе́ть (*pf.*); понести́ (*pf.*); **the enemy ~ed heavy losses** проти́вник понёс тяжёлые поте́ри; **~ an injury** перенести́ (*pf.*) тра́вму. **4.** (*keep going, maintain*): **~ a role** выде́рживать, вы́держать роль; **a ~ed effort** дли́тельное/непреры́вное уси́лие; **~ a note** (*mus.*) держа́ть (*impf.*) но́ту. **5.** (*uphold*) подтвер|жда́ть, -ди́ть; **~ an objection** прин|има́ть, -я́ть возраже́ние.

sustenance ['sʌstɪnəns] *n.* пита́ние, пи́ща.

suture ['su:tʃə(r)] *n.* **1.** (*anat.*) шов. **2.** (*surg., stitching*) наложе́ние шва.

v.t. заш|ива́ть, -и́ть (*рану*).

suzerain ['su:zərən] *n.* сюзере́н.

suzerainty ['su:zərəntɪ] *n.* сюзеренитéт.

svelte [svelt] *adj.* стро́йный, ги́бкий.

swab [swɒb] *n.* **1.** (*mop etc.*) шва́бра. **2.** (*surg.*) тампо́н. **3.** (*med., specimen*) мазо́к.

v.t. мыть, вы- шва́брой; подт|ира́ть, -ере́ть.

swaddl|e ['swɒd(ə)l] *v.t.* пелена́ть, с-; сви|ва́ть, -ть; **~ing-clothes** пелёнки (*f. pl.*), свива́льник.

swag [swæg] *n.* (*sl., booty*) награ́бленная добы́ча.

swagger ['swægə(r)] *n.* ва́жная похо́дка; **walk with a ~** расха́живать (*impf.*) с ва́жным ви́дом.

v.i. **1.** (*of walk*) расха́живать (*impf.*) с ва́жным ви́дом. **2.** (*of manner*) ва́жничать (*impf.*). **3.** (*boast*) хва́стать(ся) (*impf.*).

swallow[1] ['swɒləʊ] *n.* (*bird*) ла́сточка.

cpd. **~-tail** *n.* (*butterfly*) ба́бочка-па́русник.

swallow[2] ['swɒləʊ] *n.* (*gulp*) глото́к; **at one ~** одни́м глотко́м; за́лпом.

v.t. **1.** прогла́тывать, -оти́ть; **he ~ed the vodka at one go** он вы́пил во́дку за́лпом; **~ the bait** (*fig.*) попа́сться (*pf.*) на у́дочку; **I made him ~ his words** я заста́вил его́ взять свои́ слова́ наза́д; **he had to ~ his pride** ему́ пришло́сь проглоти́ть своё самолю́бие; **she will ~ the most outrageous tales** она́ гото́ва пове́рить са́мым фантасти́ческим ро́ссказням. **2.** (*usu.* **~ up:** *engulf, absorb*) погло|ща́ть, -ти́ть; **the expenses ~ed up the earnings** расхо́ды поглоти́ли весь за́работок.

v.i. глота́ть (*impf.*); **he ~ed** он сглотну́л.

swamp [swɒmp] *n.* боло́то.

v.t. **1.** (*fill, cover with water*) затоп|ля́ть, -и́ть; зал|ива́ть, -и́ть. **2.** (*fig., overwhelm, inundate*) навод|ня́ть, -ни́ть; зас|ыпа́ть, -ы́пать; **we were ~ed with applications** мы бы́ли зава́лены заявле́ниями.

swampy ['swɒmpɪ] *adj.* боло́тистый, то́пкий.

swan [swɒn] *n.* ле́бедь (*m.*).

v.i. шата́ться (*impf.*) (*coll.*).

cpds. **~sdown** *n.* лебя́жий пух; **~-song** *n.* лебеди́ная песнь.

swank [swæŋk] (*coll.*) *v.i.*: **~ about sth.** хва́стать (*impf.*) чем-н.

swap [swɒp] (*coll.*) *n.* обме́н.

v.t. меня́ть, с-; махну́ться (*pf.*) *+i.*; **will you ~ places with me?** вы согла́сны со мной поменя́ться места́ми?; **let's ~ watches** махнёмся часа́ми?; **they were ~ping jokes** они́ обме́нивались анекдо́тами.

swarm[1] [swɔ:m] *n.*: **~ of ants/bees** муравьи́ный/пчели́ный рой; **~ of locusts** ста́я саранчи́.

v.i. **1.** (*of bees, ants etc.*) рои́ться (*impf.*). **2.** (*of people*): **children came ~ing round him** де́ти столпи́лись вокру́г него́; **a crowd of people ~ed into the square** огро́мная толпа́ хлы́нула на пло́щадь. **3.** (*teem*) кише́ть (*impf.*) *+i.*; **the town is ~ing with tourists** го́род киши́т тури́стами.

swarm[2] [swɔ:m] *v.t. & i.* кара́бкаться, вс-; **the sailors ~ed (up) the ropes** матро́сы вскара́бкались по ва́нтам.

swarthy ['swɔ:ðɪ] *adj.* сму́глый.

swashbuckler ['swɒʃ,bʌklə(r)] *n.* сорвиголова́ (*m.*).

swastika ['swɒstɪkə] *n.* сва́стика.

swat [swɒt] *v.t.* бить (*impf.*); прихло́п|ывать, -нуть.

swatch [swɒtʃ] *n.* образе́ц, обра́зчик; образцы́ (*m. pl.*).

swath(e) [sweɪð] *n.* проко́с.

swathe [sweɪð] *v.t.* бинтова́ть, за-; заку́т|ывать, -ать.

sway [sweɪ] *n.* **1.** (*~ing motion*) кача́ние, колеба́ние. **2.** (*influence*) влия́ние; (*authority*) авторите́т; (*rule*) власть; **have, hold ~ over s.o.** держа́ть (*impf.*) кого́-н. в подчине́нии.

v.t. **1.** (*rock*) кача́ть (*impf.*); колеба́ть, по-; **~ the balance in s.o.'s favour** поколеба́ть/склони́ть (*pf.*) весы́ в чью-н. по́льзу. **2.** (*influence, move*) влия́ть, по-; колеба́ть, по-; **he cannot be ~ed by such arguments** его́ нельзя́ поколеба́ть таки́ми до́водами; **his speech ~ed votes** его́ речь повлия́ла на исхо́д голосова́ния.

v.i. кача́ться (*impf.*); колеба́ться, по-.

swear [sweə(r)] *v.t. & i.* **1.** (*pronounce, promise solemnly*) кля́сться (*impf.*); божи́ться (*impf.*); **they swore eternal friendship** они́ покляли́сь в ве́чной дру́жбе; **~ an oath** прин|оси́ть, -ести́ кля́тву; **I ~ to God (that) ...** кляну́сь (Го́сподом) Бо́гом, что... **2.** (*bind by an oath*) прив|оди́ть, -ести́ к прися́ге; **the jury was sworn in** прися́жных привели́ к прися́ге; **he was sworn to secrecy** с него́ взя́ли кля́тву о неразглаше́нии та́йны; **sworn enemies** закля́тые враги́.

v.i. **1.** (*take an oath*) кля́сться, по-; (*fig.*): **he ~s by aspirin** он мо́лится на аспири́н; **he swore to having seen the crime** он заяви́л под прися́гой, что был свиде́телем преступле́ния. **2.** (*use bad language, curse*) брани́ться (*impf.*); сквернosло́вить (*impf.*); **~ing** брань, ру́гань; **~ like a trooper** руга́ться (*impf.*) как изво́зчик.

cpd. **~-word** *n.* руга́тельство, нецензу́рное сло́во.

sweat [swet] *n.* **1.** пот; **by the ~ of one's brow** в по́те лица́ своего́; **his brows were running, dripping with ~** у него́ со лба пот ли́лся ручьём; **his shirt was dripping with ~** вся его́ руба́шка была́ по́тная, хоть выжима́й. **2.** (*state or process of ~ing*) поте́ние, пот; **he was in a ~** (*lit., fig.*) он был (весь) в поту́; **a cold ~** холо́дный пот. **3.** (*coll., drudgery*): **it is a ~ compiling a dictionary** что́бы соста́вить слова́рь, прихо́дится попоте́ть.

v.t. **1.** (*exude*) поте́ть (*impf.*) *+i.*; **~ blood** (*fig.*) рабо́тать (*impf.*) до крова́вого по́та. **2.** (*force hard work from*): **~ed labour** потого́нный труд.

v.i. (*lit., fig.*) поте́ть, вс-; **he was ~ing with fear** он был в холо́дном поту́ от стра́ха.

cpds. **~-band** *n.* (*sportsman's*) потничо́к; **~-gland** *n.* потова́я железа́; **~-shirt** *n.* бума́жный (спорти́вный) сви́тер, футбо́лка; **~-shop** *n.* предприя́тие, на кото́ром существу́ет потого́нная систе́ма; **~suit** трениро́вочный костю́м.

sweater ['swetə(r)] *n.* сви́тер.

sweaty ['swetɪ] *adj.*: **~ hands** по́тные ру́ки; **~ clothes** пропи́танная по́том оде́жда; **~ odour** за́пах по́та.

Swede [swi:d] *n.* (*pers.*) швед (*fem.* -ка); (*s~: vegetable*) брю́ква.

Sweden ['swi:dən] *n.* Шве́ция.

Swedish ['swi:dɪʃ] *n.* (*language*) шве́дский язы́к.

adj. шве́дский.

sweep [swi:p] *n.* **1.** (*with broom etc.*): **give a room a good ~** хороше́нько подмести́ (*pf.*) ко́мнату; (*fig.*): **make a clean ~** забра́ть/вы́мести (*pf.*) всё под метёлку. **2.** (*steady movement*) ше́ствие, движе́ние; (*~ing movement*) взмах, разма́х; **~ of the arm** взмах руки́; **with one ~** одни́м ма́хом. **3.** (*range, reach*) разма́х, диапазо́н. **4.** (**chimney-~**) трубочи́ст.

v.t. **1.** (*rush over*): **the waves swept the shore** во́лны набега́ли на бе́рег; **the storm swept the countryside** бу́ря пронесла́сь над всей окру́гой; **the new fashion ~ing the country** но́вая мо́да, охвати́вшая страну́. **2.** (*carry forcefully*): **a wave swept him over-**

board его́ смы́ло волно́й (за́ борт); **he swept her off her feet** (*fig.*) он вскружи́л ей го́лову. **3.** (*touch, brush*): **he swept his hand across the table** он провёл руко́й по́ столу. **4.** (*pass searchingly over*): **he swept the horizon with a telescope** он обша́рил горизо́нт подзо́рной трубо́й; **the search vessels swept the sea** разве́дывательные корабли́ борозди́ли мо́ре. **5.** (*clean*) подме|та́ть, -сти́; чи́стить, вы́-; ~ **a chimney** проч|ища́ть, -и́стить трубу́; ~ **the board** (*fig., win all stakes*) забра́ть (*pf.*) все ста́вки. **6.** (*brush*): **he swept the litter into a corner** он замёл му́сор в у́гол; **her dress swept the ground** её пла́тье волочи́лось по земле́; (*fig.*): ~ **sth. under the carpet** заме|та́ть, -сти́ что-н. под ковёр.

v.i. **1.** (*rush, dash*) прон|оси́ться, -ести́сь; **rain swept across the country** дождь прошёл по всей стране́; **fear swept over him** страх охвати́л его́. **2.** (*walk majestically*): **she swept into the room** она́ вели́чественно вошла́ в ко́мнату. **3.** (*clean, brush*) мести́ (*impf.*); подме|та́ть, -сти́.

with advs.: ~ **along** *v.t.* нести́ (*det.*); **the boat was swept along by the current** ло́дку несло́/уноси́ло тече́нием; *v.i.* проше́ствовать (*impf.*); ~ **aside** *v.t.*: **he swept the curtain aside** он ре́зко отодви́нул занаве́ску; **she swept him aside** она́ отстрани́ла его́; ~ **away** *v.t.* сме|та́ть, -сти́; **they were ~ing the snow away** они́ сгреба́ли снег; **the bridge was swept away by the rains** мост смы́ло дождя́ми; (*fig., abolish*) поко́нчить (*pf.*) с+*i.*; уничт|ожа́ть, -о́жить; ~ **off** *v.t.* срыва́ть, сорва́ть; **the roof was swept off in the gale** кры́шу сорва́ло урага́ном; ~ **out** *v.t.*: **the maid was ~ing out the cupboards** служа́нка вымета́ла шкафы́; *v.i.*: **she swept out (of the room etc.)** она́ вели́чественно удали́лась; ~ **up** *v.t.*: **I have to ~ up the kitchen** я до́лжен подмести́ ку́хню; *v.i.*: **I had to ~ up after them** мне пришло́сь по́сле них убира́ть.

cpd. **~stake** *n.* ≃ лотере́я, тотализа́тор.

sweeper ['swi:pə(r)] *n.* (*pers.*) подмета́льщик; (*device*) подмета́льная маши́на.

sweeping ['swi:pɪŋ] *adj.* **1.** (*of motion etc.*): **a ~ bow** широ́кий покло́н; ~ **gesture** разма́шистый жест. **2.** (*comprehensive*) всеобъе́млющий; (*thoroughgoing*) реши́тельный; ~ **changes** радика́льные измене́ния; (*wholesale*) огу́льный; **a ~ statement** огу́льное утвержде́ние.

sweepings ['swi:pɪŋz] *n.* му́сор, сор.

sweet [swi:t] *n.* **1.** (*~meat*) конфе́та, (*pl.*) сла́сти (*f. pl.*). **2.** (*dish*) сла́дкое, тре́тье. **3.** (*beloved*): **my ~** (мой) ми́лый, (моя́) ми́лая.

adj. **1.** (*to taste*) сла́дкий; **I am not fond of ~ foods** я не люблю́ сла́достей; **I like my tea very ~** я пью о́чень сла́дкий чай; **my brother has a ~ tooth** мой брат сластёна; **make ~** засласти́ть, по-; ~ **corn** кукуру́за; ~ **potato** бата́т; ~ (*fresh, pure*) **water** све́жая/пре́сная вода́. **2.** (*fragrant*) сла́дкий, души́стый; **how ~ the roses smell!** как сла́дко па́хнут ро́зы!; ~ **peas** души́стый горо́шек. **3.** (*melodious*): ~ **voice** прия́тный/мелоди́чный го́лос; ~ **melody** сла́дкая/преле́стная мело́дия. **4.** (*agreeable*): ~ **words** ла́сковые слова́; **a ~ face** ми́лое лицо́; **a ~** (*gentle*) **temper** мя́гкий хара́ктер; (*coll., charming, nice*) ми́лый; **a ~ little dog** симпати́чная соба́чка; **they were perfectly ~ to us** они́ бы́ли чрезвыча́йно ми́лы с на́ми.

cpds. **~-and-sour** *adj.* ки́сло-сла́дкий; **~bread** *n.* «сла́дкое мя́со»; **~heart** *n.* возлю́бленн|ый (*fem.* -ая); **~meat** *n.* = **~** *n.* **1.**; **~-shop** *n.* конди́терская; **~-tempered** *adj.* с мя́гким хара́ктером, мя́гкого нра́ва; **~-william** *n.* туре́цкая гвозди́ка.

sweeten ['swi:t(ə)n] *v.t.* подсла́|щивать, -сти́ть.

sweetener ['swi:tənə(r)] *n.* (*sugar substitute*) замени́тель (*m.*) са́хара; (*bribe*) взя́тка.

sweetness ['swi:tnɪs] *n.* сла́дость; прия́тность.

swell [swel] *n.* (*of sea*) зыбь.

adj. (*first-rate*) шика́рный, миро́вой (*coll.*).

v.t. **1.** (*increase size or volume of*) разд|ува́ть, -у́ть; **the wind ~ed the sails** ве́тер наду́л паруса́; **my finger is swollen** у меня́ па́лец опу́х/распу́х. **2.** (*increase number of*) увели́чи|вать, -ть. **3.** (*make arrogant*): **he was swollen with pride** он весь наду́лся/разду́лся от го́рдости; **~ed/swollen head** (*fig., coll.*) самомне́ние.

v.i. **1.** (*expand, dilate: also* ~ **up**) над|ува́ться, -у́ться; разд|ува́ться, -у́ться; (*of part of body*) оп|уха́ть, -у́хнуть; расп|уха́ть, -у́хнуть. **2.** (*increase in size or volume*) выраста́ть, вы́расти; разбуха́ть, -у́хнуть; взд|ува́ться, -у́ться. **3.** (*of pers., with pride etc.*) над|ува́ться, -у́ться; **my heart ~ed with pride** се́рдце моё напо́лнилось го́рдостью. **4.** (*of sound*) нараста́ть (*impf.*).

swelling ['swelɪŋ] *n.* (*on body*) о́пухоль, опуха́ние; (*on other object*) вы́пуклость.

swelter ['sweltə(r)] *v.i.* (*of pers.*) изнемога́ть (*impf.*) от жары́; **~ing** (*of atmosphere etc.*) нестерпи́мо жа́ркий.

swerve [swɜ:v] *n.* отклоне́ние, поворо́т.

v.i. (кру́то) пов|ора́чиваться, -ерну́ться; свёртывать, -ну́ть; **the car ~d to avoid an accident** маши́на кру́то сверну́ла, что́бы избежа́ть ава́рии.

swift [swɪft] *n.* (*bird*) стриж.

adj. (*rapid*) бы́стрый; (*prompt*) ско́рый; **a ~ reply** ско́рый отве́т; ~ **to anger** вспы́льчивый.

cpd. **~-acting** *adj.* быстроде́йствующий.

swiftness ['swɪftnɪs] *n.* быстрота́, ско́рость.

swig [swɪg] (*coll.*) *n.* глото́к; **have, take a ~ of sth** сде́лать (*pf.*) глото́к чего́-н.

v.t. хлеба́ть (*impf.*).

swill [swɪl] *n.* (*lit., fig.*) по́йло; (*pig-food*) помо́|и (*pl., g.* -ев).

v.t. **1.** (*wash, rinse*) мыть, вы́-; полоска́ть, вы́-. **2.** (*drink heavily*) лака́ть, хлеба́ть (*both impf., coll.*).

swim [swɪm] *n.* **1. have, go for a ~** купа́ться, ис-. **2.** (*main current of affairs*): **be in the ~** быть в ку́рсе дел; сле́довать (*impf.*) мо́де.

v.t. **1.** (*cross by ~ming*) перепл|ыва́ть, -ы́ть. **2.** (*cover by ~ming*): ~ **a mile** пропл|ыва́ть, -ы́ть ми́лю.

v.i. **1.** пла́вать (*indet.*), плыть (*det.*), по-; **he can ~ on his back** он уме́ет пла́вать на спине́; ~ **with the tide** (*lit., fig.*) плыть (*det.*) по тече́нию; ~ **against the tide** плыть (*det.*) про́тив тече́ния. **2.** (*of things: float*) пла́вать (*indet.*). **3.** (*fig., reel, swirl*): **the noise made my head ~** от шу́ма у меня́ закружи́лась голова́; **everything was ~ming before my eyes** всё поплы́ло у меня́ пе́ред глаза́ми.

swimmer ['swɪmə(r)] *n.* плов|е́ц (*fem.* -чи́ха).

swimming ['swɪmɪŋ] *n.* пла́вание.

cpds. **~-bath, ~-pool** *nn.* (пла́вательный) бассе́йн; **~-costume** *n.* купа́льный костю́м; **~-trunks** *n.* пла́в|ки (*pl., g.* -ок).

swindle ['swɪnd(ə)l] *n.* жу́льничество, моше́нничество.

v.t. обма́н|ывать, -у́ть; **you've been ~d** вас наду́ли.

v.i. жу́льничать (*impf.*); моше́нничать (*impf.*).

swindler ['swɪndlə(r)] *n.* жу́лик, моше́нник.

swine [swaɪn] *n.* (*lit., fig.*) свинья́.

cpd. **~herd** *n.* свинопа́с.

swing [swɪŋ] *n.* **1.** (*movement*) кача́ние, колеба́ние; **he took a ~ at the ball** он уда́рил по мячу́ с разма́ху; **in full ~** (*fig.*) в (по́лном) разга́ре. **2.** (*shift*): **the polls showed a ~ to the left** вы́боры показа́ли ре́зкий поворо́т вле́во. **3.** (*of gait or rhythm*) ритм; **the party went with a ~** вечери́нка вы́шла на сла́ву; **I couldn't get into the ~ of things** я ника́к не мог включи́ться в де́ло. **4.** (*seat slung on rope*) качел|и (*pl., g.* -ей); **he gave the boy a (go on the) ~** он раскача́л ма́льчика на каче́лях.

v.t. **1.** (*apply circular motion to*): **~ one's arms** разма́хивать (*impf.*) рука́ми; (*brandish*): **he swung the sword above his head** он взмахну́л шпа́гой над голово́й. **2.** (*cause to turn, pivot*) разв|ора́чивать, -ерну́ть. **4.** (*sling, hoist*) вски́|дывать, -нуть; **he swung himself into the saddle** он вскочи́л в седло́; **they swung the cargo ashore** они́ перебро́сили груз на бе́рег. **5.** (*give rhythmic motion to*) кача́ть (*impf.*); колеба́ть (*impf.*).

v.i. **1.** (*sway, oscillate*) кача́ться, колеба́ться, пока́чиваться (*all impf.*); (*dangle*) висе́ть, болта́ться (*both impf.*); **let one's legs ~** болта́ть (*impf.*) нога́ми; **he could ~ from a branch with one hand** он мог раска́чиваться на ве́тке одно́й руко́й; **a lamp swung from the ceiling** с потолка́ све́шивалась ла́мпа; **the children were ~ing in the park** де́ти кача́лись на каче́лях в па́рке. **2.** (*turn, pivot*) пов|ора́чиваться, -ерну́ться; враща́ться (*impf.*); **the door swung open in the wind** дверь распахну́лась от ве́тра. **3.** (*move rhythmically*): **the band swung down the street** орке́стр (про)ше́ствовал по у́лице; **the monkeys swung from bough to bough** обезья́ны раска́чивались на ветвя́х. **4.** (*sl., hang*): **he will ~ for this murder** его́ вздёрнут за э́то уби́йство.

cpds. **~-bridge** *n.* разводно́й мост; **~-doors** *n.* свобо́дно распа́хивающаяся дверь.

swinish ['swaınıʃ] *adj.* сви́нский, ско́тский.

swipe [swaıp] (*coll.*) *n.*: **take a ~ at s.o.** замахну́ться (*pf.*) на кого́-н.; **he took a ~ at the ball** он с сило́й/разма́ху уда́рил по мячу́.

v.t. (*steal*) сти́брить (*pf.*); стяну́ть (*pf.*) (*coll.*).

swirl [swɜːl] *n.* (*of snow*) вихрь (*m.*); **~ of dust** столб пы́ли.

v.i. (*of water*) крути́ться (*impf.*) в водоворо́те; (*of snow*) ви́хри́ться (*impf.*); (*of leaves etc.*) кружи́ться, за-; (*of dust*) подн|има́ться, -я́ться столбо́м.

swish [swıʃ] *n.* (*of whip*) свист; (*of scythe etc.*) взмах со сви́стом; (*of dress etc.*) шурша́ние, ше́лест.

adj. (*coll.*) шика́рный.

v.t. (*flick*) взма́х|ивать, -ну́ть +*i.*

v.i. (*of fabric*) шурша́ть (*impf.*); шелесте́ть (*impf.*); (*of cane etc.*) расс|ека́ть, -е́чь во́здух (со сви́стом); (*of scythe*) свисте́ть (*impf.*).

Swiss [swıs] *n.* швейца́р|ец (*fem.* -ка).

adj. швейца́рский; **~ roll** руле́т с варе́ньем.

switch [swıtʃ] *n.* **1.** (*twig, rod*) прут. **2.** (*rail.*) стре́лка. **3.** (*elec.*) выключа́тель (*m.*), переключа́тель (*m.*). **4.** (*change of position, role, tactics etc.*) поворо́т, переме́на.

v.t. (*transfer*) перев|оди́ть, -ести́; переключ|а́ть, -и́ть.

v.i.: **he ~ed from one extreme to the other** он перешёл/бро́сился из одно́й кра́йности в другу́ю.

with advs.: **~ off** *v.t.* выключа́ть, вы́ключить; **~ off a lamp** гаси́ть, по- ла́мпу; *v.i.* (*coll., withdraw one's attention*) отключи́ться (*pf.*); **~ on** *v.t.* включ|а́ть, -и́ть; (*light*) заж|ига́ть, -е́чь; **~ over** *v.t. & i.* переключ|а́ть(ся), -и́ть(ся); пере|ходи́ть, -йти́.

cpds. **~back** *n.* (*in amusement park*) америка́нские го́ры (*f. pl.*); **~board** *n.* коммута́тор; распредели́тельный щит; **~board operator** телефони́ст (*fem.* -ка); **~man** *n.* стре́лочник.

Switzerland ['swıtsər,lænd] *n.* Швейца́рия.

swivel ['swıv(ə)l] *n.* вертлю́г; (*attr.*) враща́ющийся, поворо́тный; вертлю́жный.

v.t. & i. пов|ора́чивать(ся), -ерну́ть(ся) (на шарни́рах).

cpd. **~-chair** *n.* поворо́тное/враща́ющееся сиде́нье.

swollen-headed ['swəʊlən] *adj.* чванли́вый, напы́щенный.

swoon [swuːn] *n.* о́бморок.

v.i. па́дать, упа́сть в о́бморок.

swoop [swuːp] *n.* **1.** (*of bird etc.*) паде́ние вниз. **2.** (*sudden attack*) налёт; **at one fell ~** еди́ным уда́ром/ма́хом.

v.i. (*aeron.*) пики́ровать, с-; **the eagle ~ed (down) on its prey** орёл ри́нулся на свою́ жёртву; **the enemy ~ed on the town** неприя́тель соверши́л внеза́пный налёт на го́род.

sword [sɔːd] *n.* шпа́га; (*liter., or fig.*) меч; **cross ~s with s.o.** (*lit., fig.*) скрести́ть (*pf.*) шпа́ги с кем-н.; **put to the ~** пред|ава́ть, -а́ть мечу́.

cpds. **~fish** *n.* меч-ры́ба; **~-play** *n.* фехтова́ние; **~sman** *n.* фехтова́льщик.

swot [swɒt] *n.* (*pers.*) зубри́л(к)а (*c.g.*).

v.t.: **~ up a subject** зубри́ть, под-/вы́- предме́т.

v.i. зубри́ть (*impf.*).

sybarite ['sıbə,raıt] *n.* сибари́т (*fem.* -ка).

sybaritic [,sıbə'rıtık] *adj.* сибари́тский.

sycamore ['sıkə,mɔː(r)] *n.* сикамо́р анти́чный; (*maple*) я́вор; (*US, plane-tree*) плата́н, чина́р.

sycophant ['sıkə,fænt] *n.* подхали́м, льстец.

sycophantic [,sıkə'fæntık] *adj.* подхали́мский, льсти́вый.

syllabic [sı'læbık] *adj.* силлаби́ческий, слогово́й.

syllable ['sıləb(ə)l] *n.* слог; **in words of one ~** (*fig.*) досту́пным языко́м.

syllabus ['sıləbəs] *n.* програ́мма; уче́бный план.

syllogism ['sılə,dʒız(ə)m] *n.* силлоги́зм.

syllogistic [,sılə'dʒıstık] *adj.* силлогисти́ческий.

sylph [sılf] *n.* сильф (*fem.* -и́да).

cpd. **~-like** *adj.* грацио́зный.

symbiosis [,sımbaı'əʊsıs, ,sımbı-] *n.* симбио́з.

symbiotic [,sımbaı'ɒtık, ,sımbı-] *adj.* симбиоти́ческий.

symbol ['sımb(ə)l] *n.* си́мвол; (*sign, e.g. math.*) знак.

symbolic(al) [,sım'bɒlık(ə)l] *adj.* символи́ческий, символи́чный.

symbolism ['sımbə,lız(ə)m] *n.* символи́зм.

symbolize ['sımbə,laız] *v.t.* символизи́ровать (*impf., pf.*).

symmetric(al) [,sı'metrık(ə)l] *adj.* симметри́чный, симметри́ческий.

symmetry ['sımıtrı] *n.* симметри́я, симметри́чность.

sympathetic [,sımpə'θetık] *adj.* **1.** (*compassionate*) сочу́вственный; **lend a ~ ear to** сочу́вственно выслу́шивать, вы́слушать. **2.** (*favourable, supportive*): **I am ~ towards his ideas** его́ иде́и мне близки́. **3.** (*physiol. etc.*): **~ nerve** симпати́ческий нерв.

sympathize ['sımpə,θaız] *v.i.* сочу́вствовать (*impf.*) (+*d.*); **he ~d with me in my grief** он сочу́вствовал моему́ го́рю.

sympathizer ['sımpə,θaızə(r)] *n.* сочу́вствующий, сторо́нник.

sympathy ['sımpəθı] *n.* **1.** (*compassion, commiseration, fellow-feeling*) сочу́вствие, сострада́ние; **feel ~ for s.o.** испы́тывать (*impf.*) сочу́вствие к кому́-н.; **we are in ~ with your ideas** мы сочу́вствуем ва́шим иде́ям; **my sympathies are with the miners** все мои́ симпа́тии на стороне́ шахтёров.

symphonic [sım'fɒnık] *adj.* симфони́ческий.

symphony ['sımfənı] *n.* симфо́ния; **~ orchestra** симфони́ческий орке́стр.

symposium [sım'pəʊzıəm] *n.* симпо́зиум.

symptom ['sımptəm] *n.* симпто́м; (*sign*) при́знак; **develop ~s** прояв|ля́ть, -и́ть симпто́мы.

symptomatic [,sımptə'mætık] *adj.* симптомати́чный, симптомати́ческий.

synagogue ['sınə,gɒg] *n.* синаго́га.

sync(h) [sıŋk] *n.* (*coll.*): **out of ~** несинхро́нный.

synchromesh ['sıŋkrəʊ,meʃ] *n.* синхрониза́тор; (*attr.*) синхронизи́рующий.

synchronization [,sıŋkrənaı'zeıʃ(ə)n] *n.* синхрониза́ция.

synchronize ['sıŋkrə,naız] *v.t.* синхронизи́ровать (*impf., pf.*); **~d swimming** худо́жественное пла́вание.

v.i. (*of events*) совпада́ть (*impf.*) во вре́мени; (*of clocks*) пока́зывать (*impf.*) одина́ковое вре́мя.
syncopate ['sɪŋkəˌpeɪt] *v.t.* (*gram.*, *mus.*) синкопи́ровать (*impf.*, *pf.*).
syncopation [ˌsɪŋkə'peɪʃ(ə)n] *n.* синко́па.
syncope ['sɪŋkəpɪ] *n.* (*gram.*) синко́па; (*med.*) о́бморок.
syndicate[1] ['sɪndɪkət] *n.* синдика́т.
syndicate[2] ['sɪndɪˌkeɪt] *v.t.* синдици́ровать (*impf.*, *pf.*).
syndrome ['sɪndrəʊm] *n.* синдро́м.
synod ['sɪnəd] *n.* сино́д.
synodal ['sɪnəd(ə)l] *adj.* синода́льный.
synonym ['sɪnənɪm] *n.* сино́ним.
synonymous [sɪ'nɒnɪməs] *adj.* синоними́чный; синоними́ческий; (*fig.*) равнозна́чный (+*d.*).
synopsis [sɪ'nɒpsɪs] *n.* сино́псис; ~ **of a thesis** (*acad.*) авторефера́т диссерта́ции.
syntactic(al) [sɪn'tæktɪkəl] *adj.* синтакси́ческий.
syntax ['sɪntæks] *n.* си́нтаксис.
synthesis ['sɪnθɪsɪs] *n.* си́нтез.
synthesize ['sɪnθɪˌsaɪz] *v.t.* синтези́ровать (*impf.*, *pf.*).
synthesizer ['sɪnθɪˌsaɪzə(r)] *n.* синтеза́тор.
synthetic [sɪn'θetɪk] *adj.* (*chem.*, *ling.*) синтети́ческий; (*artificial*) иску́сственный.
syphilis ['sɪfɪlɪs] *n.* си́филис.
syphilitic [ˌsɪfɪ'lɪtɪk] *adj.* сифилити́ческий.
Syria ['sɪrɪə] *n.* Си́рия.
syringe [sɪ'rɪndʒ, 'sɪr-] *n.* шприц, спринцо́вка; **hypodermic** ~ шприц для подко́жных впры́скиваний.
v.t. (*ears etc.*) спринцева́ть (*impf.*).
syrup ['sɪrəp] *n.* сиро́п; (*treacle*) па́тока; **golden** ~ све́тлая па́тока.
syrupy ['sɪrəpɪ] *adj.* (*fig.*) слаща́вый.
system ['sɪstəm] *n.* **1.** (*complex*) систе́ма; **solar** ~ со́лнечная систе́ма; ~ **analysis** систе́мный ана́лиз. **2.** (*network*) сеть; **railway** ~ железнодоро́жная сеть. **3.** (*body as a whole*) органи́зм; **get sth. out of one's** ~ (*fig.*) оч|ища́ться, -и́ститься от чего́-н. **4.** (*method*) систе́ма; ~ **of government** систе́ма правле́ния, госуда́рственный строй. **5.** (*methodical behaviour*) системати́чность.
systematic [ˌsɪstə'mætɪk] *adj.* системати́ческий.
systematize ['sɪstəməˌtaɪz] *v.t.* систематизи́ровать (*impf.*, *pf.*)
systemic [sɪ'stemɪk] *adj.* системати́ческий, сомати́ческий.
systole ['sɪstəlɪ] *n.* си́стола, сокраще́ние се́рдца.

T

T [tiː] *n.*: **this suits me to a** ~ э́то меня́ вполне́ устра́ивает.
cpds. ~**-junction** *n.* Т-обра́зный перекрёсток; ~**-shaped** *adj.* Т-обра́зный; ~**-shirt** *n.* ма́йка; ~**-square** *n.* рейсши́на.
ta [tɑː] *nt.* (*coll.*) спаси́бо.
tab [tæb] *n.* **1.** (*label on garment etc.*) наши́вка; (*for hanging clothes*) ве́шалка. **2.** (*coll.*, *check*): **the police are keeping** ~**s on him** поли́ция присма́тривает за ним.
tabby ['tæbɪ] *n.* (*also* ~ **cat**) (се́рая) полоса́тая ко́шка.
tabernacle ['tæbəˌnæk(ə)l] *n.* **1.** (*bibl.*) ски́ния; киво́т. **2.** (*place of worship*) моле́льня.
table ['teɪb(ə)l] *n.* **1.** стол; **at** ~ за столо́м; **he turned the** ~**s on his adversary** он поби́л проти́вника его́ же ору́жием; **a** ~ **for three** (*at restaurant*) сто́лик на трёх челове́к; (*fig.*, *food*) стол, ку́хня. **2.** (*tablet*) плита́. **3.** (*arrangement of data*) табли́ца; ~ **of contents** оглавле́ние, содержа́ние; **he knows his twelve times** ~ он уме́ет умножа́ть на двена́дцать.
v.t.: ~ (*propose*) **an amendment** вн|оси́ть, -ести́ попра́вку.
cpds. ~**cloth** *n.* ска́терть; ~**-lamp** *n.* насто́льная ла́мпа; ~**land** *n.* плато́ (*indecl.*), плоского́рье; ~**-linen** *n.* столо́вое бельё; ~**-mat** *n.* подста́вка (*под блюдо и т.п.*); ~**-napkin** *n.* салфе́тка; ~**spoon** *n.* столо́вая ло́жка; ~**-tennis** *n.* насто́льный те́ннис; ~**ware** *n.* столо́вая посу́да.
tableau ['tæbləʊ] *n.* жива́я карти́на; живопи́сная сце́на.
table d'hôte [ˌtɑːb(ə)l 'dəʊt] *n.* табльдо́т.
tablet ['tæblɪt] *n.* **1.** (*block for writing on*) (вощёная) доще́чка. **2.** (*inscribed plate or stone*) мемориа́льная доска́. **3.** (*of soap*) кусо́к. **4.** (*pill*) табле́тка.
tabloid ['tæblɔɪd] *n.* малоформа́тная газе́та; (*pej.*) бульва́рная газе́та.
tab|oo, -u [tə'buː] *n.* (*lit.*, *fig.*) табу́ (*nt. indecl.*); (*prohibition*) запре́т.
adj.: **the subject is** ~ э́то запрещённая те́ма.
tabular ['tæbjʊlə(r)] *adj.* в ви́де табли́ц; табли́чный.
tabulate ['tæbjʊˌleɪt] *v.t.* табули́ровать (*impf.*); сост|авля́ть, -а́вить табли́цу из+*g.*
tabulation [ˌtæbjʊ'leɪʃ(ə)n] *n.* табули́рование; составле́ние табли́ц.
tabulator ['tæbjʊˌleɪtə(r)] *n.* (*machine*) табуля́тор.
tachometer [tə'kɒmɪtə(r)] *n.* тахо́метр.
tacit ['tæsɪt] *adj.* молчали́вый; ~ **agreement** молчали́вое согла́сие.
taciturn ['tæsɪˌtɜːn] *adj.* неразгово́рчивый.
tack [tæk] *n.* **1.** (*small nail*) гво́здик; **let's get down to brass** ~**s** (*fig.*) дава́йте разберёмся, что к чему́. **2.** (*long, loose stitch*) намётка. **3.** (*direction of vessel*) галс; (*fig.*) курс, ли́ния; **he is on the wrong** ~ он на неве́рном пути́.
v.t. **1.** (*fasten*) прикреп|ля́ть, -и́ть гво́здиками. **2.** (*stitch*) сши|ва́ть, -ть; **she** ~**ed the dress together** она́ смета́ла пла́тье на живу́ю ни́тку. **3.** ~ **on** (*fig.*, *add*) доб|авля́ть, -а́вить.
v.i. пов|ора́чивать, -ерну́ть на друго́й галс.
tackle ['tæk(ə)l] *n.* **1.** (*rope-and-pulley mechanism*) полиспа́ст; сло́жный блок. **2.** (*equipment*) принадле́жности (*f. pl.*), обору́дивание; **fishing** ~ рыболо́вные сна́сти (*f. pl.*). **3.** (*football*) блокиро́вка.
v.t. (*grapple with*) бра́ться, взя́ться за+*a.*; **I went and** ~**d him on the subject** я пошёл к нему́ и возбуди́л э́тот вопро́с; (*football*) блоки́ровать.
tacky ['tækɪ] *adj.* (*sticky*) ли́пкий, кле́йкий.
tact [tækt] *n.* такт, такти́чность.
tactful ['tæktfʊl] *adj.* такти́чный.
tactic ['tæktɪk] = **tactic(s)**
tactical ['tæktɪk(ə)l] *adj.* такти́ческий.
tactician [tæk'tɪʃ(ə)n] *n.* та́ктик.
tactic(s) ['tæktɪks] *n.* та́ктика.
tactile ['tæktaɪl] *adj.* осяза́тельный, такти́льный.
tactless ['tæktlɪs] *adj.* беста́ктный.
tadpole ['tædpəʊl] *n.* голова́стик.
Tadzhikistan [ˌtædʒɪkɪ'stɑːn] *n.* Таджикиста́н.
taffeta ['tæfɪtə] *n.* тафта́; (*attr.*) тафтяно́й.
tag [tæg] *n.* **1.** (*label*) ярлы́к; **price** ~ ярлы́к с обозна́ченной цено́й, це́нник. **2.** (*child's game*) (игра́ в) са́л|ки (*pl. g.* -ок).
v.t. (*fasten* ~ *to*) наве́|шивать, -сить ярлы́к на+*a.*
v.i. (*follow*): **the children** ~**ged along behind** де́ти тащи́лись сза́ди; **he** ~**ged on to the group** он примкну́л к гру́ппе.

taiga ['taɪgə] *n.* тайгá.

tail [teɪl] *n.* **1.** (*of animal*) хвост; (*dim.*) хвóстик; **the dog wagged its ~** собáка вилЯла хвостóм; **they turned ~ and ran** онИ повернУли и брóсились наутёк. **2.** (*fig.*): **at the ~ end** в сáмом концé; **I can't make head or ~ of it** я никáк тут не разберУсь. **3.** (*of a coin*) рéшка. **4.: ~s** (*coat*) фрак.

v.t. (*follow closely*) висéть (*impf.*) на хвостé у+*g.*

v.i. **1.** (*follow*) тащИться (*impf.*) за+*i.* **2.** (*dwindle*) уб|ывáть, -Ыть; **the attendance figures ~ed off** посещáемость упáла; **his voice ~ed away into silence** егó гóлос (постепéнно) затИх.

cpds. **~back** *n.* хвост; **~-coat** *n.* фрак; **~-end** *n.* конéц, хвост; **~-gate** *n.* зáдняя двéрца; **~-lamp, ~-light** *nn.* зáдний фонáрь; стоп-сигнáл; **~plane** *n.* (*aeron.*) хвостовóй стабилизáтор; **~-spin** *n.* (*aeron.*) нормáльный штóпор.

tailor ['teɪlə(r)] *n.* портнóй.

v.t.: **a well-~ed coat** хорошó сшИтое пальтó; (*fig.*) приспос|áбливать, -óбить; **his speech was ~ed to the situation** егó речь былá состáвлена с учётом ситуáции.

cpd. **~-made** *adj.* сдéланный по закáзу.

taint [teɪnt] *n.* пятнó, изъЯн; (*trace*) налёт, прИмесь.

v.t. пóртить, ис-; **~ed meat** несвéжее мЯсо; **~ed reputation** подмóченная репутáция.

Taiwan [taɪ'wɑːn] *n.* ТайвáнЬ (*m.*).

take [teɪk] *n.* **1.** (*money taken, e.g. at box office*) сбор, вЫручка. **2.** (*cin.*) монтáжный кадр; (*repetition*) дубль (*m.*).

v.t. **1.** (*pick up, lay hold of, grasp*) брать, взять; **~ my arm!** возьмИте менЯ пóд руку!; **he took her in his arms** он её обнЯл; **he took her by the hand** он взял её зá руку; **he took me by the throat** он взял/схватИл менЯ за гóрло; (*remove*): **she took a coin out of her purse** онá вЫнула монéту из кошелькá; **~ 5 from 10** отнимИте 5 от 10. **2.** (*catch*) ловИть, поймáть; (*come upon*): **I was ~n by surprise** я был застИгнут врасплóх. **3.** (*capture*): **the city was ~n by storm** гóрод взЯли штУрмом; **he was ~n captive** он попáл в плен; (*assume*) прин|имáть, -Ять на себЯ; **you must ~ the initiative** вы должнЫ взять на себЯ инициатИву; **he took the lead** (*in an enterprise*) он взял на себЯ руковóдство; **the Italians took the lead** (*racing*) итальЯнцы вЫрвались вперёд; **he took control** он взял управлéние в своИ рУки; (*win, gain*) выИгрывать, вЫиграть; **she took first prize** онá получИла пéрвый приз; (*captivate*) нрáвиться, по- +*d.*; **that ~s my fancy** мне Это нрáвится; **I was ~n by the house** дом менЯ очаровáл. **4.** (*acquire; obtain possession of*): **he decided to ~ a wife** он решИл женИться; **he took a partner** он взял компаньóна; (*for money*): **I have ~n a flat in town** я снял квартИру в гóроде; **these seats are ~n** Эти местá зáняты; (*in payment*): **they took £50 in one evening** онИ вЫручили 50 фУнтов за одИн вéчер; (*by enquiry or examination*): определ|Ять, -Ить; **the tailor took his measurements** портнóй снял с негó мéрку; **the doctor took my temperature** дóктор измéрил мне температУру; (*unlawfully or without consent*): **the thieves took all her jewellery** вóры забрáли все её драгоцéнности. **5.** (*avail o.s. of*) воспóльзоваться (*pf.*) +*i.*; **please ~ a seat** пожáлуйста, садИтесь; **I'm taking a day's leave** я берУ выходнóй день; **~ your time!** спешИть нéкуда; не торопИтесь!; (*board, travel by*): **let's ~ a taxi** давáйте возьмём таксИ; **he took a bus to the station** он поéхал автóбусом до стáнции. **6.** (*occupy*) зан|имáть, -Ять; **will you ~ the chair?** (*at meeting*) вы не хотИте быть председáтелем?; **I am taking his place** я егó замещáю; **that ~s first place** Это (должнó быть) на пéрвом мéсте. **7.** (*adopt, choose*): **I don't wish to ~ sides** я не желáю становИться ни на чью стóрону; **I don't ~ the same view** у менЯ другáя тóчка зрéния; **~ me, for instance!** возьмИте менЯ, напримéр! **8.** (*accept*) прин|имáть, -Ять; **will you ~ a cheque?** я могУ расплатИться чéком?; **~ my advice!** послУшайте менЯ!; **I ~ responsibility** я берУ на себЯ ответственность; **he took his defeat well** он стóйко перенёс поражéние; **can't you ~ a joke?** что вы, шУток не понимáете?; **he would not ~ no for an answer** он не прИнял откáза; **~ it from me!** (*believe me!*) повéрьте мне!; Я вам говорЮ; **~ it easy!** не волнУйтесь!; осторóжно!; (*bear*) выдéрживать, вЫдержать; **he took his punishment like a man** он перенёс наказáние, как подобáет мужчИне; **I won't ~ this lying down** я не сдáмся без бóя; (*receive*) брать (*impf.*); **she ~s lessons in Spanish** онá берёт урóки испáнского языкá; **we ~ the Times** мы выпИсываем «Таймс»; **she ~s paying guests** онá дéржит постоЯльцев; **I took him into my confidence** я емУ довéрился; (*qualify for*): **he took his degree** он получИл диплóм/стéпень; (*submit to*): **when do you ~ your exams?** когдá вы сдаёте экзáмены?. **9.** (*use regularly; esp. food or drink*) прин|имáть, -Ять; **do you ~ sugar in your tea?** вы пьёте чай с сáхаром?; (*of size in clothes*): **I ~ tens in shoes** у менЯ десЯтый размéр ботИнок. **10.** (*apprehend*) пон|имáть, -Ять; **what do you ~ that to mean?** как вы Это понимáете?; (*assume*) считáть (*impf.*); **I ~ him to be an honest man** я считáю егó чéстным человéком. **11.** (*conceive, evince*) проЯв|лЯть, -Ить; **he has ~n a dislike to me** он менЯ невзлюбИл. **12.** (*exert, exercise*): **~ care!** бУдьте осторóжны!; **he took no notice** он не обратИл никакóго внимáния. **13.** (*of single finite actions: give, have, make*): **~ a look at this!** взглянИте-ка на Это!; **I took a deep breath** я сдéлал глубóкий вдох; **he took a bite out of the apple** он откусИл Яблоко; (*of longer, but finite, activity: have*): **I took a bath** я прИнял вáнну; **let us ~ a walk!** давáйте прогулЯемся!; (*partake of, consume*) есть, по-; **will you ~ tea with us?** вы вЫпьете с нáми чáю? **14.** (*make or obtain from original source*): **may we ~ notes?** мóжно нам дéлать замéтки?; **I took an impression of the key** я сдéлал óттиск ключá; **~ a letter!** (*from dictation*) я вам продиктУю письмó. **15.** (*convey*) отн|осИть, -естИ; брать (*impf.*); перед|авáть, -áть; **he took the letter to the post** он отнёс письмó на пóчту; **the train will ~ you there in an hour** пóезд довезёт вас тудá за час; **he was ~n to hospital** егó достáвили в большИцу; **she ~s the children to school** онá отвóдит/отвóзит детéй в шкóлу. **16.** (*conduct, carry out*) вестИ (*det.*); **the class was ~n by the headmaster** дирéктор вёл урóк в Этом клáссе; **the curate took the service** викáрий отслужИл молéбен. **17.** (*need, require*): **the job will ~ a long time** рабóта займёт мнóго врéмени; **how long does it ~ to get there?** скóлько (врéмени) тудá добирáться?; **that ~s courage** Это трéбует мУжества; **it ~s some doing** Это совсéм не прóсто; (*gram., govern*) управлЯть (*impf.*) +*i.*; **this verb ~s the dative** Этот глагóл трéбует дáтельного падежá.

v.i. **1.** (*~ effect; succeed*): **the vaccination has not ~n** вакцИна не привилáсь. **2.** (*become*): **he took sick** он заболéл. **3. ~ after** (*resemble*): **he ~s after his father** он похóж на отцá. **4. ~ to** (*resort to*) приб|егáть, -éгнуть к+*d.*; **she took to her bed** онá слеглá; **he took to drink** он зáпил; **he has ~n to getting up early** он стал рáно вставáть; (*feel (well-)disposed towards*) **I took to him from the start** он мне срáзу понрáвился; **she does not ~ kindly to change** онá плóхо перенóсит перемéну обстанóвки.

with advs.: **~ along** *v.t.* брать (*impf.*); прив|одИть, -естИ; (*by vehicle*) прив|озИть, -езтИ; **~ apart** *v.t.* (*dismantle*) раз|бирáть, -обрáть; **~ aside** *v.t.* отв|оди́ть, -ести́ в сто́рону; ~ **away** *v.t.* (*remove*) уб|ира́ть, -ра́ть; заб|ира́ть, -ра́ть; **the police took his gun away** поли́ция отобрала́ у него́ пистоле́т; **he was ~n away to prison** его́ отвели́ в тюрьму́; (*subtract*) вычита́ть, вы́честь; отн|има́ть, -я́ть; (~ *home*): **hot meals to ~ away** горя́чая еда́ на вы́нос; ~ **back** *v.t.* (*return*) возвра|ща́ть, -ти́ть; (*retrieve*) брать, взять обра́тно; (*retract*): **I ~ back everything I said** я беру́ наза́д всё, что сказа́л; ~ **down** *v.t.* (*remove*) сн|има́ть, -ять; (*dismantle*) сн|оси́ть, -ести́; **the shed was ~n down** сара́й снесли́; (*write down*) запи́с|ывать, -а́ть; **she took down the speech in shorthand** она́ застенографи́ровала речь; ~ **in** *v.t.* (*lit.*) вн|оси́ть, -ести́; (*give shelter to*): **they took him in when he was starving** они́ приюти́ли его́, когда́ он голода́л; (*let accommodation to*): **she ~s in lodgers** она́ берёт постоя́льцев; (*make smaller*): **she took in her dress** она́ уши́ла пла́тье; (*furl*) уб|ира́ть, -ра́ть (*napyca*); (*include, encompass*) включ|а́ть, -и́ть; **this map ~s in the whole of London** э́то ка́рта всего́ Ло́ндона; (*comprehend, assimilate*) усв|а́ивать, -о́ить; **I could not ~ in all the details** я не мог удержа́ть все подро́бности; (*deceive*) обма́н|ывать, -у́ть; **I was completely ~n in** меня́ здо́рово провели́; ~ **off** *v.t.* (*remove*) сн|има́ть, -ять; **shall I ~ off my clothes?** мне ну́жно разде́ться?; (*deduct from price*): **I will ~ 10% off for cash** е́сли вы плати́те нали́чными, я ски́ну 10%; (*lead away*) ув|оди́ть, -ести́; **she was ~n off to hospital** её увезли́ в больни́цу; (*coll., impersonate, mimic*) имити́ровать (*impf.*); *v.i.* (*become airborne*) взлет|а́ть, -е́ть; ~ **on** *v.t.* (*hire*) брать, взять; нан|има́ть, -я́ть; (*undertake*) брать, взять на себя́; (*assume, acquire*) приобре|та́ть, -сти́; **the word took on a new meaning** сло́во обрело́ но́вое значе́ние; ~ **out** *v.t.* (*extract*) вынима́ть, вы́нуть; **he had all his teeth ~n out** ему́ удали́ли все зу́бы; (*borrow from library*) брать, взять (в библиоте́ке); (*cause to go out for recreation etc.*) выводи́ть, вы́вести; **she took the baby out for a walk** она́ пошла́ с ребёнком погуля́ть; **he took his secretary out to dinner** он повёл свою́ секрета́ршу в рестора́н; (*remove*) выводи́ть, вы́вести; (*put into effect by writing*): **I must ~ out a new subscription** я до́лжен возобнови́ть подпи́ску; ~ **out a policy** брать, взять страхово́й по́лис; (*vent one's feelings*): **he took it out on his wife** он сорва́л всё на свое́й жене́; ~ **over** *v.t. & i.* (*assume control* (*of*)) прин|има́ть, -я́ть руково́дство (*+i.*); *v.i.* (*replace s.o.*): **let me ~ over!** я вас сменю́!; ~ **up** *v.t.* (*lift; lay hold of*) подн|има́ть, -я́ть; **the rebels took up arms** повста́нцы взя́ли́сь за ору́жие; (*accept*) прин|има́ть, -я́ть; (*carry upstairs*): **will you ~ up my bags, please?** пожа́луйста, отнеси́те наве́рх мои́ ве́щи; (*remove from floor*): **the carpet has been ~n up** ковёр сня́ли/сверну́ли; **wind in the rope and ~ up the slack!** смота́йте верёвку и натяни́те её!; (*occupy*): **this table ~s up too much room** э́тот стол занима́ет сли́шком мно́го ме́ста; **sport ~s up all my spare time** я спо́рту отдаю́ всё своё свобо́дное вре́мя; **he is very ~n up with his new lady-friend** он сейча́с поглощён свое́й но́вой знако́мой; (*promote*): **his cause was ~n up by his MP** депута́т поддержа́л его́ де́ло; (*pursue*): **I shall ~ the matter up with the Minister** я обращу́сь с э́тим де́лом к мини́стру; (*accept challenge or offer*): **I'll ~ you up on that!** я ловлю́ вас на сло́ве; (*interest o.s. in*) взя́ться (*impf.*) за+*a.*; **she has ~n up knitting** она́ заняла́сь вяза́нием; *v.i.* (*consort*): **he has ~n up with some dubious acquaintances** у него завели́сь подозри́тельные знако́мые.

cpds. **~-away** *adj.*: **a ~-away meal** еда́ на вы́нос; **~-home** *adj.*: **~-home pay** чи́стый за́работок; **~-off** *n.* (*impersonation*) подража́ние, паро́дия; (*of aircraft; also fig.*) взлёт; **~-over** *n.* (*comm.*) поглоще́ние (*какой-н. компании другой компанией*).

taker ['teɪkə(r)] *n.* беру́щий; **there were no ~s** никто́ не при́нял пари́; жела́ющих не́ было.

taking ['teɪkɪŋ] *n.* взя́тие; овладе́ние; (*pl., money taken*) сбор, вы́ручка.

talc(um) ['tælkəm] *n.*: (**~ powder**) тальк.

tale [teɪl] *n.* **1.** (*story*) расска́з, по́весть; **fairy ~** ска́зка. **2.** (*malicious or idle report*) спле́тни (*f. pl.*); вы́думки (*f. pl.*); **there is a ~ going about, that ...** погова́ривают, что....

cpds. **~-bearer, ~-teller** *nn.* я́бедни|к (*fem.* -ца).

talent ['tælənt] *n.* тала́нт, дар; **a man of great ~s** исключи́тельно тала́нтливый челове́к; (*persons of ability*) тала́нтливые лю́ди; **local ~** ме́стные тала́нты; **~ scout** открыва́тель (*m.*) тала́нтов.

talented ['tæləntɪd] *adj.* тала́нтливый.

talisman ['tælɪzmən] *n.* талисма́н.

talk [tɔːk] *n.* **1.** (*speech, conversation*) разгово́р, бесе́да; **we had a long ~** мы до́лго бесе́довали/разгова́ривали; **I'd better have a ~ with him** мне бы на́до с ни́м поговори́ть; **~ show** переда́ча в фо́рме бесе́ды; **small ~** све́тская болтовня́; **they became the ~ of the town** они́ сде́лались при́тчей во язы́цех. **2.** (*address, lecture*) ле́кция; докла́д; **give a ~** прочита́ть (*pf.*) ле́кцию.

v.t. **1.** (*express*) говори́ть (*impf.*); **you are ~ing nonsense** вы говори́те чепуху́. **2.** (*discuss*) обсу|жда́ть, -ди́ть; разгова́ривать (*impf.*) о+*p.*. **3.**: **~ French** говори́ть (*impf.*) по-францу́зски. **4.** (*bring or make by ~ing*): **he ~ed himself hoarse** он договори́лся до хрипоты́; **he ~ed me into it** он уговори́л меня́ сде́лать э́то; **I tried to ~ her out of it** я пыта́лся отговори́ть её от э́того; **I ~ed him round to my view** я склони́л его́ на свою́ сто́рону.

v.i. говори́ть (*impf.*); **baby is just learning to ~** ребёнок ещё то́лько у́чится говори́ть; **a ~ing parrot** говоря́щий попуга́й; **we got ~ing** мы разговори́лись; **people are beginning to ~** уже́ пошли́ разгово́ры/то́лки; **he ~ed at me for an hour** он це́лый час мне выгова́ривал; **~ing of students, how's your brother?** кста́ти о студе́нтах — как пожива́ет ваш брат?; **~ of the devil!** лёгок на поми́не!; **~ing-point** до́вод, резо́н; **I shall have to ~ to** (*reprimand*) **that boy** мне приде́тся отчита́ть э́того мальчи́шку; **now you're ~ing!** (*coll.*) вот тепе́рь вы говори́те де́ло!; **he refused to ~** (*coll., give information*) он не хоте́л ничего́ расска́зывать.

with advs.: **~ back** *v.i.* дерзи́ть, возража́ть (*both impf.*); **I gave him no chance to ~ back** я не дал ему́ возмо́жности возрази́ть; **~ down** *v.t.* (*aeron.*): **the pilot was ~ed down** пило́та напра́вили на переса́дку по ра́дио; *v.i.*: **children dislike being ~ed down to** де́ти не лю́бят, когда́ к ним подла́живаются; **~ over** *v.t.* (*discuss*) обсу|жда́ть, -ди́ть.

talkative ['tɔːkətɪv] *adj.* разгово́рчивый, болтли́вый.

talker ['tɔːkə(r)] *n.* разгово́рчивый челове́к, болту́н; **he is a great ~** он лю́бит поговори́ть.

talking-to ['tɔːkɪŋ] *n.* вы́говор.

tall [tɔːl] *adj.* **1.** высо́кий, высо́кого ро́ста; **how ~ are you?** како́го вы ро́ста?; **six feet ~** ро́стом в шесть фу́тов. **2.** (*coll., extravagant, unreasonable*) преувели́ченный; **a ~ story** небыли́ца, вы́думка; **that's a ~ order** э́то тру́дная зада́ча.

cpd. **~boy** *n.* высо́кий комо́д.

tallow ['tæləʊ] *n.* са́ло.

tally ['tælɪ] *n.* (*account, score*) счёт; (*total*) ито́г.

v.i. соотве́тствовать (*impf.*); **their versions do not ~** их ве́рсии не совпада́ют.

cpd. **~-clerk** *n.* учётчик.

tally-ho [ˌtælɪ'həʊ] *int.* ату́!

Talmud ['tælmʊd, -məd] *n.* Талму́д.

talon ['tælən] *n.* ко́готь (*m.*).

tambourine [ˌtæmbəˈriːn] *n.* тамбури́н.

tame [teɪm] *adj.* (*not wild*; *domesticated*) ручно́й, дома́шний, приручённый; (*submissive*, *spiritless*) послу́шный; (*dull*, *boring*) пре́сный, ску́чный.
v.t. приручі|а́ть, -и́ть; (*of savage animals*) укро|ща́ть, -ти́ть.

tamer [ˈteɪmə(r)] *n.* укроти́тель (*m.*).

tamper [ˈtæmpə(r)] *v.i.*: ~ **with** (*meddle in*) вмеш|ива́ться, -а́ться в+*a.*; **someone has been ~ing with the lock** кто-то ковыря́лся в замке́; **he ~ed with the document** он подде́лал докуме́нт.

tampon [ˈtæmpɒn] *n.* тампо́н.

tan [tæn] *n.* (*colour*) цвет бро́нзы; (*tint of skin*) зага́р.
v.t. **1.** (*convert to leather*) дуби́ть (*impf.*); **I'll ~ your hide** (*fig.*) я тебе́ зада́м. **2.** (*make brown*): **a ~ned face** загоре́лое лицо́.
v.i.: **she ~s easily** она́ бы́стро загора́ет.

tandem [ˈtændəm] *n.* **1.** (~ *bicycle*) па́рный велосипе́д. **2.**: **in ~** гусько́м, цу́гом.

tang [tæŋ] *n.* (*sharp taste or smell*) о́стрый/те́рпкий при́вкус/за́пах; **the ~ of sea air** за́пах мо́ря.

tangent [ˈtændʒ(ə)nt] *n.* (*geom.*) каса́тельная; (*fig.*): **he went off at a ~** он отклони́лся от те́мы; (*trig.*) та́нгенс.

tangential [tænˈdʒenʃ(ə)l] *adj.* тангенциа́льный; (*fig.*) отклоня́ющийся от те́мы.

tangerine [ˈtændʒəˌriːn] *n.* мандари́н.

tangible [ˈtændʒɪb(ə)l] *adj.* осяза́емый; (*fig.*) осяза́емый, ощути́мый; ~ **assets** осяза́емые/реа́льные сре́дства.

tangle [ˈtæŋg(ə)l] *n.* сплете́ние; (*fig.*) пу́таница.
v.t. спу́т|ывать, -ать; **the wool had got ~d up** ни́тки спу́тались; (*fig.*) запу́т|ывать, -ать.
v.i. (*coll.*) свя́з|ываться, -а́ться.

tango [ˈtæŋgəʊ] *n.* та́нго (*indecl.*).
v.i. танцева́ть, с- та́нго.

tangy [ˈtæŋɪ] *adj.* о́стрый, те́рпкий.

tank [tæŋk] *n.* **1.** (*container*) бак, цисте́рна; **petrol ~** бензоба́к; **water ~** бак для воды́. **2.** (*armoured vehicle*) танк; **the T~ Corps** бронета́нковые войска́; **~ warfare** та́нковые сраже́ния.
v.i.: ~ **up** (*with petrol*) запр|авля́ться, -а́виться.

tankard [ˈtæŋkəd] *n.* высо́кая пивна́я кру́жка.

tanker [ˈtæŋkə(r)] *n.* (*vessel*) та́нкер; (*vehicle*) автоцисте́рна.

tanner [ˈtænə(r)] *n.* (*of skins*) коже́вник, дуби́льщик.

tannery [ˈtænərɪ] *n.* коже́венный заво́д.

tannic [ˈtænɪk] *adj.* дуби́льный.

tannin [ˈtænɪn] *n.* тани́н.

tantalize [ˈtæntəˌlaɪz] *v.t.* дразни́ть (*impf.*); терза́ть (*impf.*).

tantamount [ˈtæntəˌmaʊnt] *adj.* равноси́льный.

tantrum [ˈtæntrəm] *n.* вспы́шка раздраже́ния; **he is in one of his ~s** у него́ очередно́й при́ступ раздраже́ния; **the child is in a ~** ребёнок капри́зничает.

Tanzania [ˌtænzəˈniːə] *n.* Танза́ния.

tap[1] [tæp] *n.* кран; **don't leave the ~s running** закро́йте кра́ны; **there is plenty of wine on ~** разливно́го вина́ полно́.
v.t. **1.** (*pierce to extract liquid*): **the cask was ~ped** бочо́нок откры́ли; (*fig.*); **the line is being ~ped** разгово́р подслу́шивают. **2.** (*fig.*, *use*) испо́льзовать (*impf.*).

tap[2] [tæp] *n.* (*light blow*) лёгкий уда́р; стук.
v.t. легко́ уд|аря́ть, -а́рить; сту́к|ать, -нуть; **he ~ped me on the shoulder** он тро́нул меня́ за плечо́.
v.i. стуча́ться, по-; **he ~ped on the door** он постуча́лся в дверь; **his toes were ~ping to the rhythm** он отбива́л ритм нога́ми.
with adv.: ~ **out** *v.t.*: **he ~ped out his pipe** он вы́бил тру́бку; **he ~ped out a message** он вы́стукал сообще́ние.
cpds. **~-dance, ~-dancing** *nn.* чечётка; **~-dancer** *n.* танцо́р, отбива́ющий чечётку.

tape [teɪp] *n.* (*strip of fabric etc.*) тесьма́; ле́нта; (*in race*) фи́нишная ле́нточка; **adhesive ~** ли́пкая ле́нта; (*magnetic ~*) магнитофо́нная ле́нта; плёнка; **~ deck** (магнитофо́нная) де́ка; **put sth. on ~** запи́с|ывать, -а́ть что-н. на плёнку.
v.t. **1.** (*bind with ~*) свя́з|ывать, -а́ть тесьмо́й. **2.** (*record*) запи́с|ывать, -а́ть на плёнку.
cpds. **~-measure** *n.* руле́тка, сантиме́тр; **~-recorder** *n.* магнитофо́н; **~-recording** *n.* магнитофо́нная за́пись; **~worm** *n.* ле́нточный червь.

taper [ˈteɪpə(r)] *n.* то́нкая свеча́.
v.t. & *i.* (*narrow off*) сужа́ть(ся), су́зить(ся).

tapestry [ˈtæpɪstrɪ] *n.* гобеле́н.

tapioca [ˌtæpɪˈəʊkə] *n.* тапио́ка.

tapir [ˈteɪpə(r), -pɪə(r)] *n.* тапи́р.

tar[1] [tɑː(r)] *n.* (*substance*) дёготь (*m.*).
v.t. ма́зать, на- дёгтем; смоли́ть, вы́-/о-; **a ~red road** гудрони́рованная доро́га.

tar[2] [tɑː(r)] *n.* (*coll.*, *sailor*) матро́с, моря́к.

tarantula [təˈræntjʊlə] *n.* тара́нтул.

tardiness [ˈtɑːdɪnɪs] *n.* медли́тельность; опозда́ние.

tardy [ˈtɑːdɪ] *adj.* (*slow-moving*) медли́тельный; (*late in coming*, *belated*) запозда́вший, запозда́лый.

tare [teə(r)] *n.* (*bot.*) ви́ка; (*pl.*, *weeds*) сорняк|и́ (*pl.*, *g.* -о́в).

target [ˈtɑːgɪt] *n.* (*for shooting etc.*) мише́нь, цель; **~ practice** уче́бная стрельба́; (*fig.*) **he became a ~ for abuse** он стал мише́нью для оскорбле́ний; (*objective*) цель; **we hope to reach the ~ of £1,000** мы наде́емся собра́ть наме́ченную су́мму в 1000 фу́нтов.

tariff [ˈtærɪf] *n.* **1.** (*duty*) тари́ф; **~ wall** тари́фный барье́р. **2.** (*list of charges*) тари́ф; (*for goods*) прейскура́нт.

tarmac [ˈtɑːmæk] *n.* гудрони́рованное шоссе́; (*aeron.*) предanга́рная бетони́рованная площа́дка.
v.t. гудрони́ровать (*impf.*, *pf.*).

tarnish [ˈtɑːnɪʃ] *n.* ту́склость.
v.t.: **~ed by damp** потускне́вший от вла́ги; (*fig.*) пятна́ть, за-.
v.i. тускне́ть, по-.

tarpaulin [tɑːˈpɔːlɪn] *n.* (*material*) брезе́нт.

tarragon [ˈtærəgən] *n.* полы́нь, эстраго́н.

tarry[1] [ˈtɑːrɪ] *adj.* (*of or like tar*) смоли́стый.

tarry[2] [ˈtærɪ] *v.i.* (*liter.*) (*remain*, *stay*) ост|ава́ться, -а́ться; (*delay*) заде́рж|иваться, -а́ться; ме́длить (*impf.*).

tart[1] [tɑːt] *n.* **1.** (*flat pie*) откры́тый пиро́г с фру́ктами. **2.** (*sl.*, *prostitute*) у́личная де́вка, шлю́ха.
v.t.: ~ **up** (*coll.*, *embellish*) прикра́|шивать, -сить; **she was all ~ed up** она́ была́ вся разоде́та.

tart[2] [tɑːt] *adj.* (*of taste*) ки́слый; (*fig.*) ко́лкий, ехи́дный.

tartan [ˈtɑːt(ə)n] *n.* **1.** (*fabric*) шотла́ндка. **2.** (*design*) клётчатый рису́нок.

tartar[1] [ˈtɑːtə(r)] *n.* **1.** (*incrustation from wine*) ви́нный ка́мень; **cream of ~** ки́слый ви́нный ка́мень. **2.** (*on teeth*) (зубно́й) ка́мень.

Tartar[2] [ˈtɑːtə(r)] *n.* (*also* **Tatar**) тата́р|ин (*fem.* -ка).

task [tɑːsk] *n.* зада́ча, зада́ние; **he was set a difficult ~** пе́ред ним поста́вили тру́дную зада́чу; **take s.o. to ~ for carelessness** проб|ира́ть, -ра́ть кого́-н. за хала́тность; **~ force** (*mil.*) операти́вная гру́ппа.
cpd. **~master** *n.*: **he is a hard ~master** он из тебя́ все со́ки выжима́ет.

Tasmania [tæzˈmeɪnɪə] *n.* Тасма́ния.

TASS [tæs] *n.* (*abbr. of* ***Telegraph Agency of the Soviet Union***) ТАСС, (Телегра́фное аге́нтство Сове́тского Сою́за).

tassel [ˈtæs(ə)l] *n.* ки́сточка.

taste [teɪst] *n.* (*sense*; *flavour*) вкус; **the fruit was sweet to the ~** плод был сла́док на вкус; **I have lost my ~ for whisky** я потеря́л вкус к ви́ски; **it**

leaves a bad ~ in the mouth (*fig.*) э́то оставля́ет неприя́тный оса́док; (*act of tasting*; *small portion for tasting*): **have a ~ of this!** попро́буйте э́того!; **I gave him a ~ of his own medicine** (*fig.*) я оплати́л ему́ тем же (*or* той же моне́той); (*fig.*, *liking*): **Wagner is not to everybody's ~** Ва́гнер нра́вится далеко́ не всем; **there is no accounting for ~s** о вку́сах не спо́рят; **add salt and pepper to ~** (*in recipe*) доба́вьте со́ли и пе́рца по вку́су; (*fig.*, *discernment*, *judgement*) понима́ние; **he is a man of ~** он челове́к со вку́сом; **bad ~** дурно́й вкус.

v.t. **1.** (*perceive flavour of*) различ|а́ть, -и́ть; **can you ~ the garlic in this dish?** вы чу́вствуете чесно́к в э́том блю́де? **2.** (*professionally*) дегусти́ровать (*impf.*, *pf.*). **3.** (*eat small amount of*) есть, по-; **~ this and say if you like it** попро́буйте и скажи́те, нра́вится вам или нет. **4.** (*experience*) вку|ша́ть, -си́ть; изве́д|ывать, -ать.

v.i.: **the meat ~s horrible** у мя́са проти́вный вкус; **~ of** име́ть (*impf.*) при́вкус +*g.*; отдава́ть (*impf.*) +*i.*; **what does it ~ like?** како́го оно́ на вкус?

cpd. **~-bud** *n.* вкусова́я лу́ковица.

tasteful ['teɪstfʊl] *adj.* изя́щный; со вку́сом.

tasteless ['teɪstlɪs] *adj.* (*insipid*) безвку́сный; (*showing want of taste*) безвку́сный; (*in bad taste*) беста́ктный; в дурно́м то́не.

taster ['teɪstə(r)] *n.* (*sampler of wines etc.*) дегуста́тор.

tasty ['teɪstɪ] *adj.* вку́сный.

Tatar ['tɑ:tə(r)] = **Tartar**[2]

tattered ['tætəd] *adj.* по́рванный, разо́рванный.

tatters ['tætəz] *n.* кло́чь|я (*pl.*, *g.* -ев), лохмо́ть|я (*pl.*, *g.* -ев); **his shirt was in ~** от его́ руба́хи оста́лись кло́чья.

tattle ['tæt(ə)l] *n.* спле́тня, болтовня́.

v.i. болта́ть (*impf.*); спле́тничать, по-.

tattler ['tætlə(r)] *n.* болту́н, спле́тник.

tattoo[1] [tə'tu:, tæ-] *n.* (*on skin*) татуиро́вка.

v.t. татуи́ровать, вы́-.

tattoo[2] [tə'tu:, tæ-] *n.* **1.** (*mil. signal*) сигна́л пове́стки пе́ред отбо́ем; (*fig.*) стук; **the rain beat a ~ on the roof** дождь бараба́нил по кры́ше. **2.** (*entertainment*) показа́тельные выступле́ния военнослу́жащих.

tatty ['tætɪ] *adj.* (*coll.*) потрёпанный, обша́рпанный.

taunt [tɔ:nt] *n.* насме́шка.

v.t. дразни́ть (*impf.*); **he was ~ed with cowardice** над ним насмеха́лись, называ́я его́ тру́сом.

Taurus ['tɔ:rəs] *n.* (*astron.*) Теле́ц.

taut [tɔ:t] *adj.* туго́й, ту́го натя́нутый.

tautological [,tɔ:tə'lɒdʒɪk(ə)l] *adj.* тавтологи́ческий.

tautology [tɔ:'tɒlədʒɪ] *n.* тавтоло́гия.

tavern ['tæv(ə)n] *n.* таве́рна.

tawdriness ['tɔ:drɪnɪs] *n.* крикли́вость, безвку́сица.

tawdry ['tɔ:drɪ] *adj.* крича́щий, безвку́сный.

tawny ['tɔ:nɪ] *adj.* кори́чнево-жёлтый.

tax [tæks] *n.* **1.** (*levy*) нало́г; **income ~** подохо́дный нало́г; **purchase ~** нало́г на поку́пки; **after ~** за вы́четом нало́га. **2.** (*fig.*, *strain*, *demand*) испыта́ние; нагру́зка; **it was a great ~ on her strength** э́то подрыва́ло её си́лы.

v.t. обл|ага́ть, -ожи́ть нало́гом; (*fig.*): **he ~es my patience** он испы́тывает моё терпе́ние.

cpds. **~-collector** *n.* сбо́рщик нало́гов; **~-deductible** *adj.* необлага́емый нало́гом; **~-free** *adj.* освобождённый от упла́ты нало́гов; **~man** *n.* (*coll.*) нало́говый инспе́ктор; **~payer** *n.* налогоплате́льщик.

taxable ['tæksəb(ə)l] *adj.* подлежа́щий обложе́нию нало́гов.

taxation [tæk'seɪʃ(ə)n] *n.* налогообложе́ние.

taxi ['tæksɪ] *n.* такси́ (*nt. indecl.*).

v.i. **1.** (*ride by ~*) е́хать (*det.*) на такси́. **2.** (*of aircraft*) рули́ть (*impf.*).

cpds. **~cab** *n.* такси́ (*nt. indecl.*); **~-driver** *n.* шофёр такси́; **~meter** *n.* таксо́метр; **~-rank** *n.* стоя́нка такси́.

taxidermist ['tæksɪ,dɜ:mɪst] *n.* таксидерми́ст.

taxidermy ['tæksɪ,dɜ:mɪ] *n.* таксиде́рмия.

taxonomist [tæk'sɒnəmɪst] *n.* бота́ник/зо́олог-система́тик.

taxonomy [tæk'sɒnəmɪ] *n.* таксоно́мия.

TB (*abbr. of* **tuberculosis**) туберкулёз.

tea [ti:] *n.* (*plant*, *beverage*) чай; (*meal*) чай, по́лдник; **make (the) ~** зава́р|ивать, -и́ть чай; **have, take ~** пить, вы́- ча́ю; **I have lemon with my ~** я пью чай с лимо́ном; **that's not my cup of ~** (*coll.*) э́то не в моём вку́се.

cpds. **~-bag** *n.* паке́тик с ча́ем; **~-break** *n.* переры́в на чай; **~-caddy** *n.* ча́йница; **~cloth** *n.* ча́йное полоте́нце; **~-cosy** *n.* чехо́льчик (на ча́йник); **~cup** *n.* ча́йная ча́шка; **storm in a ~cup** бу́ря в стака́не воды́; **~-house** *n.* ча́йная; **~-leaf** *n.* ча́йный лист; **~-party** *n.* зва́ный чай; **~pot** *n.* ча́йник (для зава́рки); **~-service, ~-set** *nn.* ча́йный серви́з; **~shop** *n.* кафе́ (*indecl.*); **~spoon** *n.* ча́йная ло́жечка; **~-strainer** *n.* ча́йное си́точко; **~time** *n.* ра́нний ве́чер; **~-towel** *n.* ча́йное полоте́нце.

teach [ti:tʃ] *v.t.* **1.** (*instruct*) учи́ть, на-; обуч|а́ть, -и́ть; **she taught me Russian** она́ учи́ла меня́ ру́сскому языку́; **I taught myself English** я самостоя́тельно вы́учился англи́йскому языку́. **2.** (*v.t. & i.*, *give instruction*) (*school etc.*) учи́ть (*impf.*); (*university etc.*) преподава́ть (*impf.*); **~ing staff** преподава́тельский соста́в. **3.** (*ellipt.*): **that will ~ you!** э́то вас нау́чит уму́-ра́зуму!; **I'll ~ you (a lesson)!** я вас проучу́!

cpd. **~-in** *n.* семина́р, учёбный сбор.

teacher ['ti:tʃə(r)] *n.* учи́тель (*fem.* -ница); **~ training college** педагоги́ческий институ́т.

teaching ['ti:tʃɪŋ] *n.* **1.** (*precept*) уче́ние. **2.** (*activity*) преподава́ние, обуче́ние. **3.** (*profession*) преподава́ние; **she intends to take up ~** она́ собира́ется преподава́ть.

teak [ti:k] *n.* (*wood*) тик; (*tree*) тик, ти́ковое де́рево.

team [ti:m] *n.* (*of horses etc.*) упря́жка; (*games*) кома́нда; (*representative ~*) сбо́рная; (*of workers etc.*) брига́да; **~ of scientists** гру́ппа учёных; (*of researchers etc.*) коллекти́в.

v.i.: **we ~ed up with our neighbours** мы объедини́лись с сосе́дями.

cpds. **~-spirit** *n.* коллективи́зм; **~-work** *n.* коллекти́вная рабо́та; сы́гранность.

tear[1] [tɪə(r)] *n.* **(~-drop)** слеза́; **~s ran down her cheeks** слёзы текли́ по её щека́м; **I found her in ~s** я заста́л её в слеза́х; **burst into ~s** распла́каться (*pf.*); **the audience was moved to ~s** пу́блика была́ тро́нута до слёз.

cpds. **~-duct** *n.* слёзный прото́к; **~-gas** *n.* слезоточи́вый газ.

tear[2] [teə(r)] *n.* (*rent*) разры́в, проре́ха.

v.t. **1.** (*rip*, *rend*) разрыва́ть, -орва́ть; рвать; **I tore my shirt on a nail** я порва́л руба́шку о гвоздь; **the book is badly torn** кни́га си́льно растрёпана; (*fig.*): **my argument was torn to shreds** мой аргуме́нт разби́ли в пух и прах; **a country torn by strife** страна́, раздира́емая враждо́й; **she was torn by emotions** её раздира́ли (разли́чные) чу́вства. **2.** (*snatch*; *remove by force*) от|рыва́ть, -орва́ть; срыва́ть, сорва́ть; **she tore the baby from his arms** она́ вы́рвала ребёнка у него́ из рук. **3.** (*pull violently*) вырыва́ть, вы́рвать; **it makes one ~ one's hair** (*fig.*) от э́того хо́чется рвать на себе́ во́лосы.

v.i. **1.** (*pull violently*): **he tore at the wrapping-paper** он бро́сился срыва́ть обёрточную бума́гу. **2.** (*become torn*) рва́ться (*impf.*); **this material ~s easily** э́тот материа́л легко́ рвётся. **3.** (*rush*) мча́ться, по-; нести́сь, по-; **why are you in such a**

~ing hurry? куда́ вы так спеши́те?

with advs.: **I could not ~ myself away** я не мог оторва́ться; **the notice had been torn down** объявле́ние сорва́ли; **the old buildings are to be torn down** ста́рые зда́ния бу́дут снос́ить; **he tore off on his bicycle** он помча́лся прочь на велосипе́де; **several pages had been torn out** не́сколько страни́ц бы́ло вы́рвано; **the children came ~ing out of school** де́ти стремгла́в вы́бежали из шко́лы; **the letter was torn up** письмо́ порва́ли.

cpd. **~away** *n.* сорвиголова́ (*c.g.*).

tearful ['tɪəfʊl] *adj.* по́лный слёз, запла́канный.

tease [ti:z] *n.* (*pers.*) задира (*c.g.*), насме́шни|к (*fem.* -ца).

v.t. **1.** (*make fun of, irritate*) дразни́ть (*impf.*); издева́ться (*impf.*) над+*i*. **2.** (*pester*) пристава́ть (*impf.*) к+*d*.

teat [ti:t] *n.* сосо́к.

technical ['teknɪk(ə)l] *adj.* техни́ческий; **~ college** техни́ческий вуз, те́хникум; **~ term** специа́льный те́рмин; **~ly** форма́льно.

technicality [,teknɪ'kælɪtɪ] *n.* (*detail*) техни́ческая дета́ль; форма́льность.

technician [tek'nɪʃ(ə)n] *n.* те́хник.

technique [tek'ni:k] *n.* (*skill*) те́хника, уче́ние; (*method*) техни́ческий приём, мето́дика.

technological [,teknə'lɒdʒɪk(ə)l] *adj.* технологи́ческий, техни́ческий.

technologist [tek'nɒlədʒɪst] *n.* техно́лог.

technology [tek'nɒlədʒɪ] *n.* те́хника, техноло́гия.

teddy-bear ['tedɪ] *n.* плю́шевый медвежо́нок/ми́шка.

teddy-boy ['tedɪ] *n.* стиля́га (*m.*).

tedious ['ti:dɪəs] *adj.* утоми́тельный, ску́чный.

tedi|ousness ['ti:dɪəsnɪs], **-um** ['ti:dɪəm] *nn.* ску́ка.

tee [ti:] *n.* (*peg*) ко́лышек.

v.i.: **~ off** де́лать, с- пе́рвый уда́р.

teem [ti:m] *v.i.* (*be full, swarm*) кише́ть (*impf.*); изоби́ловать (*impf.*); **the house is ~ing with ants** дом киши́т муравья́ми; **his head ~s with new ideas** он по́лон но́вых иде́й; **it was ~ing with rain** (*coll.*) лило́ как из ведра́.

teen [ti:n] *n.*: **he is in his ~s** ему́ ещё нет двадцати́ лет; он подро́сток.

cpds. **~-age** *adj.* ю́ношеский, несовершенноле́тний; **~ager** *n.* ю́ноша (*m.*)/де́вушка до двадцати́ лет.

teeny(-weeny) ['ti:nɪ] *adj.* (*coll.*) малю́сенький.

teeter ['ti:tə(r)] *v.i.* кача́ться (*impf.*); (*fig.*) колеба́ться (*impf.*).

teeth|e [ti:ð] *v.i.*: **baby is ~ing** у ребёнка ре́жутся зу́бы.

teetotal [ti:'təʊt(ə)l] *adj.* непью́щий.

teetotaller [ti:'təʊtələ(r)] *n.* тре́звенник.

telecast ['telɪ,kɑ:st] *n.* телепереда́ча.

v.t. перед|ава́ть, -а́ть по телеви́дению.

telecommunication [,telɪkə,mju:nɪ'keɪʃ(ə)n] *n.*: **~ satellite** спу́тник свя́зи; **~s** да́льняя связь.

telegram ['telɪ,græm] *n.* телегра́мма.

telegraph ['telɪ,grɑ:f, -,græf] *n.* телегра́ф.

v.t. & i. телеграфи́ровать (*impf., pf.*; *pf. also* про-).

cpds. **~-pole** *n.* телегра́фный столб; **~-wire** *n.* телегра́фный про́вод.

telegraph|er ['telɪ,grɑ:fə(r), tɪ'legrəfə(r)], **-ist** [tɪ'legrəfɪst] *nn.* телеграфи́ст (*fem.* -ка).

telegraphic [,telɪ'græfɪk] *adj.* телегра́фный.

telegraphist [tɪ'legrəfɪst] = **telegrapher**

telegraphy [tɪ'legrəfɪ] *n.* телеграфи́я.

telemeter ['telɪ,mi:tə(r), tɪ'lemɪtə(r)] *n.* телеме́тр.

telemetry [tɪ'lemətrɪ] *n.* телеметри́я.

teleological [,telɪə'lɒdʒɪk(ə)l, ,ti:-] *adj.* телеологи́ческий.

teleology [,telɪ'ɒlədʒɪ, ,ti:-] *n.* телеоло́гия.

telepathic [,telɪ'pæθɪk] *adj.* телепати́ческий.

telepathy [tɪ'lepəθɪ] *n.* телепа́тия.

telephone ['telɪ,fəʊn] *n.* телефо́н; **are you on the ~?** у вас есть телефо́н?; **he is (talking) on the ~** он разгова́ривает по телефо́ну; **~ call** телефо́нный звоно́к; **~ exchange** телефо́нная ста́нция; **~ number** но́мер телефо́на, (*coll.*) телефо́н; **~ operator** телефони́ст (*fem.* -ка); **public ~** телефо́н-автома́т.

v.t. & i. звони́ть, по- (*кому*) по телефону; телефони́ровать (*impf., pf.*) (*что кому*) (*pf. also* про-).

telephonic [,telɪ'fɒnɪk] *adj.* телефо́нный.

telephonist [tɪ'lefənɪst] *n.* телефони́ст (*fem.* -ка).

telephony [tɪ'lefənɪ] *n.* телефони́я.

telephoto(graphic) [,telɪ,fəʊtə'græfɪk] *adj.* телефотографи́ческий.

teleprinter ['telɪ,prɪntə(r)] *n.* телета́йп.

teleprompter ['telɪ,prɒmptə(r)] *n.* телесуфлёр.

telesales ['telɪ,seɪlz] *n. pl.* прода́жа по телефо́ну.

telescope ['telɪ,skəʊp] *n.* телеско́п.

telescopic [,telɪ'skɒpɪk] *adj.* **1.** телескопи́ческий. **2.** (*consisting of retracting and extending sections*) складно́й, выдвижно́й.

telethon ['telə,θɒn] *n.* (благотвори́тельный) телемарафо́н.

teletype ['telɪ,taɪp] *n.* телета́йп.

v.t. перед|ава́ть, -а́ть по телета́йпу.

televiewer ['telɪ,vjʊə(r)] *n.* телезри́тель (*m.*) (*fem.* -ница).

televise ['telɪ,vaɪz] *v.t.* пока́з|ывать, -а́ть по телеви́дению.

television ['telɪ,vɪʒ(ə)n, -'vɪʒ(ə)n] *n.* (*system, process*) телеви́дение; **what's on ~?** что пока́зывается по телеви́дению?; **(~ receiver, set)** телеви́зор; **~ programme** телевизио́нная переда́ча, телепереда́ча, телепрогра́мма; **~ studio** телесту́дия; **closed-circuit ~** ка́бельное телеви́дение.

telex ['teleks] *n.* те́лекс.

tell [tel] *v.t.* **1.** (*relate; inform of; make known*) расска́з|ывать, -а́ть; сообщ|а́ть, -и́ть; ука́з|ывать, -а́ть; **~ me all about it!** расскажи́те мне всё как есть/бы́ло; **(I'll) ~ you what, let's both go!** зна́ете что, дава́йте пойдём вме́сте!; **can you ~ me the time?** вы не зна́ете, кото́рый час? **2.** (*speak, say*) говори́ть, сказа́ть; **are you ~ing the truth?** вы говори́те пра́вду? **3.** (*decide, determine, know*) определ|я́ть, -и́ть; узн|ава́ть, -а́ть; **how do you ~ which button to press?** отку́да изве́стно, каку́ю кно́пку на́до нажима́ть?; **can she ~ the time yet?** она́ уже́ уме́ет определя́ть вре́мя?; **you never can ~** никогда́ не зна́ешь. **4.** (*distinguish*) отлич|а́ть, -и́ть; различ|а́ть, -и́ть; **I can't ~ them apart** я не могу́ их различи́ть. **5.** (*assure*) зав|еря́ть, -е́рить; **I can ~ you** поверьте мне. **6.** (*count*): **there were seven all told** в о́бщей сло́жности их бы́ло семь/се́меро. **7.** (*direct, instruct*) прика́з|ывать, -а́ть; объясн|я́ть, -и́ть; **he was told to wait outside** ему́ веле́ли подожда́ть за две́рью. **8.** (*predict*) предска́з|ывать, -а́ть; **I told you so!** я вам говори́л!; **can you ~ my fortune?** мо́жете мне погада́ть?

v.i. **1.** (*give information*) расска́з|ывать, -а́ть; **he told of his adventures** он рассказа́л о свои́х приключе́ниях; **don't ~ on me!** (*coll.*) не выдава́й меня́!; **he promised not to ~** (*divulge secret*) он обеща́л молча́ть; **time will ~** вре́мя пока́жет. **2.** (*have an effect*) ска́з|ываться, -а́ться.

with adv.: **~ off** (*coll., reprove*) отчи́т|ывать, -а́ть; **he got a good ~ing-off** его́ здо́рово отчита́ли.

cpd. **~-tale** *n.* спле́тник, я́беда (*c.g.*); (*attr.*) преда́тельский, многоговоря́щий.

teller ['telə(r)] *n.* (*narrator*) расска́зчик; (*counter of votes*) счётчик голосо́в; (*cashier*) касси́р.

telling ['telɪŋ] *adj.* си́льный; **a ~ argument** убеди́тельный до́вод; **a ~ example** нагля́дный приме́р;

a ~ blow ощути́мый уда́р.
telly ['telɪ] *n.* те́лик (*coll.*).
temerity [tɪ'merɪtɪ] *n.* сме́лость.
temp [temp] *n.* (*coll.*) рабо́тающ|ий (*fem.* -ая) вре́менно.
v.i. рабо́тать (*impf.*) вре́менно.
temper ['tempə(r)] *n.* **1.** (*disposition of mind*) нрав; настрое́ние; **he has a quick ~** он вспы́льчив(ый); **he lost his ~** он вы́шел из себя́; **I had difficulty keeping my ~** я с трудо́м сде́рживался. **2.** (*irritation, anger*) вспы́льчивость; несде́ржанность; **he flew into a ~** он вспыли́л; **he left in a ~** он разозли́лся и ушёл.
v.t. **1.** (*metall.*) зака́л|ивать, -и́ть. **2.** (*mitigate*) умеря́ть (*impf.*); смягч|а́ть, -и́ть.
tempera ['tempərə] *n.* те́мпера.
temperament ['temprəmənt] *n.* темпера́мент, нрав.
temperamental [ˌtemprə'ment(ə)l] *adj.* (*subject to moods*) неуравнове́шенный; с но́ровом; (*of a machine*) капри́зный.
temperance ['tempərəns] *n.* **1.** (*moderation*) уме́ренность. **2.** (*abstinence from alcohol*) тре́звость; воздержа́ние от спиртны́х напи́тков.
temperate ['tempərət] *adj.* уме́ренный; **the ~ zone** уме́ренный по́яс.
temperature ['temprɪtʃə(r)] *n.* температу́ра; (*fever*) жар; **he has a ~** у него́ температу́ра/жар.
tempest ['tempɪst] *n.* (*lit., fig.*) бу́ря.
tempestuous [tem'pestjʊəs] *adj.* бу́рный.
template ['templɪt, -pleɪt] *n.* шабло́н.
temple[1] ['temp(ə)l] *n.* (*relig.*) храм, святи́лище.
temple[2] ['temp(ə)l] *n.* (*anat.*) висо́к.
tempo ['tempəʊ] *n.* (*lit., fig.*) темп, ритм.
temporal ['tempər(ə)l] *adj.* (*of time*) временно́й; (*of this life; secular*) мирско́й, све́тский.
temporary ['tempərərɪ] *adj.* вре́менный.
temporize ['tempəˌraɪz] *v.i.* тяну́ть (*impf.*) вре́мя; ме́длить (*impf.*).
tempt [tempt] *v.t.* соблазн|я́ть, -и́ть; иску|ша́ть, -си́ть.
temptation [temp'teɪʃ(ə)n] *n.* собла́зн, искуше́ние; **she yielded to ~** она́ поддала́сь собла́зну.
tempter ['temptə(r)] *n.* искуси́тель (*m.*); соблазни́тель (*m.*).
temptress ['temptrɪs] *n.* искуси́тельница, соблазни́тельница.
ten [ten] *n.* де́сять; (**~** *people*) де́сятеро, де́сять челове́к; **~ each** по десяти́; **in ~s, ~ at a time** по десяти́, деся́тками; (*figure; thg. numbered 10; group of* **~**) деся́тка; **~s of thousands** деся́тки (*m. pl.*) ты́сяч; (*with var. nn. expr. or understood: cf. examples under* **five**): **~ to one** (*almost certainly*) почти́ наверняка́; **~ to ~** (*o'clock*) без десяти́ де́сять.
adj. де́сять +*g. pl.*; **~ eggs** (*as purchase*) деся́ток яи́ц; **~ threes are thirty** де́сятью три — три́дцать.
cpds. **~fold** *adj.* десятикра́тный; **~pins** *n.* ке́гл|и (*pl., g.* -ей).
tenable ['tenəb(ə)l] *adj.* **1.** (*defensible*) обороноспосо́бный; (*fig.*) здра́вый; **a ~ argument** разу́мный до́вод. **2.** (*to be held*): **the office is ~ for three years** срок полномо́чий — три го́да.
tenacious [tɪ'neɪʃəs] *adj.* це́пкий, насто́йчивый; **the dog held on ~ly** соба́ка кре́пко вцепи́лась.
tenacity [tɪ'næsɪtɪ] *n.* це́пкость, насто́йчивость.
tenancy ['tenənsɪ] *n.* **1.** (*renting*) наём помеще́ния; (*period*) срок на́йма/аре́нды; **during his ~** в пери́од его́ прожива́ния. **2.** (*ownership*) владе́ние.
tenant ['tenənt] *n.* (*one renting from landlord*) жиле́ц, кварти́рант; аренда́тор.
tend[1] [tend] *v.t.* (*look after*) присм|а́тривать, -отре́ть за+*i.*; уха́живать (*impf.*) за+*i.*; **the shepherds ~ed their flocks** пастухи́ пасли́ свои́ стада́; **the machine needs constant ~ing** маши́на тре́бует постоя́нного ухо́да.
tend[2] [tend] *v.i.* (*be inclined*) склоня́ться (*impf.*) (*к чему*); **I am ~ing towards your view** я склоня́юсь к ва́шей то́чке зре́ния.
tendency ['tendənsɪ] *n.* тенде́нция; **an upward ~ in the market** тенде́нция к повыше́нию на ры́нке.
tendentious [ten'denʃəs] *adj.* тенденцио́зный.
tender[1] ['tendə(r)] *n.* (*ship*) посы́льное су́дно; (*wagon*) те́ндер.
tender[2] ['tendə(r)] *n.* **1.** (*offer*) предложе́ние; **~s are invited for the contract** принима́ются зая́вки на подря́д. **2.** (*currency*): **legal ~** зако́нное платёжное сре́дство.
v.t. предл|ага́ть, -ожи́ть; **he ~ed his resignation** он по́дал заявле́ние об отста́вке.
v.i.: **he ~ed for the contract** он предложи́л себя́ в подря́дчики.
tender[3] ['tendə(r)] *adj.* **1.** (*sensitive*) не́жный; **of ~ years** в не́жном во́зрасте; **my finger is still ~** мой па́лец всё ещё боли́т. **2.** (*loving, solicitous*) не́жный, ла́сковый. **3.** (*not tough*): **a ~ steak** мя́гкий бифште́кс.
cpds. **~-hearted** *adj.* мягкосерде́чный; **~loin** *n.* вы́резка.
tenderness ['tendənɪs] *n.* не́жность.
tendon ['tend(ə)n] *n.* сухожи́лие.
tendril ['tendrɪl] *n.* у́сик.
tenement ['tenɪmənt] *n.* (неблагоустро́енное) жили́ще; **~ house** многокварти́рный дом.
tenet ['tenɪt, 'ti:net] *n.* до́гмат, при́нцип.
tenner ['tenə(r)] *n.* (*coll.*) деся́тка.
tennis ['tenɪs] *n.* те́ннис.
cpds. **~-court** *n.* те́ннисный корт; **~-player** *n.* тенниси́ст (*fem.* -ка); **~-racket** *n.* те́ннисная раке́тка.
tenon ['tenən] *n.* шип.
cpds. **~-joint** *n.* соедине́ние на вставны́х шпи́льках; **~-saw** *n.* шипоре́зная пила́.
tenor[1] ['tenə(r)] *n.* (*course, direction*) направле́ние; (*of speech etc.*); (*purport*) смысл, содержа́ние.
tenor[2] ['tenə(r)] *n.* (*mus.*) те́нор; **he sings ~** он поёт те́нором; (*attr.*) теноро́вый; **~ part** па́ртия те́нора; **~ saxophone** саксофо́н-те́нор; **~ voice** те́нор.
tense[1] [tens] *n.* (*gram.*) вре́мя (*nt.*).
tense[2] [tens] *adj.* натя́нутый, напряжённый; **a moment of ~ excitement** моме́нт не́рвного возбужде́ния.
v.t. натя́|гивать, -ну́ть; напр|яга́ть, -я́чь; **I was all ~d up** я был в напряжённом состоя́нии.
v.i. напр|яга́ться, -я́чься.
tensile ['tensaɪl] *adj.* растяжи́мый; **~ strength** преде́л про́чности при растяже́нии.
tension ['tenʃ(ə)n] *n.* **1.** (*stretching; being stretched*) напряже́ние; (*stretched state*) напряжённое состоя́ние; (*mental strain, excitement*) напряжённость, **racial ~** напряжённые ра́совые отноше́ния. **2.** (*voltage*): **high/low ~** высо́кое/ни́зкое напряже́ние.
tent [tent] *n.* пала́тка; шатёр.
tentacle ['tentək(ə)l] *n.* щу́пальце.
tentative ['tentətɪv] *adj.* про́бный, предвари́тельный; **~ly** ориентиро́вочно.
tenterhooks ['tentəˌhʊks] *n.*: **I was on ~** я сиде́л как на иго́лках.
tenth [tenθ] *n.* **1.** (*date*) деся́тое число́; **on the ~ of May** деся́того ма́я. **2.** (*fraction*) деся́тая часть; **one ~** одна́ деся́тая.
adj. деся́тый.
cpd. **~-rate** *adj.* ни́зшего со́рта.
tenuous ['tenjʊəs] *adj.* то́нкий; (*fig.*): **a ~ excuse** неубеди́тельная отгово́рка.
tenure ['tenjə(r)] *n.* (*of office*) пребыва́ние в до́лжности; (*of property*) усло́вия (*nt. pl.*)/срок владе́ния иму́ществом.
tepee ['ti:pi:] *n.* вигва́м.
tepid ['tepɪd] *adj.* теплова́тый; (*fig.*) прохла́дный.
tercentenary [ˌtɜ:sen'ti:nərɪ, -'tenərɪ, tɜ:'sentɪnərɪ] *n.* трёхсотле́тие.

adj. трёхсотле́тний.

term [tɜ:m] *n.* **1.** (*fixed or limited period*) перио́д; **~ of office** срок полномо́чия; **a long ~ of imprisonment** дли́тельный срок заключе́ния; (*in school, university etc.*) триме́стр, уче́бная че́тверть; (*in law courts*) се́ссия. **2.** (*math., logic*) элеме́нт, член. **3.** (*expression*) те́рмин; **~ of abuse** бра́нное выраже́ние; **contradiction in ~s** противоречи́вое поня́тие; **he spoke of you in flattering ~s** он говори́л о вас в ле́стных выраже́ниях; **in ~s of** с то́чки зре́ния +*g.*; в смы́сле +*g.*; **in metric ~s** в метри́ческом выраже́нии. **4.** (*pl., conditions*) усло́вия (*nt. pl.*); **~s of surrender** усло́вия капитуля́ции; **they came to ~s** они́ пришли́ к соглаше́нию; **~s of reference** круг полномо́чий; (*charges*) усло́вия опла́ты. **5.** (*pl., relations*) отноше́ния (*nt. pl.*); **we are on the best of ~s** мы в прекра́сных отноше́ниях; **they are not on speaking ~s** они́ не разгова́ривают друг с дру́гом.

v.t. наз|ыва́ть, -ва́ть.

termagant ['tɜ:məgənt] *n.* меге́ра, фу́рия.

terminal ['tɜ:mɪn(ə)l] *n.* **1.** (*of transport*) коне́чный пункт; (*rail*) вокза́л; **air ~** (*in city*) (городско́й) аэровокза́л. **2.** (*elec.*) зажи́м.

adj. (*coming to or forming the end point*) коне́чный; после́дний; **~ illness** смерте́льная боле́знь.

terminate ['tɜ:mɪˌneɪt] *v.t.* заверш|а́ть, -и́ть; класть, положи́ть коне́ц +*d.*; **they ~d his contract** они́ расто́ргли с ним контра́кт.

v.i. зак|а́нчиваться, -о́нчиться; заверш|а́ться, -и́ться.

termination [ˌtɜ:mɪ'neɪʃ(ə)n] *n.* заверше́ние; прекраще́ние; коне́ц; (*of a word*) оконча́ние.

terminology [ˌtɜ:mɪ'nɒlədʒɪ] *n.* терминоло́гия.

terminus ['tɜ:mɪnəs] *n.* коне́чный пункт; (*rail*) вокза́л.

termite ['tɜ:maɪt] *n.* терми́т.

tern [tɜ:n] *n.* кра́чка.

terra [ˌterə] *n.*: **~ *firma*** ['fɜ:mə] су́ша.

terrace ['terəs, -rɪs] *n.* (*raised area*) терра́са; (*row of houses*) ряд домо́в, постро́енных вплотну́ю.

v.t. терраси́ровать (*impf., pf.*).

terracotta [ˌterə'kɒtə] *n.* террако́та; (*attr.*) террако́товый.

terrain [te'reɪn, tə-] *n.* ме́стность.

terrapin ['terəpɪn] *n.* водяна́я черепа́ха.

terrestrial [tə'restrɪəl, tɪ-] *adj.* (*of the earth*) земно́й; (*living on dry land*) живу́щий на/в земле́.

terrible ['terɪb(ə)l] *adj.* (*inspiring fear*) стра́шный; (*coll., very unpleasant or bad*) ужа́сный, стра́шный.

terribly ['terɪblɪ] *adv.* ужа́сно, стра́шно.

terrier ['terɪə(r)] *n.* терье́р.

terrific [tə'rɪfɪk] *adj.* (*coll., huge*) колосса́льный; (*coll., marvellous*) потряса́ющий.

terrify ['terɪˌfaɪ] *v.t.* ужас|а́ть, -ну́ть.

territorial [ˌterɪ'tɔ:rɪəl] *n.* военнослу́жащий территориа́льной а́рмии.

adj. территориа́льный.

territory ['terɪtərɪ, -trɪ] *n.* террито́рия, райо́н.

terror ['terə(r)] *n.* (*fear*) у́жас, страх; **the thought struck ~ into me** э́та мысль привела́ меня́ в у́жас; (*pol., hist.*) терро́р; (*coll., child*) чертёнок.

cpd. **~-stricken** *adj.* объя́тый стра́хом/у́жасом.

terrorism ['terəˌrɪz(ə)m] *n.* террори́зм.

terrorist ['terərɪst] *n.* террори́ст (*fem.* -ка); (*attr.*) террористи́ческий.

terrorize ['terəˌraɪz] *v.t.* терроризи́ровать (*impf., pf.*).

terse [tɜ:s] *adj.* кра́ткий, сжа́тый.

tertiary ['tɜ:ʃərɪ] *adj.* (*geol. etc.*) трети́чный.

Terylene ['terɪˌli:n] *n.* (*propr.*) терилéн.

test [test] *n.* испыта́ние, про́ба, контро́ль (*m.*); **~ case** показа́тельный слу́чай; **endurance ~** испыта́ние выно́сливости; **his promises were put to the ~** его́ обеща́ния подве́рглись прове́рке в де́ле; **these methods have stood the ~ of time** э́ти ме́тоды вы́держали прове́рку вре́менем; (*examination*) экза́мен; контро́льная рабо́та; (*oral*) опро́с; **he took a ~ in English** он сдава́л экза́мен по англи́йскому языку́; (*chem.*) ана́лиз; о́пыт; **(nuclear) ~ ban** запреще́ние испыта́ний я́дерного ору́жия; **blood ~** ана́лиз кро́ви.

v.t. **1.** (*make trial of*) подв|ерга́ть, -е́ргнуть испыта́нию; пров|еря́ть, -е́рить. **2.** (*subject to ~s*) пров|еря́ть, -е́рить; **the pupils were ~ed in arithmetic** ученика́м да́ли контро́льную рабо́ту по арифме́тике; **his job is to ~ (out) new designs** он ведёт испыта́ния но́вых констру́кций.

cpds. **~-match** *n.* междунаро́дный кри́кетный матч; **~-pilot** *n.* лётчик-испыта́тель (*m.*); **~-tube** *n.* проби́рка.

testament ['testəmənt] *n.* (*will*) завеща́ние; (*bibl.*) заве́т; **the Old T~** Ве́тхий заве́т; **New T~** (*attr.*) новозаве́тный.

testator [te'steɪtə(r)] *n.* завеща́тель (*m.*).

testatrix [te'steɪtrɪks] *n.* завеща́тельница.

tester ['testə(r)] *n.* (*pers.*) испыта́тель (*m.*); (*device*) испыта́тельный прибо́р.

testicle ['testɪk(ə)l] *n.* яи́чко.

testify ['testɪˌfaɪ] *v.t.* & *i.* **1.** (*affirm*) свиде́тельствовать (*impf.*); да|ва́ть, -ть показа́ния; **will you ~ to my innocence?** вы подтверди́те мою́ невино́вность? **2.: ~ to** (*be evidence of*) свиде́тельствовать (*impf.*) о+*p.*

testimonial [ˌtestɪ'məʊnɪəl] *n.* (*certificate of conduct etc.*) рекоменда́ция, характери́стика.

testimony ['testɪmənɪ] *n.* показа́ния (*nt. pl.*); (*sign*) при́знак, свиде́тельство.

testis ['testɪs] = **testicle**

testy ['testɪ] *adj.* вспы́льчивый, раздражи́тельный.

tetanus ['tetənəs] *n.* столбня́к, те́танус.

tetchy ['tetʃɪ] *adj.* раздражи́тельный, оби́дчивый.

tête-à-tête [ˌteɪtɑ:'teɪt] *n.* тет-а-те́т.

adv. тет-а-те́т; с гла́зу на гла́з; вдвоём.

tether ['teðə(r)] *n.* при́вязь; **he was at the end of his ~** он дошёл до ру́чки/то́чки.

v.t. привя́з|ывать, -а́ть.

tetrahedron [ˌtetrə'hi:drən, -'hedrən] *n.* четырёхгра́нник.

tetrameter [tɪ'træmɪtə(r)] *n.* тетра́метр.

Teutonic [tju:'tɒnɪk] *adj.* тевто́нский, герма́нский.

text [tekst] *n.* (*original words*) текст; (*quoted passage*) отры́вок; (*subject, theme*) те́ма.

cpd. **~-book** *n.* уче́бник.

textile ['tekstaɪl] *n.* ткань; (*pl.*) тексти́ль (*m.*).

adj. тексти́льный; **~ workers** тексти́льщики.

textual ['tekstjʊəl] *adj.* текстово́й.

textural ['tekstʃərəl] *adj.* структу́рный.

texture ['tekstʃə(r)] *n.* (*of fabric*) строе́ние (тка́ни), тексту́ра; (*fig., structure, arrangement*) склад, строе́ние.

Thailand [taɪ] *n.* Таила́нд

thalidomide [θə'lɪdəˌmaɪd] *n.* (*pharm.*) талидоми́д; **~ babies** же́ртвы (*f. pl.*) талидоми́да.

Thames [temz] *n.* Те́мза.

than [ðən, ðæn] *conj.* чем; **he is taller ~ I** он вы́ше меня́; **can't you walk faster ~ that?** вы не мо́жете идти́ быстре́е?; **I would do anything rather ~ have him return** я гото́в на всё — лишь бы он не возвраща́лся; **I want nothing better ~ to relax** мне ничего́ так не хо́чется, как отдохну́ть.

thank [θæŋk] *v.t.* благодари́ть, от-; **~ you** спаси́бо; благодарю́ вас; **how can I ~ you?** как вы́разить вам свою́ благода́рность?; **he has only himself to ~** он сам во всём винова́т; **~ God you are safe** сла́ва Бо́гу, вы в безопа́сности.

cpds. **~-you** *n.*: **he left without as much as a ~-**

you он ушёл, да́же не сказа́в спаси́бо; *adj.*: **~-you letter** благода́рственное письмо́.
thankful ['θæŋkfʊl] *adj.* благода́рный.
thankfulness ['θæŋkfʊlnɪs] *n.* благода́рность.
thankless ['θæŋklɪs] *adj.* неблагода́рный.
thanks [θæŋks] *n. pl.* благода́рность; **~ for everything** спаси́бо за всё; **many ~** большо́е спаси́бо!; **~ to** благодаря́+*d.*; **vote of ~** вынесе́ние коллекти́вной благода́рности.
cpd. **~giving** *n.* (*expression of gratitude*) благодаре́ние; (*service*) благода́рственный моле́бен; **T~giving Day** день благодаре́ния.
that [ðæt] *pron.* **1.** (*demonstrative*) э́то; **~'s him!** вот (э́то) он!; **those are the boys I saw** э́то те ма́льчики, кото́рых я ви́дел; **those were the days!** вот э́то бы́ли времена́!; **what is ~?** что э́то тако́е?; **who is ~** кто э́то?; (*on the telephone*) кто говори́т?; **what's ~ for?** э́то к чему́?; **~'s a nice hat!** кака́я краси́вая шля́пка!; **~'s it!** (*sc. the point*) вот и́менно!; (*sc. right*) пра́вильно!; так!; **~'s just it, I can't swim** в то́м-то и де́ло, что я не уме́ю пла́вать; **it's not ~** не в э́том де́ло; **~ is how the war began** вот как начала́сь война́; **~'s right!** пра́вильно!; ве́рно!; **~'s all** вот и всё!; **~'s ~. then: now we can go** ну, всё, тепе́рь мы мо́жем идти́; **I'm going, and ~'s ~** я ухожу́, вот и всё; **with ~ he ended his speech** на э́том он ко́нчил свою́ речь; **~ is (to say)** то́ есть; **we talked of this and ~** мы говори́ли о том, о сём; **for all ~, he's a good husband** и при всём при э́том он хоро́ший муж; **the climate is like ~ of France** кли́мат тако́й же, как во Фра́нции; (*pl.*, *as antecedent*): **there are those who say ...** есть таки́е, что говоря́т...; ко́е-кто говори́т; **at ~** (*moreover*) к тому́ же; вдоба́вок; **he's only a journalist, and a poor one at ~** он всего́ лишь журнали́ст, и при э́том нева́жный. **2.** (*rel.*) кото́рый; **the book ~ I am talking about** кни́га, о кото́рой я говорю́; **the year ~ my father died** год, в кото́ром сконча́лся мой оте́ц.
adj. э́тот, тот; **I'll take ~ one** я возьму́ вот э́тот; **from ~ day forward** начина́я/впредь с того́ дня; **at ~ time** в то вре́мя.
adv.: **~ much I know** э́то-то я зна́ю; э́то всё, что я зна́ю; **I can't walk ~ far** я не могу́ сто́лько ходи́ть; **it is not all ~ cold** не так уж хо́лодно.
conj. что; (*expr. wish*) чтобы; (*expr. purpose*) (для того́) чтобы; (*var.*): **it's just ~ I have no time** де́ло в том, что у меня́ про́сто нет вре́мени; **it's not ~ I don't like him** не то, чтобы он мне не нра́вился; **now ~** раз уж; **now ~ I have more time** поско́льку у меня́ сейча́с бо́льше вре́мени; **he differs in ~ he likes reading** он отлича́ется тем, что он лю́бит чита́ть.
thatch [θætʃ] *n.* соло́ма, тростни́к.
v.t. крыть, по- соло́мой; **a ~ed roof** соло́менная/тростнико́вая кры́ша.
thaw [θɔ:] *n.* о́ттепель; **a ~ set in** начала́сь о́ттепель.
v.t. топи́ть, рас-.
v.i. та́ять, рас-/от-.
the [ðɪ, ðə, ði:] *def. art.*, *usu. untranslated*; (*if more emphatic*) э́тот, тот (са́мый); **~ one with ~ blue handle** тот, что с голубо́й ру́чкой; **something of ~ sort** что́-то в э́том ро́де; **he is ~ man for ~ job** он са́мый подходя́щий челове́к для э́той рабо́ты; **not *the* Mr Smith?** неуже́ли тот са́мый ми́стер Смит?; **Turkey is *the* place this year** в э́том году́ са́мое мо́дное ме́сто — Ту́рция.
adv.: **~ more ~ better** чем бо́льше, тем лу́чше; **that makes it all ~ worse** от э́того то́лько ху́же; **so much ~ worse for him** тем ху́же для него́.
theatre ['θɪətə(r)] *n.* **1.** (*playhouse*) теа́тр; **~ ticket** биле́т в теа́тр. **2.** (*dramatic literature*) драматурги́я; теа́тр; (*drama*) театра́льное иску́сство; **~ group** драмкружо́к. **3.** (*hall for lectures etc.*) зал; **operating ~** операцио́нная. **4.** (*scene of operation*) по́ле де́йствий; **~ of war** теа́тр вое́нных де́йствий.
cpd. **~-goer** *n.* театра́л.
theatrical [θɪ'ætrɪk(ə)l] *adj.* театра́льный.
theatricals [θɪ'ætrɪk(ə)ls] *n.*: **amateur ~** театра́льная самоде́ятельность.
theft [θeft] *n.* кра́жа.
their [ðeə(r)] *adj.* их; (*referring to gram. subject*) свой; **they lost ~ rights** они́ лиши́лись свои́х прав; **they want a house of ~ own** они́ хотя́т име́ть со́бственный дом; **they broke ~ legs** они́ слома́ли себе́ но́ги.
theirs [ðeəz] *pron.* их, свой (*cf.* **their**); **the money was ~ by right** де́ньги принадлежа́ли им по пра́ву; **it is a habit of ~** у них така́я привы́чка.
theism ['θi:ɪz(ə)m] *n.* теи́зм.
theist ['θi:ɪst] *n.* теи́ст.
theistic [θi:'ɪstɪk] *adj.* теисти́ческий.
thematic [θɪ'mætɪk] *adj.* темати́ческий.
theme [θi:m] *n.* (*subject: also mus.*) те́ма; **~ park** темати́ческий парк; **~ song, tune** лейтмоти́в.
themselves [ðəm'selvz] *pron.* **1.** (*refl.*) себя́, себе́; -ся, -сь; **they have only ~ to blame** они́ са́ми винова́ты; **they live by ~** они́ живу́т одни́; **they did it by ~** (*unaided*) они́ сде́лали э́то са́ми. **2.** (*emph.*): **they did the work ~** они́ са́ми сде́лали э́ту рабо́ту.
then [ðen] *n.*: **before ~** до э́того/того́ вре́мени; **by ~** к э́тому/тому́ вре́мени; **since ~** с тех пор; **till ~** до тех пор.
adj. тогда́шний; **the ~ king** тогда́шний коро́ль.
adv. **1.** (*at that time*) тогда́; **~ and there** тут же, сра́зу же; **now and ~** вре́мя от вре́мени. **2.** (*next*; *after that*) да́льше, да́лее. **3.** (*furthermore*) кро́ме того́; опя́ть-таки. **4.** (*in that case*) тогда́; **~ what *do* you want?** чего́ же вы в тако́м слу́чае хоти́те?; **till tomorrow, ~!** ну, тогда́ до за́втра!; (*introducing apodosis*) то. **5.** (*in resumption*) зна́чит; и так. **6.** (*emph.*) ита́к; **now ~, let's see what you've brought** ну что ж, дава́йте посмо́трим, что вы принесли́; **now ~!** (*warning*) ну-ну́!; **well ~, we can go tomorrow** зна́чит , мы мо́жем пойти́ за́втра.
thence [ðens] *adv.* (*from that place*) отту́да; (*from that source*, *for that reason*) отсю́да, из э́того.
cpds. **~forth, ~forward** *advs.* с тех пор.
theocracy [θɪ'ɒkrəsɪ] *n.* теокра́тия.
theocratic [θɪə'krætɪk] *adj.* теократи́ческий.
theologian [θɪə'ləʊdʒɪən, -dʒ(ə)n] *n.* богосло́в.
theological [θɪə'lɒdʒɪk(ə)l] *adj.* богосло́вский, теологи́ческий.
theology [θɪ'ɒlədʒɪ] *n.* богосло́вие, теоло́гия.
theorem ['θɪərəm] *n.* теоре́ма.
theoretical [θɪə'retɪk(ə)l] *adj.* теорети́ческий.
theor|etician [ˌθɪərɪ'tɪʃ(ə)n], **-ist** ['θɪərɪst] *nn.* теоре́тик.
theorize ['θɪəraɪz] *v.i.* теоретизи́ровать (*impf.*).
theory ['θɪərɪ] *n.* тео́рия; **in ~** в тео́рии; теорети́чески.
theosophical [θɪə'sɒfɪk(ə)l] *adj.* теосо́фский.
theosophist [θɪ'ɒsəfɪst] *n.* теосо́ф (*fem.* -ка).
theosophy [θɪ'ɒsəfɪ] *n.* теосо́фия.
therapeutic [ˌθerə'pju:tɪk] *adj.* терапевти́ческий.
therapeutics [ˌθerə'pju:tɪks] *n.* терапе́втика.
therapist ['θerəpɪst] *n.* терапе́вт.
therapy ['θerəpɪ] *n.* терапи́я; **occupational ~** трудотерапи́я.
there [ðeə(r)] *adv.* **1.** (*in or at that place*) там; вон; вон та́м; **hey, you ~!** эй, ты!; **he's not all ~** у него́ не все до́ма (*coll.*). **2.** (*to that place*) туда́; **when shall we get ~?** когда́ мы туда́ доберёмся?; **we went ~ and back in a day** мы съе́здили/сходи́ли туда́ и обра́тно за оди́н день. **3.** (*at that point or stage*) тут, здесь; **~ the matter ended** на э́том де́ло и ко́нчилось; **I wrote to him ~ and then** я тут же написа́л ему́. **4.** (*in that respect*) здесь; в э́том

отноше́нии; ~ **I agree with you** здесь я с ва́ми согла́сен. **5.** (*demonstr.*): ~ **goes the bell!** а вот и звоно́к!; **I don't like it, but** ~ **it is** не нра́вится мне э́то, да ничего́ не поде́лаешь; ~ **you are, take it!** вот вам, держи́те!; **oh,** ~ **you are; I was looking for you** ах, вы тут! а я вас иска́л; **~'s gratitude for you!** вот вам людска́я благода́рность! **6.** (*with v. to be, expr. presence, availability etc.*): **~'s a fly in my soup** у меня́ в су́пе му́ха; **is** ~ **a doctor here?** тут есть врач?; **~'s no time to lose** нельзя́ не теря́ть ни мину́ты; ~ **seems to have been a mistake** тут, ка́жется, произошла́ оши́бка; ~ **was plenty to eat** еды́ бы́ло полно́; **what is** ~ **to say?** что тут мо́жно сказа́ть?

int.: ~! **what did I tell you?** ну вот! что я вам говори́л?; ~, ~! (*comforting child etc.*) ну! ну!

thereabouts ['ðeərə,baʊts, -'baʊts] *adv.* (*nearby*) побли́зости; (*approximately*) о́коло э́того.

thereafter [ðeər'ɑ:ftə(r)] *adv.* по́сле того́; впредь.

thereby [ðeə'baɪ, 'ðeə-] *adv.* э́тим; таки́м о́бразом.

therefore ['ðeəfɔ:(r)] *adv.* поэ́тому, сле́довательно.

therein [ðeər'ɪn] *adv.* там; в э́том/том/них.

thereupon [,ðeərə'pɒn] *adv.* сра́зу же; тут; всле́дствие того́.

therm [θɜ:m] *n.* терм.

thermal ['θɜ:m(ə)l] *n.* (*aeron.*) восходя́щий пото́к тёплого во́здуха.

adj.: ~ **capacity** теплоёмкость; ~ **reactor** реа́ктор на тепловы́х нейтро́нах; ~ **springs** горя́чие исто́чники.

thermodynamics [,θɜ:məʊdaɪ'næmɪks] *n.* термодина́мика.

thermometer [θə'mɒmɪtə(r)] *n.* термо́метр.

thermonuclear [,θɜ:məʊ'nju:klɪə(r)] *adj.* термоя́дерный; ~ **device** термоя́дерное устро́йство.

thermos ['θɜ:məs] *n.* (~ **flask**) те́рмос.

thermostat ['θɜ:mə,stæt] *n.* термоста́т.

thesaurus [θɪ'sɔ:rəs] *n.* теза́урус.

thesis ['θi:sɪs] *n.* (*dissertation*) диссерта́ция; (*contention*) те́зис.

Thespian ['θespɪən] *n.* (*joc.*) актёр, актри́са.

they [ðeɪ] *pron.* они́; ~ **who ...** те, кото́рые/кто...; **both of them** они́ о́ба.

thick [θɪk] *n.*: **in the** ~ **of the fighting** в са́мом пе́кле бо́я; **he stood by me through** ~ **and thin** он стоя́л за меня́ гру́дью.

adj. **1.** (*of solid substance*) то́лстый; (*of liquid*) густо́й; **a** ~ **overcoat** тяжёлое пальто́; **a** ~ **coat of paint** то́лстый слой кра́ски; **the dust lay an inch** ~ пыль лежа́ла толщино́й в дюйм; ~ **soup** густо́й суп. **2.** (*close together, dense*) густо́й; (*of population*) пло́тный; ~ **hair** густы́е во́лосы; **a** ~ **forest** густо́й лес; **the air was** ~ **with smoke** стоя́л густо́й дым. **3.** (*coll., stupid*) тупо́й. **4.** (*dull, indistinct*): **I woke with a** ~ **head** я просну́лся с тяжёлой голово́й; (*pronounced, extreme*): **he has a** ~ **accent** у него́ си́льный акце́нт.

adv. гу́сто, ча́сто; **the blows came** ~ **and fast** уда́ры сы́пались оди́н за други́м.

cpds. **~head** *n.* тупи́ца (*c.g.*); **~-headed** *adj.* тупоголо́вый; **~set** *adj.* (*stocky*) корена́стый, кряжи́стый; **~-skinned** *adj.* (*lit., fig.*) толстоко́жий.

thicken ['θɪkən] *v.t.* утол|ща́ть, -сти́ть; де́лать, с- бо́лее густы́м.

v.i. утол|ща́ться, -сти́ться; усложн|я́ться, -и́ться.

thicket ['θɪkɪt] *n.* ча́ща; за́росл|и (*pl., g.* -ей).

thickness ['θɪknɪs] *n.* толщина́, густота́; (*layer*) слой.

thief [θi:f] *n.* вор; **stop** ~! держи́ во́ра!

thiev|e [θi:v] *v.i.* красть, у-; ворова́ть, у-/с-; **a ~ing fellow** ворова́тый тип.

thievery ['θi:vərɪ] *n.* кра́жа, воровство́.

thigh [θaɪ] *n.* бедро́.

cpd. **~-bone** *n.* бе́дренная кость.

thimble ['θɪmb(ə)l] *n.* напёрсток.

thimbleful ['θɪmb(ə)l,fʊl] *n.* (*fig.*) глото́чек.

thin [θɪn] *adj.* **1.** (*of measurement between surfaces*) то́нкий; **his coat had worn** ~ **at the elbows** его́ пальто́ протёрлось на локтя́х. **2.** (*not dense*) ре́дкий; жи́дкий; **your hair is getting** ~ **on top** у вас во́лосы реде́ют на маку́шке; **he vanished into** ~ **air** его́ как ве́тром сду́ло. **3.** (*not fat*) то́нкий, худо́й; ~ **in the face** с худы́м лицо́м; **she has become** ~ она́ похуде́ла. **4.** (*of liquids*) жи́дкий; разба́вленный. **5.** (*flimsy, inadequate*) сла́бый; ша́ткий; **a** ~ **excuse** неубеди́тельная отгово́рка. **6.** (*coll., uncomfortable*): **I had a** ~ **time** я скве́рно провёл вре́мя.

adv. то́нко; **don't cut the bread so** ~! не на́до ре́зать хлеб так то́нко!

v.t. де́лать, с- то́нким; разб|авля́ть, -а́вить; **these plants should be ~ned (out)** э́ти расте́ния ну́жно прореди́ть.

v.i. станови́ться (*impf.*) жи́дким; **when the fog ~s** когда́ тума́н рассе́ется; **the crowd ~ned out** толпа́ пореде́ла; **his hair is ~ning** у него́ реде́ют во́лосы.

cpd. **~-skinned** *adj.* (*lit.*) тонкоко́жий; (*fig.*) уязви́мый; оби́дчивый.

thine [ðaɪn] *pron. & adj.* (*arch.*) твой.

thing [θɪŋ] *n.* **1.** (*object*) вещь, предме́т; **what is that black ~?** что э́то за чёрная шту́ка?; **you must be seeing ~s!** (*coll.*) вам что́-то мере́щится!; **there's no such** ~ **as ghosts** привиде́ний не существу́ет. **2.** (*pl., belongings*) иму́щество; ве́щи (*f. pl.*); **pack up your ~s!** упаку́йте/собери́те свои́ ве́щи! **3.** (*pl., clothes*) оде́жда, ве́щи; **take your ~s off!** (*sc. outer clothing*) раздева́йтесь! **4.** (*pl., food*) еда́; **I don't care for sweet ~s** я не люблю́ сла́дкого. **5.** (*pl., equipment*) принадле́жности (*f. pl.*); **she got out the tea ~s** она́ вы́ставила ча́йный серви́з. **6.** (*matter, affair*) де́ло; вещь; **~s of importance** ва́жные дела́; **for one ~, he's too old** нача́ть с того́, что он сли́шком стар; **you had better leave ~s as they are** лу́чше оста́вить всё как есть; **how are ~s?** как дела́?; **other ~s being equal** при про́чих ра́вных усло́виях; **all ~s considered** принима́я во внима́ние всё; **as ~s go** при ны́нешним положе́нии дел; **above all ~s** пре́жде всего́; **among other ~s** среди́ про́чего; **she was told to take ~s easy** ей веле́ли не перенапряга́ться; **let's talk ~s over** дава́йте э́то обсу́дим; **it was just one of those ~s** (*coll.*) ничего́ нельзя́ бы́ло поде́лать; **it comes to the same** ~ э́то сво́дится к тому́ же са́мому. **7.** (*act*) де́йствие; посту́пок; **it's the worst** ~ **you could have done** э́то са́мое плохо́е, что вы могли́ сде́лать; **I have some ~s to do** у меня́ есть ко́е-каки́е дела́. **8.** (*course of action*): **the only** ~ **now is to take a cab** еди́нственное, что мо́жно сейча́с сде́лать, э́то взять такси́; **the best** ~ **for you would be to marry** лу́чше всего́ вам бы бы́ло жени́ться. **9.** (*event*) собы́тие; **what a terrible** ~ **to happen!** како́е ужа́сное несча́стье!; **first** ~ пе́рвым де́лом; **last** ~ в после́днюю о́чередь; **last** ~ **at night** пе́ред сном; **it was a close, near** ~ всё чуть не сорвало́сь. **10.** (*word, remark*): **what a** ~ **to say!** как мо́жно сказа́ть тако́е!; **he said nice ~s about you** он о́чень хорошо́ о вас отозва́лся. **11.** (*fact*): **I could tell you a** ~ **or two** я мог бы вам рассказа́ть ко́е-что. **12.** (*issue*): **the** ~ **is, can you afford it?** хва́тит ли у вас на э́то де́нег? — вот в чём де́ло. **13.** (**a** ~: *something*; *with neg.*: *nothing*): **it's a** ~ **I have never done before** я э́того никогда́ ра́ньше не де́лал; **I can't see a** ~ я ничего́ не ви́жу. **14.** (*creature*) существо́. **15.** (*emotively, of persons or animals*) созда́ние, тварь; **don't be such a mean** ~ не бу́дьте тако́й скаре́дой!; **poor** ~ бедня́га, бедня́жка; (*both c.g.*). **16.**: **the** ~ (*var. idioms*): **it's the done** ~ так при́нято; **it's not the** ~ **(to do)** так не поступа́ют; **just the** ~! то, что на́до!; **it's not quite the** ~ э́то не совсе́м то; **he did the right** ~ **by us** он с на́ми хорошо́ обошёлся; **books and** ~**s** кни́ги и тому́ подо́бное (*or* и так да́лее).

thing|amy ['θɪŋəmɪ], **-umajig** ['θɪŋəmə,dʒɪg] *nn.* (*coll.*) штуко́вина; (*of people*) как (бишь) его́/её?

think [θɪŋk] *n.*: **I must have a** ~ мне на́до поду́мать.

v.t. & i. (*opine*) ду́мать, по-; полага́ть (*impf.*); счита́ть (*impf.*); **I** ~ (я) ду́маю; ка́жется; по-мо́ему; **I don't** ~ **so** не ду́маю; **what do you** ~**?** как вы ду́маете?; **yes, I** ~ **so** да, пожа́луй; **I** ~ **I'll go** я, пожа́луй, пойду́; **how could you** ~ **that?** как вам э́то могло́ прийти́ на ум?; **when do you** ~ **you'll be back?** когда́ вы ду́маете верну́ться?; **I** ~ **I'm going to sneeze** я, ка́жется, сейча́с чихну́; (*judge*): **it suits me, don't you** ~**?** вы не нахо́дите, что э́то мне идёт?; **do you** ~ **she's pretty?** вы счита́ете её хоро́шенькой?; **do what you** ~ **fit** поступа́йте так, как вы счита́ете ну́жным; **I thought it better to stay** я реши́л, что лу́чше оста́ться; (*reflect*) ду́мать, по-; мы́слить (*impf.*); ~ **for o.s.** ду́мать самостоя́тельно; **to** ~ **that he's only 12!** поду́мать то́лько, ему́ всего́ 12 лет!; **let me** ~**, what was his name?** да́йте вспо́мнить, как же его́ зову́т?; **just** ~! вы то́лько поду́майте!; **I can't** ~ **straight today** у меня́ сего́дня голова́ не рабо́тает; (*expect*) ду́мать (*impf.*); предполага́ть (*impf.*); **I thought as much** так я и ду́мал; (*imagine*): **I can't** ~ **how he does it** я не могу́ себе́ предста́вить, как он э́то де́лает; **who would have thought it?** кто б мог поду́мать?; (*with inf.*): **I never thought to ask** мне не пришло́ в го́лову спроси́ть; (*with preps.* **about, of**): **I have other things to** ~ **about** у меня́ мно́го други́х забо́т; **what do you** ~ **about having a meal?** как насчёт того, что́бы перекуси́ть?; **it doesn't bear** ~**ing about** стра́шно поду́мать об э́том; **I was just** ~**ing of going to bed** я как раз собира́лся идти́ спать; ~ **of a number!** заду́майте число́!; **I couldn't** ~ **of letting you pay** я бы не мог допусти́ть, что́бы вы заплати́ли; **I thought of an excuse** я приду́мал предло́г; **it's not much when you** ~ **of it** э́то немно́го, е́сли вду́маться; **I can't** ~ **of anything to say** я не зна́ю, что сказа́ть; **his employers** ~ **well of him** он на хоро́шем счету́ у свои́х работода́телей; **I don't** ~ **much of him as a teacher** я невысоко́ ценю́ его́ как преподова́теля; **I was going to sell my house, but I thought better of it** я собира́лся продава́ть свой дом, а пото́м разду́мал; ~ **nothing of it!** (*in reply to thanks*) не сто́ит!; **he** ~**s nothing of a 20-mile walk** ему́ прогу́лка в 20 миль нипочём; **while I** ~ **of it** кста́ти; ме́жду про́чим.

with advs.: **the matter needs** ~**ing out** э́то де́ло на́до обмозгова́ть; **his arguments are well thought out** его́ аргуме́нты хорошо́ проду́маны; ~ **it over!** обду́майте э́то!; **he never** ~**s his ideas through** он никогда́ не доду́мывает свои́ иде́и до конца́; ~ **up** (*devise*) приду́м|ывать, -ать; (*invent*) выду́мывать, вы́думать.

cpd. ~**-tank** (*coll.*) «мозгово́й центр».

thinkable ['θɪŋkəb(ə)l] *adj.* мы́слимый; возмо́жный; **such an idea is barely** ~ э́то почти́ немы́слимо.

thinker ['θɪŋkə(r)] *n.* мысли́тель (*m.*); **he is a quick** ~ он бы́стро сообража́ет.

thinking ['θɪŋkɪŋ] *n.* **1.** (*cogitation*) размышле́ние; **we have some hard** ~ **to do** нам на́до как сле́дует поразмы́слить. **2.** (*opinion*) мне́ние; **to my way of** ~ на мой взгляд.

adj. ду́мающий; **the** ~ **public** ду́мающие/мы́слящие лю́ди.

cpd. ~**-cap** *n.*: **I must put my** ~**-cap on** (*coll.*) мне придётся пораски́нуть мозга́ми.

thinness ['θɪnnɪs] *n.* то́нкость.

third [θɜ:d] *n.* **1.** (*date*) тре́тье число́; **my birthday is on the** ~ мой день рожде́ния тре́тьего. **2.** (*fraction*) треть; **two** ~**s** две тре́ти. **3.** (*mus.*) те́рция.

adj. тре́тий; ~ **party, person** (*leg. etc.*) тре́тья сторона́; ~ **person** (*gram.*) тре́тье лицо́; **the T**~ **World** тре́тий мир.

cpds. ~**-class** *adj.* (*rail etc.*) третьекла́ссный; ~**-party** *adj.*: ~**-party insurance** страхо́вка, возмеща́ющая убы́тки тре́тьих лиц; ~**-rate** *adj.* третьесо́ртный.

thirdly ['θɜ:dlɪ] *adv.* в-тре́тьих.

thirst [θɜ:st] *n.* (*lit., fig.*) жа́жда; **they died of** ~ они́ у́мерли от жа́жды; ~ **for knowledge** жа́жда зна́ний.

v.i. (*fig.*) жа́ждать (*impf.*) (*чего*).

thirsty ['θɜ:stɪ] *adj.* испы́тывающий жа́жду; **I am, feel** ~ мне хо́чется (*or* я хочу́) пить.

thirteen [θɜ:'ti:n, 'θɜ:-] *n.* трина́дцать.

adj. трина́дцать +*g. pl.*

thirteenth [θɜ:'ti:nθ, 'θɜ:tɪnθ] *adj.* трина́дцатый.

thirtieth ['θɜ:tɪɪθ] *adj.* тридца́тый.

thirt|y ['θɜ:tɪ] *n.* три́дцать; **it happened in the** ~**ies** э́то случи́лось в тридца́тых года́х; **he is in his** ~**ies** ему́ за три́дцать.

adj. три́дцать +*g. pl.*

this [ðɪs] *pron.* э́то; ~ **is what I think** вот что я ду́маю; **are these your shoes?** э́то ва́ши ту́фли?; **we talked of** ~ **and that** мы говори́ли о том, о всём; **do it like** ~ сде́лайте э́то так (*or* сле́дующим о́бразом); **it was like** ~ вот как э́то бы́ло; ~ **is it** (*coll., the difficulty etc.*) вот и́менно!; в то́м-то и де́ло!

adj. э́тот; да́нный; ~ **book here** вот э́та кни́га; ~ **country of ours** э́та на́ша страна́; ~ **very day** сего́дня же; **come here** ~ **minute!** иди́ сюда́ сию́ же мину́ту!; **these days** (*nowadays*) в настоя́щее вре́мя, ны́нче; ~ **one or that** тот и́ли друго́й.

adv.: **about** ~ **high** приме́рно тако́й высоты́; **can you give me** ~ **much?** вы мо́жете дать мне сто́лько?; **I know** ~ **much** мне изве́стно одно́.

thistle ['θɪs(ə)l] *n.* чертополо́х.

thither ['ðɪðə(r)] *adv.* туда́.

tho' [ðəʊ] = **though**

thong [θɒŋ] *n.* реме́нь (*m.*).

thorax ['θɔ:ræks] *n.* грудна́я кле́тка.

thorn [θɔ:n] *n.* колю́чка, шип; **he is a** ~ **in my flesh** он сиди́т у меня́ в печёнках.

thorny ['θɔ:nɪ] *adj.* колю́чий; (*fig.*): **a** ~ **path** терни́стый путь; **a** ~ **problem** о́страя пробле́ма.

thorough ['θʌrə] *adj.* (*comprehensive*) подро́бный; (*conscientious*) добросо́вестный; **a** ~ **worker** добросо́вестный рабо́тник; **he made a** ~ **job of it** он тща́тельно вы́полнил свою́ рабо́ту; (*fundamental*) основа́тельный; (*out-and-out*): **he is a** ~ **scoundrel** он зако́нченный негодя́й.

cpds. ~**bred** *n.* чистопоро́дное живо́тное; *adj.* чистокро́вный, поро́дистый; ~**fare** *n.* тра́нспортная магистра́ль; **"No T~fare"** «прохо́да/прое́зда нет»; ~**going** *adj.* доскона́льный, тща́тельный.

thoroughly ['θʌrəlɪ] *adv.* вполне́, соверше́нно, по́лностью.

thou [θaʊ] *pron.* (*arch.*) ты.

though [ðəʊ] *adv. & conj.* хотя́, хоть; несмотря́ на то, что...; ~ **not a music-lover, I ...** хотя́ я и не большо́й люби́тель му́зыки, я...; ~ **severe, he is just** он строг, но справедли́в; **even** ~ **it's late** пусть уже́ по́здно, но...; **strange** ~ **it may seem** как э́то ни стра́нно; **he said he would come; he didn't,** ~ он сказа́л, что придёт; одна́ко же, не пришёл; **as** ~ как бу́дто бы; сло́вно; **it looks as** ~ **he will lose** похо́же на то, что он проигра́ет.

thought [θɔ:t] *n.* **1.** (*way, instance or body of thinking*) мысль; **modern scientific** ~ совреме́нная нау́чная мысль. **2.** (*reflection*) разду́мье, размышле́ние; **he spends hours in** ~ он прово́дит це́лые часы́ в разду́мье; **deep, lost in** ~ погружённый в мы́сли;

he acted without a moment's ~ он дéйствовал, не задýмываясь; **I gave serious ~ to the matter** я мнóго дýмал об э́том; **don't give it a ~!** вы́киньте э́то из головы́!; **collect one's ~s** соб|ирáться, -рáться с мы́слями. **3.** (*idea, opinion*) мысль, идéя; **the ~ struck me** мне пришлó в гóлову; **he keeps his ~s to himself** он дéржит свои́ мы́сли при себé; **his one ~ was to escape** он дýмал тóлько о том, как бы убежáть. **4.** (*intention*): **she gave up all ~ of marrying** онá отказáлась от вся́кой мы́сли о замýжестве; **I had some ~ of resigning** я подýмывал об отстáвке.

thoughtful ['θɔ:tfʊl] *adj.* **1.** (*meditative*) задýмчивый. **2.** (*well-considered, profound*): **a ~ essay** вдýмчивое/содержáтельное эссé. **3.** (*considerate*) внимáтельный, чýткий.

thoughtfulness ['θɔ:tfʊlnɪs] *n.* задýмчивость; внимáтельность, чýткость.

thoughtless ['θɔ:tlɪs] *adj.* (*careless*) бездýмный, неосмотри́тельный; (*inconsiderate*) невнимáтельный.

thoughtlessness ['θɔ:tlɪsnɪs] *n.* бездýмность, неосмотри́тельность; невнимáтельность.

thousand ['θaʊz(ə)nd] *n.* & *adj.* ты́сяча; **a ~ people** ты́сяча людéй; **with £1,000** с ты́сячью фýнтами; **I have a ~ and one things to do** у меня́ ты́сяча дел; **a ~ thanks!** огрóмнейшее спаси́бо!

cpd. **~fold** *adj.* тысячекрáтный; *adv.* в ты́сячу раз бóльше.

thousandth ['θaʊzəndθ] *adj.* ты́сячный.

thrall [θrɔ:l] *n.* (*liter.*): **he was in ~ to his passions** он был рабóм свои́х стрáстей.

thrash [θræʃ] *v.t.* **1.** (*beat*) порóть, вы́-; (*fig., defeat*) побе|ждáть, -ди́ть; **he got a ~ing in the final round** емý си́льно достáлось в финáльном рáунде. **2.** (*also* **thresh:** *make turbulent by beating*) колоти́ть (*impf.*); ударя́ть (*impf.*); **the whale ~ed the water with its tail** кит бил хвостóм по водé.

v.i. метáться (*impf.*); **the swimmer ~ed about in the water** пловéц колоти́л рукáми и ногáми по водé; **he ~ed about in bed** он метáлся в постéли.

with adv.: **~ out** *v.t.* (*fig.*) обстоя́тельно обсу|ждáть, -ди́ть; **they ~ed out a solution** они́ вы́работали решéние.

thread [θred] *n.* **1.** (*spun fibre; length of this*) ни́тка; **a reel of ~** катýшка ни́ток; **his life hung by a ~** егó жизнь висéла на волоскé; (*fig.*) связь; нить; **he lost the ~ of his argument** он потеря́л нить рассуждéния. **2.** (*of a screw etc.*) резьбá.

v.t. прод|евáть, -éть ни́тку в+*a.*; нани́з|ывать, -áть; **can you ~ this needle?** вы мóжете продéть ни́тку в э́ту иглý?; **she was ~ing beads** онá нани́зывала бýсы.

cpd. **~bare** *adj.* потёртый, изнóшенный, потрёпанный.

threat [θret] *n.* угрóза; **there was a ~ of rain** собирáлся дождь.

threaten ['θret(ə)n] *v.t.* & *i.* угрожáть (*impf.*) +*d.*; грози́ть, по- +*d.*; грози́ться (*impf.*); **he ~ed me with a stick** он погрози́л мне пáлкой; **I was ~ed with bankruptcy** мне грози́ло/угрожáло банкрóтство; **he ~ed to leave** он грози́лся уйти́; **war ~ed** нави́сла угрóза войны́; **rain was ~ing** надвигáлся дождь.

three [θri:] *n.* (числó/нóмер) три; (**~** *people*) трóе; **~ of us went** нас трóе пошлó; мы пошли́ втроём; **~ each** пó три; **~ at a time, in ~s** пó три/трóе; трóйками; (*figure, thg. numbered 3; group of* **~**) трóйка; (*cut, divide*) **in ~** нáтрое; **fold in ~** сложи́ть (*pf.*) втрóе; (*cf. also examples under* **two**).

adj. три +*g. sg.*; (*for people and pluralia tantum, also*) трóе +*g. pl.* (*cf. examples under* **two**); **he and ~ others** он с тремя́ други́ми; **~ fours are twelve** три́жды (*or* три на) четы́ре — двенáдцать; **~ times as much** втрóе бóльше; **~ quarters** три чéтверти (*adv.*) нá три чéтверти.

cpds. **~-cornered** *adj.* треугóльный; **~-D** (*coll.*) *adj.* трёхмéрный; **~-dimensional** *adj.* (*lit.*) трёхмéрный; в трёх измерéниях; **~fold** *adj.* тройнóй; троекрáтный; *adv.* втройнé, втрóе; **~-lane** *adj.* трёхколéйный; **~-legged** *adj.* (*of table etc.*) на трёх нóжках; **~-piece** *adj.*: **~-piece suit** (костю́м-)трóйка; **~-piece suite** ди́ван с двумя́ крéслами; **~-seater** *adj.* трёхмéстный; **~some** *n.* (*persons*) трóе, трóйка; **~-speed** *adj.*: **~-speed gear** трёхскоростнáя передáча; **~-storey** *adj.* трёхэтáжный; **~-wheel(ed)** *adj.* трёхколёсный; **~-year** *adj.* трёхлéтний; **~-year-old** *adj.* трёхлéтний.

thresh [θreʃ] *v.t.* (*beat grain from*) молоти́ть (*impf.*).

thresher ['θreʃə(r)] *n.* (*worker*) молоти́льщик; (*machine*) молоти́лка.

threshing ['θreʃɪŋ] *n.* молотьбá.

cpds. **~-floor** *n.* ток, гумнó; **~-machine** *n.* молоти́лка.

threshold ['θreʃəʊld, -həʊld] *n.* порóг; **on the ~** на порóге.

thrice [θraɪs] *adv.* (*liter.*) (*three times*) три́жды.

thrift [θrɪft] *n.* бережли́вость, эконóмность.

thrifty ['θrɪftɪ] *adj.* бережли́вый, эконóмный.

thrill [θrɪl] *n.* (*physical sensation*) дрожь, трéпет; (*excitement*) востóрг, восхищéние; **it gave me a ~** э́то привелó меня́ в востóрг.

v.t. восхи|щáть, -ти́ть; **a ~ing finish** захвáтывающий конéц.

v.i.: **we ~ed at the good news** мы обрáдовались хорóшим вестя́м; **she ~ed with delight/horror** онá затрепетáла от рáдости/ýжаса.

thriller ['θrɪlə(r)] *n.* (*coll., play or story*) приключéнческий/детекти́вный ромáн/фильм.

thrive [θraɪv] *v.i.* (*prosper*) процветáть (*impf.*); (*grow vigorously*) разраст|áться, -и́сь.

throat [θrəʊt] *n.* гóрло; (*gullet*) гортáнь, глóтка; **he took me by the ~** он схвати́л меня́ за глóтку; **you are cutting your own ~** (*fig.*) вы рýбите сук, на котóром сиди́те; **I have a sore ~** у меня́ боли́т гóрло; **he cleared his ~** он откáшлялся; **don't jump down my ~!** не затыкáйте мне рот!; **the words stuck in my ~** словá застря́ли у меня́ в гóрле.

throaty ['θrəʊtɪ] *adj.* (*guttural*) гортáнный, хри́плый.

throb [θrɒb] *n.* биéние, пульсáция.

v.i. (*beat*) стучáть (*impf.*); си́льно би́ться (*impf.*); (*fig., quiver*) трепетáть, пульси́ровать; **his heart ~bed** сéрдце егó (учащённо) би́лось; **his head ~bed** у негó гудéла головá.

throe [θrəʊ] *n.* сýдорога, спазм; **~s of childbirth** родовы́е мýки (*f. pl.*); **I was in the ~s of packing** я лихорáдочно упакóвывал вéщи.

thrombosis [θrɒm'bəʊsɪs] *n.* тромбóз.

throne [θrəʊn] *n.* (*lit., fig.*) трон, престóл; **he came to the ~** он вступи́л на престóл.

throng [θrɒŋ] *n.* толпá.

v.i. толпи́ться (*impf.*).

throttle ['θrɒt(ə)l] *n.* дрóссель (*m.*); **at full ~** на пóлном газý; **he opened the ~** он приба́вил газ.

v.t. (*strangle*) души́ть, за-/у-.

through [θru:] *adj.* **1.** прямóй; сквознóй; **~ traffic** сквознóе движéние; **"No ~ road"** «нет проéзда»; **a ~ train** прямóй пóезд. **2.** (*var. pred. uses*): **his trousers were ~** (*threadbare*) **at the knee** егó брю́ки протёрлись на колéнях; **you must wait till I'm ~** (*finished*) **with the paper** вам придётся подождáть, покá я кóнчу читáть газéту; **she told him she was ~ with him** онá емý сказáла, что мéжду ни́ми всё кóнчено.

adv. (*from beginning to end; completely*) до концá; **I was there all ~** я был там до концá; **have you read it ~?** вы всё прочитáли?; **you will get wet ~** вы промóкнете насквóзь; **the whole night ~** всю ночь напролёт; (*all the way*) прямо; **the train goes ~ to Paris** поезд идёт прямо до Парижа.

prep. **1.** (*across*; *from end to end or side to side of*) через+*a.*; (*esp. suggesting difficulty*) сквозь+*a.*; **he came ~ the door** он прошёл через дверь; **visible ~ smoke** видимый сквозь дым; (*into*, *in at*) в+*a.*; **he looked ~ the telescope** он посмотрел в телескоп; **look ~ the window!** посмотрите в окно!; **I could see him ~ the fog** я мог разглядеть его в тумане; **I don't like driving ~ fog** я не люблю ездить, когда туман; **the stone flew ~ the air** камень летел по воздуху; (*via*): **we travelled ~ Germany** мы ехали через Германию. **2.** (*from beginning to end of*): **he won't live ~ the night** он не доживёт до утра. **3.** (*during*) в течение +*g.*; **the dog doesn't bark ~ the day** днём собака не лает. **4.** (*US*, *up to and including*): **from Monday ~ Saturday** с понедельника по субботу (включительно). **5.** (*over the area of*): **the news spread ~ the town** весть распространилась по городу. **6.** (*through the medium of*): **the order was passed ~ him** приказ был передан через него; **I heard of you ~ your sister** я слышал о вас от вашей сестры. **7.** (*from*, *because of*) из-за+*g.*; по+*d.*; **~ laziness** из-за лени; **~ stupidity** по глупости; **he succeeded ~ his own efforts** он добился своего своими силами; (*of desirable result*) благодаря+*d.*

cpd. **~put** *n.* пропускная способность.

throughout [θru:'aʊt] *adv.* (*in every part*) везде; повсюду; (*in all respects*) во всех отношениях.

prep. (*from end to end of*) через+*a.*; **~ the country** по всей стране; (*for the duration of*): **it rained ~ the night** всю ночь шёл дождь.

throw [θrəʊ] *n.* **1.** (*act of ~ing*) бросание, метание; **~ of dice** бросание костей; (*distance ~n*) бросок. **2.** (*in wrestling*) бросок.

v.t. **1.** бр|осать, -осить; кидать, кинуть; **~ sth. 100 yards** бросить что-н. на сто ярдов; **he threw the ball into the air** он подбросил мяч в воздух; **his horse threw him** лошадь сбросила его; **he was thrown to the ground by the explosion** его бросило на землю от взрыва; **~ing a cloak over his shoulders ...** накинув плащ на плечи,...; **the news threw them into a panic** сообщение подвергло их в панику; **he was ~n off balance** он потерял равновесие; **the news threw me** (*coll.*) известие меня потрясло; **this ~s light on the problem** это проливает свет на проблему; **he threw himself at me** он бросился на меня; **he threw himself into the job** он с головой ушёл в работу; **he threw his arms round her** он её обнял; **he threw himself on their mercy** он сдался им на милость. **2.** (*dice*) выбрасывать, выбросить. **3. ~** (*reverse*) **a switch** повернуть (*pf.*) выключатель обратно. **4.** (*coll.*, *have*) устр|аивать, -оить; **let's ~ a party** давайте устроим вечеринку.

with advs.: **~ about** *v.t.* (*scatter*) разбр|асывать, -осить; **don't ~ litter about** не разбрасывайте мусор; (*lavish*): **he ~s his money about** он бросается деньгами; (*obtrude*): **he likes to ~ his weight about** он любит задаваться; **~ away** *v.t.* (*discard*) выбрасывать, выбросить; (*forgo*) упус|кать, -тить; **don't ~ away this chance** не упустите эту возможность (*or* этот шанс); **~ back** *v.t.* отбр|асывать, -осить назад; **he was ~n back by the explosion** его отбросило взрывом; **~ down** *v.t.* бр|осать, -осить на землю; **he threw himself down** он бросился на землю; (*fig.*): **the enemy threw down their arms** враг сложил оружие; **~ in** *v.t.* вбр|асывать, -осить; (*fig.*) (*include*) доб|авлять, -авить; **~ in one's lot with** соедин|ять, -ить свою судьбу с+*i.*; **~ in one's hand** (*surrender*) сд|аваться, -аться; **~ off** *v.t.*: **he threw off his clothes** он сбросил с себя одежду; **he threw off his pursuers** он избавился от своих преследователей; **~ on** *v.t.*: **he threw on a coat** он набросил/накинул пальто (на плечи); **~ open** *v.t.*: **the gardens were ~n open to the public** сады были открыты для публики; **he threw open the door** он распахнул дверь; **~ out** *v.t.* выбросать, выбросить; **he threw out a challenge** он бросил вызов; (*reject*) отклон|ять, -ить; **the bill was ~n out** (*parl.*) законопроект отклонили; (*expel*) исключ|ать, -ить; (*upset*) сб|ивать, -ить; путать (*impf.*); **you will ~ me out in my calculations** вы собьёте меня со счёта; **~ together** *v.t.* (*compile*) компилировать, с-; **~ up** *v.t.* (*lit.*) подбр|асывать, -осить; вски|дывать, -нуть; **he threw the ball up** он подбросил мяч; **he threw up his hands in horror** он вскинул руки от ужаса; (*give up*): **he intends to ~ up his job** он собирается бросить работу; *v.i.* (*vomit*): **he threw up** его вырвало; **I felt like ~ing up** меня тошнило.

thrower ['θrəʊə(r)] *n.* метатель (*m.*).

thrum [θrʌm] *v.i.* бренчать (*impf.*); **he ~med on the table** он барабанил пальцами по столу.

thrush[1] [θrʌʃ] *n.* (*bird*) дрозд.

thrush[2] [θrʌʃ] *n.* (*disease*) молочница.

thrust [θrʌst] *n.* толчок; (*mil.*) наступление, удар; (*in fencing*) укол.

v.t. толк|ать, -нуть; **he ~ a note into my hand** он сунул мне в руку записку; **he ~ his sword home** он вонзил меч по самую рукоятку; **they ~ their way through the crowd** они пробились сквозь толпу.

v.i. толкаться (*impf.*); пробиваться (*impf.*).

thud [θʌd] *n.* глухой звук; стук.

v.i. уд|аряться, -ариться со стуком.

thug [θʌg] *n.* бандит, головорез.

thumb [θʌm] *n.* большой палец (руки); **he was given the ~s up sign to begin** ему дали сигнал к началу; **he works by rule of ~** он работает кустарным способом (*or* на глазок); **he is completely under her ~** он у неё полностью под каблуком; **I'm all (fingers and) ~s** у меня руки как крюки.

v.t. **1.** (*turn over with ~*) перелист|ывать, -ать; **a well-~ed volume** захватанный том. **2.: ~ a lift** (*coll.*) «голосовать» (*impf.*); **he ~ed a lift in a lorry** он приехал на попутном грузовике. **3.: ~ one's nose at** показать (*pf.*) нос +*d.*

cpds. **~nail** *n.* ноготь (*m.*) большого пальца; **~nail sketch** набросок; краткое описание; **~-print** *n.* отпечаток большого пальца; **~screw** *n.* тиск|и (*pl.*, *g.* -ов) для больших пальцев (*орудие пыток*); **~-tack** *n.* (*US*) кнопка.

thump [θʌmp] *n.* (*blow*) тяжёлый удар; (*noise*) глухой стук.

v.t. бить (*impf.*); колотить (*impf.*); **he ~ed me on the back** он сильно ударил меня по спине; **she ~ed the cushion** она взбила подушку.

v.i. биться (*impf.*); колотиться (*impf.*); **my heart began to ~** у меня заколотилось сердце.

thumping ['θʌmpɪŋ] *adj. & adv.* (*coll.*) громадный, ужасающий; **a ~ lie** наглая ложь.

thunder ['θʌndə(r)] *n.* гром; **a peal, crash of ~** удар грома; (*fig.*) грохот, гром; **the ~ of the waves** шум волн; **a ~ of applause** гром аплодисментов.

v.t. греметь, про-; **'Get out!' he ~ed** «убирайтесь отсюда!», прогремел он.

v.i. (*lit.*) греметь; **it is ~ing** гром гремит; **it has been ~ing all day** весь день гремела гроза; (*fig.*) **the train ~ed past** поезд с грохотом пронёсся мимо.

cpds. **~bolt** *n.* удар молнии, гром; **~clap** *n.* удар грома; **~cloud** *n.* грозовая туча; **~storm** *n.* гроза; **~struck** *adj.* (*fig.*) ошеломлённый.

thunderous ['θʌndərəs] *adj.* (*loud*) громовой; **~ applause** бурные аплодисменты.

thundery ['θʌndərɪ] *adj.*: **it is ~ weather** погода (пред)грозовая.

Thursday ['θɜːzdeɪ, -dɪ] *n.* четве́рг.
thus [ðʌs] *adv.* (*in this way*) таки́м о́бразом; (*accordingly*) сле́довательно, таки́м о́бразом; ~ **far and no farther** до сих пор и ни ша́гу да́льше.
thwart [θwɔːt] *v.t.* меша́ть, по- *+d.*; ~ **s.o.'s plans** расстр|а́ивать, -о́ить чьи-н. пла́ны.
thy [ðaɪ] *adj.* (*arch.*) твой.
thyme [taɪm] *n.* тимья́н.
thyroid ['θaɪrɔɪd] *n.* (~ **gland**) щитови́дная железа́.
adj. щитови́дный.
tiara [tɪ'ɑːrə] *n.* тиа́ра.
Tibet [tɪ'bet] *n.* Тибе́т.
tibia ['tɪbɪə] *n.* большеберцо́вая кость.
tic [tɪk] *n.* тик.
tick[1] [tɪk] *n.* **1.** (*of clock etc.*) ти́канье; ~, **tock** тик-та́к. **2.** (*coll., moment*) секу́нда; мину́та; **just a** ~! одну́ секу́нду! **3.** (*checking mark*) га́лочка, пти́чка.
v.t. отм|еча́ть, -е́тить га́лочкой.
v.i. ти́кать (*impf.*).
with advs.: **she ~ed off the items as I read them out** я перечисля́л предме́ты, а она́ отмеча́ла га́лочками; **he got ~ed off** (*coll., reprimanded*) ему́ да́ли нагоня́й; **I left the engine ~ing over** я оста́вил мото́р на холосто́м ходу́.
tick[2] [tɪk] *n.* (*parasite*) клещ.
tick[3] [tɪk] *n.* (*coll., credit*) креди́т; **I got some groceries on** ~ я купи́л ко́е-каки́е проду́кты в креди́т.
ticker ['tɪkə(r)] *n.* (*coll.*) (*US, teleprinter*) ти́ккер; (*watch*) час|ы́ (*pl., g.* -о́в); (*heart*) се́рдце.
cpd. **~-tape** *n.* серпанти́н из ти́ккерной ле́нты.
ticket ['tɪkɪt] *n.* (*for travel, seating etc.*) биле́т; **a return ~ to London** обра́тный биле́т до Ло́ндона; (*tag*) ярлы́к; **price** ~ этике́тка с цено́й; це́нник; (*US, list of election candidates*) спи́сок кандида́тов на вы́борах; (*printed notice of offence*): **he got a ~ for speeding** он получи́л штраф за превыше́ние ско́рости.
v.t. снаб|жа́ть, -ди́ть ярлыко́м/этике́ткой.
cpds. **~-collector** *n.* контролёр; **~-machine** *n.* биле́тный автома́т; **~-office** *n.* биле́тная ка́сса; **~-punch** *n.* компо́стер.
ticking ['tɪkɪŋ] *n.* (*fabric*) тик.
tickle ['tɪk(ə)l] *n.* щекота́ние; **he felt a ~ in his throat** у него́ заперши́ло в го́рле.
v.t. щекота́ть, по-; (*fig., amuse*) смеши́ть, рас-; **it ~d my fancy** э́то дразни́ло моё воображе́ние; **I was ~d to death** (*coll.*) я чуть не ло́пнул со́ смеху.
v.i. чеса́ться (*impf.*); **this blanket ~s** э́то одея́ло шерсти́т; **my nose ~s** у меня́ щеко́чет в носу́.
ticklish ['tɪklɪʃ] *adj.* (*sensitive to tickling*) боя́щийся щеко́тки; (*requiring careful handling*) щекотли́вый.
tidal ['taɪd(ə)l] *adj.* прили́вный; ~ **river** прили́во-отли́вная река́; ~ **wave** прили́вная волна́.
tidbit ['tɪdbɪt] = **titbit**
tiddler ['tɪdlə(r)] *n.* (*small fish*) ко́люшка.
tiddl(e)y ['tɪdlɪ] *adj.* (*tipsy*) «под мухо́й» (*sl.*); (*small, trifling*) ма́ленький, малю́сенький.
tiddl(e)y-winks ['tɪdlɪwɪŋks] *n.* игра́ в бло́шки.
tide [taɪd] *n.* морско́й прили́в (и отли́в); **high** ~ вы́сшая то́чка прили́ва; **low** ~ ни́зшая то́чка прили́ва; **the ~ is coming in** начался́ прили́в; **the ~ has gone out** (*or* **is out**) сейча́с отли́в; (*fig.*) волна́, тече́ние; **the rising ~ of excitement** уси́ливающееся возбужде́ние.
v.t.: **this will ~ me over till next month** благодаря́ э́тому, я перебью́сь до сле́дующего ме́сяца.
tidiness ['taɪdɪnɪs] *n.* аккура́тность, опря́тность.
tidings ['taɪdɪŋz] *n.* (*liter. and joc.*) ве́сти (*f. pl.*), но́вости (*f. pl.*).
tidy ['taɪdɪ] *adj.* (*neat, orderly*) аккура́тный, опря́тный; (*of room etc.*) аккура́тно при́бранный; (*considerable*) поря́дочный, значи́тельный; **a ~ sum** прили́чная/кру́гленькая су́мма.
v.t. (*also* ~ **up**) прив|оди́ть, -ести́ в поря́док; при|бира́ть, -бра́ть.
v.i.: ~ **up** нав|оди́ть, -ести́ поря́док.
tie [taɪ] *n.* **1.** (**neck** ~) га́лстук. **2.** (*part that fastens or connects*) скре́па; шнур; ле́нта. **3.** (*fig., bond*) у́з|ы (*pl., g.* —); **~s of friendship** у́зы дру́жбы; **family ~s** семе́йные у́зы. **4.** (*fig., restriction*) обу́за; тягота́. **4.** (*equal score*) ра́вное число́ очко́в; **the match ended in a ~** матч зако́нчился вничью́.
v.t. **1.** (*fasten*) свя́з|ывать, -а́ть; привя́з|ывать, -а́ть; (*fig.*): **my hands are ~d** у меня́ свя́заны ру́ки. **2.** (*arrange in bow or knot*) перевя́з|ывать, -а́ть; завя́з|ывать, -а́ть; шнурова́ть, за-; **he learnt to ~ his shoe-laces** он научи́лся шнурова́ть боти́нки; **can you ~ a knot in this string?** вы мо́жете завяза́ть у́зел на э́той верёвке?
v.i. **1.** (*fasten*) завя́з|ываться, -а́ться; **does this sash ~ at the front?** э́тот по́яс завя́зывается спе́реди? **2.** (*make equal score*) равня́ть, с- счёт; игра́ть, сыгра́ть в ничью́; **we ~d with them for first place** мы подели́ли с ни́ми пе́рвое ме́сто; **the runners ~d** сопе́рники пришли́ к фи́нишу одновре́ме́нно.
with advs.: ~ **back** *v.t.* подвя́з|ывать, -а́ть; **she wore her hair ~d back** она́ зачёсывала во́лосы наза́д; ~ **down** *v.t.* (*lit.*) привя́з|ывать, -а́ть; (*fig., restrict*) свя́з|ывать, -а́ть; **I don't want to ~ myself down to a date** я не хочу́ быть свя́занным определённой да́той; ~ **in** *v.i.* соотве́тствовать (*impf.*); согласо́в|ываться, -а́ться; **this ~s in with what I was saying** э́то согласу́ется с тем, что я говори́л; ~ **on** *v.t.* привя́з|ывать, -а́ть; ~ **up** *v.t.* (*lit.*) привя́з|ывать, -а́ть; свя́з|ывать, -а́ть; **can you ~ up this parcel?** вы мо́жете перевяза́ть э́ту посы́лку?; (*fig.*): **his firm is ~d up with the Ministry** его́ фи́рма свя́зана с министе́рством; **I'm rather ~d up this week** я дово́льно си́льно за́нят на э́той неде́ле; **his capital is ~d up** его́ капита́л заморо́жен.
cpds. **~-breaker** *n.* реша́ющая игра́; **~pin** *n.* була́вка для га́лстука; **~-up** *n.* (*link*) связь.
tier [tɪə(r)] *n.* ряд; я́рус.
tiff [tɪf] *n.* размо́лвка.
tiger ['taɪgə(r)] *n.* тигр.
cpd. **~-cub** *n.* тигрёнок.
tight [taɪt] *adj.* **1.** (*closely fixed or fitting*) те́сный; облега́ющий; **the dress was a ~ fit** пла́тье бы́ло те́сно; **this knot is very ~** э́тот у́зел о́чень туго́й; **my shoes are too ~** мои́ ту́фли жмут. **2.** (*packed as full as possible*) наби́тый. **3.** (*taut*) стро́гий. **4.** (*under pressure; difficult*) тру́дный; тяжёлый; **in a ~ corner** в тру́дном положе́нии; **I have a ~ schedule** у меня́ жёсткое расписа́ние. **5.** (*miserly*) прижи́мистый, скупо́й; **he is very ~ with his money** он о́чень скуп. **6.** (*in short supply*) тру́дно добыва́емый; **money is ~** с деньга́ми ту́го. **7.** (*coll., drunk*) навеселе́; **he went out and got ~** он пошёл и напи́лся.
adv. кре́пко; пло́тно; **hold ~!** держи́тесь кре́пко!; **shut your eyes ~!** кре́пко зажму́рьте глаза́!; **the door was ~ shut** дверь была́ пло́тно закры́та; **I sat ~ and waited** я стоя́л на своём и выжида́л.
cpds. **~-fisted** *adj.* скупо́й, прижи́мистый; **~(ly)-fitting** *adj.* пло́тно облега́ющий; **~-lipped** *adj.* (*fig., secretive*) скры́тный; **~rope** *n.* натя́нутый кана́т; **he is walking a ~rope** (*fig.*) он хо́дит по острию́ ножа́; **~rope-walker** *n.* канатохо́дец.
tighten ['taɪt(ə)n] *v.t.* (*also* ~ **up**) сжима́ть (*impf.*); закрепля́ть (*impf.*); **the screws need ~ing (up)** на́до затяну́ть болты́; **we must ~ our belts** (*fig.*) мы должны́ поту́же затяну́ть поя́са́; **the rules were ~ed** пра́вила ста́ли стро́же.
tightness ['taɪtnɪs] *n.* напряжённость; стеснённость.
tights [taɪts] *n.* колго́т|ки (*pl., g.* -ок), трико́ (*indecl.*).
tigress ['taɪgrɪs] *n.* тигри́ца.

tilde ['tɪldə] *n.* ти́льда.

tile [taɪl] *n.* (*for roof*) черепи́ца; **he was (out) on the ~s last night** (*sl.*) он вчера́ кути́л; (*decorative, for wall etc.*) ка́фель (*m.*), пли́тка, изразе́ц.

v.t. крыть, по- черепи́цей/ка́фелем.

till¹ [tɪl] *n.* ка́сса.

till² [tɪl] *v.t.*: **~ the ground** обраба́тывать (*impf.*) зе́млю.

till³ [tɪl] (*see also* **until**) *prep.* до+*g.*; **~ then** до того́ вре́мени; **he will not come ~ after dinner** он придёт то́лько по́сле у́жина; **I never saw him ~ now** я его́ впервы́е ви́жу.

conj. пока́... (не); до тех пор, пока́; **~ we meet again!** до сле́дующей встре́чи!; **don't go ~ I come back** не уходи́те, пока́ я не верну́сь (*or, coll.*, пока́ я верну́сь); **not ~ Tuesday** не ра́ньше вто́рника.

tillage ['tɪlɪdʒ] *n.* обрабо́тка по́чвы.

tiller¹ ['tɪlə(r)] *n.* (*for steering*) ру́мпель (*m.*).

tiller² ['tɪlə(r)] n. (*of the soil*) земледе́лец.

tilt [tɪlt] *n.* **1.** (*sloping position*) накло́н, склон; **the table is on the ~** стол стои́т кри́во. **2.** (*attack*): **he came at me full ~** он я́ростно набро́сился на меня́.

v.t. наклон|я́ть, -и́ть; **he ~ed the chair back** он наклони́л стул наза́д.

v.i. (*slope*) наклон|я́ться, -и́ться; **the table was ~ing dangerously** стол опа́сно накрени́лся.

timber ['tɪmbə(r)] *n.* (*substance*) лесоматериа́л, древеси́на; (*trees grown for felling*) строево́й лес; (*beam of roof, ship etc.*) бревно́.

cpd. **~-yard** *n.* дровяно́й склад.

timbre ['tæmbə(r), 'tæ̃brə] *n.* тембр.

time [taɪm] *n.* **1.** вре́мя (*nt.*); **for all ~** навсегда́; **from the beginning of ~** испоко́н веко́в; **in (the) course of ~, with ~** с тече́нием вре́мени; **to the end of ~** ве́чно; **~ flies** вре́мя бежи́т; **~ hangs heavy on my hands** вре́мя тя́нется ме́дленно; **kill ~** уб|ива́ть, -и́ть вре́мя; **~ has passed him by** жизнь прошла́ ми́мо его́; **~ is running out** срок истека́ет; **~ is on our side** вре́мя рабо́тает на нас; **~ will tell** вре́мя пока́жет; **~ waits for no man** вре́мя не ждёт. **2.** (*system of measurement*): **Greenwich Mean T~** гринви́чское сре́днее вре́мя; **local ~** ме́стное вре́мя. **3.** (*duration, period, opportunity*): **after a ~** че́рез не́которое вре́мя; **all the ~** всегда́, постоя́нно; **he has done ~** (*coll., been in prison*) он своё отсиде́л; **he stayed for a ~** он про́был не́которое вре́мя; **I have been here for some ~** я здесь уже́ дово́льно до́лго; **given ~, he will succeed** дай срок, и он добьётся успе́ха; **all in good ~** всему́ своё вре́мя; **in good ~** заблаговре́менно; **I have no ~ for him** (*fig.*) мне с ним не́чего де́лать; **I have no ~ to lose** мне нельзя́ теря́ть ни мину́ты; **I shall get used to it in ~** со вре́менем я к э́тому привы́кну; **in no ~ (at all)** момента́льно; **I could do it in no ~** я бы мог э́то сде́лать в два счёта; **do it in your own ~** сде́лайте э́то в нерабо́чее вре́мя; **I haven't seen him for a long ~** я его́ давно́ не ви́дел; **long ~ no see!** (*coll.*) ско́лько лет, ско́лько зим!; **a long ~ ago** давно́; **make up for lost ~** нав|ёрстывать, -ерста́ть поте́рянное вре́мя; **he lost no ~ in reading the book** он то́тчас же при́нялся чита́ть э́ту кни́гу; **pass the ~** пров|оди́ть, -ести́ вре́мя; **play for ~** оття́|гивать, -ну́ть вре́мя; **I am pressed for ~** у меня́ ма́ло вре́мени; **for some ~ now** с не́которого вре́мени; **in one's spare ~** на досу́ге; **take your ~!** не торопи́тесь!; **it will take ~** э́то займёт вре́мя; **he asked for ~ off** он отпроси́лся с рабо́ты; **I want some ~ to myself** мне хо́чется побы́ть одному́; **your ~ is up** ва́ше вре́мя истекло́; **~ and motion study** хронометра́ж движе́ний рабо́чего. **4.** (*life-span*) пери́од жи́зни; век; **if I had my ~ over again** е́сли бы мо́жно бы́ло нача́ть жизнь сно́ва. **5.** (*measuring progress or speed*): **this watch keeps good ~** э́ти часы́ хорошо́ иду́т; **what was his ~ for the race?** за ско́лько он пробежа́л диста́нцию? **6.** (*experience*): **he gave us a bad ~** он доста́вил нам неприя́тность; **they gave us a good ~** они́ нас хорошо́ при́няли; **have a good ~!** повесели́тесь как сле́дует!; **we had the ~ of our lives** мы отли́чно провели́ вре́мя; **I had a trying ~** я пережи́л тру́дный пери́од. **7.** (**~** *of day or night*) час; **what's the ~?** кото́рый час?; **the ~ is 8 o'clock** сейча́с 8 часо́в; **we passed the ~ of day** (*greeted each other*) мы поздоро́вались; **at that ~** (*hour*) в э́тот час; **at what ~?** в кото́ром часу́? **8.** (*moment*): **I was away at the ~** меня́ тогда́ (*or* в то вре́мя) не́ было; **at the right ~** в ну́жный/подходя́щий моме́нт; **at that ~** в то вре́мя; **at the same ~** (*simultaneously*) в то же (са́мое) вре́мя; (*notwithstanding*) тем не ме́нее; вме́сте с тем; **at ~s** иногда́, времена́ми; **at all ~s** всегда́; во всех слу́чаях; **at different ~s** в ра́зное вре́мя; **at no ~** никогда́; **at other ~s** в други́х слу́чаях; **before ~** преждевре́менно; **behind ~** с опозда́нием; **from ~ to ~** иногда́, вре́мя от вре́мени; **it's ~ for bed** пора́ спать; **it's ~ I went** мне пора́ идти́; **~'s up** вре́мя истекло́; пора́ конча́ть; **will he arrive in ~ for dinner?** он поспе́ет к у́жину?; **there's no ~ like the present** ≃ лови́ моме́нт; **the train was on ~** по́езд пришёл во́время. **9.** (*instance, occasion*) раз; **~ and (~) again; ~ after ~** сно́ва и сно́ва; раз за ра́зом; **I've told you ~ and again** ско́лько раз я вам говори́л!; **nine ~s out of ten** в девяти́ слу́чаях из десяти́; **six ~s running** шесть раз подря́д; **the ~ before** в про́шлый раз; **another ~** когда́-то; когда́-нибу́дь; в друго́й раз; **one at a ~!** по одному́; не все сра́зу!; **it's the first ~ we've met** э́то на́ша пе́рвая встре́ча; **for the last ~, will you shut up?** я тебе́ в после́дний раз говорю́ — заткни́сь!/замолчи́!; **many a ~, many ~s** мно́го раз, ча́сто; **next ~** в сле́дующий раз; **there may not be a next ~** второ́го слу́чая мо́жет не предста́виться; **I'll let you off this ~** на сей раз я вас проща́ю. **10.** (*in multiplication*): **6 ~s 2 is 12** 6 (умно́жить) на 2 — 12; ше́стью два — двена́дцать; **ten ~s as easy** в де́сять раз ле́гче. **11.** (*period, age*) времена́ (*nt. pl.*), эпо́ха; **in the ~ of Queen Elizabeth** в эпо́ху короле́вы Елизаве́ты; **in olden ~s** в ста́рые времена́; в дре́вности; **at one ~** одно́ вре́мя, когда́-то, не́когда; **that was before my ~** э́то бы́ло до меня́; **at my ~ of life** в моём во́зрасте. **12.** (*circumstances*): **we have seen good and bad ~s** мы пе́режили и хоро́шее и плохо́е; **she is behind the ~s** она́ отста́ла от жи́зни. **13.** (*mus.*) такт, ритм; **in quick ~** в бы́стром те́мпе; **in double-quick ~** (*fig.*) в два счёта; **they clapped in ~ with the music** они́ хло́пали в такт му́зыке; **beat ~** (*with foot etc.*) отбива́ть (*impf.*) такт (*ногой и т.п.*); **mark ~** (*lit.*) марширова́ть (*impf.*) на ме́сте; (*fig.*) топта́ться (*impf.*) на ме́сте.

v.t. **1.** (*do at a chosen* **~**) выбира́ть, вы́брать вре́мя +*g.*; рассчи́т|ывать, -а́ть вре́мя +*g.*; **his remarks were ill ~d** его́ замеча́ния бы́ли некста́ти. **2.** (*measure* **~** *of or for*) зас|ека́ть, -е́чь вре́мя +*g.*; хронометри́ровать (*impf., pf.*); **they ~d him over the mile** они́ засекли́ вре́мя, за кото́рое он пробежа́л одну́ ми́лю.

cpds. **~-bomb** *n.* бо́мба заме́дленного де́йствия; **~-exposure** *n.* вы́держка; **~-honoured** *adj.* освящённый века́ми; **~-keeper** *n.* (*pers.*) та́бельщик, хронометри́ст; **he is a good ~-keeper** (*at work*) он то́чно прихо́дит на рабо́ту; **~-lag** *n.* запа́здывание; **~-limit** *n.* преде́льный срок; **~piece** *n.* час|ы́ (*pl., g.* -о́в), хроно́метр; **~-saving** *n.* эконо́мия вре́мени; *adj.* эконо́мящий вре́мя; **~-share** *n.* совме́стное владе́ние куро́ртным помеще́нием; тайм-шер; **~-study** *n.* хронометра́ж; **~-switch** *n.* переключа́тель (*m.*) вре́мени; **~table** *n.* расписа́ние;

гра́фик; **~-wasting** *adj.* напра́сный, ли́шний.
timeless ['taɪmlɪs] *adj.* (*eternal*) ве́чный, непреходя́щий; (*unmarked by time*) неподвла́стный вре́мени, неустарева́ющий.
timeliness ['taɪmlɪnɪs] *n.* своевре́менность.
timely ['taɪmlɪ] *adj.* своевре́менный.
timer ['taɪmə(r)] *n.* (*pers.*) хронометражи́ст; (*device*) отме́тчик вре́мени, та́ймер.
timid ['tɪmɪd] *adj.* ро́бкий; (*shy*) засте́нчивый.
timidity [ˌtɪ'mɪdɪtɪ] *n.* ро́бость; засте́нчивость.
timing ['taɪmɪŋ] *n.* вы́бор (наибо́лее подходя́щего/удо́бного) вре́мени; темп; хронометра́ж.
timorous ['tɪmərəs] *adj.* боязли́вый, пугли́вый.
timpani ['tɪmpənɪ] *n.* лита́вры (*f. pl.*)
tin [tɪn] *n.* **1.** (*metal*) о́лово; (*attr.*) оловя́нный; **~ can** консе́рвная ба́нка. **2.** (*container, can*) жестя́нка, консе́рвная ба́нка; **~ of beans** ба́нка фасо́ли.
v.t. (*pack in ~s*) консерви́ровать (*impf.*); **~ned goods** консерви́рованные проду́кты; консе́рв|ы (*pl., g.* -ов); **~ned fish** ры́бные консе́рвы.
cpds. **~foil** *n.* оловя́нная фо́льга; **~-opener** *n.* консе́рвный нож; **~-plate** *n.* бе́лая жесть; **~smith** *n.* луди́льщик; жестя́нщик.
tincture ['tɪŋktjə(r), -tʃə(r)] *n.* раство́р; тинкту́ра.
tinder ['tɪndə(r)] *n.* трут.
cpd. **~-box** *n.* тру́тница.
tine [taɪn] *n.* зубе́ц.
tinge [tɪndʒ] *n.* лёгкая окра́ска, отте́нок; (*fig.*) при́месь, налёт, отте́нок.
v.t. слегка́ окра́|шивать, -сить; (*fig.*): **her voice was ~d with regret** в её го́лосе звуча́ло лёгкое сожале́ние.
tingl|e ['tɪŋg(ə)l] *v.i.*: **the slap made his hand ~e** его́ рука́ зуде́ла от уда́ра; **they were ~ing with excitement** они́ дрожа́ли от возбужде́ния.
tinker ['tɪŋkə(r)] *n.* ме́дник; луди́льщик.
v.i. (*meddle etc.*) вози́ться (*impf.*) (*с чем*).
tinkle ['tɪŋk(ə)l] *n.* (*sound*) звон; звя́канье; (*coll., telephone call*) телефо́нный звоно́к; **give me a ~ some time** звя́кните мне ка́к-нибу́дь.
v.t.: **he ~d the bell** он зазвони́л в колоко́льчик.
v.i.: **the bell ~d** колоко́льчик зазвене́л.
tinnitus [tɪ'naɪtəs] *n.* шум в уша́х.
tinny ['tɪnɪ] *adj.* (*of sound*) металли́ческий, жестяно́й; (*of taste*) металли́ческий.
tinsel ['tɪns(ə)l] *n.* блёст|ки (*pl., g.* -ок); мишура́.
adj. (*fig.*) мишу́рный.
tint [tɪnt] *n.* отте́нок.
v.t.: **~ed glasses** тёмные очки́; **she ~s her hair** она́ подкра́шивает во́лосы.
tiny ['taɪnɪ] *adj.* кро́шечный.
tip[1] [tɪp] *n.* (*pointed end*) ко́нчик; верху́шка; **~ of the iceberg** (*lit., fig.*) верху́шка а́йсберга; **I had his name on the ~ of my tongue** его́ и́мя верте́лось у меня́ на языке́.
v.t.: **arrows ~ped with bronze** стре́лы с ме́дными наконе́чниками; **~ped cigarettes** папиро́сы с фи́льтром.
cpds. **~toe** *n.*: **on ~toe(s)** на цы́почках; *v.i.* ходи́ть (*indet.*) на цы́почках; **~-top** *adj.* первокла́ссный; **in ~-top condition** в превосхо́дном состоя́нии.
tip[2] [tɪp] *n.* (*dumping-ground*) сва́лка.
v.t. **1.** (*tilt*) наклон|я́ть, -и́ть; **he ~s the scale at 12 stone** он ве́сит 168 фу́нтов; **this will ~ the scale** (*fig.*) **in their favour** э́то склони́т ча́шу весо́в в их по́льзу. **3.** (*overturn, empty*) выва́ливать, вы́валить; **~ the rubbish into the bin!** вы́валите му́сор в я́щик!
with advs.: **~ out** *v.t.* выва́ливать, вы́валить; **~ over** *v.t. & i.* опроки́|дывать(ся), -нуть(ся); **he ~ped the cup over** он опроки́нул ча́шку; **the boat ~ped over** ло́дка переверну́лась; **~ up** *v.t. & i.* наклон|я́ть(ся), -и́ть(ся); **he ~ped his plate up** он наклони́л таре́лку.
cpd. **~-up** *adj.*: **a ~-up seat** откидно́е сиде́ние.
tip[3] [tɪp] *n.* **1.** (*piece of advice, recommendation*) сове́т; **shall I give you a ~?** хоти́те сове́т? **2.** (*gratuity*) чаев|ы́е (*pl., g.* -ы́х); **I gave the porter a ~** я дал носи́льщику на чай.
v.t. **1.** (*mention as likely winner*): **he always ~ped the winner** он всегда́ уга́дывал победи́теля; **the horse was ~ped to win** большинство́ ста́вило на э́ту ло́шадь. **2.** (*remunerate*) да|ва́ть, -ть на чай +*d.*
with adv.: **~ off** (*coll.*) предупре|жда́ть, -ди́ть.
cpd. **~-off** *n.*: **the police had a ~-off** поли́ции настуча́ли (*coll.*).
tipper ['tɪpə(r)] *n.* (*vehicle*) самосва́л.
tipple ['tɪp(ə)l] *n.* питьё, напи́ток.
v.i. выпива́ть (*impf.*).
tippler ['tɪplə(r)] *n.* пьянчу́жка (*c.g.*).
tipsy ['tɪpsɪ] *adj.* подвы́пивший, навеселе́, под хмелько́м.
tirade [taɪ'reɪd, tɪ-] *n.* тира́да.
tire[1] ['taɪə(r)] (*US*) = **tyre**
tire[2] ['taɪə(r)] *v.t.* утом|ля́ть, -и́ть; надо|еда́ть, -е́сть +*d.*; **the walk ~d me** я уста́л от прогу́лки; **you will soon get ~d of him** он вам ско́ро надое́ст; **I had a tiring day** у меня́ был тру́дный день.
v.i. утом|ля́ться, -и́ться; уст|ава́ть, -а́ть; **she ~s easily** она́ бы́стро устаёт; **I shall never ~ of that music** э́та му́зыка мне никогда́ не надое́ст.
tiredness ['taɪədnɪs] *n.* уста́лость.
tireless ['taɪəlɪs] *adj.* неутоми́мый.
tiresome ['taɪəsəm] *adj.* надое́дливый, ну́дный.
tissue ['tɪʃu:, 'tɪsju:] *n.* **1.** (*text., biol.*) ткань; **~ paper** то́нкая обёрточная бума́га; папиро́сная бума́га; **face ~** бума́жная салфе́тка; **toilet ~** туале́тная бума́га. **2.** (*fig.*) паути́на; сеть; **a ~ of lies** паути́на лжи.
tit[1] [tɪt] *n.* (*bird*) сини́ца.
tit[2] [tɪt] *n.* (*breast*) си́ська (*sl.*).
tit[3] [tɪt] *n.*: **~ for tat** «зуб за́ зуб».
titan ['taɪt(ə)n] *n.* тита́н.
titanic [taɪ'tænɪk, tɪ-] *adj.* титани́ческий.
titanium [taɪ'teɪnɪəm, tɪ-] *n.* тита́н.
titbit ['tɪtbɪt] (*US* **tidbit**) *n.* ла́комый кусо́чек; (*fig.*): **a ~ of news** пика́нтная но́вость.
titch [tɪtʃ] *n.* коро́тыш, недоро́сток.
titchy ['tɪtʃɪ] *adj.* низкоро́слый.
tithe [taɪð] *n.* десяти́на.
titillate ['tɪtɪˌleɪt] *v.t.* щекота́ть (*impf.*); прия́тно возбу|жда́ть, -ди́ть.
titillation [ˌtɪtɪ'leɪʃ(ə)n] *n.* прия́тное возбужде́ние.
titivate ['tɪtɪˌveɪt] *v.i.* прихора́шиваться (*impf.*).
title ['taɪt(ə)l] *n.* **1.** (*name of book etc.*) загла́вие; назва́ние. **2.** (*indicator of rank, occupation, status etc.*) зва́ние, ти́тул; **courtesy ~** почётный ти́тул. **3.** (*legal right or claim*) пра́во; **what is his ~ to the property?** на како́м основа́нии он претенду́ет на э́ту со́бственность?
cpds. **~-deed** *n.* докуме́нт, подтвержда́ющий пра́во со́бственности; **~-holder** *n.* чемпио́н; **~-page** *n.* ти́тульный лист; **~-role** *n.* загла́вная роль.
titled ['taɪt(ə)ld] *adj.* титуло́ванный.
titmouse ['tɪtmaʊs] *n.* сини́ца.
titter ['tɪtə(r)] *n.* хихи́канье.
v.i. хихи́кать (*impf.*).
tittle-tattle ['tɪt(ə)lˌtæt(ə)l] *n.* спле́тн|и (*pl., g.* -ен).
v.i. спле́тничать (*impf.*).
titular ['tɪtjʊlə(r)] *adj.* (*in name only*) номина́льный.
tiz(zy) ['tɪzɪ] *n.* ажиота́ж (*coll.*); **she got into a ~** она́ распсихова́лась (*coll.*).
TNT (*abbr. of* **trinitrotoluene**) ТНТ, (тринитротолуо́л).
to [tə, *before a vowel* tʊ, *emph.* tu:] *adv.* **1.** (*into closed position*): **draw the curtains ~!** задёрните занаве́ски! **2.**: **~ and fro** туда́ и сюда́; взад и вперёд.
prep. **1.** (*expr. ind. obj., recipient*): *usu. expr. by d.*

case; **a letter ~ my wife** письмо́ мое́й жене́; **it was a surprise ~ him** для него́ э́то бы́ло неожи́данностью; **~ me that is absurd** по-мо́ему э́то неле́по; **a monument ~ Pushkin** па́мятник Пу́шкину; (*expr. support*): **a toast ~ the workers** тост за рабо́тников; **here's ~ our victory** за на́шу побе́ду. **2.** (*expr. destination*) a) (*with place-names, countries, areas, buildings, institutions, places of study or entertainment*) в+*a.*; **~ Moscow** в Москву́; **~ Russia** в Росси́ю; **~ the Crimea** в Крым; **~ the theatre** в теа́тр; **~ school** в шко́лу; **he was elected ~ the council** его́ вы́брали в сове́т; (*expr. direction*): **the road ~ Berlin** доро́га на Берли́н; b) (*with islands, peninsulas, mountain areas of Russia, planets, points of the compass, left and right, places considered as activity or function, places of employment*) на+*a.*; **~ Ceylon** на Цейло́н; **~ the Caucasus** на Кавка́з; **back ~ earth** обра́тно на зе́млю; **turn ~ the right!** поверни́те напра́во!; **~ a concert** на конце́рт; **~ war** на войну́; **~ the factory** на фа́брику; **~ the station** на ста́нцию; **he set the lines ~ music** он положи́л э́ти стихи́ на му́зыку; c) (*with persons, types of shop, objects approached but not entered*) к+*d.*; **he went ~ his parents'** он отпра́вился к свои́м роди́телям; **pull the chair up ~ the table!** пододви́ньте стул к столу́! **3.** (*expr. limit or extent of movement*: *up to, as far as, until*) до+*g.*; на+*a.*; по+*a.*; **is it far ~ town?** до го́рода далеко́?; **he was in the water (up) ~ his waist** он стоя́л по по́яс в воде́; **you will get soaked ~ the skin** вы промо́кните до ни́тки; **~ the bottom** на са́мое дно; **from morning ~ night** с утра́ до́ ночи; **ten (minutes) ~ six** без десяти́ (мину́т) шесть. **4.** (*expr. end state*): **torn ~ shreds** разо́рванный в кло́чья (*or* на куски́); **from bad ~ worse** всё ху́же и ху́же. **5.** (*expr. response*) на+*a.*; к+*d.*; **an answer ~ my letter** отве́т на моё письмо́; **deaf ~ entreaty** глухо́й к мольба́м. **6.** (*expr. result or reaction*) к+*d.*; **~ my surprise** к моему́ удивле́нию; **it is ~ your advantage** э́то в ва́ших интере́сах; **~ no avail** напра́сно. **7.** (*expr. appurtenance, attachment, suitability*) к+*d.*; от+*g.*; в+*a.*; **the preface ~ the book** предисло́вие к кни́ге; **the key ~ the door** ключ от две́ри; **there's nothing ~ it** (*coll., it presents no problem*) э́то па́ра пустяко́в. **8.** (*expr. reference or relationship*): **he is good ~ his employees** он хорошо́ отно́сится к свои́м сотру́дникам; **soft ~ the touch** мя́гкий на о́щупь; **attention ~ detail** внима́ние к подро́бностям; **secretary ~ the director** секрета́рь дире́ктора; **close ~** бли́зкий к+*d.* **9.** (*expr. ratio or proportion*): **ten ~ one he won't succeed** де́сять про́тив одного́, что э́то ему́ не уда́стся; **this car does 30 (miles) ~ the gallon** э́та маши́на де́лает 30 миль на галло́н. **10.** (*expr. score*) на+*a.*; **we won by six goals ~ four** мы вы́играли со счётом 6–4. **11.** (*expr. position*): **~ my right** спра́ва от меня́; **~ the south of London** к ю́гу от Ло́ндона.

particle with v. forming inf. **1.** (*as subj. or obj. of v.*): **~ err is human** челове́ку сво́йственно ошиба́ться; **he learnt ~ swim** он научи́лся пла́вать. **2.** (*as extension of adj.*): **easy ~ read** удобочита́емый; **too hot ~ touch** тако́й горя́чий, что не дотро́нуться. **3.** (*expr. purpose*) (с тем *or* для того́), что́бы...; (*with inf. only*): **I came ~ help** я пришёл помо́чь; (*expr. result, sequel*): **he disappeared, never ~ return** он исче́з, и никогда́ уже́ не возвраща́лся. **4.** (*as substitute for rel. clause*): **he was first ~ arrive and last ~ leave** он при́был пе́рвым и уе́хал после́дним; **the captain was the next man ~ die** сле́дующим у́мер капита́н. **5.** (*as substitute for complete inf.*): **I was going ~ write but I forgot ~** я собира́лся написа́ть, но забы́л.

toad [təʊd] *n.* жа́ба.

cpd. **~stool** *n.* пога́нка.

toady ['təʊdɪ] *n.* подхали́м.

v.i. подли́зываться (*impf.*) (*к кому*).

toast[1] [təʊst] *n.* грено́к, поджа́ренный хлеб.

v.t. поджа́ри|вать, -ть; **~ed cheese** грено́к с сы́ром; **he ~ed his toes by the fire** он гре́л но́ги у ками́на.

toast[2] [təʊst] *n.* (*drinking of health*) тост; **propose a ~ to** провозгла́сить (*pf.*) тост за+*a.*; **drink a ~ to sth.** вы́пить (*pf.*) за что-н.

v.t. пить, вы́- за (*чьё-н.*) здоро́вье.

cpd. **~-master** лицо́, провозглаша́ющее то́сты.

toaster ['təʊstə(r)] *n.* (*machine*) то́стер.

tobacco [tə'bækəʊ] *n.* таба́к.

cpd. **~-pouch** *n.* кисе́т.

tobacconist [tə'bækənɪst] *n.* торго́вец таба́чными изде́лиями.

toboggan [tə'bɒgən] *n.* тобо́гган; са́н|и (*pl., g.* -е́й).

v.i. ката́ться (*impf.*) на саня́х.

tocsin ['tɒksɪn] *n.* наба́т.

today [tə'deɪ] *n. & adv.* сего́дня; **what's ~?** како́й день сего́дня?; **~'s newspaper** сего́дняшняя газе́та; **from ~ on** с сего́дняшнего дня; (*fig., the present time*) настоя́щее вре́мя; **young people of ~** совреме́нная молодёжь.

toddle ['tɒd(ə)l] *v.i.* ковыля́ть (*impf.*).

toddler ['tɒdlə(r)] *n.* ребёнок, начина́ющий ходи́ть.

to-do [tə'du:] *n.* шум; суета́; **what's all the ~?** из-за чего́ весь э́тот шум?

toe [təʊ] *n.* **1.** (*of foot*) па́лец (ноги́); **big ~** большо́й па́лец (ноги́); **tread on s.o.'s ~s** (*fig., offend*) наступи́ть (*pf.*) на люби́мую мозо́ль (*кому*); **on one's ~s** (*fig.*) начеку́. **2.** (*of shoe or sock*) носо́к.

v.t.: **~ the line** (*fig., conform*) ходи́ть (*indet.*) по стру́нке.

cpds. **~-cap** *n.* носо́к; **~-hold** *n.* опо́ра; то́чка опо́ры; **~-nail** *n.* но́готь (*m.*) на па́льце ноги́.

toffee ['tɒfɪ] *n.* ири́с(ка); тяну́чка; **a ~** ири́ска.

tofu ['təʊfu:] *n.* со́евый творо́г.

tog [tɒg] (*coll.*) *n.* (*pl. only*) оде́жда.

v.t. with advs. над|ева́ть, -е́ть; **we got him ~ged out for school** мы снаряди́ли его́ в шко́лу; **he ~ged himself up in a dinner-jacket** он вы́рядился в смо́кинг.

toga ['təʊgə] *n.* то́га.

together [tə'geðə(r)] *adv.* **1.** (*in company*) вме́сте; **they get on well ~** они́ ла́дят друг с дру́гом; **~ with** (*in addition to*) вме́сте с+*i.* **2.** (*simultaneously*) одновре́ме́нно. **3.** (*in succession*) подря́д, непреры́вно; **he was away for weeks ~** он был в разъе́здах неде́лями. **4.:** *for other phrasal vv. see relevant entries.*

toil [tɔɪl] *n.* (тяжёлый) труд.

v.i. **1.** (*work hard or long*) труди́ться (*impf.*). **2.** (*move with difficulty*) тащи́ться (*impf.*); **they ~ed up the hill** они втащи́лись на холм.

toiler ['tɔɪlə(r)] *n.* тру́жени|к (*fem.* -ца).

toilet ['tɔɪlɪt] *n.* **1.** (*process of dressing, arranging hair etc.*) туале́т; **~ articles** туале́тные принадле́жности. **2.** (*lavatory*) туале́т, убо́рная.

cpds. **~-paper** *n.* туале́тная бума́га; **~-roll** *n.* руло́н туале́тной бума́ги.

toiletries ['tɔɪlɪtrɪz] *n.pl.* туале́тные принадле́жности.

toilette [twɑ:'let] *n.* туале́т.

token ['təʊkən] *n.* **1.** (*sign, evidence, guarantee*) знак, си́мвол; **in ~ of my friendship** в знак мое́й дру́жбы; **by the same ~** по той же причи́не. **2.** (*keepsake, memento*) сувени́р. **3.** (*substitute for coin*) жето́н. **4.** (*attr.*) символи́ческий; **they put up a ~ resistance** они́ оказа́ли лишь ви́димость сопротивле́ния.

tolerable ['tɒlərəb(ə)l] *adj.* (*endurable*) терпи́мый, выноси́мый; (*fairly good*) терпи́мый, сно́сный.

tolerance ['tɒlərəns] *n.* (*forbearance*) терпи́мость; (*resistance to adverse conditions, drugs etc.*) выно́сливость; (*tech., permissible variation*) до́пуск.

tolerant ['tɒlərənt] *adj.* терпи́мый; **he is not very ~ of criticism** он не о́чень лю́бит кри́тику.

tolerate ['tɒlə,reɪt] *v.t.* (*endure*) терпе́ть (*impf.*); (*permit*) допус|ка́ть, -ти́ть; (*sustain without harm*) перен|оси́ть, -ести́.

toleration [,tɒlə'reɪʃ(ə)n] *n.* терпи́мость.

toll[1] [təʊl] *n.* (*tax*) по́шлина, сбор; **age is taking its ~** во́зраст начина́ет ска́зываться; го́ды беру́т своё; **the ~ of the road** (*accident rate*) чи́сленность жертв доро́жных происше́ствий.

cpds. **~-gate** *nn.* заста́ва; **~-bridge** *n.* мост, где взима́ется сбор.

toll[2] [təʊl] *n.* (*of bell*) колоко́льный звон.

v.t. & i. звони́ть (*impf.*) в ко́локол; **the bell ~ed the hours** ко́локол отбива́л часы́.

Tom [tɒm] *n.* **1.: any ~, Dick or Harry** ка́ждый; пе́рвый встре́чный; **peeping ~** соглята́тай. **2.** (**t~**: *male cat*) кот.

cpds. **~boy** *n.* девчо́нка-сорване́ц; **~cat** *n.* кот; **~foolery** *n.* дура́чество, шутовство́; **~tit** *n.* сини́ца.

tomahawk ['tɒmə,hɔ:k] *n.* томага́вк.

tomato [tə'mɑ:təʊ] *n.* помидо́р; **~ purée** тома́т(-пюре́); **~ sauce/juice** тома́тный со́ус/сок.

tomb [tu:m] *n.* моги́ла; (*monument*) мавзоле́й.

cpd. **~stone** *n.* надгро́бный ка́мень; надгро́бная плита́.

tombola [tɒm'bəʊlə] *n.* лотере́я.

tome [təʊm] *n.* том.

tommy ['tɒmɪ] *n.* (**T~**: *private soldier*) (англи́йский) рядово́й.

cpds. **~-gun** *n.* автома́т, пистоле́т-пулемёт; **~-rot** *n.* (*coll.*): **talk ~-rot** поро́ть (*impf.*) дичь.

tomorrow [tə'mɒrəʊ] *n. & adv.* за́втра; **~ morning** за́втра у́тром; **the day after ~** послеза́втра; **until ~** до за́втра; **~'s weather** за́втрашняя пого́да.

tomtom ['tɒmtɒm] *n.* тамта́м.

ton [tʌn] *n.* то́нна; (*fig.*): **he has ~s of money** у него́ ку́ча де́нег; **he came down on me like a ~ of bricks** он так на меня́ и обру́шился.

tonal ['təʊn(ə)l] *adj.* (*mus.*; *of colours*) тона́льный.

tonality [tə'nælɪtɪ] *n.* тона́льность.

tone [təʊn] *n.* **1.** (*quality of sound*) тон; (*mus. interval*) звук, тон; (*intonation*) го́лос, тон. **2.** (*character*) хара́ктер, стиль (*m.*); **the debate took on a serious ~** диску́ссия приобрела́ серьёзный хара́ктер. **3.** (*distinction*) тон. **4.** (*shade of colour*) отте́нок, тон (*pl.* -а́). **5.** (*med.*) то́нус.

v.i. гармони́ровать (*impf.*).

with advs.: **~ down** *v.t.* смягч|а́ть, -и́ть; осл|абля́ть, -а́бить; **~ in** *v.i.* гармони́ровать (*impf.*); **~ up** *v.t.* укреп|ля́ть, -и́ть; тонизи́ровать (*impf.*).

cpds. **~-deaf** *adj.* лишённый музыка́льного слу́ха; **~-poem** *n.* симфони́ческая поэ́ма.

toneless ['təʊnlɪs] *adj.* моното́нный.

toner ['təʊnə(r)] *n.* (*xerographic*) кра́сящий порошо́к.

tongs [tɒŋz] *n.* щипц|ы́ (*pl., g.* -о́в).

tongue [tʌŋ] *n.* **1.** (*lit., and as food*) язы́к; **put, stick one's ~ out** высо́вывать, вы́сунуть (*or* пока́з|ывать, -а́ть) язы́к; (*dim., e.g. baby's*) язычо́к. **2.** (*fig., article so shaped*) язычо́к; **the ~ of a shoe** язычо́к боти́нка. **3.** (*fig., faculty or manner of speech*) язы́к, речь; **she has a sharp ~** у неё о́стрый язы́к; **he spoke with his ~ in his cheek** он говори́л со скры́той ирони́ей; **have you lost your ~?** вы что, язы́к проглоти́ли?; **hold your ~!** молчи́те! **4.** (*language*) язы́к; **mother ~** родно́й язы́к.

cpds. **~-lashing** *n.* разно́с; **~-tied** *adj.* косноязы́чный; **he was ~-tied** он как язы́к проглоти́л; **~-twister** *n.* скорогово́рка.

tonic ['tɒnɪk] *n.* **1.** (*medicine*) тонизи́рующее сре́дство; (*fig.*) подде́ржка, утеше́ние; **the news was a ~ to us all** но́вость нас всех подбодри́ла. **2.** (**~ water**): то́ник. **3.** (*mus.*) то́ника.

adj.: **the ~ quality of sea air** тонизи́рующее сво́йство морско́го во́здуха; **~ solfa** сольфе́джио (*indecl.*).

tonight [tə'naɪt] *n.* сего́дняшний ве́чер.

adj. сего́дня ве́чером.

tonnage ['tʌnɪdʒ] *n.* (*internal capacity*) тонна́ж.

tonne [tʌn] *n.* метри́ческая то́нна.

tonsil ['tɒns(ə)l, -sɪl] *n.* минда́лина, миндалеви́дная железа́; **has he had his ~s out?** ему́ удали́ли гла́нды?

tonsillectomy [,tɒnsɪ'lektəmɪ] *n.* удале́ние минда́лин.

tonsillitis [,tɒnsɪ'laɪtɪs] *n.* воспале́ние минда́лин, тонзилли́т.

tonsorial [tɒn'sɔ:rɪəl] *adj.* парикма́херский.

tonsure ['tɒnsjə(r), 'tɒnʃə(r)] *n.* тонзу́ра.

too [tu:] *adv.* **1.** (*also*) та́кже, то́же. **2.** (*moreover*) к тому́ же; бо́лее того́; **and him a married man, ~!** а ещё жена́тый! **3.** (*US coll., indeed*) действи́тельно. **4.** (*excessively*) сли́шком; **it's ~ cold for swimming** сли́шком хо́лодно, что́бы купа́ться; **am I ~ late for dinner?** я не опозда́л к у́жину?; **I've had ~ much to eat** я объе́лся; **that is ~ much!** э́то уж сли́шком!; **he had one (drink) ~ many** он вы́пил ли́шнего. **5.** (*very*) о́чень; кра́йне; **you are ~ kind** вы о́чень добры́; **I'm not ~ sure** я бы не поручи́лся; **~ bad!** (о́чень) жаль!

tool [tu:l] *n.* **1.** (*implement*) инструме́нт, ору́дие; (*pl., collect.*) инструме́нт; **~s of one's trade** (*fig.*) ору́дия труда́; **(machine-~)** стано́к; (*cutting part of lathe etc.*) резе́ц. **2.** (*fig., means, aid*) ору́дие. **3.** (*fig., pers. used by another*) ору́дие; марионе́тка; **he was a mere ~ in their hands** он был лишь ору́дием в их рука́х.

v.t. **1.** (*ornament*) вытисня́ть, вы́тиснить узо́р на+*p.* **2.** (*equip with machinery*) обору́довать (*impf., pf.*) инструме́нтом; **the factory was ~ed up for new production** фа́брику оснасти́ли/обору́довали для вы́пуска но́вой проду́кции.

cpds. **~-bag** *n.* су́мка для инструме́нтов; **~-box, ~-chest** *nn.* я́щик для инструме́нтов; **~-shed** *n.* сара́й для инструме́нтов.

toot [tu:t] *n.* гудо́к; сигна́л.

v.t.: **he ~ed the horn** он погуде́л; он дал сигна́л.

v.i. гуде́ть (*impf.*); дать, из- гудо́к.

tooth [tu:θ] *n.* **1.** зуб; (*dim., e.g. baby's*) зу́бик, зубо́к; **false teeth** иску́сственные зу́бы; **she has a sweet ~** она́ сластёна; **I have a ~ loose** у меня́ шата́ется зуб; **he went to have a ~ out** он пошёл удали́ть зуб; **my ~ aches** у меня́ боли́т зуб. **2.** (*fig.*): **armed to the teeth** вооружённый до зубо́в; **fed up to the (back) teeth** сыт по го́рло; **he sailed into the teeth of the gale** он поплы́л пря́мо про́тив си́льного ве́тра; **I can't wait to get my teeth into the job** не те́рпится скоре́е приня́ться за рабо́ту; **he got away by the skin of his teeth** он чу́дом уцеле́л; **they were fighting ~ and nail** они́ драли́сь не на жизнь, а на смерть; **he's a bit long in the ~** он уже́ не пе́рвой мо́лодости; **it was not long before he showed his teeth** он вско́ре показа́л ко́гти. **3.** (*of a saw, gear, comb etc.*) зуб, зубе́ц.

cpds. **~ache** *n.* зубна́я боль; **~-brush** *n.* зубна́я щётка; **~paste** *n.* зубна́я па́ста; **~pick** *n.* зубочи́стка.

toothy ['tu:θɪ] *adj.* зуба́стый.

top[1] [tɒp] *n.* **1.** (*summit; highest or upper part*) верх (*pl.* -и́); верху́шка, верши́на; маку́шка; **at the ~ of the hill** на верши́не холма́; **the ~s of the trees** верху́шки дере́вьев; **they climbed to the very ~** они́ взобра́лись на са́мый верх; **at the ~ of the page** в нача́ле страни́цы; **she cleaned the house from ~ to bottom** она́ убрала́ дом све́рху до́низу; (*of the head*) маку́шка; **he has no hair on (the) ~ (of his head)** у него́ (на маку́шке) плешь; **he blew his ~** (*sl.*) он вы́шел из себя́; **from ~ to toe** с головы́ до пят. **2.** (*fig., highest rank, foremost place*) вы́сший ранг; пе́рвое ме́сто; **he came ~ of the form** он стал пе́рвым в кла́ссе; **they put him at the ~ of the table** его́ посади́ли во главе́ стола́. **3.** (*fig., utmost degree, height*) верх; **the ~ of my ambition** преде́л мои́х мечта́ний; **at the ~ of his voice** во весь го́лос. **4.** (*upper surface*) пове́рхность; верх; **wood floats to the ~** де́рево всплыва́ет наве́рх; **on ~** (*lit.*) наверху́; (*fig.*): **I feel on ~ of the world** я чу́вствую себя́ на седьмо́м не́бе; **I'm getting on ~ of my work** я начина́ю справля́ться с рабо́той; **on ~ of everything I caught a cold** вдоба́вок ко всему́ я ещё простуди́лся. **5.** (*lid, cover*) верх; кры́шка. **6.: the big ~** (*circus tent*) шапито́ (*indecl.*). **7.** (*attr.; see also cpds.*): **~ hat** цили́ндр; **~ secret** *adj.* соверше́нно секре́тный; **at ~ speed** во всю мочь.

v.t. **1.** (*serve as ~ to*): **a church ~ped by a steeple** це́рковь, уве́нчанная шпи́лем. **2.** (*reach ~ of*) дост|ига́ть, -и́гнуть верши́ны +*g.* **3.** (*be higher than; exceed*) прев|ыша́ть, -ы́сить; **the mountains ~ 5,000 ft.** го́ры вы́ше пяти́ ты́сяч фу́тов; **he ~ped 60 mph** он де́лал бо́льше шести́десяти миль в час; (*fig., surpass*): **it ~ped all my expectations** э́то превзошло́ все мои́ ожида́ния.

with adv.: **~ up** *v.t.* дол|ива́ть, -и́ть; нап|олня́ть, -о́лнить; *v.i.* запр|авля́ться, -а́виться.

cpds. **~-coat** *n.* (*garment*) пальто́ (*indecl.*); (*of paint*) ве́рхний слой; **~-flight** *adj.* первокла́ссный, наилу́чший; **~-gallant** *n.* брам-сте́ньга; **~-heavy** *adj.* неусто́йчивый; переве́шивающий в ве́рхней ча́сти; **~-knot** *n.* чуб; пучо́к воло́с/пе́рьев; **~mast** *n.* сте́ньга; **~-notch** *adj.* первокла́ссный; **~-ranking** *adj.* вы́сшего ра́нга; высокопоста́вленный; **~-sail** *n.* то́псель (*m.*); **~side** *n.* (*of beef*) говя́жья груди́нка; **~soil** *n.* па́хотный слой.

top² [tɒp] *n.* (*toy*) волчо́к; **I slept like a ~** я спал как уби́тый.

topaz [ˈtəʊpæz] *n.* топа́з (*attr.* -овый).

topiary [ˈtəʊpɪərɪ] *adj.*: **the ~ art** фигу́рная стри́жка кусто́в.

topic [ˈtɒpɪk] *n.* те́ма; предме́т обсужде́ния.

topical [ˈtɒpɪk(ə)l] *adj.* актуа́льный; злободне́вный.

topless [ˈtɒplɪs] *adj.* (*of dress*) без ли́фа, обнажа́ющий грудь; (*of pers.*) с обнажённой гру́дью.

topmost [ˈtɒpməʊst] *adj.* са́мый ве́рхний/ва́жный.

topographic(al) [ˌtɒpəˈgræfɪk(ə)l] *adj.* топографи́ческий.

topography [təˈpɒgrəfɪ] *n.* топогра́фия.

topology [təˈpɒlədʒɪ] *n.* тополо́гия.

topple [ˈtɒp(ə)l] *v.t.* вали́ть, с-; **the dictator was ~d (from power)** дикта́тора сбро́сили.

v.i. опроки́|дываться, -нуться; вали́ться, с-.

topsy-turvy [ˌtɒpsɪˈtɜːvɪ] *adj.* перевёрнутый верх дном.

adv. вверх дном; ши́ворот-навы́ворот.

toque [təʊk] *n.* (*woman's hat*) ток.

Torah [ˈtɔːrə] *n.* то́ра.

torch [tɔːtʃ] *n.* фа́кел; (*fig.*) све́точ; **(electric ~)** электри́ческий фона́рь; (*welding ~*) сва́рочная горе́лка.

cpds. **~-bearer** *n.* фа́кельщик; (*fig.*) просвети́тель (*m.*); **~light** *n.* свет фа́кела/фонаря́.

toreador [ˈtɒrɪəˌdɔː(r)] *n.* тореадо́р.

torment¹ [ˈtɔːment] *n.* муче́ние; **a soul in ~** душа́, раздира́емая му́ками.

torment² [tɔːˈment] *v.t.* му́чить (*impf.*); **he was ~ed with jealousy** он терза́лся ре́вностью.

tormentor [tɔːˈmentə(r)] *n.* мучи́тель (*fem.* -ница).

tornado [tɔːˈneɪdəʊ] *n.* торна́до (*indecl.*).

torpedo [tɔːˈpiːdəʊ] *n.* торпе́да.

v.t. (*lit.*) торпеди́ровать (*impf.*).

cpd. **~-boat** *n.* торпе́дный ка́тер.

torpid [ˈtɔːpɪd] *adj.* вя́лый, апати́чный.

torpor [ˈtɔːpə(r)] *n.* вя́лость, апа́тия.

torque [tɔːk] *n.* (*mech.*) враща́ющий моме́нт.

torrent [ˈtɒrənt] *n.* (*lit., fig.*) пото́к; **the rain fell in ~s** шёл проливно́й дождь.

torrential [təˈrenʃ(ə)l] *adj.* проливно́й.

torrid [ˈtɒrɪd] *adj.* жа́ркий, зно́йный; **~ zone** тропи́ческий по́яс.

torsion [ˈtɔːʃ(ə)n] *n.* (*process*) скру́чивание; (*state*) скру́ченность.

torso [ˈtɔːsəʊ] *n.* ту́ловище, торс.

tort [tɔːt] *n.* гражда́нско-правово́й дели́кт.

tortoise [ˈtɔːtəs] *n.* черепа́ха; (*attr.*) черепа́ший.

cpd. **~shell** *n.* (*as material*) черепа́ха; *adj.* черепа́ховый.

tortuous [ˈtɔːtjʊəs] *adj.* изви́листый.

torture [ˈtɔːtʃə(r)] *n.* (*physical*) пы́тка; **he was put to the ~** его́ подве́ргли пы́ткам; (*mental*) му́ки (*f. pl.*).

v.t. пыта́ть (*impf.*); му́чить (*impf.*); **she was ~d with anxiety** её му́чила трево́га; **a ~d expression** выраже́ние му́ки.

torturer [ˈtɔːtʃərə(r)] *n.* мучи́тель (*m.*).

Tory [ˈtɔːrɪ] *n.* (*coll.*) то́ри (*m. indecl.*); **the ~ party** консервати́вная па́ртия; **~ leaders** ли́деры то́ри.

toss [tɒs] *n.* (*throw*) бросо́к; **with a ~ of her head, she ...** тряхну́в голово́й (*or* вски́нув го́лову), она́...

v.t. **1.** (*throw*) бр|оса́ть, -о́сить; кида́ть, ки́нуть; **the horse ~ed its rider** ло́шадь сбро́сила седока́; **they ~ed a coin to decide** они́ подки́нули моне́ту, что́бы реши́ть исхо́д де́ла. **2.** (*rock, agitate*) швыр|я́ть, -ну́ть; **the ship was ~ed by the waves** во́лны подки́дывали су́дно вверх и вниз.

v.i. мета́ться (*impf.*); **the child ~ed in its sleep** ребёнок мета́лся во сне; **a ship was ~ing on the waves** кора́бль кача́лся на волна́х.

with advs.: **~ about** *v.i.* мета́ться (*impf.*); **~ away** *v.t.* отбр|а́сывать, -о́сить; **~ off** *v.t.* выпива́ть, вы́пить за́лпом; де́лать, с- на́спех; **~ up** *v.t.* подбр|а́сывать, -о́сить; *v.i.*: **shall we ~ up to see who goes?** дава́йте бро́сим жре́бий, кому́ идти́.

cpd. **~-up** *n.* нея́сный исхо́д; де́ло слу́чая.

tot¹ [tɒt] *n.* (*child*) малы́ш; (*of liquor*) глото́к.

tot² [tɒt] *v.t. with adv.* **up** сост|авля́ть, -а́вить (*сумму*); **he ~ted up the figures** он подвёл ито́г.

v.i.: **his expenses ~ted up to £50** его́ расхо́ды соста́вили 50 фу́нтов.

total [ˈtəʊt(ə)l] *n.* су́мма, ито́г; **the grand ~ came to £200** о́бщая су́мма соста́вила 200 фу́нтов.

adj. це́лый, о́бщий, по́лный; **~ eclipse** по́лное затме́ние; **~ failure** по́лный прова́л; **the ~ figure** о́бщая ци́фра; **~ war** тота́льная война́.

v.t. & i. (*reckon, also* **~ up**) подсчи́т|ывать, -а́ть; подв|оди́ть, -ести́ ито́г; **the visitors ~led several hundred** число́ посети́телей дости́гло не́скольких со́тен.

totalitarian [təʊˌtælɪˈteərɪən] *adj.* тоталита́рный.

totalitarianism [təʊˌtælɪˈteərɪənɪz(ə)m] *n.* тоталитари́зм.

totality [təʊˈtælɪtɪ] *n.* вся су́мма, всё коли́чество; тота́льность.

totalizator [ˈtəʊtəlaɪˌzeɪtə(r)] *n.* тотализа́тор.

totally [ˈtəʊtəlɪ] *adv.* соверше́нно, по́лностью.

tote¹ [təʊt] (*coll.*) = **totalizator**

tote² [təʊt] *v.t.* (*US coll.*) носи́ть, нести́ (*груз, оружие и т.п.*).

totem [ˈtəʊtəm] *n.* тоте́м.

cpd. **~-pole** *n.* тоте́мный столб.

totter [ˈtɒtə(r)] *v.i.* (*walk unsteadily*) ковыля́ть (*impf.*); (*fig.*) шата́ться, пошатну́ться.

toucan [ˈtuːkən] *n.* тука́н.

touch [tʌtʃ] *n.* **1.** (*contact; light pressure of hand etc.*) прикоснове́ние. **2.** (*sense*) осяза́ние; **the blind man recognized me by ~** слепо́й узна́л меня́ на о́щупь; **soft to the ~** мя́гкий на о́щупь. **3.** (*light stroke of* *pen or brush*) штрих; **he was putting the finishing ~es to the picture** он наноси́л после́дние мазки́ (на карти́ну). **4.** (*tinge*, *trace*) чу́точка, отте́нок, налёт; **a ~ of frost in the air** лёгкий моро́зец; **this soup needs a ~ of salt** в су́пе не хвата́ет чу́точку со́ли. **5.** (*artist's or performer's style*) стиль (*m.*); **he has a light ~ on the piano** у него́ лёгкое туше́ (на фортепья́но); (*fig.*): **you must have lost your ~** вы я́вно утра́тили (былу́ю) хва́тку. **6.** (*communication*) обще́ние; **we must keep in ~** мы должны́ подде́рживать конта́кт друг с дру́гом; **we have been out of ~ for so long** мы так до́лго не обща́лись; **how can I get in ~ with you?** как мо́жно с ва́ми связа́ться?; **we lost ~ with him** мы потеря́ли с ним конта́кт/связь.

v.t. **1.** (*contact physically*) тро́|гать, -нуть; прик|аса́ться, -осну́ться к+*d.*; **he ~ed her (on the) arm** он косну́лся её руки́; **don't ~ the paint** не дотра́гивайтесь до кра́ски; **it was ~ and go** исхо́д был неизве́стен до са́мого конца́; **~ wood!** тьфу-тьфу́, не сгла́зить! **2.** (*actuate*): **I ~ed the bell** я нажа́л звоно́к. **3.** (*reach*) дост|ига́ть, -и́гнуть +*g.*; **can you ~ the top of the door?** вы мо́жете дотяну́ться до ве́рха две́ри?; **I can just ~ bottom** я е́ле достаю́ до дна. **4.** (*approach in excellence*; *compare with*) равня́ться (*impf.*) с+*i.*; идти́ (*det.*) в сравне́ние с+*i.*; **no-one can ~ him for eloquence** никто́ не мо́жет сравни́ться с ним в красноре́чии. **5.** (*affect*) тро́гать (*impf.*); волнова́ть, вз-; **it ~ed me to the heart** я был глубоко́ тро́нут; **his remarks ~ed me on the raw** его́ замеча́ния заде́ли меня́ за живо́е; **we were very ~ed by his speech** его́ речь о́чень взволнова́ла нас. **6.** (*taste*) притр|а́гиваться, -о́нуться; **I never ~ a drop** (*of alcohol*) я совсе́м не пью. **7.** (*injure slightly*) нан|оси́ть, -ести́ уще́рб +*d.*; **the flowers were ~ed by the frost** цветы́ бы́ли тро́нуты моро́зом. **8.** (*deal with*; *cope with*) спр|авля́ться, -а́виться с+*i.*; **nothing will ~ these stains** э́ти пя́тна ниче́м не вы́ведешь. **9.** (*concern*) име́ть отноше́ние к+*d.*; каса́ться (*impf.*) +*g.*; **it ~es us all** э́то каса́ется нас всех. **10.** (*have to do with*) зан|има́ться, -я́ться +*i.*; **I refuse to ~ your schemes** я не хочу́ име́ть ничего́ о́бщего с ва́шими пла́нами. **11.** (*treat lightly*; *also v.i. with prep.* **on**) затр|а́гивать, -о́нуть; **he ~ed (on) the subject of race** он косну́лся ра́сового вопро́са.

v.i. **1.** (*make contact*) соприк|аса́ться, -осну́ться; **our hands ~ed** на́ши ру́ки встре́тились; **if the wires ~ there will be an explosion** е́сли провода́ соприкосну́тся, бу́дет взрыв. **2. ~ on:** *see v.t.* **11.**

with advs.: **~ off** *v.t.* (*cause*) вызыва́ть, вы́звать; **~ up** *v.t.* испр|авля́ть, -а́вить; **I'll just ~ it up** я чуть ко́е-где подпра́влю; **the photographs had been ~ed up** фотогра́фии бы́ли отретуши́рованы.

cpds. **~-and-go** *adj.* с непредсказу́емым исхо́дом; **~-down** *n.* (*aeron.*) поса́дка; **~line** *n.* бокова́я ли́ния по́ля; **~stone** *n.* (*fig.*) про́бный ка́мень; осело́к; **~-typist** *n.* машини́стка, рабо́тающая по слепо́му ме́тоду.

touched [tʌtʃd] *adj.* (*emotionally*) растро́ганный; (*coll.*, *mentally*) слегка́ поме́шанный, тро́нутый.

touchiness ['tʌtʃɪnɪs] *n.* оби́дчивость.

touching ['tʌtʃɪŋ] *adj.* тро́гательный.

touchy ['tʌtʃɪ] *adj.* оби́дчивый.

tough [tʌf] *adj.* **1.** (*resistant to cutting or chewing*) жёсткий; упру́гий. **2.** (*strong*, *sturdy*, *hardy*) кре́пкий; про́чный; выно́сливый; **you need a ~ pair of shoes** вам нужна́ кре́пкая о́бувь. **3.** (*difficult*) тру́дный; упря́мый. **4.** (*coll.*, *severe*, *uncompromising*) жёсткий; упря́мый; **you must take a ~ line with the children** с э́тими детьми́ ну́жно быть постро́же. **5.** (*coll.*, *painful*): **it was ~ on him when his father died** смерть отца́ была́ тя́жким уда́ром для него́; **~ luck!** вот незада́ча!

toughen ['tʌfən] *v.t. & i.* де́лать(ся), с- жёстким.

toughness ['tʌfnɪs] *n.* про́чность; выно́сливость.

toupee ['tu:peɪ] *n.* небольшо́й пари́к, накла́дка.

tour [tʊə(r)] *n.* **1.** (*extended visit*) путеше́ствие, пое́здка; экску́рсия; **we are going on a ~ of Europe** мы собира́емся путеше́ствовать по Евро́пе. **2.** (*theatr.*) турне́ (*indecl.*); гастро́ли (*f. pl.*); **the company was on ~** тру́ппа гастроли́ровала (*or* находи́лась на гастро́лях). **3.** (*period of duty*) срок слу́жбы.

v.t. & i. соверш|а́ть, -и́ть экску́рсию (по+*d.*); **we have been ~ing Scotland** мы объе́здили Шотла́ндию.

tour de force [,tʊə də 'fɔ:s] *n.* проявле́ние си́лы.

tourism ['tʊərɪz(ə)m] *n.* тури́зм.

tourist ['tʊərɪst] *n.* тури́ст; **~ agency** туристи́ческое аге́нтство, бюро́ (*indecl.*) путеше́ствий.

tournament ['tʊənəmənt] *n.* турни́р; спорти́вное соревнова́ние.

tourniquet ['tʊənɪ,keɪ] *n.* турнике́т.

tousle ['taʊz(ə)l] *v.t.* еро́шить, -взъ-.

tout [taʊt] *n.* зазыва́ла (*m.*).

v.i. навя́з|ывать, -а́ть това́р.

tow[1] [təʊ] *n.*: **can I give you a ~?** взять вас на букси́р?

v.t. букси́ровать (*impf.*); **the ship was ~ed into harbour** кора́бль вошёл в га́вань на букси́ре.

cpds. **~(ing-)path** *n.* бечевни́к; **~-rope** *n.* бечева́.

tow[2] [təʊ] *n.* (*material*) па́кля.

toward(s) [tə'wɔ:dz, twɔ:dz] *prep.* **1.** (*in the direction of*) к+*d.*; на+*a.*; по направле́нию к+*d.*; **he stood with his back ~ me** он стоя́л ко мне спино́й. **2.** (*in relation to*) по отноше́нию к+*d.*; относи́тельно+*g.*; **what is his attitude ~ education?** как он отно́сится к пробле́ме образова́ния?; **they seemed friendly ~ us** каза́лось, что они́ к нам дру́жески располо́жены; **responsibility ~ his family** отве́тственность пе́ред семьёй. **3.** (*for the purpose of*) для+*g*; **I gave him something ~ the price** я ему́ дал часть де́нег на э́ту поку́пку. **4.** (*near*) к+*d.*; о́коло+*g*; **~ evening** к ве́черу, под ве́чер; **I'm getting ~ the end of my supply** мои́ запа́сы подхо́дят к концу́.

towel ['taʊəl] *n.* полоте́нце; **throw in the ~** (*fig.*) призна́ть (*pf.*) себя́ побеждённым.

cpd. **~-rail** *n.* ве́шалка для полоте́нец.

tower ['taʊə(r)] *n.* ба́шня; (*fig.*): **a ~ of strength** надёжная опо́ра.

v.i. вы́ситься, возвыша́ться (*both impf.*); **the building ~ed above us** зда́ние уходи́ло высо́ко́ в не́бо; **a ~ing rage** неи́стовая я́рость.

cpd. **~-block** *n.* многоэта́жный/высо́тный дом.

town [taʊn] *n.* **1.** го́род; **he is out of ~** он уе́хал за́ город. **2.** (*attr.*) городско́й; **~ crier** глаша́тай; **~ hall** мэ́рия; ра́туша; **~ house** особня́к; **~ planning** градострои́тельство.

cpds. **~sfolk** *n.* горожа́не (*m. pl.*); **~sman** *n.* горожа́нин.

township ['taʊnʃɪp] *n.* (*small town*) посёлок, городо́к.

tox(a)emia [tɒk'si:mɪə] *n.* зараже́ние кро́ви.

toxic ['tɒksɪk] *adj.* ядови́тый, токси́ческий.

toxicologist [,tɒksɪ'kɒlədʒɪst] *n.* токсико́лог.

toxicology [,tɒksɪ'kɒlədʒɪ] *n.* токсиколо́гия.

toxin ['tɒksɪn] *n.* токси́н; яд.

toy [tɔɪ] *n.* игру́шка; **~ soldier** оловя́нный солда́тик.

v.i.: **I have been ~ing with the idea** я забавля́лся э́той иде́ей; **he ~ed with her affections** он игра́л её чу́вствами.

cpd. **~shop** *n.* игру́шечный магази́н.

trace[1] [treɪs] *n.* **1.** (*track*) след; отпеча́ток. **2.** (*vestige*; *sign of previous existence*) след; **he went away leaving no ~** он исче́з, не оста́вив и следа́; **the ship disappeared without ~** кора́бль пропа́л/исче́з бессле́дно. **3.** (*small quantity*) ма́лое коли́чество;

следы́ (*в анализе*); ~ **elements** микроэлеме́нты.

v.t. **1.** (*delineate*) черти́ть, на-; **he ~d (out) his route on the map** он начерти́л маршру́т на ка́рте; (*with transparent paper or carbon*) копи́ровать, с-; **tracing paper** воско́вка. **2.** (*follow the tracks of*) выsле́живать, вы́следить; **the thief was ~d to London** следы́ во́ра вели́ в Ло́ндон; **he ~s his descent from Charlemagne** он ведёт свой род от Ка́рла Вели́кого. **3.** (*discover by search; discern*) устан|а́вливать, -ови́ть; просле́|живать, -ди́ть; **I cannot ~ your letter** я не могу́ разыска́ть ва́ше письмо́.

trace[2] [treɪs] *n.* (*of harness*) постро́мка.

tracer ['treɪsə(r)] *n.* (~ **bullet**) трасси́рующая пу́ля.

trachea [trə'ki:ə, 'treɪkɪə] *n.* трахе́я.

tracheotomy [,trækɪ'ɒtəmɪ] *n.* трахеотоми́я.

trachoma [trə'kəʊmə] *n.* трахо́ма.

track [træk] *n.* **1.** (*mark of passage*) след; **the fox left ~s in the snow** лиси́ца оста́вила след на снегу́; **we followed in his ~s** мы шли по его́ следа́м; **the police were on his ~** поли́ция напа́ла на его́ след; **he covered his ~s successfully** он успе́шно замёл следы́; **make ~s** улизну́ть (*pf., coll.*). **2.** (*path*) путь (*m.*), доро́жка; **the beaten ~** проторённая доро́жка; **he is on the wrong ~** он на ло́жном пути́. **3.** (*for racing etc.*) (бегова́я) доро́жка; ~ **events** соревнова́ния по лёгкой атле́тике. **4.** (*rail*) колея́; **single ~** одноколе́йный путь. **5.** (*of tank etc.*) гу́сеница; **~ed vehicle** гу́сеничный тра́нспорт.

v.t. следи́ть за+*i.*; высле́живать, вы́следить; **~ing station** ста́нция слеже́ния.

with adv.: ~ **down** *v.t.*: **have you ~ed down the cause of the disease?** вы докопа́лись до причи́ны боле́зни?

cpds. **~-racing** *n.* го́нки по тре́ку; **~-suit** *n.* трениро́вочный костю́м.

tracker ['trækə(r)] *n.* (*hunter*) охо́тник; ~ **dog** соба́ка-ище́йка.

tract[1] [trækt] *n.* (*region*) уча́сток, райо́н; (*anat.*) тракт; **respiratory ~** дыха́тельные пути́ (*m. pl.*).

tract[2] [trækt] *n.* (*pamphlet*) памфле́т.

tractable ['træktəb(ə)l] *adj.* послу́шный, сгово́рчивый.

traction ['trækʃ(ə)n] *n.* тя́га; ~ **engine** тя́говый двига́тель (*m.*); тяга́ч.

tractor ['træktə(r)] *n.* тра́ктор.

cpds. **~-driven** *adj.* на тра́кторной тя́ге; **~-driver** *n.* трактори́ст (*fem.* -ка).

trade [treɪd] *n.* **1.** (*business, occupation*) ремесло́; профе́ссия; **the building ~** строи́тельная промы́шленность; **he is a builder by ~** он по профе́ссии строи́тель; **jack of all ~s** ма́стер на все ру́ки. **2.** (*commerce; exchange of goods*) торго́вля; **foreign ~** вне́шняя торго́вля; ~ **discount** ски́дка ро́зничным торго́вцам; ~ **figures** да́нные о торго́вле; ~ **gap** дефици́т торго́вого бала́нса; ~ **secret** профессиона́льный секре́т; ~ **price** опто́вая цена́; ~ **wind** éccaт. .

v.t. (*exchange*) меня́ть (*impf.*); обме́н|ивать, -я́ть; **they ~d furs for food** они́ меня́ли шку́ры на проду́кты.

v.i. **1.** торгова́ть (*impf.*); **he ~s in sables** он торгу́ет соболя́ми; **trading estate** промы́шленная зо́на. **2.**: ~ **on** (*take advantage of*) испо́льзовать (*impf., pf.*) в свои́х интере́сах; **he ~s on my generosity** он злоупотребля́ет мое́й ще́дростью.

with adv.: ~ **in** *v.t.*: **I ~d in my old car for a new one** я сдал ста́рую маши́ну в счёт поку́пки но́вой.

cpds. **~-mark** *n.* (*lit.*) фабри́чная ма́рка; (*fig.*) отличи́тельный знак; **~-name** *n.* назва́ние фи́рмы; торго́вое/фи́рменное назва́ние назва́ние това́ра; **~sman** *n.* торго́вец; **~(s) union** *n.* профсою́з; **~-unionist** *n.* член профсою́за.

trader ['treɪdə(r)] *n.* (*merchant*) торго́вец, купе́ц.

tradition [trə'dɪʃ(ə)n] *n.* тради́ция.

traditional [trə'dɪʃən(ə)l] *adj.* традицио́нный.

traduce [trə'dju:s] *v.t.* (*liter.*) клевета́ть (*impf.*) на+*a.*; черни́ть, о-.

traffic ['træfɪk] *n.* **1.** (*movement of vehicles etc.*) движе́ние, тра́нспорт; **heavy ~** интенси́вное движе́ние; ~ **circle** (*US*) кольцева́я развя́зка; ~ **indicator** указа́тель (*m.*) поворо́та; ~ **lights** светофо́р. **2.** (*trade*) торго́вля; **the drug ~** торго́вля нарко́тиками.

v.i. торгова́ть (*чем*).

trafficator ['træfɪ,keɪtə(r)] *n.* указа́тель (*m.*) поворо́та.

trafficker ['træfɪkə(r)] *n.* (*pej.*) торга́ш; деле́ц.

tragedian [trə'dʒi:dɪən] *n.* тра́гик.

tragedienne [trə,dʒi:dɪ'en] *n.* траги́ческая актри́са.

tragedy ['trædʒɪdɪ] *n.* (*lit. fig.*) траге́дия.

tragic ['trædʒɪk] *adj.* траги́ческий.

tragicomedy [,trædʒɪ'kɒmɪdɪ] *n.* трагикоме́дия.

tragicomic [,trædʒɪ'kɒmɪk] *adj.* трагикоми́ческий.

trail [treɪl] *n.* след; **a ~ of smoke** о́блако ды́ма; **the police were on his ~** поли́ция напа́ла на его́ след.

v.t. **1.** (*draw or drag behind*) тащи́ть (*impf.*); волочи́ть (*impf.*); **she ~ed her skirt in the mud** её ю́бка волочи́лась по гря́зи. **2.** (*pursue*) идти́ (*det.*) по сле́ду +*g.*

v.i. **1.** (*be drawn or dragged*) тащи́ться (*impf.*); волочи́ться (*impf.*); **the rope ~ed on the ground** верёвка волочи́лась по земле́. **2.** (*straggle, follow wearily*) плести́сь (*impf.*); **they ~ed along behind him** они́ плели́сь за ним; **her voice ~ed away** её го́лос постепе́нно затиха́л. **3.** (*grow or hang loosely*) све́шиваться (*impf.*); **the roses ~ed over the wall** ро́зы обвива́ли сте́ну.

trailer ['treɪlə(r)] *n.* **1.** (*vehicle*) прице́п. **2.** (*cin.*) вы́держки (*f. pl.*) из реклами́руемого фи́льма.

train [treɪn] *n.* **1.** (*rail*) по́езд; **I came by ~** я прие́хал по́ездом; **the ~ is already in** по́езд уже́ при́был. **2.** (*line of moving vehicles, animals etc.*) проце́ссия; карава́н; (*mil.*) обо́з. **3.** (*fig.*) ряд, цепь; ~ **of events** цепь/верени́ца/ряд собы́тий; **I don't follow your ~ of thought** мне тру́дно улови́ть ход ва́ших мы́слей. **4.** (*of dress etc.*) шлейф.

v.t. **1.** (*give instruction to*) обуч|а́ть, -и́ть; приуч|а́ть, -и́ть; **I have ~ed my dog to do tricks** я обучи́л соба́ку трю́кам; **he ~s horses** он дрессиру́ет лошаде́й. **2.** (*direct*) нав|оди́ть, -ести́; **they ~ed their guns on the ship** они́ навели́ ору́дия на кора́бль.

v.i. (*undertake preparation*) гото́виться (*impf.*); тренирова́ться (*impf.*); **she is ~ing to be a teacher** она́ гото́вится стать учи́тельницей.

cpds. **~-driver** *n.* машини́ст; **~man** *n.* (*US*) проводни́к; **~-ride** *n.* пое́здка по́ездом; **~-set** *n.* игру́шечная моде́ль желе́зной доро́ги.

trainee [treɪ'ni:] *n.* стажёр (*fem.* -ка); учени́|к (*fem.* -ца).

trainer ['treɪnə(r)] *n.* **1.** тре́нер; (*of horses etc.*) дрессиро́вщи|к (*fem.* -ца). **2.** (*sports shoe*) кроссо́вка.

training ['treɪnɪŋ] *n.* **1.** (*study, instruction*) подгото́вка, обуче́ние. **2.** (*physical preparation*) трениро́вка; **he went into ~** он на́чал тренирова́ться. **3.** (*of animals*) дрессиро́вка.

cpds. **~-college** *n.* педагоги́ческий институ́т; **~-ship** *n.* уче́бное су́дно.

traipse [treɪps] *v.i.* (*coll.*) таска́ться (*impf.*).

trait [treɪ, treɪt] *n.* сво́йство; черта́.

traitor ['treɪtə(r)] *n.* преда́тель (*m.*), изме́нник.

traitorous ['treɪtərəs] *adj.* преда́тельский, изме́ннический.

trajectory [trə'dʒektərɪ, 'trædʒɪk-] *n.* траекто́рия.

tram [træm] *n.* трамва́й.

cpd. **~car** *n.* трамва́йный ваго́н.

tramp [træmp] *n.* (*sound of steps*) то́пот; (*long walk*) дли́тельный похо́д; (*vagrant*) бродя́га.

v.t.: **he ~ed the streets looking for work** он исходил весь город в поисках работы; **we ~ed the hills together** мы с ним много ходили по горам.

v.i. **1.** (*walk heavily*) то́пать (*impf.*); **the soldiers ~ed down the road** солдаты громко протопали по улице. **2.** (*walk a long distance*) шагать, про-.

trample ['træmp(ə)l] *v.t.* топтать (*or* растаптывать), рас-; **the children ~d down the flowers** дети вытоптали цветы; **I was almost ~d underfoot** меня чуть не растоптали.

v.i. тяжело ступать (*impf.*); (*fig.*): **~ on** поп|ирать, -рать; **he ~d on everyone's feelings** он не считался ни с чьими чувствами.

trampoline ['træmpə,li:n] *n.* трамплин, батут.

trampolining ['træmpə,li:nɪŋ] *n.* батутный спорт.

trance [trɑ:ns] *n.* транс.

tranquil ['træŋkwɪl] *adj.* спокойный, мирный.

tranquillity [træŋ'kwɪlɪtɪ] *n.* спокойствие.

tranquillize ['træŋkwɪ,laɪz] *v.t.* успок|аивать, -оить.

tranquillizer ['træŋkwɪ,laɪzə(r)] *n.* успокаивающее средство, транквилизатор.

transact [træn'zækt, trɑ:n-, -'sækt] *v.t.* вести (*det.*) (*дела*); заключ|ать, -ить (*сделку*).

transaction [træn'zækʃ(ə)n, trɑ:n-, -'sækʃ(ə)n] *n.* **1.: ~ of business** ведение дел. **2.** (*deal*) сделка.

transatlantic [,trænzət'læntɪk, ,trɑ:n-, -sət'læntɪk] *adj.* трансатлантический.

Transcaucasia [,trænskɔ:'keɪzjə] *n.* Закавказье.

Transcaucasian [,trænskɔ:'keɪzjən] *adj.* закавказский.

transcend [træn'send, trɑ:n-] *v.t.* прев|ышать, -ысить; выходить, выйти за пределы +*g*.

transcendent [træn'send(ə)nt, trɑ:n-] *adj.* **1.** (*surpassing*) превосходный, выдающийся. **2.** (*phil.*) трансцендентный.

transcendental [,trænsen'dent(ə)l, ,trɑ:n-] *adj.* (*phil.*) трансцендентальный.

transcontinental [trænz,kɒntɪ'nent(ə)l, trɑ:nz-] *adj.* трансконтинентальный.

transcribe [træn'skraɪb, trɑ:n-] *v.t.* переписывать, -ать; транскрибировать (*impf., pf.*).

transcript ['trænskrɪpt, 'trɑ:n-] *n.* копия; расшифровка.

transcription [,træn'skrɪpʃ(ə)n, 'trɑ:n-] *n.* переписывание; копия, транскрипция; **phonetic ~** фонетическая транскрипция.

transept ['trænsept, 'trɑ:n-] *n.* трансепт.

transfer[1] ['trænsfɜ:(r), 'trɑ:ns-] *n.* **1.** (*conveyance; move*) перенесение, перенос; перевод; **~ of property** передача имущества. **2.** (*drawing etc.*) переводная картинка. **3.** (*US*, **~ *ticket***) пересадочный билет.

transfer[2] [træns'fɜ:(r), trɑ:ns-] *v.t.* **1.** (*move*) перен|осить, -ести. **2.** (*hand over*) перед|авать, -ать. **3.** (*convey from one surface to another*) перев|одить, -ести; перен|осить, -ести (*рисунок*).

v.i. (*move*) перев|одиться, -естись; пере|ходить, -йти; (*change from one vehicle to another*) перес|аживаться, -есть.

transferable [træns'fɜ:rəb(ə)l, trɑ:ns-, 'tr-] *adj.* допускающий замену; переводимый.

transference ['trænsfərəns, 'trɑ:-] *n.* перенесение.

transfiguration [træns,fɪgjʊ'reɪʃ(ə)n, trɑ:-] *n.* видоизменение; (*relig.*) **the T~** Преображение.

transfigure [træns'fɪgə(r), trɑ:-] *v.t.* видоизмен|ять, -ить; (*with joy etc.*) преобра|жать, -зить.

transfix [træns'fɪks, trɑ:-] *v.t.* **1.** (*impale*) пронз|ать, -ить. **2.** (*fig., root to the spot*) прик|о́вывать, -овать к месту; **he was ~ed with horror** он оцепенел от ужаса.

transform [træns'fɔ:m, trɑ:-] *v.t.* (*change*) измен|ять, -ить; преобраз|о́вывать, -ать; (*make unrecognizable*) менять, изменить до неузнаваемости.

transformation [,trænsfə'meɪʃ(ə)n, ,trɑ:-] *n.* превращение; метаморфоза, трансформация.

transformer [træns'fɔ:mə(r), trɑ:-, -z'fɔ:mə(r)] *n.* (*elec.*) трансформатор.

transfuse [træns'fju:z, trɑ:-] *v.t.* перел|ивать, -ить.

transfusion [træns'fju:ʒ(ə)n, trɑ:-] *n.* переливание (крови).

transgress [trænz'gres, trɑ:-, -s'gres] *v.t. & i.* (*infringe*) пере|ходить, -йти границы +*g.*; нар|ушать, -ушить (*закон и т.п.*); (*sin*) грешить, со-.

transgression [trænz'greʃ(ə)n, trɑ:-] *n.* (*infringement*) проступок; нарушение; (*sin*) грех.

transgressor [trænz'gresə(r), trɑ:-, -s'gresə(r)] *n.* правонарушитель (*fem.* -ница), грешни|к (*fem.* -ца).

tranship [træn'ʃɪp, trɑ:-, trænz-] (*also* **transship**) *v.t.* (*goods*) перегру|жать, -зить с одного судна на другое; (*persons*) перес|аживать, -дить с одного судна на другое.

transhipment [træn'ʃɪpmənt, trɑ:-] (*also* **transshipment**) *n.* (*of goods*) перегрузка; (*of persons*) пересадка.

transient ['trænzɪənt, 'trɑ:-, -sɪənt] *n.* (*US, temporary lodger*) временный жилец.

adj. (*impermanent*) временный; (*brief, momentary*) мимолётный, преходящий.

transistor [træn'zɪstə(r), trɑ:-, -'sɪstə(r)] *n.* транзистор.

transit ['trænzɪt, 'trɑ:-, -sɪt] *n.* транзит, перевозка; **lost in ~** потерянный при перевозке; **~ camp** транзитный лагерь.

transition [træn'zɪʃ(ə)n, trɑ:-, -'sɪʃ(ə)n] *n.* (*change*) переход; (*period of change*) переходный период.

transitional [træn'zɪʃənəl, trɑ:-, -'sɪʃənəl] *adj.* переходный; промежуточный.

transitive ['trænsɪtɪv, 'trɑ:-, -zɪtɪv] *adj.* переходный

transitory ['trænsɪtərɪ, 'trɑ:-, -zɪtərɪ] *adj.* преходящий, мимолётный.

translate [træn'sleɪt, trɑ:-, -'zleɪt] *v.t. & i.* **1.** (*express in another language*) перев|одить, -ести; **he ~s from Russian into English** он переводит с русского на английский. **2.** (*convert*): **promises must be ~d into action** обещания нужно претворять в жизнь.

translation [træns'leɪʃ(ə)n, trɑ:-, -z'leɪʃ(ə)n] *n.* перевод; **a novel in ~** переводный роман.

translator [træns'leɪtə(r), trɑ:-, -z'leɪtə(r)] *n.* переводчи|к (*fem.* -ца).

transliterate [trænz'lɪtə,reɪt, trɑ:-, -s'lɪtə,reɪt] *v.t.* транслитерировать (*impf., pf.*).

transliteration [trænz,lɪtə'reɪʃ(ə)n, trɑ:-, -s,lɪtə'reɪʃ(ə)n] *n.* транслитерация.

translucent [trænz'lu:s(ə)nt, trɑ:-, -'lju:s(ə)nt, -s'l-] *adj.* просвечивающий(ся), полупрозрачный.

transmigration [,trænzmaɪ'greɪʃ(ə)n, ,trɑ:-, -smaɪ'greɪʃ(ə)n] *n.* переселение.

transmission [trænz'mɪʃ(ə)n, trɑ:-, -s'mɪʃ(ə)n] *n.* передача; **there are news ~s every hour** новости передаются каждый час.

transmit [trænz'mɪt, trɑ:-, -s'mɪt] *v.t. & i.* сообщ|ать, -ить; перед|авать, -ать; **the plague was ~ted by rats** чуму разнесли крысы; **iron ~s heat** железо проводит тепло; **wires ~ electric current** электрический ток идёт по проводам.

transmitter [træns'mɪtə(r), trɑ:-, -z'mɪtə(r)] *n.* передатчик; передающая радиостанция; **portable ~** рация.

transoceanic [trænz,əʊʃɪ'ænɪk, trɑ:-, -s,əʊʃɪ'ænɪk] *adj.* заокеанский; **~ countries** заморские/заокеанские страны; **~ flight** межконтинентальный полёт.

transom ['trænsəm] *n.* фрамуга.

transparency [træns'pærənsɪ, trɑ:-, -'peərənsɪ] *n.* **1.** прозрачность. **2.** (*picture*) транспарант.

transparent [træns'pærənt, trɑ:-, -'peərənt] *adj.* прозрачный; (*fig.*) явный, очевидный.

transpire [træn'spaɪə(r), trɑ:-] *v.i.* (*come to be known*) обнаружи|ваться, -ться; (*coll., happen*) случ|аться, -иться.

transplant[1] ['trænsplɑ:nt, 'trɑ:-] *n.* **1.** рассада; (*sapling*) саженец. **2.: heart ~** пересадка сердца.

transplant[2] [træns'plɑ:nt, trɑ:-] *v.t. & i.* переса|живать, -дить; **this species does not ~ easily** этот вид плóхо перенóсит пересáдку; (*fig.*) пересел|я́ть, -и́ть; **the doctors ~ed skin from his back** врачи́ сдéлали емý пересáдку кóжи со спины́.

transplantation [træns,plɑːn'teɪʃ(ə)n, trɑː-] *n.* пересáдка, трансплантáция; (*fig.*) переселéние.

transport[1] ['trænspɔːt, 'trɑː-] *n.* **1.** (*conveyance*) перевóзка, трáнспорт. **2.** (*means of conveyance*) трáнспорт; **~ café** дорóжное кафé; **public ~** общéственный трáнспорт; **have you got ~?** вы на колёсах? **3.** (*ship*) трáнспортное сýдно; **troop ~** войсковóй трáнспорт.

transport[2] [træns'pɔːt, trɑː-] *v.t.* **1.** (*convey*) перев|o-зи́ть, -езти́; транспорти́ровать (*impf., pf.*). **2.** (*send to penal colony*) отпр|авля́ть, -áвить на кáторгу. **3.** (*of emotion*): **~ed with delight** вне себя́ от рáдости.

transportable [træns'pɔːtəb(ə)l, trɑː-] *adj.* перевози́мый; (*of a sick pers.*) транспортáбельный.

transportation [,trænspɔː'teɪʃ(ə)n, ,trɑː-] *n.* (*of goods etc.*) перевóзка, транспорти́рование; (*of a convict*) ссы́лка, транспортáция.

transporter [træns'pɔːtə(r), trɑː-] *n.* транспортёр.

transpose [træns'pəʊz, trɑː-, -z'pəʊz] *v.t.* перест|авля́ть, -áвить; меня́ть, по- местáми; (*mus.*) транспони́ровать (*impf., pf.*).

transposition [,trænspə'zɪʃ(ə)n, ,trɑː-, -zpə'zɪʃ(ə)n] *n.* перестанóвка; (*mus.*) транспози́ция.

transsexual [trænz'seksjʊəl] *n.* транссексуали́ст.

adj. транссексуáльный.

transship [træn'ʃɪp, trɑː-, trænz-], **-ment** [træn'ʃɪpmənt, trɑː-, trænz-] = **tranship, -ment**

Trans-Siberian [trænz,saɪ'bɪərɪən] *adj.*: **~ Railway** транссиби́рская желéзная дорóга.

transverse ['trænzvɜːs, 'trɑː-, -'vɜːs, -ns-] *adj.* поперéчный; косóй.

transvestism [trænz'vestɪz(ə)m, trɑː-, -s'vestɪz(ə)m] *n.* трансвести́зм.

transvestite [trænz'vestaɪt, trɑː-, -s'vestaɪt] *n.* трансвести́т.

trap [træp] *n.* **1.** (*for animals etc.*) капкáн, западня́; **I shall set a ~ for the mice** я постáвлю мышелóвку; (*fig.*) ловýшка; **he fell into the ~** он попáл в ловýшку. **2.** (*light vehicle*) рессóрная двукóлка. **3.** (*mouth*) глóтка, пасть (*sl.*); **shut your ~!** заткни́сь!; закрóй глóтку!

v.t. лови́ть, поймáть в ловýшку/западню́; (*fig., catch*): **his fingers were ~ped in the door** он защеми́л пáльцы двéрью; **he felt ~ped** он почýвствовал, что зажáт в ýгол.

cpd. **~-door** *n.* люк.

trapeze [trə'piːz] *n.* трапéция; **~ artist** акробáт.

trapezium [trə'piːzɪəm] *n.* трапéция.

trapezoid ['træpɪ,zɔɪd] *n.* трапецóид.

trapper ['træpə(r)] *n.* трáппер; охóтник, стáвящий капкáны.

trappings ['træpɪŋz] *n.* (*harness*) сбрýя; (*fig.*): **the ~ of office** внéшние атрибýты (*m. pl.*) влáсти.

trash [træʃ] *n.* **1.** (*rubbishy material, writing etc.*) халтýра, макулатýра. **2.** (*US, refuse*) мýсор, отбрóсы (*m. pl.*).

cpd. **~-can** *n.* (*US*) мýсорное ведрó.

trashy ['træʃɪ] *adj.* низкопрóбный; дряннóй.

trauma ['trɔːmə, 'traʊ-] *n.* трáвма.

traumatic [trɔː'mætɪk, traʊ-] *adj.* травмати́ческий.

traumatize ['trɔːmə,taɪz, 'traʊ-] *v.t.* травми́ровать (*impf., pf.*).

travail ['træveɪl] *n.* мýки (*f. pl.*).

travel ['træv(ə)l] *n.* **1.** (*journeying*) путешéствие, поéздка; **~ bureau** бюрó путешéствий, туристи́ческое агéнтство; **he suffers from ~ sickness** он плóхо перенóсит путешéствие/дорóгу. **2.** (*movement of a part or mechanism*) ход.

v.t. путешéствовать (*impf.*) по+*d.*; éздить (*indet.*) по+*d.*; **I have ~led the whole of England** я изъéздил всю Áнглию.

v.i. путешéствовать (*impf.*); éздить, съ-; **he has been ~ling since yesterday** он со вчерáшнего дня в пути́; (*move*) дви́гаться (*impf.*); перемещáться (*impf.*); **light ~s faster than sound** скóрость свéта превышáет скóрость звýка; **his eye ~led over the scene** он обвёл глазáми всю сцéну.

traveller ['trævələ(r)] *n.* **1.** путешéственник; **~'s cheque** тури́стский чек. **2.** (*commercial ~*) коммивояжёр.

travelling ['trævəlɪŋ] *n.* путешéствие.

adj. путешéствующий; **~ library** передвижнáя библиотéка; **~ salesman** коммивояжёр.

cpd. **~-clock** *n.* дорóжные час|ы́ (*pl., g.* -óв).

traverse ['trævəs, trə'vɜːs] *n.* (*in mountaineering*) поперéчина, трáверс.

v.t. перес|екáть, -éчь.

travesty ['trævɪstɪ] *n.* шарж, парóдия; **~ of justice** парóдия на справедли́вость.

trawl [trɔːl] *n.* **(~-net)** трал.

v.t. & i. трáлить (*impf.*); **they ~ed for herring** они́ отлáвливали сельдь (трáлом).

trawler ['trɔːlə(r)] *n.* (*vessel*) трáулер.

tray [treɪ] *n.* (*for tea etc.*) поднóс; (*for correspondence*) корзи́нка.

treacherous ['tretʃərəs] *adj.* (*lit., fig.*) предáтельский; веролóмный, ковáрный; **the roads are ~** дорóги опáсны.

treachery ['tretʃərɪ] *n.* предáтельство, веролóмство.

treacle ['triːk(ə)l] *n.* пáтока.

treacly ['triːklɪ] *adj.* ли́пкий, вя́зкий.

tread [tred] *n.* **1.** (*step*) пóступь; шаги́ (*m. pl.*). **2.** (*manner or sound of walking*) похóдка. **3.** (*of tyre*) протéктор.

v.t. **1.** (*walk on*) ступáть (*impf.*) по+*d.*; шагáть (*impf.*) по+*d*; **his ambition was to ~ the boards** (*be an actor*) он мечтáл о теáтре. **2.** (*trample on*) топтáть, по-; дави́ть, раз-.

v.i.: **don't ~ on the grass** по травé не ходи́ть; (*fig.*): **he trod in his father's footsteps** он шёл по стопáм отцá; **he ~s on everybody's toes** он вéчно наступáет лю́дям на люби́мую мозóль; **we must ~ lightly in this matter** в э́той ситуáции мы должны́ дéйствовать осторóжно.

with advs.: **he trod down the earth** он утрамбовáл зéмлю; **they trod out the fire** они́ затоптáли огóнь.

cpd. **~mill** *n.* (*lit.*) топчáк; (*fig.*) однообрáзная рабóта.

treadle ['tred(ə)l] *n.* педáль.

treason ['triːz(ə)n] *n.* (госудáрственная) измéна.

treasonable ['triːzənəb(ə)l] *adj.* измéннический.

treasure ['treʒə(r)] *n.* (*precious object or person*) сокрóвище; **(~ trove)** клад; **art ~s** сокрóвища искýсства.

v.t. (*store up, esp. in memory*) храни́ть, со-; **~d memories** дороги́е воспоминáния; (*value highly*) высокó цени́ть (*impf.*).

cpd. **~-house** *n.* сокрóвищница.

treasurer ['treʒərə(r)] *n.* казначéй.

treasury ['treʒərɪ] *n.* (*lit., fig.*) сокрóвищница; (*public revenue department*) казнá; **~ note** казначéйский билéт.

treat [triːt] *n.* **1.** (*pleasure*) большóе удовóльствие; **it's a ~ to listen to him** слýшать егó — однó удовóльствие. **2.** (*defrayal of entertainment*): **he stood ~ for them all** он всех угощáл; **it's my ~!** я угощáю!

v.t. **1.** (*behave towards*) обращáться (*impf.*) с+*i.*; **he ~s me like a child** он обращáется со мной, как с ребёнком; **how is the world ~ing you?** как жизнь?; как вы поживáете? **2.** (*deem, regard*) рассмáтривать (*impf.*); отн|оси́ться, -ести́сь к+*d.*; **he ~ed it as a joke** он отнёсся к э́тому, как к шýтке. **3.** (*deal with; discuss*) трактовáть (*impf.*); рассмáтривать (*impf.*); **he ~ed the subject in detail** он подро́бно осветил те́му. **4.** (*give medical care to*) лечи́ть (*impf.*); **he was ~ed for burns** его́ лечи́ли от ожо́гов. **5.** (*apply chemical process to*) обраб|а́тывать, -о́тать. **6.** (*make a free partaker*) уго|ща́ть, -сти́ть; **he ~ed me to a drink** он поднёс мне рю́мку; **I shall ~ myself to a holiday** я устро́ю себе́ о́тпуск.

v.i. **1.** (*give an account*): **this book ~s of many subjects** в э́той кни́ге говори́тся о мно́гих веща́х. **2.** (*negotiate*) вести́ (*det.*) перегово́ры.

treatise ['tri:tɪs, -ɪz] *n.* тракта́т; нау́чный труд.

treatment ['tri:tmənt] *n.* **1.** (*handling*) обраще́ние; тракто́вка; **the subject received only superficial ~** э́той те́мы косну́лись лишь пове́рхностно. **2.** (*chem. etc.*) обрабо́тка. **3.** (*med.*) лече́ние, процеду́ра; **she is still under ~** она́ всё ещё ле́чится.

treaty ['tri:tɪ] *n.* догово́р.

treble ['treb(ə)l] *n.* (*voice*) ди́скант; (*attr.*) дисканто́вый; **~ clef** скрипи́чный ключ.

adj. тройно́й; **he earns ~ my money** он зараба́тывает втро́е бо́льше меня́.

v.t. & i. утр|а́ивать(ся), -о́ить(ся).

tree [tri:] *n.* де́рево; **family ~** родосло́вное де́рево.

cpds. **~-surgery** *n.* обре́зка дере́вьев на омоложе́ние; **~-top** *n.* верху́шка де́рева.

treeless ['tri:lɪs] *adj.* лишённый дере́вьев.

trefoil ['trefɔɪl, 'tri:-] *n.* (*plant*) кле́вер; (*decoration*) трили́стник.

trek [trek] *n.* (*migration*) переселе́ние; (*arduous journey*) похо́д; перехо́д.

v.i. пересел|я́ться, -и́ться; тащи́ться (*impf.*).

trellis ['trelɪs] *n.* шпале́ра, трелья́ж.

cpd. **~-work** *n.* решётка.

trembl|e ['tremb(ə)l] *n.* дрожь.

v.i. дрожа́ть (*impf.*); трясти́сь (*impf.*); **he was ~ing with excitement** он дрожа́л от волне́ния; **in fear and ~ing** в стра́хе и тре́пете.

tremendous [trɪ'mendəs] *adj.* грома́дный; стра́шный; (*coll., very great; splendid*) огро́мный.

tremolo ['treməlәʊ] *n.* тре́моло (*indecl.*).

tremor ['tremə(r)] *n.* сотрясе́ние, содрога́ние, дрожь; **there was a ~ in his voice** его́ го́лос дрожа́л; **earth ~** подзе́мный толчо́к.

tremulous ['tremjʊləs] *adj.* **1.** (*trembling*) дрожа́щий. **2.** (*timid*) боязли́вый, трепе́щущий.

trench [trentʃ] *n.* ров, кана́ва; (*mil.*) око́п, транше́я; **~ coat** шине́ль; **~ warfare** око́пная война́.

trenchant ['trentʃ(ə)nt] *adj.* о́стрый, ре́зкий.

trend [trend] *n.* направле́ние, тенде́нция; **set a ~** вв|оди́ть, -ести́ но́вый стиль.

cpd. **~-setter** *n.* законода́тель (*fem.* -ница) мод.

trendy ['trendɪ] *adj.* (*coll.*) мо́дный.

trepidation [ˌtrepɪ'deɪʃ(ə)n] *n.* тре́пет, дрожь; **in ~** трепеща́.

trespass ['trespəs] *n.* **1.** (*leg., offence*) правонаруше́ние; (*intrusion on property*) наруше́ние владе́ния. **2.** (*relig.*) прегреше́ние; **forgive us our ~es** оста́ви нам до́лги на́ши.

v.i. **1.** (*intrude*) вт|орга́ться, -о́ргнуться в чужи́е владе́ния; **"No ~ing"** «вход воспрещён». **2.** (*relig.*) греши́ть, со-; **those that ~ against us** те, кто про́тив нас согреша́ют.

trespasser ['trespəsə(r)] *n.* правонаруши́тель (*fem.* -ница); лицо́, вторга́ющееся в чужи́е владе́ния; **"T~s will be prosecuted"** «наруши́тели бу́дут пресле́доваться».

tress [tres] *n.* ло́кон.

trestle ['tres(ə)l] *n.* ко́з|лы (*pl., g.* -ел).

cpds. **~-bridge** *n.* мост на деревя́нных опо́рах; **~-table** *n.* стол на ко́злах.

triad ['traɪæd] *n.* (*math.*) триа́да; (*mus.*) трезву́чие.

trial ['traɪəl] *n.* **1.** (*testing, test*) испыта́ние, про́ба; **it was a ~ of strength between them** э́то была́ про́ба их сил; **I discovered the truth by ~ and error** я откры́л пра́вду эмпири́ческим путём; **why not give him a ~?** почему́ бы не взять его́ на испыта́тельный срок? **2.** (*attr.*) про́бный; **~ balloon** про́бный шар; **~ match** отбо́рочный матч; **~ run** испыта́тельный пробе́г. **3.** (*judicial examination*) суде́бный проце́сс; **he went on ~ for murder** его́ суди́ли за уби́йство; **bring to ~** привл|ека́ть, -е́чь к суду́; **the case came up for ~** наступи́л день суда́. **4.** (*annoyance, ordeal*) пережива́ние, испыта́ние.

triangle ['traɪˌæŋg(ə)l] *n.* (*geom., mus., fig.*) треуго́льник.

triangular [traɪ'æŋgjʊlə(r)] *adj.* треуго́льный.

triangulation [traɪˌæŋgjʊ'leɪʃ(ə)n] *n.* триангуля́ция.

Triassic [traɪ'æsɪk] *adj.* триа́совый.

tribal ['traɪb(ə)l] *adj.* племенно́й.

tribe [traɪb] *n.* **1.** (*racial group*) пле́мя (*nt.*), род. **2.** (*pej., group, body*) ша́тия, компа́ния.

cpd. **~sman** *n.* член пле́мени.

tribulation [ˌtrɪbjʊ'leɪʃ(ə)n] *n.* страда́ние, беда́.

tribunal [traɪ'bju:n(ə)l, trɪ-] *n.* трибуна́л.

tribune ['trɪbju:n] *n.* (*pers.*) трибу́н; (*platform*) трибу́на, эстра́да.

tributary ['trɪbjʊtərɪ] *n.* прито́к.

tribute ['trɪbju:t] *n.* (*payment*) дань; (*token of respect etc.*) дань; до́лжное; **he paid ~ to his wife's help** он вы́разил благода́рность свое́й жене́ за по́мощь.

trick [trɪk] *n.* **1.** (*dodge, device*) шту́ка, приём, хи́трости (*f. pl.*); **he knows all the ~s of the trade** он зна́ет все ходы́ и вы́ходы; **he tried every ~ in the book** он примени́л все изве́стные приёмы. **2.** (*deception, mischievous act*) шу́тка; обма́н, трюк; **he is always playing ~s on me** он всегда́ надо мной подшу́чивает; **he is up to his old ~s again** он сно́ва приня́лся за свои́ проде́лки; **a ~ of the light** опти́ческий обма́н; **a dirty ~** по́длость; **play a dirty ~ on s.o.** подложи́ть (*pf.*) кому́-н. свинью́; **he is good at card ~s** он ло́вко де́лает ка́рточные фо́кусы. **3.** (*feat*) шту́ка; **their dog can do a lot of ~s** их соба́ка зна́ет мно́го кома́нд. **4.** (*knack*) хва́тка; **there's a ~ to operating this machine** что́бы обраща́ться с э́той маши́ной, нужна́ осо́бая сноро́вка. **5.** (*at cards*) взя́тка; **he never misses a ~** (*fig.*) он никогда́ не упу́стит слу́чая.

v.t. обма́н|ывать, -у́ть; над|ува́ть, -у́ть; **they ~ed him out of a fortune** они́ вы́манили у него́ ма́ссу де́нег.

trickery ['trɪkərɪ] *n.* обма́н, надува́тельство.

trickle ['trɪk(ə)l] *n.* стру́йка.

v.t. ка́пать (*impf.*).

v.i. сочи́ться (*impf.*); ка́пать (*impf.*); (*fig.*): **the news ~d out** но́вости просочи́лись.

trickster ['trɪkstə(r)] *n.* обма́нщик.

tricky ['trɪkɪ] *adj.* (*crafty, deceitful*) хи́трый; (*awkward*) сло́жный, мудрёный.

tricolour ['trɪkələ(r), 'traɪˌkʌlə(r)] *n.* (*flag*) трёхцве́тный флаг; (*French*) францу́зский флаг.

tricot ['trɪkəʊ, 'tri:-] *n.* трико́ (*indecl.*).

tricycle ['traɪsɪk(ə)l] *n.* трёхколёсный велосипе́д.

trident ['traɪd(ə)nt] *n.* трезу́бец.

tried [traɪd] *adj.* (*tested*) испы́танный, прове́ренный.

trier ['traɪə(r)] *n.* (*persevering person*) стара́тельный челове́к.

trifle ['traɪf(ə)l] *n.* **1.** (*thg. of small value or importance*) пустя́к, ме́лочь; **she gets upset over ~s** она́ огорча́ется по пустяка́м; (*small sum*) небольша́я су́мма. **2. a ~** (*as adv.*) немно́го; **I was just a ~ angry** я чу́точку рассерди́лся. **3.** (*sweet dish*) бискви́т со сби́тыми сли́вками.

v.i. относи́ться (*impf.*) несерьёзно к+*d.*; **he ~d with her affections** он игра́л её чу́вствами; **he is not a man to be ~d with** с ним шу́тки пло́хи.

trifling ['traɪflɪŋ] *adj.* пустяко́вый; незначи́тельный.

trigger ['trɪgə(r)] *n.* спусково́й крючо́к.

v.t. (*usu.* ~ **off**) вызыва́ть, вы́звать; да|ва́ть, -ть нача́ло +*d.*; **his action ~ed off a chain of events** его́ посту́пок повлёк за собо́й цепь собы́тий.

trigonometrical [ˌtrɪgənə'metrɪk(ə)l] *adj.* тригономе-три́ческий.

trigonometry [ˌtrɪgə'nɒmɪtrɪ] *n.* тригономе́трия.

trilateral [traɪ'lætər(ə)l] *adj.* трёхсторо́нний.

trilby ['trɪlbɪ] *n.* мя́гкая фе́тровая шля́па.

trill [trɪl] *n.* трель.

v.i.: **the birds were ~ing** пти́цы залива́лись тре́лью.

trillion ['trɪljən] *n.* (*10^{18}*) квинтильо́н; (*US*, *10^{12}*) триллио́н.

trilogy ['trɪlədʒɪ] *n.* трило́гия.

trim [trɪm] *n.* **1.** (*order*, *fitness*) поря́док; состоя́ние гото́вности; **everything was in good ~** всё бы́ло в образцо́вом поря́дке; **we must get into ~ before the race** нам ну́жно прийти́ в фо́рму пе́ред соревнова́нием. **2.** (*light cut*) подре́зка, стри́жка; **your hair needs a ~** вам ну́жно подровня́ть во́лосы.

adj. аккура́тный, опря́тный; **she has a ~ figure** у неё стро́йная фигу́рка.

v.t. **1.** (*cut back to desired shape or size*) подр|еза́ть, -е́зать; подр|а́внивать, -овня́ть; **he was ~ming the hedge** он подра́внивал и́згородь. **2.** (*decorate*) отде́л|ывать, -ать; **a hat ~med with fur** ша́пка, отде́ланная ме́хом.

with advs.: ~ **away,** ~ **off** *vv.t.* подстр|ига́ть, -и́чь; подре́з|ывать (*or* подреза́ть), -ать.

trimaran ['traɪməˌræn] *n.* тримара́н.

trimming ['trɪmɪŋ] *n.* (*on dress etc.*) отде́лка; (*pl.*, *cul.*) гарни́р, припра́ва; **roast duck and all the ~s** жа́реная у́тка с гарни́ром.

trinitrotoluene [traɪˌnaɪtrə'tɒljʊˌi:n] = **TNT**

Trinity ['trɪnɪtɪ] *n.* Тро́ица; **T~ Sunday** Тро́ицын день.

trinket ['trɪŋkɪt] *n.* безделу́шка.

trio ['tri:əʊ] *n.* (*group of three*) тро́йка; (*mus.*) три́о (*indecl.*).

trip [trɪp] *n.* **1.** (*excursion*) пое́здка, путеше́ствие; **he has gone on a ~ to Paris** он пое́хал (ненадо́лго) в Пари́ж. **2.** (*stumble*) спотыка́ние.

v.t. **1.** (*cause to stumble*; *also* ~ **up**) ста́вить, по-подно́жку +*d.*; (*fig.*) запу́т|ывать, -ать; **counsel tried to ~ the witness up** адвока́т пыта́лся сбить свиде́теля. **2.** (*release from catch*) расцепля́ть (*impf.*); выключа́ть (*impf*).

v.i. **1.** (*run or dance lightly*) пританцо́вывать (*impf.*) вприпля́ску; **she came ~ping down the stairs** она́ легко́ сбежа́ла вниз по ле́стнице. **2.** (*stumble*; *also* ~ **up**) спот|ыка́ться, -кну́ться; **he ~ped over the rug** он споткну́лся о ковёр; (*fig.*, *commit error*) ошиб|а́ться, -и́ться.

cpds. **~-hammer** *n.* па́дающий мо́лот; **~-wire** *n.* ми́нная про́волока.

tripartite [traɪ'pɑ:taɪt] *adj.* трёхсторо́нний.

tripe [traɪp] *n.* (*offal*) требуха́; (*coll.*, *rubbish*) чепуха́.

triple ['trɪp(ə)l] *adj.* тройно́й, утро́енный.

v.t. & i. утр|а́ивать(ся), -о́ить(ся).

triplet ['trɪplɪt] *n.* **1.** (*one of three children born together*) тройня́шка; **~s** (*children*) тро́йня (*sg.*). **2.** (*mus.*) трио́ль.

triplex ['trɪpleks] *adj.*: ~ **glass** три́плекс, безоско́лочное стекло́.

triplicate ['trɪplɪkət] *n.*: **in ~** в трёх экземпля́рах.

tripod ['traɪpɒd] *n.* трено́га, трено́жник.

tripper ['trɪpə(r)] *n.* экскурса́нт (*fem.* -ка).

triptych ['trɪptɪk] *n.* три́птих.

trite [traɪt] *adj.* бана́льный, изби́тый.

triumph ['traɪəmf, -ʌmf] *n.* торжество́; **they came home in ~** они́ верну́лись с побе́дой.

v.i. **1.** (*be victorious*) побе|жда́ть, -ди́ть; **justice will ~ in the end** в конце́ концо́в справедли́вость восторжеству́ет; **he ~ed over adversity** он одоле́л невзго́ды. **2.** (*exult*) ликова́ть (*impf.*); торжествова́ть (*impf.*).

triumphal [traɪ'ʌmf(ə)l] *adj.* триумфа́льный.

triumphant [traɪ'ʌmf(ə)nt] *adj.* (*victorious*) победоно́сный; (*exultant*) торжеству́ющий.

triumvir ['traɪəmvɪə(r), -'ʌmvə(r)] *n.* триумви́р.

triumvirate [traɪ'ʌmvɪrət] *n.* триумвира́т.

trivet ['trɪvɪt] *n.* (*tripod*) подста́вка; (*bracket*) тага́н.

trivia ['trɪvɪə] *n.* ме́лочи (*f. pl.*).

trivial ['trɪvɪəl] *adj.* (*trifling*) ме́лкий; незначи́тельный; (*commonplace*, *everyday*) обы́денный; (*shallow*, *artificial*) пове́рхностный.

triviality [ˌtrɪvɪ'ælɪtɪ] *n.* незначи́тельность.

trivialize ['trɪvɪəˌlaɪz] *v.t.* оп|ошля́ть, -о́шлить.

trochaic [trə'keɪɪk] *adj.* трохеи́ческий.

trochee ['trəʊki:, -kɪ] *n.* хоре́й, трохе́й.

troglodyte ['trɒgləˌdaɪt] *n.* троглоди́т.

troika ['trɔɪkə] *n.* тро́йка.

Trojan ['trəʊdʒ(ə)n] *n.* троя́н|ец (*fem.* -ка); (*fig.*): **he worked like a ~** он до́блестно труди́лся; он рабо́тал как вол.

adj. троя́нский; ~ **horse** (*fig.*) троя́нский конь.

troll[1] [trəʊl] *n.* (*myth.*) тролль (*m.*).

troll[2] [trəʊl] *v.t. & i.* (*sing*) распева́ть (*impf.*).

trolley ['trɒlɪ] *n.* (*handcart*) теле́жка; (*table on wheels*) сто́лик на колёсиках; (*US*, *street-car*) трамва́й.

cpds. **~-bus** *n.* тролле́йбус; **~-car** *n.* (*US*) трамва́й.

trollop ['trɒləp] *n.* (*slattern*) растрёпа, неря́ха; (*prostitute*) проститу́тка, шлю́ха.

trombone [trɒm'bəʊn] *n.* тромбо́н.

trombonist [trɒm'bəʊnɪst] *n.* тромбони́ст.

troop [tru:p] *n.* **1.** (*assembled group of persons*) отря́д. **2.** (*mil. unit*) батаре́я; ро́та. **3.** (*pl.*, *soldiers*) войск|а́ (*pl.*, *g.* —).

v.t.: **~ing the colour** церемо́ния вы́носа зна́мени.

v.i. дви́|гаться, -нуться толпо́й; **the children ~ed out of school** де́ти стро́ем вы́шли из шко́лы.

cpds. **~-carrier** *n.* (*mil.*) транспортёр для перево́зки ли́чного соста́ва; **~ship** *n.* тра́нспорт для перево́зки войск.

trooper ['tru:pə(r)] *n.* **1.** (*soldier*) кавалери́ст; танки́ст; **he swore like a ~** он руга́лся как изво́зчик. **2.** (*US*, *policeman*) полице́йский.

trophy ['trəʊfɪ] *n.* трофе́й; (*prize*, *also*) приз.

tropic ['trɒpɪk] *n.* тро́пик; **T~ of Cancer** тро́пик Ра́ка; **T~ of Capricorn** тро́пик Козеро́га.

tropical ['trɒpɪk(ə)l] *adj.* тропи́ческий.

trot [trɒt] *n.* **1.** (*gait*, *pace*) рысь; **at a gentle ~** лёгкой ры́сью; (*fig.*) **I have been on the ~ all day** (*moving about*) я был на нога́х це́лый день. **2.** (*run or ride at this pace*) прогу́лка, пробе́жка; **she took her horse for a ~** она́ взяла́ ло́шадь на вы́ездку.

v.t. **1.** (*exercise*) выгу́ливать (*impf.*); **he ~ted his horse in the park** он прогу́ливал ло́шадь в па́рке.

v.i. (*of a horse*) идти́ (*det.*) ры́сью; (*of pers.*) семени́ть (*impf.*).

with advs. ~ **along,** ~ **off** *vv.i.* (*coll.*) отпр|авля́ться, -а́виться; **I must be ~ting off home** мне пора́ (отправля́ться) домо́й; ~ **out** *v.t.* (*coll.*): **he ~ted out the usual excuses** он, как всегда́, вы́ставил ма́ссу отгово́рок.

trotter ['trɒtə(r)] *n.* (*horse*) рыси́стая ло́шадь; (*animal's foot*) но́жка; **pig's ~s** свины́е но́жки.

troubadour ['tru:bəˌdɔ:(r)] *n.* трубаду́р.

trouble ['trʌb(ə)l] *n.* **1.** (*grief*, *anxiety*) волне́ние, трево́га; (*misfortune*, *affliction*) го́ре, беда́; **his ~s are over** тепе́рь все его́ несча́стья позади́; **there is ~ brewing** быть беде́. **2.** (*difficulty*, *difficulties*) хло́п|оты (*pl.*, *g.* -о́т); затрудне́ние; **money ~s** де́нежные затрудне́ния; **I am having ~ with the car** у меня́ непола́дки (*f. pl.*) с маши́ной; **don't make ~**

for me не создава́йте мне ли́шних тру́дностей; **what's the ~?** в чём де́ло?; **the ~ is (that) ...** беда́ в том, что...; **that's the ~** вот в чём беда́; **without any ~** легко́. **3.** (*predicament*): **he's always getting into ~** он ве́чно попада́ет в исто́рии; **he is in ~ with the police** у него́ неприя́тности с поли́цией; **ask for ~** лезть (*det.*) на рожо́н; **that's asking for ~** э́так то́лько нарвёшься на неприя́тности. **4.** (*inconvenience*): **I don't want to put you to any ~** я не хочу́ вас затрудня́ть; **he saved me the ~** он изба́вил меня́ от э́той необходи́мости. **5.** (*pains, care, effort*) забо́та, труд, хло́п|оты (*pl., g.* -о́т); **she took a lot of ~ over the cake** она́ приложи́ла мно́го стара́ния для приготовле́ния пирога́; **thank you for all your ~** спаси́бо за все ва́ши хло́поты; **it is not worth the ~** не сто́ит хлопо́т. **6.** (*disease, ailment*) неду́г, боле́знь; **he has heart ~** у него́ больно́е се́рдце. **7.** (*unrest, civil commotion*) волне́ния (*nt. pl.*); беспоря́дки (*m. pl.*); **labour ~s** волне́ния среди́ рабо́чих; **~ spot** горя́чая то́чка.

v.t. **1.** (*agitate, disturb, worry*) трево́жить (*impf.*); волнова́ть (*impf.*); **don't let it ~ you** не принима́йте э́то бли́зко к се́рдцу; **~d times** сму́тные времена́. **2.** (*afflict*) беспоко́ить (*impf.*); му́чить (*impf.*); **he is ~d with a cough** его́ му́чит ка́шель; **my back ~s me** у меня́ боли́т спина́. **3.** (*put to inconvenience*) затрудн|я́ть, -и́ть; **may I ~ you for a match?** мо́жно попроси́ть у вас спи́чку?; **don't ~ yourself** не беспоко́йтесь; **sorry to ~ you!** прости́те за беспоко́йство!

v.i. труди́ться (*impf.*); беспоко́иться (*impf.*); **don't ~ about that** не беспоко́йтесь об э́том; **don't ~ to come and meet me** не сто́ит меня́ встреча́ть.

cpds. **~-free** *adj.* (*reliable*) надёжный; безотка́зный; **~-maker** *n.* скло́чни|к (*fem.* -ца); (*instigator of ~*) смутья́н (*fem.* -ка); **~-shooter** *n.* авари́йный монтёр; (*fig.*) уполномо́ченный по ула́живанию конфли́ктов.

troublesome ['trʌb(ə)lsəm] *adj.* тру́дный; хлопотный; **a ~ cough** мучи́тельный ка́шель.

trough [trɒf] *n.* **1.** (*for animals*) коры́то, корму́шка; (*for dough*) квашня́; (*for water*) жёлоб, лото́к. **2.** (*meteor.*) фронт ни́зкого давле́ния.

trounce [traʊns] *v.t.* (*thrash*) поро́ть, вы́-; (*defeat*) разб|ива́ть, -и́ть.

troupe [tru:p] *n.* тру́ппа.

trouser|s ['traʊzəz] *n.* штан|ы́ (*pl., g.* -о́в), брю́ки (*pl., g.* —); **a pair of ~s** па́ра брюк.

cpds. **~-leg** *n.* штани́на; **~-suit** *n.* брю́чный костю́м.

trousseau ['tru:səʊ] *n.* прида́ное.

trout [traʊt] *n.* форе́ль.

trowel ['traʊəl] *n.* (*for bricklaying etc.*) мастеро́к; (*for gardening*) (садо́вый) садо́к, лопа́тка.

truancy ['tru:ənsɪ] *n.* прогу́л.

truant ['tru:ənt] *n.* прогу́льщик; **did you ever play ~?** вы когда́-нибудь прогу́ливали уро́ки?

truce [tru:s] *n.* переми́рие; (*respite*) передышка.

truck[1] [trʌk] *n.* (*railway wagon*) откры́тая това́рная платфо́рма; (*lorry*) грузови́к; (*barrow*) теле́жка.

truck[2] [trʌk] *n.*: **I'll have no ~ with him** (*fig.*) я не жела́ю име́ть с ним никаки́х дел.

truculent ['trʌkjʊlənt] *adj.* агресси́вный, драчли́вый.

trudge [trʌdʒ] *n.* дли́нный/тру́дный путь.

v.i. тащи́ться (*impf.*).

true [tru:] *n.* (*alignment, adjustment*): **the wheel is out of ~** колесо́ пло́хо устано́влено.

adj. **1.** (*in accordance with fact*) ве́рный, правди́вый; **a ~ story** правди́вый расска́з; **is it ~ that he is married?** э́то пра́вда, что он жена́т?; **all my dreams came ~** все мои́ мечты́ сбы́лись/осуществи́лись; (*concessive*): **~, it will cost more** разуме́ется, э́то бу́дет сто́ить бо́льше. **2.** (*in accordance with reason, principle, standard; genuine*) правди́вый; настоя́щий; и́стинный; **it is not a ~ comparison** э́то ло́жное сравне́ние; **the ~ price is much higher** действи́тельная/настоя́щая цена́ намно́го вы́ше. **3.** (*conforming accurately*) пра́вильный; **~ to life** реалисти́ческий. **4.** (*loyal, faithful; dependable*) пре́данный, ве́рный; надёжный; **he was always a ~ friend to me** он был мне всегда́ пре́данным дру́гом; **he remained ~ to his word** он сдержа́л сло́во.

adv. пра́вильно, ве́рно; **his story rings ~** его́ расска́з звучи́т убеди́тельно; **he aimed ~** он то́чно прице́лился.

cpd. **~-love** *n.* (*sweetheart*) возлю́бленн|ый, -ая.

truffle ['trʌf(ə)l] *n.* трю́фель (*m.*).

truism ['tru:ɪz(ə)m] *n.* трюи́зм.

truly ['tru:lɪ] *adv.* **1.** (*accurately; truthfully*) и́скренне; правди́во. **2.** (*loyally*) ве́рно. **3.** (*sincerely*) и́скренне; **yours ~** (*at end of letter*) пре́данный Вам. **4.** (*genuinely*) и́скренне; действи́тельно; **a ~ memorable occasion** пои́стине незабыва́емое собы́тие.

trump [trʌmp] *n.* **(~ card)** ко́зырь (*m.*), козырна́я ка́рта; (*fig.*): **he played his ~ card** он вы́ложил свой ко́зырь; **the weather turned up ~s** нам (неожи́данно) повезло́ с пого́дой.

v.t. бить, по- ко́зырем.

with adv.: **~ up** *v.t.* фабрикова́ть, с-.

trumpet ['trʌmpɪt] *n.* **1.** (*instrument*) труба́; **blow one's own ~** (*fig.*) хвали́ться (*impf.*). **2.** (*object so shaped*) тру́бка; **ear-~** слухова́я тру́бка.

v.t. & i. **1.** (*proclaim*) труби́ть, про-. **2.** (*of an elephant*) реве́ть, про.

trumpeter ['trʌmpɪtə(r)] *n.* труба́ч.

truncate [trʌŋ'keɪt, 'trʌŋ-] *v.t.* ус|ека́ть, -е́чь; **a ~d cone** усечённый ко́нус; **his speech was ~d** его́ ре́чь уре́зали.

truncheon ['trʌntʃ(ə)n] *n.* полице́йская дуби́нка.

trundle ['trʌnd(ə)l] *v.t. & i.* кати́ть(ся) (*impf.*).

trunk [trʌŋk] *n.* **1.** (*of tree*) ствол. **2.** (*of body*) ту́ловище. **3.** (*box*) сунду́к. **4.** (*of elephant*) хо́бот. **5.** (*pl., garment*) пла́в|ки (*pl., g.* -ок). **6.** (*US, boot of car*) бага́жник.

cpds. **~-call** *n.* вы́зов по междугоро́дному телефо́ну; **~-line** *n.* (*rail.*) магистра́ль; (*teleph.*) междугоро́дная связь; **~-road** *n.* магистра́льная доро́га.

truss [trʌs] *n.* **1.** (*structural support*) стропи́льная фе́рма. **2.** (*surgical support*) грыжево́й банда́ж.

v.t. **1.** (*support*) укреп|ля́ть, -и́ть. **2.** (*tie up; also ~ up*) свя́з|ывать, -а́ть.

trust [trʌst] *n.* **1.** (*firm belief; confidence*) дове́рие; ве́ра; **I place perfect ~ in him** я доверя́ю ему́ по́лностью; **he takes everything on ~** он всё принима́ет на ве́ру. **2.** (*credit*) креди́т; **goods supplied on ~** това́ры, предоста́вленные в креди́т. **3.** (*responsibility*) отве́тственность; **a position of ~** отве́тственный пост. **5.** (*leg.*) довери́тельная со́бственность; **property held in ~** иму́щество, управля́емое по дове́ренности. **6.** (*association of companies*) трест.

v.t. **1.** (*have confidence in, rely on*) дов|еря́ть, -е́рить +*d.*; **he is not to he ~ed** ему́ нельзя́ доверя́ть; **I wouldn't ~ him with my money** я бы ему́ свои́х де́нег не дове́рил **2.** (*entrust*) вв|еря́ть, -е́рить. **3.** (*earnestly hope*) наде́яться (*impf.*); полага́ть (*impf.*).

v.i. **1.** (*have faith, confidence*) дов|еря́ться, -е́риться. **2.** (*commit o.s. with confidence*) наде́яться (*impf.*); **he ~ed to luck** он (по)наде́ялся на сча́стье.

trustee [trʌs'ti:] *n.* довери́тельный со́бственник; опеку́н.

trusteeship [trʌs'ti:ʃɪp] *n.* опе́ка, попечи́тельство.

trustful ['trʌstfʊl] *adj.* дове́рчивый.

trusting ['trʌstɪŋ] *adj.* дове́рчивый; наи́вный.

trustworthiness ['trʌst,wɜːðɪnɪs] *n.* надёжность.
trustworthy ['trʌst,wɜːðɪ] *adj.* надёжный.
trusty ['trʌstɪ]*adj.* ве́рный, надёжный.
truth [truːθ] *n.* пра́вда; (*verity, true saying*) и́стина; **the ~ is; to tell the ~** по пра́вде сказа́ть; **in ~** в са́мом де́ле.
truthful ['truːθfʊl] *adj.* (*of pers.*) правди́вый; (*of statement etc., also*) ве́рный, то́чный.
truthfulness ['truːθfʊlnɪs] *n.* правди́вость; ве́рность, то́чность.
try [traɪ] *n.* **1.** (*attempt*) попы́тка. **2.** (*test*) испыта́ние; про́ба; **why not give it a ~?** а почему́ бы не попро́бовать? **3.** (*Rugby football*) прохо́д с мячо́м.
v.t. **1.** (*attempt*) пыта́ться, по-; стара́ться, по-; **he tried his best** он стара́лся изо всех сил; **he tried hard** он о́чень стара́лся. **2.** (*sample*) про́бовать, по-; (*taste*) отве́д|ывать, -ать; (*experiment with*) **have you tried aspirin?** вы аспири́н про́бовали? **3.** (*leg.*): **he was tried for murder** его́ суди́ли за уби́йство; **the judge tried the case** судья́ вёл проце́сс. **4.** (*subject to strain*) утом|ля́ть, -и́ть; раздража́ть (*impf.*); му́чить (*impf.*); **he tries my patience** он испы́тывает моё терпе́ние; **a ~ing situation** тру́дное положе́ние. **5.** (*test*) испы́т|ывать, -а́ть; пров|еря́ть, -е́рить; подв|ерга́ть, -е́ргнуть испыта́нию; про́бовать, по-; **I shall ~ my luck again** я ещё раз попыта́ю сча́стья; **a tried remedy** испы́танное сре́дство.
v.i.: **~ harder next time!** в сле́дующий раз приложи́те бо́льше уси́лий!; **I tried for a prize** я добива́лся при́за; я претендова́л на приз.
with advs.: **~ on** *v.t.* прим|еря́ть, -е́рить; **~ out** *v.t.* испы́т|ывать, -а́ть; опро́бовать (*pf.*); **he tried out the idea on his friends** он подели́лся свои́м за́мыслом с друзья́ми, что́бы узна́ть их реа́кцию.
cpds. **~-out** *n.* прове́рка, про́ба; **~-square** *n.* уго́льник.
tryst [trɪst] *n.* назна́ченная встре́ча, свида́ние.
tsar, tzar [zɑː(r)] *n.* царь (*m.*).
tsarina, tzarina [zɑː'riːnə] *n.* цари́ца.
tsarism ['zɑːrɪz(ə)m] *n.* цари́зм.
tsarist ['zɑːrɪst] *adj.* ца́рский.
tsetse(-fly) ['tsetsɪ, 'tetsɪ] *n.* му́ха цеце́ (*indecl.*).
tub [tʌb] *n.* **1.** лоха́нь, уша́т. **2.** (*bath*) ва́нна. **3.** (*coll., old boat*) ста́рое коры́то.
tuba ['tjuːbə] *n.* ту́ба.
tubby ['tʌbɪ] *adj.* (*of pers.*) коротконо́гий и то́лстый.
tube [tjuːb] *n.* **1.** (*of metal, glass etc.*) труба́, тру́бка; **(test-~)** проби́рка. **2.** (*of paint, toothpaste etc.*) тю́бик. **3.** (*inner ~ of tyre*) ка́мера (ши́ны). **4.** (*organ of body*) бронх; **bronchial ~s** ме́лкие бро́нхи. **5.** (*underground railway*) метро́ (*indecl.*); **travel by ~** е́хать (*det.*) на метро́.
cpd. **~-station** *n.* ста́нция метро́.
tuber ['tjuːbə(r)] *n.* (*bot.*) клу́бень (*m.*).
tubercle ['tjuːbək(ə)l] *n.* ме́лкий клу́бень; тубе́ркул.
tubercular [tjʊ'bɜːkjʊlə(r)] *adj.* туберкулёзный.
tuberculosis [tjʊˌbɜːkjʊ'ləʊsɪs] *n.* туберкулёз.
tuberose ['tjuːbəˌrəʊs] *n.* тубero̐за.
tubular ['tjuːbjʊlə(r)] *adj.* тру́бчатый.
TUC (*abbr. of* ***Trades Union Congress***) Всебрита́нский конгре́сс тредюнио́нов.
tuck[1] [tʌk] *n.* (*fold in garment*) скла́дка, сбо́рка.
v.t. (*stow*) пря́тать, с-; под|бира́ть, -обра́ть (под себя́); **he ~ed his legs under the table** он спря́тал но́ги под стол.
with advs.: **~ away** *v.t.* запря́т|ывать, -ать; **~ in** *v.t.* запр|авля́ть, -а́вить; **~ up** *v.t.* под|вёртывать, -верну́ть; **he ~ed up his shirt sleeves** он засучи́л рукава́; **she ~ed up her skirt** она́ подобрала́ ю́бку; **they ~ed the children up (in bed)** дете́й уложи́ли в крова́ть (и подоткну́ли одея́ло).
tuck[2] [tʌk] *n.* (*coll., eatables*) сла́сти (*f. pl.*).
v.i.: **they ~ed into their supper** они́ уплета́ли у́жин за о́бе щеки́; **~ in!** нава́ливайтесь!
cpds. **~-box** *n.* коро́бка для сла́достей; **~-shop** *n.* конди́терская.
Tudor ['tjuːdə(r)] *adj.* эпо́хи Тюдо́ров; (*archit.*) позднеготи́ческий.
Tuesday ['tjuːzdeɪ, -dɪ] *n.* вто́рник.
tuft [tʌft] *n.* (*of grass, hair etc.*) пучо́к.
tufted ['tʌftɪd] *adj.*: (*of bird*) с хохолко́м.
tug [tʌg] *n.* **1.** (*pull*) рыво́к, дёрганье; **he gave a ~ at the rope** он дёрнул за верёвку. **2.** (*boat*) букси́р.
v.t. тащи́ть (*impf.*); тяну́ть (*impf.*).
v.i. дёргать; **he ~ged at my sleeve** он дёрнул меня́ за рука́в.
cpd. **~-of-war** *n.* перетя́гивание на кана́те.
tuition [tjuː'ɪʃ(ə)n] *n.* обуче́ние.
tulip ['tjuːlɪp] *n.* тюльпа́н.
tulle [tjuːl] *n.* тюль (*m.*).
tumble ['tʌmb(ə)l] *n.* **1.** (*fall*) паде́ние; **take a ~** упа́сть (*pf.*). **2.** (*acrobatic feat*) кувырка́нье.
v.t. бр|оса́ть, -о́сить; опроки́|дывать, -нуть; **we were all ~d out of the bus** нас вы́бросило из авто́буса.
v.i. **1.** (*fall*) свали́ться (*pf.*); скати́ться (*pf.*); **the child ~d downstairs** ребёнок скати́лся с ле́стницы; **he ~d into bed** он бро́сился в крова́ть. **2.** (*fig.*): **I ~d to his meaning** до меня́ дошло́, что он име́л в виду́.
with advs.: **the puppies ~d about on the floor** щеня́та кувырка́лись на полу́; **the house seemed about to ~ down** дом, каза́лось, вот-во́т развали́тся; **he often ~s over** он ча́сто спотыка́ется.
cpds. **~down** *adj.* развали́вшийся; полуразру́шенный; **~-drier** *n.* электри́ческая суши́лка для белья́.
tumbler ['tʌmblə(r)] *n.* **1.** (*drinking-vessel*) стака́н. **2.** (*mechanism*) реверси́вный механи́зм. **3.** (*acrobat*) акроба́т. **4.** (*pigeon*) ту́рман.
tumid ['tjuːmɪd] *adj.* распу́хший; (*fig.*) напы́щенный.
tummy ['tʌmɪ] *n.* (*coll.*) живо́т; (*dim., e.g. baby's*) живо́тик.
cpds. **~-ache** *n.* боль в живо́те; **~-button** *n.* пупо́к.
tumour ['tjuːmə(r)] *n.* о́пухоль.
tumult ['tjuːmʌlt] *n.* шум; сумато́ха.
tumultuous [tjʊ'mʌltjʊəs] *adj.* шу́мный, беспоко́йный; **he received a ~ welcome** ему́ устро́или бу́рную встре́чу.
tuna ['tjuːnə] *n.* (голубо́й) туне́ц.
tundra ['tʌndrə] *n.* ту́ндра.
tune [tjuːn] *n.* **1.** (*melody*) мело́дия; моти́в; **the ~ goes like this** моти́в тако́й; (*fig.*) тон; **he will soon change his ~** он ско́ро запоёт ина́че; **I paid up, to the ~ of £30** я заплати́л це́лых 30 фу́нтов. **2.** (*correct pitch; consonance*) строй; настро́енность; **you are not singing in ~** вы фальши́вите; **the piano is out of ~** фортепья́но расстро́ено; (*fig.*) согла́сие; гармо́ния.
v.t. **1.** (*bring to right pitch*) настр|а́ивать, -о́ить; **the instrument needs tuning** инструме́нт нужда́ется в настро́йке; **tuning-fork** камерто́н. **2.** (*adjust running of*) настр|а́ивать, -о́ить; регули́ровать (*impf.*).
with advs.: **~ in** *v.t. & i.* настр|а́ивать(ся), -о́ить(ся); **he ~d in to the BBC** он настро́ил свой приёмник на Би-Би-Си́; **~ up** настр|а́ивать(ся), -о́ить(ся); **he ~d up his guitar** он настро́ил гита́ру.
tuneful ['tjuːnfʊl] *adj.* музыка́льный, мелоди́чный.
tuneless ['tjuːnlɪs] *adj.* немузыка́льный, немелоди́чный.
tuner ['tjuːnə(r)] *n.* (*of pianos etc.*) настро́йщик.
tungsten ['tʌŋst(ə)n] *n.* вольфра́м; (*attr.*) вольфра́мовый.
tunic ['tjuːnɪk] *n.* (*ancient garment*) туни́ка; (*woman's blouse*) блу́зка, со́бранная в та́лии; (*part of uniform*) ки́тель (*m.*).

tuning ['tju:nɪŋ] *n.* настро́йка, регулиро́вка.
Tunisia [tju:'nɪzɪə] *n.* Туни́с.
tunnel ['tʌn(ə)l] *n.* тонне́ль (*m.*), тунне́ль (*m.*).
v.t.: **they ~led their way out (of prison)** они́ сде́лали подко́п и бежа́ли.
v.i. про|кла́дывать, -ложи́ть тонне́ль.
tunny(-fish) ['tʌnɪ] *n.* туне́ц.
tuppence ['tʌpəns] *n.* (*coll.*) два пе́нса; **I don't care ~** мне наплева́ть (*coll.*).
tuppenny ['tʌpənɪ] *adj.* (*coll.*) двухпе́нсовый.
cpd. **~-ha'penny** *adj.* (*fig.*) грошо́вый. ничто́жный.
turban ['tɜ:bən] *n.* тюрба́н, чалма́.
turbid ['tɜ:bɪd] *adj.* му́тный; (*fig.*) тума́нный.
turbidity [,tɜ:'bɪdɪtɪ] *n.* му́тность; (*fig.*) тума́нность.
turbine ['tɜ:baɪn] *n.* турби́на.
turbo-jet ['tɜ:bəʊ,dʒet] *n.* турбореакти́вный самолёт.
turbo-prop ['tɜ:bəʊ,prɒp] *n.* турбовинтово́й самолёт.
turbot ['tɜ:bət] *n.* белоко́рый па́лтус.
turbulence ['tɜ:bjʊləns] *n.* бу́рность; (*aeron.*) турбуле́нтность, (*coll.*) болта́нка; (*fig.*) беспоко́йство.
turbulent ['tɜ:bjʊlənt] *adj.* бу́рный; (*fig.*) беспоко́йный, неукроти́мый.
tureen [tjʊə'ri:n, tə-] *n.* су́пница; су́пник.
turf [tɜ:f] *n.* **1.** (*grassy topsoil*) дёрн; (*peat*) торф; **a cottage thatched with turves** до́мик под земляно́й кры́шей. **2.** (*racing*): **a devotee of the ~** завсегда́тай бего́в; **~ accountant** букме́кер.
v.t. **1.** (*cover with ~; also ~* **over**) покр|ыва́ть, -ы́ть дёрном. **2. ~ out** (*coll., eject*) вышвы́ривать, вы́швырнуть.
turgid ['tɜ:dʒɪd] *adj.* (*fig.*) напы́щенный.
Turk [tɜ:k] *n.* ту́р|ок (*fem.* -ча́нка).
Turkey ['tɜ:kɪ] *n.* **1.** (*country*) Ту́рция. **2.** (**t~**: *bird*) инд|ю́к (*fem.* -е́йка); (*as food*) индю́шка.
Turkic ['tɜ:kɪk] *adj.* тю́ркский.
Turkish ['tɜ:kɪʃ] *n.* туре́цкий язы́к.
adj. туре́цкий; **~ bath** туре́цкие ба́ни (*f. pl.*); **~ delight** раха́т-луку́м; **~ towel** махро́вое полоте́нце.
Turkmen ['tɜ:kmən] *n.* (*pers.*) туркме́н (*fem.* -ка); (*language*) туркме́нский язы́к.
adj. туркме́нский.
Turkmenistan [tɜ:kmenɪ'stɑ:n] *n.* Туркмениста́н.
turmeric ['tɜ:mərɪk] *n.* курку́ма.
turmoil ['tɜ:mɔɪl] *n.* беспоря́док; смяте́ние.
turn [tɜ:n] *n.* **1.** (*rotation*) поворо́т, оборо́т; **a ~ of the handle** поворо́т ру́чки; **the meat was done to a ~** мя́со бы́ло поджа́рено как раз в ме́ру. **2.** (*change of direction*) измене́ние направле́ния; поворо́т; **a ~ in the road** поворо́т доро́ги; **I took a right ~** я поверну́л напра́во; **he made an about ~ in policy** он сде́лал поворо́т на 180° в поли́тике; **at every ~** (*fig.*) на ка́ждом шагу́; **at the ~ of the century** в нача́ле ве́ка. **3.** (*change in condition*) переме́на; поворо́т; **his luck is on the ~** он вступа́ет в полосу́ везе́ния; **his condition took a ~ for the worse** его́ состоя́ние уху́дшилось. **4.** (*opportunity of doing sth. in proper order*) о́чередь; **it's your ~ next** вы сле́дующий; **I missed my ~** я пропусти́л свою́ о́чередь; **they all spoke in ~ (*or* took ~s to speak)** они́ выступа́ли/говори́ли по о́череди. **5.** (*service*) услу́га; **he did me a good ~** он оказа́л мне до́брую услу́гу. **6.** (*tendency, capability*): **he has a practical ~ of mind** он челове́к практи́ческого скла́да; **a witty ~ of phrase** остроу́мный оборо́т. **7.** (*short stage performance*) вы́ход; но́мер (програ́ммы); **star ~** гвоздь (*m.*) програ́ммы. **8.** (*coll., nervous shock*) потрясе́ние; припа́док; **you gave me quite a ~** вы меня́ поря́дком испуга́ли; **she had one of her ~s** с ней случи́лся припа́док.
v.t. **1.** (*cause to move round*) пов|ора́чивать, -ерну́ть; **he ~ed the key (in the lock)** он поверну́л ключ; **he ~ed his head** он поверну́л го́лову; он оберну́лся; **he ~ed his back on me** он поверну́лся ко мне спино́й; **she ~ed the pages** она́ перелиста́ла страни́цы; **he ~ed the scale at 12 stone** он ве́сил 168 фу́нтов. **2.** (*direct*) напр|авля́ть, -а́вить; **they ~ed the hose on to the flames** шланг напра́вили на пла́мя; **I ~ed my mind to other things** я сосредото́чился на друго́м; **he can ~ his hand to anything** он всё уме́ет; он ма́стер на все ру́ки; **he ~ed a blind eye** он закры́л глаза́ (на+*a.*); **he ~ed a deaf ear to my request** он игнори́ровал мою́ про́сьбу; (*adapt*): **he ~ed his skill to good use, account** он уме́ло испо́льзовал своё мастерство́; (*incline*): **the accident ~ed me against driving** катастро́фа отби́ла у меня́ охо́ту води́ть маши́ну. **3.** (*pass round or beyond*): **slow down as you ~ the corner** при поворо́те за́ угол сба́вьте ско́рость; **it has ~ed two o'clock** уже́ два часа́; **he has ~ed fifty** ему́ испо́лнилось 50 лет. **4.** (*transform*) превра|ща́ть, -ти́ть; **he ~ed the water into wine** он обрати́л во́ду в вино́; **it's enough to ~ one's stomach** от э́того мо́жет затошни́ть; **success ~ed his head** успе́х вскружи́л ему́ го́лову. **5.** (*reverse*) перев|ора́чивать, -ерну́ть; меня́ть (*impf.*) на противополо́жное; **the picture was ~ed upside down** карти́ну переверну́ли вверх нога́ми; **the room was ~ed upside down** (*ransacked*) в ко́мнате всё переверну́ли вверх дном; **I ~ed the tables on him** (*fig.*) я отплати́л ему́ то́й же моне́той; **he did not ~ a hair** он и гла́зом не моргну́л. **6.** (*send forcibly*) прог|оня́ть, -на́ть; **he was ~ed out of the house** его́ вы́гнали и́з дому; **he will not be ~ed from his purpose** его́ не собьёшь с и́збранного ку́рса. **7.** (*shape*): **the bowl was ~ed on the lathe** ку́бок/ча́шу обточи́ли на тока́рном станке́. **8.** (*execute by ~ing*): **the children were ~ing somersaults** ребяти́шки кувырка́лись; **the wheel has ~ed full circle** колесо́ сде́лало по́лный оборо́т; (*fig.*) положе́ние кардина́льно измени́лось.
v.i. **1.** (*move round*) пов|ора́чиваться, -ерну́ться; враща́ться (*impf.*); **the earth ~s on its axis** земля́ враща́ется вокру́г свое́й о́си; **the key won't ~** ключ не повора́чивается; **he ~ed on his heel** он кру́то поверну́лся; (*fig.*): **this will make him ~ in his grave** он от э́того в гробу́ перевернётся; (*depend*) зави́сеть (*impf.*); **everything ~s on his answer** всё зави́сит от его́ отве́та. **2.** (*change direction*) направля́ться (*impf.*); **we ~ (to the) left here** тут мы повора́чиваем нале́во; **right ~!** напра́во!; (*fig.*) обра|ща́ться, -ти́ться; **she hardly knew which way to ~** она́ не зна́ла, что ей де́лать; **the people ~ed against their rulers** наро́д восста́л про́тив прави́телей; **he ~ed on his attackers** он бро́сился на свои́х оби́дчиков. **3.** (*change*) превра|ща́ться, -ти́ться; **he ~ed into a miser** он стал скря́гой; (*change colour*): **the leaves have ~ed** ли́стья пожелте́ли. **4.** (*become*) ста|нови́ться, -ть; де́латься, с-; **she ~ed pale** она́ побледне́ла; **it has ~ed warm** потепле́ло; (*become sour*): **the milk has ~ed** молоко́ прокисло. *See also* **turning**
with advs.: **~ about** *v.t.* (*reverse*) пов|ора́чивать, -ерну́ть; *v.i.* (*change to opposite direction*) поверну́ться (*pf.*) на 180°; **about ~!** круго́м!; **~ aside** *v.t. & i.* отклон|я́ть(ся), -и́ть(ся); **~ away** *v.t.* (*avert*): **he ~ed his head away** он поверну́л го́лову в сто́рону; (*refuse admittance to*) прог|оня́ть, -на́ть; не пус|ка́ть, -ти́ть; *v.i.*: **she ~ed away in disgust** она́ с отвраще́нием отверну́лась; **~ back** *v.t.* (*repel*) от|сыла́ть, -осла́ть наза́д; **we were ~ed back at the frontier** нас верну́ли с грани́цы; (*fold back*) отв|ора́чивать, -ерну́ть; **he ~ed the clock back** (*lit.*) он перевёл часы́ наза́д; **we cannot ~ the clock back** (*fig.*) мы не мо́жем поверну́ть вре́мя вспять; *v.i.* пов|ора́чивать, -ерну́ть наза́д; пойти́ (*pf.*) обра́тно; **~ down** *v.t.* (*fold down*): **his collar was ~ed down**

у негó воротни́к был отвёрнут; (*reduce by* ~*ing*) уб|авля́ть, -а́вить; ~ **down the gas!** прикрути́те газ!; ~ **the volume down!** (*TV etc.*) уба́вьте звук!; (*reject*) отка́з|ываться, -а́ться от+*g*.; **I was ~ed down for the job** мне отказа́ли в рабо́те; **my offer was ~ed down** моё предложе́ние бы́ло отве́ргнуто; ~ **in** *v.t.* (*surrender*; *hand over*) сда|ва́ть, -ть; **he ~ed himself in to the police** он сда́лся поли́ции; *v.i.* (*incline inwards*) св|ёртываться, -ерну́ться внутрь; (*go to bed*) отпра́виться (*pf.*) на бокову́ю (*coll.*); ~ **inside out** *v.t. & i.* вывора́чивать(ся), вы́вернуть(ся) наизна́нку; ~ **off** *v.t.* (*e.g. light, engine*) выключа́ть, вы́ключить; гаси́ть, по-; ~ **off the light!** погаси́те/вы́ключите свет!; (*tap*) закр|ыва́ть, -ы́ть; **the water was ~ed off at the main** во́ду отключи́ли; *v.i.* (*make a diversion*) св|ора́чивать, -ерну́ть; ~ **on** *v.t.* (*e.g. light, engine, radio*) включ|а́ть, -и́ть; (*tap*) откр|ыва́ть, -ы́ть; **this music ~s me on** (*coll.*) э́то му́зыка меня́ возбужда́ет; ~ **out** *v.t.* (*expel*) прог|оня́ть, -на́ть; исключ|а́ть, -и́ть; (*switch off*) гаси́ть, по-; **the lights were ~ed out** свет был поту́шен; (*produce*) выпуска́ть, вы́пустить; произв|оди́ть, -ести́; **the factory ~s out 500 cars a day** фа́брика выпуска́ет 500 маши́н в день; (*fig.*) укра|ша́ть, -си́ть; **he is always well ~ed out** он всегда́ хорошо́ оде́т; (*empty*) вывора́чивать, вы́вернуть; **he ~ed out his pockets** он вы́вернул карма́ны; (*tidy*) уб|ира́ть, ра́ть; (*assemble for duty*) вызыва́ть, вы́звать; *v.i.* (*prove*) ока́з|ываться, -а́ться; **as it ~ed out I was not required** как оказа́лось, я не пона́добился; **he ~ed out to be a liar** он оказа́лся лжецо́м; (*become*): **after a wet morning, it ~ed out a fine day** по́сле дождли́вого у́тра день вы́дался хоро́шим; (*assemble*) соб|ира́ться, -ра́ться; (*go out of doors*): **I had to ~ out in the cold** мне пришло́сь вы́йти на хо́лод; ~ **over** *v.t.* (*overturn*) перев|ора́чивать, -ерну́ть; опроки́|дывать, -нуть; (*reverse position of*): **I ~ed over the page** я переверну́л страни́цу; (*revolve*) запус|ка́ть, -ти́ть; (*transfer*; *hand over*) перед|ава́ть, -а́ть; **he was ~ed over to the authorities** его́ пе́редали властя́м; *v.i.* (*overturn*) перев|ора́чиваться, -ерну́ться; **the boat ~ed over and sank** ло́дка переверну́лась и затону́ла; (*change position*) переверну́ться (*pf.*); **he ~ed over (in bed)** он переверну́лся на друго́й бок; ~ **round** *v.t.* (*change or reverse position of*) перев|ора́чивать, -ерну́ть; ~ **your chair round this way** поверни́те стул в э́ту сто́рону; **he ~ed his car round** он разверну́л маши́ну; *v.i.* (*change position*): **he ~ed round to look** он оберну́лся, что́бы посмотре́ть; (*revolve*) враща́ться (*impf.*); **the weather-vane ~s round in the wind** флю́гер враща́ется/ве́ртится на ветру́; ~ **to** *v.i.* (*join in, help*) бра́ться/взя́ться за де́ло; ~ **up** *v.t.* (*increase flow of*) приб|авля́ть, -а́вить; уси́ли|вать, -ть; ~ **up the gas!** приба́вьте га́зу!; (*disinter*) выка́пывать, вы́копать; (*put in higher position*) подн|има́ть, -я́ть вверх; **he ~ed his collar up** он по́днял воротни́к; **don't ~ your nose up at the offer** не вороти́те нос от тако́го предложе́ния; *v.i.* (*arrive*) появ|ля́ться, -и́ться; **look who's ~ed up!** смотри́те, кто пришёл!; (*be found*; *occur*) ока́з|ываться, -а́ться; подв|ёртываться, -ерну́ться; (*happen*; *become available*) подверну́ться (*pf.*); ~ **upside down** *v.t. & i.* перев|ора́чивать(ся), -ерну́ть(ся) вверх дном.

cpds. **~coat** *n.* ренега́т; преда́тель (*fem.* -ница); **~-down** *adj.* отложно́й; **~out** *n.* (*assembly*) собра́ние, сбор; **there was a very good ~out** собрало́сь о́чень мно́го наро́ду; (*cleaning, tidying*) чи́стка, убо́рка; **~over** *n.* (*in business*) оборо́т (капита́ла); (*rate of renewal*) теку́честь; **~pike** *n.* доро́жная заста́ва; (*road*) шоссе́ (*indecl.*); **~-round** *n.* (*reversal of policy, opinion etc.*) поворо́т на 180°; **~stile** *n.* турнике́т; **~table** *n.* (*rail.*) поворо́тный круг; (*of record player*) верту́шка; **~-up** *n.* (*of trouser*) манже́та; (*coll.*, *surprise*) неожи́данность.

turner ['tɜ:nə(r)] *n.* то́карь (*m.*).

turning ['tɜ:nɪŋ] *n.* (*bend*; *junction*) поворо́т; перекрёсток.

cpd. **~-point** *n.* (*lit.*) поворо́тный пункт; (*fig.*) кри́зис, перело́м; **it was a ~-point in his career** э́то был реша́ющий моме́нт в его́ карье́ре.

turnip ['tɜ:nɪp] *n.* ре́па, турне́пс.

turpentine ['tɜ:pən,taɪn] *n.* скипида́р.

turpitude ['tɜ:pɪ,tju:d] *n.* поро́чность, ни́зость.

turquoise ['tɜ:kwɔɪz, -kwɑ:z] *n.* бирюза́; (*colour*) бирюзо́вый цвет.

turret ['tʌrɪt] *n.* (*tower*) ба́шенка; (*of tank etc.*) ору́дийная ба́шня; **~-lathe** револьве́рный стано́к.

turtle ['tɜ:t(ə)l] *n.* черепа́ха.

cpd. **~-neck** *adj.*: **~-neck sweater** водола́зка.

turtle-dove ['tɜt(ə)l,dʌv] *n.* ди́кий го́лубь.

tusk [tʌsk] *n.* клык, би́вень (*m.*).

tussle ['tʌs(ə)l] *n.* борьба́, дра́ка.

v.i. боро́ться (*impf.*); дра́ться (*impf.*).

tussock ['tʌsək] *n.* ко́чка.

tut [tʌt] (*also* **~-tut**) *v.i.* цо́кать (*impf.*) языко́м.

int. а́х ты!; ай-яй-я́й!

tutelage ['tju:tɪlɪdʒ] *n.* попечи́тельство; опе́ка.

tutelary ['tju:tɪlərɪ] *adj.* опеку́нский, опека́ющий.

tutor ['tju:tə(r)] *n.* (*private teacher*) репети́тор; (*university teacher*) преподова́тель (*fem.* -ница).

v.t. & i. (*instruct*) дава́ть (*impf.*) ча́стные уро́ки +*d*.

tutorial [tju:'tɔ:rɪəl] *n.* ≃ семина́р, консульта́ция.

tutu ['tu:tu:] *n.* па́чка.

tuxedo [tʌk'si:dəʊ] *n.* (*US*) смо́кинг.

TV (*abbr. of* **television**) ТВ, (телеви́дение); (*set*) телеви́зор, (*coll.*) те́лик; ~ **addict** телема́н; **closed-circuit** ~ за́мкнутое телеви́дение.

twaddle ['twɒd(ə)l] *n.* чепуха́; болтовня́.

twang [twæŋ] *n.* (*sound of plucked string*) звук натя́нутой струны́; (*nasal tone of voice*) гнуса́вый го́лос.

tweak [twi:k] *n.* щипо́к.

v.t. ущипну́ть (*pf.*).

tweed [twi:d] *n.* (*material*) твид; **a ~ jacket** пиджа́к из тви́да; (*pl.*) тви́довый костю́м.

tweet [twi:t] *n.* щёбет, чири́канье.

v.i. щебета́ть (*impf.*); чири́кать (*impf.*).

tweezer ['twi:zə(r)] *n.* (*usu. pl.*) пинце́т; щи́пчик|и (*pl.*, *g.* -ов).

twelfth [twelfθ] *n.* (*date*) двена́дцатое число́; (*fraction*) одна́ двена́дцатая.

adj. двена́дцатый; **T~ Night** кану́н Креще́ния.

twelve [twelv] *n.* двена́дцать.

adj. двена́дцать +*g. pl.*; **12 times 12** двена́дцатью (*or* двена́дцать на) двена́дцать; (*with nn. expr. or understood*): ~ **(o'clock)** (*midday*) по́лдень (*m.*); (*midnight*) по́лночь; **quarter to** ~ без че́тверти двена́дцать; **quarter/half past** ~ че́тверть/полови́на пе́рвого; **a boy of** ~ двенадцатиле́тний ма́льчик.

cpd. **~month** *n.* год.

twentieth ['twentɪɪθ] *n.* (*date*) двадца́тое число́; (*fraction*) одна́ двадца́тая.

adj. двадца́тый.

twent|y ['twentɪ] *n.* два́дцать; **at (the age of) ~y** в два́дцать лет; **the ~ies** (*decade*) двадца́тые го́ды.

adj. два́дцать +*g. pl.*

twerp [twɜ:p] (*coll.*) ничто́жество.

twice [twaɪs] *adv.* два́жды; вдво́е; два ра́за; ~ **two is four** два́жды два — четы́ре; **he is ~ my age** он вдво́е ста́рше меня́; ~ **as much** в два ра́за (*or* вдво́е) бо́льше; **that made him think** ~ э́то заста́вило его́ заду́маться.

twiddl|e ['twɪd(ə)l] *v.t.* верте́ть (*impf.*); крути́ть (*impf.*); **he sat there ~ing his thumbs** он бил баклу́ши.

twig[1] [twɪg] *n.* (*bot.*) ве́тка; прут.
twig[2] [twɪg] *v.t. & i.* (*coll.*) смек|а́ть, -ну́ть.
twilight ['twaɪlaɪt] *n.* су́мер|ки (*pl.*, *g.* -ек); полумра́к.
twill [twɪl] *n.* твил, са́ржа.
twin [twɪn] *n.* близне́ц; (*pl.*) близнецы́, дво́йня (*f. sg.*); **I have a ~ sister** у меня́ сестра́ — мы с ней близнецы́; **identical ~s** однояйцевые/иденти́чные близнецы́.
adj. похо́жий; одина́ковый; **~ beds** две односпа́льные крова́ти; **~ propellers** двойно́й пропе́ллер.
v.t. (*fig.*) соедин|я́ть, -и́ть; **Cheltenham is ~ned with Sochi** Че́лтнем и Со́чи — города́-побрати́мы.
twine [twaɪn] *n.* бечёвка, шнуро́к.
v.t. & i. ви́ть(ся) (*impf.*); обв|ива́ть(ся), -и́ть(ся); **the ivy ~d round the tree** плющ ви́лся вокру́г де́рева.
twinge [twɪndʒ] *n.* при́ступ о́строй бо́ли; (*fig.*) му́ка; **a ~ of conscience** угрызе́ние со́вести.
twinkl|e ['twɪŋk(ə)l] *n.* мерца́ние; огонёк.
v.i. мерца́ть (*impf.*); сверка́ть (*impf.*); **his eyes ~ed with amusement** его́ глаза́ ве́село блесте́ли; **in the ~ing of an eye** в мгнове́ние о́ка.
twirl [twɜ:l] *n.* враще́ние.
v.t. верте́ть (*impf.*); крути́ть (*impf.*); **he ~ed his walking-stick** он верте́л тро́стью/па́лкой.
twist [twɪst] *n.* **1.** (*jerk; sharp turning motion*) круче́ние; рыво́к; **he gave the handle a ~** он поверну́л ру́чку. **2.** (*sharp change of direction*) изги́б, поворо́т; **the lane was all ~s and turns** тропи́нка была́ о́чень изви́листой; **a ~ in the plot** круто́й поворо́т сюже́та. **3.** (*sth. ~ed or spiral in shape*) пе́тля; у́зел; **the rope was full of ~s** верёвка была́ вся в узла́х.
v.t. **1.** (*screw round*) крути́ть (*or* скру́чивать), с-; **he tried to ~ my arm** (*lit.*) он пыта́лся вы́вернуть мне ру́ку; (*fig., coerce me*) он пыта́лся на меня́ дави́ть; **I ~ed my ankle** я подверну́л (себе́) но́гу. **2.** (*contort*) искрив|ля́ть, -и́ть; **a ~ed smile** крива́я улы́бка; (*fig.*) иска|жа́ть, -зи́ть; **don't try to ~ my meaning** не искажа́йте мои́ слова́! **3.** (*wind, twine*) обв|ива́ть, -и́ть; **they ~ed the flowers into a garland** они́ сплета́ли цветы́ в гирлянду; **he can ~ you round his little finger** он мо́жет из вас верёвки вить. **4.** (*coll., cheat*) обма́н|ывать, -у́ть; **are you trying to ~ me?** вы пыта́етесь меня́ наду́ть?
v.i. **1.** (*wriggle*) ко́рчиться (*impf.*); извива́ться (*impf.*); **he ~ed about, trying to get away** он извива́лся, стара́ясь вы́рваться. **2.** (*twine; grow spirally*) обв|иваться, -и́ться.
with advs.: **~ off** *v.t.* откру́|чивать, -ти́ть; отви́н|чивать, -ти́ть; **~ up** *v.t.* запу́т|ывать, -ать; **the string was all ~ed up** верёвка была́ вся в узла́х.
twister ['twɪstə(r)] *n.* обма́нщик, моше́нник.
twisty ['twɪstɪ] *adj.* изви́листый.
twit[1] [twɪt] *n.* ничто́жество, пусто́е ме́сто (*coll.*).
twit[2] [twɪt] *v.t.* поддр|а́знивать, -азни́ть.
twitch [twɪtʃ] *n.* подёргивание.
v.t. **1.** (*jerk*) дёргать (*impf.*); выдёргивать (*impf.*). **2.** (*move spasmodically*) подёргивать (*impf.*) +*i.*; **the dog ~ed its ears** соба́ка повела́ уша́ми.
v.i. дёргаться (*impf.*); **my nose is ~ing** у меня́ дёргается нос.
twitter ['twɪtə(r)] *n.* **1.** (*chirping*) щебет. **2.** (*rapid chatter*) щебет, болтовня́.
v.i. (*chirp*) щебета́ть (*impf.*); чири́кать (*impf.*); (*talk rapidly*) щебета́ть (*impf.*); болта́ть (*impf.*).
two [tu:] *n.* **1.** (число́/но́мер) два; (*~ people*) дво́е; **we ~** мы о́ба; **the ~** э́ти два/дво́е; о́ба +*g. sg.*; **there were ~ of us** нас бы́ло дво́е; **(the) ~ of us went** мы пошли́ вдвоём; **~ each, in ~s, ~ at a time, ~ by ~** по́ два/дво́е; (*cut, divide*) **in ~** на́ двое/попола́м; **fold in ~** сложи́ть (*pf.*) вдво́е; **the plate broke in ~** таре́лка разби́лась попола́м; (*figure, thg. numbered 2*) дво́йка; **~ and ~ are four** два плюс/и два — четы́ре; (*with var. nn. expr. or understood*): **chapter ~** втора́я глава́; **page ~** страни́ца два; **size ~** второ́й разме́р; **a No. ~ (bus)** дво́йка, второ́й но́мер; **at ~ (o'clock)** в два (часа́); **~ p.m.** два часа́ дня; **an hour or ~** ча́с(ик)-друго́й; **in an hour or ~** че́рез час-друго́й; (*of age*): **he is ~** ему́ два го́да; **a boy of ~** двухле́тний ма́льчик; (*idioms*): **~'s company, three's none** тре́тий — ли́шний; **~ can play at that game** ≃ я могу́ отплати́ть той же моне́той; **I put ~ and ~ together** я сообрази́л, что к чему́; **that makes ~ of us** вот и я то́же.
adj. два +*g. sg.*; (*for people and* pluralia tantum, *also*) дво́е +*g. pl.*; **~ patients** дво́е больны́х; **~ children** дво́е дете́й; два ребёнка; **~ watches** дво́е часо́в; **~ whole glasses** це́лых два стака́на; **the ~ carriages** о́ба ваго́на; **he and ~ others** он с двумя́ други́ми; **~ fives are ten** два́жды пять — де́сять; **~ coffees** (*as order*) два ра́за ко́фе.
cpds. **~-day** *adj.* двухдне́вный; **~-dimensional** *adj.* двухме́рный; **~-edged** *adj.* (*lit., fig.*) обоюдо́острый; **~-faced** *adj.* (*fig.*) двули́чный; **~fold** *adj.* двойно́й; *adv.* вдво́е; **~-lane** *adj.* двухколе́йный; **~-legged** *adj.* двуно́гий; **~pence** *n.* два пе́нса; двухпе́нсовая моне́та; *see also* **tuppence; ~penny** *adj.* двухпе́нсовый; **~penny-halfpenny** *adj.* (*coll., rubbishy*) грошо́вый; *see also* **tuppenny; ~-piece** *n.* (*suit*) (костю́м)-дво́йка; **~-ply** *adj.* двойно́й, двухсло́йный; **~-seater** *n.* двухме́стный автомоби́ль; **~-sided** *adj.* двусторо́нний; **~-storey** *adj.* двухэта́жный; **~-stroke** *adj.* двухта́ктный; **~-way** *adj.* (*e.g. traffic*) двусторо́нний; **~-year** *adj.* двухгоди́чный, двухле́тний; **~-year-old** *adj.* двухле́тний.
tycoon [taɪ'ku:n] *n.* (*business magnate*) магна́т; кру́пный заправи́ла.
type [taɪp] *n.* **1.** (*example*) тип; типи́чный образе́ц. **2.** (*class*) род, класс. **3.** (*letters for printing*) шрифт; **in large/heavy ~** кру́пным/жи́рным шри́фтом.
v.t. **1.** (*classify*) классифици́ровать (*impf., pf.*); определ|я́ть, -и́ть. **2.** (*write with ~writer*) печа́тать, от- (*or* писа́ть, на-) (на маши́нке).
v.i. печа́тать (*impf.*) (на маши́нке); **typing** (*as n.*) машинопись; **typing error** опеча́тка; **typing pool** машинопи́сное бюро́.
cpds. **~cast** *adj.*: **he is ~cast as the butler** он всегда́ игра́ет роль дворе́цкого; **~-face** *n.* шрифт; **~script** *n.* машинопи́сный текст; **~setter** *n.* (*person*) набо́рщик; (*machine*) фотонабо́рная маши́на; **~setting** *n.* типогра́фский набо́р; **~write** *v.t.* печа́тать, на- на маши́нке; **a ~written letter** письмо́, напеча́танное на маши́нке; **~writer** *n.* (пи́шущая) маши́нка.
typhoid ['taɪfɔɪd] *n.* (*also* **~ fever**) брюшно́й тиф.
adj. тифо́зный.
typhoon [taɪ'fu:n] *n.* тайфу́н.
typhus ['taɪfəs] *n.* сыпно́й тиф.
typical ['tɪpɪk(ə)l] *adj.* типи́чный; **that is ~ of him** э́то для него́ типи́чно.
typify ['tɪpɪˌfaɪ] *v.t.* быть типи́чным представи́телем +*g.*
typist ['taɪpɪst] *n.* (*fem.*) машини́стка.
typographer [taɪ'pɒgrəfə(r)] *n.* печа́тник.
typographic(al) [ˌtaɪpə'græfɪk(ə)l] *adj.* типогра́фский.
typography [taɪ'pɒgrəfɪ] *n.* книгопеча́тание.
tyrannical [tɪ'rænɪk(ə)l] *adj.* тирани́ческий.
tyrannize ['tɪrəˌnaɪz] *v.t. & i.* тира́нить (*impf.*).
tyranny ['tɪrənɪ] *n.* (*despotic power*) тирани́я; (*tyrannical behaviour*) тира́нство.
tyrant ['taɪərənt] *n.* тира́н, де́спот.
tyre ['taɪə(r)] (*US* **tire**) *n.* ши́на; **I have a flat ~** у меня́ спусти́лась ши́на.
cpd. **~-lever** *n.* монтиро́вочная лопа́тка.
tzar [zɑ:(r)] *etc.* = **tsar** *etc.*

U

U [uː] *cpds.* **~-boat** *n.* неме́цкая подво́дная ло́дка; **~-turn** *n.* разворо́т; (*fig.*) ре́зкое измене́ние поли́тики; поворо́т на 180°.
ubiquitous [juːˈbɪkwɪtəs] *adj.* вездесу́щий.
udder [ˈʌdə(r)] *n.* вы́мя (*nt.*).
UFO (*abbr. of* ***unidentified flying object***) НЛО, (неопо́знанный лета́ющий объе́кт).
Uganda [juːˈgændə] *n.* Уга́нда.
ugh [əx, ʌg, ʌx] *int.* брр!; ах!; тьфу!
ugliness [ˈʌglɪnɪs] *n.* уро́дство; некраси́вая вне́шность; безобра́зность.
ugly [ˈʌglɪ] *adj.* **1.** (*unsightly*) некраси́вый, уро́дливый, безобра́зный; ~ **duckling** га́дкий утёнок. **2.** (*unpleasant*) проти́вный, скве́рный. **3.** (*threatening*) опа́сный; **an ~ customer** гну́сный тип/субъе́кт; **he was in an ~ mood** он был в гро́зном настрое́нии.
UK (*abbr. of* ***United Kingdom***) Соединённое Короле́вство (Великобрита́нии и Се́верной Ирла́ндии).
adj. (велико)брита́нский.
ukase [juːˈkeɪz] *n.* ука́з.
Ukraine [juːˈkreɪn] *n.* Украи́на; **in (the) ~** на Украи́не.
Ukrainian [juːˈkreɪnɪən] *n.* (*pers.*) украи́н|ец (*fem.* -ка); (*language.*) украи́нский язы́к.
adj. украи́нский.
ukulele [juːkəˈleɪlɪ] *n.* гава́йская гита́ра.
ulcer [ˈʌlsə(r)] *n.* я́зва (желу́дка).
ulceration [ˌʌlsəˈreɪʃ(ə)n] *n.* изъязвле́ние.
ulcerous [ˈʌlsərəs] *adj.* я́звенный.
Ulster [ˈʌlstə(r)] *n.* (*province*) О́льстер.
ulterior [ʌlˈtɪərɪə(r)] *adj.* скры́тый, невы́раженный; ~ **motive** скры́тый моти́в; за́дняя мысль.
ultimate [ˈʌltɪmət] *adj.* после́дний, оконча́тельный; ~ **end, purpose** коне́чная цель.
ultimatum [ˌʌltɪˈmeɪtəm] *n.* ультима́тум.
ultramarine [ˌʌltrəməˈriːn] *n.* ультрамари́н.
adj. ультрамари́новый.
ultrasonic [ˌʌltrəˈsɒnɪk] *n.* ультразвуково́й.
ultra-violet [ˌʌltrəˈvaɪələt] *adj.* ультрафиоле́товый.
ultra vires [ˌʌltrə ˈvaɪəˌriːz, ˌʊltrɑː ˈviːreɪz] *adj. & adv.* вне компете́нции, за преде́лами полномо́чий (*кого*).
umber [ˈʌmbə(r)] *n.* у́мбра.
adj. тёмно-кори́чневый.
umbilical [ʌmˈbɪlɪk(ə)l, ˌʌmbɪˈlaɪk(ə)l] *adj.* пупо́чный; ~ **cord** пупови́на.
umbrage [ˈʌmbrɪdʒ] *n.* оби́да; **take ~ (at)** об|ижа́ться, -и́деться (на+*a.*).
umbrella [ʌmˈbrelə] *n.* **1.** зо́нтик, зонт. **2.** (*fig., protection*) (авиацио́нное) прикры́тие; **nuclear ~** я́дерный зо́нтик. **3.** (*fig., general heading*) ру́брика; ~ **organisation** возглавля́ющая организа́ция.
umlaut [ˈʊmlaʊt] *n.* умля́ут.
umpire [ˈʌmpaɪə(r)] *n.* (*arbitrator*) посре́дник; (*in games*) судья́ (*m.*); ре́фери́ (*m. indecl.*).
v.t. & i.: **he ~d both matches** он суди́л о́ба ма́тча.
umpteen [ʌmpˈtiːn] *adj.* (*coll.*) бесчи́сленное коли́чество +*g.*
umpteenth [ʌmpˈtiːnθ] *adj.* (*coll.*) э́нный; **I have told you for the ~ time** ско́лько раз я тебе́ говори́л!
UN (*abbr. of* ***United Nations (Organization)***): **the ~** ООН (*f. indecl.*), (Организа́ция Объединённых На́ций).
adj. (*coll.*) оо́новский.
unabashed [ˌʌnəˈbæʃt] *adj.* без смуще́ния.
unable [ʌnˈeɪb(ə)l] *adj.* неспосо́бный; **he is ~ to swim** он не уме́ет пла́вать; **I shall be ~ to come** я не смогу́ прийти́.
unabridged [ˌʌnəˈbrɪdʒd] *adj.* несокращённый, по́лный.
unaccented [ˌʌnækˈsentɪd] *adj.* безуда́рный.
unacceptable [ˌʌnəkˈseptəb(ə)l] *adj.* неприе́млемый.
unaccompanied [ˌʌnəˈkʌmpənɪd] *adj.* не сопровожда́емый; **she came ~** она́ пришла́ одна́ (*or* без сопровожде́ния); (*mus.*) без аккомпанеме́нта.
unaccountable [ˌʌnəˈkaʊntəb(ə)l] *adj.* (*inexplicable*) необъясни́мый; (*irrational*) безотчётный; (*not obliged to render an account of o.s.*) безотчётный.
unaccounted-for [ˌʌnəˈkaʊntɪd fɔː] *adj.* (*unexplained*) необъяснённый; (*not included in account*) не ука́занный в отчёте.
unaccustomed [ˌʌnəˈkʌstəmd] *adj.* **1.** (*unused*) непривы́кший; ~ **as I am to public speaking** хотя́ я и не привы́к выступа́ть. **2.** (*unusual*) необы́чный.
unacknowledged [ˌʌnəkˈnɒlɪdʒd] *adj.* **1.** (*unrecognized*) непри́знанный. **2.: my letter was ~** я не получи́л подтвержде́ния о получе́нии письма́.
unacquainted [ˌʌnəˈkweɪntɪd] *adj.* незнако́мый.
unadorned [ˌʌnəˈdɔːnd] *adj.* неприкра́шенный.
unadulterated [ˌʌnəˈdʌltəˌreɪtɪd] *adj.* настоя́щий, неподде́льный; ~ **nonsense** чисте́йший вздор; **the ~ truth** чи́стая пра́вда.
unadventurous [ˌʌnədˈventʃərəs] *adj.* непредприи́мчивый, несме́лый; (*uneventful*) без приключе́ний, споко́йный.
unaffected [ˌʌnəˈfektɪd] *adj.* **1.** (*without affectation*) непринуждённый, есте́ственный. **2.** (*not harmed or influenced*): **our plans were ~ by the weather** пого́да не измени́ла на́ших пла́нов; **he was ~ by my entreaties** он остава́лся безуча́стным к мои́м мольба́м.
unafraid [ˌʌnəˈfreɪd] *adj.* незапу́ганный.
unaided [ʌnˈeɪdɪd] *adj.* без посторо́нней по́мощи.
unaligned [ˌʌnəˈlaɪnd] *adj.*: **the ~ countries** неприсоедини́вшиеся стра́ны.
unalleviated [ˌʌnəˈliːvɪˌeɪtɪd] *adj.* несмягчённый.
unalterable [ʌnˈɔːltərəb(ə)l, ʌnˈɒl-] *adj.* неизме́нный.
unambiguous [ˌʌnæmˈbɪgjʊəs] *adj.* недвусмы́сленный.
unambitious [ˌʌnæmˈbɪʃəs] *adj.* непритяза́тельный, скро́мный.
un-American [ˌʌnəˈmerɪkən] *adj.* чу́ждый америка́нским обы́чаям и поня́тиям; антиамерика́нский.
unanimity [juːnəˈnɪmɪtɪ] *n.* единоду́шие.
unanimous [juːˈnænɪməs] *adj.* единоду́шный, единогла́сный.
unannounced [ˌʌnəˈnaʊnst] *adj.* необъя́вленный; без докла́да.
unanswerable [ʌnˈɑːnsərəb(ə)l] *adj.*: **an ~ argument** неопровержи́мый до́вод.
unanswered [ʌnˈɑːnsəd] *adj.* оста́вшийся без отве́та.
unanticipated [ˌʌnænˈtɪsɪˌpeɪtɪd] *adj.* (*unexpected*) непредви́денный, неожи́данный.
unappealing [ˌʌnəˈpiːlɪŋ] *adj.* неприя́тный, непривлека́тельный.
unappetizing [ʌnˈæpɪˌtaɪzɪŋ] *adj.* неаппети́тный.
unappreciated [ˌʌnəˈpriːʃɪˌeɪtɪd] *adj.* непри́знанный, недооценённый.
unappreciative [ˌʌnəˈpriːʃətɪv] *adj.* неблагода́рный.
unapproachable [ˌʌnəˈprəʊtʃəb(ə)l] *adj.* недосту́пный.
unarmed [ʌnˈɑːmd] *adj.* невооружённый, безору́жный; ~ **combat** самозащи́та без ору́жия; (*abbr.* са́мбо (*indecl.*)).
unashamed [ˌʌnəˈʃeɪmd] *adj.* бессты́дный; без со́вести/стесне́ния.

unassailable [ˌʌnəˈseɪləb(ə)l] *adj.*: **an ~ fortress** неприступная крепость; **an ~ argument** неопровержимый довод.
unassisted [ˌʌnəˈsɪstɪd] *adj.* без (посторонней) помощи.
unassuming [ˌʌnəˈsjuːmɪŋ] *adj.* непритязательный, скромный.
unattached [ˌʌnəˈtætʃt] *adj.* не прикреплённый (*к чему*); **she is ~** она одинока.
unattainable [ˌʌnəˈteɪnəb(ə)l] *adj.* недосягаемый.
unattended [ˌʌnəˈtendɪd] *adj.* оставленный без надзора/присмотра; **the children were left ~** детей оставили одних (без надзора); **the shop is ~** в магазине нет продавца.
unattractive [ˌʌnəˈtræktɪv] *adj.* непривлекательный, несимпатичный.
unauthorized [ʌnˈɔːθəˌraɪzd] *adj.* неразрешённый; (*pers.*) посторонний.
unavailable [ˌʌnəˈveɪləb(ə)l] *adj.* не имеющийся в наличии; **he was ~** он был недосягаем/занят.
unavailing [ˌʌnəˈveɪlɪŋ] *adj.* бесполезный, напрасный, тщетный.
unavoidabl|e [ˌʌnəˈvɔɪdəb(ə)l] *adj.* (*sure to happen*) неизбежный, неминуемый; **I was ~y detained** я не мог освободиться (раньше).
unaware [ˌʌnəˈweə(r)] *adj.* незнающий, неподозревающий; **I was ~ that he was married** я не знал, что он женат.
unawares [ˌʌnəˈweəz] *adv.* нечаянно; врасплох; **I was taken ~ by his question** его вопрос застиг меня врасплох.
unbalanced [ʌnˈbælənsd] *adj.* неравномерный, односторонний; (*mentally*) неуравновешенный.
unbearable [ʌnˈbeərəb(ə)l] *adj.* невыносимый.
unbeaten [ʌnˈbiːt(ə)n] *adj.* (*unsurpassed*) непревзойдённый.
unbecoming [ˌʌnbɪˈkʌmɪŋ] *adj.* (*inappropriate*) неподходящий; (*indecorous*) неподобающий (*+d.*), неприличный (для*+g.*).
unbeknown [ˌʌnbɪˈnəʊn] *adv.*: **he did it ~ to me** он сделал это без моего ведома.
unbelievable [ˌʌnbɪˈliːvəb(ə)l] *adj.* (*coll.*, *amazing*) невероятный.
unbeliever [ˌʌnbɪˈliːvə(r)] *n.* неверующий.
unbelieving [ˌʌnbɪˈliːvɪŋ] *adj.* неверующий.
unbend [ʌnˈbend] *v.t.* выпрямлять, выпрямить; раз|гибать, -огнуть.
unbending [ʌnˈbendɪŋ] *adj.* (*fig.*) непреклонный, суровый, негибкий.
unbiased [ʌnˈbaɪəst] *adj.* беспристрастный.
unbind [ʌnˈbaɪnd] *v.t.* развяз|ывать, -ать; (*wound*) разбинтов|ывать, -ать.
unblemished [ʌnˈblemɪʃt] *adj.* чистый; (*fig.*) незапятнанный; безупречный.
unblock [ʌnˈblɒk] *v.t.*: **the plumber ~ed the drain** водопроводчик прочистил водосток.
unbolt [ʌnˈbəʊlt] *v.t.* отп|ирать, -ереть.
unborn [ʌnˈbɔːn] *adj.*: **her ~ child** её ещё не рождённое (*or* её будущее) дитя.
unbound [ʌnˈbaʊnd] *adj.* (*of book*) непереплетённый.
unbounded [ʌnˈbaʊndɪd] *adj.* неограниченный, безмерный.
unbowed [ʌnˈbaʊd] *adj.* несогнутый; непокорённый; **his head was ~** (*fig.*) он не покорился.
unbridled [ʌnˈbraɪdəld] *adj.* (*fig.*) необузданный, разнузданный.
unbroken [ʌnˈbrəʊkən] *adj.* неразбитый, несломленный; **only one plate was ~** только одна тарелка уцелела; **an ~ record** непревзойдённый рекорд; **~ sleep** непрерывный сон.
unbuckle [ʌnˈbʌk(ə)l] *v.t.* расстёг|ивать, -нуть.
unburden [ʌnˈbɜːd(ə)n] *v.t.*: **he ~ed his soul to me** он излил мне душу.
unbutton [ʌnˈbʌt(ə)n] *v.t.* расстёг|ивать, -нуть.
uncalled-for [ʌnˈkɔːldfɔː(r)] *adj.* (*inappropriate*) неуместный; (*undeserved*) незаслуженный.
uncanny [ʌnˈkænɪ] *adj.* странный, необъяснимый.
uncared-for [ʌnˈkeədfɔː(r)] *adj.* заброшенный.
unceasing [ʌnˈsiːsɪŋ] *adj.* беспрерывный, беспрестанный.
uncensored [ʌnˈsensəd] *adj.* не прошедший цензуру.
unceremonious [ˌʌnserɪˈməʊnɪəs] *adj.* (*abrupt*, *discourteous*) бесцеремонный.
uncertain [ʌnˈsɜːt(ə)n] *adj.* **1.** (*hesitant*, *in doubt*) неуверенный, нерешительный; **he was ~ what to do** он не знал, что делать; **I am ~ what he wants** я не могу понять, чего он хочет. **2.** (*not clear*) неясный, неопределённый; **in no ~ terms** весьма недвусмысленно. **3.** (*changeable*, *unreliable*): **the weather is ~** погода изменчива; **my position is ~** (*shaky*) у меня шаткое положение.
uncertaint|y [ʌnˈsɜːtəntɪ] *n.* **1.** (*hesitation*) неуверенность, нерешительность; **be in a state of ~y** сомневаться (*impf.*); колебаться (*impf.*). **2.** (*lack of clarity*) неизвестность, неопределённость. **3.** (*unreliable or unpredictable nature*) изменчивость; **the ~ies of life** превратности (*f. pl.*) судьбы.
unchain [ʌnˈtʃeɪn] *v.t.* спус|кать, -тить с цепи; **~ the door** сн|имать, -ять цепочку с двери.
unchallengeable [ʌnˈtʃælɪndʒəb(ə)l] *adj.* неоспоримый.
unchallenged [ʌnˈtʃælɪndʒd] *adj.* всеми признанный; **I let his remark go ~** я не стал оспаривать его замечание.
unchangeable [ʌnˈtʃeɪndʒəb(ə)l] *adj.* неизменяемый, неизменный.
uncharitable [ʌnˈtʃærɪtəb(ə)l] *adj.* чрезмерно строгий, придирчивый.
uncharted [ʌnˈtʃɑːtɪd] *adj.* неисследованный.
unchecked [ʌnˈtʃekt] *adj.*: **an ~ advance** (*mil.*) беспрепятственное продвижение.
uncivil [ʌnˈsɪvɪl] *adj.* невежливый, грубый.
uncivilized [ʌnˈsɪvɪˌlaɪzd] *adj.* нецивилизованный, некультурный.
unclaimed [ʌnˈkleɪmd] *adj.* невостребованный.
unclasp [ʌnˈklɑːsp] *v.t.* (*loosen clasp of*) расстёг|ивать, -нуть; (*release grip on*) разж|имать, -ать; **he ~ed his hands** он разжал руки.
unclassified [ʌnˈklæsɪˌfaɪd] *adj.* неклассифицированный; (*without security grading*) несекретный.
uncle [ˈʌŋk(ə)l] *n.* дядя (*m.*).
unclean [ʌnˈkliːn] *adj.* (*impure*) нечистый.
uncleanness [ʌnˈkliːnnɪs] *n.* нечистота.
uncoil [ʌnˈkɔɪl] *v.t. & i.* разм|атывать(ся), -отать(ся).
uncoloured [ʌnˈkʌləd] *adj.* бесцветный, неокрашенный; **an ~ description** неприукрашенное описание.
uncomfortable [ʌnˈkʌmftəb(ə)l] *adj.* (*lit.*, *fig.*) неудобный; неловкий.
uncommitted [ˌʌnkəˈmɪtɪd] *adj.* нейтральный; (*pol.*, *unaligned*) неприсоединившийся.
uncommon [ʌnˈkɒmən] *adj.* редкий; необычный; **he showed ~ generosity** он проявил необыкновенную щедрость.
uncommunicative [ˌʌnkəˈmjuːnɪkətɪv] *adj.* неразговорчивый, сдержанный.
uncomplaining [ˌʌnkəmˈpleɪnɪŋ] *adj.* безропотный.
uncomplimentary [ˌʌnkɒmplɪˈmentərɪ] *adj.* нелестный.
uncompromising [ʌnˈkɒmprəˌmaɪzɪŋ] *adj.* бескомпромиссный, неуступчивый.
unconcealed [ˌʌnkənˈsiːld] *adj.* нескрываемый.
unconcern [ˌʌnkənˈsɜːn] *n.* беззаботность, беспечность.
unconcerned [ˌʌnkənˈsɜːnd] *adj.* (*carefree*) беззаботный, беспечный.
unconditional [ˌʌnkənˈdɪʃən(ə)l] *adj.* безусловный, безоговорочный; **~ surrender** безоговорочная капитуляция.

unconfirmed [ˌʌnkənˈfɜːmd] *adj.* неподтверждённый.
unconnected [ˌʌnkəˈnektɪd] *adj.* не свя́занный; **the wires were ~** провода́ не́ были соединены́.
unconquerable [ʌnˈkɒŋkərəb(ə)l] *adj.* непобеди́мый.
unconscionable [ʌnˈkɒnʃənəb(ə)l] *adj.*: **an ~ liar** отъя́вленный/невозмо́жный лгун.
unconscious [ʌnˈkɒnʃəs] *adj.* **1.** (*senseless*) потеря́вший созна́ние; в (глубо́ком) о́бмороке; **he was knocked ~** он потеря́л созна́ние от уда́ра. **2.** (*unaware*) не сознаю́щий; **he was ~ of having done wrong** он не сознава́л, что поступи́л пло́хо. **3.** (*unintentional*) нево́льный; **he spoke with ~ irony** он говори́л с бессозна́тельной иро́нией.
unconsciousness [ʌnˈkɒnʃəsnɪs] *n.* бессозна́тельное состоя́ние.
unconstitutional [ˌʌnkɒnstɪˈtjuːʃən(ə)l] *adj.* противоре́чащий конститу́ции.
unconstrained [ˌʌnkənˈstreɪnd] *adj.* непринуждённый.
uncontrollable [ˌʌnkənˈtrəʊləb(ə)l] *adj.*: **an ~ temper** неукроти́мый нрав; **an ~ child** неуправля́емый ребёнок.
uncontrolled [ˌʌnkənˈtrəʊld] *adj.* неконтроли́руемый, бесконтро́льный.
unconventional [ˌʌnkənˈvenʃən(ə)l] *adj.* нешабло́нный, эксцентри́чный.
unconvinced [ˌʌnkənˈvɪnsd] *adj.* неубеждённый.
unconvincing [ˌʌnkənˈvɪnsɪŋ] *adj.* неубеди́тельный.
uncooked [ʌnˈkʊkt] *adj.* сыро́й; непригото́вленный.
uncooperative [ˌʌnkəʊˈɒpərətɪv] *adj.* не проявля́ющий гото́вность помо́чь.
uncork [ʌnˈkɔːk] *v.t.* отку́пори|вать, -ть.
uncountable [ʌnˈkaʊntəb(ə)l] *adj.* (*innumerable*) бесчи́сленный, неисчисли́мый.
uncounted [ʌnˈkaʊntɪd] *adj.* (*innumerable*) несчётный, бесчи́сленный.
uncouple [ʌnˈkʌp(ə)l] *v.t.* (*rail carriages*) расцеп|ля́ть, -и́ть.
uncouth [ʌnˈkuːθ] *adj.* гру́бый, неотёсанный.
uncover [ʌnˈkʌvə(r)] *v.t.* сн|има́ть, -ять; **he ~ed his head** он обнажи́л го́лову; (*fig.*) раскр|ыва́ть, -ы́ть; обнару́жи|вать, -ть; **the conspiracy was ~ed** за́говор раскры́ли.
uncritical [ʌnˈkrɪtɪk(ə)l] *adj.* некрити́ческий.
uncrowned [ʌnˈkraʊnd] *adj.*: **~ king** (*lit.*, *fig.*) некороно́ванный коро́ль.
unction [ˈʌŋkʃ(ə)n] *n.* (*anointing*) пома́зание; **extreme ~** собо́рование.
unctuous [ˈʌŋktjʊəs] *adj.* еле́йный.
uncultivated [ʌnˈkʌltɪˌveɪtɪd] *adj.* (*of land*) необрабо́танный, невозде́ланный; (*of pers.*) некульту́рный.
uncultured [ʌnˈkʌltʃəd] *adj.* некульту́рный.
uncut [ʌnˈkʌt] *adj.* неразре́занный; неподстри́женный; **the film was shown ~** фильм показа́ли целико́м (*or* без сокраще́ний/купю́р).
undamaged [ʌnˈdæmɪdʒd] *adj.* неповреждённый.
undaunted [ʌnˈdɔːntɪd] *adj.* неустраши́мый.
undecided [ˌʌndɪˈsaɪdɪd] *adj.* нерешённый; нереши́тельный; **I am ~ whether to go or stay** я не зна́ю, идти́ мне и́ли нет.
undecipherable [ˌʌndɪˈsaɪfərəb(ə)l] *adj.* неразбо́рчивый.
undeclared [ˌʌndɪˈkleəd] *adj.* необъя́вленный; **a state of ~ war** состоя́ние необъя́вленной войны́.
undefended [ˌʌndɪˈfendɪd] *adj.* незащищённый; **they left the city ~** они́ оста́вили го́род без прикры́тия.
undemonstrative [ˌʌndɪˈmɒnstrətɪv] *adj.* сде́ржанный.
undeniable [ˌʌndɪˈnaɪəb(ə)l] *adj.* неоспори́мый, я́вный.
undependable [ˌʌndɪˈpendəb(ə)l] *adj.* ненадёжный.
under [ˈʌndə(r)] *adv.* вниз; **the ship went ~** кора́бль затону́л; **he dived and stayed ~ for a minute** он нырну́л и продержа́лся под водо́й (одну́) мину́ту.
prep. **1.** под+*i.*; (*of motion*) под+*a.*; **(out) from ~** из-под+*g.* **2.** (*less than*) ме́ньше+*g.*; ни́же+*g.*; **he earns ~ £40 a week** он зараба́тывает ме́ньше сорока́ фу́нтов в неде́лю; **children ~ 14** де́ти моло́же (*or* в во́зрасте до) четы́рнадцати лет; **I can get there in ~ an hour** я могу́ добра́ться туда́ ме́ньше, чем за час. **3.** (*var. uses*): **~ arms** под ружём; **you are ~ arrest** вы аресто́ваны; **~ oath** под прися́гой; **~ repair** в ремо́нте; **~ suspicion** под подозре́нием; **~ way** на ходу́; (**~** *authority of*): **he served ~ me** он служи́л под мои́м руково́дством; **he studied ~ a professor** он учи́лся у профе́ссора; **~ the tsars** при царя́х; **England ~ the Stuarts** А́нглия в ца́рствование Стю́артов; (*according to*): **~ the terms of the agreement** по усло́виям соглаше́ния; **~ orders** по прика́зу; **~ the rules** согла́сно уста́ву; (*classified with*): **they come ~ the same heading** они́ отно́сятся к той же ру́брике.
underarm [ˈʌndərˌɑːm] *adj.* & *adv.*: **an ~ shot** уда́р предплечьем.
undercarriage [ˈʌndəˌkærɪdʒ] *n.* шасси́ (*nt. indecl.*).
undercharge [ˌʌndəˈtʃɑːdʒ] *v.i.* брать, взять (*or* назн|ача́ть, -а́чить) сли́шком ни́зкую це́ну.
underclothes [ˈʌndəˌkləʊðz, -ˌkləʊz] *n.* ни́жнее бельё.
undercoat [ˈʌndəˌkəʊt] *n.* (*of paint*) грунто́вка.
under-cover [ˌʌndəˈkʌvə(r), ˈʌn-] *adj.* та́йный.
undercurrent [ˈʌndəˌkʌrənt] *n.* подво́дное тече́ние; (*fig.*) скры́тая тенде́нция.
under-developed [ˌʌndədɪˈveləpt] *adj.* недора́звитый; **~ countries** слабора́звитые стра́ны.
underdog [ˈʌndəˌdɒg] *n.* (*fig.*) побеждённая сторона́; обездо́ленный челове́к; неуда́чник.
underdone [ˌʌndəˈdʌn, ˈʌn-] *adj.* (*of food*) недожа́ренный, недова́ренный.
underestimate[1] [ˌʌndərˈestɪmət] *n.* недооце́нка.
underestimate[2] [ˌʌndərˈestɪˌmeɪt] *v.t.* недооце́н|ивать, -и́ть.
underestimation [ˌʌndərestɪˈmeɪʃ(ə)n] *n.* недооце́нка.
underexpose [ˌʌndərɪkˈspəʊz] *v.t.* (*phot.*) недоде́рж|ивать, -а́ть.
underexposure [ˌʌndərɪkˈspəʊʒə(r)] (*phot.*) недоста́точная вы́держка.
underfed [ˌʌndəˈfed] *adj.* недоко́рмленный.
underfelt [ˈʌndəˌfelt] *n.* грунт ковра́.
underfoot [ˌʌndəˈfʊt] *adv.* под нога́ми.
undergarments [ˈʌndəˌgɑːmənts] *n. pl.* ни́жнее бельё.
undergo [ˌʌndəˈgəʊ] *v.t.* испы́т|ывать, -а́ть; подв|ерга́ться, -е́ргнуться +*d.*; **he has to ~ an operation** ему́ предстои́т опера́ция.
undergraduate [ˌʌndəˈgrædjʊət] *n.* студе́нт (*fem.* -ка); (*attr.*) студе́нческий.
underground [ˈʌndəˌgraʊnd] *n.* **1.** (**~** *railway*) метро́ (*indecl.*); **on the U~** в метро́. **2.** (**~** *movement*) подпо́лье.
adj. подзе́мный; (*fig.*, *secret*, *subversive*) подпо́льный; **an ~ newspaper** подпо́льная газе́та.
adv. под землёй/зе́млю; (*fig.*) подпо́льно.
undergrowth [ˈʌndəˌgrəʊθ] *n.* подле́сок.
underhand [ˈʌndəˌhænd] *adj.* (*secret*, *deceitful*) закули́сный, та́йный.
adv. тайко́м.
underl|ie [ˌʌndəˈlaɪ] *v.t.* **1.** (*lit.*) лежа́ть (*impf.*) под+*i.*; **~ying stratum** ни́жний слой. **2.** (*fig.*) лежа́ть в осно́ве +*g.*; **~ying causes** причи́ны, лежа́щие в осно́ве (*чего*).
underline [ˌʌndəˈlaɪn] *v.t.* (*lit.*, *fig.*) подч|ёркивать, -еркну́ть.
underling [ˈʌndəlɪŋ] *n.* ме́лкий чино́вник.
undermine [ˌʌndəˈmaɪn] *v.t.* подк|а́пывать, -опа́ть; (*fig.*) разр|уша́ть, -у́шить; **his health was ~d by drink** алкого́ль подорва́л его́ здоро́вье; **his authority is ~d** его́ авторите́т вся́чески подрыва́ют.
underneath [ˌʌndəˈniːθ] *adv.* внизу́, ни́же.
prep. под+*i.*; (*of motion*) под+*a.*

undernourished [ˌʌndəˈnʌrɪʃt] *adj.* недокóрмленный.
underpants [ˈʌndəˌpænts] *n. pl.* (*long*) кальсóн|ы (*pl.*, *g.* —); (*short*) (мужскúе) трус|ы́ (*pl.*, *g.* -óв).
underpass [ˈʌndəˌpɑːs] *n.* проéзд под полотнóм желéзной дорóги; (ýличный) тоннéль (*m.*).
underpa|y [ˌʌndəˈpeɪ] *v.t.* слúшком нúзко оплá|чивать, -тúть; недоплá|чивать, -тúть; **the workers are ~id** рабóчим мáло плáтят.
underpayment [ˌʌndəˈpeɪmənt] *n.* слúшком нúзкая оплáта; недоплáта.
under-populated [ˌʌndəˈpɒpjʊˈleɪtɪd] *adj.* малонаселённый.
under-privileged [ˌʌndəˈprɪvɪlɪdʒd] *adj.* неимýщий; пóльзующийся мéньшими правáми.
under-production [ˌʌndəprəˈdʌkʃ(ə)n] *n.* недопроизвóдство.
underrate [ˌʌndəˈreɪt] *v.t.* недооцéн|ивать, -úть.
underripe [ˌʌndəˈraɪp] *adj.* недозрéлый, неспéлый.
underscore [ˌʌndəˈskɔː(r)] *v.t.* подч|ёркивать, -еркнýть.
under-secretary [ˌʌndəˈsekrətərɪ] *n.* заместúтель (*m.*) минúстра.
undersell [ˌʌndəˈsel] *v.t.* (*goods*) прод|авáть, -áть по понúженной ценé (*or* нúже стóимости).
undershirt [ˈʌndəˌʃɜːt] *n.* мáйка; (*with sleeves*) нúжняя рубáшка/сорóчка.
under-side [ˈʌndəˌsaɪd] *n.* низ; нúжняя сторонá.
undersign [ˈʌndəˌsaɪn, -ˌʌndəˈsaɪn] *v.t.*: **we, the ~ed** мы, нижеподписáвшиеся.
undersized [ˈʌndəˌsaɪzd, -ˈsaɪzd] *adj.* (*of pers.*) низкорóслый.
underskirt [ˈʌndəˌskɜːt] *n.* нúжняя ю́бка.
understaffed [ˌʌndəˈstɑːft] *adj.* испы́тывающий недостáток рабóчей сúлы; неукомплектóванный.
understand [ˌʌndəˈstænd] *v.t.* **1.** (*comprehend*) пон|имáть, -я́ть; **he ~s French** он понимáет по-францу́зски; **he ~s finance** он разбирáется в финáнсовых вопрóсах; **now I ~!** тепéрь всё поня́тно; **he can make himself understood in English** он мóжет объясня́ться по-англúйски; **he ~s children** он умéет обращáться с детьмú; **am I to ~ you refuse?** инáче говоря́ (*or* нáдо понимáть), вы откáзываете?; **what are we to ~ from such an act?** как мы должны́ поня́ть/истолковáть такóй постýпок? **2.** (*gather*, *be informed*): **I ~ you are leaving** я слы́шал, что вы уезжáете; **you were, I ~, alone** вы бы́ли, наскóлько я пóнял, однú. **3.** (*agree*, *accept*): **it is understood** самó собóй разумéется; установлено; (*custom*) так заведенó; **it is understood, then, that we meet tomorrow** итáк, решенó: мы встречáемся зáвтра. **4.** (*gram.*): **the verb is understood** глагóл подразумевáется.
understandable [ˌʌndəˈstændəb(ə)l] *adj.* поня́тный.
understanding [ˌʌndəˈstændɪŋ] *n.* **1.** (*intellect*) ум; **it passes my ~** э́то вы́ше моегó понимáния. **2.** (*comprehension*): **he has a clear ~ of the problem** он прекрáсно понимáет проблéму; **he has a good ~ of economics** он хорошó разбирáется в эконóмике. **3.** (*sympathy*) понимáние, отзы́вчивость; **he showed ~ for my position** он вошёл в моё положéние. **4.** (*agreement*) соглашéние, договорённость; **on the clear ~ that ...** тóлько при услóвии, что...

adj. отзы́вчивый, чýткий; **~ parents** разýмные родúтели.
understate [ˌʌndəˈsteɪt] *v.t.* преум|еньшáть, -éньшить.
understatement [ˌʌndəˈsteɪtmənt, ˈʌndə-] *n.* преуменьшéние, недоскáз.
understudy [ˈʌndəˌstʌdɪ] *n.* дублёр (*fem.* -ша).

v.t. дублúровать (*impf.*).
undertak|e [ˌʌndəˈteɪk] *v.t.* **1.** (*take on*) предприн|имáть, -я́ть; брать, взять на себя́; **he has ~en the job of secretary** он прúнял на себя́ дóлжность секретаря́. **2.** (*pledge o.s.*, *promise*) обя́з|ываться, -áться. **3.** (*guarantee*) ручáться (*impf.*).
undertaker [ˈʌndəˌteɪkə(r)] *n.* гробовщúк; завéдующий/владéлец похорóнного бюрó.
undertaking [ˌʌndəˈteɪkɪŋ] *n.* (*enterprise*) предприя́тие; (*pledge*, *guarantee*) обязáтельство, гарáнтия.
undertone [ˈʌndəˌtəʊn] *n.*: **in an ~** вполгóлоса.
undervalue [ˌʌndəˈvæljuː] *v.t.* недооцéн|ивать, -úть.
underwater [ˌʌndəˈwɔːtə(r)] *adj.* подвóдный.
underwear [ˈʌndəˌweə(r)] *n.* нúжнее бельё.
underworld [ˈʌndəˌwɜːld] *n.* (*myth.*) преиспóдняя; (*criminal society*) престýпный мир.
underwrite [ˌʌndəˈraɪt, ˈʌn-] *v.t.* **1.**: **~ a marine insurance policy** подпúс|ывать, -áть пóлис морскóго страховáния. **2.**: **~ a loan** гарантúровать (*impf.*, *pf.*) размещéние зáйма. **3.** (*support*) (финáнсово) поддéрж|ивать, -áть.
underwriter [ˈʌndəˌraɪtə(r)] *n.* (морскóй) страхóвщик.
undeserved [ˌʌndɪˈzɜːvd] *adj.* незаслýженный.
undesirable [ˌʌndɪˈzaɪərəb(ə)l] *n.* (*pers.*) нежелáтельный элемéнт.

adj. нежелáтельный.
undetected [ˌʌndɪˈtektɪd] *adj.* необнарýженный.
undetermined [ˌʌndɪˈtɜːmɪnd] *adj.* неопределённый.
undeveloped [ˌʌndɪˈveləpt] *adj.* неразвитóй; **an ~ country** слаборáзвитая странá; **~ land** необрабóтанная земля́.
undignified [ʌnˈdɪgnɪˌfaɪd] *adj.* недостóйный.
undiluted [ˌʌndaɪˈljuːtɪd] *adj.* неразбáвленный.
undiminished [ˌʌndɪˈmɪnɪʃt] *adj.* неумéньшенный.
undiplomatic [ˌʌndɪpləˈmætɪk] *adj.* недипломатúчный.
undisciplined [ʌnˈdɪsɪplɪnd] *adj.* недисциплинúрованный.
undisclosed [ˌʌndɪsˈkləʊzd] *adj.* неразоблачённый.
undiscriminating [ˌʌndɪˈskrɪmɪˌneɪtɪŋ] *adj.* недискриминúрующий, неразбóрчивый.
undisguised [ˌʌndɪsˈgaɪzd] *adj.* я́вный; **with ~ relief** с я́вным/нескрывáемым облегчéнием.
undismayed [ˌʌndɪsˈmeɪd] *adj.* неустрашúмый.
undisputed [ˌʌndɪˈspjuːtɪd] *adj.* неоспорúмый.
undistinguished [ˌʌndɪˈstɪŋgwɪʃt] *adj.* (*of pers.*) посрéдственный, невзрáчный.
undisturbed [ˌʌndɪˈstɜːbd] *adj.* невстревóженный, спокóйный.
undivided [ˌʌndɪˈvaɪdɪd] *adj.* нераздéльный; **~ attention** нераздéльное внимáние.
undo [ʌnˈduː] *v.t.* **1.** (*unfasten*) развя́з|ывать, -áть. **2.** (*annul*) уничт|ожáть, -óжить; **he tried to ~ the work of his predecessor** он пытáлся перечеркнýть рабóту своегó предшéственника. **3.** (*ruin*) губúть, по-; **drink was his ~ing** пья́нство егó погубúло.
undomesticated [ˌʌndəˈmestɪˌkeɪtɪd] *adj.* неприрýченный.
undoubted [ʌnˈdaʊtɪd] *adj.* несомнéнный; **an ~ success** несомнéнный/бесспóрный успéх; **you are ~ly right** вы несомнéнно/безуслóвно прáвы.
undreamed-of [ʌnˈdriːmd, ʌnˈdremt], **undreamt-of** [ʌnˈdremt] *adj.* не снúвшийся; невообразúмый; **~ riches** немы́слимое богáтство.
undress [ʌnˈdres] *n.*: **in a state of ~** полуодéтый; (*naked*) в гóлом вúде.

v.t. & i. разд|евáть(ся), -éть(ся).
undressed [ʌnˈdrest] *adj.* (*without clothes*) раздéтый; (*untreated*) необрабóтанный.
undrinkable [ʌnˈdrɪŋkəb(ə)l] *adj.* непригóдный для питья́.
undue [ʌnˈdjuː] *adj.* (*excessive*) чрезмéрный, излúшный; (*improper*) неподобáющий.
undulate [ˈʌndjʊˌleɪt] *v.i.* волновáться (*impf.*); колыхáться (*impf.*).
unduly [ʌnˈdjuːlɪ] *adv.* чрезмéрно; неправúльно.
undying [ʌnˈdaɪɪŋ] *adj.* бесмéртный; **he won ~ glory** он завоевáл себé вéчную слáву; **you have earned my ~ gratitude** я вам обя́зан до гробовóй доскú.
unearned [ʌnˈɜːnd] *adj.* незарабóтанный; **~ income**

нетрудовы́е дохо́ды (*m. pl.*); (*undeserved*) незаслу́женный.
unearth [ʌn'ɜ:θ] *v.t.* выка́пывать, вы́копать; (*fig.*, *discover*) раск|а́пывать, -опа́ть.
unearthly [ʌn'ɜ:θlɪ] *adj.* **1.** (*supernatural*) неземно́й. **2.** (*ghostly*) при́зрачный. **3.** (*coll.*, *unreasonable*) абсу́рдный; **why do you wake me at this ~ hour?** заче́м вы меня́ бу́дите в таку́ю рань?
uneasiness [ʌn'i:zɪnɪs] *n.* нело́вкость; беспоко́йство.
uneasy [ʌn'i:zɪ] *adj.* **1.** (*anxious*) беспоко́йный, трево́жный; **she was ~ about her daughter** она́ беспоко́илась за дочь. **2.** (*ill at ease*) стеснённый.
uneatable [ʌn'i:təb(ə)l] *adj.* несъедо́бный.
uneconomic [ˌʌni:kə'nɒmɪk, ˌʌnek-] *adj.* неэконо́мный; **an ~ rent** невы́годная ре́нта.
uneconomical [ˌʌni:kə'nɒmɪk(ə)l, ˌʌnek-] *adj.* (*wasteful*) неэконо́мный; бесхозя́йственный.
uneducated [ʌn'edjʊˌkeɪtɪd] *adj.* необразо́ванный.
unemployed [ˌʌnɪm'plɔɪd] *adj.* **1.** (*out of work*) безрабо́тный; (*as n.*: **the ~**) безрабо́тные (*pl.*). **2.** (*unused*, *e.g. resources*) неиспо́льзованный.
unemployment [ˌʌnɪm'plɔɪmənt] *n.* безрабо́тица; **~ benefit** посо́бие по безрабо́тице.
unending [ʌn'endɪŋ] *adj.* несконча́емый.
unendurable [ˌʌnɪn'djʊərəb(ə)l] *adj.* невыноси́мый, нестерпи́мый.
unenlightened [ˌʌnɪn'laɪt(ə)nd] *adj.* непросвещённый.
unenterprising [ʌn'entəˌpraɪzɪŋ] *adj.* непредприи́мчивый.
unenthusiastic [ˌʌnɪnˌθju:zɪ'æstɪk, ˌʌnɪnˌθu:-] *adj.* невосто́рженный; **he was ~ about the idea** он не́ был в восто́рге от э́той иде́и.
unenviable [ʌn'envɪəb(ə)l] *adj.* незави́дный.
unequal [ʌn'i:kw(ə)l] *adj.* нера́вный; **~ in length** разли́чной/неодина́ковой длины́; **he was ~ to the task** зада́ча была́ ему́ не по плечу́; **~ treaty** неравнопра́вный догово́р.
unequalled [ʌn'i:kw(ə)ld] *adj.* непревзойдённый.
unequipped [ˌʌnɪ'kwɪpt] *adj.* неподгото́вленный, неприспосо́бленный.
unequivocal [ˌʌnɪ'kwɪvək(ə)l] *adj.* недвусмы́сленный.
unerring [ʌn'ɜ:rɪŋ] *adj.* безоши́бочный.
unescapable [ˌʌnɪ'skeɪpəb(ə)l] *adj.* неизбе́жный.
unethical [ʌn'eθɪk(ə)l] *adj.* неэти́чный.
uneven [ʌn'i:v(ə)n] *adj.* неро́вный; неравноме́рный; **an ~ temper** неуравнове́шенный хара́ктер.
uneventful [ˌʌnɪ'ventfʊl] *adj.* ти́хий; без (осо́бых) приключе́ний/собы́тий.
unexampled [ˌʌnɪg'zɑ:mp(ə)ld] *adj.* бесприме́рный.
unexcelled [ˌʌnɪk'seld] *adj.* непревзойдённый.
unexceptionable [ˌʌnɪk'sepʃənəb(ə)l] *adj.* безупре́чный.
unexceptional [ˌʌnɪk'sepʃən(ə)l] *adj.* неисключи́тельный, зауря́дный.
unexpected [ˌʌnɪk'spektɪd] *adj.* неожи́данный.
unexplored [ˌʌnɪk'splɔ:d] *adj.* неизве́данный; неиссле́дованный.
unexposed [ˌʌnɪk'spəʊzd] *adj.* (*film*) неэкспони́рованный.
unexpressed [ˌʌnɪk'sprest] *adj.* невы́сказанный.
unexpurgated [ʌn'ekspəˌgeɪtɪd] *adj.* без купю́р.
unfailing [ʌn'feɪlɪŋ] *adj.* ве́рный, неизме́нный; **an ~ source** неиссяка́емый исто́чник.
unfair [ʌn'feə(r)] *adj.* несправедли́вый; **~ advantage** незако́нное преиму́щество; **an ~ opponent** нече́стный проти́вник.
unfairness [ʌn'feənɪs] *n.* несправедли́вость.
unfaithful [ʌn'feɪθfʊl] *adj.* неве́рный; **his wife was ~ to him** жена́ ему́ измени́ла.
unfamiliar [ˌʌnfə'mɪljə(r)] *adj.* незнако́мый; **I am ~ with the district** я не зна́ю э́того райо́на.
unfamiliarity [ˌʌnfəmɪlɪ'ærɪtɪ] *n.* незнако́мство (*с чем*).
unfashionabl|e [ʌn'fæʃənəb(ə)l] *adj.* немо́дный; старомо́дный; **~y** не по мо́де.
unfasten [ʌn'fɑ:s(ə)n] *v.t.* откреп|ля́ть, -и́ть; (*untie*) отвя́з|ывать, -а́ть; развя́з|ывать, -а́ть; (*unbutton*, *unclasp*) отстёг|ивать, -ну́ть; расстёг|ивать, -ну́ть; (*open*) откр|ыва́ть, -ы́ть.
unfathomable [ʌn'fæðəməb(ə)l] *adj.* неизмери́мый; (*incomprehensible*) непостижи́мый.
unfavourable [ʌn'feɪvərəb(ə)l] *adj.* неблагоприя́тный.
unfeeling [ʌn'fi:lɪŋ] *adj.* бесчу́вственный; жесто́кий.
unfeigned [ʌn'feɪnd] *adj.* неподде́льный, непритво́рный.
unfetter [ʌn'fetə(r)] *v.t.* (*lit.*, *fig.*) сн|има́ть, -ять око́вы с+*g.*; освобо|жда́ть, -ди́ть; **~ed** свобо́дный.
unfinished [ʌn'fɪnɪʃt] *adj.* незако́нченный.
unfit [ʌn'fɪt] *adj.* неподходя́щий, него́дный; **~ to rule** неспосо́бный пра́вить; **the doctor pronounced him ~** врач призна́л его́ больны́м (*for mil. service*: него́дным).
unflagging [ʌn'flægɪŋ] *adj.* неосла́бный.
unflappable [ʌn'flæpəb(ə)l] *adj.* (*coll.*) невозмути́мый.
unflattering [ʌn'flætərɪŋ] *adj.* неле́стный.
unfledged [ʌn'fledʒd] *adj.* (*lit.*, *fig.*) неопери́вшийся.
unfold [ʌn'fəʊld] *v.t.* развёр|тывать, -ну́ть; (*fig.*) раскр|ыва́ть, -ы́ть.
v.i. развёр|тываться, -ну́ться; расстила́ться (*impf.*).
unforced [ʌn'fɔ:st] *adj.* (*voluntary*) доброво́льный; (*spontaneous*) непринуждённый.
unforeseen [ˌʌnfɔ:'si:n] *adj.* непредви́денный.
unforgettable [ˌʌnfə'getəb(ə)l] *adj.* незабыва́емый, незабве́нный.
unforgivable [ˌʌnfə'gɪvəb(ə)l] *adj.* непрости́тельный.
unfortunate [ʌn'fɔ:tjʊnət, -tʃənət] *adj.* несча́стный, неуда́чный; **an ~ remark** неуда́чное замеча́ние.
unfortunately [ʌn'fɔ:tjʊnətlɪ, -tʃənətlɪ] *adv.* к сожале́нию, к несча́стью.
unfounded [ʌn'faʊndɪd] *adj.* необосно́ванный.
unfreeze [ʌn'fri:z] *v.t.* (*also fig.*, *of assets*) размор|а́живать, -о́зить.
unfriendliness [ʌn'frendlɪnɪs] *adj.* недружелю́бие.
unfriendly [ʌn'frendlɪ] *adj.* недружелю́бный, неприя́зненный; **an ~ act** недру́жественный посту́пок.
unfrock [ʌn'frɒk] *v.t.* лиш|а́ть, -и́ть духо́вного са́на.
unfruitful [ʌn'fru:tfʊl] *adj.* (*fig.*) беспло́дный; (*vain*) напра́сный; (*useless*) бесполе́зный.
unfulfilled [ˌʌnfʊl'fɪld] *adj.* (*of task*, *aim etc.*) невы́полненный; (*of pers.*) неудовлетворённый.
unfurl [ʌn'fɜ:l] *v.t.* развёр|тывать, -ну́ть; распус|ка́ть, -ти́ть.
unfurnished [ʌn'fɜ:nɪʃt] *adj.* немеблиро́ванный.
ungainly [ʌn'geɪnlɪ] *adj.* нело́вкий, неуклю́жий.
ungenerous [ʌn'dʒenərəs] *adj.* (*petty*) неблагоро́дный, ме́лочный; (*stingy*) нище́дрый, скупо́й.
ungentlemanly [ʌn'dʒentəlmənlɪ] *adj.* не досто́йный джентльме́на; неблагоро́дный.
ungodly [ʌn'gɒdlɪ] *adj.* непра́ведный, нечести́вый; (*coll.*, *frightful*): **an ~ noise** ужа́сный шум.
ungovernable [ʌn'gʌvənəb(ə)l] *adj.* неуправля́емый.
ungracious [ʌn'greɪʃəs] *adj.* неве́жливый, нелюбе́зный.
ungrammatical [ˌʌngrə'mætɪk(ə)l] *adj.* негра́мотный; (*of languages*, *also*) безгра́мотный.
ungrateful [ʌn'greɪtfʊl] *adj.* неблагода́рный.
ungrudging [ʌn'grʌdʒɪŋ] *adj.* ще́дрый; до́брый; **he gave ~ly of his time** он ще́дро дари́л своё вре́мя.
unguarded [ʌn'gɑ:dɪd] *adj.* (*e.g. town*) незащищённый; (*careless*) неосторо́жный, неосмотри́тельный.
unguent ['ʌŋgwənt] *n.* мазь.
ungulate ['ʌŋgjʊlət, -ˌleɪt] *adj.* копы́тный.
unhallowed [ʌn'hæləʊd] *adj.* неосвящённый.
unhampered [ʌn'hæmpəd] *adj.* беспрепя́тственный; свобо́дный (от+*g.*).
unhappily [ʌn'hæpɪlɪ] *adv.* **1.** (*without happiness*) несча́стливо; **they were ~ married** их брак был

несчастли́вый. **2.** (*unfortunately*) к несча́стью.
unhappiness [ʌn'hæpɪnɪs] *n.* несча́стье, го́ре, грусть.
unhappy [ʌn'hæpɪ] *adj.* (*sorrowful*) несчастли́вый, несча́стный, гру́стный; (*unfortunate*) неуда́чный.
unharmed [ʌn'hɑːmd] *adj.* неповреждённый; (*pred.*) цел и невреди́м.
unharness [ʌn'hɑːnɪs] *v.t.* распр|яга́ть, -я́чь.
unhealthy [ʌn'helθɪ] *adj.* **1.** (*in or indicating ill-health*) нездоро́вый, боле́зненный. **2.** (*coll., dangerous*) вре́дный.
unheard-of [ʌn'hɜːdɔv] *adj.* (*unknown*) неслы́ханный; (*unexampled, also*) беспрецеде́нтный.
unheeded [ʌn'hiːdɪd] *adj.* незаме́ченный; **his advice went ~** к его́ сове́там не прислу́шались.
unhelpful [ʌn'helpfʊl] *adj.* бесполе́зный; (*pers.*) неотзы́вчивый.
unhesitating [ʌn'hezɪˌteɪtɪŋ] *adj.* неколе́блющийся, реши́тельный.
unhinge [ʌn'hɪndʒ] *v.t.* (*lit.*) сн|има́ть, -ять с пе́тель; (*fig.*) расстр|а́ивать, -о́ить; **the tragedy ~d his mind** от пе́режи́той траге́дии он тро́нулся умо́м.
unhitch [ʌn'hɪtʃ] *v.t.* отвя́з|ывать, -а́ть; распр|яга́ть, -я́чь.
unholy [ʌn'həʊlɪ] *adj.* нечести́вый; (*coll., frightful*) ужа́сный; **an ~ row** ужа́сный/жу́ткий сканда́л.
unhook [ʌn'hʊk] *v.t.* **1.** (*unfasten hooks of*) расстё|г|ивать, -ну́ть. **2.** (*release from hook etc.*) отцеп|ля́ть, -и́ть.
unhurried [ʌn'hʌrɪd] *adj.* неторопли́вый, неспе́шный.
unhurt [ʌn'hɜːt] *adj.* невреди́мый.
unhygienic [ˌʌnhaɪ'dʒiːnɪk] *adj.* негигиени́чный.
unicorn ['juːnɪˌkɔːn] *n.* единоро́г.
unidentified [ˌʌnaɪ'dentɪˌfaɪd] *adj.* неопо́знанный; **~ flying object (UFO)** неопо́знанный лета́ющий объе́кт (НЛО).
unification [ˌjuːnɪfɪ'keɪʃ(ə)n] *n.* объедине́ние.
uniform ['juːnɪˌfɔːm] *n.* фо́рма; (*esp. mil.*) мунди́р.
adj. однообра́зный; одина́ковый; станда́ртный; **at a ~ temperature** при постоя́нной температу́рой.
uniformed ['juːnɪˌfɔːmd] *adj.* оде́тый в фо́рму; в мунди́ре.
uniformity [ˌjuːnɪ'fɔːmɪtɪ] *n.* единообра́зие.
unify ['juːnɪˌfaɪ] *v.t.* объедин|я́ть, -и́ть.
unilateral [ˌjuːnɪ'lætər(ə)l] *adj.* односторо́нний.
unimaginable [ˌʌnɪ'mædʒɪnəb(ə)l] *adj.* невообрази́мый.
unimaginative [ˌʌnɪ'mædʒɪnətɪv] *adj.* лишённый воображе́ния; прозаи́чный.
unimpeachable [ˌʌnɪm'piːtʃəb(ə)l] *adj.* безупре́чный, безукори́зненный.
unimpeded [ˌʌnɪm'piːdɪd] *adj.* беспрепя́тственный.
unimportant [ˌʌnɪm'pɔːt(ə)nt] *adj.* нева́жный, незначи́тельный.
unimpressed [ˌʌnɪm'prest] *adj.*: **I was ~ by his threats** его́ угро́зы не произвели́ на меня́ никако́го впечатле́ния.
uninformed [ˌʌnɪn'fɔːmd] *adj.* неосведомлённый, несве́дущий.
uninhabitable [ˌʌnɪn'hæbɪtəb(ə)l] *adj.* неприго́дный для жилья́.
uninhabited [ˌʌnɪn'hæbɪtɪd] *adj.* необита́емый.
uninhibited [ˌʌnɪn'hɪbɪtɪd] *adj.* нестесни́тельный.
uninitiated [ˌʌnɪ'nɪʃɪˌeɪtɪd] *adj.* непосвящённый.
uninjured [ʌn'ɪndʒəd] *adj.* непострада́вший; **he was ~ by his fall** при паде́нии он не получи́л поврежде́ний
uninspired [ˌʌnɪn'spaɪəd] *adj.* невдохновлённый.
uninsured [ˌʌnɪn'ʃʊəd] *adj.* незастрахо́ванный.
unintelligent [ˌʌnɪn'telɪdʒ(ə)nt] *adj.* неу́мный.
unintelligible [ˌʌnɪn'telɪdʒɪb(ə)l] *adj.* неразбо́рчивый, невня́тный.
unintended [ˌʌnɪn'tendɪd] *adj.* ненаме́ренный; (*unforeseen*) непредусмо́тренный.
unintentional [ˌʌnɪn'tenʃən(ə)l] *adj.* ненаме́ренный.
uninterested [ʌn'ɪntrəstɪd, -trɪstɪd] *adj.* безразли́чный (к+*d.*); не заинтересо́ванный (*чем*).
uninteresting [ʌn'ɪntrəstɪŋ, -trɪstɪŋ] *adj.* неинтере́сный.
uninterrupted [ˌʌnɪntə'rʌptɪd] *adj.* непрерыва́емый, непреры́вный.
uninvited [ˌʌnɪn'vaɪtɪd] *adj.* неприглашённый, незва́ный.
uninviting [ˌʌnɪn'vaɪtɪŋ] *adj.* непривлека́тельный; **an ~ prospect** неприя́тная перспекти́ва.
union ['juːnjən, -nɪən] *n.* **1.** (*joining, uniting*) объедине́ние, сою́з. **2.** (*association*) сою́з; **U~ of Soviet Socialist Republics** Сою́з Сове́тских Социалисти́ческих Респу́блик; **U~ Jack** госуда́рственный флаг Великобрита́нии; **students' ~** студе́нческий сою́з. **3. (trade ~)** профессиона́льный сою́з, профсою́з. **4.** (*state of harmony*) гармо́ния; согла́сие; **they live in perfect ~** они́ живу́т в по́лном согла́сии.
unique [jʊ'niːk, juː'niːk] *adj.* уника́льный, еди́нственный (в своём ро́де).
unisex ['juːnɪˌseks] *adj.*: **~ clothes** одина́ковая оде́жда для обо́их поло́в.
unisexual [ˌjuːnɪ'seksʊəl] *adj.* (*bot.*) однопо́лый.
unison ['juːnɪs(ə)n] *n.* (*mus.*) унисо́н; (*fig.*) гармо́ния.
unit ['juːnɪt] *n.* **1.** (*single entity*) едини́ца; це́лое. **2.** (*math., and of measurement*) едини́ца; **~ of length** едини́ца длины́; **~ of currency, monetary ~** де́нежная едини́ца. **3.** (*mil.*) часть; (*large ~, formation*) соедине́ние; (*small ~, sub-~*) подразделе́ние; (*detachment*) отря́д. **4.** (*of furniture etc.*) се́кция; **kitchen ~s** се́кции для ку́хонного комба́йна. **5.** (*tech.*) агрега́т.
unite [jʊ'naɪt, juː-] *v.t.* соедин|я́ть, -и́ть; объедин|я́ть, -и́ть; **a ~d family** дру́жная семья́; **they made a ~d effort** они́ объедини́лись для совме́стных уси́лий; **the U~d Nations** (*organization*) Организа́ция Объединённых На́ций; **the U~d Kingdom** Соединённое Короле́вство; **the U~d States** Соединённые Шта́ты.
v.i. соедин|я́ться, -и́ться; объедин|я́ться, -и́ться; **they ~d in condemning him** они́ единоду́шно его́ осуди́ли; **~d front** еди́ный фронт.
unity ['juːnɪtɪ] *n.* **1.** (*oneness; coherence*) еди́нство; сплочённость; **national ~** национа́льное еди́нство. **2.** (*concord*) согла́сие; **dwell in ~** жить (*impf.*) в согла́сии.
universal [ˌjuːnɪ'vɜːs(ə)l] *adj.* всео́бщий, универса́льный; **~ joint** (*tech.*) универса́льный шарни́р; **~ suffrage** всео́бщее избира́тельное пра́во.
universality [ˌjuːnɪvɜː'sælɪtɪ] *n.* универса́льность.
universe ['juːnɪˌvɜːs] *n.* вселе́нная, мир.
university [ˌjuːnɪ'vɜːsɪtɪ] *n.* университе́т; **~ town** университе́тский го́род/городо́к.
unjust [ʌn'dʒʌst] *adj.* несправедли́вый.
unjustifiable [ʌn'dʒʌstɪˌfaɪəb(ə)l] *adj.* непрости́тельный.
unjustified [ʌn'dʒʌstɪˌfaɪd] *adj.* неопра́вданный.
unkempt [ʌn'kempt] *adj.* нечёсаный, растрёпанный.
unkind [ʌn'kaɪnd] *adj.* недо́брый, нелюбе́зный; **be ~ to s.o.** пло́хо обраща́ться (*impf.*) с кем-н. (*or* относи́ться (*impf.*) к кому́-н.).
unknown [ʌn'nəʊn] *n.* неизве́стное; **fear of the ~** страх пе́ред неизве́стностью; (*math.*) неизве́стная величина́.
adj. неизве́стный; **an ~ quantity** неизве́стная величина́; **the U~ Soldier** Неизве́стный солда́т.
unlace [ʌn'leɪs] *v.t.* расшнуро́в|ывать, -а́ть.
unladylike [ʌn'leɪdɪˌlaɪk] *adj.* неподоба́ющий воспи́танной же́нщине; вульга́рный.
unlatch [ʌn'lætʃ] *v.t.* отп|ира́ть, -ере́ть.
unlawful [ʌn'lɔːfʊl] *adj.* незако́нный.
unleaded [ʌn'ledɪd] *adj.*: **~ petrol** неэтили́рованный бензи́н.

unleash [ʌn'li:ʃ] *v.t.* спус|ка́ть, -ти́ть со сво́ры (*or* с це́пи); ~ **a war** развяза́ть (*pf.*) войну́.
unleavened [ʌn'lev(ə)nd] *adj.* незаква́шенный, пре́сный.
unless [ʌn'les, ən'les] *conj.* е́сли (то́лько) не; пока́ не; ра́зве (то́лько); **I shall go** ~ **it rains** я пойду́, е́сли не бу́дет дождя́.
unlike [ʌn'laɪk] *adj. & adv.* непохо́жий, ра́зный; **they are utterly** ~ они́ соверше́нно ра́зные лю́ди (*or* не похо́жи друг на дру́га); **that** (*conduct etc.*) **is** ~ **him** э́то на него́ не похо́же; ~ **the others, he works hard** не в приме́р други́м (*or* в отли́чие от остальны́х), он усе́рдно рабо́тает.
unlikelihood [ʌn'laɪklɪhʊd] *n.* неправдоподо́бие.
unlikely [ʌn'laɪklɪ] *adj.* неправдоподо́бный; **it is** ~ **he will recover** маловероя́тно, что он попра́вится.
unlimited [ʌn'lɪmɪtɪd] *adj.* неограни́ченный.
unlined [ʌn'laɪnd] *adj.* **1.:** ~ **paper** нелино́ванная бума́га. **2.: an** ~ **coat** пальто́ без подкла́дки.
unlit [ʌn'lɪt] *adj.* неосвещённый; **the lamp was** ~ ла́мпу не зажгли́.
unload [ʌn'ləʊd] *v.t.* выгружа́ть, вы́грузить; разгру|жа́ть, -зи́ть; **she** ~**ed her worries on to him** она́ переложи́ла свои́ забо́ты на него́.
v.i. разгру|жа́ться, -зи́ться.
unloaded [ʌn'ləʊdɪd] *adj.* незаря́женный, пусто́й; **his gun was** ~ его́ ружьё не́ было заря́жено.
unlock [ʌn'lɒk] *v.t.* отп|ира́ть, -ере́ть (ключо́м).
unlocked [ʌn'lɒkt] *adj.* о́тпертый, неза́пертый.
unloved [ʌn'lʌvd] *adj.* нелюби́мый.
unluckily [ʌn'lʌkɪlɪ] *adv.* к несча́стью.
unlucky [ʌn'lʌkɪ] *adj.* неуда́чный, невезу́чий, незада́чливый; **he is** ~ **at cards** ему́ не везёт в ка́ртах; ~ **number** несчастли́вое число́.
unmade [ʌn'meɪd] *adj.*: **an** ~ **bed** незасте́ленная посте́ль.
unmanageable [ʌn'mænɪdʒəb(ə)l] *adj.* неуправля́емый; непоко́рный; не поддаю́щийся контро́лю.
unmanned [ʌn'mænd] *adj.* не укомплекто́ванный людьми́; **an** ~ **satellite** спу́тник, управля́емый автомати́чески.
unmannerly [ʌn'mænəlɪ] *adj.* невоспи́танный.
unmarked [ʌn'mɑ:kt] *adj.* неотме́ченный, неме́ченный.
unmarried [ʌn'mærɪd] *adj.* нежена́тый; незаму́жняя; **he is** ~ он не жена́т; **she is** ~ она́ не за́мужем; ~ **mother** мать-одино́чка.
unmask [ʌn'mɑ:sk] *v.t.* (*fig.*) разоблач|а́ть, -и́ть.
unmentionable [ʌn'menʃənəb(ə)l] *adj.* неприли́чный, запре́тный.
unmerciful [ʌn'mɜ:sɪˌfʊl] *adj.* немилосе́рдный, безжа́лостный.
unmindful [ʌn'maɪndfʊl] *adj.* невнима́тельный, забы́вчивый; ~ **of his duty** забы́в о до́лге.
unmistakabl|e [ˌʌnmɪ'steɪkəb(ə)l] *adj.* ве́рный, я́сный, очеви́дный; ~**y** несомне́нно, безусло́вно.
unmitigated [ʌn'mɪtɪˌgeɪtɪd] *adj.* зако́нченный, отъя́вленный, я́вный.
unmoved [ʌn'mu:vd] *adj.* бесчу́вственный; оста́вшийся равноду́шным.
unnamed [ʌn'neɪmd] *adj.* нена́званный; (*unidentified*) неизве́стный.
unnatural [ʌn'nætʃər(ə)l] *adj.* неесте́ственный; **not** ~**ly** есте́ственно.
unnavigable [ʌn'nævɪgəb(ə)l] *adj.* несудохо́дный.
unnecessary [ʌn'nesəsərɪ] *adj.* нену́жный, ли́шний; (*excessive*) изли́шний.
unnerv|e [ʌn'nɜ:v] *v.t.* обесси́ли|вать, -ть; лиш|а́ть, -и́ть (*кого*) му́жества; **an** ~**ing experience** неприя́тное/жу́ткое пережива́ние.
unnoticeable [ʌn'nəʊtɪsəb(ə)l] *adj.* незаме́тный.
unnoticed [ʌn'nəʊtɪst] *adj.* незаме́ченный.
unnumbered [ʌn'nʌmbəd] *adj.* **1.** (*countless*) бессчётный, несме́тный. **2.** (*without numbering*) без но́мера; ~ **pages** непронумеро́ванные страни́цы.
UNO ['ju:nəʊ] = **UN**
unobservant [ˌʌnəb'zɜ:v(ə)nt] *adj.* ненаблюда́тельный.
unobtainable [ˌʌnəb'teɪnəb(ə)l] *adj.* недосту́пный.
unobtrusive [ˌʌnəb'tru:sɪv] *adj.* скро́мный, ненавя́зчивый.
unoccupied [ʌn'ɒkjʊˌpaɪd] *adj.* neза́нятый, свобо́дный; **an** ~ **house** пусто́й дом.
unofficial [ˌʌnə'fɪʃ(ə)l] *adj.* неофициа́льный.
unopposed [ˌʌnə'pəʊzd] *adj.* не встреча́ющий/встре́тивший сопротивле́ния; **his candidature was** ~ он был еди́нственным кандида́том.
unorganized [ʌn'ɔ:gəˌnaɪzd] *adj.* неорганизо́ванный.
unoriginal [ˌʌnə'rɪdʒɪn(ə)l] *adj.* неоригина́льный; заи́мствованный.
unorthodox [ʌn'ɔ:θəˌdɒks] *adj.* неортодокса́льный; (*unconventional*) необщепри́нятый.
unorthodoxy [ʌn'ɔ:θəˌdɒksɪ] *n.* неортодокса́льность.
unostentatious [ˌʌnɒsten'teɪʃəs] *adj.* непоказно́й; скро́мный, ненавя́зчивый.
unpack [ʌn'pæk] *v.t. & i.* распако́в|ывать(ся), -а́ть(ся).
unpaid [ʌn'peɪd] *adj.* **1.** неопла́ченный; (*of debt, bill etc.*) неупла́ченный; ~ **work** беспла́тная рабо́та. **2.** (*of pers., unsalaried*) не получа́ющий пла́ту/жа́лованье.
unpalatable [ʌn'pælətəb(ə)l] *adj.* невку́сный; (*fig.*) неприя́тный; **an** ~ **truth** го́рькая и́стина.
unparalleled [ʌn'pærəˌleld] *adj.* несравни́мый, несравне́нный; беспода́бный.
unpardonable [ʌn'pɑ:dənəb(ə)l] *adj.* непрости́тельный.
unpatriotic [ˌʌnpætrɪ'ɒtɪk, ˌʌnpeɪt-] *adj.* непатриоти́ческий.
unpaved [ʌn'peɪvd] *adj.* немощёный.
unpersuaded [ˌʌnpə'sweɪdɪd] *adj.* неубеждённый.
unperturbed [ˌʌnpə'tɜ:bd] *adj.* невозмути́мый.
unpick [ʌn'pɪk] *v.t.* расп|а́рывать, -оро́ть.
unpin [ʌn'pɪn] *v.t.* отк|а́лывать, -оло́ть.
unplanned [ʌn'plænd] *adj.* незаплани́рованный; неожи́данный; **an** ~ **economy** непла́новая эконо́мика.
unpleasant [ʌn'plez(ə)nt] *adj.* неприя́тный.
unpleasantness [ʌn'plezəntnɪs] *n.* неприя́тность.
unplug [ʌn'plʌg] *v.t.* отключ|а́ть, -и́ть.
unpolluted [ˌʌnpə'lu:tɪd] *adj.* незагрязнённый.
unpopular [ʌn'pɒpjʊlə(r)] *adj.* непопуля́рный.
unpopularity [ˌʌnpɒpjʊ'lærɪtɪ] *n.* непопуля́рность.
unprecedented [ʌn'presɪˌdentɪd] *adj.* беспрецеде́нтный.
unprejudiced [ʌn'predʒʊdɪst] *adj.* непредвзя́тый, непредубеждённый.
unpremeditated [ˌʌnprɪ'medɪˌteɪtɪd] *adj.* непреднаме́ренный; непредуму́шленный.
unprepared [ˌʌnprɪ'peəd] *adj.* неподгото́вленный; **his speech was** ~ он произнёс свою речь экспро́мтом.
unprepossessing [ˌʌnpri:pə'zesɪŋ] *adj.* нерасполага́ющий.
unpretentious [ˌʌnprɪ'tenʃəs] *adj.* непретенцио́зный, скро́мный, просто́й.
unpreventable [ˌʌnprɪ'ventəb(ə)l] *adj.* неизбе́жный, неотврати́мый.
unprincipled [ʌn'prɪnsɪp(ə)ld] *adj.* беспринци́пный.
unprintable [ʌn'prɪntəb(ə)l] *adj.* нецензу́рный, непеча́тный.
unproductive [ˌʌnprə'dʌktɪv] *adj.* непродукти́вный, непроизводи́тельный; **an** ~**argument** бесполе́зный спор.
unprofessional [ˌʌnprə'feʃən(ə)l] *adj.* непрофессиона́льный; ~ **conduct** наруше́ние профессиона́льной э́тики.
unprofitable [ʌn'prɒfɪtəb(ə)l] *adj.* нерента́бельный,

невы́годный, неприбы́льный; (*useless*) бессмы́сленный, бесполе́зный.
unpromising [ʌn'prɒmɪsɪŋ] *adj.* малообеща́ющий.
unpronounceable [ˌʌnprə'naʊnsəb(ə)l] *adj.* непроизноси́мый.
unpropitious [ˌʌnprə'pɪʃəs] *adj.* неблагоприя́тный.
unprotected [ˌʌnprə'tektɪd] *adj.* незащищённый, беззащи́тный.
unprove|d [ʌn'pru:vd], **-n** [ʌn'pru:v(ə)n] *adjs.* недока́занный.
unprovoked [ˌʌnprə'vəʊkt] *adj.* неспровоци́рованный; ниче́м не вы́званный.
unpublished [ʌn'pʌblɪʃt] *adj.* неопублико́ванный, неи́зданный.
unpunished [ʌn'pʌnɪʃt] *adj.* безнака́занный.
unqualified [ʌn'kwɒlɪˌfaɪd] *adj.* **1.** (*without reservations*) безоговоро́чный; ~ **praise** безграни́чная хвала́. **2.** (*not competent*) неквалифици́рованный; **I am ~ to judge** я недоста́точно компете́нтен, что́бы суди́ть.
unquenchable [ʌn'kwentʃəb(ə)l] *adj.* (*of thirst*) неутоли́мый; (*of fire*) неугаси́мый.
unquestionabl|e [ʌn'kwestʃənəb(ə)l] *adj.* (*undoubted*) несомне́нный; (*indisputable*) неоспори́мый, беспо́рный; **you are ~y right** вы безусло́вно пра́вы.
unquestioned [ʌn'kwestʃ(ə)nd] *adj.* беспо́рный, при́знанный.
unquestioning [ʌn'kwestʃənɪŋ] *adj.*: ~ **obedience** безоговоро́чное/по́лное повинове́ние.
unravel [ʌn'ræv(ə)l] *v.t.* распу́т|ывать, -ать; (*fig.*) разга́д|ывать, -а́ть.
unreachable [ʌn'ri:tʃəb(ə)l] *adj.*: **he was ~ at his office** его́ нельзя́ бы́ло заста́ть в конто́ре.
unreadable [ʌn'ri:dəb(ə)l] *adj.* (*illegible*) неразбо́рчивый; (*tedious*) нечита́бельный.
unreal [ʌn'rɪəl] *adj.* нереа́льный; фантасти́ческий; ото́рванный от действи́тельности.
unrealistic [ˌʌnrɪə'lɪstɪk] *adj.* **1.** (*unpractical*, *unreasonable*) нереа́льный. **2.** (*of art*) нереалисти́ческий.
unrealizable [ʌn'rɪəlaɪzəb(ə)l] *adj.* неосуществи́мый; (*comm.*) не могу́щий быть реализо́ванным.
unreasonable [ʌn'ri:zənəb(ə)l] *adj.* безрассу́дный; не(благо)разу́мный; (*excessive*) чрезме́рный; ~ **demands** необосно́ванные тре́бования.
unreasoning [ʌn'ri:zənɪŋ] *adj.* неразу́мный, нерассужда́ющий.
unreciprocated [ˌʌnrɪ'sɪprəˌkeɪtɪd] *adj.* без (*or* не встреча́ющий) взаи́мности.
unrecognizable [ʌn'rekəgˌnaɪzəb(ə)l] *adj.* неузнава́емый.
unrecognized [ʌn'rekəgˌnaɪzd] *adj.* неу́знанный; непри́знанный; **his genius was ~** его́ ге́ний не получи́л призна́ния.
unrecorded [ˌʌnrɪ'kɔ:dɪd] *adj.* незапи́санный.
unrefined [ˌʌnrɪ'faɪnd] *adj.* неочи́щенный, нерафини́рованный; ~ **language** гру́бые выраже́ния.
unrehearsed [ˌʌnrɪ'hɜ:st] *adj.* неподгото́вленный; неотрепети́рованный.
adv. экспро́мптом; без подгото́вки.
unrelated [ˌʌnrɪ'leɪtɪd] *adj.* **1.** (*not connected*) несвя́занный (c+*i.*); не име́ющий отноше́ния (к+*d.*). **2.** (*not kin*): **he is ~ to me** он мне не ро́дственник.
unrelenting [ˌʌnrɪ'lentɪŋ] *adj.* (*inexorable*) неумоли́мый; (*assiduous*) неосла́бный.
unreliability [ˌʌnrɪˌlaɪə'bɪlɪtɪ] *n.* ненадёжность.
unreliable [ˌʌnrɪ'laɪəb(ə)l] *adj.* ненадёжный; (*of pers.*) безотве́тственный; **he is ~** на него́ нельзя́ положи́ться.
unrelieved [ˌʌnrɪ'li:vd] *adj.* **1.** не освобождённый (*от чего*); не получи́вший по́мощи. **2.** однообра́зный; ~ **gloom** беспросве́тный мрак.
unremarkable [ˌʌnrɪ'mɑ:kəb(ə)l] *adj.* невыдаю́щийся; ниче́м не примеча́тельный.
unremitting [ˌʌnrɪ'mɪtɪŋ] *adj.* неосла́бный.
unrepeatable [ˌʌnrɪ'pi:təb(ə)l] *adj.* неповтори́мый; (*improper*) нецензу́рный.
unrepentant [ˌʌnrɪ'pent(ə)nt] *adj.* нераска́явшийся.
unrepresentative [ˌʌnreprɪ'zentətɪv] *adj.* непоказа́тельный, нетипи́чный.
unrequited [ˌʌnrɪ'kwaɪtɪd] *adj.* не по́льзующийся взаи́мностью; ~ **love** любо́вь без взаи́мности.
unreserved [ˌʌnrɪ'zɜ:vd] *adj.* (*not set aside*) незаброни́рованый; (*open*, *frank*) открове́нный; (*wholehearted*) по́лный; **I agree with you ~ly** я по́лностью с ва́ми согла́сен.
unresolved [ˌʌnrɪ'zɒlvd] *adj.* нереши́тельный; **an ~ problem** нерешённая пробле́ма; **my doubts were ~** мои́ сомне́ния не рассе́ялись.
unresponsive [ˌʌnrɪ'spɒnsɪv] *adj.* неотзы́вчивый; **he was ~ to my suggestion** он не реаги́ровал на моё предложе́ние.
unrest [ʌn'rest] *n.* (*disquiet*) беспоко́йство; (*social*, *political*) волне́ния (*nt. pl.*); беспоря́дки (*m. pl.*).
unrestrained [ˌʌnrɪ'streɪnd] *adj.* несде́ржанный; необу́зданный.
unrestricted [ˌʌnrɪ'strɪktɪd] *adj.* неограни́ченный.
unrewarding [ˌʌnrɪ'wɔ:dɪŋ] *adj.* неблагода́рный.
unripe [ʌn'raɪp] *adj.* неспе́лый, незре́лый (*also fig.*).
unrivalled [ʌn'raɪv(ə)ld] *adj.* непревзойдённый; **an ~ opportunity** уника́льная возмо́жность.
unroll [ʌn'rəʊl] *v.t.* & *i.* развёр|тывать(ся), -ну́ть(ся).
unruffled [ʌn'rʌf(ə)ld] *adj.* (*fig.*) невозмути́мый.
unruly [ʌn'ru:lɪ] *adj.* непоко́рный; бу́йный.
unsaddle [ʌn'sæd(ə)l] *v.t.* рассёдл|ывать, -а́ть.
unsafe [ʌn'seɪf] *adj.* ненадёжный, опа́сный.
unsaid [ʌn'sed] *adj.*: **some things are better left ~** есть ве́щи, о кото́рых лу́чше умолча́ть.
unsatisfactory [ˌʌnsætɪs'fæktərɪ] *adj.* неудовлетвори́тельный.
unsatisfied [ʌn'sætɪsˌfaɪd] *adj.* неудовлетворённый.
unsaturated [ʌn'sætʃəˌreɪtɪd, -tjʊˌreɪtɪd] *adj.* ненасы́щенный.
unsavoury [ʌn'seɪvərɪ] *adj.* (*lit.*) невку́сный; (*fig.*) неприя́тный; **an ~ reputation** сомни́тельная репута́ция.
unscathed [ʌn'skeɪðd] *adj.* невреди́мый; (*pred.*) цел и невреди́м.
unscheduled [ʌn'ʃedju:ld] *adj.* незаплани́рованный; **an ~ flight** полёт вне расписа́ния.
unscientific [ˌʌnsaɪən'tɪfɪk] *adj.* нену́чный.
unscramble [ʌn'skræmb(ə)l] *v.t.* **1.** (*teleph. conversation*) раскоди́ровать (*impf.*, *pf.*). **2.** (*coll.*, *analyse*, *sort out*) расшифро́в|ывать, -а́ть.
unscrew [ʌn'skru:] *v.t.* & *i.* отви́н|чивать(ся), -ти́ть(ся); разви́н|чивать(ся), -ти́ть(ся).
unscrupulous [ʌn'skru:pjʊləs] *adj.* беспринци́пный, недобросо́вестный.
unseal [ʌn'si:l] *v.t.* распеча́т|ывать, -ать; вскры|ва́ть, -ть.
unseasonable [ʌn'si:zənəb(ə)l] *adj.* не по сезо́ну.
unseasoned [ʌn'si:z(ə)nd] *adj.*: ~ **food** неприпра́вленная еда́; ~ **timber** невы́держанная древеси́на.
unseat [ʌn'si:t] *v.t.* ст|а́лкивать, -олкну́ть; **the horse ~ed its rider** ло́шадь сбро́сила ездока́; (*fig.*): **he was ~ed at the last election** его́ лиши́ли парла́ментского манда́та на после́дних вы́борах.
unsecured [ˌʌnsɪ'kjʊəd] *adj.* (*of loan etc.*) необеспе́ченный, негаранти́рованный.
unseeing [ʌn'si:ɪŋ] *adj.* незря́чий, неви́дящий.
unseemly [ʌn'si:mlɪ] *adj.* неподоба́ющий, непристо́йный.
unseen [ʌn'si:n] *n.* (*translation*) перево́д с листа́.
adj. неви́димый.
unselfish [ʌn'selfɪʃ] *adj.* бескоры́стный.
unselfishness [ʌn'selfɪʃnɪs] *n.* бескоры́стие.
unsettle [ʌn'set(ə)l] *v.t.* (*fig.*) выбива́ть, вы́бить из

колей; расстр|áивать, -óить.
unsettled [ʌn'set(ə)ld] *adj.* неустóйчивый; беспокóйный; **~ weather** неустóйчивая погóда; **an ~ account** незаплáченный счёт; **~ territory** незаселённая территóрия.
unshackle [ʌn'ʃæk(ə)l] *v.t.* сн|имáть, -ять кандалы́ c+*g.*
unshakeable [ʌn'ʃeɪkəb(ə)l] *adj.* непоколеби́мый.
unshaven [ʌn'ʃeɪv(ə)n] *adj.* небри́тый.
unsheathe [ʌn'ʃi:ð] *v.t.* вынимáть, вы́нуть из нóжен; **he ~d his sword** он обнажи́л меч.
unsightly [ʌn'saɪtlɪ] *adj.* некраси́вый, непригля́дный.
unsigned [ʌn'saɪnd] *adj.* неподпи́санный.
unskilful [ʌn'skɪlfʊl] *adj.* неумéлый, неискýсный.
unskilled [ʌn'skɪld] *adj.* неквалифици́рованный.
unsociable [ʌn'səʊʃəb(ə)l] *adj.* необщи́тельный, нелюди́мый.
unsold [ʌn'səʊld] *adj.* непрóданный; залежáвшийся.
unsolicited [ˌʌnsə'lɪsɪtɪd] *adj.* предостáвленный добровóльно; непрóшенный.
unsolved [ʌn'sɒlvd] *adj.* нерешённый, неразгáданный.
unsophisticated [ˌʌnsə'fɪstɪˌkeɪtɪd] *adj.* простодýшный; безыскýсный; наи́вный.
unsought [ʌn'sɔ:t] *adj.* непрóшенный.
unsound [ʌn'saʊnd] *adj.* (*bad, rotten*) испóрченный, гнилóй; (*unwholesome*) нездорóвый; (*unstable*) непрóчный; **~ views** необоснóванные взгля́ды; **of ~ mind** душевнобольнóй; **a man of ~ judgement** человéк, лишённый здрáвого смы́сла.
unsparing [ʌn'speərɪŋ] *adj.* щéдрый; усéрдный; **~ in his efforts** не щадя́щий сил.
unspeakable [ʌn'spi:kəb(ə)l] *adj.* невырази́мый; **he is an ~ bore** он ужáсный занýда.
unspecified [ʌn'spesɪˌfaɪd] *adj.* тóчно не укáзанный/ установлéнный.
unspoil|ed [ʌn'spɔɪld], **-t** [ʌn'spɔɪlt] *adj.* неиспóрченный; (*of pers.*) неизбалóванный.
unspoken [ʌn'spəʊkən] *adj.* невы́сказанный.
unsport|ing [ʌn'spɔ:tɪŋ], **-smanlike** [ʌn'spɔ:tsmənˌlaɪk] *adjs.* нечéстный; недостóйный спортсмéна; **he behaved unsportingly** он вёл себя́ неспорти́вно.
unstable [ʌn'steɪb(ə)l] *adj.* нетвёрдый, неустóйчивый; (*fig.*) измéнчивый; **an ~ personality** неуравновéшенная ли́чность.
unstained [ʌn'steɪnd] *adj.* (*fig.*) незапя́тнанный.
unsteady [ʌn'stedɪ] *adj.* нетвёрдый; неустóйчивый, шáткий; **the table was ~** стол шатáлся; **he was ~ on his legs** он нетвёрдо держáлся на ногáх.
unstinting [ʌn'stɪntɪŋ] *adj.* (*generous*) щéдрый.
unstrap [ʌn'stræp] *v.t.* отстёг|ивать, -нýть; расстёг|ивать, -нýть.
unstressed [ʌn'strest] *adj.* (*phon.*) безудáрный.
unstuck [ʌn'stʌk] *adj.*: **the stamp came ~** мáрка отклéилась; (*fig., coll.*): **my schemes came ~** мои́ плáны провали́лись.
unsubstantiated [ˌʌnsəb'stænʃɪˌeɪtɪd] *adj.* недокáзанный, неподтверждённый.
unsuccessful [ˌʌnsək'sesfʊl] *adj.* безуспéшный, неудáчный; **he was ~ in the exam** он не вы́держал экзáмена.
unsuitability [ʌnˌsu:tə'bɪlɪtɪ, ʌn'sju:-] *n.* непригóдность.
unsuitable [ʌn'su:təb(ə)l, ʌn'sju:-] *adj.* неподходя́щий, непригóдный.
unsuited [ʌn'su:tɪd, ʌn'sju:-] *adj.* неподходя́щий; **he is ~ to the post** он не подхóдит/годи́тся для э́той дóлжности.
unsullied [ʌn'sʌlɪd] *adj.* (*fig.*) незапя́тнанный.
unsung [ʌn'sʌŋ] *adj.*: **an ~ hero** невоспéтый герóй.
unsure [ʌn'ʃʊə(r), ʌn'ʃɔ:(r)] *adj.* неувéренный; **he was ~ of his ground** он не чýвствовал себя́ компетéнтным; **I am ~ if he will come** я не увéрен, что он придёт; **~ of o.s.** неувéренный в себé.
unsurpass|able [ˌʌnsə'pɑ:səb(ə)l], **-ed** [ˌʌnsə'pɑ:st] *adjs.* непревзойдённый.
unsuspected [ˌʌnsə'spektɪd] *adj.* неподозревáемый.
unsusp|ecting [ˌʌnsə'spektɪŋ], **-icious** [ˌʌnsə'spɪʃəs] *adjs.* неподозревáющий, довéрчивый.
unswayed [ʌn'sweɪd] *adj.*: **~ by public opinion** не поддáвшийся влия́нию общéственного мнéния.
unswerving [ʌn'swɜ:vɪŋ] *adj.* (*fig.*) непоколеби́мый.
unsympathetic [ˌʌnsɪmpə'θetɪk] *adj.* несочýвствующий.
unsystematic [ˌʌnsɪstə'mætɪk] *adj.* несистемати́ческий.
untameable [ʌn'teɪməb(ə)l] *adj.* неукроти́мый.
untangle [ʌn'tæŋg(ə)l] *v.t.* распýт|ывать, -ать; **she ~d the wool** онá распýтала клубóк шéрсти.
untarnished [ʌn'tɑ:nɪʃt] *adj.* непотусклéвший; (*fig.*) незапя́тнанный.
untenable [ʌn'tenəb(ə)l] *adj.* несостоя́тельный; **~ arguments** неубеди́тельные дóводы; **an ~ position** (*mil.*) незащити́мая/невы́годная пози́ция.
untended [ʌn'tendɪd] *adj.* забрóшенный, неухóженный.
unthinkable [ʌn'θɪŋkəb(ə)l] *adj.* (*unimaginable*) невообрази́мый, немы́слимый; (*inadmissible*) недопусти́мый.
unthinking [ʌn'θɪŋkɪŋ] *adj.* (*thoughtless*) бездýмный; (*inadvertent*) нечáянный; машинáльный.
untidiness [ʌn'taɪdɪnɪs] *n.* неопря́тность.
untidy [ʌn'taɪdɪ] *adj.* неопря́тный, неаккурáтный; **an ~ person** неря́ха (*c.g.*); **his room was ~** егó кóмната былá неýбрана.
untie [ʌn'taɪ] *v.t.* развя́з|ывать, -áть; отвя́з|ывать, -áть; расшнурóв|ывать, -áть.
until [ən'tɪl, ʌn-] = **till; unless and ~** тóлько когдá/ éсли.
untimely [ʌn'taɪmlɪ] *adj.* (*premature*) преждеврéменный; (*unseasonable*) несвоеврéменный; (*ill-timed, inappropriate*) неумéстный.
untiring [ʌn'taɪərɪŋ] *adj.* неутоми́мый, неустáнный.
unto ['ʌntʊ, 'ʌntə] (*arch.*) = **to**
untold [ʌn'təʊld] *adj.* **1.** (*not told*) нерасскáзанный. **2.** (*inestimable*) бессчётный; **~ wealth** несмéтные богáтства.
untouchable [ʌn'tʌtʃəb(ə)l] *n.* неприкасáемый, хариджáн.
untouched [ʌn'tʌtʃt] *adj.* нетрóнутый.
untoward [ˌʌntə'wɔ:d, ʌn'təʊəd] *adj.* (*inconvenient; adverse*) неблагоприя́тный; **nothing ~ happened** ничегó плохóго не случи́лось.
untrained [ʌn'treɪnd] *adj.* необýченный, неподготóвленный.
untransferable [ˌʌntræns'fɜ:rəb(ə)l, ˌʌntrɑ:ns-, ʌn't-] *adj.* без прáва передáчи.
untranslatable [ˌʌntræns'leɪtəb(ə)l, ˌʌntrɑ:n-, -z'leɪtəb(ə)l] *adj.* непереводи́мый.
untried [ʌn'traɪd] *adj.* неиспы́танный, непровéренный.
untrodden [ʌn'trɒd(ə)n] *adj.* неисхóженный.
untroubled [ʌn'trʌb(ə)ld] *adj.* невозмути́мый, спокóйный.
untrue [ʌn'tru:] *adj.* (*inaccurate*) невéрный, неправи́льный; (*unfaithful*) невéрный.
untrustworthy [ʌn'trʌstˌwɜ:ðɪ] *adj.* (*unreliable*) ненадёжный; (*undeserving of confidence*) не заслýживающий довéрия.
untruth [ʌn'tru:θ] *n.* непрáвда.
untruthful [ʌn'tru:θfʊl] *adj.* (*of thg.*) невéрный, лóжный; (*of pers. or thg.*) лжи́вый.
untwist [ʌn'twɪst] *v.t.* раскрý|чивать, -ти́ть.
unusable [ʌn'ju:zəb(ə)l] *adj.* непригóдный.
unused[1] [ʌn'ju:zd] *adj.* (*not put to use*) неиспóльзованный; **my ticket was ~** я не испóльзовал свой билéт.
unused[2] [ʌn'ju:st] *adj.* (*unaccustomed*) непривы́кший (к+*d.*); **I am ~ to this** я к э́тому не привы́к.
unusual [ʌn'ju:ʒʊəl] *adj.* необыкновéнный, необы́чный; **~ly** осóбенно, исключи́тельно.

unutterable [ʌn'ʌtərəb(ə)l] *adj.* невырази́мый, неска-за́нный.
unvaried [ʌn'veərɪd] *adj.* неизме́нный, постоя́нный.
unvarnished [ʌn'vɑːnɪʃt] *adj.* (*fig.*): **the ~ truth** неприкра́шенная пра́вда.
unvarying [ʌn'veərɪɪŋ] *adj.* неизме́нный.
unveil [ʌn'veɪl] *v.t.*: **the statue was ~ed on Sunday** торже́ственное откры́тие па́мятника состоя́лось в воскресе́нье; **he ~ed his designs** он раскры́л свои́ пла́ны.
unverifiable [ʌn'verɪˌfaɪəb(ə)l] *adj.* не поддаю́щийся прове́рке.
unverified [ʌn'verɪˌfaɪd] *adj.* непрове́ренный.
unversed [ʌn'vɜːst] *adj.* несве́дущий (*в чём*).
unvoiced [ʌn'vɔɪst] *adj.* (*phon.*) глухо́й.
unwanted [ʌn'wɒntɪd] *adj.* нежела́нный; **they made me feel ~** они́ да́ли мне почу́вствовать, что я ли́шний среди́ них.
unwarranted [ʌn'wɒrəntɪd] *adj.* недозво́ленный; необосно́ванный.
unwary [ʌn'weərɪ] *adj.* неосторо́жный.
unwashed [ʌn'wɒʃt] *adj.* немы́тый; нести́ранный.
unwavering [ʌn'weɪvərɪŋ] *adj.* непоколеби́мый; неизме́нный; твёрдый.
unwearable [ʌn'weərəb(ə)l] *adj.* него́дный для но́ски.
unwedded [ʌn'wedɪd] *adj.* незаму́жняя.
unwelcome [ʌn'welkəm] *adj.* неприя́тный; нежела́тельный; **he is ~ here** он здесь ли́шний.
unwell [ʌn'wel] *adj.* нездоро́вый; **I felt ~** мне нездоро́вилось.
unwholesome [ʌn'həʊlsəm] *adj.* нездоро́вый.
unwieldy [ʌn'wiːldɪ] *adj.* громо́здкий, тяжелове́сный.
unwilling [ʌn'wɪlɪŋ] *adj.* нежела́ющий; **he was ~ to agree** он не пожела́л согласи́ться; **~ly** неохо́тно.
unwind [ʌn'waɪnd] *v.t. & i.* разм|а́тывать(ся), -ота́ть(ся); (*fig.*): **as the plot ~s** по ме́ре разви́тия сюже́та; **the drink helped him to ~** вино́ помогло́ ему́ рассла́биться.
unwise [ʌn'waɪz] *adj.* не(благо)разу́мный.
unwitting [ʌn'wɪtɪŋ] *adj.* нечая́нный.
unworkable [ʌn'wɜːkəb(ə)l] *adj.* нереа́льный, неосуществи́мый.
unworldly [ʌn'wɜːldlɪ] *adj.* неземно́й, не от ми́ра сего́.
unworthy [ʌn'wɜːðɪ] *adj.* (*undeserving*) недосто́йный (*кого/чего*); (*base*) по́длый, ни́зкий.
unwrap [ʌn'ræp] *v.t.* разв|ора́чивать, (*or* разв|ёртывать), -ерну́ть.
unwritten [ʌn'rɪt(ə)n] *adj.*: **an ~ law** непи́саный зако́н.
unyielding [ʌn'jiːldɪŋ] *adj.* непрекло́нный, упо́рный.
unzip [ʌn'zɪp] *v.t.* расстёг|ивать, -ну́ть; раскр|ыва́ть, -ы́ть.
up [ʌp] *n.*: **~s and downs** (*of fortune*) взлёты (*m. pl.*) и паде́ния (*nt. pl.*); превра́тности (*f. pl.*) судьбы́.

adv. **1.** (*in a high or higher position*) вверх, наве́рх; **high ~ in the sky** высоко́ в не́бе; **'this side ~'** «верх!»; **they live 3 floors ~ from us** они́ живу́т тремя́ этажа́ми вы́ше нас; **she had her umbrella ~** зо́нтик у неё был раскры́т; **the window was ~** окно́ бы́ло откры́то; **the blinds were ~** што́ры бы́ли по́дняты; **his spirits were ~ one minute, down the next** у него́ беспреста́нно меня́лось настрое́ние; **prices are ~** це́ны подняли́сь; (*advanced*): **he was ~ in the lead** он был среди́ пе́рвых; **he is well ~ in his subject** он прекра́сно зна́ет свой предме́т; (*with greater intensity*): **sing ~! speak ~!** гро́мче! **2.** (*into a higher position*) вверх; **hands ~!** ру́ки вверх!; (*~wards*) вы́ше, бо́льше; **children from the age of 12 ~** де́ти двена́дцати лет и ста́рше; (*expr. support*): **~ (with) the workers!** да здра́вствуют рабо́чие! **3.** (*out of bed*; *standing*; *active*): **he was ~ on his feet at once** он момента́льно вскочи́л на́ ноги; **I must be ~ and doing** мне пора́ приня́ться за рабо́ту; **he was already ~ when I called** когда́ я пришёл, он уже́ встал; **she was soon ~ and about again** она́ вско́ре опра́вилась; **I was ~ late last night** я вчера́ о́чень по́здно лёг; **the house is not ~** (*built*) **yet** дом ещё не постро́ен. **4.** (*roused*): **his blood was ~** он был взбешён; **they were ~ in arms against the new proposal** они́ встре́тили но́вое предложе́ние в штыки́. **5.** (*of agenda*): **the house is ~ for sale** дом продаётся; **he was ~ for trial** он находи́лся под судо́м. **6.** (*expr. completion or expiry*): **time's ~** вре́мя истекло́; **it's all ~ with them** с ни́ми всё ко́нчено; **the game is ~!** ка́рта би́та! **7.** (*coll.*, *happening*; *amiss*): **what's ~?** в чём де́ло?; что тут происхо́дит?; **there's something ~ with the radio** (радио)приёмник барахли́т. **8.** **~ against** (*in contact with*): **the table was (right) ~ against the wall** стол стоя́л у стены́ (*or* вплотну́ю к стене́); (*confronted by*): **you are ~ against stiff opposition** вы име́ете де́ло с упо́рным сопротивле́нием; **he was ~ against it** он был в тру́дном положе́нии. **9.** **~ to** (*equal to*): **I don't feel ~ to it** я не чу́вствую себя́ в си́лах; **he is not ~ to his work** он не справля́ется с рабо́той; (*on a par with*): **the book is ~ to expectations** кни́га оправда́ет ожида́ния; (*as far as*) до+*g.*; **~ to, ~ till now** до сих пор; **I am ~ to chapter 3** я дочита́л до тре́тьей главы́; **his work is not ~ to scratch** его́ рабо́та оставля́ет жела́ть лу́чшего; (*incumbent upon*): **it is ~ to us to help** э́то мы должны́ помо́чь; **it's ~ to you now** тепе́рь э́то от вас зави́сит; (*occupied with*): **what is he ~ to?** чем он занима́ется?; **what are the children ~ to?** что там де́ти затея́ли?; **he is ~ to no good** он замы́слил что́-то недо́брое.

prep.: **they live ~ the hill** они́ живу́т на горе́/холме́; **he ran ~ the hill** он взбежа́л на́ гору, на хо́лм; **the cat was ~ a tree** кот взобра́лся на де́рево; **he went ~ the stairs** он подня́лся по ле́стнице; **they live ~** (*further along*) **the street** они́ живу́т по/на э́той у́лице; **he is known ~ and down the land** его́ зна́ют по всей стране́.

v.i. (*coll.*): **she ~(ped) and said ...** она́ взяла́ и сказа́ла...
up-and-coming [ˌʌpən'kʌmɪŋ] *adj.* многообеща́ющий.
upbraid [ʌp'breɪd] *v.t.* укор|я́ть, -и́ть; порица́ть (*impf.*).
upbringing ['ʌpˌbrɪŋɪŋ] *n.* воспита́ние.
update [ʌp'deɪt] *v.t.* модернизи́ровать (*impf.*, *pf.*); пересмотре́ть и допо́лнить (*both pf.*) (*книгу*).
up-end [ʌp'end] *v.t.* поста́вить (*pf.*) перпендикуля́рно.
upgrade ['ʌpgreɪd] *n.* подъём; **on the ~** на подъёме.

v.t. пов|ыша́ть, -ы́сить в до́лжности; придава́ть (*impf.*) бо́льшее значе́ние +*d.*
upheaval [ʌp'hiːv(ə)l] *n.* (*fig.*) переворо́т.
uphill ['ʌphɪl] *adj.* иду́щий в го́ру; **an ~ road** крута́я доро́га; **an ~ task** тяжёлая зада́ча.

adv. в го́ру.
uphold [ʌp'həʊld] *v.t.* (*support*, *lit.*, *fig.*) подде́рж|ивать, -а́ть; отст|а́ивать, -оя́ть; (*confirm*) утвер|жда́ть, -ди́ть.
upholster [ʌp'həʊlstə(r)] *v.t.* об|ива́ть, и́ть; **an ~ed chair** кре́сло с мя́гкой оби́вкой.
upholsterer [ʌp'həʊlstərə(r)] *n.* обо́йщик, драпиро́вщик.
upholstery [ʌp'həʊlstərɪ] *n.* оби́вка.
upkeep ['ʌpkiːp] *n.* содержа́ние, ремо́нт, ухо́д (за+*i.*).
upland ['ʌplənd] *n.* наго́рье.

adj. наго́рный.
uplift[1] ['ʌplɪft] *n.* (*moral elevation*) духо́вный подъём.
uplift[2] [ʌp'lɪft] *v.t.* подн|има́ть, -я́ть.
up-market [ʌp'mɑːkɪt] *adj.* элита́рный, для шика́рной пу́блики.
upmost ['ʌpməʊst] = **uppermost**
upon [ə'pɒn] *prep.* **1.** *see* **on**. **2.**: **once ~ a time** одна́жды; **once ~ a time there lived ...** жил(и)-бы́л(и)...;

~ my word, soul! (*expr. surprise etc.*) Го́споди!; ~ my honour! че́стное сло́во!; the holidays are ~ us приближа́ются кани́кулы; the enemy is ~ us враг уже́ бли́зок.

upper ['ʌpə(r)] *n.* передо́к боти́нка; **he was on his ~s** (*coll.*) он оста́лся без гроша́.

adj. ве́рхний; вы́сший; **~ classes** вы́сшие кла́ссы; **he got the ~ hand** он одержа́л верх; **U~ House** (*in UK*) пала́та ло́рдов; (*in USA*) сена́т.

cpds. **~-case** *adj.* прописно́й; **~-class, -crust** *adjs.* относя́щийся к вы́сшему о́бществу; **~cut** *n.* апперко́т; **~most** (*also* **upmost**) *adj.* са́мый ве́рхний, вы́сший; **it was ~most in my mind** э́то бо́льше всего́ занима́ло мои́ мы́сли.

upright ['ʌpraɪt] *n.* (*beam, pillar etc.*) столб; (**~ piano**) пиани́но (*indecl.*).

adj. (*erect*) вертика́льный, прямо́й; (*honourable*) че́стный, прямо́й.

adv.: **stand ~** стоя́ть (*impf.*) пря́мо.

uprising ['ʌpˌraɪzɪŋ] *n.* восста́ние.

up-river ['ʌprɪvə(r)] = **upstream**

uproar ['ʌprɔ:(r)] *n.* (*noise*) шум, (*coll.*) гам; (*tumult, confusion*) возмуще́ние.

uproarious [ʌp'rɔ:rɪəs] *adj.* (*noisy*) шу́мный, бу́рный, бу́йный; (*funny*) ужа́сно смешно́й.

uproot [ʌp'ru:t] *v.t.* корчева́ть, вы́-; вырыва́ть, вы́рвать с ко́рнем; (*fig., displace*) выселя́ть, вы́селить; пересел|я́ть, -и́ть.

upset[1] ['ʌpset] *n.* **1.** (*physical*) недомога́ние; **stomach ~** расстро́йство желу́дка. **2.** (*emotional shock, confusion*) огорче́ние. **3.** (*unexpected result in sport*) неожи́данный результа́т.

upset[2] [ʌp'set] *v.t.* опроки́|дывать, -нуть; **he ~ the milk** он опроки́нул молоко́; **the news ~ her** но́вость её расстро́ила; **rich food ~s my stomach** от жи́рной пи́щи у меня́ расстра́ивается желу́док.

upshot ['ʌpʃɒt] *n.* развя́зка; заключе́ние.

upside down [ˌʌpsaɪd 'daʊn] *adv.* вверх дном.

upstage [ʌp'steɪdʒ] *v.t.* затм|ева́ть, -и́ть.

upstairs [ʌp'steəz] *adv.* наверху́, вве́рх; **he ran ~** он вбежа́л наве́рх; (*attr.*): **the ~ rooms** ве́рхние ко́мнаты.

upstanding [ʌp'stændɪŋ] *adj.* **1.** (*sturdy*) кре́пкий. **2.** прямо́й; **be ~!** вста́ньте!

upstart ['ʌpstɑ:t] *n.* вы́скочка (*c.g.*).

upstream ['ʌpstri:m], **up-river** ['ʌp'rɪvə(r)] *advs.* (*of place*) вверх по тече́нию; (*of motion*) про́тив тече́ния.

upsurge ['ʌpsɜ:dʒ] *n.* подъём.

uptake ['ʌpteɪk] *n.*: **quick in the ~** (*coll.*) сметли́вый, сообрази́тельный.

uptight [ʌp'taɪt, 'ʌptaɪt] *adj.* (*coll., tense, angry*) напряжённый, нерво́зный.

up-to-date [ʌptə'deɪt] *adj.* совреме́нный; нове́йший, (са́мый) после́дний.

up-to-the-minute [ˌʌptəðə'mɪnɪt] *adj.* сиюмину́тный; са́мый после́дний.

upturn ['ʌptɜ:n] *n.* (*fig.*) сдвиг (к лу́чшему); улучше́ние.

upward ['ʌpwəd] *adj.* напра́вленный верх; **an ~ trend in prices** тенде́нция к повыше́нию цен.

adv. (*also* **~s**) вверх; **~s of** (*over*) **£100** свы́ше ста фу́нтов.

Urals ['jʊər(ə)lz] *n.* Ура́льские го́ры (*f. pl.*), Ура́л.

uranium [jʊ'reɪnɪəm] *n.* ура́н; (*attr.*) ура́новый.

Uranus ['jʊərənəs, jʊ'reɪnəs] *n.* Ура́н.

urban ['ɜ:bən] *adj.* городско́й.

urbane [ɜ:'beɪn] *adj.* све́тский, учти́вый.

urchin ['ɜ:tʃɪn] *n.* **1.** мальчи́шка (*m.*). **2.** (*zool.*) морско́й ёж.

Urdu ['ʊədu:, 'ɜ:-] *n.* язы́к урду́.

urea ['jʊərɪə, -'ri:ə] *n.* мочеви́на.

urethra [jʊə'ri:θrə] *n.* уре́тра.

urge [ɜ:dʒ] *n.* побужде́ние, стремле́ние; **I felt an ~ to go back** меня́ потяну́ло верну́ться/наза́д.

v.t. **1.** (*impel*; *also* **~ on, ~ forward**) гнать (*impf.*); под|гоня́ть, -огна́ть. **2.** (*exhort*) взыва́ть, возва́ть (*кого к чему*); приз|ыва́ть, -ва́ть (*кого к чему*); угова́ривать (*impf.*).

urgency ['ɜ:dʒ(ə)nsɪ] *n.* **1.** (*need for prompt action*) сро́чность, неотло́жность; **as a matter of ~** в сро́чном поря́дке. **2.** (*importunity*) насто́йчивость.

urgent ['ɜ:dʒ(ə)nt] *adj.* **1.** (*brooking no delay*) сро́чный, безотлага́тельный, неотло́жный; **he is in ~ need of money** он кра́йне нужда́ется в деньга́х. **2.** (*pressing, importunate*) настоя́тельный, насто́йчивый.

uric ['jʊərɪk] *adj.*: **~ acid** мочева́я кислота́.

urinal [jʊə'raɪn(ə)l, 'jʊərɪn(ə)l] *n.* писсуа́р.

urinary ['jʊərɪnərɪ] *adj.* мочево́й.

urinate ['jʊərɪˌneɪt] *v.i.* мочи́ться (*impf.*).

urination [ˌjʊərɪ'neɪʃ(ə)n] *n.* мочеиспуска́ние.

urine ['jʊərɪn] *n.* моча́.

urn [ɜ:n] *n.* **1.** (*vase for ashes etc.*) у́рна, ва́за; **Grecian ~** гре́ческая ва́за. **2.** (*for tea, coffee etc.*) куб.

Ursa [ˌɜ:sə] *n.* (*astron.*): **~ Major/Minor** Больша́я/Ма́лая Медве́дица.

Uruguay ['jʊərəˌgwaɪ] *n.* Уругва́й.

US(A) (*abbr. of* **United States of America**) США (*pl., indecl.*), (Соединённые Шта́ты Аме́рики).

adj. америка́нский; **US Army** а́рмия США.

usable ['ju:zəb(ə)l] *adj.* примени́мый, (при)го́дный.

usage ['ju:sɪdʒ] *n.* **1.** (*manner of treatment*) обраще́ние; **rough ~** гру́бое обраще́ние. **2.** (*habitual process*) обыкнове́ние; **a guide to English ~** уче́бник англи́йского словоупотребле́ния.

use[1] [ju:s] *n.* **1.** (*utilization*) употребле́ние, по́льзование +*i.*; **the telephone is in ~** телефо́н за́нят; **this book is in constant ~** э́та кни́га нахо́дится в постоя́нном по́льзовании; **make good ~ of your time!** хороше́нько испо́льзуйте ва́ше вре́мя!; **he is making ~ of you** он вас испо́льзует (в свои́х це́лях); **a room for the ~ of the public** ко́мната о́бщего по́льзования; **these coins came into ~ last year** э́ти моне́ты вошли́ в обраще́ние в про́шлом году́. **2.** (*purpose*; *profitable application*) назначе́ние; примене́ние; **this tool has many ~s** э́тот инструме́нт применя́ется для разли́чных це́лей; **I have no further ~ for it** мне э́то бо́льше не пона́добится. **3.** (*value, advantage*) по́льза, толк; **this machine is no longer (of) any ~** э́та маши́на бо́льше не годи́тся; **will this be of ~ to you?** вам э́то пригоди́тся?; **it's no ~ grumbling** что то́лку ворча́ть? **4.** (*power of using*): спосо́бность по́льзования (*чем*); **he lost the ~ of his legs** он утра́тил спосо́бность ходи́ть. **5.** (*right to use*): **I gave him the ~ of my car** я разреши́л ему́ по́льзоваться мое́й маши́ной; **'with ~ of kitchen'** с пра́вом по́льзования ку́хней. **6.** (*consumption*) потребле́ние, расхо́дование.

use[2] [ju:z] *v.t.* **1.** (*make use of, employ*) употреб|ля́ть, -и́ть; по́льзоваться, вос- +*i.*; (*apply*) примен|я́ть, -и́ть; **are you using this knife?** вам сейча́с ну́жен э́тот нож?; **oil is ~d for frying potatoes** карто́фель жа́рят на расти́тельном ма́сле; **~ your eyes!** смотри́те как сле́дует!; **~ force** приб|ега́ть, -е́гнуть к наси́лию; **may I ~ your name?** могу́ я на вас сосла́ться?; **a ~d car** поде́ржанная маши́на. **2.** (**~ up**, *consume*): испо́льзовать (*impf., pf.*); расхо́довать, из-; тра́тить, по-; **the car ~s a lot of petrol** э́та маши́на берёт/расхо́дует мно́го бензи́на. **3.** (*treat*) обраща́ться (*impf.*), обходи́ться (*impf.*) с+*i.* **4.** (*exploit*): **I feel as if I have been ~d** я чу́вствую, что меня́ испо́льзовали в чьи́х-то це́лях.

use[3] [ju:z] *v.t. & i.* **1.** (*accustom*): **get ~d to** прив|ыка́ть, -ы́кнуть к+*d.*; **he is ~d to it** он к э́тому привы́к; **he is ~d to dining late** он (обы́чно) обе́дает по́здно. 2. (*be accustomed*): **he ~d to be a teacher** он ра́ньше был учи́телем; **I ~d not to like him** пре́жде он мне не нра́вился; **I ~ed to go** я пре́жде/быва́ло ходи́л.

useful ['ju:sfʊl] *adj.* поле́зный; **make yourself ~!** займи́тесь че́м-нибудь поле́зным!; **he is very ~ about the house** он о́чень мно́го помога́ет по до́му.

usefulness ['ju:sfʊlnɪs] *n.* по́льза; **this book has outlived its ~** э́та кни́га устаре́ла.

useless ['ju:slɪs] *adj.* (*worthless*) неприго́дный; (*futile*) бесполе́зный; (*coll., incompetent*): **he is ~ at tennis** он никуды́шний теннисист.

uselessness ['ju:slɪsnɪs] *n.* неприго́дность; бесполе́зность.

user ['ju:zə(r)] *n.* употребля́ющий; потреби́тель (*m.*).
cpd. **~-friendly** *adj.* удо́бный в употребле́нии; (*comput.*) дру́жественный.

usher ['ʌʃə(r)] *n.* билетёр.
v.t. (*also* **~ in**) вв|оди́ть, -ести́; **I was ~ed into his presence** меня́ ввели́ к нему́; (*fig.*) возве|ща́ть, -сти́ть; **the new year ~ed in many changes** но́вый год принёс с собо́й мно́жество переме́н.

usherette [,ʌʃə'ret] *n.* билетёрша.

USSR (*abbr. of* ***Union of Soviet Socialist Republics***) СССР, (Сою́з Сове́тских Социалисти́ческих Респу́блик).

usual ['ju:ʒʊəl] *adj.* обыкнове́нный, обы́чный; **with his ~ alacrity** со сво́йственной ему́ жи́востью; **it is ~ to remove one's hat** при́нято снима́ть шля́пу; **he is late as ~** он, по обыкнове́нию (*or* как всегда́), опа́здывает; **the bus was fuller than ~** авто́бус был перепо́лен бо́льше обы́чного.

usurer ['ju:ʒərə(r)] *n.* ростовщи́|к (*fem.*-ца).

usurious [jʊ'ʒʊərɪəs] *adj.* ростовщи́ческий.

usurp [jʊ'zɜ:p] *v.t.* узурпи́ровать (*impf., pf.*).

usurpation [,ju:zə'peɪʃ(ə)n] *n.* узурпа́ция.

usurper [jʊ'zɜ:pə(r)] *n.* узурпа́тор.

usury ['ju:ʒərɪ] *n.* ростовщи́чество.

utensil [ju:'tens(ə)l] *n.* инструме́нт; (*pl., collect.*) посу́да, у́тварь.

uterine ['ju:tə,raɪn, -rɪn] *adj.* ма́точный.

uterus ['ju:tərəs] *n.* ма́тка.

utilitarian [jʊtɪlɪ'teərɪən] *n.* утилитари́ст (*fem.* -ка).
adj. утилита́рный.

utilitarianism [jʊtɪlɪ'teərɪə,nɪz(ə)m] *n.* утилитари́зм.

utilit|y [ju:'tɪlɪtɪ] *n.* 1. (*usefulness*) поле́зность, практи́чность, вы́годность. 2.: **public ~ies** коммуна́льные услу́ги (*f. pl.*).

utilization [ju:tɪlaɪ'zeɪʃ(ə)n] *n.* испо́льзование, утилиза́ция.

utilize ['ju:tɪ,laɪz] *v.t.* испо́льзовать (*impf., pf.*); утилизи́ровать (*impf., pf.*).

utmost ['ʌtməʊst] *n.* преде́л возмо́жного; **he did his ~ to avoid defeat** орн сде́лал всё возмо́жное, что́бы избежа́ть пораже́ния; **he exerts himself to the ~** он стара́ется изо всех сил.
adjs. кра́йний; преде́льный.

Utopia [ju:'təʊpɪə] *n.* уто́пия.

Utopian [ju:'təʊpɪən] *adj.* утопи́ческий.

utter[1] ['ʌtə(r)] *adj.* по́лный, абсолю́тный, соверше́нный; **~ darkness** абсолю́тная темнота́; **an ~ scoundrel** отъя́вленный негодя́й.

utter[2] ['ʌtə(r)] *v.t.* (*pronounce, emit*) изд|ава́ть, -а́ть; произн|оси́ть, -ести́; **she ~ed a moan** она́ издала́ стон; **he could not ~ a word** он не мог вы́говорить ни сло́ва.

utterance ['ʌtərəns] *n.* 1. (*diction, speech*) произноше́ние, ди́кция; **defective ~** дефе́кт ре́чи. 2. (*expression*) выраже́ние; **he gave ~ to his anger** он вы́разил свой гнев. 3. (*pronouncement*) выска́зывание.

uvula ['ju:vjʊlə] *n.* язычо́к.

uvular ['ju:vjʊlə(r)] *adj.* язычко́вый.

Uzbek ['ʌzbek, 'ʊz-] *n.* (*pers.*) узбе́|к (*fem.* -чка); (*language*) узбе́кский язы́к.

Uzbekistan [,ʌzbekɪ'stɑ:n, ,ʊz-] *n.* Узбекиста́н.

V-neck [vi:'nek, 'vi:-] *n.* вы́рез мы́сиком; **~-neck sweater** сви́тер с вы́резом (в ви́де бу́квы «V»).

v. *abbr. of* 1. **volt(s)** [vɒlt(z), vəʊlt(z)] В, (вольт). 2. **versus** ['vɜ:səs] про́тив; **England ~ France** А́нглия про́тив Фра́нции.

vacanc|y ['veɪkənsɪ] *n.* (*job*) вака́нсия; (*place on course etc.*) ме́сто; (*room*): **'No ~ies'** «(свобо́дных) ко́мнат нет».

vacant ['veɪkənt] *adj.* 1. (*empty*) пусто́й. 2. (*unoccupied*) neза́нятый, свобо́дный; **a ~ chair** свобо́дный стул; **a ~ post** вака́нтная до́лжность, вака́нсия. 3. (*of mind, expression etc.*) отсу́тствующий.

vacate [və'keɪt, veɪ-] *v.t.* освобо|жда́ть, -ди́ть; **he ~d his chair** он встал со сту́ла; **the flat had been ~d** жильцы́ съе́хали с кварти́ры; **he will ~ the post in May** он уйдёт с до́лжности в ма́е.

vacation [və'keɪʃ(ə)n] *n.* 1. (*leaving empty*) освобожде́ние. 2. (*at university, courts etc.*) кани́кул|ы (*pl., g.* —); **long ~** ле́тние кани́кулы. 3. (*US, holiday*) о́тпуск, о́тдых; **when will you take your ~?** когда́ вы идёте в о́тпуск?; **on ~** в о́тпуске.

vaccinate ['væksɪ,neɪt] *v.t.* де́лать, с- приви́вку +*d.*; прив|ива́ть, -и́ть о́спу +*d.*

vaccination [,væksɪ'neɪʃ(ə)n] *n.* приви́вка, оспопривива́ние.

vaccine ['væksi:n] *n.* вакци́на.

vacillate ['væsɪ,leɪt] *v.i.* колеба́ться (*impf.*).

vacillation [,væsɪ'leɪʃ(ə)n] *n.* колеба́ние.

vacuity [və'kju:ɪtɪ] *n.* пустота́.

vacuous ['vækjʊəs] *adj.* пусто́й.

vacuum ['vækjʊəm] *n.* 1. (*empty or airless place*) ва́куум; безвозду́шное простра́нство; (*fig.*) пустота́; **~ flask** те́рмос. 2. (*coll.*, **~-cleaner**) пылесо́с.
v.t. & i. (*coll., clean with* **~** (2.)) пылесо́сить (*impf., pf.*).

vagabond ['vægə,bɒnd] *n.* бродя́га (*c.g.*), скита́лец.

vagary ['veɪgərɪ] *n.* причу́да, капри́з.

vagina [və'dʒaɪnə] *n.* влага́лище.

vaginal [və'dʒaɪnəl] *adj.* влага́лищный.

vagrancy ['veɪgrənsɪ] *n.* бродя́жничество.

vagrant ['veɪgrənt] *n.* бродя́га (*c.g.*).
adj. бродя́чий.

vague [veɪg] *adj.* неопределённый, сму́тный, нея́сный; **a ~ resemblance** отдалённое схо́дство; **~ rumours** сму́тные слу́хи; **I haven't the ~st idea** не име́ю ни мале́йшего поня́тия/представле́ния.

vagueness ['veɪgnɪs] *n.* неопределённость, нея́сность.

vain [veɪn] *adj.* 1. (*unavailing; fruitless*) тще́тный, напра́сный; **a ~ attempt** тще́тная попы́тка; **~ hopes** напра́сные наде́жды; **they tried in ~ to get a seat** они́ безуспе́шно пыта́лись найти́ ме́сто. 2. (*empty*) пусто́й; **~ boasts** пуста́я похвальба́. 3. (*conceited*) тщесла́вный.
cpds. **~glorious** *adj.* тщесла́вный; **~glory** *n.* тщесла́вие.

val|ance ['væləns], **-ence** ['veɪləns] *n.* (*curtain, frill*)

подзо́р, обо́рка, сбо́рка.
vale [veɪl] *n.* доли́на, дол.
valediction [ˌvælɪ'dɪkʃ(ə)n] *n.* проща́ние.
valedictory [ˌvælɪ'dɪktərɪ] *adj.* проща́льный; (*US*, *as n.*) речь на вы́пуске (*учащихся*).
valence[1] ['veɪləns] = **valance**
valenc|e[2] ['veɪləns], **-y** ['veɪlənsɪ] *nn.* (*chem.*) вале́нтность.
valentine ['vælənˌtaɪn] *n.* (*missive*) ≃ любо́вное посла́ние.
valerian [və'lɪərɪən] *n.* (*bot.*) валериа́на.
valet ['vælɪt, -leɪ] *n.* камерди́нер.
v.t. служи́ть (*impf.*) камерди́нером *+d.*
valiant ['væljənt] *adj.* до́блестный, хра́брый; (*of effort*) герои́ческий.
valid ['vælɪd] *adj.* **1.** (*sound*) ве́ский, обосно́ванный; ~ **objections** убеди́тельные возраже́ния; ~ **reasons** ве́ские до́воды. **2.** (*leg.*) действи́тельный; **a ~ claim** зако́нная прете́нзия; **a ticket ~ for 3 months** биле́т, действи́тельный на три ме́сяца.
validate ['vælɪˌdeɪt] *v.t.* утвер|жда́ть, -ди́ть; подтвер|жда́ть, -ди́ть.
validation [ˌvælɪ'deɪʃ(ə)n] *n.* утвержде́ние, подтвержде́ние.
validity [və'lɪdɪtɪ] *n.* зако́нность, ве́скость; **the ~ of his argument** ве́скость его́ до́вода.
valise [və'li:z] *n.* (*US*) саквоя́ж, чемода́н.
valley ['vælɪ] *n.* доли́на.
valorous ['vælərəs] *adj.* до́блестный.
valour ['vælə(r)] *n.* до́блесть.
valuable ['væljʊəb(ə)l] *n.* (*usu. pl.*) це́нности (*f. pl.*); драгоце́нности (*f. pl.*).
adj. це́нный, поле́зный, ва́жный.
valuation [ˌvæljʊ'eɪʃ(ə)n] *n.* оце́нка; определе́ние сто́имости.
value ['vælju:] *n.* **1.** (*worth*; *advantageousness*) це́нность, ва́жность; **his advice was of great ~** его́ сове́т о́чень пригоди́лся; **he sets a high ~ on his time** он до́рого це́нит своё вре́мя. **2.** (*in money etc.*) це́нность, сто́имость; **the ~ of the pound** покупа́тельная си́ла фу́нта; **the book is good ~ for money** э́та кни́га — вы́годная поку́пка; ~ **added tax** нало́г на доба́вленную сто́имость. **3.** (*denomination of coin, card etc.*) досто́инство. **4.** (*pl.*, *standards*) (*духовные и т.п.*) це́нности (*f. pl.*).
v.t. **1.** (*estimate ~ of*) оце́н|ивать, -и́ть; **the house was ~d at £80,000** дом оцени́ли в 80 000 фу́нтов. **2.** (*regard highly*) дорожи́ть (*impf.*); цени́ть (*impf.*); **a ~d friend of mine** друг, кото́рый мне о́чень до́рог.
valueless ['væljʊlɪs] *adj.* ничего́ не сто́ящий; бесполе́зный; **a ~ promise** пусто́е обеща́ние.
valuer ['væljʊə(r)] *n.* оце́нщик.
valve [vælv] *n.* (*tech.*) кла́пан, ве́нтиль (*m.*); (*anat.*, *mus.*) кла́пан; (*radio*) электро́нная ла́мпа.
valvular ['vælvjʊlə(r)] *adj.* кла́пановый; ~ **defect** поро́к кла́панов (се́рдца).
vamoose [və'mu:s] *v.i.* см|ыва́ться, -ы́ться (*US sl.*).
vamp[1] [væmp] *n.* (*part of shoe*) передо́к боти́нка.
vamp[2] [væmp] *n.* (*adventuress*) (же́нщина-)вамп.
v.t. соблазн|я́ть, -и́ть.
vampire ['væmpaɪə(r)] *n.* **1.** (~ **bat**) вампи́р, упы́рь (*m.*). **2.** (*human creature*) вампи́р, кровопи́йца (*c.g.*).
van[1] [væn] *n.* **1.** (*motor vehicle*) (авто)фурго́н; **furniture ~** ме́бельный фурго́н. **2.** (*railway truck*) бага́жный ваго́н.
cpd. **~-driver** *n.* води́тель (*m.*) фурго́на.
van[2] [væn] *n.* (*of army etc.*) головно́й отря́д; (*fig.*) аванга́рд.
cpd. **~guard** *n.* аванга́рд; передово́й отря́д.
vandal ['vænd(ə)l] *n.* ванда́л, хулига́н.
vandalism ['vændəˌlɪz(ə)m] *n.* вандали́зм.
vandalize ['vændəˌlaɪz] *v.t.* разр|уша́ть, -у́шить.
vane [veɪn] *n.* (*weathercock*) флю́гер; (*of windmill*) крыло́; (*of propeller*, *turbine*) ло́пасть.
vanilla [və'nɪlə] *n.* вани́ль.
vanish ['vænɪʃ] *v.i.* исч|еза́ть, -е́знуть; проп|ада́ть, -а́сть; **~ing-point** то́чка схожде́ния паралле́льных (*в перспективе*); **his hopes of success ~ed** его́ наде́жды на успе́х улету́чились.
vanity ['vænɪtɪ] *n.* **1.** (*conceit*) тщесла́вие; ~ **case** да́мская су́мочка; космети́чка. **2.** (*futility*; *worthlessness*) суета́, тщета́; ~ **of vanities** суета́ сует.
vanquish ['væŋkwɪʃ] *v.t.* побе|жда́ть, -ди́ть; поко-р|я́ть, -и́ть.
vantage ['vɑ:ntɪdʒ] *n.* преиму́щество.
cpd. **~-point** *n.* вы́годная пози́ция.
vapid ['væpɪd] *adj.* (*fig.*) пло́ский, пре́сный; ~ **conversation** пусто́й/бессодержа́тельный разгово́р.
vaporization [ˌveɪpəraɪ'zeɪʃ(ə)n] *n.* испаре́ние, парообразова́ние.
vaporize ['veɪpəˌraɪz] *v.t.* & *i.* испар|я́ть(ся), -и́ть(ся).
vaporous ['veɪpərəs] *adj.* (*lit.*, *fig.*) тума́нный; (*filmy*) прозра́чный.
vapour ['veɪpə(r)] *n.* **1.** (*steam*) пар; ~ **bath** парова́я ба́ня/ва́нна. **2.** (*mist*) тума́н. **3.** (*gaseous manifestation*) испаре́ние; ~ **trail** инверсио́нный след.
variable ['veərɪəb(ə)l] *n.* переме́нная величина́.
adj. изме́нчивый, непостоя́нный; ~ **winds** ве́тры переме́нных направле́ний; ~ **standards** меня́ющиеся крите́рии.
variance ['veərɪəns] *n.* измене́ние; расхожде́ние; **this is at ~ with what we heard** э́то противоре́чит тому́, что мы слы́шали.
variant ['veərɪənt] *n.* вариа́нт.
adj. **1.** (*different*; *alternative*) разли́чный, ино́й. **2.** (*changing*) переме́нчивый.
variation [ˌveərɪ'eɪʃ(ə)n] *n.* **1.** (*fluctuation*) измене́ние; **~s of temperature** колеба́ния (*nt. pl.*) температу́ры. **2.** (*divergence*) отклоне́ние; ~ **from the norm** отклоне́ние от но́рмы. **3.** (*variant*; *also mus.*) вариа́ция; **~s on a theme** вариа́ции на те́му.
varicoloured ['veərɪˌkʌləd] *adj.* разноцве́тный.
varicose ['værɪˌkəʊs] *adj.* варико́зный; ~ **veins** расшире́ние вен.
varied ['veərɪd] *adj.* (*diverse*) разнообра́зный, разли́чный.
variegated ['veərɪˌgeɪtɪd, -rɪəˌgeɪtɪd] *adj.* разноцве́тный, пёстрый.
variety [və'raɪətɪ] *n.* **1.** (*diversity*; *many-sidedness*) разнообра́зие. **2.** (*number of different things*) ряд; мно́жество; **for a ~ of reasons** по це́лому ря́ду соображе́ний. **3.** (**~ entertainment**) варьете́ (*indecl.*); ~ **artist** эстра́дный арти́ст; ~ **show** эстра́дное представле́ние. **4.** (*biol.*) разнови́дность.
various ['veərɪəs] *adj.* **1.** (*diverse*) разли́чный, ра́зный, разнообра́зный. **2.** (*with pl.*, *several*) мно́гие (*pl.*); ра́зные (*pl.*); **at ~ times** в ра́зное вре́мя.
varnish ['vɑ:nɪʃ] *n.* лак.
v.t. лакирова́ть, от-.
var|y ['veərɪ] *v.t.* меня́ть (*impf.*); измен|я́ть, -и́ть; разнообра́зить (*impf.*).
v.i. **1.** (*change*) меня́ться (*impf.*); **the menu never ~ies** меню́ никогда́ не меня́ется. **2.** (*differ*) ра|сходи́ться, -зойти́сь; отлич|а́ться, -и́ться; **opinions ~y** мне́ния расхо́дятся; **with ~ying success** с переме́нным успе́хом.
vascular ['væskjʊlə(r)] *adj.* сосу́дистый.
vase [vɑ:z] *n.* ва́за.
vasectomy [və'sektəmɪ] *n.* вазэктоми́я.
Vaseline ['væsɪˌli:n] *n.* (*propr.*) вазели́н.
vassal ['væs(ə)l] *n.* васса́л; (*attr.*) васса́льный.
vast [vɑ:st] *adj.* обши́рный, грома́дный; огро́мный; (*grandiose*) грандио́зный; ~ **plains** необозри́мые равни́ны.
vastly ['vɑ:stlɪ] *adv.* о́чень, кра́йне.

vastness ['vɑ:stnɪs] *n.* ширь; огро́мность; грандио́зность.

VAT [ˌvi:eɪ'ti:, væt] *n.* (*Br., abbr. of* **value added tax**) нало́г на доба́вленную сто́имость.

vat [væt] *n.* бо́чка, чан.

Vatican ['vætɪkən] *n.* Ватика́н.

adj. ватика́нский.

vaudeville ['vɔ:dəvɪl, 'vəʊ-] *n.* водеви́ль (*m.*).

vault[1] [vɔ:lt, vɒlt] *n.* **1.** (*arched roof*) свод. **2.** (*underground room or chamber*) подва́л, по́греб; (*of a bank*) храни́лище; **family ~** (*tomb*) фами́льный склеп.

vault[2] [vɔ:lt, vɒlt] *n.* (*leap*) прыжо́к, скачо́к.

v.t. & i. перепры́г|ивать, -нуть; **he ~ed (over) the fence** он перепры́гнул че́рез забо́р; **~ing-horse** гимнасти́ческий конь.

vaulted ['vɔ:ltɪd, 'vɒltɪd] *adj.* сво́дчатый.

vaunt [vɔ:nt] *v.t. & i.* хва́стать(ся), по-; похвал|я́ться, -и́ться (+*i.*).

VC = **Victoria Cross**

VCR (*abbr. of* ***video cassette recorder***) видеомагнитофо́н.

VD (*abbr. of* ***venereal disease***) венери́ческая боле́знь.

VDU (*abbr. of* ***visual display unit***) диспле́й.

veal [vi:l] *n.* теля́тина.

vector ['vektə(r)] *n.* (*math.*) ве́ктор; (*of disease*) перено́счик/носи́тель (*m.*) инфе́кции.

veer [vɪə(r)] *v.i.* измен|я́ть, -и́ть направле́ние; пов|ора́чивать(ся), -ерну́ть(ся); (*fig.*) измен|я́ть, -и́ть курс; измен|я́ться, -и́ться; **public opinion is ~ing in his favour** обще́ственное мне́ние меня́ется в его́ по́льзу.

vegan ['vi:gən] *n.* стро́гий вегетариа́нец; (*attr.*) стро́го вегетариа́нский.

veganism ['vi:gənɪz(ə)m] *n.* стро́гое вегетариа́нство.

vegetable ['vedʒɪtəb(ə)l, 'vedʒtəb(ə)l] *n.* о́вощ; **green ~s** зе́лень, о́вощи.

adj. овощно́й; **the ~ kingdom** расти́тельное ца́рство; **~ oils** расти́тельные масла́; **~ marrow** кабачо́к.

vegetarian [ˌvedʒɪ'teərɪən] *n.* вегетариа́н|ец (*fem.* -ка); (*attr.*) вегетариа́нский.

vegetarianism [ˌvedʒɪ'teərɪəˌnɪz(ə)m] *n.* вегетариа́нство.

vegetate ['vedʒɪˌteɪt] *v.i.* (*lit., fig.*) прозяба́ть (*impf.*); (*fig.*) вести́ (*impf.*) расти́тельный о́браз жи́зни.

vegetation [ˌvedʒɪ'teɪʃ(ə)n] *n.* (*plant life*) расти́тельность.

vehemence ['vi:əməns] *n.* стра́стность, я́рость.

vehement ['vi:əmənt] *adj.* стра́стный, я́ростный.

vehicle ['vi:ɪk(ə)l, 'vɪək(ə)l] *n.* **1.** (*conveyance*) тра́нспортное сре́дство; **space ~** косми́ческий кора́бль. **2.** (*fig.*) проводни́к; сре́дство распростране́ния/переда́чи.

veil [veɪl] *n.* вуа́ль; **she took the ~** (*fig.*) она́ постри́глась в мона́хини; **under a ~ of secrecy** под покро́вом та́йны.

v.t. (*lit., fig.*) вуали́ровать, за-; **~ed threat** скры́тая угро́за.

vein [veɪn] *n.* **1.** (*anat.*) ве́на. **2.** (*of leaf*) жи́лка. **3.** (*of rock*) жи́ла; **a ~ of gold** прожи́лка зо́лота. **4.** (*mood*) настрое́ние, расположе́ние; **he was in humorous ~** он был в игри́вом настрое́нии; **in the same ~** в то́м же ду́хе.

Velcro ['velkrəʊ] *n.* (*propr.*): **~ fastener** застёжка «ве́лкро», липу́чка, замо́к-отры́вок.

vellum ['veləm] *n.* то́нкий перга́мент; **~ paper** веле́новая бума́га.

velocity [vɪ'lɒsɪtɪ] *n.* ско́рость, быстрота́.

velodrome ['veləˌdrəʊm] *n.* велодро́м.

velour(s) [və'lʊə(r)] *n.* велю́р.

velvet ['velvɪt] *n.* ба́рхат; **a ~ dress** ба́рхатное пла́тье.

velveteen [ˌvelvɪ'ti:n] *n.* вельве́т.

velvety ['velvɪtɪ] *adj.* бархати́стый.

venal ['vi:n(ə)l] *adj.* прода́жный.

venality [ˌvi:'nælɪtɪ] *n.* прода́жность.

vendetta [ven'detə] *n.* венде́тта.

vending-machine ['vendɪŋ] *n.* автома́т.

vendor ['vendə(r), -dɔ:(r)] *n.* продав|е́ц (*fem.* -щи́ца).

veneer [vɪ'nɪə(r)] *n.* шпон, фане́ра; (*fig.*) вне́шний лоск; **a ~ of politeness** показна́я ве́жливость.

venerable ['venərəb(ə)l] *adj.* почте́нный; **~ ruins** дре́вние/свяще́нные разва́лины.

venerate ['venəˌreɪt] *v.t.* чтить (*impf.*); почита́ть (*impf.*); благогове́ть (*impf.*) пе́ред+*i.*

veneration [ˌvenə'reɪʃ(ə)n] *n.* благогове́ние.

venereal [vɪ'nɪərɪəl] *adj.* венери́ческий; **~ disease** венери́ческая боле́знь.

Venetian [vɪ'ni:ʃ(ə)n] *adj.* венециа́нский; **~ blinds** жалюзи́ (*nt. pl., indecl.*).

Venezuela [ˌvenɪ'zweɪlə] *n.* Венесуэ́ла.

vengeance ['vendʒ(ə)ns] *n.* месть; **he sought ~ for the wrong done him** он хоте́л отомсти́ть за причинённую ему́ оби́ду/несправедли́вость; **he swore to take ~ on me** он покля́лся отомсти́ть мне. **2.: with a ~** (*coll., in a high degree*) вовсю́, с лихво́й.

vengeful ['vendʒfʊl] *adj.* мсти́тельный.

venial ['vi:nɪəl] *adj.* прости́тельный.

Venice ['venɪs] *n.* Вене́ция.

venison ['venɪs(ə)n, -z(ə)n] *n.* оле́нина.

venom ['venəm] *n.* яд; (*fig.*) яд, зло́ба.

venomous ['venəməs] *adj.* ядови́тый; (*fig.*) ядови́тый, зло́бный.

vent [vent] *n.* **1.** (*opening*) выходно́е отве́рстие; (*flue*) дымохо́д; (*in jacket*) разре́з. **2.** (*fig., outlet*) вы́ход; выраже́ние; отду́шина; **he gave ~ to his feelings** он дал во́лю свои́м чу́вствам.

v.t. (*fig.*) изл|ива́ть, -и́ть; да|ва́ть, -ть вы́ход +*d.*; **he ~ed his ill-temper on his secretary** он сорва́л своё дурно́е настрое́ние на секрета́рше.

ventilate ['ventɪˌleɪt] *v.t.* прове́три|вать, -ть; вентили́ровать, про-; (*fig.*) обсу|жда́ть, -ди́ть.

ventilation [ˌventɪ'leɪʃ(ə)n] *n.* **1.** вентиля́ция; **~ shaft** вентиляцио́нная ша́хта. **2.** (*fig.*) (публи́чное) обсужде́ние.

ventilator ['ventɪˌleɪtə(r)] *n.* вентиля́тор (*also med.*).

ventricle ['ventrɪk(ə)l] *n.* желу́дочек (се́рдца/мо́зга).

ventriloquism [ven'trɪləˌkwɪz(ə)m] *n.* чревовеща́ние.

ventriloquist [ven'trɪləˌkwɪst] *n.* чревовеща́тель (*m.*).

venture ['ventʃə(r)] *n.* **1.** (*risky undertaking*) риско́ванное предприя́тие. **2.** (*commercial speculation*) спекуля́ция.

v.t. (*risk, bet*) риск|ова́ть, -ну́ть +*i.*; ста́вить, по- на ка́рту; **I will ~ £5** я поста́влю 5 фу́нтов.

v.i. (*dare*) осме́ли|ваться, -ться; отва́житься (*pf.*); **I ~ to suggest** я бы посове́товал/рекомендова́л; **don't ~ too near the edge** не подходи́те сли́шком бли́зко к кра́ю; **nothing ~, nothing win** попы́тка не пы́тка.

venturesome ['ventʃəsəm] *adj.* (*daring*) предприи́мчивый; (*risky*) риско́вый.

venue ['venju:] *n.* ме́сто сбо́ра/встре́чи/соревнова́ний.

Venus ['vi:nəs] *n.* (*myth., astron.*) Вене́ра.

veracious [və'reɪʃəs] *adj.* правди́вый, достове́рный.

veracity [və'ræsɪtɪ] *n.* правди́вость; достове́рность (информа́ции).

veranda(h) [və'rændə] *n.* вера́нда.

verb [vɜ:b] *n.* глаго́л.

verbal ['vɜ:b(ə)l] *adj.* **1.** (*of or in words*) слове́сный; **~ subtleties** то́нкости языка́. **2.** (*oral*) у́стный; **~ly** (то́лько) на слова́х. **3.** (*gram.*): **~ noun** отглаго́льное существи́тельное.

verbalize ['vɜ:bəˌlaɪz] *v.t.* (*put into words*) выража́ть, вы́разить слова́ми.

verbatim [vɜ:'beɪtɪm] *adv.* досло́вно; сло́во в сло́во.

verbena [vɜːˈbiːnə] *n.* вербе́на.
verbiage [ˈvɜːbɪɪdʒ] *n.* многосло́вие; пустосло́вие.
verbose [vɜːˈbəʊs] *adj.* многосло́вный.
verbosity [vɜːˈbɒsɪtɪ] *n.* многосло́вие.
verdant [ˈvɜːd(ə)nt] *adj.* зелёный.
verdict [ˈvɜːdɪkt] *n.* (*leg.*) верди́кт; **the jury brought in a ~ of guilty** суд прися́жных призна́л подсуди́мого вино́вным; (*fig., decision, judgement*) заключе́ние, пригово́р; **what's the ~?** како́в пригово́р?
verdigris [ˈvɜːdɪgrɪs, -ˌgriːs] *n.* ярь-медя́нка.
verdure [ˈvɜːdjə(r)] *n.* зе́лень.
verge [vɜːdʒ] *n.* край; (*of road*) обо́чина; **a grass ~** бордю́р из дёрна; (*fig.*): **on the ~ of destruction** на краю́ ги́бели; **on the ~ of tears** на гра́ни слёз.
v.i.: **it ~s on madness** э́то грани́чит с безу́мием.
verger [ˈvɜːdʒə(r)] *n.* (*church official*) ≃ дьячо́к.
verifiable [ˈverɪˌfaɪəb(ə)l] *adj.* поддаю́щийся прове́рке.
verification [ˌverɪfɪˈkeɪʃ(ə)n] *n.* прове́рка, подтвержде́ние.
verify [ˈverɪˌfaɪ] *v.t.* (*check accuracy of*) пров|еря́ть, -е́рить; (*bear out, confirm*) подтвер|жда́ть, -ди́ть.
verily [ˈverɪlɪ] *adv.* (*arch.*) и́стинно, пои́стине.
verisimilitude [ˌverɪsɪˈmɪlɪˌtjuːd] *n.* правдоподо́бие.
veritable [ˈverɪtəb(ə)l] *adj.* настоя́щий, су́щий.
verit|y [ˈverɪtɪ] *n.* и́стина; **eternal ~ies** ве́чные и́стины.
vermicelli [ˌvɜːmɪˈselɪ, -ˈtʃelɪ] *n.* вермише́ль.
vermiform [ˈvɜːmɪˌfɔːm] *adj.*: **~ appendix** (*anat.*) червообра́зный отро́сток, аппе́ндикс.
vermilion [vəˈmɪljən] *n.* (*pigment; colour*) вермильо́н, ки́новарь.
adj. я́рко-кра́сный.
vermin [ˈvɜːmɪn] *n.* **1.** (*animal pests*) вреди́тели (*m. pl.*); ме́лкие хи́щники (*m. pl.*). **2.** (*parasitic insects*) парази́ты (*m. pl.*).
vermouth [ˈvɜːməθ, vəˈmuːθ] *n.* ве́рмут.
vernacular [vəˈnækjʊlə(r)] *n.* **1.** (*dialect*) диале́кт; наре́чие. **2.** (*slang*) жарго́н, арго́ (*indecl*). **3.** (*homely speech*) простонаре́чие.
adj. просторе́чный.
vernal [ˈvɜːn(ə)l] *adj.* весе́нний.
versatile [ˈvɜːsəˌtaɪl] *adj.* разносторо́нний, многосторо́нний.
versatility [ˌvɜːsəˈtɪlɪtɪ] *n.* разносторо́нность, многосторо́нность.
verse [vɜːs] *n.* **1.** (*line of ~*) строка́. **2.** (*stanza*) строфа́. **3.** (*of Bible*) стих. **4.** (*sg. or pl., poems*) стихи́ (*m. pl.*); стихотворе́ния (*nt. pl.*); **prose and ~** про́за и поэ́зия; **he wrote in ~** он писа́л в стиха́х.
versed [vɜːst] *adj.* (*well-informed*) све́дующий (в+*p.*); (*skilful*) искушённый.
versification [ˌvɜːsɪfɪˈkeɪʃ(ə)n] *n.* стихосложе́ние.
version [ˈvɜːʃ(ə)n] *n.* **1.** (*individual account*) ве́рсия, расска́з; **according to his ~** по его́ слова́м. **2.** (*translation*) перево́д; **a French ~ of Shakespeare** Шекспи́р в францу́зском перево́де. **3.** (*form or variant of text etc.*) вариа́нт, текст; **original ~** по́длинник; **the Russian ~ is authentic** ру́сский текст аутенти́чен; (*adaptation*) переложе́ние, переде́лка; **silent ~** (*cin.*) немо́й вариа́нт; **screen ~** экраниза́ция; **stage ~** инсцениро́вка.
versus [ˈvɜːsəs] *prep.* **1.** (*leg.*) про́тив+*g.* **2.** (*sport*): **Manchester ~ Chelsea** матч Ма́нчестер — Че́лси. **3.** (*compared or contrasted with*) в сравне́нии с+*i.*
vertebra [ˈvɜːtɪbrə] *n.* позвоно́к.
vertebrate [ˈvɜːtɪbrət, -ˌbreɪt] *n.* позвоно́чное (живо́тное).
adj. позвоно́чный.
vertex [ˈvɜːteks] *n.* верши́на.
vertical [ˈvɜːtɪk(ə)l] *n.* вертика́ль; перпендикуля́р.
adj. вертика́льный, перпендикуля́рный; **a ~ cliff** отве́сный утёс.
vertiginous [vəˈtɪdʒɪnəs] *adj.* головокружи́тельный.
vertigo [ˈvɜːtɪˌgəʊ] *n.* головокруже́ние.
verve [vɜːv] *n.* жи́вость, эне́ргия; огонёк.
very [ˈverɪ] *adj.* **1.** (*exact; identical*) тот са́мый; **this ~ day** сего́дня же; **at that ~ moment** в тот же моме́нт; **this is the ~ thing for me** э́то как раз то, что мне ну́жно. **2.** (*extreme*) са́мый; **at the ~ end** в са́мом конце́. **3.** (*in emphasis*): **the ~ idea of it** одна́ мысль об э́том; **the ~ idea!** поду́мать то́лько!; **the ~ fact of his being there is suspicious** (уже́) оди́н факт его́ прису́тствия подозри́телен.
adv. **1.** (*exceedingly*) о́чень; **I don't feel ~ well** я чу́вствую себя́ нева́жно; **I can't sing ~ well** я дово́льно пло́хо пою́; **~ well, you can go** ну, хорошо́, мо́жете идти́. **2.** (*emph., with superl. etc.*) са́мый; **the ~ best** са́мый лу́чший; наилу́чший; **the ~ next day** на сле́дующий же день.
vespers [ˈvespə(r)s] *n.* вече́рня; вече́рняя моли́тва.
vessel [ˈves(ə)l] *n.* **1.** (*receptacle*) сосу́д. **2.** (*ship*) су́дно, кора́бль (*m.*). **3.** (*anat.*) сосу́д; **blood ~** кровено́сный сосу́д.
vest[1] [vest] *n.* (*undergarment*) ма́йка; (*US, waistcoat*) жиле́т.
v.i. (*put on robes*) облач|а́ться, -и́ться.
cpd. **~-pocket** *n.* жиле́тный карма́н.
vest[2] [vest] *v.t.* **1.** (*endow, furnish*) надел|я́ть, -и́ть; обл|ека́ть, -е́чь; **be ~ed with a right** име́ть (*impf.*) пра́во; по́льзоваться (*impf.*) пра́вом; **~ with power to act** упономо́чи|вать, -ть. **2.** (*place, establish*): **authority ~ed in him** власть, кото́рой он облечён; **~ed interest** иму́щественное пра́во, закреплённое зако́ном; кро́вная заинтересо́ванность.
vestibule [ˈvestɪˌbjuːl] *n.* вестибю́ль (*m.*).
vestige [ˈvestɪdʒ] *n.* **1.** (*trace*) след; мале́йший при́знак. **2.** (*biol.*) оста́ток.
vestigial [veˈstɪdʒɪəl, -dʒ(ə)l] *adj.* оста́точный, рудимента́рный.
vestment [ˈvestmənt] *n.* облаче́ние.
vestry [ˈvestrɪ] *n.* (*room*) ри́зница.
vet [vet] *n.* (*coll., veterinary surgeon*) ветерина́р.
v.t. (*coll., investigate*) пров|еря́ть, -е́рить.
vetch [vetʃ] *n.* ви́ка.
veteran [ˈvetərən] *n.* (*lit., fig.*) ветера́н.
adj. многоо́пытный, старе́йший; **a ~ car** автомоби́ль-ветера́н.
veterinarian [ˌvetərɪˈneərɪən] *n.* ветерина́р.
veterinary [ˈvetəˌrɪnərɪ] *adj.* ветерина́рный; **~ surgeon** ветерина́рный врач.
veto [ˈviːtəʊ] *n.* ве́то (*indecl.*); **he put a ~ on the suggestion** он наложи́л ве́то на то предложе́ние.
v.t. нал|ага́ть, -ожи́ть ве́то на+*a.*; **my proposal was ~ed** моё предложе́ние бы́ло отве́ргнуто.
vex [veks] *v.t.* доса|жда́ть, -ди́ть; раздраж|а́ть, -и́ть; **how ~ing!** така́я доса́да!; **a ~ed question** больно́й вопро́с.
vexation [vekˈseɪʃ(ə)n] *n.* доса́да; огорче́ние.
vexatious [vekˈseɪʃ(ə)s] *adj.* доса́дный.
via [ˈvaɪə] *prep.* че́рез+*a.*
viability [ˌvaɪəˈbɪlɪtɪ] *n.* жизнеспосо́бность.
viable [ˈvaɪəb(ə)l] *adj.* (*able to survive or exist*) жизнеспосо́бный; (*coll., feasible*) осуществи́мый.
viaduct [ˈvaɪəˌdʌkt] *n.* виаду́к, путепрово́д.
vibes [vaɪbz] *n.* (*coll., vibrations*) вибра́ции (*f. pl.*).
vibrant [ˈvaɪbrənt] *adj.* (*vibrating*) вибри́рующий; (*thrilling*) трепе́щущий; (*resonant*) резони́рующий.
vibrat|e [vaɪˈbreɪt] *v.t.* заст|авля́ть, -а́вить вибри́ровать (*impf.*).
v.i. вибри́ровать, дрожа́ть (*both impf.*); **the whole house ~es** весь дом сотряса́ется.
vibration [vaɪˈbreɪʃ(ə)n] *n.* вибра́ция, дрожь.
vibrato [vɪˈbrɑːtəʊ] *n. & adv.* вибра́то (*indecl.*).
vibrator [vaɪˈbreɪtə(r)] *n.* (*for massage*) вибра́тор.
viburnum [vaɪˈbɜːnəm, vɪ-] *n.* кали́на.
vicar [ˈvɪkə(r)] *n.* (*clergyman*) прихо́дский свяще́нник;

(*eccl.*, *representative*) замести́тель (*m.*); вика́рий.
vicarage ['vɪkərɪdʒ] *n.* дом свяще́нника.
vicarious [vɪ'keərɪəs] *adj.* ко́свенный; **feel ~ pleasure** пережива́ть (*impf.*) чужу́ю ра́дость.
vice[1] [vaɪs] *n.* **1.** (*evil doing*) поро́к; **~ squad** отря́д поли́ции нра́вов. **2.** (*particular fault*) поро́к, сла́бость, недоста́ток.
vice[2] [vaɪs] (*US* **vise**) *n.* (*tool*) тиск|и́ (*pl.*, *g.* -ов); клёщ|и (*pl.*, *g.* -е́й).
vice[3] [vaɪs] *n.* (*coll.*, *deputy*) замести́тель (*m.*).
cpds. **~-admiral** *n.* ви́це-адмира́л; **~chairman** *n.* замести́тель (*m.*) председа́теля; **~-chancellor** *n.* ре́ктор; **~-president** *n.* ви́це-президе́нт.
viceroy ['vaɪsrɔɪ] *n.* ви́це-коро́ль (*m.*); (*hist.*) генера́л-губерна́тор И́ндии.
vice versa [,vaɪsɪ 'vɜ:sə] *adv.* наоборо́т.
vicinity [vɪ'sɪnɪtɪ] *n.* (*nearness*) бли́зость, сосе́дство; (*neighbourhood*) окру́га, окре́стность.
vicious ['vɪʃəs] *adj.* **1.** (*spiteful*) злой, зло́бный. **2.** (*of an animal*) злой, опа́сный, норови́стый. **3.: a ~ circle** поро́чный круг.
viciousness ['vɪʃəsnɪs] *n.* (*evil*) поро́чность; (*spite*) зло́бность; (*of an animal*) но́ров, зло́бность.
vicissitude [vɪ'sɪsɪ,tju:d, vaɪ-] *n.* превра́тность.
victim ['vɪktɪm] *n.* же́ртва; (*of accident*) пострада́вший; **fall ~ to** па́|дать, -сть же́ртвой +*g.*
victimization [,vɪktɪmaɪ'zeɪʃ(ə)n] *n.* пресле́дование.
victimize ['vɪktɪ,maɪz] *v.t.* подв|ерга́ть, -е́ргнуть пресле́дованию.
victor ['vɪktə(r)] *n.* победи́тель (*m.*).
Victoria Cross [vɪk'tɔ:rɪə] (*Br.*, *mil.*) *n.* крест Викто́рии.
Victorian [vɪk'tɔ:rɪən] *adj.* викториа́нский; (*fig.*) старомо́дный.
victorious [vɪk'tɔ:rɪəs] *adj.* победоно́сный, побе́дный, торжеству́ющий.
victory ['vɪktərɪ] *n.* побе́да.
victual ['vɪt(ə)l] *n.* (*obs.*, *pl. only*) пи́ща; съестны́е припа́с|ы (*pl.*, *g.* -ов).
video ['vɪdɪəʊ] *n.*: **~ camera** видеока́мера; **~ cassette** видеокассе́та; **~ cassette recorder** видеомагнитофо́н; **~ games machine** телеавтома́т; **~ recording** видеоза́пись; **~ rental club** видеоте́ка; **~ tape** видеоле́нта; **~ telephone** видеотелефо́н.
v.t. запи́с|ывать, -а́ть на ви́део.
vie [vaɪ] *v.i.* состяза́ться (*impf.*); сопе́рничать (*impf.*); **they ~d with each other for first place** они́ боро́лись друг с дру́гом за пе́рвое ме́сто.
Vienna [vɪ'enə] *n.* Ве́на.
Vietnam [,vjet'næm] *n.* Вьетна́м.
view [vju:] *n.* **1.** (*sight*; *field of vision*) вид; по́ле зре́ния; **the mountains came into ~** показа́лись го́ры; **a ~ of the sea** вид на мо́ре; **the procession passed from ~** проце́ссия скры́лось и́з виду/глаз; **in full ~ of the audience** на виду́ у пу́блики. **2.** (*fig.*): **I want to get a clear ~ of the situation** я хочу́ соста́вить себе́ я́сное представле́ние о ситуа́ции; **look at it from my point of ~** посмотри́те на э́то с мое́й то́чки зре́ния. **3.** (*scene*, *prospect*) вид; пейза́ж; **you get a good ~ from here** отсю́да хоро́ший вид. **4.** (*mental attitude or opinion*) взгляд, мне́ние; **she has strong ~s on the subject** у неё на э́тот счёт твёрдые убежде́ния; **I take a different ~** у меня́ друга́я то́чка зре́ния. **5.** (*intention*) наме́рение; **I am saving with a ~ to buying a house** я коплю́ де́ньги, что́бы купи́ть дом; **what have you in ~?** что вы име́ете в виду́? **6.** (*consideration*): **in ~ of** ввиду́+*g.*; **he was excused in ~ of his youth** его́ прости́ли по мо́лодости; **in ~ of recent developments** в све́те после́дних происше́ствий.
v.t. **1.** (*survey*; *gaze on*) смотре́ть (*impf.*); рассм|а́тривать, -отре́ть; **he ~ed the landscape through binoculars** он обозрева́л ме́стность в бино́кль. **2.** (*inspect*) осм|а́тривать, -отре́ть. **3.** (*fig.*, *consider*) рассм|а́тривать, -отре́ть; оце́н|ивать, -и́ть; **he ~ed it in a different light** он ина́че смотре́л на э́то.
cpds. **~-finder** *n.* видоиска́тель (*m.*); **~point** *n.* то́чка зре́ния.
viewer ['vju:ə(r)] *n.* **1.** (*onlooker*) зри́тель (*fem.* -ница). **2.** (*of TV*) телезри́тель (*fem.* -ница).
vigil ['vɪdʒɪl] *n.* бде́ние; **she kept ~ over the invalid** она́ не отходи́ла от посте́ли больно́го.
vigilance ['vɪdʒɪləns] *n.* бди́тельность.
vigilant ['vɪdʒɪlənt] *adj.* бди́тельный.
vigilante [,vɪdʒɪ'læntɪ] *n.* ≃ дружи́нник.
vignette [vi:'njet] *n.* (*ornamental design*) винье́тка; (*character sketch*) набро́сок.
vigorous ['vɪgərəs] *adj.* си́льный, бо́дрый; **a ~ speech** энерги́чная речь.
vigour ['vɪgə(r)] *n.* си́ла, бо́дрость; (*of language*, *style etc.*) живость, энерги́чность.
Viking ['vaɪkɪŋ] *n.* ви́кинг.
vile [vaɪl] *adj.* гну́сный, ни́зкий, ме́рзкий.
vilification [,vɪlɪfɪ'keɪʃ(ə)n] *n.* поноше́ние.
vilify ['vɪlɪ,faɪ] *v.t.* поноси́ть (*impf.*); черни́ть, о-.
villa ['vɪlə] *n.* ви́лла.
village ['vɪlɪdʒ] *n.* дере́вня, село́; (*attr.*) деревéнский; **~ hall** се́льский клуб.
villager ['vɪlɪdʒə(r)] *n.* жи́тель (*fem.* -ница) дере́вни; крестья́н|ин (*fem.* -ка).
villain ['vɪlən] *n.* **1.** (*man of base character*) злоде́й, негодя́й; (*theatr.*) отрица́тельный геро́й; **he was the ~ of the piece** (*fig.*) он был гла́вным вино́вником. **2.** (*coll.*, *criminal*) престу́пник.
villainous ['vɪlənəs] *adj.* по́длый, ни́зкий, гну́сный.
villainy ['vɪlənɪ] *n.* злоде́йство, по́длость.
vim [vɪm] *n.* эне́ргия, си́ла.
vinaigrette [,vɪnɪ'gret] *n.* подли́вка из у́ксуса и прова́нского ма́сла.
vindicate ['vɪndɪ,keɪt] *v.t.* (*defend successfully*) отст|а́ивать, -оя́ть; защи|ща́ть, -ти́ть; (*justify*) опра́вд|ывать, -а́ть.
vindication [,vɪndɪ'keɪʃ(ə)n] *n.* защи́та; оправда́ние.
vindictive [vɪn'dɪktɪv] *adj.* мсти́тельный.
vindictiveness [vɪn'dɪktɪvnɪs] *n.* мсти́тельность.
vine [vaɪn] *n.* (*grape-~*) виногра́дная лоза́; (*any climbing or trailing plant*) вью́щееся/ползу́чее расте́ние.
cpds. **~-growing** *adj.* виноде́льческий; **~yard** *n.* виногра́дник.
vinegar ['vɪnɪgə(r)] *n.* у́ксус.
vinegary ['vɪnɪgərɪ] *adj.* у́ксусный; ки́слый (*also fig.*).
viniculture ['vɪnɪ,kʌltʃə(r)] *n.* виногра́дарство.
vintage ['vɪntɪdʒ] *n.* **1.** (*grape harvest*) сбор виногра́да; **the 1950 ~** (*sc. wine*) вино́ урожа́я (*or* из сбо́ра) ты́сяча девятьсо́т пятидеся́того го́да; **this is a good ~** э́то хоро́ший год; **~ wine** ма́рочное вино́. **2.** (*fig.*): **a ~ car** автомоби́ль (*m.*) ста́рой ма́рки; **of the same ~** (*sc. age*) того́ же вы́пуска.
vintner ['vɪntnə(r)] *n.* виноторго́вец.
vinyl ['vaɪnɪl] *n.* вини́л.
adj. вини́ловый.
viola[1] [vɪ'əʊlə] *n.* (*mus.*) альт.
viola[2] ['vaɪələ] *n.* (*bot.*) вио́ла.
violate ['vaɪə,leɪt] *v.t.* **1.** (*infringe*, *transgress*) нар|уша́ть, -у́шить; преступ|а́ть, -и́ть; **this ~s the spirit of the agreement** э́то противоре́чит ду́ху соглаше́ния; **~ one's conscience** де́йствовать (*impf.*) вопреки́ свое́й со́вести. **2.** (*rape*) наси́ловать, из-.
violation [,vaɪə'leɪʃ(ə)n] *n.* наруше́ние; **~ of territory** вторже́ние на чужу́ю террито́рию; (*rape*) изнаси́лование.
violence ['vaɪələns] *n.* си́ла, наси́лие; **he resorted to ~** он примени́л си́лу; он прибе́гнул к наси́лию; **robbery with ~** грабёж с наси́лием; **do ~ to a text** иска|жа́ть, -зи́ть смысл те́кста.
violent ['vaɪələnt] *adj.* **1.** (*strong*, *forceful*) си́льный,

неи́стовый, я́ростный; **a ~ storm** жесто́кий/си́льный што́рм; **~ pain** о́страя боль; **~ passions** неи́стовые стра́сти; **a ~ scene** бу́рная сце́на; **I took a ~ dislike to him** он вы́звал во мне ре́зкое отвраще́ние; **he was in a ~ temper** он был вне себя́ от бе́шенства; **he made a ~ speech** он произнёс горя́чую речь. **2.** (*using or involving force*): **~ blows** си́льные уда́ры; **he became ~** он на́чал бу́йствовать; **he died a ~ death** он у́мер наси́льственной сме́ртью.

violet ['vaɪələt] *n.* (*bot.*) фиа́лка; (*colour*) фиоле́товый цвет.

adj. (*of colour*) фиоле́товый.

violin [ˌvaɪə'lɪn] *n.* скри́пка.

violinist [vaɪə'lɪnɪst] *n.* скрипа́ч (*fem.* -ка).

violoncello [ˌvaɪələn'tʃeləʊ, ˌviːə-] *n.* виолонче́ль.

VIP (*abbr. of* **very important person**) высокопоста́вленное лицо́.

viper ['vaɪpə(r)] *n.* гадю́ка; випе́ра; (*fig.*) гадю́ка.

virago [vɪ'rɑːgəʊ, -'reɪgəʊ] *n.* меге́ра.

virgin ['vɜːdʒɪn] *n.* де́ва, де́вственница; (*male*) де́вственник; **the (Blessed) V~** де́ва Мари́я; **she is still a ~** она́ ещё де́вушка/деви́ца; **~ birth** рожде́ние от де́вы; (*pure*; *undefiled*) чи́стый, нетро́нутый; **~ soil** целина́; **~ forest** де́вственный лес.

virginal ['vɜːdʒɪn(ə)l] *adj.* де́вственный; непоро́чный.

virginity [və'dʒɪnɪtɪ] *n.* де́вственность, непоро́чность; **lose one's ~** теря́ть, по- неви́нность.

Virgo ['vɜːgəʊ] *n.* Де́ва.

virile ['vɪraɪl] *adj.* **1.** облада́ющий мужско́й си́лой/поте́нцией. **2.** (*manly, robust*) му́жественный, энерги́чный.

virility [vɪ'rɪlɪtɪ] *n.* му́жество; полова́я поте́нция; му́жественность, эне́ргия.

virtual ['vɜːtjʊəl] *adj.* факти́ческий; **the dress was ~ly new** э́то бы́ло практи́чески но́вое пла́тье; **he is a ~ stranger to me** я его́, в су́щности, не зна́ю; **~ reality** виртуа́льная действи́тельность.

virtue ['vɜːtjuː, -tʃuː] *n.* **1.** (*moral excellence*) доброде́тель; **his great ~ is patience** его́ гла́вная доброде́тель —терпе́ние. **2.** (*chastity*) целому́дрие; **a woman of easy ~** досту́пная же́нщина. **3.** (*good quality*; *advantage*) досто́инство, преиму́щество. **4.** (*consideration*) основа́ние; **by ~ of his long service** на основа́нии (*or* ввиду́) его́ долголе́тней слу́жбы.

virtuosity [ˌvɜːtjuː'ɒsɪtɪ, -tʃuː'ɒsɪtɪ] *n.* виртуо́зность.

virtuoso [ˌvɜːtjʊ'əʊsəʊ, -zəʊ] *n.* виртуо́з; **a ~ performance** виртуо́зное исполне́ние.

virtuous ['vɜːtjʊəs, -tʃʊəs] *adj.* доброде́тельный; (*chaste*) целому́дренный.

virulence ['vɪrʊləns, 'vɪrjʊ-] *n.* (*of disease*) вируле́нтность; (*of temper, speech etc.*) зло́ба, я́рость.

virulent ['vɪrʊlənt, 'vɪrjʊ-] *adj.* (*of disease*) вируле́нтный; (*of temper, words etc.*) зло́бный, я́ростный.

virus ['vaɪərəs] *n.* ви́рус; **a ~ disease** ви́русное заболева́ние.

visa ['viːzə] *n.* ви́за.

visage ['vɪzɪdʒ] *n.* (*liter.*) лицо́; выраже́ние лица́; вид.

vis-à-vis [ˌviːzɑː'viː] *adv.* визави́.

prep. (*in relation to*) по отноше́нию к+*d.*; в отноше́нии+*g.*; пе́ред+*i.*

viscera ['vɪsərə] *n.* вну́тренности (*f. pl.*).

visceral ['vɪsər(ə)l] *adj.* вну́тренний.

viscose ['vɪskəʊz, -kəʊs] *n.* виско́за.

viscosity [vɪ'skɒsɪtɪ] *n.* ли́пкость, вя́зкость.

viscount ['vaɪkaʊnt] *n.* вико́нт.

viscountess ['vaɪkaʊntɪs] *n.* виконте́сса.

viscous ['vɪskəs] *adj.* ли́пкий, вя́зкий.

vise [vaɪs] = **vice**[2]

visibility [ˌvɪzɪ'bɪlɪtɪ] *n.* ви́димость.

visible ['vɪzɪb(ə)l] *adj.* **1.** (*perceptible by eye*) ви́димый. **2.** (*apparent*; *obvious*) я́вный, очеви́дный; **he has no ~ means of support** у него́ нет определённых средств к существова́нию.

vision ['vɪʒ(ə)n] *n.* **1.** (*faculty of sight*) зре́ние; **field of ~** по́ле зре́ния. **2.** (*imaginative insight*) проница́тельность; **a man of ~** дальнови́дный челове́к; челове́к с широ́ким кругозо́ром. **3.** (*apparition*) при́зрак; привиде́ние. **4.** (*sth. imagined or dreamed of*) мечта́; о́браз.

visionary ['vɪʒənərɪ] *n.* мечта́тель (*fem.* -ница); прови́д|ец (*fem.* -ица).

adj. неосуществи́мый, нереа́льный.

visit ['vɪzɪt] *n.* (*call*) визи́т, посеще́ние; (*trip, stay*) пое́здка, пребыва́ние; (*of ship*) осмо́тр; **make, pay a ~ to s.o.** посе|ща́ть, -ти́ть (*or* наве|ща́ть, -сти́ть) кого́-н.; **we had a ~ from our neighbours** нас посети́ли (*or* у нас бы́ли в гостя́х) на́ши сосе́ди; **we had a ~ from a policeman** к нам приходи́л полице́йский; **~ to a museum** посеще́ние музе́я; **pay us a ~** прове́дайте нас; **he is here on a ~** он гости́т здесь; он прие́зжий; **during my ~ to the States** во вре́мя моего́ пребыва́ния в Шта́тах.

v.t. посе|ща́ть, -ти́ть; наве|ща́ть, -сти́ть; **he ~ed Europe** он побыва́л в Евро́пе; он съе́здил в Евро́пу; **I have never ~ed New York** я никогда́ не быва́л в Нью-Йо́рке; **~ing card** визи́тная ка́рточка; **~ing hours** приёмные часы́; часы́ посеще́ния.

v.i. (*US*): **~ with** вида́ться, по-, *or* бесе́довать (*impf.*) с+*i.*

visitation [ˌvɪzɪ'teɪʃ(ə)n] *n.* (*official visit*) обхо́д; (*affliction*) ка́ра, наказа́ние (бо́жье).

visitor ['vɪzɪtə(r)] *n.* гость (*m.*), посети́тель (*m.*); **the town is full of ~s** го́род по́лон прие́зжих; **~s' book** кни́га посети́телей.

vi|sor, -zor ['vaɪzə(r)] *n.* (*of cap*) козырёк; (*of windscreen*) солнцезащи́тный щито́к.

vista ['vɪstə] *n.* перспекти́ва, вид.

visual ['vɪzjʊəl, 'vɪʒj-] *adj.* (*concerned with seeing*) зри́тельный, визуа́льный; **~ image** зри́тельный о́браз; **~ aids** нагля́дные посо́бия.

visualize ['vɪzjʊəˌlaɪz, 'vɪʒj-] *v.t.* предст|авля́ть, -а́вить себе́.

vital ['vaɪt(ə)l] *adj* **1.** (*concerned with life*) жи́зненный; **~ principle** жи́зненное нача́ло; **wounded in a ~ part** получи́вший смерте́льное ране́ние. **2.** (*essential*; *indispensable*) насу́щный; (кра́йне) необходи́мый; **a ~ question** суще́ственный вопро́с; **it is of ~ importance** э́то вопро́с/де́ло первостепе́нной ва́жности; **speed was ~ to success** ско́рость была́ гла́вным зало́гом успе́ха. **3.** (*lively*; *having vitality*) энерги́чный, живо́й.

vitality [vaɪ'tælɪtɪ] *n.* (*vital power*) жи́зненная си́ла; (*energy*; *liveliness*) эне́ргия, жи́вость.

vitalize ['vaɪtəˌlaɪz] *v.t.* ожив|ля́ть, -и́ть.

vitamin ['vɪtəmɪn, 'vaɪt-] *n.* витами́н; (*attr.*) витами́нный; **V~ C** витами́н С (*pr.* це).

vitiate ['vɪʃɪˌeɪt] *v.t.* по́ртить, ис-; (*fig., invalidate*) де́лать, с- недействи́тельным; под|рыва́ть, -орва́ть.

viticulture ['vɪtɪˌkʌltʃə(r)] *n.* виногра́дарство.

vitreous ['vɪtrɪəs] *adj.* стекля́нный.

vitrify ['vɪtrɪˌfaɪ] *v.t. & i.* превра|ща́ть(ся), -ти́ть(ся) в стекло́.

vitriol ['vɪtrɪəl] *n.* **1.** купоро́с; **blue ~** ме́дный купоро́с. **2.** (*fig.*) яд.

vitriolic [ˌvɪtrɪ'ɒlɪk] *adj.* купоро́сный; (*fig.*) е́дкий, ядови́тый.

vituperation [vɪˌtjuːpə'reɪʃ(ə)n, vaɪ-] *n.* поноше́ние, брань.

vituperative [vɪ'tjuːpərətɪv, vaɪ-] *adj.* бра́нный, зло́бный.

vivacious [vɪ'veɪʃəs] *adj.* живо́й, оживлённый.

vivacity [vɪ'væsɪtɪ] *n.* жи́вость, оживле́ние.

vivid ['vɪvɪd] *adj.* **1.** (*bright*) я́ркий. **2.** (*lively*) живо́й; пы́лкий; **a ~ imagination** пы́лкое воображе́ние. **3.** (*clear and distinct*) чёткий, я́сный.

vividness ['vɪvɪdnɪs] *n.* я́ркость, жи́вость, чёткость.

vivisection [ˌvɪvɪˈsekʃ(ə)n] *n.* вивисéкция.
vivisectionist [ˌvɪvɪˈsekʃ(ə)nɪst] *n.* вивисéктор.
vixen [ˈvɪks(ə)n] *n.* лиси́ца(-сáмка); (*fig.*) мегéра.
viz. [vɪz] *adv.* а и́менно.
vizier [vɪˈzɪə(r), ˈvɪzɪə(r)] *n.* визи́рь (*m.*).
vizor [ˈvaɪzə(r)] = **visor**
vocabulary [vəˈkæbjʊlərɪ] *n.* (*range of words*) словáрь (*m.*), запáс слов; (*of a language*) словáрный состáв; (*of a subject*) номенклатýра; (*list of words*) словáрь (*m.*), спи́сок слов.
vocal [ˈvəʊk(ə)l] *adj.* **1.** (*of or using the voice*) голосовóй, речевóй; **~ cords** голосовы́е свя́зки; **~ music** вокáльная мýзыка. **2.** (*eloquent*) красноречи́вый.
vocalist [ˈvəʊkəlɪst] *n.* вокали́ст; пев|éц (*fem.* -и́ца).
vocation [vəˈkeɪʃ(ə)n] *n.* (*calling, aptitude*) призвáние; (*trade, profession*) профéссия.
vocational [vəˈkeɪʃən(ə)l] *adj.* профессионáльный.
vocative [ˈvɒkətɪv] *n.* & *adj.* звáтельный (падéж).
vociferous [vəˈsɪfərəs] *adj.* грóмкий, шýмный.
vodka [ˈvɒdkə] *n.* вóдка.
vogue [vəʊg] *n.* мóда; **in ~** в мóде.
voice [vɔɪs] *n.* **1.** гóлос; **he is in good ~** он в гóлосе; **he shouted at the top of his ~** он кричáл во всё гóрло; **keep your ~ down!** не разговáривайте так грóмко!; **I lost my ~** я потеря́л гóлос; **he raised his ~** он повы́сил гóлос. **2.** (*expression of opinion*) мнéние; гóлос; **we must speak with one ~** мы должны́ говори́ть однó и то же; **I have no ~ in the matter** моё мнéние ничегó не знáчит в э́том дéле. **3.** (*gram.*) залóг.
v.t. **1.** (*utter*) выражáть, вы́разить. **2.** (*phon.*) произн|оси́ть, -ести́ звóнко; **a ~ed consonant** звóнкий соглáсный.
cpd. **~-over** *n.* (*TV etc.*) гóлос за кáдром, закáдровый гóлос.
voiceless [ˈvɔɪslɪs] *adj.* (*mute*) безглáсный; (*phon.*) глухóй.
void [vɔɪd] *n.* пустотá; пустóе прострáнство.
adj. **1.** (*empty; bereft*) пустóй; лишённый (*чего*). **2.** (*invalid*) недействи́тельный; **the contract is null and ~** контрáкт не имéет си́лы.
v.t. (*make invalid*) аннули́ровать (*impf., pf.*); (*emit from body*) выделя́ть, вы́делить.
voile [vɔɪl, vwɑːl] *n.* вуáль.
volatile [ˈvɒləˌtaɪl] *adj.* (*of liquid*) летýчий; (*fig., of pers.*) непостоя́нный, изменчивый.
volatility [ˌvɒləˈtɪlɪtɪ] *n.* летýчесть; (*fig.*) непостоя́нство, измéнчивость.
vol-au-vent [ˈvɒləʊˌvɑ̃] *n.* воловáн (*слоеный пирожок*).
volcanic [vɒlˈkænɪk] *adj.* вулкани́ческий.
volcano [vɒlˈkeɪnəʊ] *n.* вулкáн.
vole [vəʊl] *n.* полёвка.
volition [vəˈlɪʃ(ə)n] *n.* вóля; **I went of my own ~** я пошёл по своéй вóле.
volley [ˈvɒlɪ] *n.* **1.** (*simultaneous discharge*) залп; (*fig.*): **a ~ of oaths** потóк брáни. **2.** (*tennis etc.*) удáр с лёта; **half ~** удáр с отскóка.
v.t. удáрить (*pf.*) с лёта.
cpd. **~-ball** *n.* волейбóл.
volt [vəʊlt] *n.* вольт.
voltage [ˈvəʊltɪdʒ] *n.* вольтáж; **what is the ~ here?** какóе здесь напряжéние?
volte-face [vɒltˈfɑːs] *n.* (*about-turn*) поворóт кругóм; (*fig., complete reversal*) крутóй поворóт.
voltmeter [ˈvəʊltˌmiːtə(r)] *n.* вольтмéтр.
volubility [ˌvɒljʊˈbɪlɪtɪ] *n.* говорли́вость, разговóрчивость.
voluble [ˈvɒljʊb(ə)l] *adj.* говорли́вый, разговóрчивый.
volume [ˈvɒljuːm] *n.* **1.** (*tome*) том; **it speaks ~s for his honesty** э́то лýчшее доказáтельство егó чéстности. **2.** (*size*) объём. **3.** (*of sound*) си́ла; **~ control** регуля́тор грóмкости; **turn the ~ down!** сдéлайте звук поти́ше!
voluminous [vəˈljuːmɪnəs, vəˈluː-] *adj.* огрóмный; **a ~ work** объёмистое произведéние; **a ~ writer** плодови́тый писáтель.
voluntary [ˈvɒləntərɪ] *adj.* **1.** (*acting or done without compulsion*) добровóльный; **~ worker** общéственный рабóтник. **2.** (*maintained by ~ effort*) содержáщийся на добровóльные взнóсы. **3.** (*controlled by will*) сознáтельный; **~ muscle** произвóльная мы́шца.
volunteer [ˌvɒlənˈtɪə(r)] *n.* доброво́лец, охóтник; (*attr.*) добровóльческий.
v.t. предл|агáть, -ожи́ть; дéлать, с- добровóльно; **he ~ed his services** он предложи́л свои́ услýги.
v.i. вызывáться, вы́зваться сдéлать что-н.; **no-one ~ed** охóтника не нашлóсь; **were you conscripted or did you ~?** вас призвáли на воéнную слýжбу и́ли вы пошли́ добровóльцем/сáми?
voluptuous [vəˈlʌptjʊəs] *adj.* сладострáстный; (*sensual*) чýвственный; (*luxurious*) пы́шный, роскóшный.
vomit [ˈvɒmɪt] *n.* рвóта.
v.t.: **he ~ed blood** егó вы́рвало/рвáло крóвью.
v.i.: **he ~ed** егó вы́рвало; **an attack of ~ing** при́ступ рвóты.
voodoo [ˈvuːduː], **-ism** [ˈvuːduːɪz(ə)m] *nn.* колдовствó, шамáнство.
voracious [vəˈreɪʃəs] *adj.* прожóрливый, жáдный; (*fig.*): **a ~ reader** ненасы́тный читáтель.
vortex [ˈvɔːteks] *n.* (*lit., fig.*) вихрь (*m.*), водоворóт.
vote [vəʊt] *n.* **1.** (*act of voting*) голосовáние; **shall we put it to the ~?** постáвим э́то на голосовáние?; **proxy ~** голосовáние по довéренности. **2.** (**~** *cast*) гóлос; **the chairman has the casting ~** у председáтеля решáющий гóлос; **affirmative ~** гóлос за; **negative ~** гóлос прóтив. **3.** (*affirmation*) вóтум; **the Prime Minister received a ~ of confidence** премьéр-мини́стр получи́л вóтум довéрия; **pass a ~** прин|имáть, -я́ть резолю́цию. **4.** (*right to ~*) прáво гóлоса; избирáтельное прáво. **5.** (*number of ~s cast*) коли́чество голосовáвшихся.
v.t.: **they were ~d back into power** их снóва избрáли в прави́тельство; (*allocate by ~*) ассигновáть (*impf., pf.*); **a large sum was ~d for defence** большáя сýмма былá вы́делена на оборóну; (*coll., propose*): **I ~ we go home** я предлагáю (*or* я за то, чтóбы) пойти́ домóй.
v.i. голосовáть, про-; **they are voting on the resolution** они́ голосýют резолю́цию.
with advs.: **the measure was ~d down, out** предложéние провали́ли; **they were ~d in by a large majority** их избрáли решáющим большинствóм голосóв; **the bill was ~d through** закóн прошёл (*or* был при́нят).
voter [ˈvəʊtə(r)] *n.* избирáтель (*m.*).
voting [ˈvəʊtɪŋ] *n.* голосовáние; (*attr.*): **~ paper** избирáтельный бюллетéнь.
vouch [vaʊtʃ] *v.i.* ручáться, поручи́ться; **I will ~ for the truth of his story** я могý подтверди́ть, что он говори́т прáвду.
voucher [ˈvaʊtʃə(r)] *n.* (*token*) (льгóтный) талóн; билéт; вáучер; **luncheon ~** талóн на обéд.
vouchsafe [vaʊtʃˈseɪf] *v.t.* (*accord*) удост|áивать, -óить (*кого чем*); (*condescend*) соизвóлить (*pf.*).
vow [vaʊ] *n.* обéт, кля́тва; **he broke his marriage ~s** он нарýшил брáчный обéт.
v.t. кля́сться, по-; **they ~ed obedience** они́ дáли обéт послушáния; **he ~ed not to smoke** он дал зарóк не кури́ть.
vowel [ˈvaʊəl] *n.* глáсный.
voyage [ˈvɔɪɪdʒ] *n.* путешéствие (водóй); рейс; (*by sea*) плáвание; (*by air*) полёт; **on the ~ home** на обрáтном пути́.
v.i. путешéствовать (*impf.*).

voyager ['vɔɪɪdʒə(r)] *n.* путеше́ственник; морепла́ватель (*m.*); (*in space*) воздухопла́ватель.
voyeur [vwɑː'jɜː(r)] *n.* челове́к, получа́ющий полово́е удовлетворе́ние от созерца́ния эроти́ческих сцен.
V-sign ['viːsaɪn] *n.* **1.** (*gesture of contempt*) ≃ ку́киш. **2.** (*for victory*) знак побе́ды.
vulcanite ['vʌlkəˌnaɪt] *n.* эбони́т.
vulcanize ['vʌlkəˌnaɪz] *v.t.* вулканизи́ровать (*impf.*).
vulgar ['vʌlgə(r)] *adj.* **1.** (*plebeian*) простонаро́дный; **the ~ tongue** наро́дный/родно́й язы́к. **2.** (*low, coarse, in bad taste*) вульга́рный, по́шлый, гру́бый; **~ language** гру́бый/у́личный язы́к. **3.** (*ordinary, widespread*) распространённый; **~ fraction** проста́я дробь.
vulgarism ['vʌlgəˌrɪz(ə)m] *n.* вульгари́зм.
vulgarity [vʌl'gærɪtɪ] *n.* вульга́рность, по́шлость, гру́бость.
vulgarize ['vʌlgəˌraɪz] *v.t.* вульгаризи́ровать (*impf., pf.*).
vulnerability [ˌvʌlnərə'bɪlɪtɪ] *n.* уязви́мость.
vulnerable ['vʌlnərəb(ə)l] *adj.* уязви́мый; (*defenceless*) беззащи́тный; **~ to air attack** не защищённый от нападе́ния с во́здуха.
vulture ['vʌltʃə(r)] *n.* гриф; (*fig.*) стервя́тник.
vulva ['vʌlvə] *n.* ву́льва.

wacky ['wækɪ] *adj.* (*sl.*) сумасше́дший, чо́кнутый.
wad [wɒd] *n.* **1.** (*pad, plug etc.*) комо́к; пыж. **2.** (*of papers, esp. banknotes*) па́чка.
v.t. (*line with wadding etc.*) подб|ива́ть, -и́ть ва́той; **~ded jacket** стёганый жаке́т; ва́тник.
wadding ['wɒdɪŋ] *n.* ва́та; (*sheet ~*) вати́н.
waddle ['wɒd(ə)l] *n.* похо́дка вразва́лку; **she walks with a ~** она́ хо́дит перева́ливаясь.
v.i. ходи́ть (*indet.*) вразва́лку; перева́ливаться (*impf.*) (с бо́ку на́ бок).
wade [weɪd] *v.t.* пере|ходи́ть, -йти́ вброд; **we shall have to ~ the stream** нам придётся перейти́ ре́ку вброд.
v.i. проб|ира́ться, -ра́ться; **wading bird** боло́тная пти́ца; **we ~d through the mud** мы шли, увязя́я в грязи́; (*fig.*): **I have ~d through all his novels** я (с трудо́м) одоле́л все его́ рома́ны; **I ~d into the argument** я ри́нулся в спор.
with advs.: **~ in** *v.i.* (*lit.*) входи́ть, войти́ в во́ду; (*coll.*) набр|а́сываться, -о́ситься (*на кого/что*); **~ out** *v.i.*: **we had to ~ out to the boat** к ло́дке пришло́сь добира́ться по воде́.
wader ['weɪdə(r)] *n.* (*bird*) боло́тная пти́ца; (*pl., waterproof boots*) боло́тные сапоги́ (*m. pl.*).
wafer ['weɪfə(r)] *n.* **1.** (*thin biscuit*) ва́фля. **2.** (*Communion bread*) обла́тка.
waffle[1] ['wɒf(ə)l] *n.* (*cul.*) ва́фля.
cpd. **~-iron** *n.* ва́фельница.
waffle[2] ['wɒf(ə)l] *n.* (*coll., verbiage*) вода́.
v.i. (*also* **~ on**) во́ду лить (*impf.*).
waffler ['wɒflə(r)]*n.* (*coll.*) водоле́й.
waffly ['wɒflɪ] *adj.* (*coll.*) водяни́стый.
waft [wɒft, wɑːft] *n.* (*whiff; breath*) дунове́ние.
v.t. дон|оси́ть, -ести́; **the leaves were ~ed by the breeze** ветеро́к гна́л ли́стья; **their voices were ~ed over to us** их голоса́ доноси́лись до нас.
wag[1] [wæg] *n.* (*shake*): **with a ~ of his tail** вильну́в хвосто́м.
v.t. мах|а́ть, -ну́ть +*i.*; кача́ть, по- +*i.*; **the dog ~ged its tail** соба́ка вильну́ла хвосто́м; **he ~ged his finger at me** он погрози́л мне па́льцем.
v.i.: **this will set tongues ~ging** э́то даст по́вод к спле́тням; э́то вы́зовет то́лки.
cpd. **~tail** *n.* трясогу́зка.
wag[2] [wæg] *n.* (*jocular person*) остря́к, шутни́к.
wage[1] [weɪdʒ] *n.* **1.** за́работная пла́та; (*coll.*) зарпла́та; **he gets good ~s** он хорошо́ зараба́тывает; **a living ~** прожи́точный ми́нимум; **a fair day's ~** прили́чная зарпла́та. **2.** (*pl., fig.*) возме́здие, пла́та; **~s of sin** пла́та за грехи́.
cpds. **~-earner** *n.* наёмный рабо́чий; (*breadwinner*) корми́л|ец (*fem.* -ица); **~-freeze** *n.* замора́живание за́работной пла́ты; **~-packet** *n.* (*fig.*) зарпла́та, полу́чка.
wage[2] [weɪdʒ] вести́, проводи́ть (*both impf.*).
wager ['weɪdʒə(r)] *n.* пари́ (*nt. indecl.*); **lay a ~** би́ться (*impf.*) об закла́д; держа́ть (*impf.*) пари́.
v.t.: **he ~ed £10 on a horse** он поста́вил 10 фу́нтов на ло́шадь.
waggle ['wæg(ə)l] *v.t. & i.* пома́х|ивать, -а́ть +*i.*; пока́ч|ивать, -а́ть +*i.*; **he ~d his head** он кача́л голово́й.
wag(g)on ['wægən] *n.* **1.** (*horse-drawn*) пово́зка, теле́га; фурго́н. **2.** (*on railway*) ваго́н-платфо́рма.
wag(g)oner ['wægənə(r)] *n.* во́зчик.
wagon-lit [ˌvægɔ̃'liː] *n.* спа́льный ваго́н.
waif [weɪf] *n.* бездо́мный; **~s and strays** (*children*) беспризо́рники (*m. pl.*).
wail [weɪl] *n.* (*cry, howl*) вопль (*m.*); вой; (*lament*) причита́ние; (*fig., of the wind*) завыва́ние, вой; (*of sirens etc.*) вой.
v.i. (*cry, howl*) вопи́ть (*impf.*); выть (*impf.*).
wainscot ['weɪnskət], **-ing** ['weɪnskətɪŋ] *nn.* стенна́я пане́ль; обши́вка.
waist [weɪst] *n.* (*of body or dress*) та́лия; **he stripped to the ~** он разде́лся до по́яса; **he put his arm round her ~** он обня́л её за та́лию.
cpds. **~-band** *n.* по́яс ю́бки/брюк; **~coat** *n.* жиле́т; **~-deep, ~-high** *adjs.* по по́яс; **~line** *n.*: **I must watch my ~line** мне прихо́дится следи́ть за свое́й фигу́рой.
wait [weɪt] *n.* **1.** (*act or time of ~ing*) ожида́ние; **we had a long ~ for the bus** мы до́лго жда́ли авто́буса. **2.** (*ambush*) заса́да; **the robbers lay in ~ for their victim** разбо́йники/граби́тели подстерега́ли свою́ же́ртву.
v.t. **1.** (**~** *for; await*) ждать (*impf.*); выжида́ть (*impf.*); **you must ~ your turn** ва́ша о́чередь ещё не наступи́ла. **2.** (*defer*): **don't ~ dinner for me** не жди́те меня́ с обе́дом.
v.i. **1.** (*refrain from movement or action*) ждать, подо-; **we must ~ and see what happens** подождём — уви́дим, что бу́дет да́льше; **it can/must ~ till tomorrow** э́то придётся отложи́ть до за́втра; **I could hardly ~ to ...** я сгора́л от нетерпе́ния +*inf.*; **I ~ed for the rain to stop** я ждал, когда́ око́нчится дождь; **'No W~ing'** «стоя́нка запрещена́»; **~ing-list** спи́сок (*кандидатов, очередников и т.п.*); о́чередь; **I'll put you on the ~ing-list** я вас занесу́ в о́чередь; **~ing-room** (*doctor's etc.*) приёмная; (*on station*) зал ожида́ния; **'Repairs while you ~'** «Ремо́нт в прису́тствии зака́зчика». **2.** (*act as servant*): **she ~s on him hand and foot** она́ при нём как прислу́га; **he ~ed at table** он прислу́живал за столо́м; **who is ~ing at this table?** кто обслу́живает э́тот стол? **3.**: **~ up**: **she ~ed up for him** она́ не ложи́лась (спать) до его́ прихо́да.

waiter ['weɪtə(r)] *n.* официа́нт.
waitress ['weɪtrɪs] *n.* официа́нтка.
waive [weɪv] *v.t.* (*forgo*) отка́з|ываться, -а́ться от+*g.*; (*not insist on*) воздéрж|иваться, -а́ться от+*g.*; не соблю|да́ть, -сти́ +*g.*; **on this occasion we will ~ the regulations** на сей раз мы пренебрежём пра́вилами.
waiver ['weɪvə(r)] *n.* отка́з (от+*g.*).
wake[1] [weɪk] *n.* (*funeral observance*) бдéние у гроба; поми́н|ки (*pl.*, *g.* -ок).
wake[2] [weɪk] *n.* (*track of vessel*) кильва́тер; (*fig.*): **he drove away with the police in his ~** он умча́лся, преслéдуемый поли́цией; **his action brought trouble in its ~** его́ поведéние повлекло́ за собо́й неприя́тности.
wake[3] [weɪk] *v.t.* буди́ть, раз-; **the letter woke memories of the past** письмо́ пробуди́ло/вы́звало воспомина́ния о про́шлом.
v.i. (*also* **~ up**) прос|ыпа́ться, -ну́ться; **she woke with a start** она́ внеза́пно просну́лась; **~ up!** (*lit.*, *fig.*) просни́тесь!
wakeful ['weɪkfʊl] *adj.*: **the child was ~** ребёнок то и дéло просыпа́лся; **we had a ~ night** мы провели́ бессо́нную ночь.
wakefulness ['weɪkfʊlnɪs] *n.* бессо́нница.
waken ['weɪkən] *v.t.* (*lit.*, *fig.*) буди́ть, раз-.
Wales [weɪlz] *n.* Уэ́льс.
walk [wɔːk] *n.* **1.** (*action of ~ing*) ходьба́; **a short ~ away** в нéскольких шага́х отсю́да/отту́да. **2.** (*excursion*) (пéшая) прогу́лка; **shall we take a ~?** пойдёмте гуля́ть!; хоти́те погуля́ть?; **will you take the children for a ~?** вы погуля́ете с детьми́?; вы поведёте детéй на прогу́лку?; **I went on a ten-mile ~** я прошёл дéсять миль пешко́м. **3.** (*~ing pace*) шаг; **the horse slowed to a ~** ло́шадь перешла́ на шаг. **4.** (*gait*) похо́дка, по́ступь. **5.** (*route for ~ing*): **there are some pleasant ~s round here** здесь есть прия́тные места́ для прогу́лок. **6.** (*path*) тропа́, доро́жка. **7.** (*contest*): **long-distance ~** (спорти́вная) ходьба́ на дли́нную диста́нцию. **8.** (*~ of life*, *profession*) заня́тие, профéссия; **people from all ~s of life** представи́тели всех слоёв о́бщества.
v.t. **1.** (*traverse*): **I ~ed these lanes in my youth** я исходи́л э́ти доро́ги в мо́лодости. **2.** (*cause to ~*): **he ~ed his horse up the hill** он пусти́л ло́шадь ша́гом в го́ру; **he ~ed me off my feet** он меня́ си́льно утоми́л прогу́лкой; (*accompany*) сопрово|жда́ть, -ди́ть; **he offered to ~ her home** он вы́звался проводи́ть её домо́й; (*take for a ~*) выводи́ть, вы́вести на прогу́лку; прогу́л|ивать, -я́ть.
v.i. **1.** (*go*, *come*, *move about*, *on foot*) ходи́ть (*indet.*), идти́ (*det.*); прогу́ливаться (*impf.*); **I was ~ing along the road** я шёл по доро́ге; **I ~ed ten miles** я прошёл дéсять ми́ль; **I ~ed here in an hour** я дошёл сюда́ за час; **he ~s with a stick** он хо́дит с па́лкой; **the baby is learning to ~** ребёнок у́чится ходи́ть; **I ~ed into a shop** я вошёл в магази́н; **he ~ed into a puddle** он ступи́л в лу́жу; **they ~ed into** (*entered unwarily*) **an ambush** они́ попа́ли в заса́ду; **he ~ed over the estate** он обошёл/исходи́л всё имéние. **2.** (*opp. ride*): **on fine days I ~ to the office** в хоро́шую пого́ду я хожу́ на рабо́ту пешко́м. **3.** (*opp. run*): **he ~ed the last 100 metres** послéдние сто мéтров он прошёл ша́гом; **at a ~ing pace** ша́гом. **4.** (*take exercise*, *holiday etc. on foot*) ходи́ть (*indet.*) пешко́м; гуля́ть (*impf.*), прогу́ливаться (*impf.*); **I spent 2 weeks ~ing in Scotland** я броди́л две недéли по Шотла́ндии; **a ~ing tour** туристи́ческий похо́д; **a ~ing race** соревнова́ние по спорти́вной ходьбé. **5.** (*take part in procession*) шéствовать (*impf.*).
with advs.: **~ about** *v.i.* прогу́ливаться (*impf.*); **~ away** *v.i.* уходи́ть, уйти́; **he ~ed away with several prizes** он без труда́ завоева́л нéсколько призо́в; **~ back** *v.i.* возвраща́ться, верну́ться пешко́м; **~ down** *v.i.* спус|ка́ться, -ти́ться; **~ in** *v.i.* входи́ть, войти́; **~ off with** *v.t.*: (*steal*) **someone ~ed off with my hat** кто́-то стащи́л мою́ шля́пу; (*win*) **he always ~s off with first prize** он всегда́ берёт пéрвый приз; **~ on** *v.i.* (*continue ~ing*) продолжа́ть (*impf.*) идти́; идти́ (*det.*) да́льше; (**~** *ahead*) идти́ (*det.*) вперёд; (*theatr.*) выходи́ть, вы́йти на сцéну; **~ out** *v.i.* выходи́ть, вы́йти; **the delegates ~ed out in protest** делега́ты поки́нули зал (*or* вы́шли из за́ла) в знак протéста; **the men are threatening to ~ out** (*strike*) рабо́чие грозя́т забасто́вкой; **~ out on s.o.** (*coll.*) бр|оса́ть, -о́сить кого́-н.; **~ up** *v.i.* (*approach*): **I ~ed up to him** я подошёл к нему́; (*climb*): **'Did you use the lift?' — 'No, I ~ed up'** «Вы приéхали на ли́фте?» — «Нет, я подня́лся по лéстнице».
cpds. **~about** *n.* (*fig.*, *coll.*) общéние знамени́тости с наро́дом; **~-on** *n.*: **a ~-on part** немая́ роль; **~-out** *n.* (*as protest*) демонстрати́вный ухо́д; (*strike*) забасто́вка; **~over** *n.* лёгкая побéда; **~way** *n.* широ́кая пешехо́дная доро́жка, аллéя.
walker ['wɔːkə(r)] *n.* (*one who walks*) ходо́к; (*athlete*) скорохо́д; **a hostel for ~s** общежи́тие для пéших тури́стов.
walkie-talkie [ˌwɔːkɪ'tɔːkɪ] *n.* ра́ция.
walking ['wɔːkɪŋ] *n.* ходьба́; **~ shoes** о́бувь для ходьбы́.
adj. ходя́чий, шага́ющий; **a ~ encyclopaedia** ходя́чая энциклопéдия; **~ wounded** ходя́чие ра́неные.
cpd. **~-stick** *n.* трость, па́лка.
Walkman ['wɔːkmən] *n.* (*propr.*) во́кмен, плéер.
wall [wɔːl] *n.* (*lit.*, *fig.*) стена́, стéнка; **within these four ~s** (*fig.*) (стро́го) мéжду на́ми; **~s have ears** у стен есть у́ши; **he stood with his back to the ~** (*lit.*) он стоя́л у стены́; **they had their backs to the ~** (*fig.*) их припёрли к стéнке; **go up the ~** (*coll.*) лезть, по- на стéн(к)у; **it's enough to send, drive you up the ~** (*coll.*) э́то хоть кого́ заста́вит на стéнку лезть; **it's like banging, running one's head against a brick ~** всё равно́, что прошиба́ть стéну лбом; **a mountain ~** отвéсная скала́; **~ clock** настéнные час|ы́ (*pl.*, *g.* -о́в); **~ painting** стенна́я ро́спись; фрéска.
v.t. обн|оси́ть, -ести́ стено́й; **~ed garden** обнесённый стено́й сад.
with advs.: **~ in** *v.t.* обн|оси́ть, -ести́ стено́й; **~ off** *v.t.* отгор|а́живать, -оди́ть (стено́й); **~ up** *v.t.* задéл|ывать, -ать (*дверь, окно*); замуро́в|ывать, -а́ть.
cpds. **~flower** *n.* желтофио́ль; (*at dance*) да́ма, оста́вшаяся без партнёра; **~paper** *n.* обо́|и (*pl.*, *g.* -ев); *v.t.* обклéи|вать, -ть обо́ями; **~-to-~** *adj.*: **~-to-~ carpeting** ковёр, покрыва́ющий весь пол.
wallet ['wɒlɪt] *n.* (*pocket-book*) бума́жник.
wall-eye ['wɔːlaɪ] *n.* глаз с бельмо́м.
wall-eyed ['wɔːlaɪd] *adj.* с бельмо́м на глазу́; криво́й.
wallop ['wɒləp] (*coll.*) *n.* (*blow*) уда́р.
v.t. (*thrash*) дуба́сить, от- (*coll.*); (*defeat*) разгроми́ть (*pf.*).
wallow ['wɒləʊ] *v.i.* валя́ться (*impf.*); (*fig.*) купа́ться (*impf.*) (*в чём*); **~ in luxury** купа́ться (*impf.*) в ро́скоши; **~ in grief** упива́ться (*impf.*) свои́м го́рем.
wally ['wɒlɪ] *n.* (*coll.*) дуралéй, неумёха.
walnut ['wɔːlnʌt] *n.* грéцкий орéх; (*tree*) орéховое дéрево; (*wood*) орéх.
adj. орéховый.
walrus ['wɔːlrəs, 'wɒl-] *n.* морж.
waltz [wɔːls, wɔːlts, wɒ-] *n.* вальс; **in ~ time** в ри́тме ва́льса; **a ~ tune** мело́дия ва́льса.
v.t. (*coll.*): **he ~ed her round the room** он закружи́лся с ней по ко́мнате.
v.i. танцева́ть (*impf.*) вальс; (*fig.*) пританцо́вывать (*impf.*).

wan [wɒn] *adj.* блёдный, изнурённый; **a ~ smile** сла́бая улы́бка; **his face looked ~** он осу́нулся.

wand [wɒnd] *n.* (волше́бная) па́лочка; **with a wave of his ~** по манове́нию (волше́бной) па́лочки.

wander ['wɒndə(r)] *n.*: **I had a ~ round the shops** я прошёлся по магази́нам.

v.t. броди́ть; стра́нствовать; скита́ться (*all impf.*) по+*d*.

v.i. **1.** (*roam; go aimlessly or unhurriedly*) броди́ть (*impf.*); идти́ (*det.*) неторопли́во; **a ~ing minstrel** бродя́чий певе́ц; **the car was ~ing all over the road** маши́на виля́ла из стороны́ в сто́рону; **I ~ed into the nearest pub** я забрёл в ближа́йший бар; **his mind was ~ing** (*absent-mindedly*) его́ мы́сли блужда́ли; (*in delirium*) он бре́дил. **2.** (*stray*) заблу|жда́ться, -ди́ться; (*lit., fig.*) отклон|я́ться, -и́ться; **we ~ed from the track** мы сби́лись с тропы́; **don't let your attention ~** не отвлека́йтесь; **he ~ed from the point** он отклони́лся от те́мы.

with advs.: **~ about** *v.i.* слоня́ться (*impf.*); **~ along** *v.i.* забре|да́ть, -сти́ куда́-н.; **~ away** *v.i.*: **she tried to stop the children ~ing away** она́ пыта́лась не дать де́тям разбрести́сь; **~ in** *v.i.* случа́йно за|ходи́ть, -йти́; **~ off** *v.i.* побрести́ (*pf.*) куда́-н.; **~ on** *v.i.* прод|олжа́ть, -о́лжить; **he ~ed on** (*speaking*) он продолжа́л бубни́ть; **~ over** *v.i.*: **he ~ed over to hear the news** он приплёлся узна́ть но́вости; **~ up** *v.i.*: **he ~ed up to us** он подошёл к нам вя́лой похо́дкой.

wanderer ['wɒndərə(r)] *n.* стра́нник, скита́лец.

wandering ['wɒndərɪŋ] *n.* стра́нствие.

wanderlust ['wɒndəˌlʌst, 'vændəˌlʊst] *n.* страсть к путеше́ствиям.

wane [weɪn] *n.*: **be on the ~** (*lit., fig.*) убыва́ть (*impf.*); быть на исхо́де.

v.i. (*of the moon*) убыва́ть (*impf.*); быть на уще́рбе; (*fig., decline*) ослабева́ть (*impf.*); угаса́ть (*impf.*).

wangle ['wæŋg(ə)l] *v.t.* (*obtain by scheming*) заполучи́ть (*pf.*) хи́тростью; **he ~d £5 out of me** он вы́клянчил (*coll.*) у меня́ 5 фу́нтов.

wank [wæŋk] *v.i.* (*vulg.*) дрочи́ть (*impf.*).

wanker ['wæŋkə(r)] *n.* (*vulg., fig.*) муда́к.

want [wɒnt] *n.* **1.** (*lack*) недоста́ток, отсу́тствие; **for ~ of** за неиме́нием +*g.*; **I took this for ~ of anything better** я взял э́то за неиме́нием лу́чшего. **2.** (*need*) нужда́; необходи́мость; **the house is in ~ of repair** дом нужда́ется в ремо́нте. **3.** (*penury*) бе́дность, нужда́. **4.** (*desire; requirement*) потре́бность, запро́сы (*m. pl.*), жела́ние; **they can supply all your ~s** они́ мо́гут удовлетвори́ть все ва́ши запро́сы.

v.t. **1.** (*need; require*) нужда́ться (*impf.*) в+*p.*; **we badly ~ rain** нам о́чень ну́жен дождь; **what do you ~?** что вы хоти́те?; что вам на́до?; **the floor ~s polishing** пол на́до натере́ть; **your hair ~s cutting** вам пора́ постри́чься; **I shan't ~ you today** вы мне сего́дня не пона́добитесь; **he is ~ed by the police** его́ разы́скивает поли́ция; **'W~ed: a housekeeper'** «Тре́буется эконо́мка»; **you're ~ed on the telephone** вас (про́сят) к телефо́ну; **you are ~ed at the office** вас вызыва́ют на рабо́ту. **2.** (*desire; wish for*) хоте́ть (*impf.*) +*g. or inf.*; жела́ть (*impf.*) +*g. or inf.*; **she ~s to go away** она́ хо́чет уе́хать/уйти́; **she ~s me to go away** она́ хо́чет, что́бы я уе́хал/ушёл; **I don't ~ him meddling in my affairs** я не хочу́, что́бы он вме́шивался в мои́ дела́; **I don't ~ any bread today** сего́дня мне хлеб не ну́жен; **I ~ it done immediately** я тре́бую, что́бы э́то бы́ло сде́лано неме́дленно; **what do I ~ with all these books?** заче́м (*or* для чего́) мне все э́ти кни́ги?

v.i. (*liter., be in need*): **they ~ for nothing** они́ ни в чём не нужда́ются.

wanting ['wɒntɪŋ] *adj.* (*missing*) отсу́тствующий; недостаю́щий; (*inadequate*) недоста́точный; неполноце́нный; **he was tried and found ~** он не вы́держал испыта́ния.

wanton ['wɒnt(ə)n] *adj.* **1.** (*wilful; ruthless*) своенра́вный, своево́льный; **~ cruelty** бессмы́сленная жесто́кость. **2.** (*licentious; immoral*) распу́тный.

war [wɔː(r)] *n.* **1.** война́; **the art of ~** вое́нное иску́сство; **~ of attrition** война́ на истоще́ние; **~ of nerves** война́ не́рвов; психологи́ческая война́; **civil ~** гражда́нская война́; **cold ~** холо́дная война́; **the Great W~** Пе́рвая мирова́я война́; **~ of independence** война́ за незави́симость; **a country at ~** страна́ в состоя́нии войны́; **their countries were at ~** их стра́ны воева́ли друг с дру́гом; **you've been in the ~s!** (*fig.*) ну и доста́лось же вам!; **declare ~ on** объяв|ля́ть, -и́ть войну́ +*d.*; **make, wage ~ on** вести́ (*det.*) войну́ (*or* воева́ть (*impf.*)) с+*i.* **2.** (*attr.*) вое́нный (*see also cpds.*); **~ correspondent** вое́нный корреспонде́нт; **~ criminal** вое́нный престу́пник; **~ damage** разруше́ния (*nt. pl.*) (*or* поте́ри (*f. pl.*)), нанесённые войно́й; **~ decoration** боева́я награ́да; **W~ Department** вое́нное министе́рство; **help the ~ effort** рабо́тать (*impf.*) для нужд фро́нта; **on a ~ footing** на вое́нном положе́нии; **~ graves** солда́тские моги́лы; **~ memorial** па́мятник геро́ям войны́; **W~ Office** вое́нное министе́рство; **~ service** слу́жба в де́йствующей а́рмии; **~ widow** вдова́ поги́бшего на войне́.

v.i. боро́ться (*impf.*); сража́ться (*impf.*).

cpds. **~-cry** *n.* боево́й клич; **~-dance** *n.* вои́нственный та́нец; **~-game** *n.* вое́нная игра́; **~head** *n.* боева́я часть, боеголо́вка; **~-horse** *n.* (*lit.*) боево́й конь; (*fig.*) быва́лый солда́т, ветера́н; **~like** *adj.* (*martial*) вои́нственный; (*military*) вое́нный; **~-lord** *n.* полково́дец; **~monger** *n.* поджига́тель (*m.*) войны́; **~mongering** *n.* разжига́ние войны́; **~-paint** *n.* раскра́ска; **~-path** *n.* (*lit.*) тропа́ войны́; **on the ~-path** (*fig.*) в вои́нственном настрое́нии; **~-plane** *n.* вое́нный самолёт; **~ship** *n.* вое́нный кора́бль; **~time** *n.* вое́нное вре́мя; **~-torn** *adj.* раздира́емый/опустошённый войно́й; **~-weary** *adj.* изнурённый/изму́ченный войно́й.

warble ['wɔːb(ə)l] *n.* (*song*) трель; пе́ние птиц.

v.i. (*of birds*) издава́ть (*impf.*) тре́ли; (*of pers.*) залива́ться (*impf.*) пе́сней.

warbler ['wɔːblə(r)] *n.* (*bird*) пе́вчая пти́ца.

ward [wɔːd] *n.* **1.** (*person under guardianship*) подопе́чный; **~ of court** несовершенноле́тний/душевнобольно́й под опе́кой суда́. **2.** (*urban division*) о́круг. **3.** (*in hospital etc.*) пала́та; **isolation ~** изоля́тор. **4.** (*in prison*) ка́мера.

v.t.: **~ off** (*a blow*) отра|жа́ть, -зи́ть; **~ off danger** отвра|ща́ть, -ти́ть опа́сность.

cpds. **~room** *n.* офице́рская каю́т-компа́ния; **~-sister** *n.* пала́тная сестра́.

warden ['wɔːd(ə)n] *n.* **1.** (*of college*) ре́ктор; (*of prison*) нача́льник тюрьмы́. **2.: air-raid ~** уполномо́ченный гражда́нской оборо́ны; **game ~** инспе́ктор по охра́не ди́чи; **traffic ~** контролёр счётчиков на автомоби́льных стоя́нках.

warder ['wɔːdə(r)] *n.* (*in prison*) надзира́тель (*m.*), тюре́мщик.

wardrobe ['wɔːdrəʊb] *n.* **1.** платяно́й шкаф, гардеро́б; (*stock of clothes*) гардеро́б. **2.** (*theatr.*) костюме́рная; **~ mistress** одева́льщица.

ware [weə(r)] *n.* **1.** (*collect., usu. comb. form, manufactured articles*) това́р; изде́лия (*nt. pl.*); (*pottery*): **Delft~** фая́нс. **2.** (*pl., articles offered for sale*) това́ры (*m. pl.*); изде́лия (*nt. pl.*); **peddle one's ~s** предлага́ть (*impf.*) това́ры на прода́жу.

cpds. **~house** *n.* (това́рный) склад; *v.t.* храни́ть (*impf.*) на скла́де; **~houseman** *n.* кладовщи́к.

warfare ['wɔːfeə(r)] *n.* война́; боевы́е де́йствия; **germ**

~ бактериологи́ческая война́; **guerrilla ~** партиза́нская война́.

wariness ['weərɪnɪs] *n.* осторо́жность, насторо́жённость.

warlock ['wɔ:lɒk] *n.* колду́н, маг.

warm [wɔ:m] *n.* (*act of ~ing*): **come and have a ~ by the fire** иди́те погре́йтесь у ками́на.

adj. тёплый; **a ~ day** тёплый день; **a ~ fire** жа́ркий ого́нь; **~ countries** жа́ркие/тёплые стра́ны; **I can't keep ~ in this weather** в э́ту пого́ду я ника́к не могу́ согре́ться; (*fig.*) тёплый, серде́чный; **accept my ~est thanks** приими́те мою́ горя́чую благода́рность; **his plan was ~ly approved** его́ план горячо́ поддержа́ли; **he has a ~ heart** он отзы́вчивый челове́к; **the scent was still ~** след ещё не осты́л; **am I getting ~?** (*fig.*) я бли́зок к пра́вде?

v.t. греть, со-; подогр|ева́ть, -е́ть; нагр|ева́ть, -е́ть; согр|ева́ть, -е́ть; **~ o.s. at the fire** гре́ться (*impf.*) у ками́на/огня́; **that fire will not ~ the room** э́тот ками́н не обогре́ет ко́мнату; **will you have your milk ~ed?** вам подогре́ть молоко́?

v.i. нагр|ева́ться, -е́ться; разогр|ева́ться, -е́ться; согр|ева́ться, -е́ться; (*fig.*): **I ~ed to(wards) him as I got to know him** чем бли́же я его́ узнава́л, тем бо́льше он мне нра́вился.

with advs.: **~ over** *v.t.* разогр|ева́ть, -е́ть; **~ up** *v.t.* разогр|ева́ть, -е́ть; согр|ева́ть, -е́ть; **a fire will ~ up the room** ками́н нагре́ет ко́мнату; **his dinner had been ~ed up** ему́ разогре́ли у́жин; **a drink will ~ you up** вино́ вас согре́ет; **this engine needs a lot of ~ing up** э́тот мото́р прихо́дится до́лго прогрева́ть; *v.i.* согр|ева́ться, -е́ться; отогр|ева́ться, -е́ться; **the house takes a long time to ~ up** э́тот дом тру́дно прогре́ть; **the conversation ~ed up** разгово́р оживи́лся; **he ~ed up before the race** он сде́лал разми́нку пе́ред нача́лом соревнова́ния.

cpds. **~-blooded** *adj.* теплокро́вный; **~-hearted** *adj.* серде́чный; **~-up** *n.* разми́нка.

warmth [wɔ:mθ] *n.* теплота́, тепло́; (*fig.*) серде́чность.

warn [wɔ:n] *v.t.* **1.** (*caution*) предупре|жда́ть, -ди́ть; предостер|ега́ть, -е́чь; **we were ~ed against pickpockets** нас предостерегли́ от карма́нных воро́в; **he was ~ed off drink** ему́ запрети́ли пить. **2.** (*admonish*): **I shan't ~ you again** э́то моё после́днее предупрежде́ние.

warning ['wɔ:nɪŋ] *n.* предупрежде́ние, предостереже́ние; **gale ~** штормово́е предупрежде́ние; **give ~ of** предупре|жда́ть, -ди́ть о+*p.*; **let this be a ~ to you** пусть э́то послу́жит вам предостереже́нием; **he was let off with a ~** он отде́лался (одни́м лишь) предупрежде́нием; **without ~** без предупрежде́ния; соверше́нно неожи́данно.

adj. предупрежда́ющий; предостерега́ющий; **he gave a ~ look** он бро́сил предостерега́ющий взгляд; **he fired a ~ shot** он дал предупреди́тельный вы́стрел.

warp [wɔ:p] *n.* (*weaving*) осно́ва; (*distortion*) искривле́ние; деформа́ция.

v.t. **1.** (*distort*) коро́бить, по-; искрив|ля́ть, -и́ть; **damp ~s the binding** переплёт коро́бит от сы́рости. **2.** (*fig.*) по́ртить, ис-; **a ~ed sense of humour** извращённое чу́вство ю́мора.

v.i. (*become distorted*) коро́биться, по-.

warrant ['wɒrənt] *n.* о́рдер; суде́бное распоряже́ние; **search ~** о́рдер на о́быск; **~ officer** старшина́ (*m.*); **death ~** (*fig.*) сме́ртный пригово́р.

v.t. **1.** (*justify*) опра́вд|ывать, -а́ть. **2.** (*guarantee*) гаранти́ровать (*impf., pf.*); руча́ться, поручи́ться за+*a.*; **he will be back I('ll) ~ you** он вернётся, уверя́ю вас.

warranty ['wɒrəntɪ] *n.* **1.** (*authority*) оправда́ние, руча́тельство. **2.** (*guarantee*) гара́нтия; **this watch is under ~** э́ти часы́ с гара́нтией.

warren ['wɒrən] *n.* кро́личья нора́; (*fig.*) мураве́йник, лабири́нт.

warrior ['wɒrɪə(r)] *n.* во́ин; **the Unknown W~** Неизве́стный солда́т.

Warsaw ['wɔ:sɔ:] *n.* Варша́ва; **~ Pact** Варша́вский догово́р.

wart [wɔ:t] *n.* борода́вка.

cpd. **~-hog** *n.* борода́вочник.

wary ['weərɪ] *adj.* осторо́жный, осмотри́тельный, насторо́жённый; **be ~ of** остерега́ться (*impf.*) +*g.*; относи́ться (*impf.*) насторо́жённо к+*d.*

wash [wɒʃ] *n.* **1.** (*act of ~ing*) мытьё; **I must have, get a ~** мне на́до помы́ться/умы́ться; **he gave the floor a good ~** он хороше́нько вы́мыл пол. **2.** (*laundering; laundry*) сти́рка; **send to the ~** отд|ава́ть, -а́ть в сти́рку; **my shirts are all at the ~** все мои́ руба́шки в сти́рке; **it will all come out in the ~** (*fig.*) всё ула́дится. **3.** (*motion of water etc.*) прибо́й; волна́; **the vessel made a big ~** от корабля́ пошла́ си́льная волна́. **4.** (*solution of paint*) то́нкий слой аквар́ели. **6.** (*lotion; liquid toilet preparation*) примо́чка; лосьо́н.

v.t. **1.** (*cleanse with water etc.*) мыть, по-/об-/вы́; стира́ть, вы́-; **~ one's hands and face** вы́мыть (*pf.*) ру́ки и лицо́; **~ dishes** мыть, вы́- посу́ду; **he ~ed himself in the stream** он помы́лся/обмы́лся в ручье́; **this fabric must be ~ed in cold water** э́ту ткань сле́дует стира́ть в холо́дной воде́; (*fig.*): **~ one's hands of sth.** умы́ть (*pf.*) ру́ки. **2.** (*of water; flow past*) омыва́ть (*impf.*); (*sweep away*) сн|оси́ть, -ести́; **he was ~ed overboard by a wave** его́ смы́ло волно́й за́ борт. **3.** (*coat with thin paint*) покр|ыва́ть, -ы́ть то́нким сло́ем кра́ски.

v.i. **1.** (*~ o.s.*) мы́ться, вы́-; ум|ыва́ться, -ы́ться. **2.** (*~ clothes*) стира́ть, вы́-. **3.** (*of fabric: stand up to ~ing*) стира́ться (*impf.*); (*fig.*): **that excuse won't ~** э́та отгово́рка не пройдёт. **4.** (*of water*) плеска́ться (*impf.*); **waves ~ed over the deck** во́лны перека́тывались по па́лубе.

with advs.: **~ away** *v.t.* (*remove: stains etc.*) смы|ва́ть, -ть (*пятна*); (*erode: cliffs etc.*) разм|ыва́ть, -ы́ть (*утёсы*); **~ down** *v.t.* мыть, вы́-; сн|оси́ть, -ести́; зап|ива́ть, -и́ть (*что чем*); **I had a sandwich, ~ed down with beer** я съел бутербро́д и запи́л его́ пи́вом; **~ off** *v.t. & i.* смы|ва́ть(ся), -ы́ть(ся); отсти́р|ывать(ся), -а́ть(ся); **~ out** *v.t.* (*e.g. stains*) смы|ва́ть, -ть; отм|ыва́ть, -ы́ть; (*a garment*) стира́ть, вы́-; (*a stain*) отсти́р|ывать, -а́ть; (*of colour*) линя́ть, по-/вы́-; **you look ~ed out** у вас утомлённый вид; **~ up** *v.t.* (*dishes*) мыть, вы́- (*посуду*); (*on to shore*) выбра́сывать, вы́бросить на бе́рег; **~ed up** (*exhausted*) уста́лый, разби́тый; (*ruined*) ко́нченый.

cpds. **~-basin** *n.* ра́ковина; **~board** *n.* стира́льная доска́; **~-day** *n.* день (*m.*) сти́рки; **~-house** *n.* пра́чечная; **~leather** *n.* мо́ющаяся за́мша; **~-out** *n.* (*coll., fiasco*) прова́л; (*coll., failure*) неуда́ча; **~-room** *n.* убо́рная; **~-stand** *n.* умыва́льник; **~-tub** *n.* лоха́нь; коры́то.

washable ['wɒʃəb(ə)l] *adj.* мо́ющийся.

washer ['wɒʃə(r)] *n.* (*washing-machine*) стира́льная маши́на; (*machine component*) прокла́дка.

cpd. **~woman** *n.* пра́чка.

washing ['wɒʃɪŋ] *n.* **1.** (*action*) мытьё, умыва́ние, сти́рка. **2.** (*clothes*) бельё; **hang out the ~** ве́шать, пове́сить (*or* разве́|шивать, -сить) бельё; **take in ~** брать (*impf.*) бельё в сти́рку.

cpds. **~-machine** *n.* стира́льная маши́на; **~-powder** *n.* стира́льный порошо́к; **~-up** *n.*: **do the ~-up** мыть, вы́- посу́ду.

wasp [wɒsp] *n.* оса́.

waspish ['wɒspɪʃ] *adj.* язви́тельный, ко́лкий.

wastage ['weɪstɪdʒ] *n.* убы́ток, уте́чка.

waste [weɪst] *n.* **1.** (*purposeless or extravagant use*; *failure to use*) (рас)тра́та, растра́чивание; **~ of money** пуста́я тра́та де́нег; вы́брошенные де́ньги; **it would be a ~ of time** э́то бы́ло бы напра́сной тра́той вре́мени; **go, run to ~** тра́титься (*impf.*) по́пусту. **2.** (*refuse*) отхо́ды (*m. pl.*), отбро́сы (*m. pl.*), му́сор; **~ collection** вы́воз му́сора. **3.** (*superfluous material*) отхо́ды (*m. pl.*), отбро́сы (*m. pl.*).

adj. **1.** (*superfluous, unwanted*) ли́шний, нену́жный; (*left over after manufacture*) отрабо́танный; (*rejected; thrown away*) брако́ванный; **~ products** отхо́ды (*m. pl.*); **~ paper** макулату́ра. **2.** (*of land: desolate, desert*) пусты́нный; (*uninhabited*) незаселённый, опустошённый; **~ ground** невозде́ланная земля́; **~ land** пусты́рь (*m.*), пу́стошь; **lay ~** опустош|а́ть, -и́ть.

v.t. **1.** (*make no use of, use to no purpose, squander*) тра́тить, ис-/по- да́ром/зря/по́пусту; растра́|чивать, -тить; **be ~d** проп|ада́ть, -а́сть (да́ром); **~ one's chance** упусти́ть (*pf.*) слу́чай; **~ one's breath, words** говори́ть (*impf.*) на ве́тер. **2.** (*lay ~; ravage*) опустош|а́ть, -и́ть. **3.** (*wear away*) изнур|я́ть, -и́ть; истощ|а́ть, -и́ть; **his body was ~d by sickness** его́ те́ло бы́ло истощено́/изнурено́ боле́знью; **a wasting disease** изнури́тельная боле́знь.

v.i. (*usu.* **~ away:** *become weak; wither*) исс|яка́ть, -я́кнуть; истощ|а́ться, -и́ться; ча́хнуть, за-.

cpds. **~-basket** *n.* му́сорная корзи́на; **~-bin** *n.* му́сорное ведро́; му́сорный я́щик; **~-disposal** *n.*: **~-disposal unit** мусородроби́лка; **~-paper-basket** *n.* корзи́н(к)а для бума́ги; **~-pipe** *n.* сливна́я/водоотво́дная труба́.

wasteful ['weɪstfʊl] *adj.* расточи́тельный.

waster ['weɪstə(r)] *n.* (*coll.*) никуды́шный/никчёмный челове́к; безде́льник.

wastrel ['weɪstr(ə)l] *n.* (*arch., good-for-nothing*) безде́льник; расточи́тель (*m.*).

watch[1] [wɒtʃ] *n.* **1.** (*alert state*) надзо́р, наблюде́ние; **keep ~** стоя́ть (*impf.*) на ва́хте; **the dog keeps ~ on, over the house** соба́ка карау́лит/сторожи́т дом; **on the ~** начеку́; **she is on the ~ for a bargain** она́ подстерега́ет слу́чай купи́ть по дешёвке. **2.** (*hist., night guardian or patrol (collect.)*) стра́жа; карау́л; патру́ль (*m.*). **3.** (*duty period at sea*) ва́хта; **be on ~** стоя́ть (*impf.*) на ва́хте; (*in general, e.g. for signal operators*) дежу́рство; **I was on ~ from 6 to 12** я дежу́рил с шести́ до двена́дцати.

v.t. **1.** (*look at; keep eyes on*) смотре́ть (*impf.*); **I ~ed him draw** я смотре́л, как он рису́ет. **2.** (*keep under observation*) следи́ть (*impf.*) за+*i.*; смотре́ть (*impf.*) за+*i.*; **he is being ~ed by the police** поли́ция следи́т за ним; (*be careful of*) следи́ть (*impf.*) за+*i.*; **I have to ~ my weight** мне ну́жно следи́ть за ве́сом/фигу́рой; **~ your step!** (*lit.*) не оступи́тесь!; (*fig.; also, coll.,* **~ it!**) бу́дьте осторо́жны!; осторо́жно!; берегите́сь! **3.** (*guard*) сторожи́ть; карау́лить; стере́чь (*all impf.*).

v.i. **1.** смотре́ть, наблюда́ть, следи́ть (*all impf.*); **she ~ed by his bedside** она́ дежу́рила у его́ посте́ли; **will you ~ over my things?** вы не присмо́трите за мои́ми веща́ми?; **he ~ed over her interests** он стоя́л на стра́же её интере́сов. **2.** (*be careful*): **~ how you cross the street** бу́дьте осторо́жны (*or* смотри́те) при перехо́де у́лицы.

with adv.: **~ out** *v.i.* (*beware*) остерега́ться (+*g.*); бере́чься (+*g.*) (*both impf.*); **~ out for the signal!** ждите сигна́ла!

cpds. **~-dog** *n.* сторожева́я соба́ка; **~man** *n.* сто́рож, вахтёр; **~tower** *n.* сторожева́я ба́шня; **~word** *n.* (*slogan*) ло́зунг, деви́з; (*password*) паро́ль (*m.*).

watch[2] [wɒtʃ] *n.* (*timepiece*) час|ы́ (*pl., g.,* -о́в); **two ~es** дво́е часо́в; **set one's ~** ста́вить, по- часы́; **what time is it by your ~?** ско́лько на ва́ших часа́х?

cpds. **~-chain** *n.* цепо́чка для часо́в; **~-maker** *n.* часовщи́к; **~-strap** *n.* ремешо́к для часо́в; (*metal*) брасле́т.

watcher [wɒtʃə(r)] *n.* наблюда́тель (*m.*).

watchful ['wɒtʃfʊl] *adj.* внима́тельный; бди́тельный; насторо́жённый.

water ['wɔːtə(r)] *n.* **1.** вода́; **we went there by ~** мы поéхали туда́ по воде́ (*or* во́дным путём); **at the ~'s edge** у са́мой воды́; **the ~ has been cut off** во́ду отключи́ли; **she turned on the ~** она́ пусти́ла во́ду (*or* откры́ла кран); **a house with ~ laid on** дом с водопрово́дом; **the road is under ~** доро́га зато́плена; **he spends money like ~** он сори́т деньга́ми. **2.** (*attr.*) (*see also cpds.*): **~ bus** речно́й трамва́й; **~ power** гидроэне́ргия; **~ sports** во́дный спорт; **~ supply** водоснабже́ние. **3.** (*fig. phrr.*): **in deep ~** в беде́/го́ре; в опа́сном положе́нии; **get into hot ~** вл|ипа́ть, -и́пнуть; **keep one's head above ~** св|оди́ть, -ести́ концы́ с конца́ми; **pour, throw cold ~ on** раскритикова́ть (*pf.*); **the argument won't hold ~** э́тот до́вод ни на чём не осно́ван. **4.** (*pl., areas of sea; reaches of river*) во́ды (*f. pl.*); **in Icelandic ~s** в исла́ндских во́дах; (*pl., mineral ~s*) минера́льные во́ды. **5.** (*urine*) моча́; **make, pass ~** мочи́ться, по-. **6.** (*state of tide*): у́ровень (*m.*) воды́; **high/low ~** прили́в/отли́в.

v.t. **1.** (*sprinkle ~ on*) пол|ива́ть, -и́ть водо́й. **2.** (*provide with ~*) пои́ть, на-.

v.i. (*exude ~*) слези́ться (*impf.*); **his eyes were ~ing with the wind** от ве́тра у него́ слези́лись глаза́; **the sight of food made my mouth ~** при ви́де еды́ у меня́ потекли́ слю́нки.

with adv.: **~ down** *v.t.* (*lit.*) разб|авля́ть, -а́вить; (*fig.*) смягч|а́ть, -и́ть; осл|абля́ть, -а́бить.

cpds. **~-biscuit** *n.* пече́нье на воде́; **~-bottle** *n.* (*soldier's*) фля́жка; (*carafe*) графи́н; (*for heating bed*) гре́лка; **~-buffalo** *n.* буйво́л; **~-butt** *n.* ка́дка; **~-cannon** *n.* брандспо́йт, гидропу́льт; **~-chute** *n.* водяны́е го́ры (*f. pl.*); **~-colour** *n.* (*paint*) акваре́ль; акваре́льные кра́ски (*f. pl.*); (*painting*) акваре́ль; **~-cooled** *adj.* с водяны́м охлажде́нием; **~course** *n.* пото́к; ру́сло; **~cress** *n.* кресс водяно́й; **~ed-down** *adj.* (*fig.*) осла́бленный; **~fall** *n.* водопа́д; **~fowl** *n.* водопла́вающая пти́ца; **~front** *n.* часть го́рода, примыка́ющая к бе́регу; **~-heater** *n.* кипяти́льник; **~-hole** *n.* пруд, ключ, исто́чник; **~-ice** *n.* шербе́т; **~-lily** *n.* водяна́я ли́лия, кувши́нка; **~-line** (*naut.*) *n.* ватерли́ния; **~logged** *adj.* (*of ground*) заболо́ченный; **~-main** *n.* водопрово́дная магистра́ль; **~mark** *n.* водяно́й знак; **~-meadow** *n.* заливно́й луг; **~-melon** арбу́з; **~-meter** *n.* водоме́р; **~-mill** *n.* водяна́я ме́льница; **~-pipe** *n.* водопрово́дная труба́; **~-polo** *n.* во́дное по́ло (*indecl.*); **~proof** *n.* & *adj.* непромока́емый (плащ); **~-rat** *n.* водяна́я кры́са; **~-rate** *n.* пла́та за во́ду; **~-repellent** *adj.* водоотта́лкивающий; **~side** *n.* бе́рег; **~-skiing** *n.* воднолы́жный спо́рт; **~-skis** *n. pl.* во́дные лы́жи (*f. pl.*); **~spout** *n.* (*phenomenon*) водяно́й смерч; (*conduit*) водосто́чная труба́; **~-tank** *n.* резервуа́р; бак для воды́; **~tight** *adj.* (*lit.*) водонепроница́емый; (*fig., of argument etc.*) неопровержи́мый; **~-tower** *n.* водонапо́рная ба́шня; **~way** *n.* во́дный путь; **~-weed** *n.* во́доросль; **~-wheel** *n.* водяно́е колесо́.

watering ['wɔːtərɪŋ] *n.* поли́вка; **the roses need ~** ну́жно поли́ть ро́зы.

cpds. **~-can** *n.* ле́йка; **~-place** *n.* (*for animals*) водопо́й.

watershed ['wɔːtəʃed] *n.* (*lit., fig.*) водоразде́л.

watery ['wɔːtərɪ] *adj.* водяни́стый, жи́дкий; **~ colour** бле́дный/размы́тый/водяни́стый цвет; **a ~ grave** водяна́я моги́ла.

watt [wɒt] *n.* ватт.

wattage ['wɒtɪdʒ] *n.* мóщность в ваттах.

wattle[1] ['wɒt(ə)l] *n.* (*interlaced sticks*) прýтья (*m. pl.*), плéтень (*m.*).

wattle[2] ['wɒt(ə)l] *n.* (*of bird*) борóдка.

wave [weɪv] *n.* **1.** (*ridge of water*) волнá; вал; **life on the ocean ~** морскáя жизнь. **2.** (*fig., of persons advancing*) волнá. **3.** (*fig., temporary increase or spread*) подъём, волнá; **~ of enthusiasm** волнá/взрыв энтузиáзма; **crime ~** рéзкий рост преступности; **heat ~** жарá; полосá сильной жары. **4.** (*phys.*) волнá; **short/medium/long ~s** корóткие/срéдние/длинные вóлны. **5.** (*undulation*): **her hair has a natural ~** у неё (от прирóды) вьющиеся вóлосы; **permanent ~** шестимéсячная завивка; пермaнéнт. **6.** (*gesture*) взмах, жест (руки); **she gave a ~ of her hand** онá помахáла рукóй.

v.t. **1.** (*move to and fro or up and down*) размáхивать (*impf.*) +*i.*; махáть, по- +*i.*; **the children were waving flags** дéти размáхивали флажкáми; **he ~d his hand** (*as a signal*) он пóдал знак (*or* махнýл) рукóй. **2.** (*express by hand-waving*): **~ a greeting** помахáть (*pf.*) рукóй в знак привéтствия; **~ goodbye** помахáть (*pf.*) рукóй на прощáние. **3.** (*set in ~s*) зав|ивáть, -ить; **she had her hair ~d** онá завилá вóлосы.

v.i. **1.** (*move to and fro or up and down*) развевáться (*impf.*); качáться (*impf.*); **the flags were waving in the breeze** флáги развевáлись на ветрý. **2.** (*~ one's hand*) махáть, по-; **~ at s.o.** махáть, помý-н. **3.** (*undulate; be wavy*) виться (*impf.*).

with advs.: **~ aside** *v.t.* отстран|ять, -ить жéстом; **he ~d my objections aside** он отмахнýлся от моих возражéний; **~ down** *v.t.* остан|áвливать, -овить; **the policeman ~d us down** полицéйский сдéлал знак рукóй, чтóбы мы остановились.

cpds. **~band** *n.* диапазóн волн; **~length** *n.* длинá волны; **he and I are on the same ~length** (*fig.*) мы с ним настрóены на однý волнý.

waver ['weɪvə(r)] *v.i.* **1.** (*flicker*) колыхáться (*impf.*). **2.** (*falter; become unsteady*) дрожáть, за-; дрóгнуть (*pf.*); **his voice ~ed** егó гóлос задрожáл. **3.** (*hesitate; be irresolute*) колебáться (*impf.*).

wavy ['weɪvɪ] *adj.* волнообрáзный, волнистый; **a ~ line** волнистая линия; **~ hair** вьющиеся вóлосы.

wax[1] [wæks] *n.* **1.** воск; (*in the ears*) ушнáя сéра; **paraffin ~** твёрдый парафин. **2.** (*attr.*) восковóй; *see also cpds.*

v.t. вощить, на-; нат|ирáть, -ерéть (вóском).

cpds. **~-paper** *n.* вощáнка, воскóвка; **~work** *n.* (*model*) восковáя фигýра; **~works** *n.* (*exhibition*) галерéя восковых фигýр.

wax[2] [wæks] *v.i.* **1.** (*of moon*) прибывáть (*impf.*). **2.** (*liter., grow*) дéлаться (*impf.*); становиться (*impf.*); **~ eloquent** дéлаться, с- красноречивым; **~ angry** рассердиться (*pf.*).

waxen ['wæks(ə)n] *adj.* восковóй.

waxy ['wæksɪ] *adj.* восковóй.

way [weɪ] *n.* **1.** (*road, path*) дорóга, путь (*m.*); (*track*) тропá; **Milky W ~** Млéчный путь; **over the ~** напрóтив. **2.** (*route, journey*): **which is the best ~ to London?** как лýчше пройти/проéхать в Лóндон?; **he lost his ~** он заблудился; он сбился с пути; **he went (on) his ~** он пошёл дáльше; **they went their own ~s** кáждый пошёл своим путём; **go down the wrong ~** (*of food etc.*) попáсть (*pf.*) не в то гóрло; **lead the ~** (*lit.*) идти (*det.*) вперёд; (*fig.*) под|авáть, -áть примéр; **feel one's ~** двигаться (*impf.*) осмотрительно (*or* на óщупь); **we made our ~ to the dining-room** мы прошли в столóвую; **you must make your own ~ to the station** вам придётся добирáться до стáнции самомý; **they made their ~ across mountains** они пробились чéрез гóры; **he made his ~ in the world** он пробил себé дорóгу в жизни; **pay one's ~** (*lit.*) оплá|чивать, -тить свою дорóгу; жить (*impf.*) на сóбственные срéдства (*or* по срéдствам); **he worked his ~ through college** он учился в коллéдже и одноврéменно рабóтал; (*with preps.*): **by ~ of London** чéрез Лóндон; **by the ~** по дорóге; в пути; (*incidentally*) кстáти; мéжду прóчим; **by ~ of** *see also* **11.**; **in the ~** *see* **9.**; **on the ~** по дорóге; на/по пути; **he was on his ~ to the bank** он шёл в банк; **a letter is on its ~** письмó (нахóдится) в пути; **I must be on my ~** мне порá; **I sent him on his ~** я егó отпрáвил; **they have another child on the ~** они ожидáют ещё одногó ребёнка; **be on the ~ in/out** (*of fashion*) входить (*impf.*) в мóду, выходить (*impf.*) из мóды; **the hall is well on the ~ to completion** строительство зáла близится к концý; **he went out of his ~ to help me** он проявил немáлое усéрдие, чтóбы мне помóчь; **out of the ~** (*remote*) в сторонé; далекó; *see also* **9.**; (*with adv. indicating direction*): **~ across** перехóд; **~ in** вход; **~ out** (*lit., fig.*) выход; **can you find the ~ back?** вы найдёте дорóгу назáд?; **the ~ ahead will be difficult** нам предстоит трýдная дорóга; **~ through** прохóд; **~ round** окóльный путь; (*fig., loophole*) лазéйка; **he knows his ~ around** он знáет, что к чемý. **3.** (*door*): **he came in by the front ~ and went out by the back** он вошёл с парáдного хóда, а вышел с чёрного. **4.** (*direction*) сторонá, направлéние; **which ~ did they go?** в какýю стóрону они пошли?; **this ~** сюдá; **are you going my ~?** вам со мной по пути?; **look the other ~** (*fig.*) смотрéть (*impf.*) сквозь пáльцы; **I travelled by bus both ~s** я éхал автóбусом тудá и обрáтно (*or* в óба концá); **I don't know which ~ to turn** я не знáю, что дéлать (*or* как быть). **5.** (*of reversible thgs.*): **his hat is on the wrong ~ round** он надéл шляпу зáдом напéред; **the picture is the wrong ~ up** картина повéшена вверх ногáми; **the other ~ round** наоборóт, напрóтив. **6.** (*neighbourhood, area*): **down your ~** в вáших краях; **he lives somewhere Plymouth ~** он живёт где-то в райóне Плимута. **7.** (*distance*) расстояние; **a long ~ off** (*away*) далекó; **a little, short ~** недалекó; **quite a ~** довóльно далекó; **it is only a little ~ to the shops** до магазинов совсéм недалекó; **all the ~** всю дорóгу; (*fig.*) пóлностью. **8.** (*US coll.*) (*a long ~*) далекó; **~ back** (*long ago*) давным-давнó; **~ ahead of the others** намнóго вперéди остальных. **9.** (*clear passage; space or freedom to proceed*) проéзд, прохóд; **right of ~** прáво проéзда; **clear the ~** расч|ищáть, -истить путь; **fight one's ~ through the crowd** прод|ирáться, -рáться сквозь толпý; **get in the ~** мешáть, по- (*комý*); **get out of the ~!** (прочь) с дорóги!; дáйте пройти!; **get sth. out of the ~** (*lit.*) уб|ирáть, -рáть что-н. с дорóги; (*fig., dispose of*) свáл|ивать, -ить что-н.; изб|авляться, -áвиться от чегó-н.; **make ~ for the President!** дорóгу президéнту!; **he made ~ for his successor** он уступил мéсто своемý преéмнику; **put out of the ~** устран|ять, -ить; **you are standing in the ~** вы загорáживаете дорóгу; **I shan't stand in your ~** я не бýду стоять на вáшем пути (*or* вам мешáть); **give ~** (*fail to resist*) подд|авáться, -áться; (*collapse*) провáл|иваться, -иться; раз|рывáться, -орвáться; рýхнуть (*pf.*); **his legs gave ~** у негó подкосились нóги; (*retreat*) отступ|áть, -ить; (*make concessions*) уступ|áть, -ить; (*surrender, abandon o.s.*) сд|авáться, -áться; пред|авáться, -áться; **give ~ to tears** дать (*pf.*) вóлю слезáм. **10.** (*means, method*) срéдство, мéтод, приём; **he found a ~ to keep food warm** он нашёл спóсоб/срéдство сохранять пищу горячей; **there are ~s and means** есть всякие пути и возмóжности; **you will soon get into the ~ of it** вы вскóре наýчитесь.

11. (*manner, fashion*) срéдство, спóсоб, óбраз, мéтод; **in this ~** такúм óбразом; **is this the ~ to do it?** так э́то дéлается?; **do it your own ~!** дéлайте по-своéму!; **one ~ or another** так úли инáче; тем úли иным спóсобом; **the right ~** так; прáвильно; **the wrong ~** не так, непрáвильно; **in the same ~** (тóчно) так же; такúм же óбразом; **~ of thinking** взгля́ды (*m. pl.*); **to my ~ of thinking** как мне кáжется; на мой взгляд; по-мóему; **let's put it this ~** скáжем так; **by ~ of** (*in order to*) с тем, чтóбы; с цéлью; **by ~ of a change** для разнообрáзия; **by ~ of a joke** шýтки рáди; (*in the guise of*) в вúде/кáчестве; вмéсто; взамéн (*all +g.*); (*manner of behaving*): **she has a winning ~** у неё обая́тельная манéра; **it's only his ~** у негó прóсто такáя манéра; **he has a ~ with the ladies** он умéет нрáвится дáмам; (*preference*): **have it your own ~!** будь по-вáшему!; **have, get one's own ~** доб|ивáться, -úться своегó; **things went my ~** делá сложúлись в мою́ пóльзу. **12.** (*habit, custom*) обы́чай, привы́чка; **~ of life** óбраз жúзни; **it is not my ~ to deceive** не в моём обы́чае/харáктере обмáнывать; **that's always the ~ with him** он всегдá так; **mend one's ~s** испр|авля́ться, -áвиться; **fall into bad ~s** пойтú (*pf.*) по плохóй/дурнóй дорóжке. **13.** (*state, condition*) положéние, состоя́ние; **things are in a bad ~** плóхо дéло; делá из рук вон плóхи; **she was in a terrible ~** (*ill*) онá былá óчень больнá. **14.** (*scale, degree*): **in a small ~** скрóмно; **in a big ~** в ширóком/большóм масштáбе; **he went in for photography in a big ~** он стал занимáться фотогрáфией всерьёз. **15.** (*sense, respect*) смысл, отношéние; **in a ~** в нéкотором отношéнии; **in some ~s** в нéкоторых отношéниях; **in one ~** в однóм смы́сле; **in no ~** ничýть; никóим óбразом. **16.** (*line, course*): **what have we in the ~ of food?** что у нас есть по чáсти еды́?; **he called there in the ~ of business** он зашёл тудá по дéлу. **17.** (*of ship etc.*): **under ~** на ходý, в путú; **preparations are under ~** (сейчáс) идýт приготовлéния.

cpds. **~bill** *n.* (*list of goods*) трáнспортная накладнáя; **~farer** *n.* пýтник; **~lay** *v.t.* подстер|егáть, -éчь; устр|áивать, -óить засáду *+d.*; **~side** *n.* обóчина (дорóги); (*attr.*) придорóжный; **fall by the ~side** (*fig.*) выбывáть, вы́быть из стрóя.

wayward ['weɪwəd] *adj.* своенрáвный, непокóрный.

WC (*abbr. of* **water-closet**) убóрная.

we [wi:, wɪ] *pron.* мы (*also royal, editorial*); **give us a rest!** дáйте человéку отдохнýть!; **how are ~ feeling today?** как мы сегóдня себя́ чýвствуем?; **~ don't inform on people** у нас не прúнято доносúть.

weak [wi:k] *adj.* **1.** (*infirm; feeble*) слáбый; **a ~ constitution** хрýпкое сложéние; **a ~ imagination** бéдное воображéние; **a ~ old man** дря́хлый старúк; **he's a bit ~ in the head** он придурковáт; **their cries grew ~er** их крúки слабéли/ослабевáли; **his ~ point is spelling** он слаб в орфогрáфии; орфогрáфия — егó слáбое мéсто; **the ~est go to the wall** слáбых бьют. **2.** (*unconvincing*) неубедúтельный, неосновáтельный; **they put up a ~ case** онú привелú слáбые дóводы. **3.** (*of morals or will*) безвóльный, слабовóльный; **a ~ man/character** слáбый/нерешúтельный человéк/харáктер. **4.** (*diluted; thin*) жúдкий, слáбый; **do you like your tea ~?** вы лю́бите некрéпкий/слáбый чай? **5.** (*gram.*) слáбый. **6.** (*of style*) вя́лый.

cpds. **~-spirited** *adj.* малодýшный; **~-willed** *adj.* слабовóльный.

weaken ['wi:kən] *v.t.* осл|абля́ть, -áбить.

v.i. слабéть, ослáбнуть.

weakling ['wi:klɪŋ] *n.* слáбый человéк.

weakly ['wi:klɪ] *adj.* хúлый, болéзненный.

weakness ['wi:knɪs] *n.* слáбость, хúлость; **the tests revealed ~es in the structure** испытáния вы́явили структýрные дефéкты.

weal[1] [wi:l] *n.* (*liter.*) блáго, благосостоя́ние; **the common, public ~** блáго óбщества; óбщее блáго.

weal[2] [wi:l] *n.* (*mark on skin*) рубéц.

wealth [welθ] *n.* богáтство; **a man of ~** богáч; состоя́тельный человéк; **~ tax** налóг на имýщество; (*fig., profusion*) обúлие; **a ~ of illustrations** обúлие иллюстрáций; **a ~ of detail** мнóжество подрóбностей; **a ~ of experience** богатéйший óпыт; **a ~ of material** огрóмный материáл.

wealthy ['welθɪ] *adj.* богáтый, состоя́тельный; **the ~** богачú (*m. pl.*); богáтые.

wean [wi:n] *v.t.* отн|имáть, -я́ть от грудú; отлуч|áть, -úть от мáтери; (*fig.*) отуч|áть, -úть (*от чего*).

weapon ['wepən] *n.* орýжие; **guided ~s** управля́емые снаря́ды (*m. pl.*)/ракéты (*f. pl.*); **~ of war** боевóе срéдство; (*fig.*) орýдие, срéдство.

weaponry ['wepənrɪ] *n.* орýжие, вооружéние.

wear [weə(r)] *n.* **1.** (*articles or type of clothing*) одéжда, плáтье; **children's ~** дéтская одéжда, дéтское плáтье; (*~ing of clothes*) нóска, ношéние; **a suit for everyday ~** бýдничный/повседнéвный костю́м. **2.** (*continued use as causing damage or loss of quality*) изнóс, снос; **this material stands up to hard ~** э́тот материáл прекрáсно нóсится; **show signs of ~** имéть (*impf.*) понóшенный/потрёпанный вид. **3.** (*resistance to ~*) нóскость; **these shoes have a lot of ~ left in them** э́ти ботúнки мóжно ещё дóлго носúть (*or* ещё дóлго бýдут носúться).

v.t. **1.** (*of garments or accessories*) носúть (*indet.*); над|евáть, -éть; **what shall I ~?** что мне надéть?; **she was ~ing light blue** онá былá в голубóм (плáтье); **he ~s galoshes** он нóсит галóши; **he always wore a hat** он всегдá ходúл в шля́пе; **she ~s scent** онá дýшится; **worn** (*used*) **clothes** (из)нóшенная/стáрая одéжда; (*of hair*): **~ one's hair long** носúть (*indet.*) длúнные вóлосы; **~ one's hair short** кóротко стрúчься (*impf.*); **he ~s his hair brushed back** он зачёсывает вóлосы назáд; **they all wore beards** онú все носúли бóроды; **~ mourning** ходúть (*indet.*) в трáуре; (*fig.*): **~ing a smile** с улы́бкой (на лицé); **~ing a frown** насýпившись. **2.** (*injure surface of; abrade; damage by use*) ст|ирáть, -ерéть; прот|ирáть, -ерéть; **the steps are worn** ступéни стёрлись; **he ~s his socks into holes** он изнáшивает noскú до дыр; **a well-worn suit** сúльно понóшенный костю́м; **the waves have worn the stone** вóлны обточúли/отшлифовáли кáмень; (*fig.*): **I had a ~ing day** у меня́ был тяжёлый день; **a well-worn theme** избúтая тéма. **3.** (*produce by friction*): **the stream wore a channel in the sand** потóк проры́л канáву в пескé; **you've worn a hole in your trousers** вы протёрли брю́ки (до дыр); **a well-worn track** проторённая дорóжка.

v.i. **1.** (*stand up to ~*) (хорошó) носúться (*indet.*); быть прóчным. **2.** (*show effects of ~*): **~ thin** изн|áшиваться, -осúться; истрёп|ываться, -áться; (*fig.*): **his patience wore thin** егó терпéние бы́ло на исхóде; **that excuse has worn thin** э́то оправдáние звучúт неубедúтельно.

with advs.: **~ away** *v.t. & i.* ст|ирáть(ся), -ерéть(ся); **weather had worn away the inscription** вéтры и дождú стёрли нáдпись; **~ down** *v.t. & i.* изн|áшивать(ся), -осúть(ся); **the heels have worn down very quickly** каблукú сносúлись óчень бы́стро; (*fig.*): **they wore down the enemy's resistance** онú сломúли сопротивлéние протúвника; **~ in** *v.t.* (*shoes*) разн|áшивать, -осúть (*ботинки*); **~ off** *v.t. & i.* ст|ирáть(ся), -ерéть(ся); **the pattern wore off** узóр стёрся; (*fig.*) (постепéнно) проходúть (*impf.*); **the novelty soon wore off** вскóре новизнá вы́ветрилась; **~ on** *v.i.*: **as the evening wore on** к концý вéчера;

~ **out** *v.t. & i.* изн|áшивать(ся), -оси́ть(ся); истрёп|ывать(ся), -áть(ся); **the machine wore out** маши́на срабóталась; (*fig.*) изнур|я́ть(ся), -и́ть(ся); **the children wore me out** дéти меня́ измýчили; **you look worn out** у вас измýченный вид; **worn-out** (*of clothes etc.*) изнóшенный, истёртый, потёртый.

wearer ['weərə(r)] *n.* владéлец, носи́тель (*fem.* -ница).

weariness ['wɪərɪnɪs] *n.* утомлéние; скýка.

wearing ['weərɪŋ] *adj.* утоми́тельный, надоéдливый.

wearisome ['wɪərɪsəm] *adj.* надоéдливый, скýчный.

weary ['wɪərɪ] *adj.* **1.** (*tired*) устáлый, утомлённый; ~ **of walking** устáвший от ходьбы́; **the journey made him** ~ путешéствие егó утоми́ло. **2.** (*showing tiredness*) устáвший; **he gave a ~ sigh** он устáло вздохнýл. **3.:** ~ **of** (*fed up with*) устáвший от (*чего*); **I was ~ of his complaints** мне надоéли егó жáлобы.

v.t. & i. утом|ля́ть(ся), -и́ть(ся).

weasel ['wi:z(ə)l] *n.* лáска; ~ **words** (*fig.*) обмáнчивые словá.

weather ['weðə(r)] *n.* погóда; **bad** ~ плохáя погóда, ненáстье; **rough** ~ непогóда; **wet** ~ дожли́вая погóда; **in all ~s** в любýю погóду; **what's the ~ like?** какáя сегóдня погóда?; ~ **permitting** при благоприя́тной погóде; **make heavy ~ of sth.** (*fig.*) осложн|я́ть, -и́ть дéло; **be, feel under the** ~ (*fig.*) невáжно себя́ чýвствовать (*impf.*); **keep a ~ eye open** смотрéть (*impf.*) в óба; ~ **forecast** прогнóз погóды.

v.t. **1.** (*survive*; *circumvent*) выдéрживать, вы́держать; переж|ивáть, -и́ть; ~ **a storm** вы́держать (*pf.*) штóрм; ~ **a crisis** перенести́/вы́держать (*pf.*) кри́зис. **2.** (*discolour or wear away by exposure*) изн|áшивать, -оси́ть.

cpds. **~-beaten** *adj.* обвéтренный; **~cock** *n.* флю́гер; **~man** *n.* метеорóлог; ~ **map** *n.* синопти́ческая кáрта; **~-proof** *adj.* погодоустóйчивый; **~-service** *n.* метеорологи́ческая слýжба; **~-vane** *n.* флю́гер.

weav|e [wi:v] *n.* ткáцкое переплетéние; вы́работка ткáни.

v.t. **1.** (*thread*, *flowers etc.*) плести́, с-; спле|тáть, -сти́; впле|тáть, -сти́. **2.** (*cloth*, *basket etc.*) плести́, с-; ткать, со-; (*fig.*): **~e a web of intrigue** плести́, ссеть интри́г.

v.i. **1.** (*work at loom*) ткать (*impf.*); **engaged in ~ing** занимáющийся ткáчеством. **2.** (*twist and turn*) сновáть (*impf.*), идти́ (*det.*) непрямы́м путём.

weaver ['wi:və(r)] *n.* ткач (*fem.* -и́ха).

web [web] *n.* **1. (spider's ~)** паути́на; (*fig.*) сеть, паути́на, сплетéние. **2.** (*membrane*) перепóнка.

cpd. **~-footed** *adj.* перепóнчатый.

webbing ['webɪŋ] *n.* ткáнный ремéнь; ткáная лéнта.

wed [wed] *v.t. & i.* (*liter.*) **1.** (*of man*) жени́ться (*impf.*, *pf.*) на+*p.*; **his ~ded wife** егó закóнная супрýга. **2.** (*of woman*) выходи́ть, вы́йти (зáмуж) за+*a.* **3.** (*of couple*) пожени́ться (*pf.*); вступ|áть, -и́ть в брак; **the newly ~ded pair** новобрáчные (*pl.*), молодожёны (*m. pl.*). **4.** (*fig.*): **he is ~ded to his job** он (всецéло) прéдан своéй рабóте; **he is ~ded to his opinion** он упóрно дéржится своегó взгля́да.

wedding ['wedɪŋ] *n.* свáдьба, бракосочетáние; (*in church*) венчáние; **silver/golden** ~ серéбряная/золотáя свáдьба; ~ **anniversary** годовщи́на свáдьбы.

cpds. **~-cake** *n.* свáдебный торт; **~-day** *n.* день (*m.*) свáдьбы; **~-dress** *n.* подвенéчный/свáдебный наря́д; **~-ring** *n.* обручáльное кольцó.

wedge [wedʒ] *n.* клин; **drive (in) a** ~ (*lit.*, *fig.*) вби|вáть, -ть клин (мéжду+*i.*).

v.t. закреп|ля́ть, -и́ть кли́ном; закли́н|ивать, -и́ть; **we were ~d in** нас сти́снули со всех сторóн.

cpd. **~-shaped** *adj.* клинови́дный, клинообрáзный.

wedlock ['wedlɒk] *n.* брак, супрýжество; **born in** ~ законорождённый.

Wednesday ['wenzdeɪ, -dɪ] *n.* средá.

wee [wi:] *adj.* (*Sc. & coll.*) крóшечный, малю́сенький; **she's a ~ bit jealous** онá чýточку ревнýет.

weed [wi:d] *n.* (*in garden or field*) сорня́к; **the garden ran to ~s** сад зарóс сорнякáми; (*in water*) вóдоросль.

v.t. (*clear of ~s*) полóть, вы́-; проп|áлывать, -олóть.

with adv.: ~ **out** *v.t.* (*eradicate*, *remove*) устран|я́ть, -и́ть; искорен|я́ть, -и́ть.

cpds. **~-grown** *adj.* зарóсший сорнякáми; **~-killer** *n.* гербици́д.

weeds [wi:dʒ] *n.*: **widow's** ~ вдóвий трáур/наря́д.

weedy ['wi:dɪ] *adj.* (*overgrown with weeds*) зарóсший сорнякáми; (*lanky*, *weakly*) худосóчный, слáбый.

week [wi:k] *n.* недéля; **what day of the ~ is it?** какóй сегóдня день (недéли)?; **the ~ before last** позапрóшлая недéля; **the ~ after next** чéрез две недéли; **a ~ (from) today** (*or* **today** ~, *or* **this day** ~) рóвно чéрез недéлю; **in a** ~ чéрез недéлю; **I haven't seen him in, for ~s** я егó давнó не ви́дел; **from one ~ to the next** из недéли в недéлю; ~ **in,** ~ **out** (цéлыми) недéлями; **I'm not at home during the** ~ в рабóчие дни меня́ не бывáет дóма; **~'s wages** недéльное жáлованье; **work a 40-hour** ~ рабóтать (*impf.*) сóрок часóв в недéлю; **working** ~ рабóчая недéля; **I'm off on a ~'s holiday** я уезжáю на недéлю в óтпуск.

cpds. **~day** *n.* бýдний/рабóчий день; **my ~day clothes** моя́ бýдничная одéжда; **~end** *n.* конéц недéли, уикéнд; **we get up late at the ~end** по суббóтам и воскресéньям мы встаём пóздно.

weekly ['wi:klɪ] *n.* еженедéльник.

adj. (*once a week*) еженедéльный.

adv. еженедéльно; кáждую недéлю.

weep [wi:p] *n.* плач, рыдáние; **she had a good** ~ онá как слéдует (*or* хорошéнько) вы́плакалась.

v.t. плáкать, за-; **she wept bitter tears** онá гóрько плáкала; онá пролилá гóрькие слёзы.

v.i. **1.** (*shed tears*) плáкать, за-; **she wept over her misfortune** онá оплáкивала своё несчáстье; **he was ~ing** (*mourning*) **for his mother** он горевáл по своéй мáтери. **2.:** **~ing willow** плакýчая и́ва.

weevil ['wi:vɪl] *n.* долгонóсик.

wee-wee ['wi:wi:] *n.* пи-пи́ (*nt. indecl.*) (*coll.*).

v.i. дéлать, с- пи-пи́; ходи́ть, с- по-мáленькому; пи́сать, на-/по-.

weft [weft] *n.* утóк.

weigh [weɪ] *v.t.* **1.** (*find or test weight of*) взвé|шивать, -сить; ~ **o.s.** взвé|шиваться, -ситься; (*fig.*, *consider*; *assess*; *compare*) взвé|шивать, -сить; обдýм|ывать, -ать; ~ **the consequences** взвéсить (*pf.*) послéдствия; ~ **one's words** взвéшивать (*impf.*) (свои́) словá. **2.** (*of ~ed object*: *amount to*) вéсить (*impf.*); **my luggage ~s 20 kilos** мой багáж вéсит 20 кило́; **what do you ~?** скóлько вы вéсите?; какóй у вас вес?; **I ~ too much** я вéшу сли́шком мнóго; у меня́ сли́шком большóй вес. **3.:** ~ **anchor** сн|имáться, -я́ться с я́коря.

v.i. **1.** (*indicate weight*) покáз|ывать, -áть вес; **these scales ~ accurately** э́ти весы́ тóчные; **~ing machine** весы́(-автомáт). **2.** (*fig.*, *be a burden*) дави́ть (*impf.*); **there is something ~ing on his mind** он чем-то подáвлен. **3.** (*fig.*, *have influence or importance*) имéть (*impf.*) вес/значéние.

with advs.: **~(t) down** *v.t.* (*burden*) отяго|щáть, -ти́ть; **the branches were ~ed down with, by fruit** вéтви гнýлись под тя́жестью плодóв; (*fig.*) угнетáть (*impf.*); **he was ~ed down with care** он был угнетён/подáвлен забóтой; ~ **in** *v.i.* (*be ~ed before contest*) взвé|шиваться, -ситься пéред соревновáнием; (*coll.*, *intervene forcefully*): **they ~ed in with a powerful argument** они́ вы́двинули си́льный аргумéнт/дóвод; ~ **out** *v.t.* отвé|шивать, -сить; **he**

~ed out half a pound of cheese он отвéсил полуфýнта сы́ра; **~ up** *v.t.* (*lit., fig.*) взвé|шивать, -сить; (*fig.*) оцéн|ивать, -и́ть.

cpds. **~bridge** *n.* весы́-платфóрма; **~-in** *n.* (*sport*) взвéшивание боксёра/жокéя пéред состязáнием.

weight [weɪt] *n.* **1.** (*phys., gravitational force; relative mass; this expressed on a scale*) вес; **3lbs in ~** вéсом в три фýнта; **goods sold by ~** товáр, продаю́щийся на вес; **what is your ~?** скóлько вы вéсите?; какóй у вас вес?; **I have to watch my ~** мне прихóдится следи́ть за фигýрой/вéсом; **gain, put on ~** приб|авля́ть, -áвить в вéсе; попр|авля́ться, -áвиться; **lose ~** теря́ть, по- в вéсе; **he is under/over ~** он вéсит сли́шком мáло/мнóго; **he is worth his ~ in gold** таки́е как он — на вес зóлота; **pull one's ~** (*fig.*) выполня́ть, вы́полнить свою́ дóлю рабóты; **throw one's ~ about** (*fig.*) распоряжáться (*impf.*); комáндовать (*impf.*). **2.** (*load*) тя́жесть, груз; (*fig.*) брéмя (*nt.*); **the pillars take all the ~** колóнны несýт всю нагрýзку; **that chair won't take, stand your ~** э́тот стул не вы́держит вáшего вéса; **it was a great ~ off my mind** у меня́ кáмень с души́ свали́лся; **dead ~** мёртвый груз; (*pressure*) нажи́м. **3.** (*object for weighing or ~ing*) ги́ря; **a 2lb ~** двухфунтóвая ги́ря. **4.** (*importance; influence*) вес; влия́ние; авторитéт; **his opinion carries great ~** с егó мнéнием óчень считáются; он пóльзуется больши́м влия́нием/авторитéтом; **this adds ~ to his words** э́то придаёт вес егó словáм.

v.t. **1.** (*attach a ~ to; make heavier*) утяжел|я́ть, -и́ть; **a stick ~ed with lead** пáлка, утяжелённая свинцóм. **2.** (*add compensatory factor to*): **London ~ing** тари́фная надбáвка для рабóтающих в Лóндоне; **the system was ~ed in their favour** систéма предоставля́ла им привилéгии.

with adv.: **~ down** *v.t.* = **weigh down**

cpds. **~-lifter** *n.* штанги́ст (*fem.* -ка); **~-lifting** *n.* поднятие тя́жестей.

weightless ['weɪtlɪs] *adj.* невесóмый.

weightlessness ['weɪtlɪsnɪs] *n.* невесóмость.

weighty ['weɪtɪ] *adj.* (*heavy*) тяжёлый; (*important*) вáжный, вéский, весóмый.

weir [wɪə(r)] *n.* плоти́на, водосли́в.

weird [wɪəd] *adj.* **1.** (*unearthly, uncanny*) таи́нственный, сверхъестéственный. **2.** (*strange, frightening*) стрáнный, жýткий.

weirdo ['wɪədəʊ] *n.* псих (*coll.*).

welcome ['welkəm] *n.* приём, привéтствие; **bid s.o. ~** привéтствовать (*impf.*) когó-н.; **they gave us a warm ~** они́ нас радýшно при́няли.

adj. **1.** (*gladly received*) желáнный; **a ~ guest** желáнный/дорогóй гость; **this is ~ news** э́то прия́тное извéстие; **make s.o. (feel) ~** окáз|ывать, -áть комý-н. радýшный приём. **2.** (*pred., ungrudgingly permitted*): **you are ~ to take it** пожáлуйста, бери́те!; **anyone is ~ to my share** я с удовóльствием уступлю́ свою́ дóлю комý угóдно; **you're ~!** (*esp. US: no thanks are required*) пожáлуйста!; нé за что!; на здорóвье!

v.t. привéтствовать (*impf.*); встр|ечáть, -éтить тепло́/радýшно; **she ~d her guests at the door** она́ привéтствовала гостéй в двеpя́х; **a welcoming smile** привéтливая улы́бка; **I ~ the suggestion** я привéтствую э́то предложéние; **I would ~ the opportunity** я был бы рад (такóму) слýчаю; **his arrival was ~d by all** все рáдовались егó приéзду/появлéнию.

int. добрó пожáловать!; ми́лости прóсим!

weld [weld] *n.* сварнóе соединéние; сварнóй шов.

v.t. & i. свáр|ивать(ся), -и́ть(ся); пая́ть (*impf.*); (*fig.*) спл|áчивать, -оти́ть.

with advs.: **~ on** *v.t.* припá|ивать, -я́ть; **~ together** *v.t.* (*lit., fig.*) свáр|ивать, -и́ть; спá|ивать, -я́ть; (*fig.*) спл|áчивать, -оти́ть.

welder ['weldə(r)] *n.* свáрщик.

welding ['weldɪŋ] *n.* свáрка; **arc ~** дуговáя свáрка; **~ torch** свáрочная горéлка.

welfare ['welfeə(r)] *n.* (*well-being*) благосостоя́ние; (*organized provision for social needs*) социáльное обеспéчение; **the W~ State** госудáрство всеóбщего благосостоя́ния.

well[1] [wel] *n.* (*for water*) колóдец; (*for oil*) нефтянáя сквáжина; (*mineral spring*) истóчник.

v.i. (*spring up; gush*) бить (*impf.*) ключóм; хлы́нуть (*pf.*); **tears ~ed up in her eyes** её глазá напóлнились слезáми.

cpds. **~-head** *n.* (*source*) истóчник, родни́к, ключ; **~-water** *n.* родникóвая/колóдезная водá.

well[2] [wel] *adj.* (*usu. pred.*) **1.** (*in good health*) здорóвый; **I haven't been ~** мне нездорóвилось; **I am quite ~ again** я совсéм вы́здоровел/попрáвился; **you don't look ~** вы плóхо вы́глядите. **2.** (*right, satisfactory*): **all's ~** всё хорошó/прекрáсно; всё в поря́дке. **3.** (*as n.*): **leave ~ alone** от добрá добрá не и́щут. **4.: (just) (as) ~** (*advisable*): **it would be (as) ~ to ask** не мешáло бы (*or* стóило бы) спроси́ть; **it may be as ~ to explain** пожáлуй, стóит объясни́ть; *see also adv.*, **10.. 5.: ~ enough; all very ~** (*tolerable*) вполнé гóдный; снóсный; неплохóй; **that's all very ~, but ...** всё так (*or* э́то прекрáсно), но... **6.: all very ~** (*easy, convenient*): **it's all very ~ for you, you're not a woman** вáм-то что — вы не жéнщина!; **it's all very ~ to say that afterwards** легкó говори́ть зáдним числóм.

adv. **1.** (*satisfactorily*) хорошó; **I did not sleep ~** я плóхо спал; **~ done!** здóрово!; молодéц!; **extremely ~** отли́чно; **perfectly ~** прекрáсно; **pretty ~** вполнé хорошó; (*nearly*) почти́; (*considerably*) значи́тельно. **2.** (*very, thoroughly; properly*) óчень, весьмá, хорошéнько; **I was ~ pleased** я был óчень довóлен; **~ done** (*of food*) (хорошó) прожáренный; **I am ~ aware of it** я э́то прекрáсно знáю; **~ and truly** окончáтельно, реши́тельно; **the picture was ~ worth £2,000** э́та карти́на вполнé стóила двух ты́сяч фýнтов. **3.** (*considerably: esp. with advs. & preps.*) горáздо, далекó; **~ up in the list** в сáмом начáле спи́ска; **~ over retiring age** мнóго стáрше пенсиóнного вóзраста; **~ past 40** далекó за сóрок; **~ into the night** далекó зá полночь. **4.** (*favourably*): **~ off** богáтый; состоя́тельный; **~ off for** обеспéченный +*i.*; **I wish him ~** я емý желáю благополýчия; **his teacher thinks ~ of him** учи́тель о нём хорóшего мнéния. **5.** (*fortunately, successfully*) удáчно, благополýчно; **all went ~** всё прошлó благополýчно; **he did very ~ for himself** он прекрáсно устрóил свой делá. **6.** (*comfortably, affluently*): **live ~** жить (*impf.*) в достáтке. **7.** (*wisely*) разýмно, прáвильно; **he did ~ to ask for his money back** он прáвильно сдéлал, что попроси́л дéньги назáд; **you would do ~ to insure your luggage** вам бы слéдовало застраховáть свой багáж. **8.** (*probably, indeed, reasonably*): **it may ~ be true** э́то вполнé возмóжно; **you may ~ ask** вопрóс нели́шний; **you may ~ be surprised** вы имéете все основáния удивля́ться; **we might ~ try** óчень стóит попытáться. **9.: as ~** (*in addition*) сверх тогó; тóже; тáкже; **there was meat as ~ as fish** там былá не тóлько ры́ба, но и мя́со; там бы́ли и ры́ба и мя́со. **10.: as ~** (*with equal reason or profit*) с таки́м же основáнием/успéхом; **(you, he** *etc.*) **may, might as ~** (*expr. recommendation*) не мешáло бы; пожáлуй; почемý бы не; **you may as ~ take an umbrella** на вся́кий слýчай прихвати́те зóнтик с собóй; *cf. adj.*, **5.**

int. ну; (*expr. surprise*) ну!; вот те рáз!; **~, I never!** вот те нá!; вот каки́е делá!; **~, ~!** ну и ну!; (*expr. expectation*): **~ then?** ну как?; ну так что же?; (*impatient or emphatic interrogation*): **~, what do you**

want? ну, так чего́ вы хоти́те?; **~, what's it about?** да в чём де́ло?; (*agreement*): **very ~, I'll do it** хорошо́, я э́то сде́лаю; (*concession*): **~, you can come if you like** что ж(е), е́сли хоти́те, приходи́те; **ah, ~, in that case** ах, ну, в тако́м слу́чае; (*resignation*): **oh ~, it can't be helped** (ну) что ж, ничего́ не поде́лаешь; (*summing up*) ну (вот); **~ then** (ну) так вот; (*resumption*): **~, as I was saying** ита́к, как я говори́л; (*indecision, explanation*) да...; **~, I'm not sure** ви́дите ли, я не уве́рен.

cpds. **~-balanced** *adj.* уравнове́шенный, разу́мный; **a ~-balanced diet** рациона́льная дие́та; **~-behaved** *adj.* (благо)воспи́танный; хоро́шего поведе́ния; **~-being** *n.* благополу́чие, благосостоя́ние; **~-bred** *adj.* (благо)воспи́танный; **~-built** *adj.* (*pers.*) хорошо́ сложённый; **~-deserved** *adj.* заслу́женный; **~-disposed** *adj.* благожела́тельный; благосклóнный; **~-earned** *adj.* заслу́женный; **~-educated** *adj.* образо́ванный; **~-fed** *adj.* отко́рмленный, сы́тый; **~-founded, ~-grounded** *adjs.* обосно́ванный, аргументи́рованный; **~-groomed** *adj.* ухо́женный, хо́леный; **~-grounded** *adj.* = **~-founded**; **~-heeled** *adj.* (*coll.*) состоя́тельный; **~-informed** *adj.* све́дущий; хорошо́ осведомлённый; **~-intentioned** *adj.* де́йствующий/сде́ланный из лу́чших побужде́ний; **~-kept, ~-run** *adjs.* содержа́щийся в поря́дке; **~-known** *adj.* (*of pers.*) изве́стный; (*of facts*) (обще-)изве́стный; **~-made** *adj.* хорошо́/иску́сно сде́ланный; **~-mannered** *adj.* воспи́танный; **~-meaning** *adj.* (*of pers.*) де́йствующий из лу́чших побужде́ний; **~-nigh** *adv.* (*liter.*) почти́; **~-off** *adj.* состоя́тельный; зажи́тичный; обеспе́ченный; **~-ordered, ~-run** *adjs.* хорошо́ организо́ванный; **~-paid** *adj.* хорошо́ опла́чиваемый; **~-preserved** *adj.* хорошо́ сохрани́вшийся; **~-read** *adj.* начи́танный; **~-run** *adj.* = **~-ordered, ~-kept**; **~-spoken** *adj.* учти́вый; **~-thought-of** *adj.* уважа́емый, по́льзующийся хоро́шей репута́цией; **~-to-do** *adj.* состоя́тельный; зажи́точный; обеспе́ченный; **~-trained** *adj.* вы́ученный, обу́ченный; **~-trodden** *adj.* проторённый, исхо́женный; **~-turned** *adj.* (*of speech etc.*) уда́чно вы́раженный; **~-wisher** *n.* доброжела́тель (*fem.* -ница); **~-worn** *adj.* (*lit.*) поно́шенный; (*fig., trite*) изби́тый, истáсканный.

wellington ['welɪŋt(ə)n] *n.* (*pl.*) рези́новые сапоги́ (*m. pl.*).

Welsh [welʃ] *n.* **1.: the ~** (*pl., people*) валли́йцы (*m. pl.*), уэ́льсцы (*m. pl.*). **2.** (*language*) валли́йский язы́к.

adj. валли́йский, уэ́льский; **~ rabbit, rarebit** грено́к с сы́ром.

cpds. **~man** *n.* валли́ец, уэ́льсец; **~woman** *n.* валли́йка, уроже́нка Уэ́льса.

welt [welt] *n.* (*of shoe*) рант; (*weal*) рубе́ц (*от удара плетью и т.п.*); (*border of garment*) обши́вка.

welter ['weltə(r)] *n.* (*confusion*) пу́таница; (*disorderly mixture*) мешани́на; хао́с; **a ~ of new ideas** це́лый водоворо́т но́вых иде́й.

cpd. **~-weight** *n.* боксёр/боре́ц второ́го полусре́днего ве́са.

wench [wentʃ] *n.* де́вка.

wend [wend] *v.t.*: **~ one's way** держа́ть (*impf.*) путь.

werewolf ['wɪəwʊlf, 'weə-] *n.* челове́к-волк; оборо́тень (*m.*).

west [west] *n.* за́пад; **in the ~** на за́паде; **to the ~ of** к за́паду от+*g.*; за́паднее +*g.*; **the W~** (*pol.*) За́пад; **the Wild W~** ди́кий за́пад; **W~ End** Уэст-Э́нд.

adv. к за́паду; на за́пад; **due ~ of** пря́мо на за́пад от+*g.*; **go ~** (*fig.*) (*coll., fig.*) умере́ть, исче́знуть, пропа́сть (*all pf.*).

westerly ['westəlɪ] *n.* (*wind*) за́падный ве́тер.

adj. за́падный; (*of wind*) с за́пада.

adv. (*westwards*) к за́паду, на за́пад.

western ['west(ə)n] *n.* ве́стерн, ковбо́йский рома́н/фильм.

adj. за́падный.

cpd. **~most** *adj.* са́мый за́падный.

westerner ['westənə(r)] *n.* жи́тель (*m.*) за́пада.

westernization [ˌwestənaɪ'zeɪʃ(ə)n] *n.* внедре́ние за́падного о́браза жи́зни.

westernize ['westəˌnaɪz] *v.t.* внедр|я́ть, -и́ть за́падный о́браз жи́зни в+*a.*

westward ['westwəd] *n.*: **to (the) ~** к за́паду, на за́пад.

adj. за́падный.

westwards ['westwədz] *adv.* к за́паду; на за́пад.

wet [wet] *n.* **1.** (*liquid; moisture*): **there is some ~ on the floor** на полу́ кака́я-то вода́. **2.** (*rain*): **come in out of the ~** входи́те, не сто́йте под дождём!

adj. **1.** (*covered, soaked or splashed with water etc.*) мо́крый; **~ through** (*or* **to the skin**) промо́кший до ни́тки; **her cheeks were ~ with tears** её лицо́ бы́ло мокры́м от слёз; **get ~** промо́кнуть (*pf.*); **I got my suit ~** мой костю́м промо́к; **~ suit** гидрокостю́м; **he's still ~ behind the ears** (*coll.*) у него́ молоко́ ещё на губа́х не обсо́хло. **2.** (*rainy*) дождли́вый; **we are in for a ~ spell** наступа́ет пери́од дожде́й. **3.** (*in liquid state*) сыро́й, жи́дкий; **~ paint** све́жая кра́ска; **'W~ Paint'** «осторо́жно, окра́шено!»; **the ink was still ~** черни́ла ещё не просо́хли. **4.** (*coll., inept; spineless*) вя́лый, малоду́шный.

v.t. (*make ~*) мочи́ть, на-; см|а́чивать, -очи́ть; **the child ~ itself** ребёнок обмочи́лся/опи́сался; **the child ~s its bed** ребёнок мо́чится в посте́ли.

cpd. **~-nurse** *n.* корми́лица.

whack [wæk] *n.* (*blow; sound of blow*) уда́р; звук уда́ра; (*coll., share*) зако́нная/причита́ющая до́ля.

v.t. (*coll., beat*) бить, по-; колоти́ть, от-; **I feel ~ed** (*exhausted*) я чу́вствую себя́ вконе́ц разби́тым.

whacking ['wækɪŋ] *n.* по́рка.

adj. & adv. (*sl.*) здоро́вый, здорове́нный; **a ~ (great) lie** чудо́вищная ложь.

whale [weɪl] *n.* **1.** кит. **2.: a ~ of a ...** (*coll.*) огро́мный; замеча́тельный; **we had a ~ of a time** мы потряса́юще/здо́рово провели́ вре́мя.

cpds. **~-boat** *n.* китобо́йное су́дно; **~bone** *n.* кито́вый ус; **~-oil** *n.* кито́вый жир.

whaler ['weɪlə(r)] *n.* (*man*) китобо́й; (*ship*) китобо́йное су́дно.

whaling ['weɪlɪŋ] *n.* охо́та на кито́в; китобо́йный про́мысел.

wham [wæm] *n. & int.* уда́р; бум!; хлоп!

v.t. уд|аря́ть, -а́рить в+*a.*

wharf [wɔːf] *n.* при́стань, на́бережная.

what [wɒt] *pron.* **1.** (*interrog.*) что?; что же?; **~'s that?** что э́то (тако́е)?; **~ (did you say)?** как (вы сказа́ли)?; что?; **~ is that in Russian?** как э́то по-ру́сски?; **~ is it?; ~'s the matter?** в чём де́ло?; **~ is he?** (*by occupation*) кто он?; кем он рабо́тает?; **~ is she like?** (*in appearance*) как она́ вы́глядит?; (*in character*) кака́я она́?; **~ do you want to be?** (*to a child*) кем ты хо́чешь стать?; **~ (sex) is their new baby?** кто у них роди́лся?; **~'s the weather like?** кака́я пого́да?; **~ does it look like?** как э́то вы́глядит?; **~ does it taste like?** како́во э́то на вкус?; **~ was the film like?** ну, как фильм?; **~ is the price?; ~ does it cost?** ско́лько э́то сто́ит?; **~'s the date?** како́е сего́дня число́?; **~ is his name?** как его́ зову́т?; как его́ фами́лия?; **~'s the news?** каки́е но́вости?; что слы́шно но́вого?; **~ do you think?** как вы ду́маете?; како́во ва́ше мне́ние?; **~ about money?** а де́ньги?; как насчёт де́нег?; **~ about the cat?** ну, а как ко́шка?; как быть с ко́шкой?; **~ about it?** (*what relevance has it?*) ну и что из э́того?; (*shall we?*) ну так как?; **~ about a walk?** не пройти́сь ли нам?; **~ of it?** ну и (да́льше) что?; ~ **does it matter?** какóе э́то имéет значéние?; ~ **for?** зачéм?; к чемý?; ~ **do I want this money for?** на что мне э́ти дéньги?; **I'll give you ~ for!** я вам покажý/дам!; ~**'s up?** (*coll.*) в чём дéло?; что случи́лось?; ~ **exactly?** что и́менно?; ~ **next!** ещё чегó!; до чегó дошли́!; **so ~?** (*coll.*) ну и что?; ~ **then?** (~ *do we do then*?) что тогдá (дéлать)?; (~ *happened then*?) а дáльше что?; ~ **if ...?** а что, как..?; ~ **if he refuses (after all)?** а вдруг он откáжется? **2.** (*rel.*: *that which*; *the things which*) (то), что; ~ **is so annoying is ...** что осóбенно досáдно, э́то...; **and, ~ is more ...** к томý же...; бóльше/мáло тогó,...; ~ **is missing is a guarantee** чегó нет — э́то гарáнтии; **this is ~ I mean** вот что я имéю в видý; **give me ~ you can** дáйте мнé скóлько мóжете; **she knows ~'s ~** онá знáет, что к чемý; **I'll see ~ I can do** я постарáюсь сдéлать, что могý; ~ **with one thing and another** из-за одногó, то из-за другóго. **3.** (*whatever*): **I will do ~ I can** я сдéлаю (всё), что могý; **come ~ may** что бы ни произошлó; будь что бýдет. **4.** (*exclamatory*): ~ **I wouldn't give for a cup of tea!** я бы всё отдáл за чáшку чáя; ~ **didn't we do!** чегó мы тóлько не дéлали!; ~ **a lot of ...** скóлько +*g.*!

adj. **1.** (*interrog.*) какóй; какóв?; ~ **colour are his eyes?** какóго цвéта у негó глазá?; ~ **chance is there of success?** каковы́ шáнсы на успéх?; ~ **kind of (a)** какóй; ~ **news is there?** что нóвого?; каки́е нóвости?; ~ **time is it?** котóрый час?; ~**'s the use?** какóй смысл?; **find out ~ trains there are** узнáть (*pf.*), каки́е есть поездá. **2.** (*rel.*): ~ **friends I make is no concern of yours** не вáше дéло, с кем я дружý; ~ **little he published** то немнóгое, что он напечáтал; **I gave him ~ money I had** я óтдал емý все дéньги, каки́е у меня́ бы́ли. **3.** (*exclamatory*): ~ **an idea!** что за идéя!; ~ **impudence!** какáя/каковá нáглость!; ~ **weather!** какáя (*or* что за *or* ну и) погóда!; погóда какáя!; ~ **was his surprise when ...** каковó бы́ло егó удивлéние, когдá...; ~ **lovely soup!** какóй прекрáсный суп.

cpds. ~**-d'ye-call-him,** ~**'s-his-name** *nn.* как егó там?; как бишь егó?; ~**-d'ye-call-it,** ~**'s it** *nn.* как егó; э́то сáмое...

whatever [wɒt'evə(r)] *pron.* **1.** (*anything that*): **do ~ you like** дéлайте, что хоти́те; дéлайте всё, что вам угóдно; ~ **I have is yours** всё моё — вáше. **2.** (*no matter what*): ~ **happens** что бы ни случи́лось. **3.** (*what ever*): ~ **are you doing?** чем вы там зáняты?; ~ **did you do that for?** ну, зачéм вы э́то сдéлали?; ~ **is wrong?** в чём (же) дéло?

adj. **1.** (*any*): **he took ~ food he could find** он забрáл всю пи́щу, какýю тóлько мог найти́. **2.** (*no matter what*) какóй бы ни; ~ **friends we may offend** пусть ины́е друзья́ и обижáются. **3.** (*emphasising neg. or interrog.*): **there is no doubt ~ of his guilt** в егó винóвности нет ни малéйшего сомнéния; **is there any chance ~ that he may recover?** есть ли хоть какóй-нибýдь шанс, что он попрáвится?; **he will see no one ~** он абсолю́тно никогó не принимáет.

whatsoever [ˌwɒtsəʊ'evə(r)] *pron.* = **whatever** *pron.* **1., 2.**

adj. = **whatever** *adj.*

wheat [wi:t] *n.* пшени́ца; **summer/winter ~** яровáя/ози́мая пшени́ца.

wheedle ['wi:d(ə)l] *v.t.* подоль|щáться, -сти́ться к+*d.*; ~ **sth. out of s.o.** выпрáшивать, вы́просить что-н. у когó-н.; вымáнивать, вы́манить что-н. у когó-н. лéстью.

wheel [wi:l] *n.* **1.** колесó; **spare ~** запаснóе колесó; **change a ~** (*on car*) меня́ть, по- колесó; **take the ~** сади́ться, сéсть за руль; **big ~** (*on fairground*) колесó обозрéния; чёртово колесó; (*sl.*, *bigwig*) (большáя) ши́шка; **break on the ~** колесовáть (*impf.*, *pf.*); **turn a pot on the ~** дéлать, с- горшóк на гончáрном крýге; **put a spoke in s.o.'s ~** (*fig.*) вст|авля́ть, -áвить комý-н. пáлки в колёса. **2.** (*mil.*): **they carried out a right ~** они́ сдéлали поворóт вправо.

v.t. катáть, вози́ть (*both indet.*); кати́ть (*det.*); везти́ (*det.*); **he ~ed his bicycle up the hill** он вкати́л велосипéд нá гору.

v.i. вертéться; вращáться; кружи́ть(ся) (*all impf.*); **gulls were ~ing overhead** чáйки кружи́ли(сь) над головóй; **he ~ed round to face me** он крýто повернýлся ко мне (*or* в мою́ стóрону).

cpds. ~**barrow** *n.* тáчка; ~**base** *n.* колёсная бáза; ~**-chair** *n.* инвали́дное крéсло; ~**-house** *n.* рулевáя рýбка; ~**wright** *n.* колéсник; колёсный мáстер.

wheeled [wi:ld] *adj.* колёсный, на колёсах.

wheeze [wi:z] *n.* (*chesty breathing*) хрип; сопéние; (*sl.*, *bright idea*; *scheme*) удáчная мысль; лóвкий трюк.

v.i. сопéть (*impf.*); хрипéть (*impf.*); дышáть (*impf.*) с при́свистом.

wheezy ['wi:zɪ] *adj.* хри́плый; страдáющий оды́шкой.

whelk [welk] *n.* (*mollusc*) брюхонóгий моллю́ск.

whelp [welp] *n.* (*puppy*, *also fig.*) щенóк.

v.i. щени́ться, о-.

when [wen] *adv.* **1.** (*interrog.*) когдá; **say ~!** (*to s.o. pouring a drink*) скажи́те, когдá довóльно. **2.** (*rel.*): **there have been occasions ~** бы́ли слýчаи, когдá...; **the day ~ I met you** день, когдá (*or* в котóрый) я вас встрéтил.

with preps.: ~ **do you have to be there by?** к какóму часý вам нýжно там быть?; ~ **must it be ready for?** когдá э́то должнó быть готóво?; ~ **does it date from?** к какóму врéмени э́то отнóсится?; **since ~?** с каки́х (э́то) пор?; с какóго врéмени?; **till, until ~?** до каки́х пор?; до какóго врéмени?

conj. когдá; как (тóлько); пóсле, тогó как; тогдá, когдá; (*by the time that*) покá; ~ **she saw him, she ...** уви́дев егó, онá...; ~ **he was grown up, he ...** когдá он вы́рос, он...; ~ **passing** проходя́ ми́мо; ~ **young** в мóлодости; **how can he buy it ~ he has no money?** как он мóжет э́то купи́ть, éсли у негó нет дéнег?

whence [wens] *adv. & conj.* (*liter.*) (*interrog.*) (*also* **from ~**) откýда; ~ **this confusion?** отчегó/почемý такóе смятéние.

whenever [wen'evə(r)] *adv. & conj.* **1.** (*at whatever time*) когдá; **come ~ you like** приходи́те, когдá тóлько захоти́те; ~ **he comes** когдá бы он ни пришёл. **2.** (*on every occasion when*) кáждый/вся́кий раз, когдá; ~ **he speaks he stammers** он всегдá заикáется, когдá говори́т. **3. or ~** (*coll.*, *at any time*) и́ли ещё когдá.

where [weə(r)] *adv.* **1.** (*direct or indirect question*) где; (*whither*) кудá; ~ **should we be without you?** что бы мы без вас дéлали?; ~ **did he hit you?** кудá он вас удáрил? **2.** (*rel.*) где; **the hotel ~ we stopped** гости́ница, в котóрой мы останови́лись; (*without antecedent*) там, где; **that's not ~ I left my coat** я не здесь/там остáвил пальтó; **that's ~ you're wrong** здéсь-то вы и ошибáетесь; **you can go ~ you please** мóжете идти́, кудá угóдно. **3.** (*whereas*) тогдá, как; в то врéмя как; **(in cases ~)** в тех слýчаях, когдá.

with preps.: ~ **from?** откýда; (*of origin*): ~ **does he come from?** откýда он (рóдом)?; ~ **to?** кудá?; ~ **have you got to in the story?** до какóго мéста вы дочитáли/дошли́?; **I've no idea ~ he can have got to** поня́тия не имéю, кудá он мог дéться.

whereabouts ['weərəˌbaʊts] *n.* местонахождéние.

adv. где; ~ **did you find it?** где вы э́то нашли́?

whereas [weər'æz] *conj.* **1.** (*while*) тогдá как; в то врéмя как; а; мéжду тем, как. **2.** (*leg.*, *since*) в видý того́, что; поско́льку; учи́тывая, что.

whereby [weə'baɪ] *adv.* (*liter.*) чем; посре́дством кото́рого; **there is a rule ~ ...** существу́ет пра́вило, согла́сно кото́рому...

wherefore ['weəfɔ:(r), -'fɔ:(r)] *n.*: **he wanted to know the why(s) and ~(s)** он хоте́л знать, как и почему́.
adv. (*arch.*, *why?*) почему́?

wherein [weər'ɪn] *adv.* (*interrog.*, *rel.*) где; в кото́ром; в чём.

whereof [weər'ɒv] *rel. adv.* (*liter.*) из кото́рого; о ком; о чём; **the person ~ I spoke** лицо́, о кото́ром я говори́л.

whereon [weər'ɒn] *rel. adv.* (*liter.*) на кото́ром.

whereupon [ˌweərə'pɒn, 'weər-] *adv.* (*and then*) по́сле чего́; всле́дствие чего́; на э́то.

wherever [weər'evə(r)] *adj. & conj.* где; куда́; **sit ~ you like** сади́тесь, куда́ уго́дно; **~ he goes he makes friends** где бы он ни оказа́лся, он приобрета́ет друзе́й; **or ~** (*coll.*) и́ли ещё где; (*where ever*): **~ are you going?** куда́ же вы идёте?

wherewithal ['weəwɪˌðɔ:l] *n.* (*coll.*) необходи́мые сре́дства; **I haven't the ~ to pay him** мне не́чем с ним расплати́ться.

whet [wet] *v.t.* точи́ть, на-; (*fig.*) обостр|я́ть, -и́ть; возбу|жда́ть, -ди́ть.
cpd. **~stone** *n.* точи́льный ка́мень; (*lit.*, *fig.*) осело́к.

whether ['weðə(r)] *conj.* **1.** (*introducing indirect question*) ли; **I asked ~ he was coming with us** я спроси́л, пойдёт ли он с на́ми; **the question is ~ to go or stay** вопро́с в том — идти́ и́ли остава́ться; **it depends on ~ I am free tonight** э́то зави́сит от того́, бу́ду ли я свобо́ден сего́дня ве́чером. **2.** (*introducing alternative hypotheses*): **~ you like it or not, I shall go** нра́вится вам э́то и́ли нет, а я пойду́; **~ or no** всё равно́; во вся́ком (*or* в любо́м) слу́чае.

whew [hwju:] *int.* уф!

whey [weɪ] *n.* сы́воротка.

which [wɪtʃ] *pron.* **1.** (*interrog.*) како́й, кото́рый; (*of pers.*) кто; **~ is the right answer?** како́й отве́т пра́вильный?; **~ is the way to the museum?** как пройти́ в музе́й?; **~ of you?** кто/кото́рый из вас?; **~ do you want, milk or cream?** что вы предпочита́ете — молоко́ и́ли сли́вки? **2.** (*rel.*, *in defining and non-defining senses*) кото́рый; **the book (~) I was reading has gone** кни́га, кото́рую я чита́л, пропа́ла; **the hotel at ~ we stayed** гости́ница, в кото́рой (*or* где) мы жи́ли/останови́лись; (*with adj. or descriptive n. as antecedent*): **he looked like a boxer, ~ indeed he was** он был похо́ж на боксёра, каковы́м он, со́бственно, и явля́лся; (*with clause as antecedent*) что; **he refused, ~ I had expected** он отказа́л, чего́ я, со́бственно, и ожида́л.
adj. **1.** (*direct or indirect question*) кото́рый; **~ shoes are yours?** каки́е тут боти́нки/ту́фли ва́ши?; **~ film do you mean?** како́й фильм вы име́ете в виду́?; **~ brother runs the business?** кото́рый из бра́тьев возглавля́ет де́ло?; **do you know ~ horse won?** вы (не) зна́ете, кака́я ло́шадь вы́играла? **2.** (*rel.*) како́й; кото́рый; каково́й; **10 years, during ~ time he spoke to nobody** де́сять лет, в тече́ние кото́рых он ни с кем не говори́л.

whichever [ˌwɪtʃsəʊ'evə(r)] *pron. & adj.* како́й бы ни; **take ~ book you like** бери́те любу́ю кни́гу, каку́ю хоти́те; **~ of you comes in first wins the prize** кто из вас придёт пе́рвым, полу́чит приз; **~ way you go, you'll have plenty of time** како́й бы доро́гой вы ни пошли́, вы вполне́ успе́ете.

whiff [wɪf] *n.* дунове́ние; (*pleasant smell*) лёгкий арома́т; (*unpleasant*) душо́к; (*of smoke etc.*) за́пах, дымо́к; **a ~ of chloroform** глото́к хлорофо́рма; **he stepped out for a ~ of fresh air** он вы́шел подыша́ть (све́жим во́здухом).

while [waɪl] *n.* вре́мя; **where have you been all this ~?** где вы бы́ли всё э́то вре́мя?; **after a ~** че́рез не́которое вре́мя; **I am going away for a ~** я уезжа́ю ненадо́лго (*or* на не́которое вре́мя); **I haven't seen you for a long ~** я вас давно́ не ви́дел; **a short ~ before** незадо́лго до (э́того); **a short ~ ago** неда́вно; **in a little, short ~** ско́ро, вско́ре; **once in a ~** и́зредка; вре́мя от вре́мени; **it was well worth ~** э́то сто́ило (затра́ченного вре́мени/труда́).
v.t.: **~ away:** корота́ть, с- (*время*).
conj. (*also* **whilst**) **1.** (*during the time that*) пока́; в то вре́мя, как; во вре́мя того́, как; **be good ~ I'm away!** веди́ себя́ хорошо́, пока́ меня́ нет до́ма; **~ reading he fell asleep** за чте́нием (*or* чита́я) он засну́л; **~ asleep** во сне; **write ~ I dictate** пиши́те, а я бу́ду диктова́ть; **~ in Paris I visited the Louvre** во вре́мя (моего́) пребыва́ния в Пари́же, я пошёл в Лувр. **2.** (*whereas*) а; тогда́ как. **3.** (*although*) хотя́.

whilst [waɪlst] = **while** *conj.*

whim [wɪm] *n.* при́хоть, капри́з.

whimper ['wɪmpə(r)] *n.* хны́канье.
v.t. & i. (*of pers.*) хны́кать, по-; (*of a dog*) скули́ть (*impf.*).

whimsical ['wɪmzɪk(ə)l] *adj.* прichу́дливый; капри́зный; игри́вый.

whimsy ['wɪmzɪ] *n.* при́хоть, причу́да, капри́з.

whin|e [waɪn] *n.* вой; хны́канье; нытьё; **the ~e of a shell** вой снаря́да; **the ~e of machinery** гул маши́н.
v.i. скули́ть (*impf.*); хны́кать (*impf.*); **the dog was ~ing to come in** соба́ка скули́ла у две́ри, что́бы её впусти́ли; (*fig.*, *complain*) хны́кать (*impf.*); ныть (*impf.*).

whinge [wɪndʒ] = **whine** *v.i.* (*complain*).

whinny ['wɪnɪ] *n.* ти́хое/ра́достное ржа́ние.
v.i. ти́хо/ра́достно ржать, за-.

whip [wɪp] *n.* **1.** (*lash*) кнут, хлыст; **have the ~ hand over s.o.** (*fig.*) име́ть (*impf.*) кого́-н. в по́лном подчине́нии. **2.** (*party official*) организа́тор парла́ментской фра́кции.
v.t. **1.** (*flog*) поро́ть, вы́-; хлеста́ть, от-; сечь, вы́-; **~ping-boy** (*fig.*, *scapegoat*) «ма́льчик для битья́»; козёл отпуще́ния; (*fig.*): **the wind ~ped the waves into a fury** во́лны я́ростно вздыма́лись под ве́тром. **2.** (*beat into froth*) взби|ва́ть, -ть; **~ped cream** взби́тые сли́вки. **3.** (*coll.*, *move rapidly*): **as I entered he ~ped the papers into a drawer** когда́ я вошёл, он бы́стро су́нул бума́ги в я́щик; **she ~ped the cake out of the oven** она́ бы́стро вы́тащила торт из пе́чи/духо́вки.
v.i. (*coll.*, *move rapidly*) рвану́ться, бро́ситься, (*both pf.*); **he ~ped into the shop** он влете́л в магази́н.
with advs.: **~ back** *v.i.*: **the branch ~ped back in my face** пле́тка разогну́лась и хлестну́ла меня́ по лицу́; **~ off** *v.t.* (*coll.*): **the wind ~ped off my hat** ве́тром сби́ло мою́ шля́пу; **~ out** *v.t.* (*coll.*): **~ping out a knife** выхва́тив нож; *v.i.* (*coll.*): **he ~ped out for a breath of air** он вы́скочил на мину́ту глотну́ть све́жего во́здуха; **~ round** *v.i.* (*coll.*): **he ~ped round to face me** он кру́то оберну́лся ко мне; **~ up** *v.t.* (*beat into froth*) взби|ва́ть, -ть; (*fig.*, *stimulate*): **~ up enthusiasm** возбу|жда́ть, -ди́ть энтузиа́зм; (*coll.*, *improvise*) де́лать, с- на ско́рую ру́ку; **she ~ped up a nice supper** она́ бы́стро состря́пала вку́сный у́жин.
cpds. **~lash** *n.* реме́нь (*m.*) (кнута́), бечева́ (пле́ти); **~-round** *n.* (*coll.*, *collection*) сбор де́нег (на благотвори́тельные це́ли).

whipper-snapper ['wɪpəˌsnæpə(r)] *n.* молокосо́с, щено́к.

whirl [wɜ:l] *n.* **1.** (*revolving or eddying movement*) круже́ние; (*fig.*) смяте́ние, неразбери́ха; **my brain is in a ~** у меня́ голова́ идёт круго́м. **2.** (*bustling* *activity*) водоворо́т, вихрь (*m.*).

v.t. & i. **1.** (*swing round and round*) верте́ть(ся) (*impf.*); кружи́ть(ся) (*impf.*); **the leaves ~ed about in the wind** ли́стья кружи́лись на ветру́. **2.** (*hurry; dash*) нести́сь (*impf.*); **the trees and hedges ~ed past** дере́вья и кусты́ проноси́лись ми́мо.

cpds. **~pool** *n.* водоворо́т; **~wind** *n.* вихрь (*m.*), урага́н; (*fig., attr.*) стра́стный, бу́рный.

whirligig ['wɜ:lɪgɪg] *n.* **1.** (*top*) юла́, волчо́к. **2.** (*roundabout*) карусе́ль. **3.** (*fig.*) водоворо́т, вихрь (*m.*), круговоро́т.

whirr [wɜ:(r)] *n.* жужжа́ние.

v.i. жужжа́ть (*impf.*).

whisk [wɪsk] *n.* **1.** (*small brush or similar device*) ве́ничек, метёлочка. **2.** (*for beating eggs, cream etc.*) муто́вка.

v.t. **1.** (*flap; brush*) сма́х|ивать, -ну́ть; **she ~ed the dust under the carpet** она́ бы́стро замела́ пыль под ковёр. **2.** (*beat, e.g. eggs*) взб|ива́ть, -ить.

v.i. (*move briskly*) мча́ться, по-.

with advs.: **~ about** *v.t.* (*wave; brandish*) маха́ть (*impf.*); **~ away** *v.t.*: **he ~ed away the flies with his handkerchief** он отогна́л мух платко́м; **~ off** *v.t.* (*convey quickly*) бы́стро ун|оси́ть, -ести́ (*or* ув|оди́ть, -ести́); **he was ~ed off in an ambulance** его́ умча́ла каре́та ско́рой по́мощи.

whisker ['wɪskə(r)] *n.* (*pl., facial hair*) ба́к|и (*pl., g.* —); бакенба́рды (*f. pl.*); (*of animal*) усы́ (*m. pl.*).

whiskered ['wɪskəd] *adj.* (*of pers.*) нося́щий ба́ки; с бакенба́рдами/ба́чками; (*of cat etc.*) уса́тый.

whisk(e)y ['wɪskɪ] *n.* ви́ски (*nt. indecl.*); **~ and soda** ви́ски с со́довой.

whisper ['wɪspə(r)] *n.* шёпот; **he spoke in a ~** он говори́л шёпотом; (*rumour*) слух, молва́; (*sibilant sound*) шо́рох, ше́лест.

v.t. & i. **1.** (*speak, say in ~s*) шепта́ть(ся) (*impf.*); говори́ть (*impf.*) шёпотом; **she ~ed her secret to me** она́ шепну́ла/прошепта́ла мне свою́ та́йну на́ ухо. **2.** (*make ~ing noise*) шелесте́ть (*impf.*); шурша́ть (*impf.*).

whist [wɪst] *n.* (*card game*) вист.

whistle ['wɪs(ə)l] *n.* **1.** (*sound*) свист, свисто́к. **2.** (*instrument*) свисто́к; (*factory ~*) гудо́к; **blow the/a ~** св|исте́ть, -и́стнуть. **3.** (*fig.*) **wet one's ~** (*coll.*) промочи́ть (*pf.*) го́рло.

v.t. **1.** (*call by ~ing*) сви́стнуть (*pf.*); **he ~d his dog back** он сви́стом подозва́л (к себе́) соба́ку. **2.** (*produce by ~ing*) св|исте́ть, -и́стнуть; **can you ~ the tune?** вы мо́жете насвисте́ть моти́в э́той пе́сни?

v.i. св|исте́ть, про-, сви́стнуть; да|ва́ть, -ть свисто́к; **the train ~d as it entered the tunnel** при вхо́де в тунне́ль по́езд дал свисто́к; **the wind ~s in the chimney** ве́тер завыва́ет в трубе́; **when the kettle ~s** когда́ ча́йник засвисти́т; **a bullet ~d past him** пу́ля просвисте́ла ми́мо него́.

whit[1] [wɪt] *n.* (*arch.*) ка́пля, йо́та.

Whit[2] [wɪt] *adj.*: **~ Monday** Ду́хов день; **~ Sunday** = **Whitsun**.

white [waɪt] *n.* **1.** (*colour*) бе́лый цвет; белизна́; **off ~** (*adj.*) белова́тый; (*clothes*): **she was wearing ~** она́ была́ в бе́лом; **dressed in ~** оде́тый в бе́лое; (*paint*) бе́лая кра́ска; бели́л|а (*pl., g.* —). **2.** (*of the eyes*) бело́к. **3.** (*of an egg*) бело́к. **4.** (*racial type*) белоко́жий, бе́лый. **5.** (*chess*) бе́лые (*pl.*); **it was W~'s move** был ход бе́лых.

adj. бе́лый; **grow ~** беле́ть, по-; **his hair turned ~** он поседе́л; **he turned ~** он побледне́л; **a ~ Christmas** Рождество́ со сне́гом; **~ coffee** ко́фе с молоко́м; **~ heat** бе́лое кале́ние; **the W~ House** Бе́лый дом; **~ lead** свинцо́вые бели́ла; **a ~ lie** ложь во спасе́ние; **W~ Paper** Бе́лая кни́га; **~ sugar** (са́хар-)рафина́д; рафини́рованный са́хар; **~ tie and tails** фрак.

cpds. **~bait** *n.* малёк; **~-collar** *adj.*: **~-collar worker** *n.* слу́жащий; **~-haired** *adj.* белоголо́вый; седо́й; **~-hot** *adj.* раскалённый добела́; **~wash** *n.* побе́лка; (*fig.*) обеле́ние; зама́зывание (недоста́тков); *v.t.* бели́ть, по-; (*fig.*) обел|я́ть, -и́ть; зама́з|ывать, -ать.

whiten ['waɪt(ə)n] *v.t.* бели́ть, по-.

whitener ['waɪt(ə)nə(r)] *n.*: **coffee ~** осветли́тель (*m.*) ко́фе.

whiteness ['waɪtnɪs] *n.* белизна́; бе́лый цвет.

whither ['wɪðə(r)] *adv.* (*liter.*) куда́.

whiting ['waɪtɪŋ] *n.* (*fish*) хек; мерла́нг.

whitish ['waɪtɪʃ] *adj.* белёсый; белова́тый.

Whitsun ['wɪts(ə)n] *n.* (*Whit Sunday*) Тро́ицын день, Тро́ица; *see also* **Whit**[2]

whittle ['wɪt(ə)l] *v.t.* строга́ть, вы-; **he ~d a twig into a whistle** он вы́строгал (себе́) свисто́к из ве́тки.

with advs.: **~ away** *v.t.* состру́г|ивать, -а́ть; (*fig.*) ум|еньша́ть, -е́ньшить; св|оди́ть, -ести́ на нет; **his savings were ~d away** его́ сбереже́ния постепе́нно истя́кли; **~ down** *v.t.* состру́г|ивать, -а́ть; (*fig.*) сн|ижа́ть, -и́зить.

whiz(z) [wɪz] *n.* свист.

v.i. прон|оси́ться, -ести́сь со сви́стом; мча́ться, про-; просвисте́ть (*pf.*).

cpd. **~-kid** *n.* (*coll.*) ≃ восходя́щая звезда́.

who [hu:] *pron.* **1.** (*interrog.*) кто; **~ is he?** кто он (тако́й)?; э́то кто?; **~ does he think he is?** что он о себе́ вообража́ет?; **~ am I to object?** како́е я име́ю пра́во возража́ть?; **~ goes there?** (*mil.*) кто идёт?; **~(m)ever do you mean?** кого́ же вы име́ете в виду́?; **he knows ~'s ~** он зна́ет, кто есть кто. **2.** (*rel.*) кото́рый, како́й, кто; **those ~** те, кто/кото́рые; **anyone ~** вся́кий, кто; **the sort of people ~m we need** таки́е лю́ди, каки́е нам нужны́.

whoa, wo [wəʊ] *int.* тпру!

whodunit [hu:'dʌnɪt] *n.* (*sl.*) детекти́вный рома́н/фильм.

whoever [hu:'evə(r)] *pron.* **1.** (*anyone who; no matter who; also arch.* **whosoever**) кто бы ни; **~ comes will be welcome** кто бы ни пришёл, бу́дет жела́нным го́стем. **2.** (*who ever*) кто то́лько; **~ would have thought it?** кто бы мог поду́мать?

whole [həʊl] *n.* (*single entity*) це́лое; (*totality*) все, всё; **the ~ of the audience** вся аудито́рия; **taken as a ~** в це́лом; **on the ~** в о́бщем (и це́лом).

adj. **1.** (*intact; unbroken; undamaged*) це́лый, невреди́мый. **2.** (*in one piece*) целико́м. **3.** (*full; complete; entire*) весь, це́лый, це́льный; **two ~ glasses** це́лых два стака́на; **the ~ lot** всё; (*people*) все; **a ~ number** це́лое число́; **~ milk** це́льное молоко́; **the ~ world** весь мир; **his ~ life through** на протяже́нии всей его́ жи́зни.

cpds. **~-hearted** *adj.* беззаве́тный; **~-heartedly** от всей души́; **~meal** *adj.*: **a ~meal loaf** буха́нка хле́ба из непросе́янной муки́; **~sale** *n.* опто́вая торго́вля; **sell sth. by (*US* at) ~sale** прод|ава́ть, -а́ть о́птом; *adj.* опто́вый; (*fig.*) ма́ссовый; *adv.* о́птом; (*fig.*) в ма́ссовом масшта́бе; **~saler** *n.* оптови́к.

wholefood ['həʊlfu:d] *n.* натура́льные проду́кты.

adj. натура́льный.

wholefooder ['həʊlfu:də(r)] *n.* натури́ст.

wholeness ['həʊlnɪs] *n.* (*integrality*) це́льность, це́лость.

wholesome ['həʊlsəm] *adj.* **1.** (*promoting health*) поле́зный, здоро́вый; **~ food** здоро́вая пи́ща. **2.** (*sound; prudent*) здра́вый, благотво́рный; **I gave him some ~ advice** я ему́ дал поле́зный сове́т.

wholly ['həʊllɪ] *adv.* по́лностью; целико́м; **I am ~ at a loss** я в по́лном/соверше́нном недоуме́нии.

whoop [hu:p, wu:p] *n.* во́зглас; вопль (*m.*); **with a ~ of joy** с ра́достным кри́ком.

v.i. **1.** издава́ть (*impf.*) во́пли; **~ing-cough** коклю́ш.

2.: ~ it up (*sl.*) бу́рно весели́ться (*impf.*); кути́ть (*impf.*).

whoops [wʊps] *int.* (*coll.*) оп!

whopper ['wɒpə(r)] *n.* (*sl.*) **1.** (*anything very large*) грома́дина, махи́на. **2.** (*outrageous lie*) чудо́вищная ложь.

whopping ['wɒpɪŋ] (*sl.*) *adj.* (*also* **~ great**) огро́мный, чудо́вищный, здорове́нный.

whore [hɔ:(r)] *n.* шлю́ха.

cpd. **~-house** *n.* барда́к, борде́ль (*m.*).

whorl [wɔ:l, wɜ:l] *n.* вито́к, завито́к; (*bot.*) муто́вка; (*of finger-prints*) пальцево́й узо́р.

whortleberry ['wɜ:t(ə)l,berɪ] *n.* черни́ка (*collect.*).

whose [hu:z] *pron.* (*interrog.*) чей; **~ partner are you?** чей вы партнёр?; (*rel.*) чей, кото́рого; **the people ~ house we bought** лю́ди, у кото́рых мы купи́ли дом.

whosoever [,hu:səʊ'evə(r)] *pron.* (*arch.*) = **whoever 1.**

why [waɪ] *adv.* почему́, заче́м; **'Are you married?' — 'No, ~?'** «вы жена́ты?» — «Нет, а что?»; **~ not?** почему́?; почему́ бы нет?; **~ not let me help you?** дава́йте я вам помогу́; **the reasons ~ ...** соображе́ния, по кото́рым…

int. да; ведь; **~, of course** да, коне́чно; **~, what's the harm in it?** а что в э́том плохо́го?; **~ yes, I suppose so** да наве́рное э́то так.

wick [wɪk] *n.* фити́ль (*m.*).

wicked ['wɪkɪd] *adj.* (*depraved*) гре́шный, поро́чный; (*malicious*) злой, зло́бный; (*roguish*) лука́вый; **she gave him a ~ glance** она́ лука́во взгляну́ла на него́; (*coll., disgraceful*) ужа́сный, безобра́зный; **a ~ shame** безобра́зие.

wickedness ['wɪkɪdnɪs] *n.* (*depravity*) грех, поро́чность; (*malice*) зло́ба.

wicker ['wɪkə(r)] *n.* пру́тья (*m. pl.*) для плете́ния; **~ chair** плетёное кре́сло.

cpd. **~work** *n.* плете́ние; плетёные изде́лия.

wicket ['wɪkɪt] *n.* **1. (~-gate)** кали́тка. **2.** (*at cricket*) воро́тц|а (*pl., g.* -ев).

cpd. **~-keeper** *n.* ловя́щий мяч за воро́тцами (*в крикете*).

wide [waɪd] *adj.* **1.** широ́кий; (*in measuring*) шириной в+*a.*, **the table is 3 feet ~** стол ширино́й в 3 фу́та. **2.** (*extensive*) большо́й, широ́кий, обши́рный; **~ experience** большо́й/бога́тый о́пыт; **~ interests** широ́кий круг интере́сов; **a ~ choice** широ́кий вы́бор; **the ~ world over** во всём ми́ре; по всему́ (бе́лому) све́ту. **3.** (*off target*): **his answer was ~ of the mark** он попа́л па́льцем в не́бо.

adv. **1.** (*extensively*): **far and ~** повсю́ду; вдоль и поперёк. **2.** (*to full extent*): **open the door ~!** откро́йте дверь на́стежь! **3.** (*off target*) ми́мо це́ли; **shoot ~** стреля́ть (*impf.*) ми́мо це́ли.

cpds. **~-angle** *adj.*: **~-angle lens** широкоуго́льная ли́нза; **~-awake** *adj.* бди́тельный, начеку́; **~-eyed** *adj.* (*surprised*) изумлённый; **~-ranging** *adj.* (*intellect etc.*) разносторо́нний; **~spread** *adj.* распространённый.

widely ['waɪdlɪ] *adv.* **1.** (*to a large extent*) широ́ко́; **~ differing opinions** ре́зко расходя́щиеся мне́ния. **2.** (*over a large area*) далеко́; **~ scattered** разбро́санный; **it is ~ known** широко́ изве́стно; **it is ~ believed that ...** мно́гие счита́ют, что…

widen ['waɪd(ə)n] *v.t. & i.* расш|иря́ть(ся), -и́рить(ся); **they are ~ing the road** веду́тся рабо́ты по расшире́нию доро́ги.

widow ['wɪdəʊ] *n.* вдова́; **become a ~** стать (*pf.*) вдово́й; овдове́ть (*pf.*); **war ~** же́нщина, потеря́вшая му́жа на войне́.

v.t. де́лать, с- вдово́й.

widower ['wɪdəʊə(r)] *n.* вдове́ц.

widowhood ['wɪdəʊ,hʊd] *n.* вдовство́.

width [wɪtθ, wɪdθ] *n.* **1.** (*measurement*) ширина́; **the river is 2 miles in ~** река́ име́ет 2 ми́ли ширины́ (*or* в ширину́). **2.** (*piece of material*) поло́тнище. **3.** (*wide extent*) широта́.

cpds. **~ways, ~wise** *advs.* в ширину́.

wield [wi:ld] *v.t.* держа́ть (*impf.*) в рука́х; **~ an axe** рабо́тать (*impf.*) топоро́м; **~ authority** по́льзоваться (*impf.*) вла́стью.

wife [waɪf] *n.* **1.** (*spouse*) жена́; **he made her his ~** он на ней жени́лся; **the President's ~** супру́га президе́нта; **common-law ~** гражда́нская/неве́нчанная жена́; подру́га. **2.** (*arch., old woman*) стару́ха, ба́бка; **old wives' tales** ба́бьи ска́зки (*f. pl.*).

wig [wɪg] *n.* пари́к.

wiggle ['wɪg(ə)l] *n.* пока́чивание, ёрзание.

v.t. пока́чивать (*impf.*); виля́ть (*impf.*); **the baby ~d its toes** ребёнок шевели́л па́льцами ног.

v.i. (*e.g. a loose tooth*) шата́ться (*impf.*), кача́ться (*impf.*).

wiggly ['wɪglɪ] *adj.*: **a ~ line** волни́стая ли́ния.

wigwam ['wɪgwæm] *n.* вигва́м.

wild [waɪld] *n.* **1.** (**~** *state*): **this animal is not found in the ~** э́то живо́тное не во́дится на во́ле. **2.** (*pl., desert or uncultivated tract*) де́бр|и (*pl., g.* -ей); **the ~s of Africa** де́бри А́фрики.

adj. **1.** (*not domesticated; not cultivated*) ди́кий; **~ boar** каба́н; **~ flower** полево́й цвето́к; **~ goose chase** (*fig.*) бессмы́сленное предприя́тие; **in the ~ state** в ди́ком состоя́нии/ви́де, на во́ле. **2.** (*not civilized*) ди́кий; **~ man** (*savage*) дика́рь (*m.*). **3.** (*of scenery: desolate, uninhabited*) ди́кий, пусты́нный. **4.** (*of birds etc.: easily startled*) пугли́вый. **5.** (*unrestrained, wayward, disorderly*) необу́зданный, бу́рный, бу́йный; (*dissolute*) разгу́льный; **everything was in ~ confusion** (там) цари́л стра́шный беспоря́док; **he let the garden run ~** он запусти́л сад. **6.** (*tempestuous*) бу́рный, бу́йный; **it was a ~ sea** мо́ре бушева́ло. **7.** (*excited, passionate, frantic*) вне себя́; **~ with rage/delight** вне себя́ от я́рости/восто́рга; **he drives me ~** он меня́ из себя́ выво́дит; **they were ~ about him** они́ бы́ли в (ди́ком) восто́рге от него́; **~ laughter** бе́шеный хо́хот. **8.** (*reckless; ill-considered*) безу́мный; неле́пый; **a ~ scheme** безу́мная зате́я; **a ~ shot** вы́стрел науга́д.

adv. наобу́м; науга́д.

cpds. **~-cat** *adj.*: **~-cat strike** неофициа́льная забасто́вка; **~fire** *n.*: **the news spread like ~fire** но́вость распространи́лась с молниено́сной быстрото́й; **~fowl** *n.* дичь.

wilderness ['wɪldənɪs] *n.* ди́кая ме́стность; пусты́ня; **a voice crying in the ~** (*fig.*) глас вопию́щего в пусты́не; (*neglected garden*) запу́щенный сад.

wildlife ['waɪldlaɪf] *n.* жива́я приро́да; **~ sanctuary** запове́дник; **~ photography** фотоохо́та.

wile [waɪl] *n.* (*liter.*) хи́трость, уло́вка; (*pl.*) ухищре́ния (*nt. pl.*).

wilful ['wɪlfʊl] (*US* **willful**) *adj.* **1.** (*of pers., headstrong, refractory*) своенра́вный, упря́мый. **2.** (*intentional*) умы́шленный, преднаме́ренный; **~ disobedience** созна́тельное неповинове́ние.

will[1] [wɪl] *n.* **1.** (*faculty; its exercise; determination, intent*) во́ля; **free ~** свобо́да во́ли; **he has a ~ of his own** он челове́к упря́мый/своево́льный; **against my ~** вопреки́ моему́ влия́нию; **lack of ~** безво́лие, отсу́тствие си́лы во́ли; **the ~ to live** во́ля к жи́зни; **of one's own free ~** доброво́льно, по со́бственной во́ле. **2.** (*energy; enthusiasm*) эне́ргия; **go to work with a ~** рабо́тать (*impf.*) энерги́чно. **3.** (*discretion, desire*) жела́ние, во́ля; **he came and went at ~** он приходи́л и уходи́л, когда́ хоте́л. **4.** (*disposition*) расположе́ние; **I feel no ill ~ towards him** я на него́ не в оби́де; **men of good ~** лю́ди до́брой во́ли. **5.** (*disposition of property*) завеща́ние; **last ~ and testament** после́дняя во́ля; **make, draw up**

one's ~ сде́лать (*pf.*) завеща́ние.

v.t. **1.** (*compel*) заст|авля́ть, -а́вить; **he ~ed himself to stay (*or* into staying) awake** (уси́лием во́ли) он заста́вил себя́ бо́дрствовать. **2.: God ~ing** е́сли на то бу́дет во́ля бо́жья. **3.** (*bequeath*) завеща́ть (*impf.*, *pf.*).

cpd. **~-power** *n.* си́ла во́ли.

will[2] [wɪl] *v.t. & i.* (*see also* **would**) **1.** (*expr. future*): **he ~ be president** он бу́дет президе́нтом; **in five minutes it ~ be midnight** че́рез пять мину́т насту́пит по́лночь; **tomorrow ~ be Tuesday** за́втра — вто́рник; **he said he would be back by 3** он сказа́л, что вернётся к трём; **I won't do it again** я бо́льше не бу́ду. **2.** (*expr. wish, insistence*): **let him do what he ~** пусть де́лает, что хо́чет; **he ~ always have his own way** он всегда́ настои́т на своём. **3.** (*expr. willingness*): **I ~ come with you** я пойду́ с ва́ми; **~ (*or* won't) you come in?** войди́те, пожа́луйста!; **he won't help me** он не хо́чет мне помо́чь; **the window won't open** окно́ ника́к не открыва́ется. **4.** (*expr. inevitability*): **boys ~ be boys** ма́льчики есть ма́льчики; **accidents ~ happen** несча́стных слу́чаев не избежа́ть. **5.** (*expr. habit*): **he ~/would sit there for hours on end** он проси́живает/проси́живал там часа́ми; **he would often come to see me** он ча́сто заходи́л ко мне. **6.** (*expr. surmise, probability*): **this ~ be the book you're looking for** вот, ве́рно, кни́га, кото́рую вы и́щете.

willful ['wɪlfʊl] = **wilful**

willies ['wɪlɪz] *n.* (*sl.*): **it gives me the ~** у меня́ от э́того мура́шки по спине́ (бе́гают).

willing ['wɪlɪŋ] *adj.* **1.** (*readily disposed*) скло́нный, располо́женный; **~ workers** усе́рдные рабо́тники; **I am ~ to admit ...** я гото́в призна́ть...; **show ~** прояв|ля́ть, -и́ть гото́вность; **'Will you do me a favour?' — 'W~ly!'** «Вы мо́жете сде́лать мне одолже́ние?» — «Охо́тно!». **2.** (*readily given or shown*) доброво́льный.

willingness ['wɪlɪŋnɪs] *n.* гото́вность, жела́ние.

will-o'-the-wisp [ˌwɪləðə'wɪsp] *n.* блужда́ющий огонёк.

willow ['wɪləʊ] *n.* и́ва; **pussy ~** ве́рба; **weeping ~** плаку́чая и́ва.

cpd. **~-herb** *n.* кипре́й.

willowy ['wɪləʊɪ] *adj.* то́нкий, ги́бкий, стро́йный.

willy-nilly [ˌwɪlɪ'nɪlɪ] *adv.* во́лей-нево́лей; хо́чешь не хо́чешь.

wilt [wɪlt] *v.i.* (*lit., fig.*) ни́кнуть, по-; пон|ика́ть, -и́кнуть; **~ing enthusiasm** ослабева́ющий энтузиа́зм.

wily ['waɪlɪ] *adj.* хи́трый, лука́вый.

wimp [wɪmp] *n.* слизня́к, сопля́к.

wimpish ['wɪmpɪʃ] *adj.* бесхара́ктерный.

win [wɪn] *n.* (*gain*) вы́игрыш; (*victory*) побе́да; **it was an easy ~ for them** они́ с лёгкостью вы́играли.

v.t. **1.** (*be victorious in*) выи́грывать, вы́играть; **~ a race** побе|жда́ть, -ди́ть в забе́ге; **who won the election?** кто вы́играл на вы́борах?; **~ the day** одержа́ть (*pf.*) побе́ду. **2.** (*gain*) получ|а́ть, -и́ть; выи́грывать, вы́играть; **he won £5 from me** он вы́играл у меня́ 5 фу́нтов; **~ a medal** завоёв|ывать, -а́ть меда́ль; **~ a prize** вы́играть/взять (*pf.*) приз; **~ s.o.'s heart** покор|я́ть, -и́ть чьё-н. се́рдце; **~ s.o.'s confidence** сни́ск|ивать, -а́ть (*or* войти́ (*pf.*) в) чьё-н. дове́рие.

v.i.: **~ hands down** вы́играть (*pf.*) без труда́ (*or* с лёгкостью); **~ on points** вы́играть (*pf.*) по очка́м.

with advs.: **~ back** *v.t.* оты́гр|ывать, -а́ть; **~ over, ~ round** *vv.t.* угов|а́ривать, -ори́ть; **he cannot be won round** его́ нельзя́ уговори́ть; **~ through** *v.i.* проб|ива́ться, и́ться.

wince [wɪns] *n.*: **with a ~** вздро́гнув.

v.i. содрог|а́ться, -ну́ться; мо́рщиться, по-.

winch [wɪntʃ] *n.* лебёдка, во́рот.

v.t. подн|има́ть, -я́ть с по́мощью лебёдки.

wind[1] [wɪnd] *n.* **1.** ве́тер; **high ~** си́льный ве́тер; **fair ~** попу́тный ве́тер; **strong ~** ре́зкий ве́тер; **the ~ blew hard** дул кре́пкий ве́тер; **get, catch ~ of** (*fig.*) пронюх|ивать, -ать. **2.** (*var. fig. uses*): **he ran like the ~** он мча́лся как ве́тер; **fling caution to the ~s** отбро́сить (*pf.*) вся́кую осторо́жность; **I must see how the ~ blows** мне ну́жно поня́ть, куда́ ве́тер ду́ет; **it took the ~ out of his sails** (*fig.*) э́то обескура́жило его́; **there is something in the ~** что́-то назрева́ет/затева́ется. **3.** (*breath*) дыха́ние; **out of ~** запыха́вшись; **lose one's ~** запыха́ться (*pf.*); **get back one's ~** отдыша́ться (*pf.*); **get one's second ~** обре|та́ть, -сти́ второ́е дыха́ние. **4.** (*in bowels etc.*) га́зы (*m. pl.*); **I've got ~** меня́ распира́ют га́зы; **break ~** по́ртить, ис- во́здух. **5.** (**~** *instruments*) духовы́е инструме́нты (*m. pl.*).

v.t. (*deprive of breath*): **the blow ~ed him** от уда́ра у него́ дух захвати́ло; **I was ~ed by the climb** от подъёма я запыха́лся; **he ~ed me** он уда́рил меня́ под вздох.

cpds. **~bag** *n.* (*coll.*) пустоме́ля (*c.g.*), краснобай́; **~-cheater** (*US* **-breaker**) *nn.* ветронепроница́емая ку́ртка; штормо́вка; **~fall** *n.* (*of fruit*) па́данец; (*of good fortune*) непредви́денный дохо́д; **~mill** *n.* ветряна́я ме́льница; **~pipe** *n.* дыха́тельное го́рло; **~screen** (*US* **~shield**) *nn.* пере́днее/ветрово́е стекло́; **~screen wiper** стеклоочисти́тель (*m.*), «дво́рник»; **~swept** *adj.* (*of terrain*) откры́тый ве́тру; (*of hair etc.*) растрёпанный; **~-tunnel** *n.* аэродинами́ческая труба́.

wind[2] [waɪnd] *n.* **1.** (*single turn*) вито́к. **2.** (*bend*) поворо́т, изги́б.

v.t. **1.** (*cause to encircle, curve or curl*): **she wound the wool into a ball** она́ смота́ла шерсть в клубо́к; **the thread was wound on to a reel** ни́тка была́ намо́тана на кату́шку; **the chain had wound itself round the wheel** цепь обвила́сь вокру́г колеса́; **the hedgehog ~s itself into a ball** ёжик свёртывается клубко́м (*or* в клубо́к). **2.** (*fold, wrap*) уку́т|ывать, -ать; **she wound the baby in a shawl** она́ уку́тала/заверну́ла ребёнка в плато́к; **~ing-sheet** са́ван. **3.** (*rotate*) верте́ть (*impf.*); крути́ть (*impf.*). **4.: ~ a clock** зав|оди́ть, -ести́ часы́; **~ing-engine** подъёмная маши́на.

v.i. (*twist*) ви́ться (*impf.*); извива́ться (*impf.*); **~ing staircase** винтова́я ле́стница; **a ~ing road** изви́листая доро́га.

with advs.: **~ about** *v.i.*: **the road ~s about** доро́га вьётся; **~ in** *v.t.*: **~ in a fishing line** см|а́тывать, -ота́ть у́дочку; **~ up** *v.t.*: **~ up the bucket from the well** подн|има́ть, -я́ть ведро́ из коло́дца; **~ up a clock** зав|оди́ть, -ести́ часы́; (*fig., arouse*) взви́н|чивать, -ти́ть; **he gets very wound up at times** иногда́ он ужа́сно взви́нчивается; (*fig., settle*) заверш|а́ть, -и́ть; **I am ~ing up my affairs** я свёртываю свои́ дела́; (*fig., terminate*) зак|а́нчивать, -о́нчить; *v.i.* (*conclude*) заключ|а́ть, -и́ть; **he wound up by shooting himself** он ко́нчил тем, что застрели́лся.

windlass ['wɪndləs] *n.* лебёдка, во́рот.

windless ['wɪndlɪs] *adj.* безве́тренный.

window ['wɪndəʊ] *n.* **1.** окно́; (*dim., also cashier's etc.*) око́шко; **he looked through the ~** он смотре́л в окно́; он вы́глянул из окна́; **(shop-~)** витри́на; **a ~ on the world** окно́ в мир. **2.** (*comput.*) окно́. **3.** (*attr.*) око́нный.

cpds. **~-blind** *n.* што́ра; жалюзи́ (*nt. indecl.*); **~-box** *n.* нару́жный я́щик для цвето́в; **~-cleaner** *n.* мо́йщик о́кон; **~-dressing** *n.* (*lit.*) оформле́ние витри́н; (*fig.*) очковтира́тельство; **~-ledge** *n.* (нару́жный) подоко́нник; **~-pane** *n.* око́нное стекло́; **~-shopping** *n.* рассма́тривание витри́н; **~-sill** *n.* подоко́нник.

windsurfer ['wɪndˌsɜːfə(r)] *n.* виндсёрфинги́ст.

windsurfing [ˈwɪndˌsɜːfɪŋ] *n.* виндсёрфинг.

windward [ˈwɪndwəd] *adj.* навéтренный.

windy [ˈwɪndɪ] *adj.* **1.** (*characterized by wind*) вéтреный; **a ~ night** вéтреная ночь. **2.** (*exposed to wind*) обдувáемый вéтром; откры́тый вéтрам.

wine [waɪn] *n.* винó; **dry, medium dry, sweet ~** сухóе/полусухóе/слáдкое винó; **sparkling ~** игри́стое винó.

v.t.: **he was ~d and dined** егó угости́ли на слáву.

cpds. **~-bottle** *n.* ви́нная буты́лка; **~-cellar** *n.* ви́нный пóгреб; **~-glass** *n.* бокáл, рю́мка; **~-grower** *n.* винодéл; **~-growing** *n.* виноде́лие; *adj.* виноде́льческий; **~-list** *n.* кáрта вин: **~-press** *n.* дави́льный пресс; **~skin** *n.* мех для винá; **~-tasting** *n.* дегустáция вин.

wing [wɪŋ] *n.* **1.** (*of bird, insect or aircraft*) крылó; **on the ~** в полёте; **shoot a bird on the ~** подстрели́ть (*pf.*) пти́цу на летý; **spread, stretch one's ~s** (*fig.*) распр|авля́ть, -áвить кры́лья; **take ~** (*lit.*) улет|áть, -éть; взлет|áть, -éть; **take under one's ~** (*fig.*) брать, взять под своё кры́лышко. **2.** (*of building*) крылó, фли́гель (*m.*). **3.** (*of vehicle*) крылó. **4.** (*of mil. formation*) фланг; крылó; край. **5.** (*of political party*) крылó. **6.** (*of football or hockey team*) фланг; край; (*player in this position*) крáйний нападáющий. **7.** (*pl., of stage*) кули́сы (*f. pl.*); **wait in the ~s** (*lit.*) ждать (*impf.*) своегó вы́хода на сцéну; (*fig.*) ждать (*impf.*) своегó чáса.

v.t. **1.: ~ one's way** летéть (*impf.*). **3.** (*wound in ~*) подстрéл|ивать, -и́ть.

cpds. **~-commander** *n.* подполкóвник авиáции; **~-half** *n.* полузащи́тник; **~-mirror** *n.* боковóе зéркало; **~-span, ~-spread** *nn.* размáх кры́льев.

winger [ˈwɪŋə(r)] *n.* (*player*) крáйний нападáющий.

wingless [ˈwɪŋlɪs] *adj.* бескры́лый.

wink [wɪŋk] *n.*: **give s.o. a ~** подми́г|ивать, -нýть комý-н.; **tip s.o. the ~** (*fig.*) намек|áть, -нýть комý-н.; предупре|ждáть, -ди́ть когó-н.; **I didn't sleep a ~** я всю ночь не сомкнýл глаз; **have, take forty ~s** (*coll.*) вздремнýть (*pf.*).

v.i.: **~ at s.o.** подми́г|ивать, -нýть комý-н.; **~ at sth.** (*connive at*) смотрéть (*impf.*) сквозь пáльцы на что-н.; **it's as easy as ~ing** э́то раз плю́нуть; (*of star, light etc.*) мигáть (*impf.*); мерцáть (*impf.*).

winkle [ˈwɪŋk(ə)l] *n.* морскáя ули́тка.

v.t.: **~ out** (*fig.*) извл|екáть, -éчь; выковы́ривать, вы́ковырять.

winner [ˈwɪnə(r)] *n.* победи́тель (*fem.* -ница), лауреáт (*fem.* -ка); **who was the ~?** кто вы́играл/победи́л?

winning [ˈwɪnɪŋ] *adj.* **1.** (*victorious*) вы́игравший, победи́вший; **the ~ team** комáнда-победи́тельница. **2.** (*bringing about a win*) выи́грывающий; **~ card** вы́игрышная кáрта. **3.** (*persuasive, attractive*) привлекáтельный, обая́тельный; **~ ways** прия́тные манéры; **a ~ smile** подкупáющая улы́бка.

cpd. **~-post** *n.* фи́нишный столб.

winnings [ˈwɪnɪŋz] *n. pl.* вы́игрыш.

winnow [ˈwɪnəʊ] *v.t.* вéять (*impf.*); отвé|ивать, -ять; (*fig.*) отсé|ивать, -ять.

winsome [ˈwɪnsəm] *adj.* привлекáтельный, располагáющий.

winter [ˈwɪntə(r)] *n.* зимá; **in ~** зимóй; (*attr.*) зи́мний; **~ crop** ози́мая культýра; **~ sports** зи́мные ви́ды спóрта.

v.i. зимовáть, пере-.

cpd. **~-time** *n.* зимá.

wintry [ˈwɪntrɪ] *adj.* зи́мний,морóзный.

wipe [waɪp] *n.*: **give this plate a ~!** вы́трите э́ту тарéлку!; **she gave the baby's face a ~** онá вы́терла ребёнку лицó.

v.t. **1.** (*rub clean or dry*) вытирáть, вы́тереть; прот|ирáть, -ерéть; **~ s.o.'s nose** вы́тереть (*pf.*) комý-н. нос; **~ one's eyes** утерéть (*pf.*) слёзы; **~ your shoes on the mat!** оботри́те нóги/боти́нки о кóврик! **2.** (*efface*) ст|ирáть, -ерéть.

with advs.: **~ away** *v.t.* ст|ирáть, -ерéть; ут|ирáть, -ерéть; **~ down** *v.t.* прот|ирáть, -ерéть; **~ off** *v.t.* ст|ирáть, -ерéть; **~ out** *v.t.* (*clean*) вытирáть, вы́тереть; прот|ирáть, -ерéть; (*expunge*): **I can't ~ out the memory** я не могý отогнáть воспоминáние; (*destroy*) уничт|ожáть, -óжить; **~ up** *v.t.* подт|ирáть, -ерéть.

wire [ˈwaɪə(r)] *n.* **1.** (*fine-drawn metal; a length of this*) прóволока; **barbed ~** колю́чая прóволока; **~ netting** прóволочная сéтка; **~ wool** прóволочная мочáлка. **2.** (*elec.*) прóвод; **fuse ~** плáвкий предохрани́тель; **telephone ~** телефóнный кáбель; **live ~** (*lit.*) прóвод под напряжéнием/тóком; (*fig., of pers.*) (человéк-)огóнь, жи́вчик; **get one's ~s crossed** (*fig.*) запýтаться (*pf.*); невéрно поня́ть (*pf.*) что-н. **3.** (*coll., telegram*) телегрáмма.

v.t. **1.** (*provide, strengthen or fasten with ~*) скреп|ля́ть, -и́ть прóволокой. **2.** (*coll., send telegram to*) телеграфи́ровать (*impf., pf.*) +*d.* **3.** (*elec.*): **they ~d the house** они́ сдéлали провóдку в дóме.

v.i. (*coll., telegraph*) телеграфи́ровать (*impf., pf.*).

with advs.: **~ together** *v.t.* скреп|ля́ть, -и́ть прóволокой; **~ up** *v.t.* (*connect*) подключ|áть, -и́ть.

cpds. **~-cutters** *n.* кусáч|ки (*pl., g.* -ек); **~-tapping** *n.* подслýшивание телефóнных разговóров; подслýшка.

wireless [ˈwaɪəlɪs] *n.* **1.** (*~ telegraphy*) беспрóволочный телегрáф; **~ officer** ради́ст. **2.** (*sound radio*) рáдио (*indecl.*); **~ enthusiast** радиолюби́тель (*m.*). **3.** (*broadcast receiver: also* **~ set**) (радио)приёмник; рáдио.

wiring [ˈwaɪərɪŋ] *n.* (*elec.*) электропровóдка.

wiry [ˈwaɪərɪ] *adj.* (*of pers.*) жи́листый.

wisdom [ˈwɪzdəm] *n.* мýдрость; (*prudence*) благоразýмие, разýмность; **~ tooth** зуб мýдрости.

wise [waɪz] *adj.* **1.** (*sage*) мýдрый; **~ counsel** мýдрый совéт; **get, grow ~r** умнéть, по-; **he nodded ~ly** он глубокомы́сленно ки́вал головóй. **2.** (*sensible, prudent*) ýмный, благоразýмный; **~ after the event** зáдним умóм крéпок; **he ~ly refused** он имéл мýдрость отказáться. **3.** (*well-informed*) осведомлённый; **now that you've told me I am none the ~r** дáже пóсле вáшего объяснéния я мáло чегó понимáю; **~ guy** (*US sl.*) «ýмник»; **put s.o. ~ to sth.** (*coll.*) ввести́ (*pf.*) когó-н. в курс дéла; **be ~ to sth.** (*coll.*) быть в кýрсе дел; ви́деть (*impf.*) что-н. насквóзь.

cpd. **~crack** (*coll.*) *n.* шýтка, острота́.

wish [wɪʃ] *n.* **1.** (*desire*) желáние, вóля; (*request*) прóсьба; **make a ~!** загадáйте желáние!; **he expressed the ~ that** он вы́разил желáние, чтóбы; **you acted against my ~es** вы дéйствовали прóтив моéй вóли. **2.** (*thg. ~ed for or requested*) предмéт желáний; мечтá; **he got his ~** егó желáние сбылóсь; егó мечтá сбылáсь. **3.** (*hope on another's behalf*) пожелáние; **best ~es!** всегó наилýчшего!; **with every good ~** с наилýчшими пожелáниями.

v.t. **1.** (*want, require*) желáть (*impf.*); хотéть (*impf.*) (*both +a. or g., inf. or* чтóбы). **2.** (*expr. unfulfilled desire*): **I ~ I hadn't gone there** я жалéю, что пошёл тудá; **I only ~ I knew** éсли бы я тóлько знал; хотел бы я знать; **I ~ you'd be quiet** нельзя́ ли не шумéть?; **I ~ he was alive** кабы́ он был жив!; **I ~ he hadn't left so soon** как жаль, что он ушёл так рáно. **3.** (*with double object*): **I ~ him well** я желáю емý добрá; **I ~ed him good morning** я пожелáл емý дóброго утрá; **I ~ you many happy returns** поздравля́ю вас с днём рождéния; **I ~ed him goodbye** я попрощáлся с ним. **4.** (*coll., inflict*) навя́з|ывать, -áть; **I wouldn't ~ this headache on anyone** такóй головнóй бóли и врагý своемý не пожелáю.

v.i.: **she has everything a woman could ~ for** у неё есть всё, о чём то́лько же́нщина мо́жет мечта́ть.

cpd. **~-bone** *n.* ду́жка.

wishful ['wɪʃfʊl] *adj.*: **~ thinking** самообольще́ние; приня́тие жела́емого за действи́тельное.

wishy-washy ['wɪʃɪ,wɒʃɪ] *adj.* (*of pers.*) вя́лый; (*sentimental*) сентимента́льный; (*of style*) вя́лый.

wisp [wɪsp] *n.* пучо́к, клок; **a ~ of hair** прядь воло́с; **a ~ of smoke** стру́йка ды́ма.

wist|aria [wɪ'steərɪə], **-eria** [wɪ'stɪərɪə] *n.* глици́ния.

wistful ['wɪstfʊl] *adj.* тоскли́вый; **a ~ smile** мечта́тельная улы́бка.

wit[1] [wɪt] *n.* **1.** (*intelligence*) ум, ра́зум, соображе́ние; **at one's ~'s end** в отча́янии; **I am at my ~'s end to know what to do** про́сто ума́ не приложу́, что де́лать; **he has a ready ~** он за сло́вом в карма́н не поле́зет; **keep one's ~s about one** не растеря́ться (*pf.*); **he was scared out of his ~s** он был до́ смерти напу́ган. **2.** (*verbal ingenuity*) остроу́мие. **3.** (*pers.*) остря́|к (*fem. coll.* -чка).

wit[2] [wɪt] *v.* (*arch.*): **to ~** а и́менно.

witch [wɪtʃ] *n.* **1.** (*sorceress*) ве́дьма. **2.** (*charmer*) чарови́ница. **3.** (*hag*) ве́дьма, ста́рая карга́.

v.t. (*arch.*): **the ~ing hour** глуха́я по́лночь.

cpds. **~craft** *n.* колдовство́; **~-doctor** *n.* зна́харь (*m.*); **~-hunt** *n.* (*lit., fig.*) охо́та за ве́дьмами.

with [wɪð] *prep.* **1.** (*expr. accompaniment*) *usu.* c+*i.*; **come ~ me!** пойдёмте со мной!; **she has no-one to play ~** ей не́ с кем игра́ть; **he is ~ the manager** он у заве́дующего; **~ no hat on** без шля́пы; **meat ~ tomato sauce** мя́со в тома́тном со́усе. **2.** (*expr. agreement or sympathy*): **he that is not ~ us is against us** кто не с на́ми, тот про́тив нас; **I'm ~ you** (*in understanding*) понима́ю; (*in opinion*) я с ва́ми согла́сен; (*in support*) я на ва́шей стороне́. **3.: don't be rough ~ the cat!** не обраща́йтесь так гру́бо с ко́шкой!; **are you pleased ~ the result?** вы дово́льны результа́том?; **what do you want ~ me?** что вы от меня́ хоти́те?; **what has it to do ~ him?** при чём тут он?; како́е э́то име́ет к нему́ отноше́ние?. **4.** (*expr. antagonism or separation*): **don't argue ~ me** не спо́рьте со мной; **at war ~** в состоя́нии войны́ с+*i.*; **a break ~ tradition** отхо́д от тради́ции. **5.** (*in the case of*) у+*g.*; с+*i.*; **it's a habit ~ me** у меня́ така́я привы́чка; **~ children it's different** с детьми́ совсе́м друго́е де́ло. **6.** (*denoting host or person in charge, possession etc.*): **we stayed ~ our friends** мы жи́ли у друзе́й; **I have no money ~ me** у меня́ нет с собо́й (*or* при себе́) де́нег. **7.** (*denoting instrument or means*): **I am writing ~ a pen** я пишу́ перо́м; **he walks ~ a stick** он хо́дит с па́лкой; (*by means of*) с по́мощью (*or* при по́мощи) +*g.*; посре́дством+*g.*; **the word begins/ends ~ an A** э́то сло́во начина́ется/конча́ется на «А»; **it is written ~ a hyphen** э́то пи́шется че́рез дефи́с. **8.** (*denoting cause*) от+*g.*; **she was shaking ~ fright** она́ дрожа́ла от стра́ха; **he went down ~ flu** он заболе́л гри́ппом; **I am delighted ~ him** я в восто́рге от него́. **9.** (*denoting characteristic*): **a girl ~ blue eyes** де́вушка с голубы́ми глаза́ми; **~ child** (*pregnant*) бере́менная; **a dressing-gown ~ a blue lining** хала́т на голубо́й подкла́дке; **a tie ~ blue spots** га́лстук в си́них кра́пинках. **10.** (*denoting manner etc.*): **~ pleasure** с удово́льствием; **~ care** осторо́жно. **11.** (*in the same direction or degree as*; *at the same time as*): **~ the approach of spring** с наступле́нием весны́; **one must move ~ the times** на́до идти́ в но́гу с вре́менем; **I could barely keep up ~ him** я е́ле за ним поспева́л. **12.** (*denoting attendant circumstance*): **I sleep ~ the window open** я сплю с откры́тым окно́м; **a holiday ~ all expenses paid** по́лностью опла́ченный о́тпуск; **~ your permission** с ва́шего разреше́ния. **13.** (*despite*) несмотря́ на+*a.*; при+*p.*; **~ all his faults he's a gentleman** несмотря́ на все его́ недоста́тки, он джентльме́н; **~ the best will in the world** при всём жела́нии. **14.** (*in excl. or command*): **down ~ tyranny!** доло́й произво́л!; **off ~ you!** убира́йтесь!; **out ~ it!** расска́зывайте!; не таи́те(сь)!

withdraw [wɪð'drɔː] *v.t.* отн|има́ть, -я́ть; сн|има́ть, -ять; уб|ира́ть, -ра́ть; **~ one's hand** отдёр|гивать, -нуть ру́ку; **~ a coin from circulation** из|ыма́ть, -ъя́ть моне́ту из обраще́ния; **~ money from the bank** брать, взять де́ньги из ба́нка; **~ troops** от|води́ть, -вести́ войска́; **~ an offer** брать, взять обра́тно/наза́д предложе́ние; **~ a statement** отка́з|ываться, -а́ться от заявле́ния; **a ~n character** за́мкнутый челове́к.

v.i. удал|я́ться, -и́ться; **~ from a competition** выбыва́ть, вы́быть из соревнова́ния; **~ into o.s.** зам|ыка́ться, -кну́ться в себе́; (*mil.*) от|ходи́ть, -ойти́.

withdrawal [wɪð'drɔːəl] *n.* отня́тие, сня́тие; (*of coinage*) изъя́тие; (*mil.*) отво́д; (*absenting o.s.*) вы́ход, ухо́д; (*of drugs*) прекраще́ние приёма нарко́тиков; **~ symptoms** абстине́нтный синдро́м.

wither ['wɪðə(r)] *v.t.* **1.** иссуш|а́ть, -и́ть; **~ed leaves** увя́дшие ли́стья; **a ~ed arm** суха́я рука́. **2.** (*fig.*) губи́ть, по-; **~ing scorn** убийственное презре́ние.

v.i. вя́нуть, за-; блёкнуть, по-; **the flowers ~ed in the sun** цветы́ завя́ли на со́лнце.

with advs.: **~ away** *v.i.* отс|ыха́ть, -о́хнуть; ча́хнуть, за-; (*of the state*) отм|ира́ть, -ере́ть.

withers ['wɪðəz] *n.* хо́лка, загри́вок.

withhold [wɪð'həʊld] *v.t.* **1.** (*refuse to give*) отка́з|ывать, -а́ть в (*чём*); возде́рж|иваться, -а́ться от (*чего*); **~ one's consent** не да|ва́ть, -ть согла́сия; **~ payment** уде́рж|ивать, -а́ть (*or* заде́рж|ивать, -а́ть) опла́ту; **~ information** ута́|ивать, -и́ть информа́цию. **2.** (*restrain*) уде́рж|ивать, -а́ть.

within [wɪ'ðɪn] *adv.* внутри́; **from ~** изнутри́.

prep. **1.** (*inside*) в+*p.*; внутри́+*g.*; **a voice ~ him said 'no'** вну́тренний го́лос сказа́л ему́ «нет»; **my heart sank ~ me** у меня́ упа́ло се́рдце. **2.** (*nor farther than*; *accessible to*) в преде́лах +*g.*; **the library is ~ walking distance** до библиоте́ки мо́жно дойти́ пешко́м; **~ earshot** в преде́лах слы́шимости; **~ reach** в зо́не/преде́лах достяга́емости; **~ sight** в преде́лах ви́димости. **3.** (*of time*) в тече́ние +*g.*; на протяже́нии +*g.*; за+*a.*; **~ (the next) three days** в тече́ние (ближа́йших) трёх дней; **I can finish the job ~ a week** я могу́ ко́нчить э́ту рабо́ту за неде́лю. **4.** (*~ limits of*) в преде́лах/ра́мках +*g.*; **live ~ one's income** жить (*impf.*) по сре́дствам; **~ one's rights** по пра́ву; **it is ~ his powers** э́то ему́ по си́лам; э́то вхо́дит в его́ компете́нцию; **~ limits** до изве́стной сте́пени.

without [wɪ'ðaʊt] *adv.* (*arch., liter.*) снару́жи.

prep. **1.** (*arch., outside*) вне+*g.* **2.** (*not having*; *lacking*; *free from*) без+*g.*; **~ delay** сра́зу же; **~ doubt** без сомне́ния; **~ fail** непреме́нно; **~ success** безуспе́шно; **it goes ~ saying** само́ собо́й разуме́ется; (*with gerund*): **~ thinking** не ду́мая; не поду́мав; **he left ~ so much as saying goodbye** он ушёл, да́же не прости́вшись.

withstand [wɪð'stænd] *v.t.* устоя́ть (*pf.*) пе́ред+*i.*; выде́рживать, вы́держать; **~ a siege** вы́держать (*pf.*) оса́ду; **~ temptation** устоя́ть (*pf.*) пе́ред собла́зном; не подда́ться (*pf.*) собла́зну.

witless ['wɪtlɪs] *adj.* безмо́зглый, глу́пый.

witness ['wɪtnɪs] *n.* **1.** (*eye-*) очеви́д|ец (*fem.* -ица); свиде́тель (*fem.* -ница). **2.** (*in court of law*) свиде́тель (*fem.* -ница). **3.** (*testimony*) свиде́тельство; **bear ~** свиде́тельствовать (*impf.*); **bear false ~** лжесвиде́тельствовать (*impf.*); **in ~ whereof** в подтвержде́ние/доказа́тельство чего́.

v.t. **1.** (*be spectator of*) быть свиде́телем/очеви́дцем +*g.*; **no-one ~ed the accident** никто́ не ви́дел, как произошла́ катастро́фа. **2.** (*be evidence of*) свиде́тельствовать (*impf.*) о+*p.* **3.:** ~ **s.o.'s signature** зав|еря́ть, -е́рить чью-н. по́дпись.

cpds. ~**-box,** ~**-stand** *nn.* ме́сто для да́чи свиде́тельских показа́ний.

witticism ['wɪtɪ,sɪz(ə)m] *n.* острота́.

wittiness ['wɪtɪnɪs] *n.* остроу́мие.

wittingly ['wɪtɪŋlɪ] *adv.* заве́домо, созна́тельно.

witty ['wɪtɪ] *adj.* остроу́мный.

wizard ['wɪzəd] *n.* (*magician*) колду́н; (*fig.*) волше́бник; **a financial** ~ фина́нсовый ге́ний.

wizardry ['wɪzədrɪ] *n.* колдовство́.

wizened ['wɪz(ə)nd] *adj.* вы́сохший, иссо́хший.

wobble ['wɒb(ə)l] *n.* кача́ние, поша́тывание.

v.t. (*also* ~ **about**) шата́ть (*impf.*).

v.i. (*also* ~ **about**) шата́ться; ковыля́ть; кача́ться (*both impf.*).

wobbly ['wɒblɪ] *adj.* (*lit., fig.*) ша́ткий, неусто́йчивый.

wodge [wɒdʒ] *n.* (*coll.*) ком, кусо́к.

woe [wəʊ] *n.* **1.** (*grief, distress*) го́ре; **tale of** ~ го́рестная исто́рия. **2.** (*pl., troubles*) бе́ды (*f. pl.*).

cpd. ~**begone** *adj.* удручённый, го́рестный.

woeful ['wəʊfʊl] *adj.* го́рестный, жа́лкий, уны́лый; **a** ~ **countenance** ско́рбное лицо́.

wok [wɒk] *n.* котело́к (с вы́пуклым дни́щем).

wolf [wʊlf] *n.* (*animal*) волк; **(she-**~**)** волчи́ца; **cry** ~ (*fig.*) подн|има́ть, -я́ть ло́жную трево́гу; **lone** ~ (*fig.*) единоли́чни|к (*fem.* -ца); ~ **in sheep's clothing** (*fig.*) волк в ове́чьей шку́ре.

v.t. (*coll., also* ~ **down**) прогл|а́тывать, -оти́ть с жа́дностью.

cpds. ~**-cub** *n.* волчо́нок; ~**hound** *n.* волкода́в.

woman ['wʊmən] *n.* **1.** же́нщина; **old** ~ стару́ха; **single** ~ незаму́жняя же́нщина; **Women's Lib(eration movement)** движе́ние за эмансипа́цию же́нщин; **women's rights** же́нское равнопра́вие. **2.** (*coll., charwoman*): **daily** ~ приходя́щая домрабо́тница. **3.:** ~ **doctor** же́нщина-врач; ~ **friend** подру́га, прия́тельница.

cpds. ~**-hater** *n.* женоненави́стник; ~**kind** *n.* же́нщины (*f. pl.*); ~**-servant** *n.* служа́нка.

womanhood ['wʊmən,hʊd] *n.* **1.** (*maturity*) же́нская зре́лость; **grow to** ~ созр|ева́ть, -е́ть. **2.** (*instinct*) же́нственность; же́нские ка́чества.

womanize ['wʊmə,naɪz] *v.i.* (*coll., philander*) пу́таться (*impf.*) с ба́бами.

womanizer ['wʊmə,naɪzə(r)] *n.* (*coll.*) женолю́б, ба́бник.

womanly ['wʊmənlɪ] *adj.* же́нственный; не́жный.

womb [wu:m] *n.* ма́тка; (*fig.*) утро́ба.

wonder ['wʌndə(r)] *n.* **1.** (*miracle, marvel*) чу́до; **work** ~**s** твори́ть, со- чудеса́; (*marvel*): ~**s will never cease** (*joc.*) чудеса́ в решете́; чудеса́, да и то́лько!; **that child is a little** ~ э́тот ребёнок настоя́щий вундерки́нд; (*surprising thg.*): **the** ~ **is that ...** удиви́тельно, что...; **small** ~ **that ...** неудиви́тельно, что...; **no** ~ **he was angry!** неудиви́тельно, что он рассерди́лся! **2.** (*amazement, admiration*) изумле́ние, восхище́ние; **the sight filled him with** ~ зре́лище его́ порази́ло/изуми́ло.

v.t. **1.** (*be surprised*): **I** ~ **he wasn't killed** удиви́тельно, что он оста́лся в живы́х; **I shouldn't** ~ **if it rained** я не удивлю́сь, е́сли пойдёт дождь. **2.** (*deliberate, desire to know*): **I** ~ **who that was** интере́сно (*or* хоте́лось бы знать), кто бы э́то мог быть; **you will** ~ **why I said that** вы спро́сите, почему́ я э́то сказа́л; **I was** ~**ing whether to invite him** я не мог реши́ть, приглаша́ть его́ и́ли нет; **I** ~ **if I might open the window** вы не возража́ете, е́сли я откро́ю окно́? *See also v.i.*

v.i. **1.** (*feel surprised*) удив|ля́ться, -и́ться (*чему*); пора|жа́ться, -зи́ться (*чему*); **I** ~**ed at his foolishness** я был поражён его́ легкомы́слием; **can you** ~ **that he got hurt?** неудиви́тельно, что он уши́бся. **2.** (*feel curiosity*) интересова́ться (*impf.*); **I was** ~**ing about that** я и сам разду́мывал об э́том. **3.** (*expr. doubt*): **I** ~ я не уве́рен; сомнева́юсь.

cpd. ~**land** *n.* страна́ чуде́с.

wonderful ['wʌndə,fʊl] *adj.* изуми́тельный, удиви́тельный; **what** ~ **weather!** кака́я чу́дная пого́да!; **you have a** ~ **memory** у вас замеча́тельная па́мять.

wonderment ['wʌndəmənt] *n.* удивле́ние, изумле́ние.

wondrous ['wʌndrəs] (*arch. or liter.*) *adj.* ди́вный.

wont [wəʊnt] (*arch. or liter.*) *n.* обыкнове́ние, привы́чка; **as is his** ~ по своему́ обыкнове́нию.

adj. привы́чный, обы́чный; **as he was** ~ **to say** как он люби́л говори́ть.

woo [wu:] *v.t.* **1.** (*court*) уха́живать (*impf.*) за+*i.* **2.** (*fig., coax*) обха́живать (*impf.*); **both candidates were** ~**ing the voters** о́ба кандида́та пыта́лись завоева́ть расположе́ние избира́телей.

wood [wʊd] *n.* **1.** (*forest*) лес; ~**ed country** леси́стая ме́стность; (*fig.*): **we're not out of the** ~ **yet** ещё не все опа́сности/тру́дности преодолены́. **2.** (*substance*) де́рево; **work in** ~ ре́зать (*impf.*) по де́реву; **touch** (*US* **knock on**) ~ тьфу, тьфу! (чтоб не сгла́зить!); ~ **alcohol** древе́сный спирт; ~ **block** (*for paving*) торе́ц; ~ **carving** деревя́нная резьба́; ~ **pulp** древеси́на. **3.** (*as fuel or kindling*) дров|а́ (*pl., g.* —); **I chopped some** ~ **for the fire** я наколо́л дров для ками́на.

cpds. ~**cut** *n.* гравю́ра на де́реве; ~**cutter** *n.* дровосе́к; ~**land** *n.* леси́стая ме́стность; (*attr.*) лесно́й; ~**-louse** *n.* мокри́ца; ~**man** *n.* лесни́к, лесору́б; ~**pecker** *n.* дя́тел; ~**-pigeon** *n.* вя́хирь (*m.*), го́рлица; ~**-shed** *n.* дровяно́й сара́й; ~**sman** *n.* лесно́й жи́тель; ~**-wind** *n.* (*collect.*) деревя́нные духовы́е инструме́нты (*m. pl.*); ~**work** *n.* (*carpentry*) столя́рная рабо́та; (*articles*) деревя́нные изде́лия; ~**worker** *n.* пло́тник, столя́р; ~**worm** *n.* личи́нка древото́чца; ~**-yard** *n.* дровяно́й склад.

wooded ['wʊdɪd] *adj.* леси́стый.

wooden ['wʊd(ə)n] *adj.* деревя́нный.

cpd. ~**-headed** *adj.* тупо́й, тупоу́мный.

woody ['wʊdɪ] *adj.* (*wooded*) леси́стый; (*of or like wood*) деревя́нный.

woof[1] [wu:f] *n.* (*weft*) уто́к.

woof[2] [wʊf] *n.* (*dog's bark*) га́вканье, лай.

v.t. га́вкать (*impf.*); ла́ять (*impf.*).

wool [wʊl] *n.* **1.** (*on sheep etc.*) шерсть, руно́; **pull the** ~ **over s.o.'s eyes** (*fig.*) вв|оди́ть, -ести́ кого́-н. в заблужде́ние; пус|ка́ть, -ти́ть пыль в глаза́ кому́-н.; **knitting** ~ шерсть для вяза́ния. **2.** (*similar substance*): **cotton** ~ ва́та; **steel** ~ ёжик.

woollen ['wʊlən] (*US* **woolen**) *n. pl.* шерстяна́я оде́жда.

adj. шерстяно́й; ~ **cloth** сукно́.

woolly ['wʊlɪ] *n.* сви́тер.

adj. **1.** шерсти́стый; (*furry*) мохна́тый; (*downy*) пуши́стый. **2.** (*of mind, argument etc.*) нея́сный, нечёткий, му́тный.

woozy ['wu:zɪ] *adj.* (*coll., tipsy*) косо́й, окосе́вший.

word [wɜ:d] *n.* **1.** сло́во; **he doesn't know a** ~ **of English** он совсе́м не зна́ет англи́йского; **by** ~ **of mouth** у́стно, на слова́х; **eat one's** ~**s** взять (*pf.*) свои́ слова́ наза́д; ~**s fail me** не нахожу́ слов; **from the** ~ **go** с са́мого нача́ла; **I couldn't get a** ~ **in (edgeways)** мне не удало́сь вста́вить ни слове́чка; **you can't get a** ~ **out of him** слове́чка от него́ не добъёшься; **may I have a** ~ **with you?** мо́жно вас на полсло́ва?; **beyond** ~**s** неопису́емый; **I have no** ~**s for it** я не зна́ю, как э́то назва́ть; **in a** ~ (одни́м) сло́вом; коро́че говоря́; **in a few** ~**s** в не́скольких слова́х; **in other** ~**s** и́наче говоря́, други́ми слова́ми; **in so many** ~**s** пря́мо, напрями́к; **in** ~**s of one syllable** (*fig.*) са́мыми просты́ми слова́ми; **in** ~ **and**

deed сло́вом и де́лом; **last ~s** после́дние/предсме́ртные слова́; **the last ~ in fashion** после́дний крик мо́ды; **he had the last ~** после́днее сло́во оста́лось за ним; **be at a loss for ~s** не находи́ть (*impf.*) слов; **not a ~!** ни сло́ва!; **play on ~s** игра́ слов, каламбу́р; **put into ~s** выража́ть, вы́разить слова́ми; **put in a good ~ for s.o.** замо́лвить (*pf.*) слове́чко за кого́-н.; **you took the ~s out of my mouth** э́то как раз то, что я хоте́л сказа́ть; **he is too greedy for ~s** он невероя́тно жа́ден; **~ for ~** сло́во в сло́во; **a ~ in your ear** я хочу́ вам ко́е-что сказа́ть. **2.** (*pl., disputation, quarrel*) ссо́ра; **they had ~s** они́ побрани́лись. **3.** (*pl., text set to music*) текст, слова́ (*nt. pl.*); **set, put ~s to music** положи́ть (*pf*) слова́ на му́зыку. **4.** (*news; information*) изве́стие, сообще́ние; **send ~ of sth.** изве|ща́ть, -сти́ть о чём-н.; **he sent, left ~ that he was not coming** он переда́л, что не смо́жет прийти́; **~ came that he had been killed** пришло́ сообще́ние, что он поги́б; **the ~ got round that ...** ста́ло изве́стно, что... **5.** (*promise; assurance*) сло́во, обеща́ние; **give, pledge one's ~** да|ва́ть, -ть сло́во; обеща́ть (*impf., pf.*); **keep one's ~** держа́ть, с- сло́во; **~ of honour!** че́стное сло́во!; **take s.o. at his ~** пойма́ть (*pf.*) кого́-н. на сло́ве; **you must take my ~ for it** вам придётся пове́рить мне на сло́во. **6.** (*command*) сло́во, прика́з; **at the ~ of command** по кома́нде; **give the ~** отда́ть (*pf.*) приказа́ние/распоряже́ние; **just say the ~!** то́лько прикажи́те!

v.t. формули́ровать, с-; сост|авля́ть, -а́вить; **that might have been differently ~ed** э́то мо́жно бы́ло сказа́ть/вы́разить ина́че.

cpds. **~-game** *n.* слове́сная игра́ (*скрэбл и т.п.*); **~-perfect** *adj.* зна́ющий (*что*) на зубо́к; **~-play** *n.* игра́ слов; каламбу́р; **~-processing** *n.* редакти́рование те́кста; **~-processor** *n.* (*comput., hardware*) те́кстовый проце́ссор; (*software*) те́кстовый реда́ктор.

wording ['wɜːdɪŋ] *n.* реда́кция; формулиро́вка.

wordy ['wɜːdɪ] *adj.* многосло́вный, велеречи́вый.

work [wɜːk] *n.* **1.** (*mental or physical labour, task*) рабо́та, труд; (*official, professional*) слу́жба; (*school etc.*) заня́тия (*nt. pl.*); (*activity*) де́ятельность; **job of ~** де́ло; **he is at ~** он сейча́с рабо́тает; **he is at (his place of) ~** он на рабо́те/слу́жбе; **he is at ~ on a dictionary** он рабо́тает над словарём; **all in the day's ~** в поря́дке веще́й, норма́льно; **creative ~** тво́рческая де́ятельность; **good ~s** до́брые дела́; **public ~s** обще́ственные рабо́ты (*f. pl.*); **his life's ~** де́ло его́ жи́зни; **get to ~ on** нача́ть (*pf.*) рабо́ту над+*i.*; **get down to ~** приня́ться/взя́ться (*pf.*) за рабо́ту/де́ло; **make short ~ of** бы́стро/ жи́во распра́виться (*pf.*) с+*i.* **2.** (*activity, not necessarily productive*) де́йствие, посту́пок; **it was the ~ of a moment** э́то бы́ло де́лом одно́й мину́ты; **dirty ~** (*difficult, unpleasant*) чёрная рабо́та; (*nefarious*) по́длость; **there's been some dirty ~ here** тут де́ло нечи́сто; **nice ~!** (*coll.*) отли́чно!; здо́рово. **3.** (*employment*) рабо́та, слу́жба; **it is hard to find ~** тру́дно найти́ рабо́ту; **in ~** рабо́тающий; **out of ~** без рабо́ты. **4.** (*workmanship*) мастерство́, отде́лка; **an excellent piece of ~** отли́чная рабо́та. **5.** (*finished product*) произведе́ние, изде́лие; **sale of ~** прода́жа изде́лий. **6.** (*literary or artistic composition*) произведе́ние; (*esp. academic*) труд; (*collect.*) тво́рчество; (*publication*) изда́ние; **the (complete) ~s of Shakespeare** (по́лное) собра́ние сочине́ний Шекспи́ра; **~s on art** кни́ги по иску́сству; **~ of reference** спра́вочник. **7.** (*pl., parts of machine*) механи́зм; **the ~s of a clock** часово́й механи́зм; **something is wrong with the ~s** механи́зм испо́ртился. **8.** (*pl., factory or similar installation*) заво́д, фа́брика, предприя́тие; **engineering ~s** машинострои́тельный заво́д; **steel ~s** сталелите́йный заво́д; **~s manager** дире́ктор заво́да/ фа́брики. **9.** (*pl., operations*): **public ~s** обще́ственные рабо́ты (*f. pl.*). **10.** (*pl., defensive structures; fortifications*) фортифика́ция (*f. pl.*); **defensive ~s** оборони́тельные сооруже́ния.

v.t. **1.** (*cause to ~, exact ~ from*): **he ~s his men hard** он заставля́ет люде́й рабо́тать, не поклада́я рук; **he ~ed himself to death** он извёл себя́ рабо́той; **~ one's fingers to the bone** труди́ться/рабо́тать (*impf.*) до седьмо́го по́та. **2.** (*set in motion, actuate*) прив|оди́ть, -ести́ в движе́ние/де́йствие; **~ a lever** наж|има́ть, -а́ть на рыча́г; **how do you ~ this machine?** как рабо́тает э́то маши́на? **3.** (*effect*): **~ wonders** твори́ть, со- чудеса́. **4.** (*achieve by ~ing*): **~ one's passage** отраб|а́тывать, -о́тать свой прое́зд; **he ~ed his way up to the rank of manager** из просты́х рабо́чих он проби́лся в дирекtора́; **~ one's way forward** пробира́ться (*impf.*) вперёд. **5.** (*operate, manage: a mine, land etc.*) разраба́тывать, эксплуати́ровать (*both impf.*). **6.** (*move, bring by degrees*): **~ sth. into place** вти́с|кивать, -нуть что-н. куда́-н.; **he ~ed the conversation round to his favourite subject** он постепе́нно подвёл разгово́р к свое́й излю́бленной те́ме. **7.** (*shape, manipulate*) обраб|а́тывать, -о́тать; **~ clay/dough** меси́ть, за- глину́/те́сто. **8.** (*excite*): **he ~ed the crowd into a frenzy** он довёл толпу́ до неи́стовства; **~ o.s. into a rage** дов|оди́ть, -ести́ себя́ до исступле́ния.

v.i. **1.** (*labour, be employed*) рабо́тать, труди́ться, служи́ть (*all impf.*); **he ~ed for 6 hours** он прорабо́тал 6 часо́в; **~ at a problem** рабо́тать/би́ться (*impf.*) над зада́чей; **~ for the government** рабо́тать (*impf.*) на госуда́рственной слу́жбе; **~ for peace** боро́ться (*impf.*) за мир; **~ for a living** зараба́тывать (*impf.*) себе́ на жизнь; **he ~s in oils** он пи́шет ма́слом; **~ to rule** пров|оди́ть, -ести́ италья́нскую забасто́вку; **~ with s.o.** сотру́дничать (*impf.*) с кем-н. **2.** (*operate, function*) рабо́тать (*impf.*); де́йствовать (*impf.*); **the brake won't ~** то́рмоз отказа́л; **my watch stopped ~ing** мои́ часы́ переста́ли идти́; **the machine ~s by electricity** э́тот аппара́т рабо́тает на электри́честве. **3.** (*produce desired effect*): **the plan ~ed** план уда́лся; **the medicine ~ed** лека́рство помогло́/поде́йствовало; **the method ~s well** э́тот ме́тод уда́чен. **4.** (*exert influence*) рабо́тать, де́йствовать (*both impf.*); ока́зывать (*impf.*) влия́ние; **~ against** меша́ть (*impf.*) +*d.*; служи́ть (*impf.*) поме́хой +*d.*; **~ towards** спосо́бствовать (*impf.*) +*d.*; стреми́ться (*impf.*) к+*d.* **5.** (*move gradually*): **a screw ~ed loose** винт ясла́б; **the damp ~ed through the plaster** сы́рость прошла́/прони́кла че́рез штукату́рку.

with advs.: **~ off** *v.t.*: **he ran round the house to ~ off some of his energy** он пробежа́лся вокру́г до́ма, что́бы дать вы́ход свое́й эне́ргии; **I shall never be able to ~ off this debt** я никогда́ не смогу́ погаси́ть э́тот долг; **~ out** *v.t.* (*devise*) разраб|а́тывать, -о́тать; (*calculate*) вычисля́ть, вы́числить; **you must ~ out the answer yourself** вы должны́ са́ми найти́ отве́т; (*solve*) разреш|а́ть, -и́ть; **~ things out** раз|бира́ться, -обра́ться; *v.i.* (*turn out*) ока́з|ываться, -а́ться; конча́ться, ко́нчиться; (*turn out satisfactorily*): **our marriage hasn't ~ed out** наш брак оказа́лся неуда́чным; (*be solved*) разреш|а́ться, -и́ться; **the sum won't ~ out** зада́ча не выхо́дит/получа́ется; (*of calculation*); (*train, of an athlete*) тренирова́ться (*impf.*); **~ over** *v.t.* (*beat up*): **the gang gave him a ~ing-over** (*coll.*) ша́йка его́ разби́ла до полусме́рти; **I was just ~ing round to that point** я как раз подходи́л к э́тому (вопро́су); **~ up** *v.t.* (*elaborate*) перераб|а́тывать, -о́тать; (*raise, develop*): **he**

~ed up a profitable business он развернýл прúбыльное дéло; I can't ~ up any interest in economics я никáк не могý пробудúть в себé интерéс к экономике; I went for a short walk to ~ up an appetite я вы́шел немнóго пройтúсь, чтóбы нагулять себé аппетúт; (*arouse, excite*): he ~ed himself up он взвинтúл себя́; (*pred.*): ~ed up (*excited*) взволнóван, возбуждён; (*worried*) расстрóен; get o.s. ~ed up расстр|áиваться, -óиться.

cpds. ~-bench *n.* верстáк; ~-book *n.* тетрáдь для упражнéний; ~day (*unit of payment*) трудодéнь (*m.*); ~-force *n.* рабóчие (*pl.*); рабóчая сúла; ~-horse *n.* рабóчая лóшадь; ~house *n.* (*Br.*) рабóтный дом; (*US*) исправúтельная тюрьмá; ~-load *n.* нагрýзка; ~man *n.* рабóтник; ~manlike *adj.* искýсный; ~manship *n.* искýсство, мастерствó; ~mate *n.* сотрýдни|к (*fem.* -ца), коллéга (*c.g.*); ~-out *n.* тренирóвка; ~-room *n.* рабóчая кóмната/мастерскáя; ~shop *n.* мастерскáя, цех; ~-shy *adj.* (*coll.*) ленúвый; ~-top *n.* (*surface for working*) рабóчий стол; (*in kitchen*) вéрхняя панéль; ~-to-rule *n.* ≃ итальянская забастóвка.

workable ['wɜ:kəb(ə)l] *adj.* 1. (*of mine etc.*) рентáбельный. 2. (*feasible*) выполнúмый, осуществúмый.

workaday ['wɜ:kəˌdeɪ] *adj.* бýдний, повседнéвный.

workaholic [ˌwɜ:kə'hɒlɪk]*n.* работомáн.

worker ['wɜ:kə(r)] *n.* рабóтник, трудя́щийся; (*manual*) рабóчий; hard ~ трýжени|к (*fem.* -ца), работя́га (*c.g.*); office ~ слýжащий.

working ['wɜ:kɪŋ] *n.* 1. (*mine, quarry etc.*) руднúк, вы́работки (*f. pl.*). 2. (*usu. pl.*; *operation*) рабóта, дéйствие; the ~s of the human mind мыслúтельный процéсс человéка. 3. (*attr., pert. to work*) рабóчий; ~ capital оборóтный капитáл; ~ clothes рабóчая одéжда; ~ conditions услóвия трудá; ~ day (*part of day devoted to work*) рабóчий день; (*opp. to rest day*) рабóчий/бýдний день; ~ knowledge óбщее знакóмство (c+*i.*); ~ lunch деловóй обéд; in ~ order в испрáвности.

adj. рабóчий; ~ man рабóтник, рабóчий; ~ class рабóчий класс; ~ model дéйствующая модéль.

cpd. ~-class *adj.* рабóчий, характéрный для представúтеля рабóчего клáсса; ~-class families сéмьи рабóчих.

world [wɜ:ld] *n.* 1. (*universe, system*) мир; the ancient ~ антúчный мир; new ~ нóвый мир; come into the ~ появ|ля́ться, -úться на свет; bring into the ~ (*give birth to; deliver*) произв|одúть, -естú на свет; out of this ~ (*coll., stupendous*) потрясáющий; not of this ~ не от мúра сегó; in this ~ на э́том свéте; the next ~ тот свет. 2. (*intensive and other fig. uses*): how in the ~ did you know? как вы тóлько умудрúлись (э́то) узнáть?; what in the ~ has happened? да что же, наконéц, случúлось?; why in the ~ didn't you tell me? ну почемý же вы мне не сказáли?; not for the ~ ни на что на свéте; she's all the ~ to me она для меня́ — всё; the boss thinks the ~ of him он у хозя́ина на óчень высóким счетý; I would give the ~ to know я бы всё отдáл, тóлько бы узнáть; dead to the ~ без сознáния; в пóлном изнеможéнии; I felt on top of the ~ я был на вершúне благополýчия; я был в превосхóдном настроéнии. 3. (*infinite amount or extent*) мнóго, ýйма; a ~ of difference огрóмная рáзница; it will do him a ~ of good э́то емý óчень дáже пойдёт на пóльзу. 4. (*geog.; the earth's countries and peoples*) мир, свет; a journey round the ~ путешéствие вокрýг свéта; the ~'s his oyster весь мир у егó ног; his ~ is a very narrow one у негó óчень ýзкий кругозóр; the whole (*or* all the) ~ knows всем (*or* всемý мúру) извéстно; (all) the ~ over в цéлом мúре; по всемý свéту; the Old/New W~ Стáрый/Нóвый свет; the English-speaking ~ англоязы́чные стрáны (*f. pl.*); the Third W~ трéтий мир; ~ affairs междунарóдные делá; a ~ power велúкая держáва; ~ record мировóй рекóрд; ~ war мировáя войнá. 5. (*human affairs; active life*) жизнь; a man of the ~ свéтский/бывáлый человéк; all's right with the ~ в мúре всё прекрáсно; get on in the ~ вы́йтú (*pf.*) в лю́ди; come up in the ~ сдéлать (*pf.*) карьéру. 6. (*sphere; domain*) мир; сфéра; the ~ of nature цáрство прирóды; the scientific ~ наýчные кругú (*m. pl.*); the animal ~ живóтный мир; the ~ of art мир искýсства.

cpds. ~-famous *adj.* всемúрно извéстный; ~-view *n.* мировоззрéние; ~-wide *adj.* всемúрный, мировóй; *adv.* по всемý свéту/мúру.

worldly ['wɜ:ldlɪ] *adj.* 1. (*material*) земнóй, материáльный; ~ goods имýщество. 2. (*of this world; secular*) земнóй, мирскóй; ~ wisdom житéйская мýдрость. 3.: a ~ person сýетный человéк.

cpd. ~-wise *adj.* óпытный; обладáющий жúзненным óпытом.

worm [wɜ:m] *n.* 1. (*earth* ~) червь (*m.*), червя́к. 2. (*maggot; grub*) гýсеница, личúнка. 3. (*parasite*) глист; have ~s имéть (*impf.*) глисты́. 4. (*abject person*) ничтóжный червь; раб; ничтóжество.

v.t. 1. (*insinuate*): he ~ed himself into her confidence он вкрáлся к ней в довéрие. 2. (*extract*) выпы́тывать, вы́пытать; they ~ed the secret out of him онú вы́ведали егó тáйну.

cpds. ~-eaten *adj.* червúвый; ~-hole *n.* червотóчина; ~-powder *n.* глистогóнное срéдство; ~-wheel *n.* червя́чное колесó.

wormwood ['wɜ:mwʊd] *n.* поли́нь.

worn [wɔ:n] *see* wear *v.t. and* wear out

worrier ['wʌrɪə(r)] *n.* (*pers.*) беспокóйный человéк; he's a ~ он вéчно беспокóится; он у нас паникёр.

worrisome ['wʌrɪsəm] *adj.* (*causing worry*) беспокóйный, тревóжный; (*given to worrying*) беспокóйный, мнúтельный.

worr|y ['wʌrɪ] *n.* 1. (*anxiety*) тревóга, забóта. 2. (*sth. causing anxiety*) неприя́тность, забóта; he is a ~y to me я с ним мýчаюсь; money ~ies дéнежные забóты (*f. pl.*).

v.t. 1. (*cause anxiety or discomfort to*) беспокóить (*impf.*); волновáть (*impf.*); I'm ~ied about my son я беспокóюсь за сы́на; меня́ беспокóит сын; I am ~ied about his health я озабóчен состоя́нием егó здорóвья; don't ~y yourself не беспокóйтесь. 2. (*trouble; bother*) надоедáть (*impf.*) +*d.*; приставáть (*impf.*) к+*d.*; he keeps ~ying me to read him a story он пристаёт ко мне, чтóбы я емý почитáл; the noise doesn't ~y me мне шум не мешáет. 3. (*of dog*) рвать (*impf.*) зубáми; трепáть (*impf.*).

v.i. беспокóиться, волновáться; мýчиться (*all impf.*); you are ~ying over nothing вы напрáсно (*or* по пустякáм) волнýетесь; not to ~! (*coll.*) не волнýйтесь!; не бедá!; всё устрóится.

worse [wɜ:s] *n.* хýдшее; there is ~ to come э́то ещё не всё; a change for the ~ перемéна к хýдшему; things went from bad to ~ положéние час óт часу становúлось хýже.

adj. хýдший; we couldn't have picked a ~ day трýдно бы́ло бы вы́брать бóлее неудáчный день; my trouble is ~ than yours моя́ бедá похýже вáшей; you will only make matters ~ вы тóлько ухýдшите положéние; or ~ úли ещё что-н. похýже; I can't think of anything ~ не могý себé представить ничегó хýже; ~ luck! к сожалéнию; к несчáстью; (*in health*) хýже; the patient is ~ today больнóму сегóдня хýже; his condition is ~ егó состоя́ние ухýдшилось.

adv. хýже; they are ~ off than we онú в хýдшем положéнии, чем мы; (*financially*) онú мéнее состоя́тельны, чем мы.

worsen ['wɜ:s(ə)n] *v.t. & i.* ух|удша́ться, -у́дшиться.

worship ['wɜ:ʃɪp] *n.* **1.** (*relig.*) культ, поклоне́ние, почита́ние; **act of ~** богослуже́ние, церко́вная слу́жба; **freedom of ~** свобо́да вероиспове́дания; **place of ~** це́рковь, храм. **2.** (*of pers. etc.*) поклоне́ние; **Your W~** Ва́ша ми́лость.

v.t. & i. поклоня́ться (*impf.*) +*d.*; почита́ть (*impf.*); **~ God** моли́ться (*impf.*) Бо́гу; **~ strange gods** поклоня́ться чужи́м бога́м; **he ~s the ground she treads on** он боготвори́т её.

worshipful ['wɜ:ʃɪp,fʊl] *adj.* уважа́емый, почте́нный.

worshipper ['wɜ:ʃɪpə(r)] *n.* (*person attending service*) моля́щийся; (*fig.*) покло́нни|к (*fem.* -ца).

worst [wɜ:st] *n.* наиху́дшее; са́мое плохо́е; **the ~ of it is that ...** ху́же всего́ то, что...; **that's the ~ of being clever** в то́м-то и беда́/го́ре у́мников; **if the ~ should happen** е́сли произойдёт са́мое стра́шное; **if the ~ comes to the ~** в са́мом ху́дшем слу́чае; на ху́дой коне́ц; **we must prepare for the ~** мы должны́ быть гото́вы ко всему́ (*or* к ху́дшему); **you saw him at his ~** вы ви́дели его́ в о́чень неудо́бный моме́нт.

adj. наиху́дший; са́мый плохо́й; **my ~ enemy** мой зле́йший враг; **that was his ~ mistake** э́то была́ его́ са́мая серьёзная оши́бка; **you came at the ~ possible time** вы пришли́ в са́мое неподходя́щее вре́мя.

adv. ху́же всего́/всех; **he fared ~ of all** ему́ пришло́сь ху́же, чем всем остальны́м.

worsted ['wʊstɪd] *n.* (*yarn*) гребенна́я шерсть; (*cloth*) ткань из гребенно́й ше́рсти; шерстяна́я мате́рия.

worth [wɜ:θ] *n.* (*value*) це́нность; (*merit*) досто́инство; **of great ~** значи́тельный; **of little ~** незначи́тельный; **a man of ~** досто́йный челове́к; (*quantity of specified value*): **give me a pound's ~ of sweets** да́йте мне конфе́т на (оди́н) фунт.

pred. adj. **1.** (*of value equal to*): **it's ~ about £1** э́то сто́ит о́коло одного́ фу́нта; **what is your house ~?** во ско́лько оце́нивается ваш дом?; **this isn't ~ much today** сейча́с за э́то мно́го не возьмёшь; **it's ~ a lot to me** для меня́ э́то о́чень це́нно/ва́жно (*or* мно́го зна́чит); **our money is ~ less every day** с ка́ждым днём на́ши де́ньги обесце́ниваются; **he is ~ his weight in gold** таки́е, как он, це́нятся на вес зо́лота. **2.** (*deserving of*) сто́ящий, заслу́живающий; **it's not ~ the trouble of asking** не сто́ит спра́шивать; **it is well ~ while** о́чень да́же сто́ит; **it is ~ noticing** э́то заслу́живает внима́ния; **it's well ~ the money** э́то вполне́ сто́ящая вещь; **well ~ having** о́чень сто́ящий/поле́зный. **3.** (*possessed of*): **he died ~ a million** он оста́вил миллио́н; (*fig.*): **he ran for all he was ~** он мча́лся изо всех сил.

cpd. **~while** *adj.* **a ~while person** досто́йный/сто́ящий челове́к; **a ~while undertaking** сто́ящее де́ло.

worthiness ['wɜ:ðɪnɪs] *n.* досто́инство.

worthless ['wɜ:θlɪs] *adj.* ничего́ не сто́ящий; ничто́жный, никчёмный.

worthlessness ['wɜ:θlɪsnɪs] *n.* ничто́жность.

worthy ['wɜ:ðɪ] *adj.* **1.** (*estimable; meritorious; deserving respect*) досто́йный, почте́нный; **a ~ cause** пра́вое де́ло. **2.** (*deserving*): **~ of note** досто́йный внима́ния; **a cause ~ of support** де́ло, заслу́живающее подде́ржки. **3.** (*matching up or appropriate*): **~ of the occasion** подоба́ющий слу́чаю; **he is not ~ of her** он её не сто́ит.

would [wʊd, wəd] *v.* (*see also* **will**) **1.** (*conditional*): **he ~ be angry if he knew** он бы рассерди́лся, е́сли бы узна́л; **I ~ like to know** я хоте́л бы знать; **I ~n't know** отку́да мне знать? **2.** (*expr. wish*): **I ~ rather** я бы предпочёл; **~ to God I had never seen him!** заче́м то́лько я с ним повстреча́лся! **3.** (*of typical action etc.*): **you ~ do that!** с тебя́ ста́нется!; **of course he ~ say that** ну коне́чно, он э́то ска́жет. **4.** (*of habitual action*): *see* **will[2] 5.**

cpd. **~-be** *adj.* претенду́ющий (*на что*); **a ~-be writer** мечта́ющий стать писа́телем.

wound [wu:nd] *n.* ра́на, ране́ние; **receive a ~** получи́ть (*pf.*) ране́ние; **he inflicted several knife ~s** он нанёс не́сколько ножевы́х уда́ров.

v.t. ра́нить (*impf., pf.*); **he was ~ed in the leg** его́ ра́нило в но́гу; **there were many ~ed** бы́ло мно́го ра́неных; (*fig.*) ра́нить (*impf., pf.*); об|ижа́ть, -и́деть; **~ s.o.'s feelings** оскорб|ля́ть, -и́ть чьи-н. чу́вства; **~ed pride** уязвлённое самолю́бие.

wow [waʊ] *n.* (*sl.*): **the show was a ~** спекта́кль прошёл с огро́мным успе́хом.

v.t. (*sl.*) прив|оди́ть, -ести́ в восто́рг.

int. здо́рово!; вот э́то да!; блеск!

WPC (*abbr. of* ***woman police constable***) же́нщина-полице́йский.

wrangle ['ræŋg(ə)l] *n.* препира́ние, ссо́ра, спор.

v.i. препира́ться; ссо́риться; спо́рить (*all impf.*).

wrap [ræp] *n.* **1.** (*lit.*) (*shawl*) шаль; (*cloak*) наки́дка; (*rug*) плед. **2.** (*fig., covering*): **under ~s** (*fig.*) стро́го засекре́ченный; **take the ~s off** (*fig.*) рассекре́|чивать, -тить.

v.t. **1.** (*enclose*) завёр|тывать, -ну́ть; обёр|тывать, -ну́ть; **~ o.s. in a blanket** завёр|тываться, -ну́ться (*or* заку́т|ываться, -аться) в одея́ло; **they were ~ping presents** они́ завёртывали пода́рки; (*fig.*) скры|ва́ть, -ть; **~ped in mystery** оку́танный та́йной; **the mountain was ~ped in mist** гора́ была́ оку́тана тума́ном. **2.** (*wind or fold as a covering*) свёр|тывать, -ну́ть; скла́дывать, сложи́ть; **~ one's coat round one** заверну́ться/закута́ться (*pf.*) в пальто́; **he ~ped his arms around her** он заключи́л её в объя́тия; он о́бнял её.

with adv.: **~ up** *v.t.* (*cover up*) об(в)ёр|тывать, -ну́ть; завёр|тывать, -ну́ть; запако́в|ывать, -а́ть; заку́т|ывать, -ать; (*conclude*) закругл|я́ть, -и́ть (*coll.*); (*dispose of; summarize*) кра́тко сумми́ровать (*impf.*); (*obscure*) скры|ва́ть, -ть; (*pass., be engrossed*) погрузи́ться (*pf.*) (*во что*); **he is ~ped up in his studies** он поглощён заня́тиями; *v.i.* (*put on extra clothes*) заку́таться (*pf.*); **~ up well when you go out!** оде́ньтесь потепле́е, когда́ бу́дете выходи́ть!

wrapper ['ræpə(r)] *n.* (*of foodstuff, sweet etc.*) обёртка; (*of book*) суперобло́жка; (*of newspaper sent by post*) бандеро́ль.

wrapping ['ræpɪŋ] *n.* (*cover*) обёртка, упако́вка; (*packing material*) упако́вочный/обёрточный материа́л.

cpd. **~-paper** *n.* обёрточная бума́га.

wrath [rɒθ, rɔ:θ] *n.* (*liter.*) гнев; **vent one's ~ on** обру́ши|вать, -ть гнев на+*a.*

wrathful ['rɒθfʊl] *adj.* гне́вный, я́ростный.

wreak [ri:k] *v.t.* нан|оси́ть, -ести́; **~ vengeance on** мсти́ть, ото- +*d.*

wreath [ri:θ] *n.* вено́к; **~ of roses** вено́к из роз; **lay a ~ on s.o.'s grave** возложи́ть (*pf.*) вено́к на чью-н. моги́лу; (*fig.*): **~ of smoke** кольцо́/завито́к ды́ма.

wreathe [ri:ð] *v.t.* **1.** (*encircle*) окруж|а́ть, -и́ть; об|вива́ть, -ви́ть; **the hills were ~d in mist** над гора́ми клуби́лся тума́н; **her face was ~d in smiles** её лицо́ сия́ло улы́бкой. **2.** (*twine*) спле|та́ть, -сти́; сви|ва́ть, -ть; **the snake ~d itself round his neck** змея́ обвила́сь вокру́г его́ ше́и.

v.i. (*of smoke*) клуби́ться (*impf.*).

wreck [rek] *n.* **1.** (*ruin, destruction, esp. of ship*) (кора́бле)круше́ние, ава́рия; **the gales caused many ~s** от што́рмов мно́жество судо́в потерпе́ло круше́ние; (*fig.*) ги́бель, крах, разоре́ние. **2.** (*~ed ship*) затону́вший кора́бль; **the shores were strewn with ~s** берега́ бы́ли усе́яны оста́тками кораблекруше́ний. **3.** (*damaged or disabled vehicle, building, person etc.*) разва́лина; **his car was a ~ after the collision** по́сле ава́рии его́ маши́на пришла́ в по́лную него́дность; **she became a nervous ~** у неё не́рвы совсе́м сда́ли; **I look a ~** я вы́гляжу ужа́сно.

v.t. **1.** (*sink*) топи́ть, по-; **the ship was ~ed** су́дно потерпе́ло круше́ние. **2.: ~ a train** вызыва́ть, вы́звать круше́ние по́езда; **~ a building** сн|оси́ть, -ести́ зда́ние. **3.** (*fig.*, *ruin*, *destroy*) разр|уша́ть, -у́шить; разор|я́ть, -и́ть.

wreckage ['rekɪdʒ] *n.* (*wrecking*, *lit.*, *fig.*) круше́ние; (*remains*) обло́мки (*m. pl.*) (круше́ния *и т.п.*).

wrecker ['rekə(r)] *n.* **1.** (*salvager*) спаса́тель (*m.*). **2.** (*demolition worker*) рабо́чий по сно́су домо́в. **3.** (*US*, *repairer*) рабо́чий авари́йно-ремо́нтной брига́ды; (*vehicle*) маши́на техни́ческой по́мощи.

wren [ren] *n.* вьюро́к, королёк; крапи́вник.

wrench [rentʃ] *n.* **1.** (*violent twist or pull*) дёрганье, рыво́к; **he gave his ankle a ~** он вы́вихнул но́гу. **2.** (*fig.*) тоска́, боль, надры́в; **leaving our old home was a ~** покида́я родно́й дом, мы испы́тывали о́струю боль. **3.** (*tool*) га́ечный ключ.

v.t. дёр|гать, -нуть; рвать, со-; **he ~ed the door open** он ре́зко рвану́л к себе́ дверь; **he ~ed the paper out of my hand** он вы́рвал/вы́дернул бума́гу из мои́х рук.

with advs.: **~ off, ~ out** *vv.t.* от|рыва́ть, -орва́ть; вырыва́ть, вы́рвать; выдёргивать, вы́дернуть.

wrest [rest] *v.t.* вырыва́ть, вы́рвать (си́лой); **they ~ed a confession of guilt from him** они́ принуди́ли его́ призна́ться в свое́й вине́.

wrestle ['res(ə)l] *n.* борьба́.

v.i. боро́ться (*impf.*); (*fig.*): **~ with a problem** би́ться (*impf.*) над зада́чей; **he ~d with his conscience** он боро́лся со свое́й со́вестью.

wrestler ['reslə(r)] *n.* бор|е́ц (*fem.* -чи́ха).

wrestling ['reslɪŋ] *n.* борьба́.

cpds. **~-bout, ~-match** *nn.* встре́ча/схва́тка по борьбе́.

wretch [retʃ] *n.* (*sad or unfortunate person*) несча́стный; жа́лкий челове́к; (*contemptible person*) негодя́й; **little ~** (*of a child*) чертёнок; **poor ~** бедня́га (*c.g.*).

wretched ['retʃɪd] *adj.* (*miserable*, *unhappy*) несча́стный, жа́лкий; **a ~ hovel** жа́лкая лачу́га; (*inferior*) скве́рный; **~ food** отврати́тельная еда́; (*unpleasant*): **I've had a ~ day** у меня́ был ужа́сный день; **~ weather** ме́рзкая/проти́вная пого́да; (*as expletive*): **owing to his ~ stupidity** благодаря́/из-за его́ дура́цкой ту́пости.

wretchedness ['retʃɪdnɪs] *n.* (*misery*) страда́ние, муче́ние, несча́стье; (*poor quality*) него́дность.

wrick [rɪk] = **rick**[2]

wriggle ['rɪg(ə)l] *v.t.* (*also* **~ about**): **~ one's toes** шевели́ть (*impf.*) па́льцами ног; **he ~d (himself) free** он вы́скользнул; **he ~d his way out of the cave** он ползко́м, извива́ясь, вы́брался из пеще́ры.

v.i. (*also* **~ about**) изгиба́ться (*impf.*); извива́ться (*impf.*); **don't ~ in your seat** переста́нь ёрзать!; **~ out of a difficulty** вы́вернуться (*pf.*) из затрудни́тельного положе́ния; **~ out of a responsibility** увильну́ть (*pf.*) от отве́тственности.

wring [rɪŋ] *v.t.* **1.** (*squeeze*) пож|има́ть, -а́ть; сж|има́ть, -ать; **he wrung my hand** он кре́пко пожа́л мне ру́ку; **he wrung his hands in despair** он в отча́янии лома́л ру́ки; (*squeeze out by twisting*) выжима́ть, вы́жать; отж|има́ть, -а́ть; **~ clothes dry** выжима́ть, вы́жать бельё до́суха; **~ing wet** мо́крый, хоть вы́жми; (*twist round*) скру́|чивать, -ти́ть; **I'll ~ your neck!** я тебе́ ше́ю сверну́! **2.** (*fig.*, *extract by force*) ист|орга́ть, -о́ргнуть; **I wrung a promise from him** я вы́рвал у него́ обеща́ние. **3.** (*fig.*, *torture*; *distress*) терза́ть (*impf.*); **her tears wrung his heart** её слёзы терза́ли ему́ ду́шу.

with adv.: **~ out** *v.t.*: (*clothes*) выжима́ть, вы́жать; (*water*) отж|има́ть, -а́ть; (*fig.*) **~ out a confession** вырыва́ть, вы́рвать призна́ние.

wringer ['rɪŋə(r)] *n.* пресс для отжима́ния белья́.

wrinkle ['rɪŋk(ə)l] *n.* **1.** (*on skin*) морщи́на; (*on dress*) скла́дка.

v.t.: **~ one's brow** мо́рщить, на- лоб; **~ one's nose** мо́рщить, с- нос.

v.i. мя́ться (*impf.*); **this material ~s easily** э́тот материа́л о́чень мнётся/мну́щийся.

wrinkl|ed ['rɪŋk(ə)ld], **-y** ['rɪŋklɪ] *adjs.* морщи́нистый, смо́рщенный.

wrist [rɪst] *n.* запя́стье.

cpds. **~-band** *n.* (*of watch*) брасле́т; **~-watch** *n.* нару́чные час|ы́ (*pl.*, *g.* -о́в).

writ [rɪt] *n.* **1.** (*written injunction or summons*) пове́стка; исково́е заявле́ние; **~ of execution** исполни́тельный лист; **serve a ~ on s.o.** вруч|а́ть, -и́ть кому́-н. пове́стку. **2.: Holy W~** свяще́нное писа́ние.

write [raɪt] *v.t.* **1.** писа́ть, на-; **the word is written with a hyphen** э́то сло́во пи́шется че́рез дефи́с. **2.: ~ a cheque** выпи́сывать, вы́писать чек. **3.** (*compose*) писа́ть, на-; сочин|я́ть, -и́ть; **he ~s plays** он пи́шет пье́сы; **Beethoven wrote nine symphonies** Бетхо́вен сочини́л де́вять симфо́ний. **4.** (*convey by letter*): **he wrote me all the news** он написа́л мне обо всех новостя́х. *See also* **written**

v.i. **1.** писа́ть (*impf.*); **please ~ larger/smaller** пиши́те, пожа́луйста, крупне́е/ме́льче. **2.** (*compose*) сочин|я́ть, -и́ть; писа́ть, на-; **~ for a living** зараба́тывать (*impf.*) перо́м; **she wants to ~** она́ хо́чет стать писа́тельницей; **~ for the screen/stage** писа́ть сцена́рии/пье́сы; **nothing to ~ home about** (*coll.*) ничего́ осо́бенного.

with advs.: **~ away, ~ off** *vv.i.*: **he wrote away, off for a catalogue** он вы́писал себе́ катало́г; **~ down** *v.t.* (*make a note of*): **~ the address down before you forget it** запиши́те а́дрес, а то забу́дете; **~ in** *v.t.* впис|ывать, -а́ть; вст|авля́ть, -а́вить; *v.i.* обра|ща́ться, -ти́ться с пи́сьмами (*куда-н.*); **~ in for a free sample!** закажи́те (по по́чте) беспла́тный образе́ц!; **~ off** *v.t.* (*cancel*): **~ off a debt** спис|ывать, -а́ть долг; (*recognize annulment or loss of*): **~ off £500 for depreciation** списа́ть (*pf.*) 500 фу́нтов на амортиза́цию; **I wrote him off** я на нём поста́вил крест; *v.i.* = **~ away; ~ out** *v.t.* выпи́сывать, вы́писать; **~ out your homework again!** перепиши́ дома́шнее зада́ние!; **~ up** *v.t.*: **the journalist wrote up the incident** журнали́ст подро́бно описа́л инциде́нт.

cpds. **~-off** *n.*: **the car was a ~-off** маши́ну списа́ли на слом; **~-up** *n.* отчёт в пре́ссе.

writer ['raɪtə(r)] *n.* **1.** (*person writing*) а́втор. **2.** (*author*) писа́тель (*fem.* -ница).

writhe [raɪð] *v.i.* ко́рчиться (*impf.*); извива́ться (*impf.*).

writing ['raɪtɪŋ] *n.* **1.** (*act*, *process*) (на)писа́ние. **2.** (*ability*, *art*) письмо́, гра́мота; **reading and ~** чте́ние и письмо́; **the art of ~** иску́сство сло́ва. **3.** (*written words*): **in ~** пи́сьменно; в пи́сьменном ви́де; в пи́сьменной фо́рме; **commit to ~** изл|ага́ть, -ожи́ть на бума́ге. **4.** (*script*, *system of ~*) письмо́, пи́сьменность. **5.: sacred ~s** свяще́нные кни́ги (*f. pl.*). **6.** (*literary composition*) произведе́ние, сочине́ния (*nt. pl.*). **7.** (*profession*) писа́тельский труд; **take up ~** зан|има́ться, -я́ться литерату́рой. **8.** (*style*) стиль (*m.*); язы́к; **a good piece of ~** прекра́сная про́за.

cpds. **~-case** *n.* несессе́р для пи́сьменных принадле́жностей; **~-desk** *n.* пи́сьменный стол; **~-pad** *n.* блокно́т; **~-paper** *n.* почто́вая/пи́счая бума́га; **~-table** *n.* пи́сьменный стол.

written ['rɪt(ə)n] *adj.* (*not oral*, *not typed*) пи́сьменный, рукопи́сный; **the ~ word** пи́сьменная речь; (*printed*, *typed*) печа́тное сло́во; *see also* **write**

wrong [rɒŋ] *n.* **1.** (*moral ~*) зло; **do ~** греши́ть, со-; непра́вильно/нехорошо́/пло́хо поступа́ть (*impf.*); **know the difference between right and ~** различа́ть (*impf.*) добро́ и зло; **two ~s don't make a right** злом зла не попра́вишь. **2.** (*unjust action or its result*) несправедли́вость, оби́да; **do ~ to** об|ижа́ть, -и́деть; быть несправедли́вым к+*d.*; **they did him a great ~** они́ его́ кре́пко оби́дели; **right a ~** испр|а-вля́ть, -а́вить зло/несправедли́вость; **you do ~ to accuse him** вы его́ напра́сно обвиня́ете. **3.** (*state of error*): **you are in the ~** вы непра́вы/винова́ты.

adj. **1.** (*contrary to morality*) гре́шный; **it is ~ to steal** ворова́ть нельзя́/грешно́/нехорошо́; **that was very ~ of you** э́то с ва́шей стороны́ бы́ло о́чень нехорошо́/ду́рно. **2.** (*mistaken*) непра́вый; **I was ~ to let him do it** я не до́лжен был разреша́ть ему́ э́то; **you are ~** вы непра́вы/ошиба́етесь; **prove ~** опров|ерга́ть, -е́ргнуть (*кого/что*). **3.** (*incorrect*) непра́вильный, неве́рный, оши́бочный, неподходя́щий; не тот; **in/to the ~ place** не там/туда́; **get hold of the ~ end of the stick** непра́вильно поня́ть (*pf.*) что-н.; **you're going the ~ way** вы идёте непра́вильно (*or* не туда́); **that's the ~ way to go about it** э́то де́лается не так; **this shirt is the ~ size** э́та руба́шка не того́ разме́ра; **~ side out** наизна́нку; **the ~ way round** наоборо́т; **the clock is ~** часы́ врут; **everything went ~** всё сложи́лось неуда́чно; **you have the ~ number** вы не туда́ попа́ли; **what's ~ with it?** (*what is the harm in it?*) что в э́том плохо́го? **4.** (*out of order; causing concern*) нела́дный; **is (there) anything ~?** что́(-нибудь) случи́лось?; **there's something ~ with my car** что́-то с мое́й маши́ной не в поря́дке. **5.** (*of health*): **the doctor asked me what was ~** врач спроси́л, на что я жа́луюсь; **he found nothing ~ with me** он никаки́х боле́зней у меня́ не нашёл.

adv. (*incorrectly*) непра́вильно, не так; **don't get me ~** (*coll.*) пойми́те меня́ пра́вильно; **you've got it all ~** вы всё перепу́тали; **the clock went ~** часы́ испо́ртились; **our plans went ~** на́ши пла́ны спу́тались; **where did we go ~** (*make a mistake*)? в чём мы оши́блись?; **I guessed ~** я не угада́л.

v.t. (*treat unjustly*) быть несправедли́вым к+*d.*; об|ижа́ть, -и́деть.

cpds. **~doer** *n.* гре́шни|к (*fem.* -ца); правонаруши́тель (*fem.* -ница); **~doing** *n.* грех, правонаруше́ние; **~-headed** *adj.* упо́рствующий в своём заблужде́нии.

wrongful [ˈrɒŋfʊl] *adj.* (*unjust*) несправедли́вый; (*unlawful*) незако́нный; **~ dismissal** незако́нное увольне́ние.

wrought [rɔːt] *adj.* (*cf.* **work** *v.t.* **7.**): **~ iron** сва́рочная/мя́гкая/ко́вкая сталь.

wry [raɪ] *adj.* криво́й, перекошенный; **a ~ smile** крива́я улы́бка; **make a ~ face** скриви́ться, смо́рщиться (*both pf.*).

X [eks] *n.* (*unknown quantity or person*) X, икс; **let ~ be the number of hours worked** пусть X равня́ется числу́ рабо́чих часо́в; **the correspondent, Mr ~** корреспонде́нт, г-н N; **~ marks the spot where the body was found** кресто́м обозна́чено ме́сто, где был на́йден труп; **he signed with an ~** он поста́вил кре́стик вме́сто по́дписи.

cpd. **~-ray** *n.* (*pl.*) рентге́новы лучи́; (*sg., picture*) рентгеногра́мма; рентге́новский сни́мок; *v.t.* просве́|чивать, -ти́ть рентге́новскими луча́ми; де́лать, с- рентге́н +*g.*

xenophobe [ˈzenəˌfəʊb] *n.* ксенофо́б.

xenophobia [ˌzenəˈfəʊbɪə] *n.* ксенофо́бия.

xenophobic [ˌzenəˈfəʊbɪk] *adj.* отлича́ющийся ксенофо́бией.

Xerox [ˈzɪərɒks, ˈze-] *n.* ксе́рокс, фотоко́пия.

v.t. де́лать, с- ксе́рокс +*g.*; ксерографи́ровать (*impf., pf.*).

Xmas [ˈkrɪsməs, ˈeksməs] = **Christmas**

xylophone [ˈzaɪləˌfəʊn] *n.* ксилофо́н.

Y [waɪ] *n.* (*math.*) и́грек.

cpd. **~-shaped** *adj.* вилкообра́зный, У-обра́зный.

yacht [jɒt] *n.* я́хта.

v.i. пла́вать/ходи́ть/ката́ться (*indet.*) на я́хте.

cpds. **~-club** *n.* яхт-клу́б; **~sman** *n.* яхтсме́н.

yachting [ˈjɒtɪŋ] *n.* пла́вание/ката́ние на я́хтах; па́русный/я́хтенный спорт.

yack [jæk] *v.i.* (*coll.*) болта́ть (*impf.*).

yak [jæk] *n.* як; (*attr.*) я́чий.

Yale lock [jeɪl] *n.* (*propr.*) цилиндри́ческий/автомати́ческий/америка́нский замо́к.

yam [jæm] *n.* я́мс, бата́т.

Yank[1] [jæŋk], **yankee** [ˈjæŋkɪ] (*coll.*) *n.* я́нки (*m. indecl.*); северя́нин (*в США*).

adj. америка́нский; се́верный.

yank[2] [jæŋk] (*coll., pull*) *n.* рыво́к, дёрганье.

v.t. дёр|гать, -нуть.

with advs.: **~ off** *v.t.* срыва́ть, сорва́ть; **~ out** *v.t.* вырыва́ть, вы́рвать; выта́скивать, вы́тащить.

yap [jæp] *n.* тя́вканье.

v.i. тя́вк|ать, -нуть.

yard[1] [jɑːd] *n.* **1.** (*unit of measure*) ярд; **this material is sold by the ~** э́то сукно́ продаётся на я́рды. **2.** (*naut.*) рей.

cpds. **~-arm** *n.* нок ре́я; **~stick** *n.* (*fig.*) мери́ло, ме́рка, крите́рий.

yard[2] [jɑːd] *n.* **1.** (*of house*; **court~**) двор. **2.** (*for industrial purposes*): **timber ~** лесно́й склад; **builder's ~** строи́тельная площа́дка; **railway ~** парк. **3.** (*for cattle*) заго́н.

yarmulka [ˈjɑːməlkə] *n.* ермо́лка.

yarn [jɑːn] *n.* **1.** (*spun thread*) пря́жа; (*for knitting*) ни́тка. **2.** (*coll., story*) анекдо́т, расска́з.

yashmak [ˈjæʃmæk] *n.* чадра́, яшма́к.

yawn [jɔːn] *n.* зево́к.

v.i. зев|а́ть, -ну́ть; **he was ~ing his head off** он отча́янно зева́л; (*fig, of chasm*) зия́ть (*impf.*).

ye [jiː] *pron.* (*arch.*) вы; **~ Gods!** о бо́ги!

yea [jeɪ] *n.* (*affirmative vote*): **the ~s have it** большинство́ «за».

yeah [jeə] *adv.* (*coll.*) да; ага́; **oh ~?** неуже́ли?; ну да?; ах так?

year [jɪə(r), jɜː(r)] *n.* **1.** год; **last ~** в про́шлом году́; **he was only 40 years old** ему́ бы́ло всего́ со́рок лет; **twice a ~** два ра́за в год; **~ in, ~ out** из го́да в год; **~ after ~** год за го́дом; **~ by ~** с ка́ждым го́дом; **all the ~ round** кру́глый год; **Happy New**

Y~! с Но́вым го́дом!; **New Y~'s Day** день Но́вого го́да; **New Y~'s Eve** новогóдняя ночь, кану́н Но́вого го́да; **he is in his third ~** (*as student*) он на тре́тьем ку́рсе. **2.** (*pl., a long time*): **it is ~s since I saw him** я его́ це́лую ве́чность не ви́дел. **3.** (*pl., age*): **he looks young for his ~s** он мо́лодо вы́глядит для свои́х лет; **advanced in ~s** в года́х/лета́х; **he is getting on in ~s** он (уже́) в во́зрасте; **a man of his ~s** челове́к его́ во́зраста.

cpd. **~-book** *n.* ежего́дник.

yearling [ˈjɪəlɪŋ, ˈjɜː-] *n.* годови́к; (*horse*) годова́лая ло́шадь.

yearly [ˈjɪəlɪ, ˈjɜː-] *adj.* (*happening once a year*) ежего́дный, годи́чный; (*pert. to a year*) годово́й; **~ income** годово́й дохо́д.

adv. (*once a year*) раз в год; (*every year*) ка́ждый год.

yearn [jɜːn] *v.i.* **1.: ~ for** тоскова́ть (*impf.*) по+*d.*; жа́ждать (*impf.*) +*g.* **2.: ~ to, towards: he has long ~ed to see her** он уже́ давно́ мечта́ет уви́деться с ней.

yearning [ˈjɜːnɪŋ] *n.* тоска́ (*по чему*); жа́жда (+*g.*); си́льное жела́ние (+*g.*);

yeast [jiːst] *n.* дро́жж|и (*pl., g.* -е́й); заква́ска; (*attr.*) дрожжево́й.

yell [jel] *n.* (пронзи́тельный) крик; **give a ~** вскри́к|ивать, -нуть; закрича́ть (*pf.*).

v.t. & i. кр|ича́ть, -и́кнуть.

yellow [ˈjeləʊ] *n.* жёлтый цвет; **she was dressed in ~** она́ была́ оде́та в жёлтое.

adj. **1.** жёлтый; **go, turn ~** желте́ть, по-; **~ fever** жёлтая лихора́дка. **2.** (*coll., cowardly*) трусли́вый; **there was a ~ streak in him** он был трусова́т.

v.i. желте́ть, по-; **~ed leaves** пожелте́лые ли́стья; **paper ~ed with age** бума́га, пожелте́вшая от вре́мени.

yelp [jelp] *n.* визг.

v.i. визжа́ть, взви́згнуть.

Yemen [ˈjemən] *n.* Йе́мен.

yen[1] [jen] *n.* (*unit of currency*) ие́на.

yen[2] [jen] *n.* (*coll., yearning*) тоска́ (*по чему*).

v.i. тоскова́ть (*impf.*) (*по чему*).

yeoman [ˈjəʊmən] *n.* **1.** (*hist.*) йо́мен. **2.** (*small landowner*) ме́лкий землевладе́лец, фе́рмер. **3.: Y~ of the Guard** ≃ лейб-гварде́ец. **4.: do ~ service** ока́з|ывать, -а́ть по́длинную по́мощь.

yeomanry [ˈjəʊmənrɪ] *n.* (*hist.*) сосло́вие йо́менов; (*cavalry force*) территориа́льная ко́нница.

yes [jes] *n.* (*affirmation*) утвержде́ние; (*vote in favour*) го́лос «за».

adv. да; (*in reply to neg. statement or command*) нет; **~, sir** слу́шаюсь!; (*mil.*) так то́чно!; есть!

cpd. **~-man** *n.* подпева́ла (*m.*).

yesterday [ˈjestəˌdeɪ] *n.* вчера́шний день; **~'s paper** вчера́шняя газе́та; **since ~** со вчера́шнего дня; **the day before ~** позавчера́.

adv. вчера́; **~ morning** вчера́ у́тром.

yet [jet] *adv.* **1.** (*so far, up to now, to date*) до сих пор; пока́; **as ~** пока́; **as ~ nothing has been done** ничего́ пока́ не сде́лано; (*with neg.*) ещё; **he has not read the book ~** он ещё не чита́л кни́ги; **it's not time ~** ещё ра́но; ещё не вре́мя; (*with interrog.*): **has the post arrived ~?** по́чта ещё не пришла́?; **can I come in ~?** мо́жно уже́ войти́? **2.** (*some day; before all is over*) ещё; **he will win ~** он ещё победи́т. **3.** (*still*): **he has ~ to learn of the disaster** он ещё не зна́ет о катастро́фе; **while there is ~ time** пока́ ещё есть вре́мя. **4.** (*so early*) уже́; **need you go ~?** вам уже́ пора́ (идти́)?; **let's not give up ~!** ещё ра́но отча́иваться!; **it won't happen just ~** э́то ещё не сейча́с случи́тся; **shall we go? Not just ~** пойдёмте? Чуть попо́зже. **5.** (*with comp., even*) да́же, ещё; **this book is ~ more interesting** э́та книга (да́же) ещё интере́снее. **6.** (*again, in addition*) ещё; **there is ~ another reason** есть ещё и друга́я причи́на; **he came back ~ again** он сно́ва/опя́ть (*or* ещё раз) верну́лся. **7.** (*nevertheless*) тем не ме́нее; всё-таки; всё же; **it is strange ~ true** э́то стра́нно, но тем не ме́нее ве́рно/так.

conj. но; одна́ко.

yeti [ˈjetɪ] *n.* сне́жный челове́к, йе́ти (*m. indecl.*).

yew [juː] *n.* тис.

adj. ти́совый.

Yiddish [ˈjɪdɪʃ] *n.* и́диш, евре́йский язы́к.

adj.: **a ~ newspaper** газе́та на и́дише.

yield [jiːld] *n.* **1.** (*crop*) урожа́й; **a poor ~** ску́дный урожа́й. **2.** (*return*) дохо́д. **3.** (*quantity produced*) вы́ход; (*of milk*) надо́й; (*of mine*) добы́ча.

v.t. **1.** (*bring in; produce*) прин|оси́ть, -ести́; произв|оди́ть, -ести́; (с)да|ва́ть, -ть; **this land ~s a good harvest** э́та земля́ даёт хоро́ший урожа́й. **2.** (*give up*) уступ|а́ть, -и́ть; **~ the floor** (*parl.*) уступ|а́ть, -и́ть трибу́ну; **~ ground** сда|ва́ть, -ть террито́рию; (*fig.*) сда|ва́ть, -ть (свои́) пози́ции; **he ~ed the point** в э́том пу́нкте он согласи́лся.

v.i. уступ|а́ть, -и́ть; подд|ава́ться, -а́ться; под|ава́ться, -а́ться; **the door ~ed to a strong push** под си́льным напо́ром дверь подала́сь; **he ~s to none in bravery** он никому́ не уступа́ет в хра́брости; **he ~ed to the temptation** он не смог устоя́ть пе́ред собла́зном; **we will never ~ to force** мы ни за что не подчини́мся наси́лию; **the disease ~ed to treatment** боле́знь поддала́сь лече́нию.

yippee [ˈjɪpiː, -ˈpiː] *int.* ура́!

YMCA (*abbr. of* ***Young Men's Christian Association***) Христиа́нский сою́з молоды́х люде́й.

yob(bo) [ˈjɒbəʊ] *n.* (*sl.*) хулига́н, грубия́н.

yoga [ˈjəʊgə] *n.* йо́га.

yog(h)urt [ˈjɒgət] *n.* йогу́рт.

yogi [ˈjəʊgɪ] *n.* йог.

yoke [jəʊk] *n.* **1.** (*fitted to oxen etc.*) ярмо́. **2.** (*fig.*) и́го, ярмо́; **the Ta(r)tar ~** (*hist.*) тата́рское и́го; **come under the ~** подпа́сть (*pf.*) под и́го; **shake off the ~** сбр|а́сывать, -о́сить и́го/ярмо́. **3.** (*for carrying pails etc.*) коромы́сло. **4.** (*of dress*) коке́тка.

v.t. впря|га́ть, -чь в ярмо́.

yokel [ˈjəʊk(ə)l] *n.* дереве́нщина (*c.g.*).

yolk [jəʊk] *n.* желто́к; **~ sac** (*biol.*) желто́чный мешо́к (заро́дыша).

yon(der) [ˈjɒndə(r)] *adj.* вон тот.

adv. вон там.

yore [jɔː(r)] *n.* (*liter.*): **in days of ~** давны́м-давно́; во вре́мя о́но.

you [juː] *pron.* **1.** вы; (*familiar sg.*) ты; **~ and I** мы с тобо́й/ва́ми; **~ and he** вы с ним; **this is for ~** э́то для вас, э́то вам; **~ silly fool!** (вот) дура́к!; **~ darling!** ми́лая моя́!; как ты мил(а́)!; **don't ~ go away** не взду́майте уйти́. **2.** (*one, anyone*): **~ never can tell** как знать?; **~ soon get used to it** к э́тому ско́ро привыка́ешь; **there's a book for ~!** (*sc. a fine one*) вот э́то кни́га!

cpd. **~-know-who** *n.* (*coll.*) не́кто; э́тот са́мый.

young [jʌŋ] *n.*: **the ~** молодёжь; (*~ animals*) детёныши (*m. pl.*); (*birds*) птенцы́, пте́нчики (*m. pl.*).

adj. **1.** молодо́й, ю́ный; **~ man** молодо́й челове́к, ю́ноша (*m.*); **her ~ man** (*sweetheart*) её возлю́бленный; **~** (*child*) **musicians** ю́ные музыка́нты; **~ children** ма́ленькие де́ти; **~ people** молодёжь; **~ ones** (*children*) де́т|и (*pl.*, g. -е́й); (*animals*) детёныши; **in my ~ days** в дни мое́й ю́ности; когда́ я был молоды́м/мо́лод; **he is ~er than I** он моло́же меня́; **the ~er Smith** Смит мла́дший; **the night is ~** ещё не по́здно.

cpd. **~-looking** *adj.* моложа́вый.

youngster [ˈjʌŋstə(r)] *n.* (*child*) ма́льчик, подро́сток; (*youth*) юне́ц; (*pl., collect.*) молодёжь.

your [jɔ:(r), jʊə(r)] *adj.* **1.** ваш; (*familiar sg.*) твой; (*referring to subj. of clause*) свой. **2.** (*pej.*): **that's ~ politician for you!** вот они́, (ва́ши) поли́тики!

yours [jɔ:z, jʊəz] *pron.* ваш; твой; свой; **my father and ~** мой оте́ц и ваш; **my teacher and ~** (*2 people*) на́ши с ва́ми учителя́; (*1 pers.*) наш с ва́ми учи́тель; **a friend of ~** оди́н из ва́ших прия́телей; **here is my hat — have you found ~?** вот моя́ шля́па, (а) вы свою́ нашли́?

pred. adj. ваш; **~ truly** пре́данный Вам; (*joc.*) ваш поко́рный слуга́; **what's ~?** что вы бу́дете пить?; **that cough of ~** э́тот ваш ка́шель.

yourself [jɔ:'self, jʊə-] *pron.* **1.** (*refl.*) себя́; **don't deceive ~!** не обма́нывайте (самого́) себя́!; не обма́нывайтесь! **2.** (*emph.*) сам; **you wrote to him ~** вы са́ми ему́ писа́ли. **3.** (*after preps.*): **you brought this trouble on ~** вы са́ми на себя́ навлекли́ э́ту неприя́тность; **why are you sitting by ~?** почему́ вы сиди́те в одино́честве?; **did you do it all by ~?** вы э́то сде́лали са́ми? **4.: you don't look ~ today** вы нева́жно вы́глядите сего́дня.

youth [ju:θ] *n.* **1.** (*state or period*) мо́лодость; (*liter.*) ю́ность; **in my ~** в (мое́й) мо́лодости. **2.** (*young man*) ю́ноша (*m.*). **3.** (*young people*) молодёжь; **the ~ of our country** молодёжь на́шей страны́; **~ club** молодёжный клуб; **~ hostel** молодёжная ба́за/гости́ница.

youthful ['ju:θfʊl] *adj.* ю́ный, ю́ношеский; **~ dreams** мечты́ мо́лодости; (*of face, pers. etc.*) молодо́й, ю́ный; **he had a ~ appearance** у него́ моложа́вый вид.

youthfulness ['ju:θfʊlnɪs] *n.* мо́лодость; (*of appearance*) моложа́вость.

yo-yo ['jəʊjəʊ] *n.* йо-йо́ (*indecl.*).

yucky ['jʌkɪ] *adj.* (*sl.*) гря́зный, га́дкий.

Yugoslavia [ju:gə'slɑ:vɪə] *n.* Югосла́вия.

yule [ju:l] *n.* (*arch.*) Рождество́; свя́т|ки (*pl., g.* -ок).

yummy ['jʌmɪ] *adj.* (*coll.*) вку́сный.

yum-yum [jʌm'jʌm] *int.* ням-ня́м!

yurt [jʊət] *n.* ю́рта.

Z

Z [zed] *n.*: **from A to ~** от «а» до «я»; с са́мого нача́ла до са́мого конца́.

Zaire [zɑ:'ɪə(r)] *n.* Заи́р.

Zambia ['zæmbɪə] *n.* За́мбия.

zany ['zeɪnɪ] *adj.* смешно́й, фигля́рский.

zeal [zi:l] *n.* усе́рдие, рве́ние; энтузиа́зм.

zealot ['zelət] *n.* фан|а́тик (*fem.* -ати́чка); ревни́тель (*fem.* -ница).

zealous ['zeləs] *adj.* усе́рдный, рья́ный, ре́вностный; **a ~ supporter** горя́чий сторо́нник.

zebra ['zebrə, 'zi:-] *n.* зе́бра; (*attr.*) зе́бровый; **~ crossing** перехо́д «зе́бра».

zenith ['zenɪθ, 'zi:-] *n.* (*lit., fig.*) зени́т; (*fig.*) вы́сшая то́чка; расцве́т.

zephyr ['zefə(r)] *n.* зефи́р.

Zeppelin ['zepəlɪn] *n.* цеппели́н.

zero ['zɪərəʊ] *n.* нуль (*m.*), ноль (*m.*); нулева́я то́чка; **absolute ~** абсолю́тный нуль; **ten degrees below ~** ми́нус де́сять гра́дусов; де́сять гра́дусов ни́же нуля́; **~ hour** час «Ч»; **~ option** (*pol.*) нулево́й вариа́нт.

v.i.: **~ in on a target** пристре́л|иваться, -я́ться.

zest [zest] *n.* пыл; энтузиа́зм; **add ~ to** прид|ава́ть, -а́ть вкус/пика́нтность/интере́с *+d.*; **~ for life** жизнера́достность.

zigzag ['zɪgzæg] *n.* зигза́г.

adj. зигзагообра́зный.

v.i. идти́ (*det.*) зигза́гом; де́лать, с- зигза́ги.

Zimbabwe [zɪm'bɑ:bwɪ, -weɪ] *n.* Зимба́бве (*indecl.*).

zinc [zɪŋk] *n.* цинк.

adj. ци́нковый.

Zionism ['zaɪə,nɪz(ə)m] *n.* сиони́зм.

Zionist ['zaɪənɪst] *n.* сиони́ст (*fem.* -ка).

zip [zɪp] *n.* **1.** (*~-fastener, also* **~per**) (застёжка-)мо́лния. **2.** (*sound of bullet*) свист (пу́ли). **3.** (*coll., energy*) пыл, эне́ргия. **4.: Z~ code** (*US*) (почто́вый) и́ндекс.

v.t. (*usu.* **~ up**) застёг|ивать, -ну́ть (на мо́лнию).

v.i. (*of bullet etc.*) свисте́ть, про-; прон|оси́ться, -ести́сь со сви́стом.

cpd. **~-fastener** *n.* (застёжка-)мо́лния.

zirconium [zə'kəʊnɪəm] *n.* цирко́ний.

zit [zɪt] *n.* (*coll.*) прыщ, хоти́мчик.

zither ['zɪðə(r)] *n.* ци́тра.

zodiac ['zəʊdɪ,æk] *n.* зодиа́к.

zombie ['zɒmbɪ] *n.* (*fig., coll.*) ску́чный/вя́лый челове́к; живо́й труп.

zonal ['zəʊnəl] *adj.* зона́льный.

zone [zəʊn] *n.* зо́на, по́яс, полоса́; **danger ~** опа́сная зо́на; (*geog.*): **torrid ~** тропи́ческий по́яс; **frigid ~** аркти́ческий по́яс; **temperate ~s** уме́ренные пояса́.

v.t. (*divide into ~s*) разб|ива́ть, -и́ть на зо́ны.

zoo [zu:] *n.* зоопа́рк.

zoological [,zəʊə'lɒdʒɪk(ə)l] *adj.* зоологи́ческий; **~ gardens** зоологи́ческий сад.

zoologist [zəʊ'ɒlədʒɪst] *n.* зоо́лог.

zoology [zəʊ'ɒlədʒɪ] *n.* зооло́гия.

zoom [zu:m] *n.*: **~ lens** объекти́в с переме́нным фо́кусным расстоя́нием.

Zulu ['zu:lu:] *n.* зулу́с (*fem.* -ка).

adj. зулу́сский.

Zurich ['zjʊərɪk] *n.* Цю́рих.

zygote ['zaɪgəʊt] *n.* зиго́та.